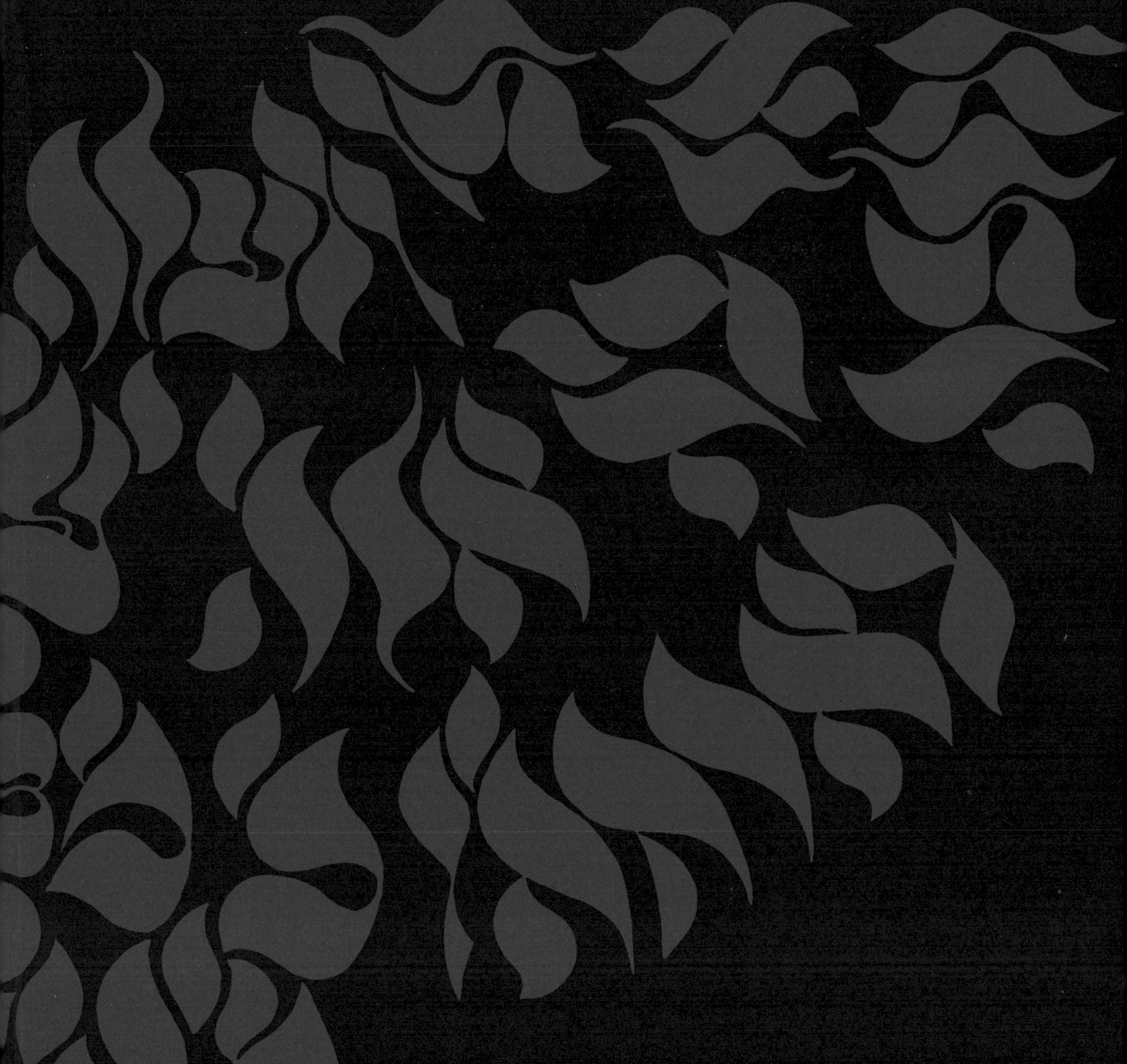

o the House of the God of Jacob and He will teach us
n shall go forth the Law and the word of the Lord from
lem

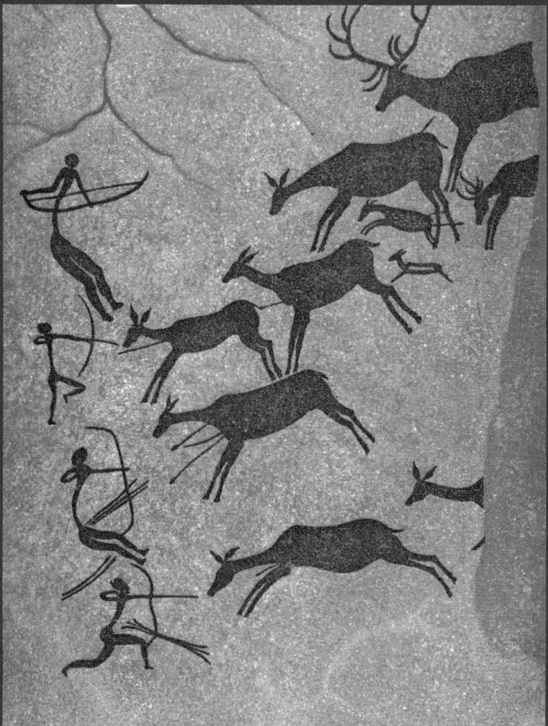

David and Ruth Livingston

ENCYCLOPAEDIA JUDAICA

VOLUME 1

INTRODUCTION · INDEX

ENCYCLOPAEDIA JUDAICA

ENCYCLOPAEDIA JUDAICA JERUSALEM

Library of Congress Catalog Card Number: 72-90254

First printing 1972
Second printing 1973
Third printing 1974
Fourth printing 1978

Computerized typesetting, printing and binding by
Keterpress Enterprises, Jerusalem

Printed in Israel

A Clal Project

TABLE OF CONTENTS

1 INTRODUCTION
17 ENCYCLOPAEDIA JUDAICA RESEARCH FOUNDATION
18 EDITORIAL BOARD
19 DIVISIONAL AND DEPARTMENTAL EDITORS
24 STAFF
27 EDITORS OF THE ENCYCLOPAEDIA
39 CONTRIBUTORS TO THE ENCYCLOPAEDIA
73 GENERAL ABBREVIATIONS
74 ABBREVIATIONS USED IN RABBINICAL LITERATURE
79 BIBLIOGRAPHICAL ABBREVIATIONS
90 TRANSLITERATION RULES
93 ILLUSTRATIONS
107 SUPPLEMENTARY LISTS
109 Hundred Year Jewish Calendar 1920–2020
160 Ḥasidism
169 Israel Place List
193 Hebrew Newspapers and Periodicals
221 Pottery
272 Synagogues
273 INDEX
275 Introduction to the Index
277 Abbreviations used in the Index
283 Index
844 Corrigenda to Color Plate Captions

Typesetting was accomplished by using a specially designed computerized system.

The index was extracted with the aid of the above system.

The computerized typesetting, printing and binding by
Keter Press Enterprises Ltd., Jerusalem.

The type face is Photon Times Roman.

The color printing is by E. Lewin-Epstein Ltd. and United Artists Ltd., Tel Aviv.

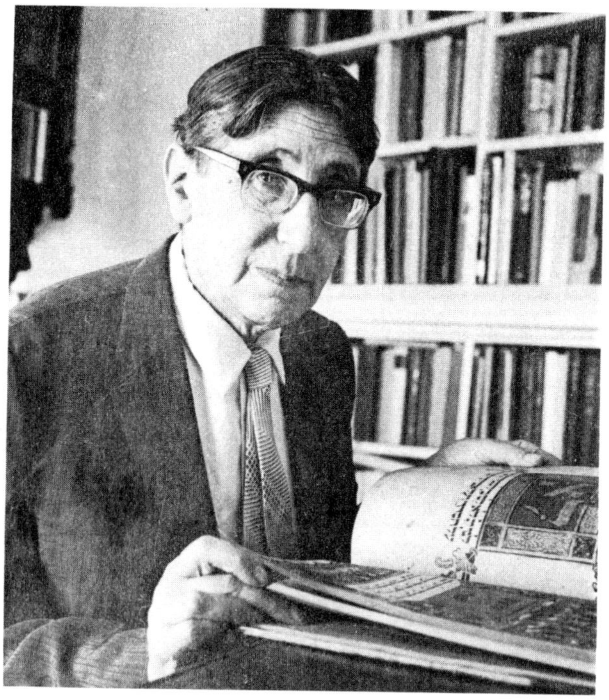

PROFESSOR CECIL ROTH (1899–1970)

Cecil Roth as editor in chief of the *Encyclopaedia Judaica* was a publisher's dream, bringing to the position not only his encyclopedic knowledge—which spanned far more than those specific subjects such as history and art to which he had made an immense contribution—but also a lifetime of close contact and wide experience in the intricacies of editing and bringing a manuscript to the press. With his facility with the pen, he had himself published more than 700 books and articles, among them some of an encyclopedic character, even if they were small by comparison to our present enterprise.

I can truly say that there was not a single request made by the publishers to Cecil Roth that he did not carry out and many of the requests were very difficult—especially in the time available. It is no secret that despite his age, his daily output in editing was several times larger than that of any other single editor and each page showed evidence of his work—corrections, questions, suggested additions. Even during times of his illness both in Jerusalem and New York the flow of work continued at least at a rate normal for any other editor. His leadership and example influenced the team as a whole; his judgment in securing the proper balance between quality of the final product and time available, was one of his finest abilities; and his resourcefulness in personally writing missing sections on a large variety of subjects helped out on numerous occasions. To stress this point—after his death we had to turn to at least 20 different individuals in similar emergencies to cover the same ground.

The assembling of the vast army of editors and contributors from the best available in Jewry today was no doubt due to his standing. He was chief architect of the determination of wordage for the various entries, so important to give balance and proportion to our encyclopedia, which he himself characterized as the "greatest Jewish literary work of scholarship of the century." In truth, it is even more than that—and the *Encyclopaedia Judaica* will be the greatest living memorial and tribute to Cecil Roth's outstanding career in Jewish scholarship.

Despite his great erudition he was a very humble man. He led the team by devotion and personal example and by gentle persuasion rather than his authority. He knew well that he was dependent on a great number of *prima donnas* but he knew how to steer an even course even in stormy waters, and he went to endless extremes to promote goodwill and peace. If he was disappointed with the quality of the work (which often happened and which imposed upon him the extra strain of rewriting), he confined his caustic remarks to paper and avoided offending the individuals involved. And these remarks were always peppered with the well-known particular Rothian sense of humor. He had the unique capacity of seeing the positive in individuals and in building on this positive basis, while ignoring their negative characteristics.

Cecil Bezalel Roth returned to Jerusalem, which he loved, in those tense days which preceded the Six-Day War. Instead of holding a scheduled reception for editors on June 5, 1967 at his home, he spent that evening in the air-raid shelter. Although he knew of the imminent danger he felt his place was among his people and he wanted to be part of the great history which was being made in Jerusalem. He witnessed from his balcony the battles which returned, after nearly 2,000 years, the Old City of Jerusalem to Israel sovereignty and the fight for Bethlehem and the surrounding area. And then with elation he watched from the same balcony the endless streams of pilgrims who came for days, weeks, and months to the Western Wall. In addition to the exaltation which soared up among the whole of Jewry everywhere during those historic days he, as a historian, could bring an extra dimension of perspective to the great events which unfolded before his very eyes. Returning to the office on the Thursday morning when the guns had fallen silent in Jerusalem he insisted on a special *kiddush* to mark the occasion and delivered a memorable moving and eloquent address to the staff. He wrote shortly after this: "The recent events in the Middle East (culminating in the amazing Israel victory in the Six-Day War) have thrown all former books of reference on the Jews completely out of focus. It is for this reason that the publication of the *Encyclopaedia Judaica* has taken on a new urgency." And then he applied himself to this task with this real sense of urgency.

Here in one man we had the unique combination of respect for tradition with a scientific approach to modern learning. From Cecil Roth's example there is much to learn, and this is reflected in the encyclopedia—*Ahavat Yisrael* (the love of Israel), the centrality of Jerusalem, the understanding of the mission of the Jewish people, all of which were so important to Cecil Roth, emerge from its pages.

Yitzhak Rischin
for the publishers

INTRODUCTION

The *Encyclopaedia Judaica* is the first Jewish encyclopedia on a major scale to be published for many decades. It represents the culmination of years of intensive work by scholars from many parts of the world and provides a comprehensive picture of all aspects of Jewish life and knowledge up to the present day, intended for both the Jewish and non-Jewish reader.

Previous Jewish Encyclopedias

The first complete work of this nature, the English-language *Jewish Encyclopedia,* appeared in New York at the beginning of the 20th century (its twelfth and final volume was published in 1906). This pioneering work summed up the state of Jewish scholarship and the condition of the Jewish world at the time. It was an extraordinary achievement—especially if one considers the relatively small numbers of the English-speaking and English-reading Jewish population at the time. It was able, however, to call upon the collaboration of Jewish scholars in many countries—in particular the representatives of the Wissenschaft des Judentums, then at its height. There were aspects that it tended to overlook or underplay, such as the world of East European Jewry, Kabbalah and Ḥasidism, Yiddish language and literature, and the life and culture of the Jews in Muslim lands, but seen as a whole, it was a monumental work incorporating many entries which became classic statements of their subject.

The 16-volume Russian Jewish encyclopedia *Yevreyskaya Entsiklopediya,* which also appeared before World War I, was well conceived and in some respects brilliantly edited. Particularly outstanding was its expertise on East European Jewish subjects. The 10-volume Hebrew *Oẓar Yisrael* (1924), an almost single-handed achievement by J. D. Eisenstein, was on a far smaller scale and had less strict standards, although in certain areas its articles presented useful material.

At the time of the revival of Jewish interest and learning in Germany after World War I, Jacob Klatzkin, Ismar Elbogen, and Nahum Goldmann planned a new encyclopedia in the German language. This was intended to incorporate the results of the intervening years of intensive scholarship and research, to reflect the intellectual attitudes which had become established during this period, and to correct certain defects of balance of the *Jewish Encyclopedia.* Around them, Klatzkin and Goldmann gathered a galaxy of scholars. The work—called *Encyclopaedia Judaica*—progressed majestically, notwithstanding the obstacles and difficulties of those troubled times, until the Nazis rose to power in Germany. Publication had to be suspended after Volume 10 (completing the letter L) leaving incomplete this last monument of the intellectual greatness of German Jewry. Under the same auspices, a Hebrew version—the *Eschkol* encyclopedia—began to appear, but only two volumes were issued. Mention should also be made of the five-volume *Juedisches Lexikon,* edited by Georg Herlitz and Bruno Kirschner, published by the Juedischer Verlag in 1927–30. Although more modest in scope than the other works mentioned, it made a useful contribution to Jewish studies and also paid more attention than its predecessors to illustrative material.

In the first years of World War II (1939–43) the *Universal Jewish Encyclopedia,* edited by Isaac Landman, was issued in the United States in ten volumes. It was able to reflect the growing importance of U.S. Jewry and to take into account late developments, especially in American Jewish history and biography. It had considerable merits but was not an ambitious work. Moreover the fact that it was published in a period of major transition in itself set a limit to its utility. It was the *Universal Jewish Encyclopedia* which constituted the basis of the ten-volume Spanish-language *Enciclopedia Judaica Castellana* produced in Mexico between 1948 and 1951. The main original achievement of the latter work was in those entries dealing with the development of Jewish life in Latin America.

After the establishment of the State of Israel, the *Encyclopaedia Hebraica* in the Hebrew language began to be published in Jerusalem by the Massada Publishing Company directed by the Peli family. This is the first large-scale general encyclopedia in the Hebrew language—and naturally it empha-

sizes the Jewish aspects of various subjects, some of them of high scholarly importance and in certain cases even pioneering studies in their field. But though it contains the elements of a Jewish encyclopedia, it is not—nor is it intended to be—a Jewish encyclopedia as such.

The Development of the Encyclopaedia Judaica

For many years, and especially since the cataclysmic events in Jewish history of the 1940s, the need has been felt for an entirely new Jewish encyclopedia, especially in the English language for English-speaking Jewry, who now account for about half of the Jews of the world. Furthermore the survivors of the editorial board of the German *Encyclopaedia Judaica* had always been determined that the Nazi attack on their work could not be accepted as a final defeat and that the unfinished publication must be completed. However, they too recognized that now only a relatively small proportion of the Jewish people had access to a work in German and that any new endeavor in this field must be, first and foremost, in English. Dr. Nahum Goldmann, the last active survivor of the original board of editors, had long had this objective.

Hence in the late 1950s two different programs emerged which eventually coalesced—the completion of the old *Encyclopaedia Judaica* and the publication of a new Jewish encyclopedia in English. At the same time the publishers of the *Encyclopaedia Hebraica* had long held hopes of producing the Judaic portions of their encyclopedia in English. These converging tendencies engendered the practical project to publish the *Encyclopaedia Judaica* in the English language.

Initial funding of the project was made possible through an allocation obtained by Dr. Goldmann from the German reparations fund earmarked for cultural purposes. The Rassco Company in Israel also became interested and provided some of the funds during the early stages. In the U.S., the Encyclopaedia Judaica Research Foundation was established to raise further support for the project.

During this early period, when the preliminary work was being centered in the U.S., Prof. Benzion Netanyahu, then editor of the *Encyclopaedia Hebraica,* served as editor in chief. The main editorial offices were established in Philadelphia in 1963. Prof. A. A. Neuman, then president of Dropsie College, became chairman of the American board of editors, later succeeded by Prof. Alexander Altmann of Brandeis University, while Prof. Benzion Dinur, formerly Israel Minister of Education and Emeritus Professor of Jewish History at the Hebrew University, became chairman of the Israel board.

In 1965 Prof. Netanyahu was compelled through pressure of work to retire from his post and it was decided to transfer the editorial center to Jerusalem. This was regarded as advisable because Jerusalem was the unquestioned pivot of Jewish studies in the world, with the greatest concentration of scholars in the subject as well as possessing unrivaled research facilities. Moreover it was now the home of Prof. Cecil Roth, who had been appointed to succeed Prof. Netanyahu as editor in chief.

The publishing responsibility was assumed by the Israel Program for Scientific Translations (at that time an Israel government corporation headed by Yitzhak Levi, now owned by CLAL Israel Investment Company Ltd.). The Israel Program for Scientific Translations had already begun diversifying its publishing program with the establishment of the Israel Universities Press and subsequently set up the Keter Publishing House Ltd. under whose imprint the Encyclopaedia now appears. In the U.S. the *Encyclopaedia Judaica* is also appearing with the imprint of Macmillan under an agreement early reached by which the Macmillan Company would distribute the Encyclopaedia in the Western Hemisphere.

The financing of the Encyclopaedia during the five years of actual work in which it has been produced in Israel was made possible initially by a generous loan from the United States government out of counterpart funds available in Israel at a nominal interest. This was supplemented by a considerable investment made by the publisher to bring the project to a successful conclusion.

Work started in earnest in 1967 and a period of five years was allocated for the completion of the entire Encyclopaedia. It was early decided that by appropriate organization and by proper exploitation of technological advances it would be possible to achieve the highly desirable goal of publishing the Encyclopaedia at one time in its entirety. This would obviate the time gap inevitable in works that

appear gradually, avoid the frustration of having the first volumes of a series but not the continuation to which references are made, and make possible the simultaneous publication of an index volume which the editors saw as the basic and indispensable key to the whole work.

To complete the Encyclopaedia within the given time, it was decided to adopt the principle of maximum subdivision so as to involve the greatest number of editors and contributors. The subject matter was broken down into some 20 divisions and these were again subdivided into departments. Some divisions had only two or three departments but others comprised many more—35 in the history division and over 70 in the division dealing with the participation of Jews in world culture. The detailed structure can be seen by consulting the editorial list.

The general flow of an entry was from the contributor to the departmental and divisional editors, then to the central office for translation (where necessary), checking, styling, transliterating and bibliographical verification, approval by the relevant associate editor and by the editors in chief, and then back to the contributor for his approval of the final version (in cases where substantial editorial changes had been inserted). Finally the entry was sent to the index department and then to press.

A number of outstanding scholars have served as consulting editors. They have advised the Encyclopaedia staff in their fields of specialization when requested but have not borne any editorial responsibility. Nor has any departmental, divisional, or associate editor or deputy editor in chief editorial responsibility for any contents of the Encyclopaedia apart from those which were his own direct responsibility. In a very few instances, an editorial stage was omitted, and in such cases the responsibility was assumed by other editors. The final responsibility for all entries rests with the editors in chief.

Dr. Geoffrey Wigoder was appointed deputy editor in chief and the various divisions were grouped into sections each headed by an associate editor. The associate editors—Prof. Louis Rabinowitz, Prof. Raphael Posner, Dr. Binyamin Eliav, and Mr. Simḥa Katz—together with the editor in chief and his deputy constituted the editorial board. After the death of Prof. Roth in 1970 the editorial board was headed by Dr. Wigoder, and Prof. Rabinowitz and Prof. Posner were appointed deputy editors in chief. The New York office was headed by Dr. Frederick Lachman, who coordinated the departments and divisions whose editors were in North America. Parallel with the preparation of the text was the work of the illustrations and graphics department headed by Mr. Moshe Shalvi. The complex administration was directed by Mrs. Rachel Sabbath. The extent of the operation can be illustrated by the fact that apart from the 300 editors and 1,800 contributors with whom contact was maintained, the Encyclopaedia employed an internal staff of 150—not including those who worked on the printing and binding stages. It was not always easy to find the specialists required and in some spheres these had to be specially trained to work on the Encyclopaedia. The entire publishing operation was directed by Mr. Yitzhak Rischin, managing director of the Keter Publishing House Ltd. and the Israel Program for Scientific Translations Ltd.

The New World of the Encyclopaedia

As a result of the unprecedented events of this century, no Jewish encyclopedia today can be merely a remodeling and updating of its predecessors. A new world has emerged—politically, culturally, scientifically, and indeed cosmically. This is especially true of any Jewish context. The following are only some of the areas in which this is exemplified:

(1) Progress of Study. At the time of the planning of the *Jewish Encyclopedia* the so-called "Science of Judaism" (Wissenschaft des Judentums) had been active for about three-quarters of a century. Since then, another three-quarters of a century has elapsed during which the most intensive research has been carried out in all branches of Jewish studies. In 1900 there were only three major Jewish learned periodicals: a larger number than this is now published in Hebrew alone and over 70 years of publications have to be taken into account. A whole library of research has to be considered and summarized in an encyclopedic work such as this one.

(2) Discoveries. Apart from the normal progress of research, new discoveries have been made in the field of Jewish studies, a number of which may be termed epoch-making. To quote three instances:

(a) Up to half a century ago, few original documents in the strict sense bearing on the history of the Hebrews in the biblical period were known. Today, a considerable body of such material is available as a result of the striking discoveries made throughout the Middle East.

(b) The discovery of the Dead Sea Scrolls and other material in the Judean Desert from 1947 onward has provided an entire corpus of religious and other literature from the late Second Temple era and the following period, regarding which formerly there was scarcely a single original document. This has thrown fascinating new light on the whole epoch. Moreover, it has provided many biblical manuscripts nearly a thousand years older than those previously known.

(c) Even before these discoveries, the revealing of the treasures of the Cairo *Genizah* especially by Solomon Schechter had shed a new light on the history and literature of the Jews in the Muslim world in the geonic period. It also furnished large numbers of hitherto unknown texts and original works by writers of the Judeo-Arabic school. This material was partially used in earlier Jewish encyclopedias but research on it has progressed continually since then and the results must now be summarized in any Jewish work of reference.

(3) New Scientific Perspectives. Inevitably scholarly perspectives change from generation to generation. Social and economic history was barely recognized as a subject for serious research three-quarters of a century ago; now it takes a foremost position in historical scholarship. The study of contemporary Jewry, whereby the tools of the modern social sciences are applied to the current situation, has been developed at various research centers over the past 20 years and its findings, which have brought new understanding of the Jewish world, have been extensively incorporated in this Encyclopaedia. The growing understanding of the full significance of East European Jewry in Jewish history has resulted in comprehensive treatment both in breadth and depth. New light has been thrown on the Jews in Muslim lands—in the old encyclopedias there tended to be a virtual blank in this field after the Middle Ages. Now, although much more research is still required, it is possible to continue the story in detail until our own day when the entire chapter has almost come to an end. The work of Prof. Gershom Scholem has opened up new vistas on Jewish mysticism, here fully reflected. The subject of Jewish law has been developed as an independent discipline (in previous encyclopedias it was regarded as a part of Talmud and Rabbinics) and is now analyzed for the first time from its essentially juridical aspects. Another field requiring special treatment is Yiddish language and literature which had such a magnificent, albeit comparatively brief, flowering, of which a certain perspective can already be obtained.

Jewish art, formerly considered almost a contradiction in terms, has now come into its own and its history taken back by many centuries as a result of archaeological discoveries. The Jewish museums which now exist in many places have helped to bring this before the public. Moreover, Jewish artists, a rare phenomenon a century ago, have begun to make a great impact on the world of art and their work must be given due consideration. These aspects too are connected with the whole new approach to the visual and illustrative material, conceived as an integral part of the Encyclopaedia.

(4) New Areas. At the beginning of the 20th century Jewish life was still largely confined to the same areas in which Jewish history had been enacted for centuries past—preeminently Europe and the Mediterranean Basin. The United States had only recently acquired a Jewish population of real significance, as yet preponderantly immigrant. Today the map of the Jewish world has changed radically. Three-quarters of world Jewry lives in communities which have emerged, or re-emerged, to prominence in the course of this century. Half the Jews of the world are now concentrated in the U.S. Significant communities have developed in other English-speaking countries—Canada, South Africa, and Australia. The important Spanish- and Portuguese-speaking Jewries of Latin America have only emerged in recent generations. The "ingathering of the exiles" in Israel has provided world Jewry with a new-old focus.

The Climacterics of the Twentieth Century

In the course of this century, the Jewish people has undergone a series of major, traumatic experiences which have profoundly affected its very nature, and this Encyclopaedia has paid special attention to all of these. In many instances, these subjects are treated for the first time in a reference work of this nature.

(a) The rise of "racial" anti-Semitism and the Holocaust. It is less than a century since the term "anti-Semitism" was coined and during this period the phenomenon took on new, ugly dimensions. Eventually this was developed into its climactic expression by the Nazis with their cold-blooded slaughter of six million Jews. This event has left an ineradicable scar on the face of Jewish existence. It brought to an end the long primacy of European Jewry and its many glorious contributions to Jewish history as well as having an untold influence on Jews everywhere. The subject is treated thoroughly in the Encyclopaedia. Apart from entries on the Holocaust and everything related, special sections in the entries on every country and community affected by the Holocaust trace the fate of the Jews there during the Nazi period. Much of this has involved original research (largely pursued at the archives of *Yad Vashem* in Jerusalem) and for the first time it is possible to obtain a picture of the fate of most communities (in some cases, notably in the Soviet Union, the documentation is still not available). The editors have consciously allotted the maximum of space to this subject in view of its unique importance.

(b) Zionism and the State of Israel. The 20th century has seen the effective development of the Zionist Movement culminating in the second climacteric—the establishment of the State of Israel in 1948. This too has revolutionized the nature and condition of the Jewish people with major ramifications in all branches of Jewish life. This Encyclopaedia has been written within the framework of the new outlooks and perspectives resulting from these developments. Israel has become the center of much of Jewish life and activity—religious, cultural, political, sociological—and must permeate any contemporary Jewish work of reference. This is expressed, for example, in the major entry "Israel"; in the space devoted to the geography and history of the country; in the emphasis given to modern Hebrew language and literature; or in the special attention in entries on Jewish law to their application in Israel; or in the sections in articles on countries devoted to their relations with and attitude to the State of Israel.

Illustrations

One of the outstanding advances of this Encyclopaedia in comparison with its predecessors is in the selection, quantity, and quality of its illustrative material. Particular attention has been paid to this aspect of the Encyclopaedia. An archive of 25,000 photographs was assembled, from which 8,000 were selected to illustrate the Encyclopaedia. The rich pictorial content reflects modern attitudes whereby visual material serves not only as an adjunct but often supplements and crystallizes the written article. In particular, the inclusion of several hundred pictures in color provides a vivid and accurate reproduction of some of the great masterpieces of Jewish art.

Special attention has been paid to the preparation of maps, charts, and diagrams. Many of these will be found throughout the Encyclopaedia presenting graphically both material contained in the relevant entries and also supplementary facts and statistics. For example, almost every country has its map showing the distribution of Jewish communities—often both historically and currently. Every place in Israel is accompanied by a small map which at a glance shows its location. The demographic entries are accompanied by charts facilitating the comprehension of the statistics.

The cover design of the Encyclopaedia by the English designer Abram Games in the form of a *menorah* contains the Hebrew and English text from Isaiah "Come ye and let us go up to the mountain of the Lord to the House of the God of Jacob and He will teach us of His ways and we will walk in His paths for out of Zion shall go forth the Law and the word of the Lord from Jerusalem." On the spine the volume is so designed that the words "Lord," "Zion," "Jerusalem" predominate.

Index

One of the highlights of the Encyclopaedia is its comprehensive index, edited by Prof. Posner. This provides the key which unlocks the Encyclopaedia so that each detail becomes readily available for consultation. Ordinarily, an encyclopedia can be consulted only through the alphabetical list of entries. In the case of the *Encyclopaedia Judaica* this would give the reader some 25,000 subjects. With the aid of the index the option is expanded tenfold to some 200,000 subjects, and the reader can at once see where he can find information on topics that have not received independent entries but have been treated under other headings. In addition he can follow a subject through all aspects of its treatment in the Encyclopaedia. For example, if he is interested in Maimonides, he will discover not only that there is a major entry on Maimonides but that there are further extensive treatments of Maimonides' thought and work in dozens of other entries—such as the entry *Mishpat Ivri* (Jewish Law), Philosophy, Medicine, Aristotle, Attributes, etc.

The index is an indispensable tool for the use of the Encyclopaedia and the editors recommend that the reader always start by turning to it. Only by consulting the Index will he grasp the full treatment of any subject. (Where a person can be referred to under various names or pseudonyms, the index will guide the reader to the relevant entry.) In planning the Encyclopaedia, the editors have endeavored to maintain an overview of the complete work and to avoid overlapping, as far as possible. Without the index, the reader would not be aware of the carefully planned structure of each subject and might conclude that certain important facets had been omitted or overlooked or that in certain cases treatment was inadequate. But by referring to the index he will immediately find out under what heading each subject is treated and where the supplementary aspects are dealt with. In order to emphasize the centrality of the role of the index, it was decided that it should constitute Volume 1 of the Encyclopaedia.

It should be noted that the captions to the illustrations have also been indexed. Thus under Chagall will be found a listing of all the reproductions of his paintings throughout the Encyclopaedia, or under Scroll of Esther complete information on all the illustrations of the Scroll. In this way, the reader has easy access to all the visual material in the Encyclopaedia.

This index far surpasses any similar index in a Jewish work and constitutes an important and pioneering guide to all fields of Jewish studies. For fuller details on the Index and its use, the reader is referred to the Introduction to the Index on page 275 of this volume.

Principles of Selection

An obvious problem in the compilation of any encyclopedia is the decision as to which entries are to be included and which excluded. Guidelines were drawn up as a result of which certain subjects were earmarked for definite inclusion while others clearly fell short. But there is always a body of "borderline" entries which potentially could fall in either category. The problem becomes particularly sensitive when dealing with biographies of contemporaries. Which scholars receive entries and which do not? Where is the line to be drawn for rabbis or businessmen or lawyers or scientists? Because of the complexity of the problems involved an extreme proposal made at the planning stage of the Encyclopaedia—which was not accepted—was to exclude living people altogether!

The Editorial Board laid down general principles but was fully aware that there was the risk of inconsistency in certain instances. Wherever the cut-off line was placed there would inevitably be problematic cases—if X, why not Y, and conversely if Y was omitted, why should X be in? The Editorial Board considered the entire entry list and paid especial attention to the "borderline" entries according to the principles of selection it had laid down.

Various methods and criteria were established. For one thing editors were circumscribed by the word allocation. For example, the editors of the section on Jews in medicine listed many hundreds of Jews who had distinguished themselves in the field. They were asked to subdivide the list into those of major importance of whose inclusion there was no doubt; those who should appear if possible; those

who could appear in the form of a "capsule" entry at the end of the main entry on medicine (see below); and those who should at least be mentioned and characterized in the main entry. In this way, the maximum of names appear in the Encyclopaedia (and by reference to the Index, information can be discovered on all of them). But at the same time, it was obvious that along the borderline, different selections would be made by different experts. In certain categories, it is impracticable to talk about objective standards and an element of subjectivity must enter the final selection. This inevitably provides a happy hunting ground for discussion and criticism, but in point of fact the editors of this and any such work have no alternative in such instances but to rely on their judgment formed after consultation with the expert editors and advisers in each field.

With contemporary scholars, the tendency was to be more generous with the older generation, whose major work had been completed, but to be more selective with younger scholars who are in the process of producing their major works and where it is therefore more difficult to reach an assessment that may not be soon outdated. In cases where younger scholars have already produced a major contribution they are of course the subject of articles, but in other instances it was decided to postpone such articles to the annual yearbook and to future editions.

In some subjects, it was possible to fix objective criteria. For example when it came to U.S. Jewish communities, it was decided to include only those numbering over 4,500 (although here too exceptions had to be made where the community had historical or other social importance). For places in Israel, it was decided that all municipalities would have their own entry as well as kibbutzim and moshavim which were in existence at the time of the establishment of the State in 1948. For those settlements founded subsequently, only those of special interest have their own entry. (A complete list of settlements, however, is to be found in this volume of the Encyclopaedia.)

In certain biographical entries a problem was to determine who was a Jew. The first principle adopted was that anyone born a Jew qualified for inclusion, even if he had subsequently converted or otherwise dissociated himself from Jewish life (where these facts are known, they are stated). The second principle was that a person with one Jewish parent would qualify for inclusion (with the relevant information stated) if he were sufficiently distinguished. A person whose Jewish origins were more remote would only be the subject of an entry in very unusual cases. However, a more generous attitude was taken in the case of Marranos, in view of the special circumstances surrounding their history.

A number of non-Jews are also the subject of entries in the Encyclopaedia. They have been included because of their relationship to Jewish life or culture (to avoid misunderstanding, the sign ° has been placed before their name at the head of the entry). These have been selected to ensure the completeness of the Encyclopaedia, for example in matters of history (e.g., Alexander the Great, Napoleon,, Balfour, Stalin), philosophy and thought (e.g., Aristotle, Avicenna, Kant), or literature (e.g., Dante, Shakespeare, Goethe). In these cases, the entry concentrates only on those elements of the subject's life and thought which are of Jewish interest, and for a biography and assessment, the interested reader should refer to a general encyclopedia.

"Capsule" Entries

To expand the scope of biographical entries, especially covering the participation of Jews in world culture, the main entries in many of these subjects are followed by a listing of the outstanding Jews in each sphere (e.g., Art, Medicine, [American] Literature). Where the person mentioned is the subject of an independent article he is merely listed and an asterisk—the regular cross-reference sign—is given. In other cases, however, a "capsule" biography is provided containing the salient details of the person in question. Each "capsule" biography is the subject of an entry in the Index.

Consistency

Notwithstanding all efforts, it has been impossible to maintain perfect consistency in the *Encyclopaedia Judaica*. For one thing, scholars who have written the entries have been allowed a certain

latitude in incorporating their own conclusions and this leads occasionally to internal contradictions. For example there are differing views about biblical chronology. It is possible that a scholar writing on a king of ancient Israel may maintain a certain year to have been that of his death; another scholar writing about his successor may be of the view that he began to reign a few years earlier or later; while the author of the general survey of the period may give still different dates. Since the entire subject is a matter of conjecture and each scholar regards his own chronology as well founded, it is impossible to compel him to use dates with which he disagrees. Wherever possible, such dates have been coordinated but the editors are aware of such discrepancies, which must be seen against the differences of opinion among the scholars.

Similarly there can be inconsistencies regarding the transliteration of places and names. The name Leib represents the accepted English version of a Yiddish name; but many with that name who lived in German-speaking countries themselves wrote it Loeb, so that both forms are to be found in the Encyclopaedia. Accepted usage is followed in most cases but there are many problems. In some instances, it is customary in English to anglicize names, such as foreign rulers: Empress Catherine—and not Yekaterina or Caterina; Frederick the Great—and not Friedrich; Victor Emmanuel—and not Vittorio Emmanuele. But usage differs in other instances: Christopher (not Cristóbal or Cristoforo) Columbus but Johann (not John) Sebastian Bach, Leo (not Lev) Tolstoy but Albrecht (not Albert) Duerer. Just as inconsistency occurs in general usage, so it occurs in specific Jewish contexts. It is common to adapt the better-known names into English and to write Salomon as Solomon or Josef as Joseph but what about Salomone and Giuseppe? Biblical names have a familiar English form that has been accepted but it would hardly be appropriate to anglicize Hebrew names in modern Israel and to refer to Moses Dayan!

Whether Slavic names should end with the form –ich, –icz, –itz, or –itch must depend on usage and not logic; and usage is sometimes confusing as, for example, when a person could have spelt his name according to German or Czech usage.

For a number of reasons (in part because of the ambiguity and interchangeability of the forms Aben and Ibn but mainly because of the sheer weight of numbers) the Encyclopaedia has generally entered persons bearing these quasi-surnames under the second name—but not in the case of accepted usage such as that of Abraham ibn Ezra who is always referred to as Ibn Ezra. Here too inconsistencies occur and again, the reader is advised to start his search for entries from the Index.

Problems have also cropped up concerning the consistency of place-names: the modern Slovakian town of Bratislava, for example, was famous in Jewish life as a center of scholarship as Pressburg, and is frequently referred to as such within a historical context. Both forms will therefore be found in the Encyclopaedia. In such instances the Index will prove an invaluable guide in coordinating the various references.

Certain concessions have led to inconsistencies with regard to Hebrew transliteration (see below). Apart from the different systems that have been employed, common English usage has been taken into consideration in some cases. According to Encyclopaedia rules, the word for commandment should be transliterated *miẓvah*—but the spelling "bar mitzvah" has in fact passed into the English language as has "kibbutz" (not *kibbuẓ*) and it is the accepted usage that has been adopted. Current Anglo-American usage refers, even in legislation, to ritually prepared food as "kosher" but in other contexts the term is transliterated according to Hebrew usage as *kasher*.

There are similar problems regarding the transliteration of terms in modern Hebrew which embody the "mobile *sheva*," which is normally not pronounced in the middle of a word in modern Hebrew. Thus the organization הִסְתַּדְּרוּת should be transliterated in accordance with the rules as *Histadderut* but it is universally known as Histadrut. The familiar "moshav ovdim" should strictly figure as *moshav ovedim*. And then there are transliterations officially adopted by various bodies—the name of the Religious Zionist movement is Mizrachi by which it appears throughout the world, and so it appears in the Encyclopaedia even though according to the rules it should appear as *Mizraḥi*.

Inconsistencies also occur with regard to italicization. Foreign words are generally italicized—but not where they have become part of the English language. But this too leads to anomalies. Yesh-

ivah by now is an English word and is not italicized; but the principal of a yeshivah is a *rosh yeshivah,* which is italicized. Ḥasidim have joyfully entered the English language but their opponents, the *Mitnaggedim,* remain italicized outsiders.

Bible

Special problems were posed in the Bible Division in view of the greatly varied and even radically opposing attitudes to the Bible and Bible scholarship. It was felt that an encyclopedia designed to reflect all aspects of knowledge relevant to Jewish culture must, in the sphere of Bible, bring to the reader all views—from the most traditional to the most critical. It was realized that the balance would be precarious and that, in view of the strong feelings held on either side, it would be difficult and probably impossible to satisfy all the readers all the time. All concerned agreed that both traditional and critical viewpoints should be fully represented. Inevitably, an individual entry may sometimes appear weighted in one direction or another, but a thorough reading of the entire Bible section will reveal the overall effort to present every aspect.

The Bible entries have been written and edited by the outstanding scholars in their field and can claim a breadth and comprehension unparalleled in any encyclopedia other than a specialized biblical one. Traditional approaches and knowledge are combined with the latest scholarship on the Ancient Middle East, its ways of life, its modes of thought, and its languages. Occasionally, an authority in dealing with a subject has stressed specific angles and overlooked other aspects which were required to present the overall picture. In all such cases, additional sections have been commissioned and edited by one of the distinguished editors of the Bible section.

The Bible entries were all edited by the appropriate departmental editors. With a few exceptions they were also seen by the divisional editor of Bible. The entire material was also gone over by the editors in chief and it is they and not the contributors or editors who bear final responsibility for the published material. No other member of the editorial staff is responsible for entries dealing with the Biblical Period.

Cross-References and Glossary

The Encyclopaedia has been planned as a unit. To avoid unnecessary duplication, cross-references are made to complementary entries and the fullest treatment of any subject will be obtained by consulting both the cross-references given in any entry together with any other references listed under the subject in the Index. However, the Encyclopaedia has avoided a plethora of text cross-references which send the reader from volume to volume (such as Ribash see Isaac ben Sheshet: Rabad see Abraham ben David, Abraham ibn Daud: Midrash Rabbah see Midrash, Genesis Rabbah, Exodus Rabbah, etc.). Such information will be found by turning to the Index Volume which gives all relevant references.

In the text, cross-references are indicated in two ways. The first is by the direct statement "See . . . . " referring to entries that have directly relevant additional information. The second is by the use of an asterisk (*). The asterisk is placed before the word under which the entry appears. Thus "Abraham *ibn Ezra" indicates that further information related to that entry is to be looked for in the article on Ibn Ezra. In occasional instances the asterisk has been used to refer the reader to an entry in the Index rather than an article in the text.

Generally speaking, asterisks indicate those further entries which, it is felt, throw additional light on the subject under discussion. For example, in the statement "Benjamin Cardozo was born in New York," there is no cross-reference to New York, both because it is unnecessary and because the entry on New York contains no supplementary information on Cardozo. But the first reference to New York in the entry on "United States" will have a cross-reference because the New York entry in many ways supplements the "United States" entry. Occasional exceptions have been made where some more obscure name or phrase is mentioned, the explanation of which would unduly complicate

the text. In most cases, only the first reference to a subject receives a cross-reference, but on occasions it is repeated for special reasons.

It is inevitable in a work of this nature to use a considerable number of Hebrew and technical terms which may not be familiar to the general reader. To explain these on every occasion would make the work far too cumbersome and where necessary the cross-reference is given. However, for the convenience of the reader a glossary has been prepared of the most frequently recurring Hebrew terms and specialized names. This glossary is printed at the front of every volume.

Transliteration

For its basic transliteration from the Hebrew, the Encyclopaedia has adopted a simplified system (see table on page 90 of this volume). It has been devised with particular regard to the usages of the English-speaking reader. However, certain exceptions have been necessary:

a) The editors of the section dealing with Hebrew and Semitic languages felt that the Encyclopaedia's simplified system could not convey all the nuances required in technical linguistic entries. All entries in this section use the transliteration adopted by the Academy of the Hebrew Language (for details see page 90). However, to avoid inconsistencies in proper names, the basic system used in the rest of the Encyclopaedia has also been retained for names in these entries.

b) The editors of the Bible section felt the need for a few modifications in the Encyclopaedia's system in order to convey certain nuances (for details see page 90). To preserve the maximum unity, these have generally been added in parentheses after the usual transliteration, although in certain cases where it makes no difference to the ordinary reader (use of ṭ in place of t), only one form has been given.

c) Other forms of transliteration will be found in some of the musical notations. This is in accordance with the system that has been developed so as best to print Hebrew transliteration together with music. Some musical examples have been photographed from a variety of printed sources and have therefore preserved other systems of transliteration.

d) As already mentioned, in a few instances, Hebrew words have become part of the English language and their spelling standardized. In such cases, the term must be regarded by now as an English word, and the spelling in Webster's New International Dictionary (Third Edition) has been followed.

For details of transliterations from other languages see tables on pages 91–92. Here, too, certain English usages have been taken into account inasmuch as certain words and names have received accepted English forms—for example Koran (rather than Qurʾān (or Saladin (rather than Salaḥ al-Dīn). In place of the umlaut in German names an "e" has been added after the accented vowel. Thus Koenigsberg, not Königsberg.

Bibliographies

The bibliographies printed at the end of each entry are integral to the treatment of the subject as a whole. On the basis of these references, the reader who wishes to pursue the subject in greater depth can turn to these basic books and articles.

A principle of selectivity has had to be adopted in view of the vast amount of material that has accumulated. It has to be recognized that the German language, in which so much of Jewish research was written, has become inaccessible to most Jewish students. On the other hand, a considerable body of scientific publication on Jewish subjects has now become available in English while the corresponding literature in Hebrew has assumed vast proportions.

A preference has been given to works in the English language provided they are of an adequate scientific standard. Moreover, where translations are available in English they have been listed in some cases in preference to a (generally German) original. However, exceptions have been made in

some cases where the English translation does not represent the entire original (e.g., in some sections of Graetz's *History of the Jews*).

Generally, only the most important and significant works are listed. Fuller bibliographies can usually be found in the works referred to and where there is a full bibliography on the subject in a work cited, this fact is mentioned.

Many problems were encountered in the course of compiling the bibliography, not all of which have found an ideal solution. For example, there is the problem of which edition to cite—the first or the latest? A book can have its first edition in England in a different year from its first U.S. edition—and even have a different name for each; an article can appear in a periodical and be reprinted as part of a book; many volumes are now being reprinted photographically and are designated as "second editions" although—where no extra material is added—this is inaccurate.

The organization of the bibliographies (basically supplied by the authors) is also not consistent. An attempt has been made to give precedence to the major works on the subject and to works in English, while generally speaking books precede articles. However, in certain cases other arrangements (e.g., chronological) have been followed. Names of articles in periodicals have not been listed for reasons of space, but the author and full details of the periodical will direct the reader to the major studies in such publications.

The standard histories—Graetz, Dubnow, Baron—have not been cited for every article but only in those cases where they provide material of special significance for the subject in hand. Similarly, as regards individual countries, the standard regional histories have been mentioned only when specially called for and the reader should remember that they must be consulted. For local conditions, statistics, etc., for the early part of the 20th century the *Jewish Encyclopedia* should be used; for the interwar period the German *Encyclopaedia Judaica* is invaluable and references to these works have been reduced to a minimum.

Most of the bibliographical checking has been done at the Jewish National and University Library, Jerusalem, whose staff has been unfailingly helpful. The unrivaled richness of its collection made possible a thorough investigation of most subjects dealt with and most works cited, but there were cases when certain works or editions were not available and the facts given by the contributor could not be verified.

To make the bibliographies less unwieldy a large number of standard works are quoted by abbreviation and a full list of these abbreviations will be found on pages 79–89. Such works can be distinguished in the bibliographies by the fact that their titles are not italicized.

Biographical Entries

The title entry for an individual is given according to the name by which he was most commonly known. Other names by which he was known or versions of the name given in the title entry follow in parentheses. All forms are listed in the index.

Wherever possible, biographical entries are given under the surname of the person if he had one. Where a combined rendering has become accepted in Europe (e.g., Abenatar) this is followed in the Encyclopaedia. In the case of Spanish and Portuguese names (e.g., Texeira de Mattos, Mendes da Costa), accepted usage is followed even though the first component of these names is the basic part.

The place of birth and death are not always given. The reason is that the information given customarily is in many cases conjectural, in others irrelevant. Places of birth are mentioned in the text when these have been found to be verifiable. Place of death is not mentioned unless there is a specific reason for giving it. Generally, it can be assumed that a subject died in the place where he is last mentioned as having resided. To keep the entries within allotted proportions, places of education have generally been omitted as have details concerning awards such as honorary degrees, visiting professorships, prizes (except for major ones such as the Nobel Prize and the Israel Prize), promotion details (e.g., for military figures only the last rank attained is usually given), etc.

Special Terminology

In a few instances, the Encyclopaedia staff had to make decisions regarding the adoption of basic terminology. One such term is "Holocaust" referring to the fate of the Jews resulting from Nazi policies, from 1933 to 1945.

Another is the use of the term Ereẓ Israel. The name Palestine was specifically created by the Romans in order to invalidate the association of the Jewish people with the country they had formerly called Judea. It was virtually unknown even when the country was under Muslim (as well as crusader) rule. The Encyclopaedia therefore terms the country by its proper name Ereẓ Israel (literally the Land of Israel) using the term "Palestine" only in certain contexts (especially with regard to the later Roman period and to the period of the British Mandate when it was the official name of the country).

Israel, on the other hand, generally implies in these pages the modern State of Israel. Since the origins of a great part of Israel institutions and life go back to the 1880s, for certain purposes the term Israel is used retrospectively to this seminal period. For example, the section of the comprehensive entry Israel (by far the largest in the Encyclopaedia) headed State of Israel covers not only the period from 1948 but also the pre-State period. According to official government usage, Israel (and not Israeli) is the adjective relating to Israel: Israeli is a citizen (or permanent resident) of the State of Israel.

It is impossible to mention all decisions regarding terminology, but use of the Index will always refer the reader to the form which has been adopted. However, to give one further example: the Encyclopaedia uses the term Jerusalem Talmud rather than Palestinian Talmud because although the latter is more accurate (the work was not written or compiled in Jerusalem) the former conveys the traditional Jewish title—*Talmud Yerushalmi.*

Place-Names

The basic guide for the form of place-names has been the *Columbia Lippincott Gazetteer of the World* (Columbia University Press, 1966) and where various alternatives are cited there, the preferred form has been adopted. Place-names occurring in the Bible are given according to *The Holy Scriptures* (according to the Masoretic text; The Jewish Publication Society of America, 1955). Other places in Israel are cited according to the Encyclopaedia's rules of transliteration. This has led to some inconsistencies in cases where ancient and modern places (not always on the same site) have identical names. Thus readers will find that some towns mentioned in the Bible will begin with Beth (e.g., Beth Shean) but others not mentioned there will begin with Bet (Bet She'arim). There will be a similar problem with "En" and "Ein." To help the reader, every place-name in Ereẓ Israel is also given in Hebrew letters.

Another problem with place-names is that in many instances, places had different names at different periods. The usage of the Encyclopaedia is that where a place is still in existence, the entry appears under its current name (in a very few cases, an exception has been made where the alternative name is so strong in Jewish tradition that any variant would look bizarre). Variants are given at the beginning of the entry on the place and all these variants are cited in their appropriate place in the index with the reference to where the article can be found. When place-names occur in the body of entries, it has often been necessary to change the usage according to the period. For example it would be absurd to talk of a person in "Leningrad" in the 19th century—he was in St. Petersburg; a book in the 18th century was published in Constantinople, not Istanbul.

A special problem was posed by East European names not to be found in the gazetteer. Many Jews were born or lived in small places which had a reputation in the Jewish world but are not large enough to figure in Western works of reference. Such places were identified in standard atlases and where necessary the Encyclopaedia's regular rules of transliteration for the appropriate language were followed.

Proper Names

Some of the problems relating to consistency in the use of proper names have already been mentioned. As noted, the tendency has been to anglicize first names where appropriate. This has been done even though in certain instances the person himself did not use the form. Thus a German Jew would have signed himself (probably in Hebrew letters) as Schlomo but—as is customary in all standard works of reference in English—these all appear as Solomon.

Every effort has been made to give the spelling of the surname as the person himself spelt it—even if this means that the more usual Berdichevski appears as Berdyczewski and Moshe Glikson appears as Glueckson, these being the forms they themselves used. However, problems remain. What about a person who never signed his name, as far as is known, in Latin characters? For example, if such a person's name was רבינוביץ, is it to be transliterated Rabinowitz, Rabbinowitz, Rabbinowicz, Rabbinovich, Rabinovitch, or any other of the known transliterations, all of which are legitimate. There is no ready-made answer. In some instances, there are precedents to follow; in others, the precedent has to be invented. We are aware that not always has consistency proved possible. Sometimes an apparent inconsistency is deliberate. A man living in a German-speaking country would have written his name Hirsch. But for a man with this name in Eastern Europe there is no reason to use a German form of transliteration; in such instances the rules of Yiddish (or familiar English) transliteration have been followed and the name appears as Hirsh.

Dates

The Hebrew year begins in the fall, three months approximately (in recent centuries) before the Gregorian year. Where the Hebrew year is known (but not the exact date) the probability is that the period in question corresponds to the last nine months rather than the first three months of the Hebrew year. So the Encyclopaedia has normally used, e.g., 1298 and not 1297/98 to correspond to the Hebrew year 5058; 1429 and not 1428/29 to correspond to 5189; and for example in dates after the invention of printing 1587 and not 1586/87 to correspond to 5347, etc. Where, however, the exact Hebrew date is known, it is possible to be more precise. Where precision is significant the form 1527/28 is used; this implies that the event took place in the Hebrew year 5388 but the period of the year cannot be determined.

Before the Gregorian reform of the calendar in 1587 the secular-Christian New Year was considered in most places to have been in March; the Gregorian reform established January 1st but this was adopted only gradually in Europe. The *Encyclopaedia Judaica* assumes, however, in most cases (in accordance with modern historical practice) the beginning of the new year in January, even before the Gregorian reform. To avoid unnecessary complications, account has not been taken of the ten- (to 12- or 13-) day discrepancy between the Gregorian and Julian calendars, which has continued in some areas until our own day. (The 1917 revolutions in Russia are mostly called the February and October Revolutions, although by Western calendars they occurred in March and November.)

Statistics

The Encyclopaedia has done its utmost to keep abreast of the rapidly changing kaleidoscope of contemporary Jewry. Population figures have been revised at the last possible moment before going to press, both in the entries and in the graphic tables, charts, and maps.

At the same time, it must be recalled that the whole area of Jewish demography is highly problematical and in most cases precise numbers cannot be determined. Only in recent years have systematic attempts been made to determine Jewish statistics. Moreover, different criteria have been adopted in different places, and results will vary with such factors as whether any sort of Jewish definition appears in an official census, whether the particular community has been subject to a scientific analysis—and how one defines a Jew! The arbitrariness involved can be gauged by comparing two excellent

sources, each regarded as the product of reliable research—the *American Jewish Year Book* and the *Jewish Year Book* published in London by the *Jewish Chronicle*. For 1969, the former gives the Jewish population of Austria as 8,200, the latter as 12,000; the former says there are 36,000 Jews in Mexico, the latter 32,000, and similar discrepancies occur regarding cities (São Paulo has 65,000 in one and 55,000 in the other).

The situation becomes complicated regarding figures in the U.S.S.R. (the above-mentioned reference works give the number of Jews in Leningrad as 165,000 and 325,000, and Moscow as 285,000 and 700,000 respectively!). The Russian census publishes figures concerning those who declare themselves to be of Jewish nationality; however the number who are registered as such in their identity papers but do not declare their "nationality" as Jewish at the census can only be guessed. Moreover, the breakdown is published only for the Soviet Republics, for a few major towns, and for provinces: figures for other towns are "guess-timates" gathered from various sources and for many of the smaller towns which were of special Jewish importance up to 1917, nothing is known of their recent Jewish history (including their fate during the Holocaust).

Every effort has been made to obtain the most up-to-date and authoritative statistics in all spheres, but in view of the difficulties—such as those described—occasional discrepancies are inevitable.

Alphabetization

Entries have been arranged (both in the body of the Encyclopaedia and in the Index) in strict alphabetical order—disregarding space and hyphens. The criterion is the order of the letters up to the first punctuation sign (comma, period, etc.). This makes for easy reference as well as facilitating the work of the computer.

For example, Ben-Gurion should be sought somewhere after Benghazi and before Benjamin; El Paso will be after Elephantine but before Elul.

The following elements are not considered in alphabetization: definite and indefinite articles; personal titles (e.g., Sir or Baron), with the exception of "Saint"; material that appears in parentheses; the ordinal number of a monarch or pope. In the event of absolutely identical title entries, the following order of precedence prevails: places, people, things. Where persons have identical names, the one who lived earlier comes first. Where the same name is used as a first and family name, entries of the first name precede those of the family name.

For example in looking for an ABRAHAM one would find the order:

ABRAHAM (the patriarch)
ABRAHAM (family name)
ABRAHAM, APOCALYPSE OF (the comma after Abraham acting as a caesura)
ABRAHAM, MAX
ABRAHAM ABELE BEN ABRAHAM SOLOMON (considered as a unit in the absence of a comma)
ABRAHAM A SANCTA CLARA
ABRAHAM BAR ḤIYYA
ABRAHAM BEN ALEXANDER (note that "bar" and "ben" are considered as spelt in full)
ABRAHAM ḤAYYIM BEN GEDALIAH
ABRAHAMITES
ABRAHAM JOSHUA HESCHEL OF APTA
ABRAHAM (ben Aaron) OF BAGHDAD (note that variants in parentheses are ignored for alphabetization purposes)
ABRAHAM OF SARAGOSSA
ABRAHAMS
ABRAHAMS, ISRAEL
ABRAHAMS, SIR LIONEL (note that titles such as Sir and Lord are ignored for alphabetization purposes)
ABRAHAMS, MOSES
ABRAHAM'S BOSOM
ABRAHAMSEN, DAVID
ABRAHAM ẒEVI BEN ELEAZAR

Family Entries

A single entry often covers various members of the same family. This has been especially the case when there are a number of members of the family who are of sufficient interest to warrant a description but where space would not allow individual entries. In such cases the various members are generally treated in chronological order within the entry. It often occurs that in such families there are several

members mentioned in the body of the entry but one or two members are of exceptional importance, warranting a separate entry. In this case they are only listed in their appropriate chronological context within the family entry, together with an asterisk by their names indicating that they are the subject of separate entries.

In certain instances, two or more members of the same family have been combined into a single entry. There are also examples of composite entries in the case, for example, of biblical persons and places where a single entry covers more than one person or place of the same name. In all such cases, each individual subject can be traced through the Index where he or it will have an individual listing. If the family name is not repeated in the article following a personal name, it is understood that the name is identical with that of the title entry.

Style

Although basing itself on standard rules of style, the Encyclopaedia has in many cases had to establish its own rules to meet its own particular requirements. Spelling was based on Webster's Third International Dictionary, except for a number of specific Jewish and Hebrew words. Italicization is used in the text for non-English words and phrases. The style rules laid down for bibliographical abbreviations are on page 79.

Familiar abbreviations of rabbinical authorities (e.g., Rif for Isaac Alfasi or Rashba for Solomon ben Adret) are not employed in the text but are used in bibliographical references in articles on rabbinical literature and Jewish law: a list of these abbreviations—which are only used in these specialized contexts—is to be found on pages 74–79. The exception here is Rashi (Rabbi Solomon Yiẓḥaki) who is so universally known by his acronym that it would be unnecessarily pedantic to insist on his full name in usual references to him. In other cases, a decision had to be made with regard to the form regularly used: thus the Encyclopaedia uses Maimonides rather than Moses ben Maimon or Maimuni and Naḥmanides rather than Moses ben Naḥman. Here again the reader should consult the Index at the outset and he will be immediately referred from every alternative form to the form used in the Encyclopaedia.

Supplementary Material

Inevitably, once a work of this nature has gone to press, additional material continues to stream in. Each day's newspaper contains information that should find a place in some entry. Every day, books or studies are published which should be listed in some bibliography. Every month new books and researches appear which require mention and in some cases even basic revision of existing material. The staff of the Encyclopaedia has kept an eagle eye open for last-minute information which has been incorporated right up to the moment of printing.

In the body of the Encyclopaedia, the following supplementary material has been incorporated:

1) Articles which for one reason or another were received too late for inclusion in their appropriate place have been printed in the special section of Supplementary Entries at the end of Volume 16. Where possible a note to that effect has been included in the appropriate place in the Encyclopaedia. However this was not always possible as the receipt of certain entries was in doubt until the last moment. All entries, without exception, can be found by turning first to the Index.

2) A number of supplementary lists, charts, diagrams, etc. have been published in this volume (starting on page 107).

3) This volume also includes various other categories of additional material including dates of death occurring after going to press, errata discovered between printing and publication, and supplementary picture credits (including all credits for Volumes 2 and 3). The reader is referred to the table of contents at the beginning of this volume for further details.

However, in the long run it is realized that there is the danger of certain entries becoming out-of-date or obsolete. The run of events and the progress of research will necessitate changes and revisions.

To answer this problem, there will be published annually (starting 1973) the ENCYCLOPAEDIA JUDAICA YEARBOOK. This will ensure that the Encyclopaedia will retain its topical usefulness and enable its users to keep apace with all developments in the Jewish world and in Jewish culture. Among other features, the yearbook will contain latest information on living people whose biographies are given in the Encyclopaedia; a summary of latest events, statistics, etc. to update all the topical entries; new entries on important subjects that emerge; surveys of research and scholarship in every sphere of Jewish studies and where this results in major changes in knowledge and perspective; new entries on subjects already dealt with in the Encyclopaedia. In this way, the Encyclopaedia and its supplements will continue to be the last word in its field.

Signatures

At the end of each entry will be found the initials of its author. Where different contributors have written sections of an entry, their initials are found at the end of the section. When two contributions have been merged into a single article a joint signature appears at the end of the entry. Entries written by internal editors are generally signed [Ed.]. The key to the initials can be found in this volume on pages 39–71.

The *Encyclopaedia Judaica* received permission to utilize entries appearing in two other encyclopedias in other languages—the German *Encyclopaedia Judaica* and the *Encyclopaedia Hebraica*. Where contributors of such entries were living, the English version was sent to them for their approval and where received, the author's initial is given. In a few cases, for one reason or another, the author was not available or not prepared to check the English version; in such cases the entries are merely signed [EJ] or [EH] to indicate that the source is to be found in these works. Where authors were no longer living and the English version required further editing or updating the author's initial was retained together with [Ed.] to indicate that certain editorial changes have been introduced into the entry. Where the editorial changes were substantial, the entry is signed [EJ/ED.] or [EH/ED.].

Production

The production of the *Encyclopaedia Judaica* has been accomplished by the publishers' own printing and binding works in Jerusalem (the only exception being the color plates which were produced by Lewin-Epstein Ltd. in Bat Yam and United Artists Ltd. in Tel Aviv). The fact that the publisher was also the printer enabled the necessary planning to produce the work in the minimum time.

Conclusion

The preparation of the *Encyclopaedia Judaica* has been a labor of devotion and dedication on the part of those responsible. It is the product of intricate work by thousands of participants, many of whom—notably the internal staff and the editors—have made very special efforts and even personal sacrifices to ensure its successful conclusion. In this, they have been motivated by an awareness of the potential historic and cultural value of this work and the significant role it can play in Jewish education and culture, in the spread of Jewish knowledge—which is such an urgent priority in the Jewish- and non-Jewish world today—and in the closer linking of Israel with Jews as well as non-Jews the world over. The editors are aware that for objective reasons, they have not always attained the desired perfection and that, as is inevitable in any work of comparable size and scope, errors have crept in. But they feel that the final product, seen in its entirety, is indeed a historical contribution to Jewish culture with which they feel privileged to have been associated.

ENCYCLOPAEDIA JUDAICA RESEARCH FOUNDATION

DIVISIONAL AND DEPARTMENTAL EDITORS*

AMERICANA

Divisional Editor:

Prof. **Lloyd P. Gartner,** New York

Assistant Divisional Editor:

Hillel Halkin, Jerusalem

BIBLE

Divisional Editor:

Prof. **Harold Louis Ginsberg,** New York

Associate Divisional Editor:

Prof. **Shalom M. Paul,** New York

Departmental Editors:

The Ancient Near East (except Egypt);
Prof. **Pinḥas Artzi,** Ramat Gan

Period of the Pentateuch, Desert, Joshua, and Judges;
Prof. **Nahum M. Sarna,** Waltham, Massachusetts

Period of the Kingdom;
Dr. **Hanoch Reviv,** Jerusalem

Period of the Second Temple;
Dr. **Bezalel Porten,** Jerusalem

Biblical Books and Literature; Bible Scholars and Research;
Prof. **Menahem Haran,** Jerusalem

Ideas and Religion;
Prof. **Shalom M. Paul,** New York

Society and Law;
Prof. **Moshe Greenberg,** Jerusalem

Realia;
Dr. **Moshe Dothan,** Jerusalem

CANADA

Departmental Editor:

Rabbi Dr. **Stuart E. Rosenberg,** Toronto

CONTEMPORARY JEWRY

Divisional Editor:

Dr. **Chaim Yahil,** Jerusalem

Departmental Editors:

Demography;
Dr. **Usiel O. Schmelz,** Jerusalem

Arab and Oriental Countries;
Dr. **Hayyim J. Cohen,** Jerusalem

East Europe;
Dr. **Binyamin Eliav,** Jerusalem

Latin America;
Dr. **Haim Avni,** Jerusalem

EREẒ ISRAEL

Departmental Editors:

Historical Geography;
Prof. **Yohanan Aharoni,** Tel Aviv
Prof. **Michael Avi-Yonah,** Jerusalem

Flora and Fauna;
Prof. **Jehuda Feliks,** Ramat Gan

MODERN EREẒ ISRAEL

Divisional Editor:

Dr. **Binyamin Eliav,** Jerusalem

Deputy Divisional Editor:

Misha Louvish, Jerusalem

Departmental Editors:

Ereẓ Israel from 1880 to 1948;
Dr. **Moshe Avidor,** Jerusalem

The State of Israel;
Edwin, Viscount **Samuel,** Jerusalem

Personalities in Modern Ereẓ Israel;
Benjamin Jaffe, Jerusalem

Places in Modern Ereẓ Israel;
Efraim Orni, Jerusalem

HEBREW AND SEMITIC LANGUAGES

Divisional Editor:

Prof. **Zeev Ben-Hayyim,** Jerusalem

Assistant Divisional Editor:

Dr. **Uzzi Ornan,** Jerusalem

HISTORY

Divisional Editors:

General topics: Central and Eastern Europe;
Prof. **Haim Hillel Ben-Sasson,** Jerusalem

* Places after the names of editors refer to their academic institutions, where appropriate. For fuller details see biographical notes on editors on pages 27–38.

Muslim Countries;
Prof. **Haïm Z'ew Hirschberg,** Ramat Gan

Western Europe and Central and East Asia;
Prof. **Cecil Roth** *(deceased)*, Jerusalem

DEPARTMENTAL EDITORS:

General articles on Jewish History;
Prof. **Haim Hillel Ben-Sasson,** Jerusalem

Anti-Semitism;
Dr. **Léon Poliakov,** Massy, France

Autonomy and Social Institutions;
Prof. **Isaac Levitats,** New York

The Church and the Jews;
Dr. **Bernhard Blumenkranz,** Paris

Economic History;
Prof. **Haim Hillel Ben-Sasson,** Jerusalem

Ḥasidism;
Dr. **Avraham Rubinstein,** Ramat Gan

Islam and Judaism;
Prof. **Haïm Z'ew Hirschberg,** Ramat Gan

The Karaites;
Dr. **Leon Nemoy,** Philadelphia

The Jewish Labor Movement;
Dr. **Moshe Mishkinsky,** Tel Aviv

The Marranos;
Prof. **Martin A. Cohen,** New York

Period 135–663 C.E.;
Prof. **Alan R. Schulman,** New York

The Samaritans;
Ayala Loewenstamm, Jerusalem

REGIONS

Arabia;
Prof. **Haïm Z'ew Hirschberg,** Ramat Gan

Austria;
Meir Lamed *(deceased)*, Kibbutz Ne'ot Mordekhai

The Balkan States;
Dr. **Simon Marcus,** Jerusalem

The Baltic States;
Dr. **Yehuda Slutsky,** Tel Aviv

Bukovina;
Dr. **Yehouda Marton,** Jerusalem

The Byzantine Empire;
Prof. **Andrew Sharf,** Ramat Gan

China;
Dr. **Rudolf Loewenthal,** Los Angeles

Czechoslovakia;
Meir Lamed *(deceased)*, Kibbutz Ne'ot Mordekhai
Dr. **Oskar K. Rabinowicz** *(deceased)*, New York

England;
Peter Elman, Jerusalem

Ereẓ Israel (640–1917);
Prof. **Haïm Z'ew Hirschberg,** Ramat Gan

Western Europe (Modern France, Switzerland, Belgium, The Netherlands, Scandinavia);
Dr. **Baruch Mevorah,** Jerusalem

Medieval France;
Dr. **Bernhard Blumenkranz,** Paris

Germany;
Prof. **Ze'ev W. Falk,** Jerusalem

Hungary;
Prof. **Alexander Scheiber,** Budapest

Hungary: Assistant Departmental Editor
Dr. **Baruch Yaron,** Jerusalem

India and Southeast Asia;
Prof. **Walter J. Fischel,** Santa Cruz, California

Italy;
Dr. **Attilio Milano** *(deceased)*, Hod Ha-Sharon, Israel

Japan;
Prof. **Hyman Kublin,** New York

Latin America (Colonial Period);
Prof. **Martin A. Cohen,** New York

The Maghreb;
David Corcos, Jerusalem

Asian Regions of the Ottoman Empire (Iraq, Syria, and Turkey);
Aryeh Shmuelevitz, Tel Aviv

Persia and Afghanistan;
Prof. **Walter J. Fischel,** Santa Cruz, California

Poland (until 1800) and Lithuania;
Prof. **Haim Hillel Ben-Sasson,** Jerusalem

Poland (from 1800);
Moshe Landau, Tel Aviv

Portugal;
Prof. **Martin A. Cohen,** New York

Rumania;
Dr. **Theodor Lavi,** Jerusalem

Russia;
Dr. **Yehuda Slutsky,** Tel Aviv

South Africa;
Gustav Saron, Johannesburg

Moslem Spain;
Prof. **Haïm Z'ew Hirschberg,** Ramat Gan

Christian Spain;
Prof. **Haim Beinart,** Jerusalem

Transylvania;
Dr. **Yehouda Marton,** Jerusalem

Yemen;
Prof. **Haïm Z'ew Hirschberg,** Ramat Gan

CONSULTING EDITOR:

Economic History;
Dr. **Nachum Gross,** Jerusalem

THE HOLOCAUST

DIVISIONAL EDITORS:

Dr. **Shaul Esh** *(deceased)*, Jerusalem

Dr. **Jozeph Michman,** Jerusalem

JEWISH LAW

DIVISIONAL EDITOR:

Prof. **Menachem Elon,** Jerusalem

DEPARTMENTAL EDITORS:

General Articles on Jewish Law; the Legal and Literary Sources of the Law; the Laws of Obligation; Public and Administrative Law; Conflict of Laws;
Prof. **Menachem Elon,** Jerusalem

Criminal Law; the Laws of Procedure and Evidence;
Justice **Haim H. Cohn,** Jerusalem

The Laws of Property; the Laws of Tort;
Prof. **Shalom Albeck,** Ramat Gan

Family Law and Inheritance;
Justice Dr. **Ben-Zion (Benno) Schereschewsky,** Jerusalem

Translator, Jewish Law;
Julius Kopelowitz, Advocate, B.A., LL.B. (Rand), Rishon le-Zion

JUDAISM

DIVISIONAL EDITOR:

Prof. **R.J. Zwi Werblowsky,** Jerusalem

DEPARTMENTAL EDITORS:

Christianity;
Dr. **Yona Malachy,** Jerusalem

Education;
Dr. **Judah Pilch,** New York

Folklore;
Dr. **Dov Noy,** Jerusalem

Judaism, Liturgy;
Rabbi Dr. **Raphael Posner,** Jerusalem

CONSULTING EDITOR:

Liturgy;
Meir Medan, Jerusalem

LITERATURE

MEDIEVAL LITERATURE

DEPARTMENTAL EDITORS:

Medieval Hebrew Poetry;
Prof. **Abraham M. Habermann,** Tel Aviv

Medieval Hebrew Prose;
Prof. **Joseph Dan,** Jerusalem

Translations and Judeo-Arabic Literature;
Prof. **Abraham S. Halkin,** Jerusalem

Christian Hebraists;
Raphael Loewe, London

MODERN HEBREW LITERATURE

DIVISIONAL EDITOR:

Prof. **Ezra Spicehandler,** Jerusalem

DEPARTMENTAL EDITOR:

Prof. **Avraham Holtz,** New York

ASSISTANT DEPARTMENTAL EDITOR:

Modern Hebrew and Yiddish Literature;
Prof. **Curt Leviant,** New Brunswick, New Jersey

RABBINICAL LITERATURE

DIVISIONAL EDITOR:

Rabbi Sir **Israel Brodie,** London

DEPUTY DIVISIONAL EDITOR:

Dr. **Yehoshua Horowitz,** Ramat Gan

ASSISTANT DIVISIONAL EDITOR:

Dr. **David Tamar,** Jerusalem

MODERN JEWISH SCHOLARSHIP

DIVISIONAL EDITOR:

Prof. **Seymour Siegel,** New York

ASSOCIATE DIVISIONAL EDITOR:

Dr. **Menahem H. Schmelzer,** New York

PHILOSOPHY, JEWISH

DIVISIONAL EDITOR:

Prof. **Arthur Hyman,** New York

SECOND TEMPLE PERIOD

DIVISIONAL EDITOR:

Prof. **Abraham Schalit,** Jerusalem

DEPARTMENTAL EDITORS:

Apocrypha and Pseudepigrapha;
Dr. **Michael E. Stone,** Jerusalem

Dead Sea Scrolls;
Prof. **Frederick F. Bruce,** Manchester

Hellenistic Literature;
Prof. **Louis H. Feldman,** New York

TALMUD

Divisional Editor:

Prof. **Yitzhak Dov Gilat,** Ramat Gan

Departmental Editor:

Midrash and Aggadah;
Dr. **Joseph Heinemann,** Jerusalem

ZIONISM

Divisional Editor:

Getzel Kressel, Ḥolon

THE PARTICIPATION OF JEWS IN WORLD CULTURE

Divisional Editor:

Israel Shamah, London

ART

Divisional Editor:

Dr. **Alfred Werner,** New York

Departmental Editors:

Illuminated Manuscripts;
Dr. **Bezalel Narkiss,** Jerusalem

Israel Art;
Yona Fischer, Jerusalem

Numismatics;
Arie Kindler, Tel Aviv

LITERATURE

Departmental Editors:

Balkan Literature;
Prof. **Zdenko Löwenthal,** Belgrade

Canadian Literature;
Prof. **Miriam D. Waddington,** Toronto

Czechoslovak Literature;
Dr. **Avigdor Dagan,** Jerusalem

Dutch Literature;
Gerda Alster-Thau, Ramat Gan

English Literature;
Prof. **Harold Fisch,** Ramat Gan

French Literature;
Dr. **Denise Goitein,** Tel Aviv

German Literature;
Prof. **Sol Liptzin,** Jerusalem

Greek Literature;
Prof. **Rachel Dalven,** New York

Hungarian Literature;
Dr. **Baruch Yaron,** Jerusalem

Italian Literature;
Dr. **Joseph B. Sermoneta,** Jerusalem

Ladino Literature and Jewish Dialects;
Prof. **Moshe Lazar,** Jerusalem

Middle Eastern Literature;
Dr. **Hayyim J. Cohen,** Jerusalem

Polish Literature;
Stanislaw Wygodzki, Givatayim, Israel

Rumanian Literature;
Abraham Feller, Tel Aviv

Russian Literature;
Prof. **Maurice Friedberg,** Bloomington, Indiana

Scandinavian Literature;
Dr. **Leni Yahil,** Jerusalem

Spanish and Portuguese Literature;
Prof. **Kenneth R. Scholberg,** East Lansing, Michigan

United States Literature;
Prof. **Milton Hindus,** Waltham, Massachusetts

Consulting Editors:

Polish Literature;
Prof. **Moshe Altbauer,** Jerusalem

Rumanian Literature;
Dora Litani-Littman, Jerusalem

MEDICINE

Departmental Editor:

Prof. **Suessmann Muntner,** Jerusalem

Consulting Editor:

Dr. **Shabbetai Ginton,** Jerusalem

MUSIC

Divisional Editors:

Dr. **Israel Adler,** Jerusalem

Dr. **Bathja Bayer,** Jerusalem

Departmental Editor:

Music Illustrations;
Avigdor Herzog, Jerusalem

THE SCIENCES

Consulting Editor:

Dr. **Harry Zvi Tabor,** Jerusalem

DEPARTMENTAL EDITORS:

Aeronautics, Astronautics, Aviation, Engineering, Invention;
Dr. **Samuel A. Miller** *(deceased)*, London

Astronomy, Chemistry, Mathematics, Physics, the History and Philosophy of Science;
Maurice Goldsmith, London

Biology, Botany, Zoology;
Prof. **Mordecai L. Gabriel,** New York

Geology;
Prof. **Leo Picard,** Jerusalem

Meteorology;
Prof. **Dov Ashbel,** Jerusalem

OTHER DISCIPLINES

Anthropology;
Prof. **Ephraim Fischoff,** Eau Claire, Wisconsin

Archaeology;
Dr. **Penuel P. Kahane,** Jerusalem

Bridge and Chess;
Gerald Abrahams, Liverpool

Criminology;
Dr. **Zvi Hermon,** Tel Aviv

Dance;
Dr. **Selma J. Cohen,** New York

Economics;
Dr. **Joachim O. Ronall,** New York

Education;
Prof. **William W. Brickman,** Philadelphia

Geography;
Prof. **Moshe Brawer,** Tel Aviv

Historiography;
Prof. **Oscar I. Janowsky,** New York

Journalism;
Kalman Seigel, New York

Law and Politics;
Peter Elman, Jerusalem

Law and Socialism in the United States;
Prof. **Milton R. Konvitz,** Ithaca, New York

Linguistics;
Prof. **Herbert H. Paper,** Ann Arbor, Michigan

Military Service;
Lt. Col. (Res.) **Mordechai M. Kaplan,** Tel Aviv

Jewish Newspapers and Periodicals;
Josef Fraenkel, London

Philosophy;
Prof. **Richard H. Popkin,** San Diego, California

Photography;
Peter Pollack, New York

Psychiatry;
Dr. **Louis Miller,** Jerusalem

Psychology;
Prof. **Helmut Adler,** New York

Public Relations;
Bernard Postal, New York

Publishing and Printing;
John M. Shaftesley, London

Social Welfare;
Dr. **Joseph Neipris,** Jerusalem

Socialism and the Labor Movement;
Dr. **S. Levenberg,** London

Sociology;
Prof. **Werner J. Cahnman,** Newark, New Jersey

Sports;
Jesse Silver, Surfside, Florida

Theater and Films;
Stewart Kampel, New York
Stephen Klaidman, Washington D.C.

STAFF

MANAGEMENT

ADMINISTRATIVE MANAGER:

Rachel Sabbath

PRODUCTION PLANNING:

Moshe Shalvi, B.A.

ASSISTANT:

Walter Zanger, M.A.

EDITORIAL STAFF

ASSISTANT EDITORS:

Rabbi Morton Mayer Berman, M.H.L.
Rabbi Alexander Carlebach, D.en D.

STAFF EDITORS:

Emanuel Beeri, M.A.
Joan Comay
Arthur Cygielman
Rabbi Michael J. Graetz, M.H.L.
Prof. Judah Rosenthal, Ph.D.
Moshe Rosetti
Rabbi Aaron Rothkoff, D.H.L.
Alexander Shapiro, Ph.D.
Godfrey Edmond Silverman, M.A.
Michael Simon, Ph.D.
Lewis Sowden, M.A.

RESEARCH EDITOR (History and Illustrations):

B. Mordecai Ansbacher, M.A.

REVISING EDITOR:

Derek Orlans

WRITERS:

Laurentino José Afonso, B.D.; Essa Cindorf, B.A.; Stuart Cohen M.A.; Jonathan Cowan, LL.M.; Abraham David, M.A.; David Goldberg, B.A.; Edward L. Greenstein, B.A., B.H.L.; Yuval Kamrat; Joseph Kaplan, M.A.; Sinai Leichter M.A.; Avital Levy B.A.; Mervyn Lewis, M.A.; Aaron Lichtenstein, Ph.D.; Esther (Zweig) Liebes, B.A.; David Maisel, M.A.; Rabbi Sefton D. Temkin, Ph.D.; Nechama Unterman, M.A.; Henry Wasserman, B.A.; Adela Wolfe, M.A.; Rabbi Meir Ydit, Ph.D.; Moshe Zeidner, B.A.

STYLISTS:

Yehuda Ben-Dror (James Marshall), B.A.; Ruth Connell Robertson, LL.B.; Ina Friedman, M.A.; Reva Garmise, B.A.; Yvonne Glikson, B.A.; Avie Goldberg, B.A.; Manya Keller; Judith Krausz, B.A.; Sandra Litt Hai, B.A.; Penina Mellick; Moira Paterson, B.A., Dip. Ed.; Jack Rosenthal, M.A.; Judith Shalowitz, M.A.; Alice Shalvi, Ph.D.; Claire Sotnick, B.A.

TRANSLATORS:

Josephine Bacon; Rabbi Chaim Brovender, Ph.D.; Rivkah Duker, M.A.; Priscilla Fishman; Rabbi David Goldstein, Ph.D.; Rabbi Barnet David Klien, M.A.; Rabbi Israel Hananiah Levine, Ph.D.; Yael Lotan-Hairston; Anita Matza, M.A.; Fern Seckback, B.A.; Rabbi Kalman Szmulewicz; Leontine Williams

BIBLIOGRAPHERS AND CHECKERS:

Shelomo Shunami, Chief Bibliographer (1967–69)
Dina Bachrach, B.A.; Martha Baraz, M.A.; Ruth Berger; Katherine Bloom, B.A.; Rabbi Judah Brumer; Claire Dienstag, M.A.; Daniel Efron, M.A.; Michael J. Frenkel, M.A., Dip. Lib.; Gideon Fuks, B.A.; Daniel Furman; Henri Guttel, B.A.; Abraham Herman; Eva Herman; Giza Kamrat; Eva Kondor; Simcha Kruger, B.S.; Benjamin Lubelski, B.A., Dip.Lib.; Samuel S. Matza, Mag. Jur., M.A.; Mirjam Mundsztuk; David M.L. Olivestone, B.A.; Miriam Prager; Benjamin Richler; Betty-Lou Rosen, M.A.; Janet (Zander) Shvili; Rabbi Andrew Silberfeld, Ph.D.; Rita Sirota, B.A.; Sophie Winston, M.L.S.; Michael Ya'akobi, Dr. jur., Dipl. sc.pol.

TRANSLITERATORS:

Hanna Avituv, B.A.; Amikam Cohen, B.A.; Uri Davis, B.A.; Leah (Rosen) Teichthal, B.A.

INDEX

EDITOR OF THE INDEX VOLUME:

Rabbi Raphael Posner, D.H.L.

DEPUTY EDITORS:

Rabbi Hayyim Schneid, M.S.; Alan Unterman, Ph.D.

EDITORS:

Peretz M. Hein; Uri Kaploun, B.A., B.Ed.; Daisy Ticho, B.A.; Naphtali Winter, B.A.; Hillel Wiseberg

INDEXERS:

Ilana (Shapira) Glickman, M.A.; Pauline (Donbrow) Moldovan, B.A., Dip. Lib.; Bernard Nissenholz, B.A.; Judith Redlich, M.A.; Bracha Rivlin, B.A.

ILLUSTRATIONS

ILLUSTRATIONS EDITOR:

Moshe Shalvi, B.A.

ILLUSTRATIONS RESEARCHERS:

Ya'ara Eisenberg, B.A.; Rabbi Shmuel Gorr, B.A.; Leorah Kroyanker, B.A.; Susan Marx Leibowitz, B.F.A.; Joan (Maisels) Maman, B.A.; Genya (Markon) Yarkoni, B.A.

Graphic Researchers:

Zvia Levy, B.A.; Jacqueline Davis, B.A.; Rina Fink, B.A.; Judith Gottschalk, B.A.; Chanah Safrai, B.A.

Graphic Design:

Haim Ron; Odeda Ben Yehuda Saguy

Graphic Artists:

Ana Cleja; Avigail Cohen, M.S.

Secretarial and Technical Staff:

Devorah Eisenman, B.A., Section Coordinator; Mia Demant-Bargiora; Lydia Ebrahimoff; Aviva Hess; Gloria Hillel; Arlene Jacobs; Gene A. Lowenthal, J.D.

ADMINISTRATION

Supervisors:

Jacob Auerbach; Hanna (Chaikin) Ben David; Georgette Corcos; Murray Crawcour; Dvora Erel; Stanley Feldman; Esther Finkelstein; Yishai Geva, B.A.; Margit Halevy; Henriette Orni; Shoshanah Shalev; Tova Wilk

Supervisor (New York Office):

Marilyn Swist

Archivist:

Yehuda Blumenfeld

Secretarial and Technical Staff:

Dorothy Aronson; Israela Abramovitz; Vera Arbel; Lorraine Astar, B.A.; Amy Byer, B.A.; Tamara Carlin; Linda Cohen; Nechamah Cohn; Meira Davidovitz; Doris Dwarka; Rachel Efrati, B.A.; Ilana (Ben-Dror) Granot; Gideon Hazor; Edna Kollet; Ursula Kroner; Belle Lerman; Rivka Marcus; Deborah Oleska; Naomi Ron; Sara Shapiro; Ella Slivkin; Adele Zion

PRODUCTION

Plant Manager:

Meir Doron

Production Coordinator:

Nissan Balaban

Typesetting and Production Manager:

Lotte Schweig

Photon and Technical Manager:

Haim Jacob Frumkin

SUPERVISORS:

Typesetting (LCC):
Allan Gewirtz

Proofreading:
Brian Streett

Page Make-up:
Yaakov Zoref

Photography:
Lily Marmelstein

Platemaking:
Avinoam Gat

Printing:
Paul Morgan, F.T.C. (Printing)

Binding:
Käte Wiener, Chanoch Ehrentreu

Computer typesetting program created and supervised by NATAM, Systems Analysis and Operational Research Ltd., Jerusalem

Paper and Binding Materials Consultant:
Frank Grunfeld, London

EDITORS OF THE ENCYCLOPAEDIA

ABRAHAMS, GERALD, born Liverpool, 1907. He was chess champion of North England three times and invented the Abrahams Defense strategy. His books include *Teach Yourself Chess* (1948), *Technique in Chess* (1961), and *The Jewish Mind* (1961).

Departmental editor: JEWS IN BRIDGE AND CHESS

ABRAHAMS, ISRAEL, born Vilna, 1903. He was rabbi in England and from 1937 in South Africa, where he became Chief Rabbi of the Hebrew Congregations of Cape Province. From 1968, he lived in Jerusalem. He was the author of books of Jewish studies and sermons.

Consulting editor

ADLER, HELMUT E., born Nuremberg, 1920. He emigrated to the U.S. in 1940 and taught at Columbia University and at Yeshiva University, where he became Professor of Psychology in 1964. Adler wrote *Bird Life* (1969) and *Development and Evolution of Behavior* (1970), and was co-author of *Bird Behavior* (1962).

Departmental editor: JEWS IN PSYCHOLOGY

ADLER, ISRAEL, born Berlin, 1925. He was director of the Hebraica–Judaica Department at the Bibliothèque Nationale, Paris. In Israel he headed the Music Department of the Jewish National and University Library, Jerusalem from 1963 and was appointed director of the Center for Research in Jewish Music in 1971. His publications include *Les Incunables hebraïques de la bibliothèque nationale* (1962) and *La Pratique musicale savante dans quelques communautés juives en Europe au XVIIe et XVIIe siècles* (1966).

Joint Divisional editor: MUSIC

AHARONI, YOHANAN, born Germany, 1919. He settled in Ereẓ Israel in 1933, taught at the Hebrew University of Jerusalem, and in 1968 became chairman of the Department of Ancient Near Eastern Studies and director of the Archaeology Institute at Tel Aviv University. His publications include *The Land of the Bible* (1967).

Joint Departmental editor:
HISTORICAL GEOGRAPHY OF EREẒ ISRAEL

ALBECK, SHALOM, born Berlin, 1931. He settled in Ereẓ Israel in 1935. From 1960 until 1963 when he became Professor of Talmud and Law at Bar Ilan University, Albeck taught at the Jewish Theological Seminary of America. He published a book on the law of torts in the Talmud (1965) and papers on the development of the talmudic laws of property.

Departmental editor:
THE LAWS OF PROPERTY; THE LAWS OF TORT

ALSTER-THAU, GERDA, born Vienna, 1930. In 1938 she was taken to Holland and from 1961 she was Lecturer in modern Hebrew Literature at the universities of Amsterdam, Leiden and Utrecht. She settled in Israel in 1964 and from 1965 was Lecturer in Hebrew and World Literature at Bar Ilan University. She wrote on language and literature in modern Israel.

Departmental editor: DUTCH LITERATURE

ALTBAUER, MOSHÉ, born Przemyśl, Poland, 1904. He was Lecturer in Ukrainian at the School of Political Science of the Research Institute for Eastern Europe, Vilna, before emigrating to Ereẓ Israel in 1935. In Israel he founded the Historical Museum of Tel Aviv, which he directed from 1957–66, and joined the teaching staff of the Hebrew University of Jerusalem, becoming Associate Professor of Slavic Linguistics and Russian Studies in 1969. He contributed to professional journals.

Consulting editor: POLISH LITERATURE

ARTZI, PINḤAS, born Budapest, 1923. He was ordained rabbi in 1949, and in 1950 settled in Israel, where he became Lecturer in Akkadian at Tel Aviv University and Associate Professor of History and Ancient Semitic Languages at Bar Ilan University. He was editor of *Beth Miqra* (translations from the Sumerian and Akkadian).

Departmental editor:
THE ANCIENT NEAR EAST (EXCEPT EGYPT)

ASHBEL, DOV, born Jerusalem, 1895. He established a network of rainfall-measuring stations throughout Ereẓ Israel, and compiled a rain map of the country (1928) and of the Near East (1940). He later investigated the effects of solar radiation. In 1954 he became Associate Professor of Meteorology and Climatology at the Hebrew University of Jerusalem.

Departmental editor: JEWS IN METEOROLOGY

AVIDOR, MOSHE, born Kiev, 1906. He was taken to Ereẓ Israel in 1912 and was director-general of the Ministry of Education and Culture from 1954 to 1960, when he became director-general of the Jewish Agency. Subsequently he was director-general of the Israel Academy of Sciences and Humanities, and Israel Ambassador to UNESCO. Avidor wrote *Self-Government of the Jews in Palestine* (1934) and *Education in Israel* (1958).

Departmental editor:
EREẒ ISRAEL FROM 1880 TO 1948

AVI-YONAH, MICHAEL, born Lemberg, Austria, 1904. He settled in Ereẓ Israel in 1921 and worked with the Palestine Department of Antiquities. He taught at the Hebrew University of Jerusalem and became Professor of Archaeology and of the History of Art in 1963. He wrote about Jewish history, historical geography, art, and archaeology, particularly in the classical period.

Joint Departmental editor:
HISTORICAL GEOGRAPHY OF EREẒ ISRAEL

AVNI, HAIM, born Vienna, 1930. He was taken to Ereẓ Israel in 1933 and became assistant director of the Institute for Youth Leaders from Abroad. In 1970 he was appointed Lecturer in Contemporary Jewry at the Hebrew University of Jerusalem, specializing in Latin American Jewry.

Departmental editor:
CONTEMPORARY JEWRY—JEWS IN LATIN AMERICA

BARON, SALO WITTMAYER, born Tarnow, Galicia, 1895. In 1926 he emigrated to the U.S. where he was Professor of History at Columbia University from 1930 and director of the Center of Israel and Jewish Studies there from 1950 to 1968. Among his works are *A Social and Religious History of the Jews* (1937: 2nd ed. 1952ff.) and *The Jewish Community* (1942).

Consulting editor

BAYER, BATHJA, born Bingen, Germany, 1928. In 1936 she went to Ereẓ Israel, where she became head of the Music Department of the Jewish National and University Library, Jerusalem in 1969. Her publications include *The Material Relics of Music in Ancient Palestine* (1963).

Joint Divisional editor: MUSIC

BEINART, HAIM, born Pskov, Russia, 1917. In 1937 he settled in Ereẓ Israel, where he became Professor of Jewish History at the Hebrew University of Jerusalem in 1971. He was honorary secretary of the World Union of Jewish Studies from 1969. He published *Anusim be-Din ha-Inkviziẓyah* (1965) and prepared the 4-volume *Corpus Actorum Inquisitionis Civitatis Regiae.*

Departmental editor:
HISTORY OF THE JEWS IN THE KINGDOMS OF CHRISTIAN SPAIN

BEN-HAYYIM, ZEEV, born Mościska, Galicia, 1907. In 1931 he settled in Ereẓ Israel, where he became vice-president of the Academy of the Hebrew Language and was appointed Professor of Hebrew Language at the Hebrew University of Jerusalem in 1955. An authority on Samaritan Hebrew, he published four volumes of his *Ivrit va-Aramit Nussaḥ Shomeron,* and other works on the Hebrew language.

Divisional editor:
HEBREW AND SEMITIC LANGUAGES

BEN-SASSON, HAIM HILLEL, born Volozhin, Russia, 1914. In 1934 he settled in Ereẓ Israel, where he was Professor of Jewish History at the Hebrew University of Jerusalem. He wrote and edited many works on Jewish history.

Divisional editor:
GENERAL TOPICS (HISTORY): JEWISH HISTORY IN CENTRAL AND EASTERN EUROPE
Departmental editor:
GENERAL ARTICLES ON JEWISH HISTORY; JEWISH ECONOMIC HISTORY; HISTORY OF THE JEWS IN POLAND AND LITHUANIA

BLUMENKRANZ, BERNHARD, born Vienna, 1913. He was Maître de Recherches at the Centre National de la Recherche Scientifique in Paris, president of the French Commission of Jewish Archives, and director of the journal *Archives Juives.* His publications include *Juifs et Chrétiens dans le monde occidental* (1960), *Bibliographie des Juifs en France* (1961), and *Le Juif médiéval au miroir de l'art chrétien* (1966).

Departmental editor:
THE CHURCH AND THE JEWS; HISTORY OF THE JEWS IN MEDIEVAL FRANCE

BRAWER, MOSHE, born Vienna, 1919; in Ereẓ Israel from 1920. In 1966 he was appointed head of the Geography Department at Tel Aviv University. Brawer produced maps and historical and geographical atlases, including an atlas of the Middle East.

Departmental editor: JEWS IN GEOGRAPHY

BRICKMAN, WILLIAM W., born New York, 1913. He was Professor of Education at New York University and from 1962 Professor of Educational History and Comparative Education at the University of Pennsylvania. He wrote *Guide to Research in Educational History* (1949) and *The Educational System in the U.S.* (1969).

Departmental editor: JEWS IN EDUCATION

BRODIE, RABBI SIR ISRAEL, born Newcastle-upon-Tyne, 1895. From 1923 to 1937 he was senior minister in Melbourne, Australia. He served as senior chaplain in World War II, and from 1948 to 1965 was Chief Rabbi of the British Commonwealth. Brodie published an edition of the *Eẓ Ḥayyim* of Rabbi Jacob ben Judah Ḥazzan of London.

Divisional editor: RABBINICAL LITERATURE

BRUCE, FREDERICK FYVIE, born Scotland, 1910. From 1949 he was Professor of Biblical Criticism and Exegesis at the University of Manchester. His publications include many studies of the New Testament and *The Hittites and the Old Testament (1948); The Teacher of Righteousness and the Qumran Texts* (1957); and *Israel and the Nations* (1963).

Departmental editor: THE DEAD SEA SCROLLS

CAHNMAN, WERNER J., born Munich, 1902. In 1939 he emigrated to the U.S., where he taught at various colleges and became Professor of Sociology at Rutgers University in 1965. He was author of *Der oekonomische Pessimismus und das Ricardosche System* (1929) and co-author of *Sociology and History* (1964) and *How Cities Grew* (1965).

Departmental editor: JEWS IN SOCIOLOGY

COHEN, HAYYIM J., born Amarah, Iraq, 1930. In 1944 he settled in Ereẓ Israel, where he worked in the research department of the Ministry for Foreign Affairs in 1957, and became Lecturer in Contemporary Jewry at the Hebrew University of Jerusalem in 1964. His publications include studies in Islamic history and on Jewish and political life in Iraq.

Departmental editor:
CONTEMPORARY JEWRY—JEWS IN ARAB AND ORIENTAL COUNTRIES; ORIENTAL LITERATURE

COHEN, MARTIN A., born Philadelphia, 1928. He was Professor of Jewish History at the New York School of the Hebrew Union College—Jewish Institute of Religion. He also served as rabbi in various communities. Cohen edited and translated Samuel Usque's *Consolation for the Tribulations of Israel* (1965).

Departmental editor:
THE MARRANOS; HISTORY OF THE JEWS IN PORTUGAL

COHEN, SELMA JEANNE, born Chicago, 1920. She taught history of the dance at the High School of Performing Arts, New York, and at the Connecticut College of Dance, and in 1965 was appointed to the advisory Dance Panel of the National Council on the Arts. She wrote *The Modern Dance—Seven Statements of Belief* (1966) and was co-founder and editor of *Dance Perspectives* magazine.

Departmental editor: DANCE

COHN, HAIM H., born Luebeck, Germany, 1911. In 1930 he settled in Ereẓ Israel, where he was Attorney General from 1950 until 1960 (except for a period as Minister of Justice in 1952–53) and Supreme Court Justice from 1960. He wrote *Foreign Laws of Marriage and Divorce* (1937), *Freedom and Freedom of Belief* (1967), and *The Trial of Jesus* (1968).

Departmental editor:
CRIMINAL LAW; THE LAWS OF PROCEDURE AND EVIDENCE

CORCOS, DAVID, born Mogador, Morocco, 1917. He settled in Israel in 1959 and contributed articles to historical journals on the history of Moroccan Jewry.

Departmental editor:
HISTORY OF THE JEWS IN THE MAGHREB

DAGAN, AVIGDOR, born Czechoslovakia, 1912. In 1949 he settled in Israel, where he joined the Foreign Office and served as ambassador to Poland, Yugoslavia and, from 1967, to Norway. Under his original name Viktor Fischl, he published poetry and a novel in Czech.

Departmental editor: CZECHOSLOVAK LITERATURE

DALVEN, RACHEL, born Preveza, Greece, 1904. In 1909 she was taken to the U.S., where she became Professor and chairman of the English Department of Ladycliff College, Highland Falls, New York. Among her publications are *Poems* (1944), dealing with the Greek Hebrew poet Joseph Eliyia, *Modern Greek Poetry* (1949), *The Complete Works of Cavafy* (1961), and *Anna Comnena* (1971).

Departmental editor: GREEK LITERATURE

DAN, JOSEPH, born Bratislava, 1935. In 1938 he was taken to Ereẓ Israel, where he became Associate Professor of Hebrew Literature at the Hebrew University of Jerusalem in 1971. He wrote extensively on medieval Hebrew literature, the *Ḥasidei Ashkenaz*, and Kabbalah.

Departmental editor: MEDIEVAL HEBREW PROSE

DAVIS, MOSHE, born Brooklyn, 1916. He was dean and provost of the Teachers' Institute of the Jewish Theological Seminary of America, New York, and from 1959 directed the Institute for Contemporary Jewry at the Hebrew University of Jerusalem. His publications include *Jewish Religious Life and Institutions in America* (1949) and *The Emergence of Conservative Judaism* (1963).

Consulting editor

DOTHAN, MOSHE, born Cracow, 1919. He settled in Ereẓ Israel in 1938, where in 1964 he became director of excavations and surveys at the government Department of Antiquities. He was also deputy director of the Department. Dothan published archaeological papers and reports on his excavations, notably at Ashdod.

Departmental editor: BIBLE REALIA

ELIAV, BINYAMIN, born Riga, 1909. He settled in Ereẓ Israel in 1925. After serving as general secretary of world Betar in Paris, he resettled in Ereẓ Israel (1935) and engaged through journalism and political activities in the struggle for Jewish independence. From 1944 to 1948 he led the Tenu'at ha-Am party. In 1953 he joined the Israel foreign service, was attached to the embassy in Buenos Aires (1954–55), served as consul general in New York (1960–61) and as political adviser. In 1966–67 he headed Israel's information services.

Associate editor
Divisional editor: MODERN EREẒ ISRAEL
Departmental editor:
CONTEMPORARY JEWRY—JEWS IN EAST EUROPE

ELMAN, PETER, born London, 1913. From 1946 he was in private practice as a barrister and in 1965 settled in Israel, where he became senior assistant to the Attorney General. He wrote *Partners and the Law* (1949) and edited *Introduction to Jewish Law* (1960).

Departmental editor:
HISTORY OF THE JEWS IN ENGLAND; JEWS IN LAW; JEWS IN POLITICS

ELON, MENACHEM, born Duesseldorf, 1923. In 1935 he settled in Ereẓ Israel, where he was ordained rabbi and practiced as a lawyer. He became adviser on Jewish law to the Ministry of Justice in 1959 and in 1966 was appointed Associate Professor of Jewish Law at the Hebrew University of Jerusalem, where he was also director of the Institute for Research in Jewish Law.

Divisional editor: JEWISH LAW
Departmental editor:
GENERAL ARTICLES ON JEWISH LAW; THE LEGAL AND LITERARY SOURCES OF LAW; THE LAWS OF OBLIGATION; PUBLIC AND ADMINISTRATIVE LAW; CONFLICT OF LAWS

ESH, SHAUL, born Hamburg, 1921, died 1968. In 1938 he settled in Ereẓ Israel, where he was editor of the *Yad Vashem* publications from 1956 to 1960, and became Senior Lecturer in Contemporary Jewry at the Hebrew University of Jerusalem. His studies on the Holocaust appeared in the *Yad Vashem Studies* (of which he edited the first four volumes) and elsewhere.

Joint Divisional editor: THE HOLOCAUST

FALK, ZE'EV WILHELM, born Breslau, 1923. He settled in Ereẓ Israel in 1939 and became legal adviser to the Finance and Interior Ministries, and in 1970 Associate Professor of Law at the Hebrew University of Jerusalem. His publications include *Halakhah and Reality in the State of Israel, Hebrew Law in Biblical Times,* and *Jewish Matrimonial Law in the Middle Ages.*

Departmental editor:
HISTORY OF THE JEWS IN GERMANY

FELDMAN, LOUIS HARRY, born Hartford, Connecticut, 1926. In 1966 he became Professor of Classics at Yeshiva University, New York. Feldman translated and edited books 18 to 20 of Josephus' *Jewish Antiquities* (Loeb Classical Library Edition, vol. 9, 1965) and published *Scholarship on Philo and Josephus 1937–1962* (1963), a critical bibliography.

Departmental editor: HELLENISTIC LITERATURE

FELIKS, JEHUDA, born Kosów-Huculski, Poland, 1922. He settled in Ereẓ Israel in 1938 and became a member of Kibbutz Sedeh Eliyahu. From 1960 he taught at Bar Ilan University, where he became Professor of Biblical and Talmudic Botany. Among his publications are *Olam ha-*

Ẓome'aḥ ha-Mikra'i (1957, 1968), *Animal World of the Bible* (1962), *Ẓimḥiyyat ha-Mishnah* (1967).

Departmental editor: Flora and Fauna

FELLER, ABRAHAM, born Botosani, Rumania, 1893. In 1950 he settled in Israel, where he became manager of *Ha-Boker* and the Rumanian weekly *Mintuirea.* Feller translated into Rumanian and published a compendium of Dubnow's *History of the Jews* (1936).

Departmental editor: Rumanian Literature

FISCH, HAROLD (HAREL), born Birmingham, England, 1923. After teaching at Leeds University he settled in Israel in 1957 and became Professor and head of the English Department at Bar Ilan University of which he was Rector (1968–71). He wrote *The Dual Image* (1959) and *Jerusalem and Albion* (1964).

Departmental editor: English Literature

FISCHEL, WALTER JOSEPH, born Frankfort, 1902. He taught at the Hebrew University of Jerusalem (1926–45) and at Berkeley (1945–70). In 1970 he became Professor of Judaic Studies and History at the University of California, Santa Cruz. Among his publications are *Jews in the Economic and Political Life of Ancient Islam* (1937) and *The Jews in India* (Heb. 1960).

Departmental editor:
History of the Jews in Persia, Afghanistan, Central Asia, and India

FISCHER, YONA, born Tel Aviv, 1932. He was art critic of the newspapers *Haaretz* and *La-Merḥav,* and curator of contemporary art at the Israel Museum, Jerusalem. Fischer edited *Qav,* a journal of modern art and contributed the chapter on painting in *Art in Israel* (1963) and the chapter on Israel art in *Art of Our Time* (1967).

Departmental editor: Israel Art

FISCHOFF, EPHRAIM, born New York, 1904. He taught at various universities and was Professor of Sociology at the University of Wisconsin. He was also ordained rabbi. His main fields of study were social theory and the sociological aspects of religion, of welfare and of medicine. He edited and translated Max Weber's *Sociology of Religion* (1962).

Departmental editor: Jews in Anthropology

FRAENKEL, JOSEF, born Ustrzyki Dolne, Poland, 1903. He emigrated to Britain in 1939. Fraenkel became director of the Press Department of the World Jewish Congress. Among his publications are several works on Herzl, *Louis D. Brandeis* (1959) and *Jewish Libraries of the World* (1959).

Departmental editor:
Jewish Newspapers and Periodicals

FRIEDBERG, MAURICE, born Rzeszow, Poland, 1929. In 1966 he joined the faculty of Indiana University where he was Professor of Slavic Languages and Literatures and director of the Russian and East European Institute. His publications include: *Russian Classics in Soviet Jackets* (1962), *The Party and The Poet in the USSR* (1963), and *The Jew in Post-Stalin Soviet Literature* (1970).

Departmental editor: Russian Literature

GABRIEL, MORDECAI L., born New York, 1918. He taught zoology at Columbia University and in 1955 was appointed Associate Professor of Biology at Brooklyn College. He was co-author of *Great Experiments in Biology* (1955) and author of *Laboratory Student in Developmental Anatomy* (1963).

Departmental editor:
Jews in Biology; Botany; Zoology

GARTNER, LLOYD P., born Brooklyn, 1927. He was Associate Professor of History at the City College, New York and at the graduate faculty of the City University of New York. He was also a research associate of the American Jewish History Center of the Jewish Theological Seminary of America where he taught from 1958 to 1967. He wrote *The Jewish Immigrant in England 1870–1914* (1960) and *Jewish Education in the United States; A Documentary History* (1969) and was co-author of *History of the Jews of Milwaukee* (1963) and *History of the Jews of Los Angeles* (1970).

Divisional editor: Americana

GILAT, YITZHAK DOV, born Lithuania, 1919. In 1935 he settled in Ereẓ Israel, where he became head of the Talmud Department of Bar Ilan University in 1961 and Associate Professor there in 1969. He was also a Senior Lecturer at Tel Aviv University. He wrote *The Teachings of Rabbi Eliezer Ben Hyrkanos and Their Position in the History of Halakhah* (Heb. 1968).

Divisional editor: Talmud

GINSBERG, HAROLD LOUIS, born Montreal, 1903. In 1936 he settled in the U.S., and from 1941 was Professor of Bible at the Jewish Theological Seminary of America, New York. He published much on Aramaic and Ugaritic philology and its application to the Bible. His works include *Kitvei Ugarit* (1936), *The Legend of King Keret* (1946), *Studies in Daniel* (1948), and *Studies in Koheleth* (1950). He was also chief editor of the Jewish Publication Society's English translation of the Prophets (1962–) and editor of *The Five Megilloth and Jonah* (1969).

Divisional editor: Bible

GINTON, SHABBETAI, born Buczacz, Galicia, 1906. In 1914 he was taken to Vienna, where he practised medicine, and in 1938 settled in Ereẓ Israel. He became public information officer, and in 1948 chief Israel government press officer. From 1953 he worked in the Ministry of Health, where he was head of international relations from 1960.

Consulting editor: Medicine

GOITEIN, DENISE R., born Paris, 1922. She moved to the U.S. and later settled in Israel, where she was Lecturer in French Literature at Tel Aviv University. She wrote papers on French literary figures such as Paul Claudel, Albert Cohen, and Nathalie Sarraute and made a study of Jewish themes in modern French literature.

Departmental editor: French Literature

GOLDSMITH, MAURICE, born London, 1913. From 1966 he was director of the Science Policy Foundation. He was author of *Careers in Technology* (1963), co-author of *Science, History and Technology,* books 1 and 2 (1965 and 1969), science editor of UNESCO (Paris), joint editor of *The Science of Science* (1964) and editor of various journals.

Departmental editor:
Jews in Astronomy; Chemistry; Mathematics; Physics; the History and Philosophy of Science

GREENBERG, MOSHE, born Philadelphia, 1928. He taught at the University of Pennsylvania and at the Jewish Theological Seminary of America. In 1970 he settled in Israel, being appointed Professor of Bible at the Hebrew University of Jerusalem. Greenberg wrote *The Ḥab/piru* (1955) and *Introduction to Hebrew* (1961), and prepared an abridged translation of Kaufmann's *The Religion of Israel* (1960).

Departmental editor: BIBLICAL SOCIETY AND LAW

GROSS, NACHUM, born Vienna, 1926. He settled in Ereẓ Israel in 1939. In 1966 he was appointed Lecturer in Economics at the Hebrew University of Jerusalem.

Consulting editor: JEWISH ECONOMIC LIFE

HABERMANN, ABRAHAM MEIR, born Zurawno, Galicia, 1901. In 1934 he settled in Ereẓ Israel, where he was director of the Schocken Library in Jerusalem until 1967, and in 1968 Professor of Medieval Hebrew Literature at Tel Aviv University. Among his publications are *Megillot Midbar Yehudah* (1959), *Ha-Sefer ha-Ivri be-Hitpatteḥuto* (1965), and *Toledot ha-Piyyut ve-ha-Shirah* (1970).

Departmental editor: MEDIEVAL HEBREW POETRY

HALKIN, ABRAHAM SOLOMON, born Mogilev, Russia, 1903. He taught at Columbia University and at the Jewish Theological Seminary of America and in 1950 became Professor of Hebrew at City College, New York. In 1970 he settled in Jerusalem. His works include an edition of Maimonides' *Epistle to the Yemen* and of *Ibn Aknin's Arabic Commentary on the Song of Songs* (1964).

Departmental editor:
MEDIEVAL TRANSLATIONS AND
JUDEO-ARABIC LITERATURE

HALKIN, HILLEL D., born New York, 1939. He worked as a free-lance writer and translator. In 1970 he settled in Israel where he translated several early 20th century Hebrew classics.

Assistant Divisional editor: AMERICANA

HARAN, MENAHEM, born Moscow, 1925. In 1934 he was taken to Ereẓ Israel. He was head of the Bible Department at Tel Aviv University from 1957 to 1962, and in 1966 was appointed Associate Professor of Bible at the Hebrew University of Jerusalem. He was an editor of *Tarbiz*, a quarterly published by the Hebrew University.

Consulting editor
Departmental editor: BIBLICAL BOOKS AND LITERATURE;
BIBLE SCHOLARS AND RESEARCH

HEINEMANN, JOSEPH, born Munich, 1915. He was ordained rabbi and moved to England in 1939. In 1949 he settled in Israel, where he became Lecturer in Talmud at Bar Ilan University and in 1967 Senior Lecturer in Hebrew Literature at the Hebrew University of Jerusalem. Heinemann published studies on Jewish prayers and on talmudic teachings.

Departmental editor: MIDRASH AND AGGADAH

HERMON, ZVI, born Duisburg, Germany, 1912. In 1938 he settled in Ereẓ Israel, where he became commissioner of prisons and scientific adviser to the Prisons Department in the Mandatory and Israel governments. He introduced modern scientific methods in prison administration and social, psychological, and psychiatric services for prisoners.

Departmental editor; JEWS IN CRIMINOLOGY

HERTZBERG, ARTHUR, born in Lubaczow, Poland, 1921. In 1926 he was taken to the U.S., where he became rabbi of Temple Emanu-El in Englewood, New Jersey in 1956, and in 1961 Lecturer in History in the graduate faculty at Columbia University. Among his publications are *The Zionist Idea* (1959) and *The French Enlightenment and the Jews* (1968).

Consulting editor

HERZOG, AVIGDOR, born Nove Zamky, Czechoslovakia, 1922. He settled in Israel in 1949. From 1955 to 1965 he was head of the ethnomusicological division of the Israel Institute of Religious Music, and in 1965 was appointed librarian in charge of the National Sound Archives at the Jewish National and University Library, Jerusalem. He also taught at Bar Ilan University from 1969.

Departmental editor: MUSIC ILLUSTRATIONS

HINDUS, MILTON HENRY, born New York, 1916. From 1962 he was Professor of English at Brandeis University. His works include *The Crippled Giant* (1950) and *The Proustian Vision* (1954), and he edited *Leaves of Grass: 100 Years After* (1955), a collection of essays in honor of Walt Whitman.

Departmental editor: UNITED STATES LITERATURE

HIRSCHBERG, HAÏM Z'EW, born Tarnopol, Galicia, 1903. He settled in Ereẓ Israel in 1943, and in 1960 was appointed Professor of Jewish History at Bar Ilan University. His writings include *Yisrael be-Arav* (1946) and *Toledot ha-Yehudim be-Afrikah ha-Ẓefonit* (1965).

Divisional editor:
HISTORY OF THE JEWS IN MUSLIM COUNTRIES
Departmental editor:
ISLAM AND JUDAISM: THE MUSLIM WORLD; ARABIA;
EREẒ ISRAEL (640–1917); MUSLIM SPAIN; YEMEN

HOLTZ, AVRAHAM, born New York, 1934. He was ordained rabbi at the Jewish Theological Seminary of America, where he was Associate Professor of Modern Hebrew Literature. Holtz was the editor and compiler of *The Holy City: Jews on Jerusalem* (1971) and of articles in Jewish and literary journals.

Departmental editor: MODERN HEBREW LITERATURE

HOROWITZ, YEHOSHUA, born Rzeszow, Poland, 1911. He moved to Vienna in 1914, was ordained rabbi, and in 1939 settled in Ereẓ Israel, where he engaged in teaching. He contributed articles on talmudic and rabbinic literature to the *Enẓiklopedyah le-Ḥakhmei ha-Talmud ve-ha-Geonim*, the *Enẓiklopedyah le-Toledot Gedolei Yisrael*, the *Encyclopaedia Hebraica*, and other publications. He also wrote papers on the *geonim* and the *rishonim*.

Deputy Divisional editor: RABBINICAL LITERATURE

HYMAN, ARTHUR, born Halle, Germany, 1921. When the Nazis came to power he emigrated to the U.S. where he became Professor of Philosophy at Yeshiva University. He was co-editor of *Philosophy in the Middle Ages: The Christian, Islamic and Jewish Tradition* (1967).

Divisional editor: JEWISH PHILOSOPHY

JAFFE, BENJAMIN, born Jerusalem, 1921. He was secretary of Youth Aliyah, legal secretary of the Supreme Court, Jerusalem, and in 1965 was appointed director of the Department for External Relations of the World Zionist Organization. Jaffe wrote *The Rabbi of Yahud* (Heb. 1957) and *Benjamin Disraeli* (Heb. 1960).

Departmental editor:
PERSONALITIES IN MODERN EREẒ ISRAEL

JANOWSKY, OSCAR ISAIAH, born Suchowola, Poland, 1900. He was taken to the U.S. in 1910 and became Professor of History at City College, New York. In 1946–47 he was director of the Jewish National Welfare Board Survey and was later chairman of the Commission for the Study of Jewish Education in the U.S. Among his publications are *The Jews and National Minorities (1892–1919)* (1933), *Nationalities and National Minorities* (1945), *Foundations of Israel* (1964), and *Education of American Jewish Teachers* (1967).

Departmental editor: JEWS IN HISTORIOGRAPHY

KAHANE, PENUEL PETER, born Berlin, 1904. He settled in Ereẓ Israel in 1938 and was director of the museum section of the Israel Department of Antiquities. From 1965 to 1969 he was chief curator of the Samuel Bronfman Biblical and Archaeological Museum at the Israel Museum, Jerusalem. He also organized several archaeological museums in Israel. His special field of study was ancient pottery and glass.

Departmental editor: JEWS IN ARCHAEOLOGY

KAMPEL, STEWART, born Brooklyn, 1938. In 1958 he joined the staff of *The New York Times* and did editorial work in the cultural and foreign news departments. From 1965 he taught courses in copy editing, news and feature writing and introductory journalism at the English department of City College, New York.

Joint Departmental editor: JEWS IN THEATER AND FILMS

KAPLAN, MORDECHAI (MAX), born Marijampole, Lithuania, 1903. In 1922 he moved to Germany and worked as an engineer, and in 1932 settled in Ereẓ Israel, where he became a military industrialist. He was appointed a senior officer of the Haganah in 1940, and in 1948, of the Israel Defense Forces. From 1963 he was an officer in the reserves in charge of the *Loḥem Yehudi* (Jewish fighting-man) section of the army journal *Ma'arakhot.*

Departmental editor: JEWS IN MILITARY SERVICE

KATZ, SIMḤA, born Dvinsk, Latvia, 1916. In 1935 he settled in Ereẓ Israel and from 1949 was general academic secretary, editor of the department of the history of the Jews in Russia and general associate editor of the *Encyclopaedia Hebraica.* He worked with the *Encyclopaedia Judaica* from 1963.

Associate editor

KINDLER, ARIE, born Berlin, 1920. In 1923 he was taken to Ereẓ Israel. He became director of the Kadman Numismatic Museum and deputy director of the Museum Ha'aretz in Tel Aviv. He was also scientific editor of the Israel Numismatic Society and the author of books and articles on numismatics.

Departmental editor: NUMISMATICS

KLAIDMAN, STEPHEN, born New York, 1938. A journalist from 1959, he worked for *The New York Times* in different editorial capacities, as foreign correspondent, and in the cultural news department. In 1969 he became day foreign editor of *The Washington Post.*

Joint Departmental editor: JEWS IN THEATER AND FILMS

KONVITZ, MILTON RIDVAS, born Safed, Ereẓ Israel, 1908. He was taken to the U.S. in 1915. He became Professor of Industrial and Labor Relations at Cornell University in 1949, and Professor of Law in 1956. Active in the struggle for civil rights, he wrote several works on the subject and edited the *Cornell Studies on Civil Liberty.*

Departmental editor:
LAW AND SOCIALISM IN THE UNITED STATES

KRESSEL, GETZEL, born Zablotów, Galicia, 1911. In 1930 he settled in Ereẓ Israel, where he was an editor of the newspaper *Davar* and founded Genazim, the Biobibliographical Institute of the Association of Israel Writers. Among his publications are *Ereẓ Israel ve-Toledoteha* (1943), a history of Hebrew journalism in Israel (1964), and a lexicon of modern Hebrew literature (1965–67).

Divisional editor: ZIONISM

KUBLIN, HYMAN, born Boston, 1919. He was Professor of History at Brooklyn College from 1961, and in 1967 became director of the University of Hawaii Summer Institute of Asian Studies. His publications include a study of Japanese trade unionism (1959), *The Rim of Asia* (1963), *The Founder of Asian Communism* (1963), and *Asian Revolutionary: The Life of Sen Katayama* (1964).

Departmental editor:
HISTORY OF THE JEWS IN JAPAN

LACHMAN, FREDERICK RICHARD, born Breslau, 1902. He settled in Ereẓ Israel in 1933 and was entrusted with academic and organizational missions abroad. From 1952 he served as the personal U.S. representative of the Israel Minister of Education. He was director of the American Friends of the Hebrew University and of the American-Israel Cultural Foundation. He wrote *Die Studentes des Christophorus Stymmelius und ihre Buehne* (1926), and *La salud y la enfermedad en la conciencia del pueblo judio* (1943).

Executive editor

LAMED, MEIR, born Ronsperg, Czechoslovakia, 1914, died 1971. In 1939 he settled in Ereẓ Israel and became a member of Kibbutz Ne'ot Mordekhai. He later did research in the history of Jewish youth movements in Czechoslovakia at the Hebrew University of Jerusalem. He also worked on the *Pinkas ha-Kehillot, Bavaria* (Register of Jewish Communities in Bavaria exterminated by the Nazis) at *Yad Vashem.* Lamed joined the staff of the *Encyclopaedia Judaica* in 1967.

Departmental editor:
HISTORY OF THE JEWS IN AUSTRIA
Joint Departmental editor:
HISTORY OF THE JEWS IN CZECHOSLOVAKIA

LANDAU, MOSHE, born Cracow, 1917. In 1936 he settled in Ereẓ Israel and worked in education. He contributed entries on Western Galicia to the *Pinkas ha-Kehillot, Polin* (Register of Jewish Communities in Poland exterminated by the Nazis), published by *Yad Vashem.*

Landau also published *Eshkolot* (1956) on educational problems.

Departmental editor: HISTORY OF THE JEWS IN MODERN POLAND

LAVI, THEODOR, born Turnu-Severin, Rumania, 1905. An educator, he was imprisoned for Zionist activities in 1950. On his release in 1955 he settled in Israel, where he worked at *Yad Vashem.* Among his writings are studies of Trumpeldor and Herzl, *Istoria Sionismului* (1934) and *Yahadut Romanyah be-Ma'avak al Hazzalatah* (1965), a history of Rumanian Jewry during the Holocaust.

Departmental editor: HISTORY OF THE JEWS IN RUMANIA

LAZAR, MOSHÉ, born Micouloi, Rumania, 1928. He settled in Israel in 1948 and from 1966 to 1971 was Associate Professor of Romance Studies at the Hebrew University of Jerusalem. Lazar wrote on French and Provençal literature of the twelfth and thirteenth centuries.

Departmental editor: LADINO LITERATURE AND JEWISH DIALECTS

LEVENBERG, SCHNEIER ZALMAN, born Kursk, Russia, 1907. He settled in England and became editor of the *Zionist Review* and later foreign correspondent of the Israel newspaper *Davar.* In 1949 he was appointed representative of the Jewish Agency in the United Kingdom. His publications include *The Jews and Palestine* (1945) and *Dubnow—The Historian of Russian Jewry* (1962).

Departmental editor: JEWS IN SOCIALISM AND THE LABOR MOVEMENT

LEVIANT, CURT, born 1932. He taught Hebraic studies at Rutgers University from 1960. He edited *Masterpieces of Hebrew Literature* (1964) and edited and translated three Shalom Aleichem treasuries and *The Jewish Government and Other Stories* (1971), a collection of the Yiddish fiction of Lamed Shapiro. He is also the author of *King Artus: A Hebrew Arthurian Romance of 1279.*

Assistant Departmental editor: MODERN HEBREW AND YIDDISH LITERATURE

LEVITATS, ISAAC, born Zagare, Lithuania, 1907. He emigrated to the U.S. in 1926 and from 1959 was educational director at the Beth El Temple, Bellmore, New York. From 1967 he was Professor of Bible at the Herzliah Jewish Teachers' Seminary, New York. Levitats wrote *The Jewish Community in Russia, 1772–1844* (1943) and *Jewish Boards of Education in America* (1952).

Departmental editor: HISTORY OF JEWISH AUTONOMY AND SOCIAL INSTITUTIONS

LIPTZIN, SOL, born Satanov, Russia, 1901. In 1910 he was taken to the U.S. and became Professor of German and chairman of the Department of German and Slavic Languages at City College, New York. In 1962 he settled in Israel and taught at the American College, Jerusalem. His works include *Historical Survey of German Literature* (1936), *The English Legend of Heinrich Heine* (1954), *The Flowering of Yiddish Literature* (1963), and *The Maturing of Yiddish Literature* (1970).

Departmental editor: GERMAN LITERATURE

LITANI-LITTMAN, DORA, born Jassy, Rumania, 1908. From 1948 she was a research worker in the Institute for Literary History of the Rumanian Academy. She settled in Israel in 1958, and became a research worker at *Yad Vashem,* where she was a major contributor to the *Pinkas ha-Kehillot, Rumania* (Register of Jewish Communities in Rumania exterminated by the Nazis).

Consulting editor: RUMANIAN LITERATURE

LOEWE, RAPHAEL, born Calcutta, 1919. He taught at Cambridge and Leeds universities and became Lecturer in Hebrew at University College, London. His special fields of study were Christian Hebraists and rabbinic and medieval Hebrew.

Departmental editor: CHRISTIAN HEBRAISTS

LOEWENSTAMM, AYALA, born Przeworsk, Poland, 1918. In 1938 she settled in Ereẓ Israel and in 1964 became a research worker on the historical dictionary project at the Academy of the Hebrew Language. She specialized in Samaritan biblical exegesis.

Departmental editor: THE SAMARITANS

LOEWENTHAL, RUDOLF, born Schwerin, Germany, 1904. He taught at Yenching University, Peiping, China, from 1934. In 1947 he emigrated to the U.S. and became Instructor in German and researcher in Far Eastern and Central Asian studies at Cornell University, New York and Lecturer at Georgetown University, Washington, D.C. Before his retirement he was active in the field of computer systems engineering and did extensive work in automated linguistic and semantic classification. He published several articles and bibliographies on Chinese Jewish history.

Departmental editor: HISTORY OF THE JEWS IN CHINA

LÖWENTHAL, ZDENKO, born Grabovac, Yugoslavia, 1914. He directed the State Publishing House for Medical Literature, and from 1959 was Lecturer in the History of Medicine at the Belgrade Medical Faculty. Löwenthal also headed the historical department of the Yugoslav Jewish Federation. He edited *Crimes of the Fascist Invaders Against the Yugoslav Jews* and *Jewish Almanac, 1954–1964.*

Departmental editor: BALKAN LITERATURE

LOUVISH, MISHA, born Bukovina, Rumania, 1909. In 1912 he was taken to Glasgow, where he lived until 1949, when he settled in Israel. From 1956 to 1967 he was director of publications of the Israel Government Press Office. From 1967 he was on the editorial staff of Israel Universities Press and Keter Books. Louvish translated Agnon's *Guest for the Night* and was the author of *The Challenge of Israel.* For several years he was editor of the series *Facts About Israel.*

Deputy Divisional editor: MODERN EREẒ ISRAEL

MALACHY, YONA, born Frankfort, 1930, died 1972. In 1945 he settled in Ereẓ Israel, where he became deputy director of the department of Christian sects at the Israel Ministry of Religious Affairs. He wrote studies on Christian sects and Christian Zionism, and from 1961 edited *Christian News from Israel.*

Departmental editor: CHRISTIANITY

MARCUS, SIMON, born Lodz, Poland, 1897. In 1949 he settled in Israel, where he was an inspector in the Ministry of Education until 1960. Among his publications are *Toledot ha-Rabbanim be-Mishpaḥat Yisrael be-Rhodos* (1935) and *Ha-Safah ha-Sefardit ha-Yehudit* (1965). He also translated works by Rabbi Elijah Benamozegh and worked for encyclopedias.

Departmental editor:
HISTORY OF THE JEWS IN THE BALKAN STATES

MARTON, YEHOUDA, born Nagyszalonta, Hungary, 1910. In 1945 he settled in Ereẓ Israel and from 1950 worked with the Israel Broadcasting Service, where he became news editor. He wrote articles on the history of the Jews in Transylvania.

Departmental editor:
HISTORY OF THE JEWS IN BUKOVINA;
HISTORY OF THE JEWS IN TRANSYLVANIA

MEDAN, MEIR, born Cracow, 1915. He settled in Ereẓ Israel in 1933 and from 1939 to 1952 was secretary of the editorial board of the nine last volumes of Ben-Yehuda's Hebrew dictionary. From 1948 he was scientific secretary of the Academy of the Hebrew Language. He compiled the Hebrew dictionary *Me-aleph ad tav* (1954), and was textual editor of the Koren Bible (1963).

Consulting editor: JEWISH LITURGY

MEVORAH, BARUCH, born Sofia, Bulgaria, 1930. He settled in Ereẓ Israel in 1945, and in 1965 became Lecturer in Jewish History at the Hebrew University of Jerusalem. From 1962 he was editorial secretary of the quarterly *Zion*. Mevorah wrote on the history of the Jews in Europe in the 18th and 19th centuries.

Departmental editor:
HISTORY OF THE JEWS IN WESTERN EUROPE:
BELGIUM; MODERN FRANCE; THE NETHERLANDS;
SCANDINAVIA; SWITZERLAND

MICHMAN (MELKMAN), JOZEPH, born Amsterdam, 1914. During World War II he was deported to Belsen. Later he became head of the Jewish Agency cultural and immigration department in Holland. In 1957 he settled in Israel, where he was director of *Yad Vashem*, and from 1960 cultural director at the Ministry of Education. Among his writings are anthologies of Hebrew poetry and prose, *Israel* (1950) and *Geliefde Vijand* (1964).

Joint Divisional editor: THE HOLOCAUST

MILANO, ATTILIO, born Rome, 1907, died 1969. He settled in Ereẓ Israel in 1939. His special field of study was the social and economic history of the Italian Jews, and their relation with the Roman Catholic Church. Among his publications are *Storia degli ebrei in Italia* (1963), *Il Ghetto di Roma* (1964), and *Bibliotheca Historica Italo-Judaica* (1954–1963).

Departmental editor:
HISTORY OF THE JEWS IN ITALY

MILLER, LOUIS, born Somerset West, South Africa, 1917. In 1948 he settled in Israel, where he established psychiatric services in the Armed Forces. In 1949 he became psychiatric director at the Ministry of Health and from 1954 developed public health facilities in the Jerusalem region. In 1970 he became chief national psychiatrist.

Departmental editor: JEWS IN PSYCHIATRY

MILLER, SAMUEL AARON, born Leeds, 1912, died 1970. He worked in chemical research. Miller was chairman of the Zionist Federation of Great Britain and chairman and vice-president of Po'alei Zion. He published *Acetylene, Its Properties, Manufacture and Uses* (1965–66) and edited *Ethylene and Its Industrial Derivatives* (1969).

Departmental editor:
JEWS IN AERONAUTICS; ASTRONAUTICS; AVIATION;
ENGINEERING; INVENTION

MISHKINSKY, MOSHE, born Bialystok, Poland, 1917. He settled in Ereẓ Israel in 1936 and became Senior Lecturer in the History of the Jewish Labor Movement at the Hebrew University of Jerusalem. He also taught at Tel Aviv University. Mishkinsky wrote on the early history of Zionism and on the labor movement among Russian Jewry.

Departmental editor:
HISTORY OF THE JEWISH LABOR MOVEMENT

MUNTNER, SUESSMANN, born Kolomea, Galicia, 1897. He settled in Ereẓ Israel in 1933 and from 1959 was Visiting Professor of the History of Medicine at the Hebrew University of Jerusalem. Muntner edited *The Medical Works of Maimonides* (1936) and wrote a *Medical Dictionary* and studies of medieval Jewish physicians.

Departmental editor: MEDICINE

NARKISS, BEZALEL, born Jerusalem, 1926. In 1969 he was appointed Senior Lecturer in the History of Art at the Hebrew University of Jerusalem. Narkiss wrote *Hebrew Illuminated Manuscripts* (1969).

Illustrations consultant
Departmental editor: ILLUMINATED MANUSCRIPTS

NEHER, ANDRÉ, born Obernai, France, 1914. In 1948 he was appointed Professor of Hebrew Language and Literature at the University of Strasbourg and later at Tel Aviv University. Among his publications are *L'Essence du prophétisme* (1955), *Moïse et la vocation juive* (1956), and *Parole et silence dans la Bible* (1969).

Consulting editor

NEIPRIS, JOSEPH, born Malden, Massachusetts, 1918. He served as a psychiatric social worker, and in 1950 settled in Israel, where in 1952 he became administrative director of the Lasker Mental Hygiene and Child Guidance Clinic. In 1968, he was appointed deputy director of the School of Social Work at the Hebrew University of Jerusalem. Neipris was co-author of *The Individual and the Group* (1953).

Departmental editor: JEWS IN SOCIAL WELFARE

NEMOY, LEON, born Balta, Russia, 1901. In 1923 he emigrated to the U.S., where he became curator of Hebrew and Arabic literature at the Sterling Memorial Library at Yale University, New Haven, and later scholar-in-residence at Dropsie University, Philadelphia. Among his works are his editions of the Arabic text of al-Kirkisānī's *Kitāb al-Anwār wa-al Maraqib* (5 vols., 1939–43), and *Karaite Anthology* (1952).

Departmental editor: THE KARAITES

NOY, DOV, born Kolomea, Galicia, 1920. In 1938 he settled in Ereẓ Israel, where he founded the Museum of Ethnology and Folklore in Haifa, of which he was director. In 1965 he was appointed Senior Lecturer in Hebrew Literature at the Hebrew University of Jerusalem. He wrote *An Index of Talmudic-Midrashic Literature* (1954) and studies on Jewish folktales and legends.

Departmental editor: FOLKLORE

ORNAN, UZZI, born Jerusalem, 1923. In 1966 he became Senior Lecturer in Hebrew Language at the Hebrew University of Jerusalem. Ornan published *Dikduk ha-Peh ve-ha-Ozen* (1953) and poems and articles on literature and linguisties. He also wrote *Shabbat Without Chains* (Heb. 1953) and *Civil Marriage* (Heb. 1955).

Assistant Divisional editor: HEBREW AND SEMITIC LANGUAGES

ORNI, EFRAIM, born Breslau, 1915. He settled in Ereẓ Israel in 1938 and worked for the Jewish National Fund. Orni was co-author of *Geography of Israel* (1971^3).

Departmental editor: PLACES IN MODERN EREẒ ISRAEL

PAPER, HERBERT HARRY, born Baltimore, 1925. He taught at Cornell University and at the University of Michigan, where he was Professor of Near Eastern Studies from 1962 and director of the Linguistic Institute from 1965. Paper wrote *The Phonology and Morphology of Royal Achaemenid Elamite* (1955), and textbooks of modern Persian, and was co-author of *English for Iranians* (1955).

Departmental editor: JEWS IN LINGUISTICS

PAUL, SHALOM MORTON, born Philadelphia, 1936. He was ordained rabbi at the Jewish Theological Seminary of America, where he was Associate Professor of Bible. In 1970 he settled in Israel and was appointed Senior Lecturer in Bible at the Hebrew University of Jerusalem and Tel Aviv University. Among his publications is *Studies in the Book of the Covenant in the Light of Cuneiform and Biblical Law* (1970).

Associate Divisional editor: BIBLE
Departmental editor: IDEAS AND RELIGION IN THE BIBLE

PICARD, LEO, born Wangen, Germany, 1900. He settled in Ereẓ Israel in 1924, and became head of the Geology Department of the Hebrew University of Jerusalem in 1936 and Professor of Geology in 1939. He later served as director of the Geological Survey of Israel.

Departmental editor: JEWS IN GEOLOGY

PILCH, JUDAH, born Vachnovka, Russia, 1903. He emigrated to the U.S. in 1923 and from 1961 until his retirement in 1967 headed the National Curriculum Research Institute of the American Association for Jewish Education. He was also president of the National Council for Jewish Education. His publications include *Jewish Life in Our Times* (1943) and *A History of Jewish Education in the U.S.* (1969).

Departmental editor: JEWISH EDUCATION

POLIAKOV, LÉON, born St. Petersburg, 1910. He was taken to Paris in 1920 and from 1945 to 1954 was head of the research department of the Centre de Documentation Juive Contemporaine, Paris. Subsequently he became Maître de Recherches at the Centre National de la Recherche Scientifique and worked at the Ecole Pratique des Hautes Etudes. His major work was his *Histoire de l'antisemitisme* in three volumes (1955–1968). Among his other publications was *Brevaire de la haine* (1952) on Nazi Germany and the Jews.

Departmental editor: ANTI-SEMITISM

POLLACK, PETER, born Wing, North Dakota, 1911. He was curator of photography at the Art Institute of Chicago from 1945, and in 1957 moved to New York, where he worked as consultant to art galleries and museums. In 1962–3 he was director of the American Federation of Arts. Pollack wrote *The Picture History of Photography* (1958; 1970^2).

Departmental editor: JEWS IN PHOTOGRAPHY

POPKIN, RICHARD H., born New York, 1923. From 1963 he was Professor of Philosophy and chairman of the Philosophy Department at the University of California at San Diego. His publications include *The History of Scepticism from Erasmus to Descartes* (1960) and *The Second Oswald* (1966) concerning the assassination of President Kennedy. He edited the *Journal of the History of Philosophy*.

Departmental editor: JEWS IN PHILOSOPHY

PORTEN, BEZALEL, born Philadelphia, 1931. He taught at the Jewish Theological Seminary of America, New York and at the College of Jewish Studies, Chicago and from 1965 to 1970 was Assistant Professor of Bible and Hebrew at the University of California at Davis. From 1970 he taught at universities in Israel. His publications include *Archives from Elephantine: The Life of an Ancient Jewish Military Colony* (1968).

Departmental editor: BIBLE—PERIOD OF THE SECOND TEMPLE

POSNER, RAPHAEL, born Liverpool, 1932. In 1955 he was appointed rabbi of the West End Great Synagogue, London, and in 1959 went to the U.S. to take up the position of Assistant Professor of Rabbinics at the Jewish Theological Seminary of America, New York. He settled in Israel in 1963 and became head of the Jerusalem branch of the Seminary.

Deputy editor in chief
Editor: INDEX
Departmental editor: JUDAISM AND LITURGY

POSTAL, BERNARD, born New York, 1905. He worked as a journalist and as editor of Jewish publications, and was associate editor of *The Jewish Week* and *The American Examiner*. From 1946 he was director of public information at the National Jewish Welfare Board and editor of the *Jewish Digest*. During World War II he was public relations consultant to the American Red Cross, and in 1945 was a member of the public relations staff of the United Jewish Delegation to the United Nations Conference at San Francisco. Postal wrote Jewish guidebooks, to the U.S. (1954), Europe (1962), and New York (1964).

Departmental editor: JEWS IN PUBLIC RELATIONS

RABIN, CHAIM MENACHEM, born Giessen, Germany, 1915. He was Lecturer in Post-Biblical Hebrew at the University of Oxford from 1942, and in 1956 settled in Israel where he was appointed Professor of Hebrew at the Hebrew University of Jerusalem. Among his publications are *Qumran Studies* (1957) and *The Zadokite Document* (1958^2).

Consulting editor

RABINOWICZ, OSKAR K., born Aspern, Austria, 1902, died 1969. A banker, he played a prominent role in the Revisionist movement in Czechoslovakia. In 1938 he moved to England and from 1956 lived in the U.S. His publications include *Fifty Years of Zionism* (1950), *Winston Churchill on Jewish Problems* (1956) and *Herzl, Architect of the Balfour Declaration* (1958).
Joint Departmental editor:
HISTORY OF THE JEWS IN CZECHOSLOVAKIA

RABINOWITZ, LOUIS ISAAC, born Edinburgh, 1906. He was a chaplain during World War II, and in 1945 moved to South Africa, where he was appointed Chief Rabbi of the United Hebrew Congregation of Johannesburg and the Federation of Synagogues in the Transvaal and the Orange Free State. In 1961 he settled in Israel. He wrote studies on medieval Jewish history, *The Social Life of the Jews in Northern France* (1938), *Ḥerem Hayyishub* (1945), *Jewish Merchant Adventures* (1948) and other works, including four volumes of sermons.
Deputy editor in chief

REVIV, HANOCH, born Plovdiv, Bulgaria, 1929. He settled in Ereẓ Israel in 1944, and in 1967 became Lecturer in Jewish History (biblical period) at the Hebrew University of Jerusalem.
Departmental editor:
BIBLE—PERIOD OF THE KINGDOM

ROBINSON, JACOB, born Serijai, Lithuania, 1889. He was a leader of the Lithuanian community and a member of Parliament. He emigrated to the U.S. in 1940 where he founded and headed the Institute of Jewish Affairs. In 1947 he became Jewish Agency adviser on International Law. From 1957 he coordinated the work of research institutions in Europe, the U.S., and Israel, dealing with the Holocaust. He wrote and edited many works in the field of international law and the Holocaust.
Consulting editor

RONALL, JOACHIM O., born Kassel, Germany, 1912. He emigrated to the U.S. in 1937. From 1945 to 1950 he worked as an economist for the Jewish Agency and the Government of Israel, and until 1957 with the Israel Government foreign service. From 1960 he was economist and research specialist of the Federal Reserve Bank, New York. He is co-author of *Industrialization in the Middle East* (1960).
Departmental editor: JEWS IN ECONOMICS

ROSENBERG, STUART E., born New York 1922. He served as rabbi of Temple Beth El, Rochester, New York until 1956, and subsequently as rabbi of Beth Tzedec synagogue, Toronto. Among his books are *The Jewish Community in Rochester* (1954), *America is Different* (1964), *The Jewish Community in Canada* (vol. 1, 1970), and *Great Religions of the Holy Land* (1971).
Departmental editor: CANADA

ROTH, CECIL, born London, 1899, died 1970. He was Reader in Jewish Studies at the University of Oxford from 1939 to 1964. In 1965 he settled in Israel and also was Visiting Professor at Queens College, New York from 1966 to 1969. Among his publications are *History of the Marranos* (1932), *The Jewish Contribution to Civilization* (1938), *History of the Jews in England* (1941), *History of the Jews in Italy* (1946), *The Jews in the Renaissance* (1959), and *Jewish Art* (1961).
Editor in chief
Divisional editor:
JEWISH HISTORY IN WESTERN EUROPE, CENTRAL AND EAST ASIA

RUBINSTEIN, AVRAHAM, born Tomaszow, Poland, 1912. In 1935 he settled in Ereẓ Israel, where he became director of the religious department of Youth Aliyah. From 1966 he was Lecturer, then Senior Lecturer in Jewish History at Bar Ilan University.
Departmental editor: ḤASIDISM

SAMUEL, EDWIN, Second Viscount Samuel, born London 1898. He joined the British colonial service in Palestine, where he was director of broadcasting from 1945 to 1948. He later established the nucleus of Israel's Institute of Public Administration and lectured at the Hebrew University of Jerusalem. Among his publications are *The Theory of Administration* (1947), *The Problems of Government in the State of Israel* (1957), *A Lifetime in Jerusalem* (1970), and books of short stories.
Departmental editor: THE STATE OF ISRAEL

SARNA, NAHUM M., born London, 1923. He emigrated to the U.S. in 1951. From 1957 he was librarian and Assistant Professor at the Teachers' Institute of the Jewish Theological Seminary of America, New York, and in 1965 was appointed Professor of Biblical Studies at Brandeis University. He is author of *Understanding Genesis* (1966).
Departmental editor:
BIBLE—PERIOD OF THE PENTATEUCH, THE DESERT, JOSHUA AND JUDGES

SARON, GUSTAV, born Johannesburg, 1905. He taught Classics and Hebrew at Witwaterstand University, and has also practiced as a barrister. From 1936 he was general secretary of the South African Jewish Board of Deputies. Saron was joint editor of *The Jews in South Africa.*
Departmental editor:
HISTORY OF THE JEWS IN SOUTH AFRICA

SCHALIT, ABRAHAM CHAIM, born Zolochev, Galicia, 1898. He settled in Ereẓ Israel in 1929 and in 1965 became Professor of History at the Hebrew University of Jerusalem. He is author of *Hordos ha-Melekh* (1960) and wrote extensively on Josephus and Jewish history in the Classical period.
Divisional editor: SECOND TEMPLE PERIOD

SCHEIBER, ALEXANDER, born Budapest, 1913. In 1945 he became Professor at the Rabbinical Seminary, Budapest, and director in 1950. During World War II he served as a rabbi and in 1949 was appointed Lecturer at Szeged University. He wrote on Jewish literature and folklore and on Hungarian Jewry.
Departmental editor:
HISTORY OF THE JEWS IN HUNGARY

SCHERESCHEWSKY, BEN ZION (BENNO), born Germany, 1907. In 1934 he settled in Ereẓ Israel, where he became a judge in 1949 and relieving president of the Jerusalem District Court in 1962.

FAMILY LAW AND INHERITANCE

SCHMELZ, USIEL OSCAR, born Vienna, 1918. He settled in Ereẓ Israel in 1939. From 1958 he headed the

demographic and social divisions of the Central Bureau of Statistics, and from 1961 was Research Fellow in Jewish Demography at the Hebrew University of Jerusalem. Among his publications are *Jewish Demography and Statistics; 1920–1960* (1961), a bibliography, and *Criminal Statistics in Israel* (1962–64). He was co-editor of *Jewish Population Studies, 1961–1968* (1970), to which he contributed *A Guide to Jewish Population Studies*.

Departmental editor: CONTEMPORARY JEWRY—DEMOGRAPHY

SCHMELZER, MENAHEM, born Kecel, Hungary, 1934. In 1944 he was deported to a concentration camp by the Nazis, and in 1952–1953 was imprisoned by the communists for illegal Zionist activities. He left Hungary in 1956, studied in Europe, and emigrated to the U.S. in 1961. He became librarian of the Jewish Theological Seminary of America, New York, where he was Assistant Professor of Medieval Hebrew Literature from 1970.

Associate Divisional editor: MODERN JEWISH SCHOLARSHIP

SCHOLBERG, KENNETH R., born La Crosse, Wisconsin, 1925. He taught at various universities and became Professor of Spanish at Michigan State University, East Lansing. He specialized in medieval and 17th century Spanish literature, and his works include *Pierre Bayle and Spain* (1958), *Metamorfosis a lo moderno y otras poesías de Francisco de Castro* (1959), *Poesía religiosa de Miguel de Barrios* (1961), and *Spanish Life in the Late Middle Ages* (1965).

Departmental editor: SPANISH AND PORTUGUESE LITERATURE

SCHOLEM, GERSHOM GERHARD, born Berlin, 1897. In 1923 he emigrated to Ereẓ Israel, where he became Professor of Jewish Mysticism at the Hebrew University of Jerusalem in 1933. Among his publications are *Bibliographia Kabbalistica* (1927), *Major Trends in Jewish Mysticism* (1941, repr. 1965), and *Shabbetai Ẓevi ve-ha-Tenu'ah ha-Shabbeta'it* (1957). From 1968 Scholem was president of the Israel Academy of Sciences and Humanities.

Consulting editor

SCHULMAN, ALAN RICHARD, born Brooklyn, 1930. He taught at Columbia University, and from 1965 was Associate Professor at Queen's College and in the doctoral faculty of the City University of New York. Among his publications was *Military Rank, Title and Organization in the Egyptian New Kingdom* (1964). Shulman was editor of the *Journal of the American Research Center in Egypt* from 1966 to 1971.

Departmental editor: JEWISH HISTORY FROM 135 TO 663

SEIGEL, KALMAN A., born Brooklyn, 1917. He joined the staff of *The New York Times* in 1939 and advanced to a number of editorial positions. In 1968 he was appointed Letters editor. For 20 years Seigel taught journalism and English composition at City College, New York. He was co-author of *This is a Newspaper* (1965).

Departmental editor: JEWS IN JOURNALISM

SERMONETA, JOSEPH BARUCH (GUISEPPE), born Rome, 1924. In 1953 he settled in Israel, where he was appointed inspector of Italian studies for the Ministry of Education in 1960, and Associate Professor of Jewish Philosophy and Senior Lecturer in Italian Literature at the Hebrew University from 1966. His special field of study was the relationship of Italian and Jewish thought in medieval Italy.

Departmental editor: ITALIAN LITERATURE

SHAFTESLEY, JOHN MAURICE, born Salford, England, 1901. He worked for the *Manchester Guardian*, and later joined the *Jewish Chronicle*, which he edited from 1946. On his retirement in 1958 he became editor of publications for the Jewish Historical Society.

Departmental editor: JEWS IN PUBLISHING AND PRINTING

SHARF, ANDREW, born Rostov-on-Don, Russia, 1915. He taught at the London and Liverpool universities, and in 1957 settled in Israel, where in 1966 he became Associate Professor of History at Bar Ilan University. Sharf wrote *The British Press and Jews Under Nazi Rule* (1964) and *Byzantine Jewry* (1971).

Departmental editor: HISTORY OF THE JEWS IN THE BYZANTINE EMPIRE

SHMERUK, CHONE, born Warsaw, 1921. He settled in Israel in 1949 and taught at the Hebrew University of Jerusalem, where he became Associate Professor and, in 1971, Professor of Yiddish. His special field of study was the Yiddish literature of Soviet Jewry. Among his writings are a study of Jewish agricultural settlements in the Soviet Union (1961), *Pirsumim Yehudiyyim bi-Verit ha-Mo'aẓot 1917–60* (1961) and *A Shpigl oyf a Shteyn* (1964), an anthology of Soviet Yiddish literature. He also compiled a bibliography of the works of Mendele Mokher Seforim.

Consulting editor

SHMUELEVITZ, ARYEH, born Ereẓ Israel, 1932. In 1960 he joined the Reuven Shiloah Research Center for Middle Eastern and African Studies. He was coordinator of the Center when it became part of Tel Aviv University in 1966. In that year he was appointed Lecturer in Middle Eastern and African History at Tel Aviv University. He edited the *Seder Eliyahu Zuta* by Elijah Capsali and wrote studies of Middle Eastern history in Ottoman and modern times.

Departmental editor: HISTORY OF THE JEWS IN THE ASIAN REGIONS OF THE OTTOMAN EMPIRE: IRAQ, SYRIA, AND TURKEY

SIEGEL, SEYMOUR, born Chicago, 1927. He was ordained rabbi at the Jewish Theological Seminary of America, New York, where he became Professor of Jewish Theology and of Ethics and Rabbinic Thought. Among his publications is *A Faithful Passion, a Theology of Judaism* (1971).

Divisional editor: MODERN JEWISH SCHOLARSHIP

SILVER, JESSE HAROLD, born New York, 1929. He was sports editor of the *Jewish Telegraphic Agency*, and co-author of the *Encyclopaedia of Jews in Sports* (1965).

Departmental editor: JEWS IN SPORTS

SLUTSKY, YEHUDA, born Snovsk, Ukraine, 1915. In 1925 he was taken to Ereẓ Israel, where in 1965 he was appointed Senior Lecturer in the History of the Israel Labor Movement at Tel Aviv University. He wrote the major part of *Toledot ha-Haganah* (1954–), the section on

Russian Hebrew publications in *Pirsumim Yehudiyyim bi-Verit ha-Mo'aẓot* (1961) and *Toledot ha-Ittonut ha-Yehudit ha-Rusit ba-Me'ah ha-19* (1970). From 1960 he edited *He-Avar* (journal devoted to the History of the Jews in Russia.
Departmental editor:
HISTORY OF THE JEWS IN THE BALTIC STATES;
HISTORY OF THE JEWS IN RUSSIA

SPICEHANDLER, EZRA, born Brooklyn, 1921. He was appointed Professor of Modern Hebrew Literature at the Cincinnati school of the Hebrew Union College–Jewish Institute of Religion in 1960. From 1966, when he settled in Israel, he was director of Jewish studies at its Jerusalem branch. Spicehandler was co-author of *The Hebrew Poem Itself* (1966) and of *Perakim be-Yahadut* (1962).
Divisional editor:
MODERN HEBREW LITERATURE

STONE, MICHAEL EDWARD, born Leeds, 1938. In 1965 he settled in Israel, and in 1966 was appointed Research Fellow and later Senior Lecturer in Jewish Hellenism at the Hebrew University of Jerusalem. He specialized in Armenian, apocryphal, and pseudepigraphal literature and was chairman of the Department of Iranian and Armenian studies at the Hebrew University.
Departmental editor:
THE APOCRYPHA AND THE PSEUDEPIGRAPHA

TABOR, HARRY ZVI, born London, 1917. He settled in Israel in 1949 and became a Research Fellow in Practical Physics at the Hebrew University of Jerusalem. In 1950 he was appointed director of the National Physics Laboratory. He was an authority on solar energy and solar radiation.
Consulting editor: THE SCIENCES

TAMAR, DAVID SHLOMO, born Breslau, 1928. He was brought to Ereẓ Israel in 1936, and taught at Tel Aviv University. He was later appointed Lecturer in Jewish History at Haifa University. Among his publications are *Meḥkarim be-Toledot ha-Yehudim be-Ereẓ Yisrael u-ve-Italyah* (1970) and articles on rabbinical literature and Jewish history, particularly the history of Jewish settlement in Safed.
Assistant Divisional editor: RABBINICAL LITERATURE

WADDINGTON, MIRIAM (DWORKIN), born Winnipeg, 1917. She spent some years as a social worker in Montreal and later became Assistant Professor of English at York University, Ontario. A poet, she published *Green World* (1945), *The Second Silence* (1955), *The Season's Lovers* (1958), and *The Glass Trumpet* (1966).
Departmental editor: CANADIAN LITERATURE

WERBLOWSKY, RAPHAEL JUDAH ZWI, born Frankfort, 1924. He taught in England, settled in Israel in 1956, was appointed Associate Professor, and in 1971 Professor of Comparative Religion at the Hebrew University of Jerusalem. From 1965 to 1969 he was Dean of the Faculty of Humanities. Among his publications is *Joseph Karo, Lawyer and Mystic* (1962).
Consulting editor
Divisional editor: JUDAISM

WERNER, ALFRED, born Vienna, 1911. He emigrated to the U.S. in 1940 and wrote widely on art. His books include *Utrillo* (1952), *Dufy* (1953), *Rousseau* (1957), *Modigliani* (1962), *Pascin* (1962), and three books on Chagall.
Divisional editor: ART

WIGODER, GEOFFREY, born Leeds, 1922. He settled in Israel in 1949 and from 1960 to 1967 was director of the external and foreign language broadcasts of the Israel Broadcasting Authority. From 1959 he was also director of the Oral History Division of the Institute of Contemporary Jewry at the Hebrew University of Jerusalem. He was joint editor of the *Standard Jewish Encyclopedia* and the *Encyclopedia of the Jewish Religion* and published *Abraham bar Ḥayya's Meditation of the Sad Soul* (1969).
Editor in chief

WYGODZKI, STANISLAW, born Bedzin, Poland, 1907. He was deported to Auschwitz during World War II and in 1968 settled in Israel. He published several volumes of prose and poetry and some translations of Yiddish literature.
Departmental editor: POLISH LITERATURE

YAHIL (HOFFMAN), CHAIM, born Velke Mezirici, Czechoslovakia, 1905. He settled in Ereẓ Israel in 1939 and from 1945 was representative of the Jewish Agency in Germany. From 1956 he was Israel ambassador to Norway, Sweden, and Iceland. In 1960 he became director-general of the Ministry for Foreign Affairs, and in 1965 head of "ha-Merkaz la-Tefuẓot." From 1965 he was chairman of the Board of Governors of the Israel Broadcasting Authority. He published a history of the Israel Labor Movement (1939) and *Scandinavian Socialism and Its Implementation* (1965).
Divisional editor: CONTEMPORARY JEWRY

YAHIL, LENI, born Germany, 1912. She settled in Ereẓ Israel in 1934, and from 1961 to 1963 was coordinator for the Institute for Research into the Holocaust, in conjunction with *Yad Vashem* and the Hebrew University of Jerusalem. In 1966 she was appointed Lecturer at the Hebrew University. She published *The Rescue of Danish Jewry* (1970).
Departmental editor: SCANDINAVIAN LITERATURE

YARON, BARUCH, born Budapest, 1920. In 1949 he settled in Israel, where he worked as a librarian in the National and University Library, Jerusalem, and in 1957 became the librarian of the Institute of Jewish Studies at the University.
Departmental editor: HUNGARIAN LITERATURE
Assistant Departmental editor:
HISTORY OF THE JEWS IN HUNGARY

CONTRIBUTORS TO THE ENCYCLOPAEDIA

A. A. **Abraham Aharoni;** Journalist, Tel Aviv
A. Ab. **Abraham Abraham,** Rabbi; Jerusalem
A. A. Ch. **Arthur A. Chiel,** M.A.,D.H.L., Rabbi; Woodbridge, Connecticut
A. Ad. **Abraham Addleson,** Attorney; Former Mayor of East London, South Africa
A. A. E. **Albert A. Ehrenzweig,** J.D., S.J.D., Dr. Utr. Jur.; Professor of Law, the University of California, Berkeley; Honorarprofessor, the University of Vienna
Aa. G. **Aaron Greenbaum,** Ph.D., Rabbi; American Joint Distribution Committee, Jerusalem
A. A. H. See **E. E. H.**
Aa. Ke. **Aaron Kempinski,** M.A., Lecturer in Ancient Near Eastern History and Archaeology; Tel Aviv University
A. Al. **Avraham Altman,** Ph.D.; Lecturer in Japanese Studies, the Hebrew University of Jerusalem
A. Alt. **Alexander Altmann,** Ph.D., D.H.L., Rabbi; Professor of Jewish Philosophy, Brandeis University, Waltham, Massachusetts
A. Am. **Aharon Amir;** Writer and editor, Tel Aviv
A. Ar. **Abraham Arzi,** Ph.D., Rabbi; Senior Teacher in Talmud, Bar Ilan University, Ramat Gan
A. As. **Alexander Astor,** B.A., O.B.E., Rabbi; Auckland, New Zealand
Aa. Sh. **Aaron Shaffer,** Ph.D.; Associate Professor of Assyriology, the Hebrew University of Jerusalem
Aa. Sk. **Aaron Skaist,** Ph.D., Rabbi; Senior Lecturer in Bible and in Semitic Languages, Bar Ilan University, Ramat Gan
A. A. W. **Aharon Arnold Wiznitzer,** Ph.D., D.H.L.; Historian, Los Angeles
A. B. **Alexander Bein,** Dr.Phil.; Former State Archivist, Former Director of the Central Zionist Archives, Jerusalem
Ab. A. **Abba Ahimeir** *(deceased)*, Ph.D.; Journalist and writer, Tel Aviv
Ab. B. **Abraham Berger,** M.A.; Former Director Jewish Division, the New York Public Library; Lecturer in Jewish History, the Academy for Jewish Religion, New York
Ab. B. Y. **Abraham B. Yoffe;** Critic and editor, Tel Aviv
A. Be. **Arthur Beer,** Ph.D., F.R.A.S.; Lately Senior Observer at the Observatories, the University of Cambridge
Ab. F. **Abraham Fellman,** F.A.C.C.A., C.P.A.; Accountant, Tel Aviv
Ab. H. **Abraham Halperin,** Ph.D.; Professor of Physics, the Hebrew University of Jerusalem
A. Bi. **Avraham Biran,** Ph.D.; Director of the Department of Antiquities and Museums, Ministry of Education and Culture, Jerusalem
Ab. K. **Abram Kanof,** M.D.; Physician and art historian; Professor of Pediatrics, the State University of New York—Downstate Medical Center at Brooklyn; Former President of the American Jewish Historical Society, New York
Ab. L. **Abraham Lebanon, M.A.;** Teacher in the Hebrew Teachers' College, Jerusalem
Ab. R. **Abraham Rutenberg,** Engineer; Former Director of the Israel Electric Company, Haifa
Ab. V. G. **Abram Vossen Goodman,** Ph.D., Rabbi; President of the American Jewish Historical Society, New York
A. B.-Y. **Abraham Ben-Yaacob,** B.A.; Researcher in Jewish History, Jerusalem
Ab. Z. **Abraham Zimels,** M.A., Rabbi; Senior Lecturer in Bible, the University of the Negev, Beersheba
A. C. **Alexander Carlebach,** D.en D., Rabbi; Jerusalem
A. Ca. **Alex Carmel,** Ph.D.; Instructor in International Relations and History, the Hebrew University of Jerusalem
A. Ch. **Anatole Chujoy** *(deceased)*; Dance critic and historian, New York
A. Cy. **Arthur Cygielman,** Cand. S.C.; Teacher in the Seminar Ha-Kibbutzim, Tel Aviv
A. D. **Abraham David,** M.A.: Jerusalem
A. D. C. **Alan D. Corré,** Ph.D., Rabbi; Professor of Hebrew Studies, the University of Wisconsin, Milwaukee
A. De. **Aaron Demsky,** M.A., Rabbi; Instructor in Jewish History, Bar Ilan University, Ramat Gan
Ad. K. **Adonijahu Krauss,** M.A., Rabbi; Jerusalem
A. Do. **Aron Dotan,** Ph.D.; Associate Professor of Hebrew Philology, Tel Aviv University
Ad. T. **Michael Adin Talbar,** B.A.; Ministry of Commerce and Industry, Jerusalem
A. E. **Abraham Erlik,** B.A.(Arch.); Architect, Tel Aviv
A. Eb. **Abba Eban,** M.A.; Minister for Foreign Affairs, Jerusalem
A. Ei. **Alfred Einstein** *(deceased)*, Dr.Phil.; Musicologist, Professor of Music, Smith College, Northampton, Massachusetts
A. E. S. **Akiba Ernst Simon,** Dr.Phil.; Emeritus Professor of Education, the Hebrew University of Jerusalem
A. F. **Aryeh Feigenbaum,** M.D.; Emeritus Professor of Ophthalmology, the Hebrew University of Jerusalem
A. Fe. **Abraham Feller;** Journalist, Tel Aviv
A. Fi. **Artur Fiszer,** B.A.; Researcher, Jerusalem
A. Fu. **Aharon Fuerst** *(deceased)*, Dr.Phil.; Historian, Jerusalem
A. G. **Abraham Goldberg,** Ph.D., Rabbi; Senior Lecturer in Talmud, the Hebrew University of Jerusalem
A. Go. **Asher Goren,** M.A.; Writer, Jerusalem
A. Gr. **Aaron Gruenhut,** M.A.; Librarian, the Jewish National and University Library, Jerusalem
A. Gu. **Aron Gurwitsch,** Ph.D.; Professor of Philosophy, the New School for Social Research, New York
A. H. **Abraham Haim,** M.A.; Assistant Lecturer, Department of Middle Eastern Studies, Tel Aviv University
A.Ha. **Amos Hakham,** B.A.; Researcher, Jerusalem
A. H. F. **Abraham Halevy Fraenkel** *(deceased)*, Dr.Phil.; Emeritus Professor of Mathematics, the Hebrew University of Jerusalem
A. H. Fo. **Abraham H. Foxman,** J.D.; Anti-Defamation League of B'nai B'rith, New York

A. Hi. **Alfred Hirschberg** *(deceased)*, Dr.Jur.; Director of the Confederação Israelita de Brasil, National Director of B'nai B'rith of Brazil, São Paulo

A. Hil. **Alter Hilewitz,** Ph.D., Rabbi; Principal, Hebrew Teachers Training College and Hebrew Training College for Ministers and Rabbis, Johannesburg, South Africa

Ah. K. **Aharon Kashtan,** Ing., M.A.; Associate Professor of Architecture and Town Planning, the Technion, Haifa

A. Ho. **Ari Hoogenboom,** Ph.D.; Professor of History, Brooklyn College of the City University of New York

A. H. R. **Abraham Hirsch Rabinowitz,** M.A., Rabbi; Senior Chaplain to the Israel Air Force, Jerusalem

A. Hu. **Abraham Huss,** Ph.D., D.I.C.; Associate Professor of Meteorology, the Hebrew University of Jerusalem

A. Hy. **Arthur Hyman,** Ph.D., Rabbi; Professor of General and Jewish Philosophy, Yeshiva University, New York

Ah. Ya. **Aharon Yadlin,** B.A.; Member of the Knesset; Deputy Minister of Education and Culture, Kibbutz Haẓerim

A. I. B. **Abraham Isaac Bromberg,** Rabbi; Writer, Jerusalem

A. I. I. See **A. L. I.**

A. J. **Alfred Joseph;** San Salvador

A. J. B. **Arnold J. Band,** Ph.D.; Professor of Hebrew Literature, the University of California, Los Angeles

A. J. Br. **Abraham J. Brawer,** Dr.Phil.; Geographer and historian, Tel Aviv

A. J. F. **Abraham J. Feldman,** B.H.L., Rabbi; Hartford, Connecticut

A. J. G. **Alex J. Goldman,** LL.B., Rabbi; Stamford, Connecticut

A. J. H. **Abel Jacob Herzberg,** Dr.J.; Attorney, Amsterdam

A. J. He. **Abraham Joshua Heschel** *(deceased)*, Ph.D., Rabbi; Professor of Jewish Ethics and Mysticism, the Jewish Theological Seminary of America, New York

A. J. K. **Abraham J. Karp,** M.H.L., Rabbi; Historian, and Visiting Associate Professor of Jewish History, the Jewish Theological Seminary of America, New York

A. Jo. **Alfred Jospe;** B'nai B'rith Hillel Foundations, Washington, D.C.

A.J.R. **Alvin J. Reines,** Ph.D., Rabbi; Professor of Philosophy, the Hebrew Union College—Jewish Institute of Religion, New York

A. J. T. **Abraham J. Tannenbaum,** Ph.D.; Professor of Education, Columbia University, New York

A. K. **Alvin Kass,** M.A., M.H.L. Rabbi; John Jay College of Criminal Justice of the City University of New York

A. Ka. **Asa Kasher,** Ph.D.; Lecturer in Mathematics and Philosophy, Bar Ilan University, Ramat Gan

A.Kar. **Alan Karpas;** Jerusalem

A. K. B. **Alan Keir Bowman,** Ph.D.; Assistant Professor of Classics, Rutgers University, New Jersey

A. Ki. **Arie Kindler,** Director of the Kadman Numismatic Museum, Tel Aviv

A. Kir. **Aaron Kirschenbaum,** Ph.D., Rabbi; Associate Professor of Jewish Law, Tel Aviv University

A. Ku. **Andreas Kubinyi,** Dr.Phil.; Lecturer in History, Eötvös Loránd University, Budapest

A. L. **Arye Lipshitz;** Writer, Jerusalem

Al. A. B. **Albert A. Blum,** Ph.D.; Professor of Labor History, Michigan State University, East Lansing

Al. A. G. **Alfred Abraham Greenbaum,** Ph.D.; Librarian of the University of Haifa

Al. A. S. **Albert A. Sicroff,** D.de l'U; Professor of Romance Languages, Queens College of the City University of New York

Al. B. **Alvin Boskoff,** Ph.D.; Professor of Sociology, Emory University, Atlanta, Georgia

Al. Ba. **Albert I. Baumgarten,** M.A.; Adjunct Lecturer in History, the Herbert H. Lehman College of the City University of New York

Al. C. **Alexander Cohn,** M.Sc.; Municipal Engineer, Bene-Berak

Al. D. **Alan Dowty,** Ph.D.; Lecturer in International Relations, the Hebrew University of Jerusalem

Al. E. **Alexander Ezer;** Editor, Jerusalem

Al.F. **Alexander Fuks,** Ph.D.; Professor of History and Classics, the Hebrew University of Jerusalem

A. L. I. **Alfred L. Ivry,** Ph.D.; Assistant Professor of Arabic and Hebrew Studies, Cornell University, Ithaca, New York

A. Li. **Aaron Lichtenstein,** Ph.D.; Researcher, Baltimore

A. L. K., A.-L. K. **Aryeh-Leib Kalish;** Jerusalem

Al. L. See **Ab. L.**

Al. L. Le. **Albert L. Lewis,** M.H.L., Rabbi; Haddonfield, New Jersey

Al. M. **Alexander Meijer,** M.D.; Lecturer in Child Psychiatry, the Hebrew University–Hadassah Medical School, Jerusalem

A. L. O. **Aryeh Leo Olitzki,** Dr.Phil.; Emeritus Professor of Bacteriology, the Hebrew University–Hadassah Medical School, Jerusalem

Al. R. S. **Alan Richard Schulman,** Ph.D.; Associate Professor of Ancient History, Queens College of the City University of New York

A. L. S. **Abram Leon Sachar,** Ph.D.; Chancellor, Brandeis University, Waltham, Massachusetts

Al. Sch. **Alexander Scheiber,** Dr.Phil., Rabbi; Director and Professor of the Jewish Theological Seminary of Hungary, Budapest

Al. W. **Alfred Witkon,** Dr. Jur.; Justice of the Supreme Court, Jerusalem

A. M. See **A. Mil.**

A. Ma. **Abraham Malamat,** Ph.D.; Professor of Ancient Jewish and Biblical History, the Hebrew University of Jerusalem

A. Man. **Arnold Mandel,** L.ès L.; Writer and critic, Paris

A. Mar. **Arthur Marmorstein** *(deceased)*, Ph.D.; Professor of Bible and Talmud, Jews' College, London

A. Maz. **Amihay Mazar,** B.A.; Jerusalem

A. M. D. **Alexander M. Dushkin,** Ph.D.; Emeritus Professor of Education, the Hebrew University of Jerusalem

A. M. F. **Abraham M. Fuss,** Ph.D., J.D.; Tax Commissioner, New York

A.M.H. **Abraham Meir Habermann;** Associate Professor of Medieval Hebrew Literature, Tel Aviv University

A. Mi. **Aharon Mirsky,** Ph.D.; Associate Professor of Hebrew Literature, the Hebrew University of Jerusalem

A. Mil., A. M. Il. **Attilio Milano** *(deceased),* Ph.D.; Historian, Hod Ha-Sharon, Israel

A. M. L. **Anne Marie Lambert;** Ministry for Foreign Affairs, Jerusalem

A. Mo. **Arnaldo Dante Momigliano,** D.Litt., F.B.A.; Professor of History, University College, London

A. M. R. **Alfredo Mordechai Rabello,** Dr.Jur.; Instructor in Roman Law and in the History of Medieval Law, the Hebrew University of Jerusalem

A. M. Rab. **Aron Moshe K. Rabinowicz,** Ph.D., M.C.J.; Secretary of the Faculty of Law, the Hebrew University of Jerusalem

Am. Sh. **Amnon Shiloah,** Ph.D.; Senior Lecturer in Musicology, the Hebrew University of Jerusalem

A. Mu. **Alan E. Musgrave,** Ph.D.; Professor of Philosophy, the University of Otago, Dunedin, New Zealand

A. N. **Aryeh Newman,** M.A.; Lecturer in English, the Hebrew University of Jerusalem

A. N. C. **André N. Chouraqui,** Ph.D.; Historian, Jerusalem

A. Ne. **Avraham Negev,** Ph.D.; Senior Lecturer in Classical Archaeology, the Hebrew University of Jerusalem

An. H. **André Hajdu,** M.A., Lecturer in Music, Tel Aviv University and Bar Ilan University, Ramat Gan

An. L. L. **Anthony Lincoln Lavine,** M.A.; Jerusalem

An. N. **André Neher,** Dr.Phil., M.D., Rabbi; Professor of Jewish History and Philosophy, the University of Strasbourg and Tel Aviv University

A. No. **Anita Novinsky,** Ph.D.; Lecturer in History, São Paulo University, Brazil

A. N. P. **Abraham N. Poliak** *(deceased),* Ph.D.; Professor of Islamic History and Research Professor of Khazar Studies, Tel Aviv University

An. R. **Anson Rainey,** Ph.D.; Associate Professor of Ancient Middle Eastern Civilization, Tel Aviv University

An. Sh. **Andrew Sharf,** Ph.D.; Associate Professor of History, Bar Ilan University, Ramat Gan

A. O. **A'hron Oppenheimer,** M.A.; Lecturer in Jewish History and Talmud, Tel Aviv University

A. P. **Akiva Posner** *(deceased),* Dr. Phil., Rabbi; Scholar and librarian, Jerusalem

A. Pa. **Arnold Paucker,** M.A.; Director of the Leo Baeck Institute, London

A. Pi. **Arieh Pilowsky,** B.A.; External Teacher in Foreign Languages, Haifa University

A. P. N. **Abraham Nasatir,** Ph.D.; Professor of History, San Diego State College, California

A. Po. **Arthur Polak,** M.D.; Amsterdam

A. R. **Alfred Rubens,** F.S.A., F.R.Hist. Soc.; Historian of Jewish Art and Costume, London

Ar. B. **Arnold Beichman,** M.A.; Lecturer in Politics, the University of Massachusetts, Boston

A. Re. **Alan Reitman,** B.A.; Associate Director of the American Civil Liberties Union, New York

Ar. G. **Arthur Aryeh Goren,** Ph.D.; Lecturer in American History, the Hebrew University of Jerusalem

Ar. H. **Arthur Hertzberg,** Ph.D., Rabbi; Associate Adjunct Professor of History, Columbia University, New York

Ar. K. **Arcadius Kahan,** Ph.D.; Professor of Economics, the University of Chicago

Ar. L. **Arye Levavi,** M.A.; Ambassador, Ministry for Foreign Affairs, Jerusalem

Ar. Lo. **Arthur Lourie,** LL.B., M.A.; Deputy Director General of the Ministry for Foreign Affairs, Jerusalem

Ar. M. **Aryeh Morgenstern,** B.A.; Teacher, Netanyah

A. Ro. **Aaron Rothkoff,** D.H.L., Rabbi and teacher; Jerusalem

Ar. R. **Arie Rafaeli-Zenziper;** Director of the Russian Zionist Archives, Tel Aviv

A. R. S. See **Al. R. S.**

Ar. St. **Arie Strikovsky,** Ph.D.; Lecturer in Talmud, the Technion, Haifa

A. Ru. **Avraham Rubinstein,** Ph.D.; Senior Lecturer in Jewish History, Bar Ilan University, Ramat Gan

Ar. W. **Aharon Weiss,** M.A.; Jerusalem

A. S. **Avrum Stroll,** Ph.D.; Professor of Philosophy, the University of California, San Diego

A. Sa. **Avrom Saltman,** Ph.D., F.R.Hist.Soc.; Professor of History, Bar Ilan University, Ramat Gan

A. Sch. **Abraham Schalit,** Dr. Phil.; Emeritus Professor of Jewish History, the Hebrew University of Jerusalem

A. Schi. **Abraham Schischa;** Letchworth, England

A. Schw. **Abraham Schwadron (Sharon)** *(deceased),* Dr. Phil.; Writer and collector, Jerusalem

A. S. D. **A. Stanley Dreyfus,** Ph.D., Rabbi; New York

A. S. E. **Abraham S. Eisenstadt,** Ph.D.; Professor of American History, Brooklyn College of the City University of New York

A. S. H. **Abraham Solomon Halkin,** Ph.D.; Emeritus Professor of History, the Jewish Theological Seminary of America, Jerusalem

A. Sh. **Aryeh Shmuelevitz,** M.A.; Senior Research Associate, the Shiloah Center for Middle East and African Studies; Lecturer in Middle Eastern and African History, Tel Aviv University

A. Sha. **Alexander Shapiro,** Ph.D., Rabbi; Lecturer in Jewish History, the University of the Negev, Beersheba

A. She. **Arnold Sherman,** M.A.; Public Relations Officer, El Al, Lydda Airport

A. Si. **Aryeh Simon,** B.A.; Educator, Youth Village, Ben Shemen, Israel

A. Sik. See **Ed.**

A. S. K. **Arvid S. Kapelrud,** Theol.D.; Professor of Biblical Language and Literature, the University of Oslo

A. S.-N. **Ana Shomlo-Ninic,** M.A.; Writer and critic, Belgrade

A. So. **Arnold Sorsby,** M.D., C.B.E., F.R.C.S.; Emeritus Research Professor of Ophthalmology, the Royal College of Surgeons of England, London

A. S. R. **Alvin S. Roth,** Ph.D., Rabbi; Albany, New York

A. St. **Adin Steinzalts,** Rabbi; Scholar, Jerusalem

A. S. V. D. W. **Adam Simon Van Der Woude,** M.A.; Professor of Old Testament, the State University of Groningen, the Netherlands

As. W. **Asher Weill;** Jerusalem

A. T. **Alexander Tobias,** Ph.D.; Librarian, the Jewish Theological Seminary of America, New York

A. Tar. **Aryeh Tartakower,** Ph.D., S.P.D.; Former Lec-

turer in the Sociology of the Jews, the Hebrew University of Jerusalem; Former Chairman of the Israel Executive of the World Jewish Congress, Jerusalem

A.T.B. **Arthur T. Buch,** D.S.Sc., Rabbi; Teacher, New York

A.Tch. **Avigdor (Victor) Tcherikover** *(deceased)*, Ph.D.; Professor of Ancient History, the Hebrew University of Jerusalem

A.To. **Ariel Toaff,** Ph.D., Rabbi; the Rabbinical College of Italy, Rome

A.U. **Alan Unterman,** Ph.D.; Jerusalem

A.Us., Au.S. **Ann Ussishkin,** M.A.; Jerusalem

Av.A.W. **Avraham A. Weiss,** Dr. Phil.; Senior Clinical Lecturer in Clinical Psychology, the Hebrew University of Jerusalem

Av.B. **Avner Bahat,** B.A.; Kefar Masaryk

Av.D. **Avigdor Dagan,** Dr.Jur.; Ambassador and author, Ministry for Foreign Affairs, Jerusalem

Av.E. **Avraham (Alfred) Engel;** Tel Aviv

Av.F. **Avyatar Friesel,** Ph.D.; Lecturer in Jewish History, the University of the Negev, Beersheba

Av.G. **Avraham Grossman,** M.A.; Instructor in History, the University of the Negev, Beersheba

Av.Go. **Avie Goldberg,** B.A.; Jerusalem

Av.H. **Avi Hurvitz,** Ph.D.; Lecturer in Bible and in Hebrew Language, the Hebrew University of Jerusalem

Av.He. **Avigdor Herzog,** B.A.; Librarian of the National Sound Archives, the Jewish National and University Library, Jerusalem; Lecturer in Jewish Ethnomusicology, Bar Ilan University, Ramat Gan

Av.Ho. **Avraham Holtz,** D.H.L., Rabbi; Associate Professor of Modern Hebrew Literature, the Jewish Theological Seminary of America, New York

Av.L. **Aviva Müller-Lancet,** L.ès L.; Curator of Jewish Ethnography, the Israel Museum, Jerusalem

Av.Le. **Avital Levy,** B.A.; Jerusalem

Av.R. **Avraham Ronen,** Dott. in lett.; Senior Lecturer in the History of Art, Tel Aviv University

Av.Ra. **Aviva Rabinovich,** M.Sc.; Jerusalem

Av.Ro. **Avshalom Rokach,** M.Sc.; Agronomist, Jerusalem

Av.S. **Avraham Soltes,** D.H.L., Rabbi; Musicologist, New York

A.W. **Alfred Werner,** J.D.; Art critic and writer, New York

A.We. **Abraham Wein,** M.A.; Historian, Jerusalem

A.Wi. **Aaron Wiener,** M.A.; Engineer, Director General of Tahal, Water Planning for Israel, Tel Aviv

A.Wo. **Adela Wolfe,** M.A.; Jerusalem

A.Y. **Abraham Yoffe;** Major General (Res.), Israel Defense Forces; Director of the Israel Nature Reserves Authority, Tel Aviv

A.Ya. **Avraham Yaari** *(deceased)*; Writer and bibliographer, Jerusalem

A.Y.G. **Abram Juda Goldrat,** Rabbi; Tel Aviv

Ay.L. **Ayala Loewenstamm,** M.A.; the Academy of the Hebrew Language, Jerusalem

A.Z. **Aharon Zwergbaum,** LL.D.; Legal Adviser, World Zionist Organization, Jerusalem

A.Z.B.-Y. **Aharon Zeev Ben-Yishai;** Writer and critic, Tel Aviv

Az.C. **Ezriel Carlebach** *(deceased)*, Dr.Jur.; Editor and writer, Tel Aviv

A.Z.E. **Arnost Zvi Ehrman,** Dr.Jur., F.J.C., Rabbi; Talmudic scholar, Ramat Gan

Az.K. See **Ab.K.**

Az.S. **Azriel Shochat,** Ph.D.; Associate Professor of the History of the Jewish People, Haifa University

Ba.K. **Batya Kedar;** Jerusalem

B.A.L. **Baruch A. Levine,** Ph.D., Rabbi; Professor of Hebrew, New York University, New York

B.B. **Bathja Bayer,** Ph.D.; Librarian of the Music Department, the Jewish National and University Library, Jerusalem

B.Ba. **Bernard Bachrach,** Ph.D.; Assistant Professor of Medieval History, the University of Minnesota, Minneapolis

B.Bl. **Bernhard Blumenkranz,** Ph.D., D.èsL.; Maître de Recherches, Centre National de la Recherche Scientifique, Paris

B.Br. **Bernhard Brilling,** Dr.Phil., Rabbi; Lecturer in Jewish History, the University of Muenster, Germany

B.Bt. See **B.Bl.**

B.D. **Benzion Dinur (Dinaburg);** Emeritus Professor of Jewish History, the Hebrew University of Jerusalem; Former Minister of Education and Culture, Jerusalem

B.D.G. **Bernard Dov Ganzel** *(deceased)*, Ph.D.; Historian, New York

B.D.K. **Barnet David Klien,** M.A., Rabbi; Jerusalem

B.D.S. **Barry Dov Schwartz,** M.H.L., Rabbi; Perth Amboy, New Jersey

B.D.-V. **Benjamin De-Vries** *(deceased)*, Ph.D., Rabbi, Professor of Talmud, Tel Aviv University

B.D.W. **Bernard Dov Sucher Weinryb;** Emeritus Professor of History and of Economics, Dropsie University, Philadelphia

B.E. **Binyamin Eliav,** Dr.Phil.; Editor and former official, Ministry for Foreign Affairs, Jerusalem

Be.A. **Benad Avital;** Ministry for Foreign Affairs, Jerusalem

Be.C. **Benjamin Cohen,** M.A., Rabbi; Jerusalem

Be.D. **Bernard Dubin,** M.S.W.; Executive Director of the Jewish Federation of Camden County, New Jersey

Be.G. **Bernard Grossfeld,** Ph.D., Rabbi; Assistant Professor of Hebrew Studies, the University of Wisconsin, Milwaukee

Be.H. **Bernard Heller,** Ph.D., Rabbi; New York

Be.K. **Benjamin Kahn,** M.H.L., Rabbi; International Director of the B'nai B'rith Hillel Foundations, Washington, D. C.

Be.S. **Bernard Semmel,** Ph.D.; Professor of History, the State University of New York, Stony Brook

Be.Sch. **Benjamin Schlesinger,** Ph.D.; Professor of Social Work, the University of Toronto

Be.W. **Bernard Wax,** M.A.; Director of the American Jewish Historical Society, Waltham, Massachusetts

Be.We. **Benjamin West;** Writer, Tel Aviv

B.F. **Bert Fireman,** B.A.; Lecturer in Arizona History, Arizona State University, Tempe

B.G. **Bernard Grebanier,** Ph.D.; Emeritus Professor of

English, Brooklyn College of the City University of New York

B. Gi. **Baruch Gilead,** M.A.; Ministry for Foreign Affairs, Jerusalem

B. G. K. **Ben G. Kayfetz,** B.A.; National Director of Community Relations, Canadian Jewish Congress–B'nai B'rith, Toronto

B. G. L. **Barton G. Lee,** M.A., Rabbi; Chicago

B. Go. **Bernard Goldman,** Ph.D.; Professor of Art History, Wayne State University, Detroit

B. G. R. **Bernard G. Rudolph;** Historian, Syracuse, New York

B. H. **Bernard Hooker,** B.A., Rabbi; Kingston, Jamaica

B. Hea. **Barth Healey,** B.A.; Journalist, New York

B. Hr. **Benjamin Hrushovski;** Associate Professor of Poetics and Comparative Literature, Tel Aviv University

B. I. **Benny Isaacson;** Tel Aviv

B. J. **Benjamin Jaffe,** M.A., M.Jur.; Writer and official, Jewish Agency, Jerusalem

B. J. B. **Bernard J. Bamberger,** D.D., Rabbi; President of the World Union for Progressive Judaism, New York

B. J. C. **Baruch J. Cohon**

B. J. K. **Benjamin J. Klebaner,** Ph.D.; Professor of Economics, City College of the City University of New York

B. J. R. **B. J. Roberts,** D.D.; Professor of Hebrew and Biblical Studies, University College of North Wales, Bangor

B. K. **Brian Knei-Paz (Knapheis),** M.A.; Instructor in Political Science, the Hebrew University of Jerusalem

B. Ke. **Benjamin Kedar,** Ph.D.; Lecturer in Biblical Studies, Haifa University

B. Kl. **Bronia Klibanski,** B.A.; Archivist, Jerusalem

B. Le. **Bernard Lewis;** Instructor in Films and Filming, New York University School of Continuing Education

B. M. **Baruch Mevorah,** Ph.D.; Senior Lecturer in Jewish History, the Hebrew University of Jerusalem

B. M. A. **B. Mordechai Ansbacher,** M.A.; Historian, Jerusalem

B. Ma. **Bernard Mandelbaum,** D.H.L., Rabbi; Chancellor, Professor of Homiletics, and Associate Professor of Midrash, the Jewish Theological Seminary of America, New York

B. Maz. **Benjamin Mazar,** Dr. Phil.; Pro-Rector, former President and Professor of Archaeology and of Jewish History, the Hebrew University of Jerusalem

B. McK. **Blake McKelvey,** Ph.D.; City Historian of Rochester, New York

B. Me. **Bent Melchior,** Rabbi; Chief Rabbi of Denmark, Copenhagen

B. M. L. **Bialik Myron Lerner,** Ph.D.; Instructor in Talmud, Tel Aviv University

B. M. Lev. **Boris M. Levinson,** Ph.D.; Professor of Psychology, Yeshiva University, New York

B. M. M. **Bruce M. Metzger,** Ph.D.; Professor of New Testament Language and Literature, Princeton Theological Seminary, New Jersey

B. Mo. **Baruch Modan,** M.D.; Tel Ha-Shomer, Israel

B. N. **Bezalel Narkiss,** Ph.D.; Senior Lecturer in the History of Art, the Hebrew University of Jerusalem

B. O. **Bustanay Oded,** Ph.D.; Lecturer in Jewish History, Haifa University

B. P. **Bernard Postal;** Author and Journalist, New York

B. Pi. **Benjamin Pinkus,** M.A.; Jerusalem

B. Po. **Bezalel Porten,** Ph.D., Rabbi; Teaching Fellow in Jewish History, the Hebrew University of Jerusalem; Senior Lecturer in Biblical Studies, Haifa University

B. R. See **B. Ri.**

B. R. G. **Bernard R. Goldstein,** Ph.D.; Associate Professor of the History of Science, Yale University, New Haven, Connecticut

B. Ri. **Benjamin Rivlin;** Writer, Jerusalem

B. Ro. **Beno Rothenberg,** Ph.D.; Senior Lecturer in Archaeology, Tel Aviv University

B. S. **Barry Spain,** Ph.D.; Head of the Department of Mathematics, City of London Polytechnic

B. Sa. **Benjamin Sagalowitz,** Dr. Jur.; Journalist, Zurich

B. Sch. **Baruch Shohetman** *(deceased),* M.A.; Bibliographer, Jerusalem

B. Se. **Bernard Segal,** D.H.L., Rabbi; Executive Vice-President, the United Synagogue of America, New York

B. Sh. **Bezalel Shachar,** M.A.; Lecturer in Adult Education, the Hebrew University of Jerusalem

B. St. **Bernard Sternsher;** Ph.D.; Professor of History, Bowling Green State University, Ohio

B. Su. **Bernard Suler** *(deceased),* Dr.Phil.; *Encyclopaedia Judaica* (Germany); Berlin

B. T. **Benyamin Tsedaka,** Writer, Ḥolon, Israel

B. U. **Baruch Uziel,** Former Member of the Knesset; Tel Aviv

Bu. B. **Burton Berinsky,** B.A.; Free-Lance Photographer, New York

B. V. **Bela Adalbert Vago,** Ph.D.; Senior Lecturer in History, Haifa University and the Hebrew University of Jerusalem

B. Va. **Benjamin (Benno) Varon (Weiser),** Abs. Med.; Ambassador, Ministry for Foreign Affairs, Jerusalem

B. W. **Brom Weber,** Ph.D.; Professor of English, the University of California, Davis

B. We. **Benjamin Weiss;** New York

B. W. K. **Bertram Wallace Korn,** D.H.L., Rabbi; Historian, Elkins Park, Pennsylvania

B. Y. **Baruch Yaron,** Dr. Phil. Librarian, the Hebrew University of Jerusalem

B. Z. **Benjamin Zvieli,** M.A., Rabbi; Director of Religious Broadcasting, Jerusalem

B.-Z. B. **Binyamin Zeev Benedikt,** Ph.D., Rabbi; Senior Lecturer in Rabbinical Literature and Halakhah, Tel Aviv University

B. Z. Bo. **Ben Zion Bokser,** Ph.D., Rabbi; Adjunct Professor of English, Queens College of the City University of New York

B. Z. S. **Bernard Zvi Sobel,** Ph.D.; Associate Professor of Sociology, Haifa University

B.-Z. Sch. **Ben-Zion (Benno) Schereschewsky,** Dr.Jur.; Judge of the District Court, Jerusalem

B.-Z. W. **Ben Zion Wacholder,** Ph.D., Rabbi; Professor of

Talmud and Rabbinics, the Hebrew Union College–Jewish Institute of Religion, Cincinnati,

C. Ab. **Claude Abravanel;** Lecturer, the Rubin Academy of Music, Jerusalem

Ca. C. **Calev Castel,** M.D.; Kibbutz Netzer Sereni

Ca. G. **Carol Gendler,** M.A.; Instructor in History, College of St. Mary, Omaha, Nebraska

C. Al. **Carl Alpert;** Executive Vice Chairman of the Board of Governors, the Technion, Haifa

C. An. **Charles Angoff,** B.A.; Professor of English, Farleigh Dickinson University, Rutherford, New Jersey

C. Ap. See **C. Al.**

Ca. S. **Catherine Silverman,** Ph.D; Lecturer in History, City College of the City University of New York

C. A. V. **Claude (André) Vigée,** Ph.D.; Professor of French Literature, the Hebrew University of Jerusalem

C. B. S. **C. Bezalel Sherman** *(deceased)*; Professor of Sociology, Yeshiva University and the Jewish Teachers' Seminary, New York

C. C. **Charles Cutter,** M.A., M.L.S.; Hebrew Bibliographer of the Library, Ohio State University, Columbus

C. C. A. **C. C. Aronsfeld;** Researcher, London

C. G. **Claude Gandelman,** M.A.; Jerusalem

Cha. B. **Chaim Brovender,** Ph.D., Rabbi; Instructor in Bible, Bar Ilan University, Ramat Gan

Ch. B. **Charles Boasson,** LL.D.; the Truman Center for the Advancement of Peace, the Hebrew University of Jerusalem

C. Her. See **J. Her.**

Ch. G. **Chaim Ivor Goldwater,** LL.M.; Ministry of Finance, Jerusalem

Ch. H. **Chaim Herzog,** LL.B.; Major General (Res.), Israel Defense Forces; Military commentator and business executive, Tel Aviv

Ch. I. K. **Charles I. Kapralik,** Dr. iur.; London

Ch. K. **Chaim S. Kazdan;** the Jewish Teachers' Seminary, New York

Ch. L. **Chaim Levanon,** Eng.Agr.; Agricultural engineer and former Mayor of Tel Aviv

Ch. M. **Chen Merchavya,** Ph.D.; Historian, Jerusalem

Ch. M. R. **Chaim M. Rabin;** D.Phil., Dipl.O.S.; Professor of Hebrew Language, the Hebrew University of Jerusalem

Ch. R. **Charles Reznikoff,** LL.B.; Author, New York

Ch. Sh. **Chone Shmeruk,** Ph.D.; Professor of Yiddish Literature, the Hebrew University of Jerusalem

Ch. S. S. **Charles Samuel Spencer;** Art critic, London

Ch. T. **Charles Touati,** Ph.D., Rabbi; Assistant Professor of Jewish Philosophy, Ecole Pratique des Hautes Etudes, Sorbonne, Paris

Ch. Tu. **Chava Turniansky,** M.A.; Instructor in Yiddish Language and Literature, the Hebrew University of Jerusalem

C. H. V. **Carl Hermann Voss,** Ph.D., Reverend; Author and lecturer, Jacksonville, Florida

Ch. W. **Chaim Wardi,** Ph.D.; Senior Lecturer in Christianity in the Middle East and Africa, Tel Aviv University

Ch. Wi. **Chaim Wirszubski,** Ph.D.; Professor of Classical Studies, the Hebrew University of Jerusalem

Ch. Y. **Chaim Yahil,** Ph.D.; Former Director General of the Ministry for Foreign Affairs; Chairman of the Israel Broadcasting Authority; Jerusalem

Ch. Z. **Charles Zibbell,** M.S.; Associate Executive Director, Council of Jewish Federations, New York

C. I. K. See **Ch. I. K.**

C. K., Cl. K. **Claude Klein,** Ph.D.; Senior Lecturer in Law, the Hebrew University of Jerusalem

C. L. **Curt Leviant,** Ph.D.; Associate Professor of Hebraic Studies, Rutgers University, New Brunswick, New Jersey

C. Pa. **Channah Palti;** Jerusalem

C. R. **Cecil Roth** *(deceased)*, D.Phil., F.R.Hist.Soc.; Reader Emeritus in Jewish Studies, the University of Oxford; Editor in Chief of the *Encyclopaedia Judaica*, Jerusalem

C. Ri. **Chanoch Rinott,** Ph.D.; Senior Teacher and Director of the Center for Jewish Education in the Diaspora, the Hebrew University of Jerusalem

C. Ro. **Cvi Rotem,** Ph.D.; Journalist, Tel Aviv

C. S. **Colette Sirat,** Ph.D.; Directeur d'Etudes de Paléographie Hebraïque à l'Ecole Pratique des Hautes Etudes, Sorbonne; Directeur du Project de Paléographie Hebraïque au Centre National de la Recherche Scientifique, Institut de Recherches et d'Histoire des Textes, Paris; Senior Lecturer in Jewish Philosophy, the University of the Negev, Beersheba

C. Sc. **Carmi Schwartz,** M.A., M.S.W.; Associated Jewish Charities and Welfare Fund, Baltimore

C. S. L. **Charles S. Liebman,** Ph.D.; Associate Professor of Political Science, Bar Ilan University, Ramat Gan

C. So. **Claire Sotnick,** B.A.; New York

C. T. **Chasia Turtel,** M.A.; Researcher in Jewish History, Jerusalem

C. W. **Charles Wengrov,** Rabbi; Jerusalem

Da. C. **David Cohen,** M.A.; Teacher in Hebrew and Semitic Languages, Bar Ilan University, Ramat Gan

Da. Co. **David Coren;** Member of the Knesset, Kibbutz Gesher Ha-Ziv

Da. H. **Dan Halperin,** B.A.; Economist and journalist, Jerusalem

Da. J. S. **Daniel Jeremy Silver,** Ph.D., Rabbi; Adjunct Professor of Religion, Case Western Reserve University, Cleveland

D. Al. **David Alcalay;** Jerusalem

D. Alm. **Dan Almagor,** Ph.D.; Writer, Haifa

Da. M. **David Mirsky,** M.A., Rabbi; Dean and Professor of English and Hebrew Literature, Yeshiva University, New York

Da. N. **David Neiman,** Ph.D., Rabbi; Associate Professor of Theology, Dean of the Academy for Higher Jewish Learning, Boston

Da. S. **David Solomon,** M.A.; Researcher in Jewish history, Jerusalem

Da. Sa. **David Saraph;** Tel Aviv

D. Ash. **Dov Ashbel,** Dr.Phil.; Emeritus Associate Professor of Meteorology, the Hebrew University of Jerusalem

D. Atz. **David Atzmon,** M.Jur.; Ministry for Foreign Affairs, Jerusalem

D. Av. **Dov Avron,** Ph.D.; Historian, Tel Aviv

Da. Y. **David Jutan**; Histadrut Ha-Ovdim Ha-Le'ummit, Tel Aviv
D.B. **David Baumgardt** *(deceased)*, Dr.Phil.; Professor of Philosophy, the University of Berlin; Consultant on Philosophy to the Library of Congress, Washington, D.C.
D.B.-G. **David Ben-Gurion;** Former Prime Minister and Minister of Defense of the State of Israel, Sedeh Boker
D. Bi. **David Bidney,** Ph.D.; Professor of Anthropology and Education, Indiana University, Bloomington
D. Bo. **Daniel Boyarin,** M.H.L.; New York
D. Br. **Dvora Briskin-Nadiv,** B.A., B.Ed.; Assistant in Biblical Studies, the University of the Negev, Beersheba
D. B.-R.-H. **David Bar-Rav-Hay,** Advocate; Former Member of the Knesset, Haifa
D. B. R. N. **Daniel Benito Rubinstein Novick;** National University of Buenos Aires
D. Bs. **Doris Bensimon-Donath,** Ph.D.; Chargé de Recherche au Centre National de la Recherche Scientifique, Paris
D. B. W. **David B. Weisberg;** Ph.D.; Assistant Professor of Bible and Semitic Languages, Hebrew Union College–Jewish Institute of Religion, Cincinnati
D. C. **Daniel Carpi,** Ph.D.; Associate Professor of Jewish History, Tel Aviv University
D. Ch. **Dov Chomsky;** Poet, General Secretary of the Hebrew Writers' Association, Tel Aviv
D. Co. **David Corcos;** Historian, Jerusalem
D. D. **David Diringer,** Litt.D.; Emeritus Reader in Semitic Epigraphy, the University of Cambridge; Director of the Alphabeth Museum, Tel Aviv
D. Da. **David Davidovitch,** Eng.; Director of the Museum of Ethnography and Folklore, Tel Aviv
D. D. L. **Donald Daniel Leslie,** D.de l'U; Fellow in Far Eastern History, Australian National University, Canberra
D. Do. **David Dori;** Kibbutz Ein Ha-Ḥoresh
De. Al. **David Algaze,** M.H.L., Rabbi; New York
De. D. **Danuta Dombrowska,** M.A.; Historian, Jerusalem
D. E. F., D. Ef. **Daniel Efron,** M.A.; Jerusalem
D. E. G. **Daniel E. Gershenson,** Ph.D.; Acting Associate Professor of Classics, the University of California, Los Angeles
D. F. **Daniel Furman;** Jerusalem
D. Fl. **David Flusser,** Ph.D.; Professor of Comparative Religion, the Hebrew University of Jerusalem
D. Fla. **Dov Shmuel Flattau (Plato),** Dr.Phil., Rabbi; *Encyclopaedia Judaica* (Germany); Teacher and scholar, Tel Aviv
D. G. **Ernst Daniel Goldschmidt,** Ph.D. *(deceased)*; Scholar and librarian, Jerusalem
D. Ga. **Daniel Gavron;** Writer, Jerusalem
D. Gam. **Denise Gamzon,** Ph.D.; Instructor in French Literature, Tel Aviv University
D. Ge. **Dov Genachowski,** B.A.; Senior Economist of the Bank of Israel, Jerusalem
D. Go. **David Goodblatt,** M.H.L., Rabbi; Providence, Rhode Island
D. H. **David Horowitz;** Former Governor of the Bank of Israel, Jerusalem
D. Ho. **David Horn,** Ph.D.; Professor of Physics, Tel Aviv University
D. H. P. **David H. Panitz,** M.A., Rabbi; Dean of the Academy for Jewish Religion, New York
D. H. W. **D.H. White** *(deceased)*, publisher, Houston
D. I. **David Ignatow;** Adjunct Professor of Writing, Columbia University; Poet-in-Residence, York College of the City University of New York
D. I. M. **Donald I. Makovsky,** M.A.; Assistant Professor of History, Forest Park Community College, St. Louis, Missouri
Di. N. **Dika Newlin,** Ph.D.; Professor of Music, North Texas State University, Denton
D. I. S. See **O. I. S.**
D. Ja. **David Jacoby,** Ph.D.; Associate Professor of History, the Hebrew University of Jerusalem
D. J. B. **David Joseph Bornstein** *(deceased)*; *Encyclopaedia Judaica* (Germany); Berlin
D. J. C. **Daniel J. Cohen,** Ph.D.; Director of the Central Archives for the History of the Jewish People, Jerusalem
D. J. E. **Daniel J. Elazar,** Ph.D.; Professor of Political Science and Director of the Center for the Study of Federalism, Temple University, Philadelphia
D. J. S. **Dirk Jan Struik,** Ph.D.; Emeritus Professor of Mathematics, Massachusetts Institute of Technology, Cambridge
D. J. Si. **David Jacob Simonsen** *(deceased)*, Ph.D., Rabbi; Chief Rabbi of Denmark, Copenhagen
D. K. **Otto Dov Kulka,** M.A.; Lecturer in Modern Jewish History, the Hebrew University of Jerusalem
D. Ka. **David Kadosh,** Ph.D., Rabbi; Assistant Professor of Jewish Philosophy, Yeshiva University, New York
D. Ko. **David Kotlar,** C.E.; Lecturer in Jewish History, Bar Ilan University, Ramat Gan
D. K. R. See **O. K. R.**
D. L. **Dora Litani-Littman,** M.A.; Researcher, Jerusalem
D. La. **Dvora Lapson,** B.A.; Instructor in Dance, the Hebrew Union College School of Education, New York
D. Le. **Dov Levin,** Ph.D.; Researcher in the Institute of Contemporary Jewry, the Hebrew University of Jerusalem
D. L. L. **David L. Lieber,** D.H.L., Rabbi; President and Professor of Bible, the University of Judaism; Lecturer in Hebrew, the University of California Los Angeles
D. L. M. O. See **D. M. L. O.**
D. L. S. **Dora Leah Sowden,** M.A.; Journalist, Jerusalem
D. L. Si. **David L. Silver,** B.A., Rabbi; Harrisburg, Pennsylvania
D. L. Z. **David L. Zielonka,** M.A.H.L., Rabbi; Professor of Religion, the University of Tampa, Florida
D. M. **David Maisel,** M.A.; Jerusalem
D. Ma. **David Margalith,** M.D.; Former Lecturer in the History of Medicine, Bar Ilan University, Ramat Gan
D. M. D. **Douglas Morton Dunlop,** M.A.; Professor of History, Columbia University, New York
D. M. E. **David Max Eichhorn,** D.H.L., Rabbi; Cape Kennedy, Florida
D. M. F. **Daniel M. Friedenberg,** B.A.; Curator of Coins and Medals, the Jewish Museum, New York

D.M.Fe. **David M. Feldman,** D.H.L., Rabbi; New York
D.Mi. **Dan Miron,** Ph.D.; Associate Professor of Modern Hebrew Literature, Tel Aviv University
D.M.L.O. **David M. L. Olivestone,** B.A.; Jerusalem
D.N. **David Niv,** M.A.; Editor and historian, Jerusalem
D.O. **David Obadia,** Rabbi; Member of the Rabbinical Council of Jerusalem
Do.L. **Doris Lankin,** M.Jur.; Legal journalist, Jerusalem
Do.N. **Dov Noy,** Ph.D.; Senior Lecturer in Folklore and in Hebrew and Yiddish Literature, the Hebrew University of Jerusalem
Do.W. **Donald Weinstein,** Ph.D.; Associate Professor of History, Rutgers University, New Brunswick, New Jersey
Do.Z. **Dov Zlotnick,** D.H.L., Rabbi; Associate Professor of Rabbinic Literature, the Jewish Theological Seminary of America, New York
D.P. **David Patterson,** Ph.D.; Lecturer in Post-Biblical Hebrew, the University of Oxford; Visiting Professor of Hebrew Studies, Cornell University, Ithaca, New York
D.Pa. **Dan Pagis,** Ph.D.; Senior Lecturer in Hebrew Literature, the Hebrew University of Jerusalem
D.P.B. **Dan P. Barag,** Ph.D.; Instructor in Archaeology, the Hebrew University of Jerusalem
D.R. **Dov Rabin;** Researcher, Jerusalem
D.R.G. **Denise R. Goitein,** Ph.D.; Lecturer in French Literature, Tel Aviv University
D.R.H. **Delbert Roy Hillers;** Ph.D.; Professor of Semitic Languages, Johns Hopkins University, Baltimore
D.Ro. **David Rokeaḥ,** Ph.D.; Lecturer in Jewish History, the Hebrew University of Jerusalem
D.Ru. **David Rudavsky,** Ph.D.; Professor of Hebrew Culture and Education, Director of the Institute of Hebrew Studies, New York University
D.S. **Daniel Sperber,** Ph.D., F.R.N.S.; Senior Lecturer in Talmud, Bar Ilan University, Ramat Gan
D.Sa. **Dov Sadan;** Emeritus Professor of Yiddish Literature and of Hebrew Literature, the Hebrew University of Jerusalem
D.S.F., D.Sf. **David Sfard,** Ph.D.; Jerusalem
D.S.L. **David S. Lifson,** Ph.D.; Professor of English and of Humanities, Monmouth College, Long Branch, New Jersey
D.S.Loe. **David Samuel Loewinger,** Dr.Phil., Rabbi; Scholar, Former Professor at the Jewish Theological Seminary of Hungary; the Jewish National and University Library, Jerusalem
D.Sp. **S(halom) David Sperling,** M.H.L., Rabbi; Instructor in Hebrew and Jewish History, State University of New York, Stony Brook
D.S.R. **Dan S. Rosenberg,** M.A.; Assistant Director of the Council of Jewish Federations and Welfare Funds, New York
D.T. **David Tanne;** Chairman of the Board of Directors, Tefaḥot-Mortgage Bank; Former Director General of the Ministry of Housing
D.Ta. **David Tamar,** Ph.D.; Lecturer in Jewish History, Haifa University
D.Te. **David Tene,** D.del'U; Senior Lecturer in Hebrew Language, the Hebrew University of Jerusalem.
D.Ts. **Dan Tsalka;** Writer and critic Tel Aviv
D.V. **David Vinitzky;** Givatayim, Israel
D.W. **David Winston,** Ph.D., Rabbi; Professor of Hellenistic and Judaic Studies, the Graduate Theological Union, Berkeley, California
D.W.-H. **David Weiss Halivni,** D.H.L., Rabbi; Professor of Rabbinics, the Jewish Theological Seminary of America; Adjunct Professor of Religion, Columbia University, New York
D.Y. **Dwight Young,** Ph.D.; Associate Professor of Ancient Near Eastern Civilization, Brandeis University, Waltham, Massachusetts
D.Z. **David Zakay,** Editor and journalist, Tel Aviv
D.Zo. **Danah Zohar,** M.A.; Jerusalem

E.A. **Eliyahu Ashtor,** Ph.D., Dr.Phil.; Professor of Moslem History and Civilization, the Hebrew University of Jerusalem
E.Ar. **Elia Samuele Artom** *(deceased)*, Dott.in lett., Rabbi; Teacher of Hebrew Language and Literature, Università degli Studi, Florence; Director and Professor of the Collegio Rabbinico Italiano, Florence and Rome
E.B. **Emmanuel Beeri,** M.A.; Jerusalem
E.B.B. **Eugene B. Borowitz,** D.H.L., Ed.D., Rabbi; Professor of Jewish Religious Thought and of Education, the Hebrew Union College–Jewish Institute of Religion, New York
E.Be. **Elieser Beck;** Kibbutz Kefar Ha-Maccabi
E.B.-G. **Emanuel Bin-Gorion;** Writer and scholar, Ḥolon, Israel
E.B.-H. **Eliashiv Ben-Horin,** LL.B.; Ambassador, Ministry for Foreign Affairs, Jerusalem
E.Bi. **Erwin Bienenstok** *(deceased)*, LL.M.; Journalist, London
E.B.J. See **E.B.**
E.Bo. **Elijah Bortniker,** Ph.D.; the Jewish Education Committee, New York
E.Br. **Emmanuel Brand,** Dipl. Archiv.; Jerusalem
E.Bu. **Emmanuel Bulz,** LL.D., Rabbi; Chief Rabbi of Luxembourg
E.C. **Elisheva Cohen;** Chief Curator of the Israel Museum, Jerusalem
E.D. **Eli Davis,** M.D.; Associate Professor of Medicine, the Hebrew University—Hadassah Medical School, Jerusalem
Ed. Editorial Staff, *Encyclopaedia Judaica*
E.D.G. See **D.G.**
Ed.H. **Edith Hirsch,** M.A.; Economist and teacher, New York
Ed.K. **Edy Kaufman,** Ph.D.; Jerusalem
Ed.L. **Edythe Lutzker,** M.A.; Writer, New York
E.D.M. **Evasio de Marcellis,** M.A.; Teacher in the Department of Ancient Near Eastern Studies, Tel Aviv University
Ed.N. **Eduard Nielson,** Dr.Theol.; Professor of Theology, Copenhagen University, Denmark
E.E. **Edna Elazary,** B.A.; Jerusalem
E.Ef. **Elisha Efrat,** Ph.D.; Senior Lecturer in Geography, Tel Aviv University
E.E.G. See **Em.G.**
E.E.H. **Elimelech Epstein Halevy,** M.A.; Visiting Senior Lecturer in Aggadah, Tel Aviv University
E.E.Hi. **Eugene B. Hibshman,** B.A., B.H., Rabbi; Sioux Falls, South Dakota

E. El. **Eliezer Eliner,** M.A.; Senior Teacher in Talmud, Tel Aviv University

E. Eli. **E. Elias;** Journalist, formerly Ernakulam, Cochin, India; Haifa

E. E. S. **Ernest E. Simke;** Honorary Consul-General of Israel, Manila, Philippines

E. E. U., **Ephraim Elimelech Urbach,** Dott.in.lett., Rabbi; Professor of Talmud, the Hebrew University of Jerusalem

E. F. **Ellen Friedman;** New York

E. F. B. **Ernest Frank Benjamin** *(deceased)*, Brigadier; Commander of the Jewish Brigade, England

E. Fi. **Ephraim Fischoff,** D.S.Sc., Rabbi; Professor of Sociology, Wisconsin State University, Eau Claire

E. Fl. **Ezra Fleischer,** Ph.D.; Senior Lecturer in Hebrew Literature, the Hebrew University of Jerusalem

E. G. **Efraim Gottlieb,** Ph.D.; Associate Professor of Jewish Philosophy and Mysticism, the Hebrew University of Jerusalem

E. Ga. See **B. D. G.**

Eg. F. **Egal Feldman,** Ph.D.; Professor of History, Wisconsin State University, Superior

E. G.-K. **Edith Gerson-Kiwi,** Dr.Phil.; Associate Professor of Ethnomusicology, Tel Aviv University

E.G.L. **Ernst Gottfried Lowenthal,** Dr.rer.Pol.; Berlin and London

E. Go. **Eric Gottgetreu;** Journalist, Jerusalem

E. Gr. **Edward L. Greenstein,** B.A., B.H.L.; New York

E. H., EH *Encyclopaedia Hebraica*

E. Ha. **Ernest Hamburger,** Ph.D.; Political Scientist, New York

E. Hi. **Eliyahu Hirschberg,** M.Jur., M.Ph.; Jerusalem

E. Hu. **Elazar Hurvitz,** Ph.D., Rabbi; Associate Professor of Bible and Midrash, Yeshiva University, New York

Ei. F. See **El. F.**

Ei. S. **Eisig Silberschlag,** Ph.D.; President and Professor of Hebrew Literature, the Hebrew College, Brookline, Massachusetts

E. J., EJ *Encyclopaedia Judaica* (Germany)

E. J. B. **Elias J. Bickerman,** Ph.D.; Emeritus Professor of Ancient History, Columbia University, New York

E. J. F. **Eugene Jacob Fleischmann,** Ph.D.; Maître de Recherche au Centre National de la Recherche Scientifique, Paris

E. J. K. **Elton J. Kerness,** M.S.W.; Executive Director of the Jewish Community Council of Eastern Union County, New Jersey

E. J. W. **Ephraim Jehudah Wiesenberg,** Ph.D., Rabbi; Reader in Hebrew, the University of London

E. K. **Ephraim Kupfer;** Research Fellow in Jewish Studies, the Hebrew University of Jerusalem

E. Kr. **Ernest Krausz,** Ph.D.; Lecturer in Sociology, the City University, London

E. Ku. **Erich Kulka,** Historian, Jerusalem

El. A. **Eliyahu Arieh,** M.Sc.; Director of the Seismological Laboratory, Geological Survey of Israel, Jerusalem

El. B. **Eliezer Bashan (Sternberg),** M.A.; Instructor in Jewish History, Bar Ilan University, Ramat Gan

El. Be. **Eliezer Berkovits,** Ph.D., Rabbi; Professor of Jewish Philosophy, the Hebrew Theological College, Skokie, Illinois

El. E. **Eli Eytan,** Ph.D.; Associate Professor of Hebrew Language, Tel Aviv University; Scientific Secretary of the Academy of the Hebrew Language, Tel Aviv

El. F. **Eliyahu Feldman,** Ph.D.; Senior Lecturer in Jewish History, Tel Aviv University

E. L. Fr. **Eric Lewis Friedland,** Ph.D.; Professor of Judaics, Wright State University, Antioch College, University of Dayton, and United Theological Seminary, Dayton, Ohio

El. G. **Elmer Gertz,** J.D.; Attorney, Chicago

El. Gl. **Eliezer Gluzberg;** Kibbutz Ḥaẓerim

E. Li. **Edward Lipinski,** D.D., D.Bibl.St.; Professor of Ancient History, of the History of Semitic Religions, and of Comparative Grammar of Semitic Languages, the Catholic University of Louvain, Belgium

E. Lif. **Ezekiel Lifschutz;** Archivist of the YIVO Institute for Jewish Research, New York

El. K. **Elieser Kagan,** Ph.D.; Lecturer in Hebrew Language and Literature, Haifa University

El. Ka. **Elias Katz,** Rabbi; Former Rabbi of Bratislava, Czechoslovakia, Beersheba

El. Li. **Elias Lipiner,** B.A.; Journalist, Tel Aviv

El. S. **Eliezer Schweid,** Ph.D.; Senior Lecturer in Jewish Philosophy and Mysticism, the Hebrew University of Jerusalem

El. Sh. **Eliyahu Shadmi;** Kibbutz Ma'anit

E. M. **Eliezer Margaliot,** Ph.D., Rabbi; Scholar and teacher, Jerusalem

E. Ma. **Eugene Markovitz,** D.H.L., Rabbi; Adjunct Professor of American History, Seton Hall University, South Orange, New Jersey

E. Me. **Ezra Mendelsohn,** Ph.D.; Lecturer in Contemporary Jewry and in Russian Studies, the Hebrew University of Jerusalem

E. Med. **Elliott Hillel Medlov,** B.A., Rabbi; Highland Park, New Jersey

Em. G. **Edwin Emanuel Gutmann,** Ph.D.; Senior Lecturer in Political Science, the Hebrew University of Jerusalem

Em. Gr. **Emanuel Green,** Ph.D., Rabbi; Associate Professor of Hebrew and Judaica, Hofstra University, Hempstead, New York

E. M. J. **Edmund Meir Jerusalem** *(deceased)*, Dr.Phil.; Historian, Jerusalem

Em.L. **Emanuel Litvinoff;** Writer and editor, London

Em. L. F. **Emil Ludwig Fackenheim,** Ph.D., Rabbi; Professor of Philosophy, the University of Toronto

Em. R. **Emanuel Rose,** D.H.L., Rabbi; Portland, Oregon

E. N. **Ellis Nassour,** M.A.; New York

E. N. S. **Edwin N. Soslow,** M.A., Rabbi; Lecturer in History and Literature, the Hebrew Union College School of Education, New York

E. O. **Efraim Orni,** M.A.; Geographer, Jerusalem

E. P. **Eliezer Palmor,** M.A.; Ministry for Foreign Affairs, Jerusalem

E. Pa. **Esther Panitz,** M.A.; Writer, Paterson, New Jersey

Eph. B. **Ephraim Broido;** Writer and editor, Jerusalem

Eph.E. **Ephraim Evron;** Ambassador and Deputy Director General, Ministry for Foreign Affairs, Jerusalem

Eph. S. **Ephraïm Schmidt;** Antwerp

E. Po. **Edward I. J. Poznański,** M.Phil.; Visiting Senior Lecturer in Philosophy, the Hebrew University of Jerusalem

E. R. **Edouard Roditi,** B.A.; Art critic, Paris

E. Ra. **Emanuel Rackman,** Ph.D., Rabbi; Professor of Judaic Studies and Consultant to the Chancellor, the City University of New York

E. R. G. **Erwin Ramsdell Goodenough** *(deceased)*, Ph.D.; Professor of the History of Religion, Yale University, New Haven, Connecticut

Er. H. **Ernest Hearst;** Editor, Wiener Library, London

E. Ri. **Elimelech Rimalt,** Ph.D.; Member of the Knesset, Former Minister of Posts, Ramat Gan

Er. K. **Ernst Kutsch,** Dr.Theol.; Professor of Old Testament Theology, Friedrich-Alexander Universität zu Erlangen-Nürnberg, Germany

E. Ro. **Ernst Roth,** Ph.D., Rabbi; Chief Rabbi of the State of Hesse, Frankfort on the Main

Er. R. **Erich Rosenthal,** Ph.D.; Professor of Sociology, Queens College of the City University of New York

Er. S. **Ernest Schwarcz,** Ph.D.; Professor of Philosophy, Queens College of the City University of New York

Er. St. **Ernest Stock,** Ph.D.; Lecturer in Politics and Director of the Jacob Hiatt Institute of Brandeis University, Jerusalem

E. S. **Edwin Samuel, Second Viscount Samuel,** C.M.G., B.A.; Emeritus Senior Lecturer in British Institutions, the Hebrew University of Jerusalem; Principal of the Israel Institute of Public Administration, Jerusalem

E. Sch. **Elias Schulman,** Ph.D.; the Jewish Teachers' Seminary, New York

Es. G. **Esther Goldenberg,** M.A.; Assistant in Hebrew Language, the Hebrew University of Jerusalem

E. Sh. **Efraim Shmueli,** Ph.D.; Professor of Philosophy; Adjunct Professor of Jewish History and Literature, Cleveland State University

E. S.-O. **Eleanor Sterling-Oppenheimer,** Ph.D.; Associate Professor of Political Science, J.W. Goethe-Universität, Frankfort on the Main

E. Sp. **Ezra Spicehandler,** Ph.D., Rabbi; Professor of Hebrew Literature and Director of Jewish Studies, the Hebrew Union College–Jewish Institute of Religion, Jerusalem

Es. R. **Esther Rosenthal (Schneiderman),** Cand. Pedag. Sci.; Jerusalem

E. St. see **El.B.**

E. Ste. **Ephraim Stern,** Ph.D.; Lecturer in Archaeology, Tel Aviv University

E. Su. **Esther Sulman;** New London, Connecticut

E. T. **Esther Tarsi-Gay,** Dr.Phil.; the Graduate Library School of the Hebrew University of Jerusalem

Eu. M. **Eugene Mihaly,** Ph.D.; Rabbi; Professor of Midrash and of Homiletics, the Hebrew Union College–Jewish Institute of Religion, Cincinnati

Ev. L. G. **Evelyn Levow Greenberg;** Journalist, Washington, D.C.

E. W. **Edith Wyschogrod,** Ph.D.; Assistant Professor of Philosophy, Queens College of the City University of New York

E. Y.-H. **Edith Yapou-Hoffmann,** Ph.D.; Instructor in Art History, Tel Aviv University

E. Y. K. **Eduard Yecheskel Kutscher** *(deceased)*, M.A.; Professor of Hebrew Philology, the Hebrew University of Jerusalem; Professor of Hebrew Language, Bar Ilan University, Ramat Gan

E. Z. **Esther (Zweig) Liebes,** B.A.; Jerusalem

F. A. R. **Fritz A. Rothschild,** D.H.L., Rabbi; Associate Professor of the Philosophy of Religion, the Jewish Theological Seminary of America, New York

F. B. **Fritz Bauer** *(deceased)*, Dr.Jur.; Prosecutor of War Criminals, Frankfort on the Main

F. Br. **Fred Bronner,** M.A.; Lecturer in Latin American History, the Hebrew University of Jerusalem

F. B. W. **Felix Bernard Wahle;** Tel Aviv

F. D. G. **Frank D. Grande,** M.A.; Lecturer in History, City College of the City University of New York

F. E. **Frank Emblen;** Journalist, New York

F. E. S. **Felix Eliezer Shinnar,** Dr.Jur.; Economist and former Ambassador, Tel Aviv

F. F. B. **Frederick Fyvie Bruce,** D.D.; Professor of Biblical Criticism and Exegesis, the University of Manchester, England

F. J. B.-J. **Frederik Julius Billeskov-Jansen,** Ph.D.; Professor of Danish Literature, Copenhagen University

F. J. H. **Frederik Jacob Hirsch,** B.A.; Librarian, Haifa

Fl. E. **Flower Elias;** London

Fl. G. **Florence Guggenheim-Gruenberg,** Dr.Sc.Nat.; Historian, Zurich

F. M. B. **Frederick M. Binder,** Ed.D.; Professor of Educational History, City College of the City University of New York

F. N. S. **Frank N. Sundheim,** M.A., Rabbi; Lecturer in Religion, the University of Tampa, Florida

F. P. **Frank Pelleg** *(deceased)*; Pianist and musicologist, Haifa

F. R. **Fred Rosner,** M.D.; Instructor in Medicine, Downstate Medical Center, Brooklyn, New York

Fr. J. **Franklin Jonas,** Ph.D.; Instructor in History, Long Island University, New York

Fr. J. H. **Frederick J. Hoffman;** the University of California, Riverside

F. R. K. **Frances R. Kallison,** B.A.; San Antonio, Texas

F. R. L. **Frederick R. Lachman,** Ph.D.; Executive editor of the *Encyclopaedia Judaica*, New York

Fr. S. **François Secret,** Directeur d'Etudes à l'Ecole Pratique des Hautes Etudes (Sciences Religieuses), Sorbonne, Paris

F. S. **Fritz Schiff** *(deceased)*, Dr.Phil.; Curator of the Museum of Modern Art, Haifa

F. T. **Frank Talmage,** Ph.D.; Assistant Professor of Medieval and Modern Hebrew, the University of Toronto

F. W. **Felix Weltsch** *(deceased)*, Writer and philosopher, the Jewish National and University Library, Jerusalem

G. A. **Gerald Abrahams,** M.A.; Barrister at Law, Liverpool

Ga. B. **Gabriel Bach,** LL.B.; State Attorney of the State of Israel, Jerusalem

Ga. C. **Gabriel H. Cohn,** Ph.D.; Lecturer in Bible, Bar Ilan University, Ramat Gan

G. A.-T. **Gerda Alster-Thau,** M.A.; Lecturer in Hebrew and World Literature, Bar Ilan University, Ramat Gan
G. Av. **Gitta (Aszkenazy) Avinor,** M.A.; Critic, Haifa
Ga. W. **Paul G. Werskey,** M.A.; Lecturer in Science Policy, the University of Edinburgh
G. B. **Günter Böhm,** B.A.; Professor of Jewish Art and Vice Director of the Institute for the Study of Judaism, the University of Chile, Santiago
G. B.-Y. **Geulah Bat Yehuda (Raphael),** M.A.; Writer, Jerusalem
G. C. **Gilbert Cahen;** Archiviste-Paléographe; Conservateur aux Archives Départementales de la Moselle, Metz, France
G. C. S. **Gertrude C. Serata,** M.L.S.; Librarian, Honolulu
G. D. C. **Gerson D. Cohen,** Ph.D., Rabbi; President and Professor of Jewish History, the Jewish Theological Seminary of America, New York
Ge. B. **Gershon Bacon,** M.H.L.; New York
Ge. C. **Georges Cattaui,** L.en D., Dip.Sc.Pol.; Paris
G. E. H. **G. Eric Hauck,** B.A.; Journalist, New York
G. El. **Gedalyah Elkoshi,** Ph.D.; Associate Professor of Hebrew Literature, Tel Aviv University
G. E. S. **Godfrey Edmond Silverman,** M.A.; Jerusalem
G. E. T. **Gerald E. Tauber,** Ph.D.; Professor of Mathematical Physics, Tel Aviv University
G. F. C. **Greer Fay Cashman;** Journalist, Sydney
G. H. **Gershon Hadas,** B.A., Rabbi; Kansas City, Missouri
G. H. F. **George H. Fried,** Ph.D.; Associate Professor of Biology, Brooklyn College of the City University of New York
G. Hi. **Gertrude Hirschler,** B.S.; Editor, New York
G. H.-R. **Galit Hasan-Rock,** B.A.; Assistant in Hebrew Literature, the Hebrew University of Jerusalem
Gi. F. **Giza Frankel,** Ph.D.; the Ethnological Museum, Haifa
Gi. K. **Gideon Katznelson,** M.A.; Lecturer in Modern Hebrew Literature, Tel Aviv University
Gi. L. **Gideon Lahav,** B.A.; Ministry of Commerce and Industry, Jerusalem
G. I. R. See **G. Lr.**
G. J. B. **Gerald J. Blidstein,** Ph.D., Rabbi; Associate Professor of Jewish Studies, McGill University, Montreal
G. J. W. **George Julius Webber,** LL.D.; Barrister at Law, Former Reader in English Law, the University of London
G. K. **Getzel Kressel;** Writer and bibliographer, Holon. Israel
G. K. G. **Gershon K. Gershony** *(deceased)*; Theater critic, Jerusalem
G. Ku. **Gilbert Kushner,** Ph.D.; Associate Professor of Anthropology, the College at Brockport of the State University of New York
G. L. **Gilbert Lazard,** D.ès L.; Professor of Iranian Language and Civilization, Sorbonne Nouvelle, Paris
G. La. **Guiseppe Laras,** Dr.Jur., Rabbi; Leghorn, Italy
G. Le. **Georges Levitte;** Writer, Paris
G. Lo. **Giora Lotan,** Dr.Jur.; Former Director General of the National Insurance Institute, of the Ministry of Social Welfare, and of the Ministry of Labor, Jerusalem
G. Lr., Gl. R. **Gladys Rosen,** Ph.D.; Historical researcher, New York
G. M. See **G. K.**
G. N. **Gérard Nahon,** Ph.D.; Chargé de Recherches au Centre National de la Recherche Scientifique, Paris
G. R. **Giorgio Romano,** LL.D.; Journalist, Tel Aviv
Gr. L. **Grete Leibowitz,** Dr.Phil.; Former editorial staff, *Encyclopaedia Hebraica,* Jerusalem
G. Ro. **Geraldine Rosenfield,** M.A.; the American Jewish Committee, New York
G. S. **George Schwab,** Ph.D.; Assistant Professor of Modern History, City College of the City University of New York
G. Sa. **Gustav Saron,** LL.B.; General Secretary of the South African Board of Deputies, Johannesburg
G. Sch. **Gershom Scholem,** Dr.Phil.; Emeritus Professor of Jewish Mysticism, the Hebrew University of Jerusalem
G. Sh. **Gershon Shaked,** Ph.D.; Associate Professor of Hebrew Literature, the Hebrew University of Jerusalem
G. T. **Guido (Gad) Tedeschi,** D.Jur.; Professor of Civil Law, the Hebrew University of Jerusalem
G. Ta. **Gad Tadmor,** M.D.; Savyon, Israel
Gu. L. **Guenter Lewy,** Ph.D.; Professor of Government, the University of Massachusetts, Amherst
G. V. **Georges Vajda,** D.ès L.; Professor of Medieval Jewish Thought, Directeur d'Etudes à l'Ecole Pratique des Hautes Etudes, Sorbonne, Paris
G. W. **Geoffrey Wigoder,** D.Phil.; Editor in Chief of the *Encyclopaedia Judaica;* the Institute for Contemporary Jewry, the Hebrew University of Jerusalem
G. We. **Georges Weill,** M.A., Archiviste-Paléographe; Directeur des Services d'Archives des Hauts-de-Seine, France
G. Y. **Galia Yardeni-Agmon** *(deceased)*, Ph.D.; Writer, Jerusalem
G. Y. O. **Gustav Yaacob Ormann,** Ph.D.; Editor, *Kirjath Sepher,* Jerusalem
G. Yo. **Gedalia Yogev,** Ph.D.; Editor, *The Weizmann Letters,* Jerusalem
G. Z. **Gershon Zilberberg,** Editor of *Olam Ha-Defuss,* Tel Aviv

H. A. **Haim Avni,** Ph.D.; Lecturer in Contemporary Jewry, the Hebrew University of Jerusalem
Ha. Al. **Harry Alter;** Editor, Youngstown, Ohio
Ha. Be. **Haïm Bentov,** M.A., Rabbi; Lecturer in Talmud, Bar Ilan University, Ramat Gan
Ha. Bl. **H. Elchanan Blumenthal,** M.A., Rabbi; Jerusalem
Ha. B.-O. **Hanan Bar-On;** Ministry for Foreign Affairs, Jerusalem
H. A. F. **Henry Albert Fischel,** Ph.D., Rabbi; Professor of Near Eastern Studies, Indiana University, Bloomington
Ha. L. **Haim Leor,** M.Jur.; Secretary of the Knesset, Jerusalem
Ha. Le. **Harold Lerner,** Ph.D.; Political scientist, New York
H. Al. S. **Herbert Allen Smith,** M.A.; Director of the Manpower Planning Authority, Jerusalem
Ha. P. **Hans Pohl,** Dr.Phil.; Professor of Constitutional,

Social and Economic History, the University of Bonn

Ha. R. **Hanna Ram,** M.A.; History Museum of Tel Aviv

H. A. S. **Herbert A. Strauss,** Ph.D.; Associate Professor of History, City College of the City University of New York

Ha. St. **Hannah Stein;** Executive Director of the National Council of Jewish Women, New York

H. Av. **Hanoch Avenary,** Dr.Phil.; Senior Lecturer in Musicology, Tel Aviv University

H. B. **Haim Beinart,** Ph.D.; Professor of Medieval Jewish History, the Hebrew University of Jerusalem

H. Bar. **Hillel Barzel,** Ph.D.; Associate Professor of Hebrew and World Literature, Bar Ilan University, Ramat Gan

H. B.-D. **Haim Bar-Dayan,** Dr.Phil.; Instructor in the History of Music and Art, the Rubin Academy of Music, Jerusalem

H. B. E. **H. Bruce Ehrmann,** M.H.L., Rabbi; Brockton, Massachusetts

H. B. G. **Hyman B. Grinstein,** Ph.D.; Professor of American Jewish History, Yeshiva University, New York

H. Bl. **Haim Blanc,** Ph.D.; Professor of Linguistics, the Hebrew University of Jerusalem

H. Blu. **Harry Bluestone,** B.A., A.C.S.W.; Former Executive Director of the Jewish Federation of Delaware, Wilmington

H. Bo. **Henriette Boas,** Ph.D.; Journalist, Amsterdam

H. B. R. **Howard B. Radest,** Ph.D.; Associate Professor of Philosophy, Ramapo College, Mahwah, New Jersey

H. Br. **Herbert Chanan Brichto,** Ph.D., Rabbi; Professor of Bible, the Hebrew Union College–Jewish Institute of Religion, Cincinnati

H. Bro. **Heinrich Haim Brody** *(deceased)*, Ph.D.; Scholar of medieval Hebrew poetry and former Chief Rabbi of Prague, Jerusalem

H. C. **Harvey A. Cooper,** B.A.; Journalist, New York

H. Ca. **Hayden Carruth,** M.A.; Poet and critic, Johnson, Vermont

H. Co. **Chayim Cohen,** B.A., B.H.L.; Columbia University, New York

H. D. **Herbert Davidson,** Ph.D.; Associate Professor of Philosophy, the University of California, Los Angeles

H.D.-D. **Haim Darin-Drapkin,** Ph.D., Scientific Director, International Research Centre for Cooperative Rural Communities, Tel Aviv

H. D. H. **Horace D. Hummel,** Ph.D.; Associate Professor of Religion, Valparaiso University, Indiana

H. D. M. **H. D. Modlinger**

H. E. A. **Helmut E. Adler,** Ph.D.; Professor of Psychology, Yeshiva University, New York

H. E. Ba. **Henry Eli Baker,** B.C.L., LL.B.; President of the District Court, Jerusalem; Research Fellow in the Law Faculty, the Hebrew University of Jerusalem

He. C. **Henri Cazelles,** D.en D.; Professor of Biblical Exegesis and Hebrew, Institut Catholique de Paris

H. E. K. **Harold E. Katz,** M.A., A.C.S.W.; Executive Director of the Jewish Community Council, Birmingham, Alabama

He. R. **Helen Rosenau,** Dr. Phil.; Art historian, London

He. S. **Heinrich Strauss,** Dr. Phil.; Art historian, Jerusalem

H. F. **Harold Harel Fisch,** B. Litt.; Pro-Rector and Professor of English, Bar Ilan University, Ramat Gan

H. Fl. **Heinrich Flesch** *(deceased)*, Ph.D., Rabbi; *Encyclopaedia Judaica* (Germany); Czechoslovakia

H. Fr., H. Ft. **Harry Freedman,** Ph.D., Rabbi; Caulfield, Victoria, Australia

H. G. **Henri Guttel,** B.A.; Jerusalem

H. G. A. **H. G. Adler,** Ph.D.; Historian, London

H. Ge. **Haim M. I. Gevaryahu,** Ph.D.; Chairman of the Israel Society for Biblical Research, Jerusalem

H. G. G. **Hans G. Güterbock,** Ph.D.; Professor of Hittitology, the University of Chicago

H. Go. **Harry Golden,** B.A.; Writer and editor, Charlotte, North Carolina

H. G. R. **Hanns G. Reissner,** Ph.D.; Professor of History, New York Institute of Technology, Old Westbury

H. H. **Hillel Halkin,** M.A.; Jerusalem

H.H.B.-S. **Haim Hillel Ben-Sasson,** Ph.D.; Professor of Jewish History, the Hebrew University of Jerusalem

H. H. C. **Haim Hermann Cohn;** Justice of the Supreme Court of Israel, Jerusalem; Associate Professor of Law, the Hebrew University of Jerusalem

H. H. P. **Herbert H. Paper,** Ph.D.; Professor of Near Eastern Languages and Linguistics, the University of Michigan, Ann Arbor

Hi. K. **Hilel Klein,** M.D.; Jerusalem

Hi. L. **Hildegard Lewy** *(deceased)*, Ph.D.; Visiting Professor, Hebrew Union College, Cincinnati, Ohio

Hi. S. **Hillel Seidman,** Ph.D.; President of the Beth Jacob Teachers' College, New York

H. J. **Howard Jacobson,** Ph.D.; Assistant Professor of Classics, the University of Illinois, Urbana

H. J. A. **Harry J. Alderman,** B.A., B.S.; the American Jewish Committee, New York

H. J. C. **Hayyim J. Cohen,** Ph.D.; Senior Lecturer in Contemporary Jewry, the Hebrew University of Jerusalem

H. J. K. **H. Jacob Katzenstein,** Ph.D.; Director of the Schocken Library, Jerusalem

H. J. P. **Hans Jacob Polotsky,** Dr.Phil.; Professor of Egyptian and Semitic Linguistics, the Hebrew University of Jerusalem

H. J. Z. **Hirsch Jacob Zimmels,** Ph.D., Rabbi; Former Principal and Lecturer in Jewish History and Rabbinics, Jews' College, London

H. K. **Hyman Kublin,** Ph.D.; Professor of History, Brooklyn College of the City University of New York

H. Ka. **Heinrich Karplus,** M.D.; Associate Professor of Forensic Medicine, the Hebrew University—Hadassah Medical School, Jerusalem; Director of the Institute of Forensic Medicine, Tel Aviv

H. K. B. **Haim Karl Blum** *(deceased)*, Dr.Phil.; Historian, Jerusalem

H. Ke. **Hermann Kellenbenz,** Dr. Phil.; Professor of Economic and Social History, the University of Cologne

H. Ki. **Herman Kieval,** M.H.L., Rabbi; Visiting Associate Professor of Practical Theology; Visiting

Assistant Professor of Liturgy, the Jewish Theological Seminary of America, New York
H. Kl. **Heszel Klepfisz,** Ph.D., Litt.D., Rabbi; Rector of the Instituto Alberto Einstein; Professor of Judaic Culture, the University of Panama
H. Kn. **Harry Knopf,** D.iur.Utr.; Advocate, Tel Aviv
H. Kr. **Helen Kragness-Romanishan,** M.A.; Educator, Wichita, Kansas
H. L. **Hans Liebeschütz,** Dr.Phil., F.R.Hist.Soc.; Professor Extraord. of Medieval Latin Literature, the University of Hamburg; Emeritus Reader in Medieval History, the University of Liverpool
H. L. A. **Howard L. Adelson,** Ph.D.; Professor of Medieval History, City College of the City University of New York
H. La. **Hermann Langbein;** Vienna
H. L. An. **Heinz L. Ansbacher,** Ph.D.; Professor of Psychology, the University of Vermont, Burlington
H. Le. **Hayim Leaf,** Ph.D.; Professor of Hebrew Language and Literature, Yeshiva University, New York
H. L. F. **Henry L. Feingold,** Ph.D.; Assistant Professor of American Diplomatic and American Jewish History, the Bernard Baruch College of the City University of New York
H. L. G. **Harold Louis Ginsberg,** Ph.D.; Professor of Biblical History and Literature, the Jewish Theological Seminary of America, New York
H. L. S. **Harry L. Shapiro,** Ph.D.; Emeritus Chairman of the Department of Anthropology, the American Museum of Natural History; Professor of Anthropology, Columbia University, New York
H. L. T. **Hans L. Trefousse,** Ph.D.; Professor of History, Brooklyn College of the City University of New York
H. Lu. **Heinz Lubacz;** Waltham, Massachusetts
H. M. **Hugo Mantel,** Ph.D., Rabbi; Associate Professor of Jewish History, Bar Ilan University, Ramat Gan
H. M. B. **Harry M. Bracken,** Ph.D.; Professor of Philosophy, McGill University, Montreal
H. M. Z. M. **Herrmann M. Z. Meyer,** M.A. *(deceased),* Scholar and Advocate, Berlin; Jerusalem
H. N. **Hugh Nibley,** Ph.D.; Professor of History and Religion, Brigham Young University, Provo, Utah
H. O. **Haim Ormian,** Ph.D.; Editor of the *Encyclopaedia of Education* (Hebrew), Jerusalem
H. P. **Hiram Peri** *(deceased),* Dr. Phil.; Professor of Romance Languages, the Hebrew University of Jerusalem
H. Pa. **Herbert Parzen,** M.A., M.H.L., Rabbi; Historian, New York
H. P. S. **Herman Prins Salomon,** Ph.D.; Professor of French Literature, the State University of New York, Albany
H. Pu. **Herbert Pundik,** Journalist, Tel Aviv
H. R. See **Ch. M. R.**
H. Ra. **Harry Rabinowicz,** Ph.D., Rabbi; Historian, London
H. Re. **Hanoch Reviv,** Ph.D.; Lecturer in Jewish History, the Hebrew University of Jerusalem
H. R. R. **Chayim Reuven Rabinowitz,** B.A., Rabbi; Writer, Jerusalem
H. S. **Henry Sosland,** M.H.L., Rabbi; New City, New York
H. Sa. **Harry Sacher** *(deceased),* M.A.; Attorney, writer, and editor, London
H. Sch. **Henri Schilli,** Chief Rabbi; Lecturer in Midrash and Director of the Seminaire Israélite de France, Paris
H. S. G. **Herman S. Gundersheimer,** Ph.D.; Professor of Art History, Temple University, Philadelphia
H. Sh. **Herzl Shmueli,** Ph.D.; Senior Lecturer in Musicology, Tel Aviv University
H. Si. **Harvard Sitkoff,** Ph.D.; Assistant Professor of American History, Washington University, Saint Louis, Missouri
H. St. **Chanan Steinitz,** Dr. Phil.; Musicologist, Ramot Hashavim, Israel
H. Sta. **Harry Starr,** B.A., LL.B.; President of the Lucius N. Littauer Foundation, New York
H. T. **Haim Toren,** M.A.; Writer, Jerusalem
H. Ta. **Hayim Tadmor,** Ph.D.; Professor of Assyriology, the Hebrew University of Jerusalem
H. To. **Henry J. Tobias,** Ph.D.; Professor of Russian History, the University of Oklahoma, Norman
Hu. K. **Hugo Knoepfmacher,** D.Jur.; Government official, Washington, D. C.
H. U. R. **Harold U. Ribalow,** B.S.; Writer, New York
H. V. **Hugo Mauritz Valentin** *(deceased),* Dr.Phil.; Professor of History, the University of Uppsala, Sweden
H. v. H. **Harold von Hofe,** Ph.D.; Professor of German Literature, the University of Southern California, Los Angeles
H. W. **Henry Wasserman,** M.A.; Jerusalem
H. We. **Hanna Weiner,** B.A.; Kibbutz Ne'ot Mordekhai
H. Wi. **Helene Wieruszowski,** Ph.D.; New York
H. Y. C. See **H. J. C.**
Hy. J. C. **Hyman Joseph Campeas,** M.A.; Educator, New York
H. Z. **Haïm Zafrani,** Ph.D., D.ès L.; Chargé de Recherche au Centre National de la Recherche Scientifique; Director of the Hebrew Department, the University of Paris-Vincennes
H. Ze. **Hanna Semer,** B.A.; Editor of *Davar,* Tel Aviv
H. Z. H. **Haïm Z'ew Hirschberg,** Ph.D., Rabbi; Professor of Jewish History, Bar Ilan University, Ramat Gan
H. Zo. **Harry Zohn,** Ph.D.; Professor of German, Brandeis University, Waltham, Massachusetts
H. Z. W. **Heinrich Zwi Winnik,** M.D.; Associate Professor of Psychiatry, the Hebrew University-Talbieh Psychiatric Hospital, Jerusalem

I. A. **Israel Adler,** Dr. du 3e cycle; Director of the Center for Research in Jewish Music, the Hebrew University of Jerusalem
I. A. A. **Irving A. Agus,** Ph.D., Rabbi; Professor of Jewish History, Yeshiva University, New York
I. Ab. **Isaac Abraham Abbady** *(deceased)*; Journalist, Jerusalem
I. Abr. **Israel Abrahams,** M.A., Rabbi; Emeritus Professor of Hebrew, the University of Cape Town; Former Chief Rabbi of Cape Province, South Africa; Jerusalem
I. Al. See **Y. Al.**

I. Av. See **Is. A.**

I. B. **Sir Israel Brodie,** B.A., B.Litt., Rabbi; Former Chief Rabbi of the British Commonwealth, London

I. Ba. **Isadore Barmash;** Journalist, New York

I. Be. **Isac Bercovici;** Journalist, Bat Yam

I. B. G. **Isaac B. Gottlieb,** M.A., Rabbi; Jerusalem

I. Bu. **Israel Burgansky,** M.A.; Instructor in Talmud, Bar Ilan University, Ramat Gan

I. C. **Israel Cohen;** Writer and editor, Tel Aviv

I. Ca. **Ivan Caine,** M.H.L., Rabbi; Associate Professor of Bible, Reconstructionist Rabbinical College, Philadelphia

I. D. **Israel Dostrovsky,** Ph.D.; Vice President and Professor of Physical Chemistry, the Weizmann Institute of Science, Reḥovot, Israel

I. Dr. **Israel Drapkin-Senderey.** M.D.; Professor of Criminology and Director of the Institute of Criminology, the Hebrew University of Jerusalem

I. Eph. **Israel Eph'al,** M.A.; Instructor in Biblical History, Tel Aviv University

I. E. S. **Ira E. Sanders,** M.A., Rabbi; Little Rock, Arkansas

Ie. Sch. **Iehuda Schuster;** Kibbutz Mefalsim

I. F. **Israel Finestein,** M.A., Q.C.; Barrister, London

I. Fr. **Israel Francus,** Ph.D., Rabbi; Associate Professor of Rabbinics, the Jewish Theological Seminary of America, New York

I. G. **Isaiah Gafni,** M.A.; Special Teacher in Jewish History, the Hebrew University of Jerusalem; Assistant in Jewish History, the University of the Negev, Beersheba

I. Ga. **Israel Galili;** Minister without Portfolio, Kibbutz Na'an

I. G.-E. **Israel Gal-Edd,** B.A., A.C.I.S.; Senior External Lecturer in International Trade Relations, the Hebrew University of Jerusalem; Former Director General, Ministry of Development, Jerusalem

I. Ge. **Israel Getzler,** Ph.D.; Professor in European History, La Trobe University, Melbourne

I. Gr. **Ithamar Gruenwald,** Ph.D.; Lecturer in Jewish Philosophy, Tel Aviv University

I. Gru. **Irene Grumach,** Ph.D.; Jerusalem

I. Gu. **Israel Gutman,** B.A.; Historian, Kibbutz Lehavot Habashan

I. H. **Isaac Harpaz,** Ph.D.; Associate Professor of Agricultural Entomology, the Hebrew University of Jerusalem

I. Ha. **Israel Halpern** *(deceased)*, M.A.; Professor of Jewish History, the Hebrew University of Jerusalem

I. Har. **Israel Harburg,** B.A., Rabbi; Lynn, Massachusetts

I. H. B. **Israel Ch. Biletzky,** B.A.; Writer, Tel Aviv

I. He. **Irene Heskes;** Musicologist, New York

I. H. P. See **E. H.**

I. H. Sh. **I. Harold Sharfman,** D.H.L., Rabbi; Los Angeles

I. I. **Israel (Ignacy) Isserles,** M.A., Advocate; Tel Aviv

I. I. K. **Irving I. Katz,** B.A., B.B.A., F.T.A.; Detroit, Michigan

I. J. **Immanuel Jakobovits,** Ph.D., Rabbi; Chief Rabbi of the British Commonwealth, London

I. J. B. **Ivan Jay Ball, Jr.,** B.A., B.D.; Foothill Community College, Los Altos Hills, California

I. J. G. **Ignace J. Gelb,** Ph.D.; Professor of Assyriology, the University of Chicago

I. J. K. **Israel J. Kapstein,** Ph.D.; Emeritus Professor of English Literature, Brown University, Providence, Rhode Island

I. K. **Israel Klausner,** Ph.D.; Historian and former Deputy Director of the Central Zionist Archives, Jerusalem

I. Ka. **Izhak Kanev,** M.A.; Director of the Social and Economic Research Institute, Tel Aviv

I. Ko. **Israel Kolatt,** Ph.D.; Senior Lecturer in Contemporary Jewry, the Hebrew University of Jerusalem

I. K. S. **Ida Kay Saks,** M.A.; Gary, Indiana

I. L. **Isaac Levitats,** Ph.D.; the Herzliah Hebrew Teachers' Seminary, New York

I.-L. G. **Inger-Lise Grusd;** Oslo

I. L. K. **Isaiah L. Kenen,** LL.B.; Executive Director of the American-Israel Public Affairs Committee, Washington, D. C.

Il. S. **Ilana Shapira,** M.A.; Jerusalem

I. L. U. **Ida Libert Uchill,** B.A.; Denver, Colorado

I. M. **Isaak Dov Ber Markon** *(deceased)*, Dr.Phil.; Historian, Ramsgate, England

I. Ma. **Irving Malin,** Ph.D.; Associate Professor of English, City College of the City University of New York

I. Mar. **Yitzhak Margowsky,** B.A.; Jerusalem

I. M. B. **Israel M. Biderman,** Ph.D.; Lecturer in Education, New York University; the Jewish Teachers' Seminary, New York

I. Me. **Itshak Meraz** *(deceased)*, M.A.; Jerusalem

I. M. F. **Isaac M. Fein,** Ph.D.; Emeritus Professor of Jewish History, Baltimore Hebrew College

I. M. G. **Israel M. Goldman,** M.A., D.H.L., Rabbi; Baltimore

I. M. S. **I. M. Salkind** *(deceased)*, Ph.D.; Scholar, London

I. N. **Isaac Newman,** B.A., Rabbi; London

I. O. L. **Israel O. Lehman,** D.Phil.; Curator of Manuscripts and Special Collections, the Hebrew Union College—Jewish Institute of Religion, Cincinnati

I. P. **Israel Porush,** O.B.E., Dr. Phil., Rabbi; Lecturer in Jewish History, Sydney University

I. Per. **Isa Perlis-Kressel,** M.A.; Ḥolon, Israel

I. Ph. **Israel Philipp,** M.A.; Central Zionist Archives, Jerusalem

I. R. **Irving Rosenthal,** M.A.; Associate Professor of Journalism, City College of the City University of New York

Ir. F. **Irving Fineman,** B.S.; Author, Shaftsbury, Vermont

Ir. G. **Irene Garbell** *(deceased)*, Dr.Phil.; Associate Professor of Semitic Linguistics, the Hebrew University of Jerusalem

I. Ri. **Israel Ritov;** Journalist, Tel Aviv

Ir. M. **Irwin L. Merker,** Ph.D.; Associate Professor of History, Rutgers University, Newark, New Jersey

I. Ro. **Isaac Rokach;** Managing Director of the Pardess Syndicate, Herzliyyah

I. S. See **I. T.-S.**

Is. A. **Isaac Avishur,** M.A.; Instructor in Bible and Biblical History, the University of the Negev, Beersheba

I. Sc. **Imre Schmelczer,** M.A., Rabbi; St. Gallen, Switzerland

Is. C. **Isaac Cohen,** Ph.D., Rabbi; Chief Rabbi of Ireland, Dublin

I. Sch. **Ignacy Yizhak Schiper** *(deceased)*, Dr.Phil.; Lecturer in Jewish Economic History, the Institute of Jewish Studies, Warsaw

I. S. E. **Isaac Samuel Emmanuel,** Sc.D., Rabbi; Historian, Cincinnati,

Is. G. **Israel Goldstein,** D.H.L., Rabbi; Former Chairman of the Board of Directors, Keren Hayesod, Jerusalem

Is. Ga. See **I. G.**

Is. Gar. **Isaac Garti,** B.A.; Teaching Assistant in Italian Literature, the Hebrew University of Jerusalem

Is. J. K. **Israel J. Katz,** Ph.D.; Assistant Professor of Ethnomusicology, Columbia University, New York

Is. K. **Isaac Kalugai,** M.Sc.; Emeritus Professor of Chemistry, the Technion, Haifa

Is. Kl. **Isaac Klein,** Ph.D., Rabbi; Lecturer in Philosophy, the State University of New York at Buffalo

I. S. M. **Isidore S. Meyer,** M.A., Rabbi; Historian, New York

I. So. **Israel Soifer,** B.A.; Jerusalem

I. Sol. **Isidor Solomon;** Toorak, Victoria, Australia

Is. S. **Isidore Simon,** M.D.; Professor of the History of Hebrew Medicine, Centre Universitaire d'Etudes Juives, Paris

Is. Sc. **Isaac Schattner,** Dr.Phil.; Emeritus Associate Professor of Geography, the Hebrew University of Jerusalem

Is. Sch. **Ismar Schorsch,** Ph.D., Rabbi; Assistant in Jewish History, the Jewish Theological Seminary of America, New York

Is. Sm. **Israel Smotricz,** Ph.D.; Tel Aviv

I. T. **Isadore Twersky,** Ph.D., Rabbi; Professor of Hebrew Literature and Philosophy, Harvard University, Cambridge, Massachusetts

It. G. **Itta Gutglück,** B.A.; Jerusalem

I. T. N. **Israel T. Naamani,** Ph.D.; Professor of Political Science, the University of Louisville, Kentucky

I. Tr. **Isaiah Trunk;** Historian, YIVO Institute for Jewish Research, New York

I. T.-S. **Israel Moses Ta-Shma,** M.A., Rabbi; Editorial staff, *Encyclopaedia Hebraica,* Jerusalem

I. T. Sp. **Irving T. Spivack,** M.A., M.S.; Margate, New Jersey

I. W. **Irwin Weil,** Ph.D.; Professor of Russian and Russian Literature, Northwestern University, Evanston, Illinois

I. Y. **Irwin Yellowitz,** Ph.D.; Associate Professor of History, City College of the City University of New York

I. Y.-K. **Itamar Yaos-Kest,** B.A.; Writer and Poet, Tel Aviv

I. Z. **Israel Sedaka;** Ḥolon, Israel

I. Z. K. **Isaac Ze'ev Kahane** *(deceased)*, Rabbi; Professor of Talmud and of Jewish History, Bar Ilan University, Ramat Gan

J. A. **Joseph Adar,** M.Sc.; Israel Atomic Energy Commission, Ramat Gan

Ja. B. **James Barr,** D.D., F.B.A.; Professor of Semitic Languages and Literatures, the University of Manchester, England

Jac. K. **Jacob Katz,** Dr.Phil.; Rector and Professor of Social Jewish History, the Hebrew University of Jerusalem

Ja. G. **Jacob Goldman,** Rabbi; Jerusalem

Ja. K. **Jacqueline Kahanoff,** M.A.; Writer, Tel Aviv

Ja. Ka. **Jacob Kabakoff,** B.A., D.H.L., Rabbi; Associate Professor of Hebrew, the Herbert H. Lehman College of the City University of New York

Ja. L. **Jacob Lassner,** Ph.D.; Professor of Near Eastern Studies, Wayne State University, Detroit

Ja. M. **Jacob Maimon;** Jerusalem

Ja. Mu. **James Muilenburg,** Ph.D.; Emeritus Professor of Old Testament, San Francisco Theological Seminary, San Anselmo, California

J. A. N. **John Alfred Nathan,** B.A., LL.B.; Tel Aviv

J. An. **Jean Ancel,** M.A.; Jerusalem

Ja. N. **Jacob Neusner,** Ph.D., Rabbi; Professor of Religious Studies, Brown University, Providence, Rhode Island

Ja. O. R. **Janice O. Rothschild,** B.A.; Atlanta, Georgia

J. Ap. **John J. Appel,** Ph.D.; Associate Professor of American Studies, the James Madison College of Michigan State University, East Lansing

Ja. P. **Jacob Picker,** Dr.Jur.; Ministry of Finance, Jerusalem

J. A. Sch. **Janos A. Schossberger,** M.D.; Psychiatric Director of Kfar Shaul Work Village, Jerusalem

J. Au. **Jacob Auerbach;** Jerusalem

J. A. W. **James A. Wax,** D.H.L., Rabbi; Memphis, Tennessee

J. B. **Joseph Bentwich,** M.A.; Former Lecturer in Education, the Hebrew University of Jerusalem

J. B. A. **Jacob Bernard Agus,** Ph.D., Rabbi; Adjunct Professor of Modern Jewish Philosophy, Dropsie University; Professor of Rabbinic Judaism, the Reconstructionist Rabbinical College, Philadelphia

J. Ba. **Jack Barbash,** M.A.; Professor of Economics, the University of Wisconsin, Madison

J. Bah. **Jacob Bahat;** Senior Lecturer in Hebrew Language and Literature, Haifa University

J. Bar. **Joel Barromi,** Dr.Jur.; Ministry for Foreign Affairs, Jerusalem

J. Bas. **Jack Bass,** B.A.; New York

J. B. F. **Julian B. Feigelman,** LL.D., Ph.D., Rabbi; New Orleans

J. Bl. See **Y. Bl.**

J. B.-M. **Jacov Benmayor,** B.A.; Salonika

J. Br. **Jehoshua Brand,** Ph.D.; Associate Professor of Talmudic Archaeology, Tel Aviv University

J. Bra. **Joseph Brandes,** Ph.D.; Professor of History, Paterson State College, Wayne, New Jersey

J. Bro. **Josef Brožek,** Ph.D.; Research Professor, Lehigh University, Bethlehem, Pennsylvania

J. B. S. **Joseph Baruch Sermoneta,** Ph.D., Dott.in Fil.; Associate Professor of Jewish Philosophy and Mysticism; Senior Lecturer in Italian Language and Literature and in Philosophy, the Hebrew University of Jerusalem

J. B. Sch. **Joseph B. Schechtman** *(deceased)*, Dr.Phil.; His-

torian and Former Member of the Jewish Agency Executive, New York

J.B.Sh. **Joseph Ben-Shlomo,** Ph.D.; Senior Lecturer in Philosophy, the Hebrew University of Jerusalem

J.C.G. **Jonas C. Greenfield,** Ph.D.; Professor of Ancient Semitic Languages, the Hebrew University of Jerusalem

J.Co. **Judith Cohen,** Ph.D.; Lecturer in Musicology, Tel Aviv University

J.D. **Jacob Dash,** B.Arch, A.M.T.P.I.; Head of the Planning Department, Ministry of the Interior, Jerusalem

J.D.F. **Jerome D. Folkman,** Ph.D., Rabbi; Adjunct Professor of Sociology, Ohio State University, Columbus

J.E.E. **Jacob Eliahu Ephrathi,** D.H.L.; Senior Lecturer in Talmud, Bar Ilan University, Ramat Gan

J.E.H. **J. Edwin Holmstrom,** Ph.D., C.Eng.; Folkestone, England

Je.Ha. **Jesaia Hadari,** Rabbi; Jerusalem

Je.P. **Jeonathan Prato,** Dr.Jur.; Ministry for Foreign Affairs, Jerusalem

J.F. **Jehuda Feliks,** Ph.D.; Professor of Botany, Bar Ilan University, Ramat Gan

J.Fa. **José Faur,** Ph.D.; Associate Professor of Rabbinics, the Jewish Theological Seminary of America, New York

J.Fi. **Jacob Finkelstein,** Ph.D.; Professor of Assyriology and Babylonian Literature, Yale University, New Haven, Connecticut

J.Fr. **Jacob Freimann** *(deceased)*, Dr.Phil., Rabbi; Lecturer in Rabbinics and Jewish History, the Berlin Rabbinical Seminary

J.Fra. **Jonathan Frankel,** Ph.D.; Senior Lecturer in Russian Studies and Contemporary Jewish Studies, the Hebrew University of Jerusalem

J.F.W. **James F. Watts Jr.,** Ph.D.; Assistant Professor of History, City College of the City University of New York

J.G. **Judah Goldin,** D.H.L.; Professor of Classical Judaica, Yale University, New Haven, Connecticut

J.Ga. **John W. Gassner** *(deceased)*, M.A.; Professor of Drama, Yale University, New Haven, Connecticut

J.Gel. See **Y.Gel.**

J.Gi. **Joseph Ginat,** B.A.; Deputy Adviser to the Prime Minister on Arab Affairs, Givatayim, Israel

J.Go. **Jacob Goldberg,** Ph.D.; Teacher in History, the Hebrew University of Jerusalem

J.Gor. **Jacob Gordin** *(deceased)*, Dr.Phil.; *Encyclopaedia Judaica* (Germany)

J.G.-R. **Judith Grunfeld-Rosenbaum,** Ph.D.; Educator, London

J.Gr. **Jack Gross,** Ph.D., M.D.C.M.; Professor of Experimental Medicine and Cancer Research, the Hebrew University-Hadassah Medical School, Jerusalem

J.Gut. **Joseph Gutmann,** Ph.D., Rabbi; Professor of Art History, Wayne State University, Detroit

J.G.W. **Joseph G. Weiss** *(deceased)*, Ph.D.; Professor of Jewish Studies, London University

J.H. **Jacob Haberman,** Ph.D., Dr.Jur., Rabbi; Attorney, New York

J.Ha. **Joseph Halpern,** M.A., Reverend; Educator and writer, Ramat Gan, Israel

J.H.C. **Jacob H. Copenhagen,** Librarian, Jerusalem

J.He., J.Hei. **Joseph Heinemann,** Ph.D.; Senior Lecturer in Hebrew Literature, the Hebrew University of Jerusalem

J. Her. **Jan Heřman, Ph.D.**; State Jewish Museum, Prague

J.H.H. **Jacob Hirsch Haberman,** M.A., Rabbi; Librarian the Jewish Theological Seminary of America, New York

J.Ho. **Josef Horovitz** *(deceased)*, Dr.Phil.; *Encyclopaedia Judaica* (Germany); Professor of Semitic Languages, the University of Frankfort; Director of the School of Oriental Studies, the Hebrew University of Jerusalem

J.Hod. **Joseph Hodara,** Ph.D.; Lecturer in Latin American History, the National Autonomous University of Mexico, Mexico City

J.Hor. See **J.Her.**

J.H.S. **Jesse Harold Silver,** Sports writer, Surfside, Florida

J.H.Sc. **John H. Scammon,** Th.D.; Emeritus Professor of Hebrew and Old Testament, Andover Newton Theological School, Newton Centre, Massachusetts

J.H.Sch. **Jefim (Hayyim) Schirmann,** Dr.Phil.; Emeritus Professor of Hebrew Literature, the Hebrew University of Jerusalem

J.H.Sh. **Joshua H. Shmidman,** B.A., Rabbi; Instructor in Philosophy, Yeshiva University; New York

J.H.T. **Jeffrey Howard Tigay,** M.H.L., Rabbi; Hamden, Connecticut

J.I. **Joseph Israeli;** Kibbutz Afikim

J.I.D. **Jacob I. Dienstag,** M.A.; Professor of Bibliography, Yeshiva University, New York

J.I.S. **Joseph I. Shulim,** Ph.D.; Professor of History, Brooklyn College of the City University of New York

J.J.C. **Jack J. Cohen,** Ph.D., Rabbi; Director of the B'nai B'rith Hillel Foundations in Israel, Jerusalem

J.J.D. **Joseph J. Darvin,** B.S.; Chemist, Spring Valley, New York

J.J.L. **Josef J. Lador-Lederer,** Dr.Jur.; Ministry for Foreign Affairs, Jerusalem

J.J.La. **Julian J. Landau,** M.I.A.; Journalist, Jerusalem

J.J.M. **Julius J. Marke,** J.D.; Professor of Law and Law Librarian, New York University School of Law

J.J.P. **Jakob J. Petuchowski,** Ph.D., Rabbi; Professor of Rabbinics and of Jewish Theology, the Hebrew Union College–Jewish Institute of Religion, Cincinnati

J.J.S. **Judah J. Shapiro,** D.Ed.; Lecturer in Jewish History and Sociology, School of Jewish Communal Service, the Hebrew Union College–Jewish Institute of Religion, New York

J.J.St. **Johann Jakob Stamm,** Dr.Phil., Dr.Theol.; Professor of Old Testament Studies and Ancient Near Eastern Languages, the University of Berne

J.K. **Jacob Klatzkin** *(deceased)*, Dr. Phil.; Philosopher

and Editor in Chief of the *Encyclopaedia Judaica* (Germany); Berlin

J. Ka. **Joseph Kaplan,** M.A., Assistant in Jewish History, the Hebrew University of Jerusalem

J. Kat. **Jacob Katsnelson;** Lecturer in Climatology, Tel Aviv University; Director of the Climatology Division, Israel Meteorological Service, Bet Dagan, Israel

J. Ke. **Jacob Kelemer;** Jerusalem

J. Kl. **Joseph Gedaliah Klausner** *(deceased),* Dr. Phil. Emeritus Professor of Hebrew Literature and of the Second Temple Period, the Hebrew University of Jerusalem

J. K. M. **Jacques K. Mikliszanski,** Ph.D., Rabbi; Professor of Halakhic Literature, the Hebrew College, Boston

J. Kr. **Joel Kraemer,** Ph.D., Rabbi; Assistant Professor of Arabic and Islamic Studies, Yale University, New Haven, Connecticut

J. L. **Jacob Licht,** Ph.D.; Associate Professor of Biblical Studies, Tel Aviv University

J. L. A. **James L. Apple,** Th.D., Rabbi; Great Lakes, Illinois

J. L. Bl. **Joseph L. Blau,** Ph.D.; Professor of Religion, Columbia University, New York

J. Le. **Joseph Leftwich;** Editor and journalist, London

J. Lev., J. Lew. **Jacob S. Levinger,** Ph.D.; Senior Lecturer in Jewish Philosophy, Tel Aviv University

J. Li. **Jacob Liver** *(deceased),* Ph.D.; Professor of Bible, Tel Aviv University

J. L. M. **Julian Louis Meltzer;** Executive Vice-Chairman, Yad Chaim Weizmann, Reḥovot, Israel

J. L. N. **Joshua Leib Ne'eman;** Lecturer in Bible Cantillation, the Rubin Academy of Music, Jerusalem

J. L. S. **J. Lee Shneidman,** Ph.D.; Associate Professor of History, Adelphi University, Garden City, New York

J. L. T. **Jacob L. Talmon,** Ph.D.; Professor of Modern History, the Hebrew University of Jerusalem

J. Lv. **Jacob Lvavi (Babitzky),** Agricultural Engineer, Tel Aviv

J. M. **Jozeph Michman (Melkman),** Ph.D.; Ministry of Education and Culture, Jerusalem

J. Ma. **Jacob Mann** *(deceased),* Ph.D., Rabbi; Professor of Jewish History and Talmud, the Hebrew Union College–Jewish Institute of Religion, Cincinnati

J. Mar. **Joseph Marcus,** M.D.; Jerusalem

J.Mei., J.Mel., **Joseph Meisl** *(deceased),* Dr.Phil.; *Encyclopaedia Judaica* (Germany); Historian and former Director of the Central Archives for the History of the Jewish People, Jerusalem

J. Mer. **Joseph Mersand,** Ph.D.; New York

J. M. F. **Joseph M. Foxman;** Research Associate, YIVO Institute for Jewish Research, New York

J. M. G. See **Y. M. G.**

J. Mi. **Jacob Milgrom,** D.H.L., Rabbi; Associate Professor of Near Eastern Languages, the University of California, Berkeley

J. M. L. **Jacob M. Landau,** Ph.D.; Associate Professor of Political Science, the Hebrew University of Jerusalem; Associate Professor of Arabic and Political Science, Bar Ilan University, Ramat Gan

J. M. M. **Jacob M. Myers,** Ph.D.; Professor of Old Testament, the Lutheran Theological Seminary, Gettysburg, Pennsylvania

J. M. M.-V. **José Maria Millas-Vallicrosa** *(deceased),* Ph.D.; Professor of Hebrew Studies, the University of Barcelona

J. M. O. **John M. O'Brien,** Ph.D.; Professor of Medieval History, Queens College of the City University of New York

J. M. R. **Judah M. Rosenthal,** Ph.D., Rabbi; Former Professor of Biblical Exegesis, the College of Jewish Studies, Chicago; Jerusalem

J. M. S. **John M. Shaftesley,** O.B.E., B.A., F.R.S.A.; Editor, London

J. M. Sch. See **J. H. Sch.**

J. M. Sn. **John M. Snoek,** Reverend; Secretary of the World Council of Churches' Committee on the Church and the Jewish People, Geneva

J. N. **Joseph Neipris,** D.S.W.; Senior Teacher in Social Work, the Hebrew University of Jerusalem

J. Na. **Jacob Nacht** *(deceased),* Dr.Phil.; Scholar, Tel Aviv

J. Ne. **Joseph Nehama** *(deceased),* Historian, Salonika

J. N. S. **Jakob Naphtali Hertz Simchoni** *(deceased),* Dr.Phil.; *Encyclopaedia Judaica* (Germany); Historian, Berlin

J. O. **Jean Ouellette,** Ph.D.; Assistant Professor of Semitic Languages, Sir George Williams University, Montreal

Jo. A. **Joseph Aviram,** M.A.; Director of the Institute of Archaeology, the Hebrew University of Jerusalem

Jo. B. **Joshua Barzilay (Folman),** M.A.; Ramat Gan

Jo. Br. **Joseph Braslavi (Braslavski)** *(deceased),* Historian, Tel Aviv

Jo. Fr. **Josef Fraenkel;** Journalist, London

Jo. Fra. **Jona Fraenkel,** Ph.D.; Lecturer in Hebrew Literature and in Talmud, the Hebrew University of Jerusalem

Jo. G. **John Gray,** Ph.D.; Professor of Hebrew and Semitic Languages, the University of Aberdeen, Scotland

Jo. Ga. Jo. Gar. **Joseph Gar;** Historian, Jerusalem

Jo. H. **Joseph Elijah Heller** *(deceased),* Dr.Phil.; *Encyclopaedia Judaica* (Germany); Lecturer in Hebrew, University College, London

J. O. Ha. **Joshua O. Haberman,** D.H.L., Rabbi; Washington, D. C.

Jo. Kl. **Joseph Klein,** M.H.L., Rabbi; Lecturer in Biblical Literature, Clark University, Worcester, Massachusetts

J. O. L. **Joshua O. Leibowitz,** M.D.; Associate Clinical Professor of the History of Medicine, the Hebrew University–Hadassah Medical School, Jerusalem

Jo. Le. **Joseph Levenson,** D.H.L., Rabbi; Instructor in Religion, Oklahoma City University

Jo. M. **Joseph Maier,** Ph.D.; Professor of Sociology, Rutgers University, Newark, New Jersey

Jo. Ma. **John Macdonald,** Ph.D.; Professor of Hebrew and Semitic Languages, the University of Glasgow, Scotland

Jo. Na. **Joseph Naveh,** Ph.D.; Research Fellow in West-Semitic Epigraphy, the Hebrew University of Jerusalem; Jerusalem District Archaeologist, Department of Antiquities, Jerusalem

J.O.R. **Joachim O. Ronall,** LL.D.; Associate Professor of Economics, Fordham University, New York
Jo.R. **Jo Ranson** *(deceased)*, Theater critic, New York
Jo.S. **Josef Segal,** M.A.; Haifa
Jo.Sch. **Joseph Schweitzer,** Ph.D., Rabbi; Chief Rabbi of Pécs; Professor of Jewish History, the Jewish Theological Seminary of Hungary, Budapest
Jos.H. **Joseph Hacker,** M.A.; Instructor in Jewish History, the Hebrew University of Jerusalem
J.P. **Jacob Petroff,** Ph.D., Rabbi; Senior Lecturer in Classics, Bar Ilan University, Ramat Gan
J.Pe. **Jean Perrot;** Directeur de Recherche au Centre National de la Recherche Scientifique, Paris; Director of the Centre de Recherches Préhistoriques Français, Jerusalem
J.Po. **Jean Poliatchek,** M.A., Rabbi; Lecturer in French Literature, the Hebrew University of Jerusalem and Bar Ilan University, Ramat Gan
J.Pr. **Joseph Prager,** M.D.; Neurologist and psychiatrist, Haifa
J.Q.R. See **J.O.R.**
J.R. **Jacob Robinson,** Dr.Jur.; Coordinator of Research Activities and Publications on the Holocaust for Yad Vashem and YIVO, New York
J.Re. **Jehuda Reinharz,** M.A.; Colonia, New Jersey
J.Ri. **Jack Riemer,** M.H.L., Rabbi; Dayton, Ohio
J.R.M. **Jacob Rader Marcus,** Ph.D., Rabbi; Professor of American Jewish History, the Hebrew Union College–Jewish Institute of Religion, Cincinnati
J.Ro. **Jacob Joshua Ross,** Ph.D., Rabbi; Senior Lecturer in Philosophy, Tel Aviv University
J.S. **Jon Silkin,** B.A.; Poet, Newcastle-upon-Tyne, England
J.Sch. **Josef Schawinski;** Author, Tel Aviv
J.Se. **Jack Segal,** D.H.L., Rabbi; Houston, Texas
J.Sh. **Jonathan Shunary,** Ph.D.; Assistant Professor of Hebrew and Biblical Studies, the University of Wisconsin, Madison
J.Sho. **Joseph Shochetman,** B.A.; Jerusalem
J.Sp. **Johanna L. Spector,** D.H.S.; Professor of Musicology, the Jewish Theological Seminary of America, New York
J.S.S. **Sergio Joseph Sierra,** M.A., Rabbi; Lecturer in Hebrew Language and Literature, the University of Turin
J.S.St. **Judith S. Stein,** Ph.D.; Assistant Professor of History, City College of the City University of New York
J.St. **John Strugnell** M.A.; Professor of Christian Origins, Harvard University
J.Sz., J.S.Z. See **J.Sch.**
J.T. **Josef Tal;** Composer and Senior Lecturer in Musicology, the Hebrew University of Jerusalem
J.To. **Jacob Toury,** Ph.D.; Associate Professor of Jewish History, Tel Aviv University
J.Ts. **Jacob Tsur;** Former Ambassador and Chairman of the Board of Directors, the Jewish National Fund, Jerusalem
Ju.G. **Julius Guttmann** *(deceased)*, Dr.Phil., Rabbi; Professor of Jewish Philosophy, the Hebrew University of Jerusalem
Ju.M. **Julius Margolinsky;** Journalist, Copenhagen
Ju.N. **Judah Nadich,** D.H.L., Rabbi; New York
Ju.P. **Judah Pilch,** Ph.D.; Jewish Teachers' Seminary and Peoples University, New York; Lecturer in Education, Dropsie University, Philadelphia
Ju.R. **Judah Rubinstein,** M.A.; Research Associate, Jewish Community Federation of Cleveland
Ju.W. **Julius Weiss,** B.A., LL.B.; New York
J.W. **Joseph Weitz** *(deceased);* Writer and Former Head of the Development Authority of the Jewish National Fund, Jerusalem
J.Wa. **Jehuda Wallach,** Ph.D.; Colonel (Res.) Israel Defense Forces; Senior Lecturer in Military History, Tel Aviv University
J.W.D. **Joseph W. Davis;** Ramat Ha-Sharon, Israel
J.W.P. **James W. Parkes,** D.Phil; Historian, Blandford, Dorset, England
J.Y. **Jacob Yardeni,** D.D.S.; Former Senior Lecturer, the School of Dentistry, the Hebrew University–Hadassah Medical School, Jerusalem
J.Ye. **Jacob Yehoshua,** M.A.; Former Director of the Moslem Department, Ministry of Religious Affairs, Jerusalem
J.Z. **Jenö Zsoldos,** Ph.D.; Educator, Budapest
J.Z.Z. **Jekutiel-Zwi Zehawi,** Ph.D.; Educator, Tel Aviv

K.B. **Konrad Bieber,** Ph.D.; Professor of French and Comparative Literature, the State University of New York, Stony Brook
K.D.R. **Kenneth D. Roseman,** Ph.D., Rabbi; Assistant Professor of American Jewish History, the Hebrew Union College–Jewish Institute of Religion, Cincinnati
K.G. **Kurt Grunwald,** Dr.rer.Pol.; Economist, Jerusalem
K.Gr. **Kurt Gruenberger,** Dr.jur.; Haifa
K.Ka. **Katriel Katz;** Ambassador, Ministry for Foreign Affairs, Jerusalem
K.L. **Kurt Loewenstein;** Tel Aviv
K.M. **Klara Maayan,** M.A.; Tel Aviv
K.N.S. **Keith N. Schoville,** Ph.D.; Assistant Professor of Hebrew and Semitic Studies, the University of Wisconsin, Madison
K.P. **Kurt Pinthus,** Ph.D.; Writer, New York
K.R.G. **Kurt R. Grossmann** *(deceased)*, Writer, New York
K.R.S. **Kenneth R. Scholberg,** Ph.D.; Professor of Romance Languages, Michigan State University, East Lansing
K.S. **Karl Schwarz** *(deceased)*, Dr.Phil.; Art historian and Curator of the Tel Aviv Museum
K.Se. **Kalman Seigel,** B.So.Sci.; Journalist, New York
K.W. **Kenneth Waltzer,** Ph.D.; Teaching Fellow in American History, Harvard University, Cambridge, Massachusetts
K.Y.B.-K. **Kurt Jakob Ball-Kaduri,** Dr.Jur.; Historian, Tel Aviv

L.A.C. **Lewis A. Coser,** Ph.D.; Professor of Sociology, the State University of New York, Stony Brook
L.A.Cr. **Lawrence A. Cremin,** Ph.D.; Professor of Education, Columbia University, New York
L.A.F. **Lillian A. Friedberg,** M.A.; Former Executive Director of the Jewish Community Relations Council of Pittsburgh, Pennsylvania
L.A.O. **Levi A. Olan,** B.A., Rabbi; Dallas, Texas

L. A. S. **Leon Aryeh Szeskin,** Ph.D.; Ministry of Housing, Tel Aviv
L. B. **Leon Boim,** Ph.D.; Associate Professor of Political Science, Tel Aviv University
L. Be. **Louis Bernstein,** B.A., Rabbi; Instructor in Bible, Hebrew, and Jewish History, Yeshiva University, New York
L. Bo. **Leah Borenstein,** B.A.; Assistant in Jewish History, Bar Ilan University, Ramat Gan
L. B. Y. **Lois Bar-Yaacov,** B.A.; Tel Aviv
L. C. **Louisa Cuomo,** Dott. in lett.; Assistant in Italian Language and Literature, the Hebrew University of Jerusalem
L. C. G. **Louisa Cuomo,** Dott. in lett.; Assistant in Judaica, New York University
L. Cz. **Leon Czertok,** Dr. Jur.; General Secretary, Centre de Documentation Juive Contemporaine, Paris
L. d. J. **Louis de Jong,** Litt. D.; Historian and Extraordinary Professor of Contemporary History, the University of Rotterdam; Director of the Netherlands State Institute for War Documentation, Amsterdam
Le. F. **Leon A. Feldman,** Ph.D., D.H.L., Rabbi; Professor of Hebraic Studies, Rutgers University, New Brunswick, New Jersey
Le. G. **Lea Goldberg** *(deceased),* Dr.Phil.; Author and Associate Professor of Comparative Literature, the Hebrew University of Jerusalem
Le. H. **Lee Healey;** New York
Le. He. **Leonardo Hellemberg;** Managua, Nicaragua
Le. L. **Lev Levite,** Kibbutz En-Harod (Me'uḥad)
Le. P. **Leon Perez,** M.D.; Professor of Social Psychiatry, National University of the Litoral, Santa Fé; Professor of Clinical Psychiatry, the University of Buenos Aires
Le. Sh. **Levi Shalit;** Editor, Johannesburg
L. F. **Louis Filler,** Ph.D.; Professor of American Civilization, Antioch College, Yellow Springs, Ohio
L. Fe. **Leon I. Feuer,** Rabbi; Toledo, Ohio
L. F. H. **Louis F. Hartman** *(deceased),* L.S.S., L.O.L.; Professor of Semitic and Egyptian Languages and Literatures, the Catholic University of America, Washington, D.C.
L. F. S. **Louis F. Sas,** Ph.D.; Professor of Romance Languages, City College of the City University of New York
L. G. **Linda Gutstein,** B.A.; Journalist, New York
L. Ga. **Leib Garfunkel,** M.A.; Attorney, Jerusalem
L. H. **László Harsányi,** D.L.; Historian, Budapest
L. Ha. **Lucien Harris,** M.A.; Hadassah Medical Organization, Jerusalem
L. He. **Leo Hershkowitz,** Ph.D.; Associate Professor of History, Queens College of the City University of New York
L. H. F. **Lawrence H. Feigenbaum,** Ph.D.; Lecturer in Education, City College of the City University of New York
L. H. Fe. **Louis Harry Feldman,** Ph.D.; Professor of Classics, Yeshiva University, New York
L. Ho. **Louis Hotz,** B.A.; Historian, Johannesburg
L. H. S. **Lou H. Silberman,** D.H.L., Rabbi; Professor of Jewish Literature and Thought, Vanderbilt University, Nashville, Tennessee
L. Hy. **Louis Hyman,** M.A.; Historian, Haifa
Li. C. **Lionel Cohen,** M.A.; Instructor in French and Classical Studies, Bar Ilan University, Ramat Gan
Li. H. **Lipman Halpern** *(deceased),* M.D.; Professor of Neurology, the Hebrew University–Hadassah Medical School, Jerusalem
Li. K. **Lionel Kochan,** Ph.D.; Lecturer in Jewish History, the University of Warwick, Coventry
L. I. R. **Louis Isaac Rabinowitz,** Ph.D., Rabbi; Deputy Editor in Chief of the *Encyclopaedia Judaica;* Former Chief Rabbi of the Transvaal and Former Professor of Hebrew, the University of the Witwatersrand, Johannesburg; Jerusalem
Li. Ro. **Livia Rothkirchen,** Ph.D.; Historian, Jerusalem
L. J. **Louis Jacobs,** Ph.D., Rabbi; Scholar, London
L. J. A. **Laurentino José Afonso,** B.D.; Jerusalem
L. J. S. **Leonard J. Stein,** M.A.; Barrister and historian, London
L. J. Sw. **Louis J. Swichkow,** D.H.L., Rabbi; Historian, Milwaukee, Wisconsin
L. Ju. **Leo Jung,** Ph.D., Rabbi; Emeritus Professor of Ethics, Yeshiva University, New York
L. J. Y. **Leon J. Yagod,** D.H.L., Rabbi; Irvington, New Jersey
L. K. **Yehudah Pinḥas Leo Kohn** *(deceased),* LL.D.; Jurist and diplomat, Jerusalem
L. Ka. **Leybl Kahn,** M.A.; Bibliographer, New York
L. Ko. **Lothar Kopf** *(deceased),* Ph.D.; the Jewish National and University Library, Jerusalem
L. L. **Lucien Lazare,** Ph.D.; Educator, Jerusalem
L. La. **Leo Landman,** Ph.D., Rabbi; Assistant Professor of Rabbinical Literature, Dropsie University, Philadelphia
L. Le. **Leo Levi,** D.Sc.; Research Fellow in Jewish Musicology, the Hebrew University of Jerusalem
L. Lew. **Louis Lewin** *(deceased),* Dr.Phil., Rabbi; *Encyclopaedia Judaica* (Germany); Historian, Breslau
L. M. **Lewis Mumford;** Professor of Humanities, Stanford University, California; Professor of City and Regional Planning, the University of Pennsylvania, Philadelphia
L. N. **Leon Nemoy,** Ph.D.; Scholar in Residence, Dropsie University, Philadelphia
L. Na. **Ludwig Nadelmann,** M.A., Rabbi; Lecturer in the Reconstructionist Rabbinical College, Philadelphia
Lo. G. **Louis Ginsberg;** Petersburg, Virginia
Lo. M. **Louis Miller,** M.B.; Chief National Psychiatrist, Ministry of Health, Jerusalem
Lo. S. **Louanna Smith,** Concord, New Hampshire
L. P. **Leonard Prager,** Ph.D.; Lecturer in English, Language and Literature, the Hebrew University of Jerusalem; Senior Lecturer in English, Haifa University
L. P.-E. **Lotte Pulvermacher-Egers,** Ph.D.; Lecturer in the History of Art, the Mannes College of Music, New York
L. P. G. **Lloyd P. Gartner,** Ph.D.; Associate Professor of History, City College of the City University of New York
L. Pi. **Leo Picard,** Dr.Phil., D.I.C., D.Sc.; Emeritus Professor of Geology, the Hebrew University of Jerusalem

L. Po. **Léon Poliakov,** D.es L.; Maitre de Recherches au Centre National de la Recherche Scientifique, Paris

L. R. **Leon Roth** *(deceased)*, D.Phil., F.B.A.; Former Rector and Professor of Philosophy, the Hebrew University of Jerusalem

L. Ro. **Lea Roth,** M.A.; Jerusalem

L. Ros. **Louis Rosenberg,** B.A., B.S.; Research Director, the Canadian Jewish Congress, Montreal, Canada

L. S. **Lewis Sowden,** M.A.; Writer and journalist, Jerusalem

L. Sch. **Lázaro Schallman;** Director of the Library of the Jewish Community of Buenos Aires

L. Sh. **Leon Shapiro;** Lecturer in Russian-Jewish History, Rutgers University, New Brunswick, New Jersey

L. S. K. **Leonard S. Kravitz,** Ph.D., Rabbi; Professor of Midrash and Homiletics, the Hebrew Union College–Jewish Institute of Religion, New York

L. Sp. **Leon H. Spotts,** Ph.D.; Executive Director, Atlanta Bureau of Jewish Education, Atlanta, Georgia

L. Sr. **Leo Srole,** Ph.D.; Professor of Social Sciences, Columbia College of Physicians and Surgeons, New York

L. St. **Lucien Steinberg,** M.A.; Research Worker, Centre de Documentation Juive Contemporaine, Paris

Lu. P. **Ludwig Pinner,** Dr.Phil., Kefar Shemaryahu, Israel

L. V. B. **Lawrence V. Berman,** Ph.D.; Associate Professor of Religious Studies, Stanford University, California

L. V. S. **Leonard V. Snowman,** M.A., M.R.C.P.; London

L. W. K. **Ludwig W. Kahn,** Ph.D.; Professor of German, Columbia University, New York

L. W. Sch. **Leo W. Schwarz** *(deceased)*, B.A., Rabbi; Author, New York

L. Wu. **Leon Wulman,** M.D.; New York

L. Y. **Leni Yahil,** Ph.D.; Historian, Jerusalem

L. Z. **Louis Zucker,** Ph.D.; Emeritus Professor of English, the University of Utah, Salt Lake City

M. A. **Moses Aberbach,** Ph.D.; Baltimore Hebrew College, Maryland

M. A. A. **Moshe A. Avnimelech** *(deceased)*, Ph.D.; Emeritus Professor of Geology and Paleontology, the Hebrew University of Jerusalem

M. Ab. **Mahmoud Abassi,** B.A.; Writer, Shfaram, Israel

Ma. B.-A. **Malachi Beit-Arié,** Ph.D.; Research Worker, the Jewish National and University Library, Jerusalem

M. A. Br. **Maury A. Bromsen,** M.A.; Boston, Massachusetts

M. A. C., Ma. C. **Martin A. Cohen,** Ph.D., Rabbi; Professor of Jewish History, the Hebrew Union College–Jewish Institute of Religion, New York

Ma. D. A. **Maurice D. Atkin,** M.A.; Economist, Washington, D. C.

Ma. D. H. **Mark D. Hirsch,** Ph.D.; Professor of History, Bronx Community College, New York

Ma. F. **Maurice Friedman,** Ph.D.; Professor of Religion, Temple University, Philadelphia

Ma. Fo. **Marvin Fox,** Ph.D., Rabbi; Professor of Philosophy, Ohio State University, Columbus

M. A. G. **Morris A. Gutstein,** Ph.D., D.H.L., Rabbi; Associate Professor of Jewish History and Sociology, the College of Jewish Studies, Chicago

Ma. G. **Max Gottschalk,** Ph.D.; Research Professor of Sociology, the Free University of Brussels

Ma. H. **Monford Harris,** D.H.L.; Professor of Religious Studies, the University of Toronto

Ma. K. **Mark Keller,** Rutgers University, New Brunswick, New Jersey

M. A. M. **Michael A. Meyer,** Ph.D.; Associate Professor of Jewish History, the Hebrew Union College–Jewish Institute of Religion, Cincinnati

Ma. M. **Matti Megged,** M.A.; Critic and Lecturer in Modern Hebrew Literature, Haifa University and the Hebrew University of Jerusalem

Ma. P. (Entry: **JOSEPH AND ASENATH) Marc Philonenko,** Th.D.; Professor of the History of Religions, the University of Strasbourg

Ma. P. **Mark Perlgut,** M.S.; Journalist, New York

Ma. Po. **Marvin H. Pope,** Ph.D.; Professor of Northwest Semitic Languages, Yale University, New Haven, Connecticut

M. A. R. **Mordechai Altshuler,** Ph.D.; Lecturer in Contemporary Jewry, the Hebrew University of Jerusalem

M. A. S. **Menaḥem Binyamin Andrew Silberfeld,** Ph.D., Rabbi; Librarian, Jerusalem

Ma. S. **Manny Sternlicht,** Ph.D.; Associate Professor of Psychology, Yeshiva University, New York

M. Av. **Moshé Avidor,** Ph.D.; Former Ambassador and Director General of the Israel Academy of Sciences and Humanities, Jerusalem

M. Avi. **Moshe Avidan,** Ambassador, Ministry for Foreign Affairs, Jerusalem

M. A. Y., M. A.-Y. **Michael Avi-Yonah,** Ph.D.; Professor of Archaeology and of the History of Art, the Hebrew University of Jerusalem

M. B. **Moshe Barasch;** Professor of Architecture and Fine Arts, the Hebrew University of Jerusalem

M. B. A. **Moses Bensabat Amzalak,** Ph.D.; Honorary Rector and Professor of the Technical University of Lisbon; Former President of the Academy of Sciences of Lisbon

M. Ba. **Menahem Banitt,** Ph.D.; Associate Professor of French, Tel Aviv University

M. B. Ah. **Miriam Ben-Aaron,** M.A.; Ministry of Health, Haifa

M. Bal. **Meir Balaban** *(deceased)*, Dr.Phil.; *Encyclopaedia Judaica* (Germany); Professor of Jewish Jewish History, Warsaw

M. Be. **Moshe Beer,** Ph.D.; Associate Professor of Jewish History, Bar Ilan University, Ramat Gan

M. B.-H. **Meir Ben-Horin,** Ph.D.; Professor of Education, Dropsie University, Philadelphia

M. Bi. **Maurice Bisgyer,** M.A.; Honorary Executive Vice President of B'nai B'rith, Washington, D. C.

M. Bil. **Max Bilen,** Ph.D.; Lecturer in French Literature, Tel Aviv University

M. B. L. See **B. M. L.**

M. Bo. **Mendel Bobe;** Engineer, Tel Aviv

M. Br. **Mordechai Breuer,** Jerusalem
M. Bre. **Mordechai Breuer,** Ph.D.; Educator, Jerusalem
M. B. S. **Marcia B. Siegel,** B.A.; Dance critic, New York
M. B.-Y. **Mordecai Ben-Yehezkiel** *(deceased),* Writer, Jerusalem
M. C. **Moshé Catane,** Dr. du 3e cycle, Archiviste Paléographe; Senior Lecturer in French Civilization and Literature, Bar Ilan University, Ramat Gan; Librarian, the Jewish National and University Library, Jerusalem
M.-C. G. **Marie Claire Galperine,** Ph.D.; Chargée de Recherches au Centre National de la Recherche Scientifique, Paris
M. Ch. **Mordecai Chenzin,** Rabbi; Columbus, Ohio
M. Co. **Michael Comay,** B.A., LL.B.; Ambassador, Ministry for Foreign Affairs, Jerusalem
M. Cr. **Mort Cornin,** B.Litt.; Journalist, Jersey City
M. C.-W. **Moshe Carmilly-Weinberger,** Ph.D., Rabbi; Professor of Jewish Studies, Yeshiva University, New York
M. Cz. **Moshe M. Czudnowski,** Ph.D.; Lecturer in Political Science, the Hebrew University of Jerusalem
M. D. **Melvyn Dubofsky,** Ph.D., Associate Professor of History, the University of Wisconsin, Milwaukee
M. Da. **Moshe Dayan;** Lieutenant General (Res.), Israel Defense Forces; Minister of Defense, Tel Aviv
M. D. F. **Morris D. Forkosch,** Ph.D., J.S.D.; Professor of Law, Brooklyn Law School; Professor of Economics, New School for Social Research, New York
M. D. G. **M. David Geffen,** Ph.D., Rabbi; Lecturer in Medieval and Modern Jewish Philosophy, the Jewish Theological Seminary of America, New York
M. D. H. **Moshe David Herr,** Ph.D.; Lecturer in Jewish History, the Hebrew University of Jerusalem
M. Do. **Moshe Dothan,** Ph.D.; Director of Excavations and Surveys and Deputy Director, Department of Antiquities and Museums, Jerusalem
M. D. S. **Meir de Shalit;** Former Director General Ministry of Tourism, Tel Aviv
M. E. **Menachem Elon,** Dr.Jur., Advocate, Rabbi; Professor of Jewish Law and Director of the Institute for Research in Jewish Law, the Hebrew University of Jerusalem
M. E. A. **Menachem E. Artom,** Ph.D., Rabbi; Civil Service Commission, Jerusalem
M. E. B. **Moshe Eliahu Berman,** M.Eng., F.I.E.E.; Director of Engineering, Ministry of Communications Tel Aviv
Me. Ba. **Menachem Babitz,** M.A., Ing.; Senior Research Fellow, the Technion Research and Development Foundation, Haifa
Me. Be. **Meron Benvenisti,** B.A.; Jerusalem
Me. K. **Meir Katz,** Ph.D.; Musicologist, Jerusalem
M. El. **Mordechai Eliav,** Ph.D.; Associate Professor of Jewish History and Education, Bar Ilan University, Ramat Gan
M. E. M. **Martin E. Marty,** Ph.D.; Professor of Modern Church History, the University of Chicago
M. Ep. **Morris Epstein,** Ph.D.; Editor and Professor of English, Stern College for Women, Yeshiva University, New York
Me. R. **Meir Ronnen,** B.F.A.; Journalist, Jerusalem
M. E. S. **Michael E. Stone,** Ph.D.; Senior Lecturer in Jewish Hellenism and in Iranian and Armenian Studies, the Hebrew University of Jerusalem
M. E. Sch. **Myron E. Schoen;** Union of American Hebrew Congregations, New York
Me. Si. **Meir Silverstone,** LL.B.; Attorney and former Director General, Ministry of the Interior, Jerusalem
M. E. Sw. **Manfred Eric Swarsensky,** Ph.D., Rabbi; Madison, Wisconsin
Me. W. **Menachem Weinstein,** M.A.; Instructor in the Institute for Research in the History and Culture of Oriental Jewry, Bar Ilan University, Ramat Gan
Me. Wa. **Meyer Waxman** *(deceased),* Ph.D., Rabbi; Professor of Jewish Philosophy and Literature, the Hebrew Theological College of Chicago
M. F. **Maurice Friedberg,** Ph.D.; Professor of Slavic Languages and Literatures and Director of the Russian and East European Institute, Indiana University, Bloomington
M. Fe. **Moshe M. Felber;** Ministry of Finance, Jerusalem
M. Fi. **Michael Fishbane,** M.A.; Instructor in Hebrew and of Biblical Studies, Brandeis University, Waltham, Massachusetts
M. Fo. **Michael Fox,** M.A., Rabbi; Jerusalem
M. Fr. **Menachem Friedman,** M.A.; Jerusalem
M. F. St. **Meyer F. Steinglass,** B.A.; New York
M. G. **Moshe Gottlieb,** Ph.D., Rabbi; Beit Berl, Ẓofit, Israel
M. Ga. **Miriam Gay,** M.A., M.Sc.; Senior Teacher in Psychology, Bar Ilan University, Ramat Gan; Ministry of Health, Tel Aviv
M. Ge. **Manfred Moshe Geis;** Theater critic, Tel Aviv
M. G. H. **Maurice Gerschon Hindus** *(deceased),* M.S.; Writer, New York
M. Gi. **Marcia Gitlin,** B.A.; Jerusalem
M. Go. **Michael Goldstein;** Professor of Music, Staatliche Hochschule für Musik und Darstellende Kunst, Hamburg
M. Gol. **Maurice Goldsmith,** B.Sc.; Director of the Science Policy Foundation and of the Science Information Service, London
M. Gr. **Michael J. Graetz,** M.A., Rabbi; Jerusalem
M. Gra. **Michael Graetz,** M.A.; Jerusalem
M. Gre. **Moshe Greenberg,** Ph.D., Rabbi; Professor of Bible, the Hebrew University of Jerusalem
M. H. **Meir Havazelet,** Ph.D., D.H.L., Rabbi; Professor of Rabbinic Literature and of Bible, Yeshiva University, New York
M. Ha. **Menahem Haran,** Ph.D.; Associate Professor of Bible, the Hebrew University of Jerusalem
M. Hal. **Morris Halle,** Ph.D.; Professor of Modern Languages, Massachusetts Institute of Technology, Cambridge
M. H. B., M. H. B.-S. **Mëir Hillel Ben-Shammai,** Dr.Phil.; Editor and writer, Jerusalem
M. H. C. **Michael Hart Cardozo,** B.A., LL.B.; Executive Director, Association of American Law Schools, Washington, D.C.
M. H. E. **Michael H. Ebner,** M.A.; Lecturer in American History, the Herbert H. Lehman College of the City University of New York

M. He. **Moshe Hesky,** Dr.Jur.; Former Adviser, Philatelic Services, Israel Ministry of Posts; England

M. H. H. **Milton Henry Hindus,** M.S.; Professor of English, Brandeis University, Waltham, Massachusetts

M. H. S. **Malka Hillel Shulewitz;** Journalist, Jerusalem

M. H. St. **Malcolm H. Stern,** D.H.L., Rabbi; New York

M. H. V. **Manfred H. Vogel,** Ph.D.; Associate Professor of the History and Literature of Religions, Northwestern University, Evanston, Illinois

Mi. A. **Miriam Arad;** Literary critic, Jerusalem

M. I. G. **Mayer Irwin Gruber,** M.A., M.H.L., Rabbi; South Orange, New Jersey

Mi. H. **Michael Heymann,** Ph.D.; Director of the Central Zionist Archives, Jerusalem

M. I. K. **Meir Jacob Kister,** Ph.D.; Professor of Arabic Language and Literature, the Hebrew University of Jerusalem

Mi. M. **Michel Mazor,** Dr.Jur.; Author, Paris

Mi. P. **Milton Plesur,** Ph.D.; Associate Professor of History, the State University of New York, Buffalo

Mi. R. See **Ed.**

M. J. G. **Michael James Goldman,** M. Phil., Minister, Newbury Park, Essex, England

M. J. Go. **M. J. Gottfarstein**

M. J. R. **Max Jonah Routtenberg,** D.H.L., Rabbi; Visiting Professor of Homiletics, the Jewish Theological Seminary of America, New York

M. J. S. **Marie Joseph Stiassny,** Lic.Th.; Ratisbonne Monastery, Jerusalem

M. Ju. **Hans Jungmann,** M.D.; London, England

M. K. **Mendel Kohansky;** Theater critic, Tel Aviv

M. Ka. **Moshe Kahanovich;** Journalist, Tel Aviv

M. Ke. **Moshe Kerem,** M.A.; Lecturer in Education, Haifa University; Kibbutz Gesher ha-Ziv

M. Ko. **Moshe Kochavi,** Ph.D.; Senior Lecturer in Archaeology, Tel Aviv University

M. Kol. **Moshe Kol;** Minister of Tourism, Jerusalem

M. Kr. **Max Kreutzberger,** Ph.D.; Former Director of the Leo Baeck Institute, New York; Ascona, Switzerland

M. L. **Misha Louvish,** M.A.; Writer and journalist, Jerusalem

M. La. **Meir Lamed** *(deceased)*; Kibbutz Ne'ot Mordekhai

M. Lan. **Moshe Landau,** M.A.; Educator, Tel Aviv

M. L. B.-D. **Molly Lyons Bar-David;** Journalist, Tel Aviv

M. L. C. **Margaret L. Coit,** Dr.of Letters; Associate Professor of Social Science, Fairleigh Dickinson University, Rutherford, New Jersey

M. Le. **Martin Levey,** Ph.D.; Professor of the History of Science, the State University of New York, Albany

M. L. G. **Mordecai L. Gabriel,** Ph.D.; Professor of Biology, Brooklyn College of the City University of New York

M. L. P. **Maurice L. Perlzweig,** Ph.D., Rabbi; Head of the International Affairs Department, World Jewish Congress, New York

M. M. **Moshe Mishkinsky,** Ph.D.; Senior Lecturer in the History of Jewish Labor Movements, the Hebrew University of Jerusalem; Senior Lecturer in Jewish History, Tel Aviv University

M. Ma. **Meir Mandel,** Ing.Agr., I.A.N.; Kibbutz Kiryat Anavim

M. Man. **Menahem Mansoor,** Ph.D.; Professor of Hebrew and Semitic Studies, the University of Wisconsin, Madison

M. Mar. **Mordecai Margaliot** *(deceased)*, Ph.D.; Professor of Geonic and Midrashic Literature, the Jewish Theological Seminary of America, New York

M. M. B. **Morton Mayer Berman,** M.H.L., Rabbi; Honorary Director, Department of English Speaking Countries, Keren Hayesod United Israel Appeal, Jerusalem

M. M. Br. **Menachem M. Brayer,** Ph.D., D.H.L., Rabbi; Clinical psychologist, Professor of Biblical Literature and Education, Yeshiva University, New York

M. Me. **Meir Medan,** M.A.; Chief Scientific Secretary of the Academy of the Hebrew Language, Jerusalem

M. M. K. **Max M. Kleinbaum,** M.A.; American Jewish Congress, Philadelphia

M. M. L. **Mervyn M. Lewis,** M.A.; Jerusalem

M. M. M. **Myriam M. Malinovich,** Ph.D.; Acting Assistant Professor of Philosophy, San Diego State College, California

M. M. S. **Morris M. Schnitzer,** B.S., LL.B.; Lecturer in Law, Rutgers University, New Jersey

M. N. **Mona Nobil,** B.A.; Netanyah

M. Na. **Mordekhai Nadav,** Ph.D.; Head of the Department of Manuscripts and Archives, the Jewish National and University Library; Lecturer in Jewish History, the University of the Negev, Beersheba

M. N. E. **Moshe Nes El,** B.A.; Reḥovot, Israel

M. Ni. **Miriam Nick,** B.A.; Curator of the Museum of Ethnography and Folklore, Haaretz Museum, Tel Aviv

M. Nu. **Mendel Nun;** Kibbutz Ein Gev

M. N. Z. **Moshe Nahum Zobel** *(deceased)*, Dr.Phil.; *Encyclopaedia Judaica* (Germany); Jerusalem

Mo. A. **Moshé Altbauer,** Ph.D.; Associate Professor of Slavic Linguistics and of Russian Studies, the Hebrew University of Jerusalem

Mo. Al. **Moshe Allon;** Jerusalem

Mo. Br. **Moshe Brawer,** Ph.D.; Associate Professor of Geography, Tel Aviv University

Mo. G. See **M. Gre.**

Mo. Ha. **Mordechai Hacohen** *(deceased)* Rabbi; Author, Jerusalem

Mo. Hal. **Moshe Hallamish,** M.A.; Instructor in Jewish Philosophy, Bar Ilan University, Ramat Gan

Mo. I. **Moshe Ishai,** Dr.Juris; Former Ambassador, Tel Aviv

Mo. K. **Mordechai Kaplan,** M.Eng.; Lieutenant Colonel (Res.), Israel Defense Forces, Tel Aviv

Mo. La. **Moshé Lazar,** Ph.D.; Associate Professor of Romance Philology, the Hebrew University of Jerusalem

Mo. M. **Moshe Medzini;** Journalist and writer, Jerusalem

Mo. Ma. See **Mo. Ha.**

Mo. N. **Mordkhai Neishtat;** Journalist, Tel Aviv

Mo. P. **Mordechai Piron,** M.A., Rabbi; Brigadier General, Israel Defense Forces; Chief Rabbi of the Israel Defense Forces, Bat Yam

Mo. Pe. **Moshe Pearlman,** B.Sc.; Writer, Jerusalem
Mo. Pr. **Moshe Prywes,** M.D.; Associate Professor of Medical Education, the Hebrew University–Hadassah Medical School, Jerusalem; Vice President of the Hebrew University of Jerusalem; President, University of the Negev
Mo. R. **Moshe Rosen;** Jerusalem
Mo. Ri. **Moses Rischin,** Ph.D.; Professor of History, San Francisco State College; Director of the Western Jewish History Center, Berkeley, California
Mor. K. **Mordechai Kamrat** *(deceased)*, Ph.D.; Educator, Jerusalem
Mo. Ro. **Morton Rosenstock,** Ph.D.; Professor of Social Studies and Librarian, Bronx Community College of the City University of New York
Mor. Sch. **Mordkhe Schaechter,** Ph.D.; Jewish Teachers' Seminary, New York
Mo. S. **Morris Silverman** *(deceased)*, D.H.L., Rabbi; Hartford, Connecticut
Mo. Sch. **Moshe Schwarcz,** Ph.D.; Associate Professor of Philosophy, Bar Ilan University, Ramat Gan
Mo. Sh. **Moshe Shapira,** B.A.; Research Assistant in the Institute for Research in the History and Culture of Oriental Jewry, Bar Ilan University, Ramat Gan
Mo. Si. **Moshe Singer;** Moshav Beit Yehoshua
Mo. Sp. **Maurice Moshe Spitzer,** Dr.Phil.; Publisher, Jerusalem
Mo. St. **Moshe Stern;** Jerusalem
Mo. W. **Moshe Weinfeld,** Ph.D.; Senior Lecturer in Bible, the Hebrew University of Jerusalem
M. P., M. Pe. **Mark Perlman,** Ph.D.; Professor of Economics, the University of Pittsburgh, Pennsylvania
M. Pel. **Moshe Peled,** B.A.; Colonel (Res.), Israel Defense Forces; Ministry of Transport, Jerusalem
M. Per. **Moshe Perlmann,** Ph.D.; Professor of Arabic, the University of California, Los Angeles
M. Pl. **Martin Meir Plessner,** Ph.D.; Emeritus Professor of Semitics and Islamic Studies, J.W. Goethe–Universität, Frankfort on the Main; Emeritus Professor of Islamic Civilization, the Hebrew University of Jerusalem
M. Pr. **Michael Pragai,** B.A.; Ministry for Foreign Affairs, Jerusalem
M. R. **Moshe Rosetti;** Former Clerk of the Knesset, Tel Aviv
M. Rab. **Mordechai Rabinson** *(deceased)*, Dr.Phil., Writer, Jerusalem
M. Rav. **Melech Ravitch;** Writer, Montreal
M. Re. **Manfred Reifer** *(deceased)*, Dr.Phil.; *Encyclopaedia Judaica* (Germany); Tel Aviv
M. Ri. **Moshe Rinott,** Ph.D.; Senior Teacher in Education, Haifa University
M. Ro. **Murray Roston,** Ph.D.; Professor of English, Bar Ilan University, Ramat Gan
M. Ros., M. Roz. **Marc Rozelaar,** Dr.Phil.; Associate Professor of Classical Studies, Tel Aviv University
M. S. **Moshe Starkman;** Writer, New York
M. Sa. **Menahem Savidor;** Lieutenant Colonel (Ret.), Israel Defense Forces; Former General Manager, Israel Railways; Director of the Citrus Products Export Board; National Chairman, Maccabi Sports Organization, Tel Aviv
M. Sam. **Moshe Shraga Samet,** Ph.D.; Lecturer in Jewish History and in Sociology, the Hebrew University of Jerusalem
M. S. C. **Michal Smoira-Cohn,** Ph.Lic.; Director of Music, the Israel Broadcasting Authority, Jerusalem
M. Sch. **Menahem Schmelzer,** D.H.L.; Librarian and Assistant Professor of Medieval Hebrew Literature, the Jewish Theological Seminary of America, New York
M. Scha. See **Mo. Sh.**
M. S. E. **Morton S. Enslin,** Th.D.; Professor of Early Christian History and Literature, Dropsie University, Philadelphia
M. S. F. **Meyer S. Feldblum,** Ph.D., Rabbi; Associate Professor of Rabbinics, Yeshiva University, New York
M. S. H. **Marshall S. Hurwitz,** M.A., Rabbi; Lecturer in Greek and Latin, City College of the City University of New York
M. Sh. **Matityahu Shelem;** Composer, Kibbutz Ramat Yoḥanan
M. Sha. **Mordechai Shalev,** M.A.; Ministry for Foreign Affairs, Jerusalem
M. Si. **Mendel Singer;** Writer, Haifa
M. Sim. **Michael Simon,** Dr.Phil.; Former Ambassador, Ministry for Foreign Affairs, Jerusalem
M. Sm. **Morton Smith,** Ph.D., Th.D.; Professor of History, Columbia University, New York
M. S. P. **Maurice S. Pitt,** M.A.; Educator and Journalist, Wellington, New Zealand
M. St. **Menahem Stern,** Ph.D.; Professor of Jewish History, the Hebrew University of Jerusalem
M. Sy. **Marie Syrkin,** M.A.; Emeritus Professor of English Literature, Brandeis University, Waltham, Massachusetts
M. T. **Marvin Tokayer,** M.A., Rabbi; Lecturer in Hebrew, Waseda University, Tokyo
M. U. **Moshe Unna,** Dipl.Agr.; Former Member of the Knesset, Kibbutz Sedeh Eliyahu
Mu. L. **Murray Lichtenstein,** B.A.; Lecturer in Jewish Studies, the State University of New York, Stony Brook
M. V. **Max Vorspan,** D.H.L., Rabbi; Associate Professor of Jewish History, the University of Judaism, Los Angeles
M. W. **Mark Wischnitzer** *(deceased)*, Dr.Phil.; Professor of Jewish History, Yeshiva University, New York
M. Wa. **Michael Wade,** B.A. (Hons.), Dipl.Ed.; Instructor in English and in African Literature, the Hebrew University of Jerusalem
M. Wad. **Miriam Dworkin Waddington,** M.A., M.S.W.; Associate Professor of English Literature, York University, Toronto
M. Wag. **Maurice Wagner,** M.A.; General Secretary of the Central African Jewish Board of Deputies, Bulawayo, Rhodesia
M. Wax. **Mordecai Waxman,** M.H.L., Rabbi; Great Neck, NewYork
M. W. G. **Morris W. Garber,** Ph.D.; Assistant Professor of History, Rutgers University, New Brunswick, New Jersey
M. Wu. **Max Wurmbrand;** Ramat Gan
M. W. W. **Meyer Wolf Weisgal;** Chancellor of the Weizmann Institute of Science, Reḥovot, Israel

M.Y. **Meir Ydit,** Ph.D.; Dr.rer.Pol., Rabbi; Perth, Australia

My.F. **Myer Feldman,** B.A., B.S., LL.B.; Attorney, Washington, D. C.

M.Yo. **Meir Yoeli,** M.Sc., M.D.; Professor of Preventative Medicine, New York University School of Medicine

My.S. **Myra J. Siff,** M.A.; Instructor in Religion and Bible, Wellesley College, Massachusetts

My.Sa. **Myron Samuelson,** Ph.B., LL.B.; Burlington, Vermont

M.Z. **Menahem Zulay** *(deceased)*, Dr.Phil.; Scholar of medieval Hebrew poetry, Jerusalem

M.Z.B. **Menahem Zvi Barkay,** M.A.; Senior Librarian, the Jewish National and University Library, Jerusalem

M.Zb. **Mark Zborowski,** Ph.D.; Research Associate in Medicine, Mount Zion Hospital and Medical Center, San Francisco, California

M.Z.Ba. See **Z.Ba.**

M.Ze. **Moshe Zeidner,** B.A.; Tel Aviv

M.Z.F. **Moshe Zvi Frank,** B.A.; LL.B.; Journalist, Tel Aviv

M.Z.H. See **H.Z.H.**

M.Z.-K. **Mordechay Zerkawod,** Dr.Phil.; Emeritus Professor of Bible, Bar Ilan University, Ramat Gan

M.Z.Ka. **Menahem Zevi Kaddari,** Ph.D.; Rector and Professor of Hebrew Language, Bar Ilan University, Ramat Gan

M.Zo. **Maurice Zolotow,** B.A.; Los Angeles

M.Z.S. **Moshe Zevi (Moses Hirsch) Segal** *(deceased)*, M.A.; Emeritus Professor of Bible, the Hebrew University of Jerusalem

M.Z.So. **Moshe Zeev Sole,** Dr.Phil., Rabbi; Chief Secretary of the Rabbinical Court, Jerusalem

M.Zu. **Moshe Zucker,** Ph.D., Rabbi; Professor of Biblical Exegesis, the Jewish Theological Seminary of America, New York

N.A. **Nachum Arieli,** B.A.; Jerusalem

Na.I. **Nahman Ingber,** M.A.; Instructor in Poetics and Comparative Literature, Tel Aviv University

N.Al. **Nehemya Allony,** Ph.D.; Associate Professor of Hebrew Language and Literature, the University of the Negev, Beersheba

Na.R. **Nahum Rakover,** Ph.D., Rabbi; Teaching Fellow in Jewish Law, the Hebrew University of Jerusalem

Na.Ro. **Nathan Rotenstreich,** Ph.D.; Professor of Philosophy and Former Rector, the Hebrew University of Jerusalem

Nat.G. **Nathan Greenbaum,** M.A.; Lecturer in Hebrew Literature and Language, Gratz College; Lecturer in Hebrew, Temple University, Philadelphia

N.Av. **Nachman Avigad,** Ph.D.; Professor of Archaeology, the Hebrew University of Jerusalem

N.B. **Nachman Blumental;** Historian, Jerusalem

N.Ben. **Norman Bentwich** *(deceased)*, Ph.D.; Emeritus Professor of International Relations, the Hebrew University of Jerusalem

N.B.-G. **Naftali Bar-Giora;** Jewish Agency, Jerusalem

N.B.-M. **Naphtali Ben-Menahem;** Executive Director of the Institute for Hebrew Bibliography, the Hebrew University of Jerusalem

N.B.S. **Norton B. Stern,** O.D.; Editor, Venice, California

N.C. **Noam Chomsky,** Ph.D.; Professor of Linguistics, Massachusetts Institute of Technology, Cambridge

N.D.L., N.De-L. **Nicholas de Lange,** D.Phil.; Lecturer in Rabbinics, the University of Cambridge

N.Dr. **Noah W. Dragoon,** M.A.; Jerusalem

N.E. **Natan Efrati,** M.A.; Ben Zvi Institute, Jerusalem

N.Eck **Nathan Eck,** Dr.Jur.; Historian, Tel Aviv

Ne.L. See **E.H.**

N.E.S. **Nisson E. Shulman,** D.H.L., Rabbi; Yonkers, New York

N.F. **Nathan Feinberg,** Dr.Jur.; Emeritus Professor of International Law, the Hebrew University of Jerusalem

N.Fe. **Nira Feldman,** Ph.D.; Research Fellow in Contemporary Jewry, the Hebrew University of Jerusalem

N.Fr. **Nathan Fried,** Rabbi; Bene-Berak

N.G. See **E.H.**

N.Gl. **Nathan Glazer,** Ph.D.; Professor of Education and Social Structure, Harvard University, Cambridge, Massachusetts

N. Gr. **Noé Gruss,** Ph.D.; Librarian, Bibliotheque Nationale, Paris

N.H. **Nathan Hochberg,** M.Sc.; Agronomist, Tel Aviv

N.H.S. **Norman Henry Snaith,** D.D.; Former Principal, Wesley College, Leeds; Former Lecturer in Hebrew and Old Testament, the University of Leeds

N.H.T.-S. **Naphtali Herz Tur-Sinai (Torczyner),** Dr. Phil.; Emeritus Professor of Hebrew Language, the Hebrew University of Jerusalem; President of the Academy of the Hebrew Language, Jerusalem

N.H.W. **Nathan H. Winter,** Ph.D., J.D.; Associate Professor of Hebrew Culture and Education, New York University

N.I. **Norman Itzkowitz,** Ph.D.; Associate Professor of Near Eastern Studies, Princeton University, New Jersey

Ni.B. **Nicolas Burckhardt;** Director of the International Tracing Service, Arolsen, Germany

Ni.O. **Nissan Oren,** Ph.D.; Lecturer in International Relations, the Hebrew University of Jerusalem

N.K. **Nathaniel Katzburg,** Ph.D.; Associate Professor of Jewish History, Bar Ilan University, Ramat Gan

N.K.G. **Norman K. Gottwald,** Ph.D.; Professor of Old Testament and of Biblical Theology and Ethics, the Graduate Theological Union, Berkeley, California

N.Ko. **Nathan Koren,** M.D.; Historian, Jerusalem

N.L. **Netanel Lorch,** M.A.; Lieutenant Colonel (Res.), Israel Defense Forces; Former Ambassador, Ministry for Foreign Affairs, Jerusalem

N.Ler. **Natan Lerner,** LL.D.; Executive Director, World Jewish Congress, Tel Aviv

N.Lev. **Norman Levin,** Ph.D.; Assistant Professor of Biology, Brooklyn College of the City University of New York

N.M.G. **Nathan Michael Gelber,** *(deceased)*, Dr.Phil.; *Encyclopaedia Judaica* (Germany); Jerusalem

N.M.S. **Nahum M. Sarna,** Ph.D.; Professor of Biblical Studies, Brandeis University, Waltham, Massachusetts

N.N. **Nissan Netzer,** M.A.; Former Scientific Secretary, the Academy of the Hebrew Language, Jerusalem

N.N.G. **Nahum N. Glatzer,** Ph.D.; Professor of Jewish History, Brandeis University, Waltham, Massachusetts

N.O. **Neil Ovadia,** M.A.; Lecturer in History, City College of the City University of New York

No.L. **Norman Lamm,** Ph.D., Rabbi; Professor of Jewish Philosophy, Yeshiva University, New York

N.P. **Natan Peled;** Minister of Absorption, Kibbutz Sarid

N.R. **Nimrod Raphaeli,** Ph.D.; Lecturer in Political Science, the Hebrew University of Jerusalem

N.Ro. **Nehemiah Robinson** *(deceased)*, Dr.Phil.; Director of the Institute of Jewish Affairs, New York

N.S. **Nicolas Slonimsky;** Musicologist, Los Angeles

N.Sch. **Nili Shupak,** B.A.; Jerusalem

N.Sk. **Nathan Skolnick,** M.A.; Bridgeport, Connecticut

N.W. See **N.H.W.**

N.W.C. **Naomi W. Cohen,** Ph.D.; Associate Professor of History, Hunter College of the City University of New York

N.Y. **Nissim Itzhak,** B.A.; Ministry for Foreign Affairs, Jerusalem

N.Z. **Natan Zach,** B.A.; Lecturer in Hebrew and Comparative Literature, Tel Aviv University

O.A. **Ora Alcalay,** B.A., Dip.Lib.; Director of the Library of Yad Vashem, Jerusalem

O.I.J. **Oscar Isaiah Janowsky,** Ph.D.; Emeritus Professor of History, City College of the City University of New York

O.I.S. **Otto Immanuel Spear;** Writer on philosophy, Ramat Gan

O.K.R. **Oskar K. Rabinowicz** *(deceased)*, Dr.Phil.; Historian, New York

O.L. **Ora Lipschitz,** M.A.; Jerusalem

O.M. **Oskar Mendelsohn,** Ph.D.; Historian, Oslo

O.R. **Omri Ronen,** Ph.D., Senior Lecturer, Russian and Comparative Literature, Hebrew University, Jerusalem

O.S. **Oskar Seidlin,** Ph.D.; Professor of German Literature, Ohio State University, Columbus

O.T. **Oded Tavor,** B.A.; the Shiloah Center for Middle Eastern and African Studies, Tel Aviv University

O.Z. **Oren Zinder,** Ph.D.; Jerusalem

P.A. **Pinḥas Artzi,** Ph.D., Rabbi; Associate Professor of Hebrew and Semitic Languages, Bar Ilan University, Ramat Gan; Associate Professor of Akkadian and Ancient Near Eastern History, Tel Aviv University

P.A.A. **Paul Awraham Alsberg,** Ph.D.; Israel State Archivist; Lecturer in Archival Management, Graduate Library School, the Hebrew University of Jerusalem

P.A.F. **Paul A. Freund,** S.J.D.; Professor of Law, Harvard University, Cambridge, Massachusetts

P.Ar. See **P.A.**

P.Au. **Pierre Aubery,** Ph.D.; Professor of French Literature, the State University of New York, Buffalo

P.B. **Paul Blau;** *Encyclopaedia Judaica* (Germany); Vienna

P.Bo. **Paul Borchardt;** *Encyclopaedia Judaica* (Germany); Munich

P.Bor. **Poul Borchsenius,** M.A., Reverend; Historian, Randers, Denmark

P.D. **Preston David,** M.S.; Executive Director, New York City Human Rights Commission

P.D.H. **Philip D. Hobsbaum,** L.R.A.M., L.G.S.M., Ph.D.; Lecturer in English Literature, the University of Glasgow

P.E. **Paul Engel,** M.D.; Professor of Biology, the Central University of Ecuador, Quito

P.E.G. **Peter Emanuel Gradenwitz,** Ph.D.; Lecturer in Musicology, Tel Aviv University

P.E.N. **Perry E. Nussbaum,** D.H.L., Rabbi; Jackson, Mississippi

P.F. **Paul Freireich,** M.S.; Journalist, New York

P.G. **Paul Glikson,** B.Sc.; Institute for Contemporary Jewry, the Hebrew University of Jerusalem

P.Go. **Paul Gottlieb,** B.A.; Jerusalem

P.H. **Pepita Haezrahi** *(deceased)*, Ph.D.; Senior Lecturer in Philosophy, the Hebrew University of Jerusalem

Ph.G. **Philip Goodman,** Rabbi; Executive Secretary of the Jewish Book Council of America, New York

P.J.D. **Paul Joseph Diamant** *(deceased)*, Dr.Phil.; Genealogist, Jerusalem

P.K. **Pawel Korzec,** Ph.D.; Research Associate of the Centre National de la Recherche Scientifique, Paris

P.L. **Pearl J. Lieff,** Ph.D.; Assistant Professor of Sociology, Borough of Manhattan Community College of the City University of New York

P.La. **Paul Lazarus** *(deceased)*, Dr.Phil., Rabbi; Historian, Haifa

P.Li. **Paul Link,** M.Sc.; Emeritus Professor of Textiles, Instituto Superior Tecnológico, Buenos Aires; Ḥavaẓẓelet Ḥa-Sharon, Israel

P.M. **Peretz Merhav;** Historian of the Labor Movement, Kibbutz Bet Zera

P.Ma. **Peter Machinist,** B.A.; New Haven, Connecticut

P.Me. **Pnina Meislish,** B.A.; Ramat Gan

P.M.G. **Perry Goldman,** Ph.D.; Assistant Professor of History, City College of the City University of New York

P.N. **Pnina Navè,** Ph.D.; Visiting Professor of Jewish Studies, Heidelberg University

P.P. **Peter Pollack;** Lecturer and writer on photography, New York

P.Pe. **Pinchas Hacohen Peli,** Ph.D.; Senior Lecturer in Jewish Philosophy, the University of the Negev, Beersheba; External Teacher in Jewish Studies, the Hebrew University of Jerusalem

P.Pi. **Walter Pinhas Pick;** Editor, the *Encyclopaedia Hebraica*, Jerusalem

P.P.K. **Penuel P. Kahane,** Ph.D.; Former Chief Curator of the Samuel Bronfman Biblical and Archaeological Museum, the Israel Museum, Jerusalem

P.R. **Pinchas Rosen;** Former Minister of Justice, Jerusalem

P.S.G. **Percy S. Gourgey,** M.B.E.; Journalist, Twickenham, Middlesex, England

P.T. **Pascal Themanlys;** Writer, Jerusalem

P.W. **Paul Weissman;** Jerusalem

P.W.-M. **Preben Wernberg-Møller,** D.Phil; Professorial Fellow of St. Peter's College and Reader in Semitic Philology, the University of Oxford

R.A. **Reuben Ainsztein;** Writer and journalist, London
Ra. C. **Richard Cohen,** B.A.; Associate Director, the American Jewish Congress, New York
Ra.K. **Raphael Kutscher,** Ph.D.; Lecturer in Mesopotamian Languages and Civilization, Tel Aviv University
Ra.L. **Raphael Loewe,** M.A.; Lecturer in Hebrew, University College, London
R.Ap. **Raymond Apple,** B.A., LL.B., Rabbi; London
R.A.S. **Robert A. Seigel,** M.A., Rabbi; Chicago
R.At. **Rachel Auerbach,** Dipl.Hist.Psych.; Historian, Jerusalem
R.Au. **Robert Attal;** Librarian, the Ben-Zvi Institute, Yad Vashem, Tel Aviv
Ra.W. **Raanan Weitz,** Ph.D.; Member of the World Zionist Executive; Director of the Settlement Study Center, Reḥovot, Israel
R.B. **Roberto Bachi,** Dr.Jur.; Professor of Statistics and Demography, the Hebrew University of Jerusalem
R.Ba. **Rivka Irene Banitt,** M.A.; Research Assistant in Sociology, the Institute of Criminology, Tel Aviv University
R.Be. **Roger Berg,** D.Econ.; Editor, Paris
R.B.M. **Richard B. Morris,** Ph.D.; Professor of History, Columbia University, New York
R.Br. **Ravelle Brickman,** B.A.; New York
R.Bro. **Rosalind Browne;** Art critic, New York
R.B.Y.S. **Robert B. Y. Scott,** Ph.D.; Emeritus Professor of Religion, Princeton University, New Jersey
R.C. **Ram Carmi,** Architect; Tel Aviv
R.Ch. **Robert Chazan,** Ph.D.; Associate Professor of History, Ohio State University, Columbus
R.Co. **Rachel Cohen,** B.A.; Jerusalem
R.D. **Rachel Dalven,** Ph.D.; Professor of English, Ladycliff College, Highland Falls, New York
R.Da. **Robert Dán,** Ph.D.; Research Fellow of Orientalia and Librarian, National Széchényi Library of Hungary, Budapest
R.E. **Rafael Edelman** *(deceased)*, Ph.D.; Director of Jewish Studies, Copenhagen University; Head of the Jewish Department, the Royal Library, Copenhagen
R.E.L. **Robert E. Levinson,** Ph.D.; San Francisco
Re.N. **Reuven Nall,** LL.B.; Ministry for Foreign Affairs, Jerusalem
R.E.O. **Ronald E. Ohl,** M.A.; Dean of Student Affairs, the Colorado College, Colorado Springs
Re.W. **Renee Winegarten,** Ph.D.; Literary critic, London
R.F. **Rachel Floersheim,** Ph.D.; New York
R.G.B. **Robert G. Boling,** Ph.D.; Professor of Old Testament, McCormick Theological Seminary, Chicago
R.G.H. **Rivka G. Horwitz,** Ph.D.; External Lecturer in Jewish Philosophy, the Hebrew University of Jerusalem and Tel Aviv University
R.Gl. **Rudolf Glanz,** Dr.Jur.; Historian, New York
R.Go. **Robert Gordis,** Ph.D., Rabbi; Professor of Religion, Temple University, Philadelphia; Professor of Bible, the Jewish Theological Seminary of America, New York
R.H.P. **Richard H. Popkin,** Ph.D.; Professor of Philosophy, the University of California, San Diego; Distinguished Professor of Philosophy, the Herbert H. Lehman College of the City University of New York
R.I. **Ruth Ivor,** Ph.D.; Former Lecturer in the History of Comparative Civilization, the University of Colorado; Siena, Italy
Ri.M. **Richard Meier,** Bach.Arch.; Professor of Architecture, the Cooper Union for the Advancement of Science and Art, New York
R.J.Z.W. **R.J. Zwi Werblowsky,** D.èsL.; Professor of Comparative Religion, the Hebrew University of Jerusalem; former dean, faculty of the humanities
R.K. **Rudolf Kayser** *(deceased)*, Dr.Phil.; Assistant Professor of Germanic Language and Literature, Brandeis University, Waltham, Massachusetts
R.Ka. **Reuben Kashani;** Journalist, Jerusalem
R.K.-G. **Ruth Kestenberg-Gladstein,** Ph.D.; External Teacher in the History of the Jewish People, Haifa University
R.K.S. **Rachel (Katznelson) Shazar,** B.A.; Wife of the President of Israel, Writer and editor, Jerusalem
R.L. **Rudolf Loewenthal,** Ph.D.; Historian, Bethesda, Maryland
R.Le. **Ralph Lerner,** Ph.D.; Associate Professor of Social Sciences, the University of Chicago
R.L.R. **Richard L. Rubenstein,** Ph.D., Rabbi; Professor of Religion, Florida State University, Tallahassee
R.Lu. **Roy Lubove,** Ph.D.; Professor of Social Welfare and History, the University of Pittsburgh
R.M. **Reuven Michael,** M.A.; Kibbutz Afikim
R.Ma. **Raphael Mahler,** Dr.Phil.; Emeritus Professor of Jewish History, Tel Aviv University
R.M.B. **Robert M. Benjamin,** M.A., Rabbi; Adjunct Assistant Professor of Humanities, Indiana State University, Terre Haute
R.Mo. **Rafael Moses,** M.D.; Senior Lecturer in Social Work, the Hebrew University of Jerusalem
R.M.W.K. **Robert M.W. Kempner,** LL.D.; Jurist and Chief Prosecutor, Nuremberg War Crimes Trials; Lansdowne, Pennsylvania
R.N.B. **Richard N. Bluestein,** LL.D.; Executive Vice President, the National Jewish Hospital, Denver, Colorado
R.N.-B. **Renée Neher-Bernheim,** Ph.D.; Research Fellow in Jewish History, University of Strasbourg and Tel Aviv University
Ro.A. **Robert Asher,** M.A.; Lecturer in History, City College of the City University of New York
Ro.B. **Rose Bieber,** B.A., Lic. en Sc. Comm.; Brussels
Ro.B.M. **Robert B. MacLeod,** Ph.D.; Professor of Psychology, Cornell University, Ithaca, New York
Ro.C. **Robert Cohen,** B.A.; Jerusalem
Ro.G. **Rosa Ginossar,** L.en D., Honorary President of WIZO, Jerusalem
Ro.K. **Roger Kamien,** Ph.D.; Assistant Professor of Music, Queens College of the City University of New York
Ro.Sh. **Robert Shosteck,** M.A.; Curator of the B'nai B'rith Museum, Washington, D. C.
R.P. **Raphael Posner,** D.H.L., Rabbi; Assistant Professor of Rabbinics, the Jewish Theological Seminary of America, Jerusalem
R.P.L. **Ruth P. Lehmann,** Dipl.O.A.S., F.L.A.; Librarian of Jews' College, London

R.P.R. **Rosa Perla Resnick,** Ph.D.; Social Scientist, Buenos Aires
R.P.Ra. **Rosa Perla Raicher,** M.A.; Tel Aviv
R.P.S. **Raymond P. Scheindlin,** Ph.D., Rabbi; Assistant Professor of Jewish Studies, McGill University, Montreal
R.R. **Raphael Rothstein,** B.A.; Journalist, New York
R.Ro. **Robert Rockaway,** Ph.D.; Assistant Professor of American Urban History, the University of Texas, El Paso
R.S. **Rinna Samuel,** B.A.; Journalist, Reḥovot, Israel
R.S.C. **Robert S. Cohen,** Ph.D.; Professor of Physics and Philosophy, Boston University, Massachusetts
R.Se. **Ralph Segalman,** Ph.D., A.C.S.W.; Associate Professor of Sociology, San Fernando Valley State College, Northridge, California
R.S.El. **Richard S. Ellis,** Ph.D.; Associate Professor of Near Eastern Archaeology, Yale University, New Haven, Connecticut
R.S.G. **Robert S. Goldman,** M.A.; New York
R.Sh. **Richard F. Shepard;** Journalist, New York
R.Sk. **Richard Skolnik,** Ph.D.; Assistant Professor of History, City College of the City University of New York
R.Sm. **Rudolf Smend,** Dr. Theol.; Professor of Old Testament, Georg-August-Universität zu Göttingen, Germany
R.Sp. **Renato Spiegel,** B.A.; Jerusalem
R.S.S. **René Samuel Sirat,** Ph.D., Rabbi; Professor of Modern Hebrew, Institut National des Langues et Civilisations Orientales; Director of the Centre Universitaire D'Etudes Juives, Paris; Director of the section for Overseas Students, the Hebrew University of Jerusalem
R.S.U. **Rivka Shatz-Uffenheimer,** Ph.D.; Senior Lecturer in Jewish Philosophy and Mysticism, the Hebrew University of Jerusalem
Ru.W. **Ruth Wisse,** Ph.D.; Assistant Professor of Yiddish Literature, McGill University, Montreal
R.W. **Robert Weltsch,** Dr.Jur.; Writer and Director of the Leo Baeck Institute, London
R.We. **Raphael Weiss,** M.A.; Instructor in Bible, Tel Aviv University
R.Wi. **Rachel Wischnitzer,** M.A., Dipl.Arch.; Emeritus Professor of Fine Arts, Yeshiva University, New York
R.Y. **Reuven Yaron,** D.Phil.; Professor of Roman Law and Ancient Near Eastern Law, the Hebrew University of Jerusalem

S.A. **Saul Aaron Adler** *(deceased)*, D.T.M., F.R.C.P., F.R.S.; Professor of Parasitology, the Hebrew University of Jerusalem
S.A.B. **Solomon Asher Birnbaum,** Dr.Phil.; Former Lecturer in Hebrew Palaeography and Epigraphy, the School of Oriental and African Studies, the University of London
Sa.B. **Saul Berman,** M.A., M.H.L., Rabbi; Brookline, Massachusetts
Sa.B.H. **Samuel B. Hurwich,** M.D., F.A.A.P.; Jerusalem
S.A.C. See **Ed.**
S.Ad. **Selig Adler,** Ph.D.; Professor of American History, the State University of New York, Buffalo
Sa.F. **Saul Friedländer,** Dr.Phil.; Professor of International Relations and Contemporary History, the Hebrew University of Jerusalem
Sa.H. **Samuel Hand,** Ph.D.; Associate Professor of History, the University of Vermont, Burlington
Sa.K. **Saul Kagan;** New York
S.A.L. **Sanford A. Lakoff,** Ph.D.; Professor of Political Science, the University of Toronto
S.A.M. **Samuel Aaron Miller** *(deceased)*, Ph.D., F.R.I.C.; Chemical Consultant and President of the British Zionist Federation, London
S.A.-R. See **Sh.A.-R.**
Sa.Ra. **Sanford Ragins,** M.A., Rabbi; Hartsdale, New York
Sa.Sch. **Samuel Scheps,** Ph.D.; Economist, Geneva
Sa.V. **Samuel Volkman,** Rabbi; Charleston, W. Virginia
Sa.W. **Salomon Wolf,** Ph.D.; Jerusalem
S.B.H. **Sidney B. Hoenig,** Ph.D., Rabbi; Professor of Jewish History, Yeshiva University, New York
S.B.L. **Seymour B. Liebman,** M.A., Lecturer in Latin American History, Florida Atlantic University, Boca Raton
S.Bo. **Frederick Simon Bodenheimer** *(deceased)*, Dr. Phil.; Emeritus Professor of General Zoology and Entomology, the Hebrew University of Jerusalem
S.B.U. **Symcha Bunim Urbach** *(deceased)*, Rabbi; Associate Professor of Jewish Philosophy, Bar Ilan University, Ramat Gan
S.C. **Shulamith Catane,** B.A.; Jerusalem
S.C.H. **Semah Cecil Hyman;** Former Minister Plenipotentiary, Ministry for Foreign Affairs, Jerusalem
S.D.B. **Sidney D. Braun,** Ph.D.; Professor of Romance Languages, the Herbert H. Lehman College of the City University of New York
S.De. **Shabbetai Devir;** Jerusalem
S.D.G. **Shelomo Dov Goitein,** Dr.Phil.; Emeritus Professor of Islamic Studies, the Hebrew University of Jerusalem; Emeritus Professor of Arabic, the University of Pennsylvania, Philadelphia
S.D.P. **Sergio Della Pergola,** Dr.Pol.Sc.; the Institute for Contemporary Jewry, the Hebrew University of Jerusalem
S.D.R. **Shmuel Dov Revital,** Dr.Jur.; State Comptroller's Office, Jerusalem
S.D.T. **Sefton D. Temkin,** Ph.D., Rabbi; New York
S.E. **Shlomo Eidelberg,** Ph.D., D.H.L.; Professor of Jewish History, Yeshiva University, New York and Haifa University
Se.Be. **Selma Berrol,** Ph.D.; Assistant Professor of History, the Bernard Baruch College of the City University of New York
S.Ei. **Sydney Eisen,** Ph.D.; Professor of History and Humanities, York University, Downsview, Ontario
S.E.K. **Samuel E. Karff,** D.H.L., Rabbi; Lecturer in Jewish Thought and American Culture, Divinity School, the University of Chicago
S.E.L. **Samuel Ephraim Loewenstamm,** Ph.D.; Professor of Bible, the Hebrew University of Jerusalem
S.Er. **Shimon Ernst** *(deceased)*, Ph.D.; Librarian, Tel Aviv
S.Ett. **Shmuel Ettinger,** Ph.D.; Associate Professor of

Jewish History, the Hebrew University of Jerusalem

S.F. **Solomon Fisch,** Ph.D., Rabbi; Leeds

S.F.C. **Stanley F. Chyet,** Ph.D., Rabbi; Professor of American Jewish History, the Hebrew Union College–Jewish Institute of Religion, Cincinnati

S.Fe. **Seymour Feldman,** Ph.D.; Associate Professor of Philosophy, Rutgers University, New Brunswick, New Jersey

S.G. **Solomon Grayzel,** Ph.D., Rabbi; Editor Emeritus of the Jewish Publication Society of America; Professor of History, Dropsie University, Philadelphia

S.Ge. **Saadia Gelb,** M.A., Rabbi; Kibbutz Kefar Blum

S.G.F.B. **Samuel G.F. Brandon** *(deceased)*, D.D.; Professor of Comparative Religion, the University of Manchester

S.Go. **Samuel Goldfeld,** M.D.; Jerusalem

S.H. **Shlomo Hasson,** B.A.; Jerusalem

S.Ha. **Saul Hayes,** M.A., Q.C.; Executive Vice President of the Canadian Jewish Congress, Lecturer in Social Work, McGill University, Montreal

Sh.A. **Shalom Albeck,** Ph.D.; Associate Professor of Talmud and Law, Bar Ilan University, Ramat Gan

Sh.Ab. **Samuel Abramsky,** Ph.D.; Senior Lecturer in Jewish History and in Bible, the University of the Negev, Beersheba

Sh.A.H. **Samuel Abba Horodezky** *(deceased)*, Ph.D.; Historian, Tel Aviv

Sh.Ahi. **Shmuel Aḥituv,** M.A.; Staff, *Biblical Encyclopedia,* Jerusalem

Sha.L. **Shaoul Langnas,** Ph.D.; Jewish Agency, Tel Aviv

Sh.Am. **Shimshon Avraham Amitsur,** Ph.D.; Professor of Mathematics, the Hebrew University of Jerusalem

Sh.Ap. **Shimon Applebaum,** D.Phil.; Associate Professor of Classical Archaeology and of Jewish History, Tel Aviv University

Sh.A.-R. **Shalom Adler-Rudel;** Director of the Leo Baeck Institute, Jerusalem

Sh.Ar. **Shlomo Aronson,** Ph.D.; Lecturer in Political Science, the Hebrew University of Jerusalem

Sh.Ash. **Shmuel Ashkenazi;** the Rabbi Kook Institute, Jerusalem

Sh.B. **Shlomo Bickel** *(deceased)*, Dr.Jur.; Writer and critic, New York

Sh.Ba. **Shlomo Balter,** Ph.D., Rabbi; Lecturer in Bible, the City University of New York

Sh.B.-C. **Schalom Ben-Chorin;** Writer and journalist, Jerusalem

Sh.Be. **Shmuel Bendor,** B.A.; Secretary of the Council for Higher Education, Ministry of Education and Culture, Jerusalem

Sh.Br. **Shlomo Breiman,** Ph.D.; Writer and scholar, Jerusalem

Sh.D. **Shlomo Derech;** Editor, Kibbutz Givat Ḥayyim

Sh.Da. **Shaul Dagoni,** M.D.; Haifa

Sh.Dy. **Shlomo Dykman** *(deceased)*; Translator, Jerusalem

Sh.E. **Shaul Esh** *(deceased)*, Ph.D.; Senior Lecturer in Contemporary Jewry, the Hebrew University of Jerusalem

Sh.Er. **Shlomo Erel;** Ministry of Defense, Tel Aviv

Sh.F. **Shamma Friedman,** Ph.D., Rabbi; Assistant Professor of Rabbinics, the Jewish Theological Seminary of America, New York

Sh.G. **Shmuel Gorr,** B.A.; Rabbi; Jerusalem

Sh.Gi. **Shabbetai Ginton,** M.D.; Ministry of Health, Jerusalem

Sh.H. **Shoshana Hareli,** M.A.; Haifa

Sh.H.B. **Samuel Hugo Bergman,** Dr.Phil.; Emeritus Professor of Philosophy, the Hebrew University of Jerusalem

Sh.Ho. **Shlomo Hofman,** D.Litt.; Lecturer in the History of Music, Tel Aviv University–Rubin Academy of Music

Sh.Hu. **Shmuel Hurwitz,** Dr.Agr.; Emeritus Professor of Agronomy, the Hebrew University of Jerusalem

Shi.A. **Shimeon Amir,** Ph.D.; Senior Lecturer in the Department of Developing Countries, Tel Aviv University; Deputy Director General, Ministry for Foreign Affairs, Jerusalem

Shi.B. **Shira Borut,** Ph.D.; Research Associate in Parasitology, the Hebrew University–Hadassah Medical School, Jerusalem

Shi.R. **Shimon Redlich,** Ph.D.; Lecturer in History, the University of the Negev, Beersheba

Sh.L. **Shalom Levin,** M.A.; Member of the Knesset, Tel Aviv

Sh.L.K. **Shimshon Leib Kirshenboim,** Ph.D.; Educator, Jerusalem

Shl.Sh. **Shlomo Shunami,** Dip.Lib.; Bibliographer and librarian, the Jewish National and University Library, Jerusalem

Sh.M. **Shmuel Moreh,** Ph.D.; Lecturer in Modern Arabic Language and Literature, the Hebrew University of Jerusalem

Sh.Mo. **Shelomo Morag,** Ph.D.; Professor of Hebrew Linguistics, the Hebrew University of Jerusalem

Sh.M.P. **Shalom M. Paul,** Ph.D., Rabbi; Senior Lecturer in Bible, the Hebrew University of Jerusalem and Tel Aviv University

S.H.-N. **Svend Holm-Nielsen,** Dr.Theol.; Professor of Old Testament, Copenhagen University

Sh.N. **Shemuel Niger (Charney)** *(deceased)*; Writer and critic, New York

Sh.Na. **Shlomo Na'aman,** Ph.D.; Associate Professor of Social History, Tel Aviv University

Sh.P. **Shlomo Pines,** Dr.Phil.; Professor of General and Jewish Philosophy, the Hebrew University of Jerusalem

Sh.Pe. **Shalom Perlman,** Ph.D.; Professor of Greek History, Tel Aviv University

Sh.R. **Shabtai Rosenne,** Ph.D.; Ambassador, Ministry for Foreign Affairs, Jerusalem

Sh.Ra. **Shaul Ramati,** M.A.; Lieutenant Colonel (Res.), Israel Defense Forces; Ministry for Foreign Affairs, Jerusalem

Sh.Ro. **Shalom Rosenberg,** M.A.; Jerusalem

Sh.S. **Shmuel Safrai,** Ph.D., Rabbi; Associate Professor of Jewish History, the Hebrew University of Jerusalem

Sh.Sch. **Simon S. Schlesinger** *(deceased)*, Dr.Phil.; Rabbi; Scholar and Educator, Jerusalem

Sh.Sh. **Shmuel Shilo,** Ph.D., Rabbi; Instructor in Jewish Law, the Hebrew University of Jerusalem

Sh.Si. **Shlomo Simonsohn,** Ph.D.; Professor of Jewish History, Tel Aviv University

Sh. So. **Shmuel Soler;** General Federation of Labor, Tel Aviv

Sh. T. **Shlomo Tal,** M.A., M.Jur., Rabbi; Director of the Ze'ev Gold Institute, Jerusalem

Sh. Ta. **Shimshon Tapuach,** Ph.D.; Ministry of Agriculture, Tel Aviv

Sh. Tu. **Shaul Tuval,** M.A.; Ministry for Foreign Affairs, Jerusalem

S. H.-W. **Sara O. Heller-Wilensky,** Ph.D.; Associate Professor of Jewish Philosophy, Bar Ilan University, Ramat Gan, Tel Aviv University and Haifa University

Sh. W. **Shillem Warhaftig,** Dr.Jur.; Ministry of Justice, Jerusalem

Sh. W.-H., Sh. W.-K. **Samuel Weingarten-Hakohen;** Jerusalem

Sh. Y. See **E. H.**

Sh. Z. **Shaul Zarhi,** M.Sc.; Economist, Tel Aviv

Si. A. **Simha Assaf** *(deceased)*, Rabbi; Rector and Professor of Rabbinical and Geonic Literature, the Hebrew University of Jerusalem; Justice of the Supreme Court of Israel

Si. B. **Simcha Berkowitz,** M.A., M.H.L., Rabbi; the College of Jewish Studies, Detroit

Si. Bl. **Simha Blass,** Engineer; Former Director General of Tahal Water Planning for Israel, Tel Aviv

Si. G. **Sidney Goldstein,** Ph.D.; Professor of Sociology and Anthropology, Brown University, Providence, Rhode Island

Si. K. **Simcha Kruger,** B.S.; Librarian, New York

Si. M. **Simha Moretzky;** Journalist, Bat Yam, Israel

S. I. P. **Sidney I. Pomerantz,** Ph.D.; Professor of History, City College of the City University of New York

Si. R. **Sidney Ratner,** Ph.D.; Professor of History, Rutgers University, New Brunswick, New Jersey

S. J. **Sara Japhet,** M.A.; Instructor in Bible, the Hebrew University of Jerusalem

S. J. C. **Selma Jeanne Cohen,** Ph.D.; Editor, New York

S. J. D. V. **Simon J. De Vries,** Th.D.; Professor of Old Testament, the Methodist Theological School in Ohio, Delaware

S. J. H. **Samuel J. Hurwitz,** Ph.D.; Professor of History, Brooklyn College of the City University of New York

S. J. K. **Sholom Jacob Kahn,** Ph.D.; Senior Lecturer in English and American Literature, the Hebrew University of Jerusalem

S. Jo. K. **S. Joshua Kohn,** D.H.L., Rabbi; Trenton, New Jersey

S. J. S. **Stanley J. Stein,** Ph.D.; Professor of History, Princeton University, New Jersey

S. K. **Simḥa Katz,** M.A.; Associate Editor, *Encyclopaedia Judaica,* and former General Associate Editor, *Encyclopaedia Hebraica,* Jerusalem

S. Ka. **Stewart Kampel,** M.S.; Lecturer in Journalism, City College of the City University of New York

S. Kay. **Stephen Kayser,** Ph.D.; Former Curator of the Jewish Museum, New York; Los Angeles, California

S. Ke. **Solomon Kerstein** *(deceased)*; Vice President, Bloch Publishing Company, New York

S. K. M. **Samuel Kalman Mirsky** *(deceased)*, Ph.D., Rabbi; Professor of Rabbinics, Yeshiva University, New York

S. Ko. **Sami Kohen,** M.A.; Journalist, Istanbul

S. Kr. **Stefan Krakowski,** M.A.; Yad Vashem, Jerusalem

S. L. **Sol Liptzin,** Ph.D.; Emeritus Professor of Comparative Literature, City College of the City University of New York; the American College in Jerusalem

S. Le. **Samuel Leiter,** D.H.L., Rabbi; Professor of Modern Hebrew Literature, the Jewish Theological Seminary of America, New York

S. Lev. **Schneier Zalman Levenberg,** Ph.D.; Jewish Agency representative and writer, London

S. L. F. **Stanley L. Falk,** Ph.D.; Associate Professor of National Security Affairs, Industrial College of the Armed Forces, Washington, D.C.

S. L. G. **Simeon L. Guterman,** Ph.D.; Professor of History, Yeshiva University, New York

S. L. K. See **Sh. L. K.**

S. L. L. **Sonia L. Lipman,** B.A.; London

S. L. R. **Sidney L. Regner,** B.A., Rabbi; Executive Vice President, Central Conference of American Rabbis, New York

S. L. S. **Samuel L. Sumberg,** Ph.D.; Professor of Germanic and Slavic Languages, City College of the City University of New York

S. L. Sk. **Solomon Leon Skoss** *(deceased)*, Ph.D.; Professor of Arabic, Dropsie College for Hebrew and Cognate Learning, Philadelphia

S. M. **Suessmann Muntner** *(deceased)*, M.D., Visiting Professor of the History of Medicine, the Hebrew University of Jerusalem

S. Ma. See **M. M. M.**

S. Mar. **Simon Marcus,** Dr.rer.Pol; Historian, Jerusalem

S. M. B. **Samuel M. Blumenfield** *(deceased)*, D.H.L., Rabbi; Professor of Hebrew Literature and Culture, Hofstra University, Hempstead, New York

S. M. I. **Salvator Marco Israel,** M.D.; Maître de Recherches Hebraïques, the Bulgarian Academy of Sciences, Sofia

S. M. L. **Sidney M. Lefkowitz,** Th.D.; Lecturer in Religion, Jacksonville University, Florida

S. Mo. **Sidney Monas,** Ph.D.; Professor of History and of Slavic Languages, the University of Texas, Austin

S. M. S. **Samuel Miklos Stern** *(deceased)*, D.Phil.; Fellow of All Souls College and Lecturer in the History of Islamic Civilization, the University of Oxford

S. N. **Sara Neshamith,** M.A.; Kibbutz Loḥamei ha-Getta'ot

S. Na. **Shulamit Nardi,** M.A.; Instructor in English and in Contemporary Jewry, the Hebrew University of Jerusalem

S. Ne. **Siegbert Neufeld,** Ph.D., Rabbi; Ramat Ḥen, Israel

S. N. K. **Samuel Noah Kramer,** Ph.D.; Emeritus Research Professor of Assyriology, the University of Pennsylvania, Philadelphia

S. O. **Shimon Oren,** M.A.; Teacher in Education, the Hebrew University of Jerusalem

So. G. **Salomon Gaon,** Ph.D., Rabbi; Chief Rabbi of the Spanish and Portuguese Associated Congregations of the British Commonwealth, London

So. H. W. **Solomon H. Waldenberg,** M.A., Rabbi; Santurce, Puerto Rico

So. R. **Sol Roth,** Ph.D., Rabbi; Lecturer in Philosophy, Yeshiva University, New York

S. O. T. See **S. D. T.**

S. P. C. **Saul Paul Colbi,** Dr.Jur.; Adviser on Christian Affairs to the Minister of Religious Affairs, Jerusalem

S. P. G. **Samuel P. Goldberg,** B.S.S., C.S.W., Lecturer in Communal Organization, Columbia University, New York

S. R. **Samuel Rosenblatt,** Ph.D., Rabbi; Associate Professor of Oriental Languages, Johns Hopkins University, Baltimore

S. Ra. **Solomon Rappaport,** Ph.D., Rabbi; Professor of Hebrew, the University of the Witwatersrand, Johannesburg, South Africa

S. R.-G. **Šarlota Rachmuth-Gerstl,** Ing.; Jerusalem

S. Ro. See **S. R.**

S. S. **Samuel Sandmel,** Ph.D., D.H.L., Rabbi; Professor of Bible and Hellenistic Literature, the Hebrew Union College–Jewish Institute of Religion, Cincinnati

S. Sch. **Simon R. Schwarzfuchs,** Ph.D., Rabbi; Associate Professor of Jewish History, Bar Ilan University, Ramat Gan

S. Si. **Seymour Siegel,** D.H.L., Rabbi; Professor of Theology and of Ethics and Rabbinic Thought, the Jewish Theological Seminary of America, New York

S. S. S. **Silvio Shalom Stoessl,** M.D.; Tel Aviv

S. St. **Sidney Steiman,** Ph.D., Rabbi; Affiliate Professor of Religion, the Christian Theological Seminary; Lecturer in Sociology, Marian College, Indianapolis, Indiana

S.Ste. **Siegfried Stein,** Ph.D.; Professor of Hebrew, University College, London

S. Sp. **Shmuel Spector,** M.A.; General Secretary of Yad Vashem, Jerusalem

S. T. **Samuel Tolansky,** Ph.D., D.Sc., D.I.C., F.R.A.S., F.R.S.; Professor of Physics, Royal Holloway College, the University of London

St. A. **Stanley Abramovitch,** M.A.; Director of the Education Department, American Joint Distribution Committee, Geneva

St. E. R. **Stuart E. Rosenberg,** Ph.D., Rabbi; Writer, Toronto

St. I. **Stanley Isser,** M.A.; Lecturer in History, Queens College of the City University of New York

St. L. **Stefan Lutkiewicz,** B.A.; Jerusalem

St. Sch. **Steven S. Schwarzschild,** D.H.L., Rabbi; Professor of Jewish Philosophy, Washington University, St. Louis, Missouri

Su. D. **Suzanne Daniel,** D.ès.L.; Associate Professor of Judeo-Hellenistic Literature, the Hebrew University of Jerusalem

S. V. **Simon Vega;** Ben Shemen, Israel

S. Va. **Samuel Vaisrub,** M.D. M.R.C.P.; Associate Professor, Chicago Medical School; Senior Editor, Journal of the American Medical Association

S. Vi. **Saul Viener,** M.A.; Richmond, Virginia

S. W. **Stanislaw Wygodzki;** Writer, Givatayim, Israel

S. W. B. **Salo W. Baron,** Ph.D., Rabbi; Emeritus Professor of Jewish History, Literature and Institutions, Columbia University, New York

S. We. **Samuel Werses,** Ph.D.; Associate Professor of Hebrew Literature, the Hebrew University of Jerusalem

Sy. R. **Sylvia Rothchild;** Writer, Brookline, Massachusetts

S. Z. See **Ed.**

S. Z. H. **Shlomoh Zalman Havlin,** Rabbi; Research Assistant, the Institute for Research in Jewish Law, the Hebrew University of Jerusalem

S. Z. L. **Shnayer Z. Leiman,** B.A.; Lecturer in Jewish History and Literature, Yale University, New Haven, Connecticut

T. Go. See **J. Go.**

Th. F. **Theodore Friedman,** Ph.D., Rabbi; the American College in Jerusalem

Th. H. **Theodore Hatalgui,** M.A.; the Jewish National Fund, Jerusalem

Th. H. G. **Theodor H. Gaster,** Ph.D.; Professor of Religion, Barnard College, Columbia University, New York

Thorkild Jacobsen, Dr. Phil.; Professor of Assyriology, Harvard University, Cambridge, Massachusetts

Th. L. **Theodor Lavi,** Dr.Phil.; Historian, Yad Vashem, Jerusalem

Th. M. G. See **Th. H. G.**

Th. S. **Theodore Schrire,** M.A., M.B., F.R.C.S., F.R.S.S.Af.; Senior Lecturer in Surgery, the University of Cape Town

Th. W. **Theodore Wiener,** M.H.L., Rabbi; Washington, D.C.

T. I. T. See **T. J. T.**

T. J. **Taeke Jansma,** Ph.D.; Professor of Hebrew and Aramaic, the State University of Leiden, the Netherlands

T. J. T. **Thomas J. Tobias,** B.S.; Charleston, South Carolina

T. K. R. **Theodore K. Rabb,** Ph.D.; Associate Professor of History, Princeton University, New Jersey

T. L. See **Th. L.**

T. M. **Torben Meyer;** Editor, Copenhagen

T. M. B. **Theodore M. Brown,** Ph.D.; Assistant Professor of History, City College of the City University of New York

T. O. **Toni Oelsner,** M.A., M.Soc.Sc.; Historian, New York

T. P. **Tovia Preschel,** Rabbi; Professor of Talmud, the Jewish Theological Seminary of America, New York

T. S. See **Y. S.**

T.-S. See **I. T.-S.**

Ts. A. **Tsevi Atsmon,** M.A.; Rishon le-Zion, Israel

T. S. F. **Tikva S. Frymer,** M.A.; Associate Professor of Near Eastern Languages, Wayne State University, Detroit

Ts. Ts. **Tsemah Tsamriyon,** Ph.D.; Educator, Haifa

Tu. M. See **Ju. M.**

U. C. **Umberto (Moses David) Cassuto** *(deceased)*, Litt.Doct., Rabbi; Professor of Bible, the Hebrew University of Jerusalem

U. D. **Uriel Dann,** Ph.D.; Senior Lecturer in the His-

tory of the Modern Middle East, Tel Aviv University

U.F. **Uzi Finerman;** Member of the Knesset, Kefar Yeḥezkel

U.N. **Uri Naor,** Dr.Phil.; Ministry for Foreign Affairs, Jerusalem

U.O. **Uriel Ofek,** M.A.; Writer and editor, Tel Aviv

U.Or. **Uzzi Ornan,** Ph.D.; Senior Lecturer in Hebrew Language, the Hebrew University of Jerusalem

U.O.S. **Usiel Oscar Schmelz,** Ph.D.; Research Fellow in Contemporary Jewry, the Hebrew University of Jerusalem

U.R. **Uriel Rappaport,** Ph.D.; Senior Lecturer in Jewish History, Haifa University

U.Ra. **Uri Ra'anan,** M.A.; Professor of International Politics, the Fletcher School of Law and Diplomacy, Tufts University, Medford, Massachusetts

U.S. **Uriel Simri,** Ed.D.; Scientific Director of the Wingate Institute for Physical Education and Sport, Netanyah

U.S.W. **Uri Shraga Würzburger,** M.Sc.; Managing Director of the Timna Copper Mines, Israel

U.T. **Uri (Erich) Toeplitz;** Musician and Teacher, Tel Aviv University–Rubin Academy of Music

U.W. **Uriel Weinreich** *(deceased)*, Ph.D.; Professor of Linguistics and of Yiddish Studies, Columbia University, New York

V.A.M. **Victor A. Mirelman,** M.A., Rabbi; Buenos Aires

V.C. **Vittore Colorni,** Ph.D.; Professor of the History of Italian Law, the University of Ferrara, Italy

V.D.L. **Vivian David Lipman,** Ph.D., F.R.Hist.Soc., F.S.A.; Historian, London

V.H. **Viveka Heyman,** M.A.; Teacher in Swedish, Tel Aviv University

V.Ha. **Vladimir Seev Halperin,** Ph.D.; Director of the World ORT Union, Geneva

V.R. See **U.R.**

V.T. See **U.T.**

V.W. **Veit Wyler,** Dr.Jur.; Attorney and editor, Zurich

W.A. **Wellesley Aron,** B.A.; Major (Ret.), British Army; Tel Aviv

Wa.B. **Walton Bean,** Ph.D.; Professor of History, the University of California, Berkeley

W.B. **Willy Bok,** M.A.; Acting Director of the Centre National des Hautes Etudes Juives, Brussels

W.Ba. **Walter Baumgartner** *(deceased)*, Dr.Phil.; Emeritus Professor of Bible and Oriental Languages, the University of Basle

W.B.E. **William B. Edgerton,** Ph.D.; Professor of Slavic Languages and Literatures, Indiana University, Bloomington

W.Ch. **William Chomsky,** Ph.D., D.H.L.; Professor of Hebrew and Jewish Education, Dropsie University, Philadelphia

W.F.A. **William Foxwell Albright** *(deceased)*, Ph.D.; Emeritus Professor of Near Eastern Studies, Johns Hopkins University, Baltimore, Maryland

W.G. **William Glicksman,** Ph.D.; Lecturer in Jewish History, Gratz College, Philadelphia

W.G.O. **Willard Gurdon Oxtoby,** Ph.D.; Associate Professor of Religious Studies, Yale University, New Haven, Connecticut

W.G.P. **W. Gunther Plaut,** Dr.Jur, Rabbi; Historian, Toronto

W.H. **Warren Harvey,** M.A.; New York

Wi.M. **Will Maslow,** B.A., LL.B.; Executive Director of the American Jewish Congress, New York

W.J.C. **Werner J. Cahnman,** Ph.D.; Professor of Sociology, Rutgers University, Newark, New Jersey; Member of the Faculty, New School for Social Research, New York

W.J.F. **Walter Joseph Fischel,** Ph.D.; Professor of Judaic Studies and History, the University of California, Santa Cruz; formerly Professor at University of California, Berkeley

W.K. **William Korey,** Ph.D.; Director of the B'nai B'rith United Nations Office, New York

W.Ke. **Wolfe Kelman,** M.H.L., Rabbi; Executive Vice President of the Rabbinical Assembly, New York

W.L. **Walter Lippmann;** Demographer, Melbourne

W.L.A. **Walter L. Arnstein,** Ph.D.; Professor of History, the University of Illinois, Urbana-Champaign

W.L.M. **William L. Moran,** Ph.D.; Professor of Assyriology, Harvard University, Cambridge, Massachusetts

W.Lo. **William (Ze'ev) Low,** Ph.D.; Professor of Physics, the Hebrew University of Jerusalem

W.M. **Werner Michaelis** *(deceased)*, Ph.D.; Professor of New Testament History, the University of Berne

W.N.S. **William N. Schoenfeld,** Ph.D.; Professor of Psychology, Queens College of the City University of New York and Cornell University Medical School, New York

W.P. (Entry: **ESSEX COUNTY**) **William Pages;** Journalist, Newark, New Jersey

W.P. **Wolfgang Paulsen,** Ph.D.; Professor of German, the University of Massachusetts, Amherst

W.P.E. **Willehad Paul Eckert,** Dr.Phil.; Professor of the History of Philosophy, Hochschule der Dominikaner, Walberberg, Germany

W.Pr. **Walter Preuss,** Dr.Phil., D.Econ.; Economist, Tel Aviv

W.R. **Wladimir Rabi,** M.A.; Judge and writer, Briançon, France

W.Sch. **Wolfgang Scheffler,** Dr.Phil.; Senior Research Fellow in Political Science, the University of Sussex Centre for Research in Collective Psychopathology, London

W.S.G. **Walter (Shlomoh) Gross,** Dr.Phil.; Journalist, Tel Aviv

W.So. **Walter Sorell,** M.A.; Associate in Dance and Theater History, Columbia University, New York

W.S.W. **Walter S. Wurzburger,** Ph.D., Rabbi; Visiting Associate Professor of Philosophy, Yeshiva University, New York

W.W. **Werner Weinberg,** Ph.D.; Professor of Hebrew Language and Literature, the Hebrew Union College–Jewish Institute of Religion, Cincinnati

W.W.B. **William W. Brickman,** Ph.D.; Professor of Educational History and Comparative Education, the University of Pennsylvania, Philadelphia

W.W.H. **William W. Hallo,** Ph.D.; Professor of Assyriol-

ogy and Curator of the Babylonian Collection, Yale University, New Haven, Connecticut
W.Z. **Walter Zanger,** M.A., Rabbi; Jerusalem
W.Z.R. **Wolf Zeev Rabinowitsch,** M.D.; Historian, Haifa

Y.A. **Yigal Allon;** Major General (Res.), Israel Defense Forces; Deputy Prime Minister and Minister of Education and Culture, Kibbutz Ginnosar
Ya.A. **Jacob Amit;** Editor, Tel Aviv
Y.A.D. **Yedidya A. Dinari,** Ph.D.; Lecturer in Talmud, Bar Ilan University, Ramat Gan
Ya.E. **Yaffa Eliach,** M.A.; Lecturer in Jewish and European History, Brooklyn College of the City University of New York
Ya.G. **Jacques Yakov Guggenheim;** Jerusalem
Y.A.H. **Yaakov Arie Hazan,** Member of the Knesset; Kibbutz Mishmar ha-Emek
Y.A.K. **Yehuda Arye Klausner** *(deceased)*, Ph.D.; Writer and scholar, Jerusalem
Y.A.L., Y.Al. **Itzhak Alfassi;** General Secretary, B'nai B'rith, Tel Aviv
Y.Am. **Yehoshua Amir (Neumark),** Dr.Phil., Rabbi; Senior Lecturer in Jewish Philosophy, Tel Aviv University
Ya.Ma. **Ja'acov Mazor,** B.A.; Teacher, the Rubin Academy of Music, Jerusalem
Y.Ar. **Yitzchak Arad;** Librarian and teacher, Jerusalem
Ya.Sh. **Yaacov Shimoni;** Deputy Director General, Ministry for Foreign Affairs, Jerusalem
Y.At. See **Y.A.L.**
Y.Av. **Yitzhak Avni;** Director of the Israel Government Coins and Medals Corporation, Jerusalem
Y.B. **Yohanan Boehm;** Music critic, Jerusalem
Y.Ba. **Yohanan Bader,** Dr.Jur.; Member of the Knesset, Ramat Gan
Y.B.-Ar. **Yehoshoua Ben-Arieh,** Ph.D.; Senior Lecturer in Geography, the Hebrew University of Jerusalem
Y.B.D., Y.B.-D. **Yehuda Ben-Dror (James Marshall),** B.A.; Jerusalem
Y.Be. **Yehuda Benari,** D.en D.; Director of the Jabotinsky Institute, Tel Aviv
Y.B.-H. **Yehoshua Bar-Hillel,** Ph.D.; Professor of Logic and the Philosophy of Science, the Hebrew University of Jerusalem
Y.Bl. **Joshua Blau,** Ph.D.; Professor of Arabic Language and Literature, the Hebrew University of Jerusalem; Professor of Hebrew and Semitic Linguistics, Tel Aviv University
Y.Bu. **Yosef Burg,** Ph.D., Rabbi; Minister of the Interior, Jerusalem
Y.C. **Yoseph Colombo,** Ph.D.; Lecturer in Jewish Studies, the Luigi Bocconi Commercial University, Milan
Y.C.-Y. **Yohanan (J.-G.) Cohen-Yashar (Kahn),** Ph.D.; Lecturer in Classical Languages and in Philosophy, Bar Ilan University, Ramat Gan
Y.D. **Joseph Dan,** Ph.D.; Associate Professor of Hebrew Literature, the Hebrew University of Jerusalem
Y.D.G. **Yitzhak Dov Gilat,** Ph.D.; Associate Professor of Talmud, Bar Ilan University, Ramat Gan; Senior Lecturer in Talmud, Tel Aviv University
Y.Di. **Yoram Dinstein,** Dr.Jur.; Senior Lecturer in Public International Law, Tel Aviv University
Y.Do. **Yaakov Dori** *(deceased)*, Dipl. Ing.; Lieutenant General (Res.), Israel Defense Forces and former chief of staff. Former President of the Technion, Haifa
Y.Du. **Yael Dunkelman;** Toronto
Y.E. **Yehudah Erez;** Editor and writer, Kibbutz Givat Ḥayyim
Ye.A. **Yehoshua Alouf;** Former Supervisor of Physical Education, Ministry of Education and Culture; Ramat Gan
Ye.B. **Yehuda Bauer,** Ph.D.; Senior Lecturer in Contemporary Jewry, the Hebrew University of Jerusalem
Ye.Bl., Ye.El. **Yehuda Elitzur,** M.A.; Associate Professor of Biblical Historiography, Bar Ilan University, Ramat Gan
Ye.G. **Yemima Gottlieb,** B.A.; Jerusalem
Y.E.-H. **Jehonatan Etz-Chaim;** Instructor in Talmud, Bar Ilan University, Ramat Gan
Y.Ei. **Yizhak Einhorn,** M.A.; Teacher, Tel Aviv
Ye.Ka. **Joshua Kaniel (Mershine),** M.A.; Instructor in Jewish History, Bar Ilan University, Ramat Gan
Y.El. **Jacob Elbaum,** M.A.; Assistant in Hebrew Literature, the Hebrew University of Jerusalem
Ye.N. **Iehiel Nahshon,** B.A.; Ministry of Education, Hod ha-Sharon, Israel
Ye.R. **Yechezkel Rottenberg,** M.Jur.; Assistant in Jewish Law, the Hebrew University of Jerusalem
Y.E.-Sh. See **E.H.**
Y.Ev. **Yakir Eventov;** Haifa
Y.F. **Yeshayahu Foerder** *(deceased)*, Dr.Phil.; Chairman of the Board of Directors, Bank Leumi le-Israel, Tel Aviv
Y.F.B. See **E.H.**
Y.Fi. **Yona Fischer;** Curator of Contemporary Art, the Israel Museum, Jerusalem
Y.G. **Joshua Gutmann** *(deceased)*; Emeritus Associate Professor of Jewish History and Jewish Hellenism, the Hebrew University of Jerusalem
Y.Ga. **Yehuda Gaulan,** Advocate; Ambassador, Ministry for Foreign Affairs, Jerusalem
Y.Ge. **Yehuda Gera,** Dr.Jur.; Ministry for Foreign Affairs, Jerusalem
Y.Gel. **Yaacov Geller,** M.A.; Research Assistant in the Institute for Research in the History and Culture of Oriental Jewry, Bar Ilan University, Ramat Gan
Y.G.G. **Yeḥiel G. Gumpertz,** M.D., Jerusalem
Y.Gl. **Yvonne Glikson,** B.A.; Jerusalem
Y.Go. **Itzhak Goldshlag;** Journalist, Jerusalem
Y.Gu. **Yosef Guri,** M.A.; Senior Teacher in Russian Language, the Hebrew University of Jerusalem
Y.H. **Yehoshafat Harkabi,** Ph.D.; Major General (Res.), Israel Defense Forces; Senior Lecturer in International Relations and Middle Eastern Studies, the Hebrew University of Jerusalem
Y.He. **Yehuda Hellman;** Executive Director of the Conference of Presidents of Major American Jewish Organizations; Secretary General of the World Conference of Jewish Organizations, New York
Y.(H.)L. **Yohanan (Hans) Lewy** *(deceased)*, Dr.Phil.; Senior Lecturer in Latin, the Hebrew University of Jerusalem

Y. Ho. **Yehoshua Horowitz,** Dr.Phil.; Educator, Ramat Gan

Y. Hu. **Jehoshua Hutner,** Rabbi; Director of the *Encyclopaedia Talmudica* and of Yad Harav Herzog, Jerusalem

Yi. E. **Yizchak Jacob Eisner,** Ph.D.; Ministry of Education and Culture, Jerusalem

Yi. N. **Yitzhak Navon;** Ministry for Foreign Affairs, Jerusalem

Yi. R. **Yitzchak Raphael,** Ph.D.; Member of the Knesset, Jerusalem

Y. J. M. **Jacob J. Maitlis,** Dr.Phil.; Scholar, London

Y. K. **Yuval Kamrat;** Jerusalem

Y. Ka. **Jacob Kaplan,** Ph.D.; Director of the Museum of Antiquities of Tel Aviv–Yaffo

Y. K. B. **Yakov K. Bentor,** Ph.D.; D.ès Sc.; Professor of Geology, the Hebrew University of Jerusalem

Y. Ke. **J. Yeshurun Kesheth;** Writer and critic, Jerusalem

Y. Ko. **Yehuda Komlosh,** Ph.D., Rabbi; Senior Lecturer in Bible, Bar Ilan University, Ramat Gan

Y. L. **Yitzhak Levi;** Former Managing Director of the Israel Program for Scientific Translations, Jerusalem

Y. La. **Yehuda Landau,** Ph.D.; Senior Lecturer in Philosophy, Tel Aviv University

Y. L. B. **Yehuda Leib Bialer;** Jerusalem

Y. Le. **Yehuda Levanon,** B.A.; Ministry of Absorption, Jerusalem

Y. Li. **Joseph Litvak,** M.A.; Researcher, Jerusalem

Y. M. **Yehouda Marton,** Dr.rer.Pol.; Journalist, Jerusalem

Y. Ma. **Yitzhak Maor,** Ph.D.; Historian, Kibbutz Ashdot Ya'akov (Iḥud)

Y. Mar. See **I. M.**

Y. Me. **Yohanan Meroz;** Ministry for Foreign Affairs, Jerusalem

Y. M. G. **Yehoshua M. Grintz,** Ph.D.; Professor of Biblical Studies, Tel Aviv University

Y. M. L. See **J. M. L.**

Y. Mo. **Yehuda Moriel,** Ph.D.; Lecturer in Talmud, Bar Ilan University, Ramat Gan

Y. N. See **Jo. Na.**

Y. Na. **Yaacov Nash,** B.A.; Ministry of Police, Tel Aviv

Y. No. **Izhak Noam;** Eilat, Israel

Y. O. **Yitzhak Ogen;** Writer, Tel Aviv

Yo. A. **Yohanan Aharoni,** Ph.D.; Professor of Archaeology and of the Historical Geography of Palestine, Tel Aviv University

Yo. B. **Yoav Biran,** B.A.; Ministry for Foreign Affairs, Jerusalem

Yo. Ba. **Yomtov Ludwig Bato,** Dr.phil,; Historian, Ramat Ḥen, Israel

Yo. D. **Yona David,** Ph.D.; Lecturer in Hebrew Literature, Tel Aviv University

Yo. E. **Yosef Ewen,** M.A.; Lecturer in Hebrew Literature, the Hebrew University of Jerusalem and the University of the Negev, Beersheba

Yo. M. **Yona Malachy** *(deceased)*, D.en D.; Research Fellow, the Institute for Contemporary Jewry, the Hebrew University of Jerusalem

Yo. Sh. **Yosef Shadur;** Midreshet Sedeh Boker

Yo. T. **Yohanan Twersky** *(deceased)*; Writer and editor, Tel Aviv

Y. P. **Yehoshua Porath,** Ph.D.; Instructor in the History of the Muslim Peoples, the Hebrew University of Jerusalem

Y. R. **Yehuda Ratzaby,** M.A.; Senior Lecturer in Medieval Hebrew Literature and in Jewish-Arabic Literature, Bar Ilan University, Ramat Gan

Y. Ra. **Yohanan Ratner** *(deceased)*, M.Sc.; Major General (Res.), Israel Defense Forces; Emeritus Professor of Architecture, the Technion, Haifa

Y. Re. **Yehuda Reshef,** LL.B.; Ministry of Justice, Haifa

Y. Ri. **Yitzhak Rischin,** B.A. (Hons.); Managing Director of Keter Publishing House Ltd., Jerusalem

Y. Ro. **Jacob Rothschild,** Dr.Phil.; Director of the Graduate Library School, the Hebrew University of Jerusalem

Y. Roi **Yaacov Ro'i,** M.A.; Visiting Researcher in Middle Eastern Studies, Tel Aviv University

Y. S. **Yehuda Slutsky,** Ph.D.; Senior Lecturer in the History of the Israel Labor Movement, Tel Aviv University

Y. Sh. **Yosef Shapiro;** Writer, Givatayim, Israel

Y. Sha. **Yehudith Shaltiel,** Ph.D.; Psychologist, Jerusalem

Y. She. **Yekhiel Sheintukh,** M.A.; Assistant in the Department of Yiddish Literature, the Hebrew University of Jerusalem

Y. T. **Yitzhak Julius Taub,** M.Jur.; Secretary General of the Bank of Israel, Jerusalem

Y.-T. L. **Yom-Tov Lewinski,** Dr.Phil.; Ethnographer, Tel Aviv

Y. To. **Jerucham Tolkes;** Writer, Tel Aviv

Yu. El. **Yuval Elizur,** M.A.; Journalist, Jerusalem

Y. Y. **Yaacov Yannai;** Commissioner General of the National Parks Authority, Tel Aviv

Y. Ya. **Yigael Yadin,** Ph.D.; Lieutenant General (Res.), Israel Defense Forces; Professor of Archaeology, the Hebrew University of Jerusalem

Y. Y. M. See **Y. J. M.**

Y. Z. B. **Yehuda Zvi Brandwein** *(deceased)*, Rabbi; Author. Jerusalem

Z. A. See **Z. Av.**

Z.A.B.-O. **Zvi Avraham Bar-On,** Ph.D.; Senior Lecturer in Philosophy, the Hebrew University of Jerusalem

Za. Ch. **Zalman Heyn;** Ministry of Labor, Jerusalem

Z. Ad. **Zvi Adiv,** M.A.; Assistant in History, the Hebrew University of Jerusalem and Tel Aviv University

Z. An. See **E. H.**

Z. Av. **Zvi Avneri (Hans Lichtenstein)** *(deceased)*, Dr.Phil.; Senior Lecturer in Jewish History, Haifa University

Z. B. **Zevi Baras;** Jerusalem

Z. Ba., Z. Be. **Zeev Barkai,** M.A.; Jerusalem

Z. B.-H. **Zeev Ben-Hayyim,** Ph.D.; Professor of Hebrew Philology, the Hebrew University of Jerusalem; Vice President of the Academy of the Hebrew Language, Jerusalem

Zd. L. **Zdenko Löwenthal,** M.D.; Professor of the History of Medicine, the University of Belgrade, Yugoslavia

Z. E. **Zeev Elyashiv,** M.A.; Ministry of Communications, Jerusalem

Z. Ef. **Zusia Efron**; Director of the Art Museum, Kibbutz Ein Ḥarod

Z. El. **Ze'ev Levin**; Former Ambassador, Tel Aviv

Z. F. **Ze'ev Wilhelm Falk,** Ph.D., Advocate; Associate Professor of Family Law, the Hebrew University of Jerusalem; Senior Lecturer in Jewish Law, Tel Aviv University

Z. Fe. **Zvi Hermann Federbush,** M.A.; Ministry of Education and Culture, Jerusalem

Z. G. **Zev Garber,** Ph.D.; Lecturer in Jewish Studies, the University of California, Riverside

Z. Gr. **Zeev Gries**; Jerusalem

Z. H. **Zvi Hermon,** Dr.Phil., Rabbi; Adjunct Professor of Criminology and Corrections, Center for the Study of Crime, Delinquency, and Corrections, Southern Illinois University, Carbondale

Z. He. **Zvi Herman,** Rabbi; Former Member of the Jewish Agency Executive; Former Managing Director of the Zim Israel Navigation Company, Haifa

Z. H. Z. **Zvi Harry Zinder,** B.A.; Jerusalem

Z. K. **Zvi Kaplan**; *Encyclopaedia Hebraica,* Jerusalem

Z. Ke. **Zvi Kedar,** M.A.; Ministry for Foreign Affairs, Jerusalem

Z. L. **Zvi Lamm,** Ph.D.; Lecturer in Education, the Hebrew University of Jerusalem

Z. Lo. **Zvi Loker,** B.A.; Ambassador, Ministry for Foreign Affairs, Jerusalem

Z. M. R. **Zvi Meir Rabinowitz,** Ph.D., Rabbi; Associate Professor of Talmud, Tel Aviv University

Z. O. **Zvi Ofer**; Ministry for Foreign Affairs, Kibbutz Yifat

Z. S. See **Ed.**

Z. Sa. **Zvi Saliternik,** Ph.D.; Ministry of Health, Jerusalem

Z. Sh. **Shneur Zalman Shazar**; President of the State of Israel, Jerusalem

Z. Si. See **Z. Z.**

Z. Sz. **Zvi H. Szubin,** Ph.D.; Assistant Professor of Classical Languages and Hebrew, City College of the City University of New York

Z. Y. **Ze'ev Yeivin,** M.A.; Department of Antiquities, Ministry of Education and Culture, Jerusalem

Z. Y. H. **Zvi Yehuda Hershlag,** Ph.D.; Professor of Economic History and the Economics of Developing Countries, Tel Aviv University

Z. Z. **Zvi Zinger (Yaron),** B.A., Rabbi; the Jewish Agency, Jerusalem

GENERAL ABBREVIATIONS

This list contains abbreviations used in the Encyclopaedia (apart from the standard ones, such as geographical abbreviations, points of the compass, etc.). For names of organizations, institutions, etc., in abbreviation, see Index. For bibliographical abbreviations of books and authors in Rabbinical literature, see following lists.

*	Cross reference; i.e., an article is to be found under the word(s) immediately following the asterisk (*).
°	Before the title of an entry, indicates a non-Jew (post-biblical times).
‡	Indicates reconstructed forms.
>	The word following this sign is derived from the preceding one.
<	The word preceding this sign is derived from the following one.

ad loc.	*ad locum,* "at the place"; used in quotations of commentaries.
A.H.	*Anno Hegirae,* "in the year of Hegira," i.e., according to the Muslim calendar.
Akk.	Akkadian.
A.M.	*anno mundi,* "in the year (from the creation) of the world."
anon.	anonymous.
Ar.	Arabic.
Aram.	Aramaic.
Ass.	Assyrian.
b.	born; *ben, bar.*
Bab.	Babylonian.
B.C.E.	Before Common Era (= B.C.).
bibl.	bibliography.
Bul.	Bulgarian.
c., ca.	circa.
C.E.	Common Era (= A.D.).
cf.	*confer,* "compare."
ch., chs.	chapter, chapters.
comp.	compiler, compiled by.
Cz.	Czech.
D	according to the documentary theory, the Deuteronomy document.
d.	died.
Dan.	Danish.
diss., dissert.	dissertation, thesis.
Du.	Dutch.
E	according to the documentary theory, the Elohist document (i.e., using Elohim as the name of God) of the first five (or six) books of the Bible.
ed.	editor, edited, edition.
eds.	editors.
e.g.	*exempli gratia,* "for example."
Eng.	English.
et al.	*et alibi,* "and elsewhere"; or *et alii,* "and others"; "others."
f., ff.	and following page(s).
fig.	figure.
fl.	flourished.
fol., fols.	folio(s).
Fr.	French.
Ger.	German.
Gr.	Greek.
Heb.	Hebrew.
Hg., Hung.	Hungarian.
ibid.	*ibidem,* "in the same place."
incl. bibl.	includes bibliography.
introd.	introduction.
It.	Italian.
J	according to the documentary theory, the Jahwist document (i.e., using YHWH as the name of God) of the first five (or six) books of the Bible.
Lat.	Latin.
lit.	literally.
Lith.	Lithuanian.
loc. cit.	*loco citato,* "in the [already] cited place."
Ms., Mss.	manuscript(s).
n.	note.
n.d.	no date (of publication).
no., nos.	number(s).
Nov.	Novellae (Heb. *Ḥiddushim*).
n.p.	place of publication unknown.
op. cit.	*opere citato,* "in the previously mentioned work."
P	according to the documentary theory, the Priestly document of the first five (or six) books of the Bible.
p., pp.	page(s).
Pers.	Persian.
pl., pls.	plate(s).
Pol.	Polish.
Port.	Portuguese.
pt., pts.	part(s).
publ.	published.
R.	Rabbi or Rav (before names); in Midrash (after an abbreviation)—*Rabbah.*
r.	*recto,* the first side of a manuscript page.
Resp.	Responsa (Latin "answers," Hebrew *She'elot u-Teshuvot* or *Teshuvot*), collections of rabbinic decisions.
rev.	revised.
Rum.	Rumanian.
Rus(s).	Russian.
Slov.	Slovak.
Sp.	Spanish.
s.v.	*sub verbo, sub voce,* "under the (key) word."
Sum.	Sumerian.
summ.	summary.
suppl.	supplement.
Swed.	Swedish.
tr., trans(l).	translator, translated, translation.
Turk.	Turkish.
Ukr.	Ukrainian.
v., vv.	*verso,* the second side of a manuscript page; also verse(s).
Yid.	Yiddish.

ABBREVIATIONS USED IN RABBINICAL LITERATURE

Adderet Eliyahu, Karaite treatise by Elijah b. Moses *Bashyazi.
Admat Kodesh, Resp. by Nissim Ḥayyim Moses b. Joseph Mizraḥi.
Aguddah, Sefer ha-, Nov. by *Alexander Suslin ha-Kohen.
Ahavat Ḥesed, compilation by *Israel Meir ha-Kohen.
Aliyyot de-Rabbenu Yonah, Nov. by *Jonah b. Abraham Gerondi.
Arukh ha-Shulḥan, codification by Jehiel Michel *Epstein.
Asayin (= positive precepts), subdivision of: (1) *Maimonides, *Sefer ha-Mitzvot*; (2) *Moses b. Jacob of Coucy, *Semag*.
Asefat Dinim, subdivision of *Sedei Ḥemed* by Ḥayyim Hezekiah *Medini, an encyclopaedia of precepts and responsa.
Asheri = *Asher b. Jehiel.
Ateret Ḥakhamim, by Baruch *Frankel-Teomim; pt. 1: Resp. to Sh. Ar.; pt.2: Nov. to Talmud.
Ateret Zahav, subdivision of the *Levush*, a codification by Mordecai b. Abraham (Levush) *Jaffe; *Ateret Zahav* parallels Tur, YD.
Ateret Ẓevi, Comm. to Sh. Ar. by Ẓevi Hirsch b. Azriel.
Avir Ya'akov, Resp. by Jacob Avigdor.
Avkat Rokhel, Resp. by Joseph b. Ephraim *Caro.
Avnei Millu'im, Comm. to Sh. Ar., EH, by *Aryeh Loeb b. Joseph ha-Kohen.
Avnei Nezer, Resp. on Sh. Ar. by Abraham b. Ze'ev Nahum Bornstein of *Sochaczew.
Avodat Massa, Compilation of Tax Law by Yoasha Abraham Judah.
Aẓei ha-Levanon, Resp. by Judah Leib *Zirelson.

Ba'al ha-Tanya = *Shneur Zalman of Lyady.
Ba'ei Ḥayyei, Resp. by Ḥayyim b. Israel *Benveniste.
Ba'er Heitev, Comm. to Sh. Ar. The parts on OḤ and EH are by Judah b. Simeon *Ashkenazi, the parts on YD and ḤM by *Zechariah Mendel b. Aryeh Leib. Printed in most editions of Sh. Ar.
Baḥ = Joel *Sirkes.
Baḥ, usual abbreviation for *Bayit Ḥadash*, a commentary on Tur by Joel *Sirkes; printed in most editions of Tur.
Bayit Ḥadash, see *Baḥ*.
Berab = Jacob Berab, also called Ri Berav.
Bedek ha-Bayit, by Joseph b. Ephraim *Caro, additions to his *Beit Yosef* (a comm. to Tur). Printed sometimes inside *Beit Yosef*, in smaller type. Appears in most editions of Tur.
Be'er ha-Golah, Commentary to Sh. Ar. by Moses b. Naphtali Hirsch *Rivkes; printed in most editions of Sh. Ar.
Be'er Mayim, Resp. by Raphael b. Abraham Manasseh Jacob.
Be'er Mayim Ḥayyim, Resp. by Samuel b. Ḥayyim *Vital.
Be'er Yiẓḥak, Resp. by Isaac Elhanan *Spector.
Beit ha-Beḥirah, Comm. to Talmud by Menahem b. Solomon *Meiri.
Beit Me'ir, Nov. on Sh. Ar. by Meir b. Judah Leib Posner.
Beit Shelomo, Resp. by Solomon b. Aaron Ḥason (the younger).
Beit Shemu'el, Comm. to Sh. Ar., EH, by *Samuel b. Uri Shraga Phoebus.
Beit Ya'akov, by Jacob b. Jacob Moses *Lorberbaum; pt.1: Nov. to Ket.; pt.2: Comm. to EH.
Beit Yisrael, collective name for the commentaries *Derishah*, *Perishah*, and *Be'urim* by Joshua b. Alexander ha-Kohen *Falk. See under the names of the commentaries.
Beit Yiẓḥak, Resp. by Isaac *Schmelkes.
Beit Yosef: (1) Comm. on Tur by Joseph b. Ephraim *Caro; printed in most editions of Tur; (2) Resp. by the same.
Ben Yehudah, Resp. by Abraham b. Judah Litsch (ליטש) Rosenbaum.
Bertinoro, Standard commentary to Mishnah by Obadiah *Bertinoro. Printed in most editions of the Mishnah.
[*Be'urei*] *Ha-Gra*, Comm. to Bible, Talmud, and Sh. Ar. by *Elijah b. Solomon Zalman (Gaon of Vilna); printed in major editions of the mentioned works.
Be'urim, Glosses to Isserles' *Darkhei Moshe* (a comm. on Tur) by Joshua b. Alexander ha-Kohen *Falk; printed in many editions of Tur.
Binyamin Ze'ev, Resp. by *Benjamin Ze'ev b. Mattathias of Arta.
Birkei Yosef, Nov. by Ḥayyim Joseph David *Azulai.
Ha-Buẓ ve-ha-Argaman, subdivision of the *Levush* (a codification by Mordecai b. Abraham (Levush) *Jaffe); *Ha-Buẓ ve-ha-Argaman* parallels Tur, EH.

Comm. = Commentary

Da'at Kohen, Resp. by Abraham Isaac ha-Kohen *Kook.
Darkhei Moshe, Comm. on Tur by Moses b. Israel *Isserles; printed in most editions of Tur.
Darkhei No'am, Resp. by *Mordecai b. Judah ha-Levi.
Darkhei Teshuvah, Nov. by Ẓevi *Shapiro; printed in the major editions of Sh.Ar.
De'ah ve-Haskel, Resp. by Obadiah Hadaya (see *Yaskil Avdi*).
Derashot Ran, Sermons by *Nissim b. Reuben Gerondi.
Derekh Ḥayyim, Comm. to *Avot* by *Judah Loew (Lob, Liwa) b. Bezalel (Maharal) of Prague.
Derishah, by Joshua b. Alexander ha-Kohen *Falk; additions to his *Perishah* (comm. on Tur); printed in many editions of Tur.
Derushei ha-Ẓelaḥ, Sermons by Ezekiel b. Judah Halevi *Landau.
Devar Avraham, Resp. by Abraham *Shapira.
Devar Shemu'el, Resp. by Samuel *Aboab.
Devar Yehoshu'a, Resp. by Joshua Menahem b. Isaac Aryeh Ehrenberg.
Dikdukei Soferim, variae lectiones of the talmudic text by Raphael Nathan *Rabbinowicz.
Divrei Emet, Resp. by Isaac Bekhor David.
Divrei Ge'onim, Digest of responsa by Ḥayyim Aryeh b. Jeḥiel Ẓevi *Kahana.
Divrei Ḥamudot, Comm. on *Piskei ha-Rosh* by Yom Tov Lipmann b. Nathan ha-Levi *Heller; printed in major editions of the Talmud.
Divrei Ḥayyim, several works by Ḥayyim *Halberstamm; if quoted alone refers to his Responsa.
Divrei Malkhi'el, Resp. by Malchiel Tenenbaum.
Divrei Rivot, Resp. by Isaac b. Samuel *Adarbi.
Divrei Shemu'el, Resp. by Samuel Raphael Arditi.

Edut be-Ya'akov, Resp. by Jacob b. Abraham *Boton.
Edut bi-Yhosef, Resp. by Joseph b. Isaac *Almosnino.
Ein Ya'akov, Digest of talmudic *aggadot* by Jacob (Ibn) *Ḥabib.
Ein Yiẓḥak, Resp. by Isaac Elhanan *Spector.
Ephraim of Lentshitz = Solomon *Luntschitz.
Erekh Leḥem, Nov. and glosses to Sh.Ar. by Jacob b. Abraham *Castro.
Eshkol, Sefer ha-, Digest of *halakhot* by *Abraham b. Isaac of Narbonne.
Et Sofer, Treatise on Law Court documents by Abraham b. Mordecai *Ankawa, in the 2nd vol. of his Resp. *Kerem Ḥamar*.
Etan ha-Ezraḥi, Resp. by Abraham b. Israel Jehiel (Shrenzl) *Rapaport.
Even ha-Ezel, Nov. to Maimonides' *Yad Ḥazakah* by Isser Zalman *Meltzer.
Even ha-Ezer, also called *Raban* or *Ẓafenat Pa'ne'aḥ*, rabbinical work with varied contents by *Eliezer b. Nathan of Mainz; not identical with the subdivision of Tur, Shulḥan Arukh, etc.
Ezrat Yehudah, Resp. by *Issar Judah b. Nehemiah of Brisk.

Gan Eden, Karaite treatise by *Aaron b. Elijah of Nicomedia.
Gersonides = *Levi b. Gershom, also called Leo Hebraeus, or Ralbag.
Ginnat Veradim, Resp. by *Abraham b. Mordecai ha-Levi.

Haggahot, another name for *Rema*.
Haggahot Asheri, glosses to *Piskei ha-Rosh* by *Israel of Krems; printed in most Talmud editions.
Haggahot Maimuniyyot, Comm. to Maimonides' *Yad Ḥazakah* by *Meir ha-Kohen; printed in most eds. of Yad.
Haggahot Mordekhai, glosses to *Mordekhai* by Samuel *Schlettstadt; printed in most editions of the Talmud after *Mordekhai*.
Haggahot ha-Rashash on Tosafot, annotations of Samuel *Strashun on the Tosafot (printed in major editions of the Talmud).
Ha-Gra = *Elijah b. Solomon Zalman (Gaon of Vilna).
Ha-Gra, Commentaries on Bible, Talmud, and Sh. Ar. respectively, by *Elijah b. Solomon Zalman (Gaon of Vilna); printed in major editions of the mentioned works.
Hai Gaon, Comm. = his comm. on Mishnah.
Ḥakham Ẓevi, Resp. by Ẓevi Hirsch b. Jacob *Ashkenazi.
Halakhot = Rif, *Halakhot*. Compilation and abstract of the Talmud by Isaac b. Jacob ha-Kohen *Alfasi; printed in most editions of the Talmud.
Halakhot Gedolot, compilation of *halakhot* from the Geonic period, arranged acc. to the Talmud. Here cited acc. to ed. Warsaw (1874). Author probably *Simeon Kayyara of Basra.
Halakhot Pesukot le-Rav Yehudai Ga'on, compilation of *halakhot*.
Halakhot Pesukot min ha-Ge'onim, Compilation of *halakhot* from the geonic period by different authors.
Ḥananel, Comm. to Talmud by *Hananel b. Ḥushi'el; printed in some editions of the Talmud.
Harei Besamim, Resp. by Aryeh Leib b. Isaac *Horowitz.
Ḥassidim, Sefer, Ethical maxims by *Judah b. Samuel he-Ḥasid.
Hassagot Rabad on Rif, Glosses on Rif, *Halakhot*, by *Abraham b. David of Posquières.
Hassagot Rabad [on Yad], Glosses on Maimonides, *Yad Ḥazakah*, by *Abraham b. David of Posquières.
Hassagot Ramban, Glosses by Naḥmanides on Maimonides' *Sefer ha-Mitzvot*; usually printed together with *Sefer ha-Mitzvot*.
Ḥatam Sofer = Moses *Sofer.
Ḥavvot Ya'ir, Resp. and varia by Jair Ḥayyim *Bacharach.
Ḥayyim Or Zaru'a = *Ḥayyim (Eliezer) b. Isaac.
Ḥazon Ish = Abraham Isaiah *Karelitz.
Ḥazon Ish, Nov. by Abraham Isaiah *Karelitz.
Ḥedvat Ya'akov, Resp. by Aryeh Judah Jacob b. David Dov Meisels (article under his father's name).
Heikhal Yiẓḥak, Resp. by Isaac ha-Levi *Herzog.
Ḥelkat Meḥokek, Comm. to Sh. Ar., EH, by Moses b. Isaac Judah *Lima.
Ḥelkat Ya'akov, Resp. by Mordecai Jacob Breisch.
Ḥemdah Genuzah, Resp. from the geonic period by different authors.
Ḥemdat Shelomo, Resp. by Solomon Zalman *Lipschitz.
Ḥida = Ḥayyim Joseph David *Azulai.
Ḥiddushei Halakhot ve-Aggadot, Nov. by Samuel Eliezer b. Judah ha-Levi *Edels.
Ḥikekei Lev, Resp. by Ḥayyim *Palaggi.
Ḥikrei Lev, Nov. to Sh. Ar. by Joseph Raphael b. Ḥayyim Joseph.
Ḥazzan (see article *Ḥazzan Family).
Hil. = Hilkhot ... (e. g., *Hilkhot Shabbat*).
Ḥinnukh, Sefer ha-, List and explanation of precepts attributed (probably erroneously) to Aaron ha-Levi of Barcelona
Ḥok Ya'akov, Comm. to Hil. Pesaḥ in Sh. Ar., OḤ, by Jacob b. Joseph *Reicher.
Ḥokhmat Shelomo (1), Glosses to Talmud, *Rashi* and Tosafot by Solomon b. Jehiel ("Maharshal") *Luria; printed in many editions of the Talmud.
Ḥokhmat Shelomo (2), Glosses and Nov. to Sh. Ar. by Solomon b. Judah Aaron *Kluger; printed in many editions of Sh. Ar.
Ḥur, subdivision of the *Levush*, a codification by Mordecai b. Abraham (Levush) *Jaffe; *Hur* (or *Levush ha-Hur*) parallels Tur, OḤ, 242-697.
Ḥut ha-Meshullash, fourth part of the *Tashbeẓ* (Resp.), by Simeon b. Ẓemaḥ *Duran.

Ibn Ezra, Comm. to the Bible by Abraham *Ibn Ezra; printed in the major editions of the Bible *("Mikra'ot Gedolot")*.
Imrei Yosher, Resp. by Meir b. Aaron Judah *Arik.
Ir Shushan, Subdivision of the *Levush*, a codification by Mordecai b. Abraham (Levush) *Jaffe; *Ir Shushan* parallels Tur, ḤM.
Israel of Bruna = Israel b. Ḥayyim *Bruna.
Ittur, Treatise on precepts by *Isaac b. Abba Mari of Marseilles.

Jacob Be Rab = *Be Rab.
Jacob b. Jacob Moses of Lissa = Jacob b. Jacob Moses *Lorberbaum.
Judah B. Simeon = Judah b. Simeon *Ashkenazi.
Judah Minz = Judah b. Eliezer ha-Levi *Minz.

Kappei Aharon, Resp. by Aaron Azriel.
Kehillat Ya'akov, Talmudic methodology, definitions etc. by Israel Jacob b. Yom Tov *Algazi.
Kelei Ḥemdah, Nov. and *pilpulim* by Meir Dan *Plotzki of Ostrova, arranged acc. to the Torah.
Keli Yakar, Annotations to the Torah by Solomon *Luntschitz.
Keneh Ḥokhmah, Sermons by Judah Loeb *Pochwitzer.
Keneset ha-Gedolah, Digest of *halakhot* by Ḥayyim b. Israel *Benveniste; subdivided into annotations to *Beit Yosef* and annotations to Tur.
Keneset Yisrael, Resp. by Ezekiel b. Abraham Katzenellenbogen (see article *Katzenellenbogen Family).
Kerem Ḥamar, Resp. and varia by Abraham b. Mordecai *Ankawa.
Kerem Shelomo, Resp. by Solomon b. Joseph *Amarillo.
Keritut, [*Sefer*], Methodology of the Talmud by *Samson b. Isaac of Chinon.
Kesef ha-Kedoshim, Comm. to Sh. Ar., ḤM, by Abraham *Wahrmann; printed in major editions of Sh. Ar.
Kesef Mishneh, Comm. to Maimonides, *Yad Ḥazakah*, by Joseph b. Ephraim *Caro; printed in most editions of *Yad Ḥazakah*.
Keẓot ha-Ḥoshen, Comm. to Sh. Ar., ḤM, by *Aryeh Loeb b. Joseph ha-Kohen; printed in major editions of Sh. Ar.
Kol Bo, [*Sefer*], Anonymous collection of ritual rules; also called *Sefer ha-Likkutim*.
Kol Mevasser, Resp. by Meshullam *Rath.
Korban Aharon, Comm. to *Sifra* by Aaron b. Abraham *Ibn Ḥayyim; pt. 1 is called: *Middot Aharon*.
Korban Edah, Comm. to Jer. Talmud by David *Fraenkel; with additions: *Shiyyurei Korban*; printed in most editions of Jer. Talmud.
Kunteres ha-Kelalim, subdivision of *Sedei Ḥemed*, an encyclopaedia of precepts and responsa by Ḥayyim Hezekiah *Medini.
Kunteres ha-Semikhah, a treatise by *Levi b. Ḥabib; printed at the end of his responsa.
Kunteres Tikkun Olam, part of *Mishpat Shalom* (Nov. by Shalom Mordecai b. Moses *Schwadron).

Lavin (negative precepts), subdivision of: (1) *Maimonides, *Sefer ha-Mitzvot*; (2) *Moses b. Jacob of Coucy, *Semag*.
Leḥem Mishneh, Comm. to Maimonides, *Yad Ḥazakah*, by Abraham [Ḥiyya] b. Moses *Boton; printed in most editions of *Yad Ḥazakah*.
Leḥem Rav, Resp. by Abraham [Ḥiyya] b. Moses *Boton.
Leket Yosher, Resp. and varia by Israel b. Pethahiah *Isserlein, collected by *Joseph (Joselein) b. Moses.
Leo Hebraeus = *Levi b. Gershom, also called Ralbag or Gersonides.
Levush = Mordecai b. Abraham *Jaffe.
Levush [Malkhut], Codification by Mordecai b. Abraham (Levush) *Jaffe, with subdivisions: [*Levush ha-*]*Tekhelet* (parallels Tur OḤ 1–241); [*Levush ha-*] *Ḥur* (parallels Tur OḤ 242–697); [*Levush*] *Ateret Zahav* (parallels Tur YD); [*Levush*] *ha-Buẓ ve-ha-Argaman* (parallels Tur EH); [*Levush*] *Ir Shushan* (parallels Tur ḤM); under the name *Levush* the author wrote also other works.
Li-Leshonot ha-Rambam, fifth part (nos. 1374–1700) of the Resp. by *David b. Solomon ibn Abi Zimra (Radbaz).
Likkutim, Sefer ha-, another name for [*Sefer*] *Kol Bo*

Ma'adanei Yom Tov, Comm. on *Piskei ha-Rosh* by Yom Tov Lip-

mann b. Nathan ha-Levi *Heller; printed in many editions of the Talmud.
Mabit = Moses b. Joseph *Trani.
Magen Avot, Comm. to *Avot* by Simeon b. Ẓemaḥ *Duran.
Magen Avraham, Comm. to Sh. Ar., OḤ, by Abraham Abele b. Ḥayyim ha-Levi *Gombiner; printed in many editions of Sh. Ar., OḤ
Maggid Mishneh, Comm. to Maimonides, *Yad Ḥazakah,* by *Vidal Yom Tov of Tolosa; printed in most editions of the *Yad Ḥazakah.*
Maḥaneh Efrayim, Resp. and Nov., arranged acc. to Maimonides' *Yad Ḥazakah,* by Ephraim b. Aaron *Navon.
Maharai = Israel b. Pethahiah *Isserlein.
Maharal of Prague = *Judah Loew (Lob, Liwa), b. Bezalel.
Maharalbaḥ = *Levi b. Ḥabib.
Maharam Alashkar = Moses b. Isaac *Alashkar.
Maharam Alshekh = Moses b. Ḥayyim *Alshekh.
Maharam Mintz = Moses *Mintz.
Maharam of Lublin = *Meir b. Gedaliah of Lublin.
Maharam of Padua = Meir *Katzenellenbogen.
Maharam of Rothenburg = *Meir b. Baruch of Rothenburg.
Maharam Shik = Moses b. Joseph Schick.
Maharash Engel = Samuel b. Ze'ev Wolf Engel.
Maharashdam = Samuel b. Moses *Medina.
Maharḥash = *Ḥayyim (ben) Shabbetai.
Mahari Basan = Jehiel b. Ḥayyim Basan.
Mahari b. Lev = *Joseph ibn Lev.
Mahari'az = Jekuthiel Asher Zalman Ensil Zusmir.
Maharibal = *Joseph ibn Lev.
Mahariḥ = Jacob (Israel) *Ḥagiz.
Maharik = Joseph b. Solomon *Colon.
Maharikash = Jacob b. Abraham *Castro.
Maharil = Jacob b. Moses *Moellin.
Maharimat = Joseph b. Moses di Trani (not identical with the Maharit).
Maharit = Joseph b. Moses *Trani.
Maharitaẓ = Yom Tov b. Akiva Ẓahalon. (See article *Ẓahalon Family).
Maharsha = Samuel Eliezer b. Judah ha-Levi *Edels.
Maharshag = Simeon b. Judah Gruenfeld.
Maharshak = *Samson b. Isaac of Chinon.
Maharshakh = *Solomon b. Abraham.
Maharshal = Solomon b. Jeḥiel *Luria.
Maharsham = Shalom Mordecai b. Moses *Schwadron.
Maharyu = Jacob b. Judah *Weil.
Maḥazeh Avraham, Resp. by Abraham Menahem b. Meir ha-Levi Steinberg.
Maḥazik Berakhah, Nov. by Ḥayyim Joseph David *Azulai.
*Maimonides = Moses b. Maimon, or Rambam.
*Malbim = Meir Loeb b. Jehiel Michael.
Malbim = Malbim's comm. to the Bible; printed in the major editions.
Malbushei Yom Tov, Nov. on *Levush,* OḤ, by Yom Tov Lipmann b. Nathan ha-Levi *Heller.
Mappah, another name for *Rema.*
Mareh ha-Panim, Comm. to Jer. Talmud by Moses b. Simeon *Margolies; printed in most editions of Jer. Talmud.
Margaliyyot ha-Yam, Nov. by Reuben *Margoliot
Masat Binyamin, Resp. by Benjamin Aaron b. Abraham *Slonik.
Mashbir, Ha- = *Joseph Samuel b. Isaac Rodi.
Massa Ḥayyim, Tax *halakhot* by Ḥayyim *Palaggi, with the subdivisions *Missim ve-Arnoniyyot* and *Torat ha-Minhagot.*
Massa Melekh, Compilation of Tax Law by Joseph b. Isaac *Ibn Ezra with concluding part *Ne'ilat She'arim.*
Matteh Asher, Resp. by Asher b. Emanuel Shalem.
Matteh Shimon, Digest of Resp. and Nov. to Tur and *Beit Yosef,* ḤM, by Mordecai Simeon b. Solomon.
Matteh Yosef, Resp. by Joseph b. Moses ha-Levi Nazir (see article under his father's name).
Mayim Amukkim, Resp. by Elijah b. Abraham *Mizraḥi.
Mayim Ḥayyim, Resp. by Ḥayyim b. Dov Beresh Rapaport.
Mayim Rabbim, Resp. by Raphael *Meldola.
Me-Emek ha-Bakha, Resp. by Simeon b. Jekuthiel Ephrati.
Me'irat Einayim, usual abbreviation: *Sma* (from: *Sefer Me'irat Einayim);* comm. to Sh. Ar. by Joshua b. Alexander ha-Kohen *Falk; printed in most editions of the Sh. Ar.
Melammed le-Ho'il, Resp. by David Ẓevi *Hoffmann.
Meisharim, [*Sefer*], Rabbinical treatise by *Jeroham b. Meshullam.
Meshiv Davar, Resp. by Naphtali Ẓevi Judah *Berlin.
Mi-Gei ha-Haregah, Resp. by Simeon b. Jekuthiel Ephrati
Mi-Ma'amakim, Resp. by Ephraim Oshry.
Middot Aharon, first part of *Korban Aharon,* a comm. to *Sifra* by Aaron b. Abraham *Ibn Ḥayyim.
Migdal Oz, Comm. to Maimonides, *Yad Ḥazakah,* by *Ibn Gaon Shem Tov b. Abraham; printed in most editions of the *Yad Ḥazakah.*
Mikhtam le-David, Resp. by David Samuel b. Jacob *Pardo.
Mikkaḥ ve-ha-Mimkar, Sefer ha-, Rabbinical treatise by *Hai Gaon.
Milḥamot ha-Shem, Glosses to Rif, *Halakhot,* by *Naḥmanides.
Minḥat Ḥinnukh, Comm. to *Sefer ha-Ḥinnukh,* by Joseph b. Moses *Babad.
Minḥat Yiẓḥak, Resp. by Isaac Jacob b. Joseph Judah Weiss.
Misgeret ha-Shulḥan, Comm. to Sh. Ar., ḤM, by Benjamin Ze'ev Wolf b. Shabbetai; printed in most editions of Sh. Ar.
Mishkenot ha-Ro'im, Halakhot in alphabetical order by Uzziel Alshekh.
Mishnah Berurah, Comm. to Sh. Ar., OḤ, by *Israel Meir ha-Kohen.
Mishneh le-Melekh, Comm. to Maimonides, *Yad Ḥazakah,* by Judah *Rosanes; printed in most editions of *Yad Ḥazakah.*
Mishpat ha-Kohanim, Nov. to Sh. Ar., ḤM, by Jacob Moses *Lorberbaum, part of his *Netivot ha-Mishpat;* printed in major editions of Sh. Ar.
Mishpat Kohen, Resp. by Abraham Isaac ha-Kohen *Kook.
Mishpat Shalom, Nov. by Shalom Mordecai b. Moses *Schwadron; contains: *Kunteres Tikkun Olam.*
Mishpat u-Ẓedakah be-Ya'akov, Resp. by Jacob b. Reuben *Ibn Ẓur.
Mishpat ha-Urim, Comm. to Sh. Ar., ḤM, by Jacob b. Jacob Moses *Lorberbaum, part of his *Netivot ha-Mishpat;* printed in major editions of Sh. Ar.
Mishpat Ẓedek, Resp. by *Melammed Meir b. Shem Tov.
Mishpatim Yesharim, Resp. by Raphael b. Mordecai *Berdugo.
Mishpetei Shemu'el, Resp. by Samuel b. Moses *Kalai (Kal'i).
Mishpetei ha-Tanna'im, Kunteres, Nov. on *Levush,* OḤ by Yom Tov Lipmann b. Nathan ha-Levi *Heller.
Mishpetei Uzzi'el (Uziel), Resp. by Ben-Zion Meir Ḥai *Ouziel.
Missim ve-Arnoniyyot, Tax *halakhot* by Ḥayyim *Palaggi, a subdivision of his work *Massa Ḥayyim* on the same subject.
Mitzvot, Sefer ha-, Elucidation of precepts by *Maimonides; subdivided into *Lavin* (negative precepts) and *Asayin* (positive precepts).
Mitzvot Gadol, Sefer, Elucidation of precepts by *Moses b. Jacob of Coucy, subdivided into *Lavin* (negative precepts) and *Asayin* (positive precepts); the usual abbreviation is *Semag.*
Mitzvot Katan, Sefer, Elucidation of precepts by *Isaac b. Joseph of Corbeil; the usual abbreviation is *Semak.*
Mo'adim u-Zemannim, Rabbinical treatises by Moses Sternbuch.
Modigliano, Joseph Samuel = *Joseph Samuel b. Isaac Rodi (Ha-Mashbir).
Mordekhai (Mordecai), halakhic compilation by *Mordecai b. Hillel; printed in most editions of the Talmud after the texts.
Moses b. Maimon = *Maimonides, also called Rambam.
Moses b. Naḥman = *Naḥmanides, also called Ramban.
Muram = Isaiah Menahem b. Isaac (from: Morenu R. Mendel).

Naḥal Yiẓḥak, Comm. on Sh. Ar., ḤM, by Isaac Elhanan *Spector.
Naḥalah li-Yhoshu'a, Resp. by Joshua Ẓunẓin.
Naḥalat Shivah, collection of legal forms by *Samuel b. David Moses ha-Levi.
*Naḥmanides = Moses b. Naḥman, also called Ramban.
Naẓiv = Naphtali Ẓevi Judah *Berlin.
Ne'eman Shemu'el, Resp. by Samuel Isaac *Modigliano.
Ne'ilat She'arim, concluding part of *Massa Melekh* (a work on Tax

Law) by Joseph b. Isaac *Ibn Ezra, containing an exposition of customary law and subdivided into *Minhagei Issur* and *Minhagei Mamon*.
Ner Ma'aravi, Resp. by Jacob b. Malka.
Netivot ha-Mishpat, by Jacob b. Jacob Moses *Lorberbaum; subdivided into *Mishpat ha-Kohanim*, Nov. to Sh. Ar., ḤM, and *Mishpat ha-Urim*, a comm. on the same; printed in major editions of Sh. Ar.
Netivot Olam, Sayings of the Sages by *Judah Loew (Lob, Liwa) b. Bezalel.
Nimmukei Menaḥem of Merseburg, Tax *halakhot* by the same, printed at the end of Resp. Maharyu.
Nimmukei Yosef, Comm. to Rif, *Halakhot*, by Joseph *Ḥabib (Ḥabiba); printed in many editions of the Talmud.
Noda bi-Yhudah, Resp. by Ezekiel b. Judah ha-Levi *Landau; there is a first collection *(Mahadura Kamma)* and a second collection *(Mahadura Tinyana)*.
Nov. = Novellae, Ḥiddushim.

Ohel Moshe (1), Notes to Talmud, *Midrash Rabbah*, Yad, *Sifrei* and to several Resp., by Eleazar *Horowitz.
Ohel Moshe (2), Resp. by Moses Jonah Zweig.
Oholei Tam, Resp. by *Tam ibn Yaḥya Jacob b. David; printed in the rabbinical collection *Tummat Yesharim*.
Oholei Ya'akov, Resp. by Jacob de *Castro.
Or ha-Me'ir, Resp. by Judah Meir b. Jacob Samson Shapiro.
Or Same'aḥ, Comm. to Maimonides, *Yad Ḥazakah*, by *Meir Simḥah ha-Kohen of Dvinsk; printed in many editions of the *Yad Ḥazakah*.
Or Zaru'a [the father] = *Isaac b. Moses of Vienna.
Or Zaru'a [the son] = *Ḥayyim (Eliezer) b. Isaac.
Or Zaru'a, Nov. by *Isaac b. Moses of Vienna.
Orah, Sefer ha-, Compilation of ritual precepts by *Rashi.
Oraḥ la-Ẓaddik, Resp. by Abraham Ḥayyim Rodrigues.
Oẓar ha-Posekim, Digest of Responsa.

Paḥad Yiẓḥak, Rabbinical encyclopaedia by Isaac *Lampronti.
Panim Me'irot, Resp. by Meir b. Isaac *Eisenstadt.
Parashat Mordekhai, Resp. by Mordecai b. Abraham Naphtali *Banet.
Pe'at ha-Sadeh la-Dinim and *Pe'at ha-Sadeh la-Kelalim*, subdivisions of the *Sedei Ḥemed*, an encyclopaedia of precepts and responsa, by Ḥayyim Hezekiah *Medini.
Penei Moshe (1), Resp. by Moses *Benveniste.
Penei Moshe (2), Comm. to Jer. Talmud by Moses b. Simeon *Margolies; printed in most editions of the Jer. Talmud.
Penei Moshe (3), Comm. on the aggadic passages of 18 treatises of the Bab. and Jer. Talmud, by Moses b. Isaiah Katz.
Penei Yehoshu'a, Nov. by Jacob Joshua b. Ẓevi Hirsch *Falk.
Peri Ḥadash, Comm. on Sh. Ar. by Hezekiah da *Silva.
Perishah, Comm. on Tur by Joshua b. Alexander ha-Kohen *Falk; printed in major edition of Tur; forms together with *Derishah* and *Be'urim* (by the same author) the *Beit Yisrael*.
Pesakim u-Khetavim, 2nd part of the *Terumat ha-Deshen* by Israel b. Pethahiah *Isserlein; also called *Piskei Maharai*.
Pilpula Ḥarifta, Comm. to *Piskei ha-Rosh*, *Seder Nezikin*, by Yom Tov Lipmann b. Nathan ha-Levi *Heller; printed in major editions of the Talmud.
Piskei Maharai, see *Terumat ha-Deshen*, 2nd part; also called *Pesakim u-Khetavim*.
Piskei ha-Rosh, a compilation of *halakhot*, arranged on the Talmud, by *Asher b. Jehiel (Rosh); printed in major Talmud editions.
Pitḥei Teshuvah, Comm. to Sh. Ar. by Abraham Hirsch b. Jacob *Eisenstadt; printed in major editions of the Sh. Ar.

Rabad = *Abraham b. David of Posquières (Rabad III).
Raban = *Eliezer b. Nathan of Mainz.
Raban, also called *Ẓafenat Pa'ne'aḥ* or *Even ha-Ezer*, see under the last name.
Rabi Abad = *Abraham b. Isaac of Narbonne.
Radad = David Dov b. Aryeh Judah Jacob *Meisels.
Radam = Dov Berush b. Isaac Meisels.
Radbaz = *David b. Solomon ibn Abi Zimra.
Radbaz, Comm. to Maimonides, *Yad Ḥazakah*, by *David b. Solomon ibn Abi Zimra.
Ralbag = *Levi b. Gershom, also called Gersonides, or Leo Hebraeus.
Ralbag, Bible comm. by *Levi b. Gershon
Rama [da Fano] = Menaḥem Azariah *Fano.
Ramah = Meir b. Todros [ha-Levi] *Abulafia.
Ramam = *Menahem of Merseburg.
Rambam = *Maimonides; real name: Moses b. Maimon.
Ramban = *Naḥmanides; real name: Moses b. Naḥman.
Ramban, Comm. to Torah by *Naḥmanides; printed in major. editions. ("Mikra'ot Gedolot")
Ran = *Nissim b. Reuben Gerondi.
Ran on Rif, Comm. on Rif, *Halakhot*, by *Nissim b. Reuben Gerondi.
Ranaḥ = *Elijah b. Ḥayyim.
Rash = *Samson b. Abraham of Sens.
Rash, Comm. to Mishnah, by *Samson b. Abraham of Sens; printed in major Talmud editions.
Rashash = Samuel *Strashun.
Rashba = Solomon b. Abraham *Adret.
Rashba, Resp., see also: *Sefer Teshuvot ha-Rashba ha-Meyuḥasot le-ha-Ramban*, by Solomon b. Abraham *Adret.
Rashbad = Samuel b. David.
Rashbam = *Samuel b. Meir.
Rashbam = Comm. on Bible and Talmud by *Samuel b. Meir; printed in major editions of Bible and most editions of Talmud.
Rashbash = Solomon b. Simeon *Duran.
*Rashi = Solomon b. Isaac of Troyes.
Rashi, Comm. on Bible and Talmud by *Rashi; printed in almost all Bible and Talmud editions.
Raviah = Eliezer b. Joel ha-Levi.
Redak = David *Kimḥi.
Redak, Comm. to Bible by David *Kimḥi.
Redakh = *David b. Ḥayyim ha-Kohen of Corfu.
Re'em = Elijah b. Abraham *Mizraḥi.
Rema = Moses b. Israel *Isserles.
Rema, Glosses to Sh. Ar. by Moses b. Israel *Isserles; printed in almost all editions of the Sh. Ar. inside the text in Rashi type; also called *Mappah* or *Haggahot*.
Remak = Moses Kimḥi.
Remakh = Moses ha-Kohen mi-Lunel.
Reshakh = *Solomon b. Abraham; also called Maharshakh.
Resp. = Responsa, *She'elot u-Teshuvot*.
Ri Berav = *Berab.
Ri Escapa = Joseph b. Saul *Escapa.
Ri Migash = Joseph b. Meir ha-Levi *Ibn Migash.
Riba = Isaac b. Asher ha-Levi; Riba II (Riba ha-Baḥur) = his grandson with the same name.
Ribam = Isaac b. Mordecai (or: Isaac b. Meir).
Ribash = *Isaac b. Sheshet Perfet (or: Barfat).
Rid = *Isaiah b. Mali di Trani the Elder.
Ridbaz = Jacob David b. Ze'ev *Willowski.
Rif = Isaac b. Jacob ha-Kohen *Alfasi.
Rif, *Halakhot*, Compilation and abstract of the Talmud by Isaac b. Jacob ha-Kohen *Alfasi.
Ritba = Yom Tov b. Abraham *Ishbili.
Riẓbam = Isaac b. Mordecai.
Rosh = *Asher b. Jehiel, also called Asheri.
Rosh Mashbir, Resp. by *Joseph Samuel b. Isaac Rodi.

Sedei Ḥemed, Encyclopaedia of precepts and responsa by Ḥayyim Ḥezekiah *Medini; subdivisions: *Asefat Dinim*, *Kunteres ha-Kelalim*, *Pe'at ha-Sadeh la-Dinim*, *Pe'at ha-Sadeh la-Kelalim*.
Semag, Usual abbreviation of *Sefer Mitzvot Gadol*, elucidation of precepts by *Moses b. Jacob of Coucy; subdivided into *Lavin* (negative precepts) and *Asayin* (positive precepts).
Semak, Usual abbreviation of *Sefer Mitzvot Katan*, elucidation of precepts by *Isaac b. Joseph of Corbeil.
Sh. Ar. = *Shulḥan Arukh*, code by Joseph b. Ephraim *Caro.

Sha'ar Mishpat, Comm. to Sh. Ar., ḤM, by Israel Isser b. Ze'ev Wolf.

Sha'arei Shevu'ot, Treatise on the law of oaths by *David b. Saadiah; usually printed together with Rif, *Halakhot;* also called: *She'arim of R. Alfasi.*

Sha'arei Teshuvah, Collection of resp. from Geonic period, by different authors.

Sha'arei Uzzi'el, Rabbinical treatise by Ben-Zion Meir Hai *Ouziel.

Sha'arei Ẓedek, Collection of resp. from Geonic period, by different authors.

Shadal [or Shedal] = Samuel David *Luzzatto.

Shai la-Moreh, Resp. by Shabbetai Jonah.

Shakh, Usual abbreviation of *Siftei Kohen,* a comm. to Sh. Ar., YD and ḤM, by *Shabbetai b. Meir ha-Kohen; printed in most editions of Sh. Ar.

Sha'ot de-Rabbanan, Resp. by *Solomon b. Judah ha-Kohen.

She'arim of R. Alfasi, see *Sha'arei Shevu'ot.*

Shedal, see Shadal.

She'elot u-Teshuvot ha-Ge'onim, Collection of resp. by different authors.

She'erit Yisrael, Resp. by Israel Ze'ev Mintzberg.

She'erit Yosef, Resp. by *Joseph b. Mordecai Gershon ha-Kohen.

She'ilat Yavez, Resp. by Jacob *Emden (Yavez).

She'iltot, Compilation arranged acc. to the Torah by *Aḥa (Aḥai) of Shabḥa.

Shem Aryeh, Resp. by Aryeh Leib *Lipschutz.

Shemesh Ẓedakah, Resp. by Samson *Morpurgo.

Shenei ha-Me'orot ha-Gedolim, Resp. by Elijah *Covo.

Shetarot, Sefer ha-, Collection of legal forms by *Judah b. Barzillai al-Bargeloni.

Shevut Ya'akov, Resp. by Jacob b. Joseph Reicher.

Shibbolei ha-Leket, Compilation on ritual by Zedekiah b. Abraham *Anav.

Shiltei Gibborim, Comm. to Rif, *Halakhot,* by *Joshua Boaz b. Simeon; printed in major editions of the Talmud

Shittah Mekubbezet, Compilation of talmudical commentaries by Bezalel *Ashkenazi.

Shivat Ẓiyyon, Resp. by Samuel b. Ezekiel *Landau.

Shiyyurei Korban, by David *Fraenkel; additions to his comm. to Jer. Talmud *Korban Edah;* both printed in most editions of Jer. Talmud.

Sho'el u-Meshiv, Resp. by Joseph Saul ha-Levi *Nathanson.

Sh[ulḥan] Ar[ukh] [of Ba'al ha-Tanya), Code by *Shneur Zalman of Lyady; not identical with the code by Joseph Caro.

Siftei Kohen, Comm. to Sh. Ar., YD and ḤM by *Shabbetai b. Meir ha-Kohen; printed in most editions of Sh. Ar.; usual abbreviation: *Shakh.*

Simḥat Yom Tov, Resp. by Yom Tov b. Jacob*Algazi.

Simlah Ḥadashah, Treatise on *Sheḥitah* by Alexander Sender b. Ephraim Zalman *Schor; see also *Tevu'ot Shor.*

Simeon b. Ẓemaḥ = Simeon b. Ẓemaḥ *Duran.

Sma, Comm. to Sh. Ar. by Joshua b. Alexander ha-Kohen *Falk; the full title is: *Sefer Me'irat Einayim;* printed in most editions of Sh. Ar.

Solomon b. Isaac ha-Levi = Solomon b. Isaac *Levy.

Solomon b. Isaac of Troyes = *Rashi.

Tal Orot, Rabbinical work with various contents, by Joseph ibn Gioia.

Tam, Rabbenu = *Tam Jacob b. Meir.

Tashbaz = Samson b. Zadok.

Tashbez = Simeon b. Zemaḥ *Duran, sometimes also abbreviation for Samson b. Zadok, usually known as Tashbaẓ.

Tashbez, [Sefer ha-], Resp. by Simeon b. Ẓemaḥ *Duran; the fourth part of this work is called: *Ḥut ha-Meshullash.*

Taz, Usual abbreviation of *Turei Zahav,* comm. to Sh. Ar. by *David b. Samuel ha-Levi; printed in most editions of Sh. Ar.

(Ha)-Tekhelet, subdivision of the *Levush* (a codification by Mordecai b. Abraham (Levush) *Jaffe); *Ha-Tekhelet* parallels Tur, OḤ 1–241.

Terumat ha-Deshen, by Israel b. Pethahiah *Isserlein; subdivided into a part containing responsa, and a second part called *Pesakim u-Khetavim* or *Piskei Maharai.*

Terumot, Sefer ha-, Compilation of *halakhot* by Samuel b. Isaac *Sardi.

Teshuvot Ba'alei ha-Tosafot, Collection of responsa by the Tosafists.

Teshuvot Ge'onei Mizraḥ u-Ma'arav, Collection of responsa.

Teshuvot ha-Geonim, Collection of responsa from Geonic period.

Teshuvot Ḥakhmei Provinẓyah, Collection of responsa by different Provencal authors.

Teshuvot Ḥakhmei Ẓarefat ve-Loter, Collection of responsa by different French authors.

Teshuvot Maimuniyyot, Resp. pertaining to Maimonides' *Yad Ḥazakah;* printed in major editions of this work after the text; authorship uncertain.

Tevu'ot Shor, by Alexander Sender b. Ephraim Zalman *Schor, a comm. to his *Simlah Ḥadashah,* a work on *Sheḥitah.*

Tiferet Ẓevi, Resp. by Ẓevi Hirsch of the "AHW" Communities (Altona, Hamburg, Wandsbeck).

Tiktin, Judah b. Simeon = Judah b. Simeon *Ashkenazi.

Toledot Adam ve-Ḥavvah, Codification by *Jeroham b. Meshullam.

Torat Emet, Resp. by Aaron b. Joseph *Sasson.

Torat Ḥayyim, Resp. by Ḥayyim (ben) Shabbetai.

Torat ha-Minhagot, subdivision of the *Massa Ḥayyim* (a work on tax law) by Ḥayyim *Palaggi, containing an exposition of customary law.

Tosafot Rid, Explanations to the Talmud and decisions by *Isaiah b. Mali di Trani the Elder

Tosefot Yom Tov, comm. to Mishnah by Yom Tov Lipmann b. Nathan ha-Levi *Heller; printed in most editions of the Mishnah.

Tummim, subdivision of the comm. to Sh. Ar., ḤM, *Urim ve-Tummim* by Jonathan *Eybeschuetz; printed in the major editions of Sh. Ar.

Tur, usual abbreviation for the *Arba'ah Turim* of *Jacob b. Asher.

Turei Zahav, Comm. to Sh. Ar. by *David b. Samuel ha-Levi; printed in most editions of Sh. Ar.; usual abbreviation: *Taz.*

Urim, subdivision of the following.

Urim ve-Tummim, Comm. to Sh. Ar., ḤM, by Jonathan *Eybeschuetz; printed in the major editions of the Sh. Ar.; subdivided in places into *Urim* and *Tummim.*

Vikku'aḥ Mayim Ḥayyim, Polemics against Isserles and Caro by Ḥayyim b. Bezalel.

Yad Malakhi, Methodological treatise by *Malachi b. Jacob ha-Kohen.

Yad Ramah, Nov. by Meir b. Todros [ha-Levi] *Abulafia.

Yakhin u-Vo'az, Resp. by Zemaḥ b. Solomon*Duran.

Yam ha-Gadol, Resp. by Jacob Moses *Toledano.

Yam shel Shelomo, Compilation arranged acc. to Talmud by Solomon b. Jehiel (Maharshal) *Luria.

Yashar, Sefer ha-, by *Tam, Jacob b. Meir (Rabbenu Tam); 1st pt.: Resp.; 2nd pt.: Nov.

Yaskil Avdi, Resp. by Obadiah Hadaya (printed together with his Resp. *De'ah ve-Haskel*).

Yavez = Jacob *Emden.

Yehudah Ya'aleh, Resp. by Judah b. Israel *Aszod.

Yekar Tiferet, Comm. to Maimonides' *Yad Ḥazakah,* by David b. Solomon ibn Zimra, printed in most editions of *Yad Ḥazakah.*

Yere'im [ha-Shalem], [Sefer], Treatise on precepts by *Eliezer b. Samuel of Metz.

Yeshu'ot Ya'akov, Resp. by Jacob Meshullam b. Mordecai Ze'ev *Ornstein.

Yiẓhak Rei'aḥ, Resp. by Isaac b. Samuel Abendanan (see article *Abendanan Family).

Ẓafenat Pa'ne'aḥ (1), also called *Raban* or *Even ha-Ezer,* see under the last name.

Ẓafenat Pa'ne'aḥ (2), Resp. by Joseph *Rozin.

Zayit Ra'anan, Resp. by Moses Judah Leib b. Benjamin Auerbach.

Ẓeidah la-Derekh, Codification by *Menahem b. Aaron ibn Zerah.

Ẓedakah u-Mishpat, Resp. by Ẓedakah b. Saadiah Huẓin.

Zekan Aharon, Resp. by *Elijah b. Benjamin ha-Levi.
Zekher Ẓaddik, Sermons by Eliezer *Katzenellenbogen.
Ẓemaḥ Ẓedek (1), Resp. by Menahem Mendel *Krochmal.
Ẓemaḥ Ẓedek (2), Resp. by Menahem Mendel Shneersohn (see under *Shneersohn Family).
Zera Avraham, Resp. by Abraham b. David *Yiẓḥaki.
Zera Emet, Resp. by *Ishmael b. Abraham Isaac ha-Kohen.
Ẓevi la-Ẓaddik, Resp. by Ẓevi Elimelech b. David Shapira.
Zikhron Yehudah, Resp. by *Judah b. Asher.
Zikhron Yosef, Resp. by Joseph b. Menahem *Steinhardt.
Zikhronot, Sefer ha-, Sermons on several precepts by Samuel *Aboab.
Zikkaron la-Rishonim . . ., by Albert (Abraham Elijah) *Harkavy; contains in vol. 1 pt. 4 (1887) a collection of Geonic responsa.
Ẓiẓ Eliezer, Resp. by Eliezer Judah b. Jacob Gedaliah Waldenberg.

BIBLIOGRAPHICAL ABBREVIATIONS

Bibliography in English has been systematically updated until 1969 (and where possible to 1970/1). Books in other languages have been substituted by a good English translation where available. In order to help the reader, the language of books or articles is given where not obvious from titles of books or names of periodicals. Titles of books and periodicals in languages with alphabets other than Latin, are given in transliteration, even where there is a title page in English. Titles of articles in periodicals are not given. Names of Hebrew and Yiddish periodicals well known in English-speaking countries or in Israel under their masthead in Latin characters are given in this form, even when contrary to transliteration rules. Names of authors writing in languages with non-Latin alphabets are given in their Latin alphabet form wherever known; otherwise the names are transliterated. Initials are generally not given for authors of articles in periodicals, except to avoid confusion. Non-abbreviated book titles and names of periodicals are printed in *italics*. Abbreviations are given in the list below.

AASOR	*Annual of the American School of Oriental Research* (1919ff.).
AB	*Analecta Biblica* (1952ff.).
Abel, Géog	F.-M. Abel, *Géographie de la Palestine*, 2 vols. (1933–38).
ABR	*Australian Biblical Review* (1951ff.).
Abr.	Philo, *De Abrahamo*.
Abrahams, Companion	I. Abrahams, *Companion to the Authorised Daily Prayer Book* (rev. ed. 1922).
Abramson, Merkazim	S. Abramson, *Ba-Merkazim u-va-Tefuẓot bi-Tekufat ha-Ge'onim* (1965).
Acts	Acts of the Apostles (New Testament).
ACUM	*Who is who in ACUM* [*Aguddat Kompozitorim u-Meḥabbrim*].
ADAJ	*Annual of the Department of Antiquities, Jordan* (1951ff.).
Adam	Adam and Eve (Pseudepigrapha).
ADB	*Allgemeine Deutsche Biographie*, 56 vols. (1875–1912).
Add. Esth.	The Addition to Esther (Apocrypha).
Adler, Prat Mus	I. Adler, *La pratique musicale savante dans quelques communautés juives en Europe au XVIIe et XVIIIe siècles*, 2 vols. (1966).
Adler-Davis	H.M. Adler and A. Davis (ed. and tr.), *Service of the Synagogue, a New Edition of the Festival Prayers with an English Translation in Prose and Verse*, 6 vols. (1905–06).
Aet.	Philo, *De Aeternitate Mundi*.
AFO	*Archiv fuer Orientforschung* (first two volumes under the name *Archiv fuer Keilschriftforschung*) (1923ff.).
Ag. Ber.	*Aggadat Bereshit* (ed. Buber, 1902).
Agr.	Philo, *De Agricultura*.
Ag. Sam.	*Aggadat Samuel*.
Ag. Song	*Aggadat Shir ha-Shirim* (Schechter ed., 1896).
Aharoni, Ereẓ	Y. Aharoni, *Ereẓ Yisrael bi-Tekufat ha-Mikra: Geografyah Historit* (1962).
Aharoni, Land	Y. Aharoni, *Land of the Bible* (1966).
Ahikar	Ahikar (Pseudepigrapha).
AI	*Archives Israélites de France* (1840–1936).
AJA	*American Jewish Archives* (1948 ff.).
AJHSP	*American Jewish Historical Society—Publications* (after vol. 50 = AJHSQ).
AJHSQ	*American Jewish Historical* (Society) *Quarterly* (before vol. 50 = AJHSP).
AJSLL	*American Journal of Semitic Languages and Literature* (1884–95 under the title *Hebraica*, since 1942 JNES).
AJYB	*American Jewish Year Book* (1899 ff.).
AKM	Abhandlungen fuer die Kunde des Morgenlandes (series).
Albright, Arch	W.F. Albright, *Archaeology of Palestine* (rev. ed. 1960).
Albright, Arch Bib	W.F. Albright, *Archaeology of Palestine and the Bible* (1935^3).
Albright, Arch Rel	W.F. Albright, *Archaeology and the Religion of Israel* (1953^3).
Albright, Stone	W.F. Albright, *From the Stone Age to Christianity* (1957^2).
Alon, Meḥkarim	G. Alon, *Meḥkarim be-Toledot Yisrael bi-Ymei Bayit Sheni u-vi-Tekufat ha-Mishnah ve-ha-Talmud*, 2 vols. (1957–58).
Alon, Toledot	G. Alon, *Toledot ha-Yehudim be-Ereẓ Yisrael bi-Tekufat ha-Mishnah ve-ha-Talmud*, 1(1958^3), 2(1961^2).
ALOR	Alter Orient (series).
Alt, Kl Schr	A. Alt, *Kleine Schriften zur Geschichte des Volkes Israel*, 3 vols. (1953–59).
Alt, Landnahme	A. Alt, *Landnahme der Israeliten in Palaestina* (1925); also in Alt, Kl Schr, 1 (1953), 89–125.
Ant.	Josephus, *Jewish Antiquities* (Loeb Classics ed.).
AO	*Acta Orientalia* (1922 ff.).
AOR	*Analecta Orientalia* (1931 ff.).
AOS	American Oriental Series
Apion	Josephus, *Against Apion* (Loeb Classics ed.).
Aq.	Aquila's Greek translation of the Bible.
Ar.	*Arakhin* (talmudic tractate).
Arist.	Letter of Aristeas (Pseudepigrapha).

ARN^{1}	*Avot de-Rabbi Nathan*, version (1) ed. Schechter, 1887.
ARN^{2}	*Avot de-Rabbi Nathan*, version (2) ed. Schechter, 1945^{2}.
Aronius, Regesten	I. Aronius, *Regesten zur Geschichte der Juden im fraenkischen und deutschen Reiche bis zum Jahre 1273* (1902).
ARW	*Archiv fuer Religionswissenschaft* (1898–1941/42).
AS	*Assyrological Studies* (1931 ff.).
Ashtor, Korot	E. Ashtor (Strauss), *Korot ha-Yehudim bi-Sefarad ha-Muslemit*, 1(1966^{2}), 2(1966).
Ashtor, Toledot	E. Ashtor (Strauss), *Toledot ha-Yehudim be-Miẓrayim ve-Suryah Taḥat Shilton ha-Mamlukim*, 3 vols. (1944–70).
Assaf, Ge'onim	S. Assaf, *Tekufat ha-Ge'onim ve-Sifrutah* (1955).
Assaf, Mekorot	S. Assaf, *Mekorot le-Toledot ha-Ḥinnukh be-Yisrael*, 4 vols. (1925–43).
Ass. Mos.	Assumption of Moses (Pseudepigrapha).
ATA	Alttestamentliche Abhandlungen (series).
ATANT	Abhandlungen zur Theologie des Alten und Neuen Testaments (series).
AUJW	*Allgemeine unabhaengige juedische Wochenzeitung* (till 1966 = AWJD).
AV	Authorized Version of the Bible.
Avad.	*Avadim* (post-talmudic tractate).
Avi-Yonah, Geog	M. Avi-Yonah, *Geografyah Historit shel Ereẓ-Yisrael* (1962^{3}).
Avi-Yonah, Land	M. Avi-Yonah, *The Holy Land from the Persian to the Arab conquest (536 B.C. to A.D. 640)* (1966).
Avot	*Avot* (talmudic tractate).
Av. Zar.	*Avodah Zarah* (talmudic tractate).
AWJD	*Allgemeine Wochenzeitung der Juden in Deutschland* (since 1967 = AUJW).
AZDJ	*Allgemeine Zeitung des Judentums.*
Azulai	Ḥ.Y.D. Azulai, *Shem ha-Gedolim*, ed. by I.E. Benjacob, 2 pts. (1852) (and other editions).
BA	*Biblical Archaeologist* (1938 ff.).
Bacher, Bab Amor	W. Bacher, *Agada der babylonischen Amoraeer* (1913^{2}).
Bacher, Pal Amor	W. Bacher, *Agada der palaestinensischen Amoraeer* (Heb. ed. *Aggadat Amora'ei Ereẓ Yisrael)*, 2 vols. (1892–99).
Bacher, Tann	W. Bacher, *Agada der Tannaiten* (Heb. ed. *Aggadot ha-Tanna'im*), vol. 1, pt. 1 and 2 (1903); vol. 2 (1890) .
Bacher, Trad	W. Bacher, *Tradition und Tradenten in den Schulen Palaestinas und Babyloniens* (1914).
Baer, Spain	Yitzhak (Fritz) Baer, *History of the Jews in Christian Spain*, 2 vols. (1961–66).
Baer, Studien	Yitzhak (Fritz) Baer, *Studien zur Geschichte der Juden im Koenigreich Aragonien waehrend des 13. und 14. Jahrhunderts* (1913).
Baer, Toledot	Yitzhak (Fritz) Baer, *Toledot ha-Yehudim bi-Sefarad ha-Noẓerit mi-Teḥillatan shel ha-Kehillot ad ha-Gerush*, 2 vols. (1959^{2}).
Baer, Urkunden	Yitzhak (Fritz) Baer, *Die Juden im christlichen Spanien*, 2 vols. (1929–36).
Baer S., Seder	S.I. Baer, *Seder Avodat Yisrael* (1868 and reprints).
BAIU	*Bulletin de l'Alliance Israélite Universelle* (1861–1913).
Baker, Biog Dict	*Baker's Biographical Dictionary of Musicians*, revised by N. Slonimsky (1958^{5}; with Supplement 1965).
I Bar.	I Baruch (Apocrypha).
II Bar.	II Baruch (Pseudepigrapha).
III Bar.	III Baruch (Pseudepigrapha).
Baron, Community	S.W. Baron, *The Jewish Community, its History and Structure to the American Revolution*, 3 vols. (1942).
Baron, Social	S.W. Baron, *Social and Religious History of the Jews*, 3 vols. (1937); enlarged, 1–2(1952^{2}), 3–14 (1957–69).
Barthélemy-Milik	D. Barthélemy and J.T. Milik, *Dead Sea Scrolls: Discoveries in the Judean Desert*, vol. 1 *Qumran Cave I* (1955).
BASOR	*Bulletin of the American School of Oriental Research.*
Bauer-Leander	H. Bauer and P. Leander, *Grammatik des Biblisch-Aramaeischen* (1927; repr. 1962).
BB	(1) *Bava Batra* (talmudic tractate). (2) *Biblische Beitraege* (1943 ff.).
BBB	Bonner biblische Beitraege (series).
BBLA	*Beitraege zur biblischen Landes- und Altertumskunde* (until 1949–ZDPV).
BBSAJ	*Bulletin*, British School of Archaeology, Jerusalem (1922–25; after 1927 included in PEFQS).
BDASI	*Alon* (since 1948) or *Hadashot Arkhe'ologiyyot* (since 1961), bulletin of the Department of Antiquities of the State of Israel.
Begrich, Chronologie	J. Begrich, *Chronologie der Koenige von Israel und Juda* (1929).
Bek.	*Bekhorot* (talmudic tractate).
Bel	Bel and the Dragon (Apocrypha).
Benjacob, Oẓar	I.E. Benjacob, *Oẓar ha-Sefarim* (1880; repr. 1956).
Ben Sira	see Ecclus.
Ben-Yehuda, Millon	E. Ben-Yehuda, *Millon ha-Lashon ha-Ivrit*, 16 vols. (1908–59; repr. in 8 vols., 1959).
Benzinger, Archaeologie	I. Benzinger, *Hebraeische Archaeologie* (1927^{3}).
Ben Zvi, Eretz Israel	I. Ben-Zvi, *Eretz Israel under Ottoman Rule* (1960; offprint from L. Finkelstein (ed.), *The Jews, their History, Culture and Religion*, vol. 1).
Ben Zvi, Ereẓ Yisrael	I. Ben-Zvi, *Ereẓ Yisrael bi-Ymei ha-Shilton ha-Ottomani* (1955).
Ber.	*Berakhot* (talmudic tractate).
Beẓah	*Beẓah* (talmudic tractate).
BIES	Bulletin of the Israel Exploration Society, see below BJPES.
Bik.	*Bikkurim* (talmudic tractate).
BJCE	Bibliography of Jewish Communities in Europe, catalog at General Archives for the History of the Jewish People, Jerusalem.
BJPES	Bulletin of the Jewish Palestine Exploration Society—English name of the Hebrew periodical known as: 1. *Yedi'ot ha-Ḥevrah ha-Ivrit la-Ḥakirat Ereẓ Yisrael va-Attikoteha* (1933–1954); 2. *Yedi'ot ha-Ḥevrah la-Ḥakirat Ereẓ Yisrael va-Attikoteha* (1954–1962); 3. *Yedi'ot ba-Ḥakirat Ereẓ Yisrael va-Attikoteha* (1962 ff.).
BJRL	*Bulletin of the John Rylands Library* (1914 ff.).
BK	*Bava Kamma* (talmudic tractate).
BLBI	*Bulletin of the Leo Baeck Institute* (1957 ff.).
BM	(1) *Bava Meẓia* (talmudic tractate). (2) *Beit Mikra* (1955/56 ff.). (3) British Museum.
BO	*Bibbia e Oriente* (1959 ff.).
Bondy-Dworský	G. Bondy and F. Dworský, *Regesten zur Geschichte der Juden in Boehmen, Maehren und Schlesien von 906 bis 1620*, 2 vols. (1906).
BOR	*Bibliotheca Orientalis* (1943 ff.).
Borée, Ortsnamen	W. Borée, *Die alten Ortsnamen Palaestinas* (1930).

Bousset, Religion	W. Bousset, *Die Religion des Judentums im neutestamentlichen Zeitalter* (1906^{2}).
Bousset-Gressmann	W. Bousset, *Die Religion des Judentums im spaethellenistischen Zeitalter* (1966^{3}).
BR	*Biblical Review* (1916–25).
BRCI	*Bulletin of the Research Council of Israel* (1951/52–1954/55; then divided).
BRE	*Biblical Research* (1956 ff.).
BRF	*Bulletin of the Rabinowitz Fund for the Exploration of Ancient Synagogues* (1949 ff.).
Briggs, Psalms	Ch. A. and E.G. Briggs, *Critical and Exegetical Commentary on the Book of Psalms*, 2 vols. (ICC, 1906–07).
Bright, Hist	J. Bright, *A History of Israel* (1959).
Brockelmann, Arab Lit	K. Brockelmann, *Geschichte der arabischen Literatur*, 2 vols. (1898–1902), supplement, 3 vols. (1937–42).
Bruell, Jahrbuecher	*Jahrbuecher fuer juedische Geschichte und Litteratur*, ed. by N. Bruell, Frankfort (1874–90).
Brugmans-Frank	H. Brugmans and A. Frank (eds.), *Geschiedenis der Joden in Nederland* (1940).
BTS	*Bible et Terre Sainte* (1958 ff.).
Bull, Index	S. Bull, *Index to Biographies of Contemporary Composers* (1964).
BW	*Biblical World* (1882–1920).
BWANT	*Beitraege zur Wissenschaft vom Alten und Neuen Testament* (1926 ff.).
BZ	*Biblische Zeitschrift* (1903 ff.).
BZAW	*Beihefte zur Zeitschrift fuer die alttestamentliche Wissenschaft*, supplement to ZAW (1896 ff.).
BŻIH	*Biuletyn Zydowskiego Instytutu Historycznego* (1950 ff.).
CAB	*Cahiers d'archéologie biblique* (1953 ff.).
CAD	*The [Chicago] Assyrian Dictionary* (1956ff.).
CAH	*Cambridge Ancient History*, 12 vols. (1923–39).
CAH^{2}	*Cambridge Ancient History*, new series (1962 ff.).
CAHJP	Central Archives for the History of the Jewish People.
Calwer, Lexikon	*Calwer Bibellexikon*.
Cant.	Canticles, usually given as Song (= Song of Songs).
Cantera-Millás, Inscripciones	F. Cantera and J.M. Millás, *Las Inscripciones Hebraicas de España* (1956).
CBQ	*Catholic Biblical Quarterly* (1939 ff.).
CCARY	Central Conference of American Rabbis, *Yearbook* (1890/91 ff.).
CD	*Damascus Document* from the Cairo *Genizah* (published by S. Schechter, *Fragments of a Zadokite Work*, 1910).
Charles, Apocrypha	R. H. Charles, *Apocrypha and Pseudepigrapha* . . ., 2 vols. (1913; repr. 1963–66).
Cher.	Philo, *De Cherubim*.
I (or II) Chron.	Chronicles, books I and II (Bible).
CIG	*Corpus Inscriptionum Graecarum*.
CIJ	*Corpus Inscriptionum Judaicarum*, 2 vols. (1936–52).
CIL	*Corpus Inscriptionum Latinarum*.
CIS	*Corpus Inscriptionum Semiticarum* (1881 ff.).
C.J.	Codex Justinianus.
Clermont-Ganneau, Arch	Ch. Clermont-Ganneau, *Archaeological Researches in Palestine*, 2 vols. (1896–99).
CNFI	*Christian News from Israel* (1949 ff.).
Cod. Just.	Codex Justinianus
Cod. Theod.	Codex Theodosianus
Col.	Epistle to the Colossians (New Testament).
Conder, Survey	Palestine Exploration Fund, *Survey of Eastern Palestine*, vol. 1, pt. 1 (1889) = C.R. Conder, *Memoirs of the . . . Survey*.
Conder-Kitchener	Palestine Exploration Fund, *Survey of Western Palestine*, vol. 1, pts. 1–3 (1881–83) = C. R. Conder and H. H. Kitchener, *Memoirs*.
Conf.	Philo, *De Confusione Linguarum*.
Conforte, Kore	D. Conforte, *Kore ha-Dorot* (1846^{2}).
Cong.	Philo, *De Congressu Quaerendae Eruditionis Gratia*.
Cont.	Philo, *De Vita Contemplativa*.
I (or II) Cor.	Epistles to the Corinthians (New Testament).
Cowley, Aramaic	A. Cowley, *Aramaic Papyri of the Fifth Century B.C.* (1923).
Cowley, Cat	A. E. Cowley, *A Concise Catalogue of the Hebrew Printed Books in the Bodleian Library* (1929).
CRB	*Cahiers de la Revue Biblique* (1964 ff.).
Crowfoot-Kenyon	J. W. Crowfoot, K. M. Kenyon and E. L. Sukenik, *Buildings of Samaria* (1942).
C.T.	Codex Theodosianus.
DAB	*Dictionary of American Biography* (1928–58).
Daiches, Jews	S. Daiches, *Jews in Babylonia* (1910).
Dalman, Arbeit	G. Dalman, *Arbeit und Sitte in Palaestina*, 7 vols. in 8 (1928–42; repr. 1964).
Dan.	Daniel (Bible).
Davidson, Oẓar	I. Davidson, *Oẓar ha-Shirah ve-ha-Piyyut*, 4 vols. (1924–33); Supplement in: HUCA, 12–13 (1937/38), 715–823.
DB	J. Hastings, *Dictionary of the Bible*, 4 vols. (1963^{2}).
DBI	F. G. Vigoureaux et al. (eds.), *Dictionnaire de la Bible*, 5 vols. in 10 (1912); Supplement, 8 vols. (1928–66).
Decal.	Philo, *De Decalogo*.
Dem.	*Demai* (talmudic tractate).
DER	*Derekh Ereẓ Rabbah* (post-talmudic tractate).
Derenbourg, Hist	J. Derenbourg, *Essai sur l'histoire et la géographie de la Palestine* (1867).
Det.	Philo, *Quod deterius potiori insidiari solet*.
Deus	Philo, *Quod Deus immutabilis sit*.
Deut.	Deuteronomy (Bible).
Deut. R.	*Deuteronomy Rabbah*.
DEZ	*Derekh Ereẓ Zuta* (post-talmudic tractate).
DHGE	*Dictionnaire d'histoire et de géographie ecclésiastiques*, ed. by A. Baudrillart et al., 17 vols. (1912–68).
Dik. Sof.	*Dikdukei Soferim*, variae lectiones of the talmudic text by Raphael Nathan Rabbinovitz (16 vols., 1867–97).
Dinur, Golah	B. Dinur (Dinaburg), *Yisrael ba-Golah*, 2 vols. in 7 (1959–68) = vols. 5 and 6 of his *Toledot Yisrael*, second series.
Dinur, Haganah	B. Dinur (ed.), *Sefer Toledot ha-Haganah* (1954 ff.).
Diringer, Iscr	D. Diringer, *Iscrizioni antico-ebraiche palestinesi* (1934).
Discoveries	*Discoveries in the Judean Desert* (1955 ff.).
DNB	*Dictionary of National Biography*, 66 vols. (1921–22^{2}) with Supplements.
Dubnow, Divrei	S. Dubnow, *Divrei Yemei Am Olam*, 11 vols. (1923–38 and further editions).
Dubnow, Ḥasidut	S. Dubnow, *Toledot ha-Ḥasidut* (1960^{2}).
Dubnow, Hist	S. Dubnow, *History of the Jews* (1967).
Dubnow, Hist Russ	S. Dubnow, *History of the Jews in Russia and Poland*, 3 vols. (1916–20).
Dubnow, Outline	S. Dubnow, *An Outline of Jewish History*, 3 vols. (1925–29).
Dubnow, Weltgesch	S. Dubnow, *Weltgeschichte des juedischen Volkes*, 10 vols. (1925–29).
Dukes, Poesie	L. Dukes, *Zur Kenntnis der neuhebraeischen religioesen Poesie* (1842).

Dunlop, Khazars	D. H. Dunlop, *History of the Jewish Khazars* (1954).
EA	El-Amarna Letters (edited by J.A. Knudtzon, *Die El-Amarna Tafeln,* 2 vols. (1907–14)).
EB	*Encyclopaedia Britannica.*
EBI	*Estudios bíblicos* (1941 ff.).
EBIB	T. K. Cheyne and J. S. Black, *Encyclopaedia Biblica,* 4 vols. (1899–1903).
Ebr.	Philo, *De Ebrietate.*
Eccles.	Ecclesiastes (Bible).
Eccles. R.	*Ecclesiastes Rabbah.*
Ecclus.	Ecclesiasticus or Wisdom of Ben Sira (or Sirach; Apocrypha).
Eduy.	*Eduyyot* (mishnaic tractate).
EG	*Enẓiklopedyah shel Galuyyot* (1953 ff.).
EH	*Even ha-Ezer.*
EḤA	*Enẓiklopedyah la-Ḥafirot Arkheologiyyot be-Ereẓ Yisrael,* 2 vols. (1970).
EI	*Enzyklopaedie des Islam,* 4 vols. (1905–14), Supplement vol. (1938).
EIS	*Encyclopaedia of Islam,* 4 vols. (1913–36).
EIS²	*Encyclopaedia of Islam,* second edition (1954–68).
EIS³	*Encyclopaedia of Islam,* New Edition (1960 ff.).
Eisenstein, Dinim	J. D. Eisenstein, *Oẓar Dinim u-Minhagim* (1917; several reprints).
Eisenstein, Yisrael	J. D. Eisenstein, *Oẓar Yisrael,* 10 vols. (1907–13; repr. with additions 1951).
EIV	*Enẓiklopedyah Ivrit* (1949 ff.).
EJ	*Encyclopaedia Judaica* (German, A-L only), 10 vols. (1928–34).
EJC	*Enciclopedia Judaica Castellana,* 10 vols. (1948–51)
Elbogen, Century	I. Elbogen, *A Century of Jewish Life* (1960²).
Elbogen, Gottesdienst	I. Elbogen, *Der juedische Gottesdienst . . .* (1931³, repr. 1962).
Elon, Mafte'aḥ	M. Elon (ed.), *Mafte'aḥ ha-She'elot ve-ha-Teshuvot, She'elot u-Teshuvot ha-Rosh* (1965).
EM	*Enẓiklopedyah Mikra'it* (1950 ff.).
I (or II) En.	I and II Enoch (Pseudepigrapha).
Eph.	Epistle to the Ephesians (New Testament).
Ephros, Cant	G. Ephros, *Cantorial Anthology,* 5 vols. (1929–57).
Ep. Jer.	Epistle of Jeremy (Apocrypha).
Epstein, Amora'im	J. N. Epstein, *Mevo'ot le-Sifrut ha-Amora'im* (1962).
Epstein, Marriage	L. M. Epstein, *Marriage Laws in the Bible and the Talmud* (1942).
Epstein, Mishnah	J. N. Epstein, *Mavo le-Nusaḥ ha-Mishnah,* 2 vols. (1964²).
Epstein, Tanna'im	J. N. Epstein, *Mevo'ot le-Sifrut ha-Tanna'im* (1947).
ER	*Ecumenical Review.*
Er.	*Eruvin* (talmudic tractate).
ERE	*Encyclopaedia of Religion and Ethics,* 13 vols. (1908–26); reprinted.
I Esd.	I Esdras (Apocrypha) (= III Ezra).
II Esd.	II Esdras (Apocrypha) (= IV Ezra).
ESE	*Ephemeris fuer semitische Epigraphik,* ed. by M. Lidzbarski.
ESN	*Encyclopaedia Sefardica Neerlandica,* 2 pts. (1949).
ESS	*Encyclopaedia of the Social Sciences,* 15 vols. (1930–35); reprinted in 8 vols. (1948–49).
Esth.	Esther (Bible).
Est. R.	*Esther Rabbah.*
ET	*Enẓiklopedyah Talmudit* (1947 ff.).
Eusebius, Onom.	E. Klostermann (ed.), *Das Onomastikon* (1904), Greek with Hieronymus' Latin translation.
Ex.	Exodus (Bible).
Ex. R.	*Exodus Rabbah.*
Exs.	Philo, *De Exsecrationibus.*
EZD	*Enẓiklopedyah shel ha-Ẓiyyonut ha-Datit* (1951 ff.).
Ezek.	Ezekiel (Bible).
Ezra	Ezra (Bible).
III Ezra	III Ezra (Pseudepigrapha).
IV Ezra	IV Ezra (Pseudepigrapha).
Finkelstein, Middle Ages	L. Finkelstein, *Jewish Self-Government in the Middle Ages* (1924).
Fischel, Islam	W. J. Fischel, *Jews in the Economic and Political Life of Mediaeval Islam* (1937; reprint with introduction "The Court Jew in the Islamic World," 1969).
FJW	*Fuehrer durch die juedische Gemeindeverwaltung und Wohlfahrtspflege in Deutschland* (1927/28).
Frankel, Mevo	Z. Frankel, *Mevo ha-Yerushalmi* (1870; reprint 1967).
Frankel, Mishnah	Z. Frankel, *Darkhei ha-Mishnah* (1923²; reprint 1959²).
Frazer, Folk-Lore	J. G. Frazer, *Folk-Lore in the Old Testament,* 3 vols. (1918–19).
Frey, Corpus	J.-B. Frey, *Corpus Inscriptionum Iudaicarum,* 2 vols. (1936–52).
Friedmann, Lebensbilder	A. Friedmann, *Lebensbilder beruehmter Kantoren,* 3 vols. (1918–27).
FRLT	Forschungen zur Religion und Literatur des Alten und Neuen Testaments (series) (1950 ff.).
Frumkin-Rivlin	A. L. Frumkin and E. Rivlin, *Toledot Ḥakhmei Yerushalayim,* 3 vols. (1928–30), Supplement vol. (1930).
Fuenn, Keneset	S. J. Fuenn, *Keneset Yisrael,* 4 vols. (1887–90).
Fuerst, Bibliotheca	J. Fuerst, *Bibliotheca Judaica,* 2 vols. (1863; repr. 1960).
Fuerst, Karaeertum	J. Fuerst, *Geschichte des Karaeertums,* 3 vols. (1862–69).
Fug.	Philo, *De Fuga et Inventione.*
Gal.	Epistle to the Galatians (New Testament).
Galling, Reallexikon	K. Galling, *Biblisches Reallexikon* (1937).
Gardiner, Onomastica	A. H. Gardiner, *Ancient Egyptian Onomastica,* 3 vols. (1947).
Geiger, Mikra	A. Geiger, *Ha-Mikra ve-Targumav,* tr. by J. L. Baruch (1949).
Geiger, Urschrift	A. Geiger, *Urschrift und Uebersetzungen der Bibel* (1928²).
Gen.	Genesis (Bible).
Gen. R.	*Genesis Rabbah.*
Ger.	*Gerim* (post-talmudic tractate).
Germ Jud	M. Brann, I. Elbogen, A. Freimann, and H. Tykocinski (eds.), *Germania Judaica,* vol. 1 (1917; repr. 1934 and 1963); vol. 2, in 2 pts. (1917–68), ed. by Z. Avneri.
GHAT	*Goettinger Handkommentar zum Alten Testament* (1917–22).
Ghirondi-Neppi	M. S. Ghirondi and G. H. Neppi, *Toledot Gedolei Yisrael u-Ge'onei Italyah . . . u-Ve'urim al Sefer Zekher Ẓaddikim li-Verakhah . . .* (1853), index in ZHB, 17 (1914), 171–83.
Gig.	Philo, *De Gigantibus.*
Ginzberg, Legends	L. Ginzberg, *Legends of the Jews,* 7 vols. (1909–38; and many reprints).
Git.	*Gittin* (talmudic tractate).

Glueck, Explorations	N. Glueck, *Explorations in Eastern Palestine*, 2 vols. (1951).
Goell, Bibliography	Y. Goell, *Bibliography of Modern Hebrew Literature in English Translation* (1968).
Goodenough, Symbols	E. R. Goodenough, *Jewish Symbols in the Greco-Roman Period*, 13 vols. (1953–68).
Gordon, Textbook	C.H. Gordon, *Ugaritic Textbook* (1965; repr. 1967).
Graetz, Gesch	H. Graetz, *Geschichte der Juden* (last edition 1874–1908).
Graetz, Hist	H. Graetz, *History of the Jews*, 6 vols. (1891–1902).
Graetz, Psalmen	H. Graetz, *Kritischer Commentar zu den Psalmen*, 2 vols. in 1 (1882–83).
Graetz-Rabbinowitz	H. Graetz, *Divrei Yemei Yisrael*, tr. by S.P. Rabbinowitz (1928–29^{2}).
Gray, Names	G.B. Gray, *Studies in Hebrew Proper Names* (1896).
Gressmann, Bilder	H. Gressmann, *Altorientalische Bilder zum Alten Testament* (1927^{2}).
Gressmann, Texte	H. Gressmann, *Altorientalische Texte zum Alten Testament* (1926^{2}).
Gross, Gal Jud	H. Gross, *Gallia Judaica* (1897; repr. with add. 1969).
Grove, Dict	*Grove's Dictionary of Music and Musicians*, ed. by E. Blum, 9 vols. (1954^{5}) and suppl. (1961^{5}).
Guedemann, Gesch Erz	M. Guedemann, *Geschichte des Erziehungswesens und der Cultur der abendlaendischen Juden*, 3 vols. (1880–88).
Guedemann, Quellenschr	M. Guedemann, *Quellenschriften zur Geschichte des Unterrichts und der Erziehung bei den deutschen Juden* (1873, 1891).
Guide	Maimonides, *Guide of the Perplexed*.
Gulak, Oẓar	A. Gulak, *Oẓar ha-Shetarot ha-Nehugim be-Yisrael* (1926).
Gulak, Yesodei	A. Gulak, *Yesodei ha-Mishpat ha-Ivri, Seder Dinei Mamonot be-Yisrael, al pi Mekorot ha-Talmud ve-ha-Posekim*, 4 vols. (1922; repr. 1967).
Guttmann, Mafte'aḥ	M. Guttmann, *Mafte'aḥ ha-Talmud*, 3 vols. (1906–30).
Guttmann, Philosophies	J. Guttmann, *Philosophies of Judaism* (1964).
Hab.	Habakkuk (Bible).
Ḥag.	*Ḥagigah* (talmudic tractate).
Haggai	Haggai (Bible).
Ḥal.	*Ḥallah* (talmudic tractate).
Halevy, Dorot	I. Halevy, *Dorot ha-Rishonim*, 6 vols. (1897–1939).
Halpern, Pinkas	I. Halpern (Halperin), *Pinkas Va'ad Arba Araẓot* (1945).
Hananel-Eškenazi	A. Hananel and Eškenazi (eds.), *Fontes Hebraici ad res oeconomicas socialesque terrarum balcanicarum saeculo XVI pertinentes*, 2 vols. (1958–60; in Bulgarian).
HB	*Hebraeische Bibliographie* (1858–82).
Heb.	Epistle to the Hebrews (New Testament).
Heilprin, Dorot	J. Heilprin (Heilperin), *Seder ha-Dorot*, 3 vols. (1882; repr. 1956).
Her.	Philo, *Quis Rerum Divinarum Heres*.
Hertz, Prayer	J.H. Hertz (ed.), *Authorised Daily Prayer Book* (rev. ed. 1948; repr. 1963).
Herzog, Instit	I. Herzog, *The Main Institutions of Jewish Law*, 2 vols. (1936–39; repr. 1967).
Herzog-Hauck	J.J. Herzog and A. Hauck (eds.), *Realencyklopaedie fuer protestantische Theologie* (1896–1913^{3}).
HḤY	*Ha-Ẓofeh le-Ḥokhmat Yisrael* (first four volumes under the title *Ha-Ẓofeh me-Ereẓ Hagar)* (1910/11–13).
Hirschberg, Afrikah	H.Z. Hirschberg, *Toledot ha-Yehudim be-Afrikah ha-Ẓefonit*, 2 vols. (1965).
HJ	*Historia Judaica* (1938–61).
HL	*Das Heilige Land* (1857ff.)
ḤM	*Ḥoshen Mishpat*.
Hommel, Ueberliefer	F. Hommel, *Die altisraelitische Ueberlieferung in inschriftlicher Beleuchtung* (1897).
Hor.	*Horayot* (talmudic tractate).
Horodezky, Ḥasidut	S.A. Horodezky, *Ha-Ḥasidut ve-ha-Ḥasidim*, 4 vols. (1923).
Horowitz, Ereẓ Yis	I.W. Horowitz, *Ereẓ Yisrael u-Shekhenoteha* (1923).
Hos.	Hosea (Bible).
HTR	*Harvard Theological Review* (1908ff.).
HUCA	*Hebrew Union College Annual* (1904; 1924ff.)
Ḥul.	*Ḥullin* (talmudic tractate).
Husik, Philosophy	I. Husik, *History of Medieval Jewish Philosophy* (1932^{2}).
Hyman, Toledot	A. Hyman, *Toledot Tanna'im ve-Amora'im* (1910; repr. 1964).
Ibn Daud, Tradition	Abraham Ibn Daud, *Sefer ha-Qabbalah—The Book of Tradition*, ed. and tr. by G.D. Cohen (1967).
ICC	International Critical Commentary on the Holy Scriptures of the Old and New Testaments (series, 1908ff.).
IDB	*Interpreter's Dictionary of the Bible*, 4 vols. (1962).
Idelsohn, Liturgy	A.Z. Idelsohn, *Jewish Liturgy and its Development* (1932; paperback repr. 1967).
Idelsohn, Melodien	A.Z. Idelsohn, *Hebraeisch-orientalischer Melodienschatz*, 10 vols. (1914–32).
Idelsohn, Music	A.Z. Idelsohn, *Jewish Music in its Historical Development* (1929; paperback repr. 1967).
IEJ	*Israel Exploration Journal* (1950ff.).
IESS	*International Encyclopedia of the Social Sciences* (various eds.).
IG	*Inscriptiones Graecae*, ed. by the Prussian Academy.
IGYB	*Israel Government Year Book* (1949/50ff.).
ILR	*Israel Law Review* (1966ff.).
IMIT	*Izraelita Magyar Irodalmi Társulat, Évkönyv* (1895–1948).
IMT	International Military Tribunal.
INB	*Israel Numismatic Bulletin* (1962–63).
INJ	*Israel Numismatic Journal* (1963ff.).
Ios.	Philo, *De Iosepho*.
Isa.	Isaiah (Bible).
IZBG	*Internationale Zeitschriftenschau fuer Bibelwissenschaft und Grenzgebiete* (1951 ff.).
JA	*Journal asiatique* (1822ff.).
James	Epistle of James (New Testament).
JAOS	*Journal of the American Oriental Society* (c. 1850ff.).
Jastrow, Dict	M. Jastrow, *Dictionary of the Targumim, the Talmud Babli and Yerushalmi, and the Midrashic literature*, 2 vols. (1886–1902 and reprints).
JBA	*Jewish Book Annual* (1942ff.).
JBL	*Journal of Biblical Literature* (1881 ff.).
JBR	*Journal of Bible and Religion* (1933 ff.).
JC	*Jewish Chronicle* (1841 ff.).
JCS	*Journal of Cuneiform Studies* (1947 ff.).
JE	*Jewish Encyclopedia*, 12 vols. (1901–05; several reprints).
Jer.	Jeremiah (Bible).

Jeremias, Alte Test — A. Jeremias, *Das Alte Testament im Lichte des alten Orients* (1930⁴).
JGGJČ — *Jahrbuch der Gesellschaft fuer Geschichte der Juden in der Čechoslovakischen Republik* (1929–38).
JHSEM — Jewish Historical Society of England, *Miscellanies* (1925 ff.).
JHSET — Jewish Historical Society of England, *Transactions* (1893 ff.).
JJGL — *Jahrbuch fuer juedische Geschichte und Literatur* (Berlin) (1898–1938).
JJLG — *Jahrbuch der juedisch-literarischen Gesellschaft* (Frankfort) (1903–32).
JJS — *Journal of Jewish Studies* (1948 ff.).
JJSO — *Jewish Journal of Sociology* (1959 ff.).
JJV — *Jahrbuch fuer juedische Volkskunde* (1898–1924).
JL — *Juedisches Lexikon*, 5 vols. (1927–30).
JMES — *Journal of the Middle East Society* (1947 ff.).
JNES — *Journal of Near Eastern Studies* (continuation of AJSLL) (1942 ff.).
J.N.U.L. — Jewish National and University Library.
Job — Job (Bible).
Joel — Joel (Bible).
John — Gospel according to John (New Testament).
I, II, and III John — Epistles of John (New Testament).
Jos., Ant. — Josephus, *Jewish Antiquities* (Loeb Classics ed.).
Jos., Apion — Josephus, *Against Apion* (Loeb Classics ed.).
Jos., index — *Josephus' Works*, Loeb Classics ed., index of names.
Jos., Life — Josephus, *Life* (ed. Loeb Classics).
Jos., Wars — Josephus, *The Jewish War* (Loeb Classics ed.).
Josh. — Joshua (Bible).
JPESB — Jewish Palestine Exploration Society Bulletin, see BJPES.
JPESJ — Jewish Palestine Exploration Society Journal —Eng. title of the Hebrew periodical *Kovez ha-Ḥevrah ha-Ivrit la-Ḥakirat Erez Yisrael va-Attikoteha.*
JPOS — *Journal of the Palestine Oriental Society* (1920–48).
JPS — Jewish Publication Society of America, *The Torah* (1962, 1967²); *The Holy Scriptures* (1917).
JQR — *Jewish Quarterly Review* (1889 ff.).
JR — *Journal of Religion* (1921 ff.).
JRAS — *Journal of the Royal Asiatic Society* (1838 ff.).
JRH — *Journal of Religious History* (1960/61 ff.).
JSOS — *Jewish Social Studies* (1939 ff.).
JSS — *Journal of Semitic Studies* (1956 ff.).
JTS — *Journal of Theological Studies* (1900 ff.).
JTSA — Jewish Theological Seminary of America (also abbreviated as JTS).
Jub. — Jubilees (Pseudepigrapha).
Judg. — Judges (Bible).
Judith — Book of Judith (Apocrypha).
Juster, Juifs — J. Juster, *Les Juifs dans l'Empire Romain*, 2 vols. (1914).
JYB — *Jewish Year Book* (1896 ff.).
JZWL — *Juedische Zeitschrift fuer Wissenschaft und Leben* (1862–75).

Kal. — *Kallah* (post-talmudic tractate).
Kal. R. — *Kallah Rabbati* (post-talmudic tractate).
Kaufmann, Schriften — D. Kaufmann, *Gesammelte Schriften*, 3 vols. (1908–15).
Kaufmann Y., Religion — Y. Kaufmann, *The Religion of Israel* (1960), abridged tr. of his *Toledot.*
Kaufmann Y., Toledot — Y. Kaufmann, *Toledot ha-Emunah ha-Yisre'elit*, 4 vols. (1937–57).
KAWJ — *Korrespondenzblatt des Vereins zur Gruendung und Erhaltung der Akademie fuer die Wissenschaft des Judentums* (1920–30).
Kayserling, Bibl — M. Kayserling, *Biblioteca Española-Portugueza-Judaica* (1890; repr. 1961).
Kelim — *Kelim* (mishnaic tractate).
Ker. — *Keritot* (talmudic tractate).
Ket. — *Ketubbot* (talmudic tractate).
Kid. — *Kiddushin* (talmudic tractate).
Kil. — *Kilayim* (talmudic tractate (T.J.)).
Kin. — *Kinnim* (mishnaic tractate).
Kisch, Germany — G. Kisch, *Jews in Medieval Germany* (1949).
Kittel, Gesch — R. Kittel, *Geschichte des Volkes Israel*, 3 vols. (1922–28).
Klausner, Bayit Sheni — J. Klausner, *Historyah shel ha-Bayit ha-Sheni*, 5 vols. (1950/51²).
Klausner, Sifrut — J. Klausner, *Historyah shel ha-Sifrut ha-Ivrit ha-Ḥadashah*, 6 vols. (1952–58²).
Klein, Corpus — S. Klein (ed.), *Juedisch-palaestinisches Corpus Inscriptionum* (1920).
Koehler-Baumgartner — L. Koehler and W. Baumgartner, *Lexicon in Veteris Testamenti libros* (1953).
Kohut, Arukh — H.J.A. Kohut (ed.), *Sefer he-Arukh ha-Shalem*, by Nathan b. Jehiel of Rome, 8 vols. (1876–92; Supplement by S. Krauss et al., 1936; repr. 1955).
Krauss, Tal Arch — S. Krauss, *Talmudische Archaeologie*, 3 vols. (1910–12; repr. 1966).
Kressel, Leksikon — G. Kressel, *Leksikon ha-Sifrut ha-Ivrit ba-Dorot ha-Aḥaronim*, 2 vols. (1965–67).
KS — *Kirjath Sepher* (1923/4 ff.).
Kut. — *Kuttim* (post-talmudic tractate).

LA — Studium Biblicum Franciscanum, *Liber Annuus* (1951 ff.).
L. A. — Philo, *Legum Allegoriae.*
Lachower, Sifrut — F. Lachower, *Toledot ha-Sifrut ha-Ivrit ha-Ḥadashah*, 4 vols. (1947–48; several reprints).
Lam. — Lamentations (Bible).
Lam. R. — *Lamentations Rabbah.*
Landshuth, Ammudei — L. Landshuth, *Ammudei ha-Avodah* (1857–62; repr. with index, 1965).
Legat. — Philo, *De Legatione ad Caium.*
Lehmann, Nova Bibl — R.P. Lehmann, *Nova Bibliotheca Anglo-Judaica* (1961).
Lev. — Leviticus (Bible).
Lev. R. — *Leviticus Rabbah.*
Levy, Antología — I. Levy, *Antología de liturgía judeo-española* (1965 ff.).
Levy J., Chald Targ — J. Levy, *Chaldaeisches Woerterbuch ueber die Targumim*, 2 vols. (1867–68; repr. 1959).
Levy J., Neuhebr Tal — J. Levy, *Neuhebraeisches und chaldaeisches Woerterbuch ueber die Talmudim . . .*, 4 vols. (1875–89; repr. 1963).
Lewin, Ozar — B.M. Lewin, *Ozar ha-Ge'onim*, 12 vols. (1928–43).
Lewysohn, Zool — L. Lewysohn, *Zoologie des Talmuds* (1858).
Lidzbarski, Handbuch — M. Lidzbarski, *Handbuch der nordsemitischen Epigraphik*, 2 vols. (1898).
Life — Josephus, *Life* (Loeb Classics ed.).
LNYL — *Leksikon fun der Nayer Yidisher Literatur* (1956 ff.).
Loew, Flora — I. Loew, *Die Flora der Juden*, 4 vols. (1924–34; repr. 1967).
LSI — *Laws of the State of Israel* (1948 ff.).
Luckenbill, Records — D.D. Luckenbill, *Ancient Records of Assyria and Babylonia*, 2 vols. (1926).

Luke	Gospel according to Luke (New Testament).
LXX	Septuagint (Greek translation of the Bible).
Ma'as.	*Ma'aserot* (talmudic tractate).
Ma'as. Sh.	*Ma'aser Sheni* (talmudic tractate).
I, II, III, and IV Macc.	Maccabees, I, II, III (Apocrypha), IV (Pseudepigrapha).
Maimonides, Guide	Maimonides, *Guide of the Perplexed.*
Maim., Yad	Maimonides, *Mishneh Torah (Yad Ḥazakah).*
Maisler, Untersuchungen	B. Maisler (Mazar), *Untersuchungen zur alten Geschichte und Ethnographie Syriens und Palaestinas,* 1 (1930).
Mak.	*Makkot* (talmudic tractate).
Makhsh.	*Makhshirin* (mishnaic tractate).
Mal.	Malachi (Bible).
Mann, Egypt	J. Mann, *Jews in Egypt and in Palestine under the Fatimid Caliphs,* 2 vols. (1920–22).
Mann, Texts	J. Mann, *Texts and Studies,* 2 vols. (1931–35).
Mansi	G.D. Mansi, *Sacrorum Conciliorum nova et amplissima collectio,* 53 vols. in 60 (1901–27; repr. 1960).
Margalioth, Gedolei	M. Margalioth, *Enẓiklopedyah le-Toledot Gedolei Yisrael,* 4 vols. (1946–50).
Margalioth, Ḥakhmei	M. Margalioth, *Enẓiklopedyah le-Ḥakhmei ha-Talmud ve-ha-Ge'onim,* 2 vols. (1945).
Margoliouth, Cat	G. Margoliouth, *Catalogue of the Hebrew and Samaritan Manuscripts in the British Museum,* 4 vols. (1899–1935).
Mark	Gospel according to Mark (New Testament).
Mart. Isa.	Martyrdom of Isaiah (Pseudepigrapha).
Mas.	Masorah.
Matt.	Gospel according to Matthew (New Testament).
Mayer, Art	L.A. Mayer, *Bibliography of Jewish Art* (1967).
MB	*Wochenzeitung* (formerly *Mitteilungsblatt*) *des Irgun Olej Merkas Europa* (1933 ff.).
MEAH	*Miscelánea de estudios árabes y hebraicos* (1952 ff.).
Meg.	*Megillah* (talmudic tractate).
Meg. Ta'an.	*Megillat Ta'anit* (in HUCA, 8–9 (1931–32), 318–51).
Me'il.	*Me'ilah* (mishnaic tractate).
MEJ	*Middle East Journal* (1947 ff.).
Mekh.	*Mekhilta de-R. Ishmael.*
Mekh. SbY	*Mekhilta de-R. Simeon bar Yoḥai.*
Men.	*Menaḥot* (talmudic tractate).
MER	*Middle East Record* (1960 ff.).
Meyer, Gesch	E. Meyer, *Geschichte des Altertums,* 5 vols. in 9 (1925–58).
Meyer, Ursp	E. Meyer, *Ursprung und Anfaenge des Christentums* (1921).
Mez.	*Mezuzah* (post-talmudic tractate).
MGADJ	*Mitteilungen des Gesamtarchivs der deutschen Juden* (1909–12).
MGG	*Die Musik in Geschichte und Gegenwart,* 14 vols. (1949–68).
MGH	*Monumenta Germaniae Historica* (1826 ff.).
MGJV	*Mitteilungen der Gesellschaft fuer juedische Volkskunde* (1898–1929); title varies, see also JJV.
MGWJ	*Monatsschrift fuer Geschichte und Wissenschaft des Judentums* (1851–1939).
MHJ	*Monumenta Hungariae Judaica,* 11 vols. (1903–67).
Michael, Or	H.Ḥ. Michael, *Or ha-Ḥayyim: Ḥakhmei Yisrael ve-Sifreihem,* ed. by S.Z. Ḥ. Halberstam and N. Ben-Menahem (1965^2).
Mid.	*Middot* (mishnaic tractate).
Mid. Ag.	*Midrash Aggadah.*
Mid. Hag.	*Midrash ha-Gadol.*
Mid. Job	*Midrash Job.*
Mid. Jonah	*Midrash Jonah.*
Mid. Lek. Tov	*Midrash Lekaḥ Tov.*
Mid. Prov.	*Midrash Proverbs.*
Mid. Ps.	*Midrash Tehillim* (Eng. tr. *The Midrash on Psalms* (JPS, 1959)).
Mid. Sam.	*Midrash Samuel.*
Mid. Song	*Midrash Shir ha-Shirim.*
Mid. Tan.	*Midrash Tanna'im* on Deuteronomy.
Miége, Maroc	J.L. Miège, *Le Maroc et l'Europe,* 3 vols. (1961–62).
Mig.	Philo, *De Migratione Abrahami.*
Mik.	*Mikva'ot* (mishnaic tractate).
Milano, Bibliotheca	A. Milano, *Bibliotheca Historica Italo-Judaica* (1954); supplement for 1954–63 (1964); supplement for 1964–66 in RMI, 32 (1966).
Milano, Italia	A. Milano, *Storia degli Ebrei in Italia* (1963).
MIO	*Mitteilungen des Instituts fuer Orientforschung* (1953 ff.).
Mish.	Mishnah.
MJ	*Le Monde Juif* (1946 ff.).
MJC	see Neubauer, Chronicles.
MK	*Mo'ed Katan* (talmudic tractate).
MNDPV	*Mitteilungen und Nachrichten des deutschen Palaestinavereins* (1895–1912).
Mortara, Indice	M. Mortara, *Indice Alfabetico dei Rabbini e Scrittori Israeliti . . . in Italia . . .* (1886).
Mos.	Philo, *De Vita Mosis.*
Moscati, Epig	S. Moscati, *Epigrafia ebraica antica* 1935–1950 (1951).
MT	Masoretic Text of the Bible.
Mueller, Musiker	[E.H. Mueller], *Deutsches Musiker-Lexikon* (1929).
Munk, Mélanges	S. Munk, *Mélanges de philosophie juive et arabe* (1859; repr. 1955).
Mut.	Philo, *De Mutatione Nominum.*
MWJ	*Magazin fuer die Wissenschaft des Judentums* (1874–93).
Nah.	Nahum (Bible).
Naz.	*Nazir* (talmudic tractate).
NDB	*Neue Deutsche Biographie* (1953 ff.).
Ned.	*Nedarim* (talmudic tractate).
Neg.	*Nega'im* (mishnaic tractate).
Neh.	Nehemiah (Bible).
Neubauer, Cat	A. Neubauer, *Catalogue of the Hebrew Manuscripts in the Bodleian Library . . .,* 2 vols. (1886–1906).
Neubauer, Chronicles	A. Neubauer, *Mediaeval Jewish Chronicles,* 2 vols. (Heb., 1887–95; repr. 1965), Eng. title of *Seder ha-Ḥakhamim ve-Korot ha-Yamim.*
Neubauer, Géogr	A. Neubauer, *La géographie du Talmud* (1868).
Neuman, Spain	A.A. Neuman, *The Jews in Spain, their Social, Political, and Cultural Life During the Middle Ages,* 2 vols. (1942).
Neusner, Babylonia	J. Neusner, *History of the Jews in Babylonia,* 5 vols. (1965–70), 2nd revised printing 1969 ff.).
Nid.	*Niddah* (talmudic tractate).
Noah	Fragment of Book of Noah (Pseudepigrapha).
Noth, Hist Isr	M. Noth, *History of Israel* (1958).
Noth, Personennamen	M. Noth, *Die israelitischen Personennamen . . .* (1928).
Noth, Ueberlief	M. Noth, *Ueberlieferungsgeschichte des Pentateuchs* (1949).

Noth, Welt	M. Noth, *Die Welt des Alten Testaments* (1957[3]).
Nowack, Lehrbuch	W. Nowack, *Lehrbuch der hebraeischen Archaeologie,* 2 vols. (1894).
NT	New Testament.
Num.	Numbers (Bible).
Num. R.	*Numbers Rabbah.*
Obad.	Obadiah (Bible).
OḤ	*Oraḥ Ḥayyim.*
Oho.	*Oholot* (mishnaic tractate).
Olmstead	H.T. Olmstead, *History of Palestine and Syria* (1931; repr. 1965).
OLZ	*Orientalistische Literaturzeitung* (1898 ff.).
Onom.	Eusebius, *Onomasticon.*
Op.	Philo, *De Opificio Mundi.*
OPD	*Osef Piskei Din shel ha-Rabbanut ha-Rashit le-Ereẓ Yisrael, Bet ha-Din ha-Gadol le-Irurim* (1950).
Or.	*Orlah* (talmudic tractate).
Or. Sibyll.	Sibylline Oracles (Pseudepigrapha).
OS	*L'Orient Syrien* (1956 ff.).
OTS	*Oudtestamentische Studien* (1942 ff.).
PAAJR	*Proceedings of the American Academy for Jewish Research* (1930 ff.).
pap 4QS[c]	A papyrus exemplar of 1QS (yet unpublished).
Par.	*Parah* (mishnaic tractate).
Pauly-Wissowa	A.F. Pauly, *Realencyklopaedie der klassischen Altertumswissenschaft,* ed. by G. Wissowa et al. (1894 ff.).
PD	*Piskei Din shel Bet ha-Mishpat ha-Elyon le-Yisrael* (1948 ff.).
PDR	*Piskei Din shel Battei ha-Din ha-Rabbaniyyim be-Yisrael.*
PdRE	*Pirkei de-R. Eliezer* (Eng. tr. 1916, 1965[2]).
PdRK	*Pesikta de-Rav Kahana.*
Pe'ah	*Pe'ah* (talmudic tractate).
Peake, Commentary	A.J. Peake (ed.), *Commentary on the Bible* (1919; rev. 1962).
Pedersen, Israel	J. Pedersen, *Israel, Its Life and Culture,* 4 vols. in 2 (1926–40).
PEFQS	*Palestine Exploration Fund Quarterly Statement* (1869–1937; since 1938—PEQ).
PEQ	*Palestine Exploration Quarterly* (until 1937 PEFQS; after 1927 includes BBSAJ).
Perles, Beitraege	J. Perles, *Beitraege zur rabbinischen Sprach- und Alterthumskunde* (1893).
Pes.	*Pesaḥim* (talmudic tractate).
Pesh.	Peshitta (Syriac translation of the Bible).
Pesher Hab.	Commentary to Habakkuk from Qumran; see 1Qp Hab.
I and II Pet.	Epistles of Peter (New Testament).
Pfeiffer, Introd	R.H. Pfeiffer, *Introduction to the Old Testament* (1948).
PG	J.P. Migne (ed.), *Patrologia Graeca,* 161 vols. (1866–86).
Phil.	Epistle to the Philippians (New Testament).
Philem.	Epistle to Philemon (New Testament).
PIASH	*Proceedings of the Israel Academy of Sciences and Humanities* (1963/4 ff.).
PJB	*Palaestinajahrbuch des deutschen evangelischen Instituts fuer Altertumswissenschaft, Jerusalem* (1905–1933).
PK	*Pinkas ha-Kehillot,* encyclopedia of Jewish communities. Manuscript material available at Yad Vashem, Jerusalem, arranged by countries, regions, and localities. Already published: *Plnkas ha-Kehillot, Romanyah,* vol. 1 (1970), on Rumania (PK Romanyah). In preparation: vol. 2 on Rumania, and volumes on Bavaria, Hungary, Poland (Lodz region), and Holland.
PL	J.P. Migne (ed.), *Patrologia Latina,* 221 vols. (1844–64).
Plant.	Philo, *De Plantatione.*
PO	R. Graffin and F. Nau (eds.), *Patrologia Orientalis* (1903 ff.).
Pool, Prayer	D. de Sola Pool, *Traditional Prayer Book for Sabbath and Festivals* (1960).
Post.	Philo, *De Posteritate Caini.*
PR	*Pesikta Rabbati.*
Praem.	Philo, *De Praemiis et Poenis.*
Prawer, Ẓalbanim	J. Prawer, *Toledot Mamlekhet ha-Ẓalbanim be-Ereẓ Yisrael,* 2 vols. (1963).
Press, Ereẓ	I. Press, *Ereẓ-Yisrael, Enẓiklopedyah Topografit-Historit,* 4 vols. (1951–55).
Pritchard, Pictures	J.B. Pritchard (ed.), *Ancient Near East in Pictures* (1954, 1970).
Pritchard, Texts	J.B. Pritchard (ed.), *Ancient Near Eastern Texts . . .* (1970[3]).
Pr. Man.	Prayer of Manasses (Apocrypha).
Prob.	Philo, *Quod Omnis Probus Liber Sit.*
Prov.	Proverbs (Bible).
PS	*Palestinsky Sbornik* (Russ. 1881–1916, 1954 ff.).
Ps.	Psalms (Bible).
PSBA	*Proceedings of the Society of Biblical Archaeology* (1878–1918).
Ps. of Sol.	Psalms of Solomon (Pseudepigrapha).
1Q Apoc	The *Genesis Apocryphon* from Qumran, cave one, ed. by N. Avigad and Y. Yadin (1956).
6QD	*Damascus Document* or *Sefer Berit Dammesek* from Qumran, cave six, ed. by M. Baillet, in RB, 63 (1956), 513–23 (see also CD).
QDAP	*Quarterly of the Department of Antiquities in Palestine* (1932 ff.).
4QDeut. 32	Manuscript of Deuteronomy 32 from Qumran, cave four (ed. by P.W. Skehan, in BASOR, 136 (1954), 12–15).
4QEx[a]	Exodus manuscript in Jewish script from Qumran, cave four (yet unpublished).
4QEx[α]	Exodus manuscript in Paleo-Hebrew script from Qumran, cave four (partially ed. by P.W. Skehan, in JBL, 74 (1955), 182–7).
4QFlor	*Florilegium,* a miscellany from Qumran, cave four (ed. by J.M. Allegro, in JBL, 75 (1956), 176–77 and 77 (1958), 350–54).
QGJD	*Quellen zur Geschichte der Juden in Deutschland* (1888–98).
1QH	*Thanksgiving Psalms* or *Hodayot* from Qumran, cave one (ed. by E.L. Sukenik and N. Avigad, *Oẓar ha-Megillot ha-Genuzot* (1954)).
1QIs[a]	Scroll of Isaiah from Qumran, cave one (ed. by M. Burrows et al., *Dead Sea Scrolls . . .,* 1 (1950).
1QIs[b]	Scroll of Isaiah from Qumram, cave one (ed. by E.L. Sukenik and N. Avigad, *Oẓar ha-Megillot ha-Genuzot* (1954)).
1QM	The *War Scroll* or *Serekh ha-Milḥamah* (ed. by E.L. Sukenik and N. Avigad, *Oẓar ha-Megillot ha-Genuzot* (1954)).
4QpNah	Commentary on Nahum from Qumran, cave four (partially ed. by J.M. Allegro, in JBL, 75 (1956), 89–95).
1QPhyl	Phylacteries *(tefillin)* from Qumran, cave one (ed. by Y. Yadin, in *Eretz Israel,* 9 (1969), 60–85).

4Q Prayer of Nabonidus	A document from Qumran, cave four, belonging to a lost Daniel literature (ed. by J.T. Milik, in RB, 63 (1956), 407–15).
1QS	*Manual of Discipline* or *Serekh ha-Yaḥad* from Qumran, cave one (ed. by M. Burrows et al., *Dead Sea Scrolls* . . ., 2, pt. 2 (1951)).
1QS^{a}	The *Rule of the Congregation* or *Serekh ha-Edah* from Qumran, cave one (ed. by M. Burrows et al., *Dead Sea Scrolls* . . ., 1 (1950), under the abbreviation 1Q28a).
1QS^{b}	*Blessings* or *Divrei Berakhot* from Qumran, cave one (ed. by M. Burrows et al., *Dead Sea Scrolls* . . ., 1 (1950), under the abbreviation 1Q28b).
4QSam^{a}	Manuscript of I and II Samuel from Qumran, cave four (partially ed. by F.M. Cross, in BASOR, 132 (1953), 15–26).
4QSam^{b}	Manuscript of I and II Samuel from Qumran, cave four (partially ed. by F.M. Cross, in JBL, 74 (1955), 147–72).
4QTestimonia	Sheet of Testimony from Qumran, cave four (ed. by J.M. Allegro, in JBL, 75 (1956), 174–87).
4QT.Levi	*Testament of Levi* from Qumran, cave four (partially ed. by J.T. Milik, in RB, 62 (1955), 398–406).
Rabinovitz, Dik Sof	See Dik. Sof.
RB	*Revue biblique* (1892 ff.).
RBI	*Recherches bibliques* (1954 ff.).
RCB	*Revista de cultura bíblica* (São Paulo) (1957 ff.).
Régné, Cat	J. Régné, *Catalogue des actes . . . des rois d'Aragon, concernant les Juifs* (1213–1327), in: REJ, vols. 60–70, 73, 75–78 (1910–24).
Reinach, Textes	T. Reinach, *Textes d'auteurs Grecs et Romains relatifs au Judaïsme* (1895; repr. 1963).
REJ	*Revue des études juives* (1880 ff.).
Rejzen, Leksikon	Z. Rejzen, *Leksikon fun der Yidisher Literatur*, 4 vols. (1927–29).
Renan, Ecrivains	A. Neubauer and E. Renan, *Les écrivains juifs français* . . . (1893).
Renan, Rabbins	A. Neubauer and E. Renan, *Les rabbins français* (1877).
RES	*Revue des études sémitiques et Babyloniaca* (1934–45).
Rev.	Revelation (New Testament).
RGG^{3}	*Die Religion in Geschichte und Gegenwart*, 7 vols. (1957–65^{3}).
RH	*Rosh Ha-Shanah* (talmudic tractate).
RHJE	*Revue de l'histoire juive en Egypte* (1947 ff.).
RHMH	*Revue d'histoire de la médecine hébraïque* (1948 ff.).
RHPR	*Revue d'histoire et de philosophie religieuses* (1921 ff.).
RHR	*Revue d'histoire des religions* (1880 ff.).
RI	*Rivista Israelitica* (1904–12).
Riemann-Einstein	*Hugo Riemanns Musiklexikon*, ed. by A. Einstein (1929^{11})
Riemann-Gurlitt	*Hugo Riemanns Musiklexikon*, ed. by W. Gurlitt (1959–67^{12}), Personenteil.
Rigg-Jenkinson, Exchequer	J.M. Rigg, H. Jenkinson and H.G. Richardson (eds.), *Calendar of the Plea Rolls of the Exchequer of the Jews*, 4 vols. (1905–1970); cf. in each instance also J.M. Rigg (ed.), *Select Pleas* . . . (1902).
RMI	*Rassegna Mensile di Israel* (1925 ff.).
Rom.	Epistle to the Romans (New Testament).
Rosanes, Togarmah	S.A. Rosanes, *Divrei Yemei Yisrael be-Togarmah*, 6 vols. (1907–45), and in 3 vols. (1930–38^{2}).
Rosenbloom, Biogr Dict	J.R. Rosenbloom, *Biographical Dictionary of Early American Jews* (1960).
Roth, Art	C. Roth, *Jewish Art* (1961).
Roth, Dark Ages	C. Roth (ed.), *World History of the Jewish People*, second series, vol. 2, *Dark Ages* (1966).
Roth, England	C. Roth, *History of the Jews in England* (1964^{3}).
Roth, Italy	C. Roth, *History of the Jews in Italy* (1946).
Roth, Mag Bibl	C. Roth, *Magna Bibliotheca Anglo-Judaica* (1937).
Roth, Marranos	C. Roth, *History of the Marranos* (2nd rev. ed. 1959; reprint 1966).
Rowley, Old Test	H.H. Rowley, *Old Testament and Modern Study* (1951; repr. 1961).
RS	*Revue sémitique d'épigraphie et d'histoire ancienne* (1893/94 ff.).
RSO	*Rivista degli studi orientali* (1907 ff.).
RSV	Revised Standard Version of the Bible.
Ruth	Ruth (Bible).
Ruth R.	*Ruth Rabbah*.
RV	Revised Version of the Bible.
Sac.	Philo, *De Sacrificiis Abelis et Caini*.
Salfeld, Martyrol	S. Salfeld, *Martyrologium des Nuernberger Memorbuches* (1898).
I and II Sam.	Samuel, books I and II (Bible).
Sanh.	*Sanhedrin* (talmudic tractate).
SBA	Society of Biblical Archaeology.
SBB	*Studies in Bibliography and Booklore* (1953 ff.).
SBE	*Semana Bíblica Española*.
SBT	*Studies in Biblical Theology* (1951 ff.).
SBU	*Svenskt Bibliskt Uppslagsverk*, 2 vols. (1962–63^{2}).
Schirmann, Italyah	J.Ḥ. Schirmann, *Ha-Shirah ha-Ivrit be-Italyah* (1934).
Schirmann, Sefarad	J.Ḥ. Schirmann, *Ha-Shirah ha-Ivrit bi-Sefarad u-vi-Provence*, 2 vols. (1954–56).
Scholem, Mysticism	G. Scholem, *Major Trends in Jewish Mysticism* (rev. ed. 1946; paperback ed. with additional bibliography 1961).
Scholem, Shabbetai Ẓevi	G. Scholem, *Shabbetai Ẓevi ve-ha-Tenu'ah ha-Shabbeta'it bi-Ymei Ḥayyav*, 2 vols. (1967).
Schrader, Keilinschr	E. Schrader, *Keilinschriften und das Alte Testament* (1903^{3}).
Schuerer, Gesch	E. Schuerer, *Geschichte des juedischen Volkes im Zeitalter Jesu Christi*, 3 vols. and index-vol. (1901–11^{4}).
Schuerer, Hist	E. Schuerer, *History of the Jewish People in the Time of Jesus*, ed. by N.N. Glatzer, abridged paperback edition (1961).
Sef. T.	*Sefer Torah* (post-talmudic tractate).
Sem.	*Semaḥot* (post-talmudic tractate).
Sendrey, Music	A. Sendrey, *Bibliography of Jewish Music* (1951).
SER	*Seder Eliyahu Rabbah*.
SEZ	*Seder Eliyahu Zuta*.
Shab.	*Shabbat* (talmudic tractate).
Sh. Ar.	J. Caro, Shulḥan Arukh. OḤ – *Oraḥ Ḥayyim* YD – *Yoreh De'ah* EH – *Even ha-Ezer* ḤM – *Ḥoshen Mishpat*.
Shek.	*Shekalim* (talmudic tractate).
Shev.	*Shevi'it* (talmudic tractate).
Shevu.	*Shevu'ot* (talmudic tractate).
Shunami, Bibl	S. Shunami, *Bibliography of Jewish Bibliographies* (1965^{2}).
Sif. Deut.	*Sifrei Deuteronomy*.

Sif. Num.	*Sifrei Numbers.*
Sifra	*Sifra* on Leviticus.
Sif. Zut.	*Sifrei Zuta.*
SIHM	Sources inédites de l'histoire du Maroc (series).
Silverman, Prayer	M. Silverman (ed.), *Sabbath and Festival Prayer Book* (1946).
Singer, Prayer	S. Singer, *Authorised Daily Prayer Book* (1943[17]).
Sob.	Philo, *De Sobrietate.*
Sof.	*Soferim* (post-talmudic tractate).
Som.	Philo, *De Somniis.*
Song	Song of Songs (Bible).
Song Ch.	Song of the Three Children (Apocrypha).
Song R.	*Song of Songs Rabbah.*
SOR	*Seder Olam Rabbah.*
Sot.	*Sotah* (talmudic tractate).
SOZ	*Seder Olam Zuta.*
Spec.	Philo, *De Specialibus Legibus.*
SRJC	Society for the Research of Jewish Communities.
Steinschneider, Arab lit	M. Steinschneider, *Die arabische Literatur der Juden* (1902).
Steinschneider, Cat Bod	M. Steinschneider, *Catalogus Librorum Hebraeorum in Bibliotheca Bodleiana,* 3 vols. (1852–60; reprints 1931 and 1964).
Steinschneider, Handbuch	M. Steinschneider, *Bibliographisches Handbuch ueber die . . . Literatur fuer hebraeische Sprachkunde* (1859; repr. with additions 1937).
Steinschneider, Uebersetzungen	M. Steinschneider, *Die hebraeischen Uebersetzungen des Mittelalters* (1893).
Stern, Americans	M.H. Stern, *Americans of Jewish Descent* (1960).
van Straalen, Cat	S. van Straalen, *Catalogue of Hebrew Books in the British Museum Acquired During the Years 1868–1892* (1894).
Suárez Fernández, Documentos	L. Suárez Fernández, *Documentos acerca de la expulsión de los Judíos de España* (1964).
Suk.	*Sukkah* (talmudic tractate).
Sus.	Susanna (Apocrypha).
SY	*Sefer Yeẓirah.*
Sym.	Symmachus' Greek translation of the Bible.
SZNG	*Studien zur neueren Geschichte.*
Ta'an.	*Ta'anit* (talmudic tractate).
Tam.	*Tamid* (mishnaic tractate).
Tanḥ.	*Tanḥuma.*
Tanḥ. B.	*Tanḥuma,* Buber ed. (1885).
Targ. Jon.	Targum Jonathan (Aramaic version of the Prophets).
Targ. Onk.	Targum Onkelos (Aramaic version of the Pentateuch).
Targ. Yer.	Targum Yerushalmi.
TB	Babylonian Talmud or Talmud Bavli.
Tcherikover, Corpus	V. Tcherikover, A. Fuks, and M. Stern, *Corpus Papyrorum Judaicorum,* 3 vols. (1957–60).
Tef.	*Tefillin* (post-talmudic tractate).
Tem.	*Temurah* (mishnaic tractate).
Ter.	*Terumah* (talmudic tractate).
Test. Patr.	Testament of the Twelve Patriarchs (Pseudepigrapha). Ash. — Asher Ben. — Benjamin Dan — Dan Gad — Gad Iss. — Issachar Joseph — Joseph Judah — Judah Levi — Levi Naph. — Naphtali Reu. — Reuben Sim. — Simeon Zeb. — Zebulun.
I and II Thess.	Epistle to the Thessalonians (New Testament).
Thieme-Becker	U. Thieme and F. Becker (eds.), *Allgemeines Lexikon der bildenden Kuenstler von der Antike bis zur Gegenwart,* 37 vols. (1907–50).
Tidhar	D. Tidhar (ed.), *Enẓiklopedyah la-Ḥalutzei ha-Yishuv u-Vonav* (1947 ff.).
I and II Timothy	Epistles to Timothy (New Testament).
Tit.	Epistle to Titus (New Testament).
TJ	Jerusalem Talmud or Talmud Yerushalmi.
Tob.	Tobit (Apocrypha).
Toh.	*Tohorot* (mishnaic tractate).
Torczyner, Bundeslade	H. Torczyner, *Die Bundeslade und die Anfaenge der Religion Israels* (1930[2]).
Tos.	*Tosafot.*
Tosef.	Tosefta.
Tristram, Nat Hist	H.B. Tristram, *Natural History of the Bible* (1877[5]).
Tristram, Survey	Palestine Exploration Fund, *Survey of Western Palestine,* vol. 4 (1884) = *Fauna and Flora* by H.B. Tristram.
TS	*Terra Santa* (1920 ff.).
TSBA	*Transactions of the Society of Biblical Archaeology* (1872–93).
TY	*Tevul Yom* (mishnaic tractate).
UBSB	United Bible Societies, *Bulletin.*
UJE	*Universal Jewish Encyclopedia,* 10 vols. (1939–43).
Uk.	*Ukẓin* (mishnaic tractate).
Urbach, Tosafot	E.E. Urbach, *Ba'alei ha-Tosafot* (1957[2]).
de Vaux, Anc Isr	R. de Vaux, *Ancient Israel: its Life and Institutions* (1961; paperback 1965).
de Vaux, Instit	R. de Vaux, *Institutions de l'Ancien Testament,* 2 vols. (1958–60).
Virt.	Philo, *De Virtutibus.*
Vogelstein, Chronology	M. Vogelstein, *Biblical Chronology* (1944).
Vogelstein-Rieger	H. Vogelstein and P. Rieger, *Geschichte der Juden in Rom,* 2 vols. (1895–96).
VT	*Vetus Testamentum* (1951 ff.).
VTS	*Vetus Testamentum* Supplements (1953 ff.).
Vulg.	Vulgate (Latin translation of the Bible).
Wars	Josephus, *The Jewish War.*
Watzinger, Denkmaeler	K. Watzinger, *Denkmaeler Palaestinas,* 2 vols. (1933–35).
Waxman, Literature	M. Waxman, *History of Jewish Literature,* 5 vols. (1960[2]).
Weiss, Dor	I. H. Weiss, *Dor, Dor ve-Dorshav,* 5 vols. (1904[4]).
Wellhausen, Proleg	J. Wellhausen, *Prolegomena zur Geschichte Israels* (1927[6]).
WI	*Die Welt des Islams* (1913 ff.).
Wininger, Biog	S. Wininger, *Grosse juedische National-Biographie . . .,* 7 vols. (1925–36).
Wisd.	Wisdom of Solomon (Apocrypha).
WLB	*Wiener Library Bulletin* (1958 ff.).
Wolf, Bibliotheca	J.C. Wolf, *Bibliotheca Hebraea,* 4 vols. (1715–33).
Wright, Atlas	G.E. Wright, *Westminster Historical Atlas to the Bible* (1945).
Wright, Bible	G.E. Wright, *The Bible and the Ancient Near East* (1961).
WWWJ	*Who's Who in World Jewry* (New York, 1955, 1965[2]).

WZJT	*Wissenschaftliche Zeitschrift fuer juedische Theologie* (1835–47).
WZKM	*Wiener Zeitschrift fuer die Kunde des Morgenlandes* (1887 ff.).
Yaari, Sheluḥei	A. Yaari, *Sheluḥei Ereẓ Yisrael* (1951).
Yad	Maimonides, *Mishneh Torah (Yad Ḥazakah)*
Yad.	*Yadayim* (mishnaic tractate).
Yal.	*Yalkut Shimoni.*
Yal. Mak.	*Yalkut Makhiri.*
Yal. Reub.	*Yalkut Reubeni.*
YD	*Yoreh De'ah.*
YE	*Yevreyskaya Entsiklopediya,* 14 vols. (c. 1910).
Yev.	*Yevamot* (talmudic tractate).
YIVOA	*YIVO Annual of Jewish Social Studies* (1946 ff.).
YLBI	*Year Book of the Leo Baeck Institute* (1956 ff.).
YMḤEY	See BJPES.
YMḤSI	*Yedi'ot ha-Makhon le-Ḥeker ha-Shirah ha-Ivrit* (1935/36 ff.).
YMMY	*Yedi'ot ha-Makhon le-Madda'ei ha-Yahadut* (1924/25 ff.).
Yoma	*Yoma* (talmudic tractate).
ZA	*Zeitschrift fuer Assyriologie* (1886/87 ff.).
Zav.	*Zavim* (mishnaic tractate).
ZAW	*Zeitschrift fuer die alttestamentliche Wissenschaft und die Kunde des nachbiblischen Judentums* (1881 ff.).
ZAWB	*Beihefte* (supplements) to ZAW.
ZDMG	*Zeitschrift der Deutschen Morgenlaendischen Gesellschaft* (1846 ff.).
ZDPV	*Zeitschrift des Deutschen Palaestina-Vereins* (1878–1949; from 1949 = BBLA).
Zech.	Zechariah (Bible).
Zedner, Cat	J. Zedner, *Catalogue of Hebrew Books in the Library of the British Museum* (1867; repr. 1964).
Zeitlin, Bibliotheca	W. Zeitlin, *Bibliotheca Hebraica Post-Mendelssohniana* (1891–95).
Zeph.	Zephaniah (Bible).
Zev.	*Zevaḥim* (talmudic tractate).
ZGGJT	*Zeitschrift der Gesellschaft fuer die Geschichte der Juden in der Tschechoslowakei* (1930–38).
ZGJD	*Zeitschrift fuer die Geschichte der Juden in Deutschland* (1887–92).
ZHB	*Zeitschrift fuer hebraeische Bibliographie* (1896–1920).
Zinberg, Sifrut	I. Zinberg, *Toledot Sifrut Yisrael,* 6 vols. (1955–60).
Ẓiẓ.	*Ẓiẓit* (post-talmudic tractate).
ZNW	*Zeitschrift fuer die neutestamentliche Wissenschaft* (1901 ff.).
ZS	*Zeitschrift fuer Semitistik und verwandte Gebiete* (1922 ff.).
Zunz, Gesch	L. Zunz, *Zur Geschichte und Literatur* (1845).
Zunz, Lit Poesie	L. Zunz, *Literaturgeschichte der synagogalen Poesie* (1865; Supplement, 1867; repr. 1966).
Zunz, Poesie	L. Zunz, *Synagogale Poesie des Mittelalters,* ed. by Freimann (1920²; repr. 1967).
Zunz, Ritus	L. Zunz, *Ritus des synagogalen Gottesdienstes* (1859; repr. 1967).
Zunz, Schr	L. Zunz, *Gesammelte Schriften,* 3 vols. (1875–76).
Zunz, Vortraege	L. Zunz, *Gottesdienstliche Vortraege der Juden . . .* (1892²; repr. 1966).
Zunz-Albeck, Derashot	L. Zunz, *Ha-Derashot be-Yisrael,* Heb. tr. of Zunz, Vortraege by H. Albeck (1954²).

TRANSLITERATION RULES

HEBREW AND SEMITIC LANGUAGES:

	General	*Scientific*
א	not transliterated[1]	ʾ
בּ	b	b
ב	v	v, ḇ
גּ	g	g
ג		ḡ
דּ	d	d
ד		ḏ
ה	h	h
ו	v—when not a vowel	w
ז	z	z
ח	ḥ	ḥ
ט	t	ṭ, t
י	y—when vowel and at end of words—i	y
כּ	k	k
כ,ך	kh	kh, ḵ
ל	l	l
מ,ם	m	m
נ,ן	n	n
ס	s	s
ע	not transliterated[1]	ʿ
פּ	p	p
פ,ף	f	p, f, ph
צ,ץ	ẓ	ṣ, ẓ
ק	k	q, k
ר	r	r
שׁ	sh[2]	š
שׂ	s	ś, s
תּ	t	t
ת		ṯ
ג׳	dzh, J	ğ
ז׳	zh, J	ž
צ׳	ch	č
◌ָ		å, o, ȯ (short); â, ā (long)
◌ַ	a	a
◌ֲ		a, ^{a}
◌ֵ		e, ẹ, ē
◌ֶ	e	æ ä, ę
◌ֱ		œ, ĕ, ^{e}
◌ְ	only *sheva na* is transliterated	ə, ĕ, e; only *sheva na* transliterated
◌ִ, ◌ִי	i	i
◌ֹ, וֹ	o	o, o, o
◌ֻ	u	u, ŭ
וּ		û, ū
◌ֵי	ei; biblical e	
‡		reconstructed forms of words

1. The letters א and ע are not transliterated.
   An apostrophe (') between vowels indicates that they do not form a diphthong and are to be pronounced separately.
2. *Dagesh ḥazak* (forte) is indicated by doubling of the letter, except for the letter שׁ
3. Names. Biblical names and biblical place names are rendered according to the Bible translation of the Jewish Publication Society of America. Post-biblical Hebrew names are transliterated; contemporary names are transliterated or rendered as used by the person. Place names are transliterated or rendered by the accepted spelling. Names and some words with an accepted English form are usually not transliterated.

YIDDISH

א	not transliterated
אַ	a
אָ	o
בּ	b
בֿ	v
ג	g
ד	d
ה	h
ו,וּ	u
וו	v
וי	oy
ז	z
זש	zh
ח	kh
ט	t
טש	tsh, ch
י	(consonant) y (vowel) i
יִ	i
יי	ey
ײַ	ay
כּ	k
כ,ך	kh
ל	l
מ,ם	m
נ,ן	n
ס	s
ע	e
פּ	p
פֿ,ף	f
צ,ץ	ts
ק	k
ר	r
ש	sh
שׂ	s
תּ	t
ת	s

1. Yiddish transliteration rendered according to U. Weinreich's *Modern English-Yiddish Yiddish-English Dictionary*.
2. Hebrew words in Yiddish are usually transliterated according to standard Yiddish pronunciation, e.g., חזנות = *khazones*.

LADINO

Ladino and Judeo-Spanish words written in Hebrew characters are transliterated phonetically, following the General Rules of Hebrew transliteration (see above) whenever the accepted spelling in Latin characters could not be ascertained.

ARABIC

ا '	a[1]	ض	ḍ
ب	b	ط	ṭ
ت	t	ظ	ẓ
ث	th	ع	c
ج	j	غ	gh
ح	ḥ	ف	f
خ	kh	ق	q
د	d	ك	k
ذ	dh	ل	l
ر	r	م	m
ز	z	ن	n
س	s	ه	h
ش	sh	و	w
ص	ṣ	ي	y
ـَ	a	ـَا ى	ā
ـِ	i	ـِي	ī
ـُ	u	ـُو	ū
ـَو	aw	ـِيّ	iyy[2]
ـَي	ay	ـُوّ	uww[2]

1. not indicated when initial
2. see note (f)

a) The EJ follows the *Columbia Lippincott Gazetteer* and the *Times Atlas* in transliteration of Arabic place names. Sites that appear in neither are transliterated according to the table above, and subject to the following notes.

b) The EJ follows the *Columbia Encyclopaedia* in transliteration of Arabic names. Personal names that do not therein appear are transliterated according to the table above and subject to the following notes (e.g., Ali rather than ʿAlī, Suleiman rather than Sulayman).

c) The EJ follows the *Webster's Third International Dictionary, Unabridged* in transliteration of Arabic terms that have been integrated into the English language.

d) The term "Abu" will thus appear, usually in disregard of inflection.

e) Nunnation (end vowels, *tanwīn*) are dropped in transliteration.

f) Gemination (*tashdīd*) is indicated by the doubling of the geminated letter, unless an end letter, in which case the gemination is dropped.

g) The definitive article *al-* will always be thus transliterated, unless subject to one of the modifying notes (e.g., El-Arish rather than al-ʿArīsh; modification according to note (a)).

h) The Arabic transliteration disregards the Sun Letters (the antero-palatals *(al-Ḥurūf al-Shamsiyya)*.

i) The *tāʾ-marbūṭa* (o) is omitted in transliteration, unless in construct-state (e.g., *Khirba* but *Khirbat Mishmish*).

These modifying notes may lead to various inconsistencies in the Arabic transliteration, but this policy has deliberately been adopted to gain smoother reading of Arabic terms and names.

GREEK

Ancient Greek	*Modern Greek*	*Greek Letter*
a	a	*Α*; α; ᾳ
b	v	*Β*; β
g	gh; g	*Γ*; γ
d	dh	*Δ*; δ
e	e	*Ε*; ε
z	z	*Ζ*; ζ
e; e	i	*Η*; η ῃ
th	th	*Θ*; θ
i	i	*Ι*; ι
k	k; ky	*Κ*; κ
l	l	*Λ*; λ
m	m	*Μ*; μ
n	n	*Ν*; ν
x	x	*Ξ*; ξ
o	o	*Ο*; ο
p	p	*Π*; π
r; rh	r	*Ρ*; ϱ; ῥ
s	s	*Σ*; σ; ς
t	t	*Τ*; τ
u; y	i	*Υ*; υ
ph	f	*Φ*; φ
ch	kh	*Χ*: χ
ps	ps	*Ψ*; ψ
o; ō	o	*Ω*; ω ῳ
ai	e	αι
ei	i	ει
oi	i	οι
ui	i	υι
ou	ou	ου
eu	ev	ευ
eu; ēu	iv	ηυ
—	j	τζ
nt	d; nd	ντ
mp	b; mb	μπ
ngk	g	γκ
ng	ng	νγ
h	—	‘
—	—	’
w	—	ϝ

RUSSIAN

А	A
Б	B
В	V
Г	G
Д	D
Е	E, Ye [1]
Ё	Yo, O[2]
Ж	Zh
З	Z
И	I
Й	Y [3]
К	K
Л	L
М	M
Н	N
О	O
П	P
Р	R
С	S
Т	T
У	U
Ф	F
Х	Kh
Ц	Ts
Ч	Ch
Ш	Sh
Щ	Shch
Ъ	omitted; see note [1]
Ы	Y
Ь	omitted; see note [1]
Э	E
Ю	Yu
Я	Ya

1. Ye at the beginning of a word; after all vowels except *Ы* ; and after *Ъ* and *Ь*.
2. O after *Ч* , *Ш* and *Щ* .
3. Omitted after *Ы*, and in names of people after *И*.

A. Many first names have an accepted English or quasi-English form which has been preferred to transliteration.
B. Place names have been given according to the *Columbia Lippincott Gazetteer*.
C. Pre-revolutionary spelling has been ignored.
D. Other languages using the Cyrillic alphabet (e.g., Bulgarian, Ukrainian), inasmuch as they appear, have been phonetically transliterated in conformity with the principles of this table.

ILLUSTRATIONS

The illustrations in the Encyclopaedia Judaica have been obtained from sources throughout the world. The Encyclopaedia is grateful to the innumerable institutions, bodies, and individuals who have helped to make this material available. Special thanks are due to the following:

American Jewish Archives on the Cincinnati campus of the Hebrew Union College—Jewish Institute of Religion.
American Jewish Historical Society, Waltham, Mass.
Armenian Patriarchate, Jerusalem.
Dr. Bathja Bayer, Jerusalem.
Trustees of the British Museum, London.
Curators of the Bodleian Library, Oxford.
Central Archives of the History of the Jewish People, Jerusalem.
Central Zionist Archives, Jerusalem.
Library of Congress, Washington, D.C.
"Dagon" Collection, Archaeological Museum of Grain Handling in Israel, Haifa.
Zusia Efron, En-Ḥarod, Israel.
I. Einhorn, Tel Aviv.
E. Ben Eliavoo, Haifa (formerly of Cochin, India).
Daniel M. Friedenberg, New York.
Genazim (Asher Barash Institute of Records, Writers' Association in Israel), Tel Aviv.
Haganah Historical Archives, Tel Aviv.
Hebrew University of Jerusalem, Public Relations Department.
Hechal Shlomo, Sir Isaac and Lady Wolfson Museum, Jerusalem.
Israel Department of Antiquities and Museums, Jerusalem.
Israel Government Press Office, Tel Aviv.
Israel Museum, Jerusalem.
Israel State Archives, Jerusalem.
Jerusalem Municipality Historical Archives.
Jewish Agency Photo Service, Jerusalem.
Jewish Museum, New York.
Jewish National Fund (Keren Kayemet le-Israel), Jerusalem.
Jewish National and University Library, Jerusalem.
Library of the Jewish Theological Seminary of America, New York.
Keren Hayesod-United Israel Appeal, Jerusalem.
Anatol Lewkowicz and Joseph Zahavi, Jerusalem.
Monastery of St. Catherine, Sinai.
Museum of Modern Art, New York.
National Archives and Records Service, Washington, D.C.
Jacques Pinto, Madrid.
Dr. Chaim Schieber, Netanyah, Israel.
Prof. Gershom Scholem, Jerusalem.
State Jewish Museum in Prague.
Weizmann Institute of Science, Reḥovot, Public Relations Department.
Yad Vashem, Jerusalem.

BLACK AND WHITE ILLUSTRATION CREDITS: VOLUMES 2 AND 3.

Article	Column	Credit
		VOLUME 2
AACHEN	1	Courtesy Municipal Archive, Aachen.
AARGAU	3	From J. C. Ulrichs, *Sammlung Juedischer Geschichte,* Basle, 1768. Jerusalem, J.N.U.L.
AARON BEN ELIJAH	10	Jerusalem J.N.U.L.
AARON OF YORK	23	London, Westminster Abbey Muniment Room.
AARONSOHN	23–29	Figures. 1, 2, 4. Zikhron Ya'akov, Beit Aaronsohn. Figure 3, London, Public Record Office.
ABDULLAH, IBN HUSSEIN	57	Courtesy State Archives, Jerusalem.
ABEL	58	Madrid, Duke of Alba Library.
ABENDANA	65	Amsterdam, Portugees-Israelitische Gemeente.
ABENSUR	69	Copenhagen, Danish National Museum.
ABERDEEN	71	Cecil Roth Collection.
ABLUTION	81–86	Figure 3. Cleveland, Ohio, Olyn and Joseph B. Horwitz Judaica Collection. Photo Helga Studio, New York. Figure 4. Jerusalem, Sir Isaac and Lady Wolfson Museum in Hechal Shlomo. Photo David Harris, Jerusalem.
ABOAB, ISAAC DE MATTATHIAS	94	London, Jewish Museum.
ABOAB DE FONSECA, ISAAC	96	Cecil Roth Collection. Photo David Harris, Jerusalem.
ABRAHAM	115–6	Figure 1. After Y. Aharoni, *Carta's Atlas of the Bible,* Jerusalem, 1964.
ABRAHAM, family	125–6	Courtesy Abraham & Straus, Brooklyn, New York.
ABRAHAM B. DAVID OF POSQUIÈRES	137	Jerusalem, J.N.U.L.
ABRAHAM B. JEHIEL MICHAL HA-KOHEN	148	Jerusalem, J.N.U.L.
ABRAHAM B. SHABBETAI HA-KOHEN	155	Jerusalem, J.N.U.L.

Article	Column	Credit
ABRAHAMS, ABRAHAM	163	London, Jews' College.
ABRAHAM'S BOSOM	166	Courtesy Caisse Nationale des Monuments Historiques.
ABRAM, MORRIS	167	Courtesy Brandeis University, Waltham, Mass. Photo Ralph Norman.
ABRAMOVITZ, MAX	168	Photo Fabian Bachrach, New York.
ABRAMOVITZ, HERMAN	169	Photo Forbath, Montreal.
ABRAMSKY, YEHEZKEL	171	Photo Yacoby, Jerusalem.
ABRAMSON	171	Bene-Berak, Israel, J. Wallersteiner Collection.
ABSALOM	175	León, Spain, Archives of Royal Collegiate Church of San Isidoro, Ms. 3.
ABU GHOSH	181–2	Courtesy Government Press Office, Tel Aviv.
ACACIA	199	Photo Yosaif Cohain.
ACADEMIES	203–4	Based on M. Avi-Yonah, *Atlas of the Period of the Second Temple, the Mishnah and the Talmud*, Jerusalem, 1966.
ACHRON, JOSEPH	211	Jerusalem, J.N.U.L., Schwadron Collection.
ACHZIB	213	Courtesy Government Press Office, Tel Aviv.
ACRE	221–9	Figures, 1, 2, 3. London, British Museum. Figure 4. Courtesy National Parks Authority, Jerusalem. Figure 5. Photo Werner Braun, Jerusalem. Figure 6. Courtesy Government Press Office, Tel Aviv.
ACROSTICS	231	New York, Jewish Theological Seminary of America.
ADAM	243	Figure 3. Madrid, Museo del Prado.
ADAR, ZVI	253	Courtesy Hebrew University, Jerusalem. Photo David Harris, Jerusalem.
ADDIR BI-MELUKHA	256–7	Example 1. Lithuania, transcribed from oral tradition. After A. Nadel in EJ, vol. 1, col. 809. Example 2. Western Ashkenazi. After A. Baer, *Baal T'fillah*, 1883[2], no. 770, and other sources. Example 3. Western Ashkenazi (Hamburg local usage), transcribed from oral tradition. After A. Nadel in EJ, vol. 1, col. 810.
ADDIR HU	257–8	Synagogal Weintraub. After setting of melody for *Hodu* for Pesaḥ, in H. Weintraub, *Schire Beth Adonai*, 1859, part 2, no. 121. Synagogal Lewandowsky. Version used by L. Lewandowsky for *Mi kamokha*, *Kiddush*, etc. on Pesaḥ in *Todah W'simrah*, part 2, 1876, nos. 7,13. Family Traditions. Three north German versions (Danzig and vicinity), as notated by H. Avenary.
ADEN	264	Courtesy Jewish Agency Archives, Jerusalem.
ADENAUER, KONRAD	265	Courtesy Government Press Office, Tel Aviv.
ADLER	271	Photo Rappaport Studios, New York.
ADLER, ALFRED	272	New York, Kurt A. Adler Collection. Photo O. Peter Radl.
ADLER, DAVID B.	274	Copenhagen, Royal Library.
ADLER, ELKAN N.	275	Courtesy Israel Museum Photo Archives, Jerusalem.
ADLER, FELIX	276	Jerusalem, J.N.U.L., Schwadron Collection.
ADLER, GUIDO	277	Jerusalem, J.N.U.L., Schwadron Collection.
ADLER, HERMANN	279	Cecil Roth Collection. Photo David Harris, Jerusalem.
ADLER, JANKEL	280	Jerusalem, Israel Museum.
ADLER, MAX	282	Courtesy Austrian National Library Photo Archives, Vienna.
ADLER, NATHAN MARCUS	286	Cecil Roth Collection.
ADLER, PAUL	287	Jerusalem, J.N.U.L., Schwadron Collection.
ADLER, SAUL	288	Courtesy Hebrew University, Jerusalem. Photo Alfred Bernheim, Jerusalem.
ADLOYADA	290	Courtesy Government Press Office, Tel Aviv.
ADOLPHUS	293	London, Alfred Rubens Collection.
ADON OLAM	297	Example 1. Ashkenazi (region not specified), after A. Baer, *Baal T'fillah*, 1883[2], no. 996. Example 2. Bukhara, after Idelsohn, *Melodien*, vol. 3, no. 154. Example 3. From Djerba, for sabbaths and festivals. Recorded by A. Herzog in Jerusalem, 1955, and transcribed in his *Renanot*, Jerusalem, n.d., fasc. 1–2.
ADRIANOPLE	309	Jerusalem, David Corcos Collection.
ADVERTISING	317	Courtesy Grey & Davis, Inc., New York. Photo Fabian Bachrach, New York.
AELIA CAPITOLINA	319	After M. Avi-Yonah, *Atlas of the Period of the Second Temple, the Mishnah and the Talmud*, Jerusalem, 1966.
AERONAUTICS	320–4	Figures 1,3. Courtesy National Air and Space Museum, Smithsonian Institution, Washington, D.C. Figure 2, Courtesy U.S. Department of the Navy, Washington, D.C.
AGAM, YAACOV	342	Photo Léon Herschtritt, Paris,

Article	Column	Credit
AGE AND THE AGED	344	Courtesy J.D.C.–Malben, Tel Aviv.
AGNON, SHMUEL YOSEF	368	Courtesy Ministry for Foreign Affairs, Jerusalem. Photo K. Meyerowitz, Jerusalem.
	370	Photo Reportagebild, Stockholm.
AGRANAT, SHIMON	373	Courtesy Government Press Office, Tel Aviv.
AGRICULTURAL METHODS AND IMPLEMENTS	375–82	Figure 1. Haifa, Dagon Collection, Archaeological Museum of Grain Handling in Israel. Figure 2. From C.R. Lepsius, *Denkmaeler aus Aegypten und Aethiopien,* Berlin, 1849. Figure 3. Courtesy New York State Board of Education. Figure 4. Photo David Eisenberg, Jerusalem.
AGRICULTURE	383–414	Figures 1, 2. Courtesy Israel Department of Antiquities, Jerusalem. Figures 3, 4, 5. Israel Museum, Jerusalem, Israel Department of Antiquities Collection. Figures 6, 10, 15, 17, 18. Haifa, Dagon Collection, Archaeological Museum of Grain Handling in Israel. Figures 7, 16. Ditto, on loan from Israel Department of Antiquities. Figure 8. From W. Wreszinski, *Atlas zur altaegyptischen Kulturgeschichte,* Leipzig, 1923–32, vol. 2. Figure 9. Haifa, Dagon Collection, Archaeological Museum of Grain Handling in Israel. Courtesy Y. Yadin. Figure 11. From *Views of the Biblical World,* Ramat Gan, 1961. Figure 12. Replica in Israel Museum, Jerusalem. Figures 13, 14. Haifa, Dagon Collection, Archaeological Museum of Grain Handling in Israel, on loan from Tel Aviv University. Figures 19,20 Courtesy M. Evenari. Figure 21. Courtesy Alliance Israélite Universelle, Jerusalem. Figure 22. Courtesy Central Zionist Archives, Jerusalem. Figures 23, 24, 25, 26. Courtesy C.A.H.J.P., Jerusalem. Photos, Figures 10, 18, Hannah Ophir-Rosenstein, Haifa.
AGRIPPINA	419–20	By M. Ben-Dov, assisted by R. Gardiner and E. Gelbron.
AGRON, GERSHON	419	Courtesy Keren Hayesod, United Israel Appeal, Jerusalem.
AGUILAR, DIEGO D'	427	Cecil Roth Collection.
AHAB	436	After Y. Aharoni, *Carta's Atlas of the Bible*, Jerusalem, 1964.
	438	Courtesy Israel Department of Antiquities, Jerusalem.
AḤAD HA'AM	442	Courtesy Central Zionist Archives, Jerusalem.
	445–6	Jerusalem, J.N.U.L., Schwadron Collection.
AHARONI, YOHANAN	452	Courtesy Hebrew University, Jerusalem. Photo K. Meyerowitz, Jerusalem.
AHLEM	468	Courtesy S. Adler-Rudel, Jerusalem.
AI	471–2	After J. Callaway, "The 1964 Ai (et-Tell) Excavations" in *Bulletin of American School of Oriental Research*, no. 178.
AKEDAH	482	Figure 2. Baltimore, Md., Walters Art Gallery.
AKZIN, BENJAMIN	505	Courtesy Hebrew University, Jerusalem. Photo R.M. Kneller, Jerusalem.
ALASHKAR, MOSES B. ISAAC	511	Jerusalem, J.N.U.L.
ALBALA, DAVID	519–20	Jerusalem, J.N.U.L.
ALBELDA, MOSES B. JACOB	529	Jerusalem, J.N.U.L.
ALBERTA	531	Photo Matthews Photo Lab. Ltd., Calgary.
ALBU, SIR GEORGE	540	Courtesy South African Jewish Board of Deputies. Photo *African World.*
ALEINU LE-SHABBE'AḤ	556	A. Western Ashkenazi. After A. Baer, *Baal T'fillah*, 1883², no. 1227. B. Eastern Ashkenazi. After H. Weintraub, *Schire Beth Adonai,* 1859, part 2, 160. C. "Acculturated" version by L. Lewandowsky, *Kol Rinnah u'T'fillah,* Frankfurt, 1921¹⁶, no. 189.
	558	Cecil Roth Collection.
ALEXANDROW	560	Jerusalem, J.N.U.L.
ALEMÁN, MATEO	562	Jerusalem, J.N.U.L.
ALEXANDER, ABRAHAM	572	Charleston, S.C., Gibbs Art Gallery. Courtesy T. J. Tobias for Estate of Rosa Hays Alexander. Photo Louis Schwartz, Charleston.
ALEXANDER, MORRIS	574	Cape Town, South African National Gallery.
ALEXANDER, MOSES	575	Courtesy American Jewish Archives, Cincinnati, O. Photo Rothschild, Los Angeles, Calif.
ALEXANDER, SAMUEL	576	Courtesy Manchester University.
ALEXANDER SUSLIN HA-KOHEN	585	Jerusalem, J.N.U.L.

Article	Column	Credit
ALFANDARI, ḤAYYIM B. ISAAC	598	Jerusalem, J.N.U.L.
ALGAZI, YOM TOV B. ISRAEL JACOB	611	Jerusalem, J.N.U.L.
ALGIERS	623–4	Jerusalem, Israel Museum. Photo David Harris, Jerusalem.
AL-ḤARIZI, JUDAH B. SOLOMON	627	Rome, Vatican Library, Ms. 4359.
AL ḤET	630	Bene-Berak, Israel, J. Wallersteiner Collection.
ALIYAH	634	Courtesy Keren Hayesod, United Israel Appeal, Jerusalem.
ALKALAI, DAVID	638	Jerusalem, J.N.U.L., Schwadron Collection.
ALKALAI, JUDAH B. SOLOMON ḤAI	638	Courtesy Central Zionist Archives, Jerusalem.
	640	Jerusalem, J.N.U.L., Schwadron Collection.
ALLENBY, EDMUND HENRY HYNMAN, VISCOUNT	647	Courtesy Central Zionist Archives, Jerusalem.
ALLGEMEINE ZEITUNG DES JUDENTUMS	648	Jerusalem, J.N.U.L.
ALLIANCE ISRAÉLITE UNIVERSELLE	649	Courtesy J.D.C., New York.
ALLON, YIGAL	655	Courtesy Government Press Office, Tel Aviv.
ALMANZI, JOSEPH	660	Jerusalem, J.N.U.L., Schwadron Collection.
ALMOG, YEHUDA	662	Courtesy Government Press Office, Tel Aviv.
ALMOLI, SOLOMON B. JACOB	664	Jerusalem, J.N.U.L.
ALMOND, GABRIEL A.	666	Photo Blackstone-Shelburne, New York.
ALMOSNINO, SOLOMON	668	London, Jews' College, Montefiore Library. Courtesy Spanish & Portugese Jews Congregation, London.
ALMOSNINO JOSEPH B. ISAAC	670	Cecil Roth Collection.
ALPHABET, HEBREW: NORTH-WEST SEMITIC	675–88	Figure 1. From F.M. Cross, "The Origin and Early Evolution of the Alphabet," *Eretz Israel,* 8, Jerusalem, 1967. Figures 2, 10, J. Naveh, Jerusalem. Figure 3. After Virolleaud, *Syria*, 28, Paris, 1951, 22. Figure 11, N. Avigad in *Scripta Hierosalymitana,* 4, 1957.
CURSIVE SCRIPT	689–702	Figures 4, 12, 14, 18, 21. London, S.A. Birnbaum Collection. Figure 7, S.A. Birnbaum, *The Hebrew Scripts,* London, 1954–57, Fig. 153. Figure 10. *Ibid.,* Fig. 187.
SQUARE SCRIPT	711–28	Figure 1. *Ibid.*, Fig. 122. Figure 9. *Ibid.*, Fig. 92. Figure 20. *Ibid.* Fig. 231. Figure 23. *Ibid.*, Fig. 241. Figure 30. *Ibid.*, Fig. 302. Figure 35. *Ibid.*, Fig. 345.
MASHAIT SCRIPT	732–42	Figures 6,9. London, S.A. Birnbaum Collection.
ALSACE	751–2	Based on J. Bloch, "Tableau Statistique du Mouvement de la Population. Juive en Alsace de 1784 à 1953" in *Bulletin de nos communautés,* 1956.
	753–4	Courtesy Baruch Mevorach, Jerusalem.
ALSHEIKH, SHALOM B. JOSEPH	758	Courtesy J. Ratzhabi, Tel Aviv.
ALTAR	760–7	Figures 1, 2, 3. Courtesy Israel Department of Antiquities, Jerusalem. Figure 4. Jerusalem, Rockefeller Museum, Israel Department of Antiquities.
ALTENBERG, PETER	772	Jerusalem, J.N.U.L., Schwadron Collection.
ALTENSTADT	773	From H. Rose, *Geschichtliches der Israelitischen Kultusgemeinde Altenstadt*, 1931.
ALTERMAN, NATHAN	774	Courtesy Genazim, Tel Aviv.
ALTMAN, NATHAN	778	Jerusalem, Israel Museum.
ALTMANN, ALEXANDER	779	Photo Alice Holz, Jerusalem.
ALTSCHULER, DAVID	783	Jerusalem, J.N.U.L.
ALVA, SOLOMON SIEGFRIED	785	Jerusalem, Alice and Moshe Shalvi Collection.
AMATUS LUSITANUS	795	Jerusalem, J.N.U.L.
	796	Jerusalem, J.N.U.L., Schwadron Collection.
AMBERG	800	Courtesy Yad Vashem Archives, Jerusalem.
AMEN	804	Example 1a. Yemen. After Idelsohn, *Melodien*, vol. 1, no. 12. Example 1b. Western Ashkenazi. After S. Naumbourg, *Zemirot Yisrael,* vol. 2, 1847, no 181. Example 2. Morocco. After Idelsohn, *Melodien,* vol. 5, nos. 29, 30.

Article	Column	Credit
AMERICA	809–16	Figures on all maps from *American Jewish Yearbook.*
AMERICAN ACADEMY FOR JEWISH RESEARCH	819	Photo John H. Popper.
AMERICAN ISRAELITE	821	Cincinnati, O., American Jewish Archives.
AMERY, LEOPOLD STENNETT	833	Courtesy Central Zionist Archives, Jerusalem.
AMIDAR	846	Courtesy Government Press Office, Tel Aviv.
AMIRAN, DAVID	849	Courtesy Hebrew University, Jerusalem.
AMMON, AMMONITES	854	Based on Y. Aharoni, *Carta's Atlas of the Bible,* Jerusalem. 1964.
AMON	864	New York, Brooklyn Museum.
AMORITES	878	Jerusalem, J.N.U.L.
AMSHEWITZ, JOHN HENRY	895	Courtesy Gresham Committee, London. Photo Jon Whitbourne.
AMSTERDAM	897–904	Figures 1, 2. Jerusalem, Israel Museum. Photos David Harris, Jerusalem. Figure 4. Courtesy Yad Vashem Archives, Jerusalem. Figure 5. Photo M. Ninio, Jerusalem.
AMULET	907–14	Figures 1–19. Tel Aviv, I. Einhorn Collection. Photos David Harris, Jerusalem.
AMZALAK, MOSES BENSABAT	916	Photo Silva Conto Studios, Lisbon.
ANACLETUS II	917	From J. Prinz, *Popes from the Ghetto,* New York, 1966.
ANAU, PHINEHAS ḤAI B. MENAHEM	935	Cecil Roth Collection.
ANAV, JEHIEL B. JEKUTHIEL	937	Leiden, Holland, Bibliotheek der Rijksuniversiteet.
ANCONA	942–3	Figures 1, 2. Photo Joseph Shaw, London.
ANCONA (D'ANCONA)	944	Jerusalem, J.N.U.L., Schwadron Collection.
ANDERNACH	946	Courtesy Andernach Municipality.
ANDRADE, EDWARD	947	Photo Walter Bird, London.
ANGRIST, ALFRED	980	Courtesy Albert Einstein College of Medicine, Yeshiva University, New York. Photo Ferdinand Vogel.
		VOLUME 3
ANIELEWICZ, MORDECAI	3	Courtesy Yad Vashem Archives, Jerusalem.
ANI MA'AMIN	5	Jerusalem, J.N.U.L.
ANIM ZEMIROT	22	Example 1. Eastern Ashkenazi, Poland. After A. Baer, *Baal T'fillah,* 1883², no. 1363. Example 2. Israel Ashkenazi version, conventionally sung by a child, as heard in a Jerusalem synagogue and transcribed by Avigdor Herzog. The source is a well-known Sephardi melody.
ANNENBERG, WALTER H.	27	Courtesy *Philadelphia Inquirer.* Photo Karsh, Ottawa.
ANSBACH	32	Courtesy Ansbach Municipality. Photo Hanns Beer.
AN-SKI	34	Courtesy YIVO, New York.
ANTHROPOLOGY, PHYSICAL	41–43	Figure 1. Courtesy Israel Department of Antiquities, Jerusalem. Figure 2. Jerusalem, Rockefeller Museum, Israel Department of Antiquities.
ANTHROPOMORPHISM	52–54	Figure 1. Jerusalem, Michael Kaufman Collection. Figure 2. Amsterdam, Oudekerk Cemetery.
ANTICHRIST	61	Cecil Roth Collection.
ANTI-FASCIST COMMITTEE	63	Courtesy B.Z. Goldberg, New York.
ANTIGONUS II	66	Jerusalem, Bank of Israel Collection.
ANTIOCHUS	75	Jerusalem, Bank of Israel Collection.
ANTIPATRIS	78	Photo Zev Radovan, Jerusalem.
ANTI-SEMITISM	91–158	Figure 1a. Photo Emil Bauer, Bamberg. Figure 3b. Cecil Roth Photo Collection. Figures 4a-c. Photos Uffizi Gallery, Florence. Figure 9c. Jerusalem, Israel Museum. Photo David Harris, Jerusalem. Figures 9h, 19. Courtesy Y. Harkabi, Tel Aviv. Figure 21. Courtesy Archivo de Prensa, Buenos Aires. Photo S. Zimberoff.
ANTOKOLSKI, MARK	161	Jerusalem, J.N.U.L., Schwadron Collection.
ANTONIA	164	Based on L. H. Vincent in, *Revue Biblique,* Jan. 1933, vol. 42, 112.
ANTONINUS PIUS	165	Jerusalem, Bank of Israel Collection.
APAM	175	Courtesy U. Nahon, Jerusalem.
APE	176	Jerusalem, Rockefeller Museum, Israel Department of Antiquities.
APOLLONIA	188	Courtesy Israel Department of Antiquities, Jerusalem.
APOSTASY	201–15	Figure 1. Basle, Kunstmuseum. Figures 2, 3, 4, 5. Cecil Roth Collection.

Article	Column	Credit
APTOWITZER, VICTOR	225	Jerusalem, J.N.U.L., Schwadron Collection.
APULIA	226	After A. Milano, *Storia degli ebrei d'Italia*, 1963.
	227	Courtesy Superintendent of Antiquities, Taranto.
ARABAH	231	Courtesy Government Press Office, Tel Aviv.
ARABIA	233	Based on J. W. Hirschberg, *Yisrael be-Arav*, 1946.
ARABIC LANGUAGE	238	Based on C. H. Vincent in *Revue Biblique*, January 1933, Vol. 42, 112.
ARAD	245–8	Figures 1, 3, 5, 6, 8, 9. Courtesy Institute of Archaeology, Tel Aviv University. Figures 2, 10. Courtesy Government Press Office, Tel Aviv. Figure 4. Jerusalem, Israel Museum, Israel Department of Antiquities Collection. Figure 7. Courtesy Israel Department of Antiquities, Jerusalem. Photos: Figure 1, David Harris, Jerusalem. Figure 5. J. Schweig, Jerusalem.
ARAM, ARAMEANS	253–4	After Y. Aharoni, *Carta's Atlas of the Bible,* Jerusalem, 1964.
ARAMA, ISAAC B. MOSES	258	Jerusalem, J.N.U.L.
ARAMAIC	261–2	J. Naveh, Jerusalem.
	284	Figures 1, 2. New York, Brooklyn Museum.
ARAM-DAMASCUS	288	From D. Abd el Kader in *Syria*, 26, Paris, 1949, pl. 8.
ARANNE, ZALMAN	289	Photo Y. Agor, Tel Aviv.
ARBEL	293	Courtesy Israel Department of Antiquities, Jerusalem.
ARCHAEOLOGY	304	After Y. Aharoni, *The Land of the Bible,* London, 1967.
	307–10	Courtesy Israel Department of Antiquities, Jerusalem.
	311–30	Figure 1. Courtesy Institute of Archaeology, Tel Aviv University. Figures 2, 3, 30, 32, 35. Courtesy Government Press Office, Tel Aviv. Figures 4, 5. From C.R. Lepsius, *Denkmaeler aus Aegypten und Aethiopia,* Berlin, 1849. Figures 7, 11, 12, 13, 14b, 17, 18, 20, 21, 23, 24, 28, 31, 34. Courtesy Israel Department of Antiquities, Jerusalem. Figures 8, 9. Jerusalem, Rockefeller Museum, Israel Department of Antiquities. Figure 10. Photo Richard Cleave, Jerusalem. Figures 14a, 19. London, British Museum. Figure 15. Courtesy Society for Near Eastern Studies in Japan, Tokyo. Figure 25. From Y. Meshorer, *Jewish Coins of the Second Temple Period,* Tel Aviv, 1966. Figure 26. Jerusalem, Israel Museum, Shrine of the Book, D. Samuel & Jeane H. Gottesman Center for Biblical Manuscripts. Figure 27. Jerusalem, Israel Museum, Israel Department of Antiquities Collection. Figure 29. Ditto, Photo David Harris, Jerusalem. 33. Courtesy Archaeological Survey of Israel, Jerusalem.
ARCHELAUS	333–4	Jerusalem, Bank of Israel Collection.
ARCHESYNAGOGOS	335	Courtesy Israel Department of Antiquities, Jerusalem. Photo David Harris, Jerusalem.
ARCHITECTURE AND ARCHITECTS	338–56	Figure 1. Jerusalem, Israel Museum, Department of Antiquities Collection. Figure 2. Jerusalem, Rockefeller Museum, Israel Department of Antiquities. Figure 3. After J.L. Starkey, *Palestine Exploration Fund*, 1936, pl. 9, 2. Figure 4. Photo Prior, Tel Aviv. Figure 5. After Bliss-Macalister, *Excavations in Palestine*, London, 1902, pl. 16. Figures 6,9, 30, Courtesy Israel Department of Antiquities, Jerusalem. Figure 7. Courtesy Ministry of Tourism, Jerusalem. Photo David Harris, Jerusalem. Figure 11. London, Royal Institute of British Architects Drawings Collection. Figure 12. Courtesy Civico Museo Revoltella, Galleria d'Arte Moderna, Trieste. Figure 13. Courtesy Mrs. E. Mendelson, San Francisco, Calif. Figure 16. Courtesy United Nations, Geneva. Figure 17. Courtesy Topografische Atlas Gemeentearchief, Amsterdam. Figure 19. Photo Chicago Architectural Photographic Co. Figure 20. Photo Gordon Sommers, Beverly Hills, Calif. Figure 21. Courtesy Yale University Art Gallery, New Haven, Conn. Figure 22. Photo Ezra Stoller (Esto), Mamaroneck, N.Y. Figure 23. Courtesy Albert Kahn Associates, Detroit, Mich. Figure 24. Photo Erich Locker, New York. Figures 25, 27, 29, 33. Courtesy Government Press Office, Tel Aviv. Figures 26, 28, 31. Courtesy Keren Hayesod, United Israel Appeal, Jerusalem. Figure 32. Photo Alfred Bernheim, Jerusalem. Figures 34, 37, 42, 50. Photo P. Gross, Tel Aviv. Figures 36, 40. Photo Werner Braun, Jerusalem.

Article	Column	Credit
		Figure 41. Photo Keren-Or, Haifa. Figure 43. Courtesy American Jewish Archives, Cincinnati, O. Figure 44. Courtesy Ministry of Tourism, Jerusalem. Photo J. Strajmayster. Figure 45. Photo David Harris, Jerusalem. Figure 46. Photo Henry Kalen, Winnipeg. Figure 47. Photo Panda Associates, Toronto. Figure 48. Photo L. Heskia. Figure 49. Photo Selwyn Pullan, N. Vancouver.
ARCHIVES	336–96	Figures 4, 5. Jerusalem, Rockefeller Museum, Israel Department of Antiquities. Figure 6. Courtesy Institute of Archaeology, Tel Aviv University. Photo Ricarda Schwerin, Jerusalem.
ARDON, MORDECAI	401	Photo Ricarda Schwerin, Jerusalem.
ARÉGA, LÉON	402	Photo Marc Foucault.
ARENDA	405	Photo David Harris, Jerusalem.
ARGENTINA	422–32	Figure 1. Courtesy Archivo de Prensa, Buenos Aires. Photo S. Zimberoff. Figures 3, 4, 5, 6, 7. Courtesy C.A.H.J.P., Jerusalem.
ARIPUL	438	Jerusalem, J.N.U.L.
ARK	451–6	Figure 1. Damascus, National Museum. Figure 2. Jerusalem, Israel Museum. Photo David Harris, Jerusalem. Figure 3. Paris, Musée de Cluny. Figure 4. (Mistakenly repeating caption for Figure 1). Ark from Urbino, Italy, first half of 16th century, with the Ten Commandments on the inside of the doors. New York, Jewish Museum. Courtesy Photographic Archive of Jewish Theological Seminary, New York. Photo Frank J. Darmstaedter. Figure 8. Photo Saul Miller, San Francisco, Calif. Figure 9. Courtesy Landesbildstelle, Berlin. Figure 11. Photo David Harris, Jerusalem.
ARK OF THE COVENANT	461–2	Figure 1. Photo Richard Cleave, Jerusalem. Figure 4. Damascus, National Museum.
	464	From Y. Aharoni, *Carta's Atlas of the Bible,* Jerusalem, 1964.
ARLOSOROFF, CHAIM	470	Courtesy Central Zionist Archives, Jerusalem.
	471	Jerusalem, State Archives.
ARMENIA	475	Photo David Harris, Jerusalem.
ARMISTICE AGREEMENTS	478–82	Figures 1, 6. Courtesy Government Press Office, Tel Aviv, Figures 2, 4, 5, 7. State Archives, Jerusalem. Figure 3. Courtesy Jewish Agency, Jerusalem.
ARNSTEIN	490–1	Figure 1. Lithograph by Franz Eybl, c. 1780. Figure 2. Mezzotint after painting by Pierre Guérin. Vienna, Historiches Museum der Stadt Wien. Photo Rudolf Stepanek.
ARONSON, NAUM LVOVICH	495	Courtesy Aimée Alexandre, Paris.
ART	501–90	Figures 1, 2, 8, 10. Jerusalem, Rockefeller Museum, Israel Department of Antiquities. Figure 3. Courtesy Jean Perrot, Paris. Figure 4. Jerusalem, Israel Museum, Israel Department of Antiquities Collection. Courtesy Pesach Bar-Adon. Figures 5, 7, 9. Jerusalem, Israel Museum, Israel Department of Antiquities Collection. Figures 6, 15, 26. Courtesy Israel Department of Antiquities, Jerusalem. Figure 11. Haifa, Dagon Collection, Archaeological Museum of Grain Handling in Israel. Figures 12, 14, 16. Courtesy Government Press Office, Tel Aviv. Figure 13. From E.L. Sukenik, *The Ancient Synagogue of Beth Alpha,* Jerusalem, 1932. Figure 17. Damascus, National Museum. Figure 20. Photo Prior, Tel Aviv. Figure 21. Courtesy Institute of Archaeology, Hebrew University, Jerusalem. Figure 22. Courtesy Sardis Expedition. Figure 27. Wuerzburg Mainfrankisches Museum. Photo Gundermann, Wuerzburg. Figure 28. Courtesy B. J. Hăba, Prague. Figure 29. Photo Fischer, Curaçao, N.A. Figures 32, 33, 40, 56, 58, 60, 62, 65, 71, 73, 74, 86, 87, 91, 92, 93, 95, 96, 99, 101, 105. Jerusalem, Israel Museum. (All photos David Harris, Jerusalem, except: Figure 33, David Harris and Ronald Sheridan. Figures 40, 95, Hillel Burger, Jerusalem. Figure 93, A. Hauser, Jerusalem.) Figure 34. Courtesy Photographic Archive of Jewish Theological Seminary of America, New York. Photo Frank J. Darmstaedter. Figures 35, 36, 37c, 37d. Jerusalem, J.N.U.L. Figures 38, 39. Formerly Detroit, Mich., Charles E. Feinberg Collection. Photo Manning Bros. Figure 42. Amsterdam, Jewish Museum. Figure. 43. Ardmore, Pa., Sigmund Harrison Collection. Figure 44. New York, Jewish Museum, Daniel M. Friedenberg Collection. Figures 45,46.

Article	Column	Credit
		Cecil Roth Collection. Figure 47. Liverpool, Williamson Gallery. Photo W. Cull, Birkenhead. Figures 48, 53, 55, 57, 59. New York, Oscar Gruss Collection. Photo Frank J. Darmstaedter. Figure 49. New York, Jewish Museum, Oscar Gruss Collection. Figure 50. Dublin, Municipal Museum of Modern Art. Photo Barry Mason. Figure 51. Beverly Hills, Calif., Norton Simon Collection. Figure 52. Formerly New York, Zagaysky Collection. Figure 54. Stockholm, National Museum. Figure 61. B'nai B'rith photo by Larry Franklin. Figure 63. London, National Portrait Gallery. Figure 64. London, William Margulies Collection. Figure 66. London, Alexander and Stella Margulies Collection. Figure 67. Courtesy Roland, Browse & Delbanco, London. Figure 68. New York, Albert A. List Collection. Photo John A. Ferrari. Figure 69. New York, Radio City Music Hall, Grand Lounge. Photo Impact, New York. Figure 70. Allentown, Pa., Allentown Art Museum, James A. Michener Foundation Collection. Photo Oliver Baker, New York. Figure 72. Cambridge, Mass., Fogg Art Museum, Harvard University. Figures 75, 81. Courtesy Yad Vashem Archives, Jerusalem. Figures 76, 79. Kibbutz Loḥamei ha-Getta'ot, Ghetto Fighters' House. Figures 77, 78, 80, 82 83. Jerusalem, Yad Vashem Museum. Figures 84, 85. Prague, State Jewish Museum. Figure 88. Courtesy Esther Pann, Jerusalem. Figures 89, 98, 107. Jerusalem, Bineth Gallery of Fine Arts. Photo David Harris, Jerusalem. Figures 90, 94, Tel Aviv Museum. Photo I. Zafrir, Tel Aviv. Figures 97, 98. Tel Aviv Museum. Figure 100. Photo Hayovel, Jerusalem. Figure 102. Haifa, Museum of Modern Art. Photo Keren-Or, Haifa. Figure 106. Tel Aviv, I. Zafrir Collection. Figure 109. Photo I. Zafrir, Tel Aviv. Figure 110.Courtesy Yona Palombo.
ART—Illustrations to Capsule Articles	613–44	Figure 1. Courtesy Mrs. Y. Dunkelman, Toronto. Figures 2, 6, 12, 13, 17, 20, 21, 24, 25, 28, 43, 44, 50, 52, 53. Jerusalem, Israel Museum. (All photos except Figures 25, 44, David Harris, Jerusalem.) Figure 4. Collection J. Achtman. Courtesy Mrs. Y. Dunkelman, Toronto. Figure 5. Photo O.E. Nelson, New York. Figures 7, 32, 33. Courtesy Marlborough Fine Art (London) Ltd. Figure 8. Philadelphia, Pa., Elizabeth C. Zeidman Collection. Figure 9. Photo P. Gross, Tel Aviv. Figure 10. Courtesy Z. Loewenthal, Belgrade. Figure 11. Courtesy Grace Borgenicht Gallery, New York. Photo O.E. Nelson, New York. Figure 16. Courtesy Robert Fraser Gallery, London. Figure 18. Atlanta, Ga., High Museum of Art. Photo Rudolph Burckhardt. Figure 19. London, Tate Gallery. Figures 22, 27. Copenhagen, Royal Museum of Fine Arts. Figure 26. New York, Whitney Museum of American Art. Photo Geoffrey Clements, New York. Figure 29. Photo Lew Rosenberg. Figure 30. London, Imperial War Museum. Figure 31. Albany, N. Y. Temple Beth Emeth. Photo David Alexander Studio, Albany. Figure 34. Philadelphia, Pennsylvania Academy of Fine Arts. Figures 35, 36. Courtesy Government Press Office, Tel Aviv. Figure 37. Courtesy J. & E. Hall, Dartford, Kent. Figures 38, 47. Courtesy Marlborough-Gerson Gallery, New York. Photo O. E. Nelson, New York. Figure 39. Photo I. Zafrir, Tel Aviv. Figure 40. New York, Solomon R. Guggenheim Museum. Figure 41. London, New Grafton Gallery. Courtesy Arts Council of Great Britain. Photo R. B. Fleming & Co., London. Figure 42. Jerusalem, Sir Isaac and Lady Wolfson Museum in Hechal Shlomo. Photo David Harris, Jerusalem. Figure 46. Courtesy Laurence Fleischmann Collection. Figure 48. Copenhagen, Churchill Park, donated by the artist's widow. Figure 51. Brookline, Mass., Temple Israel. Photo J.J. Breit, New York. Figure 54. Courtesy Leo Baeck Institute, New York. Figure 55. Haifa, Museum of Modern Art. Photo Keren-Or, Haifa. Figure 56. Courtesy, La Boetie, New York. Figure 57. Photo A. Hauser, Jerusalem. Figure 58. Courtesy Leo Castelli, New York. Photo Rudolph Burckhardt.
ARTOM, BENJAMIN	662	London, Jews' College, Montefiore Library. Courtesy Spanish & Portuguese Jews Congregation, London.

Article	Column	Credit
ARTOM, ELIA SAMUELE	663	Courtesy M.E. Artom, Jerusalem.
ASCETICISM	681–2	Photo Richard Cleave, Jerusalem.
ASCH, SHOLEM	684	Courtesy Leo Baeck Institute, New York.
ASCHAFFENBURG	687	Courtesy Aschaffenburg Municipality. Photo Fuchs.
ASCHERSON, PAUL	689	Jerusalem, J.N.U.L., Schwadron Collection.
ASCHHEIM, ISIDOR	689	Jerusalem, Israel Museum, on loan from Jerusalem Municipality. Photo David Harris, Jerusalem.
ASCOLI, ETTORE	691	Courtesy Unione Communitá Israelitiche Italiane, Rome.
ASCOLI, GRAZIADIO ISAIA	691	Jerusalem, J.N.U.L., Schwadron Collection.
ASHDOD	696–8	Figure 1. Jerusalem, Israel Museum. Photo David Harris, Jerusalem. Figure 2. From M. Avi-Yonah, *The Madaba Mosaic Map*, Jerusalem, 1954. Figure 3. Courtesy Government Press Office, Tel Aviv.
ASHDOT YA'AKOV	699	Courtesy J.N.F., Jerusalem.
ASHER	700	After Y. Aharoni in *Lexicon Biblicum*, Tel Aviv, 1965.
ASHERA	704	Courtesy Israel Department of Antiquities, Jerusalem.
ASHINSKY, AARON MORDECAI HALEVI	711	Courtesy Mrs. S.D. Ashinsky-Ebin, New York.
ASHKANASY, MAURICE	712	Courtesy The Herald & Weekly Times, Ltd., Melbourne.
ASHKELON	715–17	Figure 1. From W. Wreszinski, *Atlas zur altaegyptischen Kulturgeschichte*, 2, Leipzig, 1935. Figures 2, 3. Courtesy Israel Department of Antiquities, Jerusalem. Figure 4. From M. Avi-Yonah, *The Madaba Mosaic Map*, Jerusalem, 1954. Figures 5, 6, 7. Courtesy Government Press Office, Tel Aviv.
ASHKENAZI, SAUL B. MOSES HA-KOHEN	722	Jerusalem, J.N.U.L.
ASHTORETH	738	London, British Museum.
ASIMOV, ISAAC	749	Courtesy Marvin Sussman, *Newsday*, Long Island, N.Y.
ASSAF, SIMḤA	757	Courtesy Hebrew University, Jerusalem. Photo Prisma, Jerusalem.
ASSER	765	Jerusalem, J.N.U.L., Schwadron Collection.
ASTI	785	Photo Joseph Shaw, London.
ASTROLABE	786	Jerusalem, J.N.U.L.
ASTRONOMY	797–804	Figures 1, 2. Jerusalem, J.N.U.L. Figure 3. Prague, State Jewish Museum.
ASTRUC, JEAN	809	Courtesy Israel Medical Association, Jerusalem.
ASZOD, JUDAH B. ISRAEL	811	Jerusalem, J.N.U.L., Schwadron Collection.
ATAROT	813	Courtesy Central Zionist Archives, Jerusalem.
ATHALIAH	815–6	Paris, Musée du Louvre. Photo Arts Graphiques de la Cité, Paris.
ATHIAS	820	Jerusalem, J.N.U.L.
ATHLIT	821–2	Courtesy Archaeological Survey of Israel, Jerusalem.
ATLAN, JEAN	823	London, Alexander and Stella Margulies Collection.
ATLAS	826	Jerusalem, Israel Museum Photo Collection, Department of Ethnography. Photo Shulman, 1953.
ATLAS, JECHEZKIEL	828	Courtesy Ghetto Fighters' House, Kibbutz Loḥamei ha-Getta'ot.
ATONEMENT	831–2	Amsterdam, Stedelijk Museum.
ATRAN, FRANK Z.	832	Courtesy Anthony di Gesu.
AUB, MAX	839	Mexico City, Instituto Nacional de Bellas Artes y Letras.
AUCKLAND	839–40	Figure 1. Courtesy Lawrence D. Nathan, Auckland.
AUERBACH	841–2	After S. M. Auerbach, *The Auerbach Family*, London, 1957.
AUERBACH, ARNOLD JACOB	844	Photo Boston Celtics.
AUERNHEIMER, RAOUL	848	Courtesy Harry Zohn, W. Newton, Mass.
AUGSBURG	850	Courtesy Stadtbildstelle, Augsburg.
AUSCHWITZ	857–72	Figure 1. Based on E. Kulka, *Death Factory*, Jerusalem, 1966. Figures 2–16, Courtesy Yad Vashem Archives, Jerusalem. Figure 17. From E. Kulka, *Death Factory*.
AUSCHWITZ TRIALS	873	Courtesy Yad Vashem Archives, Jerusalem.
AUSTER, DANIEL	876	Courtesy Central Zionist Archives, Jerusalem.
AUSTERLITZ	876	Courtesy Israel Museum Archives, Jerusalem.
AUSTRALIA	879–86	Figure 1. Adelaide, Art Gallery of South Australia. By permission of the trustees. Photo Ballantyne & Partners. Figure 2. Cecil Roth Collection. Figure 3. Courtesy Israel Porush, Sydney. Figures 4, 5, 6, 9. Courtesy The Herald & Weekly Times, Ltd., Melbourne. Figures 7, 8. Photo Wolfgang Sievers, Melbourne.
AUTO DA FÉ	912	Madrid, Museo del Prado.

Article	Column	Credit
AUTOGRAPHS	913–8	Jerusalem, J.N.U.L., Schwadron Collection.
AUTONOMY	922–7	Figure 1. Courtesy Mrs. J. Szyk, New York. Figures 2, 3, 4, 5. Jerusalem, C.A.H.J.P.
AVEDAT	943–4	A. Negev, Jerusalem.
AVELIM	947	Courtesy Israel Department of Antiquities, Jerusalem.
AVIAD, YESHAYAHU	954	Courtesy Mrs. S. Aviad, Jerusalem. Photo ATP Press, Zurich.
AVI AVI	955–6	Example 1. Western Sephardi. After M.J. Benharoche-Baralia, *Chants hébraïques traditionnels en usage dans la communauté sephardie de Bayonne*, 1961, no. 131. Example 2. Eastern Sephardi, from Aleppo, as notated by A.Z. Idelsohn in Jerusalem. After his *Melodien*, vol. 4, no. 135. Example 3. Western Sephardi, from London. After E. Aguilar and D.A. de Sola, *Sephardi Melodies*, 1857, no. 59.
AVIDOV, ZVI	961	Photo Frence Grubner, Jerusalem.
AVIGAD, NAḤMAN	962	Courtesy Hebrew University, Jerusalem. Photo Moshe Ron, Jerusalem.
AVIGNON	965	Cecil Roth Collection.
AVINOAM, REUVEN	972	Photo J. Gordon, Tel Aviv.
AVINU MALKENU	973	Example 1. Yemen, after Idelsohn, *Melodien*, vol. 1, no. 99.
AVI-YONAH, MICHAEL	975	Courtesy Hebrew University, Jerusalem. Photo Ricarda Schwerin, Jerusalem.
AVODAH	978	West Ashkenazi, first version, after A. Baer, *Baal T'fillah*, 1883^2, no. 1442. Ditto, second version, as notated in Josef Goldstein's manuscript (c. 1791–99) in Idelsohn, *Melodien*, vol. 6, part 2, no. 25. East Ashkenazi, first version, after A. Marksohn and W. Wolff, *Auswahl alter Hebraeischer Synagogal-Melodien*, 1875^2, no. 9. Ditto, second version, after Idelsohn, *Melodien*, vol. 8, no. 189.
AVRIEL, EHUD	989	Courtesy Government Press Office, Tel Aviv.
AYALON, DAVID	993	Courtesy Hebrew University, Jerusalem. Photo Alfred Bernheim, Jerusalem.
AYLLON, SOLOMON B. JACOB	996	Cecil Roth Collection.
AZEKAH	1004	Courtesy Israel Department of Antiquities, Jerusalem.
AZOR	1012	Courtesy Israel Department of Antiquities, Jerusalem. Photo Benno Rothenberg, Tel Aviv.
AZULAI	1016	Photo David Harris, Jerusalem.

ADDITIONAL CREDITS

VOLUME 4

Article	Column	Credit
BARNERT, NATHAN	249	Photo Max Gavzy, New Jersey.
BARNETT, SIR LOUIS EDWARD	250	Courtesy Alexander Turnbull Library, Wellington, New Zealand. Photo S.P. Andrew, Wellington.
BAR-YEHUDAH, ISRAEL	285	Photo F. Schlesinger, Jerusalem.
BAYONNE	351	Photo Aubert, Bayonne.
BEHRMAN, SAMUEL NATHANIEL	397	Photo Lotte Jacobi, Hillsboro, N.H.
BEIT, SIR ALFRED	404	Johannesburg, Africana Museum.
BENTWICH (Herbert)	556	Courtesy Central Zionist Archives, Jerusalem.
BEN-YEHUDA, HEMDAH	569	Courtesy Central Zionist Archives, Jerusalem.
BERENSON, BERNARD	603	Courtesy *Harvard Bulletin*, Cambridge, Mass.
BERGNER, ELIZABETH	617	Courtesy BBC, London.
BERNBACH, WILLIAM	675	Photo Mottke Weissman.
BERNHEIMER, CHARLES LEOPOLD	680	Photo Pach Brothers, New York.
BESREDKA, ALEXANDER	703	Photo Institut Pasteur, Paris.
BIRTH	1050	Figure 1. Amsterdam, Bibliotheca Rosenthaliana.
BLACK, MISHA	1063	Photo Rex Coleman, Baron Studios Ltd., London.
BLAUSTEIN (Jacob)	1077	Photo Fabian Bachrach, New York.
BLOOD LIBEL	1127	Jerusalem, Yad Vashem Museum.
BLUME, PETER	1139	Photo Charles Uht, New York.
BODIN, JEAN	1162	London, British Museum.
BOHEMIA	1178	Figure 2. Courtesy State Jewish Museum, Prague.
BOLOGNA	1190	Figure 1. New York, Jewish Division, New York Public Library, Astor, Lenox and Tilden Foundations.

Article	Column	Credit
BONDI, AUGUST	1202	Topeka, Kansas State Historical Society.
BOORSTIN, DANIEL J.	1240	Courtesy Smithsonian Institution, Washington, D.C.
BRANDYS NAD LAREM	1307	Prague, State Jewish Museum.
BUDNYĚ NAD OHŘI	1458	Courtesy State Jewish Museum, Prague.
		VOLUME 5
CANADIAN JEWISH CONGRESS	114	Photo P.I.C., H.H. Deutsch, Montreal.
CAPP, AL	151	Photo New York News Inc.
CLEVELAND	612	Figure 3. Photo Rebman.
CONNECTICUT	898	Figure 1. From Morris Silverman, *Hartford Jews, 1659–1970*. Hartford, Conn., 1971.
DA COSTA, JOSEPH MENDES	1221	Amsterdam, Stedelijk Museum.
DAMASCUS, BOOK OF COVENANT OF	1247	Cambridge University Library.
DARMESTETER, ARSÈNE	1305	Jerusalem, J.N.U.L.
		VOLUME 6
DIAMOND, DAVID	3	Photo Louis Ouzer, Rochester, New York.
EBAN, ABBA	344	Figure 2. Photo United Nations, New York.
ELEAZAR BEN JAIR	591	Photo Zev Radovan, Jerusalem.
FOERDER, YESHAYAHU	1373	Photo Sam Frank, Tel Aviv.
		VOLUME 7
GERMANY	502	Figure 26. Courtesy Government Press Office, Tel Aviv.
GRATZ COLLEGE	861	Photo Sonnee Gottlieb.
HA-YOM	1500	Jerusalem, J.N.U.L.
		VOLUME 8
HENRIQUES (Sir Basil)	328	Photo Camera Press, Ltd., London.
HIGH PRIEST	473	Jerusalem, Moshe and Alice Shalvi Collection.
HOMILETIC LITERATURE	959–60	Figures 1, 2, 3. Jerusalem, J.N.U.L.
IBN ARDUT, ḤAYYIM JOSEPH B. AZRIEL	1156	Jerusalem, J.N.U.L.
		VOLUME 9
ISRAEL, STATE OF		
(Aliyah and Absorption)	522	Figure 7. Courtesy Keren Hayesod-United Israel Appeal, Jerusalem.
(Cultural Life)	1002	Figure 2. Courtesy Government Press Office, Tel Aviv.
	1020	Figure 14. Photo Werner Braun, Jerusalem.
JACOBSON, DAN	1239	Photo *Hampstead and Highgate Express*, London.
JERUSALEM	1451	Figure 41. Jerusalem, Israel Museum, Feuchtwanger Collection, donated by Baruch and Ruth Rappaport.
	1501–2	Figure 99. Photo Werner Braun, Jerusalem.
	1587	Figure 140. Photo Sadeh, Haifa.
	1588	Figure 142. Photo David Harris, Jerusalem.
		VOLUME 10
JONAH, BOOK OF	177	Figure 5. New York, Metropolitan Museum of Art, Joseph Pulitzer Bequest.
KATZ, BENZION	822	Photo I. Berez, Tel Aviv.
KLEIN, PHILIP	1101	Courtesy Elizabeth Isaacs, New York.
KOFFKA, KURT	1134	Courtesy Molly Harrower, Greenport, N.Y.
		VOLUME 11
LIEBERMAN, SAUL	219	Photo John H. Popper, New York.
LION	267	Figure 6. Photo Karel Minc, Prague.
LUZ, KADISH	594	Photo Hutman, Jerusalem.
MAINZ	789	Figure 1. Mainz, Mittelrheinisches Landesmuseum.
MANCHESTER	859	Courtesy Manchester Great and New Synagogue.
MENDEZ	1342	Photo John R. Freeman, London.
MILITARY SERVICE	1556	Figure 5. From *Russian Jews in the War*, London.
	1557	Figure 6. Nuremberg, Germanisches Nationalmuseum.

Article	Column	Credit
		VOLUME 12
MOSES, SIEGFRIED	415	Photo Alfred Bernheim, Jerusalem.
MOTION PICTURES	455–64	Figure 5. Courtesy Columbia Picture Corporation, New York. Figure 14. Courtesy United Artists Corporation, New York. Figure 16. Courtesy Twentieth Century-Fox Film Corporation, New York.
NATURE RESERVES IN ISRAEL	892	Photo Werner Braun and David Harris, Jerusalem.
NE'EMAN, YUVAL	922	Photo Nachum Gutman, Tel Aviv.
NE'ILAH	944	Photo Klaus G. Beyer, Weimar, Germany.
NETHERLANDS	978	Photo David Harris, Jerusalem.
NEW YORK CITY	1113–4	Figure 30. Courtesy State of Israel Bonds Organization, Jerusalem. Figure 33. Photo Whitestone, New York.
NIRENBERG, MARSHALL W,	1173	Courtesy N.I.H., Bethesda, Md.
OILS	1349	Figure 2. Photo David Harris, Jerusalem.
OLITZKI, A.L.	1363	Photo David Harris, Jerusalem.
OPPENHEIMER, J. ROBERT	1430	Photo David Rubinger, Jerusalem.
ORT	1483	Figure 3. Photo I. L. O., Geneva.
		VOLUME 13
PAPYRUS	71	Photo Yosaif Cohain.
PINES, SHLOMO	534	Photo J. Goren, Jerusalem.
RABBINICAL COUNCIL OF AMERICA	1462	Photo Joseph Brown, New York.
		VOLUME 14
ROMBERG, SIGMUND	240	Courtesy of The New York Public Library Astor, Lenox and Tilden Foundations.
ROSH PINNAH	312	Photo Z. Kluger, Orient Press Photo Co., Tel Aviv.
SABBATH	569	Figure 10. Photo David Harris, Jerusalem.
SALK, JONAS EDWARD	686	Courtesy The National Foundation, March of Dimes, White Plains, N.Y.
SAMARKAND	759	London, University College, Mocatta Library and Jewish Historical Society of England.
SAN ANTONIO	823	Photo Zavell Smith, San Antonio, Texas.
SAUL	915	Figure 2. London, Lambeth Palace Library, Ms. 3, fol. 51.
SCHOMBERG (English Family)	992	Figure 1. Courtesy of the Trustees, The National Gallery, London.
SCHWARZ-BART, ANDRÉ	1028	Photo Jean-Pierre Ducatez, Paris.
SEALS	1077	Figure 10. Jerusalem, Israel Museum. Photo Zev Radovan, Jerusalem.
SHRAGAI, SHLOMO Z.	1461	Photo Hutman, Jerusalem.
		VOLUME 15
SOUTH AFRICA	196	From *South African Jewry,* edited by L. Feldberg, Johannesburg, 1967–68.
SUZMAN, HELEN	541	Photo H. Koester, Johannesburg.
SWITZERLAND	559	Figure 5. Photo Diethard Koenig, Bremgarten.
SYNAGOGUE	605	Figure 3. Photo J. Ehm.
TALMON	750	Photo Frence Grubner, Jerusalem.
TALMUD	777	Cod. Or. 4720, Vol. II, F. 310[1].
TANNAIM	801	Caption omitted. Principal *tannaim* of Ereẓ Israel, c. 20–c. 200 C.E.
TEMPLE	960	Photo Werner Braun, Jerusalem.
TEMPLE MOUNT	991–2	Plan based on map published by I.D.F. Publications Department, Tel Aviv.
THEATER	1053	Figure 2. Photo David Harris, Jerusalem.
TRANSNISTRIA	1330	Courtesy Yad Vashem Archives, Jerusalem.
		VOLUME 16
VENICE	101	London, British Museum, 01903, a. 14.
WARSAW	335	Photo David Harris, Jerusalem.
	351–2	Courtesy Robert J. Milch, New York.
WEIZMANN (family)	423	Courtesy Meyer W. Weisgal.
WEIZMANN, CHAIM	423	Figure 1. Courtesy Meyer W. Weisgal.
WOLF, EDWIN	603	From *American Jewish Yearbook,* Vol. 27, 1935–36, Philadelphia, Pa.

COLOR PLATES

The majority of the color plates in the Encyclopaedia Judaica were printed by E. Lewin-Epstein Ltd., Bat Yam, Israel. The photographers have been credited in the relevant places, but the following additions have to be made:

David Harris, Jerusalem.	Volume 3 Between columns 300 and 301
	Volume 4 Between columns 844 and 845
	Volume 7 Between columns 1068 and 1069
	Volume 8 Between columns 1016 and 1017
	Volume 10 Between columns 108 and 109
	Volume 11 Between columns 748 and 749
	Volume 14 Between columns 12 and 13
INTERFOTO MTI, Budapest.	Volume 7 Between columns 748 and 749
H.R. Lippmann, New York.	Volume 3 Between columns 988 and 989

The color plates in the Israel section were printed by Keter Publishing House, Jerusalem. The remainder of the color plates in the Encyclopaedia were printed by United Artists Ltd., Tel Aviv. They appear in the volumes and between the columns specified below:

VOLUME 3	908–09	Photo Norman Kurshan Inc., New York.
VOLUME 4	364–65	
	812–13	Photo David Harris, Jerusalem.
	908–09	
	1068–69	
VOLUME 6	428–29	
	1068–69	Photo INTERFOTO MTI, Budapest.
VOLUME 7	396–97	Photo David Harris, Jerusalem.
	812–13	
	876–77	Photo David Harris, Jerusalem.
	1132–33	
	1196–97	Photo David Harris, Jerusalem.
	1324–25	
	1388–89	
VOLUME 8	1081–82	
	1145–46	
	1209–10	
	1273–74	
	1337–38	
VOLUME 9	44–45	
VOLUME 11	620–21	Photo David Harris, Jerusalem.
	684–85	Photo INTERFOTO MTI, Budapest.
	876–77	Photo David Harris, Jerusalem.
	1068–69	
	1132–33	
	1356–57	
VOLUME 12	428–29	
VOLUME 14	1324–25	Photo David Harris, Jerusalem.
	1516–17	
VOLUME 15	492–93	
VOLUME 16	616–17	
	744–45	

SUPPLEMENTARY LISTS

HUNDRED-YEAR JEWISH CALENDAR, 1920–2020

Introduction. This calendar gives the Jewish calendar and its Gregorian equivalent for a period of a century. It also marks festivals and the weekly portions of the Torah reading. Two modifications should be noted for use in Israel. The first is that Second Days of Festivals (except Rosh Ha-Shanah) are not holidays in Israel. Such days are indicated by vertical stripes. The other is that when the Second Day of a festival in the Diaspora falls on a Sabbath (in which case a special portion of the Law replaces the regular Sabbath reading), there will be a discrepancy during the following weeks between the reading in Israel and the reading outside Israel. Eventually this is compensated by having two portions read in one week in the Diaspora but not in Israel. Such variations can occur during the readings of the Books of Exodus, Leviticus, and Numbers. An Israel calendar should be consulted to discover where such discrepancies occur.

Notes. The Gregorian and the Jewish years are given at the top of each half page. The Jewish New Year (Tishri 1) falls in September/October.

The names of the Hebrew months are printed in bold type in the relevant columns. The beginning of the month (Rosh Ḥodesh) is indicated by the letters R.Ḥ.

The figures 1–31 at the extreme left of the page are the days of the Gregorian month. The corresponding days of the Hebrew months are printed in light type in the columns for each of the twelve months. The figures in heavy type in these columns indicate the Sabbath, with the appropriate weekly portion of the Law in italics in the box to the right. The major holy days are boxed on a dark background, the second day observed in the Diaspora appearing on a striped background below.

The postponement of a fast falling on the Sabbath is indicated by an arrow.

The word Omer indicates the day on which the Counting of the Omer starts.

1920

5680/81 תר״פ / תרפ״א

	January	February	March	April	May	June	July	August	September	October	November	December
1	10 **Tevet** Fast	12	11	13	**13** *Aḥarei Mot Kedoshim*	15	15	17	18	19 Ḥol ha-	20	20
2	11	13	12	14	14	16	16	18	19	**20** Mo'ed	21	21
3	**12** *Va-Yeḥi*	14	13 Ta'anit Esther	**15** Pesaḥ	15	17	**17** *Balak*	19	20	21 Hoshana Rabba	22	22
4	13	15	14 Purim	16 Omer	16	18	18 Fast	20	**21** *Ki Tavo*	22 Shemini Aẓeret	23	**23** *Va-Yeshev*
5	14	16	15 Shushan Purim	17 Ḥol ha-Mo'ed	17	**19** *Be-Ha'alotkha*	19	21	22	23 Simḥat Torah *Ve-Zot Ha-Berakhah*	24	24
6	15	17	**16** *Ki Tissa*	18	18 Lag ba-Omer	20	20	22	23	24	**25** *Ḥayyei Sarah*	25 Ḥanukkah 1
7	16	**18** *Yitro*	17	19	19	21	21	**23** *Ekev*	24	25	26	26 2
8	17	19	18	20	**20** *Emor*	22	22	24	25	26	27	27 3
9	18	20	19	21 Pesaḥ	21	23	23	25	26	**27** *Bereshit*	28	28 4
10	**19** *Shemot*	21	20	**22**	22	24	**24** *Pinḥas*	26	27	28	29	29 5
11	20	22	21	23	23	25	25	27	**28** *Niẓẓavim*	29	30 R.Ḥ.	**30** R.Ḥ. *Mi-Keẓ* 6
12	21	23	22	24	24	**26** *Shelaḥ*	26	28	29	30 R.Ḥ.	1 **Kislev** R.Ḥ.	1 **Tevet** R.Ḥ. 7
13	22	24	**23** *Va-Yakhel Pekudei* Parah	25	25	27	27	29	1 **Tishri** Rosh Ha-Shanah	1 **Ḥeshvan** R.Ḥ.	**2** *Toledot*	2 8
14	23	**25** *Mishpatim* Shekalim	24	26	26	28	28	**30** R.Ḥ. *Re'eh*	2	2	3	3
15	24	26	25	27	**27** *Be-Har Be-Ḥukkotai*	29	29	1 **Elul** R.Ḥ.	3 Fast	3	4	4
16	25	27	26	28	28	30 R.Ḥ.	1 **Av** R.Ḥ.	2	4	**4** *No'aḥ*	5	5
17	**26** *Va-Era*	28	27	**29** *Shemini*	29	1 **Tammuz** R.Ḥ.	**2** *Mattot Masei*	3	5	5	6	6
18	27	29	28	30 R.Ḥ.	1 **Sivan** R.Ḥ.	2	3	4	**6** *Va-Yelekh* Shabbat Shuvah	6	7	**7** *Va-Yiggash*
19	28	30 R.Ḥ.	29	1 **Iyyar** R.Ḥ.	2	**3** *Koraḥ*	4	5	7	7	8	8
20	29	1 **Adar** R.Ḥ.	**1** **Nisan** R.Ḥ. *Va-Yikra* Ha-Ḥodesh	2	3	4	5	6	8	8	**9** *Va-Yeẓe*	9
21	1 **Shevat** R.Ḥ.	**2** *Terumah*	2	3	4	5	6	**7** *Shofetim*	9	9	10	10 Fast
22	2	3	3	4	**5** *Be-Midbar*	6	7	8	10 Yom Kippur	10	11	11
23	3	4	4	5	6 Shavuot	7	8	9	11	**11** *Lekh Lekha*	12	12
24	**4** *Bo*	5	5	**6** *Tazri'a Meẓora*	7	8	**9** *Devarim* Tishah be-Av	10	12	12	13	13
25	5	6	6	7	8	9	10 Fast	11	**13** *Ha'azinu*	13	14	**14** *Va-Yeḥi*
26	6	7	7	8	9	**10** *Ḥukkat*	11	12	14	14	15	15
27	7	8	**8** *Ẓav* Shabbat ha-Gadol	9	10	11	12	13	15 Sukkot	15	**16** *Va-Yishlaḥ*	16
28	8	**9** *Teẓavveh* Zakhor	9	10	11	12	13	**14** *Ki Teẓe*	16	16	17	17
29	9	10	10	11	**12** *Naso*	13	14	15	17 Ḥol ha-	17	18	18
30	10		11	12	13	14	15	16	18 Mo'ed	**18** *Va-Yera*	19	19
31	**11** *Be-Shallaḥ*		12		14		**16** *Va-Etḥannan*	17		19		20

1921

5681/82 תרפ״א / תרפ״ב

	January	February	March	April	May	June	July	August	September	October	November	December
1	**21 Tevet** *Shemot*	23	21	22	23	24	25	26	28	**28** *Nizzavim*	30 R. H.	30 R. H.
2	22	24	22	**23** *Shemini Parah*	24	25	**26** *Shelah*	27	29	29	1 **Heshvan** R. H.	1 **Kislev** R. H.
3	23	25	23	24	25	26	27	28	**30** R. H. *Re'eh*	**1 Tishri** Rosh Ha-Shanah	2	**2** *Toledot*
4	24	26	24	25	26	**27** *Be-Hukkotai*	28	29	1 **Elul** R. H.	2	3	3
5	25	**27** *Mishpatim*	**25** *Va-Yakhel* Shekalim	26	27	28	29	1 **Av** R. H.	2	3 Fast	**4** *No'ah*	4
6	26	28	26	27	28	29	30 R. H.	**2** *Mattot Masei*	3	4	5	5
7	27	29	27	28	**29** *Aharei Mot*	1 **Sivan** R. H.	1 **Tammuz** R. H.	3	4	5	6	6
8	**28** *Va-Era*	30 R. H.	28	29	30 R. H.	2	2	4	5	**6** *Va-Yelekh* Shabbat Shuvah	7	7
9	29	1 **Adar I** R. H.	29	**1 Nisan** R. H. *Tazri'a* Ha-Hodesh	1 **Iyyar** R. H.	3	**3** *Korah*	5	6	7	8	8
10	1 **Shevat** R. H.	2	30 R. H.	2	2	4	4	6	**7** *Shofetim*	8	9	**9** *Va-Yeze*
11	2	3	1 **Adar II** R. H.	3	3	**5** *Be-Midbar*	5	7	8	9	10	10
12	3	**4** *Terumah*	**2** *Pekudei*	4	4	6 Shavuot	6	8	9	10 Yom Kippur	**11** *Lekh Lekha*	11
13	4	5	3	5	5	7	7	**9** *Devarim* Tishah be-Av	10	11	12	12
14	5	6	4	6	**6** *Kedoshim*	8	8	10 Fast	11	12	13	13
15	**6** *Bo*	7	5	7	7	9	9	11	12	**13** *Ha'azinu*	14	14
16	7	8	6	**8** *Mezora* Shabbat ha-Gadol	8	10	**10** *Hukkat*	12	13	14	15	15
17	8	9	7	9	9	11	11	13	**14** *Ki Teze*	15 Sukkot	16	**16** *Va-Yishlah*
18	9	10	8	10	10	**12** *Naso*	12	14	15	16	17	17
19	10	**11** *Tezavveh*	**9** *Va-Yikra* Zakhor	11	11	13	13	15	16	17 Hol ha-Mo'ed	**18** *Va-Yera*	18
20	11	12	10	12	12	14	14	**16** *Va-Ethannan*	17	18	19	19
21	12	13	11	13	**13** *Emor*	15	15	17	18	19	20	20
22	**13** *Be-Shallah*	14	12	14	14	16	16	18	19	**20**	21	21
23	14	15	13 Ta'anit Esther	**15** Pesah	15	17	**17** *Balak*	19	20	21 Hoshana Rabba	22	22
24	15	16	14 Purim	16 Omer	16	18	18 Fast	20	**21** *Ki Tavo*	22 Shemini Azeret	23	**23** *Va-Yeshev*
25	16	17	15 Shushan Purim	17 Hol ha-Mo'ed	17	**19** *Be-Ha'alotkha*	19	21	22	23 Simhat Torah *Ve-Zot Ha-Berakhah*	24	24
26	17	**18** *Ki Tissa*	**16** *Zav*	18	18 Lag ba-Omer	20	20	22	23	24	**25** *Hayyei Sarah*	25 Hanukkah 1
27	18	19	17	19	19	21	21	**23** *Ekev*	24	25	26	26 2
28	19	20	18	20	**20** *Be-Har*	22	22	24	25	26	27	27 3
29	**20** *Yitro*		19	21 Pesah	21	23	23	25	26	**27** *Bereshit*	28	28 4
30	21		20	**22**	22	24	**24** *Pinhas*	26	27	28	29	29 5
31	22		21		23		25	27		29		**30** R. H. *Mi-Kez* 6

1922

5682/83 תרפ״ב / תרפ״ג

	January	February	March	April	May	June	July	August	September	October	November	December
1	1 **Tevet** R. H. 7	3	1 **Adar** R. H.	**3** *Va-Yikra*	3	5	**5** *Korah*	7	8	9	10	11
2	2 8	4	2	4	4	6 Shavuot	6	8	**9** *Ki Teze*	10 Yom Kippur	11	**12** *Va-Yeze*
3	3	5	3	5	5	7	7	9 Tishah be-Av	10	11	12	13
4	4	**6** *Bo*	**4** *Terumah*	6	6	8	8	10	11	12	**13** *Lekh Lekha*	14
5	5	7	5	7	7	9	9	**11** *Va-Ethannan*	12	13	14	15
6	6	8	6	8	**8** *Aharei Mot Kedoshim*	10	10	12	13	14	15	16
7	**7** *Va-Yiggash*	9	7	9	9	11	11	13	14	**15** Sukkot	16	17
8	8	10	8	**10** *Zav* Shabbat ha-Gadol	10	12	**12** *Hukkat Balak*	14	15	16	17	18
9	9	11	9	11	11	13	13	15	**16** *Ki Tavo*	17 Hol ha-Mo'ed	18	**19** *Va-Yishlah*
10	10 Fast	12	10	12	12	**14** *Naso*	14	16	17	18	19	20
11	11	**13** *Be-Shallah*	**11** *Tezavveh* Zakhor	13	13	15	15	17	18	19	**20** *Va-Yera*	21
12	12	14	12	14	14	16	16	**18** *Ekev*	19	20	21	22
13	13	15	13 Ta'anit Esther	15 Pesah	**15** *Emor*	17	17 Fast	19	20	21 Hoshana Rabba	22	23
14	**14** *Va-Yehi*	16	14 Purim	16 Omer	16	18	18	20	21	**22** Shemini Azeret	23	24
15	15	17	15 Shushan Purim	**17** Hol ha-Mo'ed	17	19	**19** *Pinhas*	21	22	23 Simhat Torah *Ve-Zot Ha-Berakhah*	24	25 Hanukkah 1
16	16	18	16	18	18 Lag ba-Omer	20	20	22	**23** *Nizzavim Va-Yelekh*	24	25	**26** *Va-Yeshev* 2
17	17	19	17	19	19	**21** *Be-Ha'alotkha*	21	23	24	25	26	27 3
18	18	**20** *Yitro*	**18** *Ki Tissa* Parah	20	20	22	22	24	25	26	**27** *Hayyei Sarah*	28 4
19	19	21	19	21 Pesah	21	23	23	**25** *Re'eh*	26	27	28	29 5
20	20	22	20	22	**22** *Be-Har Be-Hukkotai*	24	24	26	27	28	29	1 **Tevet** R. H. 6
21	**21** *Shemot*	23	21	23	23	25	25	27	28	**29** *Bereshit*	1 **Kislev** R. H.	2 7
22	22	24	22	**24** *Shemini*	24	26	**26** *Mattot Masei*	28	29	30 R. H.	2	3 8
23	23	25	23	25	25	27	27	29	**1 Tishri** Rosh Ha-Shanah	1 **Heshvan** R. H.	3	**4** *Mi-Kez*
24	24	26	24	26	26	**28** *Shelah*	28	30 R. H.	2	2	4	5
25	25	**27** *Mishpatim* Shekalim	**25** *Va-Yakhel Pekudei* Ha-Hodesh	27	27	29	29	1 **Elul** R. H.	3 Fast	3	**5** *Toledot*	6
26	26	28	26	28	28	30 R. H.	1 **Av** R. H.	**2** *Shofetim*	4	4	6	7
27	27	29	27	29	**29** *Be-Midbar*	1 **Tammuz** R. H.	2	3	5	5	7	8
28	**28** *Va-Era*	30 R. H.	28	30 R. H.	1 **Sivan** R. H.	2	3	4	6	**6** *No'ah*	8	9
29	29		29	1 **Iyyar** R. H. *Tazri'a Mezora*	2	3	**4** *Devarim*	5	7	7	9	10 Fast
30	1 **Shevat** R. H.		1 **Nisan** R. H.	2	3	4	5	6	**8** *Ha'azinu* Shabbat Shuvah	8	10	**11** *Va-Yiggash*
31	2		2		4		6	7		9		12

1923

5683/84 תרפ״ג / תרפ״ד

	January	February	March	April	May	June	July	August	September	October	November	December
1	13 **Tevet**	15	13 Ta'anit Esther	15 Pesaḥ	15	17	17 Fast	19	20 *Ki Tavo*	21 Hoshana Rabba	22	23 *Va-Yeshev*
2	14	16	14 Purim	16 Omer	16	18 *Be-Ha'alotkha*	18	20	21	22 Shemini Aẓeret	23	24
3	15	17 *Be-Shallaḥ*	15 *Teẓavveh* Shushan Purim	17	17	19	19	21	22	23 Simḥat Torah *Ve-Zot Ha-Berakhah*	24 *Ḥayyei Sarah*	25 Ḥanukkah 1
4	16	18	16	18 Ḥol ha-Mo'ed	18 Lag ba-Omer	20	20	22 *Ekev*	23	24	25	26 2
5	17	19	17	19	19 *Emor*	21	21	23	24	25	26	27 3
6	18 *Va-Yeḥi*	20	18	20	20	22	22	24	25	26 *Bereshit*	27	28 4
7	19	21	19	21 Pesaḥ	21	23	23 *Pinḥas*	25	26	27	28	29 5
8	20	22	20	22	22	24	24	26	27 *Niẓẓavim*	28	29	30 *Mi-Keẓ* R. Ḥ. 6
9	21	23	21	23	23	25 *Shelaḥ*	25	27	28	29	1 **Kislev** R. Ḥ.	1 **Tevet** R. Ḥ. 7
10	22	24 *Yitro*	22 *Ki Tissa* Parah	24	24	26	26	28	29	30 R. Ḥ.	2 *Toledot*	2 8
11	23	25	23	25	25	27	27	29 *Re'eh*	1 **Tishri** Rosh Ha-Shanah	1 **Ḥeshvan** R. Ḥ.	3	3
12	24	26	24	26	26 *Be-Har Be-Ḥukkotai*	28	28	30 R. Ḥ.	2	2	4	4
13	25 *Shemot*	27	25	27	27	29	29	1 **Elul** R. Ḥ.	3 Fast	3 *No'aḥ*	5	5
14	26	28	26	28 *Shemini*	28	30 R. Ḥ.	1 **Av** R. Ḥ. *Mattot Masei*	2	4	4	6	6
15	27	29	27	29	29	1 **Tammuz** R. Ḥ.	2	3	5 *Va-Yelekh* Shabbat Shuvah	5	7	7 *Va-Yiggash*
16	28	30 R. Ḥ.	28	30 R. Ḥ.	1 **Sivan** R. Ḥ.	2 *Koraḥ*	3	4	6	6	8	8
17	29	1 **Adar** R. Ḥ. *Mishpatim* Shekalim	29 *Va-Yakhel Pekudei* Ha-Ḥodesh	1 **Iyyar** R. Ḥ.	2	3	4	5	7	7	9 *Va-Yeẓe*	9
18	1 **Shevat** R. Ḥ.	2	1 **Nisan** R. Ḥ.	2	3	4	5	6 *Shofetim*	8	8	10	10 Fast
19	2	3	2	3	4 *Be-Midbar*	5	6	7	9	9	11	11
20	3 *Va-Era*	4	3	4	5	6	7	8	10 Yom Kippur	10 *Lekh Lekha*	12	12
21	4	5	4	5 *Tazri'a Meẓora*	6 Shavuot	7	8 *Devarim*	9	11	11	13	13
22	5	6	5	6	7	8	9 Tishah be-Av	10	12 *Ha'azinu*	12	14	14 *Va-Yeḥi*
23	6	7	6	7	8	9 *Ḥukkat*	10	11	13	13	15	15
24	7	8 *Terumah* Zakhor	7 *Va-Yikra*	8	9	10	11	12	14	14	16 *Va-Yishlaḥ*	16
25	8	9	8	9	10	11	12	13 *Ki Teẓe*	15 Sukkot	15	17	17
26	9	10	9	10	11 *Naso*	12	13	14	16	16	18	18
27	10 *Bo*	11	10	11	12	13	14	15	17	17 *Va-Yera*	19	19
28	11	12	11	12 *Aḥarei Mot Kedoshim*	13	14	15 *Va-Etḥannan*	16	18 Ḥol ha-Mo'ed	18	20	20
29	12		12	13	14	15	16	17	19	19	21	21 *Shemot*
30	13		13	14	15	16 *Balak*	17	18	20	20	22	22
31	14		14 *Ẓav* Shabbat ha-Gadol		16		18	19		21		23

1924

5684/85 תרפ״ד / תרפ״ה

	January	February	March	April	May	June	July	August	September	October	November	December
1	24 **Tevet**	26	25 *Va-Yakhel* Shekalim	26	27	28	29	1 **Av** R. Ḥ.	2	3 Fast	4 *No'aḥ*	4
2	25	27 *Mishpatim*	26	27	28	29	30 R. Ḥ.	2 *Mattot Masei*	3	4	5	5
3	26	28	27	28	29 *Aḥarei Mot*	1 **Sivan** R. Ḥ.	1 **Tammuz** R. Ḥ.	3	4	5	6	6
4	27	29	28	29	30 R. Ḥ.	2	2	4	5	6 *Va-Yelekh* Shabbat Shuvah	7	7
5	28 *Va-Era*	30 R. Ḥ.	29	1 **Nisan** R. Ḥ. *Tazri'a* Ha-Ḥodesh	1 **Iyyar** R. Ḥ.	3	3 *Koraḥ*	5	6	7	8	8
6	29	1 **Adar I** R. Ḥ.	30 R. Ḥ.	2	2	4	4	6	7 *Shofetim*	8	9	9 *Va-Yeẓe*
7	1 **Shevat** R. Ḥ.	2	1 **Adar II** R. Ḥ.	3	3	5 *Be-Midbar*	5	7	8	9	10	10
8	2	3	2 *Pekudei*	4	4	6 Shavuot	6	8	9	10 Yom Kippur	11 *Lekh Lekha*	11
9	3	4 *Terumah*	3	5	5	7	7	9 *Devarim* Tishah be-Av	10	11	12	12
10	4	5	4	6	6 *Kedoshim*	8	8	10 Fast	11	12	13	13
11	5	6	5	7	7	9	9	11	12	13 *Ha'azinu*	14	14
12	6 *Bo*	7	6	8 *Meẓora* Shabbat ha-Gadol	8	10	10 *Ḥukkat*	12	13	14	15	15
13	7	8	7	9	9	11	11	13	14 *Ki Teẓe*	15 Sukkot	16	16 *Va-Yishlaḥ*
14	8	9	8	10	10	12 *Naso*	12	14	15	16	17	17
15	9	10	9 *Va-Yikra* Zakhor	11	11	13	13	15	16	17	18 *Va-Yera*	18
16	10	11 *Teẓavveh*	10	12	12	14	14	16 *Va-Etḥannan*	17	18 Ḥol ha-Mo'ed	19	19
17	11	12	11	13	13 *Emor*	15	15	17	18	19	20	20
18	12	13	12	14	14	16	16	18	19	20	21	21
19	13 *Be-Shallaḥ*	14	13 Ta'anit Esther	15 Pesaḥ	15	17	17 *Balak*	19	20	21 Hoshana Rabba	22	22
20	14	15	14 Purim	16 Omer	16	18	18 Fast	20	21 *Ki Tavo*	22 Shemini Aẓeret	23	23 *Va-Yeshev*
21	15	16	15 Shushan Purim	17	17	19 *Be-Ha'alotkha*	19	21	22	23 Simḥat Torah *Ve-Zot Ha-Berakhah*	24	24
22	16	17	16 *Ẓav*	18 Ḥol ha-Mo'ed	18 Lag ba-Omer	20	20	22	23	24	25 *Ḥayyei Sarah*	25 Ḥanukkah 1
23	17	18 *Ki Tissa*	17	19	19	21	21	23 *Ekev*	24	25	26	26 2
24	18	19	18	20	20 *Be-Har*	22	22	24	25	26	27	27 3
25	19	20	19	21 Pesaḥ	21	23	23	25	26	27 *Bereshit*	28	28 4
26	20 *Yitro*	21	20	22	22	24	24 *Pinḥas*	26	27	28	29	29 5
27	21	22	21	23	23	25	25	27	28 *Niẓẓavim*	29	30 R. Ḥ.	30 *Mi-Keẓ* R. Ḥ. 6
28	22	23	22	24	24	26 *Shelaḥ*	26	28	29	30 R. Ḥ.	1 **Kislev** R. Ḥ.	1 **Tevet** R. Ḥ. 7
29	23	24	23 *Shemini* Parah	25	25	27	27	29	1 **Tishri** Rosh Ha-Shanah	1 **Ḥeshvan** R. Ḥ.	2 *Toledot*	2 8
30	24		24	26	26	28	28	30 R. Ḥ. *Re'eh*	2	2	3	3
31	25		25		27 *Be-Ḥukkotai*		29	1 **Elul** R. Ḥ.		3		4

1925

5685/86 תרפ"ה / תרפ"ו

	January	February	March	April	May	June	July	August	September	October	November	December
1	5 **Tevet**	7	5	7	7	9	9	**11** *Va-Etḥannan*	12	13	14	14
2	6	8	6	8	**8** *Aḥarei Mot Kedoshim*	10	10	12	13	14	15	15
3	**7** *Va-Yiggash*	9	7	9	9	11	11	13	14	**15** Sukkot	16	16
4	8	10	8	**10** *Ẓav* Shabbat ha-Gadol	10	12	**12** *Ḥukkat Balak*	14	15	16	17	17
5	9	11	9	11	11	13	13	15	**16** *Ki Tavo*	17 Ḥol ha-Mo'ed	18	**18** *Va-Yishlaḥ*
6	10 Fast	12	10	12	12	**14** *Naso*	14	16	17	18	19	19
7	11	**13** *Be-Shallaḥ*	**11** *Teẓavveh* Zakhor	13	13	15	15	17	18	19	**20** *Va-Yera*	20
8	12	14	12	14	14	16	16	**18** *Ekev*	19	20	21	21
9	13	15	13 Ta'anit Esther	15 Pesaḥ	**15** *Emor*	17	17 Fast	19	20	21 Hoshana Rabba	22	22
10	**14** *Va-Yeḥi*	16	14 Purim	16 Omer	16	18	18	20	21	**22** Shemini Aẓeret	23	23
11	15	17	15 Shushan Purim	**17** Ḥol ha-Mo'ed	17	19	**19** *Pinḥas*	21	22	23 Simḥat Torah *Ve-Zot Ha-Berakhah*	24	24
12	16	18	16	18	18 Lag ba-Omer	20	20	22	**23** *Niẓẓavim Va-Yelekh*	24	25	**25** *Va-Yeshev* Ḥanukkah 1
13	17	19	17	19	19	**21** *Be-Ha'alotkha*	21	23	24	25	26	26 2
14	18	**20** *Yitro*	**18** *Ki Tissa* Parah	20	20	22	22	24	25	26	**27** *Ḥayyei Sarah*	27 3
15	19	21	19	21 Pesaḥ	21	23	23	**25** *Re'eh*	26	27	28	28 4
16	20	22	20	22	**22** *Be-Har Be-Ḥukkotai*	24	24	26	27	28	29	29 5
17	**21** *Shemot*	23	21	23	23	25	25	27	28	**29** *Bereshit*	30 R. Ḥ.	30 R. Ḥ. 6
18	22	24	22	**24** *Shemini*	24	26	**26** *Mattot Masei*	28	29	30 R. Ḥ.	1 **Kislev** R. Ḥ.	1 **Tevet** R. Ḥ. 7
19	23	25	23	25	25	27	27	29	**1 Tishri** Rosh Ha-Shanah	1 **Ḥeshvan** R. Ḥ.	2	**2** *Mi-Keẓ* 8
20	24	26	24	26	26	**28** *Shelaḥ*	28	30 R. Ḥ.	2	2	3	3
21	25	**27** *Mishpatim* Shekalim	**25** *Va-Yakhel Pekudei* Ha-Ḥodesh	27	27	29	29	1 **Elul** R. Ḥ.	3 Fast	3	**4** *Toledot*	4
22	26	28	26	28	28	30 R. Ḥ.	1 **Av** R. Ḥ.	**2** *Shofetim*	4	4	5	5
23	27	29	27	29	**29** *Be-Midbar*	1 **Tammuz** R. Ḥ.	2	3	5	5	6	6
24	**28** *Va-Era*	30 R. Ḥ.	28	30 R. Ḥ.	1 **Sivan** R. Ḥ.	2	3	4	6	**6** *No'aḥ*	7	7
25	29	1 **Adar** R. Ḥ.	29	**1 Iyyar** R. Ḥ. *Tazri'a Meẓora*	2	3	**4** *Devarim*	5	7	7	8	8
26	1 **Shevat** R. Ḥ.	2	1 **Nisan** R. Ḥ.	2	3	4	5	6	**8** *Ha'azinu* Shabbat Shuvah	8	9	**9** *Va-Yiggash*
27	2	3	2	3	4	**5** *Koraḥ*	6	7	9	9	10	10 Fast
28	3	**4** *Terumah*	**3** *Va-Yikra*	4	5	6	7	8	10 Yom Kippur	10	**11** *Va-Yeẓe*	11
29	4		4	5	6 Shavuot	7	8	**9** *Ki Teẓe*	11	11	12	12
30	5		5	6	7	8	9 Tishah be-Av	10	12	12	13	13
31	**6** *Bo*		6		8		10	11		**13** *Lekh Lekha*		14

1926

5686/87 תרפ"ו / תרפ"ז

	January	February	March	April	May	June	July	August	September	October	November	December
1	15 **Tevet**	17	15 Shushan Purim	17 Ḥol ha-Mo'ed	**17** *Emor*	19	19	21	22	23 Simḥat Torah *Ve-Zot Ha-Berakhah*	24	25 Ḥanukkah 1
2	**16** *Va-Yeḥi*	18	16	18	18 Lag ba-Omer	20	20	22	23	**24** *Bereshit*	25	26 2
3	17	19	17	**19**	19	21	**21** *Pinḥas*	23	24	25	26	27 3
4	18	20	18	20	20	22	22	24	**25** *Niẓẓavim Va-Yelekh*	26	27	**28** *Mi-Keẓ* 4
5	19	21	19	21 Pesaḥ	21	**23** *Shelaḥ*	23	25	26	27	28	29 5
6	20	**22** *Yitro*	**20** *Ki Tissa* Parah	22	22	24	24	26	27	28	**29** *Toledot*	1 **Tevet** R. Ḥ. 6
7	21	23	21	23	23	25	25	**27** *Re'eh*	28	29	1 **Kislev** R. Ḥ.	2 7
8	22	24	22	24	**24** *Be-Har Be-Ḥukkotai*	26	26	28	29	30 R. Ḥ.	2	3 8
9	**23** *Shemot*	25	23	25	25	27	27	29	**1 Tishri** Rosh Ha-Shanah	**1** R. Ḥ. *No'aḥ* **Ḥeshvan**	3	4
10	24	26	24	**26** *Shemini*	26	28	**28** *Mattot Masei*	30 R. Ḥ.	2	2	4	5
11	25	27	25	27	27	29	29	1 **Elul** R. Ḥ.	**3** *Ha'azinu* Shabbat Shuvah	3	5	**6** *Va-Yiggash*
12	26	28	26	28	28	**30** R. Ḥ. *Koraḥ*	1 **Av** R. Ḥ.	2	4 Fast	4	6	7
13	27	**29** *Mishpatim* Shekalim	**27** *Va-Yakhel Pekudei* Ha-Ḥodesh	29	29	1 **Tammuz** R. Ḥ.	2	3	5	5	**7** *Va-Yeẓe*	8
14	28	30 R. Ḥ.	28	30 R. Ḥ.	1 **Sivan** R. Ḥ.	2	3	**4** *Shofetim*	6	6	8	9
15	29	1 **Adar** R. Ḥ.	29	1 **Iyyar** R. Ḥ.	**2** *Be-Midbar*	3	4	5	7	7	9	10 Fast
16	**1 Shevat** R. Ḥ. *Va-Era*	2	1 **Nisan** R. Ḥ.	2	3	4	5	6	8	**8** *Lekh Lekha*	10	11
17	2	3	2	**3** *Tazri'a Meẓora*	4	5	**6** *Devarim*	7	9	9	11	12
18	3	4	3	4	5	6	7	8	**10** Yom Kippur	10	12	**13** *Va-Yeḥi*
19	4	5	4	5	6 Shavuot	**7** *Ḥukkat*	8	9	11	11	13	14
20	5	**6** *Terumah*	**5** *Va-Yikra*	6	7	8	9 Tishah be-Av	10	12	12	**14** *Va-Yishlaḥ*	15
21	6	7	6	7	8	9	10	**11** *Ki Teẓe*	13	13	15	16
22	7	8	7	8	**9** *Naso*	10	11	12	14	14	16	17
23	**8** *Bo*	9	8	9	10	11	12	13	15 Sukkot	**15** *Va-Yera*	17	18
24	9	10	9	**10** *Aḥarei Mot Kedoshim*	11	12	**13** *Va-Etḥannan*	14	16	16	18	19
25	10	11 Ta'anit Esther	10	11	12	13	14	15	**17** Ḥol ha-Mo'ed	17	19	**20** *Shemot*
26	11	12	11	12	13	**14** *Balak*	15	16	18	18	20	21
27	12	**13** *Teẓavveh* Zakhor	**12** *Ẓav* Shabbat ha-Gadol	13	14	15	16	17	19	19	**21** *Va-Yeshev*	22
28	13	14 Purim	13	14	15	16	17	**18** *Ki Tavo*	20	20	22	23
29	14		14	15	**16** *Be-Ha'alotkha*	17 Fast	18	19	21 Hoshana Rabba	21	23	24
30	**15** *Be-Shallaḥ*		15 Pesaḥ	16	17	18	19	20	22 Shemini Aẓeret	**22** *Ḥayyei Sarah*	24	25
31	16		16 Omer		18		**20** *Ekev*	21		23		26

1927

5687/88 תרפ״ז / תרפ״ח

	January	February	March	April	May	June	July	August	September	October	November	December
1	27 Tevet Va-Era	29	27	28	29	1 Sivan R. Ḥ.	1 Tammuz R. Ḥ.	3	4	5 Va-Yelekh Shabbat Shuvah	6	7
2	28	30 R. Ḥ.	28	29 Tazri'a Ha-Ḥodesh	30 R. Ḥ.	2	2 Ḥukkat	4	5	6	7	8
3	29	1 Adar I R. Ḥ.	29	1 Nisan R. Ḥ.	1 Iyyar R. Ḥ.	3	3	5	6 Shofetim	7	8	9 Va-Yeẓe
4	1 Shevat R. Ḥ.	2	30 R. Ḥ.	2	2	4 Naso	4	6	7	8	9	10
5	2	3 Terumah	1 R. Ḥ. Pekudei Adar II Shekalim	3	3	5	5	7	8	9	10 Lekh Lekha	11
6	3	4	2	4	4	6 Shavuot	6	8 Devarim	9	10 Yom Kippur	11	12
7	4	5	3	5	5 Emor	7	7	9 Tishah be-Av	10	11	12	13
8	5 Bo	6	4	6	6	8	8	10	11	12 Ha'azinu	13	14
9	6	7	5	7 Meẓora	7	9	9 Balak	11	12	13	14	15
10	7	8	6	8	8	10	10	12	13 Ki Teẓe	14	15	16 Va-Yishlaḥ
11	8	9	7	9	9	11 Be-Ha'alotkha	11	13	14	15 Sukkot	16	17
12	9	10 Tezavveh	8 Va-Yikra Zakhor	10	10	12	12	14	15	16	17 Va-Yera	18
13	10	11	9	11	11	13	13	15 Va-Ethannan	16	17 Ḥol ha-Mo'ed	18	19
14	11	12	10	12	12 Be-Har	14	14	16	17	18	19	20
15	12 Be-Shallaḥ	13	11	13	13	15	15	17	18	19	20	21
16	13	14	12	14 Aḥarei Mot Shabbat ha-Gadol	14	16	16 Pinḥas	18	19	20	21	22
17	14	15	13 Ta'anit Esther	15 Pesaḥ	15	17	17 Fast	19	20 Ki Tavo	21 Hoshana Rabba	22	23 Va-Yeshev
18	15	16	14 Purim	16 Omer	16	18 Shelaḥ	18	20	21	22 Shemini Aẓeret	23	24
19	16	17 Ki Tissa	15 Ẓav Shushan Purim	17 Ḥol ha-Mo'ed	17	19	19	21	22	23 Simḥat Torah Ve-Zot Ha-Berakhah	24 Ḥayyei Sarah	25 Ḥanukkah 1
20	17	18	16	18	18 Lag ba-Omer	20	20	22 Ekev	23	24	25	26 2
21	18	19	17	19	19 Be-Ḥukkotai	21	21	23	24	25	26	27 3
22	19 Yitro	20	18	20	20	22	22	24	25	26 Bereshit	27	28 4
23	20	21	19	21 Pesaḥ	21	23	23 Mattot	25	26	27	28	29 5
24	21	22	20	22	22	24	24	26	27 Niẓẓavim	28	29	30 R. Ḥ. Mi-Keẓ 6
25	22	23	21	23	23	25 Koraḥ	25	27	28	29	1 Kislev R. Ḥ.	1 Tevet R. Ḥ. 7
26	23	24 Va-Yakhel	22 Shemini Parah	24	24	26	26	28	29	30 R. Ḥ.	2 Toledot	2 8
27	24	25	23	25	25	27	27	29 Re'eh	1 Tishri Rosh Ha-Shanah	1 Ḥeshvan R. Ḥ.	3	3
28	25	26	24	26	26 Be-Midbar	28	28	30 R. Ḥ.	2	2	4	4
29	26 Mishpatim		25	27	27	29	29	1 Elul R. Ḥ.	3 Fast	3 No'aḥ	5	5
30	27		26	28 Kedoshim	28	30 R. Ḥ.	1 R. Ḥ. Av Masei	2	4	4	6	6
31	28		27		29		2	3		5		7 Va-Yiggash

1928

5688/89 תרפ״ח / תרפ״ט

	January	February	March	April	May	June	July	August	September	October	November	December
1	8 Tevet	10	9	11	11	13	13	15	16 Ki Tavo	17 Ḥol ha-Mo'ed	18	18 Va-Yishlaḥ
2	9	11	10	12	12	14 Naso	14	16	17	18	19	19
3	10 Fast	12	11 Tezavveh Zakhor	13	13	15	15	17	18	19	20 Va-Yera	20
4	11	13 Be-Shallaḥ	12	14	14	16	16	18 Ekev	19	20	21	21
5	12	14	13 Ta'anit Esther	15 Pesaḥ	15 Emor	17	17 Fast	19	20	21 Hoshana Rabba	22	22
6	13	15	14 Purim	16 Omer	16	18	18	20	21	22 Shemini Aẓeret	23	23
7	14 Va-Yeḥi	16	15 Shushan Purim	17 Ḥol ha-Mo'ed	17	19	19 Pinḥas	21	22	23 Simḥat Torah Ve-Zot Ha-Berakhah	24	24
8	15	17	16	18	18 Lag ba-Omer	20	20	22	23 Niẓẓavim Va-Yelekh	24	25	25 Va-Yeshev Ḥanukkah 1
9	16	18	17	19	19	21 Be-Ha'alotkha	21	23	24	25	26	26 2
10	17	19	18 Ki Tissa Parah	20	20	22	22	24	25	26	27 Ḥayyei Sarah	27 3
11	18	20 Yitro	19	21 Pesaḥ	21	23	23	25 Re'eh	26	27	28	28 4
12	19	21	20	22	22 Be-Har Be-Ḥukkotai	24	24	26	27	28	29	29 5
13	20	22	21	23	23	25	25	27	28	29 Bereshit	30 R. Ḥ.	30 R. Ḥ. 6
14	21 Shemot	23	22	24 Shemini	24	26	26 Mattot Masei	28	29	30 R. Ḥ.	1 Kislev R. Ḥ.	1 Tevet R. Ḥ. 7
15	22	24	23	25	25	27	27	29	1 Tishri Rosh Ha-Shanah	1 Ḥeshvan R. Ḥ.	2	2 Mi-Keẓ 8
16	23	25	24	26	26	28 Shelaḥ	28	30 R. Ḥ.	2	2	3	3
17	24	26	Va-Yakhel Pekudei 25 Ha-Ḥodesh	27	27	29	29	1 Elul R. Ḥ.	3 Fast	3	4 Toledot	4
18	25	27 Mishpatim Shekalim	26	28	28	30 R. Ḥ.	1 Av R. Ḥ.	2 Shofetim	4	4	5	5
19	26	28	27	29	29 Be-Midbar	1 Tammuz R. Ḥ.	2	3	5	5	6	6
20	27	29	28	30 R. Ḥ.	1 Sivan R. Ḥ.	2	3	4	6	6 No'aḥ	7	7
21	28 Va-Era	30 R. Ḥ.	29	1 R. Ḥ. Iyyar Tazri'a Meẓora	2	3	4 Devarim	5	7	7	8	8
22	29	1 Adar R. Ḥ.	1 Nisan R. Ḥ.	2	3	4	5	6	8 Ha'azinu Shabbat Shuvah	8	9	9 Va-Yiggash
23	1 Shevat R. Ḥ.	2	2	3	4	5 Koraḥ	6	7	9	9	10	10 Fast
24	2	3	3 Va-Yikra	4	5	6	7	8	10 Yom Kippur	10	11 Va-Yeẓe	11
25	3	4 Terumah	4	5	6 Shavuot	7	8	9 Ki Teẓe	11	11	12	12
26	4	5	5	6	7	8	9 Tishah be-Av	10	12	12	13	13
27	5	6	6	7	8	9	10	11	13	13 Lekh Lekha	14	14
28	6 Bo	7	7	8 Aḥarei Mot Kedoshim	9	10	11 Va-Ethannan	12	14	14	15	15
29	7	8	8	9	10	11	12	13	15 Sukkot	15	16	16 Va-Yeḥi
30	8		9	10	11	12 Ḥukkat Balak	13	14	16	16	17	17
31	9		10 Ẓav Shabbat ha-Gadol		12		14	15		17		18

1929

5689/90 תרפ״ט / תר״צ

	January	February	March	April	May	June	July	August	September	October	November	December
1	19 **Tevet**	21	19	20	21 Pesaḥ	**22** *Be-Ḥukkotai*	23	24	26	26	28	28
2	20	**22** *Yitro*	**20** *Ki Tissa*	21	22	23	24	25	27	27	**29** *Bereshit*	29
3	21	23	21	22	23	24	25	**26** *Mattot Masei*	28	28	30 R. Ḥ.	1 **Kislev** R. Ḥ.
4	22	24	22	23	**24** *Aḥarei Mot*	25	26	27	29	29	1 **Ḥeshvan** R. Ḥ.	2
5	**23** *Shemot*	25	23	24	25	26	27	28	30 R. Ḥ.	**1 Tishri** Rosh Ha-Shanah	2	3
6	24	26	24	**25** *Shemini* Ha-Ḥodesh	26	27	**28** *Shelaḥ*	29	1 **Elul** R. Ḥ.	2	3	4
7	25	27	25	26	27	28	29	1 **Av** R. Ḥ.	**2** *Shofetim*	3 Fast	4	**5** *Toledot*
8	26	28	26	27	28	**29** *Be-Midbar*	30 R. Ḥ.	2	3	4	5	6
9	27	**29** *Mishpatim*	**27** *Va-Yakhel* Shekalim	28	29	1 **Sivan** R. Ḥ.	1 **Tammuz** R. Ḥ.	3	4	5	**6** *No'aḥ*	7
10	28	30 R. Ḥ.	28	29	30 R. Ḥ.	2	2	**4** *Devarim*	5	6	7	8
11	29	1 **Adar I** R. Ḥ.	29	1 **Nisan** R. Ḥ.	**1** R. Ḥ. *Kedoshim* **Iyyar**	3	3	5	6	7	8	9
12	**1** R. Ḥ. *Va-Era* **Shevat**	2	30 R. Ḥ.	2	2	4	4	6	7	**8** *Ha'azinu* Shabbat Shuvah	9	10
13	2	3	1 **Adar II** R. Ḥ.	**3** *Tazri'a*	3	5	**5** *Koraḥ*	7	8	9	10	11
14	3	4	2	4	4	6 Shavuot	6	8	**9** *Ki Teẓe*	10 Yom Kippur	11	**12** *Va-Yeẓe*
15	4	5	3	5	5	**7**	7	9 Tishah be-Av	10	11	12	13
16	5	**6** *Terumah*	**4** *Pekudei*	6	6	8	8	10	11	12	**13** *Lekh Lekha*	14
17	6	7	5	7	7	9	9	**11** *Va-Etḥannan*	12	13	14	15
18	7	8	6	8	**8** *Emor*	10	10	12	13	14	15	16
19	**8** *Bo*	9	7	9	9	11	11	13	14	**15** Sukkot	16	17
20	9	10	8	**10** *Meẓora* Shabbat ha-Gadol	10	12	**12** *Ḥukkat Balak*	14	15	16	17	18
21	10	11	9	11	11	13	13	15	**16** *Ki Tavo*	17	18	**19** *Va-Yishlaḥ*
22	11	12	10	12	12	**14** *Naso*	14	16	17	18 Ḥol ha-Mo'ed	19	20
23	12	**13** *Teẓavveh*	**11** *Va-Yikra* Zakhor	13	13	15	15	17	18	19	**20** *Va-Yera*	21
24	13	14	12	14	14	16	16	**18** *Ekev*	19	20	21	22
25	14	15	13 Ta'anit Esther	15 Pesaḥ	**15** *Be-Har*	17	17 Fast	19	20	21 Hoshana Rabba	22	23
26	**15** *Be-Shallaḥ*	16	14 Purim	16 Omer	16	18	18	20	21	**22** Shemini Aẓeret	23	24
27	16	17	15 Shushan Purim	17	17	19	**19** *Pinḥas*	21	22	23 Simḥat Torah *Ve-Zot Ha-Berakhah*	24	25 Ḥanukkah 1
28	17	18	16	18 Ḥol ha-Mo'ed	18 Lag ba-Omer	20	20	22	**23** *Niẓẓavim Va-Yelekh*	24	25	**26** *Va-Yeshev* 2
29	18		17	19	19	**21** *Be-Ha'alotkha*	21	23	24	25	26	27 3
30	19		**18** *Ẓav Parah*	20	20	22	22	24	25	26	**27** *Ḥayyei Sarah*	28 4
31	20		19		21		23	**25** *Re'eh*		27		29 5

1930

5690/91 תר״צ / תרצ״א

	January	February	March	April	May	June	July	August	September	October	November	December
1	1 **Tevet** R. Ḥ. Ḥanukkah 6	**3** *Va-Era*	**1** R. Ḥ. *Mishpatim* **Adar** Shekalim	3	3	5	5	7	8	9	**10** *Lekh Lekha*	11
2	2 7	4	2	4	4	6 Shavuot	6	**8** *Devarim*	9	10 Yom Kippur	11	12
3	3 8	5	3	5	**5** *Tazri'a Meẓora*	7	7	9 Tishah be-Av	10	11	12	13
4	**4** *Mi-Keẓ*	6	4	6	6	8	8	10	11	**12** *Ha'azinu*	13	14
5	5	7	5	**7** *Va-Yikra*	7	9	**9** *Ḥukkat*	11	12	13	14	15
6	6	8	6	8	8	10	10	12	**13** *Ki Teẓe*	14	15	**16** *Va-Yishlaḥ*
7	7	9	7	9	9	**11** *Naso*	11	13	14	15 Sukkot	16	17
8	8	**10** *Bo*	**8** *Terumah* Zakhor	10	10	12	12	14	15	16	**17** *Va-Yera*	18
9	9	11	9	11	11	13	13	**15** *Va-Etḥannan*	16	17	18	19
10	10 Fast	12	10	12	**12** *Aḥarei Mot Kedoshim*	14	14	16	17	18 Ḥol ha-Mo'ed	19	20
11	**11** *Va-Yiggash*	13	11	13	13	15	15	17	18	**19**	20	21
12	12	14	12	**14** *Ẓav* Shabbat ha-Gadol	14	16	**16** *Balak*	18	19	20	21	22
13	13	15	13 Ta'anit Esther	15 Pesaḥ	15	17	17 Fast	19	**20** *Ki Tavo*	21 Hoshana Rabba	22	**23** *Va-Yeshev*
14	14	16	14 Purim	16 Omer	16	**18** *Be-Ha'alotkha*	18	20	21	22 Shemini Aẓeret	23	24
15	15	**17** *Be-Shallaḥ*	**15** Shushan Purim *Teẓavveh*	17	17	19	19	21	22	23 Simḥat Torah *Ve-Zot Ha-Berakhah*	**24** *Ḥayyei Sarah*	25 Ḥanukkah 1
16	16	18	16	18 Ḥol ha-Mo'ed	18 Lag ba-Omer	20	20	**22** *Ekev*	23	24	25	26 2
17	17	19	17	19	**19** *Emor*	21	21	23	24	25	26	27 3
18	**18** *Va-Yeḥi*	20	18	20	20	22	22	24	25	**26** *Bereshit*	27	28 4
19	19	21	19	**21** Pesaḥ	21	23	**23** *Pinḥas*	25	26	27	28	29 5
20	20	22	20	22	22	24	24	26	**27** *Niẓẓavim*	28	29	**30** R. Ḥ. *Mi-Keẓ* 6
21	21	23	21	23	23	**25** *Shelaḥ*	25	27	28	29	1 **Kislev** R. Ḥ.	1 **Tevet** R. Ḥ. 7
22	22	**24** *Yitro*	**22** *Ki Tissa* Parah	24	24	26	26	28	29	30 R. Ḥ.	**2** *Toledot*	2 8
23	23	25	23	25	25	27	27	**29** *Re'eh*	1 **Tishri** Rosh Ha-Shanah	1 **Ḥeshvan** R. Ḥ.	3	3
24	24	26	24	26	**26** *Be-Har Be-Ḥukkotai*	28	28	30 R. Ḥ.	2	2	4	4
25	**25** *Shemot*	27	25	27	27	29	29	1 **Elul** R. Ḥ.	3 Fast	**3** *No'aḥ*	5	5
26	26	28	26	**28** *Shemini*	28	30 R. Ḥ.	**1** R. Ḥ. *Mattot* **Av** *Masei*	2	4	4	6	6
27	27	29	27	29	29	1 **Tammuz** R. Ḥ.	2	3	**5** *Va-Yelekh* Shabbat Shuvah	5	7	**7** *Va-Yiggash*
28	28	30 R. Ḥ.	28	30 R. Ḥ.	1 **Sivan** R. Ḥ.	**2** *Koraḥ*	3	4	6	6	8	8
29	29		*Va-Yakhel Pekudei* **29** Ha-Ḥodesh	1 **Iyyar** R. Ḥ.	2	3	4	5	7	7	**9** *Va-Yeẓe*	9
30	1 **Shevat** R. Ḥ.		1 **Nisan** R. Ḥ.	2	3	4	5	**6** *Shofetim*	8	8	10	10 Fast
31	2		2		**4** *Be-Midbar*		6	7		9		11

1931

5691/92 — תרצ״א / תרצ״ב

	January	February	March	April	May	June	July	August	September	October	November	December
1	12 Tevet	14	12	14	14	16	16	18 Ekev	19	20 Ḥol ha-Mo'ed	21	21
2	13	15	13 Ta'anit Esther	15 Pesaḥ	15 Emor	17	17 Fast	19	20	21 Hoshana Rabba	22	22
3	14 Va-Yeḥi	16	14 Purim	16 Omer	16	18	18	20	21	22 Shemini Aẓeret	23	23
4	15	17	15 Shushan Purim	17 Ḥol ha-Mo'ed	17	19	19 Pinḥas	21	22	23 Simḥat Torah Ve-Zot Ha-Berakhah	24	24
5	16	18	16	18	18 Lag ba-Omer	20	20	22	23 Niẓẓavim Va-Yelekh	24	25	25 Va-Yeshev Ḥanukkah 1
6	17	19	17	19	19	21 Be-Ha'alotkha	21	23	24	25	26	26 2
7	18	20 Yitro	18 Ki Tissa Parah	20	20	22	22	24	25	26	27 Ḥayyei Sarah	27 3
8	19	21	19	21 Pesaḥ	21	23	23	25 Re'eh	26	27	28	28 4
9	20	22	20	22	22 Be-Har Be-Ḥukkotai	24	24	26	27	28	29	29 5
10	21 Shemot	23	21	23	23	25	25	27	28	29 Bereshit	30 R. Ḥ.	30 R. Ḥ. 6
11	22	24	22	24 Shemini	24	26	26 Mattot Masei	28	29	30 R. Ḥ.	1 Kislev R. Ḥ.	1 Tevet R. Ḥ. 7
12	23	25	23	25	25	27	27	29	1 Tishri Rosh Ha-Shanah	1 Ḥeshvan R. Ḥ.	2	2 Mi-Keẓ 8
13	24	26	24	26	26	28 Shelaḥ	28	30 R. Ḥ.	2	2	3	3
14	25	27 Mishpatim Shekalim	25 Va-Yakhel Pekudei Ha-Ḥodesh	27	27	29	29	1 Elul R. Ḥ.	3 Fast	3	4 Toledot	4
15	26	28	26	28	28	30 R. Ḥ.	1 Av R. Ḥ.	2 Shofetim	4	4	5	5
16	27	29	27	29	29 Be-Midbar	1 Tammuz R. Ḥ.	2	3	5	5	6	6
17	28 Va-Era	30 R. Ḥ.	28	30 R. Ḥ.	1 Sivan R. Ḥ.	2	3	4	6	6 No'aḥ	7	7
18	29	1 Adar R. Ḥ.	29	1 Iyyar R. Ḥ. Tazri'a Meẓora	2	3	4 Devarim	5	7	7	8	8
19	1 Shevat R. Ḥ.	2	1 Nisan R. Ḥ.	2	3	4	5	6	8 Ha'azinu Shabbat Shuvah	8	9	9 Va-Yiggash
20	2	3	2	3	4	5 Koraḥ	6	7	9	9	10	10 Fast
21	3	4 Terumah	3 Va-Yikra	4	5	6	7	8	10 Yom Kippur	10	11 Va-Yeẓe	11
22	4	5	4	5	6 Shavuot	7	8	9 Ki Teẓe	11	11	12	12
23	5	6	5	6	7	8	9 Tishah be-Av	10	12	12	13	13
24	6 Bo	7	6	7	8	9	10	11	13	13 Lekh Lekha	14	14
25	7	8	7	8 Aḥarei Mot Kedoshim	9	10	11 Va-Etḥannan	12	14	14	15	15
26	8	9	8	9	10	11	12	13	15 Sukkot	15	16	16 Va-Yeḥi
27	9	10	9	10	11	12 Ḥukkat Balak	13	14	16	16	17	17
28	10	11 Teẓavveh Zakhor	10 Ẓav Shabbat ha-Gadol	11	12	13	14	15	17 Ḥol ha-Mo'ed	17	18 Va-Yishlaḥ	18
29	11		11	12	13	14	15	16 Ki Tavo	18	18	19	19
30	12		12	13	14 Naso	15	16	17	19	19	20	20
31	13 Be-Shallaḥ		13		15		17	18		20 Va-Yera		21

1932

5692/93 — תרצ״ב תרצ״ג

	January	February	March	April	May	June	July	August	September	October	November	December
1	22 Tevet	24	23	24	25	26	27	28	30 R. Ḥ.	1 Tishri Rosh Ha-Shanah	2	2
2	23 Shemot	25	24	25 Shemini Ha-Ḥodesh	26	27	28 Shelaḥ	29	1 Elul R. Ḥ.	2	3	3
3	24	26	25	26	27	28	29	1 Av R. Ḥ.	2 Shofetim	3 Fast	4	4 Toledot
4	25	27	26	27	28	29 Be-Midbar	30 R. Ḥ.	2	3	4	5	5
5	26	28	27 Va-Yakhel Shekalim	28	29	1 Sivan R. Ḥ.	1 Tammuz R. Ḥ.	3	4	5	6 No'aḥ	6
6	27	29 Mishpatim	28	29	30 R. Ḥ.	2	2	4 Devarim	5	6	7	7
7	28	30 R. Ḥ.	29	1 Nisan R. Ḥ.	1 Iyyar R. Ḥ. Kedoshim	3	3	5	6	7	8	8
8	29	1 Adar I R. Ḥ.	30 R. Ḥ.	2	2	4	4	6	7	8 Ha'azinu Shabbat Shuvah	9	9
9	1 Shevat R. Ḥ. Va-Era	2	1 Adar II R. Ḥ.	3 Tazri'a	3	5	5 Koraḥ	7	8	9	10	10
10	2	3	2	4	4	6 Shavuot	6	8	9 Ki Teẓe	10 Yom Kippur	11	11 Va-Yeẓe
11	3	4	3	5	5	7	7	9 Tishah be-Av	10	11	12	12
12	4	5	4 Pekudei	6	6	8	8	10	11	12	13 Lekh Lekha	13
13	5	6 Terumah	5	7	7	9	9	11 Va-Etḥannan	12	13	14	14
14	6	7	6	8	8 Emor	10	10	12	13	14	15	15
15	7	8	7	9	9	11	11	13	14	15 Sukkot	16	16
16	8 Bo	9	8	10 Meẓora Shabbat ha-Gadol	10	12	12 Ḥukkat Balak	14	15	16	17	17
17	9	10	9	11	11	13	13	15	16 Ki Tavo	17 Ḥol ha-Mo'ed	18	18 Va-Yishlaḥ
18	10	11	10	12	12	14 Naso	14	16	17	18	19	19
19	11	12	11 Va-Yikra Zakhor	13	13	15	15	17	18	19	20 Va-Yera	20
20	12	13 Teẓavveh	12	14	14	16	16	18 Ekev	19	20	21	21
21	13	14	13 Ta'anit Esther	15 Pesaḥ	15 Be-Har	17	17 Fast	19	20	21 Hoshana Rabba	22	22
22	14	15	14 Purim	16 Omer	16	18	18	20	21	22 Shemini Aẓeret	23	23
23	15 Be-Shallaḥ	16	15 Shushan Purim	17 Ḥol ha-Mo'ed	17	19	19 Pinḥas	21	22	23 Simḥat Torah Ve-Zot Ha-Berakhah	24	24
24	16	17	16	18	18 Lag ba-Omer	20	20	22	23 Niẓẓavim Va-Yelekh	24	25	25 Va-Yeshev Ḥanukkah 1
25	17	18	17	19	19	21 Be-Ha'alotkha	21	23	24	25	26	26 2
26	18	19	18 Ẓav Parah	20	20	22	22	24	25	26	27 Ḥayyei Sarah	27 3
27	19	20 Ki Tissa	19	21 Pesaḥ	21	23	23	25 Re'eh	26	27	28	28 4
28	20	21	20	22	22 Be-Ḥukkotai	24	24	26	27	28	29	29 5
29	21	22	21	23	23	25	25	27	28	29 Bereshit	30 R. Ḥ.	30 R. Ḥ. 6
30	22 Yitro		22	24 Aḥarei Mot	24	26	26 Mattot Masei	28	29	30 R. Ḥ.	1 Kislev R. Ḥ.	1 Tevet R. Ḥ. 7
31	23		23		25		27	29		1 Ḥeshvan R. Ḥ.		2 Mi-Keẓ 8

1933

5693/94 — תרצ״ג / תרצ״ד

	January	February	March	April	May	June	July	August	September	October	November	December
1	3 Tevet	5	3	5 Va-Yikra	5	7	7 Hukkat	9 Tishah be-Av	10	11	12	13
2	4	6	4	6	6	8	8	10	11 Ki Teze	12	13	14 Va-Yishlah
3	5	7	5	7	7	9 Naso	9	11	12	13	14	15
4	6	8 Bo	6 Terumah	8	8	10	10	12	13	14	15 Va-Yera	16
5	7	9	7	9	9	11	11	13 Va-Ethannan	14	15 Sukkot	16	17
6	8	10	8	10	10 Aharei Mot Kedoshim	12	12	14	15	16	17	18
7	9 Va-Yiggash	11	9	11	11	13	13	15	16	17	18	19
8	10 Fast	12	10	12 Zav Shabbat ha-Gadol	12	14	14 Balak	16	17	18 Hol ha-Mo'ed	19	20
9	11	13	11 Ta'anit Esther	13	13	15	15	17	18 Ki Tavo	19	20	21 Va-Yeshev
10	12	14	12	14	14	16 Be-Ha'alotkha	16	18	19	20	21	22
11	13	15 Be-Shallah	13 Tezavveh Zakhor	15 Pesah	15	17	17 Fast	19	20	21 Hoshana Rabba	22 Hayyei Sarah	23
12	14	16	14 Purim	16 Omer	16	18	18	20 Ekev	21	22 Shemini Azeret	23	24
13	15	17	15 Shushan Purim	17	17 Emor	19	19	21	22	23 Simhat Torah Ve-Zot Ha-Berakhah	24	25 Hanukkah 1
14	16 Va-Yehi	18	16	18 Hol ha-Mo'ed	18 Lag ba-Omer	20	20	22	23	24 Bereshit	25	26 2
15	17	19	17	19	19	21	21 Pinhas	23	24	25	26	27 3
16	18	20	18	20	20	22	22	24	25 Nizzavim Va-Yelekh	26	27	28 Mi-Kez 4
17	19	21	19	21 Pesah	21	23 Shelah	23	25	26	27	28	29 5
18	20	22 Yitro	20 Ki Tissa Parah	22	22	24	24	26	27	28	29 Toledot	30 R. H. 6
19	21	23	21	23	23	25	25	27 Re'eh	28	29	1 Kislev R. H.	1 Tevet R. H. 7
20	22	24	22	24	24 Be-Har Be-Hukkotai	26	26	28	29	30 R. H.	2	2 8
21	23 Shemot	25	23	25	25	27	27	29	1 Tishri Rosh Ha-Shanah	1 R. H. Heshvan No'ah	3	3
22	24	26	24	26 Shemini	26	28	28 Mattot Masei	30 R. H.	2	2	4	4
23	25	27	25	27	27	29	29	1 Elul R. H.	3 Ha'azinu Shabbat Shuvah	3	5	5 Va-Yiggash
24	26	28	26	28	28	30 R. H. Korah	1 Av R. H.	2	4 Fast	4	6	6
25	27	29 Mishpatim Shekalim	27 Va-Yakhel Pekudei Ha-Hodesh	29	29	1 Tammuz R. H.	2	3	5	5	7 Va-Yeze	7
26	28	30 R. H.	28	30 R. H.	1 Sivan R. H.	2	3	4 Shofetim	6	6	8	8
27	29	1 Adar R. H.	29	1 Iyyar R. H.	2 Be-Midbar	3	4	5	7	7	9	9
28	1 R. H. Va-Era Shevat	2	1 Nisan R. H.	2	3	4	5	6	8	8 Lekh Lekha	10	10 Fast
29	2		2	3 Tazri'a Mezora	4	5	6 Devarim	7	9	9	11	11
30	3		3	4	5	6	7	8	10 Yom Kippur	10	12	12 Va-Yehi
31	4		4		6 Shavuot		8	9		11		13

1934

5694/95 — תרצ״ד / תרצ״ה

	January	February	March	April	May	June	July	August	September	October	November	December
1	14 Tevet	16	14 Purim	16 Omer	16	18	18 Fast	20	21 Ki Tavo	22 Shemini Azeret	23	24 Va-Yeshev
2	15	17	15 Shushan Purim	17	17	19 Be-Ha'alotkha	19	21	22	23 Simhat Torah Ve-Zot Ha-Berakhah	24	25 Hanukkah 1
3	16	18 Yitro	16 Ki Tissa	18 Hol ha-Mo'ed	18 Lag ba-Omer	20	20	22	23	24	25 Hayyei Sarah	26 2
4	17	19	17	19	19	21	21	23 Ekev	24	25	26	27 3
5	18	20	18	20	20 Emor	22	22	24	25	26	27	28 4
6	19 Shemot	21	19	21 Pesah	21	23	23	25	26	27 Bereshit	28	29 5
7	20	22	20	22	22	24	24 Pinhas	26	27	28	29	1 Tevet R. H. 6
8	21	23	21	23	23	25	25	27	28 Nizzavim	29	1 Kislev R. H.	2 Mi-Kez 7
9	22	24	22	24	24	26 Shelah	26	28	29	30 R. H.	2	3 8
10	23	25 Mishpatim Shekalim	23 Va-Yakhel Pekudei Parah	25	25	27	27	29	1 Tishri Rosh Ha-Shanah	1 Heshvan R. H.	3 Toledot	4
11	24	26	24	26	26	28	28	30 R. H. Re'eh	2	2	4	5
12	25	27	25	27	27 Be-Har Be-Hukkotai	29	29	1 Elul R. H.	3 Fast	3	5	6
13	26 Va-Era	28	26	28	28	30 R. H.	1 Av R. H.	2	4	4 No'ah	6	7
14	27	29	27	29 Shemini	29	1 Tammuz R. H.	2 Mattot Masei	3	5	5	7	8
15	28	30 R. H.	28	30 R. H.	1 Sivan R. H.	2	3	4	6 Va-Yelekh Shabbat Shuvah	6	8	9 Va-Yiggash
16	29	1 Adar R. H.	29	1 Iyyar R. H.	2	3 Korah	4	5	7	7	9	10 Fast
17	1 Shevat R. H.	2 Terumah	1 R. H. Va-Yikra Nisan Ha-Hodesh	2	3	4	5	6	8	8	10 Va-Yeze	11
18	2	3	2	3	4	5	6	7 Shofetim	9	9	11	12
19	3	4	3	4	5 Be-Midbar	6	7	8	10 Yom Kippur	10	12	13
20	4 Bo	5	4	5	6 Shavuot	7	8	9	11	11 Lekh Lekha	13	14
21	5	6	5	6 Tazri'a Mezora	7	8	9 Devarim Tishah be-Av	10	12	12	14	15
22	6	7	6	7	8	9	10 Fast	11	13 Ha'azinu	13	15	16 Va-Yehi
23	7	8	7	8	9	10 Hukkat	11	12	14	14	16	17
24	8	9 Tezavveh Zakhor	8 Zav Shabbat ha-Gadol	9	10	11	12	13	15 Sukkot	15	17 Va-Yishlah	18
25	9	10	9	10	11	12	13	14 Ki Teze	16	16	18	19
26	10	11	10	11	12 Naso	13	14	15	17	17	19	20
27	11 Be-Shallah	12	11	12	13	14	15	16	18 Hol ha-Mo'ed	18 Va-Yera	20	21
28	12	13 Ta'anit Esther	12	13 Aharei Mot Kedoshim	14	15	16 Va-Ethannan	17	19	19	21	22
29	13		13	14	15	16	17	18	20	20	22	23 Shemot
30	14		14	15	16	17 Balak	18	19	21 Hoshana Rabba	21	23	24
31	15		15 Pesah		17		19	20		22		25

1935

5695/96 תרצ״ה / תרצ״ו

	January	February	March	April	May	June	July	August	September	October	November	December
1	26 Tevet	28	26	27	28	29 Be-Midbar	30 R. Ḥ.	2	3	4	5	5
2	27	29 Mishpatim	27 Va-Yakhel Shekalim	28	29	1 Sivan R. Ḥ.	1 Tammuz R. Ḥ.	3	4	5	6 No'aḥ	6
3	28	30 R. Ḥ.	28	29	30 R. Ḥ.	2	2	4 Devarim	5	6	7	7
4	29	1 Adar I R. Ḥ.	29	1 Nisan R. Ḥ.	1 Iyyar R. Ḥ. Kedoshim	3	3	5	6	7	8	8
5	1 Shevat R. Ḥ. Va-Era	2	30 R. Ḥ.	2	2	4	4	6	7	8 Ha'azinu Shabbat Shuvah	9	9
6	2	3	1 Adar II R. Ḥ.	3 Tazri'a	3	5	5 Koraḥ	7	8	9	10	10
7	3	4	2	4	4	6 Shavuot	6	8	9 Ki Teẓe	10 Yom Kippur	11	11 Va-Yeẓe
8	4	5	3	5	5	7	7	9 Tishah be-Av	10	11	12	12
9	5	6 Terumah	4 Pekudei	6	6	8	8	10	11	12	13 Lekh Lekha	13
10	6	7	5	7	7	9	9	11 Va-Etḥannan	12	13	14	14
11	7	8	6	8	8 Emor	10	10	12	13	14	15	15
12	8 Bo	9	7	9	9	11	11	13	14	15 Sukkot	16	16
13	9	10	8	10 Meẓora Shabbat ha-Gadol	10	12	12 Ḥukkat Balak	14	15	16	17	17
14	10	11	9	11	11	13	13	15	16 Ki Tavo	17 Ḥol ha-Mo'ed	18	18 Va-Yishlaḥ
15	11	12	10	12	12	14 Naso	14	16	17	18	19	19
16	12	13 Teẓavveh	11 Va-Yikra Zakhor	13	13	15	15	17	18	19	20 Va-Yera	20
17	13	14	12	14	14	16	16	18 Ekev	19	20	21	21
18	14	15	13 Ta'anit Esther	15 Pesaḥ	15 Be-Har	17	17 Fast	19	20	21 Hoshana Rabba	22	22
19	15 Be-Shallaḥ	16	14 Purim	16 Omer	16	18	18	20	21	22 Shemini Aẓeret	23	23
20	16	17	15 Shushan Purim	17 Ḥol ha-Mo'ed	17	19	19 Pinḥas	21	22	23 Simḥat Torah Ve-Zot ha-Berakhah	24	24
21	17	18	16	18	18 Lag ba-Omer	20	20	22	23 Niẓẓavim Va-Yelekh	24	25	25 Va-Yeshev Ḥanukkah 1
22	18	19	17	19	19	21 Be-Ha'alotkha	21	23	24	25	26	26 2
23	19	20 Ki Tissa	18 Ẓav Parah	20	20	22	22	24	25	26	27 Ḥayyei Sarah	27 3
24	20	21	19	21 Pesaḥ	21	23	23	25 Re'eh	26	27	28	28 4
25	21	22	20	22	22 Be-Ḥukkotai	24	24	26	27	28	29	29 5
26	22 Yitro	23	21	23	23	25	25	27	28	29 Bereshit	30 R. Ḥ.	30 R. Ḥ. 6
27	23	24	22	24 Aḥarei Mot	24	26	26 Mattot Masei	28	29	30 R. Ḥ.	1 Kislev R. Ḥ.	1 Tevet R. Ḥ. 7
28	24	25	23	25	25	27	27	29	1 Tishri Rosh Ha-Shanah	1 Ḥeshvan R. Ḥ.	2	2 Mi-Keẓ 8
29	25		24	26	26	28 Shelaḥ	28	30 R. Ḥ.	2	2	3	3
30	26		25 Shemini Ha-Ḥodesh	27	27	29	29	1 Elul R. Ḥ.	3 Fast	3	4 Toledot	4
31	27		26		28		1 Av R. Ḥ.	2 Shofetim		4		5

1936

5696/97 תרצ״ו / תרצ״ז

	January	February	March	April	May	June	July	August	September	October	November	December
1	6 Tevet	8 Bo	7	9	9	11	11	13 Va-Etḥannan	14	15 Sukkot	16	17
2	7	9	8	10	10 Aḥarei Mot Kedoshim	12	12	14	15	16	17	18
3	8	10	9	11	11	13	13	15	16	17 Ḥol ha-Mo'ed	18	19
4	9 Va-Yiggash	11	10	12 Ẓav Shabbat ha-Gadol	12	14	14 Balak	16	17	18	19	20
5	10 Fast	12	11 Ta'anit Esther	13	13	15	15	17	18 Ki Tavo	19	20	21 Va-Yeshev
6	11	13	12	14	14	16 Be-Ha'alotkha	16	18	19	20	21	22
7	12	14	13 Teẓavveh Zakhor	15 Pesaḥ	15	17	17 Fast	19	20	21 Hoshana Rabba	22 Ḥayyei Sarah	23
8	13	15 Be-Shallaḥ	14 Purim	16 Omer	16	18	18	20 Ekev	21	22 Shemini Aẓeret	23	24
9	14	16	15 Shushan Purim	17 Ḥol ha-Mo'ed	17 Emor	19	19	21	22	23 Simḥat Torah Ve-Zot ha-Berakhah	24	25 Ḥanukkah 1
10	15	17	16	18	18 Lag ba-Omer	20	20	22	23	24 Bereshit	25	26 2
11	16 Va-Yeḥi	18	17	19	19	21	21 Pinḥas	23	24	25	26	27 3
12	17	19	18	20	20	22	22	24	25 Niẓẓavim Va-Yelekh	26	27	28 Mi-Keẓ 4
13	18	20	19	21 Pesaḥ	21	23 Shelaḥ	23	25	26	27	28	29 5
14	19	21	20 Ki Tissa Parah	22	22	24	24	26	27	28	29 Toledot	30 R. Ḥ. 6
15	20	22 Yitro	21	23	23	25	25	27 Re'eh	28	29	1 Kislev R. Ḥ.	1 Tevet R. Ḥ. 7
16	21	23	22	24	24 Be-Har Be-Ḥukkotai	26	26	28	29	30 R. Ḥ.	2	2 8
17	22	24	23	25	25	27	27	29	1 Tishri Rosh Ha-Shanah	1 Ḥeshvan R. Ḥ. No'aḥ	3	3
18	23 Shemot	25	24	26 Shemini	26	28	28 Mattot Masei	30 R. Ḥ.	2	2	4	4
19	24	26	25	27	27	29	29	1 Elul R. Ḥ.	3 Ha'azinu Shabbat Shuvah	3	5	5 Va-Yiggash
20	25	27	26	28	28	30 R. Ḥ. Koraḥ	1 Av R. Ḥ.	2	4 Fast	4	6	6
21	26	28	27 Va-Yakhel Pekudei Ha-Ḥodesh	29	29	1 Tammuz R. Ḥ.	2	3	5	5	7 Va-Yeẓe	7
22	27	29 Mishpatim Shekalim	28	30 R. Ḥ.	1 Sivan R. Ḥ.	2	3	4 Shofetim	6	6	8	8
23	28	30 R. Ḥ.	29	1 Iyyar R. Ḥ.	2 Be-Midbar	3	4	5	7	7	9	9
24	29	1 Adar R. Ḥ.	1 Nisan R. Ḥ.	2	3	4	5	6	8	8 Lekh Lekha	10	10 Fast
25	1 Shevat R. Ḥ. Va-Era	2	2	3 Tazri'a Meẓora	4	5	6 Devarim	7	9	9	11	11
26	2	3	3	4	5	6	7	8	10 Yom Kippur	10	12	12 Va-Yeḥi
27	3	4	4	5	6 Shavuot	7 Ḥukkat	8	9	11	11	13	13
28	4	5	5 Va-Yikra	6	7	8	9 Tishah be-Av	10	12	12	14 Va-Yishlaḥ	14
29	5	6 Terumah	6	7	8	9	10	11 Ki Teẓe	13	13	15	15
30	6		7	8	9 Naso	10	11	12	14	14	16	16
31	7		8		10		12	13		15 Va-Yera		17

1937

5697/98 תרצ״ז / תרצ״ח

	January	February	March	April	May	June	July	August	September	October	November	December
1	18 Tevet	20	18	20 Ḥol ha-Moʼed	20 *Emor*	22	22	24	25	26	27	27 3
2	19 *Shemot*	21	19	21 Pesaḥ	21	23	23	25	26	27 *Bereshit*	28	28 4
3	20	22	20	22	22	24	24 *Pinḥas*	26	27	28	29	29 5
4	21	23	21	23	23	25	25	27	28 *Niẓẓavim*	29	30 R. Ḥ.	30 R. Ḥ. *Mi-Keẓ* 6
5	22	24	22	24	24	26 *Shelaḥ*	26	28	29	30 R. Ḥ.	1 Kislev R. Ḥ.	1 Tevet R. Ḥ. 7
6	23	25 *Mishpatim* Shekalim	*Va-Yakhel Pekudei* 23 Parah	25	25	27	27	29	1 Tishri Rosh Ha-Shanah	1 Ḥeshvan R. Ḥ.	2 *Toledot*	2 8
7	24	26	24	26	26	28	28	30 R. Ḥ. *Reʼeh*	2	2	3	3
8	25	27	25	27	27 *Be-Har Be-Ḥukkotai*	29	29	1 Elul R. Ḥ.	3 Fast	3	4	4
9	26 *Va-Era*	28	26	28	28	30 R. Ḥ.	1 Av R. Ḥ.	2	4	4 *Noʼaḥ*	5	5
10	27	29	27	29 *Shemini*	29	1 Tammuz R. Ḥ.	2 *Mattot Masei*	3	5	5	6	6
11	28	30 R. Ḥ.	28	30 R. Ḥ.	1 Sivan R. Ḥ.	2	3	4	6 *Va-Yelekh* Shabbat Shuvah	6	7	7 *Va-Yiggash*
12	29	1 Adar R. Ḥ.	29	1 Iyyar R. Ḥ.	2	3 *Koraḥ*	4	5	7	7	8	8
13	1 Shevat R. Ḥ.	2 *Terumah*	1 R. Ḥ. *Va-Yikra* Nisan Ha-Ḥodesh	2	3	4	5	6	8	8	9 *Va-Yeẓe*	9
14	2	3	2	3	4	5	6	7 *Shofetim*	9	9	10	10 Fast
15	3	4	3	4	5 *Be-Midbar*	6	7	8	10 Yom Kippur	10	11	11
16	4 *Bo*	5	4	5	6 Shavuot	7	8	9	11	11 *Lekh Lekha*	12	12
17	5	6	5	6 *Tazriʼa Meẓora*	7	8	9 *Devarim* Tishah be-Av	10	12	12	13	13
18	6	7	6	7	8	9	10 Fast	11	13 *Haʼazinu*	13	14	14 *Va-Yeḥi*
19	7	8	7	8	9	10 *Ḥukkat*	11	12	14	14	15	15
20	8	9 *Teẓavveh* Zakhor	8 *Ẓav* Shabbat ha-Gadol	9	10	11	12	13	15 Sukkot	15	16 *Va-Yishlaḥ*	16
21	9	10	9	10	11	12	13	14 *Ki Teẓe*	16	16	17	17
22	10	11	10	11	12 *Naso*	13	14	15	17	17	18	18
23	11 *Be-Shallaḥ*	12	11	12	13	14	15	16	18 Ḥol ha-Moʼed	18 *Va-Yera*	19	19
24	12	13 Taʼanit Esther	12	13 *Aḥarei Mot Kedoshim*	14	15	16 *Va-Etḥannan*	17	19	19	20	20
25	13	14 Purim	13	14	15	16	17	18	20	20	21	21 *Shemot*
26	14	15 Shushan Purim	14	15	16	17 *Balak*	18	19	21 Hoshana Rabba	21	22	22
27	15	16 *Ki Tissa*	15 Pesaḥ	16	17	18 Fast	19	20	22 Shemini Aẓeret	22	23 *Va-Yeshev*	23
28	16	17	16 Omer	17	18	19	20	21 *Ki Tavo*	23 Simḥat Torah *Ve-Zot Ha-Berakhah*	23	24	24
29	17		17 Ḥol ha-Moʼed	18 Lag ba-Omer	19 *Be-Haʼalotkha*	20	21	22	24	24	25 Ḥanukkah 1	25
30	18 *Yitro*		18	19	20	21	22	23	25	25 *Ḥayyei Sarah*	26 2	26
31	19		19		21		23 *Ekev*	24		26		27

1938

5698/99 תרצ״ח / תרצ״ט

	January	February	March	April	May	June	July	August	September	October	November	December
1	28 Tevet *Va-Era*	30 R. Ḥ.	28	29	30 R. Ḥ.	2	2	4	5	6 *Va-Yelekh* Shabbat Shuvah	7	8
2	29	1 Adar I R. Ḥ.	29	1 R. Ḥ. *Tazriʼa* Nisan Ha-Ḥodesh	1 Iyyar R. Ḥ.	3	3 *Koraḥ*	5	6	7	8	9
3	1 Shevat R. Ḥ.	2	30 R. Ḥ.	2	2	4	4	6	7 *Shofetim*	8	9	10 *Va-Yeẓe*
4	2	3	1 Adar II R. Ḥ.	3	3	5 *Be-Midbar*	5	7	8	9	10	11
5	3	4 *Terumah*	2 *Pekudei*	4	4	6 Shavuot	6	8	9	10 Yom Kippur	11 *Lekh Lekha*	12
6	4	5	3	5	5	7	7	9 *Devarim* Tishah be-Av	10	11	12	13
7	5	6	4	6	6 *Kedoshim*	8	8	10 Fast	11	12	13	14
8	6 *Bo*	7	5	7	7	9	9	11	12	13 *Haʼazinu*	14	15
9	7	8	6	8 *Meẓora* Shabbat ha-Gadol	8	10	10 *Ḥukkat*	12	13	14	15	16
10	8	9	7	9	9	11	11	13	14 *Ki Teẓe*	15 Sukkot	16	17 *Va-Yishlaḥ*
11	9	10	8	10	10	12 *Naso*	12	14	15	16	17	18
12	10	11 *Teẓavveh*	9 *Va-Yikra* Zakhor	11	11	13	13	15	16	17	18 *Va-Yera*	19
13	11	12	10	12	12	14	14	16 *Va-Etḥannan*	17	18 Ḥol ha-Moʼed	19	20
14	12	13	11	13	13 *Emor*	15	15	17	18	19	20	21
15	13 *Be-Shallaḥ*	14	12	14	14	16	16	18	19	20	21	22
16	14	15	13 Taʼanit Esther	15 Pesaḥ	15	17	17 *Balak*	19	20	21 Hoshana Rabba	22	23
17	15	16	14 Purim	16 Omer	16	18	18 Fast	20	21 *Ki Tavo*	22 Shemini Aẓeret	23	24 *Va-Yeshev*
18	16	17	15 Shushan Purim	17	17	19 *Be-Haʼalotkha*	19	21	22	23 Simḥat Torah *Ve-Zot Ha-Berakhah*	24	25 Ḥanukkah 1
19	17	18 *Ki Tissa*	16 *Ẓav*	18 Ḥol ha-Moʼed	18 Lag ba-Omer	20	20	22	23	24	25 *Ḥayyei Sarah*	26 2
20	18	19	17	19	19	21	21	23 *Ekev*	24	25	26	27 3
21	19	20	18	20	20 *Be-Har*	22	22	24	25	26	27	28 4
22	20 *Yitro*	21	19	21 Pesaḥ	21	23	23	25	26	27 *Bereshit*	28	29 5
23	21	22	20	22	22	24	24 *Pinḥas*	26	27	28	29	1 Tevet R. Ḥ. 6
24	22	23	21	23	23	25	25	27	28 *Niẓẓavim*	29	1 Kislev R. Ḥ.	2 *Mi-Keẓ* 7
25	23	24	22	24	24	26 *Shelaḥ*	26	28	29	30 R. Ḥ.	2	3 8
26	24	25 *Va-Yakhel* Shekalim	23 *Shemini* Parah	25	25	27	27	29	1 Tishri Rosh Ha-Shanah	1 Ḥeshvan R. Ḥ.	3 *Toledot*	4
27	25	26	24	26	26	28	28	30 R. Ḥ. *Reʼeh*	2	2	4	5
28	26	27	25	27	27 *Be-Ḥukkotai*	29	29	1 Elul R. Ḥ.	3 Fast	3	5	6
29	27 *Mishpatim*		26	28	28	30 R. Ḥ.	1 Av R. Ḥ.	2	4	4 *Noʼaḥ*	6	7
30	28		27	29 *Aḥarei Mot*	29	1 Tammuz R. Ḥ.	2 *Mattot Masei*	3	5	5	7	8
31	29		28		1 Sivan R. Ḥ.		3	4		6		9 *Va-Yiggash*

1939

5699/5700 תרצ״ט / ת״ש

	January	February	March	April	May	June	July	August	September	October	November	December
1	10 Tevet Fast	12	10	12 Ẓav Shabbat ha-Gadol	12	14	14 Balak	16	17	18 Ḥol ha-Mo'ed	19	19
2	11	13	11 Ta'anit Esther	13	13	15	15	17	18 Ki Tavo	19	20	20 Va-Yeshev
3	12	14	12	14	14	16 Be-Ha'alotkha	16	18	19	20	21	21
4	13	15 Be-Shallaḥ	13 Teẓavveh Zakhor	15 Pesaḥ	15	17	17 Fast	19	20	21 Hoshana Rabba	22 Ḥayyei Sarah	22
5	14	16	14 Purim	16 Omer	16	18	18	20 Ekev	21	22 Shemini Aẓeret	23	23
6	15	17	15 Shushan Purim	17 Ḥol ha-Mo'ed	17 Emor	19	19	21	22	23 Simḥat Torah Ve-Zot Ha-Berakhah	24	24
7	16 Va-Yeḥi	18	16	18	18 Lag ba-Omer	20	20	22	23	24 Bereshit	25	25 Ḥanukkah 1
8	17	19	17	19	19	21	21 Pinḥas	23	24	25	26	26 2
9	18	20	18	20	20	22	22	24	25 Niẓẓavim Va-Yelekh	26	27	27 Mi-Keẓ 3
10	19	21	19	21 Pesaḥ	21	23 Shelaḥ	23	25	26	27	28	28 4
11	20	22 Yitro	20 Ki Tissa Parah	22	22	24	24	26	27	28	29 Toledot	29 5
12	21	23	21	23	23	25	25	27 Re'eh	28	29	30 R. Ḥ.	30 R. Ḥ. 6
13	22	24	22	24	24 Be-Har Be-Ḥukkotai	26	26	28	29	30 R. Ḥ.	1 Kislev R. Ḥ.	1 Tevet R. Ḥ. 7
14	23 Shemot	25	23	25	25	27	27	29	1 Tishri Rosh Ha-Shanah	1 Ḥeshvan R. Ḥ. No'aḥ	2	2 8
15	24	26	24	26 Shemini	26	28	28 Mattot Masei	30 R. Ḥ.	2	2	3	3
16	25	27	25	27	27	29	29	1 Elul R. Ḥ.	3 Ha'azinu Shabbat Shuvah	3	4	4 Va-Yiggash
17	26	28	26	28	28	30 R. Ḥ. Koraḥ	1 Av R. Ḥ.	2	4 Fast	4	5	5
18	27	29 Mishpatim Shekalim	27 Va-Yakhel Pekudei Ha-Ḥodesh	29	29	1 Tammuz R. Ḥ.	2	3	5	5	6 Va-Yeẓe	6
19	28	30 R. Ḥ.	28	30 R. Ḥ.	1 Sivan R. Ḥ.	2	3	4 Shofetim	6	6	7	7
20	29	1 Adar R. Ḥ.	29	1 Iyyar R. Ḥ.	2 Be-Midbar	3	4	5	7	7	8	8
21	1 Shevat R. Ḥ. Va-Era	2	1 Nisan R. Ḥ.	2	3	4	5	6	8	8 Lekh Lekha	9	9
22	2	3	2	3 Tazri'a Meẓora	4	5	6 Devarim	7	9	9	10	10 Fast
23	3	4	3	4	5	6	7	8	10 Yom Kippur	10	11	11 Va-Yeḥi
24	4	5	4	5	6 Shavuot	7 Ḥukkat	8	9	11	11	12	12
25	5	6 Terumah	5 Va-Yikra	6	7	8	9 Tishah be-Av	10	12	12	13 Va-Yishlaḥ	13
26	6	7	6	7	8	9	10	11 Ki Teẓe	13	13	14	14
27	7	8	7	8	9 Naso	10	11	12	14	14	15	15
28	8 Bo	9	8	9	10	11	12	13	15 Sukkot	15 Va-Yera	16	16
29	9		9	10 Aḥarei Mot Kedoshim	11	12	13 Va-Etḥannan	14	16	16	17	17
30	10		10	11	12	13	14	15	17 Ḥol ha-Moed	17	18	18 Shemot
31	11		11		13		15	16		18		19

1940

5700/01 ת״ש / תש״א

	January	February	March	April	May	June	July	August	September	October	November	December
1	20 Tevet	22	21	22	23	24 Be-Midbar	25	26	28	28	30 R. Ḥ.	1 Kislev R. Ḥ.
2	21	23	22 Va-Yakhel	23	24	25	26	27	29	29	1 Ḥeshvan R. Ḥ. No'aḥ	2
3	22	24 Mishpatim	23	24	25	26	27	28 Masei	30 R. Ḥ.	1 Tishri Rosh Ha-Shanah	2	3
4	23	25	24	25	26 Kedoshim	27	28	29	1 Elul R. Ḥ.	2	3	4
5	24	26	25	26	27	28	29	1 Av R. Ḥ.	2	3 Ha'azinu Shabbat Shuvah	4	5
6	25 Va-Era	27	26	27 Tazri'a Ha-Ḥodesh	28	29	30 R. Ḥ. Ḥukkat	2	3	4 Fast	5	6
7	26	28	27	28	29	1 Sivan R. Ḥ.	1 Tammuz R. Ḥ.	3	4 Shofetim	5	6	7 Va-Yeẓe
8	27	29	28	29	30 R. Ḥ.	2 Naso	2	4	5	6	7	8
9	28	30 R. Ḥ.	29 Pekudei Shekalim	1 Nisan R. Ḥ.	1 Iyyar R. Ḥ.	3	3	5	6	7	8 Lekh Lekha	9
10	29	1 Adar I R. Ḥ. Terumah	30 R. Ḥ.	2	2	4	4	6 Devarim	7	8	9	10
11	1 Shevat R. Ḥ.	2	1 Adar II R. Ḥ.	3	3 Emor	5	5	7	8	9	10	11
12	2	3	2	4	4	6 Shavuot	6	8	9	10 Yom Kippur	11	12
13	3 Bo	4	3	5 Meẓora	5	7	7 Balak	9 Tishah be-Av	10	11	12	13
14	4	5	4	6	6	8	8	10	11 Ki Teẓe	12	13	14 Va-Yishlaḥ
15	5	6	5	7	7	9 Be-Ha'alotkha	9	11	12	13	14	15
16	6	7	6 Va-Yikra	8	8	10	10	12	13	14	15 Va-Yera	16
17	7	8 Teẓavveh	7	9	9	11	11	13 Va-Etḥannan	14	15 Sukkot	16	17
18	8	9	8	10	10 Be-Har	12	12	14	15	16	17	18
19	9	10	9	11	11	13	13	15	16	17 Ḥol ha-Mo'ed	18	19
20	10 Be-Shallaḥ	11	10	12 Aḥarei Mot Shabbat ha-Gadol	12	14	14 Pinḥas	16	17	18	19	20
21	11	12	11 Ta'anit Esther	13	13	15	15	17	18 Ki Tavo	19	20	21 Va-Yeshev
22	12	13	12	14	14	16 Shelaḥ	16	18	19	20	21	22
23	13	14	13 Ẓav Zakhor	15 Pesaḥ	15	17	17 Fast	19	20	21 Hoshana Rabba	22 Ḥayyei Sarah	23
24	14	15 Ki Tissa	14 Purim	16 Omer	16	18	18	20 Ekev	21	22 Shemini Aẓeret	23	24
25	15	16	15 Shushan Purim	17 Ḥol ha-Mo'ed	17 Be-Ḥukkotai	19	19	21	22	23 Simḥat Torah Ve-Zot Ha-Berakhah	24	25 Ḥanukkah 1
26	16	17	16	18	18 Lag ba-Omer	20	20	22	23	24 Bereshit	25	26 2
27	17 Yitro	18	17	19	19	21	21 Mattot	23	24	25	26	27 3
28	18	19	18	20	20	22	22	24	25 Niẓẓavim Va-Yelekh	26	27	28 Mi-Keẓ 4
29	19	20	19	21 Pesaḥ	21	23 Koraḥ	23	25	26	27	28	29 5
30	20		20 Shemini Parah	22	22	24	24	26	27	28	29 Toledot	30 R. Ḥ. 6
31	21		21		23		25	27 Re'eh		29		1 Tevet R. Ḥ. 7

1941

5701/02 תש״א / תש״ב

	January	February	March	April	May	June	July	August	September	October	November	December
1	2 Tevet Ḥanukkah 8	4 *Bo*	2 *Terumah*	4	4	6 Shavuot	6	8	9	10 Yom Kippur	11 *Lekh Lekha*	11
2	3	5	3	5	5	7	7	9 *Devarim* Tishah be-Av	10	11	12	12
3	4	6	4	6	6 *Tazri'a Meẓora*	8	8	10 Fast	11	12	13	13
4	5 *Va-Yiggash*	7	5	7	7	9	9	11	12	13 *Ha'azinu*	14	14
5	6	8	6	8 *Ẓav* Shabbat ha-Gadol	8	10	10 *Ḥukkat*	12	13	14	15	15
6	7	9	7	9	9	11	11	13	14 *Ki Teẓe*	15 Sukkot	16	16 *Va-Yishlaḥ*
7	8	10	8	10	10	12 *Naso*	12	14	15	16	17	17
8	9	11 *Be-Shallaḥ*	9 *Teẓavveh* Zakhor	11	11	13	13	15	16	17 Ḥol ha-Mo'ed	18 *Va-Yera*	18
9	10 Fast	12	10	12	12	14	14	16 *Va-Etḥannan*	17	18	19	19
10	11	13	11	13	13 *Aḥarei Mot Kedoshim*	15	15	17	18	19	20	20
11	12 *Va-Yeḥi*	14	12	14	14	16	16	18	19	20	21	21
12	13	15	13 Ta'anit Esther	15 Pesaḥ	15	17	17 *Balak*	19	20	21 Hoshana Rabba	22	22
13	14	16	14 Purim	16 Omer	16	18	18 Fast	20	21 *Ki Tavo*	22 Shemini Aẓeret	23	23 *Va-Yeshev*
14	15	17	15 Shushan Purim	17 Ḥol ha-Mo'ed	17	19 *Be-Ha'alotkha*	19	21	22	23 Simḥat Torah *Ve-Zot Ha-Berakhah*	24	24
15	16	18 *Yitro*	16 *Ki Tissa*	18	18 Lag ba-Omer	20	20	22	23	24	25 *Ḥayyei Sarah*	25 Ḥanukkah 1
16	17	19	17	19	19	21	21	23 *Ekev*	24	25	26	26 2
17	18	20	18	20	20 *Emor*	22	22	24	25	26	27	27 3
18	19 *Shemot*	21	19	21 Pesaḥ	21	23	23	25	26	27 *Bereshit*	28	28 4
19	20	22	20	22	22	24	24 *Pinḥas*	26	27	28	29	29 5
20	21	23	21	23	23	25	25	27	28 *Niẓẓavim*	29	30 R. Ḥ.	30 R. Ḥ. *Mi-Keẓ* 6
21	22	24	22	24	24	26 *Shelaḥ*	26	28	29	30 R. Ḥ.	1 Kislev R. Ḥ.	1 Tevet R. Ḥ. 7
22	23	25 *Mishpatim* Shekalim	23 *Va-Yakhel Pekudei* Parah	25	25	27	27	29	1 Tishri Rosh Ha-Shanah	1 Ḥeshvan R. Ḥ.	2 *Toledot*	2 8
23	24	26	24	26	26	28	28	30 R. Ḥ. *Re'eh*	2	2	3	3
24	25	27	25	27	27 *Be-Har Be-Ḥukkotai*	29	29	1 Elul R. Ḥ.	3 Fast	3	4	4
25	26 *Va-Era*	28	26	28	28	30 R. Ḥ.	1 Av R. Ḥ.	2	4	4 *No'aḥ*	5	5
26	27	29	27	29 *Shemini*	29	1 Tammuz R. Ḥ.	2 *Mattot Masei*	3	5	5	6	6
27	28	30 R. Ḥ.	28	30 R. Ḥ.	1 Sivan R. Ḥ.	2	3	4	6 *Va-Yelekh* Shabbat Shuvah	6	7	7 *Va-Yiggash*
28	29	1 Adar R. Ḥ.	29	1 Iyyar R. Ḥ.	2	3 *Koraḥ*	4	5	7	7	8	8
29	1 Shevat R. Ḥ.		1 Nisan R. Ḥ. *Va-Yikra* Ha-Ḥodesh	2	3	4	5	6	8	8	9 *Va-Yeẓe*	9
30	2		2	3	4	5	6	7 *Shofetim*	9	9	10	10 Fast
31	3		3		5 *Be-Midbar*		7	8		10		11

1942

5702/03 תש״ב / תש״ג

	January	February	March	April	May	June	July	August	September	October	November	December
1	12 Tevet	14	12	14	14	16	16	18 *Ekev*	19	20 Ḥol ha-Mo'ed	21	22
2	13	15	13 Ta'anit Esther	15 Pesaḥ	15 *Emor*	17	17 Fast	19	20	21 Hoshana Rabba	22	23
3	14 *Va-Yeḥi*	16	14 Purim	16 Omer	16	18	18	20	21	22 Shemini Aẓeret	23	24
4	15	17	15 Shushan Purim	17 Ḥol ha-Mo'ed	17	19	19 *Pinḥas*	21	22	23 Simḥat Torah *Ve-Zot Ha-Berakhah*	24	25 Ḥanukkah 1
5	16	18	16	18	18 Lag ba-Omer	20	20	22	23 *Niẓẓavim Va-Yelekh*	24	25	26 *Va-Yeshev* 2
6	17	19	17	19	19	21 *Be-Ha'alotkha*	21	23	24	25	26	27 3
7	18	20 *Yitro*	18 *Ki Tissa* Parah	20	20	22	22	24	25	26	27 *Ḥayyei Sarah*	28 4
8	19	21	19	21 Pesaḥ	21	23	23	25 *Re'eh*	26	27	28	29 5
9	20	22	20	22	22 *Be-Har Be-Ḥukkotai*	24	24	26	27	28	29	1 Tevet R. Ḥ. 6
10	21 *Shemot*	23	21	23	23	25	25	27	28	29 *Bereshit*	1 Kislev R. Ḥ.	2 7
11	22	24	22	24 *Shemini*	24	26	26 *Mattot Masei*	28	29	30 R. Ḥ.	2	3 8
12	23	25	23	25	25	27	27	29	1 Tishri Rosh Ha-Shanah	1 Ḥeshvan R. Ḥ.	3	4 *Mi-Keẓ*
13	24	26	24	26	26	28 *Shelaḥ*	28	30 R. Ḥ.	2	2	4	5
14	25	27 *Mishpatim* Shekalim	25 *Va-Yakhel Pekudei* Ha-Ḥodesh	27	27	29	29	1 Elul R. Ḥ.	3 Fast	3	5 *Toledot*	6
15	26	28	26	28	28	30 R. Ḥ.	1 Av R. Ḥ.	2 *Shofetim*	4	4	6	7
16	27	29	27	29	29 *Be-Midbar*	1 Tammuz R. Ḥ.	2	3	5	5	7	8
17	28 *Va-Era*	30 R. Ḥ.	28	30 R. Ḥ.	1 Sivan R. Ḥ.	2	3	4	6	6 *No'aḥ*	8	9
18	29	1 Adar R. Ḥ.	29	1 Iyyar R. Ḥ. *Tazri'a Meẓora*	2	3	4 *Devarim*	5	7	7	9	10 Fast
19	1 Shevat R. Ḥ.	2	1 Nisan R. Ḥ.	2	3	4	5	6	8 *Ha'azinu* Shabbat Shuvah	8	10	11 *Va-Yiggash*
20	2	3	2	3	4	5 *Koraḥ*	6	7	9	9	11	12
21	3	4 *Terumah*	3 *Va-Yikra*	4	5	6	7	8	10 Yom Kippur	10	12 *Va-Yeẓe*	13
22	4	5	4	5	6 Shavuot	7	8	9 *Ki Teẓe*	11	11	13	14
23	5	6	5	6	7	8	9 Tishah be-Av	10	12	12	14	15
24	6 *Bo*	7	6	7	8	9	10	11	13	13 *Lekh Lekha*	15	16
25	7	8	7	8 *Aḥarei Mot Kedoshim*	9	10	11 *Va-Etḥannan*	12	14	14	16	17
26	8	9	8	9	10	11	12	13	15 Sukkot	15	17	18 *Va-Yeḥi*
27	9	10	9	10	11	12 *Ḥukkat Balak*	13	14	16	16	18	19
28	10	11 *Teẓavveh* Zakhor	10 *Ẓav* Shabbat ha-Gadol	11	12	13	14	15	17 Ḥol ha-Mo'ed	17	19 *Va-Yishlaḥ*	20
29	11		11	12	13	14	15	16 *Ki Tavo*	18	18	20	21
30	12		12	13	14 *Naso*	15	16	17	19	19	21	22
31	13 *Be-Shallaḥ*		13		15		17	18		20 *Va-Yera*		23

1943

5703/04 תש״ג / תש״ד

	January	February	March	April	May	June	July	August	September	October	November	December
1	24 Tevet	26	24	25	26 Aḥarei Mot	27	28	29	1 Elul R. Ḥ.	2 Rosh Ha-Shanah	3	4
2	25 Shemot	27	25	26	27	28	29	1 Av R. Ḥ.	2	3 Ha'azinu Shabbat Shuvah	4	5
3	26	28	26	27 Shemini Ha-Ḥodesh	28	29	30 R. Ḥ. Koraḥ	2	3	4 Fast	5	6
4	27	29	27	28	29	1 Sivan R. Ḥ.	1 Tammuz R. Ḥ.	3	4 Shofetim	5	6	7 Va-Yeẓe
5	28	30 R. Ḥ.	28	29	30 R. Ḥ.	2 Be-Midbar	2	4	5	6	7	8
6	29	1 Adar I R. Ḥ. Mishpatim	29 Va-Yakhel Shekalim	1 Nisan R. Ḥ.	1 Iyyar R. Ḥ.	3	3	5	6	7	8 Lekh Lekha	9
7	1 Shevat R. Ḥ.	2	30 R. Ḥ.	2	2	4	4	6 Devarim	7	8	9	10
8	2	3	1 Adar II R. Ḥ.	3	3 Kedoshim	5	5	7	8	9	10	11
9	3 Va-Era	4	2	4	4	6 Shavuot	6	8	9	10 Yom Kippur	11	12
10	4	5	3	5 Tazri'a	5	7	7 Ḥukkat	9 Tishah be-Av	10	11	12	13
11	5	6	4	6	6	8	8	10	11 Ki Teẓe	12	13	14 Va-Yishlaḥ
12	6	7	5	7	7	9 Naso	9	11	12	13	14	15
13	7	8 Terumah	6 Pekudei	8	8	10	10	12	13	14	15 Va-Yera	16
14	8	9	7	9	9	11	11	13 Va-Etḥannan	14	15 Sukkot	16	17
15	9	10	8	10	10 Emor	12	12	14	15	16	17	18
16	10 Bo	11	9	11	11	13	13	15	16	17 Ḥol ha-Mo'ed	18	19
17	11	12	10	12 Meẓora Shabbat ha-Gadol	12	14	14 Balak	16	17	18	19	20
18	12	13	11 Ta'anit Esther	13	13	15	15	17	18 Ki Tavo	19	20	21 Va-Yeshev
19	13	14	12	14	14	16 Be-Ha'alotkha	16	18	19	20	21	22
20	14	15 Teẓavveh	13 Va-Yikra Zakhor	15 Pesaḥ	15	17	17 Fast	19	20	21 Hoshana Rabba	22 Ḥayyei Sarah	23
21	15	16	14 Purim	16 Omer	16	18	18	20 Ekev	21	22 Shemini Aẓeret	23	24
22	16	17	15 Shushan Purim	17 Ḥol ha-Mo'ed	17 Be-Har	19	19	21	22	23 Simḥat Torah Ve-Zot Ha-Berakhah	24	25 Ḥanukkah (1)
23	17 Be-Shallaḥ	18	16	18	18 Lag ba-Omer	20	20	22	23	24 Bereshit	25	26 (2)
24	18	19	17	19	19	21	21 Pinḥas	23	24	25	26	27 (3)
25	19	20	18	20	20	22	22	24	25 Niẓẓavim Va-Yelekh	26	27	28 Mi-Keẓ (4)
26	20	21	19	21 Pesaḥ	21	23 Shelaḥ	23	25	26	27	28	29 (5)
27	21	22 Ki Tissa	20 Ẓav Parah	22	22	24	24	26	27	28	29 Toledot	30 R. Ḥ. (6)
28	22	23	21	23	23	25	25	27 Re'eh	28	29	1 Kislev R. Ḥ.	1 Tevet R. Ḥ. (7)
29	23		22	24	24 Be-Ḥukkotai	26	26	28	29	30 R. Ḥ.	2	2 (8)
30	24 Yitro		23	25	25	27	27	29	1 Tishri Rosh Ha-Shanah	1 Ḥeshvan R. Ḥ. No'aḥ	3	3
31	25		24		26		28 Mattot Masei	30 R. Ḥ.		2		4

1944

5704/05 תש״ד / תש״ה

	January	February	March	April	May	June	July	August	September	October	November	December
1	5 Tevet Va-Yiggash	7	6	8 Ẓav Shabbat ha-Gadol	8	10	10 Ḥukkat	12	13	14	15	15
2	6	8	7	9	9	11	11	13	14 Ki Teẓe	15 Sukkot	16	16 Va-Yishlaḥ
3	7	9	8	10	10	12 Naso	12	14	15	16	17	17
4	8	10	9 Teẓavveh Zakhor	11	11	13	13	15	16	17 Ḥol ha-Mo'ed	18 Va-Yera	18
5	9	11 Be-Shallaḥ	10	12	12	14	14	16 Va-Etḥannan	17	18	19	19
6	10 Fast	12	11	13	13 Aḥarei Mot Kedoshim	15	15	17	18	19	20	20
7	11	13	12	14	14	16	16	18	19	20	21	21
8	12 Va-Yeḥi	14	13 Ta'anit Esther	15 Pesaḥ	15	17	17 Balak	19	20	21 Hoshana Rabba	22	22
9	13	15	14 Purim	16 Omer	16	18	18 Fast	20	21 Ki Tavo	22 Shemini Aẓeret	23	23 Va-Yeshev
10	14	16	15 Shushan Purim	17 Ḥol ha-Mo'ed	17	19 Be-Ha'alotkha	19	21	22	23 Simḥat Torah Ve-Zot Ha-Berakhah	24	24
11	15	17	16 Ki Tissa	18	18 Lag ba-Omer	20	20	22	23	24	25 Ḥayyei Sarah	25 Ḥanukkah (1)
12	16	18 Yitro	17	19	19	21	21	23 Ekev	24	25	26	26 (2)
13	17	19	18	20	20 Emor	22	22	24	25	26	27	27 (3)
14	18	20	19	21 Pesaḥ	21	23	23	25	26	27 Bereshit	28	28 (4)
15	19 Shemot	21	20	22	22	24	24 Pinḥas	26	27	28	29	29 (5)
16	20	22	21	23	23	25	25	27	28 Niẓẓavim	29	30 R. Ḥ.	30 R. Ḥ. Mi-Keẓ (6)
17	21	23	22	24	24	26 Shelaḥ	26	28	29	30 R. Ḥ.	1 Kislev R. Ḥ.	1 Tevet R. Ḥ. (7)
18	22	24	23 Va-Yakhel Pekudei Parah	25	25	27	27	29	1 Tishri Rosh Ha-Shanah	1 Ḥeshvan R. Ḥ.	2 Toledot	2 (8)
19	23	25 Mishpatim Shekalim	24	26	26	28	28	30 R. Ḥ. Re'eh	2	2	3	3
20	24	26	25	27	27 Be-Har Be-Ḥukkotai	29	29	1 Elul R. Ḥ.	3 Fast	3	4	4
21	25	27	26	28	28	30 R. Ḥ.	1 Av R. Ḥ.	2	4	4 No'aḥ	5	5
22	26 Va-Era	28	27	29 Shemini	29	1 Tammuz R. Ḥ.	2 Mattot Masei	3	5	5	6	6
23	27	29	28	30 R. Ḥ.	1 Sivan R. Ḥ.	2	3	4	6 Va-Yelekh Shabbat Shuvah	6	7	7 Va-Yiggash
24	28	30 R. Ḥ.	29	1 Iyyar R. Ḥ.	2	3 Koraḥ	4	5	7	7	8	8
25	29	1 Adar R. Ḥ.	1 Nisan R. Ḥ. Va-Yikra Ha-Ḥodesh	2	3	4	5	6	8	8	9 Va-Yeẓe	9
26	1 Shevat R. Ḥ.	2 Terumah	2	3	4	5	6	7 Shofetim	9	9	10	10 Fast
27	2	3	3	4	5 Be-Midbar	6	7	8	10 Yom Kippur	10	11	11
28	3	4	4	5	6 Shavuot	7	8	9	11	11 Lekh Lekha	12	12
29	4 Bo	5	5	6 Tazri'a Meẓora	7	8	9 Devarim Tishah be-Av	10	12	12	13	13
30	5		6	7	8	9	10 Fast	11	13 Ha'azinu	13	14	14 Va-Yeḥi
31	6		7		9		11	12		14		15

1945

5705/06 תש״ה / תש״ו

	January	February	March	April	May	June	July	August	September	October	November	December
1	16 **Tevet**	18	16	18 Hol ha-Mo'ed	18 Lag ba-Omer	20	20	22	**23** *Nizzavim Va-Yelekh*	24	25	**26** *Va-Yeshev* 2
2	17	19	17	19	19	**21** *Be-Ha'alotkha*	21	23	24	25	26	27 3
3	18	**20** *Yitro*	**18** *Ki Tissa Parah*	20	20	22	22	24	25	26	**27** *Hayyei Sarah*	28 4
4	19	21	19	21 Pesah	21	23	23	**25** *Re'eh*	26	27	28	29 5
5	20	22	20	22	**22** *Be-Har Be-Hukkotai*	24	24	26	27	28	29	1 **Tevet** R. H. 6
6	**21** *Shemot*	23	21	23	23	25	25	27	28	**29** *Bereshit*	1 **Kislev** R. H.	2 7
7	22	24	22	**24** *Shemini*	24	26	**26** *Mattot Masei*	28	29	30 R. H.	2	3 8
8	23	25	23	25	25	27	27	29	1 **Tishri** Rosh Ha-Shanah	1 **Heshvan** R. H.	3	**4** *Mi-Kez*
9	24	26	24	26	26	**28** *Shelah*	28	30 R. H.	2	2	4	5
10	25	**27** *Mishpatim Shekalim*	**25** *Va-Yakhel Pekudei* Ha-Hodesh	27	27	29	29	1 **Elul** R. H.	3 Fast	3	**5** *Toledot*	6
11	26	28	26	28	28	30 R. H.	1 **Av** R. H.	**2** *Shofetim*	4	4	6	7
12	27	29	27	29	**29** *Be-Midbar*	1 **Tammuz** R. H.	2	3	5	5	7	8
13	**28** *Va-Era*	30 R. H.	28	30 R. H.	1 **Sivan** R. H.	2	3	4	6	**6** *No'ah*	8	9
14	29	1 **Adar** R. H.	29	**1** R. H. **Iyyar** *Tazri'a Mezora*	2	3	**4** *Devarim*	5	7	7	9	10 Fast
15	1 **Shevat** R. H.	2	1 **Nisan** R. H.	2	3	4	5	6	**8** *Ha'azinu* Shabbat Shuvah	8	10	**11** *Va-Yiggash*
16	2	3	2	3	4	**5** *Korah*	6	7	9	9	11	12
17	3	**4** *Terumah*	**3** *Va-Yikra*	4	5	6	7	8	10 Yom Kippur	10	**12** *Va-Yeze*	13
18	4	5	4	5	6 Shavuot	7	8	**9** *Ki Teze*	11	11	13	14
19	5	6	5	6	7	8	9 Tishah be-Av	10	12	12	14	15
20	**6** *Bo*	7	6	7	8	9	10	11	13	**13** *Lekh Lekha*	15	16
21	7	8	7	**8** *Aharei Mot Kedoshim*	9	10	**11** *Va-Ethannan*	12	14	14	16	17
22	8	9	8	9	10	11	12	13	**15** Sukkot	15	17	**18** *Va-Yehi*
23	9	10	9	10	11	**12** *Hukkat Balak*	13	14	16	16	18	19
24	10	**11** *Tezavveh* Zakhor	**10** *Zav* Shabbat ha-Gadol	11	12	13	14	15	17 Hol ha-Mo'ed	17	**19** *Va-Yishlah*	20
25	11	12	11	12	13	14	15	**16** *Ki Tavo*	18	18	20	21
26	12	13 Ta'anit Esther	12	13	**14** *Naso*	15	16	17	19	19	21	22
27	**13** *Be-Shallah*	14 Purim	13	14	15	16	17	18	20	**20** *Va-Yera*	22	23
28	14	15 Shushan Purim	14	**15** *Emor*	16	17 Fast	**18** *Ekev*	19	21 Hoshana Rabba	21	23	24
29	15		15 Pesah	16	17	18	19	20	22 Shemini Azeret	22	24	**25** *Shemot*
30	16		16 Omer	17	18	**19** *Pinhas*	20	21	23 Simhat Torah Ve-Zot Ha-Berakhah	23	25 Hanukkah 1	26
31	17		**17** Hol ha-Mo'ed		19		21	22		24		27

1946

5706/07 תש״ו / תש״ז

	January	February	March	April	May	June	July	August	September	October	November	December
1	28 **Tevet**	30 R. H.	28	29	30 R. H.	**2** *Be-Midbar*	2	4	5	6	7	8
2	29	**1** **Adar I** R. H. *Mishpatim*	**29** *Va-Yakhel* Shekalim	1 **Nisan** R. H.	1 **Iyyar** R. H.	3	3	5	6	7	**8** *Lekh Lekha*	9
3	1 **Shevat** R. H.	2	30 R. H.	2	2	4	4	**6** *Devarim*	7	8	9	10
4	2	3	1 **Adar II** R. H.	3	**3** *Kedoshim*	5	5	7	8	9	10	11
5	**3** *Va-Era*	4	2	4	4	6 Shavuot	6	8	9	**10** Yom Kippur	11	12
6	4	5	3	**5** *Tazri'a*	5	7	**7** *Hukkat*	9 Tishah be-Av	10	11	12	13
7	5	6	4	6	6	8	8	10	**11** *Ki Teze*	12	13	**14** *Va-Yishlah*
8	6	7	5	7	7	**9** *Naso*	9	11	12	13	14	15
9	7	**8** *Terumah*	**6** *Pekudei*	8	8	10	10	12	13	14	**15** *Va-Yera*	16
10	8	9	7	9	9	11	11	**13** *Va-Ethannan*	14	15 Sukkot	16	17
11	9	10	8	10	**10** *Emor*	12	12	14	15	16	17	18
12	**10** *Bo*	11	9	11	11	13	13	15	16	**17** Hol ha-Mo'ed	18	19
13	11	12	10	**12** *Mezora* Shabbat ha-Gadol	12	14	**14** *Balak*	16	17	18	19	20
14	12	13	11 Ta'anit Esther	13	13	15	15	17	**18** *Ki Tavo*	19	20	**21** *Va-Yeshev*
15	13	14	12	14	14	**16** *Be-Ha'alotkha*	16	18	19	20	21	22
16	14	**15** *Tezavveh*	**13** *Va-Yikra* Zakhor	15 Pesah	15	17	17 Fast	19	20	21 Hoshana Rabba	**22** *Hayyei Sarah*	23
17	15	16	14 Purim	16 Omer	16	18	18	**20** *Ekev*	21	22 Shemini Azeret	23	24
18	16	17	15 Shushan Purim	17 Hol ha-Mo'ed	**17** *Be-Har*	19	19	21	22	23 Simhat Torah Ve-Zot Ha-Berakhah	24	25 Hanukkah 1
19	**17** *Be-Shallah*	18	16	18	18 Lag ba-Omer	20	20	22	23	**24** *Bereshit*	25	26 2
20	18	19	17	**19**	19	21	**21** *Pinhas*	23	24	25	26	27 3
21	19	20	18	20	20	22	22	24	**25** *Nizzavim Va-Yelekh*	26	27	**28** *Mi-Kez* 4
22	20	21	19	21 Pesah	21	**23** *Shelah*	23	25	26	27	28	29 5
23	21	**22** *Ki Tissa*	**20** *Zav* Parah	22	22	24	24	26	27	28	**29** *Toledot*	30 R. H. 6
24	22	23	21	23	23	25	25	**27** *Re'eh*	28	29	1 **Kislev** R. H.	1 **Tevet** R. H. 7
25	23	24	22	24	**24** *Be-Hukkotai*	26	26	28	29	30 R. H.	2	2 8
26	**24** *Yitro*	25	23	25	25	27	27	29	1 **Tishri** Rosh Ha-Shanah	**1** R. H. **Heshvan** *No'ah*	3	3
27	25	26	24	**26** *Aharei Mot*	26	28	**28** *Mattot Masei*	30 R. H.	2	2	4	4
28	26	27	25	27	27	29	29	1 **Elul** R. H.	**3** *Ha'azinu* Shabbat Shuvah	3	5	**5** *Va-Yiggash*
29	27		26	28	28	**30** R. H. *Korah*	1 **Av** R. H.	2	4 Fast	4	6	6
30	28		**27** *Shemini* Ha-Hodesh	29	29	1 **Tammuz** R. H.	2	3	5	5	**7** *Va-Yeze*	7
31	29		28		1 **Sivan** R. H.		3	**4** *Shofetim*		6		8

1947

5707/08

תש״ז / תש״ח

	January	February	March	April	May	June	July	August	September	October	November	December
1	9 Tevet	11 *Be-Shallaḥ*	9 *Teẓavveh* Zakhor	11	11	13	13	15	16	17	18 *Va-Yera*	18
2	10 Fast	12	10	12	12	14	14	16 *Va-Ethannan*	17	18 Ḥol ha-Mo'ed	19	19
3	11	13	11	13	13 *Aḥarei Mot Kedoshim*	15	15	17	18	19	20	20
4	12 *Va-Yeḥi*	14	12	14	14	16	16	18	19	20	21	21
5	13	15	13 Ta'anit Esther	15 Pesaḥ	15	17	17 *Balak*	19	20	21 Hoshana Rabba	22	22
6	14	16	14 Purim	16 Omer	16	18	18 Fast	20	21 *Ki Tavo*	22 Shemini Aẓeret	23	23 *Va-Yeshev*
7	15	17	15 Shushan Purim	17	17	19 *Be-Ha'alotkha*	19	21	22	23 Simḥat Torah *Ve-Zot Ha-Berakhah*	24	24
8	16	18 *Yitro*	16 *Ki Tissa*	18 Ḥol ha-Mo'ed	18 Lag ba-Omer	20	20	22	23	24	25 *Ḥayyei Sarah*	25 Ḥanukkah 1
9	17	19	17	19	19	21	21	23 *Ekev*	24	25	26	26 2
10	18	20	18	20	20 *Emor*	22	22	24	25	26	27	27 3
11	19 *Shemot*	21	19	21 Pesaḥ	21	23	23	25	26	27 *Bereshit*	28	28 4
12	20	22	20	22	22	24	24 *Pinḥas*	26	27	28	29	29 5
13	21	23	21	23	23	25	25	27	28 *Niẓẓavim*	29	30 R. Ḥ.	30 R. Ḥ. *Mi-Keẓ* 6
14	22	24	22	24	24	26 *Shelaḥ*	26	28	29	30 R. Ḥ.	1 Kislev R. Ḥ.	1 Tevet R. Ḥ. 7
15	23	25 *Mishpatim* Shekalim	*Va-Yakhel Pekudei* 23 Parah	25	25	27	27	29	1 Tishri Rosh Ha-Shanah	1 Ḥeshvan R. Ḥ.	2 *Toledot*	2 8
16	24	26	24	26	26	28	28	30 *Re'eh* R. Ḥ.	2	2	3	3
17	25	27	25	27	27 *Be-Har Be-Ḥukkotai*	29	29	1 Elul R. Ḥ.	3 Fast	3	4	4
18	26 *Va-Era*	28	26	28	28	30 R. Ḥ.	1 Av R. Ḥ.	2	4	4 *No'aḥ*	5	5
19	27	29	27	29 *Shemini*	29	1 Tammuz R. Ḥ.	2 *Mattot Masei*	3	5	5	6	6
20	28	30 R. Ḥ.	28	30 R. Ḥ.	1 Sivan R. Ḥ.	2	3	4	6 *Va-Yelekh* Shabbat Shuvah	6	7	7 *Va-Yiggash*
21	29	1 Adar R. Ḥ.	29	1 Iyyar R. Ḥ.	2	3 *Koraḥ*	4	5	7	7	8	8
22	1 Shevat R. Ḥ.	2 *Terumah*	1 Nisan R. Ḥ. *Va-Yikra* Ha-Ḥodesh	2	3	4	5	6	8	8	9 *Va-Yeẓe*	9
23	2	3	2	3	4	5	6	7 *Shofetim*	9	9	10	10 Fast
24	3	4	3	4	5 *Be-Midbar*	6	7	8	10 Yom Kippur	10	11	11
25	4 *Bo*	5	4	5	6 Shavuot	7	8	9	11	11 *Lekh Lekha*	12	12
26	5	6	5	6 *Tazri'a Meẓora*	7	8	9 *Devarim* Tishah be-Av	10	12	12	13	13
27	6	7	6	7	8	9	10 Fast	11	13 *Ha'azinu*	13	14	14 *Va-Yeḥi*
28	7	8	7	8	9	10 *Ḥukkat*	11	12	14	14	15	15
29	8		8 *Ẓav* Shabbat ha-Gadol	9	10	11	12	13	15 Sukkot	15	16 *Va-Yishlaḥ*	16
30	9		9	10	11	12	13	14 *Ki Teẓe*	16	16	17	17
31	10		10		12 *Naso*		14	15		17		18

1948

5708/09

תש״ח / תש״ט

	January	February	March	April	May	June	July	August	September	October	November	December
1	19 Tevet	21	20	21	22	23	24	25	27	27	29	29
2	20	22	21	22	23	24	25	26	28	28 *Niẓẓavim*	30 R. Ḥ.	30 R. Ḥ.
3	21 *Shemot*	23	22	23 *Shemini* Parah	24	25	26 *Shelaḥ*	27	29	29	1 Ḥeshvan R. Ḥ.	1 Kislev R. Ḥ.
4	22	24	23	24	25	26	27	28	30 R. Ḥ. *Re'eh*	1 Tishri Rosh Ha-Shanah	2	2 *Toledot*
5	23	25	24	25	26	27 *Be-Ḥukkotai*	28	29	1 Elul R. Ḥ.	2	3	3
6	24	26	25 *Va-Yakhel* Shekalim	26	27	28	29	1 Av R. Ḥ.	2	3 Fast	4 *No'aḥ*	4
7	25	27 *Mishpatim*	26	27	28	29	30 R. Ḥ.	2 *Mattot Masei*	3	4	5	5
8	26	28	27	28	29 *Aḥarei Mot*	1 Sivan R. Ḥ.	1 Tammuz R. Ḥ.	3	4	5	6	6
9	27	29	28	29	30 R. Ḥ.	2	2	4	5	6 *Va-Yelekh* Shabbat Shuvah	7	7
10	28 *Va-Era*	30 R. Ḥ.	29	1 Nisan R. Ḥ. *Tazri'a* Ha-Ḥodesh	1 Iyyar R. Ḥ.	3	3 *Koraḥ*	5	6	7	8	8
11	29	1 Adar I R. Ḥ.	30 R. Ḥ.	2	2	4	4	6	7 *Shofetim*	8	9	9 *Va-Yeẓe*
12	1 Shevat R. Ḥ.	2	1 Adar II R. Ḥ.	3	3	5 *Be-Midbar*	5	7	8	9	10	10
13	2	3	2 *Pekudei*	4	4	6 Shavuot	6	8	9	10 Yom Kippur	11 *Lekh Lekha*	11
14	3	4 *Terumah*	3	5	5	7	7	9 *Devarim* Tishah be-Av	10	11	12	12
15	4	5	4	6	6 *Kedoshim*	8	8	10 Fast	11	12	13	13
16	5	6	5	7	7	9	9	11	12	13 *Ha'azinu*	14	14
17	6 *Bo*	7	6	8 *Meẓora* Shabbat ha-Gadol	8	10	10 *Ḥukkat*	12	13	14	15	15
18	7	8	7	9	9	11	11	13	14 *Ki Teẓe*	15 Sukkot	16	16 *Va-Yishlaḥ*
19	8	9	8	10	10	12 *Naso*	12	14	15	16	17	17
20	9	10	9 *Va-Yikra* Zakhor	11	11	13	13	15	16	17	18 *Va-Yera*	18
21	10	11 *Teẓavveh*	10	12	12	14	14	16 *Va-Ethannan*	17	18 Ḥol ha-Mo'ed	19	19
22	11	12	11	13	13 *Emor*	15	15	17	18	19	20	20
23	12	13	12	14	14	16	16	18	19	20	21	21
24	13 *Be-Shallaḥ*	14	13 Ta'anit Esther	15 Pesaḥ	15	17	17 *Balak*	19	20	21 Hoshana Rabba	22	22
25	14	15	14 Purim	16 Omer	16	18	18 Fast	20	21 *Ki Tavo*	22 Shemini Aẓeret	23	23 *Va-Yeshev*
26	15	16	15 Shushan Purim	17	17	19 *Be-Ha'alotkha*	19	21	22	23 Simḥat Torah *Ve-Zot Ha-Berakhah*	24	24
27	16	17	16 *Ẓav*	18 Ḥol ha-Mo'ed	18 Lag ba-Omer	20	20	22	23	24	25 *Ḥayyei Sarah*	25 Ḥanukkah 1
28	17	18 *Ki Tissa*	17	19	19	21	21	23 *Ekev*	24	25	26	26 2
29	18	19	18	20	20 *Be-Har*	22	22	24	25	26	27	27 3
30	19		19	21 Pesaḥ	21	23	23	25	26	27 *Bereshit*	28	28 4
31	20 *Yitro*		20		22		24 *Pinḥas*	26		28		29 5

1949

5709/10 תש״ט / תש״י

	January	February	March	April	May	June	July	August	September	October	November	December
1	30 Kislev R. Ḥ. Ḥanukkah 6 *Mi-Keẓ*	2	30 R. Ḥ.	2	2	4	4	6	7	8 *Ha'azinu* Shabbat Shuvah	9	10
2	1 Tevet R. Ḥ. 7	3	1 Adar R. Ḥ.	3 *Va-Yikra*	3	5	5 *Koraḥ*	7	8	9	10	11
3	2 8	4	2	4	4	6 Shavuot	6	8	9 *Ki Teẓe*	10 Yom Kippur	11	12 *Va-Yeẓe*
4	3	5	3	5	5 Yom ha-Aẓma'ut	7	7	9 Tishah be-Av	10	11	12	13
5	4	6 *Bo*	4 *Terumah*	6	6	8	8	10	11	12	13 *Lekh Lekha*	14
6	5	7	5	7	7	9	9	11 *Va-Etḥannan*	12	13	14	15
7	6	8	6	8	8 *Aḥarei Mot Kedoshim*	10	10	12	13	14	15	16
8	7 *Va-Yiggash*	9	7	9	9	11	11	13	14	15 Sukkot	16	17
9	8	10	8	10 *Ẓav* Shabbat ha-Gadol	10	12	12 *Ḥukkat Balak*	14	15	16	17	18
10	9	11	9	11	11	13	13	15	16 *Ki Tavo*	17 Ḥol ha-Mo'ed	18	19 *Va-Yishlaḥ*
11	10 Fast	12	10	12	12	14 *Naso*	14	16	17	18	19	20
12	11	13 *Be-Shallaḥ*	11 *Teẓavveh* Zakhor	13	13	15	15	17	18	19	20 *Va-Yera*	21
13	12	14	12	14	14	16	16	18 *Ekev*	19	20	21	22
14	13	15	13 Ta'anit Esther	15 Pesaḥ	15 *Emor*	17	17 Fast	19	20	21 Hoshana Rabba	22	23
15	14 *Va-Yeḥi*	16	14 Purim	16 Omer	16	18	18	20	21	22 Shemini Aẓeret	23	24
16	15	17	15 Shushan Purim	17 Ḥol ha-Mo'ed	17	19	19 *Pinḥas*	21	22	23 Simḥat Torah *Ve-Zot Ha-Berakhah*	24	25 Ḥanukkah 1
17	16	18	16	18	18 Lag ba-Omer	20	20	22	23 *Niẓẓavim Va-Yelekh*	24	25	26 *Va-Yeshev* 2
18	17	19	17	19	19	21 *Be-Ha'alotkha*	21	23	24	25	26	27 3
19	18	20 *Yitro*	18 *Ki Tissa* Parah	20	20	22	22	24	25	26	27 *Ḥayyei Sarah*	28 4
20	19	21	19	21 Pesaḥ	21	23	23	25 *Re'eh*	26	27	28	29 5
21	20	22	20	22	22 *Be-Har Be-Ḥukkotai*	24	24	26	27	28	29	1 Tevet R. Ḥ. 6
22	21 *Shemot*	23	21	23	23	25	25	27	28	29 *Bereshit*	1 Kislev R. Ḥ.	2 7
23	22	24	22	24 *Shemini*	24	26	26 *Mattot Masei*	28	29	30 R. Ḥ.	2	3 8
24	23	25	23	25	25	27	27	29	1 Tishri Rosh Ha-Shanah	1 Ḥeshvan R. Ḥ.	3	4 *Mi-Keẓ*
25	24	26	24	26	26	28 *Shelaḥ*	28	30 R. Ḥ.	2	2	4	5
26	25	27 *Mishpatim* Shekalim	25 *Va-Yakhel Pekudei* Ha-Ḥodesh	27	27	29	29	1 Elul R. Ḥ.	3 Fast	3	5 *Toledot*	6
27	26	28	26	28	28	30 R. Ḥ.	1 Av R. Ḥ.	2 *Shofetim*	4	4	6	7
28	27	29	27	29	29 *Be-Midbar*	1 Tammuz R. Ḥ.	2	3	5	5	7	8
29	28 *Va-Era*		28	30 R. Ḥ.	1 Sivan R. Ḥ.	2	3	4	6	6 *No'aḥ*	8	9
30	29		29	1 Iyyar R. Ḥ. *Tazri'a Meẓora*	2	3	4 *Devarim*	5	7	7	9	10 Fast
31	1 Shevat R. Ḥ.		1 Nisan R. Ḥ.		3		5	6		8		11 *Va-Yiggash*

1950

5710/11 תש״י / תשי״א

	January	February	March	April	May	June	July	August	September	October	November	December
1	12 Tevet	14	12	14 *Ẓav* Shabbat ha-Gadol	14	16	16 *Balak*	18	19	20 Ḥol ha-Mo'ed	21	22
2	13	15	13 Ta'anit Esther	15 Pesaḥ	15	17	17 Fast	19	20 *Ki Tavo*	21 Hoshana Rabba	22	23 *Va-Yeshev*
3	14	16	14 Purim	16 Omer	16	18 *Be-Ha'alotkha*	18	20	21	22 Shemini Aẓeret	23	24
4	15	17 *Be-Shallaḥ*	15 Shushan Purim *Teẓavveh*	17 Ḥol ha-Mo'ed	17	19	19	21	22	23 Simḥat Torah *Ve-Zot Ha-Berakhah*	24 *Ḥayyei Sarah*	25 Ḥanukkah 1
5	16	18	16	18	18 Lag ba-Omer	20	20	22 *Ekev*	23	24	25	26 2
6	17	19	17	19	19 *Emor*	21	21	23	24	25	26	27 3
7	18 *Va-Yeḥi*	20	18	20	20	22	22	24	25	26 *Bereshit*	27	28 4
8	19	21	19	21 Pesaḥ	21	23	23 *Pinḥas*	25	26	27	28	29 5
9	20	22	20	22	22	24	24	26	27 *Niẓẓavim*	28	29	30 R. Ḥ. *Mi-Keẓ* 6
10	21	23	21	23	23	25 *Shelaḥ*	25	27	28	29	1 Kislev R. Ḥ.	1 Tevet R. Ḥ. 7
11	22	24 *Yitro*	22 *Ki Tissa* Parah	24	24	26	26	28	29	30 R. Ḥ.	2 *Toledot*	2 8
12	23	25	23	25	25	27	27	29 *Re'eh*	1 Tishri Rosh Ha-Shanah	1 Ḥeshvan R. Ḥ.	3	3
13	24	26	24	26	26 *Be-Har Be-Ḥukkotai*	28	28	30 R. Ḥ.	2	2	4	4
14	25 *Shemot*	27	25	27	27	29	29	1 Elul R. Ḥ.	3 Fast	3 *No'aḥ*	5	5
15	26	28	26	28 *Shemini*	28	30 R. Ḥ.	1 Av R. Ḥ. *Mattot Masei*	2	4	4	6	6
16	27	29	27	29	29	1 Tammuz R. Ḥ.	2	3	5 *Va-Yelekh* Shabbat Shuvah	5	7	7 *Va-Yiggash*
17	28	30 R. Ḥ.	28	30 R. Ḥ.	1 Sivan R. Ḥ.	2 *Koraḥ*	3	4	6	6	8	8
18	29	1 Adar R. Ḥ. *Mishpatim* Shekalim	29 *Va-Yakhel Pekudei* Ha-Ḥodesh	1 Iyyar R. Ḥ.	2	3	4	5	7	7	9 *Va-Yeẓe*	9
19	1 Shevat R. Ḥ.	2	1 Nisan R. Ḥ.	2	3	4	5	6 *Shofetim*	8	8	10	10 Fast
20	2	3	2	3 Yom ha-Aẓma'ut	4 *Be-Midbar*	5	6	7	9	9	11	11
21	3 *Va-Era*	4	3	4	5	6	7	8	10 Yom Kippur	10 *Lekh Lekha*	12	12
22	4	5	4	5 *Tazri'a Meẓora*	6 Shavuot	7	8 *Devarim*	9	11	11	13	13
23	5	6	5	6	7	8	9 Tishah be-Av	10	12 *Ha'azinu*	12	14	14 *Va-Yeḥi*
24	6	7	6	7	8	9 *Ḥukkat*	10	11	13	13	15	15
25	7	8 *Terumah* Zakhor	7 *Va-Yikra*	8	9	10	11	12	14	14	16 *Va-Yishlaḥ*	16
26	8	9	8	9	10	11	12	13 *Ki Teẓe*	15 Sukkot	15	17	17
27	9	10	9	10	11 *Naso*	12	13	14	16	16	18	18
28	10 *Bo*	11	10	11	12	13	14	15	17 Ḥol ha-Mo'ed	17 *Va-Yera*	19	19
29	11		11	12 *Aḥarei Mot Kedoshim*	13	14	15 *Va-Etḥannan*	16	18	18	20	20
30	12		12	13	14	15	16	17	19	19	21	21 *Shemot*
31	13		13		15		17	18		20		22

1951

5711/12 תשי״א / תשי״ב

	January	February	March	April	May	June	July	August	September	October	November	December
1	23 Tevet	25	23	24	25	26	27	28	30 R. H. *Re'eh*	1 Tishri Rosh Ha-Shanah	2	2 *Toledot*
2	24	26	24	25	26	27 *Be-Ḥukkotai*	28	29	1 Elul R. H.	2	3	3
3	25	27 *Mishpatim*	25 *Va-Yakhel* Shekalim	26	27	28	29	1 Av R. H.	2	3 Fast	4 *No'aḥ*	4
4	26	28	26	27	28	29	30 R. H.	2 *Mattot Masei*	3	4	5	5
5	27	29	27	28	29 *Aḥarei Mot*	1 Sivan R. H.	1 Tammuz R. H.	3	4	5	6	6
6	28 *Va-Era*	30 R. H.	28	29	30 R. H.	2	2	4	5	6 *Va-Yelekh* Shabbat Shuvah	7	7
7	29	1 Adar I R. H.	29	1 R. H. *Tazri'a* Nisan Ha-Hodesh	1 Iyyar R. H.	3	3 *Koraḥ*	5	6	7	8	8
8	1 Shevat R. H.	2	30 R. H.	2	2	4	4	6	7 *Shofetim*	8	9	9 *Va-Yeẓe*
9	2	3	1 Adar II R. H.	3	3	5 *Be-Midbar*	5	7	8	9	10	10
10	3	4 *Terumah*	2 *Pekudei*	4	4 Yom ha-Aẓma'ut	6 Shavuot	6	8	9	10 Yom Kippur	11 *Lekh Lekha*	11
11	4	5	3	5	5	7	7	9 *Devarim* Tishah be-Av	10	11	12	12
12	5	6	4	6	6 *Kedoshim*	8	8	10 Fast	11	12	13	13
13	6 *Bo*	7	5	7	7	9	9	11	12	13 *Ha'azinu*	14	14
14	7	8	6	8 *Meẓora* Shabbat ha-Gadol	8	10	10 *Ḥukkat*	12	13	14	15	15
15	8	9	7	9	9	11	11	13	14 *Ki Teẓe*	15 Sukkot	16	16 *Va-Yishlaḥ*
16	9	10	8	10	10	12 *Naso*	12	14	15	16	17	17
17	10	11 *Teẓavveh*	9 *Va-Yikra* Zakhor	11	11	13	13	15	16	17 Ḥol ha-Mo'ed	18 *Va-Yera*	18
18	11	12	10	12	12	14	14	16 *Va-Ethannan*	17	18	19	19
19	12	13	11	13	13 *Emor*	15	15	17	18	19	20	20
20	13 *Be-Shallaḥ*	14	12	14	14	16	16	18	19	20	21	21
21	14	15	13 Ta'anit Esther	15 Pesaḥ	15	17	17 *Balak*	19	20	21 Hoshana Rabba	22	22
22	15	16	14 Purim	16 Omer	16	18	18 Fast	20	21 *Ki Tavo*	22 Shemini Aẓeret	23	23 *Va-Yeshev*
23	16	17	15 Shushan Purim	17 Ḥol ha-Mo'ed	17	19 *Be-Ha'alotkha*	19	21	22	23 Simḥat Torah *Ve-Zot Ha-Berakhah*	24	24
24	17	18 *Ki Tissa*	16 *Ẓav*	18	18 Lag ba-Omer	20	20	22	23	24	25 *Ḥayyei Sarah*	25 Ḥanukkah 1
25	18	19	17	19	19	21	21	23 *Ekev*	24	25	26	26 2
26	19	20	18	20	20 *Be-Har*	22	22	24	25	26	27	27 3
27	20 *Yitro*	21	19	21 Pesaḥ	21	23	23	25	26	27 *Bereshit*	28	28 4
28	21	22	20	22	22	24	24 *Pinḥas*	26	27	28	29	29 5
29	22		21	23	23	25	25	27	28 *Niẓẓavim*	29	30 R. H.	30 R. H. *Mi-Keẓ* 6
30	23		22	24	24	26 *Shelaḥ*	26	28	29	30 R. H.	1 Kislev R. H.	1 Tevet R. H. 7
31	24		23 *Shemini* Parah		25		27	29		1 Ḥeshvan R. H.		2 8

1952

5712/13 תשי״ב / תשי״ג

	January	February	March	April	May	June	July	August	September	October	November	December
1	3 Tevet	5	4 *Terumah*	6	6	8	8	10	11	12	13 *Lekh Lekha*	13
2	4	6 *Bo*	5	7	7	9	9	11 *Va-Ethannan*	12	13	14	14
3	5	7	6	8	8 *Aḥarei Mot Kedoshim*	10	10	12	13	14	15	15
4	6	8	7	9	9	11	11	13	14	15 Sukkot	16	16
5	7 *Va-Yiggash*	9	8	10 *Ẓav* Shabbat ha-Gadol	10	12	12 *Ḥukkat Balak*	14	15	16	17	17
6	8	10	9	11	11	13	13	15	16 *Ki Tavo*	17 Ḥol ha-Mo'ed	18	18 *Va-Yishlaḥ*
7	9	11	10	12	12	14 *Naso*	14	16	17	18	19	19
8	10 Fast	12	11 *Teẓavveh* Zakhor	13	13	15	15	17	18	19	20 *Va-Yera*	20
9	11	13 *Be-Shallaḥ*	12	14	14	16	16	18 *Ekev*	19	20	21	21
10	12	14	13 Ta'anit Esther	15 Pesaḥ	15 *Emor*	17	17 Fast	19	20	21 Hoshana Rabba	22	22
11	13	15	14 Purim	16 Omer	16	18	18	20	21	22 Shemini Aẓeret	23	23
12	14 *Va-Yeḥi*	16	15 Shushan Purim	17 Ḥol ha-Mo'ed	17	19	19 *Pinḥas*	21	22	23 Simḥat Torah *Ve-Zot Ha-Berakhah*	24	24
13	15	17	16	18	18 Lag ba-Omer	20	20	22	23 *Niẓẓavim Va-Yelekh*	24	25	25 Ḥanukkah *Va-Yeshev* 1
14	16	18	17	19	19	21 *Be-Ha'alotkha*	21	23	24	25	26	26 2
15	17	19	18 *Ki Tissa* Parah	20	20	22	22	24	25	26	27 *Ḥayyei Sarah*	27 3
16	18	20 *Yitro*	19	21 Pesaḥ	21	23	23	25 *Re'eh*	26	27	28	28 4
17	19	21	20	22	22 *Be-Har Be-Ḥukkotai*	24	24	26	27	28	29	29 5
18	20	22	21	23	23	25	25	27	28	29 *Bereshit*	30 R. H.	30 R. H. 6
19	21 *Shemot*	23	22	24 *Shemini*	24	26	26 *Mattot Masei*	28	29	30 R. H.	1 Kislev R. H.	1 Tevet R. H. 7
20	22	24	23	25	25	27	27	29	1 Tishri Rosh Ha-Shanah	1 Ḥeshvan R. H.	2	2 *Mi-Keẓ* 8
21	23	25	24	26	26	28 *Shelaḥ*	28	30 R. H.	2	2	3	3
22	24	26	25 *Va-Yakhel Pekudei* Ha-Ḥodesh	27	27	29	29	1 Elul R. H.	3 Fast	3	4 *Toledot*	4
23	25	27 *Mishpatim* Shekalim	26	28	28	30 R. H.	1 Av R. H.	2 *Shofetim*	4	4	5	5
24	26	28	27	29	29 *Be-Midbar*	1 Tammuz R. H.	2	3	5	5	6	6
25	27	29	28	30 R. H.	1 Sivan R. H.	2	3	4	6	6 *No'aḥ*	7	7
26	28 *Va-Era*	30 R. H.	29	1 Iyyar R. H. *Tazri'a Meẓora*	2	3	4 *Devarim*	5	7	7	8	8
27	29	1 Adar R. H.	1 Nisan R. H.	2	3	4	5	6	8 *Ha'azinu* Shabbat Shuvah	8	9	9 *Va-Yiggash*
28	1 Shevat R. H.	2	2	3	4	5 *Koraḥ*	6	7	9	9	10	10 Fast
29	2	3	3 *Va-Yikra*	4	5	6	7	8	10 Yom Kippur	10	11 *Va-Yeẓe*	11
30	3		4	5 Yom ha-Aẓma'ut	6 Shavuot	7	8	9 *Ki Teẓe*	11	11	12	12
31	4		5		7		9 Tishah be-Av	10		12		13

1953

5713/14 תשי״ג / תשי״ד

	January	February	March	April	May	June	July	August	September	October	November	December
1	14 Tevet	16	14 Purim	16 Omer	16	18	18	20 Ekev	21	22 Shemini Aẓeret	23	24
2	15	17	15 Shushan Purim	17	17 Emor	19	19	21	22	23 Simḥat Torah Ve-Zot Ha-Berakhah	24	25 Ḥanukkah 1
3	16 Va-Yeḥi	18	16	18 Ḥol ha-Mo'ed	18 Lag ba-Omer	20	20	22	23	24 Bereshit	25	26 2
4	17	19	17	19	19	21	21 Pinḥas	23	24	25	26	27 3
5	18	20	18	20	20	22	22	24	25 Niẓẓavim Va-Yelekh	26	27	28 Mi-Keẓ 4
6	19	21	19	21 Pesaḥ	21	23 Shelaḥ	23	25	26	27	28	29 5
7	20	22 Yitro	20 Ki Tissa Parah	22	22	24	24	26	27	28	29 Toledot	1 Tevet R. Ḥ. 6
8	21	23	21	23	23	25	25	27 Re'eh	28	29	1 Kislev R. Ḥ.	2 7
9	22	24	22	24	24 Be-Har Be-Ḥukkotai	26	26	28	29	30 R. Ḥ.	2	3 8
10	23 Shemot	25	23	25	25	27	27	29	1 Tishri Rosh Ha-Shanah	1 Ḥeshvan R. Ḥ. No'aḥ	3	4
11	24	26	24	26 Shemini	26	28	28 Mattot Masei	30 R. Ḥ.	2	2	4	5
12	25	27	25	27	27	29	29	1 Elul R. Ḥ.	3 Ha'azinu Shabbat Shuvah	3	5	6 Va-Yiggash
13	26	28	26	28	28	30 R. Ḥ. Koraḥ	1 Av R. Ḥ.	2	4 Fast	4	6	7
14	27	29 Mishpatim Shekalim	27 Va-Yakhel Pekudei Ha-Ḥodesh	29	29	1 Tammuz R. Ḥ.	2	3	5	5	7 Va-Yeẓe	8
15	28	30 R. Ḥ.	28	30 R. Ḥ.	1 Sivan R. Ḥ.	2	3	4 Shofetim	6	6	8	9
16	29	1 Adar R. Ḥ.	29	1 Iyyar R. Ḥ.	2 Be-Midbar	3	4	5	7	7	9	10 Fast
17	1 Shevat R. Ḥ. Va-Era	2	1 Nisan R. Ḥ.	2	3	4	5	6	8	8 Lekh Lekha	10	11
18	2	3	2	3 Tazri'a Meẓora	4	5	6 Devarim	7	9	9	11	12
19	3	4	3	4	5	6	7	8	10 Yom Kippur	10	12	13 Va-Yeḥi
20	4	5	4	5 Yom ha-Aẓma'ut	6 Shavuot	7 Ḥukkat	8	9	11	11	13	14
21	5	6 Terumah	5 Va-Yikra	6	7	8	9 Tishah be-Av	10	12	12	14 Va-Yishlaḥ	15
22	6	7	6	7	8	9	10	11 Ki Teẓe	13	13	15	16
23	7	8	7	8	9 Naso	10	11	12	14	14	16	17
24	8 Bo	9	8	9	10	11	12	13	15 Sukkot	15 Va-Yera	17	18
25	9	10	9	10 Aḥarei Mot Kedoshim	11	12	13 Va-Etḥannan	14	16	16	18	19
26	10	11 Ta'anit Esther	10	11	12	13	14	15	17	17	19	20 Shemot
27	11	12	11	12	13	14 Balak	15	16	18 Ḥol ha-Mo'ed	18	20	21
28	12	13 Teẓavveh Zakhor	12 Ẓav Shabbat ha-Gadol	13	14	15	16	17	19	19	21 Va-Yeshev	22
29	13		13	14	15	16	17	18 Ki Tavo	20	20	22	23
30	14		14	15	16 Be-Ha'alotkha	17 Fast	18	19	21 Hoshana Rabba	21	23	24
31	15 Be-Shallaḥ		15 Pesaḥ		17		19	20		22 Ḥayyei Sarah		25

1954

5714/15 תשי״ד / תשט״ו

	January	February	March	April	May	June	July	August	September	October	November	December
1	26 Tevet	28	26	27	28 Kedoshim	29	30 R. Ḥ.	2	3	4	5	6
2	27 Va-Era	29	27	28	29	1 Sivan R. Ḥ.	1 Tammuz R. Ḥ.	3	4	5 Va-Yelekh Shabbat Shuvah	6	7
3	28	30 R. Ḥ.	28	29 Tazri'a Ha-Ḥodesh	30 R. Ḥ.	2	2 Ḥukkat	4	5	6	7	8
4	29	1 Adar I R. Ḥ.	29	1 Nisan R. Ḥ.	1 Iyyar R. Ḥ.	3	3	5	6 Shofetim	7	8	9 Va-Yeẓe
5	1 Shevat R. Ḥ.	2	30 R. Ḥ.	2	2	4 Naso	4	6	7	8	9	10
6	2	3 Terumah	1 Adar II R. Ḥ. Shekalim Pekudei	3	3 Yom ha-Aẓma'ut	5	5	7	8	9	10 Lekh Lekha	11
7	3	4	2	4	4	6 Shavuot	6	8 Devarim	9	10 Yom Kippur	11	12
8	4	5	3	5	5 Emor	7	7	9 Tishah be-Av	10	11	12	13
9	5 Bo	6	4	6	6	8	8	10	11	12 Ha'azinu	13	14
10	6	7	5	7 Meẓora	7	9	9 Balak	11	12	13	14	15
11	7	8	6	8	8	10	10	12	13 Ki Teẓe	14	15	16 Va-Yishlaḥ
12	8	9	7	9	9	11 Be-Ha'alotkha	11	13	14	15 Sukkot	16	17
13	9	10 Teẓavveh	8 Va-Yikra Zakhor	10	10	12	12	14	15	16	17 Va-Yera	18
14	10	11	9	11	11	13	13	15 Va-Etḥannan	16	17	18	19
15	11	12	10	12	12 Be-Har	14	14	16	17	18 Ḥol ha-Mo'ed	19	20
16	12 Be-Shallaḥ	13	11	13	13	15	15	17	18	19	20	21
17	13	14	12	14 Aḥarei Mot Shabbat ha-Gadol	14	16	16 Pinḥas	18	19	20	21	22
18	14	15	13 Ta'anit Esther	15 Pesaḥ	15	17	17 Fast	19	20 Ki Tavo	21 Hoshana Rabba	22	23 Va-Yeshev
19	15	16	14 Purim	16 Omer	16	18 Shelaḥ	18	20	21	22 Shemini Aẓeret	23	24
20	16	17 Ki Tissa	15 Ẓav Shushan Purim	17	17	19	19	21	22	23 Simḥat Torah Ve-Zot Ha-Berakhah	24 Ḥayyei Sarah	25 Ḥanukkah 1
21	17	18	16	18 Ḥol ha-Mo'ed	18 Lag ba-Omer	20	20	22 Ekev	23	24	25	26 2
22	18	19	17	19	19 Be-Ḥukkotai	21	21	23	24	25	26	27 3
23	19 Yitro	20	18	20	20	22	22	24	25	26 Bereshit	27	28 4
24	20	21	19	21 Pesaḥ	21	23	23 Mattot	25	26	27	28	29 5
25	21	22	20	22	22	24	24	26	27 Niẓẓavim	28	29	30 R. Ḥ. Mi-Keẓ 6
26	22	23	21	23	23	25 Koraḥ	25	27	28	29	1 Kislev R. Ḥ.	1 Tevet R. Ḥ. 7
27	23	24 Va-Yakhel	22 Shemini Parah	24	24	26	26	28	29	30 R. Ḥ.	2 Toledot	2 8
28	24	25	23	25	25	27	27	29 Re'eh	1 Tishri Rosh Ha-Shanah	1 Ḥeshvan R. Ḥ.	3	3
29	25		24	26	26 Be-Midbar	28	28	30 R. Ḥ.	2	2	4	4
30	26 Mishpatim		25	27	27	29	29	1 Elul R. Ḥ.	3 Fast	3 No'aḥ	5	5
31	27		26		28		1 Av R. Ḥ. Masei	2		4		6

1955

5715/16 — תשט״ו / תשט״ז

	January	February	March	April	May	June	July	August	September	October	November	December
1	7 Tevet *Va-Yiggash*	9	7	9	9	11	11	13	14	15 Sukkot	16	16
2	8	10	8	10 *Ẓav* Shabbat ha-Gadol	10	12	12 *Ḥukkat Balak*	14	15	16	17	17
3	9	11	9	11	11	13	13	15	16 *Ki Tavo*	17 Ḥol ha-Mo'ed	18	18 *Va-Yishlaḥ*
4	10 Fast	12	10	12	12	14 *Naso*	14	16	17	18	19	19
5	11	13 *Be-Shallaḥ*	11 *Teẓavveh* Zakhor	13	13	15	15	17	18	19	20 *Va-Yera*	20
6	12	14	12	14	14	16	16	18 *Ekev*	19	20	21	21
7	13	15	13 Ta'anit Esther	15 Pesaḥ	15 *Emor*	17	17 Fast	19	20	21 Hoshana Rabba	22	22
8	14 *Va-Yeḥi*	16	14 Purim	16 Omer	16	18	18	20	21	22 Shemini Aẓeret	23	23
9	15	17	15 Shushan Purim	17 Ḥol ha-Mo'ed	17	19	19 *Pinḥas*	21	22	23 Simḥat Torah *Ve-Zot Ha-Berakhah*	24	24
10	16	18	16	18	18 Lag ba-Omer	20	20	22	23 *Niẓẓavim Va-Yelekh*	24	25	25 Ḥanukkah 1 *Va-Yeshev*
11	17	19	17	19	19	21 *Be-Ha'alotkha*	21	23	24	25	26	26 2
12	18	20 *Yitro*	18 *Ki Tissa* Parah	20	20	22	22	24	25	26	27 *Ḥayyei Sarah*	27 3
13	19	21	19	21 Pesaḥ	21	23	23	25 *Re'eh*	26	27	28	28 4
14	20	22	20	22	22 *Be-Har Be-Ḥukkotai*	24	24	26	27	28	29	29 5
15	21 *Shemot*	23	21	23	23	25	25	27	28	29 *Bereshit*	30 R. Ḥ.	30 R. Ḥ. 6
16	22	24	22	24 *Shemini*	24	26	26 *Mattot Masei*	28	29	30 R. Ḥ.	1 Kislev R. Ḥ.	1 Tevet R. Ḥ. 7
17	23	25	23	25	25	27	27	29	1 Tishri Rosh Ha-Shanah	1 Ḥeshvan R. Ḥ.	2	2 *Mi-Keẓ* 8
18	24	26	24	26	26	28 *Shelaḥ*	28	30 R. Ḥ.	2	2	3	3
19	25	27 *Mishpatim* Shekalim	*Va-Yakhel-Pekudei* 25 Ha-Ḥodesh	27	27	29	29	1 Elul R. Ḥ.	3 Fast	3	4 *Toledot*	4
20	26	28	26	28	28	30 R. Ḥ.	1 Av R. Ḥ.	2 *Shofetim*	4	4	5	5
21	27	29	27	29	29 *Be-Midbar*	1 Tammuz R. Ḥ.	2	3	5	5	6	6
22	28 *Va-Era*	30 R. Ḥ.	28	30 R. Ḥ.	1 Sivan R. Ḥ.	2	3	4	6	6 *No'aḥ*	7	7
23	29	1 Adar R. Ḥ.	29	1 R. Ḥ. Iyyar *Tazri'a Meẓora*	2	3	4 *Devarim*	5	7	7	8	8
24	1 Shevat R. Ḥ.	2	1 Nisan R. Ḥ.	2	3	4	5	6	8 *Ha'azinu* Shabbat Shuvah	8	9	9 *Va-Yiggash*
25	2	3	2	3	4	5 *Koraḥ*	6	7	9	9	10	10 Fast
26	3	4 *Terumah*	3 *Va-Yikra*	4	5	6	7	8	10 Yom Kippur	10	11 *Va-Yeẓe*	11
27	4	5	4	5 Yom ha-Aẓma'ut	6 Shavuot	7	8	9 *Ki Teẓe*	11	11	12	12
28	5	6	5	6	7	8	9 Tishah be-Av	10	12	12	13	13
29	6 *Bo*		6	7	8	9	10	11	13	13 *Lekh Lekha*	14	14
30	7		7	8 *Aḥarei Mot Kedoshim*	9	10	11 *Va-Etḥannan*	12	14	14	15	15
31	8		8		10		12	13		15		16 *Va-Yeḥi*

1956

5716/17 — תשט״ז / תשי״ז

	January	February	March	April	May	June	July	August	September	October	November	December
1	17 Tevet	19	18	20 Ḥol ha-Mo'ed	20	22	22	24	25 *Niẓẓavim Va-Yelekh*	26	27	27 *Mi-Keẓ* 3
2	18	20	19	21 Pesaḥ	21	23 *Shelaḥ*	23	25	26	27	28	28 4
3	19	21	20 *Ki Tissa* Parah	22	22	24	24	26	27	28	29 *Toledot*	29 5
4	20	22 *Yitro*	21	23	23	25	25	27 *Re'eh*	28	29	30 R. Ḥ.	30 R. Ḥ. 6
5	21	23	22	24	24 *Be-Har Be-Ḥukkotai*	26	26	28	29	30 R. Ḥ.	1 Kislev R. Ḥ.	1 Tevet R. Ḥ. 7
6	22	24	23	25	25	27	27	29	1 Tishri Rosh Ha-Shanah	1 Ḥeshvan R. Ḥ. *No'aḥ*	2	2 8
7	23 *Shemot*	25	24	26 *Shemini*	26	28	28 *Mattot Masei*	30 R. Ḥ.	2	2	3	3
8	24	26	25	27	27	29	29	1 Elul R. Ḥ.	3 *Ha'azinu* Shabbat Shuvah	3	4	4 *Va-Yiggash*
9	25	27	26	28	28	30 R. Ḥ. *Koraḥ*	1 Av R. Ḥ.	2	4 Fast	4	5	5
10	26	28	*Va-Yakhel Pekudei* 27 Ha-Ḥodesh	29	29	1 Tammuz R. Ḥ.	2	3	5	5	6 *Va-Yeẓe*	6
11	27	29 *Mishpatim* Shekalim	28	30 R. Ḥ.	1 Sivan R. Ḥ.	2	3	4 *Shofetim*	6	6	7	7
12	28	30 R. Ḥ.	29	1 Iyyar R. Ḥ.	2 *Be-Midbar*	3	4	5	7	7	8	8
13	29	1 Adar R. Ḥ.	1 Nisan R. Ḥ.	2	3	4	5	6	8	8 *Lekh Lekha*	9	9
14	1 Shevat R. Ḥ. *Va-Era*	2	2	3 *Tazri'a Meẓora*	4	5	6 *Devarim*	7	9	9	10	10 Fast
15	2	3	3	4	5	6	7	8	10 Yom Kippur	10	11	11 *Va-Yeḥi*
16	3	4	4	5 Yom ha-Aẓma'ut	6 Shavuot	7 *Ḥukkat*	8	9	11	11	12	12
17	4	5	5 *Va-Yikra*	6	7	8	9 Tishah be-Av	10	12	12	13 *Va-Yishlaḥ*	13
18	5	6 *Terumah*	6	7	8	9	10	11 *Ki Teẓe*	13	13	14	14
19	6	7	7	8	9 *Naso*	10	11	12	14	14	15	15
20	7	8	8	9	10	11	12	13	15 Sukkot	15 *Va-Yera*	16	16
21	8 *Bo*	9	9	10 *Aḥarei Mot Kedoshim*	11	12	13 *Va-Etḥannan*	14	16	16	17	17
22	9	10	10	11	12	13	14	15	17 Ḥol ha-Mo'ed	17	18	18 *Shemot*
23	10	11 Ta'anit Esther	11	12	13	14 *Balak*	15	16	18	18	19	19
24	11	12	12 *Ẓav* Shabbat ha-Gadol	13	14	15	16	17	19	19	20 *Va-Yeshev*	20
25	12	13 *Teẓavveh* Zakhor	13	14	15	16	17	18 *Ki Tavo*	20	20	21	21
26	13	14 Purim	14	15	16 *Be-Ha'alotkha*	17 Fast	18	19	21 Hoshana Rabba	21	22	22
27	14	15 Shushan Purim	15 Pesaḥ	16	17	18	19	20	22 Shemini Aẓeret	22 *Ḥayyei Sarah*	23	23
28	15 *Be-Shallaḥ*	16	16 Omer	17 *Emor*	18	19	20 *Ekev*	21	23 Simḥat Torah *Ve-Zot Ha-Berakhah*	23	24	24
29	16	17	17 Ḥol ha-Mo'ed	18 Lag ba-Omer	19	20	21	22	24 *Bereshit*	24	25 Ḥanukkah 1	25 *Va-Era*
30	17		18	19	20	21 *Pinḥas*	22	23	25	25	26 2	26
31	18		19		21		23	24		26		27

1957

5717/18 תשי״ז / תשי״ח

	January	February	March	April	May	June	July	August	September	October	November	December
1	28 Tevet	30 R. Ḥ.	28	29	30 R. Ḥ.	**2** *Naso*	2	4	5	6	7	8
2	29	**1 Adar I** R. Ḥ. *Terumah*	**29** *Pekudei* Shekalim	1 Nisan R. Ḥ.	1 Iyyar R. Ḥ.	3	3	5	6	7	**8** *Lekh Lekha*	9
3	1 Shevat R. Ḥ.	2	30 R. Ḥ.	2	2	4	4	**6** *Devarim*	7	8	9	10
4	2	3	1 Adar II R. Ḥ.	3	**3** *Emor*	5	5	7	8	9	10	11
5	**3** *Bo*	4	2	4	4	6 Shavuot	6	8	9	**10** Yom Kippur	11	12
6	4	5	3	**5** *Meẓora*	5 Yom ha-Aẓma'ut	7	**7** *Balak*	9 Tishah be-Av	10	11	12	13
7	5	6	4	6	6	8	8	10	**11** *Ki Teẓe*	12	13	**14** *Va-Yishlaḥ*
8	6	7	5	7	7	**9** *Be-Ha'alotkha*	9	11	12	13	14	15
9	7	**8** *Teẓavveh*	**6** *Va-Yikra*	8	8	10	10	12	13	14	**15** *Va-Yera*	16
10	8	9	7	9	9	11	11	**13** *Va-Etḥannan*	14	15 Sukkot	16	17
11	9	10	8	10	**10** *Be-Har*	12	12	14	15	16	17	18
12	**10** *Be-Shallaḥ*	11	9	11	11	13	13	15	16	**17**	18	19
13	11	12	10	**12** *Aḥarei Mot* Shabbat ha-Gadol	12	14	**14** *Pinḥas*	16	17	18 Ḥol ha-Mo'ed	19	20
14	12	13	11 Ta'anit Esther	13	13	15	15	17	**18** *Ki Tavo*	19	20	**21** *Va-Yeshev*
15	13	14	12	14	14	**16** *Shelaḥ*	16	18	19	20	21	22
16	14	**15** *Ki Tissa*	**13** *Ẓav* Zakhor	15 Pesaḥ	15	17	17 Fast	19	20	21 Hoshana Rabba	**22** *Ḥayyei Sarah*	23
17	15	16	14 Purim	16 Omer	16	18	18	**20** *Ekev*	21	22 Shemini Aẓeret	23	24
18	16	17	15 Shushan Purim	17	**17** *Be-Ḥukkotai*	19	19	21	22	23 Simḥat Torah *Ve-Zot Ha-Berakhah*	24	25 Ḥanukkah 1
19	**17** *Yitro*	18	16	18 Ḥol ha-Mo'ed	18 Lag ba-Omer	20	20	22	23	**24** *Bereshit*	25	26 2
20	18	19	17	**19**	19	21	**21** *Mattot*	23	24	25	26	27 3
21	19	20	18	20	20	22	22	24	**25** *Niẓẓavim Va-Yelekh*	26	27	**28** *Mi-Keẓ* 4
22	20	21	19	21 Pesaḥ	21	**23** *Koraḥ*	23	25	26	27	28	29 5
23	21	**22** *Va-Yakhel*	**20** *Shemini* Parah	22	22	24	24	26	27	28	**29** *Toledot*	30 R. Ḥ. 6
24	22	23	21	23	23	25	25	**27** *Re'eh*	28	29	1 Kislev R. Ḥ.	1 Tevet R. Ḥ. 7
25	23	24	22	24	**24** *Be-Midbar*	26	26	28	29	30 R. Ḥ.	2	2 8
26	**24** *Mishpatim*	25	23	25	25	27	27	29	1 Tishri Rosh Ha-Shanah	**1** R. Ḥ. Heshvan *No'aḥ*	3	3
27	25	26	24	**26** *Kedoshim*	26	28	**28** *Masei*	30 R. Ḥ.	2	2	4	4
28	26	27	25	27	27	29	29	1 Elul R. Ḥ.	**3** *Ha'azinu* Shabbat Shuvah	3	5	**5** *Va-Yiggash*
29	27		26	28	28	**30** R. Ḥ. *Ḥukkat*	1 Av R. Ḥ.	2	4 Fast	4	6	6
30	28		**27** *Tazri'a* Ha-Ḥodesh	29	29	1 Tammuz R. Ḥ.	2	3	5	5	**7** *Va-Yeẓe*	7
31	29		28		1 Sivan R. Ḥ.		3	**4** *Shofetim*		6		8

1958

5718/19 תשי״ח / תשי״ט

	January	February	March	April	May	June	July	August	September	October	November	December
1	9 Tevet	**11** *Be-Shallaḥ*	**9** *Teẓavveh* Zakhor	11	11	13	13	15	16	17	**18** *Va-Yera*	19
2	10 Fast	12	10	12	12	14	14	**16** *Va-Etḥannan*	17	18 Ḥol ha-Mo'ed	19	20
3	11	13	11	13	**13** *Aḥarei Mot Kedoshim*	15	15	17	18	19	20	21
4	**12** *Va-Yeḥi*	14	12	14	14	16	16	18	19	**20**	21	22
5	13	15	13 Ta'anit Esther	**15** Pesaḥ	15	17	**17** *Balak*	19	20	21 Hoshana Rabba	22	23
6	14	16	14 Purim	16 Omer	16	18	18 Fast	20	**21** *Ki Tavo*	22 Shemini Aẓeret	23	**24** *Va-Yeshev*
7	15	17	15 Shushan Purim	17	17	**19** *Be-Ha'alotkha*	19	21	22	23 Simḥat Torah *Ve Zot Ha-Berakhah*	24	25 Ḥanukkah 1
8	16	**18** *Yitro*	**16** *Ki Tissa*	18 Ḥol ha-Mo'ed	18 Lag ba-Omer	20	20	22	23	24	**25** *Ḥayyei Sarah*	26 2
9	17	19	17	19	19	21	21	**23** *Ekev*	24	25	26	27 3
10	18	20	18	20	**20** *Emor*	22	22	24	25	26	27	28 4
11	**19** *Shemot*	21	19	21 Pesaḥ	21	23	23	25	26	**27** *Bereshit*	28	29 5
12	20	22	20	**22**	22	24	**24** *Pinḥas*	26	27	28	29	1 Tevet R. Ḥ. 6
13	21	23	21	23	23	25	25	27	**28** *Niẓẓavim*	29	1 Kislev R. Ḥ.	**2** *Mi-Keẓ* 7
14	22	24	22	24	24	**26** *Shelaḥ*	26	28	29	30 R. Ḥ.	2	3 8
15	23	**25** *Mishpatim* Shekalim	**23** *Va-Yakhel Pekudei* Parah	25	25	27	27	29	1 Tishri Rosh Ha-Shanah	1 Heshvan R. Ḥ.	**3** *Toledot*	4
16	24	26	24	26	26	28	28	**30** R. Ḥ. *Re'eh*	2	2	4	5
17	25	27	25	27	**27** *Be-Har Be-Ḥukkotai*	29	29	1 Elul R. Ḥ.	3 Fast	3	5	6
18	**26** *Va-Era*	28	26	28	28	30 R. Ḥ.	1 Av R. Ḥ.	2	4	**4** *No'aḥ*	6	7
19	27	29	27	**29** *Shemini*	29	1 Tammuz R. Ḥ.	**2** *Mattot Masei*	3	5	5	7	8
20	28	30 R. Ḥ.	28	30 R. Ḥ.	1 Sivan R. Ḥ.	2	3	4	**6** *Va-Yelekh* Shabbat Shuvah	6	8	**9** *Va-Yiggash*
21	29	1 Adar R. Ḥ.	29	1 Iyyar R. Ḥ.	2	**3** *Koraḥ*	4	5	7	7	9	10 Fast
22	1 Shevat R. Ḥ.	**2** *Terumah*	**1** Nisan *Va-Yikra* R. Ḥ. Ha-Ḥodesh	2	3	4	5	6	8	8	**10** *Va-Yeẓe*	11
23	2	3	2	3	4	5	6	**7** *Shofetim*	9	9	11	12
24	3	4	3	4 Yom ha-Aẓma'ut	**5** *Be-Midbar*	6	7	8	10 Yom Kippur	10	12	13
25	**4** *Bo*	5	4	5	6 Shavuot	7	8	9	11	**11** *Lekh Lekha*	13	14
26	5	6	5	**6** *Tazri'a Meẓora*	7	8	**9** *Devarim* Tishah be-Av	10	12	12	14	15
27	6	7	6	7	8	9	10 Fast	11	**13** *Ha'azinu*	13	15	**16** *Va-Yeḥi*
28	7	8	7	8	9	**10** *Ḥukkat*	11	12	14	14	16	17
29	8		**8** *Ẓav* Shabbat ha-Gadol	9	10	11	12	13	15 Sukkot	15	**17** *Va-Yishlaḥ*	18
30	9		9	10	11	12	13	**14** *Ki Teẓe*	16	16	18	19
31	10		10		**12** *Naso*		14	15		17		20

1959

5719/20 תש״ט / תש״כ

	January	February	March	April	May	June	July	August	September	October	November	December
1	21 Tevet	23	21	22	23	24	25	26 *Mattot Masei*	28	28	30 R. Ḥ.	30 R. Ḥ.
2	22	24	22	23	24 *Aḥarei Mot*	25	26	27	29	29	1 Ḥeshvan R. Ḥ.	1 Kislev R. Ḥ.
3	23 *Shemot*	25	23	24	25	26	27	28	30 R. Ḥ.	1 Tishri Rosh Ha-Shanah	2	2
4	24	26	24	25 *Shemini* Ha-Ḥodesh	26	27	28 *Shelaḥ*	29	1 Elul R. Ḥ.	2	3	3
5	25	27	25	26	27	28	29	1 Av R. Ḥ.	2 *Shofetim*	3 Fast	4	4 *Toledot*
6	26	28	26	27	28	29 *Be-Midbar*	30 R. Ḥ.	2	3	4	5	5
7	27	29 *Mishpatim*	27 *Va-Yakhel* Shekalim	28	29	1 Sivan R. Ḥ.	1 Tammuz R. Ḥ.	3	4	5	6 *No'aḥ*	6
8	28	30 R. Ḥ.	28	29	30 R. Ḥ.	2	2	4 *Devarim*	5	6	7	7
9	29	1 Adar I R. Ḥ.	29	1 Nisan R. Ḥ.	1 Iyyar R. Ḥ. *Kedoshim*	3	3	5	6	7	8	8
10	1 Shevat R. Ḥ. *Va-Era*	2	30 R. Ḥ.	2	2	4	4	6	7	8 *Ha'azinu* Shabbat Shuvah	9	9
11	2	3	1 Adar II R. Ḥ.	3 *Tazri'a*	3	5	5 *Koraḥ*	7	8	9	10	10
12	3	4	2	4	4	6 Shavuot	6	8	9 *Ki Teẓe*	10 Yom Kippur	11	11 *Va-Yeẓe*
13	4	5	3	5	5 Yom ha-Aẓma'ut	7	7	9 Tishah be-Av	10	11	12	12
14	5	6 *Terumah*	4 *Pekudei*	6	6	8	8	10	11	12	13 *Lekh Lekha*	13
15	6	7	5	7	7	9	9	11 *Va-Etḥannan*	12	13	14	14
16	7	8	6	8	8 *Emor*	10	10	12	13	14	15	15
17	8 *Bo*	9	7	9	9	11	11	13	14	15 Sukkot	16	16
18	9	10	8	10 *Meẓora* Shabbat ha-Gadol	10	12	12 *Ḥukkat Balak*	14	15	16	17	17
19	10	11	9	11	11	13	13	15	16 *Ki Tavo*	17 Ḥol ha-Mo'ed	18	18 *Va-Yishlaḥ*
20	11	12	10	12	12	14 *Naso*	14	16	17	18	19	19
21	12	13 *Teẓavveh*	11 *Va-Yikra* Zakhor	13	13	15	15	17	18	19	20 *Va-Yera*	20
22	13	14	12	14	14	16	16	18 *Ekev*	19	20	21	21
23	14	15	13 Ta'anit Esther	15 Pesaḥ	15 *Be-Har*	17	17 Fast	19	20	21 Hoshana Rabba	22	22
24	15 *Be-Shallaḥ*	16	14 Purim	16 Omer	16	18	18	20	21	22 Shemini Aẓeret	23	23
25	16	17	15 Shushan Purim	17 Ḥol ha-Mo'ed	17	19	19 *Pinḥas*	21	22	23 Simḥat Torah *Ve-Zot Ha-Berakhah*	24	24
26	17	18	16	18	18 Lag ba-Omer	20	20	22	23 *Niẓẓavim Va-Yelekh*	24	25	25 Ḥanukkah *Va-Yeshev* 1
27	18	19	17	19	19	21 *Be-Ha'alotkha*	21	23	24	25	26	26 2
28	19	20 *Ki Tissa*	18 *Ẓav* Parah	20	20	22	22	24	25	26	27 *Ḥayyei Sarah*	27 3
29	20		19	21 Pesaḥ	21	23	23	25 *Re'eh*	26	27	28	28 4
30	21		20	22	22 *Be-Ḥukkotai*	24	24	26	27	28	29	29 5
31	22 *Yitro*		21		23		25	27		29 *Bereshit*		30 R. Ḥ. 6

1960

5720/21 תש״כ / תשכ״א

	January	February	March	April	May	June	July	August	September	October	November	December
1	1 Tevet R. Ḥ. 7 Ḥanukkah	3	2	4	4	6 Shavuot	6	8	9	10 Yom Kippur	11	12
2	2 *Mi-Keẓ* 8	4	3	5 *Va-Yikra*	5 Yom ha-Aẓma'ut	7	7 *Ḥukkat*	9 Tishah be-Av	10	11	12	13
3	3	5	4	6	6	8	8	10	11 *Ki Teẓe*	12	13	14 *Va-Yishlaḥ*
4	4	6	5	7	7	9 *Naso*	9	11	12	13	14	15
5	5	7	6 *Terumah*	8	8	10	10	12	13	14	15 *Va-Yera*	16
6	6	8 *Bo*	7	9	9	11	11	13 *Va-Etḥannan*	14	15 Sukkot	16	17
7	7	9	8	10	10 *Aḥarei Mot Kedoshim*	12	12	14	15	16	17	18
8	8	10	9	11	11	13	13	15	16	17 Ḥol ha-Mo'ed	18	19
9	9 *Va-Yiggash*	11	10	12 *Ẓav* Shabbat ha-Gadol	12	14	14 *Balak*	16	17	18	19	20
10	10 Fast	12	11 Ta'anit Esther	13	13	15	15	17	18 *Ki Tavo*	19	20	21 *Va-Yeshev*
11	11	13	12	14	14	16 *Be-Ha'alotkha*	16	18	19	20	21	22
12	12	14	13 *Teẓavveh* Zakhor	15 Pesaḥ	15	17	17 Fast	19	20	21 Hoshana Rabba	22 *Ḥayyei Sarah*	23
13	13	15 *Be-Shallaḥ*	14 Purim	16 Omer	16	18	18	20 *Ekev*	21	22 Shemini Aẓeret	23	24
14	14	16	15 Shushan Purim	17 Ḥol ha-Mo'ed	17 *Emor*	19	19	21	22	23 Simḥat Torah *Ve-Zot Ha-Berakhah*	24	25 Ḥanukkah 1
15	15	17	16	18	18 Lag ba-Omer	20	20	22	23	24 *Bereshit*	25	26 2
16	16 *Va-Yeḥi*	18	17	19	19	21	21 *Pinḥas*	23	24	25	26	27 3
17	17	19	18	20	20	22	22	24	25 *Niẓẓavim Va-Yelekh*	26	27	28 *Mi-Keẓ* 4
18	18	20	19	21 Pesaḥ	21	23 *Shelaḥ*	23	25	26	27	28	29 5
19	19	21	20 *Ki Tissa* Parah	22	22	24	24	26	27	28	29 *Toledot*	30 R. Ḥ. 6
20	20	22 *Yitro*	21	23	23	25	25	27 *Re'eh*	28	29	1 Kislev R. Ḥ.	1 Tevet R. Ḥ. 7
21	21	23	22	24	24 *Be-Har Be-Ḥukkotai*	26	26	28	29	30 R. Ḥ.	2	2 8
22	22	24	23	25	25	27	27	29	1 Tishri Rosh Ha-Shanah	1 Ḥeshvan R. Ḥ. *No'aḥ*	3	3
23	23 *Shemot*	25	24	26 *Shemini*	26	28	28 *Mattot Masei*	30 R. Ḥ.	2	2	4	4
24	24	26	25	27	27	29	29	1 Elul R. Ḥ.	3 *Ha'azinu* Shabbat Shuvah	3	5	5 *Va-Yiggash*
25	25	27	26	28	28	30 R. Ḥ. *Koraḥ*	1 Av R. Ḥ.	2	4 Fast	4	6	6
26	26	28	27 *Va-Yakhel Pekudei* Ha-Ḥodesh	29	29	1 Tammuz R. Ḥ.	2	3	5	5	7 *Va-Yeẓe*	7
27	27	29 *Mishpatim* Shekalim	28	30 R. Ḥ.	1 Sivan R. Ḥ.	2	3	4 *Shofetim*	6	6	8	8
28	28	30 R. Ḥ.	29	1 Iyyar R. Ḥ.	2 *Be-Midbar*	3	4	5	7	7	9	9
29	29	1 Adar R. Ḥ.	1 Nisan R. Ḥ.	2	3	4	5	6	8	8 *Lekh Lekha*	10	10 Fast
30	1 Shevat R. Ḥ. *Va-Era*		2	3 *Tazri'a Meẓora*	4	5	6 *Devarim*	7	9	9	11	11
31	2		3		5		7	8		10		12 *Va-Yeḥi*

1961

5721/22 — תשכ"א / תשכ"ב

	January	February	March	April	May	June	July	August	September	October	November	December
1	13 Tevet	15	13 Ta'anit Esther	15 Pesaḥ	15	17	17 Balak	19	20	21 Hoshana Rabba	22	23
2	14	16	14 Purim	16 Omer	16	18	18 Fast	20	21 Ki Tavo	22 Shemini Aẓeret	23	24 Va-Yeshev
3	15	17	15 Shushan Purim	17	17	19 Be-Ha'alotkha	19	21	22	23 Simḥat Torah Ve-Zot Ha-Berakhah	24	25 Ḥanukkah 1
4	16	18 Yitro	16 Ki Tissa	18 Ḥol ha-Mo'ed	18 Lag ba-Omer	20	20	22	23	24	25 Ḥayyei Sarah	26 2
5	17	19	17	19	19	21	21	23 Ekev	24	25	26	27 3
6	18	20	18	20	20 Emor	22	22	24	25	26	27	28 4
7	19 Shemot	21	19	21 Pesaḥ	21	23	23	25	26	27 Bereshit	28	29 5
8	20	22	20	22	22	24	24 Pinḥas	26	27	28	29	1 Tevet R. Ḥ. 6
9	21	23	21	23	23	25	25	27	28 Niẓẓavim	29	1 Kislev R. Ḥ.	2 Mi-Keẓ 7
10	22	24	22	24	24	26 Shelaḥ	26	28	29	30 R. Ḥ.	2	3 8
11	23	25 Mishpatim Shekalim	23 Va-Yakhel Pekudei Parah	25	25	27	27	29	1 Tishri Rosh Ha-Shanah	1 Ḥeshvan R. Ḥ.	3 Toledot	4
12	24	26	24	26	26	28	28	30 R. Ḥ. Re'eh	2	2	4	5
13	25	27	25	27	27 Be-Har Be-Ḥukkotai	29	29	1 Elul R. Ḥ.	3 Fast	3	5	6
14	26 Va-Era	28	26	28	28	30 R. Ḥ.	1 Av R. Ḥ.	2	4	4 No'aḥ	6	7
15	27	29	27	29 Shemini	29	1 Tammuz R. Ḥ.	2 Mattot Masei	3	5	5	7	8
16	28	30 R. Ḥ.	28	30 R. Ḥ.	1 Sivan R. Ḥ.	2	3	4	6 Va-Yelekh Shabbat Shuvah	6	8	9 Va-Yiggash
17	29	1 Adar R. Ḥ.	29	1 Iyyar R. Ḥ.	2	3 Koraḥ	4	5	7	7	9	10 Fast
18	1 Shevat R. Ḥ.	2 Terumah	1 Nisan Va-Yikra R. Ḥ. Ha-Ḥodesh	2	3	4	5	6	8	8	10 Va-Yeẓe	11
19	2	3	2	3	4	5	6	7 Shofetim	9	9	11	12
20	3	4	3	4 Yom ha-Aẓma'ut	5 Be-Midbar	6	7	8	10 Yom Kippur	10	12	13
21	4 Bo	5	4	5	6 Shavuot	7	8	9	11	11 Lekh Lekha	13	14
22	5	6	5	6 Tazri'a Meẓora	7	8	9 Devarim Tishah be-Av	10	12	12	14	15
23	6	7	6	7	8	9	10 Fast	11	13 Ha'azinu	13	15	16 Va-Yeḥi
24	7	8	7	8	9	10 Ḥukkat	11	12	14	14	16	17
25	8	9 Teẓavveh Zakhor	8 Ẓav Shabbat ha-Gadol	9	10	11	12	13	15 Sukkot	15	17 Va-Yishlaḥ	18
26	9	10	9	10	11	12	13	14 Ki Teẓe	16	16	18	19
27	10	11	10	11	12 Naso	13	14	15	17 Ḥol ha-Mo'ed	17	19	20
28	11 Be-Shallaḥ	12	11	12	13	14	15	16	18	18 Va-Yera	20	21
29	12		12	13 Aḥarei Mot Kedoshim	14	15	16 Va-Etḥannan	17	19	19	21	22
30	13		13	14	15	16	17	18	20	20	22	23 Shemot
31	14		14		16		18	19		21		24

1962

5722/23 — תשכ"ב / תשכ"ג

	January	February	March	April	May	June	July	August	September	October	November	December
1	25 Tevet	27	25	26	27	28	29	1 Av R. Ḥ.	2 Shofetim	3 Fast	4	4 Toledot
2	26	28	26	27	28	29 Be-Midbar	30 R. Ḥ.	2	3	4	5	5
3	27	29 Mishpatim	27 Va-Yakhel Shekalim	28	29	1 Sivan R. Ḥ.	1 Tammuz R. Ḥ.	3	4	5	6 No'aḥ	6
4	28	30 R. Ḥ.	28	29	30 R. Ḥ.	2	2	4 Devarim	5	6	7	7
5	29	1 Adar I R. Ḥ.	29	1 Nisan R. Ḥ.	1 Iyyar R. Ḥ. Kedoshim	3	3	5	6	7	8	8
6	1 Shevat R. Ḥ. Va-Era	2	30 R. Ḥ.	2	2	4	4	6	7	8 Ha'azinu Shabbat Shuvah	9	9
7	2	3	1 Adar II R. Ḥ.	3 Tazri'a	3	5	5 Koraḥ	7	8	9	10	10
8	3	4	2	4	4	6 Shavuot	6	8	9 Ki Teẓe	10 Yom Kippur	11	11 Va-Yeẓe
9	4	5	3	5	5 Yom ha-Aẓma'ut	7	7	9 Tishah be-Av	10	11	12	12
10	5	6 Terumah	4 Pekudei	6	6	8	8	10	11	12	13 Lekh Lekha	13
11	6	7	5	7	7	9	9	11 Va-Etḥannan	12	13	14	14
12	7	8	6	8	8 Emor	10	10	12	13	14	15	15
13	8 Bo	9	7	9	9	11	11	13	14	15 Sukkot	16	16
14	9	10	8	10 Meẓora Shabbat ha-Gadol	10	12	12 Ḥukkat Balak	14	15	16	17	17
15	10	11	9	11	11	13	13	15	16 Ki Tavo	17	18	18 Va-Yishlaḥ
16	11	12	10	12	12	14 Naso	14	16	17	18 Ḥol ha-Mo'ed	19	19
17	12	13 Teẓavveh	11 Va-Yikra Zakhor	13	13	15	15	17	18	19	20 Va-Yera	20
18	13	14	12	14	14	16	16	18 Ekev	19	20	21	21
19	14	15	13 Ta'anit Esther	15 Pesaḥ	15 Be-Har	17	17 Fast	19	20	21 Hoshana Rabba	22	22
20	15 Be-Shallaḥ	16	14 Purim	16 Omer	16	18	18	20	21	22 Shemini Aẓeret	23	23
21	16	17	15 Shushan Purim	17	17	19	19 Pinḥas	21	22	23 Simḥat Torah Ve-Zot Ha-Berakhah	24	24
22	17	18	16	18 Ḥol ha-Mo'ed	18 Lag ba-Omer	20	20	22	23 Niẓẓavim Va-Yelekh	24	25	25 Va-Yeshev Ḥanukkah 1
23	18	19	17	19	19	21 Be-Ha'alotkha	21	23	24	25	26	26 2
24	19	20 Ki Tissa	18 Ẓav Parah	20	20	22	22	24	25	26	27 Ḥayyei Sarah	27 3
25	20	21	19	21 Pesaḥ	21	23	23	25 Re'eh	26	27	28	28 4
26	21	22	20	22	22 Be-Ḥukkotai	24	24	26	27	28	29	29 5
27	22 Yitro	23	21	23	23	25	25	27	28	29 Bereshit	30 R. Ḥ.	30 R. Ḥ. 6
28	23	24	22	24 Aḥarei Mot	24	26	26 Mattot Masei	28	29	30 R. Ḥ.	1 Kislev R. Ḥ.	1 Tevet R. Ḥ. 7
29	24		23	25	25	27	27	29	1 Tishri Rosh Ha-Shanah	1 Ḥeshvan R. Ḥ.	2	2 Mi-Keẓ 8
30	25		24	26	26	28 Shelaḥ	28	30 R. Ḥ.	2	2	3	3
31	26		25 Shemini Ha-Ḥodesh		27		29	1 Elul R. Ḥ.		3		4

1963

5723/24 תשכ״ג / תשכ״ד

	January	February	March	April	May	June	July	August	September	October	November	December
1	5 **Tevet**	7	5	7	7	**9** *Naso*	9	11	12	13	14	15
2	6	**8** *Bo*	**6** *Terumah*	8	8	10	10	12	13	14	**15** *Va-Yera*	16
3	7	9	7	9	9	11	11	**13** *Va-Etḥannan*	14	15 Sukkot	16	17
4	8	10	8	10	**10** *Aḥarei Mot Kedoshim*	12	12	14	15	16	17	18
5	**9** *Va-Yiggash*	11	9	11	11	13	13	15	16	**17**	18	19
6	10 Fast	12	10	**12** *Ẓav* Shabbat ha-Gadol	12	14	**14** *Balak*	16	17	18 Ḥol ha-Mo'ed	19	20
7	11	13	11 Ta'anit Esther	13	13	15	15	17	**18** *Ki Tavo*	19	20	**21** *Va-Yeshev*
8	12	14	12	14	14	**16** *Be-Ha'alotkha*	16	18	19	20	21	22
9	13	**15** *Be-Shallaḥ*	**13** *Teẓavveh* Zakhor	15 Pesaḥ	15	17	17 Fast	19	20	21 Hoshana Rabba	**22** *Ḥayyei Sarah*	23
10	14	16	14 Purim	16 Omer	16	18	18	**20** *Ekev*	21	22 Shemini Aẓeret	23	24
11	15	17	15 Shushan Purim	17	**17** *Emor*	19	19	21	22	23 Simḥat Torah *Ve-Zot Ha-Berakhah*	24	25 Ḥanukkah 1
12	**16** *Va-Yeḥi*	18	16	18 Ḥol ha-Mo'ed	18 Lag ba-Omer	20	20	22	23	**24** *Bereshit*	25	26 2
13	17	19	17	**19**	19	21	**21** *Pinḥas*	23	24	25	26	27 3
14	18	20	18	20	20	22	22	24	**25** *Niẓẓavim Va-Yelekh*	26	27	**28** *Mi-Keẓ* 4
15	19	21	19	21 Pesaḥ	21	**23** *Shelaḥ*	23	25	26	27	28	29 5
16	20	**22** *Yitro*	**20** *Ki Tissa* Parah	22	22	24	24	26	27	28	**29** *Toledot*	30 R. Ḥ. 6
17	21	23	21	23	23	25	25	**27** *Re'eh*	28	29	1 **Kislev** R. Ḥ.	1 **Tevet** R. Ḥ. 7
18	22	24	22	24	**24** *Be-Har Be-Ḥukkotai*	26	26	28	29	30 R. Ḥ.	2	2 8
19	**23** *Shemot*	25	23	25	25	27	27	29	1 **Tishri** Rosh Ha-Shanah	1 **Ḥeshvan** R. Ḥ. *No'aḥ*	3	3
20	24	26	24	**26** *Shemini*	26	28	**28** *Mattot Masei*	30 R. Ḥ.	2	2	4	4
21	25	27	25	27	27	29	29	1 **Elul** R. Ḥ.	**3** *Ha'azinu* Shabbat Shuvah	3	5	**5** *Va-Yiggash*
22	26	28	26	28	28	**30** *Koraḥ* R. Ḥ.	1 **Av** R. Ḥ.	2	4 Fast	4	6	6
23	27	**29** *Mishpatim* Shekalim	**27** *Va-Yakhel Pekudei* Ha-Ḥodesh	29	29	1 **Tammuz** R. Ḥ.	2	3	5	5	**7** *Va-Yeẓe*	7
24	28	30 R. Ḥ.	28	30 R. Ḥ.	1 **Sivan** R. Ḥ.	2	3	**4** *Shofetim*	6	6	8	8
25	29	1 **Adar** R. Ḥ.	29	1 **Iyyar** R. Ḥ.	**2** *Be-Midbar*	3	4	5	7	7	9	9
26	1 **Shevat** *Va-Era* R. Ḥ.	2	1 **Nisan** R. Ḥ.	2	3	4	5	6	8	**8** *Lekh Lekha*	10	10 Fast
27	2	3	2	**3** *Tazri'a Meẓora*	4	5	**6** *Devarim*	7	9	9	11	11
28	3	4	3	4	5	6	7	8	10 Yom Kippur	10	12	**12** *Va-Yeḥi*
29	4		4	5 Yom ha-Aẓma'ut	6 Shavuot	**7** *Ḥukkat*	8	9	11	11	13	13
30	5		**5** *Va-Yikra*	6	7	8	9 Tishah be-Av	10	12	12	**14** *Va-Yishlaḥ*	14
31	6		6		8		10	**11** *Ki Teẓe*		13		15

1964

5724/25 תשכ״ד / תשכ״ה

	January	February	March	April	May	June	July	August	September	October	November	December
1	16 **Tevet**	**18** *Yitro*	17	19	19	21	21	**23** *Ekev*	24	25	26	26 2
2	17	19	18	20 Ḥol ha-Mo'ed	**20** *Emor*	22	22	24	25	26	27	27 3
3	18	20	19	21 Pesaḥ	21	23	23	25	26	**27** *Bereshit*	28	28 4
4	**19** *Shemot*	21	20	22	22	24	**24** *Pinḥas*	26	27	28	29	29 5
5	20	22	21	23	23	25	25	27	**28** *Niẓẓavim*	29	30 R. Ḥ.	**30** R. Ḥ. *Mi-Keẓ* 6
6	21	23	22	24	24	**26** *Shelaḥ*	26	28	29	30 R. Ḥ.	1 **Kislev** R. Ḥ.	1 **Tevet** R. Ḥ. 7
7	22	24	*Va-Yakhel Pekudei* **23** Parah	25	25	27	27	29	1 **Tishri** Rosh Ha-Shanah	1 **Ḥeshvan** R. Ḥ.	**2** *Toledot*	2 8
8	23	**25** *Mishpatim* Shekalim	24	26	26	28	28	**30** R. Ḥ. *Re'eh*	2	2	3	3
9	24	26	25	27	**27** *Be-Har Be-Ḥukkotai*	29	29	1 **Elul** R. Ḥ.	3 Fast	3	4	4
10	25	27	26	28	28	30 R. Ḥ.	1 **Av** R. Ḥ.	2	4	**4** *No'aḥ*	5	5
11	**26** *Va-Era*	28	27	**29** *Shemini*	29	1 **Tammuz** R. Ḥ.	**2** *Mattot Masei*	3	5	5	6	6
12	27	29	28	30 R. Ḥ.	1 **Sivan** R. Ḥ.	2	3	4	**6** *Va-Yelekh* Shabbat Shuvah	6	7	**7** *Va-Yiggash*
13	28	30 R. Ḥ.	29	1 **Iyyar** R. Ḥ.	2	**3** *Koraḥ*	4	5	7	7	8	8
14	29	1 **Adar** R. Ḥ.	1 **Nisan** *Va-Yikra* R. Ḥ. Ha-Ḥodesh	2	3	4	5	6	8	8	**9** *Va-Yeẓe*	9
15	1 **Shevat** R. Ḥ.	**2** *Terumah*	2	3	4	5	6	**7** *Shofetim*	9	9	10	10 Fast
16	2	3	3	4 Yom ha-Aẓma'ut	**5** *Be-Midbar*	6	7	8	10 Yom Kippur	10	11	11
17	3	4	4	5	6 Shavuot	7	8	9	11	**11** *Lekh Lekha*	12	12
18	**4** *Bo*	5	5	**6** *Tazri'a Meẓora*	7	8	**9** *Devarim*	10	12	12	13	13
19	5	6	6	7	8	9	10 Tishah be-Av	11	**13** *Ha'azinu*	13	14	**14** *Va-Yeḥi*
20	6	7	7	8	9	**10** *Ḥukkat*	11	12	14	14	15	15
21	7	8	**8** *Ẓav* Shabbat ha-Gadol	9	10	11	12	13	15 Sukkot	15	**16** *Va-Yishlaḥ*	16
22	8	**9** *Teẓavveh* Zakhor	9	10	11	12	13	**14** *Ki Teẓe*	16	16	17	17
23	9	10	10	11	**12** *Naso*	13	14	15	17	17	18	18
24	10	11	11	12	13	14	15	16	18 Ḥol ha-Mo'ed	**18** *Va-Yera*	19	19
25	**11** *Be-Shallaḥ*	12	12	**13** *Aḥarei Mot Kedoshim*	14	15	**16** *Va-Etḥannan*	17	19	19	20	20
26	12	13 Ta'anit Esther	13	14	15	16	17	18	**20**	20	21	**21** *Shemot*
27	13	14 Purim	14	15	16	**17** *Balak*	18	19	21 Hoshana Rabba	21	22	22
28	14	15 Shushan Purim	**15** Pesaḥ	16	17	18 Fast	19	20	22 Shemini Aẓeret	22	**23** *Va-Yeshev*	23
29	15	**16** *Ki Tissa*	16 Omer	17	18	19	20	**21** *Ki Tavo*	23 Simḥat Torah *Ve-Zot Ha-Berakhah*	23	24	24
30	16		17 Ḥol ha-Mo'ed	18 Lag ba-Omer	**19** *Be-Ha'alotkha*	20	21	22	24	24	25 Ḥanukkah 1	25
31	17		18		20		22	23		**25** *Ḥayyei Sarah*		26

1965

5725/26 תשכ"ה / תשכ"ו

	January	February	March	April	May	June	July	August	September	October	November	December
1	27 Tevet	29	27	28	29 *Aḥarei Mot*	1 Sivan R. Ḥ.	1 Tammuz R. Ḥ.	3	4	5	6	7
2	28 *Va-Era*	30 R. Ḥ.	28	29	30 R. Ḥ.	2	2	4	5	6 *Va-Yelekh* Shabbat Shuvah	7	8
3	29	1 Adar I R. Ḥ.	29	1 Nisan *Tazri'a* R. Ḥ. Ha-Ḥodesh	1 Iyyar R. Ḥ.	3	3 *Koraḥ*	5	6	7	8	9
4	1 Shevat R. Ḥ.	2	30 R. Ḥ.	2	2	4	4	6	7 *Shofetim*	8	9	10 *Va-Yeẓe*
5	2	3	1 Adar II R. Ḥ.	3	3	5 *Be-Midbar*	5	7	8	9	10	11
6	3	4 *Terumah*	2 *Pekudei*	4	4 Yom ha-Aẓma'ut	6 Shavuot	6	8	9	10 Yom Kippur	11 *Lekh Lekha*	12
7	4	5	3	5	5	7	7	9 *Devarim* Tishah be-Av	10	11	12	13
8	5	6	4	6	6 *Kedoshim*	8	8	10 Fast	11	12	13	14
9	6 *Bo*	7	5	7	7	9	9	11	12	13 *Ha'azinu*	14	15
10	7	8	6	8 *Meẓora* Shabbat ha-Gadol	8	10	10 *Ḥukkat*	12	13	14	15	16
11	8	9	7	9	9	11	11	13	14 *Ki Teẓe*	15 Sukkot	16	17 *Va-Yishlaḥ*
12	9	10	8	10	10	12 *Naso*	12	14	15	16	17	18
13	10	11 *Teẓavveh*	9 *Va-Yikra* Zakhor	11	11	13	13	15	16	17	18 *Va-Yera*	19
14	11	12	10	12	12	14	14	16 *Va-Ethannan*	17	18 Ḥol ha-Mo'ed	19	20
15	12	13	11	13	13 *Emor*	15	15	17	18	19	20	21
16	13 *Be-Shallaḥ*	14	12	14	14	16	16	18	19	20	21	22
17	14	15	13 Ta'anit Esther	15 Pesaḥ	15	17	17 *Balak*	19	20	21 Hoshana Rabba	22	23
18	15	16	14 Purim	16 Omer	16	18	18 Fast	20	21 *Ki Tavo*	22 Shemini Aẓeret	23	24 *Va-Yeshev*
19	16	17	15 Shushan Purim	17	17	19 *Be-Ha'alotkha*	19	21	22	23 Simḥat Torah *Ve-Zot ha-Berakhah*	24	25 Ḥanukkah 1
20	17	18 *Ki Tissa*	16 *Zav*	18 Ḥol ha-Mo'ed	18 Lag ba-Omer	20	20	22	23	24	25 *Ḥayyei Sarah*	26 2
21	18	19	17	19	19	21	21	23 *Ekev*	24	25	26	27 3
22	19	20	18	20	20 *Be-Har*	22	22	24	25	26	27	28 4
23	20 *Yitro*	21	19	21 Pesaḥ	21	23	23	25	26	27 *Bereshit*	28	29 5
24	21	22	20	22	22	24	24 *Pinḥas*	26	27	28	29	1 Tevet R. Ḥ. 6
25	22	23	21	23	23	25	25	27	28 *Niẓẓavim*	29	1 Kislev R. Ḥ.	2 *Mi-Keẓ* 7
26	23	24	22	24	24	26 *Shelaḥ*	26	28	29	30 R. Ḥ.	2	3 8
27	24	25 *Va-Yakhel* Shekalim	23 *Shemini* Parah	25	25	27	27	29	1 Tishri Rosh Ha-Shanah	1 Ḥeshvan R. Ḥ.	3 *Toledot*	4
28	25	26	24	26	26	28	28	30 R. Ḥ. *Re'eh*	2	2	4	5
29	26		25	27	27 *Be-Ḥukkotai*	29	29	1 Elul R. Ḥ.	3 Fast	3	5	6
30	27 *Mishpatim*		26	28	28	30 R. Ḥ.	1 Av R. Ḥ.	2	4	4 *No'aḥ*	6	7
31	28		27		29		2 *Mattot Masei*	3		5		8

1966

5726/27 תשכ"ו / תשכ"ז

	January	February	March	April	May	June	July	August	September	October	November	December
1	9 *Va-Yiggash*	11	9	11	11	13	13	15	16	17	18	18
2	10 Fast	12	10	12 *Zav* Shabbat ha-Gadol	12	14	14 *Balak*	16	17	18 Ḥol ha-Mo'ed	19	19
3	11	13	11 Ta'anit Esther	13	13	15	15	17	18 *Ki Tavo*	19	20	20 *Va-Yeshev*
4	12	14	12	14	14	16 *Be-Ha'alotkha*	16	18	19	20	21	21
5	13	15 *Be-Shallaḥ*	13 *Teẓavveh* Zakhor	15 Pesaḥ	15	17	17	19	20	21 Hoshana Rabba	22 *Ḥayyei Sarah*	22
6	14	16	14 Purim	16 Omer	16	18	18	20 *Ekev*	21	22 Shemini Aẓeret	23	23
7	15	17	15 Shushan Purim	17	17 *Emor*	19	19	21	22	23 Simḥat Torah *Ve-Zot ha-Berakhah*	24	24
8	16 *Va-Yeḥi*	18	16	18 Ḥol ha-Mo'ed	18 Lag ba-Omer	20	20	22	23	24 *Bereshit*	25	25 Ḥanukkah 1
9	17	19	17	19	19	21	21 *Pinḥas*	23	24	25	26	26 2
10	18	20	18	20	20	22	22	24	25 *Niẓẓavim Va-Yelekh*	26	27	27 *Mi-Keẓ* 3
11	19	21	19	21 Pesaḥ	21	23 *Shelaḥ*	23	25	26	27	28	28 4
12	20	22 *Yitro*	20 *Ki Tissa* Parah	22	22	24	24	26	27	28	29 *Toledot*	29 5
13	21	23	21	23	23	25	25	27 *Re'eh*	28	29	30 R. Ḥ.	30 R. Ḥ. 6
14	22	24	22	24	24 *Be-Har Be-Ḥukkotai*	26	26	28	29	30 R. Ḥ.	1 Kislev R. Ḥ.	1 Tevet R. Ḥ. 7
15	23 *Shemot*	25	23	25	25	27	27	29	1 Tishri Rosh Ha-Shanah	1 Ḥeshvan R. Ḥ. *No'aḥ*	2	2 8
16	24	26	24	26 *Shemini*	26	28	28 *Mattot Masei*	30 R. Ḥ.	2	2	3	3
17	25	27	25	27	27	29	29	1 Elul R. Ḥ.	3 *Ha'azinu* Shabbat Shuvah	3	4	4 *Va-Yiggash*
18	26	28	26	28	28	30 R. Ḥ. *Koraḥ*	1 Av R. Ḥ.	2	4 Fast	4	5	5
19	27	29 *Mishpatim* Shekalim	27 *Va-Yakhel Pekudei* Ha-Ḥodesh	29	29	1 Tammuz R. Ḥ.	2	3	5	5	6 *Va-Yeẓe*	6
20	28	30 R. Ḥ.	28	30 R. Ḥ.	1 Sivan R. Ḥ.	2	3	4 *Shofetim*	6	6	7	7
21	29	1 Adar R. Ḥ.	29	1 Iyyar R. Ḥ.	2 *Be-Midbar*	3	4	5	7	7	8	8
22	1 Shevat R. Ḥ. *Va-Era*	2	1 Nisan R. Ḥ.	2	3	4	5	6	8	8 *Lekh Lekha*	9	9
23	2	3	2	3 *Tazri'a Meẓora*	4	5	6 *Devarim*	7	9	9	10	10 Fast
24	3	4	3	4	5	6	7	8	10 Yom Kippur	10	11	11 *Va-Yeḥi*
25	4	5	4	5 Yom ha-Aẓma'ut	6 Shavuot	7 *Ḥukkat*	8	9	11	11	12	12
26	5	6 *Terumah*	5 *Va-Yikra*	6	7	8	9 Tishah be-Av	10	12	12	13 *Va-Yishlaḥ*	13
27	6	7	6	7	8	9	10	11 *Ki Teẓe*	13	13	14	14
28	7	8	7	8	9 *Naso*	10	11	12	14	14	15	15
29	8 *Bo*		8	9	10	11	12	13	15 Sukkot	15 *Va-Yera*	16	16
30	9		9	10 *Aḥarei Mot Kedoshim*	11	12	13 *Va-Ethannan*	14	16	16	17	17
31	10		10		12		14	15		17		18 *Shemot*

1967

5727/28 תשכ״ז / תשכ״ח

	January	February	March	April	May	June	July	August	September	October	November	December
1	19 Tevet	21	19	20 Shemini Parah	21 Pesah	22	23 Korah	24	26	26	28	28
2	20	22	20	21	22	23	24	25	27 Re'eh	27	29	29 Toledot
3	21	23	21	22	23	24 Be-Midbar	25	26	28	28	30 R. H.	1 Kislev R. H.
4	22	24 Mishpatim	22 Va-Yakhel	23	24	25	26	27	29	29	1 Heshvan R. H. No'ah	2
5	23	25	23	24	25	26	27	28 Masei	30 R. H.	1 Tishri Rosh Ha-Shanah	2	3
6	24	26	24	25	26 Kedoshim	27	28	29	1 Elul R. H.	2	3	4
7	25 Va-Era	27	25	26	27	28	29	1 Av R. H.	2	3 Ha'azinu Shabbat Shuvah	4	5
8	26	28	26	27 Tazri'a Ha-Hodesh	28	29	30 R. H. Hukkat	2	3	4 Fast	5	6
9	27	29	27	28	29	1 Sivan R. H.	1 Tammuz R. H.	3	4 Shofetim	5	6	7 Va-Yeze
10	28	30 R. H.	28	29	30 R. H.	2 Naso	2	4	5	6	7	8
11	29	1 Adar I R. H. Terumah	29 Pekudei Shekalim	1 Nisan R. H.	1 Iyyar R. H.	3	3	5	6	7	8 Lekh Lekha	9
12	1 Shevat R. H.	2	30 R. H.	2	2	4	4	6 Devarim	7	8	9	10
13	2	3	1 Adar II R. H.	3	3 Emor	5	5	7	8	9	10	11
14	3 Bo	4	2	4	4	6 Shavuot	6	8	9	10 Yom Kippur	11	12
15	4	5	3	5 Mezora	5 Yom ha-Azma'ut	7	7 Balak	9 Tishah be-Av	10	11	12	13
16	5	6	4	6	6	8	8	10	11 Ki Teze	12	13	14 Va-Yishlah
17	6	7	5	7	7	9 Be-Ha'alotkha	9	11	12	13	14	15
18	7	8 Tezavveh	6 Va-Yikra	8	8	10	10	12	13	14	15 Va-Yera	16
19	8	9	7	9	9	11	11	13 Va-Ethannan	14	15 Sukkot	16	17
20	9	10	8	10	10 Be-Har	12	12	14	15	16	17	18
21	10 Be-Shallah	11	9	11	11	13	13	15	16	17 Hol ha-Mo'ed	18	19
22	11	12	10	12 Aharei Mot Shabbat ha-Gadol	12	14	14 Pinhas	16	17	18	19	20
23	12	13	11 Ta'anit Esther	13	13	15	15	17	18 Ki Tavo	19	20	21 Va-Yeshev
24	13	14	12	14	14	16 Shelah	16	18	19	20	21	22
25	14	15 Ki Tissa	13 Zav Zakhor	15 Pesah	15	17	17 Fast	19	20	21 Hoshana Rabba	22 Hayyei Sarah	23
26	15	16	14 Purim	16 Omer	16	18	18	20 Ekev	21	22 Shemini Azeret	23	24
27	16	17	15 Shushan Purim	17 Hol ha-Mo'ed	17 Be-Hukkotai	19	19	21	22	23 Simhat Torah Ve-Zot Ha-Berakhah	24	25 Hanukkah 1
28	17 Yitro	18	16	18	18 Lag ba-Omer	20	20	22	23	24 Bereshit	25	26 2
29	18		17	19	19	21	21 Mattot	23	24	25	26	27 3
30	19		18	20	20	22	22	24	25 Nizzavim Va-Yelekh	26	27	28 Mi-Kez 4
31	20		19		21		23	25		27		29 5

1968

5728/29 תשכ״ח / תשכ״ט

	January	February	March	April	May	June	July	August	September	October	November	December
1	30 Kislev R. H. Hanukkah 6	2	1 Adar R. H.	3	3	5 Be-Midbar	5	7	8	9	10	10
2	1 Tevet R. H. 7	3	2 Terumah	4	4 Yom ha-Azma'ut	6 Shavuot	6	8	9	10 Yom Kippur	11 Lekh Lekha	11
3	2 8	4 Bo	3	5	5	7	7	9 Devarim Tishah be-Av	10	11	12	12
4	3	5	4	6	6 Tazri'a Mezora	8	8	10 Fast	11	12	13	13
5	4	6	5	7	7	9	9	11	12	13 Ha'azinu	14	14
6	5 Va-Yiggash	7	6	8 Zav Shabbat ha-Gadol	8	10	10 Hukkat	12	13	14	15	15
7	6	8	7	9	9	11	11	13	14 Ki Teze	15 Sukkot	16	16 Va-Yishlah
8	7	9	8	10	10	12 Naso	12	14	15	16	17	17
9	8	10	9 Tezavveh Zakhor	11	11	13	13	15	16	17 Hol ha-Mo'ed	18 Va-Yera	18
10	9	11 Be-Shallah	10	12	12	14	14	16 Va-Ethannan	17	18	19	19
11	10 Fast	12	11	13	13 Aharei Mot Kedoshim	15	15	17	18	19	20	20
12	11	13	12	14	14	16	16	18	19	20	21	21
13	12 Va-Yehi	14	13 Ta'anit Esther	15 Pesah	15	17	17 Balak	19	20	21 Hoshana Rabba	22	22
14	13	15	14 Purim	16 Omer	16	18	18 Fast	20	21 Ki Tavo	22 Shemini Azeret	23	23 Va-Yeshev
15	14	16	15 Shushan Purim	17 Hol ha-Mo'ed	17	19 Be-Ha'alotkha	19	21	22	23 Simhat Torah Ve-Zot Ha-Berakhah	24	24
16	15	17	16 Ki Tissa	18	18 Lag ba-Omer	20	20	22	23	24	25 Hayyei Sarah	25 Hanukkah 1
17	16	18 Yitro	17	19	19	21	21	23 Ekev	24	25	26	26 2
18	17	19	18	20	20 Emor	22	22	24	25	26	27	27 3
19	18	20	19	21 Pesah	21	23	23	25	26	27 Bereshit	28	28 4
20	19 Shemot	21	20	22	22	24	24 Pinhas	26	27	28	29	29 5
21	20	22	21	23	23	25	25	27	28 Nizzavim	29	30 R. H.	30 R. H. Mi-Kez 6
22	21	23	22	24	24	26 Shelah	26	28	29	30 R. H.	1 Kislev R. H.	1 Tevet R. H. 7
23	22	24	23 Va-Yakhel Pekudei Parah	25	25	27	27	29	1 Tishri Rosh Ha-Shanah	1 Heshvan R. H.	2 Toledot	2 8
24	23	25 Mishpatim Shekalim	24	26	26	28	28	30 R. H. Re'eh	2	2	3	3
25	24	26	25	27	27 Be-Har Be-Hukkotai	29	29	1 Elul R. H.	3 Fast	3	4	4
26	25	27	26	28	28	30 R. H.	1 Av R. H.	2	4	4 No'ah	5	5
27	26 Va-Era	28	27	29 Shemini	29	1 Tammuz R. H.	2 Mattot Masei	3	5	5	6	6
28	27	29	28	30 R. H.	1 Sivan R. H.	2	3	4	6 Va-Yelekh Shabbat Shuvah	6	7	7 Va-Yiggash
29	28	30 R. H.	29	1 Iyyar R. H.	2	3 Korah	4	5	7	7	8	8
30	29		1 Nisan R. H. Va-Yikra Ha-Hodesh	2	3	4	5	6	8	8	9 Va-Yeze	9
31	1 Shevat R. H.		2		4		6	7 Shofetim		9		10 Fast

1969

5729/30 תשכ״ט / תש״ל

	January	February	March	April	May	June	July	August	September	October	November	December
1	11 Tevet	13 Be-Shallaḥ	11 Tezavveh Zakhor	13	13	15	15	17	18	19 Ḥol ha-Mo'ed	20 Va-Yera	21
2	12	14	12	14	14	16	16	18 Ekev	19	20	21	22
3	13	15	13 Ta'anit Esther	15 Pesaḥ	15 Emor	17	17 Fast	19	20	21 Hoshana Rabba	22	23
4	14 Va-Yeḥi	16	14 Purim	16 Omer	16	18	18	20	21	22 Shemini Aẓeret	23	24
5	15	17	15 Shushan Purim	17 Ḥol ha-Mo'ed	17	19	19 Pinḥas	21	22	23 Simḥat Torah Ve-Zot Ha-Berakhah	24	25 Ḥanukkah 1
6	16	18	16	18	18 Lag ba-Omer	20	20	22	23 Nizzavim Va-Yelekh	24	25	26 Va-Yeshev 2
7	17	19	17	19	19	21 Be-Ha'alotkha	21	23	24	25	26	27 3
8	18	20 Yitro	18 Ki Tissa Parah	20	20	22	22	24	25	26	27 Ḥayyei Sarah	28 4
9	19	21	19	21 Pesaḥ	21	23	23	25 Re'eh	26	27	28	29 5
10	20	22	20	22	22 Be-Har Be-Ḥukkotai	24	24	26	27	28	29	1 Tevet R. Ḥ. 6
11	21 Shemot	23	21	23	23	25	25	27	28	29 Bereshit	1 Kislev R. Ḥ.	2 7
12	22	24	22	24 Shemini	24	26	26 Mattot Masei	28	29	30 R. H.	2	3 8
13	23	25	23	25	25	27	27	29	1 Tishri Rosh Ha-Shanah	1 Ḥeshvan R. Ḥ.	3	4 Mi-Keẓ
14	24	26	24	26	26	28 Shelaḥ	28	30 R. H.	2	2	4	5
15	25	27 Mishpatim Shekalim	25 Va-Yakhel Pekudei Ha-Hodesh	27	27	29	29	1 Elul R. H.	3 Fast	3	5 Toledot	6
16	26	28	26	28	28	30 R. H.	1 Av R. H.	2 Shofetim	4	4	6	7
17	27	29	27	29	29 Be-Midbar	1 Tammuz R. H.	2	3	5	5	7	8
18	28 Va-Era	30 R. Ḥ.	28	30 R. H.	1 Sivan R. Ḥ.	2	3	4	6	6 No'aḥ	8	9
19	29	1 Adar R. Ḥ.	29	1 Iyyar R. H. Tazri'a Mezora	2	3	4 Devarim	5	7	7	9	10 Fast
20	1 Shevat R. H.	2	1 Nisan R. H.	2	3	4	5	6	8 Ha'azinu Shabbat Shuvah	8	10	11 Va-Yiggash
21	2	3	2	3	4	5 Koraḥ	6	7	9	9	11	12
22	3	4 Terumah	3 Va-Yikra	4	5	6	7	8	10 Yom Kippur	10	12 Va-Yeẓe	13
23	4	5	4	5 Yom ha-Aẓma'ut	6 Shavuot	7	8	9 Ki Teẓe	11	11	13	14
24	5	6	5	6	7	8	9 Tishah be-Av	10	12	12	14	15
25	6 Bo	7	6	7	8	9	10	11	13	13 Lekh Lekha	15	16
26	7	8	7	8 Aḥarei Mot Kedoshim	9	10	11 Va-Ethannan	12	14	14	16	17
27	8	9	8	9	10	11	12	13	15 Sukkot	15	17	18 Va-Yeḥi
28	9	10	9	10	11	12 Ḥukkat Balak	13	14	16	16	18	19
29	10		10 Zav Shabbat ha-Gadol	11	12	13	14	15	17 Ḥol ha-Mo'ed	17	19 Va-Yishlaḥ	20
30	11		11	12	13	14	15	16 Ki Tavo	18	18	20	21
31	12		12		14 Naso		16	17		19		22

1970

5730/31 תש״ל / תשל״א

	January	February	March	April	May	June	July	August	September	October	November	December
1	23 Tevet	25	23	24	25	26	27	28 Mattot Masei	30 R. H.	1 Tishri Rosh Ha-Shanah	2	3
2	24	26	24	25	26 Aḥarei Mot	27	28	29	1 Elul R. H.	2	3	4
3	25 Shemot	27	25	26	27	28	29	1 Av R. Ḥ.	2	3 Ha'azinu Shabbat Shuvah	4	5
4	26	28	26	27 Shemini Ha-Ḥodesh	28	29	30 R. H. Koraḥ	2	3	4 Fast	5	6
5	27	29	27	28	29	1 Sivan R. Ḥ.	1 Tammuz R. H.	3	4 Shofetim	5	6	7 Va-Yeẓe
6	28	30 R. H.	28	29	30 R. Ḥ.	2 Be-Midbar	2	4	5	6	7	8
7	29	1 Adar I R. H. Mishpatim	29 Va-Yakhel Shekalim	1 Nisan R. H.	1 Iyyar R. H.	3	3	5	6	7	8 Lekh Lekha	9
8	1 Shevat R. H.	2	30 R. H.	2	2	4	4	6 Devarim	7	8	9	10
9	2	3	1 Adar II R. H.	3	3 Kedoshim	5	5	7	8	9	10	11
10	3 Va-Era	4	2	4	4	6 Shavuot	6	8	9	10 Yom Kippur	11	12
11	4	5	3	5 Tazri'a	5 Yom ha-Aẓma'ut	7	7 Ḥukkat	9 Tishah be-Av	10	11	12	13
12	5	6	4	6	6	8	8	10	11 Ki Teẓe	12	13	14 Va-Yishlaḥ
13	6	7	5	7	7	9 Naso	9	11	12	13	14	15
14	7	8 Terumah	6 Pekudei	8	8	10	10	12	13	14	15 Va-Yera	16
15	8	9	7	9	9	11	11	13 Va-Ethannan	14	15 Sukkot	16	17
16	9	10	8	10	10 Emor	12	12	14	15	16	17	18
17	10 Bo	11	9	11	11	13	13	15	16	17 Ḥol ha-Mo'ed	18	19
18	11	12	10	12 Mezora Shabbat ha-Gadol	12	14	14 Balak	16	17	18	19	20
19	12	13	11 Ta'anit Esther	13	13	15	15	17	18 Ki Tavo	19	20	21 Va-Yeshev
20	13	14	12	14	14	16 Be-Ha'alotkha	16	18	19	20	21	22
21	14	15 Tezavveh	13 Va-Yikra Zakhor	15 Pesaḥ	15	17	17 Fast	19	20	21 Hoshana Rabba	22 Ḥayyei Sarah	23
22	15	16	14 Purim	16 Omer	16	18	18	20 Ekev	21	22 Shemini Aẓeret	23	24
23	16	17	15 Shushan Purim	17 Ḥol ha-Mo'ed	17 Be-Har	19	19	21	22	23 Simḥat Torah Ve-Zot Ha-Berakhah	24	25 Ḥanukkah 1
24	17 Be-Shallaḥ	18	16	18	18 Lag ba-Omer	20	20	22	23	24 Bereshit	25	26 2
25	18	19	17	19	19	21	21 Pinḥas	23	24	25	26	27 3
26	19	20	18	20	20	22	22	24	25 Nizzavim Va-Yelekh	26	27	28 Mi-Keẓ 4
27	20	21	19	21 Pesaḥ	21	23 Shelaḥ	23	25	26	27	28	29 5
28	21	22 Ki Tissa	20 Zav Parah	22	22	24	24	26	27	28	29 Toledot	30 R. H. 6
29	22		21	23	23	25	25	27 Re'eh	28	29	1 Kislev R. H.	1 Tevet R. Ḥ. 7
30	23		22	24	24 Be-Ḥukkotai	26	26	28	29	30 R. H.	2	2 8
31	24 Yitro		23		25		27	29		1 Ḥeshvan R. H. No'aḥ		3

1971

5731/32 תשל״א / תשל״ב

	January	February	March	April	May	June	July	August	September	October	November	December
1	4 Tevet	6	4	6	6 Tazri'a Mezora	8	8	10 Fast	11	12	13	13
2	5 Va-Yiggash	7	5	7	7	9	9	11	12	13 Ha'azinu	14	14
3	6	8	6	8 Zav Shabbat ha-Gadol	8	10	10 Hukkat	12	13	14	15	15
4	7	9	7	9	9	11	11	13	14 Ki Teze	15 Sukkot	16	16 Va-Yishlah
5	8	10	8	10	10	12 Naso	12	14	15	16	17	17
6	9	11 Be-Shallah	9 Tezavveh Zakhor	11	11	13	13	15	16	17	18 Va-Yera	18
7	10 Fast	12	10	12	12	14	14	16 Va-Ethannan	17	18 Hol ha-Mo'ed	19	19
8	11	13	11	13	13 Aharei Mot Kedoshim	15	15	17	18	19	20	20
9	12 Va-Yehi	14	12	14	14	16	16	18	19	20	21	21
10	13	15	13 Ta'anit Esther	15 Pesah	15	17	17 Balak	19	20	21 Hoshana Rabba	22	22
11	14	16	14 Purim	16 Omer	16	18	18 Fast	20	21 Ki Tavo	22 Shemini Azeret	23	23 Va-Yeshev
12	15	17	15 Shushan Purim	17	17	19 Be-Ha'alotkha	19	21	22	23 Simhat Torah Ve-Zot Ha-Berakhah	24	24
13	16	18 Yitro	16 Ki Tissa	18 Hol ha-Mo'ed	18 Lag ba-Omer	20	20	22	23	24	25 Hayyei Sarah	25 Hanukkah 1
14	17	19	17	19	19	21	21	23 Ekev	24	25	26	26 2
15	18	20	18	20	20 Emor	22	22	24	25	26	27	27 3
16	19 Shemot	21	19	21 Pesah	21	23	23	25	26	27 Bereshit	28	28 4
17	20	22	20	22	22	24	24 Pinhas	26	27	28	29	29 5
18	21	23	21	23	23	25	25	27	28 Nizzavim	29	30 R.H.	30 R.H. Mi-Kez 6
19	22	24	22	24	24	26 Shelah	26	28	29	30 R.H.	1 Kislev R.H.	1 Tevet R.H. 7
20	23	25 Mishpatim Shekalim	23 Va-Yakhel Pekudei Parah	25	25	27	27	29	1 Tishri Rosh Ha-Shanah	1 Heshvan R.H.	2 Toledot	2 8
21	24	26	24	26	26	28	28	30 R.H. Re'eh	2	2	3	3
22	25	27	25	27	27 Be-Har Be-Hukkotai	29	29	1 Elul R.H.	3 Fast	3	4	4
23	26 Va-Era	28	26	28	28	30 R.H.	1 Av R.H.	2	4	4 No'ah	5	5
24	27	29	27	29 Shemini	29	1 Tammuz R.H.	2 Mattot Masei	3	5	5	6	6
25	28	30 R.H.	28	30 R.H.	1 Sivan R.H.	2	3	4	6 Va-Yelekh Shabbat Shuvah	6	7	7 Va-Yiggash
26	29	1 Adar R.H.	29	1 Iyyar R.H.	2	3 Korah	4	5	7	7	8	8
27	1 Shevat R.H.	2 Terumah	1 Nisan Va-Yikra R.H. Ha-Hodesh	2	3	4	5	6	8	8	9 Va-Yeze	9
28	2	3	2	3	4	5	6	7 Shofetim	9	9	10	10 Fast
29	3		3	4 Yom ha-Azma'ut	5 Be-Midbar	6	7	8	10 Yom Kippur	10	11	11
30	4 Bo		4	5	6 Shavuot	7	8	9	11	11 Lekh Lekha	12	12
31	5		5		7		9 Devarim Tishah be-Av	10		12		13

1972

5732/33 תשל״ב / תשל״ג

	January	February	March	April	May	June	July	August	September	October	November	December
1	14 Tevet Va-Yehi	16	15 Shushan Purim	17	17	19	19 Pinhas	21	22	23 Simhat Torah Ve-Zot Ha-Berakhah	24	25 Hanukkah 1
2	15	17	16	18 Hol ha-Mo'ed	18 Lag ba-Omer	20	20	22	23 Nizzavim Va-Yelekh	24	25	26 Va-Yeshev 2
3	16	18	17	19	19	21 Be-Ha'alotkha	21	23	24	25	26	27 3
4	17	19	18 Ki Tissa Parah	20	20	22	22	24	25	26	27 Hayyei Sarah	28 4
5	18	20 Yitro	19	21 Pesah	21	23	23	25 Re'eh	26	27	28	29 5
6	19	21	20	22	22 Be-Har Be-Hukkotai	24	24	26	27	28	29	1 Tevet R.H. 6
7	20	22	21	23	23	25	25	27	28	29 Bereshit	1 Kislev R.H.	2 7
8	21 Shemot	23	22	24 Shemini	24	26	26 Mattot Masei	28	29	30 R.H.	2	3 8
9	22	24	23	25	25	27	27	29	1 Tishri Rosh Ha-Shanah	1 Heshvan R.H.	3	4 Mi-Kez
10	23	25	24	26	26	28 Shelah	28	30 R.H.	2	2	4	5
11	24	26	25 Va-Yakhel Pekudei Ha-Hodesh	27	27	29	29	1 Elul R.H.	3 Fast	3	5 Toledot	6
12	25	27 Mishpatim Shekalim	26	28	28	30 R.H.	1 Av R.H.	2 Shofetim	4	4	6	7
13	26	28	27	29	29 Be-Midbar	1 Tammuz R.H.	2	3	5	5	7	8
14	27	29	28	30 R.H.	1 Sivan R.H.	2	3	4	6	6 No'ah	8	9
15	28 Va-Era	30 R.H.	29	1 R.H. Iyyar Tazri'a Mezora	2	3	4 Devarim	5	7	7	9	10 Fast
16	29	1 Adar R.H.	1 Nisan R.H.	2	3	4	5	6	8 Ha'azinu Shabbat Shuvah	8	10	11 Va-Yiggash
17	1 Shevat R.H.	2	2	3	4	5 Korah	6	7	9	9	11	12
18	2	3	3 Va-Yikra	4	5	6	7	8	10 Yom Kippur	10	12 Va-Yeze	13
19	3	4 Terumah	4	5 Yom ha-Azma'ut	6 Shavuot	7	8	9 Ki Teze	11	11	13	14
20	4	5	5	6	7	8	9 Tishah be-Av	10	12	12	14	15
21	5	6	6	7	8	9	10	11	13	13 Lekh Lekha	15	16
22	6 Bo	7	7	8 Aharei Mot Kedoshim	9	10	11 Va-Ethannan	12	14	14	16	17
23	7	8	8	9	10	11	12	13	15 Sukkot	15	17	18 Va-Yehi
24	8	9	9	10	11	12 Hukkat Balak	13	14	16	16	18	19
25	9	10	10 Zav Shabbat ha-Gadol	11	12	13	14	15	17	17	19 Va-Yishlah	20
26	10	11 Tezavveh Zakhor	11	12	13	14	15	16 Ki Tavo	18 Hol ha-Mo'ed	18	20	21
27	11	12	12	13	14 Naso	15	16	17	19	19	21	22
28	12	13 Ta'anit Esther	13	14	15	16	17	18	20	20 Va-Yera	22	23
29	13 Be-Shallah	14 Purim	14	15 Emor	16	17 Fast	18 Ekev	19	21 Hoshana Rabba	21	23	24
30	14		15 Pesah	16	17	18	19	20	22 Shemini Azeret	22	24	25 Shemot
31	15		16 Omer		18		20	21		23		26

1973

5733/34 תשל״ג / תשל״ד

	January	February	March	April	May	June	July	August	September	October	November	December
1	27 **Tevet**	29	27	28	29	1 **Sivan** R. Ḥ.	1 **Tammuz** R. Ḥ.	3	**4** *Shofetim*	5	6	**6** *Va-Yeẓe*
2	28	30 R. Ḥ.	28	29	30 R. Ḥ.	**2** *Be-Midbar*	2	4	5	6	7	7
3	29	**1** **Adar I** R. Ḥ. *Mishpatim*	**29** *Va-Yakhel* Shekalim	1 **Nisan** R. Ḥ.	1 **Iyyar** R. Ḥ.	3	3	5	6	7	**8** *Lekh Lekha*	8
4	1 **Shevat** R. Ḥ.	2	30 R. Ḥ.	2	2	4	4	**6** *Devarim*	7	8	9	9
5	2	3	1 **Adar II** R. Ḥ.	3	**3**	5	5	7	8	9	10	10
6	**3** *Va-Era*	4	2	4	4	6 Shavuot	6	8	9	**10** Yom Kippur	11	11
7	4	5	3	**5** *Tazri'a*	5 Yom ha-Aẓma'ut	7	**7** *Ḥukkat*	9 Tishah be-Av	10	11	12	12
8	5	6	4	6	6	8	8	10	**11** *Ki Teẓe*	12	13	**13** *Va-Yishlaḥ*
9	6	7	5	7	7	**9** *Naso*	9	11	12	13	14	14
10	7	**8** *Terumah*	**6** *Pekudei*	8	8	10	10	12	13	14	**15** *Va-Yera*	15
11	8	9	7	9	9	11	11	**13** *Va-Etḥannan*	14	15 Sukkot	16	16
12	9	10	8	10	**10** *Emor*	12	12	14	15	16	17	17
13	**10** *Bo*	11	9	11	11	13	13	15	16	**17** Ḥol ha-Mo'ed	18	18
14	11	12	10	**12** *Meẓora* Shabbat ha-Gadol	12	14	**14** *Balak*	16	17	18	19	19
15	12	13	11 Ta'anit Esther	13	13	15	15	17	**18** *Ki Tavo*	19	20	**20** *Va-Yeshev*
16	13	14	12	14	14	**16** *Be-Ha'alotkha*	16	18	19	20	21	21
17	14	**15** *Teẓavveh*	**13** *Va-Yikra* Zakhor	15 Pesaḥ	15	17	17 Fast	19	20	21 Hoshana Rabba	**22** *Ḥayyei Sarah*	22
18	15	16	14 Purim	16 Omer	16	18	18	**20** *Ekev*	21	22 Shemini Aẓeret	23	23
19	16	17	15 Shushan Purim	17 Ḥol ha-Mo'ed	**17** *Be-Har*	19	19	21	22	23 Simḥat Torah *Ve-Zot Ha-Berakhah*	24	24
20	**17** *Be-Shallaḥ*	18	16	18	18 Lag ba-Omer	20	20	22	23	**24** *Bereshit*	25	25 Ḥanukkah 1
21	18	19	17	**19**	19	21	**21** *Pinḥas*	23	24	25	26	26 2
22	19	20	18	20	20	22	22	24	**25** *Niẓẓavim Va-Yelekh*	26	27	**27** *Mi-Keẓ* 3
23	20	21	19	21 Pesaḥ	21	**23** *Shelaḥ*	23	25	26	27	28	28 4
24	21	**22** *Ki Tissa*	**20** *Ẓav* Parah	22	22	24	24	26	27	28	**29** *Toledot*	29 5
25	22	23	21	23	23	25	25	**27** *Re'eh*	28	29	30 R. Ḥ.	30 R. Ḥ. 6
26	23	24	22	24	**24** *Be-Ḥukkotai*	26	26	28	29	30 R. Ḥ.	1 **Kislev** R. Ḥ.	1 **Tevet** R. Ḥ. 7
27	**24** *Yitro*	25	23	25	25	27	27	29	1 **Tishri** Rosh Ha-Shanah	**1** **Ḥeshvan** R. Ḥ. *No'aḥ*	2	2 8
28	25	26	24	**26** *Aḥarei Mot*	26	28	**28** *Mattot Masei*	30 R. Ḥ.	2	2	3	3
29	26		25	27	27	29	29	1 **Elul** R. Ḥ.	**3** *Ha'azinu* Shabbat Shuvah	3	4	**4** *Va-Yiggash*
30	27		26	28	28	**30** R. Ḥ. *Koraḥ*	1 **Av** R. Ḥ.	2	4 Fast	4	5	5
31	28		**27** *Shemini* Ha-Ḥodesh		29		2	3		5		6

1974

5734/35 תשל״ד / תשל״ה

	January	February	March	April	May	June	July	August	September	October	November	December
1	7 **Tevet**	9	7	9	9	**11** *Naso*	11	13	14	15 Sukkot	16	17
2	8	**10** *Be-Shallaḥ*	**8** *Teẓavveh* Zakhor	10	10	12	12	14	15	16	**17** *Va-Yera*	18
3	9	11	9	11	11	13	13	**15** *Va-Etḥannan*	16	17 Ḥol ha-Mo'ed	18	19
4	10 Fast	12	10	12	**12** *Aḥarei Mot Kedoshim*	14	14	16	17	18	19	20
5	**11** *Va-Yeḥi*	13	11	13	13	15	15	17	18	**19**	20	21
6	12	14	12	**14** *Ẓav* Shabbat ha-Gadol	14	16	**16** *Balak*	18	19	20	21	22
7	13	15	13 Ta'anit Esther	15 Pesaḥ	15	17	17 Fast	19	**20** *Ki Tavo*	21 Hoshana Rabba	22	**23** *Va-Yeshev*
8	14	16	14 Purim	16 Omer	16	**18** *Be-Ha'alotkha*	18	20	21	22 Shemini Aẓeret	23	24
9	15	**17** *Yitro*	**15** *Ki Tissa* Shushan Purim	17 Ḥol ha-Mo'ed	17	19	19	21	22	23 Simḥat Torah *Ve-Zot Ha-Berakhah*	**24** *Ḥayyei Sarah*	25 Ḥanukkah 1
10	16	18	16	18	18 Lag ba-Omer	20	20	**22** *Ekev*	23	24	25	26 2
11	17	19	17	19	**19** *Emor*	21	21	23	24	25	26	27 3
12	**18** *Shemot*	20	18	20	20	22	22	24	25	**26** *Bereshit*	27	28 4
13	19	21	19	**21** Pesaḥ	21	23	**23** *Pinḥas*	25	26	27	28	29 5
14	20	22	20	22	22	24	24	26	**27** *Niẓẓavim*	28	29	**30** R. Ḥ. *Mi-Keẓ* 6
15	21	23	21	23	23	**25** *Shelaḥ*	25	27	28	29	1 **Kislev** R. Ḥ.	1 **Tevet** R. Ḥ. 7
16	22	**24** *Mishpatim*	**22** *Va-Yakhel* Parah	24	24	26	26	28	29	30 R. Ḥ.	**2** *Toledot*	2 8
17	23	25	23	25	25	27	27	**29** *Re'eh*	1 **Tishri** Rosh Ha-Shanah	1 **Ḥeshvan** R. Ḥ.	3	3
18	24	26	24	26	**26** *Be-Har Be-Ḥukkotai*	28	28	30 R. Ḥ.	2	2	4	4
19	**25** *Va-Era*	27	25	27	27	29	29	1 **Elul** R. Ḥ.	3 Fast	**3** *No'aḥ*	5	5
20	26	28	26	**28** *Shemini*	28	30 R. Ḥ.	**1** R. Ḥ. **Av** *Mattot Masei*	2	4	4	6	6
21	27	29	27	29	29	1 R. Ḥ. **Tammuz**	2	3	**5** *Va-Yelekh* Shabbat Shuvah	5	7	**7** *Va-Yiggash*
22	28	30 R. Ḥ.	28	30 R. Ḥ.	1 **Sivan** R. Ḥ.	**2** *Koraḥ*	3	4	6	6	8	8
23	29	**1** **Adar** *Terumah* R. Ḥ. Shekalim	**29** *Pekudei* Ha-Ḥodesh	1 **Iyyar** R. Ḥ.	2	3	4	5	7	7	**9** *Va-Yeẓe*	9
24	1 **Shevat** R. Ḥ.	2	1 **Nisan** R. Ḥ.	2	3	4	5	**6** *Shofetim*	8	8	10	10 Fast
25	2	3	2	3 Yom ha-Aẓma'ut	**4** *Be-Midbar*	5	6	7	9	9	11	11
26	**3** *Bo*	4	3	4	5	6	7	8	10 Yom Kippur	**10** *Lekh Lekha*	12	12
27	4	5	4	**5** *Tazri'a Meẓora*	6 Shavuot	7	**8** *Devarim*	9	11	11	13	13
28	5	6	5	6	7	8	9 Tishah be-Av	10	**12** *Ha'azinu*	12	14	**14** *Va-Yeḥi*
29	6		6	7	8	**9** *Ḥukkat*	10	11	13	13	15	15
30	7		**7** *Va-Yikra*	8	9	10	11	12	14	14	**16** *Va-Yishlaḥ*	16
31	8		8		10		12	**13** *Ki Teẓe*		15		17

1975

5735/36 תשל״ה / תשל״ו

	January	February	March	April	May	June	July	August	September	October	November	December
1	18 Tevet	20 Yitro	18 Ki Tissa Parah	20 Hol ha-Mo'ed	20	22	22	24	25	26	27 Hayyei Sarah	27 3
2	19	21	19	21 Pesah	21	23	23	25 Re'eh	26	27	28	28 4
3	20	22	20	22	22 Be-Har Be-Hukkotai	24	24	26	27	28	29	29 5
4	21 Shemot	23	21	23	23	25	25	27	28	29 Bereshit	30 R. H.	30 R. H. 6
5	22	24	22	24 Shemini	24	26	26 Mattot Masei	28	29	30 R. H.	1 Kislev R. H.	1 Tevet R. H. 7
6	23	25	23	25	25	27	27	29	1 Tishri Rosh Ha-Shanah	1 R. H. Heshvan	2	2 Mi-Kez 8
7	24	26	24	26	26	28 Shelah	28	30 R. H.	2	2	3	3
8	25	27 Mishpatim Shekalim	25 Va-Yakhel Pekudei Ha-Hodesh	27	27	29	29	1 Elul R. H.	3 Fast	3	4 Toledot	4
9	26	28	26	28	28	30 R. H.	1 Av R. H.	2 Shofetim	4	4	5	5
10	27	29	27	29	29 Be-Midbar	1 Tammuz R. H.	2	3	5	5	6	6
11	28 Va-Era	30 R. H.	28	30 R. H.	1 Sivan R. H.	2	3	4	6	6 No'ah	7	7
12	29	1 Adar R. H.	29	1 Iyyar R. H. Tazri'a Mezora	2	3	4 Devarim	5	7	7	8	8
13	1 Shevat R. H.	2	1 Nisan R. H.	2	3	4	5	6	8 Ha'azinu Shabbat Shuvah	8	9	9 Va-Yiggash
14	2	3	2	3	4	5 Korah	6	7	9	9	10	10 Fast
15	3	4 Terumah	3 Va-Yikra	4	5	6	7	8	10 Yom Kippur	10	11 Va-Yeze	11
16	4	5	4	5 Yom ha-Azma'ut	6 Shavuot	7	8	9 Ki Teze	11	11	12	12
17	5	6	5	6	7	8	9 Tishah be-Av	10	12	12	13	13
18	6 Bo	7	6	7	8	9	10	11	13	13 Lekh Lekha	14	14
19	7	8	7	8 Aharei Mot Kedoshim	9	10	11 Va-Ethannan	12	14	14	15	15
20	8	9	8	9	10	11	12	13	15 Sukkot	15	16	16 Va-Yehi
21	9	10	9	10	11	12 Hukkat Balak	13	14	16	16	17	17
22	10	11 Tezavveh Zakhor	10 Zav Shabbat ha-Gadol	11	12	13	14	15	17 Hol ha-Mo'ed	17	18 Va-Yishlah	18
23	11	12	11	12	13	14	15	16 Ki Tavo	18	18	19	19
24	12	13 Ta'anit Esther	12	13	14 Naso	15	16	17	19	19	20	20
25	13 Be-Shallah	14 Purim	13	14	15	16	17	18	20	20 Va-Yera	21	21
26	14	15 Shushan Purim	14	15 Emor	16	17 Fast	18 Ekev	19	21 Hoshana Rabba	21	22	22
27	15	16	15 Pesah	16	17	18	19	20	22 Shemini Azeret	22	23	23 Shemot
28	16	17	16 Omer	17	18	19 Pinhas	20	21	23 Simhat Torah Ve-Zot Ha-Berakhah	23	24	24
29	17		17 Hol ha-Mo'ed	18 Lag ba-Omer	19	20	21	22	24	24	25 Va-Yeshev Hanukkah 1	25
30	18		18	19	20	21	22	23 Nizzavim Va-Yelekh	25	25	26 2	26
31	19		19		21 Be-Ha'alotkha		23	24		26		27

1976

5736/37 תשל״ו / תשל״ז

	January	February	March	April	May	June	July	August	September	October	November	December
1	28 Tevet	30 R. H.	29	1 Nisan R. H.	1 Iyyar R. H. Kedoshim	3	3	5	6	7	8	9
2	29	1 Adar I R. H.	30 R. H.	2	2	4	4	6	7	8 Ha'azinu Shabbat Shuvah	9	10
3	1 Shevat R. H. Va-Era	2	1 Adar II R. H.	3 Tazri'a	3	5	5 Korah	7	8	9	10	11
4	2	3	2	4	4	6 Shavuot	6	8	9 Ki Teze	10 Yom Kippur	11	12 Va-Yeze
5	3	4	3	5	5 Yom ha-Azma'ut	7	7	9 Tishah be-Av	10	11	12	13
6	4	5	4 Pekudei	6	6	8	8	10	11	12	13 Lekh Lekha	14
7	5	6 Terumah	5	7	7	9	9	11 Va-Ethannan	12	13	14	15
8	6	7	6	8	8 Emor	10	10	12	13	14	15	16
9	7	8	7	9	9	11	11	13	14	15 Sukkot	16	17
10	8 Bo	9	8	10 Mezora Shabbat ha-Gadol	10	12	12 Hukkat Balak	14	15	16	17	18
11	9	10	9	11	11	13	13	15	16 Ki Tavo	17 Hol ha-Mo'ed	18	19 Va-Yishlah
12	10	11	10	12	12	14 Naso	14	16	17	18	19	20
13	11	12	11 Va-Yikra Zakhor	13	13	15	15	17	18	19	20 Va-Yera	21
14	12	13 Tezavveh	12	14	14	16	16	18 Ekev	19	20	21	22
15	13	14	13 Ta'anit Esther	15 Pesah	15 Be-Har	17	17 Fast	19	20	21 Hoshana Rabba	22	23
16	14	15	14 Purim	16 Omer	16	18	18	20	21	22 Shemini Azeret	23	24
17	15 Be-Shallah	16	15 Shushan Purim	17 Hol ha-Mo'ed	17	19	19 Pinhas	21	22	23 Simhat Torah Ve-Zot Ha-Berakhah	24	25 Hanukkah 1
18	16	17	16	18	18 Lag ba-Omer	20	20	22	23 Nizzavim Va-Yelekh	24	25	26 Va-Yeshev 2
19	17	18	17	19	19	21 Be-Ha'alotkha	21	23	24	25	26	27 3
20	18	19	18 Zav Parah	20	20	22	22	24	25	26	27 Hayyei Sarah	28 4
21	19	20 Ki Tissa	19	21 Pesah	21	23	23	25 Re'eh	26	27	28	29 5
22	20	21	20	22	22 Be-Hukkotai	24	24	26	27	28	29	1 Tevet R. H. 6
23	21	22	21	23	23	25	25	27	28	29 Bereshit	1 Kislev R. H.	2 7
24	22 Yitro	23	22	24 Aharei Mot	24	26	26 Mattot Masei	28	29	30 R. H.	2	3 8
25	23	24	23	25	25	27	27	29	1 Tishri Rosh Ha-Shanah	1 Heshvan R. H.	3	4 Mi-Kez
26	24	25	24	26	26	28 Shelah	28	30 R. H.	2	2	4	5
27	25	26	25 Shemini Ha-Hodesh	27	27	29	29	1 Elul R. H.	3 Fast	3	5 Toledot	6
28	26	27 Va-Yakhel Shekalim	26	28	28	30 R. H.	1 Av R. H.	2 Shofetim	4	4	6	7
29	27	28	27	29	29 Be-Midbar	1 Tammuz R. H.	2	3	5	5	7	8
30	28		28	30 R. H.	1 Sivan R. H.	2	3	4	6	6 No'ah	8	9
31	29 Mishpatim		29		2		4 Devarim	5		7		10 Fast

1977

5737/38 — תשל״ז / תשל״ח

	January	February	March	April	May	June	July	August	September	October	November	December
1	11 Tevet *Va-Yiggash*	13	11	13	13	15	15	17	18	19 Ḥol	20	21
2	12	14	12	14 *Ẓav* Shabbat ha-Gadol	14	16	16 *Balak*	18	19	20 ha-Mo'ed	21	22
3	13	15	13 Ta'anit Esther	15 Pesaḥ	15	17	17 Fast	19	20 *Ki Tavo*	21 Hoshana Rabba	22	23 *Va-Yeshev*
4	14	16	14 Purim	16 Omer	16	18 *Be-Ha'alotkha*	18	20	21	22 Shemini Aẓeret	23	24
5	15	17 *Be-Shallaḥ*	15 *Teẓavveh* Shushan Purim	17 Ḥol ha-Mo'ed	17	19	19	21	22	23 Simḥat Torah *Ve-Zot Ha-Berakhah*	24 *Ḥayyei Sarah*	25 Hanukkah 1
6	16	18	16	18	18 Lag ba-Omer	20	20	22 *Ekev*	23	24	25	26 2
7	17	19	17	19	19 *Emor*	21	21	23	24	25	26	27 3
8	18 *Va-Yeḥi*	20	18	20	20	22	22	24	25	26 *Bereshit*	27	28 4
9	19	21	19	21 Pesaḥ	21	23	23 *Pinḥas*	25	26	27	28	29 5
10	20	22	20	22	22	24	24	26	27 *Niẓẓavim*	28	29	30 R. Ḥ. *Mi-Keẓ* 6
11	21	23	21	23	23	25 *Shelaḥ*	25	27	28	29	1 Kislev R. Ḥ.	1 Tevet R. Ḥ. 7
12	22	24 *Yitro*	22 *Ki Tissa* Parah	24	24	26	26	28	29	30 R. Ḥ.	2 *Toledot*	2 8
13	23	25	23	25	25	27	27	29 *Re'eh*	1 Tishri Rosh Ha-Shanah	1 Ḥeshvan R. Ḥ.	3	3
14	24	26	24	26	26 *Be-Har Be-Ḥukkotai*	28	28	30 R. Ḥ.	2	2	4	4
15	25 *Shemot*	27	25	27	27	29	29	1 Elul R. Ḥ.	3 Fast	3 *No'aḥ*	5	5
16	26	28	26	28 *Shemini*	28	30 R. Ḥ.	1 Av R. Ḥ. *Mattot Masei*	2	4	4	6	6
17	27	29	27	29	29	1 Tammuz R. Ḥ.	2	3	5 *Va-Yelekh* Shabbat Shuvah	5	7	7 *Va-Yiggash*
18	28	30 R. Ḥ.	28	30 R. Ḥ.	1 Sivan R. Ḥ.	2 *Koraḥ*	3	4	6	6	8	8
19	29	1 Adar R. Ḥ. *Mishpatim* Shekalim	*Va-Yakhel Pekudei* 29 Ha-Ḥodesh	1 Iyyar R. Ḥ.	2	3	4	5	7	7	9 *Va-Yeẓe*	9
20	1 Shevat R. Ḥ.	2	1 Nisan R. Ḥ.	2	3	4	5	6 *Shofetim*	8	8	10	10 Fast
21	2	3	2	3 Yom ha-Aẓma'ut	4 *Be-Midbar*	5	6	7	9	9	11	11
22	3 *Va-Era*	4	3	4	5	6	7	8	10 Yom Kippur	10 *Lekh Lekha*	12	12
23	4	5	4	5 *Tazri'a Meẓora*	6 Shavuot	7	8 *Devarim*	9	11	11	13	13
24	5	6	5	6	7	8	9 Tishah be-Av	10	12 *Ha'azinu*	12	14	14 *Va-Yeḥi*
25	6	7	6	7	8	9 *Ḥukkat*	10	11	13	13	15	15
26	7	8 *Terumah* Zakhor	7 *Va-Yikra*	8	9	10	11	12	14	14	16 *Va-Yishlaḥ*	16
27	8	9	8	9	10	11	12	13 *Ki Teẓe*	15 Sukkot	15	17	17
28	9	10	9	10	11 *Naso*	12	13	14	16	16	18	18
29	10 *Bo*		10	11	12	13	14	15	17 Ḥol	17 *Va-Yera*	19	19
30	11		11	12 *Aḥarei Mot Kedoshim*	13	14	15 *Va-Etḥannan*	16	18 ha-Mo'ed	18	20	20
31	12		12		14		16	17		19		21 *Shemot*

1978

5738/39 — תשל״ח / תשל״ט

	January	February	March	April	May	June	July	August	September	October	November	December
1	22 Tevet	24	22	23 *Shemini* Parah	24	25	26 *Shelaḥ*	27	29	29	1 Ḥeshvan R. Ḥ.	1 Kislev R. Ḥ.
2	23	25	23	24	25	26	27	28	30 R. Ḥ. *Re'eh*	1 Tishri Rosh Ha-Shanah	2	2 *Toledot*
3	24	26	24	25	26	27 *Be-Ḥukkotai*	28	29	1 Elul R. Ḥ.	2	3	3
4	25	27 *Mishpatim*	25 *Va-Yakhel* Shekalim	26	27	28	29	1 Av R. Ḥ.	2	3 Fast	4 *No'aḥ*	4
5	26	28	26	27	28	29	30 R. Ḥ.	2 *Mattot Masei*	3	4	5	5
6	27	29	27	28	29 *Aḥarei Mot*	1 Sivan R. Ḥ.	1 Tammuz R. Ḥ.	3	4	5	6	6
7	28 *Va-Era*	30 R. Ḥ.	28	29	30 R. Ḥ.	2	2	4	5	6 *Va-Yelekh* Shabbat Shuvah	7	7
8	29	1 Adar I R. Ḥ.	29	1 Nisan R. Ḥ. *Tazri'a* Ha-Ḥodesh	1 Iyyar R. Ḥ.	3	3 *Koraḥ*	5	6	7	8	8
9	1 Shevat R. Ḥ.	2	30 R. Ḥ.	2	2	4	4	6	7 *Shofetim*	8	9	9 *Va-Yeẓe*
10	2	3	1 Adar II R. Ḥ.	3	3	5 *Be-Midbar*	5	7	8	9	10	10
11	3	4 *Terumah*	2 *Pekudei*	4	4 Yom ha-Aẓma'ut	6 Shavuot	6	8	9	10 Yom Kippur	11 *Lekh Lekha*	11
12	4	5	3	5	5	7	7	9 *Devarim* Tishah be-Av	10	11	12	12
13	5	6	4	6	6 *Kedoshim*	8	8	10 Fast	11	12	13	13
14	6 *Bo*	7	5	7	7	9	9	11	12	13 *Ha'azinu*	14	14
15	7	8	6	8 *Meẓora* Shabbat ha-Gadol	8	10	10 *Ḥukkat*	12	13	14	15	15
16	8	9	7	9	9	11	11	13	14 *Ki Teẓe*	15 Sukkot	16	16 *Va-Yishlaḥ*
17	9	10	8	10	10	12 *Naso*	12	14	15	16	17	17
18	10	11 *Teẓavveh*	9 *Va-Yikra* Zakhor	11	11	13	13	15	16	17 Ḥol ha-Mo'ed	18 *Va-Yera*	18
19	11	12	10	12	12	14	14	16 *Va-Etḥannan*	17	18	19	19
20	12	13	11	13	13 *Emor*	15	15	17	18	19	20	20
21	13 *Be-Shallaḥ*	14	12	14	14	16	16	18	19	20	21	21
22	14	15	13 Ta'anit Esther	15 Pesaḥ	15	17	17 *Balak*	19	20	21 Hoshana Rabba	22	22
23	15	16	14 Purim	16 Omer	16	18	18 Fast	20	21 *Ki Tavo*	22 Shemini Aẓeret	23	23 *Va-Yeshev*
24	16	17	15 Shushan Purim	17 Ḥol ha-Mo'ed	17	19 *Be-Ha'alotkha*	19	21	22	23 Simḥat Torah *Ve-Zot Ha-Berakhah*	24	24
25	17	18 *Ki Tissa*	16 *Ẓav*	18	18 Lag ba-Omer	20	20	22	23	24	25 *Ḥayyei Sarah*	25 Hanukkah 1
26	18	19	17	19	19	21	21	23 *Ekev*	24	25	26	26 2
27	19	20	18	20	20 *Be-Har*	22	22	24	25	26	27	27 3
28	20 *Yitro*	21	19	21 Pesaḥ	21	23	23	25	26	27 *Bereshit*	28	28 4
29	21		20	22	22	24	24 *Pinḥas*	26	27	28	29	29 5
30	22		21	23	23	25	25	27	28 *Niẓẓavim*	29	30 R. Ḥ.	30 R. Ḥ. *Mi-Keẓ* 6
31	23		22		24		26	28		30 R. Ḥ.		1 Tevet R. Ḥ. 7

1979

5739/40 תשל״ט / תש״מ

	January	February	March	April	May	June	July	August	September	October	November	December
1	2 Tevet Hanukkah 8	4	2	4	4	6 Shavuot	6	8	9 *Ki Teze*	10 Yom Kippur	11	11 *Va-Yeze*
2	3	5	3	5	5 Yom ha-Azma'ut	7	7	9 Tishah be-Av	10	11	12	12
3	4	6 *Bo*	4 *Terumah*	6	6	8	8	10	11	12	13 *Lekh Lekha*	13
4	5	7	5	7	7	9	9	11 *Va-Ethannan*	12	13	14	14
5	6	8	6	8	8 *Aharei Mot Kedoshim*	10	10	12	13	14	15	15
6	7 *Va-Yiggash*	9	7	9	9	11	11	13	14	15 Sukkot	16	16
7	8	10	8	10 *Zav* Shabbat ha-Gadol	10	12	12 *Hukkat Balak*	14	15	16	17	17
8	9	11	9	11	11	13	13	15	16 *Ki Tavo*	17 Hol ha-Mo'ed	18	18 *Va-Yishlah*
9	10 Fast	12	10	12	12	14 *Naso*	14	16	17	18	19	19
10	11	13 *Be-Shallah*	11 *Tezavveh Zakhor*	13	13	15	15	17	18	19	20 *Va-Yera*	20
11	12	14	12	14	14	16	16	18 *Ekev*	19	20	21	21
12	13	15	13 Ta'anit Esther	15 Pesah	15 *Emor*	17	17 Fast	19	20	21 Hoshana Rabba	22	22
13	14 *Va-Yehi*	16	14 Purim	16 Omer	16	18	18	20	21	22 Shemini Azeret	23	23
14	15	17	15 Shushan Purim	17 Hol ha-Mo'ed	17	19	19 *Pinhas*	21	22	23 Simhat Torah *Ve-Zot Ha-Berakhah*	24	24
15	16	18	16	18	18 Lag ba-Omer	20	20	22	23 *Nizzavim Va-Yelekh*	24	25	25 *Va-Yeshev* Hanukkah 1
16	17	19	17	19	19	21 *Be-Ha'alotkha*	21	23	24	25	26	26 2
17	18	20 *Yitro*	18 *Ki Tissa* Parah	20	20	22	22	24	25	26	27 *Hayyei Sarah*	27 3
18	19	21	19	21 Pesah	21	23	23	25 *Re'eh*	26	27	28	28 4
19	20	22	20	22	22 *Be-Har Be-Hukkotai*	24	24	26	27	28	29	29 5
20	21 *Shemot*	23	21	23	23	25	25	27	28	29 *Bereshit*	30 R. H.	30 R. H. 6
21	22	24	22	24 *Shemini*	24	26	26 *Mattot Masei*	28	29	30 R. H.	1 Kislev R. H.	1 Tevet R. H. 7
22	23	25	23	25	25	27	27	29	1 Tishri Rosh Ha-Shanah	1 Heshvan R. H.	2	2 *Mi-Kez* 8
23	24	26	24	26	26	28 *Shelah*	28	30 R. H.	2	2	3	3
24	25	27 *Mishpatim* Shekalim	25 *Va-Yakhel Pekudei* Ha-Hodesh	27	27	29	29	1 Elul R. H.	3 Fast	3	4 *Toledot*	4
25	26	28	26	28	28	30 R. H.	1 Av R. H.	2 *Shofetim*	4	4	5	5
26	27	29	27	29	29 *Be-Midbar*	1 Tammuz R. H.	2	3	5	5	6	6
27	28 *Va-Era*	30 R. H.	28	30 R. H.	1 Sivan R. H.	2	3	4	6	6 *No'ah*	7	7
28	29	1 Adar R. H.	29	1 R. H. Iyyar *Tazri'a Mezora*	2	3	4 *Devarim*	5	7	7	8	8
29	1 Shevat R. H.		1 Nisan R. H.	2	3	4	5	6	8 *Ha'azinu* Shabbat Shuvah	8	9	9 *Va-Yiggash*
30	2		2	3	4	5 *Korah*	6	7	9	9	10	10 Fast
31	3		3 *Va-Yikra*		5		7	8		10		11

1980

5740/41 תש״מ / תשמ״א

	January	February	March	April	May	June	July	August	September	October	November	December
1	12 Tevet	14	13 ↑ *Tezavveh Zakhor*	15 Pesah	15	17	17 Fast	19	20	21 Hoshana Rabba	22 *Hayyei Sarah*	23
2	13	15 *Be-Shallah*	14 Purim	16 Omer	16	18	18	20 *Ekev*	21	22 Shemini Azeret	23	24
3	14	16	15 Shushan Purim	17 Hol ha-Mo'ed	17 *Emor*	19	19	21	22	23 Simhat Torah *Ve-Zot Ha-Berakhah*	24	25 Hanukkah 1
4	15	17	16	18	18 Lag ba-Omer	20	20	22	23	24 *Bereshit*	25	26 2
5	16 *Va-Yehi*	18	17	19	19	21	21 *Pinhas*	23	24	25	26	27 3
6	17	19	18	20	20	22	22	24	25 *Nizzavim Va-Yelekh*	26	27	28 *Mi-Kez* 4
7	18	20	19	21 Pesah	21	23 *Shelah*	23	25	26	27	28	29 5
8	19	21	20 *Ki Tissa* Parah	22	22	24	24	26	27	28	29 *Toledot*	1 Tevet R. H. 6
9	20	22 *Yitro*	21	23	23	25	25	27 *Re'eh*	28	29	1 Kislev R. H.	2 7
10	21	23	22	24	24 *Be-Har Be-Hukkotai*	26	26	28	29	30 R. H.	2	3 8
11	22	24	23	25	25	27	27	29	1 Tishri Rosh Ha-Shanah	1 Heshvan R. H. *No'ah*	3	4
12	23 *Shemot*	25	24	26 *Shemini*	26	28	28 *Mattot Masei*	30 R. H.	2	2	4	5
13	24	26	25	27	27	29	29	1 Elul R. H.	3 *Ha'azinu* Shabbat Shuvah	3	5	6 *Va-Yiggash*
14	25	27	26	28	28	30 R. H. *Korah*	1 Av R. H.	2	↓ 4 Fast	4	6	7
15	26	28	27 *Va-Yakhel Pekudei* Ha-Hodesh	29	29	1 Tammuz R. H.	2	3	5	5	7 *Va-Yeze*	8
16	27	29 *Mishpatim* Shekalim	28	30 R. H.	1 Sivan R. H.	2	3	4 *Shofetim*	6	6	8	9
17	28	30 R. H.	29	1 Iyyar R. H.	2 *Be-Midbar*	3	4	5	7	7	9	10 Fast
18	29	1 Adar R. H.	1 Nisan R. H.	2	3	4	5	6	8	8 *Lekh Lekha*	10	11
19	1 Shevat R. H. *Va-Era*	2	2	3 *Tazri'a Mezora*	4	5	6 *Devarim*	7	9	9	11	12
20	2	3	3	4	5	6	7	8	10 Yom Kippur	10	12	13 *Va-Yehi*
21	3	4	4	5 Yom ha-Azma'ut	6 Shavuot	7 *Hukkat*	8	9	11	11	13	14
22	4	5	5 *Va-Yikra*	6	7	8	9 Tishah be-Av	10	12	12	14 *Va-Yishlah*	15
23	5	6 *Terumah*	6	7	8	9	10	11 *Ki Teze*	13	13	15	16
24	6	7	7	8	9 *Naso*	10	11	12	14	14	16	17
25	7	8	8	9	10	11	12	13	15 Sukkot	15 *Va-Yera*	17	18
26	8 *Bo*	9	9	10 *Aharei Mot Kedoshim*	11	12	13 *Va-Ethannan*	14	16	16	18	19
27	9	10	10	11	12	13	14	15	17 Hol ha-Mo'ed	17	19	20 *Shemot*
28	10	11 Ta'anit Esther ↑	11	12	13	14 *Balak*	15	16	18	18	20	21
29	11	12	12 *Zav* Shabbat ha-Gadol	13	14	15	16	17	19	19	21 *Va-Yeshev*	22
30	12		13	14	15	16	17	18 *Ki Tavo*	20	20	22	23
31	13		14		16 *Be-Ha'alotkha*		18	19		21		24

1981

5741/42 — תשמ״א / תשמ״ב

	January	February	March	April	May	June	July	August	September	October	November	December
1	25 Tevet	27	25	26	27	28	29	1 Av R. Ḥ. *Masei*	2	3 Fast	4	5
2	26	28	26	27	28 *Kedoshim*	29	30 R. Ḥ.	2	3	4	5	6
3	27 *Va-Era*	29	27	28	29	1 Sivan R. Ḥ.	1 Tammuz R. Ḥ.	3	4	5 *Va-Yelekh* Shabbat Shuvah	6	7
4	28	30 R. Ḥ.	28	29 *Tazri'a* Ha-Ḥodesh	30 R. Ḥ.	2	2 *Ḥukkat*	4	5	6	7	8
5	29	1 Adar R. Ḥ.	29	1 Nisan R. Ḥ.	1 Iyyar R. Ḥ.	3	3	5	6 *Shofetim*	7	8	9 *Va-Yeẓe*
6	1 Shevat R. Ḥ.	2	30 R. Ḥ.	2	2	4 *Naso*	4	6	7	8	9	10
7	2	3 *Terumah*	1 Adar II R. Ḥ. Shekalim *Pekudei*	3	3 Yom ha-Aẓma'ut	5	5	7	8	9	10 *Lekh Lekha*	11
8	3	4	2	4	4	6 Shavuot	6	8 *Devarim*	9	10 Yom Kippur	11	12
9	4	5	3	5	5 *Emor*	7	7	9 Tishah be-Av	10	11	12	13
10	5 *Bo*	6	4	6	6	8	8	10	11	12 *Ha'azinu*	13	14
11	6	7	5	7 *Meẓora*	7	9	9 *Balak*	11	12	13	14	15
12	7	8	6	8	8	10	10	12	13 *Ki Teẓe*	14	15	16 *Va-Yishlaḥ*
13	8	9	7	9	9	11 *Be-Ha'alotkha*	11	13	14	15 Sukkot	16	17
14	9	10 *Teẓavveh*	8 *Va-Yikra* Zakhor	10	10	12	12	14	15	16	17 *Va-Yera*	18
15	10	11	9	11	11	13	13	15 *Va-Etḥannan*	16	17	18	19
16	11	12	10	12	12 *Be-Har*	14	14	16	17	18 Ḥol ha-Mo'ed	19	20
17	12 *Be-Shallaḥ*	13	11	13	13	15	15	17	18	19	20	21
18	13	14	12	14 *Aḥarei Mot* Shabbat ha-Gadol	14	16	16 *Pinḥas*	18	19	20	21	22
19	14	15	13 Ta'anit Esther	15 Pesaḥ	15	17	17 Fast	19	20 *Ki Tavo*	21 Hoshana Rabba	22	23 *Va-Yeshev*
20	15	16	14 Purim	16 Omer	16	18 *Shelaḥ*	18	20	21	22 Shemini Aẓeret	23	24
21	16	17 *Ki Tissa*	15 *Ẓav* Shushan Purim	17	17	19	19	21	22	23 Simḥat Torah *Ve-Zot Ha-Berakhah*	24 *Ḥayyei Sarah*	25 Ḥanukkah 1
22	17	18	16	18 Ḥol ha-Mo'ed	18 Lag ba-Omer	20	20	22 *Ekev*	23	24	25	26 2
23	18	19	17	19	19 *Be-Ḥukkotai*	21	21	23	24	25	26	27 3
24	19 *Yitro*	20	18	20	20	22	22	24	25	26 *Bereshit*	27	28 4
25	20	21	19	21 Pesaḥ	21	23	23 *Mattot*	25	26	27	28	29 5
26	21	22	20	22	22	24	24	26	27 *Niẓẓavim*	28	29	30 R. Ḥ. *Mi-Keẓ* 6
27	22	23	21	23	23	25 *Koraḥ*	25	27	28	29	1 Kislev R. Ḥ.	1 Tevet R. Ḥ. 7
28	23	24 *Va-Yakhel*	22 *Shemini* Parah	24	24	26	26	28	29	30 R. Ḥ.	2 *Toledot*	2 8
29	24		23	25	25	27	27	29 *Re'eh*	1 Tishri Rosh Ha-Shanah	1 Ḥeshvan R. Ḥ.	3	3
30	25		24	26	26 *Be-Midbar*	28	28	30 R. Ḥ.	2	2	4	4
31	26 *Mishpatim*		25		27		29	1 Elul R. Ḥ.		3 *No'aḥ*		5

1982

5742/43 — תשמ״ב / תשמ״ג

	January	February	March	April	May	June	July	August	September	October	November	December
1	6 Tevet	8	6	8	8 *Aḥarei Mot Kedoshim*	10	10	12	13	14	15	15
2	7 *Va-Yiggash*	9	7	9	9	11	11	13	14	15 Sukkot	16	16
3	8	10	8	10 *Ẓav* Shabbat ha-Gadol	10	12	12 *Ḥukkat Balak*	14	15	16	17	17
4	9	11	9	11	11	13	13	15	16 *Ki Tavo*	17	18	18 *Va-Yishlaḥ*
5	10 Fast	12	10	12	12	14 *Naso*	14	16	17	18 Ḥol ha-Mo'ed	19	19
6	11	13 *Be-Shallaḥ*	11 *Teẓavveh* Zakhor	13	13	15	15	17	18	19	20 *Va-Yera*	20
7	12	14	12	14	14	16	16	18 *Ekev*	19	20	21	21
8	13	15	13 Ta'anit Esther	15 Pesaḥ	15 *Emor*	17	17 Fast	19	20	21 Hoshana Rabba	22	22
9	14 *Va-Yeḥi*	16	14 Purim	16 Omer	16	18	18	20	21	22 Shemini Aẓeret	23	23
10	15	17	15 Shushan Purim	17	17	19	19 *Pinḥas*	21	22	23 Simḥat Torah *Ve-Zot Ha-Berakhah*	24	24
11	16	18	16	18 Ḥol ha-Mo'ed	18 Lag ba-Omer	20	20	22	23 *Niẓẓavim Va-Yelekh*	24	25	25 Ḥanukkah 1 *Va-Yeshev*
12	17	19	17	19	19	21 *Be-Ha'alotkha*	21	23	24	25	26	26 2
13	18	20 *Yitro*	18 *Ki Tissa* Parah	20	20	22	22	24	25	26	27 *Ḥayyei Sarah*	27 3
14	19	21	19	21 Pesaḥ	21	23	23	25 *Re'eh*	26	27	28	28 4
15	20	22	20	22	22 *Be-Har Be-Ḥukkotai*	24	24	26	27	28	29	29 5
16	21 *Shemot*	23	21	23	23	25	25	27	28	29 *Bereshit*	30 R. Ḥ.	30 R. Ḥ. 6
17	22	24	22	24 *Shemini*	24	26	26 *Mattot Masei*	28	29	30 R. Ḥ.	1 Kislev R. Ḥ.	1 Tevet R. Ḥ. 7
18	23	25	23	25	25	27	27	29	1 Tishri Rosh Ha-Shanah	1 Ḥeshvan R. Ḥ.	2	2 *Mi-Keẓ* 8
19	24	26	24	26	26	28 *Shelaḥ*	28	30 R. Ḥ.	2	2	3	3
20	25	27 *Mishpatim* Shekalim	25 *Va-Yakhel Pekudei* Ha-Ḥodesh	27	27	29	29	1 Elul R. Ḥ.	3 Fast	3	4 *Toledot*	4
21	26	28	26	28	28	30 R. Ḥ.	1 Av R. Ḥ.	2 *Shofetim*	4	4	5	5
22	27	29	27	29	29 *Be-Midbar*	1 Tammuz R. Ḥ.	2	3	5	5	6	6
23	28 *Va-Era*	30 R. Ḥ.	28	30 R. Ḥ.	1 Sivan R. Ḥ.	2	3	4	6	6 *No'aḥ*	7	7
24	29	1 Adar R. Ḥ.	29	1 Iyyar R. Ḥ. *Tazri'a Meẓora*	2	3	4 *Devarim*	5	7	7	8	8
25	1 Shevat R. Ḥ.	2	1 Nisan R. Ḥ.	2	3	4	5	6	8 *Ha'azinu* Shabbat Shuvah	8	9	9 *Va-Yiggash*
26	2	3	2	3	4	5 *Koraḥ*	6	7	9	9	10	10 Fast
27	3	4 *Terumah*	3 *Va-Yikra*	4	5	6	7	8	10 Yom Kippur	10	11 *Va-Yeẓe*	11
28	4	5	4	5 Yom ha-Aẓma'ut	6 Shavuot	7	8	9 *Ki Teẓe*	11	11	12	12
29	5		5	6	7	8	9 Tishah be-Av	10	12	12	13	13
30	6 *Bo*		6	7	8	9	10	11	13	13 *Lekh Lekha*	14	14
31	7		7		9		11 *Va-Etḥannan*	12		14		15

1983

5743/44 תשמ״ג / תשמ״ד

	January	February	March	April	May	June	July	August	September	October	November	December
1	16 Tevet *Va-Yeḥi*	18	16	18 Ḥol ha-Mo'ed	18 Lag ba-Omer	20	20	22	23	24 *Bereshit*	25	25 Ḥanukkah 1
2	17	19	17	19	19	21	21 *Pinḥas*	23	24	25	26	26 2
3	18	20	18	20	20	22	22	24	25 *Niẓẓavim Va-Yelekh*	26	27	27 *Mi-Keẓ* 3
4	19	21	19	21 Pesaḥ	21	23 *Shelaḥ*	23	25	26	27	28	28 4
5	20	22 *Yitro*	20 *Ki Tissa* Parah	22	22	24	24	26	27	28	29 *Toledot*	29 5
6	21	23	21	23	23	25	25	27 *Re'eh*	28	29	30 R. H.	30 R. H. 6
7	22	24	22	24	24 *Be-Har Be-Ḥukkotai*	26	26	28	29	30 R. H.	1 Kislev R. H.	1 Tevet R. H. 7
8	23 *Shemot*	25	23	25	25	27	27	29	1 Tishri Rosh Ha-Shanah	1 Ḥeshvan R. H. *No'aḥ*	2	2 8
9	24	26	24	26 *Shemini*	26	28	28 *Mattot Masei*	30 R. H.	2	2	3	3
10	25	27	25	27	27	29	29	1 Elul R. H.	3 *Ha'azinu* Shabbat Shuvah	3	4	4 *Va-Yiggash*
11	26	28	26	28	28	30 R. H. *Koraḥ*	1 Av R. H.	2	4 Fast	4	5	5
12	27	29 *Mishpatim* Shekalim	27 *Va-Yakhel Pekudei* Ha-Ḥodesh	29	29	1 Tammuz R. H.	2	3	5	5	6 *Va-Yeẓe*	6
13	28	30 R. H.	28	30 R. H.	1 Sivan R. H.	2	3	4 *Shofetim*	6	6	7	7
14	29	1 Adar R. H.	29	1 Iyyar R. H.	2 *Be-Midbar*	3	4	5	7	7	8	8
15	1 Shevat R. H. *Va-Era*	2	1 Nisan R. H.	2	3	4	5	6	8	8 *Lekh Lekha*	9	9
16	2	3	2	3 *Tazri'a Meẓora*	4	5	6 *Devarim*	7	9	9	10	10 Fast
17	3	4	3	4	5	6	7	8	10 Yom Kippur	10	11	11 *Va-Yeḥi*
18	4	5	4	5 Yom ha-Aẓma'ut	6 Shavuot	7 *Ḥukkat*	8	9	11	11	12	12
19	5	6 *Terumah*	5 *Va-Yikra*	6	7	8	9 Tishah be-Av	10	12	12	13 *Va-Yishlaḥ*	13
20	6	7	6	7	8	9	10	11 *Ki Teẓe*	13	13	14	14
21	7	8	7	8	9 *Naso*	10	11	12	14	14	15	15
22	8 *Bo*	9	8	9	10	11	12	13	15 Sukkot	15 *Va-Yera*	16	16
23	9	10	9	10 *Aḥarei Mot Kedoshim*	11	12	13 *Va-Etḥannan*	14	16	16	17	17
24	10	11 Ta'anit Esther	10	11	12	13	14	15	17 Ḥol ha-Mo'ed	17	18	18 *Shemot*
25	11	12	11	12	13	14 *Balak*	15	16	18	18	19	19
26	12	13 *Teẓavveh* Zakhor	12 *Ẓav* Shabbat ha-Gadol	13	14	15	16	17	19	19	20 *Va-Yeshev*	20
27	13	14 Purim	13	14	15	16	17	18 *Ki Tavo*	20	20	21	21
28	14	15 Shushan Purim	14	15	16 *Be-Ha'alotkha*	17 Fast	18	19	21 Hoshana Rabba	21	22	22
29	15 *Be-Shallaḥ*		15 Pesaḥ	16	17	18	19	20	22 Shemini Aẓeret	22 *Ḥayyei Sarah*	23	23
30	16		16 Omer	17 *Emor*	18	19	20 *Ekev*	21	23 Simḥat Torah *Ve-Zot Ha-Berakhah*	23	24	24
31	17		17 Ḥol ha-Mo'ed		19		21	22		24		25 *Va-Era*

1984

5744/45 תשמ״ד / תשמ״ה

	January	February	March	April	May	June	July	August	September	October	November	December
1	26 Tevet	28	27	28	29	1 Sivan R. H.	1 Tammuz R. H.	3	4 *Shofetim*	5	6	7 *Va-Yeẓe*
2	27	29	28	29	30 R. H.	2 *Naso*	2	4	5	6	7	8
3	28	30 R. H.	29 *Pekudei* Shekalim	1 Nisan R. H.	1 Iyyar R. H.	3	3	5	6	7	8 *Lekh Lekha*	9
4	29	1 Adar I R. H. *Terumah*	30 R. H.	2	2	4	4	6 *Devarim*	7	8	9	10
5	1 Shevat R. H.	2	1 Adar II R. H.	3	3 *Emor*	5	5	7	8	9	10	11
6	2	3	2	4	4	6 Shavuot	6	8	9	10 Yom Kippur	11	12
7	3 *Bo*	4	3	5 *Meẓora*	5 Yom ha-Aẓma'ut	7	7 *Balak*	9 Tishah be-Av	10	11	12	13
8	4	5	4	6	6	8	8	10	11 *Ki Teẓe*	12	13	14 *Va-Yishlaḥ*
9	5	6	5	7	7	9 *Be-Ha'alotkha*	9	11	12	13	14	15
10	6	7	6 *Va-Yikra*	8	8	10	10	12	13	14	15 *Va-Yera*	16
11	7	8 *Teẓavveh*	7	9	9	11	11	13 *Va-Etḥannan*	14	15 Sukkot	16	17
12	8	9	8	10	10 *Be-Har*	12	12	14	15	16	17	18
13	9	10	9	11	11	13	13	15	16	17 Ḥol ha-Mo'ed	18	19
14	10 *Be-Shallaḥ*	11	10	12 *Aḥarei Mot* Shabbat ha-Gadol	12	14	14 *Pinḥas*	16	17	18	19	20
15	11	12	11 Ta'anit Esther	13	13	15	15	17	18 *Ki Tavo*	19	20	21 *Va-Yeshev*
16	12	13	12	14	14	16 *Shelaḥ*	16	18	19	20	21	22
17	13	14	13 *Ẓav* Zakhor	15 Pesaḥ	15	17	17 Fast	19	20	21 Hoshana Rabba	22 *Ḥayyei Sarah*	23
18	14	15 *Ki Tissa*	14 Purim	16 Omer	16	18	18	20 *Ekev*	21	22 Shemini Aẓeret	23	24
19	15	16	15 Shushan Purim	17 Ḥol ha-Mo'ed	17 *Be-Ḥukkotai*	19	19	21	22	23 Simḥat Torah *Ve-Zot Ha-Berakhah*	24	25 Ḥanukkah 1
20	16	17	16	18	18 Lag ba-Omer	20	20	22	23	24 *Bereshit*	25	26 2
21	17 *Yitro*	18	17	19	19	21	21 *Mattot*	23	24	25	26	27 3
22	18	19	18	20	20	22	22	24	25 *Niẓẓavim Va-Yelekh*	26	27	28 *Mi-Keẓ* 4
23	19	20	19	21 Pesaḥ	21	23 *Koraḥ*	23	25	26	27	28	29 5
24	20	21	20 *Shemini* Parah	22	22	24	24	26	27	28	29 *Toledot*	30 R. H. 6
25	21	22 *Va-Yakhel*	21	23	23	25	25	27 *Re'eh*	28	29	1 Kislev R. H.	1 Tevet R. H. 7
26	22	23	22	24	24 *Be-Midbar*	26	26	28	29	30 R. H.	2	2 8
27	23	24	23	25	25	27	27	29	1 Tishri Rosh Ha-Shanah	1 Ḥeshvan R. H. *No'aḥ*	3	3
28	24 *Mishpatim*	25	24	26 *Kedoshim*	26	28	28 *Masei*	30 R. H.	2	2	4	4
29	25	26	25	27	27	29	29	1 Elul R. H.	3 *Ha'azinu* Shabbat Shuvah	3	5	5 *Va-Yiggash*
30	26		26	28	28	30 R. H. *Ḥukkat*	1 Av R. H.	2	4 Fast	4	6	6
31	27		27 *Tazri'a* Ha-Ḥodesh		29		2	3		5		7

1985

5745/46 תשמ"ה / תשמ"ו

	January	February	March	April	May	June	July	August	September	October	November	December
1	8 Tevet	10	8	10	10	12 *Naso*	12	14	15	16	17	18
2	9	11 *Be-Shallaḥ*	9 *Teẓavveh* Ẓakhor	11	11	13	13	15	16	17	18 *Va-Yera*	19
3	10 Fast	12	10	12	12	14	14	16 *Va-Etḥannan*	17	18 Ḥol ha-Mo'ed	19	20
4	11	13	11	13	13 *Aḥarei Mot Kedoshim*	15	15	17	18	19	20	21
5	12 *Va-Yeḥi*	14	12	14	14	16	16	18	19	20	21	22
6	13	15	13 Ta'anit Esther	15 Pesaḥ	15	17	17 *Balak*	19	20	21 Hoshana Rabba	22	23
7	14	16	14 Purim	16 Omer	16	18	18 Fast	20	21 *Ki Tavo*	22 Shemini Aẓeret	23	24 *Va-Yeshev*
8	15	17	15 Shushan Purim	17	17	19 *Be-Ha'alotkha*	19	21	22	23 Simḥat Torah *Ve-Zot Ha-Berakhah*	24	25 Ḥanukkah 1
9	16	18 *Yitro*	16 *Ki Tissa*	18 Ḥol ha-Mo'ed	18 Lag ba-Omer	20	20	22	23	24	25 *Ḥayyei Sarah*	26 2
10	17	19	17	19	19	21	21	23 *Ekev*	24	25	26	27 3
11	18	20	18	20	20 *Emor*	22	22	24	25	26	27	28 4
12	19 *Shemot*	21	19	21 Pesaḥ	21	23	23	25	26	27 *Bereshit*	28	29 5
13	20	22	20	22	22	24	24 *Pinḥas*	26	27	28	29	1 Tevet R. Ḥ. 6
14	21	23	21	23	23	25	25	27	28 *Niẓẓavim*	29	1 Kislev R. Ḥ.	2 *Mi Keẓ* 7
15	22	24	22	24	24	26 *Shelaḥ*	26	28	29	30 R. Ḥ.	2	3 8
16	23	25 *Mishpatim* Shekalim	23 *Va-Yakhel Pekudei* Parah	25	25	27	27	29	1 Tishri Rosh Ha-Shanah	1 Ḥeshvan R. Ḥ.	3 *Toledot*	4
17	24	26	24	26	26	28	28	30 R. Ḥ. *Re'eh*	2	2	4	5
18	25	27	25	27	27 *Be-Har Be-Ḥukkotai*	29	29	1 Elul R. Ḥ.	3 Fast	3	5	6
19	26 *Va-Era*	28	26	28	28	30 R. Ḥ.	1 Av R. Ḥ.	2	4	4 *No'aḥ*	6	7
20	27	29	27	29 *Shemini*	29	1 Tammuz R. Ḥ.	2 *Mattot Masei*	3	5	5	7	8
21	28	30 R. Ḥ.	28	30 R. Ḥ.	1 Sivan R. Ḥ.	2	3	4	6 *Va-Yelekh* Shabbat Shuvah	6	8	9 *Va-Yiggash*
22	29	1 Adar R. Ḥ.	29	1 Iyyar R. Ḥ.	2	3 *Koraḥ*	4	5	7	7	9	10 Fast
23	1 Shevat R. Ḥ.	2 *Terumah*	1 Nisan R. Ḥ. *Va-Yikra* Ha-Ḥodesh	2	3	4	5	6	8	8	10 *Va-Yeẓe*	11
24	2	3	2	3	4	5	6	7 *Shofetim*	9	9	11	12
25	3	4	3	4 Yom ha-Aẓma'ut	5 *Be-Midbar*	6	7	8	10 Yom Kippur	10	12	13
26	4 *Bo*	5	4	5	6 Shavuot	7	8	9	11	11 *Lekh Lekha*	13	14
27	5	6	5	6 *Tazri'a Meẓora*	7	8	9 *Devarim* Tishah be-Av	10	12	12	14	15
28	6	7	6	7	8	9	10 Fast	11	13 *Ha'azinu*	13	15	16 *Va-Yeḥi*
29	7		7	8	9	10 *Ḥukkat*	11	12	14	14	16	17
30	8		8 *Ẓav* Shabbat ha-Gadol	9	10	11	12	13	15 Sukkot	15	17 *Va-Yishlaḥ*	18
31	9		9		11		13	14 *Ki Teẓe*		16		19

1986

5746/47 תשמ"ו / תשמ"ז

	January	February	March	April	May	June	July	August	September	October	November	December
1	20 Tevet	22 *Yitro*	20 *Ki Tissa*	21	22	23	24	25	27	27	29 *Bereshit*	29
2	21	23	21	22	23	24	25	26 *Mattot Masei*	28	28	30 R. Ḥ.	30 R. Ḥ.
3	22	24	22	23	24 *Aḥarei Mot*	25	26	27	29	29	1 Ḥeshvan R. Ḥ.	1 Kislev R. Ḥ.
4	23 *Shemot*	25	23	24	25	26	27	28	30 R. Ḥ.	1 Tishri Rosh Ha-Shanah	2	2
5	24	26	24	25 *Shemini* Ha-Ḥodesh	26	27	28 *Shelaḥ*	29	1 Elul R. Ḥ.	2	3	3
6	25	27	25	26	27	28	29	1 Av R. Ḥ.	2 *Shofetim*	3 Fast	4	4 *Toledot*
7	26	28	26	27	28	29 *Be-Midbar*	30 R. Ḥ.	2	3	4	5	5
8	27	29 *Mishpatim*	27 *Va-Yakhel* Shekalim	28	29	1 Sivan R. Ḥ.	1 Tammuz R. Ḥ.	3	4	5	6 *No'aḥ*	6
9	28	30 R. Ḥ.	28	29	30 R. Ḥ.	2	2	4 *Devarim*	5	6	7	7
10	29	1 Adar I R. Ḥ.	29	1 Nisan R. Ḥ.	1 Iyyar R. Ḥ. *Kedoshim*	3	3	5	6	7	8	8
11	1 Shevat R. Ḥ. *Va-Era*	2	30 R. Ḥ.	2	2	4	4	6	7	8 *Ha'azinu* Shabbat Shuvah	9	9
12	2	3	1 Adar II R. Ḥ.	3 *Tazri'a*	3	5	5 *Koraḥ*	7	8	9	10	10
13	3	4	2	4	4	6 Shavuot	6	8	9 *Ki Teẓe*	10 Yom Kippur	11	11 *Va-Yeẓe*
14	4	5	3	5	5 Yom ha-Aẓma'ut	7	7	9 Tishah be-Av	10	11	12	12
15	5	6 *Terumah*	4 *Pekudei*	6	6	8	8	10	11	12	13 *Lekh Lekha*	13
16	6	7	5	7	7	9	9	11 *Va-Etḥannan*	12	13	14	14
17	7	8	6	8	8 *Emor*	10	10	12	13	14	15	15
18	8 *Bo*	9	7	9	9	11	11	13	14	15 Sukkot	16	16
19	9	10	8	10 *Meẓora* Shabbat ha-Gadol	10	12	12 *Ḥukkat Balak*	14	15	16	17	17
20	10	11	9	11	11	13	13	15	16 *Ki Tavo*	17	18	18 *Va-Yishlaḥ*
21	11	12	10	12	12	14 *Naso*	14	16	17	18 Ḥol ha-Mo'ed	19	19
22	12	13 *Teẓavveh*	11 *Va-Yikra* Zakhor	13	13	15	15	17	18	19	20 *Va-Yera*	20
23	13	14	12	14	14	16	16	18 *Ekev*	19	20	21	21
24	14	15	13 Ta'anit Esther	15 Pesaḥ	15 *Be-Har*	17	17 Fast	19	20	21 Hoshana Rabba	22	22
25	15 *Be-Shallaḥ*	16	14 Purim	16 Omer	16	18	18	20	21	22 Shemini Aẓeret	23	23
26	16	17	15 Shushan Purim	17	17	19	19 *Pinḥas*	21	22	23 Simḥat Torah *Ve-Zot Ha-Berakhah*	24	24
27	17	18	16	18 Ḥol ha-Mo'ed	18 Lag ba-Omer	20	20	22	23 *Niẓẓavim Va-Yelekh*	24	25	25 *Va-Yeshev* Ḥanukkah 1
28	18	19	17	19	19	21 *Be-Ha'alotkha*	21	23	24	25	26	26 2
29	19		18 *Ẓav* Parah	20	20	22	22	24	25	26	27 *Ḥayyei Sarah*	27 3
30	20		19	21 Pesaḥ	21	23	23	25 *Re'eh*	26	27	28	28 4
31	21		20		22 *Be-Ḥukkotai*		24	26		28		29 5

1987

5747/48 תשמ״ז / תשמ״ח

	January	February	March	April	May	June	July	August	September	October	November	December
1	30 Kislev R. Ḥ. 6 Ḥanukkah	2	30 R. Ḥ.	2	2	4	4	6 Devarim	7	8	9	10
2	1 Tevet R. Ḥ. 7	3	1 Adar R. Ḥ.	3	3 Tazri'a Meẓora	5	5	7	8	9	10	11
3	2 Mi-Keẓ 8	4	2	4	4	6 Shavuot	6	8	9	10 Yom Kippur	11	12
4	3	5	3	5 Va-Yikra	5 Yom ha-Aẓma'ut	7	7 Ḥukkat	9 Tishah be-Av	10	11	12	13
5	4	6	4	6	6	8	8	10	11 Ki Teẓe	12	13	14 Va-Yishlaḥ
6	5	7	5	7	7	9 Naso	9	11	12	13	14	15
7	6	8 Bo	6 Terumah	8	8	10	10	12	13	14	15 Va-Yera	16
8	7	9	7	9	9	11	11	13 Va-Ethannan	14	15 Sukkot	16	17
9	8	10	8	10	10 Aḥarei Mot Kedoshim	12	12	14	15	16	17	18
10	9 Va-Yiggash	11	9	11	11	13	13	15	16	17	18	19
11	10 Fast	12	10	12 Ẓav Shabbat ha-Gadol	12	14	14 Balak	16	17	18	19	20
12	11	13	11 Ta'anit Esther	13	13	15	15	17	18 Ki Tavo	19 Ḥol ha-Mo'ed	20	21 Va-Yeshev
13	12	14	12	14	14	16 Be-Ha'alotkha	16	18	19	20	21	22
14	13	15 Be-Shallaḥ	13 Teẓavveh Zakhor	15 Pesaḥ	15	17	17 Fast	19	20	21 Hoshana Rabba	22 Ḥayyei Sarah	23
15	14	16	14 Purim	16 Omer	16	18	18	20 Ekev	21	22 Shemini Aẓeret	23	24
16	15	17	15 Shushan Purim	17 Ḥol ha-Mo'ed	17 Emor	19	19	21	22	23 Simḥat Torah Ve-Zot Ha-Berakhah	24	25 Ḥanukkah 1
17	16 Va-Yeḥi	18	16	18	18 Lag ba-Omer	20	20	22	23	24 Bereshit	25	26 2
18	17	19	17	19	19	21	21 Pinḥas	23	24	25	26	27 3
19	18	20	18	20	20	22	22	24	25 Niẓẓavim Va-Yelekh	26	27	28 Mi-Keẓ 4
20	19	21	19	21 Pesaḥ	21	23 Shelaḥ	23	25	26	27	28	29 5
21	20	22 Yitro	20 Ki Tissa Parah	22	22	24	24	26	27	28	29 Toledot	30 R. Ḥ. 6
22	21	23	21	23	23	25	25	27 Re'eh	28	29	1 Kislev R. Ḥ.	1 Tevet R. Ḥ. 7
23	22	24	22	24	24 Be-Har Be-Ḥukkotai	26	26	28	29	30 R. Ḥ.	2	2 8
24	23 Shemot	25	23	25	25	27	27	29	1 Tishri Rosh Ha-Shanah	1 Ḥeshvan R. Ḥ. No'aḥ	3	3
25	24	26	24	26 Shemini	26	28	28 Mattot Masei	30 R. Ḥ.	2	2	4	4
26	25	27	25	27	27	29	29	1 Elul R. Ḥ.	3 Ha'azinu Shabbat Shuvah	3	5	5 Va-Yiggash
27	26	28	26	28	28	30 R. Ḥ. Koraḥ	1 Av R. Ḥ.	2	4 Fast	4	6	6
28	27	29 Mishpatim Shekalim	27 Va-Yakhel Pekudei Ha-Ḥodesh	29	29	1 Tammuz R. Ḥ.	2	3	5	5	7 Va-Yeẓe	7
29	28		28	30 R. Ḥ.	1 Sivan R. Ḥ.	2	3	4 Shofetim	6	6	8	8
30	29		29	1 Iyyar R. Ḥ.	2 Be-Midbar	3	4	5	7	7	9	9
31	1 Shevat R. Ḥ. Va-Era		1 Nisan R. Ḥ.		3		5	6		8 Lekh Lekha		10 Fast

1988

5748/49 תשמ״ח / תשמ״ט

	January	February	March	April	May	June	July	August	September	October	November	December
1	11 Tevet	13	12	14	14	16	16	18	19	20 Ḥol ha-Mo'ed	21	22
2	12 Va-Yeḥi	14	13 Ta'anit Esther	15 Pesaḥ	15	17	17 Balak	19	20	21 Hoshana Rabba	22	23
3	13	15	14 Purim	16 Omer	16	18	18 Fast	20	21 Ki Tavo	22 Shemini Aẓeret	23	24 Va-Yeshev
4	14	16	15 Shushan Purim	17 Ḥol ha-Mo'ed	17	19 Be-Ha'alotkha	19	21	22	23 Simḥat Torah Ve-Zot Ha-Berakhah	24	25 Ḥanukkah 1
5	15	17	16 Ki Tissa	18	18 Lag ba-Omer	20	20	22	23	24	25 Ḥayyei Sarah	26 2
6	16	18 Yitro	17	19	19	21	21	23 Ekev	24	25	26	27 3
7	17	19	18	20	20 Emor	22	22	24	25	26	27	28 4
8	18	20	19	21 Pesaḥ	21	23	23	25	26	27 Bereshit	28	29 5
9	19 Shemot	21	20	22	22	24	24 Pinḥas	26	27	28	29	1 Tevet R. Ḥ. 6
10	20	22	21	23	23	25	25	27	28 Niẓẓavim	29	1 Kislev R. Ḥ.	2 Mi-Keẓ 7
11	21	23	22	24	24	26 Shelaḥ	26	28	29	30 R. Ḥ.	2	3 8
12	22	24	23 Va-Yakhel Pekudei Parah	25	25	27	27	29	1 Tishri Rosh Ha-Shanah	1 Ḥeshvan R. Ḥ.	3 Toledot	4
13	23	25 Mishpatim Shekalim	24	26	26	28	28	30 R. Ḥ. Re'eh	2	2	4	5
14	24	26	25	27	27 Be-Har Be-Ḥukkotai	29	29	1 Elul R. Ḥ.	3 Fast	3	5	6
15	25	27	26	28	28	30 R. Ḥ.	1 Av R. Ḥ.	2	4	4 No'aḥ	6	7
16	26 Va-Era	28	27	29 Shemini	29	1 Tammuz R. Ḥ.	2 Mattot Masei	3	5	5	7	8
17	27	29	28	30 R. Ḥ.	1 Sivan R. Ḥ.	2	3	4	6 Va-Yelekh Shabbat Shuvah	6	8	9 Va-Yiggash
18	28	30 R. Ḥ.	29	1 Iyyar R. Ḥ.	2	3 Koraḥ	4	5	7	7	9	10 Fast
19	29	1 Adar R. Ḥ.	1 Nisan R. Ḥ. Va-Yikra Ha-Ḥodesh	2	3	4	5	6	8	8	10 Va-Yeẓe	11
20	1 Shevat R. Ḥ.	2 Terumah	2	3	4	5	6	7 Shofetim	9	9	11	12
21	2	3	3	4 Yom ha-Aẓma'ut	5 Be-Midbar	6	7	8	10 Yom Kippur	10	12	13
22	3	4	4	5	6 Shavuot	7	8	9	11	11 Lekh Lekha	13	14
23	4 Bo	5	5	6 Tazri'a Meẓora	7	8	9 Tishah be-Av Devarim	10	12	12	14	15
24	5	6	6	7	8	9	10 Fast	11	13 Ha'azinu	13	15	16 Va-Yeḥi
25	6	7	7	8	9	10 Ḥukkat	11	12	14	14	16	17
26	7	8	8 Ẓav Shabbat ha-Gadol	9	10	11	12	13	15 Sukkot	15	17 Va-Yishlaḥ	18
27	8	9 Teẓavveh Zakhor	9	10	11	12	13	14 Ki Teẓe	16	16	18	19
28	9	10	10	11	12 Naso	13	14	15	17 Ḥol ha-Mo'ed	17	19	20
29	10	11	11	12	13	14	15	16	18	18 Va-Yera	20	21
30	11 Be-Shallaḥ		12	13 Aḥarei Mot Kedoshim	14	15	16 Va-Ethannan	17	19	19	21	22
31	12		13		15		17	18		20		23 Shemot

1989

5749/50 תשמ״ט / תש״ן

	January	February	March	April	May	June	July	August	September	October	November	December
1	24 Tevet	26	24	25 Shemini Ha-Ḥodesh	26	27	28 Shelaḥ	29	1 Elul R. Ḥ.	2 Rosh Ha-Shanah	3	3
2	25	27	25	26	27	28	29	1 Av R. Ḥ.	2 Shofetim	3 Fast	4	4 Toledot
3	26	28	26	27	28	29 Be-Midbar	30 R. Ḥ.	2	3	4	5	5
4	27	29 Mishpatim	27 Va-Yakhel Shekalim	28	29	1 Sivan R. Ḥ.	1 Tammuz R. Ḥ.	3	4	5	6 No'aḥ	6
5	28	30 R. Ḥ.	28	29	30 R. Ḥ.	2	2	4 Devarim	5	6	7	7
6	29	1 Adar I R. Ḥ.	29	1 Nisan R. Ḥ.	1 Iyyar R. Ḥ. Kedoshim	3	3	5	6	7	8	8
7	1 Shevat R. Ḥ. Va-Era	2	30 R. Ḥ.	2	2	4	4	6	7	8 Ha'azinu Shabbat Shuvah	9	9
8	2	3	1 Adar II R. Ḥ.	3 Tazri'a	3	5	5 Koraḥ	7	8	9	10	10
9	3	4	2	4	4	6 Shavuot	6	8	9 Ki Teẓe	10 Yom Kippur	11	11 Va-Yeẓe
10	4	5	3	5	5 Yom ha-Aẓma'ut	7	7	9 Tishah be-Av	10	11	12	12
11	5	6 Terumah	4 Pekudei	6	6	8	8	10	11	12	13 Lekh Lekha	13
12	6	7	5	7	7	9	9	11 Va-Etḥannan	12	13	14	14
13	7	8	6	8	8 Emor	10	10	12	13	14	15	15
14	8 Bo	9	7	9	9	11	11	13	14	15 Sukkot	16	16
15	9	10	8	10 Meẓora Shabbat ha-Gadol	10	12	12 Ḥukkat Balak	14	15	16	17	17
16	10	11	9	11	11	13	13	15	16 Ki Tavo	17	18	18 Va-Yishlaḥ
17	11	12	10	12	12	14 Naso	14	16	17	18 Ḥol ha-Mo'ed	19	19
18	12	13 Teẓavveh	11 Va-Yikra Zakhor	13	13	15	15	17	18	19	20 Va-Yera	20
19	13	14	12	14	14	16	16	18 Ekev	19	20	21	21
20	14	15	13 Ta'anit Esther	15 Pesaḥ	15 Be-Har	17	17 Fast	19	20	21 Hoshana Rabba	22	22
21	15 Be-Shallaḥ	16	14 Purim	16 Omer	16	18	18	20	21	22 Shemini Aẓeret	23	23
22	16	17	15 Shushan Purim	17	17	19	19 Pinḥas	21	22	23 Simḥat Torah Ve-Zot Ha-Berakhah	24	24
23	17	18	16	18 Ḥol ha-Mo'ed	18 Lag ba-Omer	20	20	22	23 Niẓẓavim Va-Yelekh	24	25	25 Ḥanukkah 1 Va-Yeshev
24	18	19	17	19	19	21 Be-Ha'alotkha	21	23	24	25	26	26 2
25	19	20 Ki Tissa	18 Ẓav Parah	20	20	22	22	24	25	26	27 Ḥayyei Sarah	27 3
26	20	21	19	21 Pesaḥ	21	23	23	25 Re'eh	26	27	28	28 4
27	21	22	20	22	22 Be-Ḥukkotai	24	24	26	27	28	29	29 5
28	22 Yitro	23	21	23	23	25	25	27	28	29 Bereshit	30 R. Ḥ.	30 R. Ḥ. 6
29	23		22	24 Aḥarei Mot	24	26	26 Mattot Masei	28	29	30 R. Ḥ.	1 Kislev R. Ḥ.	1 Tevet R. Ḥ. 7
30	24		23	25	25	27	27	29	1 Tishri Rosh Ha-Shanah	1 Ḥeshvan R. Ḥ.	2	2 Mi-Keẓ 8
31	25		24		26		28	30 R. Ḥ.		2		3

1990

5750/51 תש״ן / תשנ״א

	January	February	March	April	May	June	July	August	September	October	November	December
1	4 Tevet	6	4	6	6	8	8	10	11 Ki Teẓe	12	13	14 Va-Yishlaḥ
2	5	7	5	7	7	9 Naso	9	11	12	13	14	15
3	6	8 Bo	6 Terumah	8	8	10	10	12	13	14	15 Va-Yera	16
4	7	9	7	9	9	11	11	13 Va-Etḥannan	14	15 Sukkot	16	17
5	8	10	8	10	10 Aḥarei Mot Kedoshim	12	12	14	15	16	17	18
6	9 Va-Yiggash	11	9	11	11	13	13	15	16	17	18	19
7	10 Fast	12	10	12 Ẓav Shabbat ha-Gadol	12	14	14 Balak	16	17	18 Ḥol ha-Mo'ed	19	20
8	11	13	11 Ta'anit Esther	13	13	15	15	17	18 Ki Tavo	19	20	21 Va-Yeshev
9	12	14	12	14	14	16 Be-Ha'alotkha	16	18	19	20	21	22
10	13	15 Be-Shallaḥ	13 Teẓavveh Zakhor	15 Pesaḥ	15	17	17 Fast	19	20	21 Hoshana Rabba	22 Ḥayyei Sarah	23
11	14	16	14 Purim	16 Omer	16	18	18	20 Ekev	21	22 Shemini Aẓeret	23	24
12	15	17	15 Shushan Purim	17	17 Emor	19	19	21	22	23 Simḥat Torah Ve-Zot Ha-Berakhah	24	25 Ḥanukkah 1
13	16 Va-Yeḥi	18	16	18 Ḥol ha-Mo'ed	18 Lag ba-Omer	20	20	22	23	24 Bereshit	25	26 2
14	17	19	17	19	19	21	21 Pinḥas	23	24	25	26	27 3
15	18	20	18	20	20	22	22	24	25 Niẓẓavim Va-Yelekh	26	27	28 Mi-Keẓ 4
16	19	21	19	21 Pesaḥ	21	23 Shelaḥ	23	25	26	27	28	29 5
17	20	22 Yitro	20 Ki Tissa Parah	22	22	24	24	26	27	28	29 Toledot	30 R. Ḥ. 6
18	21	23	21	23	23	25	25	27 Re'eh	28	29	1 Kislev R. Ḥ.	1 Tevet R. Ḥ. 7
19	22	24	22	24	24 Be-Har Be-Ḥukkotai	26	26	28	29	30 R. Ḥ.	2	2 8
20	23 Shemot	25	23	25	25	27	27	29	1 Tishri Rosh Ha-Shanah	1 Ḥeshvan R. Ḥ. No'aḥ	3	3
21	24	26	24	26 Shemini	26	28	28 Mattot Masei	30 R. Ḥ.	2	2	4	4
22	25	27	25	27	27	29	29	1 Elul R. Ḥ.	3 Ha'azinu Shabbat Shuvah	3	5	5 Va-Yiggash
23	26	28	26	28	28	30 R. Ḥ. Koraḥ	1 Av R. Ḥ.	2	4 Fast	4	6	6
24	27	29 Mishpatim Shekalim	27 Va-Yakhel Pekudei Ha-Ḥodesh	29	29	1 Tammuz R. Ḥ.	2	3	5	5	7 Va-Yeẓe	7
25	28	30 R. Ḥ.	28	30 R. Ḥ.	1 Sivan R. Ḥ.	2	3	4 Shofetim	6	6	8	8
26	29	1 Adar R. Ḥ.	29	1 Iyyar R. Ḥ.	2 Be-Midbar	3	4	5	7	7	9	9
27	1 Shevat R. Ḥ. Va-Era	2	1 Nisan R. Ḥ.	2	3	4	5	6	8	8 Lekh Lekha	10	10 Fast
28	2	3	2	3 Tazri'a Meẓora	4	5	6 Devarim	7	9	9	11	11
29	3		3	4	5	6	7	8	10 Yom Kippur	10	12	12 Va-Yeḥi
30	4		4	5 Yom ha-Aẓma'ut	6 Shavuot	7 Ḥukkat	8	9	11	11	13	13
31	5		5 Va-Yikra		7		9 Tishah be-Av	10		12		14

1991

5751/52 תשנ״א / תשנ״ב

	January	February	March	April	May	June	July	August	September	October	November	December
1	15 **Tevet**	17	15 Shushan Purim	17	17	**19** *Be-Ha'alotkha*	19	21	22	23 Simḥat Torah *Ve-Zot Ha-Berakhah*	24	24
2	16	**18** *Yitro*	**16** *Ki Tissa*	18 Ḥol ha-Mo'ed	18 Lag ba-Omer	20	20	22	23	24	**25** *Ḥayyei Sarah*	25 Ḥanukkah 1
3	17	19	17	19	19	21	21	**23** *Ekev*	24	25	26	26 2
4	18	20	18	20	**20** *Emor*	22	22	24	25	26	27	27 3
5	**19** *Shemot*	21	19	21 Pesaḥ	21	23	23	25	26	**27** *Bereshit*	28	28 4
6	20	22	20	**22**	22	24	**24** *Pinḥas*	26	27	28	29	29 5
7	21	23	21	23	23	25	25	27	**28** *Niẓẓavim*	29	30 R. Ḥ.	**30** R. Ḥ. *Mi-Keẓ* 6
8	22	24	22	24	24	**26** *Shelaḥ*	26	28	29	30 R. Ḥ.	1 **Kislev** R. Ḥ.	1 **Tevet** R. Ḥ. 7
9	23	**25** *Mishpatim* Shekalim	*Va-Yakhel Pekudei* **23** Parah	25	25	27	27	29	1 **Tishri** Rosh Ha-Shanah	1 **Ḥeshvan** R. Ḥ.	**2** *Toledot*	2 8
10	24	26	24	26	26	28	28	**30** R. Ḥ. *Re'eh*	2	2	3	3
11	25	27	25	27	**27** *Be-Har Be-Ḥukkotai*	29	29	1 **Elul** R. Ḥ.	3 Fast	3	4	4
12	**26** *Va-Era*	28	26	28	28	30 R. Ḥ.	1 **Av** R. Ḥ.	2	4	**4** *No'aḥ*	5	5
13	27	29	27	**29** *Shemini*	29	1 **Tammuz** R. Ḥ.	**2** *Mattot Masei*	3	5	5	6	6
14	28	30 R. Ḥ.	28	30 R. Ḥ.	1 **Sivan** R. Ḥ.	2	3	4	**6** *Va-Yelekh* Shabbat Shuvah	6	7	**7** *Va-Yiggash*
15	29	1 **Adar** R. Ḥ.	29	1 **Iyyar** R. Ḥ.	2	**3** *Koraḥ*	4	5	7	7	8	8
16	1 **Shevat** R. Ḥ.	**2** *Terumah*	**1** R. Ḥ. *Va-Yikra* **Nisan** Ha-Ḥodesh	2	3	4	5	6	8	8	**9** *Va-Yeẓe*	9
17	2	3	2	3	4	5	6	**7** *Shofetim*	9	9	10	10 Fast
18	3	4	3	4 Yom ha-Aẓma'ut	**5** *Be-Midbar*	6	7	8	10 Yom Kippur	10	11	11
19	**4** *Bo*	5	4	5	6 Shavuot	7	8	9	11	**11** *Lekh Lekha*	12	12
20	5	6	5	**6** *Tazri'a Meẓora*	7	8	**9** *Devarim* Tishah be-Av	10	12	12	13	13
21	6	7	6	7	8	9	10 Fast	11	**13** *Ha'azinu*	13	14	**14** *Va-Yeḥi*
22	7	8	7	8	9	**10** *Ḥukkat*	11	12	14	14	15	15
23	8	**9** *Teẓavveh* Zakhor	**8** *Ẓav* Shabbat ha-Gadol	9	10	11	12	13	15 Sukkot	15	**16** *Va-Yishlaḥ*	16
24	9	10	9	10	11	12	13	**14** *Ki Teẓe*	16	16	17	17
25	10	11	10	11	**12** *Naso*	13	14	15	17	17	18	18
26	**11** *Be-Shallaḥ*	12	11	12	13	14	15	16	18 Ḥol ha-Mo'ed	**18** *Va-Yera*	19	19
27	12	13 Ta'anit Esther	12	**13** *Aḥarei Mot Kedoshim*	14	15	**16** *Va-Etḥannan*	17	19	19	20	20
28	13	14 Purim	13	14	15	16	17	18	**20**	20	21	**21** *Shemot*
29	14		14	15	16	**17** *Balak*	18	19	21 Hoshana Rabba	21	22	22
30	15		**15** Pesaḥ	16	17	18 Fast	19	20	22 Shemini Aẓeret	22	**23** *Va-Yeshev*	23
31	16		16 Omer		18		20	**21** *Ki Tavo*		23		24

1992

5752/53 תשנ״ב / תשנ״ג

	January	February	March	April	May	June	July	August	September	October	November	December
1	25 **Tevet**	**27** *Mishpatim*	26	27	28	29	30 R. Ḥ.	**2** *Mattot Masei*	3	4	5	6
2	26	28	27	28	**29** *Aḥarei Mot*	1 **Sivan** R. Ḥ.	1 **Tammuz** R. Ḥ.	3	4	5	6	7
3	27	29	28	29	30 R. Ḥ.	2	2	4	5	**6** *Va-Yelekh* Shabbat Shuvah	7	8
4	**28** *Va-Era*	30 R. Ḥ.	29	**1 Nisan** *Tazri'a* R. Ḥ. Ha-Ḥodesh	1 **Iyyar** R. Ḥ.	3	**3** *Koraḥ*	5	6	7	8	9
5	29	1 **Adar I** R. Ḥ.	30 R. Ḥ.	2	2	4	4	6	**7** *Shofetim*	8	9	**10** *Va-Yeẓe*
6	1 **Shevat** R. Ḥ.	2	1 **Adar II** R. Ḥ.	3	3	**5** *Be-Midbar*	5	7	8	9	10	11
7	2	3	**2** *Pekudei*	4	4 Yom ha-Aẓma'ut	6 Shavuot	6	8	9	10 Yom Kippur	**11** *Lekh Lekha*	12
8	3	**4** *Terumah*	3	5	5	7	7	**9** *Devarim* Tishah be-Av	10	11	12	13
9	4	5	4	6	**6** *Kedoshim*	8	8	10 Fast	11	12	13	14
10	5	6	5	7	7	9	9	11	12	**13** *Ha'azinu*	14	15
11	**6** *Bo*	7	6	**8** *Meẓora* Shabbat ha-Gadol	8	10	**10** *Ḥukkat*	12	13	14	15	16
12	7	8	7	9	9	11	11	13	**14** *Ki Teẓe*	15 Sukkot	16	**17** *Va-Yishlaḥ*
13	8	9	8	10	10	**12** *Naso*	12	14	15	16	17	18
14	9	10	**9** *Va-Yikra* Zakhor	11	11	13	13	15	16	17	**18** *Va-Yera*	19
15	10	**11** *Teẓavveh*	10	12	12	14	14	**16** *Va-Etḥannan*	17	18 Ḥol ha-Mo'ed	19	20
16	11	12	11	13	**13** *Emor*	15	15	17	18	19	20	21
17	12	13	12	14	14	16	16	18	19	**20**	21	22
18	**13** *Be-Shallaḥ*	14	13 Ta'anit Esther	**15** Pesaḥ	15	17	**17** *Balak*	19	20	21 Hoshana Rabba	22	23
19	14	15	14 Purim	16 Omer	16	18	18 Fast	20	**21** *Ki Tavo*	22 Shemini Aẓeret	23	**24** *Va-Yeshev*
20	15	16	15 Shushan Purim	17	17	**19** *Be-Ha'alotkha*	19	21	22	23 Simḥat Torah *Ve-Zot Ha-Berakhah*	24	25 Ḥanukkah 1
21	16	17	**16** *Ẓav*	18 Ḥol ha-Mo'ed	18 Lag ba-Omer	20	20	22	23	24	**25** *Ḥayyei Sarah*	26 2
22	17	**18** *Ki Tissa*	17	19	19	21	21	**23** *Ekev*	24	25	26	27 3
23	18	19	18	20	**20** *Be-Har*	22	22	24	25	26	27	28 4
24	19	20	19	21 Pesaḥ	21	23	23	25	26	**27** *Bereshit*	28	29 5
25	**20** *Yitro*	21	20	**22**	22	24	**24** *Pinḥas*	26	27	28	29	1 **Tevet** R. Ḥ. 6
26	21	22	21	23	23	25	25	27	**28** *Niẓẓavim*	29	1 **Kislev** R. Ḥ.	**2** *Mi-Keẓ* 7
27	22	23	22	24	24	**26** *Shelaḥ*	26	28	29	30 R. Ḥ.	2	3 8
28	23	24	**23** *Shemini* Parah	25	25	27	27	29	1 **Tishri** Rosh Ha-Shanah	1 **Ḥeshvan** R. Ḥ.	**3** *Toledot*	4
29	24	**25** *Va-Yakhel* Shekalim	24	26	26	28	28	**30** R. Ḥ. *Re'eh*	2	2	4	5
30	25		25	27	**27** *Be-Ḥukkotai*	29	29	1 **Elul** R. Ḥ.	3 Fast	3	5	6
31	26		26		28		1 **Av** R. Ḥ.	2		**4** *No'aḥ*		7

1993

5753/54 תשנ״ג / תשנ״ד

	January	February	March	April	May	June	July	August	September	October	November	December
1	8 Tevet	10	8	10	10 *Aḥarei Mot Kedoshim*	12	12	14	15	16	17	17
2	9 *Va-Yiggash*	11	9	11	11	13	13	15	16	17	18	18
3	10 Fast	12	10	12 *Ẓav* Shabbat ha-Gadol	12	14	14 *Balak*	16	17	18 Ḥol ha-Mo'ed	19	19
4	11	13	11 Ta'anit Esther	13	13	15	15	17	18 *Ki Tavo*	19	20	20 *Va-Yeshev*
5	12	14	12	14	14	16 *Be-Ha'alotkha*	16	18	19	20	21	21
6	13	15 *Be-Shallaḥ*	13 *Teẓavveh* Zakhor	15 Pesaḥ	15	17	17 Fast	19	20	21 Hoshana Rabba	22 *Ḥayyei Sarah*	22
7	14	16	14 Purim	16 Omer	16	18	18	20 *Ekev*	21	22 Shemini Aẓeret	23	23
8	15	17	15 Shushan Purim	17	17 *Emor*	19	19	21	22	23 Simḥat Torah *Ve-Zot Ha-Berakhah*	24	24
9	16 *Va-Yeḥi*	18	16	18 Ḥol ha-Mo'ed	18 Lag ba-Omer	20	20	22	23	24 *Bereshit*	25	25 Hanukkah 1
10	17	19	17	19	19	21	21 *Pinḥas*	23	24	25	26	26 2
11	18	20	18	20	20	22	22	24	25 *Niẓẓavim Va-Yelekh*	26	27	27 *Mi-Keẓ* 3
12	19	21	19	21 Pesaḥ	21	23 *Shelaḥ*	23	25	26	27	28	28 4
13	20	22 *Yitro*	20 *Ki Tissa* Parah	22	22	24	24	26	27	28	29 *Toledot*	29 5
14	21	23	21	23	23	25	25	27 *Re'eh*	28	29	30 R. Ḥ.	30 R. Ḥ. 6
15	22	24	22	24	24 *Be-Har Be-Ḥukkotai*	26	26	28	29	30 R. Ḥ.	1 Kislev R. Ḥ.	1 Tevet R. Ḥ. 7
16	23 *Shemot*	25	23	25	25	27	27	29	1 Tishri Rosh Ha-Shanah	1 Ḥeshvan R. Ḥ. *No'aḥ*	2	2 8
17	24	26	24	26 *Shemini*	26	28	28 *Mattot Masei*	30 R. Ḥ.	2	2	3	3
18	25	27	25	27	27	29	29	1 Elul R. Ḥ.	3 *Ha'azinu* Shabbat Shuvah	3	4	4 *Va-Yiggash*
19	26	28	26	28	28	30 R. Ḥ. *Koraḥ*	1 Av R. Ḥ.	2	4 Fast	4	5	5
20	27	29 *Mishpatim* Shekalim	27 *Va-Yakhel Pekudei* Ha-Hodesh	29	29	1 Tammuz R. Ḥ.	2	3	5	5	6 *Va-Yeẓe*	6
21	28	30 R. Ḥ.	28	30 R. Ḥ.	1 Sivan R. Ḥ.	2	3	4 *Shofetim*	6	6	7	7
22	29	1 Adar R. Ḥ.	29	1 Iyyar R. Ḥ.	2 *Be-Midbar*	3	4	5	7	7	8	8
23	1 Shevat R. Ḥ. *Va-Era*	2	1 Nisan R. Ḥ.	2	3	4	5	6	8	8 *Lekh Lekha*	9	9
24	2	3	2	3 *Tazri'a Meẓora*	4	5	6 *Devarim*	7	9	9	10	10 Fast
25	3	4	3	4	5	6	7	8	10 Yom Kippur	10	11	11 *Va-Yeḥi*
26	4	5	4	5 Yom ha-Aẓma'ut	6 Shavuot	7 *Ḥukkat*	8	9	11	11	12	12
27	5	6 *Terumah*	5 *Va-Yikra*	6	7	8	9 Tishah be-Av	10	12	12	13 *Va-Yishlaḥ*	13
28	6	7	6	7	8	9	10	11 *Ki Teẓe*	13	13	14	14
29	7		7	8	9 *Naso*	10	11	12	14	14	15	15
30	8 *Bo*		8	9	10	11	12	13	15 Sukkot	15 *Va-Yera*	16	16
31	9		9		11		13 *Va-Etḥannan*	14		16		17

1994

5754/55 תשנ״ד / תשנ״ה

	January	February	March	April	May	June	July	August	September	October	November	December
1	18 Tevet *Shemot*	20	18	20 Ḥol ha-Mo'ed	20	22	22	24	25	26 *Bereshit*	27	28 4
2	19	21	19	21 Pesaḥ	21	23	23 *Pinḥas*	25	26	27	28	29 5
3	20	22	20	22	22	24	24	26	27 *Niẓẓavim*	28	29	30 R. Ḥ. *Mi-Keẓ* 6
4	21	23	21	23	23	25 *Shelaḥ*	25	27	28	29	1 Kislev R. Ḥ.	1 Tevet R. Ḥ. 7
5	22	24 *Mishpatim*	22 *Va-Yakhel* Parah	24	24	26	26	28	29	30 R. Ḥ.	2 *Toledot*	2 8
6	23	25	23	25	25	27	27	29 *Re'eh*	1 Tishri Rosh Ha-Shanah	1 Ḥeshvan R. Ḥ.	3	3
7	24	26	24	26	26 *Be-Har Be-Ḥukkotai*	28	28	30 R. Ḥ.	2	2	4	4
8	25 *Va-Era*	27	25	27	27	29	29	1 Elul R. Ḥ.	3 Fast	3 *No'aḥ*	5	5
9	26	28	26	28 *Shemini*	28	30 R. Ḥ.	1 Av R. Ḥ. *Mattot Masei*	2	4	4	6	6
10	27	29	27	29	29	1 Tammuz R. Ḥ.	2	3	5 *Va-Yelekh* Shabbat Shuvah	5	7	7 *Va-Yiggash*
11	28	30 R. Ḥ.	28	30 R. Ḥ.	1 Sivan R. Ḥ.	2 *Koraḥ*	3	4	6	6	8	8
12	29	1 Adar R. Ḥ. *Terumah* Shekalim	29 *Pekudei* Ha-Hodesh	1 Iyyar R. Ḥ.	2	3	4	5	7	7	9 *Va-Yeẓe*	9
13	1 Shevat R. Ḥ.	2	1 Nisan R. Ḥ.	2	3	4	5	6 *Shofetim*	8	8	10	10 Fast
14	2	3	2	Yom ha-Aẓma'ut	4 *Be-Midbar*	5	6	7	9	9	11	11
15	3 *Bo*	4	3	4	5	6	7	8	10 Yom Kippur	10 *Lekh Lekha*	12	12
16	4	5	4	5 *Tazri'a Meẓora*	6 Shavuot	7	8 *Devarim*	9	11	11	13	13
17	5	6	5	6	7	8	9 Tishah be-Av	10	12 *Ha'azinu*	12	14	14 *Va-Yeḥi*
18	6	7	6	7	8	9 *Ḥukkat*	10	11	13	13	15	15
19	7	8 *Teẓavveh* Zakhor	7 *Va-Yikra*	8	9	10	11	12	14	14	16 *Va-Yishlaḥ*	16
20	8	9	8	9	10	11	12	13 *Ki Teẓe*	15 Sukkot	15	17	17
21	9	10	9	10	11 *Naso*	12	13	14	16	16	18	18
22	10 *Be-Shallaḥ*	11	10	11	12	13	14	15	17	17 *Va-Yera*	19	19
23	11	12	11	12 *Aḥarei Mot Kedoshim*	13	14	15 *Va-Etḥannan*	16	18 Ḥol ha-Mo'ed	18	20	20
24	12	13 Ta'anit Esther	12	13	14	15	16	17	19	19	21	21 *Shemot*
25	13	14 Purim	13	14	15	16 *Balak*	17	18	20	20	22	22
26	14	15 *Ki Tissa* Shushan Purim	14 *Ẓav* Shabbat ha-Gadol	15	16	17 Fast	18	19	21 Hoshana Rabba	21	23 *Va-Yeshev*	23
27	15	16	15 Pesaḥ	16	17	18	19	20 *Ki-Tavo*	22 Shemini Aẓeret	22	24	24
28	16	17	16 Omer	17	18 *Be-Ha'alotkha*	19	20	21	23 Simḥat Torah *Ve-Zot Ha-Berakhah*	23	25 Hanukkah 1	25
29	17 *Yitro*		17 Ḥol ha-Mo'ed	18 Lag ba-Omer	19	20	21	22	24	24 *Ḥayyei Sarah*	26 2	26
30	18		18	19 *Emor*	20	21	22 *Ekev*	23	25	25	27 3	27
31	19		19		21		23	24		26		28 *Va-Era*

1995

5755/56 — תשנ״ה / תשנ״ו

	January	February	March	April	May	June	July	August	September	October	November	December
1	29 Tevet	1 Adar I R. Ḥ.	29	1 Nisan R. Ḥ. Tazri'a Ha-Hodesh	1 Iyyar R. Ḥ.	3	3 Koraḥ	5	6	7	8	8
2	1 Shevat R. Ḥ.	2	30 R. Ḥ.	2	2	4	4	6	7 Shofetim	8	9	9 Va-Yeẓe
3	2	3	1 Adar II R. Ḥ.	3	3	5 Be-Midbar	5	7	8	9	10	10
4	3	4 Terumah	2 Pekudei	4	4 Yom ha-Aẓma'ut	6 Shavuot	6	8	9	10 Yom Kippur	11 Lekh Lekha	11
5	4	5	3	5	5	7	7	9 Devarim Tishah be-Av	10	11	12	12
6	5	6	4	6	6 Kedoshim	8	8	10 Fast	11	12	13	13
7	6 Bo	7	5	7	7	9	9	11	12	13 Ha'azinu	14	14
8	7	8	6	8 Meẓora Shabbat ha-Gadol	8	10	10 Ḥukkat	12	13	14	15	15
9	8	9	7	9	9	11	11	13	14 Ki Teẓe	15 Sukkot	16	16 Va-Yishlaḥ
10	9	10	8	10	10	12 Naso	12	14	15	16	17	17
11	10	11 Teẓavveh	9 Va-Yikra Zakhor	11	11	13	13	15	16	17 Ḥol ha-Mo'ed	18 Va-Yera	18
12	11	12	10	12	12	14	14	16 Va-Etḥannan	17	18	19	19
13	12	13	11	13	13 Emor	15	15	17	18	19	20	20
14	13 Be-Shallaḥ	14	12	14	14	16	16	18	19	20	21	21
15	14	15	13 Ta'anit Esther	15 Pesaḥ	15	17	17 Balak	19	20	21 Hoshana Rabba	22	22
16	15	16	14 Purim	16 Omer	16	18	18 Fast	20	21 Ki Tavo	22 Shemini Aẓeret	23	23 Va-Yeshev
17	16	17	15 Shushan Purim	17 Ḥol ha-Mo'ed	17	19 Be-Ha'alotkha	19	21	22	23 Simḥat Torah Ve-Zot Ha-Berakhah	24	24
18	17	18 Ki Tissa	16 Ẓav	18	18 Lag ba-Omer	20	20	22	23	24	25 Ḥayyei Sarah	25 Hanukkah 1
19	18	19	17	19	19	21	21	23 Ekev	24	25	26	26 2
20	19	20	18	20	20 Be-Har	22	22	24	25	26	27	27 3
21	20 Yitro	21	19	21 Pesaḥ	21	23	23	25	26	27 Bereshit	28	28 4
22	21	22	20	22	22	24	24 Pinḥas	26	27	28	29	29 5
23	22	23	21	23	23	25	25	27	28 Niẓẓavim	29	30 R. Ḥ.	30 R. Ḥ. Mi-Keẓ 6
24	23	24	22	24	24	26 Shelaḥ	26	28	29	30 R. Ḥ.	1 Kislev R. Ḥ.	1 Tevet R. Ḥ. 7
25	24	25 Va-Yakhel Shekalim	23 Shemini Parah	25	25	27	27	29	1 Tishri Rosh Ha-Shanah	1 Heshvan R. Ḥ.	2 Toledot	2 8
26	25	26	24	26	26	28	28	30 R. Ḥ. Re'eh	2	2	3	3
27	26	27	25	27	27 Be-Ḥukkotai	29	29	1 Elul R. Ḥ.	3 Fast	3	4	4
28	27 Mishpatim	28	26	28	28	30 R. Ḥ.	1 Av R. Ḥ.	2	4	4 Noaḥ	5	5
29	28		27	29 Aḥarei Mot	29	1 Tammuz R. Ḥ.	2 Mattot Masei	3	5	5	6	6
30	29		28	30 R. Ḥ.	1 Sivan R. Ḥ.	2	3	4	6 Va-Yelekh Shabbat Shuvah	6	7	7 Va-Yiggash
31	30 R. Ḥ.		29		2		4	5		7		8

1996

5756/57 — תשנ״ו / תשנ״ז

	January	February	March	April	May	June	July	August	September	October	November	December
1	9 Tevet	11	10	12	12	14 Naso	14	16	17	18	19	20
2	10 Fast	12	11 Teẓavveh Zakhor	13	13	15	15	17	18	19 Ḥol ha-Mo'ed	20 Va-Yera	21
3	11	13 Be-Shallaḥ	12	14	14	16	16	18 Ekev	19	20	21	22
4	12	14	13 Ta'anit Esther	15 Pesaḥ	15 Emor	17	17 Fast	19	20	21 Hoshana Rabba	22	23
5	13	15	14 Purim	16 Omer	16	18	18	20	21	22 Shemini Aẓeret	23	24
6	14 Va-Yeḥi	16	15 Shushan Purim	17	17	19	19 Pinḥas	21	22	23 Simḥat Torah Ve-Zot Ha-Berakhah	24	25 Ḥanukkah 1
7	15	17	16	18 Ḥol ha-Mo'ed	18 Lag ba-Omer	20	20	22	23 Niẓẓavim Va-Yelekh	24	25	26 Va-Yeshev 2
8	16	18	17	19	19	21 Be-Ha'alotkha	21	23	24	25	26	27 3
9	17	19	18 Ki Tissa Parah	20	20	22	22	24	25	26	27 Ḥayyei Sarah	28 4
10	18	20 Yitro	19	21 Pesaḥ	21	23	23	25 Re'eh	26	27	28	29 5
11	19	21	20	22	22 Be-Har Be-Ḥukkotai	24	24	26	27	28	29	1 Tevet R. Ḥ. 6
12	20	22	21	23	23	25	25	27	28	29 Bereshit	1 Kislev R. Ḥ.	2 7
13	21 Shemot	23	22	24 Shemini	24	26	26 Mattot Masei	28	29	30 R. Ḥ.	2	3 8
14	22	24	23	25	25	27	27	29	1 Tishri Rosh Ha-Shanah	1 Heshvan R. Ḥ.	3	4 Mi-Keẓ
15	23	25	24	26	26	28 Shelaḥ	28	30 R. Ḥ.	2	2	4	5
16	24	26	25 Va-Yakhel-Pekudei Ha-Hodesh	27	27	29	29	1 Elul R. Ḥ.	3 Fast	3	5 Toledot	6
17	25	27 Mishpatim Shekalim	26	28	28	30 R. Ḥ.	1 Av R. Ḥ.	2 Shofetim	4	4	6	7
18	26	28	27	29	29 Be-Midbar	1 Tammuz R. Ḥ.	2	3	5	5	7	8
19	27	29	28	30 R. Ḥ.	1 Sivan R. Ḥ.	2	3	4	6	6 Noaḥ	8	9
20	28 Va-Era	30 R. Ḥ.	29	1 Iyyar R. Ḥ. Tazri'a Meẓora	2	3	4 Devarim	5	7	7	9	10 Fast
21	29	1 Adar R. Ḥ.	1 Nisan R. Ḥ.	2	3	4	5	6	8 Ha'azinu Shabbat Shuvah	8	10	11 Va-Yiggash
22	1 Shevat R. Ḥ.	2	2	3	4	5 Koraḥ	6	7	9	9	11	12
23	2	3	3 Va-Yikra	4	5	6	7	8	10 Yom Kippur	10	12 Va-Yeẓe	13
24	3	4 Terumah	4	5 Yom ha-Aẓma'ut	6 Shavuot	7	8	9 Ki Teẓe	11	11	13	14
25	4	5	5	6	7	8	9 Tishah be-Av	10	12	12	14	15
26	5	6	6	7	8	9	10	11	13	13 Lekh Lekha	15	16
27	6 Bo	7	7	8 Aḥarei Mot Kedoshim	9	10	11 Va-Etḥannan	12	14	14	16	17
28	7	8	8	9	10	11	12	13	15 Sukkot	15	17	18 Va-Yeḥi
29	8	9	9	10	11	12 Ḥukkat Balak	13	14	16	16	18	19
30	9		10 Ẓav Shabbat ha-Gadol	11	12	13	14	15	17 Ḥol ha-Mo'ed	17	19 Va-Yishlaḥ	20
31	10		11		13		15	16 Ki Tavo		18		21

1997

5757/58 תשנ"ז / תשנ"ח

	January	February	March	April	May	June	July	August	September	October	November	December
1	22 Tevet	24 Yitro	22 Ki Tissa	23	24	25	26	27	29	29	1 R. H. Heshvan No'ah	2
2	23	25	23	24	25	26	27	28 Mattot Masei	30 R. H.	1 Tishri Rosh Ha-Shanah	2	3
3	24	26	24	25	26 Aharei Mot	27	28	29	1 Elul R. H.	2	3	4
4	25 Shemot	27	25	26	27	28	29	1 Av R. H.	2	3 Ha'azinu Shabbat Shuvah	4	5
5	26	28	26	27 Shemini Ha-Hodesh	28	29	30 R. H. Korah	2	3	4 Fast	5	6
6	27	29	27	28	29	1 Sivan R. H.	1 R. H. Tammuz	3	4 Shofetim	5	6	7 Va-Yeze
7	28	30 R. H.	28	29	30 R. H.	2 Be-Midbar	2	4	5	6	7	8
8	29	1 Adar I R. H. Mishpatim	29 Va-Yakhel Shekalim	1 Nisan R. H.	1 Iyyar R. H.	3	3	5	6	7	8 Lekh Lekha	9
9	1 R. H. Shevat	2	30 R. H.	2	2	4	4	6 Devarim	7	8	9	10
10	2	3	1 Adar II R. H.	3	3 Kedoshim	5	5	7	8	9	10	11
11	3 Va-Era	4	2	4	4	6 Shavuot	6	8	9	10 Yom Kippur	11	12
12	4	5	3	5 Tazri'a	5 Yom ha-Azma'ut	7	7 Hukkat	9 Tishah be-Av	10	11	12	13
13	5	6	4	6	6	8	8	10	11 Ki Teze	12	13	14 Va-Yishlah
14	6	7	5	7	7	9 Naso	9	11	12	13	14	15
15	7	8 Terumah	6 Pekudei	8	8	10	10	12	13	14	15 Va-Yera	16
16	8	9	7	9	9	11	11	13 Va-Ethannan	14	15 Sukkot	16	17
17	9	10	8	10	10 Emor	12	12	14	15	16	17	18
18	10 Bo	11	9	11	11	13	13	15	16	17 Hol ha-Mo'ed	18	19
19	11	12	10	12 Mezora Shabbat ha-Gadol	12	14	14 Balak	16	17	18	19	20
20	12	13	11 Ta'anit Esther	13	13	15	15	17	18 Ki Tavo	19	20	21 Va-Yeshev
21	13	14	12	14	14	16 Be-Ha'alotkha	16	18	19	20	21	22
22	14	15 Tezavveh	13 Va-Yikra Zakhor	15 Pesah	15	17	17 Fast	19	20	21 Hoshana Rabba	22 Hayyei Sarah	23
23	15	16	14 Purim	16 Omer	16	18	18	20 Ekev	21	22 Shemini Azeret	23	24
24	16	17	15 Shushan Purim	17 Hol ha-Mo'ed	17 Be-Har	19	19	21	22	23 Simhat Torah Ve-Zot Ha-Berakhah	24	25 Hanukkah 1
25	17 Be-Shallah	18	16	18	18 Lag ba-Omer	20	20	22	23	24 Bereshit	25	26 2
26	18	19	17	19	19	21	21 Pinhas	23	24	25	26	27 3
27	19	20	18	20	20	22	22	24	25 Nizzavim Va-Yelekh	26	27	28 Mi-Kez 4
28	20	21	19	21 Pesah	21	23 Shelah	23	25	26	27	28	29 5
29	21		20 Zav Parah	22	22	24	24	26	27	28	29 Toledot	30 R. H. 6
30	22		21	23	23	25	25	27 Re'eh	28	29	1 Kislev R. H.	1 Tevet R. H. 7
31	23		22		24 Be-Hukkotai		26	28		30 R. H.		2 8

1998

5758/59 תשנ"ח / תשנ"ט

	January	February	March	April	May	June	July	August	September	October	November	December
1	3 Tevet	5	3	5	5	7	7	9 Tishah be-Av Devarim	10	11	12	12
2	4	6	4	6	6 Tazri'a Mezora	8	8	10 Fast	11	12	13	13
3	5 Va-Yiggash	7	5	7	7	9	9	11	12	13 Ha'azinu	14	14
4	6	8	6	8 Zav Shabbat ha-Gadol	8	10	10 Hukkat	12	13	14	15	15
5	7	9	7	9	9	11	11	13	14 Ki Teze	15 Sukkot	16	16 Va-Yishlah
6	8	10	8	10	10	12 Naso	12	14	15	16	17	17
7	9	11 Be-Shallah	9 Tezavveh Zakhor	11	11	13	13	15	16	17 Hol ha-Mo'ed	18 Va-Yera	18
8	10 Fast	12	10	12	12	14	14	16 Va-Ethannan	17	18	19	19
9	11	13	11	13	13 Aharei Mot Kedoshim	15	15	17	18	19	20	20
10	12 Va-Yehi	14	12	14	14	16	16	18	19	20	21	21
11	13	15	13 Ta'anit Esther	15 Pesah	15	17	17 Balak	19	20	21 Hoshana Rabba	22	22
12	14	16	14 Purim	16 Omer	16	18	18 Fast	20	21 Ki Tavo	22 Shemini Azeret	23	23 Va-Yeshev
13	15	17	15 Shushan Purim	17 Hol ha-Mo'ed	17	19 Be-Ha'alotkha	19	21	22	23 Simhat Torah Ve-Zot Ha-Berakhah	24	24
14	16	18 Yitro	16 Ki Tissa	18	18 Lag ba-Omer	20	20	22	23	24	25 Hayyei Sarah	25 Hanukkah 1
15	17	19	17	19	19	21	21	23 Ekev	24	25	26	26 2
16	18	20	18	20	20 Emor	22	22	24	25	26	27	27 3
17	19 Shemot	21	19	21 Pesah	21	23	23	25	26	27 Bereshit	28	28 4
18	20	22	20	22	22	24	24 Pinhas	26	27	28	29	29 5
19	21	23	21	23	23	25	25	27	28 Nizzavim	29	30 R. H.	30 R. H. Mi-Kez 6
20	22	24	22	24	24	26 Shelah	26	28	29	30 R. H.	1 Kislev R. H.	1 Tevet R. H. 7
21	23	25 Mishpatim Shekalim	23 Va-Yakhel Pekudei Parah	25	25	27	27	29	1 Tishri Rosh Ha-Shanah	1 R. H. Heshvan	2 Toledot	2 8
22	24	26	24	26	26	28	28	30 R. H. Re'eh	2	2	3	3
23	25	27	25	27	27 Be-Har Be-Hukkotai	29	29	1 Elul R. H.	3 Fast	3	4	4
24	26 Va-Era	28	26	28	28	30 R. H.	1 Av R. H.	2	4	4 No'ah	5	5
25	27	29	27	29 Shemini	29	1 R. H. Tammuz	2 Mattot Masei	3	5	5	6	6
26	28	30 R. H.	28	30 R. H.	1 Sivan R. H.	2	3	4	6 Va-Yelekh Shabbat Shuvah	6	7	7 Va-Yiggash
27	29	1 Adar R. H.	29	1 Iyyar R. H.	2	3 Korah	4	5	7	7	8	8
28	1 R. H. Shevat	2 Terumah	1 R. H. Nisan Va-Yikra Ha-Hodesh	2	3	4	5	6	8	8	9 Va-Yeze	9
29	2		2	3	4	5	6	7 Shofetim	9	9	10	10 Fast
30	3		3	4 Yom ha-Azma'ut	5 Be-Midbar	6	7	8	10 Yom Kippur	10	11	11
31	4 Bo		4		6 Shavuot		8	9		11 Lekh Lekha		12

1999

5759/60 תשנ"ט / תש"ס

	January	February	March	April	May	June	July	August	September	October	November	December
1	13 **Tevet**	15	13 Ta'anit Esther	15 Pesaḥ	**15** *Emor*	17	17 Fast	19	20	21 Hoshana Rabba	22	22
2	**14** *Va-Yeḥi*	16	14 Purim	16 Omer	16	18	18	20	21	**22** Shemini Aẓeret	23	23
3	15	17	15 Shushan Purim	**17** Ḥol ha-Mo'ed	17	19	**19** *Pinḥas*	21	22	23 Simḥat Torah *Ve-Zot Ha-Berakhah*	24	24
4	16	18	16	18	18 Lag ba-Omer	20	20	22	**23** *Niẓẓavim Va-Yelekh*	24	25	**25** *Va-Yeshev* Ḥanukkah 1
5	17	19	17	19	19	**21** *Be-Ha'alotkha*	21	23	24	25	26	26 2
6	18	**20** *Yitro*	**18** *Ki Tissa* Parah	20	20	22	22	24	25	26	**27** *Ḥayyei Sarah*	27 3
7	19	21	19	21 Pesaḥ	21	23	23	**25** *Re'eh*	26	27	28	28 4
8	20	22	20	22	**22** *Be-Har Be-Ḥukkotai*	24	24	26	27	28	29	29 5
9	**21** *Shemot*	23	21	23	23	25	25	27	28	**29** *Bereshit*	30 R. Ḥ.	30 R. Ḥ. 6
10	22	24	22	**24** *Shemini*	24	26	**26** *Mattot Masei*	28	29	30 R. Ḥ.	1 **Kislev** R. Ḥ.	1 **Tevet** R. Ḥ. 7
11	23	25	23	25	25	27	27	29	**1 Tishri** Rosh Ha-Shanah	1 **Ḥeshvan** R. Ḥ.	2	**2** *Mi-Keẓ* 8
12	24	26	24	26	26	**28** *Shelaḥ*	28	30 R. Ḥ.	2	2	3	3
13	25	**27** *Mishpatim* Shekalim	**25** *Va-Yakhel Pekudei* Ha-Ḥodesh	27	27	29	29	1 **Elul** R. Ḥ.	3 Fast	3	**4** *Toledot*	4
14	26	28	26	28	28	30 R. Ḥ.	1 **Av** R. Ḥ.	**2** *Shofetim*	4	4	5	5
15	27	29	27	29	**29** *Be-Midbar*	1 **Tammuz** R. Ḥ.	2	3	5	5	6	6
16	**28** *Va-Era*	30 R. Ḥ.	28	30 R. Ḥ.	1 **Sivan** R. Ḥ.	2	3	4	6	**6** *No'aḥ*	7	7
17	29	1 **Adar** R. Ḥ.	29	1 **Iyyar** R. Ḥ. *Tazri'a Meẓora*	2	3	**4** *Devarim*	5	7	7	8	8
18	1 **Shevat** R. Ḥ.	2	1 **Nisan** R. Ḥ.	2	3	4	5	6	**8** *Ha'azinu* Shabbat Shuvah	8	9	**9** *Va-Yiggash*
19	2	3	2	3	4	**5** *Koraḥ*	6	7	9	9	10	10 Fast
20	3	**4** *Terumah*	**3** *Va-Yikra*	4	5	6	7	8	10 Yom Kippur	10	**11** *Va-Yeẓe*	11
21	4	5	4	5 Yom ha-Aẓma'ut	6 Shavuot	7	8	**9** *Ki Teẓe*	11	11	12	12
22	5	6	5	6	**7**	8	9 Tishah be-Av	10	12	12	13	13
23	**6** *Bo*	7	6	7	8	9	10	11	13	**13** *Lekh Lekha*	14	14
24	7	8	7	**8** *Aḥarei Mot Kedoshim*	9	10	**11** *Va-Etḥannan*	12	14	14	15	15
25	8	9	8	9	10	11	12	13	**15** Sukkot	15	16	**16** *Va-Yeḥi*
26	9	10	9	10	11	**12** *Ḥukkat Balak*	13	14	16	16	17	17
27	10	**11** *Teẓavveh* Zakhor	**10** *Ẓav* Shabbat ha-Gadol	11	12	13	14	15	17 Ḥol ha-Mo'ed	17	**18** *Va-Yishlaḥ*	18
28	11	12	11	12	13	14	15	**16** *Ki Tavo*	18	18	19	19
29	12		12	13	**14** *Naso*	15	16	17	19	19	20	20
30	**13** *Be-Shallaḥ*		13	14	15	16	17	18	20	**20** *Va-Yera*	21	21
31	14		14		16		**18** *Ekev*	19		21		22

2000

5760/61 תש"ס / תשס"א

	January	February	March	April	May	June	July	August	September	October	November	December
1	**23 Tevet** *Shemot*	25	24	**25** *Shemini* Ha-Ḥodesh	26	27	**28** *Shelaḥ*	29	1 **Elul** R. Ḥ.	2 Rosh Ha-Shanah	3	4
2	24	26	25	26	27	28	29	1 **Av** R. Ḥ.	**2** *Shofetim*	3 Fast	4	**5** *Toledot*
3	25	27	26	27	28	**29** *Be-Midbar*	30 R. Ḥ.	2	3	4	5	6
4	26	28	**27** *Va-Yakhel* Shekalim	28	29	1 **Sivan** R. Ḥ.	1 **Tammuz** R. Ḥ.	3	4	5	**6** *No'aḥ*	7
5	27	**29** *Mishpatim*	28	29	30 R. Ḥ.	2	2	**4** *Devarim*	5	6	7	8
6	28	30 R. Ḥ.	29	1 **Nisan** R. Ḥ.	1 **Iyyar** R. Ḥ. *Kedoshim*	3	3	5	6	7	8	9
7	29	1 **Adar I** R. Ḥ.	30 R. Ḥ.	2	2	4	4	6	7	**8** *Ha'azinu* Shabbat Shuvah	9	10
8	1 **Shevat** R. Ḥ. *Va-Era*	2	1 **Adar II** R. Ḥ.	**3** *Tazri'a*	3	5	**5** *Koraḥ*	7	8	9	10	11
9	2	3	2	4	4	6 Shavuot	6	8	**9** *Ki Teẓe*	10 Yom Kippur	11	**12** *Va-Yeẓe*
10	3	4	3	5	5 Yom ha-Aẓma'ut	**7**	7	9 Tishah be-Av	10	11	12	13
11	4	5	**4** *Pekudei*	6	6	8	8	10	11	12	**13** *Lekh Lekha*	14
12	5	**6** *Terumah*	5	7	7	9	9	**11** *Va-Etḥannan*	12	13	14	15
13	6	7	6	8	**8** *Emor*	10	10	12	13	14	15	16
14	7	8	7	9	9	11	11	13	14	**15** Sukkot	16	17
15	**8** *Bo*	9	8	**10** *Meẓora* Shabbat ha-Gadol	10	12	**12** *Ḥukkat Balak*	14	15	16	17	18
16	9	10	9	11	11	13	13	15	**16** *Ki Tavo*	17 Ḥol ha-Mo'ed	18	**19** *Va-Yishlaḥ*
17	10	11	10	12	12	**14** *Naso*	14	16	17	18	19	20
18	11	12	**11** *Va-Yikra* Zakhor	13	13	15	15	17	18	19	**20** *Va-Yera*	21
19	12	**13** *Teẓavveh*	12	14	14	16	16	**18** *Ekev*	19	20	21	22
20	13	14	13 Ta'anit Esther	15 Pesaḥ	**15** *Be-Har*	17	17 Fast	19	20	21 Hoshana Rabba	22	23
21	14	15	14 Purim	16 Omer	16	18	18	20	21	**22** Shemini Aẓeret	23	24
22	**15** *Be-Shallaḥ*	16	15 Shushan Purim	**17** Ḥol ha-Mo'ed	17	19	**19** *Pinḥas*	21	22	23 Simḥat Torah *Ve-Zot Ha-Berakhah*	24	25 Ḥanukkah 1
23	16	17	16	18	18 Lag ba-Omer	20	20	22	**23** *Niẓẓavim Va-Yelekh*	24	25	**26** *Va-Yeshev* 2
24	17	18	17	19	19	**21** *Be-Ha'alotkha*	21	23	24	25	26	27 3
25	18	19	**18** *Ẓav* Parah	20	20	22	22	24	25	26	**27** *Ḥayyei Sarah*	28 4
26	19	**20** *Ki Tissa*	19	21 Pesaḥ	21	23	23	**25** *Re'eh*	26	27	28	29 5
27	20	21	20	22	**22** *Be-Ḥukkotai*	24	24	26	27	28	29	1 **Tevet** R. Ḥ. 6
28	21	22	21	23	23	25	25	27	28	**29** *Bereshit*	1 **Kislev** R. Ḥ.	2 7
29	**22** *Yitro*	23	22	**24** *Aḥarei Mot*	24	26	**26** *Mattot Masei*	28	29	30 R. Ḥ.	2	3 8
30	23		23	25	25	27	27	29	**1 Tishri** Rosh Ha-Shanah	1 **Ḥeshvan** R. Ḥ.	3	**4** *Mi-Keẓ*
31	24		24		26		28	30 R. Ḥ.		2		5

2001

5761/62 תשס״א / תשס״ב

	January	February	March	April	May	June	July	August	September	October	November	December
1	6 Tevet	8	6	8	8	10	10	12	13 Ki Teẓe	14	15	16 Va-Yishlaḥ
2	7	9	7	9	9	11 Naso	11	13	14	15 Sukkot	16	17
3	8	10 Bo	8 Terumah Zakhor	10	10	12	12	14	15	16	17 Va-Yera	18
4	9	11	9	11	11	13	13	15 Va-Etḥannan	16	17	18	19
5	10 Fast	12	10	12	12 Aḥarei Mot Kedoshim	14	14	16	17	18 Ḥol ha-Mo'ed	19	20
6	11 Va-Yiggash	13	11	13	13	15	15	17	18	19	20	21
7	12	14	12	14 Ẓav Shabbat ha-Gadol	14	16	16 Balak	18	19	20	21	22
8	13	15	13 Ta'anit Esther	15 Pesaḥ	15	17	17 Fast	19	20 Ki Tavo	21 Hoshana Rabba	22	23 Va-Yeshev
9	14	16	14 Purim	16 Omer	16	18 Be-Ha'alotkha	18	20	21	22 Shemini Aẓeret	23	24
10	15	17 Be-Shallaḥ	15 Teẓavveh Shushan Purim	17	17	19	19	21	22	23 Simḥat Torah Ve-Zot Ha-Berakhah	24 Ḥayyei Sarah	25 1
11	16	18	16	18 Ḥol ha-Mo'ed	18 Lag ba-Omer	20	20	22 Ekev	23	24	25	26 2
12	17	19	17	19	19 Emor	21	21	23	24	25	26	27 3
13	18 Va-Yeḥi	20	18	20	20	22	22	24	25	26 Bereshit	27	28 4
14	19	21	19	21 Pesaḥ	21	23	23 Pinḥas	25	26	27	28	29 5
15	20	22	20	22	22	24	24	26	27 Niẓẓavim	28	29	30 R. H. Mi-Keẓ 6
16	21	23	21	23	23	25 Shelaḥ	25	27	28	29	1 Kislev R. H.	1 Tevet R. H. 7
17	22	24 Yitro	22 Ki Tissa Parah	24	24	26	26	28	29	30 R. H.	2 Toledot	2 8
18	23	25	23	25	25	27	27	29 Re'eh	1 Tishri Rosh Ha-Shanah	1 Ḥeshvan R. H.	3	3
19	24	26	24	26	26 Be-Har Be-Ḥukkotai	28	28	30 R. H.	2	2	4	4
20	25 Shemot	27	25	27	27	29	29	1 Elul R. H.	3 Fast	3 No'aḥ	5	5
21	26	28	26	28 Shemini	28	30 R. H.	1 Av R. H. Mattot Masei	2	4	4	6	6
22	27	29	27	29	29	1 Tammuz R. H.	2	3	5 Va-Yelekh Shabbat Shuvah	5	7	7 Va-Yiggash
23	28	30 R. H.	28	30 R. H.	1 Sivan R. H.	2 Koraḥ	3	4	6	6	8	8
24	29	1 Adar R. H. Mishpatim Shekalim	29 Va-Yakhel Pekudei Ha-Ḥodesh	1 Iyyar R. H.	2	3	4	5	7	7	9 Va-Yeẓe	9
25	1 Shevat R. H.	2	1 Nisan R. H.	2	3	4	5	6 Shofetim	8	8	10	10 Fast
26	2	3	2	3 Yom ha-Aẓma'ut	4 Be-Midbar	5	6	7	9	9	11	11
27	3 Va-Era	4	3	4	5	6	7	8	10 Yom Kippur	10 Lekh Lekha	12	12
28	4	5	4	5 Tazri'a Meẓora	6 Shavuot	7	8 Devarim	9	11	11	13	13
29	5		5	6	7	8	9 Tishah be-Av	10	12 Ha'azinu	12	14	14 Va-Yeḥi
30	6		6	7	8	9 Ḥukkat	10	11	13	13	15	15
31	7		7 Va-Yikra		9		11	12		14		16

2002

5762/63 תשס״ב / תשס״ג

	January	February	March	April	May	June	July	August	September	October	November	December
1	17 Tevet	19	17	19 Ḥol	19	21 Be-Ha'alotkha	21	23	24	25	26	26 2
2	18	20 Yitro	18 Ki Tissa Parah	20 ha-Mo'ed	20	22	22	24	25	26	27 Ḥayyei Sarah	27 3
3	19	21	19	21 Pesaḥ	21	23	23	25 Re'eh	26	27	28	28 4
4	20	22	20	22	22 Be-Har Be-Ḥukkotai	24	24	26	27	28	29	29 5
5	21 Shemot	23	21	23	23	25	25	27	28	29 Bereshit	30 R. H.	30 R. H. 6
6	22	24	22	24 Shemini	24	26	26 Mattot Masei	28	29	30 R. H.	1 Kislev R. H.	1 Tevet R. H. 7
7	23	25	23	25	25	27	27	29	1 Tishri Rosh Ha-Shanah	1 Ḥeshvan R. H.	2	2 Mi-Keẓ 8
8	24	26	24	26	26	28 Shelaḥ	28	30 R. H.	2	2	3	3
9	25	27 Mishpatim Shekalim	25 Va-Yakhel Pekudei Ha-Ḥodesh	27	27	29	29	1 Elul R. H.	3 Fast	3	4 Toledot	4
10	26	28	26	28	28	30 R. H.	1 Av R. H.	2 Shofetim	4	4	5	5
11	27	29	27	29	29 Be-Midbar	1 Tammuz R. H.	2	3	5	5	6	6
12	28 Va-Era	30 R. H.	28	30 R. H.	1 Sivan R. H.	2	3	4	6	6 No'aḥ	7	7
13	29	1 Adar R. H.	29	1 Iyyar R. H. Tazri'a Meẓora	2	3	4 Devarim	5	7	7	8	8
14	1 Shevat R. H.	2	1 Nisan R. H.	2	3	4	5	6	8 Ha'azinu Shabbat Shuvah	8	9	9 Va-Yiggash
15	2	3	2	3	4	5 Koraḥ	6	7	9	9	10	10 Fast
16	3	4 Terumah	3 Va-Yikra	4	5	6	7	8	10 Yom Kippur	10	11 Va-Yeẓe	11
17	4	5	4	5 Yom ha-Aẓma'ut	6 Shavuot	7	8	9 Ki Teẓe	11	11	12	12
18	5	6	5	6	7	8	9 Tishah be-Av	10	12	12	13	13
19	6 Bo	7	6	7	8	9	10	11	13	13 Lekh Lekha	14	14
20	7	8	7	8 Aḥarei Mot Kedoshim	9	10	11 Va-Etḥannan	12	14	14	15	15
21	8	9	8	9	10	11	12	13	15 Sukkot	15	16	16 Va-Yeḥi
22	9	10	9	10	11	12 Ḥukkat Balak	13	14	16	16	17	17
23	10	11 Teẓavveh Zakhor	10 Ẓav Shabbat ha-Gadol	11	12	13	14	15	17	17	18 Va-Yishlaḥ	18
24	11	12	11	12	13	14	15	16 Ki Tavo	18 Ḥol ha-Mo'ed	18	19	19
25	12	13 Ta'anit Esther	12	13	14 Naso	15	16	17	19	19	20	20
26	13 Be-Shallaḥ	14 Purim	13	14	15	16	17	18	20	20 Va-Yera	21	21
27	14	15 Shushan Purim	14	15 Emor	16	17 Fast	18 Ekev	19	21 Hoshana Rabba	21	22	22
28	15	16	15 Pesaḥ	16	17	18	19	20	22 Shemini Aẓeret	22	23	23 Shemot
29	16		16 Omer	17	18	19 Pinḥas	20	21	23 Simḥat Torah Ve-Zot Ha-Berakhah	23	24	24
30	17		17 Ḥol	18 Lag ba-Omer	19	20	21	22	24	24	25 Hanukkah Va-Yeshev 1	25
31	18		18 ha-Mo'ed		20		22	23 Niẓẓavim Va-Yelekh		25		26

2003

5763/64 תשס״ג / תשס״ד

	January	February	March	April	May	June	July	August	September	October	November	December
1	27 Tevet	29 Mishpatim	27 Va-Yakhel Shekalim	28	29	1 Sivan R. Ḥ.	1 Tammuz R. Ḥ.	3	4	5	6 No'aḥ	6
2	28	30 R. Ḥ.	28	29	30 R. Ḥ.	2	2	4 Devarim	5	6	7	7
3	29	1 Adar I R. Ḥ.	29	1 Nisan R. Ḥ.	1 Iyyar R. Ḥ. Kedoshim	3	3	5	6	7	8	8
4	1 Shevat R. Ḥ. Va-Era	2	30 R. Ḥ.	2	2	4	4	6	7	8 Ha'azinu Shabbat Shuvah	9	9
5	2	3	1 Adar II R. Ḥ.	3 Tazri'a	3	5	5 Koraḥ	7	8	9	10	10
6	3	4	2	4	4	6 Shavuot	6	8	9 Ki Teẓe	10 Yom Kippur	11	11 Va-Yeẓe
7	4	5	3	5	5 Yom ha-Aẓma'ut	7	7	9 Tishah be-Av	10	11	12	12
8	5	6 Terumah	4 Pekudei	6	6	8	8	10	11	12	13 Lekh Lekha	13
9	6	7	5	7	7	9	9	11 Va-Etḥannan	12	13	14	14
10	7	8	6	8	8 Emor	10	10	12	13	14	15	15
11	8 Bo	9	7	9	9	11	11	13	14	15 Sukkot	16	16
12	9	10	8	10 Meẓora Shabbat ha-Gadol	10	12	12 Ḥukkat Balak	14	15	16	17	17
13	10	11	9	11	11	13	13	15	16 Ki Tavo	17 Ḥol ha-Mo'ed	18	18 Va-Yishlaḥ
14	11	12	10	12	12	14 Naso	14	16	17	18	19	19
15	12	13 Teẓavveh	11 Va-Yikra Zakhor	13	13	15	15	17	18	19	20 Va-Yera	20
16	13	14	12	14	14	16	16	18 Ekev	19	20	21	21
17	14	15	13 Ta'anit Esther	15 Pesaḥ	15 Be-Har	17	17 Fast	19	20	21 Hoshana Rabba	22	22
18	15 Be-Shallaḥ	16	14 Purim	16 Omer	16	18	18	20	21	22 Shemini Aẓeret	23	23
19	16	17	15 Shushan Purim	17 Ḥol ha-Mo'ed	17	19	19 Pinḥas	21	22	23 Simḥat Torah Ve-Zot ha-Berakhah	24	24
20	17	18	16	18	18 Lag ba-Omer	20	20	22	23 Niẓẓavim Va-Yelekh	24	25	25 Ḥanukkah 1 Va-Yeshev
21	18	19	17	19	19	21 Be-Ha'alotkha	21	23	24	25	26	26 2
22	19	20 Ki Tissa	18 Ẓav Parah	20	20	22	22	24	25	26	27 Ḥayyei Sarah	27 3
23	20	21	19	21 Pesaḥ	21	23	23	25 Re'eh	26	27	28	28 4
24	21	22	20	22	22 Be-Ḥukkotai	24	24	26	27	28	29	29 5
25	22 Yitro	23	21	23	23	25	25	27	28	29 Bereshit	30 R. Ḥ.	30 R. Ḥ. 6
26	23	24	22	24 Aḥarei Mot	24	26	26 Mattot Masei	28	29	30 R. Ḥ.	1 Kislev R. Ḥ.	1 Tevet R. Ḥ. 7
27	24	25	23	25	25	27	27	29	1 Tishri Rosh Ha-Shanah	1 Ḥeshvan R. Ḥ.	2	2 Mi-Keẓ 8
28	25	26	24	26	26	28 Shelaḥ	28	30 R. Ḥ.	2	2	3	3
29	26		25 Shemini Ha-Ḥodesh	27	27	29	29	1 Elul R. Ḥ.	3 Fast	3	4 Toledot	4
30	27		26	28	28	30 R. Ḥ.	1 Av R. Ḥ.	2 Shofetim	4	4	5	5
31	28		27		29 Be-Midbar		2	3		5		6

2004

5764/65 תשס״ד / תשס״ה

	January	February	March	April	May	June	July	August	September	October	November	December
1	7 Tevet	9	8	10	10 Aḥarei Mot Kedoshim	12	12	14	15	16	17	18
2	8	10	9	11	11	13	13	15	16	17 Ḥol ha-Mo'ed	18	19
3	9 Va-Yiggash	11	10	12 Ẓav Shabbat ha-Gadol	12	14	14 Balak	16	17	18	19	20
4	10 Fast	12	11 Ta'anit Esther	13	13	15	15	17	18 Ki Tavo	19	20	21 Va-Yeshev
5	11	13	12	14	14	16 Be-Ha'alotkha	16	18	19	20	21	22
6	12	14	13 Teẓavveh Zakhor	15 Pesaḥ	15	17	17 Fast	19	20	21 Hoshana Rabba	22 Ḥayyei Sarah	23
7	13	15 Be-Shallaḥ	14 Purim	16 Omer	16	18	18	20 Ekev	21	22 Shemini Aẓeret	23	24
8	14	16	15 Shushan Purim	17	17 Emor	19	19	21	22	23 Simḥat Torah Ve-Zot ha-Berakhah	24	25 Ḥanukkah 1
9	15	17	16	18 Ḥol ha-Mo'ed	18 Lag ba-Omer	20	20	22	23	24 Bereshit	25	26 2
10	16 Va-Yeḥi	18	17	19	19	21	21 Pinḥas	23	24	25	26	27 3
11	17	19	18	20	20	22	22	24	25 Niẓẓavim Va-Yelekh	26	27	28 Mi-Keẓ 4
12	18	20	19	21 Pesaḥ	21	23 Shelaḥ	23	25	26	27	28	29 5
13	19	21	20 Ki Tissa Parah	22	22	24	24	26	27	28	29 Toledot	1 Tevet R. Ḥ. 6
14	20	22 Yitro	21	23	23	25	25	27 Re'eh	28	29	1 Kislev R. Ḥ.	2 7
15	21	23	22	24	24 Be-Har Be-Ḥukkotai	26	26	28	29	30 R. Ḥ.	2	3 8
16	22	24	23	25	25	27	27	29	1 Tishri Rosh Ha-Shanah	1 Ḥeshvan R. Ḥ. No'aḥ	3	4
17	23 Shemot	25	24	26 Shemini	26	28	28 Mattot Masei	30 R. Ḥ.	2	2	4	5
18	24	26	25	27	27	29	29	1 Elul R. Ḥ.	3 Ha'azinu Shabbat Shuvah	3	5	6 Va-Yiggash
19	25	27	26	28	28	30 R. Ḥ. Koraḥ	1 Av R. Ḥ.	2	4 Fast	4	6	7
20	26	28	27 Va-Yakhel Pekudei Ha-Ḥodesh	29	29	1 Tammuz R. Ḥ.	2	3	5	5	7 Va-Yeẓe	8
21	27	29 Mishpatim Shekalim	28	30 R. Ḥ.	1 Sivan R. Ḥ.	2	3	4 Shofetim	6	6	8	9
22	28	30 R. Ḥ.	29	1 Iyyar R. Ḥ.	2 Be-Midbar	3	4	5	7	7	9	10 Fast
23	29	1 Adar R. Ḥ.	1 Nisan R. Ḥ.	2	3	4	5	6	8	8 Lekh Lekha	10	11
24	1 Shevat R. Ḥ. Va-Era	2	2	3 Tazri'a Meẓora	4	5	6 Devarim	7	9	9	11	12
25	2	3	3	4	5	6	7	8	10 Yom Kippur	10	12	13 Va-Yeḥi
26	3	4	4	5 Yom ha-Aẓma'ut	6 Shavuot	7 Ḥukkat	8	9	11	11	13	14
27	4	5	5 Va-Yikra	6	7	8	9 Tishah be-Av	10	12	12	14	15
28	5	6 Terumah	6	7	8	9	10	11 Ki Teẓe	13	13	15	16
29	6	7	7	8	9 Naso	10	11	12	14	14	16	17
30	7		8	9	10	11	12	13	15 Sukkot	15 Va-Yera	17	18
31	8 Bo		9		11		13 Va-Etḥannan	14		16		19

2005

5765/66 תשס״ה / תשס״ו

	January	February	March	April	May	June	July	August	September	October	November	December
1	20 Tevet Shemot	22	20	21	22	23	24	25	27	27 Nizzavim	29	29
2	21	23	21	22 Shemini Parah	23	24	25 Korah	26	28	28	30 R. H.	1 Kislev R. H.
3	22	24	22	23	24	25	26	27	29 Re'eh	29	1 Heshvan R. H.	2 Toledot
4	23	25	23	24	25	26 Be-Midbar	27	28	30 R. H.	1 Tishri Rosh Ha-Shanah	2	3
5	24	26 Mishpatim	24 Va-Yakhel	25	26	27	28	29	1 Elul R. H.	2	3 No'ah	4
6	25	27	25	26	27	28	29	1 Av R. H. Masei	2	3 Fast	4	5
7	26	28	26	27	28 Kedoshim	29	30 R. H.	2	3	4	5	6
8	27 Va-Era	29	27	28	29	1 Sivan R. H.	1 Tammuz R. H.	3	4	5 Va-Yelekh Shabbat Shuvah	6	7
9	28	30 R. H.	28	29 Tazri'a Ha-Hodesh	30 R. H.	2	2 Hukkat	4	5	6	7	8
10	29	1 Adar I R. H.	29	1 Nisan R. H.	1 Iyyar R. H.	3	3	5	6 Shofetim	7	8	9 Va-Yeze
11	1 Shevat R. H.	2	30 R. H.	2	2	4	4	6	7	8	9	10
12	2	3 Terumah	1 R. H. Pekudei Adar II Shekalim	3	3 Yom ha-Azma'ut	5	5	7	8	9	10 Lekh Lekha	11
13	3	4	2	4	4	6 Shavuot	6	8 Devarim	9	10 Yom Kippur	11	12
14	4	5	3	5	5 Emor	7	7	9 Tishah be-Av	10	11	12	13
15	5 Bo	6	4	6	6	8	8	10	11	12 Ha'azinu	13	14
16	6	7	5	7 Mezora	7	9	9 Balak	11	12	13	14	15
17	7	8	6	8	8	10	10	12	13 Ki Teze	14	15	16 Va-Yishlah
18	8	9	7	9	9	11 Be-Ha'alotkha	11	13	14	15 Sukkot	16	17
19	9	10 Tezavveh	8 Va-Yikra Zakhor	10	10	12	12	14	15	16	17 Va-Yera	18
20	10	11	9	11	11	13	13	15 Va-Ethannan	16	17	18	19
21	11	12	10	12	12 Be-Har	14	14	16	17	18 Hol ha-Mo'ed	19	20
22	12 Be-Shallah	13	11	13	13	15	15	17	18	19	20	21
23	13	14	12	14 Aharei Mot Shabbat ha-Gadol	14	16	16 Pinhas	18	19	20	21	22
24	14	15	13 Ta'anit Esther	15 Pesah	15	17	17 Fast	19	20 Ki Tavo	21 Hoshana Rabba	22	23 Va-Yeshev
25	15	16	14 Purim	16 Omer	16	18 Shelah	18	20	21	22 Shemini Azeret	23	24
26	16	17 Ki Tissa	15 Zav Shushan Purim	17	17	19	19	21	22	23 Simhat Torah Ve-Zot Ha-Berakhah	24 Hayyei Sarah	25 Hanukkah 1
27	17	18	16	18 Hol ha-Mo'ed	18 Lag ba-Omer	20	20	22 Ekev	23	24	25	26 2
28	18	19	17	19	19 Be-Hukkotai	21	21	23	24	25	26	27 3
29	19 Yitro		18	20	20	22	22	24	25	26 Bereshit	27	28 4
30	20		19	21 Pesah	21	23	23 Mattot	25	26	27	28	29 5
31	21		20		22		24	26		28		30 R. H. Mi-Kez 6

2006

5766/67 תשס״ו / תשס״ז

	January	February	March	April	May	June	July	August	September	October	November	December
1	1 Tevet R. H. 7 Hanukkah	3	1 Adar R. H.	3 Va-Yikra	3	5	5 Korah	7	8	9	10	10
2	2 8	4	2	4	4	6 Shavuot	6	8	9 Ki Teze	10 Yom Kippur	11	11 Va-Yeze
3	3	5	3	5	5 Yom ha-Azma'ut	7	7	9 Tishah be-Av	10	11	12	12
4	4	6 Bo	4 Terumah	6	6	8	8	10	11	12	13 Lekh Lekha	13
5	5	7	5	7	7	9	9	11 Va-Ethannan	12	13	14	14
6	6	8	6	8	8 Aharei Mot Kedoshim	10	10	12	13	14	15	15
7	7 Va-Yiggash	9	7	9	9	11	11	13	14	15 Sukkot	16	16
8	8	10	8	10 Zav Shabbat ha-Gadol	10	12	12 Hukkat Balak	14	15	16	17	17
9	9	11	9	11	11	13	13	15	16 Ki Tavo	17	18	18 Va-Yishlah
10	10 Fast	12	10	12	12	14 Naso	14	16	17	18 Hol ha-Mo'ed	19	19
11	11	13 Be-Shallah	11 Tezavveh Zakhor	13	13	15	15	17	18	19	20 Va-Yera	20
12	12	14	12	14	14	16	16	18 Ekev	19	20	21	21
13	13	15	13 Ta'anit Esther	15 Pesah	15 Emor	17	17 Fast	19	20	21 Hoshana Rabba	22	22
14	14 Va-Yehi	16	14 Purim	16 Omer	16	18	18	20	21	22 Shemini Azeret	23	23
15	15	17	15 Shushan Purim	17	17	19	19 Pinhas	21	22	23 Simhat Torah Ve-Zot Ha-Berakhah	24	24
16	16	18	16	18 Hol ha-Mo'ed	18 Lag ba-Omer	20	20	22	23 Nizzavim Va-Yelekh	24	25	25 Hanukkah 1 Va-Yeshev
17	17	19	17	19	19	21 Be-Ha'alotkha	21	23	24	25	26	26 2
18	18	20 Yitro	18 Ki Tissa Parah	20	20	22	22	24	25	26	27 Hayyei Sarah	27 3
19	19	21	19	21 Pesah	21	23	23	25 Re'eh	26	27	28	28 4
20	20	22	20	22	22 Be-Har Be-Hukkotai	24	24	26	27	28	29	29 5
21	21 Shemot	23	21	23	23	25	25	27	28	29 Bereshit	30 R. H.	30 R. H. 6
22	22	24	22	24 Shemini	24	26	26 Mattot Masei	28	29	30 R. H.	1 Kislev R. H.	1 Tevet R. H. 7
23	23	25	23	25	25	27	27	29	1 Tishri Rosh Ha-Shanah	1 Heshvan R. H.	2	2 Mi-Kez 8
24	24	26	24	26	26	28 Shelah	28	30 R. H.	2	2	3	3
25	25	27 Mishpatim Shekalim	25 Va-Yakhel Pekudei Ha-Hodesh	27	27	29	29	1 Elul R. H.	3 Fast	3	4 Toledot	4
26	26	28	26	28	28	30 R. H.	1 Av R. H.	2 Shofetim	4	4	5	5
27	27	29	27	29	29 Be-Midbar	1 Tammuz R. H.	2	3	5	5	6	6
28	28 Va-Era	30 R. H.	28	30 R. H.	1 Sivan R. H.	2	3	4	6	6 No'ah	7	7
29	29		29	1 R. H. Iyyar Tazri'a Mezora	2	3	4 Devarim	5	7	7	8	8
30	1 Shevat R. H.		1 Nisan R. H.	2	3	4	5	6	8 Ha'azinu Shabbat Shuvah	8	9	9 Va-Yiggash
31	2		2		4		6	7		9		10 Fast

2007

5767/68 תשס"ז / תשס"ח

	January	February	March	April	May	June	July	August	September	October	November	December
1	11 Tevet	13	11 Ta'anit Esther	13	13	15	15	17	**18** *Ki Tavo*	19 Ḥol	20	**21** *Va-Yeshev*
2	12	14	12	14	14	**16** *Be-Ha'alotkha*	16	18	19	20 ha-Mo'ed	21	22
3	13	**15** *Be-Shallaḥ*	**13** *Teẓavveh* Zakhor	15 Pesaḥ	15	17	17 Fast	19	20	21 Hoshana Rabba	**22** *Ḥayyei Sarah*	23
4	14	16	14 Purim	16 Omer	16	18	18	**20** *Ekev*	21	22 Shemini Aẓeret	23	24
5	15	17	15 Shushan Purim	17	**17** *Emor*	19	19	21	22	23 Simḥat Torah *Ve-Zot Ha-Berakhah*	24	25 Ḥanukkah 1
6	**16** *Va-Yeḥi*	18	16	18 Ḥol ha-Mo'ed	18 Lag ba-Omer	20	20	22	23	**24** *Bereshit*	25	26 2
7	17	19	17	**19**	19	21	**21** *Pinḥas*	23	24	25	26	27 3
8	18	20	18	20	20	22	22	24	**25** *Niẓẓavim Va-Yelekh*	26	27	**28** *Mi-Keẓ* 4
9	19	21	19	21 Pesaḥ	21	**23** *Shelaḥ*	23	25	26	27	28	29 5
10	20	**22** *Yitro*	**20** *Ki Tissa* Parah	22	22	24	24	26	27	28	**29** *Toledot*	1 Tevet R. Ḥ. 6
11	21	23	21	23	23	25	25	**27** *Re'eh*	28	29	1 Kislev R. Ḥ.	2 7
12	22	24	22	24	**24** *Be-Har Be-Ḥukkotai*	26	26	28	29	30 R. Ḥ.	2	3 8
13	**23** *Shemot*	25	23	25	25	27	27	29	1 Tishri Rosh Ha-Shanah	**1** R. Ḥ. Ḥeshvan *No'aḥ*	3	4
14	24	26	24	**26** *Shemini*	26	28	**28** *Mattot Masei*	30 R. Ḥ.	2	2	4	5
15	25	27	25	27	27	29	29	1 Elul R. Ḥ.	**3** *Ha'azinu* Shabbat Shuvah	3	5	**6** *Va-Yiggash*
16	26	28	26	28	28	**30** R. Ḥ. *Koraḥ*	1 Av R. Ḥ.	2	4 Fast	4	6	7
17	27	**29** *Mishpatim* Shekalim	**27** *Va-Yakhel Pekudei* Ha-Ḥodesh	29	29	1 Tammuz R. Ḥ.	2	3	5	5	**7** *Va-Yeẓe*	8
18	28	30 R. Ḥ.	28	30 R. Ḥ.	1 Sivan R. Ḥ.	2	3	**4** *Shofetim*	6	6	8	9
19	29	1 Adar R. Ḥ.	29	1 Iyyar R. Ḥ.	**2** *Be-Midbar*	3	4	5	7	7	9	10 Fast
20	**1** R. Ḥ. Shevat *Va-Era*	2	1 Nisan R. Ḥ.	2	3	4	5	6	8	**8** *Lekh Lekha*	10	11
21	2	3	2	**3** *Tazri'a Meẓora*	4	5	**6** *Devarim*	7	9	9	11	12
22	3	4	3	4	5	6	7	8	10 Yom Kippur	10	12	**13** *Va-Yeḥi*
23	4	5	4	5 Yom ha-Aẓma'ut	6 Shavuot	**7** *Ḥukkat*	8	9	11	11	13	14
24	5	**6** *Terumah*	**5** *Va-Yikra*	6	7	8	9 Tishah be-Av	10	12	12	**14** *Va-Yishlaḥ*	15
25	6	7	6	7	8	9	10	**11** *Ki Teẓe*	13	13	15	16
26	7	8	7	8	**9** *Naso*	10	11	12	14	14	16	17
27	**8** *Bo*	9	8	9	10	11	12	13	15 Sukkot	**15** *Va-Yera*	17	18
28	9	10	9	**10** *Aḥarei Mot Kedoshim*	11	12	**13** *Va-Etḥannan*	14	16	16	18	19
29	10		10	11	12	13	14	15	**17** Ḥol	17	19	**20** *Shemot*
30	11		11	12	13	**14** *Balak*	15	16	18 ha-Mo'ed	18	20	21
31	12		**12** *Ẓav* Shabbat ha-Gadol		14		16	17		19		22

2008

5768/69 תשס"ח / תשס"ט

	January	February	March	April	May	June	July	August	September	October	November	December
1	23 Tevet	25	**24** *Va-Yakhel*	25	26	27	28	29	1 Elul R. Ḥ.	2 Rosh Ha-Shanah	**3** *No'aḥ*	4
2	24	**26** *Mishpatim*	25	26	27	28	29	**1** R. Ḥ. Av *Masei*	2	3 Fast	4	5
3	25	27	26	27	**28** *Kedoshim*	29	30 R. Ḥ.	2	3	4	5	6
4	26	28	27	28	29	1 Sivan R. Ḥ.	1 Tammuz R. Ḥ.	3	4	**5** *Va-Yelekh* Shabbat Shuvah	6	7
5	**27** *Va-Era*	29	28	**29** *Tazri'a* Ha-Ḥodesh	30 R. Ḥ.	2	**2** *Ḥukkat*	4	5	6	7	8
6	28	30 R. Ḥ.	29	1 Nisan R. Ḥ.	1 Iyyar R. Ḥ.	3	3	5	**6** *Shofetim*	7	8	**9** *Va-Yeẓe*
7	29	1 Adar I R. Ḥ.	30	2	2	**4** *Naso*	4	6	7	8	9	10
8	1 Shevat R. Ḥ.	2	**1** R. Ḥ. Adar II *Pekudei* Shekalim	3	3 Yom ha-Aẓma'ut	5	5	7	8	9	**10** *Lekh Lekha*	11
9	2	**3** *Terumah*	2	4	4	6 Shavuot	6	**8** *Devarim*	9	10 Yom Kippur	11	12
10	3	4	3	5	**5** *Emor*	7	7	9 Tishah be-Av	10	11	12	13
11	4	5	4	6	6	8	8	10	11	**12** *Ha'azinu*	13	14
12	**5** *Bo*	6	5	**7** *Meẓora*	7	9	**9** *Balak*	11	12	13	14	15
13	6	7	6	8	8	10	10	12	**13** *Ki Teẓe*	14	15	**16** *Va-Yishlaḥ*
14	7	8	7	9	9	**11** *Be-Ha'alotkha*	11	13	14	15 Sukkot	16	17
15	8	9	**8** *Va-Yikra* Zakhor	10	10	12	12	14	15	16	**17** *Va-Yera*	18
16	9	**10** *Teẓavveh*	9	11	11	13	13	**15** *Va-Etḥannan*	16	17	18	19
17	10	11	10	12	**12** *Be-Har*	14	14	16	17	18 Ḥol ha-Mo'ed	19	20
18	11	12	11	13	13	15	15	17	18	**19**	20	21
19	**12** *Be-Shallaḥ*	13	12	**14** *Aḥarei Mot* Shabbat ha-Gadol	14	16	**16** *Pinḥas*	18	19	20	21	22
20	13	14	13 Ta'anit Esther	15 Pesaḥ	15	17	17 Fast	19	**20** *Ki Tavo*	21 Hoshana Rabba	22	**23** *Va-Yeshev*
21	14	15	14 Purim	16 Omer	16	**18** *Shelaḥ*	18	20	21	22 Shemini Aẓeret	23	24
22	15	16	**15** *Ẓav* Shushan Purim	17	17	19	19	21	22	23 Simḥat Torah *Ve-Zot Ha-Berakhah*	**24** *Ḥayyei Sarah*	25 Ḥanukkah 1
23	16	**17** *Ki Tissa*	16	18 Ḥol ha-Mo'ed	18 Lag ba-Omer	20	20	**22** *Ekev*	23	24	25	26 2
24	17	18	17	19	**19** *Be-Ḥukkotai*	21	21	23	24	25	26	27 3
25	18	19	18	20	20	22	22	24	25	**26** *Bereshit*	27	28 4
26	**19** *Yitro*	20	19	**21** Pesaḥ	21	23	**23** *Mattot*	25	26	27	28	29 5
27	20	21	20	22	22	24	24	26	**27** *Niẓẓavim*	28	29	**30** R. Ḥ. *Mi-Keẓ* 6
28	21	22	21	23	23	**25** *Koraḥ*	25	27	28	29	1 Kislev R. Ḥ.	1 Tevet R. Ḥ. 7
29	22	23	**22** *Shemini* Parah	24	24	26	26	28	29	30 R. Ḥ.	**2** *Toledot*	2 8
30	23		23	25	25	27	27	**29** *Re'eh*	1 Tishri Rosh Ha-Shanah	1 Ḥeshvan R. Ḥ.	3	3
31	24		24		**26** *Be-Midbar*		28	30 R. Ḥ.		2		4

2009

5769/70 תשס"ט / תש"ע

	January	February	March	April	May	June	July	August	September	October	November	December
1	5 Tevet	7	5	7	7	9	9	11 Va-Ethannan	12	13	14	14
2	6	8	6	8	8 Aharei Mot Kedoshim	10	10	12	13	14	15	15
3	7 Va-Yiggash	9	7	9	9	11	11	13	14	15 Sukkot	16	16
4	8	10	8	10 Zav Shabbat ha-Gadol	10	12	12 Hukkat Balak	14	15	16	17	17
5	9	11	9	11	11	13	13	15	16 Ki Tavo	17	18	18 Va-Yishlah
6	10 Fast	12	10	12	12	14 Naso	14	16	17	18 Hol ha-Mo'ed	19	19
7	11	13 Be-Shallah	11 Tezavveh Zakhor	13	13	15	15	17	18	19	20 Va-Yera	20
8	12	14	12	14	14	16	16	18 Ekev	19	20	21	21
9	13	15	13 Ta'anit Esther	15 Pesah	15 Emor	17	17 Fast	19	20	21 Hoshana Rabba	22	22
10	14 Va-Yehi	16	14 Purim	16 Omer	16	18	18	20	21	22 Shemini Azeret	23	23
11	15	17	15 Shushan Purim	17	17	19	19 Pinhas	21	22	23 Simhat Torah Ve-Zot Ha-Berakhah	24	24
12	16	18	16	18 Hol ha-Mo'ed	18 Lag ba-Omer	20	20	22	23 Nizzavim Va-Yelekh	24	25	25 Hanukkah 1 Va-Yeshev
13	17	19	17	19	19	21 Be-Ha'alotkha	21	23	24	25	26	26 2
14	18	20 Yitro	18 Ki Tissa Parah	20	20	22	22	24	25	26	27 Hayyei Sarah	27 3
15	19	21	19	21 Pesah	21	23	23	25 Re'eh	26	27	28	28 4
16	20	22	20	22	22 Be-Har Be-Hukkotai	24	24	26	27	28	29	29 5
17	21 Shemot	23	21	23	23	25	25	27	28	29 Bereshit	30 R.H.	30 R.H. 6
18	22	24	22	24 Shemini	24	26	26 Mattot Masei	28	29	30 R.H.	1 Kislev R.H.	1 Tevet R.H. 7
19	23	25	23	25	25	27	27	29	1 Tishri Rosh Ha-Shanah	1 Heshvan R.H.	2	2 Mi-Kez 8
20	24	26	24	26	26	28 Shelah	28	30 R.H.	2	2	3	3
21	25	27 Mishpatim Shekalim	25 Va-Yakhel Pekudei Ha-Hodesh	27	27	29	29	1 Elul R.H.	3 Fast	3	4 Toledot	4
22	26	28	26	28	28	30 R.H.	1 Av R.H.	2 Shofetim	4	4	5	5
23	27	29	27	29	29 Be-Midbar	1 Tammuz R.H.	2	3	5	5	6	6
24	28 Va-Era	30 R.H.	28	30 R.H.	1 Sivan R.H.	2	3	4	6	6 No'ah	7	7
25	29	1 Adar R.H.	29	1 R.H. Iyyar Tazri'a Mezora	2	3	4 Devarim	5	7	7	8	8
26	1 Shevat R.H.	2	1 Nisan R.H.	2	3	4	5	6	8 Ha'azinu Shabbat Shuvah	8	9	9 Va-Yiggash
27	2	3	2	3	4	5 Korah	6	7	9	9	10	10 Fast
28	3	4 Terumah	3 Va-Yikra	4	5	6	7	8	10 Yom Kippur	10	11 Va-Yeze	11
29	4		4	5 Yom ha-Azma'ut	6 Shavuot	7	8	9 Ki Teze	11	11	12	12
30	5		5	6	7	8	9 Tishah be-Av	10	12	12	13	13
31	6 Bo		6		8		10	11		13 Lekh Lekha		14

2010

5770/71 תש"ע / תשע"א

	January	February	March	April	May	June	July	August	September	October	November	December
1	15 Tevet	17	15 Shushan Purim	17	17 Emor	19	19	21	22	23 Simhat Torah Ve-Zot Ha-Berakhah	24	24
2	16 Va-Yehi	18	16	18 Hol ha-Mo'ed	18 Lag ba-Omer	20	20	22	23	24 Bereshit	25	25 Hanukkah 1
3	17	19	17	19	19	21	21 Pinhas	23	24	25	26	26 2
4	18	20	18	20	20	22	22	24	25 Nizzavim Va-Yelekh	26	27	27 Mi-Kez 3
5	19	21	19	21 Pesah	21	23 Shelah	23	25	26	27	28	28 4
6	20	22 Yitro	20 Ki Tissa Parah	22	22	24	24	26	27	28	29 Toledot	29 5
7	21	23	21	23	23	25	25	27 Re'eh	28	29	30 R.H.	30 R.H. 6
8	22	24	22	24	24 Be-Har Be-Hukkotai	26	26	28	29	30 R.H.	1 Kislev R.H.	1 Tevet R.H. 7
9	23 Shemot	25	23	25	25	27	27	29	1 Tishri Rosh Ha-Shanah	1 R.H. No'ah Heshvan	2	2 8
10	24	26	24	26 Shemini	26	28	28 Mattot Masei	30 R.H.	2	2	3	3
11	25	27	25	27	27	29	29	1 Elul R.H.	3 Ha'azinu Shabbat Shuvah	3	4	4 Va-Yiggash
12	26	28	26	28	28	30 R.H. Korah	1 Av R.H.	2	4 Fast	4	5	5
13	27	29 Mishpatim Shekalim	27 Va-Yakhel Pekudei Ha-Hodesh	29	29	1 Tammuz R.H.	2	3	5	5	6 Va-Yeze	6
14	28	30 R.H.	28	30 R.H.	1 Sivan R.H.	2	3	4 Shofetim	6	6	7	7
15	29	1 Adar R.H.	29	1 Iyyar R.H.	2 Be-Midbar	3	4	5	7	7	8	8
16	1 R.H. Va-Era Shevat	2	1 Nisan R.H.	2	3	4	5	6	8	8 Lekh Lekha	9	9
17	2	3	2	3 Tazri'a Mezora	4	5	6 Devarim	7	9	9	10	10 Fast
18	3	4	3	4	5	6	7	8	10 Yom Kippur	10	11	11 Va-Yehi
19	4	5	4	5 Yom ha-Azma'ut	6 Shavuot	7 Hukkat	8	9	11	11	12	12
20	5	6 Terumah	5 Va-Yikra	6	7	8	9 Tishah be-Av	10	12	12	13 Va-Yishlah	13
21	6	7	6	7	8	9	10	11 Ki Teze	13	13	14	14
22	7	8	7	8	9 Naso	10	11	12	14	14	15	15
23	8 Bo	9	8	9	10	11	12	13	15 Sukkot	15 Va-Yera	16	16
24	9	10	9	10 Aharei Mot Kedoshim	11	12	13 Va-Ethannan	14	16	16	17	17
25	10	11 Ta'anit Esther	10	11	12	13	14	15	17	17	18	18 Shemot
26	11	12	11	12	13	14 Balak	15	16	18 Hol ha-Mo'ed	18	19	19
27	12	13 Tezavveh Zakhor	12 Zav Shabbat ha-Gadol	13	14	15	16	17	19	19	20 Va-Yeshev	20
28	13	14 Purim	13	14	15	16	17	18 Ki Tavo	20	20	21	21
29	14		14	15	16 Be-Ha'alotkha	17 Fast	18	19	21 Hoshana Rabba	21	22	22
30	15 Be-Shallah		15 Pesah	16	17	18	19	20	22 Shemini Azeret	22 Hayyei Sarah	23	23
31	16		16 Omer		18		20 Ekev	21		23		24

2011

5771/72 — תשע״א / תשע״ב

	January	February	March	April	May	June	July	August	September	October	November	December
1	**25 Tevet** *Va-Era*	27	25	26	27	28	29	**1 Av** R. Ḥ.	2	**3** *Ha'azinu* Shabbat Shuvah	4	5
2	26	28	26	**27** *Tazri'a* Ha-Hodesh	28	29	**30** R. Ḥ. *Ḥukkat*	2	3	4 Fast	5	6
3	27	29	27	28	29	**1 Sivan** R. Ḥ.	**1 Tammuz** R. Ḥ.	3	**4** *Shofetim*	5	6	**7** *Va-Yeẓe*
4	28	30 R. Ḥ.	28	29	30 R. Ḥ.	**2** *Naso*	2	4	5	6	7	8
5	29	**1 Adar I** R. Ḥ. *Terumah*	**29** *Pekudei* Shekalim	**1 Nisan** R. Ḥ.	**1 Iyyar** R. Ḥ.	3	3	5	6	7	**8** *Lekh Lekha*	9
6	**1 Shevat** R. Ḥ.	2	30 R. Ḥ.	2	2	4	4	**6** *Devarim*	7	8	9	10
7	2	3	**1 Adar II** R. Ḥ.	3	**3** *Emor*	5	5	7	8	9	10	11
8	**3** *Bo*	4	2	4	4	6 Shavuot	6	8	9	**10** Yom Kippur	11	12
9	4	5	3	**5** *Meẓora*	5 Yom ha-Azma'ut	7	**7** *Balak*	9 Tishah be-Av	10	11	12	13
10	5	6	4	6	6	8	8	10	**11** *Ki Teẓe*	12	13	**14** *Va-Yishlaḥ*
11	6	7	5	7	7	**9** *Be-Ha'alotkha*	9	11	12	13	14	15
12	7	**8** *Teẓavveh*	**6** *Va-Yikra*	8	8	10	10	12	13	14	**15** *Va-Yera*	16
13	8	9	7	9	9	11	11	**13** *Va-Etḥannan*	14	15 Sukkot	16	17
14	9	10	8	10	**10** *Be-Har*	12	12	14	15	16	17	18
15	**10** *Be-Shallaḥ*	11	9	11	11	13	13	15	16	**17** Ḥol ha-Mo'ed	18	19
16	11	12	10	**12** *Aḥarei Mot* Shabbat ha-Gadol	12	14	**14** *Pinhas*	16	17	18	19	20
17	12	13	11 Ta'anit Esther	13	13	15	15	17	**18** *Ki Tavo*	19	20	**21** *Va-Yeshev*
18	13	14	12	14	14	**16** *Shelaḥ*	16	18	19	20	21	22
19	14	**15** *Ki Tissa*	**13** *Ẓav* Zakhor	15 Pesaḥ	15	17	17 Fast	19	20	21 Hoshana Rabba	**22** *Ḥayyei Sarah*	23
20	15	16	14 Purim	16 Omer	16	18	18	**20** *Ekev*	21	22 Shemini Aẓeret	23	24
21	16	17	15 Shushan Purim	17 Ḥol ha-Mo'ed	**17** *Be-Ḥukkotai*	19	19	21	22	23 Simḥat Torah *Ve-Zot Ha-Berakhah*	24	25 Ḥanukkah 1
22	**17** *Yitro*	18	16	18	18 Lag ba-Omer	20	20	22	23	**24** *Bereshit*	25	26 2
23	18	19	17	**19**	19	21	**21** *Mattot*	23	24	25	26	27 3
24	19	20	18	20	20	22	22	24	**25** *Niẓẓavim Va-Yelekh*	26	27	**28** *Mi-Keẓ* 4
25	20	21	19	21 Pesaḥ	21	**23** *Koraḥ*	23	25	26	27	28	29 5
26	21	**22** *Va-Yakhel*	**20** *Shemini* Parah	22	22	24	24	26	27	28	**29** *Toledot*	30 R. Ḥ. 6
27	22	23	21	23	23	25	25	**27** *Re'eh*	28	29	**1 Kislev** R. Ḥ.	**1 Tevet** R. Ḥ. 7
28	23	24	22	24	**24** *Be-Midbar*	26	26	28	29	30 R. Ḥ.	2	2 8
29	**24** *Mishpatim*		23	25	25	27	27	29	**1 Tishri** Rosh Ha-Shanah	**1 Ḥeshvan** R. Ḥ. *No'aḥ*	3	3
30	25		24	**26** *Kedoshim*	26	28	**28** *Masei*	30 R. Ḥ.	2	2	4	4
31	26		25		27		29	**1 Elul** R. Ḥ.		3		**5** *Va-Yiggash*

2012

5772/73 — תשע״ב / תשע״ג

	January	February	March	April	May	June	July	August	September	October	November	December
1	**6 Tevet**	8	7	9	9	11	11	13	**14** *Ki Teẓe*	15 Sukkot	16	**17** *Va-Yishlaḥ*
2	7	9	8	10	10	**12** *Naso*	12	14	15	16	17	18
3	8	10	**9** *Teẓavveh* Zakhor	11	11	13	13	15	16	17 Ḥol ha-Mo'ed	**18** *Va-Yera*	19
4	9	**11** *Be-Shallaḥ*	10	12	12	14	14	**16** *Va-Etḥannan*	17	18	19	20
5	10 Fast	12	11	13	**13** *Aḥarei Mot Kedoshim*	15	15	17	18	19	20	21
6	11	13	12	14	14	16	16	18	19	**20**	21	22
7	**12** *Va-Yeḥi*	14	13 Ta'anit Esther	**15** Pesaḥ	15	17	**17** *Balak*	19	20	21 Hoshana Rabba	22	23
8	13	15	14 Purim	16 Omer	16	18	18 Fast	20	**21** *Ki Tavo*	22 Shemini Aẓeret	23	**24** *Va-Yeshev*
9	14	16	15 Shushan Purim	17 Ḥol ha-Mo'ed	17	**19** *Be-Ha'alotkha*	19	21	22	23 Simḥat Torah *Ve-Zot Ha-Berakhah*	24	25 Ḥanukkah 1
10	15	17	**16** *Ki Tissa*	18	18 Lag ba-Omer	20	20	22	23	24	**25** *Ḥayyei Sarah*	26 2
11	16	**18** *Yitro*	17	19	19	21	21	**23** *Ekev*	24	25	26	27 3
12	17	19	18	20	**20** *Emor*	22	22	24	25	26	27	28 4
13	18	20	19	21 Pesaḥ	21	23	23	25	26	**27** *Bereshit*	28	29 5
14	**19** *Shemot*	21	20	**22**	22	24	**24** *Pinḥas*	26	27	28	29	**1 Tevet** R. Ḥ. 6
15	20	22	21	23	23	25	25	27	**28** *Niẓẓavim*	29	**1 Kislev** R. Ḥ.	**2** *Mi-Keẓ* 7
16	21	23	22	24	24	**26** *Shelaḥ*	26	28	29	30 R. Ḥ.	2	3 8
17	22	24	**23** *Va-Yakhel Pekudei* Parah	25	25	27	27	29	**1 Tishri** Rosh Ha-Shanah	**1 Ḥeshvan** R. Ḥ.	**3** *Toledot*	4
18	23	**25** *Mishpatim* Shekalim	24	26	26	28	28	**30** R. Ḥ. *Re'eh*	2	2	4	5
19	24	26	25	27	**27** *Be-Har Be-Ḥukkotai*	29	29	**1 Elul** R. Ḥ.	3 Fast	3	5	6
20	25	27	26	28	28	30 R. Ḥ.	**1 Av** R. Ḥ.	2	4	**4** *No'aḥ*	6	7
21	**26** *Va-Era*	28	27	**29** *Shemini*	29	**1 Tammuz** R. Ḥ.	**2** *Mattot Masei*	3	5	5	7	8
22	27	29	28	30 R. Ḥ.	**1 Sivan** R. Ḥ.	2	3	4	**6** *Va-Yelekh* Shabbat Shuvah	6	8	**9** *Va-Yiggash*
23	28	30 R. Ḥ.	29	**1 Iyyar** R. Ḥ.	2	**3** *Koraḥ*	4	5	7	7	9	10 Fast
24	29	**1 Adar** R. Ḥ.	**1 Nisan** *Va-Yikra* R. Ḥ. Ha-Ḥodesh	2	3	4	5	6	8	8	**10** *Va-Yeẓe*	11
25	**1 Shevat** R. Ḥ.	**2** *Terumah*	2	3	4	5	6	**7** *Shofetim*	9	9	11	12
26	2	3	3	4 Yom ha-Azma'ut	**5** *Be-Midbar*	6	7	8	10 Yom Kippur	10	12	13
27	3	4	4	5	6 Shavuot	7	8	9	11	**11** *Lekh Lekha*	13	14
28	**4** *Bo*	5	5	**6** *Tazri'a Meẓora*	7	8	**9** *Devarim* Tishah be-Av	10	12	12	14	15
29	5	6	6	7	8	9	10 Fast	11	**13** *Ha'azinu*	13	15	**16** *Va-Yeḥi*
30	6		7	8	9	**10** *Ḥukkat*	11	12	14	14	16	17
31	7		**8** *Ẓav* Shabbat ha-Gadol		10		12	13		15		18

2013

5773/74 תשע״ג / תשע״ד

	January	February	March	April	May	June	July	August	September	October	November	December
1	19 Tevet	21	19	21 Pesaḥ	21	23 *Shelaḥ*	23	25	26	27	28	28 4
2	20	22 *Yitro*	20 *Ki Tissa* Parah	22	22	24	24	26	27	28	29 *Toledot*	29 5
3	21	23	21	23	23	25	25	27 *Re'eh*	28	29	30 R. Ḥ.	30 R. Ḥ. 6
4	22	24	22	24	24 *Be-Har Be-Ḥukkotai*	26	26	28	29	30 R. Ḥ.	1 Kislev R. Ḥ.	1 Tevet R. Ḥ. 7
5	23 *Shemot*	25	23	25	25	27	27	29	1 Tishri Rosh Ha-Shanah	1 Ḥeshvan R. Ḥ. *No'aḥ*	2	2 8
6	24	26	24	26 *Shemini*	26	28	28 *Mattot Masei*	30 R. Ḥ.	2	2	3	3
7	25	27	25	27	27	29	29	1 Elul R. Ḥ.	3 *Ha'azinu* Shabbat Shuvah	3	4	4 *Va-Yiggash*
8	26	28	26	28	28	30 R. Ḥ. *Koraḥ*	1 Av R. Ḥ.	2	4 Fast	4	5	5
9	27	29 *Mishpatim* Shekalim	27 *Va-Yakhel Pekudei* Ha-Ḥodesh	29	29	1 Tammuz R. Ḥ.	2	3	5	5	6 *Va-Yeẓe*	6
10	28	30 R. Ḥ.	28	30 R. Ḥ.	1 Sivan R. Ḥ.	2	3	4 *Shofetim*	6	6	7	7
11	29	1 Adar R. Ḥ.	29	1 Iyyar R. Ḥ.	2 *Be-Midbar*	3	4	5	7	7	8	8
12	1 Shevat R. Ḥ. *Va-Era*	2	1 Nisan R. Ḥ	2	3	4	5	6	8	8 *Lekh Lekha*	9	9
13	2	3	2	3 *Tazri'a Meẓora*	4	5	6 *Devarim*	7	9	9	10	10 Fast
14	3	4	3	4	5	6	7	8	10 Yom Kippur	10	11	11 *Va-Yeḥi*
15	4	5	4	5 Yom ha-Aẓma'ut	6 Shavuot	7 *Ḥukkat*	8	9	11	11	12	12
16	5	6 *Terumah*	5 *Va-Yikra*	6	7	8	9 Tishah be-Av	10	12	12	13 *Va-Yishlaḥ*	13
17	6	7	6	7	8	9	10	11 *Ki Teẓe*	13	13	14	14
18	7	8	7	8	9 *Naso*	10	11	12	14	14	15	15
19	8 *Bo*	9	8	9	10	11	12	13	15 Sukkot	15 *Va-Yera*	16	16
20	9	10	9	10 *Aḥarei Mot Kedoshim*	11	12	13 *Va-Etḥannan*	14	16	16	17	17
21	10	11 Ta'anit Esther	10	11	12	13	14	15	17	17	18	18 *Shemot*
22	11	12	11	12	13	14 *Balak*	15	16	18	18	19	19
23	12	13 *Teẓavveh* Zakhor	12 *Ẓav* Shabbat ha-Gadol	13	14	15	16	17	19 Ḥol ha-Mo'ed	19	20 *Va-Yeshev*	20
24	13	14 Purim	13	14	15	16	17	18 *Ki Tavo*	20	20	21	21
25	14	15 Shushan Purim	14	15	16 *Be-Ha'alotkha*	17 Fast	18	19	21 Hoshana Rabba	21	22	22
26	15 *Be-Shallaḥ*	16	15 Pesaḥ	16	17	18	19	20	22 Shemini Aẓeret	22 *Ḥayyei Sarah*	23	23
27	16	17	16 Omer	17 *Emor*	18	19	20 *Ekev*	21	23 Simḥat Torah *Ve-Zot Ha-Berakhah*	23	24	24
28	17	18	17	18 Lag ba-Omer	19	20	21	22	24 *Bereshit*	24	25 Ḥanukkah 1	25 *Va-Era*
29	18		18	19	20	21 *Pinḥas*	22	23	25	25	26 2	26
30	19		19 Ḥol ha-Mo'ed	20	21	22	23	24	26	26	27 *Mi-Keẓ* 3	27
31	20		20		22		24	25 *Niẓẓavim Va-Yelekh*		27		28

2014

5774/75 תשע״ד / תשע״ה

	January	February	March	April	May	June	July	August	September	October	November	December
1	29 Tevet	1 R. Ḥ. *Terumah* Adar I	29 *Pekudei* Shekalim	1 Nisan R. Ḥ.	1 Iyyar R. Ḥ.	3	3	5	6	7	8 *Lekh Lekha*	9
2	1 Shevat R. Ḥ.	2	30 R. Ḥ.	2	2	4	4	6 *Devarim*	7	8	9	10
3	2	3	1 Adar II R. Ḥ.	3	3 *Emor*	5	5	7	8	9	10	11
4	3 *Bo*	4	2	4	4	6 Shavuot	6	8	9	10 Yom Kippur	11	12
5	4	5	3	5 *Meẓora*	5 Yom ha-Aẓma'ut	7	7 *Balak*	9 Tishah be-Av	10	11	12	13
6	5	6	4	6	6	8	8	10	11 *Ki Teẓe*	12	13	14 *Va-Yishlaḥ*
7	6	7	5	7	7	9 *Be-Ha'alotkha*	9	11	12	13	14	15
8	7	8 *Teẓavveh*	6 *Va-Yikra*	8	8	10	10	12	13	14	15 *Va-Yera*	16
9	8	9	7	9	9	11	11	13 *Va-Etḥannan*	14	15 Sukkot	16	17
10	9	10	8	10	10 *Be-Har*	12	12	14	15	16	17	18
11	10 *Be-Shallaḥ*	11	9	11	11	13	13	15	16	17	18	19
12	11	12	10	12 *Aḥarei Mot* Shabbat ha-Gadol	12	14	14 *Pinḥas*	16	17	18	19	20
13	12	13	11 Ta'anit Esther	13	13	15	15	17	18 *Ki Tavo*	19 Ḥol ha-Mo'ed	20	21 *Va-Yeshev*
14	13	14	12	14	14	16 *Shelaḥ*	16	18	19	20	21	22
15	14	15 *Ki Tissa*	13 *Ẓav* Zakhor	15 Pesaḥ	15	17	17 Fast	19	20	21 Hoshana Rabba	22 *Ḥayyei Sarah*	23
16	15	16	14 Purim	16 Omer	16	18	18	20 *Ekev*	21	22 Shemini Aẓeret	23	24
17	16	17	15 Shushan Purim	17	17 *Be-Ḥukkotai*	19	19	21	22	23 Simḥat Torah *Ve Zot Ha-Berakhah*	24	25 Ḥanukkah 1
18	17 *Yitro*	18	16	18	18 Lag ba-Omer	20	20	22	23	24 *Bereshit*	25	26 2
19	18	19	17	19	19	21	21 *Mattot*	23	24	25	26	27 3
20	19	20	18	20 Ḥol ha-Mo'ed	20	22	22	24	25 *Niẓẓavim Va-Yelekh*	26	27	28 *Mi-Keẓ* 4
21	20	21	19	21 Pesaḥ	21	23 *Koraḥ*	23	25	26	27	28	29 5
22	21	22 *Va-Yakhel*	20 *Shemini* Parah	22	22	24	24	26	27	28	29 *Toledot*	30 R. Ḥ. 6
23	22	23	21	23	23	25	25	27 *Re'eh*	28	29	1 Kislev R. Ḥ.	1 Tevet R. Ḥ. 7
24	23	24	22	24	24 *Be-Midbar*	26	26	28	29	30 R. Ḥ.	2	2 8
25	24 *Mishpatim*	25	23	25	25	27	27	29	1 Tishri Rosh Ha-Shanah	1 R. Ḥ. *No'aḥ* Ḥeshvan	3	3
26	25	26	24	26 *Kedoshim*	26	28	28 *Masei*	30 R. Ḥ.	2	2	4	4
27	26	27	25	27	27	29	29	1 Elul R. Ḥ.	3 *Ha'azinu* Shabbat Shuvah	3	5	5 *Va-Yiggash*
28	27	28	26	28	28	30 R. Ḥ. *Ḥukkat*	1 Av R. Ḥ	2	4 Fast	4	6	6
29	28		27 *Tazri'a* Ha-Ḥodesh	29	29	1 Tammuz R. Ḥ.	2	3	5	5	7 *Va-Yeẓe*	7
30	29		28	30 R. Ḥ.	1 Sivan R. Ḥ.	2	3	4 *Shofetim*	6	6	8	8
31	30 R. Ḥ.		29		2 *Naso*		4	5		7		9

2015

5775/76

תשע"ה / תשע"ו

	January	February	March	April	May	June	July	August	September	October	November	December
1	10 **Tevet** Fast	12	10	12	12	14	14	**16** *Va-Ethannan*	17	18 Hol ha-Mo'ed	19	19
2	11	13	11	13	**13** *Aharei Mot Kedoshim*	15	15	17	18	19	20	20
3	**12** *Va-Yehi*	14	12	14	14	16	16	18	19	**20**	21	21
4	13	15	13 Ta'anit Esther	**15** Pesah	15	17	**17** *Balak*	19	20	21 Hoshana Rabba	22	22
5	14	16	14 Purim	16 Omer	16	18	18 Fast	20	**21** *Ki Tavo*	22 Shemini Azeret	23	**23** *Va-Yeshev*
6	15	17	15 Shushan Purim	17 Hol ha-Mo'ed	17	**19** *Be-Ha'alotkha*	19	21	22	23 Simhat Torah *Ve-Zot Ha-Berakhah*	24	24
7	16	**18** *Yitro*	**16** *Ki Tissa*	18	18 Lag ba-Omer	20	20	22	23	24	**25** *Hayyei Sarah*	25 Hanukkah 1
8	17	19	17	19	19	21	21	**23** *Ekev*	24	25	26	26 2
9	18	20	18	20	**20** *Emor*	22	22	24	25	26	27	27 3
10	**19** *Shemot*	21	19	21 Pesah	21	23	23	25	26	**27** *Bereshit*	28	28 4
11	20	22	20	**22**	22	24	**24** *Pinhas*	26	27	28	29	29 5
12	21	23	21	23	23	25	25	27	**28** *Nizzavim*	29	30 R. H.	**30** R. H. *Mi-Kez* 6
13	22	24	22	24	24	**26** *Shelah*	26	28	29	30 R. H.	1 **Kislev** R. H.	1 **Tevet** R. H. 7
14	23	**25** *Mishpatim* Shekalim	*Va-Yakhel Pekudei* **23** Parah	25	25	27	27	29	1 **Tishri** Rosh Ha-Shanah	1 **Heshvan** R. H.	**2** *Toledot*	2 8
15	24	26	24	26	26	28	28	**30** R. H. *Re'eh*	2	2	3	3
16	25	27	25	27	**27** *Be-Har Be-Hukkotai*	29	29	1 **Elul** R. H.	3 Fast	3	4	4
17	**26** *Va-Era*	28	26	28	28	30 R. H.	1 **Av** R. H.	2	4	**4** *No'ah*	5	5
18	27	29	27	**29** *Shemini*	29	1 **Tammuz** R. H.	**2** *Mattot Masei*	3	5	5	6	6
19	28	30 R. H.	28	30 R. H.	1 **Sivan** R. H.	2	3	4	**6** *Va-Yelekh* Shabbat Shuvah	6	7	**7** *Va-Yiggash*
20	29	1 **Adar** R. H.	29	1 **Iyyar** R. H.	2	**3** *Korah*	4	5	7	7	8	8
21	1 **Shevat** R. H.	**2** *Terumah*	**1 Nisan** *Va-Yikra* R. H. Ha-Hodesh	2	3	4	5	6	8	8	**9** *Va-Yeze*	9
22	2	3	2	3	4	5	6	**7** *Shofetim*	9	9	10	10 Fast
23	3	4	3	4 Yom ha-Azma'ut	**5** *Be-Midbar*	6	7	8	10 Yom Kippur	10	11	11
24	**4** *Bo*	5	4	5	6 Shavuot	7	8	9	11	**11** *Lekh Lekha*	12	12
25	5	6	5	**6** *Tazri'a Mezora*	7	8	**9** *Devarim* Tishah be-Av	10	12	12	13	13
26	6	7	6	7	8	9	10 Fast	11	**13** *Ha'azinu*	13	14	**14** *Va-Yehi*
27	7	8	7	8	9	**10** *Hukkat*	11	12	14	14	15	15
28	8	**9** *Tezavveh* Zakhor	**8** *Zav* Shabbat ha-Gadol	9	10	11	12	13	15 Sukkot	15	**16** *Va-Yishlah*	16
29	9		9	10	11	12	13	**14** *Ki Teze*	16	16	17	17
30	10		10	11	**12** *Naso*	13	14	15	17 Hol ha-Mo'ed	17	18	18
31	**11** *Be-Shallah*		11		13		15	16		**18** *Va-Yera*		19

2016

5776/77

תשע"ו / תשע"ז

	January	February	March	April	May	June	July	August	September	October	November	December
1	20 **Tevet**	22	21	22	23	24	25	26	28	**28** *Nizzavim*	30 R. H.	1 **Kislev** R. H.
2	**21** *Shemot*	23	22	**23** *Shemini* Parah	24	25	**26** *Shelah*	27	29	29	1 **Heshvan** R. H.	2
3	22	24	23	24	25	26	27	28	**30** R. H. *Re'eh*	1 **Tishri** Rosh Ha-Shanah	2	**3** *Toledot*
4	23	25	24	25	26	**27** *Be-Hukkotai*	28	29	1 **Elul** R. H.	2	3	4
5	24	26	**25** *Va-Yakhel* Shekalim	26	27	28	29	1 **Av** R. H.	2	3 Fast	**4** *No'ah*	5
6	25	**27** *Mishpatim*	26	27	28	29	30 R. H.	**2** *Mattot Masei*	3	4	5	6
7	26	28	27	28	**29** *Aharei Mot*	1 **Sivan** R. H.	1 **Tammuz** R. H.	3	4	5	6	7
8	27	29	28	29	30 R. H.	2	2	4	5	**6** *Va-Yelekh* Shabbat Shuvah	7	8
9	**28** *Va-Era*	30 R. H.	29	**1 Nisan** *Tazri'a* R. H. Ha-Hodesh	1 **Iyyar** R. H.	3	**3** *Korah*	5	6	7	8	9
10	29	1 **Adar I** R. H.	30 R. H.	2	2	4	4	6	**7** *Shofetim*	8	9	**10** *Va-Yeze*
11	1 **Shevat** R. H.	2	1 **Adar II** R. H.	3	3	**5** *Be-Midbar*	5	7	8	9	10	11
12	2	3	**2** *Pekudei*	4	4 Yom ha-Azma'ut	6 Shavuot	6	8	9	10 Yom Kippur	**11** *Lekh Lekha*	12
13	3	**4** *Terumah*	3	5	5	7	7	**9** *Devarim* Tishah be-Av	10	11	12	13
14	4	5	4	6	**6** *Kedoshim*	8	8	10 Fast	11	12	13	14
15	5	6	5	7	7	9	9	11	12	**13** *Ha'azinu*	14	15
16	**6** *Bo*	7	6	**8** *Mezora* Shabbat ha-Gadol	8	10	**10** *Hukkat*	12	13	14	15	16
17	7	8	7	9	9	11	11	13	**14** *Ki Teze*	15 Sukkot	16	**17** *Va-Yishlah*
18	8	9	8	10	10	**12** *Naso*	12	14	15	16	17	18
19	9	10	**9** *Va-Yikra* Zakhor	11	11	13	13	15	16	17 Hol ha-Mo'ed	**18** *Va-Yera*	19
20	10	**11** *Tezavveh*	10	12	12	14	14	**16** *Va-Ethannan*	17	18	19	20
21	11	12	11	13	**13** *Emor*	15	15	17	18	19	20	21
22	12	13	12	14	14	16	16	18	19	**20**	21	22
23	**13** *Be-Shallah*	14	13 Ta'anit Esther	**15** Pesah	15	17	**17** *Balak*	19	20	21 Hoshana Rabba	22	23
24	14	15	14 Purim	16 Omer	16	18	18 Fast	20	**21** *Ki Tavo*	22 Shemini Azeret	23	**24** *Va-Yeshev*
25	15	16	15 Shushan Purim	17 Hol ha-Mo'ed	17	**19** *Be-Ha'alotkha*	19	21	22	23 Simhat Torah *Ve-Zot Ha-Berakhah*	24	25 Hanukkah 1
26	16	17	**16** *Zav*	18	18 Lag ba-Omer	20	20	22	23	24	**25** *Hayyei Sarah*	26 2
27	17	**18** *Ki Tissa*	17	19	19	21	21	**23** *Ekev*	24	25	26	27 3
28	18	19	18	20	**20** *Be-Har*	22	22	24	25	26	27	28 4
29	19	20	19	21 Pesah	21	23	23	25	26	**27** *Bereshit*	28	29 5
30	**20** *Yitro*		20	**22**	22	24	**24** *Pinhas*	26	27	28	29	1 **Tevet** R. H. 6
31	21		21		23		25	27		29		**2** *Mi-Kez* 7

2017

5777/78 תשע״ז / תשע״ח

	January	February	March	April	May	June	July	August	September	October	November	December
1	3 **Tevet** Ḥanukkah 8	5	3	**5** *Va-Yikra*	5 Yom ha-Aẓma'ut	7	**7** *Ḥukkat*	9 Tishah be-Av	10	11	12	13
2	4	6	4	6	6	8	8	10	**11** *Ki Teẓe*	12	13	**14** *Va-Yishlaḥ*
3	5	7	5	7	7	**9** *Naso*	9	11	12	13	14	15
4	6	**8** *Bo*	**6** *Terumah*	8	8	10	10	12	13	14	**15** *Va-Yera*	16
5	7	9	7	9	9	11	11	**13** *Va-Etḥannan*	14	15 Sukkot	16	17
6	8	10	8	10	**10** *Aḥarei Mot Kedoshim*	12	12	14	15	16	17	18
7	**9** *Va-Yiggash*	11	9	11	11	13	13	15	16	**17** Ḥol ha-Mo'ed	18	19
8	10 Fast	12	10	**12** *Ẓav* Shabbat ha-Gadol	12	14	**14** *Balak*	16	17	18	19	20
9	11	13	11 Ta'anit Esther	13	13	15	15	17	**18** *Ki Tavo*	19	20	**21** *Va-Yeshev*
10	12	14	12	14	14	**16** *Be-Ha'alotkha*	16	18	19	20	21	22
11	13	**15** *Be-Shallaḥ*	**13** *Teẓavveh* Zakhor	15 Pesaḥ	15	17	17 Fast	19	20	21 Hoshana Rabba	**22** *Ḥayyei Sarah*	23
12	14	16	14 Purim	16 Omer	16	18	18	**20** *Ekev*	21	22 Shemini Aẓeret	23	24
13	15	17	15 Shushan Purim	17 Ḥol ha-Mo'ed	**17** *Emor*	19	19	21	22	23 Simḥat Torah *Ve-Zot Ha-Berakhah*	24	25 Ḥanukkah 1
14	**16** *Va-Yeḥi*	18	16	18	18 Lag ba-Omer	20	20	22	23	**24** *Bereshit*	25	26 2
15	17	19	17	**19**	19	21	**21** *Pinḥas*	23	24	25	26	27 3
16	18	20	18	20	20	22	22	24	**25** *Niẓẓavim Va-Yelekh*	26	27	**28** *Mi-Keẓ* 4
17	19	21	19	21 Pesaḥ	21	**23** *Shelaḥ*	23	25	26	27	28	29 5
18	20	**22** *Yitro*	**20** *Ki Tissa Parah*	22	22	24	24	26	27	28	**29** *Toledot*	30 R. Ḥ. 6
19	21	23	21	23	23	25	25	**27** *Re'eh*	28	29	1 **Kislev** R. Ḥ.	1 **Tevet** R. Ḥ. 7
20	22	24	22	24	**24** *Be-Har Be-Ḥukkotai*	26	26	28	29	30 R. Ḥ.	2	2 8
21	**23** *Shemot*	25	23	25	25	27	27	29	1 **Tishri** Rosh Ha-Shanah	1 **Ḥeshvan** R. Ḥ. *No'aḥ*	3	3
22	24	26	24	**26** *Shemini*	26	28	**28** *Mattot Masei*	30 R. Ḥ.	2	2	4	4
23	25	27	25	27	27	29	29	1 **Elul** R. Ḥ.	**3** *Ha'azinu* Shabbat Shuvah	3	5	**5** *Va-Yiggash*
24	26	28	26	28	28	**30** R. Ḥ. *Koraḥ*	1 **Av** R. Ḥ.	2	4 Fast	4	6	6
25	27	**29** *Mishpatim* Shekalim	**27** *Va-Yakhel Pekudei* Ha-Ḥodesh	29	29	1 **Tammuz** R. Ḥ.	2	3	5	5	**7** *Va-Yeẓe*	7
26	28	30 R. Ḥ.	28	30 R. Ḥ.	1 **Sivan** R. Ḥ.	2	3	**4** *Shofetim*	6	6	8	8
27	29	1 **Adar** R. Ḥ.	29	1 **Iyyar** R. Ḥ.	**2** *Be-Midbar*	3	4	5	7	7	9	9
28	**1 Shevat** R. Ḥ. *Va-Era*	2	1 **Nisan** R. Ḥ.	2	3	4	5	6	8	**8** *Lekh Lekha*	10	10 Fast
29	2		2	**3** *Tazri'a Meẓora*	4	5	**6** *Devarim*	7	9	9	11	11
30	3		3	4	5	6	7	8	**10** Yom Kippur	10	12	**12** *Va-Yeḥi*
31	4		4		6 Shavuot		8	9		11		13

2018

5778/79 תשע״ח / תשע״ט

	January	February	March	April	May	June	July	August	September	October	November	December
1	14 **Tevet**	16	14 Purim	16 Omer	16	18	18 Fast	20	**21** *Ki Tavo*	22 Shemini Aẓeret	23	**23** *Va-Yeshev*
2	15	17	15 Shushan Purim	17 Ḥol ha-Mo'ed	17	**19** *Be-Ha'alotkha*	19	21	22	23 Simḥat Torah *Ve-Zot Ha-Berakhah*	24	24
3	16	**18** *Yitro*	**16** *Ki Tissa*	18	18 Lag ba-Omer	20	20	22	23	24	**25** *Ḥayyei Sarah*	25 Ḥanukkah 1
4	17	19	17	19	19	21	21	**23** *Ekev*	24	25	26	26 2
5	18	20	18	20	**20** *Emor*	22	22	24	25	26	27	27 3
6	**19** *Shemot*	21	19	21 Pesaḥ	21	23	23	25	26	**27** *Bereshit*	28	28 4
7	20	22	20	**22**	22	24	**24** *Pinḥas*	26	27	28	29	29 5
8	21	23	21	23	23	25	25	27	**28** *Niẓẓavim*	29	30 R. Ḥ.	**30** R. Ḥ. *Mi-Keẓ* 6
9	22	24	22	24	24	**26** *Shelaḥ*	26	28	29	30 R. Ḥ.	1 **Kislev** R. Ḥ.	1 **Tevet** R. Ḥ. 7
10	23	**25** *Mishpatim* Shekalim	**23** *Va-Yakhel Pekudei* Parah	25	25	27	27	29	1 **Tishri** Rosh Ha-Shanah	1 **Ḥeshvan** R. Ḥ.	**2** *Toledot*	2 8
11	24	26	24	26	26	28	28	**30** R. Ḥ. *Re'eh*	2	2	3	3
12	25	27	25	27	**27** *Be-Har Be-Ḥukkotai*	29	29	1 **Elul** R. Ḥ.	3 Fast	3	4	4
13	**26** *Va-Era*	28	26	28	28	30 R. Ḥ.	1 **Av** R. Ḥ.	2	4	**4** *No'aḥ*	5	5
14	27	29	27	**29** *Shemini*	29	1 **Tammuz** R. Ḥ.	**2** *Mattot Masei*	3	5	5	6	6
15	28	30 R. Ḥ.	28	30 R. Ḥ.	1 **Sivan** R. Ḥ.	2	3	4	**6** *Va-Yelekh* Shabbat Shuvah	6	7	**7** *Va-Yiggash*
16	29	1 **Adar** R. Ḥ.	29	1 **Iyyar** R. Ḥ.	2	**3** *Koraḥ*	4	5	7	7	8	8
17	1 **Shevat** R. Ḥ.	**2** *Terumah*	**1 Nisan** *Va-Yikra* R. Ḥ. Ha-Ḥodesh	2	3	4	5	6	8	8	**9** *Va-Yeẓe*	9
18	2	3	2	3	4	5	6	**7** *Shofetim*	9	9	10	10 Fast
19	3	4	3	4 Yom ha-Aẓma'ut	**5** *Be-Midbar*	6	7	8	**10** Yom Kippur	10	11	11
20	**4** *Bo*	5	4	5	6 Shavuot	7	8	9	11	**11** *Lekh Lekha*	12	12
21	5	6	5	**6** *Tazri'a Meẓora*	7	8	**9** *Devarim* Tishah be-Av	10	12	12	13	13
22	6	7	6	7	8	9	10 Fast	11	**13** *Ha'azinu*	13	14	**14** *Va-Yeḥi*
23	7	8	7	8	9	**10** *Ḥukkat*	11	12	14	14	15	15
24	8	**9** *Teẓavveh* Zakhor	**8** *Ẓav* Shabbat ha-Gadol	9	10	11	12	13	15 Sukkot	15	**16** *Va-Yishlaḥ*	16
25	9	10	9	10	11	12	13	**14** *Ki Teẓe*	16	16	17	17
26	10	11	10	11	**12** *Naso*	13	14	15	17 Ḥol ha-Mo'ed	17	18	18
27	**11** *Be-Shallaḥ*	12	11	12	13	14	15	16	18	**18** *Va-Yera*	19	19
28	12	13 Ta'anit Esther	12	**13** *Aḥarei Mot Kedoshim*	14	15	**16** *Va-Etḥannan*	17	19	19	20	20
29	13		13	14	15	16	17	18	**20**	20	21	**21** *Shemot*
30	14		14	15	16	**17** *Balak*	18	19	21 Hoshana Rabba	21	22	22
31	15		**15** Pesaḥ		17		19	20		22		23

2019

5779/80 תשע״ט / תש״פ

	January	February	March	April	May	June	July	August	September	October	November	December
1	24 Tevet	26	24	25	26	27 *Be-Ḥukkotai*	28	29	1 Elul R. H.	Rosh Ha-Shanah 2	3	3
2	25	27 *Mishpatim*	25 *Va-Yakhel* Shekalim	26	27	28	29	1 Av R. H.	2	3 Fast	4 *No'aḥ*	4
3	26	28	26	27	28	29	30 R. H.	2 *Mattot Masei*	3	4	5	5
4	27	29	27	28	29 *Aḥarei Mot*	1 Sivan R. H.	1 Tammuz R. H.	3	4	5	6	6
5	28 *Va-Era*	30 R. H.	28	29	30 R. H.	2	2	4	5	6 *Va-Yelekh* Shabbat Shuvah	7	7
6	29	1 Adar I R. H.	29	1 Nisan *Tazri'a* R. H. Ha-Ḥodesh	1 Iyyar R. H.	3	3 *Koraḥ*	5	6	7	8	8
7	1 Shevat R. H.	2	30 R. H.	2	2	4	4	6	7 *Shofetim*	8	9	9 *Va-Yeẓe*
8	2	3	1 Adar II R. H.	3	3	5 *Be-Midbar*	5	7	8	9	10	10
9	3	4 *Terumah*	2 *Pekudei*	4	4 Yom ha-Aẓma'ut	6 Shavuot	6	8	9	10 Yom Kippur	11 *Lekh Lekha*	11
10	4	5	3	5	5	7	7	9 *Devarim* Tishah be-Av	10	11	12	12
11	5	6	4	6	6 *Kedoshim*	8	8	10 Fast	11	12	13	13
12	6 *Bo*	7	5	7	7	9	9	11	12	13 *Ha'azinu*	14	14
13	7	8	6	8 *Meẓora* Shabbat ha-Gadol	8	10	10 *Ḥukkat*	12	13	14	15	15
14	8	9	7	9	9	11	11	13	14 *Ki Teẓe*	15 Sukkot	16	16 *Va-Yishlaḥ*
15	9	10	8	10	10	12 *Naso*	12	14	15	16	17	17
16	10	11 *Teẓavveh*	9 *Va-Yikra* Zakhor	11	11	13	13	15	16	17 Ḥol ha-Mo'ed	18 *Va-Yera*	18
17	11	12	10	12	12	14	14	16 *Va-Etḥannan*	17	18	19	19
18	12	13	11	13	13 *Emor*	15	15	17	18	19	20	20
19	13 *Be-Shallaḥ*	14	12	14	14	16	16	18	19	20	21	21
20	14	15	13 Ta'anit Esther	15 Pesaḥ	15	17	17 *Balak*	19	20	21 Ḥoshana Rabba	22	22
21	15	16	14 Purim	16 Omer	16	18	18 Fast	20	21 *Ki Tavo*	22 Shemini Aẓeret	23	23 *Va-Yeshev*
22	16	17	15 Shushan Purim	17 Ḥol ha-Mo'ed	17	19 *Be-Ha'alotkha*	19	21	22	23 Simḥat Torah *Ve-Zot Ha-Berakhah*	24	24
23	17	18 *Ki Tissa*	16 *Ẓav*	18	18 Lag ba-Omer	20	20	22	23	24	25 *Ḥayyei Sarah*	25 Ḥanukkah 1
24	18	19	17	19	19	21	21	23 *Ekev*	24	25	26	26 2
25	19	20	18	20	20 *Be-Har*	22	22	24	25	26	27	27 3
26	20 *Yitro*	21	19	21 Pesaḥ	21	23	23	25	26	27 *Bereshit*	28	28 4
27	21	22	20	22	22	24	24 *Pinḥas*	26	27	28	29	29 5
28	22	23	21	23	23	25	25	27	28 *Niẓẓavim*	29	30 R. H.	30 R. H. *Mi-Keẓ* 6
29	23		22	24	24	26 *Shelaḥ*	26	28	29	30 R. H.	1 Kislev R. H.	1 Tevet R. H. 7
30	24		23 *Shemini* Parah	25	25	27	27	29	1 Tishri Rosh Ha-Shanah	1 Ḥeshvan R. H.	2 *Toledot*	2 8
31	25		24		26		28	30 R. H. *Re'eh*		2		3

2020

5780/81 תש״פ / תשפ״א

	January	February	March	April	May	June	July	August	September	October	November	December
1	4 Tevet	6 *Bo*	5	7	7	9	9	11 *Va-Etḥannan*	12	13	14	15
2	5	7	6	8	8 *Aḥarei Mot Kedoshim*	10	10	12	13	14	15	16
3	6	8	7	9	9	11	11	13	14	15 Sukkot	16	17
4	7 *Va-Yiggash*	9	8	10 *Ẓav* Shabbat ha-Gadol	10	12	12 *Ḥukkat Balak*	14	15	16	17	18
5	8	10	9	11	11	13	13	15	16 *Ki Tavo*	17	18	19 *Va-Yishlaḥ*
6	9	11	10	12	12	14 *Naso*	14	16	17	18 Ḥol ha-Mo'ed	19	20
7	10 Fast	12	11 *Teẓavveh* Zakhor	13	13	15	15	17	18	19	20 *Va-Yera*	21
8	11	13 *Be-Shallaḥ*	12	14	14	16	16	18 *Ekev*	19	20	21	22
9	12	14	13 Ta'anit Esther	15 Pesaḥ	15 *Emor*	17	17 Fast	19	20	21 Ḥoshana Rabba	22	23
10	13	15	14 Purim	16 Omer	16	18	18	20	21	22 Shemini Aẓeret	23	24
11	14 *Va-Yeḥi*	16	15 Shushan Purim	17 Ḥol ha-Mo'ed	17	19	19 *Pinḥas*	21	22	23 Simḥat Torah *Ve-Zot Ha-Berakhah*	24	25 Ḥanukkah 1
12	15	17	16	18	18 Lag ba-Omer	20	20	22	23 *Niẓẓavim Va-Yelekh*	24	25	26 *Va-Yeshev* 2
13	16	18	17	19	19	21 *Be-Ha'alotkha*	21	23	24	25	26	27 3
14	17	19	18 *Ki Tissa* Parah	20	20	22	22	24	25	26	27 *Ḥayyei Sarah*	28 4
15	18	20 *Yitro*	19	21 Pesaḥ	21	23	23	25 *Re'eh*	26	27	28	29 5
16	19	21	20	22	22 *Be-Har Be-Ḥukkotai*	24	24	26	27	28	29	1 Tevet R. H. 6
17	20	22	21	23	23	25	25	27	28	29 *Bereshit*	1 Kislev R. H.	2 7
18	21 *Shemot*	23	22	24 *Shemini*	24	26	26 *Mattot Masei*	28	29	30 R. H.	2	3 8
19	22	24	23	25	25	27	27	29	1 Tishri Rosh Ha-Shanah	1 Ḥeshvan R. H.	3	4 *Mi-Keẓ*
20	23	25	24	26	26	28 *Shelaḥ*	28	30 R. H.	2	2	4	5
21	24	26	25 *Va-Yakhel Pekudei* Ha-Ḥodesh	27	27	29	29	1 Elul R. H.	3 Fast	3	5 *Toledot*	6
22	25	27 *Mishpatim* Shekalim	26	28	28	30 R. H.	1 Av R. H.	2 *Shofetim*	4	4	6	7
23	26	28	27	29	29 *Be-Midbar*	1 Tammuz R. H.	2	3	5	5	7	8
24	27	29	28	30 R. H.	1 Sivan R. H.	2	3	4	6	6 *No'aḥ*	8	9
25	28 *Va-Era*	30 R. H.	29	1 Iyyar R. H. *Tazri'a Meẓora*	2	3	4 *Devarim*	5	7	7	9	10 Fast
26	29	1 Adar R. H.	1 Nisan R. H.	2	3	4	5	6	8 *Ha'azinu* Shabbat Shuvah	8	10	11
27	1 Shevat R. H.	2	2	3	4	5 *Koraḥ*	6	7	9	9	11	12
28	2	3	3 *Va-Yikra*	4	5	6	7	8	10 Yom Kippur	10	12 *Va-Yeẓe*	13
29	3	4 *Terumah*	4	5 Yom ha-Aẓma'ut	6 Shavuot	7	8	9 *Ki Teẓe*	11	11	13	14
30	4		5	6	7	8	9 Tishah be-Av	10	12	12	14	15
31	5		6		8		10	11		13 *Lekh Lekha*		16

Based on *150 Year Calendar*, M. Greenfield, 1963.

ḤASIDISM (Chart of the relationships of the leading Ḥasidic dynasties, from the *Ba'al Shem Tov* to the present time.)

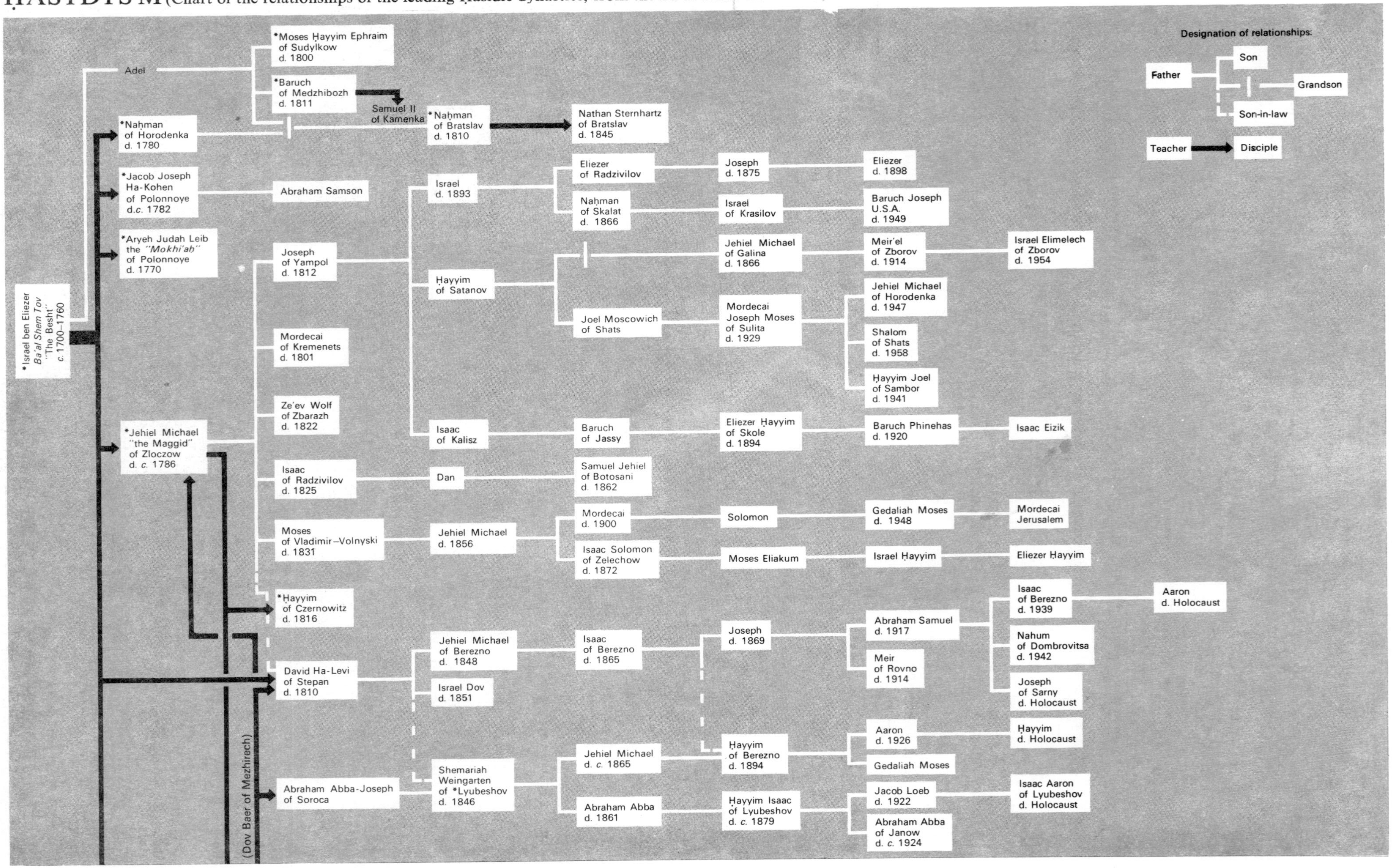

*Israel ben Eliezer Ba'al Shem Tov "The Besht" c. 1700–1760
Adel
*Moses Ḥayyim Ephraim of Sudylkow d. 1800
*Baruch of Medzhibozh d. 1811
Samuel II of Kamenka
*Naḥman of Horodenka d. 1780
*Naḥman of Bratslav d. 1810
Nathan Sternhartz of Bratslav d. 1845
*Jacob Joseph Ha-Kohen of Polonnoye d.c. 1782
Abraham Samson
*Aryeh Judah Leib the "Mokhi'ah" of Polonnoye d. 1770
Joseph of Yampol d. 1812
Israel d. 1893
Eliezer of Radzivilov
Joseph d. 1875
Eliezer d. 1898
Naḥman of Skalat d. 1866
Israel of Krasilov
Baruch Joseph U.S.A. d. 1949
Ḥayyim of Satanov
Jehiel Michael of Galina d. 1866
Meir'el of Zborov d. 1914
Israel Elimelech of Zborov d. 1954
Joel Moscowich of Shats
Mordecai Joseph Moses of Sulita d. 1929
Jehiel Michael of Horodenka d. 1947
Shalom of Shats d. 1958
Ḥayyim Joel of Sambor d. 1941
Mordecai of Kremenets d. 1801
Ze'ev Wolf of Zbarazh d. 1822
*Jehiel Michael "the Maggid" of Zloczow d. c. 1786
Isaac of Kalisz
Baruch of Jassy
Eliezer Ḥayyim of Skole d. 1894
Baruch Phinehas d. 1920
Isaac Eizik
Isaac of Radzivilov d. 1825
Dan
Samuel Jehiel of Botosani d. 1862
Moses of Vladimir-Volnyski d. 1831
Jehiel Michael d. 1856
Mordecai d. 1900
Solomon
Gedaliah Moses d. 1948
Mordecai Jerusalem
Isaac Solomon of Zelechow d. 1872
Moses Eliakum
Israel Ḥayyim
Eliezer Ḥayyim
*Ḥayyim of Czernowitz d. 1816
David Ha-Levi of Stepan d. 1810
Jehiel Michael of Berezno d. 1848
Israel Dov d. 1851
Isaac of Berezno d. 1865
Joseph d. 1869
Abraham Samuel d. 1917
Isaac of Berezno d. 1939
Aaron d. Holocaust
Nahum of Dombrovitsa d. 1942
Joseph of Sarny d. Holocaust
Meir of Rovno d. 1914
Abraham Abba-Joseph of Soroca
Shemariah Weingarten of *Lyubeshov d. 1846
Jehiel Michael d. c. 1865
Ḥayyim of Berezno d. 1894
Aaron d. 1926
Ḥayyim d. Holocaust
Gedaliah Moses
Abraham Abba d. 1861
Ḥayyim Isaac of Lyubeshov d. c. 1879
Jacob Loeb d. 1922
Isaac Aaron of Lyubeshov d. Holocaust
Abraham Abba of Janow d. c. 1924
(Dov Baer of Mezhirech)
Designation of relationships:
Father
Son
Grandson
Son-in-law
Teacher
Disciple

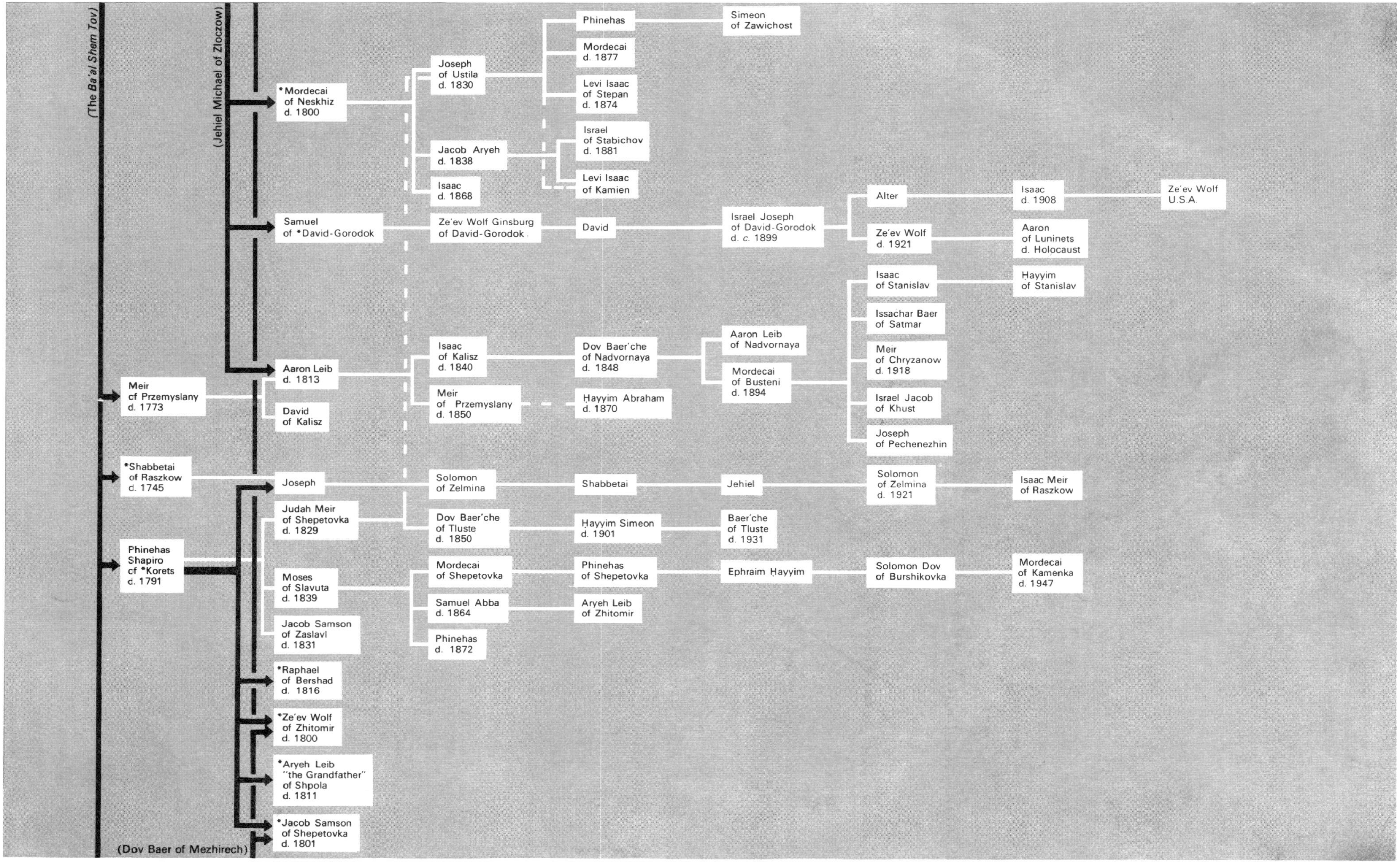
(The Ba'al Shem Tov)
(Jehiel Michael of Zloczow)
(Dov Baer of Mezhirech)
Meir cf Przemyslany d. 1773
*Shabbetai of Raszkow c. 1745
Phinehas Shapiro cf *Korets c. 1791
*Mordecai of Neskhiz d. 1800
Samuel of *David-Gorodok
Aaron Leib d. 1813
David of Kalisz
Joseph
Judah Meir of Shepetovka d. 1829
Moses of Slavuta d. 1839
Jacob Samson of Zaslavl d. 1831
*Raphael of Bershad d. 1816
*Ze'ev Wolf of Zhitomir d. 1800
*Aryeh Leib "the Grandfather" of Shpola d. 1811
*Jacob Samson of Shepetovka d. 1801
Joseph of Ustila d. 1830
Jacob Aryeh d. 1838
Isaac d. 1868
Ze'ev Wolf Ginsburg of David-Gorodok
Isaac of Kalisz d. 1840
Meir of Przemyslany d. 1850
Solomon of Zelmina
Dov Baer'che of Tluste d. 1850
Mordecai of Shepetovka
Samuel Abba d. 1864
Phinehas d. 1872
Phinehas
Mordecai d. 1877
Levi Isaac of Stepan d. 1874
Israel of Stabichov d. 1881
Levi Isaac of Kamien
David
Dov Baer'che of Nadvornaya d. 1848
Ḥayyim Abraham d. 1870
Shabbetai
Ḥayyim Simeon d. 1901
Phinehas of Shepetovka
Aryeh Leib of Zhitomir
Simeon of Zawichost
Israel Joseph of David-Gorodok d. c. 1899
Aaron Leib of Nadvornaya
Mordecai of Busteni d. 1894
Jehiel
Baer'che of Tluste d. 1931
Ephraim Ḥayyim
Alter
Ze'ev Wolf d. 1921
Isaac of Stanislav
Issachar Baer of Satmar
Meir of Chryzanow d. 1918
Israel Jacob of Khust
Joseph of Pechenezhin
Solomon of Zelmina d. 1921
Solomon Dov of Burshikovka
Isaac d. 1908
Aaron of Luninets d. Holocaust
Ḥayyim of Stanislav
Isaac Meir of Raszkow
Mordecai of Kamenka d. 1947
Ze'ev Wolf U.S.A.

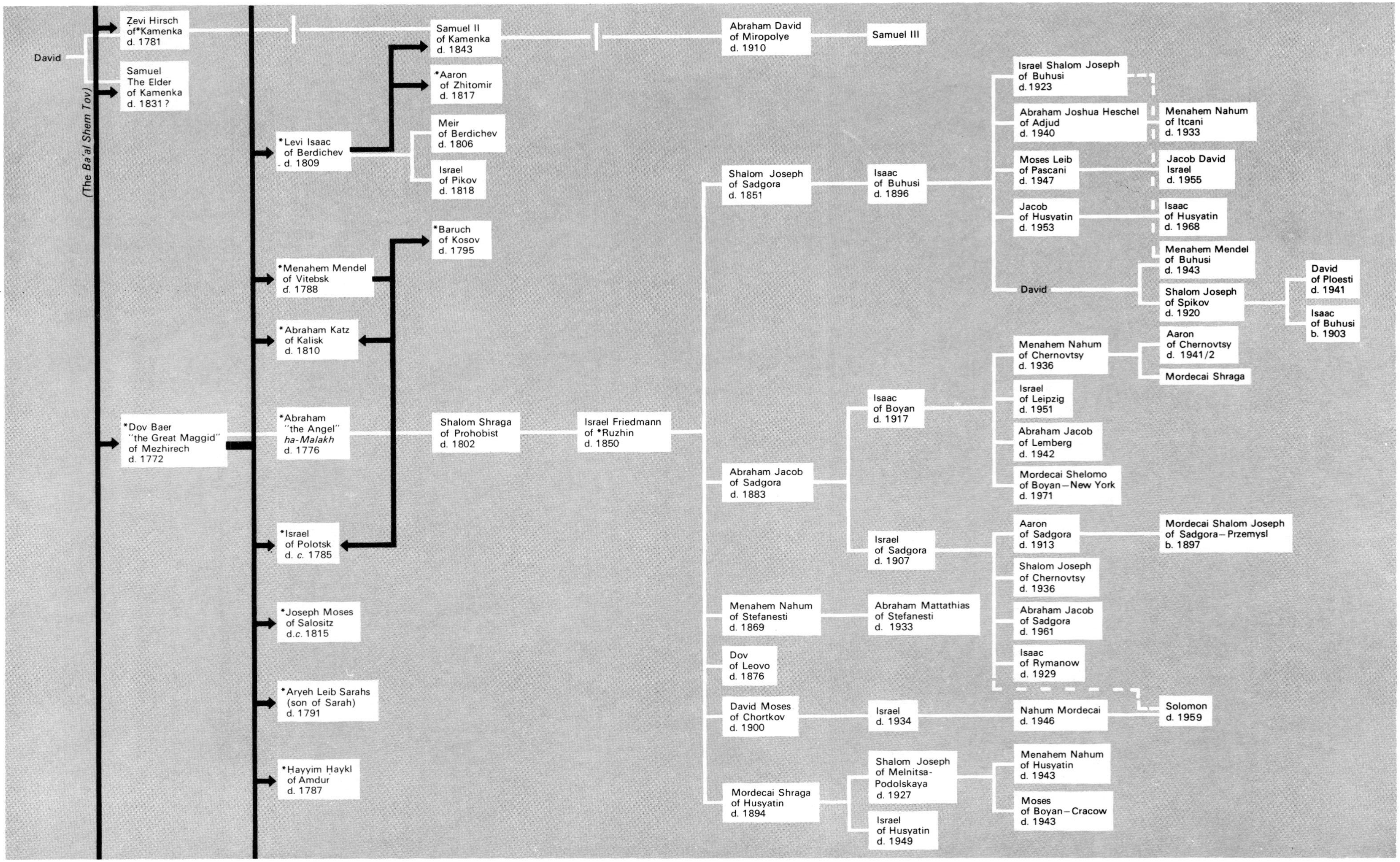
David
(The Ba'al Shem Tov)
Ẓevi Hirsch of *Kamenka d. 1781
Samuel The Elder of Kamenka d. 1831 ?
Samuel II of Kamenka d. 1843
Abraham David of Miropolye d. 1910
Samuel III
*Levi Isaac of Berdichev d. 1809
*Aaron of Zhitomir d. 1817
Meir of Berdichev d. 1806
Israel of Pikov d. 1818
*Baruch of Kosov d. 1795
*Menahem Mendel of Vitebsk d. 1788
*Abraham Katz of Kalisk d. 1810
*Dov Baer "the Great Maggid" of Mezhirech d. 1772
*Abraham "the Angel" ha-Malakh d. 1776
Shalom Shraga of Prohobist d. 1802
Israel Friedmann of *Ruzhin d. 1850
*Israel of Polotsk d. c. 1785
*Joseph Moses of Salositz d.c. 1815
*Aryeh Leib Sarahs (son of Sarah) d. 1791
*Hayyim Haykl of Amdur d. 1787
Shalom Joseph of Sadgora d. 1851
Isaac of Buhusi d. 1896
Israel Shalom Joseph of Buhusi d. 1923
Abraham Joshua Heschel of Adjud d. 1940
Menahem Nahum of Itcani d. 1933
Moses Leib of Pascani d. 1947
Jacob David Israel d. 1955
Jacob of Husyatin d. 1953
Isaac of Husyatin d. 1968
Menahem Mendel of Buhusi d. 1943
David
Shalom Joseph of Spikov d. 1920
David of Ploesti d. 1941
Isaac of Buhusi b. 1903
Abraham Jacob of Sadgora d. 1883
Isaac of Boyan d. 1917
Menahem Nahum of Chernovtsy d. 1936
Aaron of Chernovtsy d. 1941/2
Mordecai Shraga
Israel of Leipzig d. 1951
Abraham Jacob of Lemberg d. 1942
Mordecai Shelomo of Boyan–New York d. 1971
Israel of Sadgora d. 1907
Aaron of Sadgora d. 1913
Mordecai Shalom Joseph of Sadgora–Przemysl b. 1897
Shalom Joseph of Chernovtsy d. 1936
Abraham Jacob of Sadgora d. 1961
Isaac of Rymanow d. 1929
Menahem Nahum of Stefanesti d. 1869
Abraham Mattathias of Stefanesti d. 1933
Dov of Leovo d. 1876
David Moses of Chortkov d. 1900
Israel d. 1934
Nahum Mordecai d. 1946
Solomon d. 1959
Mordecai Shraga of Husyatin d. 1894
Shalom Joseph of Melnitsa-Podolskaya d. 1927
Menahem Nahum of Husyatin d. 1943
Moses of Boyan–Cracow d. 1943
Israel of Husyatin d. 1949

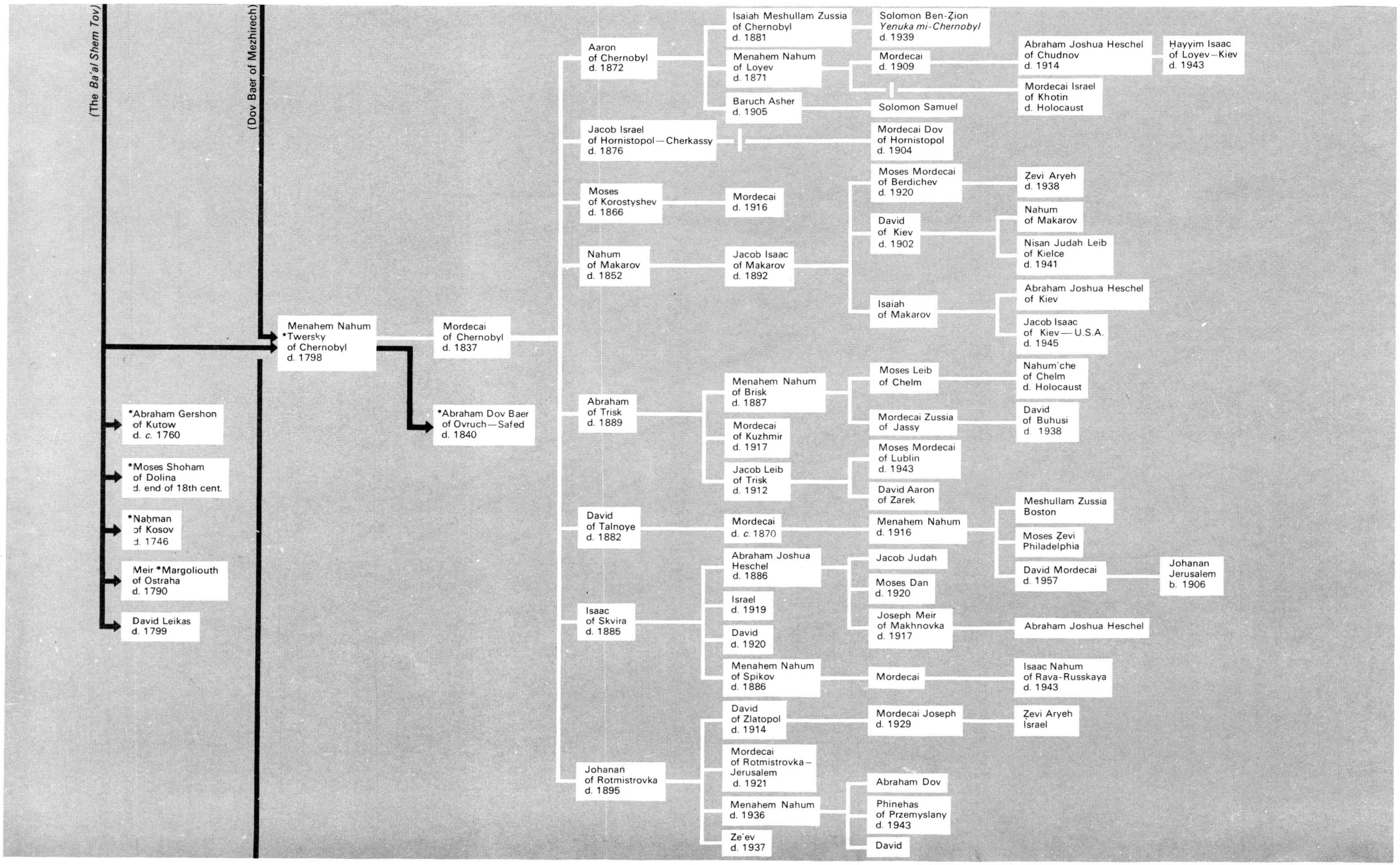
(The Ba'al Shem Tov)
(Dov Baer of Mezhirech)
*Abraham Gershon of Kutow d. c. 1760
*Moses Shoham of Dolina d. end of 18th cent.
*Nahman of Kosov d. 1746
Meir *Margoliouth of Ostraha d. 1790
David Leikas d. 1799
Menahem Nahum *Twersky of Chernobyl d. 1798
Mordecai of Chernobyl d. 1837
*Abraham Dov Baer of Ovruch—Safed d. 1840
Aaron of Chernobyl d. 1872
Isaiah Meshullam Zussia of Chernobyl d. 1881
Solomon Ben-Zion Yenuka mi-Chernobyl d. 1939
Menahem Nahum of Loyev d. 1871
Mordecai d. 1909
Abraham Joshua Heschel of Chudnov d. 1914
Hayyim Isaac of Loyev–Kiev d. 1943
Mordecai Israel of Khotin d. Holocaust
Baruch Asher d. 1905
Solomon Samuel
Jacob Israel of Hornistopol—Cherkassy d. 1876
Mordecai Dov of Hornistopol d. 1904
Moses of Korostyshev d. 1866
Mordecai d. 1916
Nahum of Makarov d. 1852
Jacob Isaac of Makarov d. 1892
Moses Mordecai of Berdichev d. 1920
Zevi Aryeh d. 1938
David of Kiev d. 1902
Nahum of Makarov
Nisan Judah Leib of Kielce d. 1941
Isaiah of Makarov
Abraham Joshua Heschel of Kiev
Jacob Isaac of Kiev—U.S.A. d. 1945
Abraham of Trisk d. 1889
Menahem Nahum of Brisk d. 1887
Moses Leib of Chelm
Nahum'che of Chelm d. Holocaust
Mordecai Zussia of Jassy
David of Buhusi d. 1938
Mordecai of Kuzhmir d. 1917
Jacob Leib of Trisk d. 1912
Moses Mordecai of Lublin d. 1943
David Aaron of Zarek
David of Talnoye d. 1882
Mordecai d. c. 1870
Menahem Nahum d. 1916
Meshullam Zussia Boston
Moses Zevi Philadelphia
David Mordecai d. 1957
Johanan Jerusalem b. 1906
Isaac of Skvira d. 1885
Abraham Joshua Heschel d. 1886
Jacob Judah
Moses Dan d. 1920
Joseph Meir of Makhnovka d. 1917
Abraham Joshua Heschel
Israel d. 1919
David d. 1920
Menahem Nahum of Spikov d. 1886
Mordecai
Isaac Nahum of Rava-Russkaya d. 1943
Johanan of Rotmistrovka d. 1895
David of Zlatopol d. 1914
Mordecai Joseph d. 1929
Zevi Aryeh Israel
Mordecai of Rotmistrovka–Jerusalem d. 1921
Menahem Nahum d. 1936
Abraham Dov
Phinehas of Przemyslany d. 1943
David
Ze'ev d. 1937

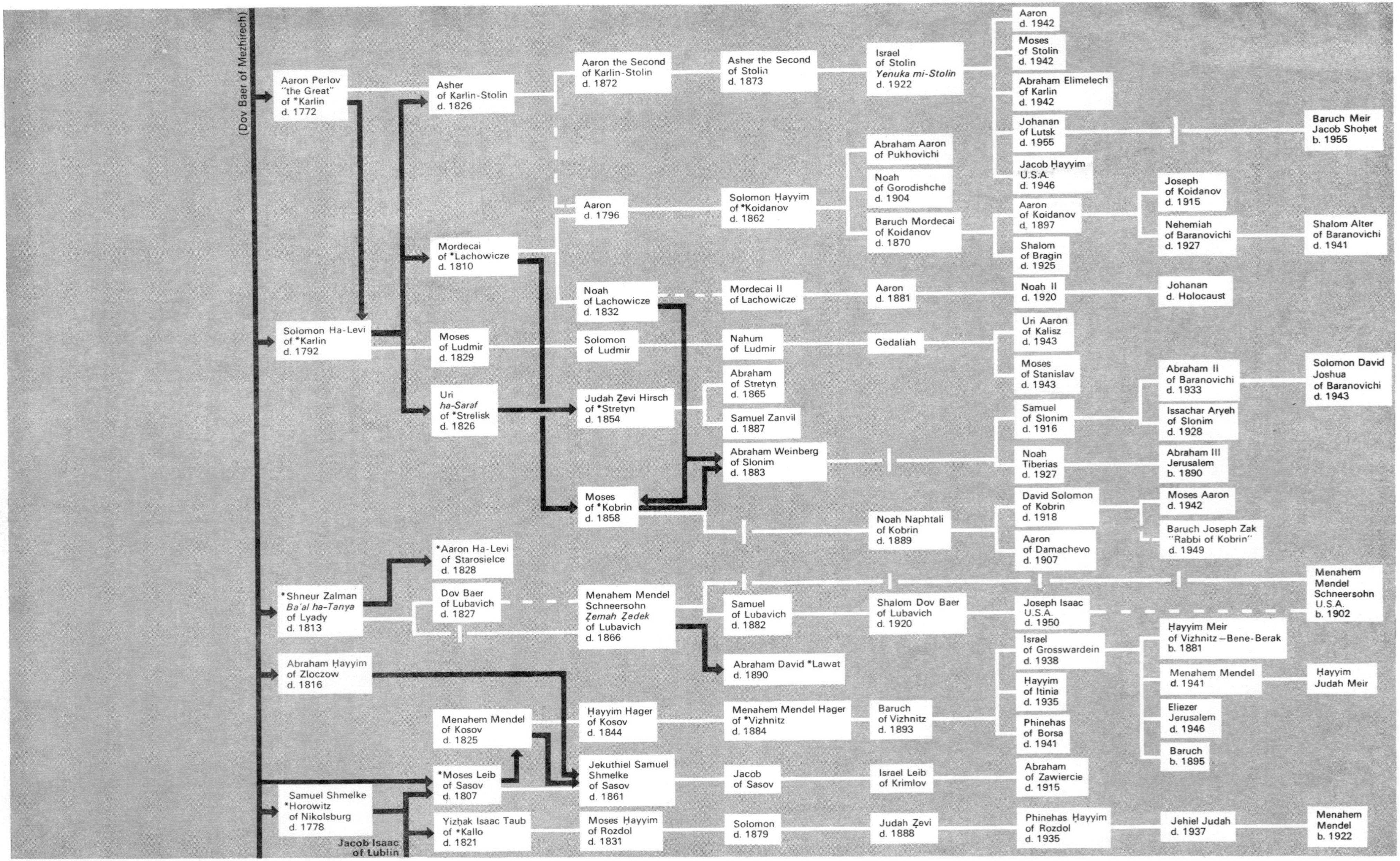
(Dov Baer of Mezhirech)
Aaron Perlov "the Great" of *Karlin d. 1772
Asher of Karlin-Stolin d. 1826
Aaron the Second of Karlin-Stolin d. 1872
Asher the Second of Stolin d. 1873
Israel of Stolin *Yenuka mi-Stolin* d. 1922
Aaron d. 1942
Moses of Stolin d. 1942
Abraham Elimelech of Karlin d. 1942
Johanan of Lutsk d. 1955
Baruch Meir Jacob Shoḥet b. 1955
Jacob Ḥayyim U.S.A. d. 1946
Aaron d. 1796
Solomon Ḥayyim of *Koidanov d. 1862
Abraham Aaron of Pukhovichi
Noah of Gorodishche d. 1904
Baruch Mordecai of Koidanov d. 1870
Aaron of Koidanov d. 1897
Joseph of Koidanov d. 1915
Nehemiah of Baranovichi d. 1927
Shalom Alter of Baranovichi d. 1941
Shalom of Bragin d. 1925
Mordecai of *Lachowicze d. 1810
Noah of Lachowicze d. 1832
Mordecai II of Lachowicze
Aaron d. 1881
Noah II d. 1920
Johanan d. Holocaust
Solomon Ha-Levi of *Karlin d. 1792
Moses of Ludmir d. 1829
Solomon of Ludmir
Nahum of Ludmir
Gedaliah
Uri Aaron of Kalisz d. 1943
Moses of Stanislav d. 1943
Uri *ha-Saraf* of *Strelisk d. 1826
Judah Ẓevi Hirsch of *Stretyn d. 1854
Abraham of Stretyn d. 1865
Samuel Zanvil d. 1887
Abraham Weinberg of Slonim d. 1883
Samuel of Slonim d. 1916
Abraham II of Baranovichi d. 1933
Solomon David Joshua of Baranovichi d. 1943
Issachar Aryeh of Slonim d. 1928
Noah Tiberias d. 1927
Abraham III Jerusalem b. 1890
Moses of *Kobrin d. 1858
Noah Naphtali of Kobrin d. 1889
David Solomon of Kobrin d. 1918
Moses Aaron d. 1942
Baruch Joseph Zak "Rabbi of Kobrin" d. 1949
Aaron of Damachevo d. 1907
*Shneur Zalman *Ba'al ha-Tanya* of Lyady d. 1813
*Aaron Ha-Levi of Starosielce d. 1828
Dov Baer of Lubavich d. 1827
Menahem Mendel Schneersohn *Ẓemah Ẓedek* of Lubavich d. 1866
Samuel of Lubavich d. 1882
Shalom Dov Baer of Lubavich d. 1920
Joseph Isaac U.S.A. d. 1950
Menahem Mendel Schneersohn U.S.A. b. 1902
Abraham David *Lawat d. 1890
Abraham Ḥayyim of Zloczow d. 1816
Menahem Mendel of Kosov d. 1825
Ḥayyim Hager of Kosov d. 1844
Menahem Mendel Hager of *Vizhnitz d. 1884
Baruch of Vizhnitz d. 1893
Israel of Grosswardein d. 1938
Ḥayyim Meir of Vizhnitz–Bene-Berak b. 1881
Menahem Mendel d. 1941
Ḥayyim Judah Meir
Eliezer Jerusalem d. 1946
Baruch b. 1895
Ḥayyim of Itinia d. 1935
Phinehas of Borsa d. 1941
*Moses Leib of Sasov d. 1807
Jekuthiel Samuel Shmelke of Sasov d. 1861
Jacob of Sasov
Israel Leib of Krimlov
Abraham of Zawiercie d. 1915
Samuel Shmelke *Horowitz of Nikolsburg d. 1778
Jacob Isaac of Lublin
Yiẓhak Isaac Taub of *Kallo d. 1821
Moses Ḥayyim of Rozdol d. 1831
Solomon d. 1879
Judah Ẓevi d. 1888
Phinehas Ḥayyim of Rozdol d. 1935
Jehiel Judah d. 1937
Menahem Mendel b. 1922

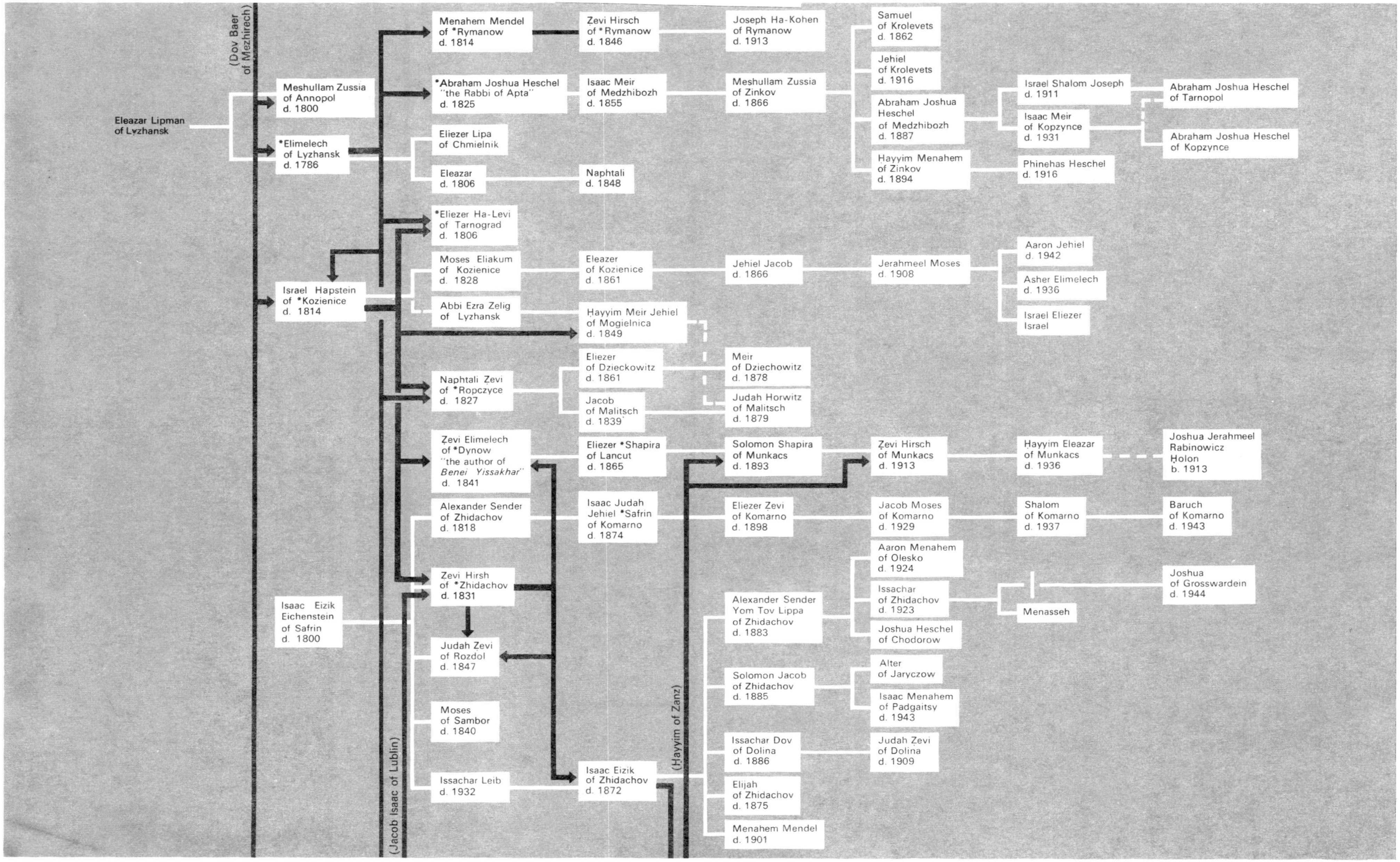

Eleazar Lipman of Lyzhansk
(Dov Baer of Mezhirech)
Meshullam Zussia of Annopol d. 1800
*Elimelech of Lyzhansk d. 1786
Israel Hapstein of *Kozienice d. 1814
Isaac Eizik Eichenstein of Safrin d. 1800
(Jacob Isaac of Lublin)
Menahem Mendel of *Rymanow d. 1814
*Abraham Joshua Heschel "the Rabbi of Apta" d. 1825
Eliezer Lipa of Chmielnik
Eleazar d. 1806
*Eliezer Ha-Levi of Tarnograd d. 1806
Moses Eliakum of Kozienice d. 1828
Abbi Ezra Zelig of Lyzhansk
Naphtali Zevi of *Ropczyce d. 1827
Ẓevi Elimelech of *Dynow "the author of Benei Yissakhar" d. 1841
Alexander Sender of Zhidachov d. 1818
Zevi Hirsh of *Zhidachov d. 1831
Judah Zevi of Rozdol d. 1847
Moses of Sambor d. 1840
Issachar Leib d. 1932
Zevi Hirsch of *Rymanow d. 1846
Isaac Meir of Medzhibozh d. 1855
Naphtali d. 1848
Eleazer of Kozienice d. 1861
Hayyim Meir Jehiel of Mogielnica d. 1849
Eliezer of Dzieckowitz d. 1861
Jacob of Malitsch d. 1839
Eliezer *Shapira of Lancut d. 1865
Isaac Judah Jehiel *Safrin of Komarno d. 1874
Isaac Eizik of Zhidachov d. 1872
(Hayyim of Zanz)
Joseph Ha-Kohen of Rymanow d. 1913
Meshullam Zussia of Zinkov d. 1866
Jehiel Jacob d. 1866
Meir of Dziechowitz d. 1878
Judah Horwitz of Malitsch d. 1879
Solomon Shapira of Munkacs d. 1893
Eliezer Zevi of Komarno d. 1898
Alexander Sender Yom Tov Lippa of Zhidachov d. 1883
Solomon Jacob of Zhidachov d. 1885
Issachar Dov of Dolina d. 1886
Elijah of Zhidachov d. 1875
Menahem Mendel d. 1901
Samuel of Krolevets d. 1862
Jehiel of Krolevets d. 1916
Abraham Joshua Heschel of Medzhibozh d. 1887
Hayyim Menahem of Zinkov d. 1894
Jerahmeel Moses d. 1908
Ẓevi Hirsch of Munkacs d. 1913
Jacob Moses of Komarno d. 1929
Aaron Menahem of Olesko d. 1924
Issachar of Zhidachov d. 1923
Joshua Heschel of Chodorow
Alter of Jaryczow
Isaac Menahem of Padgaitsy d. 1943
Judah Zevi of Dolina d. 1909
Israel Shalom Joseph d. 1911
Isaac Meir of Kopzynce d. 1931
Phinehas Heschel d. 1916
Aaron Jehiel d. 1942
Asher Elimelech d. 1936
Israel Eliezer Israel
Hayyim Eleazar of Munkacs d. 1936
Shalom of Komarno d. 1937
Menasseh
Abraham Joshua Heschel of Tarnopol
Abraham Joshua Heschel of Kopzynce
Joshua Jerahmeel Rabinowicz Holon b. 1913
Baruch of Komarno d. 1943
Joshua of Grosswardein d. 1944

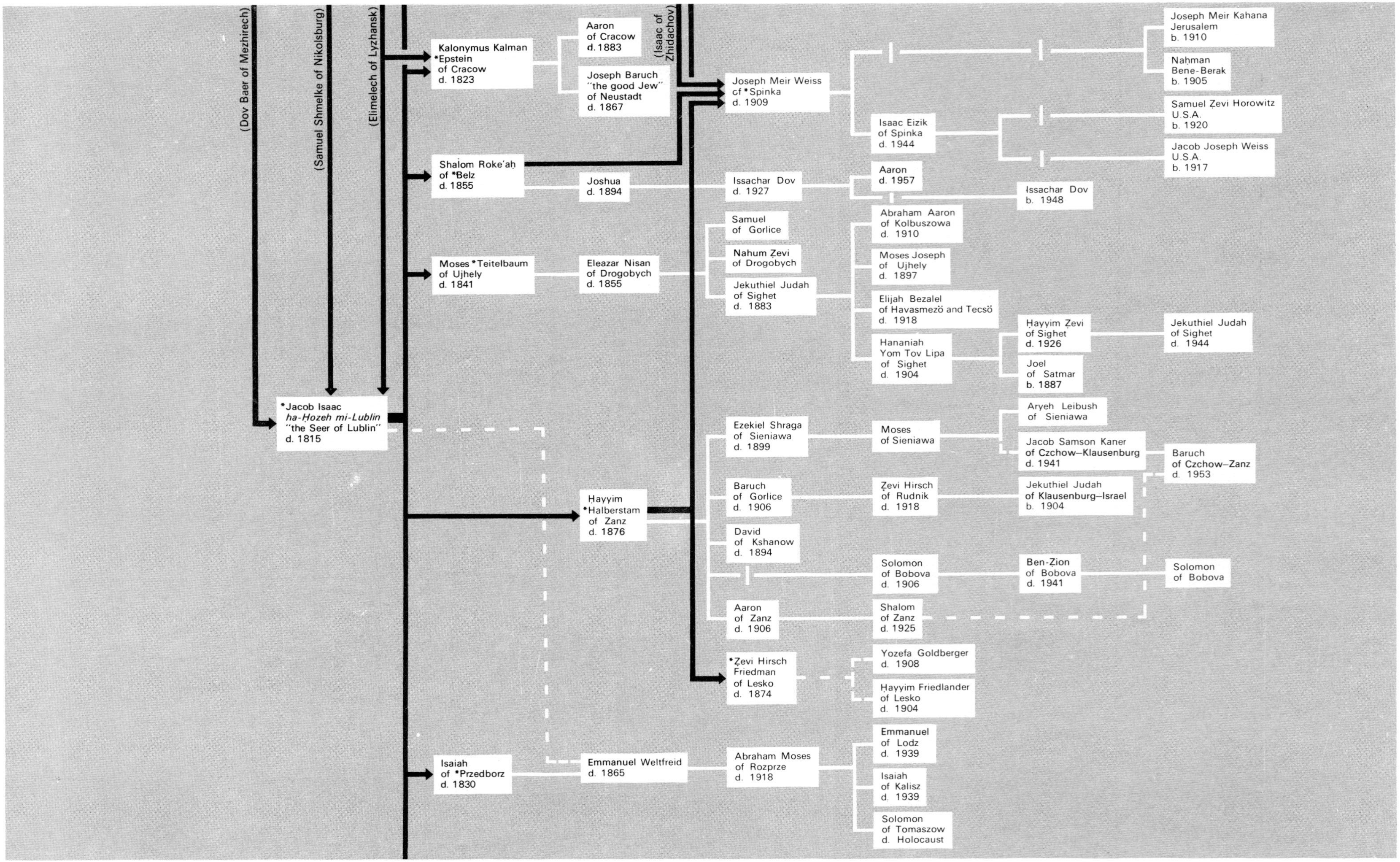
(Dov Baer of Mezhirech)
(Samuel Shmelke of Nikolsburg)
(Elimelech of Lyzhansk)
(Isaac of Zhidachov)
*Jacob Isaac ha-Hozeh mi-Lublin "the Seer of Lublin" d. 1815
Kalonymus Kalman *Epstein of Cracow d. 1823
Aaron of Cracow d. 1883
Joseph Baruch "the good Jew" of Neustadt d. 1867
Shalom Roke'aḥ of *Belz d. 1855
Joshua d. 1894
Issachar Dov d. 1927
Aaron d. 1957
Issachar Dov b. 1948
Moses *Teitelbaum of Ujhely d. 1841
Eleazar Nisan of Drogobych d. 1855
Samuel of Gorlice
Nahum Zevi of Drogobych
Jekuthiel Judah of Sighet d. 1883
Abraham Aaron of Kolbuszowa d. 1910
Moses Joseph of Ujhely d. 1897
Elijah Bezalel of Havasmezö and Tecsö d. 1918
Hananiah Yom Tov Lipa of Sighet d. 1904
Ḥayyim Ẓevi of Sighet d. 1926
Joel of Satmar b. 1887
Jekuthiel Judah of Sighet d. 1944
Joseph Meir Weiss of *Spinka d. 1909
Isaac Eizik of Spinka d. 1944
Joseph Meir Kahana Jerusalem b. 1910
Naḥman Bene-Berak b. 1905
Samuel Ẓevi Horowitz U.S.A. b. 1920
Jacob Joseph Weiss U.S.A. b. 1917
Ḥayyim *Halberstam of Zanz d. 1876
Ezekiel Shraga of Sieniawa d. 1899
Moses of Sieniawa
Aryeh Leibush of Sieniawa
Jacob Samson Kaner of Czchow–Klausenburg d. 1941
Baruch of Czchow–Zanz d. 1953
Baruch of Gorlice d. 1906
Ẓevi Hirsch of Rudnik d. 1918
Jekuthiel Judah of Klausenburg–Israel b. 1904
David of Kshanow d. 1894
Solomon of Bobova d. 1906
Ben-Zion of Bobova d. 1941
Solomon of Bobova
Aaron of Zanz d. 1906
Shalom of Zanz d. 1925
*Ẓevi Hirsch Friedman of Lesko d. 1874
Yozefa Goldberger d. 1908
Ḥayyim Friedlander of Lesko d. 1904
Isaiah of *Przedborz d. 1830
Emmanuel Weltfreid d. 1865
Abraham Moses of Rozprze d. 1918
Emmanuel of Lodz d. 1939
Isaiah of Kalisz d. 1939
Solomon of Tomaszow d. Holocaust

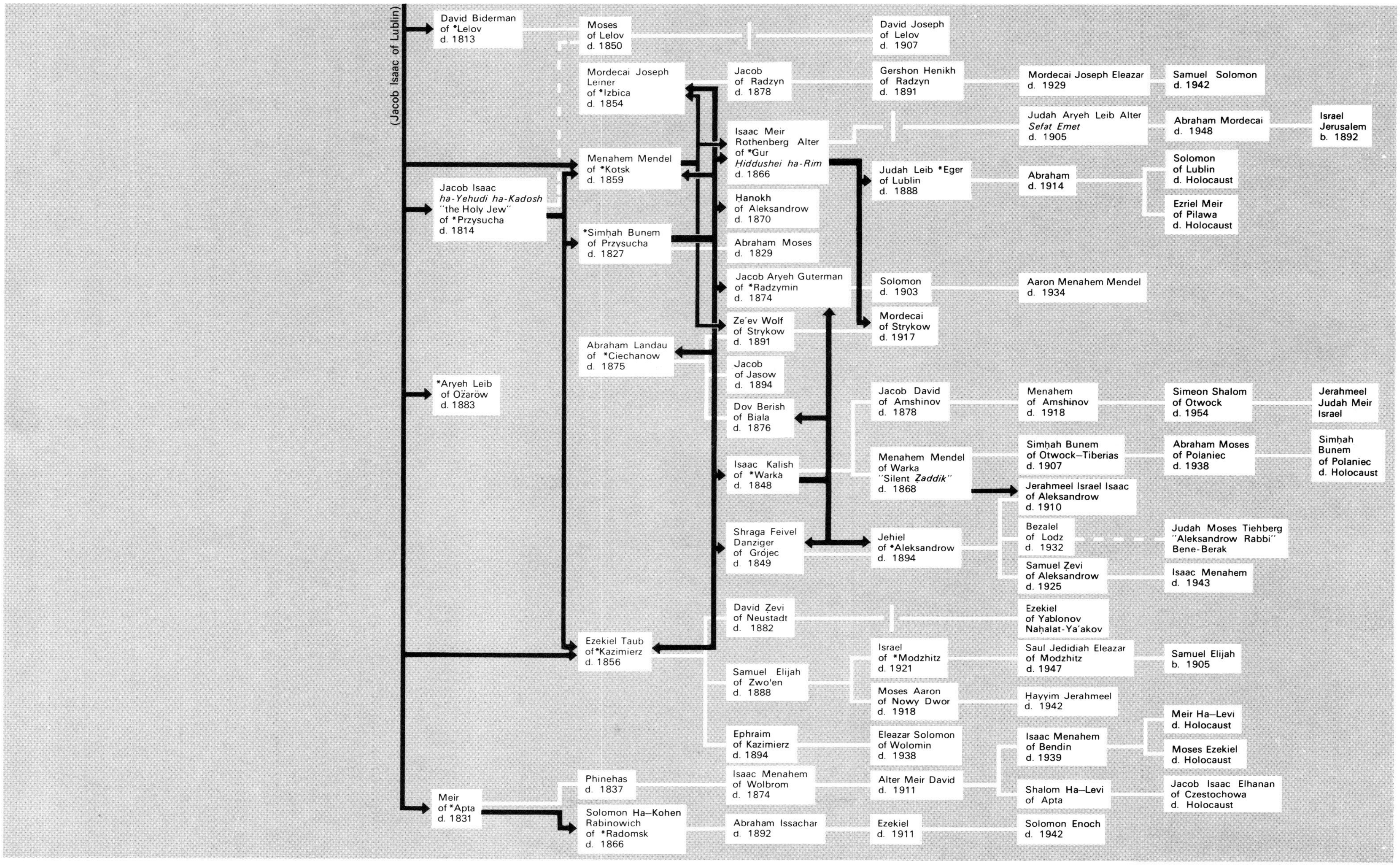
(Jacob Isaac of Lublin)
David Biderman of *Lelov d. 1813
Jacob Isaac ha-Yehudi ha-Kadosh "the Holy Jew" of *Przysucha d. 1814
*Aryeh Leib of Ożarów d. 1883
Meir of *Apta d. 1831
Moses of Lelov d. 1850
Mordecai Joseph Leiner of *Izbica d. 1854
Menahem Mendel of *Kotsk d. 1859
*Simḥah Bunem of Przysucha d. 1827
Abraham Landau of *Ciechanow d. 1875
Ezekiel Taub of *Kazimierz d. 1856
Phinehas d. 1837
Solomon Ha-Kohen Rabinowich of *Radomsk d. 1866
Jacob of Radzyn d. 1878
Isaac Meir Rothenberg Alter of *Gur Ḥiddushei ha-Rim d. 1866
Ḥanokh of Aleksandrow d. 1870
Abraham Moses d. 1829
Jacob Aryeh Guterman of *Radzymin d. 1874
Ze'ev Wolf of Strykow d. 1891
Jacob of Jasow d. 1894
Dov Berish of Biala d. 1876
Isaac Kalish of *Warka d. 1848
Shraga Feivel Danziger of Grójec d. 1849
David Ẓevi of Neustadt d. 1882
Samuel Elijah of Zwo'en d. 1888
Ephraim of Kazimierz d. 1894
Isaac Menahem of Wolbrom d. 1874
Abraham Issachar d. 1892
David Joseph of Lelov d. 1907
Gershon Henikh of Radzyn d. 1891
Judah Leib *Eger of Lublin d. 1888
Solomon d. 1903
Mordecai of Strykow d. 1917
Jacob David of Amshinov d. 1878
Menahem Mendel of Warka "Silent Ẓaddik" d. 1868
Jehiel of *Aleksandrow d. 1894
Israel of *Modzhitz d. 1921
Moses Aaron of Nowy Dwor d. 1918
Eleazar Solomon of Wolomin d. 1938
Alter Meir David d. 1911
Ezekiel d. 1911
Mordecai Joseph Eleazar d. 1929
Judah Aryeh Leib Alter Sefat Emet d. 1905
Abraham d. 1914
Aaron Menahem Mendel d. 1934
Menahem of Amshinov d. 1918
Simḥah Bunem of Otwock–Tiberias d. 1907
Jerahmeel Israel Isaac of Aleksandrow d. 1910
Bezalel of Lodz d. 1932
Samuel Ẓevi of Aleksandrow d. 1925
Ezekiel of Yablonov Naḥalat-Ya'akov
Saul Jedidiah Eleazar of Modzhitz d. 1947
Ḥayyim Jerahmeel d. 1942
Isaac Menahem of Bendin d. 1939
Shalom Ha–Levi of Apta
Solomon Enoch d. 1942
Samuel Solomon d. 1942
Abraham Mordecai d. 1948
Solomon of Lublin d. Holocaust
Ezriel Meir of Pilawa d. Holocaust
Simeon Shalom of Otwock d. 1954
Abraham Moses of Polaniec d. 1938
Judah Moses Tiehberg "Aleksandrow Rabbi" Bene-Berak
Isaac Menahem d. 1943
Samuel Elijah b. 1905
Meir Ha–Levi d. Holocaust
Moses Ezekiel d. Holocaust
Jacob Isaac Elhanan of Czestochowa d. Holocaust
Israel Jerusalem b. 1892
Jerahmeel Judah Meir Israel
Simḥah Bunem of Polaniec d. Holocaust

ISRAEL PLACE LIST (1970)

PLACES OF JEWISH HABITATION IN ISRAEL AND THE ADMINISTERED TERRITORIES

G —Gadna	IK — Iḥud ha-Kevuẓot ve-ha-Kibbutzim	M —Mapam
Ḥ —Ḥerut	KA —Ha-Kibbutz ha-Arẓi (Ha-Shomer ha-Ẓa'ir)	OẒ —Ha-Oved ha-Ẓiyyoni
H —Histadrut	KD —Ha-Kibbutz ha-Dati	PAI —Po'alei Agudat Israel
HI —Hitaḥadut ha-Ikkarim	KM —Ha-Kibbutz ha-Me'uḥad	PM —Ha-Po'el ha-Mizrachi
IḤ —Iḥud Ḥakla'i		TM —Tenu'at ha-Moshavim

Name	Geographical Region	Year of Founding	Settlement Form	Affiliation	Municipal Status	No. of inhabitants 31 Dec 70
Acre (Akko)	Acre Plain	—	Town		municipality	33,900 (thereof 8,850 non-Jews)
Adamit	Western Upper Galilee	1958	Kibbutz	KA	RC Sullam Ẓor	. .
Adanim	Southern Sharon	1950	Moshav	RC	RC Ha-Yarkon	200
Adderet	Judean Foothills (Adullam Region)	1961	Moshav	TM	RC Matteh Yehudah	255
Addirim	Jezreel Valley (Taanach Region)	1956	Moshav	TM	RC Ha-Gilboa	362
Afek	Acre Plain	1939	Kibbutz	KM	RC Na'aman	420
Afikim	Kinneret Valley	1932	Kibbutz	IK	RC Jordan Valley	1,350
Afulah (Ir Yizre'el)	Jezreel Valley	1925	Urban Settlement		local council	16,900
Agur	Southern Judean Foothills	1950	Moshav	TM	RC Matteh Yehudah	295
Aḥi'ezer	Coastal Plain (Lod Region)	1950	Moshav	PM	RC Lod Plain	875
Aḥihud	Acre Plain	1950	Moshav	TM	RC Na'aman	498
Aḥisamakh	Coastal Plain (Lod Region)	1950	Moshav	TM	RC Modi'im	660
Aḥituv	Central Sharon (Ḥefer Plain)	1951	Moshav	TM	RC Ḥefer Plain	585
Aḥuzzam	Southern Coastal Plain (Lachish Region)	1950	Moshav	OẒ	RC Lachish	525
Aḥuzzat Naftali	Eastern Lower Galilee	1949	Institution (Yeshivah)	PM	(RC) Lower Galilee	28
Allon Shevut	Hebron Hills; 67+	1971	Rural Center	PM		. .
Allonei Abba	Southern Lower Galilee	1948	Moshav Shittufi	OẒ	RC Kishon	232
Allonei Yiẓḥak	Manasseh Hills	1949	Youth Village	OẒ	(RC) Manasseh	380
Allonim	Jezreel Valley	1938	Kibbutz	KM	RC Kishon	480
Almagor	Kinneret Valley	1961	Moshav	TM	RC Jordan Valley	79
Almah	Eastern Upper Galilee	1949	Moshav	PM	RC Merom ha-Galil	640
Alumim	Northwestern Negev (Besor Region)	1966	Kibbutz	KD	RC Azzatah	76
Alummah	Southern Coastal Plain (Malakhi Region)	1965	Rural Center		(RC) Shafir	129

NOTES:
Geographical Region: The sign "67+" indicates a settlement beyond the pre-1967 borders.
Year of Founding: Where the year is not indicated, the settlement is ancient.
Where the year is given in brackets, the place was temporarily abandoned and resettled in the year given.
Form of Settlement: Only the present form of settlement is given.
Affiliation: Only the present affiliation is given.
Municipal Status: RC—the settlement is represented in the regional council indicated.
(RC)—the settlement belongs to the area of the regional council, but is not represented in it.
No. of Inhabitants: The sign . . indicates that the population figures are not available.

Name	Geographical Region	Year of Founding	Settlement Form	Affiliation	Municipal Status	No. of inhabitants 31 Dec 70
Alummot (Bitanyah)	Kinneret Valley	1941	Kibbutz	IK	RC Jordan Valley	66
Amaẓyah	Lachish (Adoraim) Region	1955	Moshav Shittufi	Ḥ	RC Lachish	. .
Amir	Ḥuleh Valley	1939	Kibbutz	KA	RC Ha-Galil ha-Elyon	400
Amirim	Eastern Upper Galilee	1950	Moshav	TM	RC Merom ha-Galil	130
Amkah	Acre Plain	1949	Moshav	TM	RC Ga'aton	585
Ammi'ad	Eastern Upper Galilee (Hazor Region)	1946	Kibbutz	IK	RC Ha-Galil ha-Elyon	251
Ammikam	Iron Hills (Northwestern Samaria)	1950	Moshav	Ḥ	RC Allonah	120
Amminadav	Jerusalem Hills	1950	Moshav	TM	RC Matteh Yehudah	255
Ammi'oz	Northwestern Negev (Besor Region)	1957	Moshav	TM	RC Eshkol	226
Arad	Northeastern Negev	1961	Urban Settlement	—	local council	4,350
Arbel	Eastern Lower Galilee	1949	Moshav	TM	RC Ha-Galil ha-Taḥton	164
Argaman	Lower Jordan Valley; 67 +	1968	Moshav (Kibbutz)	Ḥ		. .
Arugot	Southern Coastal Plain (Malakhi Region)	1949	Moshav	TM	RC Be'er Tuviyyah	250
Aseret	Coastal Plain, (Reḥovot Region)	1954	Rural Center	—	RC Gederot	480
Ashdod	Southern Coastal Plain	1955	City		Township	37,600
Ashdot Ya'akov	Kinneret Valley	1933	Kibbutz	IK	RC Jordan Valley	. .
Ashdot Ya'akov	Kinneret Valley	1933	Kibbutz	KM	RC Jordan Valley	. .
Ashkelon	Southern Coastal Plain	—	City		municipality	40,100
Athlit	Carmel Coast	1904	Urban Settlement		local council	2,170
Avdon	Western Upper Galilee	1952	Moshav	TM	RC Ma'aleh ha-Galil	319
Avi'el	Northern Sharon (Ḥaderah Region)	1949	Moshav	Ḥ	RC Allonah	212
Avi'ezer	Judean Foothills	1958	Moshav	PM	RC Matteh Yehudah	230
Avigedor	Southern Coastal Plain (Malakhi Region)	1950	Moshav	TM	RC Be'er Tuviyyah	326
Aviḥayil	Central Sharon	1932	Moshav	TM	RC Ḥefer Plain	590
Avital	Jezreel Valley (Taanach Region)	1953	Moshav	TM	RC Ha-Gilboa	370
Avivim	Eastern Upper Galilee	1960	Moshav	TM	RC Merom ha-Galil	. .
Ayanot	Coastal Plain (Rishon le-Zion Region)	1930	Agricultural School	—	—	428
Ayyelet ha-Shaḥar	Ḥuleh Valley	1918	Kibbutz	IK	Ha-Galil ha-Elyon	750
Azaryah	Judean Foothills	1949	Moshav	TM	RC Gezer	462
Azor	Coastal Plain (Tel Aviv Region)	1948	Urban Settlement	—	local council	5,250
Azri'el	Southern Sharon (Kefar Sava Region)	1951	Moshav	PM	RC Hadar ha-Sharon	485
Azrikam	Southern Coastal Plain (Malakhi Region)	1950	Moshav	TM	RC Be'er Tuviyyah	600
Baḥan	Central Sharon	1953	Kibbutz	IK	RC Ḥefer Plain	267

Name	Geographical Region	Year of Founding	Settlement Form	Affiliation	Municipal Status	No. of inhabitants 31 Dec 70
Balfouriyyah	Jezreel Valley	1922	Moshav	TM	RC Yizre'el	230
Barak	Jezreel Valley (Taanach Region)	1956	Moshav	TM	RC Ha-Gilboa	260
Baram	Eastern Upper Galilee	1949	Kibbutz	KA	RC Merom ha-Galil	310
Bareket	Coastal Plain (Petaḥ Tikvah Region)	1952	Moshav	PM	RC Modi'im	740
Bar Giora	Jerusalem Hills	1950	Moshav	Ḥ	RC Matteh Yehudah	203
Barkai	Iron Hills (Northwestern Samaria)	1949	Kibbutz	KA	RC Manasseh	330
Bat Shelomo	Manasseh Hills	1889	Moshav	HI	RC Ḥof ha-Karmel	170
Bat Yam	Coastal Plain (Tel Aviv Region)	1926	City		municipality	83,500
Be'eri	Northwestern Negev (Eshkol Region)	1946	Kibbutz	KH	RC Eshkol	500
Be'er Orah	Southern Arabah Valley	1950	Youth Camp	G	(RC) Ḥevel Eilot	. .
Be'erotayim	Coastal Plain (Ḥefer Plain)	1949	Moshav	TM	RC Ḥefer Plain	270
Be'erot Yiẓḥak	Coastal Plain (Petaḥ Tikvah Region)	1948	Kibbutz	PM	RC Modi'im	281
Beersheba (Be'er Sheva)	Northern Negev	(1948)	City		municipality	77,400
Be'er Tuviyyah	Southern Coastal Plain (Malakhi Region)	1930	Moshav	TM	RC Be'er Tuviyyah	650
Be'er Ya'akov	Coastal Plain (Lod Region)	1907	Urban Settlement		local council	4,140
Beko'a	Judean Foothills	1951	Moshav	TM	RC Matteh Yehudah	476
Ben Ammi	Acre Plain	1949	Moshav	TM	RC Ga'aton	300
Benayah	Southern Coastal Plain (Reḥovot Region)	1949	Moshav	TM	RC Brenner	280
Bene-Berak	Coastal Plain (Tel Aviv Region)	1924	City		municipality	72,100
Benei Atarot	Coastal Plain (Petaḥ Tikvah Region)	1948	Moshav	TM	RC Modi'im	291
Benei Ayish	Southern Coastal Plain (Reḥovot Region)	1958	Village	—	RC Ḥevel Yavneh	955
Benei Darom	Coastal Plain (Reḥovot Region)	1949	Moshav Shittufi	PM	RC Ḥevel Yavneh	175
Benei Deror	Southern Sharon	1946	Moshav Shittufi	TM	RC Hadar ha-Sharon	219
Benei Re'em	Coastal Plain (Reḥovot Region)	1949	Moshav	PAI	RC Naḥal Sorek	311
Benei Zion	Southern Sharon (Herzliyyah Region)	1947	Moshav	IḤ	RC Ḥof ha-Sharon	380
Ben Shemen	Coastal Plain (Lod Region)	1921	Youth Village		(RC) Modi'im	800
Ben Shemen	Coastal Plain (Lod Region)	1952	Moshav	TM	RC Modi'im	200
Ben Zakkai	Southern Coastal Plain (Reḥovot Region)	1950	Moshav	PM	RC Ḥevel Yavneh	610
Berekhyah	Southern Coastal Plain (Ashkelon Region)	1950	Moshav	TM	RC Ḥof Ashkelon	735
Berosh	Northern Negev (Gerar Region)	1953	Moshav	TM	RC Benei Shimon	369
Beror Ḥayil	Southern Coastal Plain (Ashkelon Region)	1948	Kibbutz	IK	RC Sha'ar ha-Negev	540
Bet Alfa	Harod Valley	1922	Kibbutz	KA	RC Ha-Gilboa	695
Bet Arif	Coastal Plain (Lod Region)	1951	Moshav	TM	RC Modi'im	550
Bet Berl	Southern Sharon	1947	Educational Center	H	(RC) Ha-Sharon ha-Tikhon	280
Bet Dagan	Coastal Plain (Lod Region)	1948	Urban Settlement		local council	2,740
Bet Elazari	Coastal Plain (Reḥovot Region)	1948	Moshav	TM	RC Brenner	425

Name	Geographical Region	Year of Founding	Settlement Form	Affiliation	Municipal Status	No. of inhabitants 31 Dec 70
Bet Eżra	Southern Coastal Plain (Malakhi Region)	1950	Moshav	TM	RC Be'er Tuviyyah	565
Bet Gamli'el	Coastal Plain (Reḥovot Region)	1949	Moshav	PM	RC Ḥevel Yavneh	395
Bet Guvrin	Southern Judean Foothills	1949	Kibbutz	KM	RC Yo'av	120
Bet ha-Emek	Acre Plain	1949	Kibbutz	IK	RC Ga'aton	314
Bet ha-Gaddi	Northern Negev (Gerar Region)	1949	Moshav	PM	RC Azzatah	650
Bet ha-Levi	Central Sharon (Ḥefer Plain)	1945	Moshav	TM	RC Ḥefer Plain	219
Bet ha-Shittah	Harod Valley	1935	Kibbutz	KM	RC Ha-Gilboa	870
Bet Ḥanan	Coastal Plain (Rishon le-Zion Region)	1930	Moshav	TM	RC Gan Raveh	360
Bet Ḥananyah	Northern Sharon (Ḥaderah Region)	1950	Moshav	TM	RC Ḥof ha-Karmel	260
Bet Ḥerut	Central Sharon (Ḥefer Plain)	1933	Moshav Shittufi	TM	RC Ḥefer Plain	294
Bet Ḥilkiyyah	Coastal Plain (Reḥovot Region)	1953	Moshav	PAI	RC Naḥal Sorek	262
Bet Hillel	Ḥuleh Valley	1940	Moshav	TM	RC Ha-Galil ha-Elyon	173
Beth-Shean	Beth-Shean Valley	—	Urban Settlement	—	local council	11,900
Beth-Shemesh (Formerly Hartuv)	Judean Foothills	1950	Urban Settlement	—	local council	10,200
Bet Kamah	Northern Negev (Gerar Region)	1949	Kibbutz	KA	RC Benei Shimon	250
Bet Keshet	Eastern Lower Galilee	1944	Kibbutz	KM	RC Ha-Galil ha-Taḥton	280
Bet Leḥem ha-Gelilit	Southern Lower Galilee	1948	Moshav	TM	RC Kishon	270
Bet Me'ir	Judean Hills	1950	Moshav	PM	RC Matteh Yehudah	310
Bet Neḥemyah	Northern Judean Foothills (Lod Region)	1950	Moshav	OẒ	RC Modi'im	257
Bet Nekofah	Jerusalem Hills	1949	Moshav	TM	RC Matteh Yehudah	196
Bet Nir	Southern Coastal Plain (Lachish Region)	1955	Kibbutz	KA	RC Yo'av	170
Bet Oren	Mount Carmel	1939	Kibbutz	KM	RC Ḥof ha-Karmel	200
Bet Oved	Coastal Plain (Rishon le-Zion Region)	1933	Moshav	TM	RC Gan Raveh	208
Bet Rabban	Coastal Plain (Reḥovot Region)	1946	Yeshivah	KD	RC Ḥevel Yavneh	350
Bet She'arim	Jezreel Valley	1936	Moshav	TM	RC Kishon	308
Bet Shikmah	Southern Coastal Plain (Ashkelon Region)	1950	Moshav	TM	RC Ḥof Ashkelon	550
Bet Uzzi'el	Judean Foothills (Lod Region)	1956	Moshav	PM	RC Gezer	350
Bet Yannai	Central Sharon (Ḥefer Plain)	1933	Moshav	IḤ	RC Ḥefer Plain	234
Bet Yehoshu'a	Southern Sharon (Netanyah Region)	1938	Moshav	OẒ	RC Ḥof ha-Sharon	234
Bet Yiẓḥak	Central Sharon Ḥefer Plain)	1940	Rural Settlement	—	RC Ḥefer Plain	810
Bet Yosef	Beth-Shean Valley	1937	Moshav	TM	RC Beth-Shean Valley	315
Bet Zayit	Jerusalem Hills	1949	Moshav	TM	RC Matteh Yehudah	485
Bet Zera	Kinneret Valley	1927	Kibbutz	KA	RC Jordan Valley	650
Bet Ẓevi (Kefar Sitrin)	Carmel Coast	1953	Educational Institute	—	(RC) Ḥof ha-Karmel	312
Beẓet	Acre Plain	1949	Moshav	TM	RC Sullam Ẓor	243
Binyaminah	Northern Sharon (Ḥaderah Region)	1922	Urban Settlement	—	local council	2,520

Name	Geographical Region	Year of Founding	Settlement Form	Affiliation	Municipal Status	No. of inhabitants 31 Dec 70
Biranit	Western Upper Galilee	1964	Rural Settlement	—	(RC) Ma'aleh ha-Galil	. .
Biriyyah	Eastern Upper Galilee	1945	Rural Settlement	—	RC Merom ha-Galil	335
Bitan Aharon	Central Sharon (Ḥefer Plain)	1936	Moshav	IH	RC Ḥefer Plain	100
Bitḥah	Northwestern Negev (Besor Region)	1950	Moshav	TM	RC Merḥavim	700
Biẓẓaron	Southern Coastal Plain (Malakhi Region)	1935	Moshav	TM	RC Be'er Tuviyyah	410
Boẓrah	Southern Sharon (Kefar Sava Region)	1946	Moshav	IH	RC Ḥof ha-Sharon	425
Burgetah	Central Sharon (Ḥefer Plain)	1949	Moshav	TM	RC Ḥefer Plain	333
Bustan ha-Galil	Acre Plain	1948	Moshav	IH	RC Ga'aton	320
Dafnah	Ḥuleh Valley	1939	Kibbutz	KM	RC Ha-Galil ha-Elyon	570
Daliyyah	Manasseh Hills	1939	Kibbutz	KA	RC Megiddo	600
Dalton	Eastern Upper Galilee	1950	Moshav	PM	RC Merom ha-Galil	650
Dan	Ḥuleh Valley	1939	Kibbutz	KA	RC Ha-Galil ha-Elyon	440
Daverat	Jezreel Valley	1946	Kibbutz	IK	RC Yizre'el	298
Deganim (Merkaz Shapira)	Southern Coastal Plain (Malakhi Region)	1948	Rural Center	—	(RC) Shafir	474
Deganyah (Deganiyyah) Alef	Kinneret Valley	1909	Kibbutz	IK	RC Jordan Valley	442
Deganyah (Deganiyyah) Bet	Kinneret Valley	1920	Kibbutz	IK	RC Jordan Valley	525
Devirah	Northern Negev (Beersheba Region)	1951	Kibbutz	KA	RC Benei Shimon	175
Devorah	Jezreel Valley (Taanach Region)	1956	Moshav	TM	RC Ha-Gilboa	300
Dimonah	Negev Hills	1955	City	—	municipality	22,500
Dishon	Eastern Upper Galilee	1953	Moshav	OẒ	RC Ha-Galil ha-Elyon	. .
Dor	Carmel Coast	1949	Moshav	TM	RC Ḥof ha-Karmel	170
Dorot	Southern Coastal Plain (Ashkelon Region)	1941	Kibbutz	IK	RC Sha'ar ha-Negev	410
Dovev	Eastern Upper Galilee	1963	Moshav	TM	RC Merom ha-Galil	. .
Ein Ayyalah	Carmel Coast	1949	Moshav	TM	RC Ḥof ha-Karmel	302
Efal-Bet Avot	Coastal Plain (Tel Aviv Region)	1950	Aged People's Home	—	RC Ono	350
Efal-Merkaz Seminariyyonim	Coastal Plain (Tel Aviv Region)	1950	Educational Institute	—	RC Ono	46
Eilat (Elath)	Southern Negev	1951	Town	—	municipality	14,600
Eilon	Western Upper Galilee	1938	Kibbutz	KA	RC Sullam Ẓor	590
Eilot	Eilat Hills	1962	Kibbutz	KM	RC Ḥevel Eilot	. .
Einat	Coastal Main (Petaḥ Tikvah Region)	1925	Kibbutz	IK	RC Mifalot Afek	480
Ein Ayyalah	Carmel Coast	1949	Moshav	TM	RC Ḥof ha-Karmel	302
Ein Gev	Kinneret Valley	1937	Kibbutz	IK	RC Jordan Valley	300
Ein ha-Emek	Manasseh Hills	1944	Rural Settlement	—	RC Megiddo	315
Ein ha-Ḥoresh	Central Sharon (Ḥefer Plain)	1931	Kibbutz	KA	RC Ḥefer Plain	590
Ein ha-Mifraẓ	Zebulun Valley	1938	Kibbutz	KA	RC Na'aman	600
Ein ha-Naẓiv	Beth-Shean Valley	1946	Kibbutz	KD	RC Beth-Shean Valley	354

Name	Geographical Region	Year of Founding	Settlement Form	Affiliation	Municipal Status	No. of inhabitants 31 Dec 70
Ein ha-Sheloshah	Northwestern Begev (Besor Region)	1950	Kibbutz	OẒ	RC Eshkol	242
Ein ha-Shofet	Manasseh Hills	1937	Kibbutz	KA	RC Megiddo	600
Ein Hod	Mount Carmel	1954	Artists' Village	—	(RC) Ḥof ha-Karmel	34
Ein Iron	Northern Sharon (Ḥaderah Region)	1934	Moshav	TM	RC Manasseh	192
Ein Karmel	Carmel Coast	1947	Kibbutz	KM	RC Ḥof ha-Karmel	399
Ein Sarid	Southern Sharon (Kefar Sava Region)	1950	F Settlement	—	RC Hadar ha-Sharon	500
Ein Shemer	Northern Sharon (Ḥaderah Region)	1927	Kibbutz	KA	RC Manasseh	550
Ein Vered	Southern Sharon (Kefar Sava Region)	1930	Moshav	TM	RC Hadar ha-Sharon	520
Ein Ya'akov	Western Upper Galilee	1950	Moshav	TM	RC Ma'aleh ha-Galil	281
Ein Yahav	Central Arabah Valley	1951	Moshav	TM	RC Ḥevel Eilot	. . .
Ein Zivan	Golan; 67+	1968	Kibbutz	KM	—	. .
Ein Ẓurim	Southern Coastal Plain (Shafir Region)	1949	Kibbutz	KD	RC Shafir	340
Eitan	Southern Coastal Plain (Lachish Region)	1955	Moshav	PM	RC Shafir	463
Eitanim	Jerusalem Hills	1952	Hospital	—	(RC) Matteh Yehudah	212
El Al (Naḥal El Al)	Golan; 67+	1968	Moshav	TM	—	. .
Elifelet	Eastern Upper Galilee (Hazor Region)	1949	Moshav	TM	RC Ha-Galil ha-Elyon	370
Elishama	Southern Sharon	1951	Moshav	TM	RC Ha-Yarkon	565
Elkosh	Western Upper Galilee	1949	Moshav	TM	RC Ma'aleh ha-Galil	320
Elyakhin	Central Sharon (Ḥefer Plain)	1950	Rural Settlement	—	RC Ḥefer Plain	1,785
Elyakim	Manasseh Hills	1949	Moshav	TM	RC Megiddo	640
Elyashiv	Central Sharon (Ḥefer Plain)	1933	Moshav	HI	RC Ḥefer Plain	360
Emunim	Southern Coastal Plain (Malakhi Region)	1950	Moshav	TM	RC Be'er Tuviyyah	405
Enat	Coastal Plain (Petaḥ Tikvah Region)	1925	Kibbutz	IK	RC Mifalot Afek	490
En-Dor	Eastern Lower Galilee	1948	Kibbutz	KA	RC Yizre'el	545
En-Gedi	Dead Sea Region	1953	Kibbutz	IK	RC Tamar	. .
En-Harod	Harod Valley	1921	Kibbutz	IK	RC Ha-Gilboa	690
En-Harod	Harod Valley	1921	Kibbutz	KM	RC Ha-Gilboa	755
Erez	Southern Coastal Plain (Ashkelon Region)	1949	Kibbutz	IK	RC Sha'ar ha-Negev	203
Eshbol	Northern Negev (Gerar Region)	1955	Moshav	TM	RC Merḥavim	418
Eshel ha-Nasi	Northern Negev (Besor Region)	1952	Agricultural School	—	(RC) Merḥavim	260
Eshtaol	Judean Foothills	1949	Moshav	TM	RC Matteh Yehudah	333
Even Menaḥem	Western Upper Galilee	1960	Moshav	TM	RC Ma'aleh ha-Galil	310
Even Sappir	Jerusalem Hills	1950	Moshav	TM	RC Matteh Yehudah	445
Even Shemu'el	Southern Coastal Plain (Lachish Region)	1956	Rural Center	—	RC Shafir	210
Even Yehudah	Southern Sharon (Netanyah Region)	1932	Rural Settlement	—	local council	3,950
Even Yiẓḥak (Galed)	Manasseh Hills	1945	Kibbutz	IK	RC Megiddo	261
Evron	Acre Plain	1945	Kibbutz	KA	RC Ga'aton	420

Name	Geographical Region	Year of Founding	Settlement Form	Affiliation	Municipal Status	No. of inhabitants 31 Dec 70
Eyal	Southern Sharon (Kefar Sava Region)	1949	Kibbutz	KM	RC Ha-Sharon ha-Tikhon	100
Ezer	Southern Coastal Plain (Malakhi Region)	1966	Rural Center	—	(RC) Be'er Tuviyyah	46
Ga'ash	Southern Sharon (Herzliyyah Region)	1951	Kibbutz	KA	RC Ḥof ha-Sharon	412
Ga'aton	Western Upper Galilee	1948	Kibbutz	KA	RC Ga'aton	275
Gadish	Jezreel Valley (Taanach Region)	1956	Moshav	TM	RC Ha-Gilboa	460
Gadot	Eastern Upper Galilee (Hazor Region)	1949	Kibbutz	KM	RC Ha-Galil ha-Elyon	240
Galon	Southern Judean Foothills	1946	Kibbutz	KA	RC Yo'av	340
Gan ha-Darom	Coastal Plain (Reḥovot Region)	1953	Moshav	IḤ	RC Gederot	266
Gan ha-Shomron	Northern Sharon (Ḥaderah Region)	1934	Rural Settlement	—	RC Manasseh	311
Gan Ḥayyim	Southern Sharon (Kefar Sava Region)	1935	Moshav	TM	RC Ha-Sharon ha-Tikhon	214
Gannei Am	Southern Sharon (Kefar Sava Region)	1934	Moshav	—	RC Ha-Yarkon	186
Gannei Tikvah	Coastal Plain (Petaḥ Tikvah Region)	1953	Urban Settlement	—	local council	3,140
Gannei Yehudah	Coastal Plain (Petaḥ Tikvah Region)	1951	Moshav	IḤ	RC Mifalot Afek	630
Gannei Yoḥanan (Gannei Yonah)	Coastal Plain (Reḥovot Region)	1950	Moshav	TM	RC Gezer	278
Gannot	Coastal Plain (Lod Region)	1953	Moshav	IḤ	RC Emek Lod	281
Gannot Hadar	Southern Sharon (Netanyah Region)	1964	Rural Settlement	—	RC Ha-Sharon ha-Ẓefoni	97
Gan Shelomo (Kevuẓat Schiller)	Coastal Plain (Reḥovot Region)	1927	Kibbutz	IK	RC Brenner	267
Gan Shemu'el	Northern Sharon (Ḥaderah Region)	1913	Kibbutz	KA	RC Manasseh	720
Gan Sorek	Coastal Plain (Rishon le-Zion Region)	1950	Moshav	TM	RC Gan Raveh	123
Gan Yavneh	Coastal Plain (Reḥovot Region)	1931	Rural Settlement	—	local council	2,730
Gan Yoshiyyah	Central Sharon (Ḥefer Plain)	1949	Moshav	TM	RC Ḥefer Plain	210
Gat	Southern Coastal Plain (Lachish Region)	1942	Kibbutz	KA	RC Yo'av	450
Gat Rimmon	Coastal Plain (Petaḥ Tikvah Region)	1926	Rural Settlement	—	RC Mifalot Afek	170
Gazit	Southeastern Lower Galilee	1948	Kibbutz	KA	RC Yizre'el	442
Ge'ah	Southern Coastal Plain (Ashkelon Region)	1949	Moshav	TM	RC Ḥof Ashkelon	190
Ge'alyah	Coastal Plain (Reḥovot Region)	1948	Moshav	TM	RC Gan Raveh	380
Gederah	Coastal Plain (Reḥovot Region)	1884	Urban Settlement	—	local council	5,200
Gefen	Southern Judean Foothills	1955	Moshav	PM	RC Matteh Yehudah	372
Gelil Yam	Southern Sharon (Herzliyyah Region)	1943	Kibbutz	KM	RC Ḥof ha-Sharon	250
Gerofit	Southern Arabah Valley	1963	Kibbutz	IK	RC Ḥevel Eilot	..
Gesher	Kinneret Valley	1939	Kibbutz	KM	RC Jordan Valley	..
Gesher ha-Ziv	Acre Plain	1949	Kibbutz	IK	RC Sullam Ẓor	371
Ge'ulei Teiman	Central Sharon (Ḥefer Plain)	1947	Moshav	PM	RC Ḥefer Plain	183
Ge'ulei Teiman	Central Sharon (Ḥefer Plain)	1947	Rural Settlement	—	RC Ḥefer Plain	167
Ge'ulim	Southern Sharon	1945	Moshav	TM	RC Ḥefer Plain	505
Geva	Harod Valley	1921	Kibbutz	IK	RC Ha-Gilboa	515

Name	Geographical Region	Year of Founding	Settlement Form	Affiliation	Municipal Status	No. of inhabitants 31 Dec 70
Geva Karmel	Carmel Coast	1949	Moshav	TM	RC Ḥof ha-Karmel	410
Gevaram	Southern Coastal Plain (Ashkelon Region)	1942	Kibbutz	KM	RC Ḥof Ashkelon	205
Gevat	Jezreel Valley	1926	Kibbutz	KM	RC Kishon	630
Gevim	Southern Coastal Plain (Ashkelon Region)	1947	Kibbutz	IK	RC Sha'ar ha-Negev	230
Gevulot	Northwestern Negev (Besor Region)	1943	Kibbutz	KA	RC Eshkol	129
Gezer	Judean Foothills	1945	Institution	—	RC Gezer	24
Gibbethon	Coastal Plain (Reḥovot Region)	1933	Moshav	—	RC Brenner	164
Gidonah	Harod Valley	1949	Rural Settlement	—	RC Ha-Gilboa	154
Gilat	Northern Negev (Gerar Region)	1949	Moshav	TM	RC Merḥavim	570
Gimzo	Judean Foothills	1950	Moshav	PAI	RC Modi'im	163
Ginnaton	Coastal Plain (Lod Region)	1949	Moshav	TM	RC Modi'im	250
Ginnegar	Jezreel Valley	1922	Kibbutz	IK	RC Yizre'el	418
Ginnosar	Kinneret Valley	1937	Kibbutz	KM	RC Jordan Valley	410
Givat Adah	Northern Sharon (Ḥaderah Region)	1903	Rural Settlement	—	local council	1,290
Givatayim	Coastal Plain (Tel Aviv Region)	1922	City	—	municipality	46,000
Givat Brenner	Coastal Plain (Reḥovot Region)	1928	Kibbutz	KM	RC Brenner	1,500
Givat ha-Sheloshah	Coastal Plain (Petaḥ Tikvah Region)	1925	Kibbutz	KM	RC Mifalot Afek	480
Givat Ḥayyim	Central Sharon (Ḥefer Plain)	1932	Kibbutz	IK	RC Ḥefer Plain	675
Givat Ḥayyim	Central Sharon (Ḥefer Plain)	1932	Kibbutz	KM	RC Ḥefer Plain	720
Givat Ḥen	Southern Sharon	1933	Moshav	TM	RC Ha-Yarkon	213
Givat Ko'aḥ	Judean Foothills	1950	Moshav	TM	RC Modi'im	393
Givat Nili	Northwestern Iron Hills	1953	Moshav	Ḥ	RC Allonah	195
Givat Oz	Jezreel Valley	1949	Kibbutz	KA	RC Megiddo	370
Givat Shapira	Southern Sharon	1958	Moshav	IḤ	RC Ḥefer Plain	105
Givat Shemesh	Judean Foothills	1954	Educational institution	—	(RC) Matteh Yehudah	106
Givat Shemu'el	Coastal Plain (Petaḥ Tikvah Region)	1942	Urban Settlement	—	local council	4,590
Givat Ye'arim	Jerusalem Hills	1950	Moshav	TM	RC Matteh Yehudah	515
Givat Yeshayahu	Judean Foothills (Adullam Region)	1958	Moshav	OẒ	RC Matteh Yehudah	. .
Givat Yo'av	Golan; 67+	1968	Moshav	TM		
Givati	Southern Coastal Plain (Malakhi Region)	1950	Moshav	TM	RC Be'er Tuviyyah	366
Givolim	Northern Negev (Gerar Region)	1952	Moshav	PM	RC Azzatah	210
Givot Zaid	Jezreel Valley	1943	Rural Settlement	—	(RC) Kishon	105
Gizo	Judean Foothills	1968	Rural center	—	—	40
Gonen	Ḥuleh Valley	1951	Kibbutz	IK	RC Ha-Galil ha-Elyon	250
Goren	Western Upper Galilee	1950	Moshav	TM	RC Ma'aleh ha-Galil	335
Ha-Bonim	Carmel Coast	1949	Moshav Shittufi	TM	RC Ḥof ha-Karmel	154

Name	Geographical Region	Year of Founding	Settlement Form	Affiliation	Municipal Status	No. of inhabitants 31 Dec 70
Hadar Am	Central Sharon (Ḥefer Plain)	1933	Moshav	IH	RC Ḥefer Plain	175
Ḥaderah	Northern Sharon (Ḥaderah Region)	1890	Town	—	municipality	30,700
Ḥadid	Northern Judean Foothills	1950	Moshav	PM	RC Modi'im	400
Ḥafeẓ Ḥayyim	Southern Coastal Plain (Reḥovot Region)	1944	Kibbutz	PAI	RC Naḥal Sorek	350
Ḥagor	Southern Sharon (Kefar Sava Region)	1949	Moshav	TM	RC Mifalot Afek	310
Ha-Gosherim	Ḥuleh Valley	1949	Kibbutz	KM	RC Ha-Galil ha-Elyon	420
Ha-Ḥoterim	Carmel Coast	1948	Kibbutz	KM	RC Ḥof ha-Karmel	357
Haifa	Mt. Carmel and Zebulun Valley	—	City	—	municipality	217,100 thereof 13,200 non-Jews
Ḥamadyah	Beth-Shean Valley	1942	Kibbutz	IK	RC Beth-Shean	..
Ha-Ma'pil	Northern Sharon	1945	Kibbutz	KA	RC Ḥefer Plain	446
Ḥamrah	Lower Jordan Valley; 67 +	1971	Moshav Shittufi	OẒ	—	..
Ḥanitah	Western Upper Galilee	1938	Kibbutz	IK	RC Sullam Ẓor	..
Ḥanni'el	Central Sharon (Ḥefer Plain)	1950	Moshav	TM	RC Ḥefer Plain	280
Ha-Ogen	Central Sharon (Ḥefer Plain)	1947	Kibbutz	KA	RC Ḥefer Plain	495
Ha-On	Kinneret Valley	1949	Kibbutz	IK	RC Jordan Valley	163
Harel	Judean Foothills	1948	Kibbutz	KA	RC Matteh Yehudah	147
Ḥaruẓim	Southern Sharon	1951	Rural Settlement	—	RC Ḥof ha-Sharon	570
Ha-Solelim	Western Lower Galilee	1949	Kibbutz	OẒ	RC Kishon	173
Ḥavaẓẓelet ha-Sharon	Central Sharon (Ḥefer Plain)	1935	Moshav	IḤ	RC Ḥefer Plain	170
Ḥavvat ha-Shomer	Eastern Lower Galilee	1956	Educational Institute	—	(RC) Ha-Galil ha-Taḥton	234
Ha-Yogev	Jezreel Valley	1949	Moshav	TM	RC Yizre'el	350
Ḥaẓav	Southern Coastal Plain (Malakhi Region)	1949	Moshav	TM	RC Be'er Tuviyyah	740
Ḥaẓerim	Northern Negev (Beersheba Region)	1946	Kibbutz	IK	RC Benei Shimon	327
Ḥaẓevah	Central Arabah Valley	1965	Moshav	TM	RC Tamar	..
Ḥazon	Eastern Lower Galilee	1969	Moshav	PM	RC Merom ha-Galil	100
Ḥaẓor Ashdod	Southern Coastal Plain (Malakhi Region)	1946	Kibbutz	KA	RC Be'er Tuviyyah	530
Ha-Zore'a	Jezreel Valley	1936	Kibbutz	KA	RC Megiddo	640
Ha-Zore'im	Eastern Lower Galilee	1939	Moshav	PM	RC Ha-Galil ha-Taḥton	318
Ḥaẓor ha-Gelilit	Eastern Upper Galilee (Hazor Region)	1953	Urban Settlement	—	local council	5,250
Ḥefẓi-Bah	Harod Valley	1922	Kibbutz	KM	RC Ha-Gilboa	478
Ḥeleẓ	Southern Coastal Plain (Ashkelon Region)	1950	Moshav	TM	RC Ḥof Ashkelon	555
Ḥemed	Coastal Plain (Lod Region)	1950	Moshav	PM	RC Emek Lod	530
Ḥerev le-Et	Central Sharon (Ḥefer Plain)	1947	Moshav	IḤ	RC Ḥefer Plain	227
Ḥerut	Southern Sharon (Kefar Sava Region)	1930	Moshav	TM	RC Hadar ha-Sharon	400
Herzliyyah	Southern Sharon	1924	City	—	municipality	38,500
Ḥever	Jezreel Valley (Taanach Region)	1958	Rural Center	—	(RC) Ha-Gilboa	20

Name	Geographical Region	Year of Founding	Settlement Form	Affiliation	Municipal Status	No. of inhabitants 31 Dec 70
Ḥibbat Zion	Central Sharon (Ḥefer Plain)	1933	Moshav	HI	RC Ḥefer Plain	300
Hod ha-Sharon	Southern Sharon (Kefar Sava Region)	1924	Urban Settlement	—	local council	12,700
Hodiyyah	Southern Coastal Plain (Ashkelon Region)	1949	Moshav	TM	RC Ḥof Ashkelon	420
Ḥofit	Central Sharon (Ḥefer Plain)	1955	Rural Settlement	—	RC Ḥefer Plain	420
Ḥoglah	Central Sharon (Ḥefer Plain)	1933	Moshav	TM	RC Ḥefer Plain	186
Ḥolon	Coastal Plain (Tel Aviv Region)	1933	City	—	municipality	88,500
Ḥoreshim	Southern Sharon (Kefar Sava Region)	1955	Kibbutz	KA	RC Mifalot Afek	170
Ḥosen	Western Upper Galilee	1949	Moshav	Ḥ	RC Ma'aleh ha-Galil	244
Ḥukkok	Eastern Lower Galilee	1945	Kibbutz	KM	RC Jordan Valley	225
Ḥulatah	Ḥuleh Valley	1937	Kibbutz	KM	RC Ha-Galil ha-Elyon	360
Ḥuldah	Judean Foothills	1930	Kibbutz	IK	RC Gezer	275
Ilaniyyah	Eastern Lower Galilee	1902	Moshav	IḤ	RC Ha-Galil ha-Taḥton	190
Jerusalem	Jerusalem Hills	—	City	—	municipality	291,700 thereof 76,200 non-Jews
Kabri	Acre Plain	1949	Kibbutz	KM	RC Ga'aton	540
Kadimah	Southern Sharon (Kefar Yonah Region)	1933	Urban Settlement	—	local council	3,970
Kadoorie	Eastern Lower Galilee	1931	Agricultural School	—	(RC) Ha-Galil ha-Taḥton	248
Kannot	Southern Coastal Plain (Malakhi Region)	1952	Agricultural School	—	(RC) Be'er Tuviyyah	310
Karmi'el	Western Lower Galilee	1964	Urban Settlement	—	local council	3,370
Karmiyyah	Southern Coastal Plain (Ashkelon Region)	1950	Kibbutz	KA	RC Ḥof Ashkelon	230
Kedmah	Southern Coastal Plain (Malakhi Region)	1946	Rural Settlement	—	(RC) Yo'av	—
Kefar Aḥim	Southern Coastal Plain (Malakhi Region)	1949	Moshav	TM	RC Be'er Tuviyyah	239
Kefar Aviv	Coastal Plain (Reḥovot Region)	1951	Moshav	IḤ	RC Gederot	258
Kefar Avodah	Southern Sharon (Herzliyyah Region)	1942	Educational Institution	—	(RC) Hadar ha-Sharon	20
Kefar Azar	Coastal Plain (Tel Aviv Region)	1932	Moshav	TM	RC Ono	343
Kefar Azzah	Southern Coastal Plain (Ashkelon Region)	1951	Kibbutz	IK	RC Sha'ar ha-Negev	175
Kefar Barukh	Jezreel Valley	1926	Moshav	TM	RC Kishon	212
Kefar Bialik	Zebulun Valley (Haifa Bay Area)	1934	Moshav	IḤ	RC Zebulun	550
Kefar Bilu	Coastal Plain (Reḥovot Region)	1932	Moshav	TM	RC Gezer	369
Kefar Bin Nun	Judean Foothills	1952	Moshav	IḤ	RC Gezer	140
Kefar Blum	Ḥuleh Valley	1943	Kibbutz	IK	RC Ha-Galil ha-Elyon	540
Kefar Dani'el (Bet Ḥever)	Coastal Plain (Lod Region)	1949	Moshav Shittufi	TM	RC Modi'im	123
Kefar Darom (Naḥal Kefar Darom)	Gaza Strip; 67 +	1970	Kibbutz	KD	—	. .
Kefar Eẓyon	Hebron Hills; 67 +	1967	Kibbutz	KD		
Kefar Gallim	Carmel Coast	1952	Agricultural School	—	—	440
Kefar Gidon	Jezreel Valley	1923	Moshav	PAI	RC Yizre'el	141

Name	Geographical Region	Year of Founding	Settlement Form	Affiliation	Municipal Status	No. of inhabitants 31 Dec 70
Kefar Giladi	Ḥuleh Valley	1916	Kibbutz	IK	RC Ha-Galil ha-Elyon	645
Kefar Glickson	Northern Sharon (Ḥaderah Region)	1939	Kibbutz	OẒ	RC Manasseh	247
Kefar ha-Ḥoresh	Southern Lower Galilee	1933	Kibbutz	IK	RC Kishon	249
Kefar ha-Makkabbi	Zebulun Valley (Haifa Bay Area)	1936	Kibbutz	IK	RC Zebulun	310
Kefar ha-Nagid	Coastal Plain (Rishon le-Zion area)	1949	Moshav	TM	RC Gan Raveh	344
Kefar ha-Nasi	Eastern Upper Galilee (Hazor Region)	1948	Kibbutz	IK	RC Ha-Galil ha-Elyon	417
Kefar ha-No'ar ha-Dati	Zebulun Valley (Haifa Bay area)	1937	Agricultural School	—	RC Zebulun	535
Kefar ha-Rif	Southern Coastal Plain (Malakhi Region)	1956	Moshav	IḤ	RC Yo'av	231
Kefar ha-Ro'eh	Central Sharon (Ḥefer Plain)	1934	Moshav	PM	RC Ḥefer Plain	850
Kefar Ḥabad	Coastal Plain (Lod Region)	1949	Moshav	—	RC Emek Lod	1,530
Kefar Ḥayyim	Central Sharon (Ḥefer Plain)	1933	Moshav	TM	RC Ḥefer Plain	340
Kefar Ḥasidim Alef	Zebulun Valley (Haifa Bay area)	1924	Moshav	—	RC Zebulun	400
Kefar Ḥasidim Bet	Zebulun Valley (Haifa Bay area)	1950	Rural Settlement	—	RC Zebulun	300
Kefar Hess	Southern Sharon (Kefar Sava Region)	1933	Moshav	TM	RC Hadar ha-Sharon	415
Kefar Ḥittim	Eastern Lower Galilee	1936	Moshav Shittufi	TM	RC Ha-Galil ha-Taḥton	196
Kefar Jawitz	Southern Sharon (Kefar Sava Region)	1932	Moshav	PM	RC Hadar ha-Sharon	377
Kefar Kisch	Eastern Lower Galilee	1946	Moshav	TM	RC Ha-Galil ha-Taḥton	185
Kefar Maimon	Northern Negev (Gerar Region)	1959	Moshav	PM	RC Azzatah	270
Kefar Malal (formerly Ein Ḥai)	Southern Sharon (Kefar Sava Region)	1922	Moshav	TM	RC Ha-Yarkon	251
Kefar Masaryk	Zebulun Valley (Haifa Bay area)	1938	Kibbutz	KA	RC Na'aman	510
Kefar Menaḥem	Southern Coastal Plain (Malakhi Region)	1937	Kibbutz	KA	RC Yo'av	560
Kefar Monash	Central Sharon (Ḥefer Plain)	1946	Moshav	TM	RC Ḥefer Plain	313
Kefar Mordekhai	Coastal Plain (Reḥovot Region)	1950	Moshav	IḤ	RC Gederot	210
Kefar Netter	Southern Sharon	1939	Moshav	—	RC Ḥof ha-Sharon	230
Kefar Pines	Northern Sharon (Ḥaderah Region)	1933	Moshav	PM	RC Manasseh	405
Kefar Rosenwald (Zarit)	Western Upper Galilee	1967	Moshav	TM	(RC) Ma'aleh ha-Galil	..
Kefar Rosh ha-Nikrah	Acre Plain	1949	Kibbutz	IK	RC Sullam Ẓor	..
Kefar Ruppin	Beth-Shean Valley	1938	Kibbutz	IK	RC Beth-Shean Valley	..
Kefar Sava	Southern Sharon	1903	Town	—	municipality	24,400
Kefar Shammai	Eastern Upper Galilee	1949	Moshav	PM	RC Merom ha-Galil	269
Kefar Shemaryahu	Southern Sharon (Herzliyyah Region)	1937	Rural Settlement	—	local council	1,290
Kefar Shemu'el	Judean Foothills	1950	Moshav	OẒ	RC Gezer	223
Kefar Silver	Southern Coastal Plain (Ashkelon Region)	1957	Agricultural School	—	(RC) Ḥof Ashkelon	280
Kefar Syrkin	Coastal Plain (Petaḥ Tikvah Region)	1936	Rural Settlement	—	RC Mifalot Afek	530
Kefar Szold	Ḥuleh Valley	1942	Kibbutz	KM	RC Ha-Galil ha-Elyon	450
Kefar Tavor	Eastern Lower Galilee	1901	Rural Settlement	—	local council	310
Kefar Truman	Northern Judean Foothills	1949	Moshav	TM	RC Modi'im	270

Name	Geographical Region	Year of Founding	Settlement Form	Affiliation	Municipal Status	No. of inhabitants 31 Dec 70
Kefar Uriyyah	Judean Foothills	1944	Moshav	TM	RC Matteh Yehudah	265
Kefar Vitkin	Central Sharon (Ḥefer Plain)	1933	Moshav	TM	RC Ḥefer Plain	840
Kefar Warburg	Southern Coastal Plain (Malakhi Region)	1939	Moshav	TM	RC Be'er Tuviyyah	483
Kefar Yeḥezkel	Harod Valley	1921	Moshav	TM	RC Ha-Gilboa	440
Kefar Yehoshu'a	Jezreel Valley	1927	Moshav	TM	RC Kishon	655
Kefar Yonah	Southern Sharon	1932	Rural Settlement	—	local council	2,670
Kefar Zeitim	Eastern Lower Galilee	1950	Moshav	TM	RC Ha-Galil ha-Taḥton	260
Kelaḥim	Northern Negev (Gerar Region)	1954	Moshav	IḤ	RC Merḥavim	310
Kerem Ben Zimrah	Eastern Upper Galilee	1949	Moshav	PM	RC Merom ha-Galil	304
Kerem Maharal	Mount Carmel	1949	Moshav	TM	RC Ḥof ha-Karmel	200
Kerem Shalom	Northwestern Negev (Besor Region)	1956	Kibbutz	KA	RC Eshkol	. .
Kerem Yavneh	Coastal Plain (Reḥovot Region)	1963	Educational Institution (Yeshivah)	PM	RC Ḥevel Yavneh	260
Kevuẓat Yavneh	Coastal Plain (Reḥovot Region)	1941	Kibbutz	KD	RC Ḥevel Yavneh	645
Kesalon	Judean Hills	1952	Moshav	IḤ	RC Matteh Yehudah	227
Kidron	Coastal Plain (Reḥovot Region)	1949	Moshav	TM	RC Brenner	570
Kinneret	Kinneret Valley	1908	Kibbutz	IK	RC Jordan Valley	690
Kinneret	Kinneret Valley	1909	Rural Settlement	—	local council	190
Kiryat Anavim	Jerusalem Hills	1920	Kibbutz	IK	RC Matteh Yehudah	310
Kiryat Ata	Zebulun Valley (Haifa Bay area)	1925	Town	—	municipality	25,600
Kiryat Bialik	Zebulun Valley (Haifa Bay area)	1934	Urban Settlement	—	local council	14,600
Kiryat Ekron	Coastal Plain (Reḥovot Region)	1948	Urban Settlement	—	local council	4,150
Kiryat Gat	Southern Coastal Plain (Lachish Region)	1954	Urban Settlement	—	local council	18,000
Kiryat Ḥaroshet	Zebulun Valley (Haifa Bay area)	1935	Rural Settlement	—	local council	234
Kiryat Malakhi	Southern Coastal Plain (Malakhi Region)	1951	Urban Settlement	—	local council	8,050
Kiryat Motzkin	Zebulun Valley (Haifa Bay area)	1934	Urban Settlement	—	local council	15,200
Kiryat Ono	Coastal Plain (Tel Aviv Region)	1939	Urban Settlement	—	local council	14,900
Kiryat Shemonah	Ḥuleh Valley	1950	Urban Settlement	—	local council	15,100
Kiryat Tivon	Southern Lower Galilee (Tivon Hills)	1937	Urban Settlement	—	local council	9,850
Kiryat Yam	Zebulun Valley (Haifa Bay area)	1946	Urban Settlement	—	local council	17,200
Kiryat Ye'arim	Jerusalem Hills	1952	Educational Institution	—	(RC) Matteh Yehudah	114
Kissufim	Northwestern Negev (Besor Region)	1951	Kibbutz	KM	RC Eshkol	224
Kokhav Mikha'el	Southern Coastal Plain (Ashkelon Region)	1950	Moshav	TM	RC Ḥof Ashkelon	310
Komemiyyut	Southern Coastal Plain (Malakhi Region)	1950	Moshav	PAI	RC Shafir	333
Lahav (Ẓiklag)	Northern Negev (Beersheba Region)	1952	Kibbutz	KA	RC Benei Shimon	201
Lahavot ha-Bashan	Ḥuleh Valley	1945	Kibbutz	KA	RC Ha-Galil ha-Elyon	457
Lahavot Ḥavivah	Northern Sharon (Ḥaderah Region)	1949	Kibbutz	KA	RC Manasseh	234
Lachish (Lakhish)	Southern Coastal Plain (Lachish Region)	1955	Moshav	TM	RC Lachish	222
Lavi	Eastern Lower Galilee	1949	Kibbutz	KD	RC Ha-Galil ha-Taḥton	450
Liman	Acre Plain	1949	Moshav	TM	RC Sullam Ẓor	256
Li On	Judean Foothills (Adullam Region)	1960	Rural Center	—	(RC) Matteh Yehudah	20

Name	Geographical Region	Year of Founding	Settlement Form	Affiliation	Municipal Status	No. of inhabitants 31 Dec 70
Lod (Lydda)	Coastal Plain (Lod Region)	—	Town	—	municipality	29,300 thereof 3,200 non-Jews
Loḥamei ha-Getta'ot	Acre Plain	1949	Kibbutz	KM	RC Ga'aton	341
Luzit	Southern Judean Foothills	1955	Moshav	TM	RC Matteh Yehudah	257
Ma'agan	Kinneret Valley	1949	Kibbutz	IK	RC Jordan Valley	262
Ma'agan Mikha'el	Carmel Coast	1949	Kibbutz	KM	RC Ḥof ha-Karmel	750
Ma'aleh Gilboa	Mt. Gilboa	1962	Kibbutz	KD	(RC) Beth-Shean Valley	..
Ma'aleh ha-Ḥamishah	Jerusalem Hills	1938	Kibbutz	IK	RC Matteh Yehudah	260
Ma'alot-Tarshiḥa	Western Upper Galilee	(1957)	Urban Settlement	—	local council	5,050 thereof 1,800 non-Jews
Ma'anit	Northern Sharon (Ḥaderah Region)	1942	Kibbutz	KA	RC Manasseh	420
Ma'as	Coastal Plain (Petaḥ Tikvah Region)	1935	Moshav	TM	RC Mifalot Afek	422
Ma'barot	Central Sharon (Ḥefer Plain)	1933	Kibbutz	KA	RC Ḥefer Plain	550
Mabbu'im	Northern Negev (Gerar Region)	1958	Rural Center	—	RC Merḥavim	145
Ma'gallim	Northern Negev (Gerar Region)	1958	Rural Center	—	(RC) Azzatah	56
Magen	Northwestern Negev (Besor Region)	1949	Kibbutz	KA	RC Eshkol	210
Maggal	Northern Sharon (Ḥaderah Region)	1953	Kibbutz	IK	RC Manasseh	172
Magshimim	Coastal Plain (Petaḥ Tikvah Region)	1949	Moshav	IḤ	RC Mifalot Afek	390
Maḥanayim	Eastern Upper Galilee (Hazor Region)	(1939)	Kibbutz	KM	RC Ha-Galil ha-Elyon	282
Maḥaseyah	Judean Foothills	1950	Rural Settlement	—	RC Matteh Yehudah	210
Malkiyyah	Eastern Upper Galilee	1949	Kibbutz	KM	RC Ha-Galil ha-Elyon	..
Manarah	Eastern Upper Galilee	1943	Kibbutz	KM	RC Ha-Galil ha-Elyon	..
Ma'or	Northern Sharon (Ḥaderah Region)	1953	Moshav	TM	RC Manasseh	200
Ma'oz Ḥayyim	Beth-Shean Valley	1937	Kibbutz	KM	RC Beth-Shean Valley	..
Margaliyyot	Eastern Upper Galilee	1951	Moshav	TM	RC Ha-Galil ha-Elyon	..
Mashabbei Sadeh	Negev Hills	1949	Kibbutz	KM	RC Ramat ha-Negev	300
Mashen	Southern Coastal Plain (Ashkelon Region)	1950	Moshav	TM	RC Ḥof Ashkelon	700
Maslul	Northwestern Negev (Besor Region)	1950	Moshav	TM	RC Merḥavim	177
Massadah	Kinneret Region	1937	Kibbutz	IK	RC Jordan Valley	280
Massu'ot Yiẓḥak	Southern Coastal Plain (Malakhi Region)	1949	Moshav Shittufi	PM	RC Shafir	410
Matta	Judean Hills	1950	Moshav	TM	RC Matteh Yehudah	209
Mavki'im	Southern Coastal Plain (Ashkelon Region)	1949	Moshav Shittufi	OẒ	RC Ḥof Ashkelon	132
Ma'yan Barukh	Ḥuleh Valley	1947	Kibbutz	IK	RC Ha-Galil ha-Elyon	..
Ma'yan Ẓevi	Mt. Carmel	1938	Kibbutz	IK	RC Ḥof ha-Karmel	555
Mazkeret Batyah	Coastal Plain (Reḥovot Region)	1883	Rural Settlement	—	local council	950
Maẓli'aḥ	Coastal Plain (Lod Region)	1950	Moshav	TM	RC Gezer	680

Name	Geographical Region	Year of Founding	Settlement From	Affiliation	Municipal Status	No. of inhabitants 31 Dec 70
Mazor	Coastal Plain (Petaḥ Tikvah Region)	1949	Moshav	TM	RC Modi'im	300
Maẓẓuvah	Western Upper Galilee	1940	Kibbutz	IK	RC Sullam Ẓor	347
Megadim	Carmel Coast	1949	Moshav	TM	RC Ḥof ha-Karmel	424
Mefallesim	Southern Coastal Plain (Ashkelon Region)	1949	Kibbutz	IK	RC Sha'ar ha-Negev	385
Megiddo	Jezreel Valley	1949	Kibbutz	KA	RC Megiddo	285
Meḥolah	Lower Jordan Valley; 67 +	1968	Moshav	PM	—	. .
Mei Ammi	Samaria (Iron Hills)	1963	Moshav Shittufi	OẒ	—	. .
Me'ir Shefeyah	Mt. Carmel	(1923)	Agricultural School	—	RC Ḥof ha-Karmel	450
Meishar	Coastal Plain (Reḥovot Region)	1950	Moshav	IḤ	RC Gederot	188
Meitav	Jezreel Valley (Taanach Region)	1954	Moshav	TM	RC Ha-Gilboa	472
Mele'ah	Jezreel Valley (Taanach Region)	1956	Moshav	TM	RC Ha-Gilboa	255
Melilot	Northern Negev (Gerar Region)	1953	Moshav	PM	RC Azzatah	356
Menaḥemiyyah	Eastern Lower Galilee	1902	Moshav	IḤ	local council	600
Menuḥah (Vardon)	Southern Coastal Plain (Malakhi Region)	1953	Moshav	TM	RC Lachish	565
Me'onah	Western Upper Galilee	1949	Moshav	TM	RC Ma'aleh ha-Galil	280
Merḥavyah	Harod Valley	1922	Moshav	TM	RC Yizre'el	227
Merḥavyah	Harod Valley	1911	Kibbutz	KA	RC Yizre'el	550
Merom Golan	Golan; 67 +	1967	Kibbutz	KM	—	. .
Meron	Eastern Upper Galilee	1949	Moshav	PM	RC Merom ha-Galil	280
Mesillat Zion	Judean Foothills	1950	Moshav	TM	RC Matteh Yehudah	215
Mesillot	Beth-Shean Valley	1938	Kibbutz	KA	RC Beth-Shean Valley	470
Metullah	Eastern Upper Galilee	1896	Rural Settlement	—	local council	345
Mevasseret Zion (Ẓiyyon)	Jerusalem Hills	1951	Urban Settlement	—	local council	4,250
Mevo Beitar	Jerusalem Hills	1950	Moshav Shittufi	Ḥ	RC Matteh Yehudah	198
Mevo Ḥammah	Golan; 67 +	1968	Kibbutz	IK	—	. .
Mevo Ḥoron	Judean Foothills; 67 +	1970	Kibbutz	PAI	—	. .
Mevo Modi'im	Judean Foothills	1964	Moshav	PAI	(RC) Modi'im	50
Meẓer	Northern Sharon (Ḥaderah Region)	1953	Kibbutz	KA	RC Manasseh	287
Midrakh Oz	Jezreel Valley	1952	Moshav	TM	RC Megiddo	450
Midreshet Ruppin	Central Sharon (Ḥefer Plain)	1948	Seminary	—	—	. .
Migdal	Kinneret Valley	1910	Rural Settlement	—	local council	535
Migdal ha-Emek	Southern Lower Galilee	1952	Urban Settlement	—	local council	8,800
Mikhmoret	Central Sharon (Ḥefer Plain)	1945	Moshav and Educational Institution	TM	RC Ḥefer Plain	720
Mikveh Yisrael	Coastal Plain (Tel Aviv Region)	1870	Agricultural School	—	—	950
Misgav Am	Eastern Upper Galilee	1945	Kibbutz	KM	RC Ha-Galil ha-Elyon	. .
Misgav Dov	Coastal Plain (Reḥovot Region)	1950	Moshav	Ḥ	RC Gederot	200
Mishmar Ayyalon	Judean Foothills	1949	Moshav	TM	RC Gezer	210
Mishmar David	Judean Foothills	1948	Kibbutz	IK	RC Gezer	73
Mishmar ha-Emek	Jezreel Valley	1926	Kibbutz	KA	RC Megiddo	700
Mishmar ha-Negev	Northern Negev (Gerar Region)	1946	Kibbutz	KM	RC Benei Shimon	498
Mishmar ha-Sharon	Central Sharon (Ḥefer Plain)	1933	Kibbutz	IK	RC Ḥefer Plain	390

Name	Geographical Region	Year of Founding	Settlement Form	Affiliation	Municipal Status	No. of inhabitants 31 Dec 70
Mishmar ha-Shivah	Central Coastal Plain (Lod Region)	1949	Moshav	—	RC Emek Lod	430
Mishmar ha-Yarden	Eastern Upper Galilee (Hazor Region)	(1949)	Moshav	Ḥ	RC Ha-Galil ha-Elyon	226
Mishmarot	Northern Sharon (Ḥaderah Region)	1933	Kibbutz	IK	RC Manasseh	222
Mishmeret	Southern Sharon (Kefar Sava Region)	1946	Moshav	TM	RC Hadar ha-Sharon	336
Mivtaḥim	Northwestern Negev (Besor Region)	1950	Moshav	TM	RC Eshkol	460
Mizra	Jezreel Valley	1923	Kibbutz	KA	RC Yizre'el	610
Miẓpeh	Eastern Lower Galilee	1908	Rural Settlement	—	RC Ha-Galil ha-Taḥton	42
Miẓpeh Ramon	Central Negev Hills	1954	Urban Settlement	—	local council	1,500
Miẓpeh Shalem	Dead Sea Region; 67 +	1970	Kibbutz	IK	—	. .
Moledet (B'nai B'rith)	Southeastern Lower Galilee	1937	Moshav Shittufi	TM	RC Ha-Gilboa	424
Moẓa Illit	Jerusalem Hills	1933	Rural Settlement	—	RC Matteh Yehudah	400
Moẓa Taḥtit	Jerusalem Hills	1894	Rural Settlement	—	(RC) Matteh Yehudah	40
Na'an	Coastal Plain (Reḥovot Region)	1930	Kibbutz	KM	RC Gezer	855
Naḥalah	Southern Coastal Plain (Malakhi Region)	1953	Moshav	TM	RC Yo'av	400
Nahalal	Jezreel Valley	1921	Moshav	TM	RC Kishon	1,030
Naḥalat Yehudah	Coastal Plain (Rishon le-Zion Region)	1914	Rural Settlement	—	local council	2,320
Naḥal Diklah	Northeastern Sinai; 67 +	1969	Moshav	Ḥ	—	. .
Naḥal Geshur	Golan; 67 +	1968	Kibbutz	KA	—	. .
Naḥal Gilgal	Lower Jordan Valley; 67 +	1970	Kibbutz	KM	—	. .
Naḥal Golan	Golan; 67 +	1967	Kibbutz	IK	—	. .
Naḥal Kallia	Dead Sea Region; 67 +	1968	Kibbutz	—	—	. .
Naḥal Massu'ah	Lower Jordan Valley; 67 +	1969	Kibbutz	PM	—	. .
Naḥal Naaran	Lower Jordan Valley; 67 +	1970	Kibbutz	KM	—	. .
Naḥal Oz	Northwestern Negev	1951	Kibbutz	IK	RC Sha'ar ha-Negev	279
Naḥal Sinai	Northeastern Sinai; 67 +	1968	Kibbutz	IK	—	. .
Naḥal Yam	Northwestern Sinai; 67 +	1967	Kibbutz	KM	—	. .
Naḥal Ẓofar	Central Arabah Valley	1968	Kibbutz	KA	RC Ḥevel Eilot	. .
Naḥam	Judean Foothills	1950	Moshav	PM	RC Matteh Yehudah	388
Nahariyyah	Acre Plain	1934	Town	—	municipality	21,900
Naḥsholim	Carmel Coast	1948	Kibbutz	KM	RC Ḥof ha-Karmel	253
Naḥshon	Judean Foothills	1950	Kibbutz	KA	RC Matteh Yehudah	245
Naḥshonim	Northern Judean Foothills	1949	Kibbutz	KA	RC Mifalot Afek	223
Naẓerat Illit	Southern Lower Galilee	1957	Urban Settlement	—	local council	15,000
Negbah	Southern Coastal Plain (Malakhi Region)	1939	Kibbutz	KA	RC Yo'av	402
Neḥalim	Coastal Plain (Petaḥ Tikvah Region)	1948	Moshav	PM	RC Modi'im	610
Nehorah	Coastal Plain (Lachish Region)	1956	Rural Center	—	RC Lachish	131
Ne'ot Golan	Golan; 67 +	1968	Moshav	OẒ	—	. .
Ne'ot ha-Kikkar	Northern Arabah Valley	1963	Moshav	IḤ	RC Tamar	. .
Ne'ot Mordekhai	Ḥuleh Valley	1946	Kibbutz	IK	RC Ha-Galil ha-Elyon	625
Nes Harim	Jerusalem Hills	1950	Moshav	TM	RC Matteh Yehudah	360
Nesher	Zebulun Valley (Haifa Bay area)	1925	Urban Settlement	—	local council	9,400
Nes Ẓiyyonah	Coastal Plain (Rishon le-Zion Region)	1883	Urban Settlement	—	local council	12,100
Neta'im	Coastal Plain (Rishon le-Zion Region)	1932	Moshav	TM	RC Gan Raveh	204

Name	Geographical Region	Year of Founding	Settlement Form	Affiliation	Municipal Status	No. of inhabitants 31 Dec 70
Netanyah	Southern Sharon	1929	City	—	municipality	65,400
Netiv ha-Lamed He	Southern Judean Foothills	1949	Kibbutz	KM	RC Matteh Yehudah	270
Netiv ha-Shayyarah	Acre Plain	1950	Moshav	TM	RC Ga'aton	361
Netivot	Northwestern Negev (Gerar Region)	1956	Urban Settlement	—	local council	5,350
Netu'ah	Western Upper Galilee	1966	Moshav	TM	(RC) Ma'aleh ha-Galil	. .
Ne'urim	Central Sharon (Ḥefer Plain)	1953	Educational Institution	—	(RC) Ḥefer Plain	500
Nevatim	Northern Negev (Beersheba Region)	1946	Moshav	TM	RC Benei Shimon	439
Neveh Avot	Northern Sharon (Ḥaderah Region)	1948	Aged People's Home	—	—	1,060
Neveh Efrayim (Monosson)	Coastal Plain (Petaḥ Tikvah Region)	1953	Rural Settlement	—	local council	1,150
Neveh Eitan	Beth-Shean Valley	1938	Kibbutz	IK	RC Beth-Shean Valley	234
Neveh Ilan	Jerusalem Hills	(1946)	—	—	(RC) Matteh Yehudah	. .
Neveh Mivtaḥ	Southern Coastal Plain (Malakhi Region)	1950	Moshav	TM	RC Be'er Tuviyyah	201
Neveh Ur	Northern Beth-Shean Valley	1949	Kibbutz	KM	RC Beth-Shean Valley	. .
Neveh Yam	Carmel Coast	1939	Kibbutz	IK	RC Ḥof ha-Karmel	139
Neveh Yamin	Southern Sharon (Kefar Sava Region)	1949	Moshav	TM	RC Ha-Sharon ha-Tikhon	555
Neveh Yarak	Southern Sharon (Herzliyyah Region)	1951	Moshav	TM	RC Ha-Yarkon	390
Neẓer Sereni	Coastal Plain (Rishon le-Zion Region)	1948	Kibbutz	IK	RC Gezer	515
Nir Akiva	Northern Negev (Gerar Region)	1953	Moshav	TM	RC Merḥavim	140
Nir Am	Southern Coastal Plain (Ashkelon Region)	1943	Kibbutz	IK	RC Sha'ar ha-Negev	266
Nir Banim	Southern Coastal Plain (Malakhi Region)	1954	Moshav	TM	RC Shafir	325
Nir David	Beth-Shean Valley	1936	Kibbutz	KA	RC Beth-Shean Valley	555
Nir Eliyahu	Southern Sharon (Kefar Sava Region)	1950	Kibbutz	IK	RC Ha-Sharon ha-Tikhon	230
Nir Eẓyon	Mt. Carmel	1950	Moshav Shittufi	PM	RC Ḥof ha-Karmel	450
Nir Gallim	Southern Coastal Plain (Yavneh Region)	1949	Moshav Shittufi	PM	RC Ḥevel Yavneh	408
Nir Ḥen	Southern Coastal Plain (Lachish Region)	1955	Moshav	TM	RC Lachish	80
Nirim	Northwestern Negev (Besor Region)	1949	Kibbutz	KA	RC Eshkol	280
Nir Moshe	Northern Negev (Gerar Region)	1953	Moshav	TM	RC Merḥavim	181
Nir Oz	Northwestern Negev (Besor Region)	1955	Kibbutz	KA	RC Eshkol	184
Nir Yafeh	Jezreel Valley (Taanach Region)	1956	Moshav	TM	RC Ha-Gilboa	250
Nir Yisrael	Southern Coastal Plain (Ashkelon Region)	1949	Moshav	OẒ	RC Ḥof Ashkelon	240
Nir Yiẓḥak (formerly Nirim)	Northwestern Negev (Besor Region)	(1949)	Kibbutz	KA	RC Eshkol	260
Nir Ẓevi	Coastal Plain (Lod Region)	1954	Moshav	IḤ	RC Emek Lod	510
Niẓẓanei Oz	Southern Sharon (Kefar Yonah Region)	1951	Moshav	TM	RC Ha-Sharon ha-Ẓefoni	351
Niẓẓanim	Southern Coastal Plain (Ashkelon Region)	1943	Kibbutz	OẒ	RC Ḥof Ashkelon	250
Niẓẓanim (Kefar ha-No'ar)	Southern Coastal Plain (Ashkelon Region)	1949	Agricultural School	—	RC Ḥof Ashkelon	385
No'am	Southern Coastal Plain (Lachish Region)	1953	Moshav	PM	RC Shafir	490
Nofekh	Coastal Plain (Petaḥ Tikvah Region)	1949	Rural Settlement	—	RC Modi'im	200

Name	Geographical Region	Year of Founding	Settlement Form	Affiliation	Municipal Status	No. of inhabitants 31 Dec 70
Nogah	Southern Coastal Plain (Lachish Region)	1955	Moshav	TM	RC Lachish	530
Nordiyyah	Southern Sharon (Netanyah Region)	1948	Moshav Shittufi	Ḥ	RC Ha-Sharon ha-Ẓefoni	286
Ofakim	Northwestern Negev (Besor Region)	1955	Urban Settlement	—	local council	9,200
Ofer	Mount Carmel	1950	Moshav	TM	RC Ḥof ha-Karmel	235
Ohad	Northwestern Negev (Besor Region)	1969	Moshav	TM	RC Eshkol	120
Olesh	Central Sharon (Ḥefer Plain)	1949	Moshav	TM	RC Ḥefer Plain	302
Omen	Jezreel Valley (Taanach Region)	1958	Rural Center	—	(RC) Ha-Gilboa	20
Omer	Northern Negev (Beersheba Region)	1949	Rural Settlement	—	RC Benei Shimon	1,000
Omeẓ	Central Sharon (Ḥefer Plain)	1949	Moshav	TM	RC Ḥefer Plain	207
Orah	Jerusalem Hills	1950	Moshav	TM	RC Matteh Yehudah	293
Or Akiva	Northern Sharon (Ḥaderah Region)	1951	Urban Settlement	—	local council	6,350
Oranim	Southern Lower Galilee (Tivon Hills)	1951	Kibbutz Seminary	—	RC Zebulun	350
Or ha-Ner	Southern Coastal Plain (Ashkelon Region)	1957	Kibbutz	IK	RC Sha'ar ha-Negev	284
Orot	Southern Coastal Plain (Malakhi Region)	1952	Moshav	TM	RC Be'er Tuviyyah	240
Or Yehudah	Coastal Plain (Tel Aviv Region)	1950	Urban Settlement	—	local council	12,300
Oẓem	Southern Coastal Plain (Lachish Region)	1955	Moshav	TM	RC Lachish	635
Pa'amei Tashaz	Northern Negev (Gerar Region)	1953	Moshav	TM	RC Merḥavim	330
Palmaḥim	Coastal Plain (Rishon le-Zion Region)	1949	Kibbutz	KM	RC Gan Raveh	291
Pardes Ḥannah-Karkur	Northern Sharon (Ḥaderah Region)	(1913)	Urban Settlement	—	local council	13,400
Pardesiyyah	Southern Sharon	1942	Rural Settlement	—	local council	800
Parod	Eastern Upper Galilee	1949	Kibbutz	KM	RC Merom ha-Galil	228
Pattish	Northern Negev (Besor Region)	1950	Moshav	TM	RC Merḥavim	640
Pedayah	Judean Foothills	1951	Moshav	TM	RC Gezer	458
Peduyim	Northern Negev (Besor Region)	1950	Moshav	TM	RC Merḥavim	307
Peki'in Ḥadashah	Western Upper Galilee	1955	Moshav	TM	RC Ma'aleh ha-Galil	235
Perazon	Jezreel Valley (Taanach Region)	1953	Moshav	TM	RC Ha-Gilboa	500
Petaḥ Tikvah	Coastal Plain (Petaḥ Tikvah Region)	1878	City	—	municipality	83,200
Petaḥyah	Judean Foothills	1951	Moshav	OẒ	RC Gezer	446
Peẓa'el (Ma'aleh Efrayim)	Lower Jordan Valley; 67 +	1970	Moshav	TM	—	. .
Porat	Southern Sharon (Kefar Sava Region)	1950	Moshav	PM	RC Hadar ha-Sharon	800
Poriyyah (Kefar Avodah)	Eastern Lower Galilee	1955	Moshav	—	RC Jordan Valley	120
Poriyyah (Neveh Oved)	Eastern Lower Galilee	1949	Rural Settlement	—	RC Jordan Valley	680
Ra'anannah	Southern Sharon (Herzliyyah Region)	1921	Urban Settlement	—	local council	12,700
Ramat David	Jezreel Valley	1926	Kibbutz	IK	RC Kishon	280
Ramat Efal	Coastal Plain (Tel Aviv Region)	1969	Rural Settlement	—	RC Ono	400
Ramat Gan	Coastal Plain (Tel Aviv Region)	1921	City	—	municipality	115,500

Name	Geographical Region	Year of Founding	Settlement Form	Affiliation	Municipal Status	No. of inhabitants 31 Dec 70
Ramat ha-Kovesh	Southern Sharon (Kefar Sava Region)	1932	Kibbutz	KM	RC Ha-Sharon ha-Tikhon	520
Ramat ha-Sharon	Southern Sharon (Herzliyyah Region)	1923	Urban Settlement	—	local council	17,600
Ramat ha-Shofet	Manasseh Hills	1941	Kibbutz	KA	RC Megiddo	530
Ramat Magshimim	Golan; 67 +	1968	Moshav	PM	—	. .
Ramat Pinkas	Coastal Plain (Tel Aviv Region)	1952	Rural Settlement	—	RC Ono	780
Ramat Raḥel	Jerusalem Hills	1926	Kibbutz	IK	RC Matteh Yehudah	70
Ramat Raziel	Judean Hills	1948	Moshav	Ḥ	RC Matteh Yehudah	135
Ramat Yishai	Southern Lower Galilee (Tivon Hills)	1925	Rural Settlement	—	local council	800
Ramat Yoḥanan	Zebulun Valley (Haifa Bay area)	1932	Kibbutz	IK	RC Zebulun	500
Ramat Ẓevi	Southeastern Lower Galilee	1942	Moshav	TM	RC Ha-Gilboa	180
Ramleh	Coastal Plain (Lod Region)	—	City	—	municipality	30,800 thereof 3,800 non-Jews
Ram On	Jezreel Valley (Taanach Region)	1960	Moshav	TM	RC Ha-Gilboa	215
Ramot	Golan: 67 +	1970	Moshav	TM		. .
Ramot ha-Shavim	Southern Sharon (Kefar Sava Region)	1933	Moshav	IḤ	local council	450
Ramot Me'ir	Coastal Plain (Lod Region)	1949	Moshav Shittufi	TM	RC Gezer	240
Ramot Menasheh	Manasseh Hills	1948	Kibbutz	KA	RC Megiddo	500
Ramot Naftali	Eastern Upper Galilee	1945	Moshav	TM	RC Ha-Galil ha-Elyon	. .
Rannen	Northern Negev (Besor Region)	1950	Moshav	TM	RC Merḥavim	414
Regavim	Manasseh Hills	1948	Kibbutz	KM	RC Manasseh	291
Regbah	Acre Plain	1946	Moshav Shittufi	TM	RC Ga'aton	323
Reḥov	Beth-Shean Valley	1951	Moshav	PM	RC Beth-Shean Valley	345
Reḥovot	Coastal Plain (Reḥovot Region)	1890	City	—	municipality	36,600
Re'im	Northwestern Negev (Besor Region)	1949	Kibbutz	KM	RC Eshkol	199
Rekhasim	Zebulun Valley (Haifa Bay area)	1957	Urban Settlement	—	local council	2,550
Reshafim	Beth-Shean Valley	1948	Kibbutz	KA	RC Beth-Shean Valley	442
Revadim	Southern Coastal Plain (Malakhi Region)	1948	Kibbutz	KA	RC Yo'av	251
Revaḥah	Southern Coastal Plain (Lachish Region)	1953	Moshav	PM	RC Shafir	565
Revayah	Beth-Shean Valley	1952	Moshav	PM	RC Beth-Shean Valley	322
Revivim	Negev (southern Beersheba basin)	1943	Kibbutz	KM	RC Ramat ha-Negev	429
Rinnatyah	Coastal Plain (Lod Region)	1949	Moshav	TM	RC Modi'im	437
Rishon le-Zion	Coastal Plain (Rishon le-Zion Region)	1882	City	—	municipality	46,500
Rishpon	Southern Sharon (Herzliyyah Region)	1936	Moshav	TM	RC Ḥof ha-Sharon	449
Roglit	Judean Foothills (Adullam Region)	1958	Moshav	HI	RC Matteh Yehudah	268
Rosh ha-Ayin	Coastal Plain (Petaḥ Tikvah Region)	1950	Urban Settlement	—	local council	11,600
Rosh Pinnah	Eastern Upper Galilee (Hazor Region)	1882	Rural Settlement	—	local council	805
Rosh Ẓurim	Hebron Hills; 67 +	1969	Kibbutz	KD	—	. .
Ruḥamah	Southern Coastal Plain (Ashkelon Region)	(1944)	Kibbutz	KA	RC Sha'ar ha-Negev	510

Name	Geographical Region	Year of Founding	Settlement Form	Affiliation	Municipal Status	No. of inhabitants 31 Dec 70
Sa'ad	Northwestern Negev (Gerar Region)	1947	Kibbutz	KD	RC Azzatah	530
Sa'ar	Acre Plain	1948	Kibbutz	KA	RC Ga'aton	240
Safed (Ẓefat)	Eastern Upper Galilee	—	Town	—	municipality	13,100
Sarid	Jezreel Valley	1926	Kibbutz	KA	RC Kishon	620
Sasa	Eastern Upper Galilee	1949	Kibbutz	KA	RC Merom ha-Galil	. .
Savyon	Coastal Plain (Tel Aviv Region)	1954	Rural Settlement	—	RC Mifalot Afek	1,680
Sedeh Boker	Central Negev Hills	1952	Kibbutz	IK	RC Ramat ha-Negev	. .
Sedeh Boker (Midrashah)	Central Negev Hills	1965	Educational Institution	—	RC Ramat ha-Negev	530
Sedeh David	Southern Coastal Plain (Lachish Region)	1955	Moshav	OẒ	RC Lachish	437
Sedeh Eli'ezer	Ḥuleh Valley	1952	Moshav	OẒ	RC Ha-Galil ha-Elyon	265
Sedeh Eliyahu	Beth-Shean Valley	1939	Kibbutz	KD	RC Beth-Shean Valley	375
Sedeh Ilan	Eastern Lower Galilee	1949	Moshav	PM	RC Ha-Galil ha-Taḥton	220
Sedeh Moshe	Southern Coastal Plain (Lachish Region)	1956	Moshav	TM	RC Lachish	295
Sedeh Naḥum	Beth-Shean Valley	1937	Kibbutz	KM	RC Beth-Shean Valley	290
Sedeh Neḥemyah	Ḥuleh Valley	1940	Kibbutz	IK	RC Ha-Galil ha-Elyon	304
Sedeh Uzziyyah	Southern Coastal Plain (Malakhi Region)	1950	Moshav	OẒ	RC Be'er Tuviyyah	800
Sedeh Warburg	Southern Sharon (Kefar Sava Region)	1938	Moshav	IḤ	RC Ha-Sharon ha-Tikhon	380
Sedeh Ya'akov	Jezreel Valley	1927	Moshav	PM	RC Kishon	500
Sedeh Yiẓḥak	Northern Sharon (Ḥaderah Region)	1952	Moshav	TM	RC Manasseh	150
Sedeh Yo'av	Southern Coastal Plain (Malakhi Region)	1956	Kibbutz	KA	RC Yo'av	60
Sedeh Ẓevi	Northern Negev (Gerar Region)	1953	Moshav	IḤ	RC Merḥavim	327
Sedei Ḥemed	Southern Sharon (Kefar Sava Region)	1952	Moshav	TM	RC Ha-Sharon ha-Tikhon	280
Sedei Terumot	Beth-Shean Valley	1951	Moshav	PM	RC Beth-Shean Valley	465
Sederot	Southern Coastal Plain (Ashkelon Region)	1951	Urban Settlement	—	local council	7,500
Sedom (Sodom)	Dead Sea Region	—	Industrial Site	—	—	. .
Sedot Mikhah	Southern Judean Foothills	1955	Moshav	TM	RC Matteh Yehudah	260
Sedot Yam	Northern Sharon (Ḥaderah Region)	1940	Kibbutz	KM	RC Ḥof ha-Karmel	510
Segev	Western Lower Galilee	1953	Rural Settlement	—	—	171
Segullah	Southern Coastal Plain (Malakhi Region)	1953	Moshav	TM	RC Yo'av	227
Senir (Ramat Banias, Kefar Moshe Sharett)	Ḥuleh Valley; 67 +	1967	Kibbutz	KA	(RC) Ha-Galil ha-Elyon	. .
Shaalbim	Northern Judean Foothills	1951	Kibbutz	PAI	RC Gezer	270
Sha'ar Efrayim	Southern Sharon (Kefar Yonah Region)	1953	Moshav	TM	RC Ha-Sharon ha-Ẓefoni	482
Sha'ar ha-Amakim	Southern Lower Galilee (Tivon Hills)	1935	Kibbutz	KA	RC Zebulun	580
Sha'ar ha-Golan	Kinneret Valley	1937	Kibbutz	KA	RC Jordan Valley	590
Sha'ar Ḥefer	Central Sharon (Ḥefer Plain)	1940	Moshav	IḤ	RC Ḥefer Plain	350
Sha'ar Menasheh	Northern Sharon (Ḥaderah Region)	1949	Institution (Aged People's Village)	—	(RC) Manasseh	310
Sha'arei Avraham	Coastal Plain (Reḥovot Region)	1958	Educational Institution	—	(RC) Naḥal Sorek	70

Name	Geographical Region	Year of Founding	Settlement Form	Affiliation	Municipal Status	No. of inhabitants 31 Dec 70
Shadmot Devorah	Eastern Lower Galilee	1939	Moshav	TM	RC Ha-Galil ha-Taḥton	166
Shafir	Southern Coastal Plain (Malakhi Region)	1949	Moshav	PM	RC Shafir	241
Shaḥar	Southern Coastal Plain (Lachish Region)	1955	Moshav	TM	RC Lachish	347
Shalvah	Southern Coastal Plain (Lachish Region)	1952	Moshav	PM	RC Shafir	499
Shamir	Ḥuleh Valley	1944	Kibbutz	KA	RC Ha-Galil ha-Elyon	433
Sharonah	Eastern Lower Galilee	1938	Moshav	TM	RC Ha-Galil ha-Taḥton	178
Sharsheret	Northwestern Negev (Gerar Region)	1951	Moshav	PM	RC Azzatah	545
Shavei Zion	Acre Plain	1938	Moshav Shittufi	IḤ	local council	312
She'ar Yashuv	Ḥuleh Valley	1940	Moshav	OẒ	RC Ha-Galil ha-Elyon	. .
Shedemah	Coastal Plain (Reḥovot Region)	1954	Moshav	IḤ	RC Gederot	160
Shefayim	Southern Sharon (Herzliyyah Region)	1935	Kibbutz	KM	RC Ḥof ha-Sharon	550
Shefer	Eastern Upper Galilee	1950	Moshav	TM	RC Merom ha-Galil	257
Shelomi	Acre Plain	1950	Rural Settlement	—	local council	2,020
Sheluḥot	Beth-Shean Valley	1948	Kibbutz	KD	RC Beth-Shean Valley	340
Shetulah	Western Upper Galilee	1969	Moshav	TM	RC Ma'aleh ha-Galil	. .
Shetulim	Southern Coastal Plain (Malakhi Region)	1950	Moshav	TM	RC Be'er Tuviyyah	630
Shezor	Western Lower Galilee	1953	Moshav	TM	RC Merom ha-Galil	340
Shibbolim	Northwestern Negev (Gerar Region)	1952	Moshav	PM	RC Azzatah	430
Sho'evah	Judean Hills	1950	Moshav	IḤ	RC Matteh Yehudah	179
Shokedah	Northwestern Negev (Gerar Region)	1957	Moshav	PM	RC Azzatah	337
Shomerah	Northwestern Upper Galilee	1949	Moshav	TM	RC Ma'aleh ha-Galil	263
Shomrat	Acre Plain	1948	Kibbutz	KA	RC Ga'aton	324
Shoresh	Judean Hills	1948	Moshav Shittufi	OẒ	RC Matteh Yehudah	190
Shoshannat ha-Amakim	Central Sharon (Ḥefer Plain)	1951	Rural Settlement	—	(RC) Ḥefer Plain	366
Shoshannat ha-Amakim (Ammidar)	Central Sharon (Ḥefer Plain)	1956	Rural Settlement	—	RC Ḥefer Plain	232
Shoval	Northern Negev (Gerar Region)	1946	Kibbutz	KA	RC Benei Shimon	440
Shuvah	Northwestern Negev (Gerar Region)	1950	Moshav	PM	RC Azzatah	397
Sifsufah	Eastern Upper Galilee	1949	Moshav	TM	RC Merom ha-Galil	480
Sitriyyah	Coastal Plain (Reḥovot Region)	1949	Moshav	TM	RC Gezer	407
Tal Shaḥar	Judean Foothills	1948	Moshav	TM	RC Matteh Yehudah	400
Talmei Bilu	Northern Negev (Gerar Region)	1953	Moshav	HI	RC Merḥavim	264
Talmei Elazar	Northern Sharon (Ḥaderah Region)	1952	Moshav	HI	RC Manasseh	210
Talmei Yafeh	Southern Coastal Plain (Ashkelon Region)	1950	Moshav Shittufi	OẒ	RC Ḥof Ashkelon	87
Talmei Yeḥi'el	Southern Coastal Plain (Malakhi Region)	1949	Moshav	TM	RC Be'er Tuviyyah	277
Ta'oz	Judean Foothills	1950	Moshav	PM	RC Matteh Yehudah	385
Tarum	Judean Foothills	1950	Moshav	PM	RC Matteh Yehudah	372

Name	Geographical Region	Year of Founding	Settlement Form	Affiliation	Municipal Status	No. of inhabitants 31 Dec 70
Te'ashur	Northern Negev (Gerar Region)	1953	Moshav	TM	RC Benei Shimon	188
Tekumah	Northwestern Negev (Gerar Region)	1949	Moshav	PM	RC Azzatah	234
Tel Adashim	Jezreel Valley	1923	Moshav	TM	RC Yizre'el	400
Telamim	Southern Coastal Plain (Lakhish Region)	1950	Moshav	TM	RC Lachish	555
Tel Aviv-Jaffa	Coastal Plain (Tel Aviv Region)	1909	City	—	municipality	384,000 thereof 7,200 non-Jews
Tel Kaẓir	Kinneret Region	1949	Kibbutz	IK	RC Jordan Valley	. .
Tel Mond	Southern Sharon (Kefar Sava Region)	1929	Rural Settlement	—	local council	3,060
Tel Yiẓḥak (includes Neveh Hadassah)	Southern Sharon (Netanyah Region)	1938	Kibbutz	OẒ	RC Ḥof ha-Sharon	510
Tel Yosef	Harod Valley	1921	Kibbutz	IK	RC Ha-Gilboa	515
Tenuvot	Southern Sharon	1952	Moshav	TM	RC Ha-Sharon ha-Ẓefoni	565
Tiberias (Teveryah)	Kinneret Valley	—	Town	—	municipality	23,900
Tidhar	Northern Negev (Gerar Region)	1953	Moshav	TM	RC Benei Shimon	370
Tifraḥ	Northern Negev (Besor Region)	1949	Moshav	PAI	RC Merḥavim	350
Timmurim	Southern Coastal Plain (Malakhi Region)	1954	Moshav Shittufi	OẒ	RC Be'er Tuviyyah	230
Tirat Karmel	Carmel Coast	1949	Urban Settlement	—	local council	13,300
Tirat Yehudah	Coastal Plain (Petaḥ Tikvah Region)	1949	Moshav	PM	RC Modi'im	329
Tirat Ẓevi	Beth-Shean Valley	1937	Kibbutz	KD	RC Beth-Shean Valley	. .
Tirosh	Southern Judean Foothills	1955	Moshav	PM	RC Matteh Yehudah	510
Toḥelet	Coastal Plain (Lod Region)	1951	Rural Settlement	—	RC Emek Lod	334
Tushiyyah	Northwestern Negev (Gerar Region)	1958	Rural Center	—	(RC) Azzatah	193
Udim	Southern Sharon (Netanyah Region)	1948	Moshav	IḤ	RC Ḥof ha-Sharon	369
Urim	Northwestern Negev (Besor Region)	1946	Kibbutz	IK	RC Merḥavim	384
Ushah	Zebulun Valley (Haifa Bay area)	1937	Kibbutz	IK	RC Zebulun	305
Uzzah	Southern Coastal Plain (Lachish Region)	1950	Moshav	PM	RC Shafir	700
Ya'arah	Western Upper Galilee	1950	Moshav	TM	RC Ma'aleh ha-Galil	275
Yad Binyamin	Coastal Plain (Reḥovot Region)	1949	Rural Center	—	RC Naḥal Sorek	220
Yad Ḥannah (Me'uḥad)	Central Sharon (Ḥefer Plain)	1950	Kibbutz	KM	RC Ḥefer Plain	. .
Yad Ḥannah (Semol)	Central Sharon (Ḥefer Plain)	1950	Kibbutz	—	RC Ḥefer Plain	76
Yad Mordekhai	Southern Coastal Plain (Ashkelon Region)	1943	Kibbutz	KA	RC Ḥof Ashkelon	481
Yad Natan	Southern Coastal Plain (Lachish Region)	1953	Moshav	OẒ	RC Lachish	117
Yad Rambam	Coastal Plain (Lod Region)	1955	Moshav	PM	RC Gezer	580
Yagel	Coastal Plain (Lod Region)	1950	Moshav	TM	RC Emek Lod	367
Yagur	Zebulun Valley (Haifa Bay area)	1922	Kibbutz	KM	RC Zebulun	1,150
Yakhini	Northwestern Negev	1950	Moshav	TM	RC Sha'ar ha-Negev	540

Name	Geographical Region	Year of Founding	Settlement Form	Affiliation	Municipal Status	No. of inhabitants 31 Dec 70
Yakum	Southern Sharon (Herzliyyah Region)	1947	Kibbutz	KA	RC Ḥof ha-Sharon	358
Yanuv	Southern Sharon (Kefar Yonah Region)	1950	Moshav	TM	RC Ha-Sharon ha-Ẓefoni	535
Yardenah	Beth-Shean Valley	1952	Moshav	TM	RC Beth-Shean Valley	. .
Yarḥiv	Southern Sharon (Kefar Sava Region)	1949	Moshav	TM	RC Ha-Sharon ha-Tikhon	520
Yarkonah	Southern Sharon (Kefar Sava Region)	1932	Moshav	TM	RC Ha-Yarkon	110
Yashresh	Coastal Plain (Lod Region)	1950	Moshav	TM	RC Gezer	432
Yas'ur	Zebulun Valley (Haifa Bay area)	1949	Kibbutz	KA	RC Na'aman	334
Yavne'el	Eastern Lower Galilee	1901	Rural Settlement	—	local council	1,490
Yavneh (Jabneh)	Coastal Plain (Reḥovot Region)	1949	Urban Settlement	—	local council	10,000
Yaẓiẓ	Coastal Plain (Lod Region)	1950	Moshav	TM	RC Gezer	605
Yedidah	Judean Hills	1964	Educational Institution	—	(RC) Matteh Yehudah	125
Yedidyah	Central Sharon (Ḥefer Plain)	1935	Moshav	TM	RC Ḥefer Plain	285
Yeḥi'am	Western Upper Galilee	1946	Kibbutz	KA	RC Ga'aton	415
Yehud	Coastal Plain (Petaḥ Tikvah Region)	(1948)	Urban Settlement	—	local council	8,600
Yeroḥam	Central Negev Hills	1951	Urban Settlement	—	local council	5,400
Yesha	Northwestern Negev (Besor Region)	1957	Moshav	TM	RC Eshkol	150
Yesodot	Judean Foothills	1948	Moshav Shittufi	PAI	RC Naḥal Sorek	297
Yesud ha-Ma'alah	Ḥuleh Valley	1883	Rural Settlement	—	local council	432
Yifat	Jezreel Valley	(1926)	Kibbutz	IK	RC Kishon	750
Yiftaḥ	Eastern Upper Galilee	1948	Kibbutz	IK	RC Ha-Galil ha-Elyon	. .
Yinnon	Southern Coastal Plain (Malakhi Region)	1952	Moshav	TM	RC Be'er Tuviyyah	610
Yiron	Eastern Upper Galilee	1949	Kibbutz	KM	RC Merom ha-Galil	. .
Yish'i	Judean Foothills	1950	Moshav	PM	RC Matteh Yehudah	500
Yizre'el	Mt. Gilboa	1948	Kibbutz	IK	RC Ha-Gilboa	248
Yodefat	Western Lower Galilee	1960	Kibbutz	—	RC Na'aman	47
Yokne'am	Jezreel Valley	1935	Rural Settlement	—	RC Megiddo	443
Yokne'am (Illit)	Jezreel Valley	1950	Urban Settlement	—	local council	3,650
Yoshivyah	Northwestern Negev (Besor Region)	1950	Moshav	PM	RC Azzatah	237
Yotvatah	Southern Arabah Valley	1951	Kibbutz	IK	RC Ḥevel Eilot	. .
Yuval	Ḥuleh Valley	1952	Moshav	TM	RC Ha-Galil ha-Elyon	. .
Ẓafririm	Southern Judean Foothills (Adullam Region)	1958	Moshav	TM	RC Matteh Yehudah	175
Ẓafriyyah	Coastal Plain (Lod Region)	1949	Moshav	PM	RC Emek Lod	298
Zano'aḥ	Judean Foothills	1950	Moshav	PAI	RC Matteh Yehudah	320
Zavdi'el	Southern Coastal Plain (Malakhi Region)	1950	Moshav	PAI	RC Shafir	412
Ẓe'elim	Northwestern Negev (Besor Region)	1947	Kibbutz	IK	RC Eshkol	193
Zeitan	Coastal Plain (Lod Region)	1950	Moshav	TM	RC Emek Lod	480
Zekharyah	Southern Judean Foothills	1950	Moshav	TM	RC Matteh Yehudah	575
Ẓelafon	Judean Foothills	1950	Moshav	TM	RC Matteh Yehudah	495

Name	Geographical Region	Year of Founding	Settlement Form	Affiliation	Municipal Status	No. of inhabitants 31 Dec 70
Zeraḥyah	Southern Coastal Plain (Malakhi Region)	1950	Moshav	PM	RC Shafir	450
Ẓerufah	Carmel Coast	1949	Moshav	TM	RC Ḥof ha-Karmel	430
Zeru'ah	Northwestern Negev (Gerar Region)	1953	Moshav	PM	RC Azzatah	280
Zikhron Ya'akov	Mt. Carmel	1882	Urban Settlement	—	local council	4,480
Zikim	Southern Coastal Plain (Ashkelon Region)	1949	Kibbutz	KA	RC Ḥof Ashkelon	227
Zimrat	Northwestern Negev (Gerar Region)	1957	Moshav	PM	RC Azzatah	403
Ẓippori	Western Lower Galilee	1949	Moshav	TM	RC Kishon	204
Ẓofit	Southern Sharon (Kefar Sava Region)	1933	Moshav	TM	RC Ha-Sharon ha-Tikhon	330
Ẓofiyyah	Coastal Plain (Reḥovot Region)	1955	Educational Institution	—	(RC) Ḥevel Yavneh	60
Zohar	Southern Coastal Plain (Lachish Region)	1956	Moshav	IḤ	RC Lachish	255
Ẓorah	Judean Foothills	1948	Kibbutz	IK	RC Matteh Yehudah	431
Ẓovah	Jerusalem Hills	1948	Kibbutz	KM	RC Matteh Yehudah	260
Ẓur Hadassah	Jerusalem Hills	1960	Rural Center	—	(RC) Matteh Yehudah	90
Ẓuri'el	Western Upper Galilee	1950	Moshav	PAI	RC Ma'aleh ha-Galil	228
Ẓur Moshe	Southern Sharon (Kefar Yonah Region)	1937	Moshav	TM	RC Ha-Sharon ha-Ẓefoni	412
Ẓur Natan	Southern Sharon	1966	Moshav Shittufi	Ḥ	(RC) Ha-Sharon ha-Tikhon	. .

[E.O.]

NEWSPAPERS AND PERIODICALS, HEBREW

A list of Hebrew newspapers, covering all periods of the Hebrew press, was last published in the late 1920s and about the same amount of time has elapsed since the publication of a list of the Hebrew press in Ereẓ Israel from its inception. In the last few decades the Hebrew press, particularly in Ereẓ Israel, has greatly and rapidly developed. From the point of view of quantity it exceeds, several fold, all the Hebrew press from its beginning until 40 years ago. Consequently, the following list is, of necessity, very selective and only the outstanding Hebrew newspapers and periodicals in all the countries and periods have been included. One of the aims of the list has been to provide a representative sampling of the vast professional and light literature press in the State of Israel, a sampling which is likewise very selective.

Jubilee and memorial volumes, periodicals of all types of educational institutions (from primary school to university), newspapers issued by individual settlements in Israel (of which there are hundreds), house organs of institutions, organizations, factories, and social and political movements, etc. have not been included. There is however a small sampling of Israel governmental publications: for the rest see *Reshimat Pirsumei ha-Memshalah* ("List of Government Publications") which appears quarterly.

The dates of the newspapers listed present a special problem in that it has not always been possible to translate the Hebrew date accurately because the Hebrew year starts with Rosh Ha-Shanah (which usually falls in September) whereas the secular year starts on January 1. Another problem has been that of the continuity of many of the publications; some newspapers and periodicals did (or do) not actually appear with the regularity claimed and thus many items are described as "irregular." A large number of newspapers are unavailable and have not been listed; for others of this kind, which have been listed, no exact statistics have been recorded.

Notwithstanding the above factors, however, the list does reflect the scope and nature of the Hebrew press of the last 300 years.

Abbreviations used are:

A.	= Annual	M.	= Monthly
B-M.	= Bimonthly	N.S.	= New Series
B-W.	= Biweekly	N.Y.	= New York
D.	= Daily	Q.	= Quarterly
F.	= Fortnightly	S-A.	= Semiannual
Irr.	= Irregular	T.A.	= Tel Aviv
Jer.	= Jerusalem	W.	= Weekly
Lit.	= Literary		

1901–1904 indicates that the item appeared from 1901 until 1904; 1901, 1904 indicates that the item appeared in each of these two years only.

Title	Freq.	Place of Publication	Date(s) of Appearance	Main Characteristics
A.B.	F.	Ḥolon	1969–	the first Samaritan newspaper
Adrikhalut	Q.		1966–	architecture, city planning, engineering, interior design, and construction arts
Aḥdut—see also: Ha-Aḥdut Le-Aḥdut ha-Avodah				
Aḥdut ha-Avodah	1	Jaffa	1919	the first organ of the Aḥdut ha-Avodah party
Aḥdut ha-Avodah	M.	T.A.	1930–1932	lit., Mapai
Aḥdut ha-Avodah	1–4	T.A.	1943–1946	collections of issues related to Mapai
Aḥi'asaf—see: Lu'aḥ Aḥi'asaf				
Akhsanyah	1	T.A.	1955	lit.
Akhshav	Irr.	Jer.	1957–	lit.
Akrav	W.	T.A.	1946–1947	humor and satire
Al Admat Bessarabyah	Irr.	T.A.	1959–1963	history of Bessarabian Jewry, 3 vols.
Alef	1	Lvov, Galicia	1937	lit.
Alef	Irr.	T.A.	1938–	organ of the Ha-Ivrim movement (Canaanites)
Aleh	M.	T.A.	1959–	youth organ of the Iḥud ha-Kevuẓot ve-ha-Kibbutzim; continuation of *Nivim*, 1951–59
Alei Hadas	1–4	Odessa, Russia	1865	lit.
Alei Mishmeret	Q.	T.A.	1958–	organ of the National Religious Party Youth
Alei Si'aḥ	1–3	T.A.	1966–1967	literary circles of the Iḥud ha-Kevuẓot ve-ha-Kibbutzim
Al ha-Ḥomah	M.	T.A.	1938	organ of Ha-Shomer ha-Ẓa'ir; appeared under various other titles
Al ha-Mishmar	W.	Jer.	1922–1923	nonpartisan
Al ha-Mishmar	D.	T.A.	1943–	originally *Mishmar*, organ of Ha-Kibbutz ha-Arẓi Ha-Shomer ha-Ẓa'ir; from 1948 *Al ha-Mishmar, Ḥotam* organ of Mapam; from 1970 also weekly magazine
Al ha-Saf	1	Jer.	1918	the last organ of Po'alei Zion in Ereẓ Israel before it merged with Aḥdut ha-Avodah
Al Ḥuk ha-Mikra	1–4	T.A.	1947–1954	biblical research
Alil	1–2	N.Y.	1946–1947	lit.
Alim	1	Kiev, Ukraine	1912	lit.
Alim	Irr.	Jer.	1939–1956	Youth Aliyah; ceased publication in 1956 and renewed publication in 1970
Alim	Irr.	T.A.	1951–1963	theoretical organ of the Ha-No'ar ha-Ẓiyyoni movement.
Alim le-Bibliografyah u-le-Safranut	B–M.	T.A.	1947–1948	bibliography and librarianship; first volume published under the names *Yad la-Safran* and *Ha-Safran*

Title	Freq.	Place of Publication	Date(s) of Appearance	Main Characteristics
Alim le-Bibliografyah ve-Korot Yisrael	Irr.	Vienna	1934–1937	bibliography and Jewish history
Aliyah	Irr.	Jer.	1934–1937 1969–	published by the Aliyah Department of the Jewish Agency
Almanakh ha-Ishah	A.	T.A.	1961–1965	women's almanac
Almanakh Mizpeh	1	T.A.	1930	literary almanac of the Mizpeh Publishing House
Alonekh	M.	T.A.	1950–1963	women's publication
Alon ha-Congress	Q.	T.A.	1967–	published by Israel branch of the World Jewish Congress
Alon ha-Dayyagim	Q.	Haifa	1951–1962	bulletin on fisheries; superseded by *Dayig u-Midgeh*
Alon ha-Ḥevrah ha-Numismatit	Q.	T.A.	1966–	numismatics
Alon ha-Note'a	M.	T.A.	1945–	cultivating fruit trees
Alon ha-Palmaḥ	Irr.	T.A.	1942–1950	illegal organ of the Palmaḥ; without a masthead and no mention of an address
Alon ha-Shofetim	Irr.	T.A.	1963–	bulletin of soccer referees
Alon ha-Shomerim	Irr.	T.A.	1935–1957	organ of the Association of Guards
Alon ha-Tenu'ah ha-Bein-le'ummit le-Sarevanei Milḥamah mi-Ta'amei Mazpun	Irr.	T.A.	1949–1959 1963–1964	bulletin of the international movement of conscientious objectors
Alonim (Kibbutz Dati)—see: Ammudim				
Alon Kibbutzei Ha-Shomer ha-Za'ir	M.	T.A.	1965–	economic problems of the settlements organized in Ha-Kibbutz ha-Arzi Ha-Shomer ha-Za'ir
Alon Mishkei ha-Iḥud	Irr.	T.A.	1963–	economic problems of the settlements organized in Iḥud ha-Kevuzot ve-ha-Kibbutzim
Alon Mishkei ha-Kibbutz ha-Me'uḥad	Irr.	T.A.	1961–	economic problems of the settlements organized in Ha-Kibbutz ha-Me'uḥad
Al Penei Kaddur ha-Arez	1	T.A.	1943	view of the world during World War II
Al Saf ha-Maḥar	1	T.A.	1945	problems of the post-World War II period
Alummah	1	Jer.	1936	research in Judaic studies
Ammanah	1	Jer.	1939	research in Judaic studies
Ammanah	A.	Jer.	1956–1957	Torah culture
Ammot	B–M.	T.A.	1962–1965	lit. and Jewish problems
Ammud ha-Yirah	Irr.	Jer.	1879–1880	ultra-Orthodox organ devoted to propaganda for the settlement of Erez Israel; previously published in Hungary
Ammudim	W.	T.A.	1944–1947	new Aliyah
Ammudim	Irr.	T.A.	1955–	organ of Kibbutz Dati
Am u-Medinah	W.	Jer.	1950–1951	general affairs
Am va-Sefer	Irr.	Jer.-T.A.	1936–	Hebrew culture in Erez Israel and the Diaspora; published by Brit Ivrit Olamit; continuation of *Berit Am*
Am ve-Admato	Q.	Jer.	1963–	problems of land settlement; organ of the Jewish National Fund; continuation of *Karnenu*
Anakh	1	T.A.	1954	lit.
Appiryon	M.	N.Y.	1923–1927	rabbinics; printed in Hungary
Arakhim	1	Warsaw	1919	lit.
Arakhim	Irr.	T.A.	1968–1969	collections for holidays and festivals published by the Religious Department of the Histadrut
Arakhim	Irr.	T.A.	1969–	ideological organ of the New Communist Party (Rakaḥ)
Areshet	1	Jer.	1944	lit. organ of religious writers
Aresheth	A.	Jer.	1958–	bibliography and Hebrew booklore
Ari'el	W.	Jer	1874–1877	newspaper published by former members of the editorial board of *Ḥavazzelet*
Arkhitekturah—see: Adrikhalut				
Ashmoret	W.	T.A.	1945–1952	Mapai Youth
Asefat Ḥakhamim	M.	Koenigsberg, E. Prussia	1877–1878	the second socialist periodical in Hebrew (after *Ha-Emet*); officially a supplement to *Ha-Kol.*
Aspaklaryah	M.	N.Y.	1904	lit.
Aspaklaryah	W.	Jer.	1922–1923	lit. and general affairs
Aspaklaryah	M.	T.A.	1938–1947	digest of Hebrew and non-Hebrew newspapers in Erez Israel and abroad
Aspaklaryah shel ha-Sport	W.	T.A.	1946–1948	sports
Asuppot	Irr.	T.A.	1945–	history of Erez Israel and Jewish labor movement
At	M.	T.A.	1967–	women's magazine

Title	Freq.	Place of Publication	Date(s) of Appearance	Main Characteristics
Atidenu	M.	Berlin	1924	culture and education
Atidenu	M.	Buenos Aires	1926–1927	lit. and current affairs
Atidot	Irr.	T.A.	1944–1959	lit. for youth; frequency of publication changed several times
Attikot	Irr.	Jer.	1946	archaeology
Avaryanut ve-Ḥevrah	A.	Jer.	1966–	delinquency; first year semiannually
Avodah u-Vittu'aḥ Le'ummi	M.	Jer.	1949–	labor and national insurance
Ayin	W.	T.A.	1951–1952	lit.
Ayin be-Ayin	W.	Jer.	1958–1959	religious illustrated magazine; superseded by *Panim el Panim*
Ba-Avodah	1	Jaffa	1918	first publication edited by Berl Katznelson
Ba-Derekh	F.	Vienna	1920–1921	general affairs
Ba-Derekh	W.	Warsaw	1935–1937	the last Hebrew newspaper in Poland
Ba-Derekh	A.	Givat Ḥavivah-Merḥavyah	1967–	Jewish labor movement in Israel and abroad
Ba-Derekh (Communist)—see: Zo ha-Derekh				
Ba-Histadrut	M.	T.A.	1943–1970	weekly review of all Histadrut activities; called *Pinkas li-Fe'ilei ha-Histadrut* during first year of publication; ceased publication in 1960 and renewed in 1962; ceased publication in 1970
Ba-Kefar	M.	T.A.	1947–1952	organ of agricultural workers
Ba-Kibbutz	W.	T.A.	1950–	information weekly of Ha-Kibbutz ha-Me'uḥad
Ba-Kibbutz ha-Arẓi—see: Ha-Shavu'a ba-Kibbutz ha-Arẓi				
Ba-Kur	1	T.A.	1941	Haganah lit. and current affairs
Ba-Ma'aleh	F.	T.A.	1931–	organ of Ha-No'ar ha-Oved; seven issues published 1927–30
Ba-Ma'arakhah	W.	Jer.	1931–1934	extreme anti-Mandatory publication
Ba-Ma'arakhah	Irr.	Jer.	1948, 1961–	problems of Sephardi Jews (see also: *Shevet va-Am*)
Ba-Ma'avar	1–4	Warsaw	1925	published by Hitaḥadut in Poland
Bamah	B–M.	Jer.	1933–1948 1959–	theatrical review
Ba-Maḥaneh	W.	T.A.	1948–	published by Israel Defense Forces; formerly published underground in mimeographed form
Bamat ha-Ishah	Q.	T.A.	1960–	published by WIZO
Ba-Mesillah	M.	T.A.	1946–1947	published by Mizrachi
Ba-Midgeh	M.	Nir David	1948–	fisheries; continuation of *Alon li-Megaddelei Dagim*
Ba-Mifal	M.	Haifa	1942–1950	industrial, Histadrut
Ba-Mifneh	F.	T.A.	1935–1940	published by Left Po'alei Zion; formerly collections published for special occasions under this title
Ba-Mishor	W.	Jer.	1940–1946	lit., religious
Ba-Mivḥan	M.	T.A.	1943–	published by Maḥanot ha-Olim, Deror, Tenu'at ha-No'ar ha-Ḥaluẓi; appeared irregularly from the 1930s to the 1940s
Ba-Nativ	M.	Jer.	1951–1955	aviation club publication
Ba-Nekhar	1	Alexandria, Egypt	1918	published by Palestinian refugees in Egypt during World War I
Ba-Rekhev	M.	T.A.	1955	transportation
Bar-Ilan	A.	Ramat Gan	1963	Judaica and humanities
Barkai	Irr.	Vienna	1886	lit.
Barkai	W.	Odessa, Russia	1919	lit.
Barkai	F.	Johannesburg	1933–	lit; a few first numbers called *Ba-Sad*
Ba-Sa'ar	1	T.A.	1943	lit; Hebrew writers for Jewish soldiers
Ba-Sha'ar	F.	T.A.	1947–1952	Youth Movement of Mapam
Ba-Sha'ar	M. & B–M.	T.A.	1958–	ideological organ of Mapam
Ba-Telem	Irr.	T.A.	1954–1960	published for moshavim of new immigrants
Bat Kol	D., W.	Cracow-Lvov, Galicia	1911–1914	lit., religious
Be'ad ve-Neged	B-M.	Jer.	1963–	social and political problems
Be'ayot	M.	Jer.	1944–1949	Jewish-Arab cooperation; continuation of *Be'ayot ha-Yom*
Be'ayot Beinle'ummiyyot	Q.	T.A.	1963–	international affairs, underdeveloped countries

Title	Freq.	Place of Publication	Date(s) of Appearance	Main Characteristics
Be'ayot ha-Ḥinnukh ha-Meshuttaf	Q.	T.A.	1937–	pedagogical organ of Ha-Kibbutz ha-Arẓi Ha-Shomer ha-Ẓa'ir
Be'ayot ha-Yom				Jewish-Arab cooperation, superseded by *Be'ayot*
Be-Ḥakla'ut u-va-Meshek	M.	T.A.	1960–1965	labor and output
Beḥinot	1–11	Jer.	1952–1955	literary criticism
Beḥinot	Irr.	T.A.	1970–	studies of Russian and East European Jews
Beinetayim	1	Jer.	1913	lit.
Bein ha-Meẓarim	1–2	Jer.	1915	organ of Po'alei Zion during World War I
Bein ha-Zemannim	1	Safed	1916	organ of Po'alei Zion during World War I
Bein ha-Zemannim	1–2	Kharkov, Ukraine	1918–1919	lit.
Bein Milḥamah ve-Shalom	1	T.A.	1945	post-World War II political problems
Beitar	M.	Jer.	1933–1934	lit.; Revisionist
Beit Eked	1	Berdichev, Ukraine	1892	lit.
Beit ha-Keneset	1	Jer.	1955	studies of synagogues
Beit ha-Midrash	M.	Vienna	1865	Judaic studies
Beit ha-Midrash	1	Cracow, Poland	1888	rabbinics and Judaic studies
Beit ha-Midrash he-Ḥadash	M.	Grajewo, Poland	1928–1931	Judaic studies
Beit Mikra	Q.	Jer.	1956–	Bible studies
Beit Oẓar ha-Sifrut—see: Oẓar ha-Sifrut				
Beit Talmud	1–5	Vienna	1881–1889	studies of rabbinic literature
Beit Va'ad la-Ḥakhamim	M.	Grosswardein (Oradea), Transylvania	1875	Judaic studies
Beit Va'ad la-Ḥakhamim	M.	London-Leeds	1902–1904	rabbinics and Judaic studies
Beit Va'ad la-Ḥakhamim	M.	N.Y.	1903	rabbinics
Beit Va'ad la-Ḥakhamim		SatuMare (Szatmar), Transylvania	1922–1939	rabbinics
Beit Ya'akov	M.	Jer.	1959–	education and lit., religious
Beit Yiẓḥak	A.	N.Y.	1952–1961	*halakhah*
Beivar	Q.	T.A.	1959	zoo
Be-Maḥaneh Gadna	M.	T.A.	1949–	organ of the *Gadna
Be-Maḥaneh Naḥal	M.	T.A.	1948–	organ of the *Naḥal
Be-Misholei ha-Ḥinnukh	Irr.	Kaunas (Kovno), Lithuania	1936–1940	pedagogy
Ben Ammi	M.	St. Petersburg	1887	lit.
Bereshit	1	Moscow-Leningrad	1926	lit.; printed in Berlin
Beri'ut	F.	T.A.	1933–1935	health
Beri'ut ha-Am	Q.	Jer.	1926–1927	health
Beri'ut ha-Oved	Irr.	T.A.	1924–1929	workers' health
Beri'ut ha-Ẓibbur	Q.	Jer.	1958	health
Be-Sha'ah Zu	1–3	Jaffa	1916	organ of Ha-Po'el ha-Ẓa'ir during World War I
Be-Sherut ha-Ezraḥ	Q.	T.A.	1957–	Magen David Adom in Israel
Be-Sherut ha-Ta'asukah	B–M.	Ramat Gan	1959–	problems of employment
Be-Terem	M., F., Q.	T.A.	1942–1960	semilegal organ of the Haganah; originally called *Milḥamtenu* and also known by other titles until the establishment of the State of Israel
Betiḥut	M.	T.A.	1957–	safety and hygiene at work
Be-Ẓok ha-Ittim	1	Safed	1919	lit.
Bikkoret ha-Ittim	Irr.	Leipzig, Germany	1864–1865	the first humor and satire periodical in Hebrew
Bikkoret u-Farshanut	Irr.	Ramat Gan	1970–	literary criticism
Bikkurei ha-Ittim	A	Vienna	1821–1831	lit. and Judaic studies: first few volumes partly in German
Bikkurei ha-Ittim	1	Vienna	1844	lit. and Judaic studies
Bikkurei ha-Ittim ha-Ḥadashim	1	Vienna	1845	lit. and Judaic studies
Bikkurei ha-Shanah	A	Amsterdam	1843	Hebrew and Dutch almanac
Bikkurei To'elet	A.	Amsterdam	1820	almanac
Bikkurim	A.	Vienna	1864–1865	lit.
Billui Na'im	F.	Jer.	1969–	humor, crossword puzzles, etc.
Bimat ha-Ḥovevim	Irr.	T.A.	1959–	amateur theater organ
Binyan va-Ḥaroshet	M.	T.A.	1927–1928	organ of the Engineers' Union; continuation of *Yedi'ot*
Bi-Sedeh Ḥemed		T.A.	1957–	pedagogical organ of religious teachers

Title	Freq.	Place of Publication	Date(s) of Appearance	Main Characteristics
Bi-Sedeh ha-Beniyyah	M.	Haifa	1953–	engineering
Bi-Sedeh ha-Tekhnikah	Irr.		1941–1946	technology; name changed from *Bi-Shevilei ha-Tekhnikah* to *Be-Darkhei ha-Tekhnikah* to *Bi-Netivei ha-Tekhnikah*
Bi-Tefuẓot ha-Golah	Q.	Jer.	1958–	World Jewry, published by the Zionist Organization
Bittaḥon ve-Higyenah ba-Avodah	Q.	Jer.	1949–1956	safety and hygiene at work
Bitta'on	M.	Chicago	1934–1938	pedagogy, originally mimeographed
Bitte'on Ḥabad	Irr.	T.A.	1953–	published by Ḥabad Ḥasidim
Bitte'on Ḥeil ha-Avir—see: Ḥeil ha-Avir				
Bittu'aḥ	Q.	T.A.	1967	insurance
Bitzaron	M.	N.Y.	1939–	lit. and Judaic studies
Bul	W.	T.A.	1965–	gossip and sex
Bulim—see also: Ha-Bulai	M.	T.A.	1957–1963	stamps: superseded by *Ha-Yarḥon ha-Yisre'eli le-Vula'ut*
Bulletin shel ha-Makhon le-Ḥeker ha-Kalkalah		T.A.	1937–1948	economics
Bustanai—see also: Mi-Yamim Rishonim	W.	Reḥovot	1929–1939	organ of the Hitaḥadut ha-Ikkarim (Farmers' Association); youth supplement *Bustanai la-No'ar,* 1934–37
Daf	Irr.	T.A.	1950–	information bulletin of the Hebrew Writers' Association
Daf ha-Tenu'ah	W.	T.A.	1960–	organ of Ha-No'ar ha-Ẓiyyoni
Dagesh	F., M.	T.A.	1950–1954	digest of the Hebrew press abroad
Dappei Aliyah	Irr.	Jer.	1949–	*aliyah* problems
Dappim	Q.	Jer.	1948–	Youth Aliyah
Dappim	M.	Johannesburg	1950–1953	lit.
Dappim	Irr.	Jer.	1950–1955 1964–	pedagogical and special problems
Dappim le-Fiyyut u-le-Vikkoret	1	Jer.	1916	poetry and criticism
Dappim le-Ḥeker ha-Sho'ah		T.A.	1951	Holocaust research by Isaac Katznelson House, N.S. 1970
Dappim le-Limmud Ta'amei ha-Mikra	Irr.	T.A.	1959–	biblical accents
Dappim li-Tezunah	M.	Jer.	1950–	nutrition; formerly *Yarḥon ha-Tezunah*
Dappim li-Ydi'ot ha-Sefer ve-ha-Safranut	Irr.	Jer.	1942–1943	booklore and librarianship
Dappim Refu'iyyim	B–M.	T.A.	1935	medical organ of Kuppat Ḥolim
Darkenu	1	Odessa, Russia	1917	Hebrew culture and education
Darkhei ha-Kalkalah	B–M.	T.A.	1939–1940	economics
Darkhei ha-No'ar	1	Jer.	1938	problems of youth in the Zionist framework
Darom	M.	Buenos Aires	1938	lit.; see also *Zohar*
Dat u-Medinah	1	T.A.	1949	published by religious members of the Histadrut
Davar	D.	T.A.	1925–	Histadrut daily; the first daily newspaper of Jewish workers in Ereẓ Israel
Davar la-Golah	W.	T.A.	1939–1940	*Davar* aimed at a readership abroad
Dayig u-Midgeh	Q.	Haifa	1963–	fisheries
Degel ha-Rabbanim	Irr.	Lodz, Poland	1926–1929	rabbinics
Degel ha-Torah	M.	Warsaw	1921–1922	rabbinics
De'ot	Irr.	Jer.	1957–	published for religious students
Derekh—see also: Ha-Derekh				
Derekh ha-Po'el	M.	T.A.	1934–1946	Left Po'alei Zion
Devarenu	M.	Vienna	1930–1931	lit.
Devar ha-Moreh	Irr.	Warsaw	1930–1939	pedagogy
Devar ha-Moreh	Irr.	N.Y.	1945	pedagogy
Devar ha-Po'elet	M.	T.A.	1934–	women's magazine of the Histadrut
Devar ha-Shavu'a	W.	T.A.	1946–	illustrated magazine; in the last few years the weekly supplement of *Davar*
Devar ha-Shilton ha-Mekomi—see: Ha-Shilton ha-Mekomi				
Devir	Q.	Berlin	1923	Judaic studies
Diglenu	M.	Warsaw	1920–1930	Ẓe'irei Agudat Israel
Diglenu	M.	T.A.	1939	Ẓe'irei Agudat Israel in Ereẓ Israel; irregular.
Dinei Yisrael	A.	Jer.	1970–	Jewish law and family law in Israel; partly in English
Divrei ha-Akademyah le-Madda'im	A.	Jer.	1966–	transactions of the Academy

Title	Freq.	Place of Publication	Date(s) of Appearance	Main Characteristics
Divrei ha-Keneset		Jer.	1949–	deliberations of the Knesset; preceded by deliberations of the Provisional State Council, 1948–49
Divrei Ḥakhamim	1	Metz, Lorraine	1849	collection of edited Hebrew manuscripts from the Middle Ages
Divrei ha-Yamim	1–4	Jer.	1950–1955	ancient and medieval history of the Jews in the form of a modern newspaper
Divrei Soferim	1	T.A.	1944	lit.
Diyyunim	Irr.	Ẓofit (Bet Berl)	1970–	discussions of current problems
Do'ar—see also: Ha-Do'ar	Q.	Jer.	1952–	published by the Ministry of Posts
Do'ar ha-Yom	D.	Jer.	1919–1936	newspaper published by native-born Palestinian Jews and supported by farming circles and older settlers; for some time edited by V. Jabotinsky and supported the Revisionist movement
Dorenu	M.	Chicago	1934–1935	lit.
Dorot	F.	T.A.	1949–1950	lit.
Dukhan	A.	Jer.	1960–1966	music and religion
Edot	Q.	Jer.	1945–1948	folklore and ethnology
Edut le-Yisrael	Q.	N.Y.-Lvov	1888–1898	missionary newspaper
Egel ha-Zahav	W.	T.A.	1939	humor and satire
Egoz	A.	Jer.	1968–1969	lit.
Ein ha-Kore	Q.	Berlin	1923	lit. and bibliography
Ein ha-Moreh	Irr.	Sedeh Boker	1969–	pedagogy
Ein ha-Sefer	Irr.	T.A.	1945–1947	bibliography
Eitanim—see also: Ha-Eitanim	M.	T.A.	1948–	health and hygiene; for a number of years included a youth supplement, *Eitanim li-Yladeinu*
Eked	Q.	T.A.	1960–	poetry
Emunim	1	Jer.	1955	collections of poems by religious poets
Ereẓ	1	Odessa, Russia	1919	lit.
Ereẓ Yisrael		Jer.	1923	the first morning daily in Ereẓ Israel
Eretz Israel	A.	Jer.	1951–1969	archaeology and history of the *yishuv*; each volume is dedicated to a scholar
Eshkolot	Irr.	Kishinev, Moldavia	1927–1929	lit.
Eshkolot	A.	Jer.	1954–	the classical world
Eshnav	Irr.	T.A.	1941–1947	illegal organ of the Haganah; 157 issues printed
Etgar	Irr.	T.A.	1960–1967	organ of the "Semitic movement"
Foto-Roman	M.	T.A.	1970–	picture stories
Gadish	1	T.A.	1930	lit.
Gallim	F.	Vilna	1929–1930	lit.
Gammad	M.	T.A.	1957–	humor
Gan ha-Yerek	M.	Jaffa	1917–1918	vegetable growing; published Berl Katzenelson's articles on vegetables
Gannenu	Irr.	Jer.	1919–1925	kindergarten
Gan Peraḥim	1–3	Vilna	1882–1893	lit.
Gan va-Nof	M.	T.A.	1945–	gardening and planting
Gazit	M.	T.A.	1932	lit. and art; first published in Jerusalem
Genazim—see also: Yedi'ot Genazim	A.	T.A.	1961–	collection of documents of modern Hebrew literature
Ge'on ha-Areẓ	A.	Warsaw	1893–1894	lit.
Gerizim	F.	Ḥolon	1970–	the second Samaritan newspaper
Gesher	Q.	Jer.	1954–	problems of Jews and Judaism
Gevilin	Q.	T.A.	1957–	published by the National Religious Party
Gevulot	Irr.	Vienna	1918–1920	lit.
Gilyonenu	Irr.	N.Y.	1946–1954	religious education of American Mizrachi
Gilyonot	M.	T.A.	1933–1954	lit.
Ginzei Kedem	Irr.	Jer.	1922–1944	collections of research on the geonic period
Ginzei Nistarot	Irr.	Bamberg, Germany	1868–1878	Judaic studies
Ginzei Schechter	Irr.	N.Y.	1928–1929	*genizah* studies

Title	Freq.	Place of Publication	Date(s) of Appearance	Main Characteristics
Gittit	M.	T.A.	1964–	music
Gordonyah	Irr.	Warsaw	1926–1933	published by World Center of the Gordonia movement
Goren Kiddon	M.	T.A.	1948–1951	sports; published by Hapoel
Ha-Adamah	M.	T.A.	1920, 1923	lit.; final issues appeared after its editor, J. H. Brenner, was killed
Ha-Aḥdut—see also: Aḥdut	W.	Jer.	1910–1915	first Hebrew organ of Po'alei Zion in Ereẓ Israel; a monthly in 1910
Ha-Aḥot be-Yisrael	Q.	T.A.	1948–	nursing; copies of *Ha-Aḥot* came out in Jerusalem during the 1930s and 1940s
Ha-Am	W.	Moscow	1916–1918	lit.
Ha-Am	D.	Moscow	1917–1918	the last Hebrew daily in Russia; closed by the Bolsheviks
Ha-Am	W.	N.Y.	1916	lit.
Ha-Am		Jer.	1931	Revisionist, superseded by *Ḥazit ha-Am*
Haaretz		Jer.-T.A.	1919–	until Dec. 2, 1919 called *Ḥadshot ha-Areẓ*; in Jerusalem until 1923 and from then in Tel Aviv; many supplements for youth and others; weekly magazine supplement issued since the beginning of 1963
Ha-Areẓ	Irr.	Jer.	1891	lit.
Ha-Areẓ ve-ha-Avodah	Q.	Jaffa	1918–1919	organ of Ha-Po'el ha-Ẓa'ir
Ha-Ari'el—see: Ari'el				
Ha-Asif	A.	London-Leipzig	1847, 1849	Judaic studies
Ha-Asif	A.	Warsaw	1884–1893	lit.
Ha-Be'er	Q.	Zamosc, Poland	1923–1938	rabbinics
Ha-Bimah ha-Ivrit	M.	Buenos Aires	1921–1928	lit.
Ha-Binyan	Irr.	T.A.	1934–1938	architecture; known under other names
Ha-Boker	D.	Warsaw	1909	
Ha-Boker	D.	T.A.	1935–1965	General Zionists (B), Liberals; many supplements
Ha-Boker Or	M.	Lvov-Warsaw	1876–1886	lit.
Ha-Boneh ha-Ḥofshi	B–M.	T.A.	1933–	freemasonry; began as a quarterly for a number of years
Ha-Bulai ha-Ivri	Irr.	T.A.	1950–1957	stamps; during the last year of publication known as *Ha-Bulai*
Ḥadashot	W. & D.	T.A.	1937–1940	general affairs
Ḥadashot Aḥaronot	D.	Jer.	1936–1937	general affairs
Ḥadashot Arkheologiyyot	Q.	Jer.	1962–	archaeology
Ḥadashot me-ha-Areẓ ha-Kedoshah	W.	Jer.-Cairo	1918–1919	newspaper of the British occupation autyorities; the first newspaper to appear in Palestine after the British conquest; its continuation was *Ḥadshot ha-Areẓ*, the first incarnation of *Haaretz*
Ha-Dayig ha-Yisre'eli	M.	T.A.	1950–1961	fisheries
Ha-Degel—see: Ha-Yehudi				
Ha-Derekh	M.	Frankfort Zurich-Vienna	1913–1914 1919–1924	central organ of Agudat Israel
Ha-Derekh	Irr.	Warsaw	1928	World Union of Jewish Youth
Ha-Derekh	W.	T.A.	1942–1947	Agudat Israel
Ha-Derekh	Irr.	T.A.	1951–1965	theoretical organ of the Israel Communist Party; superseded by *Zu ha-Derekh* of the New Communist List (Rakaḥ)
Ha-Deror	W.	N.Y.	1911	lit.
Ha-Devir	M.	Jer.	1919–1923	Judaic studies and rabbinics
Ha-Devorah	M.	N.Y.	1911–1912	lit. and satire
Hadoar	D.	N.Y.	1921–1923	255 issues
Hadoar	W.	N.Y.	1923–	lit.
Ha-Dor	W.	Cracow Poland	1901, 1904	lit.
Ha-Dor	D.	T.A.	1948–1955	Mapai afternoon paper
Hadorom	S–A	N.Y.	1957–	rabbinics and Judaic studies
Ḥadshot ha-Erev	D.	T.A.	1946–1947	afternoon paper of Mapai
Ḥadshot ha-Kalkalah ha-Ereẓ Yisre'elit	M.	Jer.	1945–1948	economics
Ḥadshot ha-Neft	M.	T.A.	1965–	published by the Israel Oil Institute
Ḥadshot ha-Sport	D.	T.A.	1954–	sports
Ḥadshot ha-Taḥburah	F.	Ramat Gan	1970–	air, land, and sea transportation

Title	Freq.	Place of Publication	Date(s) of Appearance	Main Characteristics
Ḥadshot ha-Yom	D.	Jer.	1943	a government newspaper in Hebrew that was published when all Hebrew newspapers were confiscated on the eve of the siege and search of Ramat ha-Kovesh by the British; eight issues published in November 1943
Ḥadshot N.C.R.	Q.	T.A.	1964–	N.C.R. news
Ḥadshot Pensyah u-Vittu'aḥ Sozyali	M.	T.A.	1968–	pension and social security
Ḥadshot Sport ve-Toto	W.	T.A.	1970–	sports and Toto (football pools)
Ha-Edah	Q.	Jer.	1966–	ultra-Orthodox community in Jerusalem
Ha-Eitanim	M.	Drohobycz, Galicia	1897–1898	the first pedagogical periodical in Hebrew; only three issues published
Ha-Emet	M.	Vienna	1877	the first Socialist periodical in Hebrew; only three issues published; two reprints
Ha-Em ve-ha-Yeled	A.	T.A.	1934–1936	child care; also under the names *Sefer ha-Shanah ha-Em ve-ha-Yeled* or *Lu'aḥ ha-Em ve-ha-Yeled*
Ha-Esh	M.	T.A.	1955–1962	published by the Fire Department; isolated pamphlets under this title came out in 1930 and 1940
Ha-Eshkol	A.	Cracow, Poland	1898–1913	Judaic studies (1–7)
Ha-Ezraḥ	M.	Jaffa	1919	lit.
Ha-Galgal	F. & W.	Jer.	1943–1948	lit. and radio; continuation of *Radio Yerushalayim*; official paper of the Mandatory government
Ha-Galil	1	Tiberias-Safed	1919	lit.
Ha-Gan	1	St. Petersburg	1899	lit.
Ha-Gat	1	St. Petersburg	1897	lit.
Ha-Gedud	Irr.	T.A.	1923–1929	published by the "Defenders of the Hebrew language"
Ha-Gesher	Q.	Chicago	1939–1940	pedagogy
Ha-Ginnah	Irr.	Odessa-Jer.	1917–1925	nursery school problems
Ha-Goren	A.	Berdichev-Berlin	1897–1928	Judaic studies
Ha-Goren	1	St. Petersburg	1898	lit.
Ha-Ḥarsa—see: Ha-Shemesh				
Ha-Ḥayyal ha-Ivri	F. & D.		1941–1946	originally mimeographed in the North African desert and later in various places in Europe; a daily under the name *La-Ḥayyal*, 1944–46
Ha-Ḥayyal ha-Meshuḥrar	Irr.	T.A.	1946–	began to appear as *Ha-Ḥayyal ha-Ivri*, the newspaper of the demobilized soldiers, and later under other names until it became the organ of disabled veterans of Israel wars; currently *Ha-Loḥem*
Ha-Ḥayyim	W.	Vilna	1920	lit.
Ha-Ḥayyim	W.	Jer.	1922	illus. lit.; one of the first illustrated weeklies.
Ha-Ḥayyim Hallalu	W.	T.A.	1935	illus.
Ha-Ḥazit	Irr.	T.A.	1943–1948	organ of Leḥi; mostly mimeographed organ
Ha-Ḥazit	M.	T.A.	1966–	organ of the extreme nationalists (formerly Leḥi) and after the Six-Day War supporting the territorial integrity of Ereẓ Israel
Ha-Hed	M.	Jer.	1926–1952	lit., religious; unofficial organ of the Department of Religion of the JNF
Ha-Ḥerut—see also: Ḥerut	F. & D.	Jer.	1909–1917	a daily from 1912; the only newspaper to appear in Jerusalem during World War I.
Ha-Ḥerut	D.	Jer.	1932	Sephardi organ
Ha-Ḥevrah	Irr.	T.A.	1940–1946	pro-Revisionist
Ha-Ḥevrah	Irr.	T.A.	1959–1964, 1969–	pro-Mapai academicians; now under the name *Akademot*
Ha-Ḥinnukh	M., B–M. Q.	Jer. T.A.	1910–	the oldest pedagogical periodical still appearing
Ha-Ḥinnukh ha-Gufani	B–M.	T.A.-Netanyah	1944–	originally published by the Va'ad Le'ummi and now published by the Wingate Institute; publication periodically interrupted
Ha-Ḥinnukh ha-Ivri	Q.	N.Y.	1938–1939	pedagogy
Ha-Hinnukh ha-Meshuttaf—see: Be'ayot ha-Hinnukh				
Ha-Ḥinnukh ha-Musikali	Irr.	Jer.	1950–	music education

Title	Freq.	Place of Publication	Date(s) of Appearance	Main Characteristics
Ha-Ḥoker	Irr.	Cracow-Vienna	1891–1893	Judaic studies
Ha-Ḥomah	Irr.	Jer.	1944–	published by the Neturei Karta under various names, including *Ḥomatenu, Mishmeret ha-Ḥomah,* etc.
Ha-Ḥozeh	W.	Berlin-Hamburg	1881–1882	lit.
Ha-Ikkar	Irr.	Jer.	1893–1895	first agricultural periodical in Hebrew—first two issues are partly in Yiddish
Ha-Ishah	M.	Jer.	1926–1929	women's magazine
Ha-Ishah ba-Medinah	M.	T.A.	1949–1953	women's magazine
Ha-Ishah be-Yisrael	Irr.	T.A.	1948–1949	WIZO organ; first issue entitled *WIZO bi-Medinat Yisrael*
Ha-Itton ha-Demokrati	Irr.	T.A.	1945	the "Third [Trotskyite] Force Movement"
Ha-Itton ha-Rasmi	F.	Jer.	1921–1948	official gazette of the British in Palestine; also in Arabic and English
Ha-Ittonai ha-Yehudi	Irr.	Jer.-T.A.	1963–	organ of the World Union of Jewish Journalists; partly in Yiddish, three in English; first 17 issues entitled *Korot*
Haivri—see also: Ivri	W.	N.Y.	1892–1898 1901–1902	lit.; with short interruptions
Ha-Ivri	W.	Berlin-N.Y.	1910–1921	Mizrachi; from 1916 in New York
Ha-Ivri	Irr.	T.A.	1935–1936	vocalized, for new immigrants
Ha-Ivri he-Ḥadash	1	Warsaw	1912	lit.
Ha-Kabbai ha-Mitnaddev	B–M.	T.A.	1938–1945	voluntary firemen
Ha-Kabbelan ve-ha-Boneh	M.	T.A.	1952–	Building Contractors' Association
Ha-Kalban	M.	Jer.	1944–1947	dog owners and trainers
Ha-Kalkalah ha-Ereẓ Yisre'elit	M.	T.A.	1935–1938	economy of Palestine
Ha-Karmel	W. & M.	Vilna	1860–1879	the first Hebrew weekly of Lithuanian Jews; a weekly until the beginning of 1871 and a monthly from the end of 1871
Ha-Karmel	D.	Haifa	1938	afternoon daily
Ha-Kaspan	M.	Jer.	1932–1934	financial and economic affairs
Ha-Kedem	Q.	St. Petersburg	1907–1909	Judaic studies
Ha-Kenes ha-Madda'i ha-Meyuḥad	Irr.	Jer.	1956–	published by the Association for the Advancement of Science in Israel
Ha-Kerem	1	Warsaw	1887	Judaic studies, lit.
Ha-Kerem	1	Vilna	1906	lit.
Ha-Kerem	1	Berdichev, Ukraine	1897	lit.
Ha-Kerem	B–M.	Boston, Mass.	1915	pedagogy
Ha-Keshet—see also: Keshet	M.	Berlin	1903	lit. and art, the first art periodical in Hebrew
Ha-Khimai be-Yisrael	Irr.	Haifa	1968–	organ of the Israel Chemistry Society
Ha-Kinnus ha-Arẓi le-Torah she-be-Al Peh	A.	Jer.	1959–	halakhic transactions
Ha-Kinnus ha-Olami le-Madda'ei ha-Yahadut	Irr.	Jer.	1952, 1967–1968	papers of the First and Fourth World Congress of Jewish studies; partly in other languages
Ḥakla'ut be-Yisrael	M.	T.A.	1956–	agriculture
Ha-Kokhavim	1	Vilna	1865	lit.
Ha-Kokhavim be-Ḥodsham	M.	Jer.	1954–	astronomy
Ha-Kol—see also: Kol	F. & W.	Koenigsberg, E. Prussia	1876–1880	the second Hebrew Socialist newspaper, *Asefat Ḥakhamim,* was published under the auspices of this paper
Ha-Kol	W. & F.	N.Y.	1889	a continuation of the previous entry
Ha-Kol	W.	Warsaw	1907	ultra-Orthodox
Ha-Kol	D.	Jer.	1949–1967	Po'alei Agudat Israel
Ha-Le'om	M. & W.	N.Y.	1901–1908	during the first years partly in Yiddish
Ha-Le'ummi	W.	N.Y.	1888–1889	lit.
Ha-Levanon	M., F. & W.	Jer., Paris-Mainz-London	1863–1886	the first newspaper published in Jerusalem (1863–64); afterward in Europe with interruptions
Halikhot—see also: Shanah be-Shanah	Q.	T.A.	1958–	religious publication
Hallel	M.	Jer.	1930	music and song
Ha-Loḥem—see: Ha-Ḥayyal ha-Meshuḥrar				
Ha-Ma'arav	F. & W.	T.A.	1950–1952	
Ha-Ma'as	Irr.	T.A.	1944–1950	organ of Leḥi during the British Mandate
Ha-Mabbit	W.	Vienna	1878	lit.; some issues under the title *Ha-Mabbit le-Yisrael*
Ha-Madda ve-ha-Tekhnikah, —Ha-Tekhnai ha-Ẓa'ir see Ha-Tekhnai ha-Ẓa'ir				

Title	Freq.	Place of Publication	Date(s) of Appearance	Main Characteristics
Ha-Maggid	W.	Lyck-Berlin-Cracow	1856–1903	the first modern newspaper in Hebrew; from the 1890s the name varies: *Ha-Maggid he-Ḥadash, Ha-Maggid le-Yisrael, Ha-Shavu'a*
Ha-Maḥar	Irr.	T.A.	1927–1931 1940	a nonconformist publication by A. Hameiri
Ha-Makkabbi	Q.	Odessa, Russia	1918	Maccabi Russia
Ha-Makkabbi	Irr.	Jer.-Jaffa-T.A.	1913–1938	various pamphlets and organs by this name were published irregularly by the Maccabi Organization
Ḥammamot u-Feraḥim	Irr.	T.A.	1968–	flower growing
Ḥamishah ha-Kunteresim	1	Vienna	1864	collection of edited ancient manuscripts
Ha-Ma'or	M.	N.Y.	1946	rabbinics
Ha-Mashkif	D.	T.A.	1938–1948	Revisionist organ; superseded by *Ḥerut*
Ha-Matos	M.	T.A.	1954	aviation
Ha-Mattarah	W.	T.A.	1933	published by the Grossman faction, which split from the Revisionist movement in the same year
Ha-Ma'yan	M. & Q.	Jer.	1952–	halakhic and Judaic studies
Ha-Mazkir	Irr.	Lvov, Galicia	1881–1886	Hebrew supplement to the Polish-Jewish Assimilations paper *Ojczyzna*
Ha-Me'ammer	Irr.	Jer.	1905–1920	collections of Palestinography
Ha-Me'assef—see also: Me'assef	Irr.	Koenigsberg-Berlin-Breslau-Altona-Dessau	1783–1811	inaugurated the Haskalah period of modern Jewish literature
Ha-Me'assef	1	Breslau, Germany	1829	lit.; partly in German
Ha-Me'assef	1	Vienna	1862	new edition of the first volume of *Ha-Me'assef* with many additions
Ha-Me'assef	1	Koenigsberg, Prussia	1879	lit. supplement to *Ha-Kol*
Ha-Me'assef	M.	Jer.	1896–1915	rabbinics
Ha-Me'assef ba-Areẓ ha-Ḥadashah	1	N.Y.	1881	organ of the first Society of Lovers of Hebrew in the United States
Ha-Me'assef li-Shenat ha-Sheloshim shel ha-Ẓefirah	1	Warsaw	1903	in honor of the 30th anniversary of *Ha-Ẓefirah*
Ha-Medinah	D.	T.A.	1948	a political newspaper
Ha-Me'ir	M.	Jaffa	1912	Palestinography
Ha-Melakhah	Irr.	Jer.	1943–1950 1958	published for craftsmen
Ha-Meliẓ—see also: Meliẓ	W. B–W. D.	Odessa-St. Petersburg	1860–1903	the first Hebrew newspaper in Russia; in St. Petersburg from 1871; a daily from 1886
Ha-Melonai	Q.	T.A.	1967	published by the Hotel Association in Israel
Ha-Melona'ut	Irr.	T.A.	1949–	published by the Union of Hotel Employees in Israel
Ha-Me'orer	M.	London	1906–1907	lit.
Ha-Me'orer	Irr.	T.A.	1953–1958	organ for Sephardim and members of Oriental communities
Ha-Meshek ha-Ḥakla'i	M.	T.A.	1940–	continuation of *Ha-Ḥaklai ha-Za'ir;* early volumes entitled *Ha-Meshek ha-Za'ir,* first volume partly in German
Ha-Meshek ha-Shittufi	F.	T.A.	1932–	cooperative economics; ceased publication in 1948 and reissued in 1953
Ha-Meshek ha-Za'ir—see: Ha-Meshek ha-Ḥakla'i				
Ha-Mesillah	M.	N.Y.	1936–1943	rabbinics; partly in Yiddish
Ha-Mesillah	Irr.	Jer.	1956–1964	organ of yeshivah students and immigrants from Yemen
Ha-Mevakker ha-Penimi	Q.	T.A.-Jer.	1963–	published by the Association of Internal Auditors
Ha-Mevasser	W.	Lvov Galicia	1861–1866	the first Hebrew newspaper in Galicia; its literary supplement was called *Ha-Nesher*
Ha-Mevasser	W.	Constantinople	1910–1911	a Zionist paper published after the revolution of the Young Turks
Ha-Mevasser	D. & W.	Jer.	1948–1952	Agudat Israel; originally an afternoon daily, later a weekly
Ha-Mevatte'aḥ ha-Yisre'eli	Irr.	T.A.	1941–1960	insurance; two issues appeared in 1932 under the title *Ha-Mevatte'aḥ*
Ha-Mifal	M.	T.A.	1953–	output and export
Ha-Minhal	Q.	T.A.	1950–1959	management
Hamisderonah	M.	Jer.	1886–1887	rabbinics and Judaic studies; the first issues were printed in Frankfort

Title	Freq.	Place of Publication	Date(s) of Appearance	Main Characteristics
Ha-Mishar	W., F. & M.	T.A.-Jaffa	1933–1940 1945–1956	trade
Ha-Mishar ba-Ammim u-ve-Yisrael	1	T.A.	1941	trade
Ha-Mishpat—see also: Mishpat	M.	Jer.-T.A.	1927–1934	law
Ha-Mishpat ha-Ivri	1	Odessa, Russia	1918	Jewish law
Ha-Mishpat ha-Ivri	A.	T.A.	1926–1939	Jewish law
Ha-Mizpeh	M.	St. Petersburg	1886	lit.
Ha-Mizpeh	W.	Cracow, Poland	1904–1914 1917–1921	S. Y. Agnon published his first literary endeavors in this paper
Ha-Mizpeh	M.	N.Y.	1910–1911	rabbinics and Judaic studies
Ha-Mizpeh	Irr.	Warsaw	1926–1936	publication of Ha-Shomer ha-Za'ir in Poland
Ha-Mizpeh	Irr.	T.A.	1945–1949	publication of Ha-Shomer ha-Za'ir in Israel
Ha-Mizpeh	S–A.	Jer.	1961–1968	organ of the National Religious Party
Ha-Mizrah	M.	Cracow, Poland	1903	first organ of Mizrachi
Ha-Mizrah	W.	T.A.	1938	affairs of the Yemenite community
Ha-Mizrah he-Hadash	Q.	Jer.	1949–	published by the Israel Oriental Society
Ha-Mizrachi	W.	Warsaw	1919–1922	organ of Mizrachi in Poland
Ha-Modi'a	W.	Poltava, Ukraine	1910–1914	ultra-Orthodox
Ha-Modi'a	D.	Jer.	1950–	Agudat Israel; supplement for children, 1952–59
Ha-Modi'a le-Hodashim	M.	N.Y.	1900–1901	lit.
Ha-Moreh	M.	N.Y.	1894	lit.
Ha-Moreh	1	N.Y.	1924	pedagogy
Ha-Moriyyah—see also: Moriyyah	F.	Jer.	1892	informative material from Erez Israel
Ha-Musakh	M.	T.A.	1954–	automobile repairs
Handasah ve-Adrikhalut	B–M.	T.A.	1931–	engineering; in the first year appeared irregularly under various names
Ha-Ne'eman	Irr.	T.A.	1945–	organ of yeshivah students
Ha-Nesher	M.	Pressburg (Bratislava), Czechoslovakia	1933–1940	rabbinics; for *Ha-Nesher* of Lvov, see *Ha-Mevasser*
Ha-Nir	1	Jer.	1909	lit.—religious
Ha-No'ar ha-Musikali	M.	T.A.	1957–1961	music education
Ha-No'ar ve-ha-Arez	B–M.	T.A.	1926–1927	for older youth
Ha-Noked	Irr.	Merhavyah Haifa	1940	published by the Association of Shepherds
Ha-Of	M.	T.A.	1939	poultry raising; superseded by *Ha-Meshek ha-Za'ir* and *Ha-Meshek ha-Hakla'i*
Ha-Ofek	Irr.	Jer.	1952–1959	published by the "Le-Ma'an ha-Tenu'ah el ha-Makor" faction of Ha-Po'el ha-Mizrachi
Ha-Ohel	Q.	Jer.	1955–	rabbinics
Ha-Ohelah	Irr.	Jer.	1925–1926	Ha-Po'el ha-Mizrachi
Haolam—see also: Olam	W.	Cologne-Vilna-Odessa-London-Berlin Berlin	1907–1914 1919–1950	organ of the World Zionist Organization
Ha-Olam ha-Zeh	W.	Jer.-T.A.	1937–	organ of Ha-Olam ha-Zeh–Ko'ah Hadash; founded as *Tesha ba-Erev*; name changed to *Ha-Olam ha-Zeh* in 1947; came under new direction in 1950; first Hebrew magazine to introduce sex
Ha-Omer	Irr.		1907–1908	lit.; S. Y. Agnon's works first appeared here under the name Agnon
Ha-Or	M.	Lvov, Galicia	1882–1883	lit.
Ha-Or—see: Ha-Zevi				
Ha-Or	W. & F.	T.A.	1925 1930–1939	Communist (Trotskyite)
Ha-Or	M.	Jer.	1956–1958	organ of the Karaite community; mimeographed
Ha-Oved	Irr.	Warsaw	1921–1922	organ of the Z. S. in Poland
Ha-Oved ha-Dati	Irr.	T.A.	1945–1967	Ha-Oved ha-Dati of the Histadrut
Ha-Oved ha-Le'ummi	M.	T.A.	1943–1959	central organ of the Histadrut ha-Ovedim ha-Le'ummit
Ha-Oved ha-Ziyyoni	M.	T.A.	1936–1955	organ of Ha-Oved ha-Ziyyoni
Ha-Pardes	M.	Several places in Poland & in the U.S.	1913–	rabbinics

Title	Freq.	Place of Publication	Date(s) Appearance	Main Characteristics
Ha-Pardes—see also: Pardes	W. & B–W.	Jer.	1909	general affairs
Ha-Pedagog	M.	Cracow, Poland	1903–1904	the first modern educational periodical
Ha-Peles	M.	Poltava-Berlin	1900–1904	ultra-Orthodox, anti-Zionist
Ha-Peraḥ	W.	Calcutta, India	1878–1889	in Hebrew and Arabic
Ha-Peraklit	Q.	T.A.	1943–	published by Israel Bar Association
Ha-Pisgah	W.	N.Y.-Baltimore-Boston-St. Louis-Chicago	1888–1900	with interruptions; from the sixth volume known as *Ha-Teḥiyyah*; Saul Tchernichowsky's first poem was published therein in 1892.
Ha-Pisgah	A.	Vilna	1895–1902	rabbinics, 9 vols., in the second volume were printed articles by Rabbi Y. L. Fishman-Maimon.
Ha-Po'el ha-Mizrachi	M.	Jer.	1923–1925	organ of Ha-Po'el ha-Mizrachi
Ha-Po'el ha-Vatik	Irr.	T.A.	1938–	organ of the older workers organized in the Histadrut; changes in title; from 1959 *Shelabbim*
Ha-Po'el ha-Ẓa'ir	F. & W.	Jaffa-T.A.	1907–1970	organ of Ha-Po'el ha-Ẓa'ir, Mapai, and Ha-Avodah; mimeographed two issues in 1907; from 1912 W.; publication interrupted from 1916 to 1918
Ha-Posek	M.	T.A.	1940–1953	rabbinics
Ha-Problemai	M.	Kabri-Givat Brenner	1954–1969	chess; originally *Problemai*
Ha-Rashut ha-Mekomit	M.	T.A.	1954–1959	municipality problems
Harefuah—see also: Refuah	Irr.–F.	Jer.-T.A.	1920	newsletter of the Medical Association, 1921–22; known as *Harefuah* from 1924
Ha-Ro'eh	Irr.	Lvov-Ofen (Budapest)	1837, 1839	pungent criticism
Ha-Rofe ba-Histadrut	Irr.	T.A.	1953–1956	problems of the physician in the Histadrut
Ha-Rofe ba-Mosad	Irr.	T.A.	1946–1968	organ of the Kuppat Ḥolim physician
Harofe Haivri	Irr.-S–A.	N.Y.	1928–1965	medicine and the history of Jewish medicine; special editions for Ereẓ Israel; irregularly from 1928 to 1933; twice annually from 1937; published partly in English
Ha-Roke'aḥ ha-Ivri	Irr., B–M.	T.A.	1940–	published by the Pharmaceutical Association; called *Ha-Roke'aḥ,* 1940–46
Ḥaroshet u-Melakhah	M.	T.A.	1965–	innovations in production in Israel industry and crafts
Ha-Sadeh	M.	T.A.	1920–	agriculture; the only publication of its kind to reach its 50th anniversary (1970)
Ha-Sadeh la-No'ar	B–M.	T.A.	1948–1958	agricultural publication for youth; superseded by *Teva va-Areẓ*
Ha-Sadeh le-Gan va-Nof —see: Gan va-Nof				
Ha-Safah	Irr.	St. Petersburg	1912	Hebrew language studies
Ha-Safran—see: Alim le-Bibliografyah u-le-Safranut				
Ha-Sanegor	Irr.	N.Y.	1890	lit.
Ha-Sefer	Irr.	Jer.	1954–1961	bibliography; superseded by *Kunteres ha-Sefer ha-Torani*
Ha-Sefer be-Yisrael	M.	T.A.	1959–	organ of publishers in Israel; continuation of *Olam ha-Sefer*
Ha-Sefer ha-Ivri—see: Jewish Book Annual				
Ha-Segullah	Irr.	Jer.	1934–1940	editions of manuscripts
Ha-Sha'ar	D.	T.A.	1964–	management and the stock market
Ha-Shaḥar	M.	Vienna	1868–1884	lit.; the leading periodical of this period
Ha-Shaḥmat—see: Shaḥmat				
Ha-Sharon	1	Cracow, Poland	1893	lit.
Ha-Sharon	F.	Lvov, Galicia	1895	lit.
Ha-Shavu'a—see: Ha-Maggid				
Ha-Shavu'a ba-Kibbutz ha-Arẓi	W.	Merḥavyah-T.A.	1950–	appeared from 1930 to 1950 as under various titles organ of the kibbutzim of Ha-Shomer ha-Ẓa'ir
Ha-Shavu'a la-Mishpaḥah	W.	T.A.	1932	entertainment
Ha-Shemesh	W.	Sighet, Transylvania-Kolomea, Galicia	1878–1892	lit.

Title	Freq.	Place of Publication	Date(s) of Appearance	Main Characteristics
Ha-Shilo'aḥ	M.	Cracow-Warsaw-Odessa-Jer.	1896–1926	lit.; the leading literary journal in Russia until World War I
Ha-Shilton ha-Mekomi be-Yisrael	M. & B–M.	T.A.	1950–	municipal problems
Hashkafah—see- Ha-Ẓevi				
Ha-Shofar	Irr.	Haifa	1914, 1923	Jewish-Arab problems; originally as supplement to an Arab newspaper
Ha-Shomer ha-Ẓa'ir	F.	Warsaw	1927–1931	organ of Ha-Shomer ha-Ẓa'ir
Ha-Shomer ha-Ẓa'ir	F.	T.A.	1931–1943	organ of Ha-Shomer ha-Ẓa'ir Ha-Kibbutz ha-Arẓi from 1934; superseded by *Mishmar*
Ha-Sifrut	Q.	T.A.	1968–	science of literature
Ha-Soker		Budapest		Judaic studies
Ha-Solel	M.	Lvov, Galicia	1933–1934	lit.
Ha-Sport—see also: Sport	Irr.	T.A.	1932, 1940–1941	sport
Ha-Sport ha-Le'ummi	W.	T.A.	1949–1950	sport; Betar
Ha-Ta'asiyyah—see also: Ta'asiyyah	M.	T.A.	1937–1938, 1941–	published by the Manufacturers' Association
Ha-Tarbut ha-Yisre'elit	1	Jaffa	1913	lit.
Ha-Tashbeẓ—see: Tashbeẓ				
Ha-Teḥiyyah—see: ha-Pisgah				
Ha-Teḥiyyah	Irr.	Berlin	1850, 1857	Judaic studies
Ha-Tekhnai be-Yisrael	Q.	T.A.	1963–1967	published by the Technicians' Organization
Ha-Tekhnai ha-Ẓa'ir	M.	Kiryat Shemonah	1945–	technical problems for youth; later changed name to *Ha-Madda ve-ha-Tekhnikah*
Ha-Tekhnion	A.	Haifa	1966–	organ of the Technion, Haifa
Ha-Tekufah	Q. & A.	Moscow-Warsaw-Berlin-T.A. - N.Y.	1918–1950	lit.
Ha-Tenu'ah le-Aḥdut ha-Avodah —see: Le-Aḥdut ha-Avodah				
Ha-Tenu'ah le-Yahadut shel Torah	A.	Jer.	1966, 1968	published by the Yahadut shel Torah movement
Ha-Te'ufah	Irr., M.	T.A.	1947–1956	aeronautics
Ha-Teva ve-ha-Arez	M.	T.A.	1932–1940 1947–1954 1959–	natural sciences, nature and geography of Israel
Ha-Tikvah	W.	N.Y.	1901	lit.; the first publication in the United States to introduce a vocalized supplement for children
Ha-Tor	M.	Sighet, Transylvania-Kolomea, Galicia-Cracow, Poland	1874–1876 1880–1882	lit.
Ha-Tor	W.	Jer.	1920–1935	organ of Mizrachi in Ereẓ Israel
Ha-Torah ve-ha-Medinah	A.	T.A.	1949–1960	religion in Israel
Ha-Toren	M. W.	N.Y.	1913–1926	lit.; weekly, 1916–19
Ha-Ummah	W.	N.Y.	1915	lit.; merged in 1916 with *Ha-Toren ha-Shevu'i*
Ha-Ummah	Q.	Jer.	1962–	lit.
Ḥavaẓẓelet	W.	Jer.	1863–1864 1870–1911	the second newspaper in Ereẓ Israel
Ha-Ya'ar	Irr.	Jer.-Netanyah	1947–1955	problems of afforestation
Ha-Yahadut	F.	Lvov, Galicia	1885	lit.
Ha-Yahalom	Irr.	T.A.	1943–1944 1947	professional and managerial problems in the diamond industry
Ha-Yahalom	Irr.	T.A.	1967–	problems in the diamond industry
Ha-Yam	Irr., M.	T.A.	1938–1963, 1969–	seamanship
Ha-Yamai ha-Yisre'eli	M.	Haifa	1951–	published by the National Union of
Ha-Yarden	Irr.	Stanislavov, Galicia	1906	lit.
Ha-Yarden	M.	Zurich-N.Y.	1919–1925	lit.
Ha-Yarden	D. & W.	Jer.-T.A.	1934–1941	Revisionist publication
Ha-Yare'aḥ	Irr.	Koenigsberg, Prussia	1871–1872	lit.
Ha-Yare'aḥ	1	Jer.	1896	lit.
Ha-Yarḥon—see also: Yarḥon ha-Yisre'eli le-Vula'ut	M.	T.A.	1966–	stamps; continuation of *Bulim*

Title	Freq.	Place of Publication	Date(s) of Appearance	Main Characteristics
Ha-Yehudi	W.	Pressburg (Bratislava), Czechoslovakia	1875–1878	lit.; the first Hebrew newspaper in Hungary
Ha-Yehudi	W.	London	1897–1913	lit.; the only Hebrew newspaper in England that enjoyed a long career
Ha-Yehudi	M.	N.Y.	1936–1938	lit.; religious
Ha-Yehudi ha-Niẓḥi	Irr.	Lvov, Galicia	1866	Judaic studies
Ha-Yekev	1	St. Petersburg	1894	lit.
Ha-Yesod	W.	T.A.	1932–1948	religious; apolitical
Ha-Yishuv	W.	T.A.	1924–1927	lit. and general affairs
Ha-Yisre'eli	W.	N.Y.	1903	lit.
Ha-Yom	D.	St. Petersburg	1886–1888	the first Hebrew daily (Feb. 12, 1886–March 12, 1888)
Ha-Yom	D.	Warsaw	1906–1907	
Ha-Yom	D.	N.Y.	1909	the first Hebrew daily in the United States (90 days); exact data on the second attempt before World War I unavailable
Ha-Yom	D.	Warsaw	1925–1926	
Ha-Yom	D.	Jer.	1948–1949	originally called *Itton ha-Yom*; began to appear in Jerusalem during the siege of the War of Independence
Ha-Yom	D.	T.A.	1966–1969	published by Gaḥal; result of merger of two papers, *Ha-Boker* and *Ḥerut*
Ha-Yonah	1	Berlin	1851	Judaic studies
Ha-Yonah	1	Odessa, Russia	1907	rabbinics and Judaica; the first editorial endeavors of Y. L. Maimon (Fishman)
Ḥayyei Olam	1	Paris	1878	collection of edited ancient manuscripts
Ḥayyei Sha'ah	W.	T.A.	1953–1958	entertainment
Ha-Ẓafon	W.	Haifa	1926–1927	lit. and general affairs
Ha-Ẓa'ir	Irr.	Zloczow (Zolochev), Ukraine	1910	lit.
Ha-Ẓa'ir	1	Jer.	1916	lit.
Ha-Ẓefirah	1	Zolkiew (Zholkva), Galicia	1823	lit.
Ha-Ẓefirah	W. & D.	Warsaw (Berlin)	1862 1874–1906 1910–1921, 1926–1928 1931	the first Hebrew newspaper in Warsaw; during the first years devoted mainly to science; 1874–75 in Berlin; from 1886 a daily and 1917–19 a weekly
Ha-Zeman	W.	N.Y.	1895–1896	lit.
Ha-Zeman	F.	Cracow, Poland	1890–1891	lit.
Ha-Zeman	1	Warsaw	1896	lit.
Ha-Zeman	Q.	St. Petersburg	1903	lit.; published Bialik's famous poem *"Be-Ir-ha-Haregah."*
Ha-Zeman	M.	Vilna	1905	lit.
Ha-Zeman	B–W., D.	St. Petersburg-Vilna	1903–1915	first 92 issues biweekly; from 1905 in Vilna; known as *Hed ha-Zeman*. 1907–11.
Ha-Zeman	D.	T.A.	1930	general
Ha-Zeman	D.	T.A.	1941–1944	a nonconformist paper edited by B. Katz, editor of *Ha-Zeman* in Vilna
Ha-Ẓevi	W. & D.	Jer.	1884–1915	a daily from 1908; sometimes called *Ha-Or, Hashkafah*; the pioneer of modern journalism in Ereẓ Israel; several interruptions in publication.
Ha-Zibbul	Q.	Jaffa-T.A.	1924	problems of agricultural fertilization
Ha-Ẓillum	M.	T.A.	1965–	originally appeared in 1947 under the title *Ẓillum*; from 1971 published by the Association of Amateur Photographers
Ha-Ẓir	Irr.	Jaffa	1919	Mizrachi
Ḥazit ha-Am	B–W.,W.	Jer.	1932–1934	Revisionist publication
Ḥazit ha-Oved	M.	T.A.	1958–	organ of Ha-Oved ha-Le'ummi in the Histadrut
Ha-Ẓiyyoni ha-Kelali	W.	Jer.	1932–1935	General Zionists (B)
Ha-Ẓiyyoni ha-Vatik	Irr.	T.A.	1940–1941	organ of the old-time Zionists; appeared under various titles
Ha-Ẓiyyonut	A.	T.A.	1970–	studies in the history of the Zionist movement and of the Jews in Ereẓ Israel
Ha-Ẓofeh	Irr.	Lvov, Galicia	1878	lit.
Ha-Ẓofeh	D.	Warsaw	1903–1905	general; the first to introduce literary contests; the first prize was won by Y. D. Berkowitz

Title	Freq.	Place of Publication	Date(s) of Appearance	Main Characteristics
Ha-Ẓofeh	D.	Jer.-T.A.	1937–	organ of Mizrachi—National Religious Party; the first issues were published in Jerusalem
Ha-Ẓofeh	Irr.	Jer.	1935–1946	scouting
Ha-Ẓofeh ba-Areẓ ha-Ḥadashah	W.	N.Y.	1871–1876	the first Hebrew newspaper in the United States
Ha-Ẓofeh le-Ḥokhmat Yisrael	M.	Budapest	1911–1915, 1921–1931	Judaic studies; originally called *Ha-Ẓofeh me-Ereẓ Hagar*
Ha-Ẓofeh le-Veit Yisrael	Irr.	London	1887	lit.
Ha-Ẓofeh le-Veit Yisrael	M.	Cracow, Poland	1890	lit.
Ḥazon	Irr.	T.A.	1943–1955	Mizrachi youth
Ḥazut	A.	Jer.	1953–1960	discussions on questions of Zionism, the Jewish People, and the State of Israel
He-Atid	Irr.	Berlin	1908–1926	six collections on matters concerning Jews and Judaism
He-Atid	F.	Warsaw	1925–1934	organ of the He-Ḥalutz World Center
He-Atid	Irr.	T.A.	1939–1941	organ of Po'alei Agudat Israel
He-Atid	Q.	T.A.	1966–	published by the West German embassy, Tel Aviv
He-Avar	Q.	Petrograd	1918	history of the Jews
He-Avar (Heawar)	Q. & A.	T.A.	1952–	history of the Jews in Russia
Hed ha-Am—see also: Ha-Hed	W.	Jer.	1924–1926	religious publication
Hed ha-Defus	Irr.	T.A.	1937–1961	published by the Organization of Printing Workers the name differs on various editions
Hed ha-Gan	B–M. & M. & Q.	T.A.	1934–	published by the Association of Nursery School Teachers
Hed ha-Ḥinnukh	F. & W.	Jer.-T.A.	1926–	published by the Teachers' Association; a weekly from 1949
Hed ha-Karmel	D.	Haifa	1940	general affairs; one of the attempts to establish a daily newspaper in Haifa
Hed ha-Kevuẓah	Irr.	Detroit, Mich.	1941–1961	lit.
Hed ha-Mizraḥ	F. & W.	Jer.	1942–1951	Oriental communities in the past and present; first issues called *Ha-Mizraḥ*
Hed ha-Moreh	M.	N.Y.	1915	the first Hebrew pedagogical periodical in the U.S.
Hed ha-Sport	W.	T.A.	1965–1966	sports
Hed ha-Zeman—see: Ha-Zeman				
Hed ha-Ẓiyyoni ha-Vatik —see: Ha-Ẓiyyoni ha-Vatik				
Hedim	B–M.	T.A.	1922–1928	the leading literary journal in the 1920s
Hedim li-She'elot ha-Ḥevrah ha-Kibbutzit	Irr. & Q.	Merḥavyah	1934	organ of Ha-Kibbutz ha-Arẓi Ha-Shomer ha-Ẓa'ir
Hed Lita	F.	Kaunas (Kovno), Lithuania	1924–1925	lit.
Hed Yerushalayim	W.	Jer.	1939–1946	general affairs; during the final year of publication called *Ha-Shavu'on ha-Ereẓ-Yisre'eli ve-Hed Yerushalayim*
Hegeh	D.	T.A.	1940–1947	vocalized daily
Hegeh	W.	T.A.	1939–1940	afternoon paper of *Davar*
Hegeh	W.	T.A.	1947–1949	Saturday evening paper
He-Hadar	M.	T.A.	1928–1940	citrus
He-Ḥalutz	Irr.	Lvov-Breslau-Prague-Frankfort-Vienna	1852–1889	Judaic studies
He-Ḥalutz ha-Ẓa'ir	Irr.	Warsaw	1926–1939	published by He-Ḥalutz ha-Ẓa'ir; partly in Yiddish
He-Ḥaver	Irr.	Berne-Berlin	1912, 1914	organ of the student Zionist organization He-Ḥaver
Heikhal ha-Ivri	W.	Chicago	1877–1879	the first Hebrew paper in Chicago
Ḥeil ha-Avir	S–A.	T.A.	1948–	air force organ
Ḥeil ha-Yam—see: Ma'arekhot Yam				
Ḥemdah Genuzah	A.	Koenigsberg, E. Prussia	1856	collection of edited ancient manuscripts
Ḥermon	A.	Lvov, Galicia	1902–1903	lit.
Ḥerut	D.	T.A.	1948–1966	organ of the Ḥerut Party; a number of editions were published earlier in Jerusalem as a weekly
Heshbona'ut u-Missim	Irr.	T.A.-Ramat Gan	1962–1967	published by the Union of Accountants and Tax Consultants

Title	Freq.	Place of Publication	Date(s) of Appearance	Main Characteristics
Heyeh Nakhon	Q.	Jer.-T.A.	1946–	scouting
Higyenah Ruḥanit	M.	Jer.	1944–1951	hygiene in the schools
Higyenah u-Veri'ut	Q.	Jer.	1940–1948	health and hygiene
Ḥikrei Avodah	Q.	T.A.	1947–1954	labor studies and social security
Ḥinnukh	Q.	N.Y.	1935–1939	education
Ḥok u-Mishpat	F.	Jer.-T.A.	1954–	law
Ḥol va-Ru'aḥ	1	Ḥolon	1964	lit. Hebrew and Yiddish
Horeb	S—A.	N.Y.	1934–1960	Judaic studies
Ḥotam	F.	T.A.	1964–	Mapam; from 1970 weekly magazine of Al ha-Mishmar
Iddan Ḥadash	M.	T.A.	1968	organ of Ha-Merkaz ha-Ḥofshi
Iggeret la-Ḥaverim	W.	T.A.	1951–	organ of Iḥud ha-Kevuẓot ve-ha-Kibbutzim. Continuation of *Iggeret*, organ of Ḥever ha-Kevuẓot
Iggeret le-Ḥinnukh	Q.	T.A.-Tel Yosef	1952	educational organ of Iḥud ha-Kevuẓot ve-ha-Kibbutzim
Iggeret li-Meḥannekhim	B–M.	T.A.	1964	educational organ of Ha-Kibbutz ha-Me'uḥad
Ikkarei Yisrael	A.	T.A.	1954–1962	annual of the Farmers' Association
Ikkarei Yisrael	M.	T.A.	1962–	organ of the Farmers' Association
Ittim	W.	T.A.	1946–1948	lit.
Itton ha-Bonim	M.	T.A.	1937–1939, 1946–1949	organ of the Association of Landlords and property owners
Itton le-Misḥar	Irr.	T.A.	1936–1939	trade
Itton Meyuḥad	W.	T.A.-Jer.	1933–1951	pioneer of sensational reportage
Ivri Anokhi	W.	Brody-Galicia	1865–1890	indirect continuation of *Ha-Mevasser*, sometimes: *Ha-Ivri*
Iyyim	1	London	1928	lit.
Iyyun	Q.	T.A.-Jer.	1945	philosophy
Iyyunim Beinle'ummiyyim	Irr.	Ramat Gan	1951–1964	international affairs—superseded by *International Outlook*
Iyyunim bi-Ve'ayot Ḥevrah	A.	T.A.	1969–	social, educational, and cultural problems
Iyyunim le-Vikkoret ha-Medinah	Q.	Jer.	1960–	Bulletin of the State Comptroller's office
Jewish Book Annual	A.	N.Y.	1942	Hebrew-English-Yiddish. Bibliography
Kadimah	M.	N.Y.	1899	lit.
Kadimah	1	Kiev, Ukraine	1920	philosophy and science of religion
Kalkelan	W., M.	Jer.	1952–	finance and economy
Kammah	A.	Jer.	1948–1952	Keren Kayemeth
Karmelit	A.	Haifa	1954–	lit.
Karmi	M.	Pressburg (Bratislava), Czechoslovakia	1881–1882	general, Hebrew and Ladino
Karmi Shelli	Irr.	Vienna	1891	general, Hebrew and Ladino
Karnenu	Q.	Jer.	1924–1963	Keren Kayemeth, superseded by *Am ve-Admato*
Katif	A.	Petaḥ Tikvah	1954	
Kav	Q.	Jer.	1965–	lit.
Kavveret	1	Odessa, Russia	1890	lit.; Ḥibbat Zion
Kaẓir	M.	T.A.	1945–1946	digest of books
Kaẓir	1	T.A.	1964	history of Zionism in Russia
Kedem	Irr.	Jer.	1942, 1945	archaeology of Palestine
Kedmah	M.	T.A.	1963–1964	organ of Betar
Kehilliyyatenu	1	T.A.-Haifa	1922	the first organ of Ha-Shomer ha-Ẓa'ir in Ereẓ Israel, new reprint
Keneset	1	Odessa, Russia	1917	lit.
Keneset	1	T.A.	1928	lit.
Keneset	A.	T.A.	1936–1946 1960	lit. Bialik and Judaic studies
Keneset ha-Gedolah	Irr.	Warsaw	1890–1891	lit.
Keneset Yisrael	A.	Warsaw	1886–1889	lit.
Keneset Yisrael	M.	Vilna	1930–1934	rabbinics
Kerem Ḥemed	A.	Vienna-Berlin	1833–1856	lit. and Judaic studies, 9 vols.
Keren Or	M.	Chicago	1889	lit.; only 2 issues
Kesafim u-Misḥar	D.	T.A.	1966–1967	finance and economy

Title	Freq.	Place of Publication	Date(s) of Appearance	Main Characteristics
Kesher ve-Elektronikah	M.	T.A.	1967–	electronics, Israel Defense Forces
Keshet	Q.	T.A.	1958–	lit.
Ketavim	Q.	Rehovot-Bet Dagon	1951–	Agricultural Research Station
Ketuvim	W.	T.A.	1926–1933	lit. organ of the young Avantgardists
Kevuẓat Ḥakhamim	1	Vienna	1861	Judaic studies
Kikyon Yonah	1	Paris	1860	Judaic studies
Kirjath Sepher	Q.	Jer.	1924–	bibliography of the Jewish National and University Library Jer., the first regular scientific publication of the Hebrew University
Kitvei ha-Universitah	1	Jer.	1924	Judaic studies, mathematics and physics. Printed in Leipzig
Ko'aḥ Ḥadash	Irr.	T.A.	1966–1967	organ of Ha-Olam ha-Zeh—Ko'aḥ Ḥadash
Kohelet	1	St. Petersburg	1881	lit.
Kohelet Musar	Irr.	Berlin	1750	the first literary-moralistic periodical in Hebrew; 2 issues, 2 reprints
Kokhevei Yiẓhak	A.	Vienna	1845–1869 1873	lit.; central organ of the Hebrew Haskalah movement; 37 vols.
Kol—see: Ha-Kol				
Kol ha-Am	D., W.	T.A.	1947–	Communist. From the 1920s in various forms, underground newspaper. 1970—weekly
Kol ha-No'ar	Irr.	T.A.	1940–1966	Communist youth
Kol ha-Shabbat	M.	Jer.	1957–	Sabbath observance
Kol Nekhei Milḥamah	M.	T.A.	1949–	war invalids
Kolno'a	F.	T.A.	1931–1935	cinema; the first of its kind
Kolot	M.	Warsaw	1923–1924	lit.
Kol Sinai	M.	Jer.	1962–	religious
Kol Torah	M.	Jer.	1929, 1932	rabbinics
Kol Ya'akov	W.	Jer.	1922–1928, 1933–1934	religious
Kol Yisrael	W.	Jer.	1921–1949	Agudat Israel
Komemiyyut	A.	T.A.	1951–1954	lit. Appeared each year on Independence Day
Ko'operaẓyah	F.	T.A.	1930–1939	cooperative affairs
Korot—see also: Ha-Ittonai ha-Ivri	Q.	T.A.	1952–	history of medicine and science
Korot	M.	T.A.	1970–	history of the yishuv and Zionism
Koveẓ al Yad (Kobez al jad)	Irr.	Berlin-Jer.	1885–	editions of ancient manuscripts. Vols. 1–10 Berlin, N.S. Jer. 1937–
Koveẓ ha-Ḥevrah la-Ḥakirat Ereẓ Yisrael	Irr.	Jer.	1921–1945	archaeology of Palestine and history of the yishuv, 4 vols. in several parts
Koveẓ Harẓa'ot ha-Ḥevrah ha-Historit	Irr.	Jer.	1964–1966	lectures on history from the annual seminar of the society
Koveẓ Harẓa'ot shel ha-Iggud ha-Yisre'eli le-Ibbud Informaẓyah	A.	Jer.	1965–	information processing—partly in English
Koveẓ ha-Tammim	Irr.	Warsaw	1935–1937	Ḥasidei Ḥabad, Ḥasidei Lubavich
Koveẓ li-Ve'ayot ha-Ḥinnukh ha-Gufani	B–M.	T.A.	1962–1965	Wingate Institute, physical education
Koveẓ Ma'amarim le-Divrei Yemei ha-Ittonut ha-Ivrit be-Ereẓ Yisrael	A.	T.A.	1935–1936	history of the Hebrew press in Ereẓ Israel
Koveẓ Schocken le-Divrei Sifrut	1	T.A.	1941	lit.; superseded by Lu'aḥ ha-Areẓ
Koveẓ Sifruti	A.	Jer.	1914	lit., ed. by Po'alei Zion
Kunteres	W.	T.A.	1919–1929, 1940–1944	organ of Aḥdut ha-Avodah; in the 1940s of Mapai
Kunteres	Irr.	Riga-Warsaw	1929–1927	Ḥasidei Lubavich
Kunteres Bibliografi	M.	T.A.	1950–1970	bibliography
Kunteres ha-Sefer ha-Torani —see: Ha-Sefer				
Kunteresim	Irr.	Jer.	1937–1942	Hebrew language studies; new ed. 1964
Lada'at	M.	Jer.	1970–	popular science
La-Gever	M.	T.A.	1963–1969	entertainment
La-Ḥayyal—see: Ha-Ḥayyal				
La-Ishah	W.	T.A.	1947–	women's magazine
La-Kore ha-Ẓa'ir	M.	T.A.	1950–1954	bibliography
La-Matḥil	W.	Jer.	1956–	easy Hebrew. For some years did not appear in order
La-Merḥav	D.	T.A.	1954–1971	organ of Aḥdut ha-Avodah, the first months as F. and W.; merged with Davar

Title	Freq.	Place of Publication	Date(s) of Appearance	Main Characteristics
La-Mishpaḥah	M.	N.Y.	1963–	general
La-Mo'ed	Irr.	Jer.	1945–1947	collections for festivals. 7 appeared
La-Ya'aran	Q.	Netanyah	1950–	forestry
La-Yehudim	A.	Jer.	1909–1912, 1921–1925	humor, the first humorist periodical in Ereẓ Israel
La-Yogev	A.	T.A.	1945–1949	cultivation problems
Le-Aḥdut ha-Avodah	W.	T.A.	1944–1948	organ of Le-Aḥdut ha-Avodah party, from its split with Mapai until its amalgamation with Mapam
Lefi Sha'ah	Irr.	Jer.	1915–1917	8 issues during World War I
Leket Amarim	1	St. Petersburg	1889	lit.
Le-Ma'an ha-Yeled ve-ha-No'ar	F.	Jer.	1942–1949	Szold Institute for chidren and youth
Le-Shabbat	W.	Jer.	1922	general
Leshonenu	Q.	Jer.	1928–	Hebrew language studies
Leshonenu la-Am	M.	Jer.	1945	Hebrew language studies in popular form
Lev Ḥadash	Irr.	T.A.-Jer.	1922–1924	critical-radical
Le-Yad ha-Hegeh	Irr.	T.A.	1952–1959	taxi drivers' bulletin
Li-Kerat	Irr.	T.A.	1952–1953	Hebrew young writers
Likkud	M.	T.A.	1946–1947	leftist
Livyat Ḥen	1	Warsaw	1887	lit.
Lu'aḥ Aḥi'asaf	A.	Warsaw	1893–1904, 1923	lit., 13 vols.
Lu'aḥ Aḥi'ever	A.	N.Y.	1918, 1921	lit., 2 vols.
Lu'aḥ Ereẓ Yisrael	A.	Jer.	1895–1915	Palestinography and lit., 21 vols.
Lu'aḥ ha-Areẓ	A.	T.A.	1941–1954	lit. almanac of *Haaretz*
Lu'aḥ ha-Em ve-ha-Yeled —see: Ha-Em ve-ha-Yeled				
Lu'aḥ ha-Me'orer	1	T.A.	1935	Ereẓ Israel labor movement
Lu'aḥ Keren Kayemet–see: Moladti				
Lu'aḥ Ko'operativi	A.	T.A.	1931–	cooperative types; now: *Lu'aḥ ha-Ko'operaẓyah*
Lu'aḥ Sha'ashu'im	1	Cracow, Poland	1902	lit.
Lu'aḥ Yerushalayim	A.	Jer.	1940–1951	history of Jerusalem and the *yishuv*. 12 vols.
Ma'anit	A.	Jer.	1926	lit. Hebrew writers for Keren Kayemeth
Ma'anit	B–M.	T.A.	1939–1954	youth of Tenu'at ha-Moshavim
Ma'anit	Irr.	T.A.	1946–1958	moshavim of Ha-Po'el ha-Mizrachi
Ma'arakhot	M., Q.	T.A.	1939–	military journal of the Haganah and the Israel Defense Forces
Ma'arekhot Ḥimmush	Q.	T.A.	1961	ammunition problems, ordinance corps
Ma'arekhot Yam	Q.	T.A.	1948–	naval organ
Ma'ariv	D.	T.A.	1948–	independent, the first issues—*Yedi'ot Ma'ariv*
Ma'avak	Irr.	T.A.	1947	organ of the Kena'anim
Ma'avak	W.	T.A.	1952–1954	party organ which separated from Mapam until its amalgamation with Mapai
Ma'barot	M.	T.A.-Jaffa	1919–1921	literary organ of Ha-Po'el ha-Ẓa'ir
Mabbat Ḥadash	W.	T.A.	1965–1968	organ of Rafi
Mabbu'a	Q.	N.Y.	1952–1954	lit.
Mabbu'a	A.	Jer.	1963–	religious literature
Madda	B–M.	Jer.	1956–	popular science
Madda'ei ha-Yahadut	A.	Jer.	1926–1927	Judaic studies of the Hebrew University, Jer. continuation of *Yedi'ot ha-Makhon le-Madda'ei ha-Yahadut*
Madrikh li-Mekomot Avodah Me'urganim	A.	T.A.	1956–1965	list of work places where work is organized by the Histadrut
Maggid Mishneh	W.	Lyck, E. Prussia	1879–1881	lit.
Maḥanayim	Irr.	T.A.	1948–	collections for the festivals and specific subjects by the army chaplaincy. The first 18 booklets called: *Yalkut ha-Rabbanut ha-Ẓeva'it*
Maḥanot	M.	T.A.	1942–1947	organ of the camp workers
Maḥazikei ha-Dat	W.	Lvov, Galicia	1879–1913	extreme Orthodox; sometimes: *Kol Maḥazikei ha-Dat*
Maḥazikei ha-Dat	W., B–M.	Jer.	1919–1924	extreme Orthodox, partly in Yiddish
Maḥbarot le-Marxizm	Irr.	Givat Ḥavivah	1950–1951	studies on Marxism
Maḥbarot le-Sifrut	B–M.,	T.A.	1940–1954	lit.
Maḥbarot le-Sozyologyah	B–M.	T.A.	1943–1945	sociology
Maḥberet	Q.	Jer.	1952–1967	lit. organ of Alliance Israelite Universelle, partly in French

Title	Freq.	Place of Publication	Date(s) of Appearance	Main Characteristics
Makkabbi—see: Ha-Makkabbi				
Marot ha-Kalkalah be-Yisrael	M.	Jer.	1955–1966	economics
Masakh	Irr.	T.A.	1954–1955	lit., theater and art
Maslul	W.	T.A.	1951–1952	for Yemenite and Eastern immigrants
Massa	F.	T.A.	1951–1954	lit., from 1954 literary supplement of *La-Merḥav* and from 1971 of *Davar*
Massad	A.	N.Y.	1933, 1936	lit.
Massad	Irr.	T.A.	1951, 1967	No'ar Dati Oved
Massekhet	1	T.A.	1951	lit.
Massu'ot	1	Odessa, Russia	1919	lit.
Mattekhet	Q.	Haifa	1958–1967, 1971	Israel metal industry in the Technion
Ma'yan ha-Ḥasidut—see also: Ha-Ma'yan	A.	Jer.	1964–	ḥasidic affairs
Ma'yanot	A.	Jer.	1952–1968	religious
Maẓpen	Irr.	T.A.	1943–1944	pro-Revisionist
Maẓpen	W.	T.A.	1954–1955	general
Maẓpen	Irr.	T.A.-Jer.	1963–	leftist
Me'assef—see also: Ha-Me'assef	1	St. Petersburg	1902	lit.
Me'assef	A.	Jer.-T.A.	1960–1968	lit. 8 vols.
Me'assefim Madda'iyyim shel ha-Tekhniyyon	Irr.	Haifa	1944–1955	science. 6 vols.
Me'assef Soferei Ereẓ Yisrael	1	T.A.	1940	lit.
Me'assef Soferei Ereẓ Yisrael	1	T.A.	1942	lit. 2 vols.
Me'at me-Harbeh	1	T.A.	1947	lit.
Me-Et le-Et	1	N.Y.	1900	lit.
Me-Et le-Et	M.	Vilna	1918	lit.
Megammot	Q.	Jer.	1949–	child problems, by Szold Institute
Meged Geresh Yeraḥim	M.	Vienna	1848	lit. supplement to the weekly *Centralorgan fuer juedische Interessen*
Meged Yeraḥim	M.	Lvov, Galicia	1855–1856	lit. 4 issues
Megillot	M.	Jer.	1950–1953	Hebrew culture and education
Me-Ḥag le-Ḥag	Irr.	N.Y.-Baltimore	1915, 1918	lit. 2 issues
Mehallekhim	Irr.	Jer.	1969–	organ of the Torah Judaism movement
Me-Havvayot ha-Zeman	M., Irr.	T.A.	1944–1946, 1952	contemporary affairs
Meḥkarim be-Geografyah shel Ereẓ Yisrael	A.	Jer.	1960–	Palestinography
Me'ir Einayim	A.	Bene-Berak	1968–1969	bibliography
Mekhes ve-Ta'avurah	Irr.	T.A.	1949–1956	organ of the Association of Customs Agents
Mekhon ha-Tekanim	Q.	T.A.	1968–	Israel Standards Institute
Melilah	A.	Manchester, England	1944–1955	Judaic studies. 5 vols. (double 3/4)
Meliẓ Eḥad Minni Elef	1	St. Petersburg	1884	lit. in honor of the 100th copy of *Ha-Meliẓ*
Menorah	F.	Lodz, Poland	1930	Judaic studies
Meshek ha-Bakar ve-ha-Ḥalav	Q.	T.A.	1952–	dairy farming
Meshek ha-Ofot	M.	T.A.-Tel Yosef	1949–	poultry farming
Mesibbah	1	T.A.	1926	lit. the first editing work in Ereẓ Israel by E. Steinman
Mesillot	M.	Warsaw	1935–1937	education and Hebrew culture
Meteorologyah be-Yisrael	Q.	Bet Dagon	1963–	meteorology
Mevasseret Ẓiyyon	M.	Jer.	1884	the first periodical edited by E. Ben-Yehuda. 4 issues
Mevo'ot	M.	T.A.	1953–1956	lit.
Meẓudah	Irr.	London	1943–1954	lit. and Judaic studies. 5 vols. (2 doubles)
Mi-Bayit	1	T.A.	1946	lit. from Ereẓ Israel authors for the remnants of the Holocaust
Mi-Bifenim	Irr., Q.	En-Harod-T.A.	1923	Organ of Ha-Kibbutz ha-Me'uḥad. New reprint of the first 28 issues.
Mifgash	Irr.	T.A.	1964	lit. first of its kind in Hebrew. Hebrew and Arabic literature. Hebrew and Arabic on parallel pages
Mi-Keren Zavit	1	Detroit, Mich.-Baltimore, Md.	1921	lit.
Mikhtav Ḥozer—see: Ha-Refu'ah				
Mikkun Ḥakla'i	Q.	T.A.	1956–	farm mechanization
Miklat	M.	N.Y.	1919–1920	lit.
Milḥamtenu—see also: Be'Terem				
Mi-Mizraḥ u-mi-Ma'arav	M., Irr.	Vienna-Berlin	1894–1899	lit. and Judaic studies
Minḥah	1	T.A.	1930	lit.

Title	Freq.	Place of Publication	Date(s) of Appearance	Main Characteristics
Min ha-Yesod	F.	T.A.	1962–1965	organ of *Min ha-Yesod faction.* two collections were issued with this name in 1962–63.
Misḥar ha-Makkolet	M.	T.A.	1940–1951	grocery business. Previously issued under: *Soḥer ha-Makkolet*
Misḥar ve-Ta'asiyyah	F.	T.A.	1923–1933	trade, factories, and agriculture
Mishmar—see: Al ha-Mishmar				
Mishpat ha-Shalom ha-Ivri	1	T.A.	1925	magistrates' court problems during the Mandate
Mishpat ve-Khalkalah	M.	T.A.	1955–1959	law and economics
Mi-Teiman	1	T.A.	1938	history of the Yemenite Jews' immigration to Israel
Mi-Tekufat ha-Even	A.	Jer.	1960	prehistoric studies in Israel
Mivrak	D.	T.A.	1947–1948	afternoon paper. Organ of Leḥi
Mi-Yamim Rishonim	M.	T.A.	1934–1935	history of Zionism and the *yishuv*
Mi-Yrushalayim	Irr.	Warsaw	1892	lit. Ereẓ Israel topics. 2 issues
Mi-Ẓiyyon	1	Warsaw	1895	lit.
Miẓpeh—see also: Ha-Miẓpeh	1	T.A.	1953	lit. *Ha-Ẓofeh* annual
Mizraḥ u-Ma'arav	M.	Jer.	1919–1932	Judaic studies, in particular on Spanish and Sephardi Jewry
Mo'adon Mekhoniyyot ve-Sayyarut be-Yisrael	M.	T.A.	1966–	automobile and touring club
Molad	M., B–M.	T.A.-Jer.	1948	lit. N.S. 1967-the last years B–M.
Moladti	A.	Jer.	1936–1968	most years on behalf of Keren ha-Kayemeth
Moriyyah	W. & D.	Jer.	1910–1915	Orthodox; from 1913, daily
Moznayim	W.	T.A.	1929–1933	lit. organ of the Hebrew Writers' Association
Moznayim	M.	T.A.	1933–1947, 1955–	lit. organ of the Hebrew Writers' Association
Moznayim	F.	T.A.	1948	lit. organ of the Hebrew Writers' Association
Muze'on ha-Areẓ	A.	T.A.	1959–	on all museums in the Tel Aviv vicinity
Naḥali'el	Irr.	Jer.	1965–	religious
Nativ	Irr.	T.A.	1934–1935	a nonconformist periodical by A. L. Yaffe, "the father of the moshavim"
Ner	F., Irr.	Jer.	1950–	Jewish-Arab relations
Ner ha-Ma'aravi	M.	N.Y.	1895, 1897	lit.
Ner Ma'aravi	A.	N.Y.	1922, 1925	rabbinics and Judaica
Nerot Shabbat	Irr.	Jer.	1943–1952	Sabbath observance
Netivah	F., Irr.	Jer.	1926–1938, 1943	Ha-Po'el ha-Mizrachi
Netivei Irgun	M., B–M.	Jer.	1954–	organization and administration, from 1969 B–M.
Netivot	1	Warsaw	1913	lit.
Netivot	A.	Jer.	1953–1968	religious education for Diaspora Jews
Nimim	1	N.Y.	1923	lit. printed in Berlin
Nir—see also: Ha-Nir	A.	N.Y.	1952	education and lit. continuation of *Ha-Nir* 1930–38
Nir	M.	T.A.	1948–1959	education through J.N.F.
Nisan	1	Warsaw	1930	lit.
Nisan	1	T.A.	1942	lit.
Niv	Irr.	N.Y.	1936–1966	lit. organ of the Young Hebrew Writers in U.S.
Niv ha-Kevuẓah	Irr., Q.	T.A.	1930–	organ of Ḥever ha-Kevuẓot and from 1952 of Ihud ha-Kevuzot ve-ha-Kibbutzim. Some interruptions
Niv ha-Midrashiyyah	A.	T.A.	1963–	lit. rabbinics, religious education
Niv ha-Moreh	M.	T.A.	1958–	teachers of Agudat Israel
Niv ha-Rofe	Q. & S-A.	T.A.	1951–	organ of the Histadrut doctors
Niẓoẓ	Irr.	Kaunas (Kovno)-Dachau-Munich	1940–1948	at the beginning in Kovno ghetto and Dachau camp, then in Munich, the only permanent Hebrew newspaper of the remnants from the Holocaust
No'am	A.	Jer.	1958–	clarification of contemporary halakhic problems
Nogah ha-Yare'aḥ	M.	Lvov-Tarnopol, Galicia	1872–1873, 1880	Judaic studies, lit.
Ofakim	Irr.	Warsaw	1932–1934	education
Ofakim	Irr.	T.A.	1943–1961	education by Ha-Shomer ha-Ẓa'ir
Ofek	1	T.A.	1970	lit.

Title	Freq.	Place of Publication	Date(s) of Appearance	Main Characteristics
Ohel—see also: Ha-Ohel	1	T.A.	1921	lit.
Ohel Mo'ed	Irr.	Cracow, Poland	1898–1900	rabbinics
Ohel Mo'ed	Irr.	Warsaw	1926–1935	rabbinics
Ohel Torah	M., Irr.	Jer.	1926–1927, 1929	rabbinics
Oholei Gadna	M.	T.A.	1952–1960	vocalized, for Gadna
Olamenu	1	Odessa Petrograd, Moscow	1917	lit.
Olam ha-Defus	M., Q.	T.A.	1956–	typography
Olam ha-Elektronikah	M.	Jer.	1962–1965	electronics, continuation of *Radio ve-Elektronikah*
Olam ha-Ishah	F.	T.A.	1940–1963	womens' magazine
Olam ha-Kolno'a	W.	T.A.	1951–	cinema
Olam ha-Mistorin	Q.	T.A.	1968–	parapsychology
Olam ha-Sefer	Irr.	T.A.	1954–1958	organ of publishers, superseded by *Ha-Sefer be-Yisrael*
Olam ha-Ẓillum	M.	T.A.	1966–1967	photography
Olamot Aḥerim	Irr.	T.A.	1970	parapsychology
Omer–see also: Ha-Omer	1	T.A.	1927	lit.
Omer	W., Irr.	T.A.	1936–1942	weekly 1936–39, from then on monthly sometimes in place of the banned *Davar*
Omer	D.	T.A.	1951–	daily, vocalized (with *Davar*)
Omer	A.	T.A.	1955–1960	rabbinics
Ommanut	Q.	Jer.	1940–1942	art
Ommanut ha-Kolno'a	Irr.	T.A.	1957–1963	cinema
Or ha-Mizraḥ	Q.	N.Y.	1954–	rabbinics, Judaic studies
Orlogin	Irr.	T.A.	1950–1957	lit. 13 issues
Orot	Irr.	T.A.	1950–1955	cultural work of the Histadrut; 3 vols.
Orot	B–M., Q.	Jer.	1950–1966, 1968	lit. and Hebrew culture, N.S. from 1968 Q., partly in English
Or Torah	Irr.	Lvov, Galicia-Frankfort, Germany	1874	lit. 4 issues
Or Torah	Q.	Jer.	1897–1901	rabbinics
Oshyot	Irr.	T.A.	1947–1957	educational problems before school
Ot	Irr. W.	T.A.	1966–1968 1971	organ of the Israel Labor Party
Ovnayim	A.	Bet Berl	1961–1966	collection—Bet Berl affairs
Oẓar Genazim	1	Jer.	1960	printed manuscript letters on history of Ereẓ Israel
Oẓar ha-Ḥayyim	Irr.	De a-Seini, Rumania	1924–1938	Judaic studies
Oẓar ha-Ḥokhmah ve-ha-Madda	Irr.	N.Y.	1894	lit. 2 issues
Oẓar ha-Sifrut	A.		1887–1896, 1902	lit. 5 vols. + 1
Oẓar Ḥokhmah	Irr.	Lvov, Galicia	1859–1865	lit. 3 issues
Oẓar Neḥmad	Irr.	Vienna-Pressburg (Bratislava), Czechoslovakia	1856–1863	Judaic studies. 4 vols.
Oẓar Tov	Irr.	Berlin	1878–1886, 1893	mainly editions of Hebrew manuscripts
Oẓar Yehudei Sefarad	A.	Jer.	1959–	research on Spanish Jewry past and present
Palmaḥ—see: Alon ha-Palmaḥ				
Pamalyah	1	T.A.	1953	lit. collection dedicated to young authors
Panim el Panim	W.	T.A.-Jer.	1954–1956, 1959–	religious ill. magazine, during the interruption appeared as *Ayin be-Ayin*—see there.
Pardes—see also: Ha-Pardes	Irr.	Odessa, Russia	1892–1896	lit. 3 vols; in the first volume Bialik's first poem was published
Pargod	Irr.	Jer.	1963, 1966	theater, 2 issues
Perakim (Peraqim)	Irr.	N.Y.	1955–1966	Judaica studies 4 vols.; organ of Hebrew Academy in N.Y.
Perakim	F.	Haifa	1958–1965	lit. continuation of the journal of the same name in Buenos Aires
Perakim	A.	Jer.	1967–1968	Judaic studies (Schocken Institute, Jer.)
Peri Eẓ Ḥayyim	Irr.	Amsterdam	1691–1807	the first rabbinical periodical
Peri To'elet	1	Amsterdam	1825	lit.
Pesi'ot	Irr.	Jer.	1926–1935	educational problems in the low grades
Petaḥ	A.	Bet-Berl	1959–1968	studies on various problems

Title	Freq.	Place of Publication	Date(s) of Appearance	Main Characteristics
Petaḥim	B–M.	Jer.	1967–	modern approach to religion
Pinkas Histadrut ha-Ovedim	Irr.	T.A.	1922–1925	the first periodical of the Histadrut. Superseded by *Davar*
Pinkas Histadrut ha-Ovedim	M.	T.A.	1936–1938	new series in another form
Pinkas le-Inyenei ha-Pekidim —see: Shurot				
Pirḥei Ẓafon	A.	Vilna	1841, 1844	lit., the first Hebrew periodical in Russia
Pirkei Bessarabyah	Irr.	T.A.	1952, 1958	history of the Bessarabian Jewry, 2 vols.
Pirsumei ha-Iggud ha-Yisre'eli le-Ibbud Informaẓyah	A.	T.A.	1968–	information processing
Praxis	Irr.	T.A.	968–	leftist
Problemai—see: Ha-Problemai				
Problemot	M., Irr.	T.A.	1962–	nonconformist-anarchist, partly in Yiddish
Perozedor	Irr.	T.A.	1962–1965, 1968–	problems of religion
Qadmoniot	Q.	Jer.	1968	archaeology of Palestine and Biblical lands
Radio	W.	Jer.	1960–1962	Kol Israel newspaper
Radio ve-Elektronikah	M.	Jer.	1957–1961	radio and electronics
Radio Yerushalayim	W.	Jer.	1938–1942	radio newspaper of the Mandate, superseded by *Ha-Galgal*. In the times of *Ha-Galgal*, supplement for few years. Partly in English
Ramah	M.	N.Y.	1937–1939	lit.
Ramzor	M.	Jer.-T.A.	1961–1962, 1965–	in the beginning, organ of the Mapai student cell in Jerusalem. From 1965, Mapai youth in Tel Aviv
Refu'ah Veterinarit	Irr., M.	T.A.-Bet Dagon	1939–	in the beginning irregular, organ of veterinary surgeons
Refu'at ha-Shinnayim	B–M.	T.A.	1944–	organ of dentists
Reshafim	W.	Warsaw	1909	lit. 50 issues
Reshimat Ma'amarim be-Madda'ei ha-Yahadut	A.	Jer.	1967–	index of articles on Jewish studies
Reshimat Pirsumei ha-Memshalah	Q.	Jer.	1956–	list of government publications
Reshit	Q.	Warsaw	1933–1934	lit.
Reshummot	Irr.	Odessa-Berlin-T.A.	1918–1930	folklore, first issued in Odessa. 6 vols.
Reshumot	A.	T.A.	1945–1953	folklore. 5 vols.
Revivim	Irr.	Lvov-Jer.-Jaffa	1908–1919	lit. 6 vols.
Rihut ve-Dekoraẓyah	Q.	T.A.	1961–	furnishing and decoration
Rimmon	Irr.	Berlin	1922–1924	lit. and art
Rimmon	W.	T.A.	1956–1957	ill. weekly
Rimmon	Irr.	Buenos Aires	1966–1968	lit.
Rivon ha-Aguddah ha-Zo'otekhnit	Q.	Reḥovot	1969–	Association of Zootechnics
Rivon Handasat Betiḥut	Q.	T.A.	1968–	security engineering
Rivon Katan	Q.	N.Y.	1944	lit. 2 issues
Rivon le-Banka'ut	Q.	T.A.	1961–	banking
Rivon le-Inyenei Missim	Q.	Jer.	1965–	taxes
Rivon le-Khalkalah	Q.	T.A.	1953–	economics
Rivon le-Matematikah	Q.	Jer.	1946–	mathematics
Rivon Merkaz ha-Beniyyah ha-Yisre'eli	Q.	T.A.	1970–	building
Rivon Mishteret Yisrael	Q.	T.A.	1956–1965	police
Ro'eh ha-Ḥeshbon	Irr., B–M.	T.A.	1939–1946, 1950–	accounting
Rotary Yisrael	Q.	Ramat Gan	1960–	Rotary
Sa'ad	B–M.	Jer.	1957–	social welfare
Saddan	Irr.	T.A.-Jer.	1924–1926	lit. organ of U. Ẓ. Greenberg
Sadot	Irr.	T.A.	1938–1945	under various names—Ha-No'ar ha-Lomed
Sarid u-Falit	1	T.A.	1945	Judaic studies (mainly editions of manuscripts)
Sedarim	1	T.A.	1942	lit. 4 vols.
Sedemot	Irr.	T.A.	1949–1954	Ha-No'ar ha-Lomed
Sedemot	Q.	T.A.	1960–	previously Iḥud ha-Kevuẓot ve-ha-Kibbutzim, later youths from all various collective settlements

Title	Freq.	Place of Publication	Date(s) of Appearance	Main Characteristics
Sefatenu	Irr.	Odessa-Berlin	1917, 1923	Hebrew language studies
Sefatenu	1	T.A.	1927	league of defenders of the Hebrew language
Sefer ha-Misḥar	A.	T.A.	1964–1967	commerce
Sefer ha-Shanah —see also: Shenaton	A.	Warsaw	1900–1906	lit. 5 vols.
Sefer ha-Shanah	A.	Chicago	1935–1959	lit. College of Jewish Studies
Sefer ha-Shanah	A.	N.Y.-Tel Aviv	1964–	history of Polish Jewry. First English, Hebrew, and Yiddish, 2–3 Yiddish and Hebrew
Sefer ha-Shanah ba-Amerikah shel Histadrut Benei Ereẓ Yisrael	A.	N.Y.	1931–1947	lit. Superseded by *Yisrael*
Sefer ha-Shanah le-Bibliografyah Yehudit be-Polanyah	A.	Warsaw	1934	Jewish bibliography in Poland. 1 vol.
Sefer ha-Shanah ha-Em ve-ha-Yeled —see: Ha-Em ve-ha-Yeled				
Sefer ha-Shanah le-Anaf ha-Beniyyah	A.	T.A.	1966, 1969–	building trade. In 1935 building annual issued
Sefer ha-Shanah li-Kehillot ve-Irgunim	A.	Jer.	1970–	world Jewish communities and organizations annual
Sefer ha-Shanah li-Melekhet ha-Defus	A.	T.A.	1938	typography and printing. 1 vol.
Sefer ha-Shanah li-Yhudei Amerikah	A.	N.Y.	1931–1949	lit. 11 vols. (2 doubles)
Sefer ha-Shanah li-Yhudei Polanyah	A.	Cracow, Poland	1938	Polish Jewry. 1 vol.
Sefer ha-Shanah shel Ereẓ Yisrael	A.	T.A.	1923–1926, 1934–1935	lit.
Sefer ha-Shanah shel ha-Ittona'im	A.	T.A.	1942–	journalists and journalism
Sefunot	A.	Jer.	1956–1966	research on the Jewish communities in the East
Sekirah Ḥodshit	M.	T.A.	1954–	monthly review of and for the Israel Defense Forces
Semol	Irr.	T.A.	1953–1954	Moshe Sneh's organ, between his leaving Mapam and joining Maki
Seneh	M.	Warsaw	1929	lit.
Senunit	M.	Lvov, Galicia	1910–1912	lit.
Sha'arei Beri'ut	M.	T.A.	1931–1932	health and hygiene
Sha'arei Halakhot	A.	Jer.	1966	rabbinics
Sha'arei Torah	M.	Warsaw	1907–1927	rabbinics
Sha'arei Ẓiyyon	W.	Jer.	1876–1884	in the first year partly in Yiddish—the first Yiddish newspaper in Ereẓ Israel
Sha'ar la-Kore he-Ḥadash	W.	Jer.	1961	easy Hebrew, vocalized
Sha'ar Ẓiyyon	B–M.	London	1946–	religious, Judaic studies, partly in English
Shaḥarit	M.	Odessa-Warsaw	1913	lit.
Shaḥmat	Irr.	T.A. Haifa-Jer.	1923, 1932, 1936–1937, 1946, 1960	chess—various newspapers under this name or *Ha-Shaḥmat*
Shai	1	Jer.	1925	lit. Hebrew writers for J.N.F.
Shallekhet	1	Lvov, Galicia	1910	lit.
Shalom	Irr.	T.A.	1953–1956	organ of the Peace Movement
Shanah be-Shanah	A.	Jer.	1960–	religious, lit. annual of Hechal Shlomo in Jer., the first volume called: Halikhot
She'arim	W., D.	T.A.	1945–	Po'alei Agudat Israel from 1939, W. from 1949, daily from 1951
Sheḥakim	Irr.	Kefar Ḥabad	1969–	organ of Aircraft Industries
She'ifoteinu	Irr., M.	Jer.	1927–1933	organ of Bet Shalom (Jewish-Arab cooperation)
Shelabbim—see: Ha-Po'el ha-Vatik				
Sheluḥot	M.	Jer.	1945–1962	religious youth department of the Jewish Agency, continuation of *Iggeret la-Golah*
Sheluḥot	F.	T.A.	1950–1955	department of Yemenites belonging to Mapai
Shelumei Emunei Yisrael	A.	Odessa, Russia	1898–1902	lit. 4 vols.
Shema'atin	Q.	Bene-Berak	1963–	organ of teachers of religious subjects in religious secondary schools
Shemoneh ba-Erev	W.	T.A.	1968–	radio and T.V.
Shenaton—see also: Sefer ha-Shabat Agudat Yisrael-Amerikah	A.	T.A.	1951, 1953	Agudat Israel-America

Title	Freq.	Place of Publication	Date(s) of Appearance	Main Characteristics
Shenaton ha-Aguddah ha-Yisre'elit le-Shikkum	A.	T.A.	1964–	rehabilitation of invalids and soldiers
Shenaton ha-Histadrut	A.	T.A.	1963–	sketches of all Histadrut activities
Shenaton ha-Hitaḥadut le-Khadduregel	A.	T.A.	1959, 1964/65	football
Shenaton ha-Memshalah	A.	Jer.	1949–	activities of the government, appears also in English as *Government Yearbook*
Shenaton ha-Po'el	A.	T.A.	1968–	sport
Shenaton ha-Sefer—see: Jewish Book Annual				
Shenaton ha-Student	A.	Jer.	1965–1966 1968–	students in Israel
Shenaton ha-Televizyah	A.	Haifa	1969–	T.V.
Shenaton Ḥerut	A.	T.A.	1953–1954	activities of Ḥerut movement
Shenaton Hidrologi	A.	Jer.	1950–	hydrology
Shenaton le-Mishpat Ivri	A.	Jer.	1970–	Jewish law
Shenaton Massadah	A.	Ramat Gan	1968	1967 events
Shenaton Statisti le-Yisrael	A.	Jer.	1950–	statistical summary
Shenaton Yedi'ot Aḥaronot	A.	T.A.	1966–	newspaper annual; also called *Yedi'on*
Shenaton Yisrael le-Ommanut ha-Ẓillum	A.	T.A.	1963–	photography
Shenayim Plus	M.	T.A.	1970–	ill. entertainment magazine
Shevet va-Am	A.	Jer.	1954–1960, 1970–	Sephardi Jews past and present
Shevilei ha-Ḥinnukh	F., Q.	N.Y.	1925–1930, 1940–	education
Shevilim	Irr.	T.A.	1955–1958	organ of Ha-No'ar ha-Ẓiyyoni
Shevilin	S–A., A.	T.A.	1962–	organ of rabbis in Mizrachi and Ha-Po'el ha-Mizrachi movement
Shevut Teiman	1	T.A.	1945	history of Yemenite Jews. Various booklets with this name concerning Yemenites issued in years 1940–44
Shibbolim	F.	N.Y.	1909	lit. The first modern lit. journal in U.S. 7 issues
Shittuf	M., B–M.	T.A.	1948–	organ of the central cooperative of the Histadrut
Shivat Ẓiyyon	A.	Jer.	1950–1956	history of Zionism and the *yishuv*, 3 vols. (one double)
Shomer Ẓiyyon ha-Ne'eman	Irr.	Altona	1846–1856	rabbinics, Orthodox; 222 issues, new reprint
Shorashim	Irr.	Jer.	1936–1953	teachers' platform for Keren ha-Kayemeth
Shoval	Q.	T.A.	1962–1967	20 issues, public council for culture and art
Shulamit	F.	Jer.	1935	women's magazine
Shurot	Irr.	Beltsy, Bessarabia	1935–1937	lit.
Shurot	Irr., M.	T.A.	1938–	organ of clerks-office workers
Si'aḥ	Irr.	T.A.	1969	New Left in Israel
Sifrei Sha'ashu'im	Irr.	Cracow-Buczacz, Galicia	1896–1899	lit.
Sifrut—see also: Ha-Sifrut	Irr.	Warsaw	1908–1909	lit. 4 issues
Sifrut Ẓe'irah	W.	Jer.	1939	lit. organ of young writers
Signon	B–M.	T.A.	1970–	architecture and interior design
Sikkot	W.	T.A.	1940–1945	humor
Sinai	A.	Bucharest	1928–1933	Judaic studies, 5 vols.
Sinai	M.	Jer.	1937–	Judaic studies, rabbinics
Sport ba-Olam—see also: Ha-Sport	M.	T.A.	1964–1965	sport
Sport ha-Boker	W.	T.A.	1936	sport. Separate sport edition of *Ha-Boker*, afterward included in *Ha-Boker*
Sport ha-Shavu'a	W.	T.A.	1947–1948	sport
Sport Kadduregel	W.	T.A.	1965–1966	soccer
Sport la-Am	B–M., W.	T.A.	1947–1959	sport; from 1951 W., from 1959 included in *Davar*
Sport ve-Toto	W.	T.A.	1968–1969	sport and Toto (lottery)
Sport Yisrael	W.	T.A.	1949–1954	sport
Sugyot	1	Givat Ḥavivah	1956	collection of studies from the Ha-Shomer ha-Za'ir seminar on Jewish and general problems
Sullam	M.	Jer.	1949–1964	Cheoretical organ of Lehi members and their adherents in Ereẓ Israel
Sura	A.	Jer.	1954–1964	Judaic studies, 4 vols.

Title	Freq.	Place of Publication	Date(s) of Appearance	Main Characteristics
Ta'asiyyah u-Mishar	M.	Jer.	1959–	industry and trade
Ta'asiyyah ve-Khalkalah	M.	Jer.	1937–1941	industry and economics
Tafrit	M.	T.A.	1949–1953	entertainment— army
Tagim	1	Bene-Berak	1969	bibliography
Taḥbiv	M.	T.A.	1962–1963, 1970–	hobbies
Taḥburah ve-Tayyarut	M.	T.A.	1962–	transport and tourism
Taḥkemoni	Irr.	Berne-Berlin-Jer.	1910–1911	Judaic studies, 2 issues
Talpiyyot	1	Berdichev, Ukraine	1895	lit. largest collection of its kind issued in those days
Talpiyyot	W.	Jassy (Iasi), Rumania	1898	lit. Zionist
Talpioth	Q.	N.Y.	1943–1963	rabbinics and Judaic studies
Tamḥir	Q.	T.A.	1960–	costing and business economics
TaRAV (Tav Resh-Ayin-Vav)	1	Jer.	1916	Ereẓ Israel and Jerusalem in World War I
Tarbiz	Q.	Jer.	1930–	Judaic studies; in the first years also humanities
Tarbut	M.	N.Y.	1919–1920	education
Tarbut	M.	Warsaw	1922–1924	Hebrew culture and education
Tarbut	B–M.	London	1944–1968	lit. from 1940 under various names
Tashbeẓ	F., Irr.	T.A.-Nahariyyah-Ramat Gan	1954–	crossword
Tav-Shin	A.	T.A.	1943–1956	lit. almanacs of *Davar*, some under different names
Taẓlil	A.	Haifa	1960–	music research and bibliography
Te'atron	M.	T.A.	1953–1954	theater
Te'atron	B–M.	Haifa	1962–1966	theater
Te'atron ve-Ommanut	M.	T.A.-Jer.	1925–1928	theater and art
Tefuẓot Yisrael	B–M.	Jer.	1962–	Jewish life in the Diaspora
Teḥiyyah—see also: Ha-Teḥiyyah	M.	N.Y.	1913	lit.
Teḥumim	Q.	Warsaw	1937–1938	lit.
Tekhnikah u-Madda	M.	T.A.	1937–1954	popular science
Tekhunat ha-Ru'aḥ ha-Yisre'eli	1	N.Y.	1889	lit.
Tekufatenu	Q.	London	1932–1933	lit.
Tekumah	Irr.	N.Y.	1938–1939	education and J.N.F.
Telamim	Irr., Q.	T.A.	1933–	organ of the moshav movement
Telegramot Aḥaronot	D.	T.A.	1941	independent afternoon paper
Tel-Talpiyyot	F., Irr.	Vac, Hungary	1892–1938	rabbinics, interruption during years 1921–22
Temurot	M.	T.A.	1938–	General Zionist Labor movement, afterward Liberal
Teraklin	M.	T.A.	1949–1965	lit. and entertainment
Terapyah Shimmushit	M.	Petaḥ Tikvah	1965–	physiotherapy
Terumah	1	T.A.	1925	lit. Hebrew writers for J.N.F.
Tesha ba-Erev—see: Ha-Olam ha-Ẓeh				
Tesha Tesha Tesha	Irr.	T.A.	1953–1957	police (named after the tel. no. 999)
Te'urah	Q.	Chicago	1944–1945	education
Tevai	Q.	T.A.	1965–	architecture, town planning, plastic art
Teva u-Veri'ut	Q.	Petaḥ Tikvah	1956–	organ of vegetarians and naturalists
Teva va-Areẓ—see: Ha-Teva ve-ha-Areẓ				
Tevunah	Irr.	Memel-Koenigsberg, E. Prussia	1861	rabbinics, organ of the Musar movement
Tevunah	Irr.	Kovno, Lithuania	1922–1924, 1928	rabbinics
Tevunah	W., F.	Jer.	1932–1933, 1941–1958	religious
Torah mi-Ẓiyyon	Irr.	Jer.	1886–1906	rabbinics
Torat Ereẓ-Yisrael	M.	Jer.	1930–1955	rabbinics, some interruptions
Torat ha-Areẓ	Irr.	Petaḥ Tikvah	1935–1938	rabbinics
Turim	W.	T.A.	1933–1934, 1938–1939	lit.
Udim	Irr.	Beltsy, Bessarabia	1939	lit.
Urim	Irr., M.	T.A.	1935–1966	education organ of Ha-Merkaz le-Ḥinnukh of the Histadrut. M. from 1953
Urim le-Horim	Irr. & M.	T.A.	1946–	education problems for parents. M. from 1954

Title	Freq.	Place of Publication	Date(s) of Appearance	Main Characteristics
Uvdot u-Misparim	M.	Jer.	1947–1969	facts and figures of the Keren Hayesod and the U.J.A.
Uzzenu	A.	T.A.	1943–1948	sport annual of Hapoel
Uzzenu	F. & M.	T.A.	1933–1935	sport organ of Hapoel
Va'ad Ḥakhamim	M.	Jer.	1923–1924	rabbinics
Va-Yelakket Yosef	F.	Bonyhad-Munkacs, Hungary	1899–1918	rabbinics
Wizo. . .–see: Ha-Ishah be-Yisrael				
Ya'ad	Irr.	T.A.	1962–	organ of Ha-No'ar ha-Oved ha-Le'ummi
Yadan Ma'ariv	A.	T.A.	1956–	*Ma'ariv* annual
Yad la-Koré	B–M.	T.A.	1943–1944	bibliography and librarianship
Yad la-Koré	Q.	T.A.-Jer.	1946–	bibliography and librarianship
Yad la-Safran—see: Alim le-Bibliografyah u-le-Safranut				
Yad Vashem—see also: Yedi'ot Yad Vashem	A.	Jer.	1957–	research on the Holocaust and Resistance
Yagdil Torah	Irr.	Odessa, Russia	1879–1885	rabbinics
Yagdil Torah	Irr.	Berlin	1890–1893	rabbinics
Yagdil Torah	W. & M. B–M. & Irr.	Slutsk, Belorussia	1908–1928	rabbinics, with interruptions. The last rabbinical periodical in Russia
Yagdil Torah	Irr.	London	1949–1959	rabbinics
Yahadut Polin	Irr.	T.A.	1962, 1965	history of Polish Jewry, Hebrew and Yiddish. 2 issues
Yaḥdav	M. & Irr.	T.A.	1953–	Ha-Kibbutz ha-Me'uḥad brigade
Yalkut ha-Mikhvarot	Irr.	T.A.	1949–1966	bee breeding
Yalkut ha-Mizraḥ ha-Tikhon	M.	Jer.	1935–1951	Middle East affairs
Yalkut ha-Re'im	Irr.	T.A.	1942–1946	lit. organ of young writers, 4 issues
Yalkut Ma'aravi	A.	N.Y.	1904	lit.
Yalkut Magen	Irr.	T.A.	1956–	organ of the Association to help Soviet Russian Jewry
Yalkut Moreshet	S–A. & A.	T.A.	1963–	research on the Holocaust, organ of the M. Anielewicz Institute for Research on the Holocaust at Yad Mordekhai
Yalkut Tekhni	B–M.	T.A.	1955–1960	institute for work productivity and production
Yalkut Vohlin	Irr.	T.A.	1945–	history of Volhynian Jews
Yarhon ha-Avodah—see also: Ha-Yarḥon	M.	T.A.	1949–1958	labor and social security (National Insurance)
Yarḥon ha-Ḥazzanim	M.	Czestochowa, Poland	1896	song, music, *ḥazzanut;* the first of its kind in Hebrew, 4 issues
Yarḥon ha-No'ar ha-Musikali be-Yisrael	M.	T.A.	1957–1961	music for youth
Yarḥon ha-Sport	M.	T.A.	1960–1961	sport
Yarḥon Statisti la-Shetaḥim ha-Muḥzakim	M.	T.A.	1971–	statistics figures on the occupied territories
Yarḥon Statisti le-Yisrael	M. & Q.	T.A.-Jer.	1949–	statistical figures on all walks of life in Israel—some appendices
Yavneh	M.	Lvov, Galicia	1929–1931	Judaic studies and lit.
Yavneh	A.	Jer.	1939–1942	Judaic studies, 3 vols.
Yavneh	Irr.	Jer.	1946–1949	organ of religious academicians
Yeda Am	Irr.	T.A.	1948–	folklore
Yedi'on–see: Shenaton Yedi'ot Aḥaronot				
Yedi'on ha-Aguddah li-Gerontologyah	Irr.	T.A.	1945–	gerontology
Yedi'ot	A.	Jer.	1959–1966	religious music. 8 vols.
Yedi'ot Aḥaronot	D.	T.A.	1939–	independent
Yedi'ot Arkhiyyon u-Muze'on ha-Avodah	Irr.	T.A.	1933–1951	history of the labor movement in Ereẓ Israel
Yedi'ot Beit Loḥamei ha-Getta'ot	Irr.	Haifa	1951–1960	Holocaust research. Organ of the Isaac Katznelson Institute for research on the Holocaust at kibbutz Loḥamei ha-Getta'ot
Yedi'ot Ereẓ ve-Emunah	Irr.	T.A.	1954–	religious J.N.F.

Title	Freq.	Place of Publication	Date(s) of Appearance	Main Characteristics
Yedi'ot Genazim	Irr.	T.A.	1962–	documentation material on the history of Hebrew literature by the Genazim Institute
Yedi'ot ha-Ḥevrah la-Ḥakirat Ereẓ Yisrael va-Attikoteha	Q.	Jer.	1933–1967	archaeology of Palestine and Bible lands. Superseded by *Kadmoniyyot*
Yedi'ot ha-Makhon le-Ḥeker ha-Shirah ha-Ivrit	Irr.	Berlin-Jer.	1933–1958	research on Hebrew poetry during the Middle Ages; from 4 vols. in Jer. 7 vols.
Yedi'ot ha-Makhon le-Madda'ei ha-Yahadut	Q.	Jer.	1925	the first publication of the Judaic Institute of the Hebrew University, 2 issues; superseded by *Madda'ei ha-Yahadut*
Yedi'ot ha-Mazkirut	Irr.	T.A.	1947–	Ha-Kibbutz ha-Me'uḥad secretariat, appeared under various names
Yedi'ot ha-Tenu'ah le-Aḥdut ha-Avodah—see: Le-Aḥdut ha-Avodah				
Yedi'ot Taḥanat ha-Nissayon	Q.	Reḥovot-T.A.	1926–1931, 1936–1938	agricultural research station of the Zionist movement. 4 vols.
Yedi'ot Yad Vashem	Q. & Irr.	Jer.	1954–	Holocaust research, Yad Vashem, Jer.
Yehudah vi-Yrushalayim	Irr.	Jer.	1877–1878	newspaper interrupted by the editors on occasion of the founding of Petaḥ Tikvah. Motif of settling Ereẓ Israel, new ed. 1955.
Yerushalayim	A.	Zolkiew-Lvov	1844–1845	lit.
Yerushalayim	A. & Irr.	Vienna-Jer.	1882–1919	Palestinography and history of Ereẓ Israel, 13 vols. The first of its kind in Hebrew bibliography
Yerushalayim	B–M.	Cracow, Poland	1900–1901	bibliography
Yerushalayim	1	Jer.	1913	lit. dedicated to Jerusalem
Yerushalayim	Q.	Jer.	1947–1955	history of Ereẓ Israel and Jerusalem
Yerushalayim	A.	Jer.	1965–	lit. The collection which was issued in 1968 was called *Ve-li-Yrushalayim*—a gift to those who fought in the Six-Day War
Yeshurun (Jeschurun)	A.	Lvov-Breslau-Bamberg	1856–1878	Judaic studies, 9 vols., partly in German
Yeshurun	M.	Bucharest	1920–1923	lit. and Judaic studies
Yokhani	Irr.	T.A.	1961–1967	lit., 7 issues
Yosef Da'at	F.	Adrianople, Turkey	1888–1889	Judaic studies, partly in Ladino
Yuval	1	Jer.	1968	studies in Jewish music
Ẓarekhanut Shittufit	M.	T.A.	1959–1969	economics and cooperatives, afterward incorporated into *Davar*
Ẓelilim	M.	Jer.	1940–1941	music and art. 6 issues
Ẓelil va-Omer	Q.	Haifa	1957–1962	music for youth. 21 issues
Zemannim	D.	Jer.	1953–1955	Progressives newspaper
Zera'im	M.	Jer.-T.A.	1936–	organ of Benei Akiva, Mizrachi youth, the first two years irregular
Zeramim	W.	Vilna	1931–1932	lit.
Ẓeror Mikhtavim	Irr.	T.A.	1933–1951	organ of Ha-Kibbutz ha-Me'uḥad, continuation of *Iggerot mi-Bifenim* 1929–1934
Ẓeror Mikhtavim li-She'elot ha-Ḥinnukh ha-Meshuttaf	Irr.	T.A.	1938–	pedagogical organ of Ha-Kibbutz ha-Me'uḥad, change of names
Zikhronot Devarim shel ha-Aguddah ha-Mediẓinit ha-Ivrit	Irr.	Jaffa	1912–1914	the first medical journal in Hebrew, 5 issues (one double)
Zikhronot ha-Akademyah la-Lashon ha-Ivrit	A.	Jer.	1949–	Hebrew language studies, until 1954, memoirs of Va'ad ha-Lashon
Ẓiklon	M.	T.A.	1953–1963	included later in *Ma'arekhet*, world newspaper translations for soldiers
Ẓillum —see: Ha-Ẓillum				
Ẓilẓelei Shama	1	Kharkov, Ukraine	1923	lit. the only literary publication in Hebrew, printed and edited in U.S.S.R.
Zimrat ha-Areẓ	Q.	Jassy (Iasi), Rumania	1872	lit.
Zion	Q.	Jer.	1936–	history of Jews
Zion, Me'assef	A.	Jer.	1926–1934	history and ethnography of Jews. 6 vols
Zion, Yedi'ot	M.	Jer.	1929–1931	folklore and ethnography of Jews. 11 issues
Ẓippor ha-Nefesh	W.	T.A.	1964–1965	humor and satire
Ẓiyyon	Irr. & M.	Drohobycz, Galicia	1885, 1888, 1896–1897	lit.
Ẓiyyon	A.	Frankfort	1841–1842	lit. 2 vols.
Ẓiyyon he-Ḥadash	1	Leipzig	1845	lit.
Zo ha-Derekh	W.	T.A.	1965–	organ of Rakaḥ
Zohar	M.	Buenos Aires	1961–1964	lit. joined later with *Darom*
Zot ha-Areẓ	F.	T.A.	1968–	organ of the Greater Israel Movement

[G. K.]

POTTERY (From the Neolithic Period to the end of the Israelite Period.)

All plate references are from R. Amiran, P. Beck and V. Zevulun, *The Ancient Pottery of Eretz Yisrael* (Hebrew Edition), Jerusalem 1963. Copyright by The Bialik Institute and The Israel Exploration Society, Jerusalem. Courtesy Ruth Amiran, Jerusalem.

PLATE I: NEOLITHIC PERIOD, c. 5500–4000 B.C.E.

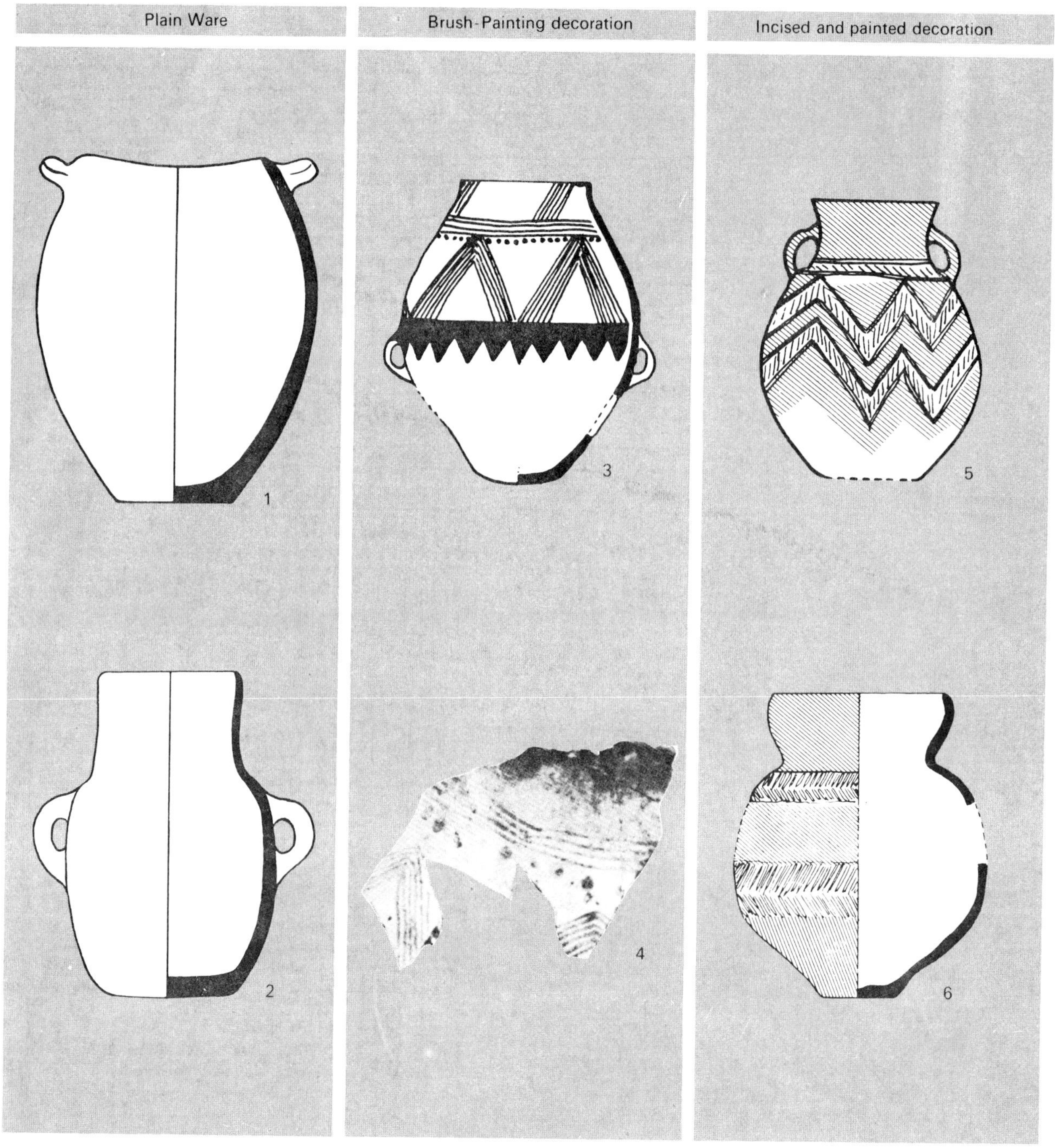

1. Brown-gray jar with two enlarged knobs and holemouth rim, from Sha'ar ha-Golan (Yarmukian cultures). [pl. 1, no. 11]

2. Jar with high neck and two loops handles, from Jericho, stratum IX. [pl. 1, no. 2]

3. Jar with red brush decoration covering the upper surface of the vessel, from Ghrubba. [pl. 1, no. 10]

4. Painted sherd, from Ghrubba. From Amiran, Beck Zevulun, p. 34.

5. Jar with incised and painted red decoration, applied before firing, composed of parallel zigzag bands and straight band around the neck, all filled with small parallel grooves, from Sha'ar ha-Golan (Yarmukian culture.) [pl. 1, no. 1]

6. Jar with incised and painted red decoration composed of bands of herringbone motif, from Jericho, stratum VIII. [pl. 1, no. 3]

PLATE II: CHALCOLITHIC PERIOD, c. 4000–3150 B.C.E.

1. V-shaped bowl with red painted band around the rim, from Ghassul. [pl. 2, no. 2]

2. Bowl with rounded sides and lug handles, from Ghassul. [pl. 2, no. 4]

3. Painted goblet from Ghassul. [pl. 2, no. 11]

4. Pedestal goblet, from Adeimeh. [pl. 2, no. 12]

5. Horn-shaped cornet with painted rim and two tiny lug handles, from Ghassul. [pl. 2, no. 6]

6. Short cornet with the pointed tip cut off to form a flat base, from Ghassul. [pl. 2, no. 8]

7. Chalice on hollow stand, from Ghassul. [pl. 2, no. 14]

8. Small jar with painted decoration and two pairs of lug handles on either side, from Ghassul. [pl. 2, no. 16]

9. Jar with holemouth rim and two lug handles, from Ghassul, stratum IVA. [pl. 2, no. 20]

10. Pithos (large container) with plastic decorations of rope-like clay bands, from a site near Ashdot Ya'akov in the Jordan Valley. Jerusalem, Israel Museum, Israel Department of Antiquities Collection.

11. Large, deep bowl with profiled rim, from Safadi. [pl. 4, no. 6]

12. Spindle-shaped goblet, from Gezer. [pl. 5, no. 3]

13. Painted goblet, from Abu-Maṭar. [pl. 5, no. 11]

14. Large jar with elongated, unpierced lug handles, from Abu-Maṭar. [pl. 6, no. 2]

15. Holemouth jar with lug handles, from Abu-Maṭar. [pl. 6, no. 11]

16. Cream-colored jar ("cream ware" type) with tiny pierced lug handles and tubular handles, from Safadi. [pl. 5, no. 8]

17. Basalt set of chalice and two bowls, from Abu-Maṭar. Jerusalem, Israel Museum, Israel Department of Antiquities Collection.

18. Small, stylized, white churn with brown decoration, from Azor. [pl. 7, no. 5]

19. Big churn, with one flat side, from Safadi. Jerusalem, Israel Museum, Israel Department of Antiquities.

20. Small churn (the so-called bird vase), from Ghassul, stratum IV. [pl. 7, no. 1]

21. Jars used as ossuaries by pinching together the neck and mouth of the vessel and cutting an opening in the wall. Jerusalem, Israel Museum, Israel Department of Antiquities Collection.

PLATE II: CHALCOLITHIC PERIOD, c. 4000–3150 B.C.E.

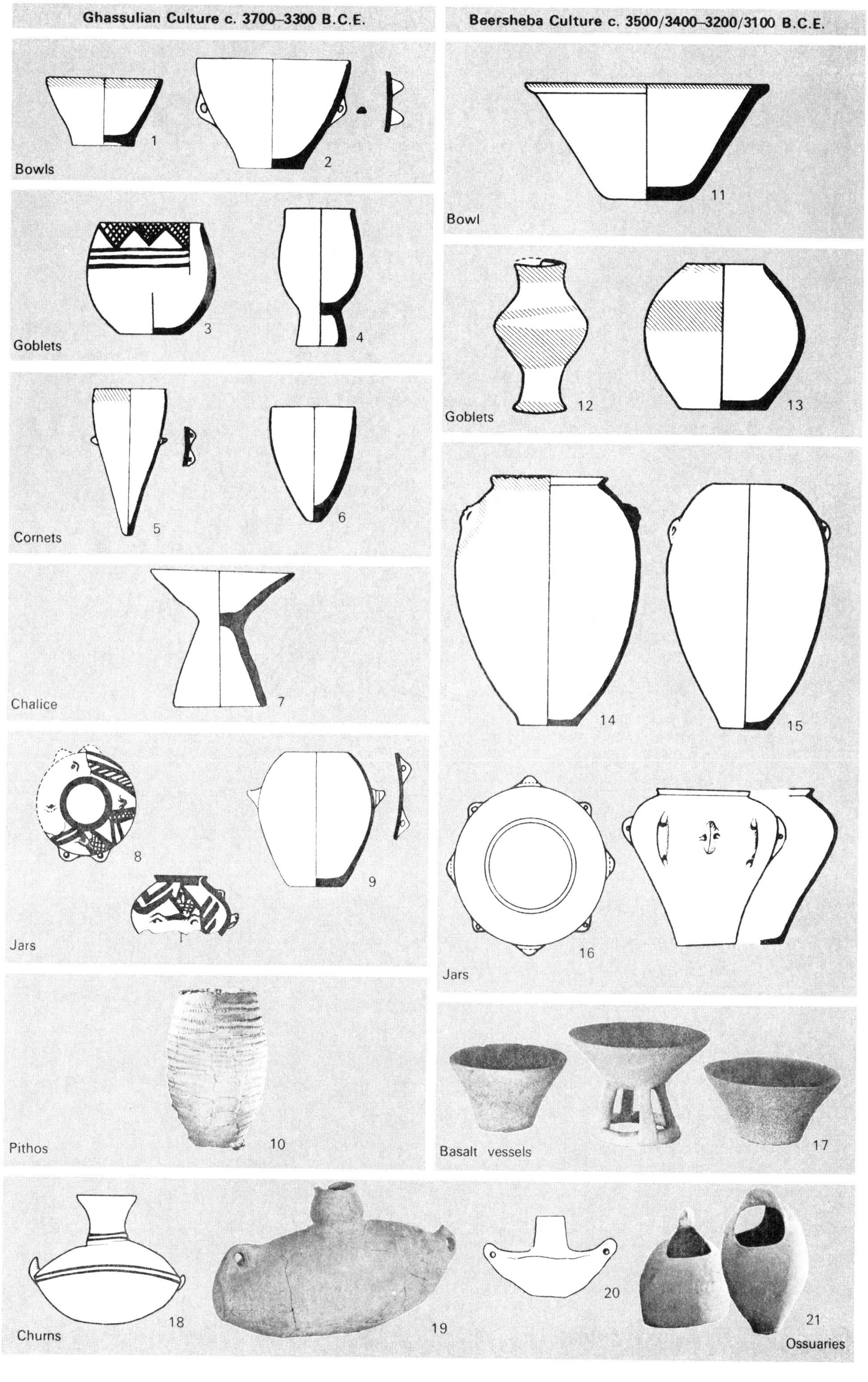

PLATE III: EARLY BRONZE PERIOD, c. 3150–2200 B.C.E.

PL. IIIa: EARLY BRONZE I, c. 3150–2900 B.C.E.

1–5. Sherds of jars with band-slip (grain-wash) technique of painting, from Afulah. *Journal of the Palestine Oriental Society,* 21 (1948), pl. XVIII.

6. Bowl with red-burnished slip and ledge handle, from a tomb at Far'ah (N). [pl. 9, no. 6]

7. Platter with brown-red burnished slip and broad, flattish base, from a stratified deposit at Far'ah (N). [pl. 13, no. 2]

8. Teapot with brown-red slip, narrow neck, and a ridge at the base of the neck, from a tomb at Asawir.[pl. 9, no. 15]

9. Teapot with pink slip and white neck, from a tomb at Far'ah (N). [pl. 9, no. 12]

10. Amphoriskos with red-burnished slip and two lug handles, from a tomb at Far'ah (N). [pl. 9, no. 19]

11. Amphoriskos with red slip, bag-shaped body, and large, diagonal lug handles, from a tomb at Megiddo. [[pl. 9, no. 17]

12. Small holemouth jar with red-burnished slip, from a tomb at Far'ah (N). [pl. 9, no. 25]

13. Jar with red-burnished slip and small ledge handles, from a tomb at Far'ah (N). [pl. 9, no. 29]

14. Juglet with red-burnished slip and high loop handle, from a tomb at Far'ah (N). [pl. 9, no. 24]

15. Juglet with red-burnished slip and high loop handle, from a tomb at Asawir. [pl. 9, no. 22]

16. Gray-burnished, wide bowl with softly carinated sides, and broad knobs placed on the line of carination, from Afulah. [pl. 10, no. 2]

17. Gray-burnished, wide bowl with softly carinated sides, and a sinuous ridge on the line of carination, from Beth-Shean, stratum XVI. [pl. 10, no. 1]

18. Gray-burnished, deep bowl with twisted clay rope applied to upper part of the wall, from a tomb at Far'ah (N). [pl. 10, no. 3]

19. The same type of bowl on a fenestrated stand (also called incense burner), from a tomb at Far'ah (N). [pl. 10, no. 7]

20. Undecorated gray-burnished bowl with rigid carination, from Far'ah (N). [pl. 10, no. 4]

PLATE III : EARLY BRONZE PERIOD, c. 3150–2200 B.C.E.

PL. IIIa: EARLY BRONZE I, c. 3150–2900 B.C.E.

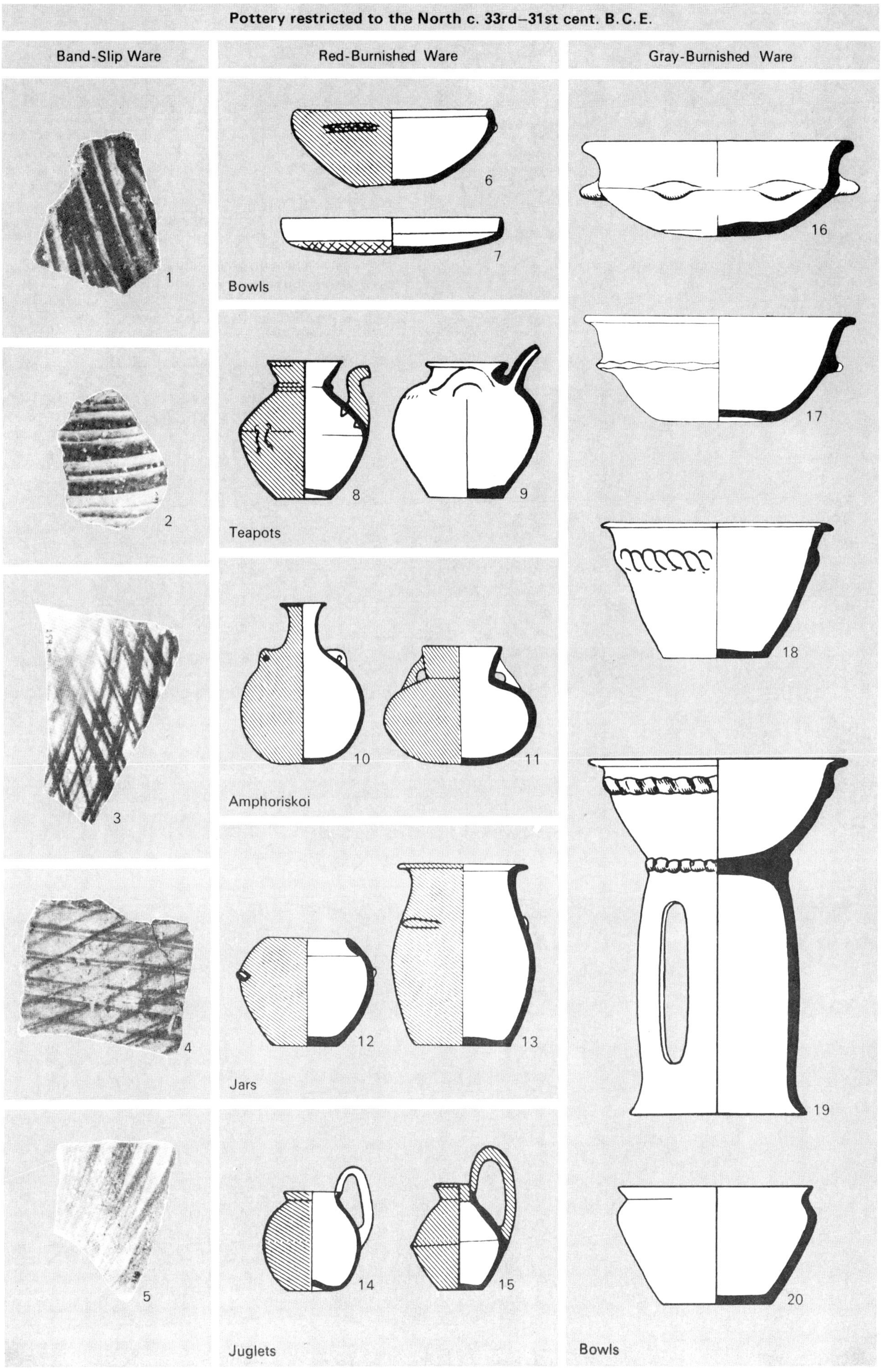

PLATE III: EARLY BRONZE PERIOD, c. 3150–2200 B.C.E.

PL. IIIa: EARLY BRONZE I, c. 3150–2900 B.C.E.

21. Hemispherical bowl with shallow omphalos and lug handle, from a tomb at Ai. [pl. 11, no. 1]

22. V-shaped bowl with painted red decoration, from a tomb at Ai. [pl. 11, no. 6]

23. Amphoriskos with red decoration and two lug handles, from a tomb at the Ophel, Jerusalem. [pl. 11, no. 8]

24. Amphoriskos with red decoration from a tomb at Ai. [pl. 11, no. 13]

25. Amphoriskos with red decoration, from Jericho, stratum VI. [pl. 13, no. 9]

26. Bottle with dark-red decoration, from a tomb at the Ophel. [pl. 11, no. 9]

27. Twin bottle with brown decoration, from a tomb at Ai. [pl. 11, no. 12]

28. Spouted bowl with red decoration, from a tomb at Ai. [pl. 11, no. 11]

29. Small jar with thumb-indented ledge handle, white slip and red decoration, from a tomb at Ai. [pl. 11, no. 24]

30. Spouted jar with plain ledge handle and traces of red decoration, from a tomb at Ai. [pl. 11, no. 25]

31. Hybrid juglet-amphoriskos with dark-red decoration, from a tomb at Ai. [pl. 11, no. 15]

32. Hybrid juglet-amphoriskos with red decoration and high loop handle, from Jericho, stratum VI [pl. 13, no. 11]

33. Spouted jug with red decoration, from a tomb at Ai. [pl. 11, no. 5]

PLATE III : EARLY BRONZE PERIOD, c. 3150–2200 B.C.E.

PL.IIIa: EARLY BRONZE I, c. 3150–2900. B.C.E.

Pottery restricted to the south c. 31st–29th cent. B.C.E.

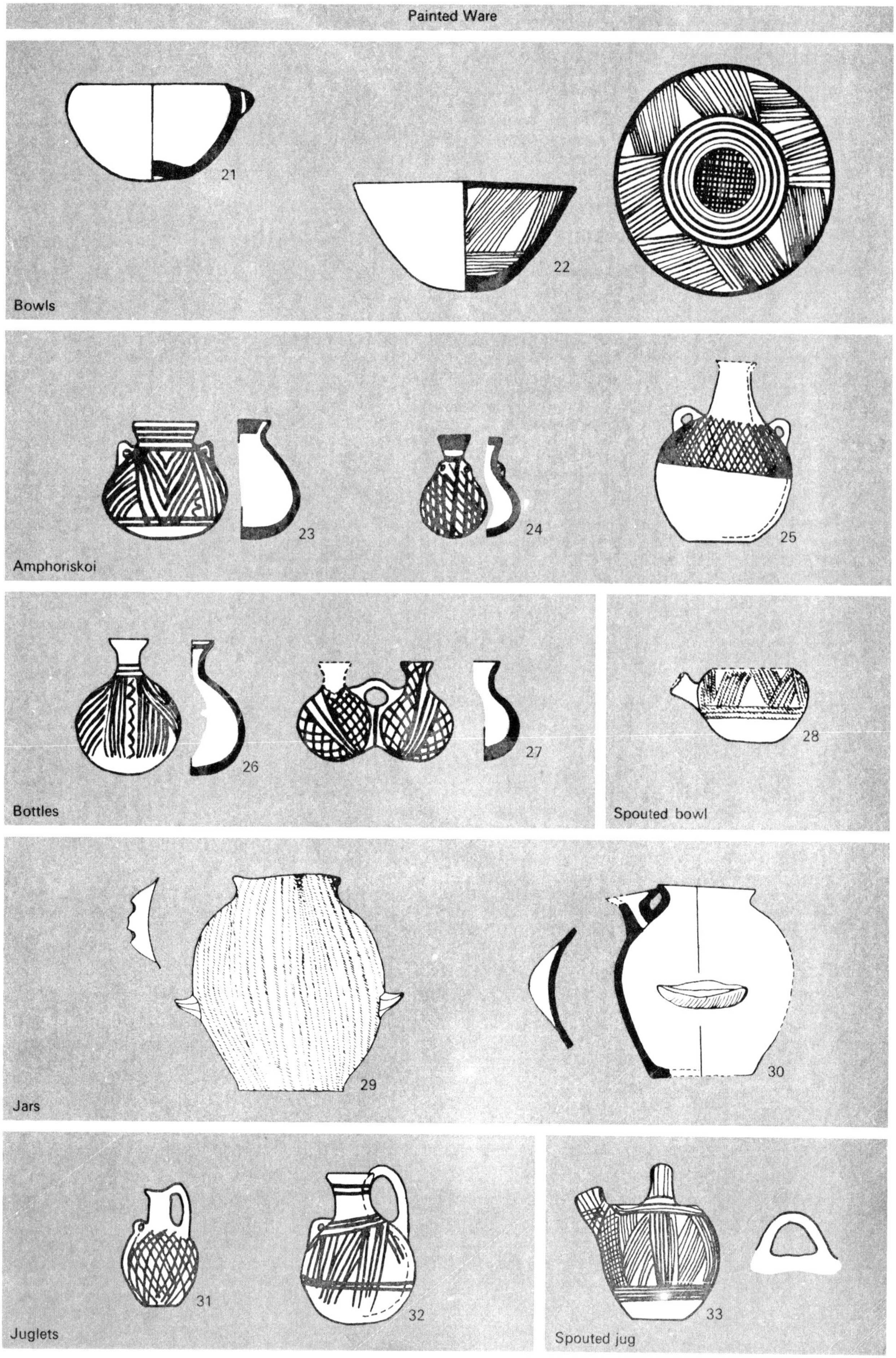

PLATE III: EARLY BRONZE PERIOD, c. 3150–2200 B.C.E.

PL. IIIb: EARLY BRONZE II, c. 2900–2600 B.C.E.

1. Large, deep bowl with white slip and sloping sides, from Megiddo, stratum XVIII. [pl. 15, no. 9]

2. Platter with flat, tray-like base, from Megiddo, stratum XVII [pl. 15, no. 8]

3. Deep platter from Megiddo, stratum XVII. [pl. 15, no. 7]

4. Chalice with red decoration, from Jericho, strata V–IV. [pl. 15, no. 10]

5. Amphoriskos with two tiny lug handles and red decoration, from Jericho, stratum IV. [pl. 15, no. 14]

6. Amphoriskos with long neck and two lug handles, from Beth-Shean. [pl. 15, no. 15]

7. Twin vessels with brown-red decoration, from Megiddo, stratum XVII. [pl. 15, no. 11]

8. Juglet of common type, from Farʿah (N). [pl. 15, no. 12]

9. Hybrid juglet-amphoriskos, from Jericho, stratum V. [pl. 15, no. 13]

10. Short jar with low neck, two ledge handles, and a spout, decorated with dark red lines on red-burnished slip, from Ai. From J. Marquet-Krause, *Les fouilles de 'Ay (Et-Tell)*, Paris, 1949.

11. Jar with elongated body and large lug handles, decorated with two-directional combed pattern, from Bet Yeraḥ, stratum XIIC. [pl. 16, no. 1]

12. Jug with oval body and one loop handle drawn from rim to shoulder, from a tomb at Kinneret. [pl. 17, no. 1]

13. Jug of similar shape, but without a handle, with brown-burnished slip, from Jericho. [pl. 17, no. 11]

14. Jug of similar shape, with two small loop handles on the body of the vessel in addition to the loop handle on the shoulder, from Farʿah (N). [pl. 17, no. 3]

15. Cylindrical jug with high stump base, loop handle drawn from the middle of the neck to the shoulder, and red-burnished slip, from Megiddo, stratum XVII. [pl. 17, no. 13]

16. Light-brown juglet with brown-black decoration, upper band alternately plain and dotted triangles, lower band, hatched triangles, from a tomb at Kinneret. [pl. 17, no. 7]

17. The same as no. 16, but lower band filled with chevrons, from Beth-Shean. [pl. 17, no. 6]

18. Light-brown juglet, with black decoration consisting of two bands of alternately plain and dotted triangles and a third band of chevrons, from a tomb at Jericho. [pl. 17, no. 9]

19. Jug with oval body, decorated with bands of dotted triangles and herringbone motif, from Saqqara, Egypt. [pl. 17, no. 10]

20. Jar with alternating bands of dotted triangles and chevrons, from Arad. Courtesy Arad Expedition.

PLATE III : EARLY BRONZE PERIOD, c. 3150–2200 B.C.E.

PL.IIIb: EARLY BRONZE II, c. 2900–2600 B.C.E.

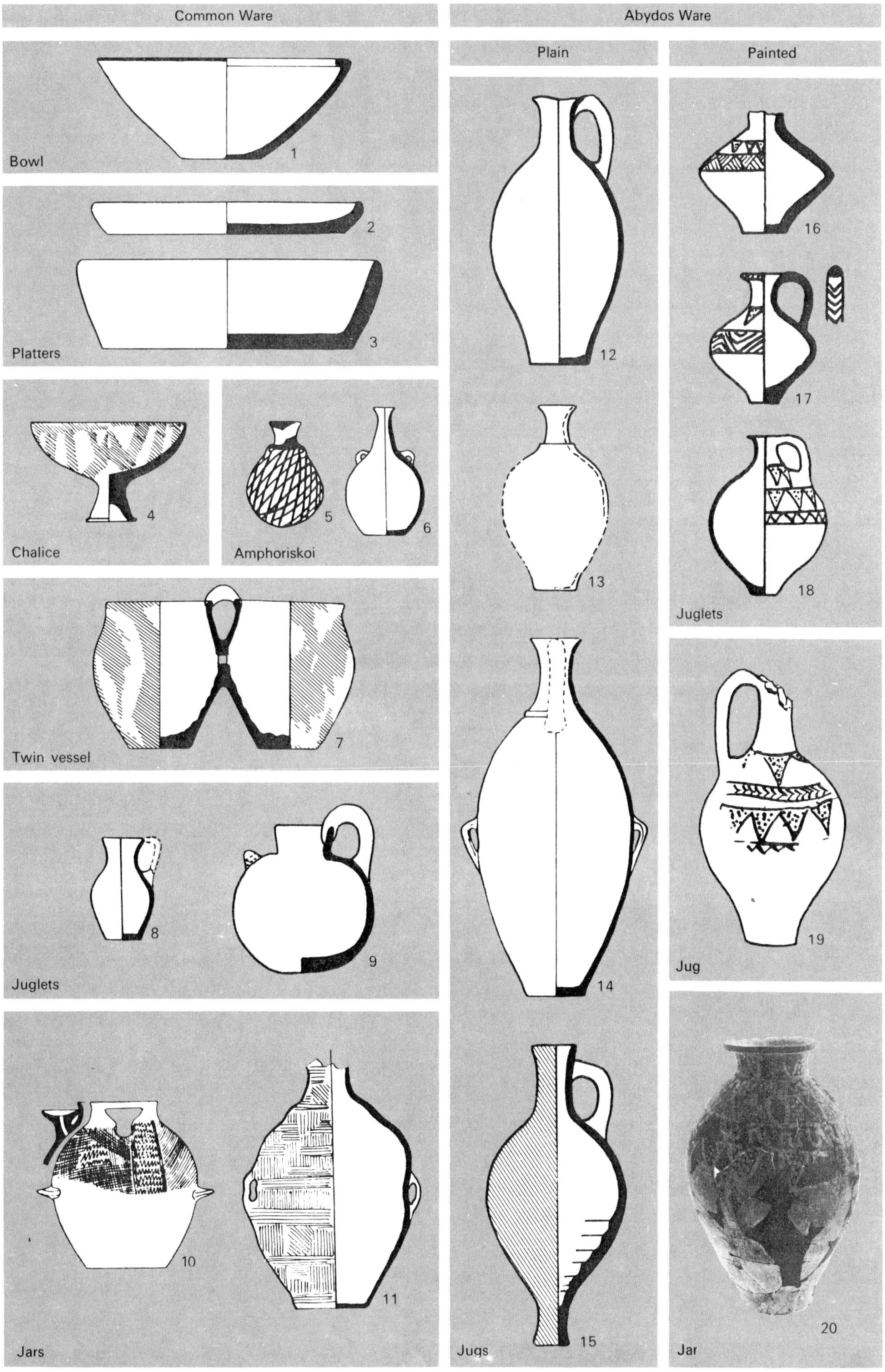

PLATE III: EARLY BRONZE PERIOD, c. 3150–2200 B.C.E.

PL. IIIc: EARLY BRONZE III, c. 2600–2300 B.C.E.

1. Deep bowl with flat base and pushed-up ledge handles, from temple A at Ai. [pl. 18, no. 6]

2. Platter with profiled rim and burnished slip, decorated with red pattern, from temple A at Ai. [pl. 18, no. 3]

3. Platter with profiled rim and burnished slip, decorated with dark-red pattern, from Beth-Shean, stratum XII. [pl. 18, no. 1]

4. Platter with plain rim and rounded base from Bet Yeraḥ, stratum XB. [pl. 18, no. 5]

5. Elongated jug (shaped like the Abydos Ware), from tomb A at Jericho. [pl. 20, no. 12]

6. Jug with stump base and red slip, from tomb A at Jericho. [pl. 20, no. 13]

7. Pear-shaped, gray-black burnished jug, from tomb A at Jericho. [pl. 20, no. 17]

8. Pear-shaped juglet with red slip, from tomb A at Jericho. [pl. 20, no. 19]

9. Pear-shaped, black juglet with decoration of white dots, from tomb A at Jericho. [pl. 20, no. 20]

10. Jar with profiled rim, wide, rope-decorated neck, and body patterned with combing decorations, from Bet Yeraḥ, stratum XB. [pl. 18, no. 13]

11. Spouted holemouth jar with pushed-up ledge handle, from temple A at Ai. [pl. 18, no. 11]

12. Jar with wide neck and pushed-up ledge handles, from tomb A at Jericho. [pl. 21, no. 4]

13a, 13b. Chalice from temple A at Ai. [pl. 18, no. 7]

14a, 14b. Cup (goblet) from temple A at Ai. [pl. 18, no. 9]

PLATE III : EARLY BRONZE PERIOD, c. 3150–2200 B.C.E.

PL.IIIc: EARLY BRONZE III, c. 2600–2300 B.C.E.

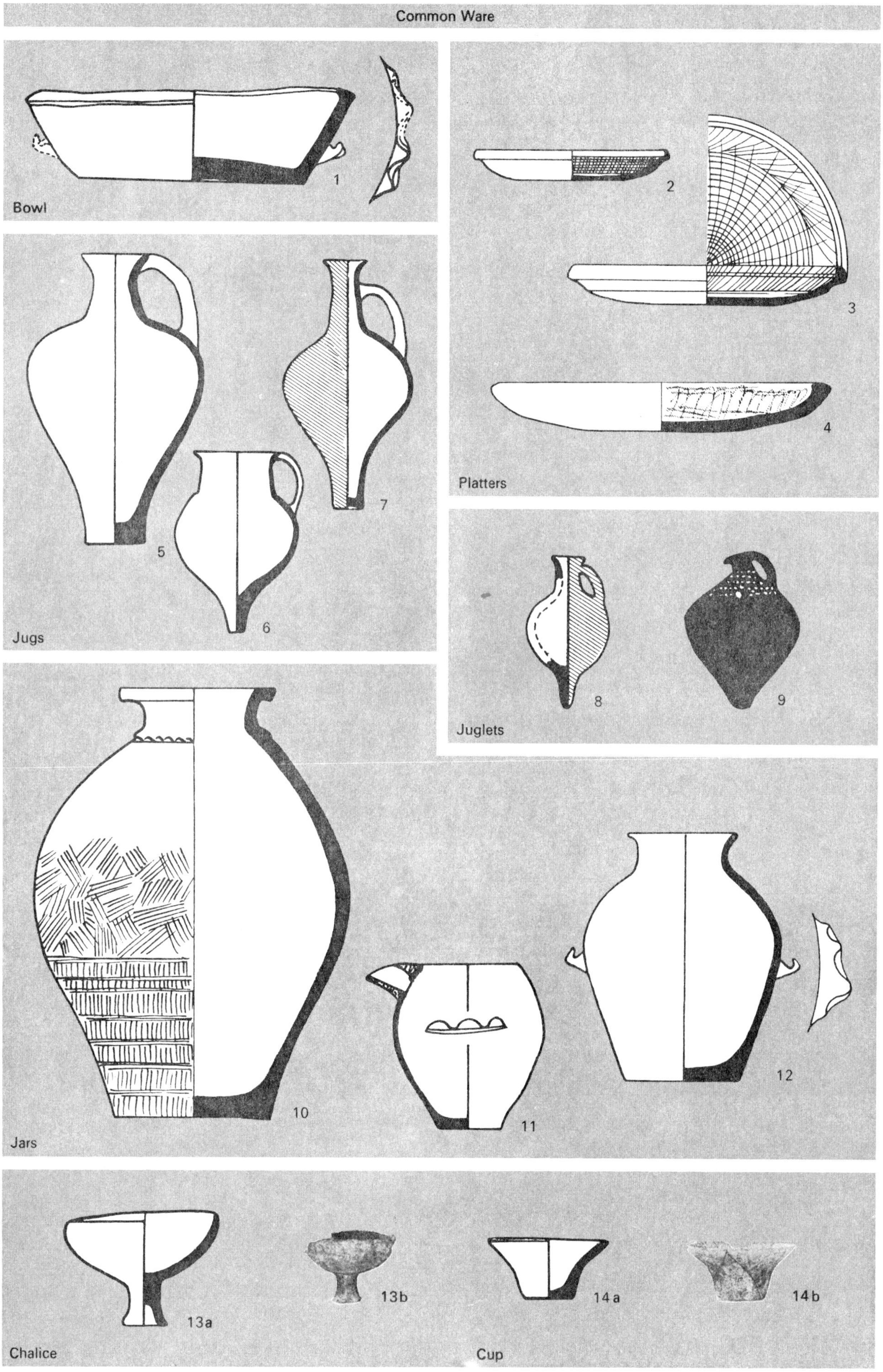

PLATE III: EARLY BRONZE PERIOD, c. 3150–2200 B.C.E.

PL. III c: EARLY BRONZE III, c. 2600–2300 B.C.E.

15. Small, delicate bowl with straight wall and omphalos base, from Beth-Shean, stratum XII. [pl. 19, no. 1]

16. Heavy-slipped, burnished bowl, black outside and red inside, with s-shaped wall and omphalos base, from Megiddo, stratum XVII. [pl. 19, no. 2]

17, 18. Small, deep bowls with small omphalos base, and pronounced s-shaped wall, from Beth-Shean, strata XI and XII [pl. 19, nos. 4, 3]

19, 20. Heavy-slipped, burnished kraters, black outside and red inside, with relief decoration, from Beth Yeraḥ strata XB and XII. [pl. 19, nos. 9, 12]

21. Mug with tiny knobs and loop handle, from Afulah. [pl. 19, no. 7]

22. Black mug with heavy slip, from Afulah. Courtesy Israel Department of Antiquities, Jerusalem.

23. Lid, from Beth-Shean, stratum XII. [pl. 19, no. 11]

24. Cylindrical stand, from Afulah. [pl. 19, no. 14]

25. Cylindrical stand with handle, from Beth-Shean. [pl. 19, no. 10]

26. Horseshoe-shaped stand from Bet Yeraḥ. Jerusalem, Israel Museum, Israel Department of Antiquities Collection.

PLATE III : EARLY BRONZE PERIOD, c. 3150–2200 B.C.E.

PL. IIIc: EARLY BRONZE III, c. 2600–2300 B.C.E.

Khirbet Kerak Ware

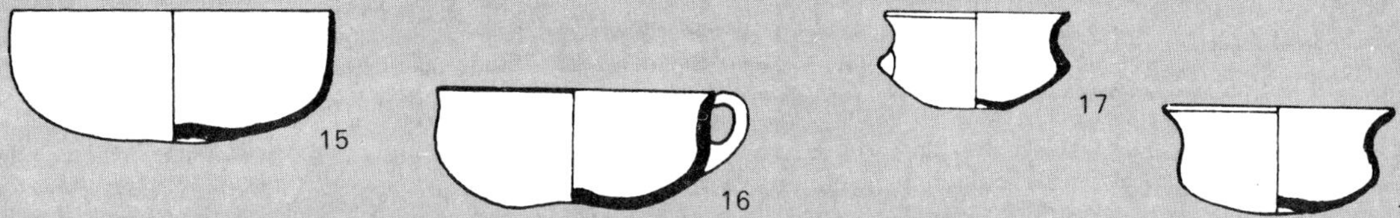

15 16 17 18

Bowls

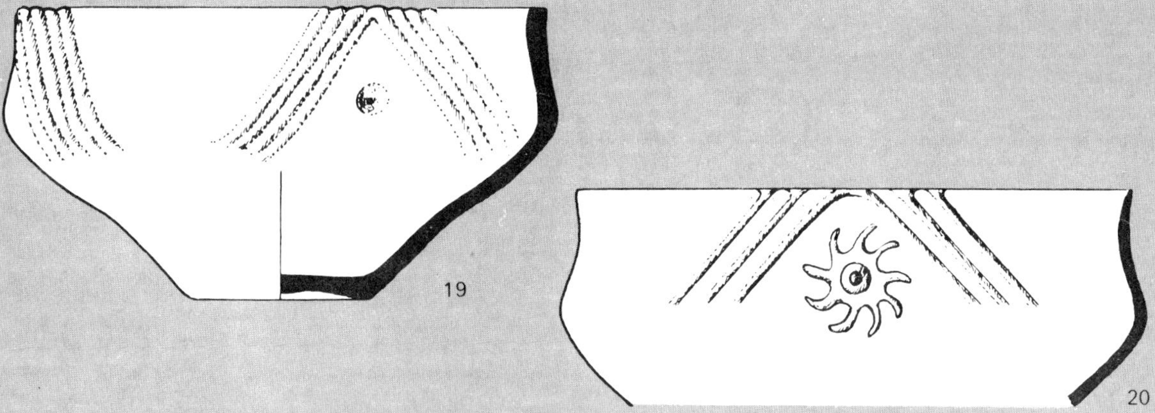

19 20

Kraters

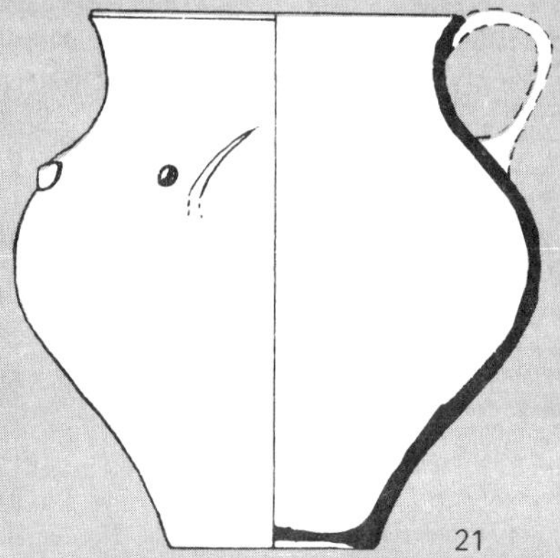

21

Mug

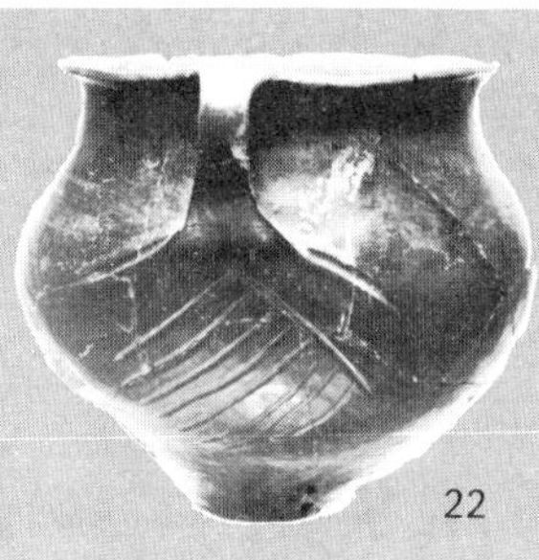

22

Pot

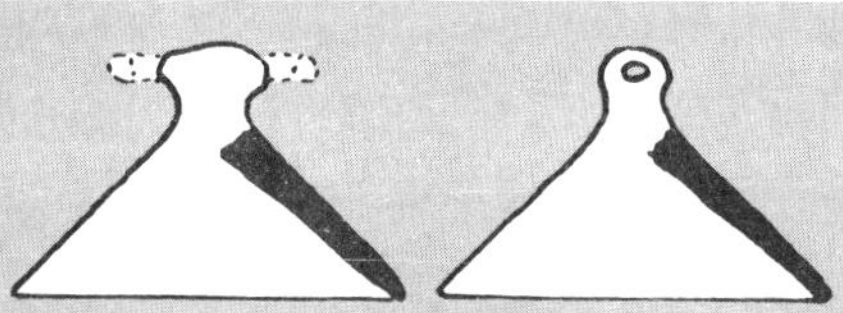

23

Lid

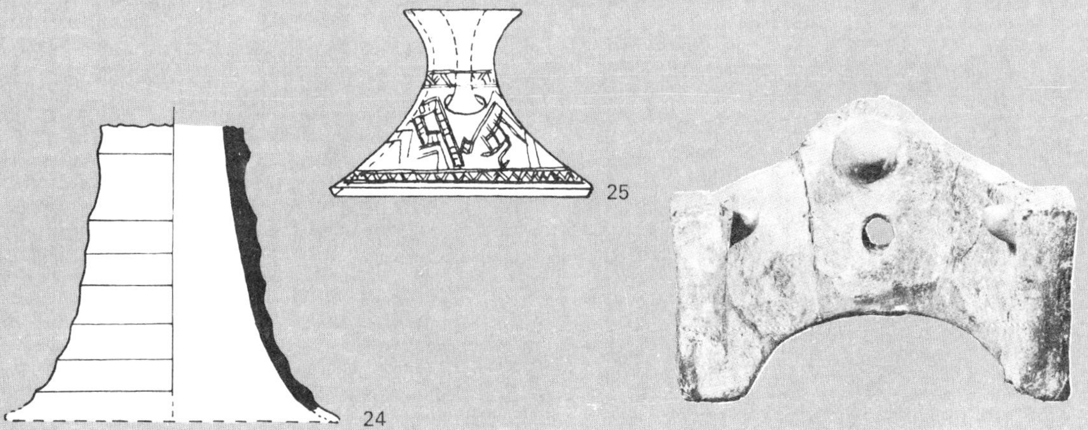

24 25 26

Stands

PLATE IV: MIDDLE BRONZE PERIOD, c. 2200–1550 B.C.E.

PL. IVa: INTERMEDIATE BRONZE AGE (MIDDLE BRONZE I), c. 2200–1950 B.C.E.

1. Barrel-shaped jar with incised decoration and degenerate ledge handle, from a tomb at Lachish [pl. 22, no. 18]

2. Barrel-shaped jar, brown-green color, with combed decoration and single knob on the shoulder, from Beth Mirsim, stratum H. [pl. 22, no. 21]

3. Light-brown amphoriskos with lug handles drawn from neck to shoulder, from Beth Mirsim, stratum H. [pl. 22, no. 12]

4. Light-brown amphoriskos, with combed and punctured decoration and high neck, from unknown location. [pl. 22, no. 13]

5. Teapot with incised decoration, from Lachish. [pl. 22, no. 6]

6. Light-brown teapot with combed decoration, from Ras Tawil [pl. 22, no. 7]

7. Goblet with ribbed walls, from Lachish. [pl. 22, no. 1]

8. Goblet with ribbed walls and tiny pierced knob at the lowest carination, from Lachish. [pl. 22, no. 2]

9. Light-brown goblet with s-shaped walls and combed decoration, from El Metaba. [pl. 22, no. 4]

10. Light-brown goblet with inverted walls, from Benayah. [pl. 22, no. 3]

11. Undecorated, barrel-shaped jar with enveloped ledge handles and pronounced shoulder. From Amiran, *Qadmoniot,* vol. II, no. 2 (6), 1969, p. 48.

12. Jar with enveloped ledge handle and incised decoration around the neck. *ibid.*

13. Amphoriskos with pronounced shoulder. *ibid.*

14. Teapot without neck and a knob opposite the spout. *ibid.*

15–20. Elongated amphoriskoi without handles, a predominant vessel in this group, *ibid.*

PLATE IV : MIDDLE BRONZE PERIOD, c. 2200–1550 B.C.E.

PL. IVa: INTERMEDIATE BRONZE AGE (MIDDLE BRONZE I), c. 2200–1950 B.C.E.

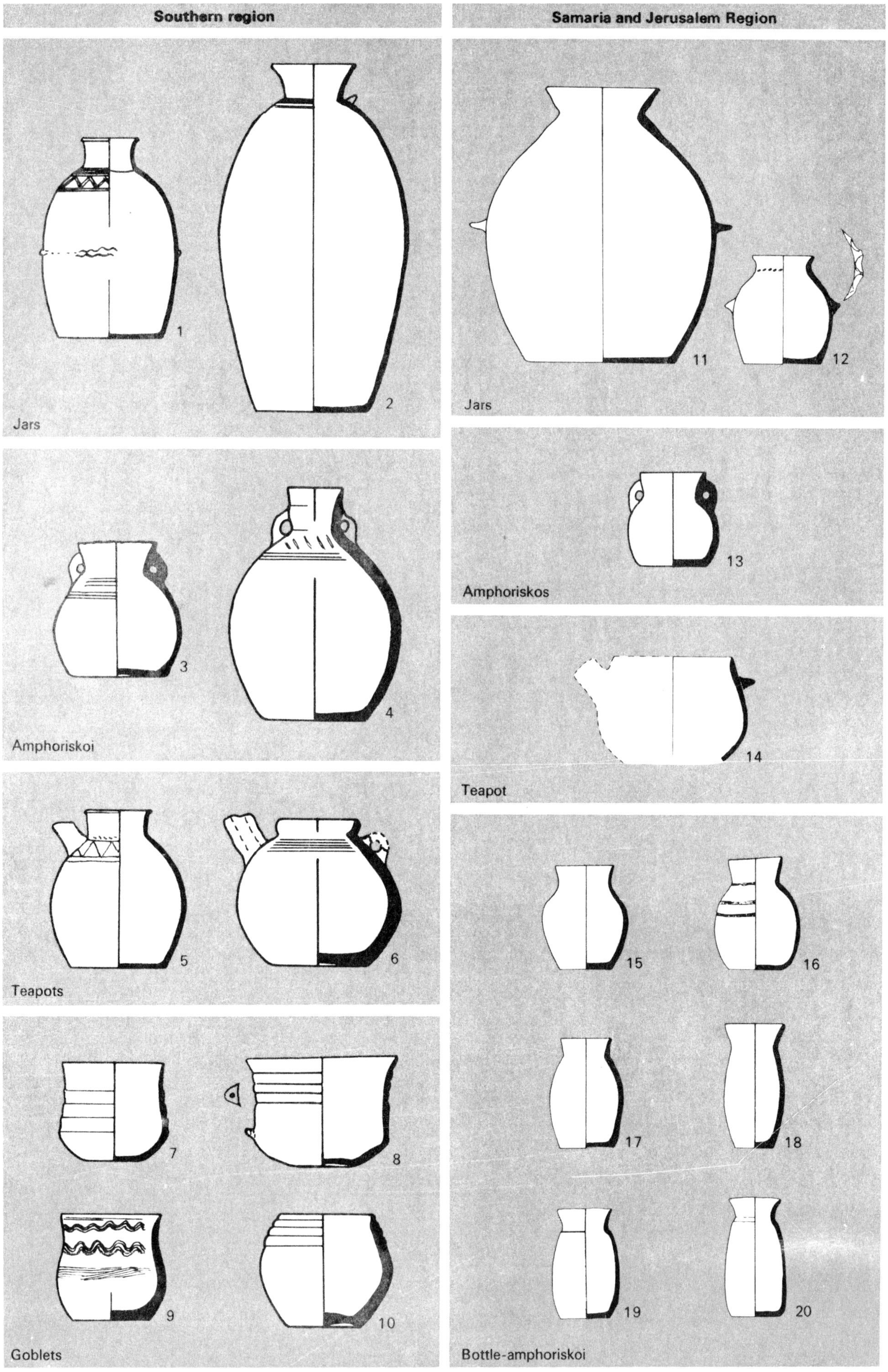

PLATE IV: MIDDLE BRONZE PERIOD, c. 2200–1550 B.C.E.

PL. IVa: INTERMEDIATE BRONZE AGE (MIDDLE BRONZE I), c. 2200–1950 B.C.E.

21. Jar with three downward-pointing, conical knobs on the neck, from a tomb at Ma'yan Barukh. [pl. 23, no. 5]

22. Spherical amphoriskos with incised decoration and lug handles around the neck and two lug handles on the body, from a tomb at Ma'yan Barukh. [pl. 23, no. 10]

23. Spherical amphoriskos with incised decoration and two lug handles around the neck, from a tomb at el-Husn. [pl. 23, no. 14]

24. Brownish-gray teapot with combed decoration, from a tomb at Ma'yan Barukh. [pl. 23, no. 1]

25. Brownish-red teapot with combed decoration, from Ma'yan Barukh. [pl. 23, no. 2]

26. Tall goblet from a tomb at Ma'yan Barukh. [pl. 23, no. 6]

27. Yellow jar with incised decoration and enveloped ledge handles, from a tomb at Megiddo. [pl. 24, no. 12]

28. Spherical jar with enveloped ledge handles, from a tomb at Megiddo. [pl. 24, no. 20]

29. Amphoriskos with red decoration, from a tomb at Megiddo. [pl. 24, no. 19]

30. Brown-ocher amphoriskos, from a tomb at Megiddo. [pl. 24, no. 10]

31. Hybrid teapot-amphoriskos, from a tomb at Megiddo. [pl. 24, no. 11]

32. Tall, narrow-necked teapot, blue-black outside, with white-yellow decoration, from a tomb at Megiddo. [pl. 24, no. 1]

33. Tall goblet, blue-black outside, with white-yellow decoration and incised zigzag, from a tomb at Megiddo. [pl. 24, no. 6]

34. Low goblet (cup), reddish-black with white-yellow decoration, from a tomb at Megiddo. [pl. 24, no. 5]

N.B. The Northern Region group (nos. 21–34) also includes the so-called "Megiddo group," see Amiran, *Atiqot* 7, Hebrew ed. (in press).

PLATE IV : MIDDLE BRONZE PERIOD, c. 2200–1550 B.C.E.

PL.IVa: INTERMEDIATE BRONZE AGE (MIDDLE BRONZE I), c. 2200–1950 B.C.E.

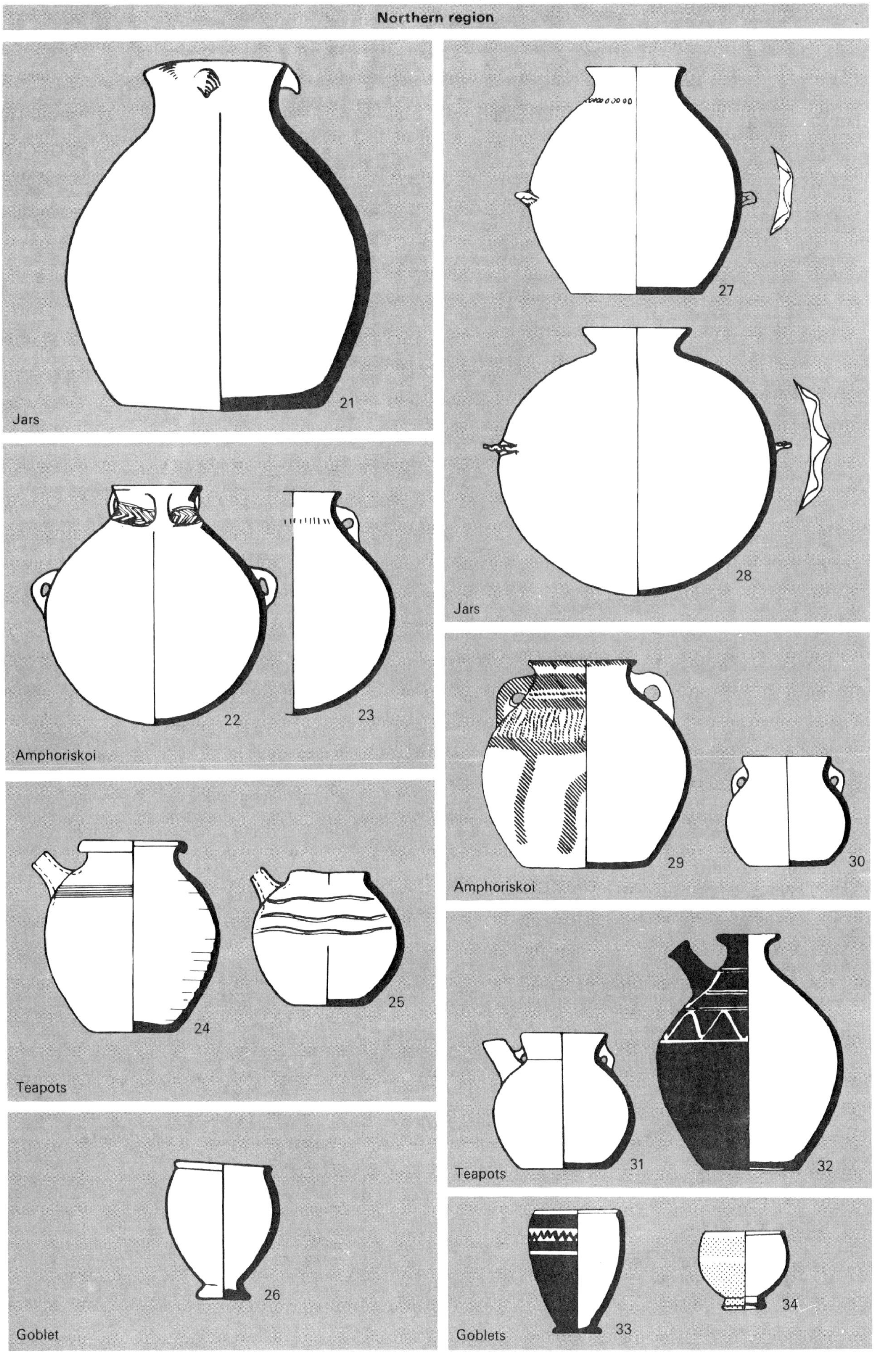

PLATE IV: MIDDLE BRONZE PERIOD, c. 2200–1550 B.C.E.

PL. IVb: MIDDLE BRONZE IIa, c. 1950– 1750 B.C.E.

1. Bowl with wide, profiled rim, bar handles, disc base and red, wheel-burnished slip, from a tomb at Megiddo, stratum XIV. [pl. 25, no. 1]

2. Bowl with turned-in rim and disc base, decorated on the inside with a red-painted cross, from Beth Mirsim, stratum F. [pl. 25, no. 2]

3. Wheel-made bowl with low disc base, sharp carination, and red, highly burnished slip, from a tomb at Megiddo, stratum XIV. [pl. 27, no. 2]

4. Wheel-made bowl with wheel combing on the outside and a gentle carination of the walls, from Rosh ha-Ayin. [pl. 27, no. 3]

5. Handmade cooking pot with straight walls, a row of punctures below the rim, and an applied rope decoration, from Megiddo, stratum XV. [pl. 30, no. 1]

6. Juglet with oval body, funnel-shaped neck, and orange, vertically burnished slip, from a tomb at Megiddo, stratum XIV. [pl. 33, no. 10]

7. Pear-shaped juglet with small flat base, a ridge below the rim, a double handle drawn from the ridge to the shoulder, and red, vertically burnished slip, from a tomb at Megiddo, stratum XV. [pl. 33, no. 11]

8. Juglet painted with red and black concentric circles on the body, from Megiddo, stratum XIII. [pl. 33, no. 14]

9. Cylindrical juglet with pyxis-like body and light-red, vertically burnished slip, from a tomb at Megiddo. [pl. 33, no. 13]

10. Jug with short, globular body, disc base, delicately profiled rim with an inner gutter lip, and a double handle on the shoulder, from a tomb at Megiddo, stratum XIV. [pl. 33, no. 7]

11. Brown-ocher jug with funnel-shaped neck, small disc base, and a triple handle drawn from the rim to the shoulder, with red and blue-black bands painted on upper part of vessel, from a tomb at Megiddo. [pl. 33, no. 2]

12. Goblet with red, vertically burnished slip, from Rosh ha-Ayin. [pl. 28, no. 1]

13. Goblet with double-loop handle, decorated with red and black bands, from a tomb at Megiddo, stratum XIII A [pl. 28, no. 4]

14. Jar without handles, relatively short oval body, flattened base, and profiled rim, decorated with combed finish and concentric circles painted in black and red, from Megiddo, stratum XIV. [pl. 31, no. 2]

15. Jar without handles, more elongated body, and profiled rim with an inner gutter, from a tomb at Megiddo, stratum XIV. [pl. 31, no. 1]

16. Large storage jar with elongated body and two handles, decorated with comb finish, from Megiddo, stratum XIII B. [pl. 31, no. 4]

PLATE IV : MIDDLE BRONZE PERIOD, c. 2200–1550 B.C.E.

PL.IVb: MIDDLE BRONZE IIa, c. 1950–1750 B.C.E.

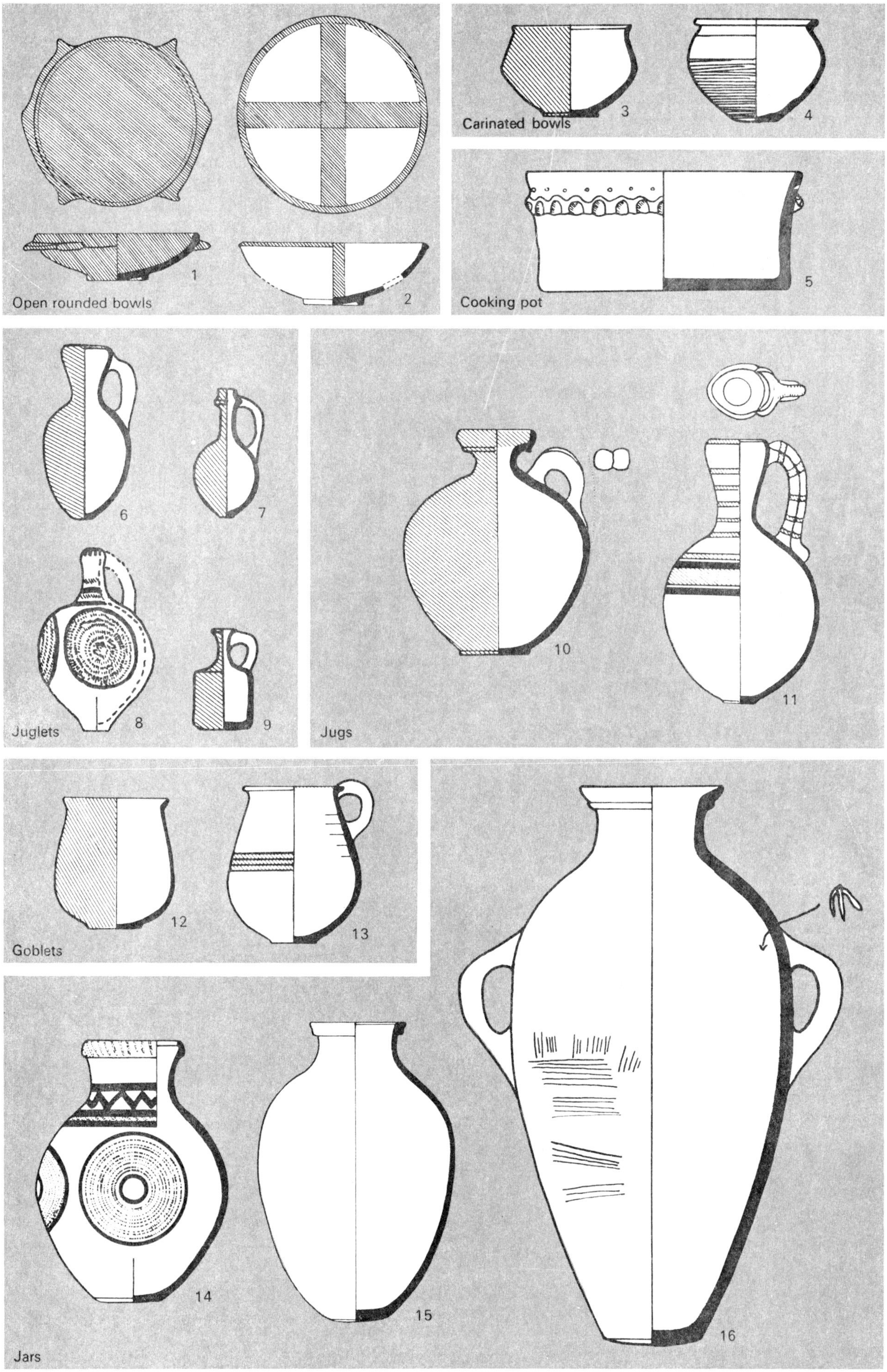

PLATE IV: MIDDLE BRONZE PERIOD, c. 2200–1550 B.C.E.

PL. IVb: MIDDLE BRONZE IIa, c. 1950–1750 B.C.E.

17. Krater with red-burnished slip and four elongated knobs placed at right angles to the rim, from a tomb at Megiddo, stratum XIII. [pl. 29, no. 1]

18. El-Yehudiyya juglet with oval body, profiled rim with a ridge below it, and double handle drawn from the ridge to the shoulder, rows of arrow-shaped punctures outlined by grooves. The punctures were filled with white chalk. From Afulah. [pl. 36, no. 1]

19. El-Yehudiyya juglet with oval body and typical decoration of vertical rows of punctures outlined by grooves, from Afulah. Courtesy Israel Department of Antiquities, Jerusalem.

20. Jar with short, oval body, decorated with parallel red bands on pink-burnished background, from a tomb at Megiddo, stratum XIV. [pl. 31, no. 3]

21. Red jug with whitish slip, painted with red and black decoration, from a tomb at Rosh ha-Ayin. Courtesy Israel Department of Antiquities, Jerusalem.

22. Child-burial in a large storage-jar with dipper juglet near the skeleton, dated to c. 1800 B.C.E., from Gezer. Courtesy William G. Dever, Hebrew Union College, Biblical and Archaeological School, Jerusalem.

PLATE IV : MIDDLE BRONZE PERIOD, c. 2200–1550 B.C.E.

PL.IVb: MIDDLE BRONZE IIa, c. 1950–1750 B.C.E.

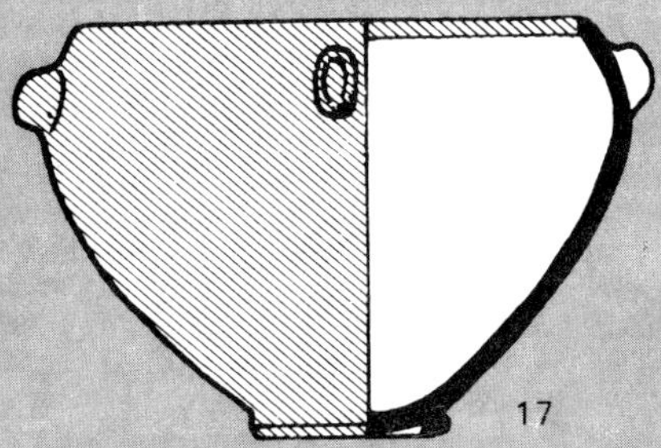

17

Krater

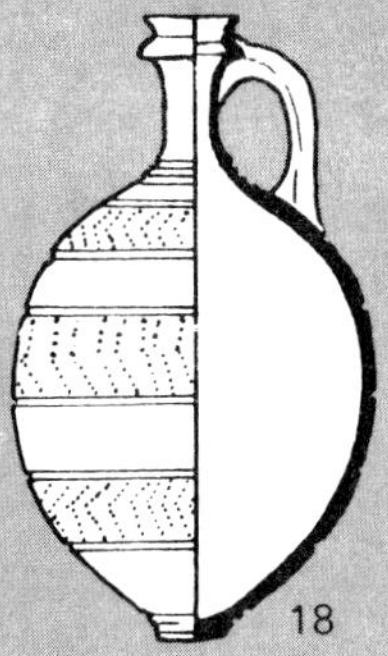

18

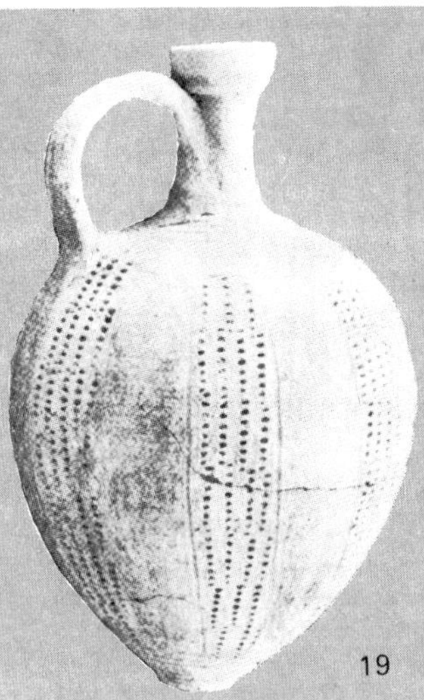

19

Jugs, El-Yehudiyya ware

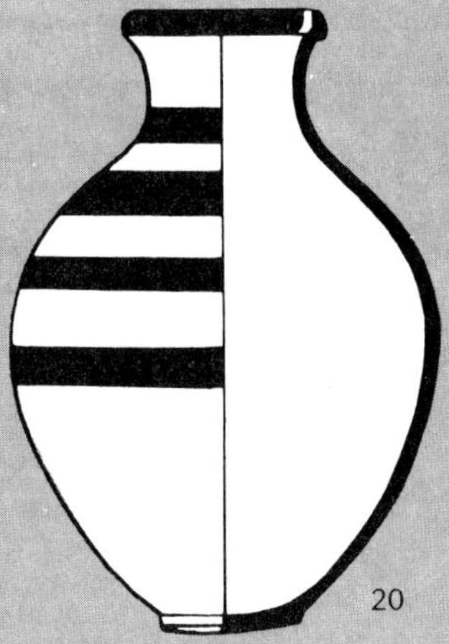

20

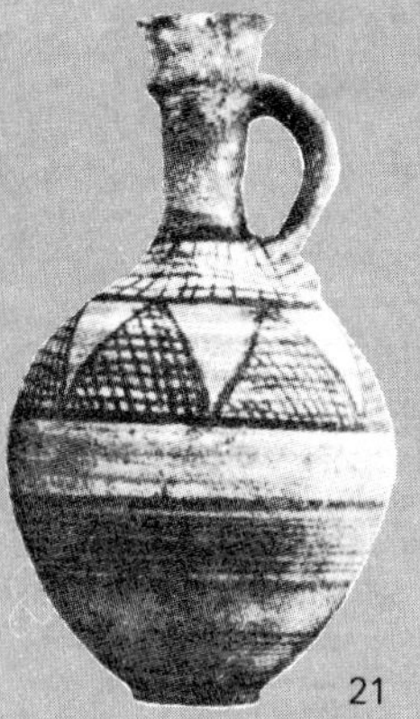

21

Khabur-Style, jar and jug

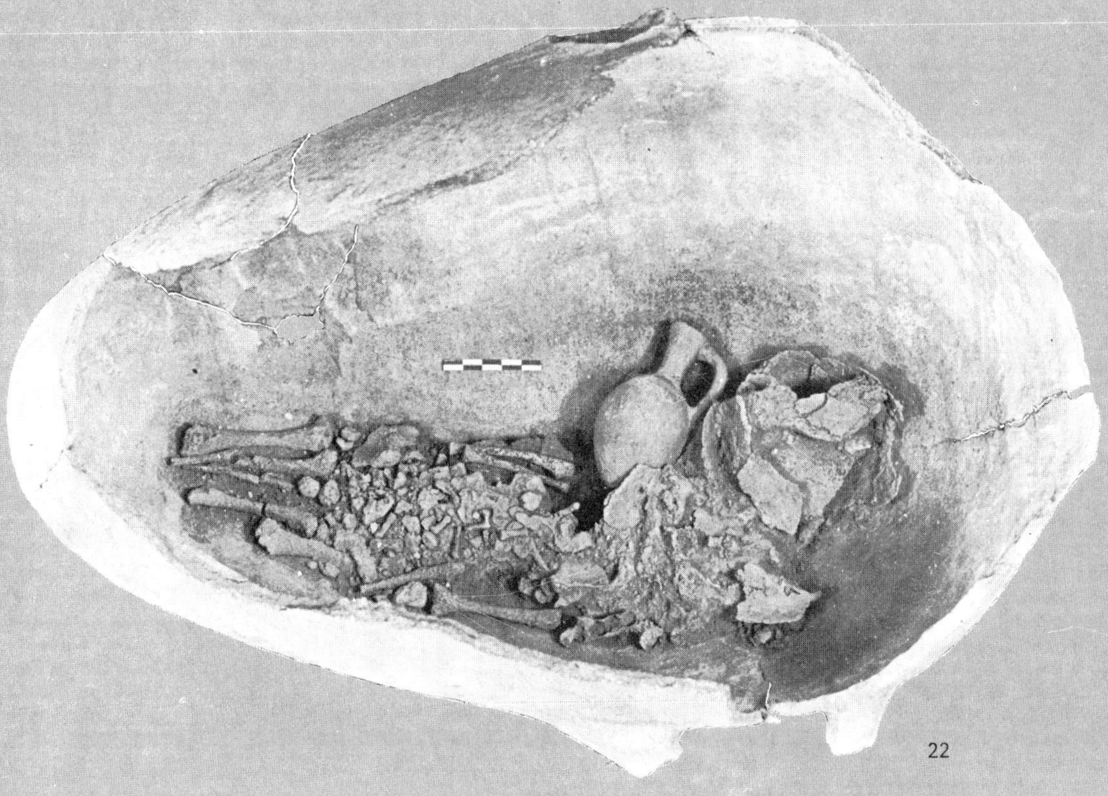

22

Jar

PLATE IV: MIDDLE BRONZE PERIOD, c. 2200–1550 B.C.E.

PL. IVc: MIDDLE BRONZE IIb, c. 1750–1550 B.C.E.

1. Bowl with ring base and profiled rim with spiral-shaped knobs, from a tomb at Megiddo, stratum XI. [pl. 26, no. 1]

2. Well-baked, thin bowl with trumpet base and flaring carination from a tomb at Megiddo. [pl. 27, no. 20]

3. S-shaped bowl with flaring carination, from Megiddo, stratum XI. [pl. 27, no. 10]

4. Similar bowl with quartrefoil mouth, from Hazor. [pl. 27, no. 12]

5. Goblet on pedestal, with red and black decoration, from a tomb at Megiddo, stratum X. [pl. 28, no. 9]

6. Goblet-chalice with trumpet base, from Megiddo, stratum XI [pl. 28, no. 10]

7. High-footed chalice with wide, slightly rounded bowl, from Ajjul, stratum I. [pl. 28, no. 16]

8. Chalice with a tube or goblet rising from the center and flaring carination, decorated in red and blue, from Megiddo, stratum X. [pl. 28, no. 11]

9. Krater standing on three loop handles, with straight neck, from a tomb at Megiddo, stratum XI. [pl. 29, no. 11]

10. Cooking pot with straight walls and applied rope decoration on rim, from Beth Mirsim, stratum D. [pl. 30, no. 3]

11. Cooking pot with s-shaped wall, from Megiddo, stratum X [pl. 30, no. 5]

12. Jar with two loop handles, decorated on shoulder with alternating straight and wavy lines in black and red over a white slip, from Ajjul. Courtesy Israel Department of Antiquities, Jerusalem.

13. Jar with elongated, elliptical body and thin walls, from Megiddo, stratum XII. [pl. 32, no. 1]

PLATE IV: MIDDLE BRONZE PERIOD, c. 2200–1550 B.C.E.

PL. IVc: MIDDLE BRONZE IIb, c. 1750–1550 B.C.E.

LOCAL WARE

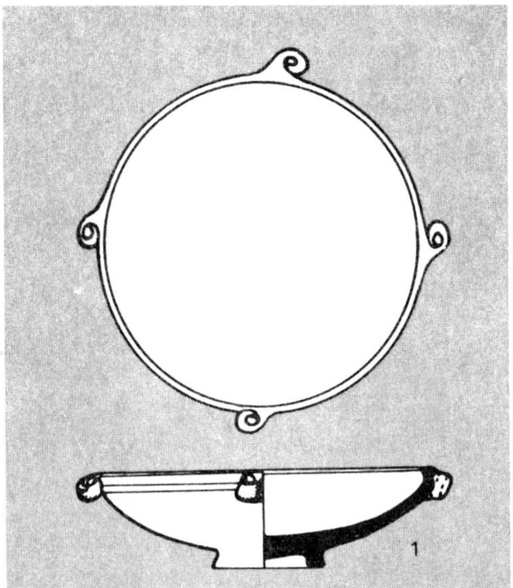

Open rounded bowl

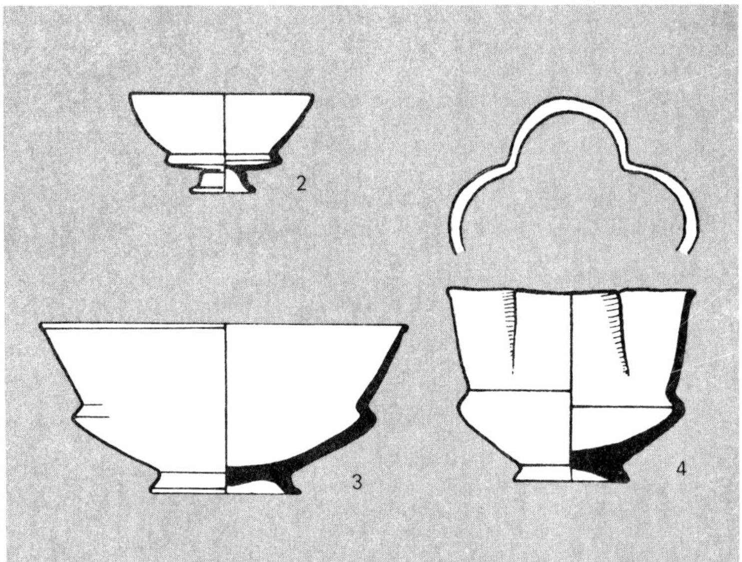

Carinated bowls

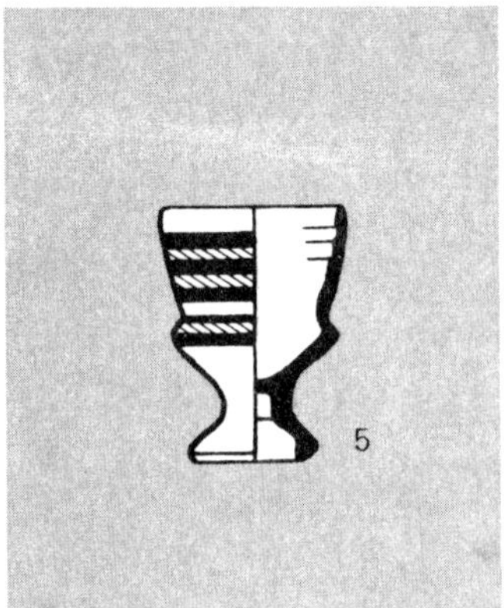

Goblet

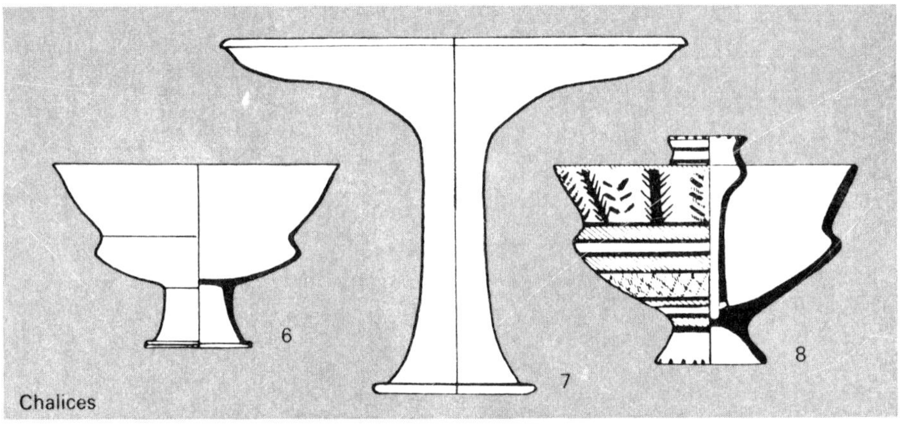

Chalices

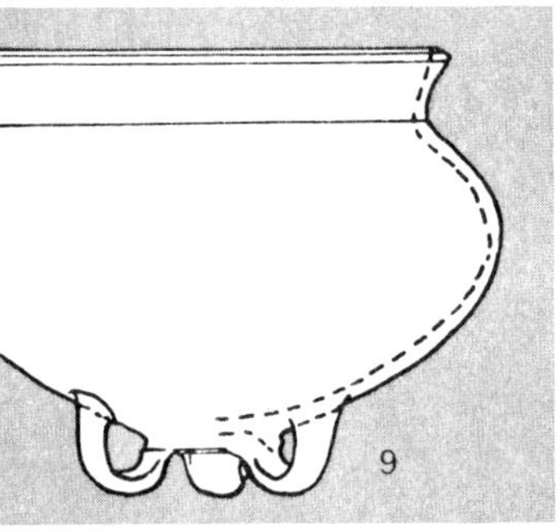

Krater

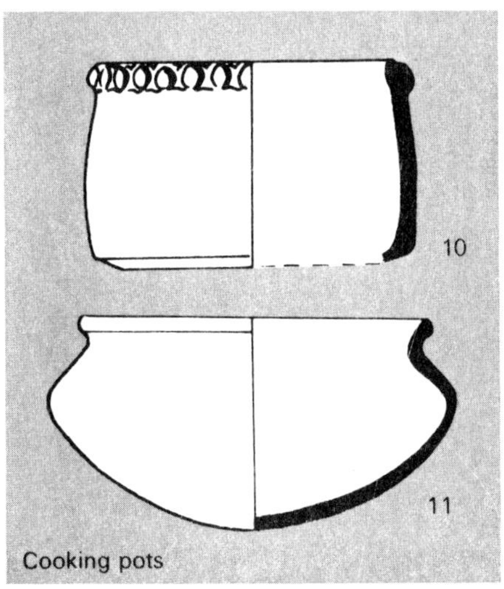

Cooking pots

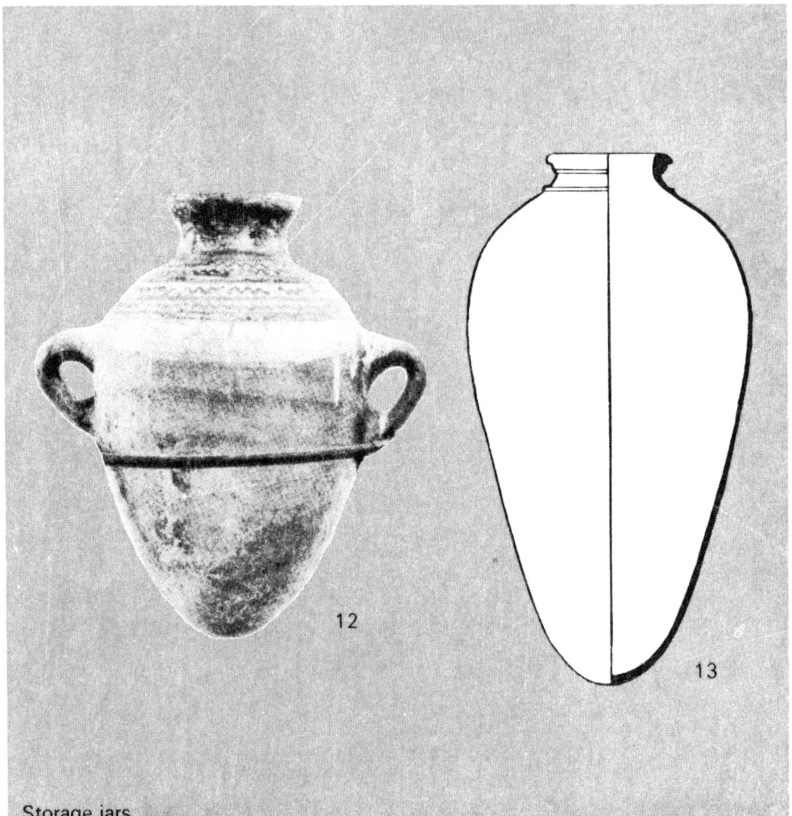

Storage jars

POTTERY

PLATE IV: MIDDLE BRONZE PERIOD, c. 2200–1550 B.C.E.

PL. IVc: MIDDLE BRONZE IIb, c. 1750–1550 B.C.E.

14. Jug with triple loop handle on shoulder and slipless surface vertically burnished to an ivory color, from a tomb at Megiddo, stratum, XI. [pl. 34, no. 8]

15. Cup-like jug with trefoil rim (continued into Late Bronze I), from a tomb at Megiddo, stratum XII. [pl. 34, no. 3]

16. Jug in form which continued in the following periods, from a tomb at Megiddo. [pl. 34, no. 4]

17. Elongated, oval dipper-juglet with orange-red, vertically burnished slip, from a tomb at Megiddo, stratum XII. [pl. 34, no. 10]

18. Pear-shaped juglet with triple handle drawn from the rim, button-base, and orange, vertically burnished slip, from a tomb at Megiddo, stratum XII. [pl. 34, no. 16]

19. Juglet with decoration of red-brown concentric circles derived from the Middle Bronze IIa tradition, from a tomb at Ajjul. [pl. 34, no. 14]

20. Cylindrical juglet with double handle, from a tomb at Megiddo, stratum XII. [pl. 34, no. 17]

21. Pear-shaped juglet with well-profiled, rounded shoulders, narrow neck, and handle attached just below the out-turned rim. Decoration of zigzag grooves and punctures, with traces of white filling. From a tomb at Megiddo. [pl. 36, no. 6]

22. Squat juglet with dark-red burnished slip and punctured decoration, from Megiddo, stratum XII. [pl. 36, no. 10]

23. Dark-gray, cylindrical juglet, with gray slip and incised and punctured decoration, from a tomb at Lachish. [pl. 36, no. 13]

24. Globular handmade jug with black-burnished slip and red decoration. Classified with "Red-on-Black" Cypriot Ware. From a tomb at Megiddo, stratum XII. [pl. 37, no. 2]

25. Globular handmade jug, with groups of brownish-black bands on a light background. Classified with "White-painted VI" Cypriot Ware. From a tomb at Megiddo, stratum XI. [pl. 37, no. 3]

26. Globular handmade jug, burnished, with black decoration. Classified with "White-painted V" Cypriot Ware. From a tomb at Megiddo, stratum XI. [pl. 37, no. 7]

27. Globular handmade jug, decorated with black, closely spaced, straight and wavy lines. Classified with "White-painted IV" Cypriot Ware. From Megiddo, stratum XII. [pl. 37, no. 9]

28. Bowl with thick, white-burnished slip and red-brown decoration. Classified with "White-slip I" Cypriot Ware. From Megiddo, stratum X. [pl. 37, no. 14]

PLATE IV : MIDDLE BRONZE PERIOD, c. 2200–1550 B.C.E.

PL.IVc: MIDDLE BRONZE IIb, c. 1750–1550 B.C.E.

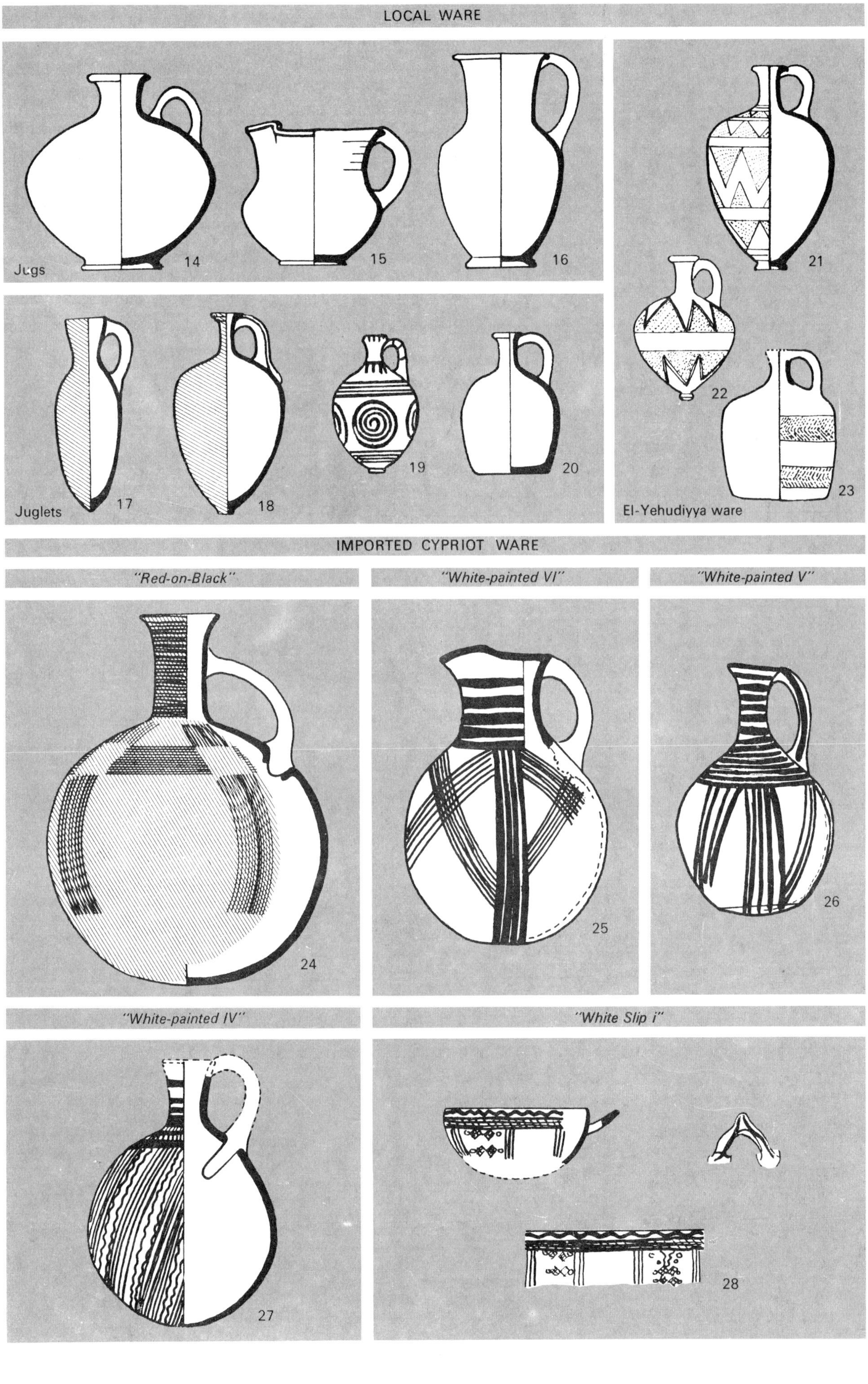

PLATE V: LATE BRONZE PERIOD, c. 1550–1200 B.C.E.

PL. Va: LATE BRONZE I, c. 1550–1400 B.C.E.

1. Bowl with gently rounded sides, from a tomb at Megiddo, stratum IX. [pl. 38, no. 1]

2. Bowl with sloping sides and red decoration, from Hazor, stratum 3. [pl. 38, no. 4]

3. Carinated bowl, a typical shape throughout the Late Bronze Age, from Temple I at Lachish. [pl. 39, no. 5]

4. Carinated bowl with two handles placed in the narrow junction of the cusps, from Hazor. [pl. 39, no. 4]

5. Goblet decorated with red horizontal bans, from Temple I at Lachish. [pl. 40, no. 1]

6. Chalice with burnished exterior, from Megiddo, stratum IX. [pl. 40, no. 3]

7. Dark-gray cooking pot with out-turned, triangular rim, from Beth-Shemesh, stratum IVa. [pl. 42, no. 2]

8. Krater shaped like the Middle Bronze ordinary krater, from Temple I at Lachish. [pl. 41, no. 1]

9. Commercial jar with thick walls and thick, button-like base, from Megiddo, stratum IX. [pl. 43, no. 2]

10. Domestic jar with thin walls, rounded base, and red decoration, from a tomb at Megiddo. [pl. 44, no. 1]

11. Jug with red and black decoration, from a tomb at Megiddo, stratum IX. [pl. 46, no. 5]

12. Dipper-juglet with shortened body and narrow, straight neck, from a tomb at Megiddo, stratum VIII. [pl. 46, no. 8]

13. Gray juglet with long, narrow neck, handle drawn from under the rim to the shoulder, spherical body, and flattened base. Wheel-made and well-burnished. From a tomb at Megiddo, stratum IX. [pl. 46, no. 5]

14. Biconical jug decorated with a large metope zone in red and black, irregularly burnished, from a tomb at Far'ah (N). [pl. 47, no. 1]

15. Pilgrim flask with wide, slightly swollen neck and decoration of brown concentric circles on the body, from a tomb in Jerusalem. [pl. 51, no. 1]

PLATE V: LATE BRONZE PERIOD, c. 1550–1200 B.C.E.

PL.Va: LATE BRONZE I, c. 1550–1400 B.C.E. LOCAL WARE

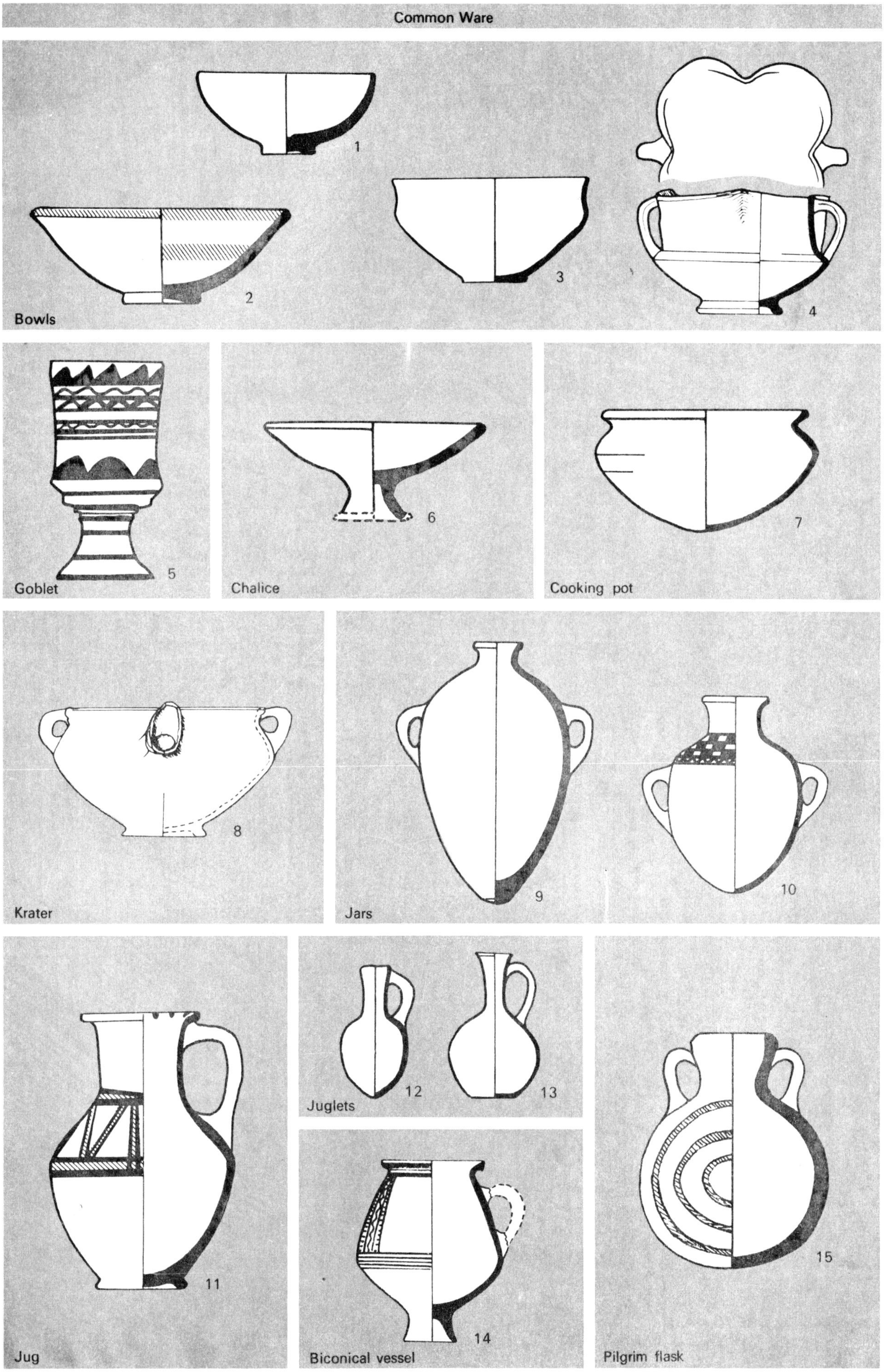

PLATE V: LATE BRONZE PERIOD, c. 1550–1200 B.C.E.

PL. Va: LATE BRONZE I, c. 1550–1400 B.C.E.

16. Krater with horizontal handle, decorated with Bichrome (red and black) metope zone, from Beth-Shemesh. [pl. 48, no. 9]

17. Bowl with one horizontal handle, imitating Cypriot bowl in shape, with Bichrome decoration, from Temple I at Lachish. [pl. 48, no. 12]

18. Spherical jug in Cypriot style, classified with "White-painted V–VI" Cypriot Ware, from Ajjul. Jerusalem, Rockefeller Museum, Israel Department of Antiquities.

19. Jug with similar body and neck, with flat base, and handle springing from rim, decorated in Bichrome style, from Ajjul. Jerusalem, Rockefeller Museum, Israel Department of Antiquities.

20. Bowl with burnished white slip inside and outside, and red decoration, from Megiddo, stratum IX. [pl. 49, no. 5]

21. Wheel-made bowl with ring base and cream, ring-burnished slip. The omphalos on the inside is encircled by a raised ring (21a). From Megiddo. From P.L.O. Guy, *Megiddo Tombs,* Chicago, 1938.

22. Large jug with wheel-made rim and white yellow, horizontally burnished slip, neatly decorated with Indian-red lines in a geometric pattern, from a tomb at Megiddo. From P.L.O. Guy, *ibid.*

23. Globular jug with white slip and red decoration of wheel-made horizontal and wavy lines, from a tomb at Jericho. [pl. 49, no. 8]

24. White amphoriskos with red decoration, from a tomb at Far'ah (N). [pl. 49, no. 10]

25. Juglet with white slip and brown-painted frieze with half circles filled with dots, from a tomb at Jericho. [pl. 49, no. 7]

PLATE V : LATE BRONZE PERIOD, c. 1550–1200 B.C.E.

PL.Va: LATE BRONZE I, c. 1550–1400 B.C.E. LOCAL WARE

Bichrome Ware

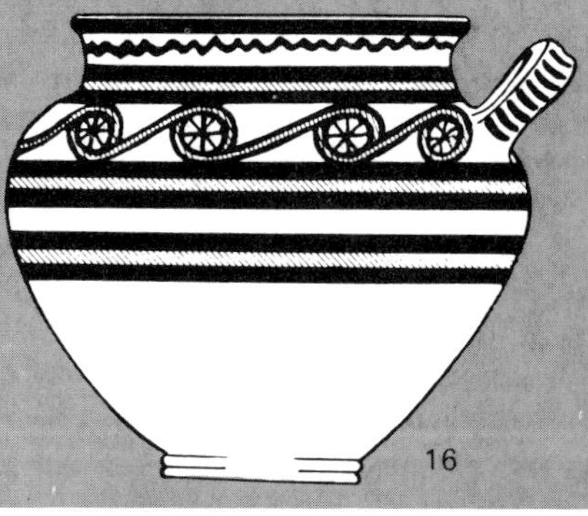

Krater 16

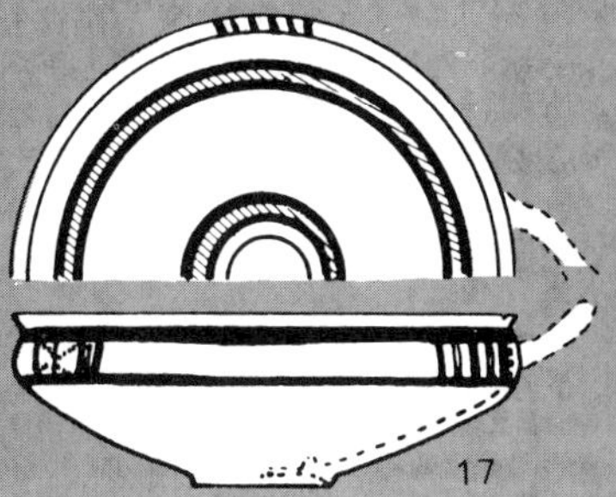

Bowl 17

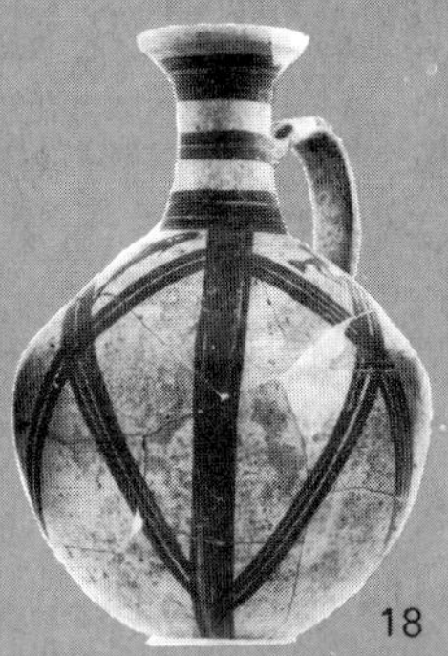

18

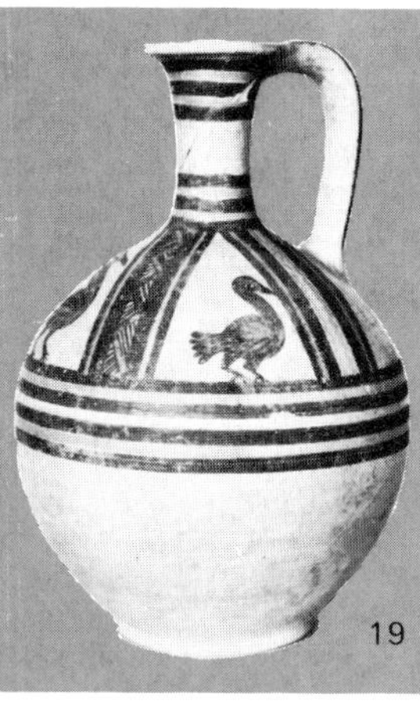

19

Jugs

"Chocolate-on-white" ware

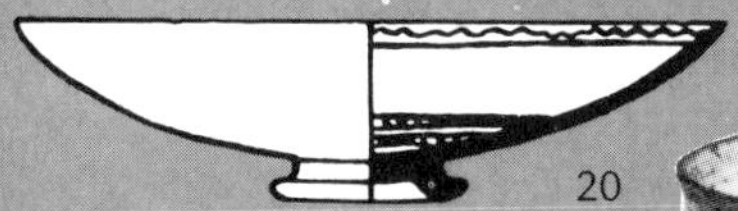

20

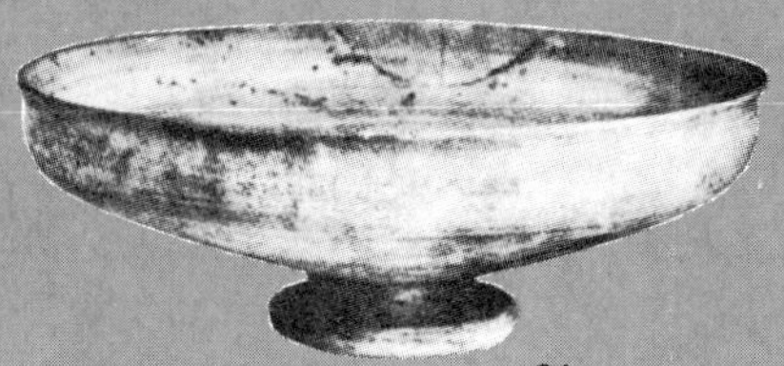

21

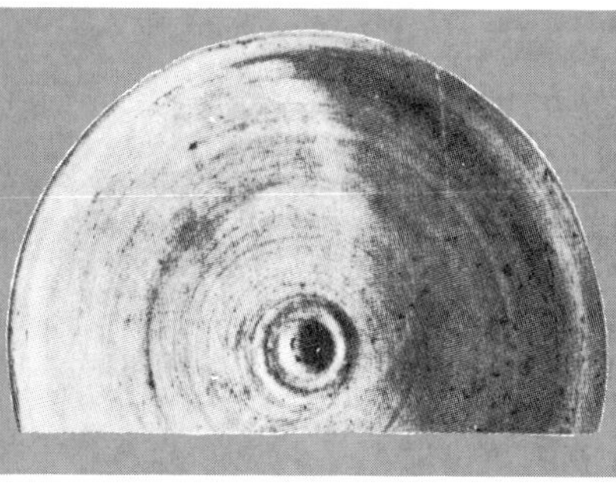

21a

Bowls

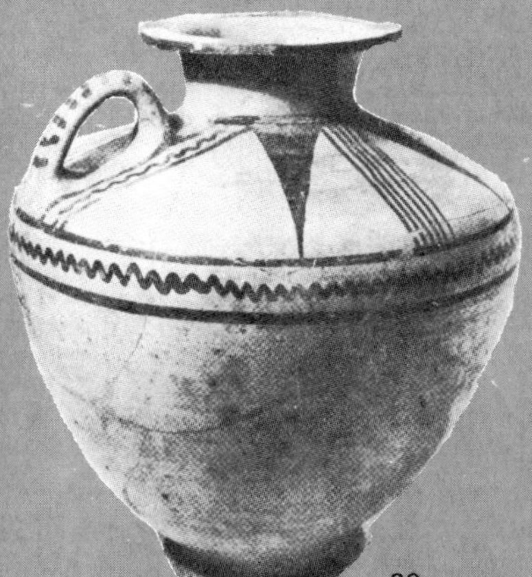

22

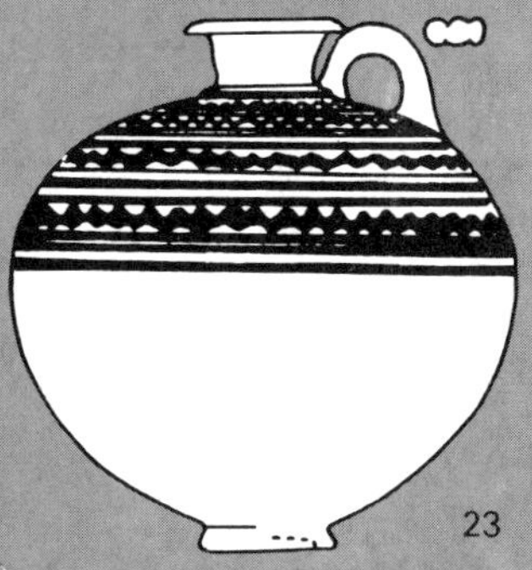

23

Jugs

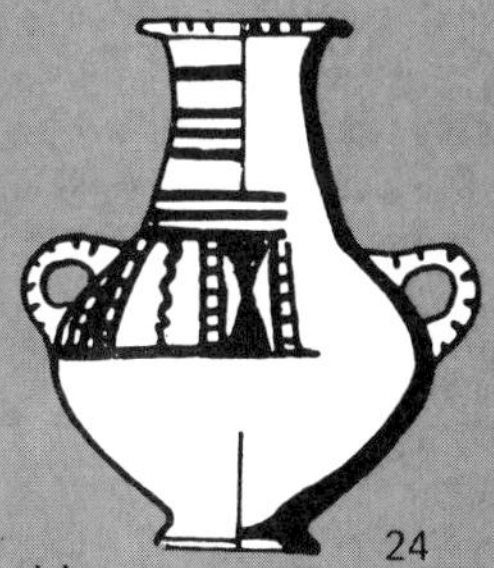

Amphoriskos 24

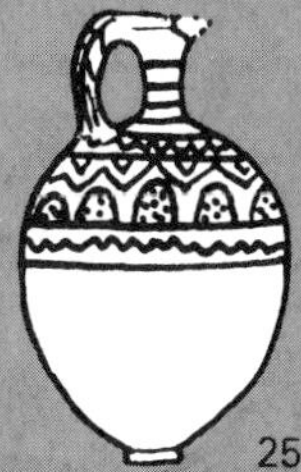

Juglet 25

PLATE V: LATE BRONZE PERIOD, c. 1550–1200 B.C.E.

PL. Vb: LATE BRONZE IIa, c. 1400–1300 B.C.E.

1. Bowl with sloping sides and disc base, decorated with red and black bands, from Megiddo, stratum VIII. [pl. 38, no. 8]

2. Degenerate carinated bowl, with a slight fold in place of the carination, from Megiddo, stratum VIII. [pl. 39, no. 8]

3. Chalice with well-burnished red slip, from Hazor, stratum 1B. [pl. 40, no. 7]

4. Chalice with metope containing schematic painting of palm tree and ibex, a characteristic Late Bronze Motif. From Megiddo, stratum VII. [pl. 50, no. 8]

5. Spherical goblet, decorated with metopes divided by straight and wavy lines and a palm-tree and ibex motif in the metope, from Temple II at Lachish. [pl. 50, no. 6]

6. Krater with two horizontal handles, painted with an uncommon pattern of red triangles and semicircles, from Temple II at Lachish. [pl. 41, no. 7]

7. Cooking pot with elongated, triangular rim, from Beth Mirsim, stratum C. [pl. 42, no. 13]

8. Domestic jar with ovoid body, red, metope-style decoration, with palm-tree and ibex motif, from Megiddo, stratum VII B. [pl. 50, no. 7]

9. Commercial jar with thick, button-like base, slanting body, and pronounced shoulders, from Abu-Hawam, stratum V. [pl. 43, no. 5]

10. Juglet developed from the gray juglet of Late Bronze I, with brown-painted decoration, from a tomb in Jerusalem. [pl. 46, no. 13] no. 13]

11. Dipper-juglet with shallow shoulder and short, wide neck, from Megiddo, stratum VIII. [pl. 46, no. 16]

12. Jug decorated with red-painted metopes, from Megiddo, stratum VIII. [pl. 46, no. 11]

13. Biconical jug with red and black metope, containing palm-tree and ibex motif in naturalisitc style, from Megiddo, stratum VIII. [pl. 50, no. 5]

14. Pilgrim flask with handles attached to neck and body in a special petal-like form, and wide, triangular rim. Decorated with concentric red circles. From Hazor, stratum 1B. [pl. 51, no. 4]

PLATE V : LATE BRONZE PERIOD, c. 1550–1200 B.C.E.

PL.Vb: LATE BRONZE IIa, c. 1400–1300 B.C.E., LOCAL WARE

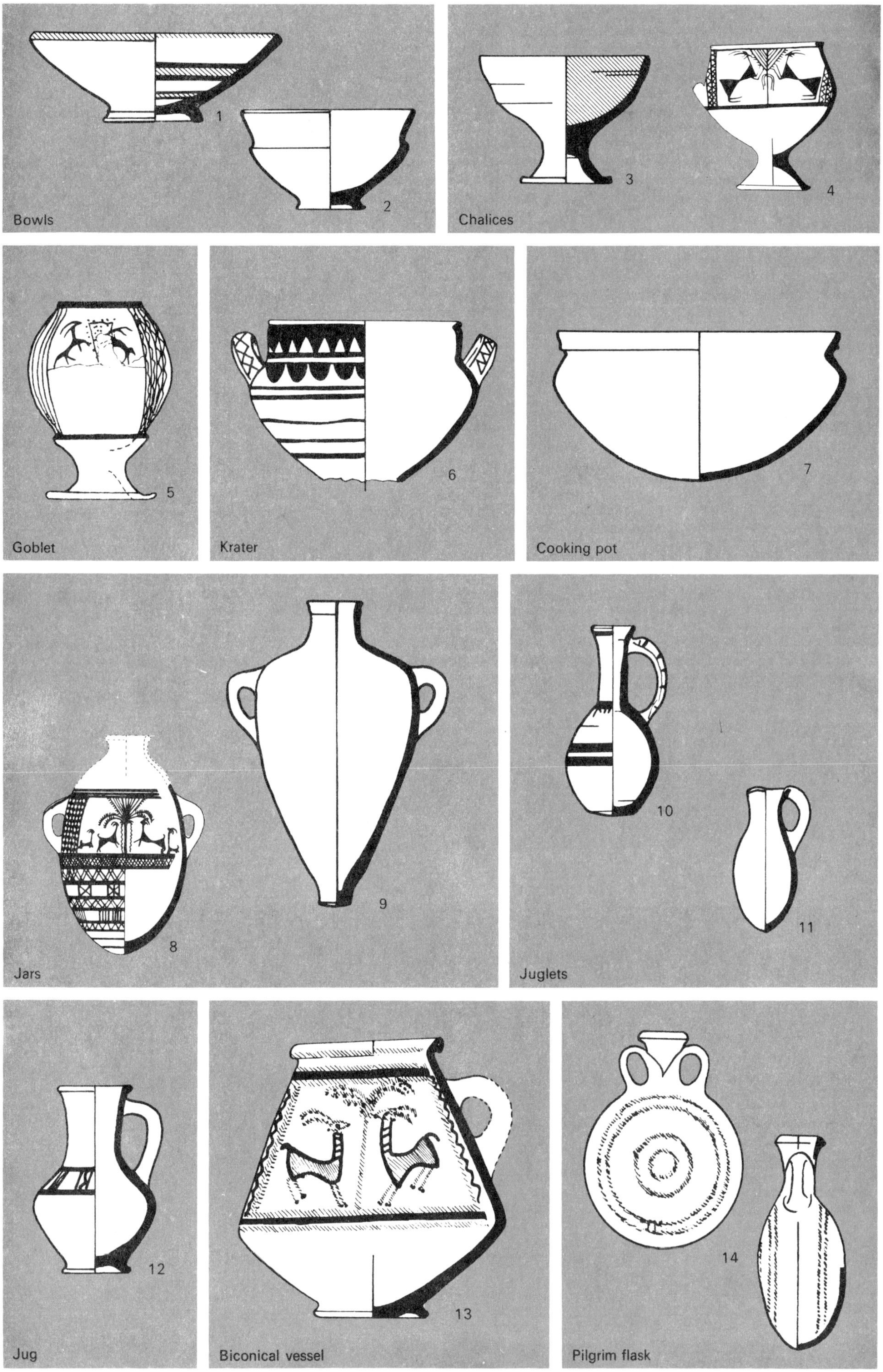

PLATE V: LATE BRONZE PERIOD, c. 1550–1200 B.C.E.

PL. Vb: LATE BRONZE IIb, c. 1300–1200 B.C.E.

15. Bowl with rounded sides and bar handles on one side. The red painting on the inside includes a palm-tree motif. From a tomb at Lachish. [pl. 38, no. 26]

16. Bowl with vestigial carination, from Hazor, stratum 1A. [pl. 39, no. 15]

17. Goblet with two rows of metope decoration, the upper row including an ibex, from Temple III at Lachish. [pl. 40, no. 10]

18. Chalice with sharply cut rim, from a tomb at Megiddo. [pl. 40, no. 15]

19. Krater with two horizontal handles, decorated with red, stylized variation of the palm-tree motif. The palm is represented by two triangles and two curls. From Megiddo, stratum VII B. [pl. 41, no. 11]

20. Krater with perpendicular loop handles and zones of red decoration, the lower one divided by diagonal triglyphs with stylized birds and ibex, from Temple II at Lachish. [pl. 41, no. 8]

21. Cooking pot with long-edged, triangular rim, from Hazor. [pl. 42, no. 17]

22. Domestic jar decorated in the metope style, from Hazor, stratum 2. [pl. 44, no. 6]

23. Commercial jar with elongated, sloping body, sharply pronounced shoulders, and button base, from Megiddo, stratum VIIB. [pl. 43, no. 9]

24. Dipper-juglet with wide, cylindrical form, from Temple III at Lachish. [pl. 46, no. 22]

25. Juglet developed from the "gray juglet" types of Late Bronze I and IIa, with red decoration, from Megiddo, stratum VII. [pl. 46, no. 21]

26. Jug with loop handle, drawn from rim to shoulder and red-burnished slip, from Hazor, stratum 1A. [pl. 46, no. 17]

27. Biconical jug with red decoration of triglyphs consisting of alternating straight and wavy lines, crisscross pattern, triangles, and a stylized palm tree, from Megiddo, stratum VIIB. [pl. 47, no. 10]

28. Small pilgrim flask with high, narrow neck and ordinary loop handles, decorated with closely spaced concentric circles in red and black, from Temple III at Lachish. [pl. 51, no. 11]

PLATE V : LATE BRONZE PERIOD, c. 1550–1200 B.C.E.

PL.Vb: LATE BRONZE IIb, c. 1300–1200 B.C.E. LOCAL WARE

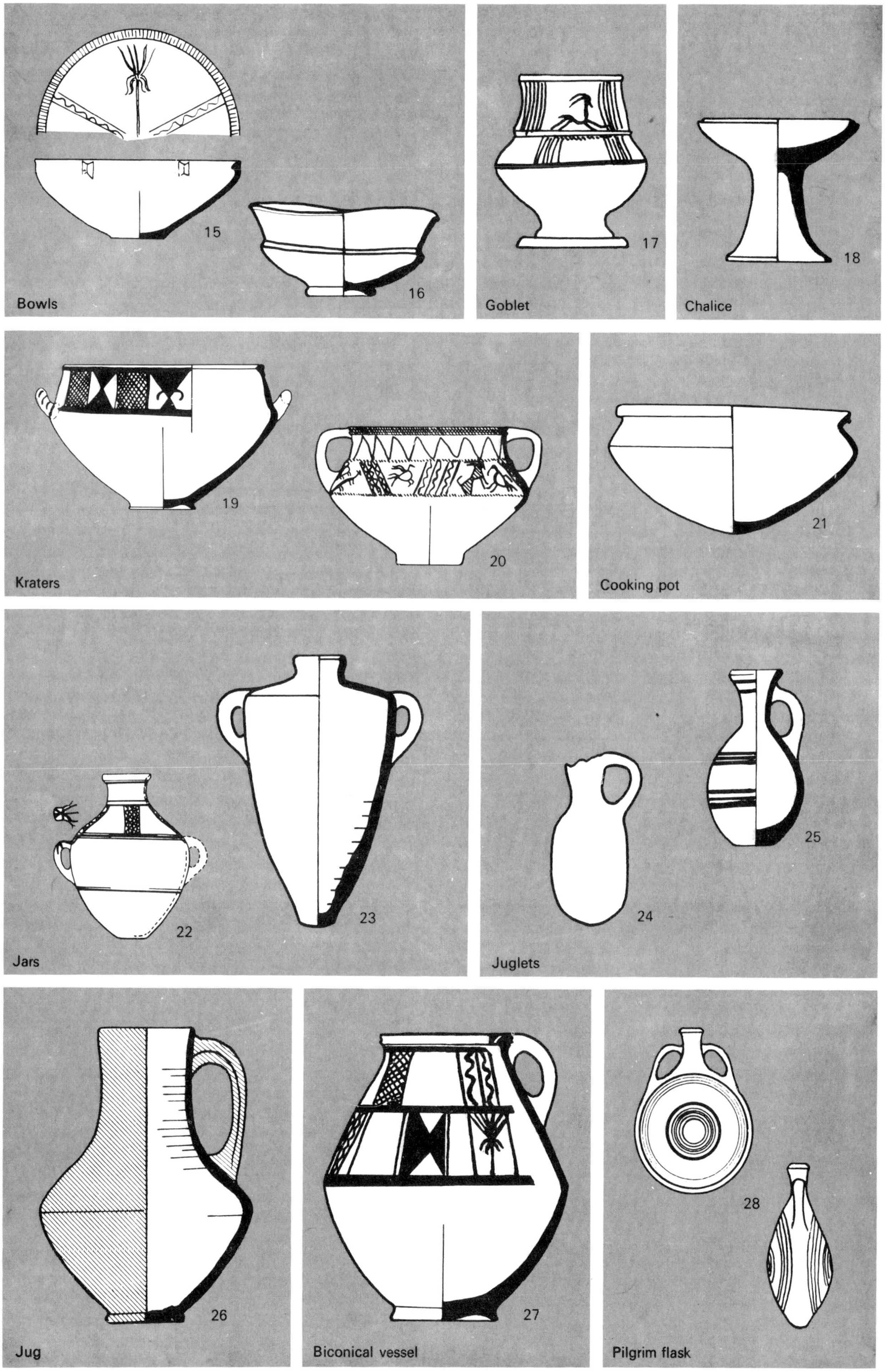

PLATE Vc: LATE BRONZE PERIOD, IMPORTED WARE

1. "Milk bowl" decorated with lozenges and delicate, embroidery-like pattern, from Ajjul. [pl. 53, no. 2]

2. "Milk bowl" decorated in more rigid, schematic style, with ladder-pattern, from a tomb at Lachish. [pl. 53, no. 4]

3. "Bilbil," burnt to a metallic clay, with brown-gray slip and plastic ornament around the neck, from a tomb in Jerusalem. [pl. 54, no. 7]

4. Jug of well-burnt, metallic clay, with brown-gray slip, from a tomb at Lachish. [pl. 55, no. 4]

5. Bowl of well-burnt, metallic clay, with horizontal handle, trough-shaped spout on the rim, and traces of black slip and red decoration, from a tomb at Lachish. [pl. 55, no. 2]

6. Juglet with black slip and incised decoration made before application of slip, from a tomb at Lachish. [pl. 55, no. 5]

7. Juglet with white-yellow slip, decorated with red and brown bands, from a tomb at Megiddo. [pl. 55, no. 6]

8. Juglet with black and white decoration, from a tomb at Megiddo. [pl. 55, no. 7]

9. "Milk bowl" with white, irregularly burnished slip, decorated with horizontal bands around the rim, enclosing a schematic ladder-pattern, and two rows of dots. From a tomb at Lachish. [pl. 53, no. 6]

10. "Bilbil" of well-burnt-metallic clay, with brown slip and white decoration, from Temple II at Lachish. [pl. 54, no. 12]

11. Yellowish-brown "Bucchero" jug with ridged decoration and brown-gray slip, from a tomb in Jerusalem. [pl. 54, no. 17]

12. Brown jug with black slip, from a tomb at Lachish. [pl. 55, no. 11]

13. Knife-shaved juglet in the form of the Canaanite dipper-juglet, from Abu-Hawam, stratum V. [pl. 55, no. 12]

14. "Milk bowl" with dark-brown sets of lines, a degenerate ladder-pattern, from a tomb at Lachish. [pl. 53, no. 9]

15. "Bilbil" with black slip and white decoration, from a tomb in Jerusalem. [pl. 54, no. 18]

16. Brown "Bucchero" jug, with black slip, from Temple III at Lachish. [pl. 54, no. 21]

17. Knife-shaved juglet in the form of the Canaanite dipper-juglet, from Megiddo, stratum VII. [pl. 55, no. 15]

PLATE Vc: LATE BRONZE PERIOD, IMPORTED WARE

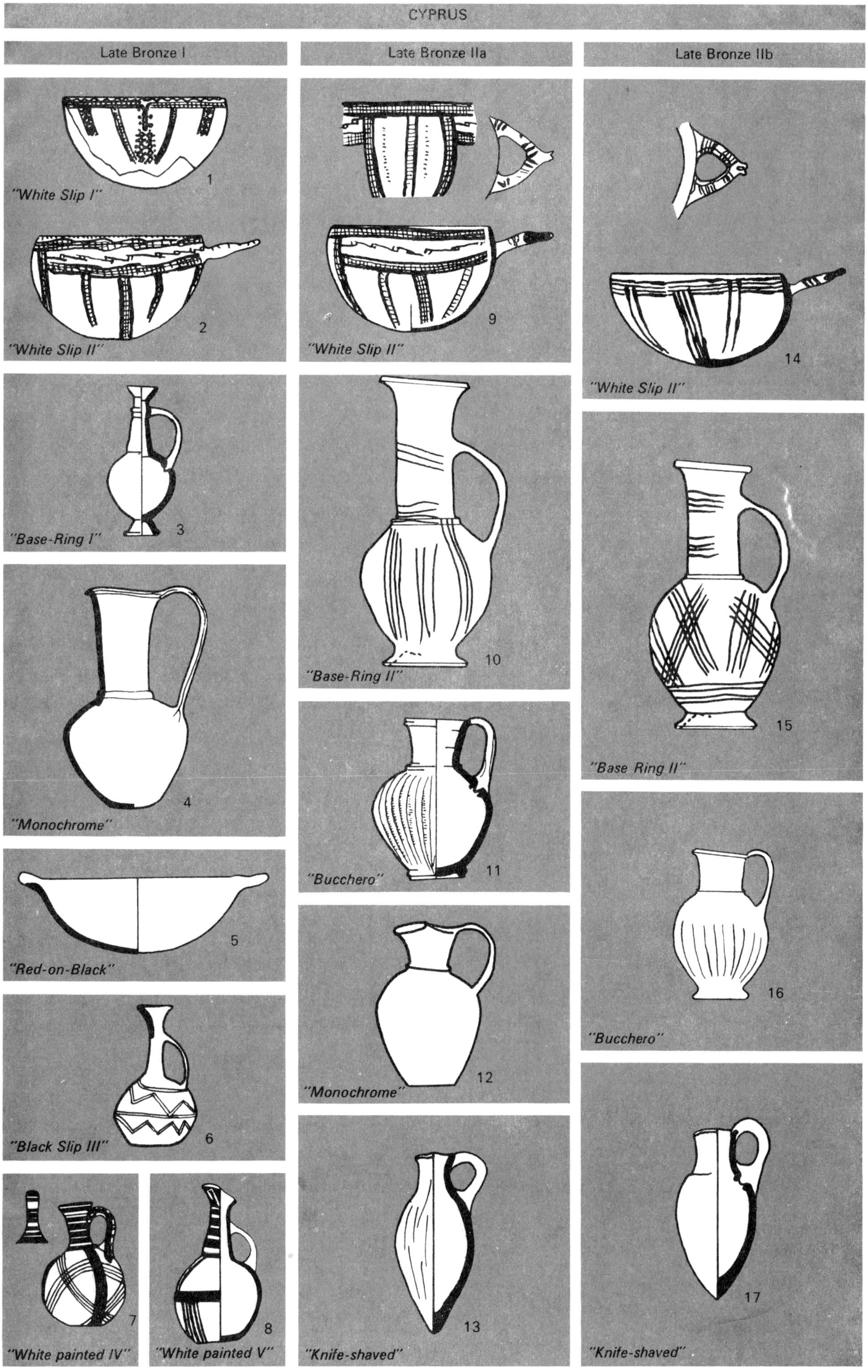

PLATE Vc: LATE BRONZE PERIOD, IMPORTED WARE

18. Fine wheel-made, well-fired kylix with high loop handle and glossy painting, from Temple I at Lachish. Courtesy Israel Department of Antiquities, Jerusalem.

19. Kylix from a tomb in Jerusalem. Courtesy Israel Department of Antiquities, Jerusalem.

20. Stirrup jar from Beth-Shemesh. Courtesy Israel Department of Antiquities, Jerusalem.

21. Juglet with pear-shaped body and high base and neck. Courtesy Israel Department of Antiquities, Jerusalem.

22. Chariot amphoriskos from Tell Dan. From V. Karageorgis, *Qadmoniot,* vol. IV, no. 1 (13) 1971, p. 12. Courtesy Dan Expedition, Israel Department of Antiquities, Jerusalem.

23. High kylix from Abu-Hawam. Courtesy Israel Department of Antiquities, Jerusalem.

24. Stirrup jar, from Gezer. Courtesy Department of Archaeology, Hebrew University, Jerusalem.

25. Jug with globular body, from Abu-Hawam. Courtesy Israel Department of Antiquities, Jerusalem.

Selection of imported ware on exhibition in the Israel Museum, Jerusalem.

1. "Syrian" flask from a tomb in Jerusalem.

2, 3. "Syrian" flask and gray-burnished juglet, from a tomb at Bahan.

4. Stirrup jar, from Gezer.

5. Globular pilgrim flask, from Gezer.

6. Pear-shaped jar, from Gezer.

7. Pyxis, from Hazor.

8. Pear-shaped jar, from Hazor.

9. Cup, upside down, from Hazor.

10. Alabaster pilgrim flask.

11. Alabaster vessel decorated with snakes in relief.

12. Stone goblet, from a tomb in Baḥan.

13. "Bucchero" jug, from Cyprus.

14. "Milk bowl" from Acre.

15. Painted juglet.

16–19. Jugs of "Base Ring" type.

20–22. Bowls of "Base Ring" type.

23, 24. Bull-shaped vessels of "Base Ring" type.

PLATE Vc: LATE BRONZE PERIOD, IMPORTED WARE

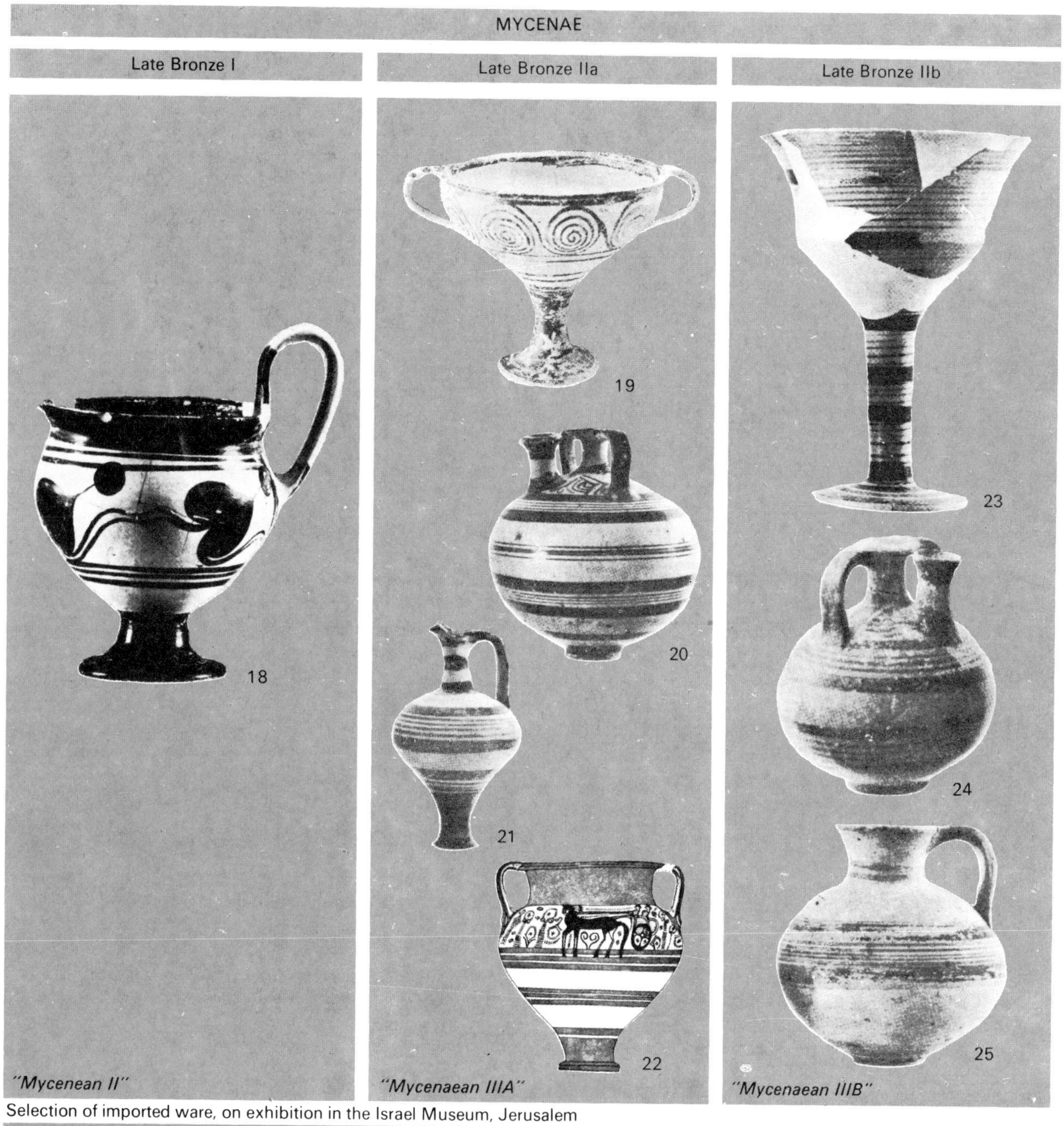

Selection of imported ware, on exhibition in the Israel Museum, Jerusalem

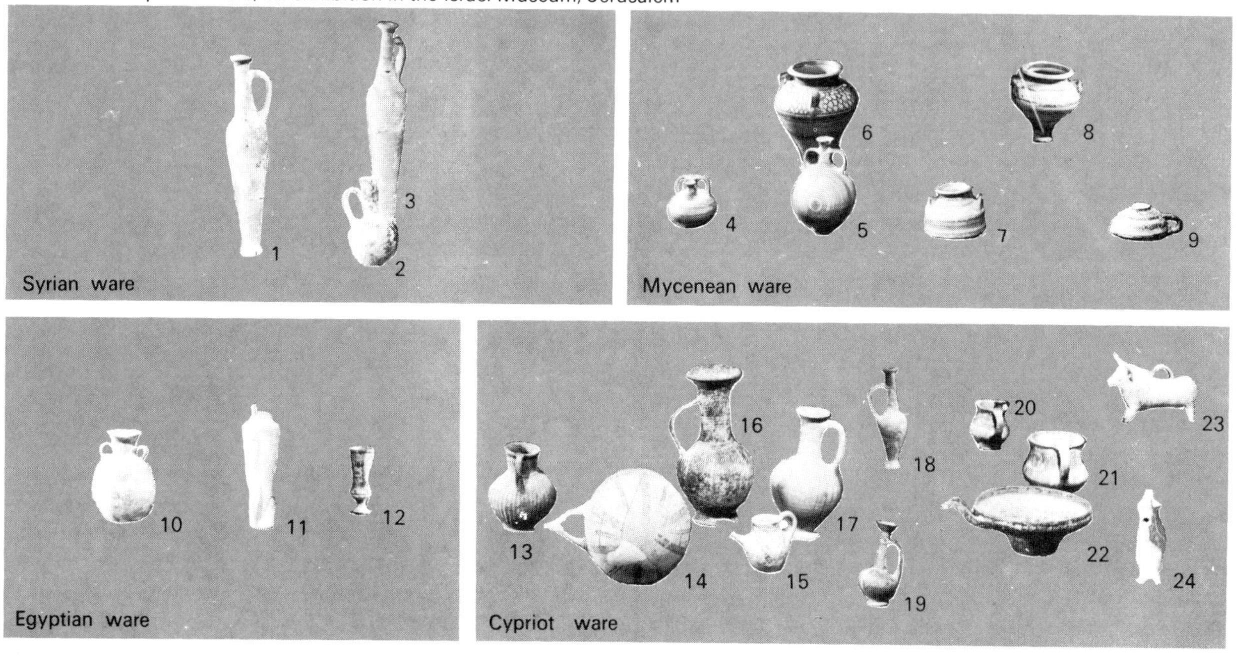

PLATE VI: IRON AGE PERIOD, c. 1200–587 B.C.E.

PL. VIa: IRON AGE Ia–b, c. 1200–1000 B.C.E.

1. Large, carinated bowl, of coarse workmanship, with thick walls, from Hazor, stratum XII. [pl. 60, no. 2]

2. Rounded bowl with red-painted bands, from Megiddo, stratum VI. [pl. 60, no. 13]

3. Chalice with a step in lower part of foot, from a tomb at Megiddo. [pl. 68, no. 1]

4. Broad, shallow cooking pot with carinated body, rounded base and elongated, triangular rim, from Megiddo, stratum VI. [pl. 75, no. 1]

5. Krater with multiple handles, rope decoration in the handle zone, and rim thickened inwards and outwards, from Beth-Shean, stratum VI. [pl. 69, no. 1]

6. Top of pithos showing the commonest pithos rim of the period: high and narrow. Usually combined with an elliptical body with two handles, from Hazor, stratum XII. [pl. 77, no. 11]

7. "Collared rim" pithos with a ridge at the base of the very short neck, decorated on the rim with three reed impressions, from Shiloh. This type, which appears also in the south, is believed to belong to the early Israelite settlers. [pl. 77, no. 4]

8. Ovoid jar with straight high neck encircled by four handles, from Megiddo, stratum VIA. [pl. 78, no. 6]

9. Jug with trough-like strainer-spout and handle at right angle to the spout, drawn from middle of neck to shoulder. Decorated with black and red metopes in Bichrome style. From Megiddo, stratum VIA. [pl. 84, no. 11]

10. Jug with biconical body from Megiddo, stratum VI. [pl. 84, no. 4]

11. Dipper-juglet with trefoil mouth, ovoid body, and slightly pointed base, from Megiddo, stratum VI. [pl. 84, no. 15]

12. Pyxis with elongated body, two carinations—one setting off the shoulder, the other near the base—and two lug handles. Decorated with red bands. From Megiddo, stratum VIIA. [pl. 96, no. 2]

13. Small flask with cup-like mouth and pierced lug handles, from a tomb at Megiddo. [pl. 93, no. 10]

PLATE VI : IRON AGE PERIOD, c. 1200–587 B.C.E.

PL. VIa: IRON AGE Ia–b, c. 1200–1000 B.C.E.

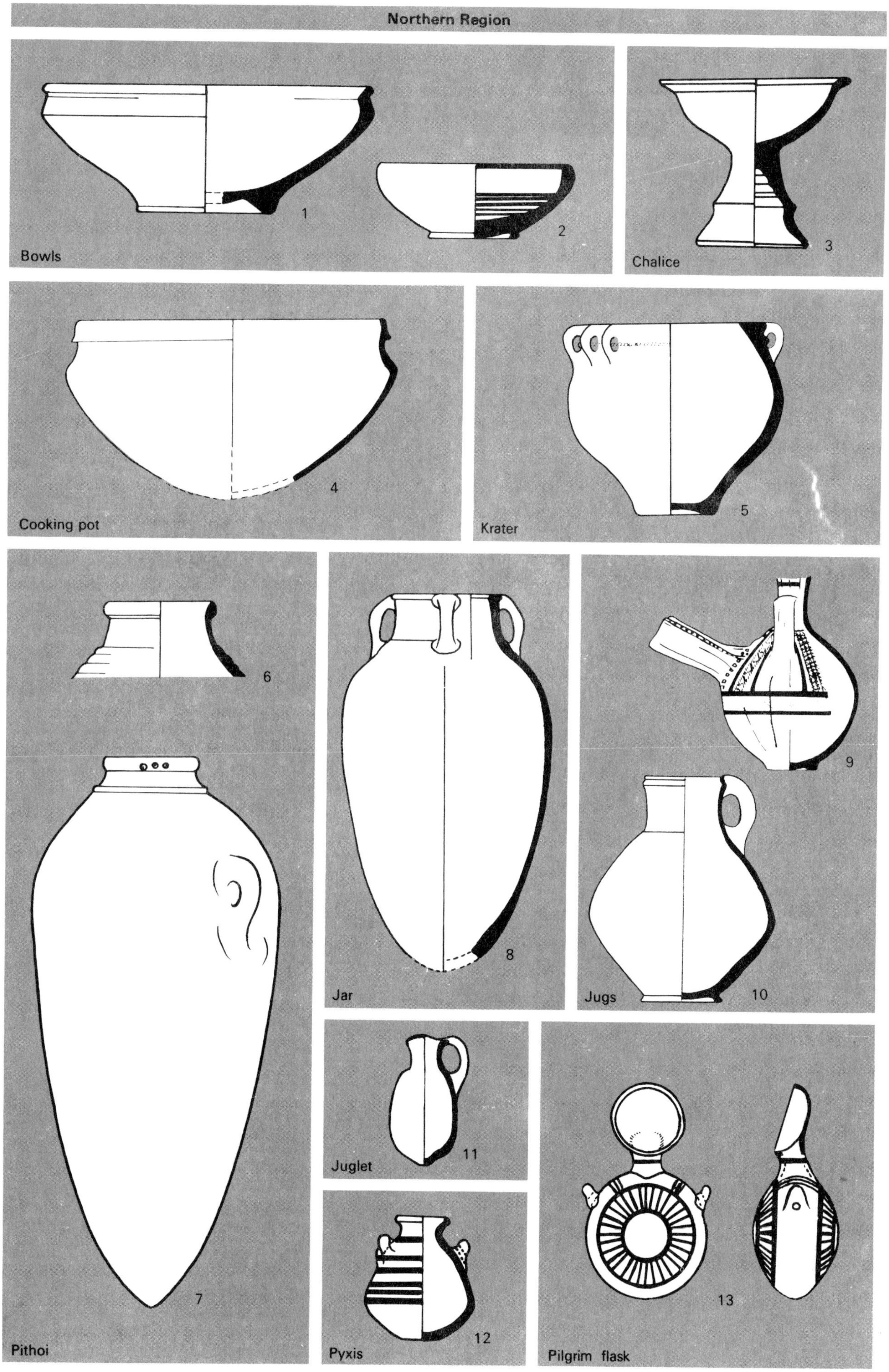

PLATE VI: IRON AGE PERIOD, c. 1200–587 B.C.E.
PL. VIa: IRON AGE Ia–b, c. 1200–1000 B.C.E.

14. Carinated bowl with purple-brown radial bands on the inside, dividing it into sectors containing representations of palm trees, from Gezer. [pl. 61, no. 4]

15. Rounded bowl decorated with irregular hand-burnishing on the inside, from Beth Mirsim, stratum B. [pl. 61, no. 6]

16. Chalice with carinated rim and stepped foot, from Qasile, stratum X. [pl. 68, no. 8]

17. Standard krater, from Beth Mirsim, stratum B. [pl. 70, no. 1]

18. Ovoid jar with slanting body, short neck, and eight handles, from Farʿah (S). [pl. 78, no. 7]

19. Cooking pot, similar to the Northern type, with two handles, from Beth-Shemesh, stratum III. [pl. 76, no. 2]

20. Pyxis shaped and decorated like the Mycenaean prototype, from Farʿah (S). [pl. 96, no. 9]

21. Jug with pear-shaped body, slightly concave neck, trefoil mouth, and handle drawn from rim to shoulder, from a tomb at Farʿah (S). [pl. 85, no. 3]

22. Squat jug with globular body, ring base, wide neck, and handle drawn from rim to shoulder, from a tomb at Farʿah (S). [pl. 85, no. 5]

23. Juglet with trefoil mouth, wide neck, and elongated cylindrical body, from a tomb at Gezer. [pl. 85, no. 13].

24. Small flask with loop handles shaped like slanting eyes, a type which appears also in the North, from a tomb at Farʿah (S). [pl. 95, no. 4]

25. Small flask with cup-like mouth and ordinary loop handles, from a tomb at Farʿah (S). [pl. 95, no. 5]

PLATE VI : IRON AGE PERIOD, c. 1200–587 B.C.E.

PL. VIa : IRON AGE Ia–b, c. 1200–1000 B.C.E.

Southern Region

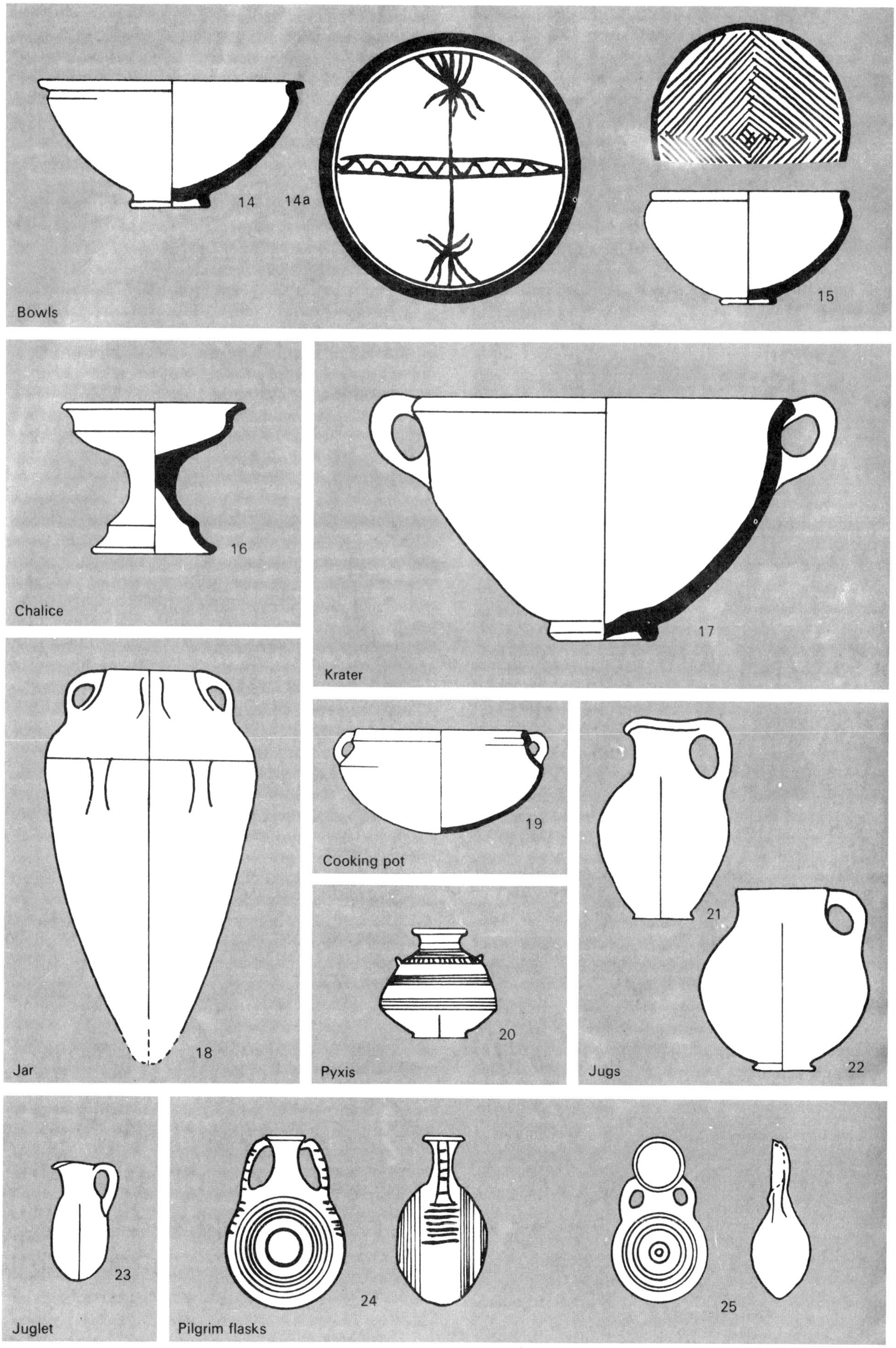

PLATE VI: IRON AGE PERIOD, c. 1200–587 B.C.E

PL. VIb: IRON AGE I, PHILISTINE WARE

1. Krater decorated with metopes in black and red on white slip. The metopes contain a checkerboard, and spirals enclosing a cross. From Gezer. [pl. 90, no. 2]

2. Bowl decorated with metopes containing motif of a stylized bird with head turned backwards, from Gezer. [pl. 90, no. 1]

3. Bowl with a frieze filled with antithetic-tongue motif in red and black on a white slip, from Ashkelon. [pl. 90, no. 4]

4. Selection of bowls with two horizontal handles, decorated with spirals and birds from Farʿah (S) and Azor. Courtesy Israel Department of Antiquities, Jerusalem.

5. Elongated pyxis, from Gezer. [pl. 90, no. 6]

6. Stirrup jar decorated in metope style with the bird motif in each metope, from Gezer. [pl. 90, no. 10]

7. Jug decorated with friezes of net-pattern motif and concentric semicircles, from a tomb at Farʿah (S). [pl. 90, no. 5]

8. Jug decorated with geometric pattern including concentric semicircle motif, from a tomb at Farʿah (S). [pl. 90, no. 9]

9, 9a. "Beer jug," decorated with two bands in red and black on a white slip. The upper band (9a) contains alternating bird and fish motifs, the lower is divided by triglyphs into metopes filled with geometric patterns, bird motifs, and checkerboard. From a tomb at Itun. Courtesy Israel Department of Antiquities, Jerusalem.

PLATE VI : IRON AGE PERIOD, c. 1200–587 B.C.E.

PL.VIb: IRON AGE I, PHILISTINE WARE

Mycenaean IIIc$_1$ character

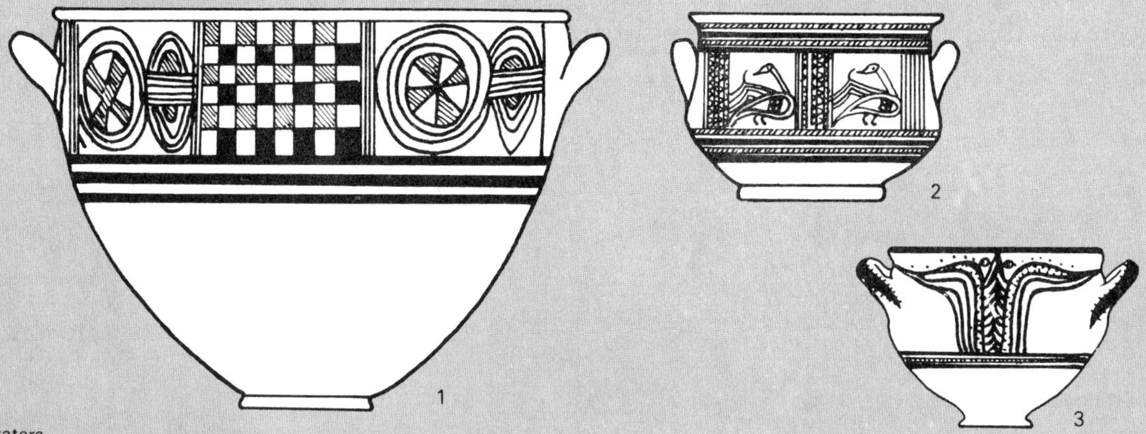

1

2

3

Kraters

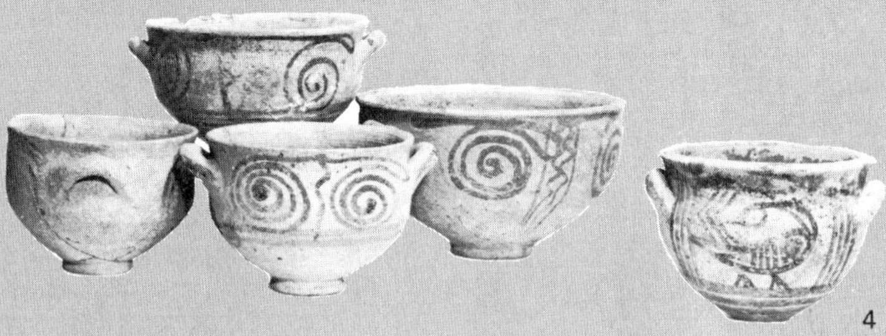

4

Bowls

5

Pyxis

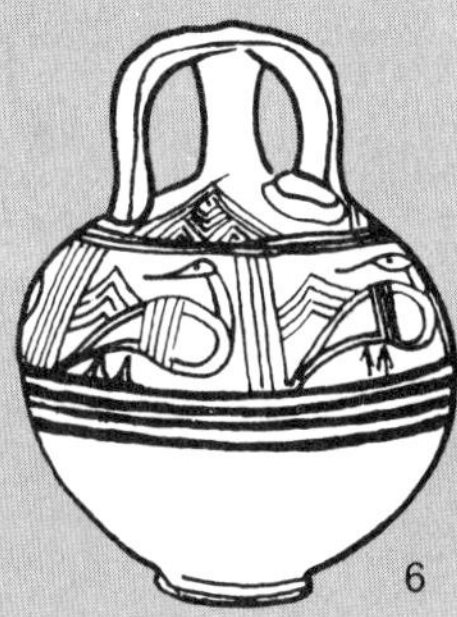

6

Stirrup jar

Local Canaanite character

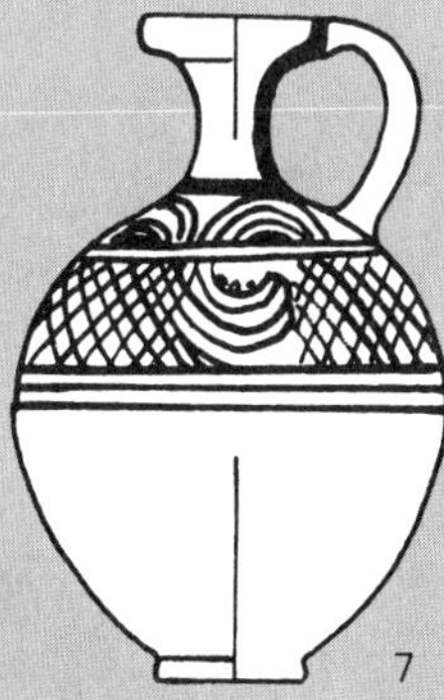

7

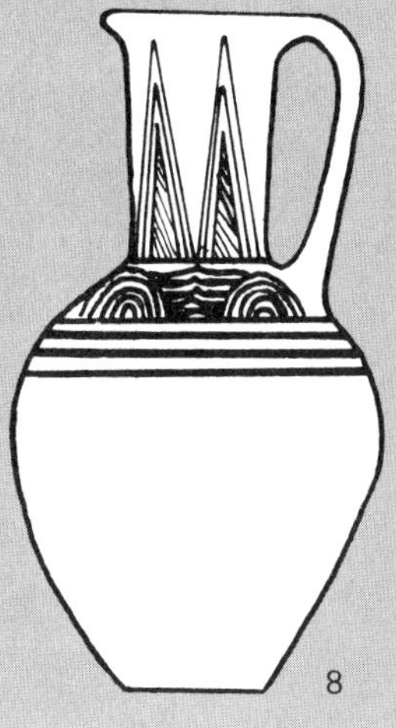

8

Jugs

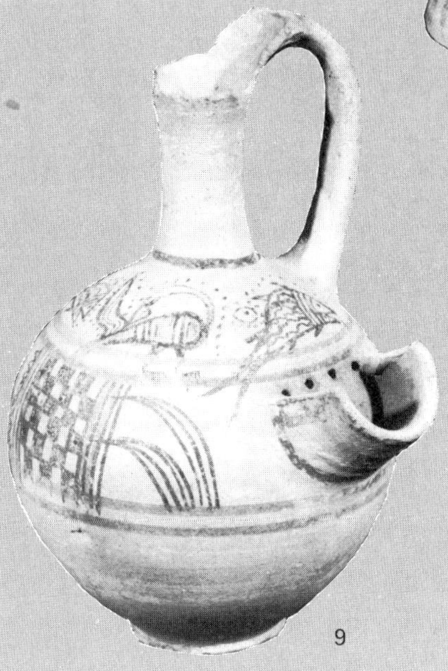

9

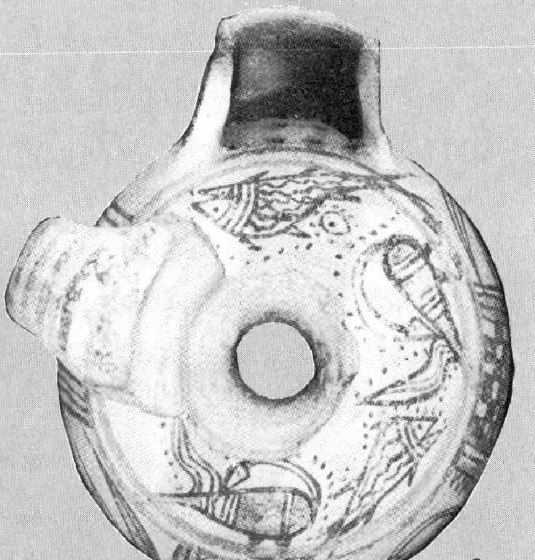

9a

Beer jug

PLATE VI: IRON AGE PERIOD, c. 1200–587 B.C.E.

PL. VIc: IRON AGE IIa–b, c. 1000–800 B.C.E.

1. Sharply-carinated bowl with low ring base, from Hazor, stratum IX. [pl. 62, no. 7]

2. Deep, rounded, small bowl with red-burnished slip applied to the entire vessel, from Hazor, stratum X. [pl. 62, no. 18]

3. Shallow, rounded bowl with a low ring base and painted red and black concentric circles in Bichrome style, from Abu-Hawam, stratum IV. [pl. 62, no. 21]

4. Bowl on three stump legs, from Hazor, stratum VIII. [pl. 62, no. 27]

5. Bowl of eggshell-thin, well-baked ware covered with thick, wheel-burnished red slip, from Samaria, stratum III. [pl. 66, no. 6]

6. Thick-walled bowl with heavy, wheel-burnished red slip, from Hazor, strata IX–X. [pl. 67, no. 1]

7. Chalice with high foot and deep bowl, and red and black decoration in Bichrome style, from Megiddo, stratum VI. [pl. 68, no. 13].

8. Krater with pronounced carination, four handles, and a molded rim, from Hazor, stratum VIII. [pl. 71, no. 5]

9. Cooking pot with carination in lower part of the vessel, two handles, and a short rim, triangular in section, from Far'ah (N), stratum III. [pl. 75, no. 11]

10. Ovoid jar with ridged neck and pronounced shoulder, from Hazor, stratum VIII. [pl. 79, no. 1]

11. Sausage-shaped jar with pronounced shoulder, from Megiddo, stratum V. [pl. 79, no. 2]

12. Juglet with burnished black slip (the so-called "black juglet") with long narrow neck, and handle attached to middle of neck, from Megiddo, stratum V. [pl. 86, no. 12]

13. Dipper-juglet with cylindrical body and trefoil mouth, from Abu-Maṭar, stratum III. [pl. 86, no. 14]

14. Jug with ridged neck and handle drawn from the ridge to the shoulder, decorated with red and black painted bands, from Megiddo, stratum V. [pl. 86, no. 4]

15. Jug with trough-like strainer spout, small body, trumpet base, wide neck, and red, irregularly hand-burnished slip, from Megiddo, stratum V. [pl. 86, no. 7]

16. Small flask, vertically burnished, from Abu-Hawam, stratum III. [pl. 94, no. 3]

17. Jug with red-burnished slip and black decoration, classified with "Black on Red I" Cypriot Ware, from Megiddo, stratum VA. [pl. 97, no. 7]

18. Decorated juglet, classified with "Black on Red II," from a tomb at Ajjul. [pl. 97, no. 23]

19. Jug defined by clear lines, with trefoil mouth and highly burnished, thick, dark-red slip, from Megiddo, stratum IV B. [pl. 92, no. 3].

PLATE VI : IRON AGE PERIOD, c. 1200–587 B.C.E.

PL. VIc: IRON AGE IIa–b, c. 1000–800 B.C.E.

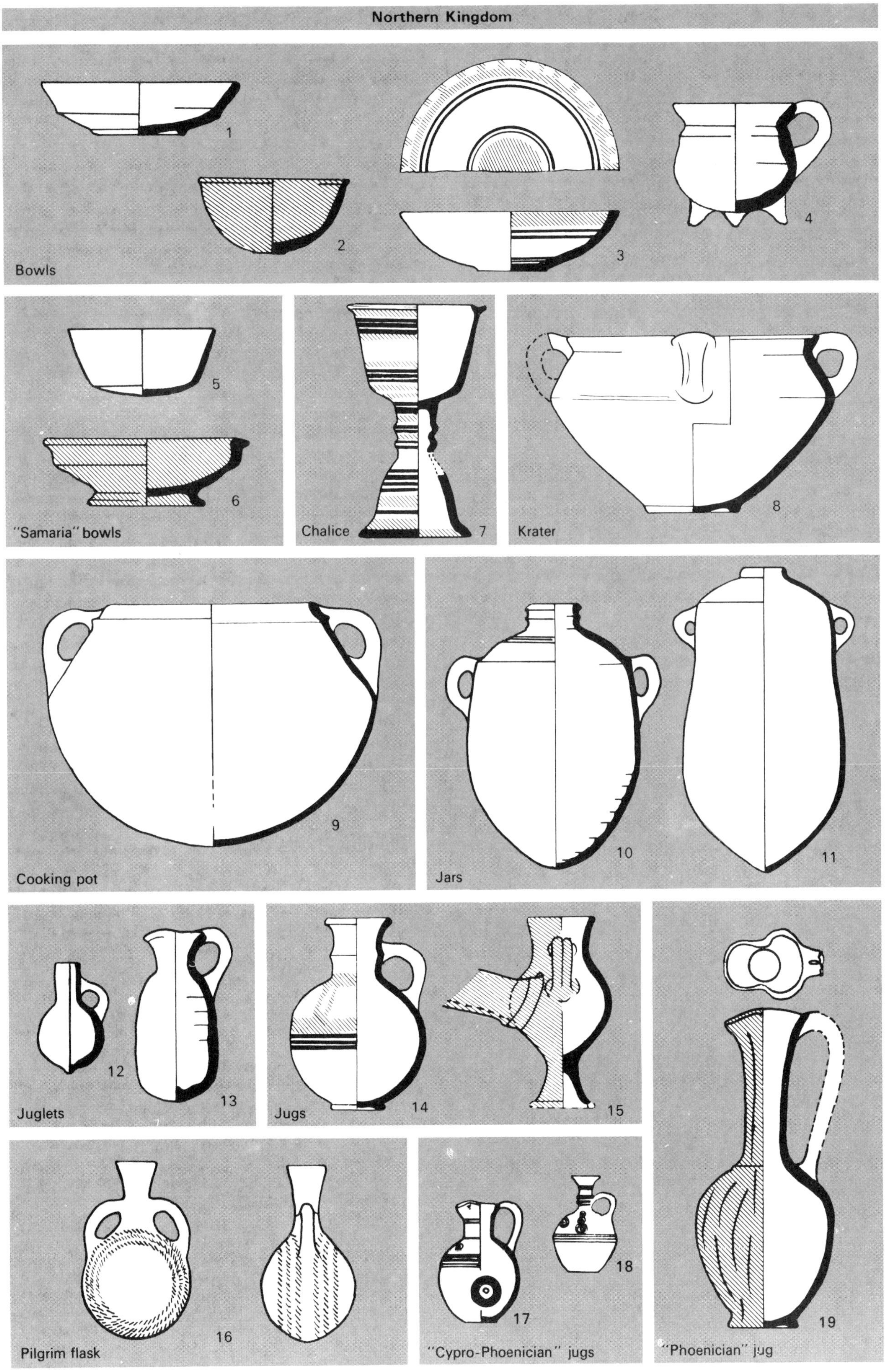

PLATE VI: IRON AGE PERIOD, c. 1200–587 B.C.E.

PL. VIc: IRON AGE IIa–b, c. 1000–800 B.C.E.

20. Bowl with obtuse carination and small ring base, from Beth-Shemesh, stratum IIa. [pl. 63, no. 2]

21. Bowl with two small, degenerate, horizontal handles, grooves on the upper part, and red, irregularly hand-burnished slip, from Jemmeh. [pl. 63, no. 7]

22. Bowl with bar handles, grooves on the upper part, and red irregularly hand-burnished slips, from a tomb at Lachish. [pl. 63, no. 8]

23. Cup-like bowl with three stump legs, from Farʿah (S). [pl. 63, no. 15].

24. Chalice with low foot, decorated with an embroidery-like pattern, from a tomb at Farʿah (S). [pl. 68, no. 15]

25. Krater with pronounced neck ridged in the middle, pear-shaped body, and relatively narrow mouth, from a tomb at Ajjul. [pl. 72, no. 4]

26. Cooking pot with rounded shape and two handles from Beth-Shemesh, stratum IIa. [pl. 76, no. 7]

27. Two fragments of a cooking pot showing carinated wall and a short rim, triangular in section, from Beth-Shemesh, stratum IIa. [pl. 76, no. 9, 10]

28. Ovoid jar with pronounced shoulder, from a tomb at Farʿah (S) [pl. 80, no. 1]

29. High-necked jar with a ridge in the middle of the neck, from which three handles, are drawn to the shoulder, and an overall burnished red-slip, from a tomb at el-Ruqeish. [pl. 80, no. 5]

30. Jug with high, ridged neck and a handle drawn from the ridge to the shoulder, from a tomb at Farʿah (S). [pl. 87, no. 6]

31. Jug with trough-like strainer spout, and dark-red vertically burnished slip, from a tomb at Lachish. [pl. 87, no. 7]

32. Brown-red vertically burnished juglet ("black juglet" type) with long neck and handle attached to the middle, from Beth Mirsim, stratum B. [pl. 87, no. 13]

33. Dipper-juglet, from Beth-Shemesh, stratum IIa. [pl. 87, no. 12]

34. Small flask from a tomb in Farʿah (S). [pl. 95, no. 9]

35. Degenerate small pyxis with black-burnished slip, from Beth-Shemesh, stratum III. [pl. 96, no. 23]

PLATE VI : IRON AGE PERIOD, c. 1200–587 B.C.E.

PL. VIc : Iron Age IIa-b, c. 1000–800 B.C.E.

Southern Kingdom

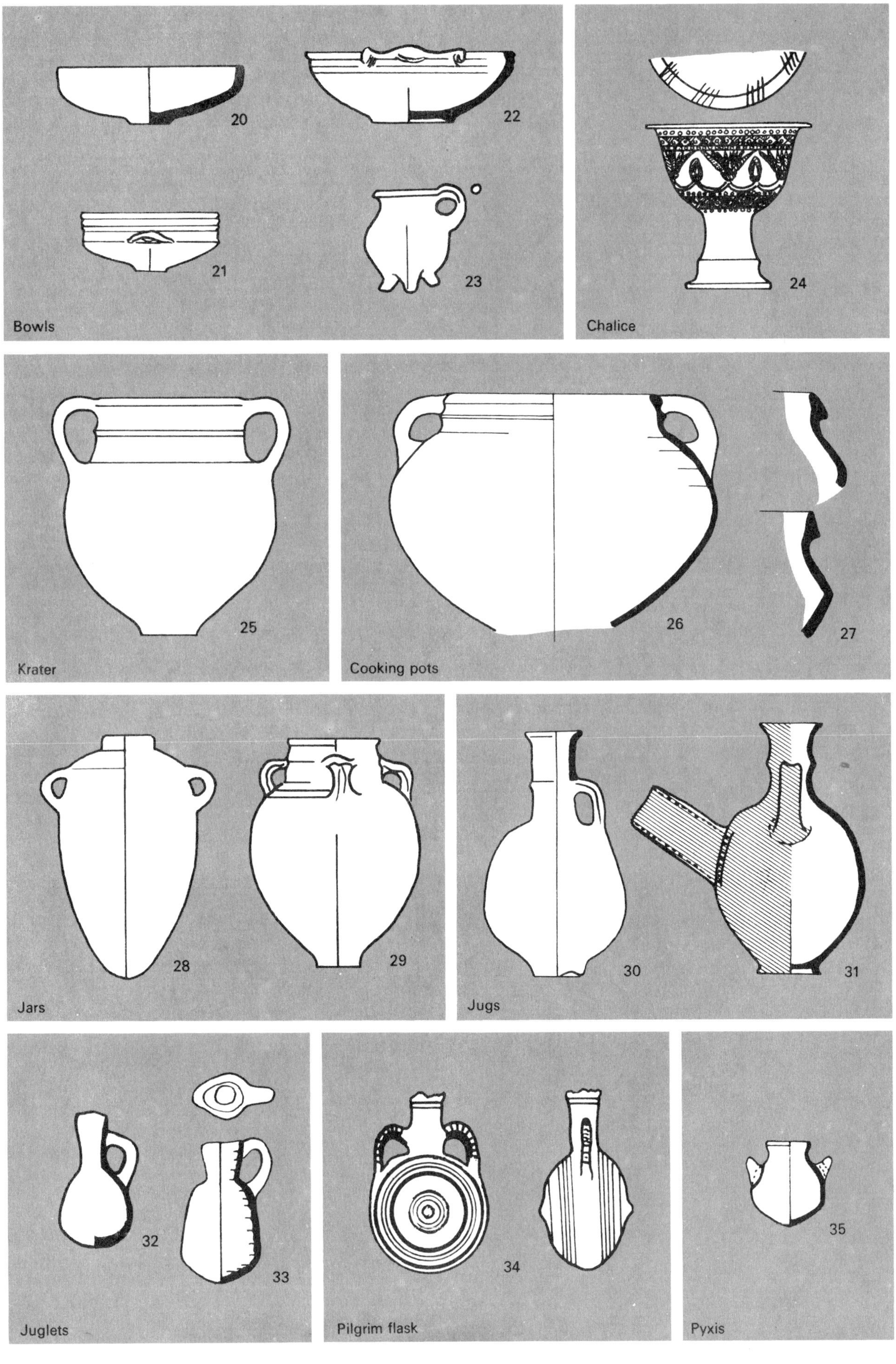

PLATE VI: IRON AGE PERIOD, c. 1200–586 B.C.E.

PL. VId: IRON AGE IIc, c. 800–586 B.C.E.

1. Bowl with carination on its lower part, profiled, red-decorated rim, and shallow disc base, from Hazor, stratum VB. [pl. 64, no. 5]

2. Bowl with bar handles serving purely as ornamentation, from Hazor, stratum IV. [pl. 64, no. 26]

3. Large, deep bowl with rounded walls, thickened, ridged rim, and red-burnished slip, from Hazor, stratum VA. [pl. 64, no. 25]

4. Small, goblet-like chalice, from Megiddo, stratum III. [pl. 68, no. 20]

5. Carinated bowl of eggshell-thin, well-baked ware covered with thick red-burnished slip, from Hazor, stratum VII. [pl. 66, no. 10]

6. Thick-walled bowl with trumpet base and heavy, red-burnished slip, from Samaria. [pl. 67, no. 15]

7. Krater with plastic decoration evolved from the bar handle and two loop handles, from Hazor, stratum VA. [pl. 73, no. 7]

8. Sausage-shaped, yellowish-pink jar of well-baked metallic clay, with pronounced shoulder and very short neck with a straight rim, from Hazor, stratum VA. [pl. 81, no. 5]

9. Jar with three handles and spout (which served as a seat for a dipper-juglet), metallic ware, decorated with grooves on the shoulder, from Hazor, stratum VA. [pl. 81, no. 13]

10. Cooking pot with slightly squat body, two handles, very gentle carination, and stepped rim with a ridge, from Hazor, stratum IV. [pl. 75, no. 19]

11. Pilgrim flask, one half almost flat, the other bulging, with incised decoration, from Megiddo, strata III–II. [pl. 94, no. 8]

12. Decanter, one of the most characteristic jug types of the period. This variant is of well-baked metallic ware with deeply grooved, funnel-like rim and a group of grooves on the shoulder. From Hazor, stratum VA. [pl. 88, no. 4]

13. Jug with short, trough-like, strainer spout, double-ridged rim, and red slip, from Hazor, stratum VA. [pl. 88, no. 11]

14. Dipper-juglet with cylindrical body, from Hazor, stratum VA. [pl. 88, no. 18]

15. Degenerate "black juglet," very small, with relatively short neck, handle drawn from rim, and vertically burnished, from Megiddo, strata IV–I. [pl. 88, no. 19]

16. Degenerate, small pyxis from Megiddo, stratum III. [pl. 96, no. 25]

17. Jugs with sharp, clear-cut form and long neck, either straight or conical. Jerusalem, Israel Museum, Israel Department of Antiquities Collection.

18. Decorated juglet, classified with "Black on Red I," from a tomb at Lachish. [pl. 98, no. 3]

19. Juglet-flask classified with "Red on Black II," from Megiddo, strata V–III. [pl. 98, no. 6]

PLATE VI : IRON AGE PERIOD, c. 1200–587 B.C.E.

PL.VId: IRON AGE IIc, c. 800–586 B.C.E.

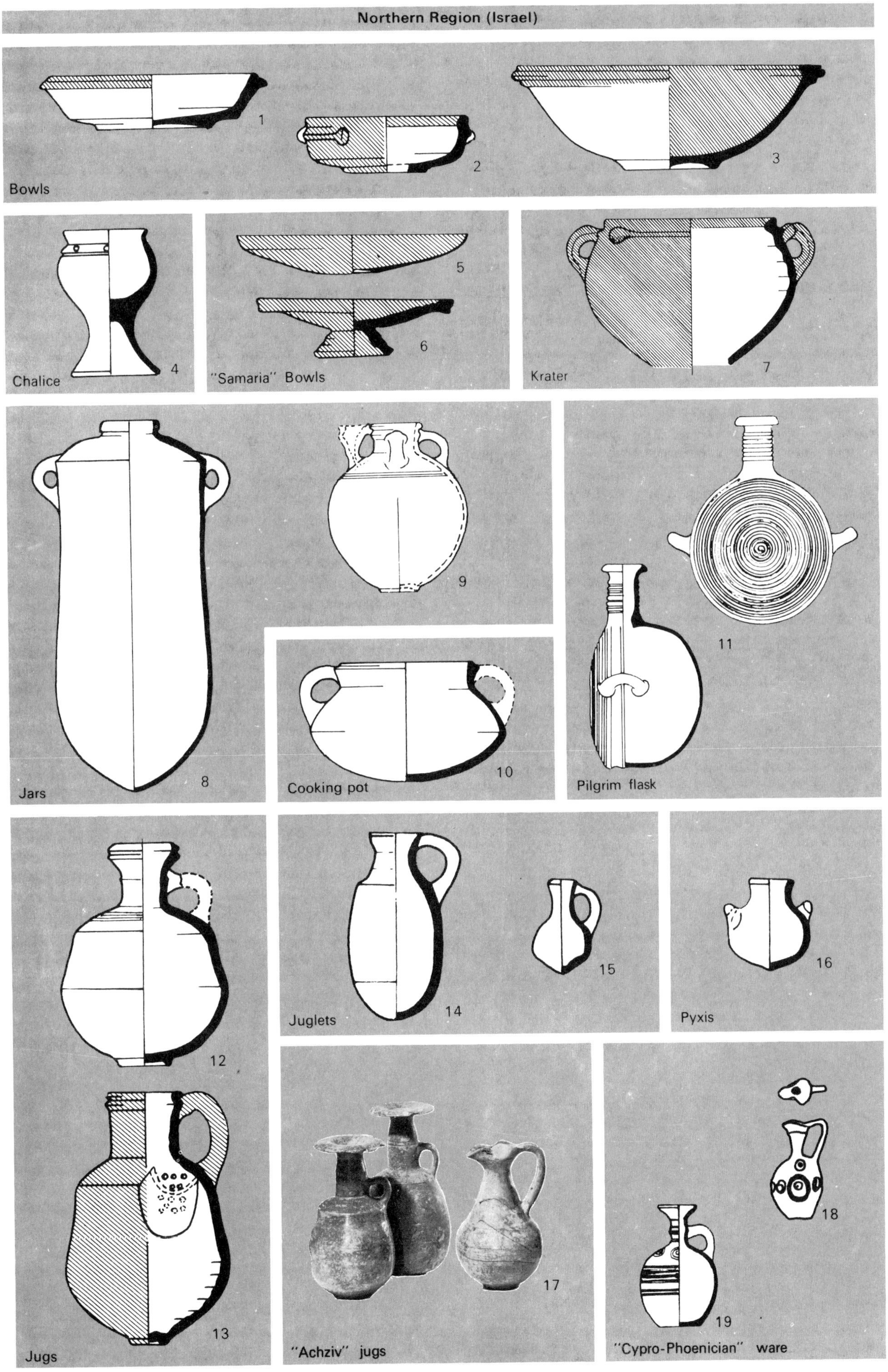

PLATE VI: IRON AGE PERIOD, c. 1200–586 B.C.E.

PL. VId: IRON AGE IIc, c. 800– 586 B.C.E.

20. Rounded bowl with holemouth rim and wheel-burnished slip, from Beth Mirsim, stratum A. [pl. 65, no. 16]

21. Small bowl with broad, flattened base, flaring walls, sharp rim, and red wheel-burnished slip, from Beth Mirsim, stratum A. [pl. 65, no. 9]

22. Bowl with turned-over rim, carinated walls, and brownish-red slip. Wheel-burnished inside. From Beth Mirsim, stratum A. [pl. 65, no. 2]

23. Bowl on three stump legs, perforated like a sieve, from Lachish, stratum III. [pl. 65, no. 21]

24. Goblet-like chalice from Qasile, stratum VII. [pl. 68, no. 22]

25. Deep cooking pot, with well-developed ridged neck and two handles drawn from rim to shoulder, from Beth-Shemesh, stratum II b–c. [pl. 76, no. 16]

26. Krater with two handles, pink slip inside, and standard Iron Age turned-over rim, from a tomb at Lachish. [pl. 74, no. 2]

27. Decanter with wheel-burnished slip, from Lachish, stratum II. [pl. 89, no. 1]

28. Jug with wide neck, handle drawn from rim to shoulder, and a ridge below the rim, from Beth Mirsim, stratum A. [pl. 89, no. 13]

29. Ovoid jar with relatively high, wide shoulder, thickened rim, and four handles, from Lachish, strata II–III. [pl. 82, no. 1]

30. Jar handle with la-Melek impression (LMLK MMST). Such handles, belonging to the type of ovoid jar illustrated (No. 29), have been found all over Judea. Courtesy Israel Department of Antiquities, Jerusalem.

31. Holemouth jar with barrel-shaped body, from Beth Mirsim, stratum A. [pl. 82, no. 8]

32. Jar with three handles and spout, in which a dipper-juglet is placed. The spout is hollow and also served to collect any liquid spilled when the juglet was used. From Arad. Jerusalem, Israel Museum. Courtesy Arad Expedition.

33. Dipper-juglet, from Beth Mirsim, stratum A. [pl. 89, no. 20]

34. Degenerate, small "black juglet" from Beth Mirsim, stratum A. [pl. 89, no. 22]

35. Degenerate, small pyxis with squat body and irregularly burnished slip, from a tomb at Lachish. [pl. 96, no. 26]

36. Grooved pilgrim flask with knobs under handles, from a tomb at Lachish. [pl. 95, no. 14]

PLATE VI : IRON AGE PERIOD, c. 1200–586 B.C.E.

PL.VId: IRON AGE IIc, c. 800–586 B.C.E.

Southern Region (Judea)

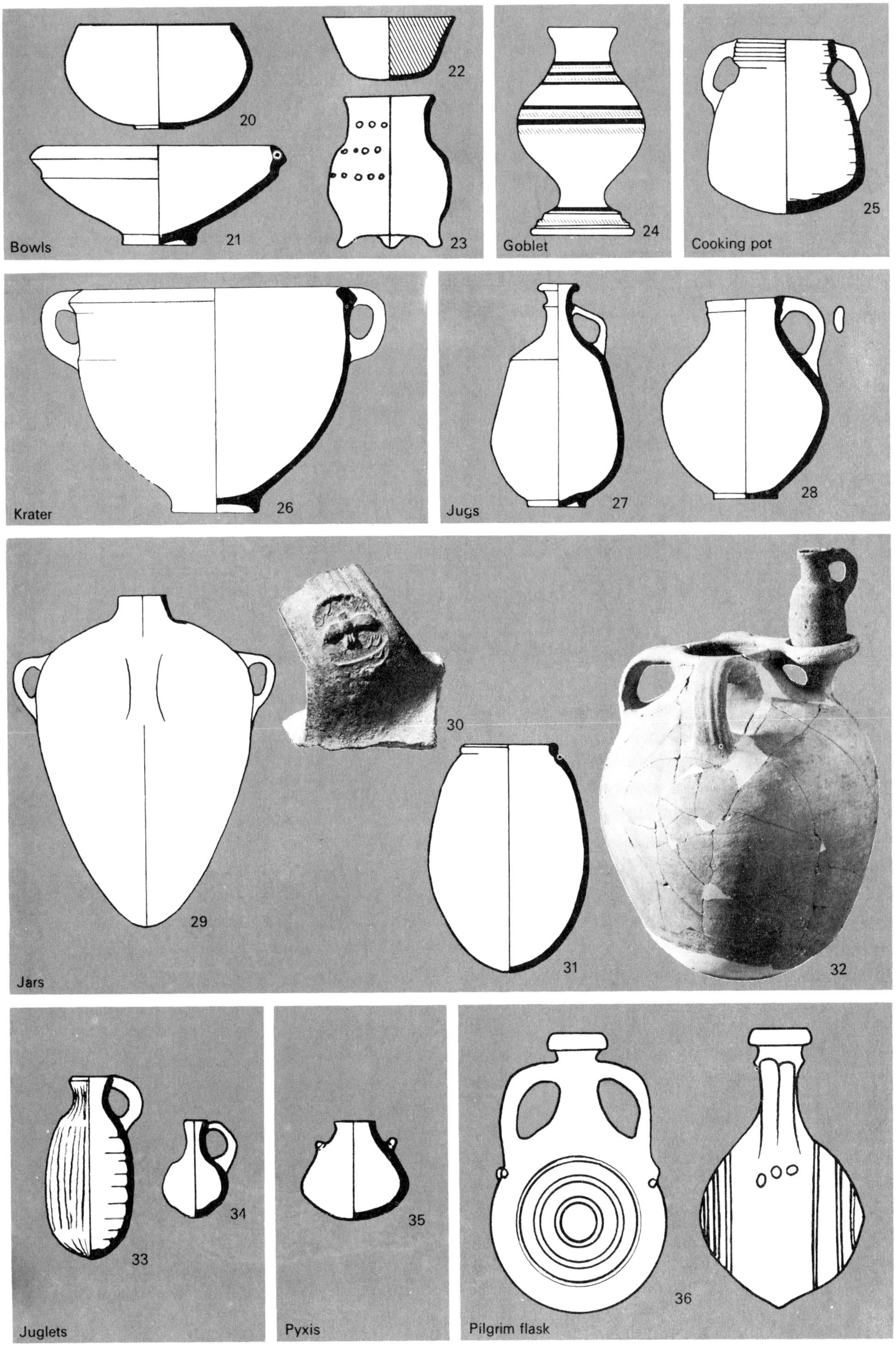

ESTIMATED NUMBER OF SYNAGOGUES ACCORDING TO COUNTRY (1971)

Country	Estimated number of synagogues	Country	Estimated number of synagogues	Country	Estimated number of synagogues	Country	Estimated number of synagogues
Afghanistan	1	Finland	2	Mexico	14	†††United States	5,500
†Algeria	5	France	187	Morocco	50	Uruguay	8
Argentina	99	Germany, East	8	New Zealand	7	††††U.S.S.R.	62
Aruba	1	Germany, West	5	Nicaragua	1	Venezuela	4
Australia	53	Gibraltar	4	Norway	2	Virgin Islands	1
Austria	10	Great Britain	399	Pakistan	1	Yugoslavia	20
Bahamas	1	Greece	4	Panama	3	Zambia	3
Belgium	19	Guatemala	1	Paraguay	3		
Bolivia	4	Holland	20	Peru	6		
Brazil	32	Hong Kong	1	Philippines	1		
Bulgaria	1	Hungary	30	Poland	1		
Burma	1	India	27	Portugal	3		
Canada	169	Iran	50	Rhodesia	8		
Channel Islands	1	Iraq	3	Rumania	3		
Chile	1	Ireland, Republic of	8	Singapore	2		
Colombia	9	††Israel	6,000	South Africa	166		
Costa Rica	1	Italy	54	Spain	3		
Cuba	1	Jamaica	1	Sudan	1		
Curacao	2	Japan	1	Surinam	2		
Czechoslovakia	2	Kenya	1	Sweden	10		
Denmark	2	Lebanon	2	Switzerland	24		
Dominican Republic	2	Libya	3	Syria	5		
Ecuador	1	Luxembourg	3	Trinidad	1		
Egypt	3	Malta	1	Tunisia	2		
Ethiopia	1			Turkey	26		

† Figures for Arab countries are estimates according to number of Jews and communities.

†† Ministry for Religious Affairs figure.

††† In 1970 the Conservatives claimed 830, the Reform 698; in 1963 the Orthodox claimed 3,900 in U.S. and Canada.

†††† AJYB estimate; Soviet sources have 97 and Rabbi Lewin of Moscow stated 102.

INDEX

INTRODUCTION TO THE INDEX

FUNCTION

The Index is the key to the Encyclopaedia. It serves five main purposes:

(a) to provide the reader with a list of titles of articles appearing in the body of the Encyclopaedia ("title entries");

(b) to refer the reader to items which do not have articles of their own, but which appear within articles on different subjects ("main entries");

(c) to gather together all the information on a given entry, whether title or main, which is scattered throughout the Encyclopaedia, and to present it under one index heading;

(d) to send the reader to the correct form of an entry by means of *see* references when he is looking under another possible form which is not an index entry, e.g. Yom Kippur, *see* DAY OF ATONEMENT;

(e) to guide the reader, through *see also* entries, to related topics which he may wish to pursue, e.g. CAMPS (Concentration and Extermination), *see also* FORCED LABOR; GHETTO; HOLOCAUST.

In addition, certain index entries are intended to serve educational and research purposes. Thus, for instance, the entry under TOSAFOT contains a list of all tosafists appearing in the Encyclopaedia.

ARRANGEMENT

The index entries are arranged alphabetically, letter by letter, up to the first comma. Thus FISCHER, SAMUEL precedes FISCHER-GRAZ, WILHELM. In the case of identical names the order is chronological; people precede places and places precede things. Thus EGLON (Moab. k.) precedes EGLON (Cana. city). The definite and indefinite articles: "the", "a", "an" are not alphabetized, nor are titles of nobility, or roman numerals following a name, e.g. Henry V, John III.

Owing to the nature of Hebrew names and their transliteration, a name including the prefix Bar, Ben, or Ibn, should also be sought, if necessary, under the the other two prefixes.

PAGE REFERENCES

The references are to volume and page (i.e., column). The volume number is printed bold and followed by a colon. Thus **10:** 1426 means that the information is to be found in volume **10** on page 1426. When different volume references follow each other, they are separated by a semi-colon (**10:** 1426; **14:** 415); when different page numbers in the same volume follow they are separated by a comma (**8**: 157,429) unless the volume number is repeated. When the page reference is followed by f. or ff., this means that relevant information is also to be found on the following pages.

Volume 1 contains lists of ḥasidic dynasties, Israel place-names, newspapers, pottery, and synagogues. Index references to this kind of information appear (e.g.) as **1**: syn. list.

TYPOGRAPHY

When an entry is printed in capital letters (upper case), this indicates that there is an article of that name in the Encyclopaedia (title entry); when it is printed in large and small letters (upper and lower case) this means that the subject is mentioned on the page recorded, but is not the subject of an article in the Encyclopaedia (main entry). Thus:

ALEXANDRIA (city, Egy.) **2:** 589
Alexandria (city, Louis.) **11:** 517

Both title and main entries are flush with the left-hand margin.

Capsule entries (i.e., subjects of brief biographies after a general entry—see Introduction to the Encyclopaedia) are printed in upper case. So are the sections of multiple articles; thus BERENICE (name of 2 women) is treated as though it were 2 separate Encyclopaedia articles.

Occasionally sections of large articles are indexed as though they were independent articles. Thus WATER AND IRRIGATION IN ISRAEL appears in the Index under the letter "W" and is followed by sub-entries as well as being part of the ISRAEL entry. This is in order to facilitate quick reference without the reader having to examine major entries.

Italics are used for names of books, newspapers, plays, ships, and certain foreign-language words. Quotation marks are used for works of art and nicknames.

Where an entry runs over onto a second line, the continuation of the entry is indented, but without indentation marks.

SUB-ENTRIES

Both title and main entries may be followed by sub-entries. The purpose of the sub-entries is to guide the reader to those places in the Encyclopaedia where the subject is discussed in other contexts. The sub-entries are listed alphabetically under the title or main entry and are indented with an indentation mark. The sub-entries may be grouped in sub-divisions, in which case the sub-divisions will be indented one space and the sub-entries two spaces. In some cases the sub-divisions are further sub-divided, and then the sub-entries are indented three spaces. The sub-divisions are not necessarily arranged in alphabetical order although the sub-entries are. Thus:

(1) ALEXANDRIA **2:**589
(2) —General

(3) ——banking **4:**166
(3) ——capitulations **5:**148
(2) —Ancient Period
(3) ——*Acts of Alexandrian Martyrs* **2:**594
(3) ——alchemy **2:**546
(3) ——Apion **3:**178
(2) —Medieval and Modern
(3) ——Almani, Aaron he-Ḥaver **2:**509
(3) ——Crusader captives **9:**271

(1) = Title entry; (2) = Sub-division;
(3) = Sub-entry
For large Encyclopaedia articles a list of contents appears immediately after the title entry. Thus:

GREECE **7:**867
—*Contents:*
——Second Temple Period **7:**868
——Early and Middle Byzantine Periods **7:**870
———Forced Conversion **7:**871
———Social and Economic Conditions **7:**872
——Fourth Crusade and Late Byzantine Period **7:**874

The article indicated by a title entry should always be consulted before the sub-entries, since it contains the main body of information on the topic concerned.

See AND *see also* REFERENCES

All *see* and *see also* references are to the Index itself. The *see* references bring the reader to the name under which the subject is treated. *See also* references guide the reader to information which is related to the subject he is studying.

The typographic system described above is also used in the *see* and *see also* references.

ILLUSTRATIONS

With the exception of photographic portraits, all illustrations in the Encyclopaedia are indexed. Illustration references are preceded by—*illus*:. The word "text" indicates that the article itself includes one or more illustrations, while the subsequent references will lead the reader to other illustrations connected with the subject. When the entry is for an artist, the illustration subdivision will list the places where his works appear in the Encyclopaedia. Illustration entries may also be arranged in subdivisions. The above system is likewise used for maps, charts, diagrams, and musical notations.

DESCRIPTIONS

Most entries, except for people, are followed by a short description in parentheses. People are only given descriptions when there is a possibility of confusion or when a name is not obviously recognizable as such.

All biblical figures are so described, as are *tannaim* (tan.) *amoraim* (amora), *geonim* (gaon), kings (k.), queens (q.), popes (pope), and tosafists (tos.). A full list of the abbreviations used in the Index follows.

ABBREVIATIONS USED IN THE INDEX

abbrev.	abbreviation, abbreviated
Aby.	Abyssinia, Abyssinian
acad.	academy, academic
act.	actor, actress
adm.	admiral
admin.	administrator
adv.	advertisement, advertiser
advent.	adventurer
Aeg.	Aegean Sea
aero.	aeronautics, aeronautical
Afg.	Afghanistan, Afghanistani
Afr.	Africa, African
agg.	aggadah, aggadic
agr.	agriculture, agricultural, agriculturist
agron.	agronomist
Akk.	Akkadian
Ala.	Alabama
Alb.	Albania
alch.	alchemy, alchemist
Alex.	Alexandria, Alexandrian
Alg.	Algeria, Algerian
Als.	Alsatian
Alsk.	Alaska, Alaskan
Als.-Lor.	Alsace-Lorraine
Alta.	Alberta
Am.	America, American
Ammon.	Ammonite
Amor.	Amorite
Amst.	Amsterdam
anat.	anatomy, anatomist, anatomical
anc.	ancient
And.	Andorra
And. Is.	Andaman Islands
Ang.	Angola
Angl.-Sax.	Anglo-Saxon
anon.	anonymous
Antarc.	Antarctica
anth.	anthology
anthro.	anthropology, anthropological, anthropologist
antiq.	antiquity, antiquities, antiquarian
anti-Sem.	anti-Semite, anti-Semitic
Apoc.	Apocrypha, Apocryphal
apos.	apostasy, apostate
Arab.	Arabia, Arabic, Arabist
Arag.	Aragon
Aram.	Aramaic, Aramean
arbit.	arbitration, arbitrator
arch.	archaeology, archaeologist, archaeological
archbp.	archbishop
archit.	architecture, architect, architectural
archiv.	archives, archivist
Arg.	Argentina, Argentinian
Ariz.	Arizona
Ark.	Arkansas
Arm.	Armenia, Armenian
art.	artist, artistic
As.	Asia, Asiatic
asc.	ascetic, asceticism
Ash.	Ashkenaz, Ashkenazi
As. M.	Asia Minor
assim.	assimilation, assimilationist
assoc.	association
Assyr.	Assyria, Assyrian, Assyriologist
astrol.	astrology, astrologer, astrological
astron.	astronomy, astronomer, astronomical
au.	author
Aus.	Austria, Austrian
Austr.	Australia, Australian
auth.	authority
Az.	Azores
Azer.	Azerbaijan
b.	born
Babyl.	Babylon, Babylonia, Babylonian
bact.	bacteriology, bacteriologist, bacteriological
Bagh.	Baghdad
Bah.	Bahamas
Bahr.	Bahrein
Bal.	Baluchistan
Bal. Is.	Balearic Islands
Barb.	Barbados
bart.	baronet
Bav.	Bavaria, Bavarian
B. C.	British Columbia
B.C.E.	Before Common Era
Belg.	Belgium, Belgian
Belor.	Belorussia
ben.	benediction
Ber.	Bermuda
Bess.	Bessarabia
Bib.	Bible
bib.	biblical
bibl.	bibliography, bibliographer, bibliographical
biblio.	bibliophile
biog.	biography, biographer, biographical
biol.	biology, biologist, biological
bk.	book
bldg.	building
bld. lib.	blood libel
bldr.	builder
bnk.	bank, banker, banking
Bohem.	Bohemia, Bohemian
Bol.	Bolivia, Bolivian
boro.	borough
Bosn.	Bosnia
bot.	botany, botanist, botanical
bp.	bishop
Br.	Britain, British
br.	brother
Braz.	Brazil, Brazilian
br.-in-l.	brother-in-law
bsmn.	businessman

bswn.	businesswoman
Buk.	Bukovina
Bukh.	Bukhara, Bukharan
Bul.	Bulgaria, Bulgarian
Bur.	Burma, Burmese
Byz.	Byzantium, Byzantine
C.	Central, center
c.	circa
Calif.	California
Can.	Canada
can.	canal
Cana.	Canaan, Canaanite
Can. Is.	Canary Islands
Cape Col.	Cape Colony
capt.	captain
card.	cardinal
Carib.	Caribbean
caric.	caricature, caricaturist
cart.	cartoon, cartoonist
cartog.	cartography, cartographer
C. As.	Central Asia
cas.	castle
Cast.	Castile
Cath.	Catholic
cath.	cathedral
Cauc.	Caucasia, Caucasus, Caucasian
C. E.	Common Era
cent.	century
cerem.	ceremonial
Cey.	Ceylon
ch.	church
chan.	channel
Chan. Is.	Channel Islands
chem.	chemistry, chemist, chemical
Chil.	Chilean
Chin.	Chinese
choreog.	choreography, choreographer
Chr.	Christianity, Christian
chron.	chronology
civ. ser.	civil servant
cler.	clergyman
clny.	colony
cmty.	community
Co.	Company
co.	county
col.	colonel
coll.	college
collec.	collector, collection
Colo.	Colorado
Colom.	Colombia, Colombian
com.	commerce, commercial, commission, commissioner, committee, commune
comm.	commander
comment.	commentary, commentator
commun.	communism, communist
comp.	composer
compil.	compilation, compiler
conc.	concept
concen.	concentration
cond.	conductor
cong.	congregation
Conn.	Connecticut
Cons.	Conservative
Const.	Constantinople
const.	constitution, constitutional
contemp.	contemporary
contr.	contractor
conv.	Converso, convert
co-op.	co-operative
Corp.	Corporation
Cors.	Corsica
court.	courtier
C. R.	Costa Rica
crftn.	craftsman
crim.	criminal
criminol.	criminology, criminologist
crit.	critic, critical
Crus.	Crusades, Crusader
cult.	culture, cultural
Cyp.	Cyprus
Cz.	Czech, Czechoslovakia, Czechoslovakian
d.	died
Dan.	Danish
dan.	dancing, dance, dancer
dau.	daughter
D. C.	District of Colombia
Del.	Delaware
Den.	Denmark
dent.	dentistry, dentist
dept.	department
des.	desert
desig.	designer
diag.	diagram
dict.	dictionary
dipl.	diplomat
dir.	director, direction
dist.	district
div.	division
doc.	document, documentation
dom.	dominion
D. P.	Displaced Person
dram.	dramatist
drg.	drawing
D. S. Scroll	Dead Sea Scroll
Du.	Dutch
dyn.	dynasty
E. (e.)	East, Eastern
Ec.	Ecuador
eccl.	ecclesiastical, ecclesiast
econ.	economics, economist
ed.	editor
educ.	education, educator
Egy.	Egypt, Egyptian
Egyptol.	Egyptology, Egyptologist
emis.	emissary
emp.	emperor, empress, empire
enc.	encyclopaedia
encyc.	encyclical
Eng.	England, English
engin.	engineer, engineering
engr.	engraving, engraver
ent.	entertainer
Er. Isr.	Ereẓ Israel
eschat.	eschatology, eschatological
Est.	Estonia, Estonian

etch.	etching
Eth.	Ethiopia, Ethiopian
ethnol.	ethnologist
Eur.	Europe, European
exct.	extinct
exec.	executive
exeget.	exegetical
exil.	exilarch
expl.	explorer
f.	father
fam.	family
fcg.	facing
fed.	federation
Fest.	Festival
fig.	figure
Fin.	Finland, Finn, Finnish
fin.	finance, financier
fl.	flourished
Fla.	Florida
Flem.	Flemish
flklr.	folklore, folklorist
fort.	fortress, fortified
found.	foundation, founder
Fr.	France, French
frsc.	fresco
fspc.	frontispiece
ftr.	fighter
Ga.	Georgia
Gal.	Galicia
gen.	general
geneal.	genealogy, genealogist, genealogical
geog.	geography, geographer, geographical
geol.	geology, geologist
Ger.	Germany, German
Gib.	Gibraltar
gov.	governor
govt.	government
Gr.	Greece, Greek
gr.	group
gram.	grammar, grammarian
Gt. Brit.	Great Britain
h.	husband
Hag.	Haggadah
hal.	halakhah, halakhic
ḥas.	ḥasidic
Hask.	Haskalah
Hasm.	Hasmonean
Heb.	Hebrew, Hebraic
Hebr.	Hebraist
Hellen.	Hellenism, Hellenist, Hellenistic
hist.	history, historian, historical
H. K.	Hong Kong
Holl.	Holland
Hond.	Honduras
h. pr.	high priest
H. Rom. Emp.	Holy Roman Empire/Emperor
Hung.	Hungary, Hungarian
I. (s.)	Island(s)
Ia.	Iowa
Ice.	Iceland

Ida.	Idaho
I. E.	Indo-European
I. F. S.	Irish Free State
Ill.	Illinois
illum.	illumination, illuminated
illus.	illustration, illustrator
Ind.	India, Indiana, Indian
Indoch.	Indochina
Indon.	Indonesia
indus.	industry, industrial, industrialist
Inq. (inq.)	Inquisition, inquisitor
inscr.	inscription
inst.	institute, institution
instr.	instrument
int.	international
interp.	interpretation, interpreter
inv.	invention, inventor
Ir.	Irish
Ire.	Ireland
Isl.	Islam, Islamic
isl.	island
Isr.	Israel
It.	Italy, Italian
J.	Jew, Jewish
Jam.	Jamaica, Jamaican
Jap.	Japan, Japanese
Jer.	Jerusalem
Jor.	Jordan
journ.	journalism, journalist, journal
jr.	junior
Jud.	Judaism, Judaic
Judaiz.	Judaizing
jur.	jurist, jurisprudence
K. (k.)	King (king)
Kab.	Kabbalah
kab.	kabbalist, kabbalistic
Kan.	Kansas
Kar.	Karaism, Karaite
kdm.	kingdom
Ken.	Kenya
kev.	kevuẓah
kib.	kibbutz
Kurd.	Kurdistan
Ky.	Kentucky
La.	Louisiana
lab.	labor
lang.	language
Lat.	Latin
Latv.	Latvia, Latvian
law.	lawyer
ldr.	leader
Leb.	Lebanon
leg.	legal, legalistic, legend, legendary
legis.	legislation, legislator, legislature
let.	letter
lev.	levitical
lexicog.	lexicographer
Lib.	Liberal
libn.	librarian
lieut.	lieutenant
ling.	linguistic(s), linguist

lit.	literature, literary
Lith.	Lithuania, Lithuanian
lith.	lithograph, lithography, lithographer
litur.	liturgical, liturgist
loc.	locality
Lond.	London
Ltd.	Limited
Lux.	Luxembourg
m.	married
Macc.	Maccabee, Maccabean
Maced.	Macedonia, Macedonian
mag.	magazine
magis.	magistrate
Maim.	Maimonides, Maimonidean
Maj.	Majorca
maj.	major
Man.	Manitoba
Mar.	Marrano
mart.	martyr
masor.	masoretic
Mass.	Massachusetts
math.	mathematics, mathematician
Md.	Maryland
mdvl.	medieval
Me.	Maine
meas.	measure
mech.	mechanics, mechanic, mechanical
med.	medicine, medicinal, medical
medal.	medallist
Medit.	Mediterranean
mer.	merchant
Mesop.	Mesopotamia
Mess.	Messiah
mess.	messianic
met.	metal, metallurgy, metallurgist
meteorol.	meteorology, meteorologist, meteorological
Mex.	Mexico, Mexican
mfr.	manufacture, manufacturer
Mich.	Michigan
Mid.	Midrash
mid.	midrashic
mil.	military
min.	mineral, mineralogy
miniat.	miniature
minis.	minister
m.-in-l.	mother-in-law
Minn.	Minnesota
Mish.	Mishnah
mish.	mishnaic
Miss.	Mississippi
miss.	missionary
Mo.	Missouri
mo.	mother
Moab.	Moabite
mod.	modern
Mold.	Moldavia, Moldavian
mon.	monument
Mont.	Montana, Montgomery
Mor.	Morocco, Moroccan
Morav.	Moravia
mosh.	moshav, moshavah
ms. (mss.)	manuscript(s)
msq.	mosque
mt.	mount, mountain
Muham.	Muhammadan
mus.	museum, music, musician, musical
musicol.	musicology, musicologist
Musl.	Muslim
mvmt.	movement
myst.	mystic, mystical
myth.	mythology, mythological
N. (n.)	North, Northern
N. Afr.	North Africa, North African
N. Am.	North America, North American
nat.	nationalism, national
natur.	naturalist, naturalism
naut.	nautical
nav.	naval
navig.	navigator
N. C.	North Carolina
N. D.	North Dakota
neg.	negative
Neth.	Netherlands
neurol.	neurologist
Nev.	Nevada
newsp.	newspaper
Nfd.	Newfoundland
N. H.	New Hampshire
nick.	nickname
Nig.	Nigeria
N. J.	New Jersey
no. (nos.)	number(s)
Nor.	Norway, Norwegian
nov.	novel, novelist
N. T.	New Testament
numis.	numismatist
N. Y. (C.)	New York (City)
N. Z.	New Zealand
O.	Ocean, Oceanic, Ohio
obs.	obsolete
of.	officer
offic.	official
Okla.	Oklahoma
Ont.	Ontario
Oreg.	Oregon
org.	organic
orgn.	organisation, organiser
orient.	oriental, orientalist
orn.	ornament
ornith.	ornithology, ornithologist
Orth.	Orthodox
O. T.	Old Testament
Ott.	Ottoman
Pa.	Pennsylvania
pac.	pacifist
Pac. O.	Pacific Ocean
paint.	painting, painter
Pak.	Pakistan
Pal.	Palestine, Palestinian
paleog.	paleography
paleont.	paleontology, paleontologist
pam.	pamphlet
Pan.	Panama
Parag.	Paraguay

parl.	parliament
Parth.	Parthia, Parthian
pass.	passage
pat.	patriot, patriotic
path.	pathology, pathologist
patr.	patriarch, patristic
penin.	peninsular
period.	periodical
Pers.	Persia, Persian
Phar.	Pharisee
pharm.	pharmacy, pharmacist, pharmaceutical, pharmacologist
Phil.	Philistine
philan.	philanthropy, philanthropist, philanthropic
philol.	philology, philologist
philos.	philosophy, philosopher
Phoen.	Phoenicia, Phoenician
phot.	photography, photographer
phys.	physics, physicist
physic.	physician
physiol.	physiology, physiologist
pion.	pioneer
Pl.	plate illustration
pl.	player
plat.	plateau
plwrt.	playwright
Pol.	Poland, Polish
polem.	polemics, polemicist
polit.	politics, politician, political
pol. sci.	political science, political scientist
pop.	population
Port.	Portugal, Portuguese
Pr. (pr.)	Prince
pr.	priest, priestly
prch.	preacher
pres.	president, presidency
prin.	prince, princess
princip.	principality
print.	printing, printer, printed
pr. min.	prime minister
prod.	produce, producer
prof.	professor
propag.	propaganda, propagandist
pros.	proselyte
Prot.	Protestant, Protestantism
prot.	protectorate
Prov.	Provence, Provençal
prov.	province, provincial
Prus.	Prussia, Prussian
ps.	pseudo
pseud.	pseudonym
pseudepig.	pseudepigrapha
psych.	psychical, psychology, psychologist, psychiatry, psychoanalysis, psychoanalyst
pub.	public, publication
publ.	publishing, publisher, published
public.	publicist
Pumb.	Pumbedita
Q. (q.)	Queen (queen)
qtr.	quarter
Que.	Quebec

R., r.	Rabbi, rabbi
rab.	rabbinic, rabbinical
rad.	radical
R. C.	Roman Catholic
rd.	road
re.	regarding
reconst.	reconstruction
Ref.	Reform, Reformation
ref.	reformer, reformist
reg.	region
rel.	religion, religious
rep.	republic
repr.	representative
resist.	resistance
revol.	revolution, revolutionary
Rhod.	Rhodesia, Rhodesian
R. I.	Rhode Island
rit.	ritual
riv.	river
rlf.	relief
rly.	railway
Rom.	Roman
Rum.	Rumania, Rumanian
Rus.	Russia, Russian
S. (s.)	San, South, Southern
s.	son, son of
S. A.	South Africa
Sadd.	Sadducee, Sadducean
Sah.	Sahara
S. Am.	South America
Samar.	Samaria, Samaritan
sanct.	sanctuary
S. Arab.	South Arabia
Sard.	Sardinia, Sardinian
Sask.	Saskatchewan
Saud. Arab.	Saudi Arabia
S. C.	South Carolina
Scand.	Scandinavia, Scandinavian
schol.	scholar, scholarly
sci.	science, scientist, scientific
Scot.	Scotland, Scottish, Scotch
sculp.	sculpture, sculptor
S. D.	South Dakota
sect.	sectarian
Sel.	Seleucid
Sem.	Semite, Semitic
Seph.	Sephardi
Serb.	Serbia, Serbian
Shab.	Shabbatean
Sib.	Siberia, Siberian
Sic.	Sicily, Sicilian
sing.	singer
sis.	sister
Slav.	Slavonia, Slavonic, Slavic
Slov.	Slovakia
Sloven.	Slovenia
soc.	society, social, socialist
sociol.	sociology, sociologist, sociological
sol.	soldier
Sov.	Soviet
Sov. Un.	Soviet Union
Sp.	Spain, Spanish
sport.	sportsman, sportswoman

sr.	senior
s.s.	steamship
S. S. R.	Soviet Socialist Republic
St.	Saint
states.	statesman
statis.	statistics, statistical, statistician
stlmt.	settlement
stlr.	settler
sub.	suburb
Sud.	Sudan
Sult. (sult.)	Sultan (sultan)
suppl.	supplement
surg.	surgery, surgeon
surv.	surveyor
Swed.	Sweden, Swedish
Switz.	Switzerland
syn.	synagogue, synagogal
Syr.	Syria, Syrian, Syriac
T.	Talmud (Babylonian Talmud—TB, Palestinian Talmud–TJ)
tab.	table
tal.	talmudic
tan.	tanna
Tas.	Tasmania
TB	Talmud Babylonian
Tenn.	Tennessee
terr.	territory
Tex.	Texas
Thai.	Thailand
theat.	theater, theatrical
theol.	theology, theological, theologian
tit.	title
TJ	Talmud Palestinian (Jerusalem)
tn.	town
tos.	tosafot, tosafist
Tosef.	Tosefta
tpst.	tapestry
tract.	tractate
trans.	translation, translator
Transj.	Transjordan
Transyl.	Transylvania
trav.	travel, traveler
trib.	tributary
Trip.	Tripoli
Tun.	Tunis, Tunisia
Turk.	Turkey
Turkest.	Turkestan
U. A. R.	United Arab Republic
U. K.	United Kingdom
Ukr.	Ukraine, Ukrainian
U. N.	United Nations
univ.	university
urb.	urban
Urug.	Uruguay
U. S.	United States (of America)
U. S. S. R.	Union of Soviet Socialist Republics
Va.	Virginia
val.	valley
Ven.	Venice, Venetian
Venez.	Venezuela
vet.	veterinary
vict.	victim
vill.	village
vol.(s)	volume(s)
Vt.	Vermont
W. (w.)	West
w.	wife
Wash.	Washington
wdct.	woodcut
Wis.	Wisconsin
wk.	work
wkr.	worker
writ.	writer
wrtg.	writing
wtrcl.	watercolor
W. Va.	West Virginia
W.W.I or II	World War I or II
Wyo.	Wyoming
Yem.	Yemen, Yemenite
Yid.	Yiddish, Yiddishist
Yug.	Yugoslavia
Zion.	Zionism, Zionist
zool.	zoology, zoologist, zoological

A

AACHEN (city, Ger.) 2:1
– *illus:* text
'Aani, Kadduri Elijah 4:312
AARGAU (canton, Switz.) 2:3
– emancipation 6:709ff
– Switzerland 15:556
– *illus:* text
Aarhus, Peter S. 8:21
Aarlen (tn.), *see* Arlon
AARON (bib. fig.) 2:4
– *Contents:*
– – General 2:4
– – Critical View 2:6
– – In Aggadah 2:7
– – In Christian Tradition 2:8
– – In Koran, Islamic Literature 2:8
– burial place 8:971
– death anniversary 3:935; 16:702
– Exodus, Book of 6:1052ff
– Golden Calf 7:709ff; 12:750
– Hārūn 13:362
– in the Arts 12:404*ff*
– kabbalistic view 10:575
– kiss of death 5:1427
– Korah 10:1190ff
– Moses 12:372
– peace 10:477; 13:197
– Plagues 13:605
– priesthood 13:1076ff
– priestly vestments 13:1064
– rod of Aaron 14:218
– sages on 14:640
– Samaritan priesthood 14:727; 14:734
– *illus:*
– – Aaron's rod 3:*fcg.* 524
– – ceremonial object motif 3:542; 4:244, 1232, 1339; 5:296; 7:1307
– – confronting Pharaoh 2:952
– – episodes 12:*fcg.* 427
– – folk-art portrait 8:1286
– – *Kaufmann Haggadah* 8:1275
– – Korah and 10:1191
– – lighting the *menorah* 11: *fcg.* 1355
– – Manna 11:885
– – Mount Sinai 2:*fcg.* 11
– – performing miracle with rod 12:379
– – Pharaoh entreating 13:605
– – pouring oil into the *menorah* 8:*fcg.* 1271
– – priestly vestments 6:277
– – rod changed into serpent 12:*fcg.* 427
– – supporting hands of Moses 2:788; 12:382
– – watching battle with Amalek 14:1258
Aaron (gaon) 7:323
– Abraham Gaon 2:158
Aaron, A. 15:830
Aaron, Barney 15:305, 306
Aaron, Coja Jacob 14:1415
Aaron, House of, *see* AARONIDES
Aaron, Israel 5:1009; 5:934
Aaron, Judah 12:1465
Aaron, S. 8:343
Aaron, Sons of, *see* AARONIDES
Aaron Abraham ben Baruch Simeon ha-Levi 8:1003; 9:1231
Aaron Araki ha-Kohen 12:199
Aaron Avuyah 14:1648
Aaron ben Abraham ben Isaac 13:1264
Aaron ben Abraham Gaon 2:158
Aaron ben Abraham of Offenbach 13:575
AARON BEN AMRAM 2:9
– economic history 16:1283
Aaron ben Asher, *see* BEN ASHER, AARON BEN MOSES
Aaron ben Baruch 16:1232
AARON BEN BATASH 2:9
– Merinids 11:1386
– Morocco 12:331
– Wattasids 16:365
AARON BEN DAVID COHEN OF RAGUSA 2:9
– on book trade 4:1238
AARON BEN ELIJAH (Kar.) 2:10
– atomism 3:830
– commandments, reasons for 5:785
– *Kalām* 10:703
– Karaites 10:771
– Luzki, Simḥah 11:595
– providence 13:1285
– philosophy 13:433
Aaron ben Elijah ha-Kohen (print.) 2:780
Aaron ben Ḥayyim of Grodno 11:918
AARON BEN ISAAC BENJAMIN WOLF 2:12
AARON BEN JACOB HA-KOHEN OF LUNEL 2:12
– codification of law 5:647
– *Haggadah* commentary 7:1092
– Isaac of Corbeil 9:22
– *Kol Bo* 10:1159ff
Aaron ben Jeshua, *see* ABU AL-FARAJ HARUN IBN AL-FARAJ
Aaron ben Jonah 6:250
AARON BEN JOSEPH HA-KOHEN SARGADO 2:13
– gaonate 7:318
– Saadiah Gaon 14:546ff
AARON BEN JOSEPH HA-LEVI 2:14
– *Ha-Ḥinnukh* 2:308; 7:1127
– Jewish literature 11:334
AARON BEN JOSEPH HA-ROFE 2:15
– *illus:*
– – *Sefer ha-Mivḥar ve-Tov ha-Mishar* (1835) 10:767
Aaron ben Joshua ibn Alamani, *see* ALAMANI, AARON HE-ḤAVER BEN YESHU'AH
AARON BEN JUDAH KUSDINI 2:16
Aaron ben Manīr 14:729; 14:753; 14:755
Aaron ben Mariyyon ha-Kohen 2:631; 13:575
Aaron ben Meir (gaon), *see* BEN MEIR, AARON
AARON BEN MEIR BRISKER 2:16
Aaron Ben-Meshal, *see* Ben-Meshal, Aaron
AARON BEN MESHULLAM OF LUNEL 2:16
– Maimonides 13:792
– Meshullam of Lunel 11:1400
AARON BEN MOSES HA-LEVI OF STAROSIELCE 2:17
– *ẓimẓum* doctrine 10:593
Aaron benMoses Rofeh 4:653
Aaron ben Moses the Scribe 11:474
– illuminated manuscripts 8:1287
AARON BEN SAMUEL (Ger.) 2:17
Aaron ben Samuel ha-Levi 13:575
Aaron ben Senton (Shemtov), *see* AARON BEN BATASH
Aaron ben Solomon ben Ḥasson 8:1170
Aaron ben Ẓevi Dessau, *see* Dessau, Aaron ben Ẓevi
AARON BERECHIAH BEN MOSES OF MODENA 2:18
– life after death 6:880ff
Aaron the Elder, *see* AARON BEN JOSEPH HA-ROFE
Aaron fil Josce of York, *see* AARON OF YORK
Aaron 'fiz Diaboli 13:916
Aaron ha-Gadol (the Great), *see* Karlin, Aaron ben Jacob of
AARON HAKIMAN 2:18
Aaron ha-Kohen (poet) 2:631
Aaron ha-Kohen (r.) 11:798
Aaron ha-Levi of Barcelona, *see* AARON BEN JOSEPH HA-LEVI
Aaron ha-Sab'uni of Salé 2:527
– Sarfaty, Aaron 14:879
– Toledano, Daniel 15:1193
AARONIDES (prs.) 2:18
– Korah 10:1191
– Messiah 11:1422
– *geneal. table:* text
– *see also:* PRIESTS AND PRIESTHOOD
Aaron Isaac (Swed.), *see* ISAAC, AARON
Aaron Leib (ḥas.) 13:277
Aaron Menahem Mendel of Radzymin 13:1508
Aaron Moses ben Joseph ha-Kohen 10:233
AARON OF BAGHDAD 2:21
– Gaeta 7:253
– Kalonymus family 10:720
– mysticism 10:510
– title 13:1446
Aaron of Barcelona, *see* AARON BEN JOSEPH HA-LEVI
Aaron of Belz 4:453
Aaron of Berdichev 13:133
Aaron of Chernobyl 15:1471
Aaron of Chernovtsy, *see* Friedmann, Aaron
Aaron of Cieszewiec 13:724
Aaron of Copenhagen, *see* AARON SIMEON BEN JACOB ABRAHAM OF COPENHAGEN
Aaron of Karlin, *see* Karlin, Aaron ben Jacob of
Aaron of Kremenets, *see* AARON SAMUEL BEN MOSES SHALOM OF KREMENETS
Aaron of Lachowicze, *see* Lachowicze, Aaron of
Aaron of Lengnau, *see* Eiron of Lengnau
AARON OF LINCOLN 2:21
– England 6:748
– Exchequer of Aaron 6:1006
– Josce of York 10:200
– Lincoln 11:256
– *illus:* text
Aaron of Lunel (12/13 cent.), *see* AARON BEN MESHULLAM OF LUNEL
Aaron of Lunel (13/14 cent.), *see* AARON BEN JACOB HA-KOHEN OF LUNEL
AARON OF NEUSTADT 2:22
– Krems 10:1258
Aaron of Nicomedia, *see* AARON BEN ELIJAH
AARON OF PESARO 2:22
Aaron of Radzymin, *see* Aaron Menahem Mendel of Radzymin
Aaron of Ragusa, *see* AARON BEN DAVID COHEN OF RAGUSA
Aaron of Starosielce, *see* AARON BEN MOSES HA-LEVI OF STAROSIELCE
Aaron of Ujhely (Satoraljaujhely) 16:1004
AARON OF YORK 2:22
– York 16:849
– *illus:* text
AARON OF ZHITOMIR 2:23

Aaron of Zolkiew, *see* AARON SELIG BEN MOSES OF ZOLKIEW
Aaron Peraḥyah ha-Kohen **14:**1648
Aarons, Charles L. **11:**1589
AARON SAMUEL BEN MOSES SHALOM OF KREMENETS **2:**23
AARON SAMUEL BEN NAPHTALI HERZ HA-KOHEN **2:**23
Aaronsburg (tn., U.S.) **11:**154
AARON SELIG BEN MOSES OF ZOLKIEW **2:**24
Aaron Setzer, *see* Aaron ben Elijah ha-Kohen
AARON SIMEON BEN JACOB ABRAHAM OF COPENHAGEN **2:**24
– *illus:*
– – *Or ha-Yashar* (1769) **5:**614
AARONSOHN (fam.) **2:**24
– *illus:*
– – Zikhron Ya'akov home **12:**1163
Aaronsohn, Aaron **2:**24
– B'nai B'rith **4:**1148
– botanical discovery **16:**480
– Feinberg, Avshalom **6:**1209
– Nili **12:**1162ff
– *illus:*
– – Zionist delegation to Palestine, 1918 **9:**336
Aaronsohn, Alexander **2:**28
– Nili **12:**1162
Aaronsohn, Efrayim Fishel **2:**24
Aaronsohn, Sarah **2:**29
– Feinberg, Avshalom **6:**1209
– Lishansky, Yosef **11:**303
– Nili **12:**1162ff
AARONSON, LAZARUS LEONARD **6:**786
Aaronson, Michael **10:**733
Aaron the Younger, *see* AARON BEN ELIJAH
A.B. (Samar. newsp., Isr.) **1:**newsp. list
Ab, Ninth of, *see* AV, THE NINTH OF
A-b-a(r.), *see* ASHER, ABRAHAM BEN GEDALIAH IBN
A-b-a (physic.), *see* Iscandari, Eleazar ben Abraham
ABADDON (conc.) **2:**30
– *see also:* NETHERWORLD
Abadi (name), *see* Abbadi
Abaelardus, Petrus, *see* ABELARD, PETER
Abag (pseud.), *see* GOTTLOBER, ABRAHAM BAER
Abailard, Pierre, *see* ABELARD, PETER
Abarbanel (fam.), *see* ABRABANEL, ABRAVANEL
Aba-Sava (vill., Cauc.) **12:**478
Abaujszanto (tn.), *see* Santo
Abayuv, Aaron **11:**1212
Aba Zabra (Falasha) **6:**1150; **6:**1151
Abazardiel, *see* ABZARDIEL, MOSES
Abba (pupil, Simeon bar Yoḥai) **16:**1198
Abba (amora), *see* RAVA
ABBA (Ba; amora) **2:**30
ABBA (Ba, the Later; amora) **2:**30
– Rabba ben Mattna **13:**1439
Abba (savora) **14:**920
ABBA (8th cent., r.) **2:**30
ABBA ("father") **2:**31
– title **15:**1164
Abba, Isaac Judah **11:**1159
Abba Arikha (amora), *see* RAV
ABBA BAR AḤA (amora) **2:**31
Abba bar Ammi (gaon) **7:**318
ABBA BAR AVINA (Binah; amora) **2:**31
Abba bar Dodai (gaon), *see* Rabbah bar Dodai
Abba bar Ḥanna (amora), *see* RABBAH BAR ḤANNA
Abba bar Huna (amora), *see* RABBAH BAR HUNA
ABBA BAR KAHANA (amora) **2:**32
– circuses and theaters **5:**577
– *Pesikta de Rav Kahana* **13:**334
ABBA BAR MARTA (amora) **2:**32
ABBA BAR MEMEL (amora) **2:**33
Abba bar Menyomi (amora) **2:**32
Abba bar Minah (amora), *see* ABBA BAR AVINA
ABBA BAR ZAVDA (amora) **2:**33
ABBA BAR ZEMINA (amora) **2:**33
– in *Shevi'it* tractate **14:**1392
ABBA BEN ABBA HA-KOHEN (tan./amora) **2:**34
Abba ben Aivu (amora), *see* RAV
Abba ben Dostai, *see* ABBA YOSE BEN DOSTAI
ABBA BENJAMIN (tan.) **2:**34
Abbad III (k., Seville) **2:**522; **15:**226
Abba Dan (amora), *see* AVDAN
Abbadi, Jacob **2:**565
Abbadi, Mordecai **2:**565
– Kabbalah **10:**553
– Song of Songs **14:**1058
Abbadi, Solomon **10:**895
Abba Elias (Falasha sermon) **6:**1150
Abba Elijah **11:**321
– *Tanna de-Vei Eliyahu* **15:**803
ABBA GULISH (mid. fig.) **2:**34
ABBA GURYON OF SIDON (tan.) **2:**35
Abba Ḥalafta (tan.), *see* ḤALAFTA
ABBA HILKIAH (tan.) **2:**35
ABBAHU (amora) **2:**35
– Abba of Akko **2:**38
– calendar **5:**49
– Christian beliefs **3:**191
– circuses and theaters **5:**577
– Greek **8:**296
– *resh kallah* **14:**83
Abbahu de-Shemu'el, *see* ABBA BEN ABBA HA-KOHEN
Abba Isi ben Ḥanin (Hanan , Johanan; tan.), *see* ABBA YOSE BEN ḤANIN
Abba Judah of Antioch **3:**71
ABBA KOHEN BARDELA (tan.) **2:**36
ABBA KOLON (mid. fig.) **2:**36
ABBA MARI BEN ELIGDOR **2:**37
ABBA MARI BEN ISAAC OF ST. GILLES **2:**37
Abba Mari of Lunel, *see* ASTRUC, ABBA MARI BEN MOSES BEN JOSEPH OF LUNEL
Abba Mari of Salon **2:**37
ABBA OF AKKO (amora) **2:**38
Abba of Glussk **6:**655
Abba of Sidon, *see* ABBA GURYON OF SIDON
Abba of Sura **13:**59
ABBA OSHAYA (Hoshaya) OF TIRIAH (amora) **2:**38
ABBAS I (shah, Pers.) **2:**38
– Persian Jews **13:**313
Abbas II (shah, Pers.) **2:**39
– Persian Jews **13:**313
ABBAS, JUDAH BEN SAMUEL IBN **2:**39
– education **6:**406ff
ABBAS, MOSES BEN SAMUEL **2:**39
– Saragossa **14:**862
ABBAS, MOSES JUDAH BEN MEIR **2:**39
Abbas, Samuel (cataloguer) **11:**196; **14:**1168
Abbas, Samuel ben Judah ibn *see* SAMAU'AL BEN JUDAH IBN ABBAS
Abba Sakkara, *see* ABBA SIKRA
ABBA SAUL (tan.) **2:**40
– embryo **4:**1020
– imitation of God **8:**1292
– trees **4:**1029
ABBA SAUL BEN BATNIT (tan.) **2:**40
– high priesthood **14:**641
Abbas Effendi, *see* ʿAbdu'l-Bahá
ABBASI, JACOB BEN MOSES IBN **2:**41
Abbāsī, Mahmud **9:**1039; **9:**1043
ABBASIDS (Arab dyn.) **2:**42
– attitude to Jews **8:**1445
– Ereẓ Israel **9:**262; **9:**265
– Jerusalem **9:**1425
– Spain **15:**226
ABBA SIKRA (1st cent. C.E., Er. Isr.) **2:**43
Abbassi, Samuel ben Joseph **15:**1425
ABBA UMANA (tal. fig.) **2:**44
– Academy on High **2:**208
– medicine **11:**1182
ABBAYE (amora) **2:**44
– Abbaye Kashisha **2:**45
– Academy on High **2:**208
– astronomy **15:**518
– decisions **5:**891
– Dimi of Nehardea **6:**49
– history chart **8:**766–767
– Palestinian *amoraim* **2:**873
– peace **13:**197
– Rava **13:**1579
– rebuke **14:**648
– righteousness **14:**181
– *ye'ush* **16:**775
ABBAYE KASHISHA (amora) **2:**45
ABBA YOSE BEN DOSTAI (tan.) **2:**45
ABBA YOSE BEN ḤANIN (Johanan; tan.) **2:**46
– *Shekalim* **14:**1346
Abba Yudan (amora), *see* AVDAN
Abbazia (tn., Croatia) **14:**185
Abbé Grégoire, *see* GRÉGOIRE, HENRI BAPTISTE
ABBELL, MAXWELL **2:**46
Abbing, Justine, *see* BRUGGEN, CARRY VAN
ABBREVIATIONS **2:**46
– *Contents:*
– – Introduction **2:**46
– – Terminology **2:**47
– – History **2:**49
– – Types **2:**49
– – Holy Name **2:**50
– – Names **2:**50
– – Town Names **2:**51
– – Book Titles **2:**51
– – In Kabbalah **2:**51
– – Misunderstandings and Misinterpretations **2:**51
– – In Jewish Folklore **2:**52
– colophons **5:**749
– greetings **7:**916
– Hebrew book titles **8:**75
– letters **11:**62
– masorah **16:**1424
– *serugin* **16:**1434
– *illus:*
– – text
– – *Shivviti* plaques **14:**1420-1421
Abbūshī, Burhān al-Dīn al- **9:**1040
Abdahali, Ḥayyim **10:**1006
ʿAbd al-ʿAzīz (sult., Mor.) **2:**517
ʿAbd al-Ghanī ben Ismāʿīl al-Nabulusi **15:**1358
ʿAbd al-Ḥāfiẓ (sult., Mor.) **2:**517
Abdal-Hagg, Aaron **11:**800
ʿAbd al-Ḥamīd II (sult.) **5:**62
– Circassian settlement **9:**921
– Ereẓ Israel **9:**322
– Herzl **8:**414; **16:**1071ff
– Ottoman Empire **16:**1553
– *illus:*
– – New Gate, Jerusalem **9:**1432
ʿABD AL-ḤAQQ AL-ISLĀMI **2:**52
Abdallah (gov., Acre) **9:**294,297
ABDALLAH, YUSUF (ps. mess.) **2:**53
Abdallah al-Mamun (caliph) **15:**1675
Abdallah ibn Khiḍer **8:**1452
ABDALLAH IBN SABĀʾ **2:**53
ABDALLAH IBN SALĀM **2:**54
– eschatology **6:**884
Abdallah ibn Wahb **7:**1051
ʾABD AL-MAJID **2:**54
– Jews' status under **16:**1538
ʿAbd al-Malik al-Muẓaffir **11:**894
ʿABD AL-MĀLIK IBN MARWĀN (caliph) **2:**55
– Dome of the Rock **9:**1424; **12:**1382; **15:**989
– Umayyads **15:**1529
ʿAbd al-Muʾmin **2:**662
– Maimonides **11:**755
– Spain **15:**226
ʿAbd al-Nabīʾ ibn Mahdī **16:**742
Abdalonymus (k., Sidon) **14:**1507
ʿAbd al-Raḥmān I **15:**224
– Umayyads **15:**1530
ʿAbd al-Raḥmān III **5:**62
– poetry **13:**682
– Spain **15:**224
– Umayyads **15:**1530
ʿAbd al-Rahmān ibn al-Lamkhānī **5:**1294
ʿAbd al-Raḥmān ibn Hishām **3:**1004
Abde (city), *see* AVEDAT
Abdel (Samar. h. pr.) **14:**728
ʿAbd-el-Kader **2:**69
Abdemon (lit. fig.) **7:**894; **7:**895
Abdera (city, Sp.), *see* Adra
Abdi-Aširta (Amor. k.) **14:**1505
Abdi Hepa (Abdihiba; k., Jer.) **2:**296, **9:**1307
– Ashkelon **3:**713
Abdi-Tirshi (k., Hazor) **7:**1535; **9:**1174
Abd-Melkarth (k., Sidon) **14:**1506
Abdon (bib. fam.) **2:**55
Abdon (city, Er. Isr.) **3:**701
ABDON SON OF HILLEL (bib. fig.) **2:**55
ABDON SON OF MICAH (bib. fig.) **2:**55
– *see also:* ACHBOR
ABDUCTION **2:**55
– punishment purpose **13:**1388
ʿAbduʾl-Bahá **9:**923
Abdul Ḥamīd II, *see* ʿAbd al-Ḥamīd II
Abdullah Bridge (Er. Isr.) **9:**1487
ABDULLAH IBN HUSSEIN (k., Jor.) **2:**56
– assassination **9:**1492
– Churchill **5:**555
– Golda Meir **11:**1243
– Husseini, Hajj Amin al- **8:**1132
– Jewish Agency **9:**347
– Palestine **9:**1031
– partition plan **16:**1085
– Sasson, Eliyahu **14:**896
– Trans-Jordan **9:**338,596
– *illus:*
– – text
– – Arab Legion and **9:**352
– – independence of Transjordan **9:**339
– – Lawrence, T.E., and **10:**1489
– – Samuel, Herbert **10:**199
ʿAbdullah ibn Muʿawiya **15:**1529
Abdullah ibn Zubayr (caliph) **15:**1529
Abdullah Yacoub, *see* QUERIDO, JACOB
Abdul Mejid (sult.), *see* ʿABD AL-MAJĪD
Abdul-Mumin, *see* ʿAbd al-Muʾmin
Abed-Nego (bib. fig.), *see*

SHADRACH, MESHACH, ABED-NEGO
Abedroth, David, see ABTERODE, DAVID BEN MOSES ELIAKIM
Abeilard, Peter, see ABELARD, PETER
ABEL (bib. fig.) 2:58
- in the Arts 5:24
- Lurianic Kabbalah 10:615
- sacrifice 14:605
- son of man 15:160
- illus:
- - episodes from life of 8:1271
- - killing of 5:21-23
- - the offering 6:980
- see also: CAIN
ABEL, AVEL (pl. name) 2:59
- Egypt 8:1064
ABEL, ELIE 10:308
ABEL, EMIL 2:59
ABEL, LOUIS FELIX 2:59
ABELARD, PETER 2:59
Abelard and Schumann (publ. co.) 12:1122
ABEL-BETH-MAACAH (city, Er Isr.) 2:60
- Testament of Levi 2:62
Abele Poswoler, see ABRAHAM ABELE BEN ABRAHAM SOLOMON
Abeles, Charles T. 3:459
Abeles, Herbert R. 6:904
Abeles, Lazar 2:61
ABELES, OTTO 2:61
ABELES, SIMON (Simele) 2:61
- Prague 13:968
ABELIOVICH, LEV MOYSSEYEVICH 12:679
Abelitas, Ishmael de, see Ibn Abbas, Ishmael
Abel-Maim, see ABEL-BETH-MAACAH
Abelman, Jonathan, see JONATHAN BEN ABRAHAM ISAAC
ABELMANN, ILYA SOLOMOVITCH 2:61
ABEL-MAUL (city, Er. Isr.) 2:61
Abel Mayin, see ABEL-BETH-MAACAH
ABEL-MEHOLAH (city, Er. Isr.) 2:62
- Abel Maul 2:62
Abelow, S. P. 8:568
ABEL-SHITTIM (tn., Moab) 2:62
- Acacia 2:198
ABELSON, HAROLD HERBERT 2:63
ABELSON, JOSHUA 2:63
ABELSON, PAUL 2:63
Abembron, David 9:1186
Abenabez, Moses, see ABBAS, MOSES BEN SAMUEL
Abenaes (fam. name), see also Yaish
Abenaes, Jacob 2:64; 16:1535
ABENAES, SOLOMON 2:63
- banking 4:171
- Benveniste, Moses 4:563
- ennobled 15:1166
- Tiberias 9:287 16:1535
ABENAFIA, JOSEPH 2:64
Abenaish, Solomon, see ABENAES, SOLOMON
Abenalazar (fam.), see ELEAZAR
Abenalazar, Abulfath 6:584; 14:859
Abenalazar, Alazrach 14:859
Abenamias, Moses 10:1359
Abenaqua, Solomon 15:1300
Abenardut, see ARDUT
Abenaso, Lunbroso 5:594
Abenatar (fam. name), see also ATAR; Benatar; Ben Attar
Abenatar, Abraham (nagid) 3:812
Abenatar, Abraham (r., Mogador) 3:813
Abenatar, Abraham (r., Fez), see Abiatar, Abraham ben Solomon
Abenatar, Ḥayyim 3:812
Abenatar, Ḥayyim ben Moses 3:812
Abenatar, Jacob 3:813
Abenatar, Joseph 3:813
Abenatar, Moses 3:812
Abenatar, Shem-Tov 3:812
ABENATAR MELO, DAVID (Mar. poet) 2:65
Abenatar Melo, David (r., Amst.) 2:65
Abenatar Melo, Immanuel 2:65
Abenavez, Moses, see ABBAS, MOSES BEN SAMUEL
Aben-Ayesh, Solomon see ABENAES, SOLOMON
Abenbenist (fam.), see BENVENISTE
Abencabra, Yucef 5:38
ABENDANA (fam.) 2:65
Abendana, Abigail 2:66
Abendana, David (Mar., Amst.) 2:66
- Homem family 8:943
Abendana, David (N.Y.) 2:66
Abendana, Ferdando 2:65
Abendana, Immanuel 2:66
ABENDANA, ISAAC 2:66
ABENDANA, ISAAC SARDO 2:66
ABENDANA, JACOB BEN JOSEPH 2:66
Abendana, Manoel 2:65
Abendana, Mordecai 2:66
ABENDANAN (Mor. fam.) 2:68
- chronicles 14:625
- Fez 6:1256
Abendanan, Asase 2:68
Abendanan, Isaac 2:68; 6:1257
Abendanan, Maimon 2:68
Abendanan, Maimon ben Moses 2:68
Abendanan, Maimon ben Saadiah 2:68
Abendanan, Moses ben Maimon 2:68
Abendanan, Saadiah, see IBN DANNAN, SAADIAH BEN MAIMUN
Abendanan, Saadiah (r.) 2:68
Abendanan, Saadiah (r., poet) 2:68
Abendanan, Samuel (r., Alg.) 2:68
Abendanan, Samuel (writ.) 2:68
Abendanan, Samuel ben Saul 2:68
Abendanan, Saul ben Solomon 2:68 12:345
Abendanan, Solomon 2:68
Abendanan, Solomon ben Saadiah 2:68
Abendblatt (newsp.) 13:1053
- Arbeiter-Zeitung 3:293
- Daily Forward 10:49
- Pinski, David 13:550
Abendheimer (stlr., U.S.) 8:1255
Abend-Post (newsp.) 7:1342; 13:1054
Aben Eleazar, Mosse 6:584
Aben Filca, Jossep 14:859
Aben Filca, Rabi Asser 14:859
Abengalel (fam.), see BENGALIL
"Abenhatens", Judas 2:612
Aben-Josef, Abraham 4:170
Abenlavi (fam.), see CAVALLERIA, DE LA
ABENMENASSE (fam.) 2:69
Abenmenasse, Judah 2:69
Abenmenasse, Samuel 2:69
Abenragel, Ali, see Ali ibn Abi al-Rijal
Aben Sheara, Jacob 15:1348
ABENSUR (fam.) 2:69
- illus: text
Abensur, Aaron 2:70
Abensur, Abraham 2:69
Abensur, Daniel 2:70
Abensur, David 2:70
Abensur, Isaac (Sp.) 2:69
Abensur, Isaac (R., Mor.) 2:69
Abensur, Isaac (dipl., Mor.) 2:69
Abensur, Isaac Leon (It.) 2:70
Abensur, Don Jacob (Sp.) 2:69
Abensur, Jacob (Fr.) 2:70
Abensur, Jacob Reuben (r.) 2:69
- Attar, Judah ibn 3:835
Abensur, Joshua 2:70
Abensur, Louis, see Abensur, Jacob
Abensur, Moses (Mor.) 2:69
Abensur, Moses (mer., Ger.) 2:70
Abensur, Moses of Salé 2:69
Abensur, Samuel (Sp.) 2:69
Abensur, Samuel (Holl.) 2:70
Abensur, Samuel (Tangier) 2:69
Abensur, Shalom 2:69
Abensur, Solomon 2:70
ABENVIVES (fam.) 2:70
- Murviedro 12:531
Abenvives, Isaac 2:70
Abenvives, Joseph (admin.) 2:70
Abenvives, Joseph (Sp.) 11:494
Abenvives, Samuel 2:70
Abenyaex, Solomon, see ABENAES, SOLOMON
Aben-Yuly (fam.), see YULY
Aben-Yuly, Joseph Levy 16:895
Aben-Yuly, Judah 16:895
Aben-Yuly, Samuel ben Baruch Levy 16:895
Aben-Yuly, Samuel Levy 16:895
Aben-Yuly, Solomon Levy 16:895
Abenzara, Judah 11:917
Abenzardel, Moses, see ABZARADIEL, MOSES
Aben Zemerro, Isaac 5:4
Aben Zemerro, Moses 5:4
ABER, ADOLF 12:679
Abercrombie, Lascelles 10:459
Abercrombie, Patrick 9:580
Aberdam, Alfred 13:117
Aberdare (tn., Wales) 16:251
ABERDEEN (city, Scot.) 2:70
- Scotland 14:1036
- illus: text
Aberdeen (city, S.D.) 15:213
Aberdeen (city, Wash.) 16:356
Aberdeen Bible (15th cent. ms. It.) 8:1270
- illus: 4:967; 8:1284
Aberg, Einar 15:551
Abergel (fam.), see BERGEL
Aberle (London), Reb, see NATHAN, ABRAHAM
Aberlin (mart., Baden) 10:227
Abernathy, Ralph D. 12:932
Abezethibod (demon) 15:119
Abgar (k., Edessa) 4:858
Abgar V (k., Edessa) 6:366
Abgar VII (k., Edessa) 6:366
Abi-Afeta Ban Ab-Ḥisdah see ABU AL-FAT
Abiatar (fam. name), see also ATAR; Benatar; Ben Attar
Abiatar, Abraham ben Solomon 3:812
Abiathar (s., Aaron) 13:1077
ABIATHAR (bib. fig.) 2:71
- priestly descent 13:1072
- Samuel, Book of 14:788
- Solomon 15:97
ABIATHAR BEN ELIJAH HA-KOHEN (gaon) 2:72
- Solomon ben Elijah 15:122
- Tripoli 15:1397
- Tyre 7:323; 15:1489
Abib (name of month) 5:48
Abiba'al (Tyrian k.), see Aviba'al
Abichabod, see ICHABOD
ABICHT, JOHANN GEORG 2:72
- Hebraists 8:21
- illus:
- - Porta Accentuum (1715) 5:128, 129
'Ābid, Ezra Menasheh 12:1464
Abidani, Simon ben Benjamin 10:1298
Abidjan (Ivory Coast) 9:440
Abiel (bib. fig.) 10:1063; 14:914
Abi-eshuh (k., Mesop.) 16:1490
ABIEZER (bib. figs.; clan) 2:73
ABIGAIL (w., David) 2:73
- in the Arts 5:1334
- geneal. table: 5:1341
- illus:
- - bearing gifts to King David 3:527
- - Nabal and 12:736
ABIGAIL (sis., David) 2:74
- Amasa 2:794
- Nahash 12:771
ABI-ḤASIRA (fam.) 2:74
Abi-Ḥasira, Ayyush 2:74
Abi-Ḥasira, David 2:75
Abi-Hasira, Isaac 2:75
Abi-Ḥasira, Jacob ben Ayyush 2:74; 5:1236
Abi-Ḥasira, Jacob ben Masoud 2:74
Abi-Ḥasira, Makhlouf 2:74
Abi-Ḥasira, Samuel 2:74
Abi-Ḥasira, Yaḥya 2:74
ABIHU (bib. fig.) 2:75
- aggadah 12:750
- cause of death 6:238
- mourning rites 13:1081
- illus:
- - consumed by fire 12:750
Abijah (s., Samuel) 14:781
ABIJAH (k., Judah) 2:75
- Ahijah the Shilonite 2:460
- chronological chart 8:766-767
- history 8:595ff
- kingship 10:1016
- geneal. table: 5:1341
Abijah (s., Jeroboam I) 2:460
Abijah (pr. clan) 12:89
Abila (tn., Coele-Syr.) 2:76
- Abel Shittim 2:62
- coinage 5:720
- Decapolis 5:1449
Abileah, A., see Niezwicski, A.
Abilene (city, Tex.) 15:1036
ABILENE (dist. Syr.) 2:76
Abimai (gaon), see Ivomai
ABIMELECH (k., Gerar) 2:76
- Abraham 13:404
- Genesis, Book of 7:389
- Gerar 7:432
- Sarah 14:866
- illus:
- - espying Isaac and Rebekah 9:3
ABIMELECH (s. of Gideon) 2:77
- Baal-Berith temple 4:1
- Bible history 8:585
- Judges, Book of 10:447
- proscription and Shechem 8:347
- war and warfare 16:277
- illus:
- - slaying his brothers 9:1342
Abimelech (pr.), see AHIMELECH
Abimelech (Apoc. fig.) 4:276
ABINADAB (bib. fig.) 2:78
- ark 13:1077
- Uzzah 16:43
Abinadab ben Saadiah Halevi of Mardin 11:951
Abinafia, Aaron 13:1581
Abinnaxim (fam.), see ABENMENASSE
Abinun, Abram 15:1360
ABIOB, AARON 2:78
Abiob, Simon David, of Hebron 12:424
Abiob, Solomon 2:78
ABIR, DAVID 2:79
Abiram (bib. fig.), see DATHAN AND ABIRAM
Abiram, Y. 6:735
Abish, Abraham 11:811
Abisha (s., Phinehas) 13:267; 14:753

ABISHAG THE SHUNAMMITE **2:**79
- Adonijah **2:**295
- in the Arts **5:**1334
- Shulammite **14:**1475
ABISHAI (bib. fig.) **2:**79
- Joab **10:**106
- Orpah **12:**1478
- *geneal. table:* **5:**1342
Abisha' Scroll (Samar. Bib.) **13:**267; **14:**753
Abishua ben Phinehas **14:**736
- *illus:*
- - Passover sacrifice **14:**743
ABITBOL (fam.) **2:**80
- Fez **6:**1257
Abitbol, Amor ben Solomon **2:**80
Abitbol, Ḥayyim Elijah **2:**80
Abitbol, Raphael (18/19 cent.) **2:**80
Abitbol, Raphael (19th cent.) **2:**80
Abitbol, Saul Jeshua ben Isaac **2:**80
Abitur, Joseph ibn **8:**533
Abi Uṣaybi'a, Ibn, *see* Ibn Abi Uṣaybi'a
Abi Zimra, Abraham ben Meir **2:**81
Abi Zimra, David ben Solomon ibn, *see* DAVID BEN SOLOMON IBN ABI ZIMRA
ABI ZIMRA, ISAAC MANDIL BEN ABRAHAM **2:**81
Abkarib As'ad, *see* As'ad, Abkarib
ABKHAZ AUTONOMOUS SOVIET SOCIALIST REPUBLIC **2:**81
Ablaccon (magician) **2:**37
Ableson, Frankie, *see* VAUGHAN, FRANKIE
ABLUTION **2:**81
- *Contents:*
- - Introduction **2:**81
- - Complete Immersion **2:**82
- - Washing the Hands and Feet **2:**84
- - Washing the Hands **2:**84
- apostasy **3:**205
- bathing **4:**319
- corpse immersion **4:**1521
- Essenes **6:**899
- Falashas **6:**1147
- Frankists **7:**64
- hemerobaptists **14:**1087
- hygiene **8:**1140
- hyssop **8:**1148
- impurity **13:**1405ff
- John the Baptist **10:**161
- Koran **10:**1198
- *mayim aḥaronim* **11:**1147
- *netilat yadayim* **12:**998
- *niddah* **12:**1142ff
- *niddui* for disregard **8:**351
- proselytes **13:**1183
- Qumran community **6:**64
- red heifer **14:**9
- Samaritans **14:**744; **14:**747
- *illus:*
- - text
- - Andernach ritual bathhouse **2:**946
- - bride's key casket, Italy **11:**1039
- - immersion in a natural pool **11:**1534
- - laver for kohanim **6:**1402
- - laver in tabernacle **15:**679
- - lion-shaped laver **11:**266
- - Masada *mikveh* **11:**1087
- - *mikveh* **11:**1535–1542
- - Padua synagogue laver **13:**11
- - ritual immersion before setting of the sun **15:**1033
- - Tedeschi laver **14:**252
- - *tohorah* plate **15:**1188
- - washing the hands **12:**999; **16:**693
- *see also* MIKVEH
Abnarrabi (fam.) **14:**864; **15:**809
Abnarrabi, Ishmael **14:**864
Abnarrabi, Joshua **14:**864
Abnarrabi, Solomon **14:**861
Abnarrabi, Vidal **14:**864
ABNER (bib. fig.) **2:**87
- Hebron **8:**226
- Joab **10:**107
- Palti **13:**49
Abner Bar Ner Ha-Sharoni, *see* BASHIRI, YAḤYA
ABNER OF BURGOS **2:**88
- Albalag **2:**521
- apostasy **3:**203ff; **15:**233
- Avila, Prophet of **3:**970
- Christian Kabbalah **10:**643
- Crescas' refutation of **5:**787
- Disputation of Valladolid **16:**60
- free will **7:**129
- philosophy **13:**445
- Pollegar **13:**835
ABOAB (fam.) **2:**89
- *geneal. table.* **2:**91
Aboab, Abraham (conv.) **2:**93
Aboab, Abraham (mer.) **2:**89
Aboab, Abraham ben Samuel (It.) **2:**95
Aboab, Daniel Semah **2:**89
Aboab, David (Mar.) **2:**95
Aboab, David (conv.) **2:**89
Aboab, David ben Samuel (It.) **2:**95
Aboab, Elias **2:**89
Aboab, Gracia **2:**90
ABOAB, IMMANUEL **2:**89
- *Nomologia* **8:**556
- *geneal. table:* **2:**91
- *illus:*
- - Nomologia (1629) **8:**566
ABOAB, ISAAC (14th cent.) **2:**90
- *Contents:*
- - General **2:**90
- - Sources **2:**91
- - Thought **2:**91
- - Al-Nakawa's *Menorat-ha-Ma'or* **2:**92
- - Other Works **2:**92
- Al-Nakawa **2:**673ff
- ethical literature **11:**344
- *geneal. table:* text
- *illus:*
- - synagogue **14:**631
ABOAB, ISAAC (15th cent.) **2:**93
- *geneal. table:* **2:**91
Aboab, Isaac (16th cent.) **2:**89
Aboab, Isaac da Fonseca, *see* ABOAB DA FONSECA, ISAAC
ABOAB, ISAAC DE MATTATHIAS **2:**93
- *geneal. table:* **2:**91
Aboab, Jacob ben Isaac **2:**93
ABOAB, JACOB BEN SAMUEL **2:**94
- *geneal. table:* **2:**92
Aboab, Joseph ben Samuel **2:**95
Aboab, Mattathias **2:**93
Aboab, Moses (Braz., N.Y.) **2:**89
Aboab, Moses (polem.) **2:**89
ABOAB, SAMUEL BEN ABRAHAM **2:**94
- Gedaliah, Abraham **7:**354
- ransom of captives **5:**155
- *geneal. table:* **2:**92
Aboab Cardozo, Abigail **3:**527; **14:**1061
ABOAB DA FONSECA, ISAAC **2:**95
- Amsterdam Talmud Torah **2:**896; **2:**897
- Bible translation **14:**1168
- bibliophiles **4:**974
- portrait **2:**148
- Recife **13:**1613
Aboaf (fam.), *see* ABOAB
Abod, Nissim Moses **11:**1159
Abolafia, *see also* Abulafia
Abolafia, Juan Fernandez **2:**184
Abolafia, Samuel **2:**184; **12:**530
ABOMINATION **2:**96
- divination **6:**115
ABOMINATION OF DESOLATION (idol) **2:**97
ABONY (city, Hung.) **2:**98
ABORTION **2:**98
- *Contents:*
- - In the Biblical Period **2:**98
- - In the Talmudic Period **2:**99
- - In the Codes **2:**100
- - In the State of Israel **2:**101
- responsa on Nazi atrocities **14:**94
- *see also:* BIRTH CONTROL
Aboulker (fam., Alg.), *see* ABULKER
ABRABANEL (fam., It.) **2:**101
- Arezzo bankers **3:**408
- Medici, Cosimo de' **6:**1359
- *geneal. table:* **2:**103
Abrabanel, Abraham **2:**102
ABRABANEL, ABRAVANEL (fam.) **2:**102
Abrabanel, Benvenida **2:**101
- Reuveni, David **14:**114
ABRABANEL, ISAAC BEN JUDAH **2:**103
- *Contents:*
- - General **2:**103
- - Biblical Exegesis **2:**105
- - Philosophy **2:**107
- Aboab, Isaac **2:**93
- Affonso V **2:**326
- angels **2:**972
- Apulia **3:**228
- Arama, Isaac **3:**258
- Arcila Jews **3:**399
- articles of faith **3:**659
- astrology **3:**793
- Averroes **3:**952; **3:**953
- banking **4:**171
- Bibago, Abraham **4:**812
- Bible exegesis **4:**894; **11:**325
- biography **4:**1011
- cosmic cycles **10:**582
- exile meaning **7:**288ff
- family **2:**101
- *Haggadah* **7:**1093
- usury and gentiles **12:**251
- kabbalist apocalypse **10:**544
- philosophy **11:**342; **13:**450ff
- tax farming **16:**1291
- Toledo **15:**1198
- Torah **15:**1238; **15:**1241
- Torquemada, Tomás de **15:**1265
- trade and commerce **15:**1300
- *geneal. table:* text
- *illus:*
- - *Perush ha-Torah* (1579) **5:**1131
Abrabanel, Isaac ben Judah (15/16 cent.) **2:**109
Abrabanel, Jacob (It.) **2:**101
Abrabanel, Jacob (bnk.) **2:**102; **3:**408
Abrabanel, Jonas **11:**856
Abrabanel, Joseph (physic.) **2:**101; **2:**105
Abrabanel, Joseph (mer.) **2:**101
Abrabanel, Joseph (It.) **2:**102
Abrabanel, Judah (fin., Port.) **2:**103
ABRABANEL, JUDAH (philos.) **2:**109
- Cervantes, Miguel de **5:**313
- cosmic cycles **10:**582
- Crescas, Ḥasdai **5:**1085
- history chart **8:**766-767
- Italian literature **9:**1107
- microcosm doctrine **11:**1503
- Neoplatonism **12:**961ff
- philosophy **11:**342; **13:**450ff
- soul **15:**174
- *geneal. table:* **2:**103
Abrabanel, Judah (bnk., It.) **2:**102
Abrabanel, Judah of Córdoba **2:**102
Abrabanel, Samuel (fin.) **2:**101ff
- Widmanstetter, J. A. **16:**487
Abrabanel, Samuel, of Seville **2:**102
Abrabanel, Solomon **4:**1270
Abrabanel, Veleida **2:**102
ABRACADABRA **2:**111
Abracasus (holy name) **7:**369
ABRAHAM (patriarch) **2:**111
- *Contents:*
- - General **2:**111
- - The Biblical Data: Genesis (11:26-25:10) **2:**112
- - The Biblical Data: In the Rest of the Bible **2:**113
- - The Image of Abraham **2:**114
- - The Critical View **2:**114
- - In the Aggadah **2:**115
- - In Jewish Philosophy **2:**117
- - In Christian Tradition **2:**119
- - In Islamic Tradition **2:**119
- - In Medieval Hebrew Literature **2:**121
- Biblical Figure
- - Abimelech **2:**76; **13:**404
- - *Akedah* **2:**480
- - God's covenant **5:**1018ff
- - Melchizedek **11:**1287
- - Nimrod **12:**1167ff
- - Isaac **9:**1ff
- - Ishmael **9:**80
- - Kedemites **10:**865
- - Lot **11:**507ff
- - patriarchs **13:**181
- - Raphael **13:**1549
- - revelation **14:**117
- - sacrifice **14:**605
- - Sarah **14:**866
- - Satan **14:**903
- - Sodom, **15:**70
- In Jewish Tradition
- - Abraham's bosom **2:**165
- - angelology **2:**961
- - ethics **6:**934, 937
- - magic **11:**707
- - marriage **8:**1316
- - morning prayer **14:**1257
- - primogeniture **6:**1307
- - proselytes named after **13:**1184
- - purity **13:**1414
- - *tashlikh* custom **15:**829
- - *zekhut avot* **16:**976
- In Jewish Literature
- - *Apocalypse of Abraham* **2:**126
- - apocalyptic literature **2:**128
- - illuminated *maḥzorim* **11:**733; **11:**735
- - Josephus **8:**298
- - Naḥmanides **12:**777
- - *Sefer Yeẓirah* **10:**508; **16:**786
- - *Testament of Abraham* **2:**129
- - *Yesod Olam* **16:**908
- In Islam **9:**93
- - eschatology **6:**885
- Modern Research
- - adoption **2:**298
- - anthropolgy **3:**41ff
- - economic history **16:**1267
- - family origin **3:**305
- - Genesis **7:**390
- - Heracles myth **8:**333
- - Hurrian customs **12:**1287ff
- - patriarchal history **8:**573ff
- *illus:*
- - "Abraham Looking at the Stars" (E. M. Lilien) Fig. 86 **3**-ART
- - cast into fire by Nimrod **8:**1217; **12:**1166
- - ceremonial object motif **4:**1231,1339
- - death **5:**1421
- - Dura-Europos wall paint. **6:**283
- - God's covenant with **5:**1014, 1016
- - meeting Melchizedek **9:**1552
- - preparing to shear Melchizedek **11:**1288
- - sacrifice of Isaac **2:**120,121,480-486; **3:**511, 615; **4:**244,880,1231,1339; **6:**285; **8:**1272, 1286; **15:**673
- - sending Hagar away **7:**1075,1076
- - separation from Lot **11:**507

– – visitation by the three angels
3:543; 4:938; 8:1031; 14:867
Abraham (Bav.) 12:521
Abraham (mintmaster, Pol.) 12:61
Abraham (15th cent., Tun.) 15:1439
Abraham (15th cent., It.) 13:122
Abraham (16th cent., physic., Rus.)
12:1245
Abraham (Musician of Mantua), *see* Abraham "Musician of Mantua"
ABRAHAM (fam.) 2:125
– *illus:* text
Abraham, Abraham 2:125
– department stores 5:1546
Abraham, Adolph 11:1561
ABRAHAM, APOCALYPSE OF 2:125
Abraham, Bernard 11:1562
Abraham, Chapman 5:1566; 15:114
ABRAHAM, DAVID 15:1077
Abraham, Don (trans., Sp.) 15:252
Abraham, Jacob 3:539; 11:1173
ABRAHAM, KARL 2:127
ABRAHAM, MAX 2:128
ABRAHAM, OTHER BOOKS OF 2:128
ABRAHAM, OTTO 12:679
Abraham, Pierre 7:147
ABRAHAM, SAMUEL 2:129
ABRAHAM, TESTAMENT OF (apoc.) 2:129
– Falashas 6:1151
– Hellenistic literature 8:304
– Origen 2:128
Abraham, Vidal 3:523
Abraham Aaron, *see* Koidanov, Abraham Aaron, of Pukhovichi
Abraham Abba-Joseph of Soroca 11:628
ABRAHAM ABELE BEN ABRAHAM SOLOMON 2:129
– *illus:*
– – *haskamah* to *Te'udah be-Yisrael* 7:1453
Abraham Abele ben Israel Isser 2:143
ABRAHAM ABUSCH (Lissa) BEN ZEVI HIRSCH 2:130
"Abraham and Isaac" (etch., Rembrandt) 9:3
ABRAHAM A SANCTA CLARA 2:130
Abraham Avigdor of Marseilles, *see* Avigdor, Abraham, of Marseilles
Abraham Axelrod, *see* ABRAHAM BEN ALEXANDER OF COLOGNE
ABRAHAM BAR ḤIYYA 2:130
– *Contents:*
– – General 2:130
– – Philosophy 2:131
– – Mathematical Works 2:132
– – Astronomical Works 2:132
– – Astrology and Eschatology 2:132
– astrology 3:791ff
– astronomy 3:801; 3:802
– *Bahir, Sefer ha-* 4:99
– Barcelona 4:209
– Creation 6:695
– Decalogue 5:1447
– evil 7:777
– geographical studies 7:420ff
– Hebrew language 16:1622
– Kabbalah 10:520
– Messiah 11:1414
– Neoplatonism 12:961
– philosophy 11:339; 13:436
– soul 15:174
– soul, immortality of 15:177
– soul in Kabbalah 10:609
– *illus.*
– – astrolabe (drawing) 3:786
– – eclipses 3:797,800
– – *Zurat ha-Areẓ ve-Tavnit Kaddurei ha-Raki'a* 4:303; 7:422
Abraham ben Aaron (gaon) 7:323
Abraham ben Abraham, *see* POTOCKI, VALENTINE
ABRAHAM BEN ALEXANDER KATZ OF KALISK 2:133
– *aliyah* 9:514
– Menaham Mendel of Vitebsk 11:1311
– Shneur Zalman of Lyady 14:1433
ABRAHAM BEN ALEXANDER OF COLOGNE 2:134
– Kabbalah 10:527
– *Sefirot* doctrine 10:568
Abraham ben Aroya 13:1038
Abraham ben Aryeh Loeb Ḥayyim ha-Kohen of Mogilev 10:214
Abraham ben Asher (of Safed) 2:564
Abraham ben Asher (emis.) 2:611
ABRAHAM BEN AVIGDOR 2:134
ABRAHAM BEN AZRIEL 2:135
– Baruch of Regensburg 4:278
Abraham ben Baḥye, *see* Abraham ibn Baḥya
ABRAHAM BEN BENJAMIN ZE'EV BRISKER 2:135
Abraham ben Bolat 11:27
ABRAHAM BEN DANIEL 2:136
ABRAHAM BEN DAVID MAIMUNI (nagid, Egy.) 2:136
ABRAHAM BEN DAVID OF POSQUIÈRES (Rabad) 2:136
– anthropomorphism 3:56
– articles of faith 10:385
– Asher ben David 3:706
– chronological chart 8:766-767
– *ḥiddushim* 8:465
– Jacob Nazir 9:1232
– Kabbalah 10:519; 10:523
– Maimonides 11:759ff
– *Mishneh Torah* 5:641,651
– Naḥmanides 12:781
– responsa 14:87
– resurrection 14:101
– Talmud commentaries 11:330
– Temple Mount 15:990
– woman 16:627
– yeshivah 16:763
Abraham ben David al-Kafrmandi 10:888
ABRAHAM BEN DOV OF MEZHIRECH (ha-Malakh) 2:140
Abraham ben Eliezer (13th cent.) 2:557
ABRAHAM BEN ELIEZER HA-LEVI (ha-Zaken; kab.) 2:140
– emissary 14:1366
– Kabbalah 10:543
– *kiddush ha-shem* 10:984
– Reformation 14:19
ABRAHAM BEN ELIEZER HA-LEVI BERUKHIM 2:141
– Falashas 6:1144
– Kabbalah 10:546
– Morocco 12:335
Abraham ben Elijah (Kar. schol.) 12:420
ABRAHAM BEN ELIJAH OF VILNA 2:142
Abraham ben Elisha ben Mattathias 10:1002
ABRAHAM BEN GARTON BEN ISAAC 2:142
– incunabula 8:1323
– *illus:*
– – Rashi's Pentateuch commentary 14:38; 15:1483
Abraham ben Ḥakun 15:1172
ABRAHAM BEN ḤALFON 2:142
Abraham ben Hananiah 12:907
Abraham ben Hassan 11:27
Abraham ben Ḥayun ben Waqqāṣa 16:265
Abraham ben Ḥayyim (Prov. paytan) 14:106
ABRAHAM BEN ḤAYYIM (Heilprin; Pol.) 2:143
ABRAHAM BEN ḤAYYIM, THE DYER (It. print.) 2:143
– incunabula 8:1323
– typography 15:1480
– *illus:*
– – Pentateuch (Bologna, 1482) 15:1483
Abraham ben Ḥayyim ha-Kohen (13th cent. r.) 14:814
Abraham ben Hezekiah 9:21
ABRAHAM BEN HILLEL (Ben Nissim) OF FOSTAT 2:143
Abraham ben Isaac (paytan, Babyl.) 13:575
Abraham ben Isaac (paytan, It.) 13:575
ABRAHAM BEN ISAAC (Gerondi; kab.) 2:144
– *Aḥot Ketannah* 2:469
Abraham ben Isaac (print., Er. Isr.), *see* Ashkenazi, Abraham ben Isaac
Abraham ben Isaac (print., Sp.) 8:474,1325
Abraham ben Isaac (cmty. ldr., Pol.) 15:815
ABRAHAM BEN ISAAC HA-KOHEN BEN AL-FURAT 2:144
– Ali ben Amram 2:631
– Solomon ben Judah 15:123
ABRAHAM BEN ISAAC HA-KOHEN OF ZAMOSC 2:144
ABRAHAM BEN ISAAC HA-LEVI 2:145
– *see also:* TAMAKH, ABRAHAM BEN ISAAC HA-LEVI
Abraham ben Isaac Nagid 12:61; 13:710
ABRAHAM BEN ISAAC OF GRANADA (kab.) 2:145
Abraham ben Isaac of Granada (au.) 2:145
ABRAHAM BEN ISAAC OF MONTPELLIER 2:146
ABRAHAM BEN ISAAC OF NARBONNE 2:146
– Abraham of Granada 2:146
– *Hadran* 7:1054
– Ibn Migash 8:1189
– Kabbalah 10:519
– responsa 14:87
Abraham ben Isaac Shalom 5:313
Abraham ben Israel (print., Ger.) 13:1106
ABRAHAM BEN ISRAEL OF BRODY (kab., It.) 2:147
Abraham ben Jacob (trav.) 7:420
Abraham ben Jacob (paytan) 13:575
Abraham ben Jacob (paytan, Ger.) 13:575
ABRAHAM BEN JACOB (engr., Holl.) 2:148
– illustrated *Haggadah* 7:1102
– mapmakers 11:918
– *illus:*
– – *Amsterdam Haggadah* (1695) 3:536
– – Ereẓ Israel, Hebrew map 11:927
– – prayer for women in childbirth 4:1050
Abraham Ben-Jalil 15:1172
ABRAHAM BEN JEHIEL MICHAL HA-KOHEN 2:148
– *gematriot* 7:373
– *illus:* text
Abraham ben Jehiel of Rome 12:859
Abraham ben Joseph ha-Kohen (paytan) 13:575
ABRAHAM BEN JOSEPH (Yoske) OF LISSA (Leszno) 2:149
Abraham ben Joseph of Orleans 4:410
Abraham ben Joshua of Worms 4:562
ABRAHAM BEN JOSIAH TROKI (Kar. physic.) 2:149
ABRAHAM BEN JOSIAH YERUSHALMI (Kar. schol.) 2:149
ABRAHAM BEN JUDAH BEN ABRAHAM (Kar. schol.) 2:150
Abraham ben Judah Berlin (r., Ger.) 7:1175
Abraham ben Judah of Narbonne 10:354
Abraham ben Mattathias 13:575
ABRAHAM BEN MAZHIR 2:150
– gaonate, Syria 7:323
Abraham ben Mereno ha-Kohen (paytan) 13:575
ABRAHAM BEN MORDECAI HA-LEVI 2:150
ABRAHAM BEN MOSES BEN MAIMON 2:150
– *Contents:*
– – General 2:150
– – Philosophy 2:152
– Isaac ibn Shuwaykh 7:321
– mysticism 10:513
– Maimonides 11:757ff
– Maimonidean controversy 11:750
– *nagid* 12:762
– philosophy 13:444
– responsa 14:86
– *illus:*
– – autograph 3:913
ABRAHAM BEN MOSES HA-KOHEN HA-SEPHARDI 2:153
– Finzi-Norsa controversy 6:1301
– Joseph ha-Kohen 10:241
Abraham ben Moses Ismail 9:1375
Abraham ben Moses of Sinzheim 14:778
Abraham ben Moses Yatom 5:31
Abraham ben Mūsā 12:335; 14:633
Abraham ben Nagid, *see* Abraham ben Isaac Nagid
ABRAHAM BEN NATHAN (11/12 cent., r., Egy.) 2:153
ABRAHAM BEN NATHAN (nagid, Tun.) 2:153
– Judah of Kairouan 10:348
– *nagid* 12:760
– Tunisia 15:1439
Abraham ben Nathan (19th cent., r., Egy.) 14:304
ABRAHAM BEN NATHAN HA-YARḤI ("of Lunel") 2:154
ABRAHAM BEN N . . . HA-BAGHDADI 2:154
Abraham ben Peraḥyah ben Yajo 7:1365; 11:681
Abraham ben Quiqui, *see* Quiqui, Abraham ben
Abraham ben Raphael 3:728
Abraham ben Sahlan 15:123
Abraham ben Samuel (paytan) 13:575
Abraham ben Samuel (Er. Isr.) 11:1453
Abraham ben Samuel (schol., Ger.) 14:809
Abraham ben Samuel ben David ha-Levi (r., Pol.) 14:806
ABRAHAM BEN SAMUEL HE-ḤASID (of Speyer) 2:155
– book collection 4:973
ABRAHAM BEN SAMUEL OF DREUX 2:155
ABRAHAM BEN SHABBETAI HA-KOHEN (Zante) 2:155
– *self-portrait:* text
Abraham ben Shabbetai (poet, Egy.) 12:425
Abraham ben Sherira (gaon) 7:320
Abraham ben Shoshan, *see* Ibn Shoshan, Abraham
ABRAHAM BEN SIMEON OF

WORMS **2**:155
Abraham ben Solomon (Pal. schol.) **15**:122
ABRAHAM BEN SOLOMON (exegete) **2**:156
Abraham ben Solomon (print., Turk.) **9**:1098
ABRAHAM BEN SOLOMON OF SAINT MAXIMIN **2**:156
ABRAHAM BEN SOLOMON OF TORRUTIEL **2**:157
- Jewish history **11**:348
- Morocco **12**:332
- *Sefer ha-Kabbalah* **8**:556
Abraham ben Solomon of Treves (kab., It.) **10**:542
Abraham ben Sur **14**:304
Abraham ben Ways (Wach) **14**:626
Abraham ben Yashar, *see* ABU SA'D AL-TUSTARI
Abraham ben Yom Tov **8**:1268
- *illus:*
- - *Bishop Bedell Bible* **4**:*fcg.* 940
Abraham ben Ẓevi Hirsch of Lissau **5**:614
Abraham David of Buczacz **12**:868; **14**:1461
Abraham David of Miropolye **10**:727
Abraham dei Tintori, *see* ABRAHAM BEN ḤAYYIM, THE DYER
Abraham de Lunel **7**:383
Abraham de Toledo, *see* Toledo, Abraham de
Abraham di Boton **11**:1212
Abraham di Tibériade **6**:1030
ABRAHAM DOV BAER OF OVRUCH **2**:157
- *aliyah* **9**:514
Abraham Dov Mikhailishker, *see* LEBENSOHN, ABRAHAM DOV
Abraham the Dyer (Jer.) **13**:340
ABRAHAM EL-BARCHILON **2**:157
- Toledo **15**:1203
Abraham the Elder (Egy.) **9**:76
Abraham Elimelech of Karlin, *see* Karlin, Abraham Elimelech of
Abraham fil'Deulecresse **12**:1226
ABRAHAM GAON **2**:158
ABRAHAM GERSHON OF KUTOW **2**:158
- *aliyah* **7**:1392; **9**:514
- Ba'al Shem Tov **9**:1053
- Beth-El yeshivah **9**:293
- Hebron **8**:233
- Kabbalah **10**:554
- travels **15**:1353
- *geneal. table:* **9**:1052
Abraham Guer of Cordova, *see* ESCUDERO, LORENZO
ABRAHAM HA-BAVLI **2**:158
- linguistics **16**:1382
Abraham ha-Bedersi **2**:231
Abraham ha-Kohen (paytan) **13**:577
Abraham ha-Kohen (11th cent., Ger.) **10**:720
Abraham ha-Kohen (14th cent., Ger.) **15**:1128
ABRAHAM HA-LEVI (emis.) **2**:158
Abraham ha-Levi (r., Ott. Emp.) **16**:1548
Abraham of Hamburg, *see* NATHAN, ABRAHAM
Abraham Ḥayyim (r., Jer.) **14**:734
ABRAHAM ḤAYYIM BEN GEDALIAH (r., Gal.) **2**:159
Abraham Ḥayyim of Zloczow **9**:1079
Abraham Ḥazzan Gerondi, *see* ABRAHAM BEN ISAAC
Abraham the Hebrew, *see* Abensur, Moses
Abraham he-Ḥasid (he-Ḥaver), *see* Abraham the Pious
Abrahami, Ẓevi (pseud.), *see* ABRAMOWITZ, GRIGORI
Abraham ibn Arama **8**:1203
Abraham ibn Baḥya **6**:574; **12**:1467
Abraham ibn Ezra (Sp.) *see* IBN EZRA, ABRAHAM
Abraham ibn Ezra (r., Turk.) **8**:1174; **9**:1163
Abraham ibn Ḥen, *see* Ḥen, Abraham ibn
Abraham ibn Ḥisdai, *see* Ibn Ḥisdai, Abraham
Abrham ibn Megas, *see* Ibn Migash, Abraham
Abraham ibn Qamni'el, *see* Ibn Qamni'el, Abraham
Abraham ibn Saba **14**:849
Abraham Israel, *see* Israel, Abraham
Abraham Issachar ha-Kohen of Radomsko, *see* Radomsko, Abraham Issachar ha-Kohen of
ABRAHAMITES (Judaiz. sect) **2**:159
Abrahamites (Frankist sect) **7**:68
Abraham Jedidiah ha-Ezraḥi **8**:1323
Abraham Jordanis **11**:180
ABRAHAM JOSHUA HESCHEL OF APTA (Opatow) **2**:159
ABRAHAM JUDAEUS BOHEMUS **2**:160
- chronological chart **8**:766-767
Abraham Kabassi Gaon **6**:117
Abraham Kahana (gaon) **7**:318
Abraham Kohen (paytan) **13**:577
Abraham Leib (r.) **4**:1213
Abraham "l'Espagnol" **5**:1074
Abraham Levi (the Elder) **15**:1005
"Abraham Looking at the Stars" (drg., E. M. Lilien) Fig. 86 **3**-ART
Abraham Maimuni, *see* ABRAHAM BEN MOSES BEN MAIMON
Abraham Meir of Bar **9**:15
Abraham Melamed of Avila **3**:969
Abraham Mordecai of Pinczow **14**:635
Abraham Moses of Mir **15**:1141
Abraham Moses of Przysucha **14**:1570
Abraham Moses of Rozprze **13**:1297
Abraham Mosse de Montepessulano **4**:370
Abraham Motal ha-Paytan, *see* Ha-Paytan, Abraham Motal
Abraham "Musician of Mantua" **3**:496
Abraham Nehemiah ben Joseph **3**:230
Abraham Nuñez Bernal **2**:67
Abraham of Apta, *see* ABRAHAM JOSHUA HESCHEL OF APTA
Abraham of Aschaffenburg **3**:687
ABRAHAM (Ben Aaron) OF BAGHDAD **2**:161
ABRAHAM OF BEJA **2**:161
- travels **15**:1349
Abraham of Béziers **8**:686
Abraham of Bohemia, *see* ABRAHAM JUDAEUS BOHEMUS
Abraham of Brody, *see* ABRAHAM BEN ISRAEL OF BRODY
Abraham of Buczacz, *see* Abraham David of Buczacz
Abraham of Cologne, *see* ABRAHAM BEN ALEXANDER OF COLOGNE
Abraham of Dreux, *see* ABRAHAM BEN SAMUEL OF DREUX
Abraham of Fostat, *see* ABRAHAM BEN HILLEL OF FOSTAT
Abraham of Granada, *see* ABRAHAM BEN ISAAC OF GRANADA
Abraham of Ishpurk **13**:1189
Abraham of Kalisk, *see* ABRAHAM BEN ALEXANDER KATZ OF KALISK
Abraham of Karlin, *see* Karlin, Abraham Elimelech of
Abraham of Kitov (Kuty) **8**:233
Abraham of Lissa, *see* ABRAHAM BEN JOSEPH OF LISSA
Abraham of Marseilles, *see* Avigdor, Abraham, of Marseilles
Abraham of Medinaceli **11**:1214; **14**:712
Abraham of Mezhirech, *see* ABRAHAM BEN DOV OF MEZHIRECH
Abraham of Miropolye, *see* Abraham David of Miropolye
Abraham of Montpellier, *see* ABRAHAM BEN ISAAC OF MONTPELLIER
Abraham of Mulhausen, *see* Breslau, Abraham of Mulhausen
Abraham of Narbonne, *see* ABRAHAM BEN ISAAC OF NARBONNE
Abraham of Ovruch, *see* ABRAHAM DOV BAER OF OVRUCH
Abraham of Perpignan, *see* BONAFOS, MENAHEM BEN ABRAHAM
Abraham of Pesaro **3**:963
Abraham of Posquières, *see* ABRAHAM BEN DAVID OF POSQUIÈRES
Abraham of Prosnitz **11**:30
Abraham of Radomsko, *see* Radomsko, Abraham Issachar ha-Kohen of
Abraham of Ragola, *see* RAGOLER, ABRAHAM BEN SOLOMON
Abraham of Saint Maximin, *see* ABRAHAM BEN SOLOMON OF SAINT MAXIMIN
Abraham of Sancta Clara, *see* ABRAHAM A SANCTA CLARA
ABRAHAM OF SARAGOSSA **2**:161
ABRAHAM OF SARTEANO **2**:161
Abraham of Siguenza **14**:1527
Abraham of Sochaczew **13**:652
Abraham of Soroca, *see* Abraham Abba-Joseph of Soroca
Abraham of Speyer, *see* ABRAHAM BEN SAMUEL HE-ḤASID
Abraham of Stretyn, *see* Stretyn, Abraham of
Abraham of Theomanari (leg. fig.) **10**:326
Abraham of Torrutiel, *see* ABRAHAM BEN SOLOMON OF TORRUTIEL
Abraham of Toul (tos.) **15**:1285
Abraham of Trisk **15**:1472
Abraham of Turisk **16**:207
Abraham of Vilna, *see* ABRAHAM BEN ELIJAH OF VILNA
Abraham of Worms, *see* ABRAHAM BEN SIMEON OF WORMS
Abraham of Zamość, *see* ABRAHAM BEN ISAAC HA-KOHEN OF ZAMOŚĆ
Abraham the Physician **4**:1289
Abraham the Pious (of Cairo) **2**:143
- library catalog **4**:1237
- Shabbetai Ẓevi **14**:1224
Abraham the Proselyte **3**:195; **13**:1188
ABRAHAMS (fam., Eng.) **2**:162
ABRAHAMS (fam., athletes, Eng.) **2**:162
ABRAHAMS, ABRAHAM (schol., Eng.) **2**:163
- *illus:* text
Abrahams, Abraham (gov't. offic.) **2**:163
ABRAHAMS, ABRAHAM (ed., Eng.) **10**:308; **14**:131
ABRAHAMS, ABRAHAM ISAAC (N. Am.) **2**:164
Abrahams, Abraham Suzman (shoḥet) **2**:162
Abrahams, Sir Adolphe **2**:162
Abrahams, A. M. (S.A.) **15**:198
Abrahams, Barnett **2**:162
ABRAHAMS, GERLAD **1**:27; **5**:408
Abrahams, Harold Maurice **2**:162
- Olympics **12**:1376
Abrahams, Henry **15**:305
ABRAHAMS, ISAAC **2**:164
- universities **15**:1677
Abrahams, Israel (mer., Can.) **7**:1191
ABRAHAMS, ISRAEL (schol.) **2**:164
- *Hebrew ethical wills* **16**:530
- historiography **8**:562
- Singer, Simeon **13**:989; **14**:1615
ABRAHAMS, ISRAEL (r., S. A.) **1**:27; **2**:165
Abrahams, Joseph (r., Austr.) **2**:162
Abrahams, Joseph B. (art., U.S.) **4**:1219
- typography **15**:1479
ABRAHAMS, SIR LIONEL **2**:165
Abrahams, Lionel **15**:209
Abrahams, Moses **2**:162
ABRAHAMS, NICOLAI CHRISTIAN LEVIN **14**:927,934
Abrahams, Rachael Beth-Zion **5**:450; **10**:308
Abrahams, Sir Sidney **2**:162
Abraham Saba **10**:541
Abraham Salomon of Amsterdam **5**:208
Abraham Samson ha-Kohen Katz **9**:1229
ABRAHAM'S BOSOM **2**:165
- *illus:* text
ABRAHAMSEN, DAVID **2**:166
Abraham Seneor, *see* SENEOR, ABRAHAM
Abraham Shalom (emis.) **14**:1358
Abraham Shem Tov of Tortosa **11**:1189
Abrahamsohn, Otto, *see* BRAHM, OTTO
Abraham Solomon ha-Kohen **6**:649
"Abraham's Sacrifice" (Rembrandt van Rijn) **2**:485
Abrahamus, Nicolaus, *see* Abram, Nicolaus
Abraham von Kreuznach, *see* Kreuznach, Abraham von
Abraham von Schlesingen **6**:1345
Abraham Yerushalmi **15**:1329
Abraham Yiju **2**:261
Abraham Zalman **14**:1228
ABRAHAM ẒEVI BEN ELEAZAR **2**:166
ABRAHÃO, COJE **2**:166
ABRAM, MORRIS BERTHOLD **2**:167
- *illus:*
- - A. J. C. delegation to Paul VI **5**:543
Abram, Nicolaus **8**:21
Abram Bonet Avigdor, *see* AVIGDOR, ABRAHAM
Abram de Sala **4**:370
Abra Melin ("The Mage") **2**:156
- book of magic **10**:636
Abramovich, Bernat **4**:1258
Abramovich, Vsevolod **2**:321
Abramovitz, David, *see* ABIR, DAVID
ABRAMOVITZ, MAX (archit.) **2**:167

- *illus:*
- - Lincoln Center Philharmonic Hall, New York **3:**346
ABRAMOVITZ, MOSES **2:**168
Abramovitz, Ze'ev **13:**663
Abramowich-Ginzburg, K. R. **6:**157; **15:**166
Abramowicz, Haim **11:**618
Abramowitsch, Shalom Jacob, *see* MENDELE MOKHER SEFORIM
ABRAMOWITZ, BINA **15:**1077
Abramowitz, David **12:**180; **16:**760
ABRAMOWITZ, EMIL **2:**168
ABRAMOWITZ, GRIGORI **2:**168
ABRAMOWITZ, HERMAN **2:**169
Abramowitz, M. (ed., Pol.) **16:**1348
Abramowitz, Max (act.) **15:**1077
ABRAMOWITZ, RAPHAEL **2:**169
Abrams, Calvin **12:**1123; **15:**301
ABRAMS, CHARLES **2:**170
Abrams, David A. **16:**476
Abrams, Harriet **15:**1054
Abrams, Harry N. **13:**1372
Abrams, Susman **11:**782
Abrams, William **12:**1024
ABRAMSKY, YEḤEZKEL **2:**170
ABRAMSON (Ger. fam.) **2:**171
Abramson, Abraham **2:**171
- art **3:**539
- medalists **11:**1173
- *illus:*
- - Itzig, Daniel (medal) **3:**545
- - medal in honor of emancipation of Westphalian Jews **16:**474
Abramson, George **15:**307
Abramson, Hirsch **2:**172
Abramson, Jacob Abraham **2:**171
Abramson, Lillian S. **5:**451
Abramson, Michael Jacob **2:**172
Abramson, S. (polit., Rus.) **6:**268
Abramson, S. (schol., Jer.) **16:**1336
ABRAMSON, SHRAGA **2:**172
ABRASS, OSIAS (Joshua) **2:**172
- *score:* text
Abravalia, Don Samuel **16:**56
Abravanel (name), *see* Abrabanel
ABRECH (Abrek; term) **2:**173
- Joseph **10:**205
Abresch, Petrus **8:**21
Abrevaya, Samuel **9:**1096
Abromowitz, Moe **15:**304
Abronah (bib. loc.) **10:**300
Abruzzi, Duke D', *see* TEPPER, KOLYA
ABSABAN, SOLOMON **2:**173
ABSALOM (bib. fig.) **2:**174
- Ahithophel **2:**465; **2:**466
- Amasa **2:**793
- Amnon **15:**783
- David **5:**1325, 1329
- Joab **10:**107
- kingship **10:**1016
- naming after **12:**808
- revolt of **5:**1325; **8:**591
- *geneal. table:* **5:**1341
- *illus:*
- - David mourning death of **5:**1326
- - tomb **3:**340
ABSALOM (2nd cent. B.C.E.) **2:**176
ABSALOM (2/1 cent. B.C.E.) **2:**176
ABSALOM (1st cent. C.E.) **2:**176
Absalom, Tomb of **2:**175ff; **9:**1398
- architecture **3:**358
- Clermont-Ganneau **9:**1535
- Herod's Jerusalem **9:**1394
- pillars **13:**522
- *illus:*
- - pilgrims' guide, 16th cent. **13:**513
ABSE, DANNIE **2:**176
Abse, Leo **2:**177
Absolution, *see* FORGIVENESS
Absolution from vows **16:**227
Absorption in Israel, *see* ALIYAH AND ABSORPTION IN ISRAEL
Abstinence, *see* ASCETICISM
Abstraction-Creation group (Fr.) **13:**350
ABT, ISAAC ARTHUR **2:**177
Abt, Ẓevi **14:**844
Abt-Ashtart (ruler), *see* Straton
ABTERODE, DAVID BEN MOSES ELIAKIM **2:**177
Abtolumus ben Reuben **14:**107
ABTSHUK, AVRAHAM **2:**177
ABU (name addition) **2:**178
Abu Aaron ben Samuel ha-Nasi, *see* AARON OF BAGHDAD
Abu-Abdullah Muhammad ibn Tumart **2:**662
Abu Alafia (fam.), *see* ABULAFIA
Abū al-Baqā' Khālid ben Īsā al-Balawī **15:**1358
Abu al-Baqā' Yaḥya ben Abbas (al-Maghribi), *see* ABBAS, JUDAH BEN SAMUEL IBN
Abu al-Barākāt **5:**984; **14:**760
Abū al-Faḍl Dā'ūd ibn Abī al-Bayān Suleimān al-Isra'īlī, *see* DAVID BEN SOLOMON
ABU AL-FAḌL HASDAY **2:**178
Abu al-Faḍl Ḥisdai ibn Ḥisdai, *see* ḤISDAI IBN ḤISDAI, ABU AL-FAḌL
Abu al-Faraj (10th cent., Alg.) **2:**612
Abū al-Faraj Furqān ibn Asad, *see* JESHUAH BEN JUDAH
ABU AL-FARAJ HARUN IBN AL-FARAJ **2:**178
- linguistics **16:**1358,1381
Abu-al-Faraj ibn-al-Ibri, *see* BAR HEBRAEUS, JOḤANAN
Abu al-Faraj ibn al-Jawzī (trav.) **15:**1358
Abu al-Faraj Nafīs al-Dīn-al Kathār **14:**755
ABU AL-FAT **2:**179
- Samaritan chronicles **6:**313; **14:**728 **14:**754; **14:**757
Abu al-Fath Eleazar ibn Azhar **14:**1201; **15:**226
Abu al-Ghaña'im ibn al-Barqūlī, *see* Ibn al Barqūlī, Abu al-Ghaña'im
Abu al-Hasan, *see* IBN AL-TAQANA, MOSES
Abu al-Hasan ibn Kamniel, *see* Kamniel, Abu al-Hasan
ABU AL-ḤASAN OF TYRE **2:**179
- al-Tabbākh **14:**749; **14:**754
- Aramaic **14:**753
Abu al-Husayn Muhammad ibn Jubayr, *see* Ibn Jubayr, Abu al-Husayn Muhammad
Abu Ali al-Hasan ibn Ali al-Lāwī al-Baṣri, *see* JAPHETH BEN ALI HA-LEVI
Abu Ali Hasan ibn Bundar, *see* Japheth (Hasan) ben Bendar
Abu Ali 'Isā ibn Zar'ah **7:**1365
Abu al-Khasīb (tn., Iraq) **8:**1450
Abū al-Mu'allim, Solomon, *see* Ibn Mu'allim, Abu Ayyub Sulayman
Abu al-Munā ibn abi Naṣr al-Kohen al-'Aṭṭār **10:**421
ABU AL-MUNAJJĀ SOLOMON BEN SHAYA **2:**180
Abu al Rabi, *see* ABULRABI
Abu al-Walid ibn Ḥasdai **8:**1182
Abu al-Walid Marwan, *see* IBN JANĀḤ, JONAH
Abu al-Walid Muhammad ibn Rushd, *see* AVERROES
Abu Amar (Joseph) ben Abi Elhassan **15:**739
Abu-ar-Rabia ben Baruch **11:**550
ABU AWEIGILA (loc., Sinai) **2:**180
- Sinai Campaign **14:**1606
- Six-Day War **9:**408; **14:**1629
- War of Independence **9:**372
Abū Ayyūb Sulaymān ibn Mu'allim, *see* Ibn Mu'allim, Abu Ayub Sulayman
Abū Ayyūb Sulymān ibn Yaḥyā ibn Gabīrūl, *see* GABIROL, SOLOMON BEN JUDAH IBN
Abu Bakr Muhammad ibn Yaḥya ibn Bajja, *see* AVEMPACE
Abu Baẓal (qtr., Jer.), *see* Sha'arei Ẓedek
Abubus (f., Ptolemy), *see* Ḥabub
Abucarat, Abraham, *see* BUKARAT, ABRAHAM BEN SOLOMON HA-LEVI
ABUDARHAM (Sp. fam.) **2:**180
Abudarham, David (13th cent.) **2:**181
Abudarham, David (15th cent.) **15:**1204
ABUDARHAM, DAVID BEN JOSEPH **2:**181
- codification of law **5:**646
- *Haggadah* commentary **7:**1092
- *illus:*
- - *Perush ha-Berakhot ve-ha-Tefilot* **11:**301
Abudarham, David ben Solomon **2:**180
Abudarham, Don Isaac (Sp.) **12:**281
- Toledo **15:**1204
Abudarham, Isaac (It.) **2:**181
Abudarham, Judah (mer., Mor.) **2:**181
Abudarham, Judah (Gib.) **2:**181
Abudarham, Judah (dipl., Mor.) **2:**181
Abudarham, Moses (It.) **2:**181
Abudarham, Moses ibn (r., Egy.) **14:**304
Abudarham ha-Shalem (bk.) **2:**182
Abudarhen (fam.), *see* ABUDARHAM
Abu Dā'ud (9th cent., Musl.) **7:**1051
Abu Dā'ūd (astrol.) **3:**790
Abudiente, Gideon, *see* GIDEON, SAMSON
Abudiente, Jose **8:**1396
Abudiente, Moses Gideon **7:**1226; **10:**9
Abudiente, Reuel Gideon **7:**560
Abudiente, Sarah **10:**9
Abu Dis (vill., Er. Isr.) **9:**1487
Abudraham, *see* Abudarham
Abu Farīd **9:**1039
Abu Fuṭrus (tn.), *see* ANTIPATRIS
Abu Ghosh (sheikh) **2:**182
ABU GHOSH (vill., Isr.) **2:**182
- Ibrahim Pasha **9:**295
- music festival **12:**672
- *illus:*
- - text
- - Crusader church **3:**329; **5:**1136
- - general view **3:**348
Abū Hanifa (Isl. jur.) **2:**920; **10:**938
Abu Ḥannā, Ḥannā **9:**1042
Abu-Ḥarb (Musl. ldr.) **9:**263
- Jerusalem attack **9:**1426
Abu Harun (mer.) **15:**1302
Abu Harūn (poet), *see* IBN EZRA, MOSES BEN JACOB
Abu Ḥasira, *see* ABI-ḤASIRA
Abu Ibrahim (paytan), *see* IBN KHALFUN, ISAAC
Abu Ibrahim ibn Sakatar (Kastar), *see* IBN YASHUSH, ISAAC ABU IBRAHIM
Abu Ibrāhīm Isaac, *see* Ibn Zadok, Isaac
Abu Imram (12th cent., Egy.) **16:**1280
Abu Imrān ibn al-Lāwi al-Ishbīlī, *see* MOSES BEN JOSEPH HA-LEVI
ABU 'IMRĀN AL-TIFLĪSĪ **2:**183
- Karaites **10:**766
ABU 'ĪSĀ, ISAAC BEN JACOB AL-IṢFAHĪNĪ **2:**183
- messianism **11:**1419,1421
- Persia **13:**308
- Umayyads **15:**1530
Abu Isḥāq (12 cent.), *see* IBN AL-RABĪB
Abū Isḥāk (13th cent., poet), *see* IBRĀHĪM IBN SAHL AL-ANDALUSĪ AL-ISRAĪ'ĪLĪ
Abu Isḥak Ibn Paquda (12th cent., poet), *see* Ibn Paquda, Abu Isḥak
Abu Isḥāq Ibrāhīm ben Faraj ben Mārūth (ling.) **8:**1185; **14:**756; **16:**1390
Abu Isḥāq Ibrahim ibn 'Aṭā', (nagid, Tun.), *see* ABRAHAM BEN NATHAN
Abu Ishaq Jekuthiel ben Isaac, *see* IBN HASAN, JEKUTHIEL BEN ISSAC
Abu-Kabir (loc., Er. Isr.) **9:**1251
Abukara, Abraham **2:**184
ABUKARA, ABRAHAM BEN MOSES **2:**184
Abukara, Jacob ben Elijah **2:**184
Abukarat, Abraham (Sp., Tun.), *see* BUKARAT, ABRAHAM BEN SOLOMON HA-LEVI
Abukarat, Abraham ben Isaac ha-Levi (schol., Egy.) **4:**1469
Abu Kathir Yaḥya ben Zechariah al-Katib of Tiberias **14:**543
Abu Khaḍra, Fahd **9:**1043
Abu Khushayba, Wadi (Isr.), *see* Wadi Abu Khushayba
Abukir (Egy.) **2:**593
ABULAFIA (Sp. fam.) **2:**184
- etymology **2:**178
- *see also:* Abolafia
ABULAFIA, ABRAHAM BEN SAMUEL **2:**185
- chronological chart **8:**766-767
- *gematria* in Kabbalah **7:**372
- Kabbalah **10:**529; **10:**541
- messianism **11:**1424
- mystical literature **11:**347
- mystical meditation **10:**630; **11:**1218
- Pope **13:**854
- Sambatyon **14:**764
- *Sefer Yeẓirah* **16:**787
- *Sefirot* doctrine **10:**569
ABULAFIA, EZEKIEL DAVID BEN MORDECAI **2:**186
ABULAFIA, ḤAYYIM BEN DAVID (r., Turk.) **2:**187
- Bikayam, Meir **4:**991
ABULAFIA, HAYYIM BEN JACOB **2:**187
- Ḥayyim ben David **2:**188
ABULAFIA, ḤAYYIM BEN MOSES(?) **2:**187
- family **2:**184
- Ibn Jamil, Isaac Nissim **8:**1181
- Isaac Abulafia **2:**188
- Ricchi, Raphael Immanuel ben Abraham Ḥai **14:**154
- Tiberias **9:**290
ABULAFIA, ḤAYYIM NISSIM BEN ISAAC **2:**188
Abulafia, Hezekiah, *see* ABULAFIA, EZEKIEL DAVID BEN MORDECAI
ABULAFIA, ISAAC **2:**188
ABULAFIA, ISAAC BEN MOSES **2:**189
Abulafia, Issachar **4:**1485
Abulafia, Jacob **2:**185
ABULAFIA, JACOB BEN SOLOMON **2:**189
- Ḥayyim Vital **16:**172
- Pinto, Josiah ben Joseph **13:**553
Abulafia, Josef (print.) **13:**1023
Abulafia, Joseph ben Meir (r., Sp.) **2:**184

Abulafia, Joseph David (r., Er. Isr., Syr.) **2:**184
Abulafia, Joseph David (r., Er. Isr.) **2:**184
Abulafia, Judah **2:**190
ABULAFIA, MEIR **2:**190
- *ḥiddushim* **8:**466
- Maimonides **15:**1203
- masorah **16:**1476
- Naḥmanides **12:**774
- responsa **14:**86
- resurrection **11:**747
- *geneal. table:* text
Abulafia, Meir ben Joseph **2:**184
Abulafia, Meir ben Solomon **2:**184
Abulafia, Moses (13th cent., philos.), *see* MOSES BEN JOSEPH HA-LEVI
Abulafia, Moses (Syr.) **2:**185
Abulafia, Moses ben Meir (physic.) **2:**184
Abulafia, Samuel (14th cent., Sp.) **2:**184
Abulafia, Samuel (15th cent., Sp.), *see* Abolafia, Samuel
ABULAFIA, SAMUEL BEN MEIR HA-LEVI **2:**193
- banking **4:**170
- Spain **15:**234
- synagogue **15:**602, 613
- Toledo **15:**1203
- *illus:*
- - text
- - El Transito synagogue **3:**520; **15:**611,1201,1205
ABULAFIA, SAMUEL HA-LEVI (sci., engin.) **2:**193
ABULAFIA, TODROS BEN JOSEPH HA-LEVI (kab.) **2:**194
- Kabbalah **10:**532; **10:**537
- *Ma'arekhet ha-Elohut* **11:**637
- *geneal. table:* **2:**190
ABULAFIA, TODROS BEN JUDAH HA-LEVI **2:**195
- Abraham el-Barchilon **2:**158
- Abu Amar ben Abi Elhassan **15:**739
- Joseph, Saul Abdallah **10:**222
- poetry **13:**688ff
- Toledo **15:**1203
Abulafia, Todros ben Meir **4:**1512
- *geneal. table:* **2:**190
Abu Lavi (fam.), *see* CAVALLERIA, DE LA
Abulefia (Sp. fam.), *see* ABULAFIA
Abulfahm, Levi, *see* IBN ALTABBAN, LEVI BEN JACOB
Abu'l-Faraj (kab.), *see* ABU-AL FARAJ HARUN IBN AL-FARAJ
Abu'l Faraj (Syr. schol.), *see* BAR HEBRAEUS, JOḤANAN
ABULKER (Alg. fam.) **2:**196
- Oran **12:**1446
Abulker, Henri-Samuel **2:**196, 616
Abulker, Isaac **2:**196
Abulker, Isaac ben Samuel (astron.) **2:**196
Abulker, Isaac ben Samuel (r.) **2:**196, 623
Abulker, José **2:**196; **2:**617
Abulker, Joseph **2:**622
Abulker, Raphael **2:**617
Abulker, Samuel **2:**196
Abulker, Stéphane **2:**617
Abu l-Khayr (fam.), *see* ABULKER
Abu 'l-Ma ālī al-Musharraf ben al-Murajja (trav.) **15:**1358
ABULRABI, AARON **2:**196
Abumai (gaon), *see* Ivomai
Abu Manṣūr (Egy. nagid), *see* SAMUEL BEN HANANIA
Abu Manṣūr al-Daimari (Yem.) **10:**423
ABUN (Abuna, Bun; name) **2:**197
ABUN (Abuna; 9th cent schol.) **2:**197
- Kalonymus family **10:**719
ABUN (12th cent.) **2:**197
ABUN (Sp. litur. poet) **2:**197
Abunaha, Solomon, *see* Solomon ha-Ma'aravi
Abu Naṣr, *see* FĀRĀBĪ, ABU NAṢR MUHAMMAD AL-
Abū Naṣr Fadl (Ḥesed; bnk., Egy.) **2:**197,198
- banking **4:**166
- diamond trade **6:**4
Abu Naṣr Samuel (Wāsiṭ), *see* Ibn al-Barqūlī, Samuel
Abu-Nawar (Jord.) **9:**389
Abu Naẓẓāra (plwrt.), *see* SANŪ, YA'QŪB
Abun ben Saul **2:**197
ABUN BEN SHARADA **2:**197
Abundachus, Joseph Barbatus Memphiticus **8:**21
Abundantius (It.) **14:**683
Abu Omar ibn Yaqūy **8:**1182
Aburbi' (fam.) **14:**682
Abu-R-Rabi', ibn (Egy.) **2:**151
ABŪ SA'D AL-TUSTARĪ (fin., Egy.) **2:**197
- banking **4:**166
- diamond trade **6:**4
- trade and commerce **15:**1302
Abu Sahl, *see* DUNASH IBN TAMIM
Abu Sa'id (masoretic schol.), *see* BEN-ASHER, AARON BEN MOSES
Abu Sa'īd (13th cent., Samar.) **2:**179
- Bible translation **4:**863
Abu Sa'īd ben abu al-Hasan ben abu Sa'īd (ling.) **16:**1390
Abu Sa'id David ben Boaz, *see* DAVID BEN BOAZ
Abu Sa'īd Ḥalfon, *see* Damietta, Abu Sa'īd Halfon (ha-Levi al-)
Abū Sa'īd Levi ben Japhet, *see* LEVI BEN JAPHET
Abusamaj (tn., Iraq) **8:**1450
Abu Samra, Alīs **9:**1039
Abu Saydā (tn., Iraq) **8:**1449
Abusch Frankfurter, *see* ABRAHAM ABUSCH BEN ẒEVI HIRSCH
Abu Shehr (port.), *see* BUSHIRE
Abu Suleiman (poet, Sp.) **8:**1191
Abu Suleiman Dā'ūd Ibn Ibrahim Al-Fasi, *see* ALFASI, DAVID BEN ABRAHAM
Abu Suleiman ibn Muhagir, *see* DAVID IBN HAJJAR
Abu Ṭahir Ismā'īl **8:**462
Abu Thawr (sheikh) **9:**1425
Abutter, *see* MAẒRANUT
Abu-Ṭūr (vill., Isr.) **9:**1507
Abu-Ṭūr (qtr., Jer.) **9:**1459,1495,1501
- Baal Perazim **4:**5
Abu Ya'qūb (Almohad sult.) **2:**663
- Waqqasa family **16:**265
Abu Ya'qūb Yūsuf ibn Nuḥ (Kar. schol), *see* JOSEPH BEN NOAH
Abu Yesha' (philos.), *see* FĀRĀBĪ, ABU NAṢR MUHAMMAD AL-
Abu-Yusef ben Mar Yusef (schol.) **14:**1528
Abu Yusuf (fin.) **16:**1279
Abu Yūsuf ben Mu'allim (physic.) **11:**777
Abu Zakaria (emir, Tun.) **15:**1437
Abu Zakariyyā Yaḥyā (r., Sp.), *see* IBN BAL'AM, JUDAH BEN SAMUEL
Abū Zakariyyā Yaḥyā al-Rāqilī (polem.) **9:**102
Abu Zakkariyya (poet, Sp.), *see* Ibn Ghayyat, Judah ben Isaac
Abu Zenima (loc., Sinai) **14:**1636
Abu-Zikrī (nagid, Egy.), *see* ZUTA
ABYAḌ, YIḤYA BEN SHALOM (Yem.) **2:**198
Abydos (loc.) **16:**273
Abydos ware (pottery) **1:**pottery chart; **13:**938
Abyssinia, *see* ETHIOPIA
ABZARDIEL, MOSES **2:**198
- Toledo **15:**1203
Açac de Çolema **4:**981
ACACIA (tree) **2:**198
- in Israel **9:**225; **9:**788
- perfume adulteration **8:**1312
- plant list **13:**615
- wood **16:**630
- *illus:* text
Academic Committee on Soviet Jewry (U.S.) **14:**500
Academic Sports Association **15:**296
"Academicus" (pseud.) *see* HERSCH, PESACH LIEBMAN
ACADEMIES IN BABYLONIA AND EREẒ ISRAEL **2:**199
- *Contents:*
- - Designations **2:**199
- - Second Temple Period **2:**199
- - Pupils **2:**201
- - To Close of Mishnah **2:**201
- - Function and Authority **2:**202
- - The *Rosh Yeshivah* and Assistants **2:**203
- - Election of *Rosh Yeshivah* **2:**204
- - Babylon in Amoraim Period **2:**204
- - Aim of Studies **2:**205
- - Method of Study **2:**205
- *alluf* **2:**657
- *aurum coronarium* **3:**854
- Babylonia **2:**39ff
- Baghdad Academy **8:**1447
- *Bei-Rav* **4:**401
- distorted image **8:**664ff
- Ereẓ Israel **9:**266
- exilarchs **6:**1028ff
- gaonate **7:**315
- historical background **8:**656ff
- Ishmael and Akiva **8:**1417; **9:**84
- Jabneh **9:**1176
- Kairouan academy **10:**697ff
- *kallah* months **10:**710
- Nehardea **12:**934
- ordination **14:**1143
- Persian financial support **13:**309
- Pumbedita **13:**1384
- *Resh Kallah* **14:**82
- Saadiah and Aaron ben Meir **14:**543
- *She'iltot* **2:**449
- Sura **15:**521
- Syria **15:**641
- Tiberias **15:**1131
- Tyre **15:**1489
- universities **15:**1674
- *map:* text
- *tables:*
- - *geonim* **7:**319-323
- - Heads of the Academies **2:**866
- - principal *amoraim* **2:**869-872
- *see also:* YESHIVOT
Academy, Kairouan **10:**697
Academy, Rome **14:**241
Academy for Jewish Scholarship, *see* AKADEMIE FUER DIE WISSENSCHAFT DES JUDENTUMS
Academy of Heaven **2:**208ff
ACADEMY OF THE HEBREW LANGUAGE **2:**205
- Ben Ḥayyim, Ze'ev **4:**519
- Ben-Yehudah **4:**568
- chronological chart **8:**766-767
- Hebrew language studies **15:**55
- Hebrew pronunciation **16:**1645ff
- Israel scholarship **9:**396
- Israel cultural life **9:**1001; **9:**999
- Jawitz, Ze'ev **9:**1304
- Shimoni, David **14:**1405
ACADEMY ON HIGH **2:**208
- Ba'al Shem Tov **9:**1050
Açan, Moses ben Joseph **2:**209
AÇAN, MOSES DE ZARAGUA **2:**209
- Moses Nathan **12:**432
Accademia degli Imperditi **5:**124; **14:**318
Accents of the Torah, *see* MASORAH (Vocalization and Cantillation)
Acco (city, Isr.), *see* ACRE
Accos (pr. fam.), *see* Hakkoẓ
Accra (city, Ghana) **9:**439
Acculturation, *see* ASSIMILATION
Achaeans **8:**792
Achaemenes (k., Pers.) **13:**304
ACHAN (bib. fig.) **2:**209
- Achor Valley **2:**207
- Jericho *Herem* **8:**345
- *illus:*
- - stoning **8:**346
Achau (vill., Aus.) **3:**890
ACHBOR (f., Baal-Hanan) **2:**210
ACHBOR (s., Micaiah) **2:**210
Achdut (U.S. period.) **13:**656
Achei Ameth (soc.) **7:**110
Achei Brith and Shield of Abraham (soc.) **7:**110
Achelous (Gr.), *see* Aphilon
Acher, Mathias (pseud.), *see* BIRNBAUM, NATHAN
Achiasaf, Schachna **13:**1378
Achior (apoc. fig.) **10:**451
ACHISH (bib. fig.) **2:**210
- David **5:**1319; **8:**588-589
ACHOR, VALLEY OF (Er. Isr.) **2:**211
Achron, Isidor **2:**212
ACHRON, JOSEPH **2:**211
- *illus:* text
ACHSAH (bib. fig.) **2:**212
- Othniel **12:**1520
ACHSHAPH (tn., Er. Isr.) **2:**212
ACHZIB (tn., Er. Isr.) **2:**213
- Gesher ha-Ziv **7:**526
- tombs **15:**1217
- *illus:* text
Acker, Aaron **2:**233
ACKERMAN, NATHAN WARD **2:**214
Ackermann, Leopold **8:**21
ACKORD, ELIAS **2:**214
"Acolo" (paint., V. Brauner) **4:**1319
A Coluna (period.) **4:**1331
Acoluthus, Andreas **8:**21
Acosta (fam. name), *see also* Costa; Da Costa
Acosta, Benjamin D' **15:**488
ACOSTA, CHRISTOBAL **2:**214
- medicine **11:**1193
ACOSTA, ISAAC (Yshak) **2:**215
Acosta, Jacob **12:**1068
ACOSTA, JOAN D' **2:**215
Acosta, Uriel da, *see* COSTA, URIEL DA
Acquaviva, Duke of *see* D'Avigdor, Count Salomon Henri
ACQUI (tn., It.) **2:**215
ACQUISITION **2:**216
- *Contents;*
- - General **2:**216
- - *Kinyan Ḥaẓer* **2:**217
- - *Arba Ammot* **2:**217
- - *Hagbahah, Meshikhah, Mesirah* **2:**218
- - *Ḥazakah* **2:**218
- - *Kinyan Kesef* **2:**219
- - *Kinyan Shetar* **2:**219
- - *Ḥalifin, Kinyan Sudar* **2:**219
- - *Agav Karka* **2:**220
- - Usage and Custom **2:**220
- - Without Formal Act **2:**220
- admission **2:**290ff

- *agav karka* and lien **11:**229
- agency **2:**351ff
- *arba ammot* **3:**292
- arbitration **3:**297
- consecration and endowment **8:**280
- custom **12:**17ff
- debt assignment **3:**768
- embryo **6:**720
- fruit with land **12:**111
- gift **7:**561
- *ḥaliẓah* **11:**126
- hired service **10:**1325
- inheritance **15:**479
- *keẓaẓah* **10:**935
- *kinyan sudar* **2:**219; **5:**925
- lease and hire **10:**1528
- lien **11:**228
- loans **11:**416ff
- Marranos **5:**885
- marriage **11:**1045
- mistake **12:**158
- *ona'ah* **12:**1391
- ownership **12:**1532
- ownership transfer **5:**880ff
- partnership **13:**149
- pledge **13:**640
- property **4:**341; **13:**1146
- public authority **13:**1353; **13:**1359
- residence rights **8:**357
- sale **14:**675
- servitudes **14:**1188
- slaves **14:**1659
- suretyship **15:**525ff
- *takkanah* **15:**717
- theft **15:**1094
- waiver form **11:**1233
- wills **16:**519ff
- Women's Equal Rights Law, 1951 **12:**146
- *ye'ush* **16:**775
- *see also:* CONTRACT

ACRA (fort., Jer.) **2:**221
- Antiochus IV Epiphanes **3:**74
- history chart **8:**766-767
- Seleucids and Judea **8:**628f

ACRABA (Samar.) **2:**221
- Flavia Neapolis **12:**744

Acrabitene (toparchy, Er. Isr.) **9:**120
- *see also:* ACRABA

ACRE (city, Isr.) **2:**221
- *Contents:*
- - Situation **2:**221
- - Ancient Acre **2:**222
- - Medieval Period **2:**223
- - Modern Acre **2:**224
- after Temple destruction **9:**245
- capitulations **5:**148
- Crusader period **9:**268
- Haifa and **7:**1134
- Hellenistic period **8:**626
- history chart (1291) **8:**766-767
- human geography **9:**580
- I.Ẓ.L. and Leḥi **9:**359
- Mamluk destruction **9:**278
- maps of Ereẓ Israel **11:**924
- Ottoman period **9:**284; **9:**285; **9:**290ff
- Ptolemy Philadelphus **13:**1348
- statistics **1:**place list **15:**330
- *illus:*
- - "English Bastion" **9:**288
- - fishermen mending nets **9:**1029
- - Haganah group in prison **9:**1182
- - old city market **9:**581
- - prison, I.Ẓ.L. and Leḥi escape **8:**1469
- - St. John's Crypt **5:**1143

Acre Plain (reg., Er. Isr.) **9:**126; **9:**571; **9:**128ff; **9:**580ff

ACRO, PSEUDO- (Rom. au.) **14:**234

Acronyms **8:**76; **12:**810
- *see also:* ACROSTICS

Acropolis **5:**589

ACROSTICS **2:**229
- *Contents:*
- - Bible **2:**229
- - Post Biblical **2:**230
- amulets **2:**912
- *Baraita of 32 rules* **4:**195
- Lamentations, Book of **10:**1372
- mnemonics **12:**187
- *illus:*
- - text
- - Andrychow tombstone **15:**1228
- - newborn child's amulet **4:**1051
- *see also:* Acronyms

ACSÁDY, IGNÁC **2:**232

Acta Appiani (wk.) **2:**595

Acta Isidori et Lamponis (wk.) **2:**595

Action (legal), *see* MA'ASEH

ACTION FRANÇAISE (mvmt.) **2:**232
- *see also:* ANTI-SEMITIC POLITICAL PARTIES AND ORGANIZATIONS

Action française, L' (newsp.) **2:**232

Actions, limitations of, *see* LIMITATION OF ACTIONS

Active Intellect (philos. conc.)
- Aristotelianism **13:**430
- Kabbalah **10:**520, 529
- *Ru'aḥ ha-Kodesh* **14:**367
- soul **15:**173

Acts of Alexandrian Martyrs, see ALEXANDRIAN MARTYRS, ACTS OF

Acts of the Pagan Martyrs, see ALEXANDRIAN MARTYRS, ACTS OF

Actuality and Potentiality, *see* FORM AND MATTER

ACZÉL, TAMÁS **8:**1084

ADA (tn., Yug.) **2:**233

Adab (city, Mesop.) **16:**1488,1507

Adab al-ʿAwda (lit.) **9:**1041

Adab al-Muqawama (lit.) **9:**1042

Adad (deity), *see* HADAD

Adadah (city, Negev), *see* AROER

Adad-Guppi (7/6 cent., Babyl.) **16:**1505

ADADI, ABRAHAM ḤAYYIM BEN MASOUD ḤAI **2:**233
- Libya **11:**204
- Tripoli **15:**1398

Adadi, Nathan **2:**233; **13:**1483
- Tripoli **15:**1398

Adad-Idri (k., Aram), *see* BEN-HADAD II

Adad-Nirari III (k., Assyr.)
- Chaldeans **5:**331
- Hazael **7:**1515
- Mesopotamia **16:**1502
- Philistines **13:**402

ADAH (bib. fig.) **2:**233

ADALBERG, SAMUEL **2:**234

Adalbert (archbp.) **14:**1661
- *illus:*
- - redeeming slaves from Jewish traders **14:**1661

ADAM (bib. fig.) **2:**234
- *Contents:*
- - General **2:**234
- - In Aggadah **2:**236
- - Medieval Jewish Philosophy **2:**238
- - In Christian Tradition **2:**240
- - In Islamic Legend **2:**241
- - Illuminated Manuscripts **2:**242
- - In the Arts **2:**242
- *Adam, Books of* **2:**245
- *Adam and Eve* **2:**246
- Aggadah **13:**960
- altar site **2:**770
- Arts **5:**1070
- Ceylon tradition **5:**316
- coats of skin **12:**1167
- Eve **6:**979
- evolution **6:**1003
- fall, caused by the angel Samael **14:**719
- fire **6:**1304
- Garden of Eden **7:**326; **13:**77
- garments **6:**1339
- gnostic interpretation **2:**248; **7:**637
- *golem* **7:**754
- *ḥuppah* **11:**1040
- Kabbalah revealed to **10:**493
- kabbalistic view of **10:**607
- labor **10:**1320, 1321
- Lilith **11:**246
- Lurianic view of **10:**615ff
- Machpelah cave **11:**673
- *Mizmor Shir le-Yom ha-Shabbat* **12:**173
- nature of man **11:**846
- oil of mercy **12:**1347
- original sin **5:**1424
- Raziel **13:**1592
- Samaritan calendar **14:**749
- sin **14:**1589, 1592
- *illus:*
- - text
- - "Adam and Eve in Paradise" (Rubens and Jan Breughel the Elder) **4:**941
- - Bamberg cathedral sculpture **4:**939
- - "Creation of Adam" (Michelangelo) **5:**1068
- - creation of Eve **4:**874
- - death **2:**247
- - dressed in animal skins **8:**1271
- - expulsion from Paradise **6:**981
- - Garden of Eden **2:**242; **4:**856,1050
- - Islamic illum. mss. **2:**237; **4:**941; **6:**981
- - naming the animals **6:**980
- - Rodin's sculpture **14:**267

ADAM (city, Er. Isr.) **2:**245

Adam (conc., man) **11:**842

"Adam" (sculp., Rodin) **14:**267

Adam (journ., Rum.) **13:**1043

ADAM, LAJOS (Louis) **11:**1205

Adam, Michael **4:**1352; **4:**867; **11:**356

ADAM, OTHER BOOKS OF **2:**245

ADAM AND EVE, BOOK OF THE LIFE OF **2:**246
- *illus:* text

"Adam and Eve in Paradise" (paint, Rubens and Jan Breughel the Elder) **4:**941

ADAM BA'AL SHEM (leg. fig.) **2:**247
- Israel Ba'al Shem Tov **9:**1052
- Joshua Heshel Ẓoref **16:**1223

Adam Elyon (kab. conc.), *see* ADAM KADMON

Adam ha-Kohen (pseud.), *see* LEBENSOHN, ABRAHAM DOV

Adami (bib. tn.) **2:**248

ADAMIT (kib., Isr.) **2:**248
- statistics **1:**place list

ADAM KADMON (kab. conc.) **2:**248
- Abraham Kohen de Herrera **8:**392
- Jesus **10:**645
- Lurianic cosmogony **10:**590; **10:**594ff
- messiah **6:**881
- mystical literature **11:**346
- providence **13:**1282
- *Sefirot* **10:**566, 579
- *Shi'ur Komah* **14:**1418
- *illus:*
- - in womb of *Ein-Sof* **10:**647

ADAMS, FRANKLIN PIERCE **10:**308

Adams, G. **16:**1154

ADAMS, HANNAH **2:**249
- history **8:**560

Adams, Henry **15:**1650

ADAMS, JOHN **2:**249

Adamus, Franz, *see* Bronner, Ferdinand

Adam ve-Ḥavah (hal. wk.) **5:**644

ADANI, DAVID BEN AMRAM **2:**250
- Yemen **16:**742,745

ADANI, DAVID BEN YESHA HA-LEVI **2:**250

Adani, Eliah **5:**626

ADANI, MAHALAL **2:**250

ADANI, MIZRAḤI SHALOM **2:**250

ADANI, SAADIAH BEN DAVID (Sa'id ibn Da'ud) **2:**250
- translations **15:**1323

Adani, Samuel *see* BARAZANI, SAMUEL BEN NETHANEL HA-LEVI

ADANI, SAMUEL BEN JOSEPH (Yeshua) **2:**251

Adani, Shalom Jacob, *see* ADANI, MAHALAL

Adani, Solomon, *see* ADENI, SOLOMON BAR JOSHUA

Adanim (mosh., Isr.) **1:**place list; **16:**718

Adar (site, Moab) **2:**538

ADAR (month) **2:**251
- *ḥevra kaddisha* **8:**444
- intercalation **10:**1528
- *kallah* month **10:**711
- Purim **13:**1390
- *Shabbat Shekalim* **14:**573
- twenty eighth of **10:**353
- *illus:*
- - fish as symbol of **6:**1327
- *see also:* CALENDAR

ADAR, THE SEVENTH OF **2:**252
- Dumuh **6:**269
- *ḥevra kaddisha* **8:**444
- Moses' birthday **12:**395
- Torah reading **15:**1247

Adar, the 28th of **10:**353

ADAR, ZVI **2:**253

ADARBI, ISAAC BEN SAMUEL **2:**254

Adarique, Isaac **4:**1469

Adarpazari (city, Turk.) **4:**1484

ʿAdas, Shafiq **4:**312; **8:**1453

ADASA (Er. Isr.) **2:**254

Adass Israel Congregation (Austr.) **11:**1283
- *illus:*
- - synagogue **11:**1284

ADASS JESHURUN, ADASS JISROEL (Orth. congs.) **2:**254
- New York City **2:**426

Adat Devorim (wk.) **16:**1386;1474

Adath Yisroel (cong., Eng.) **12:**1491
- *see also:* Union of Orthodox Hebrew Congregations

Adato, Solomon **9:**1095; **13:**816; **15:**1457

ADAV (orgn.) **10:**1443

Adbeel (bib. fig.) **9:**89

ADDA BAR AHAVAH (3rd cent., amora) **2:**255
- calendar reckoning **5:**47

ADDA BAR AHAVAH (Abba; 4th cent., amora) **2:**255
- Dimi of Nehardea **6:**49
- Mar Zutra **16:**1245

Addai (Chr. prch.) **6:**366

Adda Saba (amora) **11:**992

Adderet (mosh., Isr.) **1:**place list

Adderet Eliyahu (Kar. wk.) **4:**298

Ad Dianam (city, Er. Isr.) **10:**300

Addiel (leg. k.) **6:**576

Addir, Mount (Isr.) **9:**156

ADDIR BI-MELUKHAH (Seder hymn) **2:**256

ADDIR HU (Seder hymn) **2:**257

Addirim (vill., Er. Isr.) **1:**place list; **15:**675

Addison, Lancelot **8:**21

Additional service, *see* MUSAF

Addleson, Abraham **6**:342
Addu (deity), *see* HADAD
ADEL (dau., Ba'al Shem Tov) **2**:258
- *geneal. table:* **9**:1051
ADELAIDE (Austr.) **2**:259
ADELANTADOS *(parnasim)* **2**:259
- *berurei averah* **4**:700
- Spain **15**:230,231
- *see also:* MUQADDIM
Adelie, Jonah **2**:40
Adelkind, Baruch **4**:838
Adelkind, Daniel **2**:259
ADELKIND, ISRAEL CORNELIUS **2**:259
Adelman, A., *see* TASHRAK
ADELSON, HOWARD LAURENCE **8**:543
Adelstein, Angelica, *see* ROZEANU, ANGELICA
ADEN (Arabia) **2**:260
- *Contents:*
- - General **2**:260
- - Conflict of Religious Authority **2**:260
- - Adani and Yemenite Jews **2**:261
- - Hebrew Literature **2**:261
- - Jewish Tombstones **2**:262
- - Modern Period **2**:262
- - Recent Years **2**:263
- - Folklore **2**:263
- AJA school **2**:977
- *aliyah* **9**:512
- Cairo *genizah* **16**:1340
- demography **5**:1501
- dress **6**:219
- Madmūn ben Japheth **11**:680
- silversmiths **2**:262
- trade with India **16**:741ff
- *illus:*
- - text
- - classroom in a Jewish school **6**:398
- - immigrants to Israel **9**:502
- - Rosh ha-Ayin transit camp **9**:379
- *pop. table:* text
Adenantado *(parnas)*, *see* ADELANTADOS
ADENAUER, KONRAD **2**:264
- aid to Israel **9**:402
- Ben-Gurion **4**:512
- *illus:* text
Adeni (fam. name), *see also* Adani
ADENI, SOLOMON BAR JOSHUA **2**:265
- Yemen **16**:745
ADERCA, FELIX **2**:266
A-d-e-r-e-t, *see* RABINOWITZ-TEOMIM, ELIJAH DAVID BEN BENJAMIN
Ades, Josiah Victor **13**:115
Adhan (fam.), *see* DAHAN
Adhan, Solomon **5**:1224
Adhruḥ (place) **9**:264
ADIABENE (kdm.) **2**:267
- in Josephus **10**:261
- Kurdistan **10**:1296
- Trajan **15**:1312
Adi the Arab (tal. fig.) **12**:1319
Adibe (fam.) **3**:1004; **12**:333
Adibe, Joseph **3**:1004
Adil I, al-Malik al-(sult.) **3**:998
- Abraham Maimuni **2**:151
- David ben Solomon **5**:1356
ʿĀdil, Yusuf *see* GAMA, GASPAR DA
Adir (pseud.), see DEINARD, EPHRAIM
Adiriron (kab. name) **10**:504
Adjectives (Heb. lang.) **16**:1582
ADJIMAN (fam., Turk.) **2**:268
Adjiman, Baruch **2**:268
Adjiman, Elijah **2**:268
Adjiman, Isaiah (govt. offic.) **2**:268
Adjiman, Isaiah (bnk.) **2**:268; **9**:1094
Adjiman, Jacob **2**:268
Adjiman, Meir **2**:268
Adjiman, Yeshaya **15**:918
A-D-L (orgn.), *see* Anti-Defamation League
ADLER (Frankfort fam.) **2**:268
- *geneal. table:* text
Adler (U.S. stlr. fam.) **14**:833
ADLER (U.S. theat. fam.) **2**:269
Adler (Worms fam.) **2**:269
Adler, Abraham **3**:688
Adler, Alexander **11**:556
ADLER, ALFRED **2**:271
- psychiatry **13**:1338
Adler, Bedřich **5**:1209
Adler, Celia **2**:271
- *illus:* text
ADLER, CHARLES **8**:1430
ADLER, CYRUS **2**:272
- A.J.C. **2**:822ff
- A.J.H.S. **2**:826; **2**:827
- Cairo *genizah* **16**:1334
- Conservative Judaism **5**:902ff
- J.P.S. **10**:80
- J.T.S. **10**:96
- museums **12**:544
- *illus:*
- - autograph **3**:913
- - Joint Distribution Committee **2**:829
- - JWB committee **12**:783
ADLER, DANKMAR **2**:274
- synagogue **15**:620
- *illus:*
- - Anshe Maariv synagogue, Chicago **15**:622
- - Auditorium Building, Chicago **3**:343
ADLER, DAVID BARUCH **2**:274
Adler, E. (r., Bav.) **10**:1083
Adler, E. (cmty. ldr., Eng.) **7**:334
Adler, Egyd **16**:131
ADLER, ELKAN NATHAN **2**:275
- book collection **4**:975
- Cairo *genizah* **16**:1334
- Judeo-Persian literature **10**:438
- *geneal. table:* **2**:269
- *illus:* text
ADLER, ELMER **2**:276
ADLER, EMANUEL PHILIP **10**:307; **10**:308
ADLER, FELIX **2**:276
Adler, Frances **2**:271
ADLER, FRIEDRICH (lab. ldr.) **2**:277
Adler, Friedrich (au., Cz.) **5**:1193
Adler, Fritz Baumann **13**:820
ADLER, GEORG **2**:277
ADLER, GUIDO **2**:277
Adler, Hanna **2**:275
ADLER, HARRY CLAY **2**:278
ADLER, HELMUT E. **1**:27
Adler, Herbert Marcus **2**:269
ADLER, HERMANN **2**:278
- Buechler, Adolf **4**:1458
- history chart **8**:766-767
- rabbinate **13**:1453
- *geneal. table:* **2**:269
ADLER, HUGO CHAIM **2**:279
- *Akedah* **2**:486
- Worcester **16**:633
- *mus. notations:*
- - modern psalmody **12**:667
Adler, Isaac (r., Ger.) **2**:269, 287
Adler, Isaac L. (bsmn.) **14**:211
ADLER, ISRAEL (musicol.) **1**:27; **12**:680
Adler, Israel Judah (writ), *see* Adler, Yishai
Adler, Jacob (act.) **2**:269
- *illus:*
- - as Shylock **15**:1066
Adler, Jacob Georg Christian (Hebr.) **8**:21
ADLER, JANKEL (Jacob; paint.) **2**:279
- *illus:*
- - text
- - "Priestly Blessing" **3**:558
- - "Purim-Shpil" (paint.) **13**:1404
Adler, Jean **2**:281
Adler, Joab **2**:289
Adler, Joseph **15**:1452
ADLER, JULES **2**:280
Adler, Julia **2**:271
Adler, Julius (act., Pol.) **11**:431
ADLER, JULIUS OCHS (U.S.) **2**:281
Adler, Karl **15**:463
ADLER, LARRY (Lawrence) **2**:281
ADLER, LAZARUS LEVI **2**:281
Adler, Liebmann **2**:274
Adler, Luther **2**:271
Adler, Marcus (Mordechai) Baer **2**:268,285
Adler, Margarete **12**:1375
ADLER, MAX (mus.) **2**:282
ADLER, MAX (soc., Aus.) **2**:282
Adler, Menahem Judah **2**:289
ADLER, MICHAEL **2**:283
Adler, Mordechai *see* Adler, Marcus Baer
ADLER, MORITZ (art.) **3**:594
ADLER, MORRIS (r., U.S.) **2**:283
ADLER, MORTIMER JEROME (philos.) **2**:284
Adler, Naphtali, *see* ADLER, HERMANN
ADLER, NATHAN BEN SIMEON HA-KOHEN (r., Ger.) **2**:284
- Kabbalah **10**:555
- *geneal. table:* **2**:269
ADLER, NATHAN MARCUS (r., Eng.) **2**:285
- history chart **8**:766-767
- *geneal. table:* **2**:269
Adler, Nettie **2**:269
Adler, Norbert **5**:1190
ADLER, PAUL **2**:286
Adler, Phineḥas **2**:289
ADLER, SAMUEL (r., Ger.) **2**:287
Adler, Samuel (stlr., Ark.) **3**:459
ADLER, SAMUEL M. (paint.) **2**:287
Adler, Sarah **2**:271
ADLER, SAUL AARON **2**:288
ADLER, SELIG **2**:288
ADLER, SHALOM BEN MENAHEM **2**:288
Adler, Simon L. **12**:1127
Adler, Solomon **11**:1588
Adler, Stella **2**:271; **15**:1077
ADLER, VICTOR **2**:289
Adler, Yishai **5**:435; **13**:1538
ADLER-RUDEL, SALOMON **2**:289
Adlerstein, Frances **13**:1362
Adlgasser, Anton Cajeton **14**:785
ADLOYADA (Purim carnival) **2**:289
- *illus:* text
- - Tel Aviv parade **9**:907
Admah (bib. loc.) **15**:70
Ad Me'ah Shanah (greeting) **7**:916
Admiralty Court (Isr.) **9**:638
ADMISSION (leg. conc.) **2**:290
- agency **2**:353
- assault **3**:758
- contractual obligation **5**:925
- thief's payment **15**:1098
- types of **13**:632
- *see also:* CONFESSION
Admixture of foods, *see Bittul be-rov*
ADMON, YEDIDYAH **2**:292
ADMON BEN GADDAI (tal. fig.) **2**:292
ADMONI, VLADIMIR GRIGORYEVICH **2**:292
- Brodski's trial **4**:1395
Admont Bible **12**:407; **14**:523
- *illus:*
- - illuminated ms. (12th cent.) **14**:520
ADMOR (title) **2**:293
- titles **15**:1165
Adoba (fam., Sp.) **14**:1205
Adolescentoli (fam.), *see* Ne'arim
Adolph of Nassau (k., Ger.) **4**:675
ADOLPHUS (Eng. fam.) **2**:293
Adolphus (fam., Jam.) **2**:293
Adolphus (fam., U.S.)) **2**:293
Adolphus, Abigail **2**:293
Adolphus, Isaac **2**:293
Adolphus, Jacob (fin.) **2**:293
Adolphus, Sir Jacob (sol.) **2**:293
Adolphus, John (hist.) **2**:293
Adolphus, John Leycester(law.) **2**:293
Adolphus, Michael (Meir) **2**:293
Adolphus, Moses **2**:293
Adolphus, Simḥah (Joy) **2**:293
Adolphus, Simon **2**:293
Adon (k., Egy.) **16**:659
Adon (Phil. ldr.) **13**:403
Adon (Phoen. "Lord") **15**:788
ʾAdonai (God, name of) **7**:679
ADONAI, ADONAI, EL RAḤUM VE-ḤANNUN (litur.) **2**:294
Adonai be-Ḥokhmah Yasad Areẓ (wk.), *see Midrash Konen*
Adoni (fam., Iraq) **12**:445
ADONI-BEZEK (bib. fig.) **2**:294
- Adoni-Zedek **2**:296
ADONIJAH (s., k. David) **2**:294
- Abiathar **2**:71
- Abishag the Shunammite **2**:79
- Benaiah **4**:458
- Joab **10**:107
- kingship **10**:1016
- sacrifice by **13**:1070
- Solomon **8**:591; **15**:96ff
- *geneal. table:* **5**:1341
Adonijah (lev.) **2**:295
Adonijah (contemp., Nehemiah) **2**:295
Adonim, *see* DUNASH IBN TAMIM
ADONIM BEN NISAN HA-LEVI (paytan) **2**:295
ADONIRAM (bib. fig.) **2**:295
- death **15**:841
Adonis (deity), *see* TAMMUZ
ADONI-ZEDEK (bib. fig.) **2**:296
- Adoni-Bezek **2**:294
- Eglon **6**:477
- Jerusalem **9**:1379
ADON OLAM (litur.) **2**:296
- *Contents:*
- - General **2**:296
- - Music **2**:298
- David Aaron de Sola **15**:91
- *score:* text
ADOPTION **2**:298
- *Contents:*
- - Alleged Cases in Bible **2**:298
- - As a Metaphor **2**:300
- - Later Jewish Law **2**:301
- Ancient Israel **6**:1169
- Genesis, Book of **7**:390
- Hurrian Customs **12**:1287; **12**:1289ff
- orphan **12**:1479
- rabbinical courts (Er. Isr.) **12**:143
- State of Israel **9**:640
- *takkanot* **15**:727
- *teraphim* **15**:1015
- *see also:* APOTROPOS
ADORAIM (Adora; city, Er. Isr.) **2**:303
- Hasmoneans **8**:631
Adoram (bib. fig.), *see* ADONIRAM
"Adoration of the Golden Calf" (paint., Poussin) **7**:709; **8**:1233
ADORNO, THEODOR W. **2**:303
Adoshem Malakh (J. mus.) **14**:1464
- *mus. notations:*

- - motivic structure **14**:1464
- - psalmody (Ps. 95) **13**:1331
Adra (city, Sp.) **15**:220
Adraene, *see* EDREI
ADRAMMELECH (s., Sennacherib) **2**:304
ADRAMMELECH (deity) **2**:304
Adramythion (tn., As.M.) **3**:746; **6**:10
Adret, Cresques **5**:313
ADRET, MOSES IBN **2**:305
ADRET, SOLOMON BEN ABRAHAM (Rashba) **2**:305
- Life
- - Aaron ben Joseph ha-Levi **2**:14
- - Abulafia, Abraham **2**:185
- - Ahitub Ben Isaac **2**:467
- - Anatoli, Jacob **2**:929
- - Ashkenazi tosafists **3**:721
- - Avila, Prophet of **3**:970; **11**:1424
- - Barcelona **4**:209
- - Gerona **7**:505
- - Hayyim ben Isaac **7**:1509
- - history chart **8**:766-767
- - Ibn Gaon **8**:1174
- - Jedaiah Bedersi **9**:1310
- - Maimonidean controversy **11**:751; **15**:233
- - Meiri, Menahem **11**:1257
- - Naḥmanides **12**:775
- - Raymond Martini **11**:1066
- - Toledo **15**:1202; **15**:1203
- - Vidal, Crescas **16**:119
- As Halakhist
- - amulets **2**:911
- - Attorney and fees **3**:838
- - contractual obligation **5**:926
- - guilds **7**:972
- - judicial autonomy **3**:929
- - *kapparot* **10**:756
- - method of commentary **15**:765
- - money-lending **12**:250
- - *takkanot* **15**:715; **15**:736ff
- - taxation **15**:845f **16**:1285
- Views and Writings
- - anti-Islam polemic **3**:194
- - codification of law **5**:644
- - Habib, Hayyim **7**:1024
- - *ḥiddushim* **8**:466
- - Ibn Migash **8**:1189
- - Kabbalah **10**:535; **10**:567
- - literature **11**:332f
- - Naḥmanides' system **12**:781
- - responsa **14**:86
Adrian (pope), *see* HADRIAN I
ADRIANOPLE (Turk.) **2**:309
- *Contents:*
- - General **2**:309
- - Music **2**:311
- - Recent Times **2**:311
- Apulian exiles **3**:228
- Doenmeh **6**:148
- Ottoman Empire **16**:1530
- Shabbateanism **14**:1239
Adrichem, Christian van **9**:1543ff
- *illus:*
- - Jerusalem map **9**:1542
Adrichomius, Adrian **11**:928
ADRIEL (bib. fig.) **2**:311
Adrikhalut (journ.) **1**:newsp. list
Adrotiel, Abraham **10**:542
Adū Allah (ps. mess.), *see* ABDALLAH, YUSUF
ADULLAM (city, Er. Isr.) **2**:312
ADULLAM REGION (Isr.) **2**:312
- human geography **9**:584ff
- *illus:*
- - settlement plan **9**:586
- *map:* text
ADULT EDUCATION IN ISRAEL **9**:964
- learned societies **15**:55ff
- *illus:*
- - army sergeant teaching new immigrants **9**:964
- - Tel Aviv *ulpan* class **9**:965
- - ulpan classroom in Naẓerat Illit **15**:1526
ADULTERY **2**:313
- *Contents:*
- - Biblical Period **2**:313
- - In Jewish Law **2**:315
- abortion **2**:100
- artificial insemination **3**:660
- banishment **4**:165
- basis for suspicion **16**:891
- bigamy and poligamy **4**:985
- chastity **5**:363
- Commandments, the 613 **5**:769,781
- divorce **6**:129
- Doenmeh **6**:148ff
- duress **12**:1400; **13**:224
- ethics **6**:935
- Hurrian custom **12**:1290
- imprisonment **8**:1302
- *mamzer* **11**:840
- oath of **12**:1297
- oils **12**:1349
- ordeal of jealousy **12**:1449
- priests **13**:1089
- punishment for **10**:788; **11**:1052ff
- Salonika case **10**:239
- sin **14**:1592
- Talmud **15**:170
- wife's admission **2**:292
- *illus:*
- - ordeal of "waters of bitterness" **12**:1448
- - woman who has drunk the "bitter water" **15**:171
Adumbratio Kabbalae Christianae (bk.) **10**:1118
Adummim (city, Er. Isr.) **7**:265
Adummim, Ascent of (Er. Isr.) **10**:330
Adventists (mvmt., U.S.) **16**:1154
Adventists, Seventh Day (sect) **10**:398
ADVERTISING **2**:316
- *illus:*
- - text
- - El-Al poster **6**:562
- - *Forward,* advertisement page **15**:1619
- - IZIS, Israel tourism poster **9**:1161
- - Purim fete poster, N.Y.C. **13**:1391
Advertiser (newsp.) **13**:1031
Ady, Endre (poet) **8**:1239
A.E.C., *see* Atomic Energy Commission
Aegidius da Viterbo, *see* EGIDIO DA VITERBO
Aegidius Romanus (Aegidius of Colonna) **15**:711
Aegina (tn., Gr.) **12**:181
- synagogue **3**:521; **15**:599
Aelana, *see* AKABA
Aelfric Heptateuch (11th cent. ms., Eng.)
- *illus:* **5**:370, 1014, 1016; **9**:1193
AELIA CAPITOLINA **2**:319
- Bet Guvrin **9**:251
- description **9**:1405ff
- Hadrian **7**:1054
- history chart **8**:766-767
- Jerusalem archaeology **9**:1535
- *illus:* text (plan)
- - entrance gates **9**:1401,1402
AELIAN (Claudius, Aelianus, sophist) **7**:892
Aelius Gallus, Gaius (Rom. sol.), *see* Gallus, Gaius Aelius
Aemilius, Paulus (apos.) **11**:356; **15**:1482
Aeneas (k.), *see* ARETAS IV
AERONAUTICS, AVIATION AND ASTRONAUTICS **2**:320
- *Contents:*
- - General **2**:320
- - Interwar Period **2**:321
- - Postwar **2**:322
- - Astronautics **2**:322
- - Capsules **2**:322
- *illus:*
- - text
- - Rumpler's *Rumplertaube* **14**:429
- - Schwarz's airship **14**:1024
- *see also:* EL-AL; Israel Aircraft Industries: Israel Air Force
AESCOLY, AARON ZE'EV **2**:324
Aesop **6**:1126 **2**:357
Aesthetics
- Mendelssohn, Moses **11**:1329; **11**:1332
- nature **12**:888
Aethicus Ister (Chr. writ.) **9**:1149
Aetius of Amida (anc. au.) **11**:1183
Aetolia (Gr.) **7**:868
Af'āl al-Mushtaqqa min al-Asmā,' al-, see Kitāb al-Af'āl al-Mushtaqqa min al-Asmā
Af'āl Dhawāt al-Mithlayn, al-, see Kitab al-Af'āl Dhawāt al-Mithlayn
Af'āl Dhawāt Ḥuruf al-Līn, al-, see Kitāb al-Af'āl Dhawāt Ḥuruf al-Līn
Af Al Pi (refugee boat)
- *illus:*
- - "illegal" immigration **8**:1467
Afam (litur.), *see* APAM
Afanashewa, Tatiana **6**:508
Afarayim (tn.), *see* HAPHARAIM
Afarkeset (pseud.) **13**:137
Afarsemon (spice), *see* BALSAM
Afdal, al-Malik al (sult.) **3**:998; **14**:670
Afek (Aphek; kib., Isr.) **1**:place list; **3**:177
AFENDOPOLO, CALEB BEN ELIJAH **2**:325
Afess (tan./amora) **11**:100
Afflictions of Love **7**:776ff
- justice and mercy of God **7**:670
- Lamentations, Book of **10**:1372
- Maimonides **11**:774; **13**:442
- Saadiah Gaon **14**:136
- sages **14**:653
AFFONSO II (k., Port.) **2**:326
AFFONSO III **2**:326
AFFONSO IV **2**:326
AFFONSO V **2**:326
AFFONSO HENRIQUES (k., Port.) **2**:326
AFFORESTATION IN ISRAEL **9**:787
- early Israelite **2**:387
- flora **9**:220
- J.N.F. **10**:77
- Tu bi-Shevat **15**:1420
- *illus:*
- - text
- - Balfour Forest **9**:585,586
- - J.N.F. Galilee project **10**:79
- - Jordan gallery forest **9**:153
- - Kiryat Gat **9**:786
AFGHANISTAN **2**:326
- *Contents:*
- - General **2**:326
- - Recent Years **2**:328
- - Folklore **2**:328
- *aliyah* **9**:515
- anti-Semitism **2**:328
- Israel, State of **9**:444
- Israel community **9**:502
- marriage custom **11**:1043; **11**:1045
- spices **8**:1311
- Ten Lost Tribes **15**:1006
- *illus:*
- - Judeo-Persian inscription (8th cent.) **10**:430
- *pop. table:* text
- *see also:* KHURASAN
AFIA, AARON **2**:328
AFIKE JEHUDA (soc.) **2**:329
AFIKIM (kib., Isr.) **2**:329
- statistics **1**:place list
AFIKOMAN (Seder rit.) **2**:329
- as abbreviation **2**:52
- *illus:* text
Afisah (kab. conc.), *see* Nothingness
Aflalo (Mor. fam.) **12**:339ff
AFL-CIO, *see* American Federation of Labor
Afonso (ks.,), *see* AFFONSO
Afrahim, Vidal, *see* Ephraim, Vidal
Afriat (fam., Mor.) **12**:1340
Afriat, Judah **12**:1341
AFRICA **2**:330
- General
- - Israel **9**:433
- - socialism **15**:32
- - Ten Lost Tribes **15**:1006
- - vital statistics **16**:178f
- East Africa
- - Cush, Greek appellation for **5**:1174
- North Africa
- - Agriculture **2**:401
- - *aliyah* **9**:512
- - capitulations **5**:149
- - communal organization **5**:815
- - crime among Jews **5**:1092ff
- - demography **5**:1499
- - education **6**:459ff
- - folklore **2**:68
- - gaonate **7**:324
- - Jewish farmers **2**:401; **2**:402
- - Judaizers **10**:398
- - Judeo-Arabic **10**:409
- - liturgy **11**:400
- - nagid **12**:763
- - Ottoman period **16**:1536;1542;1550
- - rabbinical titles **13**:1449; **13**:1451
- - sickness **14**:1501
- - Zionism **16**:1127
- *illus:*
- - text
- - Demnate, heads of congregations **5**:1492
- - Djerba, al-Ghariba synagogue **6**:139
- - Fez Jewish family **6**:1255
- - Isaacs, Nathaniel, *Travels . . .* (1836) **9**:43
- - Jewish Berbers **4**:587,588
- - Jewish child bride **5**:424
- - student receiving instruction in Israel **9**:439
- - Tunisia, Jewish women **7**:234
- *pop. tables:*
- - text
- - Algeria **2**:613, 617
- - countries with 500 or more Jews, 1967, **5**:1503
- - Egypt, Hellenistic period, Middle Ages, 19th cent. **6**:486, 500
- - Jewish population, 1850-1967 **5**:1495
- - Jewish population, main concentrations **2**:333
- - Libya **11**:99
- - Morocco **12**:327
- - Muslim countries, postwar communities **5**:837
- - 19/20centuries **13**:893,898,901
- - North Africa **5**:1502
- - Ottoman Empire **16**:1533
- - postwar community developments **5**:841
- - Rhodesia (1971) **14**:148
- - South Africa **15**:183,188,206
- - total Jewish population, 1840-1969 **5**:831
- - Tunisia **15**:1431
- - type of Jewish community organization and Jewish population in 1968, **5**:841
- - vital statistics **16**:180,182,186,188
- - *see also:* AFRICA, NORTH:

MUSICAL TRADITIONS; *and under individual countries*
AFRICA, NORTH: MUSICAL TRADITIONS 16:1257
– *mus. notations:*
– – Song of the Sea 14:1070
Africa Propria (Rom. kdm.), *see* Provincia Africa
Afridi (Afg. tribe) 2:326
Afridusi, Alexander, *see* Alexander al-Afridusi
Afrikaans (lang.) 15:208
Afrikaner Yidish Tsaytung (journ.) 13:1049
Afro (tn., Transj.), *see* EPHRON
Afro-Asian Institute (Isr.) 8:540; 9:436
Afroasiatic (lang.), *see* Hamito-Semitic
AFTALION, ALBERT 2:336
AFTERLIFE 2:336
– *Contents:*
– – General 2:336
– – In Bible 2:337
– – In Second Temple Literature 2:337
– – In Talmud and Midrash 2:337
– – In Medieval Jewish Philosophy 2:338
– – In Kabbalistic Literature 2:339
– – In Modern Jewish Thought 2:339
– Concept
– – Abraham's bosom 2:165
– – academy on high 2:208
– – beatitude 4:359
– – belief, source of 10:389
– – body and soul 4:1165
– – death 5:1423
– – Garden of Eden 7:326
– – God, justice and mercy of 7:669
– – *ḥibbut ha-kever* 8:464
– – Kabbalah 10:612ff
– – life and death 11:235
– – man, nature of 11:845
– – netherworld 12:996
– – Paradise 13:77
– – philosophy 13:421; 13:424
– – resurrection 14:96
– – soul 15:172
– – soul, immortality of 15:174
– – *see also:* ESCHATOLOGY; GILGUL; OLAM HA-BA; REWARD AND PUNISHMENT
– Views on
– – Abraham bar Hiyya 13:436
– – Boethusians 4:1169
– – Gabirol, Solomon ibn 7:242
– – Jacob ben Korshai 9:1221
– – Maimonides 11:776
– – Mendelssohn 11:1330f
– – Nahmanides 10:527
– *illus:*
– – the righteous in Paradise 4:360
Afternoon Service, *see* MINḤAH
"After the Pogrom" (paint., S. Fabjanski) 13:699
AFULAH (tn., Isr.) 2:339
– statistics 1:place list
– sugar industry 15:488
– *illus:*
– – Jezreel Valley 10:102
Afulah Illit (tn., Isr.) 2:339
AGA, BENJAMIN BEN SAMUEL 2:340
Agadati, Baruch 12:460
Agade (city, Shinar), *see* AKKAD
AGADIR (tn., Alg.) 2:340
– Jewish center 16:1187
– Tlemcen Jews 15:1172
AGADIR (tn., Mor.) 2:340
AGAG (bib. fig.) 2:341
– in the Arts 14:785
– rabbinic homilies 6:857
– *see also:* AMALEKITES
AGAI, ADOLF 2:342
Against Apion (bk.) 10:262
Against the Galileans (bk.) 10:468
Against the Jews (bk.) 3:178
AGAM, YAACOV 2:342
– *illus:*
– – "Rosh ha-Shanah" Pl. 19 3-ART
Agama (fauna) 9:226
Agan, Ḥayyim Abraham, *see* GAGIN, ḤAYYIM ABRAHAM BEN MOSES
Agar, Nathan 15:300
Agasi, Eliyahu 9:1041
Agate (min.) 13:1010
AGATHARCHIDES OF CNIDUS (hist.) 7:889; 7:892
Agatir (Samar. wk.) 14:749
Agatstein, Mieczyslaw, *see* JASTRUN, MIECZYSLAW
Agau (lang., Eth.) 6:1149
Agav karka (hal. conc.) 2:220
Agazi (tribe) 7:1222
AGDE (tn., Fr.) 2:343
– camp 7:34
AGE AND THE AGED 2:343
– *Contents:*
– – Old Age 2:343
– – – Bible 2:343
– – – Talmud 2:345
– – Care of Aged 2:346
– – – Middle Ages 2:346
– – – 18/19 cents. 2:346
– – – Contemporary 2:347
– – – U.S. 2:347
– – – Israel 2:348
– criminal incapacity 13:225
– vital statistics 16:177f
– wills 16:519
– *illus:*
– – text
– – Lodz, old-age home resident 11:437
– – Rockville Home for the Aged 16:357
– – Romny old age home 14:256
– – Warsaw ghetto 16:344
Agelli, Antonio 8:21
AGEN (city, Fr.) 2:349
– *illus:*
– – Rue des Juifs 10:85
Agence Permanente de l'Organisation Sioniste auprés de la Société des Nations 7:403
AGENCY (legal conc.) 2:349
– *Contents:*
– – Definition 2:349
– – Criminal Law 2:350
– – Limitations 2:350
– – Powers 2:351
– – Revocation 2:351
– – Brokerage 2:352
– – Performance by Agent 2:352
– – Debt Recovery 2:352
– – Property Acquisition 2:353
– attorney 3:837
– biblical origin 8:1423
– civil and ritual law 12:111
– contract 5:931
– corporate body 10:1567ff
– creditors, joint 12:1315
– debt assignment 3:768ff
– divorce 6:132
– *ḥaliẓah* 11:128
– *ḥazakah* 7:1521
– marriage 11:1049
– overreaching 12:1394
– public affairs 13:1353ff
– Rabbi Nathan's lien 14:1397
– slaves 14:1659
– tort liability 11:184
– *see also:* ACQUISITION; ATTORNEY; Legal Capacity; PARTNERSHIP; SHALISH
Agency, Jewish, *see* JEWISH AGENCY
Agent (shali'ah) 2:349ff
Agga (ruler, Mesop.) 16:1483
AGGADAH 2:354
– *Contents:*
– – Definition 2:354
– – Introduction 2:354
– – Content and Form 2:356
– – Folklore 2:356
– – The Discourse 2:358
– – Methods 2:359
– – Structure and Style 2:359
– – History In 2:360
– – Doctrines 2:361
– – Aggadists 2:363
– – Islam 2:364
– – Illuminated Mss. 2:365
– Abbaye 2:45
– allegorical exegesis 4:895
– *amoraim* 2:868
– animal tales 3:20ff
– anthropomorphism 3:55
– Aptowitzer's studies 3:225
– *Baraita of 32 Rules* 4:194ff
– *Baruch, Apocalypse of* 4:271
– Ben Sira 4:552
– dogma 3:658
– Dura-Europos 6:294
– Eleazar of Modi'in 6:603
– folktale 6:1379
– *halakhah* 7:1164; 15:455
– Ibn Abi Zimra 5:1357
– importance of 11:652
– Ishmael ben Elisha 9:84
– Jerusalem Talmud 15:775
– Jewish literature 11:314ff
– kabbalistic interpretation 10:640ff
– Karaites 10:769
– Krochmal, N. 10:1272
– leprosy 11:38
– Messiah 11:1410
– *Midrash ha-Gadol* 11:1515
– mystical interpretation 10:570
– preaching 13:995
– *Pugio Fidei* 4:213
– sages' appraisal of 14:651
– Septuagint 9:243
– Talmud 15:762
– Targum as 4:842
– Targum Sheni 15:811
– Theodor, Julius 15:1100
– Wuensche's studies 16:673
– *illus:*
– – text
– – Abel, variants of killing 5:21–23
– – Abraham in Nimrod's fiery furnace 2:118; 8:1217; 12:1166
– – Abraham's bosom 2:166
– – Alexander the Great 2:580
– – Asmodeus 3:754
– – Azazel 3:999
– – *behemoth* 4:360,394,*fcg.* 907
– – Bible, translation into Greek 3:439
– – Bithiah and the infant Moses 8:1059
– – Lamech killing Cain 5:25
– – leviathan 4:360,394,*fcg.* 907
– – Nebuchadnezzar riding a lion 12:916
– – Pharaoh bathing in Hebrews' blood 13:360
– – the righteous in Paradise 4:360,*fcg.* 907
– – woman giving birth to six children 4:*fcg.* 1067
– – *ziz* 4:360 *fcg.* 907
– *see also:* MIDRASH; PREACHING; PROVERBS, TALMUDIC
Aggadat Arba Kosot (wk.) 13:69
AGGADAT BERESHIT (Mid.) 2:366
Aggadat Eikhah (Mid.), *see* LAMENTATIONS RABBAH
Aggadat Ḥazita (Mid.), *see* SONG OF SONGS RABBAH
Aggadat Proverbs, *see* MIDRASH PROVERBS
Aggadat Samuel, see MIDRASH SAMUEL
Aggadot Shir ha-Shirim 11:1515
Aggadat Tehillim, see MIDRASH TEHILLIM
Aggadic Midrash, *see Midrash Aggadah*
Aggadists 2:363
Agger, Carolyn (law.) 6:1441
Aggide (Shinar), *see* AKKAD
Aggudah (hal. wk.) 5:647
Aggudat . . . *see also* Agudat; Aguddat
Aggudat ha-Ḥazzanim (Pol.) 7:1542
Aggudat ha-Ze'irim ha-Ivriyyim (orgn., Iraq) 8:1450
Aghlab, Al- (emir) 2:366
AGHLABIDS (dyn., emirs) 2:366
– Tunisia 15:1433
Aghmāt (tn., N. Afr.) 2:667
– Jewish population 10:88
AGHMATI, ZECHARIAH BEN JUDAH (12/13 cent., Mor.) 2:367
– Morocco 12:329
Agitator (polit. term) 15:41
Agla (Khirbat ᾿Ajlān) 6:477
Aglibol (deity, Palmyra) 15:698
AGMON, NATHAN 2:367
– Drama, Hebrew 6:200
– Jerusalem 9:1566
Agnon, Esther 11:1070
AGNON, SHMUEL YOSEF 2:367
– chronological chart 8:766-767
– Hebrew literature 8:199; 8:202
– Jerusalem 9:1567
– Kurzweil, Baruch 10:1303
– Mishpat ha-Shalom ha-Ivri 12:142
– world literature 8:743
– *illus:*
– – text
– – autograph 3:913
– – *Ma'aseh ha-Ez* (1925) 5:435
– – Neher, André 12:940
– – *Temol Shilshom,* manuscript 8:208
Agnosticism 10:557
AGOBARD (archbp.) 2:371
– attitude to Jews 3:101; 8:662; 8:666
– Jewish mysticism 10:515
– Louis I 11:514
– Lyons Jews 11:623
– slave trade 14:1661; 16:1281
– Vienne 16:132
Agoin (Mor.) 3:826; 12:334
– *illus:*
– – Mellah 10:88
Agorah (coin) 5:730ff
AGORANOMOS (pub. offic.) 2:372
– Babylon 8:649
Agra (city, Ind.) 8:1356
Agram (city, Yug.), *see* ZAGREB
AGRAMUNT (tn., Sp.) 2:373
AGRANAT, SHIMON 2:373
– *illus:*
– – Eichmann trial 6:519
– – Supreme Court bench 9:637
Agranium (tn., Mesop.), *see* HAGRONIA
AGRARIAN LEAGUE (Ger.) 2:373
AGRAT BAT MAHALATH (queen of demons) 2:374
– demonology 5:1527
– Lilith 11:246; 11:247
Agricola, Michael (bp.) 4:878
AGRICULTURAL METHODS AND IMPLEMENTS IN ANCIENT EREZ ISRAEL 2:374
– *Contents:*
– – Plowing 2:374
– – Fertilization 2:376
– – Sowing and Planting 2:376
– – Hoeing and Weeding 2:376
– – Harvest 2:377

– – Winnowing 2:379
– – Irrigation 2:379
– Commandments, the 613 5:777
– *illus:*
– – text
– – harvesting 2:385
– – reaper (Antonius Pius coin) 2:395
– *see also:* AGRICULTURE; AGRICULTURE IN ISRAEL
Agricultural Museum, Jerusalem, *see* Jerusalem Agricultural Museum
Agricultural Workers' Federation (Isr.) 9:658
AGRICULTURE 2:381
– *Contents:*
– – Land of Israel 2:382
– – – Prehistory 2:382
– – – Bronze Age to Joshua 2:382
– – – Early Israelite 2:387
– – – First Temple 2:390
– – – Second Temple 2:392
– – – Hasmoneans 2:393
– – – Mishnah and Talmud 2:393
– – – Byzantine Moslem 2:397
– – Babylon 2:398
– – – Livestock 2:400
– – Middle Ages 2:401
– – – Ideals 2:401
– – – History 2:401
– – Trade 2:403
– – Modern Europe 2:406
– – – Ukraine 2:407
– – – Belorussia 2:408
– – – Poland 2:409
– – – Rumania 2:411
– – U.S. 2:411
– – Canada 2:412
– – Latin America 2:413
– *arenda* 3:402
– Austrian *Toleranzpatent* 3:892
– Bessarabia 4:705ff
– Canada 5:106
– Christian slave prohibition 8:653
– crafts 5:1040
– FAO 15:1564
– I.C.A. 10:44
– Jewish pioneers 16:1285
– Modern economic history 16:1316
– Muslim countries 8:659ff
– Russia 8:741; 14:468
– Second Temple era 16:1273
– wine trade 16:541
– Zionism 16:1068ff
– *illus:*
– – text
– – Ahlem horticultural school 2:468
– – Argentina, Jewish gauchos 3:429
– – Baron de Hirsch School, Woodbine, N.J. 10:35,47; 16:158
– – Belorussia, Emes farm members 14:470
– – Grodno training farm 13:747
– – He-Ḥalutz members on a farm near Kiev 15:1517
– – ICA colony in Bessarabia 10:45
– – Komzet report on Birobidzhan (1927) 14:470
– – Mauricio (Argentina) 3:431
– – Moisésville (Argentina) 3:427-428
– – Orgeyev training farm 12:1456
– – Russian Jewish settlement, North Dakota 12:1219
– *see also:* AGRICULTURAL METHODS AND IMPLEMENTS IN ANCIENT EREZ ISRAEL; AGRICULTURE IN ISRAEL; Kolkhozes, Jewish; *and under individual countries*
AGRICULTURE IN ISRAEL 9:773
– General
– – Arab agriculture 9:1021
– – famine and drought 6:1172ff
– – Hibbat Zion 16:1039ff
– – human geography 9:567
– – Negev 12:930ff
– – rain 13:1520
– – Yemenite Jews 16:752ff
– Historical Survey 9:392ff,773
– – ancient Israel 2:438; 8:611
– – Canaan 13:472
– – Crusaders 9:268; 9:272; 9:272
– – economic history 16:1323
– – Gezer Calendar 7:538
– – Mamluk period 9:277
– – Ottoman period 9:284; 9:291
– – 70 to 640 C.E. 9:237; 9:252; 9:254; 9:258
– – 634 to 1099 9:260; 9:264
– – tribes 8:581
– Laws of
– – Commandments, the 613 5:777
– – first fruits 6:1312
– – Kalischer, Z. H. 10:709
– – Leket, Shikhḥah, and Peah 11:3
– – mixed species 12:169
– – Omer 12:1382
– – sabbatical year 14:574
– – technology 15:896
– – *terumah* 15:1025
– – tithes 15:1156
– *illus:*
– – African student receiving instruction 9:439
– – agricultural worker 9:858
– – Arabah, intensive farming 9:*fcg.* 171
– – Avedat Farm Project 2:397, 399; 12:739
– – Givat Ye'arim 9:577
– – Givat Yo'av vegetable harvest 9:578
– – harvesting muskmelon 11:1294
– – ICA letter re Sinai (1903) 10:47
– – Kinneret region 9:582
– – loading wheat at Gederah 9:517
– – Mikveh Israel school 11:1544,1545
– – Naḥal Yam, growing tomatoes 12:767
– – olive-oil press, Arab 9:1028
– – olive press, ancient 6:1417
– – plowing at Tel Yosef 13:485
– – Rishon le-Zion, harvesting grapes 14:194
– – terracing in Judean Mountains 9:133,205
– – Tnuva central dairy 15:1175
– *tables:* text
– *see also:* JEWISH COLONIZATION ASSOCIATION; NOMADISM; WATER AND IRRIGATION IN ISRAEL
AGRIGENTO (tn., Sic.) 2:415
Agrimas (demon) 11:246
AGRIPPA I (Judea) 2:415
– bridal procession 11:1034
– Caligula and Petronius 13:346
– chronological chart 8:766-767
– coinage 5:718
– *hakhel* ceremony 7:1149
– Hellenism 8:296
– Israel history 8:638
– Jerusalem 9:1531
– Josephus on 10:261
– Kidron 10:988
– letters 11:56
– Silas 14:1532
– *geneal. table:* text; 8:377
– *illus:*
– – coins 2:392; 5:704
AGRIPPA II (Herodian k.) 2:417
– coinage 5:718
– Festus, Porcius 6:1247
– *hakhel* ceremony 7:1149
– Justus of Tiberias 10:479
– Man of Lies 11:234
– Temple 15:959
– *geneal. table:* text; 8:377
– *illus:*
– – coins 5:704-705
AGRIPPA, CAIUS JULIUS (Rom. gov.) 2:418
Agrippa, H. Cornelius of Nettesheim (philos.) 10:644
– Giorgio, Francesco 7:588
– Trithemius, Johannes 15:1400
Agrippa, Marcus Julius, *see* AGRIPPA II
AGRIPPA, MARCUS VIPSANIUS (Rom. sol.) 2:418
– Herod 8:635; 9:1394
Agrippias (city, Er. Isr.), *see* ANTHEDON
AGRIPPINA (beacon station, Er. Isr.) 2:418
– Crusader castle 3:329; 12:880
– destruction 9:269
– Ramoth 13:1543
– *illus:*
– – text
– – Crusader castle 2:419; 5:1145
Agrob (prov., Bashan), *see* TRACHONITIS
Agro-Joint, *see* American Jewish Joint Agriculture Corporation
Agron (letter) 11:59
Agron (wk., Saadiah Gaon), *see Sefer ha-Agron*
Agron, al- (wk., Alfasi), *see Kitāb Jāmi' al-Alfāz*
AGRON (Agronsky), GERSHON (Isr.) 2:419
– Jerusalem 9:1498
– *illus:*
– – Agron Road, Jerusalem
Agudat . . . *see also* Aggudat
Agudat ha-Elef (Belor.) 12:52
Agudat Harabbonim, *see* UNION OF ORTHODOX RABBIS OF THE UNITED STATES AND CANADA
AGUDAT HA-SOẒYALISTIM HA-IVRIM (Eng.) 2:420
Agudath Bnei Zion (Zion. orgn., Gr.) 14:703
Agudat Ḥovevei Sefat Ever (Rus.) 10:832
Agudath Zion (gr., Urug.) 16:1126
AGUDAT ISRAEL 2:421
– *Contents:*
– – Introduction 2:421
– – Ereẓ Israel 2:424
– – U.S. 2:426
– anti-Zionism 16:1068
– Bar-Ilan University 4:225
– Beth Jacob Schools 16:1260
– education 6:427ff
– Ḥasidim 7:1397
– Hirsch, S. R. 8:514
– history chart 8:766-767
– Israel Meir ha-Kohen 9:1070
– Israel politics 9:658ff
– Judaism 10:396
– Neturei Karta 12:1003
– Orthodoxy 12:1488
– rabbinate, Israel 13:1457
– religion in Israel 9:891ff
– Rosenheim, Jacob 14:288
– U.N. 15:1559
– U.S. Zionism 16:1145
– Va'ad Le'ummi boycott 16:50
– Warsaw 16:341
– Yemenite Jews 16:755
– yeshivot 16:772
– *see also:* PO'ALEI AGUDAT ISRAEL
Agudat Montefiore (Zion. orgn.) 10:820
Agudat Neta'im (Er. Isr.) 6:542; 9:328
Agudat Zion (Can.) 16:1109
Aguddah Ẓiyyonit le-Aram-Naharayim (Iraq) 8:1450
Aguddah (wk.) 2:585
Aguddat . . . *see also* Aggudat; Agudat
Aguddat Aḥi'ever (publ., Iraq) 8:1450
AGUDDAT AḤIM (Gal.) 2:426
– Galicia 16:1330
Aguddat Benei Yehudah (Iraq) 8:1450
Aguddat Bonei Battim (Jaffa) 15:919
– *see also:* Aḥuzzat Bayit
Aguddat ha-Koremim (Er. Isr.) 7:1494; 7:632
Aguddat Soferim Ivrim (Rus.) 14:1125
Aguilar, Antonio de 11:301
Aguilar, Benjamin d' 4:463; 8:1356
Aguilar, Sir Charles Lawrence d' 2:427
Aguilar, David de 15:487
AGUILAR, DIEGO D' 2:427
– ennobled 15:1166
– tobacco trade 15:1177
AGUILAR, EMANUEL ABRAHAM 2:428
Aguilar, Ephraim d', *see* Pereira, Ephraim Lopez
Aguilar, Sir George Charles d' 2:427
AGUILAR, GRACE 2:428
Aguilar, Joseph d' 2:427
AGUILAR, MOSES RAPHAEL D' 2:429
– Recife 13:1613
AGUILAR DE CAMPÓO (tn., Sp.) 2:429
Aguilar Samuda, Joseph d', *see* Samuda, Joseph d'Aguilar
AGUNAH 2:429
– *Contents:*
– – Definition 2:429
– – The Problem 2:429
– – Mode of Proof 2:430
– – Subject-Matter of Proof 2:431
– – Civil Marriage 2:431
– – Remarriage 2:431
– – Consequences of Remarriage 2:432
– – Precautions 2:432
– – State of Israel 2:433
– Benjamin Ze'ev of Arta 4:538
– Chmielnicki massacres 5:483
– civil marriage 5:597; 5:598
– concubine 5:865
– Conservative attitude 12:1445
– Conservative *ketubbah* 10:929
– divorce 6:127ff
– *ḥaliẓah* 11:127ff
– husband's flight 8:1301
– Judah ben Bava 10:343
– one witness 16:585
– Slonik, Benjamin Aaron 14:1670
– *takkanot* 15:719
– *Tevul Yom* (tract.) 15:1033
– tractate *Yevamot* 16:777
– woman 16:629
Agur (k.), *see* SOLOMON
Agur (mosh., Isr.) 1:place list
Agur (sand-dune) 12:926
Agur (wk.)
– codification of law 5:646
– *haskamah* 7:1452
– Landau, Jacob 10:1393
AGURSKY, SAMUEL 2:433
AGUR SON OF JAKEH (bib. fig.) 2:434
AGUS, IRVING ABRAHAM 2:434
AGUS, JACOB BERNARD 2:435
Agushaya (deity), *see* Ishtar
A Gute Vokh (Yid. greeting) 7:913
Aḥa (Babyl.), *see* AḤAI
Aḥa (of Be-Ḥozai; amora) 4:395
AḤA (Pal. amora) 2:435
– marriage dance 11:1033
Aḥa (gaon) 7:318
AHAB (k., Isr.) 2:435

- *Contents:*
- - Foreign Affairs **2:**435
- - Internal Affairs **2:**437
- - Aggadah **2:**439
- archaeology **3:**306
- Elijah **6:**632ff
- history **8:**596ff
- history chart **8:**766-767
- Hosea **8:**1014ff
- in the Arts **6:**641
- Jehoshaphat **9:**1325ff
- Karkar battle **10:**792
- Mesha of Moab **11:**1397ff
- Naaman **12:**734
- Naboth **12:**746
- Rechabites **13:**1610
- Shalmaneser III **16:**1502,1509
- *Targum Sheni* **15:**812
- trade and commerce **15:**1296
- warfare **16:**273
- Zedekiah's prophecies **16:**964
- *illus:*
- - Elijah castigating **12:**747
- - ivory house **3:**315,337,503; **5:**397,1227
- - Jezebel giving advice **10:**100
- - Megiddo (plan) **11:**1225
AHAB (false prophet, Babyl.) **2:**439
- Exile, Babylonian **6:**1037
- Jeremiah **16:**964
AḤA BAR ḤANINA (amora) **2:**439
AḤA BAR RAV (amora) **2:**440
Aḥa ben Adda (amora) **15:**1521
Aḥa ben Avira (amora) **3:**975
AḤA BEN JACOB (amora) **2:**440
Aḥa ben Rabbah ben Abuha (savora) **2:**448
Aḥadboi (3rd cent., Babyl.) **11:**1132
AḤAD HA-AM **2:**440
- Benei Moshe order **4:**492ff
- Berdyczewski **4:**593ff
- critic **5:**1119
- cultural Zionism **9:**996
- Eliasberg, J. **6:**616
- encyclopedias **6:**732
- Feuerberg, M. Z. **6:**1251
- Hebrew literature **8:**190
- Hebrew vocabulary **16:**1649
- Herzl's Zionism **16:**1151
- history chart **8:**766-767
- Judaism, essence of **10:**384
- Kurzweil **10:**1302
- Lilienblum **11:**242
- Maimonides **11:**761
- Moses **12:**401
- prophecy **13:**1180
- revelation **14:**125
- Rothschild, Baron E. **14:**343
- Simon, Sir Leon **14:**1582
- soul, immortality of **15:**180
- "spiritual" Zionism **8:**751
- Syrkin, Nachman **15:**653
- Torah **12:**1246
- Weizmann **16:**428
- Zionism **16:**1041; **16:**1078ff
- Zionist ideology **16:**1043, 1046ff
- *illus:*
- - text
- - autograph **3:**913
- - fellow Hebrew writers **8:**193
- - first Zionist Congress **16:**1165
- - *Ha-Shilo'aḥ* (Berlin, 1897) **7:**1369
- - Odessa Committee convention **12:**1329
- *see also:* HA-SHILO'AḤ
Aḥad ha-Kanna'im, *see* LESTSCHINSKY, JACOB
Aḥad ha-Medinah (chief r.) **10:**1406
AḤAI (5/6 cent., Babyl.) **2:**448
Aḥai (Pal. amora), *see* AḤA SHABḤA
Aḥai ben Huna (savora) **2:**448; **14:**920
AḤAI BEN JOSIAH (2nd cent., Babyl.) **2:**448
- Dostai ben Yannai **6:**179
Aḥai of Shabḥa, *see* AḤA OF SHABḤA
Aḥa Kahana bar Rav (gaon) **7:**318
Ahamant (city, Er. Isr.), *see* RABBATH-AMMON
Aḥa of Bei Ḥattim (savora) **2:**448; **14:**920
Aḥa of Difti (5th cent., Babyl.) **11:**940
Aḥa of Huẓal (amora) **8:**1137
AḤA OF SHABḤA (7/8 cent., Pumb.) **2:**449
- *aliyah* **9:**511
- codification of law **5:**634; **11:**330
- Talmud **15:**761
- *see also: She'iltot*
Aḥarayut nekhasim, see LIEN
Aḥarit ha-yamim, see ESCHATOLOGY
Aharon, Ezra **8:**1461
Aharoni (art.) **15:**1487
- *illus:*
- - Hebrew type face example **15:**1485
Aharoni (Zion.), *see* MAZEH, JACOB
Aharoni, Abraham (writ.) **16:**256
AHARONI, ISRAEL (zool.) **2:**451
AHARONI, YOHANAN (arch.) **1:**27; **2:**451
- archaeology **3:**303
AḤARONIM (rab. authorities) **2:**452
- definition **7:**1166
- *ḥiddushim* **8:**466
- Jewish law periods **12:**122
- responsa **14:**88ff
- *see also:* AUTHORITY, RABBINICAL; CODIFICATION OF LAW; RISHONIM
AHARONOVITCH, YOSEF **2:**452
- Ha-Po'el ha-Zair **7:**1324
- political activity **9:**657ff
Aharonowitz, Zalman, *see* ARANNE, ZALMAN
AHASUERUS (k., Pers.) **2:**453
- arts **6:**908
- Esther **6:**906
- Mordecai **12:**307
- Purim **13:**1391
- Scroll of Esther **14:**1047ff
- *Targum Sheni* **15:**812
- Vashti **16:**72ff
- wives' preparations **8:**1313
- *illus:*
- - Dura-Europos wall paint. **6:**284; **8:**649
- - Esther bowing to **6:**907,909
- - Esther scroll **14:**1053
- - twelfth cent. Bible **12:**733
Ahasuerus, *see* WANDERING JEW
AHASUERUS-XERXES (k., Pers.) **2:**454
- history **8:**616; **13:**303
- Samaritans **14:**728ff
Ahasver, *see* WANDERING JEW
Ahava (Babyl.) **8:**618
Aḥavah (contracting gr., Isr.) **5:**946; **13:**659
Ahavah ben Zeira **11:**707
AHAVAH RABBAH; AHAVAT OLAM (litur.) **2:**454
Ahavah Rabbah (shtayger) **14:**1464
Ahavath Chesed (syn., N.Y.) **12:**1079
- *illus:*
- - Huebsch's prayer book **13:**1113
- - interior **12:**1091
Ahavath Zion (Zion. orgn., Braz.) **16:**1124
Ahavat Shalom (kab. gr.) **2:**609, 611; **3:**1019
Ahavat Zion (stlmt. soc.) **4:**984
- Ḥibbat Zion **16:**1038
AHAZ (k., Judah) **2:**455
- history **8:**604ff
- history chart **8:**766-767
- Hosea **8:**1010ff
- Isaiah **9:**46
- Tabeel **15:**676
- *geneal. table:* **5:**1341
AHAZIAH (k., Isr.) **2:**456
- history **8:**598ff
- history chart **8:**766-767
- Jehoshaphat **9:**1325ff
- Moabite revolt **11:**1397
- trade and commerce **15:**1296
AHAZIAH (k., Judah) **2:**456
- history **8:**599
- history chart **8:**766-767
- *geneal. table:* **5:**1341
Aḥbār ("ḥakham") **4:**928
Aḥbār, Ka'b al- (conv.), *see* KA'B AL-AḤBĀR
Aḥdut (period., Er. Isr.) **4:**578; **13:**659
- Shazar, Zalman **14:**1326ff
Aḥdut (period., U.S.), *see Achdut*
Aḥdut (orgn., Ger.) **7:**486
Aḥdut (press, Er. Isr.) **5:**946
AḤDUT HA-AVODAH (polit. party) **2:**456
- conference, 1920 **9:**683
- Eisenhower Doctrine **9:**391
- kibbutz movement **10:**971
- labor organization **9:**848ff
- Mapai **11:**913ff
- Po'alei Zion **13:**661
- Sinai withdrawal **9:**390
- Zionist Socialists **16:**1225
- *illus:*
- - Ha-Po'el ha-Ẓa'ir **9:**660
- - Mapai and Rafi **9:**677
- *see also:* ISRAEL LABOR PARTY
AḤDUT HA-AVODAH (lab. pubs., Er. Isr.) **2:**457
- Hebrew newspapers **12:**1056
- statistics **1:**newsp. list
AḤDUT HA-AVODAH-PO'ALEI ZION (polit. party) **2:**457
- Mapam **11:**914
Aḥdut Israel (Revisionists) **3:**496; **14:**129
Ahearn, Goldie **15:**306
Aḥer (tan.), *see* ELISHA BEN AVUYAH
A-ḥ-e-r (r., Hung.), *see* CHORIN, AARON
AḤERIM (tan. pseud.) **2:**458
Aḥi'asaf (publ., Warsaw) **4:**493; **7:**632; **14:**1269
- children's literature **5:**433
- publishing **13:**1375
Aḥi'ezer (mosh., Isr.) **1:**place list
Aḥihud (mosh., Isr.) **1:**place list
AHIJAH (pr., Shiloh) **2:**459
- Ichabod **8:**1215
AHIJAH THE SHILONITE (prophet) **2:**459
- Ba'al Shem Tov's mentor **9:**1052
- Jeroboam **9:**1372
- tribal antagonism **15:**103
Ahijah son of Seraiah (bib. fig.) **14:**1042
AHIKAM (bib. fig.) **2:**460
Ahikar (leg. fig.) **2:**460,461
- *geneal. table:* text
AHIKAR, BOOK OF **2:**460
AHIMAAZ (f.-in-law, Saul) **2:**462
AHIMAAZ (s., Zadok) **2:**462
- Samuel, Book of **14:**789
AHIMAAZ (s.-in-law, Solomon) **2:**462
- *geneal. table:* **5:**1342
Ahima'az, Scroll of **2:**463
- Apulian Jewry **3:**226
- Avelei Zion **3:**946
- disputations **6:**90
- emissaries **14:**1361
- fiction, Hebrew **6:**1265
- history **8:**555
- Italian Jewry **8:**666ff
- Jewish literature **11:**348
- medieval Hebrew **16:**1633
- mystics **10:**510
- *nagid* **12:**760
AHIMAAZ BEN PALTIEL (chronicler, It.) **2:**463
- *geneal. table:* text
- *see also: Ahima'az, Scroll of*
AHIMAN, SHESHAI, TALMAI (bib. figs.) **2:**463
- *see also:* ANAK, ANAKIM
AḤIMEIR, ABBA **2:**464
AHIMELECH THE HITTITE **2:**465
AHIMELECH SON OF ABIATHAR **2:**465
AHIMELECH SON OF AHITUB **2:**465
Ahimiti (Phil.) **13:**403
Ahinoam the Jezreelitess **2:**860
Ahio (bib. fig.) **2:**78; **16:**43
Aḥiram (Tyrian name), *see* HIRAM
Aḥisamakh (mosh., Isr.) **1:**place list
Aḥisefer (publ.) **14:**1269
AHITHOPHEL THE GILONITE **2:**465
- slander **10:**1432
AHITUB (bib. fig.) **2:**466
AHITUB BEN ISAAC **2:**466
Aḥituv (mosh., Isr.) **1:**place list
Aḥiya (Temple offic.) **15:**982
Aḥiyyah ha-Shiloni ha-Ḥozeh (bk.) **1:**118
AHLAB (Cana. city) **2:**467
Ahl al-Dhimma, see DHIMMA
AHL AL-KITĀB ("people of the book") **2:**467
- Dhimma **5:**1604
- Muslim rule **8:**661
Aḥlamah (gem) **13:**1010
AHLEM (vill., Ger.) **2:**468
- *illus:* text
AHLWARDT, HERMANN **2:**469
Ahmad (ruler, Tun.) **15:**1446
Ahmad al-Ḥāfiẓ **9:**287
Ahmad al-Jazzār **2:**224; **9:**291ff; **6:**1182
Aḥmad al Mahdī (imam) **14:**821
- persecutions **16:**743
- Yemenite Jews **16:**751
Aḥmad ben Yaḥya **14:**822
Aḥmad ibn Ḥazm **2:**307; **6:**91, 1030; **8:**661
Ahmad ibn Tūlūn **9:**262
Aḥmadiyya (Musl. sect) **9:**921
AHMADNAGAR (city, Ind.) **2:**469
Ahmed I **9:**287
Ahmed III **16:**1538
Ahmed Pasha **16:**1534
Ahmedabad (city, Ind.) **8:**1358
Ahmed Kūtshuk **9:**289
Aḥonai (gaon), *see* ḤANINA KAHANA BEN HUNA
Aḥor (tan.), *see* ELISHA BEN AVUYAH
AḤOT KETANNAH (hymn) **2:**469
Ahrida synagogue (Istanbul) **15:**1460
AHRWEILER (tn., Ger.) **2:**470
Ahrweiler, Hirz **2:**470
Ahrweiler, Mattityahu **2:**470
AHU (Altona, Hamburg, Wandsbek), *see* AHW
Aḥunai Kahana bar Papa (gaon) **7:**318
Ahuramzda (Pers. deity) **13:**304
Aḥuzah (gr., Eng.) **14:**687
Aḥuzat Bayit (sub., Jaffa) **4:**575; **5:**1295; **6:**138; **16:**614
- Russian Jews **16:**1138
- Tel Aviv **15:**920
Aḥuzzam (mosh., Isr.) **1:**place list
Aḥuzzat Bayit (soc., Jaffa) **15:**919
- land acquisition **16:**337
Aḥuzzat Naftali (inst., Isr.) **1:**place list

Aḥva (Zion. mvmt., Aus.) **16:**1107
Aḥvah (qtr., Jer.) **9:**238; **9:**1462
Aḥvah, Yaakov (Can.), *see* Pruzhansky, Yaakov
AHW (Altona, Hamburg, Wandsbek) **2:**779
AHWAZ (city, Khuzistan) **2:**470
AI (loc., Er. Isr.) **2:**471
– Bible history **8:**578
– fortifications **16:**273
– Luz **11:**593
– pillars **13:**521
– proscription of **8:**345ff
– *illus:*
– – excavations **5:**584*f*
– – battle **10:**269
– *plan:* text
Aiah (bib. fig.) **14:**203
Aiarammu (k., Edom) **6:**376
Aiath (city, Er. Isr.), *see* AI
AIBU (2/3 cent., Babyl.) **2:**473
AIBU (s., Rav) **2:**473
AIBU (grands., Rav) **2:**473
AIBU (amora) **2:**473
Aich Latin Bible **8:**1267
Aigen (vill., Aus.) **14:**718
Aiguptos (name for Egy.) **12:**184
Aijah (city, Er. Isr.), *see* AI
AIJALON (city, Er. Isr.) **2:**473
– Hebron **8:**226
Aijalon Valley (Isr.) **2:**473; **9:**587; **16:**237
Aiken (city, S. C.) **15:**211
AIKEN, HENRY DAVID **2:**474
AIKHENVALD, YULI ISAYEVICH **2:**474
Aikio, Matti **14:**933
A.I.K.O., *see* Allgemeine Juedische Kolonisations-Organisation
Aila (Er. Isr.), *see* ELATH
Ailsargi (orgn., Latv.) **10:**1467
AIMÉE, ANOUK **12:**463
– *illus:*
– – in *A Man and a Woman* **12:**459
Ain... *see also under* Ein..., En . . .
Ain (tn., Er. Isr.), *see* EN-RIMMON
Ain (vill., Er. Isr.), *see* IJON
Ain Jalud (spring, Er. Isr.), *see* EN-HAROD
ʿAin Shams (loc., Er. Isr.), *see* ʿAyn Shams
AINSWORTH, HENRY (schol.) **2:**474
– Bible translation **4:**870
– Christian Hebraists **8:**21
Ain Tab (city, Turk.) **3:**58
Aiquebelle (cmty., Fr.) **14:**921
Aircraft Industry (Isr.), *see* Israel aircraft industries
Air Force, Israel, *see* Israel Air Force
Air Transport in Israel **9:**837
– historical survey **9:**393ff
Ai-Shih-Tê **12:**1465
Aït-Aouday (tribe, Mor.) **15:**182
AI T'IEN (16th cent., China) **2:**475
– Hangchow Jews **7:**1262
Aivomai (gaon), *see* Ivomai
AIX-EN-PROVENCE (tn., Fr.) **2:**475
Aix-la-Chapelle (city, Ger.), *see* AACHEN
Aix-la-Chapelle Conference (1818) **16:**132
Aizen, Adolfo **13:**1370
AIZMAN, DAVID YAKOVLEVICH **2:**476
A.J.A. (Eng.), *see* ANGLO-JEWISH ASSOCIATION
A.J.A. Quarterly (Eng.) **2:**978
ʿAjamī (Pers. J.) **9:**501
ʿAjamiya, Samuel **10:**1298
AJB, *see* Association des Juifs en Belgique
A.J.C., *see* AMERICAN JEWISH CONGRESS
Ajiman, Isaiah (Turk.), *see* Adjiman, Isaiah
AJL Bulletin (U.S.) **11:**194
ʿAjlūn (tn., Jor.) **9:**181; **9:**596
– Estori ha-Parḥi **9:**279
– Fakhr al-Din II **9:**287
– Gilead **7:**570
– *see also:* TRANSJORDAN
A.J.R.F., *see* American Joint Reconstruction Foundation
Ajtai, A. Mihály **8:**21
ʿAjūl, al-(tell), *see* Tells (al-ʿAjjūl)
Ajzenberg, Leibel **10:**1433
Ajzenman-Kaniewski, Julian **12:**1416; **13:**775
Ajzensztat, Joseph David **12:**70
Ajzensztat, Moses Abraham **12:**71
Ajzykowicz, Chaim **12:**1238
AKABA (Jor. port) **2:**477
– after Temple **9:**245
– Armistice Agreements **3:**482
– Britain **9:**307
– frontier **9:**311*ff*
– Israel shipping **15:**1553ff
– navigation rights **9:**390ff
– *illus:*
– – Eilat and Gulf of Akaba **6:**567-569
– *see also:* ELATH
Akabiah bar Elioenai (Egy.) **5:**1343
AKADEMIE FUER DIE WISSENSCHAFT DES JUDENTUMS **2:**477
Akai, Kristóf **8:**21
Akasi, Jacob, *see* ABBASI, JACOB BEN MOSES IBN
AKAVYA, AVRAHAM ARYEH LEIB **2:**478
– Samaritan calendar **14:**749
AKAVYAH BEN MAHALALEL (tan.) **2:**478
Akbara (vill., Isr.) **2:**487
AKBAR THE GREAT (Moghul emp.) **2:**479
Akbon (Samar. h. pr.) **4:**17; **7:**438
– Nablus synagogue **12:**745
AKDAMUT MILLIN (piyyut) **2:**479
AKEDAH (binding of Isaac) **2:**480
– *Contents:*
– – Critical View **2:**480
– – Liturgy **2:**481
– – Rabbinic Literature **2:**481
– – Religious Thought **2:**482
– – In the Arts **2:**484
– General
– – German Jews **7:**463
– – *Kiddush ha-Shem* **10:**983
– – Maimonides on **7:**777
– – Satan **4:**903
– – Temple **15:**943
– In Art **2:**123; **9:**6
– – Aries symbol **16:**1192
– – Bet Alfa mosaics **4:**713
– – illuminated *maḥzorim* **11:**733
– *illus:*
– – text
– – Abraham ordered to sacrifice Isaac **4:**880
– – "Abraham's Sacrifice" (Rembrandt) **2:**485
– – Abraham telling Sarah of the divine command **4:**880
– – amulet **11:**265
– – Bet Alfa mosaic **3:**511
– – *Bibliothèque Nationale Pentateuch* **11:***fcg.* 1355
– – ceremonial object motif **4:**244,1231,1339
– – Dura-Europos wall paint. **6:**285
– – folk-art portrayal **8:**1286
– – fourteenth cent. ms. **15:**673
– – Islamic version **2:**120
– – Ladino ballad (music) **12:**597
– – Portaleone seal **13:**908
– – "Sacrifice of Isaac" (D. Aronson) **3:**615
– – *Sarajevo Haggadah* **8:**1272
– *see also:* ABRAHAM; ISAAC; MORIAH
Akedat Yiẓḥak (bk.) **3:**257
– philosophic exegesis **11:**346
Akerman, J. Y. **12:**1271
Akerman, Paul **15:**319
Akhaltsikhe (city, U.S.S.R.) **7:**425
Akhamot (gnostic term) **7:**638
Akhbar, Mordecai ben Samuel, *see* MEISEL, MORDECAI BEN SAMUEL
AKHBAREI (vill., Isr.) **2:**487
AKHENATON (pharaoh) **2:**487
– history chart **8:**766-767
– social revolution **6:**481
Akhetaton (loc., Egy.), *see* EL-AMARNA
Akhmatova, Anna **4:**1395
Akhmimic (Coptic dialect) **4:**861
Akhsanyah (journ.) **1:**newsp. list
Akhshaf (Cana. tn.), *see* Achshaph
Akhshav (journ.) **1:**newsp. list
Akhumai (gaon), *see* Ivomai
Akiba (Zion. mvmt.), *see* HA-NO'AR HA-IVRI-AKIBA
Akilas (bib. trans.), *see* ONKELOS AND AQUILA
Akitu (Babyl. fest.) **4:**33
AKIVA (tan.) **2:**488
– accents of the Torah **16:**1412
– Aggadah **12:**1442
– *Avinu Malkenu* **3:**974
– Bar Kokhba War **8:**646
– calendar **5:**49
– codification of law **5:**632
– Commandments, the 613 **5:**761
– Cynic *chriae* **5:**1177
– decisions **5:**891
– *halakhah* development **7:**1163
– halakhic midrash **8:**1416; **8:**1417; **11:**1522; **14:**1520
– hermeneutics **8:**371; **14:**1394
– hero of folktales **6:**1382
– history chart **8:**766-767
– Ishmael ben Elisha **9:**84ff
– Jerusalem medallion **9:**1578
– Jesus opposed **16:**844
– Keti'a bar Shalom **10:**925
– legends **8:**302
– Lost Tribes **15:**1005
– Meir **11:**1240ff
– Mishnah **12:**101
– mode of teaching **16:**777
– mysticism **10:**499
– nature **12:**888
– *pikku'aḥ nefesh* **4:**544; **13:**509
– proselyte descent **13:**1186
– Rachel, wife of **13:**1491
– sages **14:**644ff
– *Sefer Yeẓirah* **16:**786
– *Shi'ur Komah* **3:**56; **14:**1418
– *Sifra* **14:**1518
– *Sifrei Zuta* **14:**1522
– Simeon bar Yoḥai **14:**1552
– Song of Songs **15:**147ff
– Tarfon **15:**810
– tempted by Satan **14:**903
– Tinneius Rufus **15:**1148
– Torah **15:**1236,1239
– Zohar **16:**1200
– *illus:* text
Akiva (resist. gr., Pol.) **5:**1039
AKIVA BAER BEN JOSEPH **2:**492
Akiva ben Jacob Frankfurter **6:**1345; **13:**577
– Frankfort on the Main **7:**85
– Loanz, Elijah **11:**420
Akiva ben Joseph (tan.), *see* AKIVA
AKIVA BEN MENAHEM HA-KOHEN OF OFEN **2:**493
Akiva Ettinger (clny., Arg.) **3:**430
Akiva the Jew (8th cent., C.As.) **11:**1395
Akiva of Hotzenplatz **7:**1272
Akiva of Vladimir-Volynski **11:**45
AKKAD (city, Shinar) **2:**493
– Babylon **4:**31
– dynasty **16:**1485f
– Sargon of Sumer **15:**512
– Semites **14:**1148
– Shinar **14:**1408
– Ur **16:**1
– warfare **16:**266ff
– *map:* text
AKKADIAN LANGUAGE **2:**494
– *Contents:*
– – Assyrian **2:**495
– – Babylonian **2:**495
– – Phonology **2:**496
– – Morphology **2:**497
– Aramaic **3:**265ff
– cuneiform alphabet **2:**677
– grammar **16:**1512
– Hebrew linguistics **16:**1397
– Mesopotamia **16:**1490
– mishnaic Hebrew **16:** 1604
– names **12:**804f
– poetry **13:**671ff
– pre-biblical Hebrew **16:**1560
– Semitic languages **14:**1149
– Shushan **14:**1483
– Tell El-Amarna letters **15:**933
– Ugarit **15:**1505
– *diagram:* text
– *see also:* AKKAD
Akkerman (city, Bess.), *see* BELGOROD-DNESTROVSKI
Akko (city, Isr.), *see* ACRE
Akkub ben Elioenai (bib. fig.) **5:**1343
AKKUM (idol worshiper) **2:**500
– *see also:* GENTILE; IDOLATRY
Akkush (Phil. k.), *see* ACHISH
AKLAR, MORDECAI BEN RAPHAEL **2:**501
Akmechetka (concen. camp, Ukr.) **15:**1333
AKNIN, JOSEPH BEN JUDAH BEN JACOB IBN **2:**501
– education **6:**406ff
– exegesis **10:**623
– Judeo-Arabic literature **10:**419
– philosophy **13:**443
– translations **15:**1324
AKRA (tn., Kurd.) **2:**503
– Barazani's yeshivah **4:**205
Akra (citadel of Jer.), *see* ACRA
Akrabbim, Ascent of (Er. Isr.) **10:**330
Akrav (zodiac sign), *see* Scorpio
Akrav (journ.) **1:**newsp. list
AKRISH, ISAAC BEN ABRAHAM (schol., Turk.) **2:**503
– Abraham de Camondo **16:**1539
– Nasi, Joseph **12:**839
AKRON (city, O.) **2:**504
– Ohio **12:**1344
Aksa (msq.), *see* Al-Aqṣa
Aksai, Jacob, *see* ABBASI, JACOB BEN MOSES IBN
Akselrod, L. I. (Marxist, Rus.) **5:**1434
Akshak (city, Mesop.) **16:**1488
Aksum (loc., Tigre reg.) **14:**1153
Aktion (Nazi operation) **8:**831ff
– Bernhard **5:**727
– Erntefest **8:**874
– Petliura **11:**614
– Reinhard **8:**449
– Vilna **16:**149
Aktion Reinhard Case (War Crimes Trial) **16:**299
Aktion Suehnezeichen ("Atonement Operation", Ger.) **7:**498
AKZIN, BENJAMIN **2:**504
ALABAMA (U.S.) **2:**505
– *illus:*
– – Birmingham, Jewish Community Center **4:**1037
– – civil rights march (1965) **12:**931
– *pop. table:* text

ALABARCH (fiscal tit.) 2:507
Alabaster, William 8:21
Al-Adani, David, *see* ʿADANI, DAVID BEN AMRAM
Al Admat Bessarabyah (journ.) 1:newsp. list
Al-Afʿāl al-Mushtaqqa min al-Asmāʿ (wk., Ibn Balʿam), *see Kitāb al-Afʿāl al-Mushtaqqa min al-Asmāʿ*
Al-Afʿāl Dhawāt al-Mithlayn (wk., Ḥayyuj), *see Kitāb al-Afʿāl Dhawāt al-Mithlayn*
Al-Afʿāl Dhawāt Ḥuruf al-Līn (wk., Ḥayyuj), *see Kitāb al-Afʿāl Dhawāt Ḥuruf al-Līn*
Al-ʿAfūla (vill., Isr.) 2:340
Al-Aghlab, Ibrahim ibn, *see* Ibrahim ibn al-Aghlab
ALAGÓN (tn., Sp.) 2:507
Al-Agron (wk., Alfasi), *see Kitāb Jāmiʿ al-Alfāz*
ʿAlah (covenant) 5:1013
Al-Aḥbār, Kaʿb (conv.), *see* KAʿB AL-AHBĀR
Al-ʿAʾila (period., Bagh.) 13:1042
Alais (tn., Fr.), *see* ALÈS
Al-Aksa (msq.), *see* Al-Aqṣā
Al-ʿĀl (vill., Transj.) 6:583
ALALAKH (city, Turk.) 2:508
- archives 16:1498
"Alalakh weight" 16:378
Al-ʿAlam al-Isrāīlī (newsp., Beirut), *see Et Al Salām*
ʿAl-ʿAlamot (Psalms) 13:1321
ALAMAH (city, Er. Isr.) 2:509
Al-ʿAmāla al-Tūnisiyya (newsp.) 13:1041
ALAMANI, AARON HE-ḤAVER BEN YESHU'AH (r., Alex.) 2:509
Alamani, Yeshu'ah 2:509
Alamani, Zadok 2:509
Alamanni, Elias (physic.) 15:1453
Al-ʿAmārna (loc., Egy.) 15:933
Alameda (co., Calif.) 12:1294
ʿAlamī (Musl. fam.) 9:1435
ALAMI, SOLOMON 2:509
Al-ʿAmr, Ẓāhir, *see* ʿAmr, Ẓahir al-
Al-Anbār (Iraq), *see* PUMBEDITA
Alantansi, Eliezer ben Abraham 8:474
- Hebrew printing 8:1321,1325 13:1095
- *illus:*
- - Bible (c. 1487-88) 8:1330
- - printer's mark 13:1093
Alaouites (Musl. people) 9:597
Alapin, S. 5:405
Al-ʿAqīda al-Rafīʿa (bk.), *see Ha-Emunah ha-Ramah*
Al-Aqṣā (msq., Jer.) 2:55; 8:935
- Abdullah's assassination 9:1033
- British repair of 9:919
- Crusader period 9:1416
- foundation 9:1425
- Hajj al-Husseini 9:461
- Jerusalem 9:1516
- Jerusalem in art 9:1589
- Mamluks 9:1424ff
- Mussolini 9:1473
- Rohan 9:412
- Six-Day War 14:1635
- Temple Mount 15:989
- UNESCO 15:1566
- U.N. resolution 15:1549
- *illus:*
- - aerial view 9:1413,1439
- - carved doors 9:95
- - general view 8:931
- - Ramadan prayers 9:920
- - Rohan trial 9:638
- - view from south wall of Temple Mount 9:1535
- - view from the south 9:1429
Al-ʿAraba (des., Isr.), *see* ARABAH
Al-Arbaʿīn (shrine), *see* Sittin, Al-
ALARIC II (Visigothic k.) 2:510
Al-ʿArīsh (Sinai), *see* EL-ARISH
Alasa (tn., Er. Isr.), *see* ELASA
Al-Asad, Ḥafez (Syr. polit.), *see* Asad, Ḥafez al-
Al-Asad al-Mahalli (13th cent.), *see* Jacob ben Isaac
Ala Safat (site, Transj.) 15:1316
AL-ASĀṬĪR (Sam. bk.) 2:510
- language 14:754
Alashiya, *see* CYPRUS
ALASHKAR, JOSEPH BEN MOSES 2:511
ALASHKAR, MOSES BEN ISAAC 2:511
- Tlemcen 15:1173
- Tunisia 15:1441
- *illus:*
- - text
- - *She'elot u-Teshuvot* (1553) 8:72
ALASHKAR, SOLOMON 2:513
Alashkar (fam., Alg.) 15:1172
ALASKA (state, U.S.) 2:513
- *pop. table:* text
- *see also:* AMERICA
ALATINO (fam., It.) 2:514
- tobacco 15:1178
Alatino, Azriel Pethahiah (Bonaiuto) 2:514
Alatino, Jehiel Rehabiah (Vitale) 2:514
Alatino, Moses Amram 2:514
- Elijah Da Nola 12:1206
- Spoleto 15:290
ALATRI, SAMUEL 2:514
- *illus:*
- - coat of arms 8:337
ALATRINI (Alatrino; fam., It.) 2:515
Alatrini, Angelo 2:515; 9:1108
- *paytan* 13:585
Alatrini, Isaac ben Abraham 2:515
Alatrini, Johanan Mordecai Judah, *see* Alatrini, Angelo
Alatrini, Mattathias ben Abraham 2:515
Alatrino (fam.), *see* ALATRINI
Al-Attasi, Hashem (Syr. polit.), *see* Attasi, Hashem al-
Alatzar (fam.), *see* ELEAZAR
AL-AVANI, ISAAC (poet) 2:515
Alav ha-Shalom (Heb. epitaph) 7:918
ALAWIDS (Sharif dyn.) 2:516
- Morocco 12:336*ff*
Al'ayin, Jacob 13:583
Al-ʿAyya (Samar., schol.), *see* Ibrahim ben Yakʿqub al-ʿAyya
ʿAl-ʿAyyelet ha-Shaḥar (Psalms) 13:1321
Alazar (fam.), *see* ELEAZAR
Alazar, Don Mair 6:584
Alazar, Maestre Mosse 6:584
Alazar, Todros 6:584
Al-ʿĀzariyya (vill., Er. Isr.) 4:733
- *illus:*
- - Mt. of Olives tombstones used for Arab Legion barracks 9:1485
Al-Azharī (fam.), *see* Lazari
Al-Aziz (caliph), *see* Aziz, al-
Al-ʿAzzūn (Er. Isr.), *see* ʿAzzūn, Al-
Alba, Charter of (1140) 2:518
Alba, Isaac de 14:1222
ALBA, JACOB DI 2:517
Al-Bāb (Bahai shrine, Er. Isr.) 8:936
Alba Bible (15th cent. illum. ms., Sp.) 4:879
- *illus:* 2:58; 3:498; 4:879; 5:1278; 6:854; 8:335
Alba Carolina (Transyl.), *see* ALBA IULIA
ALBA DE TORMES (city, Sp.) 2:518
ALBA IULIA (city, Transyl.) 2:518
- Transylvania 15:1341
Albala (fam., Chile) 5:464
ALBALA, DAVID 2:519
- Zionism 16:1149
- *illus:* text
Albala, Paulina Loebl 16:888
Albala de Levy, Ana 5:467
Albalag, Ḥayyim 5:194
ALBALAG, ISAAC 2:520
- allegorical exegesis 4:898
- angels 2:976
- Aristotelianism 3:446ff
- Jewish philosophy 13:445
- Kabbalah 10:530
- providence 13:1285
- Torah 15:1240
Al-Balagh, Isaac, *see* Balagh, Isaac al-
ALBALIA, BARUCH BEN ISAAC (Sp.) 2:522
ALBALIA, ISAAC BEN BARUCH 2:522
- Albalia, Baruch 2:522
- Ibn Migash 8:1188
Al-Balideh, Moses, *see* BALIDEH, MOSES
Al-Balqāʾ (district), *see* Balqāʾ, Al-
ALBANIA 2:522
- Israel's relations with 9:445
- minority rights 12:45
- U.N. resolutions 15:1557
- *pop. table:* text
Albany (city, Ga.) 7:429
ALBANY (city, N.Y.) 2:524
- Wise, Isaac Mayer 16:563
- *illus:*
- - Beth Emeth synagogue 7:782
Albany Park (sub., Chicago) 5:414
Al-Baqāʿ, Abu, *see* ABBAS, JUDAH BEN SAMUEL IBN
ALBARADANI, JOSEPH 2:525
- Joseph bar Nissan 10:225
- *piyyutim* 13:574
Albaradani, Nahum ha-Ḥazzan 2:525
- African journey 16:1258
Al-Baradani, Solomon 2:525
AL-BARGELONI, ISAAC BEN REUBEN 2:525
Al-Bargeloni, Judah (r., Sp.), *see* JUDAH BEN BARZILLAI AL-BARGELONI
Al-Barqamānī, Japheth (Kar.), *see* JAPHETH AL-BARQAMĀNĪ
ALBARRACÍN (city, Sp.) 2:526
Al-Baṣīr, Yūsuf (Kar.), *see* BASIR, JOSEPH BEN ABRAHAM HA-KOHEN HA-RO'EH AL-
AL-BAṬALYAWSI, ABU MUHAMMAD ABDALLAH IBN MUHAMMAD IBN AL-SID (Arab philos.) 2:526
Albasir, Ezekiel ben Ali ha-Kohen 13:581
Al-Bathaniyya (Er. Isr.), *see* BASHAN
Albatross (period.) 10:936; 16:816
Al-Battānī (Arab astron.), *see* Battānī, Al-
Al-Batzir, Joseph, *see* BASIR, JOSEPH BEN ABRAHAM HA-KOHEN HA-RO'EH AL-
Al-Bauli, Benayah ben Kalev ben Maḥpuẓ (scribe), *see* Benayah ben Kalev ben Maḥpuẓ al-Bauli
Al-Bayḍāʾ (dist., S. Arab.) 7:1019
Al-Baydā (Khazar city) 3:823
Al-Bayḍāʿ (site, Tranj.), *see* Baydāʿ, Al-
Al-Baytjālī, Iskandar al-Khūrī (poet), *see* Baytjālī, Iskandar al-Khūrī al-
ALBAZ, MOSES BEN MAIMON (kab.) 2:527
Albāz, Raphael Moses (Mor.) 2:516
AL-BAZAK, MAẒLIʾAḤ BEN ELIJAH IBN (Sic.) 2:527
ALBECK (fam.) 2:527
Albeck, Ḥanokh 2:528
- *Genesis Rabbah* 7:401
- *Midreshei Halakhah* 11:1522
- Theodor, Julius 15:1100
Albeck, Shalom (19/20 cent.) 2:527
- Auerbach, Benjamin 3:843
ALBECK, SHALOM (20th cent.) 1:27
Albeig, Ezekiel Hai ben Ezra 8:1452
ALBELDA, MOSES BEN JACOB (philos.) 2:529
Albemarle (tn., N. C.) 12:1218
Albemarle (city, Va.) 16:162
Albenzubron (Sp. philos.), *see* GABIROL, SOLOMON BEN JUDAH, IBN
Alber, Johann 8:21
ALBERT II (duke, Aus.) 2:529
- Augsburg Jews 3:849
- Austrian anti-Semitism 3:888
ALBERT III (duke, Aus.) 2:530
ALBERT V (duke, Aus.) 2:530
- Austrian Jews 3:889
- Vienna persecutions 16:502
ALBERT, CALVIN 3:594
ALBERTA (prov., Can.) 2:530
Albert Achill of Brandenburg (duke) 8:677
Alberta Katherina (Hebr.), *see* Albertina Katherina
Albert Einstein College of Medicine (U.S.) 8:1039; 16:761
Alberti, G. Francesco 10:459
Alberti, Paul Martin 8:21
ALBERTI-IRSA (Hung.) 2:531
Albertina Katherina 8:21
Albert Lea (tn., Minn.) 12:39
Albertus Denis (fin., Ger.), *see* DENIS, ALBERTUS
ALBERTUS MAGNUS 2:532
- Aquinas 3:229
- Ibn Yaḥya 8:1210
ALBI (tn., Fr.) 2:532
- Albigenses 2:532
ALBIGENSES (Chr. sect) 2:532
- Béziers Jews 4:792
- *gilgul* 7:574
- Judaizers 10:398
- Kabbalah 10:520
ALBINUS, LUCCEIUS (Rom. gov.) 2:534
- Anias ben Nedebus 2:923
Albinus Flaccus, *see* ALCUIN
Al-Bīra (tn., Er. Isr.) 13:1529
- Beeroth 4:383; 13:1609
- human geography of Israel 9:587
- Jerusalem boundary 9:1491
Al-Bīra (vill., Galilee) 4:375
ALBO, JOSEPH (philos.) 2:535
- *Contents:*
- - Biography 2:535
- - *Sefer ha-Ikkarim* 2:535
- - - Principles 2:535
- - - Dogmas 2:536
- - - Derivative Principles 2:536
- - - Kinds of Law 2:536
- Abraham 2:119
- Adam, views on 2:240
- allegorical exegesis 4:899
- Arama's criticism 3:257
- Aristotelianism 3:446
- articles of faith 3:657
- astrology criticised 3:792ff
- attributes of God 7:660
- commandments, reasons for 5:787
- evil 7:777
- Hell 13:84
- history chart 8:766-767
- peace 13:198
- philosophy 11:342; 13:449
- prophecy 13:1179
- revelation 14:124
- reward, punishment 14:136
- soul, immortality of 15:179
- space and place 15:219
- Spain 15:238

- time **15**:1143
- Torah **15**:1238; **15**:1241; **15**:1245
- Tortosa dispute **3**:196; **15**:1271
- usury **12**:250
- *illus:*
-*Sefer ha-Ikkarim* **2**:*fcg.* 555, 700; **5**:788
Alborada (period., Yug.) **16**:888
Alborada, La (period., Cz.), *see* La Alborada
ALBORAYCOS ("conversos") **2**:537
- conversos **5**:936
ALBOTINI, JUDAH BEN MOSES **2**:537
- Kabbalah **10**:542
Albrecht, Bruno (S.S. ldr.), *see* Katzmann, Friedrich
ALBRIGHT, WILLIAM FOXWELL **2**:538
- alphabet **2**:677
- linguistics **16**:1400
- Phoenicia **13**:472ff
Albu, Austen **15**:27
ALBU, SIR GEORGE **2**:539
ALBU, ISIDOR **2**:540
Albu, Leopold **2**:539
Albu, Margaret (S.A.), *see* Parker, Margaret
Al-Buqei'ah (loc., Er. Isr.) **2**:211
Albuquerque (city, New Mex.) **12**:1037
- *illus:*
- - Temple Albert **12**:1038
Al-Burj (loc., Er. Isr.), **14**:785
Alburji, Isaac **13**:52
Al-Bustān (period., Tun.) **13**:1041
Albutaini, Judah, *see* ALBOTINI, JUDAH BEN MOSES
Al-Buṭayḥa Valley (Er. Isr.), *see* Bet Ẓayyada
Alcabala (Sp. "indirect taxes") **6**:261
Alcalá, Luis de (Sp.) **12**:1369; **15**:1205; **16**:62
ALCALÁ DE HENARES (city, Sp.) **2**:540
Alcalai, Rachel **16**:1148
ALCALAY, ISAAC **2**:541
- Yugoslavia **16**:873
Alcalay, Leon (publ.) **13**:1369
Alcama (cmty., Sp.), *see* ALJAMA
ALCAN, ALKAN (fams., Fr.) **2**:541
Alcan, Félix **2**:541; **13**:1368
Alcan, Michel **2**:541
Alcan, Moses (bnk.) **11**:496
Alcan, Moyse (poet) **2**:541 **13**:1368
ALCAÑIZ (city, Sp.) **2**:541
- Calatrava **5**:39
Al-Carsoni, Isaac, *see* Carsoni, Isaac al-
ALCASTIEL, JOSEPH **2**:542
- Kabbalah **10**:540
ALÇEH, MATILDE (poet) **12**:1465
ALCHEMY **2**:542
- *Contents:*
- - Introduction **2**:542
- - Kabbalah **2**:544
- - Personalities **2**:546
- Christian Kabbalah **10**:646
- *Magen David* **11**:696
- practical Kabbalah **10**:635
- Vital, Ḥayyim **16**:172
- *illus:* text
ALCIMUS **2**:549
- Bacchides **4**:44ff
- Cynic philosophy **5**:1178
- Hellenism **10**:381
- history chart **8**:766-767
- Jerusalem **9**:1392
- Seleucids **8**:629
- Temple **15**:961
- Yakum of Zerorot **16**:854
Alcohol
- alcoholism **11**:1376; **14**:1503
- Ḥasidism and **7**:1407
- wine **16**:538
- *see also:* DRUNKENNESS; WINE AND LIQUOR TRADE
ALCOLEA (tn., Sp.) **2**:549
ALCONIÈRE, THEODORE **2**:549
ALCONSTANTINI (fam., Arag.) **2**:550
- Cavalleria, Judah **5**:262
- Saragossa **14**:859ff
Alconstantini, Baḥye (Baḥi'el, Bafi'el) **2**:550
- Bonsenyor, Judah **4**:1213
ALCONSTANTINI, ENOCH BEN SOLOMON **2**:551
Alconstantini, Moses **2**:550
- Saragossa **14**:860
- Valencia **16**:55
Alconstantini, Sansone (It.), *see* Constantini, Sansone
Alconstantini, Solomon (court.) **2**:550
Alconstantini, Solomon (physic.) **2**:550
ALCOPLEY (art.) **3**:594
- *illus:*
- - "Thoughts, 1964" **3**:616
Alcorsono, Jacob **3**:794
ALCORSONO, JUDAH BEN JOSEPH **2**:551
Alcostantini, Abraham **3**:946
ALCUIN (eccl.) **2**:551
Aldabi (schol.), *see* ABULRABI
ALDABI, MEIR BEN ISAAC **2**:551
- medicine **11**:1191
Āldağ, Peter (hist.), *see* Kruger,Claus
Al-Dahriyya (Jer.), *see* Gate of Mercy
Al-Ḍamārī, Manṣūr, *see* Manṣūr al-Ḍamārī
ALDANOV, MARK **2**:552
Al-Darūrī fī al-Lugha al-ʿIbrāniyya (wk., Ibn Dannan), *see Darūrī Fī al-Lugha al-ʿIbrāniyya, al-*
Al-Dayrī (fam.), *see* Dayrī, Al-
Al-Dayyan, Benveniste ben Ḥiyya **13**:577
Alderson, R. A. **9**:1549
Aldian, Benveniste ben Ḥiyya **9**:1217
Al-Dikkī (tn., Er. Isr.) **12**:181; **13**:1532
Al-Doji, Menahem (ps.-mess.), *see* ALROY, DAVID
ALDO MANUZIO **2**:553
- printing **15**:1480, 1481
Aldrich, Thomas Bailey **10**:459
ALDROPHE, ALFRED-PHILIBERT **3**:362
ALDUBI, ABRAHAM BEN MOSES BEN ISMAIL **2**:553
Alduin (bp.), *see* HILDUIN
Aldus Manutius, *see* ALDO MANUZIO
Al-Dustān (Samar. sect), *see* DUSTAN
Al-Dustāniyya (Samar. sect) **6**:313
ALECHINSKY, PIERRE **2**:553
- *illus:* text
'ALEF (Heb. let.) **2**:554
- *illus:*
- - text
- - harmonic unity of *Sefirot* **10**:614
- *see also:* ALPHABET, HEBREW
Alef (period., Isr.) **2**:848; **5**:101
- statistics **1**:newsp. list
Alef (journ., Rus.) **1**:newsp. list
"Alef, Beit, Gimmel, Dalet" (pseud.), *see* DRUYANOW, ALTER
Alefaden ben Isaac ha-Kohen **15**:1128
Alef Bet de-R. Akiva (wk.), *see Otiyyot de-R. Akiva*
Alef Bet de-Rabbi Makhir (wk.) **11**:669
ALEGRE, ABRAHAM BEN SOLOMON **2**:555
Alegre, Jacob **15**:1173
Aleguo, Moses, *see* Hallegua, Moses
Aleh (journ.) **1**:newsp. list
Aleih (loc., Leb.) **10**:1545
Alei Hadas (journ.) **4**:398
- statistics **1**:newsp. list
Aleikhem Shalom (Heb. greeting) **7**:914
Alei Mishmeret (journ.) **1**:newsp. list
Aleinikov, M. (journ.) **13**:1597
ALEINU LE-SHABBE'AḤ (prayer) **2**:555
- *Contents:*
- - Description **2**:555
- - Contents **2**:557
- - Censorship **2**:557
- - Blois Tragedy **2**:558
- - Reform Usage **2**:559
- - Music **2**:559
- Christianity **3**:197
- *illus:*
- - text
- - *Seder Rav Amram* **2**:892
- *mus. notations:*
- - text
- - *mi-Sinai niggunim* **12**:151
Alei Siʿaḥ (journ.) **1**:newsp. list
ALEKSANDRIYA (tn., Volhynia) **2**:560
ALEKSANDRIYA (tn., Ukr.) **2**:560
ALEKSANDROW (ḥas. dyn.) **2**:560
- Sochaczew, Abraham of **15**:24
- *illus:* text
Aleksandrow, Hanokh Henyekh (has. ldr.) **15**:24
ALEKSANDROW LODZKI (tn., Pol.) **2**:561
Alekser, Tuvia **3**:424
Alekseyev, Konstantin Sergeyevich, *see* Stanislavsky, Konstantin
Alem, *see* AVIGDOR BEN SIMḤAH HA-LEVI OF GLOGAU
ALEMÁN, MATEO **2**:561
- *illus:* text
Alemanno, Johanan **2**:543; **2**:548
- Kabbalah **10**:540
Alemeth (city, Er. Isr.), *see* ALMON
Alentejo (prov., Port.) **16**:135
ALEPPO (city, Syr.) **2**:562
- Altaras, Joseph **2**:772
- Aramaic inscription **16**:666
- capitulations **5**:148
- community **15**:643
- dress **6**:219
- immigration to Israel **9**:500
- Jerusalem synagogue **9**:500
- Shabbetai Ẓevi **14**:1227
- synagogue **15**:613
- *illus:*
- - text
- - David's conquest (map) **5**:1321
- - synagogue courtyard **15**:636
Aleppo Codex (bib. ms.) **2**:192
- Aaron ben Asher **16**:1472
- Lamentations, Book of **10**:1371
Aleppo Pine (bot.) **9**:221; **13**:530
- *illus:*
- - Jerusalem grove **13**:531
Aleppo rites (litur.) **2**:565; **11**:400
Aleppo synagogue (Jer.), *see* Aram Zoba synagogue
ALÈS (tn., Fr.) **2**:565
Alessandra Tornimparte (pseud.), *see* GINZBURG, NATALIA
ALESSANDRIA (tn., It.) **2**:566
- special Purim **13**:1395
illus: text
- - Holocaust memorial **9**:1137
ALETRINO, ARNOLD AÄRON **6**:320; **6**:322
ALEXANDER (s. of Herod) **2**:567
- Antipater **3**:77
- Herod I **8**:381ff
- *geneal. table:* text; **8**:377
Alexander (grands. of Herod) **7**:601
Alexander (s. of Tigranes) **5**:760
Alexander (Alabarch, br. of Philo) **15**:980
- loan to Agrippa **16**:1277
Alexander (bp.) **9**:1406
Alexander (r., U.S.) **15**:1207
ALEXANDER (fam., Eng.) **2**:571
Alexander (fam., U.S.) **12**:37
Alexander (ḥas. dyn.), *see* ALEKSANDROW
Alexander (tn., Ida.) **2**:575
ALEXANDER I (czar) **2**:569
- status of Jews **8**:716
- Velizh **16**:87
ALEXANDER II (pope) **2**:568
- attitude to Jews **13**:852
- Benevento Jews **4**:500
- Narbonne **5**:1135
ALEXANDER II (czar) **2**:570
- attitude to Jews **8**:722ff
- history chart **8**:766-767
- Pale of Settlement **13**:24
- Siberia **14**:1486
- universities **15**:1678
ALEXANDER III (pope) **2**:568
- Anau, Jehiel **2**:934
- attitude to Jews **13**:853
- Lateran Council III **10**:1445
ALEXANDER III (czar) **2**:570
- May Laws **11**:1147
- universities **15**:1678
- *illus:*
- - *Punch* cartoon **14**:437
ALEXANDER IV (pope) **2**:568
- attitude to Jews **13**:854
ALEXANDER V (pope) **2**:568
ALEXANDER VI (Borgia; pope) **2**:569
- attitude to Jews **13**:856
- Avignon Jews **3**:966
ALEXANDER VII (pope) **2**:569
- popes **13**:858
Alexander, A. (schol., Eng.) **4**:871
Alexander, Aaron **3**:824
ALEXANDER, ABRAHAM **2**:572
- *illus:*
- - text
- - handwritten *maḥzor* (1803) **5**:359
Alexander, Alexander (print.) **2**:571; **13**:1374
- *illus:*
- - Hebrew-English prayer book (1770) **3**:5
- - *Lehem Oni* **11**:476
ALEXANDER, BERNARD (S.A.) **2**:572
Alexander, Bernard **15**:1376
Alexander, D. L. **8**:398
- Jewish nationalism **6**:761
- Zionism **16**:1117
Alexander, Enid **2**:575; **15**:210
ALEXANDER, FRANZ **2**:573
ALEXANDER, HAIM **12**:680
- music **12**:670
Alexander, Isaac **14**:37
Alexander, Jack **15**:198
- Zionism **16**:1140
Alexander, James **5**:265
Alexander, Joseph (sport.) **15**:307
Alexander, Joseph Raphael **2**:572
Alexander, Levy (print.) **2**:571; **11**:481
- publishing **13**:1374
Alexander, Matthias F. **12**:895
ALEXANDER, MICHAEL SOLOMON (bp.) **2**:573
- missionary activities **9**:1450
ALEXANDER, MORRIS **2**:574
- *illus:* text
Alexander, Morton (sport.) **15**:310
ALEXANDER, MOSES (gov., U.S.) **2**:575
Alexander, Moses **15**:1181
ALEXANDER, MURIEL **15**:1077

Alexander, Ruth **2:**575
ALEXANDER, SAMUEL **2:**575
– *illus:* text
Alexander, Seymour **15:**310
Alexander, Tiberius Julius (procurator), *see* TIBERIUS JULIUS ALEXANDER
Alexander, William **9:**1343
Alexander al-Afridusi **14:**731
ALEXANDER BALAS (k., Syr.) **2:**576
– Hasmonean revolt **8:**630
– Jonathan the Hasmonean **6:**560
Alexander ben Ghiat **5:**446
ALEXANDER THE FALSE (1st cent.) **2:**577
ALEXANDER THE GREAT **2:**577
– *Contents:*
– – History and Legend **2:**578
– – Aggadah **2:**579
– – Medieval Literature **2:**579
– Babylonia **4:**36
– chronological chart **8:**766-767
– Ereẓ Israel **8:**625
– Garden of Eden **7:**327
– Hellenism **8:**292
– Jaddua **9:**1246ff
– Jerusalem **9:**1389
– Jews in Europe **6:**966
– legends **8:**302
– Maccabees, First Book of **11:**657
– Samaritans **14:**729
– Shushan **14:**1483
– Solomon's throne **15:**812
– *illus:* text
ALEXANDER JAGELLON (k., Pol.) **2:**580
– Abraham Judaeus Bohemus **2:**160
Alexander Kohut Memorial Foundation (U.S.) **10:**1151
ALEXANDER LYSIMACHUS **2:**581
– Agrippa **15:**1180
– banking **4:**167
ALEXANDER OF APHRODISIAS **2:**581
– Commandments, reasons for **5:**787
– providence **13:**1284
ALEXANDER OF HALES **2:**582
Alexander of Komarno **10:**1173
ALEXANDER POLYHISTOR **2:**583
– Eupolemus **6:**964
– Ezekiel the Poet **6:**1102
– Josephus **10:**258
Alexander Severus (Rom. emp.), *see* SEVERUS, ALEXANDER
Alexandersohn, Jonathan **13:**1554
– Schwerin-Goetz **14:**1033
ALEXANDER SON OF ARISTOBULUS II **2:**584
– Alexandra **2:**587
– Aristobulus III **3:**441
– *geneal. table:* text
ALEXANDER SUSLIN HA-KOHEN OF FRANKFORT **2:**585
– codification of law **5:**647
– trade and commerce **15:**1299
– *illus:* text
ALEXANDER SUSSKIND BEN MOSES OF GRODNO **2:**586
– ethical wills **11:**346
Alexander Susskind of Metz **10:**1417
Alexander Yannai, *see* YANNAI, ALEXANDER
ALEXANDER THE ZEALOT (1st cent. C.E.) **2:**587
ALEXANDRA (m.-in-l. Herod) **2:**587
– Aristobulus III **3:**442
– Cypros **5:**1179
– Herod I **8:**380ff
– Parthians **3:**66
– *geneal. table:* text
ALEXANDRA(Hasm. prin.) **2:**588
– Ptolemy **13:**1349
Alexandrah (Alexandrai; amora), *see* ALEXANDRI
Alexandra Salome (q., Judea), *see* SALOME ALEXANDRA
Alexandre, Aron **5:**404
Alexandre, René (sol.) **11:**1562
Alexandreion (fort., Er. Isr.), *see* SARTABA
Alexandretta (tn., Turk.), *see* ISKENDERUN
ALEXANDRI (amora) **2:**588
ALEXANDRIA (city, Egy.) **2:**589
– *Contents:*
– – Ancient Period **2:**589
– – Jerusalem **2:**590
– – Jewish Culture **2:**590
– – Byzantine Period **2:**591
– – Arab Period **2:**591
– – Mamluk/Turkish Period **2:**593
– – Recent Times **2:**593
– – Hebrew Press **2:**594
– General
– – banking **4:**166
– – capitulations **5:**148
– – community **5:**810
– – craftsmen **5:**1044
– – Diaspora **6:**9; **6:**15ff
– – Egypt **6:**485ff
– – Ereẓ Israel **9:**119
– – goldsmiths **7:**740
– – guilds **7:**971
– – history chart **8:**766–767
– – Jewish seamen's guild **16:**1276
– – magic **11:**706
– – population **13:**871ff
– – psalter **13:**1306
– – *Sefer Torah* **16:**671
– – ships and sailing **14:**1412
– Ancient Period
– – *Acts of Alexandrian Martyrs* **2:**594
– – Agrippa I **2:**416
– – alchemy **2:**546
– – Apion **3:**178
– – Claudius **5:**601
– – ethnarch **6:**946
– – Flaccus **6:**1333
– – great synagogue of **2:**803 **15:**582
– – Hebrew language **8:**303
– – Hellenistic scholarship **8:**293
– – Jewish revolt **8:**645
– – Jews and gymnasium **7:**999
– – *Letter of Aristeas* **3:**440
– – library **11:**193
– – *Maccabees, Third Book of* **11:**661
– – Philo **13:**409
– – Samaritan dispute **2:**949
– – Trajan **15:**1312
– Medieval and Modern
– – Alamani, Aaron he-Ḥaver **2:**509
– – Crusader captives **9:**271
– – Mamluk persecutions **11:**835
– – Six-Day War **14:**1630
– *illus:*
– – Eliyahu ha-Navi synagogue **6:**502
– – massacre of Jews **10:**256
Alexandria (city, Louis.) **11:**517
Alexandria (city, Va.) **16:**163
ALEXANDRIAN MARTYRS, ACTS OF **2:**594
Alexandri ben Haggai (Ḥagra; Ḥadrin; amora) **2:**589
Alexandri de-Ẓaddika (amora) **2:**589
Alexandri Kerovah (amora) **2:**589
Alexandrium (fort., Er. Isr.), *see* SARTABA
Alexandroni brigade (Isr. army) **9:**363
– Haganah **7:**1073
– War of Independence **16:**310
Alexandros (amora), *see* ALEXANDRI
Alexandros (k., Judea), *see* YANNAI, ALEXANDER
Alexandrou-Nesos (tn., Egy.) **6:**9
Alexandroupolis (city, Gr.) **7:**879
Alexandrovsk (city, Ukr.), *see* ZAPOROZHE
ALEXAS (br.-in-l. Herod) **2:**595
Alexenicer, Jose **13:**820
ALEXEYEV, ALEXANDER **2:**595
Aleyde of Brabant (prin., Neth.) **16:**1290
Alez (tn., Fr.), *see* ALÈS
Alfa Beta (acrostic) **2:**230
Alfa Beta of Ben Sira (bk.), *see* BEN SIRA, ALPHABET OF
Al-Fajr (journ.) **9:**1042
Al-Fakhar (fam. Sp.), *see* IBN ALFAKHAR
Alfakhar, Abraham, *see* Ibn Alfakhar, Abraham abu Isḥak
Al-Fakhar, Joseph, *see* Ibn Alfakhar, Joseph
Alfakhar, Judah ibn, *see* Ibn alfakhar, Judah
ALFALAS, MOSES **2:**596
Al-Falluja (tn., Iraq) **8:**1450
Al-fanājīn (game) **9:**1039
ALFANDARI (Alfanderi; fam.) **2:**596
ALFANDARI, AARON BEN MOSES **2:**597
Alfandari, Abraham **2:**597
Alfandari, David **2:**596
Alfandari, Elijah ben Jacob **2:**597
Alfandari, Ḥayyim (the Elder; Turk.) **2:**596
Alfandari, Ḥayyim (Rabbenu; Er. Isr.) **2:**597
ALFANDARI, ḤAYYIM BEN ISAAC RAPHAEL **2:**597
– Samuel Primo **13:**1092
Alfandari, Isaac (Egy.) **2:**596
Alfandari, Isaac (Turk.) **2:**597
Alfandari, Isaac ben Judah (Sp.) **2:**596
Alfandari, Isaac Raphael (Turk.) **2:**596
ALFANDARI, JACOB (17th cent.) **2:**598
Alfandari, Jacob **2:**596
Alfandari, Jacob ben Judah **2:**599
Alfandari, Jacob ben Solomon (Sp.) **2:**596
Alfandari, Joseph **2:**597
Alfandari, Moses **2:**597
Alfandari, Obadiah **2:**596
Alfandari, Raphael Hezekiah Ḥayyim **2:**597
Alfandari, Shabbetai **2:**596
Alfandari, Solomon ben Ḥayyim **2:**597
ALFANDARI, SOLOMON ELIEZER BEN JACOB **2:**599
Alfandaric; Alfandrec (fam.), *see* ALFANDARI
Alfanterin (acrostic) **2:**230
Alfaqui, Judah ben Moses (paytan) **13:**587
Al-Fara, Isaac ibn **15:**1352
Al-Fārābī, Abu Naṣr Muhammad (Musl. philos.), *see* FĀRĀBĪ, ABU NAṢR MUHAMMAD, AL-
Alfas, Benzion, *see* ALFES, BENZION
ALFASI (fam., Tun.) **2:**599
ALFASI, DAVID BEN ABRAHAM **2:**600
– diacritical marks **16:**1430
– linguistics **16:**1356;1379
– masorah **16:**1437
Alfasi, Ḥayyim ben Mas'ud Raphael **2:**600
– Tunisia **15:**1444
ALFASI, ISAAC BEN JACOB (Rif) **2:**600
– General
– – Albalia, Baruch **2:**522
– – attorneys and fees **3:**837
– – Caro's rulings **5:**197
– – chronological chart **8:**766-767
– – code, scope of **12:**132
– – codification of law **5:**638
– – Gerondi, Zerahiah **7:**510
– – *halakhah* **7:**1165
– – *ḥiddushim* **8:**465
– – Ibn Migash, Joseph **8:**1188
– – Jerusalem Talmud **15:**776
– – method **15:**766
– – Muslim Spain **8:**666
– – Naḥmanides' defense of **12:**780
– – responsa **14:**86
– – *Sha'arei Shevu'ot* **14:**1212
– – Spain **15:**242
– – Talmud commentaries **11:**329; **11:**330
– Code, Commentators on
– – Aghmati **2:**367
– – Al Madari **2:**658
– – Bachrach, Judah **4:**56
– – Ephraim Alragan **6:**814
– – Ibn Ḥaviva **8:**466
– – Jonathan ha-Kohen of Lunel **10:**186
– – Joshua Boaz **10:**285
– – Naḥmanides **8:**466
– – Nissim Gerondi **12:**1185
– – Samuel ben Meir **14:**811
– – Solomon Eger **6:**473
– – Tam ibn Yaḥya **15:**785
– – Zerahiah ha-Levi **8:**466; **16:**997
Al-Fasi, Isaac ben Joseph (13th cent.) **15:**1323
Alfasi, Jacob ben Isaac **2:**601
Alfasi, Mas'ud Raphael **2:**599
– Tunisia **15:**1444
Alfasi, Solomon ben Mas'ud Raphael **2:**600
– Tunisia **15:**1444
Al-Fataḥ, *see* Fataḥ, Al-
Al-Fayyumi, Saadiah, *see* SAADIAH GAON
Alfāẓ al-Mishna (wk.) **16:**1430
Alfāẓ al-Talmūd (wk.) **16:**1430
ALFES, BENZION **2:**604
Alfieri, Vittorio **9:**1103; **9:**1105
Alfityḥi, Ḥayyim, *see* ḤABSHUSH, ḤAYYIM
Alfonsine Tablets (astron.) **2:**605; **8:**1194
Alfonso (ks., Port.), *see* AFFONSO
ALFONSO I ("The Battler;" k., Arag.) **2:**604
ALFONSO II (k., Arag.) **2:**604
– Saragossa **14:**859
– Teruel **15:**1022
Alfonso II (k., Naples) **2:**105
Alfonso III (k., Arag.) **4:**1213
Alfonso IV (k., Arag.)
– Ardut, Eleazar ibn **3:**401
– Barbastro **4:**207
– Cagliari **5:**14
– Jewish bankers **16:**1291
Alfonso V (k., León) **15:**227
ALFONSO V (k., Arag.) **2:**604
– Majorca **11:**802
– Saragossa **14:**863
– Spain **15:**238
– Teruel **15:**1023
ALFONSO VI (k., Cast.) **2:**604
– Almoravides **2:**667
– autonomy, Jewish **3:**929
– Ferrizuel, Joseph **6:**1236ff
– Toledo **15:**1200
ALFONSO VII (k., Cast.) **2:**604
– Toledo **15:**1200; **15:**1201
ALFONSO VIII (k., Cast.) **2:**604
– church tithes **15:**1162
– Toledo **15:**1201
– *see also:* JEWESS OF TOLEDO
ALFONSO X ("the Wise"; k., Cast.) **2:**604
– Abraham el-Barchilon **2:**158

- Abulafia, Samuel **2**:193
- Abulafia, Todros **2**:194
- Jewish badge **4**:65
- Spain **15**:230
- Toledo **15**:1202
ALFONSO XI (k., Cast.) **2**:605
- Toledo **15**:1203
Alfonso XII (k., Sp.) **3**:998
Alfonso de Cartagena **8**:1382
ALFONSO DE ESPINA **2**:605
- *illus:*
- - Inquisition **8**:1382
ALFONSO DE OROPESA **2**:606
- Toledo **15**:1205
Alfonso of Burgos, *see* ABNER OF BURGOS
Alfonso of Valladolid, *see* ABNER OF BURGOS
ALFONSO OF ZAMORA **2**:606
ALFONSUS BONIHOMINIS (Buenhombre) **2**:607
ALFRINK, BERNHARDUS JOHANNES **2**:607
Alfthan, Baron (Fin.) **6**:1297
Alfual, Dulcius **15**:1270
Al-Furaydis (vill., Isr.), *see* FURAYDIS, AL-
Alga (bot.) **13**:615
Algabe, Jacob **9**:1097
Algarve (prov., Port.) **13**:925
ALGAZI (fam.) **2**:607
Algazi, Abraham ben Moses **2**:607; **15**:1497
Algazi, Abraham ben (Nissim) Solomon **2**:608
Algazi, Elijah **5**:255
Algazi, Ḥayyim ben Abraham **2**:607
Algazi, Ḥayyim ben Menahem **2**:608
Algazi, Ḥayyim Isaac **2**:608
Algazi, Isaac ben Abraham **2**:608
ALGAZI, ISAAC BEN SOLOMON **2**:608
ALGAZI, ISRAEL JACOB BEN YOM TOV **2**:609;
- Algazi, Yom Tov **2**:611
Algazi, Joseph (Turk.) **2**:607
Algazi, Joseph (Egy.) **2**:608
Algazi, Judah **2**:608
Algazi, Kamar, *see* Cattaui, Kamar
ALGAZI, LÉON (Yehudah; Fr.) **2**:610
Algazi, Moses ben Abraham **2**:607
Algazi, Moses ben Joseph (Egy.) **2**:608
Algazi, Nissim Jacob ben Ḥayyim Solomon (Turk.) **2**:608
ALGAZI, (Nissim) SOLOMON BEN ABRAHAM (Jer.) **2**:610
- Shabbetai Ẓevi **14**:1230
ALGAZI, SOLOMON BEN ABRAHAM (Egy.) **2**:610
ALGAZI, YOM TOV BEN ISRAEL JACOB (Er. Isr.) **2**:611
- emissary **14**:1360
Algazi, Yom Tov ben (Nissim) Solomon (Turk.) **2**:608
Algemeyne Entsiklopedye **2**:170; **6**:731, 735
Algemeyne Ilustrirte Entsiklopedye **6**:731
Algemeyner Yidisher Arbeter Bund in Lite, Poyln un Rusland, *see* BUND
ALGERIA **2**:612
- *Contents:*
- - History **2**:612
- - Holocaust Period **2**:616
- - Contemporary Period **2**:617
- - Relations with Israel **2**:619
- Arab League **3**:242
- Baḥuẓim **4**:102
- communal organization **5**:815; **5**:828
- demography **5**:1499; **13**:897
- dress **6**:219
- emigration **16**:1527
- history chart **8**:766-767
- immigration to Israel **9**:499,538
- Isaac ben Sheshet **13**:1449
- Jewish community **7**:28ff
- Jews, condition of **5**:679
- judicial autonomy **12**:141
- Shabbateanism **14**:1236
- Six-Day War **9**:408; **14**:1626
- synagogues **1**:syn. list
- Tunisia **15**:1430
- Zionism **2**:196; **4**:275; **16**:1127ff
- *illus:*
- - Constantine rabbi **5**:916
- - dress Pls. 5a-5d **6**-DRESS
- - Ghardaïa synagogue **15**:615
- *pop. table:* text
- *see also:* ALGIERS
Al-Gharība (syn., Djerba) **6**:139
AL-GHĀRID AL-YAHUDI **2**:620
- music **12**:596
Al-Ghazālī, *see* GHAZĀLĪ, ABU ḤAMID MUHAMMAD IBN MUHAMMAD AL-ṬŪSĪ AL-
ALGHERO (tn., It.) **2**:621
- metals and mining **11**:1438
- *illus:* text
ALGIERS (city, Alg.) **2**:621
- *Contents:*
- - History **2**:621
- - Population Statistics **2**:624
- capitulations **5**:149
- Isaac ben Sheshet Perfet **9**:32
- special Purim **13**:1395
- *illus:* text
- *see also:* ALGERIA
Algonquian (Ind. lang., N.Am.) **4**:1133
ALGUADES (Alguadez), MEIR **2**:624
- translations **15**:1322
ALGUM (bot.) **2**:625
- almug wood **16**:630
- source **8**:1311
Al-Ḥabil (tn., Yem.) **7**:1027
Alhadad, Mas'ud Kohen **10**:554
Al-Hadaf (journ.) **9**:1042
Alhadeff, Nessim **14**:1083
ALḤADIB, ISAAC BEN SOLOMON BEN ẒADDIK **2**:625
- astronomical instruments **3**:787
- astronomy **3**:803; **3**:804
Al-Ḥadītha (vill., Er. Isr.) **7**:1050
'Al-ha-Gittit (Psalms) **13**:1320
Al ha-Ḥomah (period.) **1**:newsp. list **5**:460
Al Ḥai ha-Mikra (journ.) **1**:newsp. list
Alhaiza, Adolphe **6**:1448
Al-Hajj pool (Jer.) **9**:1541
AL-ḤAKAM (fam., Iraq) **2**:625
Al-Ḥakam, David **2**:626
Al-Ḥakam, Elijah ben Ḥayyim Moses **2**:625
Al-Ḥakam, Jacob **2**:626
Al-Ḥakam, Joseph Ḥayyim ben Elijah, *see* JOSEPH ḤAYYIM BEN ELIJAH AL-ḤAKAM
Al-Ḥakam, Moses Ḥayyim **2**:625
Al-Ḥākim bi-Amr Allah (caliph), *see* ḤĀKIM BI-AMR ALLAH (AL)
Al-Hamdānī (poet), *see* Ḥusaynī, Ibn al-Fātiḥ Aḥmad ibn
Alḥāmi, Moses ben Jacob **2**:265
Al ha-Mishmar (newsp.) **1**:newsp. list; **9**:1016; **12**:1056
Al ha-Mishmar (orgn., Pol.) **13**:750
Al-Ḥamma (loc., Er. Isr.), *see* Ḥamma, El-
Alhammid (vill., Mor.) **6**:190
AL HA-NISSIM (prayer) **2**:626
- *illus:*
- - text
- - eighteenth cent. *siddur* **7**:1282
Al-Haqiqa (period.) **6**:499
Al-ḥāra, *see* JEWISH QUARTER
Al-Ḥaram al-Sharīf (Jer.), *see* Ḥaram al-Sharif
Al-Ḥarīrī (Arab. au.) **2**:627; **11**:937
- *illus:*
- - *Maqamat* **9**:98
AL-ḤARIZI, JUDAH BEN SOLOMON **2**:627
- chronological chart **8**:766-767
- David ben Zakkai **5**:1359
- Ḥarizi, Abu **7**:1339
- Hebrew language **16**:1624
- Immanuel of Rome **8**:1296
- linguistics **16**:1387
- Maimonides **11**:769
- *maqāmāt* **11**:937
- parody and satire **13**:126
- poetry **11**:327; **13**:687
- Syria **15**:641
- translations **15**:1319; **15**:1324
- travels **15**:1352
Al ha-Saf (journ.) **1**:newsp. list
Al-Ḥasan al-Barqamānī (Kar.), *see* JAPHETH AL-BARQAMĀNĪ
Al-Ḥaṣbani River (Isr.), *see* Senir
'Al-ha-Sheminit (Psalms) **13**:1320
Al-Ḥāṣid (newsp.) **13**:1041
ALḤAYK, UZZIEL BEN MORDECAI **2**:629
- Tunisia **15**:1444
AL ḤET (confession) **2**:629
- *illus:* text
Al-Ḥijr (tn., Arab.) **3**:234
Al-Ḥujja (wk.), *see Kitāb al-Ḥujja*
Ali (Muhammad's s.-in-l.) **15**:1528
Ali (Arab caliph) **16**:1414
ALI (ben David; poet) **2**:630
Ali (tn., Leb.) **10**:1544
Ali, Ṭaha M. **9**:1042
Ali al-Gharbī (tn., Iraq) **8**:1450
Aliama, *see* ALJAMA
Alias Abraham da Porto **8**:1399
ALIBAG (tn., Ind.) **2**:631
- India **8**:1358
- *illus:*
- - synagogue **8**:1351
Ali ben Abi Bakr Al-Harawi **15**:1358
ALI BEN AMRAM (Egy.) **2**:631
Ali ben Ezekiel ha-Kohen (paytan) **13**:577
Ali ben Israel (linguist) **16**:1383
Ali ben Mevasser **2**:631
ALI BEN ZECHARIAH (gaon) **2**:631
- Daniel ha-Kohen **5**:1294
- Irbil **8**:1463
Ali Bey (Egy.) **9**:291
Al-Idrīsī (geog.), *see* Idrīsī, Al-
Aliens **8**:615*ff*
- *see also:* STRANGERS AND GENTILES
Aliens Act (Eng.) **8**:766-767
Alien slaves, *see* SLAVERY
ALIGER, MARGARITA YOSIFOVNA (poet) **2**:632
Alignment (Ma'arakh; polit. party) **9**:676ff
- *see also:* ISRAEL LABOR PARTY
'Ali ibn 'Isa (10th cent., Bagh.) **16**:1283
Ali ibn Mar Ḥassān (astron.), *see* ḤASSAN IBN ḤASSĀN
ALI IBN SAHL IBN RABBĀN AL-TABARĪ **2**:632
- medicine **11**:1191
ALI IBN SULEIMAN (Kar.) **2**:632
- linguistics **16**:1383
Ali ibn Yusuf ibn Tāshfīn (Almoravide) **2**:667
- Spain **15**:226
Alil (journ., U.S.) **1**:newsp. list
Al-Ilfān (Samar.) **6**:313
Al-Ilfāniyya (Samar. sect), *see* Al-Dustaniyya
Alim (journ.) **1**:newsp. list
Alim le-Bibliografyah u-le-Safranut (journ.) **1**:newsp. list
Alim le-Bibliografyah ve-Korot Yisrael (journ.) **1**:newsp. list
Ali Muntar Hill (loc., Gaza) **14**:1629
Al-'Irāq (Moab. city), *see* HORONAIM
Al-Iscandari (fam.), *see* ISCANDARI
Al-Iṣfahānī, Isaac ben Jacob, *see* ABU'ISA, ISAAC BEN JACOB AL-ISFAHINI
Al-Iṣṭakhrī (geog.) **4**:17
ALISTĀL (vill., Slov.) **2**:633
Al-Istīfā' (wk.), *see Kitāb al-Istīfā'*
Al-Istighnā' (wk.), *see Kitāb al-Istighnā'*
Alitiens, Abraham **8**:1059
Alitiens, Eliezer **8**:1059
Al-Ittiḥād (newsp.) **9**:1041
Al-Ittiḥād al-Isrā'īlī (newsp.) **13**:1041
ALITURUS (Alityros; Rome) **2**:633
- Josephus, Flavius **10**:251
- theater **15**:1050
Aliyah (journ.) **1**:newsp. list
ALIYAH (immigration) **2**:633
- General
- - agriculture **9**:773
- - British regulations **16**:1086
- - Bulgarian Jews **14**:1172
- - chronological chart **8**:766-767
- - Churchill, Sir Winston **5**:556
- - Cochin Jews **5**:627
- - Ḥibbat Zion **8**:463; **16**:1039f
- - "illegal" immigration **4**:632; **8**:1248
- - Indian Jews **8**:1357
- - Inquiry Commissions **13**:31f
- - Iraqi Jews **5**:1098
- - Italy **16**:1123
- - Kurdistan Jews **8**:1443; **10**:1299
- - North Africa/Asia **16**:1129
- - Persian Jews **13**:318
- - Poland **13**:780; **16**:1131
- - Rumania **16**:1135
- - Ruppin, Arthur **14**:431
- - Russian Zionists **16**:1138ff
- - Salonika **14**:707
- - socialist youth movements **15**:50
- - South Africa **16**:1140
- - Tel Aviv **15**:917ff
- - "The 105" **8**:251
- - Truman's support **15**:1408
- - Turkey **15**:1460
- - U.S. Zionism **16**:1146
- - Vienna **16**:1107
- - White Paper (1939) **9**:343
- - Yemenite Jews **16**:743,751f
- - Zionist Congresses **16**:1172ff
- - Zionist movement **16**:1061ff
- History **9**:324
- - beginnings **9**:515
- - Crusader period **5**:1140; **9**:273
- - early history **9**:508
- - Ḥasidim and Mitnaggedim **9**:293
- - Mamluk period **9**:280
- - migrations **16**:1519
- - Shabbateans **14**:1247
- *illus:*
- - text
- - First Aliyah immigrants **9**:518
- - Iraqi immigrant in *ma'barah* **8**:1448
- - Israel commemorative stamp **8**:1455
- - Third Aliyah immigrants **9**:517
- *pop. tables:*
- - Asian countries, main periods of *aliyah* **3**:746
- - growth of Jewish population, 1840–1966 **3**:745
- - immigration from Iran,

1948-1968 8:1441
- see also: ALIYAH AND ABSORPTION IN ISRAEL; YOUTH ALIYAH
Aliyah (call to Torah), see TORAH, READING OF
ALIYAH AND ABSORPTION IN ISRAEL 9:515
- Ashkenazim 9:497ff
- Ben-Gurion 4:998
- El Al's role 6:560
- *haavara* 7:1012
- health 9:983ff
- historical survey 9:378; 9:393ff
- immigration and labor centers 9:849
- industry 9:819
- ingathering of exiles 8:1375
- Jewish Agency 10:27ff
- Keren Hayesod 10:914
- Law of Return 10:1485
- *ma'barah* 11:654
- migration 16:1525
- Palestine office 13:40
- population of Israel 9:472
- Sephardim 9:498f
- Six-Day War effects 9:412f
- *illus:*
- - Aden immigrants 9:502
- - appeal for allowing refugees into Palestine (1943) 8:766
- - East European immigrants 9:498
- - German refugee children 16:862
- - Ḥalutzim arriving in Jaffa 9:1258
- - Kurdistan immigrants 9:504
- - Leningrad Jews' telegram (1970) 14:503
- - North African immigrants 9:499
- - Polish refugee children 9:496
- - refugees in Venice 14:28
- - Rosh ha-Ayin transit camp 9:379
- - Russian *ḥalutzim* in Constantinople 14:465
- - Russian immigrants at Lydda airport 14:503
- - Tel Aviv tent camp 15:920
- - ulpan classroom in Naẓerat Illit 15:1526
- *tables:*
- - text
- - immigrants, up to 1948 16:1127
- - immigration figures, 1919-1970 9:473
- see also: ALIYAH
Aliyah Bet, see "ILLEGAL" IMMIGRATION
Aliyah Ḥadashah (polit. party) 8:1349; 9:662ff
- inter-communal tension 9:506
- labor movement 9:859
- Landauer, George 10:1399
- landsmannschaften 10:1415
Aliyah le-regel, see PILGRIMAGE; PILGRIM FESTIVALS
Aliyah Movement (Zion. orgn.) 9:544
Aliyyat Yeladim va-No'ar, see YOUTH ALIYAH
Al-Ja'barī, Ali, see Ja'barī, Muhammed Ali al-
Al-Jābiya, see Jābiya, Al-
Al-Jadīd (period.) 9:1042
ALJAMA (cmty., Sp.) 2:635
- Spain 15:229;233
Al-Jami'ān (stlmt.,Babyl.) 8:481
Al-Jawhar (Fatimid), see Jawhar, Al-
Al-Jazair (city, Alg.), see ALGIERS
Al-Jazzār (msq.), see Jazzār, Al-
Al-Jīb (loc., Er. Isr.), see Jīb, Al-
Al-Jibāl (reg., Isr.), see SEIR, MOUNT
Al-Jiradi (Er. Isr.), see Jiradi, Al-
Al-Jūzjāni (hist., Afg.), see Jūzjānī, Al-
Al-Kabbir, see ATTAR, JUDAH BEN JACOB IBN
ALKABEZ, SOLOMON BEN MOSES HA-LEVI 2:635
- Alcastiel, Joseph 2:542
- Hebrew printing 8:1325
- Kabbalah 10:545
- *Lekhah Dodi* 11:4
- *Sefirot* doctrine 10:578
- *illus:*
- - *Lekhah Dodi* 10:655; 11:5
Al-Kabir, Abraham Sālih, see KABIR, ABRAHAM SĀLIH AL-
Al-Kafrmandi, Abraham ben David, see Abraham ben David al-Kafrmandi
Alkaḥi, Mordekhai 8:1468
Alkala, Luis de 15:809
ALKALAI, ABRAHAM BEN SAMUEL 2:637
ALKALAI, DAVID 2:637
- Zionism 16:1148
- *illus:*
- - First Zionist Congress 16:1165
ALKALAI, JUDAH BEN SOLOMON ḤAI 2:638
- Bibas, Judah 4:813
- history chart 8:766-767
- kabbalistic influence 10:643
- messianism 16:1034ff
- redemption 14:9
- Yugoslavia 16:870
- Zemun 16:990
- Zionism 16:1148
Alkalai, Rachel 16:1165
ALKALAJ, ARON 16:886,890
- Bible 4:935
Alkalaj, Haim 16:888
Alkalay, A. 4:1312
Al-Kalīym (Kar. weekly) 5:31
Al-Kamīl (wk.), see *Kamīl, Al-*
Alkan (fam. name), see also Alcan
ALKAN, ALPHONSE 2:641
ALKAN, (Morhange) CHARLES HENRI-VALENTIN 2:641
Alkan, Napoléon 2:641
Alkar (poet) 13:737,802
Al-Karak (Jor.), see Karak, Al-
Alkaraya (J. sect). 2:671
Al-Karmil (newsp.) 9:333
Al-Katute (sub., Petra), see Katute, Al
Al-Kazzaz (fam. name), see Qazzaz
Al-Kerak (Moab), see KIR HARESETH
Al-Khaḍir (Isl. name) 9:1360
Al Khaḍr (Er. Isr.), see Khaḍr, Al-
Al-Khaḍr (Elijah), Tomb of (Zarephath, Er. Isr.) 16:936
Al-Khalaṣa (site, Er. Isr.), see ELUSA
Al-Khalīl (city, Er. Isr.), see HEBRON
Al-Khazna (bldg., Petra), see Khazna, Al-
Al-Kifl (tn., Iraq), see Kifl, Al-
Alkmaar (tn., Neth.) 12:975
Al-Komion al-Arab (nat. mvmt.), see Komion al-Arab, Al-
Al-Kufa (tn., Iraq), see KUFA
Alkum (loc., Alb.), see Dulcigno
Alkvit, B., see BLUM, ELIEZER
Allah (Isl. divine name) 9:92; 10:1196
- Solomon in Koran 15:108
Al-Lajjun (vill., Er. Isr.), see Lajjun, Al-
Allal ben Sidun Naboni, see Narboni, Allal ben Sidun ben Joshua
Allaman Oglou, see ASHKENAZI, SOLOMON
Allan, Elkan 15:930
Allariz (tn., Sp.) 12:1452
Allaun, Frank 11:860
- socialism 15:27
Al-Lawāni, Da'ud 10:1485
Alldeutscher Verband 3:83
Allegheny (tn., U.S.) 13:568
ALLEGORY 2:641
- *Contents:*
- - Bible 2:641
- - Talmud/Medieval Literature 2:643
- - Kabbalah 2:644
- - Modern Literature 2:644
- anthropomorphism 3:51f
- Arama, Isaac 3:257
- Aristobulus 3:443ff
- Bible 13:1264
- drama, Hebrew 6:194ff
- Dura-Europos 6:294
- interpretation of beliefs 3:656
- Jedaiah Bedersi 9:1310
- Jewish literature 11:313
- Koran 10:702ff.
- Levi ben Abraham 11:91
- Maimonidean controversy 11:749
- Philo 13:426
- Qumran scrolls 13:333
- Saadiah Gaon 14:550
- Song of Songs 15:147
- Throne of God 15:1125
- wisdom literature 16:561
- *illus:* text
- *see also:* BIBLE (Allegorical Interpretations); HOMILETIC LITERATURE; PARABLE
Allemania, see GERMANY
Allemanno, Isaac ben Johanan 2:646
ALLEMANNO, JOHANAN BEN ISAAC 2:645
Allen, Chesney 15:1082
Allen, Gracie 15:1080
Allen, John 8:21
Allen, Michael 11:257
ALLEN, WOODY, 15:1077
ALLENBY, EDMUND HENRY HYNMAN, VISCOUNT 2:646
- Jerusalem surrender 9:1469
- *illus:*
- - text
- - entering Old City of Jerusalem 9:1472
- - Government House party, Jerusalem 9:339
- - Hebrew University, foundation-stone ceremony 8:219
- - Hebrew University, opening ceremony 8:221
Allentown (city, Pa.) 13:230
- *illus:*
- - Temple Keneseth Israel 13:230
Allerhand, Mauryey 10:1500
Allgemeine Enzyklopaedie der Wissenschaften und Kuenste 6:731
Allgemeine Israelitische Wochenschrift (period.) 13:1032
Allgemeine Juedische Kolonisations Organisation 12:1230
- territorialism 15:1020
Allgemeine Juedische Zeitung (newsp.) 13:1035; 15:655
Allgemeiner deutscher Arbeiterverein, see ADAV
Allgemeiner Rabbinerverband in Deutschland 13:1455
Allgemeine Unabhaengige Juedische Wochenzeitung (period.) 13:1033
Allgemeine Wochenzeitung der Juden in Deutschland (newsp.) 6:263
Allgemeine Wochenzeitung des Judentums (newsp.) 7:500
ALLGEMEINE ZEITUNG DES JUDENTHUMS (period.) 2:647
- history chart 8:766-767
- Katz, Albert 10:821
- *illus: text*
Alliance Anti-Juive Universelle (anti-Sem.) 3:80
Alliance France-Israel 7:42
ALLIANCE ISRAELITE UNIVERSELLE 2:648
- activities 8:725
- Adrianople school 2:310
- Aḥad Ha-Am's criticism 2:442
- Alkalai, Judah 2:639, 640
- American settlements 2:412
- Anglo-Jewish Association 2:977
- archives 3:378,382
- Argentinian settlement 3:427
- Créhange, Alexandre 5:1072
- Crémieux, Isaac Adolphe 5:1076
- education 6:426ff; 15:53
- France 7:28
- Kurdistan 10:1298
- Lapin, Israel 10:1427
- library 11:191
- Morocco 12:340ff
- Mortara Case 12:354
- North Africa 6:459ff
- Persia 13:316ff
- philanthropy 13:387
- Rhodes 14:146
- Torah u-Melakhah school 4:393
- Tunisian schools 15:1449
- Yellin, Yehoshua 16:736
- Zionism 16:1113
- *illus:*
- - text
- - Beirut, school children 4:403; 6:400
- - Fez, Sylvain Lévy School 6:1257
- - Isfahan, school 9:79
- - Rabat, school 14:681
- - Teheran, Girls' School 8:1442
- - Tunis, school 15:1437
Alliance of German Jews, see VERBAND DER DEUTSCHEN JUDEN
ALLIANZ, ISRAELITISCHE, ZU WIEN 2:654
- history chart 8:766-767
- philanthropy 13:387
Allied Jewish Community Services, Montreal 4:368
Allioli, J. F. von 4:874
Allium cepa, see ONION
Allix, Peter 8:21
All the Nations Church (Jer.) 9:1473
ALLON, GEDALYA 2:654
- historiography 8:562
ALLON, YIGAL 2:655
- boundary plan 9:414
- Haganah 9:687
- immigrant absorption 9:413
- Palmaḥ 13:47
- *illus:*
- - Sadeh, Yiẓḥak, and 7:1070
- - staff officers, and (1948) 16:327
Allon-Bacuth (site, Er. Isr.) 5:1430
ALLONEI ABBA (mosh., Isr.) 2:656
- statistics 1:place list
ALLONEI YIẒḤAK (vill., Isr.) 2:657
- statistics 1:place list
ALLONIM (kib., Isr.) 2:657
- statistics 1: place list
Allon Plan (Isr.) 2:656; 9:414
Allon Shevut (rural center, Isr.) 1:place list
ALLOUCHE, FELIX NISSIM S'AIDOU 10:308
Allouche, Moses 5:915
ALLUF (tit.) 2:657
- Edomites 6:371ff
- gaonate 7:316
- title *ḥaver* 13:1449
- titles 15:1164
Alluf (brigadier, Isr.) 2:657
Allufi u-meyudda'i 2:657
Alluf Ẓion, see ALAMANI, AARON HE-ḤAVER BEN YESHU'AH
Al-Lugha (wk.), see *Kitāb Faṣīḥ Lughat al-Ibraniyyin*
Al-Luma' (wk.), see *Kitāb al-Luma'*

Al-Luz (loc., Isr.) **2**:666
Allweil, Aryeh **4**:1220
Allweiss, Solomon Siegfried, *see* ALVA, SOLOMON SIEGFRIED
Alma (Almah; stlmt., Er. Isr.) **2**:398; **9**:272, 285
– synagogue **15**:596
Almaçan, Pasqual Perez de **5**:38
AL-MADARI, JUDAH HA-KOHEN BEN ELEAZAR HE-ḤASID **2**:657
Al-Madrasa al-Ṣalaḥiyya (musl.), *see* Salaḥiyya Madrasa, Al-
Almagest (wk., Ptolemy) **3**:799
– illuminated manuscripts **8**:1266
– Maimonides **11**:779
Almagest (wk., Zacuto), *see Ha-Ḥibbur ha-Gadol*
Al-Maghar (vill., Er. Isr.), *see* MAGHAR, AL-
Al-Maghili (Afr.), *see* Maghili, Al-
Almagia, Giacomo **11**:1559
Almagia, Joab **13**:585
ALMAGIÀ, ROBERTO **2**:658
ALMAGOR (mosh., Isr.) **2**:658
– statistics **1**:place list
– U.N. **15**:1556
– *see also:* CHORAZIN
Almagor, David **15**:295
Al-Magribi, Samuel ibn Yahya, *see* SAMAU'AL BEN JUDAH IBN ABBAS
ALMAGRO (tn., Sp.) **2**:658
– Calatrava **5**:39
ALMAH (mosh., Isr.) **2**:659
– Manduzio's followers **14**:844
– statistics **1**: place list
Almah ("young woman") **16**:160
'Al-Maḥalat (Psalms) **13**:1320
Al-Mahdī, *see* Mahdī, Al-
Al-Malaki, Solomon, *see* Solomon al-Malaki
Almali, Ibn **11**:757
Almaliach, Abraham ben Judah **6**:1124
Al-Malik al- . . . ., *see under personal name*
Al-Malik al-Ashraf Sha'bān (Musl. ruler), *see* Sha'bān, Al-Malik al-Ashraf
Al-Malik al-Nasir...*see under personal name*
Al-Ma'mun (caliph), *see* Ma'mun, al-
ALMAN, SAMUEL **2**:659
Almanak (wk.), *see Ha-Ḥibbur ha-Gadol*
Almanakh ha-Ishah (journ.) **1**:newsp. list
Almanakh Mizpeh (journ.) **1**:newsp. list
ALMANSI (fam.) **2**:659
Almansi, Abraham **2**:659
Almansi, Baruch Ḥayyim **2**:659
Almansi, Dante **2**:660
Almansi, Emilio **2**:659
Almansi, Isaac **2**:659
Al-Mansur (caliph), *see* Mansur
Al-Manṣūr (tn., Egy.), *see* MANSURA
AL-MANSUR AL-YAHŪDĪ **2**:660
Al-Manṣūr ibn Abī 'Āmir (ruler, Sp.), *see* MANṢŪR (AL)
Al-Mansuriya (tn., Iraq), *see* Mansuriya, Al-
Almanza, Joseph d' (Ind.) **11**:681
Almanzi (fam.), *see also* ALMANSI
ALMANZI, JOSEPH (poet) **2**:661
– *illus:* text
Almanzor (ruler, Sp.), *see* MANṢUR (AL)
Almaqah (diety) **14**:588
Al-Maqdisī (geog.), *see* Maqdisī, Al-
Al-M̃arha (Sinai), *see* Marḥa, Al-
Al-Mashā'irī (fam.), *see* MASHA'IRI, AL-
Al-Maslakh (qtr., Jer.), *see* Maslakh, Al-
Al-Mawjib (riv., Transj.), *see* ARNON
Al-Mazra'a (vill., Er. Isr.), *see* Mazra'a, Al-
Almeida, Joào Ferreira d' **4**:879
Almeida, Leonor de **5**:222
Almemar (syn. part), *see* BIMAH
ALMERIA (city, Sp.) **2**:661
Al-Midya (vill., Er. Isr.), *see* Midya, Al-
Al-Mīnā (vill., Er. Isr.), *see* Mina, Al-
Al-Miṣbāh (newsp.) **13**:1041
Almog, *see* ALGUM
ALMOG, YEHUDA **2**:661
Almogen, David **8**:1130
ALMOGI, YOSEF AHARON **2**:662
– Ben-Gurion **4**:513
ALMOHADS (Musl. mvmt.) **2**:662
– African Jews **2**:332
– Almería **2**:661
– forced conversion **3**:170
– Omar covenant **12**:1380
– Spain **15**:226
– Tangier **15**:791
– Tunisia **15**:1436
ALMOLI, SOLOMON BEN JACOB **2**:663
– dreams **6**:211
– *illus:* text
ALMON (city, Er. Isr.) **2**:665
ALMOND **2**:665
– food **6**:1416; **12**:171
– plant list **13**:615
– terebinth graft **12**:171
– *illus:* text
ALMOND, GABRIEL ABRAHAM **2**:666
ALMON-DIBLATHAIM (Moab. city) **2**:667
ALMORAVIDES (Berber dyn.) **2**:667
Almoslino (dipl.) **16**:990
ALMOSNINO (fam.) **2**:667
– *geneal. table:* text
Almosnino, Abraham (mart., Sp.) **2**:667
Almosnino, Abraham (Fez) **2**:668
– emissary **14**:1366
Almosnino, Abraham (poet) **2**:669
Almosnino, Baruch **2**:668
Almosnino, Barzillai **2**:667
Almosnino, Gabriel Mercado **4**:1483; **4**:1485
Almosnino, Ḥasdai (N. Afr.) **2**:669
Almosnino, Ḥasdai (Eng.) **2**:669
Almosino, Ḥayyim **2**:668
Almosnino, Isaac (Belgrade) **2**:669
Almosnino, Isaac (Gib.) **2**:669
Almosnino, Isaac (Lond.) **2**:669
Almosnino, Isaac Ḥasdai **2**:669
Almosnino, Jacob **2**:667
Almosnino, Joseph (Arag.) **2**:667
Almosnino, Joseph (Salonika) **2**:667
– *paytan* **13**:585
Almosnino, Joseph (Sp. poet) **2**:669
ALMOSNINO, JOSEPH BEN ISAAC **2**:669
– *geneal. table* **2**:668
ALMOSNINO, MOSES BEN BARUCH **2**:669
– Aristotelianism **3**:446
– Ibn Ezra **15**:520
– informers *haskamah* **8**:1367
– Nasi, Joseph **12**:839
– *Regimento de la Vida* **10**:1349
– *geneal. table:* **2**:668
– *illus:* text
Almosnino, Samuel **2**:197; **15**:520
Almosnino, Simḥah **2**:669
Almosnino, Solomon **2**:669
– *illus:* text
Almqvist, Carl Jonas Love **14**:930
Almsgiving, *see* CHARITY
Al-Mu'allim al Fāḍil, *see* Faḍil, Al-Mu'allim al-
Al-Mu'aẓẓamiyya madrasa, *see* Mu'aẓẓamiyya madrasa, Al-
Al-Mu'azzam Turan Shah (Ayyubid), *see* Mu'azzam Turan Shah, Al-
Almudaina (Majorca) **11**:796
Al-Mudari, Judah ha-Kohen, *see* AL-MADARI, JUDAH HA-KOHEN BEN ELEAZAR HE-ḤASID
Almug (wood) *see* ALGUM
Al-Muḥāḍara... (wk.), *see Kitāb al-Muḥāḍara wa al-Mudhākara*
Al-Mu'izz, *see* Mu'izz, Al-
Al-Mujtama' (period.) **9**:1041
AL-MUKAMMIṢ, DAVID IBN MARWĀN AL-RĀQI AL-SHIRAZI **2**:671
– Christianity **3**:193
– Jewish philosophy **13**:432ff
– polemics **11**:354
– reward and punishment **14**:136
Al-Mukāwar (Transj.) *see* MACHAERUS
Almuli, Jesse **4**:1271
Almuli, Solomon ben Jacob, *see* ALMOLI, SOLOMON BEN JACOB
Al-Mundari, Judah ha-Kohen, *see* AL-MADARI, JUDAH HA-KOHEN BEN ELEAZAR HE-ḤASID
Al-Muqtadi (caliph), *see* Muqtadi, al-
Al-Murshid al-Kāfī (wk.), *see Murshid al-Kāfī, al-*
Al-Musayyab (tn., Iraq), *see* Musayyab, Al-
Al-Mushtamil 'alā . . . (wk.), *see Kitāb al-Mushtamil 'alā . . .*
Al-Mustalḥaq (wk.), *see Kitāb al-Mustalḥaq*
Al-Mustansir (caliph) **4**:167
Al-Mu'tadhid (caliph), *see* Mu'tadhid, Al-
Al-Muṭahhar (imam, Yem.), *see* Muṭahhar, Al-
Al-Mu'tamid (k., Seville), *see* Abbad III
Al-Mutawakkil (caliph), *see* Mutawakkil, Al-
'Al-Mut la-Ben (Psalms) **13**:1321
Al-Muwāzana bayn . . . (wk.), *see Kitāb al-Muwāzana bayn . . .*
Al-Nābigha al-Dhubyānī, see Dhubyānī, al-Nābigha al-
Al-Nabī-Samwīl (loc., Er. Isr.), *see* Nabī-Samuīl
Alnaes, Finn **14**:933
Al-Nahrawani, Nissi ben Berechiah, *see* NISSI BEN BERECHIAH AL-NAHRAWANI
Al-Najma (newsp.) **13**:1042
ALNAKAR, ABRAHAM BEN JOSEPH **2**:672
Al-Nakawa, Abraham (Shab.) **14**:1231
Al-Nakawa, Abraham ben Samuel **2**:672
Al-Nakawa, Ephraim **6**:298, 613, 672; **15**:1172; **16**:1187
– *illus:*
– – tomb, Tlemcen **15**:1173
AL-NAKAWA, ISRAEL BEN JOSEPH **2**:672
– Aboab, Isaac **2**:92
– ethical literature **11**:344
Al-Nakawa, Solomon **2**:672
Al-Nā'ūra (vill. Isr.), *see* Nā'ūra, Al-
Al-Nil (loc., Iraq), *see* Nil, Al-
Al-Nuqra, *see* BASHAN
Aloe (bot.) **2**:625
– plant list **13**:615
– soap **15**:18
Aloe, Louis P. **14**:666
Alonekh (journ.) **1**:newsp. list
Alon ha-Dayyagim (journ.) **1**:newsp. list
Alon ha-Ḥevrah ha-Numismatit (journ.) **1**:newsp. list
Alon ha-Kongress (journ.) **1**:newsp. list
Alon ha-Note'a (journ.) **1**:newsp. list
Alon ha-Palmaḥ (journ.) **1**:newsp. list
Alon ha-Shofetim (journ.) **1**:newsp. list
Alon ha-Shomerim (journ.) **1**:newsp. list
Alon ha-Tenu'ah ha-Beinle'ummit le-Sarvanei Milḥamah mi-Ta'amei Mazpun (journ.) **1**:newsp. list
Aloni, Joseph **5**:406
ALONI, NISSIM **2**:673
– drama, Hebrew **6**:206ff
– Hebrew literature **8**:207
Alonim (journ.), *see Ammudim*
Alon Kibbutzei ha-Shomer ha-Ẓa'ir (journ.) **1**:newsp. list
Alon Mishkei ha-Iḥud (journ.) **1**:newsp. list
Alon Mishkei ha-Kibbutz ha-Me'uḥad (journ.) **1**:newsp. list
Alonso, Hernando **5**:1146; **8**:1392
– travels **15**:1349
Alonso de Espina, *see* ALFONSO DE ESPINA
Alonso de Peralta **8**:1392
Alonso Fernandez de Cordoba, *see* CORDOBA, ALONSO FERNANDEZ DE
Alonso of Cartagena (bp.) **13**:4
Alopaeus (bp.) **6**:1297
Alouf, Yehoshua **15**:295ff
Al-Palas, Moses **13**:16
Al Penei Kaddur ha-Areẓ (journ.) **1**:newsp. list
Alper, David **13**:543
Alperovich, H. **11**:385
Alpers, Bernard **11**:1201
Alpert, Augusta **13**:1339
Alpert, Harry **15**:65
ALPHABET, HEBREW **2**:674
– *Contents:*
– – N.W. Semitic **2**:674
– – – Proto-Canaanite and Cuneiform **2**:674
– – – Phoenician **2**:678
– – – Hebrew **2**:681
– – – Paleo-Hebrew **2**:683
– – – Early Aramaic **2**:685
– – – Moabite, Edomite, Ammonite **2**:685
– – – Official Aramaic **2**:686
– – – Jewish Script **2**:688
– – Cursive Script **2**:689
– – – Types **2**:690f
– – Square Script **2**:705
– – – 6th cent. B.C.E./2nd cent. C.E. **2**:705
– – – Appearance of Letters **2**:706
– – – Basic Types **2**:707f.
– – Mashait Script **2**:729
– – – Types **2**:729f.
– – Letters as Numbers **2**:743
– – Braille **2**:744
– – Manual (Deaf) **2**:744
– – – Finger Spelling **2**:745
– – Shorthand **2**:745
– General
– – abbreviations **2**:46
– – *Al Ḥet* **2**:629
– – archaeology **3**:305
– – art **3**:521
– – as numbers **12**:1255
– – Book of Lamentations **10**:1372
– – creative powers of **7**:754

– – dictionaries 16:1364
– – Diringer, David 6:63
– – Kabbalah 16:783ff
– masorah 16:1407
– – mathematics 11:1122
– – meditation on 10:630
– – mnemonics 12:189
– – mystical alphabets 10:635
– – names of God 16:1335
– – *Sefer Torah* 14:1101
– – *tagin* 15:700
– – typography 15:1480
– – writing systems 16:654ff
– Jewish Script 2:688
– – Jewish languages 10:68
– – Judeo-Arabic usage 3:241
– – Judeo-French usage 10:424
– – Ladino 10:1347
– – Letter changes in Ereẓ Israel 15:774
– – pre-biblical Hebrew 16:1335
– – Yiddish usage 16:791
– Non-Hebrew Scripts 2:674
– – Cyrillic alphabet 4:1492
– – Hittite writing 8:790
– – Lachish ostraca 10:1335
– – ostraca 12:1509
– – Phoenician 13:480
– – pre-Islamic Arabic 3:237
– – scribal education 6:392
– – Ugarit 15:1506; 16:1498
– Letters
– – *alef* 2:554
– – *bet* 4:709
– – *gimmel* 7:578
– – *dalet* 5:1227
– – *he* 8:1
– – *waw* 16:367
– – *zayin* 16:943
– – *ḥet* 8:438
– – *tet* 15:1029
– – *yod* 16:843
– – *kaf* 10:669
– – *lamed* 10:1367
– – *mem* 11:1297
– – *nun* 12:1272
– – *samekh* 14:767
– – *ayin* 3:995
– – *pe* 13:194
– – *ṣade* 14:622
– – *kof* 10:1133
– – *resh* 14:80
– – *shin* 14:1408
– – *taw* 15:836
– *illus:*
– – text
– – abecedary (orient., 10th cent.) 8:658,1274
– – *alef*, initial (15th cent. ms.) 2:554
– – Aramaic script 3:262
– – *ayin*, initial (15th cent. ms.) 3:995
– – *bet*, initial 4:3; 8:1331
– – *dalet* (9th-8th cent. plaque) 5:1227
– – Diderot's Encyclopaedia, article on 6:24
– – Samaritan script 14:748
– – *shin*, initial 4:*fcg.* 940; 8:1281; 14:1408
– – sixteenth cent. classroom chart 6:387
– – typography 15:1483-1486
– – Yiddish, with Russian transliteration 14:489
– *tables:*
– – Arabic transliteration 3:238
– – articulation of consonants 8:81
– – Braille system, Hebrew 4:1090
– – Latin transliteration 8:79
– – letters as numerical signs 2:743
– – manual alphabet of the deaf 5:1419
– – pronunciation of consonants 8:85
– – traditional pronunciations 13:1139-1142
– *see also* GEMATRIA; HEBREW GRAMMAR; PRONUNCIATIONS OF HEBREW
ALPHABET, HEBREW, IN MIDRASH, TALMUD, AND KABBALAH 2:747
– *Contents:*
– – Rabbinic Literature 2:747
– – Jewish Mysticism 2:747
– – Letters as Structures 2:748
– – Torah and Prayers 2:748
– – Sequence 2:748
– – Final Letters 2:749
Alphabetizing compositions, *see* ACROSTICS
Alphabet of Ben Sira, *see* BEN SIRA, ALPHABET OF
Alphandery, Fernand 2:597
ALPHONSE OF POITIERS 2:749
– French Jewry 7:14
– Poitou 13:704
Alptekin (10th cent., Damascus) 9:262
Al-Pumbedita (Iraq), *see* PUMBEDITA
Al-Qaʿda (Mt. of Olives), *see* Qaʿda, Al-
Al-Qanawāt (tn., Syr.), *see* Qanawāt, Al-
Al-Qarqashandī (fam.), *see* Qarqashandī, Al-
Al-Qāsim ibn ʿAsākir, *see* Ibn ʿAsākir, al-Qāsim
Al-Qastal (vill., Er. Isr.), *see* Qastal, Al-
Al-Qatīfa (tn., Bahr.), *see* Qatīfa, Al-
Al-Quds (Turk. admin. dist.) 9:121
– Jerusalem name 9:1412,1436
Alquit, B. 8:1434
Al-Qūmisī, Daniel, *see* DANIEL BEN MOSES AL-QŪMISĪ
Al-Qūmisī, David, *see* David al-Qūmisī
Al-Qurna (tn., Iraq), *see* Qurna, Al-
Alrabi, *see* ABULRABI
Al-Rafīd (site, Golan) 13:1532
Al-Ragil, Moses, *see* ARRAGEL, MOSES
Al-Raḥbah (tn., Babyl.), *see* RAḤBAH, AL-
Al-Rām (vill., Er. Isr.), *see* Ram, Al-
Al-Raqqa (city, Syr.), *see* RAQQA
Al-Ra's (tell, Isr.) 3:696
Al-Rayna (vill., Er. Isr.), *see* Rayna, Al-
Al-Rāzī, Muhammad, *see* Rhazes
Al-Rīnā, *see* JERICHO
Al-Roḥi, David (ps. mess.), *see* ALROY, DAVID
Alron (airline, Isr.) 9:838
Alroy (fam.), *see* Arollia
ALROY, DAVID (Menahem) 2:750
– Kurdistan 10:1297
– messianism 11:1410
Alroy, Solomon 2:750
Al-Rueti (fam.), *see* ROTE
Al-Rueti, Jacob ben Samuel 14:323
Al-Ruha (city, As. M.), *see* EDESSA
Al-Rumayḥī, *see* Rumayḥī
Al-Rūz (Isr.), *see* Rūz, Al-
Al-Ṣabāḥ (newsp.) 13:1042
Al-Sabba (Masada, Isr.), *see* Sabba, Al
Al-Sabʿīn Lafẓa al-Mufrada (wk.), *see Kitāb al-Sabʿīn Lafẓa al-Mufrada*
Al-Sabʿuni (fam.), *see* SIBONI
ALSACE 2:751
– *Contents:*
– – Middle Ages 2:751
– – 15/17 centuries 2:753
– – France (Ancien Régime) 2:754
– – Emancipation (1781-1844) 2:755
– – Expansion (1844-71) 2:756
– – German Rule (1871–1918) 2:756
– – After 1918 2:756
– – Nazi Period 2:757
– – Present Conditions 2:757
– archives 3:382,387
– Assembly of Jewish Notables 3:763
– French Jewry 7:20ff
– Haskalah 7:1437
– rights to Jews 8:712
– *illus:*
– – Jewish badge (World War II) 4:72
– – Purim noisemaker 13:1393
– *see also:* LORRAINE
Al-Sadīd al-Dumyāṭī, *see* Dumyati, Al-Sadid al-
Al Safha-Maḥar (journ.) 1:newsp. list
Al-Saḥja (Arab poetry) 9:1038
Al-Ṣalaḥiyya madrasa (Musl. coll.), *see* Salaḥiyya Madrasa, Al-
Al-Ṣalāt al-Kabīra (Tun.), *see* Great Synagogue
Al-Salt (tn., Jor.), *see* Salt
Al-Sāmarī (Koran fig.) 14:757
Al-Samawʾal ("Samuel"), *see* Shamwīl
Al-Samawʾal al-Maghribī, *see* SAMAU'AL BEN JUDAH IBN ABBAS
Al-Samawʾal ben Ghārid ben ʿĀdiyā, *see* SAMUEL IBN ʿADIYĀ
Al-Samū (vill., Er. Isr.), *see* ESHTEMOA; Samūʿ, Al-
Al-Sanjari, Solomon Suleiman ben Amar 13:574
Alsari (pseud.), *see* FUERST, JULIUS
Al-Ṣawīl (tn., Yemen), *see* Ṣawil, Al-
ALSCHULER, SAMUEL 2:757
Al-Shamiya (tn., Iraq), *see* Shamiya, Al-
Al-Shams (period.) 5:31; 6:499
– press 13:1041
Al-Sharāʾ, *see* SEIR, MOUNT
ALSHEIKH, RAPHAEL BEN SHALOM 2:758
ALSHEIKH, SHALOM BEN JOSEPH 2:758
Alshekh, Ḥayyim 2:759
ALSHEKH, MOSES 2:758
– influence in Syria 15:644
– Ḥayyim Vital 16:171
– homiletical literature 8:954
– Torah 15:1238; 15:1241
– *illus:*
– – *Sefer Einei Moshe* (1601) 7:514
ʿAl-Shoshannim (Psalms) 13:1320
Al-Shūna (vill., Isr.), *see* Shuna, Al-
ʿAl Shushan ʿEdut (psalms) 13:1320
ALSHVANG, ARNOLD ALEKSANDROVICH 12:680
Alsingari, Solomon, *see* SOLOMON SULIMAN BEN AMAR
Al-Sion (newsp.) 13:1042
Al-Siq (gorge, Er. Isr.), *see* Siq, Al-
Al-Sittīn, *see* Sittin, Al-
Alsókubin (tn., Cz.), *see* DOLNI KUBIN
Alsóviso (vill., Rum.) 16:165
Alstedius, Johann H. 8:21
Alster, Y. 5:1036
ALSTER-THAU, GERDA 1:27
Alston, Abbey 4:138
ALT, ALBRECHT 2:759
Alt, L. 15:162
Al-Ṭabarī, *see* ALI IBN SAHL IBN RABBAN AL-TABARĪ
Al-Tabarī, Abu Jaʿfar Muhammad, *see* Tabarī, Abu Jaʿfar Muhammad al-
Al-Tabarī, Sahl ibn Rabbān, *see* Tabarī, Sahl ibn Rabbān al-
Al-Tābigha (site, Er. Isr.), *see* TABGHA
Al-Tadhkīr wa al-Taʾnīth (wk.), *see Kitāb al-Tadhkīr wa al-Taʾnīth*
Al-Tadmurī, Isḥāq ben Ibrāhīm 15:1358
Al-Tajnīs (wk.), *see Kitāb al-Tajnīs*
Al-Tal (vill. Isr.), *see* BETHSAIDA
Altalena (pseud.), *see* JABOTINSKY, VLADIMIR
Altalena (I.Z.L. arms ship) 9:368ff; 16:322
– Begin 4:392
– Ben-Gurion 4:509
– shelling of 8:1470
– *illus:*
– – burning 8:1470; 16:318
Al-Tanbīh (wk.), *see Risālat al-Tanbih*
Al-Tanqīḥ (wk.), *see Kitāb al-Tanqīḥ*
Al-Tanqīṭ (wk.), *see Kitāb al-Tanqīṭ*
Al-Taqrīb wa al-Tashil (wk.), *see Risālat al-Taqrib wa al-Tashil*
ALTAR 2:760
– *Contents:*
– – Definition 2:760
– – Typology 2:761
– – Sanctity and Theology 2:763
– – Incense Altar 2:765
– – Halakhah 2:767
– – Aggadah 2:770
– *aggadah* 16:1004
– ariel, hearth 3:436
– asylum 5:594
– Commandments, the 613 5:773
– divorce 6:125
– endowments 8:279
– fastdays 6:1192
– Ḥanukkah 7:1283ff
– high priest's encirclement 14:179
– *hoshanot* ceremony 8:1028
– iron tools forbidden 11:1433
– Johanan ben Zakkai 9:240
– Joshua, Book of 10:276
– lots 11:510ff
– meat and wine abstention 9:238
– *mizbeʾaḥ* 5:1167ff
– Naaman 12:733
– peace 13:197
– proscribed town 8:1471
– sacrifices 14:600ff
– Tabernacle 15:683ff
– Temple 15:949ff
– Temple priesthood 13:1071
– wood 16:630
– *illus:*
– – Balak's seven altars 4:127
– – Canaanite and Israelite 2:760-767
– – Day of Atonement service 16:845
– – high priest burning incense 7:100
– – incense 3:*fcg.* 524
– – priests performing sacrifice 3:*fcg.* 988
– – Tabernacle (model) 15:680
– *see also:* CULT PLACES-ISRAELITE; Incense altar
ALTARAS (fam.) 2:771
Altaras, David ben Solomon 2:771
ALTARAS, JACQUES ISAAC 2:771
ALTARAS, JOSEPH 2:772
Altaras, Moses 2:771
Altaras, Nissim 2:772
AL-TARAS, SIDI IBN 2:772
Altaras, Solomon 2:771
Altaras, Solomon the Elder 2:771
Al-Tasārīf (wk.), *see Kitāb al-Tasārīf*
Al-Tashḥet (Psalms) 13:1320
Al-Tashwīr (wk.), *see Kitāb al-Tashwīr*
Altasmuza (vill., Latvia) 8:253
Al-Taswiʾa (wk.), *see Kitāb al-Taswiʾa*
ALTAUZEN, YAKOV MOYSEYEVICH 14:514
Al-Tayyah, *see* IBN AL-TAQANA, MOSES
Al-Ṭayyiba (vill., Er. Isr.), *see*

TAYYIBA, AL-
ALTBAUER, MOSHE 1:27
- Tuwim, Julian 15:1470
Alt-Breisach (tn., Ger.), *see* BREISACH
Altdorfer, Albrecht 15:603
- *illus:*
- - Regensburg synagogue (etch.) 14:36
Alte Herren (Zion. orgn.) 10:805
Al Teḥi ke-Avotekha (anti-Chr. satire) 3:196; 6:299; 13:130
Al-Tell (vill., Isr.), *see* BETHSAIDA
Alten, Mark 11:545
Altenberg, H. 13:1369
ALTENBERG, PETER 2:772
Altenburg (city, Ger.) 15:1129
Al Tengiziyya Madrasa (Musl. coll.), *see* Tengiziyya Madrasa, Al-
Altenkundstadt, Jacob Koppel 10:472
ALTENSTADT (vill., Bav.) 2:773
Alter, Abraham Mordecai ben Isaac Meir 7:785; 13:2
Alter, Abraham Mordecai ben Judah Aryeh Leib 7:786
Alter, Isaac Meir of Gur 7:785
- Eger, Judah Leib 6:471
- *ḥiddushim* 8:467
- Mendel of Kotsk 10:1223
ALTER, ISRAEL (cantor) 7:1545
Alter, Israel (r., Er. Isr.) 7:786
- *illus:* text
Alter, Judah Aryeh Leib 2:425; 7:785
Alter, Leon 11:679
Alter, Mendele 13:1
ALTER, VICTOR 2:773
- Anti-Fascist Committee 3:62
- *illus:*
- - portrait 6:844
Altercatio Simonis Judaei et Theophili Christiani (bk.) 6:83
ALTERMAN, NATHAN 2:773
- drama, Hebrew 6:206
- Gronemann, Samuel 7:931
- Hebrew literature 8:201
- Tel Aviv 15:918
Alte Schul (syn., Cracow) 5:1027,1029
- *illus:*
- - interior 15:604
ALTHEIMER, BENJAMIN 2:776
Altheimer, Joseph 3:459
AL TIKREI (exeget. device) 2:776
ALTING, JACOBUS 2:776
- Christian Hebraists 8:21
Alting, Johann Heinrich 8:21
Al-Ṭīra (vill., Er. Isr.), *see* TIRA, AL-
ALTMAN, BENJAMIN 2:777
Altman, Bruno 10:817
Altman, David 2:318
Altman, Henry (polit.) 16:679
Altman, Henry (sport) 15:313
ALTMAN, MOISHE 2:777
Altman, Morris 2:777
ALTMAN, NATHAN 2:777
- *illus:*
- - text
- - Pasmanik, Daniel (drg.) 13:160
- - stage set for *Uriel Acosta* 5:989
ALTMAN, OSCAR LOUIS 2:778
Altmann, Adolf 2:779; 14:718
- Trier 15:1392
ALTMANN, ALEXANDER 2:779
- Kabbalah, studies on 10:649
Altneuland (bk.) 8:420
- "Reb Shemu'el" identified 13:1478
- utopian Zionism 16:1151
Altneuschul (syn., Prague) 15:590; 15:603
- *illus:*
- - Ark of the Law 15:*fcg.* 619
- - general view 13:966
- - interior 13:967
- - plan 15:603
- - stamp (1967) 5:1198
Alt-Ofen (Hung.), *see* Obuda
Al-Tolidah (wk.), *see Tolidah, Al-*
Alton (city, Ill.) 8:1256
ALTONA (tn., Ger.) 2:779
- archives 3:386
- Ashkenazi, Ẓevi 3:734
- Emden, Jacob 6:722
- Eybeschuetz, Jonathan 6:1074
- rabbinical jurisdiction abolished 13:1453
- Shabbateanism 14:1253
- shipbuilding 14:1413
- *illus:*
- - *Pinkas ha-Takkanot* (1726) 5:821
- *see also:* HAMBURG; WANDSBECK
Altoona (city, Pa.) 13:230
ALTSCHUL (-ER; Perles; fam.) 2:780
- special Purim 13:1396
Alt-Schul (qtr., Prague) 3:693
ALTSCHUL, AARON MEYER 2:781
Altschul, Abraham Eberle 2:780
ALTSCHUL, EMIL 2:782
ALTSCHUL, FRANK 2:782
Altschul, Ḥanokh ben Moses 2:780
ALTSCHUL, JOSEPH 2:782
ALTSCHUL, LOUIS 2:782
Altschul, Moses (Pol.) 2:780
ALTSCHUL, MOSES BEN ḤANOKH (writ.) 2:783
Altschul, Moses ben Ḥanokh (Prague) 2:780
Altschuler, Abraham 15:1215
ALTSCHULER, DAVID 2:783
- Bible exegesis 4:894
- *illus:* text
Altschuler, Jehiel Hillel 2:784
- Bible exegesis 4:894
ALTSCHULER, MODEST 12:680
Altschul Foundation (philan.) 2:783
Altschul Perles, Eliakim ben Ze'ev Wolf 2:781
Altschul Perles, Judah Aaron Moses ben Abraham Ḥanokh 2:781
Altschul Perles, Naphtali Hirsch ben Asher 2:781
Altschul Perles, Ze'ev Wolf ben Dov Baer 2:781
Altshuler, Mordecai 14:499
Altspeyer (vill., Ger.) 15:262
Al-Ṭūr (vill., Isr.), *see* Ṭūr, Al-
Al-Tustari, Abu, *see* Abū Naṣr Fadl
Al'Ubaid (vill., Mesop.), *see* Ubaid
Al-'Ubaydiyya (Er. Isr.), *see* 'Ubaydiyya, Al-
Al-'Udayma (site, Transj.), *see* 'Udayma, Al-
Al-'Ukbraī, Meshwi, *see* MESHWI AL-'UKBARI
Alula (city, Er. Isr.) 7:1188
Al-'Ulaymī, Mujīr al-Dīn, *see* Mujīr al-Dīn al-'Ulaymī
Alummah (rural center, Isr.) 1:place list
Alummah (journ.) 11:169
- statistics 1:newsp. list
Alummah Society for Jewish Studies 11:169
Alummim (kib., Isr.) 10:972
- statistics 1:place list
Alummim (orgn., Isr.) 7:252
ALUMMOT (kib., Isr.) 2:784
- statistics 1:place list
Alummot (period.) 5:458; 15:96
Al-'Uqūd fī . . . (wk.), *see Kitāb al-'Uqūd fī . . .*
Al-Urdunn (prov., Er. Isr.), *see* Urdun, Al-
Aluros (vill., Idumaea) 7:1188
Al-Uṣūl (wk.), *see Kitāb al-Uṣūl*
Al-Uṣūl wa al-Fuṣūl fī al-Lugha al-'Ibrāniyya (wk.), *see Kitāb al-Uṣūl wa al-Fuṣūl fī al-Lugha al-'Ibrāniyya*
Al-'Uthmāniyya Madrasa (Musl. coll.), *see* 'Uthmāniyya Madrasa, Al-
Al-'Uzayr (tn., Iraq), *see* 'Uzayr, Al-
ALVA, SOLOMON SIEGFRIED 2:784
- *illus:*
- - Manger, Itzik (drg.) 11:873
- - "Mitzva Tanz" 5:1265
Al-Valensi (fam.), *see* VALENSI
ALVAN BEN ABRAHAM 2:784
Alvarenga (fam.) 2:614
ALVARES (fam.) 2:785
Alvares, Duarte Henriques 2:785
Alvares, Nuño 4:1295
Alvares, Samuel Dios-Ayuda 2:785
Alvares, Solomon 2:786
Alvares Caldeira (fam.) 15:1302
Alvares de Tavara, Manuel, *see* ZACUTUS LUSITANUS
Alvarez (fam.), *see also* ALVARES
Alvarez, Fernando 2:785; 8:1399
Alvarez, Humberto 5:467
Alvarez, Isaac 2:785
Alvarez, Isabel Nuñez 12:1273
Alvarez, Jacob Jessurun, *see* FONSECA, ALVARO DE
Alvarez, Juan 8:1395
Alvarez, Luis D. 4:1099
Alvarez, Martin, *see* Bueno, Ephraim Hezekiah
Alvarez Delcon, Garcia, *see* Alvares, Samuel Dios-Ayuda
ALVAREZ GATO, JUAN 2:786
Alvaro, Paolo 4:1164; 15:224
Alvaro da Fonseca, *see* Aboab, David (Mar.)
Alvaro de Montalbán 14:225
Alvarus of Córdoba, *see* Alvaro, Paolo
Alvo (bot.) 2:625
Al-wasīṭ (period.) 9:1041
Al-Yamanī, Zechariah ben Sa'id, *see* Yamanī, Zechariah ben Sa'id al-
Al-Yamanī al-Rabbani, *see* 'ADANĪ, SAADIAH BEN DAVID
Al-Yasa' (Alyasa') 6:667
Al-Yatom, Ibn (fam.), *see* Ibn al-Yatom
Al-Yawm (newsp.) 9:1017; 9:1041
Al-Yehudiyya (vill., Golan) 13:1533
Al-Yitm River (Er. Isr.) 9:176
Alyn Hospital (Isr.), *see* ILAN
'Al-Yonat 'Elem Reḥoqim (Psalms) 13:1321
Alypius (4th cent., Rom.) 9:1406
- Temple rebuilding 2:852; 9:256 10:469
Alyussani, Isaac ben Levi, *see* IBN MAR SAUL, ISAAC BEN LEVI
Al-Ẓahir (caliph), *see* Zahir, Al-
Al-Zubayr (tn., Iraq), *see* Zubayr, Al-
ALZEY (tn., Ger.) 2:786
A.M., *see Anno mundi*
Amadio ben Moses of Rimini, *see* JEDIDIAH BEN MOSES OF RECANATI
'AMADIYA (tn., Kurd.) 2:786
- Barazani's yeshivah 4:205
AMADOR DE LOS RIOS, JOSÉ 2:787
- Baer, Yitzḥak 8:564
Amadores das Musas (lit. soc.) 7:51
Amal (school, Isr.) 8:540
- vocational training 9:881
- *illus:*
- - classes for the blind 4:1091
AMALEKITES (tribe) 2:787
- *Contents:*
- - Amalek and Israel 2:787
- - Land and People 2:790
- - Amalekites and Kenites 2:790
- - In Aggadah 2:791
- Armenia 3:473
- Commandments, the 613 5:769
- Haman 13:1392
- Ishmaelites 9:89
- Jethro 10:19
- Kenites 10:907
- proscription of 8:345ff
- Rephidim 14:80
- Saul 14:912
- term for Christians 7:411
- Timna 15:1146
- *illus:*
- - Israelites' battle with 14:1258
AMALFI (city, It.) 2:791
Amama, Sixtinus (Hebr.) 8:21
AMANA (mt., Syr.) 2:792
Amana (rd. station, Syr.) 2:792
Amanah (riv., Syr.) 2:792
Amandus van Zieriksee 8:21
Amanecer (newsp.) 13:1040
Amanus Mountains (Mesop.) 16:1497
Amar, Marshal Abdel Ḥakim 12:843
Amar, David 13:816
AMAR, LICCO 12:680
Amar, Solomon 5:1484; 11:1016
- Lara, Hiyya Kohen de 10:1429
- Morocco 12:335
'Amāra, Ibrahim 5:1250
Amaraios (residents, Madeba), see Ambri
Amarant, Shlomo 14:222
Amaranth (bot.) 13:615
Amariah (priestly clan), *see* Immer
Amariah (h. pr.) 13:1075
- Jehoshaphat 9:1327
Amarillo (city, Tex.) 15:1035,1036
AMARILLO, AARON BEN SOLOMON 2:792
AMARILLO, ḤAYYIM MOSES BEN SOLOMON 2:792
Amarillo, Isaac 4:1533
AMARILLO, SOLOMON BEN JOSEPH 2:793
AMARKAL (hal. wk.) 2:793
Amarkala, Joseph ha-Levi 12:1176
Amarkalim (temple offic.) 15:973
Amar Neke (wk.) 15:520
Amar-Sin (k., Mesop.) 16:1494
Amaru (reg., Near East), *see* Amurru
AMASA (bib. fig.) 2:793
- Joab 10:107
- *geneal. table:* 5:1342
Amasai (bib. fig.) 2:794
AMASIYA (tn., Turk.) 2:794
Amat, Felix Torres 4:879
AMATUS LUSITANUS 2:795
- anatomy 2:934
- Ibn Yahya, Gedaliah 8:1210
- medicine 11:1191
- Nasi, Joseph 12:839
- Pesaro 13:329
- Pyrrhus, D. 13:1416
- Veltwyck, G. 16:89
- *illus:* text
Amaw (nomads) 2:790
AMAZIAH (k., Judah) 2:798
- Edom 6:375
- history 8:600*ff.*
- history chart 8:766-767
- *geneal. table:* 5:1341
AMAZIAH (pr., Beth-El) 2:799
- priestly dynasty 13:1072
- *illus:*
- - thirteenth cent. Latin bible 12:1293
Amazonas (state, Braz.) 4:1328
Amazons (leg. figs.) 12:1503
- *illus:*
- - battle with Greeks 12:1504
AMAẒYAH (mosh., Isr.) 2:799
- statistics 1:place list
Amaẓyahu River (Isr.) 9:163
- *illus:*
- - canyon 9:153

Ambato (city, Ec.) **6**:359
Amber (fossil resin) **13**:1010
AMBERG (city, Ger.) **2**:800
- illus: text
Amberg, David **11**:1499
Amberg, Julius **11**:1499
Amberg, Samuel **5**:755
Ambidjan (orgn.) **4**:1047
Amboise (tn., Fr.) **15**:1288
Ambri (residents, Madeba) **10**:155
Ambrogio, Teseo **8**:21
Ambron, Ezekiel (Alessandro) **2**:800
Ambron, Sabbato Isaac **2**:800
AMBRON, SHABBETAI ISAAC **2**:800
AMBROSE (ch. f.) **2**:801
- anti-Semitism **11**:1141
- Aquileia synagogue **3**:228
- Calinicum synagogue **8**:655
- usury **12**:250
Ambrose, Alice **10**:1519
Ambrosian Bible **8**:1267
- *illus:* **4**:360, fcg. 908; **5**:1018; **8**:1279
AMEIMAR (amora) **2**:802
AMELANDER, MENAHEM MANN BEN SOLOMON HA-LEVI **2**:802
- *She'erit Yisrael* **8**:560; **16**:805
- Trebitsch, A. **15**:1363
Amēl Marduk (k. Babyl.), *see* EVIL-MERODACH
AMEN (litur. response) **2**:803
- *Barukh Shem Kevod Malkhuto Le-Olam Va-Ed* **4**:284
- *El Melekh Ne'eman* **6**:683
- influence of Judaism **10**:396
- *score:* text
- *see also:* BENEDICTIONS
AMEN, IRVING **3**:595
- *illus:*
- - "Chess Players I" **3**:615
Amenhotep III (pharaoh), *see* AMENOPHIS III
AMENITIES, COMMUNAL **2**:805
- begging **4**:388
- burial **4**:1518
- burial societies **8**:443*ff*
- care of aged **2**:346f
- charity **5**:346f
- community tokens **5**:853
- *gabbai* **7**:230
- *ḥaver ir* **7**:1492
- hospitality **8**:1030
- *mikveh* **11**:1534
- public bath **4**:320
- sick (visiting) **14**:1496
- tax **15**:841
- *illus:*
- - text
- - Dubno, Jewish Hospital **8**:1036
- - London, Jew's Hospital **8**:1036
- - London, Spitalfields soup kitchen **5**:346
- - visiting the sick **14**:1497
- *see also:* COMMUNITY
Amenophis II (pharaoh) **2**:917
AMENOPHIS III (pharaoh) **2**:807
- Egypt **6**:481
Amenophis IV (pharaoh), *see* AKHENATON
AMERICA **2**:808
- *Contents:*
- - Marranos and Inquisition **2**:808
- - First Settlements: N. America **2**:809
- - Expansion: 19th cent. **2**:811
- - North and South: 20th cent. **2**:812
- General
- - Jewish soldiers **11**:1550
- - medicine **11**:1195*ff*
- - slave trade **14**:1662*ff*
- - sociology **15**:66
- - Ten Lost Tribes **15**:1006
- Countries
- - Argentina **3**:408
- - Barbados **4**:205
- - Bolivia **4**:1187
- - Brazil **4**:1322
- - Canada **5**:102
- - Chile **5**:461
- - Colombia **5**:744
- - Costa Rica **5**:989
- - Cuba **5**:1146
- - Curaçao **12**:993
- - Dominican Republic **6**:160
- - Ecuador **6**:359
- - El Salvador **6**:687
- - Guatemala **7**:956
- - Haiti **7**:1141
- - Honduras **8**:962
- - Jamaica **9**:1272
- - Mexico **11**:1453
- - Netherlands Antilles **12**:993
- - Nicaragua **12**:1135
- - Panama **13**:53
- - Paraguay **13**:85
- - Peru **13**:322
- - Puerto Rico **16**:1555
- - Surinam **15**:529
- - Trinidad **16**:473
- - United States **15**:1585
- - Uruguay **16**:10*ff*
- - Venezuela **16**:90
- *pop. tables:*
- - text
- - Americas, Jewish population figures 1900-1968 **2**:809-816
- - Argentina
- - - Jewish population, 1869-1968 **3**:418-419
- - - Jewish settlement **3**:411
- - - major towns, 1967 **5**:1514
- - Brazil, main areas of settlement **4**:1323
- - Canada
- - - age composition, 1961 **5**:1518
- - - major Jewish communities, 1871-1969 **5**:101,105
- - - major towns, 1967 **5**:1514
- - - vital statistics **16**:180,181,184
- - Chile, Jewish communities, 1970 **5**:462
- - Colombia, Jewish settlement **5**:744
- - community organization types and population, 1968 **5**:841
- - countries with 500 or more Jews, 1967 **5**:1503
- - Dominican Republic, major centers of settlement, 1969 **6**:160
- - Ecuador, major communities, 1970 **6**:360
- - Guatemala, centers of settlement **7**:956
- - Latin America, 1960's **10**:1451
- - Latin America and Caribbean postwar communities **5**:840
- - Mexico, 1971 **11**:1454
- - 19/20 centuries **13**:893,898,899
- - population by continent 1840-1969 **5**:831
- - population, world Jewish, 1850-1967 **5**:1495
- - United States, *see* UNITED STATES OF AMERICA
- - Venezuela (1969) **16**:90
- *see also:* LATIN AMERICA
America, La (newsp.) **14**:1174
AMERICA-ISRAEL CULTURAL FOUNDATION **2**:816
- Israel Philharmonic **9**:1073
- *illus:* text
America-Israel Culture House (N.Y.) **2**:817
AMERICAN, SADIE **2**:817
"Americana" (paint., Eilshemius) **3**:623
AMERICAN ACADEMY FOR JEWISH RESEARCH **2**:818
- *illus:* text
American and Foreign Bible Society **4**:969
AMERICAN ASSOCIATION FOR JEWISH EDUCATION **2**:819
American Association of Colleges for Teacher Education **14**:201
American Bible Society **4**:969
American Board of Commissioners for Foreign Missions **4**:969
American Christian Palestine Committee **16**:1155
American Civil War
- General
- - Alabama Jews **2**:506
- - anti-Semitism **15**:1649
- - Baltimore Jews **4**:148
- - Jewish soldiers **11**:1551
- - New York **12**:1075
- - United States **15**:1601
- Jews in
- - Baruch, Simon **4**:268
- - Benjamin, Judah P. **4**:528
- - Blumenberg, Leopold **4**:1139
- - De Leon, David **5**:1470
- - Hershfield, Reuben E. **10**:739
- - Joachimson, P.J. **10**:110
- - Knefler, Frederick **11**:1574
- - Levy, Jonas P. **11**:158
- - Levy, Uriah P. **11**:164
- - Mordecai, Alfred **12**:310
- - Moses, Raphael J. **12**:414
- - Taussig, E. D. **15**:835
- - Vance, Zebulon Baird **16**:66
- - Yulee, David Levy **16**:894
- *illus:*
- - Grant's anti-Semitic general order **15**:1651
- - Jewish soldiers, casualty list **15**:1602
- - Lincoln's letter to Philadelphia Jews **11**:257
American Colony (Jer.) **9**:1459,1501
- Six-Day War **14**:1630
AMERICAN COUNCIL FOR JUDAISM **2**:819
- anti-Zionism **16**:1068,1145,1147
- State of Israel **10**:395
- U.S. Zionism **15**:1635
American Emergency Committee for Zionist Affairs **2**:832
- Z.O.A. **16**:1179
American Examiner (period.) **2**:821
AMERICAN FEDERATION OF JEWS FROM CENTRAL EUROPE **2**:820
American Federation of Labor
- anti-Nazi boycott **4**:1281
- Jewish Labor Committee **10**:66
- Potofsky, J. **13**:935*ff*
American Freeman, The (period.) **7**:702
American Fund for Palestinian Institutions **8**:254
American Guild for German Cultural Freedom **4**:668
AMERICAN HEBREW, THE (period.) **2**:820
- Lipsky, Louis **11**:296
- Mendes brothers **11**:1343
- New York **12**:1103
- press **13**:1052
- *see also:* JEWISH MESSENGER, THE
AMERICAN ISRAELITE (period.) **2**:821
- Cincinnati **5**:564
- *illus:*
- - front page (1854) **2**:821
American-Israel Paper Mills **13**:1379
AMERICAN JEWISH ARCHIVES **2**:822
- Hebrew Union College **8**:218
- historiography **8**:568
- library of **11**:191
American Jewish Archives (period.) **2**:822; **8**:218
- learned societies **15**:55
AMERICAN JEWISH COMMITTEE **2**:822
- history chart **8**:766-767
- interfaith work **13**:1253
- library **11**:191
- United States **15**:1622
- Zionism **16**:1145
- *illus:*
- - text
- - delegation, with Pope Paul VI **5**:543
- - Mikoyan, Anastas I., and **12**:1112
AMERICAN JEWISH CONFERENCE **2**:825
- U.S. diplomats and **15**:1658
- Weisgal, Meyer **16**:410
American Jewish Conference on Soviet Jewry **14**:499
AMERICAN JEWISH CONGRESS **2**:825
- anti-Nazi boycott **4**:1281
- Brandeis, Louis **4**:1297
- history chart **8**:766-767
- Jewish Committee **2**:823ff
- Labor Committee **10**:66
- rabbi's function **13**:1456
- *illus:*
- - anti-Nazi demonstration **15**:1629
American Jewish Cyclopedia **6**:734
AMERICAN JEWISH HISTORICAL SOCIETY **2**:826
- historiography **8**:568
- library of **11**:191
- U.S. Jewry **15**:55
- *illus:*
- - text
- - Waltham, Mass., library **11**:191
American Jewish Historical Society Quarterly **2**:827; **15**:55
American Jewish History Center **10**:97
American Jewish Joint Agriculture Corporation **2**:828
AMERICAN JEWISH JOINT DISTRIBUTION COMMITTEE **2**:827
- American Jewry **2**:813
- *Beriḥah* **4**:630
- British Guiana **7**:998
- Dominican Republic **6**:160
- fund-raising **13**:380
- history chart **8**:766-767
- I.C.A. **10**:44ff
- Malben **11**:821
- Persian Jewry **13**:318
- Poland **13**:779
- refugees **6**:991
- Rumania **14**:408ff
- Zionism **16**:1146
- *illus:*
- - shoemakers' cooperative, Poland **13**:781
American Jewish Periodical Center (archives) **2**:822; **8**:217
American Jewish Publication Society, *see* JEWISH PUBLICATION SOCIETY OF AMERICA
American Jewish Relief Committee **2**:823
American Jewish Yearbook **2**:273, 825
American Joint Reconstruction Foundation **10**:688; **2**:828; **10**:45
American Labor Movement **10**:65
American League for the Defense of Jewish Rights, *see* Non-Sectarian Anti-Nazi League to Champion Human Rights
American League for a Free Palestine **8**:239
American Medical Center (Colo.) **5**:352
American Palestine Committee

16:1155
American Palestine Exploration Society 9:297
American Palestine Fund, Inc. 2:816
American Peace Commission 13:30
American Psychological Association 11:1097
American Quarter (Jer.), *see* American Colony
American Red Cross 15:126
American Revolution, *see* American War of Independence
American School of Oriental Research (Jer.) 9:1462
- Albright 2:538
Americans for Progressive Israel 7:1375
American Society for Jewish Farm Settlements in Russia 2:828
American Standard Version (Bib.) 4:870
American Students for Israel (Zion. orgn.) 15:451
American War of Independence
- Alexander, Abraham 2:572
- Bush, Solomon 4:1535
- Canadian Jews 5:103
- Cardozo, David Nunez 5:162
- Cardozo, Isaac Nunez 5:162
- constitutional inequality 3:113
- Franks, David S. 7:107
- Jewish soldiers 11:1550
- Nones, Benjamin 12:1210
- Salomon, Haym 14:695
- Salvador, Francis 14:715
- Sheftall, Mordecai 14:1336
- *illus:*
- - Salomon, Haym, letterbook 15:1591
- - Salvador, Francis, commemorative plaque 14:715
American Zion Commonwealth Co. 9:341
- Afulah 2:339
American Zionist, The (period.) 16:1179
AMERICAN ZIONIST COUNCIL 2:832
- American Zionist Emergency Council 2:832; 16:1088
- *illus:*
- - rally for a Jewish Palestine 15:1659,1661
American Zionist Medical Unit 9:982
American Zionist Youth Foundation (student orgn.) 15:451
Amerikaner (period.) 12:1102
Amersfoordt, Petrus 8:21
AMERSFOORT (tn., Neth.) 2:832
AMERY, LEOPOLD STENNETT 2:832
- *illus:* text
AMES (fam.) 2:833
- *illus:* text
Amescua, Antonia Mira de 10:25
Amesquita, Luis, *see* Mesquita, Luis de
Amethyst (gem) 13:1010
AM HA-AREẒ 2:833
- *Contents:*
- - Bible 2:833
- - Mishnah 2:834
- - Later Times 2:836
- Akiva 2:488
- *demai* 5:1486
- desecration 5:1560
- economic plight of 16:1275
- high priest 11:840
- Judah ha-Nasi 10:370
- Meir 11:1241ff
- ritual purity 13:88
- role in choice of kings 10:110
- sages and 14:642ff
- Shneour's new hero 14:1431
- Torah study 15:456; 16:1278
- *see also:* ELDER; ḤAVER, ḤAVERIM; Literacy; TALMID ḤAKHAM
Amharic (Eth. lang.) 14:1153
- Bible translations 4:861
- Falashas 6:1149
Am Ha-Sefer (publ.) 13:1378
Amherst (tn., Austr.) 11:1285
Amherst (tn., Can.) 11:998
Ami (period.) 5:460
Amia (city, Cana.) 5:99
A.M.I.A. (orgn., Buenos Aires) 2:836
- fundraising 13:386
AMICHAI, YEHUDA 2:838
- Hebrew literature 6:206; 8:206; 8:207
- Jerusalem theme 9:1567
Amici Israel Association (Cath. orgn.) 13:572
Amico, Bernardino 9:1544
AMIDAH (prayer) 2:838
- *Contents:*
- - Manner of Recital 2:838
- - Types, Structure, Style 2:839
- - Evolution and Redaction 2:839
- - Weekdays 2:840
- - Additions 2:842
- - Sabbaths and Festivals 2:843
- - High Holidays 2:844
- - Havinenu 2:845
- - Music 2:845
- arranged in Talmud 11:1229
- benedictions 4:485
- *Berakhot* 4:585; 4:586
- heretics 8:359; 8:361
- Jerusalem in 9:1560
- Karaite rite 10:781
- *Kedushah* 10:875
- *kerovah* 10:920
- laborer 10:1323
- liturgy 11:394ff
- Maimon ben Joseph 11:744
- Maimonides 11:760
- Messiah 11:1409
- *min* 12:3
- *minyan* 12:67
- *Ne'ilah* service 12:943
- origin of 15:630
- prayer for rain 13:1523
- priestly blessing 13:1062
- proselytes 13:1185
- resurrection 14:98
- Simeon ha-Pakuli 14:1565
- synagogues 15:592
- *illus:*
- - Rosh ha-Shanah *Musaf* service prayer 14:306
- *see also:* BIRKAT HA-MINIM; MASHIV HA-RU'AḤ
AMIDAR (Isr. nat. housing co.) 2:846
- new immigrants 9:536
- *illus:* text
Amiel (fam.) 14:682
Amiel, J. J. 15:311
AMIEL, MOSHE AVIGDOR 2:846
- religious life in Israel 9:893
- yeshivot 16:772
Amiens, Viscomte D', *see* CALMER, MOSES ELIEZER LIEFMANN
Amiens Picture Bible (12th cent. illum. ms., Sp.) 9:1373; 10:100, 106, 1021, 1028
Amieth (city, Er. Isr.), *see* ALMON
AMIGO (fam.) 2:847
AMIGO, ABRAHAM 2:847
- Shabbetai Ẓevi 14:1225
Amigo, Isaac (paytan, Turk.) 13:581
Amigo, Isaac (Rum.) 2:847
Amigo, Joseph Meir 2:847
Amigo, Meir 2:847
Amiḥai Publishing House (Isr.) 13:1378
Amina (poet, Bukhara), *see* Benjamin ben Mishal
Amīn al-Dawla 14:618
Aminoaḥ, Nehemiah 7:1320
AMIR (kib., Isr.) 2:848
- statistics 1:place list
AMIR, AHARON 2:848
AMIR, ANDA 2:848
Amir, Menahem 5:1111
AMIRA, BINYAMIN 11:1124
AMIRAN, DAVID 2:849
AMIRAN, EMANUEL 12:680
- Jerusalem song 9:1590
- music 12:670
Amiran, Ruth 2:849
- archaeology 3:303
- Jerusalem 9:1524ff
- Tel Arad 3:244
AMIRIM (mosh., Isr.) 2:849
- statistics 1:place list
Amir Range, *see* Umm al-Faḥm (block)
Amishai, M. H., *see* MAISELS, MOSES ḤAYYIM
Amistad Judeo-Christiana (orgn., Sp.) 15:246
Amitié Judéo-Chrétienne (interfaith orgn.) 9:10
Amitiés France-Israël (journ.) 16:1115
Amittai (bib. fig.) 10:169
AMITTAI (paytan) 2:849
Amittai ben Avida Ahizedek, *see* CARO, DAVID
AMITTAI BEN SHEPHATIAH 2:850
- Jewish mysticism 10:512
- *geneal. table:* 2:463
Amiẓ Ko'aḥ (piyyut) 3:978
Amkah (stlmt., Er. Isr.) 1:place list; 9:272
Amlander, Menahem, *see* AMELANDER, MENAHEM MANN BEN SOLOMON HA-LEVI
'Ammah ("cubit"; meas.) 16:378*ff.*
Amman (city, Jor.), *see* RABBATH-AMMON
Amman, Kaspar 8:21
Ammanah (journs.) 1:newsp. list
Amman Citadel inscription 16:666
'Ammar (fam.) 4:1274
AMMATHA (anc. tn., Transj.) 2:850
AMMERSCHWIHR (tn., Fr.) 2:851
AMMIAD (kib., Isr.) 2:851
- statistics 1:place list
AMMIANUS MARCELLINUS 2:851
- Julian the Apostate 10:469
AMMI BAR NATHAN (amora) 2:852
Ammidar (rural stlmt., Isr.), *see* Shoshannat ha-Amakim
Ammiel (f., Bath-Sheba) 4:322
Ammikam (mosh. Isr.) 1:place list
AMMINADAV (mosh., Isr.) 2:853
- statistics 1:place list
Ammi'oz (mosh., Isr.) 1:place list
Ammistamru I (k., Ugarit) 15:1503
AMMON, AMMONITES (bib. people) 2:853
- *Contents:*
- - The Land 2:853
- - Culture 2:854
- - Ammon and Israel 2:856
- - Assyria and Babylon 2:857
- - Aggadah 2:859
- - Halakhah 2:860
- Bible history 8:576ff; 8:587ff
- Commandments, the 613 5:773
- David's wars 5:1321
- human geography 9:596
- Jephthah 9:1341
- Jeremiah's oracle 9:1354
- language 2:686; 14:1150
- Lot's incest 11:508
- marriage with Jews 16:776
- physiography 9:177
- proselytisation 8:1423
- Ptolemaic colony 8:627
- Solomon's concubines 15:100
- status in ancient Israel 15:420
- Transjordan 15:1316ff
- war and warfare 16:277
- Zedekiah's revolt and 16:962
- *illus:*
- - text
- - David's wars against (map) 5:1322
- - Uriah the Hittite stoned 11:633
Ammonius, Kaspar, *see* Amman, Kaspar
Ammot (journ.) 1:newsp. list
Ammudei ha-Avodah (wk.) 10:1413
Ammud ha-Yir'ah (journ.) 1:newsp. list
Ammudim (journ.) 10:973
- Aliyah Ḥadashah 10:1274
Ammud River (Isr.), *see* Naḥal Ammud
Ammunition Hill (Jer.) 9:1501
- Six-Day War 14:1630
AMNON (s., David) 2:860
- in the Arts 5:1334
- Tamar 15:783
- *geneal. table:* 5:1341
- *illus:*
- - text
- - seduction of Tamar 8:1317
AMNON OF MAINZ 2:861
- Ephraim of Bonn 6:813
- *U-Netanneh Tokef* 15:1531
Amoena Amalia of Anhalt 8:21
AM OLAM (soc., Rus.) 2:861
- Bilu ideology 4:999
- Sabsovich, H. L. 14:589
Amomum (spice) 13:615; 15:267
AMON (k., Judah) 2:862
- assassination 8:606ff
- history chart 8:766-767
- Meshullemeth 16:951
- *geneal. table:* 5:1341
AMON (deity) 2:863
- demons 5:1532
- Samael 14:721
- *illus:* text
AMORA (tal. sage) 2:863
- title 13:1445
AMORAIM 2:865
- *Contents:*
- - Authority 2:865
- - Titles 2:873
- - Social and Economic Status 2:873
- - Generations of 2:874
- academies 2:203
- *aliyah* 9:510ff
- as aggadists 2:363
- Bible interpretation 8:1418
- codification of law 5:633f
- controversy restrictions 5:891
- *halakhah* development 7:1163
- Jerusalem Talmud 15:772ff
- Jewish law periods 12:121
- law and morality 10:1481
- legal maxims 10:1565
- liturgy 11:394ff
- Mishnah text 12:106
- *savora* 14:921
- *tanna, tannaim* 15:798ff
- tradition 15:1311
- *charts:* text
- *see also:* AMORA; GAON
"*Amoraim* of Nehardea" 7:1218
AMORITES (people, Cana.) 2:875
- *Contents:*
- - Extra-Biblical Sources 2:875
- - Bible 2:877
- - Talmud 2:878
- Canaan 13:473
- Habiru 7:1034

- Hadad **7:**1040
- history, early Bible **8:**572ff
- Jebusites **9:**1308
- Mesopotamia **16:**1484
- pre-biblical Hebrew **16:**1561ff
- Semites **14:**1148
- Ur **16:**3
- *illus:* text
AMOS (prophet) **2:**879
Contents:
- - Prophet **2:**879
- - The Book **2:**881
- - Prophecies **2:**884
- - Personality and Message **2:**886
- Amaziah **2:**799
- eschatology **6:**862ff
- history chart **8:**766-767
- Minor Prophets **12:**48
- morality **10:**1480
- poetry **13:**680
- *illus:*
- - text
- - thirteenth cent. Latin bible **12:**1293
Am Oved (publ.) **5:**1316; **9:**857
- Habas, Bracha **7:**1018
- Histadrut **8:**540
- Katznelson, Berl **10:**838
- publishing **13:**1378
- Shazar, S. Z. **14:**1324
Amoz (bib. fig.) **9:**44, 67
Amozag, Abraham Ḥai **2:**599
Ampal (fin. co., Isr.) **8:**539
Amphibians **3:**18; **6:**36
Amphictyony (tribal orgn.) **8:**583,610
- Sumer **16:**1493
- Twelve Tribes **15:**1382
ʿAmqa (vill., Isr.) **4:**732
ʿAmr, Zahir al-, *see* Ẓahir al-Omar
AMRAM (bib. fig.) **2:**890
- marriage **8:**1316
- Moses **12:**372
AMRAM (3rd cent., amora) **2:**890
AMRAM (4th cent., amora) **2:**890
AMRAM (nagid) **2:**890
Amram (fam.) **13:**926
AMRAM, DAVID WERNER **2:**891
AMRAM, NATHAN BEN ḤAYYIM **2:**891
Amram, Werner David **2:**891
Amram ben Isaac **14:**736
- *illus:*
- - calendar **14:**747
- - portrait **14:**733
Amram ben Johanan **14:**617
Amram ben Meswi **2:**14
Amram ben Sarad **2:**893
Amram ben Shalma **14:**738
AMRAM BEN SHESHNA (Amram Gaon) **2:**891
- angels in *Siddur* of **2:**971
- codification of law **11:**330
- gaonate **7:**315; **7:**317
- history chart **8:**766-767
- liturgy **11:**396ff
- moneylending **12:**248
- prayer book **13:**985ff
- prayers **11:**58
- *illus:* text
Amram Columns (Isr.) **9:**592
AMRAM DARAH (Samar.) **2:**893
- Markah **11:**999
Amram Gaon, *see* AMRAM BEN SHESHNA
AMRAM ḤASIDA ("The Pious"; amora) **2:**893
Amramites (tribe of Levi) **2:**890
AMRAM OF MAINZ (leg. fig.) **2:**894
Amram "The Pious," *see* AMRAM ḤASIDA
AMRAN (tn., Yem.) **2:**894
- Yemen **16:**746
ʿAmrani (poet) **13:**318
AMRAPHEL (k., Shinar) **2:**894
- Nimrod **12:**1167
- Sodom and Gomorrah **15:**70
Amrawa (tn., Transj.) **9:**279
ʾAmr ben Dayyan, *see* ʾUmar ben Dayyan
ʿAmr ibn-Alʿāṣ (Arab comm.) **9:**260
Amron, Jacob **13:**583
Amschelberg (tn., Bohem.), *see* KOSOVÁ HORA
Amsel, Abram **13:**1344
AMSHEWITZ, JOHN HENRY **2:**894
- *illus:*
- - text
- - Alexander, Morris (portrait) **2:**574
- - Vasco da Gama and Abraham Zacuto **16:**905
Amshinov (Ḥas. dyn.) **16:**304
- dynasties **1:**ḥas. table
AMSTERDAM (city, Neth.) **2:**895
- *Contents:*
- - Until 1795 **2:**895
- - 1795-1815 **2:**900
- - 1815-1939 **2:**900
- - Holocaust **2:**901
- - Contemporary Period **2:**903
- - Music: 17/18 centuries **2:**904
- Antwerp Marranos **3:**167
- *anusim* **8:**693ff
- archives **3:**384
- art **3:**535; **3:**537
- Asser family **3:**766
- banking **4:**172ff
- Barrios' studies **4:**260
- Castilian **10:**1343
- diamond trade **6:**4
- education **6:**414ff
- emissaries **14:**1363
- *ḥalukkah* **7:**1208
- Hebrew culture **14:**1167
- India **8:**1355
- library **11:**193
- Marrano center **11:**1021; **14:**1167
- museum **12:**544
- Netherlands **12:**976ff
- seals **14:**1080
- secondhand trade **14:**1085
- Shabbateanism **14:**1234; **14:**1249
- spice trade **15:**270
- Spinoza **15:**276ff
- stock exchanges **15:**405
- sugar trade **15:**487; **16:**1298
- synagogue ark **3:**458
- synagogues **15:**612
- tobacco trade **15:**1176
- Torah study **15:**459
- trade and commerce **15:**1302ff
- typography **15:**1482
- *illus:*
- - text
- - Anne Frank House **7:**53
- - Ashkenazi marriage ceremony **11:**1030
- - Benveniste's printers' mark **13:**1094
- - *Dinstagishe Kurant* **13:**1033
- - Eleazar ben Samuel Shmelka coin **11:**69
- - Ez Ḥayyim library **12:**279
- - *Gazeta de Amsterdam* (1675) **13:**1024
- - *Het Joodsche Weekblad* **12:**982
- - *Ḥevra Kaddisha* tokens **12:**977
- - Hoshana Rabba at Portuguese Synagogue **8:**1026
- - Jewish Orphanage medal **11:**1165,1166
- - Jewish quarter **15:**499
- - Jewish Quarter established by Nazis **12:**984
- - Liberal synagogue **12:**991
- - Manasseh ben Israel's printers' mark **13:**1093
- - Mendez, Mordecai F., tombstone **15:**1224
- - Ouderkerk **2:**94; **5:**_fcg._ 321
- - Pinto home **4:**175
- - Portuguese Jewish Community seal **13:**482
- - Portuguese Synagogue **3:**452; **15:**616
- - Purim masked ball **13:**1394
- - schoolchildren wearing yellow badge **12:**987
- - Sephardi masoretic accents **11:**1109
- - Waaggebouw Jewish Museum **12:**547
- - young Zionists dancing *horah* **16:**1119
- *pop. table:* text
Amsterdam (city, N.Y.) **12:**1126
Amsterdam, Abraham (Pol.) **13:**775
AMSTERDAM, ABRAHAM MEIR (Rus.) **2:**905
Amsterdam, Anthony **10:**1505
Amsterdam, Ẓevi **10:**1179
AMSTERDAM HAGGADOT **7:**1102
- Abraham Ben Jacob **2:**148
- *illus:* **3:**536; **7:**1089; **11:**927
Amsterdam-Henrykowski, S. **5:**803
Amsterdam Portuguese Synagogue **2:**896; **2:**903
Amtan (city, Er. Isr.) **16:**934
Amtchislav (city, Belor.), *see* MSTISLAVL
AMTER, ISRAEL **2:**906
AMULET **2:**906
- *Contents:*
- - General **2:**906
- - Illuminated Amulets **2:**911
- abracadabra **2:**111
- *ba'al shem* **4:**6
- childbirth charms **4:**1051ff
- Elijah **6:**645
- evil eye **6:**999
- Eybeschuetz, J. **6:**1076
- Falashas **6:**1152
- folklore **6:**1400; **6:**1406
- Hellenism **8:**301
- Israel Ba'al Shem Tov **9:**1050
- jewelry **13:**1013
- Jewish symbolism **15:**571
- Lilith **6:**645; **11:**246ff
- Magen David **11:**687ff
- menorah **11:**1369
- *mezuzah* **11:**1476
- practical Kabbalah **10:**634
- Shabbateanism **14:**1250ff
- *shivviti* plaque **14:**1420
- *tefillin* **15:**899; **15:**903
- *illus:*
- - text
- - *Akedah* **11:**265
- - *Anna be-Kho'aḥ* **3:**26
- - Baghdad hanging lamp **4:**90
- - coins **13:**315
- - evil eye **6:**998-1000
- - *Shivviti* plaques **14:**1420-1421 **7:**676
- - *hamsa* **12:**965
- - *Kimpetbriefel* **13:**44-45
- - Lilith **5:**1525; **11:**247
- - *Magen David* **11:**691
- - Michael and Gabriel **11:**1488
- - *menorah* **11:**1363,1364
- - newborn child **4:**1051; **6:**1380
- - pregnant women **13:**1593
- - *Shivviti* plaques **14:**1420–1421
- - women in childbirth **4:**1050
- *see also:* MAGIC
AMULO (archbp.) **2:**915
Am u-Medinah (journ.) **1:**newsp. list
Amun (deity), *see* Amun-Re
Amunhotpe, Nebmare (pharaoh), *see* AMENOPHIS III
Amun-Re (deity) **2:**487ff; **2:**807
- Thebes **15:**1093
Amurru (W.Sem. tribes) **8:**577
- language **14:**1151
- Sumer **15:**513
- Tell el-Amarna letters **15:**934
- *see also:* AMORITES
Amurru (city-state, Cana.) **5:**100
- Mesopotamia **16:**1493
Amusin, Joseph Davidovich **11:**18
Amut-pi-El (k., Qatna) **16:**1496
Am va-Sefer (journ.) **1:**newsp. list **4:**1382
Am ve-Admato (journ.) **1**:newsp. list
Amyrtaeus (k., Egy.) **8:**618
Amysos (As. M.) **4:**1060
Amzalak (fam.) **14:**682
AMZALAK, ḤAYYIM **2:**915
AMZALAK, MOSES BENSABAT **2:**915
Amzi (bib. fig.) **8:**481
Amzru (vill., Mor.) **6:**190
An (deity) **15:**514 **16:**1489
ʿAna (tn., Iraq) **8:**1450 **16:**1537
ANAB (city, Er. Isr.) **2:**916
Anabaptists (Chr. sect) **3:**68; **7:**472
ANACLETUS II, PETER PIERLEONE (antipope) **2:**916
- popes **13:**853
Anaconda (city, Mont.) **12:**266
Ana de Castro (Judaiz.) **8:**1395
Anagni, Cathedral of (It.) **11:**690
Anagram **4:**195
ANAḤ (youth mvmt.), *see* Iḥud ha-No'ar ha-Ḥaluẓi
ANAHARATH (city, Er. Isr.) **2:**917
Anahory, Judah **14:**682
Anah son of Zibeon (bib. fig.) **6:**1003
Anak (wk.) **16:**1382
ANAK, ANAKIM (bib. giants) **2:**918
- Ashdod **3:**695
- *see also:* NEPHILIM
Anakah (zool.) **7:**351
Anakh (lit. mag.) **3:**435
- statistics **1:**newsp. list
Anakim (giants), *see* ANAK, ANAKIM
An Alter Bakanter (pseud.) *see* PESAḤSON, ISAAC MORDECAI
Analyticus (pseud.), *see* Wise, James
ANAMMELECH (deity) **2:**918
ANAN (amora) **2:**918
Anan (pr. fam.), *see* ANAN BEN SETH
ANAN, SON OF ANAN (Sadd. h. pr.) **2:**919
- Albinus, Lucceius **2:**534
- Sanhedrin **14:**836
Anan bar Hiyya of Ḥijra **8:**279
Anan Bar Rav (amora), *see* ANAN
ANAN BEN DAVID (Kar. ldr.) **2:**919
- biography **4:**1010
- Cairo *genizah* **16:**1335
- *gilgul,* belief in **7:**573f; **10:**493
- history chart **8:**766-767
- Nahawandi, Benjamin **12:**771
- rise of Karaism **10:**764ff; **8:**664
- Yannai **16:**712
ANAN BEN MARINUS HA-KOHEN **2:**922
ANAN BEN SETH (h. pr.) **2:**922
- Joshua, son of Seth **10:**277
- priests **13:**1086
Ananel the Babylonian (h. pr.), *see* HANAMEL
ANANIAS AND HELKIAS (gens., Egy.) **2:**922
- Cleopatra **5:**604; **6:**13; **12:**1403
- war and warfare **6:**18; **16:**278
ANANIAS BEN NEDEBEUS (h. pr.) **2:**923

– Albinus, Lucceius 2:534
– expropriation of tithes 16:1274
ANANIAS OF ADIABENE (1st cent. C.E., mer.) 2:924
– Helena 8:288
– Izates 2:267
ANANIAS SON OF ZADOK (Phar.) 2:924
Ananiev (city, Ukr.), *see* ANANYEV
Ananites (Kar. sect) 2:919,920
– Karaites 10:764
– Saul ben Anan 14:918
Ananiyyim (sect), *see* Ananites
Ananus (Sadd., h. pr.), *see* ANAN, SON OF ANAN
Ananus, son of Seth (h. pr.), *see* ANAN BEN SETH
ANANYEV (city, Ukr.) 2:924
– Dubossary 6:257
A Nap (newsp.) 7:1142
ANAPA (city, Rus.) 2:924
Anaqaura, Abraham 10:641
Anarchism 7:1407; 15:33
– London 15:46
ANASCHEHON (fam.) 2:925
Anaschehon, Joseph (r., Er. Isr.) 2:925
Anaschehon, Joseph (r., Er. Isr., Turk.) 2:925
Anaschehon, Meir (r., Syr.) 2:925; 15:643
Anaschehon, Meir (kab.) 2:925
Anaschichun (fam.), *see* ANASCHEHON
Anashikon, Meir (r., Syr), *see* Anaschehon, Meir
Anastasi I Papyrus 2:212; 6:482
Anastasis, Church of the (Jer.) 9:1416
Anastasius (Byz. emp.) 14:732
Anastasius (Chr. patr.) 3:72
ʿAnāta (vill., Isr.) 2:927
– *see also:* ANATHOTH
Anath (bib. fig.) 14:1288
ANATH (deity) 2:925
– Baal 4:11
– Ugaritic 15:1506
– *illus:* text
– *see also:* ASHTORETH
Anathbethel (deity) 6:608
Anathema, *see* BLESSING AND CURSING
ANATHOTH (city, Er. Isr.) 2:927
– Abiathar 2:71
– Arab refugee camp 9:1492
– Jeremiah 9:1346
Anatoli (r., Egy.), *see* ANATOLI BEN JOSEPH
Anatoli (paytan) 13:577
Anatoli, A., *see* Kuznetsov, Anatoli
ANATOLI, JACOB BEN ABBA MARI BEN SAMSON 2:927
– allegorical exegesis 4:898
– Aristotelianism 3:446
– Frederick II's physician 7:114
– Jewish philosophy 13:444
– *Ru'aḥ Ḥen* 14:1107
– translations 15:1321; 15:1325
– *illus:* text
Anatolia, *see* ASIA MINOR
ANATOLI BEN JOSEPH 2:929
– Alexandria 15:518
– Maimonides 11:765
– Palermo 13:29
Anatolio (philos.) 2:929
ANATOMY 2:930
– *Contents:*
– – Skeleton 2:931
– – Digestive Organs 2:931
– – Respiratory Organs 2:932
– – Heart 2:932
– – Genital Organs 2:932
– – Other Organs 2:933
– – Middle Ages 2:933
– General
– – autopsies and dissection 3:931ff
– – medicine 11:1180; 11:1184
– – rabbinic misconceptions 4:1018
– – *Sefer Yeẓirah* 16:784ff
– *illus:*
– – *Sefer Etz ha-Sadeh* 4:1016
ANAU (Anav; fam., It.) 2:934
– *geneal. tab:* text
Anau,..., *see also* Anav,...
ANAU, PHINEHAS ḤAI BEN MENAHEM 2:935
– *illus:* text
Anau, Salvatore 2:935
Anav (city, Er. Isr.), *see* ANAB
Anav, Abraham ben Jacob 2:934
– *illus:*
– – Bridegroom of the Law cantata 12:622
Anav, Abraham ben Jehiel (12th cent.) 2:934
Anav, Abraham ben Jehiel (13th cent.) 2:934
Anav, Benjamin (r.) 2:934
Anav, Benjamin (ling.), *see* Benjamin ben Judah me-ha-Anavim
ANAV, BENJAMIN BEN ABRAHAM (poet) 2:936
– Jewish badge in Rome 4:68
– prosody 13:1221
– *geneal. table:* text
Anav, Daniel (r.) 2:934
Anav, Daniel ben Jehiel (paytan) 2:934
Anav, Jehiel (cmty. ldr.) 2:934
Anav, Jehiel ben Abraham (paytan) 2:934
ANAV, JEHIEL BEN JEKUTHIEL BEN BENJAMIN HA-ROFE 2:937
– *geneal. table:* 2:935
– *illus:* text
ANAV, JUDAH BEN BENJAMIN HA-ROFE (paytan) 2:938
– *geneal. table:* 2:935
Anav, Moses ben Abraham 2:934
Anav, Nathan ben Jehiel, *see* NATHAN BEN JEHIEL OF ROME
Anav, Samuel ben Moses 13:593
ANAV, ZEDEKIAH BEN ABRAHAM 2:939
– codification of law 5:644; 11:334
– dreams 6:211
– *Haggadah* commentary 7:1092
– *geneal. table:* 2:935
Anbar (tn., Babyl.), *see* PUMBEDITA
Ancenis (tn., Fr.) 4:1383
Ančerl, Karel 13:973
ANCHEL, ROBERT 2:940
Ancherson, M. 8:21
Anchorage (city, Alsk.) 2:513
Anchor Bible 4:871
– Speiser's contribution 15:259
Ancient North-Arabian (lang.), *see* Proto-Arabic
ANCIENT OF DAYS (name for God) 2:940
Ancient Order of Maccabeans, (soc., Eng.), *see* MACCABEANS, ORDER OF ANCIENT
Ancient South-Arabian (lang.) 14:1152
ANCONA (fam.) 2:943
ANCONA (city, It.) 2:941
– Alconstantini family 2:551
– archives 3:383
– education 6:417
– elegy on martyrs 6:1175
– history chart (1427,1556) 8:766-767
– Ibn Lev's responsum 11:64
– Inquisition 8:1399; 8:1400
– Paul IV 13:189
– Pesaro 13:329
– Pius V 14:249
– Shabbateanism 14:1234
– special Purim 13:1395
– synagogue 15:597
– tax 15:839
– treatment of *anusim* 8:699
– *illus:*
– – *Gemilut Ḥasadim* regulations 7:375
– – *ketubbah* (18th cent.) 8:1285
– – synagogue 9:1128
– *see also:* SENIGALLIA
Ancona, Alessandro 2:943
– theater 15:1057
ANCONA, CESARE D' 2:945
Ancona, Jacob 16:1549
Ancona, Paolo 2:945
Ancona, Sansone 2:945
ANCONA, VITO D' 2:945
Ancyra (city, Turk.), *see* ANKARA
Andala, Ruard 8:22
Andalusia (reg., Sp.) 15:226
A.N.D.B., *see* Dutch General Diamond Workers' Guild
ANDERNACH (city, Ger.) 2:946
– *illus:* text
Andersen, Hans Christian 14:927
– Wandering Jew 16:262
Anderson (city, S.C.) 15:211
Anderson, Max 12:446
Andrada, Salvador d' 12:1063
Andrade, Abraham 4:1246
Andrade, Anna (Sarah) d' 15:912
Andrade, Diego d' 14:66
ANDRADE, EDWARD NEVILLE DA COSTA 2:947
ANDRADE, VELOSINO JACOB DE 2:947
Andrássy, Count Gyula 8:1090; 16:1120
Andrea del Monte 10:469; 14:1185; 14:879
Andreas (2nd cent. C.E., J. "king"), *see* LUCUAS
Andreas (pros.) 12:1306; 13:1187
– Cairo *genizah* 16:1341
Andreas de Leon, *see* Zamora, Andreas de Leon
Andreas of Rinn, *see* ANDREW OF RINN
Andreas of Saint-Victor, *see* ANDREW OF SAINT-VICTOR
Andrea Vanni of Siena 16:260
Andre d'Avelar 8:1407
Andrew II (k., Hung.) 12:62
Andrew, James 8:22
ANDREWES, LANCELOT 2:948
– Christian Hebraists 8:22
Andrewes, Roger 8:22
ANDREW OF RINN (Chr. "mart.") 2:948
– Tyrol 15:1491
ANDREW OF SAINT-VICTOR (Hebr.) 2:948
– Christian Hebraists 8:22
Andrews, Benjamin 8:22
Andrews, Joseph 14:696
Andrews, Lewis Yelland 9:349
Andreyev (tn., Pol.), *see* JEDRZEJOW
Andreyev, Leonid Nikolayevich 14:507
Andrić, Ivo 16:887ff
ANDROGYNOS (hermaphrodite) 2:949
– Adam 2:236
– first-fruit offering 4:993
– in Jewish tradition 4:1018
Andromachus (Maced. gov., Samar.) 2:578
Andronicus II (Byz. emp.) 11:1485
ANDRONICUS SON OF MESHULLAM (schol., Alex.) 2:949
Andruzager ben Zadi Faruch 3:802
Andrychow (tn., Pol.) 15:1228
Anello, Solomon 2:415
Anemone (bot.) 6:1365
Anenu (litur.) 2:842; 3:938
ANER, ESHKOL, AND MAMRE (bib. figs.) 2:950
– Kiriath-Arba 8:226
Anes (fam.), *see* AMES
Anfa (city, Mor.), *see* CASABLANCA
Anfang (period.) 9:1015
Anfaoui, Dinar 5:223
Anfaoui, Moses 5:223
ANGARIA (corvée) 2:950
ANGEL, BARUCH 2:951
Angel, Judy 15:309
Angel, M. (ed.) 10:40
ANGEL, MEIR BEN ABRAHAM (r.) 2:951
ANGEL, SHEMAYAHU 2:951
Angelino, Joseph 16:1211
Angelis, R. M. de 9:1106
Angell (sol.) 13:699
Angello, Mordecai, *see* Galante, Mordecai
Angelo, Aaron Vita di 14:170
Angelo ben Manuele 11:1193
Angelo d'Ascoli (paytan), *see* D'Ascoli, Jacob ben Abraham
Angelo di Gaio 11:549
"Angel of Covenant," (name for Elijah) 6:643
"Angel of Darkness" (Qumran Scrolls) 2:963
ANGEL OF DEATH 2:952
– evil inclination 8:1319
– *Ḥibbut ha-Kever* 8:464
Angels, Book of (Falasha wk.) 6:1150
ANGELS AND ANGELOLOGY 2:956
– *Contents*
– – Bible 2:956
– – – Terminology 2:957
– – – As a Group 2:957
– – – Angel of the Lord 2:958f
– – – Hagiographa 2:959
– – – Prophets' silence 2:959
– – – Ezekiel 2:959
– – – Zechariah 2:960
– – – Daniel 2:960f
– – Apocrypha 2:961
– – – Jewish sects: 962
– – – Functions 2:964
– – – Fallen Angels 2:966
– – Talmud and Midrash 2:968
– – – Origin 2:968
– – – Classification 2:968
– – Liturgy 2:971
– – – Cult of, opposed 2:972
– – Mysticism 2:972
– – Jewish Philosophy 2:973f
– – – Philo 2:973
– – – Karaites 2:974
– – – Saadiah Gaon 2:974
– – – Ibn Ezra 2:975
– – – Maimonides 2:975
– – – Aristotelianism 2:975
– – Modern Period 2:976
– General
– – Adam 2:237
– – *Addir bi-Melukhah* 2:256
– – Amen 2:804
– – amulets 2:909; 2:912
– – angelic song 12:580; 15:144
– – compared with demons 5:1521
– – created by God and Torah 15:1237
– – Death, Angel of 5:1424
– – divine messengers 7:644
– – dogma of belief in 3:656
– – host of heaven 8:1044
– – idolatry 8:1231
– – logos 11:461; 11:462
– – magic 11:710ff
– – *manna* 11:885

– – Moses 14:121
– – nature of man 11:847
– – prayer 13:982
– – providence 13:1280
– – Samson 14:771
– – source of belief 10:389
– Leading Angels
– – Belial 4:428
– – Metatron 11:1443
– – Michael, Gabriel 11:1487
– – Raphael 13:1549
– – Raziel 13:1591
– – Samael 14:719
– – Sandalfon 14:827
– – Satan 5:1525f
– – Uriel 16:7
– In Various Books
– – Apocalyptic literature 3:180ff
– – Apocrypha and Pseudepigrapha 3:182ff
– – Dead Sea Scrolls 5:1403
– – *Discipline, Manual of* 6:64
– – Enoch, Ethiopic Book of 6:795
– – Jerusalem Talmud 15:775
– – *Razim, Sefer ha-* 13:1594
– – *Solomon, Testament of* 15:118
– Views on
– – Abrabanel, Isaac 2:108
– – Al-Nahawendi 12:771
– – Al-Qūmisī, Daniel ben Moses 5:1293
– – Elimelech of Lyzhansk 6:662
– – Islamic conception of 9:100
– – Karaism 10:768
– – Maimonides 11:772
– – Philo 13:427ff
– – Sadducees 14:621
– – visions of 16:166ff
– – "watchers" 16:365
– in the Arts 5:399
– *illus:*
– – text
– – Abraham and the three angels 3:544; 4:938; 8:1031; 14:867
– – Abraham ordered to sacrifice Isaac 4:880
– – Abraham receiving souls from angels 2:166
– – Abraham rescued from fire 8:1217
– – *Akedah* 2:485; 11:*fcg.* 1355; 15:673
– – amulets 2:908-914; 4:1051
– – Angel of Death 2:952
– – Balaam 4:122; 16:685
– – Burning Bush 12:*fcg.* 427
– – circumcision by Zipporah 16:1182
– – "Daniel's Vision" (Rembrandt) 5:1287
– – expulsion from Paradise 6:981
– – invocation, in childbirth 4:1052; 6:1406
– – Jacob wrestling 4:949
– – "Jacob Wrestling with the Angel" (paint., Rembrandt) 9:1199
– – Jeroboam told of impending doom 10:1028
– – Jonah rescued 10:174
– – Judah ha-Nasi's body taken to heaven 10:368
– – Michael and Gabriel amulet 11:1488
– – Moses and the Burning Bush 12:373
– – prayer for women in childbirth 4:1050
– – Raphael and Tobit 15:1184
– – rewarding good pupils 6:387
– – St. Catherine of Alexandria's burial 14:1599
– – Satan leaving to smite Job 14:903
– – Shadrach, Meshach, and Abed-Nego 14:1256
– – Sodom and Gomorrah set on fire 15:71
– – transportation of Habakkuk 7:1018
– *see also:* CHERUB; DEMONS, DEMONOLOGY; ENOCH; KABBALAH; NEPHILIM; SATAN
ANGERS (city, Fr.) 2:977
Anghiari (vill., It.) 15:1468
Angicaymal (tn., Ind.), *see* ERNAKULAM
Angioletti, G. B. 9:1107
Anglicans (Chr. cmty., Isr.) 9:917
Anglo-American Enquiry Commission (1946) 4:509; 9:358ff; 13:33
– displaced Jews 15:1658
– Palestine proposals 16:1089ff
– settlement, Jewish 16:1175
– *illus:*
– – arrival in Jerusalem 16:1089
Anglo-Boer War, *see* Boer War
Anglo-Iranian Oil Company 9:795
Anglo-Israel Friendship Association 5:1456
ANGLO-JEWISH ASSOCIATION (Eng.) 2:977
– Aden Jewish school 2:263
– Alliance Israélite Universelle 2:650
– Benisch, Abraham 4:521
– history chart 8:766-767
– Jewish Board of Deputies 4:1151
– Persia 13:316ff
– philanthropy 13:387
Anglo-Jewish Council of Trades and Industries 4:1281
Anglo-Levantine Banking Co. (Turk.) 16:1074
Anglo-Palestine Bank 9:824
– Barth, Aharon 4:263
– Jewish Colonial Trust 10:43
– Tel Aviv, foundation 15:920
– *illus:*
– – Jaffa, 1903 9:1255
– – one-pound note (1948) 5:729
– *see also:* Bank of Israel; Bank Leumi Le-Israel
Anglo-Palestine Company 9:824ff; 10:42
ANGOFF, CHARLES 2:978
Angora (city, Turk.), *see* ANKARA
ANGOULÊME (city, Fr.) 2:978
Angoulème Psalter (13th cent. illum. ms., Fr.) 6:1
ANGRIST, ALFRED ALVIN 2:979
ANHALT (state, Ger.) 3:1
ANHALZER-FISCH, OLGA 3:595
Ani (name for God) 7:684
ANIELEWICZ, MORDECAI (Ghetto ftr.) 3:2
– Warsaw Ghetto 16:351
– *illus:* text
ANILAEUS AND ASINAEUS (Babyl. sols.) 3:3
– Jewish state in Babylonia 4:38
– Josephus' account 10:261
ANI MA'AMIN (Maim. creed) 3:4
– *illus:* text
ANIMALS, CRUELTY TO 3:5
– *sheḥitah* 14:1339
– special rules 13:796
– *see also:* HUNTING
ANIMALS OF THE BIBLE AND TALMUD 3:7
– *Contents:*
– – General 3:7
– – Classification in Bible and Talmud 3:8
– – – mammals 3:8
– – – birds 3:17
– – – reptiles and "creeping things" 3:17
– – – fish and amphibia 3:18
– – – invertebrates 3:18
– Aaron ben Elijah on 13:433
– bestiality 14:1207
– Commandments, the 613 5:767,773f
– consecration of 8:279
– dietary laws 6:27; 4:1027
– fastdays 6:1192
– firstborn 6:1306; 6:1310
– folk medicine 6:1406
– gestation 4:1021
– ḥazakah 7:1521
– *ḥerem* 8:344ff
– homicidal beasts 4:1119
– impurity 11:142; 13:1406
– *Ir ha-Niddaḥat* 8:1471
– kindness to 5:855
– mixed species 12:170ff
– nature of man 11:847
– *nevelah* 12:1019
– Noah 12:1192ff
– sacrifices 14:600ff
– *sheḥitah* 14:1337
– soul 15:172
– *terefah* 15:1016
– torts 3:986ff; 15:1273ff
– writing on hides 16:659
– *illus:*
– – ape 3:176
– – ass 2:974; 3:756; 4:122
– – bear, Syrian 4:356
– – buzzard 4:1546
– – camels 5:72
– – centipede 5:283
– – chameleon 5:334
– – clean and unclean (tables) 6:31-38
– – dove 15:145
– – fox 6:1450
– – gazelle 7:346; 15:145
– – gecko 7:351
– – goat and kid 7:640
– – hare 7:1336
– – heron, white 4:1061
– – hoopoe 8:970
– – hyena 8:1139
– – ibex 8:1150; 9:233
– – jackal 9:233
– – kite 10:1078
– – monitor 12:258
– – onager 12:1395
– – owl 12:1530
– – rabbit 7:1336
– – serpent eagle 9:230
– – skink 14:1647
– – taḥash 15:703
– – vulture, griffon 16:232
– – water buffalo 9:235
– *table:* text
– *see also:* FLORA AND FAUNA IN ISRAEL; *and under names of specific animals*
Animal Soul 15:173
ANIMAL TALES 3:19
– *Contents:*
– – Bible 3:19
– – Talmud and Midrash 3:20
– – Middle Ages 3:21
– – Modern Period 3:21
– *aggadah* 2:357
– folklore 6:1378
– Jewish literature 11:353
– parables in 13:72ff
– proverbs 13:1275
– *illus:*
– – text
– – *Meshal ha-Kadmoni* 3:19,534,791; 5:430; 6:1128; 14:657
– *see also:* EXEMPLUM; FABLE
ANIM ZEMIROT (hymn) 3:21
ANINUT (bereavement) 3:23
– see also: MOURNING
ANISIMOV, ILYA SHERBATOVICH 3:23
– Mountain Jews 12:478
Anitta (Hittite k.) 8:787
ANJOU (prov., Fr.) 3:23
– Angers 2:977
– Bonfils, Joseph ben Samuel 3:23
– Jewish culture 8:667
ANKARA (city, Turk.) 3:24
– Ottoman Empire 16:1530
– special Purim 13:1395
ANKAWA, ABRAHAM BEN MORDECAI 3:24
Ankawa, Ephraim, *see* Al-Nakawa, Ephraim
Ankawa, Jacob 9:1090
Ankawa, Mordecai 3:24
ANKAWA, RAPHAEL BEN MORDECAI 3:25
Anklet (jewelry) 2:212; 13:1013
ANKORI, ẒEVI 16:1260
Anman (Bund ldr.), *see* ROSENTHAL, PAVEL
ANNA BE-KHO'AḤ (hymn) 3:25
– Neḥunya 12:941
– *illus:* text
ANNA BE-KORENU (litur.) 3:26
Anna Ivanovna (czarina) 2:215
– Voznitsyn, Alexander 16:229
Annapolis (city, Md.) 11:1077
Ann Arbor (city, Mich.) 11:1498
Anna Sophia of Hessen 8:22
Anna Urban, *see* Urban, Anna Weissbrucker
Anne Frank House (Amst.) 2:904
Annenberg, Moses L. 3:26
ANNENBERG, WALTER H. 3:26
Annenberg Foundation (U.S.) 3:26
Annet, Peter 5:1464
Annihilation 14:4
Annis (fam., U.S.) 15:790
Anno Mundi (era) 14:1092
Annuaire parisien du culte israélite (period.) 5:1072
Annuario di Studi Ebraici (period.) 5:736
Annulment of marriage *see Hafka'at Kiddushin*
Annunciation 2:123
Annunciation, Basilica of the (ch., Nazareth) 12:902
– *illus:*
– – consecration of 8:929
– – general view 12:901
ANOINTING 3:27
– *Contents:*
– – in Bible 3:27
– – in Talmud 3:31
– altar 2:764ff
– Commandments, the 613 5:773
– Israel, kingdom of 9:1047
– kingship 10:1013ff
– Messiah 11:1408
– oils used 12:1350
– priests 13:1074
– Saul 14:910
– *illus:*
– – David anointed by Samuel 6:285,1125; 12:1351
ANOKHI, ZALMAN YIẒḤAK 3:31
Anot (mus. compil., Isr.) 14:1313
Anqawa, Efraim (Alg.), *see* Al-Nakawa, Ephraim
Anqawas (fam.) 15:1172
An San (Chin. sol.), *see* Chao Ch'eng
Ansārī (Musl. fam.) 9:1435
ANSBACH (city, Ger.) 3:32
– archives 3:387
– synagogue 15:618
– *illus:* text
Anschluss (Aus. annexed by Ger.) 3:898; 3:903
– Seyss-Inquart, Arthur 14:1209
Anschowitz, Charley, *see* White, Charley
ANSELL, DAVID ABRAHAM 3:33
ANSELM HA-LEVI (Ger.) 3:33
ANSELM OF CANTERBURY

(theol.) **3**:33
Ansgarius (Hebr.), *see* Ancherson, M.
Anshe Chesed (syn., N.Y.) **12**:1071ff
Anshei emunah (kab. term) **10**:494
Anshei Knesset ha-Gedolah, see SYNAGOGUE, THE GREAT
Anshei Targum (Kurd. Js.) **10**:1298
Anshel ha-Levi (Ger.), *see* ANSELM HA-LEVI
ANSHEL OF CRACOW (au., Pol.) **3**:34
Anshe Maariv (syn., Chicago) **2**:274; **5**:411; **15**:620
- *illus:*
- - exterior **15**:622
AN-SKI, S. **3**:34
- Engel, Joel **6**:744
- family **13**:1553
- Kacyzne **10**:657
- *illus:*
- - St. Petersburg Jewish Ethnographical Expedition **12**:541
Anslus, Gerebrard **8**:22
Anspach, Henry **12**:1375
Anspach, Paul **12**:1375
ANSPACH, PHILIPPE **3**:35
Ansud (myth. bird) **16**:1490
ANT (zool.) **3**:35
Antaki, Isaac **4**:1189
Antal, Mark **5**:618
ʿAntara ibn Shaddād **9**:1038
ANTEBI, ALBERT (Avraham; Er. Isr.) **3**:36
Antebi, Raphael **2**:565
ANTELOPE (zool.) **3**:36
- dietary laws **6**:31
- *Taḥash* identified with **15**:704
ANTHEDON (city, Er. Isr.) **3**:37
- Gaza **7**:341
ANTHEIL, GEORGE **3**:37
Anthenais Eudocia (emp.) **13**:513
ANTHONY, JOSEPH **15**:1077
ANTHROPOLOGY **3**:37
- Bogoraz, Vladimir Germanovich **4**:1171
- Jewish contributions **8**:743
- kabbalistic views **10**:606ff
- *see also:* RACE, THEORY OF; SOCIOLOGY (Jewish contributions)
ANTHROPOLOGY, PHYSICAL **3**:40
- *Contents:*
- - Theories of Origins **3**:41f
- - Development **3**:47
- - - In the Diaspora **3**:48
- Semites **14**:1148
- *illus:*
- - Algeria, Constantine Jew **5**:916
- - Baghdad rabbi **10**:242
- - Black Jew **4**:1068
- - Ḥabbān Jews **7**:1019,1020
- - Jewish child bride, North Africa **5**:424
- - Moroccan Jew **6**:380
- - Sephardi Jew from Ereẓ Israel **6**:217
- - Tang figurine **5**:470
ANTHROPOMORPHISM **3**:50
- *Contents:*
- - In Bible **3**:51f
- - Targumim **3**:53
- - Hellenistic Philosophy **3**:55
- - Aggadic Literature **3**:55
- - Middle Ages **3**:55
- - Philosophy **3**:56
- - In Kabbalah **3**:56f
- - In Jewish Art **3**:57
- General
- - *Adam Kadmon* **2**:249
- - allegorical exegesis **4**:897
- - al-Maghārrīya angelology **2**:974
- - articles of faith **3**:655ff
- - Bible **7**:650ff
- - Jewish philosophy **13**:423
- - Judaism **10**:385; **10**:391; **10**:392
- - kabbalistic imagery **10**:607
- - Koran **10**:702ff
- - personification of Torah **15**:1239
- - right, left sides **14**:178
- - *Shi'ur Komah* and mysticism **10**:502; **10**:518; **14**:1417
- - talmudic literature **7**:656
- - theology **15**:1105
- - throne **15**:1124
- - Throne of God **15**:1125ff
- Views on
- - Aristobulus of Paneas **3**:443
- - Maimonides **11**:770
- - Philo **13**:426; **14**:122
- - Rosenzweig **14**:302
- - Saadiah Gaon **14**:550
- *illus:*
text
- - creation of Man **2**:43; **4**:874; **5**:1068
- - creation of the world **5**:1066, *fcg.* 1067, *fcg.* 1070
- - David praying to God **4**:321
- - Ezekiel's first vision **6**:1084
- - God appearing to Jacob **4**:730
- - God appearing to Samuel **3**:54
- - God calling Samuel **14**:782
- - God casting Satan down **2**:970
- - God the Creator **13**:574
- - God giving the Law to Moses **5**:1436-1438
- - God's covenant with Abraham **5**:1014,1016
- - God talking to Melchizedek **14**:1266
- - hand of God inspiring Bezalel **4**:787
- - rejection of Cain's offering **2**:58
- *see also:* GOD; PRESENCE, DIVINE
Anthropopathism **3**:51
ANTIBI (fam.) **3**:58
ANTIBI, ABRAHAM BEN ISAAC **3**:59
Antibi, Elijah Raḥamim **3**:59
Antibi, Ḥayyim Judah Shabbetai Raphael **3**:58
Antibi, Isaac ben Abraham **3**:59
Antibi, Isaac ben Shabbetai **3**:58
Antibi, Jacob **3**:58
ANTICHRESIS (leg. term) **3**:59
ANTICHRIST **3**:60
- Armilus **3**:476
- description **5**:1289
- Jews as legionaries of **3**:101
- *illus:* text
Anti-Christian Polemics, *see* POLEMICS AND POLEMICAL LITERATURE
Anti-Defamation League (orgn., U.S.) **3**:200; **4**:1146
- anti-Semitic propaganda **8**:742
- history chart **8**:766-767
- Zionism **16**:1147
ANTI-FASCIST COMMITTEE, JEWISH (Sov. Un.) **3**:62
- Dobrushin, Yekhezkel **6**:144
established by Stalin **15**:327
- *Eynikeyt* **6**:1077
- Halkin, Shmuel **7**:1192
- *illus:*
- - text
- - La Guardia, Fiorello, and **12**:1110
Anti-Gallican (newsp.) **7**:737
Antigonus (k.) **13**:342; **13**:1509
ANTIGONUS (Hasm. pr.) **3**:65
- *geneal. table:* text
- *see also:* ARISTOBULUS I
Antigonus the Macedonian (k., Syr.) **12**:741
ANTIGONUS II (Hasm. k.) **3**:65
- Aristobulus II **3**:441
- coinage **5**:717
- Ereẓ Israel history **8**:635
- history chart **8**:766-767
- *geneal. table:* **7**:1457
- *illus:*
- - text
- - coins **5**:700-701; **11**:1357
ANTIGONUS OF SOKHO (tan.) **3**:67
- Boethusians **4**:1169
- fear of God **6**:1199
Anti-Goyism in Zion (bk., Bahar) **16**:1152
Anti-Jewish Congresses, International **3**:80ff
Anti-Jewish Decrees, *see* ANTI-SEMITISM
Antimony (metal) **11**:1434ff
ANTIN, MARY **3**:67
- U.S. literature **15**:1573ff
Anti-Nazi boycott, *see* BOYCOTT, ANTI-NAZI
ANTINOMIANISM **3**:68
- Abrahamic legends **2**:115
- dualism **6**:243
- Ḥasidism **7**:1407
- Jewish gnosis **10**:506
- Kabbalah **10**:639
- sages **14**:654
- Shabbateanism **14**:1245
- *shemittot* doctrine **10**:583
- *see also:* GNOSTICISM
Antioch (city, Er. Isr.), *see* DAN
ANTIOCH (city, Turk.) **3**:71
- Antiochus I Soter **3**:73
- diaspora center **6**:10
- Jewish community **15**:639,641
- John Chrysostom on Jews of **10**:162
- *plan:* text
Antioch-at-Jerusalem (Gr. polis, Jer.), *see* Antiochia
Antiochia (Antiocheia; city state, Jer.) **9**:1390
- Hellenism **8**:295
- Jason **8**:628; **9**:1292
Antiochia by Hippos (city, Er. Isr.), *see* SUSITA
Antioch on the River Chrysorrhoas (city, Transj.) *see* GERASA
Antiochus I (k., Commagene) **5**:760
Antiochus (city, Er. Isr.), *see* BANIAS
Antiochus, Scroll of, *see* SCROLL OF ANTIOCHUS
Antiochus, Valley of, *see* ḤULEH
ANTIOCHUS IX CYZICENUS (prin., Syr.) **3**:75
- history chart **8**:766-767
Antiochus XII Dionysus (k., Syr.) **12**:741
- Alexander Yannai **16**:716
- warfare **16**:279
ANTIOCHUS IV EPIPHANES (k., Syr.) **3**:74
- Acra **2**:221
- Apostomos, identified with **3**:218
- ass worship **3**:784
- circumcision prohibited **5**:568
- crucifixion of Jews **5**:1134
- Ereẓ Israel history **8**:628
- *haftarah* **16**:1343
- Hannah and her seven sons **7**:1270
- Ḥanukkah **7**:1283
- Hellenization **9**:120
- history chart **8**:766-767
- Jerusalem **9**:1390
- *kiddush ha-Shem* **10**:981
- Lion of Wrath **11**:276
- Maccabees, First Book of **11**:657
- Maccabees, Second Book of **11**:658
- "Man of Lies" **11**:234
- Menelaus **8**:295
- Polybius **7**:896
- *Scroll of Antiochus* **14**:1045
- shrine on Mount Gerizim **7**:437
- swine's flesh **13**:506; **13**:507
- Temple **15**:958
- *illus:*
- - martyrdom scenes **8**:671
Antiochus Euergetes (k., Syr.), *see* ANTIOCHUS VII SIDETES
ANTIOCHUS V EUPATOR (k., Syr.) **3**:74
- defeated at Modi'in **12**:206
- history chart **8**:766-767
- Maccabees, Second Book of **11**:660
- Seleucids and Judea **8**:629
ANTIOCHUS III THE GREAT (k., Syr.) **3**:73
- administration of Ereẓ Israel **9**:119
- Babylonia **4**:36
- Ereẓ Israel history **8**:625ff
- history chart **8**:766-767
- Jerusalem **9**:1390
- Jewish settlement in Lydia **11**:621
- Jews in Asia Minor **3**:746
- Josephus' account **10**:259
- Polybius **7**:896
- priests **13**:1086
- Simeon the Just **14**:1567
- Temple **15**:958ff
Antiochus VIII Grypus **3**:75; **14**:730
- history chart **8**:766-767
Antiochus VIII Philometor, *see* Antiochus VIII Grypus
Antiochus Philopator (prin., Syr.), *see* ANTIOCHUS IX CYZICENUS
ANTIOCHUS VII SIDETES (k., Syr.) **3**:74
- history chart **8**:766-767
- Ptolemy **13**:1349
- Seleucids and Judea **8**:630
- Simeon the Hasmonean **14**:1566
ANTIOCHUS I SOTER (k., Syr.) **3**:73
ANTIOCHUS II THEOS (k., Syr.) **3**:73
- Book of Daniel **5**:1282
Antipas, *see* ANTIPATER II
ANTIPAS, HEROD (s., Herod I) **3**:75
- Aretas IV **12**:743
- coinage **5**:718
- Herodians **8**:388
- history chart **8**:766-767
- Jesus **10**:11
- John the Baptist **10**:160
- Salome **14**:689
- tetrarch of Galilee **3**:853
- Tiberias **15**:1131
- *geneal. table:* text; **8**:377
- *illus.*
- - coins **5**:703
Antipater I (grandf., Herod) **3**:76
ANTIPATER II (Herod's f.) **3**:76
- Antipatris **3**:78
- Cypros **5**:1179
- history chart **8**:766-767
- Nabateans **12**:742
- *geneal. table:* text; **8**:377
ANTIPATER (Herod's s.) **3**:77
- Alexander **2**:567
- Doris **6**:174
- Herod I **8**:381
- *geneal. table:* text; **8**:377
ANTIPATRIS (city, Er. Isr.) **3**:78
- Alexander the Great **2**:578
- battle of Yarkon River **9**:262
- Herod **8**:636
- *see also:* APHEK; ARETHUSA; ROSH HA-AYIN
Antiphonal Psalmody, *see* MUSIC
Antiquities of the Jews (bk., Josephus), *see Jewish Antiquities*
Antisemiten-Katechismus (bk.) **7**:203
Antisemiten-Liga (orgn., Ger.) **3**:79; **11**:1015
Anti-Semitic League (orgn., Ger.),

see Antisemiten-Liga
ANTI-SEMITIC POLITICAL PARTIES AND ORGANIZATIONS **3**:79
- *Contents:*
- - Germany **3**:79
- - Hapsburg Dominions **3**:83
- - Hungary **3**:84
- - Poland **3**:84
- - France **3**:84
- - Rumania **3**:86
- - Russia **3**:86
- General
- - history **8**:738
- Various Countries
- - Argentina **3**:415ff
- - - Tacuara **12**:951
- - Austria **3**:83f **3**:896f
- - - Christian Social Party **5**:516; **11**:556ff
- - - Heimwehr **8**:270
- - - neo-Nazis **12**:955
- - - Vaterlaendische Front **5**:516
- - Canada **5**:110f
- - Czechoslovakia
- - - Slovak People's Party **15**:1155; **15**:1427
- - England **6**:763
- - - British Fascists **11**:478; **12**:952
- - France **3**:84f; **7**:29f
- - - Action Française **2**:232
- - - anti-Semitic League **6**:236f
- - - Croix du Feu **8**:741
- - - Dreyfus Affair **6**:224f
- - - neo-Fascists **12**:952
- - Germany **3**:79f; **7**:481f; **12**:954
- - - Anti-Semitic League **11**:1015
- - - Christian Social Party **15**:408ff
- - - Conservative Party **5**:906ff
- - - Deutsche Antisemitische Vereinigung **7**:203
- - - Deutsche Arbeiterpartei **8**:783
- - - NPD **12**:955
- - - NSDAP **8**:783; **12**:882
- - - Socialist Reich Party **12**:955
- - - socialists and R. Calwer **5**:69ff
- - Hungary **3**:84 **8**:1096ff
- - - Anti-Semite Party **9**:1099
- - - Arrow Cross Party **3**:499
- - - Nazi movements **15**:656
- - Italy **9**:1132ff
- - - Fascism **12**:718ff
- - - neo-Fascists **12**:951
- - Mexico **11**:1457ff
- - Poland **3**:84 **13**:737ff
- - - Endecja (ND) **6**:735f
- - - Nara (ONR) **12**:826
- - - OZON **12**:1540
- - - Rozwój **14**:363
- - Rumania **3**:86; **5**:656 **14**:390ff
- - - Iron Guard **8**:1472; **14**:1547ff
- - - National Christian Party **5**:1177
- - Russia **3**:86 **14**:436ff
- - - Beilis Case **4**:399f
- - - "Black Hundred" **4**:399f **13**:697
- - - "Chamber of Archangel Michael" **15**:1538
- - - Union of the Russian People **15**:1538
- - South Africa **15**:190
- - Sweden **12**:951
- - United States **3**:126f **12**:952
- - - Ku Klux Klan **15**:1626; **15**:1653
- - - New York City **12**:1120ff
- - - U.S. Nazis **3**:126; **5**:1571; **12**:954
- *see also;* ANTI-SEMITISM; ELDERS OF ZION, PROTOCOLS OF THE LEARNED; FASCISM; HITLER, ADOLF; NATIONAL SOCIALISM; NEO-FASCISM; NEO-NAZISM
Anti-Semitic Press
- Argentina
- - *Der Weg* **12**:956
- Austria
- - *Kikeriki* **3**:153; **5**:175
- - *Kladderdatsch* **5**:175
- - *Linzer Fliegende Blaetter* **8**:782
- - *Ostara* **8**:782
- - *Vaterland* **11**:1465
- Canada
- - *Le Goglu* **5**:110
- France **7**:29
- - *Action Française* **2**:232
- - *Aspects de la France* **2**:232
- - *La Cocarde* **4**:258
- - *La Croix* **5**:1125
- - *La Libre Parole* **6**:236f; **3**:152; **5**:175
- - *La Nation Française* **2**:232
- - *Psst* **5**:175
- - *Rivarol* **2**:232
- Germany
- - *Bayreuther Blaetter* **16**:241
- - *Der Abend* **5**:176
- - *Der Goetz* **5**:176
- - *Der Stuermer* **15**:460
- - *Deutsche National-Zeitung* **12**:955
- - *Fliegende Blaetter* **5**:175
- - *Kreuzzeitung* **5**:906
- - *National- und Soldatenzeitung* **5**:178
- - *Puck* **5**:175
- Hungary
- - *Tizenkét Röpirat* **9**:1099
- Italy
- - *Il Regime Fascista* **6**:1183
- - *La Civiltà Cattolica* **5**:599f
- Mexico **11**:1457
- Morocco
- - *al-Istiqlāl* **12**:345
- Poland
- - *Gazeta Niedzielna* **14**:363
- - *Rola* **9**:1336
- - *Rozwój* **14**:363
- - *Sztafeta* **12**:826
- Rumania
- - *Antisemitul* **3**:152
- - *Buna Vestire* **8**:1472
- - *Curantul Moldovenesc* **10**:1066
- - *Gândirea* **14**:418
- - *Gindul Neamului* **10**:1066
- - *Liga Antisemită* **3**:152
- - *Porunca Vremii* **8**:1472
- - *România Nouă* **10**:1066
- - *Scutul National* **10**:1066
- - *Vremea* **14**:418
- Russia
- - *Bessarabets* **10**:1064,1281 **10**:1065; **13**:697
- - *Drug* **10**:1281
- - *Pluvium* **3**:151; **5**:175f
- - *Russkoye Znamya* **15**:1538
- Turkey
- - *Bugun* **15**:1459
- U.S.
- - *Dearborn Independent* **4**:685; **5**:1571
- - *Jeffersonian Magazine* **7**:73
- - *Niles' Weekly Register* **15**:1648
- Yugoslavia
- - *Erwache* **16**:1224
- *illus:*
- - *Antisemitul* **3**:152
- - *Der Stürmer* **3**:154; **8**:833,835
- - *La Libre Parole* **3**:152; **6**:237
- - *L'Anti-Sémitique* **3**:151
- - *Liga Antisemită* **3**:152
- - *Pluvium* **3**:151
- - political cartoons **3**:150-156
ANTI-SEMITISM **3**:87
- *Contents:*
- - In Antiquity **3**:87
- - - In the Diaspora **3**:89
- - Early Christian Period **3**:96
- - In Islam **3**:100
- - Middle Ages **3**:101
- - The Reformation **3**:107
- - Spain After 1492 **3**:108
- - The Enlightenment **3**:111
- - Emancipation and Reaction **3**:112
- - Russia and Central Europe **3**:123f
- - Between East and West **3**:125
- - Inter-War Period **3**:135
- - Postwar Period **3**:136
- - In Arab Countries **3**:138
- - In the Soviet Bloc **3**:147
- - - After October Revolution **3**:148
- - - Black Years 1948-53 **3**:149
- - - Khrushchev Period **3**:150
- - - Under Kosygin-Brezhnev **3**:158f
- - - Poland-Czechoslovakia **3**:159
- General
- - Africa **2**:331
- - America **2**:808
- - apologetic literature **3**:199
- - Asia **3**:743
- - caricatures **5**:171f; **3**:115
- - Chosen People **5**:502
- - dualism **6**:243
- - "elder", term **6**:580
- - Europe **6**:968
- - expulsions **6**:1070
- - Gobineau's theories **7**:641
- - history chart **8**:766-767
- - humiliation of Jews **8**:654,655,661,684
- - Jewish identity **10**:55,61f
- - Jewish studies **16**:578
- - magic **11**:715
- - medals **11**:1173
- - messianism **11**:1415
- - migrations caused by **16**:1518
- - modern Jewish thought **13**:453
- - origin of term **11**:1015
- - politics, Jews in **13**:807
- - proselytizing charges **13**:1189ff
- - psychology influenced by **13**:1344
- - racism **8**:737ff; **13**:1483
- - *sheḥitah* **14**:1340
- Ancient **3**:87
- - Alexandria **2**:589
- - Antiochus Epiphanes **3**:74
- - Apion **3**:178
- - Apollonius Molon **3**:188
- - Celsus the Philosopher **5**:270
- - diaspora **3**:89
- - Egypt **6**:485
- - Ereẓ Israel **3**:87
- - Manetho **11**:873
- - Moses **12**:390ff
- - Posidonius **13**:928
- - Roman period **10**:260
- - Rome **14**:244ff
- - Rutilius Namatianus **14**:525
- - Tacitus **15**:695
- - territorial **3**:88
- Christian **3**:96; **5**:506
- - Agobard **2**:372
- - Ambrose of Milan **2**:801
- - Black Death **4**:1064ff
- - Blood Libel **4**:1120
- - Capistrano, John of **5**:141
- - Catholic Church **5**:536; **8**:913
- - Church Fathers **5**:551
- - Crusades **5**:1135
- - Damascus Affair **5**:1249
- - deicide, earliest mention **11**:1291
- - *De vita et moribus Judaeorum* **5**:158
- - disputations **6**:79
- - Dominicans **6**:161
- - Franciscans **7**:47
- - Holocaust era **8**:910
- - Host desecration **8**:1040
- - Inquisition **8**:1380
- - John Chrysostom **10**:161
- - Lateran Councils **10**:1445ff
- - Luther, Martin **11**:585ff; **14**:19
- - Pastoureaux **13**:176
- - Protestants **13**:1250ff
- - Satan and Jews **14**:905
- - *Shevet Yehudah* **8**:1203
- - Talmud, burning of **15**:768
- - Wandering Jew legend **16**:259
- Islamic **3**:100
- - Almohads **2**:662
- - Damascus Affair **5**:1249
- - Hebron massacre **8**:235
- - humiliating ceremonies **16**:1279
- - Husseini, Hajj Amīn Al- **8**:1132
- - "Jadīd al-Islām" **9**:1246
- - Mamluks **6**:494; **11**:834
- - Medina **11**:1211
- - Omar, Covenant of **12**:1378
- - Ottoman Empire **16**:1538
- Legislation, Anti-Jewish
- - Avignon (1458) **3**:966
- - Babylonia, Sasanian **4**:40
- - badge, Jewish **4**:62
- - Borromeo, Carlo **4**:1258
- - candle tax **5**:119
- - censorship **5**:276
- - Christianity **5**:512
- - church councils **5**:546
- - *de non tolerandis Judaeis* **16**:1287
- - Fascist Italy **9**:1133ff
- - *fiscus Judaicus* **6**:1325
- - ghetto **7**:542
- - in Muslim lands **3**:170; **3**:174; **5**:1604
- - Jewish dress **8**:1062
- - Jewish quarter **10**:81
- - *Judenordnung* **16**:677
- - Justinian I, Code of **10**:477
- - Lateran Councils **10**:1446ff
- - May Laws **11**:1147
- - Meaux-Paris (845-6) **2**:915
- - Nazi period **10**:1573
- - *numerus clausus* **12**:1263
- - Nuremberg Laws **12**:1281
- - oath *more Judaico* **12**:1302
- - Papacy **4**:1495ff; **5**:141; **14**:245ff
- - Philip III **13**:393
- - Roman Empire **16**:1278
- - Romans and Torah teaching **2**:489; **2**:491
- - Wenceslaus IV **16**:447
- - Zamora (1313) **16**:926
- Economic and Social **3**:101ff
- - Alexandrian Jewish bankers **16**:1277
- - boycott, anti-Jewish **4**:1277f
- - boycott, Arab **4**:1282
- - Castile and Aragon **16**:1287
- - department stores **5**:1545
- - discrimination **6**:67f
- - Fourier **6**:1447
- - Grabski taxation **7**:838
- - in backward countries **16**:1305
- - Jewish "parasitism" **10**:1323
- - law *de non tolerandis Judaeis* **16**:1287
- - Marx **8**:714; **11**:1071
- - middle class **16**:1319
- - motion pictures **12**:458
- - Proudhon **13**:1255
- - slave trade **14**:1662
- - socialism **15**:25ff
- - stock exchanges **15**:406ff
- - taxation **15**:837
- - trade and commerce **15**:1299
- - wine and liquor trade **16**:541
- Modern
- - Holocaust **8**:828
- - neo-Fascism **12**:951
- - neo-Nazism **12**:954
- - partisans **13**:140
- - pogroms **13**:694ff

- - self-defense, Jewish **14:**1124
- - socialism, Jewish **15:**38ff
- - students' movements, Jewish **15:**448
- - U.N. resolutions **15:**1558ff
- - War Crimes trials **16:**300
- In Various Countries
- - Algeria **2:**616f **14:**1172
- - - Boumédienne, Houari **2:**619
- - - Constantine **5:**915
- - - Oran **12:**1446
- - Australia **11:**1277
- - Austria **3:**888ff
- - - Graz **7:**864
- - - Innsbruck **8:**1379
- - - Lueger, Karl **11:**556
- - - Schoenerer, Georg von **14:**990
- - - Verein zur Abwehr des Antisemitismus **16:**110
- - - Vienna **16:**122ff
- - Bulgaria
- - - Belev, Alexander **4:**414
- - Canada **5:**110
- - Czechoslovakia **5:**1193
- - - campaign against archbishop Kohn **10:**1148
- - - Hilsner case **8:**496
- - - Hlinka, Andrej **8:**869
- - - Prague **13:**968
- - - Slánský trial **14:**1653
- - - Slovakia **14:**1680ff
- - - Tiso, Josef **15:**1155
- - - Tuka, Vojtech **15:**1427
- - Egypt **6:**500f
- - - Cairo martyrs **11:**1077
- - - Nasser, Gamal Abdul **12:**843
- - England **3:**125; **6:**760f
- - - Belloc, Hilaire **6:**781
- - - London **11:**380; **11:**470ff.
- - - Mosley, Sir Oswald **6:**763 **8:**741
- - France **3:**112f **7:**9ff
- - - Alliance Israélite Universelle **2:**649; **2:**653
- - - Alsace **2:**752f
- - - Barrès, Auguste Maurice **4:**258
- - - Barruel, Augustin **4:**261
- - - Daudet, Léon **5:**1314
- - - Drumont, Édouard-Adolphe **6:**236
- - - French in Algeria **2:**616f
- - - Maurras, Charles **11:**1135
- - - Paris **13:**103ff
- - - Voltaire **16:**220
- - Germany **3:**114; **7:**477ff
- - - Armleder bands **3:**483
- - - Berlin **4:**643f
- - - Bismarck's attitude **4:**1058
- - - boycott, anti-Nazi **4:**1280f
- - - Catholic Church **8:**913
- - - Chamberlain, Houston Stewart **5:**332
- - - Conservative Party **5:**906f
- - - contemporary Germany **7:**499
- - - Duehring, Karl Eugen **6:**260
- - - Eisenmenger, Johann Andreas **6:**545
- - - Frederick William III **7:**116
- - - Fries, Jakob Friedrich **7:**196
- - - Fritsch, Theodor **7:**203
- - - Hep! Hep! riots **8:**330
- - - Hitler, Adolf **8:**782ff
- - - Jewish students **10:**804
- - - Lagarde, Paul Anton de **10:**1356
- - - Marr, Wilhelm **11:**1015
- - - medals **11:**1168
- - - Prussia **13:**1287ff
- - - Rhenish Crusades **5:**1135f
- - - Rohling, August **14:**224
- - - Stoecker, Adolf **15:**408
- - - Treitschke, Heinrich von **15:**1372
- - - Verband Nationaldeutscher Juden **16:**106
- - - Verein zur Abwehr des Antisemitismus **16:**110
- - - Wagner, Richard **16:**240
- - Greece **7:**876
- - Hungary **3:**124; **8:**1088f
- - - Istóczy, Győző **9:**1099
- - - Tiszaeszlár case **15:**1155ff
- - Iraq **8:**1445f
- - - Baghdad hangings **4:**91
- - - Rashīd Ali revolt **4:**90
- - Ireland **8:**1465
- - Italy **9:**1132ff
- - - L.M. Benetelli **5:**870
- - - Mussolini **12:**718
- - Japan **9:**1281
- - - Senko, Yasue **14:**1160
- - Latin America **10:**1452
- - - Argentina **3:**414f
- - - Uruguay **16:**13
- - Libya **11:**202ff
- - - Benghazi **4:**503
- - - Tripoli **15:**1398
- - Lithuania **11:**382ff
- - Morocco **12:**338ff
- - - Fez **6:**1257
- - Palestine (Modern)
- - - Arab revolt **9:**348ff
- - - Nazi agents **15:**996
- - Persia (Iran) **8:**1442; **13:**313ff
- - - *anusim* **3:**174; **4:**16; **9:**1246
- - - Meshed **11:**1399
- - - Shahs Abbas I and II **2:**38f
- - Poland **3:**135; **13:**712ff
- - - Dmowski, Roman **6:**140
- - - Haller's Army **7:**1200
- - - Samuel commission **14:**815
- - - Warsaw **16:**333ff
- - Rumania **3:**124; **14:**386
- - - Antonescu, Ion **3:**162
- - - Antonescu, Mihai **3:**163
- - - Codreanu, C. Z. **5:**656
- - - Cuza, Alexander **5:**1176
- - - Iron Guard **8:**1472
- - - Lecca, Radú **10:**1553
- - - Transnistria **15:**1333ff
- - Russia **3:**123; **10:**991; **14:**436ff
- - - Bakunin, M. A. **4:**120
- - - cantonists **5:**130f
- - - Chmielnicki massacres **5:**480f
- - - "doctors' plot" **6:**144 **15:**328
- - - in communist theory and practice **5:**792ff
- - - Kishinev pogroms **10:**1064ff
- - - Krushevan, Pavolaki **10:**1281
- - - Kychko, Trofim **3:**150; **14:**488
- - - Leningrad trials **11:**19; **14:**493
- - - Lutostansky, Hyppolite **11:**587
- - - Moscow **12:**359
- - - Mountain Jews **12:**479
- - - Nicholas II **12:**1138
- - - Pale of Settlement **13:**25
- - - Petlyura, Simon **13:**340
- - - Soviet bloc **3:**147f
- - - Stalin **15:**327ff
- - - Steiger trial **15:**348
- - - Ukraine **15:**1517
- - - "White Army" propaganda **5:**1535
- - - *Yevsektsiya* activities **16:**780
- - South Africa **15:**187f
- - Spain **3:**108 **15:**220ff
- - - Chuetas **5:**535; **15:**822
- - - *limpieza de sangre* **11:**255
- - - Toledo **15:**1202ff; **15:**1269
- - Sweden **15:**547ff
- - Syria **15:**645f
- - - Aleppo **2:**563f
- - - Damascus **5:**1245,1249f
- - Tunisia **15:**1436ff
- - - Djerba **6:**139
- - Turkey **15:**1459
- - United States **3:**126ff; **15:**1648ff
- - - among Protestants **13:**1254
- - - banking **4:**179
- - - Coughlin, Charles E. **5:**544,1571
- - - Detroit **5:**1569f
- - - Ford, Henry **5:**1571; **15:**1653
- - - Leo Frank case **7:**73
- - - Lindbergh, Charles A. **15:**1655
- - - Negro **12:**933ff
- - - New York City **12:**1114
- - - Rockwell, Lincoln **12:**954
- - - St. Louis **14:**666
- - - Saratoga Springs case **15:**1649
- - Yemen **16:**742ff
- In Art **3:**566
- - Paris school **13:**113
- In Literature: *see* ENGLISH LITERATURE (Figure of the Jew), *etc.*
- Studies
- - Bernstein, Perez **4:**688
- - Hertzberg, Arthur **8:**399
- - Isaac, Jules **9:**10
- - Lazare, Bernard **10:**1514
- - Parkes, James **13:**121
- - Poliakov, Léon **13:**796
- - Samuel, Maurice **14:**801
- - Trachtenberg, Joshua **15:**1293
- - Valentin, Hugo **16:**59
- Views
- - Ehrenburg, Ilya **6:**505f
- - Gorki, Maxim **7:**811
- - Heine, Heinrich **8:**272f
- - Herzl, Theodor **8:**408f **16:**1044ff
- - Hess, Moses **8:**433
- - Korolenko, Vladimir **10:**1212
- - Lenin, V. I. **11:**13
- - Leskov, N.S. **11:**46
- - Lilienblum, M.L. **11:**241
- - Mann, Thomas **11:**882
- - Masaryk, Jan **11:**1091
- - Nietzsche, Friedrich **12:**1154
- - Nordau, Max **12:**1212
- - Pinsker, Leon **13:**546; **16:**1042
- - Pius XI **13:**572
- - Sartre, J.-P. **12:**1033
- - Trotsky, Lev **15:**1406
- - Yevtushenko, Yevgeni **16:**781
- - Zangwill, Israel **16:**932
- - Zola, Emile **16:**1216
- *illus:*
- - text
- - Alexander III tormenting a Jew (cartoon) **14:**437
- - Antichrist supported by Jews **3:**61
- - Armleder massacres (map) **3:**483
- - Berlin, burning of Jews (1510) **4:**642
- - Berlin, bench marked "For Aryans Only" **4:**654
- - Black Death (map) **4:**1065
- - blood libels (map) **4:**1125
- - Brothers, Richard, leading Jews to the Promised Land (caric.) **4:**1410
- - *Der Gantz Juedisch Glaub* (1530) **11:**958
- - *Der Stürmer,* ritual murder libel issue (1939) **15:**460
- - desecrated tombstone in Warsaw **13:**782
- - Desecration of the Host libels **8:**688; **8:**1039-1042
- - devil about to take hanged Jew **15:**1056
- - Dreyfus affair **6:**225-229
- - Duermenach riots **2:**753
- - Grant's general order no. 12 **15:**1651
- - greediness libels **2:**139-146
- - "Hake," 13th cent. caricature **12:**1226
- - Henry Ford's *Dearborn Independent* **15:**1653
- - Hep! Hep! riots (map) **8:**331
- - idolatry libels **3:**981
- - Jacob Henry's speech in N. Carolina House of Commons (1809) **15:**1649
- - Jew as a fighter during Napoleonic Wars (caric.) **11:**1554
- - Jewish Sow libels **5:**174
- - Jews in Polish Militia (caric.) **13:**733
- - Jews in Prussian army (caric.) **11:**1557
- - *Korn Jude* medal (1694) **11:**1170
- - major concentration, forced labor, transit, and extermination camps, World War II (map) **5:**95
- - "March of Jewish National Guard in Warsaw" **13:**733
- - National Union of Social Justice rally (1935) **15:**1655
- - oath *more judaico* **12:**1302,1304
- - Pfefferkorn's *Judenfeind* (1509) **13:**356
- - *Protocols of the Elders of Zion,* Brazilian edition **6:**583
- - *Protocols of the Elders of Zion,* French edition **6:**581
- - Soviet cartoons **14:**491,492
- - Trent blood libel **15:**1374
- - U.S. non-Jewish leaders' protest (1921) **15:**1654
- - Vienna, Christian-Socialist election poster **3:**905
- *see also:* ANTI-SEMITIC POLITICAL PARTIES AND ORGANIZATIONS; ASSIMILATION; BLOOD LIBEL; BOYCOTT, ANTI-JEWISH; CARICATURES; DISCRIMINATION; ELDERS OF ZION, PROTOCOLS OF THE LEARNED; FASCISM; HOLOCAUST; INQUISITION; HOST, DESECRATION OF; NATIONAL SOCIALISM; NEO-FASCISM; NEO-NAZISM; POGROMS; RACE, THEORY OF; TALMUD, BURNING OF; Well-poisoning libel; *and under individual countires*

Antisthenes (Gr. philos.) **3:**444
Anti-Zionism, *see* ZIONISM
ANTOINE, NICOLAS **3:**161
ANTOKOLSKI, MARK (Mordecai) **3:**161
- Guenzburg **7:**963
- stamps **15:**336
- *illus:*
- - "Ivan the Terrible" **3:**556
ANTOKOLSKI, PAVEL GRIGOREVICH **14:**514
ANTONESCU, ION **3:**162
- Iron Guard **8:**1472
- Rumania **14:**400ff
ANTONESCU, MIHAI **3:**163
Antonia (widow of Drusus) **4:**601
ANTONIA (fort., Jer.) **3:**164
- Herod **8:**636; **9:**1394
- Jerusalem archaeology **9:**1525
- storming of **9:**1398
- Temple **15:**964
- *illus:*
- - Herod's Temple (model) **15:**960
- *plan:* text
Antonia, Princess of Württemberg **8:**22
Antonin of Jerusalem **7:**405
- Cairo *genizah* **16:**1337
Antonine emperors **9:**245
Antoninus (Rom. emp. in T.) **3:**165 **10:**367
- Avidius Lassius **10:**1249
- resistance literature **8:**302
- *see also:* ANTONINUS PIUS; MARCUS AURELIUS ANTONINUS
Antoninus (trav.) **7:**340
ANTONINUS PIUS (Rom. emp.) **3:**165

- attitude to Jews **14:**230
- Erez Israel **9:**248
- history chart **8:**766-767
- *Itinerarium Antonini* **9:**1149
- Jerusalem coins **9:**1406
- Jews and **8:**647
- Judah ha-Nasi **11:**1183
- Samaritans **14:**731
- *illus:*
- - text
- - coin **2:**395
ANTONIO (Port. pretender) **3:**166
Antonio degli Angelis **9:**1544
Antonio de la Peña **8:**1396; **10:**1360
Antonius, Marcus (1st cent. B.C.E., Rom.), *see* Antony
ANTONIUS DIOGENES **7:**892
ANTONIUS JULIANUS **3:**166
Antonovsky, Aaron **15:**67; **15:**69
Antony (Marcus Antonius; 1st cent. B.C.E., Rom.) **8:**376
- Cleopatra VII **5:**604
- Gofna **7:**691
- Herod **3:**66ff; **3:**852; **8:**635
- Herod's Antonia **9:**1394
- Nabateans **12:**742
- Tyre **15:**1489
Antscher, Isaac **13:**116
ANTUÑES (fam.) **3:**166
Antuñes, Aaron (r.) **3:**167
Antuñes, Aaron ben Solomon (print.) **3:**167
Antuñes, Ana Rois **3:**166
Antuñes, David **3:**167
Antuñes, Gabriel **3:**167
Antuñes, Heitor (Hector) **3:**166; **15:**1301
Antuñes Paredes (fam.) **3:**167
ANTWERP (city, Belg.) **3:**167
- banking **4:**172ff
- diamond trade **6:**5
- Plantin press **13:**613
- spice trade **15:**270
- stock exchanges **15:**405
- sugar industry **15:**487
- trade and commerce **15:**1301ff
- *illus:*
- - Jewish Brigade Group **10:**37
Anu (deity) **2:**918; **6:**837; **16:**1490
Anuarul pentru Israeliți (annual, Rum.) **14:**399
ANUSIM (forced convs.) **3:**169
- *Contents:*
- - Early Middle Ages **3:**169f
- - Later Middle Ages **3:**170f
- - Modern Times **3:**174
- General
- - Afghanistan and Meshed Jews **2:**327
- - Apulian *neofiti* **3:**227
- - civil marriage issue **5:**596
- - conflict of laws **5:**884; **5:**889
- - Ferrara **6:**1232
- - Inquisition **8:**1381ff
- - Isfahan Jews **2:**38
- - Jewish attitude toward **3:**204
- - Jewish identity **10:**57
- - Jewish observances **8:**1400
- - Joel ibn Shuaib on **8:**1201
- - *kiddush ha-Shem* **10:**983
- - Maimonides **11:**754; **11:**755
- - Mamluk persecutions **11:**835
- - messianism **11:**1425
- - Muslim Spain **15:**227
- - sugar industry **15:**487
- - Tuscany **15:**1467
- *illus:*
- - text
- - burning at the stake **5:**221
- *see also:* CRYPTO-JEWS; MARRANO; NEW CHRISTIANS
Anville, D' (cartog.) **11:**927
Anwār (journ.) **9:**1042
Anyksciai (cmty., Lith.) **14:**769 **16:**1490
Aonde Vamos? (period.) **4:**1331
Aouste-sur-Sye (vill., Fr.) **5:**362
Apácsai, Csere János **8:**22
APAM (prayer rite) **3:**174
- Asti **3:**785
- Fossano **6:**1444
- liturgy **11:**399
- Moncalvo **12:**240
- *illus:*
- - *mahzor* (18th cent. ms.) **3:**175
APAMEA (city, Phrygia) **3:**174
- Asia Minor **3:**746ff
- Diaspora **6:**10
- Phrygia **13:**487
- synagogue **15:**600
Apamea, Treaty of (188 B.C.E.) **8:**628
Aparatorul (newsp.) **14:**398
Apáti, Miklós **8:**22
APE **3:**175
- dietary laws **6:**32
- evolution **6:**1003; **6:**1004
- Solomon's trade **15:**98
- *illus:* text
APEL, WILLI **12:**681
Apelbaum, David **16:**349
Apenszlak, Jacob, *see* Appenszlak, Jacob
ʿAperu (nation), *see* HABIRU
Aphaerema (dist., Er. Isr.) **9:**120
APHEK (loc., Er. Isr.) **3:**175
- Arbel **3:**294
- Fīq **13:**1532
Aphek (kib., Isr.), *see* Afek
Aphilon (Gr.) **7:**873
Aphraates (ch. f.) **5:**552
Aphraia (tn., Er. Isr.) **7:**1319
Aphrodite, Cyprian **3:**704
- *illus:*
- - terra-cotta statuette **3:**510
Aphtha (vill., Er. Isr.) **13:**483
APIKOROS (heretic) **3:**177
- *Birkat ha-Minim* **4:**1035
- disputes with **3:**191
- heresy **8:**359ff
- Maimonides **3:**656
- witness **16:**587
- *see also:* EPICUREANISM
APION (Gr.) **3:**178
- ass worship **3:**784
- Greek literature **7:**889; **7:**895
- source of views **13:**928
ʿApiru (nation), *see* HABIRU
Apis the Bull (deity) **3:**646
APOCALYPSE ("revelation" lit.) **3:**179
- Literature
- - *Abraham, Apocalypse of* **2:**125ff
- - *Baruch, Apocalypse of* **4:**270
- - Daniel **5:**1277; **6:**871ff
- - *Daniel, Vision of* **5:**1290
- - *Enoch, Book of* **6:**795
- - Ezekiel **6:**1094
- - Hellenistic influence **8:**304
- - pseudepigrapha **3:**185
- - resistance literature **8:**301
- - *Zerubbabel, Book of* **16:**1002
- General
- - allegory **2:**643
- - angelic song **15:**144
- - Armilus legend **3:**476
- - fasting **6:**1194
- - Ingathering of the Exiles **8:**1374
- - Jerusalem **9:**1559ff
- - messianism **11:**1418
- - Metatron **11:**1443
- - Moses **12:**392
- - mysticism **10:**497; **10:**508; **10:**543
- - paradise and hell **13:**83
- - resurrection **14:**98
- - reward and punishment **14:**136
- - sages **14:**654
- - Samaritans **14:**738; **14:**740
- - Sukkot **15:**497; **15:**499
- - visions **16:**167
- *illus:*
- - *Apocalypse of Baruch, Syriac* **4:**270
Apocalypse of Abraham, see ABRAHAM, APOCALYPSE OF
Apocalypse of Baruch (Gr.), *see* BARUCH, GREEK APOCALYPSE OF
Apocalypse of Baruch (Syr.), *see* BARUCH, APOCALYPSE OF
Apocalypse of Elias, see ELIJAH, APOCALYPSE OF
Apocalypse of Elchasai **10:**39
Apocalypse of Isaiah **6:**870*ff*
Apocalypse of John, see Revelation, Book of
Apocalypsis Moysis, see ADAM AND EVE, BOOK OF THE LIFE OF
Apocalyptic Literature, *see* APOCALYPSE
Apocalyptic movement, Jewish **5:**1408
APOCRYPHA AND PSEUDEPIGRAPHA **3:**181
- *Contents:*
- - Definition **3:**181
- - Titles and Contents **3:**182
- - "Canon" of Alexandria **3:**183
- - History of **3:**184
- - Medieval Literature **3:**186
- *Abraham, Testament of* **2:**129
- *Adam and Eve, Book of the Life of* **2:**246
- astrology **3:**788
- astronomy **3:**796
- *Baruch, Rest of the Words of* **4:**276
- *Daniel, Apocryphal Books of* **5:**1277
- Davidic Messiah **11:**1409
- Dead Sea texts **5:**1402
- dualism **6:**244
- eternity of Torah **15:**1244
- folklore **6:**1376
- *halakhah* **7:**1162; **12:**117
- Hebrew fiction **6:**1263
- Hellenistic literature **8:**303
- *Isaiah, Martyrdom of* **9:**71
- Jewish censorship **5:**280
- Jewish literature **11:**310ff
- *Joseph and Asenath* **10:**223
- *Jubilees, Book of* **10:**324
- magic **11:**705ff
- *Manasseh, Prayer of* **11:**854
- *Moses, Assumption of* **12:**411
- *Naphtali, Testament of* **12:**821
- *Patriarchs, Testament of the Twelve* **13:**184
- providence **13:**1280
- public reading of **15:**1248
- Raphael **13:**1549
- resistance literature **8:**302
- Sabbath **14:**562
- Septuagint **4:**853
- *Sifrei ha-Minim* **14:**1521
- *Solomon, Psalms of* **15:**115
- *Solomon, Wisdom of* **15:**119
- *Susanna* **15:**532ff
- Temple destruction **9:**238
- Ten Lost Tribes **15:**1004
- *Tobit* **15:**1183
- *chart:* text
- *illus:*
- - *Baruch, Book of* (Fr., c. 1300) **13:**1437
- - *Wisdom of Ben Sira* (17th cent. ms.) **4:**551
Apocryphal Ezra, *see* EZRA, GREEK BOOK OF
Apocryphal Psalms, *see* PSALMS, APOCRYPHAL
Apoda (zool.) **6:**36
Apollinaire, Guillaume **7:**144; **16:**262
- *illus:*
- - portrait **13:**114
Apollinaris of Hierapolis (ch. f.) **5:**551
Apollinopolis Magna (tn., Egy.) **6:**9
- Hebrew mss. **11:**900
Apollo (deity) **14:**81
APOLLONIA (city, Er. Isr.) **3:**187
- *illus:* text
Apollonias (tn., Egy.) **6:**9
Apollonius (royal offic.) **15:**1179; **16:**279
APOLLONIUS (fin. minis., Egy.) **3:**188
APOLLONIUS MOLON (Gr.) **3:**188
- anti-Jewish accusations **3:**190; **7:**889
- Moses **12:**390
Apollonius of Perge (Gr. schol.) **8:**293
APOLOGETICS **3:**188
- *Contents:*
- - Introduction **3:**189
- - Against Hellenism **3:**189
- - Talmud and Midrash **3:**190
- - Relation to Christianity **3:**191
- - Medieval **3:**192
- - 18th Century **3:**198
- - 19/20 Centuries **3:**199
- Christianity **5:**514
- Jewish literature **11:**310ff
- Jewish philosophy **13:**424
- Judah Halevi **10:**363
- Luzzatto, Simone **11:**608
- Mendelssohn, Moses **11:**1332ff
- Troki, Isaac **15:**1403
- *illus:*
- - Aboab's *Nomologia* (1629) **8:**566
- - *Apologie des Juifs* (1789) **8:**1048
- - *Difesa contro gli Attacchi . . .* (1784) **7:**204
- - *Kevod Elohim* (1556) **8:**1196
- *see also:* DISPUTATIONS AND POLEMICS; POLEMICS AND POLEMICAL LITERATURE
APOSTASY **3:**201
- *Contents:*
- - Definition and History **3:**201
- - To Christianity **3:**202f
- - To Islam **3:**211
- - In Jewish Law **3:**211
- - Folklore **3:**214
- General
- - *anusim* **3:**169
- - apologetics **3:**195ff
- - Catholic Church **5:**538
- - Christianity **5:**507
- - Christian Kabbalah **10:**645
- - Frederick II Hohenstaufen **7:**115
- - Haskalah **7:**1437
- - Hep! Hep! riots —;331
- - Law of Return **12:**147
- - Mamluk rule **11:**837
- - Marranos **12:**1022
- - medal, anti-Semitic **11:**1168
- - Omar, Covenant of **12:**1379
- - parodies against **13:**130ff
- - population changes caused by **13:**889
- - Protestants **13:**1249
- - Russian universities **15:**1678
- - sermons to Jews **14:**1184
- - tribute to Rome **16:**948
- - Warsaw **16:**337
- Heretical groups
- - Doenmeh **6:**148f
- - Frankists **7:**59ff
- - Jewish-Christian sects **9:**1233; **10:**38
- - *Minim* **12:**1
- in Halakhah **10:**24
- - *agunah* **2:**431
- - burial **5:**275
- - city, subverted **8:**1470

– – divorce **6:**133
– – homicide, justifiable **8:**945
– – imprisonment **8:**1302
– – informers **8:**1365
– – Jewish identity **10:**57
– – levirate marriage **11:**127
– – marriage **12:**168
– – parental responsibility **14:**93
– – proscription **8:**349
– – return from **4:**184ff
– Notable Apostates
– – ʿAbd al-Ḥaqq al-Islāmī **2:**53
– – Abdallah ibn Salām **2:**54
– – Abner of Burgos **2:**88
– – Alexander, Michael Solomon **2:**573
– – Bernays, Michael **4:**673
– – Brafman, Jacob **4:**1287
– – Brandstaetter, Roman **4:**1305
– – Carben, Victor von **5:**158
– – Cassel, Paulus Stephanus **5:**231
– – Christiani, Pablo **5:**505
– – Chwolson, Daniel **5:**558
– – Donin, Nicholas **6:**167
– – Drach, Paul **6:**191
– – Eliano, Giovanni and Vittorio **6:**615
– – Elisha ben Avuyah **6:**668
– – Fioghi, Fabiano **6:**1302
– – Frank, Jacob **7:**55
– – Gamaliel ben Pedahzur **7:**299
– – Gans, Eduard **7:**311
– – Ginsburg, Christian David **7:**581
– – Halévy, Daniel **7:**1182
– – Hirschensohn-Lichtenstein, J. Z. H. **8:**522
– – Ibrahim ibn Sahl al-Isrāʾīlī **8:**1213
– – Jona, Giovanni Battista **10:**168
– – Juan de España **10:**322
– – Klaczko, Julian **10:**1085
– – Kraus, Karl **10:**1243
– – Levertoff, Paul **11:**71
– – Lorki, Joshua (*Megadef*) **11:**494
– – Lothar, Ernst **11:**509
– – Margarita, Anton **11:**958
– – Margoliouth, George **11:**966
– – Margoliouth, Moses **11:**966
– – Maritain, Raïssa **11:**995
– – Meyer, Paulus **11:**1464
– – Mithridates, Flavius **12:**160
– – Monis, Judah **12:**256
– – Neander, August **12:**910
– – Nola, Elijah da **12:**1206
– – Nuñez, Henrique **12:**1273
– – Pablo de Santa María **13:**3
– – Pasternak, Boris **3:**208, 774 **13:**174
– – Pauli, Johannes **13:**189
– – Petrus Alfonsi **13:**347
– – Pfefferkorn, Johannes **13:**355; **14:**109
– – Pitigrilli **13:**567
– – Rabinovich, Joseph **13:**1472
– – Rashīd al-Dawla **13:**1566
– – Ratisbonne Brothers **13:**1570
– – Reuter, Paul Julius von **14:**112
– – Ricardo, David **14:**153
– – Ricius, Paulus **14:**163
– – Rosenstock-Huessy, Eugen **14:**290
– – Rufeisen, Oswald ("Brother Daniel") **3:**209; **5:**507
– – Saʿid ibn Hasan **14:**658
– – Salkinson, Isaac Edward **14:**687
– – Samau'al ben Judah ibn Abbas **14:**760
– – Schereschewsky, Samuel **14:**995
– – Schlegel, Dorothea **14:**969
– – Schumann, Maurice **14:**1008
– – Seneor, Abraham **14:**1159
– – Shabbetai Ẓevi **14:**1236ff
– – Sixtus of Sienna **14:**1641
– – Stahl, Friedrich Julius **15:**326
– – Stein, Edith **15:**350
– – Trebitsch, Siegfried and Arthur **15:**1364
– – Vambery, Arminius **16:**65
– – Veith, Johann Emanuel **16:**86
– – Weidner, Paulus **16:**375
– – Weininger, Otto **16:**402
– – Wetzlar von Plankenstern, Karl **16:**478
– – Wolff, Joseph **16:**611
– – Žídek, Pavel **16:**1017
– – Zoller, Israel **16:**1217
– Various areas
– – Ereẓ Israel (Byzantine period) **9:**255; **9:**256; **9:**259
– – Germany **7:**467; **7:**477
– – Italy **9:**1135
– – Leningrad **11:**15
– – Provence **13:**1262
– – Saragossa **14:**862ff
– – Spain **15:**220ff
– Views on
– – Dohm, Christian Wilhelm von **6:**153
– – Dubnow, Simon **6:**256
– – Heine, Heinrich **8:**272f
– – Israel Ba'al Shem Tov **9:**1051
– – Luther, Martin **11:**584
– – Mendelssohn, Moses **11:**1332ff
– – Rosenzweig, Franz **14:**299ff
– *illus:*
– – text
– – Prague blood libel (1694) **8:**700
– *see also:* ASSIMILATION; HERESY
"Apostate" City, *see* IR HA-NIDDAḤAT
APOSTLE **3:**215
– Aurum Coronarium **3:**854
– Jesus **10:**11
– New Testament **12:**1059ff
– *illus:* text
Apostole (tax) **8:**648
Apostolic Council (Chr. ch.) **3:**216
Apostolic Decree (Chr. ch.) **3:**217
Apostoloi (cmty. offics.) **8:**648
APOSTOMOS **3:**217
Apotekah (leg. term) **11:**230
Apotekev, Abraham **11:**358
APOTROPOS (guardian) **3:**218
– adopter **2:**301
– embryo **6:**720
– endowment administration **8:**285
– *ḥazakah* of property **7:**1518
– orphan **12:**12; **12:**1479
– tort liability **11:**184
– wills **16:**524
– *see also:* ADOPTION; SUCCESSION
Apparition, *see* DIVINATION
Appeal, Right of (leg.) **12:**143
Appel, Gershon **16:**633
Appel, John, J. **8:**569; **15:**1569
APPEL, JUDAH LEIB **3:**222
Appelbaum, Abraham Abba (Gal.) **14:**538
Appelbaum, M. B. **16:**823
APPELFELD, AHARON **3:**222
– Hebrew literature **8:**207
– *illus:* text
Appenszlak, Jacob **12:**844; **16:**342
Appenszlak, Paulina **12:**844
Apphus, *see* JONATHAN THE HASMONEAN
APPIAN OF ALEXANDRIA **7:**892
Appiryon (journ.) **1:**newsp. list
APPLE (bot.) **3:**223
– food **6:**1416
– plant list **13:**615
– Rosh ha-Shanah **14:**309
APPLEBAUM, LOUIS **12:**681
"Apple Gatherers" (drg., M. Gertler) **3:**557
Appleton (city, Wis.) **16:**556
Appobalsamon, *see* BALSAM
Apprenticeship **7:**971ff; **9:**880
Apsar, Herzl **14:**1523
APT (tn., Fr.) **3:**224
Apta (has. dynasty) **1:**has. table
Apta (tn., Pol.), *see* OPATOW
APTA, MEIR **3:**224
Aptekman, Joseph **13:**818; **15:**28
APTER, DAVID ERNEST **3:**224
Aptheker, Haim, *see* ATAR, HAIM
APTOWITZER, VICTOR **3:**225
Aptrod, David ben Moses Eliakim, *see* ABTERODE, DAVID BEN MOSES ELIAKIM
APULEIUS (Lat. writ.) **14:**234
APULIA (reg., It.) **3:**226
– *pop. table:* text
– *illus:* text
Apulum (Rom. city), *see* ALBA IULIA
ʿAqaba, Al- (port), *see* AKABA
ʾĀqir (vill., Er. Isr.) **6:**560; **11:**1152
Aqlīma (leg. fig.) **5:**23
ʿAqraba (vill., Isr.) **2:**221
ʿAqrah (vill., Kurd.) **10:**1297
ʿAqrī, Ibrahim (nov.), *see* Ibrāhīm, Ibrāhīm Mūsā
Aqṣā, Al-(msq., Jer.), *see* Al-Aqṣā
Aqua Bella (loc., Isr.), *see* Ein Ḥemed
Aquamarine (min.) **13:**1010
Aquarius (zodiac sign) **16:**1191
– *illus:* **11:**732; **14:**1391
AQUILA (Bib. trans.) **12:**1405
– Akivah **2:**490
– Bible translations **4:**853ff; **11:**312
– Cairo *genizah* **17:**1335
– Jabneh **9:**243
– Targum Onkelos **4:**842,843
AQUILA (tn., It.) **3:**228
AQUILEIA (tn., It.) **3:**228
Aquin, Philippe d' **11:**1129; **13:**613
AQUINAS, THOMAS **3:**229
– Albo, Joseph **2:**535ff
– Duns Scotus, John **6:**274ff
– Hillel ben Samuel **13:**444
– Jewish taxation benefits **16:**1290
– Jews **5:**512
– Maimonides **13:**451
– Taitaẓak, Joseph **15:**711
Ar (tn., Er. Isr.), *see* RABBAH
ʿĀRA (vill., Isr.) **3:**231
– human geography **9:**588
Ara (bay tree) **4:**353
ARABA (city, Er. Isr.) **3:**231
Araba (Galilean dist.) **7:**266
ARABAH (reg., Isr.) **3:**231
– definition **9:**114
– frontiers **9:**313ff
– geology **9:**194ff
– human geography **9:**589; **9:**595
– metals **11:**1431ff
– Negev 12:925
– physiography **9:**159
– Timna **14:**1192; **15:**1145
– *illus:*
– – text
– – chalk formations **9:**203
– – Ein Hazevah landscape **9:**145
– – Gerofit, settlement **12:**767
– – harvesting muskmelon **11:**1294
– – Hiyyon river exit **9:**165
– – intensive farming **9:***fcg.* 171
– – sandlands **9:**165
Arabah River (Isr.) **9:**135,160ff
ʿArab al Turkumān (tribe) **9:**1045
"Arab America" (area, Pers. Gulf) **9:**467
Arabarch (tit.), *see* ALABARCH
"Arab Club" (polit. soc.) **9:**457
Arab Higher Committee **9:**465ff; **9:**1475
Arabi, Solomon **5:**1480
Arabia (prov., Transj.) **15:**1317
ARABIA (penin.) **3:**232
– Babylonians **16:**1505
– Ḥabbān **7:**1018
– Havilah **7:**1493
– Ḥimyar **8:**498
– history chart **8:**766-767
– Jewish literature **12:**1462
– Jewish tribes **8:**656
– Mt. Sinai **14:**1599
– Sabea **14:**587
– Solomon's trade **15:**98
– spices **8:**1311
– Yemen **16:**739
– *pop. table:* text
Arabica (period.) **11:**122
ARABIC LANGUAGE **3:**237
– *Contents:*
– – Old Arabic **3:**237
– – Classical Arabic **3:**237
– – Middle- and Judeo-Arabic **3:**239
– – Modern **3:**241
– – Dialects **3:**241
– Arab education in Israel **9:**1028,1029
– Aramaic **3:**263ff
– Ashkenazic Hebrew **16:**1640
– Bible translations **4:**863
– Ereẓ Israel, 634 to 1099 **9:**264
– Hebrew poetry **13:**683f **16:**1621
– Islam **9:**96
– Israel radio broadcasts **15:**931
– Jewish linguistic source **10:**67
– Judeo-Arabic **10:**67,409
– linguistics **16:**1353
– modern Hebrew **16:**1650
– philosophy **13:**427
– preservation of **16:**1414
– Saadiah Gaon **16:**1616
– Samaritans **14:**752
– Semitic languages **14:**1149ff.
– translations **15:**1319ff
– *table:* text
– *see also:* JUDEO-ARABIC; ORIENTALISTS
Arabic Literature
– Hebrew poetry **11:**325ff
– Israel **9:**1040
– Judeo-Arabic **10:**410
– Literary Society (Baghdad) **6:**615
– oriental literature **12:**1462
– *illus:*
– – Karaite Pentateuch **8:**665
Arabites (Ishmaelites) **9:**89
– Semitic languages **14:**1152
ARAB LEAGUE **3:**242
– Arab National Movement **9:**465ff
– Arab Palestine annexation **9:**1032
– Argentinian anti-Semitism **3:**416
– boycott of Israel **4:**1282
– Eden, Anthony **3:**982
– Israel historical survey **9:**384f
– Palestinian Arabs, rights **9:**355
– War of Independence **16:**306
Arab Legion, *see* Arabs (Arab Legion)
Arab Liberation Front **9:**471
ARAB LITERATURE IN ISRAEL **9:**1040
ARAB REFUGEES **9:**446
– absentee property **9:**1031ff
– Arab National Movement **9:**466f
– Conciliation Commission
– Gaza Strip **7:**344
– Jerusalem camps **9:**1492ff
– Lebanon **10:**1545,1546 **9:**377ff
– population of Israel **9:**490
– Sidon **14:**1508
– Six-Day War **14:**1638
– social conditions **9:**412ff
– United States **15:**1666
– *illus:* text
Arab Revolt, *see* Arabs (Nationalism)
ʿArab River (Er. Isr.) **9:**178
Arabs
– General
– – Abbasids **2:**42
– – Bahuẓim **4:**102; **4:**1207
– – cartography **11:**925
– – *dhimmi* **5:**1604
– – disputations **6:**88ff.
– – emancipation **6:**717
– – Ereẓ Israel, 634-1099 **9:**259

– – identification **3**:194
– – language **14**:1149; **16**:1414
– – Mamluks **11**:834
– – Muhammad **12**:508
– – Nabateans **12**:739
– – Omar, Covenant of **12**:1378
– – Semites **14**:1148
– – Sephardim **14**:1172
– – settlement in Ereẓ Israel **9**:122
– – Spain **15**:223ff
– – Umayyads **15**:1528
– – Wellhausen **16**:444
– – *see also:* ISLAM; *and various Muslim countries*
– Nationalism **9**:453
– – Abdullah **2**:56
– – Alliance Israélite **2**:652
– – Arabic **3**:241
– – "Arab Revolt" **2**:56; **9**:348ff; **9**:460ff
– – China **5**:474ff
– – growth and spread **9**:330ff,453
– – history chart **8**:766-767
– – Hussein **8**:1131
– – inquiry commissions **13**:31
– – Jewish immigration **9**:523ff
– – liberation army **16**:307
– – liberation fronts **9**:471; **10**:200
– – liberation organization **9**:404; **9**:41,1033
– – opposition to Jews **8**:757ff
– – partition plans **13**:34; **16**:1175
– – Sykes-Picot treaty **15**:566
– – Syria **15**:647
– – terrorism (Lebanon) **10**:1546
– – terrorists in Greece **7**:882
– – Zionism **16**:1056,1075ff
– *illus:*
– – al-Fatḥ poster **9**:470
– – Arab civil disobedience campaign (1936) **9**:463
– – disturbances, 1921, commission reports **9**:339
– – Hebron riots (1929) **9**:454
– – Husseini, Hajj Amin al- **9**:460
– – Jaffa riots (1936) **9**:464
– – Jerusalem demonstration (1947) **9**:466
– – Kaukji's irregulars **9**:465
– – riots, 1936, *Palestine Post's* reporting **9**:350
– – *see also:* ARAB LEAGUE
– Arab-Jewish Relations
– – Arab Higher Committee **9**:1475
– – Arlosoroff, Chaim **3**:470
– – Balfour Declaration **2**:442; **2**:448
– – Berit Shalom **4**:632
– – Gordon, A. D. **7**:793
– – Herbert Samuel **14**:799
– – Herzl, Theodor **8**:420
– – Jerusalem, reunited **9**:1509ff
– – Jerusalem clashes **9**:1473
– – Magnes, J. L. **11**:718
– – Roosevelt, F. D. **14**:258
– – Ruppin, Arthur **14**:432
– – St. James Conference **14**:660
– – Simon, A.E. **14**:1577ff
– – U.N. **15**:1548ff
– – Weizmann, Chaim **16**:431
– – White Papers **16**:483ff
– – yishuv defense **9**:681
– – Zionism **16**:1075ff
– *illus:*
– – Feisal's letter expressing positive attitude toward Zionism **16**:1050
– – Hebron meeting (1929) **8**:232
– – London Round Table Conference **9**:353
– – Old City of Jerusalem **9**:1507
– – Ramat Eshkol housing project **9**:1510
– – Transjordan meeting (1933) **9**:346
– – Weizmann and Emir Feisal **9**:336; **16**:428
– Arab Legion
– – Abdullah ibn Hussein **2**:57
– – invasion of Israel **9**:1031
– – Jerusalem **9**:1480; **9**:1486; **9**:1497
– – Sinai Campaign **8**:1131
– – Transjordan **15**:1318
– – War of Independence **9**:366ff; **16**:310ff
– *illus:*
– – Abdullah **9**:352
– – Jerusalem position **16**:317
– – soldiers on Old City wall **9**:1483
– – tombstones from Mt. of Olives used for barracks walls **9**:1485
– In Israel **9**:1021
– – agriculture **9**:780
– – banks **9**:1023
– – communal life **9**:917ff
– – cooperatives **5**:949
– – culture, popular **9**:1038
– – economy **9**:698
– – education **9**:949
– – geographical distribution **9**:569ff
– – governance **9**:598ff
– – health services **9**:992ff
– – Histadrut **8**:540
– – history chart **8**:766-767
– – Knesset **10**:1116
– – labor movement **9**:854ff
– – labor problems **9**:329ff
– – Mapam **11**:914
– – population **9**:486ff
– – radio broadcasts **15**:931
– – Teachers' Association **15**:889
– – West Bank **9**:411ff
– *illus:*
– – Bir al-Sheikh elementary school **9**:944
– – Manaḥat village **9**:581
– – President Shazar greeted by schoolchildren in Nazareth **14**:1325
– – schoolboys at Israel Museum workshop **9**:951
– – Ṭīra medical center **9**:990
– Arab States
– – anti-Jewish discrimination **6**:71
– – anti-Semitism **3**:138,147; **6**:582
– – armistice agreements **3**:478; **9**:319
– – boycott of Israel **4**:1282; **9**:427
– – China **5**:473
– – emancipation **6**:717
– – history chart **8**:766-767
– – Jewish emigration **14**:1172
– – Hussein **10**:200
– – Israel **9**:366ff
– – Israel peace efforts **9**:422
– – Six-Day War **14**:1624
– – Sinai Campaign **14**:1600
– – socialism **15**:38
– – U.N. **15**:1543ff
– – U.S. diplomacy **15**:1662ff
– – War of Independence **16**:306
– *illus:*
– – anti-Semitic cartoons **3**:145,156
– – Baghdad hangings, protest rally **8**:1451
– – Israel (cartoons) **5**:178,217,218
– – War of Independence map **9**:373
– – *see also:* Arab Summit Conferences; *and under individual states*
Arab Summit Conferences **9**:403; **9**:414
– Jordan waters **15**:649
– Six Day War **14**:1625
Arabu, *see* Arabites
"Arab with Flower" (paint., P. Litvinovsky) Pl. 2 **3**:ART
ARAD (city, Isr.) **3**:243
– altar **2**:761; **2**:765
– Arad institute **10**:31
– archive **3**:374
– cultic center **5**:1165ff
– Edom **6**:376
– fortifications **16**:273
– *ḥerem* vow by Israel **8**:345
– Jewish Legion **12**:929
– Korahites **13**:1316
– lotteries **16**:661
– ostraca **2**:682; **16**:667
– statistics **1**:place list
– temple **15**:947
– *illus:*
– – archaeological remains **2**:389,390,762,767; **5**:586,1168
– – residential zone **9**:577
– – seal **16**:660
ARAD (city, Transyl.) **3**:250
– Hungarian massacres **8**:1103
– *illus:*
– – synagogue **15**:1341
Ar'a de Yisra'el (name, Er. Isr.) **9**:111
Arad Ḥeb/pa (ruler, Jer.) **9**:1380
Arad Institute (Isr.) **10**:31
ARADUS (Phoen. city) **3**:250
– Phoenicia **13**:475
– Sidon **14**:1506
Arafat, Yasser (Fataḥ ldr.) **9**:414
– national movement **9**:468ff
– terrorist activities **14**:1639
ARAGÃO, FERNÃO XIMENES DE **3**:251
Aragon (state), *see* SPAIN
Aragon, Estenza **15**:1300
Aragon, Louis **15**:1396
Aragon rites (litur.) **11**:400
Arakhim (journ., Isr.) **1**:newsp. list
Arakhim (journ., Pol.) **1**:newsp. list
ARAKHIN (tract.) **3**:251
Arakie ha-Kohen, Eliezer ben Aaron Saadiah **5**:626
ARAM, ARAMEANS **3**:252
– Ahab **2**:436
– Ahaz **2**:455
– Armenia **3**:473
– Ben-Hadad **4**:515
– Beth-Eden **4**:727
– David **5**:1320
– history **8**:595ff
– Hittites **8**:789; **16**:1501
– Kedemites **10**:865
– Semites **14**:1148
– Uz **16**:38
– warfare **16**:273
– *illus:*
– – Ben-Hadad stele **4**:516
– – David's wars (map) **5**:1322
– *map:* text
– *see also:* ARAM-DAMASCUS
Arama, Abraham ibn, *see* Abraham ibn Arama
ARAMA, ISAAC BEN MOSES **3**:256
– Abrabanel **2**:106
– angels **2**:976
– articles of faith **3**:658
– astrology **3**:793
– Bibago, Abraham **4**:812
– exile **7**:288ff
– Moses **12**:400
– peace **13**:198
– philosophic exegesis **11**:346
– philosophy **13**:450
– Torah **15**:1238; **15**:1241
– *illus:*
– – text
– – commentary to Deuteronomy (1546) **5**:1583
Arama, Jacob **3**:259
ARAMA, MEIR BEN ISAAC **3**:259
ARAMAIC **3**:259
– *Contents:*
– – Ancient and Official **3**:260
– – – Sources **3**:260
– – – Characteristics **3**:263
– – Ancient Aramaic **3**:265
– – Official Aramaic **3**:266
– – Middle Aramaic **3**:267
– – Late Aramaic **3**:269
– – – Western Aramaic **3**:270
– – – Eastern Aramaic **3**:275
– Arabic **3**:237; **3**:240
– Arameans **3**:255
– Bible translations **4**:841; **4**:860; **11**:312ff
– Dead Sea Scrolls **16**:1584
– divorce bill **6**:131
– Egypt **6**:487
– Ereẓ Israel letter changes **15**:774
– Ezra, Book of **6**:1111
– greetings and congratulations **7**:912
– Hebrew linguistics **16**:1393
– inscriptions **16**:666ff
– Judah ha-Nasi **10**:370
– Judea, Hellenistic period **8**:293
– Kurdistan Jews **10**:1298
– linguistic development **10**:66
– masorah terms **16**:1422
– medieval Hebrew **16**:1640
– mishnaic Hebrew **16**:1605
– mnemonic device **16**:1425
– modern Hebrew **16**:1649
– Murabba'at scrolls **12**:529
– names **12**:807ff
– papyrus **16**:659
– Persians **13**:305
– Samaritan calendar **14**:749
– Samaritans **14**:752
– script **2**:685ff
– seals **14**:1073
– Semitic languages **14**:1149
– Targum **15**:811
– *Targum Sheni* **15**:813
– Yiddish **16**:790f
– – *illus:*
– – – comparative alphabets **2**:683
– – – Elephantine papyrus **8**:617
– – – script types **2**:687,711
– – – stele of Zakir **16**:664
– – – Uzziah inscription **16**:44
– *tables:* text
– *see also:* ALPHABET, HEBREW; HEBREW GRAMMAR; HEBREW LANGUAGE; NEO-ARAMAIC; SEMITIC LANGUAGES
Aramatha (city, Er. Isr.), *see* RAMOTH-GILEAD
ARAM-DAMASCUS **3**:287
– history chart **8**:766-767
– *illus:*
– – text
– – David's conquest (map) **5**:1321
– *see also:* ARAM, ARAMEANS
Arami oved avi (Hag.) **7**:1080
Aram-Naharaim (loc.) **8**:584; **13**:6
Aram Zoba (city, Syr.), *see* ALEPPO
Aram Zoba Synagogue (Jer.) **9**:500
Aranha, Oswaldo **4**:1332; **10**:1456
Aranicus, Jacobus **2**:547
ARANNE, ZALMAN **3**:289
– Israel education **9**:395
– *illus:*
– – H. Rovina, I. Bar-Yehudah, and **4**:285
– – Labor parties merger meeting **9**:677
Aranyi, Adila D', *see* Fachiri, Adila
Aranyi, Jelly E. D' **10**:110
ʿAraq el-Emir (loc., Transj.) **16**:668
ʿARʿARA (vill., Isr.) **3**:290
– human geography **9**:588
ARARAT (land, mts.) **3**:290
– Ceylon **5**:316
– flood **6**:1351; **6**:1357
– Mesopotamia **16**:1502

- Sargon II **14:**880
- Urartian inscriptions **16:**1507
Ararat (J. state) **8:**728; **16:**1036
- *illus:*
- - foundation stone **4:**1465
Ararat (Yid. theat.) **4:**1392
Aratris (J. cmty.) **5:**1239
Aratta (city-state, Mesop.) **16:**1487
ARAUNAH (bib. fig.) **3:**290
- Jebusites **9:**1307
- Temple **15:**943
Arav (place, Er. Isr.) **10:**150
Aravah (reg., Isr.), *see* ARABAH
Aravot (willow-branches), *see* HOSHANOT
Aravot (celestial spheres) **15:**1127
ARAZI, YEHUDAH **3:**291
- *illus:*
- - Haganah High Command **7:**1070
Arba (bib. fig.) **2:**918
Arba'ah minim, see FOUR SPECIES
Arba'ah Turim (hal. wk.), *see* JACOB BEN ASHER
ARBA AMMOT (hal. meas.) **3:**291
- acquisition **2:**217; **2:**353
Arbaia, *see* Arabites
Arba kanfot, see TALLIT KATAN
ARBA KOSOT (seder cups) **3:**292
- *Haggadah* **7:**1079
- Passover **13:**167
Arba Me'ot Shekel Kesef (wk.) **16:**176
Arba Parshiyyot (four special Sabbaths) **14:**573
Arbatiao (kab. name) **10:**505
ARBATTA (city, dist., Galilee) **3:**292
- *see also:* NARBATA
Arbayter, *see also under* Arbeiter, Arbeter
Arbayter Fraynd (gr., Arg.) **3:**423
Arbayter Shtime (period.) **4:**1499
Arbeh, see LOCUST
Arbeiter Ring, *see* WORKMEN'S CIRCLE
ARBEITER-ZEITUNG (newsp.) **3:**293
Arbeitsdorf (concen. camp) **5:**78
Arbeitskreis (mvmt., Ger.) **8:**1241
Arbel (mosh., Isr.) **1:** place list
ARBEL (site, Er. Isr.) **3:**293
- flaxen cloth **6:**1339
- synagogue **15:**597
Arbel River (Isr.) **7:**579; **9:**171
Arbeter, *see also under* Arbayter, Arbeiter
Arbeter Farband (assoc., U.S.) **8:**723
Arbeter Fraynd (newsp.) **13:**1031
Arbeter Ring, *see* WORKMEN'S CIRCLE
Arbeter Tsaytung (pub.) **13:**1043
ARBIB (fam.) **3:**294
Arbib, Angelo **3:**294; **11:**1559
Arbib, Edoardo **3:**294
Arbib, Emilio **3:**294
Arbib, Esther **3:**294
Arbib, Gustavo **3:**294
Arbib, Isaac ben Arroyo, *see* AROLLIA, ISAAC BEN MOSES
Arbib, Isaiah **3:**294
Arbib, Moses **3:**294
Arbib, Vittorio **3:**294
Arbil (tn., Iraq), *see* IRBIL
ARBITRATION **3:**294
- *Contents:*
- - Function **3:**294
- - Composition **3:**295
- - Arbitrators **3:**297
- - Agreement to, and Subject Matter **3:**297
- - Decision of **3:**299
- - Modern Israel **3:**299
- law development **12:**126; **12:**137
- practice, procedure **13:**952
- *see also:* COMPROMISE
Arbitration, Deed of **3:**295ff
Arboth Moab (plain), *see* MOAB
ARBUÉS, PEDRO DE **3:**300
- Francisco de Santa Fé **11:**495
- Saragossa **14:**865
Arbus, Diane **13:**484
Arcadius (Rom. emp.) **9:**257; **14:**785
Arcand, Adrien **5:**110
ARCHA (archive, Eng.) **3:**300
- Bristol **4:**1378
- Canterbury **5:**127
- economic history **16:**1290
- Exchequer of the Jews **6:**1007
- Exeter **6:**1023
- history chart **8:**766-767
- *see also:* TAXATION
ARCHAEOLOGISTS **3:**300
ARCHAEOLOGY **3:**303
- *Contents:*
- - Methods **3:**303
- - Origins of Israel **3:**305
- - Joshua to Babylonia **3:**306
- - Return to Fall of Jerusalem **3:**327
- - Destruction of Commonwealth **3:**328
- - History in Israel **3:**330
- - Evaluation **3:**331
- altar **2:**761; **2:**766
- anthropology **3:**42
- architecture **3:**336
- Bible criticism **4:**907; **4:**912
- Bible history **8:**572ff
- chronology **16:**1261
- cistern **5:**578
- cooking, baking **5:**937
- dolmens **6:**156
- door and doorpost **6:**170
- economic history **16:**1267
- glass vessels **7:**604ff
- Hebrew linguistics **16:**1395
- Jewish symbolism **15:**568
- *menorah* **11:**1355
- Mesopotamia **16:**1485
- metals, mining **11:**1428
- musical relics **12:**557; **12:**559
- ostraca **12:**1509
- papyri **13:**70
- pillars **13:**521
- population **13:**869
- pottery **1:** pottery chart; **13:**936
- seals **14:**1072
- synagogue **15:**582ff
- Tell el-Amarna **15:**933
- Transjordan **15:**1316ff
- Ugarit **15:**1501
- urbanization **5:**583
- weights and measures **16:**378; **16:**380
- writings and inscriptions **16:**654
- Yavneh-Yam potsherd **16:**723
- *illus:*
- - text
- - Ashkelon, conquest by Ramses II **3:**715
- - Babylon, reconstructions **4:**31-33
- - Banias grotto **4:**162
- - Ben-Hadad stele **4:**516
- - Dura-Europos synagogue **3:**28, 451, 461, 515; **6:**277-294
- - Egyptian antiquities **3:**311-313; **6:**488-499
- - execration text inscription, Egyptian **8:**572
- - Esarhaddon stele **6:**853
- - Gerasa antiquities **7:**433, 434
- - Gilgamesh Epic, tablet **6:**1355
- - Hamam Lif synagogue **3:**519
- - Hammurapi stele **7:**1246
- - Hiram's sarcophagus **13:**473
- - Madaba map, fragments **3:**697,715; **7:**572; **9:**1543; **11:**677,921
- - Mari antiquities **11:**972-986
- - Merneptah stele **9:**109
- - Nuzi document **8:**575
- - oil lamps, stone and clay **7:**1293-1295
- - Ostia synagogue **12:**1507,1508
- - Ramses II and Philistines, sea battle **8:**587
- - Sardis, ruins of synagogue **3:**519; **14:**877
- - Semitic clan in Egypt **3:**311
- - Sennacherib relief **3:**319
- - Seti I stele **8:**580
- - Shalmaneser III Black Obelisk **3:**320
- - Sumerian king list **3:**367
- - Tell el-Amarna, tablet **3:**370
- - Tell Ḥalaf seraph **14:**1180
- - Tyre sarcophagus **15:**1124
- - war chariots **5:**211-213
- - Yeḥawmilk stele **13:**476
- - Zakir stele **16:**664
- - Ziggurat of Ur **16:**1
- *maps:*
- - Akkad and Sumer **2:**494
- - Alexandria, early Christian period **2:**591
- - Antioch, ancient **3:**72
- - Aramean regions and cities **3:**253
- *see also:* ALPHABET, HEBREW; COINS AND CURRENCY; Khirbat . . .; Tells; *and individual sites*
Archagathus, *see* CAECILIUS OF CALACTE
ARCHANGEL (city, Rus.) **3:**333
"Archangel" (sculp., S. Lipton) **11:**298
Archangel Michael League (Iron Guard, Rum.) **14:**394
Archangels **2:**962
Archeion, see ARCHIVES
ARCHELAIS (city, Er. Isr.) **3:**333
ARCHELAUS (s., Herod) **3:**333
- Augustus **8:**636
- coinage **5:**717
- Edom **6:**378
- history chart **8:**766-767
- *geneal. table:* **8:**377
- *illus:*
- - text
- - coins **5:**702-703
Archelaus (k., Cappadocia) **7:**601
Archenhold, Friedrich Simon **3:**806
Archimedes (Gr. schol.) **8:**293
ARCHIPHERECITES (tit.) **3:**335
- titles **15:**1164
ARCHISYNAGOGOS (tit.) **3:**335
- title **15:**1164
- *illus:* text
"Architectural Tondo" (paint., Ilya Bolotowsky) **3:**619
ARCHITECTURE AND ARCHITECTS **3:**336
- *Contents:*
- - In Antiquity **3:**336
- - Modern Period **3:**359
- - Modern Israel **3:**361
- - Capsules **3:**362
- biblical themes **4:**938
- Hellenistic influence **3:**506ff
- Hellenistic Jewish **8:**300
- Israel cultural life **9:**1012
- pillars **13:**520
- Solomon **15:**101ff
- synagogue **15:**584; **15:**591; **15:**595
- Toledo **15:**1199
- Tower of Babel **4:**22
- wooden buildings **16:**630
- *illus:*
- - text
Arab
- - - Al-Aqsa Mosque, Jerusalem **8:**931; **9:**1413
- - - Dome of the Rock, Jerusalem **9:**1413,1557
- - - *see also under individual subjects*
- - Babylonian palaces (reconst.) **4:**31-33
- - Byzantine
- - - church, Shivtah **14:**1419
- - - Church of Nativity, Bethlehem **4:**300,742
- - - city gate, Jerusalem **9:**1536
- - Canaanite
- - - Arad remains **3:**245-246
- - - Megiddo, temple **2:**760
- - Contemporary, *see under individual places and architects*
- - Crusader
- - - Abu Ghosh church **2:**181; **3:**329; **5:**1136
- - - Acre, St. John's crypt **5:**1143
- - - Apollonia ruins **3:**188
- - - Aqua Bella ruins **5:**1136
- - - Belvoir, ruins **2:**419; **3:**327; **12:**880
- - - Belvoir, sculpture **5:**1145
- - - Caesarea, city walls **5:**1142; **9:**276
- - - Caesarea, gate **5:**1138,1139
- - - Castellum Pelegrinorum, Athlit **3:**328,821; **5:**1144
- - - Holy Sepulcher, Jerusalem **9:**1418
- - - Jūdīn castle **16:**728
- - - Montfort castle **5:**1136; **9:**172-173
- - - Qalat Nimrod **9:**207
- - - St. Anne Church, Jerusalem **9:**1453
- - - Tiberias, city walls **15:**1133
- - - Tomb of Miriam, Jerusalem **9:**1417
- - Early Israelite
- - - Arad temple **5:**1168
- - - ashlar masonry, Ramat Raḥel **13:**1536
- - - Azekah fortress, plan **3:**1004
- - - Beth-Cherem citadel, plan **4:**717
- - - Gezer, city gate **7:**536
- - - Gibeon, pool staircase **7:**551
- - - Hazor, citadel **5:**588
- - - kitchen (reconst.) **5:**938
- - - Lachish, reconstructions **5:**589
- - - Laish excavations **5:**1259
- - - Megiddo **3:**316; **8:**591; **11:**1223-1226
- - - Mizpah, city gate and wall **5:**587; **12:**174
- - - Samaria antiquities **2:**438
- - - window balustrade **3:**317
- - Hasmonean
- - - city walls, Jerusalem **9:**1391
- - - fortifications, Jerusalem **9:**1533
- - - Hezir, Tomb of the Sons of **15:**1219
- - - Jason's Tomb, Jerusalem **3:**321
- - - Kidron Valley monuments **3:**509
- - - Zechariah's Tomb, Jerusalem **9:**1392
- - Hellenistic
- - - Ashkelon remains **3:**716-717
- - - Maresha, tombs **3:**321
- - - Samaria, round tower **3:**322
- - Herodian
- - - Caesarea antiquities **5:**9-11
- - - Cave of Machpelah mosque, Hebron **8:**923
- - - Herodium **8:**389
- - - Herod's palace, Jerusalem **8:**380
- - - Jerusalem citadel **9:**1397
- - - Masada **3:**383; **4:**320; **11:**1081-1088
- - - masonry **3:**324; **9:**1522
- - - Phasael Tower, Jerusalem **9:**1397,1533
- - - Robinson's Arch, Jerusalem **9:**1531,1533; **14:**205
- - - Samaria, forum **14:**724
- - - Temple **3:**511; **15:**960

--- Temple Mount wall 9:1399,1522
--- Wilson's Arch, Jerusalem 16:535
-- Mamluk
--- Antipatris fortress 3:78
--- bridge, Lydda 11:619
--- caravanserai, Gaza 9:275; 11:835
--- Cave of Machpelah mosque, Hebron 8:923
--- mausoleum, Jerusalem 9:1424
--- Ramleh tower 3:330
-- Ottoman
--- city gates, Jerusalem 9:1427-1432
--- public fountains, Jerusalem 9:1433-1434
-- Roman
--- Aelia Capitolina gates, Jerusalem 9:1401,1402
--- Beth-Shean theater 4:763
--- Bozrah, plan 4:1285
--- Gerasa antiquities 7:433
--- Petra antiquities 13:341-342
--- Samaria, theater 14:723
--- Sardis synagogue 3:519
-- Synagogue, *see* SYNAGOGUE
-- Ziggurat of Ur 16:1
- *see also:* ARCHAEOLOGY; Construction
ARCHIVES 3:366
- *Contents:*
-- Biblical Period 3:367
-- Post-Biblical Period 3:375
-- Middle Ages 3:376
-- Modern Times 3:377
--- Diaspora 3:377
--- Holocaust 3:384
--- Major Archives 3:385
--- Israel 3:388
- American Jewish 2:822
- Assemani family 3:760
- books 4:1220; 4:1237
- Cairo *genizah* 16:1338
- economic history 16:1284
- Hebrew manuscripts 11:899
- Jewish National Library 11:198
- libraries 11:190
- Mesopotamia 16:1493
- Ramat Yoḥanan 14:1355
- synagogue destruction 15:585
- Yad Vashem 16:697
- *illus:*
-- text
-- Cairo *genizah* fragments 7:405, 406
-- Eliashib archives, Arad 3:248
-- Ghetto Fighters' House 7:546
-- Mainz, name changes (1808) 7:484
-- Nuzi documents 8:575
- *see also:* PINKAS
Archives Israélites de France (period.) 2:649; 5:17; 13:108
Archives Law (1955; Isr.) 3:389
Archivolti, Carlo 11:1559
ARCHIVOLTI, SAMUEL 3:397
ARCHON (offic.) 3:397
ARCHPRESBYTER (offic.) 3:398
- autonomy, judicial 3:928
- Elias le Eveske 6:618
- Episcopus Judaeorum 6:818
- exchequer of the Jews 6:1007
Archshofen (tn., Ger.) 12:1150
ARCILA (port, Mor.) 3:399
- Morocco 12:338
ARCO, GEORG WILHELM ALEXANDER HANS, GRAF VON 8:1430
Arco-Valley, Count (assassin, Ger.) 6:557
Arct, M. (publ.) 13:1369
"Arctic Birds" (paint. J. Bornfriend) 4:1252
Arculf (bp.) 9:1425; 15:1355
Ard, Al- (party, Isr.) 9:1031
Arḍ-al-Birka (pool, Jer.), *see* Lacus Legerii
Ardashir I (k., Pers.) 6:51, 1025
ARDASHIR (city, Arm.) 3:399
ARDAVAN (Parth. ks.) 3:399
Ardavan III 2:267; 3:4
Ardeal, *see* TRANSYLVANIA
Ard'et (bk.) 6:1151
Ardi-Balit (prin., Assyr.) 2:305
ARDIT (fam.) 3:400
Ardit, Abraham 3:400
ARDIT, EPHRAIM BEN ABRAHAM 3:400
Ardit, Ḥayyim Abraham 3:400
Ardit, Ḥayyim Moses 3:400
Ardit, Ḥayyim Moses Isaac 3:400
Ardit, Isaac 3:400
Ardit, Isaac ben Solomon 3:400
Ardit, Joshua Solomon 3:400
Ardit, Raphael ben Solomon 3:400
Ardit, Raphael Solomon 3:400
Ardit, Solomon ben Jacob 3:400
ARDITI, ALBERT JUDAH 3:400
- press 13:1038
Arditti, Benjamin 4:1493; 16:1108
Arditti, Eliezer 4:1493
Ardmore (city, Okla.) 12:1353
ARDON, MORDECAI 3:401
- *illus:*
-- "Toward Jerusalem" Pl. 8 3-ART
Ardor, *see* BENJAMIN, WALTER
ARDUT (fam.) 3:401
Ardut, Eleazar ibn 3:401; 11:800
Ardut, Joseph ibn 3:401
ARÉGA, LÉON 3:402
AREIOS I (k., Sparta) 3:402
- Sparta 15:256
ARENDA (lease) 3:402
- competition restrictions 7:1463
- development 2:403
- Four Lands 5:1001
- *ma'arufya* 11:640
- Podolia 13:668
- Poland 13:724
- wine, liquor trade 16:542
- *illus:* text
-- "Dodie the Innkeeper" (illus., A. Kaplan) 10:748
- *see also:* BROKERS
ARENDT, HANNAH 3:406
ARENDT, OTTO 3:406
Areopolis (tn., Er. Isr.), *see* RABBAH
Arequipa (city, Peru) 13:324
ARES (Gr. god) 3:407
- Aelia Capitolina 9:1406
- Chemosh 5:390
Areshet (journ.) 1:newsp. list
Aresheth (journ.) 1:newsp. list
ARETAS I (Nabatean k.) 3:407
- Alexander Yannai 16:715
- Nabatea 12:741
ARETAS II (Nabatean k.) 3:407
ARETAS III (Nabatean k.) 3:407
- Alexander Yannai 16:716
- Nabatea 12:741
- Aristobulus II 3:441
ARETAS IV (Nabatean k.) 3:407
- Nabatea 12:743
ARETHUSA (tn., Judea) 3:407
Aretin, J.C. 8:561
Aretino, Leon 15:1322
Aretino, Pietro 9:1105
Aretius Benedictus 8:22
Aretomos (Nabatean k.) 12:741
Areus I (k., Sparta), *see* AREIOS I
Arévalo (city, Sp.) 10:239
AREZZO (tn., It.) 3:408
- *see also:* TUSCANY
Argaman (mosh., Isr.) 1:place list
Argaman (purple) 15:913
Argelès-sur-Mer (concen. camp, Fr.) 7:34
ARGENS, JEAN BAPTISTE DE BOYER 3:408
ARGENTINA 3:408
Contents:
-- Colonial Period 3:409
-- Modern Period 3:409
--- Legal Basis for Jewish Life 3:409
--- History 3:410
--- Demography 3:418
--- Economic, Social Status 3:419
--- Religious Life 3:421
--- Cultural Life 3:423
--- Education and Youth 3:425
--- Ties with Israel 3:426
--- Agriculture 3:427
- General
-- Eichmann abduction 15:1560
-- Entre Ríos 6:802
-- history chart 8:766-67
-- Israel 9:432
-- Latin America 10:1449ff
-- Neo-Nazism 12:956
-- synagogue 1:syn. list
-- War Crimes Trials 16:297
- Demography 2:814ff; 5:1501
-- Jewish settlement 8:742
-- migrations 16:1520
-- population 13:897
-- refugee statistics 14:30
- Jewish Activities
-- agricultural settlements 2:413
-- A.M.I.A. 2:836
-- cooperatives 5:943
-- education 6:456ff
-- Habonim 8:1243
-- ICA 10:46
-- Jewish farming 16:1317
-- Jews in politics 13:820
-- philanthropy 13:386
-- press 13:1040
-- publishing 13:1370
-- socialism 4:1500; 15:33
-- Zionism 16:1123
- *illus:*
-- text
-- anti-Jewish slogan (1961) 3:158
-- Bernasconi league 16:1124
-- Buenos Aires, memorial to heroes of Israel's wars 4:1464
-- Jewish farming cooperative 2:414
-- *pop. tables:*
-- text
-- towns with 100,000 or more Jews, 1967 5:1514
- *see also:* AMERICA
Argentiner Beymelekh (journ.) 5:459
Arghūn (emir) 9:1424
Arghūn Khān (Pers. ruler) 14:618
ARGOB (reg., Er. Isr.) 3:433
Argobba (lang.) 14:1153
Argonautica (bk.) 6:1333
Argos (city, Gr.) 7:868
Argov, Alexander 15:111
Argov, Levi, *see* Kopelevich, Levi
Argov, Meir 5:1452; 16:640
Argüeti, Isaac Behar 11:1159
Argus, The (journ.) 7:737
ARḤA, ELIEZER BEN ISAAC 3:434
Arḥa, Isaac 3:434; 8:232
Arḥei-Parḥei (beggars) 4:390
A-r-i, *see* LURIA, ISAAC BEN SOLOMON
Aria College (Eng.) 6:447,1451; 10:1099
Arianism (Chr. heresy) 4:206; 8:653; 8:657
Arias, David Dias, *see* Dias Arias, David
Arias, Diego (de Avila) 4:171
ARIAS, JOSEPH SEMAH 3:434
Arias de Enciena (Franciscan) 3:498
ARIAS MONTANO, BENITO 3:434
- Bible 13:614
- Hebraist 8:22
- Jerusalem map 9:1543
- Le Fèvre de La Boderie 10:1563
Arias Montano Institute 11:684
Aribi, *see* Arabites
Arica (tn., Chile) 5:466
ARICHA, YOSEF 3:435
Arida (kib., Isr.), *see* SEDEH ELIYAHU
ARIE, RAFAEL 12:681
ARIEL (bib. term, name) 3:436
- Uriel 16:7
Ari'el (newsp.), *see Ha-Ari'el*
ARIEL, DOV 3:436
Ariel, R. 13:298
Ariel, S. Z. 6:734
Arieli, A. L. 8:211,213
Arieli, Itzchak 15:1339
ARIELI, YEHOSHUA 8:543
Aries (star) 16:1191; 16:1490
- *illus:* 12:1175
Arieti (fam.), *see* RIETI
'Ārif, 'Ārif al- (writ.) 9:1041
Arif, Mount (Isr.) 12:927
Arignano, Benjamin 14:252; 16:487
Arik, Meir ben Aaron Judah 14:92
Arikha (J. tax) 4:404
Arikha, Amos 5:437
ARIKHA, AVIGDOR 3:437
- *illus:*
-- text
-- "High Red" Pl. 14 3-ART
Arikh anpin (kab. conc.) 10:569; 10:599
Arimanon (city, Er. Isr.), *see* RAMOTH-GILEAD
Arimathea (city, dist., Er. Isr.) 10:881
- Hasmoneans 9:120
- Ramah 13:1529
Ari Nohem (bk.) 10:550
Arinyo, Gabriel Luis 5:967
ARIOCH (bib., apoc. name) 3:437
- Nebuzaradan 12:919
Ariosto, Ludovico 9:1105
ARIPUL, SAMUEL BEN ISAAC 3:437
- *illus:* text
Arish, El- (Sinai), *see* EL-ARISH
Aristarchus 8:293
ARISTEAS (hist.) 3:438
- *Job, Testament of* 10:129
ARISTEAS, LETTER OF (wk.) 3:439
- agriculture 2:393
- allegorical exegesis 4:896
- authorship 3:438
- Azariah dei Rossi 14:315
- Biblical history 8:304
- commandments 5:784
- concept of God 7:653
- Hecataeus of Abdera 8:237
- Hellenism 8:299
- Jerusalem 9:1393
- letters 11:56
- philosophy 13:425ff
- scriptures 4:816ff
- Septuagint 4:853
- *tefillin* 15:899
- *illus:* text
Aristides of Athens (Ch. F.) 5:551
ARISTOBULUS I (k., Judea) 3:440
- Alexander Yannai 16:714
- Hasmoneans 8:631
- Hellenism 8:296
- history chart 8:766-767
- war and warfare 16:279
- *geneal. table:* 7:1457
- *illus:*
-- coin 5:700
ARISTOBULUS II (k., Judea) 3:440
- Aretas III 12:742
- Hasmoneans 8:632
- Pompey 13:846

- *geneal. table:* 7:1457
ARISTOBULUS III (Hasm. h. pr.) 3:441
- Masada 11:1078
- sages 14:640
ARISTOBULUS (s., Herod) 3:442
- Berenice 4:601
- *geneal. table:* 8:377
- *see also:* ALEXANDER (s., Herod)
ARISTOBULUS (s., Aristobulus) 3:443
- *geneal. table:* 8:377
Aristobulus of Chalcis 3:474; 12:964
- coinage 5:718
ARISTOBULUS OF PANEAS (philos.) 3:443
- allegorical exegesis 4:896
- anthropomorphisms 3:55
- concept of God 7:653
- Greek debt to Jews 13:189; 8:300
- logos 11:460ff
- Mosaic law 8:304
- philosophy 11:313; 13:425ff
- Torah translations 3:189
ARISTON OF PELLA (au.) 7:892
- work 5:551
ARISTOTLE 3:445
- Philosophy and Influences 13:428ff
- - articles of faith 3:656
- - allegorical exegesis 4:897ff
- - beatitude 4:361ff
- - commandments 5:786ff
- - cosmology 5:982
- - form and matter 6:1438ff
- - God 7:658; 7:666
- - Hellenism 8:293
- - imagination 8:1289
- - Jewish theology 15:1106
- - Kabbalah 10:537,556
- - miracles 12:77
- - nature 12:889ff
- - Neoplatonism 12:959; 12:961ff
- - physics 13:488
- - Platonism 13:629
- - soul 15:172ff
- - space and place 15:217ff
- - substance, definition of 5:253
- - substance and accident 15:473
- - time 15:1142ff
- - translations of works 15:1321
- - usury 12:246
- Philosophers on
- - Aaron ben Elijah 2:11ff
- - Abrabanel, Judah 2:110
- - Arama, Isaac 3:258
- - Averroes 3:949ff
- - Avicenna 3:957ff
- - Bar Hebraeus 4:222
- - Bibago, Abraham 4:812ff
- - Cherniss's studies 5:392
- - Crescas, Ḥasdai 5:1081ff
- - Ḥibat Allah 8:462
- - Ibn Da'ud 8:1161
- - Israeli, Isaac 9:1063ff
- - Judah Halevi 10:363ff
- - Levi ben Gershom 11:93
- - Maimonides 11:769
- - Themistius 15:1099
Ariya (Hurrian name) 16:5
Arizi, Samuel 3:670
ARIZONA (U.S.) 3:449
ARK (in syn.) 3:450
- *Anim Zemirot* 3:23
- Av, Ninth of 3:938
- Bet Alfa mosaics 4:713
- ceremonial art 5:288
- Commandments, the 613 5:774
- Falasha tradition 6:1151
- fastdays 6:1192
- *ḥerem* pronouncement 8:355
- lion motif 11:262
- priestly blessing 13:1062
- symbolism 15:570
- synagogue 15:584; 15:592ff
- Torah ornaments 15:1255
- *illus:*
- - text
- - Amsterdam, Liberal Synagogue 12:991
- - Ancona synagogues 2:942,943
- - Athens synagogue 7:873
- - Baghdad, New Synagogue 8:1459
- - Bedzin, Great Synagogue 4:374
- - Belfast synagogue 8:1466
- - Beth-Shean synagogue mosaic 13:905
- - Bet She'arim catacomb, bas-relief 4:769
- - Bombay, Kneseth Elijah synagogue 4:1193
- - Bombay, Magen David synagogue 4:1193
- - Boston, Mishkan Tefilla synagogue 4:1266
- - Bremgarten synagogue 15:560
- - bronze, by Luise Kaish 3:627
- - Carpentras synagogue 5:207
- - ceremonial object motif 3:542; 5:307; 11:1475
- - Charleston, W. Va., Temple Israel 4:787
- - Chicago, South Shore Temple 5:1445
- - Copenhagen, Great Synagogue 15:621
- - Cracow, doors (17th cent.) 5:1035
- - Craiova, Sephardi synagogue 5:1058
- - Dallas, Tex., Shearith Israel synagogue 5:1231
- - Florence, Great Synagogue 15:620-621
- - Fribourg synagogue 7:170
- - Geroda synagogue 6:1403
- - Isfahan, faience-tiled 15:620-621
- - Israel stamp 9:844-845
- - Istanbul, Yambol synagogue 14:1169
- - Jerusalem, Bukharan synagogue 4:1472
- - Jerusalem, Conegliano synagogue 5:869
- - Jerusalem, Ḥurvah synagogue 9:1445
- - Jerusalem, Johanan ben Zakkai synagogue 9:1444
- - Lazne Kynzvart synagogue 10:1520
- - London, Bevis Marks Synagogue 14:1167; 15:620-621
- - London, Great Synagogue 15:619
- - London, St. John's Wood synagogue 11:480
- - Mantua, Scuola Norsa 11:896
- - Newark, N.J., Temple B'nai Abraham 12:1029
- - Novogrudok synagogue 12:1238
- - Nuremberg *Judenstain* 12:1275
- - Oporto, Kadoorie Synagogue 12:1417
- - Paris, Rue de la Victoire Synagogue 15:620-621
- - Paris, Rue Pavée synagogue 13:108
- - Pesaro, Sephardi Synagogue 13:330
- - Pinsk, Great Synagogue 13:540
- - Ponta Delgada synagogue 13:925
- - Prague, Altneuschul 15:*fcg.* 619
- - Rawicz synagogue 13:1587
- - Reggio Emilia synagogue 14:39
- - Rhodes synagogue 14:145
- - Rome, Great Synagogue 14:250
- - Safed, Ha-Ari synagogue 11:572; 14:629
- - St. Louis, Mo., U.H.C. synagogue 12:157
- - Saint Paul, Minn., Temple of Aaron 12:38
- - Salisbury, Sephardi Hebrew Congregation 14:685
- - San Daniele del Friuli 15:1255
- - Santiago, Temple Magen David 14:848
- - Siena synagogue 14:1514
- - Springfield, Mass., Beth El synagogue 15:319
- - Sulzbach synagogue 15:507
- - Tallinn synagogue 15:742
- - Tykocin synagogue 15:1475
- - Venice, Canton synagogue 5:295; 16:98
- - Venice, Great German Synagogue 16:97
- - Venice, Italian Synagogue 16:100
- - Verona synagogue 16:114
- - Vezaitiai synagogue 11:371
- - Villa Torlonia catacombs, Rome 9:1582
- - Vilna, Great Synagogue 16:142
- - Vittorio Veneto synagogue 3:*fcg.* 462
- - Westheim synagogue 4:344
- - Wlodawa synagogue 16:598
- - wooden doors (18th cent., Pol.) 3:*fcg.* 459
- - Wyszogrod synagogue 16:682
Ark, Opening of, *see* PETIḤAH
ARKANSAS (U.S.) 3:458
- *pop. table:* text
Arka'ot shel goyim, *see* Courts, non-Jewish
Arkhangelsk (city, Rus.), *see* ARCHANGEL
Arkhitekturah (journ.), *see* *Adrikhalut*
Arkia (airline) 9:838
- *illus:*
- - airplane in Eilat 9:839
ARKIN, ALAN W. 12:463
- *illus:*
- - in *Popi* 12:463
Arkin, Arseni 14:479
ARK OF THE COVENANT 3:459
- Abinadab 2:78
- cherubim 5:397
- decalogue 5:1436
- divine presence 13:1015ff
- Pentateuch 13:244
- priests 13:1077
- Samuel, Book of 14:792
- sanctity 10:868
- Sukkot 15:497
- symbolism 14:1526
- tabernacle 15:682
- tablets of Law 15:691
- temple 15:943ff
- Temple rock 6:985
- Twelve Tribes 15:1383
- Uzzah 16:43
- *illus:*
- - text
- - *Ambrosian Bible* 5:1018
- - Basnage's *République des Hébreux* 8:1235
- - Capernaum synagogue 3:461; 5:138
- - capture of Jericho 10:264
- - carried across the Jordan 11:72
- - carried into battle against Philistines 14:781
- - ceremonial object motif 4:1339
- - cherubs 14:1395
- - Dura-Europos wall painting 6:277, 284, 291
- - *First Leningrad Bible* 3:*fcg.* 524
- - *Joshua Roll* 3:517
- - *Sarajevo Haggadah* 7:*fcg.* 1131
- - Samuel, sleeping by 14:782
- - twelve tribes and 15:1381
ARK OF MOSES 3:466
- Moses 12:372
- *illus:* text
ARK OF NOAH 3:467
- Adam's body 2:245
- Ceylon legend 5:316
- folklore 6:1395
- ships 14:1411
- synagogue art 15:598
- *illus:*
- - text
- - after Flood 12:1197
- - Gerasa synagogue mosaic 7:434
- - *Golden Haggadah* 6:980
- - Kufic script 12:1193
- - "Noah and the Ark" (Jean David) 5:1346
- - Noah building 12:1192
- *see also:* NOAH
ARLEN, HAROLD 12:681
ARLES (tn., Fr.) 3:468
- archives, notarial 3:376
- museums 12:543
Arles-sur-Tech (vill., Fr.) 14:353
Arlington (sub., Chicago) 5:415
Arlon (tn., Belg.) 4:423; 11:590
ARLOSOROFF, CHAIM 3:470
- Aḥimeir, Abba 2:464
- Jewish Agency 16:1083ff
- Revisionists 9:347; 14:129
- Zionist Congress 16:1172; 16:1174
- *illus:*
- - text
- - with Transjordan Arab leaders 9:346
- - Wauchope's letter re settlement in Transjordan 9:343
Arlosoroff, Eliezer 14:256
Arluck, Hyman, *see* ARLEN, HAROLD
ARMAGEDDON (eschat.) 3:472
- Thutmose III 16:1499
Armée Juive, *see* Organisation Juive de Combat
Armengaud, Blasius 8:22
ARMENIA 3:472
- Ardashir 3:399
- Bible translations 4:861
- Trajan captures 15:1312
- *illus:* text
Armenian Quarter (Jer.) 3:475; 9:1516
- *illus:*
- - aerial view 9:1439
Armenians (cmty., Isr.) 9:911,1441
- *illus:*
- - celebrating Christmas 9:914
Armhold (cantor) 13:568
Armia Krajowa (Pol. orgn.) 16:350
ARMILUS (Armilgos; leg. fig.) 3:476
- Antichrist's form 3:61
- Heraclius 8:333
- *Zerubbabel, Book of* 11:1412; 16:1002
Armistead, Samuel G. 10:1353
ARMISTICE AGREEMENTS, ISRAEL-ARAB 3:478
- Bāqā al-Gharbiyya 4:188
- Bet Iksa 4:750
- frontiers 9:319
- Gaza Strip 7:343ff
- historical survey 9:377ff
- Jerusalem frontiers 9:1484
- Lebanese border 10:1545
- negotiations 9:422
- Sinai Campaign 14:1600
- Syria 15:647
- U.N. 15:1546ff
- Vatican 16:77
- *illus:*
- - text
- - Egyptians evacuating Faluja 16:330
- - Israel negotiators, Rhodes 9:375
- *maps:*
- - armistice demarcation lines, 1949 9:318
- - Jerusalem boundary 9:1505
Armitage, Norman C. 12:1376

Armiya, *see* JEREMIAH
ARMLEDER (anti-Sem. bands) **3:**483
- history chart **8:**766-67
Armoni (bib. fig.) **14:**203
Armor **15:**108; **16:**269
Arms, Coats of, *see* HERALDRY
Armstrong-Jones, Anthony **11:**1407
Army, Israel, *see* DEFENSE FORCES OF ISRAEL
Army Education School (Isr.) **9:**694
Army Orchestra (Isr.) **9:**1008
ARNALDO OF VILLANOVA **3:**484;
- Christian Hebraists **8:**22
Arnaud, François-Thomas d' **10:**1375
Arnd, Carol **8:**22
Arnd(ius), Joshua **8:**22
Arnd ben Isaac, *see* AARON BEN ISAAC BENJAMIN WOLF
ARNDT, ADOLF **3:**484
ARNDT, ERNST MORITZ **3:**485
- Hep! Hep! riots **8:**330
Arne, Thomas Augustine **10:**460
Arnér, Sivar **14:**931
ARNHEIM, FISCHEL **3:**485
ARNHEIM, HEYMANN **3:**485
Arnheim, Selma **15:**552
ARNHEM (city, Holl.) **3:**485
Arnhold, Eduard **11:**1440
Arnhold, Georg **3:**648
Arnhold, Hans **3:**648
Arnim, Achim von **7:**444; **14:**709
Arnold, Henryk **7:**811
Arnold, Matthew **6:**781
ARNOLD, PAULA **10:**308
Arnold, Rachel P., *see* Lit, Rachel P.
Arnold, Robert F. **7:**451
Arnold, Stanley **2:**318
Arnold, Victor **15:**1056
Arnoldi, Michael **8:**22
Arnold of Vilanova, *see* ARNALDO OF VILLANOVA
Arnoldovich, Mikhail, *see* MILNER, MOSES MICHAEL
ARNON (riv., Transj.) **3:**486
- Moab **12:**191
- Moabite revolt **11:**1397
- papyrus **16:**658
- physiography **9:**164ff; **9:**178
- Transjordan **15:**1316
ARNON, DANIEL ISRAEL **3:**487
ARNONA (Rom. tax) **3:**487
Arnonah (sub., Jer.) **9:**1472
Arnovich, Morris **15:**301
ARNSTADT (city, Ger.) **3:**488
- Thuringia **15:**1128
ARNSTEIN (fam., Aus.) **3:**488
- banking **3:**894
- railroads **13:**1517ff
- title of nobility **15:**1166
Arnstein (fam., print.), *see* Frankel-Arnstein
Arnstein, Adam Isaac (Asher Anshel) **3:**489
- *illus:*
- - decree of appointment **5:**1008
Arnstein, Benedict David **3:**491
Arnstein, Fanny **3:**490
- Hofer, Andreas **8:**807
- salons **14:**708
Arnstein, Henrietta (Judith) **3:**490
Arnstein, Isaac Aaron **3:**489
Arnstein, Joseph Michael **3:**489
Arnstein, Karl **2:**321
- *illus:*
- - *Los Angeles,* U.S. Navy dirigible **2:**321
- - U.S. Navy decoration **2:**322
Arnstein, Mark **16:**151
Arnstein, Max B. **15:**1009
Arnstein, Nathan Adam **3:**490
- *illus:*
- - decree of barony **7:**46
ARNSTEIN, WALTER LEONARD **8:**544
Arnsteiner (fam. name), *see under* Arnstein
Arnswalde, Moses, *see* Philippson, Moses
Arnuwanda (Hittite k.) **8:**789
AROCH, ARIE **3:**491
- *illus:*
- - "The High Commissioner" Pl. 12 3-ART
AROER (city, Er. Isr.) **3:**492
- Arnon **3:**487
- Moabite revolt **11:**1397
Aroiio, Abraham ibn **13:**652
Arollia (fam.) **3:**492
- *see also:* ARBIB (fam.)
AROLLIA, ISAAC BEN MOSES **3:**492
ARON (fam., J. medal.) **3:**492
Aron, Abraham **3:**492; **11:**1165
Aron, Adolphe **11:**1562
Aron, Alexandre **4:**1100
Aron, Arnaud **7:**49
Aron, Emanuel, *see* EMANUEL
Aron, Esther, *see* Liebmann, Esther
Aron, Israel **12:**64
- Prussia **11:**225; **13:**1288
Aron, Philipp **3:**492
ARON, RAYMOND **3:**492
ARON, ROBERT **8:**544
Aron Czenstochower, *see* SYNGALOWSKI, ARON
Aron ha-Edut (wk.) **2:**551
ARONIUS, JULIUS **3:**493
Aron Kodesh (Holy Ark), *see* ARK
Aronova, Raisa **14:**479
ARONOVICH, YURI MIKHAYLOVICH **12:**681
Aronow, Donald **15:**312
Aronowicz, Józef **10:**201
Aronowitz, Abe **11:**1479
Aronowski, Eliezer **5:**1149
ARONS, LEO **3:**494
Aronsohn, Louis (polit.) **4:**1547
Aronsohn, Zalman Isaac, *see* ANOKHI, ZALMAN YIZḤAK
ARONSON, BORIS **3:**494
ARONSON, DAVID (r.) **3:**494
ARONSON, DAVID (art.) **3:**595
- *illus:*
- - "Sacrifice of Isaac" **3:**615
ARONSON, GRIGORI **3:**495
Aronson, Louis (bsmn.) **6:**903
Aronson, Max, *see* Anderson, Max
ARONSON, NAUM LVOVICH **3:**495
ARONSON, SOLOMON **3:**496
- Erez Israel **9:**893
Aroostook County (Maine) **11:**782
Aroti (fam.), *see* ROTE
Aroti, Isaac **14:**323
Arouet, François-Marie, *see* VOLTAIRE
Arovas, Moses **12:**959; **13:**629; **15:**1322
Arpa, Abramino dall' **3:**496
ARPA, ABRAMO DALL' **3:**496
Arpa, Giovanni Leonardo dall' **3:**496
Arpachshad (bib. fig.) **12:**884
ARPAD (city, Syr.) **3:**497
- Arameans **3:**255
ʿARRĀBA (vill., Isr.) **3:**497
ʿArrābat al-Baṭṭūf (vill., Isr.) **3:**231
ARRABY MOOR (tit.) **3:**497
- Lisbon **11:**299
- rabbi, rabbinate **13:**1447
- seals **14:**1079
- *illus:*
- - portrait **13:**922
ARRAGEL, MOSES **3:**498
Ar-Rakka (city, Syr.), *see* Callinicum
Arrapha (kdm.) **16:**1498
Arrebo, Anders **5:**1071
Arrest **13:**959
- Inquisition **8:**1400
ARRIAN (Arrianus, Flavius; hist.) **7:**892
Arricha de Tolvens (pseud.), *see* Hollaender, Victor
Arrogance, *see* ETHICS; HUMILITY
Arrow (weapon) **16:**266
ARROW CROSS PARTY (Hung.) **3:**499
- Budapest **4:**1453
Arrowsnake, *see Kippod*
ʿArrūb River (Er. Isr.) **9:**1540
Arrueti (fam.), *see* ROTE
Arrueti, Juce (Joseph) **14:**323
Arsaces (k., Arm.) **3:**399
Arsames (satrap, Egy.) **16:**659
Arṣay (deity) **6:**339
Arsene, Maria **14:**424
Arsenius (bp.) **6:**216
Arsham letters **16:**669
Arslan Tash (loc., Syr.) **16:**662; **16:**666
Arsuf (site), *see* Tells (Arshaf)
Arsur (city, Er. Isr.), *see* APOLLONIA
ART **3:**499
- *Contents:*
- - Antiquity to 1800 **3:**500
- - - Introduction **3:**500
- - - Biblical Period **3:**505
- - - First Temple **3:**505
- - - Second Temple **3:**506
- - - Post Fall of Jerusalem **3:**507
- - - Relation to Christian **3:**508
- - - Roman Empire **3:**521
- - - Under Islam **3:**521
- - - Northern Europe **3:**522
- - - Illuminated Manuscripts **3:**522
- - - Crafts **3:**523
- - - Renaissance **3:**523
- - - Ritual **3:**524
- - - Funerary **3:**535
- - - Printed Books **3:**538
- - - Revival of Manuscripts **3:**538
- - 18th Century **3:**539
- - Age of Emancipation **3:**540
- - 20th Century **3:**567
- - Concentration Camps **3:**568
- - Post World War II **3:**576
- - Modern Israel **3:**576
- - - Introduction **3:**576
- - - Bezalel School **3:**576
- - - Tower of David Exhibition **3:**591
- - - 1923-1945 **3:**591
- - - New Horizons **3:**592
- - - Painters **3:**592
- - Investigation of **3:**593
- - Capsules **3:**594
- General
- - Bet Alfa mosaics **4:**710
- - Bezalel art academy **4:**788
- - Bible in **4:**937
- - collectors, dealers **3:**647
- - Dura-Europos **6:**276
- - *ecclesia et synagoga* **6:**346
- - folklore **6:**1389
- - Hellenistic period **8:**293; **8:**300; **15:**568
- - historians, critics **3:**649
- - image of Jew **8:**669
- - Israel **9:**1009
- - Jewish contributions **8:**743
- - Mesopotamia **16:**1486
- - Paris School **13:**112
- - Phoenicia **13:**479
- - synagogue destruction **15:**585
- - Yemenite Jews **16:**755ff
- Themes
- - anthropomorphism **3:**57
- - Jerusalem **9:**1578
- - lion **11:**275ff
- - Passover in **13:**172
- - tombstones **15:**1221
- Forms
- - bibles **4:**942; **4:**950
- - book covers **4:**1230
- - bookplates **4:**1219
- - caricatures **5:**171
- - cartoons **5:**215
- - ceremonial **5:**288
- - *Haggadot,* illuminated **7:**1095
- - heraldry **8:**334
- - iconography **8:**1216
- - illuminated manuscripts **8:**1257
- - *ketubbot* **10:**930
- - medals **11:**1165; **11:**1168
- - *menorah* **11:**1355,1368
- - *mizraḥ* plaques **12:**181
- - paper-cuts **13:**60
- - pillar motif **13:**523
- - portal **13:**905
- - sculpture **14:**1059
- - spice-box **7:**1482ff
- - tombs, ancient **9:**1532
- *illus:* text
- *illus:* Biblical Themes
- - Aaron
- - - Aaron's Rod **3:***fcg.* 524
- - - ceremonial object motif **3:**542; **4:**244,1232,1339; **5:**296; **7:**1307
- - - confronting Pharaoh **2:**952
- - - distributing manna **11:**885
- - - episodes **12:***fcg.* 427
- - - folk-art portrait **8:**1286
- - - *Kaufmann Haggadah* **8:**1275
- - - lighting the *Menorah* **11:***fcg.* 1355
- - - Mount Sinai **2:***fcg* 11
- - - performing miracle **12:**379
- - - pouring oil into the *menorah* **8:***fcg.* 1271
- - - priesthood vestments **6:**277
- - - supporting hands of Moses **2:**788; **12:**382
- - - *Venice Haggadah* **10:**211
- - - watching battle with Amalek **14:**1258
- - Abel and Cain **2:**58; **5:**21-23; **6:**980; **8:**1271
- - Abigail **12:**736
- - - bearing gifts to David **3:**527
- - Abimelech espying Isaac and Rebekah **9:**3
- - Abimelech slaying his brothers **9:**1342
- - Abraham
- - - "Abraham and Isaac" (etch., Rembrandt) **9:**3
- - - "Abraham Looking at the Stars" (E. M. Lilien) Fig. 86 3-ART
- - - "Abraham's Bosom" **2:**166
- - - cast into fire by Nimrod **2:**118; **8:**1217; **12:**1166
- - - ceremonial object motif **4:**1231, 1339
- - - covenant with God **5:**1014,1016
- - - death **5:**1421
- - - Dura-Europos painting **6:**283
- - - Melchizedek **2:**122; **9:**1552; **11:**1288
- - - sacrifice of Isaac **2:**120,121,480-486; **3:**511, 615; **4:**244, 880, 1231, 1339; **6:**285; **8:**1272,1286; **15:**673
- - - sending Hagar away (Rembrandt) **7:**1075,1076
- - - separation from Lot **11:**507
- - - telling Sarah of command to sacrifice Isaac **4:**880
- - - the three angels **3:**544; **4:**938 **8:**1031; **14:**867
- - Absalom
- - - death of **2:**175
- - - mourned by David **5:**1326
- - Achan, stoning of **8:**346
- - Adam
- - - "Adam" (sculp., Rodin) **14:**267

– – – Bamberg cathedral sculpture **4:**939
– – – "Creation of Adam" (Michelangelo) **5:**1068
– – – creation of Eve **4:**874
– – – death of **2:**247
– – – expulsion from Paradise **6:**981
– – – in Islamic mss. **2:**237; **4:**941; **6:**981
– – – in Paradise **2:**237,242,243; **4:**856,941,1050
– – – naming the animals **6:**981
– – – Seth's birth **14:**1191
– – – story of Adam and Eve **6:**980; **8:**1271
– – "Adoration of the Golden Calf" (Poussin) **7:**709; **8:**1233
– – Agag slain by Samuel **2:**341
– – Ahab
– – – castigated by Elijah **12:**747
– – – ivory house **3:**315, 337, 503; **5:**397, 1227
– – – Jezebel giving advice **10:**100
– – – speaking to Naboth **10:**100
– – Ahasuerus and Esther **2:**453; **6:**284,907,909; **12:**733
– – Ai, battle **10:**269
– – *Akedah* **2:**120,121,480-486; **3:**511, 615; **4:**244, 880, 1231, 1339; **6:**285; **8:**1272,1286; **11:***fcg.* 1355; **15:**673
– – – ceremonial object motif **4:**244,1231,1339; **11:**265
– – – Islamic version **2:**120
– – Altar (in illum. mss.) **2:**58 **3:***fcg.* 524, *fcg.* 988; **4:**127; **7:**100
– – Amaziah the priest **12:**1293
– – Amnon and Tamar **2:**860; **8:**1317
– – Amon (Egy. deity) **2**:864
– – Amos the shepherd **2:**880
– – Angels
– – – *Akedah* **11:***fcg.* 1355; **15:**673
– – – as Jacob's messengers **2:**956
– – – barring Balaam's way **2:**974; **4:**122; **16:**685
– – – calling to Moses **12:***fcg.* 427
– – – leading Moses to Mt. Sinai **2:**965
– – – ordering Abraham to sacrifice Isaac **4:**880
– – – Sodom and Gomorrah **15:**71
– – – visiting Abraham **3:**544; **4:**938
– – – watching over Shadrach, Meshach and Abed-nego **2:**960
– – – Zipporah circumcising **16:**1182
– – Ark of the Covenant **3:**461-462, 517, *fcg.* 524; **5:**138, 1018; **6:**277, 284, 291; **7:** *fcg.* 1131; **8:**1235; **9:**1582; **10:**264; **11:**72
– – – carried into battle against Philistines **14:**781
– – – ceremonial object motif **4:**1339
– – Ark of Moses **3:**466
– – Ark of Noah **3:**467; **5:**1346; **6:**980; **7:**434; **12:**1192-1197
– – Asenath and Joseph **3:**693
– – Asher, banner and emblem **8:**335
– – Asherah figurine **3:**704
– – Ashkelon, conquest by Ramses II **3:**715
– – Asmodeus carrying Sarah **3:**754
– – Astarte **3:**318,504,738
– – "Athaliah's Downfall" (A. Coypel) **3:**815
– – Azazel (15th cent. ms.) **3:**1000
– – Baal
– – – Baal of the lightning **4:**8
– – – prophets of **6:**289
– – Babylonian exiles bewailing their lot (Elkan) **6:**1037,1039
– – Balaam
– – – holding an astrolabe **3:**787
– – – meeting the angel **2:**974; **4:**122
– – – riding on ass **16:**685
– – – seven altars of Balak **4:**127
– – Balak's seven altars **4:**127
– – Banners with tribe emblems **4:**181
– – Bath-Sheba
– – – "Bat-Sheba at the Fountain" (Rubens) **4:**322
– – – espied by David **4:**321
– – Behemoth **4:**360, 394, *fcg.* 907
– – Belshazzar's feast **4:**449; **5:**1278; **11:**1349
– – Benjamin
– – – birth **4:**523
– – – brought before Joseph **10:**207
– – – Chagall's stained glass window **4:**526
– – – entrusted to Judah **4:**524; **10:**329
– – Ben Sira holding his Book **4:**551
– – Bezalel
– – – inspired by hand of God **4:**787
– – – stretching hides for Tabernacle **4:**786
– – Bithiah with the infant Moses **4:**1059
– – "bitter water" administered to adulterous woman **15:**171
– – Boaz
– – – Ruth and Naomi :1154; **9:**1
– – – Ruth in tent of **14:**520
– – Burning Bush **4:**1529; **5:**1448; **12:**373,379, *fcg.* 427
– – Cain
– – – killed by Lamech **5:**25; **10:**1365
– – – the killing of Abel **2:**58; **5:**21-23; **6:**980
– – – the rejected offering **2:**58
– – Cedars of Lebanon **5:**268
– – ceremonial objects, biblical themes **3:**451-453,531,542,627; **4:**244,374,1231, 1339-1344; **5:**296, *fcg.* 299, 300, 302, 661, 1035, 1042, 1058, 1381,1385,1444,1445,1448; **6:**1391; **7:**170,611, *fcg* 1259, 1295, 1297, 1300, 1301, 1307, 1309, 1346, 1485; **11:**265-270, 1475; **12:**1385; **14:**564,1420-1421,1649; **15:**1256,1257
– – Chedorlaomer's wars **5:**370
– – Cherubim **4:**787; **5:**397-400; **7:***fcg.* 1131; **8:**1235
– – Copper Serpent **5:**958
– – Cozbi slain by Phinehas **13:**467; **16:**1027
– – "Creation of Adam" (Michelangelo) **5:**1068
– – Creation of Man **2:**43; **4:**874; **5:**1062,1068
– – Creation of the World **5:**1062, 1066, *fcg.* 1067, *fcg.* 1070; **13:**574
– – Dagon temple and the Ark **6:**284
– – Dan
– – – emblem **5:**1258; **12:***fcg.* 1259
– – Daniel **5:**1280
– – – "Daniel in the Lions' Den" (Rubens) **5:**1283
– – – "Daniel's Vision" (Rembrandt) **5:**1287
– – – Susanna and the elders **15:**533
– – – the winged lion **5:**1217
– – Dathan and Abiram **5:**1311
– – David
– – – admonished by Nathan **12:**846
– – – anointed by Samuel **3:**28,30; **6:**285,1125; **12:**1351; **14:**793
– – – approaching Jesus **15:**1497
– – – Bath-Sheba, Uriah and Nathan **11:**633
– – – *Bohum Psalter* **14:**541
– – – bringing the Ark to Jerusalem **6:**288
– – – crowned and sceptered **5:**1336
– – – "David's Entry into Jerusalem" (Gobelin; Chagall) **5:***fcg.* 334
– – – death **10:**106
– – – entering the house of the Lord **13:**1304
– – – espying Bath-Sheba **4:**321
– – – folk-art portrait **8:**1286
– – – hiding from Saul **13:**1326
– – – in Islamic ms. **5:**1334
– – – Jonathan and **7:**196
– – – Michal being promised to **11:**1493
– – – mourning death of Absalom **5:**1326
– – – playing the harp before Saul **14:**911
– – – playing the lyre **4:**947; **7:**341
– – – praying to God **4:**321
– – – refraining from killing Saul **6:**293
– – – Saul and David greeted with songs and dances **5:**1263
– – – scorning fool **6:**1
– – – slaying Goliath **4:**1; **5:**1326,1330; **7:**757; **8:**1283; **14:**793
– – – slaying 200 Philistines **11:**1493
– – Deborah Pl. 2 **10**-KETUBBAH
– – Delilah cutting off Samson's hair **5:**1473
– – "Deluge" (Michelangelo) **6:**1353
– – Dinah abducted by Shechem **6:**56
– – *Duda'im* (18th cent. engr.) **4:**257
– – Eben-Ezer, battle at **6:**292
– – *'Eglah 'arufah* ceremony **6:**476
– – Egypt
– – – brickmaking (fresco, Thebes) **3:**311
– – – Exodus **6:**281,1045, *fcg.* 1067; **7:**119, 1084
– – – Israelite male children thrown into the Nile **7:**1084
– – – Semitic nomads **3:**311
– – – taskmaster **4:***fcg.* 1067
– – – working in the fields **2:**377, 385
– – Ehud stabbing Eglon **10:**447
– – Eldad and Medad **6:**575
– – Eli
– – – instructing the child Samuel **6:**614
– – – woken by Samuel **14:**781
– – Elijah
– – – Ahaziah's men **6:**636
– – – castigating Ahab **12:**747
– – – fed by the ravens **6:**633
– – – heralding Messiah **6:**863; **11:**1409-1412
– – – humiliating prophets of Baal **6:**289
– – – in Islamic ms. **6:**639
– – – reviving the widow's dead child **6:**283
– – Elisha
– – – mocking boys and the bears **6:**666
– – – Naaman **10:**1021
– – Elkanah and his family **6:**676; **7:**1270
– – Enoch, Death turning away **6:**793
– – Ephod, high priest's **6:**805; **7:**100
– – Ephraim
– – – emblem **12:***fcg.* 1259
– – – Manasseh and, birth of **6:**808
– – – Manasseh and, blessed by Jacob **6:**281, 809; **7:**1084
– – Esarhaddon stele **6:**853
– – Esau
– – – birth of **6:**859; **13:**1602
– – – burying Isaac **3:**515
– – – the hunter **13:**1602
– – – Jacob and, in Islamic ms. **6:**858
– – – Jacob and Esau story **6:**855
– – – selling his birthright **4:**943; **6:**859
– – Esther
– – – Ahasuerus and **2:**453; **6:**284,907,909
– – – eighteenth cent. *ketubbah* Pl. 2 **10**-KETUBBAH
– – – scenes from Book of **6:**911
– – – twelfth century Bible **12:**733
– – Eve **4:**939; **6:**984
– – – Adam and, story of **6:**980-982
– – – creation of **2:**243; **4:**874
– – – in Islamic mss. **2:**237; **4:**941; **6:**981
– – – Seth's birth **14:**1191
– – Exodus from Egypt **6:**281, 1045, *fcg.* 1067; **7:**119, 1084, *fcg.* 1195; **11:**1532
– – Expulsion from Paradise **6:**981
– – Ezekiel
– – – first vision **6:**1084
– – – the resurrection **3:**515; **4:**945; **6:**291,1093,1096
– – Ezra the Scribe **6:**1105
– – – holding a scroll **8:**1149
– – – kneeling before Darius **5:**1304
– – – reading the Torah **6:**286,384
– – Firstborn, redemption of **4:**409; **6:**1309
– – First Fruit offering **4:**993; **6:**1313
– – Flogging (18th cent. engr.) **6:**1349
– – Garden of Eden **2:**243; **4:**856,1050
– – Gaza, "City of Samson" (16th cent. ms.) **7:**342
– – Gedaliah "In Charge of the House", seal **7:**351
– – Gibeah, concubine of (13th cent. ms.) **5:**863
– – Gideon selecting soldiers **7:**559
– – Gilgal and the twelve stones **7:**572
– – Giving of the Law **2:***fspc.* **3:***fcg.* 907 **4:**430; **5:**1436-1438; **7:***fcg.* 875, *fcg.* 1131; **8:**1218; **14:***fcg.* 1323
– – God
– – – appearing to Jacob **3:**52; **4:**730
– – – appearing to young Samuel **3:**54
– – – casting Satan down **2:**970
– – – covenant with Abraham **5:**1014,1016
– – – creating man **2:**43; **4:**874; **5:**1068
– – – creating the world **5:**1066, *fcg.* 1067, *fcg.* 1070
– – – giving the law to Moses **5:**1436-1438
– – – rejecting Cain's offering **2:**58
– – – Samuel called by **14:**781
– – – talking to Melchizedek **14:**1266
– – Gog and Magog, a warrior **6:**863
– – Golden Calf **7:**709
– – Golden Table **5:**398; **14:**139
– – Goliath slain by David **4:**1; **5:**1326,1330; **7:**757; **8:**1283; **14:**793
– – Habakkuk **7:**1015
– – – transportation to Babylon **7:**1018
– – Hagar
– – – in the wilderness **9:**81
– – – sent away by Abraham **7:**1075,1076
– – Haggai prophesying **7:**1113
– – *ḥaliẓah* ceremony **11:**123; **16:**776
– – Haman
– – – hanging of **10:**1313; **12:**733
– – – leading Mordecai on the horse **6:**283; **7:**1223; **12:**308
– – – sons, hanged **13:**64; **14:**1049
– – Hannah, mother of Samuel **6:**676; **7:**1270
– – Harvesting (Egy. paint.) **2:**385
– – *Ḥerem* of Jericho **8:**346

– – Hezekiah **8:**451
– – – Sennacherib's campaign **3:**319; **5:**213
– – – warned by Isaiah **9:**68
– – High Priest **8:**473
– – – burning frankincense **7:**100
– – – wearing the ephod **6:**805; **7:**100
– – Hittite art (Beth Shean) **3:**503
– – Hoeing (Egy. fresco) **2:**377
– – Hur and Aaron supporting hands of Moses **2:**788; **12:**382; **14:**1258
– – Idol Worship **3:**981
– – Isaac
– – – about to be sacrificed **2:**121
– – – "Abraham and Isaac" (etch., Rembrandt) **9:**3
– – – blessing Esau **6:**856
– – – blessing Jacob **13:**1602
– – – death **3:**515
– – – espied by Abimelech with Rebekah **9:**3
– – – "Isaac Blessing Jacob" (drg., Rembrandt) **9:**6
– – – marriage to Rebekah **13:**1601
– – – reaping the hundredfold harvest **4:**486
– – – sacrifice of **2:**120, 121, 480-486; **3:**511, 615; **4:**244, 880, 1231, 1339; **6:**285; **8:**1272,1286
– – Isaiah **9:**45
– – – fourteenth cent. ms. **9:**57
– – – prophesying to Hezekiah **8:**451; **9:**68
– – Ishmael
– – – in the wilderness **9:**81
– – – Islamic version of the *Akedah* **2:**120
– – Israelite male children thrown into the Nile **7:**1084
– – Israelites' battle with Amalek **14:**1258
– – Issachar, tribe (Chagall's stained glass window) **9:**1077
– – Jacob
– – – at the deathbed of Isaac **3:**515
– – – at the deathbed of Rachel **4:**523
– – – Benjamin taken to Egypt **10:**329
– – – birth of **6:**859; **13:**1602
– – – blessing his sons **6:**281; **9:**1208
– – – blessing Joseph's sons **6:**281, 809; **7:**1084; **14:**67
– – – blessing Pharaoh **7:**1084
– – – confronting Laban **10:**1316
– – – death and burial of **3:**516; **5:**1423; **7:**1084
– – – dream at Beth-El **3:**52, 636; **4:**244; **6:**291; **8:**1286; **9:**1193,1205; **13:**63
– – – embraced by Laban **10:**1074
– – – entrusting Benjamin to Judah **4:**524
– – – Esau and, in Islamic ms. **6:**858
– – – going down to Egypt **7:**1001
– – – Isaac blessing Jacob (drg. Rembrandt) **9:**6
– – – Islamic depiction **9:**1203
– – – "Jacob by the Well" (paint., Lorenzo Lippi) **9:**1197
– – – "Jacob's dream" (paint., Ribera) **9:**1205
– – – "Jacob Wrestling with the Angel" (paint., Rembrandt) **9:**1199
– – – Joseph telling his dreams **10:**204, 215
– – – journey to Beth-El **4:**730
– – – leading household across Jabbok river **9:**1171
– – – meeting Rachel **13:**1487
– – – meeting with Esau **6:**854, 858
– – – mourning Joseph's death **10:**206
– – – reunion with Joseph **13:**1103
– – – the scholar **13:**1602
– – – sending messengers to Esau **2:**956
– – – sons **9:**1202
– – – wrestling with the angel **4:**949
– – Jael slaying Sisera **9:**1247; **14:**1622
– – Jehu paying tribute to Shalmaneser III **3:**320
– – Jephthah story **9:**1342
– – Jeremiah **3:***fcg.* 575; **4:**940; **9:**1353, 1358; **10:**1
– – – mourning Jerusalem **9:**1349; **13:**1417
– – Jericho, capture of **3:**517; **9:**1369; **10:**264
– – Jeroboam **10:**1028
– – – golden calves **9:**1373
– – Jethro's daughters (frsc., Botticelli) **10:**18
– – Jewish gold glass **7:***fcg.* 619 and 622
– – Jezebel
– – – advising Ahab **10:**100
– – – stoning of Naboth **12:**747
– – Joab slain at the altar **10:**106
– – Job **4:**934,1184; **6:**337; **10:**112-28
– – – comforters **15:**1522
– – – wealth of **10:***fcg.* 107
– – Joel the Prophet **4:**64; **10:**133
– – Jonah
– – – beside the walls of Nineveh **12:**1169
– – – "Jonah Preaching to the Ninevites" (U. Birnbaum) **4:**1043
– – – story of **10:**170-77
– – – the whale **4:**966; **5:**369; Pl. 9 **10**-KETUBBAH; **11:**90; **15:**1
– – Jonathan
– – – David and **7:**196
– – – fighting the Philistines **4:**879
– – – various episodes **10:**184
– – Joseph
– – – Asenath and **3:**693; **10:**223
– – – Benjamin brought by brothers **10:**207
– – – binding of Simeon **14:**1550
– – – brothers of Joseph **6:**281; **10:**207, 210
– – – dream of the sheaves **6:**209; **10:**204
– – – in prison **2:**364
– – – interpreting the dreams of the cupbearer and the baker **5:**1172; **10:**206
– – – interpreting Pharaoh's dream **6:**211; **8:**1218; **13:**363
– – – Islamic depiction **9:**1203; **10:**214
– – – "Joseph Telling His Dreams" (etch., Rembrandt) **10:**215
– – – Judeo-Persian ms. (15th cent.) **10:**434
– – – Potiphar's wife **13:**354,934
– – – "Potiphar's Wife Accusing Joseph" (engr., van Leyden) **10:**217
– – – remains carried across Red Sea **7:**211
– – – repulsing Potiphar's wife Pl. 2 **10**-KETUBBAH
– – – rescued by Ishmaelites **9:**88
– – – reunion with Jacob **13:**1103
– – – sold into slavery **13:**354
– – – story of **6:**944; **10:**206
– – – telling his dreams **6:**209; **10:**204
– – Joshua
– – – at Mount Sinai **7:***fcg.* 1131
– – – building an altar on Mount Ebal **5:**1020
– – – capture of Jericho **10:**264
– – – meeting captain of the Lord of Hosts **10:**267
– – – Moses **10:**266
– – Josiah, burial **10:**289
– – Jubal (Giotto and Pisano) **10:**323
– – Judah
– – – Benjamin taken to Egypt **10:**329
– – – Benjamin taken under Judah's protection **4:**524
– – – emblem **12:***fcg.* 1259
– – – "King Judah" (Levin) **10:**331
– – Kinneret, Lake of (W. R. Wilson) **15:**1134
– – Korah, Dathan and Abiram **5:**1311; **10:**1191
– – Laban and Jacob **4:**949; **10:**1074,1316
– – Lachish, siege (rlf., Nineveh) **3:**319; **5:**590
– – Lamech killing Cain **5:**25; **10:**1365
– – Leah
– – – given in marriage to Jacob **4:**949
– – – Jacob, and their four sons **10:**1526
– – Leviathan **4:**360, 394, *fcg.* 907
– – Lot
– – – "Drunken Lot" **14:**67
– – – made drunk by his daughters **6:**240
– – – separation from Abraham **11:**507
– – – taken into captivity **5:**370
– – Machpelah, Cave of **5:**58; **6:**1385
– – Malachi **11:**814
– – Manna Jar (*First Leningrad Bible*) **3:***fcg.* 524
– – Manasseh
– – – Ephraim and, birth of **6:**808
– – – Ephraim and, blessed by Jacob **6:**281, 809; **7:**1084
– – Manna and Quail **7:***fcg.* 875
– – Melchizedek
– – – God talking with **14:**1266
– – – meeting with Abraham **2:**122; **9:**1552; **11:**1288
– – *Menorah* **2:**642; **3:**66, *fcg.* 524; **4:**977; **6:** 277, 285, 743; **8:**1274,1275; **11:**1355-1366
– – – ceremonial object motif **2:**913; **3:**452; **4:**244,1340; **5:**296,1035
– – Michal
– – – being promised to David **11:**1493
– – – David and **14:**541
– – Miriam dancing **12:**83; **13:**166
– – Moloch, human sacrifice **8:**1237
– – Mordecai
– – – led on horse by Haman **6:**283; **7:**1223
– – – on the king's horse **12:**308
– – – triumph of **12:**994
– – Moses
– – – Aaron and, before Pharaoh **2:**952
– – – Aaron and Hur supporting hands **2:**788; **12:**382
– – – ark of Moses, making of **3:**466
– – – blessing children of Israel **12:**386
– – – blessing Phinehas **13:**467
– – – the burning bush **4:**1529; **6:**282; **12:**373,379
– – – ceremonial object motif **3:**542; **4:**244
– – – death **5:**1426
– – – dividing the waters **6:**281
– – – Dura-Europos painting **6:**283
– – – episodes **12:***fcg.* 427
– – – facing Korah, Dathan and Abiram **5:**1311; **10:**1191
– – – finding of **12:**407
– – – folk-art portrait **8:**1286
– – – found by Pharaoh's daughter **6:**285
– – – handing down the Law **5:**1441; **8:**1218; Pl. 5 **10**-KETUBBAH
– – – holding the Decalogue **12:**400
– – – in the bulrushes **4:**932
– – – infant Moses before Pharaoh **4:**1059
– – – Joshua and **10:**266
– – – *Kaufmann Haggadah* **8:**1275
– – – killing the Egyptian **12:**410
– – – led by angel to Mt. Sinai **2:**965
– – – ordeal by fire **12:**395
– – – ordering the return of the waters **6:**1045
– – – Pisano's statue of **12:**406
– – – Plagues of Egypt **13:**605-610
– – – pointing at the Torah **4:**1161
– – – providing water in the desert **6:***fcg.* 302
– – – putting the Tablets of the Law into the Ark **5:**1018
– – – reading the Torah **6:**286
– – – receiving the Tablets of the Law **2:***fcg.* 11; **4:**430; **5:**1436–1438; **12:**376; **14:**1597
– – – teaching the Ten Commandments **12:**1
– – – *Venice Haggadah* **10:**211
– – – watching battle with Amalek **14:**1258
– – Mount of Ebal, Joshua's altar **5:**1020
– – Mount of Olives (primitivist) **4:**115; **13:**513
– – Mount Sinai **2:***fcg.* 11, 965; **4:**430; **5:**59; **14:**1597
– – Naaman
– – – bathing in the Jordan **11:**34
– – – before Elisha **10:**1021
– – Nabal and Abigail **12:**736
– – Naboth
– – – listening to Ahab **10:**100
– – – stoning of **12:**747
– – Nadab and Abihu **12:**750
– – Naomi
– – – Naomi, Ruth and Boaz **9:**1
– – – Naomi in the field of Boaz **4:**1154
– – – Ruth and **12:**818
– – Nathan
– – – admonishing David **12:**846
– – – David and Bath-sheba **11:**633
– – – reassuring David **12:**846
– – Nebuchadnezzar
– – – Blake's watercolor **12:**918
– – – riding a lion **12:**916
– – Nehemiah **12:**937
– – Nephilim **12:**963
– – Nimrod
– – – Abraham delivered to **2:**118
– – – fiery furnace **2:**120; **12:**1166
– – Nineveh **12:**1169
– – Noah
– – – leaving the ark **6:**980
– – – lying drunk and naked **6:**238; **7:**1217; **9:**1285; **12:**1196
– – – "Noah and the Ark" (J. David) **5:**1346
– – – offering a sacrifice **12:**885
– – – rainbow **13:**1525
– – – the returning dove **6:**184
– – – Shem and Japheth covering drunken father **14:**1369
– – – supervising building of the ark **12:**1192
– – Oholiab building the Tabernacle **4:**787
– – "Orpah the Moabite" (Abel Pann) Fig.88 3-ART
– – Paradise **2:**237, 242, 243; **4:**360, 856, 874, *fcg.* 907, 941, 1050; **5:**1062; **6:**980–984; **7:**325; **8:**1271
– – Passover lamb **13:**165
– – Pharaoh
– – – baker and cupbearer **5:**1172
– – – bathing in Hebrew's blood

13:360
- - - dream of the seven cows **13:**361
- - - Joseph interpreting dream of **6:**211
- - - Moses and Aaron **2:**952; **4:**1059; **12:***fcg.* 427
- - - sending the Israelites out of Egypt **2:**952; **6:**1045
- - - Shiphrah and Puah **6:**285
- - Philistines
- - - ark carried into battle against **14:**781
- - - David fighting **11:**1493
- - - female deity **3:**696
- - - returning the Ark of the Covenant **3:**461
- - Phinehas slaying Zimri and Cozbi **13:**467; **16:**1027
- - Pilgrimage to Jerusalem **7:**1116
- - Pillar of Fire **6:**1303
- - Pithom and Ramses **13:**1544
- - Plagues of Egypt **2:**952; **6:**1045,1369; **7:**205; **11:**423; **13:**605-612
- - Plants of Palestine (rlf., Karnak) **2:**385
- - Potiphar's wife **2:**364; **10:**206, 214, 217, 434, Pl. 2 **10**-KETTUBAH; **13:**934
- - Priestly Vestments (12th cent. ms.) **4:**786
- - Priests performing the sacrifice **3:***fcg.* 988
- - "Prophet at Night" (Ben-Zion) (paint.) **4:**574
- - Purim scenes **8:**649
- - Queen of Sheba meeting Solomon **13:**1425; **15:**103
- - Rachel
- - - death **4:**523
- - - given in marriage to Jacob **4:**949
- - - meeting Jacob **13:**1487
- - - Nice portrayal **12:**1135
- - Rahab and two Israelite spies **13:**1514
- - Rebekah
- - - birth of Jacob and Esau **13:**1602
- - - espied by Abimelech **9:**3
- - - giving birth to Esau and Jacob **4:**943
- - - marriage to Isaac **13:**1601
- - - "Rebekah and Eliezer" (Murillo) **6:**619
- - "Redemption of the Firstborn" (B. Picart) **6:**1309
- - Red heifer **14:***fcg.* 11
- - - burning of **13:**87
- - Rehoboam **14:**43
- - Resurrection of the Bones **3:**515; **4:**945; **6:**291, 1093, 1096
- - Reuben
- - - asking Jacob to allow Benjamin to go to Egypt **14:**105
- - - emblem **12:***fcg.* 1259
- - Ritual immersion **15:**1033
- - Ruth
- - - Boaz and Naomi **9:**1
- - - gleaning in the fields of Boaz **4:**1154; **14:**520
- - - in tent of Boaz **14:**520
- - - Naomi and **12:**818
- - Sabbatical year **14:**1392
- - "Sacrifice of Ishmael" (15th cent.) **2:**482
- - Sacrificial animals **6:**277
- - Samson
- - - killing Philistines **14:**775
- - - rending the lion **14:**772
- - - "Samson and Delilah" (Mantegna) **5:**1473
- - - Solomon J. Solomon's painting **15:**118
- - - with the gates of Gaza **7:**1088
- - Samuel
- - - anointing David **3:**28,30; **6:**285,1125; **12:**1351; **14:**793
- - - asleep next to the Ark **14:**781
- - - Eli **6:**614
- - - God appearing to **3:**54
- - - slaying Agag **2:**341
- - Sarah
- - - carried by Asmodeus **3:**754
- - - in entrance to tent **14:**867
- - - preparing food for the angels **4:**938
- - - told of the command to sacrifice Isaac **4:**880
- - Satan
- - - departing from the Lord to smite Job **14:**903
- - - fall from heaven **2:**970
- - - tempting Adam and Eve **6:**981
- - Saul
- - - David and, greeted with songs and dances **5:**1263
- - - David playing the harp **14:**911
- - - death of **7:**567
- - - in the wilderness of Ziph **6:**294
- - - promising Michal to David **11:**1493
- - - sending messengers after David **7:**229
- - - suicide of **14:**915
- - - threatening David with spear **7:**196
- - Scapegoat cast over the cliff **3:**1000
- - Semitic clan in Egypt (19th cent. B.C.E.) **3:**311
- - Sennacherib's campaign against Hezekiah **3:**319; **5:**213
- - Serpent tempting Eve **2:**242; **4:**856,1050
- - Seth
- - - at Adam's deathbed **2:**247
- - - birth of **14:**1191
- - Shadrach, Meshach, and Abed-nego in fiery furnace **2:**960; **14:**1256
- - Shiphrah and Puah before Pharaoh **6:**285
- - *Shofar,* blowing the **3:**834; **5:**1524; **7:**468; **14:**1444
- - Sihon's defeat **2:**878
- - Simeon
- - - binding of **14:**1550
- - - Levi, and, avenging Dinah **7:**1250
- - Sisera slain by Jael **9:**1247
- - Six Days of Creation (17th cent. Arm. Bible) **5:***fcg.* 1070
- - Sodom and Gomorrah **15:**71
- - Sodom men calling upon Lot **4:**943
- - Solomon
- - - entering Jerusalem **10:**1024
- - - enthroned **2:**355; **5:**1
- - - folk-art portrait **8:**1286
- - - holding a Bible **6:**351
- - - holding scepter **16:**901
- - - in Islamic ms. **5:**1334
- - - the judgment **3:**527; **4:**968; **5:**1130; **8:***fcg.* 1271; **11:***fcg.* 683 and 1355; **13:**354,1269; **14:**1061; **15:**103
- - - minstrel **15:**99
- - - Queen of Sheba **13:**1425; **15:**103
- - *Sukkah* **15:**495
- - Susanna and the Elders **3:**184; **15:**533,534
- - Tabernacle
- - - animals brought for sacrifice **16:**1003
- - - Bezalel stretching hides for **4:**786
- - - building of **4:**787
- - - implements **3:***fcg.* 524; **4:**957, 963, 977; **6:***fcg.* 1195; **8:**1275
- - - sacrifice of birds **10:**1037
- - Tablets of the Law handed to Moses **2:***fcg.* 11; **3:***fcg.* 555; **4:**430
- - Tamar, rape of **2:**860; **8:**1317
- - Temple
- - - Ark of the Covenant **3:**462; **6:**277
- - - attacked by Nebuchadnezzar's army **15:**985
- - - daily sacrifices **15:**786
- - - Day of Atonement service **16:**845
- - - eighteenth cent. engraving **11:**1505
- - - medieval depictions **9:**1581,1582
- - - Mount **4:**115
- - - payment of half-shekel tax **14:**1346
- - - Perugino's painting **9:**1585
- - - sacrifices brought to **13:**327
- - - Samaritan depiction of vessels **14:**739
- - - seventeenth cent. engraving **15:**984
- - - twelfth cent. illumination **15:**987
- - - weighing of shekels **11:***fcg.* 619
- - Temptation of Adam and Eve **2:**242; **4:**856,1050; **6:**981
- - Terah delivering Abraham to Nimrod **2:**118
- - Tithing of Produce **5:**1487
- - Tobias
- - - finding himself blind **16:**689
- - - "Return of Tobias" (M. Oppenheim) **15:**1185
- - - "Tobit and the Angel Raphael" (Pollaiuolo) **15:**1184
- - Tower of Babel **4:**23,24,27
- - Tribes' Emblems **4:**181
- - "Universal Peace" (J. L. Butensky) **4:**1538
- - *Urim* and *Thummim* **6:**112
- - War chariots, Egyptian and Assyrian **5:**211-214
- - Zechariah **16:**954
- - - vision **2:2642; 16:***fcg.* 935
- - Zimri slain by Phinehas **13:**467; **16:**1027
- - Zipporah **12:***fcg.* 427
- - - circumcising sons **16:**1182
- - - *see also:* ARCHAEOLOGY; BIBLE; ILLUMINATED MANUSCRIPTS; Mosaics
- *illus:* Book Illustrations
- - children's literature **5:**430-458
- - "Climax" (A. Beardsley) **6:**775
- - "Dodie the Innkeeper" (A. Kaplan) **10:**748
- - *Ḥad Gadya* (J. Steinhardt) **7:**1050
- - *Haggadah* (S. Raskin) **6:**504, 1037
- - H.M.S. "*Pinafore*" (L. Corcos) **3:**620
- - *In the Wilderness* (A. Appelfeld) **3:**223
- - *Ivanhoe,* Rebecca (S.A. Hart) **6:**779
- - *Jerusalem* (W. Blake) **4:**1070
- - *Job of Mr. Green* **14:**490
- - *Khurbn Vilne* (1947) **10:**659
- - *Les Tireurs de Langue* (P. Alechinsky) **2:**553
- - longing for Zion (S. Raskin) **6:**1037
- - *Ma'aseh Tuviyyah* **3:**804; **5:**983; **7:**416, 419
- - "Man Like Me Won't Flee" (J. Budko) **3:***fcg.* 575
- - *Merchant of Venice* **14:**1262
- - *Meshal ha-Kadmoni* **3:**19,534, 791; **5:**430; **6:**1128
- - *Mishlei Shu'alim* **4:**597; **5:**431
- - *Oliver Twist,* Mr. Fagin (G. Cruikshank) **6:**781
- - Psalms, 126 (Saul Raskin) **6:**103f
- - Rabbi of Bacharach (J. Budko) **4:**45
- - *Salomé,* the dance (A. Beardsley) **6:**775
- - *Shirei Yeladim* (L. Pasternak) **12:**659
- - Sholem Aleichem, Gorshman's illustration **14:**1469
- - *Siḥat Ḥulin* (E. Lissitzky) **4:**1392
- - Song of Songs **15:**145,149
- - "The Warden" (J. Kramer) **10:**1237
- - *see also:* BIBLE; BOOKPLATES; BOOKS; HAGGADAH, PASSOVER; ILLUMINATED MANUSCRIPTS; MAḤZOR; PRINTING, HEBREW
- *illus:* Fine Art
- - "Acolo" (V. Brauner) **4:**1319
- - "Arctic Birds" (J. Bornfriend) **4:**1252
- - "Chess Players" (I. Kaufman) **5:**403
- - "Chess Players" (I. Amen) **3:**615
- - color print (S. Delaunay-Terk) **5:**1468
- - "Constructor" (El Lissitzky) **11:**306
- - "Cow with a Parasol" (M. Chagall) **5:**321
- - drawing (M. Band) **4:**158
- - etching (F. M. Kempf) **10:**903
- - Ethel Waters (caric., A. Hirschfeld) **8:**523
- - "Excavation" (P. Blume) **4:**1139
- - "Farmers" (A. Kolnik) **10:**1169
- - "Fish" (J. Chapiro) **5:**338
- - "Flute Player" (Z. Menkes) **11:**1354
- - "Hanging Turkey" (C. Soutine) **15:**214
- - Hannah Rovina in *Dybbuk* (M. Sima) **6:**19
- - "Hillel" (J. Levine) **11:**114
- - "Irrigation, Zionist Development, Palestine" (D. Bomberg) **4:**1196
- - Jewish cemetery at Ouderkerk **2:**94; **5:***fcg.* 331
- - "Jewish Holidays" (A. Gottlieb) **7:**822
- - "Jews at the Wailing Wall" (L. Pasternak) **16:**470
- - *"Kodashim"* (H. Lerner) **10:**1125
- - landscape (A. Stematsky) **15:**379
- - "Les Français chez les dames juives à Alger" (E. Delacroix) **6:**217
- - Messiah entering Jerusalem (S. Forst) **11:**1412
- - "Mother Russia" (M. Chagall) **5:**319
- - "Night over Vitebsk" (M. Chagall) **16:**191
- - "Old Tree and Old People" (W. Gropper) **7:**932
- - "On the Way to Jerusalem" (A. Ticho) **15:**1136
- - "Opening of the Hebrew University of Jerusalem" (L. Pilichowski) **13:**519
- - "Painting of a Girl" (I. Paldi) **13:**29
- - "Parchemin Rouge" (M.E. Castel) **5:**236
- - Paris School of Art **13:**113-119
- - "Pipe Smoker" (M. Kisling) **10:**1072
- - portrait (J. Pascin) **13:**159
- - "Portrait of the Young Girl Elvira" (Modigliani) **12:**205
- - "Quiet Scene" (E. Baizerman) **4:**111
- - "Rabbi" (P. Litvinovsky) **11:**407
- - "Rabbi with Torah"

(Mane-Katz) **11:**871
-- "Reclining Woman" (J. Iser) **9:**77
-- "Resting at the Bazaar" (M. Sterne) **15:**397
-- "Russian Village" (M. Chagall) **5:***fcg.* 334
-- "Russian Village" (I.I. Levitan) **11:**135
-- "Sitting Old Man" (J. Budko) **4:**1456
-- "Still Life" (L. Marcousis) **11:**943
-- "Sunday Afternoon" (A. Bihari) **4:**990
-- "Synagogue in Safed" (N. Gutman) **7:**988
-- "Tanit" (J. Atlan) **3:**823
-- "Three Calabrian Laborers" (C. Levi) **11:**78
-- "Tiergarten, Berlin" (Lesser Ury) **16:**16
-- "Village East" (R. Soyer) **12:**1116
-- Watercolor (Y. Zaritsky) **16:**938
-- watercolor landscape (A. Milich) **11:**1549
-- "Western Wall" (S. S. Alva) **2:**785
-- "Young Woman with Mandolin" (M. Kikoine) **10:**999
-- see also: BOOKPLATES; MEDALS; PORTRAITS OF JEWS; POTTERY; SCULPTURE
- *illus:* Holocaust
-- Anielewicz memorial (N. Rapaport) **3:**3
-- camp and ghetto drawings **3:***fcg.* 568f; **5:**95
-- concentration and extermination camp horrors (M. Hoffman) **5:**79-94
-- concentration and extermination camps (A. Games) **5:**79
-- concentration camp scenes (E. Lieberman) **8:**881
-- Dachau camp memorial (N. Glid) **7:**620
-- "*Hashoah*" memorial (B. Lishansky) **3:**633
-- "Homage to Six Million" (L. Nevilson) **3:**635
-- "Kaddish" (A. Krol) **10:**662
-- *Khurbn Vilna* (1947) **10:**659
-- Lodz ghetto **14:**428
-- "Main Gate of Kaunas Ghetto" (E. Lurie) **10:**849
-- Nazi Drawing No. 25 (M. Lasansky) **10:**1431
-- "Ruins of Synagogue" (A. Bogen) **3:**620
-- Warsaw ghetto uprising memorial **16:**351
- *illus:* Jerusalem
-- city of Shalem **14:**1266
-- craftsmen **9:**1468
-- eighteenth cent. ms. **9:**1562
-- Elijah riding into the city **7:**1086
-- festival pilgrimage **7:**1115
-- folkloristic depictions **9:***fcg.* 1531
-- Golden Gate **6:**863
-- "Heavenly Jerusalem" (14th cent.) **9:**1582
-- Hezekiah's Pool **9:**1460
-- Holy Sepulcher church **9:**1418-1420
-- "Jerusalem" (Y. Zaritsky) Pl. 3 **3**-ART
-- "Jerusalem: Mount Scopus..." (D. Bomberg) **3:**555
-- Jerusalem from the Mount of Olives (E. Lear) **9:**1585
-- "Jerusalem Hills" (A. Ticho) Fig. 95 **3**-ART
-- "Jerusalem Landscape" (L. Engelsberg) **3:**619
-- "King David's Entry" (M. Chagall) **5:***fcg.* 334
-- "King George Avenue" (H. Gliksberg) Pl. 5 **3**-ART
-- maps **9:**1542-1548
-- Messiah entering the city **6:**863; **11:**1409-1412
-- mourned by Jeremiah **13:**1417
-- Mount of Olives **4:**115
-- pilgrims eating second tithe **11:**653
-- Pool of Siloam **14:**1400
-- prayers at Western Wall **9:**1467
-- public fountains **9:**1433
-- Renaissance representations **9:**1583-1586
-- Robinson's Arch **14:**205
-- seventeenth-twentieth cent. portrayals **9:**1587,1588
-- Solomon entering the city **10:**1024
-- "Street in Jerusalem" (J. Steinhardt) Fig. 93 **3**-ART
-- "Synagogue in Jerusalem" (S. Hirshenberg) **3:**627
-- Temple **9:**1581
-- Temple Mount **4:**115
-- "Toward Jerusalem" (M. Ardon) Pl. 8 **3**-ART
-- "Western Wall" (S. Alva) **2:**785
-- Western Wall (primitivist) **4:**115
- *illus:* Jewish History
-- General
--- anti-Semitic caricatures **3:**93, 121-156; **5:**171-178
--- erotica libel **3:**127-134
--- greediness libel **3:**139-146
--- "Out of Bondage" (A. Bayefsky) **3:**613
--- rapacity libel **3:**135, 150-156
-- Ancient
--- Akiva (14th cent. *Haggadah*) **2:**490
--- Alexander the Great **2:**580
--- Antiochus IV Epiphanes, martyrdom scenes **8:**671
--- apostles, Jesus' **3:**217
--- Gamaliel teaching (14th cent. ms.) **7:**297, 1085
--- Hananiah ben Teradyon **7:**1255
--- Hannah and her seven sons **5:**458; **7:**1271
--- Ḥanukkah, appeal of Jerusalem Jews to Jews of Egypt **7:**1
--- Hasmoneans (B. Elkan) **7:**1459
--- Hasmoneans and Seleucid armies **7:**1457
--- Jesus flagellated by Jews **8:**660
--- Judah ha-Nasi (sculp., M. Horn) **10:**368
--- Judah Maccabee **10:**380, 383
--- Judith and Holofernes **3:**1; **8:**917; **10:**453-8
--- Mary Magdalene and apostles **3:**217
--- massacre of Alexandria Jews **10:**256
--- Mattathias the Hasmonean **6:**292
--- Nebuchadnezzar's army attacking the Temple **15:**985
--- Ptolemy ordering translation of Bible **3:**439
--- Ptolemy VI sacking the Temple **10:**256
--- Rome, Via Appia catacomb paintings **5:**250-252
--- St. Paul disputing with the Jews **8:**662
--- Salome with head of John the Baptist (A. Beardsley) **6:**775
--- Wandering Jew **16:**260,262
-- Middle Ages
--- Alfonso X of Castile **2:**605
--- Arragel and Luis de Guzman **3:**498
--- Constantinople, Jewish quarter **5:**917
--- Desecration of the Host Libel **3:**103-110
--- Dialogue between a bishop and a Jew **6:**82
--- disputation between Jewish and Christian scholars **6:**86
--- Ecclesia et Synagoga **3:**91-94; **6:**346-348; **8:**670
--- Henry VII granting charter of privileges **7:**465
--- Jewish Sow libel **3:**117-122; **5:**174
--- Jews burning at the stake **8:**675
--- Martin V and Jews at Constance **5:**913
--- martyrs, Jewish (15th cent. ms.) **7:**466,467
--- oath *more judaico* **12:**1302
--- Simon of Trent libel **3:**97
--- Statute of Kalish (A. Szyk) **3:**922
--- "Vicente Ferrer Preaching" (D. Morone) **6:**1235
-- Sixteenth to Eighteenth Centuries
--- auto da fé **3:**171, 912; **8:**1401
--- *Anusim* procession **3:**171
--- burning at the stake **3:**105; **4:**642; **5:**221
--- Canto de Fe (A. Berruguete) **3:**912
--- Chmielnicki, Bogdan (statue) **5:**481
--- Dutch Jewish quarter (J. van der Velde) **10:**87
--- "Expulsion of the Jews from Prague, 1745" (etch.) **13:**968
--- Fettmilch, Vincent, execution **6:**1248
--- Frankfort, expulsion of 1614 **7:**474
--- Frankfort riots, August 1614 **7:**85, 472
--- Gregoire, Henri Baptiste **7:**918
--- Jews asking Helvetia for protection **15:**557
--- Maharal mi-Prag (L. Saloun) **10:**376
--- Nathan of Gaza **12:**862
--- Prague, community banner **6:**1334
--- Prague, revocation of expulsion edict (medal) **11:**991
--- Rome, liberation of ghetto **9:**1106
--- Shabbetai Ẓevi **14:**1225,1239,1243
--- "Spinoza" (S. Hirszenberg) **8:**350
-- Nineteenth and Twentieth Centuries
--- "After the Pogrom" (S. Fabjanski) **13:**699
--- Alexander III tormenting a Jew **14:**437
--- Christian-Socialist election poster (1920) **3:**905
--- conversion sermon (Hier. Hess) **3:**201
--- "Cossacs are Coming" (A. Pann) **8:**736
--- Dreyfus, Alfred (cartoon) **3:**115
--- Dreyfus' trial **6:**227
--- Duermenach riots **2:**753
--- emancipation rejoicings **6:**705
--- England, emancipation discussed **6:**714
--- England, medal for tercentary of re-settlement **6:**772
--- French Sanhedrin **14:**841
--- "Grand Sanhedrin des Israélites de France" (E. Verner) **8:**704
--- Hep! Hep! riots **8:**332
--- "Jewish Refugees from Russia..." **12:**1084
--- Jewish soldiers (cartoon) **3:**905
--- kidnapping of Edgardo Mortara **12:**354
--- Kishinev pogrom (E.M. Lilien) **10:**1065
--- Rome ghetto (E. Roesler Franz) **10:**83
--- Warsaw, Jewish Municipal Guard **16:**355
-- *see also:* ARCHAEOLOGY; BIBLE; HERALDRY; MEDALS; *and under individual names, movements and events*
- *illus:* Jewish Life
-- Family Joys and Sorrows
--- *Ashkavah* recited at a grave **3:**713
--- *badḥan* **4:**74
--- "Bar Mitzvah Speech" (M. Oppenheim) **4:**245
--- betrothal ceremony (18th cent.) **4:**754
--- blessing of children **4:**1088
--- bride in wedding garments **11:***fcg.* 1070
--- burial scenes **4:**1522; **5:**308; **7:**609, 1153; **8:**443
--- childbirth scenes (18th cent.) **4:**1052; **6:**1406
--- "Child Entering the Covenant" (M. Oppenheim) **5:**573
--- circumcision ceremony **5:**573; **12:**30; **14:**827
--- divorce procedure (18th cent. engr.) **6:**126; **7:**592
--- "Examination" (M. Oppenheim) **6:**393
--- *hakkafot* around a coffin (B. Picart) **7:**1153
--- *ḥaliẓah* ceremony **11:**123; **16:**776
--- *ḥevra kaddisha* burial implements **4:**1519-1521
--- "Jewish Wedding" (M. Gottlieb) **3:**554
--- "Jewish Wedding" (M. Oppenheim) **11:***fcg.* 1067
--- "Joy" (M. Chagall) **14:**1467
--- Kimpetbriefel **13:**44-45
--- marriage ceremony **10:**986; **11:***fcg.* 1003; **12:**602,622; **16:***fcg.* 615
--- "Marriage Ceremony of Portuguese Jews" (B. Picart) **11:**1030
--- marriage ceremony platter **11:***fcg.* 1070
--- "Mitzva Tanz" (S. S. Alva) **5:**1265
--- "Noce Juive dans le Maroc" (E. Delacroix) **11:**1037
--- Persian bridal couple **11:**1035
--- "Rabbi's Blessing" (M. Oppenheim) **4:**1087
--- "Redemption of the Firstborn" (B. Picart) **6:**1309
--- "Return of the Volunteer" (M. Oppenheim) **11:**1561
--- Rothschild marriages **14:**339,341
--- Venice wedding **11:**1033
--- "Wedding in Shtetl" (S. Raskin) **14:**1467
--- "Woman of Valor" wedding plate **6:**887
--- women mourning over a coffin **12:**486
-- Religious Observance
--- ablution, ritual **2:**85
--- benedictions before eating fruit and vegetables **6:**1423
--- blessing of the moon **12:**292

--- circumcision **5**:573; **12**:30; **14**:827
--- dough-offering *(hallah)* **7**:1196
--- examination of a chicken (J.M. De Haan) **5**:1459
--- *Havdalah* ceremony **7**:1483, 1488
--- *Havdalah* ceremony articles **3**:529; **5**:118, 300; **6**:1390; **7**:1260-1261,1485-1488
--- "Jew at Prayer" (L. Segall) **14**:1108
--- *"Kapparot"* (J. D. Kirszenbaum) **10**:1053
--- *mazzah* baking **11**:1155,1157
--- *mezuzah*, touching of **11**:1474
--- *omer* counting chart **12**:1385; **13**:*fcg.* 46
--- passover *kashering* **13**:164
--- *pe'ot*, medieval Jew **4**:357
--- ritual slaughter **14**:1339
--- scroll of the Law, hugging of **8**:*fcg.* 1015
--- *Shema*, reciting of **8**:*fcg.* 1015
--- "Slaughterhouse" (M. Chagall) **14**:1341
--- three commandments incumbent on woman **11**:1039
--- visiting the sick **14**:1497
--- washing of hands **16**:694
--- "*Yahrzeit* at the front" (M. Oppenheim) **11**:1563
-- Shtetl **14**:1467-1470
-- Study of the Torah
--- angel rewarding good pupils **6**:387
--- children introduced to Torah study **6**:386
--- "Examination" (M. Oppenheim) **6**:393
--- "Ḥasid Studying" (L. Krestin) **7**:1403
--- "*Ḥeder*" (E. Brandon) **6**:390
--- Rabban Gamaliel teaching **7**:297, 1085
--- "Talmudists" (L. Reiss) **3**:639
--- teacher admonishing pupil **4**:967; **6**:*fcg.* 427
--- "Teacher and Young Pupil" (I. Kaufman) **3**:553
--- women pupils (15th cent.) **7**: *fcg.* 811
-- Synagogue
--- Amsterdam, Portuguese Synagogue (E. de Witte) **15**:616
--- Bridegroom of the Law cantata **12**:622
--- Bridegroom of the Law chairs **4**:1370
--- Chairs of Elijah **5**:306; **6**:643-645
--- *Haggadah* read in synagogue **2**:806; **7**:*fcg.* 1323
--- *ḥazzan*, and choir **5**:487; **7**:1543,1545; **12**:617
--- Lancut synagogue (Z. Vogel) **15**:607
--- London, Great Synagogue (engr.) **15**:609
--- "Old Synagogue" (S. Judovin) **14**:1469
--- on way to Sabbath prayers **14**:1216
--- priestly blessing (B. Picart) **13**:1061
--- raising of the Torah scroll (B. Picart) **7**:1077
--- "Rejoicing of the Law . . ." (S.A. Hart) **3**:547
--- "Rosh Ha-Shanah in Synagogue" (B. Picart) **13**:497
--- Rozdol synagogue (Marburg) **13**:497
--- "Synagogue" (H. Bloom) **4**:1132
--- synagogue attire, Germany, 18th cent. **7**:483
--- "Synagogue in Safed" (N. Gutman) **7**:988
--- worshippers (14th cent. ms.) **7**:1199
--- Zholkva synagogue (N. Pohlenberg)**15**:608
-- Trades and Professions
--- *arendar* (jug) **3**:405
--- Cracow goose market (engr.) **11**:1003
--- Jews in Tartar market **14**:437
--- moneylenders **4**:171, 173; **7**:462; **8**:674
--- Monmouth Street, London **11**:475
--- musicians **12**:568-622
--- Nuremberg hawker **12**:1277
--- old clothes men (caric.) **6**:249
--- "Old Jewish Pedlar" (G. Salomon) **3**:639
--- peddlers **3**:639; **6**:761; **12**:1277
--- physicians **11**:1182,1192-1195; **13**:708
--- "Shoemaker" (S. Judovin) **14**:1468
--- "Water-Carrier at the Town Well" (M. Minkowski) **8**:755
-- Types of Jews
--- beggar and child (E.M. Lilien) **4**:389
--- "Blind Violinist" (I. Ryback) **14**:533
--- Brody Jews (J. Pennell) **4**:1399
--- "Chess Players" (I. Kaufmann) **5**:404
--- Cracow merchants **5**:1039
--- "Descendant of the High Priest" (I. Kaufmann) **15**:*fcg.* 491
--- Drogobych market place (E. M. Lilien) **6**:233
--- emigrants (F. Villiers) **8**:739
--- "Exchange of Opinions" (J. Morvay) **15**:471
--- Frankfort couple, 18th cent. **7**:86
--- Ḥasidic dance (J. Steinhardt) **7**:1415
--- ḥasidic joy (Ch. Lieberman) **10**:320
--- "Ḥasidim in a *Bet Midrash*" (I. Kaufmann) **7**:1395
--- Houndsditch, London, a scene **6**:764
--- "In the Market of Lemberg" (J. Pennell) **11**:1001
--- Jewish quarter of Máramaros-Sziget (J. Pennell) **8**:1105
--- "Jewish Refugees from Russia . . ." **12**:1084
--- "Lithuanian Stock Exchange" (Bisson) **4**:1404
--- Marrakesh household **12**:326
--- Petticoat Lane **6**:769; **11**:1004
--- Polish Ḥasid **6**:*fcg.* 238
--- Prague Jew (caric.) **5**:172
--- shtetl scenes **14**:1467-1470
--- "Sitting Old Man" (J. Budko) **7**:1456
--- Spitalfields soup kitchen, London **5**:346
--- young Jewish woman (paint., I. Kaufmann) **10**:845
-- *see also:* CRAFTS; DRESS
- *illus:* Sabbath and Festivals
-- Av, the Ninth of **3**:937; **6**:1190
-- Day of Atonement
--- "*Ashamnu*" (A. Levy) **2**:630
--- eve of **5**:1385
--- flogging on eve of **5**:1385
--- in a Dutch synagogue (B. Picart) **3**:831
--- *kapparot* ceremony **5**:1385
--- "Yom Kippur in the Country" (A. Levy) **5**:1383
-- Ḥanukkah
--- *dreidls* **6**:1398; **7**:1286, 1287
--- games and gambling **7**:306
--- lamps **2**:335, 626, 1299; **4**:1462; **5**:301; **6**:1395; **7**:1293-1314; **11**:624
--- lighting Ḥanukkah lamp (15th cent. ms.) **2**:626
--- "Lighting of the Ḥannukah Candles" (M. Oppenheim) **7**:1281
-- Hoshana Rabba (B. Picart) **8**:1026
-- Passover
--- customs **13**:164-168
--- *Haggadah* read in synagogue **2**:806; **7**:*fcg.* 1323
--- hiding the *afikoman* **2**:330
--- *mazzah* baking **3**:*fcg.* 555; **11**:1155,1157; **12**:26
--- *mazzot* and *ḥaroset* **3**:530
--- *omer* counting chart **12**:1385; **13**:*fcg.* 46
--- "Passover Meal" (M. Oppenheim) **10**:1079
--- search for leaven **4**:*fcg.* 363, 371
--- *seder*, order of procedure **2**:47; **7**:1081
--- *seder*, washing of the hands **2**:83
--- *seder* articles **13**:172-173
--- *seder* plates **3**:531; **5**:304, 661; **6**:1391; **7**:1049; **13**:353
--- *seder* table **2**:83, 330; **3**:*fcg* 299; **4**:3; **6**:1165; **7**:*fcg.* 811, *fcg.* 1003,1067; **13**:172-173; **14**:1193
-- Purim
--- actors and musicians **12**:618
--- Dura-Europos paintings **8**:649
--- embroidered hand towel **13**:1388-1389
--- jesters **13**:1402
--- "Masked Ball" (engr.) **13**:1394
--- masked players (wdct.) **13**:1401
--- merrymakers **12**:28
--- New York ball (drg.) **12**:1081
--- pewter plate **13**:353
--- "Purim at Home" (M. Oppenheim) **13**:1403
--- "Purim-Shpil" (J. Adler) **13**:1404
--- reading of the *megillah* **11**:1229
--- Scrolls of Esther **13**:1388-1389; **14**:1049-1056
-- Rosh Ha-Shanah
--- blowing the *shofar* **3**:834; **5**:1524; **7**:468; **11**:734; **14**:306,1444
--- "Rosh Ha-Shanah in the Synagogue" (B. Picart) **13**:497
-- Sabbath
--- "Blessing over the Candles" (I. Kaufmann) **4**:487
--- blessing the lights (15th cent.) **11**:1039
--- candlesticks **5**:*fcg.* 299; **11**:269; **14**:564-568
--- "Conclusion of the Sabbath" (M. Oppenheim) **7**:1483
--- *eruv tavshilin* **6**:851
--- *eruv tavshilin* tablet (1806, Ger.) **7**:*fcg.* 843
--- *ḥallah* cover **6**:1385; **14**:572
--- *ḥallah* platter, silver **7**:1194
--- *Havdalah* ceremony **7**:1483, 1488
Havdalah ceremony articles **3**:529; **5**:118, 300; **6**:1390; **7**:1260-1261,1485-1488
--- *Havdalah* prayer **14**:569
--- Jewish quarter, Morocco **12**:331
--- *Kiddush* plate, pewter **13**:353
--- *Lekhah Dodi* wall plaque **10**:655
--- "Lighting the Sabbath Candles" (I. Szigeti) **14**:567
--- on way to prayers **14**:1276
--- Sabbath plate (16th cent.) **3**:1016
--- "Shabbat in Safed" (M. Castel) Pl. 7 3-ART
--- "Ushering In the Sabbath" (M. Oppenheim) **14**:560
-- "Shavuot" (M. Oppenheim) **6**:1368
--- paper-cut for **6**:1394
-- Simḥat Torah **14**:1571
--- Bridegroom of the Law cantata **12**:622
--- Bridegroom of the Law chairs **4**:1370
-- Sukkot
--- Amsterdam Jewish quarter **15**:499
--- German *sukkot* scene **15**:493
--- "In the Sukkah" (M. Oppenheim) **3**:548
--- papercuts **13**:44-45
--- *sukkah*, embroidered hanging for **7**:1385
--- *sukkah* meal **15**:496
--- *sukkah* wall paintings **9**:1588
- *illus:* Synagogal
-- General
--- Ark of the Law **2**:942, 943; **3**:451-456, *fcg.* 459, *fcg.* 462, 627; **4**:344,374,769,787, 1193, 1266, 1472; **5**:207, 295, 869,899,1035,1058,1231, 1445; **6**:1403; **7**:170, 873; **8**:1459,1466; **9**:1443-1445; **10**:1520; **11**:371,480,572,896; **12**:38,157,1029,1238,1417; **13**:108,330,540,1587; **14**:39,250,629,685,835,848, 1167,1169,1514; **15**:318,507,560,605,620-621, 622, 625, 742, 1255, 1460, 1461, 1469 1475; **16**:96 98,100,107,114,142,506,598, 682
--- *bimah* **2**:563; **3**:326; **4**:1002-1005, 1193; **5**:471, 625; **6**:903; **7**:927; **9**:1135; **9**:1443-45; **11**:365,545; **13**:9; **14**:631,1514; **15**:507,604-626,820,1469; **16**:99,927,1014
--- lion motif **11**:263-274
--- *mashiv ha-ru'aḥ* plaque **11**:1094
--- *Shulklapper's* mallet **14**:1477
--- *tal u-matar* plaque **13**:1523
-- Ancient and Medieval
--- Ashkelon *menorah* **3**:716
--- Ashkelon stone screen **12**:569
--- Ben Ezra synagogue doors, Cairo **5**:29
--- Bet Alfa Mosaics **3**:511, 513; **4**:711; **5**:45; **8**:651; **11**:268,989
--- Beth-Shean mosaics **13**:905
--- Caesarea stone *menorah* **11**:1359
--- Capernaum archaeological remains **5**:137-138; **6**:948; **11**:689; **13**:44
--- Chorazin **5**:493
--- Dabbûra *bet-midrash* lintel **13**:1533
--- Dura-Europos **3**:28, 451, 461,515; **6**:277-294:*fcg.* 299 and 302; **8**:649; **15**:571
--- El Transito, Toledo, stucco **3**:520
--- En-Gedi, *menorah* **6**:743
--- Eshtemoa sculpture **12**:569
--- Gaza mosaic **7**:340, 341
--- Gerasa mosaic **7**:434

– – – Gush Ḥalav synagogue, sculptured lintel **6:**337
– – – Hamam Lif mosaic **3:**519; **15:**572
– – – Ḥammat Geder mosaic **7:**249, 251
– – – Hammath mosaic floor **3:**325; **7:**1243-1244; **15:**574,575
– – – Hammath stone *menorah* **11:**1357
– – – Jericho mosaic floor **9:**1370; **11:**1360
– – – Kefar Baram sculpture **3:**517; **10:**878
– – – Ma'on synagogue mosaic **6:**604; **11:**908
– – – Naarah mosaic **12:**737
– – – Nuremberg *Judenstain* **12:**1275
– – – Ostia synagogue antiquities **12:**1507
– – – Peki'in, frieze fragment **5:**202
– – – Priene marble *menorah* **11:**1361
– – – Qasrayn portal **13:**1534
– – – Rambam synagogue, Cordoba, stucco **5:**964
– – – Regensburg synagogue (etch.) **14:**36
– – – Sardis synagogue, table support **6:**338
– – – Toledo, El Transito **15:**613
– – – Toledo, Santa Maria la Blanca **15:**612
– – Renaissance and Modern
– – – Amsterdam, new Sephardi synagogue (B. Picart) **2:**897
– – – Bechhofen wall paintings (1733) **4:**346
– – – Beth Aaron synagogue doors, Detroit **5:**1567
– – – Bridegroom of the Law chairs (18th cent.) **4:**1370
– – – Casa Sefardita candlesticks, Barcelona **4:**212
– – – Chairs of Elijah **5:**306; **6:**643-645; **9:**1140
– – – Conegliano synagogue, Jerusalem **5:**870
– – – Essen synagogue **6:**897
– – – Florence, Great Synagogue **6:**1361; **15:**620-621
– – – Horb, paintings **15:***fcg.* 622
– – – Isfahan, tiled wall **15:**620-621
– – – Istanbul, Karaite synagogue **9:**1092
– – – "Jerusalem Windows" (M. Chagall) **4:**526; **5:**1258; **9:**1077
– – – Jonah's "great fish", Checiny **5:**369
– – – London, Bevis Marks **11:**471
– – – London, Great Synagogue **11:**475
– – – London, St. Albans Place Synagogue **6:**757
– – – Mantua, Scuola Norse **11:**806
– – – Paris, Rue de la Victoire Synagogue **15:**620-621
– – – Przedborz synagogue **11:**693; **12:**621
– – – *menorah* **6:**1226; **7:**934; **10:**1445; **16:**465
– – – San Mateo synagogue sculpture (V. Ries) **5:**59
– – – *Shivviti* papercut **13:**44-45
– – – *Shivviti* plaques **13:***fcg.* 1390; **14:**1420-1421
– – – stained glass windows and Tablets of the Law (Ben Shahn) **4:**1466
– – – Tarrytown, N.Y., Temple Beth Abraham sculpture **16:**465
– – *see also:* CEREMONIAL OBJECTS; CRAFTS; Mosaics; SYNAGOGUE; TORAH ORNAMENTS
– *illus:* Miscellaneous
– – Antichrist supported by Jews **3:**61
– – *bet din* **4:***fcg.* 715; **6:**126
– – Bezalel Academy, a students' show **4:**789
– – bride's comb **11:***fcg.* 1070
– – calendars, medieval **4:**46-51
– – charity boxes **5:**339-353
– – cholent pot, cast bronze **5:**489
– – costume design for ballet (L. Bakst) **3:**554; **4:**118
– – First Zionist Congress membership card **3:**388
– – Mendelssohn playing for Goethe **11:**1327
– – Mendelssohn, Moses, with Lessing and Lavater **11:**1331
– – Nablus, a scene **12:**744
– – papercuts **6:**1394; **8:**973; **11:**271; **13:**44-45,61-65
– – pilgrims on their way to Jerusalem **13:**511
– – posters and designs (A. Games) **3:**624
– – Rothschild, Lionel, taking seat in House of Commons **14:**340
– – Saint-Léon and Fanny Cerito **14:**662
– – *Shulamis*, poster **7:**716
– – street in Brody (drg.) **16:**1327
– – Yemenite Torah scribe (E.M. Lilien) **14:**1044
– – Zacuto, Abraham, and Vasco da Gama **16:**905
– – *see also:* ADVERTISING; HERALDRY; SEAL, SEALS
Art (journ.) **7:**824
ARTA (tn., Gr.) **3:**645
– Greece **7:**873ff
Artabanus (Parth. ks.), *see* ARDAVAN
Artafernes, *see* HOLOFERNES
Artapan (Parth. ks.), *see* ARDAVAN
ARTAPANUS (Hellen. au.) **3:**645
– apologetics **3:**189
– biblical history **8:**304
– Greek debt to Jews **8:**300
– Moses **12:**390
ARṬAS (vill., Er. Isr.) **3:**646
– Millennarian settlement **9:**296
– Wadi Arṭās **9:**140
Artaxata (city), *see* ARDASHIR
ARTAXERXES I (k., Pers.) **3:**646
– head tax **6:**1027
– history **8:**616ff
– history chart **8:**766-767
– Nehemiah **8:**620ff
– Samaritans **14:**729
– Scroll of Esther **14:**1052ff
ARTAXERXES II (k., Pers.) **3:**647
– Ezra **8:**618
– history chart **8:**766-767
ARTAXERXES III (Ochus; k., Pers.) **3:**647
– Babylonian Jews **4:**36
– history chart **8:**766-767
ART COLLECTORS AND ART DEALERS **3:**647
Artef (theat.) **11:**1428
ARTEMION (revol. ldr.) **3:**649
ARTEMOVSK (city, Ukr.) **3:**649
Artephius (alch.) **2:**547ff
ART HISTORIANS AND ART CRITICS **3:**649
– *illus:*
– – Berenson, Bernard **4:**603
ARTHURIAN LEGENDS **3:**652
– fiction, Hebrew **6:**1266
– *illus:* text
Artichoke (bot.) **16:**82
– plant list **13:**615
– *illus:*
– – *maror zeh* **11:***fcg.* 939
– – *Sarajevo Haggadah*, **11:**1014
ARTICLES OF FAITH **3:**654
– *Contents:*
– – Rabbinic Literature **3:**654
– – Maimonides **3:**655
– – 13/14 Centuries **3:**656
– – 15/16 Centuries **3:**657
– – Spinoza **3:**659
– – Modern Period **3:**659
– – 19/20 Centuries **3:**659
General
– – *aggadah* **2:**361
– – *Ani Ma'amin* hymn **3:**4
– – dogma in Judaism **10:**385ff
– – eternity of Torah **15:**1244
– – Frankists **7:**58
– – Judaism **10:**385ff
– – Koran **10:**1197ff
– – resurrection **14:**96
– – reward and punishment **14:**134
– – Samaritans **14:**740
– – theology **15:**1103; **15:**1106
– – *Yigdal* hymn **16:**835
– Views on
– – Ahitub ben Isaac **2:**467
– – Albo Joseph **2:**535ff; **13:**449
– – Arama, Isaac **3:**257
– – Crescas, Ḥasdai **5:**1083; **13:**448
– – Ibn Abi Zimra **5:**1357
– – Jabez, Joseph **9:**1173
– – Maimonides **11:**759; **11:**776ff
– – Mendelssohn **11:**1337ff
– – Nahmanides **11:**1418
– – Philo **4:**432
– *illus:*
– – English translation (1770) **3:**5
– *see also:* BELIEF; HERESY
ARTIFICIAL INSEMINATION **3:**660
– paternity **16:**892
– science **15:**895
Artisans, *see* CRAFTS
Artishevski, Thea **15:**1072
Artistic crafts **5:**1041
Artists, Jewish, *see* ART
"Artist's Mother" (paint., M. Gertler) **7:**521
"Artist's Mother (paint., L. Gottlieb) **7:**826
Art Music, *see* MUSIC
ARTOM (fam.) **3:**661
– *illus:* text
Artom, Alessandro **3:**662
Artom, Benjamin **3:**662
Artom, Camillo **3:**662
ARTOM, CESARE **3:**663
ARTOM, ELIA SAMUELE **3:**663
Artom, Emanuel **3:**663
Artom, Emanuele **3:**662
– partisans **13:**147; **15:**1455
Artom, Ernest **3:**662
Artom, Eugenio **3:**662
Artom, G. **11:**101
Artom, Giulia **5:**453
Artom, Isaac **3:**661; **15:**1455
Artom, Ruben **3:**663
Artopaeus Petrus **8:**22
Artuković, Andrija **13:**192
Artus Hof (Yid. wk.) **16:**806
ARTZI, PINḤAS **1:**27
Artzi, Yiẓḥak **16:**863
Aruba (country) **12:**993
– synagogues **1:**syn. list
Arubboth (city, Er. Isr.) **3:**497; **11:**851
Arueste (fam.) **5:**464
Aruety (fam.), *see* ROTE
Aruety, Habran (Abraham) **14:**323
Arugat ha-Bosem (rab. wk.) **2:**135
Arugat ha-Bosem (gram. wk.) **3:**397
Arugot (mosh., Isr.) **1:**place list
Arugot River, *see* Naḥal Arugot
'Arukh, He- (wk., Ibn Dannan), *see* *Sefer he-'Arukh*
Arukh ha-Shalem (wk.; ed., Kohut) **3:**278
Arukh ha-Shulḥan (hal. wk.) **6:**831
Arukh la-Ner (wk.), *see* ETTLINGER, JACOB
Arumah (tn.), *see* RUMAH
Arumiyat (vill., Mor.) **6:**190
Aruna Valley (Er. Isr.) **11:**1227; **16:**270
ARUNDI, ISAAC (Ibn) **3:**663
ARUSI, ABRAHAM **3:**664
Arvad (Phoen. city) *see*, ARADUS
Arvaẓ, Samuel **3:**722
ARVEY, JACOB M. **3:**664
Arvic (lang.), *see* JUDEO-ARABIC
Arvieux, L. de **15:**1357
ARVIT (litur.) **3:**664
– *Ahavat Olam* **2:**454
– liturgy **11:**393ff
– *ma'aravot* (piyyut) **11:**637
– Samaritan Sabbath **14:**741
– *illus:*
– – text
– – *Barekhu* (1816) **4:**219
– – Roman Rite, Sabbath Service **11:**395
– *see also:* AMIDAH
Aryanization **8:**839
Aryan race theory **13:**1485
Aryeh (tos.), *see* JUDAH BEN ISAAC
Aryeh (zodiac sign), *see* Leo
ARYEH JUDAH HARRARI (ha-Yarḥi) **3:**666
ARYEH JUDAH LEIB BEN EPHRAIM HA-KOHEN **3:**667
ARYEH JUDAH LEIB (the "Mokhi'aḥ") OF POLONNOYE **3:**667
Aryeh Leib ben Asher, *see* GUNZBERG, ARYEH LEIB BEN ASHER
ARYEH LEIB BEN ELIJAH **3:**667
Aryeh Leib ben Joseph ha-Kohen, *see* HELLER, ARYEH LEIB BEN JOSEPH HA-KOHEN OF STRY
Aryeh Leib Ben Judah **10:**350
Aryeh Leib ben Nathan of Slutsk **6:**824
ARYEH LEIB BEN SAMUEL ẒEVI HIRSCH **3:**668
Aryeh Leib of Bendery, *see* Bendery, Aryeh Leib of
ARYEH LEIB OF OŻARÓW **3:**668
ARYEH LEIB OF SHPOLA **3:**668
– Naḥman of Bratslav **12:**783
Aryeh Leib of Woloczyska **9:**514
ARYEH LEIB SARAHS **3:**669
Aryeh Leibush Bolekhover, *see* ARYEH LEIB BEN ELIJAH
Aryeh Loeb ben Joseph Samuel **10:**247; **13:**1106
Aryeh of Metz **5:**615
Arzhak, Nikolai, *see* DANIEL, YULI MARKOVICH
Arzila (tn.), *see* ARCILA
ARZIN, JOSEPH BEN JACOB **3:**669
ARZT, MAX **3:**670
– *illus:*
– – JPS Torah translation committee **10:**80
ASA (k.,Judah) **3:**670
– Baasha **4:**13
– chronological chart **8:**767
– *corvée* workers **5:**977
– Geba **7:**349
– history **8:**595ff
– *geneal. table:* **5:**1341
– *illus:*
– – Mizpeh fortifications **12:**174
Asa, Abraham ben Isaac **9:**1094; **14:**1169
As'ad, Abkarib (k., Ḥimyar) **3:**234; **8:**499
Asad, Ḥafez al- **15:**649
Asad, Judah **8:**1092
Asad brothers (Isr.) **9:**1038
Asael (fallen angel), *see* Aza'el

Asael, Azriel **15:**1143
Asael, Benjamin **3:**672
ASAEL, ḤAYYIM BEN BENJAMIN **3:**671
Asaf (name) *see also* Asaph; Assaf
Asaf (physic.), *see* ASAPH HA-ROFE
Āṣāf ben Barakhyā (Koran fig.) **13:**1424; **15:**108
Asaf ha-Levi Ish Yerushalayim, *see* LEVIN, ALTER ISAAC
Asafoetida (spice) **15:**267
- plant list **13:**615
ASAHEL (br., Joab) **3:**672
- Abner **2:**87
- Joab **10:**106; **10:**107
ASAHEL (Lev.) **3:**672
ʿAsākir, al-Qāsim ibn, *see* Ibn ʿAsākir, al-Qāsim
Asalluhi (deity) **11:**952
Asamonius (pr., Er. Isr.) **11:**1127
Asaph (name), *see also* Asaf; Assaf
ASAPH (lev. singer) **3:**672
- Asaphites **7:**513
- Psalms, Book of **13:**1318
ASAPH (Temple offic.) **3:**673
ASAPH (f.,Joah) **3:**673
ASAPH (royal offic.) **3:**673
Asaph ben Berechiah (ha-Yehudi; ha-Yarḥoni; Judaeus), *see* ASAPH HA-ROFE
ASAPH HA-ROFE (physic.) **3:**673
- fennel **6:**1224
- medicine **11:**1186
- psychiatry **13:**1337
- *illus:* text
Asaph ha-Rofe Hospital (Isr.) **3:**676
Asaphites (sing.), *see* ASAPH
Asaph Judaeus, *see* ASAPH HA-ROFE
Asʿar, Yusuf Musuf (k. Arab.), *see* YUSUF ʾASʾAR YATHʿAR DHU NUWĀS
Asarah Batlanim (tit.), *see* BATLANIM
Asarah Harugei Malkhut, see TEN MARTYRS, THE
ASARAMEL (tit., place) **3:**676
Asarch, R. **16:**1165
Asaria, Zvi **5:**743
Asāṭīr (Samar. bk.), *see* AL-ASĀṬĪR
Asbury Park (city, N. J.) **12:**1030
Ascalon (city), *see* ASHKELON
ASCAMA (Ascamot; cmty. rules) **3:**677
- *illus:*
- - taxes on trading in jewels (London, 1809) **6:**1283
- *see also:* TAKKANOT HA-KAHAL
Ascandarani (fam.), *see* ISCANDARI
Ascandarani, Joseph ben Abraham **9:**75
Ascania (As. M.) **3:**718
Ascarelli, Deborah **9:**1109
- Italy **9:**1127
- Rieti, Moses **14:**171
ASCARELLI, TULLIO **3:**677
"Ascension" (sculp., Freudlich) **7:**169
Ascension, Church of (Jer.) **9:**1407
Ascension of Moses (Apoc. wk.), *see* MOSES, ASSUMPTION OF
ASCETICISM **3:**677
- *Contents:*
- - Introduction **3:**677
- - Motivations **3:**679
- - Sectarian **3:**680
- - Medieval Philosophy **3:**682
- Abraham Maimuni **2:**152
- as sin **10:**319
- Ba'al Shem Tov **9:**1054
- Baḥya **4:**107; **13:**436
- dualism **6:**242
- Elimelech of Lyzhansk **6:**661
- Essenes **6:**899
- ethics **6:**934,941
- fasting **6:**1191ff
- Halberstam, Ḥayyim **7:**1177
- *ḥasidim rishonim* **7:**1387ff
- Ḥasidism **7:**1391
- Mar bar Ravina **11:**940
- marital relations **5:**364
- Mendel of Kotsk **10:**1223
- mysticism **10:**497
- Nazirite **12:**907
- *Perushim* **3:**945
- sages **14:**652
- Shabbetai Ẓevi **14:**1222
- soul **15:**173
- sumptuary laws **15:**515
- Therapeutae **15:**1111
- *illus:* text
- *see also:* ATONEMENT
Asch (abbrev.), *see* ASH
Asch, Joel Meyer **15:**1415
Asch, Judah **15:**1415
Asch, Meir, *see* EISENSTADTER, MEIR BEN JUDAH LEIB
Asch, Moses **13:**1618
Asch, Rose **12:**1095
ASCH, SHOLEM **3:**684
- Hirschbein, Peretz **8:**517
- Jehiel Meir of Gostynin **9:**1313
- Kisling, Moise **10:**1071
- Ladino **10:**351
- Reisen, Abraham **14:**62
- *illus:*
- - text
- - advertisement of concert for **12:**660
- - Joint Distribution Committee **2:**829
- - Peretz, Isaac Leib, and **16:**814
Asch, Solomon **13:**1344
ASCHAFFENBURG (city, Ger.) **3:**687
ASCHAFFENBURG, GUSTAV **3:**688
Aschenhausen (loc., Ger.) **15:**1129
Ascher, Anton **15:**1056
Ascher, Georges **13:**117
ASCHER, SAUL **3:**688
Aschersleben (city, Ger.) **3:**1; **14:**923
ASCHERSON, PAUL FRIEDRICH AUGUST **3:**689
ASCHHEIM, ISIDOR **3:**689
- *illus:* text
Aschheim-Zondek test (med.) **16:**1220
Asch Record Company, (N.Y.) **13:**1618
ASCOLI (fam.) **3:**690
Ascoli, Albert Abram **3:**690
Ascoli, Aldo **3:**690; **11:**1559
Ascoli, Alfredo **3:**690
Ascoli, David d' **3:**692
- anti-Jewish legislation **3:**196; **4:**68
- *Apologia Hebraeorum* **3:**690
Ascoli, Emilia **3:**690
ASCOLI, ETTORE **3:**691
Ascoli, Giulio (math.) **3:**690
Ascoli, Giulio (phys.) **3:**690
ASCOLI, GRAZIADIO ISAIA **3:**691
- Italian Literature **9:**1110
- *illus:* text
Ascoli, Guido **3:**690
Ascoli, Maurizio **3:**690
Ascoli, Max **3:**690
Ascoli, Moise **3:**690
Ascoli, Saladino Ferro d' **11:**1194
Ascoli, Vittorio **3:**690
ASCOLI PICENO (city, It.) **3:**692
ASEFAT ḤAKHAMIM (period.) **3:**692
- Hebrew newspapers **12:**1046; **12:**1050
- statistics **1:** newsp. list
Asefat ha-Nivḥarim (legis., Er. Isr.) **9:**607ff; **16:**49ff
- Assaf, Simḥa **3:**757
- *Keneset Yisrael* **10:**906
- *yishuv* politics **9:**659ff
A-Sela (fort.), *see* Sela
ASENAPPER (k., Mesop.) **3:**692
- *see also:* Ashurbanipal
ASENATH (bib. fig.) **3:**693
- in the arts **10:**214
- Joseph **10:**205; **10:**211; **10:**223
- Manasseh **11:**850
- *illus:*
- - text
- - Joseph and **10:**223
Asenov, Dragomir **4:**1494
Aseo, Mordecai **14:**1186
Aseret (rural center, Isr.) **1:**place list
Aseret ha-Dibbrot, *see* DECALOGUE
Aseret yemei teshuvah (penitential period), *see* TEN DAYS OF PENITENCE
Asfi (tn., Mor.), *see* SAFI
Asgeirsson, Asgeir **9:**445
ASH (abbrev.; fam. name) **3:**693
ASH (r. fam.) **3:**693
Ash, Abraham **3:**693
Ash, Abraham ben Joseph **3:**694
Ash, Abraham Joseph **3:**694
Ash, Joel ben Meir Joseph **3:**694
Ash, Meir, *see* EISENSTADTER, MEIR BEN JUDAH LEIB
Aṣḥāb ʿAnān wa-Binyāmīn, *see* KARAITES
ʾAsham (offering) **14:**600ff
- cult **5:**1158
- Leviticus **11:**141
- priest's use **13:**1079
Aʿshā Maymūn **15:**874
Ashambethel (deity) **6:**608
ASHAMNU (litur.) **3:**694
- sins confession **5:**879
- *see also:* AL ḤET
"*Ashamnu*" (drg., Levy) **2:**630
ASHANSKI, ABEL-AARON ITSKOVICH **11:**1572
Ashʿarites (Isl. theo.) **10:**702ff
- Jewish philosophy **13:**429
Ashaʿyā, Najīb **12:**1464
ASHBEL, DOV **1:**27; **3:**695
Ashburnham Pentateuch (7th cent. illum. ms.) **2:**365; **8:**1258; **9:**1579; **12:**407
- *illus:* **2:**952; **4:**943; **8:**1271; **12:**1197
ASHDOD (city, Isr.) **3:**695
- harbor **9:**832
- human geography **9:**575
- Ponevezh *yeshivah* **10:**684
- Roman use of **9:**241
- Sargon II **14:**881
- Sargon inscription **16:**656
- Sargon steles **16:**1504
- statistics **1:**place list
- *illus:*
- - text
- - harbor **9:**837
- - housing **9:**566
- - *mikveh* **11:**1541
- - Sargon stele fragments **14:**881
- - *Shabbetai Lozinski* "illegal" immigrants **9:**361
- - Tel Ashdod excavations **3:**311
Ashdod Yam (port, Er. Isr.) **3:**696
ASHDOT YA'AKOV (kib., Isr.) **3:**698
- statistics **1:**place list
- *illus:* text
ASHENDORF, ISRAEL **3:**699
- Saul in art **14:**917
- *illus:*
- - with fellow writers **7:**616
- - Yiddish writers group, Paris **16:**821
ASHENHEIM (fam.) **3:**699
- Jamaica **9:**1274
Ashenheim, Louis **3:**699
Ashenheim, Michael **3:**699
Ashenheim, Sir Neville Noel **3:**699
ASHER (bib. fig.) **3:**699
ASHER (tribe) **3:**699
- breastplate stone **13:**1009
- Egyptian documents **3:**305
- settlement **8:**579; **8:**582
- *illus:*
- - banner and emblem **8:**335
- *map:* text
Asher (13th cent., Eng.) **16:**537
Asher (bk. firm) **3:**702; **4:**1239
Asher, Abraham (emis.) **3:**1017
ASHER, ABRAHAM (publ.) **3:**702
ASHER, ABRAHAM BEN GEDALIAH IBN (Aba) **3:**702
Asher, Adolph (publ.), *see* ASHER, ABRAHAM
ASHER, DAVID **3:**703
Asher, Gad (Philan.) **13:**542
ASHER, ISAIAH BEN MOSES HA-LEVI **3:**703
Asher, Jacob **16:**634
ASHER, JOSEPH MICHAEL **3:**703
Asher, Testament of (Pseudepig.), *see* PATRIARCHS, TESTAMENTS OF THE TWELVE
ASHERAH (deity) **3:**703
- Anath **2:**926
- idolatry **8:**1227ff
- name origin **3:**700
- Samarian worship **2:**438
- ritual impurity **13:**1408
Asher Anschel ben Eliezer Shoḥet **13:**1105
ASHER ANSCHEL BEN ISAAC OF PRZEMYŚL **3:**705
Asher Anshel ben Joseph Mordecai of Posen **3:**34
Asher Barash Bio-Bibliographical Institute (Isr.) **15:**56
Asher ben Aaron of Karlin, *see* Karlin, Asher ben Aaron of
Asher ben Abraham **5:**1079
ASHER BEN DAVID **3:**706
- *Ein-Sof* **10:**557ff
- *menorah* **11:**1367
Asher ben Isaac ha-Levi **13:**577
ASHER BEN JEHIEL (Rosh) **3:**706
- Adret, Moses ibn **2:**305
- Aldabi, Meir **2:**551
- Caro's rulings **5:**197
- chronological list **8:**766-767
- codification of law **5:**642; **5:**643; **7:**1165; **11:**334
- ethical wills **11:**345; **16:**532
- *halakhah* **11:**648
- Ḥayyim ben Isaac **7:**1509
- *hilkheta ke-vatra'ei* **3:**911
- imprisonment for debt **8:**1304; **8:**1306
- Israeli, Israel **9:**1066
- Maimonides **15:**1198
- *niddui* **8:**354
- responsa **11:**337; **14:**86
- Rosh *tosafot* **15:**1281
- Spain **15:**233
- Talmud commentaries **11:**332
- tax law **15:**867
- topics in works **12:**125; **12:**132
ASHER BEN MESHULAM HA-KOHEN OF LUNEL **3:**708
- Benjamin of Tudela **11:**1400
Asher ben Moses **15:**1328
Asher ben Nehemiah **16:**1416
Asher ben Perez Minz **8:**1319
ASHER BEN SAUL **3:**709
- *minhagim* books **12:**27
Asher the Elder (masor.) **4:**468
- Jewish literature **11:**324
- masorah **16:**1417,1472
Asher of Berlin **16:**965
Asher of Cracow, *see* ANSHEL OF CRACOW

Asher of Ropczyce **14**:259
Asher the Second of Karlin, *see* Karlin, Asher the Second of
Asheville (city, N.C.) **12**:1220
Ashguza (anc. people), *see* Ashkuza
ASHI (amora) **3**:709
- Abba the Later **2**:30
- chronological chart **8**:766-767
- Huzal **8**:1137
- marriage glass breaking **11**:1033
- Talmud redaction **11**:319; **15**:760
ASHIMA (deity) **3**:711
- Samaritans **14**:740
ASHINSKY, AARON MORDECAI HALEVI **3**:711
ASHKANASY, MAURICE **3**:712
- Melbourne **11**:1279
ASHKAVAH (litur.) **3**:712
- *piyyutim* **13**:599
- *illus:*
- - *El Male Raḥamim* **6**:682
- - for *Anusim* burned at the stake (1687) **8**:1406
- - *Hazkarat Neshamot* (Prague, 1909) **7**:1532
- *see also:* EL MALE RAḤAMIM; HAZKARAT NESHAMOT; YIZKOR
ASHKELON (city, Isr.) **3**:713
- *Contents:*
- - Ancient Period **3**:713
- - Medieval Period **3**:714
- - Modern **3**:717
- 323 B.C.E. to 70 C.E. **8**:626; **8**:635
- 70 to 634 **9**:245
- 634 to 1099 **9**:261; **9**:262; **9**:263
- 1099 to 1291 **5**:1140; **9**:267ff
- 1291 to 1517 **9**:278
- bronze weights **16**:661
- Garstang, John **7**:330
- Hebrew language **16**:1636
- human geography **9**:589ff
- Joseph son of Tobiah **15**:1179
- oil exploration **9**:795
- Silas **14**:1532
- statistics **1**:place list
- *illus:*
- - text
- - Antoninus Pius coin **3**:165
- - Egyptian record of name **3**:313
- - national park **12**:878
- - synagogue stone screen **12**:569
Ashkeloni, Joseph ben Isaac **12**:839
ASHKENAZ (bib. name) **3**:718
- Armenia **3**:473
- biblical nations **12**:882
ASHKENAZ (reg. Eur.) **3**:719
- Apulian Jewry **3**:227
- cooking, food **6**:1421ff
- culture **8**:666; **8**:691ff
- economic history **16**:1297
- Hebrew pronunciation **14**:1154; **13**:1126ff; **16**:1645ff.
- immigration to Israel **9**:378
- in Israel **9**:497ff; **9**:887ff
- Jerusalem **9**:1438; **9**:1462
- Kabbalah, halakhah **10**:640
- Lithuanian Orthodoxy **10**:395
- masoretic tradition **11**:1100ff
- musical traditions **12**:559
- Ottoman Empire **16**:1548
- rabbinical office **13**:1447,1449
- sickness **14**:1500ff
- Spain **3**:707
- tombstones **15**:1223
- widow **16**:495
- *illus:*
- - text
- - Jerusalem synagogues **9**:1445,1446
- - Pentateuch cantillation **11**:1100-1107
- - Prophets cantillation **11**:1111
- - psalmody, Ps. 95 (mus. notations) **13**:1331
- *see also:* GERMANY
Ashkenaz, Isaac ben Jacob **9**:1156
Ashkenazi (fam., It.), *see* TEDESCHI
Ashkenazi (fam. print.) **13**:1377
Ashkenazi, Aaron ben Moses Judah Zevi **8**:1155
Ashkenazi, Abraham ben Isaac **14**:631
- Eliezer ben Isaac **6**:623
- Mocha, Yemen **12**:199
- publishing **13**:1377
- sons **5**:1242
- Usque, Salomon **16**:22
ASHKENAZI, ABRAHAM BEN JACOB **3**:722
Ashkenazi, Abraham Meshullam Zalman **3**:735
Ashkenazi, Abraham Nathan ben Elisha Ḥayyim, *see* NATHAN OF GAZA
Ashkenazi, Asher **3**:730
Ashkenazi, Asher Judah ben Nathan, *see* WEIDNER, PAULUS
Ashkenazi, Azariah Joshua **9**:1162
Ashkenazi, Azriel, *see* Gunzenhauser, Azriel
Ashkenazi, Azriel ben Moses ha-Levi **15**:815
Ashkenazi, Baruch **4**:268
ASHKENAZI, BEḤOR **3**:723
Ashkenazi, Benjamin ha-Levi **4**:1482
ASHKENAZI, BEZALEL BEN ABRAHAM **3**:723
- *ḥiddushim* **8**:467
- Jerusalem **9**:1437
- Talmud commentaries **11**:333
- *illus:*
- - text
- - *Shitah Mekubbeẓet* (1721) **8**:465
Ashkenazi, Boula **3**:732
ASHKENAZI, DAN **3**:725
Ashkenazi, Eliezer Baruch, *see* MEYER, PAULUS
ASHKENAZI, ELIEZER BEN ELIJAH THE PHYSICIAN **3**:725
- Esther commentary **13**:1102
- *Haggadah* commentaries **7**:1093
- Prague **8**:443
Ashkenazi, Eliezer Isaac, *see* ELIEZER BEN ISAAC
Ashkenazi, Eliezer Susman **11**:61
Ashkenazi, Elisha **15**:1194
ASHKENAZI, GERSHON **3**:726
Ashkenazi, Ḥayyim (print., It.), *see* Ḥayyim ben Isaac ha-Levi Ashkenazi
Ashkenazi, Ḥayyim ben Samuel (print., Pol.) **7**:1190
Ashkenazi, Hillel **14**:154
Ashkenazi, Isaac (print., Syr.) **5**:1242
Ashkenazi, Isaac (r., Er. Isr.) **3**:722
Ashkenazi, Israel **13**:866
Ashkenazi, Jacob (print., Syr.) **5**:1242
Ashkenazi, Jacob (kab., Pol.), *see* TEMERLS, JACOB BEN ELIEZER
Ashkenazi, Jacob ben Ḥayyim (r., Ger.) **7**:1510
Ashkenazi, Jacob ben Isaac (r.) **9**:1278
- Jewish literature **11**:357
- Yiddish literature **16**:801
- *Ze'enah u-Re'enah* **16**:967
Ashkenazi, Jacob Moses ben Abraham Helin **11**:570
Ashkenazi, Jacob Vilna **10**:1008
Ashkenazi, Jehiel, *see* Saks, Jehiel ben Moses
Ashkenazi, Jehiel ben Israel, *see* LURIA, JEHIEL BEN ISRAEL ASHKENAZI
Ashkenazi, Joel, *see* Katzenellenbogen, Joel
Ashkenazi, Jonah **9**:1086
ASHKENAZI, JONAH BEN JACOB **3**:727
- printing **9**:1098
ASHKENAZI, JOSEPH (r., Safed) **3**:727
Ashkenazi, Joseph (r., Latv.) **9**:1333
Ashkenazi, Joseph ben Jacob, *see* GUNZENHAUSER, JOSEPH BEN JACOB
Ashkenazi, Joseph ben Jacob Padua **14**:586
Ashkenazi, Joseph ben Moses, *see* JOSEPH BEN MOSES DARSHAN OF PRZEMYSLANY
Ashkenazi, Joseph ben Shalom, *see* JOSEPH BEN SHALOM ASHKENAZI
Ashkenazi, Joseph ben Solomon **16**:1536
ASHKENAZI, JUDAH BEN JOSEPH **3**:728
ASHKENAZI, JUDAH BEN SIMEON **3**:728
ASHKENAZI, JUDAH SAMUEL **3**:729
- Kabbalah, liturgy **10**:641
ASHKENAZI, MALKIEL **3**:729
- Hebron **8**:232
ASHKENAZI, MEIR BEN BENJAMIN WOLF **3**:729
Ashkenazi, Menahem, *see* Bekemoharar, Menahem ben Isaac
Ashkenazi, Meshullam Zalman **11**:1492
Ashkenazi, Mordecai **11**:700; **14**:355
- Shabbateanism **14**:1246
ASHKENAZI, MORDECAI BEN ISAAC KOHEN **3**:730
Ashkenazi, Mordecai ben Judah Leib **5**:278
Ashkenazi, Moses (r., Candia), *see* MOSES ESRIM VE-ARBA
Ashkenazi, Moses (print., Turk.) **3**:727
ASHKENAZI, MOSES DAVID **3**:730
ASHKENAZI, NAPHTALI BEN JOSEPH **3**:730
Ashkenazi, Nathan **3**:733
Ashkenazi, Nissim **3**:727
- - *Me'am Lo'ez* (1764) **13**:1108
ASHKENAZI, NISSIM ABRAHAM BEN RAPHAEL **3**:731
- Izmir **9**:1163
Ashkenazi, Rachel **11**:61
Ashkenazi, Raphael **3**:728
Ashkenazi, Reuben **3**:727
Ashkenazi, Saadiah ha-Levi **13**:1109
- *illus:*
- - *Sefer Hikrei Lev* (1806) **13**:1109
Ashkenazi, Samuel (Switz.) **5**:1481
ASHKENAZI, SAMUEL JAFFE BEN ISAAC (r., Const.) **3**:731
- Jerusalem Talmud **15**:778
ASHKENAZI, SAUL BEN MOSES HA-KOHEN **3**:731
Ashkenazi, Shalom **4**:1482
- Vidin **16**:121
Ashkenazi, Simeon **12**:30
ASHKENAZI, SOLOMON **3**:731
- Coat of Arms **8**:340
- Istanbul **9**:1088
- Ottoman Empire **16**:1552
- Venice **16**:98
Ashkenazi, Zechariah, *see* Zechariah Zaksel Ashkenazi
ASHKENAZI, ẒEVI HIRSCH BEN JACOB (Ḥakham Ẓevi) **3**:733
- Amsterdam **2**:897; **2**:899
- Aylion, Solomon **3**:996
- chronological chart **8**:766-767
- festivals **6**:1245
- *golem* **7**:755
- Hagiz, Moses **7**:1122
- Ḥayon, Nehemiah **7**:1502
- Loewenstamm, Aryeh Loeb **11**:450
- Oppenheim, David **12**:1421
- *Peri Ḥadash* **8**:458
- portrait **3**:539
- Shabbateanism **14**:1249
- *illus:*
- - text
- - portrait **7**:478
Ashkenazi brothers (16th cent., print.) **14**:628
Ashkenazim, *see* ASHKENAZ
Ashkenazi Rite (litur.) **11**:399ff
ASHKENAZY, VLADIMIR DAVIDOVICH **3**:735
ASHKHABAD (city, Rus.) **3**:735
Ashkuza (anc. people) **3**:718
ASHLAG, YEHUDAH **3**:735
- Zohar **16**:1213
ASHMAN, AHARON **3**:736
- drama, Hebrew **6**:198; **6**:204
- *illus:*
- - *Ha-Adamah ha-Zot* in Habimah **6**:196
Ashman, Y. **5**:458
Ashmedai (spirit), *see* ASMODEUS
Ashmedai (opera) **15**:111
Ashmoret (period.) **1**:newsp. list **12**:1469
Ashmorot (prayer meetings) **13**:1333
Ashmun (deity) **3**:711
Ashpenaz (bib. fig.) **13**:1481
Ashraf, Malik al- (ruler) **14**:755
Ashraf Barsbay, al-Malik al- (sult., Egy.) **11**:836
- Ereẓ Israel **9**:274
- Jerusalem **9**:1424
Ashraf Khalīl, al-Malik al- (sult., Egy.) **11**:835
- Acre **9**:271; **9**:274
ASHREI (litur.) **3**:736
ASHRIKI, MORDECAI **3**:737
Ash-Shafi'i (Musl. jur.) **16**:1279
Ashtamker, Benjamin Samson **8**:1360
- homiletic literature **8**:957
- Oriental literature **12**:1465
Ashtar (deity), *see* ASHTORETH
ASHTAROTH, ASHTEROTH-KARNAIM, KARNAIM (city) **3**:737
ASHTOR, ELIAHU **3**:737
- Cairo *genizah* **16**:1339
ASHTORETH (deity) **3**:738
- Anath **2**:926
- Baal **4**:12
- Chemosh **5**:390; **8**:348
- dysphemism **6**:961
- figurines **3**:306
- idolatry **8**:1227ff
- Sidon **14**:1507
- *illus:*
- - text
- - figurines **3**:318,504
- - ivory carving **3**:317,738
- *see also:* Ishtar
Ashtriel (kab. name) **10**:504
Ashtumker, B. S., *see* Ashtamker, Benjamin Samson
Ashur, see ASSUR; Assyria
'ĀSHŪRA' (fast day) **3**:739
- Muhammad **12**:510
Ashurbanipal (k., Assyr.)
- Asenapper **3**:692
- Kedarites **16**:1351
- Library **3**:371
- Mesopotamia **16**:1504
- Nineveh **12**:1170
- Shushan **14**:1483
- treasury **15**:1362
- warfare **16**:273
- *illus:*

- - feasting in garden **12:**1169
Ashurnaṣirpal II (k., Assyr.) **16:**272ff,1502
Ashur-uballit (k., Assyr.) **12:**1170
- Mesopotamia **16:**1500
Ashworth, Caleb **8:**22
Ashworth, Gerald **12:**1377
ASIA **3:**739
- *Contents:*
- - History **3:**739
- - Demography **3:**745
- chronological chart **8:**766-767
- Israel's relations **9:**432
- Socialism **15:**32
- vital statistics **16:**178ff
- Zionism **16:**1127
- *pop. tables:*
- - text
- - Aden, 1839-1967 **2:**263
- - Afghanistan, Middle Ages and modern times **2:**327
- - Arabian peninsula, pre-Islamic settlement **3:**233
- - Asia Minor, ancient settlement **3:**747
- - Asia's population, 19/20 centuries **13:**893,898,901
- - Birobidzhan, 1928-59 **4:**1045,1049
- - Burma, 19th and 20th cent. **4:**1526
- - Byzantine Empire, major centers of settlement **4:**1551
- - China, major communities 8/20 cent. **5:**469
- - countries with 500 or more Jews, 1967 **5:**1503
- - Cyprus, major communities **5:**1180
- - Georgia, Jewish communities **7:**424
- - India, Jewish settlements **8:**1350
- - Iran (Persia)
- - - emigration to Israel, 1948-1968 **8:**1441
- - - jewish communities **13:**303
- - - Jewish settlements, 1967 **8:**1440
- - Iraq, major settlements, 1947 **8:**1449,1459
- - - Kurdistan (1920-1947) **10:**1296
- - Israel
- - - immigrants, up to 1948 **16:**1127
- - - Jewish population, 1856-1967 **5:**1502; **9:**473-496,533-545
- - - major towns, 1967 **5:**1514
- - - non-Jewish population **9:**1024, 1025
- - Jewish population, 1850-1967 **5:**1495
- - Muslim countries, postwar communities **5:**837
- - Ottoman Empire **16:**1531,1533
- - postwar communities **5:**841
- - Russia **14:**450,471,483,484
- - total Jewish population, 1840-1969 **5:**831
- - Turkey **15:**1457,1459
- - vital statistics **16:**180-183,186,188
- *see also individual countries, peoples*
ASIA MINOR **3:**746
- *archisynagogos* **3:**335
- Bithynia **4:**1060
- Cappadocia **5:**151
- Caria **5:**170
- Cilicia **5:**562
- Galatia **7:**262
- Herod I **8:**384; **8:**635
- Hittites **8:**786
- Ionia **9:**1301
- Jewish settlement plans **16:**287
- Lydia **11:**620
- Miletus **11:**1547
- Pergamum **13:**286
- Phrygia **13:**487
- population **13:**871
- Sardis **14:**876
- Solomon's trade **15:**97ff
- war and warfare **16:**268
- *pop. table:* text
- *see also:* BYZANTINE EMPIRE; OTTOMAN EMPIRE; TURKEY
Asiatic Brethren (freemasons) **8:**523
Asiatics (people) **16:**1499
Asiel, Nelson **15:**311
Asila (port), *see* ARCILA
Asili (kindergarten, It.) **6:**421
ASIMOV, ISAAC **3:**748
Asinaeus (Babyl.), *see* ANILAEUS AND ASINAEUS
ASINIUS POLLIO, GAIUS **3:**749
'Asīra al-Shamāliyya (vill., Samar.) **7:**1531
Asir ha-Tikvah, Isaac ha-Levi, *see* Isaac ha-Levi Asir ha-Tikvah
Asiriyyah (poem type) **13:**1204
Āsiya (w. Pharaoh) **13:**362ff
Aṣiya ben Manasseh **15:**640
Askama, *see* ASCAMA
Askar (vill., Er. Isr.) **7:**436; **14:**1493
ASKENASY, EUGEN **3:**749
ASKENASY, PAUL **3:**749
Askenazi, Léon **14:**1038
AŠKENAZY, LUDVÍK **3:**749
ASKENAZY, SIMON **3:**750
Askelon (city), *see* ASHKELON
Aškerc, Anton **16:**886
Askhabad (city), *see* ASHKHABAD
ASKNAZI, ISAAC LVOVICH **3:**750
ASLAKSSEN, CORT (Aslacus, Conrad) **3:**751
- Hebraists **8:**22
ASMAKHTA (tal. term) **3:**751
- Amoraim **2:**867
- betrothal breach **4:**755
- consecration **8:**282
- contractual obligation **5:**932
- halakhic Midrash **8:**1414
- *notarikon* **12:**1231
- public affairs **13:**1353; **13:**1359
- sharecropping **10:**1535
- surety **15:**525
- *see also:* CONDITIONS; MISTAKE
ASMODEUS (spirit) **3:**754
- Academy on High **2:**208
- *Ashmedai* opera **15:**111
- Ben Temalyon **4:**555
- demon **5:**1526
- Lilith **11:**247
- newly married **2:**954
- Raphael **13:**1549
- Solomon **15:**107; **2:**954
- *Solomon, Testament of* **15:**119
- *illus:* text
Asmonean (period.) **12:**1074; **13:**1050
Asochis (city, Er. Isr.), *see* SHIḤIN
Asociación Cultural Jaim Zhitlowsky (orgn., Urug.) **16:**12
Asociación de Industriales de la Madera y del Hierro (Arg.) **3:**420
Asociación de Sociedades Israelitas (Peru) **13:**325
Asociación Filantrópica Israelita (Arg.) **3:**416; **3:**430
Asociación Mutual Israelita Argentina, *see* A.M.I.A.
Asóka inscriptions (India) **3:**267
Asolo (tn., It.) **15:**1380; **5:**122
Asophon (city, Er. Isr.), *see* ZAPHON
Asor (string instr.) **12:**564
Asp, Matthias **8:**22
Aspaklaryah (journ., U.S.) **1:**newsp. list
Aspamia, *see* SPAIN
Aspects de la France (period.) **2:**232
Asper (coin) **5:**721
Asqanu (city), *see* ASHKELON
Asriel (bib. fig.) **11:**668; **11:**851
Asriel (fam.), *see* Santa Fé
ASS **3:**755
- dietary laws **6:**32
- fauna of Israel **9:**225
- Jewish badge **4:**63
- *illus:*
- - text
- - Balaam **2:**974; **4:**122; **16:**685
- - Messiah led into Jerusalem **11:**1409,1410
- - onager **12:**1395
- *see also:* ASS WORSHIP
Assa (bib. pr.) **4:**858
Assa (Pal. amora), *see* ASSI
Assa, Abraham ben Isaac **10:**1349; **4:**866
Assaban (fam.) **12:**334
Assaf (name), *see also* Asaf; Asaph
Assaf, Ami **16:**253
ASSAF, MICHAEL **10:**309
ASSAF, SIMḤA **3:**756
- Cairo *genizah* **16:**1339
- historiography **8:**562; **8:**564
- Mishpat ha-Shalom ha-Ivri **12:**142
- *illus:*
- - Supreme Court bench **9:**637
ASSAULT **3:**758
- arbitration **3:**298
- imprisonment **8:**1302
- punishment **13:**224
- rescue from **13:**227
Assayay, Pinhas **15:**792
ASSCHER, ABRAHAM **3:**760
- Amsterdam **2:**902
Asscher-Pinkhof, Clara **5:**448; **6:**321
ASSEMANI (fam.) **3:**760
Assemani, Joseph Simon **3:**760; **8:**22
Assemani, Stephanus Evodius **3:**760
Assembly, *see* CONGREGATION
Assembly, the Great, *see* SYNAGOGUE, THE GREAT
Assembly, Sukkot, *see* HAKHEL
Assembly of Deputies (Isr.) *see* Asefat ha-Nivḥarim
ASSEMBLY OF JEWISH NOTABLES (Fr.) **3:**761
- Alsace-Lorraine **2:**755
- consistory organization **5:**907
- history **8:**713ff
- history chart **8:**766-767
- Napoleon **7:**23; **12:**824
- Sinzheim, Joseph David **14:**1616
- *map:* text
- *see also:* SANHEDRIN, FRENCH
ASSEO, DAVID BEN ISAAC **3:**765
- Turkey **15:**1460
ASSER (fam.) **3:**765
Asser, Carel (18/19 cent.) **3:**766
Asser, Carel (19th cent.) **3:**766
Asser, Moses Solomon **3:**765; **13:**815
Asser, Tobias Michaël Carel **3:**766
Asseraf, Issachar **3:**25
Assessment, *see* DAMAGES
Asshur, *see* ASSUR; Assyria
ASSI (Pal. amora) **3:**766
- Ammi bar Nathan **2:**852ff
ASSI, RAV (amora) **3:**767
- Huẓal **8:**1137
Assideans (anc. sect), *see* HASSIDEANS
ASSIGNMENT (OF DEBT) **3:**768
- acquisition by *kinyan* **2:**216
- agency inapplicable **2:**351
- promissory note **11:**838
- Rabbi Nathan's lien **14:**1397
shetar **14:**1388
- suretyship **15:**524
- trustees **14:**1267
ASSIMILATION **3:**770
- *Contents:*
- - Introduction **3:**770
- - Antiquity, Middle Ages **3:**771
- - From Enlightenment Period **3:**772
- - Modern Period **3:**773
- - United States **3:**775
- - Other Western Countries **3:**779
- - The Soviet Union **3:**780
- General
- - Cairo *genizah* **16:**1342
- - community **5:**843; **5:**846ff
- - economic life **16:**1311
- - *galut* **7:**280ff
- - intermarriage **12:**164
- - Jewish identity **10:**60; **10:**61
- - monotheism **3:**44
- - names **12:**807ff
- - 19th century **8:**722
- - Roman culture **14:**243
- - Society for the Promotion of Culture **15:**58ff
- - vital statistics **16:**182ff
- - *see also:* ANTI-SEMITISM; EMANCIPATION
- In Halakhah **7:**412
- - non-Jewish bread **4:**1335
- - wife's ransom **8:**1124
- Trends, Movements
- - Agudat Israel **2:**421
- - Aguddat Aḥim **2:**426
- - American Council for Judaism **2:**819
- - Communism **5:**792ff
- - Haskalah **7:**1433; **7:**1437ff
- - Hellenism **3:**47ff; **8:**294
- - New Christians **12:**1022ff
- - Socialism **15:**28ff
- - Socialism, Jewish **15:**38ff
- - Verband Nationaldeutscher Juden **16:**106
- - Zionism **16:**1031
- - *see also:* SHOMER ISRAEL
- Central Europe
- - Austrian *Toleranzpatent* **3:**892
- - Čechů-Židů, Svaz **5:**266
- - Court Jews **5:**1008
- - Familiants Laws **6:**1163
- - German Jews **2:**648; **7:**476
- - German students **10:**804
- - Hep! Hep! riots **8:**331
- - *Mischlinge* **16:**677
- - Prague **13:**970
- - Slovakia **14:**1680
- Eastern Europe
- - *Izraelita* **9:**1165
- - Poland **13:**735
- - Russia **14:**436, 442, 460, 480, 481
- - Warsaw **16:**337
- - *Yevsektsiya* conflicts **16:**780
- Western Europe
- - Amsterdam **2:**900
- - France **7:**24
- Other Places
- - Mountain Jews **12:**480
- - Uruguay **16:**13
- Views on
- - Aḥad Ha-Am **2:**443ff
- - Borochov, Ber **4:**1255
- - Brandes, Georg **4:**1304
- - Byk, Emil **4:**1547
- - Dubnow, Simon **6:**254
- - Geiger, Abraham **7:**358
- - Goldmann, Nahum **7:**725
- - Herzl, Theodor **8:**411
- - Kaufmann, Y. **16:**1351
- - Kohn, Jindřich **10:**1146
- - Lenin **16:**779
- - Mendelssohn, Moses **11:**1333; **11:**1334ff
- - Trotski, Leon **15:**1406
- - Wassermann, Jakob **16:**363
Associated Israel Press **9:**1017
Association des Juifs en Belgique (Judenrat) **4:**420ff
Association for Adult Education (Isr.) **9:**965
Association for Combating Anti-Semitism, *see* VEREIN ZUR ABWEHR DES

ANTISEMITISMUS
Association for Jewish Demography (Isr.) **15:**56; **15:**347
Association for Promoting Jewish Settlement in Palestine **16:**1154
Association for the Promotion of Agriculture and Crafts in Palestine (Ger.) **16:**1115
Association for Relief and Protection of Jewish Immigrants (U.S.) **11:**160
Association of Banks in Israel **9:**825
Association of Jewish Artists (Er. Isr.) **9:**1011
Association of Jewish Book Publishers (U.S.) **13:**1377
Association of Jewish Libraries (U.S.) **11:**193; **15:**55
Association of National-German Jews, *see* VERBAND NATIONALDEUTSCHER JUDEN
Association of Orthodox Jewish Scientists **15:**1002
Association of Painters and Sculptors in Israel **9:**1011
Association of Religious Scientists (Isr.) **9:**903
Association of Societies for Jewish History and Literature, *see* VERBAND DER VEREINE FUER JUEDISCHE GESCHICHTE UND LITERATUR
Association of Wine Growers (Er. Isr.) **5:**946
Association of Young Zionist Societies (Eng.) **15:**448
Assuan (tn., Egy.), *see* Syene
ASSUMPÇÃO, DIOGO DA (mart.) **3:**783
Assumptionist Fathers (rel. order) **5:**1125
Assumption of Moses (Apoc.), *see* MOSES, ASSUMPTION OF
ASSUR (city, Assyr.) **3:**783
- Akkadian **2:**495
- excavation **16:**1507
- inscriptions **16:**667
- Mesopotamia **16:**1500
Assur, Marx **5:**1009
Assus (art.) **13:**118
Assusi, Joseph **15:**1439
ASS WORSHIP **3:**784
- Apion **3:**178
- in Temple **7:**895
- Plutarch **13:**654
Assyria (kdm.)
- Ahab **2:**437
- Ahaz **2:**455
- Akkadian **2:**495
- Arameans **3:**255
- Assur **3:**783
- Assyriology **16:**1506
- Babylonia **4:**31, 34
- calendar **17:**1262
- excavations **16:**1506ff
- exile **6:**1034
- Hurrians **16:**1498
- Judah, Kingdom of **11:**852
- kingship **10:**1011ff
- Kittim **10:**1080
- Lebanon **10:**1542
- Mari **11:**978
- Mesopotamia **16:**1500ff
- Nimrod **12:**1166
- Qumran scrolls **13:**332
- Samaritans **14:**728; **14:**736
- Sargon II **14:**880
- Semites **14:**1148
- virginity laws **16:**160ff
- warfare **16:**272
- *illus:*
- - Black Obelisk **3:**320
- - dynasties (table) **11:**980
- - Esarhaddon stele **6:**853
- - exile (map) **8:**607
Assyrian Camp (place, Jer.) **9:**1400; **15:**1168
Assyriology **16:**1506
Astaribo (angel) **11:**249
Astarot (demon) **5:**1532
Astarté (deity), *see* ASHTORETH
ASTI (city, It.) **3:**785
- *illus:* text
- *see also.* APAM
Astier (10th cent., Fr.) **16:**133
Astor, Alexander **3:**839; **6:**273
Astor, John Jacob **12:**1075
ASTORGA (city, Sp.) **3:**785
Astori, Vidal **12:**532; **16:**61
ASTRAKHAN (city, Rus.) **3:**786
Astray, Pilar Millán **14:**523
Astriga (enchantress), *see* Striga
ASTROLABE **3:**786
- nautical aid **14:**1413
- *illus:*
- - text
- - *Guide to the Perplexed* **8:***fcg.* 1143
- - *Ma'aseh Tuviyyah* **3:**804
- *see also:* ASTRONOMY
ASTROLOGY **3:**788
- *Contents:*
- - Bible and Apocrypha **3:**788
- - Talmud and Midrash **3:**789
- - Dark Ages **3:**790
- - Middle Ages **3:**791
- - Jewish Court Astrologers **3:**794
- - Jewish Folklore **3:**795
- General
- - Borsippa school **4:**1259
- - chiromancy **5:**477
- - divination **6:**115ff
- - magic **11:**710
- - microcosm **11:**1502
- - Nostradamus **12:**1230
- - practical Kabbalah **10:**636
- - seals **14:**1080
- - *Sefer Yeẓirah* **13:**1026; **16:**784ff
- - zodiac **16:**1191
- Views on
- - Gersonides **13:**446
- - Ibn Ezra, Abraham **8:**1164,1169
- - Ibn Waqār **8:**1206
- - Maimonides **11:**780
- - Zacuto, Abraham **16:**903
- *illus:*
- - text
- - Nostradamus **12:**1231
- - *Reshit Ḥokhmah* (13th cent. ms.) **2:**738
- - *see also:* ZODIAC
ASTRONOMY **3:**795
- *Contents:*
- - In Bible **3:**795
- - In Apocrypha **3:**796
- - In Talmud, Midrash **3:**796
- - In Middle Ages **3:**799
- - In Late Renaissance **3:**805
- - Modern Astronomy **3:**806
- Abraham bar Ḥiyya **2:**132
- Apocrypha, Pseudepigrapha **3:**183
- Chaldean **16:**1503ff
- Gersonides **11:**98
- Jewish calendar **5:**44f
- Maimonides **11:**779
- nautical aid **14:**1413
- rabbinical literature **13:**1462
- sages **14:**650
- sun blessing **15:**518
- Zacuto, Abraham **16:**903
- zodiac **16:**1191
- *illus:*
- - astrolabe **3:**786
- - calendar conversion chart (1568) **5:**33
- - *Guide to the Perplexed* **8:***fcg.* 1143
- - Levi ben Gershom's "Jacob's staff" **8:**1430
- - moon, areas named after Jews **12:**290
- - Zacuto, Abraham **16:**905
- - *Ẓurat ha-Areẓ ve-Tavnit Kaddurei ha-Raki'a (1546)* **3:**786,797,800; **4:**303; **13:**1102
- - *see also:* ZODIAC
ASTRUC, ABBA MARI BEN MOSES BEN JOSEPH OF LUNEL **3:**807
- Abraham of Montpellier **2:**146
- articles of faith **3:**656
- Maimonidean controversy **11:**751
- Toledo **15:**1203
ASTRUC, ELIE-ARISTIDE **3:**808
Astruc, Isaiah ben Abba Mari **15:**1378
ASTRUC, JEAN **3:**809
Astruc, Mardochée **5:**207; **7:**146
- Judeo-Provençal **6:**910; **10:**441
- Lunel, Jacob de **11:**567
ASTRUC, SAUL HA-KOHEN **3:**809
- Algiers **2:**622
- Bougie **4:**1274
- Isaac Perfet **9:**32
Astruc, Solomon, of Barcelona **7:**336
ASTRUC, ZACHARIE **3:**810
Astruc de Noves (Sen Negre), *see* ABBA MARI BEN ELIGDOR
ASTRUC HA-LEVI **3:**810
- Tortosa dispute **15:**1271ff
Astruc of Béziers **4:**793
Astrug de Porta **4:**564
Astyages (k., Media) **11:**1177
- Cyrus **5:**1184
- Nabonidus **12:**746
- Persia **13:**302
Asufi (foundling) **11:**841
Asuppot (journ.) **1:** newsp. list
Asuta (greeting) **7:**914
Asveiros (Rom.), *see* QUINTILIUS VARUS
Aswān (t., Egy.), *see* Syene
Asylum **2:**764,769
- *see also:* CITY OF REFUGE
Aszkenazy, F. **4:**885; **13:**798
ASZOD (tn., Hung.) **3:**810
Aszod, Aaron Samuel **3:**811
ASZOD, JUDAH BEN ISRAEL **3:**811
- yeshivah
- Deutsch, Eliezer Ḥayyim **5:**1587
- Pollak, Moses Ha-Levi **10:**699; **13:**834
At (mag.) **1:**newsp. list
'Atāba (Arab poetry) **9:**1038
ATAKI (vill., Bess.) **3:**812
'Aṭallah (Chr. fam.) **9:**1435
Atallef (zool.), see BAT
ATAR (fam.) **3:**812
- Meknès **11:**272
- *see also:* Abenatar; Ben Atar
ATAR, HAIM **3:**813
Atar, Moses ben **4:**539
Atarah (kab. conc.), *see Malkhut*
'Aṭarah (headdress) **5:**1130ff
- *tallit* and **15:**743
- Torah ornaments **15:**1256
- *illus:*
- - Israel Ba'al Shem Tov's tallit **9:**1057
Atargatis (Atar'ata; Syr. deity) **8:**468
- Ashtoreth and **3:**738
- Ashtaroth temple **3:**737
- Hadad's consort **7:**1040
ATAROT (moshav, Isr.) **3:**813
- airfield **9:**837
- Jerusalem development **9:**1473; **9:**1487
ATAROTH (bibl. stlmts.) **3:**814
Atartoros, Solomon **2:**564
Ata Textile Company (Isr.) **12:**229
Atatürk, Kemal **15:**1457
Atbaḥ (lit. style) **2:**230
Atbash (lit. devic; *gematria*) **7:**370
- acrostics **2:**230
- *Baraita of 32 Rules* **4:**195
- *mene, mene, tekel, u-farsin* **11:**1350
- - *illus:*
- - cryptographic letter combinations **2:**148
Ateret Ẓion (Tun. mvmt.) **3:**994
Aṭfīr (bib. fig.), *see* POTIPHAR
ATHALIAH (q., Judah) **3:**814
- Ahab **2:**435
- history chart **8:**766-767
- Jehoiada **9:**1319
- Jerusalem Baalism **9:**1383
- Phoenician cult **8:**599,600
- *geneal. table:* **5:**1342
- *illus:* text
"Athaliah's Downfall" (paint., Coypel) **3:**815
Athanasius (6/7 cent. Chr. patr.) **4:**860
'Athar (deity) **14:**588
Atheism **7:**670
- *minut* **8:**359
Athena (deity) **2:**926
ATHENS (city, Gr.) **3:**815
- diaspora **6:**9
- Greece **7:**879
- ostracism **16:**660
- P.F.L.P. **9:**416
- *Yahud* coins **8:**627
- *illus:*
- - synagogue **7:**873
Athens (city, Ga.) **7:**429
AT(H)IAS (fam.) **3:**819
- typography **15:**1487
Athias, Abraham (mart., Sp.) **3:**819
Athias, Abraham ben Raphael Hezekiah **13:**1104
Athias, David (r., Fr.) **3:**819; **4:**1244
Athias, David ben Moses (writ. It.) **3:**819
Athias, David Israel (r., Holl.) **3:**819
ATHIAS, IMMANUEL **3:**819
Athias, Jacob Ḥayyim **3:**819; **4:**1244
ATHIAS, JOSEPH (print., Holl.) **3:**819
- *illus:*
- - text
- - Auerbach's *Seliḥot* **13:**1103
- - Bible (1661) **15:**1484
Athias, Joseph (It.) **3:**819
Athias, Moses (writ., It.) **3:**819
Athias, Moses (Isr.) **3:**819
Athias, Moses Israel (Eng.) **3:**819
Athias, Solomon da Costa, *see* COSTA ATHIAS, SOLOMON DA
Athias, Yom Tov **3:**819; **16:**21
Athias Pereira (fam.), *see* AT(H)IAS
Athletics **15:**315
ATHLIT (port, Er. Isr.) **3:**821
- archaeology **3:**327ff
- foundation **9:**269
- Mamluks **9:**274
- Palmaḥ **9:**357
- salt works **9:**341
- statistics **1:**place list
- tombs **15:**1218
- *illus:*
- - text
- - Crusader castle **3:**328; **5:**1143
- - Haifa-Tel Aviv highway **9:**836
Athlit Agricultural Experimental Station **2:**26; **6:**1209
ATHRIBIS (anc. city, Egy.) **3:**822
- Diaspora **6:**9
ATHRONGES (1st cent. B.C.E.) **3:**822
Atid (orgn., U.S.) **15:**450
Atid (Cargo Lines; oil co.) **4:**1241; **9:**328; **9:**835
Atidenu (period., Arg.) **13:**1040
- statistics **1:**newsp. list
Atidenu (journ., Ger.) **1:** newsp. list
Atidot (journ.) **4:**201
- statistics **1:**newsp. list
Atidot Israel (orgn., Fr.) **4:**1446
Atika (loc.) **15:**1146

ATIL (Itil; Khazar capital) **3**:823
- Khorezm **10**:955
- Uzbekistan Jews **16**:40
Atirat (deity), *see* ASHERAH
Atkins, Larry **15**:305
ATLAN, JEAN **3**:824
- *illus:* text
ATLANTA (city, Ga.) **3**:824
Atlantic (refugee boat) **11**:1133
ATLANTIC CITY (N.J.) **3**:825
- *illus:*
- - Federation of American Zionists convention (1908) **15**:1623
Atlantic Provinces (Can.), *see* MARITIME PROVINCES
Atlas (map) **11**:927
ATLAS (mt. range, N. Afr.) **3**:826
- *illus:*
- - text
- - Agoin Jews **12**:334
- - Berber Jewish women **4**:587
- - Demnate, heads of congregation **5**:1492
ATLAS, DAVID **3**:827
ATLAS, ELEAZAR **3**:828
Atlas, Jacob **15**:817
ATLAS, JECHEZKIEL **3**:828
- partisan unit **13**:146
Atlas, Meir **16**:361
ATLAS, SAMUEL **3**:829
'Atnaḥah (cantillation sign), *see 'Etnaḥ*
Atom **3**:829
Atomic Energy **6**:537
Atomic Energy Commission **9**:969; **11**:79
ATOMIC ENERGY IN ISRAEL **9**:795
- I.A.E.A. **15**:1565
- *illus:* text
ATOMISM (theory) **3**:829
- Aaron ben Elijah **2**:12
- Karaite Kalam **13**:433
- space and place **15**:218
- time **15**:1142
Aton (animal), *see* ASS
Aton (Egy. deity) **2**:487; **2**:807
- hymn **6**:484
ATONEMENT **3**:830
- altar **2**:770
- death **5**:1423
- *eglah arufah* **6**:475
- fasting **6**:1191
- Hermann Cohen **13**:461
- Johanan ben Zakkai **9**:242; **10**:153
- *kittel* **10**:1079
- leper **11**:36
- Messiah **16**:237
- punishment as **13**:1386; **14**:136
- purity **13**:1406
- ransom **5**:856ff
- repentance **14**:75
- sacrifice **14**:600ff
- *illus:* text
- *see also:* CONFESSION OF SINS; DAY OF ATONEMENT; FORGIVENESS; KIPPER; REPENTANCE
Atonement, Day of, *see* DAY OF ATONEMENT
Atorcar, Yuce **15**:836
Atrahasis, Epic of (Mesop. leg.) **6**:1353; **12**:1192;
ATRAN, FRANK Z. **3**:832
Atrani, Samuel **5**:915
Atrato (refugee boat) **9**:521
Atriplex (flora) **9**:225
Atropatene (kdm.) **5**:1284
Atroth-Addar (city, Er. Isr.) **3**:814
Atroth-Beth-Joab (loc., Er., Isr.) **3**:814
Atroth-Shophan (city, Er., Isr.) **3**:814
Atsiz (Seljuk) **9**:263,1414
Attachment to God, *see* DEVEKUT
ATTAH EḤAD (litur.) **3**:833
ATTAH HORETA LADA'AT (prayer) **3**:833
Attah Konanta Olam (piyyut) **3**:977
ATTAH ZOKHER (litur.) **3**:833
- *illus:* text
Attal (Mor. fam.) **12**:337ff
Attal, Jacob **15**:792
Attali, E. **16**:1165
'Attar (deity) **3**:738
ATTAR, ḤAYYIM BEN MOSES (IBN) **3**:833
- Azulai, Ḥayyim **3**:1019
- Elbaz, Samuel **6**:572
- Hezekiah da Silva **8**:458
ATTAR, JUDAH BEN JACOB IBN **3**:835
- Sarfati, Elijah **14**:880
Attar, Judah ben Obed ibn **3**:835
'Attār, Moses ben **2**:516; **13**:816
Attasi, Hashem al- **15**:646; **16**:654
Attell, Abe **15**:305
Attel, Jonny **15**:306
Attell, Monte **15**:306
Attencammul (loc., Ind.) **5**:621
ATTIA, ISAAC BEN ISAIAH **3**:836
ATTIA, SHEM-TOV **3**:836
Attia, Solomon **16**:1533
Attias (name), *see* Athias
Attica (loc., Gr.) **6**:10; **7**:868
Attika Kaddisha (kab. term) **10**:561
Attikot (journ.) **1**:newsp. list
Attik yomayya (yomin), see ANCIENT OF DAYS
Attitudes, (Zion. pam.) **16**:641
ATTLEE, CLEMENT RICHARD, EARL **3**:836
- Israel immigration **9**:357ff
- Jewish refugees **16**:1088
Atto di Fede, *see* AUTO DA FÉ
ATTORNEY (leg. repr.) **3**:837
- appointed by court **13**:956; **13**:960; **13**:961
- *see also:* AGENCY; BET DIN AND JUDGES
Attorney, power of (leg. term) **2**:352ff
- assignment of debt **3**:769
Atz, Jacob **15**:301
Aualis (dist., Aby.) **7**:1493
Aub, Hirsch **3**:838
AUB, JOSEPH **3**:838
- affirmation of Judaism **3**:660
AUB, MAX **3**:838
- *illus:* text
Aubagne (loc., Provence) **13**:1259
Aubier, Dominique **5**:313
Aubigné, Agrippa d' **7**:139; **5**:1071
Aubriot, Hugues **13**:106
Aubry, Esaias **8**:22
AUCKLAND (city, N. Z.) **3**:839
- *illus:* text
Audoin (Audouin; bp.), *see* HILDUIN
Audran, Prosper Gabriel **8**:22
AUER, LEOPOLD **3**:840
- Achron, Joseph **2**:211
- Davydov, Karl **5**:1370
AUERBACH (fam.) **3**:840
- *geneal. table:* text
AUERBACH, ABRAHAM BEN SELIG AVI'EZRI **3**:844
- family **3**:842; **3**:843
- Sinzheim, Joseph **14**:1616
- *geneal. table:* **3**:841
Auerbach, Abraham ben Isaac **3**:842
- *illus:*
- - *Seliḥot* **13**:1103
Auerbach, Abraham Samuel **3**:844
Auerbach, Akiba **10**:846
Auerbach, Arieh Leibush ben Mordecai Mardush **3**:843
AUERBACH, ARNOLD JACOB ("Red") **3**:844
- sport **15**:304
AUERBACH, BERTHOLD **3**:845
- Oppenheim's illustrations **12**:1424
AUERBACH, ELIAS **3**:846
Auerbach, Eliezer ben Ḥayyim **3**:843
Auerbach, Emil Isaac **3**:844
AUERBACH, EPHRAIM **3**:846
AUERBACH, FRANK **3**:595
- *illus:*
- - "Mornington Crescent. . ." **3**:618
Auerbach, Ḥayyim ben Isaac **3**:843
Auerbach, Isaac **14**:398
AUERBACH, ISAAC EISIG BEN ISAIAH **3**:846
Auerbach, Isaac Itzik ben Ḥayyim **3**:843
AUERBACH, ISAAC LEVIN **3**:847
AUERBACH, ISRAEL **3**:847
Auerbach, Israel Mattathias **3**:843
Auerbach, Jacob (Pol. r.) **3**:842
Auerbach, Jacob (print.) **15**:817
Auerbach, Jacob (Bib. trans.) **4**:875
Auerbach, Judah **3**:842
Auerbach, Judah Leib ben Israel **3**:843
AUERBACH, LEOPOLD **3**:847
AUERBACH, MEIR BEN ISAAC **3**:848
Auerbach, Menahem **3**:843
Auerbach, Menahem ben Ḥayyim **3**:843
Auerbach, Menahem Mendel ben Meshullam **3**:841; **10**:1280
Auerbach, Menahem Mendel ben Moses **3**:841
Auerbach, Meyer **3**:843
Auerbach, Moses (court J.) **3**:840
Auerbach, Moses (r.) **3**:844
Auerbach, Moses Judah Leib ben Benjamin **14**:92
Auerbach, Naphtali Herz **7**:112
Auerbach, Nathan of Satanov **3**:841
Auerbach, Perez ben Menahem Nahum **3**:843
Auerbach, Philip **4**:346; **7**:497; **7**:499
Auerbach, Segismundo **3**:410
Auerbach, Selig (Pol.) **3**:842
Auerbach, Selig Avi'ezri (Fr.) **3**:842
Auerbach, Selig Avi'ezri (Ger.) **3**:844
Auerbach, S. H. (Bib. trans.) **4**:875
Auerbach, Simeon (16th cent.) **5**:371
Auerbach, S. Mortimer **15**:312
Auerbach, Solomon Zalman **11**:289
Auerbach, Yuri Lvovich **5**:408
Auerbach, Ẓevi Benjamin (17/18 cent.) **3**:842
Auerbach, Ẓevi Benjamin (19th cent.) **3**:843; **7**:81; **8**:956
- *Sefer ha-Eshkol* **2**:147
Auerbach, Ẓevi Hirsch ben Menahem **3**:843
Auerbacher, Israel, *see* Wolf, Israel
Auerbach-Fishhof (fam.), *see* AUERBACH
Auerbach-Levy, William **5**:220
AUERNHEIMER, RAOUL **3**:848
Auerswald, Heinz **8**:880; **16**:347
Aufbau (period.) **7**:423; **13**:1053
Aufhauset, Siegfried **15**:28
AUFRUFEN (Torah aliyah) **3**:849
- synagogue **15**:584
- *see also:* TORAH, READING OF
AUGSBURG (city, Ger.) **3**:849
- history chart (1439,1555) **8**:766-767
- seal **14**:1079
- synod **13**:1461; **15**:633
- *illus:*
- - community seal **14**:1078
"Augsburg *ḥillukim*" (method of study) **3**:849
Augury, *see* DIVINATION
August II (k., Pol.) **3**:809
August III (k., Pol.), *see* Frederick Augustus II
August, C. F., **15**:1128
Augusta (city, Ga.) **7**:429
Augusta (city, Me.) **11**:782
Augusta Victoria hospital (Jer.) **9**:1462; **12**:482; **12**:484
- *illus:*
- - British high commissioner's residence **9**:1475
Auguste Baumier School (Mogador, Mor.) **12**:332
Augusti, J. C. W. **4**:873
AUGUSTINE (Ch. F.) **3**:851
- Apocrypha **3**:186
- Church Fathers **5**:553
- golden calf **7**:712
- Jerome **9**:1378
- role of Jews **8**:654ff
- Seneca the Younger **14**:1158
AUGUSTOW (tn., Pol.) **3**:852
AUGUSTUS (Rom. emp.) **3**:852
- Agrippa, Marcus Vipsanius **2**:418
- Alexander the False **2**:577
- Archelaus **3**:334
- Aristobulus' trial **3**:442
- Cyrene Jews **5**:1184
- Herod I **8**:376ff; **8**:635
- Herod and Nabateans **12**:743
- Herod's palace **9**:1394
- history chart **8**:766-767
- Jews in Egypt **6**:488
- on Judaism **14**:232
- Sanhedrin **14**:836
- slaves **16**:1276
- Temple tax **15**:980
Augustus II (the Strong; Ger. k.) **10**:1579
Augustus II (k., Pol.), *see* August II
Augustus III (k., Pol.), *see* Frederick Augustus II
Augustus Frederick, Prince (Duke of Sussex, Eng.) **4**:976; **6**:756
- Hebraists **8**:61
'Auja al-Ḥafīr, *see* NIẒẒANAH
Aumeier, Hans **6**:917
"Aunt Naomi" (writ.), *see* Landa, Gertrude
Auping, Samuel **15**:1300
'Auran (Hasm.), *see* ELEAZAR BEN MATTATHIAS
Aurangzeb (Moghul ruler) **12**:897
Auranitis (reg.), *see* HAURAN
Aurelia Esbus (city, Provincia Arabia), *see* HESHBON
Aurelian (Rom. emp.) **12**:1318
- history chart **8**:766-767
Aurelius, Marcus (Rom. emp.), *see* MARCUS AURELIUS ANTONINUS
AURICH (tn., Ger.) **3**:853
Aurivillius, Carl **8**:22
"Aurivius Family" (paint., J. Israels) **3**:550
Aurogallus, M. **8**:22
Aurora (city, Ill.) **8**:1255
Aurora (newsp.), *see La Alborada*
AURUM CORONARIUM (Rom. tax) **3**:854
- taxation **15**:838
Auscha (tn., Cz.), *see* USTEK
Auschwitz (tn., Pol.), *see* OSWIECIM
AUSCHWITZ (concen. camp) **3**:854
- Amsterdam Jews **2**:903
- Frank, Anne **7**:53
- gassing **16**:1332
- Heschel A. J. **7**:778
- history chart **8**:766-767
- Hoess, Rudolf **8**:806
- Holocaust **8**:871,894
- Mengele, Josef **11**:1353
- *illus:*
- - text
- - Eban, Abba, official visit **13**:782
- - faces of victims **8**:875-880
- - "Loading a Transport. . ." (L.

Haas) Fig. 81 **3**-ART
- - suicide of inmates **8:**885
- - transport of women and children **8:**875
- *see also:* OSWIECIM
AUSCHWITZ TRIALS **3:**873
- *illus:* text
AUSLAENDER, NAHUM **3:**874
AUSLANDER, JOSEPH **15:**1579
Auslandsorganisation der NSDAP (Nazi orgn.) **15:**996
AUSPITZ (fam.) **3:**875
Auspitz, Abraham Shaye **3:**875
Auspitz, Heinrich **3:**875; **11:**1196
Auspitz, Lazar **3:**875
Auspitz, Rudolph **3:**875
Aussee (vill., Morav.) **6:**311
Aussenkommandos (Ger. squads) **3:**856
Aussig (tn., Bohem.), *see* USTI NAD LABEM
AUSTER, DANIEL **3:**875
- Eliash, Mordecai **6:**617
- Jerusalem mayor **9:**1476;1498
Austerberg-Verakoff, Max **16:**1152
AUSTERLITZ (tn., Morav.) **3:**876
- museum **12:**543
- Tachov **15:**694
- *illus:* text
Austerlitz, Friedrich **13:**809
Austerlitz, Leopold **11:**1556
Austin (city, Minn.) **12:**39
Austin (vill., Nev.) **12:**1017
Austin (city, Tex.) **15:**1034ff
Austin, Alfred **6:**775
AUSTRALIA **3:**877
- *Contents:*
- - 19th Century **3:**878
- - Contemporary Jewry **3:**883
- - Community Life **3:**884
- - Community Organization and Services **3:**885
- - Jews in Public Life **3:**886
- - Israel Relations **3:**886
- - Aliyah **3:**886
- Ashkenazim **3:**721
- assimilation **3:**779
- demography **5:**1498ff; **8:**733; **13:**887ff
- divorce statistics **6:**136
- education **6:**451ff
- Executive Council of Jewry **3:**712
- Habonim **8:**1243
- Ha-Shomer ha-Ẓa'ir **7:**1376
- immigration to **14:**32
- intermarriage rates **12:**166
- Isaacs, Isaac Alfred **9:**40
- Israel's relations **9:**432
- law **10:**1491ff
- military **11:**1554
- Monash, Sir John **12:**237
- Montefiore, Joseph **12:**270
- politics **13:**808ff
- press **13:**1025
- Sha'arei Emunah Synagogue **4:**1376
- Six-Day War **9:**543
- socialism **15:**27
- Soviet Jewry **14:**500
- students' movements **15:**453
- synagogues **1:**syn. list
- U.N.S.C.O.P. **15:**1688
- vital statistics **16:**183ff
- War Crimes Trials **16:**291ff
- Zionist Movement **4:**1377; **16:**1105
- *illus:*
- - text
- - Mount Scopus Memorial College, Melbourne, Victoria **6:**426
- - Israel-Australia soccer match, 1969 **9:**1019
- *pop. tables:*
- - text
- - Jewish community organization, and population, 1968 **5:**841
- - Jewish population, 1840-1969 **5:**831,1495
- - Melbourne (1933, 1961) **11:**1278,1279
- - nineteenth-twentieth cents. **13:**893,898,901
- - postwar communities **5:**839
- - Total number of Jews, 1967 **5:**1503
- - Victoria (1861,1961) **11:**1279
- - vital statistics **16:**184
Australian Hebrew (newsp.) **3:**880
Australian Jewish Herald (newsp.) **13:**1056
Australian Jewish Historical Society **12:**724
Australian Jewish News (newsp.) **13:**1025
Australian Jewish Post (newsp.) **13:**1025
Australian Jewish Times (newsp.) **13:**1056
Australian Zionist Federation **16:**1106
AUSTRIA **3:**887
- *Contents:*
- - Middle Ages **3:**887
- - Reformation—19th Century **3:**890
- - 19th Century **3:**893
- - After 1918 **3:**869
- - Holocaust **3:**898
- - Postwar **3:**902
- - Israel Relations **3:**904
- General
- - archives **3:**381
- - capitulations **5:**150
- - Middle East interests **9:**305ff
- - newspapers **12:**1048
- - press **13:**1033
- - stamps **15:**330
- - Vienna **16:**122
- Cultural Life
- - Chajes, Hirsch Perez **5:**325
- - Freud, Sigmund **7:**161f
- - Haskalah **7:**1434
- - Hebrew MSS **11:**906
- - Jellinek, Adolf **9:**1337
- - Reinhardt, Max **14:**59
- - Schnitzler, Arthur **14:**985
- - Straus, Oscar **15:**432
- - Werfel, Franz **16:**450
- - Zweig, Stefan **16:**1248
- History
- - annexation to Germany **7:**490
- - Court Jews **5:**1009
- - emancipation **6:**707ff
- - Francis Joseph I **7:**48
- - French Revolution **7:**157
- - Gestapo **7:**529
- - history chart **8:**766-767
- - Hitler, Adolf **8:**782
- - Holocaust **8:**885
- - *Iudex Judaeorum* **9:**1152
- - Kreisky, Bruno **10:**1254
- - League of Nations **10:**1523
- - markets and fairs **11:**1002ff
- - minority rights **12:**43ff
- - neo-Nazism **12:**955
- - Rudolf I of Hapsburg **14:**381
- - *semikhah* **8:**683
- - socialism **15:**26
- - socialism, Jewish **15:**42
- - Vienna, Congress of **16:**132
- - War Crimes Trials **16:**296ff
- - *see also:* HAPSBURG MONARCHY
- Anti-Semitism
- - Aaron of Neustadt **2:**22
- - Abraham a Sancta Clara **2:**130
- - Albert III **2:**530
- - Albert V **2:**530
- - anti-Semitic parties **8:**738
- - Christian Social Party **5:**516
- - Dollfuss, Engelbert **6:**155
- - Lueger, Karl **11:**556
- - 19th century **3:**124
- - *see also:* ANTI-SEMITIC POLITICAL PARTIES AND ORGANIZATIONS
- Zionism **16:**1106
- - Abeles, Otto **2:**61
- - Bato, Ludwig Yomtov **4:**326
- - Bernfeld, Siegfried **4:**675
- - Bierer, Rubin **4:**984
- - Birnbaum, Nathan **4:**1041
- - Herzl, Theodor **8:**407f
- - Po'alei Zion **13:**657ff
- Community Life and Statistics
- - communal organization **5:**825
- - crime **5:**1091
- - demography **5:**1499ff
- - divorce statistics **6:**135
- - education **6:**423ff
- - Frankl, Ludwig August **7:**100
- - *Landjudenschaft* **10:**1405
- - migration trends **8:**720; **9:**531ff **16:**1523
- - population **13:**880ff
- - refugees **14:**33
- - Rothschild family **14:**338
- - status of Jews **8:**716ff
- - students' movements **15:**448
- - synagogues **1:**synagogue list
- - universities **15:**1677
- - Volkspartei, Juedische **16:**213
- - *yeshivot* **16:**764ff
- - Youth Aliyah **16:**862
- Occupations
- - banking **4:**168
- - journalism **10:**304ff
- - military service **11:**1555
- - law **10:**1490ff
- - medicine **11:**1196ff
- - politics **13:**809ff
- - publishing **13:**1366
- - railroads **13:**1518
- - silver purveyors **12:**63
- - tobacco trade **15:**1176
- *illus:*
- - Jewish badge, decree by Ferdinand I **4:**69
- - Levant stamp **15:**331
- - medieval pointed hat **10:**405
- - *Toleranzpatent* **15:**1210
- *table:* anti-Semitic parties, 1882-1910 **3:**81
- *see also:* GALICIA
Austrian (fam.) **12:**39
Austrian hospice (Jer.) **9:**1455
Austrian Literature, *see* GERMAN LITERATURE
Austrian rite (litur.), *see* Polish rite
Austrittsgemeinde (cmty.) **12:**956,1488
- Adass Jeshurun **2:**254
- Bamberger, Seligman Baer **4:**155
- Breuer, Isaac **4:**1364
- Frankfort **7:**88
- Hildesheimer, Azriel **8:**476
- Hirsch, S.R. **8:**512
- Horovitz, Jacob **8:**980
- Reform and Orthodox **8:**723
- Secession Law **7:**478
Austro-Hungary, *see* HAPSBURG MONARCHY
Austro-Israelitic Union (J. orgn.), *see* UNION, OESTERREICH-ISCH-ISRAELITISCHE
AUSUBEL, DAVID PAUL **3:**906
AUSUBEL, NATHAN **3:**907
Authorities, *see* RESHUT
Authority, public, *see* PUBLIC AUTHORITY
AUTHORITY, RABBINICAL **3:**907
- *Contents:*
- - Development of Law **3:**907
- - Authority of Scholars **3:**908
- - Authority in Decisions **3:**908
- - Authority of Generations **3:**909
- - Evolution of Halakhah **3:**909
- - "Hilkheta Ke-Vatra'ei" **3:**910
- Assembly of Jewish Notables **3:**763
- chief rabbi, chief rabbinate **5:**418
- custom **12:**13
- decisions of halakhah **14:**192ff
- fines **6:**1288
- *geonim* **7:**316
- hakham bashi **7:**1147ff
- halakhic classification **7:**1159
- Ḥasidism **7:**1418
- interpretation of law **14:**1196
- *Kelal Israel* **10:**898
- law and morality **10:**1480
- marriage invalidation **11:**1047; **15:**726
- Meir of Rothenburg **11:**1247
- oaths **12:**1300
- rabbi, rabbinate **13:**1446
- responsa **14:**86
- sages **14:**645
- Sheshet of Saragossa **11:**748
- source of **12:**120
- *takkanah* **15:**713
- *takkanot* interpretation **8:**1427
- *tannaim* **15:**798
- *see also:* CODIFICATION OF LAW; MA'ASEH; SYNODS; TAKKANOT HA-KAHAL
Authorized Version of English Bible, *see* King James' Version
Authorship **2:**230
Autobiography, *see* BIOGRAPHIES AND AUTOBIOGRAPHIES
AUTO DA FÉ **3:**911
- Abenatar Melo, David **2:**65
- America **2:**808
- Inquisition **8:**1383, 1404ff
- Latin America **10:**1448
- Peru **13:**322
- Portugal **13:**922ff
- Saragossa **14:**865
- *illus:*
- - text
- - Fonseca, Miguel Henriques **8:**1389
- - Madrid, June 30, 1680 **8:**1401
- - Marranos procession **3:**171
- - procession, Goa **8:**1393
- - *sanbenito* garment **15:**236
"Auto da Fé" (paint., Rizi) **8:**1401
Autoemancipation (wk.) **13:**546; **16:**1039
AUTOGRAPHS **3:**912
- *illus:*
- - text
- - Adler, Felix **2:**276
- - Aḥad Ha-Am **2:**445
- - Asch, Sholem **3:**685
- - Ascoli, Graziadio Isaia **3:**691
- - Bamberger, Ludwig **4:**154
- - Barnay, Ludwig **4:**248
- - Bendemann, Eduard Julius Friedrich **4:**475
- - Benedict, Moritz **4:**489
- - Bialik, Ḥayyim Naḥman **14:**1431
- - Birnbaum, Nathan **4:**1040
- - Capp, Al **5:**217
- - Carigal, Raphael Ḥayyim Isaac **5:**179
- - Cohn, Albert **5:**687
- - d'Ancona, Alessandro **2:**944
- - Dayan, Moshe **3:**480
- - Disraeli, Benjamin **3:**914; **6:**105
- - Donath, Adolph **6:**165
- - Einstein, Albert **6:**573
- - Erter, Isaac **6:**847
- - Eytan, Walter **3:**479
- - Golomb, Eliyahu **9:**331
- - Herzl, Theodor **8:**416; **16:**1048
- - Hirsch, Solomon **8:**516
- - Hos, Dov **9:**331
- - Huberman, Bronislaw **8:**1056

- - Imber, Naphtali Herz **7:**1472
- - Israel Meir ha-Kohen (Ḥafeẓ Ḥayyim) **9:**1069
- - Jabotinsky, Vladimir **9:**1183
- - Karelitz, Avraham Yeshayahu (Ḥazon Ish) **13:**1182
- - Maimonides **11:**758
- - Makleff, Mordecai **3:**482
- - Marks, Samuel **13:**1058
- - Pelman, Joshua **3:**482
- - Rosenne, Shabtai **3:**481-482
- - Sasson, Eliyahu **3:**479
- - Sharett (Shertok), Moshe **3:**478; **9:**331
- - Shiloah, Reuven **3:**480
- - Shneour, Zalman **14:**1432
- - Spiro, Eugene **8:**1056
- - Tchernichowsky, Saul **14:**1431
- - Yadin, Yigael **3:**479
Automatic writing **10:**637
Automobile racing **15:**300
AUTONOMISM (theory of J. nat.) **3:**919
- Agudat Israel **2:**421
- autonomy **3:**927
- Bund **4:**1497ff
- Folkspartei, Russia **6:**1411
- minority rights **12:**43ff
- Silberfarb, Moses **14:**1533
- Zhitlowksy, Chaim **16:**1011
- *see also:* COMMUNITY
AUTONOMY **3:**921
- *Contents:*
- - Definition and Survey **3:**921
- - Centralization **3:**922
- - Organs of Self-Rule **3:**924
- - Local Community **3:**924
- - Association **3:**925
- - Decline **3:**926
- - Voluntary Community **3:**927
- Historical Aspects
- - Antiochus III **3:**73
- - Assembly of Jewish Notables **3:**761
- - assimilation and abolition of **3:**772
- - conferences **5:**874
- - *episcopus judaeorum* **6:**818
- - exilarch **6:**1023
- - French Revolution **7:**152ff
- - *geonim* **7:**315
- - *ḥevrah* **8:**440
- - informers **8:**1365
- - *Landjudenschaft* **10:**1405
- - Mandate for Palestine **11:**862
- - millet **11:**1582
- - *nasi* **12:**835
- - Second Temple period **8:**626; **8:**637
- - socialism **15:**42ff
- - Vozrozhdeniye **16:**229
- - *see also:* ACADEMIES; COUNCILS OF THE LANDS; MARKET DAYS AND FAIRS; SYNODS
- Theory
- - Abenaes, Solomon **2:**64
- - Adret, Solomon **2:**306
- - communism **5:**793ff
- - Hasidism **7:**1417
- - minority rights **12:**43
- - reason for possibility of **12:**129
- - *see also:* AUTONOMISM
- Communal Rule
- - banishment **4:**164
- - documents **14:**1390
- - economic life **16:**1307
- - endowments **8:**284ff
- - fines **6:**1289
- - *ḥazakah* **7:**1522
- - *ḥerem bet din* **8:**355
- - *ḥerem ha-yishuv* **8:**356
- - imprisonment **8:**1306
- - *niddui* and *ḥerem* **8:**353
- - *pinkas* **13:**537
- - price fixing **7:**1062
- - *takkanot ha-kahal* **15:**728
- - trespass **7:**1462ff
- - *see also:* AUTONOMY, JUDICIAL; DINA DE-MALKHUTA DINA; FINANCES, AUTONOMOUS JEWISH
- Places
- - Alexandria **2:**589
- - Amsterdam **2:**900
- - Ashkenaz **3:**721
- - Berdichev **4:**589
- - Birobidzhan **4:**1044
- - Bucharest **4:**1439
- - Diaspora **6:**13
- - Ereẓ Israel, pre-state **12:**145
- - France, consistory **5:**907
- - Great Poland **7:**865
- - Latvia **10:**1465
- - Ottoman Empire **16:**1547
- - Padua **13:**11
- - Persia **13:**309ff
- - Poland **13:**726
- - Portugal **13:**919
- - Russia **7:**1397; **16:**780ff
- - Salonika **2:**670
- - Spain **15:**23
- - Stockholm **15:**407
- - Volhynia **16:**209
- - Warsaw **16:**335
- *illus:*
- - text
- - Birobidzhan **4:**1045-1049
- - Council of the Four Lands (map) **5:**497
- - Maria Theresa's *Juden-Ordnung* **3:**903
- *see also:* COMMUNITY; PINKAS
AUTONOMY, JUDICIAL **3:**928
- arbitration **3:**295ff
- Assembly of Jewish Notables **3:**761
- Austria **3:**888; **3:**891; **3:**892
- *Bittul ha-tamid* **4:**1061ff
- Catania **5:**252
- codification of law **5:**655
- compromise **5:**857
- divorces **7:**594
- Ereẓ Israel, eleventh century **9:**267
- Ereẓ Israel, 70 to 640 C.E. **9:**241ff
- exilarchate **6:**1025; **6:**1031
- fines **6:**1288
- Germany **7:**460
- *ḥerem bet din* **8:**355
- *ḥerem ha-yishuv* **8:**356
- imprisonment **8:**1300
- informers **8:**1365
- Jewish law **12:**123ff
- Keneset Israel **10:**906
- Mamluks **11:**837
- Mandate for Palestine **11:**862
- punishments **13:**1388
- rabbinate decline **13:**1452
- Sanhedrin **14:**836ff
- *takkanot ha-kahal* **15:**728
- *illus:*
- - *arraby moor* **13:**922
- *see also:* AUTONOMY; BET DIN AND JUDGES; DINA DE-MALKHUTA DINA; OATH MORE JUDAICO
AUTOPSIES AND DISSECTION **3:**931
- Amatus Lusitanus **2:**796
- anatomy **2:**931
- cornea transplant **4:**1092
- Israel controversy **9:**901
- responsa on **14:**91; **14:**93
- *see also:* EMBALMING; TRANSPLANTS
AUVERGNE (prov., Fr.) **3:**934
AUXERRE (tn., Fr.) **3:**934
Auxonne (tn., Fr.) **4:**1514
Av (tit.), *see* AV BET DIN
AV (Heb. month) **3:**934
- Chieri celebration **5:**422
- Torah reading **15:**1386
- *illus:* text
- *see also:* CALENDAR
AV, THE FIFTEENTH OF **3:**935
- kibbutz festival **10:**962
- wood offerings **16:**630
AV, THE NINTH OF (fast day) **3:**936
- *Contents:*
- - Historical Background **3:**936
- - Mourning Rites **3:**937
- - Liturgy **3:**938
- - In Israel **3:**939
- - Reform Judaism **3:**939
- General
- - Frankist custom **7:**69
- - *Shabbat Ḥazon* and *Shabbat Naḥamu* **14:**573
- - Shabbetai Ẓevi **14:**1222; **14:**1235
- Historical Background
- - Crusader massacre **5:**1142
- - Hadrian's decree **9:**248
- - Temple destruction **15:**945
- - Titus **15:**1169
- Mourning Rites
- - dancing **5:**1268
- - fast days **6:**1191; **6:**1194; **6:**1237
- - food **6:**1425
- - pregnant and nursing women **8:**1053
- - Torah study **15:**456
- Liturgy **3:**938; **11:**394ff
- - *Avi Avi* refrain **3:**955
- - Doenmeh **6:**151
- - *Eli Ẓiyyon ve-Areha* **6:**672
- - Falashas **6:**1148
- - *Haggadah le-Tishah be-Av* **13:**131
- - Jerusalem in **9:**1560
- - *kinot* **10:**1010
- - Lamentations **10:**1371 **14:**1058
- - *tallit* **15:**743
- In Israel **3:**939; **9:**903
- *illus:*
- - text
- - Betar members at Western Wall **9:**1478
mus. notations:
- - *Avi Avi* refrain **3:**955
- - *Eli Ẓiyyon ve-Areha* **6:**672
- - *kinah*, oriental chant **12:**627
- *see also:* NINE DAYS; TAMMUZ, FAST OF; THREE WEEKS
Avadim (tract.) **12:**49
Avadim Hayinu (litur.) **7:**1080; **11:**728
- *illus:*
- - *Joel ben Simeon Haggadah* **3:**995
Avahu (amora), *see* ABBAHU
Avana (tn., Babyl.) **15:**1512
Avangard (Bundist orgn.) **3:**423
Avangard (pub.) **16:**1126
Avante (journ.) **13:**1038
Avar (metal), *see* Lead
ʿAvārid (tax, Ott. Emp.) **16:**1532
Avaris (anc. city, Egy.) **16:**1191
Avaryanut ve-Ḥevrah (journ.) **1:**newsp. list
Avazim (Chr. reform mvmt.), *see* HUSSITES
AV BET DIN (tit.) **3:**940
- geonic period **7:**316
- triumviral leadership **9:**250
- *zugot* **16:**1233
AVDAN (amora) **3:**941
Avdat I (Nabatean k.), *see* OBEDAS I
Avdat II (Nabatean k.), *see* OBEDAS II
Avdat III (Nabatean k.), *see* Obedas III
AVDIMI BAR ḤAMA (amora) **3:**941
Avdimi Naḥota (amora), *see* DIMI
AVDIMI OF HAIFA (amora) **3:**942
Avdon (mosh., Isr.) **1:**place list
Avedah, *see* LOST PROPERTY
AVEDAT (anc. city, Negev) **3:**942
- Obedas III of Nabatea **12:**743
- Nabateans **12:**929
- *plan:* text
- *illus:*
- - Avedat Farm Project **2:**397,399; **12:**739
Avedon, Richard **13:**484
Avel (tn., Isr.), *see* ABEL
AVÉ-LALLEMANT, FRIEDRICH CHRISTIAN BENEDICT **3:**945
Avelei Beit Olamim (J. rel. gr.) **3:**946
Avelei ha-Heikhal (J. rel. gr.) **3:**946
AVELEI ZION **3:**945
- angels as mourners **2:**973
- Daniel ben Moses al-Qūmisi **5:**1292ff
- exile **7:**283
- Karaites **9:**273
AVELIM or OVELIM (val., vill., Er. Isr.) **3:**946
- *illus:* text
Aveling, Edward **11:**1075 **15:**25
Avelut, *see* MOURNING
AVEMPACE (Musl. philos.) **3:**947
Avenarius (Hebr.), *see* Habermann, Johannes
AVENARY, HANOCH **12:**681
Avencebrol (Sp. philos.) *see* GABIROL, SOLOMON BEN JUDAH, IBN
AVENDAUTH (trans.) **3:**948
- astrolabe **3:**787
Avend Kurier (newsp.) **13:**1042
Avenger, *see* BLOOD-AVENGER
Aven Gilyon (libelous misnomer) **2:**915
Avenpesat (fam.) **7:**507
Aventurine (mineral) **13:**1010
AVERAH (transgression) **3:**948
- *see also:* SIN
AVERBAKH, LEOPOLD LEONIDOVICH **3:**948
Averbuch, Manya *see* Bialik, Manya
Avernas de Gras, Baron of, *see* Suasso, Antonio Lopez
AVERROES (Isl. philos.) **3:**949
- *Contents:*
- - Philosophic Teachings **3:**949
- - Role in Jewish Philosophy **3:**950
- - Hebrew Translations **3:**950
- - Influence on Jewish Philosophy **3:**951
- - Medical Writings **3:**952
- Albalag **2:**520
- Albo, Joseph **2:**536
- angels **2:**976
- Aristotelianism **3:**446
- attributes of God **7:**666ff
- Delmedigo **3:**658; **5:**1477
- intellect, doctrine of **2:**581
- Levi ben Gershom **11:**94
- logic **11:**460
- Maimonides **11:**769
- Moses of Beaucaire **4:**363
- Platonism **13:**629
- psychology **11:**340
- substance and accidents **15:**475
- Themistius **15:**1099
- translations **13:**443; **15:**1321
- Wolfson's Studies **16:**618
Av Gillugah (Samar.) **14:**753
Av ha-Mishnah (tit.) **12:**1495
AV HA-RAḤAMIM (prayer) **3:**953
- Crusader massacres **5:**1142
AVIA (amora) **3:**954
AVIAD, YESHAYAHU **3:**954
AVI AVI (kinnah refrain) **3:**955
Avianus (fabulist) **3:**21
Aviation, *see* AERONAUTICS, AVIATION, AND ASTRONAUTICS
Aviba'al (Tyrian k.) **8:**501; **13:**476
Avicebron, *see* GABIROL,

SOLOMON BEN JUDAH IBN
AVICENNA (Musl. philos.) **3:**955
- *Contents:*
- - Works **3:**955
- - Influence on Jewish Philosophy **3:**957
- - Influence on Maimonides **3:**958
- - Medical Writings **3:**959
- Albalag's opposition **2:**520
- Alconstantini, Enoch **2:**551
- angels **2:**975f
- attributes of God **7:**666ff
- Avendauth's translation **3:**948 **2:**520
- Averroes **3:**949ff
- cause and effect **5:**259
- existence of God **8:**1161
- Ḥibat Allah **8:**462
- logic **11:**460
- Maimonides **11:**769
- medical work **11:**1189
- substance and accidents **15:**475
- *illus:*
- - Canon of Avicenna **11:**1192
AVIDA, YEHUDA LEIB **3:**960
- South Africa **15:**197
Avidan (amora), *see* AVDAN
Avidan, David (poet) **8:**206
Avidius Cassius (Rom. comm.) **9:**249; **10:**1249
AVIDOM, MENAHEM **3:**960
AVIDOR, MOSHE **1:**27
- UNESCO **15:**1565
Avidor, Yosef **15:**885
AVIDOV, ZVI **3:**961
Avi'el (mosh., Isr.) **1:** place list
Avi'ezer (mosh., Isr.) **1:** place list
Aviezer Zelig **5:**503
AVIGAD, NAḤMAN **3:**961
- archaeology **3:**302
- Bet Alfa **4:**710
- Jerusalem archaeology **9:**1524ff
AVIGDOR (mosh., Isr.) **3:**962
- statistics **1:** place list
Avigdor (stlmt., Arg.) **3:**429; **6:**802
AVIGDOR, ABRAHAM (philos.) **3:**962
- translations **15:**1324; **15:**1328
- universities **15:**1675
Avigdor, Abraham, of Marseilles (15th cent.) **2:**157
Avigdor, Jacob (19th cent., r.) **16:**1539
Avigdor, Jacob (19/20th cent., r.) **14:**93
Avigdor, Solomon (trans.) **2:**157; **3:**963
Avigdor ben Abraham (Rum.) **6:**1135; **10:**1279
AVIGDOR BEN ELIJAH HA-KOHEN **3:**963
- Anav, Judah **2:**939
AVIGDOR BEN JOSEPH ḤAYYIM (r., Rus.) **3:**963
- Shneur Zalman of Lyady **8:**1369; **14:**1433
Avigdor ben Paltiel (Morav.) **4:**1448
Avigdor ben Samuel (Lith.) **14:**526; **14:**804
AVIGDOR BEN SIMḤAH HA-LEVI OF GLOGAU **3:**964
Avigdor ha-Ẓarefati (schol.) **7:**1378; **10:**239
Avigdor-Moisésville (stlmt., Arg.) **3:**429
Avigedor (mosh., Isr.), *see* AVIGDOR
AVIGNON (city, Fr.) **3:**964
- archives **3:**387
- Boniface VIII **4:**1209
- bookbinders **4:**1230
- Church Council **2:**534; **5:**548
- special Purim **13:**1395
- *illus:*
- - baptism of Jewish children, prohibition edict (1776) **3:**213
Avignon *Maḥzor* **2:**258
AVIGUR, SHAUL (Haganah ldr.) **3:**968
Avi ha-Ezri (bk.), *see Ravyah*
AVIḤAYIL (mosh., Isr.) **3:**968
- statistics **1:** place list
Avikhavod (bib. fig.), *see* ICHABOD
AVILA (city, Sp.) **3:**968
- Holy Child of La Guardia **10:**1360
AVILA, DE (fam.) **3:**969
Avila, Diego Arias de **3:**969
AVILA, ELIEZER BEN SAMUEL BEN MOSES DE **3:**969
Avila, Isaac de (Mor.) **3:**969
Avila, Juan Arias D' **3:**969
Avila, Meir ben Joseph de **3:**969
Avila, Moses de **3:**969
Avila, Pedro de **3:**969
AVILA, PROPHET OF (Sp.) **3:**970
- Abner of Burgos **2:**88
- Kabbalah **10:**532
AVILA, SAMUEL BEN MOSES (r., Mor.) **3:**970
- family **3:**969
Avila, Samuel de (au.) **3:**969
Avila, Solomon de **3:**969
AVIMI (amora) **3:**970
Avimi (Pers. schol.) **4:**395
AVIMI BEN ABBAHU (amora) **3:**971
AVIN (amora) **3:**971
- *neḥutei* **12:**943
AVINA (amora) **3:**972
AVIN THE CARPENTER (Babyl.) **3:**972
AVINOAM, REUVEN **3:**972
AVINU MALKENU (litur.) **3:**973
- opening Ark **3:**457
AVINU SHE-BA-SHAMAYIM (prayer formula) **3:**974
- names of God **7:**684
AVIRA (amora) **3:**975
Avir kadmon (kab. conc.) **10:**590
Avirom (airline co., Er. Isr.) **9:**838
Avishai, M. *see* MAISELS, MOSES ḤAYYIM
Avisha Ba'al ha-Mēmar (Samar.) **14:**753; **14:**755
AVI-SHAUL, MORDEKHAI **3:**975
- drama, Hebrew **6:**204
Avishur, Abraham, *see* Werber, Abraham
Avital (vill., Er. Isr.) **1:**place list; **15:**675
Avith (tn., Edom) **6:**378
AVITUS (bp.) **3:**975
Avivah-Barisia (Zion. mvmt., Transyl.) **15:**814
Avivim (mosh., Isr.) **1:**place list; **10:**1547
Aviv Publishing House (Pol.) **5:**455
Avi Yetomim (inst.) **8:**285
AVI-YONAH, MICHAEL **1:**27 **3:**975
- Jerusalem archaeology **9:**1536; **9:**1537
- *illus:*
- - Herodian Jerusalem (model) **3:**340; **15:**960
- - Nicanor's Gate model **12:**1134
Avlona (city, Alb.), *see* VALONA
Avner (writ., Rus.), *see* ROSENFELD, AHARON
Avner (ftr.), *see* Zelikovich, Elimelekh
AVNERI, URI **3:**976
AVNI, AHARON **3:**976
AVNI, HAIM **1:**27
Avni, Ẓevi **12:**670
Avni Institute, Tel Aviv (art school, Isr.) **3:**592
Avnimos ha-Gardi **12:**1332
AVODAH (Temple rit., litur.) **3:**976
- Commandments, the 613 **5:**763
- high priest **10:**1322
- sacrifices **14:**608
- temple **15:**952ff
- *illus:*
- - priests performing the sacrifice **3:** *fcg.* 988
- - scapegoat cast over the cliff **3:**1000
- *score:* text
- *see also:* DAY OF ATONEMENT; WORSHIP
Avodah (Amidah ben.) **2:**841
Avodah (polit. party), *see* ISRAEL LABOR PARTY
Avodah u'Vittuaḥ Le'ummi (journ.) **1:** newsp. list
AVODAH ZARAH (tract.) **3:**980
- *illus:*
- - text
- - title page detail (18th cent.) **8:**1237
Avodah Zarah (idol worship), *see* AKKUM; IDOLATORY
Avodat ha-Bore (bk.) **2:**492
Avodat ha-Kodesh (bk.) **2:**308
Avodat Massa (wk.) **15:**872
Avodat Yisrael (prayer bk.) **4:**81
AVON, ANTHONY ROBERT EDEN, EARL OF (Br. states.) **3:**982
- Arab-Israel settlement **9:**388
- Arab League and **3:**242
- Israel armistice lines **9:**424
AVOT (Mish. tract.) **3:**983
- Calimani, Simon **5:**61
- Djerba recitation tradition **15:**753
- ethical instruction **6:**940
- Jewish literature **11:**316
- *Magen Avot* (comm.) **4:**992
- *illus:*
- - fifteenth century ms. (Ger.) **2:**727
- - Moses receiving the Tablets of Law **3:** *fcg.* 907; **4:** 320
- *see also:* AVOT DE-RABBI NATHAN; MIDRASH; PROVERBS, TALMUDIC
Avot (Amidah ben.) **2:**840
AVOT DE-RABBI NATHAN (tract.) **3:**984
- Jewish literature **11:**316
- *Midrash ha-Gadol* **11:**1515
- *see also:* AVOT; MIDRASH; PROVERBS, TALMUDIC
AVOT NEZIKIN (J. law) **3:**986
- *Bava Kama* **4:**339
- Bible and cuneiform law **4:**1215
- consecrated property **8:**280
- domains **14:**83
- *Nezikin* **12:**1132
- *see also:* DAMAGES; TORTS
Avraham Avinu (syn., Hebron) **15:**610
Avraham David of Buczacz, *see* Abraham David of Buczacz
Avram Ḥoza'ah (amora) **4:**395
AVRIEL, EHUD **3:**989
- Slánský trials **14:**1654
Avromarin, Y.B., *see* PERLOV, YIZḤAK
Avronah (loc., Isr.) **12:**927
AVRUNIN, ABRAHAM **3:**990
Avrutick, Abraham N. **7:**1360
Av-Sakhva ben Asad ha-Danfi (Samar.) **14:**754; **14:**757
Avshalom Bar-Deroma *see* Melamed, Abraham Shelomo
AVSHALOMOV, AARON **12:**681
Avshalom, Jacob **13:**911
Avshalom, Hizgil (Ezekiel) **12:**481
AVTALYON (tan.) **3:**990
- chronological chart **8:**766-767
- proselyte **13:**1186
- sages **14:**640
- Sennacherib **14:**1163
- Shemaiah **14:**1374
- siege of Jerusalem **3:**67
Avtalyon ben Mordecai (paytan) **13:**577
AVTINAS (fam.) **3:**991
- crafts **5:**1043
Avukah (student orgn., U.S.) **15:**450
- Wise, James **16:**568
Avun (amora), *see* AVIN
Avuyah, I., *see* ELAZARI-VOLCANI YIZḤAK
Avva (reg., Assyr. emp.) **3:**991
Avvakum (archpr.) **14:**507
Avvat Nefesh (bk.) **5:**1078
AVVIM (bib. people) **3:**991
- *ḥaẓerim* **7:**1531
Awana (tn., Babyl.), *see* Avana
Awangarda (period.) **16:**348
ʿAwjâ al-Fawqā (vill., Isr.) **3:**814
ʿAwjâ al-Ḥafīr (loc., Er. Isr.) **9:**322
ʿAwja Maṣrî (loc., Sinai) **14:**1606
ʿAwjâ River (Er. Isr.) **9:**168
ʿAwnî ʿAbd-al Hâdî (Arab ldr.) **9:**341; **9:**464
Aws (tribe, Arab.) **12:**509ff
ʾAwwad, Menahem **2:**260
Ax (weapon) **16:**266ff
AXELRAD, AVRAM **14:**420; **14:**425
- children's literature **5:**453
Axelrod, Albert (sport) **12:**1377
Axelrod, Benedict Alexander **15:**1380
AXELROD, GEORGE **12:**451; **12:**463
AXELROD, JULIUS (physiol.) **11:**1205
Axelrod, Nadezhda **3:**991
Axelrod, Natan **12:**460; **13:**228
AXELROD, PAVEL BORISOVICH **3:**991
- Zuckermann **16:**1230
AXELROD, SELIK **3:**992
Axenfeld, Auguste Alexander **3:**993
Axenfeld, Henri **3:**993
AXENFELD, ISRAEL **3:**992
Ayacucho (city, Peru) **13:**324
Ayalah (writ.), *see* HOROWITZ, AARON JUDAH LOEB
AYALON, DAVID **3:**993
Ayalon Valley (Isr.), *see* Aijalon Valley
AYALTI, HANAN J. (writ.) **3:**993
Ayaluna (city, Er. Isr.), *see* AIJALON
AYANOT (agr. school, Isr.) **3:**994
- statistics **1:** place list
Ayanot (publ. co.), *see* Ayyanot
AYASH (fam.) **3:**994
Ayash, Abraham **3:**994
Ayash, Ḥayyim Judah (emis.) **14:**1366
Ayash, Isaac **3:**994
Ayash, Jacob Moses **3:**994
Ayash, Joseph **3:**994
Ayash, Judah (r.) **3:**1015; **3:**994
Ayash, Judah-Leon(sol.) **3:**994
AYDAN, DAVID **3:**994
Aydelotte, F. **13:**33
- *illus:*
- - Enquiry Committee **16:**1089
AYDIN (city, Turk.) **3:**995
- Diaspora **6:**10
Ayelet (city, Er. Isr.) **4:**1539
Ayin (journ.) **1:** newsp. list
ʿAYIN (Heb. let.) **3:**995
- suspended in Bible **16:**1408
- *see also:* ALPHABET, HEBREW
Ayin (kab. conc.), *see* Nothingness
Ayin, Hillel (poet), *see* OMER, HILLEL
Ayin be'Ayin (journ.) **1:** newsp. list
Ayir (zool.), *see* ASS
AYLLON, SOLOMON BEN JACOB **3:**996
- Ashkenazi, Ẓevi Hirsch **3:**734
- chronological chart **8:** 766-767

– emissaries **14:** 1366
– Shabbateanism **14:** 1245
– *illus:* text
Ayna (city, Er. Isr.), *see* AI
ʾAyn (part of name), *see also* Ein; En
ʿAyn al-Dûk (vill., Er. Isr.) **6:** 153
ʿAyn al-Ḥadra (oasis, Sinai) **7:** 1531
ʿAyn al-Ḥuṣb (spring, Isr.), *see* ʿAyn Ḥuṣub
ʿAyn al-Qudayrât (spring, Er. Isr.), *see* Ayn Qudayrat
Ayn al-Quṣayma (loc., Er. Isr.) **3:** 1010
ʿAyn al-Sulṭân (spring, Er. Isr.) **2:** 394; **9:** 1365
Ayn al-Wayba (loc., Isr.), *see* EIN YAHAV
ʾAyn al-Zarqâʿ (spring, Er. Isr.) **9:** 1170
ʿAyn ʿArrûb (spring, Er. Isr.) **9:** 1541
ʿAyn Fara (spring, Er. Isr.) **2:** 665; **9:** 1472; **9:** 1542
ʿAyn Fashkhah (oasis, Er. Isr.), *see* EIN FASHḤAH
ʿAyn Fatīr (spring, Isr.) **6:** 741
ʿAyn Fawwâr (spring, Er. Isr.) **9:** 1472
ʿAyn Ghadyan (loc., Isr.) **10:** 300
ʿAyn Ḥuṣub (spring, Isr.) **7:** 1531; **9:** 371
ʿAyn-Jâlût (loc., Er. Isr.) *see* EN-HAROD
ʿAyn Karm (vill., Er. Isr.), *see* EIN KEREM
ʿAyn Qudayrat (spring, Er. Isr.) **7:** 432; **8:** 972; **10:** 664
ʿAyn Qudays (spring, Er. Isr.) **10:** 664
ʿAyn Rogel (Jer.), *see* EN-ROGEL
Aynsa (tn., Sp.) **6:** 1236
ʿAyn Ṣarida (spring, Er. Isr.) **16:** 999
ʿAyn Shams (loc., Er. Isr.) **4:** 773; **13:** 399
Ayn Shoyn Mayse Bukh (wk.) **11:** 649
– *illus:*
– – title page (Basle, 1602) **11:** 650
ʿAyntâb (city, Turk.) **15:** 643
ʿAyn Zaytûn (loc., Er. Isr.), *see* EIN ZEITIM
Ayr (city, Scot.) **14:** 1036
AYRTON, HERTHA **3:** 997
Ayrton, Michael (art.) **3:** 997
Ayrton, W. E. (phys.) **3:** 997
Ayrton Gould, Barbara (polit.) **3:** 997
ʾAyûn valley (Er. Isr.), *see* Ijon River
Ayyah (zool.) **4:** 1546
Ayyal, Ayyalah (zool.), *see* DEER
Ayyalon (city, Er. Isr.), *see* AIJALON
Ayyanot (publ. co.) **7:** 189; **13:** 1374
Ayyâsh (fam.), *see* AYASH
AYYELET HA-SHAḤAR (kib., Isr.) **3:** 997
– statistics **1:** place list
– *illus:*
– – children's dining room **10:** 970
– – communal dining hall **10:** 971
Ayyelet ha-Shaḥar (newsp.), *see Jutrzenka*
Ayyûb (fam.) **3:** 998
AYYUBIDS (sults.) **3:** 998
– Ismail **9:** 269
– Jerusalem **9:** 1423
– Jewish banking **4:** 167
– Syrian Jews **15:** 641
– Yemen **16:** 742
ʿAyyûn (vill., Er. Isr.) **8:** 1244; **13:** 1533
ʿAyyûn River (Isr.), *see* Ijon River
Ayzland, R. (poet) **16:** 815
Aza (angel) **10:** 633
Azaar, Samuel (Isr. spy) **11:** 1078
– chronological chart **8:** : 766-767
Azael (angel) **2:** 967; **10:** 633; **16:** 43
Azalai, Masyud **16:** 1549
Azaliah (bib. fig.) **14:** 1042,1295
Azan, Moses de Zaragua, *see* AÇAN, MOSES DE ZARAGUA
AẔANCOT (fam.) **3:** 998
Aẓancot, David **3:** 998
Aẓancot, Moses **3:** 998
Aẓancot, Saadiah ben Levi **3:** 998
A-z-a-r (pseud.), *see* RABINOVITZ, ALEXANDER SISKIND
Azar, Samuel Bekhor **6:** 501
Azarch, Abraham, *see* GRANOVSKY, ALEXANDER
Azardel, Moses, *see* ABZARADIEL, MOSES
Azariah (k., Judah), *see* AHAZIAH
Azariah (k., Judah), *see* UZZIAH
Azariah (h. pr.) **13:** 1075
Azariah (bib. fig.), *see* SHADRACH, MESHACH, ABED-NEGO
AZARIAH (tan.) **3:** 999
– Kefar Hattin **10:** 885
AZARIAH (amora) **3:** 999
Azariah (gaon) **14:** 803
Azariah ben Abba Mari **15:** 1324
Azariah ben Hosea **15:** 428
Azariah ben Joab **14:** 586
Azariah ben Moses Halevi **14:** 889
AZARIAH BEN SOLOMON (exil.) **3:** 999
– Hezekiah ben David **8:** 456
Azariah ben Zechariah, *see* JOSEPH and AZARIAH BEN ZEHARIAH
Azariah ha-Kohen (gaon) **7:** 317; **9:** 1059; **15:** 523
Azariah Ḥayyim Ashkenazi **6:** 670
Azariah Ze'evi **13:** 866
Azario, Bahor **10:** 1351
ʿÂzariyya, al- (vill., Er. Isr.) **9:** 1491
AZARKH, RAISA MOYSEYEVNA **14:** 514
Azaryah (mosh., Isr.) **1:** place list
AZAZEL (bib. loc.) **3:** 999
– *Abraham, Apocalypse of* **2:** 126; **2:** 127
– *Avodah* **3:** 977
– demon **5:** 1524
– *eglah arufah* **6:** 476
– *kipper* **10:** 1040
– lots **11:** 510
– sin **14:** 1590
– *illus:* text
– *see also:* ATONEMENT; BET ḤARODON
ʿAzāzma, al- (Bedouin tribe) **9:** 593
"Az be-Kol" (music) **14:** 1465
Azbogah (kab. name) **10:** 504
AZEFF, ZEVNO FISHELEVICH **3:** 1002
AZEGLIO, MASSIMO TAPARELLI, MARCHESE D' **3:** 1003
– Cantoni, Lelio **5:** 130
– Cattaneo, Carlo **5:** 255
Azeglio, Roberto ' (Piedmont) **3:** 1003; **5:** 130; **5:** 255
Aẓei Ḥayyim (Torah handles) **15:** 1256
AZEKAH (tn., Er. Isr.) **3:** 1003
– Sargon II **14:** 881
– *illus:* text
ʾAzel (cantillation sign), *see ʾAzlaʾ*
AZEMMOUR (city, Mor.) **3:** 1004
– Arcila **3:** 399
AZERBAIJAN (prov.) **3:** 1005
– Neo-Aramaic **12:** 948
AẒERET (bib. term) **3:** 1006
– *see also:* SHAVUOT
AZEVEḌO (fam.) **3:** 1006
Azevedo, Belchior Vaz d' (dipl.), *see* Azevedo, Melchior Vaz d'
Azevedo, David Salom d' (r., Amst.) **3:** 1007
Azevedo, Francisco Lopes d' (Lond.) **3:** 1007
– Viera, Antonio **16:** 122
Azevedo, Henrico d' (dipl.) **3:** 1007
Azevedo, Joseph Cohen d' (Lond.) **3:** 1007
Azevedo, Melchior Vaz d' (dipl.) **3:** 1006
AZEVEDO, MOSES COHEN D' (Eng.) **3:** 1007
Azhar, Abu al-Fatḥ Eleazar ibn, *see* Abu al-Fatḥ Eleazar, Ibn Azhar
Azharah, see Warning
AZHAROT, AZHARAH (litur. poems) **3:** 1007
– Abraham ben Daniel **2:** 136
– *Amidah* additions **2:** 843
– Commandments, the 613 **5:** 761
Azhayev, Vasili **14:** 512
AZIKRI, ELEAZAR BEN MOSES **3:** 1008
– Jerusalem Talmud **15:** 778
– Safed **10:** 546
Aẓilei Benei Israel (orgn., Rum.) **16:** 1133
AẒILUT (bk.) **3:** 1009
– kabbalistic pantheism **10:** 606ff
– *Sefirot* doctrine **10:** 567
– Worlds, the Four **16:** 641
Azitawadda (k., Danunians) **14:** 1149; **16:** 666
AZIZ (k., Emesa) **3:** 1010
– Drusilla **6:** 241
– Emesa **6:** 725
– *geneal. table:* **8:** 377
ʿAzīz, al- (caliph, Egy.) **6:** 1197; **9:** 262
Aziz ben Jonah Naim, *see* Naim, Aziz ben Jonah
Aziz Mehmed Effendi, *see* SHABBETAI ẒEVI
Azkari, Eleazar ben Moses (kab.), *see* AZIKRI, ELEAZAR BEN MOSES
ʿAzlaʿ (cantillation sign) **16:** 1455
AZMON (loc., Er. Isr.) **3:** 1010
Aznati, Solomon **8:** 1463
AZNOTH-TABOR (loc., Er. Isr.) **3:** 1011
AZOR (loc., Isr.) **3:** 1011
– inscription **16:** 666
– settlement **1:** place list
– *illus:*
– – text
– – ossuaries **12:** 1504
Azor (mt., Er. Isr.), *see* BAAL-HAZOR
AZORES **3:** 1012
– São Miguel **4:** 546
– sugarcane **15:** 487
– *illus:*
– – Ponta Delgada, synagogue **13:** 925
Azotus (tn., Er. Isr.) **3:** 696
ʾAz Qoẓeẓ (piyyut lang.) **16:** 1609
Azrail (angel), *see* ANGEL OF DEATH
Azriel (kab.) **2:** 134; **13:** 1608
Azriel (gram.) **16:** 140
Azri'el (mosh., Isr.) **1:** place list
Azriel, Aaron **14:** 92
Azriel ben Joseph **13:** 577
Azriel ben Meir ha-Levi Ashkenazi **3:** 1020
Azriel Dov **14:** 922
AZRIEL OF GERONA **3:** 1012
– Asher ben David **3:** 706
– *Ein-Sof* **10:** 557ff
– Ezra ben Solomon **6:** 1123
– Kabbalah **10:** 525ff
– meditation **11:** 1218
– mystical prayer **10:** 629; **11:** 347
– Neoplatonism **12:** 960
– *Sefer Yeẓirah* **16:** 787
– Worlds, the Four **16:** 641
Azriel of Polotsk, *see* ISRAEL BEN PEREẒ OF POLOTSK
Azriel of Shklov, *see* ISRAEL BEN SAMUEL OF SHKLOV
Azrikam (mosh., Isr.) **1:** place list
AZ ROV NISSIM (piyyut) **3:** 1014
– *illus:* text
Azubah (bib. fig) **12:** 84
Azubah (dau., Shilhi) **9:** 1325
AZUBIB (fam.) **3:** 1015
Azubib, David ben Abraham **14:** 708
Azubib, Joseph ben Nehorai (17th cent.) **3:** 1015
Azubib, Joseph ben Nehorai (18th cent.) **3:** 1015
Azubib, Nehorai ben Saadiah **2:** 623; **3:** 1015
Azubib, Saadiah ben Nehorai **3:** 1015
AZUBY, ABRAHAM **3:** 1015
AZULAI (fam., crftn.) **3:** 1016
– *illus:* text
AZULAI (fam., rs., kab.) **3:** 1016
– *geneal. table:* text
Azulai, Abraham ben Ḥayyim **3:** 1017
AZULAI, ABRAHAM BEN ISRAEL **3:** 1018
– Buzaglo **4:** 1544
– Marrakesh **11:** 1016
AZULAI, ABRAHAM BEN MORDECAI **3:** 1018
– alchemy **2:** 545
– Vital, Hayyim **16:** 174ff
– Zohar **16:** 1213
– *geneal. table:* text
AZULAI, ḤAYYIM JOSEPH DAVID **3:** 1019
– Alnakar **2:** 672
– Attia **3:** 836
– Bacharach, Naphtali **4:** 50
– Berlin, Saul **4:** 663
– Beth-El yeshivah **9:** 293
– bibliography **11:** 350
– Bolzano **4:** 1192
– Bouchara dispute **4:** 1273
– emissary **14:** 1362ff
– family **3:** 1017
– *Haggadah* commentary **7:** 1093
– *haggahot* **7:** 1110
– Hebrew fiction **6:** 1271
– *Ḥomat Anakh* **2:** 266
– Papo, Samuel Shemaiah **13:** 68
– philosopher's stone **2:** 545
– Tunisia **15:** 1444
– *geneal. table:* **3:** 1017
– *illus:*
– – autograph **3:** 913
– – *Avodat ha-Kodesh* **9:** 1449
Azulai, Isaac **3:** 1016
Azulai, Isaac ben Abraham **3:** 1016
Azulai, Isaac Zerahiah ben Isaiah **3:** 1016
Azulai, Isaiah **3:** 1016; **8:** 458
Azulai, Jacob (16th cent.) **3:** 1016
Azulai, Jacob (17th cent.) **3:** 1016
Azulai, Jacob (18th cent.) **3:** 1016
AZULAI, MASʿUD **3:** 1020
Azulai, Moses **3:** 1017
Azulai, Nissim **3:** 1017
Azulai, Raphael Isaiah **3:** 1017
Azuri (Phil. Idr.) **13:** 403; **14:** 881
Aẓvut, see Melancholy
Azzach (notable, Sp.) **8:** 967
Azzam Pasha **14:** 896
Azzaouia (tn., Mor.) **6:** 572
ʿAzziyya River (Leb.) **9:** 155
ʿAzzūn, al- (loc., Er. Isr.) **14:** 1635
Azzūnī, ʿArif al- **9:** 1041
Azzuri, Ab-Ḥisda, *see* ABU AL-HASAN OF TYRE

B

Ba (amora), *see* ABBA
Baal (deity), *see* BAAL WORSHIP
BAALAH (loc., Er. Isr.) 4:1
- Jabneel 9:1175
Baalat-Beer (deity) 4:7
Baalat-Gebal (deity) 4:7
Baalath (city, Er. Isr.) 4:1
Ba'albaki, Meshwi (sect., Iraq), *see* MESHWI AL-ʿUKBARI
Baalbek (anc. city, Leb.) 7:1040; 15:640
Baal Berit (name of God) 6:678
BAAL-BERITH (deity) 4:1
- etymology 4:7
Ba'al berit milah (godfather), *see* SANDAK
Ba'alei ha-avodah (kab. term) 10:495
Ba'alei ha-Nefesh (bk.) 2:138
- *illus:*
- - title page (Berlin, 1762) 2:138
Ba'alei ha-sod (kab. term) 10:494
Ba'alei ha-Tosafot (wk.) 16:4
Ba'alei ha-yedi'ah (kab. term) 10:494
Ba'alei Mikra, *see* KARAITES
Ba'alei Sefirot (theoretical kab.) 4:6
Ba'alei Shem (tit.), *see* BA'AL SHEM
Baal-Ezer (k., Tyre) 8:501
Baal-Gad (deity) 4:7
- etymology 4:7
BAAL-GAD (loc., Er. Isr.) 4:3
- Gad 7:249
BA'AL HA-BAYIT (householder) 4:3
- *illus:* text
Baal-Hadad (deity) 14:186
Ba'al ha-Kelim, *see* LANIADO, SAMUEL BEN ABRAHAM
Ba'al ha-Ma'amarim, *see* BACHRACH, JACOB BEN MOSES
Baal-Hamon (deity) 4:7
Baal-Hanan (k., Edom) 2:210
Ba'al ha-Turim, *see* JACOB BEN ASHER
Baal-Ḥazor (deity) 4:7
BAAL-HAZOR (loc., Er. Isr.) 4:3
Baal-Hermon (deity) 4:7; 8:374
BAALIS (k., Ammon) 4:4
Ba'al keri'ah (scroll reader) 15:583
Ba'al kiyyum (protected J.) 14:1013
Ba'al Lashon (wk.) 16:1388
BAAL-MAKHSHOVES (lit. crit.) 4:4
BAAL-MEON (city, Transj.) 4:5
Baal-Peor (deity) 4:11
- Maiumas 11:793
- Simeonites 14:1550
BAAL-PERAZIM (loc., Er. Isr.) 4:5
Baal Rosh (mt.) 16:656
Baal Ṣapān (deity) 4:8ff
Baalshamin (deity) 2:98; 7:1040
BA'AL SHEM (tit.) 4:5
- Jewish mysticism 10:511
- magic 11:708; 11:710
- practical Kabbalah 10:632; 10:634
- Shabbateanism 14:1251
- *illus:*
- - text
- - Ba'al Shem of London 6:1160
- - Ba'al Shem of Michelstadt 16:649
Ba'al Shem of Bingen (leg. fig.), *see* ADAM BA'AL SHEM
Ba'al Shem of London, *see* FALK, SAMUEL JACOB ḤAYYIM
Ba'al Shem of Michelstadt, *see* WORMSER, SECKEL
Ba'al Shem Tov (found., Ḥas.), *see* ISRAEL BEN ELIEZER BA'AL SHEM TOV
Ba'al Tamar (bib. loc.) 13:43
BAAL WORSHIP 4:7
- Contents:
- - Etymology 4:7
- - Ugaritic Myths 4:9
- Ahab 2:438
- Ahaziah 2:456
- Anath 2:925ff
- Asherah 3:704ff
- Ashtoreth 3:738
- Athaliah 3:814
- Baal-Berith 4:1
- dysphemism 6:960
- Elijah 6:632ff
- Hadad cult 7:1040
- Hosea 8:1011ff
- idolatry 8:1227ff
- Jehu 9:1329
- Jezebel 10:100
- mythology 12:730
- Sidon 14:1507
- Temple 15:944
- Ugaritic 15:1506
- *illus:*
- - text
- - Baal of the lightning 4:8
- - message to Anath 4:11
Baal Zebub (deity) 4:9
- Ahaziah 2:456
- Ekron 6:559
- plague of flies 6:1369
- *Solomon, Testament of* 15:119
Baal-Zebul (deity) 4:9; 5:1526
Baal Zephon (deity) 16:934
BAAL-ZEPHON (sanct., Egy.) 4:13
- Baal's residence 4:9
Baana, Son of Ahilud (bib. fig.) 11:1227; 15:674
Baana, Son of Hushai (bib. fig.) 8:1128
Baanah (bib. fig.) 9:80
BAARS, JACOB 3:362
- synagogue 15:620
BAASHA (Baasa; k., Isr.) 4:13
- history 8:595ff
- history chart 8:766-767
- Moabite revolt 11:1397
Ba'ath (Arab polit. party) 9:466,467,471ff; 15:647
Ba-Avodah (publ.) 1:newsp. list
Ba'ayot (period.) 4:633
Ba'az (metal) 11:1436
Baazov, David (Zion.) 4:13
BAAZOV, HERZL 4:13
Baazov, Meir 4:14
BAB, JULIUS 4:14
Baba, Sons of (anti-Herodians) 5:990
BABAD (fam.) 4:14
- Brody 4:1397
Babad, Dov 4:1397
Babad, Jacob Jekel 4:14
Babad, Joseph (Aus.) 10:1086
BABAD, JOSEPH BEN MOSES (Pol.) 4:15
- *illus:* text
Babad, Joshua Heschel 15:816
Babad, Joshua Heschel ben Isaac (r.) 4:14; 4:16
- Tarnopol 15:816
Babad, Joshua Hoeschel (19/20th cent., r.) 4:16; 13:670
Babad, Judah Leibush 13:670
Babad, Menachem Munish ben Joshua Heschel 4:14
Babad, Simeon 4:16
Baba ha-Gadol (h. pr.), *see* BABA RABBAH
Bābā Ibn Nuriel 9:77; 12:756
Babai ibn Farḥād 2:39; 4:16
BABAI IBN LUṬF 4:16
BAB AL-ABWAB (pass, tn., Cauc.) 4:16
- Derbent 5:1550
- Judeo-Tāt 10:442
Bāb al-ʿAmūd (Jer.), *see* Damascus Gate
Bāb al-Dhrāʿ (loc., Jor.), *see* Dhrāʿ
Babalikashvili, Nissan 7:427
Bāb al-Khalīl (Jer.), *see* Jaffa Gate
Bāb al-Maghāriba (Jer.), *see* Dung Gate
Bāb al-Nabī Dā'ūd (Jer.), *see* Zion Gate
Bāb al-Raḥma (Jer.), *see* Gate of Mercy
Bāb al-Sāhira (Zahra; Jer.), *see* Herod's Gate
Bāb al-Silsila (Jer.), *see* Chain Gate
Bāb al-Tawba (Jer.), *see* Gate of Repentance
BABA RABBAH (Samar. h. pr.) 4:17
- Amram Darah 2:893
- chronology 14:751
- history 14:731
- Shalem Rabta synagogue 14:1266
Ba bar Huna (amora), *see* RABBAH BAR HUNA
BABEL, ISAAC EMMANUILOVICH 4:18
- students' movements, Jewish 15:448
- *illus:*
- - text
- - father's tombstone 12:1320
BABEL, TOWER OF 4:22
- *Contents:*
- - The Story 4:25
- - In Aggadah 4:26
- - In Arts 4:26
- Borsippa tower 4:1259
- Genesis, Book of 7:393
- kabbalistic view 10:616
- Nimrod 12:1167
- Sumer 15:515
- *illus:*
- - text
- - tombstone ornamentation 15:1231
- - Ziggurat of Ur 16:1
BABILEE, JEAN 5:1271
Ba'bi' religion (Bahá'í faith) 9:924
BABI YAR (loc., Rus.) 4:27
- Ivan Ozyuba 15:1519
- Kuznetsov's novel 14:511
- Pronicheva 10:995ff
- Yevtushenko 16:781
- *illus:* text
BABOVICH, SIMḤAH BEN SOLOMON 4:30
- Firkovich 6:1305ff
Babrius (Lat. au.) 3:20
Bāb Sitt Maryam (Jer.), *see* Lions Gate
BABYLON (anc. city, Mesop.) 4:30
- Garden of Eden 13:78
- Hammurapi 7:1245
- Marduk 11:951
- Mesopotamia 16:1485
- Rome 8:302
- Sennacherib 14:1161
- Tower of Babel 4:22
- Zedekiah 16:961ff
- *illus:* text
- - Ḥammurapi stele 7:1246
- *see also:* BABYLONIA
BABYLONIA 4:34
- *Contents:*
- - Introduction 4:34
- - Archaemenid Period 4:34
- - Seleucid Period 4:36
- - Parthian Period 4:36
- - Sasanian Period 4:39
- General
- - Akkadian language 2:495
- - Assyriology 16:1506

– – astrology 3:789
– – coinage 5:722
– – Greek 8:293
– – Ḥanukkah lamp 7:1289
– – history 8:651ff
– – history chart 8:766-767
– – Jeremiah 9:1350ff
– – magic 11:706
– – Mari 11:981
– – oils 12:1352
– – polygamy 12:259
– – population 13:871
– – Semites 14:1148
– – Tigris 15:1139
– – Ur 16:1
– Religion
– – angelology 10:389
– – belief in afterlife 12:996
– – Tammuz 15:787
– Trades
– – agriculture 2:399
– – banking and bankers 4:166
– – crafts 5:1045ff
– – textiles 15:1037
– Jewish Community
– – academies 2:203ff
– – *agoranomos* 2:372
– – *aliyah* 9:510
– – *amoraim* 2:868ff
– – Anilaeus and Asinaeus 3:3
– – Avimi ben Abbahu 3:971
– – *baraita* origin 4:190
– – Cairo *Genizah* 16:1333
– – communal organization 5:810; 5:813
– – diaspora 6:11,17
– – economic life 16:1270ff
– – education 6:403ff
– – exilarch 6:1023
– – flogging 13:1389
– – gaonate 7:315; 8:696ff; 15:1530
– – genealogy 7:382
– – Hebrew pronunciation 13:1122
– – judgment restrictions 5:1236
– – Masorah 16:142
– – Mesene Jews 11:1396
– – mysticism 10:508
– – *neḥutei* 12:942
– – ordination 14:1141
– – Persian community 13:309
– – Pethahiah of Regensburg 13:339
– – Pumbedita 13:1384
– – purity ritual 13:1407; 13:1413
– – responsa 14:84ff
– – Sephardi links 14:1164
– – Sura 15:521
– – Torah reading 15:1247; 16:1407
– *maps:*
– – exile 8:607
– – main academies 2:203
– *tables:*
– – exilarchs 6:1024,1026
– – *geonim*, chronological lists 7:319
– – Heads of the Academies 2:866
– – principal *amoraim* 2:869
– *see also:* BABYLON; CHALDEA, CHALDEANS; EXILE, BABYLONIAN; MESOPOTAMIA; SHAPUR
Babylonian, the (tan.), *see* NATHAN HA-BAVLI
Babylonian Aramaic 3:277
Babylonian Chronicle 12:912; 16:1503,1509ff
– *illus:* 12:914
Babylonian dialect, *see* AKKADIAN LANGUAGE
Babylonian exile, *see* EXILE, BABYLONIAN
Babylonian Masorah 16:1423ff
– biblical Hebrew 16:1571
– *mus. notations:*
– – masoretic accents 11:1109
– *see also:* MASORAH
Babylonian Pioneer Movement (J. underground mvmt.) 8:1450
Babylonian rites (litur.) 11:394ff; 16:1333
Babylonian Talmud, *see* TALMUD, BABYLONIAN
Baca (tn., Er. Isr.) 13:216
BACAU (city, Rum.) 4:43
Bacchelli, Riccardo 9:1107
Bacchi, Samson 11:575; 16:907
Bacchi, Ventura 14:590
BACCHIDES (Syr. gen.) 4:44
– history chart 8:766-767
Bacchus, *see* DIONYSUS, CULT OF
Bach, Carl Philipp Emanuel 5:1071
Bach, H. 4:1013
Bach, Johann Sebastian 10:1376
Bach, Wilhelm Friedmann 12:633
Bachad (pion. mvmt.), *see* Baḥad
Bacharach (name), *see also under* Bachrach
BACHARACH (Eur. fam.) 4:45
BACHARACH (U.S. fam.) 4:46
BACHARACH (tn., Ger.) 4:44
– *illus:* text
Bacharach, Abraham Samuel ben Isaac 4:46; 4:49
BACHARACH, ALFRED LOUIS 4:46
Bacharach, Benjamin 4:46
BACHARACH, BURT 12:682
– motion pictures 12:451
Bacharach, Ephraim Gumbrecht 4:45
Bacharach, Eva (Ḥavvah) 4:46; 4:49
Bacharach, Gottschalk of 4:45
Bacharach, Harry 4:46
Bacharach, Isaac 4:46
Bacharach, Israel 4:45
Bacharach, Jacob 4:45
BACHARACH, JAIR ḤAYYIM BEN MOSES SAMSON 4:46
– taxation 15:846
– Worms 16:646
– *illus:* text
Bacharach, Judah Loeb ben Aaron 4:45
Bacharach, Menahem (Man) 4:45
BACHARACH, MOSES SAMSON BEN ABRAHAM SAMUEL 4:49
– Worms 16:646
BACHARACH, NAPHTALI BEN JACOB ELHANAN 4:49
– *illus:*
– – *Emek ha-Melekh* 4:49; 10:597
Bacharach, Samuel 16:646
Bacharach, Simon, *see* BACHER, SIMON
Bacharach, Tobias ben Joseph Solomon 4:45
BACHE (fam.) 4:50
Bacher (fam.), *see* BACHARACH
Bacher, Aron 15:307
BACHER, EDUARD 4:50
BACHER, ROBERT FOX 13:491
BACHER, SIMON 4:51
BACHER, WILHELM 4:51
– *aggadah* 2:364
– Cairo *Genizah* 16:1339
– history chart 8:766-767
– Judeo-Persian literature 10:438
– linguistic literature 16:1376
– rabbinical seminary 13:1464
Bacherach (fam.), *see* BACHARACH
BACHI, ARMANDO 4:52
Bachi, E. D. 14:714
Bachi, Felice 15:1455
BACHI, RAPHAEL 3:595
BACHI, RICARDO 4:53
BACHI, ROBERTO 4:53
Bachi, Samson, *see* Bacchi, Samson
Bachman, Felix 11:498
BACHMANN, JACOB 4:54
Bachrach (fam.) 16:163
Bachrach (name), *see also:* BACHARACH
Bachrach, Edel 4:56
Bachrach, Emil 13:395
Bachrach, Israel ben Moses 4:56
BACHRACH, JACOB BEN MOSES 4:54
BACHRACH, JUDAH BEN JOSHUA EZEKIEL 4:56
Bachrach, Menahem 12:66
BACHRACH, MOSES BEN ISAIAH MENAHEM 4:56
Bachrach, Naphtali Herz 16:171
Bachrach, Walton 5:565
Bachrach, William 15:313
Bachrich (fam.), *see* BACHARACH
Back (fam.), *see* BAK
BACK, SAMUEL 4:57
Bačka (reg., Serb.) 8:1097; 16:872; 16:878
BACKER, GEORGE 4:57
Backofen, Jacob, *see* REISCHER, JACOB BEN JOSEPH
Bacon, Francis 6:776
BACON, ROGER 4:57
– Andrew of Saint-Victor 2:948
– Hebraists 8:23
– medicine 11:1185
BACON, YEHUDA 3:595
– *illus:*
– – "Girl's Head" 3:617
– – *In the Wilderness*, jacket design 3:223
Bacrat, Abraham ben Solomon, *see* LEVY-BACRAT, ABRAHAM BEN SOLOMON
BACRI (fam.) 4:58
Bacri, David Coen 4:58
– Bensamon 4:1207
– Duran, David 6:299
Bacri, Jacob Coen 4:58
– Algiers 2:623; 5:816
Bacri, Joseph Coen 4:58
– Abulker, Isaac 2:196
– Busnach, Naphtali 4:1536
– Duran, David 6:299
Bácska, *see* Bačka
Bacteriology 11:1197
Baculus Jacobi (astron. instr.) *see* Jacob's staff
BADAJOZ (city, Sp.) 4:59
Badal (tax, Turk.) 2:54
Bad Cannstatt (sub., Stuttgart), *see* Cannstatt
Baddiel, David 7:334
BADÈ, WILLIAM FREDERIC 4:59
BADEN (state, Ger.) 4:59
– rabbinical office 13:1454
Baden-Baden (city, Ger.) 4:60ff
– *illus:*
– – *Kristallnacht*, Jews rounded up 8:845
– – Nazi sadism 8:845-848
BADEN BEI WIEN (spa, Aus.) 4:61
Baden-Durlach (city, Ger.) 4:60
BADER, GERSHOM (Gustav) 4:62
Bader, Menaḥem 6:204
Baderej (journ.) 5:990
Ba-Derekh (journ., Aus.) 1:newsp. list
Ba-Derekh (period., Holl.), *see Ḥerutenu*
Ba-Derekh (journ., Isr.) 1:newsp. list
Ba-Derekh (commun. journ., Isr.), *see Zu ha-Derekh*
Ba-Derekh (period., Pol.) 7:1499; 12:1047; 12:1051
– statistics 1:newsp. list
BADGE, JEWISH 4:62
– *Contents:*
– – Muslim World 4:62
– – Christendom 4:63
– – – England 4:64
– – – France 4:65
– – – Spain 4:65
– – – Italy 4:67
– – – Germany 4:68
– – Discontinuance 4:70
– – Nazi Period 4:71
– General
– – Catholic Church 5:538
– – chronological chart 8:766-767
– – Dhimmi 5:1605
– – Holocaust 8:893
– – Lateran Council IV 10:1446
– – Mamluk decrees 11:835; 11:837
– – Omar, Covenant of 12:1378; 12:1379ff
– – *shikla* 2:663
– – travelers 16:1287
– Cities and Countries
– – Anjou 3:24
– – Arnhem 3:485
– – Austria 3:890; 3:892
– – Avignon 3:966
– – Bavaria 5:141
– – England 6:749
– – France 7:18
– – Germany 7:467
– – Rome 14:246
– – Spain 15:234
– – Turin 15:1453
– – Venice 16:95
– Personalities
– – Abraham ben Solomon 2:157
– – Al-Ḥākim B'ámr Allah 8:661
– – Aquinas, Thomas 3:229
– – Benedict XIV 4:482
– – Bernardino da Siena 4:672
– – Boniface IX 4:1209
– – Joseph II 10:218
– – Louis IX 11:516
– – Philip III 13:393
– – Philip V 13:394
– *illus:*
– – text
– – Amsterdam children 12:987
– – Auschwitz camp inmates 8:875-880
– – Bohemia (16th cent.) 5:172
– – England (1277) 3:93
– – Germany (18th cent.) 7:483
– – "illegal" immigrant to Ereẓ Israel 11:694
– – Venice charter 9:1132
– *see also:* ANTI-SEMITISM; DRESS; HERALDRY
Badge of Shame, *see* BADGE, JEWISH
Badger (zool.) 9:225
Badges, Family 3:522
Badges of craftsmen 5:1044
BADḤAN (ent.) 4:73
– Broder, Berl 4:1390
– Ḥasidic music 7:1424
– *marshalek* 7:304
– musicians 12:678
– parody 13:134
– punishment 13:1389
– *illus:*
– – Purim 13:1402
– – wedding ceremony 11:*fcg.* 1067
BADHAV, ISAAC BEN MICHAEL 4:75
– *illus:* text
Bad Homburg (city, Ger.), *see* HOMBURG
Badia Polesine (tn., It.) 14:354
BADIḤI, YAḤYA BEN JUDAH 4:76
Bad Kissingen (tn., Bav.), *see* KISSINGEN
Bad Koenigswart (tn., Bohem.), *see* LAZNE KYNZVART
Bad Kreuznach (city, Ger.), *see* KREUZNACH
Bad Mergentheim (city, Ger.), *see* MERGENTHEIM
Bad Nauheim (tn., Ger.), *see* NAUHEIM

Badt, Benno 4:76
BADT, HERMANN 4:76
Badt, Milton 12:1017
Bad-tibira (city, Mesop.) 16:1485
Baeck, J.W. 5:456
BAECK, LEO 4:77
- commandments 5:789
- Jewish representative 13:1455
- Judaism 10:386
- *illus:*
- - Warburg, Otto, and 16:287
BAECK, SAMUEL 4:78
- Leszno 11:53
Baeck (Leo) Institute for German Jews (Jer.) 2:289
BAENA, JUAN ALFONSO DE (poet) 4:79
Baena, Juan de (court.), *see* PINEDA, JUAN DE
BAER, ABRAHAM 4:79
- *score:*
- - *Aleinu Le-Shabbe'aḥ* 2:556
Baer, Buddy 4:80
Baer, Fritz, *see* BAER, YITZHAK
Baer, Issachar Falkensohn, *see* BEHR, ISSACHAR FALKENSOHN
Baer, Joseph 4:1239
BAER, MAXIMILIAN ADELBERT (Max) 4:79
- *illus:* text
Baer, Mordecai 10:1207
Baer, Ray 15:307
BAER, SELIGMAN ISAAC 4:80
- Bible edition 4:839
- Masorah 16:1479
- *illus:* text
Baer, Shabbetai 14:1358
Baer, Simeon Akiva, *see* AKIVA BAER BEN JOSEPH
BAER, YITZHAK 4:82
- historiography 8:562; 8:565
Baer Frankfurter, *see* JOSEPH ISSACHAR BAER BEN ELHANAN
Ba'er Heitev (*Sh. Ar.* comment.), *see* ISAIAH BEN ABRAHAM
Baer-Schlesinger, Issachar 4:992
BAERWALD, ALEX 4:83
- *illus:*
- - text
- - Anglo-Palestine Bank, Haifa 3:348
- - Merḥavya building 9:554
- - Technion Building, Haifa 3:348
BAERWALD, MORITZ 4:84
BAERWALD, PAUL 4:84
- *illus:*
- - Joint Distribution Committee 2:829
BAETHGEN, FRIEDRICH WILHELM ADOLPH 4:85
BAEYER, ADOLF VON 4:85
- *illus:*
- - stamp 12:1203
Bafrayung (period.) 16:348
B-a-g, *see* GOLDBERG, BAER (Dov) BEN ALEXANDER
Bagatti, P.G. 9:1535; 9:1537
Bagdade, Benjamin 15:317
Bâgé (vill., Fr.) 4:1358
Baggesen, Jens Immanuel 14:926ff
BAGHDAD (city, Iraq) 4:86
- *Contents:*
- - Early History 4:86
- - Community Leaders 4:89
- - World War I and After 4:89
- - Community Life—1917–1970 4:91
- - Hebrew Printing 4:93
- Aaron Ḥakiman's *kinah* 2:18
- Abbasids 2:42ff
- al-Ḥakam family 2:625ff
- Alroy, David 2:750
- banking 4:167
- Bushire Jews 4:1535
- Ezra ben Ezekiel ha-Bavli 6:1123
- gaonate 7:315ff
- goldsmiths 7:741
- marriage custom 11:1043
- Ottoman period 16:1536
- population 13:873
- Purim, special 13:1396
- synagogues 15:612
- *illus:*
- - text
- - *geonim,* chronological list 7:321
- - hangings protest rally 8:1451
- - New Synagogue 8:1459
Baghdadali, Ezekiel ben Joseph Nissim Menahem, *see* Gabbai, Ezekiel ben Joseph Nissim Menahem
Baghdad Pact 15:1463,1664
BAGINSKY, ADOLF ARON 4:93
Bagish, Z. 16:819
Bagitto (dialect) 9:1146
Bagliar, Joseph 16:1535
Bagoas (bib. fig.), *see* BAGOHI
BAGOHI (satrap, Judea) 4:94
- chronological chart 8:766-767
- Elephantine Temple 6:605; 8:624
-Ezra 6:1118
- *Jewish Antiquities* 10:259
- sacrifice 14:606
- Sanballat 14:824
Bagrat (fam.) 3:474; 7:423
Bagrianov, Ivan 4:1488
Bagris (sol.) 14:1046
BAGRIT, SIR LEON 4:95
BAGRITSKI, EDUARD GEORGIYEVICH 4:95
Bagster, Samuel 4:840
B-a-ḥ (comment.), *see* SIRKES, JOEL
Bahā' Allāh (Bahai found.) 9:923
- Acre grave 8:936
Baḥad (pion. mvmt.)
- *aliyah* 9:520
- Dutch Zionism 16:1120
- Germany 7:493
- Ha-Kibbutz ha-Dati 10:972
- Ha-Po'el ha-Mizrachi 7:1321
- *see also:* BENEI AKIVA
BAHAI RELIGION IN ISRAEL 9:923
- Acre 2:226
- Haifa 7:1139
- holy places 8:936
- *illus:*
- - Bahai Shrine, Haifa 8:933; 9:924
Bahamas (isl., W. Indies) 16:473
- synagogue 1:synagogue list
Baḥan (kib., Isr.) 1:place list
Bahar, Blanche 16:1165
Baḥar, Jacques 16:1152
Bahat (gem) 13:1011
Baḥer (fam.), *see* EZRA
BAHIA (reg., Braz.) 4:95
- Brazil 4:1327
- conversos 8:1391
Bahi el-Adgham (polit.) 15:1451
BAHIR, SEFER HA- (bk.) 4:96
- *Contents:*
- - Titles 4:97
- - Contents 4:97
- - Ideas 4:98
- - Place in Kabbalah 4:99
- - Influence 4:100
- - Editions and Commentaries 4:100
- commandments 5:790
- Elijah ben Eliezer 4:647
- *gilgul* 7:574ff
- Isaac the Blind 9:35
- Jewish gnosis 10:506; 10:509; 10:518ff
- kabbalistic doctrine 10:556ff
- Meir ben Simeon 11:1256
- mystical literature 11:347
- Neḥunya 12:941
- *Raza Rabba, Sefer* 13:1591
- sacrifices 14:615
- *illus:* text
Ba-Histadrut (journ., Isr.) 1:newsp. list
Bahjí (Bahai shrine) 9:923
BAHLUL (fam.) 4:101
- *illus:* text
Bahlul, Daniel ben Judah 4:101
Bahlul, Eleazar 4:101
Bahlul, Joseph 4:101
Bahlul, Samuel 4:101
Bahr, Hermann 4:381
Baḥr al-Ṭabariya, *see* KINNERET, LAKE
Bahrdt, Carl Friedrich 8:23
BAHREIN (terr., Pers. Gulf) 4:101
- Jewish community 16:741
Baḥris (Mamluk dyn.) 11:834
Baḥr Lūṭ, *see* DEAD SEA
Baḥr Manzala (lagoon, Medit.) 14:16
Baḥr Zuʿār, *see* DEAD SEA
BAḤUR ("young man") 4:102
- *betullah* and 16:160
- yeshivot 16:768
Baḥur (wk.) 16:1390
Baḥur, Elijah, *see* LEVITA, ELIJAH
BAHURIM (bib. loc.) 4:102
BAḤUẒIM (J. tribes) 4:102
- Bône 4:1207
- Tunisia 15:1431
BAḤYA (Pseudo; au.) 4:103
- philosophy 13:436
- soul 15:172
Baḥya, Abraham ibn, *see* Abraham ibn Baḥya
BAḤYA BEN ASHER BEN ḤLAVA 4:104
- cosmic cycles 10:582
- ethical literature 11:344
- exegesis 4:899; 10:623
- *gilgul* 7:575
- homiletical literature 8:954
- Naḥmanides' commentary 12:778
- Rashba 2:307
- *Ẓe'enah u-Re'enah* 16:967
- Zohar 16:1211
- *illus:*
- - text
- - *Be'ur al ha-Torah* (1544) 5:751
Baḥya ben Joseph (r., It.) 9:1108
BAḤYA BEN JOSEPH IBN PAQUDA (Sp.) 4:105
- alchemy 2:547
- anti-legalism 10:639
- attributes of God 7:665; 10:392
- beatitude 4:359ff
- categories 5:254
- chronological chart 8:766-767
- commandments, reasons for 5:785
- ethical literature 6:927ff; 11:343
- existence of God 7:658ff
- free will 7:127
- homiletical literature 8:949
- Jewish mysticism 10:513
- Judeo-Arabic literature 10:417
- microcosm doctrine 11:1502
- nature 12:889
- Neoplatonism 12:960; 12:961
- philosophy 11:339; 13:435
- repentance 14:76
- reward and punishment 14:137
- soul 15:173
- substance and accident 15:474
- sufism 15:487
- Ẓaddik, Joseph ben Jacob ibn 16:913
- *illus:*
- - text
- - *Ḥovot ha-Levavot* (1489) 5:785
Baḥye Alfakim (inter.) 9:1299
Baḥye ben Joseph ibn Paquda ,*see* BAḤYA BEN JOSEPH IBN PAQUDA
BAIA-MARE (tn., Rum.) 4:108
- *illus:* text
Baibars I (Mamluk sult.) 11:835
BAIERSDORF (vill., Bav.) 4:109
- *illus:* text
BAIERSDORF, SAMSON SOLOMON 4:109
- Court Jews 5:1010
Baiersdorf, Veit, *see* Samson, Veit
Baig, Michael M. 11:997
BAIGNEUX-LES-JUIFS (vill., Fr.) 4:110
Baiji (loc., Iraq) 8:1449
Bail, *see* SURETYSHIP
BAIL, CHARLES-JOSEPH 4:110
- *illus:* text
Bailee, *see* APOTROPOS; SHOMERIM
Bailees' oath 8:280; 14:1455
Bailey, Sidney 16:157
Bailey Gatzert (steamboat) 14:1083
Baillie, William 8:23
BAILYN, BERNARD 8:544
- education 6:465
Bainville, Jacques 2:232
Bairaki Hurei (newsp.) 15:828
Bairam-Alī (city, Rus.), *see* MERV
BAITLER, ZOMA 3:595
Baito Anaia (site, Isr.), *see* BET(H)-ANATH
BAITOS BEN ZONIN 4:111
- biblical books 4:1226
Baiz, Jacob 11:1551
BAIZERMAN (fam.) 4:111
Baizerman, Eugenie 4:112
- *illus:* text
Baizerman, Saul 4:111
BAJA (tn., Hung.) 4:112
- *illus:* text
Bajarski, Meir Isaac 11:918
Bajaya (tn., Alg.), *see* BOUGIE
Bajjāna (vill., Sp.), *see* PECHINA
Bajulnaya, Moses ben Isaac 10:1298
BAK (fam., It., Prague) 4:113
- Prague 13:976
BAK (fam., Er. Isr.) 4:114
- publishing 13:1377
- *illus:*
- - text
Bak, Gerson 4:113
Bak, Hirsch 15:659
Bak, Israel 4:114
- Damascus Affair 5:1251
- Frumkin 7:210
- *Ḥavaẓẓelet* 7:1479
- publishing 13:1377
- *illus:*
- - *Avodat ha-Kodesh* (1841) 9:1449
Bak, Jacob (print.) 4:113; 13:976
- Prague 13:976
Bak, Jacob (17th cent., print.) 4:113
Bak, Joseph (17th cent., print.) 4:113
Bak, Joseph (d. 1696, print.) 4:113
Bak, Judah (17th cent., print.) 4:113
- *illus:*
- - *Bak Maḥzor* (1680) 5:753
Bak, Judah (18th cent., print.) 4:114
Bak, Moses 4:114
Bak, Nisan 4:115
- *illus:*
- - Tiferet Yisrael synagogue, Jerusalem 9:1445,1480
Bak, Yomtov Lipmann 4:114
Bak'ah (qtr., Jer.) 9:1496
BAKAN, DAVID 13:1345
Ba-Kefar (journ.) 1:place list
Baker, David M. 16:476
BAKER, EDWARD MAX 4:115
Baker, Maclyn 15:303
Baker, Newton D. 5:611
BAKHCHISARAI (tn., Rus.) 4:116
Bakhmut (city, Ukr.), *see* ARTEMOVSK
Bakhshseyev, Mishi (Moshe) 12:480
BAKI ("expert") 4:116
Ba-Kibbutz (journ.) 10:972

- statistics 1:newsp. list
Ba-Kibbutz ha-Arẓi (journ.), *see* *Ha-Shavu'a ba-Kibbutz ha-Arẓi*
Baking, *see* COOKING AND BAKING
Bakish (govt. offic., Bul.) 4:1483
BAKKASHAH (litur.) 4:116
- *maqāmāt* 11:937; 11:938
- prayer 13:982
- Saadiah Gaon 14:553
- *see also:* ZEMIROT
BAKKER-NORT, BETSY 13:825
Bakl, Mania 2:862
Bak Maḥzor (1680, print, Wekelsdorf)
- *illus:* 4:114; 5:753
Bakri (fam.), *see* BACRI
Bakrī (Arab geog.) 16:741
Baksheesh (bribe) 9:325; 13:305
Bakst, Aaron 4:1401; 11:469
BAKST, LEON 4:117
- *illus:*
- - text
- - costume design for ballet 3:554
Bakst, Moses 16:1013
BAKST, NICOLAI (Noah) IGNATYEVICH 4:118
Bakstansky, Lavy 16:1118
- *illus-*
- - protest against Passfield White Paper 16:1118
BAKU (city, Azer., Rus.) 4:119
- Azerbaijan 3:1005ff
- mountain Jews 12:480
- *illus:* text
BAKUNIN, MIKHAIL ALEKSANDROVICH 4:120
- socialism 15:34
Ba-Kur (journ.) 1:newsp. list
BAKY, LÁSZLO 4:120
- War Crimes Trial 16:296
BALAAM (bib. fig.) 4:120
- *Contents:*
- - Biblical Account 4:120
- - Critical View 4:121
- - In the Aggadah 4:123
- - In Islam 4:124
- - In the Arts 4:124
- ass story 3:6; 3:756
- astronomer 3:788
- Islam 15:1531
- Israel's tents 12:25
- Jesus 10:16
- Jethro 10:19
- poetry 13:677
- prophecy 13:1176
- Spinoza 15:283
- *illus:*
- - text
- - angel barring way 2:974; 16:685
- - Balak's seven altars 4:127
- - holding an astrolabe 3:787
BALABAN, BARNEY 4:125
Balaban, J. L. 11:613
BALABAN, MEIR (Majer) 4:125
Balabanov, Angelica 15:26
Balabanov, Nikola 4:1488
Baladan (k., Mesop.) 16:1513
Baladī (litur., Yem.) 9:500; 14:542
Balagh, Isaac al- 15:1323
BALAGUER (tn., Sp.) 4:126
Balah (city, Er. Isr.) 4:1
BALAK (k., Moab) 4:127
- Balaam 4:120ff
- in the arts 4:124
- *illus:* text
Bal'am, Judah ben Samuel ibn, *see* IBN BAL'AM, JUDAH BEN SAMUEL
Balan (city, Transyl.) 8:915
BALANCE 4:127
- *see also:* WEIGHTS AND MEASURES
BALANJAR (tn., Khazaria) 4:128
Balansi (fam.), *see* VALENSI
Balansi, Isaac ben David 4:965
Balās, Shimon, *see* Ballas, Shimon
Balassa, Balint 4:883
BALASSAGYARMAT (city, Hung.) 4:128
Balat (dist., Turk.) 9:1087
Balawī, Abū al-Baqā' Khalid ben Īsā al-, *see* Abū al-Baqā' Khalid ben Īsā al-Balawī
BALÁZS, BELA 4:129
Balbo, Cesare 9:1128
BALBO, MICHAEL BEN SHABBETAI COHEN 4:129
BALCON, SIR MICHAEL 4:129
Baldi, Bernardino 8:23
Bal-Dimyen, *see* SHTIF, NAHUM
Baldovius, J. 8:23
Balduin, Dorothea 8:23
Baldwin IV (Crus. k., Er. Isr.) 9:268
Bâle (city, Switz.), *see* BASLE
Bale, John 6:774
Balearic Islands, *see* Majorca; MINORCA
BALFOUR, ARTHUR JAMES, EARL OF 4:130
- Balfour Declaration 4:131ff
- Christian Zionism 16:1153
- Hebrew University 8:220
- Weizmann, Chaim 16:426
- *illus:*
- - text
- - Balfour Declaration 4:131
- - Government House party, Jerusalem 9:339
- - *Haggadah shel ha-Bayit ha-Le'ummi* 13:139
- - Hebrew University, opening ceremony 8:221
- - Israel stamp 9:*fcg.* 843
- - Rothschild's reply to Declaration 4:135
- - Schuster, Sir Arthur and 14:1012
- - Weizmann, Chaim and 16:429
Balfour, Robert Arthur, Earl of, *see* Lytton, Robert Arthur
Balfour-Beatty Company (Isr.) 9:792
BALFOUR DECLARATION 4:131
- AJA 2:978
- American Jewish Committee 2:823
- American Jewry 2:813
- Amery, Leopold 2:833
- Arab National Movement 9:457ff
- Balfour, Arthur James 4:130
- Basle Program 4:307
- Brandeis, Louis Demitz 4:1297
- British military hostility 16:1163
- Churchill 5:556
- Cowen, Joseph 5:1024
- Ettinger, Akiva Jacob 6:953
- historical survey 9:337
- history, chronological chart 8:766-767
- Kook, Abraham Isaac 10:1183
- Lloyd George 11:413; 11:414
- mandate for Palestine 11:862
- Montagu, Edwin Samuel 12:264
- Samuel Herbert 14:798
- San Remo conference 14:845
- Simon, Sir Leon 14:1581
- Sokolow, Nahum 15:87
- Twelfth Zionist Congress 16:1171
- Weizmann, Chaim 16:428
- White Papers 16:483ff
- Zionism 16:1080
- *illus:*
- - text
- - *Ha-Am* 12:361
- - jubilee medal 16:155
Balfour Forest (Isr.) 7:578; 9:789
- *illus:* 9:585-586
- statistics 1:place list
BALFOURIYYAH (mosh., Isr.) 4:136
Balgley (art.) 13:116
Bali (Arab tribe) 15:874
BALI, ABRAHAM BEN JACOB 4:136
BALI, MOSES BEN ABRAHAM 4:137
BALIDEH, MOSES 4:137
Baline, Israel, *see* BERLIN, IRVING
Bálint, Lajos 8:1079
BALINT, MICHAEL 4:137
Balk, Henryk 13:803
Balkan Peninsula
- General
- - education 6:426ff
- - emancipation 6:709ff
- - journalism 10:304
- - messianism 7:882ff; 16:1034
- - music 7:882ff
- - Shabbateanism 14:1240; 14:1243
- Countries
- - Albania 2:522
- - Bulgaria 4:1480
- - Greece 7:868
- - Rumania 14:386
- - Turkey 15:1456
- - Yugoslavia 16:868
- *pop. table:*
- - major communities 13:901
BALKH (tn., Afg.) 4:137
- Afghanistan 2:326
Ball, Rudolf 12:1376
BALLAGI, MÓR 4:138
- Bible translations 4:884
BALLARAT (city, Austr.) 4:138
Ballas, Shimon 12:1464
Ballet Rambert (Eng.) 13:1539
BALLIN, ALBERT 4:139
- *illus:* text
BALLIN, JOEL 4:139
BALLIN, MOEGENS 3:596
BALLIN, SAMUEL JACOB 4:140
BALLY, DAVICION 4:140
Balm, *see* BALSAM
BALMES, ABRAHAM BEN MEIR DE 4:140
- linguistics 16:1360,1374
- *illus:* text
Balmes, Abraham de 4:140
BALOGH, THOMAS, BARON 4:142
Balomancy (divination) 6:114
Balqā', Al- (dist., Transj.) 9:261; 9:295; 15:1318
BALSAM (spice) 4:142
- cosmetic uses 5:980
- economic history 16:1273
- incense and perfumes 8:1311ff
- Jewish War 9:237
- plant list 13:615
- Pliny's description 2:394
- storax 15:415
- *illus:* text
Balsam oil 4:142ff; 12:1352
BALTA (city, Ukr.) 4:143
- pogrom, 1882 13:668
- self-defense 14:1124
Baltassar (bib. fig.), *see* BELTESHAZZAR
BALTAZAR, CAMIL 4:144
- *illus:* text
Balter, Samuel 12:1376
Bălti (city, Rus.), *see* BELTSY
Baltiansky, Mauricio 16:1125
Baltic States
- General
- - communal organizations 5:826
- - emancipation 6:716ff
- - journalism 10:304
- Countries
- - Estonia 6:916
- - Latvia 10:1462
- - Lithuania 11:361
BALTIMORE (city, U.S.) 4:145
- *Contents:*
- - Synagogues 4:145
- - Charities 4:145
- - Education 4:145
- - Publications 4:146
- - Zionism 4:146
- - Economics 4:147
- - Areas of Residence 4:148
- - Cultural Life 4:148
- - Politics 4:148
- - Armed Forces 4:148
- - Jews and Non-Jews 4:148
- *illus:*
- - text
- - *Sinai* (1858) 15:1600
Baltimore Hebrew College 4:146
Balua stele 16:654
Balut (Baluty; vill., Pol.) 11:426
Balyash (fam.), *see* PALACHE
Ba-Ma'aleh (period.) 5:460
Ba-Ma'arakhah (journ.) 1:newsp. list
Ba-Ma'avar (journ.) 1:newsp.
Bamah ("high place"), *see* CULT PLACES, ISRAELITE
Bamah (journ.) 1:newsp. list
Ba-Maḥaneh (period.) 9:693; 14:1289
- statistics 1:newsp list
Bamako (city, Mali) 9:440
Bamat ha-Ishah (journ.) 1:newsp. list
BAMBERG (city, Ger.) 4:149
- archives 3:387
- synagogue 15:604
- *illus:*
- - text
- - Synagoga statue (13th cent.) 6:347
Bamberg, Israel of (tos.), *see* ISRAEL OF BAMBERG
BAMBERG, SAMUEL BEN BARUCH 4:150
Bamberger (bk. trade firm) 4:1239
BAMBERGER, BERNARD JACOB 4:150
- New York 12:1118
- *illus:*
- - JPS Torah translation committee 10:80
BAMBERGER, EDOUARD-ADRIEN 4:151
BAMBERGER, EUGEN 4:151
BAMBERGER, FRITZ 4:151
BAMBERGER, HEINRICH VON 4:152
- *illus:* text
Bamberger, Henri 4:175
Bamberger, Isaac 10:1129
Bamberger, Isaac Dov ha-Levi, *see* BAMBERGER, SELIGMANN BAER
BAMBERGER, LOUIS 4:153
BAMBERGER, LUDWIG 4:153
Bamberger, Moses Loeb (1838-1899) 4:155
Bamberger, Moses Loeb (1869-1924) 4:156
Bamberger, Moses Loeb (1902-1960) 4:156; 7:334
Bamberger, Nathan 4:155
Bamberger, Nathan Wolf 4:156; 4:973
BAMBERGER, RACHEL RUTH 3:596
Bamberger, Seckel 4:155
Bamberger, Seckel Isaac 4:155
Bamberger, Selig 4:156
BAMBERGER, SELIGMANN BAER 4:154
- Hirsch, S. R. 8:510
- Orthodoxy 12:1488ff
- Wuerzburg activities 16:676
BAMBERGER, SIMON 4:156
- Cheyenne 16:679
- Utah 16:33
Bamberger, Simon Simḥah (1832-1897) 3:688; 4:155

Bamberger, Simon Simḥah (1871-1961) 4:156
Bamberger, Simon Simḥah (1899-1957) 4:156
Bamberger, Solomon 4:155
Bamberger, Solomon Menahem 4:156; 10:464
BAMBUS, WILLY 4:157
BA-MEH MADLIKIN (mish. pass.) 4:158
Ba-Mesillah (journ.) 1:newsp. list
Ba-Midbar (Bib.), *see* NUMBERS, BOOK OF
Ba-Midgeh (journ.) 1:newsp. list
Ba-Mif'al (journ.) 1:newsp. list
Ba-Mifneh (journ.) 1:newsp. list
Ba-Mishor (journ.) 1:newsp. list
Ba-Mivḥan (journ.) 1:newsp. list
Ban, *see* ḤEREM
Bana'ah (amora) 10:145
Bana'im (J. sect, Er. Isr.) 14:1087
Banat (reg., Serb.) 16:872; 16:874
Banat, R. 3:362
Ba-Nativ (journ.) 1:newsp. list
Banchi del ghetto (Ven.) 16:1291
Banco Israelit del Uruguay (Urug.) 16:13
Banco Mercantil (Mex.) 11:1457
Banco Palestino-Uruguayo (Urug.) 16:13
Band, Abraham 8:214
Band, B. 8:568
BAND, MAX (Mordecai) 4:158
- School of Montparnasse 13:116
- *illus:* text
Bandar Abbas (tn., Pers.) 8:977
- Inquisition 8:1406
- Lisbon 11:301
Band-e Kong (tn., Pers.) 8:977
Bandera, Stefan 15:1421
Bandes, Louis E., *see* MILLER, LOUIS E.
Bandman, Daniel 12:266
Bandung Conference (1955) 4:511
Ba-Nekhar (journ.) 1:newsp. list
BANET (fam.) 4:159
Banet (fam. name), *see also* Baneth; Panet; Paneth
Banet, Aber (Aberl) 4:159
Banet, Fradl 4:159
Banet, Jacob 4:159
Banet, Jacob Abraham 4:159
Banet, Johanan 4:159
BANET, MORDECAI BEN ABRAHAM 4:159
- Aszod, Judah 3:811
- Berlin, Saul 4:664
- Brill, Azriel 4:1374
- Chorin, Aaron 5:495
- historical chart 8:766-767
- *illus:* text
Banet, Mordecai ben Yom Tov 4:159
BANET, NAPHTALI BEN MORDECAI 4:160
BANETH (fam.) 4:161
Baneth (fam. name), *see* also Banet; Panet; Paneth
Baneth, David Hartwig (Zvi) 4:161; 16:1339
Baneth, Eduard Ezekiel 4:161
BANETH, EZEKIEL BEN JACOB 4:161
Baneth, Jerachmeel Bernhard 4:162
Baneth, Menahem Mendel 14:1535
Bang, Thomas 8:23
Bang-Hansen, Odd 14:933
Bangkok (city, Thai.) 15:1044
Bangor (city, Me.) 11:782ff
Bangor (tn., Wales) 16:251
Bangui (tn., Cen. Afr. Rep.) 9:438
BANIAS (city, Er. Isr.) 4:162
- coins 5:720
- Crusades 9:269; 9:272
- Diocletian 6:60
- frontier, Palestine 9:312
- history chart 8:766-767
- Huleh 8:1064
- Ramat Banias 13:1534
- Six-Day War 14:1638
- *illus:* text
Bani Hasan tomb (Egy.) 3:305; 6:480; 16:267
Banin (Benjamin), Messa (Mūsā, Moses; fam., Aden) 2:262
Banī Sa'ab (loc., Er. Isr.) 9:284
BANISHMENT 4:163
- *Contents:*
- - Second Temple and Talmud Periods 4:164
- - Middle Ages to 18th Century 4:164
- *see also:* CITY OF REFUGE; EXPULSIONS
Bāniyās River, *see* Hermon River
BANJA LUKA (city, Yug.) 4:165
Bank Hapoalim B.M. (Isr.) 9:828
- economic activities 9:716
- Histadrut 8:539
- labor economy 9:850; 9:855
BANKING AND BANKERS 4:166
- *Contents:*
- - Antiquity 4:166
- - Middle Ages 4:167
- - 19th and 20th centuries 4:173
- - Assessment of Influence 4:179
- Alexandrian Jews 16:1277
- Amsterdam Jews 2:899
- Austrian Jews 3:894ff
- Babylonian Jews 16:1271
- bills of exchange 14:1389
- caliphate 8:659
- Diaspora 6:11
- goldsmithery 7:743
- history 8:719ff
- I.C.A. 10:45
- Islamic lands 16:1282ff
- Lebanon 10:1545
- legal person 10:1569
- loan-bankers 9:1121
- money-changers 16:1273
- Padua 13:8
- Persian Jews 13:310
- railroads 13:1517
- *sarrāf* 14:886
- Speyer family 15:266
- Turin 15:1455
- Vercelli 16:107
- *illus:*
- - text
- - Hart's Bank, Canada 7:1351
- - promissory note, Hebrew (Vienna, 1337) 3:893
- *see also:* COINS AND CURRENCY; COURT JEWS; MINTMASTERS AND MONEYERS; MONEY CHANGERS; MONEYLENDING; MONTI DI PIETÀ; NUMISMATICS; STOCK EXCHANGES; USURY
BANKING IN ISRAEL 9:824
- Arabs' role 9:1022
- coins and medals 6:1309; 11:1173ff
- currency 5:727
- *illus:*
- - text 3:348
- - Anglo-Palestine Bank, Jaffa, 1903 9:1255
- - Bank Leumi-Israel 5:729
- - Bank of Israel 5:730-731
- - Neturei Karta scrip 12:1003
Bank Leumi le-Israel B.M. (Isr.) 9:827
- Barth, Aharon 4:263
- Foerder, Yeshayahu 6:1374
- Jewish Colonial Trust 10:44
- Levontin, Zalman David 11:152
- *illus:*
- - one-pound note (1952) 5:729
- *see also:* Anglo-Palestine Bank; Bank of Israel
Bankoff, Milton 8:1361
Bank of Israel 9:824
- currency 5:727
- Horowitz, David 8:988
- *illus:*
- - one-pound notes (1955 and 1958) 5:730-731
- *see also:* Anglo-Palestine Bank; Bank Leumi le-Israel
Bankruptcy
- Council of the Lands 13:729
- Joseph ben Elijah 10:227
- *niddui* 8:354
- Polish communities 16:1304
- punishment 13:1389
- *see also:* EXECUTION (Civil); IMPRISONMENT FOR DEBT
Banks, David 15:303
Banks, Lynne Reid 6:782
BANNER 4:181
- Herzl and Jewish State flag 16:1045
- tailoring guild's flag 15:705
- *illus:*
- - Israel flag on U.N. headquarters 14:1312
- - Israel stamp 9:844-845
- - Molcho, Solomon 12:226
- - Prague community 13:967
- - tribes' banners and emblems 4:181; 5:57; 6:1450; 8:335; 12:*fcg.* 1259
- *see also:* FLAG
Banner Records (co.) 13:1618
Bannmeile (area, Nazi Ger.) 4:648
Bannock (tn., Mont.) 12:266
Bannus (1st cent. C.E., asc.). *see* BANUS
BÁNÓCZI (fam.) 4:182
Bánóczi, Jozsef 4:182
- Bible translations 4:884
- *Magyar Zsidó Szemle* 11:721
Bánóczi, László 4:182
Banon, Jacob 12:345; 13:816
Banquet, *see* SE'UDAH
BANSKA BYSTRICA (tn., Slov.) 4:183
- Reik, Ḥavivah 14:54
Bantock, Granville 9:69
Bàntolmács (vill., Rum.), *see* TALMACIU
Banū al-Aḥmar (Isl. ruler, Sp.) 15:227
Banu al-Aws (tribe, Arab.) 3:234; 3:235
Banu al-Safīr (fam.) 2:180
Banu 'Amr (tribe, Arab.) 13:1436
Banū-Isrā'īl (J. tribe) 16:703
Banū Janbā (J. tribe) 9:264
Banū Jarrāḥ (Bedouin tribe) 9:262
Banu Ka'b (tribe, Arab.) 13:1436
Banu Khazraj (tribe, Arab.) 3:234
Banu Nadīr (J. tribe), *see* NADIR
Banu Qaynuqā' (tribe, Arab.), *see* QAYNUQĀ'
Banu Qurayẓa (tribe, Arab.), *see* QURAYZA
BANUS (1st cent. C.E., asc.) 4:183
- asceticism 3:682
- Bana'im 14:1087
- Josephus 10:251
BANUŞ, MARIA 4:183
- literature 14:414
Banū Sa'd (sharifs, Mor.), *see* SA'DIS
Banū Waṭṭās (Mor. dyn.), *see* WATTASIDS
Banya Luka (city, Yug.), *see* BANJA LUKA
Banyuls-sur-Mer (loc., Fr.) 14:353
BAPTISM, FORCED 4:184
- Aquinas, Thomas 3:229
- Benedict XIV 4:482
- bull *Sicut Judaeis* 5:1141
- Christianity 5:511
- Finaly case 6:1279
- Heraclius 8:333
- Martin V 11:1064
- Mortara Case 12:354
- New Christians 12:1022
- Polotsk Jews 13:837
- Roman Jews 14:250
- Spain 15:220ff
- *illus:*
text
- - conversion sermon 3:201
- - Edgardo Mortara 12:354
- - Florence, prohibition edict re children 9:1131
Baptista de Este, João 15:251
Baptist Missionary Society (bib. soc.) 4:969
BĀQĀ AL-GHARBIYYA; BĀQĀ AL-SHARQIYYA (vill., Isr.) 4:188
Bāqillānī (Arab theol.) 9:101
Baqṣard (Baqsarin; loc., Iraq) 8:1447
BA'QŪBA (tn., Iraq) 4:188
BAR (tn., Rus.) 4:188
- Podolia 13:668
- Transnistria 15:1335
Bar (vill., Fr.) 11:497
BARA, THEDA 12:463
Barabbas (N.T. fig.) 16:949
Barachel the Buzite (bib. fig.) 6:632
Baradani, Naḥum al-, *see* Albaradani, Naḥum ha-Hazzan
Barada River (Er. Isr.) 9:181
Baradoi ben Bustanai (exil.) 7:1365
Bar-Adon, P. 10:404
BARAITA, BERAITOT ("outside" Mish.) 4:189
- *Contents:*
- - Date 4:189
- - Mishnah-Baraita 4:189
- - Origin 4:190
- - Types 4:190
- - Terms 4:191
- - Memra 4:192
- - Compilations 4:192
- *amoraim* 2:865; 5:891
- codification of law 5:631
- law source 12:117
- *Midreshei Halakhah* 11:1521
- Mishnah compilation 10:372
- mishnaic Hebrew 16:1591
- Oshaiah Rabba 12:1495
- *Sifra* 14:1517
- *Sifrei* 14:1519
- *see also:* MISHNAH; TOSEFTA
BARAITA DE-MELEKHET HA-MISHKAN (mish. collect.) 4:193
- *illus:* text
BARAITA DE-NIDDAH 4:194
- development of laws 12:1145
Baraita de-Rabbi Eliezer (agg. bk.), *see* PIRKEI DE-RABBI ELIEZER
Baraita de-Rabbi Pinḥas ben Ya'ir (wk.), *see Midrash Tadshe*
Baraita de-Rabbi Yosef ben Uzziel 10:517
Baraita (Tekufah) de-Rav Adda (bk.) 2:255
Baraita de Shemuel (astron. Mid.)
- *anno mundi* 14:1092
- astrology 3:791
- astronomy 3:802
- calendric data 5:49
Baraita de-Sifrei, *see* SIFREI ZUTA
Baraita of 49 Rules (wk.) 4:194
Baraita of Samuel, *see Baraita de-Shemuel*
BARAITA OF 32 RULES (mish. collec.) 4:194
- Bible interpretation 8:1418
- commentary 10:830
- Eliezer ben Yose ha-Gelili 6:630
- *see also:* GEMATRIA;

HERMENEUTICS
BARAK (bib. fig.) **4**:195
- Bible history **8**:584
- Deborah **5**:1430
- Judges, Book of **10**:445
Barak (vill., Er. Isr.) **1**:place list **15**:675
Barakar of Shechem **14**:755
Baram (kib., Isr.) **1**: place list; **10**:878
Bar Am, Micha **13**:487
- *illus:*
- - "Mr. Rubin, Farmer from Metullah" (phot.) **13**:483
BARANGA, AUREL **4**:196
BARANOVICHI (city, Rus.) **4**:197
- ghetto **13**:770
BARANOWICZ, DAVID ELIEZER **4**:198
- *illus:* text
Baranowicze (city, Rus.), *see* BARANOVICHI
Barany, Joseph **10**:862
BÁRÁNY, ROBERT **4**:199
BARASCH, JULIUS (Judah) **4**:199
- - Rumania **14**:398,399
BARASH, ASHER **4**:200
- Barash Institute **15**:56
- Hebrew literature **8**:203
- *illus:*
- - Writers Association **16**:653
BARASH, EPHRAIM **4**:203
- Bialystok **4**:807ff
Barash, Naḥman ben Simḥah **12**:956
Barash, Zanvel **10**:1179
Baratier (-us), Johann Philip **8**:23
BARATZ, HERMANN (Hirsch) **4**:203
BARATZ, JOSEPH **4**:203
Baratz, Miriam **4**:204
Barazan (vill., Kurd.) **4**:205
BARAZANI, ASENATH BAT SAMUEL **4**:204
Barazani, David **4**:204
Barazani, Elijah **12**:445
Barazani, Moshe **8**:1468; **11**:465; **15**:490
- *illus:*
- - suicide report, *Palestine Post* **11**:463
Barazani, Samuel **4**:204
BARAZANI, SAMUEL BEN NETHANEL HA-LEVI **4**:205; **16**:1537
- Barazani, Asenath **4**:204;
Barazani, Solomon **12**:445
Barb, L. **14**:1264
BARBADOS (isl., W. Indies) **4**:205
- Israel relations **9**:443
- Marrano diaspora **11**:1021
- origin **2**:809
- slave trade **14**:1663
- sugar trade **15**:488
- West Indies **16**:473
- *see also:* AMERICA
BARBARIANS **4**:205
- writing material **16**:659
- *illus:* text
Barbaro, Marcantonio **3**:732
Barbarossa, *see* Frederick I (H. Rom. Emp.)
Barbary States, *see* AFRICA (North)
Barbatus, Joseph, *see* Abundachus, Joseph Barbatus Memphiticus
Barbasch, Boris **16**:1165
BARBASH, SAMUEL **4**:206
- *illus:*
- - Odessa Committee **12**:1329
BARBASTRO (city, Sp.) **4**:207
Barbelo (gnostic fig.) **7**:638
Barbé Marbois, Sophie **3**:817
Barberini Triglot (Samar. targum) **14**:753
Barbers (hairdressers) **5**:1051; **5**:982
Barbur (loc., Isr.) **9**:795
BARBY, MEIR BEN SAUL **4**:207
Barcares (concen. camp, Fr.) **7**:34
BARCELONA (city, Sp.) **4**:208
- *Contents:*
- - Communal Life **4**:209
- - The Decline **4**:210
- - Conversos **4**:212
- - 20th Century **4**:212
- archives **3**:376
- host desecration **8**:1043
- Inquisition **8**:1384
- Jewish landowners **16**:1286
- museums **12**:544
- Pedro IV **8**:1366
- Rashba **2**:305; **2**:307
- *shtadlanut* **14**:1462
- silversmiths **7**:741
- Spain **15**:228ff
- *takkanot* **15**:735
- *illus:* text
Barcelona (city, Venez.) **16**:90
BARCELONA, DISPUTATION OF **4**:213
- Christiani, Pablo **5**:505
- history, chronological chart **8**:766-767
- Jewish literature **11**:354
- Naḥmanides **6**:92ff; **12**:775
- Spain **15**:232
- *illus:* text
Barcelona, Isaac ben Reuben of, *see* AL-BARGELONI, ISAAC BEN REUBEN
Barcelona Haggadah (14th cent., illum. ms., Sp.) **2**:83; **7**:119, 1081,1199; **8**:1264; **11**:*fcg.*1131; **12**:602; **13**:1544
Barceloni, Isaac ben Judah **16**:1365
Barchilon, Abraham el **12**:62
Barclays Bank D.C.O. (Isr.) **9**:824
Barclay's Gate (temple Mt.) **15**:963
BARD, BASIL JOSEPH ASHER **4**:216
BARDACH, ISRAEL (Isaac ben Ḥayyim Moses) **4**:216
- *illus:* text
Bardach, Meir **4**:217
Bardakh (cmty. ldr., Rus.) **10**:996
BARDAKI, ISAIAH BEN ISSACHAR BER **4**:217
- capitulations **5**:150
- Jerusalem **9**:1448ff
- Russian Jews' status **9**:298
Bardawil (lake, Sinai) **9**:787
Bar-Dayyan (edit., Ger.), *see* Borodianski
BARDEJOV (tn., Slov.) **4**:217
- Czechoslovakia **5**:1202
- *illus:* text
Bar-Deroma, Avshalom, *see* Melamed, Abraham Shelomo
Bar Derora, *see* LIEBERMANN, AARON SAMUEL
Bardiya (br., Cambyses) **5**:71
Bárdossy, László **8**:1098; **16**:296
Bards, Jewish **14**:1426
Bar ʿEbhrāyā, Johanan, *see* BAR HEBRAEUS, JOHANAN
"Barefooted" (Cath. order) **7**:47
Bareheadedness, *see* HEAD, COVERING OF THE
Bareket (mosh., Isr.) **1**:place list
Ba-Rekhev (journ.) **1**:newsp. list
BAREKHI NAFSHI (Psalm 104) **4**:218
BAREKHU (litur.) **4**:218
- *illus:*
- - text
- - *Leipzig Maḥzor* **12**:601
- *scores:*
- - Rosh ha-Shanah liturgy **10**:663
Barel, Isaac (polit.) **8**:1443
BARENBOIM, DANIEL **4**:220
Bareqet (gem) **13**:1009
BARGAS, ABRAHAM DE **4**:220
Bargeloni, Judah ben Barzillai al-, *see* JUDAH BEN BARZILLAI AL-BARGELONI
Bar Giora (mosh., Isr.) **1**:place list
Bar-Giora (soc., Er. Isr.) **16**:1148
- Ha-Shomer **7**:1370
- Shochat, Israel **14**:1440
- Zeid, Alexander **16**:969
BAR GIORA, SIMEON **4**:220
- Edomites, command **6**:378
- Hebron **8**:228
- Lion of Wrath **11**:276
- Man of Lies **11**:234
- Masada **11**:1079
- messianism **11**:1421
- revolt against Romans **8**:639
- Titus **15**:1169
- warfare **16**:280
Bar Giora Club (Jer.) **15**:294
Bar Ḥama (4th cent., Babyl.) **13**:67
Bar-Ḥanina (4th cent., Er. Isr.) **9**:1376
Bar Harbor (tn., Me.) **11**:782
Barḥon, Hananiah **14**:761
BAR HEBRAEUS, JOHANAN **4**:222
- Roman census of Jews **13**:871
BAR HEDYA **4**:222
BAR-HILLEL, YEHOSHUA **4**:223
Barhun ben Sahalan **13**:577
BARI (city, It.) **4**:223
- anti-Jewish riots **3**:228
- origin of community **3**:226
Bari, Eleazar **5**:627
Bar-Ilan (journ.) **1**:newsp. list
BAR-ILAN, MEIR **4**:224
- Bar-Ilan University **4**:225
- Mizrachi **12**:177
- U.S. Zionism **16**:1142
- *illus:*
- - Bar-Ilan University **4**:225
- - Joint Distribution Committee **2**:829
- - Zionist Congress **16**:1173
BAR-ILAN UNIVERSITY (Isr.) **4**:225
- Bar-Ilan, Meir **4**:225
- higher education **9**:957
- *illus:*
- - campus **9**:955
- - computer **9**:971
- - library **9**:963,1003
Baring, Sir Evelyn **9**:308; **16**:1072
Baring, Francis **4**:174
Barissia (soc., Cz.) **16**:1112
BARIT, JACOB **4**:226
- Vilna **16**:144
BARKAI (kib., Isr.) **4**:226
- statistics **1**:place list
Barkai (journ., S.A.) **13**:1049
- statistics **1**:newsp. list
Barkai (journ., Aus.) **1**:newsp. list
Barkai (newsp., Rus.) **13**:1047
- statistics **1**:newsp. list
Bar Kalba Savu'a, *see* BEN KALBA SAVU'A
Bar Kamẓa (agg. fig.), *see* KAMẒA AND BAR KAMẒA
BAR KAPPARA **4**:227
- Eleazar ha-Kappar **6**:601
- fables **13**:125
- Judah ha-Nasi **10**:371; **10**:372
- *Sifrei Zuta* **14**:1522
Barkatt, Reuven **10**:1114
Barker, Samuel **8**:23
Barker, William Higgs **8**:23
Barki, Isaac **7**:1512
BAR KOCHBA ASSOCIATION (Cz.) **4**:228
- *illus:*
- - members **16**:1105
BAR KOKHBA (2nd cent. C.E., pat.) **4**:228
- *Contents:*
- - The Leader **4**:228
- - The Revolt **4**:231
- - Judean Desert Documents **4**:237
- Akiva **2**:489
- Bethar **4**:733; **4**:735
- chronological chart **8**:766-767
- coins **5**:719; **9**:1578; **13**:523
- Eleazar of Modi'in **6**:603
- Julius Severus **10**:471ff
- Lag ba-Omer **10**:1358
- letters **11**:56; **16**:1592, 1602
- messianism **11**:1412; **11**:1410; **11**:1409
- Murabba'at scrolls **12**:528
- sages **14**:644
- *illus:*
- - text
- - Bethar, and Roman camps **4**:734
- - Bethar fortress (map) **4**:735
- - coins **5**:708-710; **6**:1448; **12**:569
- - Dead Sea caves **8**:645
- - land-lease deed **3**:375
- - Naḥal Ḥever papyrus **8**:647
- - period objects **3**:325
- - script type of letters **2**:687
- *see also:* HADRIAN, PUBLIUS AELIUS
Bar Kokhba (club, Ger.) **11**:664; **15**:293
Bar Kokhba Association (Cz.), *see* BAR KOCHBA ASSOCIATION
Bar Kokhba Revolt (132 C.E., Judea)
- agriculture affected by **2**:396
- Bar Kokhba **4**:231
- circumcision prohibition **5**:570
- coinage **5**:719
- Dio Cassius' account **6**:59
- fasting **6**:1192
- history **8**:646ff; **9**:245
- Jerusalem battles **9**:1405
- Murabba'at scrolls **12**:528
- Samaritan tradition **14**:730
- Sikarikon **14**:1529
- warfare **16**:280
Bar Kozeva (2nd cent. C.E., pat.), *see* BAR KOKHBA
Barlaam and Josaphat (Joasaph; Hindu tale), *see* BEN HA-MELEKH VE-HA-NAZIR
BARLAD (tn., Rum.) **4**:240
BAR-LE-DUC (tn., Fr.) **4**:240
Barles (loc., Fr.) **14**:1623
BAR-LEV, HAIM **4**:240
- war of attrition **14**:1640
Bar-Lev Line (Suez Canal zone) **9**:416; **14**:1640
BARLEY **4**:241
- bread **4**:1333
- economic life **16**:1268ff
- food **6**:1416
- plant list **13**:615
- suitable fields for **16**:372
- *illus:* text
- *see also:* FIVE SPECIES
BARLIN, FREDERICK WILLIAM **4**:243
- *illus:*
- - text
- - Hirschel, Solomon **8**:520
Barlow, Samuel **7**:1349
BARMAS, ISSAY **12**:682
Barmen (tn., Ger.) **16**:677
BAR MITZVAH, BAT MITZVAH **4**:243
- *Contents:*
- - Called to the Torah **4**:244
- - Putting on Tefillin **4**:245
- - Bar Mitzvah Derashah **4**:245
- - Confirmation **4**:246
- - Bat Mitzvah **4**:246
- *Barukh she-petarani* **4**:285
- folklore **6**:1405
- *haftarah* reading **16**:1344
- responsum **14**:93
- Samaritans **14**:744
- *tefillin* **15**:901
- *illus:*
- - text
- - *ḥallah*, traditional shape **6**:1419

– – Kefar Ḥabad celebration for orphans **9**:904
– – service at Masada **5**:460
– – Six-Day War orphans **10**:883
– – Torah reading **15**:1248
– *see also:* CHILD MARRIAGE; PUBERTY
"Bar Mitzvah Speech" (paint., Oppenheim) **4**:245
Barna, Gyozo Viktor **15**:314
Barnabas, Saint **3**:71; **4**:924
Barnabas of Terni **4**:672
BARNACLE GOOSE MYTHS **4**:247
Barnard, Samuel **8**:23
Bar-Nash, *see* SCHAPIRA, NOAH
BARNATO, BARNEY **4**:247
– automobile racing **15**:298
Barnato, Henry **4**:247
Barnato, Woolf **15**:300
BARNAY, LUDWIG **4**:248
– *illus:* text
Barnea, Aviassaf, *see* Bernstein, Aviassaf
BARNERT, NATHAN **4**:249
– Paterson **13**:179
Barnet, Jacob **4**:463
BARNET, WILL **3**:596
– *illus:*
– – "Ona" **3**:617
Barnet, Zeraḥ, *see* BARNETT, ZERAḤ
Barnett (fam.) **3**:450
Barnett, Bernhard, *see* Beer, Bernhard
Barnett, Charles **13**:820
Barnett, C.Z. **15**:1053
Barnett, George **14**:843
BARNETT, JOHN **12**:682
BARNETT, JOHN FRANCIS **12**:682
BARNETT, LIONEL DAVID **4**:250
BARNETT, SIR LOUIS EDWARD **4**:250
– New Zealand **12**:1130
Barnett, Morris **15**:1054
Barnett, Richard David **3**:302; **4**:250
Barnett, W. **6**:342
BARNETT, ZERAḤ **4**:251
– Tel Aviv **15**:919
BARNOWSKY, VIKTOR **15**:1077
Barnston, Henry **8**:1051
Baroca (fam.) **14**:633
Barocius, Francesco, *see* Barozzi, Francesco
Baroda (physic.) **8**:694
Baroja y Nessi, Pío **15**:250
Baron, Aaron **15**:34
BARON, BERNHARD **4**:251
– tobacco trade **15**:1178
Baron, Bertram Benjamin **4**:465
Baron, David, *see* PINTER, HAROLD
BARON, DEVORAH **4**:252
– Aharonovitch, Yosef **2**:453
– Hebrew literature **8**:203
– *illus:*
– – writers' group **16**:813
Baron, Fanya **15**:34
Baron, Howard **15**:790
BARON, JOSEPH ALEXANDER **6**:785; **6**:786
BARON, JOSEPH LOUIS **4**:253
– Milwaukee **11**:1590
Baron, Louis Bernhard **4**:252
Baron, Milton **15**:315
Bar-on, M. Y. **13**:138
BARON, SALO (Shalom) WITTMAYER **1**:28; **4**:253
– American Academy for Jewish Research **2**:819
– American Jewish Historical Society **2**:827
– history **8**:562; **8**:569
– Jewish Cultural Reconstruction **10**:49
Baron, Sydney S. **13**:1362
Baron d'Auvernas le Gras, *see* Suasso, Antonio Lopez
Baron de Hirsch Agricultural School (Woodbine, N.J.) **2**:412 **16**:157
– *illus:* **10**:35,47; **16**:158
BARON DE HIRSCH FUND **4**:254
– Allianz, Israelitische, zu Wien **2**:654
– B'nai B'rith **4**:1145
– Galician agricultural movement **2**:410
– Hirsch, Baron Maurice de **8**:506
– I.C.A **10**:46
– Mexico **11**:1456
– *illus:*
– – agricultural school, Woodbine, N. J. **10**:35,47
– – Hirsch, Baron Maurice de **8**:506
Baron de Hirsch Trade School (N.Y.) **12**:1079
BARONDESS, JOSEPH **4**:255
– *illus:* text
Baron Ginzburg (loc., Arg.) **6**:802
Barón Hirsch (clny., Arg.) **3**:429; **3**:430
Baron von Sparzenstein, *see* RICIUS, PAULUS
Baroto (city, Leb.), *see* BEIRUT
BAROU, NOAH **4**:256
– *illus:*
– – Ukrainian Council **15**:1515
Baroukh (fam.) **14**:1293
Barozzi, Francesco **8**:23; **13**:1259
Bar Pada (Pedaya; amora), *see* JUDAH BEN PEDAYA
Barrakab (k., Samal) **15**:1125; **16**:663
Barranquilla (city, Colom.) **5**:745ff
Barras, Abraham D. **16**:515
BARRASSA, JACOB **4**:256
BARRENNESS AND FERTILITY **4**:256
– Arabs in Israel **9**:1023
– Ashtoreth **3**:738
– birth control **4**:1053
– castration **5**:242
– folklore **6**:1401
– gentiles **12**:1189
– Israel **9**:481
– Naḥmanides **12**:781
– polygamy **12**:259
– vital statistics **16**:177
– *illus:*
– – text
– – amulet **2**:909
– – Israel, fertility of Jewish women 1965-68 (table) **9**:482
– – Israel fertility rates 1948-1968 (table) **9**:482
– – *ketubbah* with fertility symbols **6**:1375
BARRÈS, AUGUSTE MAURICE **4**:258
Barrett, David **4**:1380; **16**:67
Barrie, James **6**:776
Barrington (tn., R. I.) **14**:143
BARRIOS, DANIEL LEVI (Miguel) DE **4**:259
– Amsterdam **2**:897
– Brussels **4**:1422
– Enríquez, Isabel **6**:800
– Sephardi literature **14**:1169
– *illus:* text
Barrois (loc., Fr.) **11**:496
Barron, Harry I. **12**:871
Barron, Herman **15**:309
BARRON, JENNIE LOITMAN **4**:260
Barron, Milton **15**:68
Barron, Moses **11**:1200; **12**:38
Barros, Manoel Alvares de **15**:912
BARROS BASTO, ARTURO CARLOS DE **4**:261
– Vila Real **16**:135
– *illus:*
– – Marrano meeting (1936) **11**:1021
Barrouch, André **13**:817; **15**:1448
BARRUEL, AUGUSTIN **4**:261
Barry, Claude **12**:453
Barryville (loc., N.Y.) **18**:860
Bar-Saliba (bk.) **3**:218
Bar-Samson, Jacob **11**:1550
Bar Sauma (monk) **9**:255; **13**:1440
Barsbā (Barsabey, Barsbay; sult., Egy.), *see* Ashraf Barsba, Al-Malik al-
Barsha, John **15**:308
Barshān, Yehuda (Jūrj) **9**:1041; **12**:1464
BARSIMSON, JACOB **4**:262
– New Amsterdam **12**:1063
Barsky, Joseph **15**:35
BART, LIONEL **6**:787
– theater **15**:1068
Barta, Istvan **12**:1376
Barter, *see* ACQUISITION; *Ḥalifin*
Barter trade **15**:99ff
Bártfa (Bartfeldt; tn., Slov.), *see* BARDEJOV
Bartfield, Jacob **15**:306
Barth, Aharon **4**:263
– *illus:*
– – Va'ad Leummi **16**:50
Barth, Eliezer (Lazar) **4**:262
– *illus:*
– – Passfield White Paper Protest **16**:1118
BARTH, JACOB **4**:262
– *illus:* text
BARTH, KARL **4**:263
Bartha, Miklós **15**:470
BARTHOLDY, JACOB **4**:264
Bartholemew map **11**:931
Bartholomé, Paul Albert **6**:674
Bartholomeu da Fonseca **8**:1391
Bartholomew (apostle) **4**:555
Bartish, L. **16**:819
Bartlett, Washington **5**:57; **14**:833; **14**:834
BARTOLOCCI, GIULIO **4**:264
– Christian Hebraists **8**:23
Bartolommeo, Fra **9**:69
Barton, Clara **15**:126
Bartos, Armand P. **12**:552
BARTOV, HANOCH **4**:265
– Hebrew literature **8**:207
Bar Tuviah, *see* FRAENKEL, FAIWEL
BARUCH (Jeremiah's scribe) **4**:266
– Hellenistic Jewish literature **8**:304
– Jeremiah **9**:1350ff
– wisdom literature **16**:560
– Books on
– – *Baruch, Apocalypse of* (Syriac) **4**:270
– – *Baruch, Book of* **4**:272
– – *Baruch, Greek Apocalypse of* **4**:273
– – *Baruch, Rest of the Words of* **4**:276
BARUCH (kab.) **4**:267
BARUCH (fam.) **4**:268
Baruch (sol.) **11**:1566
BARUCH, APOCALYPSE OF (Syr.) **4**:270
– *Baruch, Rest of the Words of* **4**:276
– Davidic Messiah **11**:1409
– *illus:* text
Baruch, Bernard Manners **4**:269; **15**:311; **15**:312
– *illus:* text
BARUCH, BOOK OF (apoc. bk.) **4**:272
– *Baruch, Rest of the Words of* **4**:276
– Falashas **6**:1151
– Septuagint **4**:853
– *illus:*
– – fourteenth cent. ms. **13**:1437; **14**:1
Baruch, Franziska **15**:1488
– *illus:*
– – type **15**:1485,1486
BARUCH, GREEK APOCALYPSE OF **4**:273
– *Baruch, Rest of the Words of* **4**:276
Baruch, Hartwig **4**:269; **15**:312
Baruch, Herman Benjamin **4**:269
Baruch, Isobel **4**:269
Baruch, Jacob **16**:132
BARUCH, JACOB BEN MOSES ḤAYYIM **4**:274
– *illus:*
– – *Shivḥei Yerushalayim* (1785) **4**:275
Baruch, Javer **14**:872
BARUCH, JOSEPH MARCOU **4**:275
Baruch, Joshua Boaz **14**:586
Baruch, L. **16**:498
Baruch, Paul, *see* BEKKER, PAUL
BARUCH, REST OF THE WORDS OF (ps. bk.) **4**:276
Baruch, Sailing Wolfe **4**:269
Baruch, Samuel **14**:871
Baruch, Simon (court J.) **4**:1211; **5**:1010
Baruch, Simon (physic.) **4**:268; **15**:212
Baruch, Xaver (polit.), *see* Baruch, Javer
BARUCH BEN DAVID YAVAN **4**:277
Baruch ben Habib **2**:593
Baruch ben Isaac di Trani, *see* Trani, Baruch ben Isaac di
BARUCH BEN ISAAC OF ALEPPO **4**:277
– Aleppo **2**:562
– Obadiah of Normandy **12**:1306
BARUCH BEN ISAAC OF REGENSBURG **4**:278
– Baruch ben Isaac of Worms **4**:278
– seals **14**:1079
BARUCH BEN ISAAC OF WORMS (tos.) **4**:278
– Baruch ben Isaac of Regensburg **4**:278
– codification of law **11**:331
– Maḥzor Vitry **11**:736
– synods **15**:633
– Worms Maḥzor **11**:736
BARUCH BEN JEHIEL OF MEDZIBEZH **4**:279
– Aryeh Leib of Shpola **3**:669
– Hershele Ostropoler **12**:1516
– Tulchin **15**:1428
– *geneal. table* **9**:1052
Baruch ben Leib
– proselytism **13**:1191
– Russia **14**:434
– Smolensk **15**:7
– Voznitsyn, Alexander **16**:229
Baruch ben Samson **2**:470
BARUCH BEN SAMUEL **4**:279
– Judah ben Kalonymus **10**:349
– Ten Lost Tribes **15**:1005
BARUCH BEN SAMUEL OF ALEPPO **4**:280
– Baruch ben Isaac of Aleppo **4**:277
BARUCH BEN SAMUEL OF MAINZ **4**:280
– Bamberg, Samuel **4**:150
Baruch Gad of Jerusalem **8**:1181; **13**:315; **15**:1005
Baruchia (Russo; Shabbatean) **12**:797
– providence **13**:1283
Baruch ibn Ya'ish ibn Isaac *see* YA'ISH BARUCH BEN ISAAC IBN
Baruch the Kabbalist **4**:267
Baruch of Arezzo **14**:1246
Baruch of Benevento **16**:487

Baruch of Chernobyl **15:**1472
Baruch of Greece, *see* BARUCH BEN SAMUEL OF ALEPPO
BARUCH (ben Abraham) OF KOSOV **4:**281
Baruch of Medzibezh (ḥas. ldr.), *see* BARUCH BEN JEHIEL OF MEDZIBEZH
Baruch of Narbonne **4:**268
Baruch of Ostrava **8:**234
Baruch of Salonika **11:**64
Baruch of Shklov **6:**655
Baruch of Wesel, *see* WESEL, BARUCH BENDET b. REUBEN
Baruch of Worms **11:**1247
Baruch the Sephardi, *see* BARUCH BEN SAMUEL OF ALEPPO
Baruch Sheli'aḥ-Ẓibbur Togarmi **4:**267; **2:**185; **10:**529
Baruch the Teuton **15:**1286
Baruch Tulchiner, *see* BARUCH BEN JEHIEL OF MEDZIBEZH
BARUH, BORA **3:**596
- *illus:*
- - self-portrait **3:**618
Baruh, Kalmi **16:**888
BARUK, HENRI **4:**281
- *illus:* text
BARUKH (litur.) **4:**282
- *illus:* text
- *see also:* BENEDICTIONS
Barukh, Armand **4:**1494
Barukh, Viktor **4:**1494
Barukh, Yavok Effendi, *see* Effendi Barukh, Yavok
Barukh Adonai le-Olam (ben.) **3:**665
Barukh ha-Ba (Heb. greeting) **7:**914
Barukh ha-Nimẓa (Heb. greeting) **7:**914
Barukh ha-Yoshev (Heb. greeting) **7:**914
BARUKH SHE-AMAR (ben.) **4:**283
Barukh she-Amar Society (Prague) **4:**284
BARUKH SHEM KEVOD MALKHUTO LE-OLAM VA-ED (litur.) **4:**284
- inclusion in *Shema* **14:**1370
BARUKH SHE-PETARANI (ben.) **4:**285
Barukh Tihyeh (Heb. greeting) **7:**916; **7:**1516
Barwin, Victor **15:**209
BAR-YEHUDAH, ISRAEL **4:**285
- Jewish registration problem **9:**396
- *illus:*
- - Ukrainian Provisional National Council **15:**1515
Bar Yoḥai (11th cent., r.) **15:**123
Bar-yokhani (myst. bird), *see* Ziz
BAR-YOSEF, YEHOSHUA **4:**286
- drama, Hebrew **6:**205
- Jerusalem theme **9:**1566
Bar-Yosef, Yosef **4:**286; **6:**207
Barzaeus, Gaspar **8:**976
Barzapharnes (Parth. satrap) **11:**627
Barzel (metal), *see* Iron
Barzel, Barukh **14:**631
BARZILAI (fam.) **4:**286
Barzilai, Benveniste **15:**1270
Barzilai, Elijah (Eliahu) **3:**818; **7:**879
Barzilai, Giuseppe **4:**286
Barzilai, Israel **9:**671,677ff
- *illus:*
- - envoy to Poland **9:**425; **13:**781
Barzilai, Nehama **13:**1340
Barzilai, Salvatore **4:**286
Barzilai, Yehoshua **6:**203
- Benei Moshe **4:**492
- newspapers **12:**1055
Barzilai-Folman, Joshua **7:**1369; **7:**1469
BARZILLAI THE GILEADITE (bib. fig.) **4:**287
BARZILLAI OF ABEL-MEHOLAH (bib. fig.) **4:**287
Barzio, Giuseppe **8:**875
Basa (Jaffa qtr.) **15:**924
Basaam ben Simeon **8:**1058
Ba-Sa'ar (journ.) **1:**newsp. list
Ba-Sad (journ.), *see Barka'i*
Basar, see FLESH
Basar, Mount (Mesop.), *see* Jabel Bishri
Basar be-Ḥalav, see DIETARY LAWS; MEAT; MILK
Basar va-Dam, see FLESH
Basātīn (loc., Egy.) **5:**30
Basch, E. **4:**1480
Basch, Henry **13:**161
Basch, Jacob **13:**161
Basch, Samuel **11:**1456
BASCH, VICTOR GUILLAUME **4:**287
Baschko, Judah Loeb **4:**289
Baschko, Moses **4:**289
BASCHKO, ẒEVI HIRSCH BEN BENJAMIN **4:**288
- *illus:* text
Baschwitz, Baruch **8:**258; **15:**1487
- *illus:*
- - *Maḥzor Minhag Ashkenazi* **15:**1485
Baschwitz, Hirsch **7:**94
Baseball **15:**300
- *illus:*
- - Gordon, Sid **15:**300
- - Rosen, Albert Leonard **15:**299
Basel (city, Switz.), *see* BASLE
Basemath (bib. fig.) **2:**234; **5:**1340; **12:**910; **16:**996
BASEVI (fam.) **4:**289
- Ashkenazi, Solomon **3:**731
- printing **13:**1095; **13:**1104
- *illus:*
- - printers' mark **13:**1093
Basevi, Abraham **4:**289; **8:**340
Basevi, Abramo **4:**289
Basevi, George **4:**290
- *illus:* **4:**289
Basevi, Gioacchino **4:**289
Basevi, James Palladio **4:**290
Basevi, Joseph **4:**289
Basevi, Joshua **4:**290
Basevi, Maria, *see* Disraeli, Maria
Basevi, Nathan (Naphtali) **4:**290; **8:**339
Basevi, Nathaniel **4:**290
Basevi Cervetto (fam.), *see* BASEVI
Basevi Cervetto, Jacob *see* CERVETTO, JACOB BASEVI
Basevi della Gondola (fam.), *see* BASEVI
Basewi, Josef **4:**291
Bash (fam.), *see* BASEVI
Ba-Sha'ar (journ.) **1:**newsp. list
BASHAN (reg., Er. Isr.) **4:**291
- Ashtaroth **3:**737
- Herod's kingdom **8:**635
- Hittites and Israel **8:**577
- human geography **9:**595ff
- physiography **9:**181
- Trachonitis **15:**1293
- *map:* text
- *see also:* BATHYRA; RAMAT HA-GOLAN
Bashan (mt., Sinai), *see* SINAI, MOUNT
BASHEVIS SINGER, ISAAC **4:**293
- Yiddish literature **16:**820; **16:**824
BASHIRI, YAḤYA **4:**296
- Masorah **16:**1477
Bashiya (tn., Iraq) **8:**1450
Bashkala (vill., Kurd.) **10:**1297
Bash Kharāj (poll tax) **16:**1532
Bashkir (rep., Rus.) **15:**1500
BASHUYSEN, HEINRICH JACOB VAN **4:**296
- Christian Hebraists **8:**23
- Hanau **7:**1257
- *illus:* text
BASHYAZI (Bashyatchi; fam., Turk.) **4:**297
- Adrianople **2:**310
Bashyazi, Elijah ben Moses **4:**297; **5:**785
Bashyazi, Menahem ben Joseph **4:**297
Bashyazi, Moses (14/15 cent.) **4:**297
Bashyazi, Moses (16th cent.) **4:**298
Basic Jewish Encyclopedia **6:**734
BASIL I (Byz. emp.) **4:**298
- disputations **6:**90
- forced conversions **3:**170; **3:**226
- Greece **7:**872
- *Vision of Daniel* **5:**1290
Basilea, Menaḥem Samson ben Solomon **4:**299
Basilea, Simone **11:**898
BASILEA, SOLOMON AVIAD SAR-SHALOM **4:**299
BASILICA (build.) **4:**299
- *illus:* text
Basilicata (reg., It.) **9:**1118
Basilikai Trapezai (royal bank) **12:**243
Basily, C. M. **9:**1448
BAṢIR, JOSEPH BEN ABRAHAM HA-KOHEN HA-RO'EH AL- **4:**301
- atomism **3:**830
- commandments **5:**785
- philosophy **13:**433
- problem of evil **7:**777
Basīsū, Saʿīd **9:**1041
Basketball **15:**302
- *illus:*
- - Israel at eighth European Championship Games **15:**295
- - Rosenbluth, Leonard **15:**302
Baskin, Bernard **7:**1239
Baskin, Israel **14:**479
BASKIN, LEONARD **4:**303
- medals **11:**1167
- *illus:*
- - "Crow" (sculp.) **4:**302
Baskin, Samuel **4:**303
BASLE (city, Switz.) **4:**303
- banking **4:**168
- chronological chart (1431-49) **8:**766-767
- museums **12:**544
- Switzerland **15:**555ff
- Zionist Congress **16:**1096
- *illus:*
- - text
- - athletes at Sixth Zionist Congress **15:**291
- - First Zionist Congress, invitation **16:**1045
- - Froben's printers' mark **13:**1093
- - Second Zionist Congress **16:**1169
- - tombstones **15:**555
Basle-Ferrara-Florence, Council of (1431-45) **5:**548; **15:**1676
BASLE PROGRAM **4:**306
- Basle **4:**304
- Kharkov conference **10:**941
- Zionism **16:**1033ff
- Zionist Congresses **16:**1164; **16:**1167; **16:**1176
- *illus:* text
Basloe, Frank **15:**302
Basman, Rivka **16:**825
BASNAGE, JACQUES CHRISTIAN (Basnage de Beauval) **4:**309
- Christian Hebraists **8:**23
- history **8:**560
- *illus:*
- - text
- - *La République des Hébreux* engravings (1713) **3:**981; **4:**257; **5:**400; **6:**112,1349; **7:**100; **8:**1235; **12:**1448
Basner, Hyman **13:**820
Basola, Moses (kab.) **4:**310
Basola, Moses (schol.) **4:**310; **12:**202
BASOLA, MOSES BEN MORDECAI **4:**310
- Jerusalem *takkanot* **9:**281
- Joseph ibn Shraga **10:**243
- Sidon **14:**1508
- travels **15:**1352
BASRA (port, Iraq) **4:**310
- Iraq **8:**1447ff
- Sura **15:**523
- *illus:* text
Bas Rhin (reg., Fr.) **3:**382
Baṣrī, Joseph **8:**1453
Baṣri, Meer **12:**1464ff
- Shaul, Anwar **14:**1319
Bass, Alfie **15:**1054
Bass, Benny **15:**305
BASS, HYMAN B. **4:**313
- encyclopedia **6:**735
Bass, Josef (cart.), *see* Bass, Yoseph
Bass, Joseph (print.) **6:**330
BASS, SHABBETAI BEN JOSEPH **4:**313
- bibliography **4:**971; **11:**350
- censorship **5:**278
- Dyhernfurth **6:**330
- Sephardim **14:**1167
- Slatkine, Menahem Mendel **14:**1655
Bass, Yoseph (cart.) **5:**219; **11:**1167
Bassan (fam., It.), *see* BASSANO
BASSAN, ABRAHAM HEZEKIAH BEN JACOB **4:**313
Bassan, Jacob **4:**313
Bassan, Samuel **16:**67
Bassani (fam., It.), *see* BASSANO
BASSANI, GIORGIO **4:**314
- Italian literature **9:**1113
BASSANI, MORDECAI (Marco) **4:**315
BASSANO (fam., It.) **4:**315
BASSANO (tn., It.) **4:**315
Bassano, Isaiah ben Israel Hezekiah **4:**315
- Bachrach, Naphtali **4:**50
- Benjamin ben Eliezer ha-Cohen Vitale **4:**532
- Luzzatto, Moses Ḥayyim **11:**599
Bassano, Israel Benjamin **4:**315; **5:**187; **9:**1109
Basser, Sir Adolph **15:**311
Bassermann, Albert **4:**1290
Bassermann, E. **10:**1342
Bassevi, Samuel **4:**316
BASSEVI OF TREUENBERG (Treuenburg), JACOB **4:**316
- coat of arms **8:**334
- ennobled **15:**1165
- *illus:*
- - text
- - coat of arms **8:**335
BASSIN, MOSHE **4:**317
Bassista, Shabbetai ben Joseph, *see* BASS, SHABBETAI BEN JOSEPH
Bassola, Moses ben Mordecai, *see* BASOLA, MOSES BEN MORDECAI
Bassora (port, Iraq), *see* BASRA
BASSUS, LUCILIUS (Rom. gov., Judea) **4:**317
Basta (tn., Sp.), *see* BAZA
Bastard, *see* MAMZER
Bastia (city, Cors.) **5:**975
Bastomski, S. **5:**440; **5:**459
BAS-TOVIM, SARAH **4:**318
- *Teḥinnot* **11:**358
Bastrop (tn., La.) **11:**520
BAT (zool.) **4:**318
- dietary laws **6:**32
- evolution **6:**1003
- reproduction **4:**1017
Bataiḥa Valley (Er. Isr.) **9:**591; **10:**1032

Baṭalyawsī, Abū Muḥammad Abdallah al-, *see* AL-BAṬALYAWSĪ, ABU MUḤAMMAD ABDALLAH IBN MUHAMMAD IBN AL-SĪD
Batanea (prov., Er. Isr.), *see* BASHAN
Bataril, Moses **16:**1552
Batas (shoe factory, Lith.) **14:**1485
Batavia (city, Indon.), *see* Jakarta
Bat-Dor Dance Company, *see* BATSHEVA AND BAT-DOR DANCE COMPANIES
BATE, JULIUS **4:**319
- Christian Hebraists **8:**23
Bateiḥa Valley (Er. Isr.), *see* Bataiḥa Valley
Batei Ungarn (qtr., Jer.), *see* Battei Ungarn
Ba-Telem (journ.) **1:**newsp. list
Bat Galim (loc., Isr.) **7:**1133
Bat Gallim (Isr. boat) **9:**387; **15:**1553
BATH (city, Eng.) **4:**319
Bath (city, Me.) **11:**782
Baʿth (Arab soc. party, Syr.), *see* Ba'ath
BATH, BATHING **4:**319
- ablution **2:**82f
- Banna'im **14:**1087
- Hammath **7:**1242ff
- *mikveh* **11:**1533, 1534
- mourning **12:**489
- Omar, Covenant of **12:**1379
- purity and impurity **13:**1405
- Three Weeks **15:**1124
- *illus:*
- - ritual immersion before sunset **15:**1033
Bath (meas.) **16:**380ff
Bathbasi (city, Er. Isr.) **14:**1565
Báthori, G. Mihály **8:**23
Bathory, Stephen (k., Pol.) **14:**537
- chronological chart **8:**766-767
Baths, public **4:**319
BATH-SHEBA (bib. fig.) **4:**321
- David's behavior **5:**1328
- in the Arts **5:**1334
- Nathan and **12:**846ff
- Solomon **15:**96ff
- *geneal. table:* **5:**1341
- *illus:*
- - text
- - David **11:**633
Bath-Sheba (fam.), *see* BASEVI
Bath-Sheba, Sabbatai Mattathias **4:**289
"Bath-Sheba at the Fountain" (paint., Rubens) **4:**322
BATHYRA (vill., Bashan) **4:**323
- Bathyra, Sons of **4:**323
BATHYRA, SONS OF (fam., Er. Isr.) **4:**323
- Bathyra **4:**323
- Hillel and **8:**482
- Paschal lamb tradition **15:**1309
- Zamaris **16:**922
- *illus:* text
Batista, Fulgencio **5:**1147; **5:**1150
Batito, Naḥman **9:**889
BAT KOL (heavenly voice) **4:**324
- *Bet Hillel* **4:**741
- in *halakhah* **12:**119
- Joshua ben Hananiah **10:**280
- Mt. Horeb **14:**1600
- prophecy **13:**1176
- rabbinical authority **3:**908ff
- *Ru'aḥ ha-Kodesh* **14:**366
- visions **16:**167
- *see also:* REVELATION
Bat Kol (journ.) **1:**newsp. list
BATLANIM (cmty. offic.) **4:**325
- "seven good men" **6:**580
Batle y Ordoñez, José **16:**10
BAT-MIRIAM, YOKHEVED **4:**325
- *illus:* text
Bat Mitzvah, *see* BAR MITZVAH, BAT MITZVAH
BATO, LUDWIG YOMTOV **4:**326
Baton Rouge (city, U.S.) **11:**517
BATSHAW, HARRY **4:**327
- Canada **5:**112
- *illus:*
- - Zionist Organization of Canada convention **16:**1110
BAT SHELOMO (mosh., Isr.) **4:**327
- statistics **1:**place list
Bat-Sheva (fam.), *see* BASEVI
BATSHEVA AND BAT-DOR DANCE COMPANIES (Isr.) **4:**327
- culture in Israel **9:**1008
- dance in Israel **5:**1271
- *illus:* text
Battānī, Al- (astron.) **3:**801
BATTAT, REUBEN **4:**328
Battei Ungarn (Jer. qtr.) **9:**325; **15:**155
Battei Varsha (qtr., Jer.) **9:**1462
- *illus:*
- - *sukkot* **15:**501
- - water ration card (1920) **9:**1476
Battering ram **16:**274
Battīr (vill., Isr.) **4:**733
Battle-ax **16:**266ff
Battle Creek (city, Mich.) **11:**1500
Battle of the Books (controversy, Ger.) **14:**108ff
Bat-Tovim, Sarah, *see* BAS-TOVIM, SARAH
BATUMI (Batum; city, Rus.) **4:**328
Bat Ya'anah (zool.) **12:**1531
BAT YAM (city, Isr.) **4:**328
- statistics **1:**place list
- Tel Aviv **15:**924
- *illus:*
- - text
- - housing project **3:**350
- - Ramat Yosef residential area **9:**567
Bat Zion (Jer.) **11:**1481
Batzir, Joseph al-, *see* BASIR, JOSEPH BEN ABRAHAM HA-KOHEN HA'RO'EH AL-
BAUDISSIN, WOLF WILHELM, GRAF VON **4:**329
Baudoin (k., Belg.) **4:**425
Bauen (seder night) **2:**258
Bauer (fam., Sp.) **11:**684
Bauer, A. **11:**684
BAUER, BRUNO **4:**329
- attitude to Jews **8:**714
- chronological chart **8:**766-767
- Jewish question **11:**1074
- Steinthal, Hermann Heymann **15:**377
BAUER, HANS **4:**330
- linguistics **16:**1397
BAUER, JACOB **4:**330
Bauer, Lina, *see* MORGENSTERN, LINA
Bauer, Norman **11:**520
BAUER, OTTO **4:**331
- socialism **15:**26,43
BAUER, SIMON HARVEY **5:**379
Bauer-Mayer, Joanne **4:**1219
Bauernfreund, Jakub, *see* BORNFRIEND, JACOB
Baugé (tn., Fr.) **3:**23
Bauli, Benayah ben Kalev ben Maḥpuẓ al-, *see* Benayah ben Kalev ben Maḥpuẓ al-Bauli
Baum, Harry **15:**302
Baum, Henrik **12:**454
BAUM, HERBERT **4:**332
Baum, Julius **15:**1525
Baum, Karl **13:**1029
BAUM, MORTON **15:**1077
- New York City **12:**1122
BAUM, OSCAR **4:**332
Baum, Samuel **3:**199
BAUM, VICKI **4:**332
Baumann, Albert **11:**1562
Baumann, Gustav **4:**1112; **12:**1447
Baumann, Isaac **4:**1111 **13:**803
Baumann, Kurt **10:**462
Baumatz, Yeshayahu **13:**1340
BAUMGARDT, DAVID **4:**333
BAUMGARTEL, ELISE J. **4:**334
- archaeology **3:**302
BAUMGARTEN, EMANUEL MENDEL **4:**334
- Ruth poem **14:**523
Baumgarten, Izidor **10:**1497
Baumgarten, Károly **10:**1497
Baumgarten, Morris **5:**411
BAUMGARTNER, WALTER **4:**334
- linguistics **16:**1399
Bauminger, H. **5:**1039
Baumritter, Ephraim **16:**248
Baunacht (seder night) **2:**258
Baur, André **15:**1535
BAUR, HARRY **4:**335
BAUSKA (tn., Rus.) **4:**335
Bava, Sons of (Jer.) **4:**338
BAVA BATRA (tract.) **4:**336
- Helena of Adiabene **8:**288
- *illus:* text
BAVA BEN BUTA (sage) **4:**338
- sacrifices **10:**918
BAVA KAMMA (tract.) **4:**338
- *illus:* text
BAVA MEẒIA (tract.) **4:**341
- *illus:* text
Bava(h) Rabbah (Samar. h. pr.), *see* BABA RABBAH
BAVARIA (state, Ger.) **4:**343
- Albany and **2:**524
- chronological chart (1551, 1813) **8:**766-767
- horse trading **2:**204
- host desecration charge **8:**1043
- migration trends **8:**720
- peddling **13:**206
- rabbinical office **13:**1454
- Vienna, Congress of **16:**132
- *illus:*
- - text
- - customs ordinance of Raffelstetten **15:**869
BAVLI, HILLEL **4:**347
- Hebrew literature **8:**212
- *illus:*
- - Hebrew Pen Club, N.Y. **8:**211; **12:**1109
- - Hebrew writers' convention, 1943 **8:**213
BAVLI, MENAHEM BEN MOSES **4:**349
Bavli, Reuben **4:**349
Bavlim (Iraqi cmty., Isr.) **9:**499
Baxa, Karel **8:**496
BAYAZID II (sult., Turk.) **4:**349
- attitude towards Jews **16:**1532
Baybars (13th cent., Egy.) **9:**271; **9:**1424
- *illus:*
- - Lydda bridge **11:**619
Bay City (city, Mich.) **11:**1499
Bay City (tn., Tex.) **15:**1036
Bayḍāʿ, Al- (site, Transj.) **15:**1316
Baydas, Khalīl **9:**1040
BAYEFSKY, ABA **3:**596
- *illus:*
- - "Out of Bondage" **3:**613
BAYER, BATHJA **1:**28
Bayer, F. Perez **12:**1271
BAYHAN (terr., S. Arab.) **4:**349
- Albright's excavations **2:**539
- Habban Jews **7:**1019
Bayit Ḥadash (hal. comment.) **5:**647; **14:**1620
- *illus:*
- - title page (1697) **14:**1619
Bayit va-Gan (tn., Isr.), *see* BAT YAM
Bayit va-Gan (suburb, Jer.)
- development **9:**1472; **9:**1496
- topography **9:**1516
- *illus:*
- - Kol Torah Yeshivah **16:**766
Bayle, Pierre **5:**1463
Bayley, Cornelius **8:**23
BAYLIS, LILIAN MARY **4:**350
Baylon (cmty. offic.) **3:**966
Bayly, Anselm **8:**23
Bay Nakht Oyfn Altn Mark (play) **13:**282; **16:**813
Baynes, Ralph **8:**23
BAYONNE (tn., Fr.) **4:**350
- archives **3:**382
- museums **12:**543
- *illus:* text
Bayonne (city, N.J.) **8:**1057; **12:**1028
Bayons (loc., Fr.) **14:**1623
Bay Psalm Book (17th cent.) **15:**1487
Bayrakdar Pasha (vizier) **16:**1538
BAYREUTH (city, Ger.) **4:**352
- archives **3:**387
Bayside Land Corporation **13:**39
Bayswater (dist., London) **6:**447,449; **11:**479
Bayt al-Hikma, *see* House of Wisdom
Bayt al-Maqdis (tn., Er. Isr.) **9:**1360
Bayt Iksā (vill., Isr.),*see* BET IKSA
Baytin (vill.) **4:**728
- *illus:*
- - Beth-El ruins **4:**729
Bayt Jālā (tn., Er. Isr.) **4:**745; **9:**587
Baytjālī, Iskandar al-Khūrī al- **9:**1040
Bayt Jann (vill., Isr.), *see* BEIT JANN
Bayt Nabālā (Arab legion camp), *see* Beit Nabālā
BAY TREE **4:**353
- Flora **9:**221
Bayt Ṣāfāfā (vill., Isr.), *see* Beit Ṣāfāfā
Bayt Sāḥūr (tn., Er. Isr.), *see* Beit Sāḥūr
Bayudaya (Judaiz. sect.) **10:**398
Bayuk, Moses **16:**157
BAZA (tn., Sp.) **4:**353
Baẓal Yarok (theat.) **9:**1005
Bazard, Saint Armand **14:**667 **15:**25
BAZELON, DAVID L. **4:**353
Baẓer (metal) **11:**1429
Bazín (tn., Slov.), *see* PEZINOK
Bazirkan (Turk. tit.) **6:**498
Bazna (vill., Rum.) **8:**1089
B.B.C., *see* British Broadcasting Corporation
BDELLIUM (Bdéllion) **4:**354
- plant list **13:**615
- source **8:**1311
Bé, Guillaume le, *see* LE BÉ, GUILLAUME
BEA, AUGUSTIN **4:**354
- *illus:* text
Beaconsfield, Benjamin Disraeli, Earl of, *see* DISRAELI, BENJAMIN
Beadle, *see* SHAMMASH
Beadle, George **4:**1031
Be'ad ve-Neged (journ.) **1:**newsp. list
Beame, Abraham D. **12:**1113
BEANS (bot.) **4:**355
- food **6:**1416
- *kapparot* **10:**756
- plant list **13:**615
- *see also:* LEGUMES
BEAR (zool.) **4:**355
- dietary laws **6:**32
- Elisha and mocking boys **6:**667
- *illus:*
- - text
- - Book of Esther in micrographic writing **14:**1055
BEARD AND SHAVING **4:**356

- Commandments, the 613 **5:**772,777
- Jacob David of Amshinov **16:**304
- Lag ba-Omer **10:**1356
- Omer period **12:**1386
- punishment **3:**759
- *sheli'aḥ ẓibbur* **14:**1356
- Three Weeks **15:**1124
- *illus:*
- - text
- - Frederick II's decree **13:**1291
- *see also:* PE'OT
"Bearded Man in a Cap" (paint., Rembrandt) **14:**68
Bearsted, Marcus Richard Samuel, Third Viscount **4:**359
BEARSTED, MARCUS SAMUEL, FIRST VISCOUNT **4:**358
Bearsted, Walter Horace Samuel, Second Viscount **4:**359
- *illus:*
- - Marks, Simon, and **11:**1009
Beasts, *see* ANIMALS OF THE BIBLE AND TALMUD
Beating, *see* FLOGGING
BEATITUDE **4:**359
- Israeli, Isaac ben Solomon **9:**1064
- Kabbalah **10:**613
- *illus:* text
- *see also:* AFTERLIFE; OLAM HA-BA; PARADISE; REWARD AND PUNISHMENT
Beatitudes, Mount of (Er. Isr.) **8:**922
- *illus:*
- - Church of Beatitudes **8:**928
Beatrice de Luna, *see* NASI, GRACIA
BEAUCAIRE (tn., Fr.) **4:**363
Beaufort (city, S. C.) **15:**211
Beaufort (Crus. fort.) **9:**269
Beaumont (city, Tex.) **15:**1034ff
Beaune la Rolande (concen. camp, Fr.) **7:**35; **8:**858
Beausang, J. J. **7:**1257
Beausobre, Julia de, *see* Namier, Julia
Beautiful Gate (Temple), *see* NICANOR'S GATE
Beauty **5:**978ff; **6:**998
Be'ayot (journ.) **1:**newsp. list
Be'ayot Beinle'ummiyyot (journ.) **1:**newsp. list
Be'ayot ha-Ḥinnukh ha-Meshuttaf (journ.) **1:**newsp. list
Be'ayot ha-Yom (journ.) **1:**newsp. list
BEBAI (amora) **4:**364
BEBAI BAR ABBAYE (amora) **4:**364
Bebai ha-Levi bar Abba of Nehar-Pekod (gaon) **2:**399; **7:**318
Bebel, August **15:**26
Becher (bib. fig.) **14:**1329
Becher, Johann **8:**703
Becher, Kurt **8:**907; **10:**816
BECHER, SIEGFRIED **4:**364
Becher, Vilmos **4:**884
Bechhoefer, Charles **12:**37
Bechhofen (vill., Bav.) **15:**611
- *illus:*
- - synagogue, wall paintings **4:**346; **15:**609
BECHHOLD, JACOB HEINRICH **5:**379
BECHYNE (Bechin; tn., Bohem.) **4:**365
Beck, Adolf **11:**1204
Beck, Fulop O. **11:**1167
Beck, Hugo **10:**1498
Beck, Julian **12:**1121; **15:**1578
BECK, KARL ISIDOR **4:**365
BECK(IUS), MATTHIAS FRIEDRICH **4:**365
- Christian Hebraists **8:**23
Beck, Meir, *see* BECK, MORITZ
BECK, MICHAEL **4:**366
- Christian Hebraists **8:**23
BECK, MORITZ **4:**366
Beck, Samuel **13:**1340,1345
BECK, WILLY **3:**596
Beck de Madarassy, Ferdinand **4:**176
BECKELMAN, MOSES W. **4:**366
BECKER (fam.) **4:**367
Becker, Abraham G. **4:**367
BECKER, AHARON **16:**1260
Becker, Harry **12:**1222
Becker, Helen, *see* TAMIRIS, HELEN
Becker, Howard **15:**67
Becker, Idel **15:**255
Becker, Israel **7:**1033
Becker, James Herman **4:**367
Becker, Jillian **15:**209
BECKER, JULIUS (journ.) **4:**367
BECKER, LAVY MORDECAI **4:**368
Becker, Lazar **7:**591
Becker, Sam **15:**306
Beckerle, Adolf **4:**1486
Beckermann, Henrietta, *see* Diamond, Henrietta
Beckhofen (vill., Bav.), *see* Bechhofen
Beckius, Matthias Friedrich, *see* BECK(IUS), MATTHIAS FRIEDRICH
Beckley (city, W. Va.) **16:**475
Beckmann, J.C. **7:**93; **8:**23
Becov (tn., Bohem.) **5:**184
- *illus:*
- - Jewish quarter (1726) **4:**1175
Bécsi Magyar Ujság (newsp.) **10:**1175
BEDA (journ.) **4:**368
BEDACHT, MAX **4:**368
Bedan (bib. fig.) **14:**744; **14:**1621
Bedanite (lang.) **14:**1152
Bedarida (fam., It.) **4:**370
BEDARIDA, GUIDO **4:**369
BÉDARRIDE, ISRAEL (Isaiah) **4:**369
Bédarride, Jassuda (Judah) **4:**369
BÉDARRIDES (vill., Fr.) **4:**369
Bédarrides, Gad ben Judah of, *see* Gad ben Judah of Bédarrides
Bédarrides, Gustave Emanuel **4:**369
BEDDINGTON (fam., Eng.) **4:**370
Beddington, Alfred Henry **4:**370
Beddington, Claude **4:**370
Beddington, Sir Edward Henry Lionel **4:**370
Beddington, William Richard **4:**370
Bede (8th cent., St.) **8:**11
Bedeken (veiling of bride) **4:**74; **7:**1150; **11:**1036,1037
Bedek Institute (Isr.), *see* Israel Aircraft Industries
Bedell, William **4:**888
Beders, Vidal de **16:**136
Bedersi (natives of Béziers) **4:**792
BEDERSI, ABRAHAM BEN ISAAC **4:**370
- linguistics **16:**1360,1387
- poetry **13:**689
Bedersi, Jedaiah ha-Penini, *see* JEDAIAH BEN ABRAHAM BEDERSI
BEDFORD (tn., Eng.) **4:**371
BEDIKAT ḤAMEẒ (searching for leaven) **4:**372
- *illus:*
- - text
- - *First Cincinnati Haggadah* **4:***fcg.* 364
- *see also:* ḤAMEẒ, SALE OF; PASSOVER
Bedil (metal), *see* Tin
Bedouin
- Arabic vocabulary **3:**239
- Arab period **9:**259ff
- camel **5:**73
- Ishmaelites **9:**89
- life of **12:**1209
- Mamluks **9:**279
- Ottoman period **9:**284ff
BEDOUIN IN ISRAEL **9:**1043
- Defense Forces **9:**692,715
- general survey **9:**1021ff
- geographical distribution **9:**569ff
- health standards **9:**991
- land distribution **9:**338
- *illus:*
- - text
- - children in the Negev **12:**930
- - plowing in the Negev **9:**782
- - Samuel, Herbert **9:**1021
- - settlement figures **9:**485
Bedwell, William **8:**23
BEDZIN (tn., Pol.) **4:**373
- He-Ḥalutz training farm **8:**252
- Holocaust **13:**752
- *illus:* text
BEE (zool.) **4:**374
- *nahalolim, na'aẓuẓim* **15:**1119
- ownership **12:**1533
- *see also:* HONEY
BEEK, MARTINUS ADRIANUS **4:**375
Beekman, Jacob **8:**23
Beelen, J. Theodor **8:**23
Beelitz (tn., Ger.) **8:**1043
Beelmaus (vill., Er. Isr.) **4:**5
Beelzebub (deity), *see* Baal Zebub
Beelzebul (deity), *see* Baal-Zebul
Beer (fam.) **10:**1108
BEER (Bib. loc.) **4:**375
Beer (beverage)
- Babylonian economy **2:**400; **16:**1276
- barley **4:**242
- ceremonies **16:**539
- cult **5:**1161
- *illus:*
- - beer jug (Israelite) **2:**397
BEER, AARON (cantor) **4:**375
- music **12:**633
- *illus:* text
Beer, Aaron (bnk.) **4:**173; **5:**1009
Beer, Alexander, *see* BEHR, ALEXANDER
Beer, Arthur **3:**807
Beer, Benjamin ben Elijah **11:**1168
- *illus:*
- - medal **11:**1169
BEER, BERNHARD (Ger.) **4:**376
Beer, Bernhard (Eng.) **12:**682
Beer, Frédéric (Paris) **16:**1165
Beer, Frederick Arthur (Lond.) **4:**380
BEER, GEORGE LOUIS **4:**377
BEER, ISRAEL **4:**377
Beer, Jacob Hertz **9:**1241; **11:**1465
Beer, Jacob Liebmann, *see* MEYERBEER, GIACOMO
BEER, MAX **4:**378
BEER, MICHAEL **4:**378
- *illus:* text
BEER, PETER (Pereẓ) **4:**379
- history **8:**560
- *illus:*
- - *Toledot Yisrael* (1796) **7:**1440
BEER, RACHEL (Richa) **4:**380
- Sassoon family **14:**900
BEER, SAMUEL FRIEDRICH **4:**380
- *illus:* text
Beer, Solomon **13:**16
Beer, S. Piperno **9:**1139
BEER, WILHELM **4:**380
- astronomy **3:**806
Beera (bib. fig.) **14:**106
BEER-BING, ISAIAH **4:**381
- Abbé Grégoire **4:**1007
Beer-Elim (loc., Moab) **4:**375
Be'er Gannim (vill., Isr.) **6:**987
Be'er ha-Golah (Shulḥan Arukh comment.) **14:**197
Be'er ha-Golah (bk.) **8:**697
BEER-HOFMANN, RICHARD **4:**381
BE'ERI (kib., Isr.) **4:**382
- - statistics **1:**place list
Beer-Lahai-Roi (loc., Er. Isr.) **9:**3
Be'er Mayim Ḥayyim (wk.) **7:**1508 **15:**520
Be'er Moshe (Bib. trans.) **11:**357
BE'ER ORAH (training camp, Isr.) **4:**382
- statistics **1:** place list
- *illus:* text
Be'erotayim (mosh., Isr.) **1:**place list
BEEROTH (city, Er. Isr.) **4:**382
- Benjamin tribe **8:**579
- el-Bire **13:**1609
BE'EROT YIẒḤAK (kib., Isr.) **4:**383
- Ha-Poel ha-Mizrachi **7:**1322
- statistics **1:**place list
BEERSHEBA (city, Isr.) **4:**383
- basin **9:**136; **12:**925ff
- Genesis, Book of **7:**389
- human geography **9:**575ff
- inter-communal conflict **9:**395ff
- population **12:**930
- statistics **1:**place list
- tribal center **15:**1383ff
- War of Independence **16:**327
- *illus:*
- - text
- - capture of (October 21, 1948) **16:**324
- - I.D.F.'s artillery **16:**322
- - I.D.F. soldiers relaxing after capture of **16:**325
- - Negev Brigade memorial **12:**931
- - Negev Institute for Arid Zone Research **9:**966
- - Shikkun Alef project **9:**564
Beersheba Culture (arch.) **3:**505
Beersheba River, *see* Naḥal Be'er Sheva
BE'ER TOVIYYAH (mosh., Isr.) **4:**386
- Arab attacks on **9:**344
- Emica reconstruction **10:**48
- statistics **1:** place list
BE'ER YA'AKOV (tn., Isr.) **4:**386
- Jacob Yiẓḥaki **12:**479
- statistics **1:**place list
Be'er Ya'akov Pittu'aḥ (mosh., Isr.) **4:**387
Beeshterah (Cana. city), *see* ASHTAROTH
Beeston, William **8:**23
BEET (bot.) **4:**387
Beethoven, Ludwig van **10:**461; **15:**1186
Beet spinach **13:**615
BEGGING AND BEGGARS **4:**387
- *illus:* text
- *see also:* CHARITY; POVERTY
BEGHI (fam., Turk.) **4:**391
Beghi, Elijah Afidah (Afdah) **4:**391
Beghi, Joseph ben Moses **4:**391
Beghi, Moses ben Benjamin **4:**391
BÉGIN, ÉMILE-AUGUSTE **4:**391
BEGIN, MENAḤEM **4:**392
- Gaḥal **7:**255
- Ḥerut **8:**400
- I.Ẓ.L. **8:**1467
- National Unity government **9:**408; **14:**1626
- politics in Israel **9:**663
- *illus:*
- - Ḥerut Central Committee meeting **9:**679
- - Six-Day War, with soldiers **9:**409
Begun, Jack **15:**306
B-e-h-a-b (2nd, 5th, and 2nd days), *see* MONDAY AND THURSDAY
Be-Hadragah (mosh., Isr.), *see* MA'AS
Behagaon, Issachar Baer ben

Tanḥum *see* ISSACHAR BAER BEN TANḤUM
BEHAK, JUDAH **4**:393
- Lebensohn, Abraham Dov **10**:1548
Be-Ḥakla'ut u-va-Meshek (journ.) **1**:newsp. list
Behar, Josef **16**:1149
Behar, J. S. **5**:446
BEHAR, NISSIM **4**:393
- press **13**:1039
Beharav, Dmitri, *see* BOGROV, DMITRI
Beharav, Grigori Isaakovich, *see* BOGROV, GRIGORI ISAAKOVICH
Behard, Yiẓḥak Isaac **16**:191
Behavior, Rules of, *see* DEREKH EREẒ; ETHICS; ETIQUETTE
Behelfer (educ.), *see* Belfer
BEHEMOTH (leg. animal) **4**:394
- iconography **8**:1222
- resurrection **14**:100
- *illus:*
- - text
- - *Ambrosian Bible* **4**:360, *fcg.* 907
- - Leviathan and **11**:89
Beḥinat Olam (bk.) **9**:1308; **11**:353
- incunabula **8**:1342
Beḥinot (period.) **13**:1378; **16**:984
- statistics **1**:newsp. list
Beḥinot (kab. conc.) **10**:577
Beḥirta, see EDUYYOT
Behistun (loc., Mesop.) **16**:669; **16**:1506
Behmer, Markus **15**:143; **15**:1488
Behor, Yakim **10**:1351
Beḥor Effendi, *see* ASHKENAZI, BEḤOR
BE-ḤOZAI (dist., anc. Pers.) **4**:395
BEHR, ALEXANDER **4**:395
Behr, David **12**:1541
BEHR, ISSACHAR FALKENSOHN **4**:395
BEHREND, JACOB FRIEDRICH **4**:396
Behrend, M. **11**:499
Behrends, Genendl, *see* Oppenheim, Genendl
Behrends, Jacob **11**:558
BEHRENDS (Behrens), LEFFMANN **4**:396
- Hanover **7**:1279
Behrens, Jacob **15**:1042
Behrens, Peter **15**:620; **15**:624
Behrman, Jacob **13**:1377
Behrman, Louis **13**:1377
BEHRMAN, MARTIN **4**:396
BEHRMAN, SAMUEL NATHANIEL **4**:397
- U.S. literature **15**:1575
- Worcester **16**:634
Behrman House (publ., U.S.) **13**:1377
BEI AVIDAN (loc., Er. Isr.) **4**:397
BEIDERMAN, BERNARDO **5**:1112
- law **10**:1503
Beihan (S. Arab.), *see* BAYHAN
Beilenson, Edna **15**:1479
Beilenson, Peter **15**:1479
Beilin, Arkadi **4**:119
BEILIN, ASHER **4**:398
BEILINSON, MOSES ELIEZER **4**:398
- *Kol Mevasser* **10**:1165
BEILINSON, MOSHE **4**:399
Beilinson Hospital (Isr.) **9**:989
BEILIS, MENAHEM MENDEL **4**:399
- Aronson, Solomon **3**:496
- chronological chart **8**:766-767
- Dashewski, Pinḥas **5**:1310
- *The Fixer* **11**:820
- Israelsohn, Jacob **9**:1074
- Motzkin, Leo **12**:477
- Nathan, Paul **12**:855
- *illus:*
- - text
- - under arrest **14**:447
Beim, Abraham **4**:401
Beim, Isaac ben Abraham **4**:401
BEIM, SOLOMON BEN ABRAHAM **4**:401
BEIMEL, JACOB **7**:1546
- choir **5**:487
BEIN, ALEXANDER **4**:401
BEINHART, HAIM **1**:28
Being (philos. conc.)
- Aristotelianism **13**:430
- Hermann Cohen **13**:461
- Jewish philosophy **13**:421
Bein ha-Mezarim (journ.) **1**:newsp. list
Bein ha-mezarim, see NINE DAYS; TAMMUZ, FAST OF; THREE WEEKS
Bein ha-Shemashot, see TWILIGHT
Bein ha-Zemannim (journs.) **1**:newsp. list
Bein Milḥamah ve-Shalom (journ.) **1**:newsp. list
Beintayim (journ.) **1**:newsp. list
Beir, Joseph **14**:210
Beira (prov., Port.) **16**:135
Beirat (orgn., Pol.) **11**:432
BEI-RAV (tal. acad.) **4**:401
Beirav, Jacob, *see* BERAB, JACOB
Beirav, Jacob ben Ḥayyim, *see* BERAB, JACOB BEN ḤAYYIM
BEIRUT (city, Leb.) **4**:402
- Agrippa I **2**:416; **8**:296
- Crusader period **9**:268ff
- French protectorate **15**:645
- Israel raid **9**:416
- - U.N. censure **15**:1558
- - Vatican censure **16**:78
- Lebanon **10**:1544ff
- *illus:*
- - Alliance school **6**:400
Beisan (tn., Isr.), *see* BET(H)-SHEAN
Beit..., *see also under* Bayt; Bet; Beth
BEIT, SIR ALFRED **4**:404
Beit, Otto John **4**:405
Beit Aharon (enc.) **6**:735
Beit al-Maqdis (tn., Er. Isr.), *see* Bayt al-Maqdis
Beit al-Rās (loc., Transj.) **15**:1317
Beitar (period.) **14**:132
- statistics **1**:newsp. list
Beit-Ardeshir (city, Babyl.) **5**:1146
Beit Aronson (archive) **3**:390
Beit Dagan (tn., Isr.), *see* Bet Dagan
Beit Dajan (vill., Er. Isr.) **4**:719
Beit Eked (mag.) **8**:1119
- statistics **1**:newsp. list
Beit-El (fam.), *see* PISA, DA
Beit-El, Jehiel bar Mattathias, *see* Pisa, Vitale da
Bei-Ter (city, Er. Isr.) **4**:734
Beit Eshel (stlmt., Isr.), *see* BET ESHEL
Beit Gan, *see* Bet Gan
Beit Gefen Center (Isr.) **9**:1039
Beit Gubrin (city, Er. Isr.), *see* BET GUVRIN
Beit ha-Am (bldg., Jer.) **9**:1496
- *illus:*
- - Eichmann trial **9**:405
Beit ha-Beḥirah (Tal. comment.) **11**:1258
Beit ha-Keneset (journ.) **1**: newsp. list
Beit ha-Kerem (sub., Jer.), *see* Bet ha-Kerem
Beit ha-Midrash (period., Aus.) **16**:578
- statistics **1**:newsp. list
Beit ha-Midrash (journ., Pol.) **1**:newsp. list
Beit ha-Midrash he-Ḥadash (journ.) **1**:newsp. list
Beit Ḥanīnā (vill., Er. Isr.) **9**:1491; **9**:1515
Beit Ḥānūn (tn., Gaza Strip) **14**:1607
Beit ha-Oẓar Publishing House **5**:432
Beit ha-peras (meas.), *see Beit peras*
Beit ha-Talmud (period.) **16**:578
Beit-Ḥisda Pool (Jer.), *see* Sheep's Pool
Beit Iksā' (vill., Isr.), *see* BET IKSĀ
Beit Ilfa (site, Isr.) **4**:710
Beitin, *see* BET(H)-EL
Beit Jālā (tn., Er. Isr.), *see* Bayt Jala
BEIT JANN (vill., Isr.) **4**:405
- human geography **9**:589
BEIT JIMĀL (monastery, Isr.) **4**:405
- Kefar Gamala **10**:881
Beit kav (meas.) **16**:390
Beit kor (meas.) **2**:395; **16**:390
Beit (Bayt) Laḥm (city, Er. Isr.), *see* BETHLEHEM
Beit letekh (meas.) **16**:390
Beit Mikra (journ.) **1**:newsp. list
Beit Mirsim (site, Er. Isr.), *see* Tells, Beit Mirsim
Beit (Bayt) Nabālā (Arab legion camp) **4**:752
Beit Nattif (toparchy, Er. Isr.), *see* BETHLEPTEPHA; BET NETOFAH
Beit Nuba (loc., Er. Isr.) **9**:272
Beit Oẓar ha-Sifrut (annual), *see Oẓar ha-Sifrut*
Beit peras (meas.) **2**:396; **16**:390
Beitraege zur biblischen Landes-und Altertumskunde (journ.) **5**:1595
Beit rova (meas.) **16**:390
Beit Ṣāfāfā (vill., Isr.) **9**:1496; **9**:1515
Beit Sāḥūr (tn., Er. Isr.) **4**:745; **9**:1487;1507; **9**:587
Beit se'ah (meas.) **16**:390
Beit Talmud (journ.) **1**:newsp. list
Beit ʿUr al-Fawqā (vill., Isr.) **4**:748
Beit ʿUr al-Taḥta (vill., Isr.) **4**:748
Beit Va'ad le-Ḥakhamin (journ., Eng.) **1**:newsp. list
Beit Va'ad le-Ḥakhamim (journs., Transyl.) **1**:newsp. list
Beit Va'ad le-Ḥakhamim (journ., U.S.) **1**:newsp. list
Beit Ya'akov (qtr.,Jer.) **9**:1459
Beit Ya'akov (newsp.) **8**:521
- statistics **1**:newsp. list
Beit Ya'akov synagogue (Jer.), *see* Ḥurbat R. Yehudah he-Ḥasid
Beit Ya'ar ha-Levanon, see HOUSE OF THE FOREST OF LEBANON
Beit Ya'azek (courtyard, Jer.) **12**:1039
Beit Yisrael (qtr., Jer.) **9**:1461,1515
Beit Yisrael (newsp.) **4**:407
Beit Yiẓḥak (journ.) **1**:newsp. list
Beit Yosef (wk.) **5**:195
- codification of law **5**:648; **11**:335
- Hanneles **7**:1272
Beit-ẓemed (meas.) **16**:390
Beivar (journ.) **1**:newsp. list
Beiẓah (meas.) **16**:388,389
BEJA (tn., Port.) **4**:405
Beja (lang.) **14**:1149
Beja, Ḥayyim of Salonika **4**:406
Beja, Isaac **4**:406
BEJA, ISAAC BEN MOSES **4**:406
- Beja **4**:406
Bejar, Francisco Nuñes de **15**:1301
BEJERANO (fam.) **4**:406
BEJERANO, BEKHOR ḤAYYIM BEN MOSES **4**:406
- Turkey **15**:1460
Bejerano, Moshe **4**:406
Bejerano, Shimon **4**:406
BEKACHE, SHALOM **4**:407
Bekah (weight, coin) **5**:696; **16**:381ff
- *illus:*
- - dome-shaped unit **16**:385
Beke, M. **8**:23
BEKEMOHARAR (fam.) **4**:407
- Adrianople **2**:310
Bekemoharar, Joseph Raphael ben Mordecai **4**:408
Bekemoharar, Menahem **4**:408
Bekemoharar, Menahem ben Isaac Ashkenazi **2**:310; **4**:407
Bekemoharar, Menahem ben Mordecai **4**:407
Bekemoharar, Menahem ben Mordecai Simeon **4**:408
Bekemoharar, Mordecai **4**:407
Bekemoharar, Mordecai ben Menahem (18th cent.) **4**:407
Bekemoharar, Mordecai ben Menahem (19th cent.) **4**:408
Bekemoharar, Mordecai Simeon **4**:408
Bekemoharar, Mordecai Simeon ben Nissim Solomon **4**:408
Bekemoharar, Moses Raḥamim **4**:408
Bekemoharar, Nissim Solomon ben Mordecai **4**:407
Bekemoharar, Raphael **4**:408
Bekemoharar, Solomon **4**:407
Bekemoharar, Yom Tov **4**:408
Bekennende Kirche (Ger.), *see* Confessing Church
Békés, János **8**:23
BÉKÉSCSABA (city, Hung.) **4**:408
Békessy, János, *see* HABE, HANS
Bekhar, Bucha **4**:1493
Bekher, see CAMEL
Bekhor, see FIRSTBORN
Bekhor, David Jacob **16**:1538
BEKHOROT (tract.) **4**:409
- *illus:*
- - text
- - title page (Frankfort, 1720) **13**:1106
BEKHOR SHOR, JOSEPH BEN ISAAC **4**:410
- apologetics **3**:195
- Bible exegesis **4**:893
- *gematria* **7**:371
Bekhu Immi Benei Immi (piyyut) **2**:295
Bekker, Georges Joseph **8**:25
Bekker, Henryk **11**:545
BEKKER, PAUL **4**:411
Bekker, Petrus, *see* Artopaeus, Petrus
Beklemishev, Yuri Solomonovich, *see* KRYMOV, YURI
Beko'a (mosh., Isr.) **1**:place list
Bel (deity), *see* MARDUK
Bél, Mátyás **8**:25
Bela (bib. fig.) **6**:515
Bela (fam.) **12**:911
Bela (bib. loc.) **15**:70
Béla IV (k., Hung.) **8**:1088
Belaish, Abraham (ben Jacob) **4**:412
BELAIS(H), ABRAHAM BEN SHALOM **4**:412
BEL AND THE DRAGON (Apoc. stories) **4**:412
- Hellenistic literature **8**:304
Be Lapat (city, Pers.) **13**:308
Belasco, Abraham (stlr., Can.) **4**:1380
Belasco, Abraham (sport.) **15**:303
BELASCO, DAVID (theat.) **4**:413
- U.S. literature **15**:1575
Belasco, David (act.), *see* JAMES, DAVID
Belasco, Israel **15**:303
Belasco, John **15**:303
Belasco, Samuel **15**:303
BELAYA TSERKOV (tn., Ukr.) **4**:413

Belaya Vezha (loc., Rus.), *see* SARKIL
Belcari, Feo **9:**1102
BELCHATOW (tn., Pol.) **4:**413
Belchira (fig.) **9:**72
Belco (petroleum co.) **9:**795
BELED (vill., Hung.) **4:**414
Belém (city, Braz.) **4:**1328
BELEV, ALEXANDER **4:**414
BELFAST (city, N. Ire.) **4:**415
- Jaffe family **9:**1265
- *illus:*
- - text
- - synagogue, Ark of the Law **8:**1466
Belfer (educ.) **8:**241
Belfer Graduate School of Science (N.Y.C.) **16:**761
BELFORT (tn., Fr.) **4:**415
- Alsace-Lorraine **2:**756
- *illus:* text
BELFORTE, SOLOMON **4:**416
- Leghorn **10:**1573
- typography **15:**1482
Belgian Congo, *see* CONGO, DEMOCRATIC REPUBLIC OF
Belgisch Israelietisch Weekblad (journ.) **13:**1026
BELGIUM **4:**416
- *Contents:*
- - Medieval Community **4:**416
- - Resettlement Period **4:**417
- - Holocaust Period **4:**418
- - Contemporary Period **4:**423
- - Relations with Israel **4:**424
- Alliance Israélite Universelle **2:**650
- Antwerp **3:**168
- capitulations **5:**150
- Church and Nazism **8:**914
- communal organization **5:**824
- Holocaust **8:**842 **8:**889
- journalism **10:**304
- population **13:**885ff
- press **13:**1026
- refugees, Jewish **14:**30
- students' movements **15:**453
- synagogues **1:** synagogue list
- War Crimes Trials **16:**289
- *illus:*
- - text
- - Jewish partisans **13:**147
- *pop. tables:* text
- *see also:* BRUSSELS
BELGOROD-DNESTROVSKI (city, Rus.) **4:**425
BELGRADE (city, Yug.) **4:**426
- museum **12:**543
- special Purim **13:**1395
- Yugoslavia **16:**868
- Zemun **16:**989
- *illus:*
- - text
- - Jewish badge (World War II) **4:**72
- - museum **12:**545
- - synagogue **16:**879
Belgrado, Kalonymus **3:**730
BELIAL ("worthlessness"; Satan) **4:**428
- Dead Sea Scrolls **13:**333; **15:**1046
- demonology **5:**1525
- *Isaiah, Ascension of* **9:**71
- Mastema **11:**1119; **11:**1120
- netherworld **12:**996
- Samael **14:**719
Beliar (Satan), *see* BELIAL
BELIEF **4:**429
- *Contents:*
- - The Bible **4:**429
- - Hellenistic Literature **4:**432
- - Rabbinic Literature **4:**432
- - Medieval Jewish Philosophy **4:**434
- - Modern Jewish Philosophy **4:**436
- General
- - *Aleinu le-Shabbe'aḥ* **2:**559
- - Commandments, the 613 **5:**763
- - ethics **6:**933
- - Jewish Aristotelianism **3:**446; **3:**447
- - Judaism **10:**385ff
- - kabbalistic influence **10:**641ff
- - Maimonidean controversy **11:**745
- - providence **13:**1279
- - resurrection **14:**96
- - Samaritan **14:**738; **14:**740
- - theology **15:**1105; **15:**1106
- Views on
- - Arama, Isaac ben Moses **3:**257
- - Kant **10:**742
- - Kaspi, Joseph ibn **10:**810
- - Luzzatto, S.D. **13:**459
- - Maimonides **11:**775
- - Mendelssohn **3:**659; **11:**1330ff
- - Naḥman ben Simḥah of Bratslav **12:**785
- - Saadiah **13:**431
- - Spinoza **3:**659
- *illus:* text
- *see also:* ARTICLES OF FAITH; HERESY; PHILOSOPHY, JEWISH; THEOLOGY
Belilia, Levi **5:**626
Belilios (fam.) **8:**339
Belin, Moses **5:**935
Belinas (city, Er. Isr.), *see* BANIAS
BELINFANTE (fam.) **4:**436
Belinfante, Elijah Hezekiah **4:**437
BELINFANTE, ISAAC **4:**437
Belinfante, Jacob **4:**437
Belinfante, Joseph Cohen **4:**436
Belinfante, Meir Ḥayyim **4:**437
Belinfante, Moses **4:**437
Belinfante, Moses ben Ẓaddik **4:**437
Belinfante, Ẓaddik **4:**437
Belinson, Moses Eliezer, *see* BEILINSON, MOSES ELIEZER
Belisarius (Rom. gen.) **10:**478
BELISHA (fam.) **4:**437
Belisha, Barrow **4:**437
Belisha, Isaac **4:**437
Belisha, Jacob Isaac **8:**974
Belisha, Jeshua **4:**437
Belisha, Moses **4:**437
Belisha, Solomon **4:**437
Belitsa (tn., Belor.) **7:**767
BELKIN, ARNOLD **3:**596
BELKIN, SAMUEL **4:**437
- universities **15:**1679
- *illus:*
- - S.C.A. celebration **15:**631
BELKIND (fam.) **4:**438
- *geneal. table:* text
- *illus:* text
Belkind, Fania **6:**1209
Belkind, Israel **4:**438; **4:**999ff
Belkind, Meir **4:**438
Belkind, Na'aman **4:**440; **12:**1164
Belkind, Shimshon **4:**440
BELKOWSKY, ẒEVI HIRSCH (Grigori) **4:**440
- Zionism **16:**1108; **16:**1156
- *illus:*
- - F.Z.C. **16:**1165
Bell, Daniel **14:**500; **15:**63
Bella bat Menaḥem **9:**24
Bellachini, Samuel **15:**1061
Bellaire (city, Tex.) **15:**1036
Bellamy, Edward **16:**1152
Bellarmino, Roberto Francesco Romolo **8:**25
Bellermann, J. Joachim **8:**25
Belleville (city, Ill.) **8:**1256
Belleville (tn., Ont.) **12:**1408
Bellevue (city, Wash.) **16:**356
Belli, Giuseppe Gioacchino **9:**1105, 1107
Bellingham (city, Wash.) **16:**356
BELLISON, SIMEON **12:**682
Bellman, Carl Mikael **14:**928
Belloc, Hilaire **6:**781
BELLOW, SAUL **4:**441
- U.S. literature **15:**1576
Bells **13:**1013
- *illus:*
- - bronze, Megiddo **12:**561
- - high priest's vestments **13:**1065
Bells (mus. instr.), *see Pa'amon*
Belmain (city, Er. Isr.), *see* IBLEAM
Belmont (t., Mass.) **11:**1112
BELMONT, AUGUST (19th cent.) **4:**442
- banking **4:**178
- Rothschild family agent **14:**342
Belmont, August (19/20 cent.) **4:**442
Belmont, Elijah Simeon **2:**786
Belmont, Jessel **2:**786
Belmont, Leo **13:**802
Belmont, Perry **4:**442
BELMONTE (fam.) **4:**442
- *see also:* ABENDANA
BELMONTE (tn., Port.) **4:**442
Belmonte, Diego Nuñez, *see* Belmonte, Jacob Israel
Belmonte, Baron Francisco (Isaac) Ximenes **4:**443
Belmonte, Isaac Nuñez (dipl.) **4:**443
- Dutch-Moroccan treaty **4:**1461
- ennobled **15:**1165
- Gomez de Sossa, Isaac **7:**770
- politics **13:**814
Belmonte, Isaac Nuñez (r.) **4:**443; **9:**1331
Belmonte, Jacob Israel **4:**442
Belmonte, Manoel (Manuel) de, *see* Belmonte, Isaac Nuñez
Belmonte, Manuel Ximenes 4:443
Belmonte, Moses **4:**443
BELOFF, MAX **4:**443
Belogorsk (city, Rus.), *see* KARASUBAZAR
Beloit (city, Wis.) **16:**556
BELORUSSIA **4:**443
- *Contents:*
- - Up to Soviet Rule **4:**444
- - Under Soviet Rule (until 1941) **4:**446
- - Under Polish and Soviet Rule **4:**447
- agricultural settlements **2:**408
- Ḥasidism **7:**1392
- partisans **13:**140ff
- self-defense **14:**1125
- South Africa and **15:**186
- theater **15:**1075
- *illus:*
- - emblem with Yiddish inscription **14:**469
- - Emes farm members **14:**470
- *see also:* LITHUANIA; POLAND; RUSSIA
Belostok (city, Pol.), *see* BIALYSTOK
Bēl-šar-uṣur (Babyl. regent) **4:**448
BELSHAZZAR (k., Babyl.) **4:**448
- Babylon revolt **16:**1505
- Daniel **5:**1279
- feast **11:**1348
- in the arts **5:**1276
- Vashti **16:**72
- *illus:*
- - feast **11:**1349
- - writing on the wall **5:**1278
"Belshazzar's Feast" (paint., Rembrandt) **4:**449; **11:**1349
Belski, Tuvia (Tuvyah) **11:**213; **12:**1238; **14:**478
Belskie, Abram **11:**1167
Belt, Yellow, *see* BADGE, JEWISH
BELTESHAZZAR (Babyl. name; Daniel) **4:**450
- *see also:* DANIEL
Belth, Norton **5:**452
BELTSY (city, Bess.) **4:**450
Belus River (isr.), *see* Na'aman
Belvoir (Crus. cas.), *see* AGRIPPINA
BELY, VICTOR ARKADYEVICH (Aronovich) **12:**682
BELZ (ḥas. dyn.) **4:**452
- communal role **16:**1328
- dynasties **1:**ḥas. table
- Issachar Dov of Belz **14:**325, 1296
- Joshua of Belz **11:**730; **14:**1459; **16:**1329
- Shalom Roke'ah **16:**1328
BELZ (tn., Rus.) **4:**451
- Maḥzike Hadas **11:**730
Belza, Wladislaw **13:**798,799
BELZEC (tn., concen. camp, Pol.) **4:**453
- gassing **16:**1332
- Komarno **10:**1173
Belzec, Israel ben Benjamin of, *see* ISRAEL BEN BENJAMIN OF BELZEC
Belzer, Nissi, *see* SPIVAK, NISSAN
BELZYCE (tn., Pol.) **4:**455
Belz Yeshivah (Jer.) **4:**453; **9:**1495
Be-Maḥaneh Gadna (journ.) **1:**newsp. list; **7:**253
Be-Maḥaneh Naḥal (journ.) **1:**newsp. list
Bembrunn, Karl von **16:**479
Be-Midbar, *see* NUMBERS, BOOK OF
Be-Misholei ha-Ḥinnukh (journ.) **1:**newsp. list
Bemoras, Irving **15:**303
BE-MOẒA'EI MENUḤAH (piyyut) **4:**455
BEMPORAD, AZEGLIO **4:**456
BEMPORAD, ENRICO **4:**456
Bemporad, Roberto **13:**1368
BENA'AH (Pal. schol.) **4:**456
BEN-ADIR (writ.) **4:**457
BENADOR, URY **14:**421; **14:**425
Benadov, Haim **4:**1493; **4:**1494
BEN-AHARON, YIẒḤAK **4:**457
BENAIAH (bib. sol.) **4:**458
- Joab **10:**108
- Kabbalah **10:**623
- Solomon **15:**96
Benaiah (Pal. schol.), *see* BENA'AH
BENAIM (fam.) **4:**458
Benaim, David **4:**459
Benaim, Gilbert **15:**306
Benaim, Jacob Ḥayyim **2:**672; **4:**458
Benaim, Joseph **4:**459
Benaim, Makhluf **4:**459
Benaim, Moses **4:**459
Benaim, Raphael Ḥayyim Moses **4:**459
BEN 'ALĀN, JOSHUA **4:**459
Ben'Alān, Judah **4:**459
Ben Allans (clan, Tun.) **15:**1435
Benallell, Solomon ben Abraham **11:**800
Ben-Ami (hist.), *see* Eliav, Arie L.
BEN-AMI, JACOB **4:**459
- Mestel, Jacob **11:**1428
- wandering Jew **16:**262
Ben-Ami, Operation (War of Indep.) **16:**310
BEN-AMI, OVED **4:**460
BEN-AMITAI, LEVI **4:**461
Ben-Ammi (bib. fig.) **2:**853; **11:**508
Ben Ammi (mosh., Isr.) **1:**place list
Ben-Ammi (journ., Rus.) **10:**744
- statistics **1:**newsp. list
BEN-AMMI, MORDECAI **4:**461
- self-defense **14:**1124
- *illus:*
- - First Zionist Congress **16:**1165
- - Odessa Committee **12:**1329
- - with writers **16:**809
Benamor, Abraham **15:**791
BEN-AMOTZ, DAHN **4:**462
BENAMOZEGH, ELIJAH BEN ABRAHAM **4:**462
- chronological chart **8:**766-767

- ethics **6**:940
- Kabbalah **10**:648
Benaras (city, Ind.), *see* BENARES
BENARDETE, MAIR JOSÉ **4**:463
BENARES (city, Ind.) **4**:463
Ben-Aroloyo (fam.), *see* Arollia
BEN-AROYA, AVRAHAM (soc.) **4**:463
BENAROYA, AVRAM (journ.) **10**:309
Benaroya, Moise **4**:1493
Benarroch, Jacob **15**:1031
BENARUS, ADOLFO **4**:464
BENAS, BARON LOUIS **4**:465
Benas, Bertram Benjamin Baron **4**:465
Benas, Henriette, *see* GOLDSCHMIDT, HENRIETTE
Ben Asher (writ.), *see* WARSHAWSKY, ISAAC
BEN-ASHER, AARON BEN MOSES **4**:465
- Cairo *genizah* **16**:1336
- Jekuthiel ben Judah ha-Kohen **9**:1335
- linguistics **16**:1353
- masorah **16**:1472
- *illus:*
- - *Keter Aram Ẕova* **11**:901
- - masoretic differences, list **4**:541,959,967
BEN-ASHER, MOSES **4**:467
- *illus:* text
Ben-Asher, Naomi **5**:452; **6**:734
Benatar (fam.), *see* ATAR
Benatar, Joseph **14**:682
Ben Atar, Judah, *see* ATTAR, JUDAH BEN JACOB IBN
Ben Attar, Jacob **2**:594
BENATZKY, RALPH **4**:469
BEN-AVI, ITHAMAR **4**:469
- Hebrew language **16**:1644
- Hebrew newspapers **12**:1055ff
Ben-Avigdor (au.), *see* SHALKOVICH, ABRAHAM LEIB
Ben-Avram, Shalom **16**:1152
BENAYAH (fam.) **4**:470
- *illus:* text
Benayah (scribe) **4**:470
- *illus:*
- - illuminated Bible (1475) **4**:963
Benayah (mosh., Isr.) **16**:723
- statistics **1**:place list
Benayah ben Kalev ben Maḥpuẓ al-Bauli **4**:471
Benayah ben Saida ben Joseph **4**:471
BENAYAHU, MEIR **4**:471
- Cairo *genizah* **16**:1340
Ben-Ayon (ed.) **15**:792
Benazareff (Benazeraf), David **12**:344; **13**:816
Ben Azzai, *see* EPSTEIN, ZALMAN
BEN AZZAI, SIMEON (tan.) **4**:472
- Eliezer Ben Jacob **6**:624
- ethics **6**:941
- reward and punishment **14**:135
- the five sages **14**:1566
Ben Baboi, *see* PIRKOI BEN BABOI
BEN BAG BAG (tan.) **4**:472
- Ben He He **4**:520
Ben Bathyra (tan.), *see* JUDAH BEN BATHYRA
Ben Batiaḥ (zealot), *see* ABBA SIKRA
Ben Battas, Aaron, *see* AARON BEN BATASH
Ben Belimah (kab. fig.) **10**:525
Ben Bella, Ahmed **2**:619
Benbeniste, Immanuel, *see* BENVENISTE, MANUEL
Ben ben Sheth (fam.) **8**:679
Ben Bundār, Madmun ben Japheth, *see* MAḌMŪN BEN JAPHETH BEN BUNDĀR
Bençao ("bless") **4**:548
BEN CHANANJA (period.) **4**:473
- Loew, Leopold **11**:445
BENCHETRIT, AARON **4**:473
BENCHIMOL (fam.) **4**:473
Benchimol, Abraham **4**:473
Benchimol, Ḥayyim **4**:473
Ben-Chorin, Shalom **9**:906
BENDA, JULIEN **4**:474
Bendahan (fam.), *see* DAHAN
Bendahan, Jacob **5**:1224
Bendahan, Joseph **5**:1224
Bendahan, Joseph Nissim **5**:1224
Bendahan, Maimon **5**:1224
Bendahan, Moses **5**:1224
BENDAVID, LAZARUS (Eleazar) **4**:474
Ben-David, Ruth, *see* Blau, Ruth
Ben-David, Yoseph **15**:69
Bendelac (fam.) **15**:1030
Bendell, Herman **13**:481
BENDEMANN, EDUARD JULIUS FRIEDRICH **4**:475
- art **3**:565
Bendemann, Felix **4**:476
Bendemann, Rudolf **4**:476
BENDER, ALFRED PHILIP **4**:476
Bender, Charles **14**:1474
Bender, General **12**:956
Bender, Ḥayyim Ze'ev **12**:1229
Bender, Joseph **16**:502
Bender, Jules **15**:303
BENDER, LAURETTA **4**:476
Bender, Louis **15**:302
BENDER, MORRIS BORIS **4**:477
BENDERLY, SAMSON **4**:477
- Baltimore **4**:146
- New York City **12**:1097
Bendersky, Mario **10**:1503
Bendery (ḥas. dyn.), *see* SAVRAN
BENDERY (city, Bess.) **4**:477
- Tighina agreement **15**:1333
- *illus:* text
Bendery, Aryeh Leib of **14**:922
Bendery, Isaac of **14**:922
Bendery, Joseph of **14**:922
Bendery, Simeon Solomon of (19th cent.) **14**:922
Bendery, Simeon Solomon of (19/20 cent.) **14**:922
Bendet, Baruch **11**:1310
Bendig, Meir **3**:469
Bendigo (city, Austr.) **3**:878
Bendin (Pol.), *see* BEDZIN
Bendin (ḥalutzim gr.) **8**:251
Bendit, Axelrod ben Eleazar **6**:1302
BENDIX, BENEDICT HEINRICH **4**:478
- *illus:*
- - Beer, Aaron (portrait) **4**:376
BENDIX, OTTO **12**:682
BENDIX, REINHARD **4**:479
- sociology **15**:65,67
BENDIX, VICTOR EMANUEL **12**:682
- Denmark **5**:1537
BEN-DOR, IMMANUEL **4**:479
Ben Dov, Yaakov **13**:486
Bene Ammon, *see* AMMON
BENE-BERAK (city, Er. Isr.) **4**:479
- Akiva's academy **2**:202; **2**:488; **2**:489
- *illus:*
- - text
- - ossuaries **12**:1504
BENE-BERAK (tn., Isr.) **1**:place list; **4**:479
- Ḥasidim **7**:1398
- Kahaneman, Joseph **10**:683; **10**:684
- religious life **9**:895
- Slobodka Yeshivah **14**:1669
- Tel Aviv **15**:925
- *illus:*
- - Ponevezh Yeshivah **10**:711
- - yeshivah (1927) **9**:895
BENEDEK, THERESE F. **4**:481
Benedetti, Giovanni Batista **14**:874
Benedetti, Padre (pr.), *see* MARIE-BENOIT
Benedict (fam.), *see* BANET
Benedict (13th cent., Eng.) **16**:537
BENEDICT VIII (pope) **4**:481
- attitude to Jews **13**:852
BENEDICT XII (pope) **4**:481
- attitude to Jews **13**:855
BENEDICT XIII (antipope) **4**:482
- attitude to Jews **13**:855
- Jews in Christian art **3**:523
- papal bull **4**:1496
- Tortosa disputation **15**:238; **15**:1271
BENEDICT XIII (pope) **4**:482
- attitude toward Jews **13**:859
- chronological list **8**:766-767
BENEDICT XIV (pope) **4**:482
- attitude toward Jews **13**:859
- Polish blood libel **5**:602
BENEDICT XV (pope) **13**:860; **16**:75
Benedict, Fred, *see* DOLBIN, B.F.
Benedict, Israel **7**:623
BENEDICT, SIR JULIUS (Isaac) **4**:483
- *illus:* text
BENEDICT BEN MOSES OF LINCOLN **4**:483
Benedict fil' Abraham of Winchester **15**:210; **16**:537
Benedicti, Jean **8**:25
Benediction, Priestly, *see* PRIESTLY BLESSING
BENEDICTIONS **4**:484
- *Contents:*
- - Origins **4**:484
- - Formula **4**:485
- - Laws **4**:486
- ablution **2**:83
- Abudarham, David ben Joseph **2**:182
- *Ahavah Rabbah, Ahavat Olam* **2**:454
- *Amen* **2**:803
- *Barukh she-Petarani* **4**:285
- *Berakhot* **4**:585; **4**:586
- cemetery **5**:275
- colophons **5**:749ff
- death **5**:1425
- firstborn redemption **6**:1309
- gambling gains **7**:301
- Grace after Meals **7**:838
- Grace before Meals **7**:841
- Great Synagogue **15**:630
- *haftarah* **16**:1344
- *hakhel* ceremony **7**:1149
- Hebrew language **16**:1591
- holiness **10**:872
- *hoshannah* **12**:10
- *kiddush ha-Shem* **7**:464; **10**:979,984
- liturgy **11**:394
- *lulav* **15**:499
- *omer*, counting **12**:1384
- rainbow **4**:552; **13**:1525
- Sabbath candles **15**:735
- *sheḥitah* **14**:1338
- sick, prayer for **14**:1496
- *sukkah* **15**:494
- sun **15**:518
- synagogue **15**:592
- *tallit* **15**:743
- *tefillin* **15**:901ff
- Tigris **15**:1139
- Torah study **15**:456
- travel **15**:1347
- washing hands **12**:999
- wine **16**:540
- woman's head covering **8**:6
- *illus:*
- - text
- - classroom wall chart (1590) **6**:387
- - fruit and vegetables **6**:1423; **15**:1419
- - Grace after Meals, short form **7**:*fcg.* 846
- - marriage ceremony **11**:1026
- - moon **12**:292
- - *omer* **12**:1383,1385
- - *Seder Birkat Ha-Mazon* **12**:303
- - spices **8**:1315; **15**:268
- - wine **13**:353; **16**:539
- *see also:* AMIDAH; BAREKHU; BARUKH; BLESSING AND CURSING; MORNING BENEDICTIONS; PRAYER
Benedictions, The Seven, *see* Seven Benedictions
Benedict Jonah of Gerona **7**:505
Benedict le Puncteur, *see* Benedictus le Puncteur
Benedict of Talmont **6**:1007
Benedict of Winchester, *see* Benedict fil' Abraham of Winchester
Benedictus (philos.), *see* SPINOZA, BARUCH DE
Benedictus filius Mossei de Lincolnia, *see* BENEDICT BEN MOSES OF LINCOLN
Benedictus le Puncteur **4**:596; **12**:1534
Benedictus of Soest **15**:74
BENEDIKT, MORITZ (physic.) **4**:489
- *illus:* text
BENEDIKT, MORITZ (journ.) **4**:489
Benefactions, *see* GIFT
Bene ha-Nevi'im ("sons of the prophets") **6**:396
Bene Heẓir tomb (Jer.), *see* Heẓir, Tomb of sons of
Benei adam, *see* SON OF MAN
BENEI AKIVA (youth mvmt.) **4**:490
- Great Britain **6**:449,768
- Ha-Po'el ha-Mizrachi **7**:1321
- Israel **9**:895; **9**:898; **9**:981
- kibbutz movement **10**:973
- U.S. Zionism **16**:1146
- yeshivot **16**:772
- *illus:*
- - text
- - badge **9**:977
- *see also:* Baḥad
Benei Anak, *see* ANAK, ANAKIM
Benei Atarot (mosh., Isr.) **1**:place list **3**:813
Benei Ayish (vill., Isr.) **1**:place list
Benei Bathyra, *see* BATHYRA, SONS OF
BENEI BINYAMIN (assoc., Er. Isr.) **4**:491
Benei Binyamin (stlmt., Er. Isr.) **13**:1534
Benei Bundār (fam.) **16**:741
BENEI DAROM (mosh., Isr.) **1**:place list **4**:492
- Kefar Darom **10**:880
BENEI DEROR (mosh., Isr.) **1**:place list **4**:492
Benei ha-Ir (municipal cmty.) **10**:1568
Benei ha-Medinah, *see* LANDJUDENSCHAFT
Benei heikhala de-malka (kab. conc.) **10**:495
Benei Ḥoshekh, *see* SONS OF LIGHT
Benei Hushim (Chr. mvmt.), *see* HUSSITES
Benei Kedem (people Syr.), *see* KEDEMITES
Benei Mikra, *see* KARAITES
BENEI MOSHE (mvmt.) **4**:492
- Aḥad Ha-Am **2**:441

- chronological chart **8:**766-767
- emissaries **14:**1366
Benei Or, see SONS OF LIGHT
Benei Re'em (mosh., Isr.) **1:**place list
Benei Roma (syn. Jer.) **15:**588
Benei Shim'on (stlmt., reg., Isr.) **9:**594; **12:**930
Benei Soncino (print.) **8:**1324
- *illus:*
- - *maḥzor* **15:**141,1483
BENE ISRAEL (J. cmty., Ind.) **4:**493
- *Contents:*
- - In India **4:**493
- - In Israel **4:**496
- Divekar, Samuel Ezekiel **6:**111
- India **8:**1356ff
- Israel **9:**399; **9:**505
- Rajpurkar, Joseph Ezekiel **13:**1526
- *illus:* text
Bene Israelite (period.) **13:**1036
Benei Yehudah (stlmt., Er. Isr.)
- Bashan **4:**293
- Galilee **7:**267
- human geography **9:**596
- Ramat ha-Golan **13:**1534
- Safed **14:**630
BENEI ZION (mosh., Isr.) **1:**place list **4:**498
Benei Zion (assoc., Rus.) **11:**151
- *illus:*
- - meeting **12:**359
Benei Zion (soc., Er. Isr.) **15:**919
Benei Zion (catechism) **8:**942
Ben-Elasah (tal. fig.) **13:**125
BEN ELIEZER, MOSHE **4:**499
- *illus:*
- - text
- - Writers' Association **16:**653
- - Vilna **16:**813
Beneš, Edvard **5:**1193
BENESCH, ALFRED ABRAHAM **4:**499
BENEŠOV (Beneschau; tn., Bohem.) **4:**500
Benet (fam.), *see* BANET
Benet, Ezekiel ben Jacob, *see* BANETH, EZEKIEL BEN JACOB
Benet, Mordecai ben Abraham, *see* BANET, MORDECAI BEN ABRAHAM
Benet, Naphtali ben Mordecai, *see* BANET, NAPHTALI BEN MORDECAI
Benetelli, Luigi Maria **4:**315
BENEVENTO (tn., It.) **4:**500
- Inquisition **8:**1398
BENEVENTO, IMMANUEL BEN JEKUTHIEL **4:**500
BENEVENUTUS GRAPHEUS HIEROSOLYMITANUS **4:**500
Bene Yonah, see DOVE
Ben-Ezer, B. **13:**1437
Ben-Ezer, Judah, *see* RAAB, JUDAH
Ben-Ezra, Akiva **5:**438
BENFELD (tn.,Fr.) **4:**501
- Alsace-Lorraine **2:**752
BENFEY, THEODOR **4:**501
Bengal (prov., Ind.) **8:**1356
BENGALIL (fam.) **4:**502
Bengalil, Abraham **2:**612; **4:**502
Bengalil, Joseph **4:**502
Bengalil, Samuel **2:**612; **4:**502
Ben Gamala (tal. fig.) **15:**980
Ben Gan (mosh., Isr.) **9:**1175
BEN-GAVRIEL, MOSHE YA'AKOV **4:**502
- German literature **7:**452
BENGHAZI (city, Libya) **4:**503
- diaspora **6:**10; **6:**16
- *illus:* text
Benghi, Elijah Afeda **10:**426
Bengio, Mordecai **12:**340; **15:**792
Ben-Giora, Simeon, *see* BAR-GIORA, SIMEON
BENGIS, SELIG REUBEN **4:**504
Benguiat, Ephraim **5:**311; **12:**544
BEN-GURION, DAVID **4:**505
- *Contents:*
- - Early Years **4:**505
- - 1914-1921 **4:**506
- - Building the Histadrut **4:**507
- - Toward the Founding of the Jewish State **4:**508
- - War of Independence **4:**509
- - 1948-1956 **4:**510
- - 1956-1963 **4:**512
- - In Retirement **4:**512
- Aḥdut ha-Avodah **2:**456; **2:**457
- Arab National Movement **9:**463
- Biltmore conference **4:**998
- Dayan, Moshe **5:**1373
- Declaration of Independence **5:**1451
- Eshkol, Levi **6:**889ff
- Fourteenth Zionist Congress **16:**1172; **16:**1177
- Goldmann, Nahum **7:**724
- Haganah policy **9:**687,688
- Hecht, Ben **8:**239
- He-Ḥalutz **8:**254
- Histadrut policy **9:**851; **9:**855ff
- Israel-German relations **9:**402ff
- Israel's foreign policy **9:**423; **9:**428
- Jabotinsky, Vladimir **14:**129
- Jewish Legion **10:**69; **10:**73
- Jewish military units **16:**1050
- Karelitz, Avraham Yeshayahu **10:**788
- Katznelson, Berl **10:**837
- Lavon affair **9:**398; **10:**1478ff
- Mapai **11:**912ff
- Palmaḥ command problem **9:**371; **13:**48
- politics **9:**657ff
- Rafi **13:**1512
- resignation, 1953 **9:**384
- Sharett conflict **9:**389
- Silver, Abba Hillel **16:**1061
- Spinoza *ḥerem* **15:**282
- United Nations **16:**1092ff
- U.S. Zionism **16:**1145
- *illus:*
- - text
- - autograph **3:**913
- - Adenauer and Goldmann **2:**265
- - Ben-Zvi, Izhak, and Raḥel **4:**580
- - Biltmore conference **15:**1633
- - Dayan, Moshe (cartoon) **5:**1373
- - Dori, Ya'akov, and Chaim Weizmann **6:**173
- - Eilat Road, opening of **9:**380
- - *Ha-Aḥdut* board **16:**999
- - Jewish Agency Executive **10:**28
- - London Round Table Conference **9:**353
- - National Council meeting **9:**365
- - Roosevelt, Eleanor **14:**258
- - Shochat, Israel **14:**1441
- - Silberschlag, Eisig **14:**1535
- - soldiers, Haifa **9:**379
- - Va'ad Le'ummi **16:**50
Ben-Gurion, Paula **4:**506
- *illus:*
- - with David Ben-Gurion **4:**513
BEN-HADAD I (k., Aram) **4:**515
- chronological chart **8:**766-767
- history **8:**595ff
- *illus:* text
BEN-HADAD II (k., Aram) **4:**515
- Ahab **2:**436ff
- chronological chart **8:**766 767
- Hazael **7:**1515
- history **8:**597ff
- warfare **16:**273
BEN-HADAD III (k., Aram) **4:**515
- chronological chart **8:**766-767
BEN-HAIM, PAUL **4:**517
Ben Ḥakhinai (tan.), *see* HANANIAH BEN ḤAKHINAI
Ben Ḥakola (amora), *see* ISAAC BEN ELEAZAR
BEN HA-MELEKH VE-HA-NAZIR (bk.) **4:**518
- Jewish literature **11:**352
- translations **15:**1321
- *illus:* text
Ben-Ḥayyim, Jacob, *see* JACOB BEN ḤAYYIM BEN ISAAC IBN ADONIJAH
BEN ḤAYYIM, ZE'EV **1:**28 ;**4:**519
- linguistic literature **16:**1398
BEN HE HE (tan.) **4:**520
- Ben Bag Bag **4:**473
Ben-Hinnom, Valley of, *see* GEHINNOM
BEN-HORIN, MEIR **4:**520
- historiography **8:**569
Ben-Hur, Elijah **7:**1068
Ben-Hur, Ithamar **6:**205
Benicrescas (13th cent., Fr.) **14:**666
BENIDER (fam.) **4:**520
Benider, Abraham **4:**520
Benider, Jacob **4:**520
Beni Hassan tomb, *see* Bani Hasan tomb
BENIOFF, HUGO **4:**520
BENISCH, ABRAHAM **4:**521
- Ereẓ Israel settlement **9:**299
Ben Israel, Manasseh, *see* MANASSEH BEN ISRAEL
Benivieni, Girolamo **8:**25; **6:**1360
Ben Jacob (mintmaster) **12:**61
Ben-Jacob, A. **8:**563
BENJACOB, ISAAC **4:**521
- Rabbinovicz, R. N. **13:**1465
Benjacob, Jacob **4:**521
Ben-Jacob, Ẓevi, *see* Rosenblatt, Ẓevi
Ben-Jalil, Abraham, *see* Abraham Ben-Jalil
BENJAMIN (bib. fig.) **4:**522
- *Contents:*
- - Genealogies **4:**523
- - Tribal Territory **4:**523
- - History of the Tribe **4:**524
- - In the Aggadah **4:**525
- - In Islam **4:**526
- The Man **4:**522
- - Genesis, Book of **7:**389
- - Jacob **9:**1193ff
- - Joseph **10:**206
- - Judah **10:**332
- - Rachel **13:**1486ff
- The Tribe **15:**1385
- - Armenian Jewry **3:**473
- - Bible history **8:**579
- - breastplate stone **13:**1009
- - coercive *ḥerem* **8:**345
- - David **5:**1325
- - Gibeah **7:**549
- - Jabesh-Gilead **9:**1171
- - Judahites **10:**329
- - Kurdish Jews **10:**1297
- - settlement **9:**115
- - Shiloh **14:**1401
- - south **14:**178
- *illus:*
- - text
- - brought before Joseph **10:**207
- - taken to Egypt **10:**329; **14:**105
- - tribal symbol **6:**1450
BENJAMIN II (Israel Joseph; trav.) **4:**526
- historiography **8:**568
- Zionism **16:**1132
BENJAMIN, BARUCH BEN ISRAEL (r., Er. Isr.) **4:**527
BENJAMIN, BARUCH BENZION (Ind.) **13:**825
Benjamin, Sir Benjamin **3:**880; **8:**339
- *illus:*
- - caricature **11:**1282
Benjamin, D. **15:**831
BENJAMIN, ERNEST FRANK **4:**527
Benjamin, Eugene Simeon **10:**35
Benjamin, Henry M. **11:**1589
BENJAMIN, ISRAEL **4:**528
- Shabbetai Ẓevi **14:**1225
Benjamin, Israel Joseph (trav.), *see* BENJAMIN II
Benjamin, Jacob **4:**1203
Benjamin, Joe **15:**306
BENJAMIN, JUDAH PHILIP **4:**528
- anti-Semitism **15:**1649
- *illus:*
- - Bellechasse home **12:**1042
BENJÁMIN, LÁSZLO **4:**529
Benjamin, Lewis Saul, *see* MELVILLE, LEWIS
Benjamin, Louis (U.S.) **5:**1567
Benjamin, Louis (S.A.) **10:**1502
Benjamin, Messa (fam.), *see* Banin (Benjamin), Messa
BENJAMIN, MOSES **4:**529
- *illus:* **9:**1098
Benjamin, Samuel **15:**830
Benjamin, Testament of (Pseudepig.), *see* PATRIARCHS, TESTAMENT OF THE TWELVE
BENJAMIN, WALTER **4:**530
Benjamin Aaron of Tykocin ,*see* SLONIK, BENJAMIN AARON BEN ABRAHAM
Benjamin Beinisch ha-Kohen of Krotoszyn **4:**6
BENJAMIN BEN AARON OF ZALOZCE **4:**531
BENJAMIN BEN AZRIEL **4:**531
BENJAMIN BEN ELIEZER HA-KOHEN VITALE OF REGGIO **4:**531
- Abraham ben Michael Rovigo **14:**356
- emissaries **14:**1362
- Kabbalah **10:**553
- Shabbateanism **14:**1245
- Zacuto, Moses **16:**907
BENJAMIN BEN ELIJAH **4:**532
- travels **15:**1353
Benjamin ben Elijah ben Shabbetai Be'er **6:**649
BENJAMIN BEN ḤIYYA (Jehiel) **4:**533
Benjamin ben Isaac **5:**160
BENJAMIN BEN JAPHET (amora) **4:**533
Benjamin ben Jehiel *see* BENJAMIN BEN ḤIYYA
Benjamin ben Jonah, *see* BENJAMIN (BEN JONAH) OF TUDELA
Benjamin ben Joseph d'Arignano, *see* Arignano, Benjamin
Benjamin ben Judah me-ha-Anavim **16:**1387
Benjamin ben Mishal **10:**436
Benjamin ben Samuel (Crimea) **12:**65
BENJAMIN BEN SAMUEL HA-LEVI (litur. poet) **4:**533
Benjamin ben Saul Katzenelbogen, *see* Katzenelbogen, Benjamin ben Saul
Benjamin Benush of Brest-Litovsk **11:**290
BENJAMIN BEN ZERAH **4:**534
Benjamin ha-Levi (kab.) **2:**925; **8:**321 **16:**174; **16:**176; **16:**907
Benjamin Isaiah ben Jeroham Fishel ha-Kohen **7:**314
Benjamin Krotoschin, *see* Benjamin Beinisch ha-Kohen of Krotoszyn
BENJAMIN NEHEMIAH BEN ELNATHAN **4:**534
- historiography **8:**558

Benjamin of Béziers **13:**931
BENJAMIN OF BRODY **4:**534
BENJAMIN OF CAMBRIDGE **4:**534
- Kimhi, Joseph **10:**1006
- linguistics **16:**1367
Benjamin of Canterbury, *see* BENJAMIN OF CAMBRIDGE
Benjamin of Caunbrigge, *see* BENJAMIN OF CAMBRIDGE
Benjamin of Rome **8:**1323
Benjamin of Silesia **14:**1536
BENJAMIN OF TIBERIAS **4:**534
- Heraclius **8:**334; **9:**259
BENJAMIN (BEN JONAH) OF TUDELA **4:**535
- Baghdad synagogue **15:**612
- chronological chart **8:**766-767
- Falashas **6:**1152
- Georgia **7:**423
- population **13:**873ff
- Ten Lost Tribes **15:**1005
- Torah-reading customs **15:**1247
- travel book **11:**350
- travels **15:**1349; **15:**1351
- *map:* text
Benjamin the Righteous (tan.), *see* ABBA BENJAMIN
Benjamin the Scribe **8:***fcg.* 1271
Benjamin the Second, *see* BENJAMIN II
BENJAMIN ZE'EV BEN MATTATHIAS OF ARTA **4:**538
- David ben Ḥayyim of Corfu **5:**1350
- taxation **15:**845
- *Tohorot ha-Kodesh* **15:**1191
BEN KALBA SAVUA **4:**538
- Akiva **2:**488
Ben Kattin (tal. fig.) **15:**980
Ben keyama, see Viable embryo
BEN-KIKI (fam.) **4:**539
Ben-Kiki, Eleazar **4:**539
Ben-Kiki, Reuben **4:**539
Ben Kozevah (Koziva), *see* BAR KOKHBA
BEN LA'ANAH **4:**539
Benlevi, M. **8:**956
Ben-Mahiya (fam.) **15:**1173
Ben Malca (fam.), *see* MALCA
Ben Māmān (fam.), *see* Maman
Ben Manlin, *see* MAGNUS, MARCUS
Ben Meir (gaon) **7:**323
BEN MEIR, AARON **4:**539
- Aaron ben Amram **2:**9
- Cairo *Genizah* **16:**1336
- calendar **5:**50
- gaonate **7:**322
- Saadiah Gaon **14:**543
Ben-Menahem, N. **4:**972; **14:**273; **16:**1377
Ben-Meshal, Aaron **12:**336
Ben-Moha, Mas'ud **12:**340
BENN, BEN **3:**596
- *illus:*
- - Baruk, Henri (portrait) **4:**282
Ben Nanas (tan.), *see* SIMEON BEN NANAS
Ben-Naphtali, Jacob ben David, *see* BEN-NAPHTALI, MOSES BEN DAVID
BEN-NAPHTALI, MOSES BEN DAVID **4:**540
- masorah **16:**1423,1464,1473ff
- *illus:*
- - *Aberdeen Bible* **4:**967
- - masoretic differences, list **4:**959
Ben-Nathan, Asher **4:**630
- Germany **7:**502
- *illus:*
- - German president **9:**406
Ben Naẓer (tal. fig.) **12:**1318
Bennet, Max **11:**1077
Bennet, Thomas **8:**25
BENNETT, ARCHIE (Aaron Baehr) **4:**541
Bennett, Arnold **6:**776; **10:**459
Bennett, Cyril **15:**930
Bennett, H. **5:**377
Bennett, James Gordon **10:**306
BENNETT, SALOMON YOM TOV **4:**543
- art **3:**540
- *illus:* text
Bennike, General **9:**385
Bennington (city, Vt.) **16:**112
BENNY, JACK **15:**1078
- television **15:**928
Benois, Alexander **4:**117
Benôit, Jean, *see* Benedicti, Jean
Benoit, Marie, *see* MARIE-BENOÎT
BENOIT-LEVY, JEAN **12:**464
BENOLIEL (fam.) **4:**544
Benoliel, Eliezer **4:**544
BENOLIEL, JOSEPH (José) **4:**544
- family **4:**544
- Tangiers **15:**792
Benoliel, Judah **4:**544; **5:**163
Ben-Oni (bib. fig.), *see* BENJAMIN
Benoni (tn., Trans.) **15:**1340
Benot Shu'aḥ (bot.) **4:**1021
Benot Ya'akov Bridge (Isr.) **8:**1064
BEN PETURA (Ben Peturi, Ben Peturin; tan.) **4:**544
- *pikku'aḥ nefesh* **13:**509
Ben Quiqui (fam.) **11:**1272
Ben-Ram Joseph **13:**587
BENREMOKH (fam.)**4:**544
Benremokh, Abraham ben Ḥayyim **4:**545
Benremokh, Ḥayyim ben Shem Tov **4:**545
Benremokh, Saul ben Shem Tov **4:**545
Benremokh, Shem Tov **4:**545
Benremokh, Shem Tov ben Abraham **4:**545
Benremokh, Solomon **4:**544
Benremokh, Yamin **4:**545
BENRUBI, ISAAC **4:**545
Bensabat, David **4:**464
Bensabat, Salomon **10:**1492; **12:**345
Bensadon, Joseph **11:**519
Bensamon (dipl.) **4:**1207
BENSANCHI, MENTESH (Mordecai) **13:**825
Ben Sarah, *see* AHARONOVITCH, YOSEF
BEN-SASSON, HAIM HILLEL **1:**28; **4:**546
- historiography **8:**565
BENSAUDE (fam.) **4:**546
Bensaude, Abraham (Port.) **4:**546
Bensaude, Abraham (19th cent.) **4:**546
Bensaude, Elias **4:**546
Bensaude, Joaquim **4:**546
Bensaude, José **4:**546
Bensaude, Solomon **4:**546
Ben Senior (print.) **9:**1165
Ben Senton, Aaron, *see* AARON BEN BATASH
Benshalom, Benzion, *see* KATZ, BENZION
Ben-Sha'ul, M. **5:**437
BEN SHEMEN (mosh., youth vill., Isr.) **4:**547
- olive groves **12:**1365
- statistics **1:**place list
- Youth Aliyah **16:**864
- *illus:*
- - text
- - Ben-Gurion and Eleanor Roosevelt **14:**258
Ben Shemtov, Aaron (vizier, Mor.), *see* AARON BEN BATASH
BENSHEN ("bless") **4:**548
- children **5:**428
- Sabbath lights **14:**566; **15:**735
- *see also:* GRACE AFTER MEALS; MOON, BLESSING OF THE
Ben-Shlomo, Y. **10:**648
Ben Simeon, David **4:**548
BEN SIMEON, RAPHAEL AARON **4:**548
Bensimon, Raphael **14:**1039
Bensinger, Maier (Ger.) **11:**1558
Bensinger, Moses **15:**304
Ben-Sion, E., *see* Priluker, Jacob
BEN SIRA, ALPHABET OF (pseudepig.) **4:**548
- fiction, Hebrew **6:**1264
- Joseph ben Uzziel **10:**238
- Lilith's legends **11:**246
- Queen of Sheba **13:**1424
- *Toledot Yeshu* **15:**1209
BEN SIRA, SIMEON BEN JESUS **4:**550
- *Ben Sira, Alphabet of* **4:**549
- Cairo *Genizah* **16:**1334
- Ecclesiastes **6:**352
- Joseph ben Uzziel **10:**238
- Minor Prophets **12:**49
- on Enoch **6:**793
- *see also:* BEN SIRA, WISDOM OF
BEN SIRA, WISDOM OF (Apoc.) **4:**550
- Abbaye's views **2:**45
- benedictions **4:**484
- Ben Sira, Simeon **4:**550
- Ben Ze'ev's translation **4:**573
- Bible interpretation **8:**1417
- Cairo *Genizah* **7:**406
- calendar **5:**49
- canon, Bible **4:**825
- chronological chart **8:**766-767
- Dead Sea scrolls **5:**1402
- Hebrew linguistic research **16:**1398
- Hellenism **8:**298; **8:**300
- Hellenistic Jewish literature **8:**304
- magic **11:**705
- prosody **13:**1210
- salvation **11:**1408
- Septuagint **4:**853,854
- Torah **15:**1236,1238
- wisdom literature **16:**557; **16:**558ff
- "yeshivah" **2:**200; **2:**201
- *illus:*
- - text
- - fragment **12:**574
Bensman, Joseph **15:**63
Ben Solomon, Joel M. **12:**1054
Bensonhurst (section, N.Y.C.) **12:**1107
Ben sorer u-moreh, see REBELLIOUS SON
Bensoussan, Edgar **11:**1567
Bensoussan, Raoul **11:**1567
BEN STADA (tal. fig.) **4:**554
- Jesus **10:**16
Ben Susan, *see* SUSAN, ISSACHAR BEN MORDECAI
BENSUSAN (fam.) **4:**554
Bensusan, Nathan Levi **4:**554
Bensusan, Samuel Levy **4:**555
Bensussan, Ḥayyim **5:**224
Ben-Sussan, René **15:**1479
Benswanger, William **6:**230; **15:**301
Ben Tabeel, *see* TABEEL, THE SON OF
BEN TEMALYON (demon) **4:**555
Ben-Thoa Synagogue (Alg.) **4:**407
Ben-Tobo (fam.) **14:**682
Benton (city, Ill.) **8:**1256
Benton Harbor (city, Mich.) **11:**1500
BENTOV, MORDEKHAI **4:**555
- *illus:*
- - proclamation of the State of Israel **4:**513
BENTWICH (fam.) **4:**556
Bentwich, Herbert **4:**556; **11:**656
Bentwich, Joseph **4:**557
Bentwich, Margery **4:**557
Bentwich, Norman de Mattos **4:**556; **9:**892
Bentwich, Thelma **4:**557; **12:**669
BENTZEN, AAGE **4:**558
Benvenist (fam.), *see* BENVENISTE
Benvenist, Adzay (Ḥasdai) **4:**558
Benvenist, Ḥayyim ben Israel ,*see* BENVENISTE, ḤAYYIM BEN ISRAEL
Benvenist, Profet **11:**39; **14:**859
BENVENISTE (fam.) **4:**558
- printing **13:**1095
- Saragossa **14:**860
BENVENISTE, ABRAHAM **4:**559
- chronological chart **8:**766-767
- Spain **15:**239
- *takkanot* **15:**725; **15:**735
- Valladolid regulations **8:**1367; **16:**61
BENVENISTE, ABRAHAM (Turk.) **4:**559
Benveniste, Asher **13:**1039
Benveniste, Benveniste ibn, *see* Benveniste ibn Benveniste
Benveniste, David ibn Vidal **16:**1533
Beneveniste, Ezra **13:**1040
BENVENISTE, ḤAYYIM BEN ISRAEL **4:**559
- Shabbetai Ẓevi **14:**1228
Benveniste, Immanuel, *see* BENVENISTE, MANUEL
BENVENISTE, ISAAC BEN JOSEPH **4:**561
Benveniste, Ishmael, *see* Benveniste, Izmel
Benveniste, Israel **4:**561
Benveniste, Izmel **4:**558
BENVENISTE, JOSEPH BEN MOSES DE SEGOVIA **4:**561
BENVENISTE, JOSHUA RAPHAEL BEN ISRAEL **4:**561
- Jerusalem Talmud **15:**778
Benveniste, Judah ben Abraham **4:**558; **16:**1533
BENVENISTE, MANUEL **4:**562
- printing **13:**1105
- *illus:* **13:**1094
BENVENISTE, MOSES **4:**562
- Ottoman Empire **16:**1553
Benveniste, Nissim **4:**558
BENVENISTE, SAMUEL **4:**563
- linguistics **16:**1388
BENVENISTE, SHESHET BEN ISAAC BEN JOSEPH **4:**563
Benveniste, Vidal Joseph **13:**690
BENVENISTE DE PORTA **4:**563
- Barcelona **4:**209
Benveniste ibn Benveniste **4:**558
Benvenisti, Simon **13:**1369
Benvenutus Grapheus, *see* BENEVENUTUS GRAPHEUS HIEROSOLYMITANUS
Benvoir, Aachel **16:**549
BENWAISH, ABRAHAM **4:**564
Benwaish, Samuel **4:**564
Ben-Walid, Isaac **12:**340
Ben-Yakir (tos.), *see* EPHRAIM BEN ISAAC
Benyamin the Third (folk hero) **6:**1382
BEN-YEḤEZKI'EL, MORDEKHAI **4:**564
Ben-Yehuda, Ehud **4:**568
BEN-YEHUDA, ELIEZER **4:**564
- chronological chart **8:**766-767
- *halukkah* **9:**326ff
- *Ḥavaẓẓelet* **7:**1480
- Hebrew language **2:**205; **8:**752; **16:**1642, 1644
- Hebrew literature **8:**197
- Hebrew newspapers **12:**1054
- Israel cultural life **9:**998
- linguistics **16:**1399
- *illus:*
- - Ben-Yehuda Street, Jerusalem **9:**1488

- - Israel stamp **9**:844-845
BEN-YEHUDA, HEMDAH **4**:569
- *illus:*
- - text
- - Ben-Yehuda, Eliezer **4**:565
BEN-YEHUDAH, BARUKH **4**:569
BEN YIZHAK, AVRAHAM **4**:570
- prosody **13**:1233
Ben-Yosef, Avraham **5**:74
BEN-YOSEF, SHELOMO **4**:571
- I.Z.L. **8**:1467
- *illus:*
- - text
- - court session **9**:632
Ben zakhar (custom), *see* SHOLEM ZOKHOR
Ben Zakkai (mosh., Isr.) **16**:723
- statistics **1**:place list
BENZAMERO (fam.) **4**:571
- Safi **14**:633
Benzamero, Aaron **4**:572
Benzamero, Abraham (interp.) **4**:572
Benzamero, Abraham ben Meir (physic.) **4**:572
Benzamero, David **4**:572
Benzamero, Ephraim **4**:571
Benzamero, Isaac (fin.) **4**:571
Benzamero, Isaac (r.) **4**:572
Benzamero, Ismael **4**:572
Benzamero, Joseph **4**:572
Benzamero, Judah (mer., Mor.) **4**:572
Benzamero, Judah ben Ephraim (Sp.) **4**:571
Benzamero, Meir **4**:571
Benzamero, Moses (fin.) **4**:571
Benzamero, Moses (royal offic.) **4**:571
Benzamero, Samuel **4**:572
Benzamero, Sliman **4**:572
Benzamero, Solomon (physic.) **4**:571
Benzamero, Solomon (dipl.) **4**:572
BEN ZAQEN (fam.) **4**:572
Ben Zaqen, Isaac ben Vidal **4**:572
Ben Zaqen, Jacob ben Samuel **4**:572
Ben Zaqen, Joseph **4**:572
Ben Zaqen, Leon **4**:572
Ben Zaqen, Samuel **4**:572
BEN ZE'EV, JUDAH LEIB **4**:573
- parody **13**:131
Benzelin (Hebr.) **8**:25
Benzelius, Ericus **8**:25
BENZER, SEYMOUR **4**:574
Ben Ẓerifa, *see* JUDAH, SON OF ẒIPPORAI
BENZINGER, IMMANUEL **4**:574
Ben-Ẓion (r., Egy.), *see* ALAMANI, AARON HE-ḤAVER BEN YESHU'AH
BEN-ZION (Weinman; paint.) **4**:574
- Moses paintings **12**:408
- *illus:*
- - text
- - Jeremiah (etch.) **9**:1358
BEN-ZION, S. **4**:575
- Moriah **12**:325
- *illus:*
- - Bialik and **4**:802
- - Mendele Mokher Seforim and **11**:1322
Benzion ben Raphael (It.) **13**:12
Benzion Katz Institute (Isr.) **15**:926
Ben-Zissi, Fordhaus, *see* Fordhaus Ben-Zissi
Ben Zita Abu al-Surrī, *see* BEN ZUTA ABU AL-SURRI
BEN ẒIẒIT HA-KASSAT **4**:576
Ben zokhor (custom), *see* SHOLEM ZOKHOR
BEN ZOMA, SIMEON (tan.) **4**:576
- five sages **14**:1566
BEN ZUTA,ABU AL-SURRI **4**:576
Ben-Ẓvi, Isser **4**:630
BEN-ZVI, IZHAK **4**:577
- Basola, Moses **4**:310
- He-Ḥalutz **8**:254
- historiography **8**:565
- Jewish Legion **10**:69,73; **16**:1050
- Po'alei Zion **13**:659
- president **13**:1021
- Samaritans **14**:735
- Va'ad Le'ummi **16**:51
- *illus:*
- - text
- - autograph **3**:913
- - *Ha-Aḥdut* board **16**:999
- - Jewish Legion **10**:74
- - Keren Hayesod cornerstone ceremony **10**:916
- - Liberia visit **9**:436
- - National Council meeting **9**:365
- - Shochat, Israel, and **14**:1441
- - 13th Zionist Congress **16**:1173
- - Transjordan Arab leaders **9**:346
- - Tsedaka, Japheth ben Abraham, and **14**:235
BEN-ZVI, RAḤEL YANAIT **4**:581
- Ein Karem **16**:1325
- *illus:*
- - *Ha-Aḥdut* board **16**:999
- - Ha-Shomer group **7**:1371
- - Leopoldville, 1962 **4**:579
BEN-ZVI, ZEEV **4**:582
- *illus:*
- - Meskin, Aharon (sculp.) Fig. 92 **3**-ART
Ben-Zvi Institute (Isr.)
- Ben-Zvi, Izhak **4**:580
- historiography **8**:565
- Ladino **10**:1348
- learned societies **15**:55
- Sephardi cultural research **14**:1176
BEOBACHTER AN DER WEICHSEL (newsp.) **4**:582
Beograd (city, Yug.), *see* BELGRADE
Beon (city, Transj.), *see* BAAL-MEON
Beor (bib. fig.) **10**:1317
Beqa' (tn., Isr.) **13**:216
Bequests, *see* WILLS
Ber, Peter Peretz **16**:124
Ber, Samuel ben Issachar **13**:836
- Berdichev **4**:591
BERAB, JACOB **4**:582
- Alashkar, Moses ben Isaac **2**:512
- chronological chart **8**:766-767
- Ḥaver, Isaac **7**:1489
- Kabbalah **10**:545
- Levi ben Ḥabib **11**:99
- Marranos **10**:58
- ordination dispute **9**:286; **14**:1144
- Trani, Moses ben Joseph **15**:1315
Berab, Jacob ben Abraham **4**:584
BERAB, JACOB BEN ḤAYYIM **4**:584
Berab, Moses **4**:584
Beracah, Valley of (Er. Isr.) **9**:1327
BERAḤ DODI (piyyut) **4**:584
Berai (tn., Isr.), *see* BIRIYYAH
Beraita, see BARAITA, BERAITOT
Berakhah Aharonah ("final benediction"), *see* GRACE AFTER MEALS
Berakhah, Elijah **4**:585
Berakhah, Hayyim **4**:585
BERAKHAH, ISAAC **4**:585
Berakhah ben Aaron of Cieszewiec **13**:724
Berakhah Me'ein Shalosh ("Benediction Summarizing the Three") **7**:841
Berakhias (clan, Tun.) **15**:1435
BERAKHOT (tract.) **4**:585
- synagogue service **15**:583
- *illus:* text
Berakhot, see BENEDICTIONS
Berakhyahu, A. M. **12**:1324
Berat (city, Alb.) **2**:522
- Shabbetai Ẓevi **14**:1241
Berat (Ott. letter of protection) **5**:148
Berāt Humayun (authorization of appointment) **9**:1453
Berav, Jacob, *see* BERAB, JACOB
BERBERS (N. Afr. tribes) **4**:587
- African Jews **2**:332
- Baḥuẓim **4**:102
- Semitic languages **14**:1149
- Spain **15**:225
- Tlemcen **15**:1172
- Toledo **15**:1200
- Tunisia **15**:1432
- Umayyads **15**:1531
- Zirids **16**:1183ff
- *illus:* text
- *see also:* ATLAS; JUDEO-ARABIC (and Judeo-Berber)
Berceo, Gonzalo de **15**:249
Berchin, M. **13**:1598
BERCOVICI, KONRAD **15**:1579
- Moses novel **12**:406
BERCOVITCH, PETER **4**:588
BERDICHEV (tn., Rus.) **4**:589
- Levi Isaac of **11**:102
- self-defense unit **14**:1127
- *illus:*
- - text
- - *ḥalutzim* **14**:458
- - Levi Isaac's tombstone **11**:103
Berdichevsky, Bernardo **5**:467
Berdiczew, Abba **2**:656
BERDUGO (Mor. fam.) **4**:591
Berdugo, Jacob **4**:592
Berdugo, Joseph **4**:592
Berdugo, Judah **4**:591
Berdugo, Maimon **4**:592
Berdugo, Mordecai **4**:591
Berdugo, Moses **4**:591
- Toledano, B. **15**:1194
Berdugo, Pethahiah Mordecai **4**:592
Berdugo, Raphael **4**:592
- Toledano, B. **15**:1196
Berdugo, Yaḥya **4**:591
Berdyczewski, Emmanuel, *see* Bin-Gorion, Immanuel
BERDYCZEWSKI, MICHA JOSEF **4**:592
- Aḥad Ha-Am **2**:441
- critic **5**:1119
- Ḥasidism **7**:1419
- Hebrew literature **8**:194
- *illus:* text
Berdyczewski, Rahel **4**:594
Berechiah (bib. fig.) **16**:953
BERECHIAH (amora) **4**:596
Berechiah (fam.) **10**:698
BERECHIAH BEN NATRONAI HA-NAKDAN **4**:596
- animal tales **3**:21; **11**:353
- Benedict le Puncteur of Oxford **12**:1534
- translations **15**:1324
- *illus:*
- - text
- - *Mishlei Shu'alim* **4**:597; **5**:431
BERECHIAH BERAKH BEN ELIAKIM GETZEL **4**:598
- Kabbalah **4**:50
- Yavorov **16**:724
BERECHIAH BERAKH BEN ISAAC EISIK **4**:598
Berechiah ha-Kohen (amora), *see* BERECHIAH
Berechiah of Mlawa **12**:186
Berechiah of Nicole, *see* BENEDICT BEN MOSES OF LINCOLN
Berechiah Sabba (amora) **4**:596
Bered (bib. loc.) **6**:690
BEREGI, ARMIN BENJAMIN **4**:599
BEREGI, OSZKÁR **15**:1078
BEREGOVO (city, Ukr.) **4**:599
BEREGOWSKI, MOSES YAKOVLEVICH **4**:599
Beregszász (city), *see* BEREGOVO
Beregszászi, Pál **8**:25
Berehovo (city), *see* BEREGOVO
Berek, Aaron **14**:831
Berekhyah (mosh., Isr.) **1**:place list
"Berele Bunes", *see* ISSACHAR BAER BEN TANḤUM
Berelson, Bernard R. **15**:68
BERENBLUM, ISAAC **4**:600
BERENDT, GOTTLIEB MICHAEL **4**:601
Berenguer IV, Ramón **15**:1268
Berenice (3rd cent. B.C.E. Egy.) **13**:1348
BERENICE (1st cent., B.C.E., dau. of Salome) **4**:601
- *geneal. table:* text; **8**:377
BERENICE (1st cent., C.E., dau. of Agrippa I) **4**:601
- Agrippa II **2**:418
- arts **15**:1170
- Gessius Florus **7**:527
- Herodian dynasty **8**:385
- Polemo, king of Cilicia **5**:562
- Titus **15**:1169; **15**:1170
- *geneal. table:* text; **8**:377
Berenice (city, Er. Isr.), *see* ELATH
Berenice (city, Libya), *see* BENGHAZI
Berenice-Hormos (tn., Egy.) **6**:9
BERENIKE (Ptolemaic cities) **4**:602
BERENSON, BERNARD **4**:602
- art collection **3**:648
BERENSON, LEON **4**:604
Berenson, L. Stanley **15**:311
Berenson, Richard I. **15**:311
Berenstain, Stan **5**:220
Berenstein, Issacher Baer **6**:1157
BERÉNY, RÓBERT **4**:604
- *illus:* text
Bererah (leg. principle) **2**:867
Bere'shit, see GENESIS, BOOK OF
Bereshit (journ.) **1**:newsp. list
Bereshit de-Rabbi Oshaya Rabbah, see GENESIS RABBAH
Bereshit Rabbah, see GENESIS RABBAH
Bereshit Rabbah (mid. wk., Moses ha-Darshan) **12**:429
Bereshit Zuta (wk.) **16**:1518
BERESTECHKO (tn., Volhynia) **4**:605
Berestovitsa, (tn., Rus.) **6**:824
BERETTYÓUJFALU (tn., Hung.) **4**:605
Beretvas, Leopold **13**:29
BEREZA (tn., Rus.) **4**:606
Berezan (tn., Rus.) **13**:839
BEREZHANY (tn., Gal.) **4**:606
BEREZINO (tn., Rus.) **4**:607
BEREZOVKA (tn., Rus.) **4**:607
BERG (duchy, Ger.) **4**:607
- *see also:* JUELICH
Berg, Alban **2**:304
Berg, Carl Nathanael **10**:461
BERG, GERTRUDE **15**:1078
Berg, Jackie **15**:306
Berg, Joseph **3**:811
BERG, LEO **4**:607
Berg, Morris **15**:301
Berg, Nissen, *see* LEVINE, EUGENE
Berg, Sidney **16**:1140
Bergama (city, Turk.) **13**:286
BERGAMO (city, It.) **4**:608
Bergeisen, Ze'ev **16**:621
BERGEL (fam.) **4**:608
Bergel, Bernard **9**:1205
BERGEL, JOSEPH **4**:608
Bergel, Moses **4**:608
Bergel, Moses (ben Yom-Tov) **4**:608
Bergel, Yom Tov **4**:608
BERGELSON, DAVID **4**:608
- Gurshtein, Aaron **7**:982
- Hofstein, David **8**:813
- Jewish Anti-Fascist Committee

3:62
- Segall, Lasar 14:1108
Bergen (Belg.), *see* Mons
BERGEN-BELSEN (concen. camp) 4:610
- Auschwitz trials 3:873
- Jewish survivors conference (1946) 4:509
- *illus:*
- - text
- - corpses of victims 8:887
- - S.S. on trial 16:295
BERGEN COUNTY (dist., N. J.) 4:612
Berger, A. 16:822
Berger, Elmer 2:820
- anti-Zionism 16:1145
Berger, Henry 3:459
Berger, Isaac 12:1377
Berger, Israel 15:439
Berger, J.L. 16:1165
Berger, M. (plwrt.) 6:205
Berger, Maxie (sport.) 15:306
BERGER, MEYER (journ.) 10:307; 10:309
Berger, Sam
- sport 15:308
- Olympics 12:1375
BERGER, VICTOR 4:613
BERGGRÜN, HEINRICH 7:1546
Bergh, Arnold van den 4:614
Bergh, George van den 4:614
Bergh, Henry van den 4:614
BERGH, HERMAN VAN DEN 4:614
Bergh, Isaac van den 4:614
Bergh, Jacob van den 4:614
Bergh, Samuel van den 4:614
Bergh, Sidney J. van den 4:614
Bergh, Simon van den 4:614
BERGH, VAN DEN (fam.) 4:614
Berghausen (vill., Ger.) 15:265
BERGHEIM (vill., Fr.) 4:614
Bergman (Judenrat dir., Ukr.) 14:358
Bergman, B. 14:931
Bergman, Eliezer 9:1464
- *aliyah* 9:515
Bergman, Hjalmar Fredrik Elgérus 14:930ff
Bergman, Judah, *see* Berg, Jackie
BERGMAN, SAMUEL HUGO 4:614
- religious life in Israel 9:900
- Zionism 16:1112
- *illus:* text
BERGMANN, ERNST DAVID 4:616
- atomic energy in Israel 9:796
BERGMANN, FELIX ELIEZER 5:379
BERGMANN, JUDAH 4:616
BERGMANN, MAX 4:617
Bergmann, Richard 15:314
BERGNER, ELIZABETH 4:617
- *illus:* text
BERGNER, HERZ 4:618
Bergner, Hinde 13:1586
Bergner, Nathan 15:412
BERGNER, YOSSI (Yosef L.) 4:618
- art 3:593
- *illus:*
- - "Well Furnished Desert" Fig. 107 3-ART
Bergner, Zekharye Khone, *see* RAVITCH, MELECH
BERGSON (fam.) 4:618
BERGSON, ABRAM 4:619
BERGSON, HENRI LOUIS 4:619
- ancestry 16:945
- family 4:619
- nature 12:891
- philosophy 13:418
- stamps 15:335
- *illus:*
- - text
- - portrait 8:750
Bergson, Joseph 4:618
BERGSON, MICHAEL 4:621
- family 4:619
Bergson, Peter, *see* Kook, Hillel
Bergson Group (Zion., U.S.) 16:1144
BERGSTEIN, FANIA 4:621
Bergstein, Lea 14:1355
BERGSTRAESSER, GOTTHELF 4:622
- linguistics 16:1397
BERGTHEIL, JONAS 4:622
- politics 13:820
Be'r Ḥindīs (vill., Er. Isr.), *see* Bīr Ḥindīs
Beria, Lavrentii P. 6:145
Beriaan, Adolf 8:894
Beriah (bib. clan) 4:523
Beribbi (amora), *see* HEZEKIAH
BERIḤAH (J. underground mvmt.) 4:622
- Avigur 3:968
- Haganah 9:687, 688
- history 8:769
- Jewish brigade group 10:37
- partisan activity 13:149
- U.S. help 16:1144
- *illus:* text
- *see also:* DISPLACED PERSONS; HOLOCAUST, RESCUE FROM
Berikh Shemei (prayer) 15:1253
Beri'on (lab. orgn.) 8:542
Berison, Joe 15:27
Berit ... *see also* Brit ..., Brith
Berit (covenant) 5:1012
Berit Avraham (bk.) 7:354
Berit ha-Biryonim (clandestine gr., Pal.) 2:464; 3:471
Berit ha-Ḥayyal (army veterans) 14:129
Berit ha-Kannaim (Jewish State Party, Fr.) 16:1114
Berit Ḥalutzim Datiyyim (pion. mvmt.), *see* Baḥad
Berit ha-No'ar ha-Ẓiyyoni ha-Soẓyalisti (Zion. mvmt., Rus.) 16:1225
Berit ha-Olamit shel Torah va-Avodah, *see* HA-PO'EL HA-MIZRACHI
Berit ha-Olim (Zion mvmt., Ger.) 8:1241
Berit Ḥerut ha-Ẓohar (Revisionists) 14:131
Berit Ivrit Olamit (World Association for Hebrew), *see* BRIT IVRIT OLAMIT
Berit Menuḥah (bk.) 2:145
- Kabbalah 10:538
Berit Nashim Le'ummiyyot (Revisionists) 14:129
Berit Po'alei Ereẓ Israel, *see* Palestine Labor League
BERIT SHALOM (Peace Assoc., Er. Isr.) 4:632
- Arab-Jewish relations 9:662; 16:1057,1084
- Ruppin, Arthur 14:432
Berit Trumpeldor, *see* BETAR
Beri'ut (journ.) 1:newsp. list
Beri'ut ha-Am (journ.) 1:newsp. list
Beri'ut ha-Oved (journ.) 1:newsp. list
Beri'ut ha-Zibbur (journ.) 1:newsp. list
BERK, FRED 5:1271
Berkeley, George 8:25
Berkelhammer, Wilhelm 12:1245
Berkelhammer, Ze'ev 5:558
BERKMAN, ALEXANDER 4:633
Berkman, Harvey 15:309
Berkooz, M. 16:1509
BERKOVITS, ELIEZER 4:633
Berkowicz, Abraham Dov 10:1341
Berkowicz, Isaac 10:1341
BERKOWICZ, JOSEPH (Józef) 4:634
Berkowicz, Leon 4:634
Berkowitz, Leonard 13:1345
Berkowicz, Michael 4:982
BERKOWITZ, HENRY 4:634
Berkowitz, Irma Mirjam 5:453
Berkowitz, Michael 16:1165
Berkowitz, William 14:162
BERKOWITZ, YITZHAK DOV 4:635
- drama, Hebrew 6:202
- Elisheva's Russian translation 6:671
- Hebrew literature 8:212,213
- Shalom Aleichem translation 14:1276
- *illus:*
- - Slutsk association 14:1682
Berkson (fam.), *see* BERGSON
BERKSON, ISAAC BAER 4:637
- *illus:*
- - Transjordan Arab leaders 9:346
Berkuz, S. H. 5:435
BERL, EMMANUEL 7:149
BERL, ERNST 5:380
Berlad (tn., Rum.), *see* BARLAD
BERLE, MILTON 15:1078
Berleburg Bible 4:873
BERLEWI, HENRYK 4:638
BERLIAND, SHLOMO MEIR 4:638
- *illus:*
- - Odessa Committee 12:1329
BERLIGNE, ELIYAHU MEIR 4:639
- *illus:*
- - National Council meeting 9:365
BERLIJN, ANTON (Aron Wolf) 4:639
BERLIN (city, Ger.) 4:639
- *Contents:*
- - Old Community (1295-1573) 4:639
- - Till 1812 4:640
- - Internal Life 4:643
- - Edict of Equality till Nazis 4:643
- - Internal Life (1812–1933) 4:644
- - 1933-1939 4:647
- - 1939-1945 4:648
- - Jewish Population 4:650
- - Contemporary Period 4:650
- - Hebrew Printing 4:653
- archives 3:387
- history chart (1712, 1872, 1873) 8:766-767
- museum 12:538
- Prussia 13:1287ff
- *sheḥitah* tax 14:1343
- stock exchange 15:406
- Zionist movement 16:1077; 16:1097
- *illus:*
- - text
- - Fasanenstrasse Community House 15:628
- - Fasanenstrasse synagogue 10:1264
- - *Gemeindeblatt* (1932) 13:1037
- - Grenadierstrasse (caric.) 5:177
- - Hochschule fuer die Wissenschaft des Judentums 8:800
- - *Kristallnacht* 10:1264
- - Nazi mass rallies 7:490; 8:829
- - Oranienburgerstrasse synagogue 15:621
- - World War II refugees 7:498
- - University students' society 16:1115
- - Wertheim department store 16:454
- - Zionist Office clerk and prospective immigrant 9:521
- *pop. table:* text
Berlin (city, N.H.) 12:1024
Berlin, Abraham Meir 4:662
BERLIN, ARYEH LOEB BEN ABRAHAM MEIR 4:654
Berlin, Batyah Miriam 16:216
BERLIN, CONGRESS OF (1878) 4:655
- Alliance Israélite Universelle 2:650
- Allianz, Israelitische 2:654
- Bismarck 4:1058
- Bleichroeder, Gerson von 4:1081
- history chart 8:766–767
- *illus:*
- - Disraeli, Benjamin 6:107
BERLIN, DAVID BEN (Judah) LOEB 4:657
Berlin, Ḥayyim (Lith.) 4:662
- religious life in Ereẓ Israel 9:890
BERLIN, IRVING 4:657
- theater 15:1059
BERLIN, SIR ISAIAH 4:658
BERLIN, ISAIAH BEN JUDAH LOEB 4:659
- *haggahot* to *Nedarim* 10:748
BERLIN, ISRAEL 4:660
Berlin, Judah, *see* LIEBMANN, JOST
Berlin, Leib Meir 15:369; 16:474
Berlin, Meir, *see* BAR-ILAN, MEIR
BERLIN, MOSES 4:660
BERLIN, NAPHTALI ẒEVI JUDAH (Ha-Naẓiv) 4:660
- history chart 8:766-767
- Soloveichik, Joseph Baer 15:131
- Volozhin yeshivah 16:215; 16:769
BERLIN, NOAH ḤAYYIM ẒEVI HIRSCH 4:662
BERLIN, SAUL BEN ẒEVI HIRSCH LEVIN (Saul Hirschel) 4:663
- Hahn, Joseph 7:1128
- Kohen, Raphael 10:1139
Berlin, Ze'ev 3:361
Berlin, Ẓevi Hirsch 7:1128
Berliner (cantor) 4:243
BERLINER, ABRAHAM 4:664
- Auerbach, Ẓ. B. 3:843
- historiography 8:562
- history chart 8:766-767
- Rashi's work 13:1563
Berliner, David 8:521
BERLINER, EMILE 4:665
- aviation 2:320; 2:321
- gramophone 13:1617
- television and radio 15:928
Berliner, H. (ed., Switz.) 13:1049
Berliner, Henry Adler (eng.) 4:665
- aviation 2:321
Berliner, H.W. (Braz.) 13:1370
Berliner, Meir 15:1369
BERLINER, YIẒḤAK 4:666
Berliner Bewegung (anti-Sem. orgn.), *see* Berlin Movement
Berliner Juedisches Gemeindeblatt (weekly) 4:648
- *illus:* 13:1037
Berliner Tageblatt (newsp.) 4:668
Berliner Volkszeitung (newsp.) 4:682
Berlinger, E. (Holl.) 16:37
Berlinger, Milton, *see* BERLE, MILTON
Berlin Movement (anti-Sem. orgn., Ger.) 4:643
- Agrarian League 2:374
Berlin Period (Zion.) 16:1171
Berlin-Pick, Isaiah, *see* BERLIN, ISAIAH BEN JUDAH LOEB
Berlin Reformgemeinde (Ger. soc.) 14:24
BERLINSKI, HERMAN 12:683
- choirs 5:488
Berlinski, Hersz 16:351
Berlinsky, S. 16:825
Berlin Talmudic Society 4:664
Berlin Unterstuetzungsverein (soc.) 5:350

Berl Katznelson (refugee boat) **9:**357
Berlyne, Alex **11:**1167
Berman, A. (Rum.) **13:**1369
BERMAN, ADOLF ABRAHAM (Zion.) **4:**666
Berman, Adolfo (polit., Chil.) **13:**821
BERMAN, EUGENE **3:**596
BERMAN, JACOB **4:**666
Berman, Leon **11:**249
BERMAN, LEONID **3:**596
BERMAN, LOUIS **4:**667
Berman, M. **8:**1362
BERMAN, MORTON MAYER **4:**667
Berman, Myron (r., Va.) **14:**162
Berman, Natalio **5:**467
BERMAN, PANDRO S. **12:**464
Berman, S. (au.) **5:**433
BERMAN, SIMEON (pion., Er. Isr.) **4:**667
Berman, Wolf **14:**1673
Berman, Ze'ev, *see* BERMANN, VASILI
Berman Ashkenazi, *see* ISSACHAR BERMAN BEN NAPHATALI HA-KOHEN
Bermann, Adolf, *see* KÓBOR, TAMÁS
Bermann, Eliezer **4:**668
Bermann, Gottfried (-Fischer) **6:**1323
Bermann, Issachar, *see* LEHMANN, BEHREND
Bermann, M. **10:**1033
BERMANN, RICHARD ARNOLD **4:**668
BERMANN, VASILI (Ze'ev Wolf) **4:**668
– Druskieniki Conference **16:**1041
– *illus:*
– – Odessa Committee **12:**1329
Bermann-Fischer, Gottfried, *see* Bermann, Gottfried
BERMANT, CHAIM ICYK **6:**785; **6:**787
Bermuda (isl., W. Indies) **16:**473
BERMUDA CONFERENCE (1943) **4:**668
– American Jewish Committee **2:**824
– Inter-Governmental Committee **6:**991
– refugees **14:**29
– *illus:*
– – Taylor's memo re failure **8:**906
Bermuda grass (bot.) **13:**615
BERNADOTTE, FOLKE **4:**669
– assassination **9:**1484
– Israel-Arab negotiations **9:**367ff
– Jerusalem **9:**1484
– Leḥi **11:**465
– mediation attempts **9:**422
– Palestine problem **16:**1096
– U.N. **15:**1545ff
– unification plan **9:**1032
– War of Independence **16:**322
– Yellin-Mor, Nathan **16:**738
– *illus:*
– – *Maariv* report, Sept. 1948 **11:**639
BERNAL (fam.) **4:**670
Bernal, Abraham (Manuel Nuñes) **4:**670
– Antuñes, David **3:**167
Bernal, Ishac de Almeida, *see* Bernal, Marco
Bernal, Jacob (Holl.) **4:**670
Bernal, Jacob (Eng.) **4:**670
Bernal, Jacob Israel (Eng.) **4:**670
Bernal, John Desmond **4:**670
Bernal, Manuel Nuñes *see* Bernal, Abraham
Bernal, Marco (Ishac de Almeida) **4:**670
– Barrios, Daniel Levi de **4:**259
Bernal, Mestre **4:**670
Bernal, Ralph **4:**670
Bernaldez, Andres **15:**240
Bernal-Osborne, Ralph **4:**670
Bernard, Edouard (Fr.) **4:**677
BERNARD, EDWARD (Orient.) **4:**670
– Christian Hebraists **8:**25
BERNARD, ḤAYYIM DAVID **4:**671
Bernard, Hermann Hedwig **8:**25
Bernard, Jean-Jacques **4:**671
Bernard, Jesse (writ.) **3:**777
Bernard, Rosine, *see* BERNHARDT, SARAH
BERNARD, TRISTAN **4:**671
BERNARDI, HERSCHEL **15:**1078
BERNARDINO DA FELTRE **4:**672
– Aquila Jews **3:**228
– Brescia **4:**1353
– history chart **8:**766-767
– sermons at Bergamo **4:**608
BERNARDINO DA SIENA **4:**672
– Aquila Jews **3:**228
– Ferrer, Vicente **6:**1236
– Rimini Jews **14:**186
Bernard Lyons Community Centre (Eng.) **15:**627
BERNARD OF CLAIRVAUX **4:**672
– Anacletus II **2:**917
– attitude towards Jews **5:**512; **8:**668ff
– Crusades **5:**1139
– Rudolph, and **14:**380
Bernard of Cluny **9:**1577
Bernard of Piotrkow **11:**9
Bernard Revel Graduate School (N.Y.) **16:**760
Bernartice (vill., Cz.) **4:**365
Bernasconi (tn., Arg.) **3:**432
– *illus:*
– – League for Ereẓ Israel Labor **16:**1124
Bernáth, István **4:**884
BERNAYS (fam.) **4:**673
Bernays, Berman **4:**673
Bernays, Edward L. **4:**674
– public relations **13:**1360
Bernays, Isaac ben Jacob **4:**673
– Hirsch, S.R. **8:**508
– history chart **8:**766-767
– homiletic literature **8:**956
Bernays, Jacob **4:**673
Bernays, Martha **4:**674
Bernays, Michael **4:**673; **7:**451
Bernays, Paul Isaac **4:**674
BERNBACH, WILLIAM **4:**674
– advertising **2:**317
Bernburg (city, Ger.) **3:**1
BERNE (city, Switz.) **4:**675
– Switzerland **15:**555
Berneri, G. **9:**1105
– *illus:*
– – liberation of Roman Ghetto **9:**1106
– – *Meo Patacca* illustration **14:**246
Bernfeld, Isaac Aaron **15:**445
BERNFELD, SIEGFRIED (psych.) **4:**675
BERNFELD, SIMON **4:**676
– historiography **8:**564
Bernhard, Emil, *see* COHN, EMIL MOSES
BERNHARD, GEORG **4:**676
– journalism **10:**305; **10:**309
– *illus:* text
Bernhard, Isaac
– Moses Mendelssohn **11:**1329
– textiles **15:**1041
Bernhard, Lazarus **7:**1348
Bernhard, Lucian **15:**1479
Bernhard of Breidenbach **15:**1356
BERNHARDT, SARAH **4:**677
– stamps **15:**336
– *illus:*
– – text
– – autogaraph **3:**913
– – in *Queen Elizabeth* **12:**447
Bernheim (fam.) **16:**546
Bernheim, Alexander **3:**566
Bernheim, Alfred **13:**486
Bernheim, Franz **4:**681; **5:**759
– League of Nations **10:**1523
Bernheim, Henry **12:**873
BERNHEIM, HIPPOLYTE **4:**678
– psychiatry **13:**1338
BERNHEIM, ISAAC WOLFE **4:**679
Bernheim, Léonce **7:**922
– Zionism **16:**1114
BERNHEIM, LOUIS **4:**679
BERNHEIMER, CARLO **4:**679
BERNHEIMER, CHARLES LEOPOLD (U.S.) **4:**680
– explorations **15:**1351
– *illus:* text
BERNHEIMER, CHARLES SELIGMAN (soc. wkr.) **4:**680
Bernheim-Jeune (publ. firm, Fr.) **13:**1368
BERNHEIM PETITION (1933) **4:**681
– Comité des Délégations Juives **5:**759
– League of Nations **10:**1523
Berniker, Pinchas **5:**1149
Bernstein (fam., Rus.) **4:**1397
Bernstein (informer, Rus.) **8:**1369
BERNSTEIN, ABRAHAM MOSHE **7:**1546
Bernstein, Alan **15:**312
Bernstein, Alexander **4:**689
BERNSTEIN, ALINE **15:**1078
BERNSTEIN, ARNOLD (shipbldr.) **4:**682
BERNSTEIN, ARON DAVID **4:**682
BERNSTEIN, ARYEH LEIB **4:**683
Bernstein, Aviassaf **7:**1546
BERNSTEIN, BÉLA **4:**683
Bernstein, Berush **4:**686
Bernstein, Boris **11:**1167
Bernstein, Cecil **4:**689
Bernstein, Charles **3:**450
Bernstein, David **16:**35
BERNSTEIN, EDUARD (soc.) **4:**684
– socialism **15:**26
Bernstein, Edward (U.S.) **12:**37
Bernstein, Elmer **12:**451
Bernstein, Fritz, *see* BERNSTEIN, PEREZ
BERNSTEIN, HAROLD JOSEPH (chem.) **5:**380
BERNSTEIN, HARRY (hist.) **8:**544
Bernstein, Harry "Czar" (U.S.) **5:**609
Bernstein, Heinrich **15:**1350
BERNSTEIN, HENRI-LEON **4:**684
BERNSTEIN, HERMAN (journ.) **4:**685
– Untermeyer, Samuel **15:**1690
Bernstein, Herman (trans.) **14:**775
BERNSTEIN, IGNATZ **4:**685
Bernstein, Isaiah **7:**1320
Bernstein, Issachar Ber (r., Gal.) **4:**683
BERNSTEIN, ISSACHAR BERUSH BEN ARYEH LOEB (r., Ger.) **4:**685
Bernstein, Jack **15:**306
BERNSTEIN, JACOB NAPHTALI HERZ **4:**686
– Kohn, Abraham **10:**1144
Bernstein, Joe **15:**306
Bernstein, John **15:**1539
BERNSTEIN, JULIUS **4:**686
Bernstein, Karl **10:**1501
Bernstein, L.E. (sol.) **11:**1558
Bernstein, Lena (pilot) **2:**322
BERNSTEIN, LEONARD (comp.) **4:**686
– Koussevitzky, Serge **10:**1227
– *illus:* text
Bernstein, Louis **11:**783
Bernstein, Luca (poet), *see* Luca, B.
BERNSTEIN, LUDWIG BEHR **4:**687
Bernstein, Meyer Yefimovich, *see* MEDVEDEV, MIKHAIL
Bernstein, Morris, *see* LOUIS, MORRIS
BERNSTEIN, NATHAN OSIPOVICH **11:**1206
BERNSTEIN, OSIP SAMOILOVICH **5:**408
BERNSTEIN, PEREZ **4:**688
– Zionism **16:**1119
– *Ha-Boker* **7:**1036
Bernstein, Philip, *see* HUGÓ, KÁROLY
BERNSTEIN, PHILIP SIDNEY **4:**688
– *Beriḥah* **4:**630; **4:**631
Bernstein, Samuel **4:**686
– *illus:*
– – portrait **6:**218
Bernstein, Saul **4:**148
BERNSTEIN, SIDNEY LEWIS, LORD **4:**689
– publishing **13:**1371
– television and radio **15:**930
BERNSTEIN, SIMON **4:**689
– *illus:*
– – Hebrew Pen Club, N.Y. **8:**211
– – Histadruth Ivrith of America **13:**371
BERNSTEIN, THEODORE **10:**309
Bernstein, Uri **16:**903
Bernstein, Y. (ed.) **7:**1534
Bernstein, Yehuda David (r., U.S.) **16:**760
BERNSTEIN, ZVI HIRSCH **4:**690
– press **13:**1053
BERNSTEIN-COHEN, MIRIAM **4:**690
– *illus:* text
BERNSTEIN-KOGAN (Cohen), JACOB **4:**691
– Berliand, Shlomo Meir **4:**638
– *illus:*
– – First Zionist Congress **16:**1165
– – Odessa Committee convention **12:**1329
Bernstein-Namierowski, Lewis, *see* NAMIER, SIR LEWIS
BERNSTEIN-SINAIEFF, LEOPOLD **4:**691
Bernstone, Zachariah **7:**334
Bernstorff, Count **16:**1078
Beroea (city, Gr.), *see* VEROIA
Ber of Bolechow, *see* BIRKENTHAL, DOV BER
Beroka (anc. schol.) **4:**395
Berolzheimer, Solomon **7:**215
Beronius, Magnus Olai **8:**25
BEROR ḤAYIL (loc., Isr.) **4:**692
– Johanan ben Zakkai's academy **2:**202; **10:**153
Beror Ḥayil (kib., Isr.) **4:**692
– statistics **1:**place list
Berosh (mosh., Isr.) **1:**place list
Berosh (tree), *see* CYPRESS
Berosus (3rd cent. B.C.E., Babyl) **10:**258
Berr, George **15:**1055
BERR, JACOB **4:**692
BERR (de Turique), MICHEL **4:**692
– notables' assembly **3:**763
Berre (loc., Prov.) **13:**1259
BERR ISAAC BERR DE

TURIQUE **4:**693
- Alsace Jews **2:**755
- notables' assembly **3:**763
BERRI, CLAUDE **12:**464
Berry, Caroline (Maria Carolina Ferdinanda Luisa; Duchess de Berry) **5:**1598
BERSHAD (tn., Ukr.) **4:**693
- Podolia **13:**668,669
- self-defense **14:**1127
- *illus:*
- - "Potato Vendor at Bershad Camp" (A. Daghani) Fig. 80 3-ART
BERSHADSKI, SERGEY ALEXANDROVICH (hist.) **4:**693
BERSHADSKY, ISAIAH **4:**694
BERSOHN, MATTHIAS **4:**695
- museums **12:**539
- *illus:*
- - collection, Warsaw Jewish Museum **12:**545
BERSON, ARTHUR JOSEPH STANISLAV **4:**696
- aviation **2:**320
Bertelsen, Aage **14:**927
BERTHOLD OF FREIBURG **4:**696
BERTHOLD OF REGENSBURG (Ratisbon) **4:**696
- Jew as usurer **7:**443
BERTHOLET, ALFRED **4:**697
Bertig, Sol **3:**459
Bertini, Gary **4:**698
- music **12:**669; **12:**672
BERTINI, K. AHARON **4:**697
BERTINORO, OBADIAH BEN ABRAHAM YARE **4:**698
- *aliyah* **9:**512
- descriptions of Ereẓ Israel **9:**280ff
- Hebrew language **16:**1634
- history chart **8:**766-767
- Jarè family **9:**1287
- Jerusalem **9:**1426
- Mamluk rule **11:**837
- messianism **11:**1425
- Mishnah commentary **11:**333
- *Tosefot Yom Tov* **8:**312
- travel book **11:**351; **15:**1352
Bertinoro *Maḥzor* (illum. ms., It.) **11:**733
Bertoletti (fam.) **7:**612
Bertonoff, Deborah **4:**699
BERTONOFF, YEHOSHUA **4:**699
- *illus:*
- - text
- - in *Genesis* **15:**1063
Berukhim, Abraham ben Eliezer ha-Levy *see* ABRAHAM BEN ELIEZER HA-LEVI BERUKHIM
BERUREI AVERAH (magis. for misdemeanors, Sp.) **4:**700
- Alconstantini, S. **2:**550
- Barcelona **4:**209
- Spain **15:**235
Berurei tevi'ot (magis. for claims, Sp.) **4:**210
BERURYAH (w., R. Meir) **4:**701
Beryl (gem) **13:**1010
Berytus (tn., Leb.), *see* BEIRUT
BESALU (tn., Sp.) **4:**701
BESANÇON (city, Fr.) **4:**702
- Alsace-Lorraine Jews **2:**756
- archives **3:**382
- *illus:* text
Besange, Hieronymus von **8:**25
Besanti (Gr.) **7:**879
Besara (city, Er. Isr.), *see* BET SHE'ARIM
BESEKOW, SAMUEL **4:**703
Besem, *see* BALSAM
Be-Sha'ah Zu (journ.) **1:**newsp. list
Be-Sherut ha-Ezraḥ (journ.) **1:**newsp. list
Be-Sherut ha-Ta'asukah (journ.) **1:**newsp. list
Be-shogeg, see Shogeg
B-e-sh-t (found. of Ḥas.), *see* ISRAEL BEN ELIEZER BA'AL SHEM TOV
BESICOVITCH, ABRAM SAMOILOVITCH **4:**703
Be-Siman Tov (greeting) **7:**916
Beskin, I. S. **11:**1557
Besnyei, György **8:**25
Besodo, Moses **2:**189
BESOR, BROOK OF (Er. Isr.) **4:**703
- Israel **9:**592
- Negev **12:**926
- *illus:*
- - loess soil **9:**573
Besor region (Isr.) **9:**594; **9:**576
BESREDKA, ALEXANDER **4:**703
BESSARABIA **4:**704
- *Contents:*
- - Up to 1812 **4:**704
- - 1812-1918 **4:**704
- - 1918-1941 **4:**707
- - From 1941 **4:**708
- agricultural settlements **2:**411
- Balta **4:**144
- deportation of Jews **3:**164
- massacre of Jews **3:**163
- Rumania **14:**387ff
- Transnistria **15:**1330ff
- *illus:*
- - text
- - ICA agricultural colony **10:**45
- *pop. table:* text
BESSELS, EMIL **4:**708
- travellers **15:**1350
Bessin, Hyman **12:**1522
BESSIS, ALBERT **4:**709
- Tunisia **15:**1448
BESSIS, JESHUA **4:**709
Best, Werner **5:**1539
Besterman, Harry, *see* Lewis, Harry
Bestiaries **3:**21
Best of Days (bk.), *see* ḤEMDAT YAMIM
Beszterce (tn., Transyl.), *see* BISTRITA
Besztercebánya (tn., Slov.), *see* BANSKA BYSTRICA
Bet . . ., Bet (h) . . ., *see also* Bayt; Beit; Beth
BET (Heb. letter) **4:**709
- *illus:*
- - initial (18th cent. wdct.) **4:**3
- *see also:* ALPHABET
Betabris (vill., Er. Isr.) **4:**731
Beta Esrael (Falashas) **6:**1145
BET AGLAYIM (place, Er. Isr.) **4:**710
- Old Gaza **7:**341
BET ALFA (Isr.) **4:**710
- anthropomorphism **3:**57
- art in synagogue **3:**508
- calendar **5:**50
- Jerusalem in art **9:**1579
- pillars **13:**523
- symbolism **15:**570ff
- synagogue **15:**598ff
- *illus:*
- - text
- - mosaics, synagogue **3:**511,513; **5:**45; **8:**651; **11:**268,989
Bet Alfa (kib., Isr.) **1:**place list **4:**713
- - Mount Gilboa **7:**568
Bet(h)-Anath (J. cmty., Syr.) **5:**1239
BET(H)-ANATH (city, Er. Isr.) **4:**713
Bet Aniya, *see* BETHANY
Betar (tn., Er. Isr.), *see* BETHAR
BETAR (Zion. mvmt.) **4:**714
- *Contents:*
- - 1923-1935 **4:**714
- - In Palestine **4:**714
- - Post-Holocaust **4:**715
- Begin's leadership **4:**392
- Ben-Yosef **4:**571
- "illegal" immigration **8:**1249
- naval school in Italy **16:**1123
- Yugoslavia **16:**1150
- Zionism **16:**1114ff
- *illus:*
- - badge **9:**977
- - guard duty at Western Wall **9:**1478
- - Latvia group **10:**1468
- *see also:* REVISIONISTS, ZIONIST
BET(H)-ARABAH (loc., Er. Isr.) **4:**716
- Judah boundary **10:**330
- *illus:* text
Bet(h)-Arbel (site, Er. Isr.) **3:**293
Bet Arif (mosh., Isr.) **1:**place list
Bet(h)-Aven, *see* BET(H)-EL
Bet(h)-Baal-Meon (city, Transj.), *see* BAAL-MEON
Bet Berl (cult. center, Isr.) **1:**place list; **3:**390; **10:**834; **16:**1193
BET(H)-CHEREM (stlmt., Er. Isr.) **4:**716
- Ein Karem **16:**1324
- vine **16:**155
Bet(h)-Cherem Valley (Isr.) **2:**768; **4:**717; **9:**152
Bet Dagan (tn., Isr.) **1:**place list **4:**719; **15:**1565
Bet Degana (bib. city), *see* BET(H) DAGON
BET(H) DAGON (bib. places) **4:**719
Bet(h)-Diblathaim (Moab. city) **2:**667
BET DIN AND JUDGES **4:**719
- *Contents:*
- - Definition **4:**719
- - Jewish Law **4:**720
- - - Origins **4:**720
- - - Jurisdiction **4:**720
- - - Appointment of Judges **4:**722
- - - Qualifications **4:**723
- - - Judicial Conduct **4:**724
- - Talmudic Period **4:**724
- - Medieval and Modern **4:**725
- General
- - ancient Israel **8:**610
- - autonomy **3:**923, 928ff
- - Christians (jurisdiction) **3:**928
- - Commandments, the 613 **5:**771f, 779
- - Councils of the Lands **5:**995; **5:**999
- - Ereẓ Israel (20th century) **12:**142
- - exilarch **6:**1031
- - gentile courts **14:**1387
- - geonic academies **7:**316
- - halakhic midrash and judgment **8:**1415
- - Israel, State of **9:**642ff; **9:**889ff
- - Jewish autonomy **12:**124; **12:**125; **12:**126
- - *Landrabbiner* **10:**1409
- - Mishnah, source material of **12:**96
- - non-Jewish law **6:**51; **6:**54
- - Palestine gaonate **12:**483
- - Philo (Pseudo-) **13:**408
- - priests **13:**1079
- - proceedings **2:**202ff
- - public authority **13:**1352
- - rabbinical authority **3:**908; **3:**911
- - sages **14:**637ff
- Jurisdiction and Function
- - abortion **2:**100
- - admission **2:**290
- - adoption **2:**301
- - apotropos **3:**219ff
- - compromise **5:**857
- - conversion before **13:**1183
- - divorce coercion **6:**127
- - documents **14:**1387ff
- - endowment administration **8:**285
- - execution forms **5:**142
- - expropriatory powers **5:**880ff
- - extreme measures **13:**227
- - firstborn redemption **6:**1309
- - *ḥaliẓah* **11:**130
- - *ḥerem bet din* **8:**355
- - imprisonment **8:**1300ff
- - informers **8:**1365ff
- - judges' names in verdict **11:**804
- - loan cases **11:**419
- - misrulings of **13:**227
- - *niddui* **8:**352; **8:**353
- - obligations, oral **12:**1314
- - perjury **13:**288
- - practice and procedure **13:**952
- - *prosbul* **13:**1181
- - status of ruling **7:**1159ff
- - *takkanot* **15:**712
- - *takkanot ha-kahal* **15:**728
- - tax case disqualification **15:**865
- - vows **16:**228
- - wills **16:**525
- - years counted by **14:**575
- - *zaken mamre* **16:**920
- Qualifications and Structure
- - abstinence from wine **6:**238
- - *av bet din* **3:**940
- - blindness **4:**1091
- - gambler, disqualified **7:**302
- - hatred, disqualification of judge **7:**1473
- - lay tribunals **12:**137; **12:**127
- - ordination required **14:**1140
- - scribe, role of **14:**1044
- - *soferim* **15:**80
- *illus:*
- - text
- - Debdou, register of transactions, 1947 **3:**930
- - fifteen cent. illum. ms. **4:***fcg.* 716
- - process of divorce **6:**126
- - Sanhedrin **14:**839
- *see also:* ARBITRATION; BRIBERY; CONTEMPT OF COURT; DAYYAN; EXTRAORDINARY REMEDIES; MAJORITY RULE; POLICE OFFENSES; RABBINICAL CONFERENCES; SANHEDRIN; SYNODS
Bet Din Gadol (great court) **2:**199
BET(H)-EDEN (Aramean kdm.) **4:**727
Bet Eked Sefarim (wk.) **4:**972
BET(H)-EL (tn., Er. Isr.) **4:**728
- Ai **2:**471; **2:**472
- Bible history **8:**578; **8:**579
- calf worship **8:**1020; **9:**1372
- cultic center **5:**1163ff
- Genesis, Book of **7:**389
- Jacob **9:**1192ff
- mountains **9:**141
- proscription **8:**346
- tribal center **15:**1383
- *illus:* text
- *see also:* LUZ
Bet El, Jehiel ben Mattathias **8:**1269
Bet El, Jekuthiel **8:**1269
Bet Elazari (mosh., Isr.) **1:**place list
Bet Elisheva (cmty. center, Jer.) **12:**212
Bet El Yeshivah (Jer.) **14:**1360
- Abraham Gershon of Kotow **7:**1392
- Kabbalah **10:**553
- Shar'abī **16:**746
Bet(h)-Emek (Bib. loc., Er. Isr.) **4:**732
Be-Terem (journ.) **1:**newsp. list
Be-Terem Har ve-Givah (litur.) **4:**280
Be-Terem Noledu Harim (litur.) **4:**280
Bet-ʿEshda (place, Er. Isr.) **5:**956

BET ESHEL (stlmt., Er. Isr.) **4**:730
- Negev **12**:929
Bet Ezra (mosh., Isr.) **1**:place list
Bet Gamli'el (mosh., Isr.) **1**:place list **16**:723
Bet Gan (vill., Er. Isr.) **9**:325
- ICA's activity **10**:48
BET GARMU (fam., Temple bakers) **4**:731
Bet Gefen (J.-Arab center, Haifa) **7**:1140
Bet Genizah (treasury) **16**:1333
Bet Gerem (loc., Arab.) **7**:327
Bet(h)-Gilgal (place, Er. Isr.) **7**:573
Bet Gufnin (tn., Judea), *see* GOFNAH
BET GUVRIN (city, kib., Isr.) **4**:731
- Arab settlement **9**:261
- Crusader period **9**:272
- Septimius Severus **9**:251
- *illus:* text
Beth . . ., *see also* Bayt; Beit; Bet(h)
Bet ha-Aravah (kib., Pal.) **4**:716
- Gesher ha-Ziv **7**:526
Bet ha-Aravah (loc., Er. Isr.) *see* BET(H)-ARABAH
Beth Abraham Hospital (U.S.) **8**:1039
Bet ha-Elohim, see Bet YHWH
BET HA-EMEK (kib., Isr.) **4**:732
Bet ha-Gaddi (mosh., Isr.) **1**:place list
Bet ha-Gedudim (mus., Isr.) **3**:968
Beth Ahabah (syn., Richmond, Va.) **14**:160
- *illus:*
- - interior **14**:161
Beth Aharon (syn., China) **14**:1293
Bet ha-Jeshimot (oasis, Er. Isr.) **5**:1394
Bet ha-Kerem (sub., Jer.) **4**:719
- ancient vegetation **9**:1515
- development **9**:1472
- housing **9**:563
- Silman, Kadish **14**:1540
- Yellin, David **16**:737
- *illus:*
- - in 1928 **9**:1477
Bet ha-Kerem (stlmt., Er. Isr.), *see* BET(H)-CHEREM
Bet ha-Kerem Seminary (Jer.), *see* Hebrew Teachers' Seminary
Bet ha-Kerem Valley (Isr.) **9**:588
Bet ha-Levi (fam., Salonika), *see* LEVI
BET HALEVI (mosh., Isr.) **4**:733
- statistics **1**:place list
Bet ha-Levi, Abraham ben Joseph, *see* LEVI, ABRAHAM BEN JOSEPH
Bet ha-Levi, Isaac ben Solomon, *see* LEVI, ISAAC BEN SOLOMON
Bet ha-Levi, Jacob ben Israel, *see* LEVI, JACOB BEN ISRAEL
Bet ha-Levi, Solomon ben Isaac, *see* LEVI, SOLOMON BEN ISAAC
Bet Halevi yeshivah (Ott. Emp.) **16**:1549
Bet ha-Midrash de-Parnas (rab. seminary, Lublin) **2**:143
Bet ha-Midrash Lilmod u-Lelamed (acad., Vienna) **16**:577
Bet ha-Mikdash, see TEMPLE
BET ḤANAN (mosh., Isr.) **4**:733
- statistics **1**:place list
Bet Ḥananya, *see* BETHANY
Bet Ḥananyah (mosh., Isr.) **1**:place list
Bet Ḥanin, *see* ANAN BEN SETH
BETHANY (vill., Er. Isr.) **4**:733
BETHAR (city, Er. Isr.) **4**:733
- Av, The Ninth **3**:936
- Bar Kokhba revolt **4**:235ff; **9**:247; **10**:471; **16**:577
- commemoration in Grace **7**:838
- history chart **8**:766-767
- marriage custom **11**:1040
BET(H)-HARAM (Haran; tn., Er. Isr.) **4**:736
- Antipas, Herod **3**:76
Betharamphtha (tn., Er. Isr.), *see* BET(H)-HARAM
BET ḤARODON (loc., Er. Isr.) **4**:736
Bet ha-Shittah (kib., Isr.) **1**:place list; **4**:775
- *illus:*
- - Passover *seder* **10**:961
Bet Ḥatunot ("wedding hall"), *see* TANZHAUS
BETHBASI (Judea) **4**:736
- battle of **16**:279
Beth David Hospital (N.Y.C.) **12**:1094
Beth-El (rel. sect, Mex.) **11**:1460
- *illus:*
- - congregants **11**:1459
Beth El (syn., Mass.) **15**:318
- *illus:*
- - interior **15**:319
Beth El Hospital (N.Y.C.) **12**:1116
Beth Elohim (syn., S.C.) **15**:620
Bethel-Sarezer (bib. fig.) **14**:34
BET ḤERUT (mosh., Isr.) **4**:736
Bethesda (place, Er. Isr.), *see* Bet-ʿEshda
Bethesda Pool (Jer.), *see* Sheep's Pool
Bet Ḥever (mosh., Isr.), *see* Kefar Dani'el
Beth Hamidrash Hagadol (syn., N.Y.C.) **12**:1094
Bet Ḥilkiyyah (mosh., Isr.) **1**:place list
BET HILLEL (mosh., Isr.) **4**:737
- statistics **1**:place list
BET HILLEL AND BET SHAMMAI (two rab. schools) **4**:737
- ablution of hands **2**:84; **13**:1410; **13**:1411
- academy pupils **2**:201
Adar, the Ninth of **2**:252
- *Baraita de-Niddah* **4**:194
- civil and ritual law **12**:112
- disputes **8**:361
- Eliezer ben Hyrcanus **6**:621
- *eruv tavshilin* **6**:850
- *halakhah*, determination of **6**:852; **9**:243
- *halakhah* and custom **12**:6
- *halakhah* development **7**:1162
- *hefker* **8**:244
- interpretation of law **11**:315
- Jesus **10**:13
- marriage **14**:647
- Mishnah, arrangement of **12**:97
- *nasi* (title) **12**:835
- resurrection **14**:100
- sages **14**:643ff
- stringency and leniency **16**:777
- *see also:* HILLEL; SHAMMAI
Beth Israel (syn., Calif.) **14**:829
- *illus:*
- - exterior **14**:830
Beth Israel (syn., Mass.) **16**:633
Beth Israel (syn. Nebr.) **12**:1374
Beth Israel (syn., Portland, Oreg.) **13**:911
Beth Israel Hospital (U.S.) **8**:1039
- New York City **12**:1098; **12**:1116
Bet(h)-Hoglah (city, Er. Isr.) **4**:710
- Judah boundary **10**:330
Beth Jacob Journal (period.) **16**:1260
BETH JACOB SCHOOLS **16**:1260
- Agudat Israel **2**:423
- education **6**:427ff
Beth Judah (syn. Mass.) **16**:633
BETHLEHEM (city, Er. Isr.) **4**:741
- Crusades **9**:267,269
- dyeing **6**:328
- human geography of Israel **9**:587ff
- Jesus **10**:11
- Judah territory **8**:579
- Ottoman period **9**:285; **9**:293
- population, Fatimid period **9**:264
- Rachel **13**:1489
- Ruth **14**:518ff
- Six-Day War **14**:1635
- *illus:*
- - text
- - Church of the Nativity **4**:300; **8**:927; **9**:912,914
- - Rachel's tomb **8**:925; **13**:1489
- *see also:* EPHRATH
Bethlehem (city, Pa.) **13**:230
Bethlehem (Templer clny., Er. Isr.) **4**:750; **15**:995
Bethlehem (tn., S.A.) **12**:1448
Bethlehem of Judea (J. stlmt., U.S.) **2**:862
Bethlen, Stephen **8**:1095
BETHLEPTEPHA (Judean tn.) **4**:747
BET(H)-HORON (tns., Er. Isr.) **4**:747
Bethmaela (city, Er. Isr.) **2**:62
Beth Mikra (period.) **15**:55
Bethnambris (loc., Er. Isr.) **4**:752
Betholeptephon (Judean tn.), *see* BETHLEPTEPHA
BETHPHAGE (vill., Er. Isr.) **4**:748
- inscription **16**:669
Beth Rivkah Ladies' College (Austr.) **11**:1282
BETHSAIDA (vill., Er. Isr.) **4**:748
Bethsaida Valley (Isr.) **9**:171; **10**:1035; **13**:1534
Beth Shalom (syn., Phila.) **13**:375; **15**:626
- *illus:*
- - exterior **13**:375
- - interior **15**:625
BETHUEL (bib. fig.) **4**:748
BETHULIA (city in Apoc.) **4**:749
- *Judith, Book of* **10**:451
Bethzeita Valley (Er. Isr.) **10**:987
Betiḥut (journ.) **1**: newsp. list
BET (Bayt) IKSĀ (vill., Isr.) **4**:749
- Six-Day War **14**:1630
Bet Ilnis (site, Er. Isr.) **4**:1539
Bet Israel (Jer. qtr.) **9**:325
Bet Kamah (kib., Isr.) **1**:place list
Bet keneset, see SYNAGOGUE
BET KESHET (kib., Isr.) **4**:750
- statistics **1**:place list
Bet Leḥem (city, Er. Isr.), *see* BETHLEHEM
BET(H) LEḤEM (Ha-Gelilit) (loc., Er. Isr.) **4**:750
- moshav statistics **1**: place list
Bet(h)-Leḥem Ẓeriyah (loc., Er. Isr.), *see* BET(H) LEḤEM (Ha-Gelilit)
Bet le-Tappu'aḥ (tn., Er. Isr.), *see* Bet(h) Tappu'ah
Bet Leviyyim (mus. school, Er. Isr.) **9**:1006
Betman, Victor **2**:321
Bet(h)-Maacah (reg., Er. Isr.) **2**:60
BET(H)-MAON (loc., Er. Isr.) **4**:750
Bet Mashiko (vill., Judea) **12**:528
BET MEIR (mosh., Isr.) **4**:751
- statistics **1**: place list
Bet(h)-Meon (city, Transj.), *see* BAAL-MEON
BET (Ha-) MIDRASH ("house of study") **4**:751
- academies **2**:199
- Ereẓ Israel history **9**:243ff
- Issachar in *aggadah* **9**:1076
- preaching, in **13**:995
- Shem **14**:1369
- synagogue **15**:584; **15**:593
- *takkanot* **15**:735
- *illus:*
- - Medzibezh, Israel Ba'al Shem Tov's **9**:1053
- - Ostroleka **12**:1515
- - Rashi, Worms **13**:1561
- - Žydikiai, Lithuania **11**:373
- *see also:* ḤEDER; STUDY; YESHIVOT
BET NEḤEMYAH (mosh., Isr.) **4**:752
- statistics **1**:place list
Bet Nekofah (mosh., Isr.) **1**: place list
BET NETOFAH (vill., Er. Isr.) **4**:752
- Israel **9**:152
- toparchy **9**:121
BET(H)-NIMRAH (loc., Er. Isr.) **4**:752
- Essenes **5**:1394
Bet Nir (kib., Isr.) **1**: place list
Bet Nissuim, see TANZHAUS
Bet Nubi (Nuba; dyeing center, Er. Isr.) **6**:328
Betomarsea (loc., Moab) **11**:793
Betomesthaim (tn., Er. Isr.) **10**:451
BET OREN (kib., Isr.) **4**:753
- statistics **1**: place list
BET OVED (mosh., Isr.) **4**:753
- statistics **1**: place list
Bet(h)-Pelet (city, Er. Isr.) **14**:1317
Bet(h)-Peor (bib. loc.) **12**:398
Bet Rabban (yeshivah, Isr.) **1**: place list
Bet Rabban (tal. acad.) **4**:401
BET(H)-REḤOB (bib. city; dyn.) **4**:753
- Banias **4**:162
Bet Reisha (city, Er. Isr.), *see* CAPITOLIAS
Bet Rimmon (loc., Er. Isr.) **9**:249
BETROTHAL **4**:753
- *Contents:*
- - Definition **4**:753
- - Gifts **4**:753
- - Tena'im **4**:754
- - Breach of Shiddukhin **4**:755
- - Validity of Tena'im **4**:756
- - Customs **4**:756
- adultery **2**:314
- agency **2**:349
- *asmakhta* **3**:753
- documents **14**:1388
- maintenance **11**:784
- ring **15**:735
- Samaritans **14**:745
- virginity **16**:162
- *illus:* text
- *see also:* DOWRY; MARRIAGE
Bet Ṣāfāfā (vill., Isr.), *see* Beit Ṣāfāfā
Betsalel (period.) **5**:457
Bet sefer (Bib. school) **6**:401ff
Bet Sefer Ivri (Heb. School) **6**:425ff
Bet Shammai, *see* BET HILLEL AND BET SHAMMAI
BET(H)-SHEAN (tn., Isr.) **4**:757
- after Temple destruction **9**:245
- Dionysus **6**:62
- dyeing center **6**:327
- Ereẓ Israel, 634 to 1099 **9**:260ff
- Ereẓ Israel, 1099 to 1291 **9**:267ff
- "gate" of Garden of Eden **7**:327
- goldsmiths and silversmiths **7**:738
- Hebrew pronunciation **16**:1586
- Israel tribes **8**:581
- Jezreel valley **10**:102
- Joseph son of Tobiah **15**:1179
- linen **6**:1339; **16**:1275
- Mamluk provincial organization **9**:274
- pillars **13**:523
- Saul's body **14**:914
- statistics **1**: place list
- tombs **15**:1218
- valley **9**:147; **9**:589ff
- *illus:*
- - text
- - archaeological remains **2**:761; **3**:314,503
- - synagogue mosaic **13**:905

- *see also:* DECAPOLIS
Bet(h) Shean Valley (Isr.) 9:147; 9:589ff
- *illus:*
- - Nir David 12:1173
- - land registration certificate 9:557
Bet She'arim (mosh., Isr.) 4:772
- statistics 1: place list
BET SHE'ARIM (city, Er. Isr.) 4:765
- art 3:508
- glass vessels 7:609
- Ḥimyarite graves 3:235
- history chart (170,351) 8:766-767
- Judah ha-Nasi 2:202; 10:367
- *menorah* 11:1368
- pillars 13:522
- symbolism 15:568ff
- synagogue 15:597
- Syrian Jews 15:639
- *illus:*
- - archaeological remains 2:687; 3:518, 528; 5:658; 7:605; 8:1007
- - Helios head on sarcophagus 15:568
BET(H)-SHEMESH (bib. cities) 4:772
- Bible history 8:578
- pictographic scripts 16:654
- sacrifice at 13:1070
- Solomon's buildings 15:102ff
- *illus:* text
Bet(h)-Shemesh (city, Egy.) 4:774
Bet(h)-Shemesh (tn., Isr.) 4:774
- statistics 1: place list
- *illus:*
- - turbo engines exhibit 9:818
Bet Shikmah (mosh., Isr.) 1: place list
Bet(h) Shittah (bib. loc.) 2:198
BET(H)-SHITTAH (loc., Er. Isr.) 4:775
Bet Sturman (mus., Isr.) 15:940
- En-Harod 6:792
Bet talmud (Talmud school) 6:401ff
BETTAN, ISRAEL 4:775
Bet(h)-Tappuah (city, Er. Isr.) 4:747; 15:806
BETTAUER, HUGO 4:775
BETTELHEIM (fam.) 4:776
BETTELHEIM, ALBERT (Aaron) SIEGFRIED 4:776
BETTELHEIM, BRUNO 4:776
Bettelheim, Félix Albert 4:776
Bettelheim, Fülöp 4:776
Bettelheim, Karl 4:776
Bettelheim, Lipót-Leopold 4:776
Bettelheim, Loeb 4:776
Bettelheim, Meyer Leb, *see* Bettelheim, Lipot-Leopold
Bettelheim, Moses 4:776
Bettelheim, Raphael, *see* Bettelheim, Fülöp
BETTELHEIM, SAMUEL 4:777
- Zionism 16:1120
Bettelheim, Selig 13:60
Bettel-Juden (J. beggars) 4:390
- *illus:*
- - Carl Wilhelm Ferdinand's order against 4:388
Bet-Ter (city, Er. Isr.) 4:734
Betterton, Sir H. 13:31
Bettman, Gilbert 5:565
Bettman, Gilbert, Jr. 5:565
Bet Trumpeldor (archive, Isr.) 15:940
Betulah, see VIRGIN, VIRGINITY
Betulah (zodiac sign), *see* Virgo
Bet-Unyaki (loc., As.M.) 4:1060
Bet Ussishkin (mus., Isr.) 5:1260
Bet Uzziel (mosh., Isr.) 1: place list
Bet Va'ad (meeting house) 2:199
Bet Ya'akov synagogue (Jer.), *see* Ḥurbat R. Yehudah he-Ḥasid
BET YANNAI (mosh., Isr.) 4:777
- statistics 1: place list
BET YEHOSHU'A (mosh., Isr.) 4:778
- statistics 1: place list
BET YERAḤ (Cana. city) 4:778
- fortifications 16:273
- pottery type 13:938
- *illus:*
- - archaeological remains 2:383
Bet YHWH 5:1162ff
BET YIZḤAK (mosh., Isr.) 4:781
- statistics 1: place list
BET YOSEF (mosh., Isr.) 4:781
- statistics 1: place list
Bet Yosef (yesh., Jer.) 6:311
BET ZAYIT (mosh., Isr.) 4:781
- statistics 1: place list
Bet Ẓayyada (vill., Er. Isr.), *see* BETHSAIDA
BET ZEKHARYAH (site, Isr.) 4:782
BET ZERA (kib., Isr.) 4:782
- statistics 1: place list
BET ẒERIFA (anc. fam.) 4:782
Bet Ẓevi (educ. inst., Isr.) 1: place list
Bet Zikha (rab. acad., Bagh.) 6:1101; 8:1451
BET(H)-ZUR (anc. city, Er. Isr.) 4:782
- Simeon the Hasmonean 14:1565
Bet-Zuri, Eliahu 11:465
BEUGNOT, AUGUSTE ARTHUR 4:783
Beula (watchnight) 5:576
Beur (bib. trans.), *see Biur*
Be'urim al Perush Rashi (wk.) 15:520
Be'ur Luḥot (wk.), *see Ha-Ḥibbur ha-Gadol*
Beuthen (tn., Pol.), *see* BYTOM
Beutler, Ernest 11:1200
Bevan, Aneurin 2:458
Bevan, Anthony Ashley 4:784
BEVAN, EDWYN ROBERT 4:784
Beverage industry (Isr.) 9:823
Beverly (city, Mass.) 11:622
Beverly Hills (city, Calif.) 11:503
Beverly Hills (sub., Chicago) 5:415
Beverungen (tn., Ger.) 13:7
Beverwijk (tn., Neth.) 7:1008
BEVIN, ERNEST 4:784
- Attlee 3:836
- Churchill 5:556
- history 8:768
- history chart 8:766-767
- immigration 9:357ff
- Palestine policy 16:1089ff
Bevingrad (area, Jer.) 9:1478
- *illus:*
- - Princess Mary Avenue 9:1481
Bevis Marks (syn., Lond.) 6:754; 11:473
- history chart 8:766-767
- *illus:*
- - Belisario's painting 15:620-621
- - Bicentenary Service invitation 11:471
- - plan 15:615
- - silver salver presented to Lord Mayor of London 11:472
Bevis of Hampton (romance), *see Sir Bevis of Hampton*
Bey (tit., Tun.) 15:1445ff
Beylin, Arkadi 13:345
Beyrouth (city, Leb.), *see* BEIRUT
BEYTH, HANS 4:785
BEẒAH (Tal. tract.) 4:785
BEZALEL (bib. fig.) 4:786
- alchemy 2:542
- art 3:506
- goldsmith 7:738
- letter combination 2:747
- magical power 16:784
- tabernacle 15:683
- tomb 14:1508
- *illus:* text
Bezalel (orgn., Hol.) 12:1397
BEZALEL (acad., Isr.) 4:788
- art 3:576
- cultural life in Israel 9:1009
- cultural reconstruction 10:49
- goldsmiths 7:743
- Ḥanukkah lamps 7:1315
- history chart 8:766-767
- *illus:*
- - text
- - Ben Shemen workshop 4:547
- - Schwarz, Boris, and students 9:331
Bezalel ben Ḥayyim 10:375
BEZALEL BEN MOSES HA-KOHEN 4:789
Bezalel ben Nathan 16:1014
BEZALEL BEN SOLOMON OF KOBRYN 4:790
- Kabbalah 10:552
Bezalel National Museum 12:551
- *illus:*
- - Israel stamp 9:844–845
Bezalel School of Arts and Crafts (Jer.), *see* BEZALEL (acad., Isr.)
Bèze, Théodore de 2:484; 11:1381
BEZEK (place-name, Er. Isr.) 4:790
BEZEM, NAPHTALI 3:597
- *illus:*
- - "Return" 3:618
Bezer (city, Er. Isr.) 5:591
- Reuben 14:105
Bėẓet (mosh., Isr.) 1: place list
Bezetha (qtr., anc. Jer.) 9:1398; 9:1405
Beẓet River (Isr.) 9:152
BEZIDUL NOU (vill., Transyl.) 4:790
BÉZIERS (city, Fr.) 4:792
- Council (1255) 5:549
- massacre 2:534
- yeshivah 16:763
- *illus:* text
Be-Ẓok ha-Ittim (journ.) 1: newsp. list
Bezprozvany, Hyman B., *see* BASS, HYMAN B.
Bezruč, Petr 5:1207
Bezymenski, Alexander 14:513
Bhamdoun (resort, Leb.) 10:1545
B.H.J. (neo-Nazi orgn.), *see* Bund Heimattreuer Jugend
Bia, Abraham 4:159
Bia, Fradl, *see* Banet, Fradl
Biafra (reg., Afr.) 9:441
BIALA (tn., Pol.) 4:793
- archives 3:387
Biala (city, Pol.), *see* ZUELZ
Biala, Dov Berish ben Abraham of 5:561; 16:304
Biala-Bielsko, *see* BIALA
BIALA PODLASKA (tn., Pol.) 4:793
Bialeh, Abraham 4:795
Bialeh, Israel ben Naphtali Herz 4:795
Bialeh, Naphtali Herz 4:795
Bialeh, Samuel 4:795
Bialeh, Simḥah 4:795
Bialeh, Solomon Dov Berush 4:795
BIALEH, ẒEVI HIRSCH BEN NAPHTALI HERZ 4:794
Bialer, Joseph 16:839
Bialer, Tuvia 11:426
Bialik, Dinah Priva 4:795
BIALIK, ḤAYYIM NAḤMAN 4:795
- *Contents:*
- - Childhood Period (1880-1890) 4:795
- - Volozhin Period 4:796
- - Ahad Ha-Am's influence 4:796
- - First Stay in Odessa 4:797
- - Return to Zhitomir 4:797
- - 1893–1896 4:798
- - 1897-1900 4:798
- - Settling in Odessa 4:799
- - Kishinev 4:800
- - Influence of Warsaw 4:800
- - Silence 4:801
- - Berlin and Palestine 4:801
- - Essays 4:801
- - Cultural Role 4:801
- - Editor and Translator 4:801
- - Evaluation 4:802
- Berdyczewski, Micha Josef 4:594
- Berkowitz, Yitzhak Dov 4:635; 4:637
- critic 5:1120
- Hebrew literature 8:195; 8:199
- Hebrew vocabulary 16:1649ff
- Hershele 8:395
- Kurzweil, Baruch 10:1303
- Lachower, Yeruḥam Fishel 10:1338; 10:1339
- *Maqāma* 10:937
- Mayakovski, Vladimir 14:510
- Oneg Shabbat meetings 9:902
- prosody 13:1225
- Rawnitzky, Ḥana 13:1588
- *Sefer ha-Aggadah* 2:364
- Shimoni, David 14:1405
- Shneour, Zalman 14:1428
- stamps 15:336
- Vogel, David 16:203
- Volozhin yeshivah 4:661
- wine and liquor trade 16:545
- Writers' Association 16:652ff
- Zionist Congress 16:1167; 16:1171
- *illus:*
- - text
- - autographs 3:913; 4:796,798
- - fellow writers and 8:193; 16:809
- - Mendele Mokher Seforim and 11:1322
- - Rawnitzki, Y.H., and 13:1589
- - Shneour, Zalman, and 14:1431
- - with *ḥalutzim* in Constantinople 14:465
Bialik, Isaac Joseph 4:795
Bialik, Jacob Moses 4:795
Bialik, Manya 4:798
Bialik Exhibition (bk. fair, Er. Isr.) 9:765
Bialik Institute (publ. firm, Isr.), *see* Mosad Bialik
BIALOBLOCKI, SAMUEL SHERAGA 4:803
BIALOBLOTZKY, CHRISTIAN HEINRICH FRIEDRICH 4:804
- Christian Hebraists 8:25
Bialoslowsky de Chazan, Sara 10:1503
BIALOSTOTZKY, BENJAMIN JACOB 4:804
Bialowieza (tn., Pol.) 10:1123
BIALYSTOK (city, Pol.) 4:805
- art in ghetto 3:568
- Duma, First 6:267
- ghetto 13:769
- pogroms 13:698
- Poland 13:768
- textiles 15:1040
- *illus:* text
- *pop. table:* text
Bialystoker Telegraf (newsp.) 13:1042
BIARRITZ (tn., Fr.) 4:811
BIBAGO, ABRAHAM BEN SHEM TOV 4:811
- Averroes 3:952
- conversos 10:322
- Maimonidean controversy 11:753
BIBAGO, ISAAC 4:812
BIBAS (fam.) 4:813
Bibas, Abraham (16th cent.) 4:813
Bibas, Abraham (20th cent.) 15:1030
Bibas, Ḥayyim 4:813; 15:1030
Bibas, Joseph 4:813
Bibas, Judah 4:813
Bibas, Samuel 4:813
Bibas, Shem Tov 4:813

Bibbero, Marquis **15**:313
Bibbiena (tn., It.) **15**:1468
Biber, Y. **5**:437
Bibi bar Abbaye (amora) **10**:710
BIBLE **4**:814
- *Contents:*
- - The Canon, Text, and Editions **4**:816
- - Translations **4**:841
- - Exegesis and Study **4**:889
- - Religious Impact **4**:915
- - In the Arts **4**:932
- This entry is divided according to the following sub-divisions: (1) General (2) Canon (3) Texts and Editions (4) Translations, Ancient (5) Translations, Modern (6) Exegesis and Study (7) Concordances and Dictionaries (8) Commentators (9) Concepts and Ideas (10) Religious Impact (11) In the Arts
(1) **General**
- afforestation **9**:787
- *akedah* **2**:480
- alchemy **2**:542ff
- *animals* **3**:19
- archives **3**:367
- astrology **3**:788
- astronomy **3**:795
- books **4**:1225ff
- education **6**:382f
- kissing of **10**:1074
- family **6**:1165ff
- food **6**:1414ff
- genealogy **7**:377
- greetings **7**:912
- history, patriarchal period **8**:572
- king, kingship **10**:1016ff
- letters **11**:55
- lots **11**:510ff
- medicine **11**:1178
- *Melokhim Bukh* **11**:1292
- mental illness **11**:1372
- metals and mining **11**:1428
- Moses **12**:394
- names **12**:803
- nomadism **12**:1207ff
- numbers **12**:1254
- oils **12**:1347ff
- pottery **13**:943
- psychology **13**:1341
- rain **13**:1520ff
- sculpture forbidden **14**:1059
- strangers' status **15**:419ff
- sun **15**:516
- taxation **15**:840
- tombstones **15**:1218
- trade and commerce **15**:1293
- visions **16**:166ff
- weights and measures **16**:376
- woman **16**:623
- yeshivah curriculum **16**:767
- *illus:*
- - animals (table) **3**:9-16
- - biblical themes as ceremonial object motif **2**:542; **3**:451-453, 531,627; **4**:244,374,1231, 1339-1344; **5**:296, *fcg.* 299, 300 302, 661, 1035, 1042, 1058, 1381, 1444, 1445, 1448; **6**:1391; **7**:170, 611, *fcg.* 1259, 1295, 1297, 1300, 1301, 1307, 1309, 1346, 1485; **14**:564
- - biblical themes as *ketubbah* ornamentation **10**:*fcg.* 939
- - cantillation, Abicht's *Porta Accentuum* **5**:128-129
- - cantillation, musical notations **11**:1100,1112
- - manuscript, script types **2**:711-728
- - plants and products of plants (table) **13**:615-626
- - Psalm Books and Psalters **2**:702, 878, 970; **3**:217; **4**:1, 321; **5**:22,757,1558; **6**:1; **8**:660,1317; **10**:1361; **11**:1,633; **12**:1351; **14**:541; **15**:103,1497
- *see also:* ARCHAEOLOGY; ISRAEL (Archaeology); ISRAEL, (History); *and under individual names of biblical figures and places*
(2) **Canon** **4**:816
- *Contents:*
- - General Titles **4**:816
- - The Canon **4**:817
- - The Tripartite Canon **4**:821
- - The Hellenistic Canon **4**:825
- - The Number of Books **4**:826
- - The Order of the Books **4**:827
- - The Languages of Scripture **4**:831
- - The History of the Biblical Text **4**:832
- Tripartite Canon **4**:821
- - Pentateuch **13**:231
- - - Deuteronomy **5**:1573
- - - Exodus **6**:1050
- - - Genesis **7**:386ff
- - - Holiness Code **8**:820
- - - Leviticus **11**:138ff
- - - Numbers **12**:1249
- - Prophets **13**:1151
- - - Ezekiel **6**:1078
- - - Isaiah **9**:44ff
- - - Jeremiah **9**:1345; **9**:1351ff
- - - Joshua **10**:271
- - - Judges **10**:442
- - - Kings **10**:1021
- - - Samuel **14**:788ff
- - Minor Prophets **12**:48
- - - Amos **2**:881
- - - Habakkuk **7**:1014
- - - Haggai **7**:1112
- - - Hosea **8**:1010
- - - Joel **10**:131
- - - Jonah **10**:171
- - - Malachi **11**:812
- - - Micah **11**:1483
- - - Nahum **12**:793
- - - Obadiah **12**:1304
- - - Zechariah **16**:953
- - - Zephaniah **16**:994
- - Hagiographa **4**:824
- - - Chronicles **5**:517
- - - Daniel **5**:1277
- - - Ecclesiastes **6**:349
- - - Esther **14**:1055
- - - Ezra and Nehemiah **6**:1111
- - - Job **10**:111
- - - Lamentations **10**:1371
- - - Proverbs **13**:1268
- - - Psalms **13**:1305ff
- - - Ruth **14**:522ff
- - - Scrolls, The Five **14**:1057
- - - Song of Songs **15**:144
- *tables:*
- - Apocrypha books, attitude of canonizing authorities **3**:181
- Hellenistic Canon **4**:825
- - Hellenistic Jewish literature **8**:303
- - Ben Sira, Wisdom of **4**:552
- - codex **16**:1416ff
- Language of Scripture **4**:831
- - Aramaic **3**:260
- - Hebrew **16**:1569
- - linguistics **16**:1348
- - *nasi*, usage of **12**:833
- - parables **13**:72
- - poetry **13**:671
- - pronunciations **13**:1121
- - prosody **13**:1200
(3) **Texts and Editions** **4**:836
- Antwerp Polyglot **13**:613
- Arias Montano **3**:434; **10**:1563
- Baer, Seligman Isaac **4**:80
- *Bible de Jérusalem* **4**:871
- *Biblia Hebraica* **10**:1080
- *Biblia Regia* **3**:434
- Bologna Pentateuch **4**:1190
- Complutensian Polyglot **16**:688
- Ferrara (1553) **6**:1234
- Ginsburg, C.D. **7**:581
- *Hexapla* **12**:1467
- Jacob ibn Adonijah **9**:1217
- Letteris, Meir **11**:55
- London Polyglot (1654-57) **13**:666; **16**:258
- *Mikra'ot Gedolot* **4**:1195; **11**:324
- Postel Polyglot **13**:933
- printing **13**:1096ff
- Soncino **15**:142
- typography **15**:1480ff
- *illus:*
- - text
- - Alantansi, Eliezer ibn, incunabulum **8**:1330
- - Athias edition **15**:1484
- - *Bible Historiée le Roy* (c. 1479) **6**:676
- - *Cologne Bible* (1478-80) **5**:1304
- - Dead Sea Scrolls **2**:684, 687, 689, 711-714; **3**:323; **5**:956, 1399-1406, 1413-1418
- - early print (1482) **2**:726
- - Exodus (14th cent.) **16**:1479
- - Gacon, Samuel, incunabulum **8**:1331
- - Isaiah, Dead Sea Scroll fragment **2**:711
- - Kings, Book of (12th cent. ms.) **10**:1021
- - *Koberger Bible* (15th cent.) **4**:787; **8**:473
- - Koren Bible **15**:1486
- - Nash Papyrus **12**:834
- - *Ninth German Bible* (15th cent.), *see Koberger Bible*
- - *Soncino Bible* (15th cent.) **4**:840
- - Stephanus edition **15**:1484
(4) **Translations, Ancient** **4**:841
- Arabic **4**:863
- - Abu al-Faraj **2**:178
- - Ibn Ghayyat **8**:1176
- - Japheth ben Ali ha-Levi **9**:1286
- - Judeo-Arabic **10**:413
- - Saadiah Gaon **14**:553
- Aramaic (Targumim) **4**:841; **15**:811
- - Aquila and Onkelos **12**:1405
- - Hagiographa **4**:848
- - Jewish literature **11**:312ff
- - Jonathan ben Uzziel **10**:188
- - Joseph ben Ḥiyya **10**:230
- - language **3**:263
- - masoretic notes **16**:1428ff
- - names of God **7**:655
- - Pentateuch **4**:842
- - Prophets **4**:846
- Armenian **4**:861
- Egyptian (Coptic) **4**:861
- Ethiopic **4**:860
- Greek (Septuagint) **4**:851
- - anthropomorphisms **3**:53
- - Aristobulus of Paneas **3**:444
- - Dead Sea Scrolls **5**:1404
- - Jewish literature **11**:312ff
- - Judeo-Greek **10**:425
- - Justinian I **8**:656; **10**:478
- - messianic interpretation **11**:1410
- - Scroll of Esther **14**:1055
- Ladino **10**:1347,1348
- Latin **4**:856
- - Jerome **9**:1377
- - Muenster's Old Testament **12**:506
- - Pagnini, Santes **13**:14
- Syriac (Peshitta and other versions) **4**:858
- - Dead Sea Scrolls **5**:1404
(5) **Translations, Modern** **4**:864
- General
- - Psalms, Book of **13**:1327
- - translators **15**:1318ff
- Arabic **4**:887; **10**:415
- - Susan, Issachar ben Mordecai **15**:532
- Bulgarian **4**:1492; **4**:886
- Catalan **4**:879
- Church Slavonic **4**:884
- Czech and Slovak **4**:884
- Danish **4**:876
- - Wolff, Abraham Alexander **16**:610
- Dutch **4**:876; **6**:316
- English **4**:868
- - Jewish Publication Society of America **10**:81
- - Leeser, Isaac **10**:1562
- - Tyndale, William **15**:1477
- Finnish **4**:878
- French and Provençal **4**:880; **7**:139ff; **10**:424
- - Wogue, Lazare Eliezer **16**:599
- German **4**:872
- - Buber, Martin **4**:1430
- - Haskalah **7**:1433; **7**:1437
- - Herxheimer, Solomon **8**:401
- - Hirsch, S.R. **8**:514ff
- - Luther, Martin **11**:585
- - Mendelssohn, Moses **11**:1339
- - Rosenzweig, Franz **14**:302ff
- Hungarian **8**:1077; **4**:883
- Icelandic **4**:877
- Italian **4**:878; **9**:1101
- - Castelli, David **5**:238
- - Luzzatto, Samuel David **11**:604
- - Pagnini, Santes **13**:14
- - Reggio, Isacco Samuel **14**:38
- Judeo-Italian **9**:1101; **10**:428
- Judeo-Persian **4**:864; **10**:433ff
- - Bābā ibn Nuriel **12**:755
- - Hakham, Simon **7**:1146
- - Jacob ben Joseph Tavus **15**:836
- Judeo-Romance **4**:865
- Judeo-Tatar **4**:865
- Ladino **4**:865; **10**:1343
- Norwegian **4**:877
- Polish **4**:885; **13**:797
- - Neufeld, Daniel **12**:1009
- Portuguese **4**:879
- Romansh (Raeto-Romance) **4**:882
- Rumanian **4**:882; **14**:417
- - Galaction, Gala **7**:256
- Russian and Ukrainian **4**:886; **14**:506
- Serbian and Croatian Wendish **4**:885; **16**:885
- Slavonic **4**:884
- Spanish **4**:878; **15**:247
- - Arragel, Moses **3**:498
- - Usque, Abraham **16**:21
- Swedish **4**:877
- Yiddish **4**:866; **11**:356ff; **16**:798
- - Isaac ben Samson ha-Kohen **9**:28
- - Levita, Elijah **11**:132
- - *Shmuel Bukh* **14**:1426
- - Yehoash **16**:729
- - *Ze'enah u-Re'enah* **16**:967
- Other Languages **4**:887
- - Hebrew **8**:179
- - Judeo-Greek **10**:425
- *illus:*
- - text
- - Arragel, Moses **3**:498
- - Esther, Book of, Yiddish version (17th cent.) **2**:702
- - German translation (1687, Amst.) **3**:820
- - Italian translation **9**:1103
- - JPS Torah translation committee **10**:80
- - Judeo-Persian paraphrase of the Pentateuch (17th and 18th cent.) **2**:733
- - Shaḥin Shirazi's paraphrase of

the Pentateuch **2**:733
-- Targum Onkelos, first edition of Pentateuch with (1482) **4**:1190
(6) **Exegesis and Study 4**:889
- *Contents:*
-- Talmudic Literature **4**:889
-- Medieval Rabbinic Commentaries **4**:890
-- Allegorical Interpretations **4**:895
-- Exegesis Among Jews in Modern Period **4**:899
-- Bible Research and Criticism **4**:903
- General
-- acrostics **2**:229ff
-- *al tikrei* **2**:776
-- antinomian view **3**:68ff
-- Apocrypha and Pseudepigrapha **3**:181; **3**:184ff
-- Assyriology **16**:1509
-- Ben-Asher, Aaron **4**:465ff
-- Ben-Asher, Moses **4**:467ff
-- Cairo *genizah* **16**:1333,1335
-- changes in text **15**:1139
-- Christian Hebraists **2**:948; **8**:9
-- Dead Sea Scrolls **5**:1399
-- Egyptian literature **6**:484
-- Gershom ben Judah Me'or ha-Golah **7**:513
-- glosses **10**:1314
-- *haggahot* **7**:1105
-- *Hapax Legomena* **7**:1318
-- Haskalah **7**:1436
-- Hebrew mss. **11**:900ff
-- historiography **8**:551
-- Josephus **3**:184
-- *Kanah, Book of* **10**:734
-- Karaites **10**:768
-- Mari **11**:981
-- masorah **11**:324; **16**:1401
-- mnemonics **12**:187
-- myth, mythology **12**:729; **12**:730
-- *Okhlah ve-Okhlah* **12**:1353
-- Pentateuch, Samaritan **13**:264
-- Psalms, Apocryphal **13**:1302
-- Samaritans **14**:755
-- Samuel ben Meir **14**:811
-- signs and symbols **14**:1524
-- Sumer **15**:515
-- Synagogue, The Great **15**:630
-- Temple texts **15**:983
-- *tokheḥah* **15**:1192
- Talmudic Literature **4**:889
-- Abba bar Kahana **2**:32
-- Akiva's system **2**:491
-- amoraim's use of **2**:867
-- Bet Hillel and Bet Shammai **4**:740
-- Eleazar ben Azariah **6**:587
-- *halakhah* **7**:1158; **7**:1161
-- halakhic midrash **8**:1414ff; **11**:1521
-- Jewish literature **11**:313ff
-- Johanan ben Zakkai **10**:150
-- Mishnah, use of **12**:95
-- *peshat* **13**:329
-- sages **14**:637
-- *Sifra* **14**:1517
-- *Sifrei* **14**:1519
-- *Sifrei Zuta* **14**:1522
-- *soferim* **15**:79
-- *see also:* AGGADAH; HERMENEUTICS
- Allegorical Interpretations **4**:895
-- Aristobulus of Paneas **3**:443ff
-- Augustine **3**:851
-- Ibn Latif **10**:529
-- Jewish literature **11**:346
-- Jewish philosophy **13**:421; **13**:421ff
-- kabbalistic view **10**:619ff
-- Levi ben Abraham ben Ḥayyim **11**:91
-- Maimonides **11**:773; **12**:78
-- messianic interpretation **11**:1410
-- metaphysics **11**:1442
-- mystical interpretation **10**:570ff
-- Neoplatonic influence **12**:958
-- Philo **3**:184; **13**:426ff
-- Song of Songs **15**:147
-- Therapeutae **15**:1111
-- Zohar **16**:1194ff
-- *see also:* ALLEGORY
- Exegesis among Jews in the Modern Period **4**:899
-- Aḥad Ha-Am **2**:447
-- Buber, Martin **4**:1430
-- Kahana, Abraham **10**:678
- Bible Research and Criticism **4**:903
-- Astruc, Jean **3**:809
-- Bendavid, Lazarus **4**:475
-- Book of the Covenant **4**:1216
-- Cassuto, Umberto **5**:235
-- Chistianity **5**:514
-- Deuteronomy **5**:1573
-- evolution **6**:1000
-- Exodus, Book of **6**:1063ff
-- Geiger, Abraham **16**:575
-- Genesis, Book of **7**:389ff
-- Ginsberg, Harold Louis **7**:580
-- Gunkel, Hermann **7**:977
-- *Hapax Legomena* **7**:1318
-- Hebrew linguistics **16**:1393ff
-- Hoffmann, David Ẓevi **8**:809
-- Holiness Code **8**:820
-- Ibn Ezra, Abraham **8**:1167
-- Isaiah authorship **9**:45
-- Israelite social structure **8**:609
-- Kant, Immanuel **10**:741
-- Kaufmann, Yeḥezkel **16**:1349ff
-- La Peyrère, Isaac **10**:1426
-- miracles **12**:74
-- Numbers, Book of **12**:1252
-- Nuzi tablets **12**:1287ff
-- Protestant universities **13**:1249
-- Psalms, Book of **13**:1311
-- Segal, Moses Hirsch Ẓevi **14**:1107
-- Schorr, Joshua Heschel **14**:997
-- Shazar, Zalman **14**:1326
-- Speiser, Ephraim Avigdor **15**:259
-- Spinoza **13**:454; **15**:279; **15**:282
-- Tur-Sinai **15**:1466
-- Wellhausen, Julius **16**:443
- *illus:*
-- Ben-Asher, Aaron, masoretic lists **4**:466, 541
-- Ben-Naphtali, masoretic lists **4**:541
-- Commandments, the 613 (lists) **5**:761-782
-- Decalogue, Exodus and Deuteronomy versions (table) **5**:1439
-- *Du rappel des Juifs* (1643) **10**:1425
-- Exodus, analysis of the Book (table) **6**:1057
-- Genesis, analysis of the Book (table) **7**:391
-- Genesis, chronology in the Book of (tables) **7**:397-398
-- Genesis, contents of the Book (table) **7**:387
-- Ezra and Nehemiah, contents and historical order of the Book (tables) **6**:1112, 1113
-- Ezekiel, Book of, contents and dates (tables) **6**:1079,1081
-- masoretic lists **4**:466, 541
(7) **Concordances and Dictionaries**
- *Heikhal ha-Kodesh* **11**:865
- Judeo-French **10**:424
- *Kitāb Jāmiʿ al-Alfāẓ* **2**:600; **16**:1356, 1380
- *Makrei Dardekei* **10**:427
- *Mirkevet ha-Mishneh* **3**:34
- *Sefer ha-Meliẓah* **15**:1337
- *see also* Concordances; Dictionaries; ENCYCLOPEDIAS
(8) **Commentators**
- Aaron ben Joseph ha-Kohen Sargado **2**:13
- Abiob, Aaron *(Korban Aharon)* **2**:78
- Abraham ben Dov of Mezhirech *(Ḥesed le-Avraham)* **2**:140
- Abraham ben Solomon *(Midrash Alẓiʾani)* **2**:156
- Abulafia, Abraham *(Mafte'aḥ)* **2**:186
- ʿAdani, Saadiah **2**:250
- Allemanno, Johanan *(Einei ha-Edah)* **2**:646
- Alshekh, Moses *(Torat Moshe)* **2**:759
- Altschuler, Jeḥiel Hillel *(Meẓudat David; Meẓudat Ẓion)* **2**:784
- Anan ben David **2**:921
- Ardit, Solomon *(Leḥem Shelomo)* **3**:400
- Attar, Ḥayyim *(Or ha-Ḥayyim)* **3**:835
- Azikri, Eleazar *(Kol Bokhim)* **3**:1009
- Azulai, Abraham *(Ba'alei Berit Avraham)* **3**:1019
- Baḥya ben Asher ben Ḥlava **4**:104
- Bar Hebraeus, Johanan *(Oẓar Razei)* **4**:222
- Bekhor Shor, Joseph **4**:410
- Ben Zaqen, Samuel *(Peri Eẓ ha-Gan)* **4**:572
- Berdugo, Judah *(Mayim Amukkim; Mikveh Mayim)* **4**:591
- Berdugo, Moses *(Kenaf Renanim)* **4**:591
- Berdugo, Raphael *(Mei Menuḥot)* **4**:592
- Berlin, Naphtali Ẓevi Judah *(Ha'amek Davar)* **4**:661
- Bloch, Mattathias **4**:1108
- Boskowitz, Ḥayyim *(Toẓe'ot Ḥayyim)* **4**:1263
- Bukarat, Abraham *(Sefer ha-Zikkaron)* **4**:1469
- Caro, Isaac *(Toledot Yiẓḥak)* **5**:193
- David ben Boaz **5**:1349
- Della Torre, Lelio **5**:1476
- Duran, Profiat *(Ma'aseh Efod)* **6**:301
- Ehrlich, Arnold Bogumil **6**:512
- Eliezer ben Reuben Kahana *(Si'aḥ Sefunim)* **9**:1295
- Eliezer of Beaugency **6**:630
- Elijah ben Solomon Zalman **6**:657
- Epstein, Kalonymus Kalman *(Ma'or va-Shemesh)* **6**:834
- Ettinger, Joseph *(Edut bi-Yhosef)* **6**:952
- Farissol, Abraham **6**:1184
- Ferber, Ẓevi Hirsch *(Kerem ha-Ẓevi)* **6**:1226
- Foa, Eliezer Naḥman *(Goren Ornan)* **6**:1369
- Gibbor, Judah *(Minḥat Yehudah)* **7**:549; **10**:620
- Gordon, Samuel Leib **7**:805
- Hananel ben Hushiel **7**:1253
- Hezekiah ben Manoah *(Ḥizzekuni)* **8**:459
- Hirsch, S. R. **8**:513
- Hirschler, Pal **8**:528
- Hoeshke, Reuben *(Yalkut Re'uveni)* **10**:640
- Homberg, Naphtali Herz *(Ha-Korem)* **8**:942
- Ibn Balʿam, Judah *(Kitab al-Tārjiḥ)* **8**:1156
- Ibn Ezra, Abraham **8**:1166
- Ibn Yaḥya, David **8**:1207
- Jacob ben Asher **9**:1214
- Jacob of Vienna **9**:1234
- Jeiteles, Aaron ben Baer *(Zera Aharon)* **9**:1330
- Joel ibn Shuaib *(Doresh Tov)* **8**:1201
- Joseph Moses of Salositz *(Berit Avraham)* **10**:246
- Kara, Joseph **10**:759
- Kimḥi, Joseph *(Sefer ha-Torah)* **10**:1006
- Kirimi, Abraham *(Sefat Emet)* **10**:1046
- Krengel, Menahem Mendel **10**:1260
- Laniado, Abraham **10**:1422
- Levi ben Gershom **11**:94
- Luzzatto, Samuel David **11**:605
- Malbim **11**:823
- Mat, Moses *(Ho'il Moshe)* **11**:1121
- *Me-Am Lo'ez* **5**:1154; **11**:1158
- Meklenburg, Jacob Ẓevi *(Ha-Ketav ve-ha-Kabbalah)* **11**:1271
- Melamed, Raḥamim Reuven *(Kisse Raḥamim)* **11**:1276
- Menahem ben Helbo **11**:1304
- Mendelssohn, Moses *(Biur)* **7**:1438
- Moses ben Jacob of Coucy *(Peshatei ha-Ram mi-Coucy)* **12**:420
- Naḥmanides **12**:777
- Najara, Moses *(Lekaḥ Tov)* **12**:797
- Nathanson Joseph Saul **12**:868
- Nissim ben Reuben Gerondi **12**:1186
- Norzi, Jedidiah *(Minḥat Shai)* **12**:1229; **16**:1477
- Philo **13**:410ff
- Porto, Abraham Menahem *(Minḥah Belulah)* **13**:913, 915
- Rashi **13**:1559ff
- Samuel ben Meir (Rashbam) **14**:810
- Sforno **14**:1210
- Shalom ben Joseph Shabbazi *(Midrash Ḥemdat Yamim)* **10**:553
- Silberstein, David Judah Leib *(Shevilei David)* **14**:1535
- Solomon Astruc of Barcelona *(Midrashei ha-Torah)* **7**:336
- Solomon ibn Melek *(Lekket Shikḥah; Mikhlal Yofi)* **2**:67
- Sorotzkin, Zalman *(Oznayim la-Torah)* **15**:167
- Spinka, Joseph Meir Weiss of *(Imrei Yosef)* **15**:275
- Spira, Nathan **15**:284
- Tanhum ben Eliezer *(Menuhat Emet)* **15**:796
- Tanḥum ben Joseph ha-Yerushalmi **15**:797
- Teomim, Aryeh Leib *(Ya'alat Ḥen)* **15**:1010
- Tibbon, Moses ben Samuel ibn **15**:1130
- Tibbon, Samuel ben Judah ibn **13**:444; **15**:1130ff
- Toledano, Jacob **15**:1195
- Trunk, Isaac Judah *(Mikra Meforash)* **15**:1414
- Vivanti, David Abraham **16**:197
- Wessely **16**:462ff
- Zechariah al-Dāhiri *(Ẓeidah la-Derekh)* **15**:959
- *Ẓe'enah u-Re'enah* **16**:967
- *see also:* LA'AZ; SUPERCOMMENTARIES ON THE PENTATEUCH
- *illus:*
-- text
-- Arama, Isaac ben Moses, Deuteronomy (1521) **5**:1583
-- *Ḥizzekuni* (1559) **8**:459
-- Ibn Ezra, Abraham, Exodus (1488) **8**:1332
-- Kimḥi, David, Book of Psalms (1487) **8**:1329
-- Levi ben Gershom
--- Deuteronomy (1546) **5**:1580
--- Exodus (1546) **6**:1065
--- Kimḥi, David, and: Former Prophets (1495) **8**:1334
-- *Me-Am Lo'ez* (1751) **5**:1154;

13:1108
-- *Megillat Setarim* (1553) **8:**1190
-- Naḥmanides' *Ḥiddushei ha-Torah* (1489) **8:**1329; **12:**775
-- Rashi, first edition of Pentateuch (1482) **4:**1190; **14:**38; **15:**1483
-- *Sefer ha-Mivḥar ve-Tov ha-Misḥar* (1835) **10:**767
-- *Ẓemaḥ David* (1785) **8:**1156
(9) **Concepts and Ideas**
- adultery **2:**313
- anthropomorphism **3:**51ff
- Commandments, the 613 **5:**760f
- cruelty to animals **3:**5;
- death **2:**952
- demons, demonology **5:**1522
- economic history **16:**1267
- ethics **6:**922
- evil **7:**775
- eschatology **6:**861ff
- holiness **10:**866
- Jewish identity **10:**53
- idolatry **8:**1227ff
- *kiddush* and *ḥillul ha-Shem* **10:**977
- justice and mercy of God **7:**669
- love **11:**523
- magic **11:**703; **11:**711
- miracles **12:**73ff
- monotheism **12:**260ff
- oaths **12:**1297ff
- prophets and prophecy **13:**1151ff
- providence **13:**1279
- repentance **14:**73
- resurrection **14:**97
- revelation **14:**117
- *Ru'aḥ ha-Kodesh* **14:**364ff
- Sabbath **14:**558
- sacrifices **14:**605ff
- *shikkuẓ shomem* **2:**98
- sin **14:**1587
- soul, immortality of **15:**174
- theology **15:**1104ff
- wisdom **16:**557ff
- *see also under individual biblical themes*
(10) **Religious Impact 4:**915
- In Judaism **4:**915; **10:**387
-- age for study **15:**456
-- Ashkenazi outlook **3:**720
-- education **6:**399ff
-- Greek philosophy **3:**444ff
-- homiletics **8:**948ff
-- Jewish tradition **8:**714; **15:**1309ff
-- Karaites **10:**761; **10:**768; **10:**777
-- liturgy **11:**392
-- *mishpat ivri* **12:**110; **12:**116
-- Orthodoxy **12:**1489ff
-- prayer **13:**978ff
-- preaching **13:**994
-- Reform Judaism **13:**571; **14:**25ff
-- Samaritans **14:**739
- In Christianity **4:**922; **5:**508
-- Paul of Tarsus **13:**190; **13:**191ff
-- Reformation **14:**19
- In Islam **4:**927
-- Islamic polemics **9:**101
-- Koran **10:**1196
-- Muhammad **12:**508
- *see also under individual biblical figures and themes*
(11) **In the Arts 4:**932
- Literature **4:**932
-- *akedah* **2:**484
-- Arthurian legends **3:**653ff
-- Blake, William **4:**1070
-- Bulgarian literature **4:**1492
-- Canadian literature **5:**115
-- children's literature **5:**429
-- Czechoslovak literature **5:**1205
-- drama, Hebrew **6:**195
-- Dutch literature **6:**316
-- English literature **6:**773
-- fiction, Hebrew **6:**1262
-- folklore **6:**1376
-- French literature **7:**139ff
-- German and Austrian literature **7:**439ff
-- Hebrew literature **8:**179
-- Hungarian literature **8:**1077
-- Italian literature **9:**1101
-- Jewish literature **11:**308
-- Judeo-Persian literature **10:**433ff
-- Ladino literature **10:**1343
-- Lamentations **10:**1375
-- *Maccabees, Fourth Book of* **11:**662
-- Polish literature **13:**797
-- Proverbs **13:**1264ff
-- Psalms **13:**1325
-- Rumanian literature **14:**417
-- Russian literature **14:**506
-- Scandinavian literature **14:**928ff
-- Song of Songs **15:**151
-- South African literature **15:**207
-- Spanish and Portuguese literature **15:**247
-- theater **15:**1049
-- U.S. literature **15:**1568ff
-- Yiddish literature **16:**800; **16:**802
- Music **4:**937
-- musical sources **12:**559,577
- Art **4:**937
-- Dura-Europos **6:**276
-- iconography **8:**1216ff
-- Psalms, Book of **13:**1326
- Islamic Art **4:**941
- Illustrated Bibles **4:**942
- Illuminated Hebrew Manuscripts **4:**950
-- *Aberdeen Bible* **8:**1270
-- *Aich Latin Bible* **8:**1267
-- *Ambrosian Bible* **8:**1267
-- artistic representation **3:**508ff
-- *Ashburnham Pentateuch* **8:**1258
-- *Bible of Borso d'Este* **8:**1270
-- *Bible of the Hispanic Society of America* **8:**1265
-- *Bible of Jean de Papeleu* **14:**524
-- *Bishop Bedell Bible* **8:**1268
-- *Cervera Bible* **8:**1260
-- *Damascus Keter* **8:**1261
-- *Haggadot* **7:**1096
-- Hebrew MSS **11:**900ff
-- *Kennicott Bible* **8:**1260
-- *Keter* **4:**465
-- *Lisbon Bible* **8:**1261
-- *Reuchlin Bible* **8:**1261
-- *Second Gaster Bible* **8:**1263
-- *Second Leningrad Bible* **8:**1261
-- Yemenite Bibles **8:**1263
-- *see also:* ILLUMINATED MANUSCRIPTS, HEBREW
- *illus:*
-- text
-- *Aberdeen Bible* (15th cent.) **8:**1284
-- *Admont Bible* (12th cent.) **14:**520
-- *Aelfric Heptateuch* (11th cent.) **5:**370,1014,1016; **9:**1193; **12:**963
-- *Aelfric Paraphrase* (11th cent.), *see Aelfric Heptateuch*
-- *Alba Bible* (15th cent.) **2:**58; **3:**498; **5:**1278; **6:**854; **8:**335
-- *Ambrosian Bible* (13th cent.) **4:**360; **5:**1018; **8:**1279
-- *Amiens Picture Bible* (12th cent.) **9:**1373; **10:**100,106,1021,1028
-- Amos, Book of *(Conradin Bible)* **2:**880; **12:**1293
-- *Ashburnham Pentateuch* (7th cent.) **2:**952; **8:**1271; **12:**1197
-- Baruch, Book of **14:**1
-- *Bible of Charles the Bald* (9th cent.) **9:**1
-- *Bible of Citeaux* (12th cent.) **8:**1149
-- *Bible of Erzwka* (1269) **5:**1437
-- *Bible of Saint Martial of Limoges* (12th cent.) **5:**1
-- *Biblia Pauperum* (15th cent.) **4:**523
-- *Bibliothèque Nationale Pentateuch* **11:***fcg.* 1355
-- *Bishop Bedell Bible* (1284) **5:**523; **8:**1281
-- *Cervera Bible* (14th cent.) **2:**642; **5:**313, 1002; **16:***fcg.* 935
-- Chronicles I *(Lisbon Bible)* **5:**519
-- Chronicles II *(Bible of Saint Martial of Limoges)* **5:**1
-- *Coburg Pentateuch* (14th cent.) **6:***fcg.* 427; **12:**1251
-- *Coimbra Bible* (14th cent.) **5:**695
-- *Cologne Bible* **10:**289; **13:**361
-- *Conradin Bible* (14th cent.) **2:**880; **7:**113,1270; **8:**1013 **11:**659,814
-- *Damascus Keter* (1260) **5:**1238
-- Daniel, Book of (1331) **5:**1280
-- *De Castro Pentateuch* (14th cent.) **7:**396; **10:**1371
-- Deuteronomy *(Ambrosian Bible)* **5:**1018,1575
-- *Duke of Sussex Pentateuch* (c. 1300) **4:**181; **5:***fcg.* 1323; **12:***fcg.* 1259
-- Ecclesiastes, opening page *(Duke of Sussex Pentateuch)* **5:***fcg.* 1323; **6:**350
-- eleventh cent. illum. ms., Cairo **3:***fcg.* 524
-- *Erzwka Bible* **15:**533
-- *Espejo de Vidas* (1720) **10:**1361
-- Esther Scrolls, illuminated **3:**541,543, **6:**1399; **9:**1101; **10:**1313; **13:**1388-1389; **14:**1049-1056
-- Exodus, opening page (13th cent.) **8:**1271
-- Ezra, Book of (12th cent.) **8:**1149
-- *Farḥi Bible* (14th cent.) **6:***fcg.* 1195; **8:**1277
-- fifteenth cent. Dutch illum. ms. **10:**447
-- *First Gaster Bible* **8:***fcg.* 951
-- *First Leningrad Bible* (10th cent.) **3:***fcg.* 524
-- Genesis, first page of the Book *(De Castro Pentateuch)* **7:**396
-- Genesis ms., Yemen 1496 **11:**903
-- *Hispanic Society Bible* (15th cent.) **13:**923
-- *Holkham Bible* (14th cent.) **5:**1066; **10:**1365
-- Hosea, Book of, a page (13th cent.) **8:**1013
-- Isaiah, Book of **9:***fcg.* 43
-- Job, Book of **10:***fcg.* 107
-- Jonah, Book of **15:**1
-- Joshua, Book of, opening page (1442) **5:**159
-- Joshua ben Abraham ibn Gaon's Bible (14th cent.) **5:**47,48
-- *Joshua Roll* (10th cent.) **3:**517; **10:**267,269
-- Judeo-Persian Pentateuch **12:**395
-- Karaite (10th cent.) **8:**1273
-- *Kennicott Bible* (15th cent.) **3:**525,787; **5:***fcg.* 971,1336; **10:**171
-- *Keter Aram Ẓova* **11:**901
-- *Lambeth Bible* (12th cent.) **14:**915
-- Lamentations, Book of **10:**1371
-- Latin Bible (1197) **13:**467; **12:**733
-- *León Bible* (1162) **2:**175; **3:**461; **5:**1328,1426,1436; **6:**633,636,666; **9:**1349,1369; **10:**1024; **12:**386
-- Leviticus, Book of (1290) **11:**145
-- *Lisbon Bible* (15th cent.) **4:**541; **5:**519,862; **8:**1278; **11:***fcg.* 299
-- *Morgan Picture Bible* (13th cent.) **2:**860; **3:**30; **7:**567; **9:**1342; **10:**184; **11:**1493; **12:**736,818; **14:**781
-- *Moulins Bible* (12th cent. illum. ms., Fr.) **10:**1313
-- *Moutier-Grandval Bible* (9th cent.) **10:**266
-- ninth century ms. **11:**900
-- Numbers, Book of **12:***fcg.* 1259
-- Octateuchs, Byzantine (11th and 12th cent.) **3:**439 **4:**122,786; **5:**1020,1172; **6:**476,575,1369, **10:**1526; **13:**1514
-- *Parma Bible* (14th cent.) **9:***fcg.* 43
-- *Perpignan Bible* (13th cent.) **4:**977; **13:**300
-- *Regensburg Pentateuch* (c. 1300) **3:**754; **4:**67; **14:***fcg.* 1323
-- *Reuchlin Bible* (13th cent.) **8:**1271
-- *San Isidoro Bible* (12th cent.), *see León Bible*
-- *Schocken Bible* (13th cent.) **7:***fcg.* 395
-- Scroll of Esther, paper-cuts **13:**63
-- *Second Leningrad Bible* (11th cent.) **5:***fcg.* 43; **8:**1273; **11:**904
-- Simon ben Samuel's Bible (1442) **5:**159
-- Song of Songs, opening page *(Tripartite Maḥzor)* **2:**355; **11:***fcg.* 683; **15:**99,145
-- *Stavordale Bible* (12th cent.) **4:**64
-- *Veleslavinova Bible* **8:**1135
-- *Vienna Genesis* (6th cent.) **2:**122,364,956; **3:**515; **4:**524, 730; **5:**1423; **6:**209,240,809; **9:**3,1171,1208; **10:**329; **13:**363,934,1525, **14:**105
-- *Winchester Bible* (12th cent.) **8:**1
-- Yemenite Pentateuch (1469) **8:**1273; **16:***fcg.*743
-- Zephaniah, Book of **16:**49
-- *see also under individual biblical figures and themes*
-- *see also* ANIMALS OF THE BIBLE AND TALMUD; ART (Biblical Themes); BIBLE SOCIETIES; BOOK OF THE COVENANT; ILLUMINATED MANUSCRIPTS, HEBREW; PENTATEUCH; TORAH
Bible, Lost Books of
- Book of Jashar **4:**1217
- Book of the Wars of the Lord **4:**1218
- Books of the Chronicles of the Kings of Judah and Israel **4:**1236
Bible as Read and Preached in the Old Synagogue (wk.) **16:**1338
Bible Contest for Jewish Youth, International (Isr.), *see* International Bible Contest for Jewish Youth
Bible de Jérusalem **4:**871
Bible Historiée le Roy (c. 1479, illum. print, Lyons)
- *illus:* **6:**676
Bible Masorah, *see* MASORAH
Bible of Charles the Bald (9th cent. illum. ms., Rheims) **9:**1
Bible of Citeaux (12th cent. illum. ms.)
- *illus:* **8:**1149
Bible of Erzwka (Arm. illum. ms., 1269)
- *illus:* **5:**1437; **15:**533
Bible of Saint Martial of Limoges (12th cent., illum. ms., Fr.)
- *illus:* **5:**1
BIBLE SOCIETIES **4:**969
Bible study **4:**917ff
Bible Study Association (Isr.) **9:**900
Bible Translation Society **4:**969
Biblia Hebraica **4:**840
BIBLIANDER, THEODOR **4:**970
- Christian Hebraists **8:**25
Biblia Pauperum (15th cent. illum. ms.)
- *illus:* **4:**523

Biblia Pentapla **4:**875
Biblia Regia (16th cent.) **3:**434
Biblical Hebrew, *see* HEBREW LANGUAGE
Biblical Research Society (Isr.) **9:**965
Biblical theology **4:**909ff
Biblical Zoo (Jer.) **9:**1496
Bibliographia Kabbalistica (wk.) **7:**1413
BIBLIOGRAPHY **4:**970
- Aguilar, Moses Raphael d' **2:**429
- auxiliary law literature **12:**118
- Bartolocci, Giulio **4:**265
- Ḥasidism **7:**1413
- Jewish literature **11:**350
- *see also:* ENCYCLOPEDIAS; KIRJATH SEPHER
Bibliography of Jewish Bibliographies (wk.) **4:**972; **16:**1156
BIBLIOPHILES **4:**973
- Adler, Elkan Nathan **2:**275
- Almanzi, Joseph **2:**661
- Bamberger, Fritz **4:**152
- Chasanowich, Joseph **5:**362
- Oppenheim, David ben Abraham **12:**1421
- Sassoon, David Solomon **14:**899
- Schocken, Salman **14:**986
Biblioteca Judía Contemporanea **14:**498 (publ., Arg.)
Biblioteca Nazionale (Turin) **8:**1322
Bibliotheca Friedlandiana (Rus.) **8:**1322
Bibliotheca Hebraea (wk.) **4:**265; **4:**971; **12:**1421
Bibliotheca Judaica (wk.) **4:**971
Bibliotheca Latina-Hebraica (wk.) **4:**265
Bibliotheca Magna Rabbinica (wk.) **4:**265; **4:**970
Bibliotheca Palatina (It.) **8:**1322
Bibliotheca rabbinica ordine alphabetico disposita (wk.) **4:**970
Bibliotheca Rosenthaliana (library, Amst.) **2:**903; **2:**904; **14:**294
BIBLIOTHÈQUE NATIONALE (library, Fr.) **4:**976
- incunabula **8:**1322
Bibliothèque Nationale Pentateuch (ms.) **11:***fcg.* 1355; **15:**110
Bibo, Solomon **12:**1038
Bibring, Greta **13:**1340
Bick (fam.) **4:**1398
BICK, JACOB SAMUEL **4:**977
Bickel, Alexander **4:**977; **10:**1505
BICKEL, SHLOMO **4:**977
BICKELS-SPITZER, ZVI **4:**978
BICKERMAN, ELIAS JOSEPH **4:**978
- Hellenism **8:**291
Bicurim (publ. house, Rum.) **5:**454; **14:**414; **16:**1135
BIDACHE (vill., Fr.) **4:**978
- Bayonne community **4:**351
Biddeford (city, Me.) **11:**782
Biddū (loc., Er. Isr.) **14:**1630
Biddūn (mus., Iraq) **8:**1461
Biden, Louis H. **2:**821
Biderman, Morris **15:**1263
Bidermanas, Israel, *see* IZIS
Bidermann, J. Gottlieb **8:**25
BIDNEY. DAVID **4:**979
- anthropology **3:**40
BIE, OSCAR **12:**683
BIEBER, HUGO **4:**979
Bieber, Isadore **15:**311
BIEBER, MARGARETE **4:**979
Bieber, Philip **15:**310
Bieberstein, Marek **5:**1038
Biebrich (tn., Ger.) **16:**507
Biecz (tn., Pol.) **7:**812
BIEDERMANN, MICHAEL LAZAR **4:**980
- textiles **15:**1040
BIEGELEISEN, HENRYK **4:**980
Biegeleisen-Zelazowski, Bronislaw **4:**980
BIEL (tn., Sp.) **4:**981
BIEL (tn., Switz.) **4:**981
Bielchowsky (mfr., Pol.) **15:**1040
BIELEFELD (city, Ger.) **4:**981
Bielitz (tn., Pol.), *see* BIELSKO
Biella (loc., It.) **16:**108
Bielschowsky, Albert **7:**451; **7:**690
BIELSK (Bielsk Podlaski; tn., Pol.) **4:**981
Bielski brothers (partisans) **13:**146
BIELSKO (tn., Pol.) **4:**982
- *see also:* BIALA
Bien, Herman M. **4:**983; **5:**988; **12:**1017
BIEN, JULIUS **4:**982
BIENENFELD, FRANZ RUDOLF **4:**983
Bienenfeld, Von (fam.) **7:**68
BIENENSTOCK, MAX **4:**983
- Jewish National Assembly **15:**445
Bienne (tn., Switz.), *see* BIEL
BIENSTOK, JUDAH LEIB **4:**984
Bienveniste (fam.), *see* BENVENISTE
Bien Venu Raffe, *see* BENEVENUTUS GRAPHEUS HIEROSOLYMITANUS
BIERER, RUBIN **4:**984
- Birnbaum, Nathan **4:**1040
- Shomer Israel **14:**1458
Bierkamp, Walter **8:**869
BIESENTHAL, JOHANN HEINRICH **4:**985
Biesheim (tn., Fr.) **2:**754
Biez, Jacques de **3:**85
BIGAMY AND POLYGAMY **4:**985
- Bulgarian Romaniots **4:**1482
- concubine **5:**864
- Gershom ben Judah **7:**512
- *ḥaliẓah* in Ashkenaz **11:**127
- legal and illegal relationship **5:**363
- levirate liability **11:**123
- reasons for disuse **14:**1356
- Sanhedrin, French **14:**841
- *takkanah* **15:**725
- woman's place **16:**626
- *see also:* MONOGAMY
Bigman, Stanley **15:**68
Bigthan (bib. fig.) **12:**308
Bigvai (bib. fig.) **6:**1040
Bigvai (satrap, Judea), *see* BAGOHI
Bihalji, Pavle **4:**990; **16:**889
BIHALJI MERIN, OTO **4:**990
BIHARI, ALEXANDER **4:**990
- *illus:* text
Bijeljina (tn., Yug.) **16:**872
Bijo, Ezra **2:**564
BIJUR, NATHAN **4:**991
- *The American Hebrew* **2:**821
Bik, Abraham **14:**1531
Bikat Bet Netofah (valley, Isr.) **9:**589
Bikat Iksalo (Er. Isr.), *see* Plain of Exaloth
BIKAYAM, MEIR BEN ḤALIFA **4:**991
- Shabbateanism **14:**1245
BIKEL, THEODORE MEIR **15:**1078
- recordings **13:**1617
BIKERMAN, JACOB JOSEPH **4:**992
BIKERMAN, JOSEPH **4:**992
Bikhowsky (indus.) **4:**119
Bikhowsky, Elisheva (poet), *see* ELISHEVA
Bikhowsky, Simeon (writ.) **6:**671
Bikhrah, *see* CAMEL
Bikhri, Judah **16:**1552
Bikhri, Moses ibn Judah **16:**1552
Bikkoret ha-Ittim (period.) **1:**newsp. list
Bikkoret u-Farshanut (journ.) **1:**newsp. list
Bikkure Hayam, The First Fruits of the West (monthly, Jam.) **3:**699
BIKKUREI HA-ITTIM (annuals) **4:**992
- statistics **1:**newsp. list
- Cohen, Shalom **5:**685
- Hebrew literature **8:**183
- Hebrew newspapers **12:**1048
- *Me'assef* **11:**1161
Bikkurei ha-Ittim ha-Ḥadashim (journ.) **1:**newsp. list
Bikkurei ha-Shanah (almanac) **1:**newsp. list
Bikkurei Ribal (wk.) **11:**119
Bikkurei To'elet (almanac) **1:**newsp. list
Bikkur Ḥolim (hospital, Isr.) **14:**674
- *illus:*
- - Jerusalem Old City **9:**983
- - newborn babies **9:**993
Bikkur ḥolim, *see* SICK, VISITING THE
Bikkurim (period.) **1:**newsp. list **12:**1048
BIKKURIM (tract.) **4:**993
- *illus:* text
Bikkurim, *see* FIRST FRUITS
Bikur Cholim (syn., N.Y.C.) **12:**1081
Bikurim (publ. house), *see* Bicurim
Bilad (Bilar; demon) **5:**1531
- *illus:*
- - seal (print., 1807) **5:**1527
BILBEIS (tn., Egy.) **4:**994
- forced conversions **11:**835
Bibūl, Ya'qûb **12:**1464; **12:**1465
Bildad (bib. fig.) **10:**113
- *illus:*
- - consoling Job (W. Blake) **4:**934
BILDERSEE, ADELE **4:**994
Bileam (city, Er. Isr.), *see* IBLEAM
BILETZKI, ISRAEL ḤAYYIM **4:**995
Bilgah (Bilgai, pr. fam.) **9:**1390; **12:**89; **12:**91; **13:**1087
BILGORAJ (tn., Pol.) **4:**995
Bilgradi, Jacob Israel **13:**583
BILHAH (bib. fig.) **4:**996
- Jacob **9:**1192ff
- *Naphtali, Testament of* **12:**821
- Rachel **13:**1487ff
- Reuben **14:**106
- tribes of **15:**1384
- *see also:* PATRIARCHS
Bilhah (city, Er. Isr.) **4:**1
Bilharzia (disease), *see* Schistosomiasis
Bilia, David ibn, *see* IBN BILIA, DAVID BEN YOM TOV
Bilid (demon), *see* Bilad
Bilitz (tn., Pol.), *see* BIELSKO
Bilitz, Samuel **8:**421
BILL-BELOTSERKOVSKI, VLADIMIR NAUMOVICH **4:**996
Billiards **15:**304
BILLIG, LEVI **4:**997
Billik, Jacob **5:**1036
BILLIKOPF, JACOB **4:**997
Billingkoff, Morris **15:**306
Billings (city, Mont.) **12:**266
Bill of exchange **14:**1389
BILLROTH, THEODOR **4:**997
- Verein zur Abwehr **16:**111
Billui Na'im (journ.) **1:**newsp. list
Billy Rose Art Garden (Jer.) **2:**817; **3:**649; **9:**1013; **12:**552; **14:**267
Biloxi (city, Miss.) **12:**154
Bilquis (Isl. name) **13:**1424
Bilshan (bib. fig.) **6:**1040; **12:**309; **15:**629; **16:**1000
Bilsky, Lillian, *see* Freiman, Lillian
Bilsky, Moses **7:**135; **12:**1521
Bilthoven (vill., Holl.) **16:**37
BILTMORE PROGRAM **4:**997
- American Jewish Committee **2:**824
- Ben-Gurion **4:**509
- Histadrut controversy **9:**859
- Israel historical survey **9:**354
- U. S. Zionism **16:**1144
- Zionism **16:**1059
- Zionist Congress **16:**1175
- Zionist General Council **9:**662
- *illus.*
- - conference **15:**1633
Biltu (coin), *see* Talent
BILU (mvmt.) **4:**998
- absorption in Israel **9:**515ff
- Belkind, Israel **4:**438ff
- charter of **16:**1038
- historical list **8:**766-767
- Idelovitch, David **8:**1223
- philanthropy **13:**389
- *illus:*
- - Belkind, Israel **4:**439
- - Belkind, Shimshon **4:**439
- - Ḥisin, Ḥayyim **8:**534
- - Meerovitch, Menashe **2:**833
- - stamp **9:***fcg.* 843
Bilu (training farm, Rus.) **8:**250
Bilu'im Ḥadashim (orgn., Rus.) **16:**971
BIMAH (syn. platform) **4:**1002
- synagogue **15:**593; **15:**601ff
- Torah reading **15:**1253
- *illus:*
- - text
- - Aleppo synagogue **2:**563
- - Amsterdam Liberal synagogue **12:**991
- - Amsterdam Portuguese synagogue **15:**616
- - B'nai Israel synagogue **15:**626
- - Bombay, Kneseth Elijah Synagogue **4:**1193
- - Bombay, Magen David Synagogue **4:**1193
- - Chorazin synagogue **3:**326
- - Cracow Alte Schul **15:**604
- - Ernakulam, Theckoobagam synagogue **5:**625
- - Fez synagogue **14:**1183
- - Florence synagogue **15:**620-621
- - Ghardaia synagogue **15:**615
- - Grodno wooden synagogue **7:**927
- - Ḥurvah Synagogue, Jerusalem **9:**1445
- - Istanbuli Synagogue, Jerusalem **9:**1444
- - Johanan ben Zakkai Synagogue, Jerusalem **9:**1444
- - Jurbarkas synagogue **11:**365
- - Kaifeng synagogue **5:**471
- - Kingston (Jam.) **9:**1274
- - Lancut synagogue **15:**607
- - Leghorn, old synagogue **9:**1139
- - Livingston, Essex County, Temple Beth Shalom **6:**903
- - London, Bevis Marks **15:**620-621
- - Lublin, Maharshal Shul **11:**545
- - Oklahoma synagogue **12:**1354
- - Padua synagogue **13:**9; **15:**616
- - Pesaro synagogue **15:**617
- - Pinsk synagogue **15:**609
- - Porat Joseph Synagogue, Jerusalem **13:**329
- - Safed synagogue **14:**631
- - Santiago synagogue **14:**848
- - Siena synagogue **14:**1514
- - Sulzbach synagogue **15:**507
- - Tarnow synagogue **15:**820
- - Venice synagogue **9:**1135; **16:**99
- - Wolpa synagogue **15:**610
- - Zabludow synagogue **15:**611
- - Zamosc synagogue **16:**927
- - Zholkva synagogue **16:**1014
Bimat ha-Ḥovevim (period.) **1:**newsp. list

Bimat ha-Saḥkanim (theat., Isr.) **15:**1062
BIMKO, FISHEL **4:**1006
Binah (*Amidah* ben.) **2:**840
Binah (kab. conc.) **10:**570ff
Binans, Jean François de **8:**25
Binder (Torah orn.) **5:**288
BINDER, ABRAHAM WOLF **4:**1006
Binder, Alexander, *see* PANA, ȘASA
Binding of Isaac, *see* AKEDAH
Bindings, Book, *see* BOOKS
Bindrim, Johann Georg **8:**25
Binet (Bineter; fam.), *see* BANET
BING (fam.) **4:**1006
Bing, Abraham **4:**1007
Bing, Abraham (19th cent., r.) **14:**156
Bing, Albert **4:**1007
Bing, Andrew, *see* Byng, Andrew
Bing, Baer **8:**258
Bing, Herman **14:**928
Bing, Isaac (print.) **7:**216
Bing, Isaac ben Baruch (Safed) **4:**1007
BING, ISAAC BEN SAMUEL **4:**1007
– Elisha Ḥayyim ben Jacob Ashkenazi **6:**670
– printing **13:**1108
Bing, Joseph **4:**1007
Bing, Richard **11:**1200
Bing, Seligmann **4:**1007
– Luria family **11:**569
– Mintz, Moses **12:**66
– Oppenheim family **12:**1419
Bing, Solomon **4:**1007
Binge (court Js.), *see* BING
Binge, Andrew, *see* Byng, Andrew
BINGEN (tn., Ger.) **4:**1007
– Adam Ba'al Shem **2:**247
– archives **3:**387
– Bing family **4:**1006
– Mintz, Moses **12:**66
– *illus:* text
– – *traustein* ("marriage stone") **11:**1041
Bingen, Jacques **13:**148
Binghamton (city, N.Y.) **12:**1126
Bingo (game) **7:**301
Bin-Gorion, Emanuel **4:**595ff; **6:**734
Bin-Gorion, Micha Josef, *see* BERDYCZEWSKI, MICHA JOSEF
Binnenstock, M., *see* BIENENSTOCK, MAX
Bin-Nun, Yoḥai **13:**48
"Binocle" (writ.), *see* SOBEL, JACOB ẒEVI
Binswanger, Harry S. **4:**1009
BINSWANGER, ISIDORE **4:**1009
Binswanger, Lewis **4:**1009
Binswanger, Samuel **4:**1009
Binyamin, H. **16:**825
BINYAMINAH (vill., Isr.) **4:**1009
– statistics **1:**place list
Binyan (fam.) **13:**918
Binyan (pub., Isr.) **8:**1241
Binyan av (hermeneutical rule) **8:**368
Binyenei ha-Ummah (convention center, Jer.) **9:**1494; **9:**1519
– *illus:*
– – exhibitions and concert hall **9:**1488
– – main auditorium **3:**353
– – Zionist Congress **16:**1175
Binyan ha-Bayit (wk.) **2:**784
Binyan va-Ḥaroshet (journ.) **1:**newsp. list
"Binyominke Moser", *see* Goldberg, Benjamin
Biogeography **7:**422
BIOGRAPHIES AND AUTOBIOGRAPHIES **4:**1010
– *Contents:*
– – Medieval Literature **4:**1010
– – Hagiography **4:**1010
– – Historiography **4:**1011
– – Legendary Autobiography **4:**1011
– – Modena, Leone **4:**1012
– – Other Elements **4:**1012
– – Memoirs **4:**1012
– – Modern Times **4:**1012
– – Lexicons **4:**1013
– auxiliary law literature **12:**118
– Haskalah **7:**1444
– Hosea **8:**1011ff
– Jewish literature **11:**351ff
– *see also:* FICTION, HEBREW; HEBREW LITERATURE, MODERN
BIOLOGY **4:**1015
– *Contents:*
– – Bible and Talmud **4:**1015
– – – Reproduction **4:**1015
– – – Embryology **4:**1019
– – – Heredity **4:**1021
– – – Ecology **4:**1027
– – Middle Ages and Modern **4:**1030
– – – 19th Century **4:**1030
– – – Modern Period **4:**1031
– evolution **6:**1000
– research in Israel **16:**438
– *illus:* text
Biona del Maestre, *see* DESMAESTRE, JONAH
Biow, Milton H. **2:**317
Biqā', al- (loc., Leb.) **9:**924
Bira (fam.), *see* ADOLPHUS
Bīra (loc., Iraq) **8:**1447
Bira (tn., Er. Isr.), *see* Al-Bira
BIRAM, ARTHUR (Yiẓḥak) **4:**1033
Biran, Abraham **3:**303; **5:**1260
BIRANIT (kib., Isr.) **4:**1033
– Galilee **7:**270
– statistics **1:**place list
– *illus:*
– – land reclamation project **9:**559
Birat Satia (vill., Er. Isr.) **12:**317
Bīr Ayyūb (well, Er. Isr.) **6:**800
Bircherod, J. **8:**25
Birck, Sixtus **10:**459; **15:**533
Birds
– Commandments, the 613 **5:**767ff
– consecration **8:**279
– dietary laws **6:**30,32
– eggs **6:**474
– fauna of Israel **3:**17; **9:**226
– Jewish symbolism **15:**569
– *illus:*
– – *Shivviti* **13:**44-45; **14:**1420-1421
– *table:* animals of the Bible and Talmud **3:**9-16
"Birds, The Language of" **6:**117
BIRDS' HEAD HAGGADAH (illum. ms., Ger.) **7:**1098
– Jerusalem in art **9:**1580
– Menahem, the scribe **11:**734
– *illus:* **2:**330,480; **7:***fcg.* 875,1081, 1543; **9:**1582; **13:**168
Birea (loc., Er. Isr.) **4:**382
Birer, Reuben **11:**612
Bi'r Gafgafa (loc., Sinai) **14:**1606,1636
Bi'r Ḥamma (loc., Sinai) **14:**1606
Bi'r Hassneh (loc., Sinai) **14:**1636
Bīr Hindis (loc., Isr.), *see* Be'er Orah
Biridya (k., Megiddo) **11:**1227
Biritaro, Samuel ben Joshua Minz **13:**593
BIRIYYAH (loc., mosh., Isr.) **4:**1034
– Crusader period **9:**272
– Ottoman period **9:**285; **9:**286
– Safed **14:**630
– – statistics **1:**place list
– *illus:* text
Birk, Alma **13:**812
Birkat al-Ḥamrā' (pool, Jer.), *see* SHILOAH, SILOAM
Birkat al-Sultan (Jer.), *see* Snake Pool
Birkat Avot (Amidah ben.), *see Avot*
Birkat Avraham (wk.) **4:**1414
Birkat Avraham (Festschrift) **4:**665
Birkat David (Amidah ben.) **2:**841
Birkat ha-Ḥodesh, see NEW MOON, ANNOUNCEMENT OF
Birkat ha-Levanah, see MOON, BLESSING OF THE
Birkat ha-Mazon, see GRACE AFTER MEALS
Birkat Ḥammām al-Biṭrīq (Jer.), *see* Hezekiah, Pool of
BIRKAT HA-MINIM (Amidah ben.) **4:**1035
– Amidah **2:**841
– effect on Judeo-Christians **9:**244
– historical background **8:**643
– informers **8:**1364
– *luz* of the spine **11:**595
– Samuel ha-Katan **14:**815
– Valladolid Disputation **16:**60
Birkat ha-Shalom (Amidah ben.) **2:**841; **2:**842
Birkat ha-Shanim (Amidah ben.) **2:**840
Birkat ha-Shir (prayer), *see* NISHMAT KOL ḤAI
BIRKAT HA-TORAH (blessing over the Law) **4:**1036
– *Ahavah Rabbah* **2:**454
Birkat Kohanim, see PRIESTLY BLESSING
Birkat Mishpat (Amidah ben.) **2:**840
Birkat Ram (lake, Golan) **9:**180, 597
– *illus:* **9:**169
Birkat Yerushalayim (Amidah ben.) **2:**841
Birkat Ẓadikim (Amidah ben.) **2:**841
Birkenau (concen. camp) **3:**855ff; **8:**871
– *illus:*
– – the barracks **3:**859
– – plan **3:**871
Birkenfeld (tn., Ger.) **6:**531
Birkenhead, 1st Baron of, *see* COHEN, HENRY BARON
Birkenstadt, Gershon ben Abraham, *see* CHAJES, GERSHON BEN ABRAHAM
BIRKENTHAL, DOV BER **4:**1036
– apologetics **3:**198
Birkhot ha-mitzvot (ben.) **4:**487
Birkhot ha-nehenin (ben.) **4:**487
– *illus:*
– – benediction over spices **8:**1315
– – benedictions before eating fruit and vegetables **6:**1423
– – grace after meals, short form **7:** *fcg.* 846
Birkhot ha-Shahar, see MORNING BENEDICTIONS
Birlad (tn., Rum.), *see* BARLAD
Bi'r Laḥfān (loc., Sinai) **14:**1629
Birman, Lejb **13:**775
BIRMINGHAM (city, Ala.) **4:**1037
– Alabama Jewry **2:**505; **2:**506
– *illus:* text
BIRMINGHAM (city, Eng.) **4:**1038
– Cohen, Abraham **5:**664
– England **6:**754f
– Gordon, Lord George **7:**795
– *illus:* text
Birnbaum (fam., Ger.), *see* FLESCH
Birnbaum, Abe **5:**220
BIRNBAUM, ABRAHAM BAER **4:**1039
BIRNBAUM, EDUARD **4:**1039
– Altschul, Joseph **2:**782
– Beer, Aaron **4:**376
– music, Jewish **12:**651; **12:**656
– Oko, Adolph S. **12:**1355
Birnbaum, Ferdinand **6:**464
Birnbaum, Joshua **15:**1040
BIRNBAUM, MENACHEM **3:**597
BIRNBAUM, NATHAN (philos.) **4:**1040
– Basle Program **4:**306
– Birnbaum, Solomon **4:**1042
– *Selbstemanzipation* **14:**1119
– Vienna **16:**127
– Yiddishists **8:**760
– Zionism **16:**1032; **16:**1105
– Zionist circle in Vienna **4:**440
– *illus:* text
Birnbaum, Nathan (comedian), *see* BURNS, GEORGE
Birnbaum, Norman **15:**68
BIRNBAUM, PHILIP **4:**1042
– encyclopedias **6:**734
Birnbaum, R. (polit.) **10:**89
BIRNBAUM, SOLOMON ASHER **4:**1042
BIRNBAUM, URIEL **4:**1043
– *illus:* text
BIRNBOIM, MOSES JOSEPH **4:**1044
Birnholz, Marco **4:**1219
– *illus:*
– – bookplate **4:**1221
Birnzweig, Isaac **11:**426
BIRO, LAJOS **4:**1044
BIROBIDZHAN (reg., Rus.) **4:**1044
– assimilation **3:**781
– autonomy **3:**927
– communism **5:**793; **5:**799
– Dimanstein, Simon **6:**48
– historical list **8:**766-767
– Kazakevich, Emmanuil **10:**856
– Siberia **14:**1488
– theater **15:**1076
– *Yevsektsiya* propaganda **16:**780
– Zhitlowsky, Chaim **16:**1009
– *illus:*
– – text
– – a street **8:**742
– *pop. tables:* text
Biro-Bidzhan (journ.) **13:**1048
Biro-Bidzhaner Shtern (newsp.) **13:**1048; **14:**471
Biron, Count **11:**282
Birs Nimrud (mound, Iraq), *see* BORSIPPA
Birstein, Y. **16:**825
Birta (tn., Babyl.) **4:**42
"Bīr Ta'abya" (well, Er. Isr.) **4:**386
Bir Taba (frontier point, Gulf of Akaba) **9:**311
BIRTH **4:**1050
– ablution **2:**83
– abortion **2:**100
– amulets **13:**62
– astrology **3:**790
– cemetery custom **5:**272
– Commandments, the 613 **5:**766
– death in childbirth **14:**135
– folklore **2:**264; **6:**1399
– impurity period **13:**1406; **13:**1407
– life before birth **12:**1149
– Lilith **11:**246ff
– male birth custom **14:**1453
– *niddah* **12:**1146
– *pikku'aḥ nefesh* **13:**510
– sacrifice following **11:**143; **14:**601; **14:**602
– Samaritan purity **14:**744
– vital statistics **16:**177ff
– *illus:*
– – text
– – amulets for protection of newborn **2:**910
– – invocation of angels **4:**1052; **6:**1406
– – *Kimpetbriefel* **13:**44-45
– – *Magen David* amulet **11:**691
– – protective prayer **4:**1050

- - sword for protection against demons 6:1406
- - Torah scroll in delivery room 6:1406
- - woman giving birth to six children (*Dragon Haggadah*) 4:*fcg.* 1068
- *see also:* CIRCUMCISION
Birtha of the Ammanitis (anc. city, Transj.) 15:1490
BIRTH CONTROL 4:1053
- conjugal obligations 5:364
- Guttmacher, Alan F. 7:990
- Holocaust 8:731
- onanism 12:1396ff
- rabbinic views 15:895
- vital statistics 16:179
- *see also:* BARRENNESS AND FERTILITY; CASTRATION
BIRTHDAY 4:1054
- birth 4:1051
Birth pangs of the Messiah, *see* MESSIAH
Birth rate
- Arabs in Israel 9:1023ff
- Israel, General 9:984
- vital statistics 16:177ff
- *see also:* DEMOGRAPHY
Birthright 2:508; 6:1306ff
Birtum (deity) 16:1490
Bīryā, *see* BIRIYYAH
BIRZAI (Birzhi; city, Rus.) 4:1055
- Samogitia 14:768
- *illus:*
- - shoemakers' synagogue 11:372
Bi'r Zayt (loc., Samaria) 9:583
BIRZULA (tn., Rus.) 4:1055
Bisa (2nd cent. C.E., schol.) 7:1218; 12:1495
BISCHHEIM (tn., Fr.) 4:1055
- Alsace-Lorraine 2:754; 2:757
BISCHOFF, ERICH 4:1055
- *Sefer Yezirah* 16:788
BISCHOFFSHEIM (fam.) 4:1056
- Bamberger, Ludwig 4:154
- Cassel 5:230
- railroads 13:1519
- *geneal. tab:* text
Bischoffsheim, Amalia 4:1057
Bischoffsheim, Ellen Odette 4:1057
Bischoffsheim, Henry Louis 4:1057
Bischoffsheim, Jonathan Raphael 4:1056
Bischoffsheim, Louis (Ludwig) Raphael 4:1056
Bischoffsheim, Raphael (Nathan) 4:1056
Bischoffsheim, Raphael Louis 4:1057
Bischofsheim on the Tauber (tn., Ger.), *see* TAUBERBISCHOFSHEIM
Bischofszell (tn., Switz.) 15:554
Bischwiller (tn., Fr.) 2:757
Biscioni (us), Antonio Maria 8:25
Bi-Sedeh ha-Beniyyah (journ.) 1: newsp. list
Bi-Sedeh ha-Tekhnikah (journ.) 1:newsp. list
Bi-Sedeh Hemed (journ.) 1:newsp. list
Bi-Sedeh Kozerim (kib. litur.) 10:960
Bisenc, Israel ben Judah Aryeh 4:1213
Bisenz (tn., Cz.), *see* BZENEC
Bisguier, Arthur 5:407
Bishop Bedell Bible (1284, illum. ms., Rome) 8:1268
- *illus:* 4:*fcg.* 940; 5:523; 8:1281
Bishop of the Jews, *see* EPISCOPUS JUDAEORUM
Bishop of Salvador (Inqu.) 8:1391
Bishops' Bible 4:869
Bishr ben Aaron 2:14; 14:547
Bishr Ibn Samʿān 3:445
Bislad (tn., Rum.) 8:1043
BISLICHES, MORDECAI LEIB 4:1057
Bismarck (city, N.D.) 12:1221
BISMARCK, PRINCE OTTO VON 4:1058
- Bamberger, Ludwig 4:154
- Bleichroeder, Gerson von 4:1081
- Lasker, Eduard 10:1436ff
Bison 3:7, 16; 16:510
Bisseliches, Marcus, *see* BISLICHES, MORDECAI LEIB
Bissinger (fam.) 5:56; 14:834
BISTRITA (Bistritz; tn., Transyl.) 4:1058
Bistritski, Nathan, *see* AGMON, NATHAN
Bisuldun (Bisuldunum; tn., Sp.) *see* BESALU
Bīt Adini (Aram. kdm.), *see* BET(H)-EDEN
BITAN AHARON (mosh., Isr.) 4:1059
- statistics 1:place list
Bitanura (vill., Kurd.) 10:1297
Bitanyah (kib., Isr.), *see* ALUMMOT
Bitas, Abraham 5:239
Bit-Daganna (bib. city), *see* BET(H) DAGON
Bit Dakkuri (tribe) 5:331
Bi-Tefuzot ha-Golah (journ.) 1: newsp. list
Bithah (mosh., Isr.) 1:place list
BITHIAH (Pharaoh's dau.) 4:1059
- *illus:* text
BITHYNIA (dist., As. M.) 4:1060
- Asia Minor 3:747
- Roman province 8:292
Bit-Iakin (anc. kdm.) 11:1389
Bitola (Bitolj; tn., Yug.), *see* MONASTIR
Bitran, Albert 13:117
Bīt Šilāni (Chaldean state) 5:331
Bittahon ve-Higyenah ba-Avodah (journ.) 1: newsp. list
Bittaon (journ.) 1: newsp. list
Bittaon Habad (journ.) 1: newsp. list
Bittaon Heil ha-Avir (journ.), *see Heil ha-Avir*
BITTELMAN, ALEXANDER 4:1060
Bitter herb, *see* MAROR
Bitter Lake (Egy.) 14:1636
BITTERN (Heron) 4:1061
- dietary laws 6:34
- *illus:* text
- *see also: Kippod*
Bittoon, Isaac 15:305
Bittu'ah (journ.) 1:newsp. list
Bittul be-rov (conc., dietary laws) 6:39
BITTUL HA-TAMID (interruptionof synagogue service) 4:1061
- synagogue 15:584
Bittul ha-yesh (has. conc.) 7:1393; 7:1404
- *Ahikar, Book of* 2:461
Bittul Ikkarei ha-Nozerim (wk.) 3:195
BITUMEN 4:1062
Bit Yakin (tribe) 5:331
Bitzaron (period.) 1:newsp. list; 8:213; 12:1053; 15:884
Biuletin (period.) 16:348
Biur (wk.) 4:875; 7:1438
Bi'ur Hamez (Passover) 4:373
"Biurists" (followers of Mendelssohn) 4:875
Bivach, Abraham, *see* BIBAGO, ABRAHAM BEN SHEM TOV
Bivach, Isaac, *see* BIBAGO, ISAAC
Bivi Gaon (Bivoi'), *see* Bebai ha-Levi bar Abba of Nehar-Pekod
Bizerta (loc., Tun.) 15:1431ff
Biz Hundert un Tsvantsik (greeting) 7:914
BIZTHA (bib. fig.) 4:1062
Bizur Ltd. (fin. co., Isr.) 9:828
BIZZARON (mosh., Isr.) 4:1062
- statistics 1: place list
Bjorneboe, Jens Ingvald 14:933
B-k-m-o-h-r-r, *see* BEKEMOHARAR
Blace, Samuel 3:450
Black, Alexander 15:1206
Black, Louis 5:609
BLACK, MAX 4:1062
BLACK, MISHA 4:1063
"Black Abomination" (Rus. tn.), *see* BELAYA TSERKOV
Blackbird (bird) 6:30
Black Bureau (orgn., Rus.), *see* Ha-Lishkah ha-Sheḥorah
Black cumin 6:1416
BLACK DEATH 4:1063
- *Contents:*
- - Well Poisoning Libel 4:1064
- - Outbreak of Persecutions 4:1065
- - The Martyrs 4:1067
- Basle 4:303
- Berne Jews 4:675
- Bingen 4:1007
- Brunswick massacres 4:1421
- Cervera Jews 5:314
- Dueñas Jews 6:261
- France 7:16
- historical list 8:766-767
- *kiddush ha-Shem* 10:984
- papal bulls 4:1496
- persecutions 8:676ff
- population changes 13:877
- Saragossa 14:861
- Speyer 15:264
- Strasbourg 15:422
- Tárrega 15:824
- Vienna 16:122
- Worms 16:645
- Zurich 16:1241
- *map:* text
- *see also:* Well-poisoning libel
Black Hole of Calcutta (Ind.) 5:39
Black Hundreds (orgn., Rus.) 3:86, 123; 13:697; 15:1538
BLACK JEWS IN AMERICA 4:1068
- negro proselytes 13:1192
- *illus:* text
- *see also:* NEGRO-JEWISH RELATIONS IN THE U.S.
Black Jews in India 5:390; 6:1213; 6:845
Black magic, *see* MAGIC
Black Obelisk 16:1502
"Black Saturday" (Isr.) 7:1072; 9:358; 9:688
- *illus:*
- - Zionist leaders released from detention 9:362; 10:31
"Blackshirts" (Eng.), *see* ANTI-SEMITIC POLITICAL PARTIES AND ORGANIZATIONS (England)
Blacksmiths 5:1044
- *illus:*
- - Jewish blacksmiths, Lithuania 11:384
BLACKSTONE, WILLIAM E. 4:1069
- Zionism 16:1154
Black Stone of Mecca, *see* Ka'ba
"Black Years, The" (1949-1953, Rus.) 5:984
Blada (custom), *see* SHOLEM ZOKHOR
Blado, Antonio 13:1100; 14:252
Blaeu (cartog.) 11:927
Blahoslav, Jan 4:884
BLAKE, WILLIAM 4:1070
- English literature 6:776
- Jerusalem poem 9:1577
- Nebuchadnezzar 12:917
- *illus:*
- - text
- - Job (engr.) 4:934; 10:115
Blancaccius, Benedictus 8:25
BLANCKENHORN, MAX 4:1071
Bland, Maria 15:1053
BLANES, JACOB 4:1071
Blank, Aristide 4:1072; 4:176
BLANK, LEON 15:1079
BLANK, MAURICE 4:1071
BLANK, SAMUEL LEIB 4:1072
BLANK, SHELDON HAAS 4:1072
Blankenburg (tn., Ger.) 4:1421
Blankenburg (ius), Fridericus 8:25
BLANKENSTEIN, MARCUS VAN 10:306; 10:309
Blankestein, Solomon, *see* SCHILLER, SOLOMON
BLANKFORT, MICHAEL S. 15:1572; 15:1579
BLANKSTEIN, CECIL N. 3:363
- *illus:*
- - Winnipeg, air terminal building 3:355
BLANTER, MATVEY ISAAKOVICH 12:683
Blantes, Leon de, *see* Lavi ha-Levi
Blantyre (tn., Malawi) 9:440
Blasco Ibáñez, Vicente 15:250
BLASER, ISAAC 4:1072
- Musar Movement 12:535ff
BLASPHEMY 4:1073
- Commandments, the 613 5:773
- cuneiform law 16:1490
- euphemism and dysphemism 6:959
- gentiles 12:1189; 12:1191
- Ḥasidism 7:1407
- Leviticus, Book of 11:146
- Shabbetai Zevi 14:1223
- Titus 15:1169
- *see also:* BLESSING AND CURSING
Blass, Moses 15:302
Blatas, Arbit 13:117
Blatt, Joseph 12:1354
Blatt, Solomon 15:213
BLAU, AMRAM 4:1074
- Blau, Moshe 4:1076
BLAU, BRUNO 4:1074
BLAU, FRITZ 4:1075
BLAU, HERBERT 15:1058; 15:1079
BLAU, JOSEPH LEON 4:1075
BLAU, JOSHUA 4:1075
Blau, Lajos, *see* BIRO, LAJOS
BLAU, LUDWIG LAJOS 4:1076
BLAU, MOSHE 4:1076
- Agudat Israel 2:424
Blau, Peter 15:68
Blau, Ruth 4:1074
Blaue Reiter (art school) 13:115
BLAUSTEIN (fam.) 4:1076
BLAUSTEIN, ABRAHAM 7:1546
BLAUSTEIN, DAVID 4:1078
Blaustein, Gerson 12:53
Blaustein, Jacob 4:1077; 16:1145
- *illus:* 12:1112
Blaustein, Louis 4:1076
Blauwatt, Isaac 11:426
BLAU-WEISS (mvmt., Ger.) 4:1078
Blayney, Benjamin 8:25
BLAZKO, MARTIN 3:597
Blebelius, Thomas 8:25
BLECH, LEO 4:1079
Blech, Wilhelm Philipp 8:25
BLECHER, MARCEL 4:1079
- *illus:* text
BLEEK, FRIEDRICH 4:1080
Bleichrode, I. 4:876
BLEICHROEDER (fam.) 4:1081
Bleichroeder, Adolf 4:1081
Bleichroeder, Gerson von 4:1081
- Ahlwardt, Hermann 2:469
- banking and finance 4:174; 8:719

- railroads **13:**1517ff
Bleichroeder, Hans **4:**1081
Bleichroeder, James **4:**1081
Bleichroeder, Samuel **4:**1081; **4:**174
BLEJER, DAVID **4:**1081
- Argentina **3:**418
BLEMISH **4:**1081
- priests **13:**1078
- sacrifice **12:**1189; **14:**600; **14:**603
Blessedness, *see* BEATITUDE
Blessing, Priestly, *see* PRIESTLY BLESSING
BLESSING AND CURSING **4:**1084
- *Amen*, response to **2:**803
- cursing **10:**425
- commandments, the 613 **5:**781
- euphemism and dysphemism **6:**959
- flogging **6:**1349
- informers **8:**1364; **8:**1367
- oath **12:**1295
- ordeal of jealousy **12:**1449
- priestly blessing **13:**1060; **13:**1076
- Solomon **15:**104
- *illus:*
- - Balaam's seven altars **4:**127
- - Isaac blessing Esau **6:**856
- - Isaac blessing Jacob (14th cent. ms.) **13:**1602
- - "Isaac blessing Jacob" (drg., Rembrandt) **9:**6
- - Jacob blessing his sons **9:**1208
- - Jacob blessing Joseph's sons **6:**281,809; **7:**1084; **14:**67
- - Jacob blessing Pharaoh **7:**1084
- - Job cursing the day he was born **10:**115
- - Moses blessing Children of Israel **12:**386
- - Moses blessing Phinehas **13:**467
- *see also:* BLASPHEMY; CONTEMPT OF COURT
BLESSING OF CHILDREN **4:**1087
- kissing **10:**1074
- *illus:*
- - text
- *see also:* BLESSING AND CURSING; CHILDREN
Blessing of Jacob, *see* JACOB, BLESSING OF
"Blessing over the Candles" (paint., I. Kaufmann) **4:**487
Blessings, *see* BENEDICTIONS
Bleter far Geshikhte (period.) **15:**54
Bleter far Yidishe Demografye, Statistik un Ekonomik (period.) **4:**1426; **11:**51
Bleu-Blanc (mvmt., Fr.) **16:**1114
Bleuler, Eugen **7:**163
Blicher, Steen Steensen **14:**927
Blick, A. **4:**1309
Blick, Elsa, *see* TRIOLET, ELSA
Blim, Moses **15:**424
BLINDMAN, YERUḤAM **4:**1088
- Altschul, Joseph **2:**782
- *illus:*
- - contract with Berdichev community **12:**642
BLINDNESS **4:**1088
- *Contents:*
- - Incidence and Causes **4:**1089
- - Effects **4:**1089
- - Metaphoric Uses **4:**1090
- - In Talmud and Law **4:**1090
- - Care of **4:**1092
- - Modern Incidence **4:**1093
- Hebrew Braille **2:**744
- legal incapacity **13:**226
- *niddui* and misleading **8:**352
- witness **16:**586
- *illus:*
- - text
- - "Blind Violinist" (ceramic, I. Ryback) **14:**533
- - Braille geography textbook **9:**950
- - Tobit finding himself blind **16:**689
Blinov, N. **16:**1012
BLIOKH, IVAN STANISLAVOVICH **4:**1094
- Fried, Alfred **7:**171
BLIS, DAVID **4:**1094
Bliss, *see* BEATITUDE
Bliss, Frank C. **15:**1569
BLISS, FREDERICK JONES **4:**1095
- Jerusalem **9:**1521ff
Blitman, Harry **15:**306
Blitz, Gerard **12:**1375
Blitz, Jekuthiel ben Isaac **2:**899; **4:**867; **11:**357
Blitz, L. **11:**684
Blitz, Maurice **12:**1376
BLITZSTEIN, MARC **4:**1095
Blobel, Paul **8:**856
BLOC, ANDRÉ **4:**1095
Bloch (fam., Bav.) **15:**507
Bloch (fam., Braz.) **13:**1370
BLOCH (fam., U.S.) **4:**1096
- book trade **4:**1239
- publishing **13:**1376
Bloch, A. (Austr.) **11:**1284
Bloch, A. (r., Fr.) **11:**1569
Bloch, Abraham Isaac (r., Lith.) **4:**1103; **15:**938
Bloch, Adolfo **13:**1370
BLOCH, ANDRE **12:**683
Bloch, Arnaldo **13:**1370
Bloch, Boris **13:**1370
Bloch, Bruno **11:**1196
BLOCH, CAMILLE **4:**1096
Bloch, Charles **4:**1096
BLOCH, CLAUDE **4:**1096
Bloch, Darius Paul, *see* DASSAULT, DARIUS PAUL
Bloch, Edward (publ.) **4:**1096; **13:**1376
Bloch, Edward H. (publ.) **4:**1096; **13:**1376
BLOCH, ELIJAH MEYER **4:**1097
- Bloch, Joseph **4:**1103
BLOCH, ERNEST (comp.) **4:**1097
BLOCH, ERNST (philos.) **4:**1098
- Antheil, George **3:**37
Bloch, Feivel **4:**1107
BLOCH, FELIX (phys.) **4:**1099
Bloch, Felix (art.) **3:**575
- *illus:*
- - old people in the Theresienstadt Ghetto Fig. 82 **3**-ART
Bloch, Friedrich **7:**203
Bloch, Gilbert **14:**1039
BLOCH, GUSTAVE **4:**1100
Bloch, Ḥayyim ben Ẓevi, *see* BLOCH, HERMANN
BLOCH, ḤAYYIM ISAAC BEN ḤANOKH ZUNDEL HA-KOHEN **4:**1100
Bloch, Herbert A. **5:**1109
BLOCH, HERMANN (r., Ger.) **4:**1101
BLOCH, HERMAN SAMUEL (chem.) **5:**380
BLOCH, HYMAN MORRIS **10:**1502; **10:**1506
BLOCH, ISSACHAR BAER BEN SAMSON **4:**1101
Bloch, Ivan Stanislavovich, *see* BLIOKH, IVAN STANISLAVOVICH
BLOCH, IWAN **4:**1102
Bloch, J. (publ.) **13:**1032
BLOCH, JEAN-RICHARD **4:**1102
BLOCH, JOSEPH (journ.) **4:**1103
Bloch, Joseph C. (jur.) **5:**609
BLOCH, JOSEPH LEIB (r., Lith.) **4:**1103
- Broida, Simḥah **4:**1401
- Tels **15:**938
BLOCH, JOSEPH SAMUEL (r., Aus.) **4:**1103
- apologetics **3:**199
- historical chart **8:**766-767
- Rohling **14:**224
BLOCH, JOSHUA **4:**1105
BLOCH, JULES **4:**1105
BLOCH, KONRAD **4:**1105
BLOCH, MARC **4:**1106
Bloch, Marcel, *see* DASSAULT, MARCEL
BLOCH, MARCUS (Mordecai) ELIEZER **4:**1107
- as biologist **4:**1030
BLOCH, MARTIN **4:**1107
BLOCH, MATTATHIAS BEN BENJAMIN ZE'EV ASHKENAZI **4:**1107
- Shabbetai Ẓevi **14:**1225; **14:**1236
BLOCH, SIR MAURICE **4:**1108
Bloch, Mór, *see* BALLAGI, MOR
Bloch, Moses (print.) **13:**1107ff
Bloch, Moses (Pol.) **4:**1110
BLOCH, MOSES (Bohem.) **4:**1108
Bloch, Pedro **5:**456; **5:**255
BLOCH, PHILIPP **4:**1109
BLOCH, PIERRE **4:**1109
BLOCH, RENE **2:**322
BLOCH, ROSINE **12:**683
BLOCH, SAMSON BEN MOSES **4:**1110
BLOCH, SAMSON HA-LEVI (Simson) **4:**1110
Bloch, Simon **2:**649
Bloch, Solomon ben Ephraim **13:**137
Bloch, Søren Niklas Johan **8:**25
Bloch, Zielo **15:**1370
Bloch-Dessault (sol., Fr.) **11:**1563
BLOCH-MICHEL, JEAN **4:**1110
Block (tn., Pol.) **13:**711
Block, Adolph **11:**1167
Block, Benjamin **15:**311
Block, Ezekiel **12:**156
BLOCK, HERBERT LAWRENCE ("Herblock") **4:**1111
- cartoons **5:**216
- *illus:* text
BLOCK, PAUL **10:**307; **10:**309
Bloemendaal (tn., Neth.) **7:**1008
BLOEMFONTEIN (city, S.A.) **4:**1111
- *illus:*
- - text
- - communal hall **12:**1448
BLOGG, SOLOMON BEN EPHRAIM **4:**1113
BLOIS (city, Fr.) **4:**1113
- *Aleinu* **2:**558; **2:**559
- Baruch of Mainz **4:**280
- blood libel **5:**1142
- historical chart (1171) **8:**766-767
- *kiddush ha-Shem* **10:**984
Blom, Abraham **12:**907
Blom, N.S. **13:**34
Blond, Anthony **13:**1371
Blond, Maurice **13:**116
BLONDES, DAVID **4:**1114
BLONDHEIM, DAVID SIMON **4:**1114
Blondheim, Solomon Hillel **4:**1115
Blondzhende Shtern (bk.) **14:**1283
Blonie (tn., Pol.) **13:**950
BLOOD **4:**1115
- altar **2:**765
- cult **5:**1157
- *eglah arufah* **6:**475ff
- folk medicine **6:**1406
- gentiles **12:**1190
- Jewish types **3:**49
- Judaizers **10:**398
- kashering **6:**28
- *kipper* **10:**1041
- Pentateuch **13:**245
- plagues of Egypt **13:**604
- prohibition of **6:**28
- sacrifices **14:**600ff
- *sheḥitah* **14:**1338
- woman's menses **12:**1141ff
BLOOD-AVENGER **4:**1116
- compounding homicide **5:**856
- elders **6:**578
- family solidarity **6:**1166
- participation in execution **5:**143
- prosecutor **13:**959
- *illus:*
- - cities of refuge (map) **5:**593
- *see also:* BLOODGUILT; CITY OF REFUGE
BLOODGUILT **4:**1118
- *eglah arufah* **6:**475
- elders **6:**578
- *see also:* BLOOD-AVENGER; HOMICIDE
BLOODLETTING **4:**1119
- crafts **5:**1052ff
BLOOD LIBEL **4:**1120
- *Contents:*
- - Origins **4:**1120
- - Middle Ages **4:**1121
- - Modern Times **4:**1124
- - - In Russia **4:**1128
- General
- - Alfonso X **2:**605
- - Benedict XIV **4:**482
- - Catholic Church **5:**538
- - Clement XIII **5:**602
- - Councils of the Lands **5:**1002
- - Crusades' effect **5:**1142
- - Damocritus and Apion **3:**178; **7:**893
- - Donin, Nicholas **6:**167
- - Frankists **7:**66
- - Frederick II Hohenstaufen **7:**114
- - Gregory of Tours **7:**921
- - historical chart **8:**766-767
- - Jews defended by Trithemius **15:**1400
- - Kohn's comment on **10:**1148
- - Levinsohn's refutation **11:**118; **3:**200
- - papal bull against **4:**1494
- - Reformation **14:**19
- - Rindfleisch massacres **14:**188
- - Rudolf I of Habsburg **14:**380
- Cases
- - Andrew of Rinn **2:**948
- - Beilis, Mendel **4:**399
- - Blondes, David **4:**1114
- - Buschoff case **16:**685
- - Damascus Affair **5:**1249
- - first reported case **6:**747
- - Hilsner Case **8:**496
- - Jewish tax-collectors **4:**1258
- - La Guardia **10:**1359; **3:**969
- - Lévy, Raphaël **11:**162ff
- Places
- - Amasya **2:**795; **15:**504
- - Austria **3:**888
- - Berne **4:**675
- - Endingen **6:**736
- - France **7:**13
- - Germany **7:**467ff
- - Kolin **10:**1161
- - London **11:**470; **11:**471
- - Majorca **15:**238
- - Malta **11:**831
- - Ottoman Empire **16:**1543
- - Paris **13:**104
- - Pezinok **13:**352
- - Rome **14:**250
- - Russia **14:**487
- - Sandomierz **14:**831
- - Saragossa **14:**860
- - Tirgu Neamt **15:**1152
- - Tiszaeszlar **15:**1155
- - Treviso **15:**1380
- - Troyes **15:**1407
- - Valréas **16:**64
- - Velizh **16:**87
- - Venice **16:**95
- - Volhynia **16:**209
- - Yemen **14:**822

- Literature
- - Alfonso de Espina **2:**606
- - apologetic literature **3:**197ff
- - cartoons, anti-Semitic **5:**177
- - *Civiltà Cattolica, La* **5:**599
- - folktales **6:**1382
- - German stories **7:**443
- - *Stuermer, Der* **15:**460
- *illus:*
text
- - Beilis under arrest **14:**447
- - Damascus Affair, commemorative medal **5:**1250
- - *Der Stürmer,* "ritual murder number" (May, 1934) **3:**154; (May, 1939) **15:**460
- - Frankl-Gruen, Adolf Abraham **7:**103
- - Simon of Trent **3:**97,119; **7:**467; **15:**1374
- - Stoeritz's broadsheet (1694) **8:**700
- *see also:* HOST, DESECRATION OF
"Bloody Oskar", *see* BLUMENTHAL, OSKAR
BLOOM, BENJAMIN SAMUEL **4:**1131
BLOOM, CLAIRE **12:**464
BLOOM, HAROLD (crit.) **15:**1579
Bloom, Harry (writ.) **15:**1060; **15:**209
Bloom, H. J. (hist.) **15:**271
BLOOM, HYMAN (paint.) **4:**1131
- *illus:* text
Bloom, Meyer **15:**303
Bloom, Moses **8:**1438
Bloom, Phil **15:**306
BLOOM, SOL **4:**1132
BLOOM, SOLOMON FRANK **8:**544
Bloomberg, Abe **5:**140; **13:**820; **15:**311
Bloomberg, Sol L. **14:**162
Bloomfield, Jack **15:**306
Bloomfield, Joseph **11:**1551
BLOOMFIELD, LEONARD **4:**1133
BLOOMFIELD, MAURICE **4:**1133
BLOOMFIELD-ZEISLER, FANNY **12:**683
Bloomgarden, Yehoash Solomon, *see* YEHOASH
BLOOMINGDALE (fam.) **4:**1133
- department stores **5:**1546; **12:**1082
Bloomingdale, Alfred S. **4:**1134
Bloomingdale, Emanuel Watson **4:**1133
Bloomingdale, Hiram C. **4:**1134
Bloomingdale, Joseph Bernhardt **4:**1133
Bloomingdale, Lyman Gustavus **4:**1133
Bloomingdale, Samuel Joseph **4:**1134
Bloomington (city, Ill.) **8:**1255
Bloom's syndrome (disease) **14:**1501
Blount, Charles **5:**1463
Bloustein, Edward J. **15:**1679
BLOWITZ, HENRI GEORGES STEPHANE ADOLPHE OPPER DE **4:**1134
- *illus:* text
BLOY, LÉON **4:**1135
Bludenz (tn., Aus.) **16:**223
Blue, *see* TEKHELET
Blue Army, *see* HALLER'S ARMY
Bluefield (city, W. Va.) **16:**475
Blue Rider (art school), *see* Blaue Reiter
BLUESTONE, JOSEPH ISAAC **4:**1135
Bluethenthal, Arthur **15:**307
Blue-White Workers' Association (mvmt., Isr.) **9:**861
Bluhm, Arthur **10:**1252
Blum, A. (Bund ldr.) **4:**1505
Blum, Abraham (r.) **11:**499
Blum, Abraham (Warsaw ghetto) **16:**349
Blum, Adrien (Switz.) **13:**1049
BLUM, AMRAM BEN ISAAC JACOB **4:**1135
Blum, Arnold (sport.) **15:**309
Blum, Bela Benzion **4:**1136; **4:**605
Blum, Carol **15:**745
Blum, Charles Eduard **2:**125
BLUM, ELIEZER **4:**1136
Blum, Isaac Jacob **4:**1136
BLUM, JEROME **8:**544
Blum, Judah Ẓevi **4:**1136
BLUM, JULIUS **4:**1136
BLUM, LÉON **4:**1136
- Gide, André **8:**744
- historical chart **8:**766-767
- *illus:*
- - Jarblum, Marc **9:**1287
BLUM, LUDWIG **3:**597
Blum, Moses Nahum **4:**1136
Blum, Peter **15:**210
Blum, R. (r., Slov.) **10:**1216
BLUM, RENÉ (impresario) **4:**1138
Blum, Robert Léon (engin.) **4:**1138
Blum, S. **10:**89
Blum, Walter **15:**310
Blumberg, Alfred **15:**312
Blumberg, Ḥayyim, *see* HARARI, ḤAYYIM
Blumberg, Isaac **15:**311
Blumberg, Isabel **15:**309
Blumberg, Jack **16:**551
BLUME, PETER **4:**1139
- *illus:* text
Blumel, André **16:**1115
BLUMENBERG, LEOPOLD **4:**1139
- Baltimore **4:**148
- *illus:*
- - Lincoln, Abraham, letter re **15:**1603
Blumenfeld, Aharon, *see* ROMAN-RONETTI, MOÏSE
Blumenfeld, Diana **12:**454; **15:**1464
Blumenfeld, Dov Ber **4:**1398
BLUMENFELD, EMANUEL **4:**1139
Blumenfeld, Feitel **4:**1140
BLUMENFELD, FELIX MIKHAYLOVICH **12:**684
BLUMENFELD, HERMANN FADDEYEVICH **4:**1140
Blumenfeld, Jules, *see* PERACHIM, JULES
BLUMENFELD, KURT YEHUDAH **4:**1140
Blumenfeld, Leopold, *see* Belmont, Leo
Blumenfeld, M. Joseph **5:**900; **7:**1360
BLUMENFELD, RALPH DAVID **4:**1141
BLUMENFELD, WALTER **13:**1345
BLUMENFIELD, SAMUEL **4:**1141
BLUMENKRANZ, BERNHARD **1:**28; **4:**1141
- historiography **8:**562
Blumenstein, Harry **10:**1494
Blumenthal, Abraham **10:**733
BLUMENTHAL, GEORGE **4:**1141
BLUMENTHAL, JACOB (Jacques) **12:**684
BLUMENTHAL, JOSEPH (bsmn.) **4:**1142
- New York City **12:**1103ff
BLUMENTHAL, JOSEPH (print.) **4:**1142
- *illus:* text
Blumenthal, M. **5:**453
BLUMENTHAL, NISSAN **4:**1143
- Gerowitsch, Eliyezer **7:**510
BLUMENTHAL, OSKAR **4:**1143
- theater **15:**1057
BLUMENTHAL, WERNER MICHAEL **4:**1144
"Blumke's Kloyz" (yeshivah, Belor.) **12:**52
Blumlein, Aaron, *see* AARON OF NEUSTADT
Blum Pasha, *see* BLUM, JULIUS
Blut fuer Ware ("blood for goods") **10:**815
Bluwstein, Raḥel (poet), *see* RAḤEL
B'nai Abraham (syn., N.J.) **6:**903
- *illus:*
- - Ark of the Law **12:**1029
B'nai Amoona (syn., U.S.) **15:**625
B'nai B'rith (mosh., Isr.), *see* MOLEDET
B'NAI B'RITH (orgn.) **4:**1144
- America **2:**811
- American Jewish Conference **2:**825
- Anti-Defamation League **13:**1253
- Bien, Julius **4:**983
- Hillel Foundation **4:**1146; **14:**590; **15:**449ff
- historical chart (1843) **8:**766-767
- library **11:**195
- New York City **12:**1072
- publishing **13:**1376
- Timendorfer, Berthold **15:**1143
- U.S. Zionism **16:**1147
- Wexler, William **16:**479
- *illus:*
- - text
- - Eisenhower presenting a citation **6:**544
- - Melbourne, B'nai B'rith House **3:**885
- - protest against Grant's anti-Semitic order **15:**1652
B'nai B'rith Blaetter (period.) **13:**1029
B'nai B'rith Magazine (period.) **13:**1051
B'nai B'rith Monatsblaetter fuer den čechoslovakischen Staat (period.) **15:**1117
B'nai B'rith Museum (Wash. D.C.) **12:**551
B'nai B'rith News (period.), *see B'nai B'rith Magazine*
B'nai El (syn., Mo.) **14:**663ff
- *illus*
- - exterior **14:**663
B'nai Israel (syn., Calif.) **15:**1604
B'nai Israel (syn., N.J.) **15:**625
- *illus:*
- - exterior **15:**625
B'nai Israel (syn., N.Y.) **12:**1071ff
B'nai Israel (syn., R.I.) **15:**626
B'nai Israel (syn., Texas) **15:**1035
B'nai Jeshurun (syn., N.Y.) **12:**1071ff; **16:**566
- *illus:* **12:**1072
B'nai Yeshurun (syn., O.) **5:**562
- *illus:*
- - exterior **12:**1345
- - interior **5:**562
B'nai Zion (soc., U.S.) **4:**1135; **4:**499
Boar **13:**506
- dietary laws **6:**32
BOARD OF DELEGATES OF AMERICAN ISRAELITES **4:**1149
BOARD OF DEPUTIES OF BRITISH JEWS **4:**1150
- Anglo-Jewish Association **2:**977f
- archives **3:**382
- autonomy **3:**927
- communal organization **8:**723
- Congress of Berlin **2:**650
- English Jewry **6:**755
- historical chart **8:**766-767
- *illus:*
- - text
- - celebration in honor of the State of Israel **6:**773
- - Duke of Edinburgh at bicentenary celebration **9:**1276
- - session **6:**771
Board of Guardians for the Relief of the Jewish Poor (Eng.), *see* Jewish Welfare Board
Board of Scientific and Industrial Research (Er. Isr.) **9:**967; **14:**767
BOAS (fam.) **4:**1151
Boas, Abraham (bnk.) **4:**1152
Boas, Abraham (mer.), *see* Boas, Hyman
BOAS, ABRAHAM TOBIAS (r.) **4:**1152
Boas, C. **13:**1373
BOAS, FRANZ **4:**1152
- anthropology **3:**38
BOAS, FREDERICK SAMUEL **6:**784; **6:**787
BOAS, GEORGE **4:**1153
Boas, Guy **6:**787
Boas, Hyman **4:**1151
Boas, Isaac Herbert **4:**1152
Boas, Simon **4:**1152; **7:**1008
Boas, Tobias (bnk.) **4:**1151; **7:**1124 **13:**1515
Boas, Tobias (schol.) **5:**625
Boate, Arnold, *see* Boote, Arnold
Boat Owners' Society (Turk.) **9:**1093
BOAZ (bib. fig.) **4:**1154
- in the Arts **14:**523
- levirate marriage **11:**122
- Naomi **12:**818
- Ruth, Book of **14:**518ff
- *geneal. table:* **5:**1341
- *illus:*
- - text
- - ninth cent. Bible **9:**1
- - Ruth in the tent of **14:**520
Boaz (Temple pillar), *see* JACHIN AND BOAZ
BOBE-MAYSE (story) **4:**1155
- Jewish literature **11:**359
Boberg, Andreas **8:**25
Bobov (ḥas. dyn.) **7:**1425; **9:**899
Bobovich, Simḥah, *see* BABOVICH, SIMḤAH BEN SOLOMON
Bobowa (tn., Pol.) **7:**812
BOBROVY KUT (stlmt., Rus.) **4:**1155
BOBRUISK (city, Belor.) **4:**1155
Bobsledding **15:**317
BOBTELSKY, MORDEKHAI (Max) **5:**380
Bocarro, Ferdinand **14:**260
Bocarro, Immanuel, *see* ROSALES, JACOB HEBRAEUS
BOCCACCIO, GIOVANNI **4:**1156
- Italian literature **9:**1104
Boccara, Abraham **15:**1444
Bochart, Samuel **8:**25
BOCHNER, LLOYD **15:**1079
BOCHNIA (tn., Pol.) **4:**1157
- ghetto **13:**766
Bocholt (city, Ger.) **15:**1042
Bochstein, Gershon, *see* CHAJES, GERSHON BEN ABRAHAM
BOCHUM (city, Ger.) **4:**1158
- *illus:* text
Bocian (15th cent., physic.) **5:**1028
Bock, H. M. **4:**645
Bock, Jerry **15:**1060
Bock, Tobias **10:**1137
Bockstadt, Gershon, *see* CHAJES, GERSHON BEN ABRAHAM
Bodansky, Meyer **5:**380
BODANSKY, OSCAR **5:**380
BODANZKY, ARTHUR **12:**684
Bod'ashteret (Sidonian k.) **16:**668
Bodecker, Stephan **3:**197
- Hebraist **8:**25
BODEK, JACOB **4:**1158
- Trebitsch, Abraham **15:**1363
BODENHEIM, MAXWELL

4:1159
BODENHEIMER, FREDERICK SIMON 4:1159
- Avidov, Zvi 3:960
Bodenheimer, Loeb 10:1252
BODENHEIMER, MAX ISIDOR 4:1160
- Basle Program 4:306
- *illus:*
- - First Zionist Congress 16:1165
BODENSCHATZ, JOHANN CHRISTOPH GEORG 4:1161
- *illus:*
- - text
- - *Kirchliche Verfassung der heutigen Juden,* engravings (1748) 3:937; 4:754,1052,1161,1522; 5:1385; 6:126,1190; 11:123,1031; 12:292,622; 14:1497
BODIAN, DAVID 11:1206
Bodiker, Stephan, *see* Bodecker, Stephan
Bodiman (orient., Ger.) 15:699
BODIN, JEAN 4:1161
- Jewish religion 8:701
- *illus:* text
BODKY, ERWIN 12:684
BODLEIAN LIBRARY 4:1163
- Cairo *genizah* 16:1334
- incunabula 8:1322
- *illus:* text
BODLEY, SIR THOMAS 4:1164
- Hebraist 8:25
Bodmer, J. J. 16:1242
BODO (9th cent., pros.) 4:1164
- proselytes 13:1187
- Spain 15:224
Bodor, Odon 12:1375
BODROGKERESZTUR (tn., Hung.) 4:1164
Body, human
- autopsies 3:931
- biology 4:1015
- death 5:1425
- hanging 5:142
BODY AND SOUL 4:1165
- afterlife 2:336
- bodily enjoyment 4:433
- death 5:1423
- Gabirol 7:241
- ḥasidic worship 7:1408
- Maimonides 11:775
- Mendelssohn 11:1330
- Neoplatonism 13:430
- netherworld 12:996
- resurrection 14:98
- reward and punishment 14:136
- Saadiah Gaon 14:551; 15:172
- soul immortality 15:174
- theology 15:1107
- Torah 15:1240ff
- *see also:* FLESH; PARADISE; SOUL
Body tax, *see* LEIBZOLL
Boeckel, Ernst G. Adolf 8:24
Boeckel, Otto 3:80
Boegner, Marc 8:915
BOEHM, ADOLF 4:1166
Boehm, Aryeh 11:1203
Boehm, Franz 14:72
Boehm, Guenther 5:467
Boehm, Johann 8:24
Boehm, Samuel 5:1038; 5:1077; 13:1102ff
Boehme, Jacob 10:645; 10:646
- Knorr von Rosenroth 10:1117
- Spaeth, Johann Peter 15:219
Boehmen, *see* BOHEMIA
Boehmer, Johann 4:886
Boehmische Landesjudenschaft (orgn.), *see* LANDESJUDENSCHAFT, BOEHMISCHE
Boehmisch-Leipa (tn., Cz.), *see* CESKA LIPA
Boendale, Jan van 12:975
Boeotia (loc. Gr.) 6:10; 7:868
Boerhaven (physic.) 11:1192
BOERNE, LUDWIG (Loeb Baruch) 4:1166
- German literature 7:444ff
- Heine and 8:272
- *illus:*
- - text
- - portrait 8:709
Boer van Rijk, Esther de 12:984
Boer War
- East London Jews 6:342
- Marks, Samuel 11:1009
- South Africa 15:184ff
BOESCHENSTEIN, JOHANN 4:1168
- Oeglin, Erhard 3:850
- *illus:* text
Boesing (tn., Cz.), *see* PEZINOK
Boethus (pr.) 4:1169; 6:18
- high priesthood 8:474
- priest 13:1087
- Simeon ben Boethus 14:1554
Boethus ben Zonin, *see* BAITOS BEN ZONIN
BOETHUSIANS (sect) 4:1169
- *am ha-areẓ* 2:835
- Antigonus of Sokho 3:67
- calendar 5:50
- *ḥaliẓah* 11:126
- Karaites 10:764
- *omer* 12:1383
- Sadducees 14:621
Boétie, Etienne de la, *see* LA BOÉTIE, ETIENNE DE
Boettcher, Julius Friedrich 8:24
Boetticher, Paul Anton de, *see* LAGARDE, PAUL ANTON DE
Bofilh (13th cent., Fr.) 12:830
Bogalusa (city, Louis.) 11:517
Bogáthi, Fazekas Miklós 8:24
Bogazköy (anc. city, As. M.), *see* Hattusas
Bogdanovka (concen. camp) 12:1326; 15:1333
Bogdányi, Moritz 6:478
Bogen (fam.), *see* KATZENELLENBOGEN
BOGEN, ALEXANDER 3:597
- *illus:*
- - "Rahel" (drg.) 13:1516
- - "Ruins of Synagogue" (etch.) 3:620
BOGEN, BORIS DAVID 4:1169
- *illus:*
- - Joint Distribution Committee 2:829
BOGER, ḤAYYIM 4:1170
Boghayla (tn., Iraq) 8:1450
Boghazköy (anc. city, As. M.), *see* Hattusas
BOGHEN, FELICE 12:684
Bogomil movement (Chr. sect) 4:1481
Bogopol (tn., Ukr.) 4:144; 13:326; 13:668
BOGORAZ, VLADIMIR GERMANOVICH 4:1171
Bogorodsk (city, Rus.) 12:364
Bogos, Arap Oglu 9:1098
BOGOTÁ (city, Colom.) 4:1171
- Colombia 5:745ff
Bograd, Shimon 14:479
Bograshov, Ḥayyim, *see* BOGER, ḤAYYIM
BOGROV, DMITRI 4:1172
BOGROV, GRIGORI ISAAKOVICH 14:509; 14:514
- Haskalah 7:1449
Bogucice (loc., Pol.) 10:817
BOGUSLAV (city, Rus.) 4:1172
Boguslaw of Mlawa, *see* Berechiah of Mlawa
Bogusze (concen. camp) 3:852
Bogutschuetz (loc., Pol.), *see* Bogucice
Bohairic (dialect) 4:861
Bohan (bib. fig.) 14:105
BOHEMIA 4:1173
- *Contents:*
- - Early-Medieval Periods 4:1173
- - 16/17 centuries 4:1175
- - Familiant Laws 4:1177
- - Toleranzpatent 4:1177
- - 19/20 centuries 4:1178
- Abrahamites 2:159
- Albert V 2:530
- Amigo, Meir 2:847
- Ashkenaz Jewry 3:721
- banking 4:168,169
- Crusades 5:1138;1139
- Familiants Laws 6:1162
- glass 7:613
- gold and silversmithery 7:742
- guilds 7:972ff
- Haskalah 7:1441
- illuminated manuscripts 8:1287
- peddling 13:204
- Shabbateanism 14:1250
- *shtetl* 14:1471
- synagogues 15:604
- textiles 15:1040ff
- tobacco trade 15:1177
- *illus:*
- - text
- - Familiants Law, certificate of marriage 8:702
- - Jewish badge (World War II) 4:72
- - Pinkas Synagogue memorial wall, Prague 13:976
- *pop. tables:* text
- - *see also:* CZECHOSLOVAKIA; MORAVIA; PRAGUE
Bohemian rite (litur.), *see* Polish rite
Bohemus, Johann, *see* Boehm, Johann
Boḥen Ẓaddik (wk.) 8:184
Boḥer (term), *see* BAḤUR
BOHLE (Bohlius), SAMUEL 4:1181
- Hebraist 8:24
BOHM, DAVID 4:1182
Böhm, Vilmos 11:1556
Bohne, Samuel A. 15:301
Bohnen, Eli A. 13:1278
Bohoreta, Laura Papo 16:888
Bohr, Harald 15:299
BOHR, NIELS HENRIK DAVID 4:1182
- Adler, David 2:275
- soccer 15:299
- stamps 15:335
- *illus:*
- - medal 11:1167
- - stamp, Denmark 12:1203
Bohum Psalter (illum. ms.) 14:541
Bohush (ḥas. dyn.) 14:531
Bohybryszcze (tn., Ukr.), *see* POGREBISHCHENSKI
Boiarsky, Ivor F. 16:476
Boieldieu, François Adrien 3:815
Boils (plague) 13:604
Bois, John 8:24
Boise (city, Ida.) 8:1222
- Alexander, Moses 2:575
BOJAN (vill., Ukr.) 4:1183
- ḥasidic dynasty 7:1422; 14:531
- *illus:*
- - *ẓaddik* with Ḥasidim 7:1406
BOJANOWO (tn., Pol.) 4:1183
Bojer, Johan 14:933
BOKANOWSKI, MAURICE 4:1183
- politics 13:813
Bokczánski, Benjamin 13:543
Bokek (loc., Er. Isr.), *see* Boqeq
Boker (newsp.), *see* HA-BOKER
Boker Avraham (bk.) 14:1244
Bokhara (reg., Rus.), *see* BUKHARA
Bokharian quarter (Jer.), *see* Bukharan Quarter
Bokher (term), *see* BAḤUR
Bokher, Elye, *see* LEVITA, ELIJAH
BOKROS-BIRMAN, DEZSŐ (Desiderius) 4:1184
- *illus:* text
Boksburg (tn., S.A.) 15:1340
Bokser (bot.), *see* CAROB
BOKSER, BEN ZION 4:1184
Bokshorn, P. 5:803
Bolaffi(-o; fam. name) 2:185
Bolaffi, Ezekiel (Hezekiah), *see* ABULAFIA, EZEKIEL DAVID BEN MORDECAI
Bolaffi, Giulio 13:147; 15:1455
BOLAFFI, MICHELE 4:1185
Bolaffio, Giacomo 15:1455
BOLAFFIO, LEONE 4:1185
- law 10:1498
Boldogasszony (tn., Aus.), *see* FRAUENKIRCHEN
Bolduc, Jacques 8:24
BOLEKHOV (Bolechów; city, Gal.) 4:1185
Bolekhovski, Leib 9:1166
Boleslav IV (k., Pol.) 12:61
BOLESLAV V (k., Pol.) 4:1186
- history chart 8:766-767
Boleslav of Kujawy 12:61
BOLESLAVSKI, ISAAC 4:1187
Boletín (period.) 15:1022
Bolingbroke, Henry St. John, Viscount 5:1464
Bolivar, Simón 8:1395
BOLIVIA 4:1187
- Latin America 10:1450ff
- refugees, Jewish 14:30
- synagogues 1:syn. list
- *see also:* AMERICA
Bollettino Della Comunitá Israelitica di Milano (period.) 13:1037
BOLM, ADOLPH RUDOLPHOVICH 4:1189
BOLOGNA (city, It.) 4:1190
- Bible 4:837
- library 11:193
- synod 15:634
- Tuscany 15:1467
- *illus:* text
BOLOTOWSKY, ILYA 3:597
- *illus:*
- - "Architectural Tondo" (paint.) 3:619
Bols, L.J. (sol., Eng.) 3:392
Bolshaya Seidemenukha (vill., Ukr.), *see* KALININDORF
Bolsheviks, Bolshevism 5:792; 5:794ff
- assimilation 3:780
- Gershenzon, Mikhail 7:511
- Hebrew parodies 13:137
- Mussolini 12:718
- Rosenberg 14:275
- socialism, Jewish 15:48
- Stalin 15:327
- Trotsky 15:1404
- U.S. Jews 15:1653
BOLZANO (city, It.) 4:1192
- Palágyi's work 13:20
- Tyrol 15:1491
Bomash, M. 6:268
BOMBAY (city, Ind.) 4:1192
- Bene Israel 4:498
- India 8:1356ff
- Sassoon family 14:896
- *illus:* text
Bomberg, Cornelius 4:1195
BOMBERG, DANIEL 4:1195
- Ben-Ḥayyim's masorah 16:1427
- Bible editions 4:838ff
- Hebraists 8:16
- Plantin, Christophe 13:613
- Postel, Guillaume 13:932
- typography 15:1481
- *illus:*

-- *Kiddushin* (1520-23) **15:**757
-- *Leviticus Rabbah* (1545) **13:**1096
-- *Midrash Ḥamesh Megillot* **11:**1507
-- *Numbers Rabbah* (1545) **12:**1262
-- *Song of Songs Rabbah* (1545) **15:**153
BOMBERG, DAVID **4:**1196
- *illus:*
-- "Jerusalem: Mount Scopus and Government House" **3:**555
Bombrac (city, Isr.), *see* BENE-BERAK
Bomeisler, Louis **14:**662
BOMZE, NAHUM **4:**1197
Bona (q., Volhynia) **16:**206
Bona (city, Alg.), *see* BÔNE
Bonacosa, Jacob, *see* Jacob Bonacosa
BONAFED, SOLOMON BEN REUBEN **4:**1197
- Botarel, Moses **4:**1269; **4:**1268
- poetry **11:**327; **13:**690
BONAFOS, MENAHEM BEN ABRAHAM **4:**1198
Bonafos, Shealtiel Isaac **2:**373; **14:**187
Bonafos, Solomon **16:**54
Bonafos bar Judah **15:**822
Bonafoux, Azariah **15:**1326
BONAFOUX, DANIEL BEN ISRAEL **4:**1198
- Shabbateanism **14:**1244
Bonafoux, Menahem ben Abraham, *see* BONAFOS, MENAHEM BEN ABRAHAM
Bonafoux Abraham of Perpignan, *see* BONAFOS, MENAHEM BEN ABRAHAM
BONALD, LOUIS GABRIEL AMBROISE, VICOMTE DE **4:**1199
BONAN (fam.) **4:**1199
- Tunisia **15:**1444
Bonan, David **4:**1200
Bonan, Ḥayyim Mordecai **4:**1200
Bonan, Isaac (18/19 cent.) **4:**1200
Bonan, Isaac (19th cent.) **4:**1200
Bonan, Mas'ud **4:**1199
Bonaparte, Jerome Napoleon **13:**1492
- Westphalia **16:**474
Bonaparte, Joseph **8:**1389
Bonaparte, Louis (k., Holl.) **2:**900
- Dutch Jews **12:**981
Bonaparte, Napoleon, *see* NAPOLEON BONAPARTE
Bonastruc, En Samuel **15:**1299
BONASTRUC, ISAAC **4:**1200
Bonastrug da Porta, *see* NAḤMANIDES
Bonaventura, Arnaldo **4:**1201
BONAVENTURA, ENZO JOSEPH **4:**1200
Bonaventura di Manuele, *see* VOLTERRA, MESHULLAM BEN MENAHEM DA
Bonaventura Consiglio **6:**1437
BONAVOGLIA, MOSES DE MEDICI **4:**1201
BONCIU, H. **14:**425
Bondage, *see* SLAVERY
BONDAVIN, BONJUDAS (Bonjusas) **4:**1201
- Marseilles **11:**1057
BONDI (fam.) **4:**1201
Bondi, Abraham **4:**1202
Bondi, Abraham ben Yom Tov **4:**1202
Bondi, Adam Raphael **4:**1202
BONDI, ARON **5:**380
BONDI, AUGUST **4:**1202
Bondi, Eliezer **4:**1202
Bondi, Elijah ben Selig **4:**1202
Bondi, George **13:**1366
Bondi, Ḥananiah Mazzal Tov **4:**1202
BONDI, SIR HERMANN **4:**1203
Bondi, Inge **13:**484
Bondi, Isaac of Prague **12:**1420
BONDI, JONAS **4:**1203
Bondi, Meshullam **4:**1202
Bondi, Mordecai **4:**1202
Bondi, Nehemiah Feivel **4:**1202
Bondi (Wise), Selma **4:**1204; **16:**565
Bondi, Shifrah, *see* Oppenheim, Shifra
Bondi, Simeon ben Isaac **4:**1202
Bondi, Solomon Zalman **4:**1202
Bondi, Yom Tov ben Abraham **4:**1202
Bondia (fam.), *see* BONDI
Bondoa, Todros Moses **15:**1328
Bonds (legal), *see* SHETAR
BONDS, STATE OF ISRAEL **4:**1204
- Ben-Gurion **4:**510
- Boyar, Louis H. **4:**1277
- Rosenblatt, Bernard **14:**281
- *illus:*
-- Eshkol, Levi, N.Y. **12:**1113
-- function, Montreal **5:**110
-- Israel stamps **9:**844-845
-- Meir, Golda, addressing dinner **15:**1668
Bondsman, *see* SLAVERY
Bondy (fam. name), *see also* Bondi
BONDY, BOHUMIL (Gottlieb) **4:**1205
BONDY, CURT **4:**1206
BONDY, FILIP **4:**1206
- Svaz Čechů-Židů **5:**267
Bondy, Jonah **4:**1202
Bondy, Joseph **15:**635
Bondy, Leo J. **15:**301
BONDY, MAX **4:**1207
Bondy, Samuel **4:**1202
BÔNE (city, Alg.) **4:**1207
- Tunisia **15:**1431; **15:**1439
Bone, Sir Muirhead **4:**1197
Boneh (disciple, Jesus) **10:**15
Boneh, Shmuel **3:**593
Bones, gathering of, *see* LIKKUT AẒAMOT
Bonet, Jacob **4:**1210
Bonet ben Meshullam ben Solomon Avigdor (philos.), *see* AVIGDOR, ABRAHAM
Bonet de Lattes, *see* LATTES, BONET
Bonfed, Solomon ben Reuben, *see* BONAFED, SOLOMON BEN REUBEN
Bonfiglioli, R. **9:**1139
Bonfil, R. **15:**1455
BONFILS, IMMANUEL BEN JACOB **4:**1207
- *Gests of Alexander* **2:**580
BONFILS, JOSEPH BEN ELIEZER **4:**1208
- David ben Joshua **4:**1351
BONFILS, JOSEPH BEN SAMUEL **4:**1208
- Anjou and Limousin **3:**23
- moneylending **12:**248
- takkaot **15:**736
Bonfils de Narbonne **7:**146
BONFRÈRE, JAQUES **4:**1209
Bongetius, J. **8:**24
Bongiorno, Bonat (David) **13:**130
Boni, Albert **13:**486; **13:**1371
Boni, Charles **13:**1372
BONIFACE VIII (pope) **4:**1209
- popes **13:**854
BONIFACE IX (pope) **4:**1209
- popes **13:**855
- Rome Jews **14:**247
Bonifaci, Natale **9:**1544
Bonifazio da Ragusa **7:**47
Bonirac, Solomon **7:**264; **15:**1326
BONJORN, BONET DAVI(D) (astron.) **4:**1210
Bonjorn, Davi(d) Bonet (physic.) **4:**1210
- *Al Tehi ke-Avotekha* **3:**196
- Duran **3:**196
Bonjudas Miles, *see* Samuel ben Judah of Marseilles
Bonjuhes, Jacob **14:**353
BONN (city, Ger.) **4:**1210
- *illus:* text
BONN, HANUŠ **5:**1208
- Prague **13:**974
Bonn, Herb **15:**301
BONN, MORITZ JULIUS **4:**1212
Bonn, Moses **2:**780
Bonn, Sebastian **6:**321
Bonnard, August **13:**1340
Bonne (cartog.) **11:**927
BONNÉ, ALFRED ABRAHAM **4:**1212
Bonnet, Charles **11:**1332ff
Bonnet, Georges **11:**679
Bonnier, Adolf **13:**1368
Bonnier, Albert **13:**1368
Bonnier, Karl Otto **13:**1368
Bonnom (mintmaster) **12:**62
Bono, David **4:**1238
Bon Senior ibn Ḥisdai, *see* Ibn Ḥisdai, Bon Senior
Bonsenyor, Astruc ben Judah **4:**1213
- Cavalleria, Judah de la **5:**261
- Murcia **12:**530
BONSENYOR, JUDAH (Jafuda) **4:**1213
- Barcelona **4:**209
Bonte (fam.), *see* BONDI
BONYHAD (tn., Hung.) **4:**1213
Bonysach (landowner) **5:**158
Boochever, Louis **13:**1361
Böök, Fredrik **14:**931
Bookbinding **5:**1048
- books **4:**1230
- Jewish artists **3:**536
- *illus:*
-- Bible bindings **4:**244, 1228
-- prayer book bindings **4:**1230, 1231
Book collectors, *see* BIBLIOPHILES
Book of..., *see also Sefer ..., and under keyword*
Book of the Acts of Solomon (Bib. source) **8:**552
BOOK OF THE COVENANT **4:**1214
- *Contents:*
-- Introduction **4:**1214
-- Cuneiform Laws **4:**1214
-- Distinguishing Features **4:**1215
-- Date **4:**1216
- Deuteronomy, Book of **5:**1573
- Exodus, Book of **6:**1059
- Hurrian laws **12:**1289
- moneylending **12:**244; **12:**245
- Pentateuch **13:**254
Book of the Covenant of Damascus, *see* DAMASCUS, BOOK OF THE COVENANT OF
Book of Creation (kab. wk.), *see* YEẒIRAH, SEFER
Book of the Dead (anc. Egy.) **6:**938; **12:**996
BOOK OF JASHAR **4:**1217
- poetry **13:**677
Book of Jewish Concepts **6:**734
Book of Jewish Knowledge **6:**734
BOOK OF LIFE **4:**1217
Book of the Religion, Ceremonies, and Prayers of the Jews **7:**299
Book of the Sacred Magic of Abra-Melin **10:**636
BOOK OF THE WARS OF THE LORD **4:**1218
- historiography **8:**551
- poetry **13:**677
BOOKPLATES **4:**1219
- Widmanstetter's trilingual **16:**487
- *illus:*
-- text
-- Adler, Elkan Nathan **2:**275
-- Friedenwald, Harry **7:**176
-- Heller, James Gutheim **8:**305
-- Liebman, Joshua Loth **11:**225
Book Publishers' Association of Israel **13:**1379
BOOKS **4:**1220
- *Contents:*
-- Production, Treatment **4:**1220
-- Bindings **4:**1229
-- Illustrations **4:**1233
- archives **3:**366
- art **3:**536
- bibliography **4:**970
- binding **5:**1048
- bookplates **4:**1219
- book trade **4:**1237
- cartoons **5:**177
- censorship **5:**276
- colophon **5:**748
- copyright safeguards **7:**1464
- *haskamah* **7:**1452
- heresy **8:**361
- illuminated manuscripts **8:**1259ff
- incunabula **8:**1319
- investigation of **14:**921
- Jewish National Library **11:**197
- *kunteres* **10:**1292
- letter writing **11:**55
- libraries **11:**190
- Louis IX **11:**515
- manuscripts **11:**899
- Markl and Bernstein **8:**1369
- pledge **13:**641
- prayer **13:**985
- prefaces **7:**1144
- printing **13:**1096
- sages **14:**639
- seals **14:**1080
- Sefer Torah **14:**1100
- tax **15:**847,850
- yeshivot **16:**768
- *illus:* text
- *see also:* WRITING, SCRIPTS, MATERIALS AND INSCRIPTIONS
BOOKS OF THE CHRONICLES OF THE KINGS OF JUDAH AND ISRAEL (Bib. source) **4:**1236
- Chronicles **5:**517
- historiography **8:**552
Bookstaber, Philip D. **7:**1348
BOOK TRADE **4:**1237
- *illus:*
-- *Aggadat Shemu'el* (1576) **3:**438
-- Jerusalem, Third International Book Fair **9:**766
- *see also:* BIBLIOGRAPHY; BOOKS; LIBRARIES
Boone, Daniel **10:**909; **15:**1305,1595
BOORSTIN, DANIEL J. **4:**1240
Boote, Arnold (Arnt) **8:**24
Booths, Feast of, *see* SUKKOT
Booty **11:**510
Bopp, Franz **4:**1335
BOPPARD (tn., Ger.) **4:**1240
- Baruch ben Samuel **4:**280
- history chart (1195-96) **8:**766-767
Boqeq (loc., Er. Isr.) **5:**1394
Bor (damages category) **3:**988ff; **15:**1272ff
Bor, Josef **5:**1208
Borach, Fanny, *see* BRICE, FANNY
BORAH, WOODROW WILSON **8:**544
BORAISHA, MENAHEM **4:**1241
Borak (tn., Yug.) **14:**869
Boras (city, Swed.) **15:**550
Borba (gov., Arcila) **3:**399

Borchardt, Georg, *see* HERMANN, GEORG
Borchardt, Jens **4:**1241; **14:**1414
Borchardt, Karl **4:**1241
BORCHARDT, LUCY **4:**1241
- shipping **14:**1414
BORCHARDT, LUDWIG **4:**1241
- archaeology **3:**302
Borchardt, Richard **4:**1241
Borchardt, Rudolf **7:**441
BORCHSENIUS, POUL **4:**1242
BORDEAUX (city, Fr.) **4:**1243
- archives **3:**387
- *illus:* text
Bordeaux Itinerary (bk.), *see* ITINERARIUM HIEROSOLYMITANUM
"Bordeaux Pilgrim" (Chr. trav.) **15:**1355
BORDJEL (fam.) **4:**1247
- Tunisia **15:**1444
Bordjel, Avraham **4:**1247; **15:**1444
Bordjel, Elijah Ḥai **4:**1247; **15:**1444
Bordjel, Joseph **4:**1247
Bordjel, Moses **4:**1247
Bordjel, Nathan **2:**629; **4:**1247
Bordjel, Solomon **4:**1247
Bordon, Abraham S. **5:**900; **7:**1360
Boré, Eugène **8:**24
Boreel, Adam, *see* Borel, Adam
Borei Nefashot (blessing) **7:**841
Borejsza, J. **13:**1370
Borel, Adam **8:**24
BORGE, VICTOR **15:**1079
Borgel, Elie **5:**817
Borgen, Johan **14:**933
Borgenicht, Louis **12:**1085
Borgentreich (tn., Ger.) **13:**7
Borges, Jorge Luis **15:**255
Borgese, Giuseppe **9:**1107
Borghese, Valerio **12:**952
BORGHI, LAMBERTO **4:**1247
Borgia, Rodrigo (pope), *see* ALEXANDER VI
BORGIL, ABRAHAM BEN AZIZ **4:**1248
Borgo San Sepolcro (tn., It.) **15:**1468ff
Borgwall, A. **8:**24
BORINSTEIN, LOUIS J. **4:**1248
Borion (loc.) **15:**1432
Boris I (Bulg.) **4:**1480
Boris III (k., Bulg.) **4:**1488
Boris, Pierre **11:**1562
BORIS, RUTHANNA **5:**1271
Borishanski, R. **7:**767
BORISLAV (city, Rus.) **4:**1248
BORISOV (tn., Rus.) **4:**1250
BORISOV, ANDREY YAKOVLEVICH **4:**1250
Borjel, *see* Bordjel
Borkum, Kalman **9:**1336
Borkum, Samson **9:**1336
BORMANN, MARTIN **4:**1250
Born (loc., Neth.) **12:**974
Born, Gustav **4:**1251
BORN, MAX **4:**1251
- *illus:* text
BORNFRIEND, JACOB **4:**1251
- *illus:* text
Bornstein, Abraham ben Ze'ev Nahum, *see* SOCHACZEW, ABRAHAM BEN ZE'EV NAHUM BORNSTEIN OF
Bornstein, Bertha **13:**1339
Bornstein, David (mfr.) **15:**1215
Bornstein, David (r.) **16:**682
BORNSTEIN, ELI **4:**1252
BORNSTEIN, ḤAYYIM JEHIEL **4:**1252
- translator **14:**1264
Bornstein, Samuel **15:**24
Bornsztejn, Rachmiel **10:**1554
BOROCHOV, BER (Dov) **4:**1253
- Vozrozhdeniye **16:**230
- Zionist socialism **15:**45
BORODAVKA, ISAAC **4:**1257
Borodianski (ed.) **10:**1137
BORODIN, MICHAEL MARKOVITSCH **4:**1258
Boro Park (section, N.Y.C.) **12:**1082; **12:**1107
Borough (dist., London) **6:**447
BOROVSKY, ALEXANDER **12:**684
Borrell, Jaime **4:**879
Borrha (us), Martin, *see* Cellarius, Martin
BORROMEO, CARLO **4:**1258
Borrow, George Henry **2:**296; **6:**780
BORSA (vill., Transyl.) **4:**1258
Borshchov (tn., Pol.) **13:**768
BORSIPPA (city, Babyl.) **4:**1259
- excavation **16:**1507
Borso (Duke of Ferrara) **12:**1137
Borsodi, Joseph **10:**862
BORSOOK, HENRY **4:**1259
Bortniker, Elijah **6:**904
Boruch, Behn **5:**452
Borwicz (Boruchowicz), Michal Maksymilian **13:**803
Boryslaw (city, Rus.), *see* BORISLAV
Borzenburg (tn., Ger.) **11:**1163
Borzykowski, Tuvia **13:**1503
Bosai (gaon) **7:**324
BOSAK, MEIR **4:**1260
Bosch, Hieronymus **9:**1580
- *illus:*
- - Jerusalem landscape **9:**1583
- - "The Garden of Eden" **2:**243
Bosch, Jacobus **8:**24
Böschenstein, Johann **8:**24
BOSCOVITCH, ALEXANDER URIYAH **4:**1260
Bosem (spice), *see* BALSAM
BOSHAL, MOSES BEN SOLOMON **4:**1261
BOSHAM, HERBERT DE **4:**1261
- Hebraist **8:**24
Boshes, Benjamin **11:**1201
BOSKOFF, ALVIN **4:**1261
BOSKOVICE (Boskowitz; tn., Morav.) **4:**1261
- archives **3:**387
- Slovakia **14:**1679
- *illus:*
- - text
- - Jewish quarter **10:**86
Boskovitz, David **13:**1554
Boskovitz, Feivel ben Asher **7:**999
BOSKOWITZ, BENJAMIN ZE'EV (Wolf) HALEVI **4:**1263
BOSKOWITZ, ḤAYYIM BEN JACOB **4:**1263
Bosna-Serai (city, Yug.), *see* SARAJEVO
Bosnian-Herzegovinian Republic **14:**869; **16:**868ff
Bosora (city, Er. Isr.), *see* BOZRAH
BOSPHORUS, KINGDOM OF **4:**1263
BOSSUET, JACQUES BENIGNE **4:**1264
- Bible translations **4:**881
- French literature **7:**140
Bostal, Moses ben Solomon, *see* BOSHAL, MOSES BEN SOLOMON
BOSTON (city, Mass.) **4:**1264
- Benei Zion **6:**1337
- Brandeis, Louis **4:**1296
- Friedman, Lee Max **7:**186
- library **11:**193
- Massachusetts **11:**1112ff
- Soloveitchik, Joseph Dov **15:**132
- *illus:*
- - text
- - Hebrew Teachers' College **8:**215
- - synagogue **11:**1115
- - Teachers' minute book **3:**384
- - Zionist Organization of America convention (1915) **15:**1623
Botahari (lang.) **14:**1153
Botany, *see* Afforestation in Israel; Flora and Fauna; FLORA AND FAUNA IN ISRAEL; FLOWERS; SPICES
BOTAREL, MOSES BEN ISAAC **4:**1268
- Baruch, the Kabbalist **4:**268
- Kabbalah **10:**539
- *Sefer Yeẓirah* **16:**787
Botein, Bernard **12:**1127
Botha, Louis **16:**1140
Bothe, Walter **4:**1251
Bothmann, Hans **5:**374
Botius, Arnold, *see* Boote, Arnold
BOTKIN, HENRY **3:**597
Botna (fort., Er. Isr.) **8:**228
Boton, Abraham ben Jacob di **4:**1270
BOTON, ABRAHAM BEN JUDAH DI **4:**1269
BOTON, ABRAHAM BEN MOSES DI **4:**1269
- Salonika **14:**702
Boton, David di **4:**1269
BOTON, ḤIYYA ABRAHAM BEN AARON DI **4:**1270
BOTON, JACOB BEN ABRAHAM DI **4:**1270
BOTON, MEIR BEN ABRAHAM DI **4:**1270
Boton, Moses de **3:**24
BOTOSANI (tn., Rum.) **4:**1271
- Rumania **14:**397,398
BOTOSHANSKY, JACOB **4:**1272
- theater **15:**1073
Botswana (rep., Afr.) **9:**438
Botta, Paul-Emile **16:**1506
Botticelli **10:**460
- *illus:*
- - Jethro's daughters (frsc.) **10:**18
BOTVINNIK, MIKHAIL **4:**1272
- chess **5:**404ff
BOUCHARA (fam.) **4:**1273
Bouchara, Abraham (18th cent.) **4:**1273
Bouchara, Abraham (d. 1801) **4:**1273
Bouchara, Isaac **4:**1273
Bouchara, Jacob Raphael **4:**1273
Bouchara, Joseph **4:**1273
BOUDIN, JEAN-FRANÇOIS **4:**1273
Boudin, Leonard **10:**1505
Boudin, Louis **15:**30
Bouget, Jean **8:**24
BOUGIE (tn., Alg.) **4:**1273
- Tunisia **15:**1439
Boujad (tn., Mor.) **12:**344
Boulaese, Jean **8:**24
Boulanger, Georges Ernest Jean Marie **3:**85
Boulanger, Nadia **2:**292; **14:**1190
BOULAY (tn., Fr.) **4:**1274
Boulder (city, Colo.) **5:**753
Boulder City (vill., Nev.) **12:**1018
Boulduc, Jacques, *see* Bolduc, Jacques
BOULE (council) **4:**1274
Boumédienne, Houari **2:**619
BOUNDARIES OF ISRAEL (ancient, medieval) **9:**112
- Gerar, Land of **7:**432
- Solomon's division **15:**102ff
- twelve tribes **15:**1381
- *illus:*
- - border police **9:**695
- - Lebanese frontier at Rosh ha-Nikrah **10:**1547
- *maps:*
- - Alexander Yannai's kingdom **9:**118; **16:**715
- - armistice demarcation lines, 1949 **9:**318
- - British Mandate, 1922 **9:**317
- - Canaan, borders **9:**112
- - David, limits of kingdom **9:**115
- - eighteenth century **11:**930
- - Franco-British agreements, 1920-23 **9:**316
- - Gaza Strip **7:**344
- - Hebrew map, 17th cent. **11:**927
- - Herod, borders of kingdom **9:**118
- - Herod, divided kingdom **8:**375
- - Hittite empire **8:**788
- - Jordan River **10:**191
- - Judah and Israel, divided kingdom **9:**116,117
- - Judges, period of, limits of Israelite control **9:**113
- - Moab, time of Mesha **12:**193
- - Near East, 3rd millennium B.C.E. **15:**513
- - non-Ptolemaic design, 14th cent. **11:**925
- - Philistine Pentapolis **13:**400
- - pictorial map, 12th cent. ms. **11:**923
- - Plan C, Woodhead Commission **13:**38
- - Saul, limits of kingdom **9:**114; **14:**910
- - Six-Day War cease fire lines **9:**318
- - Solomon, limits of kingdom **9:**115; **15:**97
- - Sykes-Picot agreement, 1916 **9:**315
- - tribal territories **3:**700; **4:**522; **5:**1256; **6:**807; **7:**247; **9:**1075; **10:**327; **11:**137,852; **12:**820; **14:**104,1548; **16:**951
- - UNSCOP partition plan, 1947 **9:**317
- - Yehud province **9:**119
- - Zionist Movement frontier proposals, 1919 **9:**316
Bound Brook (loc., N.J.) **11:**1504; **12:**1030
Bouquett, Philip **8:**24
Bourassé, J.J.B. **4:**881
Bourdeillette, Jean **7:**42
Bourdelot, Jean **8:**24
BOURG-EN-BRESSE (city, Fr.) **4:**1275
- Bresse **4:**1358
BOURGEOIS, JEAN **4:**1275
BOURGES (city, Fr.) **4:**1275
Bourguiba, Habib **12:**346; **15:**1450ff
Bourgogne (reg., Fr.), *see* DIJON
Bouriron (tn., Er. Isr.), *see* BEROR ḤAYIL
Boutedieu, *see* WANDERING JEW
Bouwmeester (fam.) **15:**1057
Bouwmeester, Frederik Christianus **15:**1058
Bouwmeester, Lily **15:**1058
Bouwmeester, Louise Francina Maria **15:**1057
BOUWMEESTER, LOUIS FREDERICK JOHANNES **15:**1079
Bouwmeester, Theodora Antonia Louis **15:**1058
Bouxwiller (tn., Alsace) **2:**752; **2:**754
BOVE-BUKH (bk.) **4:**1276
- Jewish literature **11:**359
- Levita, Elijah **11:**133
- Yiddish literature **16:**807
- *illus:* text
- *see also:* BOBE-MAYSE
Bover, J.M. **4:**879
Bovo D'Antona (bk.), *see* BOVE-BUKH
BOVSHOVER, JOSEPH **4:**1276
- Shakespeare **14:**1265
Bow (weapon) **16:**266ff
Bowling (sport) **7:**300; **15:**305

- illus:
- - Lindsey, Mortimer 15:304
Bowls, Lawn (sport), see Lawn Bowls
Bowman, Thomas 8:24
BOX (bot.) 4:1277
- plant list 13:615
Box, G. H. 12:1332
Boxer, Oswald 4:1325
Boxing (sport) 15:305
- illus:
- - Elias, Samuel 15:305
- - Kaplan, Louis "Kid" 15:310
- - Mendoza, Daniel 11:1348
Boxthorn (bot.) 13:615
Boyan (ḥas. dyn.) 7:1422; 14:531
- illus:
- - tish 7:1406
Boyan (vill., Buk.), see BOJAN
BOYAR, LOUIS H. 4:1277
Boyarski, B. 13:145
BOYCOTT, ANTI-JEWISH 4:1277
- Agobard 2:372
- Galicia 16:1330
- Germany 7:489
- Toledo 15:1203
- universities 15:1676
- Warsaw 8:735
- illus:
- - text
- - Berlin (1933) 8:837
- - Hamburger Tageblatt 7:1229
- - Magdeburg, 1938 8:849
BOYCOTT, ANTI-NAZI 4:1280
- A.J.C. 10:66
- Haavara 7:1012
- illus:
- - American Jewish Congress demonstration 15:1629
- - New York pickets 15:1631
- table: text
BOYCOTT, ARAB 4:1282
- economic warfare 9:427
- Olympic games 15:296
Boycott, Jewish (Ancona) 2:942
Boye, Karin 14:930
Boykoff, Harry 15:303
Boymvol, Rachel 5:440; 16:826
Boys, John, see Bois, John
Boysk (tn., Rus.), see BAUSKA
Bozecco (fam.) 2:934
BOZECCO (Bozecchi), BENJAMIN BEN JUDAH 4:1283
Bozeman (city, Mont.) 12:266
Bozhilov, Dobri 4:1488
Bözödújfalú (vill., Transyl.), see BEZIDUL NOU
BOZRAH (city, Bashan) 4:1284
- Halakhot Gedolot 7:1169
- Teman 15:941
BOZRAH (city, Edom) 4:1284
- Edom 6:370
BOZRAH (vill., Trachonitis) 4:1284
- Trachonitis 15:1293
- plan: text
BOẒRAH (mosh., Isr.) 4:1285
- statistics 1: place list
BOZYK, MAX 15:1079
BOZZOLO (tn., It.) 4:1287
Brabanel, see ABRABANEL
Brabant (prov., Belg.) 4:416; 12:974
Bracelet 13:1013
BRACH, SAUL 4:1287
Brack, Viktor 5:85
- euthanasia 16:1332
Bracon (tn., Fr.) 7:45
Braddock (boro., Pa.) 13:230
BRADFORD (city, Eng.) 4:1287
Bradlaugh, Charles 5:667
Bradlow, Henry 4:1112
Brady, Adolph 3:824
Braemsonius, Anders Henrikson, see Brunchmann, Anders Henriksen
BRAFMAN, JACOB 4:1287
- apostasy 3:207
- Vilna 16:144
Braga, Isaac ben Don Solomon de 4:960
- Kennicott Bible 5:976
Braga, Solomon de 5:976
BRAGADINI (fam.) 4:1288
- Haggadah, illustrated 7:1102
- haskamah development 7:1452
- printing 13:1095
Bragadini, Alvise 4:1288
- Venice 16:101
- illus:
- - printer's mark 13:1093
Bragadini, Giovanni 4:1288
BRAGANZA (tn., Port.) 4:1288
- Moncorvo 12:241
- Vila Real 16:135
Bragin (tn., Belor.) 10:1153
Bragin, Abraham 5:1107
- Birobidzhan 4:1046
Braham, Francis Elizabeth (Countess Waldegrave) 4:1290
BRAHAM, JOHN 4:1289
- Isaac Nathan 12:853
- illus:
- - text
- - caricature 12:629
Braham, Louis 10:1492
Brahe, Tycho 3:793
Brahinsky, Mani-Leib, see MANI-LEIB
BRAHM, OTTO 4:1290
- Hirschfeld, Georg 8:524
Brahms, Johannes 4:1416; 12:704
BRAILA (city, Rum.) 4:1290
Braille, Hebrew alphabet 2:744
- illus:
- - Israel, geography textbook 9:950
BRAILOV (tn., Rus.) 4:1291
Brainin, Joseph 4:1292
BRAININ, REUBEN 4:1291
- archives 3:387
- critic 5:1118
- Hebrew literature 8:213
- illus:
- - text
- - First Zionist Congress 16:1165
Brain tumors 14:1503
Brakpan (tn., S.A.) 15:1340
Bramble (bot.) 15:1119
Brambling (bird) 6:30
BRAMPTON, EDWARD 4:1293
- Duarte Brandao 14:326
- illus: text
BRAMSON, LEON (Leonty) 4:1293
- politics 13:819
- relief work 16:734
Branche française de la Jewish Trust Corporation, see Jewish Trust Corporation
BRAND, JOEL JENŐ 4:1294
- Holocaust 8:907
- Zionism 16:1122
- illus:
- - Hull's cable re negotiations with Eichmann 8:909
- see also: KASZTNER, REZSO RUDOLF
Brand, Solomon 8:1055
BRANDÃO, AMBRÓSIO FERNANDES 4:1295
Brandao, Duarte 14:326
Brandão, Edward, see BRAMPTON, EDWARD
Brandeis (fam.) 13:1399
Brandeis, Adolph Dembitz 4:1295
Brandeis, David 12:184
Brandeis, Frederika 4:1295
Brandeis, Jacob 13:158; 13:1368
Brandeis, Jonas L. 12:1378
BRANDEIS, LOUIS DEMBITZ 4:1295
- Frankfurter, Felix 7:95
- history chart 8:766-767
- United States 15:1617ff
- Wilson, Woodrow 16:535
- Wise, Stephen 16:566
- Zionism 16:1081ff
- Zionist Congress 16:1171
- Z.O.A. 16:1179
- illus:
- - text
- - autograph 3:914
- - Brandeis University 4:1300-1301
- - Zionist Organization of America convention (1915) 15:1623
Brandeis, Salomon 15:1041
Brandeis an der Elbe (tn., Bohem.) see BRANDYS NAD LABEM
BRANDEIS UNIVERSITY 4:1300
- Abramovitz, Max 2:167
- illus: text
BRANDENBURG (state, city, Ger.) 4:1301
- history chart (1510,1671) 8:766-767
- host desecration 8:1043
- Prussia 13:1287ff
Brandenstein (fam.) 5:56
BRANDES, CARL EDVARD 4:1302
- Scandinavian Literature 14:927
BRANDES, GEORG 4:1302
- Scandinavian literature 14:927ff
Brandes, J. (hist.) 8:568
Brandes, Johann Christian (dram.) 10:26
BRANDES, LUDWIG ISRAEL 4:1304
Brandes, Marge 15:1055
Brandon (tn., Can.) 11:879
Brandon, Edward, see BRAMPTON, EDWARD
BRANDON, OHEB ISAAC 7:1546
BRANDSTAEDTER, MORDECAI DAVID 4:1304
BRANDSTAETTER, ROMAN 4:1305
Brandstein, M.J. 14:834
BRANDT, BORIS (Baruch) 4:1305
Brandwein, Eliezer 15:439
Brandwein, H. 9:1568
Brandwein, Judah Ẓevi (ḥas. ldr.), see STRETYN, JUDAH ẒEVI HIRSCH
BRANDWEIN, YEHUDAH ẒEVI (kab.) 4:1306
BRANDYS, KAZIMIERZ 4:1306
- Samson 14:775
Brandys, Marian 4:1307
BRANDYS NAD LABEM (tn., Bohem.) 4:1307
- illus: text
Branicki (Pol. sol.) 7:1133
Branisteanu, B. 14:399
BRANN, MARCUS 4:1307
- historiography 8:561
- Kaufmann, David 10:843
BRANT, HENRY DREYFUS 12:684
Brantford (tn., Ont.) 12:1408
Brasca, Santo 15:1356
Brasília (city, Braz.) 4:1329
BRASLAV (tn., Belor.) 4:1308
- ḥasidic music 7:1425
BRASLAVI (Braslavski), JOSEPH 4:1309
- Cairo genizah 16:1339
BRAȘOV (city, Transyl.) 4:1309
Brass (metal) 11:1435; 15:102
Brassai, Viktor 14:673
Brassó (city, Transyl.), see BRASOV
Bratianu, Ion 3:86
Bratianu, Ionel 14:393ff; 16:1133
BRATISLAVA (city, Cz.) 4:1309
- Alistál 2:633
- Shabbateanism 14:1253
- William of Austria 14:1079
- illus:
- - text
- - bet din, the old, entrance 4:721
- - street in Jewish quarter 5:1192
Bratring, Friedrich Wilhelm August 13:882
BRATSLAV (tn., Rus.) 4:1313
- Naḥman of Bratslav 12:782ff
- pogroms, 1919 13:669
Bratslav Ḥasidism, see NAḤMAN OF BRATSLAV
Brattelli, Trygve 12:1225
Braude, Aryeh Leib 11:612
BRAUDE, ERNEST ALEXANDER 4:1314
BRAUDE, MARKUS (Mordekhai Ze'ev) 4:1314
- Lodz 11:431
- illus:
- - First Zionist Congress 16:1165
BRAUDE, MAX A. 4:1315
- ORT 12:1485
BRAUDE, WILLIAM GORDON 4:1315
Braudes (fam.) 2:586
BRAUDES, REUBEN ASHER 4:1315
- Haskalah, Russia 8:188
BRAUDO, ALEXANDER ISAYEVICH 4:1317
Braudo, Benjamin 7:925
Braudo, Lazar 15:198
BRAUDO, YEVGENI MAXIMOVICH 12:684
Brauer, A., see Graur, A.
BRAUN, ABRAHAM (Bund ldr.) 4:1317
Braun, Abraham (Adolf; Pol.) 10:1241
BRAUN, ADOLF 4:1318
BRAUN, FELIX 4:1318
- illus:
- - portrait (Stumpp) 4:1319
Braun, Heinrich (Bib. schol.) 4:874
Braun, Heinrich (writ.) 4:1318
Braun, Johannes 8:24
Braun, Karl 11:1203
Braun, Lily 4:1318
BRAUN, MIECZYSLAW 13:803
Braun, Sergei, see BRAUN, ABRAHAM
Braun, Werner 13:487
BRAUN, YEHESKIEL 12:684
BRAUNER, VICTOR 4:1319
- Paris 13:114
Braunroth, Ḥayyim Benjamin 5:560
Braunschweig (city, Ger.), see BRUNSWICK
Braunstein (fam.) 16:534
BRAUNSTEIN, MENAHEM MENDEL 4:1320
Braunstein, Mieczyslaw, see BRAUN, MIECZYSLAW
Braunstein, Terry 15:317
BRAUNTHAL, JULIUS 4:1320
Braunwald, Eugene 11:1200
Braverman, Zerah 9:891
Bravo, Carlos Vergara 5:468
BRAWER, ABRAHAM JACOB 4:1321
BRAWER, MOSHE 1:28
Brawerman, Yehiel 13:775
BRAY-SUR-SEINE (vill., Fr.) 4:1321
- Philip II 13:392
Braz (fam.), see Braudes
Brazen Serpent, see COPPER SERPENT, THE
BRAZIL 4:1322
- Contents:
- - Colonial Period 4:1322
- - Agricultural Colonies 4:1325
- - Modern Period 4:1328
- - Communal Life 4:1329
- - Education and Culture 4:1330
- - Jews in National Life 4:1331
- - Ties with Israel 4:1332
- America 2:808; 2:816
- demography 5:1508

- education 6:457
- history chart 8:766-767
- I.C.A. 10:46
- Inquisition 8:1391
- Latin America 10:1450ff
- Noronha, Fernão de 12:1216
- politics 13:820
- population 13:883ff
- press 13:1040
- publishing 13:1370
- Raffalovich, Isaiah 13:1511
- Recife 13:1613
- refugees, Jewish 14:30
- slave trade 14:1662
- sugar 15:487ff
- synagogues 1:syn. list
- trade and commerce 15:1301ff
- War Crimes Trials 16:298
- Zionism 16:1124
- *illus:* text
- - Protocols of the Elders of Zion (1937) 6:583
- *pop. table:* text
- *see also:* RIO DE JANEIRO; SÃO PAULO
Brazilianer Yidishe Presse (journ.) 4:1331
Brazilianer Yidishe Tsaytung (journ.) 4:1331
Brazzaville (city, Congo) 9:438
BREAD 4:1333
- baking 5:939ff
- *cumin* 15:267
- fennelflower 15:268
- gentile 7:413
- grace after meals 7:838
- *ḥallah* 7:1194
- heretics 8:360
- *Kiddush* 10:974
- *manna* 11:884
- Rosh ha-Shanah 14:309
- shewbread 14:1394
- tares 15:809
- unleavened bread 11:1155
- washing hands 12:998
- *illus:*
- - *ḥallah*, traditional shapes 6:1419
- - *pittah* baking 4:1427
- *see also:* FOOD
Bread, Meat, and Coal society (Eng.) 13:377
"Bread and Knowledge" (slogan) 8:1347
BRÉAL, MICHEL 4:1335
Breasla Ovreilor ("J. Corp.," Rum.) 4:1439
Breast 8:7
BREASTPLATE (Torah ornament) 4:1335
- art 5:288
- precious stones 13:1007
- *illus:*
- - text
- - Bohemian, 18th cent. 5:296
- - German, 19th cent. 3:542
- - precious stones in High Priest's breastpiece (chart) 13:1007
- - silver 15:1260-1261
- *see also:* PRIESTLY VESTMENTS; URIM AND THUMMIM
Breche (loc., Fr.) 13:1397
Brecher, Adolph 13:1243
BRECHER, GIDEON 4:1336
- Prossnitz 13:1243
BRECHER, GUSTAVE 12:685
Brecht, J. Reinhart 8:24
Breck, A.D. 8:568
Breckenridge (city, Tex.) 15:1036
BRECLAV (tn., Cz.) 4:1336
Breda, H. L. van 8:1134
BREDIG, GEORGE 5:380
Breendonck (concen. camp) 4:421; 8:858
Bregenz (city, Aus.) 16:223
Breger, Dave 5:220
Breger, Irving 5:220
Bregman, J. (Rus.) 16:229
Bregman, James (sport., U.S.) 12:1377; 15:311
BREGMAN, SIDNEY 3:363
- *illus:*
- - Niagara Falls tower 3:355
BREGSTEIN, MARCEL HENRI 10:1507
Breidenbach, Julius 4:1345
Breidenbach, Moritz 4:1345
BREIDENBACH, WOLF 4:1336
Breier, Eduard 16:917
BREISACH (tn., Ger.) 4:1345
- *illus:* text
Breisch, Mordecai Jacob 14:93
Breit, Barbara 15:315
Breitbart, Josef 15:1061
Breitbart, Siegmund 15:1061
Breitenbach, Bernard 11:928
Breitenstein, M. 8:411
Breiter, Emil 13:803
BREITHAUPT, JOHANN FRIEDRICH 4:1345
- Hebraist 8:24
BREITNER, HUGO 4:1346
BREMEN (city, Ger.) 4:1346
- Vienna, Congress of 16:132
- *illus:* text
Bremer, Fredrika 14:929
Bremerton (city, Wash.) 16:356
Bremgarten (tn., Switz.) 15:560
Brenner, Arvid 14:931
BRENNER, JOSEPH ḤAYYIM 4:1347
- Berdyczewski, Micha 4:594
- Berkowitz, Yitzhak 4:637
- critic 5:1121
- drama, Hebrew 6:202
- Hebrew literature 8:198
- Jerusalem theme 9:1566
- *illus:*
- - Givat Brenner 7:597
- *see also:* HA-ME'ORER
Brenner, Uri 13:47
BRENNER, VICTOR 4:1351
BRENTANO (fam.) 4:1351
Brentano, Arthur 4:1351; 15:307
Brentano, August (1831-1886) 4:1351
Brentano, August (1853-1899) 4:1351
Brentano, C.M. 4:874
Brentano, Franz Clemens 10:1245
Brentano, Lowell 4:1352
Brentano, Simon 4:1351
BRESCH (Bres), JUDAH LOEB (Leo) BEN MOSES NAPHTALI 4:1352
- Bible translations 4:867
BRESCIA (city, It.) 4:1352
- *illus:* text
Brescia Bible 4:837; 13:1306
Breshk (tn., Alg.) 2:613
BRESLAŞU, MARCEL 14:418; 14:425
- literature 4:935; 5:453
BRESLAU (city, Pol.) 4:1353
- archives 3:380
- Council of (1266) 5:548
- history chart 8:766-767
- host desecration 8:1043
- Lesser Poland 11:48
- museum 12:538
- rabbinical conference 13:1461; 14:24
- Silesia 14:1536ff
- *illus:*
- - text
- - Juedisch-Theologisches Seminar 10:465
Breslau, Abraham of Muelhausen 4:1357
BRESLAU, ARYEH LOEB BEN ḤAYYIM 4:1356
Breslau, David 12:505; 16:302
Breslau, Isadore 2:819
- *illus:*
- - protest against 1940 White Paper 15:1632
BRESLAU, JOSEPH MOSES BEN DAVID 4:1357
Breslau, Michael Meyer 12:505; 16:302
Breslauer, Bernhard 16:105; 16:110
Breslau Juedisch-Theologisches Seminar, *see* JUEDISCH-THEOLOGISCHES SEMINAR, BRESLAU
BRESLAW, JOSEPH 4:1357
Bresler, Charles E. 5:1567
Bresmes (vill., Fr.) 4:1322
Bresnitz-Lokschan (tn., Bohem.), *see* BREZNICE
BRESSE (reg., Fr.) 4:1358
Bresselau, Mendel 11:1161
BRESSELAU, MEYER ISRAEL 4:1358
BRESSLAU, ERNST 4:1358
BRESSLAU, HARRY 4:1359
Bresslau, Helena 4:1359
Bresslau, Israel 12:1421
Bresslau, Mendel ben Ḥayyim Judah 6:195
Bresslau, M.H. 10:40
BRESSLER, DAVID MAURICE 4:1359
Bressuire (tn., Fr.) 13:704
Brest (city, Fr.) 4:1383
Brest (city, Rus.), *see* BREST-LITOVSK
Brest Kujavsk (tn., Pol.), *see* BRZESC KUJAWSKI
BREST-LITOVSK (city, Rus.) 4:1359
- dyeing center 6:328
- history chart 8:766-767
- Saul Wahl 16:242
- Slonim 14:1672
BRETHOLZ, BERTHOLD 4:1363
Brethren (Hussites) 8:1136
BRETHREN OF SINCERITY, EPISTLES OF (philos. treatises) 4:1364
- microcosm doctrine 11:1502
Breton, André 4:1319
Brett, Richard 8:24
BREUER, ISAAC 4:1364
- Agudat Israel 2:422; 2:424
- apologetics 3:200
- Orthodoxy 12:1488
- S.R. Hirsch 8:514
BREUER, JOSEPH (physic.) 4:1365
BREUER, JOSEPH (r.) 4:1365
BREUER, RAPHAEL 4:1365
BREUER, SOLOMON 4:1366
- S.R. Hirsch 8:514
Breviarium Alaricianse (Visigothic laws) 2:510
Breviary of Philip the Fair (13th cent. illum. ms., Fr.) 14:793
Brews, Sidney 15:309
BREYER, JULIUS (Gyula) 5:408
Breyter, Isaac 13:820
Brezhnev, Leonid I. 3:158
Brezhover, Dov Ber, *see* BIRKENTHAL, DOV BER
Březina, Otakar 5:1207
Brezis (fam., Rum.) 13:650
Brezis, Judah Aryeh 13:650
BREZNICE (tn., Bohem.) 4:1366
- museum 12:543
- *illus:* text
Briançon (tn., Fr.) 5:1315
BRIBERY 4:1367
- ethics 6:933,936
- fines 6:1288
BRICE, FANNY 15:1079
- Rose, Billy 14:267
Briceni (tn., Bess.), *see* BRICHANY
BRICEVA (stlmt., Bess.) 4:1368
BRICHANY (tn., Bess.) 4:1369
BRICK, DANIEL 4:1369
- Sweden 15:551
BRICKMAN, WILLIAM W. 1:28
Brickner, Balfour 4:1370
BRICKNER, BARNETT ROBERT 4:1369
- Cleveland 5:610; 5:612
- Toronto 15:1260; 15:1261
Brickner, Max 14:211
Bride and Bridegroom
- Arta controversy 3:645
- *aufrufen* 3:849
- bridal veil 16:84
- Commandments, the 613 5:770,781
- confession of sins 5:880
- folklore 6:1398; 6:1400; 6:1404
- hairstyle 5:982
- *hakhnasat kallah* 7:1149
- *ḥakkafot* 7:1153
- *ketubbah* 10:927
- maintenance 11:784
- *niddui* as compulsory measure 8:354
- Samaritans 14:745
- vineyard dances 5:1263
- wreaths, wearing of 5:1133
- *illus:*
- - Amsterdam marriage ceremony 11:1029
- - Arab village wedding 9:1027
- - Bukharan bridal gown Pl. 9 6-DRESS
- - comb, decorative 11:*fcg.* 1070
- - fifteenth cent. marriage scene 11:*fcg.* 1003
- - Frankfort bridal procession 11:1027
- - German wedding, 18th cent. 11:1031
- - *Hamburg Halakhah Miscellany* 16:*fcg.* 615
- - Italian couple, 15th cent. 4:66
- - marriage belts, Germany 11:1043
- - *mezuzah* cover gift 11:1475
- - Moroccan bridal costume 11:1044
- - Moroccan bride's "Grand Costume" Pl. 6 6-DRESS
- - painting by I. Kaufmann 11:*fcg.* 1070
- - Portuguese marriage ceremony 11:1030
- - *Shabbat ha-Gadol piyyut* 14:1217
- *see also:* BETROTHAL; DOWRY; MARRIAGE
BRIDEGROOMS OF THE LAW 4:1370
- Simḥat Torah 14:1573; 15:502
- *illus:*
- - cantata 12:622
Bridge (period.) 3:885; 13:1025
BRIDGEPORT (city, Conn.) 4:1371
- *illus:* text
Bridger, D. 6:734
Bridgetown (Barb.) 4:205
Bridie, James 6:776; 15:533
BRIE, LUIS HARTWIG 4:1372
Brie-Comte-Robert (vill., Fr.) 4:1322; 13:392
Brieg (tn., Pol.), *see* BRZEG
Brieger, Lothar 3:652
BRIEL, JUDAH BEN ELIEZER 4:1372
- Hayon, Nehemiah 7:1502
- Mantua 11:898
- *illus:* text
Brifnshteler (bk.) 6:433
Brighenti, Giovanni Antonio 8:24
Bright (fam.) 14:1336
Bright, John 4:908
Bright, Myron 12:1221
BRIGHTON (tn., Eng.) 4:1373
- *illus:* text
Brighton (dist., Boston) 11:1112
Briks, R. 16:813

Bril, A., *see* PERLOV, YIZḤAK
Bril, Slavko **16:**918
Brilin, Eliezer Sussmann ben Isaac **4:**47
Brilin, Fani, *see* WOLF, FRUMET
Brill (pseud.), *see* LOEWE, JOEL
BRILL, ABRAHAM ARDEN **4:**1374
BRILL, AZRIEL **4:**1374
Brill, Hirsh, of Kovno **14:**917
BRILL, JEHIEL **4:**1374
– *see also:* HA-LEVANON
BRILL, JOSEPH **4:**1375
– parody **13:**135
Brill, Samuel Loew **4:**1374
– Hirsch, Markus **8:**505
BRILLING, BERNHARD **4:**1375
Brimanus (anti-Sem., Rum.) **14:**224
Brin, Arthur **12:**38
BRINDISI (seaport, It.) **4:**1375
– *illus:* text
BRINIG, MYRON **4:**1376
Brisac (math.), *see* ENSHEIM, MOSES
Brisac, Gabriel Gustave **11:**1562
Brisac, Pierre **11:**1562
Brisack, Abraham **11:**568
BRISBANE (city, Austr.) **4:**1376
Briscoe, Abraham **11:**1554
Briscoe, Benjamin **4:**1378; **13:**812
BRISCOE, ROBERT **4:**1377
– Dublin **6:**249
– *illus:* text
Brisk (city, Rus.), *see* BREST-LITOVSK
Brisk, Issar Judah of, *see* ISSAR JUDAH BEN NEHEMIAH OF BRISK
Brisk, Nathan **14:**709
Brisker, Abraham ben Benjamin Ze'ev, *see* ABRAHAM BEN BENJAMIN ZE'EV BRISKER
Brisker, Ḥayyim, *see* SOLOVEICHIK, ḤAYYIM
Brisker, Yehuda, *see* HAEZRAḤI, YEHUDA
"Brisker Rebbetzin", *see* Rattner, Sarah
"Brisker Rov", *see* DISKIN, MOSES JOSHUA JUDAH LEIB
BRISTOL (city, Eng.) **4:**1378
– Jacobs, Lazarus **9:**1236
– *illus:*
– – text
– – Jewry Lane **10:**85
Bristol (tn., R. I.) **14:**143
Bristol (city, Tenn.) **15:**1009
Bristol County (R. I.) **14:**143
BRISZK (fam., Transyl.) **4:**1379
Briszk, Mordecai ben Joshua **4:**1379
Briszk, Nathan Ẓevi ben Joshua **4:**1379
Britain, *see* ENGLAND; SCOTLAND; WALES
Britenstool, Hirsch **14:**210
B'rith, B'rit . . ., *see also* Berit . . .
BRITH ABRAHAM (U.S. orgn.) **4:**1379
British and Foreign Bible Society **4:**969; **15:**1487
British Anti-War Council (boycott gr.) **4:**1281
British Army
– Haganah **9:**681f
– Jewish regiments **11:**1553
– *illus:*
– – Palestinian volunteers **9:**358
– – *see also:* JEWISH BRIGADE GROUP; Zion Mule Corps
British Association for the Jewish National Home **5:**1456
British Broadcasting Corporation **15:**930
BRITISH COLUMBIA (prov., Can.) **4:**1380
British consulate (Jer.) **14:**1639
British Guiana (state, S. Am.), *see* GUYANA
British Intelligence **9:**687
BRITISH ISRAELITES **4:**1381
– Brothers, Richard **4:**1409
– *illus:*
– – text
– – Brothers, Richard, *A Revealed Knowledge* . . . (1794) **4:**1409
British Mandate, *see* MANDATE FOR PALESTINE
British Museum, Hebraica collection
– Costa Athias, Solomon da **5:**989
– incunabula **8:**1322
– library **11:**193
– Zedner, Joseph **16:**965
British Museum Miscellany (Fr. ms.) **8:**1266
– Samson **14:**775
– Solomon **15:**110
– *illus:* **2:**341,453,788; **3:**788; **5:**398,958,1130; **6:**907; **7:**757; **8:***fcg.* 1271,1279; **14:**772
British Museum Mishneh Torah (ms., Port.) **8:**1265ff
British National Party **12:**952
British Palestine Exploration Fund, *see* PALESTINE EXPLORATION FUND
British Palestine Society **16:**1155
British Royal Commission, *see* PEEL COMMISSION
British School of Archaeology, Jerusalem **5:**1129; **7:**329
British Union of Fascists **11:**478 **12:**952
British Zionist Federation **5:**1024
BRIT IVRIT OLAMIT (assoc.) **4:**1382
– *illus:* text
Brito, David de Souza **10:**1429
Brito, Rui Mendes de, *see* Mendes, Rui
BRITTANY (reg., Fr.) **4:**1383
– Jews **7:**14ff
Britten, Benjamin **12:**918
Britto, Manuel de **11:**518
BRIVIESCA (city, Sp.) **4:**1383
BRNO (city, Cz.) **4:**1384
– Frankists **7:**67; **14:**1253
– Holocaust period **5:**1199
– Moravia **12:**296ff
– textiles **15:**1041
– *illus:*
– – ruins of synagogue **5:**1196
– – synagogue **12:**299
Broad, Thomas, *see* Brodaeus, Thomas
Broadcasting, Israel, *see* TELECOMMUNICATIONS IN ISRAEL
Broadcasting, Jews in, *see* TELEVISION AND RADIO
Broadcasting Services Orchestra (Isr.) **9:**1496
Brocchi, Virgilio **9:**1106
BROCH, HERMANN **4:**1385
– *illus:* text
Broches, Z. **3:**387
Brociner (fam.) **4:**1397
BROCINER, JOSEPH **4:**1386
Brociner, Marco **4:**1386
Brociner, Mauriciu (Moritz) **4:**1386; **11:**1565
Brockelmann, Carl **16:**1399
Brockfliess (vill., Aus.) **3:**890
Brockhaus, F. A. **11:**1325
BROCKTON (city, Mass.) **4:**1386
Brod (fam.) **8:**1136
BROD, DOVIDL **7:**1546
BROD, MAX **4:**1387
– apologetics **3:**200
– Baum, Oscar **4:**332
– German literature **7:**450ff
– Kafka, Franz **10:**672; **10:**673
– *illus:* text
BRODA (fam.) **4:**1388
Broda (tn., Morav.), *see* UHERSKY BROD
Broda, Aaron **4:**1388
Broda, Aaron ben Israel **4:**1388
Broda, Abraham Aaron ben Shalom **4:**1389
BRODA, ABRAHAM BEN SAUL **4:**1390
– Malakh **11:**819
Broda, Abraham ben Solomon Zalman **4:**1389
– *illus:* text
Broda, Aryeh Leib **12:**1474
Broda, Benjamin **4:**1388
Broda, Dov Ber **4:**1388
Broda, Ḥayyim (r., Lith.) **4:**1388
Broda, Ḥayyim (r., Rus.) **4:**1388
Broda, Joseph **4:**1389
Broda, Mordecai ben Nathan Nata **4:**1389
Broda, Moses **4:**1390
Broda, Phinehas Illowy **8:**1257
Broda, Saul **4:**1390
Broda, Ẓevi Hirsch **5:**1564; **11:**279
Broda, Ẓevi Hirsch ben David **4:**1389
Brodaeus, Thomas **8:**24
Brodavka, Isaac, *see* BORODAVKA, ISAAC
Brodberg, Nicholas **8:**24
BRODER, BERL **4:**1390
– Broder Singers **4:**1391
– theater **15:**1064
BRODER SINGERS (gr.) **4:**1391
– Broder, Berl **4:**1391
– theater **15:**1064
BRODERZON, MOSHE **4:**1391
– *illus:*
– – text
– – *Yung Vilne* group **16:**821
Broderzon, Sheyne Miriam **4:**1392
BRODETSKY, SELIG **4:**1392
– Board of Deputies of British Jews **4:**1151
– Maccabeans, Ancient Order **11:**656
– *illus:*
– – London Round Table Conference **9:**353
– – protest against Passfield White Paper **16:**1118
BRODIE, SIR ISRAEL **1:**28; **4:**1393
– Jacobs, Louis **9:**1236
– Melbourne **11:**1281; **11:**1283
– Zionist Federation **16:**1106
Brodnitz, Julius **5:**287
BRODSKI (fam.) **4:**1394
– Zlatopol **16:**1188
Brodski, Abraham **4:**1394
BRODSKI, ALEKSANDER ILICH **4:**1394
Brodski, Arieh Leibush (Lev) **4:**1394
Brodski, Eliezer (Lazar) **4:**1394
Brodski, Israel **4:**1394; **15:**488
Brodski, Samuel **4:**1394
BRODSKI, YOSIF **4:**1395
– Russian literature **14:**507,512
BRODSKY, ADOLF **4:**1395
– *illus:* text
BRODSKY, ISAAC ISRAELEVICH **4:**1395
BRODSKY, STANLEY L. **5:**1112
BRODY (city, Gal.) **4:**1396
– Broder Singers **4:**1391
– Teomim, Aryeh Leib **15:**1010ff
– *illus:*
– – text
– – street scene (drg.) **16:**1327
BRODY, ALTER **15:**1579
Brody, Eugene **13:**1340
Brody, Gyorgy **12:**1376
BRODY, HEINRICH (Ḥayyim) **4:**1399
– Brody, Solomon **4:**1400
– Cairo *Genizah* **16:**1338
BRÓDY, LÁSZLÓ **8:**1084
BRODY, LILI **8:**1084
Brody, Maggid of, *see* KLUGER, SOLOMON BEN JUDAH AARON
BRÓDY, SÁNDOR **4:**1400
– Hungarian literature **8:**1079ff
BRODY, SOLOMON ZALMAN BEN ISRAEL **4:**1400
Brody, Talbot **15:**303
BRÓDY, ZSIGMOND **4:**1401
Brodziński, Kazimierz **13:**798
Broese, Mendel **4:**1355
Brofferio, Angelo **5:**255
BROGLIE, VICTOR-CLAUDE, PRINCE DE **4:**1401
BROIDA, SIMḤAH ZISSEL BEN ISRAEL **4:**1401
BROIDES, ABRAHAM **4:**1402
– *illus:*
– – Writers' Assoc. in Isr. **8:**205
BROIDO, EPHRAIM **4:**1402
BROIDO, LOUIS **4:**1402
Broido, Lucy Kaufmann **4:**1402
Broken Hill (tn., Zambia) **16:**922ff
"Broken Man 3" (sculp., A. Kahane) **3:**616
BROKERS **4:**1403
– agency **2:**352
– *illus:*
– – text
– – "Lame Duck" (18th cent. caric.) **5:**173
– – Nazi caricature **3:**146
Brokman, Waclaw **10:**1500
Bromberg (city, Pol.), *see* BYDGOSZCZ
Bromberg, Gabriel **15:**307
Bromberg, John **15:**303
Bromberg-Bytkowsky, Sigmund **16:**1165
Bromide Company (Isr.) **15:**72
Bron, Vladimir **5:**407
BRONFENBRENNER, MARTIN **4:**1405
BRONFMAN (Can. fam.) **4:**1405
Bronfman, Abe **4:**1405
Bronfman, Allan **4:**1407
Bronfman, Charles **4:**1407; **15:**302
Bronfman, Edgar **4:**1407
Bronfman, Gerald **4:**1405
Bronfman, Harry **4:**1405
Bronfman, Minnie **4:**1405
Bronfman, Samuel **4:**1406
– *illus:*
– – Canadian Jewish Congress leaders **5:**114
Bronfman, Yehiel **4:**1405
Broniewski, Wladyslaw **13:**801
Bronna Góra (loc., Pol.) **10:**1123
Bronnen, Arnolt **7:**450
Bronner, Ferdinand (Franz Adamus) **7:**450
BRONOWSKI, JACOB **4:**1407
Bronson, S. Jerome **5:**1572
BRONSTEIN, DAVID **4:**1407
Bronstein, Lev Davidovich, *see* TROTSKY, LEV DAVIDOVICH
Bronstein, Mordecai, *see* ARDON, MORDECAI
Bronx (boro. N.Y.C.) **12:**1077ff,1106
– *illus:*
– – Albert Einstein College of Medicine **8:**1037
– – Shalom Aleichem Folk Institute **12:**1105
Bronx-Harlem Presse (newsp.) **13:**1055
Bronx-Lebanon Hospitals (U.S.) **8:**1039
Bronzaft, M. **14:**766
Bronze (metal) **11:**1431
– *illus:*
– – musical instruments **12:**561
– – oil lamp **12:**1349
BROOK, BARRY SHELLEY

12:685
Brookdale Hospital (U.S.) 8:1039
Brookings (city, S.D.) 15:213
Brookline (tn., Mass.) 4:1265; 11:1112
Brooklyn (boro., N.Y.C.) 12:1077ff, 1106
- *illus:*
- - night patrol by Jewish volunteer organization 15:1646
Brooklyn Jewish Hospital (N.Y.C.) 12:1116
Brooks, Fanny 16:33
Brooks, Julius Gerson 16:33
BROOKS, RICHARD 12:464
BROOM (bot.) 4:1407
- flora of Israel 9:225
- plant list 13:615
- *illus:* text
Bror (loc., Isr.) 9:794
Broshah (demon) 4:1052
Bross, Ignatius 4:1408
BROSS, JACOB 4:1408
Brot, David 15:506
Brot, Samuel ha-Levi 15:1215
Brother 6:1167
Brother Daniel, *see* Rufeisen, Oswald
Brotherhood, *see* COMPASSION; Love of neighbor
Brotherhood of São Diogo (Mar. assoc.) 3:783
Brotherhood of Zion Society 14:390
"Brotherhood Sabbath" 14:574
BROTHERS, RICHARD 4:1409
- British Israelites 4:1381
- *illus:* text
Brotmanville (vill., N.J.) 16:157
Brotzlewsky, Ḥaim, *see* BAR-LEV, HAIM
BROUDY, HARRY SAMUEL 4:1410
BROUGHTON, HUGH 4:1410
Browe, Peter 8:562
Brown (Browne; fam.), *see* PARDO
Brown, Aika 3:593
- *illus:*
- - "Composition with Heads of Dolls" (paint.) Fig. 109 3-ART
BROWN, BENJAMIN 4:1411
BROWN, DAVID ABRAHAM 4:1411
- public relations 13:1362
BROWN, HERBERT CHARLES 5:380
Brown, H. Maurine, *see* Neuberger, H. Maurine
Brown, Johnny 15:306
Brown, Lawrence 12:1377
Brown, Manny 16:556
Brown, "Newsboy", *see* Montrose, Dave
BROWN, SAUL PARDO 4:1411
- family 13:93
Brown, William 8:26
Browne, Edward B. M. 11:1590
BROWNE, LEWIS 15:1579
BROWNING, ROBERT 4:1411
- English literature 6:781
Brownlow, "Parson" William 15:1649
Brownsville (section, N.Y.C.) 12:1081, 1107
Brownsville (city, Tenn.) 15:1009
Brownsviller Post (newsp.) 13:1055
Brown University 15:1677
BRUCE, FREDERICK FYVIE 1:28
Bruce, James 6:1153
BRUCE, LENNY 15:1079
Bruce, Leslie 15:1577
Bruch, Max 10:1168; 12:153
BRUCHSAL (tn., Ger.) 4:1412
Brucioli, Antonio 4:878; 9:1101; 13:14
Brucioli, Francesco 16:101
BRUCK, GRIGORI 4:1413
BRUCK, LAJOS 3:598
BRUCK, MIKSA 3:598
Bruck, Ẓevi Hirsch, *see* BRUCK, GRIGORI
BRUCKNER, FERDINAND 4:1413
Brudny, I. 11:382
BRUDO, ABRAHAM BEN ELIJAH 4:1414
BRUDO, MANUEL 4:1414
- *illus:* text
Brudus, Dionysus 11:1191
Bruecke, Ernst 7:161
Brueckmann, Arthur 5:41
Brueghel, Peter 4:27
- *illus:*
- - "The Tower of Babel" (paint.) 4:27
Bruehl, Herz 5:1597
BRUELL (fam.) 4:1415
Bruell, Adolf (Elhanan) 4:1415
- homiletic literature 8:956
Bruell, Franz 13:1340
BRUELL, IGNAZ 4:1416
BRUELL, JACOB 4:1416
- family 4:1415
Bruell, Nehemiah (Nahum) 4:1415; 7:89
- homiletic literature 8:956
Bruenn (city, Cz.), *see* BRNO
Bruerne, Richard 8:26
Bruex (city, Cz.), *see* MOST
Bruges (Brugge; city, Belg.) 4:417
BRUGGEN, CARRY VAN 4:1416
- Amsterdam 2:901
Bruggen, Kees van 4:1416
Brugmans, H. 8:563
Bruin, Cornelis de, *see* Cornelis de Bruin
Brukstein, Ludovic (Leibush) 14:414; 15:1071
Brull, Alfred 15:317
Bruller, Jean, *see* VERCORS
Brun, Antoinette 6:1279
BRUNA, ISRAEL BEN ḤAYYIM 4:1417
- Colon's rebuke 5:748
- *ḥerem* impositions 8:354
- horseracing 15:292
- responsa 11:337
Brunchmann, Anders Henriksen 8:26
Brunea-Fox, Filip 14:424
BRUNETTI, ANGELO 4:1417
Brunn, Felix 15:1509
Brunner, Alois 4:649
BRUNNER, ARNOLD 4:1418
- synagogues 15:620
- *illus:*
- - text
- - Shearith Israel synagogue 12:1070
BRUNNER, CONSTANTIN 4:1418
Brunner, Sir John 5:376; 12:241
Brunner, Jožef, *see* DEBRECENJI, JOŽEF
BRUNNER, SEBASTIAN 4:1419
- Abraham a Sancta Clara 2:130
Brunnerus, J. 8:26
BRUNSCHVICG, LÉON 4:1419
BRUNSCHVIG, ROBERT 4:1420
- underground activity 15:425
Brunschwig, Josephine, *see* Brandes, Marge
BRUNSWICK (city, Ger.) 4:1421
- rabbinical conference 13:1460
- - Hirsch, S. R. 8:511
- - Maharam Schick 14:958
- - Reform Judaism 14:24
- *illus:* text
Brunswick (city, Ga.) 7:429
Brunswick, John M. 15:304
Brunswick, Karl Wilhelm Ferdinand, *see* Charles William Ferdinand
BRUNSWIG, ALFRED 4:1422
Brusa (city, Turk.), *see* BURSA
Brusilov, N. 16:823
BRUSSELS (city, Belg.) 4:1422
- Belgium 4:416ff
- host desecration 8:1043
- Soviet Jewry conference 14:505
- *illus:* text
BRUSSILOVSKY, YEVGENI GRIGORYEVICH 4:1425
BRUSTEIN, ROBERT SANFORD 4:1425
BRUTZKUS, BORIS DOV 4:1425
Brutzkus, David Anatol 4:1426
BRUTZKUS, JULIUS 4:1426
- relief work 16:734
BRYANSK (city, Rus.) 4:1427
Bryant, David 8:497
Bryant, Lane, *see* HIMMELSTEIN, LENA
Bryant, William Cullen 15:1570
Bryant Malsin, Raphael 8:497
BRYER, MONTE 4:1427
*Bryusov, Valeri 14:507
BRZECHWA, JAN 13:803
BRZEG (tn., Pol.) 4:1428
- Silesia 14:1536ff
Brzeg Dolny (tn., Pol.), *see* DYHERNFURTH
Brześć (Radziwill) Bible 13:797
BRZESC KUJAWSKI (tn., Pol.) 4:1428
Brześć nad Bugiem (city, Rus.), *see* BREST-LITOVSK
Brzezany (tn., Gal.), *see* BEREZHANY
Brzezinka (concen. camp), *see* Birkenau
BRZEZINY (tn., Pol.) 4:1429
- Strykow 15:447
B.S.I.R. (Er. Isr.), *see* Board of Scientific and Industrial Research
Buʿāth battle (6th cent., Arab.) 13:1470
Buban (loc., Yug.) 12:1175
BUBER, MARTIN 4:1429
- General
- - Agnon, Shmuel Yosef 2:369
- - Bar Kochba Association 4:228
- - *Der Jude* 10:402
- - Holocaust reaction 14:138
- - Rosenzweig, Franz 14:300ff
- - Schmidt, Karl Ludwig 6:100ff
- - Simmel, Georg 15:65
- Ideas
- - creation, theory of 5:1070
- - ethical and metaethical 6:942
- - evil 7:777
- - existentialism 6:1042ff
- - faith 4:436
- - free will 7:130
- - God 7:664
- - Ḥasidism 7:1419
- - messianism 11:1427
- - miracles 12:80
- - Moses 12:402
- - nature 12:891
- - neo-Ḥasidism 7:1399; 10:396
- - philosophy 13:462
- - prophecy 13:1180
- - redemption 14:7
- - Reform Judaism 14:27
- - repentance 14:78
- - revelation 14:125
- - *Shekhinah* 14:1353
- - Torah 15:1242
- - truth 15:1415
- *illus:*
- - text
- - *Der Jude* (Berlin, 1927) 10:402
Buber, R. 10:90
BUBER, SOLOMON 4:1433
- *illus:* text
BUBLICK, GEDALIAH 4:1435
BUCER, MARTIN 4:1435
- Joseph of Rosheim 15:424
- Reformation 14:19
Buch, Abba Isaac 15:109
BUCHACH (city, Gal.) 4:1436
- Shabbateanism 14:1251
BUCHALTER, LOUIS ("Lepke") 4:1437
BUCHANAN, CLAUDIUS 4:1437
- Hebraist 8:26
Buchanan, George 6:774; 9:1343
BUCHAREST (city, Rum.) 4:1438f
- anti-Semitism 14:389ff
- Barasch, Julius 4:200
- Holocaust pogrom 14:400
- Malbim, Meir Loeb 11:822
- museums 12:543
- stock exchange 15:406
- Templul Coral (Choir Synagogue) 14:399
- *illus:*
- - Choir Synagogue, service 14:411
- - Israel Embassy, celebration 14:415
- - Jewish Parliamentary Club 14:393
- *pop. table:* text
Buchbinder, Baruch 4:653; 13:1107
Buchbinder, Isaac ben Loeb 7:216
BUCHBINDER, NAHUM 4:1442
Buchelin, Paul, *see* FAGIUS, PAULUS
BUCHENWALD (concen. camp, Ger.) 4:1442
- Amsterdam Jews 2:902
- Wuppertal "branch" 16:678
Bucher, Samuel Friedrich 8:26
BUCHHOLZ, CARL AUGUST 4:1445
Buchmann, Theodor, *see* BIBLIANDER, THEODOR
BUCHMIL, JOSHUA HESHEL 4:1446
- *illus:*
- - First Zionist Congress 16:1165
BUCHNER, ABRAHAM 4:1446
- H. Nussbaum 12:1285
- *illus:*
- - *Der Talmud in seiner Nichtigkeit* (1848) 7:1437
Buchner, J. K. 13:1053
BUCHNER, ZE'EV WOLF BEN DAVID HA-KOHEN 4:1447
BUCHWALD, ART 10:309
BUCHWALD, NATHANIEL 4:1447
BUCHWALD, THEO 12:685
Buckingham (fam.) 5:56
Bucks (co., Pa.) 13:368
Buckwheat (bot.) 16:481
Buckwold, Sydney 14:892
BUCKY, GUSTAV 4:1447
BUCOVICE (tn., Morav.) 4:1448
București (city, Rum.), *see* BUCHAREST
Buczacz (city, Gal.) *see* BUCHACH
Buda (city, Hung.), *see* BUDAPEST
Budanov (vill., Rus.) 4:14
BUDAPEST (city, Hung.) 4:1448
- *Contents:*
- - Buda 4:1448f
- - Obuda 4:1450
- - Pest 4:1450f
- - Holocaust Period 4:1453
- - Contemporary Jewry 4:1454
- *aliyah* center 9:513
- Buda 5:548; 8:1089
- Eichmann deportations 8:1099f
- history chart (1877) 8:766-767
- Jewish population (1914) 8:732
- library 11:193
- museums 12:538ff
- nationalism and Jews 8:726
- Ottoman period 16:1536
- seal 14:1080
- stock exchange 15:406
- Ujpest 11:457
- *illus:*

- - text
- - Jewish Museum **12**:542
- - remains of 15th cent. synagogue **8**:1091
- *pop. table:* text
Budapest Jewish Relief Committee **4**:1294
Budaspitz, Samuel **3**:811
Buday, Leo **15**:1040
Budde (Buddeus), J. Franz **8**:26
BUDDE, KARL FERDINAND REINHARD **4**:1455
- poetry **13**:676
Buddha **3**:20
Budějovice (city, Cz.), *see* ČESKÉ BUDĚJOVICE
Budin (tn., Bohem.), *see* BUDYNĚ NAD OHŘÍ
BUDKO, JOSEPH **4**:1455
- bookplates **4**:1220
- *illus:*
- - text
- - bookplate **4**:1224
- - Birnbaum, Nathan (portrait) **4**:1040
- - "Man Like Me Won't Flee" Fig. 87 **3**-ART
- - "Market Place in Town" **14**:1470
- - Peretz, Isaac Leib (draw.) **13**:280
- - Rabbi of Bacharach **4**:45
Budnaeus (Budnée), Simon, *see* BUDNY, SZYMON
BUDNY, SZYMON **4**:1456
- Bible translations **4**:885
- Hebraists **8**:26
- Polish literature **13**:798
Budon (city, Hung.), *see* BUDAPEST
Budushchnost (period.) **16**:227
Budweis (city, Cz.), *see* ČESKÉ BUDĚJOVICE
Budweiser, Karl **5**:1038
BUDYNĚ NAD OHŘÍ (tn., Bohem.) **4**:1457
- *illus:* text
Budzanow (vill., Rus.), *see* Budanov
Budzyn (concen. camp, Pol.) **4**:455; **8**:1055
Buechelin, Paul, *see* FAGIUS, PAULUS
BUECHLER, ADOLF **4**:1458
- *am ha-arez* **2**:835
- historiography **8**:562
- history chart **8**:766-767
- Torah-reading **15**:1247ff
BUECHLER, ALEXANDER **4**:1459
Buechler, Siegmund **2**:532
BUEDINGER, MAX **4**:1459
BUEHLER, JOSEF **4**:1460
Bu'eina (site, Isr.) **4**:713
Buel (angel), *see* RAPHAEL
Buelow, Bernhard von **8**:414; **16**:1071
Buenger (Nazi crim.) **11**:389
BUENO (fam.) **4**:1460
- *see also:* MESQUITA
Bueno, Ephraim Hezekiah **4**:1461
- Amsterdam **2**:896
- Rembrandt painting **12**:978; **13**:917
- *illus:*
- - portrait **12**:975; **13**:917
BUENO, ISAAC ABRAHAM **4**:1461
Bueno, Joseph **4**:1460; **12**:978
Bueno, Moses **8**:943
Bueno, Solomon **5**:1077; **13**:1102
Bueno de Mesquita (fam.) **4**:1461
Bueno de Mesquita, David (dipl., Holl.) **4**:1461
Bueno de Mesquita, David (cantor, Eng.) **4**:1461
Bueno de Mesquita, Isaac (dipl., Holl.) **4**:1461
Bueno de Mesquita, Isaac (dipl., Mor.) **4**:1461
Bueno de Mesquita, Jacob **4**:1461
Bueno de Mesquita, Joseph **4**:1461
BUENOS AIRES (prov., city, Arg.) **4**:1461
- A.M.I.A. **2**:836ff
- Argentina **3**:409ff
- demography **5**:1513
- I.C.A. **10**:46
- Jewish education **6**:456ff
- museums **12**:551
- Sociedad Hebraica Argentina **15**:52
- *illus:*
- - text
- - Jewish Book Month exhibits **3**:424; **4**:1464; **5**:845
- - Liberty Street Synagogue **3**:422
- - Sephardi synagogue **14**:1173
Buercklin, Georgius Christianus **8**:26
Bueren (dist., Ger.) **13**:7
BUERGER, LEO **4**:1464
Buerger, Victor **5**:406
Buerger's Disease **14**:1502
Bueschenthal, Lippmann Moses **15**:109
BUFFALO (city, N.Y.) **4**:1465
- *illus:* text
BUFFALO (zool.) **4**:1467
- dietary laws **6**:31
- wild ox **16**:510
- *illus:*
- - water buffalo **9**:235
Buffalo Jewish Review (period.) **4**:1466
Bug (riv., Ukr.) **15**:1330ff
Bugalho, Gil Vaz **6**:8
BUGENHAGEN, JOHANN **4**:1467
Bugojno (tn., Yug.) **14**:869
Bugun (newsp.) **15**:1459
Buḥayrat Sadūm Wa'Amūra, *see* DEAD SEA
Buhen (site, Nubia) **16**:274
BUHL, FRANZ PEDER WILLIAM MEYER **4**:1467
- Bible translations **4**:877
BÜHLER, CHARLOTTE **4**:1468
Buhrīz (tn., Iraq) **8**:1449
Buhusi (ḥas. dyn.) **14**:531
BUHUSI (tn., Rum.) **4**:1468
Building trade, *see* CONSTRUCTION
Buinaksk (tn., Rus.) **14**:488
BUITRAGO (tn., Sp.) **4**:1469
Bujumbura (city, Burundi) **9**:438
Buk (tn., Pol.) **16**:672
BUKARAT, ABRAHAM BEN SOLOMON HA-LEVI **4**:1469
Bukarester Tageblatt (newsp.) **14**:403, 407; **16**:1135
Bukayy'a (vill., Isr.), *see* PEKI'IN
BUKHARA (reg., city, Rus.) **4**:1470f
- *Contents:*
- - History **4**:1470f
- - Population **4**:1472
- - Economy **4**:1472
- - Culture and Administration **4**:1473
- - Costume **4**:1475
- - Jewelry **4**:1476
- *aliyah* **9**:515
- cooking and food **6**:1422ff
- dress **6**:219
- Erez Israel community **9**:502
- Jerusalem **9**:1465
- *jizya* tax **10**:937
- Judeo-Persian literature **10**:435
- Meshed *anusim* **2**:327
- Samarkand **14**:759
- Uzbekistan **16**:39
- *illus:*
- - text
- - bridal gown Pl. 9 **6**-DRESS
- - Israel community celebrating Simḥat Torah **14**:1573
Bukharan Quarter (Jer.) **9**:325,502ff,1461
- *illus:*
- - Porat Yosef yeshivah **16**:765
Bukhari, Al-(Musl.) **7**:1051
Bukharic (lang.) **10**:67
- *see also:* JUDEO-PERSIAN
Bukhbaza, Isaac Ḥai **11**:204
Bukhtanaṣar (Isl. fig.) **12**:916
Buki ben Yogli, *see* KATZENELSON, JUDAH LEIB BENJAMIN
BUKOFZER, MANFRED **12**:685
BUKOVINA (reg.) **4**:1476
- Holocaust period **3**:163
- Israelitische Allianz zu Wien **2**:654
- Rumania **14**:387ff
- *shtetl* **14**:1471ff
- *illus:*
- - Franz Joseph I medal **11**:1170
Bukrat, Abraham ben Solomon ha-Levi, *see* BUKARAT ABRAHAM BEN SOLOMON HA-LEVI
Bul (Bab. k.), *see* Tiglath-Pileser III
Bul (name of month) **5**:48; **16**:725
Bul (journ.) **1**:newsp. list
BULA, RAPHAEL MOSES **4**:1477
Bula, Solomon **4**:1478
Bulak-Balachowicz (anti-Sem., Rus.) **13**:700
BŪLĀN (Khazar k.) **4**:1478
- Khazar conversion **10**:950
- Khorezm **10**:955
Bulat, Abraham **11**:483
BULAT, JUDAH BEN JOSEPH **4**:1478
BULAWAYO (city, Rhod.) **4**:1479
- Rhodesia **14**:148
- *illus:*
- - synagogue **14**:149
Bulganin, Nikolai A. **9**:390
BULGARIA **4**:1480
- *Contents:*
- - Ancient Period **4**:1480
- - Byzantine and Bulgar Rule **4**:1480
- - Turkish Rule **4**:1482
- - Independent Bulgaria **4**:1483
- - Pre-World War II **4**:1484
- - - Zionist Movement **4**:1484
- - - Community Organization **4**:1484
- - - Education **4**:1484
- - - Rabbis and Scholars **4**:1485
- - - Journalism **4**:1485
- - In World War II **4**:1485
- - - Deportations Program 4:1486
- - - Opposition to Deportations **4**:1486
- - - Abolishment of Anti-Jewish Policies **4**:1488
- - Postwar Period **4**:1489
- - - Economic Restitution **4**:1490
- - - Exodus to Israel **4**:1490
- - - Contemporary Life **4**:1491
- - Relations with Israel **4**:1491
- General
- - Alliance Israélite Universelle **2**:651
- - Berlin, Congress **4**:655
- - communal organization **5**:827
- - communism **5**:805
- - cooperatives **5**:942
- - emancipation **6**:710
- - Ladino press **13**:1038
- - literature **4**:1492
- - military service **11**:1565
- - minority treaty **12**:45
- - ORT **12**:1482
- - socialism **4**:1500
- - synagogues **1**:synagogue list
- - Zionism **16**:1108
- Holocaust period **8**:851
- - Church and Nazism **8**:915
- - partisans **13**:147
- - survival of Sephardim **14**:1172
- Relations with Israel **9**:428
- - U.N. debates **15**:1556
- *illus:*
- - text
- - Jewish badge (World War II) **4**:72
- *pop. tables:* text
Bulgarian Language **4**:886
- Ladino *Haggadah* **7**:1103
BULGARIAN LITERATURE **4**:1492
- *Contents:*
- - Figure of the Jew **4**:1492
- - Jewish Contribution **4**:1493
"Bulgar" Tune (ḥas. mus.) **7**:1425
Bulim (journ.) **1**:newsp. list
"Bull" (wdct., J. Pins) **3**:636
Bull, *see* CATTLE
Bull, Francis **12**:1225
Bull, Odd **12**:1226; **14**:1629
Bull, Wild, *see* WILD BULL
Bull cult, *see* GOLDEN CALF
Bulletin du Cercle Juif (period.) **13**:1026
Bulletin shel ha-Makhon le-Ḥeker ha-Kalkalah (journ.) **1**:newsp. list
Bullfighting (sport) **15**:306
Bullinger, Heinrich **11**:585
Bullman, E. **8**:26
BULLS, PAPAL **4**:1494
- Benedict XIII **4**:482
- *Bulle de Perdao* (1533) **8**:1386
- Calixtus II **5**:62
- Catholic Church **5**:538
- Clement III **5**:601
- Clement IV **5**:601
- Gregory IX **7**:919
- Gregory XIII **7**:920
- Jewish physicians **11**:1186ff
- *Pastoris aeterni* (1539) **8**:1386
- Paul IV **2**:404; **13**:189
- Perugian Jews banished **13**:325
- *Turbato corde* (1267) **8**:1399
- *illus:* text
- *see also:* TALMUD, BURNING OF
BULOFF, JOSEPH **4**:1497
- theater **15**:1072
- *illus:*
- - in *Shabbetai Zevi* **15**:1067
Buloff, Max **15**:1074
Bulrush, *see* PAPYRUS
Bulz, Emmanuel **11**:591
Bumsla (city, Cz.), *see* MLADA BOLESLAV
Bumsla, Moses Simḥah **8**:366
Bun (amora), *see* AVIN
Bun (schols., poets), *see* ABUN
Buna (amora), *see* ABBA BAR AVINA
Bunche, Ralph **3**:478; **9**:1497
- Israel-Arab negotiations **9**:371,374,422; **15**:647
- U.N.-Israel relations **15**:1546
- *illus:*
- - civil rights march (1965) **12**:931
- - Rhodes, April 1949 **3**:479
BUND (J. soc. party) **4**:1497
- *Contents:*
- - Beginnings (Pre-Bund) **4**:1407
- - The Bund **4**:1499
- - 1907-1917 **4**:1501
- - The 1917 Revolutions and Aftermath **4**:1502
- - Polish Bund **4**:1503
- - International Jewish Labor Bund **4**:1506
- General
- - archives **3**:384
- - Duma **6**:267

- - Esther (M. Lifschitz) **6:**913
- - history chart **8:**766-767
- - Kopelson, Ẓemaḥ **10:**1188
- - Kremer, Arkadi **10:**1257
- - Medem, Vladimir **11:**1175
- - Mutnik, Abraham **12:**721
- - self-defense **14:**1125ff
- - socialism **15:**29ff
- - socialism, Jewish **15:**41ff
- - Tshemeriski, Alexander **15:**1417
- - *Yevsektsiya* joined by **16:**779
- - Zhitlowsky, Chaim **16:**1010
- - Zionism **16:**1067ff
- - Zygelbojm, Samuel Mordecai **16:**1251
- Opposition to
- - Agudat Israel **2:**421
- - Communist Party **5:**792f
- - - Lenin **11:**13ff
- - - Trotsky **15:**1406
- - Independent Jewish Workers' Party **8:**1348
- - Zionism **16:**1137
- In Various Countries
- - Argentina **3:**414
- - Belorussia **4:**445
- - Lithuania **11:**371
- - - Vilna **16:**144
- - Poland **13:**738
- - - Warsaw **16:**338
- - Russia **14:**452ff
- - - Bobruisk **4:**1156
- - - Borisov **4:**1250
- - United States **4:**1506
- - - Workmen's Circle **16:**635
- - Uruguay **16:**12
- *illus:*
- - Bundist youth rally, Warsaw **13:**741
- - 30th anniversary celebrations **13:**912
- - papers and pamphlets **15:**40
- *see also:* JEWISH SOCIAL DEMOCRATIC PARTY
Bund der Kommunisten, *see* League of the Communists
Bund der Landwirte (Ger. orgn.), *see* AGRARIAN LEAGUE
Bunderker, S. R. **12:**1465
Bundesentschaedigungsgesetz, *see* REPARATIONS, GERMAN; RESTITUTION AND INDEMNIFICATION
Bundesrueckerstattungsgesetz, *see* REPARATIONS, GERMAN; RESTITUTION AND INDEMNIFICATION
Bund Heimattreuer Jugend (neo-Nazi orgn.) **12:**955
Bund Juedischer Akademiker (orgn., Ger.) **7:**486
Bund Juedischer Corporationen (Zion. mvmt) **10:**805
Bund Werktaegiger Juden (orgn., Aus.) **16:**1108
Bund Zionistischer Korporationen (orgn.) **10:**805
Bunim, Shemuel **5:**74
BUNIN, ḤAYYIM ISAAC **4:**1507
Bunin, Ivan **14:**507
Bunsen (Bib. trans.) **4:**873
BUNSHAFT, GORDON **4:**1507
- *illus:*
- - Chase Manhattan Bank, New York City **3:**346
BUNZEL, RUTH LEAH **4:**1508
BUNZL (fam.) **4:**1508
Bunzl, Emil **4:**1508
Bunzl, Felix **4:**1508
Bunzl, George **4:**1508
Bunzl, Hugo **4:**1508
Bunzl, Martin **4:**1508
Bunzl, Robert **4:**1508
Bunzlau, Jonah ben Elijah, *see* LANDSOFER, JONAH BEN ELIJAH
Buonaccorsi, Filippo **5:**1027
Buqarat, *see* BUKARAT
Buqei'a (loc., Er. Isr.) **5:**955
Burack, A. D. **12:**1118
BURCHARD OF WORMS **4:**1508
BURCHARDT, HERMANN **4:**1508
- travelers **15:**1351
BURCHARDUS DE MONTE SION **4:** 1509
- travelers **15:**1355
BURCKHARDT, JOHANN LUDWIG **4:**1509
Burden of Proof, *see* EVIDENCE
BURDUJENI (tn., Rum.) **4:**1509
Bureau for Jewish Social Research (U.S.) **6:**192
Bureau fuer Statistik der Juden (Berlin) **14:**430; **15:**346
Bureau of Jewish Education (N.Y.) **4:**477; **6:**440
Burg, Abraham **4:**1510
Burg, Meno **11:**1560
BURG, YOSEF **4:**1510
Burge, Bella (U.S.) **15:**306
Burgel (fam.), *see* BORDJEL
BURGENLAND (reg., Aus.) **4:**1511
- archives **3:**381
- Nazi deportations **3:**899
Burger, Anton **15:**1115
Burger, Fritzi (sport.) **12:**1376
Burger, N. **8:**26
Burgetah (mosh., Isr.) **1:**place list
Burggraben (concen. camp, Pol.) **15:**464
Burgh, William **8:**26
Burgheim, David **3:**824
Burgil, Abraham Azuz (Bul.), *see* BORGIL, ABRAHAM BEN AZIZ
Burgil, Nathan ben Abraham (Tunis) *see* Bordjel, Nathan
Burglary, *see* THEFT AND ROBBERY
Burgonovo, Archangelus de **8:**26
BURGOS (city, Sp.) **4:**1512
- Spain **15:**234
Burg Starkenberg (fort.), *see* Montfort
BURGUNDY (duchy, Fr.) **4:**1514
- Besançon **4:**702
- French Jewry **7:**20
Burgundy (Fr. co.), *see* FRANCHE-COMTÉ
Burhān al-din Ibrāhīm ibn al-Firkāh, *see* Ibn al-Firkah, Burhan al-Din Ibrāhīm
Burhān al-Falak, *see* Joseph (12th cent., Iraq)
BURIAL **4:**1515
- *Contents:*
- - In the Bible **4:**1515
- - Post-Biblical Times **4:**1516
- - Reform Jewish Practice **4:**1521
- - Sephardi Practice **4:**1521
- General
- - *aliyah* **9:**509
- - anthropoid coffins **3:**306
- - catacombs **5:**249
- - death **5:**1421
- - demons, demonology **5:**1530
- - endowment funds **8:**284
- - epitaphs **6:**818
- - Ereẓ Israel as altar **2:**770
- - folklore **6:**1404
- - *Genizah* and **16:**1333
- - Hebron **8:**230
- - *ḥibbut ha-kever* **8:**464
- - Holocaust (mass graves) **8:**856
- - in Ereẓ Israel **9:**889
- - *likkut aẓamot* **11:**238
- - music at **12:**579
- - perfection of God's world **7:**776
- - resurrection **14:**99
- - taxation **13:**21
- - Tobit, Book of **15:**1184
- - tombs, Second Temple period **9:**1532
- In Various Communities
- - Falashas **6:**1146
- - Phoenicians **13:**480
- - Roman Jews **14:**250
- - Samaritans **14:**747
- Laws and Customs
- - ablution of corpse **2:**83
- - *aninut* **3:**23
- - area impurity **13:**1409
- - *ashkavah* **3:**712
- - by fence **13:**1389
- - *gemilut ḥasadim* **7:**376
- - *hakkafot* **7:**1153
- - Ḥasidim, assistance forbidden to **7:**1396
- - *ḥevra kaddisha* **8:**442
- - husband's obligation **8:**1124
- - Jerusalem **9:**1553; **13:**1411
- - kabbalistic influence **10:**642
- - *keri'ah* **10:**916
- - *kitel* as shroud **10:**1079
- - *niddui* and *ḥerem* **8:**351ff
- - postponement of **3:**932
- - priests **13:**1089ff
- - rites against Angel of Death **2:**955
- - *Sefer Torah* **14:**1103
- - *sha'atnez* **14:**1214
- - suicides **15:**490
- - *tallit* **15:**744
- - washing dead before **15:**1188
- - washing hands after **12:**998
- Views on
- - Altschul, Emil **2:**782
- - Ash, Abraham **3:**694
- - Maimonides **11:**759ff
- - Mendelssohn, Moses **11:**1334
- *illus:*
- - text
- - Absalom's Tomb, Jerusalem **3:**340
- - anthropoid coffin lid, Beth-Shean **3:**314; **4:**761
- - catacombs, Bet She'arim **4:**767-770
- - Cave of Nicanor ossuary **12:**1133
- - *El Male Raḥamim* (score) **6:**682
- - Eshmunezer's sarcophagus **13:**480
- - grave digging (18th cent. engr.) **8:**443
- - *hakkafot* around a coffin (18th cent. engr.) **7:**1153
- - hearse and *ḥevra kaddisha* members **12:**185
- - Hellenistic burial cave, Mareshah **3:**321
- - Hiram's sarcophagus **13:**473
- - Jacob, death and burial of **3:**515; **5:**1423
- - Japanese prisoner-of-war camp (1905) **14:**445
- - Jason's Tomb, Jerusalem **3:**322
- - Jericho tomb chamber **15:**1220
- - Josiah **10:**289
- - lead sarcophagus, Bet She'arim **5:**658
- - mass grave of Nazi victims **8:**763
- - Middle Bronze Age tomb, Jericho **8:**57
- - Mount of Olives cemetery, Jerusalem **5:**273
- - Odessa pogrom victim's funeral **13:**698
- - ossuaries **3:**321,513,1012; **4:**769-770,1517; **7:**1047; **12:**1504,1505
- - Philistine coffin lid **13:**401
- - *tohorah* plate **15:**1188
- - Tombs of the Sanhedrin, Jerusalem **3:**340
- - Uzziah burial inscription **16:**44
- - Via Appia catacomb, Rome **5:**249-252
- - Vigna Randanini sarcophagus **11:**1361
- - Villa Torlonia catacomb, Rome **9:**1582; **11:**1361
- - Zechariah's Tomb, Jerusalem **3:**339
- *see also:* CEMETERY; COFFIN; CREMATION; DEATH; DISINTERMENT; HESPED; LIKKUT AẒAMOT; MOURNING; OSSUARIES AND SARCOPHAGI; TOHORAH; TOMBS AND TOMBSTONES; ẒIDDUK HA-DIN
Burial society, *see* ḤEVRA KADDISHA
Burj (fort., Er. Isr.) **7:**1135
Burkhard, Willy **9:**69
BURLA (fam.) **4:**1523
Burla, Ḥayyim Jacob **4:**1524
Burla, Israel Jacob **4:**1523
Burla, Jacob Ḥai ben Judah **4:**1524
Burla, Joseph Nissim ben Ḥayyim Jacob **4:**1523
Burla, Joshua ben Bekhor Judah **4:**1524
Burla, Judah Bekhor ben Israel Jacob (Er. Isr.) **4:**1523
Burla, Judah ben Joshua (nov.), *see* BURLA, YEHUDA
Burla, Menahem ben Jacob **4:**1523
Burla, Oded **5:**437
Burla, Samuel **4:**1523
BURLA, YEHUDA **4:**1524
- Alkalai, Judah **2:**640
- family **4:**1524
- Hebrew literature **8:**203
BURLE-MARX, ROBERTO **3:**363
BURLE MARX, WALTER **12:**685
Burleigh (Burley), Francis **8:**26
Burlington (city, Ia.) **8:**1437
Burlington (city, Vt.) **16:**112
Burlington (co., N. J.) **13:**368
BURMA **4:**1526
- Israel cooperation **9:**391
- Israel's relations with **4:**1527; **9:**433ff
- medical training in Israel **9:**991
- synagogue **1:** synagogue list
- *illus:* text
- *pop. table:* text
Burman, Frans **8:**26
Burman, Henry L. **5:**416
"Burma Road" (Isr., 1948) **10:**1458
- Haganah strategy **7:**1074
- Jerusalem siege **9:**1480; **16:**319
- Orthodox Jews **9:**895
- Wingate **9:**367
Burney-C.F. **13:**674
Burnham (fam.), *see* LAWSON
Burnham, Baron, *see* Levy-Lawson, Sir Edward
Burnham, Viscount, *see* Levy-Lawson, Sir Harry Lawson Webster
Burning, *see* CAPITAL PUNISHMENT
BURNING BUSH **4:**1528
- in the Arts **12:**408
- Moses **12:**374
- Sinai etymology **14:**1597
- *illus:*
- - text
- - Dura-Europos wall paint. **6:**282
- - Knesset *Menorah* (sculp., Elkan) **5:**1448
- - Moses hiding face **12:**fcg. 427
- - sculpture at B'nai Israel Synagogue, N.J. **15:**625
- - thirteenth and 14th cent. mss. **12:**373,379
"Burning Bush" (sculp., D. Palombo) **13:**49
Burning Bush Press (U.S.) **13:**1376
BURNS, ARTHUR FRANK

4:1530
Burns, E. L. 16:1261
BURNS, GEORGE 15:1079
Burns, Tiger, *see* Levine, Dan
Burnshaw, Stanley 13:1371
Burnstone, David 5:169
Burnt offering 14:600ff
- Leviticus 11:140
- place in cult 5:1159
- priestly blessing 13:1061
- Temple 15:974ff
Buros (fam.) 3:1004
Burrell, Andrew 8:26
BURRIANA (city, Sp.) 4:1530
Burrows, Abe 15:1079
Burrows, M. 5:1396
Burs (city, Babyl.), *see* BORSIPPA
BURSA (city, Turk.) 4:1531
- Ottoman Empire 16:1530
Burschenschaft (mvmt., Ger.) 15:1129
BURSTEIN (fam.) 4:1531
- theater 15:1074
BURSTEIN, ABRAHAM 4:1532
- encyclopedias 6:734
- Salit, Norman 14:686
BURSTEIN, ISRAEL 4:1532
Burstein, Lilian, *see* Lux, Lilian
Burstein, M. (au.), *see* BURSZTYN, MICHAL
Burstein, Michael (Mordecai; sing.) 4:1531
Burstein, Pesach 4:1531
Burstein, Pinchas, *see* MARYAN
BURSZTYN, MICHAL 4:1532
BURTON, SIR MONTAGUE 4:1533
- Leeds 10:1560
- tailoring 15:707
Burundi (kdm., Afr.) 9:438
Buryat-Mongol Republic (Rus.) 14:1488; 16:111ff
BURY ST. EDMUNDS (tn., Eng.) 4:1533
- Crusades 5:1141
- *illus:*
- - Moyse's Hall 6:751
Busach, Master 13:29
Busaglo, Shalom ben Moses, *see* BUZAGLO, SHALOM BEN MOSES
BUSAL, ḤAYYIM BEN JACOB OBADIAH DE 4:1533
Busch, Adolf 12:707
Busch, Isidor, *see* BUSH, ISIDOR
Buschoff, Adolf Wolff 16:685
Busel, Hayyuta 4:1534
BUSEL, JOSEPH 4:1534
Bush, George 8:26
BUSH, ISIDOR 4:1535
Bush, Mathias 4:1535; 5:935
BUSH, SOLOMON 4:1535
- military service 11:1550
- Washington, George 16:360
BUSHIRE (port, Pers. Gulf) 4:1535
Business, *see* CRAFTS; INSURANCE; PEDDLING; TRADE AND COMMERCE
Business Ethics 16:1276ff
- Commandments, the 613 5:777
- *hafka'at she'arim* 7:1061f
- *ona'ah* 12:1391
BUSK (tn., Gal.) 4:1536
- Holocaust period 2:1536 10:728
- Shabbateanism 14:1251
BUSNACH (fam.) 4:1536
Busnach, Naphtali 4:1536
Busnach, Naphtali ben Moses 2:615, 623; 4:1536
- Bacri, David ben Joseph Coen 4:58
- Duran, David 6:299
Busra (tn., Babyl.) 15:1512
Busrā-Aski Shām (vill., Jor.), *see* BOZRAH
Buṣr al-Harīrī (vill., Syr.), *see* BOZRAH
Bus services, Israel 9:832
BUSTANAI BEN ḤANINAI (exil.) 4:1537
- seal 14:1074
- Sherira Gaon 14:1381
Bustanai (period.), *see* BUSTENAI
Bustan ha-Galil (mosh., Isr.) 1:place list
Bustānī, Wadīʿal- 9:1040; 9:1041
Bustard (ornith.) 9:220
- fauna of Israel 9:226
BUSTENAI (period.) 4:1537
- Ben-Zion, S. 4:575
- Smilansky, Moshe 15:3
- statistics 1:newsp. list
Bustenai la-No'ar (period.) 4:1538
Butchers 5:1050
- Alsace Jews 2:775
- economic life 16:1287ff
- guilds 7:972
- *sheḥitah* 14:1342
- *takkanot ha-kahal* 15:732
Buteiḥa Valley (Isr.), *see* Bethsaida Valley
Butelbroit, Israel, *see* GILADI, ISRAEL
BUTENSKY, JULES LEON 4:1538
- *illus:* text
Butler (city, Pa.) 13:230
Butler, Benjamin F. 15:1649
BUTNAH (site, Er. Isr.) 4:1538
- Mamre 11:839
Butnan (Er. Isr.), *see* BUTNAH
Buton, Abraham ben Judah di 12:239
BUTRYMOWICZ, MATEUSZ 4:1539
Butschko, E. 10:1472
Butschowitz (tn., Morav.), *see* BUCOVICE
Buttadeo (Buttadeus), *see* WANDERING JEW
Butte (city, Mont.) 12:266
Buttenwies(en) Henle, Jacob, *see* Henle, Jacob
BUTTENWIESER (fam.) 4:1539
Buttenwieser, Benjamin Joseph 4:1540
Buttenwieser, Helen, *see* Lehman, Helen
Buttenwieser, Joseph Leon 4:1539
BUTTENWIESER, MOSES 4:1540
- H.U.C.-J.I.R. 8:218
Butter 6:1417; 11:1577
- Gentiles 7:413
- marriage custom 11:1043
Büttner, Christoph Andreas 8:26
Buttner, Victorinus, *see* Bythner (Buttner), Victorinus
Button making 5:1052
BUTTONS, RED 12:464
Buttrio, Abraham ben Daniel 13:575
BUTZEL (fam.) 4:1541
Butzel, Fred M. 4:1542
Butzel, Henri M. 4:1541
Butzel, Leo M. 4:1541
Butzel, Magnus 4:1541
Butzel, Martin 4:1541
Butzel, Martin L. 4:1541
Butzer, Martin, *see* BUCER, MARTIN
Buwayhid (dyn., Iraq) 8:1446
Buxbaum, Edith 13:1339
BUXBAUM, NATHAN 4:1542
Buxton, Angela 15:314
Buxton, W. 13:33
- *illus:*
- - Anglo-American Committee of Enquiry 16:1089
Buxtorf, Jacob, *see* Buxtorf, Johann (Jacob)
Buxtorf, Johann (Jacob) (Hebr.) 8:26
BUXTORF, JOHANNES (The Elder) 4:1543
- *Aleinu le-Shabbe'aḥ* 2:557
- Aslakssen, Cort 3:751
- Basle 4:304
- bibliography 4:970
- Christian Hebraists 8:26
- Hebrew linguistics 16:1392
BUXTORF, JOHANNES (The Younger) 4:1543
- Archivolti, Samuel de 3:397
- Basle 4:304
- Christian Hebraists 8:26
- Hebrew linguistics 16:1392
- Jewish law 8:702
Buxtorf, Johann Jacob 8:26
Buxy (vill., Fr.) 4:1514
Buying and Selling, *see* SALE
Buz (bib. fig.) 6:632
Buzagli(o), Shalom ben Moses, *see* BUZAGLO, SHALOM BEN MOSES
BUZAGLO (fam.) 4:1544
Buzaglo, Abraham 4:1544
- *illus:* text
Buzaglo, Joseph 4:1544
Buzaglo, Moses 4:1544
BUZAGLO, SHALOM BEN MOSES 4:1544
- Zohar commentary 16:1213
Buzaglo-Azulay, Abraham 4:564
BUZAU (tn., Rum.) 4:1545
Buzruna (city, Er. Isr.), *see* BOZRAH
BUZZARD (ornith.) 4:1546
- dietary laws 6:34
- *illus:* text
BYADULYA-YASAKAR, ZMITROK 4:1546
- Belorussia 4:446
Byala, *see* Biala
Byblos (anc. city, Leb.), *see* JUBAYL
Bychowski, Zygmunt 11:1204
- *illus:*
- - First Zionist Congress 16:1165
BYDGOSZCZ (city., Pol.) 4:1547
- Baerwald, Moritz 4:84
Byer, Frank 15:310
Byer, Jacob 15:310
Byer, Nathaniel 15:310
BYK, EMIL 4:1547
Byk, J. 14:399
BYKHOV (city, Belor.) 4:1548
Bynaeus, Antonius 8:26
Byng, Andrew 8:26
Byoir, Carl 13:1360
BYRON, GEORGE GORDON, LORD 4:1549
- Heine 8:274
- Nathan, Isaac 12:853
- Rothschilds 8:719
- *illus:* text
Byrsa (loc., Tun.) 15:1430
Bythner, Victorinus 8:26
BYTOM (tn., Pol.) 4:1549
Bytown (city, Can.), *see* OTTAWA
BYZANTINE EMPIRE 4:1549
- *Contents:*
- - From Constantine to the Iconoclastic Period 4:1550
- - From the Iconoclastic Period to the 4th Crusade 4:1553
- - From the 4th Crusade to 1453 4:1554
- General
- - African Jews 2:332
- - *anusim* 3:170
- - autonomy 3:923
- - disputations 3:170
- - Jewish lands confiscated 16:1284
- - Jewish population 13:872
- - Khazars 10:945
- - Leo VI 11:23
- - Romanus I Lecapenus 14:239
- - synagogues 15:598
- - taxes 10:937
- - trade and commerce 15:1297
- - *Vision of Daniel* 5:1290
- Various Countries
- - Ereẓ Israel 2:397; 9:258; 9:259; 9:262; 9:264
- - - Jerusalem 9:1406ff
- - - Samaritan revolts 14:736
- - Greece 7:869
- - - Salonika 14:699
- - Transjordan 15:1317
- - Tunisia 15:1432
- *illus:*
- - Jerusalem boundaries (map) 9:1403
- - Shivtah, church 14:1419
- *pop. table:* text
- *see also:* ASIA MINOR; CONSTANTINOPLE; GREECE; OTTOMAN EMPIRE; TURKEY
Byzantine Octateuchs (11th and 12th cent. Gr.)
- *illus:* 3:439; 4:122,786,856; 5:1020,1172; 6:476,575,1369; 10:1526; 13:1514
BZENEC (tn., Morav.) 4:1556
- postwar community 10:1308
Bzheg (tn., Pol.), *see* BRZEG
Bzoza, H. 13:1376

C

Caballeria, de la (fam.), *see* CAVALLERIA, DE LA
CABBAGE **5:**1
- plant list **13:**615
Cabbalah, *see* KABBALAH
CABESSA (Cabeça, Cabeçao; fam.) **5:**1
Cabessa, Aaron **5:**1
Cabessa, Abraham (Mor.) **5:**1
Cabessa, Abraham (Fr.). **5:**1
Cabessa, David **5:**2
Cabessa, Isaac (Mor.) **5:**1
Cabessa, Isaac (Amst.) **5:**1
Cabessa, Moses (Ger.) **5:**1
Cabessa, Moses (Amst.) **5:**1
Cabessa, Samuel **5:**1
Cabessa, Solomon **5:**1
Cabicho, António **11:**301
Cabor (city, Er. Isr.), *see* CABUL
Cabra, Leonor de la **5:**263
Cabra, Martin de la, *see* Abencabra, Yucef
CABUL (city, Er. Isr.) **5:**2
- Ottoman period **9:**285
CACERES, ABRAHAM **5:**3
- *mus. notations:*
- - adaptation from **12:**625
Cáceres, Catalina de **5:**222
Caceres, Daniel de **5:**3
Caceres, Diego García de **5:**461
CACERES, FRANCISCO DE **5:**3
- literature **15:**254
Cáceres, Leonor de (Mex.) **5:**222
Caceres, Samuel de **5:**3
CACERES, SIMON (Jacob) DE (mer.) **5:**4
Cachet, Jan Lion **15:**210
Caddick, Richard **8:**26
Cademannus, J. R. **8:**26
CADENET (vill., Fr) **5:**4
Caderousse, Davin de **13:**1096
Cadmus (leg. hero) **7:**893
CADIZ (city, Sp.) **5:**4
CAECILIUS OF CALACTE **5:**5
Caedmon (poet) **6:**773
CAEN (city, Fr.) **5:**5
Caenaculum (Jer.), *see* Last Supper, Church of the
CAESAR, SEXTUS JULIUS **5:**6
- history chart **8:**766-767
CAESAR, SID **15:**1080
CAESAREA (city, Er. Isr.) **5:**6
- academy **2:**202
- Ekron **6:**559
- emperor worship **6:**729
- 70 to 640 **9:**239ff
- 634 to 1099 **9:**261; **9:**263
- 1099 to 1291 **9:**267ff
- Herod and Roman period **8:**636; **8:**639
- Jaffa **9:**1250
- Jerusalem Talmud **15:**773; **15:**773ff
- oil exploration **9:**795
- Samaritan community **5:**1140
- synagogue **15:**595
- *illus:*
- - text
- - concert at Roman theater **9:**1007; **12:**673
- - Crusader city wall **9:**276
- - Crusader town ruins **5:**1138-1142
- - golf match **15:**309
- - *menorah* from synagogue **11:**1359
- - principal *amoraim* (table) **2:**871
- - sarcophagus **12:**1504
CAESAREA IN CAPPADOCIA **5:**13
- history of Jews **8:**649; **8:**650
- Rabbi Akiva **5:**152
Caesarean section **4:**1051; **11:**1184
Caesarea Philippi (city, Er. Isr.), *see* BANIAS
Caesarius of Arles **5:**553
Cafersi (vill., Er. Isr.), *see* KEFAR YASIF
Caffa (port, Ukr.), *see* FEODOSIYA
Cafman, Berekhiel ben Meshullam of Mantua **10:**542
Cafritz, Morris (U.S.) **16:**358
Cafsuto, Moses **12:**864
CAGLI, CORRADO **5:**14
CAGLIARI (city, Sard.) **5:**14
CAHAN, ABRAHAM **5:**14
- *Jewish Daily Forward* **10:**50
- literature **15:**1570ff
- New York **12:**1102ff
- socialism **15:**31; **15:**35
- socialism, Jewish **15:**47,51
CAHAN, JUDAH LOEB (Lewis) **5:**15
CAHAN, YAAKOV **5:**16
- drama, Hebrew **6:**197
- Hebrew literature **8:**197
- Jerusalem theme **9:**1566
Cahana-Carmon, Amaliah **8:**207
Cahen, Alfred **5:**612; **13:**1372
CAHEN, ISIDORE **5:**17
- *illus:* text
Cahen, Samuel **4:**882
- press **13:**1032
Cahiers du Centre Communautaire Laïc Juif (jorn.), *see Regards*
C.A.H.J.P., *see* Central Archives for the History of the Jewish People
Cahn, Aaron (mer.) **12:**1373; **12:**911
CAHN, EDMOND NATHANIEL **5:**17
Cahn, Ernst **2:**902
Cahn, H. **3:**301
Cahn, Sir Julian **15:**307
Cahn, Julius **15:**310
CAHN, MARCELLE **5:**19
Cahn, Michael **7:**219
- *Freie Vereinigung* **16:**105
Cahn, Moïse, *see* CROHMALNICEANU, OVID S.
CAHNMAN, WERNER J. **1:**28; **5:**19
Cahokia (vill., U.S.) **8:**1255
Cahun, Léon **2:**756
CAIAPHAS, JOSEPH **5:**19
Cailingold, M. **4:**1239; **13:**1374
CAIMIS, MOISIS **5:**20
Caimont (Cana. city), *see* JOKNEAM
CAIN (bib. fig.) **5:**20
- *Contents:*
- - In the Aggadah **5:**21
- - In Christian Tradition **5:**22
- - In Islamic Literature **5:**23
- - In the Arts **5:**24
- Lurianic Kabbalah **10:**615ff
- sacrifice **14:**605
- Sumer **15:**515
- Wandering Jew legend **16:**259
- *illus:*
- - text
- - episodes from life of **8:**1271
- - rejected offering **2:**58; **6:**980
- - slain by Lamech **10:**1365
- - slaying of Abel **2:**58
- *see also:* ABEL
Cain and Abel, Adam's sons, History of (Apoc. bk.) **2:**245
Caine, Thomas Henry Hall **6:**780
CAIRO (city, Egy.) **5:**25
- Aden rabbinical court **2:**260
- capitulations **5:**148
- Fostat **6:**491
- *Genizah* **16:**1333
- geonic academy **7:**323
- Israel air attacks **14:**1640
- Jewish international trade **16:**1280
- Jewish quarter **10:**86
- Maimonides **11:**756
- Mamluk persecutions **11:**835
- mintmasters **12:**64
- Samaritans **14:**733
- Shabbetai Ẓevi **14:**1223
- special Purim **13:**1397
- synagogue **15:**613
- Torah-reading customs **15:**1247
- Yemen Jews **16:**741
- *illus:*
- - text
- - *mikveh* pumping system **11:**1537
- - *Misraim* (1904) **13:**1042
Cairo (city, Ill.) **8:**1255
Cairo *Genizah*, *see* GENIZAH, CAIRO
CAISERMAN, HANANE MEIER **5:**32
CAISERMAN-ROTH, GHITTA **3:**598
Caisse de secours et de bienfaisance israélite de Tunis (orgn.) **15:**1450
Caitung (journ.) **13:**1031
Caius Suetonius Tranquillus ,*see* Suetonius
Cajetan, Count of Berchem-Haimhausen, *see* Haimhausen, Cajetan of Berchem-
Cajetan, Tommaso Vio **16:**1290
Calabrese, Ḥayyim, *see* VITAL, ḤAYYIM BEN JOSEPH
Calabrese, Joseph Vital, *see* Vital, Joseph
Calabresi, Anche Oreste **15:**1057
CALABRIA (reg., It.) **5:**33
- *illus:* text
- *see also:* APULIA
Calah (city, Assyr.)
- archives **3:**369
- Esarhaddon **16:**1504
- excavations **16:**1508
- ivory inscription **16:**662; **16:**663
- Mesopotamia **16:**1507
- war, warfare **16:**277
CALAHOR(R)A (fam., Pol.) **5:**34
Calahora, Aaron **5:**34
Calahora, Abraham **5:**34
Calahora, Aryeh Loeb **5:**34
Calahora, David **5:**34
Calahora, Israel Samuel ben Solomon, *see* CALAHORRA, ISRAEL SAMUEL BEN SOLOMON
CALAHORA, JOSEPH BEN SOLOMON **5:**35
- *illus:* text
Calahora, Jutta, *see* Jekeles, Jutta
Calahora, Mattathias **5:**34
Calahora, Mendel (d. 1772) **5:**34
Calahora, Mendel (d. 1779) **5:**34
Calahora, Michael **5:**34
Calahora, Moses **5:**34
Calahora, Nata **5:**34
Calahora, Solomon (physic.) **5:**34
Calahora, Solomon (r.) **5:**34
CALAHORRA (city, Sp.) **5:**36
CALAHORRA, ISRAEL SAMUEL BEN SOLOMON **5:**36
Calais (city, Me.) **11:**782
Calamani, Joshua Abraham, *see* Calimani, Joshua Abraham
CALAMUS, SWEET (spice) **5:**37
- incense and perfumes **8:**1311ff
- plant list **13:**615
Călărasi (tn., Mold.), *see* KALARASH
Calas(c)io (-ius), Mario di **8:**26 **12:**854
CALATAYUD (city, Sp.) **5:**37
- Spain **15:**231
CALATRAVA (Sp. knights) **5:**39
Calcar, J. D. Van **14:**917
Calcio, Ignazio **8:**26

Calcol (bib. fig.) **16:**662
CALCUTTA (city, Ind.) **5:**39
- India **8:**1356
- *illus:*
- - text
- - Maghen David Synagogue **8:**1353
Caldeira, Antonio Nuñes **15:**1301
Calderón de la Barca, Pedro **15:**248
Caldwell (city, Ida.) **8:**1223
CALÊ, WALTER **5:**41
CALEB, CALEBITES **5:**41
- Ahiman, Sheshai, Talmai **2:**464
- Moses **12:**377
- Rechabites **13:**1610
- *geneal. table:* **7:**379
Caleb, Yehoshua **16:**1108
- *illus:*
- - F.Z.C. **16:**1165
Caleb Afendopolo (philos.) **14:**740; **14:**742; **14:**748
Caleb ben Said **13:**577
CALENDAR **5:**43
- *Contents:*
- - Fixing Rosh Ha-Shanah **5:**44
- - The Year **5:**44
- - *Tekufot* **5:**46
- - Historical **5:**48
- - Early Indications of Intercalation **5:**48
- - Regularization of Intervals of Intercalation **5:**49
- - Development of the Present Order of Intercalation **5:**50
- - Sectarian Calendars **5:**50
- History
- - chronological chart **8:**766-767
- - documents **14:**1386
- - intercalation, Babylonian **6:**1023; **6:**1032
- - *niddui* **8:**351
- - post Temple destruction **9:**241,250; **9:**256
- - Seleucid era **4:**36; **14:**1123
- Judaism
- - Academies controversy **4:**39; **4:**539
- - *Baraita de-Rav Adda* **2:**255
- - *bet din* rulings **2:**202
- - cultural activities **8:**655
- - Day of Atonement **5:**1377; **14:**311
- - mnemonics **12:**189
- - New Year **12:**1061
- - Omer **12:**1385
- - reason for lunar calendar **15:**517
- - *Seder Olam Rabbah* **14:**1092
- - study of the calendar **3:**796
- - sun blessing **15:**518
- - tithe cycle **15:**1025
- Other systems
- - Apocrypha **3:**183ff
- - Babylon **16:**1503
- - Dead Sea texts **5:**1403
- - *Enoch, Ethiopic Book of* **6:**795
- - Falashas **6:**1148
- - Islam **9:**98
- - *Jubilees, Book of* **10:**325
- - Karaite calendar **10:**778
- - Mesopotamia **16:**1490
- - Samaritans **14:**740; **14:**742; **14:**748
- Studies and Views
- - Abraham Bar Ḥiyya **2:**132
- - Abudarham's tables **2:**182
- - Akavya, Avraham **2:**478
- - Azariah dei Rossi **14:**317ff
- - Bornstein, Ḥayyim **4:**1252
- - Cohn, Berthold **5:**688
- - Dustan sect reforms **6:**313
- - Hahn, Joseph Yuspa **7:**1129
- - Hillel II **9:**256
- - Isaac ben Solomon's reform **9:**33
- - Johanan ben Zakkai **9:**241
- - Judah ha-Nasi **10:**369
- - Kornik, Meir **10:**1210
- - Meshwi al-ʿUkbrī **11:**1405
- - Nahshon bar Zadok **12:**793
- - Saadiah Gaon **14:**544
- - Slonimski, Ḥayyim **14:**1675
- - Tykocinski, Jehiel **15:**1477
- *illus:*
- - text
- - festivals and fasts (table) **6:**1239
- - Gezer Calendar **2:**386; **7:**537
- - leap years calculation table (1649) **10:**1527
- - *Omer* chart **12:**1383,1385
- - *Orden De Bendiciones* (1687) **11:**1019
- - *Or ha-Levanah* (1872) **9:**33
- - Samaritan **14:**747
- - *Sefer ha-Mahbarot* **16:**1191,1192
- - Yiddish (Russia, 1959) **14:**489
- *see also:* Hundred Year Calendar, vol. **1**; CHRONOLOGY; DAY AND NIGHT; LEAP YEAR; NEW MOON; SABBATICAL YEAR AND JUBILEE; YEAR; ZODIAC; *and under individual months*
CALENDAR REFORM **5:**53
- League of Nations **10:**1524
Calendula (bot.) **6:**1365
Calepinus, Ambrosius **8:**26
Calf, Golden, *see* GOLDEN CALF
Calfo, Moses **4:**223
CALGARY (city, Can.) **5:**54
- *illus:*
- - text
- - House of Jacob Synagogue **2:**531
Cali (city, Colom.) **5:**745ff
CALICUT (city, Ind.) **5:**55
- India **8:**1355
Calid Hebraeus (alch.), *see* Khalid ben Jasikhi
CALIFORNIA (U.S.) **5:**56
- *illus:*
- - text
- - Keysville tombstone **15:**1599
- *pop. table:* text
Caligniis, Alanus Refaut De **8:**26
CALIGULA, CAIUS CAESAR AUGUSTUS (emp.) **5:**60
- attitude to Jews **14:**229
- emperor worship **6:**729
- history chart **8:**766-767
- Roman-Jewish relations **8:**638
Calimani, Joshua Abraham **13:**130
CALIMANI, SIMON (Simḥah) **5:**61
Calimano da Treviso (It.) **15:**1380
CĂLIN, VERA **14:**423; **14:**425
Călinescu, George **12:**1327; **14:**420
CALIPH **5:**61
- Jewish community under **5:**813
- Samaritans **14:**732
- Umayyads **15:**1528
Calisch, Edith L. (writ.) **5:**451
CALISCH, EDWARD NATHAN **5:**62
Calisthenics, *see* Gymnastics
CALIXTUS II (pope) **5:**62
- attitude to Jews **13:**853
- papal bull **4:**1495; **5:**1141
CALIXTUS III (pope) **5:**62
- attitude to Jews **13:**856
Call (period.) **16:**636
Callahan, Mushy **15:**306
CALLENBERG, JOHANN HEINRICH **5:**63
- Hebraist **8:**26
CALLIGRAPHY AND WRITING MASTERS **5:**63
- typography **15:**1480
- *illus:*
- - Noah's ark, Kufic script **12:**1193
Callinicum (city, Syr.) **2:**801; **8:**655
Callimanni, Joshua Abraham, *see* Calimani, Joshua Abraham
CALLISTHENES **5:**64
Callman, Rudolf **2:**820
Callmeyer, Hans **12:**988
"Call of the Shofar" (mosaic mural, B. Shahn) **14:**1259
Callot, Jacques **9:**1544
Call's Fort (Ida., U.S.) **8:**1222
Calman (15th cent., Ger.) **14:**108
Calman, Samson **3:**853
CALMANSON, JACOB (Jacques) **5:**64
Calmat, Alain **15:**317
Calmenson, Jessie **12:**38
Calmenson, Moses **12:**36
Calmer, Antonine Louis Isaac **5:**64
CALMER, MOSES ELIEZER LIEFMANN **5:**64
- title **15:**1166
CALNEH (city, Mesop.) **5:**65
CALNEH (Calno; city, Syr.) **5:**65
- Raqqa (al-) **13:**1557
Calo, Eugenio **13:**147
Calomiti, Nehemiah ben Menahem **13:**591
Calonges, Madam De **8:**27
Calov (-ius) (Kalau), A. **8:**27
Calsena (tn., Sp.) **13:**202
CĂLUGĂRU, ION **5:**65
Calumny, *see* SLANDER
Calvary (loc., Jer.), *see* Golgotha
Calvert (city, Tex.) **15:**1035
Calvert, James **8:**27
Calvert, Thomas **8:**27
Calvin, Jean **8:**27
CALVIN, JOHN **5:**66
- Calvinism **3:**107; **8:**701
- history chart **8:**766-767
- usury **12:**252
- Reformation **14:**19
- *see also;* PROTESTANTS
CALVIN, MELVIN **5:**68
Calvo, Daniel **15:**1455
Calvo, Joseph **15:**1455
Calvo, Solomon **14:**1083
Calvoër (Calvor), Kaspar **8:**27
Calwary (fam.) **5:**34
CALWER, RICHARD **5:**69
Calycotome thorn bush **9:**221
Camagüey (prov., Cuba) **5:**1148
Cámara Comercial Industrial Israelita (Arg.) **3:**420
Cámara de Comercio Israelita (Mex.) **11:**1457
Cambodia **9:**444
CAMBRIDGE (city, Eng.) **5:**69
- university **5:**666; **15:**1677
- university library **8:**1322; **11:**193; **16:**1333
Cambridge (city, Mass.) **11:**1112
Cambridge Platonists (kabs.) **10:**646
CAMBYSES (k., Pers.) **5:**70
- history chart **8:**766-767
CAMDEN (city, county, N.J.) **5:**71
- Philadelphia **13:**368
Camden de Leon, David **6:**1362
Camden Town (dist., London) **6:**449
- *illus:*
- - J.F.S. comprehensive school **11:**478
CAMEL **5:**72
- dietary laws **6:**32
- migrations and dialects **14:**1153
- *illus:*
- - text
- - Israel stamp **12:**927
Camel-hair **15:**1037
CAMERI (theat., Isr.) **5:**73
- theater, Israel **15:**1061
- *illus:*
- - text
- - Meron, Hanna, in *Hedda Gabler* **11:**1392
- - *Saint Joan* **15:**1062
Caminero, Francisco Xavier **8:**27
Camerini, Donato **13:**122
CAMERINI, EUGENIO SALOMONE **5:**74
Camerino, Manuele da **12:**280
Cameroon (rep., Afr.) **9:**438
Camillari, M.A. **4:**887
Cammeo, Abraham di **2:**548
CAMMEO, FEDERICO **5:**75
CAMONDO (De) (fam.) **5:**75
Camondo, Abraham de **5:**75; **9:**1094; **16:**1539
Camondo, Isaac (fin.) **5:**75
Camondo, Isaac de (art collec.) **5:**76
Campana, Israel of, *see* Israel Jonah of Campana
Campanal (fam.) **11:**782
Campanall, Mordecai **7:**124
Campania (reg., It.) **9:**1121
Campanton, Isaac ben Jacob, *see* CANPANTON, ISAAC BEN JACOB
Campbell, Gay **5:**452
Camp du Richard (concen. camp, Fr.) **16:**166
Campe, Joachim **7:**1447; **8:**1118
Campe, Julius **8:**275
CAMPEN (Campensis), JOHANNES VAN **5:**76
- Hebraist **8:**27
CAMPEN, MICHEL HERMAN VAN **6:**320; **6:**322
Campinas (city, Braz.) **4:**1329
Campo de Calatrava (dist., Sp.) **5:**594
Camp of Israel (bib. and tal. term) **14:**10
Campoi, János **8:**27
Campos (city, Braz.) **14:**190
CAMPS (Concentration and Extermination) **5:**77
- *Contents:*
- - Protective Custody of Enemies of the State (1933-39) **5:**77
- - World War II **5:**78
- - Structure and Administration **5:**87
- - End of the Camps **5:**88
- General
- - art **3:**568ff
- - children's literature **5:**446
- - currency **5:**725
- - gassing **16:**1332
- - history chart **8:**766-767
- - Kapo **10:**754
- - Nazi criminals **16:**993
- - Pohl, Oswald **13:**701
- - Poland **13:**765ff
- - responsa **14:**94
- - survivors' periodicals **4:**610,612
- - tracing of inmates **8:**1412
- Main Camps
- - Austria
- - - Ebensee **11:**1137
- - - Gusen **5:**78; **11:**1137
- - - Mauthausen **11:**1136
- - Belgium
- - - Breendonck **4:**421; **8:**858
- - - Malines (Dossin, Mechelen, Mechlin) **11:**826
- - Bulgaria
- - - Somovit **4:**1488
- - Czechoslovakia
- - - Novaky **13:**147
- - - Patronka **4:**1312
- - - Petržalka **4:**1312
- - - Theresienstadt (Terezin) **15:**1112
- - - Zilina **16:**1022
- - Estonia
- - - Aigali **6:**917
- - - Ereda **6:**917
- - - Goldfield **7:**619
- - - Kalevi Liiva **6:**917
- - - Klooga **6:**917
- - - Lagedi **6:**917
- - - Vaivara **6:**917
- - France
- - - Agde **2:**343; **7:**34
- - - Argelès-Sur-Mer **7:**34
- - - Barcares **7:**34

- - - Beaune la Rolande **7:**35; **8:**858
- - - Camp du Richard **16:**166
- - - Compiègne **7:**35
- - - Drancy **6:**207; **7:**35
- - - Fort-Barraux **7:**34
- - - Gurs **7:**982
- - - Les Milles **2:**476; **7:**34
- - - Natzweiler-Struthof **12:**892
- - - Nexon **7:**34
- - - Pithiviers **7:**35
- - - Saint-Cyprien **7:**34; **7:**982
- - - Vittel **10:**830; **16:**820
- - Galicia
- - - Borislav **4:**1249
- - - Buchach **4:**1437
- - - Janowska Road Camp (Lvov) **11:**615
- - - Plaszow **13:**627, 766; **14:**534; **16:**1189
- - Germany
- - - Arbeitsdorf **5:**78
- - - Bergen-Belsen **4:**610
- - - Bochum **4:**1158
- - - Brunswick **4:**1422
- - - Buchenwald **4:**1442
- - - Cottbus **5:**992
- - - Dachau **5:**1218
- - - Dora **4:**1445
- - - Esterwegen **5:**77
- - - Flossenbuerg **5:**86
- - - Grossrosen **5:**78
- - - Lichtenburg **5:**77; **13:**1583
- - - Neuengamme **5:**95
- - - Niederhagen **5:**78
- - - Ravensbrueck **13:**1583
- - - Sachsenhausen-Oranienburg **14:**597
- - - Wells **7:**366
- - Greece
- - - Haidon **3:**818; **7:**879
- - Hungary
- - - Kistarcsa **10:**1076
- - Italy
- - - Bolzano **4:**1192
- - - Carpi **2:**567
- - - Fossoli **6:**1444
- - - Mantua **11:**897
- - - Raab **13:**147
- - Latvia
- - - Kaiserwald **10:**1467; **14:**175
- - - Salaspils **10:**1467
- - Libya
- - - Giado **11:**202
- - - Homs **11:**202
- - Lithuania
- - - Kauen (Kaunas) **10:**849
- - - Ponary **13:**847
- - Netherlands **12:**987
- - - Amersfoort **2:**832
- - - Vught (KL Herzogenbusch) **16:**232
- - - Westerbork **16:**466
- - Poland
- - - Auschwitz **3:**854
- - - Belzec **4:**453
- - - Belzyce **4:**455
- - - Birkenau **3:**855
- - - Bogusze **3:**852
- - - Bronna Gora **10:**1123
- - - Budzyn **4:**455; **8:**1055
- - - Burggraben **15:**464
- - - Chelmno **5:**374
- - - Chodosy **10:**1123
- - - Chryzanow **5:**534
- - - Cieszanow **5:**1212
- - - Elbing **15:**464
- - - Gerdauen **15:**464
- - - Heiligenbeil **15:**464
- - - Jaktorów **16:**1218
- - - Jesau **15:**464
- - - Karczew **12:**1526
- - - Kelbasin **13:**770; **15:**84
- - - Kielce **10:**990
- - - Kosaki **16:**1218
- - - Kulmhof, *see* Chelmno (above)
- - - Lackie Wielkie **16:**1218
- - - Majdanek **11:**794
- - - Miedzyrzec Podlaski **11:**1524
- - - Mielec **11:**1525
- - - Mlyniewo **16:**672
- - - Nisko **8:**854,857; **12:**1512
- - - Peikinia **14:**538
- - - Plew **16:**1218
- - - Pomiechowek **12:**1245
- - - Praust **15:**464
- - - Radomsko **5:**1213
- - - Sasov **16:**1218
- - - Schippenbeil **15:**464
- - - Seerappen **15:**464
- - - Skarzysko-Kamienna **5:**1214; **13:**767; **14:**1644
- - - Sobibor **15:**21
- - - Stolp **15:**464
- - - Stutthof **15:**464
- - - Thorn **15:**464
Treblinka **15:**1365,1368
- - - Tyszowce **12:**1526
- - - Zagłebia **10:**1309
- - - Zaprudy **10:**1123
- - - Zaslaw **14:**844
- - - Zawarnice **16:**1218
- - - Zbaszyń **16:**166
- - Rumania
- - - Caracal **6:**1371
- - - Marculesti **11:**944
- - Russia
- - - Akmechetka **15:**1333
- - - Bogdanovka **12:**1326; **15:**1333
- - - Bratslav **4:**1313
- - - Domanevka **12:**1326; **15:**1333ff
- - - Golta **12:**1326
- - - Kamenka-Bugskaya **10:**728
- - - Koldychevo **10:**1160
- - - Maly Trostinec **8:**871
- - - Odessa **12:**1326
- - - Pechora (Peczara) **15:**1335, 1428
- - - Sekiryany **14:**1118
- - - Târgu-Jiu **6:**1371; **15:**1336
- - - Tiraspol **12:**1457
- - - Vapnyarka **15:**1333; **15:**1335
- - - Volkovysk **16:**212
- - - Yedintsy **16:**727
- - - Zborov **16:**945
- - Yugoslavia
- - - Ada **2:**233
- - - Djakovo **12:**1498; **14:**872
- - - Jadovna **16:**877
- - - Jasenovac **14:**872; **15:**290
- - - Loborgrad **14:**872
- - - Saymishte **4:**428; **15:**290
- *illus:*
- - text
- - Auschwitz **3:**857-872
- - - Abba Eban's visit **13:**782
- - - suicide of inmates **8:**885
- - - transport and faces of victims **8:**875-880
- - Bergen-Belsen **4:**610-611
- - - corpses of victims **8:**887
- - Birkenau **3:**859, 871
- - Buchenwald **4:**1443-1445
- - crematorium **3:**868
- - Dachau **5:**1218-1219; **7:**620
- - Drancy, deportation **7:**31
- - drawings by camp artists Figs. 75-85 3-ART; **5:**95, 1203; **8:**881
- - Dutch deportation **12:**990
- - forced labor **6:**1429
- - Himmler's visit to Auschwitz **3:**861
- - inmates on their way to death **3:**863-866
- - Jews herded by Nazis into mass grave **8:**763
- - Ka-Zetnick's testimony **3:**857
- - Lodz children on their way to death **8:**873
- - Majdanek commemorative stamp **11:**794
- - Mauthausen **11:**1137,1138
- - memorials, East German stamp **4:**1445
- - Natzweiler-Struthof postcard and stamp **12:**893
- - Sachsenhausen, roll call **8:**761
- - scenes of daily existence (drg., E. Lieberman) **8:**881
- - Sobibor camp plan **15:**22
- - storerooms, shoes and eyeglasses of victims **3:**869
- - Theresienstadt, children's drawings **5:**1203
- - Theresienstadt deportations **15:**1113
- - Transnistria (map) **15:**1331
- - - Cihrin-Berezovca report **15:**1330
- - Treblinka camp model **15:**1368
- - Westerbork **16:**466
- - Yad Vashem shrine **16:**697
- - Zyklon B cylinders **3:**868
- *see also:* FORCED LABOR; GHETTO; HOLOCAUST

CAMPULUNG MOLDOVENESC (tn., Rum.) **5:**97
Campus, Eugen **5:**454
Campus Fabae (val., Er. Isr.), *see* JEZREEL, VALLEY OF
Campus Maximus Legionis (plain, Er. Isr.), *see* LEGIO
Cana (vill., Er. Isr.), *see* KEFAR KANNA
CANAAN (bib. fig.) **5:**97
CANAAN, CURSE OF **5:**97
CANAAN, LAND OF **5:**98
- General
- - anthropology, physical **3:**42ff
- - Bible history **8:**574ff
- - Chedorlaomer **5:**370ff
- - demons, demonology **5:**1522
- - dress **6:**214
- - economic history **16:**1267,1269
- - Genesis, Book of **7:**389ff
- - Hadad, deity **7:**1040
- - *ḥerem* **8:**345ff
- - Jerusalem **9:**1379
- - king, kingship **10:**1012ff
- - names of God **7:**674
- - priesthood **13:**1069
- - Russians identified with **14:**433
- - Semites **14:**1148
- - war and warfare **16:**269
- - weights and measures **16:**388
- Conquest and Settlement
- - Bible history **8:**577; **8:**579
- - biblical borders **10:**1551
- - Commandments, the 613 **5:**770, 774
- - Israelites **9:**115
- - Joshua **10:**265
- - Judah, tribe of **10:**328
- - Levites **13:**1072
- - Samaritan chronology **14:**750; **14:**751
- - Simeon (Simeonites) **14:**1548
- - Twelve Tribes **15:**1381
- Language and Script
- - alphabet **2:**677
- - Canaanite-Phoenician script **2:**674ff; **4:**773
- - cuneiform script **16:**661
- - Hebrew language **16:1398, 1569**
- - poetry **13:**671ff
- - Semitic languages **14:**1149
- Ugaritic **15:**1507
- - writing systems **16:**654ff
- *illus:*
- - Arad antiquities **3:**245-248
- - Ashcrah **3:**704
- - Astarte figurines **3:**318, 504
- - Beth-Shean, brick altar **2:**761
- - Bet Yeraḥ, Canaanite city (map) **4:**778
- - boundaries **9:**112
- - Megiddo, temple **2:**760
- *map:* text
- *see also:* PHOENICIA, PHOENICIANS

Canaanites (anc. people), *see* CANAAN, LAND OF
"CANAANITES" (mvmt., Isr.) **15:**101
- Ben-Avi, Ithamar **12:**1056
- Kurzweil, Baruch **10:**1303
- Ratosh, Yonathan **13:**1574
"Canaanites" (J. gr., Rus) **7:**424
Canaan Jordanis (fin.) **11:**180; **13:**720
CANADA **5:**102
- *Contents:*
- - Early Settlement **5:**102
- - Population Growth **5:**104
- - Farming **5:**106
- - Religious Life **5:**107
- - Jewish Education **5:**108
- - Major Community Organizations **5:**108
- - Zionist Organizations **5:**108
- - Jewish-Gentile Relations **5:**109
- - Anti-Semitism **5:**110
- - Political Views and Public Office **5:**111
- - Literary Activity **5:**112
- - Press **5:**113
- agriculture **2:**412
- divorce statistics **6:**136
- education **6:**452
- Habonim **8:**1241
- ICA **10:**46
- Israel **9:**432
- Jewish farming **16:**1317
- law **10:**1494
- literature **5:**114
- longevity **14:**1499ff
- migrations **16:**1520
- military **11:**1554
- museums **12:**551
- ORT **12:**1483
- Orthodoxy **12:**1490
- philanthropy **13:**385
- Po'alei Zion **13:**659
- politics **13:**810
- press **13:**1026ff
- Protestants and Jews **13:**1252
- rabbinate **13:**1252; **13:**1453
- refugees, Jewish **14:**30
- Six-Day War volunteers **9:**543
- socialism **15:**27
- statistics **13:**897; **15:**345; **16:**183ff
- students' movement **15:**450
- synagogues **1:**syn. list
- trade and commerce **15:**1305
- U.N.E.F. **15:**1554ff
- UNSCOP **15:**1688
- War Crimes Trials **16:**291
- Yiddish education **6:**436ff
- Zionism **16:**1109
- *illus:*
- - Hart's Bank, bank note **7:**1351
- - Zionist convention **16:**1110
- *pop. tables:*
- - text
- - age composition, 1961 **5:**1518
- - major towns, 1967 **5:**1514
- - postwar communities **5:**839

CANADA'S RELATIONS WITH ISRAEL **16:**1261
Canadian Israel Association **16:**1111
Canadian Jewish Chronicle **5:**113
Canadian Jewish Chronicle—Review (newsp.) **5:**113; **13:**1026
CANADIAN JEWISH CONGRESS **5:**113
- history chart **8:**766-767
- Jewish Labor Committee **10:**66
- Zionism **16:**1111
- *illus:* text
Canadian Jewish Eagle (newsp.), *see* KANADER ADLER
Canadian Jewish News (period.) **5:**113; **13:**1026
Canadian Jewish Review (newsp.) **5:**113

Canadian Jewish Times (newsp.) 5:113; 13:1026
Canadian Jewish Weekly (newsp.) 13:1026
CANADIAN LITERATURE 5:114
Canadian Zionist (period.) 13:1026; 16:1110
CANAKKALE (tn., Turk.) 5:116
Canarsie (section, N.Y.C.) 12:1107
CANARY ISLANDS 5:116
- Inquisition 8:1396
Cañas (tn., Sp.) 12:800
Canatha (city, Hauran), *see* KENATH
Canberra (city, Austr.) 3:884
Cancer (zodiac sign) 15:788; 16:1191
Cancer (disease) 14:1503
- *illus:*
- - Israel stamp 9:844-845
Cancionere de Baena (bk.) 2:785; 4:79
Candelabro Publishing House (Arg.) 5:456
Candelabrum, *see* MENORAH
Candia, *see* CRETE
Candia, Isaac 12:405
Candia, Salamone 11:61
Candioti, Teodoro 13:322
CANDLES 5:117
- candle-making 5:1051
- Day of Atonement 5:1380
- death 5:1425; 5:1426
- donation to avert danger 5:272
- *ḥerem* pronouncement 8:355
- *ḥuppah* ceremony 11:1042
- Meir Ba'al ha-Nes 11:1246
- Sabbath 14:570
- *illus:*
- - text
- - "Blessing over the Candles" (Kaufmann) 4:487
- - *ḥerem* 3:930
- - Sabbath candlesticks 14:564-568
- *see also:* POTTERY
CANDLE TAX 5:119
- *see also:* TAXATION
Candrea, I.A. 14:399,421
Cane, Biflorate (bot.) 13:615
CANEA (city, Crete) 5:119
CANETTI, ELIAS 5:120
Canini(-us), Angelo 8:27
Cannibalism 11:708
CANNSTADT, KARL FRIEDRICH 11:1206
Cannstatt (sub., Stuttgart) 15:462
Canoeing 15:307
Canoga, Na Floreta 14:846
Canon (med. bk.; Avicenna) 8:1270
Canon, Bible, *see* BIBLE (Canon, Texts and Editions)
Canon law 15:1162
Canon of Alexandria (collec. of works) 3:184
Canon of Avicenna (15th cent. illum. ms., It.)
- *illus:* 3:*fcg.* 955; 8:1283; 11:1192
Canopus inscription (Ptolemaic period) 9:108
CANPANTON, ISAAC BEN JACOB 5:120
- Naḥmanides 12:780
- Zarza, Samuel 16:939
CANPANTON, JUDAH BEN SOLOMON 5:121
CANSINO (fam.) 5:121
- *geneal. table:* text
Cansino, Aaron 5:122
Cansino, Abraham (16/17 cent.) 5:122
Cansino, Abraham (17/18 cent.) 5:121
Cansino, Ḥayyim 5:121
Cansino, Isaac (interp.) 5:121
Cansino, Isaac (emis.) 11:1149
Cansino, Isaac (apos.) 5:121
Cansino, Isaac (publ.) 5:121
Cansino, Isaac (poet) 5:122
Cansino, Jacob (gram.) 5:121
Cansino, Jacob (interp.) 5:121
Cansino, Jacob (dipl.) 2:670; 5:122
- *illus:*
- - *Extremos y Grandezas de Constantinopla* (1638) 2:670
Cansino, Jonah 5:121
Cansino, Moses 5:121
Cansino, Pedro Fernandez 5:121
Cansino, Samuel 5:122
Cansino, Solomon 5:121
Cansinos-Assens, Rafael 15:248
Cansteinsche Bibelanstalt (soc., Ger.) 4:969
CANTARINI (fam.) 5:122
Cantarini, Angelo di Grassin 5:122
Cantarini, Ḥayyim Moses 5:122
CANTARINI, ISAAC VITA HA-KOHEN 5:122
- *Paḥad Yiẓḥak* 8:558
Cantarini, Judah ben Samuel 13:12
Cantarini, Leone di Simone 5:122
CANTATAS AND CHORAL WORKS, HEBREW 5:123
- *illus:* text
CANTERA BURGOS, FRANCISCO 5:127
- Madrid university 11:684
CANTERBURY (city, Eng.) 5:127
- *map:* text
Cantheras, Simeon (h. pr.), *see* SIMEON BEN BOETHUS
Canticle of Canticles, *see* SONG OF SONGS
Canticum Canticorum, *see* SONG OF SONGS
CANTILLATION 5:128
- Babylonian system 12:585; 16:1445
- Buxtorf 4:1543
- Decalogue 5:1446
- graphic systems 16:1433
- *haftarah* 16:1342
- *maqāma* 11:937ff
- masorah 16:1412,1413
- masoretic accents 11:1098
- music 12:577ff
- *nusaḥ* 12:1283ff
- Palestinian system 16:1433,1437
- right hand 14:177
- Samaritan masorah 14:757; 16:1470
- Samuel ben Meir 14:810
- *shtayger* 14:1463
- Tiberian system 12:585; 16:1453, 1571
- Yemenite Jews 16:756ff
- *illus:* text
- *mus. notations:*
- - Ashkenazi Bible chant 12:583
- - Bukhara psalmodic pattern 12:577
- - choir development 12:663
- - German style 12:617
- - *haftarah,* Karaite 10:784
- - Italian rite 9:1143
- - Kurdistan rite 10:1299-1300
- - Pentateuch, comparative table 11:1101
- - Pentateuch, Western Ashkenazi 11:1100
- - San'a rite 16:749
- - table of accents 11:1103,1105
- *see also:* PSALMS, BOOK OF; TORAH, READING OF
"Canto de Fe" (paint., A. Berruguete) 3:912
CANTON (city, China) 5:129
Cantone, Aiolfo de 8:1321
Cantone, Aldo 14:197
CANTONI, ALBERTO 5:130
- Italian literature 9:1111
CANTONI, LELIO (Hillel) 5:130
CANTONI, RAFFAELE 5:130
- Italy 9:1139
CANTONISTS (conscripts) 5:130
- community problems 8:721ff
- history chart 8:766-767
- Levinsohn, Isaac Baer 11:116
- military service 11:1554
- Moscow settlers 12:363
- Siberia 14:1486
- *illus:*
- - recruits oath 14:439
Canton Synagogue (It.) 15:329
- *illus:*
- - Ark 5:295; 16:98
- - *bimah* 4:1003
Cantor, *see* ḤAZZAN
Cantor, Bernard 2:828; 7:180
CANTOR, EDDIE 5:133
CANTOR, JACOB AARON 5:134
CANTOR, MORITZ BENEDICT 5:134
Cantor, Nathaniel F. 5:1110
CANTOR, NORMAN FRANK 8:545
Cantor, Sol M. 11:47
Cantori, Joshua de 12:1525
Cantorial Academy, Tel Aviv 7:600
Cantorial Music, *see* ḤAZZAN; MUSIC
Cantors Assembly (U.S.) 15:1674
Cantors' Association (Pol.), *see* Aggudat ha-Ḥazzanim
Capa, Cornell 5:134; 13:484
CAPA, ROBERT 5:134
Capadose, Abraham 6:320
Caparcotnei (vill., Er. Isr.), *see* KEFAR OTNAY
Çapata, Garcia 7:955
Cape Cod (penin., Mass.) 11:1113
Cape Girardeau (city, Mo.) 12:157
Čapek, Karel 5:1193
Capel(le), Jacques 8:27
Capelus, Ludovicus, *see* Cappel, Louis
Cape of Good Hope (prov., S.A.) 15:184ff
CAPE PROVINCE (S.A.) 5:135
CAPER (bot.) 5:135
- plant list 13:615
- spices 15:267
CAPERNAUM (vill., Er. Isr.) 5:136
- holy places 8:922
- Joseph the Apostate 9:255
- pillars 13:523
- synagogue 11:687; 15:595ff
- *illus:*
- - text
- - archaeological remains 2:394; 3:461; 11:689; 13:44
- - millstone 11:1585
- - synagogue plan 15:596
CAPESTANG (tn., Fr.) 5:139
CAPE TOWN (city, S.A.) 5:139
- museum 12:551
- *illus:*
- - museum publication 12:549
- - "Old" synagogue 15:192
- - record of first *minyan* 15:185
Cape Verde Islands 15:487
Capharecho (loc. Er. Isr.) 10:877
CAPHTOR (bib. loc.) 5:140
- Philistines 13:399
CAPISTRANO, JOHN (Giovanni) OF 5:141
- Aquila Jews 3:228
- Austrian Jews 3:889
- Brno Jews 4:1384
- disputation in Rome 14:248
- history chart 8:766-67
Capitalism 16:1298,1311
- Amsterdam merchants 2:897
- Karl Marx 11:1074
- Vozrozhdeniye, ideas on 16:229
CAPITAL PUNISHMENT 5:142
- *Contents:*
- - In the Bible 5:142
- - Talmudic Law 5:142
- - In Practice in the Talmud 5:145
- General and Historical
- - autonomy, judicial 3:929ff
- - cemeteries 5:272
- - community 5:812
- - divine punishment 6:121
- - *jus gladii* 13:1117
- - informers 8:1365; 8:1366; 8:1370ff; 15:239
- - Inquisition 8:1383; 8:1401; 8:1404ff
- - literary use 10:1484
- - *nagid* 12:762
- - *nasi* 9:251
- - Parthia 6:1025
- - pre- 70 C.E. period 12:124
- - Sadducees 14:621; 14:639
- - Sanhedrin's fast 6:1196
- - Schlettstadt affair 14:974
- - Spain 15:234; 15:235
- Legal Aspects
- - abortion 2:98
- - animals 3:987
- - assault on parents 3:758
- - bail 13:959
- - bloodguilt 4:1118
- - circumstantial evidence 14:1564
- - Commandments, the 613 5:772, 779
- - compounding offenses 5:856
- - confession 5:877
- - court of 23 14:840
- - cremation 5:1072
- - extraordinary remedies 6:1073ff
- - flogging 6:1348
- - gentiles 12:1191
- - *ḥazakah* in cases of 7:1522
- - hermeneutics 13:222ff
- - *ḥillul ha-Shem* 10:980
- - impalement 8:1298
- - imprisonment 8:1300
- - *karet* 10:788
- - modes of 14:840
- - preliminaries 13:962
- - punishment 13:1386ff
- - stoning 16:161
- - *takkanah* 15:718
- - wills 16:521
- - witness 16:585
- - *zaken mamre* 16:920
- *illus:*
- - stoning of Achan 8:346
CAPITO, MARCUS HERENNIUS 5:147
CAPITO, WOLFGANG FABRICIUS 5:147
- Hebraist 8:27
- Reformation 14:19
CAPITOLIAS (city, Er. Isr.) 5:148
- Transjordan 15:1317
CAPITULATIONS 5:148
- *Contents*
- - Aleppo 5:148
- - Egypt 5:149
- - North Africa 5:149
- - Ereẓ Israel 5:150
- Ereẓ Israel history 9:298
- Jerusalem 9:1441ff
- Jewish settlers 8:727
- Suleiman the Magnificent 16:1535
Caplan, Fred H. 16:476
CAPLAN, RUPERT 15:1080
Caplin, Alfred Gerald, *see* CAPP, AL
Caplovitz, David 8:648
Capnion (Hebr.), *see* REUCHLIN, JOHANNES
Capon, Abraham 10:1351
CAPON, AUGUSTO 11:1572
CAPP, AL 5:151
- *illus:*
- - Li'l Abner sketch 5:217
CAPPADOCIA (As. M.) 5:151
- Caphtor 5:141
Cappel(le) (-lus), Louis 8:27;

4:1543; 16:1393
Cappellanus, Claude 8:27
Cappellus, Ludwig, *see* Cappel, Louis
"Capriccio" (sculp., S. Etrog) 2:622
Capricornus (zodiac sign) 16:1191
- *illus:* 11:732; 15:1032
Capriles (fam.) 16:90
CAPSALI, ELIJAH 5:152
- history 8:559; 8:697; 11:350
Capsali, Elkanah 5:152
CAPSALI, MOSES BEN ELIJAH 5:153
- chief rabbinate 13:1450
- history chart 8:766-767
- Istanbul 9:1087
- Karaites 16:1547
- Mizraḥi, Elijah 12:182
- Moses Esrim ve-Arba 12:428
"Captain Philippe," *see* Gustman, Ze'ev
Captain Weber Boycott Organization (anti-Nazi) 4:1281
CAPTIVES, RANSOMING OF 5:154
- Crusades 9:271
- endowment funds 8:284
- exilarchic dues 6:1032
- husband's obligations 6:187; 13:1024
- Istanbul Jews 9:1091
- Malta, Jewish prisoners 11:831
- paid agent captive 10:1330
- surety for 15:524
- Venice 10:1330
- *illus:*
- - Florence, *Ḥevrat Mattir Asurim* 9:1136
- *see also:* RANSOM
Captivity 5:769; 16:162
CAPUA (tn., It.) 5:156
CAPUSI, ḤAYYIM 5:156
Capuzato, Moses ha-Yevani 4:136
Caracal (concen. camp, Rum.) 6:1371
CARACALLA, MARCUS AURELIUS ANTONINUS 5:156
- attitude toward Jews 8:648
- history chart 8:766-767
- Judah ha-Nasi 9:251
- *illus:* text
CARACAS (city, Venez.) 5:157
Caracas, Nicolai 10:703
Caracciolo, Fra Roberto 10:1554
Caracosa, Yom Tov 12:289
Caraffa, Cardinal Giovanni Pietro, *see* PAUL IV
CARASSO, EMMANUEL 5:157
Caravaggio (art.) 10:460
Caravan, Danny 12:931
Caravita, Joseph 4:836; 8:1323
Caraway (bot.) 13:617; 15:267
CARBEN, VICTOR VON 5:158
Carbondale (city, Ill.) 8:1256
Carcassona (fam.) 2:621; 14:876
Carcassone, Pierre 2:617
Carcassone, Roger 2:617; 11:1563
Carcassone, Sandela, *see* Oppenheimer, Sandela
CARCASSONNE (city, Fr.) 5:158
- *illus:* text
CARCHEMISH (city, Syr.) 5:160
- Assyrians 10:292
- battle 16:1505,1509
- Mesopotamia 16:1497
"Carchemish weight" 16:378
Carcossa, Samuel 13:300
CARDIFF (city, Wales) 5:161
- *see also:* WALES
Cardinal Offenses, *see* Offenses, Cardinal
Cardon, Abraham 8:216
CARDOSO (fam.) 5:161
- *see also:* Cardozo
Cardoso, Abraham 5:161
Cardoso, Abraham Michael, *see* Cardozo, Abraham
Cardoso, David 5:161
Cardoso, Eugenio 16:135
Cardoso, Isaac, *see* CARDOZO, ISAAC
Cardoso, Jacob 5:161
Cardoso, Ruy Fernando 5:1535
CARDOZO (fam.) 5:162
- *geneal. table:* text
CARDOZO, AARON NUÑEZ 5:163
Cardozo, Abraham (U.S.) 5:162
CARDOZO, ABRAHAM MIGUEL (Shab.) 5:163
- Alfandari, Ḥayyim 2:597
- Ayllon's support 3:996
- Bonafoux, Daniel 4:1198,1199
- Primo, Samuel 13:1092
- Shabbateanism 14:1234; 14:1243
- Shabbatean Kabbalah 10:551
Cardozo, Albert Jacob 5:162; 12:1075; 12:1103
CARDOZO, BENJAMIN NATHAN 5:166
- *geneal. table* 5:162; 12:849
Cardozo, David Nunez 5:162
Cardozo, Efraim 15:255
Cardozo, Ernest Abraham 5:162
Cardozo, Fernando, *see* CARDOZO, ISAAC
Cardozo, Gonçalo, *see* Aboab, Abraham
CARDOZO, ISAAC (philos.) 15:168
Cardozo, Isaac M. (U.S.) 12:37
Cardozo, Isaac Nunez (pat.) 5:162
Cardozo, Jacob Newton 5:162
Cardozo, Jacob of Bayonne 11:803
Cardozo, Lodewijk Lopes 4:1219
Cardozo, Michael Hart 5:162
Cardozo, Moses 5:162
CARDS AND CARDPLAYING 5:168
- condemnation 7:305
- gambling 7:300
- Israel 11:513
CAREGAL, ḤAYYIM MOSES BEN ABRAHAM 5:169
CAREI (Carei-Mare; tn., Transyl.) 5:169
CARIA (dist., As. M.) 5:170
Caribbean Islands 10:1451
- Inquisition 8:1395
- population 13:883
Caribou (tn., Me.) 11:782
CARICATURES 5:171
- *Contents:*
- - After World War I 5:176
- - Nazi Cartoons 5:176
- - After the Establishment of Israel 5:178
- *illus:*
- - text
- - "Aaron Son of the Devil" 3:93
- - anti-Semitic, Soviet 3:150; 14:491,492
- - Benjamin, Sir Benjamin 11:1282
- - Braham, John 12:629
- - Brothers, Richard 4:1410
- - Buzaglo's treatment for gout 4:1544
- - Cassel, Sir Ernest Joseph 5:230
- - Crémieux, Isaac Adolphe 5:1075
- - *Der Stürmer* cartoons 3:154 8:833
- - Disraeli, Benjamin 6:106
- - Dublin Jewish old clothes men 6:249
- - Elias, Samuel 15:309
- - Goldsmid, Sir Isaac Lyon 7:734
- - Gordon, Lord George 7:796
- - "Hake" (13th cent.) 12:1226
- - Hore-Belisha 8:975
- - Jew and clergyman 6:714
- - Jew as a fighter 11:1554
- - Jewish soldiers 3:905
- - Jewish Sow (14/18 cent.) 3:117-122
- - Jews dancing around statue of Robert Grant 6:705
- - Jews in Polish militia 13:733
- - Jews in Prussian army 11:1557
- - Le Péril Juif 6:581
- - "March of the Jewish National Guard in Warsaw" 13:733
- - Mastbaum, Joel 11:1119
- - Monmouth Street, London (G. Cruikshank) 11:475
- - Motzkin, Leo 12:476
- - Naquet, Alfred Joseph 12:826
- - Nathan, Isaac 12:852
- - Nicholas I extracting money from Jews 12:1138
- - Opatoshu, Joseph 12:1409
- - Prylucki, Noah 13:1295
- - Reuter, Baron von 14:112
- - Rothschild, Karl Meyer 14:338
- - Solomon, Saul 15:112
- *see also:* ANTI-SEMITISM; CARTOONISTS
CARIGAL, RAPHAEL ḤAYYIM ISAAC 5:179
- Barbados 4:205
- Newport, R.I. 8:959
- Stiles, Ezra 15:403
- *illus:* text
CARINTHIA (prov., Aus.) 5:181
- Crusades 5:1139
Carissimi, Giacomo 9:1344
Caritas Humanitas (orgn., Rum.) 9:1294
Carites (anc. people) 13:404
Carl, Carl, *see* Bembrunn, Karl von
Carl, Howard 15:303
Carlburg, Judah Loeb 10:1251
Carlebach, Alexander 4:415
Carlebach, Emanuel
- *geneal. table:* 4:182
- *illus:*
- - Kohn, Pinchas 10:1147
Carlebach, Ephraim 10:1591
CARLEBACH, EZRIEL 5:181
- Hebrew newspapers 12:1057
- *geneal. table:* text
Carlebach, Hartwig Naphtali 12:685
CARLEBACH, JOSEPH 5:182
- *geneal. table:* text
CARLEBACH, SHLOMO 12:685
- recordings 13:1617
- *illus:*
- - Mt. Zion wedding 11:1048
Carlebach, Solomon 5:182
- homiletic literature 8:958
Carlosburg (city, Transyl.), *see* ALBA IULIA
CARLSBAD (tn., Cz.) 5:183
- Frankist center 7:69
- *illus:*
- - text
- - Thirteenth Zionist Congress 16:1173
Carlyle, Thomas 4:1533
Carmagnola (tn., It.) 13:502
Carmel (stlmt., Arg.) 6:802
CARMEL (city, Judah) 5:184
Carmel (clny., N.J.) 12:1029; 16:157
Carmel (soc., Bul.) 16:1108
Carmel (newsp.) 13:652
CARMEL, MOSHE 5:185
- Haganah 9:687
CARMEL, MOUNT (Isr.) 5:186
- Baal altar 2:438
- Bahai shrine 9:923ff
- Carmel National Park 12:879
- Coastal Plain 9:126; 9:128ff; 9:579
- forest 9:787
- geography 9:588ff
- geology 9:200ff
- Haifa 7:1133
- physiography 9:143
- prehistoric settlement 2:382
- *illus:*
- - text
- - archaeological remains 3:510
- - Bahai Temple 9:924
- - Elijah's cave 6:641; 8:925
- - oak and terebinth 9:235
- - prehistoric remains 2:383; 3:43
- - 'Usifiyyā village 16:20
Carmel, Ẓefania 15:298, 317
Carmel College (Eng.) 6:450
Carmel Company (Isr.) 7:702
Carmeli Brigade (Isr.)
- Haganah 7:1073
- Israel historical survey 9:363
- War of Independence 16:321
Carmelite Order (Isr.) 7:1134
Carmel Oriental (wine cellars, Isr.) 14:194
Carmen Sylva, *see* Elizabeth (q., of Rumania)
Carmi, David ben Joseph 5:207
CARMI, ISAIAH ḤAI BEN JOSEPH 5:187
Carmi, Isaiah Nathan 5:187
Carmi, Jacob Israel 3:763
CARMI, JOSEPH JEDIDIAH 5:187
- *illus:* text
CARMI, T. 5:188
- Hebrew literature 8:206
- translator 14:1264
Carmichael, Joel, *see* Lipsky, Joel
CARMOLY, ELIAKIM 5:189
- book collection 4:974
- *illus:*
- - text
- - poem on inauguration of synagogue in Brussels 4:419
CARMOLY, ISSACHAR BAER BEN JUDAH LIMA 5:189
Carmon, Amaliah, *see* Cahana-Carmon, Amaliah
CARMONA (city, Sp.) 5:190
CARMONA, BEKHOR ISAAC DAVID 5:190
- Istanbul 9:1094
Carmona, Daniel 13:816
Carmona, Elijah (Elia) 10:1351; 5:446
Carmona, Isaac 13:1038
Carnelian sard (gem) 13:1009
CARNIVAL (Chr. fest.) 5:191
CARNOVSKY, MORRIS 15:1080
CARO, ANTHONY 5:191
- *illus:* text
CARO, DAVID 5:192
- Haskalah activities 13:948
Caro, Ephraim 5:194; 16:1533
Caro, Ezekiel
- Caro, Joseph Ḥayyim 5:200
- Lvov 11:612
CARO, GEORG MARTIN 5:193
- historiography 8:562
CARO, HEINRICH 5:193
CARO, ISAAC BEN JOSEPH 5:193
Caro, Isaac Zelig 16:1232
Caro, Jacob 5:200
CARO, JOSEPH BEN EPHRAIM 5:194
- *Contents:*
- - Life 5:194
- - As a Halakhist 5:195
- - As a Kabbalist 5:199
- *Bedek ha-Bayit haskamah* 7:1452
- Ben Susan's works 15:532
- codification 5:642ff; 7:1165; 11:335
- history chart 8:766-767
- Kabbalah 10:545
- maggid 11:700
- Nikopol 12:1160
- Rashi and Naḥmanides 15:521
- Saks, Jehiel 5:237
- *sefirot* doctrine 10:567

- Sephardic usage 3:721
- sport on Sabbath 15:292
- Taitazak, Joseph 15:711
- tradition 15:1310
- Trani, Moses 15:1315
- *illus:*
- - text
- - autograph 3:914
- - Maran Beit Yosef synagogue, Nikopol 12:1161
- - portrait 14:1476
- *see also: Beit Yosef;* SHULḤAN ARUKH
CARO, JOSEPH ḤAYYIM BEN ISAAC 5:200
Caro, Judah ben Joseph 5:193,194,198
CARO, NIKODEM 5:201
Caro, Samuel 14:682
Caro, Solomon ben Joseph 5:194
CAROB (bot.) 5:201
- afforestation 9:788
- Jerusalem flora 9:1515
- plant 9:221; 1:617
- *illus:* text
CARO-DELVAILLE, HENRI 3:598
Carolina Israelite (newsp.) 7:708
Carolingian Empire 8:662ff; 16:1280
Carouge (tn., Switz.) 7:403
Carp (fish) 6:36
CARP, HORIA (Jehoshua) 5:202
Carpathia(reg., Ukr.), *see* SUBCARPATHIAN RUTHENIA
Carpatho-Russia (reg., Ukr.), *see* SUBCARPATHIAN RUTHENIA
Carpatho-Ukraine (reg., Ukr.), *see* SUBCARPATHIAN RUTHENIA
Carpatiero, Joseph 2:161
CARPENTRAS (tn., Fr.) 5:203
- *Contents:*
- - History of the Community 5:203
- - Statutes and Synagogues 5:206
- - Rabbis and Scholars 5:207
- museums 12:543
- special Purim 13:1397
- synagogue 15:614
- *illus:*
- - text
- - *maḥzor* (1739) 11:403
- - *maẓẓah* bakery 11:1156
- - *mikveh* 11:1540
Carpentras *Maḥzor* 11:401
Carpentry 5:1042ff
Carpet-Viper (fauna) 9:226
Carpi, Jacob 3:648
CARPI, LEONE 5:208
- Zionism 16:1123
Carpi, Solomon Joseph 14:154
Carpzov, J. B. 8:27
Carpzov, J. Gottlob 8:27
Carrascon, Fray 5:209
CARRASCON, JUAN 5:209
Carregal, Raphael Ḥayyim Isaac, *see* CARIGAL, RAPHAEL ḤAYYIM ISAAC
Carrera, José Miguel 5:461
CARRION DE LOS CONDES (city, Sp.) 5:209
- Sahagun 14:655
Carsinet, Aaron 12:336; 13:103
Carson City (city, Nev.) 12:1017
Carsoni, Isaac al- 15:252
Carta (publ., Isr.) 13:1378
Cartagena (city, Colom.) 5:744ff
- Inquisition 8:1395; 10:1448
CARTAGENA (Cartageni; city, Sp.) 5:209
CART AND CHARIOT 5:210
- Solomon's trade 15:98
- war and warfare 16:266
- *illus:* text
Cartaphilus (lit. fig.), *see* WANDERING JEW
Carter, H. G. 15:1488
CARTER, VICTOR M. 5:213
Carter, Sir W. M. 13:32
CARTHAGE (Phoen. city) 5:214
- catacombs 5:252
- inscriptions 16:668
- language 14:1149
- merchant proselytes 16:1277
- Phoenician colonization 13:479
- Tunisia 15:1430ff
Cartier, G. 4:874
Cartigena (city, Sp.), *see* CARTAGENA
Cartography, *see* GEOGRAPHY; JERUSALEM (Cartography); MAP MAKERS; MAPS OF EREẒ ISRAEL
CARTOONISTS 5:215
- *illus:*
- - text
- - Bass, Y., Ben-Gurion and Dayan 5:1373
- - Block, H. L., Six-Day War 4:1111
- - Capp, Al 5:151
- - Gardosh, Six-Day War 7:328
- - Kelen, Imre 10:898
- - Langdon, David 10:1418
- - Steinberg, Saul 15:336
- *see also:* CARICATURES
Cartoons, Political 5:176ff
Cartwright, Christopher 8:27
CARVAJAL (fam.) 5:220
- *geneal. table:* text
CARVAJAL, ABRAHAM ISRAEL (Antonio Fernandez) 5:222
Carvajal, Ana de 5:222
Carvajal, Baltasar de 5:222
Carvajal, Francisca Núñez de 5:221
Carvajal, Francisco Henríquez y 6:160
Carvajal, Gaspar de 5:222
Carvajal, Guiomar de 5:221
Carvajal, Mariana de 5:222
Carvajal, Micael de 15:248
Carvajal, Miguel de 5:222
Carvajal el Mozo, Luis de 5:221
Carvajal y de la Cueva, Luis de 5:220
Carvalho, Isaac 5:222
Carvalho, Judah 14:633
Carvalho, Mas'ud 14:633
CARVALHO, MORDECAI BARUCH 5:222
- Tunisia 15:1444
Carvalho, Naomi Nunes, *see* Nunes Carvalho, Naomi
CARVALHO, SOLOMON NUNES 5:223
Carvalho de Mello, Sebastian José de, *see* Mello, Sebastian José de Carvalho de
CARVALLO, JULES 5:223
Casa, Joseph ben Abraham, *see* CASE, JOSEPH BEN ABRAHAM
CASABLANCA (city, Mor.) 5:223
- Jewish quarter 10:87
- special Purim 13:1397
- *illus:*
- - text
- - group of Jews 12:333
- - immigrants to Israel 9:499
- - J.D.C. school 2:831
Casa de Dios (sect, Mex.), *see* Beth-El
Casa dei catecumeni (miss., Rome), *see* CATECHUMENS, HOUSE OF
Casal des Plains (fort., Er. Isr.) 3:1011
CASALE MONFERRATO (tn., It.) 5:225
- *illus:* text
Casal Imbert (Crus. camp) 2:213
Casal Soque (loc., Er. Isr.) 15:69
Casanowicz, I. M. 5:311; 12:544
Casdin, Joseph C. 16:634
CASE, JOSEPH BEN ABRAHAM 5:227
CASES (fam.) 5:227
CASÈS, BENJAMIN BEN DAVID 5:227
Cases, Hananiah (r.) 8:458
Casès, Isaac, *see* Kagig, Isaac
Cases, Israel Gedalliah 5:277
Cases, Joseph Baruch 5:227
Cases, Luliano Shalom 5:227
Cases, Menahem ben Elhanan 5:227
Cases, Moses ben Samuel 5:227
Cases, Samuel ben Moses 5:227
CASIMIR III ("The Great"; k., Pol.) 5:228
- history chart 8:766-767
Casimir IV (k., Pol.) 5:141
Casius (Hellen.-Rom. city) 4:13
Caslari, Abraham 11:1191
Caslari, Crescas, *see* Israel ben Joseph ha-Levi
Caslari, David ben Abraham (Maestro David de) 7:264; 12:830; 15:1326
Casluhim (bib. loc.) 7:432
Casola, Pietro 15:1356
Caspari, C. P. 4:877
CASPARY, EUGEN 5:228
CASPER, BERNARD MOSES 5:228
Caspi, Joseph ben Abba Mari ,*see* KASPI, JOSEPH BEN ABBA MARI IBN
Caspi, Nethanel 6:1185
CASPI, SAUL 5:228
Cass, Moses 15:27
CASSAB, JUDY 5:229
Cassel (city, Ger.), *see* KASSEL
CASSEL, DAVID 5:229
- *illus:*
- - *Kore ha-Dorot* (1846) 5:892
CASSEL, SIR ERNEST JOSEPH 5:230
- railroads 13:1519
- *illus:* text
CASSEL, PAULUS STEPHANUS (Selig) 5:231
Cassells, Miguel 8:1384
Casseres, Abraham, *see* CACERES, ABRAHAM
Casseres, de (fam.) 5:1009
Casseres, Joseph, *see* CACERES, FRANCISCO DE
Casseres, Samuel de, *see* Gomez, Gabriel
Cassia bat Shephatiah 2:850
Cassia-cinnamon (bot.) 8:1315
CASSIAN, NINA 14:425
CASSIN, RENÉ SAMUEL 5:231
Cassiodorus (Rom. writ.) 10:263
Cassirer, Bruno 13:1366
CASSIRER, ERNST 5:232
- antiquity 3:301
CASSIRER, PAUL 5:233
- Chagall, Marc 5:318
- publishing 13:1366
Cassius, Avidius *see* Avidius Cassius
Cassius, Dio, *see* DIO CASSIUS
CASSIUS LONGINUS 5:234
- Antipater 8:635
Cassulo, Andrea(s) 8:875; 14:403, 408; 15:1335
Cassuto, Giulia, *see* Artom, Giulia
CASSUTO, UMBERTO (Moses David) 5:234
- Artom, Elia Samuele 3:663
- historiography 8:564
Castanho, Isaac 13:1613
CASTEL, MOSHE ELAZAR 5:236
- *illus:*
- - text
- - "Shabbat in Safed" (paint.) Pl. 7 3-ART
Castelbolognesi, Gustavo 13:12
Castel Hill (Er. Isr.), *see* Qastal, Al-
CASTELL, EDMUND 5:236
- Hebraist 8:27
- Hebrew linguistics 16:1394
Castellane (loc., Prov.) 13:1259
Castellani, C. 14:197
CASTELLAZZO (fam.) 5:237
Castellazzo, Avigdor 5:237
Castellazzo, Moses 5:237
CASTELLAZZO, MOSES DA 5:237
Castellazzo, Simeon 5:237; 11:573
CASTELLI, DAVID 5:238
Castellio, Sebastian 4:881
CASTELLO, ABRAHAM ISAAC 5:238
Castello-Branco, Camillo 5:240
CASTELLÓN DE LA PLANA (city, Sp.) 5:239
Castellum Beleismum (Crus. cas.), *see* IBLEAM
Castellum Belveer (Crus. fort.) 11:1453
Castellum Dok (fort.), *see* DOK
Castelnuova, G. 9:1141
CASTELNUOVO, ENRICO 5:239
- Italian literature 9:1111
Castelnuovo, Jedidiah 5:239
CASTELNUOVO, MENAHEM AZARIAH MEIR (Menahem Ḥayyim) BEN ELIJAH 5:239
Castelnuovo, Samuel ben Moses 9:1109; 14:171; 14:170
CASTELNUOVO-TEDESCO, MARIO 5:240
CASTELO BRANCO (city, Port.) 5:240
Castelo Branco, Camilo 15:251
Castelo Branco, João Rodrigues de, *see* AMATUS LUSITANUS
CASTELSARRASIN (tn., Fr.) 5:240
Castiel (fam.) 5:623
Castiel, David 5:623
Castiel, Samuel 5:623
Castiglion Fiorentino (tn., It.) 15:1467
Castiglioni, Arturo 11:1198
CASTIGLIONI, CAMILLO 5:241
CASTIGLIONI, ḤAYYIM (Vittorio) 5:241
- Dante 5:1297
- Tedeschi, Marco 15:897
Castile (prov., Sp.) 15:227ff
- capital punishment 13:1389
- history chart 8:766-767
- informers 8:1366; 8:1372
- silversmithery 7:741
- special Purim 13:1397
- yeshivot 16:763
Castile, *Takkanot* of 15:735; 15:725
Castilian (lang.) 10:1343
Castilian rite, *see* LITURGY (Rite, Babylonian, Sephardi)
Castillo, El (Sp. game) 14:1167
Castillo Solórzano, Alonso de 15:250
Castleman, Benjamin 11:1202
Castles, Crusader, *see* CRUSADES (Castles)
Castor (resist.), *see* Gamzon, Robert
Castoria (tn., Gr.), *see* KASTORIA
CASTOR-OIL PLANT 5:241
- oils 12:1352
- plant list 13:617
Castra (fort., Er. Isr.) 7:1134
Castra, Ana de 13:323
CASTRATION 5:242
- Commandments, the 613 5:242
- gentiles 12:1189
- Hadrian's laws 9:246
- medicine in the Bible 11:1180
- punishment 14:1208
- *see also:* BARRENNESS AND FERTILITY

CASTRO (fam.) **5:**243
CASTRO, ABRAHAM (Egy.) **5:**244
Castro, Abraham (Beirut) **4:**402
Castro, Américo **5:**312
Castro, Ana de, *see* Castra, Ana de
Castro, Andre (Daniel Nehamias) de **5:**245
Castro, Angelo di **15:**627
- *illus:*
- - Leghorn synagogue **15:**627
Castro, Bendito (Benedict; Baruch Nehamias) de **5:**244
- medicine **11:**1192
Castro, Daniel de **5:**243
Castro, David de **5:**243
Castro, David Henriques de **5:**243
- historiography **8:**564
Castro, David Isaac de **5:**243
CASTRO, DE (fam.) **5:**244
- medicine **11:**1191
Castro, Ezekiel de, *see* CASTRO, PEDRO DE
Castro, Fidel **5:**1147; **5:**1150
Castro, F. Perez **11:**684
Castro, Hananneel de **5:**243
Castro, Henry(-i) (de) **8:**1050; **13:**1360; **15:**1035
Castro, Isaac (Egy.) **5:**30
Castro, Isaac de (Ind.) **5:**243
Castro, Isaac ben Abraham de (Turk.) **5:**244; **9:**1098
CASTRO, JACOB BEN ABRAHAM **5:**245
- *haggahot* **7:**1108
Castro, Jacob de (1691-1762), *see* CASTRO SARMENTO, JACOB DE
Castro, Jacob de (1704-1789) **5:**243
CASTRO, JACOB DE (1758-1824) **5:**245
Castro, Joseph de **5:**243
Castro, J. (José) Rodriguez de **8:**27
Castro, Leon de **3:**435
Castro, Manoel Mendes de **4:**1323
Castro, Mordochay Namias de **12:**994
Castro, Moses de **5:**243
Castro, Moses Woodrow de **5:**244
- law **10:**1503
Castro, Orobio de, *see* OROBIO DE CASTRO, ISAAC
CASTRO, PEDRO DE **5:**245
Castro, Rodrigo de **5:**244
- Hamburg **7:**1226
- medicine **11:**1192
Castro, Samuel de **5:**243
Castro, Solomon de **5:**243
Castro Alves, Antônio de **15:**251
Castrocaro (vill., It.) **15:**1467ff
CASTROJERIZ (tn., Sp.) **5:**246
Castronovate, J. de **8:**27
CASTRO QUESADA, AMERICO **5:**246
CASTRO SARMENTO, JACOB (Henrique) DE **5:**246
- medicine **11:**1192
- - *illus:* text
CASTRO TARTAS, DAVID DE **5:**247
- press **13:**1034
CASTRO TARTAS, ISAAC DE **5:**248
Castro Tartas, Jacob **5:**248
Castroville (tn., Tex.) **15:**1035
Castrum Regis (Crus. fort.), *see* Chasteau du Roi
CAT **5:**248
- dietary laws **6:**32
CATACOMBS **5:**249
- Bet She'arim **4:**771
- epitaphs **6:**819
- glass vessels **7:**604ff
- Rome **14:**242
- symbolic decoration **15:**568ff
- *illus:*
- - text
- - Bet She'arim necropolis **3:**528; **4:**767-770
- - Magna Graecia, epitaph **2:**698
- - Monteverde, epitaph **2:**723
- - Rabat, Malta **11:**831
- - Rome, Villa Torlonia **9:**1582; **11:**1361; **15:**569
- *see also:* TOMBS AND TOMBSTONES
Catalan (lang.) **4:**879
- Judeo-Catalan **10:**67
Catalan, Abraham **8:**558
Catalan Atlas (naut. world atlas) **3:**523
- *illus:*
- - East, the **11:**915
- - Europe and Africa **8:**681
- - Mediterranean **5:**1086
Catalani, Perez, *see* Trabot, Perez
Catalanic (J. lang.) **10:**67
- Judeo-Provençal **10:**439
Catalano, Moses Ḥayyim ben Abraham **13:**591
Catalina (regent, Cast.) **6:**1235
Catalogs **11:**195
- *see also:* ARCHIVES; BIBLIOGRAPHY
Catalogus Librorum Hebraeorum in Bibliotheca Bodleiana **4:**971; **15:**369
Catalonia (prov., Sp.) **15:**227
- rites **11:**400
CATANIA (city, Sic.) **5:**252
- catacombs **5:**251
CATANZARO (tn., It.) **5:**252
Catapulte (writ.), *see* EYDOUX, EMMANUEL
Cate, Gerhardus ten **8:**27
Catechism, Jewish, *see* ARTICLES OF FAITH; BELIEF
CATECHUMENS, HOUSE OF (miss., Rome) **5:**253
CATEGORIES (philos.) **5:**253
- *see also:* ARISTOTLE; FORM AND MATTER; METAPHYSICS; PHILOSOPHY, JEWISH; SUBSTANCE AND ACCIDENT
Caterpillar, *see* WORM
Catfish **6:**36
Cathari (Chr. sect), *see* ALBIGENSES
CATHERINE II (emp., Rus.) **5:**254
- autonomy, judicial **3:**931
- Karaite community **2:**340
- St. Petersburg Jews **11:**14
- Sanchez, Antonio **11:**1192
- status of Jews **8:**716
Catherine de Fernandés **14:**661
Catholic Church, *see* CHURCH, CATHOLIC
Catholic Hospice (Jer.) **9:**1460
Catholici (temple offics.) **15:**973
Catholicism, *see* CHURCH, CATHOLIC
Catholic Israel (theol. term) **14:**949
Catholic Monarchs, *see* FERDINAND AND ISABELLA
Catholic People's Party (polit. parties, Aus., Hung.) **3:**84
Catholics, *see* CHURCH, CATHOLIC
Cattail (flora) **9:**225; **13:**617
CATTAN (fam.) **5:**255
Cattan, Abraham (17th cent.) **5:**255
Cattan, Abraham (18th cent.) **5:**255
Cattan, Jacob **5:**255
Cattan, Joseph **5:**255
CATTANEO, CARLO **5:**255
CATTAUI (fam.) **5:**255
Cattaui (Bey), Aslan **5:**256; **6:**499; **13:**816
Cattaui, Elijah Hadar **5:**255
Cattaui, Georges **5:**256
Cattaui, Jacob **5:**255
Cattaui, Joseph **14:**887
Cattaui, Joseph Aslan **5:**256
Cattaui, Joseph Edmund **5:**256
Cattaui, Kamar **5:**255
Cattaui, Moses **5:**255
Cattaui, René **5:**256; **6:**502
Cattaui, Shalom **5:**255
CATTLE **5:**256
- cattle-raising **16:**1273
- dietary laws **6:**27ff
- eclipse omen **12:**291
- sacrifice **14:**601ff
- symbolism **14:**1526
- torts **15:**1272ff
- *illus:*
- - Ephraim emblem **12:***fcg.* 1259
- - *Shivviti* plaque **14:***fcg.* 1422
- *table:* animals of the Bible and Talmud **3:**9-16
Cauca (tn., Sp.), *see* COCA
Caucasian Quarter (Tel Aviv) **9:**503
CAUCASUS **5:**257
- *aliyah* **9:**515
- Judaizers **10:**401
- Mountain Jews **12:**478
- Ten Lost Tribes **15:**1006
- *illus:*
- - Baku conference, Caucasus Zionists, 1917 **4:**119
Căuşani (vill., Bess.), *see* KAUSHANY
CAUSE AND EFFECT **5:**259
- Aristotelianism **13:**430
- free will **7:**125
- miracles **12:**74ff
- *see also:* EMANATION; NATURE
Cause of World Unrest (wk.) **15:**1653
Cautín (prov., Chile) **10:**398
Cavafy, Konstantinos **7:**887
CAVAILLON (tn., Fr.) **5:**260
- museums **12:**543
- special Purim **13:**1397
- *illus:*
- - text
- - special Purim *piyyutim* **7:**15
- - synagogue **7:**23
Cavaillon, Durand de **12:**1447
Cavalaria, Abraym **11:**39
Cavalleria, Abraham de la **5:**262
Cavalleria, Alfonso de la **5:**264
- Leon, Isaac de **11:**27
- Saragossa **14:**865
Cavalleria, Astruc de la **5:**262
Cavalleria, Benveniste de la **5:**262
Cavalleria, Bonafos de la (physic.) **5:**263
Cavalleria, Bonafos (Ferdinand) de la (tax farmer) **5:**262; **5:**263; **14:**862
Cavalleria, Bonfilla de la **5:**262
CAVALLERIA, DE LA (fam.) **5:**261
- Saragossa **14:**859ff
- *geneal. table:* text
Cavalleria, Ferdinand de la, *see* Cavalleria, Bonafos de la
Cavalleria, Gaspar de la, *see* Cavalleria, Judah de la
Cavalleria, Gonzalo de la, *see* Cavalleria, (Don) Vidal Joseph de la
Cavalleria, Ḥasdai de la **5:**262
Cavalleria, James de la **5:**264
Cavalleria, Judah Benveniste de la **5:**262; **14:**861
Cavalleria, Judah de la (13th cent.) **5:**261
- Alconstantini and **2:**550
- economy **16:**1291
- salt contractor **14:**712
- Saragossa **14:**860
Cavalleria, Judah de la (14th cent.) **5:**262
Cavalleria, Judah de la (14/15 cent.) **5:**263
Cavalleria, Leonardo de la **5:**263
Cavalleria, Luis de la **4:**170
Cavalleria, Orovida de la **5:**262; **14:**861
Cavalleria, Pablo de la **5:**265
Cavalleria, Pedro de la (jur.) **5:**264, **14:**865
Cavalleria, Pedro de la (dipl.) **5:**264
Cavalleria, Reina de la **5:**263
Cavalleria, Salomon (Solomon) de la (14th cent.) **5:**262
- Saragossa **14:**861
- Villafranca **16:**136
Cavalleria, Solomon de la (13th cent.) **5:**262
Cavalleria, Tolosana de la **5:**263
Cavalleria, Vidal de la (14th cent.) **5:**262; **14:**861
Cavalleria, (Don) Vidal Joseph de la (14/15 cent.) **5:**264; **14:**862; **14:**863
Cavalleros, *see* Izmirlis (Doenmeh sect)
Cavedoni, C. **12:**1271
Cave of Horror (Judea) **10:**404
Cave of the Letters (Judea) **10:**404
- *illus:*
- - Bar Kokhba period objects **4:**237-239
Cave of Nicanor (Jer.) **12:**1134
Cave of Treasures (bk.) **2:**245
Caxton Press (Aden) **2:**262
Cayenne (city, Fr. Guiana) **15:**529ff
Cayet, Pierre Victor Palma **8:**27
CAZALET, EDWARD **5:**265
- Zionism **16:**1155
Cazalet, Victor Alexander **5:**265
Cazani, Anatoli ben David **13:**577
Cazès (fam.) **15:**1030
CAZÈS, DAVID **5:**266
Cazi (Bene Israel ldr.) **4:**495
Cazotte, Jacques **10:**26
C.B.F., *see* CENTRAL BRITISH FUND
C.B.S.-Israel (record co.) **13:**1618
C.C.A.R., *see* CENTRAL CONFERENCE OF AMERICAN RABBIS
C.C.I. (orgn., Urug.), *see* Comité Central Israelita
C.C.J.P., *see* Committee on the Church and the Jewish People
C.D.J. (Belg. resist. gr.), *see* Comité de Défense Juive
C.D.J.C. (Holocaust doc. center), *see* CENTRE DE DOCUMENTATION JUIVE CONTEMPORAINE
CEA (city, Sp.) **5:**266
Čech, Svatopluk **5:**1206
ČECHŮ-ŽIDŮ, SVAZ (league, Cz.) **5:**266
- Benesov **4:**500
CECIL, HENRY **6:**787
Cecil, Lord Robert **4:**132
CEDAR **5:**268
- Bethar *ḥuppah* **11:**1040
- plant list **13:**617
- Solomon's trade **15:**99
- wood **16:**630
- *illus:* **10:**1544
Cedar Rapids (city, Ia.) **8:**1437
Cedars of Lebanon Hospital (U.S.) **8:**1039
Cedars-Sinai Medical Center (U.S.) **8:**1039
Cederbaum, Sophia N. **5:**451
Cejwin Camps (U.S.) **6:**444
Celan, Paul **7:**454
Celebi (tit.), *see Chelebi*
Celebi, Evliya **15:**1359
Celery (bot.) **13:**617; **16:**83
Celestial chariot (kab. conc.), *see* Chariot, celestial
Celestial spheres, *see* Spheres,

celestial
CELIBACY **5:**268
- Israel **9:**481
Cella (vill., Sp.) **8:**1384
Cellada, Diego (Didacus) de **8:**27
Cellarius, C. **8:**27
Cellarius, J. **8:**27
Cellarius (Borrha(us)), Martin **8:**27
Celle (city, Ger.) **3:**694
CELLER, EMANUEL **5:**269
Celsius, Olaus, S. **8:**27
CELSUS (Gr. philos.) **5:**270
- critique of Christianity **3:**191; **6:**86ff
- Judaism, attitude to **7:**891
CELSUS, AULUS CORNELIUS **14:**234
Cema, Jacob, *see* Ẓemaḥ, Jacob
CEMETERY **5:**271
- community, provision for **5:**812
- custom of visiting grave **8:**922
- dedication ceremony **7:**1153
- *Genizah* and **16:**1333
- *kever avot* **10:**934
- Mount of Olives **12:**484ff
- priest **13:**1089
- sanctity **14:**616
- suicides **15:**490
- tombs **15:**1216
- washing hands **12:**998
- *illus:*
- - text
- - Amsterdam (Ouderkerk) **2:**94; **5:***fcg.* 321
- - Coro, Venezuela **16:**91
- - Endingen and Lengnau **6:**738
- - Fuerth **7:**215
- - Gorlice, entrance **7:**812
- - Gruzdžiai, Lithuania **11:**365
- - Haga, Sweden **15:**549
- - Jassy **9:**1293
- - Jerusalem
- - - desecrated graves in Mt. of Olives cemetery **9:**1485
- - - military cemetery **9:**368, 1493
- - - Mount of Olives **12:**481
- - Johannesburg, West Park memorial **10:**157
- - Karaite, Crimea **5:**1105
- - London, Karl Marx's grave **11:**1073
- - Los Angeles, commemorative plaque **11:**498
- - Minsk **12:**52
- - Newport, R.I. deed **15:**1587
- - New York, Chatham Sq. **12:**1063
- - Novi Sad, Yugoslavia **12:**1236
- - Odessa **12:**1320
- - Paris, Montparnasse **11:**1344
- - Prague **11:**1262
- - praying in, eve of Day of Atonement **5:**1385
- - Qumran **13:**1434
- - Sarajevo **16:**874
- - Strasbourg **15:**422
- - Stuttgart **15:**463
- - Tauberbischofsheim **15:**833
- - Tel Ḥai **15:**932
- - Tetuan **15:**1030
- - Tlemcen **15:**1173
- - Warsaw **13:**782; **15:**1227,1228
- - Worms **11:**1250; **16:**645
- - Zemun **16:**990
- *see also:* BURIAL; Necropolis; TOMBS AND TOMBSTONES
Cencio Savelli (pope), *see* HONORIUS III
Cendebaeus (sol.) **14:**1566
Ceneda (tn., It.), *see* VITTORIO VENETO
CENSORSHIP **5:**276
- *Akkum* used in **2:**500
- *Aleinu le-Shabbe'aḥ* **2:**557
- Alexander of Hales **2:**583
- *Avodah Zarah* **3:**982
- Benedict XIII **4:**482
- Dominicans **6:**162
- *haskamah* **7:**1452
- heresy **8:**361
- history chart (1554) **8:**766-767
- Talmud **10:**14
- *Yevsektsiya* **16:**780
- *illus:*
- - text
- - *Aleinu le-Shabbe'aḥ* **2:**558, 892
- - *Guzmán de Alfarache*, imprimatur **2:**562
- *see also:* TALMUD, BURNING OF
CENSUS **5:**281
- Jerusalem polis **9:**1391
- Mari **11:**985; **16:**1510
- population **13:**866ff
- vital statistics **16:**177ff
Center Bladet (journ.) **13:**1048
Center City (Pa.) **13:**374
Center for Latin American Cooperation Studies (Isr.) **9:**436
Center for Scientific and Technological Information (Isr.) **9:**975
CENTIPEDE (zool.) **5:**283
- *illus:* text
CENTO (tn., It.) **5:**283
- special Purim **13:**1397
CENTOS (orgn., Pol.) **5:**284
- Warsaw ghetto **16:**348
Centra (Lat. Am. orgn.) **10:**1454
Centraal Blad voor Israëlieten in Nederland (newsp.) **13:**1035
Central (journ.) **13:**1026
Centrala Evereilor (orgn.; Rum.) **14:**407
Central African Republic **9:**438
Central Agency for the Care of War Refugees (Aus.), *see* ZENTRALSTELLE DER FUERSORGE FUER KRIEGSFLUECHTLINGE
Central Agency of the Ministries of Justice of the States (Ger.), *see* ZENTRALE STELLE DER LANDESJUSTIZVERWALTUNGEN
Central America, *see* LATIN AMERICA
Central Archives for the History of the Jewish People (Jer.) **3:**377,385
- historiography **8:**564
Central Bank of Cooperative Institutions Ltd. (Isr.) **9:**824 **13:**39
CENTRAL BRITISH FUND **5:**285
- history chart **8:**766-767
- philanthropy **13:**388
Central Bureau of Statistics (Isr.) **15:**346
Central Committee for Jewish Education (Eng.) **6:**448ff
Central Committee for the Jewish Victims of the War (Arg.) **3:**414
Central Committee for Jewish Welfare (Belg.) **7:**980
Central Committee for Relief and Reconstruction (Ger.), *see* Zentralausschuss fuer Hilfe und Aufbau
Central Committee for the Relief of Jewish War Sufferers, *see* YEKOPO
Central Committee of the Jews in Poland, *see* Jewish Committee
CENTRAL CONFERENCE OF AMERICAN RABBIS **5:**285
- Christian Science **5:**514
- Conservative Judaism **5:**906
- history chart **8:**766-767
- proselytizing **13:**1193
- Zionism **16:**1141; **16:**1145
- *illus:* text
Central Conference of American Rabbis Journal **15:**1110
Central Conference of Grands Rabbins (Fr.) **15:**1523
Central Council of Jewish Religious Education (Eng.) **6:**449ff
Centrale Israëlietische Ziekenverpleging (hospital, Amst.) **2:**904
Central Farband (lab. orgn., U.S.) **4:**1499
CENTRAL GOVERNMENT IN STATE OF ISRAEL **9:**610
- historical survey **9:**365ff
- Ottoman and Mandatory periods **9:**598
- *illus:*
- - land registration certificate **9:**557
- - National Council meeting, May 14, 1948 **9:**365
Centralia (city, Ill.) **8:**1255
Centralia (city, Wash.) **16:**356
Central Institute for Cultural Relations between Israel and Iberoamerica, Spain, and Portugal (orgn., Isr.) **10:**1456
Central Jewish Historical Society, *see* JEWISH HISTORICAL INSTITUTE, WARSAW
Central Jewish Institute (N.Y.) **6:**440ff
Central Office for the Boycott of Israel (Syr.) **4:**1282
Central Press (print. firm) **13:**1379
Central Relief Committee (U.S.) **2:**827
Central Sephardic Jewish Community of America **14:**1174
Central Synagogue (London) **15:**620
Central Synagogue (N.Y.C.), *see* Ahavath Chesed
Central Theater (Pol.) **15:**1072
CENTRAL-VEREIN DEUTSCHER STAATSBUERGER JUEDISCHEN GLAUBENS (orgn., Ger.) **5:**286
- defense of Jews **3:**200
- history chart **8:**766-767
- Philo Verlag **13:**465
- *illus:*
- - first report (1893) **7:**486
Central-Vereins-Zeitung (journ., Ger.), *see* C.V.-ZEITUNG
Central Welfare Bureau (Office, Orgn.) of German Jews, *see* ZENTRAL WOHLFAHRTSTELLE DER DEUTSCHEN JUDEN
Central Yiddish Culture Organization (U.S.) **5:**897
Central Yiddish School Organization (Pol.)
- Bund **4:**1505
- education **6:**435
- history **8:**743
- Warsaw **16:**341
Central Zionist Archives (Jer.) **3:**378,387ff; **11:**195
CENTRE DE DOCUMENTATION JUIVE CONTEMPORAINE (Holocaust doc.) **5:**287
- archives **3:**385
- historiography **8:**566
- learned societies **15:**54
- library **11:**191
- *illus:*
- - Memorial to Unknown Jewish Martyr **13:**112
Centre Universitaire d'Études Juives (Fr.) **13:**111
Centrist Faction (polit. orgn.) **7:**1323
Centro Commercial y Industrial Israelita del Uruguay (bnk., Urug.), *see* Banco Palestino-Uruguayo
Centro Deportivo Israelita (orgn., Mex.) **10:**1454; **11:**1458
Centro Universitario Peruano-Israelita (J. students' orgn., Peru), *see* Movimiento Universitario Peruano-Israelita
Cepeda, Luis **9:**1344
Cephas (apostle), *see* Peter
Ceporinus, Jakob, **8:**27
Ceramic and Silicate Institute (Isr.) **9:**970
Ceramics, *see* POTTERY
Cerealius (Rom. sol.) **8:**228
Cereal-Offering, *see Minḥah*
Cereals, *see* FIVE SPECIES
Ceremonial Law, *see* Law, Ceremonial
CEREMONIAL OBJECTS **5:**288
- folklore **6:**1389
- iconography **8:**1221
- leather **10:**1536
- *mezuzah* **11:**1477
- Michael, Jacob, collection **11:**1486
- Passover **13:**173
- Sabbath **14:**570
- *Sefer Torah* **14:**1104
- *sheḥitah* **14:**1338
- spice-box **7:**1482ff
- symbolism **15:**568ff
- *illus:*
- - text
- - biblical themes as ornamentation motif **3:**451-453,531,627; **4:**244,374,1231,1339-1344; **5:**296, *fcg.* 299, 300, 302, 661, 1035, 1042, 1058, 1381, 1385, 1444, 1445, 1448; **6:**1391; **7:**170, 611, *fcg.* 1259, 1295, 1297, 1300, 1301, 1307, 1309, 1346, 1485; **11:**265-270,1475; **12:**1385; **14:**564,1420-1421,1649; **15:**1256,1257
- - Chairs of Elijah **5:**306; **6:**643-645
- - crown-like cult object (Chalcolithic) **3:**501
- - *etrog* box **6:**949
- - folk art **6:**1381-1403
- - goblets, glass **3:**452,713; **4:**1181
- - *ḥallah* platter, silver **7:**1194
- - Ḥanukkah lamps **2:**335,626; **4:**1462; **6:**1395; **7:**1293-1314; **11:**624, 1016; **12:**343,976; **13:**309; **15:**232; **16:**1326
- - *havdalah* ceremony articles **3:**529; **5:**118; **6:**1390; **7:**1485-1488
- - *kahal maẓẓah* holder **11:**694
- - Klaus Synagogue exhibition **13:**973
- - lion motif **11:**265-274; **14:**252
- - marriage cup **11:***fcg.* 1067
- - *mashiv ha-ru'aḥ* plaque **11:**1094
- - *menorah* **11:**1355
- - *mezuzah* **11:**1474,1475
- - *ner tamid* **12:**965
- - *omer* scroll **12:**1383,1385
- - *parokhet* (needlework) **3:**531; **5:**297,961; **15:**1256
- - Rosh Ha-Shanah plate **14:**308
- - Sabbath lamps **14:**561-568
- - *seder* plate **3:**531
- - *sheḥitah* knife **14:**1339
- - *shofarot* **14:**1445
- - Torah breastplates **3:**542; **4:**1337-1344; **5:**296
- - Torah crowns **3:**640; **5:**293; **14:**1649; **15:**1257
- - Torah finials **4:**1527; **5:**291,1444; **7:**740; **11:**269; **12:**725; **13:**311
- - Torah mantle **5:**291
- - Torah pointers **16:**693
- - Torah scroll binders **5:**291; **6:**386; **15:**1258
- - Torah scroll cases, Chinese

5:472-473
- see also: CRAFTS; CROWNS, DECORATIVE HEADDRESSES AND WREATHS; GOLDSMITHS AND SILVERSMITHS
Cerenkov, Pavel Alekseevich 15:787
Céret (tn., Fr.) 14:353
CERF, BENNETT ALFRED 5:312
Cerf, Carl Friedrich 15:1057
Cerfberr, Baruch 5:312
CERFBERR, HERZ 5:312
- Alsace-Lorraine 2:755
- Strasbourg 15:424
Cerfberr, Martin 11:1561
Cerfberr, Max 5:312
CERFBERR, MAXIMILIEN-CHARLES ALPHONSE 5:312
Ceriani, M. 12:411
Cerito, Fanny 14:661
- illus:
- - Saint-Leon, Arthur, and 14:662
Cernauţi (city, Buk.), see CHERNOVTSY
Ceruti (print.) 14:252
CERVANTES SAAVEDRA, MIGUEL DE 5:312
- Spanish literature 15:250
Cerveny Kostelec (tn., Cz.) 12:749
Cervera (Inq., Sic.) 8:1397
CERVERA (city, Sp.) 5:313
- illus: text
Cervera Bible (14th cent. illum. ms., Sp.) 8:1264
- illus: 2:642, 5:313; 10:1002; 16:fcg. 935
CERVETTO, JACOB BASEVI 12:685
- family 4:290
Cervetto, James (17/18 cent., comp.), see CERVETTO, JACOB BASEVI
Cervetto, James (18/19 cent., mus.) 4:290; 12:686
Cesarec, August 16:886
CESENA (tn., It.) 5:314
ČESKA LÍPA (tn., Cz.) 5:314
Česká Skalice (tn., Cz.) 12:749
ČESKÉ BUDĚJOVICE (city, Cz.) 5:315
- Holocaust period 5:1199
Českožidovské Listy 5:267
- press 13:1026
Českožidovský Kalendár (almanac) 5:267
Český Těšín (tn., Silesia), see TESCHEN
Cesna, David 6:1371
CESTIUS GALLUS (Rom. gov.) 5:315
- defeat 8:639
- Eleazar ben Simeon 6:598
- Galilean revolt 8:655
- Jerusalem attack 9:1398
- revolt against 9:256
Cetatea-Alba (city, Bess.), see BELGOROD-DNESTROVSKI
CEUTA (port, N. Afr.) 5:316
Cevallerius, A. R., see Chevalier A. R.
Cevallerius, Petrus 8:27
CEYLON (Sri Lanka) 5:316
- Aden rabbinical court 2:260
- spices 8:1311
Chabot, Leopoldine, see Dobruschka-Schoenfeld, Leopoldine
Chachik, Joshua 13:1378
Chacon, Sir Augustin Coronel, see CORONEL CHACON, SIR AUGUSTIN
Chad (rep., Afr.) 9:438
Chaderton, Laurence, see Chatterton, Laurence
Chadic languages 14:1149
Chadwick, George W. 10:461
CHAEREMON (1st cent., C.E., hist.) 5:317
Chaffinch (bird) 6:30
CHAGALL, MARC 5:318
- contribution to art 8:743
- Hofstein, David 8:813
- stamps 15:336
- illus:
- - text
- - autograph 3:914
- - "Jerusalem Windows" (stained glass) 4:526; 5:1258; 9:1077
- - "Joy" 14:1467
- - "King David's Entry into Jerusalem" (tpst.) 5:fcg. 334
- - "Night over Vitebsk" 16:191
- - "Russian Village" (paint.) 5:fcg. 334
- - "The Slaughterhouse" 14:1341
Chagall Museum (Fr.) 5:323
Chagar Bazar (city, Mesop.) 7:1036
CHAGY, BERELE 7:1547
"Chaider" (drg., Epstein) 12:1090
Chaikin, Benjamin 3:363
- illus:
- - Daniel Sieff Institute 16:440
Chaikin, Joseph 12:1121; 15:1578
Chaim Arlosoroff (ship) 8:1250
Chaimov, Yakub 10:436
Chaim Weizmann Institute for Zionist Research (Isr.) 15:926
CHAIN, SIR ERNST BORIS 5:324
Chain Gate (Jer.) 9:1434,1540
Chajes, Abraham 5:326
Chajes, Eliezer 5:326
CHAJES, GERSHON BEN ABRAHAM 5:324
Chajes, Ḥayyim 5:328
CHAJES, HIRSCH (Ẓevi) PEREZ 5:325
- Austrian Jewry 3:896
- Rivista Israelitica 14:197
- seminary 16:1105
- Zionism 16:1107
Chajes, Isaac 5:325,327; 5:329
CHAJES, ISAAC BEN ABRAHAM 5:326
Chajes, Joachim 5:328
Chajes, Julius 9:1206
Chajes, Leon 5:328
Chajes, Monish 5:326
CHAJES, SAUL 5:327
Chajes, Solomon 5:325,328
Chajes, Wolf 5:329
CHAJES, ẒEVI HIRSCH 5:327
- ḥiddushim 8:467
- illus: text
Chajidhimiou, P. 7:887
CHAJN, LEON 10:1500; 10:1507
Chaki, H.Y. 10:1351
Chalcedony (mineral) 5:329; 13:1010
CHALCIS (stlmt., Euboea) 5:329
- Greece 7:873
Chalcous (coin) 5:717
CHALDEA, CHALDEANS 5:330
- Habakkuk's prophecy 7:1014ff
- Ur 16:3
- War of the Kittim 10:1081; 13:332
- see also: BABYLONIA; MESOPOTAMIA
Chaldeans (astrols.) 3:789ff
Chalfan (fam.), see HALFANUS
Challenge, (journ.), see Etgar
CHÂLONS-SUR-MARNE (tn., Fr.) 5:331
CHALON-SUR-SAÔNE (tn., Fr.) 5:332
- Cluny abbey 5:619
Chaltay (Kar. lang.) 10:68
Cham (5th cent., knight, It.), see Ḥayyim
CHAMBERLAIN, HOUSTON STEWART 5:332
- anti-Semitism 3:115
- history chart 8:766-767
- Wagner, Richard 16:241
- Zollschan, Ignaz 16:1217
CHAMBERLAIN, JOSEPH 5:333
- Greenberg, L. J. 7:905
- Herzl, Theodor 8:415
- Sinai controversy 9:308
- Uganda Scheme 15:1500; 16:1072
Chamberlain, Neville 5:333
- settlement in Guyana 7:998
- illus:
- - London Round Table Conference 9:353
"Chamber of the Archangel Michael" (anti-Sem. mvmt.) 15:1538
Chamber of the Exiles (Temple) 15:968
Chamber of Hewn Stone (Temple) 15:968
- Sanhedrin 2:200
- Temple court 16:920
Chamber of Vessels (Temple) 15:981
CHAMBERS OF COMMERCE IN ISRAEL 9:828
Chamber Theater (Isr.), see CAMERI
CHAMBÉRY (tn., Fr.) 5:333
- Savoy 14:921
Chameau, see Hammel, Shimon
CHAMECKI, SAMUEL 8:1431
Chamejdes (r., Pol.) 10:818
CHAMELEON 5:333
- dietary laws 6:36
- illus: text
Chamisso, Adelbert von 6:1382; 7:442; 8:791
Chamorro (15th cent., Sp.) 15:1205
Chamoun, Camille 14:1624
CHAMPAGNE (reg., Fr.) 5:334
- Jews in 7:14ff
- Philip II 13:392
- synod 15:632
Champaign (city, Ill.) 8:1256
Champlitte-et-le-Prélot (vill., Fr.) 7:45
Chancellor, Sir John Herbert 8:470; 9:601
- illus:
- - Ruppin, Arthur, and 8:471
Chanin, N. 4:1500
CHANNEL ISLANDS 5:334
- Brampton, Sir Edward 4:1293
- synagogues 1:syn. list
Chanting, Synagogal 13:1063
- see also: CANTILLATION; ḤAZZAN; LITURGY; MUSIC
Chants séphardis (collec. Sephardi melodies) 2:610
CHAO (fam., China) 5:336
- geneal. table: text
Chao Ch'eng (An San) 5:336
Chao Ch'eng-Chi 5:337
Chao Kuang-Yü (Abram) 5:337
Chao Liang-Ching (son of Adam) 5:336
Chao Ying-Ch'eng (Moses) 5:337
Chao Ying-Kun 5:337
Chao Ying-Tou 5:337
- Oriental literature 12:1465
CHAPBOOKS (pamphlet lit.) 5:337
Chapí, Ruperto 9:1344
CHAPIRO, JACQUES 5:338
- illus: text
Chaplaincy, Jewish 11:1568
- Germany 13:1455
Chapoval (art.) 13:118
Chappaqua (tn., N.Y.) 16:464
Characene (Mesop.), see MESENE
Charachmoba (city, Er. Isr.), see KIR HARESETH
Character, Human 11:846
- Utitz's studies 16:35
Charata (tn., Arg.) 3:430
Charax (site, Er. Isr.), see KERAK
CHARAX OF PERGAMUM (2nd cent. C.E., writ.) 7:892
Charbona, M. S., see STEINSCHNEIDER, MORITZ
Charchoune, Serge 13:113
Charcot, Jean 7:161
CHARES (1st cent. C.E., sol.) 5:338
Chariot, see CART AND CHARIOT
Chariot, Celestial 11:1386
- cherubim 3:460
- emanation 10:574
- Jewish philosophy 13:423
- illus:
- - Ezekiel's first vision 6:1084
Charisma 14:365
- sages 14:638
- Saul 14:910
- see also: PROPHETS AND PROPHECY
CHARITY 5:338
- Contents:
- - In Bible 5:338
- - Rabbinic Literature 5:340
- - - Ẓedakah 5:340
- - - Givers and Receivers 5:341
- - - Allocation 5:342
- - - Charity Wardens 5:343
- - - Acceptance 5:344
- - Middle Ages 5:345
- - - Charitable Associations 5:346
- - Modern Times 5:348
- - - Social Welfare 5:348
- - - Local 5:348
- - - Central 5:350
- - - National 5:351
- - - International 5:352
- - - Conclusion 5:352
- General
- - Benjamin the Righteous 2:34
- - Dostai ben Yannai 6:179
- - ḥibbut ha-kever 8:464
- - honor, reward of 8:966
- - Koran 10:1198
- - Muslim institutions in Israel 9:918
- - righteousness 14:182
- - Sodomites 15:71ff
- - U.S. Jews 8:742
- - Venice 16:99
- Economic Life 16:1303
- - finances, autonomous 6:1281
- - pletten (meal tickets) 13:645
- - societies for 8:441
- - tax 15:841ff
- - tokens 5:854
- Types
- - beggars 4:387
- - consecration and endowment 8:281ff
- - gemilut ḥasadim 7:374
- - hakhnasat kallah 7:1150
- - ḥalukkah 7:1207
- - Meir Ba'al ha-Nes 11:1246
- - me'ot ḥittim 11:1379
- - old people 2:343
- - orphan 12:1478
- - orphans' debts 13:1182
- - pe'ah 13:201
- - poor, provision for 13:850
- - ransom of captives 5:154ff
- - sick care 14:1498
- - Temple 15:981
- - yeshivot 16:766
- Halakhic Aspects
- - burial and 4:1515
- - Commandments, the 613 5:770
- - Day of Atonement 5:1380
- - death 5:1424
- - domicile and obligation 6:159ff
- - fines payable to 6:1288
- - firstborn redemption 6:1309
- - fund as legal person 10:1569
- - gambling and gamblers 7:299,301

-- gentiles **7**:412; **12**:1189
-- *ḥazakah* on property of **7**:1519
-- *ḥevra kaddisha* **8**:442
-- interest on loans **12**:12
-- lending considered as **11**:415
-- minor's maintenance **12**:111
-- Purim **13**:1392
-- wills **16**:524
- *illus:*
-- *ḥevra kaddisha* charity boxes **8**:444,445
- *see also:* HOSPITALITY; PHILANTHROPY; POVERTY
CHARLEMAGNE **5**:353
- Alcuin **2**:551
- French Jewry **7**:11
- history chart **8**:766-767
- Jerusalem **9**:1572
- Jewish interpreter **16**:1281
- Machir ben Judah **12**:828
Charleroi (tn., Belg.) **3**:168; **4**:423
Charles (pr. of Wales) **6**:463
Charles I (k., Naples)
- Faraj da Agrigento **2**:415
- Inquisition **8**:1398
- Provence Jews **13**:1260
- *illus:*
-- Faraj ben Solomon da Agrigento and **6**:1179
Charles I (k., Sp.), *see* CHARLES V (Holy Rom. Emp.)
Charles II (k., Eng.) **11**:473
- Coronel Chacon **5**:975
Charles II (Holy Rom. Emp.) **2**:915; **7**:10
- *illus:*
-- prayerbook binding **13**:1304
Charles II (k., Naples)
- Angers **2**:977
- Anjou **3**:24
- Apulian Jewry **3**:227
- Provence **13**:1260
Charles III (k., Hung.), *see* CHARLES VI
CHARLES IV (Holy Rom. Emp.) **5**:354
- Austrian Fredericianum **3**:888
- history chart **8**:766-767
- Strasbourg **15**:423
CHARLES IV (k., Fr.) **5**:354
CHARLES V (k., Fr.) **5**:355
CHARLES V (Holy Rom. Emp.) **5**:355
- Antwerp Marranos **3**:167
- Crusade invitation **9**:287
- Gelderland Jews **3**:486
- Inquisition **8**:1388
- *illus:*
-- charter of privileges to Jews of Worms (1552) **7**:470
-- Molcho's banner **12**:226
CHARLES VI (k., Fr.) **5**:356
- *illus:*
-- Cresques' Catalan Atlas **5**:1086; **8**:681; **11**:915
CHARLES VI (k., Hung.) **5**:356
- Arnstein's influence **3**:489
- familiants laws **6**:1162
Charles VIII (k., Fr.)
- Apulian Jews **3**:228
- Provence Jews **13**:1261
- Tarascon expulsion **15**:807
Charles X (k., Fr.) **4**:58
CHARLES, GERDA **6**:785; **6**:787
Charles the Bald (Holy Rom. Emp.), *see* Charles II
Charles the Fat Bible (9th cent.) **15**:109
Charles of Anjou, *see* Charles I (k., Naples)
Charles of Luxemburg (Holy Rom. Emp.), *see* CHARLES IV
CHARLESTON (city, S.C.) **5**:356
- Azuby, Abraham **3**:1015
- Harby, Isaac **7**:1332
- history chart **8**:766-767
- South Carolina **15**:211ff
- Wise, Isaac M. **16**:563
- *illus:*
-- text
-- Hebrew Benevolent Society seal **7**:376
-- Salvador, Francis, plaque **14**:715
-- synagogue **15**:212
Charleston (city, W.Va.) **16**:475
illus:
-- Temple Israel, Ark **4**:787
Charles William Ferdinand (duke of Brunswick) **4**:1421
CHARLEVILLE (tn., Fr.) **5**:360
Charlot le Juif (troubadour) **7**:146
Charlotte (city, N.C.) **12**:1218ff
Charlottesville (city, Va.) **16**:163
Charms
- Hellenism **8**:301
- *mezuzah* **11**:1477
- practical Kabbalah **10**:634
- scarab seals **14**:1073
- *see also:* AMULET; DIVINATION; MAGIC
CHARNA, SHALOM YONAH **5**:360
Charney, Carmi, *see* CARMI, T.
CHARNEY, DANIEL **5**:361
- *illus:*
-- *Yung Vilne* group **16**:821
Charney, David B. **13**:1362
Charney, Samuel, *see* NIGER, SAMUEL
CHAROUSEK, RUDOLPH **5**:408
Charpentier, Marc-Antoine **10**:1376; **10**:460
Chartiner, Meir **7**:1316
CHARTRES (tn., Fr.) **5**:362
CHASANOWICH, JOSEPH **5**:362
CHASANOWICH, LEON **5**:362
Chasbi (city, Er. Isr.). *see* ACHZIB
Chased El (syn., Singapore) **14**:1608
CHASINS, ABRAHAM **12**:686
Chasteau de Roi (fort., Isr.) **11**:1529
CHASTITY **5**:363
- adultery **2**:313
- civil marriage **5**:595ff
- cosmetics **5**:980
- covering of head **8**:6
- divorce **6**:129
- incest **8**:1316
- *ketubbah* deprivation **8**:1127
- onanism **12**:1396
- prohibited marriages **11**:1051
- virginity **16**:160
- *illus:*
-- Joseph and Potiphar's wife **10**:206
- *see also:* SEX; SEXUAL OFFENSES
CHATEAUBRIAND, FRANÇOIS RENÉ, VICOMTE DE **5**:364
- Jerusalem **9**:1573
CHÂTEAU-LANDON (vill., Fr.) **5**:365
Château Pèlerins **9**:269
Châteaurenard (reg., Prov.) **13**:1259
CHÂTEAU-THIERRY (tn., Fr.) **5**:365
Châtelain, Isaac **9**:1220; **15**:1407
CHATHAM (city., Eng.) **5**:365
Chatham (tn., Ont.) **12**:1408
Chattanooga (city, Tenn.) **15**:1009
Chattanooga Times (newsp.) **2**:281
Chatterton, Laurence **8**:27
CHATZKELS, HELENE **5**:366
Chatzmann, Vera, *see* Weizmann, Vera
Chatzner, Alfred **10**:1492
CHAUCER, GEOFFREY **5**:366
- English literature **6**:776
Chaul (port, Ind.) **2**:469
CHAVEL, CHARLES (Dov) BER **5**:366
- Naḥmanides **5**:521
CHAVES (fam.) **5**:367
CHAVES (city, Port.) **5**:367
Chaves, Aaron de **5**:367
Chaves, Captain (sol.) **5**:367
Chaves, David de **5**:367
Chaves, Isaac de **5**:367
Chaves, Jacob de **5**:367
Chaves, Mozes de **5**:367
CHAYEFSKY, PADDY **5**:367
- U.S. literature **15**:1578ff
Chayes (fam.,) **4**:1397
Chayes, O. **4**:176
Chazan, Sara Bialoslowsky de, *see* Bialoslowsky de Chazan, Sara
CHEB (tn., Bohem.) **5**:368
CHEBAR (canal, Mesop.) **5**:368
- Nippur community **16**:1270
CHECINY (tn., Pol.) **5**:369
- *illus:* text
Checkers (game) **7**:303*f*
CHEDORLAOMER (k., Elam) **5**:370
- Ashtaroth **3**:737
- *illus:* text
CHEESE **5**:371
- cheese-making **2**:401ff; **5**:104ff
- food **6**:1417
- *illus:*
-- Tnuva dairy **15**:1175
Cheetah (fauna) **3**:7; **9**:226
Chehalis (city, Wash.) **16**:356
CHEIN, ISIDOR **13**:1346
Cheironomy (method of instruction) **12**:577
Chekhov, Anton **14**:509
- Kaganowski, E. **10**:675
Chekhov, Michael **7**:1030
Chelebi (head of J. cmty., Egy.) **3**:723; **6**:496
- Ottoman Empire **16**:1534
Chelebi, Abraham, *see* BRUDO, ABRAHAM BEN ELIJAH
Chelebi, Elijah, *see* ELIJAH CHELEBI HA-KOHEN OF ANATOLIA
Chelebi, Raphael Joseph, *see* Raphael Joseph
CHELM (city, Pol.) **5**:371
- *illus:* text
Chelm, David **5**:374
Chelm, Ḥayyim **5**:374
CHELM, SOLOMON BEN MOSES **5**:373
Chelmer Ḥakhomim ("Wise Men of Chelm") **5**:373
CHELMNO (camp, Pol.) **5**:374
- gassing **16**:1332
- Holocaust **8**:894
CHELOUCHE (fam.) **5**:375
Chelouche, Aharon **15**:919
Chelouche, Avraham **5**:375
Chelouche, Moshe **5**:375
Chelouche, Yosef Eliyahu **5**:375
Chelouche, Zaddok **5**:375
Chelovecheski Prava (newsp.) **4**:1485
Chelsea (city, Mass.) **4**:1265; **11**:1112
Chelyabinsk (city, oblast, Rus.) **14**:482
Chemerinsky, Barukh **7**:1031
- *illus:*
-- Brod, Max, and **4**:1388
Chemeriski, Alexander, *see* TSHEMERISKI, ALEXANDER
CHEMICAL CRAFTS AND INDUSTRIES **5**:375
- dyeing **6**:329
- Israel **5**:377
-- industry **9**:823
-- oil and gas **9**:795
- Mesopotamia **16**:1490
- *illus:* text
CHEMISTRY (Jews in) **5**:379
CHEMNITZ (city, Ger.), *see* KARL-MARX-STADT
CHEMOSH (deity) **5**:390
- dysphemism **6**:960
- idolatry **8**:1227
- Judges, Book of **10**:449
- Moab **12**:192
Chemoshyat (k., Moab) **11**:1397
Chemotherapy **11**:1199
Chemtou (loc., Tun.) **15**:1431
Chenaanah (bib. fig.) **16**:964
Chenery, Thomas **8**:29
Chenkin, Alvin **15**:68
CHENNAMANGALAM (Chennotty; isl., Ind.) **5**:390
- India **8**:1355
- *illus:*
-- synagogue **8**:1351
Chephirah (city, Er. Isr.) **4**:382; **7**:550
- Benjamin tribe **8**:579
Cher, Hugh of, *see* Hugh of St. Cher
Chéradame, Jean **8**:29
Cherasco (vill., It.) **13**:502
CHERCOVER, MURRAY **15**:1080
Cherethites (bib. people) **13**:402ff
- Crete **5**:1088
- Solomon **15**:96
CHERITH (brook, Er. Isr.) **5**:390
CHERKASKY, MARTIN **11**:1206
CHERKASSY (city, Rus.) **5**:391
Cherkess (Mamluk faction) **6**:495
Cherkizovo (tn., Rus.) **12**:366
Chermela (vill., Er. Isr.), *see* CARMEL
Cherniack, Saul **5**:112; **11**:879; **16**:551
- socialism **15**:27
Cherniak, Nathalie, *see* SARRAUTE, NATHALIE
CHERNIAVSKY (fam.) **12**:686
Cherniavsky, Alexander **12**:686
Cherniavsky, Boris **12**:686
Cherniavsky, Jan **12**:686
Cherniavsky, Leo **12**:686
Cherniavsky, Marion **12**:686
Cherniavsky, Michael **12**:686
CHERNIGOV (city, prov., Rus.) **5**:391
Chernikhov, Yosef, *see* Tschernikhov, Joseph
Chernis (mart.) **12**:55
CHERNISS, HAROLD **5**:392
CHERNOBYL (tn., Rus.) **5**:392
- ḥasidic dynasty **15**:1472
Chernobyl, Nahum of, *see* Nahum of Chernobyl
Chernomorski, Benzion, *see* ISRAELI, BENZION
CHERNOVTSY (city, Buk.) **5**:393
- Transylvania **15**:1333
- Yedintsy Jews **16**:727
- *illus:*
-- text
-- cemetery **5**:276
CHERNY, SASHA **5**:396
CHERNYAKHOVSKI, IVAN DANILOVICH **5**:396
Chernyostrov, Israel Abraham of, *see* Israel Abraham of Chernyostrov
Cherokees (Ind. tribe, N. Am.) **4**:888; **12**:1218
Cherry Hill (loc., N.J.) **13**:374
Chersonese (penin., Rus.) **5**:1104
CHERUB **5**:397
- *Contents:*
-- Bible **5**:397
-- Description of **5**:398
-- Etymology **5**:398
-- In Aggadah **5**:399
-- In the Arts **5**:399
- Antioch legend **3**:71
- Ark **3**:460ff
- art **3**:506
- Jeroboam's golden calves **7**:711
- Jewish mysticism **10**:516
- legitimate iconolatry **8**:1229ff
- Tabernacle **15**:682
- Temple **15**:948; **15**:950ff

- *illus:*
- - text
- - Ark curtain **14:**1396
- - Basnage's *République des Hébreux* **8:**1235
- - Bezalel sculpting the (M. Horn) **4:**787
- - *Perpignan Bible* **4:**977
- - *Sarajevo Haggadah* **7:***fcg.* 1131
- *see also:* ANGELS AND ANGELOLOGY
Chervonenkis, M. **6:**267
Chervonoarmeisk (tn., Ukr.), *see* RADZIWILLOW
CHESS **5:**401
- Açan, Moses de Zaragua **2:**209
- gambling **7:**301
- game of **7:**305
- Israel **9:**1020
- *illus:*
- - "Chess Players I" (wdct., I. Amen) **3:**615
- - Fischer, Robert, at tournament **6:**1322
- - Israel Chess Olympics medal **11:**1174
- - Israel stamp **9:**844-845
- - Reshevsky playing Lasker **14:**82
- - Tel Aviv Olympics, 1964 **7:**307
Chess, Stella **13:**1339
Chesselius, Ahenarius, *see* Kesler, J. Conrad
"Chess Players" (paint., I. Kaufman) **5:**403
"Chess Players I" (wdct., I. Amen) **3:**615
Chester (co., Pa.) **13:**368
Chester, Greville **16:**1334
Chesterton, G. K. **6:**781
Chestnut (tree) **13:**613
Chevalier, A. R. **8:**29
Chevalier, Petrus, *see* Cevallerius, Petrus.
Chevalier von Geldern, *see* GELDERN, SIMON VON
Cheyenne (city, Wyo.) **16:**679
CHEYNE, THOMAS KELLY **5:**409
Chezib (city, Er. Isr.), *see* ACHZIB
Chezib River (Isr.) **9:**152
Chezighin, Ḥayyim **5:**125
CHIARINI, LUIGI **5:**409
- Buchner, A. **4:**1447
- Christian Hebraists **8:**29
- Talmud in French **15:**768
CHICAGO (city, U.S.) **5:**410
- *Contents:*
- - Early Settlement **5:**410
- - After 1860 **5:**412
- - Economic Activity **5:**413
- - Population **5:**414
- - Post-World War II **5:**414
- - Contemporary Community **5:**415
- - Education and Culture **5:**416
- - Press **5:**417
- demography **5:**1513
- history chart (1841) **8:**766-767
- Jewish population **8:**732
- museums **12:**544ff
- tailors **15:**708
- *illus:*
- - text
- - Anshe Maariv synagogue **15:**622
- - Hebrew Theological College **8:**216
- - Michael Reese Hospital **14:**18
- - milk distribution outside Hebrew Institute **15:**1611
- - South Shore Temple, Ark **5:**1445
Chicago Daily Courier (newsp.) **13:**1055
Chicago Heights (sub.) **5:**415
Chicago Israelite, The (newsp.) **4:**1096
Chicago school (economics, U.S.) **7:**187
Chichester Psalms (mus. wk.) **13:**1328
CHICKEN **5:**418
- Jerusalem **13:**1411
- ownership **12:**1533
- sacrificed in Temple **10:**766
- *illus:*
- - text
- - slaughtering of **14:**1343
Chick-pea (bot.) **13:**617
Chicory (bot.) **13:**617
Chicory, wild (bot.) **13:**617
Chicoutimi (city and co., Can.) **13:**1423
CHIEF RABBI, CHIEF RABBINATE **5:**418
- autonomy, judicial **3:**928
- *ḥakham bashi* **7:**1146; **16:**1540
- in England **2:**278,286
- in Ereẓ Israel **9:**891ff
- Israel election controversy **9:**399
- rabbinate **13:**1448
- rabbinical courts' unification **12:**142
- U.S. Sephardim **14:**1174
- *illus:*
- - Heikhal Shlomo, Jerusalem **9:**1488
- *see also:* RABBINICAL CONFERENCES; SYNODS
CHIEFTAIN **5:**420
- Ezekiel's prophecy **6:**1089
Chiera (name, Turk.), *see* KIERA
CHIERI (tn., It.) **5:**422
- special Purim **13:**1397
- *illus:* text
Child, Rebellious, *see* REBELLIOUS SON
Childbirth, *see* BIRTH
CHILDEBERT I (ruler, Neustria) **5:**422
"Child Entering the Covenant" (paint., M. Oppenheim) **5:**573
Childlessness, *see* BARRENNESS AND FERTILITY
CHILD MARRIAGE **5:**423
- *Contents:*
- - Contracted by Child **5:**423
- - Contracted by Parents **5:**423
- - Me'un **5:**425
- - State of Israel **5:**425
- orphan **12:**1479
- puberty **13:**1350
- *takkanah* 1950 **12:**143
- *takkanah* regarding *me'un* **11:**1312
- *illus:* text
CHILDREN **5:**426
- adoption **2:**301ff
- embryology **4:**1019ff
- employment in Israel **9:**880ff
- family **6:**1166ff
- fasting **6:**1192
- infant burial **4:**1519
- infanticide **10:**978
- Inquisition **8:**1403
- kibbutz movement **10:**967
- knowledge of good and evil **13:**79
- maintenance **11:**784
- Marranos' halakhic status **12:**1023
- *mishmarot* and prayers for **12:**92
- slavery **14:**1656
- *zekhut avot* **16:**976ff
- *illus:*
- - at play in kindergarten **9:**937
- - babies' house, Menarah **10:**967
- - Bedouin in the Negev **12:**930
- - *bikkurim* festival **6:**1315; **10:**962
- - blessing of at leaving synagogue **4:**1088
- - boy from Warsaw Ghetto **13:**757
- - celebrating Shavuot in Jerusalem **14:**1321
- - child bride, North Africa **5:**424
- - "Children in Kovno Ghetto School" (drg., J. Lifschitz) Fig. 3-ART 77
- - dining room, Ayyelet ha-Shaḥar **10:**970
- - edict prohibiting baptism of Jewish children (Avignon, 1776) **3:**213
- - Florence, proclamation re baptism of (1668) **9:**1131
- - Israel, children per married woman, 1961 (table) **9:**484
- - Italian Jewish school children **9:**1138
- - Jewish boy from Munkacs region **8:**1107
- - kibbutz shelter during artillery attack **9:**419
- - Korczak, Janusz, stamp **10:**1200
- - Lodz, transport to extermination camp **8:**873
- - Lodz ghetto, child workers **11:**433
- - maintenance of converted, petition to Parliament (1702) **3:**206
- - mass execution by Nazis **8:**861
- - OSE summer camp **12:**1537
- - Polish, 19th cent. **6:***fcg.* 238
- - Polish *ḥeder* **13:**741
- - Polish refugee children **9:**496
- - Purim kindergarten party **11:**365
- - "Rabbi's Blessing" (paint., M. Oppenheim) **4:**1087
- - refugees in Europe, 1940s **14:**32
- - Simḥat Torah, distributing sweetmeats to **14:**1572
- - summer camp, Poland **13:**747
- - Theresienstadt Ghetto children's drawings **5:**1203
- - Tu bi-Shevat celebration **9:**907; **15:**1420
- - Warsaw Ghetto choir **12:**657
- - Wizo's Jerusalem Baby Home **16:**595
- - World War I orphans **8:**745
- - Yemenite *ḥeder*, Jerusalem **9:**897, 942
- - young chess players **5:**406
see also: PARENTS, HONOR OF; PARENT AND CHILD
Children and Youth Aliyah, *see* YOUTH ALIYAH
"Children in Kovno Ghetto School" (drg., J. Lifschitz) Fig. 77 3-ART
Children of the Ghetto (bk.,) **16:**930
- Imber as Melchitsedek **8:**1290
CHILDREN'S LITERATURE **5:**428
- *Contents:*
- - Hebrew **5:**429
- - - Early Period **5:**429
- - - Haskalah **5:**430
- - - Ḥibbat Zion Period **5:**432
- - - In Ereẓ Israel **5:**434
- - - State of Israel **5:**437
- - - U.S. **5:**437
- - Yiddish **5:**439
- - Ladino **5:**445
- - Holocaust **5:**446
- - English **5:**449
- - French **5:**452
- - German **5:**452
- - Italian and Dutch **5:**453
- - Rumanian **5:**453
- - Hungarian **5:**454
- - Russian **5:**454
- - Polish **5:**455
- - Czech and Serbo-Croatian **5:**455
- - Latin American **5:**455
- - Magazines **5:**456
- - - Early non-Hebrew **5:**456
- - - Hebrew **5:**457
- - - Yiddish **5:**458
- - - Non-Hebrew Today **5:**459
- - - Student Papers **5:**459
- Goldberg, Lea **7:**704
- Hebrew newspapers **12:**1051
- Kassel, David **10:**813
- Korczak, Janusz **10:**1200
- *illus:* text
- - *Ha-Peraḥim* **11:**151
CHILDREN'S SERVICES **5:**460
- *illus:*
- - text
Child Sacrifice **2:**918
- *see also:* AKEDAH; MOLOCH, CULT OF
CHILE **5:**461
- *Contents:*
- - Colonial Period **5:**461
- - 19-20th Centuries **5:**463
- - Contemporary Period **5:**465
- - Jews in Public Life **5:**467
- - Relations with Israel **5:**467
- Judaizing sects **10:**398
- Latin America **10:**1449ff
- politics **13:**820
- refugees **14:**30
- socialism **15:**32
- synagogues **1:**syn. list
- U.N. **15:**1560
- Zionism **16:**1125
Chileab (s., David), *see* DANIEL
Chilia-Nova (city, Bess.) *see* KILIYA
Chilinowicz, Nathan **11:**811
Chilion, *see* MAHLON AND CHILION
Chilius, A. **8:**29
CHILKOVSKY, NADIA **5:**1271
Chillicothe (city, Miss.) **2:**575
CHILLÓN (tn., Sp.) **5:**468
- Jews and Calatrava Order **5:**39
Chillon (cas., Switz.) **15:**554
Chilperic (ruler, Neustria) **5:**423
- forced conversions **3:**170
- Jews and **7:**9
- Priscus **13:**1116
Chim (phot.), *see* SEYMOUR, DAVID
Chimavir (aviation company, Isr.) **9:**838
Chimene, Eugene **8:**1050; **15:**1034
Chimham (bib. fig.) **4:**287
Chin (fam.) **12:**1171
CHINA **5:**468
- *Contents:*
- - Early Jewish Contacts **5:**468
- - Modern Jewish Communities **5:**470
- - China and Israel **5:**472
- *aliyah* **9:**512
- Hong Kong community **8:**963
- Israel's relations with **9:**433; **9:**444
- Joseph, Saul Abdallah **10:**222
- Kaifeng Jews **10:**695
- population **13:**872ff
- refugees **14:**30
- Sallam the interpreter **16:**1280
- spices **8:**1311
- ten lost tribes **15:**1006
- trade and commerce **15:**1297ff
- U.N. and Jewish state **16:**1092
- Uzbekistan Jews **16:**40
- War Crimes Trials **16:**291
- Zionism **16:**1127
- *illus:*
- - text
- - Karl Marx stamp **15:**335
- - Tang figurine of Semitic appearance **5:**470
- *pop. tables:* text
- *see also:* AI TI'EN; CHAO; HANGCHOW; MONGOLIA; NINGPO; SHANGHAI
China, *see* Porcelain
Chindaswinth (k., Sp.) **15:**221
Chingola (tn., Zambia) **16:**922
Chinillo, Azarias **14:**847
Chinillo, Noah **4:**171
CHINNERETH (city, Er. Isr.) **5:**474
Chinnereth, Sea of, *see* KINNERET,

LAKE
CHINON (tn., Fr.) 5:474
- Tours 15:1288
Chintila (k., Sp.) 15:220
CHIOS (Aeg. isl.) 5:475
- Cardozo, Abraham 14:1244
- Greece 7:872ff
- special Purim 13:1396
CHIPKIN, ISRAEL 5:475
Chiquatilla, Isaac ibn (gram., Sp.), *see* GIKATILLA, ISAAC IBN
Chiquatilla, Joseph, *see* GIKATILLA, JOSEPH BEN ABRAHAM
Chiquatilla, Moses, *see* GIKATILLA, MOSES BEN SAMUEL HA-KOHEN
Chirikov, Yevgeni 14:509
CHIRINO (fam.) 5:476
Chirino, Alonso 5:476
Chirino, Diego 5:476
Chirino, Diego de Valera 5:476
Chirino, Juan Garcia 5:476
Chirino, Sebastian 5:476
CHIROMANCY (palmistry) 5:477
- magic 11:712
- mysticism 10:500
- practical Kabbalah 10:637
- *illus:* text
- *see also:* DIVINATION
Chisinau (city, Mold.), *see* KISHINEV
Chislon (tn., Er. Isr.) 10:330
Chiun (deity), *see* SIKKUTH AND CHIUN
Chizbatron (ents.) 9:1005
CHIZHIK (fam.) 5:479
Chizhik, Barukh 5:479
Chizhik, Efraym 5:480; 8:1064
Chizhik, Ḥannah 5:479
Chizhik, Sarah 5:480
Chizhik, Yiẓḥak 5:480
Chlumec (vill., Cz.) 4:352
CHMELNITZKI, MELECH 5:480
CHMIELNICKI, BOGDAN 5:480
- massacres
- - Amsterdam community 2:898
- - Auerbach, Samuel of Lublin 3:841
- - Austrian Jews 3:890
- - Belaya Tserkov 4:413
- - Haidamacks and 7:1132
- - Hannover, Nathan N. 7:1273ff
- - *ḥerem ha-yishuv* 8:358
- - history chart 8:766-767
- - influence on Ḥasidism 7:1391
- - Israel of Belzec 9:1049
- - Kamenets-Podolski 10:725
- - law codification influenced by 5:655
- - Lvov 11:610
- - migration 3:721
- - Nemirov 12:947
- - Podolia 13:668
- - ransom of captives 5:155
- - Tulchin massacre 15:1428
- - Volhynia 16:208
- - Wiśniowiecki 16:570
CHMIELNIK (tn., Pol.) 5:484
- Podolia 13:668
Chmiel the Wicked, *see* CHMIELNICKI, BOGDAN
Chmurner (soc. ldr.), *see* LESTCHINSKY, JOSEPH
Chodorov (tn., Lith.) 15:610
CHODOROV, EDWARD 15:1080
Chodorov, Jerome 15:1080
Chodosy (camp. Pol.) 10:1123
CHODOVA PLANA (tn., Bohem.) 5:485
- synagogue 15:607
Chodowiecki, Daniel N. 4:1219
Chodowski, A. T. 6:273
Chodziesner, Gertrud, *see* KOLMAR, GERTRUD
Choele Choel (clny., Arg.) 3:431
CHOERILOS OF SAMOS (Gr. poet) 7:893
Choice, free, *see* FREE WILL
Choice of Pearls (bk.), *see* MIVḤAR HA-PENINIM
Chiński, Theodor Jeske 9:1336
CHOIRS 5:486
- Korahites in Temple 10:1191
- S.R. Hirsch's innovation 8:510
- *illus:*
- - text
- - Bucharest, students' chorus 14:412
- *see also:* CANTATAS AND CHORAL WORKS, HEBREW
CHOJNICE (tn., Pol.), *see* KONITZ
CHOLENT (stew) 5:489
- Sabbath 6:1422
- *illus:* text
Cholera 9:984
Cholojow (city, U.S.S.R.) 10:728
Chomedy (sub., Montreal) 12:287
Chomet, Abraham 15:821
CHOMSKY, DOV 5:490
CHOMSKY, NOAM AVRAM 5:490
- linguistics 16:1378
CHOMSKY, WILLIAM 5:491
CHOMUTOV (city, Cz.) 5:491
Chopin, Frédéric François 4:621
CHORAZIN (tn., Er. Isr.) 5:492
- synagogue 3:508; 15:595ff
- synagogue pillars 13:523ff
- *illus:*
- - synagogue *bimah* 3:326
Chorażycki, Julian 15:1361ff
Choreb (bk.) 8:509
Chorev (publ.) 13:1374
Choreography, *see* DANCE
CHORIN, AARON 5:495
- Grishaber, Isaac 7:924
- history chart 8:766-767
- Loew, L. 11:444
- oral law 12:1442
- *illus:* text
CHORNY, JOSEPH JUDAH 5:496
Choroszcz (tn., Pol.) 15:1475
CHORTKOV (city, Ukr.) 5:496
Chortkov (ḥas. Dyn.) 2:368
CHORZOW (city, Pol.) 5:498
CHOSEN PEOPLE 5:498
- *Contents:*
- - Bible 5:498
- - Rabbinic Literature 5:500
- - Medieval Thought 5:500
- - Modern Views 5:501
- General
- - *Aleinu le-Shabbe'aḥ* 2:557
- - apologetics 3:191; 3:199
- - denial of as heresy 8:359
- - Genesis, Book of 7:395
- - God and Israel 7:646; 11:524ff
- - Israel, People of 9:106
- - Jewish philosophy 13:421
- - Judaism and nationalism 10:387ff
- - *kiddush ha-Shem* 10:982
- - law and morality 10:1480
- - meaning of exile 7:283ff
- - nations of the world 7:410
- - Pentateuch 13:247
- - providence 13:1279
- - remnant of Israel 14:70
- - responsibility of election 4:431
- Views On
- - Abraham bar Ḥiyya 13:437
- - Cohen, Hermann 5:674; 7:777
- - Hirsch, S.R. 8:514
- - Judah Halevi 3:193; 8:684; 10:357ff; 13:439
- - Julian the Apostate 10:468
- - Kabbalah 10:608ff
- - Krochmal 13:458
- - Maimonides 8:684ff
- - Rosenzweig 14:301
- - sages 14:654
- - Zangwill, Israel 16:932
Chosroes (k., Parthia) 15:1312
Chosroes II (k., Pers.), *see* Khosroes II
CHOTSH, ẒEVI HIRSCH BEN JERAHMEEL 5:502
- Shabbateanism 14:1248
Chotzner, Alfred James 5:503
- India 8:1357
CHOTZNER, JOSEPH 5:503
Chou En-Lai 5:472ff
CHOURAQUI (fam.) 5:503
CHOURAQUI, ANDRÉ 5:504
- *illus:*
- - Kessel, Joseph 10:922
Chouraqui, David 5:503
Chouraqui, Elijah 5:503
Chouraqui, Ephraim 5:503
Chouraqui, Isaac 5:503
Chouraqui, Jacob 5:503
Chouraqui, Judah 5:503
Chouraqui, Mas'ud 5:503
Chouraqui, Mordecai 5:504
Chouraqui, Moses (15th cent.) 5:503
Chouraqui, Moses (18th cent.) 5:503
Chouraqui, Moses (19th cent.) 5:504
Chouraqui, Saadiah 5:503
Choynski, Joe 15:306
Chreia (Gr. maxim) 5:1177ff
Chrétien, Florent 9:1343
Chriqui, *see also* Shriqui
CHRIQUI (fam.) 5:504
- Safi 14:633
Chriqui, Joseph Ben Mas'ud 5:504
Chriqui, Mordecai 5:504
Christadelphians (sect) 16:1153
CHRISTCHURCH (city, N. Z.) 5:504
Christian IV (k., Den.) 5:1536
Christian X (k., Den.) 4:73
Christiana pietas (papal bull 1568) 4:1496
CHRISTIAN COMMUNITIES IN ISRAEL 9:909
- *Contents:*
- - Greek Orthodox 9:910
- - Armenians 9:911
- - Ethiopians 9:912
- - Latins 9:912
- - Uniates 9:915
- - Melkites 9:915
- - Anglicans and Protestants 9:917
- geographical distribution 9:569ff
- Jerusalem 9:1439ff
- religious courts 9:638ff
- *illus:*
- - Armenian bishop's throne 3:475
- - Basilica of the Agony, Jerusalem 9:1455
- - Basilica of the Annunciation 12:901
- - Christian Quarters, Jerusalem 9:1439
- - Church of Jesus the Child 12:903
- - Church of St. Anne 9:1453
- - Copts in Holy Sepulcher 9:913
- - Eshkol, Levi, meeting with leaders after Six-Day War 9:410
- - Franciscans in the Via Dolorosa 9:916
- - Garden Tomb, Jerusalem 9:1461
- - Greek Orthodox monk 9:913
- - Greek Orthodox patriarch enthroned 9:912
- - holy places 8:927-930
- - Holy Sepulcher and Christian Quarter 9:1460
- - Monastery of Notre-Dame de France, Jerusalem 9:1463
- - Mount Zion 9:1465
- - pilgrims in the Via Dolorosa 9:916
- - Protestant tourists at Jerusalem Garden Tomb 9:916
- - Russian Church of Gethsemane 9:1462
- - Russian Church property 9:1457
- - Russian Orthodox priests 9:914
- - Syrian Orthodox Church 9:914
- *pop. tables* 9:491
Christian Council of Palestine 16:1155
Christian Crusader (mvmt., U.S.) 12:952
Christian Democratic Movement (Fr.) 3:85
Christian Front (anti-Sem. mvmt., U.S.) 12:1114
Christian Greek (lang.) 16:1589
Christian Hebraists, *see* HEBRAISTS, CHRISTIAN
Christiani, F. A. 10:1592
CHRISTIANI, PABLO 5:505
- Abraham of Dreux 2:155
- Barcelona 4:209
- Barcelona disputation 4:213; 11:354
- Naḥmanides 5:601; 6:92ff; 12:775
- Spain 15:232
CHRISTIANITY 5:505
- *Contents:*
- - The Term 5:505
- - Background 5:506
- - Severance from Judaism 5:507
- - Jesus 5:508
- - Ritual and Liturgy 5:510
- - Missions to Jews 5:511
- - Attitudes to Jews 5:511
- - Orthodox Church 5:513
- - Jewish Attitudes 5:513
- - Comparison 5:514
- General
- - Calvin, John 5:66
- - Eusebius 6:977
- - Freemasons 7:122
- - Hemerobaptists 14:1088
- - Jerusalem holy sites 9:1540ff
- - Jerome 9:1376
- - Jesuits 10:8
- - Jesus 10:10ff
- - Judaizers 10:397
- - Luther, Martin 11:584
- - Paul of Tarsus 13:190
- - pilgrimages to Ereẓ Israel 13:514ff
- - Sibyl 14:1490ff
- - Somrei Sabat 15:139
- History 8:652ff
- - Aelia Capitolina community 9:1406ff
- - Agrippa II and spread of 2:418
- - Barbarians, converted to 4:206ff
- - Bar Kokhba War 8:647ff
- - Claudius 5:601
- - Crusades 5:1141
- - Egypt 6:490
- - Ereẓ Israel, 70 to 640 C.E. 9:244; 9:255; 9:258
- - Frankists 7:58ff; 14:1252
- - Hellenizers 8:297
- - holy places in Israel 8:920ff
- - Hussites 8:1134
- - Jerusalem: early community 9:1394
- - Jerusalem: Arab period 9:1426
- - Reformation 14:18ff
- - Roman Empire 9:1119
- - Rome 14:241ff
- - Transjordan 15:1317
- - Zealots 16:948
- Thought and Literature
- - Aaron 2:8
- - Adam's role 2:240
- - *Akedah* 2:481
- - antinomianism 3:68
- - Bible 4:922
- - Bible translations 4:853ff
- - Burchard's *Decretum* 4:1508
- - David, view of 5:1331
- - edict of Milan 8:652ff
- - *Enoch, Ethiopic Book of* 6:796

– – gnosticism 7:637
– – Isaac 9:5
– – *Isaiah, Ascension of* 9:71
– – Jerusalem 9:1568
– – Jewish apologetics 3:189
– – Kabbalah 10:643ff; 16:1214
– – *Maccabees, Fourth Book of* 11:662
– – Manichaeism 11:876
– – marriage, views on 5:364; 11:1027
– – Melchizedek, tradition of 11:1289
– – messianism 11:1421
– – Moses 12:402,406
– – Neoplatonism 12:958ff
– – Noah 12:1195
– – pantheistic mysticism 10:601
– – polygamy 12:259
– – prophecy 13:1176
– – Psalms 13:1327
– – redemption 14:5
– – Song of Songs 15:147
– – Temple 15:984
– – term "Jew" 10:22
– – theology 15:1103; 15:1104
– – Therapeutae 15:1112
– – Trinity 7:671,672
– – *see also:* NEW TESTAMENT
– Judaism and 10:387,390,396
– – *Aleinu le-Shabbe'aḥ* 2:557
– – *Amen* in liturgy 2:803
– – apologetics 3:191
– – Augustine 3:851
– – *avodah zarah* 3:981
– – *Birkat ha-Minim* 4:1035
– – censorship 5:276ff
– – circumcision 5:570
– – disputations 6:80ff
– – excommunications 8:353
– – festivals, Jewish 6:1244
– – halakhic attitude 7:412ff
– – homiletics 8:954ff; 13:999
– – illuminated manuscripts 8:1258ff
– – influence 13:416
– – Jacob of Kefar Sakhnayya 9:1233
– – Jewish Christian sects 10:38
– – Jewish dogma 3:656
– – Jewish martyrology 8:302
– – Jewish messianism 11:1413
– – Jewish philosophy 13:421; 13:426; 13:428; 13:451ff
– – Jewish proselytism 13:1186ff
– – Kabbalah and Christian mysticism 10:490; 10:506ff
– – kabbalistic trinity 10:563
– – *kiddush ha-Shem* interpretation 10:977ff
– – Maimonidean controversy 11:747
– – *minim* 8:359
– – music influenced by 12:556; 12:577
– – Noachide Laws 12:1189
– – original sin 10:608
– – parodies 13:130ff
– – Pharisee doctrines 13:366
– – polemical literature 11:310ff
– – Postel, Guillaume 13:932
– – *shema* 14:1373
– – synagogues 15:601
– – Talmud terminology 7:411
– Muslims and Samaritans
– – eschatology and Islam 6:883ff
– – Islam 9:92
– – Islamic polemics 9:101ff
– Mount Gerizim 7:438
– – Muhammad 12:509
– – Samaritans 14:731
– Views on
– – Abulafia, Abraham 2:185; 2:186
– – Aḥa 2:435
– – Akiva 16:844
– – Buber, Martin 4:1433; 13:463
– – Celsus the philosopher 5:270
– – Crescas, Hasdai 5:1079
– – Duran's epistle 3:196; 6:304
– – Emden, J. 3:198
– – Formstecher 13:456
– – Grayzel's studies on 7:863
– – Judah Halevi 10:363ff
– – Julian the Apostate 10:468
– – Kant 10:742
– – Kaufmann, Y. 16:1350
– – Klausner's studies 10:1094
– – Levinsohn 11:118ff
– – Maimonides 8:685
– – Mendelssohn 11:1338; 13:455
– – Montefiore, C.J. 12:269
– – Naḥmanides 4:214
– – Nietzsche, F. 12:1154
– – Pico della Mirandola 13:501
– – Porphyry 13:905
– – Rosenberg's anti-Semitism 14:275
– – Rosenzweig 13:462; 14:299ff
– – Spinoza 13:454
– – Yūsuf As'ar 16:897
– *illus:*
– – *De arcanis catholicae veritatis* (1550) 7:261 (1518); 8:10
– – Spain, Jewish and Converso communities, 1474 (map) 15:237
– *see also:* ANTISEMITISM (Christian); BULLS, PAPAL; CHURCH, CATHOLIC; CHURCH FATHERS; INQUISITION; JEWISH CHRISTIAN SECTS; POPES; PROTESTANTS; REFORMATION
Christian-Jewish Relations
– General
– – Anti-Semitism 3:96ff
– – apostates 3:202ff
– – autonomy 3:921
– – blood libel 4:1120
– – censorship 5:276
– – correspondence 11:61
– – Dominicans 6:161
– – dress 6:216ff
– – forced conversion 3:169
– – Franciscans 7:47
– – Hebrew studies 8:9ff; 16:1391
– – Host desecration 8:1040
– – informers 8:1365ff
– – isolation of Jews 10:82
– – Jew in *Galut* 7:281ff
– – Jewish identity 10:56
– – Jewish Quarter 10:81
– – *limpieza de sangre* 11:255
– – oath *more Judaico* 12:1302
– – pig 13:507
– – Protestants 13:1247, 1252ff
– – Sadducees 14:622
– – seals 14:1081
– – sermons 8:654; 14:1184
– – Sisters and Fathers of Sion 13:1571ff
– – tithes, church 15:1162
– – universities 15:1674ff
– – Vatican 16:74ff
– – Zionism 16:1152
– Historical Aspects
– – African Jews 2:332
– – agriculture, restrictions on 2:401
– – Amsterdam and Nazi occupation 2:902
– – Assembly of Jewish Notables 3:763
– – Church councils 5:546
– – disputations 6:80ff
– – Ereẓ Israel, 70 to 640 C.E. 9:244; 9:255; 9:257ff
– – European Jews 6:968
– – expulsions of Jews 6:1069ff
– – Holocaust and the Churches 8:910
– – Holocaust and theology 14:138
– – *Iudex Judaeorum* 9:1152
– – Kingdom of Jerusalem 9:272
– – Lateran Councils 10:1445ff
– – Meaux and Paris Councils 2:915
– – Reformation 14:18
– – segregation in Nuremberg 12:1277
– – slave trade 14:1660
– – Spain 15:220ff
– – Talmud, burning of 15:768
– – Toledo 15:1201ff
– – Tortosa disputation 15:1270ff
– – usury 16:32
– – Vannes council 4:1383
– Views on
– – Abrabanel, Isaac 2:104
– – Agobard 2:372
– – Alexander of Hales 2:582
– – Aquinas 3:229
– – Bernardino da Siena 4:672
– – Bernard of Clairvaux 4:672
– – Brunetti, Angelo 4:1417
– – Crispin, Gilbert 5:1113
– – Justinian 10:477
– – Odo of Sully 12:1331
– – Rivkes 14:198
– *illus:*
– – disputations 6:82-90
– – Frankfort, *Staettigkeit* (1614) 7:84
– – "Judenbuch der Scheffstrasse" (Vienna, 1389-1420) 3:901
– *see also:* CHRISTIANITY; CHURCH, CATHOLIC; PROTESTANTS
Christian Kabbalah 10:643ff; 16:1214
– *illus:*
– – *De arcanis catholicae veritatis* (1550) 7:261; (1518) 8:10
– – *Der Spinozismus im Judenthum* (1699) 10:647
– – *Kabbala Denudata* (17th cent.) 10:558
– – *Or Nerot ha-Menorah* (1548) 10:625
– – *Portae Lucis* (1516) 10:635
– *see also:* HEBRAISTS, CHRISTIAN; KABBALAH (Christian Kabbalah); POSTEL, GUILLAUME; REUCHLIN, JOHANNES
Christian Missionaries, *see* Missionaires, (non-J.)
Christian Quarter (Jer.) 9:1516
– *illus:*
– – aerial view 9:1439
– – City wall and Quarter 9:172-173
– – Hezekiah's Pool 9:1460
Christian Religious Courts in Israel 9:638ff
Christian religious drama 6:89
CHRISTIAN SCIENCE CHURCH (U.S.) 5:515
Christiansen, Sigurd 14:933
CHRISTIAN SOCIAL PARTY (Aus.) 5:516
– Austrian Jewry 3:897
– Seipel, Ignaz 14:1115
– *illus:*
– – anti-Semitic election poster, 1920 3:905
CHRISTIAN-SOCIAL PARTY, GERMAN 5:517
– Stoecker 15:408
Christian Zionists and Friends of Israel 16:1152
– Amery, Leopold 2:832
– Balfour, Arthur James 4:130f; 16:426
– Blackstone, William E. 4:1069; 16:1154
– Borchsenius, Poul 4:1242
– Borges, Jorge Luis 15:255
– Cazalet, Edward 5:265; 16:1155
– Cazalet, Victor Alexander 5:265
– Churchill, Winston 5:555
– Conder, Claude Regnier 5:865; 16:1155
– Darby, John N. 16:1153
– Deedes, Sir Wyndham 5:1455
– Dugdale, Blanche 4:131; 6:263
– Dunant, Jean Henri 6:270; 16:1155
– Eliot, George 6:663
– Elisabeth, Queen of the Belgians 4:424
– Elisheva (Zhirkova) 6:671
– Evatt, Herbert 3:886
– Finch, Sir Henry 6:1285
– Finn, James 6:1300 13:518
– Frederick, duke of Baden 7:113
– Galaction, Gala 7:256
– Gawler, George 7:338; 16:1154
– Gawler, John Cox 7:339
– Hechler, William Henry 8:237
– Hyde, Orson 16:1154
– Koenig, Marie-Pierre 7:42
– Laharanne, Ernest 10:1361
– Langallerie, Philippe Gentil de 10:1417
– Lie, Trygve 12:1225
– Lloyd George, David 11:413
– McDonald, James Grover 11:666
– Masaryk, Jan 11:1091
– Masaryk, Thomas 11:1092
– Meinertzhagen, Richard 11:1239
– Mickiewicz, Adam 11:1500
– Monk, Henry Wentworth 16:1154
– Mordovtsev, Daniil 12:316
– Musolino, Benedetto 12:716; 16:1155
– Newlinski, Philipp Michael 12:1034
– Niebuhr, Reinhold 12:1149
– Oliphant, Lawrence 9:324; 12:1362
– Patterson, John Henry 13:186
– Paulli, Holger 14:926
– Roosevelt, Eleanor 14:258 16:865
– Russell, Charles Edward 16:1155
– Scott, C. P. 4:132; 14:1036
– Shaftesbury, Earl of 8:727; 16:1154
– Smuts, Jan 15:13; 15:190ff
– Soustelle, Jacques 7:42
– Spaak, Paul-Henri 4:424
– Suttner, Berta von 12:1286
– Thomas, John 16:1153
– Toland, John 5:1464; 15:1193
– Truman, Harry S. 15:1408; 16:1176
– Van Paassen, Pierre 16:68
– Wedgwood, Josiah Clement 16:371
– Wilson, Woodrow 16:535
– Wingate, Charles Orde 16:547
Christina (q., Swed.) 5:244
– Abraham Teixeira De Sampaio 15:912
Christmann, Jacob 8:29
Christmas 9:912
– *illus:*
– – Armenians celebrating 9:914
– – Greek Orthodox patriarch enthroned 9:912
Christoph, Ernst Friedrich (Nazi offic.), *see* SAUCKEL, FRITZ
Christopherson, John 6:774; 9:1343
CHRONEGK, LUDWIG 15:1056 15:1080
Chronicle Adler (wk.), *see Chronicles, Samaritan*
Chronicle of Ahimaaz (bk.), *see Ahimaaz, Scroll of*
Chronicle of Joshua the Stylite, see Joshua the Stylite, Chronicle of
CHRONICLES, BOOK OF 5:517
– *Contents:*
– – Place in Canon 5:517
– – Contents 5:518

- - Sources **5:**527
- - Aim and Purpose **5:**529
- - Composition **5:**531
- - Author and his Time **5:**533
- Bible history **8:**577
- *Books of the Chronicles of the Kings of Judah and Israel* **4:**1237
- canon **4:**824,830
- Hebrew **16:**1588
- Joseph ben Ḥiyya **10:**230
- Nehemiah **12:**937
- satan **14:**903
- Spinoza **15:**283
- Targum **4:**849
- *illus:*
- - Latin ms. **12:**1
Chronicles. News of the Past (bib. newsp.) **5:**450
Chronicles, Samaritan (bk.) **6:**313; **14:**727; **14:**728; **14:**754; **14:**750
- *illus:*
- - beginning of eras **14:**749
Chronicles of Jerahmeel **13:**408
Chronicles of Jeremiah (Pseudepig.), *see* BARUCH, REST OF THE WORDS OF
Chronic renal disease **14:**1503
Chronik, Isaac Loew **5:**412
Chronography, *see* HISTORIOGRAPHY
Chronologica mystica (wk.) **15:**1400
CHRONOLOGY **16:**1261
- Babylonian Chronicle **16:**1509ff
- Bible history **8:**574ff
- Demetrius **5:**1490
- rabbinical literature **13:**1462
- Samaritans **14:**748
- ***Seder Olam*** **9:**1223; **14:**1091
- *illus:*
- - Genesis, Book of (table) **7:**397,398
- - Jewish history (chron. chart) **8:**766-767
- - *Kore ha-Dorot* (1846) **5:**892
- - Mari and Assyrian dynasties (table) **11:**980
- - *Me'or Einayim* (1574) **8:**567
- - *Seder Olam Rabbah* (1514) **8:**559
- - *Sefer ha-Kabbalah* (1514) **8:**1160
- - *tannaim* (table) **15:**801
- *see also:* CALENDAR
Chrysococca, Georgios, *see* Georgios Chrysococca
Chrysography (gold wrtg.) **4:**1227
Chrysolite (gem) **13:**1009
Chrysorhoas (Syr. riv.), *see* Amanah
Chrystostum Dudulaeus Westphalus (au.) **16:**261
CHRYZANOW (tn., Pol.) **5:**534
- *illus:*
- - text
- - tombstones **15:**1225,1226,1231
Chuadit (Prov. dialect), *see* JUDEO-PROVENCAL
Chüanchow (Zayton, China) **5:**469
Chubb, Thomas **5:**1464
Chudin (has. dyn.) **15:**417
CHUDNOV (tn., Ukr.) **5:**535
Chudnovsky, S. **14:**1487
CHUETAS (Mar. cmty., Maj.) **5:**535
- *limpieza de sangre* **11:**255
- New Christians **12:**1022
- *illus:* text
- *see also:* MAJORCA; MARRANO
CHUFUT-KALE (tn., Crimea) **5:**536
- Isaac ben Solomon **9:**33
CHUJOY, ANATOLE **5:**1272
Chukar partridge (zool.) **9:**226
Chukovski, Kornei **4:**1395
Chumaceiro, Aron Mendes **12:**993
Chumash (Bib.), *see* ḤUMMASH
CHURCH, CATHOLIC **5:**536
- *Contents:*
- - Under Roman Empire **5:**536
- - Early Middle Ages **5:**537
- - Later Middle Ages **5:**538
- - Renaissance and Counter-Reformation **5:**539
- - Modern Times **5:**539
- - In the U.S. **5:**542
- General
- - Church Councils **5:**546
- - Church Fathers **5:**550
- - Eve compared with **6:**983
- - excommunications **8:**353
- - livestock trade **11:**410
- - "New Jerusalem" **9:**1569ff
- - tithes, church **15:**1162
- - universities **15:**1676
- - usury **16:**32
- - wine and liquor trade **16:**541ff
- Church and Jews
- - anti-Semitism **3:**101
- - blood libel **4:**1120
- - censorship **5:**276
- - circumcision **3:**216
- - Frankists **7:**58ff; **14:**1252
- - Hebrew parodies **13:**130ff
- - Holocaust **8:**840,874,913
- - Host desecration **8:**1040
- - isolation of Jews **10:**82
- - Jewish apologetics **3:**191
- - Jewish martyrology **8:**302
- - Jews in Galut **7:**281ff
- - Judaism **10:**396
- - *limpieza de sangre* **11:**255
- - Nazism, attitude to **8:**910
- - *Nostra aetate* **10:**159
- - Sadducees **14:**622
- - Satan **14:**905
- - sermons to Jews **14:**1184
- - Zionism **16:**74ff
- History
- - Crusades **5:**1135
- - 4-7th centuries **8:**652ff
- - holy places in Israel **8:**920ff; **9:**1439
- - Jesus **10:**10
- - Justinian **10:**478
- - Reformation **14:**18ff
- Orders and Movements
- - Dominicans **6:**161
- - Franciscans **7:**47
- - Freemasons **7:**122
- - Hemerobaptists **14:**1088
- - Jesuits **10:**8
- - Judaizers **10:**398
- Regions
- - France **7:**9ff
- - Israel **9:**912
- - Jerusalem **9:**1439ff
- - Poland **13:**713
- - Spain **15:**221,221f
- - Toledo **15:**1202
- *illus:* text
- *see also:* CHRISTIANITY; Christian-Jewish Relations; HOLOCAUST AND THE CHRISTIAN CHURCHES; INQUISITION; POPES; TALMUD, BURNING OF
Church, Greek Orthodox, *see* Greek Orthodox Church
Church, Protestant, *see* PROTESTANTS
Church and Synagogue, *see* ECCLESIA ET SYNAGOGA
CHURCH COUNCILS **5:**546
- attitude to Jews **8:**673ff
- Basle **4:**304
- Elvira **6:**691
- French Jewry **7:**10ff
- Gratian **7:**857
- history chart **8:**766-767
- Meaux **2:**915
- Paris **13:**103
- Toledo **15:**220,1198
- Vatican II **3:**137
- Zamora (1313) **16:**926
- *see also:* BULLS, PAPAL; CHURCH, CATHOLIC; LATERAN COUNCILS III, IV; POPES; TALMUD, BURNING OF
Churches (ancient) **3:**329
Churches (of; of the)
- All the Nations (Jer.) **9:**1473
- Anastasis (Jer.) **9:**1416
- Annunciation (Nazareth) **12:**900
- Ascension (Jer.) **9:**1406
- Dormition (Jer.) **16:**1031
- El Transito (Toledo) **15:**611
- Gethsemane (Jer.) **9:**1406; **9:**1460
- Holy Cross (Jer.) **9:**1416
- Holy Sepulcher (Jer.) **8:**922,936; **9:**1570ff
- Last Supper (Jer.) **9:**1424,1441; **16:**1030
- Mary (Jer.) **9:**1425
- Mt. Zion (Jer.) **9:**1407
- Multiplication (Tabgha) **15:**689
- Nativity (Bethlehem) **4:**742 **8:**922,935
- Nea (Jer.) **9:**1407
- St. Andrew (Jer.) **9:**1473
- St. Anne (Jer.) **9:**1416; **9:**1455
- St. Catherine (Bethlehem)
- St. Chef **9:**1580
- St. Etienne (Jer.) **9:**1461
- St. George (Jer.) **9:**1462
- St. James (Jer.) **9:**1407
- St. John (Jer.) **9:**1459
- St. Mark (Ven.) **12:**407
- St. Mary of the Spasm (Jer.) **9:**1460
- St. Nicholas (Bet Jala) **4:**745
- St. Peter Galicante (Jer.) **9:**1473
- St. Pudenziana (Rome) **9:**1579
- St. Sophia (Jer.) **9:**1407
- St. Stephen (Jer.) **9:**1406
- *illus:*
- - Basilica of the Agony, Jerusalem **9:**1455
- - Church of the Nativity **9:**912,914
- - Church of St. Anne, Jerusalem **9:**1453
- - El Transito, Toledo **15:**613
- - Holy Sepulcher **9:**913,914,1418,1439,1460
- - Jesus the Child, Nazareth **12:**903
- - Multiplication, Tabgha **15:**689
- - Russian church, Jerusalem **9:**914,1457
- - Russian Church of Gethsemane **9:**1462
- - S. Anna, Trani **15:**1314
- - Santa Maria la Blanca, Toledo **15:**612, 1199
- - Shivtah **14:**1419
- - "The Synagogue," Nazareth **12:**900
- - Tomb of Miriam **9:**1417
- - 'Usifiyyā **16:**20
- *see also:* HOLY PLACES; and *under individual names*
CHURCH FATHERS **5:**550
- anti-Jewish sermons **8:**654
- Apocrypha and Pseudepigrapha **3:**185ff
- Christianity **5:**509
- folkloric material **6:**1376
- Herodians **8:**388
- Jerusalem **9:**1569ff
- Julian the Apostate **10:**469
- Nineveh gentiles **3:**192
- Philo **13:**427
- *illus:* text
Churchill, Charles Henry **9:**299
Churchill, John **11:**1214
CHURCHILL, SIR WINSTON LEONARD SPENCER **5:**555
- Abdullah ibn Hussein **2:**56
- *aliyah* **9:**523
- Cassin, René **5:**232
- chronological chart **8:**766-767
- Israel history **9:**340
- war crimes trials **16:**289
- White Papers **16:**483
- Wingate, Orde, and **16:**548
- *illus:*
- - in Jerusalem, 1921 **2:**57
- - letter to Weizmann re Jewish Fighting Force (August 1944) **3:**394
- - speaking at Hebrew University site **9:**1474
Churchill White Paper **16:**483ff
Church Missionary Society (bib. soc.) **4:**969
Church music, *see* MUSIC
Church of . . . *see under keyword; see also* Churches
Church Slavonic (lang.) **4:**884
Church tithes, *see* TITHES, CHURCH
CHURGIN, PINKHOS **5:**557
- Bar-Ilan University **4:**225
- *illus:*
- - Histadruth Ivrith of America **13:**371
CHURGIN, YA'AKOV YEHOSHUA **5:**558
Chush, J. C. **15:**307
Chust (city, Ukr.), *see* KHUST
Chuvakhin, Dmitri **9:**407
CHWILA (newsp.) **5:**558
- Lvov **11:**613
- press **13:**1042
- Zionism **16:**1132
- *illus:*
- - masthead **11:**615
- - Zipper, G. **16:**1182
CHWISTEK, LEON **5:**558
CHWOLSON, DANIEL **5:**558
- Society for the Promotion of Culture **15:**58ff
- universities **15:**1678
Chwolson, Orest **5:**560
Chydenius, Anders **14:**930
Chyet, S. F. **8:**568
Chytraeus, A. **8:**29
Chytraeus, David **8:**29
Cialente, Fausta **9:**1107,1113
Cibo (duchess of Camerino) **8:**29
Cibo, Giovanni Battista (pope), *see* INNOCENT VIII
CICERO, MARCUS TULLIUS **5:**560
- attitude towards Jews **14:**232
- defense of Flaccus **16:**1273
Ciceruacchio, *see* BRUNETTI, ANGELO
Cicurel (fam.) **5:**31
Cicurel, Salvador **5:**32
Cid, El (11th cent., Sp.) **15:**228
- bankers, Jewish **4:**169
Cidellus, *see* FERRIZUEL, JOSEPH HA-NASI
CIECHANOW (tn., Pol.) **5:**560
- Wegrow **16:**372
- *illus:* text
CIECHANOW, ABRAHAM BEN RAPHAEL LANDAU OF **5:**561
Ciechanowski (law., Belor.) **12:**1238
Cieszyn (tn., Silesia), *see* TESCHEN
Ciezler, Shmuel **5:**445
Cigarette industry **15:**1177
Cigar industry **15:**1177
Cihrin-Berezovca (concen. camp) **15:**1330
CILIBI, MOÏSE **5:**561
CILICIA (reg., As. M.) **5:**562
- Hattusilis I **16:**1497
- Sea Peoples **16:**1501
- *see also:* QUE
Cimara, C. de (duchess) **16:**788
Cimarosa, Domenico **10:**460 **14:**880
CINCINNATI (city, O.) **5:**562
- history chart (1817; 1875) **8:**766-767
- museum **12:**544; **12:**538

- Ohio **12:**1344
- Wise, Isaac Mayer **16:**564
- *illus:*
- - *Deborah* (1885) **13:**1052
- - Hebrew Union College **8:**217
- - Isaac Mayer Wise Temple **12:**1345

CINCINNATI HAGGADAH (15th cent. ms.) **7:**1099
- Jaffe, Meir of Ulm **9:**1263
- *illus:* **4:***fcg.* 364; **7:**1083

Cinema, *see* MOTION PICTURES
Cinfa, Moses, *see* MOSES BEN SOLOMON BEN SIMEON OF BURGOS
CINNAMON (spice) **5:**565
- incense and perfumes **8:**1311ff
- *illus:* text

Cinnamon, Ceylonese (bot.) **13:**617
Cinnamon, Chinese (bot.) **13:**617
Cinnamon, Indo-Chinese (bot.) **13:**617
Cinqarbres, Jean, *see* Quinquarboreus, Johannes
Ciorhei, I. **13:**1369
Cippola, Carlo **13:**866
C.I.R.A., *see* Congregacion Israelita de la República Argentina
Circassians (ethnic gr.)
- human geography of Israel **9:**597
- Mamluks **11:**834
- Muslim life in Israel **9:**921
- Transjordan **15:**1318
- *illus:*
- - Kafr Kamā mosque **9:**920

Circle City (cmty., Ariz.) **13:**482
Circles, Socialist (orgn., E. Eur.), *see* Kruzhki
Circumcisi (Judaizing sect) **10:**398
- *see also:* ALBIGENSES

CIRCUMCISION **5:**567
- *contents:*
- - Introduction **5:**567
- - History **5:**568
- - Laws **5:**570
- - Ritual **5:**571
- - Medical Considerations **5:**572
- - Effect on Jewry **5:**575
- - Folklore **5:**576
- General
- - *Baruch, Rest of the Words of* **4:**276
- - birth **4:**1051
- - circumcision instruments **5:**309
- - Marranos **12:**1024
- - Mountain Jews **12:**479
- - oral promises **12:**18
- - Pentateuch **13:**241
- - practical Kabbalah **10:**637
- - Reform Judaism **12:**1443
- - sign of covenant **5:**1013
- - *talmid ḥakham* **15:**746
- - Talmud **12:**920
- - taxation **13:**21
- Individuals and
- - Abraham **2:**116
- - Ambrose of Milan's attack on **2:**801
- - Hadrian **7:**1054; **9:**246,248
- - Hagozer, Jacob and Gershom **7:**1123
- - Moses **12:**395
- - Tinneius Rufus **15:**1148
- Laws and Customs
- - astrological influence **3:**795
- - Commandments, the 613 **5:**769
- - commandment validity **12:**120
- - dances **5:**1265
- - Elijah's chair **6:**643
- - folklore **6:**1399
- - grace after meals **7:**840
- - impurity **13:**1406
- - *niddui* **8:**353
- - priestly blessing **13:**1063
- - proselytes **13:**1183
- - *sholem zokhor* custom **14:**1453
- Medicine
- - cancer **14:**1503
- - Nunbergs' psychiatric studies **12:**1272
- - talmudic medicine **11:**1184
- Forms and Attitudes
- - Christian Church **3:**216
- - Falashas **6:**1146
- - Islamic conception **9:**98
- - Judaizers **10:**397
- - Karaites **10:**780
- - Samaritans **14:**744
- *illus:*
- - text
- - *Amsterdam Minhagim Book* (1662) **12:**30
- - benediction, *Seder Berakhot* (1687) **4:**486
- - Chairs of Elijah **5:**306; **6:**643-645
- - embroidered binder **5:**291
- - *ḥallah*, traditional shape **6:**1419
- - Jesus submitting to **8:**1135
- - *mohel's* box **6:**1381
- - *sandak* **14:**827
- - Zipporah circumcising her sons **16:**1182

"Circumcision" (drg., de Hooghe) **14:**827
CIRCUSES AND THEATERS **5:**577
- sport **15:**291
- *illus:*
- - Samaria theater **14:**723

CIRCUS PARTIES (Byz. Emp.) **5:**578
"Circus Woman I" (sculp., Nadelman) **12:**754
Cirrhosis (disease) **14:**1503
Cirta (tn.), *see* Constantine
Ciselius, P. **8:**29
- *see also:* CHILDREN; SANDAK

Cisneros, Francisco, *see* XIMENZ DE CISNEROS, FRANCISCO
CISTERN **5:**578
- *illus:* text

Cistus (bot.) **9:**222
Citadel of David (Jer.), *see* David, Tower of
"Cities of the Plain", *see* SODOM AND GOMORRAH
Citium (city, Phoen.) **13:**478
CITROËN, ANDRÉ GUSTAVE **5:**579
CITROEN, PAUL **5:**580
- *illus:* text

Citron (law., Ger.) **10:**1497
Citron (bot.) **13:**617
Citron, William M. (polit.) **5:**899
CITRUS **5:**580
- flora of Israel **9:**222
- Israel **9:**706ff; **9:**345
- Judean Plain **9:**576
- rue **15:**269
- *illus:*
- - text
- - Haifa, loading Jaffa oranges **9:**763
- - Ramat Gan bottling plant **9:**817

Citrus-growers' Association (coop., Er. Isr.), *see* Pardes
CITY **5:**583
- ancient Israel **8:**611ff
- economic life, ancient **16:**1268
- Hillel's *takkanah* **8:**484
- levitical cities **11:**136
- Mesopotamia **16:**1490
- property in walled city **14:**675
- Sumer **15:**513; **16:**1484
- taxation **15:**841
- Volhynia **16:**208
- war and warfare **16:**273
- *illus:*
- - text
- - Arad, citadel and temple **3:**246; **5:**1168
- - Avedat (plan) **3:**943
- - Azekah, fortress **3:**1004
- - Beth-Cherem, citadel (plan) **4:**717
- - Canaanite and Israelite cult places **5:**1163-1168
- - Israelite house **3:**338; **5:**938
- - Lachish **3:**337; **10:**1333
- - Megiddo **3:**316; **11:**1223-1226
- - *see also:* COMMUNITY; ELDER

City, Apostate, *see* IR HA-NIDDAḤAT
City, Greek, *see* Polis
City, Levitical, *see* LEVITICAL CITIES
City College (N.Y.) **12:**1085
City-kingdom, *see* City-state
City of David, *see* David, City of
CITY OF HOPE NATIONAL MEDICAL CENTER (U.S.) **5:**590
- *illus:* text

CITY OF REFUGE **5:**591
- banishment **4:**163
- blind exempt from **13:**226
- Commandments, the 613 **5:**769
- Davidic levitical cities **9:**116
- elders **6:**578
- hospitality **8:**1030
- Joshua, Book of **10:**276
- *Makkot* tractate **11:**808
- manslaughter **13:**227
- Pentateuch **13:**250
- perjurers exempt from **13:**289
- Philo **13:**414
- *illus:* text
- *see also:* BLOOD-AVENGER; LEVITICAL CITIES

City-state **5:**584
CIUDAD REAL (tn., Sp.) **5:**594
- Burriana **4:**1530
- Inquisition **8:**1383

CIUDAD RODRIGO (city, Sp.) **5:**594
Cividal, Abigdor **5:**595
CIVIDALE (tn., It.) **5:**595
Civil Court (Isr.) **9:**631ff
Civilização, A (period.) **4:**1331
Civilization, Beginnings of **13:**49
Civil law, *see Dinei Mamonot*
CIVIL MARRIAGE **5:**595
- *Contents:*
- - Jewish Law **5:**595
- - Differences of Opinion **5:**596
- - Halakhah in Practice **5:**597
- - State of Israel **5:**598
- *agunah* **2:**431
- conflict of laws **5:**885
- *see also:* MARRIAGE

Civil Rights, *see* EMANCIPATION; MINORITY RIGHTS
Civil Rights Movement (U.S.)
- New Left **12:**1031
- Protestant attitude toward **13:**1254
- *illus:*
- - Selma-Montgomery march **12:**931
- *see also:* MINORITY RIGHTS; NEGRO-JEWISH RELATIONS IN THE U.S.

CIVIL SERVICE IN ISRAEL **9:**623
- foreign service **9:**627
- governmental system **9:**617ff
- Palestine civil service **9:**603
- *tables:* text

CIVILTÀ CATTOLICA, LA (period.) **5:**599
CIVITA, DAVIT (David) **5:**600
Civitavecchia (tn., It.) **9:**1118
- Betar nautical school **9:**835

Civray (tn., Fr.) **15:**1288
C.I.Z. (hospital, Amst.), *see* Centrale Israëlietische Ziekenverpleging
Claims, *see* PLEAS
Claims Conference, *see* CONFERENCE ON JEWISH MATERIAL CLAIMS AGAINST GERMANY
Clairvoyance **13:**1158
Clajus, Johannes **8:**29
Clan **5:**894
Clanner, J. G. **8:**29
Clapp, Gordon **9:**447
- Arab Refugees **9:**378
- Middle East water **9:**385
- U.N. **15:**1550

Clara (tn., Arg.) **3:**431
- *illus:*
- - *Fondo Communal* management **3:**432

Clara de Hirsch Home for Working Girls (N.Y.) **12:**1079
Claremont (city, N.H.) **12:**1024
Claretie, Jules **15:**1055
Clark, A.P.S. **9:**828
Clark, Richard **8:**29
Clark, Samuel **8:**29
Clarke, Louis A. **12:**1376
Clarke, Orme **9:**632
Clarksburg (city, W. Va.) **16:**475
Clarksdale (city, Miss.) **12:**156
Clary (fam.) **15:**1012
Classen, David **9:**1450
Classes, social
- Second Temple era **16:**1275
- socialism **15:**41

Clauberg, Karl **5:**85
- Auschwitz experiments **3:**855
- Ravensbrueck experiments **13:**1583

CLAUDEL, PAUL **5:**600
CLAUDIAN (Claudius Claudianus; poet) **14:**234
CLAUDIUS (Rom. emp.) **5:**600
- *Acts of Alexandrian Martyrs* **2:**595
- Agrippa I **2:**416
- Alexandrian Jews **2:**589
- anti-Semitism **3:**90
- chronological chart **8:**766-767
- Dorotheus' mission **6:**176
- Greek education in Egypt **8:**297
- population **13:**871
- Rome and Judea **8:**638
- Tiberias **15:**1132
- vestments of high priest **6:**1135

CLAUDIUS IOLAUS (Julius; Phoen. hist.) **7:**893
- Dor in writing of **6:**172

Claudius Tiberius Policarmos **16:**872
- *illus:*
- - Stobi synagogue **12:**238

Clauser, Jacob **9:**1543
Clava (fam.) **5:**226
Clavering, Robert **8:**29
Clavicula Salomonis (wk.) **10:**635
Clay **9:**810ff; **16:**661
- *illus:*
- - chemical composition **9:**811
- - Qumran pen cases **16:**668

Claymond, John **8:**29
Cleanliness, *see* HYGIENE
Cleanliness, ritual, *see* PURITY AND IMPURITY, RITUAL
Cleanliness Society (Jer.) **9:**1450
CLEARCHUS OF SOLI **7:**893
- Jews, reference to **7:**888
- Jews in Asia Minor **3:**746

Clejan, Vera, *see* CALIN, VERA
Clemenceau, Georges **9:**310
CLEMENT III (antipope) **5:**601
- forced converts **5:**1138

CLEMENT III (pope) **5:**601
CLEMENT IV (pope) **5:**601
- Avignon **3:**964; **3:**965
- censorship in Aragon **4:**215
- Jews, attitude to **13:**854
- Meir ben Simeon **12:**249
- Naḥmanides **12:**776
- papal bull **4:**1496

- Spain **15:**232
Clement V (pope) **13:**855
CLEMENT VI (pope) **5:**601
- Black Death **4:**1066
- history chart **8:**766-767
- Jews, attitude to **13:**855
- papal bull **4:**1496
CLEMENT VII (pope) **5:**601
- Giovanni, Maria **7:**588
- history chart **8:**766-767
- Jews, attitude to **13:**856
- Mantino, Jacob **11:**895
- Reuveni, David **14:**114; **14:**248
CLEMENT VIII (pope) **5:**602
- censorship **10:**1503
- Jews, attitude to **13:**858
Clement IX (pope) **13:**858
CLEMENT X (pope) **5:**602
- Jews, attitude to **13:**858
CLEMENT XII (pope) **5:**602
- Jews, attitude to **13:**859
CLEMENT XIII (pope) **5:**602
- Jews, attitude to **13:**859
CLEMENT XIV (pope) **5:**602
- Jews, attitude to **13:**859
Clemente, Francisco **15:**1270
Clementis, Vlado **14:**1654
CLEMENT OF ALEXANDRIA (Ch.F.) **5:**602
Clenardus, Nicolaus **8:**29
CLEODEMUS MALCHUS **5:**603
- biblical history **8:**304
- Greek literature **7:**893
- Greeks and Jews **8:**300
CLEOPATRA I (q., Egy.) **5:**603
CLEOPATRA II (q., Egy.) **5:**603
CLEOPATRA III (q., Egy.) **5:**603
- Aristobulus III **3:**442
- Costobar **5:**990
- Jewish generals **2:**922
- Nabatea **12:**742
- Samaritans **14:**730
CLEOPATRA VII (q., Egy.) **5:**604
- Alexandra **2:**587
- Herod I **3:**853; **8:**379
CLEOPATRA OF JERUSALEM (w. of Herod) **5:**604
- *geneal. table:* **8:**377
Clerc, Jean Thomas **3:**809; **8:**29
Clericus, David **8:**29
Clericus, Samuel, *see* Clark, Samuel
Clerke, Richard, *see* Clark, Richard
CLERMONT-FERRAND (city, Fr.) **5:**604
- forced conversion **3:**169
- *illus:*
- - Rue des Quatre Passeports **7:**20
CLERMONT-GANNEAU, CHARLES **5:**605
- Jerusalem **9:**1521ff
- Qumran **13:**1430
- Shapira fragments **14:**1302
CLERMONT-TONNERRE, COUNT STANISLAS DE **5:**605
CLEVELAND (city, O.) **5:**606
- *Contents:*
- - Early Life **5:**606
- - Early Employment **5:**607
- - Social and Cultural Life **5:**608
- - Mass Immigration **5:**609
- - Post-World War I **5:**610
- - Religious Life: 20th Century **5:**610
- - Post-World War II **5:**611
- - Movement to Suburbs **5:**611
- - Influence of Israel **5:**612
- - Cultural Life **5:**612
- history chart (1837; 1855) **8:**766-767
- museum **12:**538
- Ohio **12:**1344ff
- *illus:*
- - text
- - N.U.S.J. Rally **15:**1655
Cleveland (city, Miss.) **12:**156
Cleveland Conference (rab.) **8:**766-767
Cleveland Jewish World (newsp.) **13:**1055
CLEVES (tn., Ger.) **5:**612
CLEVES GET (divorce controversy) **5:**613
- Aaron Simeon of Copenhagen **2:**24
- Abraham Abusch ben Ẓevi Hirsch **2:**130
- *illus:* text
Cleynaerts, Nicolaus, *see* Clenardus, Nicolaus
Clichy, council of (626-627) **5:**547
Clifton (city, N. J.), *see* PASSAIC-CLIFTON
CLIMATE OF ISRAEL **9:**181
- human geography **9:**571ff
- Jerusalem **9:**1514
- *illus:*
- - flash flood in the Negev **9:**185
- - rain clouds, Beth-Shean valley **9:**187
- - snowfall, Jerusalem **9:**188
- *maps:*
- - dew nights, annual number **9:**187
- - potential evaporation **9:**184
- - rainfall, 1921-60 means **9:**186
- - temperature
- - - annual means **9:**190
- - - January means **9:**192
- - - July means **9:**193
- *tables:*
- - dew nights, average values 1945-52 **5:**1601
- - rainfall **13:**1521,1522
- - temperatures, Tel Aviv and Jerusalem means **9:**189
Climate Research in Israel **9:**193ff
"Climax" (drg., Beardsley) **6:**775
Clinical medicine **11:**1197
Clisson (tn., Fr.) **4:**1383
Clodius, David **8:**29
Clodius, J. C. **8:**29
Clogory (tn., Pol.) **3:**842
CLOOTS, JEAN BAPTISTE DU VAL-DE-GRÂCE, BARON DE **5:**615
- *illus:* text
CLORE, CHARLES **5:**616
CLOTHAIRE II (k. of the Franks) **5:**616
- anti-Jewish legislation **13:**103
Clothes, clothing, *see* DRESS; TAILORING; TEXTILES
Clouts, Sydney **15:**209
Club Démocratique des Fidèles (Fr.) **5:**1072
CLUJ (city, Rum.) **5:**617
- Transylvania **15:**1342ff
- *illus:*
- - text
- - *ḥevra kaddisha* minutes **15:**1343
CLUNY (tn., Fr.) **5:**619
Cluny, Disputation of **5:**619
Cluny, Statutes of (1301) **5:**619
CLURMAN, HAROLD **5:**619
Cluverus, J. **8:**29
Clysma, Gulf of (Egy.) **14:**15
Cnidus (anc. city, Gr.) **7:**868
Cnollen, Adam Andreas **8:**29
Cnollen, J.N. **8:**29
Coal **9:**814; **11:**1439ff
Coalition government, Israel **9:**613ff
Coastal Plain (Isr.) **9:**570ff
Coats of arms, *see* HERALDRY
COBB, LEE J. **12:**465
Cobbling **5:**1051
Coblentz, Adolphe **16:**549
Coblentz, Edmond **16:**549
Cobra (art. gr., Belg.) **2:**553
Cobra (zool.) **6:**36; **9:**226
COBURG (city, Ger.) **5:**619
- *illus:* text
Coburg Pentateuch (14th cent. illum. ms.) **4:**967; **6:***fcg.* 427; **12:**1251
COCA (tn., Sp.) **5:**620
Cocceians (theol. school) **5:**620
COCCEIUS, JOHANNES **5:**620
- Hebraists **8:**41
Cochabamba (city, Bol.) **4:**1188
COCHEM (tn., Ger.) **5:**620
COCHIN (city, state, Ind.) **5:**621
- *Contents:*
- - Antiquities of Jews **5:**621
- - Rajahs and Jewish Mudaliar **5:**623
- - Dutch Period 1663-1795 **5:**623
- - Religious Works **5:**625
- - Contacts with Oriental Diaspora **5:**626
- - Hebrew Printing **5:**626
- - Holy Land **5:**627
- - In Israel **5:**627
- - Contemporary Period **5:**628
- Al-Raḥbah **13:**1516
- Amsterdam delegation **13:**272
- Bene Israel **4:**498
- Buchanan, Claudius **4:**1437
- Divekar, Samuel Ezekiel **6:**111
- dress **6:**219
- Feinstein, H. J. **6:**1213
- Ḥanukkah lamps **7:**1315
- India **8:**1350ff
- Israel community **9:**503
- sickness **14:**1501
- *illus:*
- - text
- - Ḥanukkah lamps **7:**1310,1314
- - manumission bill **14:**1663
- - Paradesi synagogue **8:**1352
- - record of privileges **8:**1351
- - Simḥat Torah service **11:**401
- - synagogue stamp **15:**335
- - wedding, Israel **11:**1049
Cocula (vill., Mex.) **11:**1460
Cocumbriel, Abraham **2:**668
Cocumbriel, Asach (Isaac) **2:**668
Codde (Coddaeus), G. Van Der **8:**28
Coddon, Samuel **12:**36
Code of Hammurapi, *see* HAMMURAPI (Code)
Codes of Jewish law, *see* CODIFICATION OF LAW
Codex, Bible, *see* BIBLE, (Canon)
Codex Alexandrinus (ms.) **15:**147
Codex Amiatinus (mss.) **3:**508
Codex Neofiti I (Targum) **4:**845
Codex Reuchlinianus (ms.) **16:**1461
Codex Sinaiticus (ms.) **15:**147
Codex Theodosianus (ms.) **9:**257; **9:**258
CODIFICATION OF LAW **5:**628
- *Contents:*
- - Concept and Other Legal Systems **5:**629
- - In Jewish Law **5:**630
- - In the Mishnah **5:**631
- - The Talmud and Post-Talmudic Halakhic Literary Forms **5:**633
- - Variety of Literary Forms **5:**634
- - Geonic Period **5:**634
- - The Rif (Alfasi) **5:**637
- - Maimonides' Method **5:**638
- - Reactions to Maimonides' Approach **5:**641
- - To Compilation of Turim **5:**643
- - Ba'al ha-Turim **5:**645
- - Joseph Caro **5:**647
- - Shulḥan Arukh **5:**649
- - Moses Isserles (Rema) **5:**650
- - Reactions to Shulḥan Arukh **5:**651
- - Acceptance of Shulḥan Arukh **5:**653
- - After the Shulḥan Arukh **5:**655
- Development **12:**118; **12:**122; **12:**132
- - Bet Hillel and Bet Shammai **4:**740ff
- - conflict of laws **5:**882ff
- - *geonim* **7:**316
- - methods **2:**200,202; **5:**890ff
- - Middle Ages **10:**392
- - Mishnah redaction **10:**372
- - Poland **13:**730
- - Pumbedita **13:**1384
- - rabbinate decline **13:**1452
- - *rishonim* **14:**192ff
- - Sanhedrin, post-Temple **9:**243
- - *savoraim* **14:**921
- - *she'iltot* **2:**449
- - tradition **15:**1310
- - Usha, Synod of **16:**18
- - *see also:* HALAKHAH; MA'ASEH; MISHPAT IVRI; SHULḤAN ARUKH; TAKKANOT
- Literature **11:**330; **11:**333
- - codes **11:** 330ff
- - *issur ve-hetter* **9:**1086ff
- - Mishnah **12:**93
- - responsa **14:**83ff
- - *sheiltot* **2:**449
- - *tosafot* **15:**1278
- - Talmud, Babylonian **15:**755
- - Talmud, Jerusalem **15:**776
- Movements
- - Islam **9:**100
- - Kabbalah **10:**639ff
- - Pharisees **13:**364-5
- - Samaritans **14:**1605; **14:**1607; **14:**727
- Personalities
- - Abraham B. Isaac of Narbonne **2:**146
- - Caro, Joseph **5:**195
- - Crescas, Ḥasdai **5:**1081
- - Eliezer ben Hyrcanus **6:**621
- - Hillel **8:**482
- - Jacob ben Asher **9:** 1214
- - Maimonides **11:1214**
- - Meir **11:**1241
- - Naḥmanides **12:**780
- - Rabad **2:**138
- - Shammai **14:**1292
- - Shneur Zalman of Lyady **14:**1432
- - Sirkes, Joel **14:**1620
CODREANU, CORNELIU ZELEA **5:**656
Cody (tn., Wyo.) **16:**680
COELE-SYRIA **5:**656
COEN, ACHILLE **8:**545
Coen, C. **5:**453
COEN, GIUSEPPE (art.) **3:**598
Coen, Giuseppe (It.) **9:**1129
COEN, GRAZIADIO VITA ANANIA **5:**657
- Carmi, Isaiah Hai **5:**187
Coen, Hannaniah Elhanan, *see* COEN, CRAZIADIOVITA ANANIA
Coenaculum, *see* Last Supper, Church of the
Coesfeld (tn., Ger.) **3:**842
Coffee (r., U.S.) **15:**1207
COFFIN **5:**657
- ancient use of **4:**1518
- funerary reliefs **8:**653
- types of **4:**1519
- *illus:*
- - anthropoid lid **3:**314; **4:**761
- - Philistine coffin lid **13:**401
- *see also:* BURIAL; OSSUARIES AND SARCOPHAGI
Cohabitation, Sexual, *see* SEX
Cohan, Charles S. **12:**266
COHEN (Br. fam.) **5:**658
- *geneal. table:* text
COHEN (Br. mer. fam.) **5:**661
Cohen (Du. fam.) **3:**486; **12:**980
Cohen (Ger. fam.) **7:**1279
COHEN (It. fam.) **5:**661
- Azulai family **3:**1016
COHEN (U.S. fam.) **5:**662
Cohen (fam., N. C., U.S.) **12:**1218
Cohen (U.S. sol., trav.) **15:**1350

Cohen, Aaron **12:**1218
Cohen, Abner **15:**1340
Cohen, Abraham (stlr., Utica) **16:**34
Cohen, Abraham (bsmn., U.S.) **15:**329
COHEN, ABRAHAM (r., Eng.) **5:**663
– sermons **8:**957
Cohen, Abraham Hyam (cantor, U.S.) **5:**679
Cohen, Abraham Myers (bsmn., N.Y.) **12:**1067
Cohen, Ada **16:**819
Cohen, Albert (Er. Isr.) **11:**194
Cohen, Albert (Fr.) **7:**184
Cohen, Albert (It.) **11:**1173
COHEN, ALBERT (nov.) **5:**664
Cohen, Albert K. (criminol.) **5:**1109; **15:**68
COHEN, ALEXANDER H. **15:**1080
COHEN, ALFRED MORTON **5:**665
Cohen, Alroy **10:**1492
Cohen, Andrew (sport., U.S.) **15:**301
COHEN, SIR ANDREW (Br. govt. offic.) **5:**665
– *geneal. table* **5:**659
Cohen, Armond **5:**610
COHEN, ARTHUR (law., Eng.) **5:**666
– family **5:**658
– *geneal. table* **5:**659
COHEN, ARTHUR (econ., Ger.) **5:**666
Cohen, Arthur A. (publ., U.S.) **13:**1377
Cohen, Astruc, *see* ASTRUC SAUL HA-KOHEN
Cohen, Barrow E. **12:**1071
Cohen, Barry **15:**27
Cohen, Ben (racing exec., U.S.) **15:**310; **15:**311
Cohen, Benjamin (mer., Mor.) **14:**681
COHEN, BENJAMIN (Du. fin.) **5:**666
Cohen, Benjamin (U.S. r.) **10:**1561
Cohen, Benjamin I. (bnk., U.S.) **5:**662
Cohen, Sir Benjamin Louis (Br. cmty. fig.) **5:**661
Cohen, Benjamin S. (bsmn., Eng.) **10:**44
COHEN, BENJAMIN VICTOR (law., U.S.) **5:**667
Cohen, Bernard (art., Br.) **5:**671
Cohen, Bernard (Kimberley) **10:**1011
Cohen, Sir Bernard Waley **5:**685
Cohen, Bezalel **14:**387
COHEN, BOAZ **5:**667
– responsa studies **14:**87
Cohen, Carl Edward, *see* BRANDES, CARL EDVARD
COHEN, CHAPMAN **5:**667
COHEN, DAVID (Du. hist.) **5:**668
– Committee for Special Jewish Affairs **2:**902; **3:**760
– Holocaust **8:**897
– Joodse Raad **2:**902
– Wiener Library **16:**503
Cohen, David (Fr. anthro.) **3:**39
Cohen, David (educ., U.S.) **16:**760
Cohen, David (r., Isr.) **12:**910
Cohen, David I. (U.S. bnk.) **5:**662
Cohen, David Isaac (14th cent.) **8:**1260
Cohen, David of Corfu (r.) **13:**1449
Cohen, Dennis David Myer **15:**1479
Cohen, D. J. **3:**385
Cohen, E. (sport., U.S.) **15:**317
Cohen, Edward (polit. Austr.) **13:**808
Cohen, Edward (bnk., U.S.) **14:**161
Cohen, Elḥanan **7:**980
COHEN, ELI **5:**668
– history chart **8:**766-767
COHEN, ELLIOT ETTELSON **10:**310
– *Commentary* **5:**792
– public relations **13:**1362
Cohen, Emanuel **12:**38
COHEN, EMIL WILHELM (Dan. min.) **5:**669
Cohen, Ephraim **14:**1005
COHEN, ERNST JULIUS **5:**669
Cohen, Esperance **12:**1464
Cohen, Ethel A. Waley **10:**1059
Cohen, Felix (philos., U.S.) **5:**683
Cohen, Florence Friedlander **5:**113
COHEN, FRANCIS LYON **5:**670
– chaplaincy, Jewish **11:**1568 **4:**1219
– Syndey **15:**565
Cohen, Fré **4:**1219
Cohen, Frederick E. **5:**1567
Cohen, Friedrich **13:**1366
Cohen, G. (sport., U.S.) **15:**313
Cohen, Gabriel (publ., U.S.) **8:**1362
Cohen, Gershom (print.), *see* Kohen, Gershom ben Solomon ha-
Cohen, George (publ., Can.) **5:**113
Cohen, George Judah (mer., Austr.) **3:**880
COHEN, GERSON D. **16:**1266
Cohen, Gustav (Zion.) **16:**287
COHEN, GUSTAVE (hist., Belg.) **5:**670
– theater **15:**1055
Cohen, H. (arch., Fr.) **3:**301
Cohen, H. (cmty. ldr., Sp.) **11:**684
Cohen, H. A. (ed.) **6:**734
Cohen, Ḥaim **14:**256
Cohen, Hal **13:**1361
Cohen, Hannah, *see* Rothschild, Hannah
Cohen, Hannah Floretta **5:**661
Cohen, Harlan **15:**316
COHEN, HAROLD (art., Br.) **5:**671
Cohen, Harold Edward (polit., Austr.) **13:**809
Cohen, Harold Leopold (mer., Br.) **5:**661
COHEN, HARRIET **5:**671
COHEN, HARRY **5:**671
Cohen, Haskell **13:**1361
Cohen, Ḥayyim (r., Ger.) **7:**86
Cohen, Hayyim (r., Belor.) **15:**13
Cohen, Ḥayyim (indus., Baku) **4:**119
COHEN, HAYYIM J. (schol.) **1:**28
Cohen Henriques, Jacob, *see* Henriques, Jacob Cohen
Cohen, Henry (jur., Austr.) **10:**1492
COHEN, HENRY (r., U.S.) **5:**671
– Texas **15:**1035
COHEN, HENRY BARON (physic., Eng.) **5:**672
Cohen, Henry Isaac (polit.,Austr.) **10:**1492; **13:**809
Cohen, Herman (racing exec., U.S.) **15:**311
Cohen, Herman M. (r., U.S.) **12:**38
COHEN, HERMANN (philos., Ger.) **5:**673
– *Contents:*
– – General **5:**673
– – Kant and Marburg System **5:**673
– – Defense of Judaism **5:**674
– – God in Marburg System **5:**674
– – Religion **5:**675
– – Correlation **5:**676
– apologetics **3:**200
– Atlas, Samuel **3:**829
– commandments, reasons for **5:**789
– evil **7:**777
– existentialism **6:**1042ff
– free will **7:**130
– God **7:**664; **7:**668
– holiness **10:**874
– justice **10:**476
– Kant, Immanuel **10:**743
– Kantian ethics **6:**323
– letters **11:**61
– nature **12:**890
– Neo-Kantianism **13:**418
– philosophy **13:**452; **13:**460ff
– prophecy **13:**1179
– redemption **14:**7
– revelation **14:**124
– Rosenzweig, Franz **14:**300ff
– *Ru'aḥ ha-Kodesh* **14:**367
– Sabbath 10:321
– soul's immortality **15:**180
– Torah **15:**1242
– truth **15:**1414
– *illus:*
– – portrait (etch., H. Struck) **8:**749
Cohen, H.P. (print., Isr.) **2:**564
COHEN, I. BERNARD **5:**676
COHEN, IRVIN J. **11:**1206
Cohen, Irwin **15:**311
Cohen, Isaac (It. ceramist) **5:**662
Cohen, Isaac (physic., U.S.) **13:**229
Cohen, Isaac (stlr., Scot.) **7:**602
Cohen, Isaac (theat. owner, Eng.) **15:**1086
Cohen, Isaac (Ir. r.) **6:**249; **8:**1466
Cohen, Isaac ben Abraham (kab.) **10:**542
COHEN, ISAAC KADMI (Fr. Zion.) **5:**677
Cohen, Isaac Seligman (Ger.) **12:**1421
Cohen, Isadore (Los Angeles) **11:**499
Cohen, Isidor (Miami) **11:**1477
Cohen, Israel (It.) **16:**115
COHEN, ISRAEL (au., Eng.) **5:**677
Cohen, Israel (mer.) **15:**1044
COHEN, ISRAEL (lit. crit.) **5:**678
Cohen, Israel I. (U.S.) **5:**662
Cohen, Jack (Br. philan.), *see* COHEN, SIR JOHN EDWARD
Cohen, Sir Jack Brunel **5:**661
Cohen, Jacob (It. ceramist) **5:**662
Cohen, Jacob (magis., U.S.) **14:**160
Cohen, Jacob (r., Ger.) **8:**827
Cohen, Jacob (au., Tun.) **15:**1449
Cohen, Jacob (law., Can.) **10:**1494
Cohen, Jacob I. (mer., U.S.) **5:**662; **16:**163
Cohen, Jacob I. (bnk., U.S.) **5:**662
COHEN, JACOB RAPHAEL (U.S. cantor) **5:**678
– Montreal **12:**284
Cohen, Jacques **5:**669
Cohen, J. J. (jur., Austr.) **10:**1492
COHEN, SIR JOHN EDWARD **5:**679
COHEN, JOHN MICHAEL **6:**785; **6:**787
Cohen, Jonah **15:**1394
COHEN, JOSEPH (Fr. law.) **5:**679
Cohen, Joseph (nov., Holl.) **6:**321
Cohen, Joseph (racing exec., U.S.) **15:**311
Cohen, Joseph H. (mfr., N.Y.) **12:**1085
Cohen, Joseph Simon (law., U.S.) **10:**1503
Cohen, Joshua I. **5:**663
Cohen, Josiah **13:**568
Cohen, Judah (Port.) **3:**498
COHEN, JUDAH (dipl., Alg.) **5:**680
– Algiers **2:**622
– Tunisia **15:**1444
Cohen, Judith **5:**662
Cohen, Julia Matilda (née Waley) **16:**251
COHEN, JULIUS BEREND **5:**381
Cohen, Lazar **6:**1411
Cohen, Leo **9:**1018
COHEN, LEONARD (Can. au.) **5:**115
Cohen, Sir Leonard Lionel (Eng.) **5:**661
COHEN, LEVI-ABRAHAM **5:**680
– Tangier **15:**792
Cohen, Levi Barent **5:**658; **14:**337
Cohen, Lewis **13:**808
COHEN, LIONEL LEONARD, BARON **5:**680
– family **5:**661
– sport **15:**308
– *geneal. table* **5:**659
Cohen, Lionel Louis **5:**658
– politics **13:**820
Cohen, Louis (Br. bnk.) **5:**658
Cohen, Louis Samuel (Br. mer.) **5:**661
COHEN, LYON **5:**680
Cohen, M. (sport.) **15:**314
COHEN, MARCEL **5:**681
– anthropology **3:**39
Cohen, Marco (Mordecai) **5:**122
Cohen, Mark **6:**274; **12:**1130
COHEN, MARTIN A. **1:**28
Cohen, Mattiyahu (Zion.) **9:**556
COHEN, MAXWELL **5:**681
– Canada **5:**111
Cohen, Menaḥem Raphael **4:**633
Cohen, Mendes (U.S. engin.) **5:**663
Cohen, Mendes I. (U.S. bnk.) **5:**662
Cohen, Meyer (Egn. fin.) **13:**42
Cohen, Meyer (r., U.S.) **15:**1538
Cohen, M. Henry **15:**790
Cohen, Michael **9:**1014
– *Ha-Levanon* **4:**1374; **7:**1178
COHEN, MORRIS (U.S. met.) **5:**381
Cohen, Morris (Dan. au.), *see* BRANDES, GEORG
COHEN, MORRIS ABRAHAM (sol., China) **5:**682
COHEN, MORRIS RAPHAEL (U.S. philos.) **5:**682
– U.S. literature **15:**1573
COHEN, MORTIMER JOSEPH **5:**683
Cohen, Moses (r., U.S.) **5:**359
Cohen, Moses (Zion.) **16:**1099
Cohen, Moses Isaac (r., Rhod.) **4:**1479
Cohen, Moshe (Isr. journ.) **7:**1316
Cohen, M. R. (r., U.S.) **4:**1380
Cohen, Mula, *see* Cohen, Shemu'el
Cohen, Myer M. **6:**1362
Cohen, Naphtali (nov., Fr.), *see* NEYRAC, PIERRE
Cohen, Naphtali (kab.), *see* KATZ, NAPHTALI BEN ISAAC
Cohen, Nat **15:**311
Cohen, Nathan **15:**1264
COHEN, NATHAN EDWARD **5:**683
Cohen, Nathaniel **5:**661; **5:**684; **16:**251
Cohen, Nina **12:**38
Cohen, N. W. **8:**569
COHEN, PAUL JOSEPH **11:**1124
Cohen, Peter **5:**411
Cohen, Philip Joseph **3:**878
– Sydney **15:**564
COHEN, PHILIP MELVIN **5:**684
Cohen, Philipp Abraham **11:**1438
COHEN, PHILIP PACY **5:**381
Cohen, Sir Rex Arthur Louis **5:**661
COHEN, ROBERT (Fr. hist.) **5:**684
Cohen, Robert (sport.) **15:**305
COHEN, SIR ROBERT WALEY **5:**684
– petroleum **13:**346
– United Synagogue **15:**1673
– *geneal. table* **5:**659
– *illus:*
– – Board of Deputies **6:**771
COHEN, RUTH LOUISA **5:**685
– family **5:**661
– *geneal. table* **5:**659
Cohen, S. (indus., U.S.) **5:**377
Cohen, Sam (S.W.Afr. mer.), *see* COHEN, SIMON
Cohen, Samuel (physic., Ger.) **5:**244

Cohen, Samuel (interp., Curacao) 12:993
Cohen, Samuel (Austr.) 15:564
Cohen, Samuel (sport.) 15:312
Cohen, Samuel (comp., Er. Isr.) 7:1471
Cohen, Samuel A., *see* Bohne, Samuel A.
COHEN, SAMUEL HERBERT 5:685
Cohen, Samuel Raphael, *see* COHEN, MARCEL
Cohen, Sir Samuel Sydney 8:339
COHEN, SELMA JEANNE 1:28; 5:1272
COHEN, SEYMOUR STANLEY 5:381
COHEN, SHALOM BEN JACOB 5:685
- Hebrew literature 8:183
Cohen, Shemu'el 13:47
COHEN, SIMON 5:686
- department stores 5:1546
Cohen, S. Joe 11:1203
Cohen, Solomon (Maharshakh) 7:876; 14:89
Cohen, Solomon Solis 16:533
Cohen, Toviah, *see* COHN, TOBIAS BEN MOSES
COHEN, WILBUR JOSEPH 5:686
Cohen, William 7:1360
Cohen, Woolf 11:1553
Cohen, Zalman 4:1417
Cohen, Ẓevi Hirsch, *see* HIRSCHKAHN, ẒEVI
Cohen and Isaacs (firm, U.S.) 15:1305
Cohen-Bacri (Alg. fam.) 4:1274
Cohen ben Maknin (fam.), *see* MACNIN
Cohen de Lara, Isaac 15:254
Cohen ibn Sūsān (fam.), *see* BENSUSAN
Cohen Lobato (fam.), *see* LOBATO
Cohen Melamed, Nissan 9:1591
Cohen Modon, Samson 11:898
Cohen-Scali, David 5:1428
Cohenstam, Aaron 6:425
Cohen-Tanoudjis (fam.), *see* TANUJI
COHN (Swiss fam.) 5:687
Cohn (U.S. fam.), *see* Kaspare Cohn
Cohn, A. (publ., Ger.) 13:1373
Cohn, Abraham 11:1551
COHN, ALBERT 5:687
Cohn, Arthur 5:687
COHN, BENEDICT 2:323
- aerodynamics 2:322
COHN, BERTHOLD 5:688
Cohn, Curt 10:1497; 10:795
COHN, EDWIN JOSEPH (U.S. chem.) 5:688
Cohn, E.J. (educ., Eng.) 10:1495
COHN, ELKAN 5:688
Cohn, Emil Ludwig, *see* LUDWIG, EMIL
COHN, EMIL MOSES 5:689
- dismissal 13:1455
- *JuedischeABC* 6:734
Cohn, Erich 5:405
COHN, FERDINAND JULIUS 5:689
- bacteriology 11:1197
COHN, FRITZ 5:689
Cohn, Georg 5:1537
COHN, GUSTAV 5:690
COHEN, HAIM 1:29; 5:690
COHN, HARRY 5:690
Cohn, Heinrich, *see* CONRIED, HEINRICH
Cohn, Herman (art., Hung.), *see* ALCONIÈRE, THEODORE
Cohn, Herman (plwrt., Ger.) 6:912
Cohn, I.J. (bibl., Isr.) 14:1426
Cohn, Isaac (polit., Aus.) 5:689
Cohn, Isaac Jojade (writ., Ger.) 14:523
Cohn, John 13:1587
COHN, JONAS 5:691
COHN, LASSAR 5:381
Cohn, Léo 15:425
- scouting 14:1038
COHN, LEOPOLD 5:691
Cohn, Manfred, *see* GEORGE, MANFRED
Cohn, Marcus (Mordecai) 5:687
- Basle 4:305
Cohen, Mark 15:309
COHN, MESHULLAM ZALMAN BEN SOLOMON 5:691
COHN, MILDRED 5:692
COHN, MORRIS MANDEL 8:1431
COHN, OSCAR 5:692
- textiles 15:1040
Cohn, Paul, *see* Cornea, Paul
Cohn, Raphael 12:140
COHN, TOBIAS BEN MOSES 5:692
- anatomy 2:930
- bloodletting 4:1119
- Conegliano, Solomon 5:871
- medicine 11:1194
- universities 15:1677
- *illus:*
- - text
- - *Ma'aseh Tuviyyah* 3:804; 5:983; 7:416,419
Cohn, William 3:650
Cohn-Bendit, Daniel 12:1034
- Israel 7:39
COHNHEIM, JULIUS 5:693
Cohn-Oppenheimer (apos.) 15:1166
COHN-REISS, EPHRAIM 5:693
COHN-WIENER, ERNST 3:598, 652
COHON, SAMUEL SOLOMON 5:694
COIMBRA (city, Port.) 5:694
- *illus:* text
Coimbra Bible (14th cent. illum. ms., Sp.) 5:695
Coin-clipping 6:751,1007; 12:1226
- *illus:*
- - Norwich account roll 12:1226
COINS AND CURRENCY 5:695
- *Contents:*
- - Ancient Palestine 5:696
- - - Pre-monetary Period 5:696
- - - Coinage Introduction 5:696
- - Judea, 5/4 Centuries 5:715
- - - Hellenistic Period 5:716
- - Jewish Coinage 5:716
- - - Hasmonean 5:716
- - - Herodian Dynasty 5:717
- - - Jewish War 5:719
- - - Bar Kokhba 5:719
- - Roman rule 5:720
- - - Procurators 5:720
- - - Judea Capta and Later 5:720
- - - City Coins 5:720
- - Talmudic Literature 5:721
- - - Metrology5:721
- - - Halakhah 5:722
- - Post-Talmudic Literature 5:722
- - - Halakhic 5:722
- - - Lexicographic-Metrological 5:722
- - - Incidental References 5:722
- - Palestine 5:723
- - - Ottoman Rule 5:723
- - - British Mandate 5:723
- - Camps and Ghettos 5:725
- - - Paper Currency 5:725
- - - Coins 5:726
- - - Theresienstadt 5:726
- - - Forgeries 5:727
- - State of Israel 5:727
- - - Law and Administration 5:727
- - - Mils of 5708/09 5:727
- - - Perutah Series 5:729
- - - Agorah Series 5:730
- - - Commemorative Coins 5:730
- - - Bank Notes 5:731
- General
- - banking 4:168
- - Israel exchange rates 9:758
- - *jahbadh* (coin tester) 14:886
- - jewelry 13:1013
- - medals 11:1168
- - mintmasters 12:60ff
- - silver 11:1431
- - weights 16:381ff
- - *see also:* NUMISMATICS
- History
- - community tokens 5:853
- - eonomic life 16:1269
- - Ereẓ Israel, 70 to 640 C.E. 9:238; 9:246
- - Hellenism 8:296
- - Khirbet Qumran 13:1432
- - Zealot ideals 16:949
- Types
- - Aelia Capitolina 9:1405
- - Bar Kokhba 4:229ff
- - "Ephraimiten" 6:811
- - Jerusalem coin 9:1578
- - *Judenpfennige* 10:406
- - Phoenician 13:471
- - Tiberias 15:1132
- - *Yahud* coins 8:627
- - *see also:* SHEKEL
- Motifs and Inscriptions
- - *etrog* 6:950
- - Greek influence 3:327; 3:506ff
- - inscriptions 16:668ff
- - names of Israel 12:809
- - Paleo-Hebrew script 2:684
- - pillar motif 13:523
- - Polish coins 12:61
- Halakhah
- - non-Jewish law, force of 6:55
- - overreaching 12:1392
- *illus:*
- - text
- - Acre city coins 2:222,223
- - Agrippa I 2:392
- - Alexander Yannai 3:509; 8:630
- - Antigonus II 3:66
- - Antiochus VII, for JohnHyrcanus 3:75
- - Antoninus Pius Ashkelon coin 3:165
- - Archelaus 3:333
- - Bar Kokhba 4:229-231; 6:1448
- - Caracalla 5:157
- - Danish ducat, Hebrew letters 5:1538
- - Hadrian 7:1055
- - Hasmonean shekel 3:322
- - Israel, firstborn redemption coin 6:1311
- - *Israel Liberata* 11:1169
- - *Judaea Capta* 9:110
- - Mattathias Antigonus 11:1357
- - musical instruments 12:569
- - Neapolis city coin 5:157
- - Neturei Karta monetary scrip 12:1003
- - Polish, Hebrew inscriptions 12:61; 13:727
- - Pontius Pilate 13:848
- - *shekel*, bronze 14:1348
- - *Shekel Yisrael* (68 C.E.) 9:109
- - Templers' coins 15:995
- - *Yahud* coin 3:322; 8:625
- - *see also:* NUMISMATICS
Coins and Medals Corporation (Isr.) 11:1174
Coition 4:1018
COJO, *see* WORLD CONFERENCE OF JEWISH ORGANIZATIONS
Cok Hagin son of Deulecresse 3:398; 6:748; 13:1015
COLBERT, JEAN BAPTISTE 5:733
COLCHESTER (tn., Eng.) 5:733
Colchicum (bot.) 6:1365
Cole, Louis M. 11:501
Colegio Israelita (instit., Mex.) 11:1457
COLEMAN, EDWARD DAVIDSON 5:734
COLENSO, JOHN WILLIAM 5:734
Coleridge, Samuel Taylor 6:775
- *illus:*
- - *Kinat Yeshurun* 12:641
Colin, Vladimir 14:423
Colitis (disease) 14:1503
Collateral, *see* SURETYSHIP
COLLATIO LEGUM MOSAICARUM ET ROMANARUM (bk.) 5:734
Collection of Israel Writers (journ.) 16:653
Collective, The (pion. gr., Sejerah) 5:946
Collectivism 10:969
Collectors Record Guild 13:1618
COLLEGE OF JEWISH STUDIES (Ill.) 5:735
College of Physicians and Surgeons (N.Y.) 15:1677
Collegiate School (S.A.) 12:1473
Collegiate Zionist League (U.S.) 15:450
Collegio Foa (rab. coll.) 16:107
COLLEGIO RABBINICO ITALIANO (rab. coll.) 5:736
- history chart 8:766-767
- library 11:192
- rabbinical seminaries 13:1464
Collegium Neophytorum (Rome) 4:265
Collem, A. van 6:320
Colle Val d'Elsa (tn., It.) 15:1467
Collier, William 8:28
Collin, C.E. 8:28
Collins, Anthony 5:1464
Collins, José 15:1081
COLLINS, LOTTIE 15:1080
Collioure (tn., Fr.) 14:353
COLM, GERHARD 5:736
Colman, George 10:1502
Colman, Jesse 14:834
Colman, Nathan 15:213
COLMAR (city, Fr.) 5:736
- Alsace 2:752ff
- archives 3:382
- Armleder 3:484
Colocasia (bot.) 13:617; 16:83
COLOGNA (DE), ABRAHAM VITA 5:737
- Notables Assembly 3:763
- *illus:* text
COLOGNE (city, Ger.) 5:738
- *Contents:*
- - History 5:738
- - Communal Structure 5:741
- - Printing 5:741
- - Modern Period 5:742
- commerce 15:1298
- Crusades 5:1135
- Germany 7:458ff
- history chart (321,1424) 8:766-767
- Jewish community 8:657
- library 11:192
- synagogue 15:620
- Zionism 16:1107
- *illus:*
- - text
- - medal for opening of synagogue 16:498
- - medieval *mikveh* 11:1538
Cologne Bible (15th cent.) 5:1304; 10:289
- *illus:* 13:361
Coloma (vill., Calif.) 5:56
COLOMBIA (rep.) 5:744
- *Contents:*
- - History 5:744
- Contemporary Period 5:746

- Latin America **10:**1451ff
- synagogues **1:**syn. list
- Zionism **16:**1124
- *pop. table:* text
Colombo, Perez **9:**281
COLOMBO, SAMUEL **5:**747
- *Rivista Israelitica* **14:**197
COLOMBO, YOSEPH **5:**747
Colomiès, Paul **8:**28
Colon (city, Pan.) **13:**53
COLON, JOSEPH BEN SOLOMON (Maharik) **5:**747
- Bertinoro, Obadiah **4:**698
- Caro, Joseph **5:**196
- *ḥiddushim* **8:**467
- Isaac of Corbeil **9:**22
- Judah ben Jehiel **10:**347
- Moses Esrim ve-Arba **12:**428
- Nathan, Mordechai **12:**854
- responsa **11:**337
- usury **12:**251
Colon, Joshua **15:**1455
Colon, Perez ben Joseph **5:**748
- Capsali, Moses ben Elijah **5:**153
Colonia (vill., Er. Isr.), *see* MOZA
Colonia Belez (stlmt., Arg.) **3:**421
Colonia Clara (stlmt., Arg.) **10:**750
Colonia Claudia Ptolemais Germanica (city, Er. Isr.) **2:**222
Colonia Lucia Septimia Severa Diospolis (city, Er. Isr.) **11:**619
Colonies and Colonization Schemes (pre-State), *see* Settlements and Colonization Schemes (pre-State)
Colonna, E. D. **9:**1111
COLONNE, JULES (Judah) EDOUARD **12:**686
Colono Cooperador (period.) **3:**432; **10:**750
COLOPHON **5:**748
- *Contents:*
- - Description **5:**748
- - Blessings **5:**749
- - Origin, Dates **5:**749
- - Felicitations **5:**750
- - Concluding Formulas **5:**751
- - Oldest Colophon **5:**752
- - Printed Books **5:**752
- *illus:*
- - text
- - Ben-Asher, Moses (896) **4:**468
- - David ben Benayah **4:**471
- - 14th cent. mss: **2:**734; **4:**1423
- - *Hovot ha-Levavot* (1489) **5:**785
- - Isaac ben Abraham ha-Levi (1106) **4:***fcg.* 812
- - Joel ben Simeon (1478) **8:**1271
- - Joseph ha-Zarefati (14th cent.) **4:**961
- - Joshua ben Abraham ibn Gaon **8:**1272
- - *Lehem Shelomo* (1597) **5:**279
- - Luzzatto, Israel David, *sheḥitah* and *bedikah* rules (1804) **6:**43
- - *Mantua Haggadah* (1560) **7:**1087
- - *Meshivat Nefesh* (1748) **10:**1347
- - *Mishneh Torah* (1475) **8:**1328
- - Pentateuch with Targum Onkelos (15th cent.) **4:**843
- - Rashi's Pentateuch commentary **14:**38
- - *Sefer ha-Ikkarim* (15th cent.) **2:**700
- - *Sefer Jossipon* (1475) **5:**861 **8:**1331
- - *Sha'ar ha-Gemul* (1490) **8:**1334
- - Solomon bar Raphael (1249) **13:**300
- *see also:* BOOKS; HAKDAMAH; INCUNABULA; MANUSCRIPTS, HEBREW
COLORADO (U.S.) **5:**753
- universities **15:**1680
- *illus:* text
- *pop. table:* text
Colorado Springs (city, U.S.) **5:**753
Colorni, Abraham **11:**898; **15:**462
COLORNI, VITTORE **5:**754
Colquhoun, Patrick **16:**68
Colton (city, Calif.) **8:**254
Columbia (city, Mo.) **12:**158
Columbia (city, S.C.) **15:**211
Columbia Haus (concen. camp) **5:**77
Columbia University (N.Y.C.) **12:**1120; **15:**1677
- bookplates, Hebrew **4:**1219
Columbus (city, Ga.) **7:**429; **12:**156
COLUMBUS (city, Ohio) **5:**755
- Ohio **12:**1344
COLUMBUS, CHRISTOPHER **5:**756
- America **2:**808
- Santangel, Luis de **4:**171; **14:**847
- Torres, Luis de **15:**1266
- Vecinho, Joseph **16:**82
- Zacuto, Abraham **16:**904
Columbus, Samuel **14:**928
Columbus Platform (Ref. Judaism, U.S.) **14:**26
- U.S. Zionism **16:**1145
Column, *see* PILLAR
Colunga, A.D. **4:**879
Colvill, A. **8:**28
COMA, HERZ **5:**757
Comando, Solomon **16:**1552
COMAY, MICHAEL SAUL **5:**758
Combund (orgn.), *see* Kombund
COMDEN, BETTY **15:**1081
Comentario (period.) **3:**424; **13:**1040
Comes Joseph **15:**1132
Comestor, Pierre **4:**881
Comfarband (orgn.) **5:**799
Comintern (orgn.) **5:**792; **5:**801ff
Comisión Coordinadora (Arg.) **16:**1124
Comitato Italia-Palestina **16:**1122
Comité Central Israelita (Urug.) **16:**12; **16:**1126
Comité Central Israelita de Méjico (Mex.) **11:**1458; **16:**1126
Comité Central Judío de Bolivia **4:**1189
Comité Contra el Nazismo y el Antisemitismo (Urug.) **16:**12
Comité Contra el Nazismo y el Antisemitismo (Arg.), *see* DAIA
Comité Cultural Uruguay-Israel **16:**1126
Comité de Bienfaisance Israélite de Paris **13:**378
Comité de Coordination des Organisations Juives en France **16:**1115
Comité de Défense des Juifs Persécutés en Allemagne (Fr.) **4:**1281
Comité de Défense Juive (Belg.) **4:**421
COMITÉ DES DÉLÉGATIONS JUIVES **5:**758
- history chart **8:**766-767
- Motzkin, Leo **12:**477
- Zionism **16:**1134
Comité Juif d'Action Sociale et de Reconstruction **5:**351
Comité pro-Palestina (Peru) **16:**1125
Comitetul Democrat Evreesc (Rum.) **14:**412; **16:**1135
Comité Uruguayo pro-Palestina **16:**1126
Comitiano, Mordecai, *see* COMTINO, MORDECAI BEN ELIEZER
COMMAGENE (state) **5:**760
Commandments, *see* MITZVAH
COMMANDMENTS, THE 613 **5:**760
- *azharot* **3:**1007
- bar mitzvah **4:**243
- Decalogue **5:**1435
- ethics **6:**933*f*
- God, existence of **5:**1081
- *Ha-Hinnukh* **7:**1126
- Karaism **10:**778
- Leviticus **11:**138
- Maimonides **11:**766ff
- Micah **11:**1483
- Saadiah Gaon **14:**551
- Samaritans **14:**741; **14:**755
- *Sefer ha-Mitzvot* **8:**242
- *Sefer Mitzvot Katan* **9:**22
- *Sefer Torah* **14:**1103
- Tablets of Law **15:**690
- *ẓiẓit* **16:**1187
- *illus:*
- - woman, three commandments **11:**1039
- *see also:* COMMANDMENTS, REASONS FOR; JUDAISM; MITZVAH; ORAL LAW
COMMANDMENTS, REASONS FOR **5:**783
- *Contents:*
- - General **5:**783
- - Hellenistic Literature **5:**784
- - Medieval Philosophy **5:**784
- - Modern Jewish Thought **5:**788
- - Kabbalah **5:**789
- Abrabanel **2:**107
- *Bahir, Sefer ha-* **4:**99
- Baḥya ibn Paquda **4:**106ff
- dogma **3:**658ff
- *Haec Sunt Verba Dei* **6:**1228
- *Hasidei Ashkenaz* **10:**531,570
- Kalam **13:**429
- Lazarus **13:**460
- Levi ben Gershom **11:**97
- Maimonides **11:**775
- Mendelssohn, Moses **13:**455
- Naḥmanides **12:**777
- Saadiah Gaon **13:**431; **14:**122
- Shammai **14:**1291
- *illus:* text
- *see also:* MITZVAH; THEOLOGY
Commandments, the Ten, *see* DECALOGUE
Commemorative coins **5:**730
Comment (period.) **12:**1003
Commentaries on the Bible, *see* BIBLE (Commentators)
COMMENTARY (period.) **5:**792
- publishing **13:**1376
Commentary to the Mishnah (Maim.) **11:**745ff
Commerce, *see* TRADE AND COMMERCE
Commercial center (Jer.) **9:**1472
Commercial Court (Isr.) **9:**631
Commercial law, *see Dinei mammonot*
Commissariat General aux Questions Juives **7:**34
Commission for Hebrew Nomenclature (Er. Isr.) **12:**811
Commission for Jewish Settlement (Komzet; U.S.S.R.) **4:**1044; **14:**468
Commission for Revision of Jewish Legislature (Rus.), *see* Pahlen Commission
Commission of Inquiry (Pal.), *see* PALESTINE, INQUIRY COMMISSIONS
Committee for Jewish Affairs (Pol.), *see* Jewish Affairs, Committee for
Committee for Jewish Affairs in Berlin **4:**656
Committee for Jewish Defence (Belg.), *see* Comité de Défense Juive
Committee for the propagation of Hebrew **2:**205
Committee for rescue from Nazi Terror **7:**761
Committee of Assistance (Rum.) **14:**408
Committee of Jewish Delegations, *see* COMITÉ DES DÉLÉGATIONS JUIVES
Committee of the National Institutions for Matters Pertaining to Jerusalem, *see* Jerusalem Emergency Committee
Committee on the Christian Approach (Prot. orgn.) **13:**1251
Committee on the Church and the Jewish People (Prot. orgn.) **13:**1249; **13:**1251
Committee on Jewish Law and Standards (U.S.) **13:**1460
- oral law **12:**1445
Commodiana (name for Jer.) **9:**1406
Commodus (Rom. emp.) **9:**251
- *Acts of Alexandrian Martyrs* **2:**595
- Samaritans **14:**731
Common law wife **5:**865
Common Market **9:**764
Communal Amenities, *see* AMENITIES, COMMUNAL
Communal autonomy, *see* COMMUNITY (Autonomy)
Communal center, *see* SYNAGOGUE (as communal center)
Communal law, *see* Public Law
Communal Regulations, *see* TAKKANOT; TAKKANOT HA-KAHAL
Communion with God, *see* DEVEKUT
COMMUNISM **5:**792
- *Contents:*
- - General **5:**792
- - Bolshevik Theory **5:**794
- - Soviet Practice **5:**797
- - World Movement **5:**801
- - Post World War II **5:**805
- anti-Semitism **3:**136
- Bund **4:**1502
- Israel **9:**398
- Israel Arabs **9:**1030
- Lenin **11:**13
- Marx **11:**1072
- New Left **12:**1031
- partisans **13:**148
- Po'alei Zion **13:**656
- Prague takeover **13:**975
- Protestants **13:**1254
- socialism, Jewish **15:**48
- Soviet Jews **16:**779ff
- Stalin **15:**326ff
- Trotski **15:**1405
- U.S. Jews **15:**1630
- Vatican **8:**912
- *illus:*
- - 'Jew and Angel of Death' (cartoon) **3:**153
- - Vitebsk *ḥeder* trial **16:**780
- *see also:* SOCIALISM
Communist Bund (Rus.), *see* Kombund
Communist International, *see* Comintern
Communist Manifesto **11:**1072
Communist Parties in Israel **5:**807
- Israel Arabs **9:**466
- labor movement **9:**853ff
- politics **9:**660ff
- Sneh, Moshe **15:**16
- *illus:*
- - Arab and Druze districts, votes cast, 1949-69 (table) **9:**1031
Communist University of the National Minorities of the West (K.U.N.M.Z.) **6:**913
COMMUNITY **5:**808
- *Contents:*
- - Antiquity **5:**809
- - Middle Ages **5:**810
- - - Character **5:**811
- - - Functions **5:**812

- - - Individual Centers **5**:813
- - Modern Variations **5**:823
- - - Introduction$5;823
- - - West Europe **5**:823
- - - Central Europe **5**:824
- - - East Europe **5**:826
- - - N. Africa **5**:827
- - - U.S. **5**:829
- - Post World War II **5**:832
- - - Introduction **5**:832
- - - Types **5**:836
- - - In Voluntaristic Environment **5**:851
- - - Polity **5**:852
- General
- - Baer, Yitzhak **4**:82
- - Cairo *Genizah* **16**:1342
- - Commandments, the 613 **5**:769*f*
- - ethics in Bible **6**:933*f*
- - fairs **4**:1353; **11**:1000
- - intermarriage **12**:164
- - Medina, Samuel de **11**:1213
- - pious **13**:504
- - titles **15**:1163
- - Tobias ha-Avel **15**:1183
- - *see also:* PHILANTHROPY
- History, Development **8**:722ff
- - Dead Sea sect **5**:1412
- - diaspora, Greco-Roman **6**:16
- - Essenes **6**:899
- - exilarchate **6**:1023
- - French Revolution **7**:152ff
- - Ḥasidism **7**:1397,1400
- - kibbutz movement **10**:965
- - *Memorbuch* **11**:1299
- - Omar, Covenant of **12**:1379
- - *pinkas* **13**:537
- - Politische Gemeinde **13**:832
- - seals **14**:1079
- - *see also:* AUTONOMISM; CITY; COUNCILS OF THE LANDS; DIASPORA
- Autonomy **3**:924; **3**:925
- - amenities **2**:805
- - documents **14**:1390
- - employment **16**:1302
- - enactments **11**:805
- - finances **6**:1280
- - fines **6**:1289
- - *ḥerem bet din* **8**:355; **8**:358
- - heretics **8**:360
- - *ḥezkat ha-yishuv* **8**:357
- - informers **8**:1365
- - millet **11**:1582
- - public authority **13**:1351
- - punishment **13**:1389
- - responsa **14**:88
- - *sheḥitah* **14**:1342
- - *takkanot* SHUM **14**:1479; **15**:264
- - taxation **15**:841ff
- - tax evasion **8**:1306
- - wills **16**:528
- Structure
- - *batlanim* **4**:325
- - *bet din* **4**:726
- - B'nai B'rith **4**:1144
- - chief rabbinate **5**:418
- - *gabbai* **7**:230
- - ḥakham bashi **7**:1146
- - *haver ir* **7**:1492
- - *ḥazzan* **7**:1542
- - *ḥevra kaddisha* **8**:442ff
- - Kultusverein **10**:1290
- - Landjudenschaft **10**:1405
- - matchmakers **14**:1254
- - nagid **12**:758
- - preacher **13**:998
- - rabbi **13**:1446ff
- - scribes **14**:1041
- - self-defense **14**:1124
- - *shamash* **14**:1292
- - *shtadlan* **14**:1462
- - Shtetl **14**:1466
- - *shulklapper* **14**:1477
- - sick care **14**:1498
- - sick, visiting of **14**:1497
- - societies, learned **15**:53
- - synagogue **15**:583
- - Tanzhaus **15**:805
- - yeshivot **16**:766ff
- - *see also:* ḤEVRAH, ḤAVURAH
- Various Countries
- - Algeria **2**:614
- - Czechoslovakia **5**:1189
- - Egypt **6**:487ff
- - Germany **7**:465
- - Greece **7**:868
- - Hungary **12**:952
- - Istanbul **9**:1088
- - Italy **9**:1118
- - Kurdistan **10**:1298
- - Latin America **10**:1452ff
- - London **11**:479ff
- - Majorca **11**:799
- - Netherlands **12**:990
- - New York City **12**:1091
- - Ottoman Empire **16**:1538,1547
- - Persia **13**:314
- - Poland **7**:865; **13**:725
- - Rumania **14**:387ff
- - Salonika **14**:701
- - South Africa **15**:191ff
- - Spain **15**:226ff
- - Toledo **15**:1202
- - Turkey **15**:1460
- - Valencia **16**:55
- - Venice **16**:99
- - *see also under various towns,countries*
- Israel
- - ancient Israel **8**:610ff
- - 70 to 640 C.E. **9**:243ff
- - eleventh century **9**:267
- - 1099 to 1291 **9**:272
- - governance **9**:606
- - Israel communities **9**:495
- - Israel population **9**:472; **9**:495
- - religious life **9**:888ff
- *Halakhah*
- - as legal person **10**:1568
- - family purity **15**:703
- - Jewish identity **10**:53; **10**:60
- - morality **10**:1481ff
- - suretyship **15**:525
- - *takkanot ha-kahal* **15**:728
- - *takkanot* interpretation **8**:1427
- *illus:*
- - text
- - Ancona, *Gemilut Ḥasadim* regulations (1746) **7**:375
- - Bratislava *bet din* **4**:721
- - contract with *ḥazzan* (1861) **12**:642
- - Council of the Four Lands, map of communities **5**:997
- - Cracow, Yiddish statute book (1595) **5**:1031
- - Dublin, *Takkanot u-Minhagim* **6**:248
- - Ferrara, tax collection regulations **6**:1233
- - Florence, *Hevrat Mattir Asurim* **9**:1136
- - Frankfort a/M, *Staettigkeit* **7**:84
- - Frankfort council **15**:516
- - Frankfort *Memorbuch* **11**:1300
- - Hartford, Conn., appointment of *shoḥet* and *ḥazzan* (1847) **7**:1360
- - Hesse-Darmstadt, register of assessment and taxes (1723-40) **6**:1281
- - Jewish Commissariat order re closing of central office **14**:461
- - Koblenz *Memorbuch* **10**:1120
- - Konice, *ḥerem* text **8**:347
- - Lima, marriage register **3**:386; **13**:324
- - Maria Theresa's *Juden-Ordnung* (1753) **3**:903
- - New York, Judah L. Magnes' letter re community debts **6**:1284
- - Plunge, Jewish fire brigade **11**:379
- - Poznan community register (1651) **3**:381
- - Pressburg, peace treaty with city of Tyrnau, 1717 **4**:1312
- - *Schulklapper's* mallet **14**:1477
- - Statute of Kalish (A. Szyk) **3**:922
- - *takkanot* of Ancona charitable society **15**:713
- - Venice region, register of circumcisions **3**:383
- - Western Wall on Jerusalem community seal **16**:469
- - Worms, register of financial transactions (1657-58) **6**:1280
- *maps:*
- - Afghanistan, Middle Ages and modern times **2**:327
- - Africa **2**:333
- - Albania **2**:523
- - Algeria **2**:613
- - Alsace **2**:751
- - Arabian Peninsula **3**:233
- - Argentina **3**:411
- - Asia, 1700 to 1945 **3**:741
- - Australia **3**:877
- - Austria **3**:887
- - Baden **4**:60
- - Bavaria, 10th-20th cent. **4**:347
- - Belgium **4**:418
- - Benjamin of Tudela, map of travels **4**:535
- - Bertinoro, Obadiah, map of travels **4**:698
- - Bohemia **4**:1173
- - Brazil **4**:1323
- - Bulgaria, 1878-1967 **4**:1481 **4**:1513
- - Burma **4**:1526
- - Byzantine Empire **4**:1551
- - Canada **5**:101
- - Chile **5**:462
- - China **5**:469
- - Columbia **5**:744
- - Crete, major medieval communities **5**:1089
- - Cyprus **5**:1180
- - Czechoslovakia **5**:1189
- - Denmark **5**:1536
- - Dominican Republic **6**:160
- - Ecuador **6**:360
- - Egypt
- - - end of 19th cent. **6**:500
- - - Hellenistic Period and Middle Ages **6**:486
- - England, Jewish settlements before 1290 **6**:749
- - Estonia **6**:917
- - Europe, Ashkenazi settlement, 6th-16th cent. **3**:719
- - expulsions, 100-1500 C.E. **8**:689
- - Finland **6**:1296
- - France
- - - Middle Ages and 1968 **7**:11
- - - Provence, medieval **13**:1261
- - Germany
- - - thirteenth cent. **7**:463
- - - twentieth cent. (1933 and 1970) **7**:487
- - Greece **7**:869
- - Guatemala **7**:956
- - Hungary **8**:1093
- - India **8**:1350
- - Iran **8**:1440; **13**:303
- - Iraq **8**:1459
- - Ireland **8**:1464
- - Italy
- - - major communities, 1450-1550, 1931 and 1970 **9**:1117;1113
- - - Southern, 12th cent. **3**:226
- - Latvia **10**:1463
- - Libya **11**:199
- - Lithuania **11**:363
- - Mexico **11**:1454
- - Moravia **12**:297
- - Morocco **12**:327
- - Netherlands **12**:973
- - New Zealand **12**:1128
- - Norway **12**:1222
- - Ottoman Empire **16**:1531,1533
- - Persia, *see* Iran
- - Poland **13**:715,719
- - Portugal **13**:920
- - Prussia **13**:1287
- - Rhodesia **14**:148
- - Roman Empire, mishnaic and talmudic periods **8**:643
- - Rumania **14**:391
- - Russia
- - - Bessarabia, 1897 **4**:707
- - - Birobidzhan **4**:1045
- - - Crimea **5**:1104
- - - Georgia **7**:424
- - - main communities outside Pale of Settlement **14**:453
- - - major centers of settlement, 1959 **14**:485
- - - Pale of Settlement **13**:25
- - South Africa **15**:183
- - Spain
- - - Burgos province, before 1492 **4**:1513
- - - Jewish and Converso communities, 1474 **15**:237
- - - Muslim rule period (11th cent.) **15**:223
- - Sweden **15**:546
- - Switzerland **15**:561
- - Tasmania **3**:877
- - Tunisia **15**:1431
- - Turkey **15**:1457
- - United States, *see* UNITED STATES OF AMERICA *(pop. tables)*
- - Venezuela **16**:90
- - Yugoslavia **16**:875

Community chest (Rus.) **5**:346
Community News (newsp.) **13**:1056
Community of Evangelian Jews (Rus.) **8**:522
COMMUNITY TOKENS (currency) **5**:853
- *illus:*
- - Amsterdam *ḥevra kaddisha* **12**:977
- - *kofer ha-yishuv* coupons **9**:355
- - Korets, monetary scrip **10**:1203

COMO (city, It.) **5**:855
Compagnia dei Musici (It.) **5**:124
Compass **14**:1413
Compass (orgn.), *see* Maẓpen
COMPASSION **5**:855
- forgiveness **6**:1433ff
- *see also:* LOVE

Compensation
- *ha'anakah* **7**:1003
- on divorce **12**:143
- wage delay **10**:1327
- *see also:* DAMAGES

Competition, Commercial **16**:1301
Compiègne (concen. camp) **7**:35; **8**:858
- art **3**:575

Complainte de Troyes (poem) **15**:1407
Complas (poems) **15**:1419
Complete Dictionary of Ancient and Modern Hebrew (Eliezer Ben-Yehuda) **4**:568
Complutensian Polyglot (Bib.) **4**:838
- Alfonso of Zamora **2**:607
- Ximenes de Cisneros **16**:688

Composing Room Incorporated (firm) **11**:47
"Composition" (lith., J. Friedlaender) **3**:625
"Composition in Brown" (paint., R. Lavie) Fig. 106 **3**-Art
"Composition with Heads of Dolls"

(paint., Aika Brown) Fig. 109
3-Art
COMPOUNDING OFFENSES **5**:856
– homicide, unintentional **5**:594
Comprad d'Arles (schol.) **13**:1264
COMPROMISE **5**:857
– *Contents:*
– – General **5**:857
– – *Pesharah and Biẓẓu'a* **5**:857
– – Desirability **5**:857
– – Nature **5**:858
– – Validity **5**:858
– actions delay **11**:253
– court practice **13**:954
– duress **12**:1399
– *see also:* ARBITRATION
Compsus ben Compsus **10**:732
COMPTROLLER, ISRAEL STATE **9**:619
Comrade Arthur, *see* ZYGELBOJM, SAMUEL MORDECAI
COMTAT VENAISSIN (terr.) **5**:859
– Avignon Jews **3**:964ff
– Beaucaire Jews **4**:363
– French Jewry **7**:16ff
– Jewish dialect **10**:440
– Pastoureaux **5**:1141
– *illus:*
– – baptism edict **3**:213
– – *Seder ha-Kunteres* (1765) **3**:965
COMTINO, MORDECAI BEN ELIEZER **5**:859
– Bashyazi, Elijah **4**:298
– Mizraḥi, Elijah **12**:182
Conakry (city, Guinea) **9**:439
Conant, Thomas Jefferson **8**:28
CONAT, ABRAHAM BEN SOLOMON **5**:861
– Ferrara **6**:1234
– incunabula **8**:1320ff
– typography **15**:1479
– *illus:*
– – text
– – *Beḥinat ha-Olam* **15**:1483
– – *Josippon* **8**:1331
Conat, Estellina **5**:861; **8**:1323
– *illus:*
– – *Beḥinat ha-Olam* **15**:1483
Concentration camps (Nazi Ger.), *see* CAMPS (Concentration and Extermination)
Concepción (city, Chile) **5**:465
Conception (biol.) **4**:1019ff
– *see also:* BIRTH CONTROL
Conceptions of God **7**:669ff
Concessions (Pol.), *see* ARENDA
Conciliation Internationale (orgn.) **7**:171
Concio, Abraham **5**:862
CONCIO, JOSEPH BEN GERSON **5**:862
Concise Dictionary of Judaism **6**:734
Concluding Celebration, *see* AẒERET
"Conclusion of the Sabbath" (paint., M. Oppenheim) **7**:1483
Concord (tn., Mass.) **11**:1112
Concord (city, N.H.) **12**:1024
Concordances, Hebrew
– *Concordantiae Bibliorum Hebraicae* **4**:1543
– *Erkhei Kinnu'yim* **8**:268
– *Heikhal ha-Kodesh* **11**:865
– Kasovsky **10**:809
– *Mirkevet ha-Mishneh* **3**:34
– *Oẓar Leshon ha-Kodesh* **7**:213
– *Oẓar Ma'amarei Ḥazal* **6**:553
– *Oẓar Ma'amarei Tanakh* **6**:553
– *Sefer ha-Zikhronot* **11**:134
– *Sefer shel R. Anshel* **3**:34
– *Tavnit Heikhal* **11**:865
– *Toledot Aharon* **2**:22
– *see also:* Dictionaries; ENCYCLOPEDIAS
Concordantiae Bibliorum Hebraicae (wk.) **4**:1543
CONCUBINE **5**:862
– adoption **2**:298
– civil marriage **5**:596
– Genesis, Book of **7**:390
– Hurrian customs **12**:1288
– Solomon **15**:100ff
– *illus:* text
CONDER, CLAUDE REGNIER **5**:865
– survey maps **11**:931
– Zionism **16**:1155
CONDITIONS (terms of contract) **5**:865
– civil and ritual law **12**:112
– contractual obligation **5**:928ff
– customs **12**:13
– divorce **6**:133
– gift **7**:562
– imprisonment for debt **8**:1304
– lease and hire **10**:1528
– loan **11**:415ff
– marriage **11**:1049
– oaths **12**:1295
– overreaching **12**:1392
– sale **14**:676ff
– suretyship **15**:526
– *Tevul Yom* **15**:1033
– *see also:* ASMAKHTA
Condottas (fin. privileges, It.) **12**:255; **16**:1290
Conduct, Rules of, *see* DEREKH EREẒ; ETIQUETTE
CONE (U.S. fam.) **5**:868
Cone, Caesar **5**:868
Cone, Claribel **5**:868
Cone, Etta **5**:869
Cone, Herman **5**:868
Cone, Marcus **15**:635
Cone, Moses Herman **5**:868
– *illus:* text
CONEGLIANO (fam.) **5**:869
– *illus:*
– – Jewish badge charter **9**:1132
CONEGLIANO (tn., It.) **5**:869
– synagogue **5**:618
– *illus:* text
Conegliano, Abraham Joel **5**:870
Conegliano, Carlo **12**:201
Conegliano, Emanuel, *see* DA PONTE, LORENZO
Conegliano, Geremia **15**:1678
Conegliano, Israel (physic.) **2**:660; **5**:870
Conegliano, Israel di (bnk.) **16**:196
Conegliano, Judah **5**:870
Conegliano, Rachele **15**:1678
Conegliano, Solomon **5**:870
Coneso, Aviasa, *see* Ha-Cohen, Aviasa
Coneso, Estenza, *see* Aragon, Estenza
Coney Island (section, N.Y.C.) **12**:1082; **12**:1107
Confederação Israelita do Brasil **4**:1330
Confederación Agrícola Israelita Argentina **3**:432
Confederación Juvenil Judeo Argentina **3**:426
Confederate States of America, *see* American Civil War
Conference for a New Politics (New Left) **12**:1032
Conference of Jewish Organizations (U.S.) **10**:66
CONFERENCE OF PRESIDENTS OF MAJOR AMERICAN JEWISH ORGANIZATIONS **5**:871
– Goldmann, Nahum **7**:725
– Jewish Labor Committee **10**:66
– Wexler, William **16**:479
CONFERENCE ON JEWISH MATERIAL CLAIMS AGAINST GERMANY **5**:872
– reparations **9**:383
– *see also:* REPARATIONS, GERMAN; RESTITUTION AND INDEMNIFICATION
CONFERENCE ON JEWISH SOCIAL STUDIES (U.S.) **5**:874
– scientific research **15**:55
Conference on Science, Philosophy, and Religion (U.S.) **10**:96
Conference on the Status of Soviet Jews (U.S.) **14**:499
Conférence Permanente des Oeuvres Sociales Juives de Bélgique **4**:424
CONFERENCES **5**:874
– *illus:*
– – Biltmore Hotel **15**:1633
– – Helsingfors **16**:1137
– – Mizrachi, Lida **16**:1099
– – U.J.A. **15**:1541
– – Ukrainian Council **15**:1515
– – Warsaw, rabbinical **16**:341
Confessing Church (Ger.) **8**:840; **8**:874
CONFESSION (leg. and crim.) **5**:877
– divorce **6**:130
– extra-legal execution **6**:1073
– informers **8**:1364; **8**:1372
– Inquisition **8**:1400ff
CONFESSION OF SINS **5**:878
– Abba bar Avina **2**:32
– *Al Ḥet* formula **2**:629ff
– *Amidah* **2**:844
– Bratslav Ḥasidim **12**:782ff
– Commandments, the 613 **5**:765
– Day of Atonement **5**:1379ff
– death **5**:1425
– execution **13**:962
– fast days **6**:1192
– forgiveness **6**:1433ff
– *Ne'ilah* service **12**:944
– repentance **14**:75
– sacrifice **14**:601
– *seliḥot* **14**:1134
– sin **14**:1590
– *illus:*
– – *"Ashamnu"* (drg., Levy) **2**:630
– *see also:* ATONEMENT; SELIḤOT; TAḤANUN
CONFINO, MICHAEL **5**:545
Confirmation, *see* BAR MITZVAH, BAT MITZVAH
CONFISCATION, EXPROPRIATION, FORFEITURE **5**:880
– *angaria* **2**:950
– despair of property **16**:774
– *ḥerem* **8**:344
– lease and hire **10**:1528
– loan cases **11**:416
– non-Jewish law, force of **6**:54
– *Sikarikon* **14**:1529
– talion **15**:741
– *illus:*
– – Majorcan Jews, account of confiscated property **11**:796
– *see also:* TAKKANOT
CONFLICT OF LAWS **5**:882
– *Contents:*
– – Definition **5**:882
– – Jewish Law **5**:882
– – Multiplicity of Rules **5**:883
– – Factual-Legal Nature **5**:886
– – Jewish and non-Jewish **5**:888
– – Foreign Law Applicability **5**:889
– autonomy, judicial **3**:928
– civil marriage **5**:598
– custom **12**:23
– Jewish Law development **12**:134
– *see also:* DINA DE-MALKHUTA DINA; MINHAG
CONFLICT OF OPINION **5**:890
– Academy on High **2**:208
– codification of law **5**:632ff
– custom **12**:11
– *halakhah* development **7**:1162
– Hillel and Shammai **4**:737; **8**:483; **14**:1291
– Ibn Abi Zimra **5**:1356
– Joshua ben Koraḥ **10**:282
– Mishnah **10**:1483; **12**:98
– peace **13**:198
– rabbinical authority **3**:910
– resolution of **14**:192ff
– responsa **14**:84ff
– sages **14**:647
Conford, Milton **15**:1534
CONFORTE, DAVID **5**:891
– Iscandari, Abraham **9**:76
– Jewish history **11**:349
– *Kore ha-Dorot* **8**:560
– Sambari, Joseph **14**:761
Conforte, Gabriel **5**:893
Confraternidad Judeo-Cristiana (orgn., Arg.) **3**:418
CONGO, DEMOCRATIC REPUBLIC OF **5**:893
– Corfu immigrants **14**:1172
– Israel's relations **9**:438
– Zionism **16**:1140
– *illus:*
– – Ben-Zvi, state visit **4**:579
– – paratroopers training in Israel **9**:443
Congregación Israelita de la Republica Argentina **3**:410
CONGREGATION (Assembly; bib. term) **5**:893
– Chieftain **5**:420ff
Congregation (inst., conc.), *see* COMMUNITY; Jewish People; SYNAGOGUE
Congress, General Jewish (Hung.) **8**:1092
Congress Bi-Weekly (period.) **2**:826
Congress Bulletin (period.) **13**:1026
CONGRESS FOR JEWISH CULTURE **5**:896
– Niger, Samuel **12**:1156
Congress of Argentinian Jewry (1916) **3**:414
Congress of Berlin (1878), *see* BERLIN, CONGRESS OF
Congress of Madrid (1880) **2**:650
Congress of National Minorities **12**:478
Congress of Vienna, *see* VIENNA, CONGRESS OF
Congress Weekly (period.) **13**:1051
Coniah (k., Judah), *see* JEHOIACHIN
Coniah ben Elnathan **6**:686
Conian (fam.), *see* CONEGLIANO
Conian, Israel (cmty. fig.) **13**:12
Conjeturas Sagradas (wk.) **2**:215
Conjoint Foreign Committee, *see* ANGLO-JEWISH ASSOCIATION
Conki, Abraham **8**:233
CONNECTICUT (state, U.S.) **5**:897
– intermarriage **15**:1590
– Ribicoff, Abraham **14**:152
– *illus:* text
– *pop. table:* text
Connecticut Jewish Ledger (period.) **5**:899
Connely, Thaddeus **8**:28
Connely, T.E. **8**:568
CONON I (Gr. au.) **7**:893
CONON II (mythographer) **7**:893
Conotou (tn., Dahomey) **9**:438
Conque, Abraham of Malaga **6**:307
Conquest of Canaan, *see* CANAAN, LAND OF
Conquest of the Desert International Exhibition and Fair (Isr.) **9**:765
Conquest of labor (lab. conc.), *see* *Kibbush ha-avodah*
CONRAD, VICTOR **5**:900
Conradin Bible (illum. ms.)

– *illus:* **2:**880; **7:**1113,1270; **8:**1013; **11:**659,814
Conrad Montferrat (Crus.) **9:**269
Conradus Aslacus Bergensis, *see* ASLAKSSEN, CORT
CONRIED, HEINRICH **12:**686
Cons, Emma **4:**350
Conscription of labour **10:**1320
Consecration, *see* HEKDESH
Conseil Représentatif des Juifs de France **7:**38
Consejo Central Sionista (Arg.) **16:**1124
Consejos y Documentos al Rey Don Pedro, see Proverbios Morales
Conservateur des Juifs (offic., Fr.) **13:**1260
CONSERVATIVE JUDAISM **5:**901
– General
– – Agus, Jacob **2:**435
– – America **2:**813
– – autonomy **3:**928
– – Finkelstein, Louis **6:**1293
– – Israel **9:**905ff
– – Jewish-Christian understanding **13:**1253
– – Jewish thought **13:**453
– – Kaplan, Mordecai **10:**751
– – Lieberman, Saul **11:**218
– – modern Judaism **10:**395; **10:**396
– – Music, Jewish **12:**650
– – Orthodoxy's opposition **12:**1489
– – Rabbinical Assembly **13:**1460
– – rabbi's office **13:**1448
– – Schechter, Solomon **14:**949ff
– – South Africa **15:**200
– – United Synagogue of America **15:**1673
– – U.S. **15:**1642ff
– – U.S. Zionism **16:**1145
– *Halakhah* **7:**1166
– – additional prayer **12:**534
– – dietary laws **6:**45
– – Jewish tradition **15:**1311
– – *ketubbah* formula **10:**929
– – non-Jewish wine **16:**540
– – oral law **12:**1444
– – organ in synagogue **12:**1454
– – prayer books **13:**991
– – proselytes **13:**1192; **13:**1193ff
– – sacrifices **14:**614
– – Torah reading **15:**1253
– *see also:* JEWISH THEOLOGICAL SEMINARY OF AMERICA, THE
Conservative Judaism (period.) **13:**1051; **13:**1460; **15:**1110
CONSERVATIVE PARTY, GERMAN **5:**906
Considerations and Opinions (pam.) **16:**641
Consigli(o) (fam.) **14:**354
CONSIGLI(O), AVTALYON (Ottavio) BEN SOLOMON **5:**907
– Rovigo controversy **14:**354
Consiglio, Jekuthiel **14:**354
Consistoire Central Israélite de Belgique (orgn.) **4:** 418ff
– Antwerp Jews **3:**169
CONSISTORY (orgn., Fr.) **5:**907
– Alsace-Lorraine **2:**756
– archives **3:**378; **3:**382
– Assembly of Jewish Notables **3:**764
– Besançon **4:**702
– Club Democratique des Fidèles **5:**1072
– Cohen, Joseph **5:**680
– community organization **5:**823; **5:**840
– Crémieux, Isaac Adolphe **5:**1075
– Dreyfus Affair **6:**229
– France **7:**24ff
– Napoleon **12:**824
– Paris **13:**108ff
– Rome **14:**251
– *illus:* text
Consolaçam as Tribulaçoens de Israel (bk.) **8:**557; **14:**1168; **16:**21
CONSOLO, FEDERICO **12:**686
Consonants (Heb. lang.) **16:**1572,1595
– *tables:*
– – articulation **8:**81
– – Latin transliteration **8:**79
– – pronunciation **8:**85
Constable (offic., Crete) **5:**152
CONSTANCE (city, Ger.) **5:**912
– council of **5:**548
– host desecration **8:**1043
– *illus:*
– – text
– – seal **14:**1077
Constant, Alphonse Louis, *see* Levi, Eliphas
CONSTANTA (city, Rum.) **5:**914
Constantia Neapolis (city, Er. Isr.) **11:**793
Constantin Brunner International Institute (The Hague) **4:**1419
Constantin Brunner Society, Berlin **4:**1419
Constantine (the Great; Rom. emp.)
– Aelia Capitolina status **9:**1405
– crucifixion abolished **5:**1134
– Ereẓ Israel **9:**255
– Greece **7:**871
– history chart **8:**766-767
– "New Jerusalem" **9:**1570
– protection of apostates **8:**653
– Samaritans **14:**731
– *illus:*
– – Mamre basilica **11:**839
Constantine II (Rom. emp.) **8:**653
Constantine (monk), *see* Cyril
CONSTANTINE (tn., Alg.) **5:**915
– Alconstantini family **2:**550
– Bonastruc, Isaac **4:**1200
– Church of Eleyona **12:**483
– Ereẓ Israel Jewry **9:**511
– Tunisia **15:**1431
– *illus:* text
CONSTANTINE VII PORPHYROGENITUS (emp., Byz.) **5:**915
– *Vision of Daniel* **5:**1290
Constantini, Sansone **2:**551, 942
CONSTANTINOPLE (city, Byz.) **5:**916
– Apulian exiles **3:**228
– dress **6:**216
– dyeing center **6:**328
– *ḥalukkah* **7:**1208
– Hebrew printing **8:**1326
– history chart (1453) **8:**766-767
– Jerusalem administration **9:**1438ff
– Jewish quarter **10:**87
– Ottoman Empire **16:**1531
– pilgrimage to Israel **11:**351
– Provence Jews **13:**1262
– Shabbetai Ẓevi **14:**1223; **14:**1243
– shipping **14:**1413
– *illus:*
– – text
– – *Extremos y Grandezas de Constantinopla* **2:**670
– – Russian *ḥalutzim* **14:**465
– – Shabbetai Ẓevi **14:**1241
– *see also:* ISTANBUL
Constantinus Afer (Africanus; monk) **6:**461; **11:**1187
Constantius (name; Rom. emps.), *see* Constantine
Constitution of Israel
– basic laws **9:**618
– historical survey **9:**374
– legislation **9:**650ff
– religious parties **9:**896
CONSTRUCTION **5:**919
– use of wood **16:**630
– *see also:* ARCHITECTURE; SYNAGOGUE
"Construction in Space . . ." (sculp., A. Pevsner) **3:**564
"Constructor" (paint., E. Lissitzky) **11:**306
Consultative Council of Jewish Organizations **2:**653
Contemplation, *see* MEDITATION
Contemporary Jewish Library (publ.) **14:**498
CONTEMPT OF COURT **5:**922
– *see also:* PRACTICE AND PROCEDURE
Conti, Vincenzo **5:**1077; **16:**1019
– *illus:*
– – *Kiẓẓur Mordekhai ve-Simanav (1557)* **5:**1078
– – *Pirkei de-Rabbi Eliezer* (1567) **13:**559
CONTINI, GIANFRANCO **5:**923
– Italian literature **9:**1114
Contra Celsum (wk.) **5:**270
Contraception, *see* BIRTH CONTROL
Contra Costa (co., Calif.) **12:**1294
CONTRACT **5:**923
– *Contents:*
– – Creation of Ties **5:**924
– – Consideration **5:**924
– – Obligations by Admission and Deed **5:** 925
– – Obligations on Something Not Yet in Existence **5:**926
– – Change in Jewish Law **5:**927
– – Influence of Custom **5:**928
– – Freedom of Stipulation **5:**928
– – Illegal Contracts **5:**930
– – Third Party Stipulations **5:**931
– – Specific Performance **5:**931
– – Breach of Contract **5:**932
– – in Israel **5:**933
– *asmakhta* **3:**751
– civil and ritual law **12:**112
– conditions **5:**865
– customs **12:**13; **12:**18ff
– gift **7:**560
– imprisonment for debt **8:**1304
– interest **16:**31
– labor law **10:**1325
– lease and hire **10:**1529ff
– loan **11:**414ff
– maintenance **11:**784
– Marranos **5:**885
– marriage stipulations **8:**1127ff
– mistake **12:**158
– non-Jewish law **6:**52
– obligations **12:**1311
– overreaching **12:**1392
– partnership **13:**149
– promissory note **11:**838
– public body **13:**1353
– sale **14:**675
– surety **15:**525
– transfer **3:**768
– waiver **11:**1232ff
– *see also:* ACQUISITION; SHETAR
CONTRACTORS **5:**933
– Alsace Jews **2:**754
– economic history **16:**1301
– labor law **10:**1325
– *Muenzjuden* **12:**63
– Portugal **15:**270
Contradictory Admissions **2:**290
Contra la Verdad no hay Fuerça (wk.) **14:**1169
Contra perfidiam Judaeorum (wk.) **13:**338
Controversy, *see* CONFLICT OF OPINION
Convegno (journ.) **5:**1428
Conventional Law, *see* Law, Conventional
Conventional Lies of Our Civilization (bk.) **12:**1211ff
Convergence Theory (psych.) **10:**1134
Conversion, Forced
– General
– – Amittai ben Shephatiah **2:**850
– – *kiddush ha-Shem* **10:**981
– History
– – Abrabanel family **2:**102
– – *anusim* **3:**169
– – Benedict XIII **4:**482
– – Cantonists **5:**130
– – Catechumens, House of **5:**253
– – chronological chart **8:**766-767
– – Crusades **5:**1137
– – *dhimma, dhimmi* **5:**1605
– – Falashas **6:**1144ff
– – Inquisition **8:**1381ff
– – Mamluk persecutions **11:**835
– – *Wiener gesera* **16:**503
– Places
– – Africa **2:**332
– – Alsace **2:**753
– – Anjou **3:**23
– – Apulia **3:**226ff
– – Arcila **3:**399
– – Barcelona **4:**211
– – Basle **4:**303
– – Benevento **4:**500
– – Bezidul Nou **4:**791
– – Capula **5:**156
– – Clermont-Ferrand **3:**975
– – Germany **7:**467
– – Greece **7:**871
– – Israel, Byzantine period **9:**259
– – Jerusalem **9:**1571ff
– – Rome **14:**248; **14:**249
– – Spain **14:**1621; **15:**220ff
– – Toledo **15:**1205
– – Tortosa **15:**1269
– Views on
– – Abner of Burgos **2:**88
– – Agobard **2:**372
– – Alami, Solomon **2:**510
– – Aquinas **3:**230
– – Berthold of Freiburg **4:**696
– – Maimon ben Joseph **11:**744
– – Maimonides **11:**754ff
– *see also:* APOSTASY; BAPTISM, FORCED
Conversion from Judaism, *see* APOSTASY
Conversion to Judaism, *see* PROSELYTES
CONVERSOS (conv. to Chr.) **5:**936
– *illus:*
– – Spain, major communities (map) **15:**237
– *see also:* CRYPTO-JEWS; MARRANO; MARRANO DIASPORA; NEW CHRISTIANS
"Converts of lions" **11:**275
Convocation, *see* CONGREGATION
Conzio, Abraham **5:**422
Conzio, Joseph **13:**587
Cook, James **8:**766-767
COOK, STANLEY ARTHUR **5:**936
COOKE, GEORGE ALBERT **5:**937
COOKING AND BAKING **5:**937
– crafts **5:** 1044ff
– dietary laws **6:**40
– guilds **7:**971
– spices **15:**267
– *illus:*
– – text
– – Bedouin, preparation of bread **9:**1044
– – cholent pot (16th cent., Ger.) **5:**489
– – Cracow bakery **16:**1331
– – girls learning to make *ḥallah* **7:**1195
– – J.F.S. baking class **11:**475

- - *mazzah* bakery, Carpentras **11:**1156; Ostia **12:**1508
- - *mazzah* machine, New York **11:**1157
- - *mazzot*, baking of **11:**1155-1157; **12:**26
- - Purim **13:**1393
- - Sabbath oven **14:**1571
- - traditional *hallah* shapes **6:**1419
- *see also:* FOOD
Coolus, Romain **7:**147
Cooney, José, *see* Collins, José
Coons, Joseph **16:**515
COOPER, ALEXANDER **5:**941
Cooper, Anthony Ashley, Earl of Shaftesbury, *see* Shaftesbury, Anthony Ashley, Earl of
Cooper, Bruce E. **7:**1349
COOPER, EMIL ALBERTOVICH **12:**686
Cooper, Irving **11:**1201
Cooper, Samuel (art.) **5:**941
Cooper, Samuel (U.S.) **16:**476
Cooperativa de Cooperativas (Arg.) **3:**432
Cooperativas de Crédito (Arg.) **3:**420
Co-operative body (leg. term) **13:**150
COOPERATIVES **5:**941
- *Contents:*
- - Russia **5:**941
- - Poland **5:**942
- - Other European Countries **5:**942
- - Argentina **5:**943
- - Postwar Poland **5:**944
- - Israel **5:**944
- - - Background **5:**944
- - - Beginnings **5:**945
- - - 1918–1939 **5:**947
- - - 1948–1970 **5:**948
- - - Structure **5:**949
- - - Agricultural Villages **5:**950
- - - Consumer Societies **5:**950
- - - Productive and Service Cooperatives **5:**950
- *illus:*
- - text
- - Argentina, Jewish cooperative farm **2:**414
- - *Fondo Communal* management **3:**432
- - Tnuva central dairy **15:**1175
- *see also:* EGGED; HISTADRUT; KIBBUTZ MOVEMENT
Cooperative Society for Agricultural Settlement, *see* Nir
Coopersmith, Harry **5:**452
Coordination (orgn., Pol.) **13:**783
Copateiro, Joseph **15:**1349
Copeland, Lillian **12:**1376
- *illus:* 15:315
COPENHAGEN (city, Den.) **5:**952
- library **11:**193
- museums **12:**544
- shipbuilding **14:**1413
- Zionism **16:**1097
Copenhagen, Aaron Simeon **5:**615
"Copenhagen manifesto" **9:**1243
Copenhagen Moreh Nevukhim (illum. ms.), *see Moreh Nevukhim, Copenhagen*
Copiapó (tn., Chile) **5:**466
Copilul Evreu (period.) **5:**453; **5:**457
Copin (bld. lib. vict.) **8:**1061
COPISAROW, MAURICE **5:**953
COPLAND, AARON **5:**954
Coplas de Yoçef ha-Zaddik (Ladino poem) **10:**1349
Copley, Alfred L., *see* ALCOPLEY
Copley, John Singleton **14:**785
- *illus:*
- - Baal Shem of London **6:**1160
COPONIUS (Rom. gov.) **5:**955
Coponius' Gate (Temple Mt.) **15:**963
Coppel, Elias **10:**1492
Copper (metal) **11:**1431
- Arabah mines **3:**232
- Israel **9:**813
- Timna mine **15:**1146ff
- *illus:*
- - Timna **9:**172-173
COPPER SCROLL (D. S. Scroll) **5:**955
- treasures **15:**1361
- writing surface **16:**661
- *illus:* text
- *see also:* DEAD SEA SCROLLS
COPPER SERPENT, THE (bib. symbol) **5:**957
- idolatry **8:**1228
- Moses **12:**384
- Timna **15:**1146
- *illus:* text
- *see also:* NEHUSHTAN
Coptic (lang.) **4:**861; **14:**1149
Copts (Chr. cmty., Isr.) **9:**912, 1441
- *illus:*
- - Holy Sepulcher **9:**913
Copyright (on bks.) **7:**1452
- encroachment safeguards **7:**1463
- *illus:*
- - Castellazzo's petition to the Venetian Council of Ten (1521) **5:**238
Coqui, Adolph **12:**1447; **13:**820
Coquimbo (tn., Chile) **5:**466
CORAL **5:**959
- jewelry **13:**1012
- *illus:*
- - text
- - Gulf of Eilat corals **6:**570; **9:**172-173
Coral Gables (city, Flor.) **6:**1363
CORALNIK, ABRAHAM **5:**960
- Anti-Nazi Boycott **4:**1281ff
CORBEIL (tn., Fr.) **5:**960
Corbo, V. (arch.) **9:**1537
CORCOS (fam.) **5:**960
- Marrakesh **11:**1016
- politics **13:**816
Corcos, Abraham (13th cent.) **5:**960
Corcos, Abraham (16th cent.) **5:**960
Corcos, Abraham (19th cent.) **5:**961
Corcos, Abraham ben Moses (18th cent.) **5:**961
CORCOS, DAVID **1:**29
Corcos, Fernand **5:**963
Corcos, Ḥayyim (16th cent.) **5:**960
Corcos, Hezekiah Ḥayyim the Elder **5:**963
CORCOS, HEZEKIAH MANOAH ḤAYYIM THE YOUNGER **5:**963
Corcos, Isaac **5:**961
Corcos, Jacob **5:**961
Corcos, Joseph (16th cent.) **5:**961
Corcos, Joseph (Mor.) **5:**961; **14:**633
Corcos, Joseph ben Joshua (Gib.) **5:**961
Corcos, Joshua (Mor. r.) **5:**960
Corcos, Joshua ben Ḥayyim (bnk.) **5:**962
Corcos, Judah ben Abraham **5:**960
CORCOS, LUCILLE **3:**598
- *illus:*
- - book illustration **3:**620
Corcos, Maimon ben Isaac **5:**961
Corcos, Meir ben Abraham **5:**962
Corcos, Moses (20th cent.) **5:**962
Corcos, Moses ben Abraham (16th cent.) **5:**961
Corcos, Solomon (Sp.) **5:**960
Corcos, Solomon (Isr.) **5:**961
Corcos, Solomon ben Abraham (Mor.) **5:**961
Corcos, Stella **5:**962
Corcos, Tranquillo Vita, *see* CORCOS, HEZEKIAH MANOAH ḤAYYIM THE YOUNGER
CORCOS, VITTORIO **3:**598
Corcos, Yose **5:**960; **11:**1200
Corday, Eliot **11:**1200
Cordilha (fam.) **3:**1004
CÓRDOBA (city, Sp.) **5:**963
- Albalia, Baruch **2:**522
- banking **4:**167
- Palma, La **13:**45ff
- Spain **15:**225
- trade **15:**1299ff
- Umayyads **15:**1530
- *illus:*
- - text
- - Maimonides' birthplace **11:**756
CÓRDOBA (prov., city, Arg.) **5:**966
- Argentina **3:**409ff
CÓRDOBA, ALONSO FERNANDEZ DE **5:**967
- engravings **8:**1321; **8:**1325
Córdoba, Gonzalvo de, *see* Gonsalvo de Córdoba
Cordova (city, Sp.), *see* CÓRDOBA
Cordova, Francisco de **5:**935
Cordova, Isaac de **13:**1105
Cordova, Moses ben Isaac of Constantinople **4:**562
CORDOVERO, GEDALIAH BEN MOSES **5:**967
- emissary **14:**1365
- Lonzano, Menahem **11:**487
CORDOVERO, MOSES BEN JACOB **5:**967
- Abulafia, Joseph **2:**195
- Alcastiel **2:**542
- Alkabez, Solomon **2:**636
- Emanation **6:**696
- imitation of God **8:**1293
- Kabbalah **10:**545ff; **11:**347
- Luria, Isaac **11:**573ff
- *Ma'arekhet ha-Elohut* **11:**637
- pantheistic tendency **7:**641
- *Sefer Yezirah* **16:**787
- Worlds, the Four **16:**643
- Yom Kippur Katan **16:**846
- Zohar **16:**1213
- *illus:*
- - text
- - harmonic unity of *Sefirot* **10:**614
- - *Pardes Rimmonim* (1592) **10:**502,584
- - *Sefirot* diagram **10:**502
- - seventy-two-lettered Holy Name **10:**584
Cordovi, Abraham **12:**333; **16:**366
Cordoza Nunes, Isaac **12:**337
Cordubo (city, Sp.), *see* CÓRDOBA
CORFU (isl. Gr.) **5:**970
- Apulian exiles **3:**228
- Arta Jews **3:**645
- Greece **7:**873
- Judeo-Greek dialect **10:**425
- Toledo, Moses de **15:**1207
- *illus:* text
CORIANDER (bot.) **5:**972
- food **6:**1416
- plant list **13:**617
CORIAT (fam.) **5:**973
Coriat, Abraham (18th cent.) **5:**973
Coriat, Abraham (18/19 cent.) **5:**973
Coriat, Abraham (19th cent.) **5:**973
Coriat, Isaac (16th cent.) **5:**973
Coriat, Isaac (18th cent., It.) **5:**973
Coriat, Isaac (18th cent., Mor.) **5:**973
Coriat, Isaac (19th cent.) **5:**973
Coriat, Judah (18th cent.) **5:**973
Coriat, Judah (18/19 cent.) **5:**973
Coriat, Nissim **5:**973
Coriat, Samuel **5:**973
Coriat, Solomon **5:**973
Corinaldi, David **13:**93
Corinne (city, Utah) **16:**33
CORINTH (city, Gr.) **5:**973
- diaspora **6:**10
- Greece **7:**868
Corinthian architecture **15:**596
Corinthian Gate (Temple), *see* NICANOR'S GATE
Corizzi, Menahem ben Mordecai ha-Parnas **13:**589
Cork (co., Ire.) **8:**1464
Cormorant, *see Shalakh*
Corn, *see* FIVE SPECIES
Cornaro-Piscopia, Cornelia L. Helena **8:**28
CORNBLAT, ISODORE CYRIL **5:**974
Corn Bunting (bird) **6:**30
Cornea, Paul **14:**423
Corneille, Pierre **15:**1170
Cornelio de Montalcino **8:**1399; **10:**469
Cornelis de Bruin (Cornellius le Bruya) **9:**1543; **9:**1549; **15:**1357
Corneliu Zelea-Codreanu, *see* Zelea-Codreanu, Corneliu
Cornerbrook (tn., Can.) **11:**997
Corner of field, *see* LEKET, SHIKHḤAH, AND PE'AH
Cornfeld, G. **6:**734
CORNILL, CARL HEINRICH **5:**974
Cornwall (tn., Ont.) **12:**1408
Coro (city, Venez.) **16:**90
Coron (port, Gr.), *see* KORONE
Coronary heart disease **14:**1502
Coronation of kings **10:**1013
Coronel, David Senior **13:**1613
Coronel, Fernando Nuñez, *see* SENEOR, ABRAHAM
Coronel, Fernando Peréz, *see* MELAMED, MEIR
Coronel (Coronello), Francisco **12:**838; **14:**1160
CORONEL, NAḤMAN NATHAN **5:**974
CORONEL CHACON, SIR AUGUSTIN **5:**975
Corporal punishment, *see* EXTRAORDINARY REMEDIES; FLOGGING; IMPRISONMENT; PUNISHMENT; TAKKANOT
Corporal toll (tax) **15:**424
Corporation (leg. body), *see* LEGAL PERSON
Corpse
- autopsies and dissection **3:**931
- impurity **13:**1405ff
- odour **5:**1424
Corpus Christi (city, Tex.) **15:**1034
Corpus Iuris Canonici (ch. law) **2:**568
Corpus Juris Civilis (anti-J. law) **10:**477
- Byzantine Empire **4:**1551
- circumcision **5:**570
- on the Jews **5:**512
Correa (16th cent., hist.) **5:**55
CORREA, ISABEL REBECCA DE **5:**975
Correa, Manuel Alvares **14:**1662
Correspondance de l'Est (newsp.) **12:**1034
Corruption **5:**856
Corsia (art.) **13:**118
CORSICA (Medit. I.) **5:**975
Corsicana (city, Tex.) **15:**1036
Corsono, Judah, *see* ALCORSONO, JUDAH BEN JOSEPH
Cortemaggiore (tn., It.) **13:**493
Cortés, Hernán (expl.) **2:**808
Cortes, Pedro Onofri (converso) **11:**801
Cortis, C. **4:**887
Cortissos, Joseph **5:**935
Cortona (tn., It.) **15:**1468
Cortot, Alfred **12:**697
CORUNNA (Coruniya; city, Sp.)

5:975
Corvallis (city, Ore.) 12:1451
CORVÉE (forced labor) 5:976
- Adoniram 2:295
- ancient Israel 16:1269
- history 8:590; 8:592
- Solomon 15:102ff
Corvida (fam.) 4:701
CORWIN, NORMAN LEWIS 5:977
Cos (isl.), *see* KOS
COSAŞU, RADU 14:423; 14:425
COSENZA (city, It.) 5:977
COSER, LEWIS A. 5:978
- sociology 15:65
Cosgrove, I.K. 7:603
Cosigner (on loan), *see* SURETYSHIP
Cosimo I (duke), *see* Medici, Cosimo I de'
Cosimo III (duke), *see* Medici, Cosimo III de'
Cosman, I. 4:876
COSMETICS 5:978
- Akiva's ruling 2:491
- finery 13:1012ff
- *foliatum* 10:343
- jewelry 13:1012
- soap 15:18
- *illus:*
- - bride's comb 11:*fcg.* 1070
- - perfume bottle (14th cent. B.C.E.) 8:1311
- - Persian bride 11:1035
- *see also:* INCENSE AND PERFUMES; OILS; SPICES
Cosmic cycles (kab. conc.), *see* SABBATICAL YEAR AND JUBILEE
Cosmogony, *see* CREATION AND COSMOGONY
Cosmography 11:928
Cosmological argument 7:657; 10:742; 11:772
COSMOLOGY 5:982
- Baruch Togarmi 4:267
- earth 6:339
- Gabirol 7:240; 7:245
- Jacob ben Jacob 9:1219
- Jewish philosophy 13:424ff
- Kabbalah 10:493; 10:556; 10:579
- sun blessing 15:518
"COSMOPOLITANS" (intellectuals, Rus.) 5:984
- cartoons 5:178
- Soviet press 15:328
Cossack massacres, *see* CHMIELNICKI, BOGDAN
"Cossacks are Coming" (drg., A. Pann) 8:736
Cossey, Henry of 8:28
Costa (fam. name), *see also:* Acosta; Da Costa
COSTA (Eng. fam.) 5:985
- coat of arms 8:339
- *illus:* text
Costa, Abraham da (mer.), *see* Costa, John da
Costa, Abraham da (sport.) 15:305
Costa, Alvaro da 5:985
Costa, Anthony da 5:985; 11:1343
- coat of arms 8:339
COSTA, CATHERINE DA 3:598
- family 5:986; 11:1343
- *illus:*
- - Mendes, Fernando (paint.) 11:1342
Costa, David Mendes da 11:1552
Costa, Duarte Nunes da 15:1303
COSTA, EMANUEL MENDES DA 5:986
- correspondence of 11:62
COSTA, ISAAC DA 5:986
- Amsterdam 2:900
Costa, Israel 5:747
Costa, Jacob da (17th cent.), *see* Costa, Alvaro da
Costa, Jacob da (18th cent.), *see* Costa, Philip da
Costa, James Lopes da, *see* TIRADO, JACOB
Costa, Jeronimo (Nunez) da 5:1010; 15:1303
Costa, John da 5:986
Costa, José da 16:137
Costa, Joshua Mendes da 8:1410
Costa, Leonor da 8:339
Costa, Lionel Gomez da 11:1553
Costa, Manuel da 5:1010
Costa, Moses da, *see* Costa, Anthony da
Costa, Philip da 11:61; 16:137
COSTA, URIEL DA 5:987
- Amsterdam 2:897
- history chart 8:766-767
- philosophy 13:417
- Silva, Samuel da 14:1542
- *Yesod Olam* 16:909
- *illus:*
- - autograph 3:914
COSTA ATHIAS, SOLOMON DA 5:989
- family 3:819
COSTA DE MATTOS, VICENTE DA 5:989
Constantini, Samson, *see* Constantini, Sansone
COSTA RICA (rep.) 5:989
- Latin America 10:1450ff
- synagogues 1:syn. list
- Zionism 16:1127
Costa Villareal, Catherine da, *see* Villareal, Catherine da Costa
Costessey, Henry of, *see* Cossey Henry of
COSTOBAR (gov., Idumea) 5:990
- Berenice 4:601
- Idumea 6:378
- *geneal. table:* 8:377
Costume, *see* DRESS
Costus (spice) 8:1315; 15:267
Costus, Petrus 8:28
Cota, Alonso 14:882
COTA DE MAGUAQUE, RODRIGO DE 5:991
- Spanish literature 15:253
Cote Dove 6:184
Cote St. Rue (sub., Montreal) 12:287
Cothino (Cotinio; Cotinsio), *see* COUTINHO
Cotignac (loc., Prov.) 13:1259
Cotta, J. F. 8:28
COTTBUS (city, Ger.) 5:991
- *illus:* text
COTTON 5:992
- Chinese Jews 5:469
- plant list 13:617
- textiles 15:1038
- *illus:*
- - Jerusalem cotton-cleaner 9:1468
- - Neveh Ur fields 10:966
Cotton Genesis (5th cent. Gr. illum. ms.) 4:943
Cottonseed Oil, *see* CASTOR-OIL PLANT
COUDENHOVE-KALERGI, HEINRICH VON 5:993
Coudenhove-Kalergi, Richard Nicholas von 5:993
Coughlin, Charles E. 12:1114
- anti-Semitism 15:1629; 15:1655
- Boston 4:1265
- Church, Catholic 5:544
- Detroit 5:1571
- hatred of Jews 8:741
- *illus:*
- - addressing meeting 15:1655
Council Bluffs (city, Ia.) 8:1437ff
Council for the Defense of Rumanian Jews in Berlin 4:655
Council for the Sabbath (Isr.) 9:905
Councils of all Lithuanian Karaites 15:1402
Council of Christians and Jews 5:684
COUNCIL OF FOUR LANDS 5:993
- *see also:* COUNCILS OF THE LANDS
Council of Jewish Communities of Spain 15:245
COUNCIL OF JEWISH FEDERATIONS AND WELFARE FUNDS 5:993
COUNCIL OF JEWS FROM GERMANY 5:994
Council of the Land of Lithuania 5:995ff
- *arenda* 3:403
- Poland 13:726
- sermons 13:1001
Council of Progressive Rabbis, *see* Mo'eẓet ha-Rabbanim ha-Mitkaddemim
Council of Rumanian Jewish Communities 15:1333
Council of the Sephardi Community (Isr.) 14:1176
Council of Thirty (Sp.) 4:209; 11:799
Council of Torah Sages, *see* Mo'eẓet Gedolei ha-Torah
Council of Vannes, *see* Vannes Church Council
Council of Young Men's Hebrew and Kindred Associations (U.S.) 12:874
Council on the Rights of Jewish Minorities, *see* COMITE DES DELEGATIONS JUIVES
Council Woman (period.) 12:870
COUNCILS OF THE LANDS 5:995
- *Contents:*
- - Constituents 5:996
- - Congresses 5:996
- - Implementation of Decisions 5:999
- - Competence 5:999
- - Leadership Structure 5:1000
- - Economic Guidance 5:1001
- - Torah Study 5:1002
- - Social Problems 5:1002
- autonomy 3:923
- autonomy, judicial 3:931
- Elder, title 6:580
- finances 6:1281
- fines imposition 6:1289
- *ḥerem ha-yishuv* 8:358
- history chart 8:766-767
- imprisonment for debt 8:1307
- informers 8:1368
- Jaroslaw 9:1288ff
- Kalisz 16:1347
- lease ordinance 7:1523
- Lesser Poland 11:48ff
- Lvov 11:610
- market days 11:1001
- Poland 13:726
- ransom of captives 5:155
- Samogitia 14:768
- *shtadlanim* 14:1463
- sumptuary laws 15:516
- *takkanot* 15:725
- tax 15:840
- Vilna 16:139
- Volhynia 16:209
- *map:* text
- *see also:* COMMUNITY; GREAT POLAND
Counter-Reformation 5:539
- anti-Semitism 14:19
- Paul IV 13:188
- Roman Jews 14:248
Counting the Omer, *see* OMER
Couperin, François 10:1376
Couplad, r. 13:32
COURANT, RICHARD 5:1003
COURLAND (reg., Latv.) 5:1004
- Jelgava 9:1336ff
- Latvia 10:1462
COURNOS, JOHN 15:1580
Court astrologers 3:794
Court Fees 15:727
- *see also:* PRACTICE AND PROCEDURE
Courthézon (tn., Fr.) 12:1447
COURT JEWS 5:1006
- economic role 16:1299
- Germany 7:476
- Haskalah 7:1434
- informers 8:1366
- Lippe 11:285
- mintmasters 12:60ff
- moneylenders 12:252
- *Oberparnas* 10:1406
- railroads 13:1517
- Spain 15:231ff
- *illus:* text
- *see also:* BANKING AND BANKERS; SHTADLAN
Court of Appeal, Rabbinical Supreme (Isr.) 12:143
Court of Peace (Isr.) 9:892
Court Rabbi (offic., Sp.), *see* RAB DE LA CORTE
Courts, Israel, *see* JUDICIARY IN ISRAEL
Courts, Jewish, *see* BET DIN AND JUDGES
Courts, Labor, *see* Labor Courts
Courts, Mixed (J. - Chr.) 3:928
- Augsburg 3:849
Courts, non-Jewish
- bills, force of 6:51; 6:54
- discouragement of use 6:1288
- divorce 7:594
- prohibition of litigation 12:125
- thieves 15:1098
Courts, Rabbinical, *see* BET DIN AND JUDGES; JUDICIARY IN ISRAEL
COUTINHO (fam.) 5:1012
Coutinho, Francisco de Sousa 5:1012
Coutinho, Gonsalvo Lopes 5:1012
Coutinho, Lourença 5:1012; 14:1541
Coutinho, Manoel Pereira 5:1012
Coutinho, Moses 5:1012
Coutinho, Sebastian 5:1012
Couty, Rabba (pion., N.Y.) 12:1067
Couzens, Isaac 5:1568
Covell, John 8:28
COVENANT 5:1012
- *Contents:*
- - God and Israel 5:1013
- - Abraham and David 5:1018
- - Theology 5:1019
- - In Prophecy 5:1020
- - Origins 5:1021
- Chosen People 5:498
- Decalogue 5:1436
- Divine forgiveness 6:1434ff
- Divine purpose 7:646
End of Days 6:864; 6:868
Ezekiel 6:1093
- Genesis 7:395
- Holiness Code 8:820; 8:821
- Hosea 8:1011
- idolatry 8:1232
- illuminated *maḥzorim* 11:733
- Israel and God 12:376
- justice and mercy of God 7:669
- Mari parallel 11:985
- monarchy 10:1019
- Noah 13:1524
- oath 12:1296
- Pentateuch 13:237; 13:242
- prophets 13:1173
- Qumran community 6:64
- sages on 14:654
- sin 14:1589ff

- Sukkot **15:**497
- *illus:* text
Covenant of Omar, *see* OMAR, COVENANT OF
Coverdale, Miles **4:**869
COVETOUSNESS **5:**1022
Covici, Pascal **13:**1371
COVILHÃ (city, Port.) **5:**1022
Covington (city, Ky.) **10:**909
COVO (fam.) **5:**1023
Covo, Elijah **5:**1023
Covo, Isaac ben Hezekiah Joseph **5:**1023
Covo, Isaac ben Joseph Hezekiah **5:**1023
Covo, Jacob Hananiah **5:**1024
Covo, Jacob Joseph **5:**1023
Covo, Joseph ben Shemaiah **5:**1023
Covo, Joseph Hezekiah ben Isaac **5:**1023
Covo, Judah (17th cent.) **5:**1023
Covo, Judah (19/20 cent.) **5:**1024
Covo, Raphael Asher **5:**1023
Covo, Raphael Ḥayyim Abraham **5:**1023
Cow, *see* CATTLE
Cow, Red, *see* RED HEIFER
Cowan, Paul **12:**1032
COWEN, SIR FREDERIC HYMEN **12:**686
COWEN, JOSEPH **5:**1024
- Zionism **16:**1117
COWEN, PHILIP **5:**1024
COWEN, ZELMAN **5:**1024
Cowley, Abraham **6:**774; **14:**784
COWLEY, SIR ARTHUR ERNEST **5:**1025
- Hebrew linguistics **16:**1396
Cowpea (bot.) **13:**617
Cowpea, Nile (bot.) **13:**617
"Cow with a Parasol" (paint., M. Chagall) **5:**321
Coypel, Antoine **9:**1344
COZBI (bib. fig.) **5:**1025
- daughter of Zur **14:**1549
- Phinehas **16:**1026
- *illus:*
- - slain by Phinehas **13:**467; **16:**1027
COZEBA (locs., Isr.) **5:**1025
Crabbe, Elisha **15:**305
Crac du Désert (Crus. fort.) **9:**268; **9:**596
CRACOW (city, Pol.) **5:**1026
- *Contents:*
- - 15th Century **5:**1026
- - Kazimierz **5:**1027
- - 16th Century **5:**1028
- - 17th Century **5:**1028
- - Communal Organization **5:**1029
- - 18th Century **5:**1031
- - Polish Partition **5:**1032
- - Republic **5:**1033
- - Under Austria **5:**1034
- - National Awakening **5:**1034
- - World War I **5:**1036
- - Hebrew Printing **5:**1037
- - Holocaust **5:**1038
- - Resistance **5:**1039
- - Contemporary **5:**1039
- Adalberg, Samuel **2:**234
- archives **3:**380
- Auschwitz trials **3:**873
- Beth Jacob Schools **16:**1261
- education **6:**413
- history chart (1454,1682) **8:**766-767
- Lesser Poland **11:**48
- museums **12:**539
- Poland **13:**712ff
- synagogues **15:**606
- *takkanot* **8:**1307; **15:**736
- university **15:**1677
- *illus:*
- - text
- - Alte Schul **15:**604
- - bakery **16:**1331
- - cemetery **5:**275
- - Franz Joseph I medal **11:**1170
- - goose market **11:**1003; **16:**1329
- - Isaac Jacobowicz synagogue **15:**606
- - Jewish badge, 1939 **4:**69
- - museum **12:**541
- - Rema synagogue **9:**1083
- *pop. table:* text
CRAFTS **5:**1040
- *Contents:*
- - In the Bible **5:**1040
- - Post-Biblical **5:**1042
- - Middle Ages **5:**1045
- - Modern Times **5:**1052
- art **3:**523
- ceremonial objects **5:**288
- diaspora **6:**11
- dress **6:**212
- economic role **16:**1302
- education **6:**388ff
- Falashas **6:**1152
- freemasons **7:**122
- Greece **7:**874
- guilds **7:**970ff
- *ḥazakah* of property **7:**1518ff
- *ḥerem ha-yishuv* **8:**358
- hostility to Jews **16:**1449
- Israel, ancient **8:**611, 614
- Israel, 634 to 1099 **9:**265
- Israel, 1099 to 1291 **9:**274
- Israel culture **9:**1012
- Kenite **10:**906
- Muslim lands **8:**659; **16:**1283
- socialism, Jewish **15:**41
- trespass **7:**1462
- Wadi Al-Nattuf **16:**238
- Yemen **16:**744ff
- *illus:*
- - text
- - baking **11:**1155-1157
- - Bar Kokhba period objects **4:**238
- - Bezalel and Oholiab building the Tabernacle **4:**787
- - Bezalel School **4:**789
- - bookbinding **2:**344; **4:**244, 1228–1232
- - cartwright **13:**745
- - coppersmithing **2:**86; **5:**339, 344,489; **12:**335; **14:***fcg.* 1422
- - cotton-cleaning **9:**1468
- - dyeing plants (6th cent. B.C.E.) **6:**327
- - gauchos, Jewish (Arg.) **3:**429,431
- - glassblowing **7:**605-612
- - gold and silversmithing **3:**529,530,542,640;**4:**244, 1228, 1230–1232, 1337–1345, 1462 1527; **5:**118,289-307,324,347,353,567, 569,1047,1444; **6:**1383; **7:**738-744,1194-1300,1307, 1039 1313, 1485–1488; **8:**445, 446; **10:**975 **11:**265–271, *fcg.* 1067, 1475, 1532; **12:**725; **13:**311, 315; **14:**561, 564, 568, 1649; **15:***fcg.* 494, 899, 1257, 1260–1261; **16:**693
- - locksmiths **16:**1013
- - London's Royal Exchange, plan **11:**470
- - maritime symbols (1st cent.) **3:**333
- - mortar and pestle on a Prague tombstone **7:**973
- - needlework **3:**531; **5:**291,297, *fcg.* 302,961,1377; **6:**911,1243,1385; **7:***fcg.* 1262; **9:**1187,1468,*fcg.* 1531; **11:**273,1475; **13:**172-173,1388-1389; **15:***fcg.* 619,1256,1258,1260-1261; **16:**469
- - "pearl making" **2:**543
- - pewter plates **13:**353
- - pottery **3:** 531, 1016
- - printing, blind youths **4:**1091
- - printing, main locations (map) **13:**1097
- - scribes **14:**1043-1045
- - shoemaking
- - - cooperative, Poland **13:**781
- - - *ḥaliẓah* shoe **11:**123,126
- - - Jerusalem shop **9:**1468
- - - Jewish shoemaker, Poland **10:**1241; **13:**746
- - - sandals, Masada **11:**1090
- - - "Shoemaker" (wdct.) **14:**1468
- - - Ukmerge school **15:**1513
- - tailor **13:**746
- - tailor's scissors on a Prague tombstone **7:**971
- - tanners **15:**446
- - weaving **12:**338
- - woodcarving **3:***fcg.* 459, 462; **4:**787; **11:**371, 572, 1474
- - Yemenite silversmith **16:**750
- *see also under individual crafts*
CRAIOVA (city, Rum.) **5:**1057
- *illus:* text
Cramer (Nazi crim.) **4:**71
Cramer, Anna Maria **8:**28
Cramer, Dan **8:**28
Cramer, Gabriel (Elisée) **8:**28
Cramer, J. Jacob **8:**28
Cramer, J. Rudolph **8:28**
Cramoisy, S. **13:**109
Crampon, J. T. **4:**881
Cranach, Lucas **10:**460
- *illus:*
- - Eve (paint.) **6:**984
- - "Judith with the Head of Holofernes" (paint.) **8:**917
CRANE (zool.) **5:**1058
- dietary laws **6:**34
Crane, C. R. **13:**30
Crane, Ralph **13:**484
Cranford (tn., N.J.) **15:**1534
CRANGANORE (port, Ind.) **5:**1059
- India **8:**1350,1355
Cranston (city, R. I.) **14:**143
CRASSUS, MARCUS LICINIUS **5:**1059
- Temple **15:**959
Crasto (fam.), *see* CASTRO
Crato, Prior of (Port. Pretender), *see* ANTONIO
Crawcour, Zillah **11:**1285
Crawford, Francis **8:**28
Creamridge (loc., N.J.) **8:**254
Creation, Book of (kab. wk.), *see* YEẒIRAH,SEFER
CREATION AND COSMOGONY **5:**1059
- *Contents:*
- - In the Bible **5:**1059
- - - Conception of God **5:**1060
- - - Mesopotamian Prototypes **5:**1061
- - - *Enuma Elish* **5:**1062
- - - Egyptian Analogues **5:**1062
- - - Other Traditions **5:**1063
- - Rabbinic View **5:**1063
- - - Bible Commentators **5:**1065
- - In Philosophy **5:**1065
- - - Philo Judaeus **5:**1065
- - - Medieval Philosophy **5:**1066
- - In Modern Thought **5:**1070
- - In the Arts **5:**1070
- General
- - Adam **2:**234ff
- - anniversary **14:**307
- - calendar **16:**1264
- - chronological dating **14:**751
- - Du Bartas' *Semaine* **6:**245
- - Eve **6:**979
- - Garden of Eden **7:**326
- - *imitatio Dei* **8:**1292
- - letters of alphabet **2:**747ff
- - nature **12:**888
- - Paradise **13:**77
- - pre-Sabbath creations **15:**691
- - Rock of **6:**985
- - sun and moon **12:**290
- Philosophy and Theology **13:**421ff; **15:**1107
- - Aristotelianism **3:**447
- - dogma **3:**654ff
- - emanation **6:**694
- - eschatology **6:**882
- - Evolution **6:**1000
- - God the Creator **7:**643; **7:**658ff
- - Islamic conception **9:**99
- - Kabbalah **10:**506; **10:**557; **10:**588ff
- - Karaite theory **10:**768
- - labor of God **10:**1320
- - logos **11:**461ff
- - miracles **12:**74ff
- - nature of man **11:**846
- - Neoplatonism **12:**958; **12:**959
- - Providence **13:**1282
- - Sabbath **14:**565
- - *sefirot* **14:**1105
- - time **15:**1142
- - Torah **14:**119; **15:**1238
- - Worlds, the Four **16:**641
- *Ex Nihilo*
- - Aristotelianism **3:**447ff
- - articles of faith **3:**656ff
- - Bible **7:**643
- - Crescas **12:**78
- - denial **8:**359
- - Kabbalah **10:**562ff
- - Levi ben Gershom **12:**890
- - Maimonides **11:**773
- - philosophy **13:**422; **13:**431; **13:**441; **13:**447
- Views on
- - Abraham bar Ḥiyya **2:**131,133
- - Albalag, Isaac **2:**521
- - Albo, Joseph **2:**536
- - Al-Farabi **6:**1176
- - Aristobulus of Paneas **3:**444ff
- - Asher ben David **3:**706
- - Azriel of Gerona **3:**1014
- - Crescas **3:**657
- - Friedman, Ẓevi Hirsch **16:**1004
- - Heraclitus **7:**894
- - Ibn Da'ud **8:**1162
- - Ibn Ezra, Abraham **8:**1169; **13:**438
- - Israeli, Isaac **13:**433
- - Jacob Gerondi **7:**508
- - Jacob Koppel of Mezhirech **9:**1231
- - Karaite Kalaam **13:**433
- - Levi ben Gershom **11:**96; **13:**447ff
- - Maimonides **11:**771; **11:**772ff; **13:**441
- - Philo **13:**426ff
- - Rosenzweig **13:**462
- - Saadiah Gaon **13:**431; **14:**550
- - Ẓaddik, Joseph ibn **16:**913
- In Literature
- - apocalypse **3:**180
- - Babylonian myth **11:**952; **16:**1490
- - *Barekhi Nafshi* **4:**218
- - Enuma Elish **12:**729ff
- - Genesis **7:**389ff
- - leviathan myth **11:**89
- - *Perek Shirah* **13:**274
- - *Rosh Ha-Shanah* **14:**311
- - *Seder Olam Rabbah* **14:**1092
- - *Sefer Yeẓirah* **10:**507; **16:**782
- - Sumerian legends **15:**515
- *illus:*
- - text
- - *Harrison Miscellany* (18th cent.) **13:**574
- *see also:* COSMOLOGY
"Creation of Adam" (frsc., Michelangelo) **5:**1068
Credibility (leg. conc.) **6:**994ff

Crédit Mobilier (bnk., Fr.) **13:**1518ff
Creditor, *see* MONEYLENDING
Creed, *see* ARTICLES OF FAITH; BELIEF
Creek (Ind. tribe, N.Am.) **16:**359
- language **4:**888
Creglingen (tn., Ger.) **12:**1150
Cregut(-us), A. **8:**28
CRÊHANGE, ALEXANDRE **5:**1072
- Bible translation **4:**882
CREIZENACH, MICHAEL **5:**1072
- Hirsch, S. R. **8:**510
- Oral Law **12:**1442
Creizenach, Theodor **7:**449
Creizenach, Wilhelm **7:**449
CREMATION **5:**1072
- ancient Israel **4:**1516
- catacombs **5:**250
- concentration camps **5:**81
- Lerner, Mayer **11:**44
- Titus **15:**1170
- *illus:*
- - Nazi extermination camp crematorium **3:**868
- *see also:* BURIAL; DEATH
CRÉMIEU (vill., Fr.) **5:**1073
Crémieu, Jassuda **5:**205
Crémieux (fam.), *see* KARMI
Crémieux (stlmt., Dakota) **14:**293
Crémieux (publ.), *see* Rieder
Crémieux, Adolphe, *see* CRÉMIEUX, ISAAC ADOLPHE
CRÉMIEUX, BENJAMIN **5:**1074
Crémieux, David ben Joseph, *see* Carmi, David ben Joseph
Crémieux, Hector Jonathan **7:**146
CRÉMIEUX, ISAAC ADOLPHE **5:**1074
- Algerian Jews **2:**335
- chronological chart **8:**766-767
- Damascus Affair **5:**1251; **12:**525
- emissary,**11:**448
- equality of Jews **8:**713
- Persian Jews **13:**316
- *illus:*
- - text
- - autograph **3:**914
- - Damascus Affair, commemorative medal **5:**1250
Crémieux, Moses **15:**520
CREMIN, LAWRENCE ARTHUR **5:**1076
CREMONA (city, It.) **5:**1077
- *illus:* text
Cremona Nuova (newsp.) **6:**1183
Crenius, T. **8:**28
Crescas (name), *see also:* Cresques
CRESCAS (name) **5:**1078
Crescas, Abraham, *see* CRESQUES, ABRAHAM
CRESCAS, ASHER (Bonan) BEN ABRAHAM **5:**1078
Crescas, Don Bonet, *see* Meshullam ben Machir
Crescas, David **13:**300
Crescas, Elisha **4:**958
- *illus:*
- - *Farḥi Bible* **6:***fcg.* 1195
Crescas, Ḥasdai (court J.) **11:**800
CRESCAS, ḤASDAI (philos.) **5:**1079
- *Contents:*
- - Biography **5:**1079
- - Works **5:**1080
- - *Or Adonai* **5:**1081
- - Fundaments **5:**1083
- - Other Dogmas **5:**1084
- - Influence and Criticism **5:**1085
- angels **2:**976
- Aristotelianism **3:**445
- articles of faith **3:**657
- astrology **3:**792ff
- atomism **3:**830
- attributes of God **7:**660; **7:**668
- beatitude **4:**363
- chronological chart **8:**766-767
- Commandments **5:**787
- cosmology **5:**984
- Creation **5:**1069ff
- free will **7:**129
- Ibn Shem Tov **8:**1199
- love of God **11:**529
- messianism **11:**1410
- miracles **12:**78
- nature **12:**890
- philosophy **11:**341; **13:**447ff
- Providence **13:**1286
- resurrection **14:**102
- revelation **14:**123
- reward, punishment **14:**136
- Saragossa **14:**861
- soul **15:**173,178
- space and place **15:**219
- Spain **15:**237
- substance and accidents **15:**475
- time **15:**1142
- Torah **15:**1237,1241,1245
- Villafranca **16:**136
- Wolfson's studies **16:**617
- *illus:* text
Crescas, Judah, *see* Cresques, Judah
Crescas, Meir (15th cent.) **6:**301
Crescas du Caylar (trans.) **10:**439
Crescas Elijah, *see* Elijah, Crescas
Crescas Solomon, *see* Solomon, Crescas
Crespin, Elia M. **13:**1038
Cresques (name), *see also* Crescas
CRESQUES, ABRAHAM **5:**1086
- cartography **3:**523; **11:**917; **11:**920
- *illus:*
- - text
- - Catalan Atlas **8:**681; **11:**915
Cresques, Judah **5:**1086
- art **3:**523
- cartography **11:**917; **11:**920
- nautical academy **14:**1413
- Majorca **11:**800; **11:**802
- *illus:*
- - Catalan Atlas **5:**1086; **8:**681; **11:**915
CRESQUES DE VIVERS **5:**1086
- astrolabes **3:**787
Cress (vegetable) **16:**83
- plant list **13:**617
Cress, garden (bot.) **13:**617
Cresselin of Provins **5:**334
CRESSON, WARDER **5:**1087
- Jerusalem **9:**1450
- proselytes **13:**1192
CRESTOHL, LEON DAVID **5:**1088
- *illus:*
- - Zionist convention **16:**1110
CRETE **5:**1088
- Cardozo, Abraham **14:**1244
- Cherethites **13:**404
- enactments **7:**1462; **7:**1522
- Greece **13:**1395
- special Purim **13:**1397
- spices **8:**1311
- sugar **15:**487
- synod **15:**633
- *takkanot* **15:**736
- taxes **15:**853
- *pop. table:* text
Cretensis, Elijah, *see* DELMEDIGO, ELIJAH BEN MOSES ABBA
Creuz (tn., Aus.), *see* DEUTSCHKREUTZ
Creuzer, Friedrich **5:**789
Crick, W. F. **13:**33
- *illus:*
- - Anglo-American Committee of Enquiry **16:**1089
Cricket (sport) **15:**307
Crimchak (J. lang.), *see* Krimchak
CRIME **5:**1091
- *Contents:*
- - Introduction **5:**1091
- - In the Diaspora **5:**1093
- - In Palestine **5:**1095
- - In State of Israel **5:**1096
- abduction **2:**55
- abortion **2:**98
- adultery **2:**313
- assault **3:**758
- bribery **4:**1367
- cuneiform law **16:**1490
- false measures **16:**390
- forgery **6:**1432
- fraud **7:**110
- homicide **8:**944
- homosexuality **8:**961
- imprisonment **8:**1299ff
- incest **8:**1316
- mental illness **11:**1377
- police offenses **13:**796
- rape **13:**1548
- sexual offenses **14:**1207
- slavery **14:**1655
- theft **15:**1094
- *illus:* text
- *tables:* Palestine and Israel crime statistics, 1940-1965 **5:**1095-1098
- *see also:* CAPITAL PUNISHMENT; PUNISHMENT
CRIMEA (penin., Rus.) **5:**1103
- *Contents:*
- - Late Antiquity **5:**1103
- - Tatar Times **5:**1105
- - Czarist Rule **5:**1106
- - Soviet Rule **5:**1107
- agricultural settlement **8:**741
- history chart **8:**766-767
- Jewish immigration to Ereẓ Israel **9:**503
- minority rights **12:**48
- *illus:*
- - text
- - Tartar market **14:**437
- - Tel Ḥai farm **14:**469
- *pop. table:* text
- *see also:* RUSSIA
Crimea (stlmt., U.S.) **2:**862
Crimea Affair **3:**64, 149
Crimean War **9:**1455; **14:**1198
Crimes, War, *see* WAR CRIMES TRIALS
Criminal law, *see* PENAL LAW
CRIMINOLOGY **5:**1108
- *Contents:*
- - Schools of Thought **5:**1108
- - Study in U.S. **5:**1110
- - British Contribution **5:**1111
- - In Israel **5:**1111
- - Capsules **5:**1112
- *illus:* text
CRIMSON WORM **5:**1113
- *tekhelet* **15:**914
Crisana (reg., Transyl.) **15:**1344
Crispia (gram.), *see* Krespia
CRISPIN, GILBERT (Gislebertus) **5:**1113
- disputation **6:**88ff
Crispin, Judah **14:**304
Cristall, Abraham **6:**368
Criticism, Biblical, *see* BIBLE
CRITICISM, HEBREW LITERARY **5:**1114
- *Contents:*
- - Beginnings **5:**1114
- - 18th Century **5:**1115
- - 19th Century **5:**1116
- - Late 19th Century **5:**1118
- - Early 20th Century **5:**1120
- - Mid-20th Century **5:**1123
- Klausner, Joseph **10:**1092
- Lachower, Yeruḥam **10:**1338
- *see also:* HAKDAMAH; HASKAMAH; HEBREW LITERATURE, MODERN; LITERATURE, JEWISH
C.R.J.F., see Conseil Representatif des Juifs de France
Croatia (rep., Yug.) **16:**868ff
Crocius, L. M. **8:**28
CROCODILE **5:**1124
- dietary laws **6:**34
- leviathan **11:**89
Crocodilopolis (city, Egy.) **6:**9
Crocus (bot.) **6:**1365; **8:**1315
- plant list **13:**617
Croesus (Lydian k.) **5:**1184; **11:**621
CROHMĂLNICEANU OVID S. **14:**423; **14:**425
CROHN, BURRILL BERNARD **5:**1125
CROISSET, FRANCIS DE **7:**149
Croitoru, Ion, *see* CĂLUGĂRU, ION
Croius, J. **8:**28
CROIX, LA (newsp.) **5:**1125
Croix du Feu (party, Fr.) **8:**741
CROLL, DAVID ARNOLD **5:**1126
- politics **13:**826
Croly, George **16:**262
Cromer, Lord, *see,* Baring, Sir Evelyn
CROMWELL, OLIVER **5:**1126
- attitude toward Jews **14:**20
- Manasseh ben Israel **15:**1006
CRONBACH, ABRAHAM **5:**1129
Cronbach, S. **13:**1366
CROOL, JOSEPH **5:**1129
Crops, doubtfully tithed, *see* DEMAI
Cross (amulet) **2:**912
- *illus:*
- - cross and crescent amulet (Morocco) **2:**913
Cross, Frank **4:**911
Cross, Leach **15:**306
Cross, True (Chr. relic) **9:**1406,1407ff
Cross, Valley of the (Jer.), *see* Valley of the Cross
Cross, Walter **8:**28
Crossbreeding **12:**170ff
Crossman, R. H. S. **13:**33 **16:**1089
Crow (bird) **6:**34
Crowfoot, Grace Mary **5:**1129
CROWFOOT, JOHN WINTER **5:**1129
- Jerusalem **9:**1522ff
Crowley (city, La.) **11:**520
Crowley, Aleister, *see* Perdurabo, Frater
CROWN, HENRY **5:**1130
Crown Heights (section, N.Y.C.) **12:**1107
- *illus:*
- - night patrol **15:**1646
CROWNS, DECORATIVE HEADDRESSES AND WREATHS **5:**1130
- jewelry **13:**1012
- kingship **10:**1013
- synagogue art **15:**597
- *illus:*
- - text
- - Baghdad, turbaned rabbi **10:**242
- - *kupke* **6:***fcg.* 238
- - Morocco, woman's headdress Pl. 7 **6**-DRESS
- - Polish *sterntichl* **6:***fcg.* 238
- - priestly vestments **13:**1065
- - Tunisia, woman's headdress Pl. 10 **6**-DRESS
- - Yemen, bridal hood **6:***fcg.* 235
- *see also:* CEREMONIAL OBJECTS; DRESS; TORAH ORNAMENTS
Crows (Ind. tribe, N.Am.) **11:**535
- sociology **15:**66
Crozier, W. P. **6:**782
CRUCIFIXION **5:**1133
- *Akedah* **2:**481; **2:**484ff
- blood libel **4:**1121

- halakhah 10:15
Crucifix manufacturing 7:741
Crudo (fam.) 15:1030
Crum, B. C. 13:33
CRUSADES 5:1135
- Contents:
- - First Crusade 5:1135
- - Second Crusade 5:1139
- - Third Crusade 5:1140
- - Significance 5:1142
- Historical Aspects 8:662; 8:668ff
- - anti-Semitism 3:101
- - archaeological remains 3:329
- - Caesarea 5:11
- - Cairo genizah 16:1340
- - debts to Jews 8:1376; 12:249
- - Erez Israel 9:267
- - European Jewry 6:969
- - freedom of holy places 8:936
- - Germany 7:461ff
- - Greece 7:872ff
- - history chart 8:766-767
- - Jerusalem 9:1415,1573
- - Lateran Council IV 10:1446
- - organization of kingdom 9:121
- - papal bulls 4:1495
- - Pastoureaux 13:176
- - pilgrimage of armies 13:515
- - Prague 13:964
- - Shum 14:1480
- - Speyer 15:263
- - Transjordan 15:1318
- - Worms 16:644
- Effects and Influences
- - agriculture in Israel 2:398
- - El Male Rahamim 6:683
- - ethnographic elements 9:122
- - French Jewry 7:13ff
- - Hep! Hep! cry 8:330
- - Jerusalem in art 9:1579
- - kiddush ha-Shem 10:983
- - messianism 11:1422
- - travel literature 15:1355
- Castles
- - Agrippina 3:329
- - Athlit 3:821
- - Belvoir 2:418
- - Carmel 5:185
- - Casal des Plains 3:1011
- - Castellum Beleismum 8:1151
- - Castellum Belveer 11:1453
- - Castellum Dok 9:1371
- - Chasteau du Roi 11:1529
- - Crac du Désert 9:596
- - Jūdīn 16:728
- - Latrun 10:1457
- - Le Toron aux Fontaines Sourdes 3:78
- - Montfort 11:1529
- - Montreal 15:1318
- illus:
- - text
- - Abu Ghosh, Hospitaler Knights' church 2:181; 3:329
- - Acre (plan of sites) 2:225
- - Apollonia ruins 3:188
- - Athlit 3:328,821; 5:1144
- - Belvoir 2:419; 3:327; 5:1145; 12:880
- - Caesarea 5:13; 9:276
- - Hittin, battle site 9:275
- - Jerusalem, Church of St. Anne 9:1453
- - Jerusalem, Holy Sepulcher 9:1418
- - Jerusalem boundaries (map) 9:1421
- - Jūdīn castle 16:728
- - Kingdom of Jerusalem (map) 9:270
- - Montfort 5:1136; 9:172-173
- - Qal'at Nimrod 9:207
- - Tiberias city walls 15:1133
- - Tomb of Miriam 9:1417
CRYPTO-JEWS 5:1145
- Inquisition 8:1381ff
- Peru 13:322
- Portugal 13:921ff
- Vila Real 16:134
- see also: ANUSIM; BAPTISM, FORCED; CONVERSOS; MARRANO
Crystal (mineral) 13:1011
Crystal, Morris 10:50
Crystal Night, see KRISTALLNACHT
Csak, Ibolya K. 12:1376
Csécsi, János 8:28
Csekei, Pál 8:28
Cselebi, Evlia 13:203
Csepregi, Ferenc 8:28
Csere, János Apáczai 2:518
CSERGÖ, HUGÓ 8:1083,1084
CSERMELY, GYULA 8:1080,1084
Csillag, István 11:1167
Csipkés, György 4:883
C. S. J. C. A., see Central Sephardic Jewish Community of America
Csokonai, Vitéz Mihály 8:1079
Csomos, János 8:28
CTESIPHON (city, Babyl.) 5:1146
- Trajan 15:1312
Cub (anc. Libya) 13:1415
CUBA 5:1146
- Israel's relations 9:432
- Latin America 10:1450ff
- synagogues 1:syn. list
- illus: text
Cubit (meas.), see 'Ammah
Cubo, Samuel 7:1345
Cuckoo (bird) 9:226
CUCUMBER 5:1151
- dill 15:268
- food 6:1416
- plant list 13:617
- illus: text
CUDWORTH, RALPH 5:1152
- Hebraists 8:28
C. U. E. J. (Fr.), see Centre Universitaire d'Études Juives
Cuenca (city, Ec.) 6:359
CUENCA (city, Sp.) 5:1152
CUENQUE (Cuenca), ABRAHAM BEN LEVI 5:1153
Cuenteniks (peddlers, S. Am.) 3:419,420
CUKIERMAN, ITZHAK (Antek) 5:1153
- Berihah 4:629,630
- Cracow ghetto 5:1039
CUKOR, GEORGE 12:451; 12:465
Çulema, Don (13th cent., court.), see IBN ZADOK, SOLOMON
Çulema, Don (14th cent., r.), see Ibn Alfakhar, Solomon
CULI, JACOB 5:1154
- Ladino literature 10:1349
- Me-Am Lo'ez 11:1159ff
- Rosanes, Judah 14:262
- illus:
- - text
- - Me'am Lo'ez 13:1108
CULLMAN, HOWARD S. 5:1155
CULT 5:1155
- Contents:
- - Animal Sacrifices 5:1156
- - Grain Offerings 5:1161
- - Other Sacrifices 5:1161
- altar 2:760
- art 3:500ff
- Ezekiel's vision 6:1089
- Genesis 7:390
- moon 12:290
- prophecy 13:1161; 13:1172
- sun 15:516
- teraphim 15:1015
- Timna temple 15:1146
- twelve tribes 15:1383
- illus:
- - text
- - Tabernacle and implements 3:fcg. 524
- see also: CULT PLACES, ISRAELITE; SACRIFICE
CULT PLACES, ISRAELITE 5:1162
- Contents:
- - Bet YHWH 5:1162
- - Mikdash 5:1164
- - Bamah 5:1165
- - Mizbe'ah 5:1167
- Arad 3:244
- Asherah 3:705
- Micah 11:1480
- Pentateuch 13:236,239
- Teacher of Righteousness 13:333
- Temple 15:954
- illus:
- - Tel Dan bamah 8:594
- see also: CULT
Cultural League, Jewish (Kiev, Rus.) 8:813; 14:1533
CULTURAL LIFE IN ISRAEL 9:996
- America-Israel Cultural Foundation 2:817
- art 3:576ff
- - Bezalel Academy 4:788
- - sculpture 14:1069
- B'nai B'rith 4:1148
- book bindings 4:1232
- children's literature 5:434; 5:457
- dance 5:1270
- drama, Hebrew 6:205ff
- - Milo, Josef 11:1584
- film industry 12:456ff
- folklore 6:1403
- food and cooking 6:1422ff
- Hebrew literature 8:203
- Hebrew newspapers 12:1053
- Histadrut 9:868
- historical survey 9:396
- inter-communal relations 9:506ff
- kibbutz movement 10:966; 10:972ff
- libraries 11:194ff
- Mifal ha-Payis 11:513
- newspapers, non-Hebrew 12:1058
- radio and TV 15:931ff; 16:1646
- recording companies 13:1618
- Yemenite Jews 16:755ff
- Zionism 16:1064
- illus:
- - Bar Ilan University library 9:963
- - basketball, European Championship games 15:296
- - Cameri production of Saint Joan 15:1062
- - Chess Olympics medal 11:1174
- - concert at Caesarea Roman theater 12:673
- - Four-Day March 15:297
- - golf match at Caesarea 15:309
- - Habimah production of Genesis 15:1063
- - International Paraplegic Olympics 15:297
- - Israel Museum 11:1460; 14:1061-1068
- - Israel Philharmonic Orchestra 9:1071
- - Jerusalem College for Women library 9:899
- - Maariv (Sept. 1948) 11:639
- - Maccabiah 11:633
- - Ohel production of Ammekha 12:1343
- - Ohel production of A Streetcar Named Desire 15:1063
- - Palestine Post: establishment of State 9:364
- - protest poster against Technion re language of instruction 9:1000
- - Rockefeller Museum 14:212
- - sailing, world championships, Tel Aviv 15:317
- - Schocken Institute 14:987
- - soccer game, Israel-Australia 15:298
- - swimming, annual crossing of Lake Kinneret 15:297
- - Tel Aviv bulletin board 15:921
- - Tel Aviv University library 9:956
- - Three-Day March 11:694
- - Uj Kelet, first issue 15:1510
- - Writers' Association 16:653
- - Yad Mordekhai Museum 16:696
- see also: DANCE; EDUCATION; LIBRARIES; MUSEUMS; MUSIC; SPORTS; THEATER
Cultural pluralism 3:777
Cultural-Social Association of the Jews in Poland 13:784
Cultural Zionism, see ZIONISM
Culture-League (Rum.) 3:86
CUMANUS VENTIDIUS (Rom. gov.) 5:1169
- Alexander the Zealot 2:587
CUMBERLAND, RICHARD 5:1169
CUMIN (spice) 5:1170
- food 6:1416
- plant list 13:617
- spices 15:267
- illus: text
Cum Nimis Absurdum (papal bull) 4:1496
CUNAEUS (Van der Cun), PETRUS 5:1171
- Hebraists 8:28
- illus: text
Cuneiform script 2:677
- decipherment 16:1506ff
- Hebrew 16:1562
- Mesopotamia 16:1499ff
- seals 14:1072
- Sumer 15:515
- writing systems 16:654
- illus:
- - Gilgamesh Epic tablet 6:1355
- - Sennacherib prism 14:1162
- - Sumerian King list 3:367
- - Tell el-Amarna tablet 3:370
- - Ugarit abecedary 2:678
- - see also: Inscriptions (Cuneiform)
Cuneo (prov., It.) 13:502
Cuneo (tn., It.) 13:1397
Cunitzen (Cunitia), Maria 8:28
Cunningham, Sir Alan 8:470; 9:365,601
- illus:
- - Weizmann, Chaim, and 8:472
CUPBEARER (royal offic.) 5:1171
- illus: text
Cuperman (publ.) 13:1369
Cup of Elijah, see ELIJAH, CUP OF
Cup of Salvation (newsp.) 13:1031
Curaçao (isl., Neth. Antilles)
- Antuñes Paredes family 3:167
- Carigal, Raphael 5:179
- funerary art 3:535
- Jewish community 2:809
- Latin America 10:1451
- Netherlands 12:993
- slave trade 14:1662
- sugar trade 15:488
- synagogues 1:syn. list
- illus:
- - Temple Emanu-el 12:995
- - tombstone of Abigail Aboab Cardozo (1747) 3:527; 14:1061
- - tombstone of Mordochay Namias de Castro 12:994
Curcos, Mordecai 10:638
CURIEL (fam.) 5:1172
Curiel (Du. firm) 14:713
Curiel, Abraham 16:195
Curiel, Elías David 16:90
CURIEL, ISRAEL BEN MEIR DI 5:1173
Curiel, Jacob 5:1172; 16:195
Curiel, Moses 5:1172; 14:713

Curiel, Moses di (Safed) 5:1173
Curiel, Solomon 5:1172
Curierul Israelit (newsp.) 5:202; 13:1043; 14:399
Curitiba (city, Braz.) 4:1329
Curling (sport) 15:317
Curran, Edward Lodge 12:1062,1114
Currency, *see* COINS AND CURRENCY
Current History (mag.) 12:1317
Cursing, *see* BLESSING AND CURSING
Cursing God, *see* BLASPHEMY
Cursive script 2:689ff
Curtis, Mary Louise 16:1024
CURTIS, TONY 12:465
Curtius, Sebastian 8:28
Curtius Rufus 2:578
Curtiz, Michael 12:451
Curzon, G. K. 15:905
CUSA, NICHOLAS OF 5:1173
- Reuchlin, Johannes 14:110ff
CUSH (bib. fig.) 5:1174
CUSH (anc. kdm., Afr.) 5:1174
- Garden of Eden 13:78
- Midian 11:1506
- Nimrod 12:1166
- Tirhakah 15:1152
CUSHAN-RISHATHAIM (k.) 5:1174
- Bible history 8:584
- Laban 10:1317
Cushi (bib. fig.) 16:994
Cushi (state), *see* COCHIN
Cushi (Heb. term for Negro) 5:1174
Cushitic languages 14:1149
Cusi, Meshullam 8:1323; 13:557
Cusi, Moses 13:557
Cusi, Solomon 13:557
Cusi Rafa, Meshullam ben Moses Jacob, *see* Cusi, Meshullam
Custodian, *see* APOTROPOS
Customs (duties) 3:402; 9:749
- *illus:*
- - Eichstaett tariffs list 15:870
- - Raffelstetten ordinance 15:869
Customs (usages), *see* MINHAG
Customs Agents' Objection Committee (Isr.) 9:640
CUTH, CUTHAH (city, Mesop.) 5:1175
Cutheans (sect), *see* SAMARITANS
Cutinho (fam.), *see* COUTINHO
CUTLER, HARRY 5:1176
- *illus:*
- - American Jewish Committee 2:823
- - Joint Distribution Committee 2:829
- - JWB committee 12:873
Cut-outs (folkart), *see* PAPER-CUTS
CUZA, ALEXANDER C. 5:1176
- Jassy 9:1293,1294,1295
- Rumania 14:394ff
- *illus:*
- - League of National Christian Defense campaign poster 14:395
C. V. (orgn., Ger.), *see* CENTRAL-VEREIN DEUTSCHER STAATSBUERGER JUEDISCHEN GLAUBENS
C. V.-ZEITUNG (period.) 5:1177
- Germany 7:493
- press 13:1032
Cyaxares (k., Media) 2:454; 11:1177
Cybernetics 16:502
Cybis, Levi 16:946
Cyclamen (bot.) 6:1365
Cycling (sport) 15:307
C.Y.C.O., *see* Central Yiddish Culture Organization
Cylkow, Isaac 16:338
Cylkow, J. 4:885
Cymbals 12:564
- *illus:*
- - bronze, Hazor 12:561
CYNICS AND CYNICISM 5:1177
- Oenomaus of Gadara 12:1332
CYON, ELIE DE 5:1178
Cyper, Elie 15:425
CYPRESS (bot.) 5:1178
- plant list 13:617
- Solomon's trade 15:99
- wood 16:630
- *illus:* text
Cyprian of Carthage (ch. F.) 5:553
CYPROS (m. of Herod) 5:1179
- henna 8:326
- *geneal. table:* 8:377
CYPROS (w. of Agrippa I) 5:1179
- Drusilla 6:241
- *geneal. table:* text; 8:377
Cypros (fort., Er. Isr.) 5:1179; 8:382
CYPRUS (isl., Medit.) 5:1180
- Greece 7:869ff
- I.C.A.'s activity 10:48
- ILO 15:1564
- Israel's relations 9:433
- Jewish revolt 8:645
- Jewish settlement 8:415
- population 13:872
- pottery 13:940
- Safed expulsion 9:289
- slave trade 14:1662
- Solomon's trade 15:99
- Trajan 15:1312
- Trietsch 15:1394
- Warburg 16:287
- Youth Aliyah 16:863
- *illus:*
- - text
- - deportation of "illegal" immigrants to 8:1252
- - escape tunnel at detention camp 9:526
- - refugees leaving detention camp 8:1253
- - *Unafraid* and "illegal" immigrants 9:361
- *pop. table:* text
- *see also:* KITTIM
Cyrenaica (reg. N. Afr.) 6:9,15ff
- Libya 11:198
- Trajan 15:1312
- Tunisia 15:1430ff
CYRENE (anc. tn., Cyrenaica) 5:1183
- catacombs 5:252
- Diaspora settlement 8:640
- Jewish revolt 2:331; 8:654
- Josephus 10:254
- *see also:* LIBYA
Cyril (bp.) 9:1406
Cyril (monk) 4:1481; 4:884; 16:885
Cyril II (Chr. patriarch) 9:1450
Cyril of Alexandria (ch. F.) 4:1550
CYRUS (k., Pers.) 5:1184
- Babylonia 16:1505
- chronology 16:1265
- conquests 4:34
- declaration of 9:1390
- history chart 8:766-767
- Nabonidus 12:746
- Persia 13:302ff
- return of exiles 8:1374
- Samaritan exile 14:728
- Sheshbazzar 14:1382
- Solomon's throne 15:812
- Tema 15:940
- Temple 15:955
C.Y.Sh.O., *see* Central Yiddish School Organization
Cytryn, Abraham 16:680
C.Z.A., *see* Central Zionist Archives
CZACKI, TADEUSZ 5:1186
Czaczkes, Samuel Josef, *see* AGNON, SHMUEL YOSEF
Czapek, Joseph 4:79
CZARNIECKI, STEFAN 5:1187
- Tykocin 15:1475
Czarnoloz (tn., Pol.) 10:1242
Czarny Las (loc., Pol.) 5:497
CZARTORYSKI, PRINCE ADAM JERZY 5:1187
Czartoryski, Joseph 10:1202
Czech (lang.) 4:884; 5:1204ff
CZECH, LUDWIG 5:1187
Czechanower, Abraham ben Raphael Landau, *see* CIECHANOW, ABRAHAM BEN RAPHAEL LANDAU OF
CZECHOSLOVAKIA 5:1188
- *Contents:*
- - Demography 5:1188
- - Communal Structure 5:1189
- - Political Affiliation 5:1190
- - Education 5:1191
- - Economic Life 5:1192
- - Cultural Sphere 5:1192
- - Anti-Semitism 5:1193
- - Emigration and Exile 5:1194
- - Holocaust Period 5:1195
- - Contemporary Jewry 5:1199
- - And Israel 5:1202
- anti-Semitism 3:159
- archives 3:381
- Bar Kochba Association 4:228
- cooperatives 5:942
- divorce statistics 6:135
- Egypt arms deal 14:1602
- history chart 8:766-767
- Holocaust 8:838ff
- Israel 9:694 9:428
- journalism 10:304
- literature 5:1204f
- migrations from 16:1523
- minority treaty 12:45
- nationalism 8:726ff
- petroleum 13:345
- population 13:885ff
- press 13:1026
- publishing 13:1368
- Slánský trials 14:1653
- Subcarpathian Ruthenia 15:470
- synagogues 1:syn. list; 15:607
- textiles 15:1041
- UNSCOP 15:1688
- War Crime Trials 16:288ff
- Youth Aliyah 16:862
- Zionism 16:1111
- *illus:*
- - text
- *pop. tables:*
- - text
- - Bohemia, 1754-1930 4:1180
- - Moravia 1908 12:297
- - Prague, 1880-1930 13:970
- *see also:* BOHEMIA; MORAVIA; SLOVAKIA
CZECHOSLOVAK LITERATURE 5:1204
- *Contents:*
- - Biblical Influences 5:1205
- - Jewish Themes 5:1205
- - Anti-Semitism 5:1206
- - Objective Treatment 55:1207
- - Jewish Contribution 5:1208
- - Capsules 5:1209
- *see also:* GERMAN LITERATURE
Czechowic, Marcin 3:197; 14:22
Czepielow (loc., Belor.) 14:1673
Czerewacha (loc., Ukr.) 10:1229
Czerkaski, Asher 13:1507
Czerkowicz, Itzhak 10:1107
CZERNIAK, MOSHE 5:1210
CZERNIAKOW, ADAM 5:1210
- Holocaust 8:897
- Warsaw Ghetto 16:347
Czernitz, Karl 15:27
Czernowitz (city, Buk.), *see* CHERNOVTSY
CZERNOWITZ YIDDISH LANGUAGE CONFERENCE 5:1211
- Yiddish literature 16:814
Czerny (fam.), *see* SHAḤOR
Czerwinsk (tn., Pol.) 16:682
CZESTOCHOWA (city, Pol.) 5:1212
- Frank, Jacob 7:66
- Poland 13:767
- *illus:* text
Czinner, Paul 4:617
CZOBEL, BÉLA 5:1214
Czortków (city, Ukr.), *see* CHORTKOV
Czuppon, György 8:28
Czuwak, Tuwia 15:1421
Czynsky, Jean 15:25

D

Da'at (sefirah) **10:**571
Dabah, Isaiah **3:**59
D'Abbadie, Antoine **6:**1153
Dabber El Benei Yisrael Ve-Yissa'u (orgn.) **4:**999
Dabbūra (vill., Golan) **13:**1532
– *illus:*
– – lintel **13:**1533
DABBŪRIYYA (vill., Isr.) **5:**1217
Dabella, Abraham **11:**302
Daberath (bib. loc.) **5:**1217
DABROWA GORNICZA (tn., Pol.) **5:**1217
DACHAU (concen. camp) **5:**1218
– Austrian Jews **3:**898
– gassing **16:**1332
– Hoess, Rudolf **8:**806
– War Crimes Trials **16:**294
– *illus:* **7:**620
Dachowitz, H. **12:**1118
Dachs, F. B. **8:**30
Dacia, *see* RUMANIA
Dack, Simon **11:**1200
Da Costa (D'Acosta; fam. name), *see also:* Acosta; Costa
DA COSTA, ISAAC **5:**1220
– slave trade **14:**1663
Dacosta, Jan **11:**14
DA COSTA, JOSEPH MENDES **5:**1220
– *illus:* text
Da Costa, Uriel, *see* COSTA, URIEL DA
Da Costa Athias (fam.), *see* AT(H)IAS
Da Costa Athias, Solomon, *see* COSTA ATHIAS, SOLOMON DA
Da Costa d'Andrade, Benjamin **16:**473
Dacqué, E. **7:**706
Daf (journ.) **1:**newsp. list
Daffodil, Sea (bot.) **13:**617
Daf Ḥaddash (mag.) **14:**1289
Daf ha-Tenu'ah (journ.) **1:**newsp. list
Dafina (stew), *see* CHOLENT
DAFNAH (kib., Isr.) **5:**1220
– statistics **1:**place list
Daftar (prayer bk.) *see Defter*
Daf Yomi (tal. study) **14:**1299
Dagan (deity), *see* DAGON
DAGAN, AVIGDOR **1:**29; **5:**1222
– Czech literature **5:**1209
Dagani, Arnold **14:**424
Dageš (gram. term) **16:**1422
Dagesh (journ.) **1:**newsp. list
Dagestan (reg., Rus.)
– immigration to Israel **9:**503
– marriage custom **11:**1043
– Mountain Jews **12:**478
– synagogue **15:**589
Daghani, Arnold **3:**575
– *illus:*
– – "Potato Vendor at Bershad Camp" (drg.) Fig. 80 **3**-ART
Dagim (zodiac sign), *see* Pisces
Dagobert I (7th cent., k.) **7:**9
– history chart **8:**766-767
Dagon (fort., Isr.), *see* DOK
DAGON (deity) **5:**1222
– Beth Dagon **4:**719
– father of Baal **4:**9ff
– Mari **11:**975
– *illus:*
– – bronze lion **11:**976
DAGON, BARUKH (Asher David) **5:**1223
Dagon silo (Haifa) **7:**1139; **8:**240
D'Aguilar (fam. name), *see under* Aguilar
DAHAN (fam.) **5:**1224
Dahan, Mas'ūd **5:**1224
Dahan, Saadiah **5:**1224
Dahan, Solomon **5:**1224
Dahir al-'Amr, *see* Ẓahir al-Omar
Dahīsha (vill., Er. Isr.) **9:**1492
Dāhiya al-Kāhina (leg. q.), *see* KĀHINA
Dahl, Basil, *see* BOVSHOVER, JOSEPH
DAHLBERG, EDWARD **5:**1224
Dahn, Felix **7:**444
Dahomey (rep., W. Afr.) **9:**438
Dahood, Mitchell **4:**913; **16:**1399
Dahriyya, Al- (Jer.), *see* Gate of Mercy
DAIA (orgn., Arg.) **5:**1225
– defense activities **3:**416ff
– Latin America **10:**1454
DAICHES (fam.) **5:**1226
Daiches, Aryeh Ẓevi ben David, *see* Daiches, Loeb Hirsh
DAICHES, DAVID **5:**1226
Daiches, Israel Ḥayyim **5:**1226; **15:**778
Daiches, Loeb Hirsh **5:**1226
Daiches, M. I. **5:**454
Daiches, Salis **5:**1226
Daiches, Samuel **5:**1226
Dailing, S. **8:**30
Daily Express (newsp.) **4:**1141
Daily Mail (newsp.) **4:**470
Daily Telegraph (newsp.) **10:**1489
"Daily Ticket" (anti-J. law) **16:**334
DAINOW, ẒEVI HIRSCH BEN ZE'EV WOLF **5:**1227
Dairen (city, China) **5:**470; **11:**860
Dairy foods **6:**1417ff
– dietary laws **6:**40
– *see also:* MILK
Daitch, Mendel **14:**1126
Dajjāl (Isl. fig.) **6:**884ff
Dajjānī (Musl. fam.) **9:**1435
Dakar (city, Senegal) **9:**441
Ḍāla' (tn., Yem.) **16:**741
Dalāl, Sasson **8:**1453
Dalālat al-Ha'irīn (wk.), *see* MAIMONIDES *(Guide of the Perplexed)*
Dalāyika (farm, Isr.) **9:**548
DALET (Heb. let.) **5:**1227
– *illus:* text
Dalgard, Olav **14:**933
Daliah (Samar. h. pr.) **14:**729
Dalin (ship) **8:**1250
Dalinsky, Gamliel **5:**447
DALIYAT AL-KARMIL (vill., Isr.) **5:**1228
– *illus:*
– – text
– – first-grade class **9:**926
Dāliyat al-Rūḥa (vill., Isr.) **5:**1229
DALIYYAH (kib., Isr.) **5:**1228
– folk-dance festival **10:**667
– statistics **1:**place list
– *illus:*
– – dance festival **9:**1010
Daliyyah River (Isr.) **9:**144
DALLAS (city, Tex.) **5:**1229
– Texas **15:**1034ff
– *illus:*
– – an "aleph class" **6:**410
– – Passover *seder* **15:**1611
Dallāta (vill., Isr.) **5:**1232
D'allemand, J. D. **8:**29
Dalmaki, Laurentius **8:**30
DALMAN, GUSTAF HERMANN **5:**1232
Dalmanutha (city, Isr.), *see* MAGDALA
Dalmatia (prov., Yug.) **12:**719; **16:**868ff
Dalmatin, Juri **16:**885
Dalnik (loc., Ukr.) **12:**1326
Dalston (sub., Lond.) **11:**479
Dalta (stlmt., Er. Isr.) **9:**272
Daltaban Pasha (vizier, Ott. Emp.) **16:**1538
DALTON (mosh., Isr.) **5:**1232
– statistics **1:**place list
Dal'ūna (Arab poetry) **9:**1038
DALVEN, RACHEL **1:**29
DAMA, SON OF NETINA (tal. fig.) **5:**1233
DAMAGES **5:**1233
– assault **3:**758ff
– *avot nezikin* **3:**986ff
– bailments **14:**1457ff
– consecrated property **8:**280
– domains **14:**83
– gentile's ox **7:**412
– *halakhah le-Moshe* **7:**1167
– liability under labor law **10:**1329ff
– oaths **12:**1299
– Pharisee approach **13:**365
– rape **13:**1548ff
– ransom **5:**856
– Samaritan divorce **14:**747
– transfer of **3:**768
– *illus:* text
– *see also:* FINES; GERAMA AND GARME; TORTS
DAMANHŪR (cities, Egy.) **5:**1236
Ḍamārī, Manṣūr al-, *see* Manṣūr al-Ḍamārī
DAMARI, SHOSHANA **12:**687
– recordings **13:**1617
Damascene, John **5:**551
– Domninus of Larissa **6:**164
DAMASCUS (city, Syr.) **5:**1237
– *Contents:*
– – In the Bible **5:**1237
– – Second Temple Period **5:**1238
– – Muslim Rule **5:**1240
– – Since 1948 **5:**1245
– Abulafia-Alfandari **2:**189
– Ahab **2:**436ff
– ancient dialect **14:**1151
– Angel, Shemayahu **2:**951
– Arab National Movement **9:**455
– Ben Hadad **4:**515f
– *Book of Convenant* **5:**1248ff
– Crusades **9:**268
– Decapolis **5:**1449
– diaspora center **6:**10
– gaonate **7:**315; **7:**323ff
– Hadad cult **7:**1040
– Jeremiah's oracle **9:**1354
– Mamluk riots **11:**835; **11:**836
– Ottoman organization **9:**284
– *Provincia Judaea* **9:**239
– Samaritans **14:**733; **14:**734
– synagogue **15:**613
– *illus:*
– – text
– – Damascus Affair, commemorative medal **5:**1250
– – *Damascus Keter* **4:** *fcg.* 844
– *see also:* ARAM-DAMASCUS; DAMASCUS AFFAIR; SYRIA
DAMASCUS, BOOK OF COVENANT OF (wk.) **5:**1246
– *Contents:*
– – The Admonition **5:**1246
– – The Laws **5:**1248
– – The Sect **5:**1248
– asceticism **3:**680
– calendar **5:**51
– Dead Sea Scrolls **5:**1396
– Dead Sea Sect **5:**1408
– Karaites **10:**762
– *Naphtali, Testament of* **12:**822
– Pesher **13:**333
– Teacher of Righteousness **15:**885
– Yaḥad **16:**699
– *illus:* text
DAMASCUS AFFAIR (bld. lib.) **5:**1249

– Abulafia family 2:184
– Antibi, Jacob 3:58ff
– French Jewry 7:26
– history chart 8:766-767
– Judaism defended 13:1249
– messianism 16:1034
– Munk, Solomon 12:526
– Ottoman Empire 16:1543
– world Jewry 8:727
– *illus:* text
Damascus Document (wk.), *see* DAMASCUS, BOOK OF COVENANT OF
Damascus Gate (Jer.) 9:1407; 9:1434
– *illus:*
– – Aelia Capitolina ruins 9:1407
– – city wall and Christian Quarter 9:172-173
Damascus Keter (illum. Bible, 1260, Burgos) 8:1261
– *illus:* 4:*fcg.* 844; 5:1238
Damascus Letters (wk., Heine) 8:274
Damaskinos, S. B. 8:875
– Greek Jews 7:879
– Nazism 8:915
DAMAVAND (tn., Iran) 5:1252
Damavandi, Samuel ben Aaron 5:1252
DAMESHEK, WILLIAM 5:1252
– medicine 11:1200
DAMIAN, PETER (Petrus Damiani) 5:1252
Damian, Samuil 14:423
DAMIETTA (city, Egy.) 5:1253
Damietta, Abu Saʿīd Ḥalfon ha-Levi al, *see* ḤALFON BEN NETHANEL HA-LEVI ABU SAʿĪD
DAMĪRA (city, Egy.) 5:1253
Dāmiya bridge (Isr.) 14:1335
Dammesek (city, Syr.), *see* DAMASCUS
Dammesek Eliezer (steward of Abraham), *see* ELIEZER
Damnate (loc., Mor.) 12:338
DAMOCRITUS 7:893
– ass worship 3:784
DAMPIERRE-DE-L'AUBE (loc., Fr.) 5:1254
– yeshivah 16:764
DAMROSCH (fam.) 5:1254
Damrosch, Frank Heino 5:1254
Damrosch, Leopold 5:1254
Damrosch, Walter Johannes 5:1254
Damski, Paul 15:306
Damwa (vill., Egy.), *see* DUMUH
DAN (bib. fig., tribe) 5:1255
– *Contents:*
– – The Name 5:1255
– – The Tribe 5:1255
– – History of Tribe 5:1256
– – In the Aggadah 5:1258
– Antichrist 3:62
– Beth-Shemesh 4:772
– breastplate stone 13:1009
– Genesis 7:389
– Kurdish Jews 10:1296
– legendary kingdom 6:576
– settlement 8:581; 8:585; 9:115
– shipping 14:1411
– twelve tribes 15:1383
– *illus:*
– – text
– – banner and emblem 4:181; 8:335
DAN (bib. city, Isr.) 5:1259
– calf worship 9:1372
– cultic center 5:1165
– Laish 8:1064
– *leshem* stone 13:1010
– Mari 11:980
– proscription 8:346
DAN (kib., Isr.) 5:160
– statistics 1:place list
– *illus:*
– – text
– – excavations 5:1259
Dan (riv., Isr.), *see* Dan River
Dan (coop., Isr.) 5:949; 5:951
DAN, FYODOR ILYICH 5:1260
– politics 13:819
DAN, JOSEPH 1:29
– *Shi'ur Komah* 14:1418
DAN, SERGIU 5:1261
Dan, Testament of (Pseudepig.), *see* PATRIARCHS, TESTAMENTS OF THE TWELVE
Dananians (anc. people) 14:215
Danaoi (anc. people) 5:1257
Danby, Frank, *see* Frankau, Julia
DANBY, HERBERT 5:1261
DANCE 5:1262
– *Contents:*
– – In Ancient Israel 5:1262
– – In the Diaspora 5:1264
– – Circumcisions 5:1267
– – Ḥasidism 5:1267
– – Renaissance 5:1268
– – Contemporary Period 5:1268
– – In Modern Period 5:1270
– – Capsules 5:1271
– Angel of Death 2:955
– *Haggadah* reading 7:1103
– Ḥasidism 7:1402; 7:1423ff
– Inbal 8:1309
– Israel 9:1008
– Kadman, Gurit 10:667
– marriage 11:1033
– Niggunim 7:1425
– Saint-Léon 14:661
– *Tanzhaus* 15:805
– Yemenite Jews 16:756; 16:758
– *illus:*
– – Arab dance group 9:1039
– – Brainin, David, in *Swan Lake* 5:1264
– – Daliyyah dance festival 5:1229; 9:1010
– – embroidered *sukkah* hanging 15:*fcg.* 494
– – *Endor* ballet 4:327
– – German refugees dancing *horah* 9:526
– – Guglielmo da Pesaro 7:969
– – Habban immigrants 9:1007
– – Hasidic Dance (paint., Ch. Lieberman) 10:320
– – Ḥasidic Dance (wdct., J. Steinhardt) 7:1415
– – Ḥasidim at the tomb of Bar Yoḥai 7:1419
– – Hasidim at Western Wall 12:672
– – *horah* 8:973
– – Inbal company in *Wild Rose* 8:1309
– – Inbal theater 16:747
– – Ivory engraving, Tel Far'eh 12:567
– – "Joy" (drg., Chagall) 14:1467
– – Kaye, Nora, in *Pillar of Fire* 10:854
– – *Klezmer* repertoire 12:597,599
– – Markova, Alicia, in *The Dying Swan* 11:1007
– – Miriam dancing 12:83; 13:166
– – Nikova, Rira in *Swan Lake* 5:1264
– – Purim play 12:618
– – Saint-Léon and Fanny Cerito 14:662
– – Wadi Kudeirat Graffito 12:568
"Dancing Clown" (paint., U. Lifschitz) Pl. 15 3-ART
"Dancing Girl" (sculp., W. Zorach) 3:560
"Dance of Salome" (paint., Gozzoli) 14:691
D'Ancona (fam.), *see* ANCONA
D'Ancona, Vito (art.), *see* ANCONA, VITO D'
Dandelion (bot.) 6:1365
D'Andrade, Anna (Sarah), *see* Andrade, Anna d'
D'Andrade, Isaac Teixeira, *see* Teixera d'Andrade, Isaac
Dane, Maxwell 2:317
Danfī, Murjān al- 14:749
Danger to life, *see* PIKKU'AḤ NEFESH
DANGLOW, JACOB 5:1274
– Melbourne 11:1283
Dangoor, Elisha 7:1181
DANGOOR, EZRA SASSON BEN REUBEN 5:1274
– Zilkha, Na'īm 16:1023
Dan ha-Shomer (Heb. opera) 7:1267
Dani, Operation (War of Indep.) 11:620; 16:323
Daničić, G. 4:885
DANIEL (pre-Mosaic St.) 5:1274
DANIEL (s. of David) 5:1275
– Absalom's succession 2:174
DANIEL (prophet) 5:1275
– *Contents:*
– – In the Aggadah 5:1275
– – In Islam 5:1276
– – In the Arts 5:1276
– – In Music 5:1277
– in the Arts 4:448; 15:534
– Susa tomb 13:315
– synagogues 15:591; 15:598
– tomb of 14:1483
– Watchers 16:365
– writing on the wall 11:1349
– *illus:*
– – Armenian missal (1331) 5:1280
– – "Daniel in the Lion's Den" (paint., Rubens) 5:1283
– – "Daniel's Vision" (paint., Rembrandt) 5:1287
– – Susa tomb 13:302
– – Susanna and the elders 15:533
– *see also:* DANIEL, BOOK OF
DANIEL (pr., postexilic times) 5:1275
Daniel (9th cent., exil. candidate) 6:1028
Daniel (12th cent., exil.) 6:1031
Daniel (12th cent., abbot) 14:506; 15:1355
DANIEL, BOOK OF 5:1277
– *Contents:*
– – Divisions 5:1277
– – Composition 5:1281
– – Genre and Motifs 5:1286
– – Language Problem 5:1288
– Ancient of Days 2:940
– angels 11:1408ff
– Apocalyptic literature 3:179
– *Book of Baruch* 4:272
– canon 4:824
– Driver's studies 3:266
– eschatology 6:871
– *kiddush ha-Shem* 10:981
– magic 11:704ff
– messianic speculation 2:109
– resistance literature 8:302
– resurrection 14:97
– Septuagint version 4:852ff
– Spinoza 15:283
– Susanna 15:532
– War Scroll 16:1559
– wisdom literature 16:557; 16:560
– *illus:*
– – "Belshazzar's Feast" (paint., Rembrandt) 4:449
– – Shadrach, Meshach, and Abed-Nego in the fiery furnace 2:960
– *see also:* SHADRACH, MESHACH, ABED-NEGO
DANIEL, BOOKS OF (Apoc.) 5:1289
– messianism 11:1418
Daniel, Brother, *see* Rufeisen, Oswald
Daniel, Ezra Menaḥem 5:1290; 13:802
Daniel, The History of (apoc. wk.) *see History of Daniel*
Daniel, Larissa Bogoraz 5:1291
DANIEL, M. 5:1289
DANIEL, MENAHEM SALIH 5:1290
– politics 13:816
Daniel, The Seventh Vision of (Arm. apocalypse), *see Seventh Vision of Daniel*
DANIEL, VISION OF (Heb. apocalypse) 5:1290
– Leo VI 11:23
DANIEL, YULI MARKOVICH 5:1290
Daniel bar Samuel, *see* Daniel ben Samuel ha-Rofe
DANIEL BEN AZARIAH (gaon) 5:1291
– Fostat community 2:631
– gaonate 7:322
– gaonate controversy 6:651
– patriarchate 9:273
DANIEL BEN ELEAZAR BEN NETHANEL ḤIBAT ALLAH (gaon) 5:1291
– Baghdad 16:361
– gaonate 7:321ff
Daniel ben Eleazar he-Ḥasid (gaon) 5:1292
DANIEL BEN ḤASDAI 5:1292
– gaonate dispute 6:1123
DANIEL BEN JEHIEL OF ROME 5:1292
Daniel ben Judah (9th cent.) 5:1351
Daniel ben Judah (13/14 cent.) 3:656; 16:833
DANIEL BEN MOSES AL-QŪMISĪ 5:1292
– Avelei Zion 3:946
– Hebrew language 16:1634
DANIEL BEN PERAḤYAH HA-KOHEN 5:1293
DANIEL BEN SAADIAH HA-BAVLI 5:1294
– Maimonides 11:766
Daniel ben Samuel ha-Rofe 8:1269; 11:733
DANIEL BEN SAMUEL IBN ABĪ RABĪ ʿHA-KOHEN 5:1294
– gaonate 5:321
Daniel ben Samuel of Rossena, *see* ROSSENA, DANIEL BEN SAMUEL OF
Daniel de Pisa 14:115
Daniel Deronda (lit. wk.) 6:664,780
Danielevitz, Hersh (poet), *see* HERSHELE
Daniel ha-Bavli, *see* DANIEL BEN SAADIAH HA-BAVLI
DANIEL ḤAYYATA (amora) 5:1295
Danieli, J. (polit., Rus.), *see* Tschernikhov, Joseph
Daniel ibn al Amshata, *see* DANIEL BEN SAADIAH HA-BAVLI
"Daniel in the Lions' Den" (paint., Rubens) 5:1283
Daniel Ish Ḥamudot, *see* LIEBERMANN, AARON SAMUEL
Daniel-Meyerovich, Mark Naumovich, *see* DANIEL, M.
Daniel of Camerino 2:936
Daniel of Meshed 10:245
Daniel of Viterbo 16:4
Danieloshvili, Moshe 7:427
DANIEL-ROPS, HENRI 5:1295
Daniels, Jacob 4:168; 16:1291
– *illus:*
– – legal document 4:170
Daniels, Michael 16:1291
Daniels, Muskin 4:168
Daniel Sieff Research Institute (Isr.), *see* WEIZMANN INSTITUTE

OF SCIENCE
"Daniel's Vision" (paint., Rembrandt) 5:1287
Daniel the Tailor (amora), *see* DANIEL ḤAYYATA
Daniilovich, Issur, *see* DOUGLAS, KIRK
Danilowitz, Abraham 15:312
Danin, Ezra 5:1295
DANIN, YEḤEZKEL 5:1295
Danish (lang.) 4:876
Danish Literature, *see* SCANDINAVIAN LITERATURE
Danishevsky, Moses 11:1260
Dankner, Oved, *see* BEN-AMI, OVED
Dankovich, Simon 5:1034; 15:817
Dannecker, Theodor 4:1486; 14:253
Dannenbaum, Henry J. 8:1051
Danning, Harry 12:1124
D'Annunzio, Gabriele 5:1428
Danon, Abraham (17th cent., r.) 16:705
DANON, ABRAHAM (schol.) 5:1295
- Adrianople 2:310ff
Danon, Joseph 2:311
Danon, Meir 2:608; 14:871; 16:888
Danon, Moses 14:871
Danon, Nissim Yehudah 9:890
- *illus:*
- - Allenby and 2:647
Danon, Samuel 13:18
Danon, Vitalis 14:537
Dános, Béla 16:1122
Dan River (Isr.) 10:192,197
- Ha-Gosherim 7:1123
- physiography 9:172
- Syrian clashes 15:649
- *illus:*
- - riverside vegetation 9:231
- *see also:* BANIAS
Danson, Barnet 15:1264
DANTE ALIGHIERI 5:1296
- biblical themes 9:1102
- Italian literature 9:1102,1104
Danville (city, Ill.) 8:1256
Danville (city, Va.) 16:163
DANZ, JOHANN ANDREAS 5:1297
- Hebraists 8:30
- *illus:*
- - *Compendium Grammaticae Ebraeo-Chaldaicae* (1765) 8:12
Danzig (fam.) 13:1399
Danzig (port., Pol.), *see* GDANSK
DANZIG (Danziger), ABRAHAM BEN JEHIEL MICHAL 5:1297
Danzig, Samuel 14:1523
Danziger (fam.) 15:635
Danziger (ḥas. dyn.), *see* ALEKSANDROW
Danziger, Bernard 10:1179
Danziger, Isaac Menahem 2:561
Danziger, Jehiel 2:561
Danziger, Jerahmeel Israel Isaac 2:561
- *illus:* text
Danziger, Samuel Ẓevi 2:561
Danziger, Shraga Feivel 2:560
DANZIGER, YITSHAK 5:1298
- *illus:*
- - text
- - sculpture, concrete Fig. 103 3-ART; 14:1064
Danzius, Johann Andreas, *see* DANZ, JOHANN ANDREAS
Daoud (16th cent., physic.) 12:838
- Castellazzo, Simeon 5:237
Da-Oz, Ram 12:671
Daphne (loc., Antioch) 15:1005
Daphne (port, Egy.), *see* Tahpanhes
DA PIERA, MESHULLAM BEN SOLOMON 5:1299
- Isaac ben Judah ha-Seniri 9:22
- Maimonidean controversy 11:749
- messianism 11:1424
- poetry 13:688ff
Da Piera, Solomon ben Immanuel 13:595
DA PIERA, SOLOMON BEN MESHULLAM 5:1299
- Abbas, Moses ben Samuel 2:39
- Alguades, Meir 2:624
- Astruc ha-Levi 3:810
- Saragossa 14:862
Da Pisa (fam.) *see* PISA, DA
DA PONTE, LORENZO 5:1300
- Italian literature 9:1110
- universities 15:1678
Dappei Aliyah (journ.) 1:newsp. list
Dapper, Olaf 15:1357
Dappim (journ., Isr.) 1:newsp. list
Dappim (journ., S. A.) 1:newsp. list
Dappim le-Fiyyut u-le Vikkoret (journ.) 1:newsp. list
Dappim le-Heker ha-Sho'ah (journ.) 1:newsp. list
Dappim le-Limmud Ta'amei ha-Mikra (journ.) 1:newsp. list
Dappim li-Tezunah (journ.) 1:newsp. list
Dappim li-Ydi'ot ha-Sefer ve-ha-Safranut (journ.) 1:newsp. list
Dappim Refu'iyyim (journ.) 1:newsp. list
Daqaqāt (mus. gr.) 8:1461
D'Aquin, Philippe, *see* Aquin, Philippe d'
Daqūqā (loc., Iraq) 8:1447
Dar (gem) 13:1011
Darʿa (reg., Mor.), *see* DRA
Darʿā (tn., Syr.) 6:381; 9:597
DARABANI (tn., Rum.) 5:1301
Darah, Amram 14:748; 14:753
Dār al-Shiknaz (syn., Jer.), *see* Menahem Ẓiyyon Synagogue
Darazī, al- (found., Druze sect) 9:924
Darband (tn., Cauc.), *see* BĀB AL-ABWĀB
Darbashiyya (loc., Golan) 14:1638
Darby, John N. 16:1153
Darda'im (mvmt., Yem.) 10:670; 16:746
Dardanelles (loc., Turk.) 11:1553
- *illus:*
- - Zion Mule Corps 11:555
Dardara (dye plant), *see Koẓah*
Dardeiro (fam.) 12:333
Dar el Beida (city, Mor.), *see* CASABLANCA
Dar e Nashir el Arabi 13:1378
Dar-es-Salaam (tn., Tanzania) 9:441
Darga' (cantillation sign) 16:1413,1455
Dari, Moses 11:744
- messianism 11:1422
DARʿĪ, MOSES BEN ABRAHAM 5:1302
Da Rieti (fam.), *see* RIETI
DARIUS I (6/5 cent., k.) 5:1303
- history 8:616
- northern India 4:34
- Shushan 14:1483
- Tattenai 15:831
- Temple 6:1041; 9:1389; 15:979
- throne 15:1125
- Zerubbabel 16:1001
DARIUS II (Nothus) 5:1304
- historical chart 8:766-767
- Samaritans 14:729
DARIUS III (Codomanus) 5:1304
- Samaritans 14:743
DARIUS THE MEDE (k., Pers.) 5:1304
- Daniel 5:1279
Darkenu (journ.) 1:newsp. list
Darkhei ha-Emori (customs), *see* ḤUKKAT HA-GOI
Darkhei ha-Kalkalah (journ.) 1:newsp. list
Darkhei ha-Nikkud ve-ha-Neginot (bk.) 16:1386, 1474
Darkhei ha-No'ar (journ.) 1:newsp. list
Darkhei ha-Talmud (wk.) 5:120
Darkhei Moshe (wk.) 9:1083
- codification of law 5:650
- Shulḥan Arukh 14:1475
Darkhei No'am (wk.) 16:1376
Darkness, plague of 13:606
- *illus:*
- - Moses pleads with Pharaoh 13:605
Darkness, Sons of (D.S. Scrolls), *see* SONS OF LIGHT
Darlan, Jean Louis Xavier François 2:617
Darmesek (city, Syr.), *see* DAMASCUS
DARMESTETER, ARSÈNE 5:1304
- *Complainte de Troyes* 15:1407
- *illus:* text
Darmesteter, James 5:1305
DARMON (fam.) 5:1306
- Tunisia 15:1444
Darmon, David 5:1306
Darmon, Isaac 5:1306
Darmon, Jacob ben Isaac 5:1306
Darmon, Jacques 5:1306
Darmon, Joseph 5:1306
Darmon, Judah 5:1306
Darmon, Masʿūd 5:1306
Darmon, Mordecai (Tun.) 5:1306
Darmon, Mordecai (Alg.) 5:1306
Darmon, Moses 5:1306
Darmon, Nehorai 5:1306
Darmon, Pierre 15:314
Darmon, Raoul 15:1449
Darmon, Victor-Ḥayyim 5:1306
DARMSTADT (city, Ger.) 5:1306
- archives 3:387
- *illus:*
- - text
- - synagogue 7:492
Darmstadt, Jacob 16:163
DARMSTADT, JOSEPH 5:1307
- Richmond 14:160
Darmstadt, Joseph Hirschel 8:523
DARMSTADT HAGGADAH (15th cent. illum. ms., Ger.) 7:1099
- Israel of Heidelberg 9:1263
- *illus:* 3:1014; 7: *fcg.* 811, 1085
Darmstadt Maḥzor (illum. ms.) 11:732
Darnel (bot.), *see* TARES
Darnell, Felix 4:788
DAROCA (city, Sp.) 5:1308
DAROFF, SAMUEL H. 5:1308
Darom (reg., Er. Isr.) 4:731
Darom (period.) 1:newsp. list; 3:424; 13:1040
Darom, Abraham S., *see* DRAPKIN, ABRAHAM
Daron (tn., Er. Isr.), *see* DEIR-AL-BALAH
DARQUIER DE PELLEPOIX, LOUIS 5:1309
Darrow, Clarence 11:441
DARSHAN (prch.) 5:1309
- fable 6:1131
- *see also:* HOMILETIC LITERATURE; MAGGID; PREACHING
Darshan, Joseph, *see* CALAHORA, JOSEPH BEN SOLOMON
Darshan, Joseph ben Moses, *see* JOSEPH BEN MOSES DARSHAN OF PRZEMYSLANY
Darshan Zaken (pseud.), *see* LEWINSKY, ELHANAN LEIB
Dar-Ṭanṭūra (loc., Er. Isr.) 9:290
Dartmouth College (U.S.) 4:1219; 15:1656; 15:1681
Dārūm (vill., Er. Isr.), *see* KEFAR DAROM
Darūrī fī al-Lugha al-ʿIbrāniyya, al- (wk.) 16:1389
Darvan (punctuation sign), *see Maqqel*
DARVAS, LILI 15:1081
Darwish, Maḥmud 9:1042
DARWĪSH, SHALOM 12:1464; 12:1466
- Iraq 8:1452
- Israel 9:1041
Da San Miniato (fam.) 2:934
Das Arbeitende Eretz Yisrael (period.) 14:1326
D'Ascoli (fam. name), *see also under* Ascoli
D'Ascoli, Angelo, *see* D'Ascoli, Jacob ben Abraham
D'Ascoli, Jacob ben Abraham 3:690, 13:583
DASHEWSKI, PINḤAS 5:1310
DA SILVA, HOWARD 12:465
Das Juedische ABC (encyc.) 6:734
Das Juedische Heim (period.) 13:1049
Das Juedische Nachrichtenblatt (period.) 4:648
Das Kapital (wk., Marx) 11:1072
Daskarta (tn., Babyl.), *see* DESKARTA
Das Leben Jesu nach juedischen Quellen (wk.) 15:1208
Das Neue Israel (journ.) 13:1049
Das Reich Judaea im Jahre 6000 (wk.) 16:1152
DASSAULT, DARIUS PAUL 5:1310
DASSAULT, MARCEL 5:1310
- aviation 2:321
DASSIN, JULES 5:1311
Dassin-Malines (internment camp) 8:858
Dassow (-vius), T. 8:30
Datafernes (name), *see* HOLOFERNES
Dates (fruit) 6:1416; 16:1276
Date tree, *see* PALM
DATHAN AND ABIRAM (bib. figs.) 5:1311
- Korah 10:1190ff
- Moses 12:377
- *illus:* text
Dating, *see* CALENDAR; CHRONOLOGY; SELEUCID ERA
Da Tivoli (fam.) 2:934
Da Tivoli, Serafino (art.), *see* TIVOLI, SERAFINO DA
Datner, Maurycy 5:1035
DATO, MORDECAI BEN JUDAH 5:1313
- Kabbalah 10:548
Dattilo (15th cent.) 2:646
Dat u-Medinah (journ.) 11:newsp. list
Dat Yehudit (legal term) 10:383; 12:9
Daube, Dave (philan.) 12:1353
DAUBE, DAVID (schol.) 5:1313
Daube, Sam 12:1353
Daud, Abraham ibn, *see* IBN DAUD, ABRAHAM BEN DAVID HA-LEVI
DAUDET, LÉON 5:1314
Daufman, Harold 12:1408
DAUGAVPILS (city, Latv.) 5:1314
- self-defense 14:1126
- *illus:*
- - synagogue 10:1464
Daughter, *see* PARENT AND CHILD
"Daughter of Pharaoh" (paint., S. Solomon) 15:117

Daughters of Zion (orgn., U.S.) 7:1041
DAUPHINÉ (reg., Fr.) 5:1315
- Jewry 7:16ff
Davan, Abraham, *see* VAEZ, ABRAHAM
DAVAR (newsp.) 5:1316
- Alterman's political verse 2:774
- newspapers 12:1047; 12:1056ff
- Shazar, Zalman 14:1324ff
- statistics 1:newsp. list
- *illus:* text
Davar (period., Arg.) 3:424; 13:1040; 15:52
Davar la-Golah (newsp.) 1:newsp. list
Davar li-Yladim (period., Isr.) 5:458; 9:1016
Davar she-lo ba la-olam (leg. term) 2:217; 5:926ff
- custom as acquisition mode 12:17
- gift 7:561
- obligation method 12:111; 12:133
- public body 13:1353; 13:1359
- waiver 11:1232ff
Davenport (city, Io.) 8:1437
DAVENPORT, MARCIA 5:1317
Daverat (kib., Isr.) 1:place list
DA VERONA, GUIDO 5:1318
- Italian literature 9:1112
Davey, Jocelyn, *see* RAPHAEL, CHAIM
Davičo, Benko 16:888
DAVIČO, HAJIM S. 16:888; 16:890
DAVIČO, LUJO 5:1272
DAVIČO, OSCAR 5:1318
DAVID 5:1318
- *Contents:*
- - In the Bible 5:1318
- - In the Aggadah 5:1326
- - Tomb of 5:1329
- - In Liturgy 5:1329
- - In Kabbalah 5:1331
- - In Christianity 5:1331
- - In Islam 5:1332
- - In Hebrew Literature 5:1333
- - In the Arts 5:1334
- General
- - abstinence example 6:1189ff
- - articles of faith 10:385
- - calendar 5:49
- - Eupolemus 6:964
- - historical chart 8:766–767
- - kabbalistic view 10:575
- - king, kingship 10:1012ff
- - kingdom of 13:237ff
- - Messiah 11:1407
- - messiah's soul 6:881
- - Micah 11:1481; 11:1483ff
- - poetry 13:672
- - population 13:867
- - priestly divisions 12:89
- - priestly ritual 13:1083
- - Psalms, Book of 13:1313; 13:1317
- - Ruth, Book of 14:518ff
- - sacrifice 14:606
- - Temple music 12:559
- Associates and Life
- - Abiathar 2:71ff
- - Abigail 2:73
- - Abishag 2:79
- - Abishai 2:79ff
- - Abner 2:87ff
- - Absalom 2:174
- - Achish 2:210
- - Adonijah 2:294
- - Ahithophel 2:465
- - Amasa 2:793ff
- - Amnon 2:860
- - ancestry of 15:782ff
- - anointing 3:31
- - Araunah 3:290
- - Bath-Sheba 4:321
- - Gihon tunnel 9:1525
- - God's covenant 5:1018ff
- - Goliath 7:756
- - Hebron 8:226
- - Hiram 8:501
- - Hushai 8:1128
- - Jebus, Jebusite 9:1307
- - Jerusalem 9:1381
- - Joab 10:106ff
- - Jonathan 10:183
- - Mephibosheth 11:1379
- - Nahash 12:770
- - Nathan 12:846
- - old age 2:344
- - Palti 13:49
- - Philistine idols 8:349
- - Rechab and Baanah 13:1609
- - Samuel, Book of 14:789
- - Saul 8:587ff; 14:911; 14:913ff
- - Sheba ben Bichri 14:1329
- - Shimei 14:1402
- - Solomon 15:96ff
- - Temple 15:943ff
- - war dress 16:271ff
- - Ziba 16:1016
- Foreign Relations
- - Amalekites 2:790
- - Ammonites 2:856
- - borders of Israel 9:115
- - Edom 6:374ff
- - Egypt 6:483
- - Transjordan 15:1317
- House of
- - Bustanai legend 4:1537
- - genealogy 7:382
- - Jesus 10:10
- - Jerusalem graves 9:1553
- - Moabite ancestry 8:1423
- - Romans 9:238
- - *see also:* DAVID, DYNASTY OF
- Legend
- - alchemist 2:543
- - Arthurian legends 3:653; 3:654
- - Ḥijāz Jews 3:233
- - Satan 14:903,904
- - Shavuot 14:1057
- - *Shmuel Bukh* 14:1426
- - tomb 8:921; 9:1496; 13:514
- In the Arts 2:175; 13:1325; 14:784,917
- *illus:*
- - text
- - Abigail bearing gifts to 3:527; 12:736
- - admonished by Nathan 12:846
- - anointing of 3:28,30; 6:285, 1125; 12:1351; 14:793
- - Bath-Sheba and 11:633
- - *Bohum Psalter* 14:541
- - bringing the Ark to Jerusalem 6:288
- - death 10:106
- - dynasty (geneal. table) 5:1341
- - entering the House of the Lord 13:1304
- - espying Bath-Sheba at her bath 4:321
- - folk-art portrait 8:1286
- - friendship with Jonathan 7:196
- - greeted by women of Israel 5:1263
- - hiding from Saul 13:1326
- - *Kaufmann Mishneh Torah* 7:*fcg.* 747
- - killing 200 Philistines 11:1493
- - "King David's Entry into Jerusalem" (tpst., M. Chagall) 5:*fcg.* 334
- - kingdom, limits of (map) 9:115
- - mourning death of Absalom 2:175; 5:1326
- - playing the harp before Saul 14:911
- - playing the lyre 4:1,947; 7:341
- - praying to God 4:321
- - refraining from killing Saul 6:293
- - *St. Albans Psalter* 15:1497
- - slaying Goliath 4:1; 8:1283; 14:793
- - threatened by Saul 7:196
- - tomb (alleged) 8:924
David (12th cent., exil. candidate) 6:1029
David (12th cent., nasi) 12:444
David (13th cent., Fr.) 15:1290
David (15/16 cent., scribe) 4:470
David II (nagid, Egy.) 11:837
David (court J. fam.) 5:1009; 7:1279
DAVID (fam., Can.) 5:1338
- Canada 5:109
David, Aaron Hart 5:1338
David, Alexander 5:1009; 12:538
- art collector 5:310
David, Benjamin 13:812
David, City of (Jer.) 9:1381; 9:1521
- *illus:*
- - site and city wall 9:1381, 1382
David, David (bnk.) 5:109; 5:1338
- Montreal 12:284
- *illus:*
- - portrait 12:285
David, David (U.S.) 12:1217
DAVID, DYNASTY OF 5:1339
- genealogy 7:382
- Hillel dynasty 14:644
- Talmud 15:1000
- *geneal. table:* text
- *see also:* DAVID
David, Sir E. (mayor) 3:840
DAVID, ERNEST (musicol.) 12:687
DAVID, FERDINAND 5:1345
David, Ferenc 8:30
DAVID, FILIP 16:890
David, Hans (ed.) 12:700
David, Hirsch 16:85
David, House of, *see* DAVID, DYNASTY OF
David, Ismar 11:47; 15:1488
- *illus:*
- - Hebron type faces 15:1486
David, Israel 5:952
David, Janina (writ.) 6:785
DAVID, JEAN (art.) 5:1346
- *illus:* text
David, J. J. (writ.) 8:1053
David, Johanan (butcher) 13:301
DAVID, JOSEPH (plwrt.) 5:1346
David, Kingdom of (Crus. kdm.), *see* Jerusalem, Kingdom of
David, Lazarus 5:1338; 12:284
David, Louise, *see* Dulcken, Louise
David, M. (r., Ger.) 4:1158
DAVID, MARTIN (orient.) 16:1266
David, Moses 5:1567
David, Samuel (sol.) 5:1338; 12:284
DAVID, SAMUEL (comp.) 12:687
David, Solomon Michael 5:934
David, Tomb of 5:1329
- holy places 8:921
- Jerusalem 9:1496
- Mt. Zion 16:1031
- pilgrimage 13:514
- *illus:*
- - Mount Zion 9:1465
David, Tower of (Jer.) 9:1394,1416; 9:1526
- *illus:*
- - Citadel entrance 9:1397
- - Hasmonean wall 9:1391
- - Johns' excavations 9:1533
- - Palestine stamp 15:332
- - *Shivviti* plaque 14:*fcg.* 1422
- - Simḥat Torah procession 9:907
- - western part of Old City wall 9:1518
- *see also:* Phasael, Tower of
David Alfasi, *see* ALFASI, DAVID BEN ABRAHAM
David al-Qūmisī 5:1293
Davidashvili, Rosa 7:427
Davidashvili, Yiẓhak 7:427
David Bacri of Algiers 4:1274
DAVID BEN AARON IBN ḤASSIN (Ḥussein) 5:1346
David ben Abraham Alfasi, *see* ALFASI, DAVID BEN ABRAHAM
David ben Abraham Caslari, *see* Caslari, David ben Abraham
DAVID BEN ABRAHAM HA-LAVAN 5:1347
- Kabbalah 10:563
David ben Abraham ha-Nagid 14:1531
DAVID BEN ABRAHAM MAIMUNI 5:1347
- Acre 9:274
David ben Amram Adani, *see* ADANI, DAVID BEN AMRAM
DAVID BEN ARYEH LEIB OF LIDA 5:1348
- Amsterdam community 2:899
- *illus:*
- - *Yad Kol Bo* (1727) 8:75
David ben Benjamin of Montalcino 7:407
David ben Ben-Zion Jehezkel 11:811
DAVID BEN BOAZ 5:1349
DAVID BEN DANIEL (exil., Egy.) 5:1349
- Abiathar ha-Kohen 2:72
- gaonate 7:323; 7:324
- sovereignty struggle 6:1033
DAVID BEN DANIEL (exil., Iraq) 5:1349
David ben Elazar ha-Levi 8:1324
David ben Eliezer ibn Pakuda, *see* IBN PAQUDA, DAVID BEN ELEAZAR
David ben Gedaliah 13:579
David ben Ḥasan (Ḥassūn), Abu Suleiman, *see* DAVID BEN HUSSEIN, ABU SULEIMAN
David ben Ḥasdai 7:1366; 15:122
David ben-Ḥayyim (Ind.) 13:1036
DAVID BEN ḤAYYIM OF CORFU 5:1350
DAVID BEN HEZEKIAH (11th cent.) 5:1350
- Hezekiah 8:457
- Iraq 8:1446
David ben Hezekiah (12th cent.) 5:1350
David ben Hodayyah 8:1447; 14:974
David ben Huna 13:579
DAVID BEN HUSSEIN, ABU SULEIMAN 5:1350
David ben Isaac 2:466
David ben Jacob ha-Ivri 12:62
David Benjamin Leib 11:213
David ben Joab 11:549
David ben Joseph Abudarham, *see* ABUDARHAM, DAVID BEN JOSEPH
David ben Joseph of Narbonne 3:803
David ben Joshua (nagid, Damascus) 4:1208
DAVID BEN JOSHUA (Kar.) 5:1351
- Zerah ben Nathan 16:996
David ben Joshua ha-Ḥazzan, *see* Ḥazzan, David ben Joshua
DAVID BEN JOSHUA MAIMUNI (nagid, Egy.) 5:1351
DAVID BEN JUDAH 5:1351
- gaonate 7:316
David ben Judah, Messer Leon, *see* LEON, MESSER DAVID BEN JUDAH
DAVID BEN JUDAH HE-HASID 5:1351
- Kabbalah 10:534; 10:563
- Zohar 16:1211
David ben Kalonymus 14:1480
DAVID BEN LEVI OF NARBONNE 5:1352

David ben Maimon (br., Maim.) **11:**755ff
David ben Maimun (schol.) **10:**278
DAVID BEN MANASSEH DARSHAN **5:**1352
David ben Meir Kalonymus **15:**1326
David ben Menahem ha-Kohen **2:**779; **4:**867; **11:**357
David ben Menahem Mendel of Kotsk **10:**1223
DAVID BEN MESHULLAM OF SPEYER **5:**1353
- Speyer **15:**263
David ben Moses of Reindorf **7:**310
David ben Moses of Zuelz (kab.) **15:**284
David ben Nasi **13:**579
DAVID (Tevele) BEN NATHAN OF LISSA **5:**1353
- Leszno **11:**53
- Wessely **16:**463
DAVID BEN SAADIAH (Sp.) **5:**1354
David ben Saadiah ha-Kohen (Yem.) **13:**579
David ben Sa'del al-Hīti **10:**422
David ben Samson **13:**579
DAVID BEN SAMUEL (exil.) **5:**1354
DAVID BEN SAMUEL HA-LEVI (Taz) **5:**1354
- Isaac ha-Levi **9:**28
- Jewish literature **11:**336
- Lvov **11:**610
- Shabbetai ha-Kohen **14:**1218
- *illus:*
- - Taz synagogue, Lvov **11:**609
DAVID BEN SAUL **5:**1355
David ben Shabbetai
- *Regensburg Pentateuch* **3:**754; **4:**67,963; **14:***fcg.* 1323
DAVID BEN SOLOMON (Kar., Egy.) **5:**1356
David ben Solomon ha-Kohen of Lunel **11:**565
DAVID BEN SOLOMON IBN ABI ZIMRA (Radbaz) **5:**1356
- articles of faith **10:**386
- Berab, Jacob **4:**583
- Egypt **6:**496
- *hiddushim* **8:**467
- Jerusalem **9:**1436
- Kabbalah **10:**545; **10:**640
- Karaite marriage **11:**842
- responsa **11:**337
- Temple Mount **15:**990
- *illus:* text
David ben Solomon of Seville **15:**1322
David ben Yaḥya **8:**1170
David ben Yom Tov, *see* IBN BILIA, DAVID BEN YOM TOV
DAVID BEN ZAKKAI **5:**1358
- Kohen Ẓedek **10:**1141
- Mubashir ha-Kohen **12:**497
- Saadiah Gaon **14:**545ff
DAVID BEN ZAKKAI II **5:**1359
- David ben Daniel **5:**1349
David ben Zimra, *see* DAVID BEN SOLOMON IBN ABI ZIMRA
DAVID D'BETH HILLEL **5:**1360
- Beirut **4:**402
- Bushire **4:**1535
- Iraq **8:**1451
- Sidon **14:**1508
- travels **15:**1350,1353
David de Caderousse, *see* DAVIN DE CADEROUSSE
David de la Hija **4:**1469
David de la Motta **8:**1396
David de Rossi, *see* Rossi, David de
David Don Çag Merdohay **6:**261
David the Elder (bnk., Ger.) **4:**168
DAVID-GORODOK (tn., Rus.) **5:**1360
David ha-Bavli, *see* AL-MUKAMMIS, DAVID IBN MARWAN AL-RAQI AL-SHIRAZI
David ha-Dayyan (gram.), *see* DAVID IBN HAJJAR
David ha-Ḥazzan, *see* Ḥazzan, David ben Joshua
David Ḥai ben Meir **10:**242
David ha-Kohen (mintmaster) **12:**63
David ha-Kohen (paytan) **13:**579
David ha-Kohen (r.) **3:**24
David ha-Kohen (au.) **14:**263
David ha-Lavan, *see* DAVID BEN ABRAHAM HA-LAVAN
David ha-Levi of Stepan **11:**628
David ha-Nasi (Kar.), *see* DAVID BEN BOAZ
David Hebrew (type let.) **15:**1488
David he-Ḥasid, *see* DAVID BEN JUDAH HE-ḤASID
Davidhof, Karl Yulyevich, *see* DAVYDOV, KARL YULYEVICH
David ibn Abi Zimra, *see* DAVID BEN SOLOMON IBN ABI ZIMRA
David ibn Bilia, *see* IBN BILIA, DAVID BEN YOM TOV
DAVID IBN HAJJAR **5:**1361
- linguistics **16:**1358,1382
- Seville **14:**1201
- Spain **15:**226
David ibn Ḥassin, *see* DAVID BEN AARON IBN ḤASSIN
David ibn Pakuda, *see* IBN PAQUDA, DAVID BEN ELEAZAR
David Joseph of Lelov **11:**9
David Kohn Ḥassid, *see* Kohn Ḥassid, David
Davidman, Eleazar **15:**315
David of Dessau **5:**615
Davidoff, Hyman **13:**820
Davidoff, Ken **15:**310
DAVIDOFF, LEO MAX **5:**1362
David of Hamadan **13:**310
David of Lelov, *see* Lelov, David of
David of Lida, *see* DAVID BEN ARYEH LEIB OF LIDA
David of Lissa, *see* DAVID BEN NATHAN OF LISSA
DAVID OF MAKOW **5:**1362
David of Metz **11:**1450
David of Minzburg **10:**349
David of Montalcino, *see* David ben Benjamin of Montalcino
David of Narbonne (12th cent.), *see* David ben Joseph of Narbonne
David of Narbonne (13th cent.), *see* DAVID BEN LEVI OF NARBONNE
David of Oxford **12:**1534
David of Ploesti, *see* Friedmann, David
David of Schweidnitz **4:**1417; **14:**1536
David of Seville, *see* David ben Solomon of Seville
David of Speyer, *see* DAVID BEN MESHULLAM OF SPEYER
DAVID OF TALNA **5:**1363
- Talnoye **15:**779
- Vasilkov **15:**1472
David Onkinerah **13:**579
Davidov, David **4:**691; **9:**1004; **15:**1061
Davidovic, E. (Cz.) **13:**975
Davidovich (soc. ldr.), *see* LVOVICH, DAVID
Davidovich, Harry Z. **14:**1264
Davidovitch, David (hist.) **3:**652
Davidow, David (art.) *see* Davidov, David
Davidowicz, David (art.) **4:**1220
"David playing the Harp before Saul" (paint., Rembrandt) **14:**911
David Reuveni, *see* REUVENI, DAVID
David River, *see* Naḥal David
DAVIDS, AARON ISSACHAR (Bernard) BEN NAḤMAN **5:**1363
- Rotterdam **14:**350
Davids, Louis **12:**984
David Savran, *see* Savran, David
David Schmelka ben Judah Loebush **10:**288
Davidsohn, Bogumil, *see* DAWISON BOGUMIL
DAVIDSOHN, ISRAEL (path.) **11:**1207
DAVIDSOHN, ROBERT **5:**1364
David Solomon of Sorki **9:**514
Davidson, Benjamin **14:**834
Davidson, Bruce **13:**484
Davidson, Cecilia, *see* RAZOVSKY, CECILIA
Davidson, Charles **5:**487
Davidson, E. **16:**1165
DAVIDSON, ISRAEL (schol.) **5:**1364
- Cairo *Genizah* **16:**1338
Davidson, Jacob **13:**1374
DAVIDSON, JO **5:**1365
DAVIDSON, LIONEL **6:**785; **6:**787
Davidson, Paul **12:**453
DAVIDSON, SAMUEL **5:**1366
David's Tower (Jer.), *see* David, Tower of
David Tevele of Lissa, *see* DAVID BEN NATHAN OF LISSA
David Uziel ben Ḥayyim *see* Uziel, David ben Hayyim
David-Weill, Pierre **10:**1513
David Ẓevi of Neustadt **10:**858
David Ẓevi of Shargorod **15:**398
Davies, Benjamin **8:**30
D'AVIGDOR (fam.) **5:**1367
- *geneal. table:* text; **7:**735
D'Avigdor, Elim **5:**1367; **6:**760
D'Avigdor, Isaac Samuel **5:**1367
D'Avigdor, Countess Rachel **5:**1367
D'Avigdor, Count Salomon Henri **5:**1367
D'Avigdor Goldsmid (fam.), *see* D'AVIGDOR
D'Avigdor-Goldsmid, Sir Henry Joseph **3:**962; **5:**1368
D'Avigdor-Goldsmid, James Arthur **5:**1368
D'Avigdor-Goldsmid, Sir Osmond **5:**1368
- English Jewry **6:**762
D'Avila (fam.), *see* AVILA, DE
D'Avila, Juan Arias, *see* Avila, Juan Arias d'
DAVIN DE CADEROUSSE **5:**1368
- Avignon **3:**967
DAVIO (orgn.) **4:**999
DAVIS, ABEL **11:**1552; **11:**1572
Davis, Al (sport.) **15:**308
DAVIS, ALEXANDER BARNARD **5:**1368
- Sydney **15:**564
Davis, Ansley **14:**1664
Davis, Mrs. Barnett **13:**569
Davis, Benjamin **14:**1664
Davis, Sir David **4:**1039
Davis, David **15:**311
DAVIS, SIR EDMUND **5:**1368
DAVIS, EDWARD (Austr. convict) **5:**1369
Davis, Edward (lit. crit.) **15:**210
Davis, Emily **12:**944
DAVIS, SIR ERNEST HYAM **5:**1369
- New Zealand **12:**1130
Davis, G. (offic., India) **8:**1357
Davis, George (U.S.) **14:**1664
Davis, Israel **6:**734
Davis, J. (Hebr.) **8:**30
Davis, James (plwrt.), *see* HALL, OWEN
Davis, Jefferson **4:**529
Davis, Lew W. **15:**1423
Davis, Mortimer B. **15:**1177
DAVIS, MOSHE **1:**29; **5:**1369
- history **8:**568
Davis, Myer David **10:**98
Davis, S. (au., Eng.) **5:**450
Davis, Sammy, Jr. **12:**451
Davis, Solomon (U.S.) **14:**1664
Davke (period.) **3:**424; **13:**1040
DAVYDOV, KARL YULYEVICH **5:**1370
Dawidgródek (tn., Rus.), *see* DAVID-GORODOK
DAWIDSOHN, ḤAYYIM **5:**1370
- Ostrog **12:**1514
DAWIDSOHN, JOSEPH **5:**1370
Dawidson, Abraham Abele **5:**1370
Dawidson, Naphtali **5:**1370
DAWISON, BOGUMIL **5:**1370
Day, *see* DAY AND NIGHT; YEAR
Day, The (newsp.), *see* JEWISH DAY
DAYAN (fam.) **5:**1371
Dayan, Assaf **5:**1371
Dayan, Devorah **5:**1371
DAYAN, MOSHE **5:**1372
- Ben-Gurion **4:**513
- Haganah **9:**687
- Jerusalem reunification **9:**411
- Mapai **11:**913
- politics **9:**669
- Rafi **13:**1512
- Six-Day War **14:**1627,1638
- unity government **9:**408ff
- *illus:*
- - text
- - autograph **3:**480
- - "Hitler's able pupil" (E. Ger. cart., 1967) **3:**155
- - Israel-Jordan Armistice Agreement **9:**375
- - Knesset Session **10:**1113
- - Rhodes, April 1949 **3:**479
- - Sadeh, Yiẓḥak, and **7:**1070
- - Six-Day War, entering Jerusalem **9:**409
- - Six-Day War orphans bar-mitzvah **10:**883
- - U.J.A. National Conference **15:**1541
- - "vying with Hitler for fame" (Rus. cart., 1967) **3:**155
Dayan, Ruth **5:**1371
Dayan, Shemuel **5:**1371
Dayan, Yael **5:**1371
Dayan, Zohar **5:**1371
DAY AND NIGHT **5:**1374
- Jewish philosophy **13:**421
- *see also:* CALENDAR; TWILIGHT
Dayaukku (bib. fig.) **11:**1176
Dayig u-Midgeh (journ.) **1:**newsp. list
Day-Jewish Journal (U.S.) **6:**1212
Daylesford (tn., Austr.) **11:**1286
Day-Morning Journal (newsp.), *see* JEWISH MORNING JOURNAL
DAY OF ATONEMENT **5:**1376
- *Contents:*
- - In the Bible **5:**1376
- - In Second Temple **5:**1377
- - In the Halakhah **5:**1377
- - Prayers **5:**1378
- - Torah reading **5:**1379

- - Customs 5: 1379
- - Eve 5: 1381
- - Termination 5: 1381
- - Meaning 5: 1382
- - Annual Day of Purgation 5: 1384
- General
- - 'Āshūrā' 3:739
- - atonement 10: 1040
- - calendar 5:44
- - Commandments, the 613 5:764,768ff
- - Days of Penitence 15: 1001
- - Gottlieb, Maurycy 7:827
- - Hoshana Rabba 8: 1027ff; 15:501
- - illuminated *maḥzorim* 11:733
- - *Jubilees, Book of* 10:325
- - magical practices 10:508
- - *pikku'ah nefesh* 13:510
- - Purim 13: 1395
- - Ramadan 10: 1198
- - repentance 14:75
- - Satan on 14:904
- - sins forgiven 14: 1592
- - synagogue 15:582,585
- - tabernacle 15:687
- Customs and Observance
- - ablution 2:83
- - *Avodah* 3:976
- - Azazel ritual 3:999
- - blessing of children 4: 1087, 1088
- - confession of sins 5:878; 5:879
- - dancing 5: 1264
- - Falashas 6: 1148
- - fasting and abstinence 6: 1189ff; 6: 1425
- - greetings 7:915
- - incense 8: 1314
- - *kapparot* 10:756
- - Karaites 10:779
- - *kotevet* 16:389
- - priestly blessing 12: 11
- - Qumran community 15:887
- - religion in Israel 9:902
- - sacrifice 14:600ff
- - Samaritans 14:742; 14:743
- - *shofar* 6: 1392
- - *sukkah* 15:493
- - *tallit* 15:743
- - *tashlikh* 15:829
- - Ungar, Joel of Rechnitz 15: 1532
- Liturgy
- - *Al Ḥet* 2:629
- - *Amidah* 2:844ff
- - *Anna be-Korenu* 3:26
- - *Ashamnu* 3:694
- - *Avinu Malkenu* 3:974
- - *Avodah* 3:976
- - *haftarah* 16: 1342
- - *Hakhel* benedictions 7: 1149
- - *ha-Mavdil* 7: 1225
- - *Kol Nidrei* 10: 1166
- - *musaf* 12:532ff
- - *Ne'ilah* 12:943
- - *Shir ha-Yiḥud* 14: 1416
- - *u-Netanneh Tokef* 15: 1531
- *illus:*
- - text
- - *"Ashamnu"* (drg., A. Levy) 2:630
- - *Ne'ilah* service, a page 12:944
- - prayer in a Dutch synagogue (drg., B. Picart) 3:831
- - salutations (table) 7:915
- - scapegoat cast over the cliff 3: 1000
- - Temple service 16:845
- - Verdun synagogue, U.S. troops 16: 109
- *mus. notations:*
- - *Avodah* 3:978
- - *El Male Raḥamim* 6:682
- - *Kol Nidrei* 10: 1168
- - *Mi-Sinai niggunim* 12: 151
- - *Yigdal* 16:835
- *see also:* FESTIVALS

DAY OF THE LORD 5: 1387
- Abraham 2: 124
- Amos' oracles 2:887
- Joel, Book of 10: 131ff
- Kabbalah 10:587
- Muslim thought 9: 1576ff
- ordeal 12: 1448
- Rosh ha-Shanah 14:307ff
- Samaritans 14:740
- tractate *Rosh ha-Shanah* 14:311
- *see also:* ESCHATOLOGY

Dayqa Pass (loc., Sinai) 14: 1606

Dayr al-Balaḥ (tn., Isr.), *see* DEIR AL-BALAḤ

Dayr al-Qamar (tn., Leb.) 10: 1544; 15:644

Dayrī, Al- (Musl. fam.) 9: 1425

Dayr Naḥḥās (vill., Isr.), *see* Deir Naḥḥās

Dayr Yāsīn (Arab. vill.), *see* Deir Yāsīn

DAYTON (city, Ohio) 5: 1388
- Agus, Jacob 2:435
- Ohio 12: 1344
- *illus:* txt

Dayton (vill., Nev.) 12: 1017

Daytona Beach (city, Fla.) 6: 1363

DAYYAN (fam.) 5: 1389

DAYYAN (judge) 5: 1390
- appointment and qualifications 9:643ff
- arbitrator 3:297
- election of 2:200
- *ḥaver* 7: 1492
- *maggid* 11:699
- sages 14:646
- title 15: 1164
- *see also:* BET DIN AND JUDGES; RABBI, RABBINATE

Dayyan, Aaron 5: 1390

Dayyan, Abraham 5: 1389

Dayyan, Hiyya al- 10:278

Dayyan, Ḥiyya ben Joseph 5: 1390; 14: 1366

Dayyan, Isaac 5: 1390

Dayyan, Isaiah 2:564

Dayyan, Isaiah ben Mordecai (r.) 5: 1390

Dayyan, Isaiah Ḥakham (scribe) 5: 1389

Dayyan, Joseph (17/18 cent.) 13: 1105

Dayyan, Joseph ben Ezra (19/20 cent.) 5: 1390

Dayyan, Mordecai 5: 1389

Dayyan, Moses (19th cent.) 5: 1390

Dayyan, Moses ben Saadiah (16th cent.) 5: 1389

Dayyan, Saul 5: 1390

Dayyan, Solomon 5: 1390

Dayyan al-Yahud (J. judge) 2: 153

Dayyanei de-Bava (tit., geonic period) 7:316

DAYYEINU (litur.) 5: 1391
- *illus:*
- - text
- - *Birds' Head Haggadah* 7:*fcg.* 875
- - *Mocatta Haggadah* 7:*fcg.* 1451
- - oriental *Haggadah* (12th cent.) 8: 1274
- - *Ryland's Spanish Haggadah* 5:*fcg.* 1387
- - *Ryland's Spanish Haggadah*, "Brother" to 7: 1083
- - *Venice Haggadah* 10:211

Dayyena, Azriel, *see* DIENNA, AZRIEL BEN SOLOMON

Da Zara, Leonino 2:321

D'Azeglio, Massimo Taparelli, Marchese, *see* AZEGLIO, MASSIMO TAPARELLI, MARCHESE D'

D'Azevedo (fam.), *see* AZEVEDO

Dead, communion with 6: 1190

Dead, respect for 5: 1425
- autopsies 3:931
- burial 4: 1517ff

"Dead" Ḥasidim, *see* NAḤMAN OF BRATSLAV

DEAD SEA 5: 1391
- consecrated property 8:281
- geology 9: 194ff
- human geography 9:589
- mineral deposits 9:801
- oil explorations 9:793
- physiography 9: 164
- Sodom, Gomorrah 15:70
- *illus:*
- - text
- - Gemini II photograph 14: 15
- - Madaba map 11:677
- - Masada 11: 1079
- - Moab plateau 9: 172-173
- - potash works 9:805; 15:73
- - quantities of ions (chart) 9:806
- - Ra's Fashkha 9: 161
- - salt composition (chart) 9:806
- - salt formations 14:710
- - Sodom mount 9: 161
- - water composition (chart) 9:807
- - western shore cliffs 9: 161

Dead Sea Potash Works (Isr.) 9:821; 15:72
- *illus:*
- - aerial view 15:73
- - bromine and carnallite plants 5:376-377
- - employees 5: 1394
- - evaporation pans 9: 157
- - potash works 9:805

DEAD SEA SCROLLS 5: 1396
- *Contents:*
- - Qumran Discoveries 5: 1396
- - Description 5: 1398
- - Biblical Manuscripts 5: 1399
- - Apocrypha 5: 1402
- - Community Documents 5: 1403
- - Khirbat Mird 5: 1404
- - Language, Orthography 5: 1404
- - Materials Used 5: 1406
- - Other Discoveries 5: 1407
- - Qumran List 5: 1407
- General
- - *Amidah* 2:839
- - benediction forms 4:486
- - chronological chart 8:766-767
- - Edom and Babylon 8:302
- - Ein Feshkha 6:527
- - Essenes 6:899ff
- - Hebrew language 16: 1583*ff*
- - Kittim 10: 1081
- - leather 16:660
- - linguistics 16: 1398
- - Qumran 13: 1429
- - *Yaḥad* 16:698
- - Zadokites 16:915
- Concepts
- - calendar 15:887
- - destiny 15: 1046
- - eschatology 6:876ff
- - gnosticism 7:638
- - Lion of Wrath 11:276
- - Man of Lies 11:233
- - messianic figures 11: 1409
- - Moses 12:393
- - mysticism 10:499
- - Ru'aḥ ha-Kodesh 14:367
- - Seekers after Smooth Things 14: 1096
- - Son of Man 15: 160
- - Sons of Light 15: 160
- - Teacher of Righteousness 15:885
- - Wicked Priest 16:485
- Literature
- - apocalyptic writings 3: 179; 3: 180
- - Aramaic texts 3:268
- - Daniel apocrypha 5: 1277
- - Esther, Book of 4:825
- - Hebrew mss. 11:900
- - Hellenistic literature 8:303
- - Jewish literature 11:310ff
- - pseudepigraphy 13: 185ff
- - Samuel, Book of 14:789
- - *Tobit, Book of* 15: 1185
- - Zadokite document 16: 1335
- Major Texts
- - *Copper Scroll* 5:955
- - *Damascus, Book of the Covenant of* 5: 1246ff
- - *Isaiah Scroll* 4:835
- - *Manual of Discipline* 6:63
- - *Naphtali, Testament of* 12:821
- - *Pesher Habakkuk* 3:331*ff*
- - *Psalms Scroll* 13: 1302
- - *Thanksgiving Psalms* 15: 1045
- Modern Scholarship
- - Albright 2:539
- - Bible redaction 4:832ff
- - Christianity 5:508
- - Crowfoot, Grace 5: 1130
- - Del Medico 5: 1477
- - Dupont-Sommer 6:275
- - Hebrew script 2:689
- - Shapira fragments 14: 1302
- - Yadin, Yigael 16:695
- *illus:*
- - text
- - copper scroll 5:956
- - Khirbat Qumrân 5: 1409
- - Paleo-Hebrew script 2:684
- - *Pesher Habakkuk* 13:332
- - Qumran caves 13: 1433
- - Qumran excavations 3:681
- - script types 2:687,689,711-714; 5: 1413-1418
- - scroll jars 3:371; 15:492
- - *tefillin* parchment 15:903
- - Temple Scroll 15:997
- - War Scroll fragment 3:323
- - *see also:* JUDEAN DESERT CAVES; MURABBA'AT SCROLLS

DEAD SEA SECT 5: 1408
- *Contents:*
- - Views 5: 1408
- - Modes of Life 5: 1412
- - Teacher of Righteousness 5: 1417
- - Essenes 5: 1418
- asceticism 3:680
- calendar 5:51,52
- dualism 6:243; 6:244
- eschatology 11: 1409
- *halakhah* 7: 1162
- *kipper* 10: 1043
- legal person 10: 1569
- Maghâriya sect 14: 1088
- messianism 11: 1421
- mystical tendencies 10:496
- old age 2:345
- oral law 12: 1441
- origin 10:390
- polygamy 12:259
- providence 13: 1280
- Pythagoreanism 8:299
- redemption 14:4
- sages 14:640
- *tefillin* 15:903ff
- Temple Scroll 15:996
- violators of rules 8:361
- *illus:*
- - text
- - Qumran excavations 3:681

Dead Sea Works (Isr.), *see* Dead Sea Potash Works (Isr.)

De Adventu Messiae (anti-J. epistle), *see Epistola Samuelis maroccani*

Deadwood (city, U.S.) 15:213

DEAF-MUTE 5: 1419
- agency 2:351
- alphabet 2:744
- gifts 7:562
- *ḥaliẓah* 11: 126
- hearing aid on Sabbath 14:94
- liability 11: 184
- property rights 15: 1095
- torts 15: 1273
- wills 16:523
- *illus:* text

– *see also:* Legal Capacity; PENAL LAW
Deak, Andrija **16:**890
DEÁK, FERENCZ **5:**1420
– Falk, Miksa **6:**1159
Deal, G.G. **6:**342
Dearborn Independent (mag.) **15:**1653
De arcanis catholicae veritatis (wk.) **7:**262
De Arignano, Benjamin ben Joseph, *see* Arignano, Benjamin
De Arte Cabalistica (wk.) **10:**644
DEATH **5:**1420
– *Contents:*
– – In the Bible **5:**1420
– – In Talmud and Midrash **5:**1422
– – Laws and Customs **5:**1425
– General
– – Altschul's view **2:**782
– – Biblical conception **11:**845
– – body and soul **4:**1165
– – crucifixion **5:**1134
– – David **5:**1328
– – euphemisms **6:**959; **6:**962
– – Kabbalah **10:**630
– – Naḥmanides **12:**781
– – netherworld **12:**996
– – personification **2:**952
– – rate in Israel **9:**1023ff; **9:**984
– – resurrection **14:**97
– – righteous **14:**182
– – Samael, angel of **14:**720
– – sin **14:**1589ff
– – *Solomon, Wisdom of* **15:**120
– – soul immortality **15:**174ff
– – tombs **15:**1216; **15:**1224
– – vital statistics **16:**177ff
– – wills **16:**519ff
– *Halakhah* and Custom
– – admissions **2:**291
– – *aninut* **3:**23
– – autopsies **3:**931ff
– – blessing of children **4:**1087
– – confession of sins **5:**879
– – embalming **6:**718
– – euthanasia **6:**978ff
– – fasting **6:**1190
– – *gemilut ḥasadim* **7:**375
– – *hakkafot* **7:**1154
– – impurity **13:**1405
– – mourning **12:**485
– – night prayers **12:**1157
– – *Oholot* **12:**1346
– – proof of **2:**431
– – shofar **14:**1446
– – *takkanot* **15:**719
– – washing of corpse **15:**1188
– – *see also:* ATONEMENT; BURIAL; MOURNING
– *illus:*
– – text
– – Angel of Death **2:**952
– – fallen tree as symbol **15:**1229
– – turning away from Enoch **6:**793
– *see also:* AFTERLIFE; CEMETERY; LIFE AND DEATH
DEATH, KISS OF **5:**1427
Death penalty, *see* CAPITAL PUNISHMENT
De Avila (fam.), see AVILA, DE
De Barrio, *see* BONJORN, BONET DAVI(D)
Debash, Isaiah **9:**15
DEBDOU (tn., Mor.) **5:**1427
– *illus:*
– – text
– – register of financial transactions **3:**930
De Beauvais, Vincent **2:**547
DE BENEDETTI, ALDO **5:**1428
– Italian literature **9:**1111
DEBENEDETTI, GIACOMO **5:**1428
– Italian literature **9:**1114
Debica (ghetto, Pol.) **13:**766
DEBIR (k.) **5:**1429
DEBIR (city, Cana.) **5:**1429
DEBIR (loc., Judah) **5:**1429
– proscription **8:**345
Debka (dance) **9:**1008
Deborah (Rebekah's nurse) **13:**1603
DEBORAH (prophetess) **5:**1429
– *Contents:*
– – War of **5:**1430
– – Song of **5:**1431
– – In the Aggadah **5:**1432
– – In the Arts **5:**1432
– chronological chart **8:**766-67
– Jabin **9:**1174
– Judges **10:**445
– poetry **13:**671ff
– settlement of tribes **8:**581; **8:**584
– *illus:*
– – eighteenth century *ketubbah* Pl. 2 **10**-KETUBBAH
Deborah (period.) **5:**564
– *illus:*
– – masthead (1885) **13:**1052
DEBORIN, ABRAM MOISEYEVICH **5:**1433
De Bourgneuf, Salvet **11:**1190
DEBRECEN (city, Hung.) **5:**1434
DEBRECENJI, JOZEF **5:**1435
Debreczeni, Petkó János **8:**30
Debreczeni, Szücs János **8:**30
De Brito (fam.), *see* ABENDANA
De Britto, Manuel, *see* Britto, Manuel de
Debt
– actions delay **11:**253
– admission **2:**290
– agency **2:**352
– assignment of **2:**768
– custom and recovery **12:**15
– disposition by heir **5:**880
– firstborn inheritance **6:**1312
– gambling **7:**300
– gaonic *takkanah* **15:**723
– *ḥazakah* **7:**1521
– lien **11:**227; **12:**1310
– maintenance **11:**786
– *niddui* **8:**351
– non-Jewish bills **6:**51
– protection of debtor **16:**723
– slavery **14:**1656
– suretyship **15:**524
– waiver **11:**1232; **11:**1234
– *see also:* EXECUTION (civil); LOAN
Debt imprisonment, *see* IMPRISONMENT FOR DEBT
Deburau, Jean Charles **15:**1055
Deburau, Jean Gaspard **15:**1055
Deburau, Philippe Germain **15:**1055
De Calderio, Luca **10:**459
DECALOGUE **5:**1435
– *Contents:*
– – Problems of Setting **5:**1435
– – Versions **5:**1438
– – Division **5:**1441
– – Original Form **5:**1443
– – Structure **5:**1444
– – Setting in Life **5:**1445
– – Rabbinical Literature **5:**1446
– – In the Liturgy **5:**1446
– – In Philosophy **5:**1447
– abduction **2:**56
– adultery **2:**313
– anthropomorphism **3:**52
– art **3:**500
– classification of Commandments **5:**762; **5:**784
– covenant with God **12:**376
– Doenmeh's precepts **6:**148
– Exodus, Book of **6:**1059ff
– honor of parents **13:**100
– *Midrash Aseret ha-Dibberot* **11:**1514
– philosophy **13:**422
– ritual and legal commandments **12:**123
– Samaritans **11:**1476; **14:**740
– *shema* **14:**1370
– stone inscription **16:**656
– tabernacle **15:**682
– Tablets of Law **15:**690
– *tefillin* **15:**904
– *illus:*
– – text
– – *British Museum Miscellany* **8:**1279
– – *mizraḥ* paper-cut **13:**64
– – Moses teaching the **12:**1
– – Moses with **12:**400
– – opening words (11/12th cent. ms.) **4:**956
De Campo, Johannes, *see* CAMPEN, JOHANNES VAN
Decapitation, *see* Slaying
DECAPOLIS **5:**1449
– Beth-Shean **4:**758
– history **8:**632; **8:**634
– *Provincia Judaea* **9:**239
– *map:* text
De Carpentras, Mordecai Cresque, *see* Aquin, Philippe d'
DE CASSERES, BENJAMIN **15:**1580
Decastro, Jacob (act.), *see* CASTRO, JACOB DE
De Castro Pentateuch (14th cent. illum. ms., Ger.)
– *illus:* **7:**396; **10:**1371
Decatur (city, Ill.) **8:**1256
Decatur, Martin **15:**310
Decebalus (k., Dacia) **15:**745
DECEMBRISTS (Rus. revols.) **5:**1451
DE CHAVES, AARON **3:**599
– *illus:*
– – Barrios, Daniel Levi de (allegorical portrayal) **4:**259
Děčín (city, Bohem.) **16:**27
Decius, Trajan (Rom. emp.) **9:**1406
DECKERT, JOSEPH **5:**1451
– Abraham a Sancta Clara **2:**130
DECLARATION OF INDEPENDENCE, ISRAEL **5:**1451
– historical survey **9:**365ff
– ingathering of exiles **9:**534
– *illus:* text
– *see also:* INDEPENDENCE DAY, ISRAEL
Declaration on the Elimination of All Forms of Racial Discrimination **15:**1559ff
Decorative headdresses, *see* CROWNS, DECORATIVE HEADDRESSES AND WREATHS
De Córdoba, Gonsalvo (viceroy of Naples), *see* Gonsalvo de Córdoba
DE CORDOVA, JACOB **5:**1455
– Texas **15:**1035
De Cordova, Phineas **5:**1455
De Corneille, Roland **5:**110
Decoster (fam.) **11:**782
De Courtenay, Baudouin **12:**844
Decrees, Anti-Jewish, *see* ANTI-SEMITISM
Decrees, the eighteen **13:**1409
Decrees, legal (rab.), *see* TAKKANOT
Décret Cremieux (Fr. law) **5:**1076
Décret Infâme (Fr. law) **2:**755; **7:**25; **16:**335
– history chart **8:**766-767
Decretum (canon laws) **4:**1508
Decsey, Sigismund **10:**1498
Decter, Moshe **14:**499
Dedan (bib. fig.) **11:**1506
Dedan (city, Edom) **6:**370
Dedeagach (city, Gr.), *see* Alexandroupolis
Dedicatory offering **14:**601
De Dieu, Louis **8:**30
Deed, *see* SHETAR
Deed, Acquisition by, *see* ACQUISITION
DEEDES, SIR WYNDHAM **5:**1455
– *illus:*
– – Abdullah ibn Hussein, and **10:**199
Deen, Van **11:**1198
DEEP, THE **5:**1456
DEER **5:**1457
– dietary laws **6:**31
– *illus:*
– – text
– – Chrizanow tombstone **15:**1232
– – Israel stamp **12:**819
– – Jerusalem emissary's seal **14:**1359
– – Lubaczow tombstone **15:**1229
– – *Shivviti* plaques **14:**1420-1421
– – Torah crown **15:**1260-1261
– *see also:* GAZELLE
Deerfield (sub., Chicago) **5:**415
Defamation, *see* LASHON HA-RA; SLANDER
Defamation of the Divine Name, *see* KIDDUSH HA-SHEM AND ḤILLUL HA-SHEM
Default proceedings **13:**959
Defecation, *see* Excretion
Defects, *see* BLEMISH
Defendant
– admission of debt **2:**290
– custodian and ward **3:**220
Defense (leg.), *see* PRACTICE AND PROCEDURE
Defense, Jewish self-, *see* SELF-DEFENSE
DEFENCE FORCES OF ISRAEL **9:**681
– Ottoman and Mandatory periods **9:**681
– – Haganah **7:**1064
– – historical survey **9:**350ff
– – Irgun **8:**1470
– – Jewish Brigade **10:**35
– – Loḥamei Ḥerut Israel **11:**463
– – Maḥal **11:**722
– – problems in *yishuv* **9:**328ff
– – War of Independence **16:**306
– 1948–1970 **9:**689
– – Adar, the Seventh of **2:**253
– – adult education **9:**964
– – Arab guerrilla **9:**469ff
– – archives **3:**395
– – disinterment **6:**73
– – Druze **9:**927
– – Egyptian cease-fire violations **9:**418ff
– – Gadna **7:**252
– – historical survey **9:**350ff; **9:**366*ff*
– – Israel Defense Forces (Ẓahal) **9:**689
– – Kafr Qâsim case **10:**674
– – ministry **9:**690
– – – Ben-Gurion **4:**505ff
– – – Dayan, Moshe **5:**1372
– – – Eshkol, Levi **6:**885
– – Naḥal **12:**766
– – radio broadcasts **15:**931
– – religious life **9:**903
– – science **9:**971
– – Six-Day War **14:**1624
– – sports events **15:**297
– – synagogue **15:**587
– *illus:*
– – army sergeant teaching new immigrants **9:**1964
– – Ben-Gurion with soldiers **9:**379
– – Cherbourg boats **9:**431
– – Congolese soldiers training **9:**443
– – Druze honor guard for Levi Eshkol **9:**927
– – Gadna **7:**252

- - Gerofit, hoisting of the flag **6:**1337
- - *Haggadah* **7:**1090,1094
- - Ha-Shomer groups **7:**1371
- - Ha-Shomer mounted guards **9:**517
- - Hawk missiles **9:**430
- - homemade armor **16:**320
- - Israel soldier at Suez Canal **9:**420
- - Israel stamps **9:**844-845
- - Jerusalem fighting, 1948 **9:**366
- - military cemetery, Jerusalem **9:**368, 1493
- - Negev Brigade memorial **12:**931
- - Paratroopers at Mitla Pass **9:**379
- - Sinai Campaign **14:**1601,1603
- - Six-Day War **9:**409; **14:**1627*ff*
- - Soldiers on parade **8:**775
- - Tampaler mortar and bomb **9:**818
- - tanks in tenth Independence Day celebration **9:**405
- - Tel Ḥai cemetery **15:**932
- - Umm Rashrash (Eilat), hoisting of the flag **6:**567
- - War of Independence **9:**373; **16:**307-330
- - wounded soldier's arrival at Hadassah Hospital **9:**990

Defense levy (Isr.) **9:**755,757
Defense literature, *see* APOLOGETICS
Defense loan (Isr.) **9:**758
Defensorium unitatis Christianae (wk.) **8:**1382
Defoe, Daniel **6:**778
Defter (prayer bk.) **4:**18; **14:**753
Deganim (rural center, Isr.) **1:**place list
DEGANYAH (kib., Isr.) **5:**1458
- Baratz, Joseph **4:**203
- Deganyah Alef, Bet **1:**place list
- Eshkol, Levi **6:**888
- history chart **8:**766-767
- War of Independence **16:**320
- *illus:* text

Degas, Edgar **9:**1344
De Gaulle, Charles
- anti-Semitism **3:**137
- arms embargo **9:**694; **9:**418
- assimilation in France **3:**779
- Ben-Gurion **4:**512
- Cassin, René **2:**652; **5:**232
- French aid **9:**402
- Jews and Israel **7:**39ff
- Six-Day War **16:**1062
- *illus:*
- - at a Jewish soldiers' memorial **7:**41

Degel (flag) **6:**1335
Degel ha-Rabbanim (journ.) **1:**newsp. list
Degel ha-Torah (period.) **1:**newsp. list; **16:**165
Degel Yerushalayim (mvmt.) **10:**1183
Degel Ẓiyyon (newsp.) **11:**204
Degeneration (bk.) **12:**1211ff
DEGGENDORF (city, Ger.) **5:**1459
De Groot, Hugo, *see* GROTIUS, HUGO
DE GRUNWALD, ANATOLE **12:**466
De Haan, Jacob Israël, *see* HAAN, JACOB ISRAËL DE
DE HAAN, JACOB MEIJER **5:**1460
- *illus:*
- - "Maternity" (paint.) **3:**549

DE HAAS, JACOB **5:**1461
- Brandeis, Louis **4:**1297
- Wise, Stephen **16:**568
- Zionism **16:**1141
- *illus:*
- - F.Z.C. **16:**1165

De Heredia, Paul, *see* Heredia, Paul de
Deḥi (cantillation sign) **16:**1457
Deḥiyyah (calendar deferment) **5:**44
DEHOK (tn., Iraq) **5:**1461
Deidesheimer, Philip **12:**267
De Idolatria (wk.,) **3:**982
DEINARD, EPHRAIM **5:**1462
- satirist **13:**136
- *illus:*
- - text
- - *Sefer ha-Ployderzakh* **13:**130

Deinard, S.N. **12:**37; **12:**38
Deioces (anc. k.), *see* Dayaukku
Deir Abu Tor, *see* Abu Ṭūr
DEIR AL-BALAḤ (tn., Isr.) **5:**1463
- Crusades **9:**268
- Six-Day War **14:**1629

Deir ʿAllā (site, Isr.) **7:**604; **15:**481; **16:**654; **16:**666
Deir el-Qamer (loc., Leb.), *see* Dayr al-Qamar
Deir Ghassāna (vill., Isr.) **16:**999
Deir Krūḥ (vill., Isr.) **13:**1532
Deir Naḥḥās (vill., Isr.) **8:**1471
Dei Rossi, Azariah ben Moses, *see* ROSSI, AZARIAH BEN MOSES DEI
Deir Yasin (vill., Isr.)
- I.Z.L. and Leḥi **8:**1469; **9:**363,1479; **11:**465
- War of Independence **16:**310

Deism **7:**673
- freemasons **7:**122
- Haskalah **7:**1436
- Nieto, David **12:**1152

De Israëlietische Letterbode (period.) **14:**221
DEISTS **5:**1463
Deitsch, Lev **15:**28
Deitscher. S.N. **5:**1038
Deitz, David **5:**612
DEJ (tn., Transyl.) **5:**1465
De Joodse Wachter (period.) **13:**1035; **16:**1118
De Jouvenel (offic., Syr.) **9:**1474
Dekabrists (Rus. revols.), *see* DECEMBRISTS
Dekalo, Albert **4:**1494
Dekel, *see* PALM
Dekel, Ephraim **4:**631ff
- *illus:*
- - forged identity documents **4:**627

Dekel, Operation (War of Indep.) **16:**324
DEKKER, MAURITS **5:**1465
Dekker, Thomas **9:**1343
DE KLERK, MICHEL **5:**1466
- *illus:*
- - text
- - Spaarndammerplantsoen housing project, Amsterdam **3:**343

Delacroix, Ferdinand V.E. **3:**998
- *illus:*
- - "Noce juive dans le Maroc" (paint.) **11:**1037

Delacrut, Ḥayyim **5:**1467
DELACRUT, MATTATHIAS BEN SOLOMON **5:**1466
- burning of Talmud **15:**771
- Jaffe, Mordecai **9:**1263
- Recanati, Menahem **13:**1608

Delahaye, Jules **3:**85
Delaiah (bib. fig.) **8:**624
- sacrifice **14:**606
- Sanballat **14:**824

De la Mar (fam.), *see* DELMAR
DE LA MOTTA, JACOB **5:**1467
De Lancey, Phila **7:**108; **12:**1068
De Lara, Manrique **10:**1352
De Lattes, Bonet *see* LATTES, BONET
Delaunay, Robert **5:**1468
DELAUNAY-TERK, SONIA **5:**1468
- *illus:*
- - text
- - "Young Girl Asleep" (paint.) **13:**113

DELAWARE (state, U.S.) **5:**1468
- *pop. table:* text

Delaware (co., Pa.) **13:**368
Del Banco (fam.) **4:**173
Del Banco, Abraham **4:**173
DEL BANCO, ANSELMO (Asher Levi Meshullam) **5:**1469
- Venice **16:**96

Del Banco, Vita (Ḥayyim) **5:**1469
DEL BENE, ELIEZER DAVID BEN ISAAC **5:**1469
DEL BENE, JUDAH ASAHEL BEN DAVID ELIEZER **5:**1470
Delcón, Garcia Alvarez, *see* Alvares, Samuel Dios-Ayuda
De Leao, Samuel **12:**993
DE LEE, JOSEPH B. **5:**1470
Delegación de Asociaciones Israelitas Argentinas (orgn.), *see* DAIA
Delek (petroleum co., Isr.) **9:**795
De Lemos, Henriette, *see* HERZ, HENRIETTE
De Leon (name), *see also* Leon
DE LEON (fam.) **5:**1470
De Leon (fam., Jam.) **9:**1274
DE LEON, DANIEL **5:**1472
- Barondess, Joseph **4:**255

De Leon, David Camden **5:**1470
- *illus:* text

De Leon, Edwin **5:**1471
De Leon, Mordecai H. **5:**1470
De Leon, Thomas Cooper **5:**1471
Delevante (fam.), *see* CHRIQUI
Delevante, Abraham-Ḥayyim **5:**504
Delevante, Jacob Addy, *see* Shriqui-Delevante, Jacob Addy
De-Levayah, Isaac, *see* Delouya, Isaac
DELFONT, BERNARD **15:**1081
- television **16:**930

Delft (tn., Neth.) **14:**308
Delgado (fam., Jam.) **9:**1274
Delgado, Gonçalo **13:**554
Delgado, Isaac **11:**520; **12:**1042
Delhi, New (city, Ind.) **8:**1358
Delhi, Old (loc., Ind.) **8:**1356
Deli (zodiac sign), *see* Aquarius
DE LIEME, NEHEMIA **5:**1472
- Zionism **16:**1118

DELILAH (bib. fig.) **5:**1473
- in the Arts **14:**775
- descendants **6:**576
- Samson **14:**773
- *illus:* text

De Lima (fam.) **5:**1537
DE LIMA, JOSEPH SUASSO **5:**1474
DELITZSCH, FRANZ (Julius) **5:**1474
- Akkadian **16:**1507
- Ehrlich, Arnold **6:**512
- Einhorn, David **6:**531
- Hebraist **8:**30

DELITZSCH, FRIEDRICH **5:**1475
Delitzschianum (miss. inst., Leipzig), *see* INSTITUTUM JUDAICUM
Dell, Edmund **15:**27
Della Genga, Annibale Sermattei (pope), *see* LEO XII
Della Marca, Giacomo **2:**941; **3:**228
Della Reyna, Joseph, *see* JOSEPH DELLA REINA
Della Rocca, *see* Basola, Moses
Della Rovere Francesco (pope), *see* SIXTUS IV
DELLA SETA, ALESSANDRO **5:**1476
DELLA SETA, UGO **13:**826
Della Sinagoga (fam.), *see* Min ha-Keneset
DELLA TORRE, LELIO (Hillel) **5:**1476
Delli Mansi (fam.) **2:**934; **12:**859
Delli Piatelli (fam.) **2:**934
Delli Putti (fam.) **4:**1190
Delly, Mount (loc., Ind.) **8:**1355
DELMAR (fam.) **5:**1476
- Busnach, Naphtali **4:**1536

Delmar-Lebhar, Abraham **5:**1477
Delmar-Lebhar, Joseph **5:**1476
Delmar-Lebhar, Masʿūd **5:**1476
Delmar-Lebhar, Mordecai **5:**1476
Delmar-Lebhar, Shalom **5:**1476
DEL MEDICO, HENRI E. **5:**1477
Delmedigo, Aba **5:**120
Delmedigo, Elijah ben Eliezer **13:**575
DELMEDIGO, ELIJAH BEN MOSES ABBA **5:**1477
- Aristotelianism **3:**446
- articles of faith **3:**658
- chronological chart **8:**766–767
- philosophy **13:**450

DELMEDIGO, JOSEPH SOLOMON **5:**1478
- alchemy **2:**548
- *Almagest* **3:**805
- Aristotelianism **3:**446
- Bacharach, Naphtali **4:**49
- book collection **4:**974
- Ibn Yahya **8:**1208
- Jewish history **11:**350
- Karaites **15:**1402
- medicine **11:**1194
- philosophy **13:**450
- *Sefirot* doctrine **10:**568
- travels **15:**1349
- Vital, Ḥayyim **16:**173
- Zeraḥ of Troki **16:**996
- *illus:*
- - text
- - *Sefer Elim* (1629) **3:**801

Delmedigo, Menahem **13:**12
DEL MONTE, CRESCENZO **5:**1481
Delo (period.) **5:**1318
Deloncle, Eugène **13:**110
De Lonzano, Menahem, *see* LONZANO, MENAHEM BEN JUDAH DE
Delo Pomoshchi (period.), *see* *Pomoshch*
DELOS (isl., Gr.) **5:**1482
- Greece **7:**868ff
- synagogue **15:**582; **15:**599
- *illus:* text

DELOUGAZ, PIERRE PINCHAS **5:**1483
DELOUYA (fam.) **5:**1484
Delouya, Isaac **5:**1484
Delouya, Jacob **5:**1484
Delouya, Jaki (Isaac) **5:**1484
Delouya, Judah **5:**1484
Delouya, Meir **5:**1484
Delouya, Mordecai ben Isaac **5:**1484
Delouya, Moses **5:**1484
De Loya (fam.), *see* DELOUYA
Delphi (city, Gr.) **6:**10; **7:**868ff
Del Rio, Martin A. **8:**30
Delson, Max **15:**31
Delson, Robert **15:**31
DE LUCENA (fam.) **5:**1484
De Lucena, Abraham Haim **5:**1484
De Lucena, Samuel **5:**1484
Deluge, *see* FLOOD, THE
"Deluge" (frsc., Michelangelo) **6:**1353
DELVALLE, MAX **5:**1484
- politics **13:**821

DEL VECCHIO (fam.) **5:**1484
Del Vecchio, Abraham ben Shabbetai **5:**1485
Del Vecchio, Samuel Mahalalel **5:**1485
DEL VECCHIO, SHABBETAI ELHANAN BEN ELISHA **5:**1485
Del Vecchio, Solomon David ben Moses **5:**1485

Del Vecchio, Solomon Moses **5:**1485
D'ELVERT, CHRISTIAN RITTER VON **5:**1485
Delyatin (tn., Gal.) **16:**1325
De Lyre, Nicholas, *see* NICHOLAS DE LYRE
DEMAI (doubtfully tithed crops) **5:**1486
- *am ha-arez* **2:**834
- laws **5:**1486
- soldiers' exemption **6:**850
DEMAI (tal. tract.) **5:**1486
Dembat (brs., Rus.), *see* Dembot
DEMBER, HARRY L. **13:**491
Dembitz, Arthur Aaron **7:**860
DEMBITZ, LEWIS NAPHTALI **5:**1487
- Brandeis, Louis **4:**1297
DEMBITZER, HAYYIM NATHAN **5:**1488
DEMBLIN, BENJAMIN **5:**1488
Dembo, A. **4:**119; **13:**345
DEMBO, ISAAC **5:**1489
Dembot (brs., Rus.) **4:**119; **13:**345
Dembowski, Andreas **7:**69
Dembowski, Nicolas **7:**57ff; **15:**771
Demei Kelila (contributions) **3:**854
De Mejo (law., Yug.) **16:**873
Demeter-Persephone (deity) **15:**572
DEMETRIUS (Gr.-J. writ.) **5:**1490
- apologetics **3:**189
- biblical history **8:**304
- dating by creation **14:**752
- on Moses **12:**390
- Septuagint **8:**299
DEMETRIUS (1st cent. B.C.E., Alex.) **5:**1491
DEMETRIUS I (Soter) **5:**1489
- Alcimus **2:**549
- chronological chart **8:**766–767
- festivals, Jewish **6:**1242
- Judah Maccabee **10:**381
- Seleucids and Judea **8:**629
DEMETRIUS II (Nicator) **5:**1489
- *angaria* **2:**950
- Hasmoneans **3:**71; **8:**630
- Simeon the Hasmonean **14:**1565
DEMETRIUS III (Eukarios Theos Philopater Soter) **5:**1490
- Alexander Yannai **16:**716
- chronological list **8:**766–767
- warfare **16:**279
Demetrius Hatzis (Gr. writ.) **7:**900
De Meza (fam.) **5:**1537; **12:**978
Demievka (tn., Rus.) **6:**434
Demiurge **6:**243
DEMNATE (tn., Mor.) **5:**1491
Democracy, *see* MAJORITY RULE
DEMOCRATIC FRACTION, **5:**1492
- Feiwel, Berthold **6:**1215
- Juedischer Verlag **10:**463
- Warsaw **16:**337
- Weizmann, Chaim **16:**424
- Zionist Congress **16:**1168
Democratic party (Turk.) **15:**1463
Democratic Party (U.S.) **13:**821
Democratic Popular Front for the Liberation of Palestine **9:**471; **10:**200
Democritus (5/4 cent., philos.) **3:**829; **13:**488
DEMOGRAPHY **5:**1493
- *Contents:*
- - Introduction **5:**1493
- - Distribution of Jewry **5:**1493
- - Population Characteristics **5:**1514
- General
- - Association for Jewish Demography and Statistics **15:**56
- - census in Bible **5:**281
- - Crusades **5:**1141, 1143
- - expulsions **6:**1071
- - Falashas **6:**1145
- - Greco-Roman Diaspora **6:**8
- - history **8:**676ff
- - intermarriage **12:**165ff
- - Jewish farming **16:**1316
- - medicine **11:**1198ff
- - 19/20 century shifts **5:**833
- - politics **13:**823
- - population resettlement **3:**45, 47
- - refugees, Jewish **14:**30
- - Samaritans **14:**736
- - *see also:* DIASPORA; MIGRATION; POPULATION; STATISTICS; VITAL STATISTICS
- Africa **2:**335ff
- - South Africa **15:**188ff
- America **2:**811ff
- - Latin America **10:**1451ff
- - New York City **12:**1076ff
- - United States **15:**1608ff
- Asia **3:**745
- - Israel
- - - Arab, general survey **9:**1023ff
- - - Galilee **7:**270
- - - Gaza Strip **7:**344ff
- - - health standards **9:**984
- - - human geography **9:**567
- - - Israel association **15:**56; **15:**347
- - - Jerusalem **9:**1470
- - - Jewish communities **9:**497ff
- - - non-Ashkenazi **14:**1176
- - - *see also:* POPULATION OF ISRAEL
- - Turkey **15:**1462
- Australia **3:**878
- Europe
- - Germany **7:**481; **7:**485; **7:**499
- - London **11:**478ff
- - Netherlands **12:**989, 990
- - Pale of Settlement **13:**27
- - Paris **13:**110
- - Poland **13:**735; **13:**739
- - Portugal **13:**920ff
- - Prussia **13:**1291ff
- - Rumania **14:**416ff
- - Russia **14:**483ff
- - Silesia **14:**1537
- - Spain **14:**1171
- *pop. tables:* text
- *pop. tables:* General
- - distribution of Jews by 1937 **8:**733
- - English-speaking communities, postwar changes **5:**839
- - intercontinental migrations, 1881-1914 **8:**729
- - intercontinental migrations, 1915-30 and 1931-39 **8:**753
- - Muslim countries, postwar communities **5:**837
- - total Jewish population, by continents, 1840-1969 **5:**831
- - type of community organization and population in 1968 **5:**841
- - vital statistics **16:**179-188
- - world Jewish communities, 1968 **5:**834
- *pop. tables:* Africa
- - Algeria **2:**613, 617
- - Egypt, Hellenistic period, Middle Ages and 19th cent. **6:**486, 500
- - Libya **11:**199
- - main concentrations **2:**333
- - Morocco **12:**327
- - 19/20 centuries **13:**893, 898, 901
- - Ottoman Empire **16:**1533
- - postwar communities **5:**841
- - Rhodesia **14:**148
- - South Africa **15:**183, 188, 206
- - Tunisia **15:**1431
- *pop. tables:* America
- - General (19/20 cent.) **13:**893, 898, 899
- - Argentina
- - - Jewish population, 1869-1968 **3:**418-419
- - - Jewish settlements **3:**411
- - Brazil **4:**1323
- - Canada, 1871-1969 **5:**101, 105
- - Chile, 1970 **5:**462
- - Colombia **5:**744
- - Dominican Republic, 1969 **6:**160
- - Ecuador, 1970 **6:**360
- - Guatemala **7:**956
- - Jewish population, 1900-1968 **2:**809-816
- - Latin America, 1960s **10:**1451
- - Latin American and Caribbean communities, postwar **5:**840
- - Mexico (1971) **11:**1454
- - United States
- - - General (1800-1968) **15:**1593, 1605, 1613, 1637
- - - Alabama, 1969 **2:**506
- - - Alaska, 1969 **2:**513
- - - Arizona, 1969 **3:**449
- - - Arkansas, 1969 **3:**459
- - - California, 1969 **5:**59
- - - Colorado, 1969 **5:**754
- - - Connecticut, 1969 **5:**897
- - - Delaware, 1969 **5:**1469
- - - Florida, 1970 **6:**1363
- - - Georgia, 1968 **7:**429
- - - Hawaii **7:**1495
- - - Idaho, 1968 **8:**1222
- - - Illinois, 1970 **8:**1255
- - - Indiana, 1968 **8:**1360
- - - Iowa, 1968 **8:**1438
- - - Kansas **10:**738
- - - Kentucky, 1968 **10:**909
- - - Louisiana, 1968 **11:**518
- - - Maine, 1968 **11:**783
- - - Maryland **11:**1077
- - - Massachusetts, 1968 **11:**1113
- - - Michigan, 1968 **11:**1499
- - - Minnesota, 1968 **12:**155
- - - Mississippi **12:**155
- - - Missouri, 1968 **12:**157
- - - Montana, 1968 **12:**267
- - - Nebraska, 1968 **12:**911
- - - Nevada, 1968 **12:**1017
- - - New Hampshire **12:**1024
- - - New Jersey, 1968 **12:**1028
- - - New Mexico, 1968 **12:**1037
- - - New York City **12:**1077, 1078
- - - New York State, 1968 **12:**1125
- - - North Carolina, 1968 **12:**1218
- - - North Dakota, 1968 **12:**1221
- - - Ohio, 1968 **12:**1344
- - - Oklahoma, 1968 **12:**1353
- - - Oregon **12:**1451
- - - Pennsylvania, 1968 **13:**229
- - - Rhode Island, 1968 **14:**143
- - - South Carolina, 1968 **15:**211
- - - South Dakota, 1968 **15:**213
- - - Tennessee, 1968 **15:**1009
- - - Texas **15:**1034
- - - Utah, 1968 **16:**34
- - - Vermont, 1968 **16:**112
- - - Virginia, 1968 **16:**163
- - - Washington, 1968 **16:**356
- - - West Virginia, 1968 **16:**475
- - - Wisconsin, 1968 **16:**557
- - - Wyoming, 1968 **16:**680
- - Venezuela, 1969 **16:**90
- *pop. tables:* Asia
- - General (19/20 cent.) **3:**743; **13:**893, 898, 901
- - Aden, 1839-1967 **2:**263
- - Afghanistan **2:**327
- - Arabian peninsula **3:**233
- - Asia Minor **3:**747
- - Birobidzhan, 1928-59 **4:**1045, 1049
- - Burma **4:**1526
- - Byzantine Empire **4:**1551
- - China **5:**469
- - Cyprus **5:**1180
- - dispersion of Jews from the 1700s to 1945 **3:**741
- - Georgia **7:**424
- - India **8:**1350
- - Iran
- - - emigration to Israel, 1948-1968 **8:**1447
- - - Jewish settlements, 1967 **8:**1440
- - Iraq, 1947 **8:**1449, 1459
- - - Kurdistan, 1920-1947 **10:**1296
- - Israel
- - - *aliyah,* main periods **3:**746
- - - immigrants, up to 1948 **16:**1127
- - - Jewish population **3:**745; **9:**473-496, 533-545; **13:**869
- - - non-Jewish population **9:**1024-1025
- - - twentieth cent. **13:**901
- - Ottoman Empire **16:**1531, 1533
- - Persia **13:**303
- - postwar communities **5:**841
- - Russia **14:**450, 471, 483, 484
- - Turkey **15:**1457, 1459
- - Yemenite refugee influx into Aden, 1946-47 **2:**263
- *pop. tables:* Australia
- - General (19/20 cent.) **13:**893, 898, 901
- - Jewish Communities **3:**877
- - Jewish population, 1841-1968 **3:**879
- - Melbourne (1933, 1961) **11:**1278, 1279
- - Tasmania **3:**877
- - Victoria (1861–1961) **11:**1279
- *pop. tables:* Europe
- - General
- - - 1300/1490 **13:**877
- - - 19/20 centuries **6:**971-978; **13:**893, 898, 899
- - Albania **2:**523
- - Alsace **2:**751
- - Ashkenazi settlement and emigration **3:**719
- - Austria **3:**887
- - Austrian provinces, 1910-1934 **3:**897
- - Baden **4:**60
- - Bavaria, 10th cent. to 1932-33 **4:**347
- - Belgium **4:**418
- - Bessarabia, 1897 **4:**707
- - Bohemia
- - - Jewish communities **4:**1173
- - - Jewish population, 1754-1930 **4:**1180
- - - percentage of mixed marriages, 1881-1930 **4:**1179
- - Bulgaria, 1878-1967 **4:**1481, 1485
- - Byzantine Empire **4:**1551
- - Crete **5:**1089
- - Czechoslovakia **5:**1189
- - - Bohemia **4:**1173
- - - Moravia **12:**297
- - - Prague, 1880-1930 **13:**970
- - Denmark **5:**1536
- - England, before 1290 and in 1969 **6:**749
- - Estonia, 1918-1940 **6:**917
- - expulsions, 1000 to 1500 C.E. **8:**689
- - Finland, 1970 **6:**1296
- - France
- - - Middle Ages and 1968 **7:**11
- - - Provence, medieval **13:**1261
- - Germany
- - - Berlin, 1816-1945 **4:**650
- - - Jewish population, 1871-1969 **7:**481
- - - major communities, 13th cent. **7:**463
- - - major communities, 1933 and 1970 **7:**487
- - Greece **7:**869
- - Hungary
- - - Budapest, 1813-1967 **4:**1449
- - - Jewish communities, 1910 and 1946 **8:**1093
- - Ireland **8:**1464
- - Italy

- - - major communities, 1450-1550, 1931 and 1970 **9:**1117,1133
- - - Southern, 12th cent. **3:**226
- - Latvia, 1935 **10:**1463
- - Lithuania **11:**363
- - Netherlands **12:**973,985,989
- - - Amsterdam, 1610-1967 **2:**901
- - Norway **12:**1222
- - Ottoman Empire **16:**1531,1533
- - Poland
- - - Bialystok, 1765-1948 **4:**811
- - - Cracow, 1900-1955 **5:**1027
- - - Lodz, 1793-1931 **11:**425; **13:**736
- - - Warsaw, 1781-1897 **13:**735
- - Portugal **13:**920
- - postwar communities **5:**835
- - Prussia, 1871 **13:**1287
- - Rumania **14:**391
- - - Bucharest, 1800-1969 **4:**1438
- - Russia **14:**450-453,471-473,483-485
- - - Bessarabia, 1897 **4:**707
- - - Birobidzhan **4:**1045
- - - Crimea, 1970 **5:**1104
- - - Georgia **7:**424
- - - Pale of Settlement **13:**25
- - Spain
- - - Burgos province, before 1492 **4:**1513
- - - Jewish and Converso communities, 1474 **15:**237
- - - Muslim rule period (11th cent.) **15:**223
- - Sweden **15:**546
- - Switzerland, 1960 **15:**561
- - Turkey **15:**1457,1459
- - Yugoslavia, 1931 **16:**876
- *pop. tables:* New Zealand **12:**1128
- - 19/20th centuries **13:**893,898
- *see also under individual countries*

DEMONS, DEMONOLOGY **5:**1521
- *Contents:*
- - Ancient Near East **5:**1521
- - In the Bible **5:**1522
- - Specific Demons **5:**1523
- - Intertestamental Literature **5:**1525
- - New Testament **5:**1526
- - In the Talmud **5:**1526
- - In Kabbalah **6:**1528
- abracadabra **2:**111
- Adam **2:**246
- Agrat bat Mahalath **2:**374
- amulet **2:**906ff
- Angel of Death **2:**953
- angelology **2:**961
- Azazel **3:**1001
- cemeteries **5:**272
- evil spirits **6:**1397
- fiction, Hebrew **6:**1268
- *hakkafot* **7:**1154
- illuminated *maḥzorim* **11:**733
- Jerusalem Talmud **15:**775
- Kabbalah **10:**505; **10:**509; **10:**551; **10:**633
- Lilith **11:**245
- netherworld **12:**997ff
- red heifer **14:**13
- Samael **14:**719
- *Solomon, Testament of* **15:**118
- visions **16:**168ff
- *illus:*
- - Asmodeus **3:**754
- - Azazel **3:**1000
- - the devil in libelous illuminations **3:**109, 119
- - Lilith, protective prayer against **4:**1050
- - *sanbenito* garb **15:**236
- - Satan fallen from heaven **2:**970
- - "Story of Job" (paint., 15th cent.) **10:**126
- - sword for protection of mother and newborn **6:**1406
- - *see also:* DIBBUK; MAGIC; SATAN

De Morpurgo, Baron H.L. **12:**1376
Demotika (city, Gr.), *see* DIDYMOTEIKHON
Den (newsp.) **12:**1480; **15:**59
Denarius (coin), *see Zuz*
DENAZIFICATION **5:**1533
- War Crimes Trials **16:**297ff
Denck, Johann **4:**873
Den Dolder (vill., Holl.), *see* Dolder
DÉNES, BÊLA (physic.) **5:**1533
Den Finski Juden (period.) **13:**1048
Den Haag (city, Neth.) *see* HAGUE, THE
DENIA (city, Sp.) **5:**1534
De Nida, Johannes, *see* PISTORIUS, JOHANNES
DENIKIN, ANTON IVANOVICH **5:**1535
- Aleksandriya **2:**560
- Churchill, Winston **5:**555
DENIS, ALBERTUS **5:**1535
- Denmark **5:**1536
Denis the Carthusian, *see* DIONYSIUS VAN RYCKEL
Denison (city, Tex.) **15:**1035
Denker, Arnold **5:**407
Denker, David N. **15:**1679
DENMARK **5:**1536
- *Contents:*
- - General History **5:**1536
- - Holocaust Period **5:**1538
- - Contemporary Period **5:**1540
- - Relations with Israel **5:**1541
- Church and Nazism **8:**915
- court Jews **5:**1007ff
- emancipation **6:**702ff
- Hebrew MSS **11:**906
- Holocaust **8:**842; **8:**876
- homiletic literature **8:**957
- Melchior family **11:**1286
- press **13:**1048
- Scandinavian literature **14:**925ff
- synagogues **1:**syn. list
- underground **8:**907
- U.N. Security Council **15:**1556ff
- War Crimes Trials **16:**291
- *illus:* text
- *pop. table: text*
- *see also:* NORWAY
D'ennery, Adolphe Philippe **7:**146
Dennery, Justin **11:**1562
De Non Tolerandis Judaeis (Papal Bull)
- Austrian Jews **3:**890
- Brno Jews **4:**1384
- economic history **16:**1287
- Warsaw **16:**334
Denouncers, *see* INFORMERS
Densing, Herman **8:**30
DENVER (city, Colo.) **5:**1542
- *illus:* text
Denyen (anc. people) **13:**399
De Occulta Philosophia (wk.) **10:**644,**15:**1400
De Oliviera, Jacob **15:**1181
De'ot (journ.) **1:**newsp. list; **15:**1110
De'ot ha-Filosofim (wk.) **6:**730
Department of Posts (Isr.) **15:**931
DEPARTMENT STORES **5:**1545
- *illus:*
- - Schocken store, Chemnitz **11:**1323
- - Spiegelberg store, Santa Fe **12:**1038
- - Wertheim store, Berlin **16:**454
DE PASS (fam.) **5:**1547
- shipping trade **14:**1414
- South Africa **15:**203
De Pass, Aaron **5:**1547
De Pass, Alfred **5:**1547
De Pass, Daniel **5:**1547
De Pass, Elias **5:**1547
De Pass, Frank Alexander **11:**1553
De Paz, *see* Buzaglo, Joseph
DE PHILIPPE, EDIS **5:**1548
- music **12:**669
De Piera, Solomon ben Meshullam, *see* DA PIERA, SOLOMON BEN MESHULLAM
De Pinna, David **12:**558
De Pinto (fam.), *see* PINTO, DE
De'Pomi (fam.), *see* POMI(S), DE
De Porta, Astrug, *see* Astrug de Porta
De Porta, Benveniste, *see* BENVENISTE DE PORTA
DEPORTATION, *see* EXILE, ASSYRIAN; EXILE, BABYLONIAN; EXPULSIONS; HOLOCAUST
Deportees (W.W. II), *see* REFUGEES
Deportment, *see* ETIQUETTE
Deposits, depositaries (fin.), *see* SHALISH
DEPPING, GEORGES-BERNARD **5:**1548
DEPUTIES OF THE JEWISH PEOPLE (Rus.) **5:**1548
Deputy (play), *see Der Stellvertreter*
Dêr (loc., Mesop.) **16:**1504
Der Afrikaner Israelit (period.) **13:**1049
Der Alter Yisrolik (mag.) **7:**715
Der Arbayter Fraynd (period.) **9:**1278; **14:**213; **14:**687
Der Arbeiter (period., U.S.) **13:**550
Der Arbeter (newsp., Eng.) **13:**1031
Der Arbeter (period., Pol.) **13:**528
DERASH (exegesis) **5:**1549
- ḥasidic literature **7:**1413
- homiletical literature **8:**950ff
- Kabbalah **10:**623ff
- *see also:* MAGGID; PREACHING
Derashah (sermon), *see* HOMILETIC LITERATURE; PREACHING
Der Ashmeday (period., U.S.) **14:**285
DERASHOT HA-RAN (bk.) **5:**1549
Der Aufstieg (period.) **4:**1040
DERAZHNYA (tn., Ukr.) **5:**1550
DERBENT (city, Cauc.) **5:**1550
- Mountain Jews **12:**478ff
- *see also:* BĀB AL-ABWĀB
Der Beobakhter an der Weykhsel (period.) **16:**340
Der Birodidzhaner Shtern (newsp.) **4:**1049
Der Blufer (period., Pol.) **13:**1043
Der Bluffer (period., Eng.) **13:**1031
Der Byalistoker Arbeiter (newsp.) **4:**806
Der Doktor (period.) **13:**1043
Derekh (journs.), *see Ha-Derekh*
Derekh Emunah (bk.) **4:**812
DEREKH EREẒ (behavior) **5:**1551
- legal capacity **16:**587ff
- modern Judaism **10:**396
- sages **14:**650
- *talmid ḥakham* **15:**747
- *see also:* ETIQUETTE
DEREKH EREẒ (tract.) **5:**1551
- *see also:* PROVERBS, TALMUDIC
Derekh ha-Poel (journ.) **1:**newsp. list
Derekh la'Asot Ḥaruzim (wk.) **16:**1378
Der Emes (newsp., Rus.) **6:**48; **13:**1048; **14:**464; **16:**780
Der Emes (mag., U.S.) **16:**154
Der Emigrant (newsp.) **14:**399
Derenbourg (fam.), *see* DERENBURG
Derenbourg, Hartwig **5:**1553
Derenbourg, Joseph Naphtali **5:**1553
DERENBURG (fam.) **5:**1553
Derenburg, Ẓevi Hirsch **5:**1553
Dereser, T.A. **8:**30
Deretschin, Maggid of, *see* EZEKIEL FEIVEL BEN ZE'EV WOLF
Der ewige Jude, *see* WANDERING JEW
Der Eybiker Yid (play), *see Eternal Jew*
Der Folksfraynd (newsp.) **15:**834
Der Fraynd (newsp., Pol.) **5:**804
Der Fraynd (newsp., Rus.) **7:**582; **11:**16; **13:**1045; **14:**455
Der Fraynd (period., U.S.) **16:**636
Der Freund Israels (period.) **13:**1052
Der Gantz Juedisch Glaub (wk.) **11:**958
"Der Grosse Michel" (16th cent., sol.) **8:**475
Der Groyser Kibitser (mag., U.S.) **13:**1055
Der Groyser Kundes (period., U.S.) **11:**955; **12:**755; **13:**1055
Der Hamer (period., U.S.) **12:**1361
Der Hamoyn (journ.) **15:**653
Der Hohe Rabbi Loew, *see* JUDAH LOEW BEN BEZALEL
Dering, Zigmund **15:**29
Derishat Ẓiyyon (wk.) **10:**708
Der Israelit (weekly, Ger.), *see* ISRAELIT, DER
Der Israelit des neunzehnten Jahrhunderts (period., Ger.) **8:**431; **15:**1128
Der Jude (period., Ger.), *see* JUDE, DER
Der Judenstaat (bk.,) **8:**409,410
- Vatican **16:**73
- Zionism **16:**1043ff,1151
Der Juedische Arbeiter (period., Aus.) **10:**754; **13:**658
Der Juedische Kantor (journ., Ger.) **7:**1548
Der Kamf (newsp., Can.) **5:**113
Der Karmel (period.) **4:**1316
Der Keneder Odler (pub.), *see* KANADER ADLER
Derketa (Syr. diety), *see* Atargatis
Derkheim, Myer **16:**163
Der Kindergarten (period.) **16:**1260
Der Klayner Bund (orgn.) **4:**1500
Der Kolonist (journ.) **16:**1041
Der Kriegstaphet (newsp.) **13:**1049
Der Kundes (period.,) **7:**987
Der Kval (pub. firm, U.S.) **13:**1377
Der Landsman (period.) **3:**886; **13:**1025
D'Erlanger (fam.), *see* ERLANGER
Der Ligner (period.) **13:**1031
Der Makkabi (journ.) **11:**664
Dermatology **11:**1201
Der Moment (newsp., Pol.) **7:**1498
- Nomberg **12:**1210
- press **13:**1023
- Revisionists **14:**131
Der Moment (period., Urug.) **16:**15
Der Morgen (period., Ger.) **13:**1033; **13:**1373
- Central-Verein **5:**287
- Germany **7:**487
- Goldstein, Julius **7:**748
Der Morgen (newsp., Pol.) **13:**1042
Der nationaldeutsche Jude (period.) **16:**106
Der Nayer Moment (newsp., Braz.) **4:**1331; **13:**1040
Der Nayer Veg (period.) **13:**1046; **14:**131
DERNBURG (fam.) **5:**1554
Dernburg, Bernhard **5:**1554
Dernburg, Friedrich **5:**1554
Dernburg, Heinrich **5:**1554
Der Neue Club (Ger.) **8:**491
Der Neue Merkur (period., Ger.) **7:**197

Der Neue Weg (period., Cz.) **13:**1029
DER NISTER (Yid. au.) **5:**1554
- Birobidzhan propaganda **4:**1048
- Gurshtein, Aaron **7:**982
- Yiddish literature **16:**818
De Rocamora (fam.) **12:**978
Der Odesser Arbeter (newsp.) **13:**1048
Der Offenbacher, *see* OFFENBACH, ISAAC
Der Onheyb (period.) **12:**1180; **16:**404
Deror (youth mvmt.) **9:**981
Deror (period., Er. Isr.) **4:**470
Deror (period., Pol.) **16:**348
Der Orient (period.) **16:**576
De'Rossi (fam. name), *see also under* Rossi
DE' ROSSI, GIOVANNI BERNARDO **5:**1557
- book collection **4:**974
- Hebraist **8:**54
- incunabula **8:**1322
- Segre **14:**1113
- translation **4:**878
De'Rossi, Solomon Ben Moses **2:**935
Deroulede, Paul **3:**85
- Dreyfus Affair **6:**227
Derp, Clothilde von **5:**1273
Der Parizer Haynt (newsp.) **6:**1295
Der Proletarisher Gedank (newsp.) **13:**1046; **14:**1323
Der Rabbi von Bacharach (wk.) **8:**272
Der Royter Shtern (newsp.) **16:**192
Der Ruf (period.) **4:**1040
Der Schild (period.) **7:**487; **13:**1033; **14:**50
Der Shtern (newsp., Kharkov) **13:**1048
Der Shtern (journ., Kiev) **13:**1048
Der Shtern (newsp., Minsk) **10:**939; **12:**53
Derso, Aloysius **10:**899
Der Stalindorfer Emes (newsp. Ukr.) **2:**408
Der Stellvertreter (play) **8:**798
- Mengele, Josef **11:**1353
Der Stern der Erloesung (bk.), *see Star of Redemption*
Der Stuermer (journ.), *see* STUERMER, DER
Der Telegraf (newsp.) **15:**650
Der Tog (orgn., Urug.) **16:**15
Der Tog (newsp., Arg.) **3:**423
Der Tog (newsp., Pol.) **13:**1042
Der Tog (newsp., Rus.) **6:**836
Der Tog (newsp., U.S.) **4:**685 **8:**517
- *see also* JEWISH DAY
Dertsik, János **8:**30
Dertsiungs-Entsiklopedye (wk.) **6:**735
Der Tunkeler (pseud.), *see* TUNKEL, JOSEPH
Der Ungarische Israelit (period.) **6:**533; **13:**1035
Derush (exegesis), *see* DERASH
Der Vayter Mizrokh (newsp. China) **7:**1332
Der Veg (period., Mex.) **11:**1459; **13:**1046
Der Veg (newsp., Pol.) **13:**1046
Der Veker (period., Belor.) **4:**445; **12:**53; **13:**1047
Der Veker (newsp., Eng.) **13:**1031
Der Veker (period., Rum.) **7:**540; **16:**371
Der Veker (period., U.S.) **13:**1056
Der Vekker (period., Gal.), *see Der Karmel*
Der Vider-Kol (period.) **3:**423
Dervish Effendi (Doenmeh ldr.) **6:**149
Der Weg (newsp., Can.) **4:**1292
Derwish Aḥmed, *see* Habillo, Moses
DÉRY, TIBOR **5:**1558
Der Yid (period., Belor) **4:**445
Der Yid (newsp., Pol.), *see Dos Yidishe Vort*
Der Yiddisher Kemfer (period., U.S.), *see* YIDISHER KEMFER
Der Yidishe Gazlen (newsp., U.S.) **12:**755
Der Yidishe Proletarier (newsp., Rus.) **13:**1046
Der Yidisher Arbayter (period., Bund) **4:**1499; **12:**721
Der Yidisher Arbayter (newsp., Pol.) **4:**1542; **5:**1036; **5:**362
Der Yidisher Ekspres (period., S. A.) **7:**7
Der Yidisher Emigrant (period.) **14:**1323
Der Yidisher Farmer (newsp., U.S.) **14:**293
Der Yidisher Fonograf (period., Arg.) **3:**423
Der Yidisher Gezelshaftlekher un Handels Buletin (period., Braz.) **4:**1331
Der Yidisher Landvirt (period., Gal.) **2:**410
Der Yidisher Progres (period., U.S.) **7:**1342
Der Yidisher Veker (period., Pol.) **4:**1436
Der Yidisher Veker (newsp., Stanislav) **15:**338
Der Yidishe Tog (newsp., U.S.), *see* JEWISH DAY
"Der Zeyde" *(writ.)*, *see* VINCHEVSKY, MORRIS
DERZHAVIN, GABRIEL ROMANOVICH **5:**1559
Dés (tn., Transyl.), *see* DEJ
De Sacris Palestinae Locis (papal bull.) **16:**77
De Saint Gilles (name), *see under* Saint Gilles
DESALINATION IN ISRAEL **9:**771
- Johnson-Eshkol Agreement **9:**400
- Tahal **15:**701
- U.S.-Israel negotiations **9:**430
- *illus:*
- - Eshkol meeting with U.S. ambassadors **9:**427
- - Negev Institute for Arid Zone Research **9:**966
De Sanctis, Francesco **5:**1428
Desart, Lady, *see* Bischoffsheim, Ellen Odette
De Saulcy (arch.), *see* SAULCY, LOUIS FELICIEN DE JOSEPH CAIGNART
Descartes, René **4:**905
"Descendant of the High Priest" (paint., I. Kaufmann) **15:***fcg.* 491
Descent, *see* GENEALOGY
Deschin, Jacob **13:**486
DESECRATION **5:**1559
- Titus **15:**1170
Desertion (marital) **11:**785
"Desert—Summer Vision" (Mairovich) Pl. 11 **3**-ART
DE-SHALIT, AMOS **5:**1560
De Shira, Myer, *see* HART, MYER
De Singoga, Joab Ben Nathan Ben Daniel **13:**585
- *see also:* Mi-Bet el (fam.)
DESKARTA (tn., Babyl.) **5:**1561
Desmaestre, Bonastruc **14:**862
DESMAESTRE, JONAH **5:**1561
- Majorca **11:**800
Desmarchais, D. **10:**1375
Des Moines (city, Ia.) **8:**1437ff
- *illus:*
- - B'nai Jeshurun synagogue **8:**1439
De Sola (fam., Can.) **5:**1562, *see also* SOLA, DE
DE SOLA (fam., Can.) **5:**1562
De Sola, Aaron David Meldola (Can.) **5:**1563
- *illus:*
- - portrait **12:**285
De Sola, Abraham **5:**1562; **12:**285
- *illus:*
- - portrait **12:**285
De Sola, Clarence Isaac **5:**1563
- Zionist **16:**1109
Despair **7:**1404
D'Espence, Claude, *see* Espencaeus, Claude
D'Espina, Alfonso, *see* ALFONSO DE ESPINA
D'Espinoza, Abraham, *see* Espinoza, Abraham d'
Des Plaines (sub., Chicago) **5:**415
Des Portell, Abraham **5:**313
Dessau (city, Ger.) **3:**1; **4:**657
Dessau, Aaron ben Ẓevi **8:**942; **13:**1107
DESSAU, BERNARDO **13:**491
- Perugia **13:**325
Dessau, Emma **13:**325
DESSAU, HERMANN **5:**1563
Dessau, Mordecai, *see* MAGNUS, MARCUS
DESSAU, PAUL **5:**1564
DESSAUER, FRIEDRICH **5:**1564
Dessauer, Jacob **2:**905
Dessauer, Leopold, *see* DESSOIR, LUDWIG
DESSLER, ELIJAH ELIEZER **5:**1564
Dessler, Reuben Baer **5:**1564
DESSOIR, LUDWIG **5:**1565
DESSOIR, MAX **5:**1565
D'Estella, David ben Samuel, *see* KOKHAVI, DAVID BEN SAMUEL
Destiny **11:**848
- *see also:* PROVIDENCE
De Successione Generationum (agg. wk.), *see* PHILO (Pseudo)
De Synagoga (fam.), *see* Mi-Bet El
Detention, *see* IMPRISONMENT
Determinability Law (philos. conc.), *see* Law of Determinability
Determinism, *see* FREE WILL; PROVIDENCE
Detmold (tn., Ger.) **11:**285
DETROIT (city, Mich.) **5:**1566
- *Contents:*
- - 1769-1840 **5:**1566
- - 1840-1880 **5:**1567
- - 1880-1914 **5:**1568
- - 1915-1940 **5:**1570
- - Post World War II **5:**1571
- museum **12:**551
- secondhand goods **14:**1086
- *illus:* text
Detroiter Vokhenblat (newsp.) **14:**281
Detroit Jewish Chronicle (newsp.) **5:**1571
Dettensee (tn., Ger.) **8:**816
De Turique, Michel, *see* BERR, MICHEL
DEUEL, HANS ERWIN **5:**1572
Deul, Subatol **5:**463
Deus absconditus (conc.) **10:**558
Deuster, Joseph, *see* ANTHONY, JOSEPH
Deutero-Isaiah (prophet) **8:**1016; **9:**48; **12:**262
DEUTERONOMY **5:**1573
- *Contents:*
- - Contents **5:**1573
- - Critical Assessment **5:**1574
- - Discovery, Book of Law **5:**1577
- - Provenance **5:**1578
- - Relation to Tetrateuch **5:**1579
- - Traditional View **5:**1582
- *ḥerem* **8:**348
- Hilkiah **8:**481
- Holiness Code **8:**820
- Hosea **8:**1012; **8:**1022ff
- Hoshana Rabba **15:**501
- Hurrian customs **12:**1290
- Kings, Book of **10:**1030
- *Law of the Lord* **9:**1327
- Magic **11:**704ff
- Micah **11:**1483
- *Midrash Tannaim* **11:**1518
- Pentateuch **13:**232ff
- *Sifrei* **14:**1519
- *Tokheḥah* **15:**1192
- *illus:*
- - text
- - initial *Elleh* **5:**1018
- *see also:* BIBLE
DEUTERONOMY RABBAH (Mid.) **5:**1584
- *Tanḥuma* **15:**794
- *illus:* text
- *see also:* MIDRASH
Deuterosis, *see* MISHNAH
Deutero-Zechariah **6:**869
Deutsch, Aaron David (Hung.) **4:**128; **8:**1092
Deutsch, Abraham **5:**1590
DEUTSCH, ALADAR **5:**1586
Deutsch, Alexander **5:**1593; **13:**346
Deutsch, André **13:**1370
DEUTSCH, BABBETTE **5:**1586
- literature **15:**1578
Deutsch, Benjamin, *see* NEMTEANU, BARBU
DEUTSCH, BERNARD SEYMOUR **5:**1586
Deutsch, Bernát **7:**1474
Deutsch, David (Ger.) **5:**1590
Deutsch, David (Hung.) **4:**128
DEUTSCH, DAVID BEN MENAHEM MENDEL **5:**1586
- Nove Mesto nad Vahom **12:**1234
DEUTSCH, ELIEZER ḤAYYIM BEN ABRAHAM **5:**1587
DEUTSCH, EMANUEL OSKAR **5:**1587
DEUTSCH, ERNST **5:**1588
- Germany **7:**500
- theater **15:**1057
DEUTSCH, FELIX (psych.) **5:**1588
Deutsch, Felix (indus.) **4:**644
DEUTSCH, GOTTHARD **5:**1588
- Academy for Research **2:**818
Deutsch, H. (Bib. trans.) **4:**884
DEUTSCH, HELENE (psych.) **5:**1589
Deutsch, Hermann Bacher D. **5:**1589
Deutsch, Ignac (Hung.) **7:**1474; **15:**488
DEUTSCH, IGNAZ (Aus.) **5:**1590
DEUTSCH, ISRAEL **5:**1590
- *illus:* text
Deutsch, Joel **11:**1532
Deutsch, Joseph Israel **4:**128
Deutsch, Józef **7:**1474
DEUTSCH, JUDAH JOEL **5:**1591
DEUTSCH, LEO (Lev Grigoryevich) **5:**1591
Deutsch, Martin **13:**1339
Deutsch, Menahem (orient.), *see* DEUTSCH, EMANUEL OSKAR
Deutsch, Menahem (r.) **5:**1587
Deutsch, Mordecai **8:**797
DEUTSCH, MORITZ **5:**1592
- Beer **4:**376
Deutsch, Moses **5:**1591
DEUTSCH, OTTO ERICH **5:**1592
Deutsch, Sandra de Hatvan **15:**488
Deutsch, Simeon (r.) **13:**1509
DEUTSCH, SIMON (revol.) **5:**1593
Deutsch, Stanley E. **16:**476
Deutsch, Tibor, *see* DÉRY, TIBOR
Deutsch de la Meurthe, Émile **5:**1593; **13:**346
DEUTSCH DE LA MEURTHE, HENRI **5:**1593
- petroleum **13:**346

Deutsch de la Meurthe, Suzanne 2:320
Deutsche Arbeiterpartei, *see* NATIONAL SOCIALISM
Deutsche Arbeitsfront (orgn., Ger.) 3:83
Deutsche Konservative Partei, *see* CONSERVATIVE PARTY, GERMAN
Deutsche Nationalsozialistische Arbeiterpartei (mvmt., Cz.) 3:84
DEUTSCHER, ISAAC 5:1594
DEUTSCHER PALAESTINA-VEREIN (orgn.) 5:1595
- Gilead survey 11:931
Deutsches Central Komitee fuer die Russischen Juden 4:1325
Deutsches Evangelisches Institut (Jer.) 2:759
DEUTSCH-ISRAELITISCHER GEMEINDEBUND (orgn.) 5:1595
- historical chart 8:766-767
- philanthropic work 13:379
- Prussia 13:1293
Deutsch-Israelitisch-Osmanische Union (orgn., Ger.) 15:1021
DEUTSCHKREUTZ (tn., Aus.) 5:1596
DEUTSCHLAENDER, LEO 5:1596
Deutschlaender, M. 9:1067
Deutschnationaler Handlungsgehilfenverband (union) 3:83
DEUTZ (tn., Ger.) 5:1597
Deutz, Emmanuel 5:1597
- *illus:*
- - portrait 7:30
DEUTZ, SIMON 5:1597
- Chateaubriand 5:364
- Drach 6:191
Devarenu (journ.) 1:newsp. list
Devar ha-Moreh (journn., U.S.) 1:newsp. list
Devar ha-Moreh (journ., Pol.) 1:newsp. list
Devar ha-Po'elet (mag.) 1:newsp. list
Devar ha-Shavu'a (period.) 1:newsp. list; 7:1018
Devar ha-Shilton ha-Mekomi (journ.), *see Ha-Shilton ha-Mekomi be-Yisrael*
Devarim (Bib.), *see* DEUTERONOMY
Devarim (prayers), *see* TEḤINNAH
Devarim Rabbah, Devarim Rabbati (Mid.), *see* DEUTERONOMY RABBAH
Devash, Meir 14:1516
De Vaux, Roland, *see* VAUX, ROLAND DE
DEVEKUT (conc.) 5:1598
- Azikri, Eleazar 3:1008ff
- Ba'al Shem Tov 9:1053
- Dov Baer of Mezhirech 6:180
- ḥasidic thought 7:1405ff
- Heschel, Abraham Joshua 2:160
- Jehiel of Zloczow 9:1314
- Kabbalah 10:613ff
- Menahem Mendel of Vitebsk 11:1311
- Neoplatonism 12:960
- piety 13:505
- *Shekhinah* 14:1354
- *Ẓaddik's* life 6:662
- *see also:* MEDITATION; PRAYER
Devenishski, Eisik Meir, *see* WEITER, A.
Dever (demon) 5:1524
Deverish Effendi (Doenmeh ldr.) 6:149
De Versamelaar (newsp.) 5:1474
De Vidas, Elijah 10:624; 10:642
Devil, *see* DEMONS, DEMONOLOGY; MASTEMA; SAMAEL; SATAN
Devil's Lake (N.D.) 12:39
Devine, Harry 12:1376
Devir (jounr.) 1:newsp. list
Devir (publ. house), *see* DVIR
Devirah (kib., Isr.) 1:place list
De Vita Mosis (bk.) 12:392ff
Devonport (tn., Eng.), *see* PLYMOUTH
DEVONS, ELY 5:1600
D'Evora, Rodrigues (fam.), *see* Rodrigues d'Evora
Devorah (vill., Isr.) 1:place list; 15:675
"Devotion" (sculp., W. Zorach) 16:1221
Devoutness in prayer, *see* KAVVANAH
Devrient, Eduard 15:1055
DE VRIES, ANDRÉ 5:1600
- medicine 11:1204
DE VRIES, BENJAMIN 5:1600
De Vries, Jacob 15:1340
DE VRIES, M. 10:1507; 13:1058
De Vrijdagavond (journ.) 13:1305
DEW 5:1600
- Duvdevani's research 6:324
- *illus:*
- - dew nights, annual number 9:187
DEW, PRAYER FOR 5:1602
- *see also:* MASHIV HA-RU'AḤ; RAIN, PRAYER FOR
De Wette, Wilhelm Martin Lebrecht, *see* WETTE, DE, WILHELM MARTIN LEBERECHT
Dewey, John 5:904
Dewey, Thomas 15:1409
Deyer, Leon 14:834
Deyling, S. *see* Dailing S.
De Young (fam.) 5:56
De Young, Michael 15:1034
Deza, Francisco Diego 5:116; 8:1387
Dhafrān (vill., Yem.) 14:1396
Dhahrat el-Humraiya (site. Isr.) 7:604
DHAMĀR (city, Yem.) 5:1603
- Yemen 16:746
DHAMĀRI, MANṢUR SULEIMAN 5:1603
DHAMĀRI, SA'ID BEN DAVID 5:1604
Dhānā (vill., Transj.) 9:596
Dhiban (vill., Jor.) 6:21
DHIMMA, DHIMMI (Musl. conc.) 5:1604
- Ahl al-Kitāb 2:468
- al-Ḥākim 9:265
- anti-Semitism 3:100
- Cairo *Genizah* 16:1340
- history 8:611
- Mamluk persecutions 11:836
- Seljuk 14:1136
- Tunisia 15:1440
- *see also:* OMAR, COVENANT OF
Dhorme, E. 4:881
Dhrā' (loc., Jor.) 2:538; 15:70
Dhū al-Kifl (Isl. fig.) 6:667
Dhubyani, Al-Nabigha al 13:1470
Dhu Nuwās (k., Arab.), *see* YŪSUF AS'AR YATH'AR DHU NUWĀS
Dhū Yazan, Sayf Ibn (k., Arab.), *see* Sayf ibn Dhūi Yazan
D.H.V. (trade union), *see* Deutschnationaler Handlungsgehilfsverband
Diacritical marks 16:1429
Diadochi (rulers) 8:625
Diabetes Melitus (disease) 11:1185; 14:1502
Diaghilev, Serge 4:117; 14:376
"Dial" (paint., P. Guston) 3:625
Di Algemeyne Yidishe Entsiklopedye 6:731
Dial of Ahaz (sundial) 15:519
Dialoghi di Amore (bk.) 2:109ff; 8:1210
Dialogue, Jewish-Christian 13:1251ff
- secular nationalism 5:514
Dialogue, Philosophy of 4:1432ff; 13:462ff
DIAMAND, HERMAN 6:1
- P.P.S. 13:951
Diamant, Hermann 8:420
DIAMANT, PAUL JOSEPH 6:2
- archives 3:388
- menorah 11:1370
Diamant, Wilhelm 8:420
Diamante, Juan Bautista 9:1343; 10:25; 15:250
Diamond (gem), *see* DIAMOND TRADE AND INDUSTRY
Diamond, A. Philip 6:1362
Diamond, Arthur Sigismund 6:3
DIAMOND, DAVID 6:2
Diamond, Henrietta 6:3
- *illus:*
- - WIZO executive 16:594
DIAMOND, I.A.L. 12:466
Diamond, Jacob Lion 2:530; 5:54
DIAMOND, JOHN, BARON 6:3
DIAMOND, LOUIS KLEIN 6:3
DIAMOND, SIGMUND 6:3
Diamond, William 2:530; 6:369
DIAMOND TRADE AND INDUSTRY 6:4
- Israel industry 9:393; 9:821
- South Africa 15:203
- *yahalom* 13:1010
- *illus:*
- - Israel postage stamp (1968) 9:763
- - Netanyah factory 9:817
- - regulations re taxes on trade (London, 1809) 6:1283
- *tables:* text
Diary of Anne Frank (bk.) 7:53
Dias, André 12:1273
Dias, Branca, *see* Fernandes, Branca
Dias, Duarte, *see* Aboab, Abraham
Dias, Jeronimo, *see* Diaz, Jeronimo
Dias, Juan 7:1291
DIAS, LUIS 6:7
Dias Arias, David 11:527
DIASPORA 6:8
- *Contents:*
- - Definition 6:8
- - Hellenistic-Roman 6:8
- - - Distribution of Population 6:8
- - - Occupations 6:11
- - - Jewish Life 6:12
- - - Roman Rule 6:13
- - - Trajanic Revolt 6:15
- - - Community Organization 6:16
- - - Links with Israel 6:18
- - - culture 6:18
- General
- - *aliyah le-regel* 13:511
- - anthropology 3:48
- - autonomy, judicial 3:928f
- - education 8:688
- - emissaries 14:1364
- - Hirsch, S.R. 8:514
- - philosophy 13:424
- - law 12:123; 12:130; 12:134; 12:141
- - messianism 11:1409
- - music 12:555
- - Shabbateanism 14:1231ff
- - *shtadlan* 14:1462
- - socialism, Jewish 15:44; 15:45
- - synagogue 15:581ff
- - tractate *Pesaḥim* 13:328
- - vital statistics 16:178ff
- - world table 8:733
- Greco-Roman
- - Augustus 3:853
- - Bar Kokhba war 8:647
- - Egypt 6:485ff
- - Hellenism 8:296
- - history, Second Temple 8:639
- - history, 70 to 640 C.E. 9:242ff
- - Jewish slaves 16:1275
- - Josephus, Flavius 10:258
- - Julius Caesar 10:470
- - religion as mysticism 10:495
- Modern Period
- - Agudat Israel 2:424
- - Hebrew language 8:760
- - immigration 9:534ff
- - Israel ties 9:402
- - Six-Day War 9:412ff; 16:1062
- - Zionism 9:540; 16:1167; 16:1176
- *maps:*
- - Asia Minor 3:747
- - Byzantine Empire 4:1551
- - Egypt 6:486
- - Roman Empire 8:643
- *see also:* ALIYAH AND ABSORPTION IN ISRAEL; COMMUNITY; DEMOGRAPHY; EXILE,ASSYRIAN; EXILE, BABYLONIAN; GALUT; HALUKKAH; MIGRATION; POPULATION; POPULATION OF ISRAEL
Diaspora, Marrano, *see* MARRANO DIASPORA
Diaspora, Sephardi, *see* SEPHARDIM
Diaspora nationalism (anti-Zion. mvmt.) 3:927; 4:1041
Diaz, Duarte, *see* Aboab, Abraham
Diaz, Jeronimo 7:639; 8:1391
DIBBUK (spirit) 6:19
- *Toledot ha-Ari* 15:1208
- *illus:* text
- *see also:* GILGUL
Dibdin, Charles 6:778
Di Bin (mvmt., Pol.) 16:405
Diblaim (bib. fig.) 8:1010
DIBON (bib. city, Transj.) 6:21
- Jahaz 9:1269
- Mesha 11:1397ff
- Ramses II 15:1316
- *illus:*
- - Moabite stone 3:319
DIBON (tn., Er. Isr.) 6:21
Di Capua, Alberto 6:361
Dice (game) 7:300
Dichter, Ernest 2:318
DICK, ISAAC MEIR 6:21
- parody 13:135
- stories 16:810
Dickdook Leshon Gnebreet (wk.) 12:257
- *illus:* 12:257
DICKENS, CHARLES 6:22
- English literature 6:780
- *illus:*
- - "Mr. Fagin and Morris Bolter..." (drg., G. Cruikshank) 6:781
Dicker, Samuel B. 14:211
Dickie, A.C. 9:1521ff
Dickinson, Emily 15:1569
Dickman, Adolfo 13:820
Dickman, Elsa 14:934
Dickmann, Max 10:307; 15:255
Dickstein, M. 16:1109
DICKSTEIN, SAMUEL (math.) 6:22
DICKSTEIN, SAMUEL (polit.) 6:23
DICKSTEIN, SZYMON 6:23
Dickstein-Wielezynska (poet) 13:802
"Dictatorship of the Proletariat" (Leninist term) 16:779
Dictionaries
- *Alef Bet de-Rabbi Makhir* 11:669
- Arabic-Hebrew (Ayalon and Schusser) 3:993
- Arabic-Hebrew (Elmaleh) 6:682

- *Aramaeisch-Neuhebraisches Woerterbuch* **5:**1232
- *Aramaic Hebrew Dictionary of the Babylonian Talmud* **11:**1275
- *Arukh (ibn Danan)* **8:**1159
- *Ba'al ha-Lashon* **16:**939
- *Beit Aharon* **2:**17
- *Beit Aharon ve-Hosafot* **2:**17
- *Beit David* **10:**1428
- Bible Aramaic **12:**417
- *Biblisches, Kirchenhistorisches . . .* **4:**985
- *Chaldaeisches Woerterbuch* **11:**158
- *Chrestomathia rabbinica* **4:**985
- *Complete Dictionary of Ancient and Modern Hebrew* **4:**568
- *De'ot ha-Pilosofim* (Shem Tov ben Joseph Falaquera) **6:**1142
- *Dictionarium Syro-Chaldaicum* **10:**1563; **11:**134
- *Dictionary of the Targumim* (Jastrow) **9:**1297
- *Dictionary of Terms in Photography* **16:**1650
- *Dos Yidish Verterbukh* **16:**729
- English and Hebrew dictionary (Danby and Segal) **5:**1261
- English-Hebrew (Even-Shmuel, Silkiner and Efros) **6:**469
- *English-Yiddish Dictionary* **7:**1342
- *Even Boḥan* **16:**1367
- French-Hebrew **6:**682
- *Galut Yehudah* **12:**202
- *Griechische und Lateinische . . .* **10:**1248
- *Ha-Meliẓ* **14:**752; **14:**756
- *Handwoerterbuch der deutschen Sprache* **7:**451
- *Ha-Oẓar* **7:**213
- *He-Arukh* **3:**278
- *He-Arukh u-Musaf he-Arukh* **10:**1397
- *Hebraeisch-deutsches Handwoerterbuch* **7:**524
- *Hebraeisch-deutsches Woerterbuch* **5:**229
- *Hebraeisches und aramaeisches Lexikon* **16:**1399
- *Hebraeisches und chaldaeisches* (Fuerst) **7:**213
- *Hebraeisches und chaldaeisches* (Gesenius) **7:**524
- *Hebrew and Chaldaic Vocabulary* **4:**985
- *Hebrew and English and English and Hebrew Vocabulary* **11:**260
- Hebrew-Arabic (Elmaleh) **6:**682
- Hebrew-Arabic (ibn Danan) **8:**1158
- *Hebrew-Aramaic-English Dictionary* **9:**1297
- Hebrew-English (Avinoam and Sachs) **3:**973
- Hebrew-English (Goor) **7:**783
- Hebrew-French **6:**682
- Hebrew-Hebrew **7:**783
- *Historical Dictionary of the Hebrew Language* **2:**207
- *Ḥotam Tokhnit* **4:**371
- *Kedem Taschen-Woerterbuch* **4:**1402
- *Kitāb al-Ḥāwī* **16:**1381
- *Kitab al-Istighnā'* **16:**1357
- *Kitāb al-Muwazana...* **8:**1157
- *Kitāb al-Tajnīs* **8:**1156
- *Kitāb al-Uṣul* **8:**1182
- *Kitāb Jāmiʿ al-Alfāz* **2:**600; **16:**1356
- Ladino-Hebrew-Spanish **10:**1348
Leksikon le-Millim Zarot **7:**783
- *Ma'arikh* **11:**486
- *Maḥberet* **16:**1356
- *Makrei Dardekei* **10:**427; **16:**1388
- *Marpe Lashon* **10:**1397
- *Menorat ha-Ma'or* **16:**1388
- *Meturgeman* **11:**134
- *Mikhlal Yofi* **4:**1198
- *Millon ha-Aramit ha-Ḥayyah* **10:**805
- *Millon Ḥadash Menukkad* **6:**986 **16:**1650
- *Millon ha-Safah ha-Ivrit* **7:**783
- *Millon le-Munaḥei ha-Politikah* **4:**546
- *Millon Shimmushi la-Talmud* **10:**805
- *Mishpat ha-Urim* **15:**363
- *Murshid al-Kāfī, al-* **16:**1360
- *Musaf he-Arukh* **12:**717
- *Neuhebraeisches und chaldaeisches . . .* **11:**158
- *Ohel Mo'ed* **16:**1360
- *Rattukot ha-Kesef* **16:**1360
- *Risāla* **8:**1193
- *Ru'aḥ Ḥen* **14:**1107
- Russian-Hebrew dictionary **15:**363
- Russian-Hebrew pocket dictionary **15:**363
- *Schulwoerterbuch der hebraeischen Sprache* **5:**229
- *Sefer ha-Agron* **14:**552
- *Sefer ha-Gedarim* **4:**1198
- *Sefer ha-Meliẓah* **15:**125; **15:**1337
- *Sefer ha-Munaḥim li-Refu'ah u-le-Madda'ei ha-Teva* **15:**881
- *Sefer ha-Shorashim* **14:**905
- *Sharshot Gavlut* **12:**1366
- *Shemot Devarim* **11:**134
- special, of the Hebrew language Committee **2:**206
- supplement to the *Arukh* **9:**1271
- technical, of the Academy of the Hebrew Language **2:**207
- technological, of the Academy of the Hebrew Language **2:**207
- *Thesaurus philologicus . . .* **7:**524
- *Tishbi* **11:**134
- *Tosefot he-Arukh ha-Shalem* **3:**278 **10:**1248
- *Yiddish-English Dictionary* **7:**1342
- *Yiddish-English-Hebrew Dictionary* **7:**1342
- *Ẓemaḥ David* **13:**844
- *illus:*
- - *Dictionary of the Yiddish Language* (New York, 1898) **7:**1342
- - *Ẓemaḥ David* (1587) **13:**845
- *see also:* Concordances; ENCYCLOPEDIAS
Didache (Ch. manual)
- *Al Ḥet* **2:**630
- Grace after Meals **7:**839
- Pseudo-Phocylides **13:**1335
Didactic literature (J.) **11:**353ff
Didacus Pyrrhus (humanist) **6:**258
Didascalia Apostolorum (Ch. wk.) **11:**855
DIDEROT, DENIS **6:**23
Didrachm (coin) **16:**381
DIDYMOTEIKHON (Didymotica; city, Gr.) **6:**24
Die Arbeiter Zeitung (newsp.) **11:**1581
Diecinueve de Abril (stlmt., Urug.) **16:**13
Die Deborah (period.) **2:**821; **13:**1052
Diederichs, J.C.W. **8:**30
Die Folkstsaytung (newsp.) **6:**844
Die Fraye Gezelshaft (monthly) **9:**1278
Die Gemeinde (newsp.) **13:**1034
Diego de Barros, *see* BARRASSA, JACOB
Diego de Marchena (pros.) **7:**955
Diego de Valencia (monk) **4:**79
Diego Roderigo, *see* ZACUTO, ABRAHAM BEN SAMUEL
Die gottesdienstlichen Vortraege der Juden (wk.) **16:**1238
Die juedische Front (newsp.) **13:**1034
Die Kalischer Vokh (newsp.), *see* *Kalischer Vokh, Die*
Diels, Rudolf **5:**77
Dien (newsp.), *see* RAZSVET
Diena, Sergio **15:**1455
DIENCHELELE (judge, Sic.) **6:**24
DIENEMANN, MAX **6:**25
Die Neue Welt (newsp.) **13:**1033, **15:**440
Die Neuzeit (weekly), *see* NEUZEIT, DIE
DIENNA, AZRIEL BEN SOLOMON **6:**25
Dienna, David **6:**25
Dienna, Jacob **6:**25
Dienna, Menahem **6:**25
Dienna, Samson **6:**25
Dienstfertig, Marcus **5:**991
Dienststelle des Sonderbeauftragten der R.R.S.S. . . . (orgn.) **13:**756
Die Ovent Zeitung (newsp.) **9:**1278
Die Palaestina-Literatur (wk.) **16:**1156
Die Roze (period.) **7:**1479
Di Ershte Algemeyne un Yudishe Hand-Entsiklopedye **6:**731
DIESENDRUCK, ZEVI **6:**26
Diest, H. Van **8:**30
Diest, Samuel Van **8:**30
Die synagogale Poesie des Mittelalters (bk.) **16:**1238
Die Synagoge (period.) **2:**282
Diet, *see* FOOD
DIETARY LAWS **6:**26
- *Contents:*
- - Permitted Foods **6:**26
- - Sheḥitah **6:**27
- - Koshering **6:**28
- - Other Meat Laws **6:**39
- - Milk and Meat **6:**40
- - Milk **6:**40
- - History **6:**40
- - Explanations of **6:**42
- General
- - abomination concept **2:**97
- - biblical animals **3:**8
- - Conservative Judaism **5:**901
- - evolution **6:**1002
- - Falashas **6:**1146ff
- - Hirsch, S.R. **8:**512
- - Islam **9:**93; **10:**1198
- - Karaites **10:**780
- - Maimonides **11:**761
- - Pentateuch **13:**248
- - Reform Judaism **14:**26
- - Shabbateanism **14:**1251
- - technology **15:**895
- *Halakhah*
- - blood **4:**1115
- - Commandments, the 613 **5:**777
- - *halakhah le-Moshe mi-Sinai* **7:**1167
- - *ḥazakah* of meat **7:**1521
- - *hekhsher* **8:**287
- - *issur ve-hetter* **9:**1085
- - Leviticus **11:**142
- - *mashgi'aḥ* **11:**1094
- - *nevelah* **12:**1019
- - ritual slaughter **3:**5,6
- - *sheḥitah* **14:**1337
- - slaughter by scythe **4:**737
- - *terefah* **6:**47
- - traditions **15:**1309
- Food Types **6:**1414
- - eggs **6:**474ff
- - fish **6:**1326
- - honey **4:**375
- - living limb **6:**987
- - meat **11:**1162
- - milk **11:**1577
- - *parveh* **13:**157
- - pig **13:**506
- - sturgeon **7:**924
- *illus:*
- - text
- - rabbinical examination of chicken (J. M. de Haan) **5:**1459
Die Taube (period.) **5:**456
Dietenberger, Johann **4:**874
Dieterich, J. C. **8:**30
Dietrich, Franz E.C. **8:**30
Dietz, Howard **13:**1361; **15:**1959
Dieuze (tn.,Fr.) **11:**496
Die Wahrheit (period, Aus.) **13:**1033; **15:**1533
Die Wahrheit (newsp., U.S.), *see* *Warheit*
Die Welt (newsp.), *see* WELT, DIE
Die Yidishe Velt (newsp. U.S.) **11:**1097
Diez (tn., Ger.) **12:**841
DIEZ, MACHO ALEJANDRO **6:**45
Die Zeit (period., Egy.) **5:**31
Die Zeit (period., Eng.) **12:**722
Die Zukunft (newsp., Eng.) **13:**1031
Die Zukunft (period., Ger.), *see* ZUKUNFT
Di Folkshtime (pub.) **13:**1043
Di Fraye Arbayter Shtime (weekly) **9:**1278
DI GARA, GIOVANNI **6:**46
- *Haggadah* **7:**1101
- Hebrew printing **16:**101
D.I.G.B., *see* DEUTSCH-ISRAELITISCHER GEMEINDEBUND
Di Genarte Velt (comedy) **16:**808
Diglat (river), *see* TIGRIS
Diglenu (journ., Pol.) **1:**newsp. list
Diglenu (journ., Isr.) **1:**newsp. list
DIGNE (tn., Fr.) **6:**46
Di Goldene Keyt (period.) **15:**539; **16:**825
Di Goldgreber (wk.) **14:**1284
Digra (masor. term) **16:**1432
Di Groyse Velt (anth.) **10:**856
Di Hofnung (period.) **13:**494; **14:**399
Dihok (tn., Iraq), *see* DEHOK
Di Ibergekhapte Briv oyf der Post (wk.) **14:**1279
Dijla (river), *see* TIGRIS
DIJON (city, Fr.) **6:**47
Dikduk, ha- (wk., Ibn Janaḥ), *see* *Kitāb al-Tanqīḥ*
Dikduk, ha- (wk., Tibbon), *see* *Sefer ha-Dikduk*
Dikdukei ha-Te'amim (wk.) **16:**1354,1472
Dikdukei Soferim (wk.) **13:**1466; **15:**80
Di Khazonim Velt (journ.) **7:**1551
Diki, Alexander **7:**1030
Di Kopeke Bibliotek (publ. house) **14:**856
Dikow (tn., Pol.), *see* TARNOBRZEG
Dikstein, Paltiel, *see* DYKAN, PALTIEL
Dilepton (coin), *see* *Perutah*
Dilherr, J.M. **8:**30
Di Literarishe Velt (period.) **14:**198
Dill (spice) **13:**617; **15:**268
Dillingham, Francis **8:**30
DILLMANN, AUGUST **6:**47
DILLON, ABRAHAM MOSHE **6:**48
Dillon, Eliezer **5:**1548; **12:**967
Dillon, Mark **10:**1500
"Dilly Tante" (poet), *see* KUNITZ, STANLEY JASSPON
Dilmun (loc., Pers.) **13:**78
Diltāwa (tn., Iraq) **8:**1449
DIMANSTEIN, SIMON **6:**48
- *Yevsektsiya* **16:**779
Dimantstein, N. **16:**819
Di Maske (theat. gr., Fr.) **15:**1071
Di Medina, Abraham **13:**577
Di Menshheyt (period.) **4:**1331
Dimensions in American Judaism (period.) **13:**1051
DIMI (amora) **6:**48
- on vows **16:**228

Dimi bar Ḥama (amora), *see* AVDIMI BAR ḤAMA
Dimi of Ḥaifa (amora), *see* AVDIMI OF ḤAIFA
DIMI OF NEHARDEA (amora) **6:**49
Dimitrov, Emanuil Pop **14:**523
Dimitrov, Georgi **4:**1490
DIMITROVSKY, CHAIM ZALMAN **6:**49
DIMONAH (tn., Isr.) **6:**50
- statistics **1:**place list
- *illus:* text
Dimonah (bib. tn., Judah) **6:**21; **6:**50
Dimona Nuclear Research Center (Isr.) **9:**797ff
Dimond, Abraham J. **6:**904
Dimyati, Ḥalfon, *see* ḤALFON BEN NETHANEL HA-LEVI ABU SAʿĪD
Din (sefirah), *see Gevurah*
Din, Muhammad Hasan ʿAlāʾ al **9:**1040; **9:**1041
Dina, Giacomo **10:**306; **15:**1455
Dinaburg, Ben Zion, *see* DINUR, BENZION
DINA DE-MALKHUTA DINA (hal. rule) **6:**51
- *Contents:*
- - Historical Background **6:**51
- - In Talmud **6:**51
- - Legal Basis **6:**52
- - Nature of Government **6:**52
- - Scope of Laws **6:**53
- - Taxes **6:**54
- - Non-Jewish Courts **6:**54
- - Value of Coinage **6:**55
- - Appointment to Office **6:**55
- autonomy, judicial **3:**928
- book copyright **7:**1466
- conflict of laws **5:**883; **5:**889
- Jewish law **12:**126ff
- legal status **8:**678
- public authority **13:**1354
- Roman taxation **14:**242
- Samuel **8:**650
- tax **15:**842
- tax evasion **8:**1306
DINAH (bib. fig.) **6:**55
- Asenath **10:**223
- Jobab **10:**129
- *illus:*
- - slaying of Hamor and Shechem **7:**1250
Din al-Tawḥīd (Druze rel.) **9:**928
Di Naye Tsayt (journ.) **16:**1123; **16:**640
Di Naye Velt (newsp.) **13:**1031
Din benei ḥalof (gilgul) **7:**574ff
Dindorf, T.I. **8:**30
DINE, JIM **3:**599
- *illus:*
- - portrait **3:**621
Dinei di-Gerameí (wk.) **12:**780
Dinei kenasot, *see* OBLIGATIONS, LAW OF
Dinei mamonot (law of civil claims)
- admission **2:**291
- agency **2:**349ff
- assault **3:**758ff
- bailees **14:**1455
- *Bava Kamma* **4:**338
- custom **12:**9
- eligible age **13:**1357
- lease and hire **10:**1528
- loans **11:**414
- majority rule **11:**805
- marriage stipulations **8:**1126,1127
- *mishpat Ivri* **12:**110ff
- non-Jewish law **6:**53
- oaths **12:**1298ff
- pleas **13:**631
- property **13:**1146
- Rabbi Nathan's lien **14:**1397
- rabbinical enactment **7:**1159
- redemption **14:**1
- *sevarah* **14:**1196
- surety **15:**524
- trustee **14:**1267
- waiver of claim **11:**1233ff
- witnesses **16:**585ff
- *see also:* PRACTICE AND PROCEDURE
Dinei nefashot, *see* CAPITAL PUNISHMENT; PENAL LAW
Dineir (tn., Turk.) **3:**174
Dinei Yisrael (journ.) **1:**newsp. list
Diner, Isaac **11:**299
DINESON, JACOB **6:**56
Di New Yorker Yidishe Tsaytung (newsp.) **14:**873
Dīn ibn Abī Sharīf, Kamāl al- **9:**1425
Dinim (laws) **12:**110
DININ, SAMUEL **6:**57
Dinis, Alvaro, *see* DENIS, ALBERTUS
DINITZ, SIMON **5:**1110; **5:**1112
Dinkelspiel, Max **11:**520
Dinkelspiel, Moses **5:**56
Dinner, Y.Z., *see* DUENNER, JOSEPH ẒEVI HIRSCH
Dinstagishe Kurant (newsp.) **13:**1034; **13:**1056
- *illus:*
- - masthead (1687) **13:**1033
Dinstagishe un Fraytagishe Kurant (newsp.) **2:**899; **16:**6
Dinter, Artur **7:**445
Din Torah (J. relig. law) **12:**110
DINUR, BENZION **6:**57
- historiography **8:**564
- *illus:*
- - with *ḥalutzim* in Constantinople **14:**465
Dinur, Jehiel (poet), *see* K. ZETNICK
Diocaesarea (city, Er. Isr.) **14:**1177
DIO CASSIUS **6:**58
- Jews **7:**891
- weapons **11:**1441
DIOCLETIAN, CAIUS VALERIANUS (Rom. emp.) **6:**60
- chronological era **14:**752
- Ereẓ Israel **9:**254
- historical chart **8:**766-767
- in Talmud **15:**1024
- Jewish privileges **8:**649
- Palaestina **9:**121
Diodati, Giovanni **4:**878; **4:**881; **9:**1101
Diodore of Tarsus (Ch. F.) **5:**552
DIODORUS OF SICILY **7:**894
- Greek literature on Jews **7:**890
DIODOTUS-TRYPHON (sol., Syr.) **6:**60
- Simeon the Hasmonean **14:**1565
Diogenes Grammaticus **14:**145
DIOGENES LAERTIUS **7:**894
Diogo da Silva **8:**1386
Dion (city, Transj.), *see* DIUM
Diono (writ.), *see* SHKLOVSKI ISAAC VLADIMIROVICH
Dionis, Albert, *see* DENIS, ALBERTUS
Dionysias-Soada (city, Syr.) **7:**1476
DIONYSIUS VAN RYCKEL **6:**61
DIONYSUS, CULT OF **6:**61
- ass worship **3:**784
- Hellenism **8:**293
- Jewish symbolism **15:**570ff
- *Maccabees, Third Book of* **11:**661
- *illus:* text
DIO OF PRUSA **7:**893
Dioqni (fin. deed) **16:**1282
DIOS (Gr. hist.) **7:**894
DIOSCORIDES PEDANIUS **7:**894
- Asaph ha-Rofe **3:**674
Dioscuri (deity) **9:**1406
Diospolis (Rom. city) **5:**720; **9:**252
- *see also:* LYDDA
Diószegi, Kalmár Pál **8:**30
Diphtheria (disease) **11:**1184
Diplomat Hotel (Jer.) **9:**1496
Diplomaticus, *see* WOLF, LUCIEN
Di Post (newsp.) **4:**690
Di Presse (newsp.) **3:**423; **13:**1040
Direchsen, Paul, *see* Absensur, Moses (Ger.)
Diret el-Sunbul (city, Syr.), *see* TADMOR
Di Rieti (It. fam.), *see* RIETI
DIRINGER, DAVID **6:**63
Di Rossi, David *see* Rossi, David de
Di Roze (period.) **16:**825
Dirsztay, Baron **15:**1166
Di San Pauler Yidishe Tsaytung (newsp.) **4:**1331
DISCHE, ZACHARIAS **6:**63
Disciplina Clericalis (wk.) **6:**1379
Discipline
- Durkheim on **6:**310
- education **6:**387ff
DISCIPLINE, MANUAL OF (D.S. Scroll) **6:**63
Contents:
- - Description **6:**63
- - Contents **6:**64
- - Language and Date **6:**65
- - Life and Identity **6:**66
- - Related Documents **6:**67
- alternative titles **14:**1180; **16:**699
- cleansing rites **13:**1431
- Dead Sea sect **5:**1409
- initiation rites **16:**916
- Second Temple **6:**796
- Thanksgiving Psalms **15:**1046
- *see also:* DAMASCUS, BOOK OF COVENANT OF; DEAD SEA SCROLLS
DISCRIMINATION **6:**67
- *Contents:*
- - Soviet Union **6:**68
- - United States **6:**69
- - England **6:**70
- - Arab Countries **6:**71
- cooperatives **5:**941
crime rates **5:**1091ff
dhimmi **5:**1605
Holocaust **8:**838ff
- law, Jewish and foreign **12:**139
- migrations **16:**1519ff
- Muslim taxation **16:**1279
- New Christians **12:**1022
- *numerus clausus* **12:**1263
- Omar, Covenant of **12:**1378
- Ottoman Empire **16:**1538
- P.P.S. **13:**951
- self-defense **14:**1124
- Seljuks **14:**1136
- Umayyads **15:**1529
- universities **15:**1675ff
- U.N. subcommission **15:**1559
- *see also:* ANTI-SEMITISM; RACE, THEORY OF; *and under individual countries and places*
Diseases, Study of, *see* Pathology
Diseases and remedies **11:**1179ff
- leprosy **11:**36
- priests **13:**1078
- *illus:*
- - prayer for health **11:**1196
- *see also:* SICKNESS
DISEGNI, DARIO **6:**72
Dishon (mosh., Isr.) **1:**place list
Di Shtime (period.) **11:**1459; **13:**1040
Dishze, Simeon **11:**964
Disinfectants **15:**267
DISINTERMENT **6:**72
- mourning **11:**239
- responsa on mass graves **14:**94
- *see also:* BURIAL; LIKKUT AẒAMOT
Diskarta (tn., Babyl.), *see* DESKARTA
DISKIN, CHAIM **11:**1572
Diskin, Isaac Jeroham **6:**75; **9:**892
DISKIN, MORDEKHAI **6:**73
DISKIN, MOSES JOSHUA JUDAH LEIB **6:**74
Diskin orphanage (Jer.) **6:**74; **9:**1460
Diskursen fun di Alte Kehile (newsp.) **13:**1034
Diskursen fun di Naye Kehile (newsp.) **13:**1034
Disma, P. **8:**30
Dismissal (labor) **10:**1326ff
DISNA (tn., Belor.) **6:**75
Disney, William **8:**30
Dispersion, *see* DIASPORA; GALUT
DISPLACED PERSONS **6:**75
- Augsburg camp **3:**850
- Austria **3:**902
- autonomy, communal **3:**925
- Beriḥah **4:**622
- Evian Conference **6:**987
- Franklin Roosevelt **14:**257
- Germany **7:**496
- Holocaust **8:**884
- Israel survey **9:**357
- J.D.C. **2:**830
- Jewish refugees **14:**28
- Kasztner, Rezso **10:**815
- Rosensaft, Josef **14:**290
- tracing of **8:**1412
- UNRRA **15:**1688
- War Refugee Board **16:**332
Dispossession **10:**1533ff
Disputation of Barcelona, *see* BARCELONA, DISPUTATION OF
Disputation of Lemberg, *see* Lvov, Disputation of
Disputation of Paris, *see* Paris, Disputation of
Disputation of Rimini, *see* RIMINI
Disputation of Tortosa, *see* TORTOSA, DISPUTATION OF
DISPUTATIONS AND POLEMICS **6:**79
- *Contents:*
- - In Pagan Environment **6:**80
- - Christian Environment **6:**82
- - Medieval Milieu **6:**88
- - Renaissance **6:**94
- - Modern Times **6:**96
- General
- - apologetics **3:**189; **3:**192
- - burning of the Talmud **5:**538
- - Catholic Church **5:**538
- - conversions **3:**173
- - Dominicans **6:**163
- - emissaries **14:**1366
- - Frankists **7:**58; **7:**61ff
- - historical chart **8:**766-767
- - Jewish literature **11:**354
- - linguisitics **16:**1361
- - messianism **11:**1424
- - mutual influence **5:**514
- - Reformation **14:**22
- Locations
- - Barcelona **4:**213
- - Cluny **5:**619
- - Ferrara **12:**251
- - France **7:**19
- - Kamenets-Podolski **10:**725
- - Lvov **4:**1037
- - Paris **13:**105
- - Rimini **11:**873
- - Rome **14:**248
- - Tortosa **15:**1270
- Personalities
- - Abbas, Moses **2:**39
- - Abraham of Dreux **2:**155
- - Alatino, Azriel **2:**514
- - Albo, Joseph **2:**535; **2:**536
- - Astruc ha-Levi **3:**810
- - Benedict XIII **4:**482
- - Bibago, Abraham **4:**811

– – Celsus 5:270
– – Crispin, Gilbert 5:1113
– – Donin, Nicholas 6:167
– – Ferrer, Vicente 6:1236
– – Grayzel 7:863
– – Ḥasan ben Mashi'aḥ 7:1365
– – Jacob of Belzyce 9:1232
– – Justin Martyr 4:924
– – Lorki, Joshua 11:494
– – Muelhausen 12:500
– – Naḥmanides 12:775
– – Priscus 8:658
– – Samuel ben Meir 14:809
– – Wagenseil, J.C. 16:239
– *illus:*
– – text
– – *Pugio Fidei* (1687) 4:214,215
– – St. Paul 8:662
– *see also:* APOLOGETICS; SERMONS TO JEWS
Disputes (legal), *see* CONFLICT OF OPINION
DISRAELI, BENJAMIN 6:103
– Basevi, Maria 4:290
– caricatures 5:175
– coat of arms 8:339
– England 6:756,780
– historical chart 8:766-767
– stamps 15:335
– Villareal 16:137
– *geneal. table:* text
– *illus:*
– – text
– – autograph 3:914; 6:105
– – coat of arms 8:338
D'ISRAELI, ISAAC 6:109
– apostasy 3:205
– community service 8:722ff
– historians 8:543
– *illus:* text
Disraeli, Maria 4:290
Dissection, *see* AUTOPSIES AND DISSECTION
Dissentchik, A. 11:640
– *illus:*
– – *Brit Trumpeldor* 10:1468
Distenfeld, Hanoch, *see* YALON, HANOCH
Distilling trade 4:1258
– *see also:* WINE AND LIQUOR TRADE
District Courts (Isr.) 9:632ff
District of Columbia, *see* WASHINGTON, D. C.
D'Italia (fam.) 11:898
– printing 13:1101ff
Di Tat (newsp.) 16:738
Ditfurt (Nazi crim.) 11:389
Dithmar, Justus C. 8:30
Di Trani, Baruch ben Isaac, *see* Trani, Baruch ben Isaac di
Di Trani, Isaiah (Younger), *see* ISAIAH BEN ELIJAH DI TRANI
Di Trani, Isaiah (Elder), *see* ISAIAH BEN MALI DI TRANI
Di Trani, Joseph, *see* TRANI, JOSEPH BEN MOSES
Di Trani, Moses, *see* TRANI, MOSES BEN JOSEPH
Di Trani, Solomon, *see* Trani, Solomon ben Moses
Di Trento (tn., It.), *see* RIVA
Di Tribune (period.) 10:70
Di Tsayt (period., Rus.) 11:1176; 12:1361
Di Tsayt (period., U.S.) 13:1053
DITTENHOEFER, ABRAM JESSE 6:110
Dittenhoefer, Isaac 4:1145
Dittenhoefer, "Navajo Sam" 12:1038
Dittenhofer, Jacob 12:38
DIUM (city, Transj.) 6:110
– *see also:* DECAPOLIS
Dius (Gr. hist.), *see* DIOS
Divan, Yahuda Amram, *see* DIWAN, JUDAH BEN AMRAM
Di Varhayt (newsp., Rus.) 13:1048
DIVEKAR, SAMUEL EZEKIEL 6:111
– Bene Israel 4:498
Divier, Anton 11:14
DIVIN (tn., Rus.) 6:111
DIVINATION 6:111
– *Contents:*
– – Prophet as Mantic 6:112
– – Foretelling, Bible 6:113
– – Biblical Attitude 6:115
– – In Talmud 6:116
– – In Middle Ages 6:118
– astrology 3:788
– Commandments, the 613 5:771
– elipse 12:291; 15:517
– ephod 6:804
– lots 11:511
– prophets 13:1153ff
– right-left 14:179
– Samuel, Book of 14:791
– sorcery 15:163
– *urim* and *thummim* 16:8
– *illus:* text
– *see also:* MAGIC
Divine Chariot, *see* MERKABAH MYSTICISM
Divine epithets, *see* GOD, NAMES OF
Divine judgment, *see* DAY OF THE LORD
Divine law, *see* DIVINE PUNISHMENT
Divine Presence, *see* PRESENCE, DIVINE; SHEKHINAH
DIVINE PUNISHMENT 6:120
– anti-Semitic legends 3:95
– assault 3:759
– banishment 4:163
– compounding offenses 5:856
– flogging 6:1349; 13:1388
– *ḥillul ha-Shem* 10:980
– imprisonment 8:1300
– Job 10:121
– *karet* 10:788
– legal compulsion 10:1482
– meaning of exile 7:283ff
– moral force 12:113
– oath, false 12:1300
– self-affliction 15:491
– *see also:* REWARD AND PUNISHMENT
Divine Will, *see* GOD
DIVORCE 6:122
– *Contents:*
– – In the Bible 6:123
– – Later Law 6:125
– – – Mutual Consent 6:125
– – – Without Consent 6:126
– – – Prohibited Marriage 6:130
– – – Will of Parties 6:130
– – – Execution 6:131
– – – Agency 6:132
– – – Conditional 6:133
– – – Consequences 6:134
– – – State of Israel 6:134
– – Statistics 6:135
– – – Europe 6:135
– – – British Commonwealth 6:136
– – – Muslim Lands 6:136
– – – United States 6:136
– General
– – Commandments, the 613 5:769,781
– – concubine 5:865
– – *Gittin* 7:592
– – *ḥaliẓah* 11:122
– – Israel 9:481
– History 11:1031
– – Akiva 2:491
– – Ash, Abraham 3:694
– – Assembly of Notables 3:763
– – Cleves *get* 5:613
– – emancipation era 12:140
– – ghetto origin 7:542
– – Hillel of Erfurt 8:490
– – Malachi 11:813ff
– – Rabbah 13:1440
– – vital statistics 16:177ff
– Legal Aspects
– – *agunah* 2:429ff
– – apostates 3:212
– – child marriage in Israel 11:1051
– – civil marriage 5:595
– – conflict of laws 5:885
– – crucified man 5:1134
– – duress 12:1398
– – embryo 6:719
– – *ḥazakah* 7:1521
– – intermarriage 12:167; 12:168
– – *mamzer* 11:840ff
– – non-Jewish bills 6:51
– – priest 13:1088ff
– – prohibited marriage 11:1052ff
– – *takkanot* 15:722
– – virgin 16:161ff
– – Woman's Equal Rights Law 16:629
– Grounds for 8:1121ff
– – bigamy and polygamy 4:985ff
– – childless wife 5:426
– – dispute 7:1162
– – head covering 8:6
– – marriage to a tanner 10:1537
– – *niddah* 12:1144
– – prostitution 13:1246
– – self evidence 14:1196
– Bill of
– – abbreviations 2:51
– – Conservative attitude 12:1445
– – kohen 13:1090
– – laws of writing 14:1044; 16:670ff
– – *meḥamat mitah* 16:521
– – preparation 11:643
– – waiver 11:1234
– Execution of 6:131
– – agency 2:349
– – imprisonment 8:1301
– – use of *niddui* 8:352; 8:354
– Consequences 6:134
– – compensation innovation 12:143
– – custody 13:95ff
– – dowry 6:185
– – father's responsibility 8:1125
– – inheritance rights 15:477
– – *ketubbah* 10:927
– – maintenance alternative 11:788
– – rabbinic office 13:1446
– Various Usages
– – Bene Israel 4:498
– – Conservative Judaism 5:904ff
– – Elephantine 6:606
– – Falashas 6:1146
– – Islam 10:1198
– – Karaites 11:841
– – Samaritans 14:745; 14:747
– *illus:*
– – text
– – bill of divorce (14th cent. ms.) 7:592
– – *Get Pashut* (1719) 7:1025
– – handing the bill of divorce 7:592
– – London *bet din* minute book (1830) 3:880
– – *Or ha-Yashar* (1969) 5:614
– – *Rei'aḥ Sadeh* (1738) 6:326
– *see also:* CHILD MARRIAGE; HUSBAND AND WIFE
Divre (Divrei) ha-Yamim (Bib.), *see* CHRONICLES, BOOK OF
Divrei David (wk.) 15:520
Divrei Ge'onim (bk.) 10:680
Divrei ha-Akademyah le-Madda'im (journ.) 1:newsp. list
Divrei ha-Ḥakhamim (chronicle; Sambari) 14:761
Divrei Ḥakhamim (ms. collec.) 1:newsp. list
Divrei ha-Keneset (journ.) 1:newsp. list
Divrei ha-Me'orot (Qumran) 4:272
Divrei ha-Yamim (newsp.) 1:newsp. list
Divrei ha-Yamim le-Araẓot Rumanyah (wk.) 13:1334
– *illus:*
– – title page (1872) 14:388
Divrei ha-Yamim le-Malkhei Ẓarefat (wk.) 8:558
Divrei ha-Yamim le-Malkhut Venezia (bk.) 5:153
Divrei ha-Yamim le-Moshe Rabbenu, *see* MOSES, CHRONICLES OF
Divrei Kabbalah (wk.) 15:1309
Divrei Neḥemyah (bk.) 14:1249
Divrei Soferim (wk.) 15:80
Divrei Soferim (journ.) 1:newsp. list
Divrei Yosef (bk.) 11:349; 14:761ff
Dibrei Ẓaddikim (bk.) 10:680; 11:116
DIWAN, JUDAH BEN AMRAM 6:137
– Persian communities 13:315
– Tabriz 15:694
Diwaniya (tn., Iraq) 8:1450
Di Welt (journ., Lith.) 16:833
Diwinski, Alter 9:1154
DIYALA (prov., Iraq) 6:137
– Gihon 13:78
– Kurdish Jews 10:1295
Diyala River (Mesop.) 16:1490
Diyarbakir (prov., Turk.) 8:1450; 9:504
Di Yidishe Bibliotek (period., Pol.) 13:281
Di Yidishe Folksbibliotek (lit. period.) 14:1274
Di Yidishe Folkshtime (period., Arg.) 3:423
Di Yidishe Folkstsaytung (newsp., Braz.) 4:1331
Di Yidishe Gazeten (period., U.S.) 14:873
Di Yidishe Poste (period., Gal.) 16:1330
Di Yidishe Shprakh (period., Rus.) 13:1048; 14:1474
Di Yidishe Shriftn (pub., Pol.) 13:1043
Di Yidishe Shtime (newsp.), *see* YIDISHE SHTIME
Di Yidishe Tsaytung (newsp., Arg.) 3:423; 13:1040
Di Yidishe Velt (period., Lith.) 12:1155; 13:1047
Di Yugend (pub., N.Y.) 16:814
Di Yugendshtime (newsp., Den.) 13:1049
Di Yunge (lit. mvmt.), *see* YUNGE, DI
Diyyunim (journ.) 1:newsp. list
DIZENGOFF, MEIR 6:138
– Tel Aviv 15:922
– *illus:*
– – laying the Habimah Theater cornerstone 7:1028
– – Mond, Alfred, and 12:242
Dizengoff, Zina 6:138
Djaen, Joseph 10:1351
Djakmak (sult.) 11:837
Djakovo (concen. camp) 12:1498; 14:872
Djanet (anc. city, Egy.), *see* ZOAN
Djavid Bey, *see* JAVID BEY
Djefti (anc. loc.) 16:270
Djelfa (tn., Alg.) 7:35
Djérada (tn., Mor.) 7:35; 12:344
DJERBA (isl., Tun.) 6:139
– Ibadids 8:1149
– marriage custom 11:1043
– Temple door legend 15:1430
– Tunisia 15:1437,1438
– *illus:*
– – Ḥāra al-Ṣeghira synagogue 15:1434
– – psalmody (mus.) 13:1329,1331
Djeridie y Lesan (journ.) 13:1038

Djian, Judah (of Jaén) **11:**1015
Djian, Nathan **15:**1173
Djian, Suzanne **13:**110
Djobar (vill., Syria), *see* JUBAR
Djubayl (tn., Leb.), *see* JUBAYL
DLUGOSZ, JAN **6:**140
DLUZHNOWSKY, MOSHE **6:**140
DMOWSKI, ROMAN **6:**140
- politics **13:**800
DNEPROPETROVSK (city, Ukr.) **6:**141
- self-defense **14:**1125
- *illus:*
- - pogrom victims **14:**445
Dniester (riv., Ukr.) **15:**1330
Do'ar (publ.) **1:**newsp. list
DO'AR HA-YOM (newsp.) **6:**142
- Ben-Avi, Ithamar **4:**470
- Elmaleh, Abraham **6:**681
- Hebrew newspapers **12:**1056; **12:**1057
- Jabotinsky **9:**1180
- Jerusalem **9:**1473
- Revisionists **14:**131
- statistics **1:**newsp. list
Do'ar Ivri (stamp label, Isr.) **15:**333
DOBIN, SHIMON (Shimoni) **6:**142
Dobisov, E. I. **7:**1331
DOBKIN, ALEXANDER **3:**599
DOBKIN, ELIYAHU **6:**143
- *illus:*
- - "Black Saturday" **10:**31
- - Jewish Agency Executive **10:**28
Dobraczyński, Jan **13:**798
DOBRATH (Lev. tn.) **6:**143
Dobrin (loc., Pol.) **3:**843
Dobrinsky, Isaac **13:**116
Dobruschka, Jacob Moses **6:**143
- Brno **4:**1384
Dobruschka, Schoendl **6:**143
Dobruschka, Solomon **6:**143
DOBRUSCHKA-SCHOENFELD (fam.) **6:**143
- Frank, Jacob **7:**68
Dobruschka-Schoenfeld, Emanuel (David) **6:**144
Dobruschka-Schoenfeld, Franceska **6:**144
Dobruschka-Schoenfeld, Leopoldine **6:**144
Dobruschka-Schoenfeld, Moses **6:**144; **7:**68
DOBRUSHIN, YEKHEZKEL **6:**144
"Dobruska" (pseud.), *see* FRANK, JACOB
Dobruska, Jacob Moses, *see* Dobruschka, Jacob Moses
Dobson, Thomas **8:**209
Dobzhinsky, Abraham ben Raphael, *see* CIECHANOW, ABRAHAM BEN RAPHAEL LANDAU OF
Dr. Beham's Pasteur Institute (Jer.) **9:**989
Dr. Blochs Oesterreichische Wochenschrift (period.) **4:**1104
Dr. Herzl (gr., Urug.) **16:**1126
Dr. L. Gelehrter Hospital (Rum.) **9:**1294
"DOCTORS' PLOT" (Rus.) **6:**144
- cartoons, anti-Semitic **5:**178
- Israel **9:**429
- Mikhoels, Solomon **11:**1531
- Slansky trials **14:**1654
- Soviet anti-Semitism **3:**149
- Stalin **15:**328
- U.N. General Assembly **15:**1562
Dr. Theodor Herzl League (Zion. gr., Arg.) **16:**1123
Doctrines, Theological, *see* ARTICLES OF FAITH; BELIEF
Documents, *see* SHETAR
DÓCZY, LAJOS **6:**145
Dodai bar Naḥman (gaon) **7:**318
Dodanim (bib. fig.), *see* RODANIM
Dodder (bot.) **15:**268
Dodekapylon (arches, Jer.) **9:**1406
Dodick, John, *see* Bernstein, Jack
"Dodie the Innkeeper" (illus., A. Kaplan) **10:**748
Dodo of Beth-Lehem (bib. fig.) **6:**611
DOEBLIN, ALFRED **6:**146
Doederlein, J. C. **8:**30
- Isaiah authorship **9:**45; **9:**61
DOEG (bib. fig.) **6:**146
- Saul **14:**914
- status of *gerim* **15:**420
Doehle, Walter **15:**996
Doelake, W. H. **8:**30
Doellinger, Johannes von **3:**485
Doenburg (city, Ger.) **15:**1128
DOENMEH (Shab. sect) **6:**148
- Ayllon, Solomon **3:**996
- Jewish status of **10:**58
- Querido, Jacob **13:**1426
- Shabbateanism **14:**1245
- Turkey **15:**1458
Doenitz, Karl **16:**289
Doerpfeld, Wilhelm **3:**301
Doetus (sol., Er. Isr.) **13:**1420
DOG **6:**152
- behavior with **6:**1288
- hunting **8:**1111
Dogliani (vill., It.) **16:**1004
Dogmas, *see* ARTICLES OF FAITH; BELIEF
Dohany, Julius **16:**1150
DOHM, CHRISTIAN WILHELM VON **6:**152
- Cerfberr **2:**755; **5:**312
- chronological chart **8:**766-767
- defense of Jews **3:**198
- Moses Mendelssohn **11:**1334
- toleration of Jews **8:**711ff
DOK (fort., Er. Isr.) **6:**153
- Jericho **9:**1371
DOKSHITSY (Dokszyce; tn., Belor.) **6:**154
Dol (tn., Fr.), *see* Dol-De-Bretagne
Dolabella, Publius Cornelius (Rom. gen.) **6:**41
Dolan Bellon **5:**160
DOLBIN, B. F. **3:**599
Dol-De-Bretagne (tn., Fr.) **4:**1383
Dolder (vill., Holl.) **16:**37
DOLGINOVO (Dolhínow; tn., Rus.) **6:**154
DOLINA (tn., Ukr.) **6:**154
DOLITZKI, MENAHEM MENDEL **6:**154
- Hebrew literature **8:**210
DOLLFUSS, ENGELBERT **6:**155
Dollis Hill Synagogue (Lond.) **15:**620
DOLMATOVSKI, YEVGENI ARONOVICH **14:**515
DOLMENS (burial chambers) **6:**156
DOLNI KOUNICE (tn., Morav.) **6:**156
DOLNI KUBIN (tn., Cz.) **6:**157
Dolp, Hermann **4:**455
Dolphins **4:**1017
- *illus:*
- - catacombs **15:**569
Dolzenovsky, Moshe **15:**1215
Domain, *see* RESHUT
Domanevka (vill., concen. camp, Ukr.) **12:**1326; **15:**1333ff
Domashevitzky, Isaiah, *see* BERSHADSKY, ISAIAH
DOMBROVENI (J. agr. clny., Bess.) **6:**157
Dombrowsky, V. **16:**342
DOMENICO GEROSOLIMITANO (apos.) **6:**158
Dome of the Rock (mosque, Jer.) **9:**1416; **9:**1516
- ʿAbd al-Mālik **2:**55; **9:**1425
- attendance in **9:**264
- Hajj Amīn al-Husseini **9:**461
- holy places **8:**935
- Jerusalem in art **9:**1579
- Ka'b al-Aḥbar **10:**488
- Mamluks **9:**1424
- Omar **12:**1382
- Suleiman's alterations **9:**1460
- Temple Mount **15:**989
- Temple rock **6:**986
- Umayyads **15:**1529
- *illus:*
- - aerial view **9:**1413
- - *even shetiyyah* **9:**1555
- - Palestine stamp **15:**332
- - printer's mark **9:**1586
- - special service **8:**931
- - Temple Mount area **15:**988
- - thirteenth cent. icon **9:**1581
- - view from al-Aqṣā mosque **9:**920
- - view from the north **9:**1431
Dom Henrique (Inq., Port.) **8:**1386
DOMICILE **6:**158
- banishment **4:**165
- conflict of laws **5:**882ff
- custom conflict **12:**23
- election rights **13:**1358
- festivals **6:**1245
- lease and hire **10:**1528
- residence laws **15:**841ff
- Sabbath **6:**849
Domínguez (tn., Arg.) **3:**432
DOMINIC, ALEXANDRU **14:**420; **14:**426
Domini canes (Cath. order), *see* DOMINICANS
DOMINICAN REPUBLIC **6:**160
- Holocaust **8:**905
- Latin America **10:**1451
- refugees **6:**991
- synagogues **1:**syn. list
- *pop. table:* text
Dominican Republic Settlement Association Inc. **6:**160
DOMINICANS (Cath. order) **6:**161
- Hebrew interests **8:**13
- Naḥmanides **12:**775
- *illus:* text
Dominici, Itek, *see* DIAMOND, I. A. L.
Dominoes (game) **7:**305
Dominus Flevit (site, ch., Jer.) **9:**1491; **12:**484
DOMITIAN (Rom. emp.) **6:**164
- Akiva's deputation **2:**489
- arch of Titus **15:**1167
- chronological list **8:**766-767
- Flavius Clemens **6:**1338
- Keti'a bar Shalom **10:**925
- tax on Jews **8:**644
- *illus:*
- - coins, Judean **5:**714
Domitilla Flavia *see* Flavia, Domittilla
DOMNINUS OF LARISSA **6:**164
Domus Boni Latronis (fort., Er. Isr.), *see* LATRUN
DOMUS CONVERSORUM (inst., Lond.) **6:**165
- chronological list **8:**766-767
Don (Sp. tit.) **15:**236
Donaldsonville (city, La.) **11:**519
Donatello (art.) **9:**1360; **10:**460
- *illus:*
- - Habakkuk (*Lo Zuccone;* statue) **7:**1015
- - Jeremiah (sculp.) **9:**1353
- - "Judith and Holofernes" (sculp.) **10:**453
DONATH, ADOLPH **6:**165
- *illus:* text
DONATH, EDUARD **6:**166
Donath, Leo **15:**314
DONATH, LUDWIG **15:**1081
DONATI, ANGELO **6:**166
DONATI, ENRICO **6:**166
- *illus:* text
Donati, Francesco, *see* Franciscus Donatus
DONATI, LAZZARO **3:**599
Donations, *see* CHARITY; HEKDESH; WILLS
Donatus, F. **8:**30
Don Bendit (tos.), *see* JOSEPH BEN MOSES OF TROYES
Don Çaq de la Maleha *see* Ibn Zadok, Isaac
Donchin, Yehudah Leib, *see* DON-YAḤIA, YEHUDAH LEIB
Don Don, Isaac **16:**1533
DONETSK (city, Ukr.) **6:**167
DONIN, NICHOLAS **6:**167
- Paris disputation **6:**92
Don Isaac ben Don Solomon Zadok, *see* Ibn Zadok, Isaac
Don Isaac de la Maleha, *see* Ibn Zadok, Isaac
Don Judah (physic.) **6:**261
Don Judah (off., Port.) **13:**920
Donkey, *see* ASS
Donkey-drivers **7:**971
Donkhin, Max **12:**405; **14:**917
Dönme(h) (Shab. sect), *see* DOENMEH
Don Mossé **4:**79
Donne, Francesco Delle **16:**114
Donnelly, Ignatius **15:**1650
DONNOLO, SHABBETAI **6:**168
- Apulia **3:**227
- astrology **3:**791
- Hebrew language **16:**1634
- Jewish mysticism **10:**511
- medicine **11:**1187
- psychiatry **13:**1337
- *Sefer Yeẓirah* **16:**786
- Taranto **15:**806
- *illus:*
- - *Sefer ha-Yakar* **11:**1189
Donolo Institute for Physiological Hygiene (Isr.) **15:**926
Don Pacifico, *see* PACIFICO, DAVID
Don Quixote (bk.) **5:**312
Donreich, Albert **16:**1165
Don Salomon ben Labi, *see* LABI, SOLOMON
Don-Yaḥia, Shabbetai **6:**170
DON-YAḤIA, YEHUDAH LEIB **6:**170
Don Yaḥya (fam.) **11:**555
Don Yaḥya, Ben Zion **11:**555
Don Yaḥya, Eliezer **11:**555
Donyel, M., *see* DANIEL, M.
Don Zag, *see* IBN SA'ID, ISAAC
DOOR AND DOORPOST **6:**170
- *menorah* position **7:**1289
- *mezuzah* **11:**1475
- Passover Seder **13:**168
- *illus:*
- - text
- - Avelim **3:**947
- - Ben Ezra synagogue, Cairo **5:**29
- - Beth Aaron synagogue, Detroit **5:**1567
- - Bet She'arim catacomb **4:**768
- - Dabbūra *bet-midrash* lintel **13:**1533
- - Eshtemoa synagogue **6:**893
- - Gush Ḥalav synagogue **6:**337
- - Karaite Synagogue, Jerusalem **10:**782
- - Khirbat Kānif synagogue **13:**1532
- - Qasrayn synagogue lintel **13:**1534
- - Shiloah lintel inscription **15:**1220
- - Yad Vashem Memorial Hall Fig. 110 3-ART
Doppelt, Frederick A. **8:**1361
DOR (tn., Er. Isr.) **6:**172
- Phoenicia **7:**613
- statistics **1:**place list
- *see also:* Dora

Dor (mosh., Isr.) **6**:172
Dor, Abraham Leon **6**:433
Dor, Hirsh Leon **6**:433
Dora (city, Er. Isr.)
- coins **5**:720
- Greek temple **3**:327
- Petronius Publius **13**:346
Dora (clny., Arg.) **3**:429; **3**:430
Dora (concen. camp, Ger.) **4**:1445
Dorban (agr. implement) **2**:390
Dorcas (N.T. fig.), *see* Tabitha
Dorchester (dist., Boston, Mass.) **4**:1265; **11**:1112
Dorchester (U.S. boat) **11**:1570
- *illus:*
- - memorial stamp **11**:1571
Dorczyn, Aaron **15**:412
Dor-De'ah (mvmt., Yem.) **2**:198
Dor Dor ve-Dorshav (wk.) **16**:413ff
Doré, Gustav **16**:261
- *illus:*
- - "The Eternally Wandering Jew" (caric.) **5**:173
Dorenu (period.) **1**:newsp. list; **15**:96
Dorenu Afrike (period.) **13**:1049
Doresh, Abraham ben Moses **13**:575
Doreshei Ḥalakot (D.S. Scrolls) *see* SEEKERS AFTER SMOOTH THINGS
Doreshei Leshon Ever (Heb. lang. soc.), *see* Ḥevrat Doreshei Leshon Ever
Doreshei Shalom (assim. soc.) **11**:612; **14**:1458
Doreshei Zion (soc., Bul.), *see* Dorshei Zion
Doreshei Zion (orgn., Rum.) **4**:1320; **9**:1294
Doreshin lashon hedyot (leg. conc.) **12**:21
Doresh le-Zion (orgn., Rum.), *see* Doreshei Zion
Doresh Shalom (assim. soc.), *see* Doreshei Shalom
Doresh Tob (Tov) le-Ammo (period., Ind.) **13**:1036; **14**:897
Doresh Tov le-Ammo (newsp., Bagh.) **13**:1041
DORFMAN, JOSEPH **6**:173
DORFMAN, RALPH ISADORE **5**:381
DORI, YA'AKOV **6**:173
- Haganah **9**:687
- *illus:*
- - text
- - Haganah High Command **7**:1070
Doria (fam., Genoa) **13**:1260
DORIAN, DOREL **14**:423; **14**:426
DORIAN, EMIL **6**:174
DORIS (w. of Herod) **6**:174
- *geneal. table:* **8**:377
Dor le-Dor (orgn., Isr.) **8**:539
Dorls, Fritz **12**:954
Dorman, Henry **16**:556
DORMIDO, DAVID ABRABANEL (Manuel Martinez) **6**:174
- Manasseh ben Israel **11**:857
Dormido, Solomon (Antonio) **6**:175
Dormition Abbey (Jer.) **8**:935; **9**:1461 **16**:1031
- *illus:*
- - crypt **8**:930
- - Mount Zion **9**:1465
Dormitzer (fam.) **13**:969
Dornach (loc., Fr.) **2**:757
Dornhan *Memorbuch* **3**:380
DOROHOI (tn., Rum.) **6**:175
- Romania **14**:390, 397, 398
Doros (Cana. city-state), *see* DOR
Doros (tn., Rus.) **5**:1105
DOROT (kib., Isr.) **6**:176
- statistics **1**:place list
Dorot (paperback series) **13**:1378
Dorot (journ.) **1**:newsp. list
Dorot ha-Rishonim (bk.) **7**:1184
Dorothea Maria (wife of John Duke of Saxe-Weimar) **8**:30
DOROTHEUS (polit. ldr.) **6**:176
Dorotheus (Gr. writ.) **13**:1150
Dorozhka, Joseph Ḥayyim **10**:707
Dorpat (city, Est.), *see* TARTU
DORSA, *see* Dominican Republic Settlement Association Inc.
Dorsen, Norman **10**:1505
Dorshei Ḥalakot (D.S. Scrolls) *see* SEEKERS AFTER SMOOTH THINGS
Dorshei Zion (soc., Bul.) **16**:1108
Dort, Leopold I.J. van **5**:316
Dort, wo die Zeder (song) **6**:1217; **16**:835
DORTMUND (city, Ger.) **6**:176
- *illus:* text
Dosa ben Eleazar (masor.) **16**:1471
DOSA BEN HARKINAS (tan.) **6**:178
Dosa ben Joshua ha-Ḥazzan **13**:579
DOSA BEN SAADIAH (gaon) **6**:178
- gaonate **7**:317
- Sura **15**:522
Dosa ha-Yevani (the Greek; r., Bul.) **4**:1482; **16**:121
Dos Folk (period.) **16**:1011
Dos Fraye Vort (newsp.) **16**:999
Dos Groyse Gevins (comedy) **14**:1284
Dosh (Isr. cart.), *see* GARDOSH, KARIEL
Dos Idishe Vort (newsp.) **5**:1149
Dosithean Sect(s), *see* DUSTAN
Dositheos (Samar.) **6**:313
Dositheus ben Drimylus
- diaspora **6**:17
- Egypt **6**:487
- Hellenism **8**:301
- military commander **13**:1348
Dos Mlaver Lebn (period.) **12**:186
Dos Morgenblat (newsp.) **13**:1042
Dos Naye Land (period.) **14**:198
Dos Naye Lebn (newsp., Pol, 1919) **13**:1042; **16**:1348
Dos Naye Lebn (journ., Pol., 1945) **13**:1043; **13**:779; **15**:137
Dos Naye Lebn (U.S. period.) **16**:1011
Dos Naye Vort (period.) **8**:315
Dos Plotsker Vort (monthly) **13**:648
Dossetai (tan.), *see* JUDAH BEN DOSOTHEOS
Dos Shedletser Lebn (journ) **14**:1509
Dossin (concen. camp, Belg.), *see* MALINES
DOSTAI BEN YANNAI (tan.) **6**:179
- Akhbarei, burial place **2**:487
- *tanna* **15**:800
Dosthes (Samar.), *see* Dositheos
Dostoyevski, Fyodor **14**:508
DOSTROVSKY, ARYEH **11**:1207
Dostrovsky, Israel **9**:796
Dostrovsky, Ya'akov, *see* DORI, YA'AKOV
Dostrzegacz Nadwislański (newsp.) *see* BEOBACHTER AN DER WEICHSEL
Dos Volk (period.) **4**:1041
Dos Vort (pub., Can.) **16**:1110
Dos Vort (period., Mex.) **11**:1459; **16**:1126
Dos Vort (newsp., Rus.) **13**:1046
Dos Yidishe Bukh (publ. firm, Pol.) **13**:1376
Dos Yidishe Folk (newsp., Pol.) **6**:1295; **7**:1498
Dos Yidishe Folk (period., U.S.) **16**:1142; **16**:1179
Dos Yidishe Folksblat (period.), *see Yidishe Folksblat, Dos*
Dos Yidishe Likht (newsp.) **13**:1055
Dos Yidishe Morgen Zhurnal (newsp.), *see* JEWISH MORNING JOURNAL
Dos Yidishe Vokhenblat (journ.), *see Brazilianer Yidishe Presse*
Dos Yidishe Vort (newsp., Pol.) **13**:1042; **15**:339; **16**:1132
Dos Yidishe Vort (period., U.S.) **2**:426
Dos Yidishe Vort—Israelite Press (newsp., Can.) **13**:1026; **16**:640
Dotan Valley (Er. Isr.) **9**:588
Dothan (bib. fig.) **12**:377
DOTHAN (city, Er. Isr.) **6**:179
DOTHAN, MOSHE **1**:29
- Hammath synagogue **7**:1243
- Tel Mor excavations **3**:697
Dothan, Trude **4**:912
Dots, Masoretic, *see* Masoretic dots
Douaumont (fort, Fr.) **16**:109
Double Gate (Jer.)
- Jerusalem wall **9**:1433
- Temple **15**:963
- *illus:*
- - general view **9**:1429
Double-Headed Eagle Society (anti-Sem., Rus.) **13**:697
Double Loyalty, *see* Loyalty, Double
Double Maḥzor (illum. ms.) **11**:732ff
DOUDTCHITZKY, DINORA **3**:599
Dough **7**:1194
Doughty, C.M. **6**:775
DOUGLAS, KIRK **6**:180
- *illus:* text
DOUGLAS, MELVYN **12**:466
Dounie, Gita, *see* Weizmann, Gita
D'Ovadia, David **4**:1494
Dovator, Lev **11**:1557; **14**:479
Dov Baer ben Samuel of Linits **9**:1056
Dov Baer ben Shneur Zalman **14**:1434
- Ḥasidism **7**:1411
- Hebron settlement **9**:297
DOV BAER OF MEZHIRECH **6**:180
- Aaron Samuel ha-Kohen **2**:23
- ecstasy **10**:631
- ḥasidic leader **7**:1392ff
- Ḥayyim Ḥaikel of Amdur **7**:1510
- history chart **8**:766-767
- Israel of Polotsk **9**:1059
- *Ẓavva'at ha-Ribash* **16**:531
- Zusya of Hanipoli **16**:1243
Dov Baer of Ruzhyn, *see* Friedmann, Dov Baer
Dov Berish ben Abraham of Byala, *see* Biala, Dov Berish ben Abraham of
DOVE **6**:184
- dietary laws **6**:33
- Noah **12**:1195
- ownership **12**:1533
- Samaritan belief **14**:740
- *illus:*
- - Chryzanow tombstone **15**:1226
- - marriage cup **11**:*fcg.* 1067
- - Song of Songs **15**:145
- *see also:* TURTLE DOVE
Dove, John **8**:30
Dover (city, N.H.) **12**:1024
Dover, John **12**:1521
Dover Mesharin (newsp.), *see Ha-Dover*
Dovev (mosh., Isr.) **1**:place list
Dov Hos (refugee boat) **9**:358
- hunger strike **3**:291
- "illegal" immigration **8**:1250
"Dovidl" Karliner, *see* FRIEDMANN, DAVID BEN SAMUEL
Dov of Leovo, *see* Friedmann, Dov Baer
Dovrat (tn., kib.), *see* DOBRATH
Dovrei Sefat-Ever (orgn., Arg.) **3**:424
Doweik ha-Cohen (fam.), *see* DUWAYK
Dower, John **6**:369
Dowling, E. Dowman **8**:30
DOWRY **6**:185
- conflict of laws **5**:883; **5**:884
- contract, oral **5**:925
- Elephantine usage **6**:124
- endowment funds **8**:284
- father's provision of **13**:97
- *Gemilut ḥasadim* **7**:375
- *hakhnasat kallah* **7**:1149
- *ḥazakah* rights **7**:1523
- head covering **8**:6
- inheritance rights to **15**:478ff
- jewelry **13**:1012
- *ketubbah* **10**:928
- *moredet* **8**:1123
- *nedunya* **10**:928; **10**:929
- Samaritans **14**:745
- usufruct waiver **11**:1232
- virgins **16**:160
- *see also:* BETROTHAL; MAINTENANCE
Doyigkeyt (conc.) **8**:765
Doyle, Ned **2**:317
DOZY, REINHART PIETER ANNE (orient.) **6**:189
D.P.F.L.P., *see* Democratic Popular Front for the Liberation of Palestine
DP's, *see* DISPLACED PERSONS
DRA (Draa; reg., Mor.) **6**:190
- *illus:* text
DRABKIN, ABRAHAM **6**:190
Drabkin, Moshe David, *see* REMEZ, MOSHE DAVID
Drabkin, S., *see* Gusev, S.
DRACH, PAUL-LOUIS-BERNARD (David) **6**:191
- Alsatian apostasy **2**:756
Drachler, Norman **5**:1571
Drachm (coin) **5**:715
Drachman (fam.) **3**:450
DRACHMAN, BERNARD **6**:191
Drachman, Philip **15**:1423
Drachman, Samuel **15**:1423
DRACHSLER, JULIUS **6**:192
Draconi, Cristoforo **5**:1077
Draenger, Laban **5**:1039
Draenger, Szymon (Shimon) **5**:1039
Draghi, A. **9**:1344
Dragon **5**:1533
Dragon Haggadah (13th cent. illum. ms., Fr.) **4**:*fcg.* 1067; **7**:1098
Dragon's Well (Isr.) **6**:800
DRAGUIGNAN (tn., Fr.) **6**:192
DRAGUNSKI, DAVID ABRAMOVICH **11**:1557; **11**:1558; **11**:1572
- Russia **14**:479
Drai, Désiré **2**:619
Drainage, swamp, *see* LAND RECLAMATION IN ISRAEL
DRAMA (city, Gr.) **6**:192
- Greece **7**:873; **7**:879
DRAMA, HEBREW **6**:193
- *Contents:*
- - Introduction **6**:193
- - Early Beginnings **6**:193
- - Haskalah Drama **6**:195
- - National Renaissance Period (1880-1947) **6**:196
- - Drama in Israel **6**:205
- folk drama **6**:1389
- Jerusalem **9**:1566
- poetry **13**:691
- *Purim-shpil* **13**:1396
- Sommo, Judah **15**:137
- Song of Songs **15**:147ff
- Yiddish plays **11**:359ff
- *illus:*
- - text
- - "Habimah," Nikolayev **12**:1160
- - *Melukhat Sha'ul* (1829) **7**:1057
- - Ohel production of *Ammekha*

12:1343
– *see also:* HEBREW LITERATURE, MODERN; THEATER
Dramer, Shalom **15:**1152
DRANCY (tn., concen. camp, Fr.) **6:**207
– art **3:**575
– history chart **8:**766-767
DRAPKIN, ABRAHAM **5:**1112
DRAPKIN, ISRAEL **6:**208
Drapkin, Zilla (poet) **16:**822
"Draussige" (Bohem. Jewry) **4:**1176
Drayton, R.H. **9:**602
DREAMS **6:**208
– *Contents:*
– – In the Bible **6:**208
– – In the Talmud **6:**209
– – In Medieval Thought **6:**210
– *aḥlamah* stone **13:**1010
– divine revelation **6:**113ff
– fastday **6:**1196
– magic **11:**710
– *Pitron Ḥalomot* (Almoli) **2:**664
– priestly blessing **13:**1062
– prophets and prophecy **13:**1153ff
– psychology **13:**1342
– Saul **14:**913
– Sumer **15:**515
– visions **16:**168ff
– *illus:*
– – text
– – amulet against bad dreams (16/17 cent.) **2:**908
– – Jacob's dream at Beth-El **3:**52,636; **4:**244; **6:**291; **8:**1286; **9:**1205
– – Joseph interpreting dreams **5:**1172; **6:**211; **8:**1218; **13:**363
– – Joseph's dreams **6:**209; **10:**204
– – Pharaoh's dreams **13:**361
– – *Pitron Ḥalomot* (1623) **2:**664
Dream Visions, the, see SEVENTY SHEPHERDS, VISION OF
DREBEN, SAM **11:**1551; **11:**1573
Drehem (city, Mesop.) **16:**1493
Dreiblatt, Yoel **7:**1272
Dreidl (game) **6:**1393; **7:**306
– *illus:*
– – lead, handmade **6:**1398
– – lead, with casting mold **7:**1287
– – silver **7:**1286
Dreiser, Theodore **15:**1571
DRESDEN (city, Ger.) **6:**211
– Saxony **14:**924
– *illus:*
– – synagogue **14:**924
DRESDEN, SEM **12:**687
– Netherlands **12:**984
Dresden Maḥzor (14th cent. illum. ms., Ger.) **2:**251; **6:**690
Dresdner, A. **3:**494
Dresler, Salek **12:**1497
Dresner, Samuel H. **4:**1013; **6:**45
Dresnitz, Samuel **3:**539
Dresnitz (Dreshnitz), Solomon Shlomel, *see* Dreznitz, Solomon Shlomel
DRESS **6:**212
– *Contents:*
– – In the Bible **6:**212
– – Types of Garment Shown on Monuments **6:**213
– – Talmudic Times **6:**214
– – Hellenistic and Persian Periods **6:**215
– – The Post-Talmudic Era **6:**216
– – Early Middle Ages **6:**216
– – The Orient **6:**216
– – Western Europe **6:**219
– – Rabbinical Dress **6:**220
– – Eastern Europe **6:**220
– – Modern **6:**223
– Algeria **2:**614
– al-Ḥākim **9:**265
– Almohads **2:**663
– cleanliness **10:**1484
– Estori ha-Parḥi **6:**918
– etiquette **6:**946
– Falashas **6:**1146
– folklore **6:**1395
– *ḥukkat ha-goi* **8:**1061
– Israel Defense Forces **9:**697
– jewelry **13:**1012ff.
– marriage **11:**1036
– mourner **10:**1484
– Muslim countries **5:**1605ff
– Nuremberg **12:**1278
– Ottoman Empire **16:**1538ff
– priestly vestments **13:**1063
– Purim **13:**1395
– rabbinate **13:**1452; **13:**1453
– Samaritans **14:**741; **14:**746
– Seljuks **14:**1136
– *talmid ḥakham* **15:**747
– *tekhelet* **15:**913
– tombs **15:**1218
– Tunisia **15:**1440; **15:**1446
– veil **16:**83ff
– Venice **16:**95
– *ẓiẓit* **16:**1187
– *illus:* text
– Africa
– – Algerian Jews (19th cent.) Pls. 5a-5d **6**-DRESS
– – Algiers Jews (19th cent.) **2:**623
– – Berber Jewish Women **4:**587
– – Berbers, Jewish, from Tikrit **4:**588
– – Morocco
– – – bridal costume Pl. 6 **6**-DRESS, 1378 **11:**1044
– – – Casablanca Jews **12:**333
– – – Debdou Jewish woman **5:**1427
– – – Dra Jewish women **6:**190
– – – Erfoud, woman's mourning attire **12:**492
– – – Fez Jewish family **6:**1255
– – – Goulmina woman **8:**5
– – – Marrakesh women **12:**340
– – – Mogador Jews **12:**213
– – – Ofran woman and child **12:**1340
– – – scholar (19th cent.) **6:**380
– – – Tangier woman **15:**791
– – North Africa, Jewish child bride **5:**424
– – Tunisia
– – – Gabès, Jewish women **7:**234
– – – Jewish woman **15:**1436
– – – man's scullcap Pl. 11 **6**-DRESS
– – – woman's headdress Pl. 10 **6**-DRESS
– Asia
– – Bukhara
– – – bridal gown Pl. 9 **6**-DRESS
– – – community leaders 4:1471
– – – woman's ceremonial coat **4:**1475
– – Ḥabbān woman **7:**1020
– – India, Bene Israel family **4:**496
– – Iraq, Baghdad rabbi **10:**242
– – Israel
– – – Bukharan Jews **9:**503
– – – Cochin Jews wedding **11:**1049
– – – *ḥakham bashi's* traditional garb **12:**1182
– – – Ḥasidim in beaver hats **7:**1410
– – – Ḥasid in *kaftan* and *shtreyml* **7:**1414
– – – Jaffa rabbi (19th cent.) **9:**1252
– – – Jerusalem emissary **14:**1363
– – – Maskit oriental gown **9:**822
– – – Yemenite bride **11:**1046
– – – Yemenite couple **11:**1047
– – Persia
– – – bride and bridegroom **11:**1035
– – – Samarkand Jews **14:**759
– – Turkey
– – – Adrianople Jewish woman (16th cent.) **2:**309
– – – Constantinople woman (19th cent.) Pl. 8 **6**-DRESS
– – – Istanbul woman (17th cent.) **9:**1089
– – – Izmir Jewish woman (19th cent.) **9:**1162
– – Yemen
– – – bridal hood, dress articles and jewels **6:***fcg.* 235
– Europe
– – Austria
– – – medieval pointed hat **10:**405
– – England, Jewish hood (13th cent.) **4:**63
– – France
– – – Jew **4:**64,65; **5:**159
– – – medieval pointed hat **13:**1
– – Germany
– – – Frankfort, discussion of sumptuary laws **15:**516
– – – Frankfort Jews (18th cent.) **7:**86
– – – Jew and Jewess (16th cent.) **4:**68
– – – Jew's hat **15:**484
– – – Landshut *Stadtbuch* (1361) **10:**1412
– – – Nuremberg Jews **12:**1276
– – – synagogue attire with Jewish badge (18th cent.) **7:**483
– – Italy, bride and bridegoom (15th cent.) **4:**66
– – Lithuania
– – – Jewish family (19th cent.) **6:***fcg.* 238
– – – "Lithuanian Stock Exchange" (1846) **4:**1404
– – Middle Ages **4:**63–67
– – Netherlands Jews (19th cent.) **6:***fcg.* 238
– – Poland
– – – bride with *Brusttuch* **11:***fcg.* 1070
– – – Cracow merchants (19th cent.) **5:**1039
– – – Galician Jews **4:**74
– – – Gur Ḥasidim in Sabbath attire **7:**1399
– – – ḥasidic couple (19th cent.) **6:***fcg.* 238
– – – Jewish children (19th cent.) **6:***fcg.* 238
– – Spain, Jewish hat (13th cent.) **4:**66
– – Russia
– – – Crimean Karaite women and children **10:**775
– – Yugoslavia, Sarajevo woman **14:**870
– *see also:* BADGE, JEWISH; CROWNS, DECORATIVE HEADDRESSES AND WREATHS; DYEING; TAILORING
Dressing of the dead **4:**1519
DRESSLER, WILLIAM **6:**223
DREUX (tn., Fr.) **6:**223
Dreydel (game), *see Dreidl*
Dreyer, Kurt **5:**407
DREYFUS (fam.) **6:**223
DREYFUS, ALFRED **6:**224
– *illus:*
– – text
– – anti-Semitic cartoon **3:**115
– *see also:* Dreyfus Affair
DREYFUS, CAMILLE **5:**381
Dreyfus, Françoise, *see* AIMÉE, ANOUK
DREYFUS, HENRY (chem.) **5:**381
Dreyfus, Henry (print.) **15:**1479
Dreyfus, Isaac (1786-1845, bnk.) **4:**177; **6:**223
Dreyfus, Isaac (1849-1909, bnk.) **6:**224
Dreyfus, Jack Jr. (U.S.) **15:**311
Dreyfus, Jacques (Ger.) **6:**223
Dreyfus, Jean **2:**617
Dreyfus, John Gustave (print.) **15:**1479
Dreyfus, Louis **4:**176
Dreyfus, Marcus **11:**1566
Dreyfus, René **15:**300
Dreyfus, Samuel **6:**223
Dreyfus, Simone **3:**39
Dreyfus, Willy **6:**224
Dreyfus, Yves **12:**1377
Dreyfus Affair **6:**224
– Alsace Jews **2:**756
– anti-Semitic parties **3:**85
– Bahar's utopia **16:**1152
– Drumont, Edouard-Adolphe **6:**237
– French literature **7:**143,144
– Herzl, Theodor **8:**408
– history chart **8:**766-767
– Jaurès, Jean Léon **9:**1301
– Kahn, Zadoc **10:**693
– Levaillant, Isaïe **11:**65
– Reinach, Joseph **14:**56
– repercussions in France **7:**29
– Zola, Emile **16:**1216ff
– *illus:*
– – the judges (caric.) **5:**175
– – snakes-and-ladders game **8:**739
Dreyfus-Brodsky, Jules **6:**224
Dreyfus-Brodsky, Paul **6:**224
Dreyfuss (fam.), *see* TRÈVES
DREYFUSS, BARNEY **6:**230
– sport **15:**300, 308
Dreyfuss, Paul Maria **9:**1207
Dreyfuss-Brodsky, Z. **4:**304
Dreyfus-Straus, Isaac **6:**224
Drezner, Yeḥiel **8:**1468
Dreznitz, Solomon Shlomel **3:**1020; **4:**116; **11:**351; **14:**890; **15:**1208; **16:**172ff
Driebergen (vill., Holl.) **16:**37
Driesche, Johann II, *see* Drusius, Johann II
Driesche, Johann Clemens van der, *see* DRUSIUS, JOHANN CLEMENS
Drifzan (fam.), *see* TRÈVES
Drifzan, Eliezer **7:**85; **15:**1377
Drifzan, Joseph **15:**1377
Drifzan, Naphtali Herz **10:**543; **15:**1377
Drifzan, Samuel, *see* Ẓevi, Samuel
Drinja (vill., Yug.) **16:**877
Drinking, *see* DRUNKENNESS
Drink offering **14:**603
Driver, Sir Godfrey Rolles **6:**231
– linguistics **16:**1394
DRIVER, SAMUEL ROLLES **6:**230
– Aramaic in Ezra, Daniel **3:**266
– Book of Exodus **6:**1063
Driver documents (Aram.) **3:**265
Drmoul (tn., Bohem.) **5:**486
DROB, MAX **6:**231
DROBNER, BOLESLAW **6:**231
DROGOBYCH (Drohobycz; city, Gal.) **6:**232
Drohobitzer Zeitung (period.) **6:**233
DROPSIE, MOSES AARON **6:**234
– *illus:* text
DROPSIE UNIVERSITY (U.S.) **6:**235
– Cairo *genizah* **16:**1334
– history chart **8:**766-767
– *illus:*
– – Meir, Golda, honorary doctorate **10:**818
DROSDOFF, MATTHEW **6:**236
Drought, *see* FAMINE AND DROUGHT
Droysen, J. G. **8:**291
Drozed, S. J. **16:**1099
Druck, Kalman **13:**1360
DRUCKER, DANIEL CHARLES

8:1431
Drucker, Norman **15**:304
Druckman, Samuil, *see* Damian, Samuil
Drugs **5**:1097; **5**:1102; **11**:1376
Drugulin, W. **10**:1592
Druion, L. **15**:193
Druja (tn., Belor.), *see* DRUYA
Drujan, S. **16**:1165
Drukarnia Diecezjalna (print. firm, Lith.) **16**:148
Drukeret (tn., Babyl.) **8**:1074
DRUMONT, EDOUARD-ADOLPHE **6**:236
- anti-Jewish agitation **3**:116; **8**:738
- Dreyfus Affair **6**:226
- history chart **8**:766-767
- *illus:* text
"Drunken Lot" (drg., Rembrandt) **14**:67
DRUNKENNESS **6**:237
- *aḥlamah* stone **13**:1010
- blessing at *minḥah* **12**:11
- drinking **14**:182
- Jerusalem Christians **9**:1440
- legal incapacity **13**:226
- Purim **13**:1392
- satirized **13**:127
- talmudic view **16**:539
- *illus:* text
- *see also:* WINE AND LIQUOR TRADE
DRUSILLA (J. prin.) **6**:241
- Aziz **3**:1010
- Emesa proselytes **6**:725
- Epiphanes' engagement **5**:760
- *geneal. table:* **8**:377
Drusius, Johann II **6**:241; **8**:30
DRUSIUS, JOHANN CLEMENS **6**:241
- Hebraist **8**:30
Drusus (s. of Agrippa I) **5**:1179
DRUYA (tn., Belor.) **6**:241
DRUYANOW, ALTER (Asher, Avraham Abba) **6**:242
- *illus:*
- - fellow Hebrew writers **4**:499
- - in Constantinople **14**:465
Druze (Leb.) **15**:640
Druze, Mt. (Er.Isr.), *see* Jebel ed-Druze
DRUZE IN ISRAEL **9**:924
- Defense Forces **9**:692
- demography **9**:570ff
- *Gadna* **7**:253
- Galilee **7**:269
- general survey **9**:1026ff
- Ḥākim bi-Amr Allah, Al- **7**:1152
- historical survey **9**:397ff
- holy places in Israel **8**:936
- Jethro **10**:20
- Knesset **10**:1116
- Lebanon **10**:1543-5
- Nabī Shu'ayb **10**:886
- Ottoman period **9**:287; **9**:289; **9**:296
- religious court **9**:641ff
- *illus:*
- - Beit Jann village **4**:405
- - Ben Gurion with Druze leaders **9**:925
- - border police members **9**:928
- - Dāliyat al-Karmil village **5**:1228
- - Eshkol, inspecting honor guard **9**:927
- - first judge sworn in **9**:925
- - Ma'sada village **9**:214
- - Nabī Shuʿayb celebration **8**:933
- - Tomb of Nabī Shu'ayb **10**:20,886
- - 'Usifiyyā village **16**:20
- *tables:* **9**:491
Dryan, David **7**:334
Dryden, John **6**:774
Dryfoos, Orvil Eugene **15**:508
DRZEWIECKI, HENRYK **13**:803
Dua-Bogen, Gershon **5**:803
DUALISM **6**:242
- *Contents:*
- - Philosophical Dualism **6**:242
- - Moral Dualism **6**:243
- - in Jewish History **6**:243
- - in Jewish Mysticism **6**:244
- - Prophetic Dualism **6**:245
- Dead Sea sect **5**:1409
- demons **5**:1525
- *Discipline, Manual of* **6**:64
- Elisha ben Avuyah **6**:669
- God **7**:671
- good and evil inclination **8**:1318
- heresy **8**:359
- Jewish gnosis **10**:506ff
- Manichaeism **11**:876
- problem of evil **7**:775ff
- pseudepigrapha **13**:185
- theology **15**:1107
Duarte da Paz **8**:1386
Duarte da Silva **8**:1387
Duarte Sanitorium (U.S.), *see* CITY OF HOPE NATIONAL MEDICAL CENTER
Dub (fam.) **8**:1136
DU BARTAS, GUILLAUME DE SALLUSTE **6**:245
- Creation epic **5**:1071
Dubator (sol., Rus.) **14**:479
Dubček, Alexander **5**:1201
Dubelman, A.I. **5**:1149
DUBERMAN, MARTIN **6**:245
Dubiel (angel) **2**:969
DUBIN, MORDECAI **6**:246
- Riga **14**:174
Dubin, Robert **15**:68
Dubin-Johnson's Disease **14**:1501
DUBINSKY, DAVID **6**:246
- Breslaw, Joseph **4**:1358
- labor and socialism **15**:46
Dubinsky, Justin Louis **10**:1494; **11**:998
DUBISLAV, WALTER ERNST OTTO **6**:247
DUBLIN (city, Ire.) **6**:248
- Briscoe, Robert **4**:1377
- Ireland **8**:1463f
- *illus:* text
Dublin, Louis I. **8**:1410
DUBNO (city, Ukr.) **6**:249
- *illus:*
- - Jewish Hospital **8**:1036
DUBNO, SOLOMON BEN JOEL **6**:251
- Altschuler, Jeḥiel Hillel **2**:784
- book collection **4**:974
- Haskalah in Russia **7**:1445
- Mendelssohn, Moses **11**:1339
- *illus:* text
Dubno Maggid (prch., E. Eur.), *see* KRANZ, JACOB BEN WOLF
DUBNOW, SIMON **6**:252
- *Contents:*
- - Life and Career **6**:252f
- - Historian and Political Ideologist **6**:255
- archives **3**:387
- civil rights society **15**:56
- Diaspora nationalism **16**:1066ff
- Folkspartei (Russia) **6**:1411ff
- history **8**:564
- minority rights **12**:43
- *Voskhod* **16**:225
- Zhitlowsky, Chaim **16**:1010
- *illus:*
- - autograph **3**:914
- - first Duma electors **14**:445
DUBNOW, ZE'EV **6**:257
- Bilu ideology **4**:1000
Dubnow-Erlich, Sophia **6**:844
Dubofsky, Maurice **15**:308
Du Bois, W.E.B. **10**:1298; **9**:433
Dubos, Marcus **16**:1328
DUBOSSARY (tn., Rus.) **6**:257
Dubrovensky, Moshe **14**:1127
Dubrovin, A. **15**:1538
DUBROVNIK (tn., Yug.) **6**:257
- Pyrrhus, Didacus **13**:1416
- special Purim **13**:1397
- Yugoslavia **16**:870; **16**:880
- *illus:*
- - Jews' street **16**:871
DUBROVNO (tn., Belor.) **6**:259
Dubuque (city, Ia.) **8**:1437
Duccio (art.) **9**:69
Duchen, David **15**:315
Duck (zool.) **6**:34
DUCKESZ, EDUARD (Yecheskel) **6**:260
Duclou, Luigi **10**:459
Duda'ei ha-Sadeh (wk.) **5**:1587
Dudai Ben Nahman (gaon) **16**:731
Dudenhofen (vill., Ger.) **15**:265
DUEHRING, KARL EUGEN **6**:260
- Jewish question **8**:853
- Wagner, Richard **16**:241
Duelling **8**:958
Duenaburg (city, Latv.) *see* DAUGAVPILS
DUEÑAS (city, Sp.) **6**:261
DUENNER, JOSEPH ẒEVI HIRSCH **6**:261
- Amsterdam **2**:900
- Netherlands **12**:982
- Zionism **16**:1118
DUEREN, ISAAC BEN MEIR **6**:261
- codification of law **5**:647
- *illus:*
- - *Issur ve-Hetter* **2**:740
- - *Sha'arei Dura* and *Hilkhot Niddah* **16**:*fcg.* 615
Duerer, Albrecht **4**:1219; **12**:1279
- *illus:*
- - bookplate for Willibald Pirkheimer **4**:1221
- - "Job and His Wife" (paint.) **10**:128
Duerrmaul (tn., Bohem.), *see* Drmoul
DUESSELDORF (city, Ger.) **6**:262
- *illus:* text
Duesseldorf, Mordecai **13**:988
Dufay, Guillaume **10**:1375
Duff, Mickey **15**:306
Dufour, T. **8**:31
Duga (fam.) **10**:1298
DUGDALE, BLANCHE ELIZABETH CAMPBELL **6**:263
Dugi, Menahem ben Solomon ibn, *see* ALROY, DAVID
DUHM, BERNHARD **6**:264
- Isaiah authorship **9**:45ff
Dühren, Eugen, *see* BLOCH, IWAN
DUISBURG (city, Ger.) **6**:264
- *illus:* text
Du Jon, François, *see* Junius, François
DUJOVNE, LEON **6**:265
DUKAS, PAUL **6**:265
- stamps **15**:336
Duke of Sussex Pentateuch (illum. ms.)
- *illus:* **4**:181; **5**:*fcg.* 1323; **12**:*fcg.* 1259
DUKER, ABRAHAM GORDON **6**:266
Dukes, Ashley **13**:1539
DUKES, LEOPOLD (Judah Loeb) **6**:266
- linguistics **16**:1390
Duke's Place Synagogue (Lond.), *see* Great Synagogue (Lond.)
Dukhan (tit., Babyl.) **15**:1164
Dukhan (journ.) **1**:newsp. list
DUKHAN (platform) **6**:267
- priestly blessing **13**:1061
Dukhenen (Yid., pr. blessing) **13**:1061
Dukhovno-Bibliyskoye Bratstvo **7**:787
Dukla (tn., Pol.) **10**:1278
Dukovani, Moshe **16**:338
Dukwitz, F. G. **5**:1539
Dulcigno (loc., Alb.) **14**:1240
Dulcinorella (d. of Paragonis) **12**:828
Dulcken, Louise **5**:1345
Duldig, Ignacy **13**:1299
Dulitzki, M. **12**:658
Dulles, John Foster **9**:388; **9**:424
Dultzin, Aryeh L. **9**:680
Duluth (city, Minn.) **12**:39
Duma (angel) **8**:464
DUMA (Imp. Rus. legis.) **6**:267
- Abramowitz, Raphael **2**:169
- Bruck, Grigori **4**:1413
- Civil Rights Society **15**:56
- Fourth Imperial Duma **16**:336
- Octobrists **12**:1318
- Pale of Settlement **13**:27
- *illus:*
- - Jewish electors **14**:445
Dumah (bib. fig.) **9**:89
Dumas, Alexandre *(père)* **3**:998
- Wandering Jew **16**:261
Dumas, Alexandre *(fils)* **14**:342
Dumashevsky, Arnold **10**:1500
Dumaskanin (Mesop.) **7**:327
Dumisch, Lenhardi Georg **4**:885
Dummesek (city, Syr.), *see* DAMASCUS
Du Monin, Jean Edouard **8**:31
DUMUH (vill., Egy.) **6**:268
Dumyāṭ (city, Egy.), *see* DAMIETTA
Dumyati, Al-Sadid al- **5**:1253
Duna (angel) **16**:909
Dunajewski, A. **12**:656
DUNAJSKA STREDA (tn., Cz.) **6**:269
- Czechoslovakia **5**:1200
DUNANT, JEAN HENRI **6**:270
- Zionism **16**:1070; **16**:1155
Dunant, Paul **13**:966
Dunash ben Judah **13**:579
DUNASH BEN LABRAT **6**:270
- Bible exegesis **4**:892
- Hayyuj, Judah **7**:1513
- Hebrew poetry **16**:1617
- history chart **8**:766-767
- Ibn Kafrun, Isaac **8**:1187
- Ibn Saruq **11**:1306
- linguistics **16**:1356,1380
- prosody **13**:1211
- Samuel ben Meir **14**:811
- Spain **15**:225
DUNASH IBN TAMIM **6**:271
- Islam **11**:754
- linguistics **16**:1356
- *Sefer Yeẓirah* **16**:786
- Tunisia **15**:1434
Dunaszerdahely (tn., Cz.), *see* DUNAJSKA STREDA
DUNAYEVSKI, ISAAC OSIPOVICH **6**:273
DUNAYEVTSY (tn., Rus.) **6**:273
Duncan, J. G. **9**:1522ff
Duncan, William Wallace **8**:31
Dundee (tn., Scot.) **14**:1035
DUNEDIN (city, N.Z.) **6**:273
Dung Gate (Jer.) **9**:1433
- *illus:* **9**:1427
Dunitz, Ellis **2**:321
Dunkelblum, Arthur **5**:406
Dunkelman, Rose **5**:113
Dunkelsbueler, A. **4**:175
Dunlop, D. M. **8**:562
Duński, Ẓevi **15**:170
Dunsky, Samson **5**:113
DUNS SCOTUS, JOHN **6**:274
- Hebraist **8**:31
- Jedaiah ben Abraham Bedersi **9**:1309
Dunstable (tn., Eng.) **6**:748
Dunster, Henry **8**:31

Du Paty de Clam (Fr. sol.) **8**:851
Du Plessis-Mornay, *see* Mornay, Philippe de
DUPONT-SOMMER, ANDRÉ **6**:275
DUQUE, SIMON DAVID **7**:1547
Dūrā al-ʿAmiriyya (vill., Isr.) **2**:303
Dūrā al-ʿArajān (vill., Isr.) **2**:303
DURA-EUROPOS (city, Mesop.) **6**:275
- anthropomorphisms **3**:57
- Aramaic inscriptions **3**:268-70
- art in synagogue **3**:508; **3**:538
- frescoes **8**:1258
- head covering **8**:2
- Hellenistic art **8**:301
- history chart (245) **8**:766-767
- Holy Ark **3**:457
- Jerusalem **9**:1579
- *menorah* **11**:1364
- pillars **13**:523
- Saul **14**:917
- symbolism **15**:570ff
- synagogue **15**:600
- *illus:*
- - text
- - anointing of David **3**:28
- - Aramaic script **2**:687
- - Ark of the Law **3**:451
- - Ezekiel's vision of the resurrection **3**:515
- - Orpheus **15**:571
- - Philistines returning the Ark **3**:461
- - Purim scenes **8**:649
- - Temple facade **9**:1581
- - wall paintings **6**:*fcg.* 299
DURAN (fam.) **6**:298
Duran, Aaron (17th cent.) **6**:298
Duran, Aaron ben Solomon (15th cent.) **6**:298; **6**:307
Duran, David **2**:623; **6**:299; **4**:58
Duran, Ḥayyim Jonah **6**:298
Duran, Isaac, *see* DURAN, PROFIAT
Duran, José **14**:785
Duran, Joseph Benjamin **6**:298
Duran, Judah **6**:299
Duran, Moses **6**:298
DURAN, PROFIAT (Profayt) **6**:299
- Almoli, Solomon **2**:664
- Christianity **6**:93ff
- defense of Judaism **3**:196
- Hebrew grammar **11**:324
- history **8**:556
- Ibn Abū al-Ṣalt **8**:1152
- linguistics **16**:1360,1388
- parody **13**:130
- polemical literature **11**:355
DURAN, SIMEON BEN SOLOMON (ben Simeon) **6**:301
- family **6**:298
DURAN, SIMEON BEN ẒEMAḤ (Rashbaẓ) **6**:302
- Albo, Joseph **2**:535; **2**:536
- alchemy opposed by **2**:548
- appointment as rabbi **13**:1447
- Aristotelianism **3**:446
- articles of faith **3**:657
- Avicenna's influence **3**:959
- Bonastruc, Isaac **4**:1200
- Christianity and Islam **3**:194 **3**:196
- commandments, reasons for **5**:788
- *Haggadah* commentary **7**:1092
- Isaac ben Sheshet Perfet **9**:32
- Majorca **11**:800; **11**:803
- philosophy **11**:341; **13**:449ff
- polemical literature **11**:355
- responsa **11**:337; **14**:86
- *Shi'ur Komah* **14**:1418
- *takkanah* **15**:726
- *illus:*
- - *Sefer ha-Tashbeẓ* **12**:978
DURAN, SOLOMON BEN SIMEON (N. Afr.) **6**:306
- Alashkar, Joseph ben Moses **2**:511
- responsa **14**:86
Duran, Solomon ben Ẓemaḥ **6**:298
- Algiers **2**:623
- Khalaẓ, Judah **10**:936
Duran, Stella, *see* Corcos, Stella
Duran, Ẓemaḥ Astruc **6**:298
Duran, Ẓemaḥ ben Benjamin **6**:298
Duran, Ẓemaḥ ben Simeon ben Ẓemaḥ **6**:298
DURAN, ẒEMAḤ BEN SOLOMON (15th cent.) **6**:307
- family **6**:298
- Marranos in *halakhah* **10**:58
Duran, Ẓemaḥ ben Solomon (16/17 cent.) **6**:298
Durand de Cavaillon, *see* Cavaillon, Durand de
Durango (city, Colo.) **5**:753
Duration, *see* TIME AND ETERNITY
DURAZZO (city, Alb.) **6**:307
- Byzantine Jews **4**:1554
DURBAN (city, S.A.) **6**:308
- *illus:*
- - Jewish club **15**:204
- *see also:* NATAL
D'urbino, Manfredo **3**:360; **15**:627
"Durch" (Berlin lit. gr.) **4**:607
Duress, *see* ONES
Durham (city, N.C.) **12**:1220
Durham (Eng.) University of, **15**:1677
DURKHEIM, EMILE **6**:308
- anthropology **3**:37
- Kaplan, Mordecai Menahem **13**:1615
- mental illness **11**:1370
- sociology **15**:64ff
Dûr-Kurigalzu (fort., Mesop.) **16**:1499
Durlacher (fam.) **13**:1112
Durlacher, E. **13**:109
- publishing **13**:1374
Durmenach (vill., Fr.) **2**:754
- *illus:*
- - anti-Jewish riots, 1848 **2**:753
Durra (bot.) **13**:617
Durrani (Afg. tribe) **2**:326
Durrës (Durrësi; city, Alb.), *see* DURAZZO
Durry, Marie-Jeanne **7**:148
Dûr-Sharrukin (city, Assyr.) **16**:1505
- excavations **16**:1506
- Philistines **13**:403
- Sargon II **14**:881
DUSCHAK, MORDECAI(Moritz) **6**:311
DUSCHINSKY, CHARLES (Jacob Koppel) **6**:311
DUSCHINSKY, JOSEPH ẒEVI BEN ISRAEL **6**:311
Duschinsky, Moses Israel **6**:311
DUSHKIN, ALEXANDER MORDECHAI **6**:312
Dushman, Israel **5**:435
DUSHMAN, SAUL **6**:313
Dūsīs ben Fufti (found. of Samar. sect) **6**:314
DUSTAN (Samar. sect) **6**:313
- Aramaic **14**:753; **14**:755
- Samaritans **14**:739
Dustes ben Pilpeloy **6**:314
Duszenko, P. **15**:1372
Dutch (lang.)
- Bible translations **4**:876
- children's literature **5**:453
- children's magazines **5**:456ff
- Jewish encyclopedias **6**:734
Dutch Antilles *see* NETHERLANDS ANTILLES
Dutch East India Company **2**:898
Dutch General Diamond Workers Guild (A.N.D.B.) **2**:901; **13**:708
Dutch Guiana, *see* SURINAM
Dutch Israelite Seminary **14**:1097
Dutch Labor Federation **13**:708
DUTCH LITERATURE **6**:316
- *Contents:*
- - Influence of the Bible **6**:316
- - Hebraic Linguistic Influences **6**:317
- - Figure of the Jew **6**:317
- - Jewish Contribution **6**:319
"Dutch Masters President's Relief" (paint, L. Rivers) **3**:638
Dutch Reform Church **2**:895
Dutch West Indies, *see* NETHERLANDS ANTILLES
DUTY **6**:323
- Baḥya ibn Paquda **13**:435
- rebuke and reproof **13**:1605
Duty, optional, *see* RESHUT
Duvdevani (cart.) *see* KIRSZENBAUM, JESEKIEL DAVID
DUVDEVANI, SHMUEL **6**:324
DUVEEN, JOSEPH, LORD **6**:324
- art collection **3**:648
- Berenson **4**:602
DUVERNOIS, HENRI **7**:149
DUWAYK (fam.) **6**:325
Duwayk, Abraham **6**:325
Duwayk, Ḥayyim **5**:32
Duwayk, Jacob Saul **6**:325
Duwayk, Saul **6**:325
Duwayk, Simeon ben Samuel **6**:325
Duwayk ha-Cohen, Elijah ben Moses **5**:40
Duwayk ha-Cohen, Moses ben Simon **5**:40
Dux, Lajos, *see* DÓCZY, LAJOS
Dux neutrorum (bk.), *see* MAIMONIDES *(Guide of the Perplexed)*
Dvinsk (city, Latv.), *see* DAUGAVPILS
DVIR (publ. house) **6**:325
- foundation **13**:1589
- *see also:* MORIAH
DVORETSKY, ARYEH **11**:1124
"Dwelling for the Feebleminded" (drg., Fritta) Fig. 84 **3**-ART
Dwight, Timothy **15**:1569
Dworkin, Dorothy Goldstick **15**:1262
Dworkin, Martin **13**:485
Dworsky, Daniel **15**:308
Dyadya Misha, *see* Gildenman, Misha
Dyakonov, I. M. **16**:1508
DYATLOVO (tn., Rus.) **6**:325
- resistance fighters **13**:146
- Sorotzkin, Zalman **15**:167
Dybbuk (spirit), *see* DIBBUK
Dybbuk, The (pl., S. An-ski) **3**:35
- Chapiro, Jacques **5**:338
- Justman's parody **10**:479
- Yiddish theater **15**:1069
- *illus:*
- - Moscow performance **14**:465
- - Rovina, Hanna **14**:356
DYCHE, JOHN ALEXANDER **6**:326
Dyck, Christopher van (typographer) **15**:1482
Dyck, C.V.A. van (Bib. trans.) **4**:887
DYEING **6**:327
- Amalfi **2**:791
- Apulian Jews' monopoly **3**:227
- Chalcis **5**:329
- craft **5**:1044
- dye tax **15**:838
- guilds **7**:971ff
- Jewish pioneers **16**:1286
- *tekhelet* **15**:914
DYE PLANTS **6**:329
- crimson worm **5**:1113
- spices **15**:269ff
- *see also:* DYEING
Dyer, Isidore **15**:1034
Dyer, Leon **6**:1362; **15**:1034
DYHERNFURTH (tn., Pol.) **6**:330
Dyhernfurther Privilegierte Zeitung (period.) **13**:1032
Dyk, Salmon **11**:679
DYKAN, PALTIEL **6**:330
DYKMAN, SHLOMO **6**:331
DYLAN, BOB **12**:687
Dymant, Dora **10**:672; **10**:673
DYMOV, OSSIP **6**:331
DYMSHYTS, VENIAMIN E. **6**:331
DYNOW, ẒEVI ELIMELECH **6**:332
Dysphemism, *see* EUPHEMISM AND DYSPHEMISM
Dyte, Charles **4**:138; **13**:808
Dywin (tn., Rus.), *see* DIVIN
Dzaudhikau (city, Rus.) *see* ORDZHONIKIDZE
Dzerzhinsk (city, Rus.), *see* KOIDANOVO
Dzerzhinski, Feliks **11**:186
Dzhugashvili, Joseph Vissarionovich, *see* STALIN, JOSEPH VISSARIONOVICH
Dzhurin (vill., Ukr.) **15**:1334
Dziadowice (Pol.) **10**:1109
DZIALOSZYCE (Dzialoshitz; tn., Pol.) **6**:332
Dzialynski, Morris A. **6**:1362; **9**:1191
Dzieckowitz (Dzikow), Eliezer of, *see* Eliezer of Dzieckowitz
Dzierzoniow (city, Silesia), *see* Reichenbach
Dzierzyński, Feliks, *see* Dzerzhinski, Feliks
Dzigan, S. (film prod.) **12**:454
DZIGAN, SHIMON **15**:1081
Dzisna (tn., Belor.), *see* DISNA
Dzykow (ḥas. dynasty) **7**:1422
Dzyuba, E. G., *see* BAGRITSKI, EDUARD GEORGIYEVICH

E

Ea (deity) **6:**1355
- *see also:* Enki: Ningursag
EAGLE **6:**337
- dietary laws **6:**34
- Edom identified with **6:**379
- Jewish symbolism **15:**572
- synagogue art **15:**597ff
- *illus:*
- - text
- - Augsburg seal **14:**1078
- - emblem of Reuben **12:***fcg.* 1259
- - Lublin tombstone **15:**1229
- - *Menorah* **16:**1326
- - *mizraḥ* paper-cut **13:**61
- - serpent eagle **9:**230
- - *Shivviti* **14:**1420-1421
Eagle, Harry **11:**1199
Eagle, S.P., *see* SPIEGEL, SAMUEL P.
Eagle Pass (city, Tex.) **15:**1036
Eannatum of Lagash **11:**974; **16:**3
Ear **13:**1119
Eardley, Lord, *see* Gideon, Samson
Early Hebrew, *see* HEBREW LANGUAGE
Ear piercing **14:**1657ff
Ear-ring **13:**1013
EARTH **6:**338
- Garden of Eden **13:**77
- geography **7:**417ff
Earth, Navel of, *see Tabbur ha-areẓ*
EARTHQUAKE **6:**340
- Ereẓ Israel **9:**583
- - 363 **9:**1046
- - 1927 **9:**1473
- - Tiberias **15:**1133
Easaca (lease ordinance) **7:**1523
East, The (period.), *see Rasaritul*
Eastchester (tn., U.S.) **16:**464
East End (dist., Lond.) **6:**759,763; **11:**477*ff*
- illus:
- - J.F.S. cookery class **11:**475
- - Petticoat Lane **11:**1004
Easter (Chr. festival)
- Ammerschwihr Jews **2:**851
- Béziers Jews **4:**792
- calendar calculation **14:**752
- Jerusalem Christian immorality **9:**1440
- Meaux and Paris Church Council **2:**915
- passion plays **3:**107
"Eastern Mediterranean School" (mus.) **4:**517
Eastern Neo-Aramaic (lang.) **12:**949
Eastern Parkway (section, N.Y.C.) **12:**1082
East Galician Federation (Gen. Zion. faction) **16:**1131
East Germany, *see* German Democratic Republic
East Greenwich (tn., R. I.) **14:**143
East India Companies **8:**1356ff
- Bushire trading post **4:**1535
- Navarro, Abraham **12:**897
- *see also:* Dutch East India Company
East Indies, *see* INDONESIA; PHILIPPINES
EAST LONDON (port, S. A.) **6:**342
East London Fund for the Jews (Chr. conv. soc.), *see* London Diocesan Council for Work amongst the Jews
EASTON (city, Pa.) **6:**342
Easton, Adam **8:**31
East Providence (tn., R. I.) **14:**143
East St. Louis (city, U.S.) **8:**1255
Eastwards (mag.) **5:**457
Eath, Augustinus **8:**31
Eating **15:**593ff
- *see also:* FOOD
EATON, JOSEPH W. **6:**343
Eau Claire (city, Wis.) **16:**556
Ebal, Mount (Er. Isr.) **9:**142; **9:**284; **9:**580
- *illus:*
- - Joshua building an altar **5:**1020
- - Nablus view **12:**745
- *see also:* GERIZIM, MOUNT
EBAN, ABBA (Aubrey) **6:**343
- Israel-Syrian conflict **9:**404
- Six-Day War **9:**407ff; **14:**1626
- U.N. General Assembly **15:**1547
- U.N. Security Council **9:**415
- Warsaw diplomatic convention **13:**787
- *illus:*
- - Auschwitz visit **13:**782
- - Jarring, Gunnar, and **9:**410
- - Johnson, Lyndon, and **10:**165
- - Knesset session **10:**1113
- - Sharett, Moshe, and **14:**1312
Ebed-Melech (6th cent. B.C.E., Eth.) **4:**266
- Jeremiah's oracle **9:**1355
EBEN-EZER (bib. loc., object) **6:**344
- *illus:*
- - battle (Dura-Europos) **6:**292
Ebenfurth (tn., Aus.) **3:**890
Ebensee (concen. camp, Aus.) **11:**1137
EBER (bib. figs.) **6:**344
- Jacob **9:**1198
- Semites **14:**1148
- Shem **14:**1368
Eberls, Moses **9:**1333
Ebers (fam.), *see* EPHRAIM
EBERS, GEORG MORITZ **6:**345
EBERSBERG, (Joseph) SIEGMUND **6:**345
Eberst, Isaac ben Judah, *see* OFFENBACH, ISAAC
Ebert (us), J. **8:**31
Ebert (us), T. **8:**31
Ebiasaph (bib. fig.) **3:**673
Ebionites (J. Chr. sect) **11:**1409
- *see also:* JEWISH-CHRISTIAN SECTS
EBNER, MEIR (Mayer) **6:**345
- *illus:*
- - 1st Zionist Congress **16:**1165
- - Parlialmentary Club, Bucharest **14:**393
Eboda (anc. city, Er. Isr.), *see* AVEDAT
EBONY (wood) **6:**346
- plant list **13:**617
Eborensis, Flavius, *see* PYRRHUS, DIDACUS
Ebreo, Leone, *see* ABRABANEL, JUDAH
Ebron (Evron; tn., Er. Isr.) **6:**1005
ECA (U.N. Commission) **15:**1563
Eça de Queirós, José Maria de **15:**251
ECAFE (U.N. Commission) **15:**1563
Ecbatana (bib. city), *see* HAMADAN
"Ecce Homo" (sculp., J. Epstein) **6:**829
Ecce Homo arch (Jer.) **9:**1406
- *illus:*
- - Via Dolorosa **9:**1401
ECCLESIA ET SYNAGOGA (Chr. symbol) **6:**346
- *illus:*
- - text
- - Bamberg Cathedral **3:**91
- - Lincoln Cathedral **4:**63
- - Rheims ms. **14:**142
- - St. Severin Church, Bordeaux **3:**93
- - thirteenth cent. Bible **3:**91
- - Trier **8:**670
- - twelfth cent. ms. **16:**237
ECCLESIASTES (bk., hagiographa) **6:**349
- General
- - ethical teaching **6:**937
- - Hellenistic Jewish literature **8:**303
- - musical rendition **14:**1058
- - old age **2:**344
- - Scrolls, The Five **14:**1058
- - Septuagint **4:**855
- - Shemini Aẓeret **15:**501
- - Solomon **15:**105
- - vows **16:**228
- - wisdom literature **16:**557
- Commentaries On
- - Abrahams, Abraham **2:**163
- - *Or ha-Ḥozer* (ʿAdanī, Mahalal) **2:**250
- - *Porat Yosef* (Taitazak, Joseph) **15:**711
- *illus:*
- - text
- - *Be'ur Sefer Kohelet* (1578) **7:**274
- - *Duke of Sussex Pentateuch* **5:***fcg.* 1323
- - *see also:* BIBLE
ECCLESIASTES RABBAH (agg. Mid.) **6:**355
- *see also:* MIDRASH
Ecclesiastic tithes, *see* TITHES, CHURCH
Ecclesiasticus (Apoc. work), *see* BEN SIRA, WISDOM OF
Echo Sioniste, L' (period.) **11:**1013
Echternach (city, Lux.) **11:**590
ÉCIJA (city, Sp.) **6:**355
ECIJA, JOSEPH (Yuçaf) DE **6:**356
- Toledo **15:**1203
Eck, Johann **4:**874
- A. Osiander **13:**352
Eckenstein, Lina **12:**405
Ecker (anti-Sem.) **14:**224
Ecker, Hans von (mason, Ger.) **8:**524
ECKARDT, ROY A. **6:**356
- on missions to Jews **13:**1252
Eckart, Dietrich **8:**783
Eckhardt (fam.) **5:**394
ECKHART, MEISTER **6:**357
- Cusa, Nicholas of **5:**1173
ECKMAN, JULIUS **6:**357
Eckstein, A. **4:**149
Eckstein, Nathan **14:**1083
Eckstein, Simon **12:**1522
ECLA (U.N. Commission) **15:**1563
Éclaireurs Israélites (mvmt., Fr.) **14:**1038; **13:**148
Eclipse, *see* MOON; SUN
École de Pédogogie et de Liturgie (Fr.) **14:**1148
École Rabbinique, *see* SÉMINAIRE ISRAÉLITE DE FRANCE
École Rabbinique d'Algérie **2:**617
Ecology **4:**1027ff
Economic and Social Council (ECOSOC) **15:**1547; **15:**1559ff
Economic Board for Palestine **5:**684
ECONOMIC DEVELOPMENT OF ISRAEL **9:**697
- Agriculture **9:**773
- historical survey **9:**392ff
- industry **9:**815ff
- tailoring **15:**709
- U.S. aid **15:**1665ff
- War of Independence **9:**370ff
- Yemenite Jews **16:**753ff
- *illus:*
- - text
- - Bonds dinner, N.Y. **12:**1113

– – ration books (1950-58) **9:**375
– – State of Israel bonds **4:**1204-1205
– *tables:*
– – text
– – cooperative societies in Israel, 1967 **5:**949
– – labor-affiliated cooperative sector **5:**951
ECONOMIC HISTORY **16:**1266
– *Contents:*
– – First Temple Period **16:**1267
– – Second Temple Period **16:**1272
– – Exile and Restoration **16:**1270
– – Talmudic Era **16:**1275
– – Muslim Middle Ages **16:**1278
– – Medieval Christendom **16:**1284
– – Economic Doctrines **16:**1291
– – Early Modern Period **16:**1296
– – – Sephardim and Ashkenazim **16:**1297
– – – Economic Environment **16:**1297
– – – Jewish Migration **16:**1298
– – – Employment Patterns **16:**1299
– – – Resource Endowment and Income Sources **16:**1304
– – – Society at Large **16:**1305
– – – Jewish Community Organization **16:**1306
– – – Social Stratification **16:**1307
– – Transition Period **16:**1309
– – Modern Period **16:**1311
– – – Jewish Migrations **16:**1312
– – – Industrial Employment **16:**1313
– – – Service Sector **16:**1315
– – – Agricultural Sector **16:**1316
– – – Income **16:**1317
– – – Western Europe **16:**1318
– – – Eastern Europe **16:**1319
– – – United States **16:**1321
– – – Palestine **16:**1322
– – Epilogue **16:**1323
– General
– – agriculture **2:**381
– – *arenda* **3:**402
– – Bachi's studies **4:**53
– – banking **4:**166
– – Cairo *genizah* **16:**1339
– – candle tax **5:**119
– – Christian slaves **8:**653
– – Court Jews **5:**1006
– – crafts **5:**1040
– – Crusades **5:**1143
– – debt and bankruptcy **8:**1307
– – Diaspora **6:**11
– – guilds **7:**970
– – liquor trade **16:**541
– – markets and fairs **11:**1000
– – Marks and Spencer **11:**1009
– – Marx's views on **11:**1074
– – May Laws **11:**1147
– – mercantilist absolutism **8:**703
– – moneylending **12:**244
– – peddling **13:**203
– – Radhanites **13:**1495
– – responsa **14:**88
– – *Schutzjuden* **14:**1013
– – slave trade **14:**1660
– – socialism, Jewish **15:**41
– – Soviet policy toward Jews **16:**779ff
– – tailoring **15:**704
– – taxation **15:**837
– – textile trade **15:**1036
– – trade and commerce **15:**1293
– – U.S. depression **15:**1628
– – vital statistics **16:**179ff
– – wood trade **16:**630
– Ereẓ Israel
– – Solomon **15:**100ff
– – 70 to 640 C.E. **9:**244ff
– – 634 to 1099 **9:**265
– – Crusader period **9:**272; **9:**274
– – Muslim conquest **8:**659
– – Mamluk period **9:**277; **9:**281
– – Ottoman period **9:**284, 300,
– *illus:*
– – coins and currency, 4th cent. B.C.E./1968 **5:**697–733
– – financial release, Hebrew, 13th cent. **4:**167
– – impounding of pledge (7th cent. B.C.E. ostracon) **3:**317
– – Jewish moneylenders **4:**171, 173; **8:**674
– – land lease contract, Bar-Kokhba administration **4:**237
– – Poland, coins minted by Jews **13:**727
– – prosbul document **13:**1182
– – promissory notes transfer, 14th cent. **4:**170
– – weights, 8/7 cent. **16:**377–374
– *see also:* HISTORY; *and under individual countries, cities, crafts, and trades*
Economic Reconstruction Association (Neo-Nazi orgn.) **12:**954
Economic Survey Mission **9:**378; **15:**1550
"Economists", *see* INDEPENDENT JEWISH WORKERS PARTY
ECOSOC (U.N. council), *see* Economic and Social Council
ECSTASY **6:**358
– Ḥasidism **7:**1391ff
– Kabbalah **10:**630
– mantic **6:**112
– Neoplatonism **12:**958
– *Ru'aḥ ha-Kodesh* **14:**366
ECUADOR **6:**359
– Latin America **10:**1450ff
– Quito **15:**1350
– synagogue **1:** synagogue list
– Zionism **16:**1125
– *pop. table:* text
Ecumenical Councils **5:**546ff
Ecumenical Movement **5:**545
– Protestant-Jewish relations **13:**1250
E.C.Z.A., *see* American Emergency Committee for Zionist Affairs
Edah, see COMMUNITY; JEWISH COMMUNITIES IN ISRAEL
Edah Ḥaredit (Orth. cmty., Isr.) **9:**892
Eddy (Baker-Eddy), Mary Morse **5:**515
EDEL, YIZHAK **12:**687
Edelberg, A. **12:**1109
Edelheim, M. **5:**1177
Edelman, A. W. **11:**499; **11:**501
Edelman, David W. **11:**501
Edelman, Marek **4:**1505; **16:**351
EDELMAN, MAURICE **6:**787
Edelmann, Mordecai Isaac **6:**362
EDELMANN, RAPHAEL **6:**362
EDELMANN, SIMḤAH REUBEN **6:**362
EDELMANN, ẒEVI HIRSCH **6:**362
Edels, Israel ben Joseph **6:**1158
EDELS, SAMUEL ELIEZER BEN JUDAH HA-LEVI (Maharsha) **6:**363
– codification of law **5:**653
– exile **7:**291ff
– *ḥerem,* opposed by **15:**737
– *ḥiddushim* **8:**467; **11:**333
– history chart **8:**766-67
EDELSTADT, DAVID **6:**364
– socialism **15:**34
Edelstein, Bertalan **4:**1449
Edelstein, Hyman **5:**115
Edelstein, J. (publ.) **10:**1137
EDELSTEIN, JACOB (Zion.) **6:**365
– Prague **13:**974
– Zionism **16:**1113
Edem (gnos. term, Eden) **7:**638
Eden (bib. city) **2:**260
Eden (Aram. kdm.), *see* BET(H)-EDEN
Eden (period.) **5:**457
Eden, Anthony Robert, *see* AVON, ANTHONY ROBERT EDEN, EARL OF
Eden, Avraham **13:**48
Eden, Garden of, *see* GARDEN OF EDEN
Edenbridge (stlmt., Can.) **14:**891
Edenkoben (vill., Ger.) **3:**842
Eder (city, Er. Isr.) **3:**244
Eder, Edith, *see* Low, Edith
EDER, MONTAGUE DAVID **6:**365
– *illus:*
– – Allenby, and **2:**647
– – Rothschild, James de, and **14:**346
– – Zionist delegation to Palestine (1918) **9:**336
Edersheim, Alfred **13:**1249; **16:**787
Edersheim, Henri **7:**1125
EDESSA (city, As. M.) **6:**366
– massacre **10:**469
– Osroene **12:**1502
– Peshitta origin **4:**858
Edfu (tn., Egy.), *see* Apollinopolis Magna
Edgeworth, Maria **6:**779
Edgware (sub., London) **6:**449; **11:**479
– *illus:*
– – shift of population **11:**479
Edict of Grace (Inq.) **8:**1400
Edicts, Anti-Jewish, *see* Legislation, Anti-Jewish
EDINBURGH (city, Scot.) **6:**367
– Daiches family **5:**1226
– Scotland **14:**1035, 1036
– *illus:*
– – synagogue **14:**1035
Edinburgh, Duke of, *see* Philip, Duke of Edinburgh
Edineti (tn., Rum.) **14:**402
EDINGER, LUDWIG **6:**368
EDINGER, TILLY **6:**368
Edirne (tn., Turk.), *see* ADRIANOPLE
"Editors' Meeting" (illus. E. Dienard) **13:**130
Edler von Liebenberg, *see* Liebmann, Israel
Edler von Neuwall, *see* Leidesdorf, Markus
EDMAN, IRWIN **6:**368
EDMONTON (city, Can.) **6:**368
EDOM (anc. people, country) **6:**369
– *Contents:*
– – The Country **6:**369
– – The People **6:**370
– – Bible **6:**371
– – Until Davidic Conquest **6:**371
– – Until Destruction of Judah **6:**374
– – Religion and Culture **6:**376
– – Second Temple Period **6:**377
– – In Aggadah **6:**378
– General
– – administration **9:**121
– – Antipater **3:**76
– – Bar Giora, Simeon **4:**220
– – *Bet Shammai* **4:**739
– – Christianity, symbolized by **5:**514
– – Costobar, governor **5:**990
– – destruction, post-Temple **9:**239; **9:**251; **9:**254
– – forced conversion **7:**1456
– – Frankists **7:**60
– – geology **9:**201
– – Hasmoneans **8:**631; **8:**633; **8:**635
– – Hebron **8:**227
– – Herod's retreat **3:**66
– – history **8:**587ff
– – human geography **9:**596ff
– – Hyrcanus, John **8:**1147
– – Jacob ben Sosas **9:**1224
– – language **14:**1150
– – language of DSS **16:**1585
– – metal mines **15:**103
– – mishnaic Hebrew **16:**1605
– – Niger of Perea **12:**1156
– – physiography **9:**175ff
– – Rome identified with **8:**302
– – swine identified with **13:**507
– – *Targum Sheni* **15:**813
– – Transjordan **15:**1316ff
– Bible
– – Amaziah **2:**798
– – Esau, ancestor **6:**854
– – Genesis, Book of **7:**389; **7:**394
– – history **8:**576ff
– – Israelites **12:**377
– – Jeremiah's oracle **9:**1354
– – Seir **14:**1116
– – Solomon's concubines **15:**100
– – status in ancient Israel **15:**420
– – Uz **16:**38
– *illus:*
– – David's conquest (map) **5:**1323
– – Petra antiquities **13:**341, 342
Edot (journ.) **1:**newsp. list
EDREHI, MOSES BEN ISAAC **6:**380
– Maimon ben Joseph **11:**744
– *illus:* text
EDREI (bib. tn.) **6:**381
– Estori ha-Parḥi **9:**279
EDUCATION **6:**381
– *Contents*
– – Biblical Period
– – – Nature of Sources **6:**382
– – – Historical Survey **6:**383
– – – Goals and Orders of Instruction **6:**385
– – – Institutions **6:**386
– – – Specific Training **6:**389
– – In the Talmud **6:**398
– – Middle Ages **6:**403
– – 16th-18th Centuries **6:**413
– – 1800-1939 **6:**420
– – Europe (War and Postwar) **6:**430
– – Yiddish **6:**433
– – U.S. **6:**437
– – Great Britain **6:**446
– – Australia **6:**451
– – Canada **6:**452
– – South Africa **6:**455
– – Argentina **6:**456
– – Brazil **6:**457
– – Uruguay **6:**457
– – Mexico **6:**458
– – North Africa **6:**459
– – Iran **6:**460
– General
– – alphabet letters and honey **8:**963
– – *apotropos'* responsibility **3:**220
– – camping **6:**443
– – children **5:**427ff
– – community and **6:**412; **3:**926; **5:**812
– – Falashas **6:**1146
– – Haskalah **7:**1433
– – intermarriage **12:**167
– – Jewish Colonization Association **10:**45
– – married students **10:**1161
– – minority rights **12:**45ff
– – Musar movement **12:**534
– – music **12:**600
– – Nazi cartoons **5:**177
– – parents' duty **13:**95ff
– – physical **15:**295ff
– – preaching **13:**994
– – rabbinical, *see* RABBINICAL SEMINARIES
– – rabbi's role **13:**1456
– – *Sefer Ḥukkei ha-Torah* **6:**410; **14:**1099
– – Sumerian system **15:**515
– – *talmid ḥakham* **15:**746
– – tax **15:**848
– – UNESCO **15:**1565

– – Yiddish **6**:433
– Biblical Aspects **6**:382f
– – ethical teaching **6**:935f
– – Levites **11**:138
– – Leviticus, Book of **11**:139
– – parables **13**:72
– – priests **13**:1080
– – Proverbs, Book of **13**:1268
– Talmud and Middle Ages **6**:398f; **8**:687; **15**:767
– – *dukhan* **6**:267
– – Hellenism **8**:297
– – homiletic literature **8**:947ff
– – Joshua ben Gamala **10**:278
– – psychology **13**:1341
– – sages **13**:366; **14**:638; **14**:643
– – Simeon ben Shetaḥ **14**:1564
– Views on
– – Ben-Gurion, David **4**:512
– – Elijah of Vilna **6**:657
– – Grodzinski, Ḥayyim Ozer **7**:928
– – Horowitz, Isaiah **8**:993
– – Judah Loew ben Bezalel **8**:696
– – Levin, Menahem Mendel **11**:108
– – Lilienblum, Moses **11**:240
– – Lilienthal, Max **11**:243
– – Rosenzweig, Franz **14**:300
– – Shapira, Ẓevi Hirsch **14**:1296
– Institutions **6**:386f
– – Agudat Israel **2**:423
– – Alliance Israélite Universelle **2**:651ff
– – associations **8**:441
– – Beth Jacob schools **16**:1260
– – College of Jewish Studies **5**:735
– – Hebrew Teachers College **8**:215
– – *Ḥeder* **8**:241
– – Hochschule fuer die Wissenschaft des Judentums **8**:799
– – HUC-JIR **8**:216
– – JTS **10**:95
– – Jews' College **10**:98
– – ORT **12**:1481
– – Ozar Hatorah **12**:1537
– – Rabbiner-Seminar fuer das Orthodoxe Judentum **13**:1459
– – Séminaire Israélite de France **14**:1147
– – Society for the Promotion of Culture, Russia **15**:58ff
– – Tarbut schools **15**:809
– – Torah Umesorah **15**:1259
– – Ulpan **15**:1525
– – Wolfenbuettel school **16**:609
– – Yeshiva University **16**:760
– – yeshivot **16**:762ff
– – – Abraham Isaac Kook's program **10**:1183
– – – Volozhin program **16**:216
– – Youth Aliyah **16**:863ff
– – *see also individual institutions*
– Countries and Cities
– – Amsterdam **2**:896ff
– – Argentina **6**:456
– – Australia **6**:451
– – – Melbourne **11**:1277
– – Babylonia **6**:403f
– – Bessarabia **4**:708
– – Brazil **6**:457
– – Canada **6**:452; **5**:108
– – – Montreal **12**:286
– – – Toronto **15**:1262
– – Czechoslovakia **5**:1191
– – England **6**:446,769
– – – London **11**:477ff
– – Europe **6**:411,413,423; **5**:1002
– – France **6**:405,408,420; **7**:26
– – – Paris **13**:107ff
– – Galicia **16**:1327
– – Germany **6**:408,415,422; **7**:465
– – – Berlin **4**:645,647
– – Greece **7**:877
– – Iran **6**:460; **13**:318ff
– – Iraq **8**:1451; **8**:1454
– – Israel, *see* EDUCATION IN ISRAEL
– – Italy **6**:405,417,420
– – Latin America **6**:437
– – Latvia **10**:1466
– – Lithuania **11**:361ff
– – Mexico **6**:458
– – North Africa **6**:419,459
– – Poland **6**:414,423,435; **13**:738
– – – Poznan **13**:949
– – – Warsaw **16**:338,341ff
– – Rumania **6**:428,435; **14**:397; **14**:414
– – Russia **6**:411,413,423; **8**:734ff; **14**:436ff
– – – Haskalah **7**:1449
– – – UNESCO conference **15**:1565
– – – *Yevsektsiya* **16**:780
– – – Yiddish **6**:433; **14**:464
– – South Africa **6**:455; **15**:194
– – Spain **6**:405; **15**:245
– – Turkey **6**:426; **15**:1460
– – U.S. **6**:437ff; **15**:1589ff
– – American Association for Jewish Education **2**:819
– – – camping **6**:443
– – – curriculum **6**:444
– – – day schools **6**:443; **14**:1174
– – – New York City **12**:1074; **12**:1094; **12**:1110ff
– – – synagogue school **6**:442
– – – United Synagogue of America **15**:1673
– – Uruguay **6**:457; **16**:14
– – *see also under individual countries and towns*
– Secular
– – Agudat Israel's attitude **2**:422ff
– – Austrian Jews **3**:892ff
– – ḥasidic rejection **7**:1400
– – *numerus clausus* **12**:1263
– – Prague **13**:970
– *illus:*
– – abecedary (10th cent.) **8**:658, 1274
– – Agoin (Atlas Mountains), rabbi and pupils **3**:826
– – Alliance Israélite Universelle, educational network, 1968 (table) **2**:653
– – Baghdad, Jewish pupils, 1920 and 1950 (table) **4**:92
– – Baron de Hirsch Agricultural School, Woodbine, N.J. **10**:35,47
– – Beirut, Alliance Israélite Universelle girls' school **4**:403
– – Bene Israel, *The Elementary Hebrew Reader* **4**:498
– – Benghazi, Jewish Brigade Hebrew School **4**:504
– – Berlin, Hochschule fuer die Wissenschaft des Judentums **8**:800
– – Boston, Hebrew Teachers' College **8**:215
– – Boston Jewish Teachers' Association, minute book **3**:384
– – Buenos Aires, Bialik and Ramat Shalom schools **4**:1463
– – Camp Morasha, Yeshiva University **8**:773
– – Casablanca, child learning to read Hebrew **5**:224
– – Casablanca, J.D.C. school **2**:831
– – Chicago, Hebrew Theological College **8**:216
– – "Children in Kovno Ghetto School" (drg., J. Lifschitz) Fig. 77 **3**-ART
– – Cincinnati, Hebrew Union College **8**:217
– – Fez, Sylvain Lévy School **6**:1257
– – Frankfort a/M, medal for 100th anniversary of the Philanthropin **7**:88
– – Gateshead, yeshivah **7**:334
– – Geneva, ORT Central Institute for Teacher and Technician Training **15**:560
– – Hamadan, Alliance Israélite Universelle school **2**:649
– – *ḥeder*, Poland **13**:741
– – *Ḥevrat Tarbut*, central committee **4**:706
– – Isfahan, Alliance school **9**:79
– – Italian Jewish school **9**:1138
– – Jewish Commissariat order forbidding the teaching of Hebrew **14**:462
– – Johannesburg, King David Day School **15**:196
– – Kaisiadorys, *Tiferet Baḥurim* **11**:375
– – Kaunas, Taḥkemoni school **10**:847
– – Kovel, Jewish gymnasium staff **10**:1228
– – *Lesebuch fuer Juedische Kinder* (1779) **5**:433
– – Lomza, yeshivah **16**:762
– – London, Jews' College **10**:99
– – London, Jews' Free School **11**:475, 478
– – Melbourne, Mount Scopus War Memorial College **3**:884
– – Melbourne, Bet Rivkeh Ladies College **3**:886
– – Melbourne, Lubavich Yeshivah College **11**:1285
– – Mogador, Auguste Baumier school **12**:332
– – Molodechno, boys' boarding school **12**:233
– – Montevideo, Sholem Aleichem School **16**:12
– – Moscow, Hebrew teacher's advertisement (1970) **14**:504
– – Netherlands, schoolchildren wearing yellow badge **12**:987
– – New York, Jewish Theological Seminary **10**:97
– – New York, teachers' strike rally **12**:1114
– – New York, Yeshiva University **16**:760,767
– – ORT schools **12**:1482-1485
– – Paris, Merkaz de Montmartre community center **5**:427
– – Pentateuch cantillation table **11**:1103,1105
– – Pereyaslav-Khmelnitski, kindergarten **13**:283
– – Philadelphia, Pa., Dropsie University **6**:236
– – Prague universities, percentage of Jewish students (table) **13**:971
– – Rabat, Alliance girls' school **14**:681
– – Shalom Aleichem Folk Institute **12**:1105
– – Tarbut kindergarten for World War I refugee children **14**:447
– – teacher admonishing pupil (14th cent. ms.) **4**:967; **6**:*fcg.* 427
– – Teheran, Alliance School for Girls **8**:1442
– – Teheran, Jewish day school pupils **15**:905
– – Toronto, Associated Hebrew Schools building **5**:107
– – Tunis, Alliance school **15**:1437
– – Ukmerge, School for shoemakers **15**:1513
– – women pupils and teachers (15th cent.) **7**:*fcg.* 811
– – Yiddish abecedary with Russian translation **14**:489
– *see also:* CHILDREN'S LITERATURE; LIBRARIES; STUDY; UNIVERSITIES
EDUCATION (Jews in) **6**:461
Education, Independent, *see* Ḥinnukh Aẓma'i
Educational Alliance (N.Y.C.) **12**:1093ff
Educational and Cultural Union (Pol.) **6**:435ff
Educational Training Institute (Isr.) **9**:693
Education and Publications **11**:1202
EDUCATION IN ISRAEL **9**:928
– agricultural **9**:777
– Agudat Israel **2**:423
– Arab education **9**:1023ff; **9**:949
– biblical **6**:382
Hebrew language **16**:1642
– Hebrew schools **9**:326ff
– higher education **9**:952
– Histadrut **9**:867
– history **9**:384; **9**:394ff
– integration **9**:507
– Jerusalem **9**:1465
– Muslim religious education **9**:917
– population **9**:477
– religious education **9**:894
– sport **15**:294
– Teachers' Association **15**:888
– UNESCO **15**:1565
– *illus:*
– – Bar-Ilan University, Ramat Gan **4**:225
– – Bedouin school class **9**:1044
– – Bezalel Academy, Jerusalem, a students' show **4**:789
– – Bezalel School of Arts and Crafts, Jerusalem **4**:789
– – Bir al-Sheikh elementary-school **9**:944
– – Braille geography textbook **9**:950
– – Daliyat-al-Karmil school **9**:926
– – Eẓ Ḥayyim Yeshivah, talmud lesson (Jer.) **16**:764
– – Gaza Strip, 1967-70 (table) **9**:1037
– – Ha-Ogen school **9**:938
– – Hebrew University buildings, Jerusalem **3**:349, 351, 354
– – Herzlia Gymnasia, first graduating class **9**:931
– – hygiene class in Arab school **9**:1030
– – income of Jewish school system (chart) **9**:935
– – Jaffa, girls' school **9**:1253
– – Jerusalem *ḥeder* **9**:897,942
– – Jerusalem school, chemistry class **9**:948
– – Jewish schools, pupils (chart) **9**:946
– – Judea and Samaria (table) **9**:1037
– – kindergarten **9**:937
– – Kiryat Noar (Boys' Town), Jerusalem **6**:436; **9**:900,943
– – Kol Torah Yeshivah (Jer.) **16**:766
– – Laemmel school (Jer.) **9**:929
– – Midreshet Sedeh Boker **14**:1090
– – Mikveh Israel, agricultural school **11**:1544,1545
– – music, recorder lesson **12**:671
– – Naẓerat Illit, ulpan classroom **15**:1526
– – ORT vocational high school, Holon **12**:1485
– – Porat Yosef Yeshivah (Jer.) **16**:765
– – school population, 1948-70 (chart) **9**:939
– – schools in educational system 1948-70 (chart) **9**:940
– – Siloam, Yemenite class **16**:749
– – state budget 1971/72 (chart) **9**:941
– – Tu bi-Shevat celebrations **9**:907
– – University of the Negev, Beersheba **4**:385
– – years of schooling (table) **9**:479
– – Yemin Orde, high school class **9**:949
Educatore Israelita (journ.) **16**:107
Educators' Assembly (U.S.) **15**:1674
ʿ*Edut* (covenant) **5**:1012

Edut (leg. term), *see* EVIDENCE; WITNESS
Edut le-Yisrael (newsp.) **1**:newsp. list
EDUYYOT (Mish. tract.) **6**:466
- arrangement of **12**:100
- codification of law **5**:632
Edward I (k., Eng.) **11**:471
- Bordeaux Jews **4**:1243
- Cambridge Jews **5**:69
- debts to Jews **16**:1285
- Domus Conversorum **6**:165
- Jewish badge **4**:64
Edward II (k., Eng.) **4**:1243
Edward III (k., Eng.) **4**:1243
EDWARDS, PAUL **6**:467
Edzardus, Esdras **8**:31
Eel **6**:36
EERDMANS, BERNARDUS DIRKS **6**:468
Efal-Bet Avot (old age home, Isr.) **1**:place list
Efal-Merkaz Seminariyyonim (educ. inst., Isr.) **1**:place list
Efeh (snake) **15**:15
Efer (fam.) **3**:693
Efes Damim (bk.) **11**:118
- blood libel **3**:200
Effendi, Boaz **14**:146
Effendi, Yiḥya **13**:798
Effendi Barukh, Javer, *see* Baruch, Javer
Effendi Shalom, Isaac **14**:871; **16**:872
Effendi Shalom, Solomon **14**:872; **16**:872
"Efod" (schol., Sp.), *see* DURAN, PROFIAT
Efrat, Yiẓḥak **14**:1673
Efrati (fam.), *see* Afriat
Efron, Elias **3**:432
EFRON, ILYA **6**:468
- publishing **13**:1370
Efron, Z. **3**:652
EFROS, ISRAEL ISAAC **6**:468
- Hebrew literature **8**:211; **8**:212
- *illus:*
- - Hebrew writers' convention **8**:213
Efroymson, G.A. **8**:1362
Egalitatea (period.) **13**:1043ff; **14**:399,1029
Egán, E. **15**:470
Egelbert (archbp.) **15**:1390
Egel ha-Zahav (journ.) **1**:newsp. list
EGER (city, Hung.) **6**:469
- synagogue **15**:602
Eger (tn., Bohem.), *see* CHEB
Eger, Abraham **6**:471
EGER, AKIVA ("The Younger") BEN MOSES GUENS **6**:469
- *ḥiddushim* **8**:467
- history chart **8**:766-767
- *Tiferet Yisrael* **11**:294
- *illus:* text
EGER, AKIVA BEN SIMḤAH BUNIM ("The Elder") **6**:471
Eger, Benjamin Wolf **6**:469
Eger, Ezriel Meir **6**:471
Eger, Jacob Moses **13**:948
EGER, JUDAH LEIB OF LUBLIN **6**:471
Eger, Judah Loeb (Ger.) **6**:471
Eger, Judith, *see* Leidesdorfer, Judith
Eger, Meshullam **13**:294
Eger, Moses **6**:472
EGER, SAMUEL (Perez Sanwel) BEN JUDAH LOEB **6**:472
EGER, SIMḤAH BUNIM BEN MOSES **6**:472
Eger, Solomon (Rus.) **11**:1206
Eger, Solomon (Pol.) **6**:471
EGER, SOLOMON BEN AKIVA (Ger.) **6**:472
Eger, Wolf **6**:471
Egert, Roman B. **15**:210
Egesippus, see Hegesippus
EGGED (Isr. coop.) **6**:473
- cooperative **5**:949; **5**:951
- *illus:*
- - text
- - headquarters, Tel Aviv **5**:952
Eggers, J. **8**:31
EGGS **6**:474
- dietary regulations **6**:27
- food **6**:1416
- *illus:*
- - mourner's pewter plate **12**:489
Egibi (bnk., Babyl.) **16**:1271
Egica (k., Sp.) **15**:222
EGIDIO DA VITERBO **6**:475
- Hebraist **8**:65
- Kabbalah **10**:645
- Levita, Elijah **11**:132
Egilsson, S. **4**:877
Eglah (w. of David), *see* MICHAL
EGLAH ARUFAH **6**:475
- Commandments, the 613 **5**:781
- discontinuation **6**:588
- elders **6**:578
- Jerusalem **9**:1553
- *illus:* text
EGLON (Moab. k.) **6**:478
- Benjamin **4**:525
- Ehud **6**:515
- Jericho captured **9**:1368
- Orpah **12**:1478
- *illus:*
- - stabbed by Ehud **10**:447
EGLON (Cana. city) **6**:477
- Bible history **8**:578
- proscription by Israel **8**:345
Egoist, The (period.) **14**:218
Egoz (journ.) **1**: newsp. list
EGOZI (fam.) **6**:478
Egozi, David **6**:478
Egozi, Ḥayyim **6**:478
Egozi, Menahem ben Moses **6**:478
Egozi, Nissim ben Ḥayyim **6**:478
Egron (wk.), *see Sefer ha-Agron*
EGYENLŐSÉG (weekly) **6**:478
- Szabolcsi family **15**:654
EGYPT **6**:479
- *Contents:*
- - Ancient Egypt **6**:479
- - Literature **6**:484
- - Hellenistic Period **6**:485
- - Roman Period **6**:488
- - Second Temple to Moslem Conquest **6**:490
- - Arab Period **6**:491
- - Contemporary Period **6**:500
- - Relations with Israel **6**:502
- General
- - abomination of **2**:97
- - agriculture **2**:402; **6**:11
- - banking **4**:167
- - burial customs **15**:1216
- - capitulations **5**:149
- - chronological chart **8**:766-767
- - Commandments, the 613 **5**:773
- - communal organization **5**:814
- - demography **5**:1497
- - diaspora **6**:9ff; **16**:1270
- - discrimination **6**:71
- - divorce statistics **6**:136
- - goldsmithery **7**:740
- - Ham, identified with **7**:1216
- - Jewish source of culture **3**:645
- - ritual purity **13**:1407
- - Samaritan community **14**:734; **14**:737
- - Shabbetai Ẓevi's mission **14**:1223
- - synagogues **1**:syn. list; **15**:581
- - term for Christian **7**:411
- - yeshivot **16**:762
- Ancient and Biblical Periods **6**:479f; **8**:573ff
- - Aaronides **2**:20
- - Athribis **3**:822
- - dress **6**:213
- - ethical values **6**:938
- - Hittites **8**:788
- - Hyksos **8**:1141
- - Judah, fall of **6**:1090
- - kingship **10**:1011ff
- - Levites **11**:74; **13**:1083
- - Manetho **11**:872
- - Mesopotamian migrants **3**:42
- - mining **11**:1432
- - Moses **12**:371
- - netherworld, belief in **12**:996
- - ostraca **12**:1510
- - papyrus **13**:70ff; **16**:658
- - Pharaoh **13**:359ff
- - population **13**:866
- - pottery types **13**:938; **13**:939
- - Ramses **13**:1545
- - Resheph (deity) **14**:81
- - Sargon II **14**:880
- - seals **14**:1072
- - Seti I **14**:1192
- - Shishak **14**:1416
- - Sinai **14**:1595
- - Solomon's concubines **15**:100
- - Solomon's trade **15**:98
- - status in Israel **15**:420
- - stone monuments **16**:656
- - Tell el-Amarna **15**:933
- - Timna **15**:1146ff
- - Tobiads **15**:1179ff
- - trade and commerce **15**:1293ff
- - war and warfare **16**:267
- - weights and measures **16**:376
- - wisdom literature **16**:559
- - writing implements **16**:664ff
- - *see also:* MIẒRAYIM
- Hellenistic Period **6**:485
- - Ananias and Helkias **2**:922
- - anti-Semitism **7**:888
- - Diaspora **8**:640
- - *fiscus judaicus* **6**:1325
- - Hellenism **8**:290ff
- - papyri **13**:70ff
- - Septuagint **4**:851
- - Trajan **15**:1312
- Arab and Ottoman Periods **6**:491; **16**:1534,1550
- - Abraham Maimonides **2**:150
- - Alashkar and academies **2**:513
- - Ashkenazi, Bezalel **3**:723
- - banking **4**:167
- - blood libel **16**:1544
- - Crusades **9**:267ff
- - David ben Daniel **5**:1349
- - David ibn Abi Zimra **5**:1356
- - *Divrei Yosef* **14**:761
- - gaonate **7**:315; **7**:323ff
- - Jerusalem community **9**:1436
- - Jewish farmers **2**:402
- - Jewish settlement **3**:998
- - *nagid* **12**:760
- - Mamluk rule **11**:834
- - Omar, Covenant of **12**:1378
- - population **13**:873
- - rabbinical titles **13**:1449; **13**:1451
- - textiles **15**:1038
- Modern Period **6**:497f
- - Arab League **3**:242ff
- - Baruch, Joseph Marcou **4**:275
- - Blum, Julius (Blum Pasha) **4**:1136
- - cartoons, anti-Semitic **5**:179
- - emigration **16**:1527
- - Ereẓ Israel **9**:294; **9**:298
- - Gaza Strip constitution **9**:1035
- - Jews in **15**:1561
- - Jews in politics **13**:816
- - Lebanon and **10**:1542
- - Muhammad Ali **12**:511
- - Nasser **12**:841
- - Neo-Nazism **12**:956
- - population **9**:1023
- - press **13**:1041
- - synagogues **1**:syn. list
- - vital statistics **16**:188ff
- - Zionism **16**:1127,1128ff
- Israel-Egypt Conflict **6**:502; **9**:391
- - Armistice Agreements **3**:478
- - border clashes **14**:1624
- - Gaza Strip **7**:343ff; **9**:1034ff
- - German aid controversy **9**:403
- - immigration to Israel **9**:538
- - Rhodes talks **9**:374ff
- - Security Council resolution, 1967 **9**:415
- - shipping ban **9**:386
- - Six-Day War **9**:404ff; **14**:1624
- - Syrian Jews **15**:646
- - U.N. resolutions **15**:1546ff
- - War of Independence **9**:366ff; **16**:306ff
- *illus:* text
- *illus:* General
- - Hebrew script types **2**:691-693,715-716,731-732
- *illus:* Ancient
- - Alexandria in early Christian times (plan) **2**:591
- - Amon **2**:864
- - brickmaking **3**:311
- - clay tablet, Tell el-Amarna **3**:370
- - execration text inscription **8**:572
- - granaries, model **2**:383
- - harvesting **2**:385
- - hoeing **2**:377
- - Jerusalem Jews' appeal to Jews of Egypt re Ḥanukkah **7**:1
- - "Karnak Botanical Garden" **2**:385
- - massacre of Alexandrian Jews **10**:256
- - Merneptah stele **3**:313
- - Ramses III and Philistines, sea battle **8**:587
- - Semitic semi-nomads **3**:311
- *illus:* Medieval
- - Cairo, Jewish quarters, Fatimid period (plan) **5**:26
- - Fostat, Jewish quarter (plan) **5**:27
- *illus:* Modern Period
- - Faluja evacuation **16**:330
- - Israel-Egypt General Armistice Agreement, 1949 **3**:479
- - Nasser stamp **12**:842
- - Sinai campaign **14**:1601,1603
- - Six-Day war **14**:1627ff
- - Spitfire shot down **16**:328
- *pop. tables:* text
EGYPT, BROOK OF (s. border, Er. Isr.) **6**:503
- *see also:* EL-ARISH
Egypt, History of (wk.), *see History of Egypt*
Egyptian (lang.) **14**:1149
- Bible translations **4**:861
- Hebrew linguistics **16**:1398
- names **12**:804
- poetry **13**:676
- *see also:* HEBREW LANGUAGE (Pre-Biblical)
Egyptian Exile **7**:275
Egyptian Expeditionary Forces **2**:646
Egyptian *Hallel* (litur.) **13**:1322
EḤAD MI YODE'A (Passover song) **6**:503
- *illus:* text
Ehal (Holy Ark) **3**:450
EHRENBERG, RICHARD **6**:504
Ehrenberg, Joshua Menahem **14**:94
EHRENBERG, VICTOR LEOPOLD **6**:505
EHRENBURG, ILYA GRIGORYEVICH **6**:505
- Grossman, Vasili **7**:939
- Jewish anti-Fascist Committee **3**:62ff
Ehrenburg, S.M. **16**:1236; **16**:609
EHRENFELD (fam.) **6**:507

Ehrenfeld, David Ẓevi **6:**507
Ehrenfeld, Edith, *see* Patai, Edith
Ehrenfeld, Isaiah **6:**507
EHRENFELD, NATHAN **6:**507
Ehrenfeld, Samuel (U.S., Isr.) **6:**508; **9:**899
EHRENFELD, SAMUEL BEN DAVID ẒEVI (Hung.) **6:**508
Ehrenfeld, Saul **6:**507
Ehrenfeld, Simeon (Hung.) **6:**507; **11:**1494
Ehrenfeld, Simḥah Bunim **6:**508
EHRENFEST, PAUL **6:**508
EHRENKRANZ, BENJAMIN (Wolf) ZEEB **6:**509
- Broder's influence **4:**1391
Ehrenpreis, Ernestine **16:**1165
EHRENPREIS, MARCUS (Mordecai) **6:**509
- Scandinavian literature **14:**931
- Zionism **16:**1148
- *illus:*
- - F.Z.C. **16:**1045,1165
EHRENREICH, ḤAYYIM JUDAH BEN KALONYMUS **6:**510
Ehrenreich, Hirsch **15:**1633
Ehrenreich, Moses **5:**736; **14:**251
Ehrenreich, Samuel **14:**1575
Ehrenreich, Solomon Zalman **10:**819
EHRENSTAMM (fam.) **6:**510
Ehrenstamm, Feith **6:**511; **15:**1041
Ehrenstamm, Solomon Jacob **6:**510
EHRENSTEIN, ALBERT **6:**511
Ehrental, A. **10:**756
Ehrenteil, A. **8:**958
Ehrentreu, Ernst (Jonah) **6:**512
EHRENTREU, HEINRICH **6:**511
- Auerbach, Ẓ. B. **3:**843
Ehrenzweig, Armin **10:**1493
EHRLICH, ABEL **12:**670; **12:**688
EHRLICH, ARNOLD BOGUMIL **6:**512
- Bible exegesis **4:**901ff
Ehrlich, Elma **5:**451; **11:**115
EHRLICH, EUGEN **6:**513
EHRLICH, GEORG **6:**513
Ehrlich, Hamilton **4:**175
Ehrlich, Henryk, *see* ERLICH, HENRYK
EHRLICH, HERMANN **7:**1547
EHRLICH, JACOB **6:**513
- Zionism **16:**1107
Ehrlich, Jeshajahu **4:**374
EHRLICH, LEONARD **15:**1580
EHRLICH, LUDWIK **10:**1507
Ehrlich, Moses **15:**318
EHRLICH, PAUL **6:**514
- stamps **15:**335
- *illus:*
- - stamp **12:**1203
Ehrlich, Wolf **4:**1112; **12:**1448
Ehrlich, Zvi, *see* EHRLICH, HERMANN
Ehrmann, František **5:**1201
EHUD (bib. fig.) **6:**515
- Bible history **8:**584
- Eglon **6:**478
- Geba, family seat **7:**349
- Judges **10:**444
- lefthandedness **14:**178
- *illus:*
- - stabbing Eglon **10:**447
Eibenschitz (tn., Morav.), *see* IVANCICE
Eibenschutz, David Solomon **4:**704; **15:**166
EIBESCHUETZ, SIMON AARON **6:**516
Eibeschutz, Jonathan, *see* EYBESCHUTZ, JONATHAN
Eichel, Isaac (educ.) **7:**1441ff
EICHELBAUM, SAMUEL **6:**516
- literature **15:**255
EICHENBAUM (Gelber), JACOB **6:**516
Eichenstein, E. **10:**1216
Eichenstein, Isaac Izak **10:**681
Eichenstein, Menachem **14:**665
Eichenstein, Ẓevi Hirsch **16:**1008; **16:**1009
Eichenwald, Julius Isayevich, *see* AIKHENVALD, YULI ISAYEVICH
EICHHORN, JOHANN GOTTFRIED **6:**517
- Genesis theory **8:**1248
- Isaiah authorship **9:**45
- Jean Astruc **3:**809
- mythology **12:**729
EICHMANN, ADOLF OTTO **6:**517
- Arendt, Hannah **3:**406
- Argentina **12:**956
- Auschwitz **3:**855
- Austrian Jewry **3:**899ff
- Brand's negotiations **4:**1294
- euthanasia **16:**1332
- extermination camps **5:**85
- Gestapo **7:**529
- Heydrich, Reinhard **8:**448
- history chart **8:**766-767
- Holocaust **8:**841ff
- Hungary **8:**1098
- Madagascar Plan **11:**679
- Mengele's association **11:**1353
- synagogue destruction **15:**586
- Szálasi, Ferenc **15:**656
- Transnistria **15:**1335ff
- U.N. resolution **15:**1560
- Vienna forced emigration **16:**128
- *illus:*
- - text
- - Brand, Joel, Hull's cable **8:**909
- - Graz Gestapo, instructions re concentration camp **7:**528
- - trial **9:**405
Eichmann Trial **6:**521
- Israel public **9:**399ff
- K. Zetnick testimony **10:**1310
- Uruguay **16:**14
- War Crimes Trials **16:**296
- *illus:*
- - Auschwitz camp, K. Zetnick's testimony **3:**857
- - Brand, Joel, testifying **4:**1294
- - documentary film showing **9:**405
Eichmann-Transports, *see* R.S.H.A.
Eichrodt, Walther **4:**909
Eichstaett (tn., Bav.) **8:**1375
- *illus:*
- - customs tariff **15:**870
Eichthal, Baron of, *see* Seligmann, Aron Elias
EICHTHAL, GUSTAVE D' **6:**523
EICHTHAL-SELIGMANN (fam.) **6:**523
Eichthal-Seligmann, Adolph von, *see* Eichthal-Seligmann, Louis Aron
Eichthal-Seligmann, Arnold von **6:**524
Eichthal-Seligmann, Bernhard von **6:**524
Eichthal-Seligmann, Carl von **6:**524
Eichthal-Seligmann, David von **6:**524
Eichthal-Seligmann, Leonhard von, *see* Eichthal-Seligmann, Simon von
Eichthal-Seligmann, Louis Aron von **6:**524
Eichthal-Seligmann, Simon von **6:**524
Eicke, Theodor **5:**87
Eideles, Israel ben Joseph **16:**1218
Eidlitz (vill., Cz.), *see* UDLICE
EIDLITZ, LEOPOLD **6:**524
illus:
- - text
- - Temple Emanu-El (old building), N.Y.C. **3:**344
EIDLITZ, (Abraham Moses) ZERAH BEN MEIR **6:**525
EIG, ALEXANDER **6:**525
Eiger, Akiva ben Moses Guens, *see* EGER, AKIVA BEN MOSES GUENS
Eiger, Stefan Marek, *see* Napierski, Stefan
Eiges, Sydney **13:**1361
Eighteen Benedictions, *see* AMIDAH
Eighth Armored Brigade (Isr. army) **16:**323
Eighth Near East International Fair (Isr.) **9:**765
Eikhah, *see* LAMENTATIONS, BOOK OF
Eikhah Rabbah, Rabbati, Rabbeta (agg. Mid.), *see* LAMENTATIONS RABBAH
Eikhah Zuta (wk.) **16:**1515
Eikh Narim Rosh be-Ereẓ Oyevim (litur.) **2:**850
Eilat (city, Isr.), *see* ELATH
Eilat (Isr. boat) **9:**367; **9:**414; **14:**1639; **15:**1557
Eilberg, Joshua **13:**230
Eilenburg, Eliezer ben Abraham **10:**543
Eilenburg, Isaac **3:**1
Eilenburg, Judah Leib ben Obadiah **2:**134; **4:**1361
EILON (kib., Isr.) **6:**526
- statistics **1:** place list
Eilonit (sterile woman) **4:**1018; **4:**258
EILOT (kib., Isr.) **6:**526
- statistics **1:** place list
- *illus:* text
EILSHEMIUS, LOUIS **3:**599
- *illus:*
- - "Americana" (paint.) **3:**623
Eimeric, Alfonso de, *see* Abnarrabi, Vidal
Ein..., *see also under* En
Eina (savora) **14:**1584
EINAEUGLER, KAROL (Hayyim) **6:**526
Einat (kib., Isr.) **7:**597
- statistics **1:** place list
Ein Avedat (spring, Isr.) **12:**879
Ein Ayyalah (mosh., Isr.) **1:** place list
EINBECK (tn., Ger.) **6:**527
Einem, J. Justs von **8:**31
Ein Etam (spring, Er. Isr.) **3:**646; **9:**1540
EIN FASHKHAH (oasis, Er. Isr.) **6:**527
- Dead Sea scrolls **5:**1397
- *illus:* text
Einfeld, Charles **13:**1361
Einfeld, Sidney **3:**886
Ein Feshkha (oasis, Er. Isr.), *see* EIN FASHKHAH
Ein Gannim (stlmt., Er. Isr.) **9:**329; **9:**548; **13:**338
Ein-Gedi (site, Er. Isr.), *see* EN-GEDI
EIN GEV (kib., Isr.) **6:**528
- Aphek, suggested site **3:**177
- music festival **12:**672
- statistics **1:**place list
- *illus:* text
EIN HA-EMEK (mosh., Isr.) **6:**529
- statistics **1:** place list
EIN HA-ḤORESH (kib., Isr.) **6:**529
- statistics **1:** place list
Ein Ḥai (mosh., Isr.), *see* KEFAR MALAL
Ein ha-Kore (kib., Isr.), *see* SHA'AR HA-GOLAN
Ein ha-Kore (masoretic wk.) **16:**1476
Ein ha-Kore (period.) **1:**newsp. list **4:**973; **7:**189
EIN HA-MIFRAẒ (kib., Isr.) **6:**529
- statistics **1:** place list
Ein ha-Moreh (journ.) **1:** newsp. list
EIN HA-NAẒIV (kib., Isr.) **6:**529
- statistics **1:** place list
Ein ha-Oved (mosh., Isr.) **3:**968
Ein ha-Sefer (bibl.) **1:** newsp. list
EIN HA-SHELOSHAH (kib., Isr.) **6:**529
- statistics **1:** place list
Ein ha-Shivah (site, Er. Isr.), *see* TABGHA
EIN HA-SHOFET (kib., Isr.) **6:**530
- Abu Ghosh festival **12:**672
- statistics **1:**place list
- *illus:*
- - text
- - planting first trees **9:**554
Ein ha-Tannim, *see* Dragon's Well
Ein Ḥaẓevah (mosh., Isr.), *see* ḤAẒEVAH
Einheit, Die (J. soc.) **4:**521
Ein Ḥemed National Park (Isr.) **2:**183; **12:**879
- *illus:*
- - Crusader ruins **5:**1136
EIN HOD (vill., Isr.) **6:**530
- statistics **1:** place list
- *illus:* text
Einhorn, Aaron **7:**1499
EINHORN, DAVID (r.) **6:**531
- articles of faith **3:**660
- Baltimore **4:**145
- history chart **8:**766-767
- oral law **12:**1443
- prayer books **13:**990
- Reform Judaism **14:**26
- slavery debate **4:**148; **12:**932; **15:**1601
- Wise, Isaac Mayer **16:**564
- *illus:*
- - text
- - *Sinai* (1858) **15:**1600
- - writers' group **16:**813
EINHORN, DAVID (poet) **6:**532
EINHORN, IGNAZ **6:**533
- Slovakia **14:**1680
EINHORN, MAX **11:**1207
EINHORN, MOSES **6:**533
Einhorn, Yitzhak **5:**311
Ein Huṣb (spring, Isr.), *see* 'Ayn Huṣub
Einiklakh (ḥas. term) **7:**1402
EIN IRON (mosh., Isr.) **6:**533
- statistics **1:**place list
Ein Karmel (kib., Isr.) **1:**place list
EIN KE-ELOHENU (hymn) **6:**534
- *illus:* text
EIN KEREM (vill., Isr.) **16:**1324
- Beth-Cherem identified with **4:**718
- churches and monasteries **9:**583
- Jerusalem municipality **9:**1496
- vegetation, ancient **9:**1515
- War of Independence **9:**369
- *illus:*
- - Church of John the Baptist **10:**160
Ein Kerem Agricultural School (Isr.) **16:**1325
Ein Mishpat (hal. index) **10:**285
Ein Mishpat (responsa) **2:**305
Ein Sarid (stlmt., Isr.) **1:**place list
Einsatzgruppen (Nazi murder units) **14:**364; **15:**323
- Gestapo **7:**529
- Holocaust **8:**869
- War Crimes Trial **16:**293ff
Einsatz Reinhard (orgn.) **13:**764
Ein Schoen Christlich neu Spil von Kinderzucht (play) **15:**1055
Einser (Pol. Bund) **4:**1504
Ein shali'aḥ li-devar averah (leg. conc.) **2:**349; **2:**350

EIN SHEMER (kib., Isr.) **6**:534
– statistics **1**:place list
Einsiedel, M. Sybilla **8**:31
EIN-SOF (kab. term) **6**:535
– *Adam Kadmon* **2**:248
– Ba'al Shem Tov's mysticism **9**:1054
– Cordovero's system **10**:546
– dualism in Kabbalah **6**:244
– Ḥabad Hasidism **14**:1438
– Isaac the Blind **9**:35
– Kabbalah **7**:661; **10**:523; **10**:557
– Kabbalah and philosophy **10**:392
– Lurianic cosmogony **10**:589
– *Ma'arekhet ha-Elohut* **11**:638
– Nahman of Bratslav **12**:785
– philosopher's stone **2**:546
– providence **13**:1283
– Shabbatean doctrine **10**:586; **14**:1241ff
– *Sefirot* **14**:1104
– theology **15**:1108
– *illus:*
– – *Adam Kadmon* **10**:647
– – development of *Sefirot* **10**:558
– – *ẓimẓum* **10**:574
Einstaedter, Heinrich **5**:453
EINSTEIN, ALBERT **6**:535
– Hebrew University **8**:220
– Jewish Council for Russian War Relief **3**:62
– stamps **15**:335
– Watters, Leon **16**:366
– *illus:*
– – text
– – autographs **3**:914; **6**:537
– – Bronx, Albert Einstein College of Medicine **8**:1037
– – portrait (drg., H. Struck) **8**:749
– – stamp **12**:1203
– – Tchernowitz, Chaim **15**:884
– – Ussishkin, Menahem **16**:24
EINSTEIN, ALFRED **6**:538
Einstein, Berthold **10**:1384
Einstein, Carl **3**:652; **14**:1069
EINSTEIN, LEWIS **6**:539
Einstein, Max **11**:1551
EIN VERED (mosh., Isr.) **6**:540
– statistics **1**: place list
Ein Ya'akov (mosh., Isr.) **1**: place list
Ein Ya'akov (wk.) **8**:1177
– history chart **8**:766-767
– *illus:*
– – title page (Venice, 1546) **8**:73
EIN YAHAV (mosh., Isr.) **6**:540
– *illus:* text
EIN ZEITIM (loc., Isr.) **6**:540
– Ottoman period **9**:284; **9**:285; **9**:286
– Safed **14**:630
EINZIG, PAUL **6**:541
Ein Zivan (kib., Er. Isr.) **13**:1534
– statistics **1**:place list
Ein Zukunftsbild (bk.) **6**:554; **16**:1151
EIN ẒURIM (kib., Isr.) **6**:541
– statistics **1**: place list
Eire, *see* IRELAND
Eiron of Lengnau **16**:1242
EIS, ALEXANDER VON **6**:541
Eisen, Jacob J. **6**:369
Eisenbach (city, Ger.) **15**:1129
Eisenbach, Joshua, *see* Joshua of Pristik
EISENBAUM, ANTON **6**:542
Eisenberg, A. (medal.) **11**:1167
EISENBERG, AHARON ELIYAHU (Er. Isr.) **6**:542
Eisenberg, Akiva (r.) **3**:904
Eisenberg, Alfredo (law.) **10**:1503
Eisenberg, Azriel Louis (au.) **5**:451
Eisenberg, Barney, *see* Wilshur, Curley
Eisenberg, Jacob **4**:1536
Eisenberg, Philip **5**:1035
EISENBERG, SHOUL **6**:542
Eisendrath, David B. **13**:486
EISENDRATH, MAURICE NATHAN **6**:543
– Toronto **15**:1260; **15**:1261
EISENHOWER, DWIGHT DAVID **6**:543
– Israel-U.S. relations **9**:391; **9**:671
– Israel water resources **15**:1665
– Sinai withdrawal **9**:390
illus:
– – inauguration of John F. Kennedy **10**:908
EISENMAN, CHARLES (philan.) **6**:544
Eisenmann, Charles (Fr.) **10**:1496
Eisenmann, H. **14**:288
EISENMANN, LOUIS **6**:544
EISENMENGER, JOHANN ANDREAS **6**:545
– *Aleinu le-Shabbe'aḥ* **2**:557
– Hebraists **8**:31
– history chart **8**:766-767
– Wertheimer, Samson **16**:458
Eisenschimel, Jindřich **13**:346
EISENSTADT (city, Aus.) **6**:546
– "Ash," abbreviation for **3**:693
– museums **12**:539
– *illus:* text
EISENSTADT, ABRAHAM SELDIN **8**:545
Eisenstadt, Abraham Ẓevi **6**:549
EISENSTADT, ABRAHAM ẒEVI HIRSCH BEN JACOB **6**:548
– *Shulḥan Arukh* **14**:1477
Eisenstadt, Benjamin **6**:549
Eisenstadt, David **7**:1550; **14**:1620
EISENSTADT, ISAIAH (Isay) **6**:549
Eisenstadt, I. T. **14**:526, 1491
EISENSTADT, MEIR (Maharam Esh) **6**:549
– *ḥiddushim* **8**:467
– Prossnitz, Judah Leib **13**:1241
– Shabbateanism **14**:1246
EISENSTADT, MENAHEM ẒEVI **6**:550
– Naḥmanides **15**:521
Eisenstadt, Michael (polit.) **5**:1549
Eisenstadt, Michael (r., Belor.) **10**:1106
Eisenstadt, Moses **10**:1106
EISENSTADT, MOSES ELEAZAR **6**:550
Eisenstadt, Samuel **3**:395
EISENSTADT, SAMUEL NOAH **6**:551
Eisenstadt, Yehoshua, *see* Barzillai, Yehoshua
Eisenstadt, Ẓevi Hirsch (r., Belor.) **12**:70
EISENSTADTER, MEIR BEN JUDAH LEIB **6**:551
– Silberstein, David Judah Leib **14**:1535
Eisenstadter, Menahem **6**:552
Eisenstadt-Levinson, Lyuba **6**:549
EISENSTAEDT, ALFRED **6**:552
Eisenstat, Harry **15**:301
EISENSTEIN, FERDINAND GOTTHOLD **11**:1124
Eisenstein, Ikey **13**:1617
EISENSTEIN, IRA **6**:552
EISENSTEIN, JUDAH DAVID **6**:552
– Hebrew literature **8**:210
Eisenstein, Pesach **12**:1514
EISENSTEIN, SERGEI MIKHAILOVICH **6**:553
Eisentraut, Alexius, *see* Sancto, Aquilino
Eisiba (anc. site, Isr.) **7**:1531
Eisik, Moses ben Yiẓḥak, *see* Moses ben Yiẓḥak Eisik
Eisikovits, Max **14**:415
Eisinger, Roger, *see* EYDOUX, EMMANUEL
Eisiskes (city, Lith.) **11**:367
Eisland, R. **14**:1214
EISLER, EDMUND MENAHEM **6**:553
– utopian Zionism **16**:1151
EISLER, GERHART **6**:554
EISLER, HANNS **6**:554
EISLER, MÁTYÁS **6**:555
EISLER, MORITZ **6**:555
EISLER, ROBERT **6**:555
EISLER, RUDOLF **6**:555
Eisler, Ruth, *see* FISCHER, RUTH
Eisman, David Yakovlevich, *see* AIZMAN, DAVID YAKOVLEVICH
Eisman, Hy **5**:216
Eismann, David, *see* AIZMAN, DAVID YAKOVLEVICH
Eismann, David **6**:556
EISMANN, MOSES **6**:556
Eisner, A. **7**:1058
EISNER, KURT **6**:556
– German politics **8**:737
EISNER, MARK **6**:557
Eisner, Pavel **5**:1193; **5**:1209
Eisner, Will **5**:216
EISSFELDT, OTTO **6**:557
– Genesis, Book of **7**:390
– Numbers, Book of **12**:1253
EISSLER, KURT R. **6**:558
Eissler, Ruth **6**:558
Eitan, A. **9**:1254ff
Eitan, Yisrael **16**:1653
Eitanim (hospital, Isr.) **1**:place list
Eitanim (journ.)**1**:newsp. list
EITINGER, LEO S. **6**:558
EITINGON, MAX **6**:559
– psychiatry **13**:1338
Eitingon Psychoanalytical Institute, *see* Psychoanalytical Institute
Eitington, Motty **7**:225
Eitington-Schild (bsmn.) **7**:225
Eizel Ḥarif, *see* SHAPIRA, JOSHUA ISAAC BEN JEHIEL
E. J. Korvette (store, U.S.) **5**:1546
Ekallâtum (Mesop.) **16**:1495
Ekdippa (loc., Er. Isr.), *see* ACHZIB
Eked (period.) **1**: newsp. list
Eked (publ. firm, Isr.) **13**:1378
Ekelung, Vilhelm **14**:930
Ekphonesis (pub. reading, Scriptures) **9**:1145
EKRON (Phil. city) **6**:559
– Beth-Shemesh, road **4**:773
– Hasmoneans **8**:630
Ekron (stlmt., Er. Isr.), *see* MAZKERET BATYAH
Ekron (tn., Kurd.), *see* AKRA
Eksati, Boula, *see* Ashkenazi, Boula
Ekstein, Rudolf **13**:1340
El (name of God) **7**:674
El (deity) **4**:9
– Asherah, consort of **3**:704
ELAH (bib. fig.) **6**:560
– Gibbethon **7**:549
– history **8**:595
– history chart **8**:766-767
Elah valley (Isr.) **9**:587; **14**:911
El Al (mosh., Isr.) **1**:place list
EL AL (airline) **6**:560
– Israel **9**:837, 840
– P.F.L.P. **2**:620; **9**:416
– *illus:* text
– – Boeing 707 **9**:838
– – stamp **9**:844-845
El Al (period.) **16**:348
Elam (fam.) **6**:1040
ELAM (reg., Iran) **6**:562
– Chedorlaomer **5**:370
– cuneiform script **16**:661
– diaspora **6**:11
– Jeremiah's oracle **9**:1351
– Mesopotamia **16**:1484
– Persians **13**:302,308
– Sargon II **14**:880
– Semites **14**:1148
– Shushan **14**:1482
– Ur **16**:3
– *see also:* PERSIA
EL-AMARNA (city, Egy.) **6**:564
– *see also:* TELL EL-AMARNA LETTERS
El Amigo de la Familia (period.) **13**:1038
El Amigo del Pueblo (period.) **4**:427; **16**:888
Elamite (lang.) **6**:562; **13**:302
El-Aqsa (msq.) *see* Al-Aqsa
EL-ARISH (tn., Sinai) **6**:564
– Chamberlain, Joseph **4**:949
– Sinai campaign **14**:1606
– Six-Day War **9**:408; **14**:1629
– Yannai, Alexander **9**:120
– *illus:* text
– – Jewish Legion, 1918 **9**:335,517
– *see also:* EGYPT, BROOK OF
El-Arish Project (for settlement of Jews) **6**:565
– Greenberg, Leopold **7**:905
– settlement plan **10**:141; **16**:1072
– Zionist Congress **16**:1168
– *illus:*
– – Herzl with commission **16**:1072
ELASA (tn., Er. Isr.) **6**:566
ELASAH (s., Shaphan) **6**:566
– Ahikam **2**:460
ELATH (Eilat; tn., Er. Isr.) **6**:566
– airport **9**:837
– Arab conquest of Ereẓ Israel **9**:260; **9**:264
– Aramaic ostraca **16**:668
– Crusades **9**:268
– distillation plant **9**:771
– Eilot **6**:526
– El-Paran **13**:88
– Ezion-Geber **6**:1103
– geology **9**:194
– harbor **9**:832
– ibex **9**:226
– Mamre **11**:839
– mountains **9**:132
– Operation Uvdah **9**:377
– power station **9**:793
– Red Sea **14**:15
– Sinai campaign **14**:1605; **14**:1607
– statistics **1**: place list
– stone corals **5**:959
– War of Independence **16**:331
– *illus:*
– – text
– – Amudei Amram **9**:213
– – Arkia airplane **9**:839
– – Ben-Gurion opening road **9**:380
– – coast, aerial view **9**:129
– – coral fauna **9**:172-173
– – Gemini II photograph **14**:15
– – Zarchin desalination plant **9**:772
– *see also:* AKABA
ELATH, ELIAHU **6**:570
– Magen David Adom **11**:697
– *illus:*
– – Board of Deputies celebration **6**:773
Elath Mountains (Isr.) **9**:592; **12**:925
– *illus:*
– – canyon **9**:149
El Avenir (journ.) **13**:1039
Elazar, David **13**:48; **14**:1630
Elazari-Volcani, Meir, *see* Wilkansky, Meir
ELAZARI-VOLCANI, YIẒḤAK **6**:571
– moshav **12**:435
El-Azariyya (vill., Er. Isr.), *see* Azariyya, al-
El Azno (journ.) **13**:1038
El-Barchilon, Abraham, *see* ABRAHAM EL-BARCHILON
El Barukh (litur.) **12**:187
Elbasan (city, Alb.) **2**:522
ELBAZ (fam.) **6**:572

- Fez **6:**1257
Elbaz, Amram **6:**572
Elbaz, André **13:**118
Elbaz, Jacob **6:**572
Elbaz, Jekutiel Michael **2:**80
Elbaz, Judah **6:**572
Elbaz, Moses ben Maimon of Tarudant **6:**572
Elbaz, Raphael Moses **2:**516; **6:**572
Elbaz, Samuel **6:**572
Elbaz, Samuel ben Isaac (16th cent.) **6:**572
Elbaz, Samuel ben Isaac (17/18 cent.) **6:**485
Elberfeld (tn., Ger.) **16:**677
Elberfeld Bible **4:**873
El Berit (name of God) **7:**678
El-Beth-El (loc., Er. Isr.), *see* BET(H)-EL
El-Bina (site, Isr.) **4:**713
Elbing (concen. camp) **15:**464
El-Bire (vill., Isr.), *see* Al-Bīra
ELBLAG (Elbing; city, Pol.) **6:**572
Elbogen (name), *see also* Katzenellenbogen
ELBOGEN, ISMAR **6:**573
El-Burj (loc., Er. Isr.) **6:**172
El Burlon (journ.) **13:**1039
ELCAN, MARCUS **6:**574
Elcan, Phila **6:**574
Elchanowicz, Aba, *see* ELHANANI, ABA
Elchasai (J.-Chr. ldr.), *see* Elxai
Elchasaites (J. Chr. sect) **10:**39
ELCHE (city, Sp.) **6:**574
El Cid, *see* Cid, El
ELDAD, ISRAEL **6:**574
- Leḥi **11:**464
ELDAD AND MEDAD (bib. figs.) **6:**575
- Moses **12:**388
- *illus:* text
ELDAD HA-DANI (trav.) **6:**576
- African Jews **2:**332
- Falashas **6:**1153
- Hebrew fiction **6:**1262
- Jewish literature **11:**350
- Sambatyon **14:**763
- Ten Lost Tribes **15:**1005
- Ẓemaḥ ben Ḥayyim **7:**317; **16:**985
ELDER **6:**578
- *eglah arufah* **6:**475ff
- endowments **8:**284
- fast proclamation **6:**1189; **6:**1192
- *gerusia* **8:**626; **9:**1389
- *ḥaliẓah* **11:**122
- legal traditions **15:**1311
- Moses **12:**377
- ordination **14:**1140
- *soferim* **15:**80
- structure of ancient Israel **8:**610ff
- tax evasion judgement **8:**1306
- *tovei ha-ir* court **12:**128
- *see also:* AGE AND THE AGED; AM HA-AREẒ; BATLANIM; TITLES
Elder, Rebellious, *see* ZAKEN MAMRE
Elders of Bathyra (fam.), *see* BATHYRA, SONS OF
Elders of Israel (clan ldrs., kdm. of Israel) **2:**438
ELDERS OF ZION, PROTOCOLS OF THE LEARNED **6:**581
- A.J.C. **2:**823
- Alliance Israélite Universelle **2:**653
- Arab anti-Semitism **3:**138
- Barruel, Augustin **4:**262
- Berne trial **4:**675
- "elders" anti-Semitic term **6:**580
- United States **15:**1653
- *illus:*
- - text
- - Egyptian pamphlet (1967) **3:**156
Eldridge, P. **16:**262
Eleagabalus (Rom. emp.) **9:**1406
ELEALEH (bib. tn., Transj.) **6:**583
Eleasah (tn., Er. Isr.), *see* ELASA
Eleazar (name), *see also* Eliezer
ELEAZAR (s. of Aaron) **6:**583
- Moses **12:**383
- Samaritan priesthood **14:**727; **14:**734
Eleazar (Pharisee ldr.) **14:**730
ELEAZAR (2nd cent. B.C.E., mart.) **6:**584
- *kiddush ha-Shem* **10:**981
- *illus:*
- - temptation and death **8:**671
Eleazar (tan.), *see* ELEAZAR BEN SHAMMUA
Eleazar (amora), *see* ELEAZAR BEN PEDAT
Eleazar (s. of Haggai) **7:**1114;
Eleazar (of Saragossa; 12th cent.) **14:**859
ELEAZAR (fam.) **6:**584
- Jacob ben Eleazar **9:**1216
Eleazar, Alaçar (12th cent.) **6:**584
Eleazar, Alaçar ben Alazrach (13th cent.) **6:**584
Eleazar, Ezdra **6:**584
Eleazar, Judah **6:**584
Eleazar, Solomon **6:**584
Eleazar Bartukha **14:**1508
Eleazar ben Abun **13:**579
Eleazar ben Amram **14:**754
ELEAZAR BEN ANANIAS **6:**585
- Bet Shammai **4:**739
- Kamẓa legend **10:**732
- Menahem **11:**1313
- Wicked Priest **16:**486
ELEAZAR BEN ARAKH (1st cent., tan.) **6:**585
Eleazar ben Arakh (2nd cent., tan.), *see* NEHORAI
ELEAZAR BEN AZARIAH (tan.) **6:**586
- pig **13:**507
- *illus:*
- - *Rylands Spanish Haggadah* **6:** *fcg.* 619
Eleazar ben Boethus (h.pr.) **4:**1169; **14:**1554
ELEAZAR BEN DAMMA (tan.) **6:**587
ELEAZAR BEN DINAI **6:**588
- Alexander the Zealot **2:**587
- *Ḥullin* **8:**1070
- magic **11:**706
Eleazar ben Enoch **13:**1410
ELEAZAR BEN ḤALFON HA-KOHEN **6:**588
ELEAZAR BEN HANANIAH BEN HEZEKIAH (tan.) **6:**589
- *Megillat Ta'anit* **11:**1230
- Roman sacrifices **8:**639
ELEAZAR BEN ḤARSOM (h. pr.) **6:**589
- Bar Kokhba **11:**1424
- riches **2:**395
Eleazar ben Hillel (gaon) **7:**321
Eleazar ben Ḥisma (tan.), *see* ELEAZAR ḤISMA
ELEAZAR BEN JACOB HA-BAVLI **6:**590
- Daniel Ibn Abī Rabī' **5:**1294
- Hebrew dialect **16:**1595, 1606
- Saruj **14:**890
ELEAZAR BEN JAIR **6:**590
- Hezekiah the Zealot **8:**455
- Sicarii **14:**1492
- Teacher of Righteousness **15:**887
- Zealot dynastic leadership **16:**949
- *illus:*
- - text
- - Masada ostracon **11:**513
- *see also:* MASADA
ELEAZAR BEN JUDAH OF BARTOTA (tan.) **6:**592
ELEAZAR BEN JUDAH OF WORMS **6:**592
- Aaron of Baghdad **2:**21
- Abulafia, Abraham **2:**186
- agriculture **2:**401
- chronicle **5:**1145
- codification of law **11:**331
- *gematria* **7:**372
- history chart **8:**766-767
- Jewish mysticism **10:**516; **10:**517ff
- Kalonymus **10:**719
- learning and merits **8:**688
- mystical literature **11:**347
- *Sefer Yeẓirah* **16:**787
- self-punishment **13:**1389
- Worms **16:**645
Eleazar ben Judan (3rd cent. C.E.) **10:**878
ELEAZAR BEN MATTATHIAS (Hasm.) **6:**594
ELEAZAR BEN MATYA (tan.) **6:**594
Eleazar ben Meir ben Isaac **12:**1470
ELEAZAR BEN MOSES HA-DARSHAN OF WUERZBURG **6:**595
ELEAZAR BEN PARTA (tan.) **6:**595
ELEAZAR BEN PEDAT (amora) **6:**596
- Yose ben Zimra **16:**857
Eleazar ben Pinḥas ben Joseph **14:**753; **14:**757
Eleazar ben Samuel of Brody **2:**899
- medal **11:**1173
- portrait painting **3:**539
- *illus:*
- - Amsterdam medal **11:**1169
ELEAZAR BEN SHAMMUA (tan.) **6:**598
- Torah **15:**1239
ELEAZAR BEN SIMEON (Zealot) **6:**598
- Menahem the Galilean **16:**949
ELEAZAR BEN SIMEON (tan.) **6:**599
- Akhbarei **2:**487
- Lag ba-Omer **8:**495
- Meron tomb **8:**921; **11:**1391
- Simeon bar Yoḥai **14:**1552
- Zohar **16:**1200
Eleazar ben Solomon of Virbalis **7:**924
ELEAZAR BEN YOSE (tan.) **6:**599
- Samaritans **13:**791
ELEAZAR BEN YOSE (amora) **6:**600
ELEAZAR BEN ZADOK (1/2 cent., tan.) **6:**600
ELEAZAR BEN ZADOK (2nd cent., tan.) **6:**601
Eleazar ben Ẓemaḥ **8:**1458
Eleazar ha-Bavli, *see* ELEAZAR BEN JACOB HA-BAVLI
Eleazar ha-Darshan, *see* ELEAZAR BEN MOSES HA-DARSHAN OF WUERZBURG
Eleazar ha-Ḥazzan **13:**579
Eleazar ha-Kallir, *see* KALLIR, ELEAZAR
ELEAZAR HA-KAPPAR (tan.) **6:**601
- *aggadah* **12:**906
Eleazar ha-Kappar Beribbi, *see* BAR KAPPARA
Eleazar ha-Kohen (the Pious; 10th cent.) **10:**720
Eleazar ha-Moda'i (tan.), *see* ELEAZAR OF MODI'IN
Eleazar he-Ḥazzan of Speyer **10:**719
ELEAZAR ḤISMA (tan.) **6:**602
Eleazar ibn Ardut of Huesca, *see* Ardut, Eleazar ibn
Eleazar Nisan of Drogobych, *see* Teitelbaum, Eleazar Nisan
Eleazar of Bartota, *see* ELEAZAR BEN JUDAH OF BARTOTA
Eleazar of Brody, *see* Eleazar ben Samuel of Brody
ELEAZAR OF MODI'IN (tan.) **6:**603
- Bar Kokhba revolt **4:**236
Eleazar of Worms, *see* ELEAZAR BEN JUDAH OF WORMS
Eleazar of Wuerzburg, *see* ELEAZAR BEN MOSES HA-DARSHAN OF WUERZBURG
Eleazar Solomon ben Ephraim Taub (of Wolomin) **10:**859
Eleazar son of Onias I (h. pr.) **12:**1402; **14:**1568
El Eco Judaico (period.) **13:**1039
Elected Assembly (legis., Er. Isr.), *see* Asefat ha-Nivḥarim
Election of Israel, Doctrine of, *see* CHOSEN PEOPLE
Electoral system in Israel **9:**615
- *illus:*
- - Jewish and Arab voters, 1949-69 (table) **9:**1025
- - Knesset, results of elections, 1949-69 (table) **9:**667
- - polling committee **9:**619
- *see also:* KNESSET
Electricity **14:**567
ELECTRICITY IN ISRAEL **9:**790
- historical survey **9:**393ff
- industry **9:**823
Electricity Corporation (Isr.) **9:**821
Elef Alfin (poem) **2:**231; **4:**371; **10:**1140; **11:**326
Elegy, *see* KINAH
ELEK, ARTUR **8:**1084
Elek, Paul **13:**1371
El Elyon (name of God) **7:**675
Elements, four **13:**422
- Aristotelianism **13:**430
- nature **12:**888ff
- *Ru'aḥ ha-Kodesh* **14:**366
- *Sefer Yezirah* **16:**783
- *Sefirot* **10:**575
- *illus:*
- - *Ma'aseh Tuviyyah* (1721) **5:**983
Eleona church (Jer.) **9:**1406
ELEPHANT **6:**603
- dietary laws **6:**32
- fauna of Israel **9:**225
- Hellenistic army **8:**294
- *illus:* text
- *see also:* IVORY
Elephantiasis (disease), *see* Filariasis
ELEPHANTINE (city, Egy.) **6:**604
- *Contents:*
- - History, Jewish Colony **6:**605
- - Legal Papyri **6:**606
- - Religion of the Jews **6:**608
- - Military Colony Organization **6:**609
- African Jews **2:**331
- *Aḥikar, Book of* **2:**460
- Aramaic documents **3:**265
- Aramaic language **2:**686
- Aramean religion **3:**256
- Artaxerxes **8:**618ff
- divorce **6:**124
- economic life **16:**1270,1271
- Hebrew mss **11:**900
- history chart **8:**766-767
- letters **11:**56
- Manasseh's army **11:**852
- mercenaries, Jewish **16:**278
- Mond, Sir Robert **12:**241
- moneylending **12:**246
- papyri **13:**70; **16:**659
- sacrifices **14:**606
- Yeb archive **3:**374
- *illus:*
- - text
- - deed, Aramaic **3:**284;**8:**617
- - papyri script **2:**684
Elesh (r., Babyl.) **12:**774
Eleutheropolis (anc. city, Isr.) **5:**720
- Bet Guvrin **4:**731

Elezar bar Itzhak Segal, *see* Isaacs, Lazarus
Elfelt (fam.) **12:**39
ELFENBEIN, ISRAEL **6:**610
ʾElgavish (gem) **13:**1011
Elgin (city, Ill.) **8:**1256
El Greco museum (Toledo, Sp.) **2:**193
Elḥa ben David, *see* GAFFAREL, JACQUES
El ha-Makor (polit. orgn.) **7:**1322
El Ḥammah (Hamme; site, Er. Isr.), *see* HAMMAT-GADER
ELHANAN (bib. fig.; s., Dodo) **6:**611
ELHANAN (bib. fig.; s., Jaare-Oregim) **6:**611
Elhanan (gaon) **7:**323
Elḥanan (J. pope) **6:**1384; **13:**853; **14:**1551
ELHANAN (apos.) **6:**611
Elhanan "Ba'al ha-Kabbalah" of Vienna **4:**6; **16:**907
Elhanan Ba'al Shem Tov **4:**7
ELḤANAN BEN HUSHIEL **6:**611
ELHANAN BEN ISAAC OF DAMPIERRE (tos.) **6:**612
ELḤANAN BEN SHEMARIAH **6:**612
– gaonate, Egypt **7:**323
– Solomon ben Judah **15:**123
ELḤANAN BEN YAKAR **6:**612
– Jewish mysticism **10:**517
– *Sefer Yeẓirah* **16:**787
Elhanan ben Ẓevi **10:**244
Elhanan de Candida **15:**1380
ELHANANI, ABA **3:**363
Elḥanani, Aryeh **16:**697
Elhanan of Dampierre, *see* ELHANAN BEN ISAAC OF DAMPIERRE
Elhanan of Danzig **5:**615
Elhanan of London, *see* ELHANAN BEN YAKAR
Elhanan Sagi Nahor **13:**1608
ʾEl-ha-Neḥilot (Psalm superscription) **13:**1321
El Heraldo (pub.) **16:**1126
ELI (pr.) **6:**613
– Hophni and Phinehas **8:**970
– in the Arts **14:**784
– priesthood **13:**1072ff
– Samaritans **14:**727
– Samuel **14:**780
Eli II (gaon) **7:**321
Elia (tn., Er. Isr.), *see* JERUSALEM
Elia, Raoul **13:**1037
Eliab (bib. fig.) **5:**1311
Eliab of Norwich, *see* JURNET OF NORWICH
Eliachar (fam.), *see also* Elyashar
Eliachar, Eliyahu **6:**693
Eliachar, Menashe **9:**829
Eliachar, Yiẓḥak **9:**829
Elia di Sabato of Fermo, *see* ELIJAH BEN SHABBETAI BE'ER
Eliah (cmty. ldr., Kurd.) **16:**920
Eliakim (bib. fig.) **8:**481; **14:**1330
Eliakim (k. of Judah), *see* JEHOIAKIM
Eliakim (h. pr.), *see* ALCIMUS
Eliakim (14th cent., Ger.) **15:**264
Eliakim (paytan, Crimea) **13:**579
Eliakim, Moses **5:**224
Eliakim Alkimos (h. pr.), *see* ALCIMUS
Eliakim ben Abraham (paytan) **13:**579
Eliakim ben Abraham (kab.), *see* HART, JACOB
Eliakim ben Joseph **3:**522
Eliakim ben Meshullam ha-Levi **9:**18; **15:**263
ELIAKIM GOETZ BEN MEIR **6:**614
Eliam (bib. fig.) **4:**322
ELIANO, GIOVANNI BATTISTA **6:**615
– Hebrew printing **14:**252
Eliano, Vittorio **6:**615; **11:**133
– Ottolenghi dispute **5:**1077; **12:**1525
– Zohar **16:**1212
Elias (15th cent., Ger.) **6:**736
Elias (fam.) **5:**40
Elias, Abraham **8:**1356
ELIAS, EDUARD **10:**306; **10:**310
Elias, Henry Hart **15:**302
Elias, Jacob **11:**498
ELIAS, JOSEPH **6:**615
Elias, Judah (of Hanover) **12:**558; **12:**633; **12:**752
Elias, Julius **7:**452
Elias, Meir **4:**92
ELIAS, NEY **6:**615
– travels **15:**1351
Elias, Samuel **15:**305
– *illus:*
– caricature **15:**305
Eliasaph ben Samuel ha-Nagid **2:**631; **14:**818
Elias ben Sabbetai of Bologna **11:**472
Eliasberg, Alexander **7:**452
Eliasberg, Jonathan **6:**616
Eliasberg, Joseph Elijah **15:**426
ELIASBERG, MORDECAI **6:**615
– Salanter, Israel **11:**280
Eliaschoff, J. **16:**1165
ELIASH, MORDECAI **6:**616
– Kefar Mordekhai **10:**889
ELIASHIB (bib. name) **6:**617
– Jerusalem's wall **8:**621ff
– Kanah **10:**733
– Sanballat **14:**824
– Temple **15:**957
– Tobiads **15:**1179
Eliashib, son of Eshyahu **3:**249
– *illus:*
– – Arad seal **16:**660
– – Ostracon **3:**248,373
Eliashiv, Shmuel **7:**191
ELIASHOV, SOLOMON BEN ḤAYYIM **6:**617
Eliashov, Y. A. **7:**1534
ELIAS LE EVESKE **6:**618
– Archpresbyter **3:**398
Elias of Chippenham **16:**1289
Elias Sabot, *see* ELIJAH BEN SHABBETAI BE'ER
Eliav, Arie L. **14:**499, 505
ELIAV, BINYAMIN **1:**29
– Revisionist Party **14:**131
– *illus:*
– – Brit Trumpeldor **10:**1468
Eliaz, Raphael **14:**1264
Eli ben Ezekiel, *see* Eli ha-Kohen ben Ezekiel of Fostat
Eli ben Judah ha-Nazir **10:**344
Eli ben Jafni **14:**751
Eli ben Zechariah (gaon), *see* ALI BEN ZECHARIAH
Eliberis (tn., Sp.), *see* ELVIRA
ELIEL, ERNEST LUDWIG **5:**381
Eliezer (name), *see also* Eleazar
ELIEZER (steward of Abraham) **6:**618
– adoption **2:**298
– *aggadah* **4:**195
– in the Arts **9:**7
– Bethuel **4:**749
– Og **12:**1341
– Rebekah **13:**1602
Eliezer (s., Moses) **12:**374; **16:**1182
Eliezer (prophet, s., Dodavahu) **11:**954; **15:**1296
Eliezer (of Sens; tos.) **14:**1163
Eliezer (r., Mor.) **14:**682
Eliezer ben Abraham Ḥayyim **7:**929
Eliezer ben David, *see* BEDARIDA, GUIDO
Eliezer ben Elijah ha-Rofeh Ashkenazi **7:**876
Eliezer ben Ephraim **13:**579
Eliezer ben Faruch **3:**802
ELIEZER BEN HYRCANUS (tan.) **6:**619
– Akiva **2:**488; **2:**489
– cynic *chriae* **5:**1177
– dispute **15:**1024
– Johanan ben Zakkai **9:**242
– laws for goldsmithery **7:**739
– lost tribes **15:**1005
– Lydda academy **2:**202
– magic **11:**706
– Mishnah **12:**99
– proselytes **13:**1185
– views not usually followed **5:**891
ELIEZER BEN ISAAC (print.) **6:**623
– publisher **13:**1377
Eliezer ben Isaac of Krotoszyn **12:**1244
ELIEZER BEN ISAAC OF WORMS **6:**623
– ethical wills **11:**345
– Kalonymus **10:**719
– *Orḥot Ḥayyim* **12:**1457; **16:**531
ELIEZER BEN JACOB (1st cent., tan.) **6:**624
– decision in accord with **5:**891
– *Kilayim* **10:**1000
– Temple **15:**969
ELIEZER BEN JACOB (2nd cent., tan.) **6:**624
ELIEZER BEN JACOB HA-LEVI OF TARNOGROD **6:**625
ELIEZER BEN JOEL HA-LEVI OF BONN **6:**625
– codification of law **5:**643
– *ḥiddushim* **8:**467
Eliezer ben Joseph **5:**475
Eliezer ben Judah **5:**332
ELIEZER BEN MANASSEH BEN BARUCH **6:**626
ELIEZER BEN MEIR HA-LEVI OF PINSK **6:**626
– Pinsk **13:**541
ELIEZER BEN NATHAN OF MAINZ **6:**626
– "Ashkenazim" **3:**720
– Baruch of Regensburg **4:**278
– economic life **16:**1289
– responsa **14:**86
– Rhineland massacres **8:**555
Eliezer ben Po'irah **14:**640
Eliezer ben Rabbenu Gershom **7:**512
ELIEZER BEN SAMSON **6:**628
Eliezer ben Samuel (11th cent.) **11:**1449
Eliezer ben Samuel (15th cent.) **8:**1325
Eliezer ben Samuel (18th cent.) **16:**1232
ELIEZER BEN SAMUEL HA-LEVI **6:**628
– ethical wills **11:**346
ELIEZER BEN SAMUEL OF METZ **6:**628
– codification of law **11:**331
ELIEZER BEN SAMUEL OF VERONA **6:**629
– Avigdor ha-Kohen **3:**963
Eliezer ben Shabbetai Don Yaḥya, *see* Don Yaḥya, Eliezer
Eliezer ben Solomon, *see* ELIEZER OF TOUQUES
ELIEZER BEN YOSE HA-GELILI (tan.) **6:**629
– Bible interpretation **8:**1418
– Torah **15:**1236
Eliezer ben Zadok (tan.), *see* ELEAZAR BEN ZADOK
Eliezer ben Ẓevi Hirsch **15:**796
Eliezer de Mordo **13:**579
ELIEZER FISCHEL BEN ISAAC OF STRZYZOW **6:**630
Eliezer the Great (tan.), *see* ELIEZER BEN HYRCANUS
Eliezer the Great, Testament of (wk.), *see Orḥot Ḥayyim*
Eliezer ha-Gadol, *see* ELIEZER BEN ISAAC OF WORMS
Eliezer ha-Levi of Pinsk, *see* ELIEZER BEN MEIR HA-LEVI OF PINSK
Eliezer ha-Levi of Tarnograd, *see* ELIEZER BEN JACOB HA-LEVI OF TARNOGROD
Eliezer ha-Kappar (tan.), *see* ELEAZAR HA-KAPPAR
Eliezer ibn Nahum **13:**93
Eliezer Leizer ben Judah Loeb **13:**579
Eliezer Maẓli'aḥ ben Abraham Kohen **14:**171
Eliezer Mendel ben Mordecai **12:**424
ELIEZER OF BEAUGENCY **6:**630
– apologetics **3:**195
– Bible exegesis **4:**893
– meaning of exile **7:**284ff
Eliezer of Bonn, *see* ELIEZER BEN JOEL HA-LEVI OF BONN
Eliezer of Damascus (steward of Abraham), *see* ELIEZER
Eliezer of Dzieckowitz (Dzikow) **14:**260
Eliezer of Krotoszyn, *see* Eliezer ben Isaac of Krotoszyn
Eliezer of Mainz (11th cent.), *see* ELIEZER BEN NATHAN OF MAINZ
Eliezer of Mainz (14th cent.), *see* ELIEZER BEN SAMUEL HA-LEVI
Eliezer of Mareshah, *see* Eliezer (prophet, s., Dodavahu)
Eliezer of Metz, *see* ELIEZER BEN SAMUEL OF METZ
Eliezer of Muehlhausen **12:**498
Eliezer of Ozopol **15:**439
Eliezer of Passua **6:**660
Eliezer of Pinsk, *see* ELIEZER BEN MEIR HA-LEVI OF PINSK
Eliezer of Sens, *see* Eliezer (of Sens; tos.)
Eliezer of Strzyzow, *see* ELIEZER FISCHEL BEN ISAAC OF STRZYZOW
Eliezer of Tarnograd, *see* ELIEZER BEN JACOB HA-LEVI OF TARNOGROD
ELIEZER OF TOUL (tos.) **6:**631
ELIEZER OF TOUQUES (tos.) **6:**631
– *tosafot* **15:**1281
Eliezer of Verona, *see* ELIEZER BEN SAMUEL OF VERONA
Eliezer of Viterbo **9:**1108
Eliezer of Worms, *see* ELIEZER BEN ISAAC OF WORMS
Eliezer Ẓedakah ha-Kohen **14:**747
Elifelet (mosh., Isr.) **1:** place list
Eli ha-Kohen ben Ezekiel of Fostat **15:**122
Eli ha-Levi (gaon) **7:**321
Eli Hashiveni me-Anaḥah u-Mehumah (poem) **2:**295
Elihoreph (bib. fig.) **14:**1042
ELIHU (bib. fig.) **6:**632
– Balaam **4:**123
– Job **10:**118
ELIJAH **6:**632
– *Contents:*
– – In the Bible **6:**632
– – In the Aggadah **6:**635
– – In Mysticism **6:**638
– – In Jewish Folklore **6:**638
– – In Islam **6:**640
– – In the Arts **6:**641
– Ahab **2:**438

- alchemy **2:**544
- Anan **2:**919
- circumcision **5:**568
- circumcision ceremony chair **6:**644
- Elisha **6:**665ff
- extraordinary legislation **7:**1159
- folktales **6:**1382
- Haifa cave **8:**921
- history **8:**596
- history chart **8:**766-767
- Jonadab **13:**1610
- kabbalistic view **10:**613
- Kings, Book of **10:**1027ff
- Lilith **11:**248
- messianism **6:**873ff
- Mordecai **12:**309
- Mt. Sinai pilgrimage **14:**1598
- Naboth **12:**747
- Raziel **13:**1592
- resurrection **14:**97
- social origins **7:**571
- *takkanot* **15:**718
- visions **16:**167; **16:**168
- zeal **9:**1306
- *illus:*
- - text
- - castigating Ahab **12:**747
- - cave, Mount Carmel **8:**925
- - fed by the ravens **6:**633;**7:**1300
- - heralding the Messiah **6:**863
- - humiliating prophets of Baal **6:**289
- - Messiah led into Jerusalem **11:**1409
- - reviving the widow's dead child **6:**283
- - riding into Jerusalem **7:**1086

Elijah (mart., Baden) **10:**227
Elijah (oratorio) **6:**642
ELIJAH, APOCALYPSE OF **6:**643
Elijah, Cave of **5:**186; **8:**921
ELIJAH, CHAIR OF **6:**643
- circumcision **5:**570
illus:
- - text
- - German, 18th cent. **5:**306
- - Italian, 17/18 cent **9:**1140

Elijah, Crescas (physic.) **5:**1078
ELIJAH, CUP OF (seder rit.) **6:**645
- *see also:* PASSOVER

Elijah, Synagogue of (Isr.) **15:**610
Elijah Ba'al Shem of Chelm **4:**6; **5:**371
Elijah Baḥur, *see* LEVITA, ELIJAH
ELIJAH BEN AARON BEN MOSES **6:**646
Elijah ben Abiathar **7:**323
ELIJAH BEN ABRAHAM (12th cent.) **6:**646
Elijah ben Abraham (15th cent.?) **13:**579
Elijah ben Asher, *see* LEVITA, ELIJAH
Elijah ben Azriel **16:**140
ELIJAH BEN BARUCH THE ELDER **6:**646
ELIJAH BEN BENJAMIN HA-LEVI **6:**646
- Sirillo, Solomon **14:**1618

Elijah ben Berechiah ha-Kohen, *see* ELIAS LE EVESKE
Elijah ben Berechiah ha-Nakdan **4:**597
ELIJAH BEN ELIEZER PHILOSOPH **6:**647
- *Bahir, Sefer ha-* **4:**100

ELIJAH BEN ḤAYYIM (Turk.) **6:**647
Elijah ben Ḥayyim ha-Kohen of Hochheim (Ger.) **3:**806
Elijah ben Joseph **3:**1009
ELIJAH BEN JUDAH OF PARIS **6:**648
ELIJAH BEN KALONYMUS OF LUBLIN **6:**648
ELIJAH BEN LOEB OF FULDA **6:**648
- Talmud **15:**778

Elijah ben Menahem ha-Zaken **13:**579
Elijah ben Mordecai (It.) **13:**579
Elijah ben Mordecai Ẓevi (Turk.) **14:**1222; **14:**1227; **14:**1243
ELIJAH BEN RAPHAEL SOLOMON HA-LEVI **6:**648
Elijah ben Samuel **13:**579
ELIJAH BEN SHABBETAI BE'ER **6:**649
- Pavia **13:**193
- Pope Martin V **14:**247

Elijah ben Shalom **13:**581
ELIJAH BEN SHEMAIAH **6:**649
ELIJAH BEN SOLOMON ABRAHAM HA-KOHEN OF SMYRNA **6:**649
- Bonafoux, Daniel **4:**1199
- chess **5:**403
- Kabbalah **10:**552
- Shabbateanism **14:**1244
- *illus:*
- - *Shevet Musar* (1734) **8:**959

ELIJAH BEN SOLOMON HA-KOHEN **6:**650
- David ben Daniel **5:**1349
- gaonate **7:**323
- Solomon ben Judah **15:**122

ELIJAH BEN SOLOMON ZALMAN ("Vilna Gaon") **6:**651
- *aliyah* **9:**293; **9:**514
- amulets **2:**911
- *Anim Zemirot* **3:**22
- Bacharach, Naphtali **4:**50
- Bachrach, Judah **4:**56
- disciple's travels **15:**1353
- ethical will **16:**532
- *haggahot* **7:**1109
- Ḥasidism **7:**1395ff
- Haskalah in Russia **7:**1445
- history chart **8:**766-767
- Issachar Baer ben Tanḥum **9:**1078
- Jerusalem Talmud **15:**778
- Judaism trends **10:**393
- language **16:**1399
- Lithuanian yeshivot **16:**768
- Mendel of Kotsk **10:**1223
- *Mitnaggedim* **12:**161ff
- Rivkes, Moses **14:**198
- *Sefer Yeẓirah* **16:**787
- Shneur Zalman of Lyady **14:**1432
- *Tiferet Yisrael* **11:**294
- Vilna **16:**140
- *ẓimẓum* **10:**593
- Zohar **16:**1213
- *illus:*
- - text
- - *Kol Nehi* (1798) **6:**1201
- - portrait **8:**717
- - Vilna synagogue **16:**141

ELIJAH CHELEBI HA-KOHEN OF ANATOLIA **6:**658
Elijah Cohen of Constantinople **5:**166
Elijah the Elder, *see* ELIJAH BEN BARUCH THE ELDER
Elijah Gaon, *see* ELIJAH BEN SOLOMON ZALMAN
Elijah ha-Kohen ha-Ittamari, *see* ELIJAH BEN SOLOMON ABRAHAM HA-KOHEN OF SMYRNA
Elijah ha-Kohen of Banias **4:**163
Elijah ha-Levi ha-Zaken **9:**1088
Elijah Ḥasid **14:**199
Elijah Ḥayyim ben Benjamin of Gennazano, *see* GENNAZANO, ELIJAH ḤAYYIM BEN BENJAMIN OF
ELIJAH MENAHEM BEN MOSES **6:**658
- Jacob ben Judah **9:**1220
- *geneal. table:* text

Elijah Obadiah ben Abraham ha-Levi **10:**859
Elijah of Anatolia, *see* ELIJAH CHELEBI HA-KOHEN OF ANATOLIA
Elijah of Buttrio **13:**581
Elijah of Candia, *see* ELIJAH BEN ELIEZER PHILOSOPH
Elijah of Chelm **7:**755
ELIJAH OF FERRARA **6:**659
- *aliyah* **9:**512
- Ereẓ Israel **9:**281

Elijah of Fulda, *see* ELIJAH BEN LOEB OF FULDA
Elijah of Lublin, *see* ELIJAH BEN KALONYMUS OF LUBLIN
Elijah of Montalto **13:**107
Elijah of Paris, *see* ELIJAH BEN JUDAH OF PARIS
ELIJAH OF PESARO **6:**659
- travels **15:**1352

ELIJAH OF PRAGUE **6:**660
Elijah of Smyrna, *see* ELIJAH BEN SOLOMON ABRAHAM HA-KOHEN OF SMYRNA
Elijah of Vesoul, *see* Héliot of Vesoul
Elijah of Vilna, *see* ELIJAH BEN SOLOMON ZALMAN
Elijah Perez **15:**796
ELIJAH PHINEHAS BEN MEIR **6:**660
ELIMELECH (bib. fig.) **6:**661
- Ruth, Book of **14:**518

Elimelech of Grodzisk **7:**929; **11:**1260
ELIMELECH OF LYZHANSK **6:**661
- doctrine of *ẓaddikism* **7:**1406
- grave in Lezajsk **11:**184ff
- Zusya of Hanipoli **16:**1243

ELION, JACQUES **6:**663
- *illus:*
- - Amsterdam Jewish Orphanage medal **11:**1165,1166

Elion, Samuel Cohen **6:**663; **11:**1167
ELIONAEUS, SON OF CANTHERAS (h. pr.) **6:**663
- Kimḥit **10:**1009
- Simeon ben Boethus **14:**1554

ELIOT, GEORGE **6:**663
- Guedalla, Haim **7:**957
- history chart **8:**766-767
- Zionism **16:**1070
- *illus:* text

Eliot, John **4:**888
Eliot, T. S. **6:**781; **15:**1571
Eliowitz, Abraham **15:**308
ELIPHAZ (bib. figs.) **6:**664
- Job, Book of **10:**113
- *illus:*
- - consoling Job **4:**934

Eliran, Ran (sing.) **12:**693
Eliraz, Yisrael **6:**206
Elisabeth (m., John the Baptist) **16:**1324
Elisabeth (q. of the Belgians) **4:**421
Elisabeth, Abbess of Pfalz **8:**31
Elisabeth Amalie Eugenie (emp. of Aus.) **6:**1159
Elisabethville (city, Congo), *see* Lubumbashi
Elis bat Mordecai of Slutzk **11:**358
ELISHA (bib. prophet) **6:**665
- Abel-Meholah **2:**62
- Elijah **6:**634ff
- in the Arts **6:**640
- Kings, Book of **10:**1027ff
- Naaman **12:**733
- *illus:*
- - text
- - Naaman **10:**1021
- *see also:* GEHAZI

Elisha, Spring of (Er. Isr.), *see* ʿAyn al-Sulṭān
ELISHA BA'AL KENAFAYIM **6:**667
Elisha ben Abraham (ling., Turk.) **16:**1361
ELISHA BEN ABRAHAM (r.) **6:**668
ELISHA BEN AVUYAH **6:**668
- apostasy cause **14:**135
- *Avot de-Rabbi Nathan* **3:**985
- gnostic dualism **10:**506
- Greek influence **8:**298
- in drama **6:**196, 200
- Jacob ben Korshai **9:**1221
- Meir **11:**1241
- pseudonym *aḥerim* **2:**459
- views on logos **11:**462

ELISHAH (bib. fig., loc.) **6:**670
ELISHA ḤAYYIM BEN JACOB ASHKENAZI **6:**670
- emissary **14:**1366

Elishama (mosh., Isr.) **1:** place list
ELISHEBA (bib. fig.) **6:**671
ELISHEVA (poet) **6:**671
Elisofon, Eliot **13:**484
El Israelita Argentino (period.) **3:**424
Elissen, G. J. **4:**174
Elitzur (sport orgn.), *see* ELIẒUR
Elius, M. **8:**31
Eliyahu Golomb (refugee boat) **3:**291; **8:**1250; **9:**358
Eliyahu ha-Navi Synagogue (Jer.) **9:**1486
Eliyahu Margalit (wk.) **16:**982
ELIYIA, JOSEPH **6:**671
Elizabeth (czarina, Rus.) **11:**1192
Elizabeth (q. of Rum.) **14:**418
Elizabeth I (q. of Eng.)
- Añes, Gonsalvo **2:**833
- England **6:**752
- Lopez, Roderigo **3:**166; **11:**1191
- Shakespeare **14:**1262
- *illus:*
- - Lopez, Roderigo, plot to poison the Queen **11:**489

Elizabeth II (q., Eng.) **5:**230; **11:**1407; **15:**1672
Elizabeth (city, N.J.) **12:**1027; **15:**1533
Elizaphan ben Uzziel (bib. fig.) **10:**1192
ELI ẒIYYON VE-AREHA (acrostic elegy) **6:**672
- Av, The Ninth **3:**939
- *score:* text

ELIẒUR (orgn., Isr.) **6:**674
- Mizrachi **12:**180
- sports **15:**296

El Jalil (publ., isr.) **13:**1378
El-Jish (vill., Isr.), *see* GISCALA
Eljowicz, Jehiel Meir (Max) **13:**648
El Judio (journ.) **13:**1039
Elk (tn., Pol.), *see* LYCK
Elk, Max **15:**400
ELKAN, BENNO **6:**674
- Ḥanukkah lamps **7:**1315 **11:**1370
- *illus:*
- - Knesset *menorah*, details **5:**1448; **6:**384,1039,1096; **7:**1255,1459; **8:**483,683; **10:**120,149; **12:**382,750
- - Mahler medal **11:**726

ELKAN, SOPHIE **6:**675
- education **6:**464
- Scandinavian literature **14:**931

ELKANAH (bib. fig.) **6:**676
- grave **14:**785
- Hannah **7:**1269
- Samuel **14:**780
- *illus:*
- - text
- - Hannah and Peninnah **7:**1270

El-Kerak (tn., Transj.), *see* KIR-HARESETH
ELKES, ELHANAN **6:**677
ELKIN, ADOLPHUS PETER **6:**677
Elkin, Moses **3:**839
ELKIND, ARKADI DANILOVICH **6:**677

Elkind, M. 7:355ff
Elkind, Z. 14:1263
El Kirbatj (journ.) 13:1039
Elko (city, Nev.) 12:1018
Elkosh (mosh., Isr.) 1: place list
Elkumsi, Daniel, *see* DANIEL BEN MOSES AL-QŪMISĪ
El-Kuntilla (loc., Sinai), *see* Kuntilla, El-
ELKUS, ABRAM ISAAC 6:678
'Ella Aṣbaḥa (k., Eth.), *see* Kaleb 'Ella Aṣbaḥa
Elleh Ezkerah (litur.) 15:1008
Elleh ha-Massa'ot (bk.) 11:351
Ellen (tn.) 5:1137
Ellenbogen (fam.), *see* KATZENELLENBOGEN
Ellenbogen, H. B. (Rhod.) 4:1480
Ellenbogen, Henry (U.S.) 13:230
ELLENBOGEN, WILHELM (polit.) 6:678
ELLENSTEIN, MEYER C. 6:678
Ellenville (tn., N.Y.) 12:1127
Eller (tn.) 5:1134
El Levi, Samuel *see* Levi, Samuele
Ellinger, Alfred 10:1129
ELLINGER, MORITZ 6:678
Elliott-Automation Company (Eng.) 4:95
Ellis, Sir Barrow 8:1357
Ellis, Edmund Helbert 11:1553
ELLIS, VIVIAN 15:1081
Ellis Island (N.Y.) 15:1609
Ellison (fam.) 15:266
Ellison, James 15:1569
ELLSBERG, EDWARD 6:679
ELLSTAETTER, MORITZ 6:680
ELLSTEIN, ABRAHAM (Abe) 12:688
El Luzero (period., U.S.) 13:1039
El Luzero de la Paciencia (newsp., Rum.) 13:1038
ELMALEH (fam.) 6:680
Elmaleh, Aaron ben Reuben 6:680
ELMALEH, ABRAHAM 6:681
- *illus:*
- - Transjordan Arab leaders and 9:346
Elmaleh, Abraham ben Joseph 6:681
Elmaleh, Amram 6:680
Elmaleh, Elijah ben Abraham 6:681
Elmaleh, Elijah ben Jacob 6:681
Elmaleh, Ḥayyim 5:224
Elmaleh, Jacob (journ.) 13:1041
Elmaleh, Jacob ben Joseph (r.) 6:680
Elmaleh, Joseph (mer.) 6:680
Elmaleh, Joseph ben Aaron (r.) 6:681
Elmaleh, Joseph ben Ayyush (kab.) 6:680
Elmaleh, Judah ben Mordecai 6:681
Elmaleh, Moses ben Don David 6:680
Elmaleh, Reuben 6:681
Elmaleh, Victor 15:315
EL MALE RAḤAMIM (memorial prayer) 6:682
- *score;* text; 12:627
- *see also:* ASHKAVAH; HAZKARAT NESHAMOT
Elmali, Aaron ben Gershon 6:680
Elmalik, Abraham ben Judah 6:680
ELMAN, MISCHA 6:683
- Auer, Leopold 3:840
ELMAN, PETER 1:29
El Mansura (tn., Egy.), *see* MANSURA
El-Matariyeh (tn., Egy.) 4:774
- Heliopolis 8:290
EL MELEKH NE'EMAN (prayer) 6:683
- Amen 2:803
EL MELEKH YOSHEV (prayer) 6:684
El Messerret (newsp.) 9:1165
Elmira (city, N.Y.) 12:1126
El-Modari, Judah, *see* AL-MADARI, JUDAH HA-KOHEN BEN ELEAZAR HE-ḤASID
Elmosnino, Hasdai 13:118
Elmwood Park (sub., Chicago) 5:415
Elnathan (bib. fig.) 6:684
ELNATHAN BEN ACHBOR (bib. fig.) 6:684
- Achbor 2:210
Elne (tn., Fr.) 14:353
Elnecave, David 3:424; 13:1039
Elnecave, Nissim 3:424; 13:1039
EL NORA ALILAH (hymn) 6:684
El Novelista (newsp.) 9:1165
El Nuevo Kirbatj (journ.) 13:1039
El 'Obeid (vill., Mesop.), *see* Ubaid
ELOESSER, ARTHUR 6:685
'Eloha (name of God) 7:679
Elohai Basser (prayer) 6:624
Elohei Yisrael (wk.) 14:1223
'Elohim (name of God) 7:679
Eloise (Abelard's mistress), *see* Héloïse
Elokim (name for God) 7:683
El Olam (name of God) 7:675
Elon (bib. fig.) 2:234
Elon, Amos 9:1567
ELON, MENACHEM 1:29
Elon-Bezaananim (loc., Er. Isr.) 10:665; 14:1622
Eloth (loc., Er. Isr.), *see* EILOT
Eloul, Kosso 14:1070
Elousa (Nabatean city), *see* ELUSA
El-Paran (Sinai), *see* PARAN
EL PASO (city, U.S.) 6:686
- Texas 15:1036
El Progreso (coop., Arg.) 3:432
El Progresso (period., Turk.), *see Yosef ha-Da'at*
El Progresso (journ., U.S.), *see La Epoca de New York*
El-Qom (site, Er. Isr.), *see* Qom, El-
El-Quds (Jer.), *see* Al-Quds
El-Quseima (loc., Sinai), *see* Quseima, El-
El Roi (name of God) 7:677
Elrom, Ephraim 15:1463
"El Ropero" (15th cent., Sp.) 12:596
El sábado secreto (period.) 11:1456
EL SALVADOR 6:687
- Latin America 10:1451
- Zionism 16:1127
- *illus:* text
Elsberg, Charles 11:1201
El Shaddai (name of God) 7:676
'El Shoshannim 'Edut (Psalm superscription) 13:1320
Elsner, C. F. 7:94
Elsner, John 5:1543
El Sol (period.) 13:1038
Elster, Pola 16:353
ELTE, HARRY 6:688
- synagogue 15:620
- *illus:* text
ELTEKEH (bib. city) 6:688
El Tiempo (journ., Isr.) 13:1040
El Tiempo (period., Turk.) 13:1038
ELTON, GEOFFREY RUDOLPH 6:688
El Transito (church, Sp.) 15:611
- *illus:* 15:613,1201,1205
El Tresoro (period.) 4:1487
El-Tur (loc., Sinai) *see* Tur, El-
Elu-Eli (k. of Tyre) 14:1506
ELUL (month) 6:689
- first of 12:1061
- *kever avot* 10:934
- *seliḥot* 14:1134
- *shofar* 14:1444
- *illus:* text
- *see also:* CALENDAR
ELUSA (Nabatean city) 6:690
- Negev 12:929
- *illus:*
- - relief fragment 12:929
Elvas, Luis Gomes d' (fam.) 15:1301
El Viego (writ.) 15:253
Elvin, B. 14:423
Elvina (grandau. of Rashi) 10:351
ELVIRA (tn., Sp.) 6:691
Elvira, Council of (305) 5:546; 6:691; 15:220
Elwert, C. Gottlieb 8:31
Elxai (1/2 cent.) 10:39
Elyakhin (mosh., Isr.) 1: place list
Elyakim (mosh., Isr.) 1: place list
El-Yam (shipping co., Isr.) 9:836
ELYAN, SIR ISADORE VICTOR 10:1491; 10:1507
Elyashar (fam., Er. Isr.) 13:1399
- *see also:* Eliachar
Elyashar, Ḥayyim Moshe 6:693
ELYASHAR, JACOB BEN ḤAYYIM JOSEPH 6:691
ELYASHAR, JACOB SAUL BEN ELIEZER JEROHAM 6:692
- controversy over succession 9:889
Elyashev, Israel Isidor *see* BAAL-MAKHSHOVES
ELYASHIV (mosh., Isr.) 6:693
- Ge'ulei Teiman 7:531
- statistics 1: place list
Elyashiv, A. 16:833
Elyehoenai (h. pr.), *see* ELIONAEUS, SON OF CANTHERAS
Elyon, Meliẓ u-Mastin (cantata) 5:125
ELZAS, BARNETT ABRAHAM 6:693
Elzet, Yehuda, *see* AVIDA, YEHUDA LEIB
El Zhurnal Izraelit (newsp.) 7:231
Elzisher, Ẓevi Hirsch 9:1082
EMANATION (myst. theory) 6:694
- General
- - creation 3:447
- - *Ein-Sof* 10:559ff
- - God 7:661
- - hasidic thought 7:1403
- - holy sparks 9:1054
- - intellect 8:1411ff
- - Kabbalah 10:531; 10:563ff
- - Lurianic cosmogony 10:588ff
- - mysticism 10:496; 10:507; 10:524
- - nature 12:889
- - neoplatonism 12:958; 12:961; 13:429
- - *Sefirot* 14:1104
- - soul 15:172
- - Worlds, the Four 16:641
- Views on
- - Avicenna 3:957
- - Ba'al Shem Tov 9:1054
- - Cordovero 10:546
- - Gabirol, Solomon ibn 7:242; 13:434
- - Hillel ben Samuel 13:445
- - Ibn Da'ud 8:1162; 13:440
- - Ibn Ezra, Abraham 8:1169
- - Israeli, Isaac 9:1064ff
- - Krochmal 13:458
- - Latif, Isaac 10:1447
- - Philo 13:426
- *see also:* CAUSE AND EFFECT
EMANCIPATION 6:696
- *Contents:*
- - Definitions and Dialectics 6:696
- - The Three Periods in the History of Jewish Emancipation 6:697
- - Emancipation in Various Countries 6:700
- General
- - Aescoly's studies 2:325
- - Alkalai, Judah 2:639
- - Allgemeine Zeitung des Judentums 2:648
- - Alliance Israélite 2:649ff
- - apologetic literature 3:197ff
- - apostasy 3:205
- - assimilation 3:772
- - autonomy 3:921; 3:926
- - Balfour Declaration 4:131
- - Bund 4:1498
- - crime rates 5:1091ff
- - defense of civil rights 3:927
- - Dhimma 5:1604
- - European economic history 16:1319
- - Ḥasidic reaction to 7:1397
- - Haskalah 7:1433ff
- - history chart 8:766-767
- - Jewish identity 10:59
- - Jewish law 12:123ff
- - Jewish nationalism 16:1034
- - Judaism 10:386; 10:394
- - liberalism 6:973
- - Lilienblum, Moses Leib 11:241ff
- - marriage 11:1028
- - *Me'assef* 11:1161
- - medals 11:1171,1173
- - Napoleon Bonaparte 12:825
- - Pinsker, Leon 13:545
- - politics, Jews in 13:805
- - Protestants' attitude 13:1248
- - rabbinate 13:1452
- - Vienna, Congress of 16:132ff
- - Voltaire's influence 16:220
- - Wissenschaft des Judentums 16:570
- Countries
- - Arab States 6:717
- - - Arab Higher Committee 9:465
- - - Iraqi Jewish women 8:1454
- - Austria 6:707ff
- - - Hirsch, S. R. 8:509
- - - Israelitische Allianz 2:654
- - - *Judenordnungen* 3:890ff
- - - Sofer, Moses 15:78
- - - *Toleranzpatent* 15:1209
- - Belgium
- - - Antwerp 3:167
- - England 6:698; 6:700ff
- - - history 8:714
- - - Lewis Way 13:1248
- - - Van Oven, Barnard 16:68
- - France 6:702ff; 7:22
- - - Assembly of Jewish Notables 3:761
- - - Carvallo, Jules 5:223
- - - Cerfberr, Herz 5:312
- - - French Revolution 7:152; 7:153ff
- - - Gregoire, Henri Baptiste 7:917
- - - history 8:712
- - - Law of September 27, 1791 2:755
- - Germany 6:704ff; 7:476ff
- - - Auerbach, Berthold 3:845
- - - Brunswick 4:1422
- - - Eger, Akiva 6:469
- - - Eger, Solomon 6:473
- - - Hep! Hep! riots 8:330; 8:331
- - - history 8:714ff
- - - Riesser, Gabriel 14:167
- - Italy 6:704ff
- - - Camerini, Eugenio 5:75
- - - Napoleon Bonaparte 12:823
- - - Tuscany 15:1468
- - Latin America
- - - Congress of Argentinian Jewry 3:414
- - Netherlands 6:703ff; 12:980
- - - Amsterdam 2:900
- - - Arnhem 3:486
- - - Felix Libertate 6:1219
- - - Friedrichsfeld, David 7:194
- - Poland 6:711ff
- - - Butrymowicz, Mateusz 4:1539
- - - Wojda's proposals 16:601
- - Russia 6:713ff
- - - Bolshevik Revolution 5:798
- - Switzerland 6:709ff
- - - Aargau Jews 2:3
- - U.S.A. 6:700ff
- - - American Jewish committee 2:824

- - - history **8:**712ff
- - - Virginia Bill **2:**810
- *illus:*
- - *Des Juifs au Dix-Neuvième Siècle* (1816) **4:**110
- - "Grand Sanhedrin des Israélites de France" **8:**704
- - Itzig, Daniel, *Naturalisationspatent* **9:**1150
- - Jews petitioning Helvetia **15:**557
- - Prussia, edict of 1812 **3:**927
- - Westphalian medal **16:**474
- *see also:* HASKALAH; *and under individual countries*
Emanuel (name), *see also* Emmanuel; Immanuel
Emanuel (k., Port.) **3:**166
EMANUEL (offic., Turk.) **6:**718
- Ashkenazi, Solomon **3:**732
Emanu-El (period., U.S.) **16:**223
Emanuel, Albert **15:**1034
Emanuel, George J. **4:**1038
Emanuel, Giovanni **15:**1057
Emanuel, Samuel **13:**918
EMANUEL, WALTER LEWIS **6:**787
Emanuel de Foralto, *see* Foralto, Emanuel de
Emanuel ha-Russi **9:**1590
EMBALMING **6:**718
- dissection **3:**931
- Jacob and Joseph **10:**208; **10:**212
- tombs **15:**1216
Embassy to Gaius (wk.) **8:**304
EMBDEN, GUSTAV **6:**719
EMBER, AARON **6:**719
Emblem, *see* FLAG; SEAL, SEALS
Embroidery **7:**972; **16:**756
- *illus:*
- - *see* CRAFTS (Needlework)
EMBRYO **6:**719
- beneficiaries of wills **16:**524
- embryology **4:**1019ff
- firstborn **6:**1309
- marriage prohibition **7:**1461
- medicine **11:**1183
- *mishmarot* and prayer **12:**92
- *see also:* ABORTION; BIRTH CONTROL; PARENT AND CHILD
EMDEN (city, Ger.) **6:**721
- *illus:* text
Emden, Frans van de **14:**66
Emden, H. van **13:**1143
EMDEN, JACOB **6:**721
- abortion **2:**100
- Abraham of Lissa **2:**149
- Abraham of Zamosc **2:**145
- alchemy **2:**548
- amulet controversy **2:**911; **6:**1076
- Anav's *Ma'alot ha-Middot* **2:**938
- *Anim Zemirot* **3:**22
- apologetics **3:**198
- Ashkenazi, Ẓevi Hirsch **3:**734
- Baruch ben David Yavan **4:**277
- blessing of children **4:**1087
- Buzaglo, Shalom **4:**1544
- Chajes, Gershon **5:**324
- chronological chart **8:**766-767
- emissaries **14:**1366
- Epstein, Aryeh Leib **6:**825
- Eybeschuetz, Jonathan, dispute with **6:**1074
- Falk, Samuel **6:**1160
- Frankists **3:**198
- *golem* **7:**755
- Kabbalah **10:**648
- Landau, Ezekiel **10:**1389
- onanism **12:**1396
- Shabbateanism **14:**1250ff
- Torah study **15:**459
- Zohar **16:**1214
- *illus:* text
Emek ha-Bakha (bk.) **8:**558; **10:**241 **11:**349
Emek ha-Melekh (kab. wk.) **10:**549
- *illus:*
- - *hitnoẓeẓut* diagram **10:**597
Emek ha-Yarden (Er. Isr.), *see* Jordan Valley
Emek Ḥefer, *see* ḤEFER PLAIN
Emek Refaim (Er. Isr.), *see* Refa'im Valley
Emek Refa'im (sub., Jer.), *see* German Colony
Emek Refa'im (bk.) **11:**117
Emek Yizre'el (Isr.), *see* JEZREEL, VALLEY OF
Emek Yizre'el (newsp.) **14:**399
Emerson, Sir Herbert **6:**991; **14:**33
EMERY, RICHARD WILDER **6:**724
EMESA (city, Syr.) **6:**725
Em ha-Banim (educ. orgn.) **12:**343
Emica (orgn.) **10:**48
Emicho of Leiningen **5:**1137
- Mainz **11:**789
Emig-direkt (orgn., Ger.) **10:**44; **13:**388
Emigration, *see* MIGRATION
EMIN PASHA (Emin Effendi) **6:**725
- traveler **15:**1350
EMIOT, ISRAEL **6:**726
Emissaries Institute (Isr.) **10:**31
Emissaries of Ereẓ Israel, *see* SHELUḤEI EREẒ ISRAEL
Emmanuel (name), *see also* Emanuel; Immanuel
Emmanuel, David **7:**428; **10:**1503
EMMANUEL, ISAAC SAMUEL **6:**726
- historiography **8:**564
Emmanuel, Samuel **6:**726
Emmanuel, Suzanne A. **6:**726
Emmanuel of Lodz **13:**1297
Emmatha (site, Er. Isr.), *see* ḤAMMAT GADER
EMMAUS (tn., Er. Isr.) **6:**726
- Arab settlement **9:**261
- Eleazar ben Arakh **6:**586
- Hammath **7:**1242
- Kiriath-Jearim **10:**1046
- Moza **12:**494
- Roman city status **9:**252
Emmaus, Neḥunya ben ha-Kanah of (tan.), *see* NEḤUNYA BEN HA-KANAH
Emmer (bot.) **13:**617
Emmeram of Mainz, *see* AMRAM OF MAINZ
Emmerich (fam., Eng.), *see* GOMPERTZ
Emmerkar (ruler, Mesop.) **16:**1487
Emmich, Z. **8:**1050
EMŐD, TAMAS **6:**727
EMOTIONS **6:**727
- good and evil inclination **8:**1318
- heart **8:**7
- Spinoza **15:**174
EMPEDOCLES (philos.) **6:**729
- neoplatonism **12:**959
Empereur, Constantin L', *see* L'EMPEREUR, CONSTANTIN
EMPEROR WORSHIP (Rom. cult.) **6:**729
- Eleazar ben Ananias **6:**585
- *halakhah* purpose **8:**302
- Petronius Publius **13:**346
- Roman anti-Semitism **3:**89
- Roman-Jewish relations **8:**639
Empire Loyalists (orgn., Br.) **12:**952
Employment, *see* LABOR
Employment in Israel, *see* LABOR EMPLOYMENT IN ISRAEL
Employment Service Supreme Objection Committee **9:**640
Empoli (tn., It.) **15:**1467ff
EMSHEIMER, ERNST **12:**688
Emunah (Zion. assoc.) **14:**47
Emunah (belief), *see* ARTICLES OF FAITH; BELIEF
Emunah Omen (wk.) **2:**150
- *illus:*
- - title page (1846) **13:**1111
Emunim (mosh., Isr.) **1:** place list
Emunim (collec.) **1:** newsp. list
Emunot ve-De'ot (bk.) **14:**548
- apologetics **3:**193
- Jewish literature **11:**338
- Jewish philosophy **13:**431
- translation **15:**1129
Emutbal (anc. kdm.) **16:**1496
Ena (savora) **14:**921
Enat (kib., Isr.), *see* Einat
En Bonafoux de l'Argentière, *see* KASPI, JOSEPH BEN ABBA MARI IBN
Encaoua, Raphael **12:**340; **14:**682
Encausse, Gérard, *see* Papus
Enciclopedia . . . *see also* Encyclopaedia . . .; Encyclopedia . . .; Enẓiklopedyah
Enciclopedia Judaica Castellana **6:**733; **11:**1459
Enciclopedia Judaica Resumida **6:**735
Enckell, Rabbe Arnfinn **14:**930
En Crescas of Orange, *see* Ezovi, Mordecai ben Isaac
Encroachment, *see* HASSAGAT GEVUL
Encyclopaedia . . . *see also* Enciclopedia . . .; Encyclopedia . . .; Enẓiklopedyah . . .
Encyclopaedia Britannica **6:**733
Encyclopaedia Judaica (Ger.) **6:**732
- Goldmann, Nahum **10:**1089 **7:**723
- Klatzkin, Jacob **10:**1088
Encyclopaedia Sefardica Neerlandica **6:**734
Encyclopedia of Jewish Knowledge **6:**734
Encyclopedia of the Jewish Religion **6:**734
Encyclopedia of Jews in Sports **6:**734
ENCYCLOPEDIAS **6:**730
- *Contents:*
- - Encyclopedias of General Content in Hebrew and Yiddish Outside of Israel **6:**730
- - Encyclopedias of Jewish Content Only **6:**731
- - Encyclopedias in Israel **6:**733
- - Jews and Judaism in General Encyclopedias **6:**733
- - Jewish Encyclopedias **6:**734
- - Israel Encyclopedias **6:**735
- law source **12:**118
- Lifshits, Shiye-Mordkhe **11:**237
- *Naḥalat Yosef* **2:**251
- Russian **14:**455
- *see also:* Concordances, Hebrew; Dictionaries; *and under individual names*
Encyclopedia Talmudica (trans.) **6:**734
ENDECJA (Endeks; polit. party, Pol.) **6:**735
- anti-Semitic parties **3:**84
- boycott, anti-Jewish **4:**1278
Endelman, Halina, *see* GÓRSKA, HALINA
Enden. Van den (Du. Schol.) **15:**276
ENDINGEN (tn., Ger.) **6:**736
ENDINGEN AND LENGNAU (vill., Switz.) **6:**737
- Aargau **2:**3
- Switzerland **15:**556
- *illus:*
- - Lengnau synagogue **2:**3; **15:**558
Endinger Judenspiel (Ger. play) **6:**737
Endler, W. **12:**1279
ENDLICH, QUIRIN **6:**738
End of Days, *see* ESCHATOLOGY
EN-DOR (city, Er. Isr.) **6:**738
En-Dor (kib., Isr.) **6:**739
- statistics **1:** place list
EN-DOR, WITCH OF **6:**739
- Abner **2:**87
- in the Arts **14:**785,917
- Saul **14:**913; **14:**916
Endowment, *see* HEKDESH
ENDRE, LÁSZLÓ **6:**740
ENELOW, HYMAN (Hillel Gershom) **6:**740
Enesco, Georges **12:**692
- Saul **14:**918
Enfantin, Barthelemy Prosper **14:**667; **15:**25
Engagement, *see* BETROTHAL; MARRIAGE
EN-GANNIM (sites, Er. Isr.) **6:**741
EN-GEDI (site, kib., Er. Isr.) **6:**741
- Aramaic ostraca **16:**668
- Bar Kokhba **4:**239
- ibex **9:**226
- Murabba'at scrolls **12:**528
- Qumran **13:**1430
- statistics **1:** place list
- *illus:*
- - text
- - ibex **9:**233
- - Masada view **11:**1079
- - spring at nature reserve **12:**892
Engel (fam., Hung.) **13:**203
Engel, Eduard **7:**690
Engel, Irving M. **12:**1112
Engel, Jacob Shalom **16:**1348
ENGEL, JOEL (Yuli Dimitriyevich) **6:**744
- *Dibbuk* **6:**20
- Jerusalem songs **9:**1590
- Society for Folk Music **15:**57
- *illus:*
- - *Shirei Yeladim* **12:**659
ENGEL, JOSEPH BEN JUDAH **6:**745
ENGEL, JÓZSEF **6:**745
- *illus:* text
Engel, Judah Leib **4:**128
Engel, Paul **6:**361
Engel, Samuel ben Ze'ev Wolf **14:**91
Engel, Yuli Dimitriyevich, *see* ENGEL, JOEL
ENGELBERG, ḤAYYIM OF **6:**746
Engelberg, Louis **5:**611
Engelberger, Ferdinand Franz, *see* ENGELBERG, ḤAYYIM OF
Engelman, Uriah Z. **9:**1279
ENGELMANN, GABRIEL **6:**746
ENGELMANN, SUSANNE CHARLOTTE **6:**747
Engels, Friedrich (philos.) **11:**1071ff
Engels, Joseph **15:**778
ENGELSBERG, LEON **3:**599
- *illus:*
- - "Jerusalem Landscape" (paint.) **3:**619
Engestroem, J. **8:**31
Engineers, *see* INVENTORS AND ENGINEERS
Englaender, Richard, *see* ALTENBERG, PETER
ENGLAND **6:**747
- *Contents:*
- - The Medieval Period **6:**747
- - The Expulsion **6:**751
- - The Resettlement Period **6:**752
- - The 19th Century **6:**755
- - Modern Period **6:**758
- - Contemporary Period **6:**765
- - Relations with Israel **6:**770
- General
- - archives **3:**382
- - British Israelites **4:**1381
- - capitulations **5:**148
- - dress **6:**219
- - history chart **8:**766-767
- - immigration (refugees) **14:**30
- - London **11:**469

-- socialism **15:**25ff
-- stamps **15:**330
-- tax **15:**838
-- Ten Lost Tribes **15:**1006
- Medieval Period
-- Aaron of Lincoln **2:**21
-- Aaron of York **2:**22
-- agricultural trade **2:**404
-- anti-Semitism **16:**849; **12:**1217
-- archae **3:**300
-- archpresbyters **3:**398
-- blood libel **4:**1121; **8:**1061
-- coin clipping **16:**1289
-- Crusades **5:**1139
-- *Domus Conversorum* **6:**165
-- Elias le Eveske **6:**618
-- Exchequer of the Jews **6:**1006
-- Henry III tax assessment **8:**1365
-- Jews in feudal system **16:**1285
-- moneylending **12:**249; **12:**254ff
-- York massacre **16:**848; **16:**849
- Resettlement Period
-- Cromwell **5:**1126
-- Lopez, Roderigo **11:**489
-- Manasseh Ben Israel **11:**856
-- Marrano Diaspora **11:**1020; **13:**924
-- Naturalization Bill (1753) **13:**1248
-- Robles case **14:**208
- Contemporary Period
-- Israel arms purchases **9:**391ff; **9:**695
-- neo-Fascism **12:**952
-- neo-Nazism **12:**954
-- New Left **12:**1033
-- peace guarantees for Israel **9:**384
-- relations with Israel **6:**770; **9:**432
-- Six-Day War volunteers **9:**543
-- Suez Campaign **9:**389ff; **14:**1605
-- War Crimes Trials **16:**289ff
- Community and Jewish Life
-- Anglo-Jewish Association **2:**977
-- assimilation **3:**779
-- B'nai B'rith **4:**1148
-- Board of Deputies **4:**1151
-- community organization **5:**824; **8:**723
-- demography **5:**1498ff; **6:**767
-- emancipation **6:**698; **6:**700ff; **8:**714
-- fraternal societies **7:**110
-- freemasons **7:**122ff
-- Goldsmid family **7:**733f
-- hospitals **8:**1034
-- Laski family **10:**1438
-- Montagu family **12:**264
-- Montefiore, Sir Moses **12:**270
-- organizations **6:**767
-- philanthropy **13:**379
-- population **8:**733ff; **13:**872
-- Rothschild family **14:**337ff
-- scouting **14:**1037ff
-- Shabbateanism **14:**1233
-- students' movements **15:**448ff
-- United Synagogue **15:**1672
-- Wolfson, Sir Isaac **16:**619
- Culture and Scholarship
-- Abrahams, Israel **2:**164
-- Berlin, Sir Isaiah **4:**658
-- Buechler, Adolf **4:**1458
-- children's literature **5:**449
-- Cohen, Abraham **5:**663
-- Daiches family **5:**1226
-- Disraeli, Benjamin **6:**103f
-- education **6:**421ff **6:**768
-- Elijah Menahem ben Moses **6:**658
-- English literature **6:**773f
-- Epstein, Isidore **6:**826
-- Gaster, Haham Moses **7:**332
-- Gollancz family **7:**760
-- Hebrew mss. **11:**906
-- *Jewish Chronicle* **10:**40
-- Jewish Historical Society **10:**53
-- *Jewish Quarterly Review* **10:**88
-- Jews' College **10:**98
-- Klein, Hyman **10:**1099
-- Loewe family **11:**447; **11:**448
-- ORT **12:**1484
-- poetry **13:**692
-- press **6:**769; **13:**1030
-- Roth, Cecil **14:**326
-- Roth, Leon **14:**329
-- Sola, David Aaron de **15:**91
-- theater **15:**1049
-- universities **15:**1677
-- Zangwill, Israel **16:**930
- Religion
-- Abramsky, Yeḥezkel **2:**170
-- Adler, Nathan Marcus **2:**285
-- Adler, Hermann **2:**278
-- Brodie, Israel **4:**1393
-- chaplaincy **11:**1564
-- Gateshead Yeshivah **7:**334
-- Grunfeld, Isidor **7:**949
-- Hertz, Joseph Herman **8:**397
-- homiletic literature **8:**957
-- Jacobs, Louis **9:**1236
-- Judaizers **10:**398
-- Lopian family **11:**491
-- Orthodoxy **12:**1491
-- rabbi's function **13:**1452
-- Reform Judaism **14:**24
-- religious life **6:**768
-- *sheḥitah* **14:**1341
-- synagogues **1:**synagogue list; **15:**618; **15:**107
- Occupations, Trade and Industry **6:**767; **15:**1302ff
-- banking **4:**168
-- glassmaking **7:**613
-- journalism **10:**303ff
-- law **10:**1491ff
-- metals and mining **11:**1438
-- military service **11:**1552ff
-- moneylending **12:**249; **12:**254ff
-- peddling **13:**206
-- petroleum, oil products **13:**346
-- politics **13:**811ff
-- psychology **13:**1344
-- publishing **13:**1370
-- secondhand goods trade **14:**1085ff
-- shipping **14:**1413
-- tailoring **15:**706
-- television and radio **15:**929ff
-- textiles **15:**1042
-- tobacco industry **15:**1177
-- trade with India **8:**1356
-- typographers **15:**1478ff
- Zionism and Palestine
-- Arab terrorists **9:**416
-- Balfour Declaration **4:**131f
-- Brodetsky, Selig **4:**1392
-- Churchill, Sir Winston **5:**555
-- Ereẓ Israel protection rights **9:**296; **9:**298
-- Greenberg, L.J. **7:**905
-- Jabotinsky and Jewish Legion **8:**756
-- Jerusalem consulate **9:**1448
-- Lloyd George, David **11:**413
-- Loḥamei Ḥerut Israel **11:**464ff
-- Maccoby, Ḥayyim Zundel **11:**665
-- mandate for Palestine **11:**861ff; **15:**1543ff
-- Marks, Simon **11:**1009
-- Middle East interests **9:**305ff
-- Palestine partition **13:**34
-- policy in Palestine **10:**1521
-- Rabinowitz, Samuel Jacob **13:**1478
-- restoration of Ereẓ Israel **8:**727
-- Revisionists, Zionist **14:**128ff
-- Sacher family **14:**591
-- St. James's Conference **14:**660
-- Samuel, Herbert **14:**797ff
-- Sieff, Israel **14:**1510
-- Sieff, Rebecca **14:**1511
-- Simon, Sir Leon **14:**1581
-- Sykes-Picot treaty **15:**565ff
-- Territorialism **15:**1020ff
-- Uganda Scheme **15:**1500
-- Weizmann, Chaim **16:**425ff
-- White Papers **16:**482ff
-- Wingate, Orde **16:**547
-- Youth Aliyah blocked **16:**862ff
-- Zionism **16:**1116
-- Zionist congress **16:**1168
-- Zionist political campaign **16:**1078
- Jewish-Christian Relations
-- anti-Semitism **6:**763
-- caricatures **5:**171ff
-- Church and Nazism **8:**916
-- discrimination **6:**70
-- Parkes, James **13:**121
-- race, theory of **13:**1484
-- Reformation, influence of **14:**20
- *illus:*
-- text
-- "Aaron Son of the Devil" (caric.) **3:**93
-- Board of Deputies **4:**1150
-- Bristol, Jewish quarter, 1250 (plan) **4:**1378
-- Canterbury, medieval Jewish quarter (plan) **5:**127
-- Carmel College synagogue, Wallingford **6:**419
-- Churchill's letter to Weizmann re Jewish Fighting Force (August, 1944) **3:**394
-- converted children, petition to Parliament (1702) **3:**206
-- exemption re arms on Sabbath in Jamaica **9:**1272
-- Francia, Francis, report of trial (1717) **7:**45
-- Jew and clergyman (caric.) **6:**714
-- Jewish badge (13th cent.) **4:**63
-- Jewish dress (13th cent. caric.) **4:**63
-- Jews attempting to enter Parliament (caric.) **5:**174
-- Jews dancing around statue of Robert Grant (caric.) **6:**705
-- London protest against Passfield White Paper **16:**1118
-- *Managem,* yacht used for Nili information **12:**1164
-- "Mr. Fagin . . ." (G. Cruikshank) **6:**781
-- petition to Oliver Cromwell re religious services **5:**1127
-- regulations re taxes on trade in jewels (1809) **6:**1283
-- Rothschild, Lionel, taking seat in House of Commons **14:**340
- *pop. tables:*
-- text
-- major towns, 1967 **5:**1514
-- postwar communities **5:**839
Englander, Daniel **11:**1115
Englander, Oskar **13:**973
Englewicz, Eliezer **16:**1328
Englewood (city, N.J.) **4:**612ff; **12:**1028
- *illus:*
-- Temple Emanu-El **12:**1030
Englisch, Berthold **5:**405
English East India Company, *see* East India Companies
English Electric Company **4:**95
English Hospital (Jer.) **9:**1491
English Language
- Bible translations **4:**868
- children's literature **5:**449
- encyclopedias, Jewish **6:**732ff
- Semitic languages **14:**1154
ENGLISH LITERATURE **6:**773
- *Contents:*
-- Biblical and Hebraic Influences **6:**773
-- The Figure of the Jew **6:**776
-- Palestine and Israel in English Literature **6:**782
-- The Jewish Contribution **6:**782
-- Capsules **6:**786
- *illus:*
-- text
-- *Fables of a Jewish Aesop* **4:**597
-- *Hebrew Melodies* (1815) **4:**1548
-- *Journey to Jerusalem* (1786) **15:**1004
-- *Merchant of Venice,* scene **14:**1262
English Mission of Jerusalem **4:**774
English rites (litur.) **11:**399
Englishtown (boro., N.J.) **12:**1030
English Zionist Federation **6:**760; **16:**1117
Engnell, I. **4:**908
Engotler, J. **8:**31
Engraving **5:**1048ff
Engürüz (city, Turk.), *see* ANKARA
En-Hakkore (spring, Er. Isr.) **14:**772
En Hakore (period.), *see Ein ha-Kore*
EN-HAROD (spring, kib., Isr.) **6:**791
- battle camp **16:**271
- Goliath **7:**758
- Mongol defeat **9:**271,1423
- Napoleon's victory **9:**291
- statistics **1:**place list
- *illus:*
-- text
-- Mishkan le-Ommanut Museum **12:**549
En-Harod Art Museum (Isr.) **3:**813; **6:**792
- *illus:*
-- folk art section **12:**549
Enheduanna (h. pr., Mesop.) **16:**1489
Enid (city, Okla.) **12:**1354
Enims (anc. people) **15:**1316
Enki (deity) **16:**1486
- Babel, Tower of **4:**25
- Babylonia **11:**951
- Eve **6:**979
- Flood **6:**1353
- Sumer **15:**514
- *see also:* Ea
Enkin, Naum **2:**837
Enkomi (site, Cyp.) **13:**400
Enlightened absolutism **8:**706
Enlightenment, Jewish, *see* HASKALAH
Enlil (deity)
- Babel, Tower of **4:**25
- flood **6:**1353
- Marduk **11:**951
- Mesopotamia **16:**1486
- Sumer **15:**514
Enmebaragesi (ruler, Mesop.), *see* Mebaragesi
En-Mishpat (loc., Cana.), *see* KADESH-BARNEA
Ennery, Adolphe Philippe d' **15:**1054
ENNERY, JONAS D' **6:**792
Enns (tn., Aus.) **2:**530
ENOCH (bib. figs.) **6:**793
- Elijah **6:**638
- *Ethiopic Book of Enoch* **6:**795
- Hellenistic Jewish literature **8:**304
- kabbalistic view of **10:**613
- legend **2:**961
- Metatron **10:**504; **11:**1444ff
- oil of life **12:**1347
- Reuben **14:**104
- *Slavonic Book of Enoch* **6:**797
- son of man **15:**160
- Uriel **16:**7
- *illus:* text
Enoch (publ., Ger.) **13:**1366
ENOCH, ETHIOPIC BOOK OF **6:**795
- astrology **3:**789
- *Baruch, Greek Apocalypse* **4:**274

- calendar **5**:48, 51
- date and contents **3**:180ff
- Dead Sea Scrolls **5**:1402
- Jewish literature **11**:311
- Kabbalah **10**:493,497ff
- Samael **14**:719
- *Slavonic Book of Enoch* **6**:797,798
- *Vision of 70 Shepherds* **14**:1198
- visions **16**:167
ENOCH, SLAVONIC BOOK OF (II Enoch) **6**:797
- astronomy **3**:796
- Jewish literature **11**:311
- magic **11**:705
- mysticism **10**:496,502
- *Shiur Komah* **14**:1418
- Uzza, Aza'el **16**:43
ENOCH BEN ABRAHAM **6**:799
Enoch ben Judah, *see* Ḥanokh Enoch ben Judah Leib ben Enoch Zundel
Enoch ben Moses, *see* ḤANOKH BEN MOSES
Enoch ha-Levi **11**:61
Enoch Zondel ben Joseph, *see* ḤANOKH ZUNDEL BEN JOSEPH
ENOSH (bib. fig.) **6**:799
Enosh ("human race") **11**:842
Enquist, Per-Olov **14**:931
EN-RIMMON (tn., Er. Isr.) **6**:799
Enrique Enríquez de Paz, *see* GÓMEZ, ANTONIO ENRÍQUEZ
Enriques, B. **5**:163
ENRIQUES, PAOLO **6**:800
ENRÍQUEZ, ISABEL **6**:800
ENRÍQUEZ BASURTO, DIEGO **6**:800
Enriquez Gómez, Antonio, *see* GÓMEZ, ANTONIO ENRIQUEZ
EN-ROGEL (spring, Jer.) **6**:800
Ens, Petrus **8**:31
Enselberg, Otto, *see* FERARU, LEON
ENSHEIM, MOSES **6**:800
ENSISHEIM (tn., Fr.) **6**:801
- Armleder massacre **3**:483
- Meir of Rothenburg **14**:381
Enslavement, *see* SLAVERY; SLAVE-TRADE
En-Tappuah (city, Er. Isr.), *see* TAPPUAH
Entdecktes Judenthum (bk.) **6**:542
Entelar, *see* ATTORNEY
Entelman, Remo **10**:1503
Enterprise, business **16**:1301
Entertainment tax (Isr.) **9**:757
Entezam, N. **13**:34
Entin, David **11**:1558
ENTIN, JOEL **6**:801
Entin, Moses **6**:1161
Entràdàm (vill., Rum.) **13**:1605
Entrepreneurs, industrial **16**:1313ff
- *see also:* CONTRACTORS; RAILROADS; TRADE AND COMMERCE
ENTRE RÍOS (prov., Arg.) **6**:802
- Gerchunoff's *Los Gauchos Judíos* **7**:434
- ICA's aid **10**:46
- Jewish colonies **3**:413ff
Enuma Elish (Babyl. epic) **5**:1061; **12**:729ff
En Vidas de Gerona, *see* DA PIERA, MESHULLAM BEN SOLOMON
Envy, *see* COVETOUSNESS; JEALOUSY
Enẓiklopedyah . . . *see also* Enciclopedia . . . ; Encyclopaedia . . . ; Encyclopedia . . .
Enẓiklopedya Ḥinnukhit (Isr.) **6**:730; **14**:1577
Enẓiklopedyah Historit shel Medinot ha-Olam **6**:735
Enẓiklopedyah Kelalit (Pal.) **6**:733
Enẓiklopedyah Kelalit Massadah (Isr.) **6**:733
Enẓiklopedyah Kelalit Yizre'el (Isr.) **6**:733
Enẓiklopedyah la-Am **6**:735
Enẓiklopedyah le-Geografyah Mikra'it **6**:734
Enẓiklopedyah le-Ḥaluẓei ha-Yishuv u-Vonav **16**:1160
Enẓiklopedyah le-Historyah **6**:735
Enẓiklopedyah le-Ishim ba-Tanakh **6**:734
Enẓiklopedyah le-Madda'ei ha-Ḥevrah **6**:735; **10**:905
Enẓiklopedyah le-Musikah **6**:735
Enẓiklopedyah le-Sifrut Yisre'elit u-Khelalit **6**:735; **10**:805
Enẓiklopedyah le-To'orei-Kavod be-Yisrael **6**:735
Enẓiklopedyah le-Ẓiyyonut **10**:1104
Enẓiklopedyah li-Sport u-le-Tarbut ha-Guf **6**:735
Enẓiklopedyah Ma'yan **6**:735
Enẓiklopedyah Me'ir Netiv le-Halikhot, Minhagim, Darkhei Musar u-Ma'asim Tovim **6**:734
Enẓiklopedyah Mikra'it **6**:734
Enẓiklopedyah shel ha-Mikra vi-Ymei Bayit Sheni **6**:734
Enẓiklopedyah shel Havai u-Masoret ba-Yahadut **6**:734
Enẓiklopedyah shel ha-Yahadut **6**:734
Enẓiklopedyah Talmudit **6**:734
- Zevin, Solomon Joseph **16**:1005
Enẓiklopedyah Yehudit **6**:734
Enẓiklopedyah Yuda'ikah **6**:734
Eössi(-y), András **13**:202; **15**:139
EÖTVÖS, BARON JÓZSEF **6**:803
- Hungarian literature **8**:1079
Eötvös, Károly **15**:1156
Eperjes (tn., Cz.), *see* PRESOV
ÉPERNAY (tn., Fr.) **6**:803
Ephah (bib. fig.) **11**:1506
Ephah (meas.) **16**:377,380ff
EPHESUS (city, As. M.) **6**:803
- diaspora **6**:10
EPHOD (sacred garment) **6**:804
- Commandments, the 613 **5**:773
- reminder **13**:1077
- Urim and Thumim **16**:9
- *illus:*
- - priestly vestments **13**:1065
- *see also:* PRIESTLY VESTMENTS
EPHRAIM (bib. fig.; tribe) **6**:806
- Biblical Figure
- - Jacob's hands **14**:177
- - Joseph **10**:206
- Tribe
- - Aaronides **2**:20
- - Benjamin, tribe of **10**:329
- - Bible history **8**:579ff
- - David, opposition to **5**:1325
- - geology of region **9**:202ff
- - Hebrew dialect **16**:1571
- - Jephthah, war with **9**:1342
- - Manassseh **11**:850
- - Samaritans **14**:727
- - settlement **9**:115
- - tribal authority **15**:1384
- *illus:*
- - banner and emblem **4**:181
- - Jacob's blessing **6**:281; **7**:1084
EPHRAIM (fam.) **6**:809
Ephraim (physic.) **11**:1183
- *illus:*
- - St. Basil and **11**:1182
Ephraim (city, Er. Isr.), *see* OPHRAH
Ephraim, Belshom **3**:787
Ephraim, Benjamin Veitel **6**:810; **15**:1041
Ephraim, David **6**:809
Ephraim, Forest of (Isr.) **9**:787
EPHRAIM, VEITEL HEINE (Ḥayyim) **6**:811
- family **6**:809
- mintmaster **12**:64
- *geneal. table:* **6**:810
Ephraim, Vidal **3**:787
Ephraim, Zacharias **6**:810
Ephraim Alnakawa, *see* Al-Nakawa, Ephraim
Ephraim ben al Zafān **10**:420
Ephraim ben Azariah ("the Jerusalemite") **2**:750
Ephraim ben Buya'a **11**:900
Ephraim ben Gerson **16**:113
EPHRAIM BEN ISAAC (of Regensburg; tos.) **6**:812
- art, view of **3**:522
- Naḥmanides **12**:780
- poetry **13**:692
Ephraim ben Israel Alnakawa, *see* Al-Nakawa, Ephraim
EPHRAIM BEN JACOB HA-KOHEN **6**:812
- Aryeh Judah Leib **3**:667
EPHRAIM BEN JACOB OF BONN **6**:813
- history of persecutions **8**:556
- martyrdom of Blois Jews **2**:558
- poetry **13**:692
Ephraim ben Jerahmeel **12**:216
Ephraim ben Joab **13**:581
Ephraim ben Judah **9**:513
Ephraim ben Meir Bums (Bimes) Margolioth of Bunzlau **6**:1317
EPHRAIM BEN SHEMARIAH **6**:813
- Ali ben Amram **2**:631
- Cairo *genizah* **16**:1338
- Solomon ben Judah **15**:122
Ephraim ben Zafran **11**:1188
Ephraim ha-Kohen **6**:812
EPHRAIM IBN AVI ALRAGAN **6**:813
Ephraim Moses ben Sender, *see* CILIBI, MOÏSE
Ephraim Mountains (Er. Isr.), *see* SAMARIA
Ephraim of Gaza **7**:342
EPHRAIM SOLOMON BEN AARON OF LUNTSHITS (Leczyca) **6**:814
- exile as social problem **7**:291ff
- *maggid* **11**:698
- social problems **8**:698
- *illus:* **8**:960
Ephrath (bib. fig.) **6**:815
EPHRATH (tn., Er. Isr.) **6**:815
Ephrati, Amram Merovas **2**:613
EPHRATI, DAVID TEVELE BEN ABRAHAM **6**:815
Ephrati, Simeon ben Yekutiel **14**:94
Ephrem the Syrian **5**:552
EPHRON (bib. fig.) **6**:816
- Abraham **2**:113
- Machpelah, Cave of **11**:670
Ephron (city, Er. Isr.), *see* OPHRAH
EPHRON (tn., Transj.) **6**:816
EPHRON (mount., Isr.) **6**:816
EPHROS, GERSHON **7**:1547
Ephros, Israel **14**:1264
EPHRUSSI, BORIS **6**:816
Ephrussi, Charles **3**:566
Epic, Sumerian **16**:1504
"Epicier" (paint., Mané-Katz) **13**:119
Epic of Creation, *see* Gilgamesh, Epic of
Epic of Gilgamesh, *see* Gilgamesh, Epic of
EPICTETUS (philos.) **6**:816
EPICUREANISM (philos.) **6**:817
- atomism **3**:829
- gods and man **8**:294
- Hellenistic period **8**:293,298
- Jewish philosophy **13**:423
Epigraphy, *see* Inscriptions
Epilepsy **6**:127,129; **16**:586
Epinal (tn., Fr.) **2**:756; **11**:497
Epiphanius (ch. f.) **3**:69,191; **9**:255
EPIRUS (prov., Gr.) **6**:818
EPISCOPUS JUDAEORIUM (tit.) **6**:818
- Worms **16**:645
Epistle, *see* LETTERS AND LETTER-WRITERS
Epistle of Barnabas (Apoc. wk.) **5**:551
Epistle of Jeremy (Jeremiah; Apoc. wk.), *see* JEREMIAH, EPISTLE OF
Epistle to Yemen (bk.), *see Iggeret Teiman*
Epistolae obscurorum virorum (bk.) **13**:357; **14**:109
Epistola Samuelis Maroccani (anti-J. epistle) **2**:607
EPITAPHS **6**:818
- Bet She'arim **4**:771
- Rome catacombs **14**:242
- *illus:*
- - text
- - Andrychow tombstone **15**:1228
- - Chryzanow tombstone **15**:1225
- - France, memorial to Jewish soldiers **7**:41
- - Narbonne (688/689 C.E.) **12**:828
- - Orléans tombstone **12**:1469
- - Tortosa, trilingual **15**:1270
- *see also:* TOMBS AND TOMBSTONES
EPPENSTEIN, SIMON **6**:822
Eppinger, William **8**:1256
Eppstein, Gottfried von, *see* Gottfried von Eppstein
Eppstein, Louis B. **15**:1035
EPPSTEIN, PAUL **6**:822
Epshtein, Mikhail Semyonovich, *see* GOLODNY, MIKHAIL
Epstein (fam., Cz.) **13**:969
Epstein, A. (indus., U.S.) **5**:377
Epstein, Aaron **6**:834
EPSTEIN, ABRAHAM (schol.) **6**:822
EPSTEIN, ABRAHAM (lit. crit.) **6**:823
- *illus:*
- - Hebrew Pen Club, N.Y. **8**:211
- - Hebrew writers convention, 1943 **8**:213
EPSTEIN, ABRAHAM (econ.) **6**:824
EPSTEIN, ABRAHAM MEIR BEN ARYEH LEIB **6**:824
EPSTEIN, ALVIN **15**:1081
Epstein, Arnold L. **3**:39
EPSTEIN, ARYEH LEIB BEN MORDECAI **6**:824
Epstein, B. **16**:1165
Epstein, Barbara **15**:1578
EPSTEIN, BARUCH HA-LEVI **6**:825
Epstein, Benjamin Wolf **12**:1419
EPSTEIN, BRIAN **15**:1081
Epstein, Chaim, *see* Epstein, Henri
Epstein, Charlotte **15**:313
Epstein, David A. **6**:465
Epstein, Eliahu, *see* ELATH, ELIAHU
Epstein, Ephraim (Chicago) **8**:216
Epstein, Ephraim (St. Louis) **14**:665
Epstein, Hayim Fischel **14**:665
Epstein, Henri **13**:117
Epstein, Herman **15**:488
EPSTEIN, ISAAC BEN MORDECAI (tal.) **6**:825
EPSTEIN, ISIDORE **6**:826
- Jews' College **10**:98
EPSTEIN, IZHAC **6**:826
Epstein, Jacob (collec.) **4**:148
EPSTEIN, SIR JACOB (sculp.) **6**:827
- portraits **13**:917
- *illus:*

- - text
- - Alexander, Samuel (bust) **2**:576
- - New York drawings **12**:1089,1090
- - Oved, Moshe (bust) **12**:1528
- - "Portrait of Winston Churchill" (sculp.) **14**:1062
- - Rosenfeld, Morris (drg.) **14**:285
- - Shaw, George Bernard (bust) **3**:555
Epstein, Jacob (au.) **15**:1573
EPSTEIN, JACOB NAHUM **6**:830
- *Sifrei Zuta* **14**:1522
- *Tarbiz* **15**:809
Epstein, Jacques **16**:917
Epstein, Jason **12**:1122; **13**:1373
EPSTEIN, JEAN **12**:453; **12**:466
EPSTEIN, JEHIEL MICHAL BEN AARON ISAAC HALEVI **6**:831
- codification of law **5**:655
EPSTEIN, JEHIEL MICHAL BEN ABRAHAM HA-LEVI **6**:832
- Shabbateanism **14**:1248
- *illus:* text
Epstein, Jehudo **3**:566
Epstein, Joseph **13**:148
Epstein, Joseph Baruch of Neustadt **6**:834
Epstein, Judah **16**:449
EPSTEIN, JUDITH **6**:833
Epstein, Julius (mus.) **16**:918
EPSTEIN, JULIUS J. (writ.) **12**:467
EPSTEIN, KALONYMUS KALMAN OF CRACOW **6**:834
EPSTEIN, LOUIS M. **6**:834
EPSTEIN, MELECH **6**:834
Epstein, Menahem Nahum **14**:1671
Epstein, Michael (trans.) **11**:357
Epstein, Michael P. (sport.) **15**:301
Epstein, Mieczyslaw **4**:176
Epstein, Morris **5**:451
Epstein, Moses Henry **15**:307
Epstein, Moses Jehiel of Ozárów **3**:668
EPSTEIN, MOSES MORDECAI **6**:835
- Broida, Simḥah Zissel **4**:1401
- Slobodka yeshivah **14**:1668
- *illus:*
- - Ḥafeẓ Ḥayyim's letter re Radun yeshivah **9**:1069
Epstein, M. S. **6**:465
EPSTEIN, PAUL SOPHUS **6**:836
Epstein, Philip G. **12**:467
Epstein, Robert **11**:1200
Epstein, S. (ed., U.S.) **5**:804
EPSTEIN, SEYMOUR **15**:1580
Epstein, Shakhne **3**:63; **6**:1077
Epstein, Shlomo **4**:982
Epstein, Vladimir **11**:1558
Epstein, Y., *see* Yakovlev, Y.
EPSTEIN, ZALMAN **6**:836
Epstein Training College for Kindergarten Teachers (Jer.) **2**:324
'Eqdaḥ (gem) **13**:1011
Equatorial Guinea (rep., Afr.), *see* Guinea, Equatorial
ER (bib. fig.) **6**:837
- Onan **12**:1395
Erasmus (schol.)
- Pfefferkorn, Johannes **13**:356
- population **13**:879
- Reuchlin, Johannes **14**:109
ERATOSTHENES OF CYRENE **7**:894
- Hellenistic literature **8**:293
Erbil (tn.,Iraq), *see* IRBIL
Ercole I (It. prin.), *see* Este, Ercole I
Ercole II (It. prin.), *see* Este, Ercole II
Ercole dei Fideli (crftn.), *see* SESSO, SALAMONE DA
Ercsei, Daniel **8**:31
Erdberg (tn., Ger.) **8**:1043
Erdman, Allan **11**:743; **12**:1377; **15**:313
Erdmann, J.F. **12**:1377
Erdösi, Sylvester János **8**:31
ERECH (city, Sumer) **6**:837
- Babylon **4**:31
- city structure **5**:584
- Edessa **6**:367
- excavations **16**:1507
Mesopotamia **16**:1487ff
- Sumer **15**:512
Ereda (concen. camp) **6**:917
Erekh Millim (tal. dict.) **6**:731
Erel, Shlomo **14**:1630
Erenberg, Philip **12**:1376; **15**:309
Ereshkigal (deity) **12**:996
Eretz-Israel (journ.) **1**: newsp. list
Erez (pseud.), *see* ZEDERBAUM, ALEXANDER
Erez (kib., Isr.) **1**: place list
Ereẓ (journ.) **1**: newsp. list **12**:1051; **13**:1047
Ereẓ Canaan (Slav. countries) **3**:720
EREẒ ISRAEL **6**:837
- *see also:* CANAAN, LAND OF; ISRAEL
Ereẓ Israel Worker's Fund **9**:853; **10**:754
Ereẓ Yisrael (period., Isr.) **1**: newsp. list **15**:55
Ereẓ Yisrael; Enziklopedyah Topografit-Historit (enc.) **6**:734
Ereẓ Yisrael ha-Shelemah, *see* Greater Land of Israel Movement
Erfûd (city, Mor.) **14**:1529
- *illus:*
- - widow in mourning attire **12**:492
ERFURT (city, Ger.) **6**:837
- Arnstadt **3**:488
- synagogue **15**:604
- synod **15**:633
- Thuringia **15**:1127
ERGAS, JOSEPH BEN EMANUEL **6**:839
- Pinheiro, Moses **13**:537
- Shabbateanism **14**:1249
- *ẓimẓum* **10**:593
- *illus:* text
Ergas, Judah **12**:897
Ergas, Raphael **5**:239
Erhard, T.A. **4**:874
Erholz, Nathan **4**:207
Erība-Marduk (k., Babyl.) **11**:1389
Erich, Aron-Hertz, *see* Serbu Ieronim
Ericson, Walter, *see* FAST, HOWARD MELVIN
Eridu (city, Mesop.) **16**:2, 1484
Erie (city, Pa.) **13**:230
Erigena, Johannes (John) Scotus **3**:1013
ERIK, MAX **6**:841
ERIKSON, ERIK HOMBERGER **6**:841
Eritrea (Afr.) **8**:1467; **9**:356
- Semitic languages **14**:1149
ERLANGEN (city, Ger.) **6**:842
Erlangen Haggadah (illum. ms.) **8**:1031
ERLANGER (fam., bnks.) **6**:842
Erlanger, Arlene **15**:311
ERLANGER, CAMILLE **12**:688
Erlanger, Frederic-Emile **6**:842
ERLANGER, JOSEPH **6**:842
- biology **4**:1032
Erlanger, Ludwig **6**:842
ERLANGER, MICHEL **6**:843
Erlanger, Milton **15**:312
Erlanger, Raphael **6**:842
Erlanger, Victor **6**:842
Erlau (city, Hung.), *see* EGER
ERLICH, HENRYK **6**:844
- Anti-Fascist Committee **3**:62
- *illus:*
- - text
- - Warsaw Bund demonstration **4**:1506
Erlich, Sophia, *see* Dubnow-Erlich, Sophia
ERLICH, VERA STEIN **6**:845
Erlich, Wolf Hersh, *see* ERLICH, HENRYK
Erlick, David **11**:1204
ERMAN, JOHANN PETER ADOLF **6**:845
Ermengaud, Matfre d', *see* Matfre d'Ermengaud
Ermler, Friedrich **12**:456
ERNAKULAM (tn., Ind.) **6**:845
- Cochin **5**:624
- India **8**:1355
- *illus:*
- - text
- - Theckobagam synagogue **5**:625
Erna Michael College of Hebraic Studies **16**:761
Erna Michael Haggadah (illum. ms.) **7**:1098; **8**:1267
- *illus:* **2**:554; **7**:*fcg.* 1067,1299; **8**:1280
Ernst, Max **13**:114
Ernst Thaelmann district (underground orgn.) **12**:56
Ernuszt, János **11**:1316; **13**:963
Erotic symbolism **10**:613; **10**:642
ERPENIUS, THOMAS **6**:846
- Christian Hebraists **8**:31
Errera, Abraham Kohen de, *see* HERRERA, ABRAHAM KOHEN DE
ERRERA, CARLO **6**:846
Errera, Jacques (bnk.) **4**:177
ERRERA, JACQUES (chem.) **5**:381
ERRERA, LÉO **6**:846
ERRERA, PAUL JOSEPH **6**:847
Error, *see* MISTAKE
Er-Routi (fam.), *see* ROTE
Érsekújvár (tn., Cz.), *see* NOVE ZAMKY
Erstein (tn.,Fr.) **2**:757
Ertel, János **8**:31
ERTER, ISAAC **6**:847
- Haskalah **8**:184
- Levinsohn **6**:849 **11**:116
- *illus:* text
Erusin, *see* BETROTHAL
ERUV (leg. device) **6**:849
- Commandments, the 613 **5**:781
- communal amenities **2**:807
- Sabbath **14**:566
- *see also:* DOMICILE
Eruv Ḥaẓerot (leg. device) **6**:849
- *illus:*
- - *Bava Batra* **4**:336
ERUVIN (tal. tract.) **6**:850
- Sabbath **14**:1216
- *illus:* text
Eruv Tavshilin (leg. device) **6**:849
- *illus:*
- - tablet (1806, Ger.) **7**:*fcg.* 843
Eruv Teḥumim (leg. device) **6**:849
Erwache (newsp.) **16**:1224
Erwig (k., Sp.) **15**:221
Erwin, Egon **13**:973
Erwitt, Elliott **13**:484
Eryngo (bot.) **13**:617
Erythrea (Afr.), *see* Eritrea
Erythrean (lang.), *see* Hamito-Semitic
Esagila (temple, Babyl.) **4**:23; **4**:33; **11**:952
Esagny, A. D. **11**:303
ESARHADDON (Assyr. k.) **6**:852
- Aḥikar **2**:460
- Deuteronomy, Book of **5**:1577
- Ekron **6**:560
- Mesopotamia **16**:1504
- Ur **16**:3
- *illus:* text
ESAU (bib. fig.) **6**:854
- Adah **2**:233
- Amalek **2**:790
- Christianity **5**:514
- Commandments, the 613 **5**:773
- Edomites **6**:370ff
- Frankists **7**:60
- Genesis, Book of **7**:389
- Haman **12**:309
- in the Arts **9**:7, 1202f
- Isaac **9**:4; **9**:5ff
- Jacob **9**:1191ff
- Leah **10**:1526
- Machpelah, Cave of **11**:673
- Nimrod **12**:1167
- Nuzi documents **16**:1510
- Rachel **13**:1487ff
- Rebekah **13**:1601ff
- Reuben **14**:106
- Samael **14**:720
- sun **12**:291; **15**:517
- Titus **15**:1169
- *illus:*
- - text
- - at Isaac's deathbed **3**:515
- - birth **4**:943; **13**:1602
- - birthright sale **4**:943
- - Jacob's messengers **2**:956
Esbus (city, Transj.), *see* HESHBON
ESCALONA (tn., Sp.) **6**:859
ESCAPA, JOSEPH BEN SAUL **6**:859
- Benveniste, Ḥayyim **4**:559
- Izmir **9**:1162
- Shabbetai Ẓevi **14**:1222
- taxation **15**:872
ESCHATOLOGY **6**:860
- *Contents:*
- - Bible **6**:861
- - Intertestamental Literature **6**:872
- - Talmudic Period **6**:879
- - Kabbalah **6**:880
- - Islam **6**:883
- General
- - Antiochus IV Epiphanes **8**:629
- - Ḥasidism **14**:1436ff
- - Hebrew fiction **6**:1261ff
- - illustrated *haggadot* **7**:1097
- - Judaism **10**:388; **10**:390
- - *kaddish* **10**:661
- - man, the nature of **11**:845
- Bible
- - Apocalypse **3**:179ff
- - apocalyptic literature **11**:311
- - Balaam's oracles **4**:123
- - Isaiah **9**:47
- - Melchizedek **11**:1288
- - Messiah **11**:1408
- - Micah **11**:1481ff
- Apocrypha and Pseudepigrapha **3**:183
- - *Abraham, Apocalypse of* **3**:127
- - *Moses, Assumption of* **12**:411
- - *Solomon, Wisdom of* **15**:119
- - son of man **15**:159
- - *Testament of the Patriarchs* **13**:186
- - *Ẓerubbabel, Book of* **16**:1002
- Qumran community
- - *Discipline, Manual of* **6**:64
- - Pesher **13**:331ff
- - Teacher of Righteousness **15**:886
- - Thanksgiving Psalms **15**:1046
- - War Scroll **16**:1559
- - Yaḥad **16**:700
- Kabbalah **6**:880 **10**:541; **10**:612ff
- - evil **10**:587
- - mystical speculation **10**:497
- - netherworld **12**:996
- - resurrection **14**:96
- - reward and punishment **14**:134
- - Zohar **16**:1208
- Views
- - Abrabanel, Isaac **2**:108
- - Abraham bar Ḥiyya **2**:132ff
- - Judah Loew ben Bezalel of Prague **10**:377
- - Judah Halevi **10**:359
- - Levi ben Gershom **11**:97

-- Luria, Isaac ben Solomon **11:**578
-- Maimonides **11:**776
-- Philo **13:**411
-- Saadiah **13:**432
- Islam **6:**883 **9:**92
-- Jerusalem **9:**1424; **9:**1576ff
- *illus:*
- *Fin de los Dias* (1666) **14:**1233
- *see also:* AFTERLIFE; ANTICHRIST; BEATITUDE; DAY OF THE LORD; GOG AND MAGOG; OLAM HA-BA; PARADISE; REVELATION; RIGHTEOUSNESS
ESCHELBACHER, JOSEPH **6:**886
Eschelbacher, Max (r.) **6:**886
Eschkol Verlag (publ. firm) **13:**1373
Esch-sur-Alzette (tn., Lux.) **11:**591
Escorting the dead **4:**1518ff
ESCUDERO, LORENZO **6:**886
Escuela Integral (educ. inst.) **16:**14
Esdraelon, Plain of (Isr.), *see* JEZREEL, VALLEY OF
Esdras, Book of, *see* EZRA, GREEK BOOK OF
Esek (loc., Er. Isr.) **7:**432
Esenwein, M. **8:**31
Esfa, see Midrash Esfa
Esgers, J. **8:**31
Esh (leg. conc.), *see* AVOT NEZIKIN; FIRE; TORTS
ESH, SHAUL **1:**29
Eshbaal (k., Isr.), *see* ISH-BOSHETH
Eshbol (mosh., Isr.) **1:** place list
Eshel ha-Nasi (agr. school, Isr.) **1:** place list
ESHET ḤAYIL (song, Proverbs) **6:**886
- *illus:* text
Esh ha-Mazref (bk.), *see Esh Mezaref*
Eshkero'a (bot.) *see* BOX
Eshkol (bib. fig.), *see* ANER, ESHKOL AND MAMRE
Eshkol (tn., Isr.) **12:**930
Eshkol, Enziklopedyah Yisre'elit (enc.) **6:**732
ESHKOL, LEVI **6:**887
- Aḥdut ha-Avodah **2:**456
- Ben-Gurion **4:**512
- chronological chart **8:**766-767
- holy places **8:**940; **9:**411
- Israel historical survey **9:**398ff
- Mapai **11:**913ff; **13:**1512
- nuclear development **9:**403
- politics **9:**666ff
- Six-Day War **9:**407ff **14:**1626
- Writers' Association **16:**653
- *illus:*
-- text
-- autograph **3:**915
-- inspecting Druze honor guard **9:**927
-- Israel Bonds dinner, N.Y. **12:**1113
-- Labor parties' merger meeting **9:**677
-- Ramot Eshkol housing project, Jerusalem **2:**846
-- Six-Day War, meeting religious leaders **9:**410
-- Six-Day War, with soldiers **9:**409
-- Texas visit, 1968 **9:**405
-- U.S. ambassadors and **9:**427
Eshkol development region (Isr.) **9:**576; **9:**594
Eshkol ha-Kofer (bk.) **7:**1046; **16:**1417
Eshkolot (journ., Isr.) **1:** newsp list
Eshkolot (journ., Rus.) **1:** newsp. list
Esh Mezaref (bk.) **2:**545; **10:**1117
Eshmunʿazar (k., Phoen.) **14:**79
- Dor **6:**172
- inscription **16:**668
- *illus:*
-- Phoenician inscription **2:**680
-- sarcophagus **13:**480
Eshna (bib. fig.) **2:**455
Eshnav (journ.) **1:** newsp. list
Eshnav la-Olam (U.N.period.) **15:**1566
Eshnunna (kdm., Mesop.) **16:**1496
- Hammurapi **7:**1247
- virgin **16:**161
Esh-Sheikh Madhkur (vill., Isr.) **2:**312
ESHTAOL (tn., mosh., Isr.) **6:**892
- Samson **14:**773
- statistics **1:** place list
ESHTEMOA (city, Er. Isr.) **6:**892
- Socoh **15:**69
- synagogue **15:**597
- *illus*
-- text
-- synagogue plan **15:**597
-- synagogue sculpture **12:**569
Eshtori ha-Farḥi, *see* ESTORI HA-PARHI
ESKELES (fam., Aus.) **6:**893
- banking **3:**894
- railroads **13:**1517ff
- title of nobility **15:**1166
Eskeles, Bernard Gabriel, *see* Eskeles, Issachar Berush
Eskeles, Bernhard **4:**176; **6:**894
Eskeles, Cecily **6:**894
Eskeles, Denis (Daniel) **6:**894
Eskeles, Eleanore, *see* Eskeles, Lea
Eskeles, Gabriel ben Judah Loew **6:**893
Eskeles, Issachar Berush **2:**427
Eskeles, Lea **6:**894
Eskeles-Stiftung, (found.) **6:**894
Eskimo (N. Am. people) **4:**1152
Esoterics, *see* KABBALAH
España, Juan de, *see* JUAN DE ESPAÑA
Espencaeus (d'Espence), Claude **8:**31
Esperança de Israel (wk.) **11:**856; **14:**1168
- *illus:* **11:**856
Esperanto **16:**925
Esperanza (Zion.soc.) **16:**1148
Esperanza, Gabriel **6:**919; **12:**314
Espés (fam.) **15:**1300
Espina, Alfonso de, *see* ALFONSO DE ESPINA
ESPINOSA, EDOUARD (dan.dir.) **5:**1272
Espinosa, Leon **5:**1272
Espinoza, Abraham d' **12:**817
ESPINOZA, ENRIQUE **10:**310
- literature **15:**255
Espionage
- Bible
-- Caleb **5:**41
-- Jericho **9:**1366
-- Joshua **10:**265
-- spies, the twelve **12:**377
- Beer, Israel **4:**377
- Cohen, Eli **5:**668
- Eskeles, Lea **6:**894
- Ḥabad ḥasidim **7:**1397
- London, Jacob ben Moses Judah **11:**483
- Nathan, Mulla Ibrahim **12:**854
- Rosenberg case **14:**280
- Rosenblum, Sigmund **14:**283
- Salomon, Hayim **14:**695
- Trebitsch-Lincoln, Ignatius Timothy **15:**1364
- *illus:*
-- Rahab and two Israelite spies **13:**1514
Espir, Elie **12:**1166
Esplugas (fam.) **15:**1300
ESRA (orgn., Ger.) **6:**895
- Allianz, Israelitische, zu Wien **2:**654
- Erez Israel settlement **16:**1041
- Zemach, Shlomo **16:**982
- Zionism **16:**1115
Esrim ve-Arba, Moses, *see* MOSES ESRIM VE-ARBA
Ess, Leander van **4:**875
Es-Salt (tn., Jor.), *see* Salt
ESSELIN, ALTER **6:**896
ESSEN (city, Ger.) **6:**896
- synagogue **15:**620
- *illus:* text
ESSENES (sect) **6:**899
- General
-- Abba title **2:**31
-- Angelology **2:**962
-- Apocalyptic movement **3:**180
-- Dead Sea sect **5:**1418
-- Hellenism **8:**295; **8:**299
-- Jesus **10:**13
-- *Jubilees, Book of* **10:**325
-- minor sects **14:**1087ff
-- origin **10:**390
-- Pseudepigrapha **3:**185
-- sages' associations **14:**642ff
- Rites, Practices, and Doctrines
-- ablution **2:**82; **13:**1412
-- acceptance rites **7:**1490
-- asceticism **3:**678ff
-- ethics **6:**941
-- free will **7:**129
-- *ḥerem* **8:**361
-- legal person example **10:**1569
-- medicine **11:**1181
-- mystical tendencies **10:**496
-- providence **13:**1289
- *see also:* PHARISEES; QUMRAN; THERAPEUTAE; YAḤAD
Essen-teg (eating days) **8:**1033; **16:**768
Essequibo (reg., Guiana) **15:**529
ESSEX COUNTY (N.J.) **6:**902
- *illus:* text
Essingen, Samuel Michel **4:**6; **16:**302
ESSLINGEN (city, Ger.) **6:**905
Estado da Bahia (reg., Braz.), *see* BAHIA
Estate, *see* APOTROPOS; SUCCESSION; WILLS
Este (fam.) **6:**1231ff
Este, Ercole I (prin., It.) **6:**1231; **6:**1232
Este, Ercole II (prin., It.) **6:**1232
Este, Isaac ben Aaron d' *see* Isaac ben Aaron d'Este
ESTE, JOÃO BAPTISTA DE (apos.) **6:**905
ESTELLA (city, Sp.) **6:**905
Estella, David ben Samuel, *see* KOKHAVI, DAVID BEN SAMUEL
Ester, Samuel **12:**1360
Esterhazy, Ferdinand Walsin **6:**226ff
Esterka of Opoczno **5:**228
ESTERMANN, IMMANUEL **6:**906
- Pittsburgh **13:**570
Esterwegen (concen. camp) **5:**77
ESTEVENS, DAVID **6:**906
- art **3:**539
ESTHER (bib. fig.) **6:**906
- Ahasuerus-Xerxes **2:**454
- Hamadan tomb **7:**1220
- Haman **7:**1222
- in the Arts **13:**1401
- moon comparison **12:**291
- Mordecai **12:**307
- *Scroll of Esther* **14:**1048ff **14:**1058
- *Targum Sheni* **15:**812
- tax **15:**841
- *illus:*
-- Ahasuerus **14:**1054
-- before Ahasuerus **2:**453
-- Dura-Europos **6:**284; **8:**649
-- eighteenth cent. *ketubbah* Pl. 2 **10**-KETUBBAH
-- twelfth cent. Bible **12:**733
ESTHER (commun.) **6:**913
Esther (Eth. q.), *see* Judith
ESTHER, ADDITIONS TO THE BOOK OF **6:**913
- Haman **7:**1223
- textual insertions **8:**304
Esther, Book of, *see* SCROLL OF ESTHER
ESTHER, FAST OF **6:**914
- calendar **5:**47
- Falashas **6:**1148
- Karaites **10:**779
ESTHER RABBAH (agg. Mid.) **6:**915
- Talmud **15:**762
- *see also:* MIDRASH
Esthersohn, U., *see* GNESSIN, URI NISSAN
Estienne (Stephanus), Robert **13:**1099ff
- Bibles **7:**404; **13:**109
- Le Bé, Guillaume **10:**1547
- typography **15:**1482
- *illus:*
-- Bible edition (1544-46) **15:**1484
ESTONIA **6:**916
- emancipation **6:**716
- minority rights **12:**45
- population **14:**482
ESTORI (ISAAC BEN MOSES) HA-PARḤI **6:**918
- agriculture **2:**398
- Beth-Shean **4:**760
- *Kaftor va-Feraḥ* **9:**281
- travel book **11:**351
- travels **15:**1352; **15:**1354
- *illus:* text
Estremadura (dist., Port.) **14:**847
ESTROSA, DANIEL **6:**919
- Istrumsa, Ḥayyim Abraham **9:**1100
Estrosa, Ḥayyim Abraham, *see* ISTRUMSA, ḤAYYIM ABRAHAM
Eszek (tn., Yug.), *see* OSIJEK
ESZTERGOM (city, Hung.) **6:**920
Étain (tn., Fr.) **11:**497
Et al-Salām (newsp.) **4:**403; **13:**1041; **15:**645
ETAM (locs., Er. Isr.) **6:**920
- Samson **14:**772
ÉTAMPES (tn., Fr.) **6:**920
Etana (k., Mesop.) **16:**1486; **16:**1490
Eternal creation, *see* CREATION AND COSMOGONY
Eternal Jew, *see* WANDERING JEW
Eternal Jew (play) **13:**550; **16:**262
- *illus:*
-- Vilna ghetto performance **16:**145
Eternal lamp, *see* NER TAMID
Eternal Light (radio and television series) **10:**96
Eternity, *see* TIME AND ETERNITY
Etgar (period.) **5:**102; **16:**738
ETHAN (bib. fig.) **6:**921
- Jeduthun **9:**1311
- Psalms, Book of **13:**1318
Ethanim (bib. month) **5:**48; **16:**725
Ethausen, Isaac Saeckel **3:**687
ETHBAAL (10th cent. B.C.E., k., Phoen.) **6:**921
ETHBAAL (9th cent. B.C.E., k., Phoen.) **6:**921
- Omri's treaty **8:**596; **12:**1391
- Sidon **13:**477; **14:**1506
ETHBAAL (6th cent. B.C.E., k., Phoen.) **6:**921
Ethereal body (kab. conc.) **10:**611
ETHERIDGE, JOHN WESLEY **6:**921
- Christian Hebraists **8:**31
ETHICAL CULTURE (mvmt.,

U.S.) 6:922
- Adler, Felix 2:276
- Neumann, Henry 12:1012
Ethical Idealism (phil. system) 6:1260
Ethical letters 6:924; 11:59
ETHICAL LITERATURE 6:922
- *Contents:*
- - Literary Form and Purpose 6:923
- - Philosophical-Ethical 6:925
- - Rabbinic-Ethical 6:927
- - Ashkenazi-Ḥasidic 6:928
- - Kabbalistic-Ethical 6:930
- General
- - dualism 6:243
- - Ḥasidei Ashkenaz 7:1377
- - Hebrew fiction 6:1267
- - homiletics 8:947ff; 13:999
- - Jewish literature 11:343ff
- - Kabbalah 10:539; 10:642
- - Musar movement 12:536
- - wills 16:530ff
- - Yiddish literature 11:358; 16:803
- Works
- - *Gei Ḥizzavon* 9:1267
- - *Ḥemdat Yamim* 8:320ff
- - *Ḥovot ha-Levavot* 4:105f
- - *Iggeret ha-Kodesh* 8:1237
- - *Iggeret ha-Musar* 6:1142
- - *Menorat ha-Ma'or* 2:672
- - *Meshal ha-Kadmoni* 5:430 14:656
- - *Mesillat Yesharim* 11:602
- - *Midrash Aseret ha-Dibberot* 11:1515
- - *Mivḥar ha-Peninim* 12:163
- - *Musar Haskel* 12:534
- - *Nezed ha-Dema* 14:1107
- - *Orḥot Hayyim* 12:1457
- - *Orḥot Zaddikim* 12:1458
- - *Sefer Ḥasidim* 6:1268; 7:1388; 11:343
- - *Sefer ha-Yashar* 14:1099
- - *Sha'arei Teshuvah* 10:179
- - *Tikkun Middot ha-Nefesh* 7:243; 11:343
- - *Tohorot ha-Kodesh* 15:1191
- - *Ẓori ha-Yagon* 6:1142
- *illus:*
- - *Catechismus Judaeorum* (1679) 9:1268
- - *Ḥovot ha-Levavot* 4:106; 5:785
- - *Meshal ha-Kadmoni* 3:19,534,791; 5:430
- - *Mesillat Yesharim* (1740) 11:600
- - *Orḥot Ẓaddikim* (1581) 12:1458
- - *Sefer Ḥasidim* (1685) 7:1389
- - *Sha'arei Teshuvah* (1595) 10:179
- - *Tikkun Middot ha-Nefesh* (1562) 6:933
- *see also:* DEVEKUT; ETHICS; HAGIOGRAPHY; HEBREW LITERATURE, MODERN; MUSAR MOVEMENT
Ethical Wills, *see* WILLS
ETHICS 6:932
- *Contents:*
- - Bible 6:932
- - Ancient Near East 6:938
- - Later Jewish Thought 6:940
- Concepts
- - animals, kindness to 3:6
- - compassion 5:855
- - *derekh ereẓ* 5:1551
- - duty 6:323
- - emotions 6:727
- - etiquette 6:947
- - free will 7:125
- - hospitality 8:1030
- - knowledge 16:561
- - redemption 14:3
- - righteousness 14:184
- - soul 15:173
- - vengeance 16:93
- Bible
- - abomination 2:97
- - Achan 2:209
- - *Akedah* 2:482
- - Decalogue 5:1435ff
- - dietary laws 6:42
- - Divine origin 7:652
- - fear of God 6:1198
- - Genesis 7:395
- - law and morality 10:1480ff
- - lost property 11:504
- - monotheism 12:261
- - Noachide laws 12:1189
- - prophecy 13:1161; 13:1172
- - Proverbs 13:1268
- - woman 16:626
- New Testament 12:1061
- Later Jewish Thought
- - *aggadah* 2:355
- - Aristotelianism 13:430ff
- - *Avot* 3:983
- - Ben Sira, Wisdom of 4:551
- - gentiles 7:410ff
- - Ḥasidei Ashkenaz 7:1381
- - Ḥasidism 7:1397
- - Jewish mysticism 10:512; 10:513ff
- - Jewish philosophy 13:421
- - Kabbalah 10:640
- - Kantianism 10:743
- - Karaite Kalam 13:433
- - Reform Judaism 14:25ff
- - sages 14:646
- Views On
- - Baḥya 13:435
- - Cohen, Hermann 13:460
- - Gabirol, Solomon ibn 7:243ff
- - Graetz, Heinrich 10:385
- - Ibn Daud 8:1163
- - Lazarus, Moritz 10:1518; 13:460
- - Maimonides 11:774ff
- - Philo 13:427ff
- - Spinoza, Baruch 15:279ff
- *illus:* text
- *see also:* ETHICAL LITERATURE; ETIQUETTE; FRIENDSHIP; ḤASIDIM, SEFER; IMITATION OF GOD; MUSAR MOVEMENT; TORAH
Ethics, Business, *see* Business Ethics
Ethics, Medical, *see* Medical Ethics
Ethics of the Fathers (Mish. tract.), *see* AVOT
Ethik des Judentums (bk.) 10:1517
ETHIOPIA 6:943
- Cush 5:1174
- Falashas 6:1143ff
- India 8:1349
- Jerusalem community 9:1441
- language 14:1153
- population 13:871ff
- Solomon 13:1424
- synagogues 1:syn. list
- Wingate, Charles Orde 16:548
- *illus:* text
Ethiopian Church (Jer.) 6:943; 9:912
Ethiopic (lang.) 4:860; 14:1149; 16:1394
ETHNARCH (tit.) 6:945
- Alexandria 2:589
- Hasmoneans 8:631; 8:632
- *see also:* ALABARCH
Ethnic-Folkways Records (co., N.Y.) 13:1618
Ethnology 3:38ff; 12:882
- *illus:*
- - St. Petersburg expedition 12:541
Ethnomusicology, *see* MUSIC
Étienne, Robert, *see* Estienne, Robert
Etienne de la Boétie, *see* LA BOÉTIE, ETIENNE DE
ETIQUETTE 6:946
- *derekh ereẓ* 5:1551
- meals 14:1193
- *talmid ḥakham* 15:747
- *see also:* ETHICS
Etkind, Y.G. 4:1395
Et Livnot (Gen. Zion. faction, Pol.) 16:1132
'Etnaḥ (*'etnaḥta'*; cantillation sign) 16:1439,1455
- *mus. notations:*
- - masoretic accents 11:1107
Etoile, Meir 15:124
Etoile du Lévant (period.) 15:1461
ETROG (citron) 6:947
- Bet Alfa mosaics 4:713
- citrus 5:580
- containers 15:502
- German community 7:470
- *hakkafot* 7:1153
- kibbutz 10:1570
- ownership 12:1531
- right hand 14:180
- sacrifice 14:612
- size, minimum 6:474
- synagogue art 15:597ff
- *illus:*
- - text
- - Dura-Europos wall paint. 6:265
- - Ḥasidic boy 15:*fcg.* 491
- - oil lamp 12:1349
- - Ostia synagogue 12:1508
- - Roman catacomb 15:569
- - 2/3 cent. bas-relief 3:716
- - silver container 5:305; 15:*fcg.* 494
- *see also:* FOUR SPECIES
ETROG, SOREL 3:599
- *illus:*
- - "Capriccio" (sculp.) 3:622
Etruria, *see* TUSCANY
Et Sha'arei Raẓon le-Hippate'aḥ (litur. poem) 2:39
Ets-Ḥayyim (yeshivah, Amst.) 13:287; 16:766
Etsi doctoribus gentium (papal bull) 4:1496
Etsi Judaeorum (papal bull) 4:1495
Etsi non displiceat (papal bull) 4:1495
Et Sofer (wk.) 16:1386
Ettelsohn, Nachman Baer 5:417
ETTENDORF (tn., Fr.) 6:951
ETTING (U.S. fam.) 6:951
Etting, Benjamin 12:1067
Etting, Elijah (mer.) 6:951
Etting, Elijah Gratz (law.) 10:1503
Etting, Frances, *see* Gratz, Frances
Etting, Reuben 6:951
Etting, Samuel 6:951
Etting, Shinah 6:951
Etting, Solomon 6:951
- *illus:* text
ETTINGER (fam.) 6:952
Ettinger, Aaron 6:952
ETTINGER, AKIVA JACOB 6:953
Ettinger, Baruch Mordecai 6:952
Ettinger, Eliezer ha-Levi 6:1074
Ettinger, Elijah 5:783
Ettinger, Ḥayyim Judah Leib 6:952
Ettinger, Isaac Aaron 6:952,954; 12:866
Ettinger, Jehiel Michel 10:1392
Ettinger, Joseph (schol.) 6:952
Ettinger, Joseph (writ.) 5:1034; 16:1328
Ettinger, Joseph ha-Levi (r.) 5:484
Ettinger, Max 6:21; 10:461
ETTINGER, MORDECAI ZE'EV BEN ISAAC AARON SEGAL 6:953
- family 6:952
- Nathanson, Joseph 12:867
Ettinger, Samuel 6:952
Ettinger, Sarah Idel 12:866
ETTINGER, SOLOMON 6:954
- *Kol Mevasser* 10:1166
- *illus:* text
Ettinger, W. 6:954
Ettinghausen, Jean-Maurice, *see* SACHS, MAURICE
Ettinghausen, Maurice L. 6:1078
Ettinghausen, Richard 3:650; 12:1461
Ettinghausen, Walter, *see* EYTAN, WALTER
Ettingon brothers 11:426; 11:432
Ettlingen (fam.), *see* OTTOLENGHI
ETTLINGEN (tn., Ger.) 6:955
- special Purim 13:1397
Ettlinger, Aaron 6:955
Ettlinger, B. A. 10:1502
ETTLINGER, JACOB 6:955
- Ash, Abraham Joseph 3:694
- *ḥiddushim* 8:467
- Hirsch, S. R. 8:508
- *illus:* text
Etwas ueber die rabbinische Literatur (pam.) 16:572
Etz Chaim (yeshivah, Lond.) 6:448,450
Etz Haim (yeshivah, Braz.) 4:1324
Etzion Bloc (Er. Isr.), *see* Eẓyon Bloc
Etzioni, Amitai 15:68
Euboea (Gr. port), *see* CHALCIS
Euboea (isl., Gr.) 5:329; 6:10; 7:868
Eucalyptus (bot.) 6:1366; 9:788
Eucharist (Chr. rite) 2:123; 10:12
EUCHEL, ISAAC ABRAHAM 6:956
- Haskalah comedy 16:807
- universities 15:1677
Euchomenoi (sect) 14:1087
Euclid (Gr. schol.) 8:293; 15:1130
Eudes of Châteauroux, *see* ODO OF CHÂTEAUROUX
Eudes of Sully, *see* ODO OF SULLY
Eudocia (emp.) 11:57
- Jerusalem 9:1406; 9:1537; 9:1540
Eudoxios (paint.) 3:508; 13:916
Eugene (city, Oreg.) 12:1451
Eugenio Maria, *see* ZOLLER, ISRAEL
EUGENIUS III (pope) 6:957
- Crusades 5:1139
EUGENIUS IV (pope) 6:957
- attitude to Jews 13:856
- Roman Jews 14:247
Eugubinus (Hebr.), *see* Steuco, Agostino
EUHEMERUS (writ.) 7:894
- gods 8:294
EULAU, HEINZ 6:958
Eullenburg, Abraham Moses Israel 6:958
EULENBURG, ERNST 12:688
EULENBURG, ISAAC BEN ABRAHAM MOSES ISRAEL 6:958
Eulenburg, Issachar Baer 5:237
EULENBURG, KURT 12:688
Eulogy, *see* HESPED
Eumenes II (k., Pergamum) 16:659
EUNUCH 6:959
- castration 5:242
- Commandments, the 613 5:781
- trade restrictions 16:1281
- *see also:* RAB-SARIS
Eupatoria (city, Rus.), *see* YEVPATORIYA
EUPHEMISM AND DYSPHEMISM 6:959
- abomination 2:96f
- blasphemy 4:1073
- *derekh ereẓ* 5:1551
- God, names of 7:655
- masorah 16:1421ff
- profanity 13:1119
- *tikkun soferim* 15:1139
- *see also:* IDOLATRY; KIDDUSH HA-SHEM AND ḤILLUL HA-SHEM
Euphemitai (sect) 14:1087
EUPHRATES (riv., As.) 6:962

- Aram-Naharaim **3**:252f
- Assur **3**:783
- Babylonia **4**:34
- Garden of Eden **13**:78
- Mesopotamia **16**:1490
- *illus:*
- - text
- - Sumer **15**:513
EUPOLEMUS (Gr. hist.) **6**:964
- apologetics **3**:189
- biblical history **8**:304
- Greek debt to Jews **8**:300
Eupolemus ben Johanan (John; pr.)
- Eupolemus identification **6**:964
- priests **13**:1086
- Rome delegation **8**:627; **14**:240
Eureka (vill., Nev.) **12**:1017
Euripides (plwrt., Gr.) **6**:1103; **8**:293
EUROPA, MADAMA **6**:965
EUROPA PLAN **6**:966
- Jewish councils **8**:883
- Wisliceny, Dieter **16**:569
EUROPE **6**:966
- *Contents:*
- - Antiquity **6**:966
- - Rise of Christianity and Islam **6**:968
- - Medieval Period **6**:969
- - Renaissance and Counter-Reformation **6**:970
- - Emancipation **6**:972
- - World War I **6**:975
- - Anti-Semitism and Nazism **6**:975
- agriculture **2**:401
- Ashkenaz **3**:719ff
- autonomy **3**:924
- beriḥah **4**:622ff
- concentration and extermination camps **5**:77
- demography **5**:1494
- economic environment **16**:1297ff
- history chart **8**:676-677
- hospitals **8**:1034
- migrations **16**:1522
- moneylending **12**:254
- secondhand goods trade **14**:1085ff
- socialism **15**:27ff
- statistics **15**:344; **16**:177ff
- *illus:*
- - anti-Semitic parties, 1870-1914 (table) **3**:81
- - Austria, first record of Jews in (c. 903-906) **3**:889
- - Black Death (map) **4**:1065
- - blood libels (map) **4**:1125
- - Jewish badges decreed by the Nazis **4**:72
- - refugee children **14**:32
- *pop. tables:*
- - text
- - General
- - - 1300/1490 **13**:877
- - - 19/20 centuries **13**:893,898,899
- - Albania **2**:523
- - Alsace **2**:751
- - Ashkenazi settlement and emigration **3**:719
- - Austria **3**:887
- - - Austrian provinces, 1910-1934 **3**:897
- - Baden **4**:60
- - Bavaria, 10th cent. to 1932-33 **4**:347
- - Belgium **4**:418
- - Bessarabia, 1897 **4**:707
- - Bohemia
- - - Jewish communities **4**:1173
- - - Jewish population, 1754-1930 **4**:1180
- - - mixed marriages, 1881-1930 **4**:1179
- - Bulgaria, 1878-1967 **4**:1481,1485
- - Byzantine Empire **4**:1551
- - countries with 500 or more Jews, 1967 **5**:1503
- - countries with 5,000 or more Jews, 1939 and 1967 **5**:1500,1507
- - Crete, medieval communities **5**:1089
- - Czechoslovakia **5**:1189
- - - Moravia, 1908 **12**:297
- - - Prague, 1880-1930 **13**:970
- - Denmark **5**:1536
- - England
- - - before 1290 and in 1969 **6**:749
- - - major towns, 1967 **5**:1514
- - Estonia, 1918-1940 **6**:917
- - expulsions, 1000 to 1500 C.E. **8**:689
- - Finland, 1970 **6**:1296
- - France
- - - main communities, Middle Ages and 1968 **7**:11
- - - major towns, 1967 **5**:1514
- - - Provence, medieval **13**:1261
- - Germany
- - - Berlin, 1816 **4**:650
- - - Jewish population, 1871-1969 **7**:481
- - - major communities, 13th cent. **7**:463
- - - major communities, 1933 and 1970 **7**:487
- - - Prussia, 1871 **13**:1287
- - Greece **7**:869
- - Hungary
- - - Budapest, 1813-1967 **4**:1449
- - - 1910 and 1946 **8**:1093
- - Ireland **8**:1464
- - Italy
- - - major communities, 1450-1550, 1931 and 1970 **9**:1117,1133
- - - Southern, Jewish communities, 12th cent. **3**:226
- - Jewish community organization, and population in 1968 **5**:841
- - Jewish population, 1850-1967 **5**:1495
- - Latvia, 1935 **10**:1463
- - Lithuania **11**:363
- - migrations to other continents
- - - 1881-1914 **8**:729
- - - 1915-30 and 1931-39 **8**:753
- - Netherlands **12**:973,985,989
- - - Amsterdam 1610-1967 **2**:901
- - Norway **12**:1222
- - Ottoman Empire **16**:1531,1533
- - Pale of Settlement **13**:25
- - Poland
- - - Bialystok, 1765-1948 **4**:811
- - - Cracow, 1900-1955 **5**:1027
- - - Lodz, 1820-1931 **11**:425
- - Portugal **13**:920
- - postwar communities **5**:835
- - Rumania, Bucharest, 1800-1969 **4**:1438; **14**:391
- - Russia **14**:450,451,453,471-472,473,483,484,485
- - - Crimea, 1970 **5**:1104
- - - Georgia **7**:424
- - - major towns, 1967 **5**:1514
- - - Soviet republics, 1959 **5**:1510
- - Spain
- - - Burgos province, before 1492 **4**:1513
- - - Jewish and Converso communities, 1474 **15**:237
- - - Muslim period **15**:223
- - Sweden **15**:546
- - Switzerland, 1960 **15**:561
- - total Jewish population, 1840-1969 **5**:831
- - Turkey **15**:1457,1459
- - Yugoslavia, 1931 **18**:876
- - Vital statistics **16**:179-181,183-184
- *see also under individual countries*
European Market **9**:764
EUSEBIUS (Ch.F.) **6**:977
- apologetics **3**:189ff
- Ashkenaz **3**:719
- Church Fathers **5**:552
- En-Dor **6**:738
- Madaba map **11**:677
Eusebius Sophronius Hieronymus, *see* JEROME
Eustachio, Giovanni Paolo, *see* NOLA, ELIJAH BEN MENAHEM DA
Eustachius (patr., Jer.) **9**:1407
Eusthatius (archit.) **9**:1406
Eustochium (Rom. woman) **9**:1378
EUTHANASIA **6**:978
- gassing **16**:1332
- Nazi program **5**:81
- proscribed **4**:1166
- *see also:* DEATH
EUTROPIUS (Rom. au.) **14**:235
Eutychius (Arab. hist.) **9**:1423
Eva (period.) **12**:844
Evalenko, A.M. **5**:1211
Evaluation, Laws of **3**:251
Evangelion (bk.) **14**:1521
Evangelism, Jewish **7**:1399
Evans, Madge **10**:1031
Evans, Mary Ann, *see* ELIOT, GEORGE
Evanston (city, Ill.) **8**:1256
Evanston (city, Wyo.) **16**:680
Evanston (sub., Chicago) **5**:415
Evansville (city, Ind.) **8**:1361
- *illus:*
- - Temple B'nai Israel **8**:1361
Evatt, Herbert V. **3**:886; **16**:1106
EVE (bib. fig.) **6**:979
- *ḥuppah* **11**:1040
- in the Arts **2**:242
- Lilith **11**:246
- Machpelah, Cave of **11**:673
- woman **16**:626
- *illus:*
- - text
- - Bamberg cathedral sculpture **4**:939
- - creation **2**:243; **4**:874
- - "Creation of Adam" (frsc. Michelangelo) **5**:1068
- - Garden of Eden **4**:856, 1050
- - "in Paradise" (Rubens and Jan Breughel the Elder) **4**:941
- - Islamic illum. ms. **2**:237; **4**:941
- - Seth and **14**:1191
- - the temptation **2**:237,242; **4**:1050
- *see also:* ADAM
Eved Ivri, *see* SLAVERY
Evel (rab. treatise), *see* SEMAHOT
Evelina de Rothschild school (Jer.) **2**:977; **9**:1458
'Even (weight) **16**:381
Even, Abba, *see* EBAN, ABBA
EVENARI, MICHAEL **6**:983
- Avedat **3**:945
- *illus:*
- - Avedat farm **12**:739
Even Boḥan (wk.; Immanuel of Rome) **16**:1388
Even Boḥan (wk.; Kalonymus ben Kalonymus) **11**:353
Even Boḥan (wk., Menahem ben Solomon) **16**:1285,1302
Even ha-Ezer (code), *see* SHULHAN ARUKH
Even ha-Ezer (wk.) **6**:627
Even ha-Shoham (wk.) **16**:943
EVEN HA-TO'IM (stone, Jer.) **6**:985
- lost articles **9**:1554
Evening Prayer, *see* ARVIT
Even Menaḥem (mosh., Isr.) **1**: place list
Even Reshef (Kar.), *see* FIRKOVICH, ABRAHAM
Even Sappir (mosh., Isr.) **1**: place list
Even Sappir (wk.) **14**:853
Even Shemu'el (rural center, Isr.) **1**: place list
EVEN SHEMUEL, JUDAH **6**:985
EVEN SHETIYYAH (world found. rock) **6**:985
- Dome of the Rock **15**:989
- Jerusalem **9**:1559
- Muslim thought **9**:1575ff
- Omar **9**:1423
- Temple **15**:951
- *illus:*
- - view from above **9**:1557
Even Shetiyyah (bk.) **13**:132
EVEN-SHOSHAN, AVRAHAM **6**:986
- Hebrew vocabulary **16**:1650
Even-Shoshan, Shelomo **6**:986
Even Yaish, Solomon, *see* ABENAES, SOLOMON
Even Yehoshu'a (qtr., Jer.) **9**:1462
EVEN YEHUDAH (stlmt., Isr.)
- statistics **1**: place list
Even Yisrael (qtr., Jer.) **9**:1459
EVEN YIẒHAK (kib., Isr.) **6**:987
- statistics **1**: place list
Ever (bib. fig.) **8**:1057
Everett (city, Wash.) **16**:356
EVER HADANI (writ.) **6**:987
EVER MIN HA-ḤAI ("Limb from a Living Animal") **6**:987
- animals, cruelty to **3**:6
- Commandments, the 613 **5**:778
- Noachide laws **12**:1189ff
- source **12**:120
Every Friday (period.) **5**:564
EVIAN CONFERENCE **6**:987
- history chart **8**:766-767
- Holocaust **8**:905
- refugees **6**:160ff; **9**:531
- *illus:* text
Evian-Les-Bains (tn., Fr.) **6**:988
Eviction **10**:1533ff
EVIDENCE **6**:991
- General
- - admission **2**:290ff
- - confession **5**:877
- - gambler **7**:302
- - heretics **8**:359
- - Inquisition **8**:1400
- - Israel **12**:146
- - king, kingship **10**:1013
- - Sabbath violators ruling **12**:144
- - Simeon ben Shetaḥ **14**:1564
- - Torah reading as **15**:1254
- - *Yevamot* **16**:776ff
- Criminal Law
- - assault **3**:758
- - confession **5**:877
- - criminal ignorance **13**:227
- - extra-legal dispensation **6**:1073
- - homicide **13**:1387
- - informer rules **8**:1372
- - oppression **12**:1436
- Civil Law
- - actions delay **11**:253
- - admission **2**:290
- - agent **2**:350
- - *agunah* **2**:430ff; **10**:343
- - attorney **3**:837
- - conflict of laws **5**:889
- - contract, illegal **5**:931
- - court handling of **13**:956; **13**:960ff
- - custom **12**:20
- - divorce **6**:129
- - eclipse omen **12**:291
- - endowments **8**:285
- - lease cases **10**:1534ff
- - loans **11**:414ff
- - marriage **11**:1049
- - *niddui* proclamation **8**:352
- - oath **12**:1297; **12**:1298
- - self testimony **14**:1196
- - takkanot **15**:719
- - *takkanot ha-kahal* **15**:732
- - tax **15**:865
- - waiver of testimony **11**:1233
- *see also:* HAZAKAH; WITNESS

Evil, *see* GOOD AND EVIL
EVIL EYE **6:**997
- amulets **2:**906ff
- change of name **6:**1328
- *ḥinnah* ceremony **11:**1044
- Lilith **11:**249
- Torah reading **15:**1254
- *illus:*
- - text
- - amulets **2:**907-914
- - bride's comb **11:***fcg.* 1070
Evil inclination, *see* INCLINATION, GOOD AND EVIL
EVIL MERODACH (k., Babyl.) **6:**1000
- Jehoiachin **16:**1270
Evil speech, *see* LASHON HA-RA
Evil spirits, *see* DEMONS, DEMONOLOGY
Evlad-i Musa (fam.) **7:**1248
EVOLUTION **6:**1000
- Holocaust **8:**853
- Kook, Abraham Isaac **10:**1186
- Lessing-Mendelssohn controversy **11:**1340
- nature **12:**891
- reproduction **4:**1016
- *Ru'aḥ ha-kodesh* **14:**368
EVORA (city, Port.) **6:**1005
Evora, Rodrigues d' (fam.), *see* Rodrigues d'Evora
E.V.O.S.M., *see* United Federation of Zionist Youth in Russia
Evrard (royal offic.) **11:**514
Evreiskaya Letopis (journ.) **13:**1047
Evreiskaya Mysl (journ.) **13:**1047
Evreiskaya Proletarskaya Mysl (period.) **13:**1047
Evreiskaya Rabotchaya Khronika (period.) **13:**1046
Evreiskaya Shkola (mag.) **13:**1046
Evreiskaya Starina (journ.) **13:**1047; **15:**54
Evreiskaya Zhizn (period.) **13:**1046
Evreiski Medizinski Golos (journ.) **13:**1047
Evreiski Mir (newsp.) **13:**1046
ÉVREUX (city, Fr.) **6:**1005
- tosafot **15:**1280
Evreyskaya Biblioteka (journ.) **15:**53
Evreyskaya Starina (journ.), *see* *Evreiskaya Starina*
Evreyski Vesti (newsp., Bul.) **4:**1489; **4:**1491
EVRON (kib., Isr.) **6:**1005
- statistics **1:**place list
- *illus:* text
Evyonah (bot.) **5:**135
Ewald (philos.), *see* FRIEDLAENDER, OSKAR EWALD
EWALD, HEINRICH GEORG AUGUST **6:**1006
- Bible research **4:**906
- Bible translations **4:**874
- Christian Hebraists **8:**33
Ewing, Alexander **9:**1590
Ewold, F. C. **15:**768
Exagoge (Gr. tragedy) **3:**189; **6:**1102; **12:**404
Exaloth (loc., Er. Isr.) **10:**102
"Examination" (paint., M. Oppenheim) **6:**393
Examination of witnesses, *see* WITNESS
"Excavation" (paint., P. Blume) **4:**1139
Excavations, *see* ARCHAEOLOGY
EXCERPTA VALESIANA (wk.) **14:**235
Exchange, Bill of, *see* SHETAR
"Exchange of Opinions" (cut, J. Morvay) **15:**471
Exchanges, *see* STOCK EXCHANGES
EXCHEQUER OF THE JEWS (Eng.) **6:**1006
- archae **3:**300
- banking **4:**169
- Irish branch **6:**248
- seals **14:**1079
- taxation **15:**839
Excise duty **9:**749
Excommunication, *see* HEREM
Excretion **8:**1140
- washing hands **2:**85; **12:**998
Execration texts (Egy.) **6:**480
- Hebrew language **16:**1561
- patriarchal history **8:**572; **8:**573
- *illus:*
- - Thebes bowl **8:**572
EXECUTION (CIVIL) **6:**1007
- bankruptcy and charity **10:**227
- divorce **6:**131
- imprisonment for debt **8:**1303
- judicial autonomy **12:**125
- lien rights **11:**228
- loan cases **11:**416ff
- maintenance and custody **13:**95ff
- rabbinical law **12:**115
- Sanhedrin **9:**243
- theft **15:**1098
Execution, *see* CAPITAL PUNISHMENT
Executive (aviation co., Isr.) **9:**839
Exegesis, Biblical, *see* BIBLE (Exegesis and Study)
EXEMPLA OF THE RABBIS (collec., stories) **6:**1020
- exemplum **6:**1021
- fiction, Hebrew **6:**1265
EXEMPLUM (leg.) **6:**1020
- animal tales **3:**19
- hagiography **7:**1116
- ḥasidic literature **7:**1415
- Hebrew fiction **6:**1261
- Ma'aseh Book **11:**649
- Yiddish **16:**804
- *see also:* EXEMPLA OF THE RABBIS; HEBREW LITERATURE, MODERN; LITERATURE, JEWISH
EXETER (tn., Eng.) **6:**1022
EXHIBITIONS IN ISRAEL **9:**764
- *illus:*
- - text
- - Binyenei ha-Ummah **9:**1488
- - International Trade Fair, 1967 **9:**818
- - Israel Museum, opening of a Chagall exhibition **9:**1010
Exhumation, *see* DISINTERMENT
EXILARCH (cmty. head, Babyl.) **6:**1023
- General
- - Babylonia **5:**813
- - David ben Zakkai **10:**1141
- - history **8:**649ff
- - history chart **8:**766-767
- - Judah ha-Nasi **10:**369
- - Persia **13:**309
- - Samuel ben Ali **11:**746
- - seals **14:**1074
- - *Seder Olam Zuta* **14:**1093
- - Sura **15:**522
- Power and Functions
- - autonomy **3:**922
- - autonomy, judicial **3:**929
- - *geonim* **7:**315
- - *ḥazakah* of property **7:**1518
- - leadership **8:**663ff
- - ordination **7:**424; **14:**1142
- - powers of kingship **12:**136
- - rabbinical appointments **13:**1448
- - sages **14:**645
- - titles **2:**873ff; **15:**1164
- *lists:* text
- *see also:* BABYLONIA; DAVID, DYNASTY OF; NAGID
Exile *see* BANISHMENT; DIASPORA; EXPULSIONS; GALUT
EXILE, ASSYRIAN **6:**1034
- Habor district **7:**1037
- Samaritans **14:**727; **14:**728; **14:**736
- *illus:*
- - route of the exiled (map) **8:**607
EXILE, BABYLONIAN **6:**1036
- courts **4:**725
- Daniel apocrypha **5:**1277
- economic consequences **16:**1270
- exilarch **6:**1023
- Ezekiel **6:**1091
- Ezra and Nehemiah **6:**1114ff
- history **8:**615ff
- Jeremiah **9:**1350ff
- Jerusalem hope **9:**1384
- Judah ha-Nasi **10:**369
- Nehemiah **12:**936
- Second Temple period **8:**640
- synagogue **15:**580
- *illus:*
- - text
- - route of the exiled (map) **8:**607
- - synagogue mural **12:**621
Exiles, Ingathering of the, *see* INGATHERING OF THE EXILES
Existence of God **7:**657ff
- General
- - anthropomorphism **3:**56
- - commandment **5:**1081ff
- - dogma **3:**654ff
- - Jewish Aristotelianism **3:**447
- - Jewish philosophy **13:**422
- Views on
- - Aaron ben Elijah **2:**11; **2:**12
- - Albo **2:**536
- - Baḥya **13:**435
- - Crescas, Ḥasdai **13:**448ff
- - Ibn Daud **13:**440
- - Levi ben Gershom **11:**95
- - Mendelssohn, Moses **11:**1330ff
- - Moses ben Joseph ha-Levi **12:**422
EXISTENTIALISM (philos. mvmt.) **6:**1041
- Hegel, G. W. F. **8:**245
- Jewish contribution **13:**419
- Jewish philosophy **13:**461
- Job, Book of **10:**123
- Reform Judaism **14:**27
- revelation **14:**125
- right and wrong **13:**223
- Rosenzweig, Franz **14:**300
- theology **15:**1109
EXODUS **6:**1042
- Bible history **8:**575; **12:**375
- Exodus, Book of **6:**1054ff
- festivals **6:**1238
- *Haggadah,* Passover **7:**1097
- Hyksos **6:**481; **8:**1142
- in the Arts **12:**404f
- libelous versions **3:**88
- Lysimachus of Alexandria **11:**627
- *manna* **11:**883
- Mt. Sinai **14:**1599
- Pharaoh **13:**360
- pillar of cloud, fire **13:**523
- Red Sea **14:**16
- Rephidim **14:**80
- Samaritan custom **14:**743
- ten plagues **13:**604
- *illus:*
- - text
- - Dura-Europos wall paint. **6:**281
- - Israelites passing from slavery to freedom **7:**119
- - Moses leading the Israelites out of Egypt **7:**1086
- - Pharaoh sending the Israelites out of Egypt **6:**1045
- - Pillar of Fire **6:**1303
- - Plagues of Egypt **13:**605-612
- - *Second Nuremberg Haggadah* **7:** *fcg* 1195
- - *seder* plate **11:**1532
- - stopping places of Israelites (18th cent. map) **11:**930
Exodus (Gr. tragedy), *see* *Exagoge*
Exodus (bk., Leon Uris) **16:**10
Exodus (motion picture) **12:**461; **13:**1014
- *illus:*
- - scene **12:**456
EXODUS, BOOK OF **6:**1050
- Hurrian customs **12:**1289ff
- *Mekhilta of R. Ishmael* **11:**1268
- *Mekhilta of R. Simeon ben Yoḥai* **11:**1269
- Pentateuch **13:**231
- *illus:*
- - text
- - 14th cent. ms. **16:**1479
- - incunabulum (1488) **8:**1332
- *see also:* BOOK OF THE COVENANT
Exodus 1947 (refugee ship)
- *beriḥah* **4:**632
- history **9:**359
- illegal immigration **8:**1254
- UNSCOP **16:**1093
- *illus:*
- - arrival in Haifa **9:**525
- - refugees herded off **8:**1253
EXODUS RABBAH (agg. Mid.) **6:**1067
- *Tanḥuma* **15:**794
- *illus:* text
- *see also:* MIDRASH
Exorcism **6:**20; **4:**7; **15:**118
- *see also:* AMULET; DEMONS, DEMONOLOGY; DIVINATION; GILGUL; MAGIC
Experiments, Pseudo-medical **8:**872
Expiation, *see* ATONEMENT
Expiation-offering, *see* Asham
Explorers, *see* TRAVELERS AND EXPLORERS
Export Institute (Isr.) **15:**709
Exports, Israel, *see* FOREIGN TRADE, ISRAEL
Expropriation, *see* CONFISCATION, EXPROPRIATION, FOREFEITURE
"Expulsion of the Jews from Prague, 1745" (etch.) **13:**968
EXPULSIONS **6:**1069
- General
- - anti-Semitism **3:**102
- - Barbarians **4:**206
- - history **8:**676ff
- - history chart **8:**766-767
- - Luther, Martin **11:**585
- - punishment **13:**1389
- - *Shevet Yehudah* **8:**1204
- Cities and Countries
- - England **6:**751ff
- - Ereẓ Israel **15:**920
- - France **7:**13ff
- - - Paris **13:**104ff
- - - Philip IV **13:**392ff
- - - robbery of Jews **16:**1284
- - Rome **14:**240ff
- - Russia **14:**436ff
- - - Moscow **12:**364ff
- - Spain **15:**221ff
- - - edict repealed (1968) **15:**245
- - - Ferdinand and Isabella **6:**1228
- - - Inquisition **8:**1403
- - - official justification **3:**173
- - - robbery of Jews **16:**1284
- - - Toledo **15:**1198,1205
- - Vienna 1670 **10:**1164
- *illus:*
- - eleventh to fifteenth centuries (map) **8:**689
- - England, tercentenary of resettlement, medal **6:**772

-- Ferdinand and Isabella's edict **15:**239
-- Frankfort, 1614 **7:**474
-- London, first synagogue after resettlement, plaque **6:**754
-- Prague (1745) **13:**968
-- Prague, Maria Theresa's edict **11:**991
- *see also:* HOLOCAUST; *and under individual countries*
Extended Physical Training, *see* Ḥagam
Extermination Camps (Nazi Ger.), *see* CAMPS (Concentration and Extermination)
Extermination Policy, Nazi **8:**853
Extracts from Gregory the Great (12th cent. illum. ms., Fr.) **4:**1
EXTRAORDINARY REMEDIES **6:**1071
- blinding **4:**1092
- compulsion by imprisonment **8:**1305
- cutting nose off adulteress **5:**620
- evidence, laws of **6:**992
- forgery **6:**1432
- *ḥerem* and *niddui* **8:**350ff
- judicial prerogative **13:**222ff
- moral compulsion **10:**1483
- *ona'ah* **12:**1393
- suicide **15:**491
- witches **14:**1564
Extra-sensory perception **10:**637
EYAL (kib., Isr.) **6:**1074
- statistics **1:**place list
EYBESCHUETZ, JONATHAN **6:**1074
- General
-- chronological chart **8:**766-767
-- controversy **2:**911; **11:**58
-- emissaries **14:**1366
-- messiah **9:**74
-- Shabbateanism **14:**1249ff
- Views
-- alchemy **2:**549
-- *ḥiddushim* **8:**467
-- imprisonment for debt **8:**1308
-- providence **13:**1283
-- *sefirot* **10:**568
-- Torah study **15:**459
- Contemporaries
-- Abraham ben Joseph of Lissa **2:**149
-- Ashkenazi, Ẓevi Hirsch **3:**734
-- Buzaglo, Shalom **4:**1544
-- Emden, Jacob **6:**722
-- Epstein, Aryeh Leib **6:**824
-- Falk, Jacob Joshua **6:**1156
-- Heilprin, Samuel Helmann **8:**269
-- Landau, Ezekiel **10:**1389
-- Prossnitz, Judah Leib **13:**1241
- *illus:*
-- autograph **3:**915
-- portrait **7:**475
Eybeschuetz, Wolf **4:**685; **6:**143, 1075
EYDOUX, EMMANUEL **6:**1076
Eye **11:**1179ff
- responsa on grafting **14:**93
- *see also:* BLINDNESS
Eygns (period.) **4:** 609; **16:**816
EYLENBURG, ISSACHAR BAER BEN ISRAEL LEISER PARNAS **6:**1077
EYNIKEYT (newsp.) **6:**1077
- Birobidzhan propaganda **4:**1048
- Jewish Anti-Fascist Committee **3:**63; **3:**64
Eyrieu (tn., Fr.) **7:**17
Eysenck, H. J. **13:**1340
EYTAN, WALTER **6:**1078
- *illus:*
-- Israel-Egypt Armistice Agreement, 1949 **3:**479
Eyüp (dist., Turk.) **9:**1086
ʾEẓbaʿ (meas.) **16:**378ff
Eẓbe'oni (period.) **5:**458
Ezechiels, Moses **4:**177
Ezekias (h. pr.) *see* HEZEKIAH, THE HIGH PRIEST
EZEKIEL (bib. fig.) **6:**1078
- *Contents:*
-- The Book **6:**1078
-- Aggadah **6:**1095
-- Tomb **6:**1096
-- Islam **6:**1097
-- Arts **6:**1097
- allegory **2:**642
- altar **2:**763
- Babylonia **4:**35
- Balkh **4:**137
- cherubim **5:**397ff
- Day of Atonement **5:**1387
- dead bones vision **15:**899
- dietary laws **6:**40
- eschatological writings **6:**867ff
- ethics **6:**934
- Exile, Babylonian **6:**1037
- history chart **8:**766-767
- Holiness Code **8:**820
- Lost Tribes **15:**1004
- magic **11:**705
- *merkabah* mysticism **11:**1386
- Mount of Olives **12:**484
- Tribes, the Twelve **15:**1385
- usury **16:**28
- wooden inscription **16:**662
- *illus:*
-- text
-- passage **15:**1484
-- vision of the resurrection **3:**515; **4:**945; **6:**291
Ezekiel (fam.) **3:**539
Ezekiel (Neth. Antilles) **12:**995
Ezekiel, Abraham (silversmith) **6:**1098
EZEKIEL, ABRAHAM EZEKIEL **6:**1098
- bookplates **4:**1219
EZEKIEL, APOCRYPHAL BOOKS OF **6:**1099
Ezekiel, Ben (U.S.) **12:**266
Ezekiel, Benjamin (Eng.) **6:**1098
Ezekiel, Ezekiel (law.) **10:**1492
Ezekiel, Ḥakham **14:**760
EZEKIEL, JACOB **6:**1099
EZEKIEL, MORDECAI JOSEPH BRILL **6:**1100
EZEKIEL, MOSES (bot.) **6:**1100
EZEKIEL, MOSES JACOB **6:**1101
- Richmond **14:**161
- *illus:*
-- Jefferson, Thomas (statue) **11:**521
-- "Religious Liberty" (sculp.) **3:**556
EZEKIEL, NISSIM **12:**1466
Ezekiel, Solomon (Isaac) **6:**1099; **13:**269
Ezekiel, Tomb of **6:**1097
Ezekiel ben Avigdor **12:**1517
Ezekiel ben Meir Jehiel ha-Levi **11:**1260; **12:**840
EZEKIEL BEN REUBEN MANASSEH **6:**1101
Ezekiel ben Shemtov David **4:**863
Ezekiel ben Ẓevi-Hirsch Taub, *see* Taub, Ezekiel ben Ẓevi-Hirsch
EZEKIEL FEIVEL BEN ZE'EV WOLF **6:**1101
Ezekiel ha-Kohen of Radomsko, *see* Radomsko, Ezekiel ha-Kohen of
Ezekiel of Merseburg **11:**1393
Ezekiel of Radzymin **5:**1363
Ezekiel of Sieniawa **14:**1295
Ezekiel of Yablonov **10:**858
EZEKIEL THE POET (Hellen. plwrt) **6:**1102
- election of Israel **3:**189
- Greek influence **8:**300
- Hellenistic Jewish literature **8:**304
- Moses **12:**391; **12:**404
- theater **15:**1081
Eẓel (underground orgn.), *see* IRGUN ẒEVA'I LE'UMMI
Ezer (rural center, Isr.) **1:**place list
Ežerenai (city, Lith.), *see* ZARASAI
Eẓ ha-Ḥayyim (wk.) **10:**590; **16:**173ff
Eẓ ha-Ḥayyim Society (print.) **14:**708
Eẓ Ḥayyim (library, Amst.) **2:**903; **12:**279
Eẓ Ḥayyim (school, Jer.) **7:**1479
Eẓ-Ḥayyim (yeshivah, Amst.), *see* Ets-Ḥayyim
Eẓ Ḥayyim (yeshivah, Isr.) **16:**771
- Kotler, Aaron **10:**1222
- Melzer, Isser Zalman **11:**1295
- Salant, Samuel **14:**674
- *illus:* **16:**764
Eẓ Ḥayyim (yeshivah, Switz.) **10:**1472
Eẓ ḥayyim (Torah ornament) **14:**1102
Eẓ Ḥayyim (wk.; Aaron ben Elijah) **2:**11
Eẓ Ḥayyim (wk.; Jacob ben Judah of London) **9:**1220; **11:**399
Eẓ Ḥayyim (wk.; Ḥayyim Vital), *see Eẓ ha-Ḥayyim*
Eẓ Ḥayyim (period.) **6:**816
Ezida, Tower of (Babyl.) **4:**23
Ezion, Isaac Raphael, *see* Holzberg, Isaac Raphael
Eẓion Bloc (Er. Isr.), *see* Eẓyon Bloc
EZION-GEBER (Bib. loc.) **6:**1103
- shipping **14:**1411; **15:**98
- trade and commerce **15:**1295; **16:**1269
Ezkerah Elohim ve-Ehemayah (piyyut) **2:**850
Ezmel ben Juceph de Ablitas **16:**1291
Ezobi, Eleazar **4:**793; **6:**1104
Ezobi, Ḥanan ben Nathan **5:**207
EZOBI, JEHOSEPH BEN HANAN BEN NATHAN **6:**1104
Ezobi, Meshullam **4:**793; **6:**1104
Ezobi, Solomon **5:**207; **13:**613
Ezobi of Orange, *see* Ezovi, Mordecai ben Isaac
Ezofovich (fam.), *see* JÓZEFOWICZ
Ezofovich, Abraham (bnk.) **10:**322
Ezofovich, Abraham Jan **10:**321
Ezofovich, Chemio **10:**322
Ezofovich, Ducko (David) **10:**322
Ezofovich, Isaac **10:**321
Ezofovich, Michael (bnk.) **4:**1360; **7:**74; **10:**321
Ezofovich, Moses(r.) **10:**322
Ezovi, Mordecai ben Isaac **5:**160
EZRA (bib. fig.) **6:**1104
- General
-- *Ezra, Apocalypse of* **3:**179; **3:**180; **6:**1108
-- *Ezra, Greek Book of* **6:**1109
-- Hillel **8:**485
-- history chart **8:**766-767
-- Johanan **10:**144
-- Lost Tribes **15:**1004
-- population **13:**870
-- Spinoza **15:**283
-- Tobiah **8:**627
-- Uriel **16:**7
- Role and Institutions
-- ablution **2:**83
-- Aramaic script **2:**688
-- Bible interpretation **8:**1416
-- courts **3:**295, **15:**636
-- education **6:**384
Great Synagogue **15:**629
-- *ḥerem* **8:**347; **8:**350
-- Jerusalem **9:**1389
-- Nethinim **7:**554
-- pharisaism **13:**363
-- purity regulation **13:**1411
-- return of the exiles **8:**616ff
-- Samaritans **14:**729
-- scribes **4:**889
-- *tikkun soferim* **15:**1139
-- Torah reading **4:**823; **11:**394; **15:**1246
-- war and warfare **16:**278
-- wisdom tradition **16:**558
- Identifications
-- Jeremiah **9:**1360
-- Malachi **11:**812
-- Teacher of Righteousness **15:**887
- *illus:*
-- text
-- holding a scroll **8:**1149
-- kneeling before Darius **5:**1304
-- reading the Torah **6:**286,384
- *see also:* EZRA AND NEHEMIAH, BOOK OF
Ezra (amora) **3:**999
Ezra (kab.), *see* Azriel
EZRA (fam., Ind.) **6:**1107
Ezra (orgn., Ger.), *see* ESRA
Ezra (youth mvmt.)
- Agudat Israel **2:**421
- education **9:**895
- Po'alei Agudat Israel **13:**655
- youth movements **9:**981
- *illus:*
-- badge **9:**977
EZRA, APOCALYPSE OF (IV Ezra) **6:**1108
- *Baruch, Apocalypse of* **4:**271
- Davidic Messiah **11:**1409
- Jewish literature **11:**311
Ezra, Apocryphal, *see* EZRA, GREEK BOOK OF
Ezra, David (18/19 cent.) **6:**1108
Ezra, David (19/20 cent.) **6:**1108
Ezra, Elias David **6:**1108
Ezra, Ezekiel **6:**1107
Ezra, IV (bk.), *see* EZRA, APOCALYPSE OF
EZRA, GREEK BOOK OF **6:**1109
- *Ezra, Apocalypse of* **6:**1109
- Ezra, Book of **6:**1113
- Hellenistic Jewish literature **8:**304
- Septuagint **4:**853
- textual insertions **8:**304
- wisdom literature **16:**560
Ezra, Joseph ben Ezra ben Joseph Khlef **6:**1107
Ezra, Muzli (Mazal-Tov) **6:**1108
Ezra, Rachel **6:**1108
EZRA AND NEHEMIAH, BOOK OF **6:**1111
- *am ha-areẓ* term **2:**834
- canonization **4:**824
- Chronicles **5:**531ff
- Driver's studies **3:**266
- Rechabites **13:**1611
- Spinoza on **15:**283
- *see also:* EZRA; HISTORY (Destruction to Alexander); NEHEMIAH
Ezra and Nehemiah, Operation (Iraqi Aliyah) **8:**1453; **9:**534
- *illus:*
-- commemorative stamp **8:**1455
EZRA BEN ABRAHAM BEN MAZHIR (gaon) **6:**1123
- gaonate **7:**323
Ezra ben Avigdor **10:**1556
EZRA BEN EZEKIEL HA-BAVLI **6:**1123
- Iraq **8:**1452
Ezra ben Isaac of Fano **10:**830
Ezra ben Nissan **15:**1402
EZRA BEN SOLOMON **6:**1123
- Kabbalah **10:**525ff
Ezrah (orgn. Arg.) **3:**414
Ezraḥ (orgn., Lith.) **11:**381
Ezraḥi, M. **2:**207
Ezra Ibn al-Barqūlī (govt. offic.), *see* Ibn al-Barqūlī, Ezra

Ezra of Gerona (kab.), *see* EZRA BEN SOLOMON
EZRA OF MONTCONTOUR (tos.) **6:**1124
– Jewish mysticism **10:**514
Ezras Torah (philan. orgn.) **8:**324; **14:**278
Ezra Synagogue (Cairo, Egy.) **7:**406
Ezrat Aḥim (soc., Bul.) **16:**1108
Ezrat Israel (soc., Er. Isr.) **14:**224; **15:**919
Ezrat Nashim (Temple) **15:**966
– *illus:*
– Avi-Yonah's model of Jerusalem **12:**1134
– *see also: Weibershul*
Ezrat Nashim (assoc., Arg.) **3:**415
Eẓyon Bloc (kib. gr., Er. Isr.)
– Ein Ẓurim **6:**541
– Kefar Eẓyon **10:**880
– Massu'ot Yiẓḥak **11:**1118
– Six-Day War **14:**1635
– War of Independence **6:**314
– *illus:*
– – supply convoy **16:**307
Eẓyoni Brigade (Isr. army) **7:**1073; **9:**363; **16:**314

F

Fabbri, Diego **9:**1107
Faber, Boderianus, *see* LE FÈVRE DE LA BODERIE, GUY
Faber, George **8:**33
Fabian, Hans Erich **4:**650
Fabian, László **12:**1377; **15:**307
Fabian Society **13:**708
FABLE **6:**1125
– *Contents:*
– – Introduction **6:**1125
– – In the Bible **6:**1127
– – In Talmud **6:**1127
– – In Middle Ages **6:**1128
– – Post-Medieval Period **6:**1131
– – Modern Literature **6:**1131
– Aesop **3:**20ff
– Aggadah **2:**357
– Bible **13:**1264
– evolution **6:**1002ff
– flood **6:**1351
– folklore **6:**1374
– ḥasidic literature **7:**1415
– illustrations **4:**1234
– Jewish literature **11:**352ff
– Jotham **10:**301
– *Kalila and Dimna* **10:**705
– *Ma'aseh Yerushalmi* **2:**152; **6:**1266
– parable **13:**72
– parody **13:**124
– Sahula, Isaac ibn **14:**656ff
– Yiddish literature **16:**804
– *illus:*
– – text
– – *Meshal ha-Kadmoni* **3:**19,534, 791; **5:**430; **6:**1128; **14:**657
– – *Mishlei Shu'alim* **4:**597;**5:**431
– *see also:* ETHICAL LITERATURE; PROVERBS, TALMUDIC
Fables of Marie de France **3:**21
Fabregat, Enrique Rodriquez **10:**1456; **13:**34
FABRI, FELIX **6:**1133
– travels **15:**1356
FABRICANT, SOLOMON **6:**1133
Fabricius, E. C. **8:**33
Fabricius, F. **8:**33
Fabricius, Guido, *see* LE FÈVRE DE LA BODERIE, GUY
Fabricius, János **8:**33
Fabricius, Laurentius **8:**33
Fabricius, P. J. **8:**33
Fabricius, T. **8:**33
Fabrikant, V. (Zion., Rus.) **10:**91; **14:**1126
Fabritius, Barent **14:**784
Fachiri, Adila **10:**110
FACKENHEIM, EMIL LUDWIG **6:**1133
– God **7:**670; **7:**673
– Holocaust **14:**138ff
Factor, Davis (Rus., U.S.) **6:**1134
Factor, Davis (U.S.) **6:**1134
Factor, Louis **6:**1134
FACTOR, MAX **6:**1134
Factor, Max, Jr. **6:**1134
Factor, Sam (Can.) **5:**112
Factor, Sidney (indus.) **6:**1134
Fadak (loc., Arab.) **3:**235
Faddeyev, Alexander **14:**511
FADENHECHT, YEHOSHUA **6:**1134
Fadil, Al-Mu'allim al- **9:**74
FADIMAN, CLIFTON **15:**1580
Faḍl Allah ibn Abi al-Khayr ibn Ali al-Hamadhānī, *see* RASHĪD AL-DAWLA
Faḍl inscriptions, *see* Sheikh Faḍl inscriptions
FADUS, CUSPIUS **6:**1135
FAENZA (city, It.) **6:**1135
FAGARAS (tn., Transyl.) **6:**1135
Fagin (Dickens character) **6:**22; **12:**459; **15:**1053
– *illus:*
– – Moody, Ron, in *Oliver* **12:**461
FAGIUS, PAULUS **6:**1136
– Hebraist **8:**33
– Levita, Elijah **11:**134
– printers' marks **13:**1096
– Strasbourg **15:**424
– typography **15:**1482
– *illus:*
– – text
– – printer's mark **13:**1094
Fagure, E. **14:**399
Fahd Abu Khaḍra (nov.), *see* Abu Khaḍra, Fahd
Faḥl (tn., Transj.), *see* PELLA
Fahländer, J. **8:**33
FAHN, REUBEN **6:**1137
Fainzilberg, Ilya Arnoldovich, *see* ILF, ILYA
Fairbanks (city, Alsk.) **2:**513
Fairclough, Richard **8:**33
Fair Lawn (boro., N.J.) **4:**612 **13:**179
Fairmont (city, W. Va.) **16:**475
Fairs, *see* MARKET DAYS AND FAIRS
Fairy tale, *see* FABLE; FICTION, HEBREW
Faisal I (k., Syr.-Iraq) **8:**1449
– Abdullah ibn Hussein **2:**56
– Arab National Movement **9:**458
– Churchill **5:**555
– Lawrence, T. E. **10:**1488
– Sasson, Eliyahu **14:**895
– Sonneborn, Rudolf **15:**155
– Weizmann **16:**1081
– Zionist Commission **9:**337
– *illus:*
– – Weizmann, Chaim, and **9:**336; **16:**428
Faisal II (k., Iraq) **14:**1624
Faith, *see* ARTICLES OF FAITH; BELIEF
FAÏTLOVITCH, JACQUES **6:**1137
– Falashas **6:**1153ff
FAITUSI, JACOB BEN ABRAHAM **6:**1138
FAIVOVICH HITZCOVICH, ANGEL **6:**1138
– Chile **5:**467
FAIYŪM (city, Egy.) **6:**1139
– documents **6:**9, 11; **16:**663
FAJANS, KASIMIR **6:**1139
Fajner, Leon **16:**353
Fajnsztat, Zalman **6:**334; **13:**775
Fajwlowicz, Shlomo, *see* SHRAGAI, SHLOMO ZALMAN
Fakhar, al (fam., Sp.), *see* Al-Fakhar
Fakhr al-Dawla Abu al-Fatḥ Isḥaq, *see* ISAAC BAR ISRAEL IBN AL-SHUWAYK
Fakhr al-Dīn (16th cent. Druze) **9:**924
Fakhr al-Din II (16/17 cent., Druze) **9:**287
FALAISE (tn., Fr.) **6:**1140
FALAQUERA (fam.) **6:**1140
Falaquera, Joseph ben Isaac **6:**1140
Falaquera, Joseph ben Judah **6:**1140
Falaquera, Joseph ben Shem Tov ibn **6:**1140
– Tudela **15:**1425
Falaquera, Nathan ben (14th cent., fin.) **6:**1140
FALAQUERA, NATHAN BEN JOEL (physic.) **6:**1140
– medicine **11:**1190
FALAQUERA, SHEM TOV BEN JOSEPH **6:**1140
– Aristotelianism **3:**446
– astrology **3:**793
– Avicenna **3:**793
– beatitude **4:**362
– didactic literature **11:**353
– Neoplatonism **12:**960ff
– philosophy **13:**444
– psychology **11:**341
– *ru'aḥ ha-kodesh* **14:**367
– translations **15:**1322
– *illus:* text
Falaquera, Solomon ben Moses **6:**1140
FALASHAS **6:**1143
– *Contents:*
– – History **6:**1143
– – Ethnology **6:**1145
– – Religion **6:**1147
– – Language **6:**1149
– – Literature **6:**1150
– – Folklore **6:**1151
– – Research **6:**1152
– – Relations with Jewry **6:**1153
– Aescoly's studies **2:**325
– Alliance Israélite Universelle **2:**653
– Faïtlovitch's studies **6:**1137
– Jewish traditions **2:**332
– *Jubilees, Book of* **10:**326
– Lost Tribes **15:**1005
– *niddah* laws **12:**1147
– Yusuf As'ar **16:**900
Falcini, Natale **10:**459
FALCO, MARIO **6:**1154
Falcon (fam.) **12:**336
Falcon, Elijah **3:**669
Falcon, Jacob (Mor.) **15:**791
Falcon, Joseph (r., Fr.) **4:**1244
Falcon, Shem Tov, *see* Falkon, Shem Tov
Faleiro, Antonio **15:**1302
FALESHTY (tn., U.S.S.R.) **6:**1154
Falik, Fernando, *see* KOSICE, GYULA
Falikman, Yehiel **10:**997
FALK (family) **6:**1155
Falk, Aryeh Leib **6:**1157
FALK, BERNARD **10:**310
Falk, Issachar Berish (r., Ger.) **6:**1157
Falk, Issachar Dov (r., Pol.) **6:**1157
FALK, JACOB JOSHUA BEN ẒEVI HIRSCH **6:**1155
– novellae **8:**467; **11:**333
Falk, Joshua (U.S.) **8:**209
FALK, JOSHUA BEN ALEXANDER HA-KOHEN **6:**1158
– codification of law **5:**647,654
– *illus:*
– – commentary on *Arba'ah Turim* **9:**1215
FALK, KAUFMAN GEORGE (chem.) **5:**382
Falk, Leon (philan.) **6:**1155
Falk, Leon Jr. (philan.) **6:**1155
Falk, Maurice (indus.) **6:**1155
FALK, MIKSA (polit.) **6:**1159
Falk, Samuel (r., Neth.) **6:**1157
FALK, SAMUEL JACOB ḤAYYIM **6:**1159
– Shabbateanism **14:**1251
– *illus:*
– – London monument **11:**473
FALK, ZE'EV WILHELM **1:**29
Falkbeer, Ernest Karl **5:**405
Falke (16th cent., Ger.) **10:**811
Falken, David **11:**180
Falkensohn, Issachar Baer, *see* BEHR, ISACHAR FALKENSOHN
Falker, Joseph **15:**635
Falkind, David **15:**553
Falkland, Samuel, *see* HEIJERMANS, HERMAN

Falk Library (Austr.) **15:**565
Falk of Kalisz (14th cent.) **16:**1346
Falkon, Shem Tov **2:**13; **11:**798
FALKOWITSCH, JOEL BAERISCH **6:**1160
FALL, LEO **12:**688
Falleiro, Andreas **5:**1535
Fallek, Wilhelm **13:**803
FALL RIVER (city, Mass.) **6:**1160
Falmouth (tn., Eng.) **6:**754
Falsehood **16:**585
- *see also:* FRAUD; OATH
FALTICENI (tn., Rum.) **6:**1161
- Rumania **14:**397
FALUDY, GYÖRGY **6:**1162
Faluja pocket (Isr.) **9:**371ff; **16:**328
Famagusta (city, Cyp.) **5:**1182
Familial Disautonomia (disease) **14:**1501
Familial Mediterranean Fever **14:**1501
Familiantenbuch (register) **6:**1163
FAMILIANTS LAWS (Familiantengesetze) **6:**1162
- Austrian Jews **3:**891; **3:**895
- history **8:**705
- history chart **8:**766-767
- *illus:*
- - certificate of marriage **8:**702
FAMILY **6:**1164
- *Contents:*
- - In the Bible **6:**1164
- - Post-Biblical **6:**1169
- adoption **2:**298
- Ancient Israel **8:**610ff
- Arab social structure **9:**1022
- Babylon **10:**369
- barrenness and fertility **4:**256
- biblical terms **5:**894
- blessing of children **4:**1087
- children **5:**426
- civil marriage **5:**597; **5:**598
- Commandments, the 613 **5:**769
- craft industries **8:**614ff
- *derekh ereẓ* **5:**1551
- documents **14:**1388
- educational influence **6:**387ff
- etiquette **6:**947
- familiants laws **6:**1162
- firstborn **6:**1306
- genealogy **7:**377
- Ḥasidism **7:**1407
- health services **9:**988
- honor of parents **13:**100
- Israel settlement unit **8:**582
- *niddah* **12:**1141
- northern France **8:**667
- parent and child **13:**95
- peace **14:**1356
- purity **14:**1206
- redemption **14:**1
- severance with member **10:**935
- *takkanot* **15:**726ff
- woman **16:**623; **16:**627
- Yemenite Jews **16:**753ff
- *yiḥus* **16:**835
- *illus:* text
- *see also:* YUḤASIN
Family Badges, *see* Badges, Family
Family Location Service (orgn., U.S.) **5:**351
Family purity, *see* NIDDAH; TAHARAT HA-MISHPAḤAH
FAMINE AND DROUGHT **6:**1172
- anti-hoarding laws **7:**1062
- fasting **6:**1190; **15:**675
- *see also:* CLIMATE OF ISRAEL; DEW, PRAYER FOR; RAIN, PRAYER FOR
Fangen, Ronald August **14:**933
Fanjawīn (tn., Iraq) **15:**504
FANO (tn., It.) **6:**1174
FANO (fam.) **6:**1174
Fano, Abraham Ḥayyim da (print.) **6:**1234
Fano, Avigdor **6:**1174
Fano, Ezra ben Isaac **6:**1174
Fano, Giorgio Voghera, *see* Triestino, Anònimo
FANO, GUIDO ALBERTO **12:**689
Fano, Ippolito da, *see* Fano, Joseph
Fano, Isaac Berechiah ben Judah Aryeh **6:**1175; **14:**890
Fano, Jacob ben Joab Elijah da **6:**1174
Fano, J. Nisim da **6:**1234
Fano, Joseph da **6:**1175
- ennobled **15:**1165
Fano, Judah ben Moses **13:**12
FANO, MENAHEM AZARIAH DA **6:**1175
- *Ein-Sof* **7:**661
- Italy **9:**1127
- Kabbalah **10:**548
- responsa **14:**89
Fantle (fam.) **15:**213
Fanto, David **13:**346
Fao (tn., Iraq) **8:**1450
FAO (U.N. orgn.), *see* Food and Agricultural Organization
Faquim, Jucef (Joseph) **11:**801; **15:**1349
Fara, Isaac ibn al-, *see* Al-Fara, Isaac ibn
FĀRĀBĪ, ABU NAṢR MUHAMMAD, AL- **6:**1176
- *Contents:*
- - Philosophy **6:**1176
- - Political Theory **6:**1177
- - Influence on Jewish Thought **6:**1177
- - Hebrew Translations **6:**1178
- - Musician **6:**1178
- attributes of God **7:**666
- Avempace **3:**947
- Avicenna **3:**957
- logic **11:**460
- Maimonides **11:**769
- Platonism **13:**629
- revelation **14:**123
- translations **15:**1130
Farafonte (spring, Er. Isr.), *see* ʿAyn Fâra
Faraḥ, Yusuf **9:**1039
FARAJ, MURĀD **6:**1178
- Oriental literature **12:**1464ff
Faraj, Samuel ben Nissim al-, *see* MITHRIDATES, FLAVIUS
FARAJ BEN SOLOMON (Salim) DA AGRIGENTO **6:**1179
- medicine **11:**1190
Faraji, Isaac **5:**70
Faraji, Jacob **11:**756
Faraynigte, *see* UNITED JEWISH SOCIALIST WORKERS PARTY
Faraynikte Partizaner Organizatsye (orgn.), *see* Fareinikte Partizaner Organizatsie
Farband (orgn., U.S.) **6:**801
- Zuckerman, Baruch **16:**1229
Farber, Leah **12:**454
FARBER, MARVIN **6:**1180
Farber, Rudolph **11:**501
Farberov, Nahum Pavlovich **10:**1501
Farbman, W. (Michael), *see* ABRAMOWITZ, GRIGORI
FARBSTEIN, DAVID ẒEVI **6:**1180
FARBSTEIN, JOSHUA HESCHEL **6:**1181
- *illus:*
- - F.Z.C. **16:**1165
- - Va'ad Le'ummi **16:**50
Farbstein, Max **13:**808
Farda (collec. for Isr.) **11:**1455
Fard Zavneh, *see* Pinḥas ben Yisḥak
Fareinikte, *see* UNITED JEWISH SOCIALIST WORKERS PARTY
Fareinikte Partizaner Organizatsie **13:**144; **16:**149ff
Farer, Louis **15:**301
Fargo (city, N. D.) **12:**1221
FARḤI (fam.) **6:**1181
Farhi, Eliezer **15:**1449
Farḥi, Ḥayyim Aaron **16:**1108
Farḥi, Hayyim Salim **2:**224; **6:**1182; **9:**297; **15:**644
Farḥi, Hillel ben Jacob **6:**1183 **12:**1464
Farḥi, Isaac ben Abraham **10:**542
Farḥi, Isaac ben Solomon **6:**1183
Farhi, Jacob **13:**1039
Farḥi, Joseph (Syr.) **6:**1182
Farḥi, Joseph David (Leb.) **6:**1183
Farḥi, Joseph Shabbetai **10:**214
Farḥi, Meir **5:**1250
Farḥi, Menahem **14:**262
Farḥi, Moses **6:**1182
Farḥi, Nuri **6:**1183
Farḥi, Raphael **6:**1182; **15:**644
Farḥi, Saul (Shilada) **6:**1182; **15:**644
Farḥi, Solomon (Salmon) **6:**1182
Farḥi Bible (illum. ms.)
- illuminated mss. **8:**1265
- *illus:* **4:**957; **6:***fcg.* 1195; **8:**1277
Fāriʿa (site, Isr.), *see* Tells (Sharuḥen)
Fariʿa (val., Isr.), *see* Wadi (Fariʿa)
FARIA, FRANCISCO DE **6:**1183
- *illus:* text
FARINACCI, ROBERTO **6:**1183
FARISSOL, ABRAHAM BEN MORDECAI **6:**1184
- Calicut Jews **5:**55
- disputations **6:**94ff
- history chart **8:**766-767
- Kaspi, Nethanel **10:**811
- lost tribes **15:**1005
- Luther, Martin **11:**585
- usury **8:**675ff; **12:**251
FARISSOL, JACOB BEN ḤAYYIM (Comprat; Vidal) **6:**1185
FARJEON, BENJAMIN LEOPOLD **6:**1185
- Dunedin **6:**273
Farjeon, Eleanor **6:**1186
Farjeon, Herbert **6:**1185
Farjeon, Joseph Jefferson **6:**1185
Farkas, E. **13:**975
Farkas, György **8:**33
Farkas, Imre **12:**1377; **15:**307
Farkas, Istvan **13:**113
Farkas, Jakab **8:**33
FARKAS, LADISLAUS (Wilhelm) **6:**1186
- *illus:* text
Farkas, Yaacov (Ze'ev) **5:**220
Farmer, J.D. **8:**1222
"Farmers" (paint., A. Kolnik) **10:**1169
FARMERS' FEDERATION OF ISRAEL **6:**1186
- Va'ad Le'ummi boycott **16:**50
Farmest (period.) **13:**1048
Farming, *see* AGRICULTURE
Farmingdale (boro., N.J.) **12:**1030
Farming in Israel, *see* AGRICULTURE IN ISRAEL
Far'n Folk (newsp.) **13:**1047
FARO (city, Port.) **6:**1187
- Hebrew printing **8:**1325
Faro (city, Sp.), *see* HARO
Faro, Abraham Rodriguez **16:**52
Faro, Jacome **6:**248
Faro, Moses ("Musi") **12:**598
Faro Pentateuch **4:**837
Farouk (k., Egy.) **12:**842
Farrar, Abraham, *see* Azevedo, Francisco Lopes d'
Farrar, Abraham "The Elder", *see* Lopez Rosa, Simon
Farrar, David **11:**491
Farri brothers (prints.) **16:**101
- *Be'ur al ha-Torah* (1554) **5:**5751
Fars (prov., Pers.) **13:**309; **14:**1415
Faruk (Egy. flagship) **9:**371
Farukh, Muhammad ibn, *see* Muhammad ibn Farukh
Farʿūn (bay, Isr.), *see* Jazīrat Farʿūn
Farwa (loc., Arab) **13:**156
Fasanenstrasse Community House (Ger.) **15:**627
FASCISM **6:**1187
- England **6:**763
- Italy **9:**1132
- Mussolini, Benito **12:**718
- Neo-Fascism **12:**951
- Wiener Library **16:**503
- *see also:* ANTI-SEMITISM; NATIONAL SOCIALISM; RACE, THEORY OF
Fasi, Joseph **5:**1173; **16:**1533
Faṣīḥ Lughat al-ʿIbrāniyyīn (wk.), *see Kitāb Faṣīḥ Lughat al-ʿIbrāniyyīn*
Fassel, H.B. **8:**957; **12:**765
FASSUTA (vill., Isr.) **6:**1188
- human geography **9:**589
FAST, HOWARD MELVIN **6:**1188
Fasting, Claus **14:**932
Fasting, Scroll of, *see* MEGILLAT TA'ANIT
FASTING AND FAST DAYS **6:**1189
- *Contents:*
- - In the Bible **6:**1189
- - Second Temple **6:**1191
- - Laws and Customs **6:**1192
- - Purpose and Conception **6:**1194
- - Classification **6:**1195
- General
- - Anan ben David **2:**921
- - Ba'al Shem Tov **9:**1051; **9:**1054
- - Babylonian Exile **6:**1038
- - calendar **5:**47
- - Ḥasidism **7:**1391
- - Jabneh **9:**243
- - Karaites **10:**779
- - *Megillat Ta'anit* **11:**1230
- - punishment for assault **3:**759
- - Purims, special **13:**1396
- - sages **14:**653ff
- - *Ta'anit* **15:**675ff
- - *talmid ḥakham* **15:**747
- - Temple **15:**953
- - Temple *mishmarot* **12:** 92
- - Ungar, Joel of Rechnitz **15:**1532
- Fast Days
- - Adar, The Seventh **2:**252
- - Av, the Ninth **3:**936
- - Day of Atonement **5:**1376
- - Esther **6:**914
- - firstborn **6:**1310
- - Gedaliah **7:**352
- - Monday and Thursday **12:**243
- - "plum fast" **4:**149
- - Shevat, 22nd of **11:**817
- - *Ta'anit ḥalom* **6:**209
- - Tammuz, the 17th **15:**789
- - *yahrzeit* **16:**703
- - Yom Kippur Katan **16:**846
- Halakhah and Custom
- - Ashi's innovations **3:**710
- - asceticism **3:**678ff
- - cemetery visiting **5:**272
- - covering of head **8:**2
- - drought **13:**1524
- - *hadran* exemption **7:**1053
- - *ḥaliẓah* **11:**130
- - marriage **11:**1043
- - New Moon **12:**1040
- - rabbinical enactment **7:**1159
- - sermons **13:**995
- - woman's work **12:**24
- Liturgy **11:**393
- - *Adonai, Adonai* **2:**294
- - *Akedah* **2:**481
- - *Anenu* **2:**842
- - *Avinu Malkenu* **3:**973; **3:**974

– – *haftarah* **16:**1342*ff*
– – *maftir* **11:**685
– – *selihot* **14:**1133ff
– *illus:*
– – text
– – Day of Atonement customs **5:**1385
– – Day of Atonement prayer (drg., B. Picart) **3:**831
– – Frankfort, service for special fast day **6:**1193
– – Ninth of Av scenes **3:**937
– – "Yom Kippur in the Country" (lith., A. Levy) **5:**1383
– *see also:* DAY AND NIGHT
Fastio, Isaac Henriques **11:**518
Fastov (city, Ukr.) **7:**1132
– pogroms **13:**700; **14:**459
Fataḥ, Al- (Fatḥ; Arab terrorist mvmt.)
– general survey **9:**1033
– Hussein **8:**1131
– Lebanon **10:**1546
– National Movement **9:**467
– sabotage raids **9:**404; **9:**414
– Six-Day War **14:**1639
– Syrian support **15:**649
– *illus:*
– – military court trial **9:**639
– – poster **9:**1470
– *see also:* Fedayeen; Palestine Liberation Organization
Fatalis, T-Cl. (Rom. sol.) **9:**1405
Fataw, Ṣaliḥ Raḥmūn **8:**1461
Fate
– folktale **6:**1380,1381
– philosophy **13:**424
– providence **13:**1280
– Sadducees **14:**622
– *see also:* FREE WILL
Fatehpur (tn., Ind.) **8:**1356
Father, *see* PARENT AND CHILD; PARENTS, HONOR OF
Father Jahn (Ger.), *see* Jahn, Father
Father Justin, *see* BOUDIN, JEAN-FRANÇOIS
Fatherland Front (orgn., Isr.) **9:**371
Father of the Prague Enlightenment, *see* Jeiteles, Jonas
Fathers according to Rabbi Nathan, *see* AVOT DE-RABBI NATHAN
Fathers of Sion (Chr. cong.), *see* Sion, Fathers of
Fātima (dau., Muhammad) **2:**516, 912; **9:**81; **12:**508
FATIMIDS (Musl. dyn.) **6:**1196
– Ashkelon, battle of **9:**267; **9:**271
– banking **4:**167
– Egypt **6:**491
– Ereẓ Israel history **9:**262ff
– Jerusalem rule **9:**1426
– Samaritans **14:**732
– Syrian Jews **15:**640
– Tunisia **15:**1433
– *see also:* ABBASIDS
Fats, *see* OILS
Fats, forbidden **6:**39
Fatt, Arthur C. **2:**317
Fattāḥ, Ibrahim ʿAbd al- **9:**1040
Faulquemont (vill., Fr.) **11:**496
Fauna in Israel, *see* FLORA AND FAUNA IN ISRAEL
Faust (leg. mag.) **7:**690; **15:**1400
Faust (-ius), J.F. **8:**33
Faustbuch (bk.) **7:**443
Faustina (1/2 cent., act.) **15:**1050
Fauvism (art) **3:**591
Fava, Abraham **15:**1440
Favir, Eliezer **16:**1014
Faʾw (tn., Iraq), *see* Fao
Fawzi al- Kaukji, *see* Kaukji, Fawzi al-
Fáy, András **8:**1079
Fay, Stanley **10:**98
Faya, Aaron Cohen, *see* Aguiar, Antonio de
Fayetteville (city, N.C.) **12:**1220
Fayfer, Shayke **7:**633
Fayln (anths., U.S.) **15:**676
Faynān (site, Isr.) **11:**1431
Faytun (k., Arab.) **11:**1212
Fayyāẓ, Tawfīq **9:**1042ff
Fayyum (city, Egy.), *see* FAIYŪM
FAZ, *see* Federation of American Zionists
Fazāz (reg., Mor.) **14:**1528
Fazekas, Miklós Bogáti **4:**883
Fazekas, Stephan **5:**406
FEARING, KENNETH **6:**1198
FEAR OF GOD **6:**1198
– *hakhel* commandment **7:**1149
– love and fear **11:**528
– Philo **13:**414
– *see also:* LOVE
Feast, *see* SE'UDAH
Feast of Fools, *see* Fools, Feast of
Feast of Fruits, *see* TU BI-SHEVAT
Fedayeen (Arab terrorist gr.) **9:**1034
– attacks on Israel **9:**387ff
– Sinai Campaign **14:**1601
– U.N. **15:**1555
– *see also:* Fatah, Al; Palestine Liberation Organization
Feder (print.) **11:**544
Feder, Adolf **13:**116
– art **3:**575
– *illus:*
– – "Landscape" (paint.) **13:**118
FEDER, ERNST **6:**1199
FEDER, RICHARD **6:**1200
FEDER, TOBIAS **6:**1200
– Bick's controversy **4:**977
Federación (inst., Arg.) **16:**1123
Federación de Comunidades de América Central (orgn.) **16:**1127
Federación de Sociedades Judías (Mex.) **11:**1457
Federación Entrerriana de Cooperativas (agr. coop., Arg.) **3:**432
Federación Juvenil Sionista (Mex.) **16:**1125
Federación Juvenil Sionista (Urug.) **16:**14; **16:**1126
Federación Sionista (Colom.) **16:**1125
Federación Sionista (Mex.) **16:**1125
Federación Sionista Argentina **16:**1123
Federación Sionista de Méjico (Mex.) **16:**1126
Federación Universitaria Sionista Sudamericana **16:**1126
Federal Indemnifaction Law, *see* REPARATIONS, GERMAN; RESTITUTION AND INDEMNIFICATION
Federalists (polit. party, U.S.) **15:**1648
Federal Restitution Law, *see* REPARATIONS, GERMAN; RESTITUTION AND INDEMNIFICATION
Federated Zionist Organization of Canada **6:**454; **16:**1109
Federation Chronicle (journ.) **13:**1049
Fédération de la Jeunesse Sioniste et Pro-Palestinienne (Fr.) **16:**1114
Fédération des Communautés Israélites d'Algérie **2:**617
Fédération des Sociétés Juives de France **7:**32; **7:**35
Federation of American Zionists **16:**1141
– history chart **8:**766-767
Federation of Communities of the Mosaic Religion (Rum.) **14:**413
Federation of General Zionists (polit. party, Er. Isr.) **9:**661
Federation of Jewish Communities (Aus.) **3:**903
Federation of Jewish Community Services and the Allied Jewish Community Services (Can.), *see* Federation of Jewish Philanthropies
Federation of Jewish Farmers (U.S.) **14:**589
Federation of Jewish Philanthropies (Montreal, Can.) **13:**385
Federation of Jewish Philanthropies (Toronto, Can.) **13:**385
Federation of Jewish Philanthropies of New York **12:**1099ff
– hospitals **8:**1039
– Willen, Joseph **16:**516
Federation of Oriental Jews (soc., U.S.) **14:**1174
Federation of Reconstructionist Congregations and Fellowships (U.S.) **13:**1616
Federation of Synagogues (Eng.) **6:**758
– Orthodoxy **12:**1491
– synagogue **15:**590
– United Synagogue **15:**1673
Federation of Synagogues of South Africa **15:**194
Federation of Zionist Societies (Can.) **16:**1109
Fédération Sioniste de France **16:**1114
FEDERATIONS OF COMMUNITIES, TERRITORIAL **6:**1201
FEDERBUSCH, SIMON **6:**1202
Federjude (medal, Ger.) **11:**1168
FEDERMAN, MAX **6:**1203
FEDERN, PAUL **6:**1203
Feet, Washing of **2:**84
Fefer, Eliezer **10:**954
FEFER, ITZIK **6:**1204
– anti-Fascist Committee **3:**63; **3:**64
– *illus:*
– – Jewish anti-Fascist Committee **3:**63; **6:**1204
– – La Guardia, Fiorello, and **12:**1110
FEIBELMAN, JULIAN BECK **6:**1205
FEIBUSCH, HANS **3:**600
Feibush Ashkenazi, *see* JOEL BEN SIMEON
Feierberg, M.Z., *see* FEUERBERG, MORDECAI ZE'EV
Feiffer, Jules **5:**216
Feiga, Wilfred B. **16:**634
Feigel, A. M. **4:**119; **13:**345
FEIGENBAUM, ARYEH **6:**1205
FEIGENBAUM, BENJAMIN **6:**1206
– *illus:*
– – Workmen's Circle leader **12:**1096
Feigenbaum, David **13:**1294
FEIGENBAUM, ISAAC HA-KOHEN **16:**1325
FEIGIN, DOV **6:**1207
– *illus:*
– – sculpture at Miẓpeh Ramon **6:**1206
FEIGIN, SAMUEL ISAAC **6:**1207
Feiginsohn, Samuel Shraga **14:**255
FEIGL, BEDRICH (Friedrich) **6:**1207
– *illus:*
– – text
– – Wassermann, August von (etch.) **16:**362
FEIGL, FRITZ **6:**1208
FEIGL, HERBERT **6:**1208
Feiglin, Abe **11:**1284
Feiglin, Baer **11:**1286
Feiglin, David **11:**1284
Feiglin, Joseph **11:**1284
Feiglin, Moses **11:**1286
Feilchenfeld **9:**1296
FEILER, ARTHUR **6:**1209
Feilmoser, A. Benedict **8:**33
Fein (r., Serb.) **16:**1224
Fein, Ḥayyim **10:**1106
– Radzyn **13:**1509
Fein, Judah Leib **12:**1497
Fein, Maria **15:**1056
FEINBERG (fam.) **6:**1209
FEINBERG, ABRAHAM (bsmn.) **6:**1210
– *illus:*
– – Israel-Bonds-UJA dinner **15:**1668
FEINBERG, ABRAHAM L. (r.) **6:**1211
Feinberg, Avshalom **6:**1209
– Aaronsohn, Aaron **2:**27
– Belkind, Na'aman **4:**440
– Lishansky, Yosef **11:**303
– Nili **12:**1162ff
– *geneal. table* **4:**439
– *illus:*
– – portrait **12:**1163
Feinberg, Benjamin **12:**1127
Feinberg, Charles E. **5:**311; **5:**1572
FEINBERG, DAVID **6:**1211
– relief work **16:**734
Feinberg, Elijah **16:**1013
Feinberg, H. **16:**1165
Feinberg, Israel (Lolik) **6:**1209
FEINBERG, LEON **6:**1212
Feinberg, Louis **5:**563
FEINBERG, NATHAN **6:**1212
– Bernheim petition **4:**681
Feinberg, Robert **15:**28
FEINBERG, SAMUEL YEVGENYEVICH **12:**689
Feinberg, Yosef **6:**1209
Feinberg, Zelda, *see* Popkin, Zelda Feinberg
Feiner, Ḥayim, *see* HEFER, ḤAYIM
Feiner, Yehiel (Dinur), *see* K. ZETNICK
Feiner, L. **4:**1505; **10:**89
Feinerman, Aaron S. **7:**1348
Feingold, George **11:**1115
Feingold, Hersz, *see* Stur, Jan
Feininger, Lyonel **5:**216
Feinkind, Joshua Alter **11:**918
Feinman, Dinah **15:**1082
FEINMAN, SIGMUND **15:**1081
Feinsilberg, Ilya Arnoldovich, *see* ILF, ILYA
FEINSINGER, JOSHUA **7:**1547
Feinsinger, Pesaḥ **4:**330
Feinsinger, Shaye, *see* FEINSINGER, JOSHUA
FEINSTEIN, ARYEH LOEB **6:**1212
Feinstein, Elijah **13:**1294
– Soloveitchik, Joseph Dov **15:**132
FEINSTEIN, ḤAYYIM JACOB HA-KOHEN **6:**1212
Feinstein, Isidore, *see* STONE, I.F.
Feinstein, Meir **8:**1468; **11:**465; **15:**490
– *illus:*
– – suicide report, *Palestine Post* **11:**463
FEINSTEIN, MOSES (r.) **6:**1213
– conversion to Judaism **10:**24
– transplants **15:**1338ff
FEINSTEIN, MOSES (poet) **6:**1213
– *illus:*
– – Hebrew Pen Club, N.Y. **8:**211; **12:**1109
– – Hebrew writers' convention **8:**213
FEINSTONE, MORRIS **6:**1213
FEIS, HERBERT **6:**1214
Feisal I (k., Syr., Iraq), *see* Faisal I
Feisal II (k., Iraq), *see* Faisal II
Feischel Buntzl, Mayer, *see* FISCHELS, MEIR BEN EPHRAIM

FEITELSON, MENAHEM MENDEL **6:**1214
Feivish, Samuel **12:**1410
FEIWEL, BERTHOLD **6:**1215
- Zionism **16:**1111
- *illus:*
- - F.Z.C. **16:**1165
- - protest against Passfield White Paper **16:**1118
FEJÉR, LEOPOLD **6:**1216
FEJTŐ, FRANÇOIS **6:**1216
FEKETE, MICHAEL **6:**1216
Fekler, Ignaz Aurel **8:**33
FELD, ISAAC **6:**1217
FELD, JACOB **8:**1431
Feld, M. **8:**1052
Feldbau, Jacques **2:**757
Feldberg, Jacob **12:**266
FELDBERG, LEON **6:**1217
Feldheim, Juliusz **13:**798,802
Feldheim, Philipp **13:**1377
Feldkirch (vill., Aus.) **16:**223
FELDMAN, ABRAHAM JEHIEL **6:**1217
- Connecticut **5:**899
Feldman, Aharon, *see* EVER HADANI
Feldman, Esther **14:**502
FELDMAN, GRIGORY PETROVICH **12:**689
Feldman, Harry **15:**311
FELDMAN, HERMAN **11:**1573
FELDMAN, IRVING **15:**1578; **15:**1580
Feldman, Israel, *see* PALDI, ISRAEL
Feldman, J. (r.) **7:**1359
Feldman, Joseph (mil. ldr.), *see* Pasenko, George
Feldman, Józef (hist.) **6:**1218
Feldman, L.A. **15:**782
FELDMAN, LOUIS HARRY **1:**29
FELDMAN, MIROSLAV **16:**889; **16:**890
Feldman, Roberto **10:**307
Feldman, Saul (polit.) **12:**1025
Feldman, S. B. (journ.) **7:**1534
FELDMAN, WILHELM **6:**1217
Feldmann, F. **4:**875
Feldsberg, Ernst **3:**904
FELEKY, GÉZA **10:**310
Felice Perette da Montalto, *see* Sixtus V
Felice Umano, *see* ANAU, PHINEHAS ḤAI BEN MENAHEM
Felici (monsignor) **16:**78
Felicity, *see* BEATITUDE
FELIKS, JEHUDA **1:**29
FELIX, ANTONIUS (Rom. gov., Judea) **6:**1218
- Aziz **3:**1010
- crucifixion of zealots **5:**1134
- Drusilla **6:**241
- procuratorial period **8:**639
- *illus:*
- - coins, Judean **5:**712
Felix, Dinah **13:**1492
Felix, Eliza Rachel (act.), *see* RACHEL
Felix, Jacob **13:**1492
Felix, Lia **13:**1492
Felix, Raphael **13:**1492
Felix, Rebecca **13:**1492
Felix, Sarah **13:**1492
FELIX LIBERTATE (Du. soc.) **6:**1218
- Amsterdam **2:**900
Felix of Galicia, *see* Selig, Gabriel
Fell, John **8:**33
Fell, Margaret **8:**33
Fellaḥin (Arab farmers) **9:**1038
FELLER, ABRAHAM (Rum.) **1:**30
FELLER, ABRAHAM HOWARD (U.S.) **6:**1219
Feller, Harry S. **12:**1021
FELLER, SHNEYUR ZALMAN **6:**1219
Fellheim (vill., Ger.) **11:**1299
Fellner, Hermann **12:**453
FELLNER, WILLIAM JOHN **6:**1220
Fellowship offering **14:**603
FELMAN, AHARON LEIB **6:**1220
FELS (fam., U.S.) **6:**1220
Fels, Joseph **6:**1220
Fels, Mary **6:**1221
Fels, Samuel Simon **6:**1221
Felsenstein, Samson **7:**1257
Felsenthal, Adolph **3:**459
FELSENTHAL, BERNHARD **6:**1221
- Historical Society **2:**826; **2:**827
- Oral Law **12:**1443
Felshtin (vill., Ukr.) **13:**668
- pogroms **13:**699
Felson, Edgar M. **9:**1191
Felsövisó (vill., Rum.), *see* VIŞEUL DE SUS
Feltsman, O. B. **13:**1340
Felvidek (S. Slov.), *see* SLOVAKIA
Female Hebrew Benevolent Society (N.Y.) **12:**1071
Fence to law, *see* TAKKANOT
Fencing **15:**292; **15:**307
FENICHEL, OTTO **6:**1222
FENICHEL, SAMUEL **6:**1223
- travels **15:**1351
FENNEL (bot.) **6:**1223
- plant list **13:**619
- spice **15:**268
- *illus:* text
Fenugreek (bot.) **13:**619
FÉNYES, ADOLF **6:**1224
Fenyes, E. **15:**1235
FENYŐ, LÁSZLÓ **8:**1084
FENYŐ, MIKSA **6:**1224
Feodor (bld. lib. vict., Rus.) **16:**87
Feodor the Jew (trans.) **14:**506
FEODOSIYA (port, Ukr.) **6:**1224
FERARU, LEON **14:**422; **14:**426
FERBER, EDNA **6:**1225
FERBER, HERBERT (sculp.) **6:**1226
- *illus:*
- - text
- - B'nai Israel synagogue, N.J. **15:**625
Ferber, H.J. (writ.) **5:**445
FERBER, ẒEVI HIRSCH (r.) **6:**1226
Ferdinand (infante of Port.) **2:**103
Ferdinand I (k., Arag.) **6:**1235ff
- Spain **15:**238
- Tortosa **15:**1270
FERDINAND I (H. Rom. Emp.) **6:**1227
- Arpa, Abramo dall' **3:**496
- Austrian Jews **3:**890
- *illus:*
- - Jewish badge, decree **4:**69
Ferdinand I (Naples) **2:**105
Ferdinand I (duke of Tuscany), *see* Medici, Ferdinand I de'
FERDINAND II (H. Rom. Emp.) **6:**1227
- Prague seal privilege **14:**1080
Ferdinand II (Naples) **3:**228
FERDINAND III (H. Rom. Emp.) **6:**1227
- *illus:*
- - Prague Jewish community banner **13:**967
Ferdinand III (Castile) **4:**1512
- Briviesca Jews **4:**1383
- Dueñas Jews **6:**261
- Seville **14:**1202
- *illus:*
- - key given by Seville Jews **14:**1203
Ferdinand IV (k., Castile) **2:**102
- Cartagena Jewry **5:**209
- Toledo **15:**1203
Ferdinand IV (k., Sicily) **8:**1397
Ferdinand VII (k., Sp.) **8:**1389
- Aẓancot, Moses **3:**998
FERDINAND, PHILIP **6:**1227
FERDINAND AND ISABELLA (Sp. monarchs) **6:**1228
- Abrabanel, Isaac **2:**104
- Barcelona inquisition **4:**212
- Cagliari Jews **5:**14
- Granada Jewry **7:**852
- Inquisition **8:**1382
- Saragossa **14:**863
- Spain **15:**240
- Toledo **15:**1204ff
- Torquemada **15:**1264
- *illus:*
- - Edict of Expulsion **15:**239
Ferencz, Benjamin **15:**1568
FERENCZI, SÁNDOR **6:**1229
- psychiatry **13:**1338
Ferenczi, Tobias **8:**33
FERKAUF, EUGENE **6:**1230
Ferkauf Graduate School of Humanities and Social Sciences **16:**761
Ferme, Moses Cohen, *see* AZEVEDO, MOSES COHEN D'
Fermented dough, *see* ḤAMEẒ
Fermi, Enrico **4:**1099
Fermi (Fermo), Joseph **2:**943; **7:**43
Fermosa, *see* JEWESS OF TOLEDO
Fern (bot.) **13:**619
Fernandes, Branca **8:**1391
Fernandes, Diego **8:**1391
- Recife **13:**1613
- sugar industry **15:**487
- trade and commerce **15:**1301
FERNANDES VILLAREAL, MANOEL **6:**1230
- Villareal family **16:**136ff
Fernandez, Diego (Diogo), *see* Fernandes, Diego
Fernandez, Simon **14:**1413
Fernández de Villanova, Alfonso *see* Abravalia, Don Samuel
Fernand-Halphen, Alice **7:**1206
Fernando VII (k., Sp.), *see* Ferdinand VII
Fernando de Zárate, *see* GÓMEZ, ANTONIO ENRÍQUEZ
FERNBERGER, SAMUEL **13:**1346
FERNHOF, ISAAC **6:**1230
- utopian Zionism **16:**1152
- *illus:*
- - F.Z.C. **16:**1165
Ferragut, *see* FARAJ BEN SOLOMON DA AGRIGENTO
Ferrand, Louis **8:**33
Ferrante I (k., Naples),*see* Ferdinand I
FERRARA (city, It.) **6:**1231
- history chart (1624) **8:**766-767
- Jewish censorship **5:**280
- synod **15:**634
- tax **15:**839
- *illus:*
- - text
- - Usque's printers' mark **13:**1094
Ferrara, David de **12:**1062
Ferrara Bible **4:**866
- Usque, Abraham **6:**1234; **16:**21
Ferrarius Saladi, *see* ZERAHIAH BEN ISAAC HA-LEVI
Ferreira, Abraham Kohen de, *see* HERRERA, ABRAHAM KOHEN DE
Ferrer, Bonifacio **4:**879
FERRER, VICENTE **6:**1235
- Barbastro Jews **4:**207
- Burgos Jews **4:**1513
- conversionist sermons **15:**237
- history chart **8:**766-767
- Jewish badge **4:**66
- Teruel **15:**1023
- Toledo **15:**1204
- Tortosa **15:**1270
- *illus:* text
FERRIS, IRIS **6:**1236
Ferrizuel (fam., Sp.) **15:**1201
FERRIZUEL, JOSEPH HA-NASI **6:**1236
- Al-Tarās, Sīdī ibn **2:**772
- Toledo **15:**1200
Fertile Crescent (reg., Middle E.) **3:**739
- Mesopotamia **16:**1495
Fertility, *see* BARRENNESS AND FERTILITY
Fessler, I. Aurelius **8:**33
Festinger, Leon **13:**1345
FESTIVALS **6:**1237
- *Contents:*
- - Introduction **6:**1237
- - In the Bible **6:**1237
- - Source of Festivals **6:**1238
- - Celebration of Festival **6:**1241
- - Apocrypha and Hellenistic Jewish Literature **6:**1242
- - Talmudic Literature **6:**1242
- - Intermediate Days **6:**1244
- - Second Days **6:**1244
- - Liturgy **6:**1245
- General
- - altar **2:**769ff
- - Ashi's innovations **3:**710
- - calendar **5:**43
- - dating according to Meshwi **11:**1405
- - dogma **3:**658
- - fast days **6:**1193
- - greetings **7:**914
- - Jabneh **9:**243
- - Jewish religious life in Israel **9:**902*ff*
- - *Jubilees, Book of* **10:**324
- - Judaism **10:**388
- - Justinian **10:**478
- - Karaites **10:**779
- - Leviticus, Book of **11:**146
- - Pentateuch **13:**248; **13:**256
- - pilgrimage **13:**510ff
- - purity for **13:**1412
- - rejoicing **10:**1566
- - sermons **13:**994
- - *Temple Scroll* **15:**997
- - Torah ornaments **15:**1257
- Attitudes to
- - Conservative Judaism **5:**906; **12:**1445
- - Maimonides on Karaites **11:**760
- - Reform Judaism **14:**26
- - Samaritans **14:**741
- - Shabbetai Ẓevi **14:**1223
- Major Festivals
- - Day of Atonement **5:**1376
- - Passover **13:**163
- - Rosh Ha-Shanah **14:**305
- - Shavuot **14:**1319
- - Shemini Aẓeret **15:**501
- - Simḥat Torah **14:**1571ff
- - Sukkot **15:**495
- Minor Festivals
- - Av, the Fifteenth of **3:**935
- - Ḥanukkah **7:**1280
- - Hoshana Rabba **8:**1026
- - Independence Day, Israel **8:**1344
- - Intermediate Days **6:**1244
- - Lag ba-Omer **10:**1356
- - New Moon **12:**1039; **12:**290
- - Purim **13:**1390; **14:**1054
- - Second Passover **13:**173
- - *Shabbat Ḥol ha-Mo'ed* **14:**573
- - Shushan Purim **13:**1390
- - Tu bi-Shevat **15:**1419
- Laws and Observances
- - *Beẓah* **4:**785
- - burial **4:**1518
- - Commandments, the 613 **5:**763,767f
- - cooking and food **6:**1422

-- court action **13:**958
-- fire **6:**1304
-- *Havdalah* **7:**1482
-- *hedkesh* vows **8:**281
-- hunting **8:**1111
-- Israel law, 1948 **12:**147
-- *mishmarot* Temple service **12:**91
-- mourning **12:**490
-- *mukzeh* **12:**515
-- *niddui* and second Diaspora day **8:**351
-- sacrifices **7:**1115
-- second day **6:**159
-- *tefillin* **15:**901
-- Temple **15:**977*ff*
-- work customs **12:**22; **12:**24
-- *Yaknehaz* **16:**705
- Liturgy
-- additional prayer (*Musaf*) **12:**532ff
-- *Amidah* **2:**843ff
-- *Arvit* **3:**665
-- *azharot* **3:**1008
-- *haftarah* **16:**1342
-- *Hallel* **7:**1198
-- Jerusalem in **9:**1561
-- *Kiddush* **10:**974
-- Torah reading **15:**1246; **15:**1248
- Sects
-- Elephantine **6:**609
-- Falashas **6:**1148
- Islam **9:**98
- *illus:*
-- text
-- *bikkurim* **6:**13-15
-- Day of Atonement service, Verdun **16:**109
-- day of week calculation table (1649) **10:**1527
-- *Eruv Tavshilin* tablet (1806, Ger.) **7:***fcg.* 843
-- Hanukkah, Modi'in torch **12:**207
-- Hanukkah, Westerbork Nazi camp **16:**466
-- Independence Day celebration **8:**1345-1347
-- Jerusalem Day **9:**1503
-- Lag ba-Omer **10:**1357,1358
-- Marrakesh, women's festive dress **12:**340
-- Mogador, woman's traditional dress **12:**213
-- Ofran, woman and child in holiday dress **12:**1340
-- Passover **13:**164-171
--- *seder* in Dallas, Texas **15:**1611
--- *se'udah* **14:**1193
-- Purim **13:**1391ff
--- Adloyada parade **9:**907
--- kindergarten party **11:**365
--- New York ball **12:**1081
-- Rosh Ha-Shanah
--- in Riga synagogue **14:**176
--- *Musaf* service, *Amidah* **14:**306
--- "Rosh Ha-Shanah in the Synagogue" **13:**497
--- *tashlikh* ceremony in Tel Aviv **15:**829
-- salutations (table) **7:**915
-- scriptural readings (chart) **15:**1251,1252
-- Shavuot
--- Jerusalem children **14:**1321
--- *piyyut* **14:**1320
-- Simhat Torah **14:**1571ff
--- procession **9:**907
-- Sukkot
--- Amsterdam Jewish quarter **15:**499
--- meal in *sukkah* **15:**496
--- prayers in trenches of Kibbutz Sa'ad (1948) **16:**323
--- scene, Germany **15:**493
-- Tu bi-Shevat celebrations **9:**907; **15:**1420
-- U.S. army chaplain and serviceman **11:**1553
- *mus. notations:*
-- *Mi-Sinai niggunim* **12:**151
- *see also:* ART (Sabbath and Festivals); DANCE; DAY AND NIGHT; DOMICILE; FASTING AND FAST DAYS; FOLKLORE; PILGRIM FESTIVALS; SE'UDAH
Festivals, Kibbutz, *see* KIBBUTZ FESTIVALS; Hag...
FESTSCHRIFTEN (jubilee vols.) **6:**1246
FESTUS, PORCIUS (Rom. gov.) **6:**1247
Fetaya, Aaron **4:**93
Fetaya, Moses **4:**93
"Fettling Shop I" (rlf., Ghisha Koenig) **3:**634
FETTMILCH, VINCENT **6:**1248
- chronological chart **8:**766-767
- Hahn, Joseph Yuspa **7:**1129
- *illus:*
-- expulsion of Frankfort Jews, 1614 **7:**474
Fetya, Judah Moses **6:**20
Feuardent, François **8:**33
FEUCHTWANG, DAVID **6:**1248
Feuchtwang, Meir **6:**1248
Feuchtwanger, Heinrich **5:**311
FEUCHTWANGER, LION **6:**1248
- *illus:* text
Feuchtwanger seals collection **14:**1081
Feudalism **16:**1285*ff*
FEUER, HENRY **5:**382
FEUER, LEON I. (Ger.) **6:**1250
FEUER, LEWIS SAMUEL **6:**1250
Feuerbach (Ger.) **8:**714
FEUERBERG, MORDECAI ZE'EV **6:**1250
- Berdyczewski, Micha Josef **4:**594
- Hebrew literature **8:**195
Feuering, Yizhak **4:**781
Feuerlicht, Morris **8:**1362
FEUERMANN, EMANUEL **12:**689
FEUERRING, MAXIMILIAN **3:**600
- *illus:*
-- "Memorial" (paint.) **3:**623
Feuerstein, Avigdor, *see* HAMEIRI, AVIGDOR
FEUERSTEIN, BEDŘICH **6:**1254
FEUERSTEIN, MOSES I. **6:**1254
FEUERSTEIN, REUVEN **13:**1346
Feugerons, Ponce **14:**922
Feyge (granddau., Baal Shem Tov) **16:**628
FEYGENBERG, RAKHEL **6:**1254
FEYNMAN, RICHARD PHILLIPS **6:**1254
FEZ (city, Mor.) **6:**1255
- Abendanan family **2:**68
- Jewish quarter **10:**87
- special Purim **13:**1397
- *takkanot* **15:**725
- *illus:*
-- text
-- synagogue *bimah* **14:**1183
Fezzan (reg., Libya) **11:**198
Fiammetta, Joseph **13:**587; **2:**943; **13:**67
Fiano, Isaac Shabbetai **13:**68
Fibetim (acrostics) **2:**230
Fichel, Hayyim **11:**938
Fichman, Meyer E. **11:**502
FICHMANN, JACOB **6:**1258
- critic **5:**1122
- Hebrew literature **8:**197
- Jerusalem theme **9:**1566
- *illus:*
-- Writers' assoc. in Israel **8:**205
FICHTE, JOHANN GOTTLIEB **6:**1260
Ficino, Marsilio **8:**33
- Abrabanel, Judah **2:**109
- Kabbalah **10:**540
FICTION, HEBREW **6:**1261
- *Contents:*
-- Talmudic-Midrashic **6:**1261
-- Midrashic Motifs **6:**1261
-- Bible Stories **6:**1262
-- Apocrypha, Pseudepigrapha **6:**1263
-- First Collections **6:**1264
-- Historiography **6:**1265
-- Romance Literature **6:**1265
-- Ethical Literature **6:**1267
-- Ashkenazi-Hasidic **6:**1267
-- Kabbalah **6:**1268
-- Italian Renaissance **6:**1269
-- Palestine, 16th Century **6:**1269
-- 17/18 Centuries **6:**1270
-- Hasidic **6:**1271
- aggadah **2:**354
- allegory **2:**643; **2:**644
- animal tales **3:**19
- biographies **4:**1010
- children's literature **5:**428
- exemplum **6:**1020
- fable **6:**1125
- folklore **6:**1374
- hagiography **7:**1116
- Hebrew literature **8:**77
- historiography **8:**551
- Jewish literature **11:**352ff
- *Moses, Chronicles of* **12:**413
- myth and mythology **12:**729
- visions **16:**167
- wisdom literature **16:**561
- Yiddish literature **16:**798
- *illus:*
-- Arthurian legends **3:**653
-- *Ben ha-Melekh ve-ha-Nazir* **4:**518
-- *Lesebuch fuer Juedische Kinder* **5:**433
-- *Ma'aseh ha-Ez* **5:**435
Fiction, Legal, *see* Legal fiction
Fidangue de Castro, Morris **16:**165
Fiddler on the Roof (play) **12:**1121
- *illus:*
-- Mostel, Zero, as Tevye **12:**443
Fiddletown (Calif.) **5:**56
Fideles (offic., Catalonia) **2:**259
FIEDLER, ARTHUR **12:**689
FIEDLER, LESLIE AARON **6:**1271
- literature **15:**1577ff
Field, Claud **5:**450
Field, Frederick **8:**33
Fielding, Henry **6:**775
Fields, Jackie **15:**305 **12:**1376
Field squads (defense force), *see* *Peluggot Sadeh*
Fiersohn, Reba, *see* GLUCK, ALMA
Fieschi, Sinibaldo (pope), *see* INNOCENT IV
FIG **6:**1272
- food **6:**1416
- plant list **13:**619
- Tree of Good and Evil **2:**238
- wood offering **16:**630
- *illus:* text
Fig, sycamore (bot.) **13:**619
Figdor, Jehiel Michael ben Samuel, *see* KITTSEE, JEHIEL MICHAEL BEN SAMUEL
Fighters' List (polit. party, Isr.) **9:**374; **9:**664
Fig marigold (bot.) **9:**222
FIGO, AZARIAH **6:**1274
Figueiredo, Antonio Pereira de **4:**879
Figueiro, Petrus **8:**33
Figueres, José **10:**1455
Fihl (tn., Transj.), *see* PELLA
Fiji (isls., Pac. O.) **9:**444
Filālī (Musl. dyn.), *see* ALAWIDS
Filariasis (disease) **14:**1502
Filastīn, *see* PALESTINE
Filastīn (newsp.) **9:**333
Filca, Jossep Aben, *see* Aben Filca, Jossep
Filca, Rabi Asser Aben, *see* Aben Filca, Rabi Asser
FILDERMAN, WILHELM **6:**1274
FILENE (fam.) **6:**1275
Filene, A. Lincoln **6:**1275
Filene, Edward Albert **6:**1275
Filene, William **6:**1275
Filipović, Frida **16:**890
Filipowicz, Jan **14:**63
FILIPOWSKI, ZEVI HIRSCH **6:**1277
Filippo (It. apos.) **13:**1606
Filipponi (fam.) **7:**1101
FILLER, LOUIS **8:**545
Film Industry (Isr.) **9:**1006
Filoni, Girolamo **6:**1234
Filosof, Esther, *see* Zevi, Esther
Filosof, Joseph **13:**1425; **14:**1240; **14:**1244
Filov, Bogdan **4:**1485; **4:**1486
FIMA (art.) **6:**1277
- *illus:*
-- text
-- painting Pl. 18 **3**-ART
FINALE (tn., It.) **6:**1278
FINAL SOLUTION (Nazi plan) **6:**1278
- Auschwitz **3:**855ff
- Bormann **4:**1250
- Eichmann **6:**517
- forced labor **6:**1429
- Frank, Hans **7:**54
- gassing **16:**1332
- Germany **7:**495
- Gestapo **7:**527ff
- ghettos **7:**543ff
- Globocnik, Odilo **7:**622
- Goebbels **7:**688
- Heydrich, Reinhard **8:**448
- Himmler **8:**498
- Hitler **8:**782
- Hoess **8:**806
- Holocaust **8:**842ff
- *judenrein* **10:**408
- Kaltenbrunner, Ernst **10:**722
- Madagascar Plan **11:**678ff
- Mueller, Heinrich **12:**503
- *Nazi-Deutsch* **12:**904
- Poland **13:**755ff
- Rauter, Hanns **13:**1576
- *Reichsvereinigung* **14:**51
- *Reichszentrale* **14:**51
- Ribbentrop **14:**150
- Rumania **14:**403
- Schellenberg, Walter **14:**953
- SS and SD **15:**322; **15:**324
- Streicher, Julius **15:**436
- Szalasi, Ferenc **15:**656
- Sztójay, Döme **15:**670
- Tuka, Vojtech **15:**1428
- War Crimes Trials **16:**291ff
- *illus:*
-- Wannsee Conference minutes **16:**264
- *see also:* CAMPS; WANNSEE CONFERENCE
Finaly, Fritz **6:**1279
Finaly, Gerald **6:**1279
Finaly, Robert **6:**1279
FINALY CASE **6:**1279
Finance, *see* BANKING AND BANKERS; ECONOMIC HISTORY; INSURANCE; TRADE AND COMMERCE
FINANCES, AUTONOMOUS JEWISH **6:**1280
- endowments **8:**284ff
- millet **11:**1583
- tax evasion **8:**1306
- *illus:* text
- *see also:* AUTONOMY; PHILANTHROPY
Finberg, Joe **15:**25

FINBERT, ELIAN-J. **7:**149
FINCH, SIR HENRY **6:**1285
Fincherri, Ephraim **16:**172
Finchley (sub., Lond.) **11:**479
- *illus:*
- - shift of population **11:**479
Finci, David **16:**1224
FINCI, ELI **10:**310
"Finding of Moses" (paint., Veronese) **12:**407
Fine, Benjamin **6:**465
FINE, LOUIS **6:**1285
FINE, REUBEN **6:**1285
- chess **5:**407
FINE, SIDNEY **8:**546
Fine, Solomon **8:**1438
Fine, Sylvia **10:**853
FINEBERG, SOLOMON ANDHIL **6:**1285
Fineman, Daniel **6:**1286
FINEMAN, ḤAYYIM **6:**1286
- Shazar, Zalman **14:**1324
FINEMAN, IRVING **6:**1286
FINER, HERMAN **6:**1286
FINES **6:**1287
- *asmakhta* **3:**751
- assault **3:**758; **8:**1302
- confession **5:**877
- divine retribution **6:**122
- flogging **6:**1351
- gambling **7:**300
- *garme* damage **7:**431
- *ḥaẓi nezek* **3:**986
- individual's transgression **12:**139
- informers **8:**1372
- inhospitality **13:**645
- Inquisition **8:**1403
- insult **8:**1409
- liability **12:**1311
- rape **13:**1548ff
- sex offenses **13:**1245
- slander **14:**1652
- theft **15:**1098
- Toledo **15:**1200
- warning required **13:**222
- *see also:* DAMAGES
FINESHRIBER, WILLIAM HOWARD **6:**1289
Fingerbreadth (meas.), *see 'Ezba'*
FINGERMAN, GREGORIO **13:**1346
Fingers
- rabbinic explanation of shape **13:**1119
- right hand **14:**179
- spelling **2:**744
Fingesten, Michel **4:**1219
Finials (Torah orn.) **5:**288; **15:**1256
- *illus:*
- - Baghdad, silver (19th cent.) **15:**1260-1261
- - Burma, in shape of hand (19th cent.) **4:**1527
- - Germany, lion-topped (19th cent.) **11:**269
- - Germany, silver (19th cent.) **15:**1260-1261
- - Holland, silver (18th cent.) **5:**291; **15:**1260-1261
- - India, silver (19th cent.) **15:**1260-1261
- - Italy, silver (18th cent.) **15:**1260-1261
- - Morocco, wood (18th cent.) **15:**1260-1261
- - Myer Myers', silver (18th cent.) **12:**725
- - North Africa, silver (19th cent.) **15:**1260-1261
- - Persia, incised silver **13:**311
- - Persia, Ten Commandments motif (20th cent.) **5:**1444
- - Sicily, silver filigree (15th cent.) **7:**740
FININBERG, EZRA **6:**1290
- Gurshtein, Aaron **7:**982
Fink, Leo **11:**1284
Fink, Ludwig **5:**1110
- *illus:*
- - talking to a prison inmate **5:**1111
FINK, THEODORE **6:**1290
FINKEL, ELIEZER JUDAH **6:**1290
- Mir **12:**71ff
FINKEL, JOSHUA **6:**1291
Finkel, Moses **6:**1292; **14:**1669
FINKEL, NATHAN ẒEVI BEN MOSES **6:**1291
- yeshivah **14:**1668
Finkel, Samuel **6:**1292
Finkel, Shimon **7:**1033
- *illus:*
- - in *Inherit the Wind* **7:**1032
- - in *Peer Gynt* **7:**1031
Finkel, Simḥah Zissel **12:**535
FINKELMAN, JACOB **6:**1293
Finkelscherer, H. **15:**400
Finkelstein, A. A. **14:**1520
Finkelstein, E. **11:**382ff
Finkelstein, Ḥayyim **16:**637
FINKELSTEIN, HEINRICH **6:**1293
Finkelstein, J., *see* Finot, Jean
Finkelstein, Jacob, *see* Fields, Jackie
FINKELSTEIN, LOUIS **6:**1293
- Academy for Jewish Research **2:**819
- Jewish Theological Seminary **10:**96
- *illus:*
- - Lieberman, Saul, and **2:**819
- - Synagogue Council of America celebration **15:**631
Finkelstein, Moses **16:**551
Finkelstein, Nehemiah **6:**1295; **7:**1498
FINKELSTEIN, NOAH **6:**1295
- Brest-Litovsk **4:**1362
- *illus:*
- - First Zionist Congress **16:**1165
Finkelstein, Simon J. **12:**1094; **12:**1118
FINLAND **6:**1295
- emancipation **6:**716
- Holocaust **8:**852
- press **13:**1048
- *sheḥitah* **14:**1341
- synagogues **1:**syn. list
- *illus:* text
- *pop. table:* text
Finland, Maxwell **11:**1199
FINLAY-FREUNDLICH, ERWIN **6:**1299
Finleyson, John **4:**1410
Finn, Elizabeth Anne **6:**1300
FINN, JAMES **6:**1300
- Ereẓ Israel missions **9:**299
- Jewish settlement **13:**518
- Samaritans **14:**738
- *illus:* text
Finnish (lang.) **4:**878
Finot, Jean **7:**147
FINZI (fam., It.) **6:**1300
Finzi (fam., Yug.), *see* Penso
Finzi, Abraham Raphael **6:**1301
- Abraham ha-Sephardi **2:**153
Finzi, Aldo **13:**815
Finzi, Angelo, *see* Finzi, Mordecai ben Abraham
Finzi, Gerald **6:**1301
Finzi, Gur Aryeh ben Benjamin **6:**1301
Finzi, Gur Aryeh ha-Levi **6:**1301
Finzi, Hezekiah of Ferrara **5:**907
Finzi, Isaac **14:**317
Finzi, Isaac Raphael ben Elisha **6:**1301
Finzi, Jacob (r.) **8:**1208
Finzi, Jacob (cantor) **9:**1145; **13:**1329
Finzi, Joseph (polit., It.) **6:**1301
Finzi, Joseph (r., Yug.) **14:**871
Finzi, Moise **14:**197
Finzi, Mordecai ben Abraham **6:**1301
- Finzi, Solomon **4:**974
- translations **15:**1325
Finzi, Moses Abraham (dipl.) **9:**1448
Finzi, Moses ben Israel (paytan) **13:**591
Finzi, Samuel **6:**1301
Finzi, Solomon ben Eliakim **6:**1301
- library **4:**974
FINZI-NORSA CONTROVERSY **6:**1301
- Abraham ha-Sephardi **2:**153
FIOGHI (Fiocchi), FABIANO **6:**1302
Fiorentino, Giovanni Ser **9:**1104
FIORENTINO, SALOMONE **6:**1302
- Italian literature **9:**1110
- *illus:*
- - poem on coronation of Leopold II **6:**1358
Fiorenzuola d'Arda (tn., It.) **13:**493
Fiorino (fam.) **8:**1287
Fīq (tn., Isr.) **3:**176; **13:**1532
Fiqh (Isl. jur.) **7:**1051
FIRE **6:**1302
- *avot nezikin* **3:**988ff
- Gabriel **11:**1490
- netherworld **12:**997
- plagues of Egypt **13:**604
- Samaritans **14:**741
- torts **15:**1272ff
- *illus:*
- - text
- - Moses' ordeal **12:**395
- - Nadab and Abihu **12:**750
- - signaling appearance of new moon **14:**310
Firer, Ben-Zion **12:**406
Firestein, Alfred **6:**1134
Firestein, Chester **6:**1134
Firestein, Max **6:**1134
Firestone, Milton **12:**38
FIRKOVICH, ABRAHAM (Even Reshef) **6:**1305
- Cairo *genizah* **16:**1334
- forgeries **6:**1431
- Harkavy, Albert **7:**1340
- Karaite works **16:**778
- Medini, Ḥayyim **11:**1216
- Mehlsack **11:**1236
- *illus:* text
Firmicus Maternus, Julius (Ch. F.) **5:**552
Firmon, Joseph **12:**896
Firoz Koh (city, Afg.) **2:**326
Firsov, Avraami **4:**886
FIRSTBORN **6:**1306
- *Contents:*
- - In the Bible **6:**1306
- - Redemption **6:**1308
- - Fast of **6:**1310
- - Legal Aspects **6:**1310
- birthright **7:**390
- Commandments, the 613 **5:**766, 774
- embryo **6:**720
- Exodus **12:**375
- first fruits **6:**1312
- Hesse **11:**411
- Hurrian customs **12:**1288
- inheritance rights **15:**476ff
- levirate marriage **11:**122; **11:**124
- levite service **11:**139
- lots, casting of **11:**512
- Mari primogeniture **11:**977
- plagues of Egypt **13:**604
- Pentateuch **13:**241; **13:**254
- priest and redemption of **13:**1088ff
- women and redemption **10:**1566
- *illus:*
- - text
- - *ḥallah* for redemption ceremony **6:**1419
- - plagues of Egypt **13:**605
- - redemption of **4:**409
First Cincinnati Haggadah (illum. ms.), *see* CINCINNATI HAGGADAH
FIRST FRUITS **6:**1312
- Agrippa I **2:**416
- *bikkurim* **4:**993
- incense offering **8:**1314
- Jericho *ḥerem* **8:**347
- leap year **10:**1528
- non-ownership of land **12:**111
- ownership **12:**1531
- pilgrimage **13:**512
- proscribed **8:**1471
- recitation **11:**392
- *illus:*
- - procession to Jerusalem **4:**993
First Fruits Festival, *see* SHAVUOT
First Gaster Bible (illum. ms., Egy.), *see Gaster Bible, First*
First International, *see* International Workingmen's Association
First Joshua Ibn Gaon Bible (14th cent. illum. ms., Sp.) **4:**958
First Judeans (Pal. battalion), *see* Judeans, First
First Kennicott Bible, see Kennicott Bible
First Leningrad Bible (10th cent. illum. ms.) **3:***fcg.* 524
Firuz (Sassanian ruler) **4:**42
FĪRŪZ (fam.) **6:**1316
Fīrūz, Al-Shams al Karīm ibn **6:**1316
Fīrūz, Daniel ben Moses **6:**1316
Fīrūz, Moses ben Isaiah (Kar. schol.) **6:**1316
Fīrūz, Moses ben Isaiah (ḥazzan) **6:**1316
Firuzkuh (vill., Iran) **8:**340
Firuz Shapur (loc., Babyl.) **13:**1384
Fisanovich, Israel **3:**62; **11:**1558; **14:**479
FISCH, HAROLD (HAREL) **1:**30
Fischach *sukkah* **9:**1589
Fischboeck, Hans **14:**937
Fischel (fam.), *see* FISHEL
FISCHEL, HARRY **6:**1316
- Goldstein, Herbert S. **7:**746
- *illus:*
- - J.D.C. **2:**829
Fischel, Karl **5:**1189
Fischel, Moses, *see* Fishel, Moses
Fischel, Sarah *see* Fishel, Sarah
FISCHEL, WALTER JOSEPH **1:**30; **6:**1317
Fischeles, Leib **14:**814
Fischel-Freind (sol.) **11:**1567
Fischels, Judith, *see* Leidesdorfer, Judith
FISCHELS, MEIR BEN EPHRAIM **6:**1317
FISCHER (fam., Cz.) **6:**1318
Fischer (fam., U.S.) **14:**833
Fischer, Artúr, *see* ELEK, ARTÚR
Fischer, Benjamin **15:**1373
Fischer, Bobby, *see* FISCHER, ROBERT
FISCHER, CAROLUS (Karl) **6:**1318
Fischer, Emil, *see* MAKAI, EMIL
Fischer, Enoch **11:**806; **11:**811
Fischer, Franz **7:**1125
Fischer, Gustav **15:**818
FISCHER, GYULA **6:**1319
Fischer, Harold **15:**304
Fisher, J., *see* Piscator, J.
FISCHER, JEAN **6:**1320
FISCHER, JOSEF (Den.) **6:**1320
- Salomon, Julius **14:**697
- Zionism **16:**1114
Fischer, Joseph (print., Pol.) **5:**1038
Fischer, Julius, *see* FISCHER, GYULA
Fischer, Leo (Den.) **6:**1320
Fischer, Leo (sport., U.S.) **15:**304

FISCHER, LOUIS **6:**1320
Fischer, Ludwig **16:**295
Fischer, Marcus (Meir, Maier) **6:**1318
Fischer, Maurice **6:**1320; **16:**78
Fischer, Michael **15:**135
Fischer, Moses **6:**1318
FISCHER, OTOKAR **6:**1321
- Prague University **13:**973
Fischer, Reuven **16:**633
FISCHER, ROBERT **6:**1322
- chess **5:**407
FISCHER, RUTH **6:**1322
FISCHER, SAMUEL **6:**1323
FISCHER, YONA **1:**30
Fischer-Graz, Wilhelm **7:**864
FISCHHOF, ADOLF **6:**1323
- 1848 revolution **3:**894
- *illus:*
- - portrait **8:**707
Fischhof, Jacob Eleazar **16:**1223
Fischhof, Meshullam Zalman (cmty. ldr.) **3:**841
Fischhof, Meshullam Zalman (mart.) **3:**841
Fischhof, Simeon **3:**841
Fischl, Otto **14:**1653
Fischl, Viktor, *see* DAGAN, AVIGDOR
Fischman, William **12:**1085
FISCHMANN, NAḤMAN ISAAC **6:**1324
Fischmann, Simeon **10:**862
FISCHOFF, EPHRAIM **1:**30
FISCUS JUDAICUS (Rom. tax) **6:**1325
- Bassus, Lucilius **4:**317
- Domitian **6:**164
- economic history **16:**1278
- First Roman War **8:**644
- taxation **15:**838
- *illus:* text
"Fish" (paint., J. Chapiro) **5:**338
FISH AND FISHING **6:**1326
- dietary regulations **6:**36; **15:**1309
- food **6:**1422
- *kapparot* **10:**757
- Krochmal's responsum **14:**90
- oil **12:**1351
- reproduction **4:**1017
- sturgeon **7:**924
- wedding custom **11:**1044
- *illus:*
- - ceremonial object motif **6:**1385
- - *mishloaḥ manot* plate **13:**1393
- - symbol of fertility **4:**258
- - Tobit and the angel Raphael **15:**1184
- - wooden *mezuzah* **11:**1474
- *table:* **3:**9-16
- *see also:* ANIMALS OF THE BIBLE AND TALMUD; FISHERIES IN ISRAEL
FISHBEIN, MORRIS **6:**1328
Fishberg, Arthur Maurice **11:**1200
FISHBERG, MAURICE **6:**1328
Fishdar (tn., Iraq) **15:**504
FISHEL (fam.) **6:**1329
Fishel, Arnold **11:**257
Fishel, Chwalka **6:**1330
Fishel, Ephraim (15th cent.) **6:**1329
Fishel, Ephraim (15/16 cent.) **6:**1330
Fishel, Ephraim (18th cent.) **13:**556
Fishel, Ephraim ben Isaac (kab.) **15:**446
Fishel, Esther **6:**1329; **13:**833
Fishel, Falka, *see* Fishel, Chwalka
Fishel, Franczek, *see* Fishel, Ephraim (15/16 cent.)
Fishel, Hendel **6:**1329
Fishel, Jacob **6:**1329
Fishel, Jan **6:**1329
Fishel, Moses (bnk.) **6:**1329; **13:**833
Fishel, Moses (r.) **6:**1330; **11:**48; **15:**1676
Fishel, Rachel **6:**1329; **13:**833
Fishel, Robert **13:**1361
Fishel, Roesil **11:**359
Fishel, Sarah **6:**1329; **13:**833
Fishel, Stanislaw **6:**1329
Fishel, Stephan **6:**1329
Fishel of Rozdol **14:**359
Fishel of Strykow **5:**561
Fisher, Annie **7:**1360
Fisher, C. S. **11:**1222
FISHER, EDDIE (Edwin) **15:**1082
Fisher, H.J. **10:**1404
FISHER, MAX M. **6:**1330
- *illus:*
- - text
- - Israel Bonds-U.J.A. dinner **15:**1668
- - U.J.A. National Conference **15:**1541
FISHER, SIR WOOLF **6:**1331
FISHERIES IN ISRAEL **9:**784ff
- fish and fishing **6:**1326
- fauna **9:**226
- science **9:**969
- *illus:*
- - Acre fishermen **9:**1029
- - Ma'agan Mikha'el fishponds **11:**635
Fish Gate (Jer.) **3:**18
Fishko, Asher David, *see* DAGON, BARUKH
Fishleder, I.M. **6:**735
Fishman, Ada, *see* MAIMON, ADA
Fishman, Alfred P. **11:**1200
Fishman, I. **5:**450
FISHMAN, JACOB **6:**1331
FISHMAN, JOSHUA AARON **6:**1331
- psychology **13:**1345
Fishman, Judah Leib, *see* MAIMON, JUDAH LEIB
FISHMAN, WILLLAM HAROLD **11:**1207
Fishpond Institute (Isr.) **9:**969
Fishson, Abraham **15:**1072
Fiszel (fam.), *see* FISHEL
Fiszelson, Abram **16:**349
Fiszlewicz, Mendel **5:**1213
Fi Tadbir al-Siḥḥa (wk.) **11:**779
Fitch, Louis **13:**803
Fitchburg (city, Mass.) **11:**1115
FITELBERG, GRZEGORZ (Gregor) **12:**689
Fitelberg, Jerzy **12:**590
Fitzgerald, F. Scott **15:**1571ff
Fitz-Gerald, Gerald **8:**33
Fitzgerald, G. M. **9:**1522ff
Fitzgerald, Sir Maurice **4:**1057
Fiume (port, Croatia), *see* RIJEKA
Five Books of Moses, *see* BIBLE; PENTATEUCH
Five Scrolls, *see* SCROLLS, THE FIVE
FIVE SPECIES (grain types) **6:**1332
- first fruit **6:**1313
- *ḥallah* **7:**1194
- *ḥameẓ* **7:**1236
- *maẓẓah* **11:**1155
- mixed species **12:**170
- wheat **16:**480
- *illus:* text
Five Worlds (myst. theory) **10:**517
Fixer, The (bk.) **11:**820
Flaccus (Asian pro-consul, B.C.E.) **5:**560
Flaccus (Rom. gov., Syr.) **3:**443
FLACCUS, AVILLIUS AULUS (Rom. gov., Egy.) **6:**1333
- Alexandria **2:**589
- economics **16:**1278
FLACCUS, VALERIUS **6:**1333
- Temple offerings **16:**1273
FLAG **6:**1334
- Herzl, Theodor **8:**411; **16:**1045
- Simḥat Torah **13:**62
- tailoring guild **15:**705
- Twelve Tribes **13:**1008ff
- Zionism **16:**613
- *illus:*
- - text
- - Israel Three-Day March **11:**694
- - Jabotinsky and Kovno Revisionist youth **16:**1098
- - U.N. headquarters, hoisting of Israel banner **14:**1312
- - U.S., Hebrew inscription **15:**1601
- *see also* BANNER; MAGEN DAVID
Flam, Bernard **11:**998
Flam, Herbert **15:**315
Flam, Ihiel **6:**1155
FLANAGAN, BUD **15:**1082
Flanders (reg., Belg.,Fr.) **8:**1043
Flandrina (tn., Ind.) **5:**55; **8:**1349
Flatau, Isaac **16:**336
Flatbush (section, N.Y.C.) **12:**1082,1107
Flatow, Alfred **12:**1375; **15:**309
Flatow, Felix **12:**1375; **15:**309
Flatow, Max **12:**1038
Flatworms **6:**38
Flaut, Hezekiah Feivel, *see* PLAUT, HEZEKIAH FEIVEL
Flavia, Domitilla **6:**1338
Flavia Ioppe (city, Isr.), *see* JAFFA
Flavia Neapolis (city, Er. Isr.), *see* NABLUS
Flavian Emperors **9:**238; **9:**242
Flavigny, Valérian de **8:**33
FLAVIUS, CLEMENS **6:**1338
- Judaic practices **8:**644
- *see also:* KETI'A BAR SHALOM
Flavius, Josephus, *see* JOSEPHUS FLAVIUS
Flavius Claudius Julianus, *see* JULIAN THE APOSTATE
Flavius Petrus Sabbatius Justinianus, *see* JUSTINIAN I
Flavius Silva, *see* SILVA FLAVIUS
Flavius Theodosius Junior, *see* THEODOSIUS II
FLAX **6:**1338
- plant list **13:**619
- textiles **15:**1037ff
- third century C.E. **9:**252
Flaxman, Carl **5:**1232
FLEA **6:**1339
FLECKELES, ELEAZAR BEN DAVID **6:**1340
Fleckman, Martin **15:**309
FLEG, EDMOND (Flegenheimer) **6:**1340
- defense of Judaism **3:**200
- French literature **7:**141ff
- *sotah* theme **15:**984
- Wandering Jew **16:**262
FLEGENHEIMER, JULIEN **3:**363
- *illus:*
- - Palace of Nations, Geneva **3:**343
Fleischberger, Leopold **16:**1224
Fleischer, Charles **4:**1265
Fleischer, Ernö, *see* EMÖD, TAMAS
Fleischer, Ezra **6:**1342; **15:**809; **16:**1338
FLEISCHER, JUDAH LOEB **6:**1342
Fleischer, Leopold **15:**520
Fleischer, Levi Isaac **16:**946
Fleischer, Max (archit.) **15:**620
FLEISCHER, MAX (cart.) **12:**467
- cartoons **5:**220
FLEISCHER,MICHAEL **6:**1343
FLEISCHER, NATHANIEL STANLEY **6:**1343
Fleischer, Victor **13:**1367
Fleischman, Lawrence **5:**1572
Fleischmann, Charles **6:**1343; **15:**310
FLEISCHMANN, GISI **6:**1343
- Reik, Ḥavivah **14:**54
Fleischmann, Gustav **13:**1028
Fleischmann, Ivo **5:**1208
Fleischmann, Johann Michael **15:**1482
FLEISCHMANN, JULIUS **6:**1344
- sports **15:**312
Fleischmann, Karel **7:**203
Fleischmann, Max **15:**312
Fleischmann, Miksa, *see* FENYO, MIKSA
FLEISHER (fam.) **6:**1344
Fleisher, Alfred W. **6:**1344
Fleisher, Benjamin Wilfred **6:**1344
Fleisher, Benjamin Wolf **6:**1344
Fleisher, Bruce **15:**309
Fleisher, Edwin Adler **6:**1344
Fleisher, Moyer **6:**1344
Fleisher, Samuel Stuart **6:**1344
Fleisher, Simon B. **6:**1344
Fleishhacker (fam.) **5:**56; **14:**834
Fleishig, see DIETARY LAWS; MEAT
Fleishman, A. **7:**1036
Fleishman, Jerry **15:**303
Fleishman, William **15:**303
Flemings (Belg. people) **3:**168
Flemington (boro., N.J.) **12:**1030
Flersheim, L.H. **4:**1465
FLESCH (fam.) **6:**1345
Flesch, Abraham (16/17 cent.) **6:**1345
Flesch, Abraham (18/19 cent.) **6:**1345
Flesch, Adolph **6:**1345
FLESCH, CARL **12:**689
Flesch, Carl Jr. **12:**689
Flesch, Gumpel, *see* Flesch, Mordecai
Flesch, Heinrich **6:**1345
Flesch, Joseph (mer., Morav.) **6:**1345
Flesch, Joseph (publ., Cz.) **6:**1345; **13:**1368
Flesch, Mordecai **6:**1345
Flesch, Philip (Solomon) **6:**1345
Flesch, Siegfried **12:**1375
Flesch-Birnbaum (fam.), *see* FLESCH
Flesh (biol.), *see* MEAT
FLESH (man) **6:**1345
- afterlife **2:**336
body and soul **4:**1165
- hasidic worship **7:**1408
- inclination, good and evil **8:**1318
- nature of man **11:**843
- spirit **6:**243
Fletcher, Charles A. **14:**829
Flexer, A.L., *see* VOLYNSKI, AKIM LEVOVICH
FLEXNER (fam.) **6:**1346
FLEXNER, ABRAHAM **6:**1347
Flexner, Bernard **6:**1346
Flexner, Jacob **6:**1347; **10:**910
Flexner, James Thomas **6:**1346; **6:**1347
Flexner, Jennie Maas **6:**1346
Flexner, Morris **6:**1346
Flexner, Simon **15:**1679
Flexner, Washington **6:**1346
Fleysher (mart., Minsk) **12:**55
Fleytsinger, Isaiah, *see* Fayfer, Shayke
Fliegel, Bernard **15:**303
Flin Flon (tn., Can.) **11:**879
Flinker, Moshe **5:**448
Flint (city, Mich.) **11:**1500
Flint, George **9:**1497
F.L.N. (Alg. mvmt.), *see* Front de Liberation Nationale
Floch, Joseph **13:**115
FLOGGING **6:**1348
- *Contents:*
- - In Biblical Law **6:**1348
- - In Talmudic Law **6:**1348
- - Punishable Offenses **6:**1349
- - Disciplinary Flogging **6:**1350

- assault **3:**758ff
- Castile regulation **8:**1372
- Commandments, the 613 **5:**771
- confession **5:**877
- contempt of court **5:**922
- custom transgression **12:**9
- Day of Atonement custom **5:**1381
- forgery **6:**1432
- gambling **7:**300
- incest **8:**1317
- Inquisition **8:**1402
- insult **8:**1409
- *karet* **6:**122; **10:**788
- *Makkot* **11:**808
- Marranos **12:**1023
- marriage acquisition modes **11:**1046
- *niddui* **8:**353; **8:**355
- oath **12:**1301
- penal law **13:**222ff
- perjury **13:**289
- prostitution **13:**1245
- punishment **13:**1388
- slander **14:**1652
- sorcery **15:**163
- suicide **15:**491
- *takkanah* **15:**718
- talion **15:**742
- theft **15:**1097
- thorns **15:**1118
- Tunis **15:**1444
- usury **16:**29
- virginity **16:**161
- weights and measures **16:**391
- *illus:*
- - text
- - Day of Atonement eve **5:**1385
- - Jesus **8:**660
- - *Makkot* **11:**809
- - teacher punishing a bad pupil **6:**387

FLOHR, SALO **6:**1351

FLOOD, THE **6:**1351
- *Contents:*
- - Biblical Narrative **6:**1351
- - Extra-Biblical Accounts **6:**1352
- - Mesopotamian Parallels **6:**1356
- - In Aggadah **6:**1358
- cuneiform records of **10:**1491
- Daniel Apocrypha **5:**1277
- Genesis **7:**389; **7:**393
- in the Arts **12:**1196
- Mesopotamia **16:**3, 1485
- myth **12:**730
- Sumerian themes **15:**515
- *illus:*
- - animals entering the ark 7:434
- - "Noah and the Ark" (paint., J. David) **5:**1346
- - Noah and the returning dove **6:**184
- - Noah leaving the Ark **6:**980
- - Noah's Ark **3:**467; **12:**1197
- *see also:* NOAH

Flora and Fauna
- cruelty to animals **3:**5
- fish and fishing **6:**1326
- incense and perfumes **8:**1311ff
- reproduction **4:**1018

FLORA AND FAUNA OF ISRAEL **9:**220
- afforestation **9:**787
- early Israelite period **2:**388
- Estori ha-Parḥi **6:**918
- evolution **6:**1002*ff*
- Jerusalem **9:**1515
- nature reserves **12:**891
- spice route **8:**1312
- *illus:*
- - acacia **2:**199
- - afforestation in Galilee **10:**79
- - Aleppo pine **13:**531
- - almond blossom **2:**665
- - animals of the Bible and Talmud (list) **3:**9-16
- - balsam tree **4:**143
- - barley **2:**392
- - bitter cucumber **5:**1151
- - bittern **4:**1061
- - broom shrub **4:**1408
- - buzzard **4:**1546
- - carob **5:**202
- - castor-oil plant **5:**242
- - centipede **5:**283
- - chameleon **5:**334
- - citrus fruit and blossoms **5:**581
- - cotton plant **5:**992
- - cumin **5:**1170
- - cypress **5:**1179
- - Dan riverside vegetation **9:**231
- - dove **15:**145
- - Eilat Gulf, coral fauna **9:**172-173
- - En-Gedi, nature reserve **12:**892
- - fennel **6:**1223
- - fig **6:**1273
- - flowers, shrubs and trees **6:**1388-1389
- - fox **6:**1450
- - garlic **7:**328
- - gazelle **7:**346; **15:**145
- - gecko **7:**351
- - grapevine **16:**156
- - griffon vulture **16:**232
- - hare **7:**1336
- - henna **8:**326
- - hoopoe **8:**970
- - hyena **8:**1139
- - hyssop **8:**1148
- - ibex **8:**1150; **9:**233
- - jackal **9:**233
- - jujube **10:**467
- - juniper **10:**473
- - kingfisher **9:**232
- - kite **10:**1078
- - lentil **11:**21
- - lettuce **11:**1014
- - "Little Switzerland" vegetation **9:**235
- - locust **11:**422
- - mallow **11:**830
- - mandrake **11:**870
- - marjoram **9:**233
- - monitor **12:**258
- - Mt. Gilboa vegetation **9:**231
- - myrrh **12:**727
- - myrtle **12:**728
- - oak maquis, Wadi al-Nimr **9:**229
- - olive treee in Garden of Gethsemane **9:**1514
- - onager **12:**1395
- - owl **12:**1530
- - palm, branching **9:**236
- - papyrus **9:**227; **13:**71
- - pelicans **9:**235
- - Phoenician seal **14:**1076
- - pine, Aleppo **9:**236
- - plants and products of plants mentioned in the Bible and Mishnah (list) **13:**615-626
- - plants brought by Thutmose III from Palestine **2:**385
- - pomegranates **3:**322
- - rabbit **7:**1336
- - ritual impurity **15:**1520
- - rocket **14:**213
- - serpent eagle **9:**230
- - skink **14:**1647
- - soap plant **15:**19
- - squill **15:**321
- - squirrel **14:**1078
- - storax **15:**415
- - tamarisk **9:**230,234; **15:**784
- - terebinth **9:**234; **15:**1016
- - thorn **15:**1119
- - tragacanth **15:**1312
- - vegetation of Israel (map) **9:**223
- - water buffalo **9:**235
- *see also:* ANIMALS OF THE BIBLE AND TALMUD; FLOWERS

Floravanti, Gerónimo **8:**33

FLORENCE (city, It.) **6:**1358
- archives **3:**383
- banking **4:**169
- Inquisition **8:**1400
- library **11:**193
- special Purim **13:**1937
- synagogue **15:**620
- *illus:*
- - text
- - Great Synagogue **15:**620-621
- - *Ḥevrat Mattir Asurim*, receipt **9:**1136
- - Jewish peddlers **13:**205
- - proclamation re. ill-treatment of Jews (1668) **9:**1131
- *see also:* TUSCANY

Florence (city, S.C.) **15:**211

Florentin (fam.) **14:**707

Florentin, David **13:**1039

Florentin, Isaac **2:**951

Florentin, Samuel **7:**1511

Florentin, Solomon
- Angel, Baruch **2:**951
- Doenmeh **6:**148; **14:**1245
- Estrosa **6:**919
- Querido, Jacob **13:**1426

Flores, Giorgio, *see* MOMIGLIANO, ATTILIO

Florian, Jean **10:**1351

Floriánski Psalter **13:**797

FLORIDA **6:**1361
- *pop. table:* text

Florina (Gr. city), *see* PHLORINA

Florio, John (Giovanni) **9:**1110

Florsheim, Leonard **15:**311

Florstedt, Hermann **11:**794

Florus, Gessius **5:**315
- crucifixion of Jewish judges **5:**1134
- procurator **8:**639,641; **13:**1118

FLORUS OF LYONS **6:**1364

Floryjanowa (stlmt., Pol.), *see* NAROL

FLOSS (vill., Ger.) **6:**1364
- archives **3:**387

Flossenbuerg (concen. camp) **5:**86

Flour **8:**279
- bread **4:**1333
- *maẓẓah* **11:**1155
- *see also:* FIVE SPECIES; ḤALLAH

Flower Gate (Jer.), *see* Herod's Gate

Flowerman, Samuel **8:**975

FLOWERS **6:**1364
- *illus:* text
- *see also:* Flora and Fauna

Floyar-Reichman, Colonel **11:**1564

Fludd, Robert **10:**646

Flug, Mary **7:**1261

Flus, Shalom **13:**1483

FLUSSER, DAVID **16:**1325

"Flute Player" (paint., Z. Menkes) **11:**1354

FLY **6:**1368
- exilarch seal **14:**1074
- *nahalolim, na'aẓuzim* **15:**1119
- *illus:* text

F.M.F. (disease), *see* Familial Mediterranean Fever

FOA (fam.) **6:**1369
- printing **13:**1095
- *illus:* text

Foa, Carlo **6:**1370

Foa, Cesare **6:**1370

Foa, Edouard **15:**1350 **6:**1370

Foa, Elia Emanuel **6:**1370

Foa, Eliezer (print.) **6:**1371

Foa, Eliezer Naḥman (r.) **6:**1369

FOA, ESTHER EUGÉNIE REBECCA **7:**149
- children's literature **5:**452

Foa, Gad (ben Isaac) **6:**1371

Foa, Gad (ben Samuel) **6:**1371

Foà, Graziadio **9:**1111

Foa, Isaac ben Gad **6:**1371

Foà, Isaiah **15:**1455

Foa, Mordecai **6:**1371

Foa, Moses Benjamin **6:**1369

Foa, Nathanel ben Jehiel **6:**1371

Foa, Pio **6:**1370

FOA, RAIMONDO **11:**1573

Foa, Salvatore **6:**1370

Foa, Samuel **6:**1371

Foa, Tobias ben Eliezer **2:**260; **6:**1370
- *illus:*
- - *Sefer Ya'ir Nativ* (1533) **14:**586

Foa, Uriel **15:**69

Foà Fusinato, Erminia **9:**1110

Fockens, Herman F.T. **8:**33

FOCSANI (tn., Rum.) **6:**1371

FODDER **6:**1372

FODOR, ANDOR **6:**1373

Foecklerus, J. **8:**33

Foehrenwald (D. P. camp) **4:**346

FOERDER, YESHAYAHU (Herbert) **6:**1373

Foerster, Bernhard **3:**80; **12:**1153

Foerster, Elizabeth **12:**1153

Foester, Johann, *see* FORSTER, JOHANN

Fogaras (tn., Transyl.), *see* FAGARAS

Fogel, Dvoyre **16:**819

Fogelman, Herschel **16:**633

Fogelman, Lazar **10:**50

Fogelman, Mordecai **14:**94

Fogelson, Dr. **16:**1348

Fohs, F.J. **9:**793

Foi (fam.), *see* FOA

Foiano (tn., It.) **15:**1468

FOIX (co., Fr.) **6:**1374

FÖLDES, JOLÂN **8:**1084

FOLIGNO, HANANEL (DA) **6:**1374

Folk dances, *see* DANCE

Folkistishe Heftn (period.) **6:**1411

Folkist Party, see FOLKSPARTEI (POLAND)

FOLKLORE **6:**1374
- *Contents:*
- - Introduction **6:**1375
- - Audio-Oral Transmission (Folk Literature) **6:**1376
- - - Narrative **6:**1377
- - - Song **6:**1384
- - - Proverb **6:**1388
- - - Riddle **6:**1389
- - - Drama **6:**1389
- - Visual **6:**1389
- - - Ceremonial Life Cycle **6:**1391
- - - Ceremonial Jewish Year Cycle **6:**1391
- - - Varia: Synagogal and Home Ceremonial and Non-Ceremonial Objects **6:**1394
- - Cogitative **6:**1396
- - - Direct (face to face) Combat **6:**1397
- - - Compromise (Agreement and Treaty) **6:**1400
- - - Deceptive Stratagem **6:**1401
- - - Varia: Beliefs and customs not related to Cycles **6:**1406
- General
- - Bergmann, Judah **4:**617
- - Crowfoot, Grace **5:**1130
- - Falashas **6:**1151
- - Hersh Danielevitz **8:**395
- - *ḥukkat ha-goi* **8:**1061
- - Justman, Moshe **10:**479
- - Kurdistan **10:**1299
- - Prohovnik, Abraham **13:**1119
- - societies **15:**55*ff*
- Subject Matter
- - Adam Ba'al Shem **2:**248
- - amulet **2:**906
- - *afikoman* **2:**329
- - Angel of Death **2:**953
- - animal tales **3:**19
- - Asmodeus **3:**755
- - astrology **3:**795

-- Belaya Tserkov 4:413
-- Chelm 5:373
-- chiromancy 5:477
-- demons 5:1521
-- flood epics 6:1351
-- Hoshana Rabba 8:1027
-- lion 11:275ff
-- *kazyonny ravvin* 10:862
-- oaths 14:1394
-- paradise 13:79
-- Rachel 13:1487ff
- Literature
-- *aggadah* 2:356
-- *Akdamut Millin* 2:479
-- *badḥan* 4:75
-- fable 6:1125
-- *Melokhim Bukh* 11:1292
-- proverbs 13:1265
-- *Razim, Sefer ha-* 13:1594
-- *Shmuel Bukh* 14:1426
-- Yiddish 16:804
- *illus:*
-- text
-- Elijah coming on Passover Eve 6:*fcg.* 651
-- Esther, embroidered scenes from Book of 6:911
-- Galician *badḥan* 4:74
-- *ḥallah* cloth 14:572
-- *ḥallah* shapes 6:1419
-- Jerusalem and other holy sites 9:*fcg.* 1531
-- *kimpetbriefel* 13:44-45
-- *Lekhah Dodi* wall plaque 10:655
-- leviathan and *shor ha-bar* 11:89
-- Maimuna celebration 11:782
-- *mizraḥ* 11:1365; 12:*fcg.* 171, 173; 13:44-45
-- Moscow Jewish folk music society, minute book 3:380
-- *omer* counting chart 12:1385; 13:44-45
-- paper-cuts 6:1394; 8:973; 11:271; 12:*fcg.* 173; 13:44-45, 61-65
-- *Shivviti* plaques 13:*fcg.* 1390; 14:1420-1421
-- Western Wall on embroidered Sabbath cloth 16:469
- *see also:* DIVINATION; MAGIC; MUSIC; PAPER-CUTS; PROVERBS, TALMUDIC
"Folk-polyphonies" (mus. term) 12:668
Folksadvokat (newsp.) 13:1053
Folksbihne (theat.) 16:636
Folksblat (period., Pol.) 4:1542; 16:641
Folksblat (newsp., Urug.) 16:15
Folksfarband (gr., Chile) 16:1125
Folksfraynd (period.) 14:844
Folksgezunt (period.) 13:1043; 15:1292
FOLKSPARTEI (POLAND) 6:1410
- Agudat Israel 2:423
- Nomberg, Hersh 12:1209
- Prylucki, Noah 13:1295
- Shtif, Nahum 14:1474
- Zionism challenged 16:1130
FOLKSPARTEI (RUSSIA) 6:1411
Folks Shtime (newsp., Arg.) 13:1040
Folksshtime (newsp., Pol.) 13:784
Folksshtime (period., Rus.) 6:142; 10:90
Folks-Theater (Arg.) 15:1073
Folkstsaytung (newsp.) 4:1500; 13:1046; 13:1047
Folkstsenter (newsp.) 5:1149
Folk Tales, *see* FOLKLORE
Folsom (city, Calif.) 5:56
Folush (loc., Iraq) 8:1447
Folz, Hans 6:94; 7:443
Folz, Samuel 11:1499
Fomento Agrario (orgn., Arg.) 3:431
FOMIN, YEFIM MOISEYEVICH 11:1573
- Russia 14:479
FONDANE, BENJAMIN 6:1412
- Rumanian literature 14:423
- Schwarzfeld 14:1029
Fond Du Lac (city, Wis.) 16:556
FONDILLER, WILLIAM 8:1431
Fondo Comunal (co-op., Arg.) 3:431; 10:750
- *illus:*
-- management 3:432
Fonds Social Juif Unifié 5:352; 7:38; 13:1032; 13:111
Foner, Meir 14:784
Fonseca, Abraham de 7:1226; 7:631
FONSECA, ALVARO DE 6:1413
Fonseca, Alvaro da (Mar.), *see* Aboab, David
FONSECA, DANIEL DE 6:1414
Fonseca, Diaz de 15:467
Fonseca, Isaac Aboab da, *see* ABOAB DA FONSECA, ISAAC
Fonseca, Joseph Nuñez de, *see* Nuñez de Fonseca, Joseph
Fonseca, Miguel Henriques da (Isaac) 11:301
- *illus:*
-- Inquisition sentence 8:1389
Fonseca, Moses 12:1068
Fonseca, Rodrigo Henriquez de 5:461; 11:1194
Fonseca, Salomón López 15:255; 16:90
Fons Vitae (wk., Gabirol), *see Mekor Ḥayyim*
FONTAINEBLEAU (tn., Fr.) 6:1414
Fontanella, F. 8:33
Fontanella, Israel Berechiah 13:583
Fontanella, Judah 13:587
Fontenoid (site, Er. Isr.), *see* KIRIATH-JEARIM
FOOD 6:1414
- *Contents:*
-- Biblical Period 6:1414
-- Post-Biblical Period 6:1418
-- Festival Cookery 6:1422
- dietary laws 6:26
- FAO 15:1564
- ḥasidic thought 7:1405
- heretics 8:360
- hygienic regulations 8:1140ff
- impurity 13:1408; 15:1190
- interest 12:245
- Israel industry 9:823
- medicine 11:1184
- paradise 4:1027
- righteousness 14:182
- *Sefer Asaf ha-Rofe* 3:675
- Spanish converts 15:221
- spices 15:267
- *illus:*
-- cooking and baking 5:937-940
-- Passover *se'udah* 14:1193
-- ration books, Israel 9:376
-- Tnuva central dairy 15:1175
- *see also:* COOKING AND BAKING; FLORA AND FAUNA OF ISRAEL; *and under individual foods*
Food and Agricultural Organization (U.N. orgn.) 15:1564
Food Industries Advisory Service (Isr.) 9:970
Fooks, E. 11:1284
Fools, Feast of (mdvl. fest.) 3:756
Foot (leg. conc.), *see* AVOT NEZIKIN; TORTS
Football (Am.) 15:307
Foote, Henry S. 15:1649
Foralto, Emanuel de 2:832
Forb, Nathan 6:944ff
- Finland 6:1298
- France 7:40
Forbach (tn., Fr.) 11:1452; 11:497
3:842
Forbelet, Battle of (1182) 9:268
Forbert, Leo 12:454
Forbes (municipality, Austr.) 3:878
Forbin (fam.) 13:1260
FORCALQUIERS (vill., Fr.) 6:1428
- Provence 13:1259
Forced conversion, *see* APOSTASY; BAPTISM, FORCED
FORCED LABOR (W.W. II) 6:1429
- concentration camps 5:86f
- Holocaust 8:852
- SS plan 13:701
- Wannsee Conference 16:264
- *see also:* CORVÉE
Force majeure (leg. conc.), *see* ONES
FORD, ALEXANDER 12:467
Ford, Henry I 5:1571
- American Jewish Committee 2:823
- anti-Semitism 15:1626; 15:1653
- Bernstein lawsuit 4:685
- chronological chart 8:766-767
- *illus:*
-- *The Dearborn Independent*, anti-Semitic article 15:1653
Fordhaus Ben Zissi 9:1006; 12:669
Foreigners, *see* STRANGERS AND GENTILES
FOREIGN EXCHANGE RATES IN ISRAEL 9:758
FOREIGN POLICY AND INTERNATIONAL RELATIONS OF ISRAEL 9:421
- Algeria 2:619
- Argentina 3:426ff
- Asia 2:336; 9:391ff
- Australia 3:886
- Austria 3:904
- Belgium 4:424
- Bolivia 4:1189
- Brazil 4:1333
- Bulgaria 4:1491
- Burma 4:1527
- Canada 16:1261
- Ceylon 5:317
- Chile 5:467
- China 5:472
- Colombia 5:747
- Costa Rica 5:990
- Cuba 5:1150
- Cyprus 5:1182
- Czechoslovakia 5:1202
- Denmark 5:1541
- developing countries 9:391ff
- Dominican Republic 6:161
- Ecuador 6:361
- Egypt 6:500
- El Salvador 6:687
- England 6:770
- Ethiopia 6:944ff
- Finland 6:1298
- France 7:40
- Germany 7:501
- Greece 7:881
- Guatemala 7:957
- Guyana 7:998
- Haiti 7:1142
- historical survey 9:402*ff*
- Honduras 8:962
- Hungary 8:1108; 9:402*ff*
- India 8:1359
- Iran 8:1443
- Iraq 8:1456
- Ireland 8:1466
- Italy 9:1141
- Jamaica 9:1274
- Japan 9:1282
- Jerusalem 9:1495
- Jordan 10:198
- Kenya 10:910
- Latin America 10:1451; 10:1455
- Lebanon 10:1546
- Libya 11:205
- Luxembourg 11:591
- Madagascar 11:677
- Malta 11:831
- Mexico 11:1460
- Morocco 12:346
- Netherlands 12:992
- New Zealand 12:1130
- Nicaragua 12:1135
- Norway 12:1225
- Panama 13:53
- Paraguay 13:85
- Peru 13:322
- Philippines 13:395
- Poland 13:785
- Portugal 13:926
- Rumania 14:411; 14:415ff
- Russia 14:487ff
- Singapore 14:1609
- South Africa 15:198ff
- Spain 15:246
- Sweden 15:552
- Switzerland 15:561
- Syria 15:647
- Thailand 15:1044
- Tunisia 15:1450
- Turkey 15:1460 15:1462
- Uruguay 16:15
- U.S. 15:1658ff
- Vatican 16:78
- Venezuela 16:90
- Yemen 16:752
- Yugoslavia 16:868
- *illus:*
-- text
-- Barzilai, Israel, envoy to Poland 13:781
-- Ben-Nathan and German president 9:406
-- German reparations agreement 14:72
-- Gromyko's speech at U.N. (May, 1947) 14:493
-- Israel diplomatic corps' visit to Auschwitz 13:782
-- McDonald, J. G., presenting credentials 11:666
-- Meir, Golda, ambassador to Russia 11:1243
-- Moscow, Israel Embassy 12:362
-- Moscow, Israel youth delegation welcomed 14:490
-- Philippine ambassador 13:396
-- President Shazar addressing diplomatic corps 14:1327
-- Soviet ambassador's greetings on Independence Day 14:497
FOREIGN SERVICE OF ISRAEL 9:627
- foreign trade 9:759
- international relations 9:421
- Jewish Agency 10:26
FOREIGN TRADE, ISRAEL 9:759
- African trade 9:434
- agricultural exports 9:774
- Austria 3:904
- Canada 16:1261
- customs duties 9:749
- economic development 9:710ff
- Foreign Ministry 9:627
- foreign relations 9:421
- industrial exports 9:815ff
- investment policy 9:823
- Japan 9:1283
- oil and gas 9:795
- Poland 13:788
- Red Sea route 14:14
- tailoring 15:704
- Turkey 15:1463
- West Bank 14:1638; 14:1640
- *illus:*
-- text
-- clothing exports (table) 15:710
-- cultivation of roses for export 9:781
-- Gaza Strip (table) 9:1037
-- industry (chart) 9:819
-- Judea and Samaria (table) 9:1037
-- minerals (chart) 9:813

FOREIRO, FRANCISCO **6:**1430
- Hebraist **8:**33
Foreman, Al **15:**306
FOREMAN, CARL **12:**467
FOREMAN, MILTON J. **6:**1430
Forest Hills (section, N.Y.C.) **12:**1108
Forest Park (loc., Mass.) **15:**319
Forestry (lumbering) trade **16:**1314
- *see also:* WOOD
Forests, *see* AFFORESTATION IN ISRAEL
Forewords and Introductions, *see* HASKAMAH
Forfeiture, *see* CONFISCATION, EXPROPRIATION, FORFEITURE
FORGERIES **6:**1431
FORGERY **6:**1432
- eclipse omen **12:**291
- *haskamah* **7:**1452
- *niddui* **8:**354
- *shetar* **14:**1387
FORGIVENESS **6:**1433
- *Contents:*
- - In Bible **6:**1433
- - In Talmud **6:**1435
- *Al Ḥet* **2:**630
- confession of sins **5:**878
- Day of Atonement **5:**1379; **5:**1378
- *kipper* **10:**1042
- repentance **14:**73
- *seliḥot* **14:**1133
- sin **14:**1590
Forgotten sheaf, *see* LEKET, SHIKHḤAH, AND PE'AH
Forkel, Johann Nikolaus **12:**558
FORLI (city, It.) **6:**1437
Forli Maḥzor (14th cent. ms.) **11:**733
Forma, Moses ibn, *see* Moses ibn Forma
Forman, Allen S. **15:**301
Forman, Donald **15:**303
FORMAN, MILOS **12:**467
FORMAN, PHILLIP **6:**1438
- Trenton **15:**1376
FORM AND MATTER **6:**1438
- Aaron ben Elijah **2:**12
- Gabirol, Solomon ibn **7:**240ff; **13:**435
- hasidic teachings **7:**1408
- Ibn Ezra, Abraham **8:**1169
- Ibn Ẓaddik **12:**889
- Kabbalah **10:**586
- Neoplatonism **12:**958; **13:**429
- philosophy **13:**422
- primordial will **10:**561; **10:**586
Form criticism (Bib.) **4:**907; **12:**1233
- Isaiah **9:**62
Formgeschichte (bib. research) **9:**45
FORMIGGINI, ANGELO FORTUNATO **6:**1439
Formiggini, Isaac **2:**186; **15:**1455
Formiggini, Moses **12:**201
Formiggini, S. **5:**1297
Formon, Ẓaddik ben Joseph **13:**92
FORMSTECHER, SOLOMON **6:**1439
- concept of God **7:**663
- nature **12:**890
- philosophy **13:**456
- revelation **14:**124
Fornication
- adultery **2:**313
- chastity **5:**363
- incest **8:**1316
- prostitution **13:**1243
- sexual offenses **14:**1207
Forois (period.) **11:**1459
Forrest, A.C. **5:**110
Försammlingsblad (period.) **13:**1048
Forschungen zur Judenfrage (Nazi studies) **8:**566
Forshpil (entertainment) **4:**74
Forst, Abraham **7:**124
Forst, Eduard **10:**1242; **13:**775
Forst, Sigmund **11:**1412
Forster, Albert **7:**348
Forster, Edward Morgan **6:**782
FORSTER, JOHANN (Forsthemius) **6:**1440
- dictionary **16:**1392
Fortalitium Fidei (wk.) **8:**1382
Fort Arthur-Port William (dist., Ont.), *see* Thunder Bay
FORTAS, ABE **6:**1441
- *illus.* text
Fort-Barraux (detention camp) **7:**34
Fort Collins (city, Colo.) **5:**753
FORTES, MEYER **6:**1442
FORTI, BARUCH UZZIEL BEN BARUCH **6:**1442
FORTI, JACOB RAPHAEL HEZEKIAH BEN ABRAHAM ISRAEL **6:**1443
Fortifications **16:**273
FORTIS, ABRAHAM ISAAC **6:**1443
Fort Lamy (tn., Chad) **9:**438
Fort Lauderdale (city, Fla.) **6:**1363
Fort Leonard Wood (loc., Mo.) **12:**158
Fort Qu'Appelle (vill., Can.) **14:**891
Fort St. George (city, Ind.), *see* MADRAS
Fortschritt (period.) **12:**1102
Fortunatus (16th cent., Hung.), *see* SZERENCSÉS, IMRE
Fortune (deity), *see* Tyche
Fortune-tellers **6:**112ff
Fort Wayne (city, Ind.) **8:**1361
Fort Worth (city, Tex.) **15:**1034ff
"Forum Judeorum" (tn., Aus.), *see* Voelkermarkt
Forverts (newsp.), *see Der Proletarisher Gedank*
Forward (*Forverts;* newsp.), *see* JEWISH DAILY FORWARD
Foscolo, Ugo **9:**1105; **9:**1128
FOSS, LUKAS **6:**1443
FOSSANO (tn., It.) **6:**1444
- *see also:* APAM
FOSSOLI (concen. camp) **6:**1444
Fostat (Egy.), *see* CAIRO
Foto-Roman (journ.) **1:**newsp. list
FOULD (fam.) **6:**1445
- politics **13:**812
- railroads **13:**1518
Fould, Achille **4:**175; **6:**1445
Fould, Achille Charles **6:**1445
Fould, Benoît (Benedict) **6:**1445
Fould, Ber Leon (bnk.) **6:**1445
Fould, B. L. (r.) **5:**606
Fould, Edouard Mathurin **6:**1445
Fould, Ernest Adolphe **6:**1445
Fould, Gustave Eugène **6:**1445
Fould-Oppenheim (bnk. house, Fr.) **6:**1445
FOUNDATIONS **6:**1445
Foundling, *see Asufi*
Fouquet, Jean **10:**264; **15:**986
- *illus:*
- - Nebuchadnezzar's army attacking the Temple **15:**985
Four (no.) **3:**292
FOUR CAPTIVES, THE (story) **6:**1446
- Cairo *genizah* **16:**1336
- Hanokh ben Moses **7:**1276
- Hushiel ben Elhanan **8:**1129
- Ibn Daud **8:**1159
- Moses ben Hanoch **12:**417
- Shemariah ben Elhanan **14:**1375
Four Cups (Passover), *see* ARBA KOSOT
Four-Day March (Isr.), *see* Three-Day March
Four Elements, *see* Elements, Four
FOURIER, FRANÇOIS MARIE CHARLES **6:**1447
- socialism **15:**25
Four Lands, Council of, *see* COUNCIL OF FOUR LANDS
"Four lands of holiness" **8:**728
Fourmont, Etienne **8:**32
Four Questions (Passover litur.), *see* MAH NISHTANNAH
FOUR SPECIES (rel. objects) **6:**1448
- categories for Jews **10:**898
- Commandments, the 613 **5:**767
- *etrog* **6:**947
- in *maḥzorim* **11:**733
- myrtle **12:**728
- ownership **12:**1531
- palm **13:**43
- position during blessing **14:**180
- Sukkot **15:**498
- willow **16:**517
- *illus:*
- - text
- - *etrogim and lulavim* **6:**948-950; **11:**512
- - German Sukkot scene **15:**493
- - myrtle**12:**728
"Fourth Philosophy" (sect, Er. Isr.) **7:**118; **13:**1118
Four Worlds, *see* WORLDS, THE FOUR
Fowl, *see* CHICKEN
FOX **6:**1450
- Akiva's parable **2:**491
- animal tales **3:**20ff
- Arthurian legends **3:**653
- dietary laws **6:**32
- fables **2:**357; **6:**1127ff
- *illus:* text
- *see also:* JACKAL
FOX, BERNARD JOSHUA **10:**1507
FOX, CHARLES **6:**1450
Fox, George **8:**32
FOX, ḤAYYIM LEIB **6:**1451
Fox, Henry S. **8:**1050
Fox, Isaac Solomon **6:**1451
FOX, JACOB SAMUEL **6:**1451
Fox, Joe **15:**306
FOX, SIR JOHN JACOB **6:**1452
FOX, WILLIAM film prod.) **6:**1452
- Los Angeles **11:**503
Foy (fam.), *see* FOA
F.P.O., *see* Fareinikte Partizaner Organizatsie
Fradkin, Irving **6:**1161
Fraenckel (fam.), *see* FRAENKEL
Fraenckel, Jonas **7:**2; **10:**465
FRAENCKEL, LIEPMANN **3:**600
- *illus:*
- - Frederick II of Denmark (miniat.) **3:**626
FRAENKEL (fam.) **7:**1
- printing **13:**1107
Fraenkel (bk. trade firm) **4:**1239
Fraenkel, Aaron Levi **7:**2
Fraenkel, Abraham (mer.) **7:**2
FRAENKEL, ABRAHAM ADOLF (math.) **11:**1124
Fraenkel, Baermann **7:**2
Fraenkel, David ben Moses **7:**2
- *Sulamith* **15:**502
FRAENKEL, DAVID BEN NAPHTALI HIRSCH **7:**3
- homiletical literature **8:**956
- Jerusalem Talmud **15:**778
- Moses Mendelssohn **11:**1329
- Prussia **13:**1290
Fraenkel, David Isaac **7:**1
FRAENKEL, EDUARD **7:**3
FRAENKEL, ELKAN **7:**4
- Model, Marx **12:**201
Fraenkel, Enoch **7:**1
Fraenkel, Esaja **7:**4
FRAENKEL, FAIWEL **7:**4
Fraenkel, Gabriel **7:**1
Fraenkel, Hoenig, *see* Fraenkel, Enoch
FRAENKEL, ISAAC SECKEL **7:**5
Fraenkel, Israel **7:**1
Fraenkel, Issachar Berman **7:**2
Fraenkel, Jacob **11:**1569
Fraenkel, Jesse, *see* Fraenkel, Esaja
FRAENKEL, JONAS (hist.) **7:**5
Fraenkel, Jonas (bsmn., Ger.), *see* Fraenckel, Jonas
FRAENKEL, JOSEF **1:**30
Fraenkel, Joseph Jonas **4:**1355
Fraenkel, Judah Loeb **7:**2
FRAENKEL, LEVI BEN SAUL **7:**5
FRAENKEL, LOUIS (fin.) **7:**5
Fraenkel, Louis (ed., Den.) **13:**1048
Fraenkel, Moses **7:**2
Fraenkel, Naphtali Hirsch **7:**3
FRAENKEL, OSMOND K. **10:**1505; **10:**1508
Fraenkel, S. (orient.) **12:**1461
Fraenkel, S.A. (fin., Pol.) **13:**1518
Fraenkel, Sándor (psych.), *see* FERENCZI, SÁNDOR
Fraenkel, Seckel, *see* Fraenkel, David Isaac
Fraenkel, Simon (physic.) **11:**1203
Fraenkel, Solomon (print.) **7:**3
Fraenkel, Zacharias (court J.) **7:**1
Fraenkel, Zacharias (bnk.) **6:**810
Fraenkel, Ẓevi Hirsch **7:**4
Fraenkel ha-Levi, Koppel **7:**4
FRAENKEL-TEOMIM, BARUCH BEN JOSHUA EZEKIEL FEIWEL **7:**6
Fraenkel-Teomim, Ezekiel Joshua Feivel **14:**537
Fraenkel-Teomim, Joshua Hoeschel **7:**6
Fraenkl, Pavel **5:**1209
FRAGA (city, Sp.) **7:**7
Fraind (period.) **11:**1459
FRAM, DAVID **7:**7
Framingham (tn., Mass.) **11:**1112
Franca (city, Braz.) **4:**1329
FRANCE **7:**7
- *Contents:*
- - Until the Revolution **7:**8
- - Modern Period **7:**22
- - Holocaust Period **7:**32
- - Contemporary Period **7:**36
- - Relations with Israel **7:**40
- General
- - Alsace **2:**751
- - Ashkenaz **3:**719ff
- - banking **4:**168
- - capitulations **5:**148
- - demography **5:**1499ff
- - dress **6:**219
- - history **8:**712ff
- - history chart **8:**766-767
- - journalism **10:**304ff
- - law **10:**1495
- - military service **11:**1560
- - oil products **13:**346
- - Paris **13:**103
- - politics **13:**812ff
- - population **13:**875ff
- - press **13:**1031
- - "promised land" **5:**616
- - Provence **13:**1259
- - publishing **13:**1368
- - race theory **13:**1484
- - railroads **13:**1517ff
- - socialism **15:**25
- - stamps **15:**330ff
- - synods **15:**632ff
- - tailoring **15:**706
- - *takkanot* **15:**723
- - tax **15:**839
- - theater **15:**1054,1071
- - trade and commerce **15:**1297ff
- - vital statistics **16:**188ff
- - *see also:* LOUIS; PHILIP
- Until Revolution
- - agriculture **2:**402
- - *aliyah* **9:**511
- - Charlemagne **5:**353

-- communities 5:818; 5:824
-- Crusades 5:1135ff
-- culture 8:667
-- expulsion 16:1284
-- gaonate 7:324
-- German Jews 7:460
-- *hiddushim* 8:465ff
-- Jerusalem 9:1441ff
-- market days 11:1000; 11:1003
-- Marrano Diaspora 11:1023
-- medicine 11:1188ff
-- moneylending 12:254
-- Pastoureaux 13:176
-- Shum 14:1480
- Modern Period
-- Algeria 2:615
-- Alliance Israélite Universelle 2:648
-- Alsace-Lorraine 2:756
-- archives 3:382
-- Assembly of Notables 3:761
-- Blum, Léon 4:1136
-- Catholic Church 5:541
-- community 11:65
-- Congress of Vienna 16:132
-- Consistory 5:907
-- Damascus Affair 5:1249
-- emancipation 6:702ff
-- Erez Israel missions 9:296
-- German Jews 7:476
-- homiletic literature 8:957
-- Napoleon 12:823
-- philanthropy 13:378
-- revolution 7:151
-- Rothschild family 14:339ff
-- Sanhedrin, French 14:840
-- Tunisia 15:1446
- Holocaust Period 8:842,883
-- Centre de Documentation 5:287
-- Church and Nazism 8:914; 8:915
-- Drancy 6:207
-- Laval, Pierre 10:1475
-- partisans 13:140,148
-- War Crimes Trials 16:289ff
- Contemporary Period
-- assimilation 3:779
-- Cassin, René 5:231
-- Mendès-France 11:1346
-- neo-Fascism 12:952
-- New Left 12:1033ff
-- ORT 12:1482
-- scouting 14:1037ff
-- Sinai Campaign 14:1605
-- statistics 14:30
-- students' movements 15:449
-- television and radio 15:929
- Cultural and Religious Life
-- Bergson, Henri 4:619
-- Bernhardt, Sarah 4:677
-- Chagall, Marc 5:318
-- education 6:405ff
-- Fleg, Edmond 6:1340
-- French literature 7:138
-- Haskalah 7:1438
-- Hebrew language 16:1635
-- Judeo-French 10:424
-- Levi ben Gershom 11:92
-- liturgy 11:399
-- manuscripts 8:1266; 11:906
-- museums 12:543
-- poetry 13:692
-- rabbinate 13:1447; 13:1452ff
-- Rachel 13:1492
-- Rashi 13:1558
-- Séminaire Israélite 14:1147
-- Société des Etudes Juives 15:52
-- synagogues 1:syn. list
-- tosafists 15:1278ff
-- yeshivot 16:763ff
- Anti-Semitism
-- Agobard 2:371
-- Barrès, Auguste 4:258
-- Chateaubriand, François 5:364ff
-- Drumont, Edouard 6:236
-- *La Croix* 5:1125
-- L'Action Française 2:232
-- Maurras, Charles 11:1135
-- 19th century 3:116
-- Zola, Emile 16:1216
-- *see also* ANTI-SEMITIC POLITICAL PARTIES AND ORGANIZATIONS
- Zionism and Relations with Israel 9:431ff; 16:1113
-- arms deal 9:388ff,694
-- Middle East 9:305ff
-- peace guarantees 9:384
-- Rothschild, Edmond de 14:342
-- Six-Day War 9:543; 14:1626
-- Spire, André 15:284
-- Suez Campaign 9:389ff; 15:1554ff
-- Sykes-Picot agreement 15:565ff
- *illus:*
-- anti-Semitic parties, 1870-1901 (table) 3:81
-- Assembly of Jewish Notables (map) 3:761
-- Cherbourg boats in Haifa 9:431
-- Cloots' *Lettre sur les Juifs* 5:615
-- Consistories of France, 1808 (map) 5:908
-- Dreyfus, Alfred, cartoon 3:115
-- Dreyfus Affair 6:225-229
-- Dürmenach riots, 1848 2:753
-- French Jew (14th cent.) 4:65
-- "Grand Sanhedrin des Israélites de France" 8:704
-- Jewish badge decreed by the Nazis 4:72
-- Jewish bankers in the Seine department, list (1817) 4:179
-- Jewish deputation to the National Assembly (1789) 4:1246
-- Jewish hat (12th cent.) 4:64
-- *La Libre Parole* 3:152; 6:237
-- *Law relating to Jews* (1791) 6:697
-- Levant stamp 15:331
-- Louis XVI's Letters Patent re Portuguese Jews (1776) 3:926
-- Mandel, Georges, memorial plaque 11:863
-- Memorial to the Unknown Jewish Martyr, Paris 3:112
-- Napoleonic decree on adoption of surnames 12:811
-- ORT school 12:1484
-- Paris war crimes trial 16:301
-- *Protocols of the Elders of Zion* 6:581
-- *Recueil des Lois concernant les Israélites* (1851) 7:1205
- *pop. tables:*
-- text
-- major towns, 1967 5:1514
-- Provence, medieval 13:1261
France, Anatole
- on Jews 7:144
- Proust, Marcel 13:1257
Frances (fam.) 11:572
FRANCES, IMMANUEL BEN DAVID 7:43
- Italian literature 9:1109
- Jewish literature 11:328
- parody 13:131
- Shabbateanism 14:1234
Frances, Immanuel Bocarro, *see* ROSALES, JACOB HEBRAEUS
FRANCES, ISAAC 7:43
FRANCES, JACOB BEN DAVID 7:44
- Italian literature 9:1109
- Jewish literature 11:328
- parody 13:131
- Shabbateanism 14:1234
Frances, Karl 16:1328
Frances, Mordecai 11:572; 11:573
Franceso della Rovere (pope), *see* SIXTUS IV
FRANCHE-COMTÉ (reg., Fr.) 7:44
- France 7:16ff
Franchetti, Judith 8:1400
Franchetti, Major 11:1561
FRANCHETTI, RAIMONDO 7:45
- travels 15:1351
Francia, Domingo Rodrigues Isaac 7:45
FRANCIA, FRANCIS 7:45
FRANCIS I (Aus. emp.) 7:46
- Austrian Jews 3:894
- Haskalah 7:1442
- holy places in Israel 8:936
- Jerusalem 9:1441
- Mantua, prayer for 7:836
"Francis Bacon" (paint., L. Freud) 3:622
FRANCISCANS 7:47
- David's tomb 9:279
- Ein Kerem 16:1325
- Hebrew interests 8:13
- Jerusalem community 9:1441
- Jerusalem map 9:1544
- Mount Zion 16:1031
- Muslim attacks 9:1425
- *illus:*
-- First Station of the Cross 9:916
-- Terra Sancta College, Jerusalem 9:1487
Francisco de Santa Fé, *see* Santa Fé, Francisco de
Franciscus, Magister 11:1215
Franciscus, Maria 8:32
Franciscus de Sant Jordi, *see* RIMOCH, ASTRUC
Franciscus Donatus 6:163
- *illus:*
-- *Tappuhei Zahav* (1618) 6:162
Franciscus Georgius Venetus, *see* GIORGIO, FRANCESCO
FRANCIS JOSEPH I OF HAPSBURG (emp.) 7:48
- Aszod, Judah 3:811
- Jerusalem 9:1458
- Jewish education fund 13:1464
- rabbi regulation 13:1464
- training of rabbis 13:1452
- *illus:*
-- medal 11:1170
Francis of Assisi 7:47; 9:1101
FRANCK, ADOLPHE 7:48
- history chart 8:766-767
FRANCK, HENRI 7:49
Franck, Isaac 16:358
Franck, Jacob, *see* FRANCK, ADOLPHE
FRANCK, JAMES 7:50
- biology 4:1032
Franck, Melchior 9:1589
Franck, Sebastian 8:32 8:701
FRANCO (fam., Eng.) 7:50
- *illus:*
-- coat of arms 8:336
Franco (fam., Sp.) 10:1359
Franco (fam., Turk.) 13:1109
Franco, Alexander 8:1362
Franco, Daniel 8:1362
Franco, David 2:94
Franco, Francisco (Sp. gen.) 4:213; 8:741
FRANCO, GAD 7:51
Franco, Hayyim 7:51
Franco, Hezekiah 7:51
Franco, Isaac (Gr. r.) 6:919
Franco, Isaac (Neth.) 12:976
Franco, Jacob de Moses 7:50; 8:339
Franco, Joseph 5:239
Franco, Juan 8:1384
Franco, Ralph, *see* Lopes, Sir Ralph
Franco, Raphael 7:50
Franco, Samuel 14:261
Franco, Solomon (stlr U.S.) 4:1264
Franco, Solomon (mer., Eng.) 7:50; 8:1356
Franco, Yuce (of Tembleque) 10:1359
Franco-British Convention 9:312
Francolm, Isaac Asher 10:1129
FRANCO-MENDES, DAVID 7:51
Franconia (reg., Ger.) 3:483; 4:343
Franco-Prussian War (1870-71) 7:28; 11:1560,1561
- *illus:*
-- medal in memory of French victims 15:91
-- "*Yahrzeit* at the Front" 11:1563
FRANCOS (Franji; term, Eur.) 7:51
- capitulations 5:148
- Laniado, Raphael 10:1423
Francus, Gregorius, *see* Franke, Gregorius
Frank (fam., U.S.) 3:450
Frank, A. (hist., Holl.) 8:563
Frank, Aaron 12:1451
Frank, Albert 13:1360
FRANK, ALBERT RUDOLPH 7:52
FRANK, ANNE 7:52
- Amsterdam 2:904
- Bergen-Belsen 4:610
- children's literature 5:448; 5:453
- Goslar, Hans 7:817
Frank, Bernard 7:148
FRANK, BRUNO 7:54
Frank, Daniel (r., Bohem.) 10:1162
Frank, Daniel (sport.) 12:1375
FRANK, ELI 7:54
Frank, Ephraim 4:630
Frank, Eva 7:67,69ff
Frank, Faivel 11:1295
FRANK, HANS MICHAEL (Nazi) 7:54
- Gestapo 7:527
- Poland 13:753
- Warsaw ghetto 16:347
- *illus:* 16:290
Frank, Henry (print.) 13:1113
Frank, Henry I. (U.S.) 12:266
Frank, Isaiah (Joszua) 16:917
FRANK, JACOB, AND THE FRANKISTS 7:55
- *Contents:*
-- Shabbatean Association 7:56
-- In Podolia 7:56
-- Disputations 7:58
-- Iwanie 7:59
-- Disputation in Lvov 7:61
-- Social Structure 7:65
-- Arrest 7:65
-- In Czestochowa 7:66
-- In Bruenn 7:67
-- Literature 7:69
-- In Prague 7:70
- antinomianism 3:70
- Ba'al Shem Tov 9:1051
- Baruch ben David Yavan 4:277
- Birkenthal 4:1037
- birth of Hasidism 7:1391,1395
- Brody 4:1397
- Busk 4:1536
- Dembowski, Nicholas 15:771
- Dobruschka-Schoenfeld 6:143
- Doenmeh 6:149
- history chart 8:766-767
- messianism 11:1426
- Nahman of Bratslav 12:783ff
- Podolia 13:668
- Polish Jewry 3:198; 6:97
- Schiller 14:965
- Shabbateanism 14:1252ff
- slander 8:1368
- Wolowski family 16:621
Frank, Jacob Elijah 7:1447
FRANK, JEROME NEW 7:72
Frank, Josef (s. of Jacob) 7:69

FRANK, JOSEF (archit.) **3:**363
Frank, Joseph (stlr., Vt.) **16:**112
FRANK, KARL HERMANN **7:**73
FRANK, LEO MAX **7:**73
– anti-Semitism **15:**1652
– Atlanta Jewry **3:**825
Frank, Leonard **15:**307
Frank, Louis **12:**177
FRANK, MENAHEM MENDEL **7:**74
Frank, Moses (indus.) **7:**73
Frank, Moses (sport., U.S.) **15:**300
Frank, Nathan **14:**666
Frank, P. A. (r., Neth.) **7:**1008
FRANK, PHILIPP (philos.) **7:**74
Frank, Raphael **10:**1592; **15:**1487
Frank, René **11:**1562
Frank, Robert **13:**484
Frank, Rochus (s. of Jacob) **7:**69
FRANK, SEMYON LYUDVIGOVICH **7:**75
Frank, Sydney **15:**300
Frank, Victor **15:**307
FRANK, WALDO DAVID **7:**75
Frank, Ẓevi Henri **11:**1142
FRANK, ẒEVI PESAḤ **7:**76
– autopsies **2:**932
– responsa **14:**93
FRANKAU (fam.) **7:**77
Frankau, Gilbert **7:**77
Frankau, Julia **7:**77
Frankau, Pamela **7:**77
Franke, Gregorius **8:**32
Frankel, Dr. (physic., Jer.) **9:**1455
Frankel, Benjamin F. **8:**1255
Frankel, Gene **12:**1121
Frankel, Harold L. **16:**476
FRANKEL, HEINRICH WALTER **5:**382
FRANKEL, HIRAM D. **7:**77
Frankel, Isaac **14:**958
Frankel, Jacob Arye **15:**521
FRANKEL, LEE KAUFER **7:**78
FRANKEL, LEO **7:**78
Frankel, Levin Saul **10:**791
FRANKEL, NAOMI **7:**79
FRANKEL, SALLY HERBERT **7:**79
FRANKEL, SAMUEL BENJAMIN **7:**79
FRANKEL, WILLIAM **10:**41; **10:**310
FRANKEL, ZACHARIAS **7:**80
– approach to Judaism **8:**726
– Breslau Seminary **10:**465
– civil rights of Jews **2:**649
– Hirsch, S. R. **8:**512
– history chart **8:**766-767
– *Monatsschrift* **12:**240
– oral law **12:**1444
– Orthodoxy **12:**1489
– rabbinical conferences **13:**1460ff
– Rapoport, S.I.L. **13:**1556
– Reform Judaism **14:**24
– Schwarz, Adolf **14:**1022
– Wissenschaft des Judentums **16:**574
Frankel-Arnstein (fam.) **15:**507
Frankenberg, Abraham von **10:**646
Frankenburger, Paul, *see* BEN-HAIM, PAUL
FRANKENBURGER, WOLF **7:**8
FRANKENHEIMER, JOHN MICHAEL **12:**467
FRANKENSTEIN, CARL **7:**82
Frankenthaler, Alfred **10:**1508
FRANKENTHALER, GEORGE **10:**1508
FRANKENTHALER, HELEN **3:**600
– family **10:**1508
– *illus:*
– – ark curtain **12:**38
– – "Sagittarius" (paint.) **3:**621
Frankfort (city, Ky.) **10:**909
FRANKFORT, HENRI **7:**82
Frankfort, Jacob **11:**498
Frankfort, Moses ben Simeon **2:**90; **3:**729
Frankfort an der Oder, *see* FRANKFORT ON THE ODER
FRANKFORT ON THE MAIN **7:**83
– *Contents:*
– – Early History **7:**83
– – 15/17 Centuries **7:**84
– – 18th Century **7:**87
– – 19/20 Centuries **7:**87
– – Holocaust Period **7:**90
– – Post-World War II **7:**91
– – Printing **7:**91
– – Music **7:**92
– Auschwitz trials **3:**874
– book trade **4:**1238
– ghetto **14:**1004
– Hirsch, S.R. **8:**510
– history chart (1603) **8:**766-767
– Kann family **10:**737
– museum **12:**538
– rabbinical conference **13:**1460
– Reform Judaism **14:**24
– special Purim **13:**1397
– stock exchange **15:**406
– tax **15:**839
– trade and commerce **15:**1299ff
– Vienna, Congress of **16:**132
– *illus:*
– – text
– – B'nai B'rith commemoration medal **4:**1147
– – bridal procession **11:**1027
– – community council discussing sumptuary laws **15:**516
– – expulsion of Jews in 1614 **7:**474
– – Fettmilch, Vincent, execution **6:**1248
– – *Memorbuch* **11:**1300
– – pewter Purim plate **13:**353
– – plundering of the ghetto in 1614 **7:**472
– – psalmody, Ps. 105 (mus. notation) **13:**1329
– – receipt for street lamps payment **15:**871
– – Rothschild house **14:**337
– – service for fast day after the 1711 fire **6:**1193
Frankfort Mishneh Torah (15th cent., illum. ms., It.) **3:***fcg.* 988
FRANKFORT ON THE ODER **7:**92
– archives **3:**387
– universities **15:**1677
– *illus:* text
Frankfort, Synod of **2:**404; **15:**633
Frankfurt, Moses ben Mendel, *see* MENDELSOHN, FRANKFURT MOSES
Frankfurt am Main, *see* FRANKFORT ON THE MAIN
Frankfurter, Akivah, *see* Akiva ben Jacob Frankfurter
Frankfurter, Baer, *see* JOSEPH ISSACHAR BAER BEN ELHANAN
FRANKFURTER, DAVID **7:**94
FRANKFURTER, FELIX **7:**94
– *Contents:*
– – Early Years **7:**94
– – Professor **7:**95
– – Zionist **7:**95
– – Politics **7:**96
– – Supreme Court **7:**97
– – Retrospect **7:**98
– – Writings **7:**98
– Brandeis, Louis **4:**1298
– Wise, Stephen **15:**566
Frankfurter, Hirsch **7:**216;
– Fuerth press **13:**1108
Frankfurter, Mendel **8:**508
FRANKFURTER, MOSES **7:**98
– printing **13:**1105
Frankfurter, Raphael, *see* Hirsch, Raphael
Frankfurter, Simon **11:**358
FRANKFURTER, SOLOMON FRIEDRICH **7:**99
FRANKINCENSE **7:**99
– impurity **13:**1079
– incense and perfumes **8:**1311ff
– plant list **13:**619
– sacrifice **14:**603ff
– *illus:* text
Frankists, *see* FRANK, JACOB, AND THE FRANKISTS
Frankl (fam.), *see* FRAENKEL
FRANKL, ADOLF **7:**100
Frankl, Liselotte **13:**1340
Frankl, Lothar **7:**101
FRANKL, LUDWIG AUGUST **7:**100
– Abulafia, Ḥayyim **2:**188
– Beirut Jews **4:**402
– Ereẓ Israel history **9:**299
– flag, colors of **6:**1337
– *illus:* text
Frankl, Oscar Benjamin **7:**103
Frankl, Paul **3:**650
FRANKL, PINKUS FRITZ (Pinḥas) **7:**102
FRANKL, VICTOR E. **7:**102
FRANKL-GRUEN, ADOLF ABRAHAM **7:**102
Frankl-Hochwart, Ludwig August, Ritter von, *see* FRANKL, LUDWIG AUGUST
FRANKLIN (fam.) **7:**103
Franklin, Abraham **7:**103
Franklin, Andrew **16:**261
Franklin, Arthur Ellis **7:**103
Franklin, Beatrice **7:**103
Franklin, Benjamin **7:**103
Franklin, Benjamin Wolf **7:**103
Franklin, Collin Ellis **15:**1478
Franklin, Ellis **7:**104
Franklin, Ellis Abraham **7:**103
Franklin, Fabian **15:**1678
Franklin, Harold **5:**169
Franklin, Harvey **11:**485
Franklin, Jacob **13:**1028; **7:**103
– *illus.*
– – *The Voice of Jacob* **13:**1027
FRANKLIN, LEO MORRIS **7:**104
Franklin, Sir Leonard **7:**103
Franklin, Lewis **14:**829
Franklin, Lumley **4:**1380; **7:**104; **16:**119
Franklin, Rosalind **7:**104
FRANKLIN, SELIM **7:**104
– British Columbia **4:**1380
FRANKLIN, SIDNEY **7:**105
– bullfighting **15:**306
– *illus:* text
Frank-Ruehl (type let.) **15:**1487
– *illus:*
– – Hebrew typefaces **15:**1485
Franks (anc. people) **3:**169; **7:**9; **8:**766-767
FRANKS (fam.) **7:**105
– *geneal. table:* text
Franks, Aaron **7:**105
Franks, Abigail Bilhah **7:**108
– New York City **12:**1068
Franks, Abraham (Eng.) **7:**105
Franks, Abraham (Can.) **10:**219; **12:**284; **13:**1423
Franks, Benjamin **4:**1192; **7:**105
Franks, Bobby **11:**441
FRANKS, DAVID **7:**106
– banking **4:**178
– family **7:**108; **11:**162
– military contractor **5:**935
– New York City **12:**1067ff
– Philadelphia **13:**368; **13:**369
– slave trade **14:**1663
– trade **15:**1305
– Washington, George **16:**359
– *geneal. table:* text
– *illus:* text
FRANKS, DAVID SALISBURY **7:**107
– Canada **5:**103
– Washington, George **16:**359
– *illus:*
– – text
– – portrait **12:**1064
Franks, Henry **12:**1074
Franks, Isaac W. **16:**360
FRANKS, JACOB (N.Y.C.) **7:**107
– family **7:**105
– New York City **12:**1067ff
– trade **15:**1305
– *geneal. table:* **7:**106
– *illus:* text
FRANKS, JACOB (Mich.) **7:**108
– Michigan **11:**1498
– Wisconsin **16:**555
– *illus:*
– – portrait **12:**285
Franks, John **13:**1423
Franks, Michael **16:**162
Franks, Moses (mer.) **4:**178
– family **7:**108; **11:**162
– Philadelphia **13:**368
– Siprutini, Emanuel **14:**1617
Franks, Naphtali (U.S.) **7:**108
Franks, Naphtali Hart (Eng.), *see* Franks, Abraham
Franks, Phila, *see* De Lancey, Phila
Franks, Rachel **14:**695
Franz, Wolfgang **8:**32
FRANZBLAU, ABRAHAM NORMAN **7:**109
Franz Joseph (Aus. emp.), *see* FRANCIS JOSEPH I OF HAPSBURG
FRANZOS, KARL EMIL **7:**109
Franz Wolf of Poesing **13:**352
Fraštak (tn., Cz.), *see* HLOHOVEC
FRATERNAL SOCIETIES **7:**110
– Sephardi (U.S.) **14:**1174
– *see also:* ḤEVRAH, ḤAVURAH; PHILANTHROPY
Fraternidad Agraria (orgn., Arg.), *see* Cooperativa de Cooperativas
Fraternitatea (period.) **14:**398,1029
Frat Maimon **6:**1185; **10:**811; **15:**124
Fratriarchate **12:**1288
Frauberger, Heinrich **3:**594, 651; **12:**538
FRAUD **7:**110
– actions delay **11:**253
– fines **6:**1288
– forgery **6:**1432
– reparation-offering **11:**141
– sages **14:**650
– sacrifice **14:**601
– supervision of prices **13:**796
– weights and measures **16:**390
– *see also:* ONA'AH; OPPRESSION
Frauenberg (loc., Fr.) **11:**496
Frauenberger, Heinrich **12:**538
Frauen Buchlein (manual), *see* *Mitzvot ha-Nashim*
FRAUENKIRCHEN (tn., Aus.) **7:**111
FRAUENSTAEDT, JULIUS (Christian Martin) **7:**112
Frauenthal, Sam **3:**459
Frau Venus (Ger. myth. fig.) **11:**248
Fraydorf (stlmt., Rus.) **14:**468
Fraye Arbayter Shtime (period.) **13:**1053,1056
Fraye Geselshaft (period.) **13:**1053
Fraye Yidishe Folks-Bihne (theat., Fr.) **15:**1071
Fraye Yidishe Folksbine (theat., U.S.) **6:**801
Frayhayt (mvmt., Arg.) **8:**1243
Frayland (vill., Ukr.) **2:**408
Fred, Benedict, *see* DOLBIN, B.F.

Fredericianum (edict) **3**:888; **7**:114
Frederick I (H. Rom. Emp.)
- attitude to Jews **8**:677
- Avignon **3**:964
- Crusades **5**:1140
Frederick I (the Peaceful; Ger.) **15**:1128
FREDERICK I (Duke, Baden) **7**:113
- Herzl **8**:412
- *illus:*
- - Hechler, William Henry **8**:238
Frederick II (the Grave; Ger.) **15**:1128
FREDERICK II (the Great; k., Prus.) **7**:113
- Adolphus, Simḥah **2**:293
- debasement of currency **12**:64
- Prussia **13**:1289
- *illus:*
- - decree concerning beards **13**:1291
Frederick II (duke, Wuerttemberg) **10**:846
Frederick III (13/14 cent., k., Ger.) **3**:888
Frederick Augustus I (elector, Saxony), *see* Augustus II (the Strong)
Frederick Augustus II (elector, Saxony) **14**:924
Frederick Augustus III (elector, Saxony) **14**:924
Frederick the Belligerent, *see* FREDERICK II OF BABENBERG
Frederick the Great (k., Prus.), *see* FREDERICK II
Frederick of Austria, *see* Frederick III
FREDERICK II OF BABENBERG **7**:114
- charter **3**:888
- history chart **8**:766-767
- *illus:*
- - "Fredericianum" (charter, 1244) **3**:892
FREDERICK III OF HAPSBURG (H. Rom. Emp.) **7**:115
Frederick II of Hesse **8**:942
FREDERICK II OF HOHENSTAUFEN **7**:114
- Anatoli, Jacob **2**:928ff
- attitude to Jews **8**:677
- badge, Jewish **4**:68
- Capua **5**:156
- Crusade **9**:269
- history chart **8**:766-767
- Jerusalem **3**:998
- Viennese Jews' charter **3**:888
Fredericksburg (city, Va.) **16**:162
- *illus:*
- - Union Army, Jewish casualties (list) **15**:1602
Frederick William (elector, Prus.) **7**:474; **13**:1287; **15**:1677
Frederick William I (k., Prus.) **2**:293; **13**:1289
- *illus:*
- - Jewish deceit edict (1726) **7**:479
Frederick William II (k., Prus.) **13**:1290
FREDERICK WILLIAM III (k., Prus.) **7**:115
- Eger, Akiva **6**:470
- Prussia **13**:1291
FREDERICK WILLIAM IV (k., Prus.) **7**:116
- Eger, Solomon **6**:472
- Prussia **13**:1292
Fredericton (city, Can.) **11**:997
Free, J. P. **6**:180
Free Academy of Art (Rus.) **5**:318
Free Center (party, Isr.) **9**:678
- establishment **7**:255
- Histadrut elections **9**:861
- Tamir, Shemuel **10**:840
FREED, ARTHUR **12**:449; **12**:467
FREED, ISADORE **12**:689
- *mus. notations:*
- - composition for synagogue **12**:665
Freed, Moshe David **7**:334
Freedman, Andrew **15**:299
FREEDMAN, BARNETT **7**:116
Freedman, David Isaac (Austr.) **3**:881
Freedman, David Noel (arch.) **3**:697
Freedman, Elisha **7**:1360
Freedman, Frank **15**:319
Freedman, H. (Austr.) **11**:1284
- *illus:*
- - JPS Torah translation committee **10**:80
Freedman, Herman (U.S.) **5**:1568
Freedman, J. (Can.) **11**:880
Freedman, Jacob (U.S.) **15**:1206
Freedman, Jacob (r., U.S.) **6**:1161
Freedman, Joseph **5**:1568
Freedman, Maurice **3**:39
FREEDMAN, SAMUEL **7**:117
- Manitoba university **16**:551
Freedman, Simon **5**:1567
FREEDOM **7**:117
- articles of faith **3**:654
- Brandeis, Louis Dembitz **4**:1299
- censorship **5**:276
- freemasons **7**:122
- from slavery **14**:1655
- heresy **8**:360
- Lessing, Gotthold **11**:49
- London Jews **5**:4
- Mendel of Kotsk **10**:1126
- Mendelssohn **11**:1337
- redemption **14**:3
- Saadiah Gaon **14**:551
- Spinoza **15**:280
- *takkanot ha-kahal* **15**:734
- *illus:*
- - text
- - man leaving prison (14th cent. ms.) **7**:*fcg.* 1387
Freehof, Lillian B. **5**:437
FREEHOF, SOLOMON BENNETT **7**:121
- Job **10**:123
- Oral Law **12**:1444
- *illus:* text
Freehold (boro., N.J.) **12**:1030
Freeland (period., Mex.) **11**:1459; **15**:1022
Freeland League (orgn.) **15**:1021
Freeman, Arthur, *see* LIEBERMANN, AARON SAMUEL
Freeman, Charles **15**:308
Freeman, David **15**:308
Freeman, Frank S. **6**:465
Freeman, George **15**:635
Freeman, Harry **14**:823
Freeman, Joe (agr.) **14**:823
FREEMAN, JOSEPH (au.) **7**:121
Freeman, Julian **8**:1362
FREEMASONS **7**:122
- Christian Kabbalah **10**:646
- *see also:* FRATERNAL SOCIETIES
Freemesser, Bernard **13**:485
Freeport (loc., Bahamas) **16**:473
Freeson, Reginald **15**:27
FREE SONS OF ISRAEL **7**:125
Free Synagogue (N.Y.) **12**:1092; **16**:567
Free Synagogue's Child Adoption Committee (N.Y.) **16**:568
Freethinker (period.) **5**:668
Freetown (city, Sierra Leone) **9**:441
FREE WILL **7**:125
- *Contents:*
- - Philosophy **7**:125
- - Talmud and Midrash **7**:129
- - Modern Thought **7**:130
- General
- - Aristotelianism **3**:448
- - articles of faith **3**:656ff
- - belief **4**:429
- - cause and effect **5**:259
- - Divinely granted **7**:649
- - *Ein-Sof* **10**:557; **10**:559; **10**:560ff
- - fear of God **6**:1199
- - Kalam **13**:429
- - man in Kabbalah **10**:607
- - man's nature **11**:844
- - penal law **13**:223
- - Pharisee ideology **13**:365
- - philosophy **13**:423; **13**:424
- - rape **13**:1548
- - theology **15**:1107ff
- Views on
- - Aaron ben Elijah **2**:12
- - Abner of Burgos **13**:445ff
- - Akiva ben Joseph **2**:492
- - Arama, Isaac ben Joseph **3**:258
- - Baruch of Kosov **4**:281
- - Crescas, Ḥasdai **5**:1083; **13**:448
- - Hirsch, Samuel **13**:457
- - Ibn Daud **8**:1162; **13**:440
- - Ibn Ezra, Abraham **8**:1169
- - Levi ben Gershom **11**:95ff
- - Mendelssohn, Moses **11**:1330ff
- - Pollegar, Isaac **13**:835
- - Saadiah **13**:432
- *see also:* PROVIDENCE; REWARD AND PUNISHMENT
Freewill offering **14**:603; **16**:227
FREIBERG (fam.) **7**:131
Freiberg, Aaron Note **11**:561
Freiberg, Albert Henry **7**:132
Freiberg, Joseph A. **7**:132
Freiberg, Julius **7**:131
Freiberg, Julius Walter **7**:131
Freiberg, Maurice J. **7**:132
Freiberg, Stella **7**:131
Freiberger, Shalom **16**:918
FREIBURG IM BREISGAU (city, Ger.) **7**:132
- Baden **4**:60; **4**:61
- *illus:* text
Freiburger Rundbrief (journ.) **7**:133
FREIDLINA, RAKHIL KHATSKELEVNA **7**:133
Freidorf (dist., Crimea) **5**:1107
FREIDUS, ABRAHAM SOLOMON **7**:134
Freie Arbeiter Stimme (period.) **12**:1102
Freie Buehne (theat. orgn.) **4**:1290
Freie Buehne fuer Modernes Leben (period., Ger.) **4**:1290
Freie Juedische Folksbuehne (J. theat. gr.) **11**:1428
FREIER, RECHA **7**:134
- Jerusalem in music **9**:1589
- Youth Aliyah **16**:862
Freies Juedisches Lehrhaus (Ger.) **7**:488
- Rosenzweig **14**:301
Freie Vereinigung fuer die Interessen des orthodoxen Judentums **8**:512; **14**:287; **16**:105
FREIFELD, ABRAHAM **3**:600
FREIFELDER, MORRIS **5**:382
Freiheit (U.S. newsp.), *see* MORNING FREIHEIT
FREILICH, MAX MELECH **7**:134
FREIMAN (fam.) **7**:135
Freiman, Archibald (Aharon) Jacob **7**:135
- Bitan Aharon moshav **4**:1059
- Ottawa **12**:1521; **12**:1522
Freiman, Lawrence **5**:108; **12**:1522; **7**:132
Freiman, Lillian **7**:135; **12**:1522
FREIMANN (fam.) **7**:135
FREIMANN, ABRAHAM ḤAYYIM (Alfred) **7**:136
FREIMANN, ARON **7**:136
- Posnanski **13**:930
Freimann, Isaac **7**:135
Freimann, Israel Meir **7**:135
FREIMANN, JACOB **7**:137
Freischule (school, Berlin) **7**:1439
Freistadt (tn., Slov.), *see* HLOHOVEC
Freistaedtl (fam.) **11**:909
Freistaedtl, Michael Lazar, *see* BIEDERMANN, MICHAEL LAZAR
Freitagishe Kuranten (newsp.) **16**:6
Frejka, Ludwik (Cz.) **14**:1653
Fréjus (loc., Prov.) **13**:1259
Frejus, Roland **13**:103
Fremantle (port, Austr.) **13**:321
French Hill (sub., Jer.) **9**:1515
French Hospital (Jer.) **9**:1491
French Language **7**:138; **10**:432,1346; **16**:1635
FRENCH LITERATURE **7**:138
- *Contents:*
- - Biblical and Hebraic Influences **7**:138
- - Image of the Jew **7**:142
- - Jewish Contribution **7**:146
- - Capsules **7**:148
- Bible translations **4**:880
- children's literature **5**:452; **5**:456; **5**:460
- Ladino literature **10**:1350
FRENCH REVOLUTION **7**:151
- *Contents:*
- - Status of Jews **7**:151
- - Era of Revolution **7**:153
- - Effects Outside France **7**:156
- Alsace **2**:755
- Bayonne **4**:351
- Brittany **4**:1383
- equality of rights **8**:712ff
- European Jewry **6**:972
- French Jewry **6**:702; **7**:22
- Grégoire, Henri **7**:917
- history chart **8**:766-767
- Jewish badge **4**:71
- Paris **13**:107
- Rome **14**:251
- Strasbourg **15**:424
Frenel (art.) **13**:118
FRENK, BEER (Issachar Dov) **7**:158
FRENK, EZRIEL (Azriel) NATHAN **7**:159
Frenkel (art.), *see* Frenel
Frenkel, Bernát **4**:884
Frenkel, J. (r.) **15**:659
FRENKEL, JACOB ILICH (phys.) **7**:159
Frenkel, S. **6**:267
Frenkel, Yitzḥak **3**:592
- *illus:*
- - "Interior of a Synagogue at Safed" Fig. 99 3-ART
Frenkel-Brunswik, Else **13**:1344
Frenkiel, Pawel **16**:351
Frenkl, Ḥayyim **14**:1485
FRENSDORFF, FERDINAND **10**:1508
- law **10**:1497
FRENSDORFF, SOLOMON **7**:159
Féret, Nicolas **5**:1464
FRESCO, DAVID **10**:310
- children's literature **5**:446
- Ladino literature **10**:1351
Fresco, Moses **16**:1538
Frescobaldi, Lionardo **15**:1356
Frese, Jacob **14**:930
FREUD, ANNA **7**:160
FREUD, LUCIEN **3**:600
- *illus:*
- - "Francis Bacon" (paint.) **3**:621
FREUD, SIGMUND **7**:161
- Bernfeld, Siegfried **4**:675
- Moses **12**:401
- psychiatry **13**:1338

- Rank, Otto, and **13:**1545
- Rodker, John **14:**218
- Stekel, Wilhelm **15:**377
- *illus:*
- - autograph **3:**915
FREUDEMANN, SIMHAH **7:**165
Freudenberg, Adolf **8:**916
Freudenberg, A. I. **10:**862
FREUDENTHAL, ALFRED MARTIN **8:**1431
FREUDENTHAL, JACOB **7:**165
FREUDENTHAL, MAX **7:**166
- Gompers family **7:**773
Freudenthal, Sigmund **12:**1218
Freudiger, Philipp von, *see* Von Freudiger, Philipp
Freud-Marlé, Lilli **15:**1088
Freund (r., U.S.) **15:**1207
Freund, Alexander **6:**687
FREUND, ERNST **7:**167
FREUND, ISMAR **7:**167
- archives **3:**387
Freund, Leopold **11:**1197
FREUND, MARTIN **5:**382
FREUND, MIRIAM KOTTLER **7:**167
FREUND, PAUL ABRAHAM **7:**168
FREUND, SAMUEL BEN ISSACHAR BAER **7:**168
- Afike Jehudah **2:**329
- Wessely, W. **16:**464
FREUND, WILHELM (philol.) **7:**168
Freund, Wilhelm (physic.) **11:**1197
FREUNDLICH, OTTO **7:**169
Frey, Emanuel, *see* Dobruschka-Schoenfeld, Emanuel
FREY, JEAN BAPTISTE **7:**169
- historiography **8:**564
Frey, J.L. (Hebr.) **8:**32
Frey, J.S.C.F. (apos.) **13:**1248
Frey, Siegmund Gottlob Junius Brutus, *see* Dobruschka-Schoenfeld, Moses
Frey, William **2:**862
Freyland (period., U. S.) **15:**1022
Freystaedtler, A. **10:**756
Freytag, Gustav (au.) **7:**444; **16:**111
Freytag, G. W. F. (Hebr.) **8:**32
FRIBOURG (city, Switz.) **7:**170
- *illus:* text
Fribourg, E.E. **15:**26
Frick, Wilhelm **15:**1129
- *illus:*
- - Nuremberg Trial **16:**289
Frida, Emil, *see* VRCHLICKÝ, JAROSLAV
Fridericianum (edict), *see* Fredericianum
Fridkin, A. **14:**64
Fridman, Isaac **4:**1183
FRIED, AARON **7:**170
FRIED, ALFRED HERMANN **7:**171
Fried, Eliezer Isaac **16:**215
Fried, Klara **15:**307
FRIED, LAZAR **15:**1082
FRIED, MORTON HERBERT **7:**171
Frieda (dau., Shneur Zalman of Lyady) **16:**628
FRIEDBERG (tn., Ger.) **7:**171
- *illus:*
- - text
- - medieval *mikveh* **11:**1539
FRIEDBERG, ABRAHAM SHALOM **7:**173
FRIEDBERG, BERNARD (Ḥayyim Dov) **7:**173
Friedberg, Heinrich von **13:**813
Friedberg, J. Benjamin **12:**1522
FRIEDBERG, MAURICE **1:**30
Friedberg, Paul **3:**361
Friedburg, Samson (Aryeh) **14:**1608
Friede, Donald **13:**1371
Friede, Leo **15:**307
FRIEDE, SHALOM **7:**1547
FRIEDELL, EGON **7:**174
Friedell, Hymer **11:**1201
FRIEDEMANN, ADOLF **7:**174
FRIEDEMANN, ULRICH **7:**174
FRIEDENBERG, ALBERT MARX **7:**175
- historiography **8:**568
Friedenberg, A. Y. **14:**1126
Friedenberg, Daniel M. **7:**175; **12:**544
FRIEDENBERG, SAMUEL **7:**175
Friedenthal, Aaron **11:**612
Friedenthal, J. H. (Aus.) **16:**504
Friedenthal, J. M. (S.A.) **15:**210
Friedenthal, Karl Rudolf **13:**813
Friedenthal, Marcus **4:**1355
FRIEDENWALD (fam.) **7:**175
Friedenwald, Aaron **7:**175
Friedenwald, Harry **7:**176; **16:**1141
- *illus:* text
Friedenwald, Jonas (bsmn.) **7:**175
Friedenwald, Jonas (physic.) **7:**176
FRIEDER, ARMIN **7:**176
Friedgood, David **5:**407
Friediger, Moses **5:**1538
FRIEDJUNG, HEINRICH **7:**177
- Austrian Jewry **3:**896
Friedlaender, Bluemchen **7:**177
Friedlaender, D. (bkdealer.) **4:**1239
Friedlaender, Daniel (mus.) **16:**1020
FRIEDLAENDER, DAVID **7:**177
- history chart **8:**766-767
- purveyor **12:**64
- Wessely's writings **5:**1353
Friedlaender, Elfriede, *see* FISCHER, RUTH
Friedlaender, Henry (art.) **15:**1488
- *illus:*
- - Hebrew typefaces **15:**1486
Friedlaender, H. J. (Prus.) **10:**1129
FRIEDLAENDER, ISRAEL **7:**179
- Zionism **16:**1141
Friedlaender, Joachim Moses **7:**177
FRIEDLAENDER, JOHNNY **3:**600
- Paris school of art **13:**118
- *illus:*
- - "Composition" (lith.) **3:**625
Friedlaender, Julius **3:**650
- art **3:**566
Friedlaender, Lillian Bentwich **7:**179
Friedlaender, M. (publ.) **7:**183
FRIEDLAENDER, MAX (mus.) **12:**690
Friedlaender, Max I. (art hist.) **3:**650
FRIEDLAENDER, MICHAEL **7:**180
Friedlaender, Mordecai Ẓevi **5:**37
FRIEDLAENDER, MORITZ **7:**181
Friedlaender, Morris **15:**1303
Friedlaender, Moses (18th cent.) **12:**371
Friedlaender, Moshe (20th cent.) **10:**1216
Friedlaender, Nathan **5:**1465
FRIEDLAENDER, OSKAR EWALD **7:**181
Friedlaender, Ruth, *see* FISCHER, RUTH
FRIEDLAENDER, SAUL **7:**182
FRIEDLAENDER, SOLOMON JUDAH **7:**182
Friedlaender, Walter **3:**650
Friedlaender-Fuld, Fritz **11:**1440; **15:**1166
Friedland (tn., Ger.) **11:**1163
FRIEDLAND (fam.) **7:**183
- Leningrad **11:**15
FRIEDLAND, ABRAHAM HYMAN (Ḥayyim) **7:**183
- *illus:*
- - Hebrew Pen Club **12:**1109
Friedland, B. **10:**90
Friedland, Guenther **5:**467
Friedland, Joseph **11:**198
Friedland, Judah Aryeh (au.), *see* FRIEDLAENDER, SOLOMON JUDAH
Friedland, Lazar **11:**485
Friedland, Meir **7:**183
Friedland, Meshullam Feivel **7:**183
Friedland, Moses Aryeh Leib **7:**183
- Leningrad **11:**17
- Wiener, Samuel **16:**502
FRIEDLAND, NATAN (r.) **7:**184
Friedland, Nathan (Bohem.) **7:**183
Friedland, Pesaḥ **16:**1099
Friedland, Raḥel, *see* SHALON, RAḤEL
Friedland, Solomon Judah, *see* FRIEDLAENDER, SOLOMON JUDAH
Friedland, Ẓevi **7:**1031
- *illus:*
- - Brod, Max, and **4:**1388
Friedlander (fam.) **5:**56
Friedlander, Alfred **13:**820
Friedlander, David **15:**1233
- *illus:*
- - Shmulovicz's mausoleum **15:**1231
- - Wyszogrod synagogue **16:**682
Friedlander, Emmanuel **11:**1440
Friedlander, Gerald **5:**450
Friedlander, Ḥayyim of Lesko, *see* Ḥayyim Friedlander of Lesko
FRIEDLANDER, ISAAC **7:**184
FRIEDLANDER, KATE **7:**185
FRIEDLANDER, WALTER **7:**185
Friedlender, Oskar **15:**339
Friedman (fam., Can.) **5:**104
Friedman (fam., Rum.) **15:**348
Friedman, A. (print.) **14:**631
Friedman, A. A. (writ., Rus.) **10:**993
Friedman, Abraham (r., Transyl.) **2:**519; **11:**210
Friedman, Abraham Mattathias **15:**348
FRIEDMAN, BENJAMIN (Benny) **7:**185
FRIEDMAN, BRUCE JAY **15:**1577; **15:**1580
FRIEDMAN, DÉNES **7:**185
Friedman, Feliks **3:**575
Friedman, Florence Louie **15:**209
Friedman, Frantisek **13:**1028
Friedman, Harry (stlr., U.S.) **13:**482
Friedman, Harry G. (philan., U.S.) **5:**311; **12:**544; **12:**538
FRIEDMAN, HERBERT A. **7:**186
- *illus:*
- - U.J.A. National Conference **15:**1541
FRIEDMAN, JACOB (poet) **7:**186
Friedman, Jacob (U.S.) **11:**485
Friedman, Jacob K. (Hung.) **12:**1292
Friedman, J. J. (law., S. A.) **10:**1502; **12:**845
FRIEDMAN, LEE MAX **7:**186
- historiography **8:**568
Friedman, Leonard **14:**599
Friedman, Matatias **16:**1134
Friedman, Max **15:**302
FRIEDMAN, MILTON **7:**187
Friedman, M. L. (Rum.) **13:**158
Friedman, Moshal (S. A.) **10:**156; **15:**191
FRIEDMAN, NAPHTALI **7:**188
Friedman, Nathan, *see* YELLIN-MOR, NATHAN
Friedman, Noah **12:**1408
FRIEDMAN, PHILIP **7:**188
Friedman, Samuel **5:**110
Friedman, Shraga **7:**1033
- *illus:*
- - in *Hello Dolly* **15:**1063
- - in *Inherit the Wind* **7:**1032
Friedman, Szajko, *see* SZAJKOWSKI, ZOSA
FRIEDMAN, THEODORE **7:**189
Friedman, William S. **5:**1545; **12:**872
Friedman, Ẓevi Hirsch of Lesko, *see* ẒEVI HIRSCH FRIEDMAN OF LESKO
Friedmann, Aaron (19/20 cent.) **14:**531
Friedmann, Aaron (20th cent.) **14:**531
FRIEDMANN, ABRAHAM (r.) **7:**189
Friedmann, Abraham (ḥas. ldr.) **14:**526
Friedmann, Abraham Heschel **14:**531
Friedmann, Abraham Jacob (19th cent.) **14:**531
Friedmann, Abraham Jacob (1884-1961) **14:**531
Friedmann, Abraham Jacob (1886-1942) **14:**531
Friedmann, Abraham Mattathias **14:**532
FRIEDMANN, ARON **7:**1547
Friedmann, D. (Hung.) **11:**721
Friedmann, David (19th cent., ḥas. ldr.) **14:**531
Friedmann, David (19/20 cent., ḥas. ldr.) **14:**531
FRIEDMANN, DAVID ARYEH **7:**189
FRIEDMANN, DAVID BEN SAMUEL **7:**190
Friedmann, David Moses **5:**497; **14:**532
FRIEDMANN, DESIDER **7:**191
- Austrian Jews **3:**898**16:**127
- Theresienstadt currency **5:**726
Friedmann, Dov Baer **11:**32; **14:**532
Friedmann, Efraim **5:**467
Friedmann, Egon, *see* FRIEDELL, EGON
Friedmann, František **13:**972; **16:**1018
FRIEDMANN, GEORGES **7:**191
- sociology **15:**65
Friedmann, Isaac (Buhusi; 19th cent.) **4:**1468; **14:**531
Friedmann, Isaac (1850-1917, ḥas. ldr.) **14:**531
Friedmann, Isaac (1887-1929, ḥas ldr.) **14:**531
Friedmann, Isaac (20th cent., ḥas. ldr.) **14:**531
Friedmann, Isaac ben Jacob **14:**531
Friedmann, Israel (18/19 cent.), *see* RUZHIN, ISRAEL
Friedmann, Israel (1853-1907) **14:**531
Friedmann, Israel (1854-1934) **14:**532
Friedmann, Israel (1856-1949) **14:**532
Friedmann, Israel (1879-1951) **14:**531
Friedmann, Israel Shalom Joseph **14:**531
Friedmann, Jacob **14:**531
Friedmann, Jacob David **14:**531
FRIEDMANN, JANE **15:**1082
Friedmann, Joseph **7:**190
Friedmann, L. **16:**1165
Friedmann, Leon **16:**1165
FRIEDMANN, MEIR **7:**192
- Bruell, Nehemiah **4:**1415
- Passover *Haggadah* **7:**1093
- *Sifra* **14:**1519
Friedmann, Menahem Mendel **4:**1469; **14:**531
Friedmann, Menahem Nahum (of Stefanesti) **14:**532
Friedmann, Menahem Nahum (of Czernowitz) **14:**531
Friedmann, Menahem Nahum (of Itzkani) **14:**531

Friedmann, Menahem Nahum (of Husyatin) **14:**532
Friedmann, Mordecai Shalom Joseph **14:**531
Friedmann, Mordecai Shelomo **14:**531
Friedmann, Mordecai Shraga (19th cent.) **14:**532
Friedmann, Mordecai Shraga (20th cent.) **14:**532
FRIEDMANN, MORITZ **7:**193
Friedmann, Moses **14:**532
Friedmann, Moses Leib **14:**531
Friedmann, Nahum Mordecai **14:**532
FRIEDMANN, PAUL **7:**193
- Midian plan **14:**1315
Friedmann, Shalom Joseph (19th cent.) **14:**531
Friedmann, Shalom Joseph (d. 1927) **14:**531
Friedmann, Shalom Joseph (1879-1936) **14:**531
Friedmann, Shalom Joseph of Spikov **14:**531
Friedmann, Shalom Shakhna **14:**527
Friedmann, Shmuel, *see* Eliashiv, Shmuel
Friedmann, Siegwart **15:**1056
Friedmann, Solomon **14:**532
Friedmann, William Henry **15:**1480
FRIEDRICHSFELD, DAVID **7:**194
Friedrichson, D. **8:**32
Friedrichstadt (city, Latv.), *see* JAUNJELGAVA
FRIEDSAM, MICHAEL **7:**194
Friend, Aaron **5:**411
Friend, Fred **13:**162
FRIEND, HUGO MORRIS **7:**194
Friend, Lawrence **15:**303
Friendly, Edwin S. **10:**307
FRIENDLY, FRED W. **7:**195
Friendly, Samson **12:**1451
FRIENDSHIP **7:**195
- *illus:* text
Friends of New Germany (Nazi orgn., U.S.) **12:**1114
Friends of Pioneeing Israel (orgn., Can.) **16:**1110
FRIES, JAKOB FRIEDRICH **7:**196
- Burschenschaft **15:**1129
- Hep! Hep! riots **8:**330
Friesach (tn., Aus.) **5:**181; **14:**717
FRIGEIS, LAZARO DE **7:**197
- anatomy **2:**934
Friman, Abraham **14:**463, 502
Frimorgn (newsp.) **8:**315; **14:**175
FRISCH, DANIEL **7:**197
FRISCH, EFRAIM (au., Aus.) **7:**197
FRISCH, EPHRAIM (r., U.S.) **7:**197
Frisch, Leo **12:**37
FRISCH, OTTO ROBERT **7:**198
Frischer, Arnošt **13:**974; **16:**1018
Frischlin, Nicodemus **8:**32
FRISCHMANN, DAVID **7:**198
- *Contents:*
- - Early Career **7:**198
- - Short Stories **7:**198
- - Literary Critic **7:**199
- - Iconoclast Poet **7:**199
- - European Culture **7:**199
- - Hebrew Journalist **7:**200
- - Editor and Publisher **7:**200
- - In Yiddish **7:**201
- - Visits to Palestine **7:**201
- - In Russia **7:**201
- - Conversations and Letters **7:**202
- Akavya, Avraham **2:**478
- as critic **5:**1118
- Berdyczewski, Micha **4:**593
- *Ha-Tekufah* **7:**1469
- Hebrew literature **8:**192
- *illus:*
- - text
- - *Ha-Zeman,* first issue **13:**1046
Frischmuth, J. **8:**32
Fritsch, Ernst Augustus **8:**32
FRITSCH, THEODOR **7:**203
FRITTA (Cz. paint.) **7:**203
- art **3:**575
- *illus:*
- - "Dwelling for the Feebleminded" (drg.) Fig. 84 **3-**ART
Fritz, Johann Gottlieb **4:**885
Fritzsche, Hans **16:**289
FRIULI (reg., It.) **7:**203
FRIZZI, BENEDETTO **7:**204
- *illus:* text
Froben, Ambrosius **4:**304; **16:**1019
Froben, Jerome (Hieronymus) **4:**304
- *illus:*
- - printer's mark **13:**1093
Froben, Johannes **4:**304; **13:**1095; **15:**1482
Fröding, Gustaf **14:**929
FROEHLICH, ALFRED **7:**205
Froehlich, Joachim, *see* GAY, PETER JACK
Froehlich, Samson Levi **10:**466
FROG (zool.) **7:**206
- dietary laws **6:**36
- plagues of Egypt **13:**606
- *illus:*
- - text
- - plagues of Egypt **13:**610
FROHLICH, HERBERT **13:**491
FROHMAN (fam.) **7:**206
Frohman, Charles **7:**206
Frohman, Daniel **7:**206
Frohman, Gustave **7:**206
Fromann, Gottlieb **15:**1527
Frome, Anthony (U.S. sing.), *see* FEINBERG, ABRAHAM L.
Fromenson, Abraham H. **13:**1362
FROMM, ERICH **7:**206
- anthropology **3:**39
- Rosenzweig **14:**301
FROMM, HERBERT **12:**690
- choirs **5:**487
Frommann, Erhard (Frommannus) **8:**32
FROMM-REICHMANN, FRIEDA **7:**207
Frondel (14th cent., Ger.) **10:**794
Frondizi, Arturo **10:**1503
- Blejer, David **4:**1081
Fronmüller, Conrad **8:**32
Front de Libération Nationale (F.L.N.) **2:**618
Frontiers of Israel (anc., mdvl. period), *see* BOUNDARIES OF ISRAEL
FRONTIERS OF ISRAEL (mod. period) **9:**311
- armistice agreements **3:**478; **9:**374ff
- demarcation lines **9:**374ff; **9:**423ff
- Gaza Strip **7:**343
- Goldmann, Nahum **7:**724
- in international affairs **9:**304
- Mapai **11:**913
- *illus:*
- - Jerusalem boundaries before and after 1967 **9:**1505
- - Jerusalem stamp **15:**333
- - Mandelbaum Gate **9:**1490
- - Musrarah quarter warning notice **9:**1489
- - Negev **12:**926
- - Sinai peninsula **14:**1594
- - Sykes-Picot treaty **15:**566
Frontiger (bnk.) **12:**899
FRONTO, MARCUS CORNELIUS **14:**235
Frost, Robert
- Job theme **10:**125
- Jonah theme **10:**175
Frucht, Ludwik **15:**1215
FRUG, SHIMON SHMUEL **7:**208
- prosody **13:**1225
- Yiddish literature **16:**811
Frugoni, P.F. **9:**1105
Fruit **6:**1416ff
- Commandments, the 613 **5:**773
- eclipse **12:**291
- economic life **16:**1268ff
- Ginnosar plain **7:**579
- grafting prohibition **12:**170ff
- *orlah* **12:**1467
- *sukkah* **15:**502
- Tu bi-Shevat **15:**1419
- *illus:*
- - grapevine **16:**156
- - *orlah* **12:**1468
- - *sukkah* decoration **15:***fcg.* 491
- - Tu bi-Shevat plate **15:**1419
Fruit Carriers, Ltd. (Isr.) **9:**836
FRUMKIN, ALEKSANDR NAUMOVICH **7:**209
FRUMKIN, ARYEH LEIB **7:**209
- Ashkenazi, Abraham **3:**722
FRUMKIN, BORIS MARKOVICH **7:**210
Frumkin, Elias ben Jacob **7:**210
FRUMKIN, GAD **10:**1508
- *Ḥavazzelet* **7:**1479
FRUMKIN, ISRAEL DOV **7:**210
- Bak, Israel **4:**115
Frumkin, Malkah, *see* ESTHER
Frumkin, Sidney, *see* FRANKLIN, SIDNEY
Fry, Christopher **6:**776; **12:**405
FRÝD, NORBERT (Nora) **7:**211
Frydlender, David **16:**681
Frydman, A. Zisha **15:**24
Frydman, Paulin **5:**406
Frye, Peter **12:**1343
F.S.J.U., *see* Fonds Social Juif Unifié
Fubini, Abraham Sanson ben Jacob ha-Levi **15:**1455
FUBINI, GUIDO **7:**211
FUBINI, MARIO **7:**211
- Italian literature **9:**1114
Fuchs, A. (r., Hung.) **16:**117
FUCHS, ABRAHAM MOSHE (writ.) **7:**212
FUCHS, ALFRED (journ.) **7:**212
- press **13:**1026
Fuchs, Benjamin Ze'ev Wolf **7:**212
Fuchs, Bina, *see* ABRAMOWITZ, BINA
FUCHS, DANIEL **15:**1580
Fuchs, Emil (sport., U.S.) **15:**301
Fuchs, Emil (medal., Aus.) **11:**1167
- *illus:*
- - Duveen, Joseph (portrait) **6:**324
Fuchs, Eugen **5:**287
Fuchs, František **5:**1201
Fuchs, Franz Eugen **5:**287
Fuchs, Ḥayyim-Leib, *see* FOX, ḤAYYIM-LEIB
Fuchs, Jacob Samuel, *see* FOX, JACOB SAMUEL
Fuchs, James **12:**1376
Fuchs, Jenő **12:**1375
Fuchs, Leo **10:**794
Fuchs, Lukas, *see* FOSS, LUKAS
FUCHS, MOSES ẒEVI **7:**212
Fuchs, Rudolf **5:**1209
Fuchs, Samuel Jacob **5:**1036
Fuchs, William, *see* FOX, WILLIAM
Fuel
- Israel taxation **9:**757
- thorns **15:**1118
Fuenfkirchen (tn., Hung.), *see* PECS
FUENN, SAMUEL JOSEPH **7:**213
- critic **5:**1116
- *Ha-Karmel* **7:**1143
- Hebrew letters **11:**62
- Pinsker, Leon **13:**546
- press **13:**1044
- Russo-Jewish Cultural Society **15:**58ff
- Vilna **16:**148
Fuenten, Ferdinand aus der **16:**296
Fueredi, Ignác **4:**884
Fuero de los Españoles (law, Sp.) **15:**244
Fuerst (fam., Ger.) **5:**1010
Fuerst, Eleazar **7:**999
Fuerst, Israel **5:**1010
Fuerst, Jeremiah **5:**1010
FUERST, JULIUS **7:**213
- Eger, Akiva **6:**470
Fuerst, Milán, *see* FÜST, MILÁN
Fuerst, Samuel **5:**1010
FUERSTENBERG, CARL **7:**214
Fuerstenberg, Hans **7:**214
Fuerstenfeld (tn., Aus.) **8:**1043
- Jewish massacre **15:**465
Fuerstenthal, Raphael **11:**1162
FUERTH (city, Ger.) **7:**214
- seal **14:**1080
- *illus:*
- - text
- - main synagogue **4:**344
FUERTH, HENRIETTE **7:**216
Fuerth, Julius **13:**1369
Fugger, W. **12:**1279
Fuks, Abraham Leib **16:**597
FUKS, ALEXANDER **7:**216
Fuks, Elhanan **13:**1300
Fuks, Jurek **3:**575
- *illus:*
- - "Jews in Line for a Meal at Przyglow" Fig. 76 **3-**ART
FUKS, LAJB **7:**216
FULBERT OF CHARTRES **7:**217
FULD, AARON BEN MOSES **7:**217
FULD, STANLEY HOWELLS **7:**218
FULDA (city, Ger.) **7:**218
- blood libel **7:**114
- historical chart (1235) **8:**766-767
- *illus:* text
FULDA, LUDWIG **7:**219
Fulda, Reuben **7:**310
Fullenius, Bernardus **8:**32
Fuller, Jake **15:**302
Fuller, Nicholas **8:**32
Fuller, Thomas **9:**1543
- *illus:*
- - Paran Desert map **13:**89
Fuller's Quarter (Jer.) **16:**1031
FULVIA (1st cent. C.E., pros.) **7:**220
Fundam (Fundão), Isaac, of Amsterdam **4:**1238
Fundamentals of Belief, *see* ARTICLES OF FAITH
Fundoianu, Barbu, *see* FONDANE, BENJAMIN
Fund-raising, *see* PHILANTHROPY
Funeral, *see* ANINUT; BURIAL; MOURNING
Funerary inscriptions, *see* EPITAPHS
Funerary rites, *see* BURIAL
FUNES (tn., Sp.) **7:**220
FUNK, CASIMIR **7:**220
Funk, Moritz von **11:**1556
FUNK, SOLOMON **7:**221
Funk, Walter **16:**289
Funkelmann, Jacob **4:**591
Fun'm Yarid (bk.) **14:**1284
FURAYDIS, AL- (vill., Isr.) **7:**221
- human geography **9:**572
Furaykh, Al- (Bedouin fam.) **9:**289
Furman, Joseph **11:**1556
Furniture **16:**630
Furrow Press (U.S.) **13:**1377
Furrows (period., U.S.) **8:**1242
FURST, MORITZ **7:**221
- *illus:* text
Furstman, Jake, *see* Fuller, Jake
FURTADO, ABRAHAM **7:**222
- historical chart **8:**766-67
- notables' assembly **3:**763

– *illus:* text
Furtado de Mendoza, Duarte **15:**270,1301
FUR TRADE AND INDUSTRY **7:**223
– crafts **5:**1048
– guilds **7:**972
– textiles **15:**1036ff
– *illus:* text
Furtseva, Yekaterina **6:**69
FURTUNA, ENRIC **7:**226
Furtwaengler, Adolf **3:**301
FÜST, MILÁN **8:**1085
Fustat (Egy.), *see* CAIRO
Fuṣūl Mūsā (wk.), *see Pirkei Moshe*
Future life, *see* AFTERLIFE; BEATITUDE; DEATH; ESCHATOLOGY; GILGUL; LIFE AND DEATH; OLAM HA-BA; PARADISE; RESURRECTION; SOUL, IMMORTALITY OF
F.Z.O.C., *see* Federated Zionist Organization of Canada

G

GAAL (bib. fig.) **7:**229
- Abimelech **2:**77
Ga'ash (kib., Isr.) **1:**place list
GA'ATON (kib., Isr.) **7:**229
- statistics **1:**place list
Ga'aton River (Isr.) **9:**152
Gabai, Isaac **10:**1351
Gabais, Menahem ben Zalman **16:**599
Gabara (city, Er. Isr.), *see* ARABA
Gabata (kib., Isr.), *see* GEVAT
GABBAI (cmty. offic.) **7:**230
- charity wardens **5:**343
- *hekdesh* institutions **8:**286
- Ḥasidism **7:**1400
- title **15:**1164
- *see also:* COMMUNITY
GABBAI (fam., Iraq, Ind.) **7:**231
- *aliyah* **9:**513
GABBAI (fam., Heb. prints.) **7:**232
- printing **13:**1109ff
- *illus:* text
Gabbai, Aaron **7:**231
Gabbai, Abraham **7:**233
Gabbai, Abraham ben Jedidiah **9:**1165
- *illus:*
- - *Ein Yosef* (1860) **9:**1164
Gabbai, ʿAzīza **7:**231
Gabbai, David **7:**231
Gabbai, Elijah **7:**231
Gabbai, Ezekiel (army paymaster, Turk.) **5:**190
- Ottoman Empire **16:**1552
Gabbai, Ezekiel (jur., Turk.) **7:**231
Gabbai, Ezekiel ben Joseph Nissim Menahem (bnk., Bagh.) **7:**231
- *ṣarrāf* **14:**887
Gabbai, Ezekiel ben Joshua **7:**231
Gabbai, Ezekiel ben Ṣāliḥ (cmty. treasurer, Ind.) **7:**231
Gabbai, Ezra ben Joseph **4:**89
- *ṣarrāf* **14:**887
Gabbai, Ezra ibn Ṣāliḥ **7:**231
Gabbai, Flora (Farḥa) **7:**231
Gabbai, Isaac (publ.) **7:**231
Gabbai, Isaac ben David ben Yeshu'ah **7:**231
Gabbai, Isaac ben Solomon **7:**232; **9:**1098; **14:**633
Gabbai, Jacob **7:**970
Gabbai, Jedidiah **7:**232; **10:**1573
- Gediliah, Abraham ben Samuel **7:**354
Gabbai, Joshua ben Simeon **7:**232
Gabbai, Judah **11:**166
GABBAI, MEIR BEN EZEKIEL IBN **7:**233
- Alcastiel, Joseph **2:**542
- Kabbalah **10:**542
GABBAI, MOSES BEN SHEM-TOV **7:**233
- Abulrabi **2:**197
Gabbai, Raphael ben Aaron **7:**232
Gabbai, Sasson ben Ezekiel Mordecai **7:**232
Gabbai, Shalom **7:**231
Gabbai, Shem-Tov **3:**834
Gabbai, Solomon ben David **7:**233
Gabbai, Solomon Ṣalaḥ **7:**232
Gabbai Ereẓ Israel (title) **14:**1364
GABBAI IZIDRO (Ysidro), ABRAHAM **7:**233
Gabba'im (Rom. tax agents), *see* TAX GATHERERS
Gabbai ẓedakah (cmty. offic.), *see* GABBAI
Gabbay, Isaac, *see* Gabbai, Isaac ben Solomon
Gabé, Dora **4:**1493
Gabel, Heinrich **13:**809
GABEL, MAX **15:**1082
Gabela (meat tax, Turk.) **2:**310; **14:**1342
- Ottoman Empire **5:**818
GABÈS (tn., Tun.) **7:**234
- Tunisia **15:**1434
- *illus:*
- - Great Synagogue **15:**1438
GABIN (tn., Pol.) **7:**235
Gabiniana (city, Hauran), *see* KENATH
GABINIUS, AULUS (1st cent. B.C.E., Rom. Gov.) **7:**235
- Ashdod **3:**696
- historical chart **8:**766-767
- Nabateans **12:**742
- Pompey **13:**846
- Rafa **13:**1509
GABIROL, SOLOMON BEN JUDAH, IBN **7:**235
- *Contents:*
- - Life **7:**235
- - Works **7:** 237
- - Poetry **7:**237
- - Philosophy **7:**240
- Literature
- - *Adon Olam* **2:**296
- - Alexander the Great tale **3:**579
- - Ibn Al-Taqana, Moses **8:**1155
- - Jewish literature **11:**327
- - Judeo-Arabic literature **10:**417
- - *Keter Malkhut* **4:**1185
- - linguistics **16:**1382
- - *Mivḥar ha-Peninim* **12:**163
- - poetic influence **13:**681ff
- - prosody **13:**1218
- - secular poetry **16:**1619
- - translations, early **15:**1129
- - Wise, Stephen, translations **16:**566
- Philosophy **13:**434
- - Albertus Magnus **2:**532
- - Alconstantini, Enoch **12:**551
- - Alexander of Hales **2:**583
- - angels **2:**976
- - Aristotelianism and Neoplatonism **3:**445
- - astrology **3:**791
- - attributes of God **7:**665
- - beatitude **4:**359ff
- - categories **5:**254
- - Christian thought **13:**451
- - cosmology **5:**983
- - Creation **5:**1067ff
- - Divine will **10:**561
- - Duns Scotus **6:**274
- - emanation and will **6:**695
- - ethical literature **6:**925; **11:**343
- - Falaquera, Shem Tov **6:**1142
- - form and matter **6:**1438
- - kabbalistic poem **16:**787
- - literature **11:**338
- - microcosm doctrine **11:**1503
- - Munk's studies **12:**526
- - mysticism **10:**513
- - Neoplatonism **12:**959; **12:**960ff
- - pantheistic tendency **7:**672
- - Plato **13:**629
- - soul **14:**172
- - soul, immortality of **15:**177
- - space and place **15:**218
- - substance and accident **15:**474
- - *Tikkun Middot ha-Nefesh* **6:**940
- - William of Auvergne **16:**517
- *illus:*
- - *Mivḥar ha-Peninim* (1484) **8:**1332
- - *Tikkun Middot ha-Nefesh* (1562) **6:**933
Gabler, Johann **4:**905
Gablonz an der Neisse (city, Bohem.), *see* JABLONEC NAD NISOU
Gabo, Naum, *see* PEVSNER, ANTON AND NAUM NEHEMIA
Gabon (rep., Afr.) **9:**439
GÁBOR, ANDOR **8:**1085
GABOR, DENNIS **7:**246
GÁBOR, IGNÁC **7:**246
Gabriel (angel), *see* MICHAEL AND GABRIEL
Gabriel, Abraham **4:**584
Gabriel, Dan, *see* GORDON, JUDAH LEIB
GABRIEL, GILBERT W. **15:**1082
GABRIEL, MORDECAI L. **1:**30
Gabriel ben Aaron Strasbourg **8:**1324
Gabriel de Téllez, *see* Tirso de Molina
GABRIELOVITCH, OSIP SOLOMONOVICH **12:**690
- orchestras **5:**1572
Gabrovski (polit., Bulg.) **4:**1486
Gacon, Samuel **8:**1325
- *illus:*
- - Pentateuch (1487) **8:**1331
GAD (Isr. tribe) **7:**246
- breastplate stone **13:**1009
- legal conditions **5:**866
- settlement **8:**579 ; **9:**115
- Transjordan **15:**1317
- Twelve Tribes **15:**1383
- *illus:*
- - text
- - banner and emblem **8:**335
GAD (deity) **7:**249
- Baal-Gad **4:**3
GAD (prophet) **7:**250
- Samuel, Book of **14:**784
Gad (Isr. archit.) **3:**362
- *illus:*
- - Israel Museum **3:**354
Gad (bot.), *see* CORIANDER
Gad, Baruch **14:**1366
Gad, Testament of (Pseudepig.), *see* PATRIARCHS, TESTAMENT OF THE TWELVE
Gada (*savora*) **14:**920
Gadal-Yama (Gedaliah; 5th cent. B.C.E., sol.) **13:**306
GADARA (Gadar, Gader; city, Gilead) **7:**251
- Alexander Yannai **8:**632
- Avdat I and Yannai **12:**74J
- *illus:*
- - synagogue (plan) **7:**249
- *see also:* DECAPOLIS; HAMMAT GADER
Gad ben Judah of Bédarrides **4:**369
Gad-Bernard, Esther **14:**1538
Gaddiel Na'ar (kab. fig.) **2:**208
Gadella, Jacob **5:**63; **12:**979
Gadish (vill., Er. Isr.) **15:**675
- statistics **1:**place list
Gadish (journ.) **1:**newsp. list
GADNA (Isr. youth mvmt.) **7:**252
- Biram, Arthur **4:**1033
- Haganah **9:**688
- Israel Defense Forces **9:**691,692
- orchestra **9:**1008; **12:**669
- *illus:*
- - text
- - Be'er Orah training camp **4:**382
Gadol, Moshe **13:**1039
Gadot (kib., Isr.) **1:**place list; **14:**1631
Gadot (shipping Co., Isr.) **9:**836
Gadres (city, Er. Isr.), *see* GAZA
GADYACH (city, Ukr.) **7:**253
Gaer, Joseph **13:**1372
GAETA (tn., It.) **7:**253
Gafat (lang.) **14:**1153
Gafeniyyah (tn., Judea), *see* GOFNAH

GAFFAREL (Gaffarellus), JACQUES 7:253
– Hebraist 8:32
Gafsa (loc., Tun.) 15:1435
– prohibited to Jews 10:88
Gagin (fam., Er. Isr.) 7:254
GAGIN, ḤAYYIM 7:254
– Wattasids 16:366
GAGIN, ḤAYYIM ABRAHAM BEN MOSES 7:254
GAGIN, SHALOM MOSES BEN ḤAYYIM ABRAHAM 7:255
Gagnier, John 8:32
GAḤAL (polit. party, Isr.) 7:255
– Begin 4:392
– General Zionists 7:385
– Ḥerut 8:401
– Histadrut elections 9:861ff
– Israel boundaries, 1967 9:413ff
– Israel historical survey 9:398ff
– politics in Israel 9:677ff
– resignation over withdrawal 9:418
– Sapir, Joseph 14:856
– *see also:* REVISIONISTS, ZIONIST
Gaieté Tunisienne, La (period.) 7:1143
Gain (*lucrum*) 12:249
Gainesville (city, Tex.) 15:1035
Gainsborough (art.) 3:540; 13:917
– *illus:*
– – Sequeira, Isaac Henrique (paint.) 13:918
Gaio, Maestro, *see* Rieti, Isaac
GAISIN (city, Ukr.) 7:255
– Auerbach family 3:842
Gaison, Abraham 16:42
Gaitskell, Dora 13:812
Gajda, Radola 5:1193
Gakon, Isaac 2:140
Galaaditis (Galaditis; reg., Transj.) 7:571; 9:120
– Seleucids 4:292
GALACTION, GALA 7:256
– Rumania 14:420
GALAI, BINYAMIN 7:256
GALANT, ELIAHU (Ilya) VLADIMIROVICH 7:256
GALANTA (tn., Cz.) 7:257
– post-war organization 5:1200
GALANTE (fam.) 7:257
Galante, Abraham (r., Syr.) 7:257
GALANTÉ, ABRAHAM (hist.) 7:258
– Turkey 15:1461
GALANTE, ABRAHAM BEN MORDECAI 7:258
GALANTE, JEDIDIAH BEN MOSES 7:258
– Gershon, Isaac 7:515
Galante, Jonathan 2:925; 7:257
Galante Joseph 7:257
Galante, Mordecai (16th cent.) 7:257
Galante, Mordecai (18th cent.) 7:257
– Syria 15:644
MORDECAI (Mokhiaḥ) BEN JONATHAN 7:259
– *illus:* text
GALANTE, MOSES BEN MORDECAI(16th cent.) 7:260
– *illus:* text
Galante, Moses ben Mordecai (18th cent.) 7:257
Galata (dist., Turk.) 9:1086; 9:1087
Galʿat Hammad (loc., Tun.) 15:1434
GALATI (Galatz; port, Rum.) 7:261
GALATIA (reg., As. M.) 7:262
– synagogues 15:604
– *see also:* ASIA MINOR
GALATINUS, PIETRO (Petrus) COLUMNA 7:262
– Hebraist 8:32
– Kabbalah and alchemy 2:545
– Reuchlin, Johannes 14:109
– *illus:*
– – *De arcanis catholicae veritatis* (1518) 8:10
Galatz (port., Rum.), *see* GALATI
Galba, Publius Servilius, *see* Servilius Galba, Publius
Galbanum (bot.) 7:263
– incense and perfumes 8:1311ff
– plant list 13:619
Galczynski, Konstanty Ildefons 13:801
Galdston, Iago 3:40
– psychiatry 13:1340
Gal-ed (reg., Transj.), *see* GILEAD
Gal'ed (kib., Isr.), *see* EVEN YIẒHAK
GALEN (Galenus), CLAUDIUS 7:263
– Asaph ha-Rofe 3:674
– fennel 6:1224
– Jews in Greek literature 7:891
– Samaritans 14:731
Galesburg (city, U.S.) 8:1256
Galewski (resist., Pol.) 15:1370
Galgal (bot.) 15:1120
Galgal (cantillation sign), *see Yeraḥ ben yomo*
Galgameš (city, Syr.), *see* CARCHEMISH
Galgóc (tn., Cz.), *see* HLOHOVEC
Galgur, Oscar 10:1502
Galia (reg., As. M.) 7:262
Galich (tn., Gal.), *see* HALICZ
GALICIA (introductory article) 7:265
GALICIA (reg., Pol.) 16:1325
– agriculture 2:405; 2:410
– anti-Semitism 3:124
– Austrian annexation 3:892
– Braude, Markus 4:1314
– Byk, Emil 4:1547
– dress 6:222
– education 10:45
– emancipation 6:712ff
– Ḥasidism 7:1392
– Haskalah 7:1434ff
– Israelitische Allianz zu Wien 2:654
– Jewish socialism 15:39; 15:46
– migrations from 16:1520
– nationalism and Jews 8:726
– petroleum and oil products 13:345
– Po'alei Zion 13:658
– Podolia 13:668
– *shtetl* 14:1471
– Volhynia 16:210
– Zionism 16:1130
– *illus:*
– – Drogobych marketplace (etch., E. M. Lilien) 6:233
– – Franz Joseph I medal 11:1170
– – *Shivviti* plaque 14:1420-1421
– *see also:* LESSER POLAND; LITHUANIA; POLAND; UKRAINE
Galicia District (Pol.) 13:767
Galicja (reg., Pol.), *see* GALICIA
Galilean Coastal Plain (reg., Er. Isr.), *see* Acre Plain
GALILEE (reg., Er. Isr.) 7:265
– Agriculture, Second Temple period 2:393
– Aramaic language 3:270; 16:1591
– Crusades 5:1139; 9:269ff
– Druze 9:924; 9:927
– early history 9:239ff
– *Gelil ha-Goyim* 16:1272
– geology 9:200ff
– hasidic aliyah 7:1392
– Hasmoneans 8:631ff
– Hebrew pronunciation 15:774; 16:1595
– human geography 9:588ff
– Israelite settlement 9:115; 9:122
– Lower, geography 9:588ff
– mishnaic Hebrew 16:1591
– mountains 9:148
– olive cultivation 12:1365
– Ottoman period 9:285ff
– Qaysites 9:261
– red heifer 13:1413
– Safed 14:626
– settlement of tribes 8:580
– Tiberias 15:1131ff
– Upper, geography 9:589ff
– *illus:*
– – Biranit land reclamation project 9:559
– – Druze population (map) 9:925
– – Ha-Shomer mounted guards 9:517
– – Kinneret early settlers 9:554
– – Lake Kinneret 9:172-173
– – National Water Cartier 11:1274
Galilee, Sea of, *see* KINNERET, LAKE
Galileo, Giovanni Battista, *see* JONA, GIOVANNI BATTISTA
GALILI, ISRAEL 7:270
– *illus:*
– – Haganah High Command 7:1070
– – Labor parties merging meeting 9:677
Galil Publishing House (Rum.) 5:453
Galinski, Heinz 4:651
GALIPAPA, ELIJAH MEVORAKH 7:271
GALIPAPA, ḤAYYIM BEN ABRAHAM 7:271
GALIPAPA, MAIMON 7:272
Galitsiya (Galizien; reg., Pol.), *see* GALICIA
Galkin, Joseph 14:145
Gall, Matei 14:424
Galla (lang.) 14:1149
Galland (Ger. pilot) 12:956
Galland, Caroline Kline 14:1083
Gallant (fam., Jam) 9:1274
GALLEGO, JOSEPH SHALOM 7:272
– paytanim 13:587
Gallei Rezayya (kab. wk.) 10:546
Gallei Ẓahal (radio station, Isr.) 9:693,1018
– television and radio 15:930; 15:931
Gallena, Elijah ben Moses 5:479
Gallery of Jewish Art (Tulsa, Okl.) 12:551
Galleys (Inq.) 8:1402
Gallia, Béla 10:1498
Gallia Judaica (hist. dictionary) 8:563
Gallicciolli, J. Baptist 8:32
Gallichi (fam.), *see* GALLICO
Gallichi, Volunio 5:125; 5:126
– psalmody 13:1330
– *illus:*
– – *Bi-Mekom Hukhan Lihyot Mishkan* 5:125
GALLICO (It. fam.) 7:272
– *illus:* text
Gallico, Abraham Jagel 13:913
Gallico, Angelo, *see* Gallico, Malachi
GALLICO, ELISHA BEN GABRIEL 7:273
– *illus:* text
Gallico, Malachi 7:272
Gallico, Samuel 7:272
Gallim (journ.) 1:newsp. list
GALLING, KURT 7:273
– Deutscher Palaestina-Verein 5:1595
GALLIPOLI (Turk. port) 7:274
– Ottoman Empire 16:1530
– Shabbetai Ẓevi 14:1231
– Zion Mule Corps 10:70; 11:1553
– *illus:*
– – Zion Mule Corps 11:1555
Gallizur (angel), *see* RAZIEL
Gallo, *see* Sarfati, Samuel
Gallo, Giuseppe, *see* Sarfati, Joseph
Gallus Caesar 16:281
Gallus, Cestius, *see* CESTIUS GALLUS
Gallus, Gaius Aelius 3:234
GALON (kib. Isr.) 7:275
– statistics 1:place list
Galperin, A. 13:819
Galperin, Simon H., Jr. 16:476
Galpern, Myer 7:603
Galsworthy, John 6:782
– Wandering Jew 16:262
Galter, Samuel 5:591
Galt-Preston (tn., Ont.) 12:1408
Galui, ha-(wk., Kimḥi), *see Sefer ha-Galui*
GALUT (exile) 7:275
– *Contents:*
– – The Concept 7:275
– – Diaspora Pattern 7:275
– – Second Temple and Mishnah Period 7:277
– – Ideology in the Medieval World 7:281
– – Ideology in Modern Times 7:292
– Concepts
– – Amos 2:887
– – ingathering of exiles 8:1373
– – kabbalistic doctrine 10:617ff
– – prophets' attitude 5:1560
– – redemption and 14:5
– – remnant of Israel 14:70
– – Shekhinah and Hasidic thought 7:1406
– – Spanish *anusim* 3:173
– Views
– – Borochov, Ber 4:1255
– – Dubnow, Simon 6:253ff
– – Haskalah 7:1445
– – Judah Loew ben Bezalel 10:378
– – Reform Judaism 10:394
– – *Shevet Yehudah* 8:1204
– – Zhitlowsky, Chaim 16:1009
– Miscellaneous
– – influence on language 16:1361
– – Lost Tribes 15:1003
– *see also:* DIASPORA; EXILE, ASSYRIAN; EXILE, BABYLONIAN; EXPULSIONS; JEWISH IDENTITY
GALVESTON PLAN (stlmt. project, U.S.) 7:294
– Hilfsverein der Deutschen Juden 8:480
– Houston 8:1050
– territorialism 15:1020
– Texas 15:1034
Galvez, Josè 10:1455
GAMA, GASPAR DA 7:295
– Vasco da Gama 8:1355; 15:1349
Gama, Vasco da 7:295; 8:1355; 15:1349
– Zacuto, Abraham 16:904
GAMALA (city, Golan) 7:295
– Chares 5:338
– Nabateans 12:743
Gamaliel (15th cnet., It. fig.) 14:248
GAMALIEL (HA-ZAKEN), RABBAN (1st cen. C.E., nasi, Er. Isr.) 7:295
– Job Targum 5:1401
– Johanan ben Zakkai 9:241
– letters from Sanhedrin 11:57
– Paul 13:190; 13:366
– sages 14:643
GAMALIEL, RABBAN II (of Jabneh; 1/2 cent., nasi, Er. Isr.) 7:296
– Akiva ben Joseph 2:489,490
– apologetics 3:191
– Baitos ben Zonin 4:111
– benedictions 4:485
– *Birkat ha-Minim* 8:1364
– calendar 5:49
– disputation on idolatry 6:81
– Eleazar ben Azariah 6:586
– Flavius Clemens and Domitilla

6:1338
- friendship with Onkelos **12:**1406
- Hellenism **8:**297
- history chart **8:**766-767
- presidency **9:**242ff
- Tabi the slave **15:**690
- *illus:*
- - text
- - teaching students **7:**1085
- *see also:* NASI
GAMALIEL III, RABBAN (be-Rabbi; 3rd cent., nasi, Er. Isr.) **7:**298
- history chart **8:**766-767
- study and labor **10:**1322
GAMALIEL IV, RABBAN (3rd. cent., nasi, Er. Isr.) **7:**298
GAMALIEL V, RABBAN (4th. cent., nasi, Er. Isr.) **7:**298
- history chart **8:**766-767
- letters **11:**57
- Libanius **8:**655
GAMALIEL VI, RABBAN (4/5 cent., nasi, Er. Isr.) **7:**298
- deposition **9:**257
- history chart **8:**766-767
- Theodosius II **15:**1101
Gamaliel ben Moses **13:**581
GAMALIEL BEN PEDAHZUR **7:**299
GAMARNIK, YAN BORISOVICH **11:**1573
- Russia **14:**460
Gamart (loc., Tun.) **15:**1430
Gambetta, Léon **11:**65
Gambia (state, W. Afr.) **9:**439
GAMBLING **7:**299
- *asmakhta* **3:**753
- banishment punishment **13:**1389
- card playing **5:**168
- fines **6:**1288
- imprisonment **8:**1302
- prohibited in Koran **10:**1198
- reclaim of losses **12:**1312
- supervision **13:**796
- testimony **16:**586
- *see also:* GAMES; LOTS
GAMES **7:**303
- Ḥanukkah **6:**1393
- *illus:* text
- *see also:* GAMBLING; HUNTING
GAMES, ABRAM **3:**600
- *illus:*
- - Concentration and Extermination Camps (poster) **5:**79
- - emblems and posters **3:**624
Gam le-Mar (Heb. greeting) **7:**916
Gammad (journ.) **1:**newsp. list
GAMORAN, EMANUEL **7:**308
Gamoran, M.G. **5:**451
Gamsy, Dennis **15:**307
Gamzon, Robert **7:**35
- *Maquis* **13:**148
- scouting movement **14:**1038ff
- *illus:*
- - partisans **13:**148
GAMZU, ḤAYYIM **7:**308
Gance, Abel **12:**453
Gancheshty (tn., Bess.), *see* KOTOVSKOYE
Gand (city, Belg.), *see* GHENT
Gandj Danesh (educ. mvmt.), *see* OẒAR HA-TORAH
Gandoor, Samuel **12:**863
GANDZ, SOLOMON **7:**309
Gan Eden, see GARDEN OF EDEN
Gan Eden (tract.) **13:**84
Ganehn, Sholom Izrailovich **6:**464
Ganganelli, Giovanni Vincenzo Antonio, *see* CLEMENT XIV
Ganges Valley (Ind.) **7:**1493; **13:**78
Gan ha-Darom (mosh., Isr.) **1:**place list
Gan ha-Sheloshah (nat. park., Isr.) **12:**879
Gan ha-Shomron (stlmt., Isr.) **1:**place list
Gan ha-Yerek journ.) **1:**newsp. list
GAN ḤAYYIM (mosh., Isr.) **7:**309
- statistics **1:**newsp. list
Gan Na'ul (philol. wk.) **16:**461
Gannei Am (mosh., Isr.) **1:** place list
Gannei Tikvah (stlmt., Isr.) **1:**place list
GANNEI YEHUDAH (mosh., Isr.) **7:**309
- statistics **1:**place list
Gannei Yoḥanan (Yonah; mosh., Isr.) **1:**place list
Gannenu (publ.) **1:**newsp. list
Gannot (mosh., Isr.) **1:**place list
Gannot Hadar (stlmt., Isr.) **1:**place list
Gan Peraḥim (journ.) **1:**newsp. list
Gans (fam., Ger.) **7:**1279
GANS, BIRD STEIN **7:**309
GANS, DAVID BEN SOLOMON **7:**310
- history **8:**697; **11:**349
- history chart **8:**766-767
- messianism **11:**1409
- *Ẓemaḥ David* **8:**268, 559
- *illus:*
- - text
- - tombstone, Czechoslovak stamp (1967) **5:**1198
GANS, EDUARD **7:**311
Gans, Herbert **15:**63,68
Gans, Isaac **11:**1551
Gans, Zalman ben Zeligman **7:**337
Gan Sha'ashu'im (period.) **5:**432
GAN SHELOMO (kib., Isr.) **7:**312
- statistics **1:**place list
GAN SHEMU'EL (kib., Isr.) **7:**313
- *illus:*
- - text
- - Shavuot celebrations **6:**1314
GAN SHOMRON (mosh., Isr.) **7:**313
GANSO, JOSEPH **7:**313
Gan Sorek (mosh., Isr.) **1:**place list
Gantz, Mieczyslaw **11:**1204
Gan va-Nof (journ.) **1:**newsp. list
Ganya (tn., Hung.) **5:**1591
GAN YAVNEH (mosh., Isr.) **7:**313
- statistics **1:**place list
Gan Yoshiyyah (mosh., Isr.) **1:**place list
Ganz, Benjamin **10:**739
Ganz, Emil **13:**482
Ganz, Herman **10:**739
Ganz, Isaac **10:**1154
GANZFRIED, SOLOMON BEN JOSEPH **7:**313
GAON (acad. head, Babyl.) **7:**315
- *Contents:*
- - Sura and Pumbedita **7:**315
- - Baghdad after the Geonic Period **7:**321
- - Gaonate in Ereẓ Israel **7:**321
- - Damascus and Egypt **7:**323
- - Other Countries **7:**324
- General
- - Cairo *genizah* **16:**1336
- - history chart **8:**766-767
- - Islamic codification **9:**103
- - Maimonides on gaonate **11:**745
- - mysticism **10:**508ff
- The Institution
- - autonomy, judicial **3:**929
- - Babylonian community **5:**814
- - communal standing **13:**1448
- - exilarchs **6:**1028ff
- - genealogy **7:**382
- - national leadership **8:**696ff
- - rabbinical authority **3:**910
- - Saadiah Gaon **14:**543
- - seals **14:**1074
- - yeshivah title **16:**762
- Activities
- - Jerusalem Talmud **15:**775
- - laws on gentiles **7:**1163
- - legal development **12:**122
- - literature **12:**132
- - liturgy **11:**395
- - Mt. of Olives proclamation **12:**483ff
- - polemics **13:**791
- - prayer books **13:**985ff
- - responsa **14:**84ff
- - *takkanot* **15:**721
- - *tosafot* **15:**1278ff
- - tradition **15:**1311
- *see also:* PUMBEDITA; SURA
GAON, MOSES DAVID **7:**324
GAON, SOLOMON **7:**325
Gaon of Vilna, *see* ELIJAH BEN SOLOMON ZALMAN
Gaponov, Boris **7:**427
Gara (bloodletter) **4:**1119
Gara, Giovanni di, *see* DI GARA, GIOVANNI
Garai, Janos **12:**1376
Garamond, Claude **10:**1547
Garbell, Alexander **13:**117
Garber, Joseph **15:**310
GARBER, MICHAEL **7:**326
Garcia, Alvar **13:**4
García, Benito **10:**1359
Garcia Blanco, Antonio **8:**32
García de la Huerta, Vicente **15:**250
Garcia de Orta, *see* ORTA, GARCIA DE
Garcian, Vidal **4:**1531
Gard, Isaac **9:**105
Gard, Jacob **9:**105
GARDEN OF EDEN **7:**326
- Abraham **2:**165
- Adam **2:**234
- entry of righteous **15:**175
- etymology **13:**78
- Messiah **6:**881
- mystical speculation **10:**497
- oil of life **12:**1347
- Philo **13:**413
- Tigris **15:**1139
- Zohar **16:**1195
- *illus:*
- - text
- - Adam and Eve **4:**856; **6:**981
- - "Garden of Delights" (Hieronymus Bosch) **2:**243
- *see also:* ADAM; EVE; OLAM HA-BA; PARADISE
Garden of God, *see* GARDEN OF EDEN
Garden Tomb (Jer.) **9:**1459
- *illus:*
- - Jesus' burial place **9:**1461
- - Protestant tourists visit **9:**916
Garden warbler (ornith.) **6:**30
Gardiner, Sir Alan **2:**674
Gardner (tn., U.S.) **11:**782
Gardner, Isabella Stewart **4:**602
Gardner, Nicholas **5:**169
GARDOSH, KARIEL (Charles; "Dosh") **7:**327
- editorial cartoons **5:**219
- *illus:*
- - political cartoon **5:**217
Gareb (bib. loc.) **11:**1483
Gareš (cantillation sign), *see Gereš*
Garfiel, Evelyn **10:**669
GARFIELD, JOHN (Jules) **12:**468
Garfield, Sid **13:**1361
Garfinkel, Jack **15:**303
Garfunkel, Beni **15:**445
Garfunkel, L. **11:**382
- *Yidishe Shtime, Di* **16:**833
Garganay (ornith.) **6:**30
Garganin (Sov. rep.), *see* GEORGIA
Garibaldi, Giuseppe **4:**275
Garigue (flora) **9:**221
Garis (loc., Er. Isr.) **10:**887
Garji (fam., Er. Isr.) **10:**437
Garji, Mattathias **2:**327
Garji, R. **8:**340
GARLIC (bot.) **7:**328
- food **6:**1416
- plant list **13:**619
- *illus:* text
GARLOCK, JOHN HENRY **7:**329
Garman-Horodisch, Alice **4:**1219
Garme (indirect damage), *see* GERAMA AND GARME
Garment Industry, *see* TAILORING; TEXTILES
Garments, rending of, *see* KERI'AH
GARMISON, SAMUEL **7:**329
- Shabbetai Ẓevi **14:**1225
Garmon (N. Afr. fam.), *see* DARMON
Garmu, Bet (fam., Temple bakers), *see* BET GARMU
Garnier, Robert **12:**917
Garrett, Visconde de Almeida **15:**251
Garrod, Dorothy **3:**45; **16:**237
Garša (cantillation sign), *see Gereš*
GARSTANG, JOHN **7:**329
Gartel, Moshe **15:**314
Garter, Thomas **15:**533
GARTNER, LLOYD P. **1:**30
Garvey, Marcus **9:**433
Garvey, Robert **5:**451
GARY (city, U.S.) **7:**330
GARY, ROMAIN **7:**330
Garzias, Dominicus **8:**32
Garzon, B. **11:**684
Gas chamber, *see* GASSING
GASCONY (prov., Fr.) **7:**331
Gashmu (k., Kedar), *see* Geshem
GAS IN ISRAEL **9:**393; **9:**576; **9:**793
GASKELL, SONJA **7:**331
Gasom, ibn (N. Afr. schol.), *see* Ibn Gasom
Gaspar d'Almeida, *see* GAMA, GASPAR DA
Gaspar de Leão, *see* LEÃO, GASPAR DE
Gasparri, Cardinal **16:**75; **16:**76
Gassel, Samuel **16:**158
GASSER, HERBERT SPENCER **7:**332
GASSING (Holocaust) **16:**1332
- camps (concentration and extermination) **5:**82ff
- race, theory of **13:**1485
Gassiteron (metal), *see* Tin
Gassmann, Florian **10:**461
GASSNER, JOHN **7:**332
"Gas Station" (sculp., G. Segal) **14:**1106
Gastabled, Franciscus, *see* Vatable, François
GASTER, MOSES **7:**332
- book collection **4:**975
- history chart **8:**766-767
- Rumania **14:**399
- Rumanian literature **14:**421
- *illus:* text
Gaster, Theodor Herzl **7:**333
Gaster Bible, First (illum. ms.) **8:***fcg* 951
Gaster Bible, Second (illum. Bib.) **8:**1263
- *illus:* **4:**953
Gastonia (city, N.C.) **12:**1220
GASTON-MARIN, GHEORGHE **13:**826
Gastroenterology **11:**1200
Gasur (anc. city, Iraq), *see* NUZI
GAT (kib., Isr.) **7:**334
- statistics **1:**place list
Gataker, Thomas **8:**32
Gategno, Abraham **14:**1266
Gategno, Benvenisti **2:**792
- *see also:* Gatigno, . . .
Gatekeepers (Temple) **10:**1191
Gatenio, Joseph **13:**17
Gatenyo (Turk. fam.) **11:**1393

Gate of the Lady Mary (Jer.), *see* Lions Gate
Gate of Mercy (Jer.) **9:**1434; **15:**964
- *illus:*
- - two views **9:**1429,1430
Gate of the Pillar (Gate of the Column; Jer.), *see* Damascus Gate
Gate of Repentance (Jer.) **9:**1434
Gateshead Foundation for Torah (soc.) **7:**335
GATESHEAD ON TYNE (tn., Eng.) **7:**334
- yeshivah **6:**448,450,763
- *illus:*
- - text
- - Talmud students **6:**421
- *see also:* NEWCASTLE-UPON-TYNE
Gates of Jerusalem **9:**1433ff
GATH (cities, Er. Isr.) **7:**335
- Achish **2:**210
- Ramleh **13:**1540
- *see also:* GITTAIM
Gath-Gittaim (tn., Er. Isr.) **7:**335
GATH-HEPHER (tn., Er. Isr.) **7:**336
- Hepher **8:**333
GATH-RIMMON (city, Er. Isr.) **7:**336
- Ramleh **13:**1540
GATIGNO (fam.) **7:**336
- *see also:* Gategno, . . .
Gatigno, Abraham ben Benveniste **7:**337
Gatigno, Benveniste (Mercado) **7:**337
Gatigno, Benveniste ben Moses **7:**337
Gatigno, Eliakim ben Isaac **7:**337
Gatigno, Ezra ben Solomon **7:**336
Gatigno, Ḥayyim Abraham ben Benveniste **7:**337
Gatigno, Ḥayyim ben Samuel **7:**337
Gatigno, Isaac ben Eliakim **7:**337
Gatigno, Judah ben Benveniste **7:**337
Gatigno, Samuel ben Judah **7:**337
Gato, Juan, *see* ÁLVAREZ GATO, JUAN
Gatooma (city, Rhod.) **14:**148
Gat Rimmon (stlmt., Isr.) **1:**place list
Gattendorf (stlmt., Aus.) **7:**112
Gatti, A. **9:**1107
Gatzert, Bailey **14:**1082
Gaucher's Disease **14:**1501
Gaudia, Barthol. Valverdio **8:**32
Gaudiocus (9th cent., Fr.) **5:**158
Gauguin, Eugène Henri Paul **5:**323; **5:**1460
Gaul, *see* FRANCE
Gaulanitis (prov., Er. Isr.) **4:**291
- *Provincia Judaea* **9:**239
Gaulmin, Gilbert **8:**32 **14:**1583
Gaum, Percy **11:**998
GAUNSE, JOACHIM **7:**337
- metals **11:**1438
Gaunz (fam. name), *see* GUENZBURG
Gauss, Karl Friedrich **9:**1226
Gautier (Walterius; 10th cent., apos.) **12:**1469
Gavel, Heinrich **16:**1331
Gavish, Yeshayahu **13:**48
- Six-Day War **14:**1629
GAVISON (Gavishon; Sp. fam.) **7:**338
- Tlemcen **15:**1173
Gavison, Abraham (15th cent. Alg.) **7:**338
Gavison, Abraham (16th cent., poet, Alg.) **7:**338
Gavison, Abraham (18th cent., publ.) **7:**338
Gavison, Abraham ben Jacob (physic. Alg.) **2:**623; **7:**338
- paytan list **13:**575
Gavison, Jacob (16th cent., poet) **7:**338
Gavison, Jacob ben Joseph (15th cent., physic.) **7:**338
Gavison, Joseph **7:**338
Gavison, Meir **7:**338
Gavison, Moses **7:**338
Gavison, Solomon **7:**338ff
Gavison, Vidal **7:**338
Gavla (stlmt., Er. Isr.) **8:**796
Gavnunim (mt.), *see* SINAI, MOUNT
Gavronsky, Helen, *see* SUZMAN, HELEN
Gavronsky, Liebe Miriam **13:**56
GAVSIE, CHARLES **7:**338
GAWLER, GEORGE **7:**338
- settlement plan **9:**299
- Zionism **16:**1154
Gawler, John Cox **7:**339
Gay, Miriam **13:**1340
GAY (Froehlich), PETER JACK (Joachim) **7:**339
Gaya (tn., Morav., Cz.), *see* KYJOV
Gaʿyah (gram. sign) **16:**1451
Gaysin (city, Ukr.), *see* GAISIN
GAZA (city, Er. Isr.) **7:**339
- History
- - Aretas and Yannai **12:**741
- - battles, 1099-1291 **9:**269; **9:**271
- - Costobar **5:**990
- - eleventh century **9:**264
- - Hellenistic Roman period **8:**626
- - Mamluk period **9:**277; **9:**278; **9:**280
- - Ottoman period **9:**283*ff*
- - Samaritans **14:**733; **14:**734; **14:**737
- - Samson **14:**772
- - Seleucid battle **14:**1123
- - Shabbetai Ẓevi **14:**1224
- - synagogue **15:**598ff
- Israel
- - settlement south of **12:**929
- - Sinai Campaign **14:**1607
- - Six-Day War **9:**408; **14:**1635
- - U.N. censure **15:**1553
- *illus:*
- - text
- - Mamluk architecture **9:**275; **11:**835
- *see also:* GAZA STRIP
Gazai (savora), *see* Gada
Gazaria (Crimea) **5:**1104
GAZA STRIP **7:**343
- agriculture **9:**784
- Arab refugees **9:**451; **9:**466
- armistice agreement **3:**481; **9:**321
- fisheries **9:**787
- health services **9:**993
- population **9:**492; **9:**575ff **9:**1034
- Sinai Campaign **9:**389ff; **14:**1607
- Six-Day War **14:**1629
- terrorism **9:**412
- U.N. negotiations **15:**1552ff
- *illus:*
- - text
- - education, 1967-70 (table) **9:**1037
- - external trade 1968-69 (table) **9:**1037
- - mobile medical unit **9:**987
- - U.N.E.F. evacuation, 1967 **9:**406
- *see also:* GAZA
GAZELLE **7:**345
- dietary laws **6:**31
- fauna of Israel **9:**225f
- *illus:*
- - text
- - *Pesaro Maḥzor* **11:**735
- - Song of Songs **15:**145
- *see also:* DEER
Gazelle Nose, Land of (reg.), *see* Land of Gazelle Nose
Gazeta de Amsterdam (period.) **2:**899; **13:**1023; **13:**1034
- *illus:*
- - masthead (1675) **13:**1024
Gazeta Romana Evreească (newsp., Rum.) **14:**398
Gazetta del Popolo (newsp., It.) **3:**294
Gazette de Jérusalem (period.) **7:**1479; **13:**1041
Gaziantep (city, Turk.), *see* ʿAyntāb
GAZIT (kib., Isr.) **7:**346
- statistics **1:**place list
Gazit (journ.) **1:**newsp. list
GDANSK (Danzig; port, Pol.) **7:**346
- archives **3:**387
- Hep! Hep! riots **8:**331
- museum **12:**538
- slave trade **14:**1662
Ge'ah (mosh., Isr.) **1:**place list
Ge'alyah (mosh., Isr.) **1:**place list
GEBA (anc. city, Benjamin) **7:**348
- *see also:* GIBEAH
GEBA (anc. city, Kutim) **7:**350
Gebal (city-state, Cana.) **5:**100
Gebal-Byblos (tn., Leb.), *see* JUBAYL
Gebalim (loc., Croatia) **16:**870
GEBA-PARASHIM (city, Er. Isr.) **7:**349
Gebelev, M. **12:**56
Gebetbuch (Hamburg prayer bk.), *see Hamburg Gebetbuch*
Gebhardi, Brandanus **8:**32
GEBIHA OF BE-KATIL (amora) **7:**350
GEBINI (1st. cent., Temple offic.) **7:**350
Gebini ben Harsom (mid. fig.) **6:**599
GEBIRTIG, MORDECAI **7:**350
GECKO (reptile) **7:**350
- dietary laws **6:**36
- fauna of Israel **9:**226
- *illus:* text
GEDALGE, ANDRÉ **12:**690
GEDALIAH (bib. fig.) **7:**351
- Ahikam **2:**460
- Exile, Babylonian **6:**1038
- governor of Judeans **8:**609
- history chart **8:**766-767
- in the Arts **9:**1360
- *illus:* text
Gedaliah, Fast of **6:**1195; **7:**352 **10:**779
Gedaliah (5th cent.B.C.E., sol.), *see* Gadal-Yama
GEDALIAH, JUDAH **7:**352
- Lisbon **11:**303
GEDALIAH, JUDAH BEN MOSES **7:**352
GEDALIAH HA-LEVI (kab.) **7:**353
GEDALIAH OF SIEMIATYCZE **7:**353
- Jerusalem **9:**1440
- Siemiatycze **14:**1512
- travels **15:**1353
GEDDES, ALEXANDER **7:**353
Geddes, Sir Patrick **15:**922
Geder (city, Gilead) **7:**251
Geder (city, Simeon), *see* GEDOR
GEDERAH (mosh., Isr.) **7:**354
- Bilu **4:**1002
- Hildesheimer, Azriel **8:**477
- history chart (1884) **8:**766-767
- ICA **10:**47
- statistics **1:**place list
- *illus:*
- - loading wheat **9:**517
GEDERAH, GEDEROTH (places, Er. Isr.) **7:**354
- Gedor **7:**355
Gedi (zodiac sign), *see* Capricornus
Gediliah, Abraham **7:**355
GEDILIAH, ABRAHAM BEN SAMUEL **7:**354
GEDOR (city, Er. Isr.) **7:**355
Gedudei Noar (Ẓahal), *see* GADNA
GEDUD HA-AVODAH (orgn.) **7:**355
- Ha-Shomer **9:**683
- Jewish labor organization **9:**848ff
- Sadeh, Yiẓḥak **14:**623
- youth movements **9:**976
Gedud Meginnei ha-Safah (orgn., Isr.) **9:**1000
Gedullah (kab. conc.) **10:**570ff
Gee, Robert **11:**1553
Geelong (city, Austr.) **3:**878; **11:**1285
Geese **12:**1533
Ge'ez (Eth. lang.) **6:**943
- Falashas **6:**1149
- Semitic languages **14:**1153
Gefen (mosh, Isr.) **1:**place list
Gefen, Ḍov **7:**1066
GEFFEN, TOBIAS **7:**356
- Atlanta **3:**825
Geffin, Aaron ("Okey") **15:**313
- *illus:*
- - rugby **15:**312
GEGELLO, ALEXANDER IVANOVICH **3:**363
Ge-Harashim (bib. place) **10:**906; **11:**619
GEHAZI (bib. fig.) **7:**356
- Naaman **12:**734
Geheime Staatspolizei, *see* GESTAPO
GEHINNOM (Gehenna) **7:**357
- Abaddon **2:**30
- eschatology **6:**875
- Jerusalem topography **9:**1515
- Judah boundary **10:**330
- Kidron **10:**988
- Moloch **12:**233
- mystical speculation **10:**497
- necropolis **9:**1398
- paradise **13:**82*ff*
- soul of wicked **15:**175
- *see also:* AFTERLIFE; BEATITUDE; NETHERWORLD; OLAM HA-BA
Geidels (fam.), *see* JEITELES
Geier, Martin, *see* Geyer, Martin
GEIGER, ABRAHAM **7:**357
- apologetics **3:**199
- articles of faith **3:**659
- commandments, reasons for **5:**789*ff*
- Eger, Solomon **6:**473
- Einhorn, David **6:**531
- Hirsch, S. R. **8:**508
- history chart **8:**766-767
- Jewish scholarship **16:**574
- mishnaic Hebrew **16:**1592
- Nassau **12:**841
- Oral Law **12:**1442
- Orthodoxy **12:**1489
- prayer books **13:**990
- rabbinical conferences **13:**1460
- rabbi type struggle **13:**1454
- Reform Judaism **14:**24ff
- Tiktin, Solomon **15:**1140
- Torah **15:**1242
- Wiesbaden **16:**507
- *illus:*
- - portrait **8:**718
GEIGER, BERNHARD **7:**360
GEIGER, LAZARUS (Eliezer Solomon) **7:**360
Geiger, Leo **2:**524
GEIGER, LUDWIG **7:**360
- *Allgemeine Zeitung des Judentums* **2:**648
GEIGER, MORITZ **7:**361
GEIGER, SOLOMON ZALMAN (ben Abraham) **7:**362
Geigerman, Bonnie **15:**306
Gei Ḥizzayon (wk.) **9:**1267
- Abraham Jagel **4:**1011
- fiction, Hebrew **6:**1269
Gei Oni (mosh., Er. Isr.), *see* ROSH PINNAH

GEIRINGER, KARL **12:**690
Geis, Gilbert **5:**1110
Geismar, Alain **12:**1034
Geismar, Gédéon **11:**1562
Geisser, Irving **15:**319
Geissmann, Raymond **15:**1536
Geitler, Leopold, *see* Jeiteles, Leopold
Geitler, Sigmund Christian, *see* Jeiteles, Samuel
Geitlin, Gabriel **8:**32
Gejerus, Martin **8:**32
Geker, N. **14:**1487
GELASIUS I (pope) **7:**362
- *Job, Testament of* **10:**130
- medicine **11:**1183
- popes **13:**852
Gelb, Adhémar **7:**749; **13:**1344
GELB, IGNACE JAY **7:**362
Gelb, Jan **3:**605
Gelbart, M. **6:**912
Gelbe, H. **8:**32
GELBER (Can. fam.) **7:**363
Gelber, Arthur E. **7:**363; **15:**1264
Gelber, Edward Elisha **7:**363
- *illus:*
- - Bonds Drive function, Montreal **5:**110
- - Zionist Organization of Canada convention **16:**1110
GELBER, JACK **15:**1578; **15:**1580
Gelber, Jacob, *see* EICHENBAUM, JACOB
Gelber, Lionel Morris **7:**363
Gelber, Louis **7:**363
Gelber, Marvin **7:**363; **15:**1264
Gelber, Moses **7:**363
GELBER, NATHAN MICHAEL **7:**363
- archives **3:**388
Gelber, Sholome Michael **7:**363
Gelber, Sylva **5:**112; **7:**363
GELBHAUS, SIGMUND (Joshua Samuel) **7:**364
GELBRUN, ARTUR **12:**690
Gelder, Leon van **6:**464
Gelderland (prov., Neth.) **3:**485; **3:**486; **12:**974
Gelderland, Duke of **3:**485
Geldern (tn., Ger.) **5:**1137
Geldern, Gottschalk Van **7:**365
Geldern, Joseph Jacob (Juspa) Van **7:**365
Geldern, Lazarus Van **7:**365
GELDERN, SIMON VON **7:**364
- Cairo *genizah* **16:**1334
- family **7:**365
- *illus:* text
GELDERN, VAN (fam.) **7:**365
- Court Jews
Geleitbriefe (letter of safe-conduct) **14:**1013
Geleitzoll (tax, Rus.) **10:**1589
GELERTER, LUDWIG LITMAN **7:**365
GELFAND, IZRAIL MOISEVICH **11:**1124
GELFOND, ALEKSANDR OSIPOVICH **11:**1125
Gelilah (rolling together of Torah scroll), *see* HAGBAHAH, GELILAH
Gelil ha-Goyim (reg., Er. Isr.), *see* GALILEE
Geliloth (place, Er. Isr.) **7:**573
GELIL YAM (kib., Isr.) **7:**366
Gelin, Daniel **15:**1055
Gell, Rose, *see* JACOBS, ROSE GELL
Geller, Eleazar **7:**806; **16:**351
Geller, L. **11:**563
Geller, Samuel **16:**537
Geller, Sandor **12:**1376; **15:**299
Geller, Todros **4:**1219
GELLER, YEFIM PETROVICH **5:**408
Geller, Yonah H. **13:**911
GELLÉRI, ANDOR ENDRE **7:**366
Gellert, Imre **12:**1375; **15:**309
GELLÉRT, OSZKÁR **8:**1085
Gelles, M. S. **16:**41
GELLMAN, LEON **7:**366
- *illus:*
- - protest against 1940 White Paper **15:**1632
GELL-MANN, MURRAY **7:**367
GELLNER, FRANTIŠEK **7:**367
GELMAN, MANUEL **7:**368
Gelman, Polina **11:**1558; **14:**479
GELNHAUSEN (tn., Ger.) **7:**368
GELSENKIRCHEN (city, Ger.) **7:**368
GEMARA (tal.) **7:**368
- *see also:* TALMUD
Gemar Ḥatimah Tovah (greeting) **7:**916
GEMARIAH SON OF HILKIAH (bib. fig.) **7:**369
- Hilkiah **8:**481
GEMARIAH SON OF SHAPHAN (bib. fig.) **7:**369
Gemariah son of Ḥizziliahu **7:**369
GEMATRIA (hermeneutical rule) **7:**369
- Abd al-Ḥaqq al-Islāmī **2:**53
- *aggadah* **2:**356
- alchemy, Christian **2:**545
- *Aleinu le-Shabbe'ah* **2:**557ff
- apologists' use of **3:**195
- *Baraita of 32 Rules* **4:**195
- Baruch Togarmi **4:**267
- Hebrew book titles **8:**75
- Ibn Abi Zimra **5:**1358
- Jewish mysticism **10:**510,516,531
- mathematics **11:**1122
- Muhammad **9:**101
- Satan **14:**904
- word games **7:**307
- *illus:*
- - letters as numerical signs **2:**743
- *see also:* ABBREVIATIONS; NOTARIKON; NUMBERS, TYPICAL AND IMPORTANT
Gemeindeblatt (newsp.), *see Berliner Juedisches Gemeindeblatt*
GEMEN (tn., Ger.) **7:**374
GEMILUT ḤASADIM (charity) **7:**374
- *ḥevra kaddisha* **8:**442
- sages on **14:**645
- *Shekhinah* **14:**1351
- sick, visiting of **14:**1496
- *see also:* CHARITY; HOSPITALITY; POOR, PROVISION FOR THE
Gemilut Hasadim Society (print. firm, Gr.) **14:**708
Geminder, Bedrich **14:**1653; **14:**708
Gemini (zodiac sign) **16:**1191
- *illus:* **14:**1624
Gemirat ha-da'at (leg. conc.) **12:**18; **12:**25; **15:**525
Gemmeker, A. K. **16:**467
Gemmingen, Christopher von **15:**740
Gems, *see* PRECIOUS STONES AND JEWELRY
Gemser, B. **15:**208
Gemul (fin. co., Isr.) **8:**539; **9:**867
Genadios (bp., Salonika) **8:**915
Genazim (inst., Isr.) **10:**1260
- archives **3:**395
- Burla, Yehuda **4:**1524
Genazim (period., Isr.) **15:**56; **16:**653
- statistics **1:**newsp. list
- *see also: Yediot Genazim*
Gendelman (cmty. ldr., Rus.) **10:**996
Genealogies, Scroll of (wk.), *see Ahimaaz, Scroll of*
GENEALOGY **7:**377
- *Contents:*
- - In the Bible **7:**377
- - Second Temple Period **7:**379
- - Modern Period **7:**383
- Aaronides **2:**20
- Benjamin's tribe **4:**523
- Ezra **8:**617ff
- firstborn **6:**1307
- settlement of tribes **8:**581
- Twelve Tribes **15:**1384
- *tables:*
- - Aaronides **2:**19
- - Aboab **2:**91
- - Abrabanel **2:**103
- - Abulafia **2:**190
- - Adler **2:**269
- - Ahikar **2:**461
- - Ahimaaz **2:**463
- - Alkabez **2:**635
- - Almosnino **2:**668
- - Anau **2:**935
- - Arnstein **3:**489
- - Auerbach **3:**841
- - Azulai **3:**1017
- - Belkind **4:**439
- - Benveniste and Nasi **12:**838
- - Bischoffsheim **4:**1056
- - Calebites **7:**379
- - Cardozo **5:**162
- - Carlebach **5:**182
- - Carvajal **5:**220
- - Cavalleria, de la **5:**263
- - Chao (Kaifeng) **5:**335
- - Cohen (Waley) **5:**659
- - David, House of **5:**1341
- - Disraeli **6:**109
- - Elijah Menahem ben Moses **6:**658
- - Ephraim (German family) **6:**810
- - Eskeles **6:**895
- - exilarchs **6:**1024-1026
- - Franks **7:**106
- - Goldsmid **7:**735
- - Gomperz **7:**771
- - Gratz **7:**858
- - Guggenheim **7:**967
- - Hart **7:**1353
- - ḥasidic dynasties **1:**has. table
- - Hasmoneans **7:**1457
- - Herod, House of **8:**377
- - Herzl **8:**409
- - Israel Ba'al Shem Tov **9:**1051
- - Itzig **9:**1151
- - Jaffe **9:**1259
- - Jeiteles **9:**1331
- - Kook **9:**1259
- - Levi (Bet ha-Levi) **11:**76
- - Mendelssohn **11:**1325
- - Montefiore-Sebag-Montefiore **12:**1273
- - Nathan (U.S.) **12:**849
- - Rashi **13:**1559
- - Rothschild **14:**335
- - Ruzhin **14:**529
- - Sassoon **14:**897
- - Schneersohn **14:**981
- - scribal family, Kingdom of Judea **14:**1042
- - Sofer **15:**76
- - Solis-Cohen **15:**96
- - Soloveichik **15:**127
- - Soncino **15:**141
- - "Table of Nations" **12:**885
- - Toledano **15:**1195
- - Yellin **16:**736
- *see also:* FAMILY; YUḤASIN
GÉNÉBRARD, GILBERT **7:**383
- Albo, Joseph **2:**537
- Antwerp Polyglot Bible **13:**614
- Hebraist **8:**32
- *Seder Olam Rabbah* **14:**1093
General Archive of German Jewry, *see* Gesamtarchiv der Deutschen Juden
General Association of Native Israelites (Rum.) **14:**390
General Cooperative Association of Jewish Labor in Palestine, *see* ḤEVRAT HA-OVEDIM
General Federation of Labor in Israel, *see* HISTADRUT
General Gouvernement (Nazi-occupied Pol.) **8:**498; **13:**763ff
General Jewish Council (U.S.A.) **2:**825; **10:**66
General Jewish Historical Archives, *see* Jewish Historical General Archives
General Jewish Workers' Union, *see* BUND
General Mortgage Bank Ltd. (Isr.) **9:**824,827
General Pinedo (tn., Arg.) **3:**430
Generalproveditеur, *see* COURT JEWS
General Roca (clny., Arg.) **3:**430
GENERAL ZIONISTS (party) **7:**384
- Ḥerut movement **8:**401
- Israel survey **9:**382ff
- origin **16:**1099
- Poland **13:**749
- Sapir, Joseph **14:**856
- Va'ad Le'ummi boycott **16:**50
- workers' faction in Histadrut **9:**861
- *see also:* HA-OVED HA-ẒIYYONI
GENESIS, BOOK OF **7:**386
- *Contents:*
- - Contents of Book **7:**386
- - Composition-Critical View **7:**388
- - Distinctiveness **7:**390
- - Antiquity of the Material **7:**393
- - Major Themes **7:**394
- *Abraham, Apocalypse of* **2:**127
- *Aggadat Bereshit* **2:**366
- Hurrian customs **12:**1287ff
- patriarchs **8:**572; **13:**181
- Pentateuch **13:**232
- Simḥat Torah **14:**1571
- *illus:*
- - text
- - Yemenite ms. (1496) **11:**903
Genesis Apocryphon (D.S. Scroll), *see* Lamech Scroll
GENESIS RABBAH (agg. Mid.) **7:**399
- justice and mercy of God **7:**669
- Monobaz and Izates **2:**267
- *illus:*
- - text
- - 11th cent. ms. **2:**737
- *see also:* MIDRASH; *Midrash Rabbah*
GENESIS RABBATI (mid. bk.) **7:**401
- Apocalypse influence **3:**181
GENEVA (city, Switz.) **7:**402
- library **11:**191
- Switzerland **15:**558f
- *illus:*
- - text
- - ORT Central Institute for Teacher and Technician Training **12:**1483; **15:**560
- - World Jewish Congress **16:**638
Genfer, Solomon **15:**1072
Genga, Annibale Sermattei della (pope), *see* LEO XII
Genis, Dionis, *see* Aboab, Abraham
Geniva (Babyl. schol.) **3:**972
- exilarch **6:**1025
GENIZAH (archive) **7:**404
- Bet Alfa **4:**710
- books **4:**1228
- historical discoveries **16:**1338
- Maḍmūn ben Japheth **11:**680
- spice trade **15:**270
- synagogue **15:**598
- *illus:* text
- *see also:* GENIZAH, CAIRO; MANUSCRIPTS, HEBREW

GENIZAH, CAIRO **16:**1333
- *Contents:*
- - Introduction **16:**1333
- - Collections of Documents **16:**1333
- - Languages **16:**1334
- - Writing Materials **16:**1334
- - History of Discoveries **16:**1334
- - Liturgy and Poetry **16:**1337
- - Documents on Europe **16:**1338
- - Illuminated Fragments **16:**1341
- - Historical Geography **16:**1342
- Abdallah ibn Salām **2:**54
- Adler, Elkan **2:**275
- African Jews **2:**332
- agricultural records **2:**402
- *Amidah* texts **2:**840
- archives **3:**375
- Baneth, David **4:**161
- economic history **16:**1280
- Egyptian Jewry **11:**834
- *Ein k-Elohenu* **6:**534
- *geonic* responsa **14:**84ff
- historiography **8:**564
- Ifriqiya **15:**1434
- Joseph Rosh Ha-Seder **10:**246
- letters **11:**57
- libraries **11:**190
- linguistics **16:**1398
- Masorah fragments **16:**1428
- notated musical sources **12:**558
- Oriental manuscripts **8:**1262
- *piyyutim* **15:**915
- prayer books **13:**985
- Schechter, Solomon **14:**948
- Simeon ben Megas ha-Kohen **14:**1561
- *Toledot Yeshu* **15:**1208
- Yannai **16:**713
- *Yoẓerot* **16:**865
- *illus:*
- - Damascus Document **5:**1247
- - *Ketubbah*, 12th cent. **10:**926
- - Khazar correspondence **10:**952
- - Maimonides' responsum **11:**758
- - page from the Prophets (895 C.E.) **11:**900
- *see also:* CAIRO; GENIZAH
Gennadi (15th cent., archbp.) **4:**884; **4:**886; **10:**399
Gennaro, Sisti **8:**34
GENNAZANO, ELIJAH ḤAYYIM BEN BENJAMIN OF **7:**407
Gennesar, Gennesareth (loc., Er. Isr.), *see* CHINNERETH; GINNOSAR, PLAIN OF
Gennesar, Water of, *see* KINNERET, LAKE
GENOA (city, It.) **7:**407
- Greece **7:**874
- history chart (1550,1567) **8:**766-767
- *illus:* text
Genocide **7:**409
- Eichmann, Adolf Otto **6:**517
- Nazi extermination camps **5:**77
- *illus:*
- - Auschwitz trial **3:**873
- - concentration camp inmates on their way to death **3:**863-866
- - Eichmann trial **6:**519
- - extermination camp crematorium **3:**868
- - Jews herded by Nazis into mass grave **8:**763
- - mass execution of Jews by Nazis **8:**861-866
- - poison gas for extermination camps, delivery note and correspondence **3:**861-862
- - Wannsee Conference minutes **16:**264
- - Zyklon B cylinders **3:**868
- *see also:* ANTI-SEMITISM; HOLOCAUST; RACE, THEORY OF; WAR CRIMES TRIALS
GENOCIDE CONVENTION **7:**409
- U.N. **15:**1558
Genootschap voor de Joodsche Wetenschap in Nederland (orgn.) **14:**1097; **16:**238
Gens, Jacob **13:**770; **16:**149ff
- Oshmyany **12:**1497
- Wittenberg, Yiẓḥak **16:**591
Genser, Joseph **12:**1295
Gent (city, Belg.), *see* GHENT
GENTILE **7:**410
- ablution **2:**84
- abortion **2:**99
- agriculture in Ereẓ Israel **2:**395
- *agunah* **2:**431
- *akkum* **2:**500
- Ashi on **10:**710
- *avodah zarah* **3:**980
- bear sale forbidden **4:**356
- blessing of **2:**803
- courts of **14:**1387
- Day of Judgment **6:**883
- Eden **13:**84
- Eleazar ben Ananias **6:**585
- Eliezer ben Hyrcanus **6:**622
- *geonim* **7:**1164
- *ḥazakah* of property **7:**1518ff
- *hefker* declaration **8:**244
- *ḥukkat ha-Goi* **8:**1061
- idolatry **8:**1236ff
- imprisonment **8:**1302
- impurity, ritual **13:**1408; **13:**1409
- intermarriage **12:**168
- Jewish courts **5:**888
- Jewish identity **10:**53; **10:**56
- *kiddush ha-Shem* **10:**979
- love of neighbor **11:**529
- Meir's attitude **11:**1241
- moneylending **12:**247f
- *niddui* **8:**351,353
- offspring of mixed marriage **11:**840ff
- Paul of Tarsus **13:**190ff
- Pharisees **9:**244
- prophets **13:**1176
- righteous Gentiles **7:**1383
- sacrifices **14:**612
- sages on **14:**640; **14:**641
- *Sefer Torah* **14:**1103
- seventy nations **12:**882
- *Temple Scroll* **15:**998
- Temple service **15:**979
- usury **16:**28ff
- wine of **16:**540
- witness **16:**586
- World To Come **4:**434; **10:**391
- Zohar on **10:**610
- *illus:*
- - Temple restriction plaque **15:**964
- *see also:* STRANGERS AND GENTILES
Gentile, E. **15:**627
Gentiles, Righteous, *see* RIGHTEOUS OF THE NATIONS
GENTILI (It. fam.) **7:**414
Gentili (Ḥefeẓ), Eliezer **13:**579
Gentili, Gershom ben Moses **7:**415
Gentili, Manasseh **12:**350
Gentili, Moses ben Gershom **7:**414
- *illus:* text
Gentilli, Joseph Hefetz **7:**422
Gentilomo, Eugenia **13:**12
Gentius, Georg **8:**34
Gentry (minor nobility) **16:**1305
Gentz, Friedrich von **11:**1449
Gentz, Georg, *see* Gentius, Georg
Geographical Survey of Israel **9:**108
GEOGRAPHY **7:**415
- *Contents:*
- - In the Bible **7:**415
- - In the Talmud **7:**415
- - Medieval **7:**420
- - Textbooks **7:**421
- - Modern **7:**421
- Canaan **13:**472
- economic life **16:**1268
- Jewish literature **11:**350
- maps of Ereẓ Israel **11:**918
- Transjordan **15:**1316
- *illus:* text
- *see also:* Cartography; MAP MAKERS; MAPS OF EREẒ ISRAEL
GEOGRAPHY, HUMAN, OF ISRAEL **9:**567
Geological Institute (Isr.) **9:**967
GEOLOGY OF ISRAEL **9:**194
- Arabah **3:**231
- earthquake **6:**340
- general survey **9:**970
- human geography **9:**571ff
- Negev **12:**925
- oil and gas **9:**793
- *illus:*
- - Cenomanian chalk cliffs, Rosh ha-Nikrah **9:**205
- - Cenomanian landscape, Levona basin **9:**209
- - Cenomanian rocks and terra-rossa soil, Judean Hills **9:**205
- - chalk formations, Safed region **9:**208
- - columnar basalt, Hameshushim pool **9:**213
- - Cretaceous cuestas, Hermon slope **9:**214
- - geological map of Israel **9:**195
- - Ḥuleh Rift Valley and Naphtali Mountains **9:**207
- - Jurassic cuestas, Hermon slope **9:**214
- - Jurassic formations, Makhtesh Ramon **9:**209
- - Jurassic limestone rocks, Hermon mt. **9:**205
- - Lashon formations, Jordan Hermon mt. **9:**217
- - loess badlands, Beersheba area **9:**203
- - Mesozoic formation, Gilead **9:**205
- - Paleozoic Nubian sandstone, Edom **9:**207
- - Paleozoic Nubian sandstone, Eilat region **9:**213
- - Pleistocene formations, Dead Sea Rift Valley **9:**217
- - Senonian and Eocene chalk formations, Arabah Valley **9:**203
- - Timna, schematic columnar section of area **9:**799
- *see also:* PHYSIOGRAPHY OF ISRAEL
Geometry, *see* MATHEMATICS
Ge'on ha-Areẓ (journ.) **1:**newsp. list
Geon Teveryah (geonic tit.) **7:**322
Geonim, *see* GAON
George I (George Louis; k., Eng.) **3:**812
George II (k., Eng.) **15:**1588
George III (k., Eng.) **4:**1378; **15:**110
George, Henry **8:**399
GEORGE, MANFRED **7:**423
GEORGE, WALTER LIONEL **6:**787
Georgetown (city, Guyana) **7:**997
Georgetown (city, S.C.) **15:**211
GEORGIA (Sov. repub.) **7:**423
- Ḥasidism **14:**1435
- Jewish immigration **9:**501ff
- marriage custom **11:**1043
- population statistics **14:**397
- synagogue **15:**589
- U.N. **15:**1562
- *illus:* text
- *pop. table:* text
- *see also:* CAUCASUS
GEORGIA (state, U.S.) **7:**428
- history chart (1733) **8:**766-767
- *illus:* text
- *pop. table:* text
Georgians (cmty., Jer.) **9:**1441; **9:**1465
Georgiopolis (tn.), *see* LYDDA
Georgios, Chrysococca **8:**34
Georgius Florentius, *see* GREGORY OF TOURS
Gephrous (tn., Transj.), *see* EPHRON
Gepstein, David **16:**1179
Gepstein, Moses **16:**1179
Gepstein, S. **13:**1597
- *illus:*
- - *Razsvet* staff **13:**1596
Ger (tn., Pol.), *see* GORA KALWARIA
Gera (f., Ehud) **6:**151
Gera (f., Shimei) **14:**1402
Gerabronn (tn., Ger.) **12:**1150
Geradike (dist., Er. Isr.), *see* GERAR
Gerah (coin, weight) **16:**381ff
- coins **5:**696ff; **14:**1347
GERAMA AND GARME (leg. conc.) **7:**430
- bonds, trustees **14:**1268
- contract liability **5:**932
- lien cancellation **11:**230
- torts **15:**1276ff
GERAR (tn., reg., Er. Isr.) **7:**432
- Abimelech **2:**76
- human geography **9:**594
- Ziklag **16:**1021
- *see also:* GEDOR
Gerar, Nahal (wadi, Isr.), *see* Naḥal Gerar
Gerard of Cremona **8:**34
GERASA (city, Transj.) **7:**432
- Crowfoot, J. W. **5:**1129
- synagogue **15:**598
- *illus:* text
- *see also:* DECAPOLIS
Gerasa (tn., Golan) **13:**1533
Gerbasi, Vicente **15:**256
Gerber, Samuel H. **5:**611
GERCHUNOFF, ALBERTO **7:**434
- *illus:* text
Gerd, Levi **12:**64
Gerdauen (concen. camp) **15:**464
Gerde, Dr. Oszkar **12:**1375
Ger de Cordova, Abraham, *see* ESCUDERO, LORENZO
Ger dynasty (ḥas.), *see* Gur Dynasty
Gereben, E. **5:**406
Gerekhtigkeyt (period.) **9:**1278
Gerer Rebbe (ḥas. ldr.), *see* Gur Dynasty
Gereš (cantillation sign) **16:**1440,1454
Gereš gadol, see Geršayim
GEREZ, JOSEF HABIB **7:**435
- Turkey **15:**1461
Gerhard, J. E. G. **8:**34
Gerhard, J. G. **8:**34
Gerhardsen, Einar **12:**1225
GERHARDT, CHARLES FREDERIC **7:**435
Geri, Ya'akov **9:**665; **15:**199
Geriatrics, *see* AGE AND THE AGED
Gerica (J., Sp.) **12:**532
Gerim (tract.) **12:**49
Gering, Bernard **15:**198; **16:**1140
Gerizim (newsp.) **1:**newsp. list
GERIZIM, MOUNT (Er. Isr.) **7:**436
- Alexander the Great **2:**577
- *Copper Scroll* **5:**956
- Decalogue **5:**1438
- holy place **8:**936
- Ottomans **9:**284
- physiography of Israel **9:**142

- Samaritan temple **8:**631; **14:**729f
- Simeonite blessing on **14:**1548
- *illus:*
- - Nablus view **12:**745
- - Samaritan paschal sacrifice **8:**934; **13:**169
- *see also* Ebal, Mount
Germa (Galatia) **7:**262
German, Daniel Aleksandrovich, *see* GRANIN, DANIEL ALEKSANDROVICH
GERMAN, YURI PAVLOVICH **7:**438
German-American Bund (Nazi orgn.) **5:**1571; **12:**1114
- anti-Semitism **3:**126
German Colony (qtr., Jer.) **9:**1476
- ancient vegetation **9:**1515
- Jerusalem development **9:**1496
- Turkish period **9:**1458
German Democratic Republic
- Arab relations **7:**501ff
- Jewish Population **7:**500
German Hebrew Benevolent Society (N.Y.) **12:**1072
German Hospital (Jer.) **9:**1458,1461
Germania Judaica (wk.) **8:**563; **15:**54
Germanicus (soc.), *see* WECHSLER, MAX
Germanius (slave) **10:**333
German language
- Hebraic influences on **7:**439
- influence on Hebrew **16:**1636
- influence on Yiddish **16:**791ff
- Nazi-Deutsch **12:**904
- Yiddish influences on **7:**442
GERMAN LITERATURE **7:**439
- *Contents:*
- - Biblical, Hebraic Influences **7:**439
- - Hebrew, Yiddish Influences **7:**442
- - Image of Jew **7:**442
- - Jewish Contribution **7:**446
- - Holocaust and Aftermath **7:**452
- - List of Authors **7:**454
- Austria **3:**894
- Bible translations **4:**872
- children's literature **5:**452; **5:**456ff
- Jewish encyclopedias **6:**731ff
- Mendelssohn, Moses **11:**1331
- *Shmuel Bukh* **14:**1426ff
- *teḥinnah* **15:**907
- Yiddish **16:**791ff
- *see also:* GERMANY (Cult. Life)
German Orthodoxy, *see* NEO-ORTHODOXY
German Quarter (Jaffa) **9:**1256
Germanus (patr., Const.) **9:**1541
Germanus, Bishop **14:**731
Germanus, Moses **13:**1191
GERMANY **7:**457
- *Contents:*
- - Middle Ages **7:**458
- - - First Crusade **7:**461
- - - Spiritual Life **7:**463
- - - Social Life **7:**465
- - - 13th Century **7:**467
- - - 14th Century **7:**468
- - - 15th Century **7:**469
- - To World War I **7:**471
- - - Absolutist Principalities **7:**473
- - - Social, Spiritual Life **7:**474
- - - Court Jews **7:**476
- - - Haskalah **7:**476
- - - French Revolution Effects **7:**476
- - - Post-Napoleonic Reaction **7:**477
- - - Assimilation, Reform **7:**477
- - - Economic, Social Life **7:**479
- - - Emancipation **7:**480
- - - Anti-Semitism **7:**481
- - - Internal Life **7:**481
- - 1914 to 1933 **7:**482
- - - Communal Organization **7:**485
- - - Cultural Life **7:**487
- - 1933 to 1939 **7:**488
- - World War II **7:**493
- - Contemporary Period **7:**496
- - Relations with Israel **7:**501
- General
- - Berlin **4:**639f
- - Breslau **4:**1353
- - Cologne **5:**738f
- - Frankfort **7:**83f
- - Hamburg **7:**1225
- - history chart **8:**766-767
- - Munich **12:**521
- - Posen **13:**947
- - Prague **13:**965ff
- - Prussia **13:**1287
- - SHUM **14:**1479
- - *see also individual towns, states*
- Statistics
- - crime among Jews **5:**1091ff
- - demography **5:**1499
- - divorce **6:**135
- - migration trends **8:**720; **16:**1523
- - population **13:**872ff
- - refugees from **14:**28ff
- - vital statistics **16:**185ff
- Movements
- - Emancipation **6:**704ff; **8:**713ff
- - Haskalah **7:**1434ff
- - New Left **12:**1033ff
- - Socialism **15:**25ff
- - Territorialism **15:**1020ff
- - Zionism **16:**1115
- Communal Life
- - *Domus Hospitale Judaeorum* **8:**1033
- - fairs **11:**1000
- - Jewish society **8:**736ff
- - organization, communal **5:**820,824
- - philanthropy **13:**379
- - Protestant-Jewish relations **13:**1252
- - synods **15:**633ff
- - *takkanot* **15:**723
- - taxation **15:**857
- Cultural Life
- - *Allgemeine Zeitung des Judentums* **2:**647
- - archives **3:**378
- - book-cover art **4:**1230
- - dress **6:**219
- - education **6:**408ff,422ff
- - Graetz, Heinrich **7:**845f
- - Ḥanukkah lamps **7:**1291
- - Hebrew language **16:**1636
- - Hebrew MSS **8:**1267; **11:**906
- - Hebrew newspapers **12:**1045ff
- - Heine, Heinrich **8:**270f
- - Kulturverein **16:**109
- - learned societies **15:**54
- - libraries **11:**193
- - literature, German **7:**439
- - poetry **13:**692
- - Steinschneider, Moritz **15:**374
- - universities **15:**1677; **15:**1678
- - Wissenschaft des Judentums **16:**571
- - Yiddish literature **16:**820
- - Zunz, Leopold **16:**1236
- Religious Life
- - Agudat Israel **2:**421f
- - Avelei Zion **3:**946
- - Baeck, Leo **4:**77
- - Bamberger, S.B. **4:**154
- - Buber, Martin **4:**1431
- - Carlebach family **5:**181f
- - Frankel, Zacharias **7:**80
- - Geiger, Abraham **7:**357
- - Ḥasidei Ashkenaz **7:**1377, **8:**687ff
- - *Ḥasidim, Sefer* **7:**1389
- - Hildesheimer, Azriel **8:**476
- - Hirsch, S.R. **8:**508f
- - homiletical literature **8:**956
- - Mendelssohn, Moses **11:**1328
- - *mikveh* **11:**1541
- - Neo-Orthodoxy **12:**956
- - Orthodoxy **12:**1487ff
- - *piyyut* **13:**597
- - rabbinical conferences **13:**1460ff
- - Reform Judaism **14:**23
- - responsa **11:**337ff
- - Rosenzweig, Franz **14:**299
- - Shabbateanism **14:**1233; **14:**1250
- - synagogues, East and West Germany (contemporary) **1:**synagogue list
- - yeshivot **16:**764ff
- Trades, Professions
- - agriculture **2:**404
- - banking **4:**168
- - commerce **15:**1297f,1303
- - contractors **5:**934
- - cooperatives **5:**943
- - Court Jews **5:**1007ff
- - department stores **5:**1545
- - gold- and silversmiths **7:**742
- - journalism, press **10:**304ff; **13:**1032ff
- - law **10:**1491ff
- - medicine **11:**1196
- - military service **11:**1559
- - mining **11:**1438
- - mintmasters **12:**62ff
- - moneylending **12:**254ff
- - peddling **13:**205
- - politics **13:**813ff
- - publishing **13:**1366
- - rabbinical office **13:**1452; **13:**1453
- - salt **14:**713
- - stock exchange **15:**405ff
- - tailoring **15:**706
- - textiles **15:**1041
- - theater **15:**1055
- Organizations
- - Berit Ḥalutzim Datiyyim **7:**1321
- - Blau-Weiss **4:**1078
- - B'nai B'rith **4:**1147
- - Central-Verein Deutscher Staatsbuerger Juedischen Glaubens **5:**286
- - Deutsch-Israelitischer Gemeindebund **5:**1595
- - freemasons **7:**123
- - Habonim **8:**1241
- - *Landjudenschaft* **10:**1405
- - Mizrachi **12:**177
- - ORT **12:**1482,1484
- - students' movements **15:**448
- - Youth Aliyah **16:**861
- Personalities
- - Aronius **3:**493
- - Berthold of Regensburg **4:**697
- - Eisner, Kurt **6:**556
- - Eleazar ben Judah of Worms **6:**592
- - Glueckel of Hameln **7:**629
- - Hess, Moses **8:**431
- - "Jew Suess" **12:**1428
- - Joselmann of Rosheim **10:**227
- - Lassalle, Ferdinand **10:**1441
- - Marx, Karl **11:**1071
- - Rathenau, Walter **13:**1569
- - Riesser, Gabriel **14:**166
- Anti-Semitism **3:**101f
- - Agrarian League **2:**373
- - Armleder **3:**483
- - badge, Jewish **4:**68f
- - Black Death **4:**1064
- - blood libel **4:**1120f
- - caricatures **5:**171ff
- - Crusades **5:**1135ff
- - disputations **6:**94
- - forced conversions **3:**170
- - Hep! Hep! riots **8:**330
- - Luther, Martin **11:**584
- - medals **11:**1168
- - military service **11:**1560
- - Pfefferkorn, Johannes **13:**355
- - political parties **3:**79; **8:**738
- - race theory **13:**1484ff
- - Rindfleisch massacres **14:**188
- - *sheḥitah* **14:**1341
- - Stoecker, Adolf **15:**408
- Nazi Period
- - Austria, migration to **3:**897
- - Bernheim Petition **4:**681
- - Bormann, Martin **4:**1250
- - concentration camps **5:**77
- - denazification **5:**1533
- - Evian Conference **6:**988
- - forced labor **6:**1429
- - Gestapo **7:**527
- - ghetto **7:**543
- - Himmler **8:**497
- - Hitler **8:**782
- - Holocaust, rescue from **8:**905
- - League of Nations **10:**1523ff
- - legislation, anti-Jewish **10:**1573
- - National Socialism **12:**882
- - Neo-Nazism **12:**954
- - partisans **13:**140ff
- - Protestant Church **8:**915
- - Reich Association of Jews **14:**50
- - reparations **14:**72
- - Rumania **14:**395,399
- - Schacht plan **14:**937
- - Stalin **15:**327
- - *Stuermer, Der* **15:**460
- - War Crimes Trials **16:**289ff,297ff
- - *see also:* HOLOCAUST
- Israel **7:**501; **9:**445
- - Adenauer, Konrad **2:**264
- - *aliyah* **9:**512,514
- - Arab terrorists **9:**416
- - Ben-Gurion **4:**510ff
- - claims against Germany **5:**873ff
- - Ereẓ Israel community **9:**506ff; **9:**891
- - Ereẓ Israel immigration **9:**528ff
- - Goldmann, Nahum **7:**724
- - Herut **4:**392
- - military, economic aid **9:**391; **9:**402ff
- - reparations **9:**382ff
- - Sykes-Picot treaty **15:**565ff
- Miscellaneous
- - Ashkenaz as **3:**719ff
- - Middle East interests **9:**307ff
- - Provence **13:**1263
- - South Africa **15:**185ff
- - Swabian League **15:**544
- *illus:*
- - text
- - anti-Semitic parties, 1878-1914 (table) **3:**81
- - anti-Semitic representatives in the *Reichstag*, 1912-1933 (table) **3:**114
- - Armleder massacres (map) **3:**483
- - Ben-Nathan and H. Luebke **9:**406
- - Bergen-Belsen Trial **16:**295
- - Berlin, Jewish community center **4:**652
- - Berlin, University students' society **16:**1115
- - Berlin, Zionist Office **9:**521
- - Bonn, synagogue destroyed by Nazis, plaque **4:**1211
- - Cologne, medieval Jewish quarter (plan) **5:**739
- - Desecration of the Host libel, broadsheet **8:**1041
- - East Germany, stamp for concentration camp memorials **4:**1445
- - Fettmilch, Vincent, execution **6:**1248
- - Frankfort Jewish costume (18th cent.) **7:**86
- - Frankfort riots, 1614 **7:**85
- - Heinrich Heine stamp **15:**334
- - Hep! Hep! riots, 1819 (map) **8:**331

- - Jewish badge, 16th cent. **4**:68
- - Jewish badge decreed by Nazis **4**:72
- - Jewish hat **4**:67
- - *Kornjude* medal **11**:1170
- - marriage belts, 17th cent. **11**:1043
- - *Monumenta Judaica* exhibition **5**:743
- - Nuremberg Laws **12**:1281
- - Nuremberg Trial **16**:289,293
- - refugees dancing *hora*, 1939 **9**:526
- - reparations agreement **14**:72
- - *takkanot* issued by Orthodox rabbinate **15**:716
- - Wannsee Conference minutes **16**:264
- - wedding ceremony, 18th cent. **11**:1031
- - Worms Jew and Jewess, 16th cent. **4**:68
- *pop. tables:*
- - text
- - Baden **4**:60
- - Bavaria, 10th cent. to 1932-33 **4**:347
- - Berlin, 1816-1945 **4**:650
- - Prussia, 1871 **13**:1287
- *see also various cities, states, provinces*
German Yiddish Theater (Pol.) **15**:1072
Germber, Hermann **8**:34
Germer-Durand, J. **9**:1537
Germinal (newsp.) **13**:1031; **14**:213
Germiston (city, S.A.) **15**:1340
- South Africa **15**:186
GERNSHEIM, FRIEDRICH **7**:504
- *illus:* text
Gernsheim, Helmut **13**:486
Gernstein, Michael **6**:818
Gerö, Attila **4**:884
Gero, Henry **15**:1074
Gerofit (kib., Isr.) **1**:place list
- *illus:*
- - founder-members **9**:980
- - Naḥal settlement **12**:767
Gerogeret (meas.) **16**:389
Geron, Joseph **8**:915
GERONA (city, Sp.) **7**:505
- Béziers Jews **4**:793
- Kabbalah **10**:525
- *illus:* text
Gerona, Councils of **5**:548
- church tithes **15**:1162
- Spain **15**:228
Gerondi, Abraham (Ḥazzan) ben Isaac, *see* ABRAHAM BEN ISAAC (Gerondi)
Gerondi, Ben Zion Aryeh **13**:577
Gerondi, Berechiah ben Isaac ha-Levi **7**:510
GERONDI, ISAAC BEN JUDAH (poet) **7**:507
Gerondi, Isaac ben Perez **4**:500
Gerondi, Isaac ha-Yizhari ben Zerahiah ha-Levi **7**:509
- *paytanim* list **13**:581
GERONDI, JACOB BEN SHESHET **7**:507
Gerondi, Jonah ben Abraham, *see* JONAH BEN ABRAHAM GERONDI
Gerondi, Joseph ben Moses de **16**:60
GERONDI, MOSES BEN SOLOMON D'ESCOLA **7**:508
Gerondi, Nissim ben Reuben (Ran), *see* NISSIM BEN REUBEN GERONDI
Gerondi, Reuben **12**:1185
GERONDI, SAMUEL BEN MESHULLAM **7**:509
GERONDI, SOLOMON BEN ISAAC **7**:509
Gerondi, Vidal Ephraim **11**:800; **11**:801
GERONDI, ZERAHIAH BEN ISAAC HA-LEVI **7**:509
- Alfasi **11**:330
- Moses ben Joseph ha-Levi **12**:421
- Naḥmanides **12**:781
Geronimo de Santa Fé, *see* LORKI, JOSHUA
Gerousia (council), *see* GERUSIA
GEROVICH, ELIEZER MORDECAI BEN ISAAC **7**:510
Gerrans, R. **8**:34
Gerśayim (cantillation sign) **16**:1455
Gersdorff, Henrietta K. Friesen **8**:34
Gershenson, Jacob **12**:1516
GERSHENZON, MIKHAIL OSIPOVICH **7**:511
Gershfield, Edward **5**:905
Gershkovitz, Jacques **13**:911
GERSHOM (bib. fig.) **7**:511
- Moses **12**:374
- Zipporah **16**:1182
Gershom (priestly fam.) **13**:466
Gershom ben Jacob Hagozer, *see* HAGOZER, JACOB AND GERSHOM
GERSHOM BEN JUDAH ME'OR HA-GOLAH **7**:511
- Ashkenazi families **8**:667
- chronological chart **8**:766-767
- deaf-mute **11**:1050
- divorce **6**:125ff
- Eliezer ben Isaac of Worms **6**:623
- *ḥerem bet din* **8**:356
- Jacob ben Yakar **9**:1224
- Judeo-French glosses **10**:424
- *ketubbah* **10**:927
- lease **7**:1522
- letters **11**:62
- Mainz yeshivah **16**:764
- polygamy **4**:986
- polygyny **12**:259
- responsa **14**:86
- SHUM **14**:1480
- synodal resolutions **15**:632
- *takkanot* **3**:721; **15**:724; **15**:725
- Talmud commentaries **11**:329
- taxation **15**:863ff
Gershom ben Moses **10**:782
GERSHOM BEN SOLOMON (schol.) **7**:513
Gershom ben Solomon ben Isaac (paytan) **13**:581
Gershom ben Solomon ha-Kohen (print., Prague), *see* Kohen, Gershom ben Solomon ha-
Gershon (mintmaster) **12**:63
Gershon, David **14**:304
GERSHON, GERSHONITES (bib. fig.; clan) **7**:513
GERSHON, ISAAC **7**:514
- Treves family **15**:1377
- *illus:* text
GERSHON, KAREN **6**:785; **6**:788
Gershon ben Eliezer of Prague **11**:351
- pilgrimage **13**:514
- Sambatyon **14**:764
Gershon ben Hezekiah **12**:1447
Gershon ben Rahamim **10**:1298
GERSHON BEN SOLOMON OF ARLES **7**:515
- alchemy **2**:548
- biology **4**:1030
- Hebrew encyclopedia **6**:730
- Hebrew language **16**:1631
- *illus:* text
Gershon Enoch of Radzyn **7**:1415
Gershoni, Ẓevi Hirsch, *see* GERSONI, HENRY
Gershon Menaḥem of Minsk **15**:131
Gershon of Frankfort **7**:93
Gershon of Kitov, *see* ABRAHAM GERSHON OF KUTOW
GERSHOVITZ, SAMUEL **7**:517
GERSHOY, LEO **8**:546
GERSHUNI, GRIGORI ANDREYEVICH **7**:517
Gershuni, Yehuda **15**:1339
GERSHWIN, GEORGE **7**:518
- theater **15**:1059
- *illus:*
- - rehearsal of *Rosalie* **16**:1018
Gershwin, Ira **7**:518
- theater **15**:1059
Gerson, George **11**:1197
Gerson, Jack **15**:303
Gerson, Samuel **12**:1375
GERSONI, HENRY **7**:518
- press **13**:1053
Gersonides, *see* LEVI BEN GERSHOM
Gersonides (printers) **13**:967; **13**:976
GERSON-KIWI, EDITH (Esther) **7**:519
GERSTEIN, BERTA **15**:1082
Gerstein, Ḥayyim Baruch **14**:1513
Gerstein, J. **15**:60
GERSTEIN, KURT **7**:520
- gassing **16**:1332
- Hochhuth's play **8**:798
Gerstein, L.C. **12**:1119
Gerstenfeld, Norman **16**:357
Gerstenkorn, Y. **4**:480
Gerstle (U.S. fam.) **5**:56
GERSTLE, LEWIS **7**:520
- Alaska **2**:514
Gerstle, S. **8**:1438
Gerstle River (Alsk.) **2**:514
Gerszonowicz, S. **12**:1519
Gertler, David **11**:435
GERTLER, MARK **7**:520
- *illus:*
- - text
- - "Apple Gatherers" (drg.) **3**:557
Gertner, Ala **4**:374
Gertner, Jacob **10**:1217
Gertner, Levi **6**:451
GERTSA (tn., Buk.) **7**:521
- Rumania **14**:387, 397
GERTZ, ELMER **7**:522
Gerunda (city, Sp.), *see* GERONA
Gerundi, Isaac ben Judah, *see* GERONDI, ISAAC BEN JUDAH
Gerupina (beacon station), *see* AGRIPPINA
Gerushin (myst. doctrine) **2**:636
GERUSIA (council) **7**:522
- ethnarch **6**:946
- Hellenistic period **9**:1389ff
- *Ḥever ha-Yehudim* **8**:438
- Second Temple period **8**:626ff
Geruzyah (rep.), *see* GEORGIA
Ger Ẓedek, *see* PROSELYTES
Gesamtarchiv der Deutschen Juden **3**:378; **5**:1595
GESANG, NATHAN-NACHMAN **7**:523
Geschwind, Moses David **14**:538
Gesellschaft der Freunde (soc.) **12**:371
GESELLSCHAFT DER JUNGEN HEBRAEER (Cz.) **7**:523
Gesellschaft fuer Sammlung und Konservierung von Kunst- und historischen Denkmaelern des Judentums (Vienna) **12**:538
Gesellschaft zur Erforschung juedischer Kunstdenkmaeler (Ger.) **3**:594; **3**:651; **12**:538
GESELLSCHAFT ZUR FOERDERUNG DER WISSENSCHAFT DES JUDENTUMS **7**:523
- publishing **15**:54
- *see also:* WISSENSCHAFT DES JUDENTUMS
Gesem, Land of (reg., Arab.) **7**:816
GESENIUS, HEINRICH FRIEDRICH WILHELM **7**:524
- Christian Hebraists **8**:34
- Hebrew linguistics **16**:1395
Geshem (k., Kedar) **7**:620ff
- inscription **16**:669
GESHER (kib., Isr.) **7**:525
- statistics **1**:place list
- *illus:*
- - Israel stamp **9**:844-845
Gesher (journ.) **1**:newsp. list
GESHER BENOT YA'AKOV (bridge, Isr.) **7**:525
- *illus:* text
GESHER HA-ZIV (kib., Isr.) **7**:526
- statistics **1**:place list
- *illus:*
- - text
- - Shavuot festival **10**:962
Geshtinanna (deity) **16**:1490
GESHURI, MEIR SHIMON (comp.) **12**:691
Geshuri, Shimon (lab. ldr.) **7**:1320
Gesius (philos.) **6**:165
Gesiv (city, Er. Isr.), *see* ACHZIB
Gesner, Konrad **4**:973
GESSIUS FLORUS (procurator) **7**:526
Gessner, Salomon **6**:775
Gestalt psychology **10**:1133; **16**:456ff
GESTAPO **7**:527
- *Contents:*
- - General **7**:527
- - Political Police **7**:528
- - From 1938 **7**:528
- - Einsatzgruppen **7**:530
- concentration camps **5**:77
- Eichmann **6**:517
- Goering **7**:688
- Heydrich **8**:448
- Himmler **8**:498
- Mueller, Heinrich **12**:503
- *illus:* text
- *see also* RSHA
Gestation of animals **4**:1021
GESTETNER, DAVID **7**:530
Gestetner, Sigmund **7**:530
GESUNDHEIT, JACOB BEN ISAAC **7**:531
- Warsaw **16**:338
Get (bill of divorce), *see* DIVORCE
Gethsemane, Church of (Jer.) **9**:1407,1460
- - Russian Church **9**:1462
Gethsemane, Garden of (Er. Isr.) **8**:935
- Mount of Olives **12**:483; **12**:484
- *illus:*
- - ancient olive tree **9**:1514
- - Basilica of the Agony **9**:1455
Geto Tsaytung (newsp.) **13**:1044
Geto Nuovo (Venice) **16**:96
Getz, Eliakim **13**:556
Getz, Stan **12**:1122
Geula (soc.) **14**:871
Ge'ulah (qtr., Jer.) **9**:1472
Geulah Company (Pol.) **6**:138; **7**:632
- Aḥuzzat Bayit **16**:337
- Goldberg, Isaac Leib **7**:702
GE'ULEI TEIMAN (mosh., Isr.) **7**:531
GE'ULIM (mosh., Isr.) **7**:531
- statistics **1**:place list
Ge'ulim (qtr. Jer.), *see* Bak'ah
Ge'ullah (qtr., Tel Aviv) **15**:920
GE'ULLAH (litur.) **7**:531
- *Amidah* **2**:840
- *arvit* **3**:665
- *Hashkivenu* **7**:1370
GEVA (kib., Isr.) **7**:532
- statistics **1**:place list
- *illus:*
- - sheepshearing festival **10**:962
Geva Karmel (mosh., Isr.) **1**:place list
GEVARAM (kib., Isr.) **7**:532
- Lachish region **10**:1336

- Negev water supply **12:**929
- statistics **1:**place list
Gevartil, Elijah **16:**840
GEVAT (kib., Isr.) **7:**532
- statistics **1:**place list
GEVAUDAN (reg., Fr.) **7:**533
Gevelber, Avraham **9:**678
Geviha of Argiza (savora) **14:**920
Gevilin (publ.) **1:**newsp. list
GEVIM (kib., Isr.) **7:**533
- statistics **1:**place list
GEVULOT (kib., Isr.) **7:**533
- Negev **12:**929
- statistics **1:**place list
Gevulot (journ.) **1:**newsp. list
Gevurah (sefirah) **10:**570ff
Gevurot (Amidah ben.) **2:**840
Gewitsch (tn.), *see* JEVICKO
GEWITSCH, AARON WOLF **7:**533
- *illus:* text
Gewuertz, J. C. **3:**360
Gewuerz, T. (publ., firm) **4:**1239
Geyer, Ludwig **16:**241
Geyer, Martin **8:**34
Gezang, Nathan **16:**1123
Gezelius, J. **8:**34
GEZER (city, Er. Isr.) **7:**534
- altar **2:**761
- anthropology **3:**45; **3:**46
- Clermont-Ganneau's identification **5:**605
- Crusader battle **9:**268
- Hasmoneans **8:**630; **14:**1565
- pictographic scripts **16:**654
- seal **14:**1074
- settlement of tribes **8:**581
- Siamun **14:**1416
- Solomon's constructions **15:**102
- Solomon's dowry **6:**483; **15:**100
- *illus:*
- - text
- - Egyptian record of name **3:**313
- *see also:* GEZER CALENDAR
GEZER (kib., Isr.) **7:**536
- statistics **1:**place list
Gezerah, see TAKKANOT
Gezerah shavah (hermeneutical rule) **8:**367
- levirate marriage **11:**124
Gezerat ha-Sheniyyot, see FAMILIANTS LAW
GEZER CALENDAR **7:**538
- alphabetic script **2:**681
- inscriptions **16:**658; **16:**665
- Old-Hebrew inscription **16:**1569
- Rosh ha-Shanah **14:**306
- seasons **2:**390
- year **16:**725
- *illus:* **2:**386
- - script type **2:**684
Gezerot taḥ ve-tat (massacres, 1648-49) **5:**481
Gezerot tatnav (massacres, 1096) **7:**461
Gezund (period.) **15:**1292
Ghafirs (police, Er. Isr.) **9:**351
Ghana (rep.) **9:**391; **9:**435; **9:**439
- War Crimes Trials **16:**298
Ghariba synagogue (Djerba) **6:**139
- *illus:*
- - exterior **15:**1434
- - interior **6:**139
Ghassulian culture **9:**591; **15:**1316
- *illus:*
- - grain-storage jug **2:**383
Ghatafān (tribe, Arab.) **13:**1436
Ghauer (reg., Jor.) **9:**1370
Ghaymen (loc., Yem.) **16:**809
GHAZALI, ABU ḤAMID MUHAMMAD IBN MUHAMMAD AL-TŪSĪ AL- **7:**538
- Albalag **2:**520
- attributes of God **7:**666ff
- Averroes **3:**949
- Avicenna **3:**958
- Neoplatonism **12:**960
- *illus:* text
Ghazis, V. **7:**887
Ghazni (tn., Afg.) **10:**958; **13:**310
- Afghanistan **2:**326
Ghazza-al-Shallāla (wadi, Er. Isr.) **4:**703
Ghazzāl (Samar.) **14:**756
Ghazzāl ibn Abu al-Sarūr al-Ghāzī **14:**756
GHELERTER, LITMAN **7:**540
GHENT (city, Belg.) **7:**541
GHEREA-DOBROGEANU, CONSTANTIN **7:**541
- socialism **15:**29
- *illus:* text
Gherla (tn., Hung.), *see* Szamosujvár
Gheron, Abraham **2:**310; **4:**410
Gheron, Eliakim **7:**542
Gheron, Yakir **10:**1009
GHERON, YAKKIR MORDECAI BEN ELIAKIM **7:**542
GHETTO **7:**542
- *Contents:*
- - General **7:**542
- - Muslim Countries **7:**543
- - Holocaust Period **7:**543
- Catholic anti-Semitism **3:**108
- currency **5:**725ff
- forced labor **6:**1429
- France **7:**18
- Holocaust **8:**852
- Italy **9:**1126ff
- Philip IV **13:**393
- Poland **13:**755
- Venice **16:**96
- *illus:*
- - text
- - Amsterdam, tokens **12:**977
- - Barcelona, ghetto wall **4:**210
- - Cavaillon, entrance **5:**260
- - Chieri **5:**421
- - Dutch Jewish quarter **10:**87
- - Eisenstadt **6:**547
- - Holocaust
- - - Bialystok, 1941-1943 **4:**805
- - - drawings by ghetto artists Figs. 75-85 **3**-ART; **5:**95; **8:**881
- - - "Kaunas ghetto, main gate of" (drg., E. Lurie) **10:**849
- - - Lodz **5:**726; **8:**871; **11:**427,431-436; **13:**1044
- - - Lodz, Rumkowski, Chaim Mordechai **14:**428
- - - Opole, postmark **12:**1416
- - - residents assembling for deportation **8:**763
- - - Riga **14:**175
- - - Theresienstadt deportations (map) **15:**1113
- - - Theresienstadt ghetto "bank note" (1943) **5:**726
- - - Transnistria (map) **15:**1331
- - - Vilna, performance of *The Eternal Jew* **16:**145
- - - Vilna, sports festival poster **16:**145
- - - Warsaw **7:**544; **8:**869; **13:**757
- - - Warsaw, children's choir **12:**657
- - - Warsaw, commemorative stamp **15:**336
- - - Warsaw, plan of Ghetto **16:**347
- - - *see also:* CAMPS (Concentration and Extermination)
- - Prague, Three Fountain Square **5:**1191
- - Rome **10:**83; **14:**243,246
- - Venice **9:**1127; **10:**82
- *see also:* JEWISH QUARTER; *and individual towns*
Ghetto, Warsaw, *see* Warsaw Ghetto
GHETTO FIGHTERS' HOUSE (memorial, Isr.) **7:**546
- Loḥamei ha-Geta'ot **11:**463
- *illus:* text
GHEZ (fam., Tun.) **7:**546
Ghez, David **7:**546
Ghez, Ḥayyim **7:**547
Ghez, Joseph **7:**546
Ghez, Mathilda **7:**547
Ghez, Moses **7:**546
Ghez, Paul **15:**1447
GHILLANY- FRIEDRICH WILHELM **7:**547
Ghirat, Alexander ibn **10:**1351
GHIRON (fam.) **7:**547
Ghiron, Isaiah **7:**548
Ghiron, Johanan **7:**547
Ghiron, Judah Ḥayyim **7:**547
Ghiron, Judah Ḥayyim Leonti **7:**547
Ghiron, Samuel Ḥayyim **7:**548
Ghirondi, Benzion **13:**12
Ghirondi, Ephraim Raphael **13:**12; **7:**548
Ghirondi, Mazal-Tov Benvenida **7:**548
Ghirondi, Mordecai **7:**548
GHIRONDI, MORDECAI SAMUEL BEN BENZION ARYEH **7:**548
Ghirondi, Solomon Eliezer **13:**12
GHIRSHMAN, ROMAN **7:**548
- archaeology **3:**302
Ghislieri, Cardinal, *see* Pius V, Pope
Ghiyyat (fam.), *see* IBN GHAYYAT
Ghor (val., Er. Isr.) **9:**167
Ghouri, E. **16:**1092ff
Ghriba (syn., Tun.) **15:**1430
Ghūlambar (tn., Iraq) **15:**504
Ghūr (Ghuristan; dist., Afg.) **2:**327
Ghuta (reg., Syr.) **9:**597
Giacobb (15th cent., physic.) **13:**122
Giacomo della Marca **4:**672
Giacomo Marchi, *see* BASSANI, GIORGIO
Giacomo of Verona **15:**1356
Giacomo Savelli, *see* HONORIUS IV (pope)
Giacon, Isaac **11:**27
Giado (vill., Libya) **11:**202
Gianetti (fam.), *see* Zanetti
Giants, *see* ANAK, ANAKIM; NEPHILIM
GIBBETHON (tn., Er. Isr.) **7:**549
GIBBETHON (mosh., Isr.) **7:**549
- statistics **1:**place list
GIBBOR, JUDAH BEN ELIJAH **7:**549
Gibborei Ẓiyyon (milit. unit, Belor.) **14:**1125
GIBEAH (tn., Isr.) **7:**549
- concubine of **5:**862
- fortifications **16:**275
- Geba **7:**349
- Philistines attack **13:**401
- Saul **3:**336; **14:**909
- tribal organization **8:**583
- *illus:*
- - ravishing of the concubine **5:**863
Gibeath-Benjamin (Isr.), *see* GIBEAH
Gibeath ha-Elohim (bib. loc., Er. Isr.) **7:**349
Gibeath-Moreh (bib. loc.) **10:**102
- battle camp **16:**272
Gibeath-Shaul (Isr.), *see* GIBEAH
Gibelius, A. **8:**34
GIBEON (city, Er. Isr.) **7:**550
- Adoni-Zedek **2:**296
- Eglon **6:**477
- Geba **7:**349
- Gibeonites **7:**552
- Gibeonites and Benjamin **4:**523
- pottery inscriptions **16:**660
- *illus:* text
GIBEONITES AND NETHINIM (pariah gr.) **7:**552
- *Contents:*
- - Introduction **7:**552
- - Post-Biblical Period **7:**554
- - Gibeonites in the Aggadah **7:**554
- Israel's conquest **8:**348; **8:**349
- Ophel **12:**1413
- Saul **14:**912
- Servants of Solomon **15:**116
- social structure of ancient Israel **8:**613
- sons of Sisera **14:**1622
- Temple **15:**954
Gibiletto (tn., Leb.), *see* JUBAYL
Gibitsh, Abraham Katz **14:**1106
GIBRALTAR (Br. crown clny.) **7:**555
- Hassan, Sir Joshua **7:**1467
- synagogues **1:**syn. list
- *illus:*
- - text
- - *Shivviti* plaque **14:**1420-1421
Gibson, Mrs. M.D. **16:**1334
GIDDAL (amora) **7:**556
Gide, André **7:**141 **8:**744
- Blecher, Marcel **4:**1080
- Debenedetti's analysis **5:**1428
GIDEON (bib. fig.) **7:**557
- *Contents:*
- - Introduction **7:**557
- - In the Aggadah **7:**558
- - In the Arts **7:**559
- Abiezrites **2:**73
- Bible history **8:**585
- En-Dor **6:**738
- history chart **8:**766-767
- Judges, Book of **10:**446
- Midian **16:**950
- Ophrah **12:**1414
- proscription in war **8:**347
- sacrifice **13:**1070
- warfare **16:**271
- *illus:* text
Gideon (Falasha k.) **6:**1144
Gideon (period., Yug.) **5:**457; **16:**888
Gideon (Zion. youth orgn., Serb.) **2:**519
- Zionism **16:**1149
Gideon, David (Ger.) **14:**139
Gideon, David (sport., U.S.) **15:**310
GIDEON, SAMSON (fin., Eng.) **7:**560
- chronological chart **8:**766-767
Gideon, Samson (Lord Eardley) **7:**560
Gid ha-Nasheh (anat.) **6:**39
Gidonah (rural stlmt., Isr.) **1:**place list
Gidonim (gr., Pal.) **2:**28
Gieldzinski, Jesser (Isser) **12:**538
GIESSEN (city, Ger.) **7:**560
Giesser, Moshe David **5:**445
GIFT **7:**560
- acquisition **2:**216
- duress **12:**1399
- firstborn inheritance **6:**1312
- *ḥazakah* plea for property **7:**1516
- *maẓranut* **11:**1154
- non-Jewish bill **6:**51; **6:**54
- ownership, temporary **12:**1533
- public body **13:**1353
- surety on **15:**527
- Temple **8:**1069; **11:**147
- wills **16:**519ff
- *illus:*
- - Abigail and David **3:**527; **12:**736
- - marriage belts, Germany **11:**1043
- - *mezuzah* cover **11:**1475
- *see also:* SALE
GIFTER, MORDECAI **7:**563
Gifts, priestly **13:**1088
- firstborn **6:**1308
- first fruits **6:**1313; **6:**1315
- *ḥallah* **7:**1195
- *ḥerem* property **8:**345
- tithes **5:**1486
Gigen (vill., Bul.) **4:**1480

Giggeius, A. **8**:34
Giguet, P. **4**:881
Gihon (Jer.) **9**:1524ff
- Hezekiah's tunnel **9**:1398
- Jerusalem location **9**:1380
- Jerusalem water supply **9**:1537ff
- Kidron **10**:988
- *illus:*
- - Hezekiah's tunnel **9**:1539
- *see also:* SHILOAH, SILOAM
Gihon (riv.) **13**:78
Gi-im-tu (city, Er. Isr.) **7**:591
GIKATILLA, ISAAC IBN **7**:563
- linguistics **16**:1380
GIKATILLA, JOSEPH BEN ABRAHAM **7**:564
- de Leon and Zohar **10**:534; **16**:1211
- practical Kabbalah **10**:635
- *Sefirot* doctrine **10**:576
- *illus:*
- - *Portae Lucis* (1516) **10**:635
GIKATILLA, MOSES BEN SAMUEL HA-KOHEN **7**:565
- Bible exegesis **4**:892
- Hebrew translations **15**:1319; **15**:1329
- linguistics **16**:1357,1382
Gikow, Ruth **11**:114
Gil, Geulah **12**:368; **14**:177
Giladi, Aharon **3**:592
- *illus:*
- - "Kinneret" (paint.) Fig. 98 3-ART
GILADI, ISRAEL **7**:566
Gilat (mosh., Isr.) **1**:place list
GILAT, YITZHAK DOV **1**:30
Gilbert, Abraham **14**:1509
GILBERT, FELIX **7**:566
GILBERT, INA **3**:601
GILBERT, MILTON **7**:567
Gilbert, Pierre **7**:42
GILBERT, SHLOMO **7**:567
Gilbert Crispin, *see* CRISPIN, GILBERT
GILBOA (mt. ridge, Er. Isr.) **7**:567
- geography **9**:588
- physiography **9**:143
- Saul **14**:913
- *illus:*
- - mountain slopes **9**:145
- - vegetation **9**:231
GILBOA, AMIR **7**:569
- Hebrew literature **8**:205
Gilboa, David **7**:1103
Gildenman, Misha **10**:1203; **13**:146; **14**:478
- *illus:*
- - partisans **13**:145
Gildesgame, Pierre **11**:665
Gilead (bib. fig.) **7**:570
GILEAD (reg., Transj.) **7**:569
- affiliation with Judah **8**:582
- afforestation **9**:787
- Ezekiel **12**:804
- geography **9**:596ff
- physiography **9**:178
- Solomon **15**:1317
- Tobiads **8**:627; **15**:1179
- Transjordan **15**:1316
- *illus:*
- - text
- - hieroglyphic record of mountains' name **8**:580
- - Jordan Valley **9**:169
Gilead, Shelomo **3**:362
GILEAD, ZERUBAVEL **7**:572
Gileadites **7**:571
GILELS, EMIL GRIGORYEVICH **7**:572
GILGAL (loc., Er. Isr.) **7**:572
- Bible history **8**:579
- Saul **14**:789; **14**:910ff
- tribal center **15**:1383
- *illus:* text
Gilgamesh, Epic of (Mesop. leg.) **6**:1354ff
- Nebuchadnezzar I **16**:1502
- netherworld **12**:996
Gilgil (detention camp, Ken.) **10**:910
GILGUL (metempsychosis) **7**:573
- *Contents:*
- - Introduction **7**:573
- - In Early Kabbalah **7**:574
- - In Later and Safed Kabbalah **7**:575
- - Ibbur **7**:576
- Abraham bar Ḥiyya **13**:436
- Balbo, Michael **4**:129
- Bikayam, Meir **4**:992
- cosmic cycles **10**:583
- *dibbuk* **6**:19
- Gan Eden and Gehinnom **13**:85
- Gehinnom **6**:881ff
- Ibn Abi Zimra **5**:1358
- Jewish myshicism **10**:509; **10**:519; **10**:536
- kabbalistic psychology **10**:613ff
- Lurianic Kabbalah **10**:548
- Naḥmanides **12**:778
- Neoplatonism **12**:958
- punishment for sins **8**:464
- soul of Messiah **6**:881
- *see also:* AFTERLIFE; SOUL, IMMORTALITY OF
Gill, Eric **14**:212; **15**:1488
- *illus:*
- - Hebrew type face **14**:212; **15**:1485
Gill, John **8**:34
Gilles, Colonel, *see* Epstein, Joseph
Gillis, Bernard **10**:1495
Gillman, Henry **15**:1572
Gillman, Sidney **15**:308
Gillui arayot, *see* SEXUAL OFFENSES
Giluni (tn., Er. Isr.), *see* GOLAN
Gilyonenu (journ.) **1**:newsp. list
GILYONOT (period.) **7**:577
- statistics **1**:newsp. list
Gilzenberg, Willie **15**:306
Gimar, Simḥah, *see* Vaz, Simḥah
GIMBEL (mer. fam.) **7**:577
- department stores **5**:1546
Gimbel, Adam (mer.) **7**:577; **8**:1361
Gimbel, Adam (sport.) **15**:312
Gimbel, Bernard F. **7**:578
Gimbel, Bruce A. **7**:578
Gimbel, Charles **7**:577
Gimbel, Ellis **7**:577
Gimbel, Isaac **7**:577
Gimbel, Jacob **7**:577
GIMMEL (Heb. let.) **7**:578
Gimzo (mosh., Isr.) **1**:place list
Ginaea (city, Er. Isr.), *see* EN-GANNIM
Ginastera, Alberto **10**:1376
Ginath (bib. fig.) **15**:1135
Gincberg brothers **16**:942
Ginczanka, Zuzanna **13**:802
Ginger (bot.) **6**:1417; **13**:619; **15**:267; **15**:268; **16**:83
GINGOLD, PINCHAS M. **7**:578
- *illus:*
- - Yiddish writers, New York **16**:823
GINIEWSKI, PAUL **10**:310
Ginjalek (port, Ind.), *see* CRANGANORE
Ginnabris (loc., Er. Isr.), *see* SENNABRIS
Ginnat Bitan (wk.) **10**:542
Ginnat Egoz (wk.) **7**:564; **10**:534
Ginnaton (mosh., Isr.) **1**:place list
GINNEGAR (kib., Isr.) **7**:578
- statistics **1**:place list
- *illus:*
- - Balfour Forest **9**:585,586
GINNOSAR (kib., Isr.) **7**:578
- statistics **1**:place list
GINNOSAR, PLAIN OF (Isr.) **7**:579
- Agriculture **2**:394
- Kinnarot Valley **10**:1032
- *illus:*
- - Kinneret region **9**:582
Ginsberg (fam. name), *see* GUENZBURG
GINSBERG, ALLEN **7**:579
- U.S. literature **15**:1578
Ginsberg, Asher Hirsch, *see* AḤAD HA-AM
GINSBERG, EDWARD **7**:580
- *illus:*
- - Israel Bonds-U.J.A. dinner **15**:1668
- - U.J.A. National Conference **15**:1541
Ginsberg, F. (mfr., S. A.) **5**:377
Ginsberg, Franz (polit., S.A.) **13**:820
Ginsberg, George Joel **11**:520
GINSBERG, HAROLD LOUIS **1**:30; **7**:580
- *illus:*
- - JPS Torah translation committee **10**:80
Ginsberg, Louis **7**:580; **13**:179
GINSBERG, MITCHELL I. **7**:581
GINSBERG, MORRIS **7**:581
Ginsberg, Myron (Joe) **15**:301
GINSBERG, NORTON SIDNEY **7**:581
Ginsburg (fam. name), *see* GUENZBURG
Ginsburg (fam., Lith.) **14**:769
Ginsburg, A. **16**:1165
Ginsburg, B. J. **16**:551
GINSBURG, CHRISTIAN DAVID (schol.) **7**:581
- Shapira Fragments **14**:1302
Ginsburg, David (ḥas. ldr.) **5**:1361 **5**:1361
GINSBURG, DAVID **5**:382
Ginsburg, Eliezer ben Simeon **9**:1082
Ginsburg, Isaac **5**:1361
Ginsburg, Israel Joseph ha-Levi **5**:1361
GINSBURG, JEKUTHIEL **7**:582
- *illus:*
- - Hebrew Pen Club, N.Y. **8**:211
GINSBURG, SAUL **7**:582
- *Voskhod* **16**:225
Ginsburg, Shimon, *see* GINZBURG, SIMON
Ginsburg, Ze'ev Wolff **5**:1361
Ginsburger (fam. name), *see* GUENZBURG
Ginsburger, Elie **4**:351
GINSBURGER, ERNEST **7**:583
Ginsburg Publishing House **4**:1156
Ginti (city, Er. Isr.) **7**:335
GINTON, SHABBETAI **1**:30
Gintzburger, Samuel **16**:67
Ginz, Joseph **6**:472
Ginz, Samuel **6**:472
Ginz, Simḥah Bunim ben Moses, *see* EGER, SIMḤAH BUNIM BEN MOSES
Ginzak (tn., Media) **2**:358
Ginzberg (fam. name), *see also* GUENZBURG
Ginzberg, Dov **8**:185
GINZBERG, ELI **7**:583
Ginzberg, Hana **4**:1363
GINZBERG, LOUIS **7**:584
- *aggadah* scholarship **2**:364
- Cairo *genizah* **16**:1336
- Oral Law **12**:1444
- Szold, Henrietta **15**:666
Ginzberg Microfilm Collection (U.S.), *see* Louis Ginzberg Microfilm Collection
Ginzburg (r., Ostrog) **12**:1514
Ginzburg (fam. name), *see also* GUENZBURG
Ginzburg, Ḥayyim **13**:647
Ginzburg, I. (publ.) **1**:1375
Ginzburg, Ilya Yakovlevich (sculp.), *see* GUENZBURG, ILYA YAKOVLEVICH
GINSBURG, ISER (au.) **7**:585
GINZBURG, NATALIA **7**:586
- Italian literature **9**:1113
Ginzburg, Pesaḥ **7**:587
- *Bustenai* **4**:1538
- Ginsburg, Jekuthiel **7**:582
- *illus:* **16**:653
GINZBURG, SIMON **7**:586
- *illus:*
- - Writers' Assoc. in Israel **8**:205 **16**:653
- - Hebrew Writers' convention, 1943 **8**:213
- - Histadruth Ivrith of America **13**:371
GINZBURG, VITALII LAZAREVICH (phys.) **7**:587
- research **3**:807
Ginzburger (fam. name), *see* GUENZBURG
Ginzei Kedem (collec.) **1**:newsp. list
Ginzei Nistarot (journ.) **1**:newsp. list
Ginzei Schechter (journ.) **1**:newsp. list
Gioberti, Vincenzo **9**:1128; **13**:502
- Cattaneo, Carlo **5**:255
Giora Godik Theater (Isr.) **15**:1062
GIORGIO, FRANCESCO **7**:587
- Christian Hebraists **8**:34
- Christian Kabbalah **10**:645
- Le Fèvre de la Boderie, Guy **10**:1563
Giorgione (paint.) **10**:460
Giotto (art.) **8**:386
Giovanni Ambrogio, *see* GUGLIELMO DA PESARO
Giovanni di Giovanni **8**:560
GIOVANNI MARIA **7**:588
- lute player **12**:616
Giovanni Maria Ciocchi del Monte (pope), *see* JULIUS III
Giovanni Pietro Caraffa (pope), *see* PAUL IV
Gipstein, Yaacov, *see* AGAM, YAACOV
Giraffe (zool.) **15**:704
- dietary laws **6**:31
Giraud, Henri Honoré **2**:617
Giraud, L'Abbé **8**:34
Giraudoux, Jean **7**:141; **10**:459
- Sodom and Gomorrah **15**:73
Girdle poems **13**:1217
Gireandeau, Bonar **8**:34
Girgan, *see* GEORGIA (Rus.)
GIRGASHITES (bib. people) **7**:588
Girgasite, Land of, *see* GEORGIA (Rus.)
Girgenti (tn., Sic.), *see* AGRIGENTO
Girgisiya (tn., Syr.), *see* Kirkisiya
"Girl's Head" (Lith., Y. Bacon) **3**:617
Girzengal (vill., Kurd.) **10**:1297
GISCALA (city, Er. Isr.) **7**:589
- Crusader period **2**:398; **9**:272
- Estori ha-Parḥi **9**:279
- Galilean district **7**:266
- population **9**:589
- synagogues **15**:595
- Titus **15**:1168
- *illus:*
- - synagogue lintel **6**:337
GISER, MOSHE DAVID **7**:589
GISSIN, AVSHALOM **7**:590
Gissin, Ephraim **7**:590
GISZKALAY, JÁNOS **7**:590
Gitelewitz, Gustav **16**:1165
Gitelewitz, Sara **16**:1165
Gitin, Joseph **14**:843
Giti-Padalla (city, Er. Isr.) **7**:335
Giti-Rimunima (city, Er. Isr.) **7**:336

Gitlin, A. **13:**1376
GITLIN, JACOB **7:**590
GITLOW, BENJAMIN **7:**591
Gitta (tn., Er. Isr.) **7:**335; **7:**591
GITTAIM (city, Er. Isr.) **7:**591
- *see also:* GATH
GITTELSOHN, ROLAND BERTRAM **7:**591
GITTIN (tract.) **7:**591
- *illus:* text
Gittit (journ.) **1:**newsp. list
Gittleman, Len **13:**485
Giudecca (isl, Ven.) **16:**94
- *see also:* JEWISH QUARTER
Giuseppe Gallo, *see* Sarfati (Ẓarefati), Joseph
Giusti, Giuseppe **9:**1104
GIUSTINIANI, AGOSTINO (Pantaleone) **7:**595
- Christian Hebraists **8:**34
- *illus:*
- - polyglot Psalter (1516) **7:**408
GIUSTINIANI, MARCO ANTONIO **7:**596
- dispute with Bragadini **4:**1288
- *haskamah* issue **7:**1452
- Le Bé, Guillaume **10:**1547
- printers' marks **13:**1093; **13:**1095
- Venice **16:**101
GIVAT ADA (mosh., Isr.) **7:**596
- statistics **1:**place list
Givat Aliyah (Jaffa qtr.) **15:**924
GIVATAYIM (tn., Isr.) **7:**596
- housing **9:**564
- statistics **1:**place list
- Tel Aviv **15:**924
GIVAT BRENNER (kib., Isr.) **7:**596
- founders **8:**1241
- Sereni, Enzo **14:**1182
- statistics **1:**place list
- *illus:* text
Givat ha-Mivtar (qtr., Jer.) **9:**1496
- inscriptions **16:**669
- Six-Day War **14:**1635
Givat ha-Moreh (mt., Er. Isr.) **9:**148
Givat Hananiah (qtr. Jer.), *see* Abu Ṭūr
GIVAT-HASHELOSHAH (kib., Isr.) **7:**597
- statistics **1:**place list
Givat ha-Temarim (housing zone, Tel Aviv) **15:**924
GIVAT ḤAYYIM (kib., Isr.) **7:**597
- statistics **1:**place list
GIVAT ḤEN (mosh., Isr.) **7:**598
- statistics **1:**place list
Givati (mosh., Isr.) **1:**place list
Givati Brigade **7:**1073; **9:**363
- Abba Kovner **10:**1232
- War of Independence **16:**310
Givat Koaḥ (mosh., Isr.) **1:**place list
Givat Mordekhai (sub., Jer.) **9:**1496
Givat Nili (mosh., Isr.) **1:**place list
Givat Olam (Samar. holy place) **14:**743
Givat Oz (kib., Isr.) **1:**place list
Givat Ram (hill, Jer.) **9:**1494
- *illus:*
- Hebrew University campus **3:**351; **8:**223; **9:**955
Givat Shapira (mosh., Isr.) **1:**place list
Givat Shaul (qtr., Jer.) **9:**1462
- religious concentration **9:**1495
- topography **9:**1516
Givat Sha'ul (bk.) **10:**222
Givat Shemu'el (urb. stlmt., Isr.) **1:**place list
Givat Washington (vill., Isr.) **16:**722
Givat Ye'arim (mosh., Isr.) **1:**place list
- *illus:*
- - Yemenites pruning trees **9:**577
Givat Yesha'yahu (mosh., Isr.) **1:**place list; **2:**312
Givat Yo'av (stlmt., Er. Isr.) **1:**place list **13:**1534
- *illus:*
- - vegetable harvest **9:**578
GIVENS, PHILIP S. **7:**598
- Toronto **15:**1264
Givers of Smooth Interpretations (D.S. Scrolls), *see* SEEKERS AFTER SMOOTH THINGS
GIVET, JACQUES **7:**149
Givolim (mosh., Isr.) **1:**place list
Givon, A. Z. **13:**930
Givon, Uri **5:**1433
Givot Zaid (rural stlmt., Isr.) **1:**place list
Givton (mosh.), *see* GIBBETHON
Giza (savora) **14:**1584
Gizbar (cmty. offic.) **8:**285
- Temple **15:**973
Gizrites (des. tribe) **2:**790
Gjørup, Knud **9:**1360
Glace Bay (tn., Can.) **11:**998
GLADIATOR **7:**598
Gladiolus (bot.) **6:**1365
GLADSTONE, GERALD **3:**601
Gladstone, Jacob, *see* GLATSTEIN, JACOB
Glaeser, J. **8:**34
Glagolitsa (Slav. script) **4:**1481
Glaire, Jean Baptiste **4:**881
- Christian Hebraists **8:**34
Glaisher, G. **9:**194
Glan, A., *see* OSHEROWTICH, MENDL
Glanc, Ẓevi Hirsch **4:**1164
GLANVILLE, BRIAN LESTER **7:**599
Glanz, A., *see* GLANZ-LEYELES, AARON
GLANZ, JACOB **7:**599
GLANZ, LEIB **7:**599
Glanz, Michael **14:**1643
Glanz, R. (hist.) **8:**568
GLANZ-LEYELES, AARON **7:**600
- *illus:* **16:**823
GLAPHYRA (1st cent. B.C.E.) **7:**601
- *geneal. table:* **8:**377
Glasberg, Abraham **4:**1398
Glaser, Daniel **5:**1109
GLASER, DONALD ARTHUR **7:**601
GLASER, EDUARD **7:**602
- travels **15:**1351
GLASER, JULIUS ANTON (Joshua) **7:**602
- Vogelsang, Karl von **16:**204
Glaser, Samuel **15:**626
GLASGOW (city, Scot.) **7:**602
- Bloch, Sir Maurice **4:**1108
- Scotland **14:**1036
- *illus:*
- - J.L.B. **14:**1038
Glasgow Hebrew College (Scot.) **12:**351
GLASMAN, BARUCH **7:**603
Glasner, Abraham **5:**617
GLASNER, MOSES SAMUEL **7:**604
GLASS **7:**604
- *Contents:*
- - Earliest Times **7:**604
- - Hellenistic/Roman Periods **7:**605
- - Third Century On (E. Med.) **7:**609
- - Medieval to Modern (E.) **7:**611
- - Medieval to Modern (W.) **7:**612
- craft **5:**1045
- glass sand **9:**813
- Jewish pioneers **16:**1286
- ritual purity **10:**900; **13:**1408; **14:**1565
- Sidon **14:**1506
- *illus:*
- - Chagall's "Jerusalem Windows" **4:**526; **5:**1258; **9:**1077
- - Ereẓ Israel vessels (1st and 4th cent.) **5:**1041
- - goblet, gold glass (c. 4th cent.) **3:**452
- - Jewish gold glass **7:***fcg.* 619 and 622
- - *hevra kaddisha* wine beaker **5:**308; **12:**185
- - *Kiddush cup* (19th cent.) **4:**1181
- - Mears, Otto, stained glass portrait **11:**1160
- - *mizraḥ* (17th cent.) **12:***fcg.* 171
- - *ner tamid* **12:**965
- - perfume bottle (14th cent. B.C.E.) **8:**1311
- - Shahn, Ben, stained glass windows, Buffalo **4:**1466
- - stamp **9:**844-845
Glass, Grzegerz **10:**1500
Glass, John **12:**1408
Glass, Louis **4:**1039
GLASS, MONTAGUE MARSDEN **7:**614
Glass, Solomon (Glassius) **8:**34
Glass-breaking ceremony **6:**1405; **11:**1028ff; **14:**746
Glasser, Stanley **15:**209
GLATSTEIN, JACOB **7:**614
- Katz, Aleph **10:**821
- *illus:*
- - writers' group **16:**821
Glatz (tn., Pol.) **14:**1536
GLATZER, NAḤUM NORBERT **7:**616
- Rosenzweig **14:**301
Glaubenswaechter (Hung.), *see* Shomrei Hadass Society
Glazer, B. Benedict **7:**618
Glazer, Moses **15:**412
GLAZER, NATHAN **7:**617
Glazer, N.B. **8:**1410
GLAZER, SIMON **7:**618
- Toledo **15:**1206
Glaziers, *see* GLASS
Glazman, B., *see* GLASMAN, BARUCH
Glazman, Josef **13:**145; **16:**149
Glazunov, A. K. (music.) **14:**918
Gleaner, The (period.) **6:**357
- San Francisco **14:**834
Gleanings, *see* LEKET, SHIKHḤAH, AND PE'AH
Gleb (pseud.), *see* MUTNIK, ABRAHAM
Glebokie (tn., Belor.), *see* GLUBOKOYE
Glebovitch, M., *see* OSHEROWITCH, MENDL
Gleich, Henryk **16:**724
Gleichenberg-Trautmannsdorf (vill., Aus.) **15:**466
Gleichgross, György **8:**34
Gleisner, J. **16:**1165
Gleiwitz (city, Pol.), *see* GLIWICE
Glencoe (sub., Chicago) **5:**415; **8:**1256
- *illus:*
- - North Shore Congregation synagogue **8:**1256
Glenn, Menachem G. **8:**211,213
Gleser, Jorge **15:**311
GLICENSTEIN, ENRICO **7:**618
- *illus:*
- - text
- - "Jimmy Walker" (sculp.) **14:**1061
- - Leivick, H. (drg.) **10:**1594
Glicenstein, Helen **7:**619
Glicenstein, Henoch, *see* GLICENSTEIN, ENRICO
GLICK, DAVID **11:**1208
GLICK, HIRSH **7:**619
Glickberg, S.J. **8:**958
Glickman, Itzchak **15:**1337
Glickman-Porush, Menahem **14:**1545
Glickson, Moshe, *see* GLUECKSOHN, MOSHE
Glickstein, Hyman N. **15:**311
GLID, NANDOR **7:**619
- *illus:* text
GLIÈRE, REINHOLD MORITZEVICH **7:**620
GLIKIN, MOSHE **7:**620
Glikovski, Moses **4:**666
Gliksberg, Haim **3:**591
- *illus:*
- - "King George Avenue. . . " Pl.5 3- ART
Gline (tn., Ukr.), *see* GLINYANY
Glinn, Bert **13:**484
GLINYANY (tn., Ukr.) **7:**621
- Shabbateanism **14:**1251
GLIWICE (city, Pol.) **7:**621
Glixman, Louis **16:**634
Globke, Hans **5:**1533
GLOBOCNIK, ODILO **7:**622
- Bialystok ghetto **4:**810
- gassing **16:**1332
- Wirth, Christian **16:**553
Glock, Ch. Y. **13:**1251
GLOGAU (tn., Pol.) **7:**622
- Host desecration charge **8:**1043
- Silesia **14:**1536ff
GLOGAU, JEHIEL MICHAEL BEN ASHER LEMMEL HA-LEVI **7:**623
Glogau, M. (publ.) **13:**1366
Glogau, Moses Ben Jehiel Michael **7:**623
Glogauer, Avigdor ben Simḥah ha-Levi, *see* AVIGDOR BEN SIMḤAH HA-LEVI OF GLOGAU
Glogauer, Israel, *see* LOVY, ISRAEL
Glogau-Schlesinger, Ezekiel **12:**185
Głogó (tn., Pol.), *see* GLOGAU
Glogowski, Herman **15:**790
Glory **10:**869
Glory of God **15:**1127
Glosk, Abraham Abba, *see* GLUSK, ABRAHAM ABBA
Glossary, Judeo-French **10:**424
Glosses, *see* LA'AZ
GLOTZ, GUSTAVE **7:**623
GLOUCESTER (city, Eng.) **7:**624
Gloucester (co., N.J.) **13:**368
Gloversville (city, N.Y.) **12:**1126
Glowno (tn., Pol.) **15:**447; **16:**1007
Glubb, Sir John Bagot ("Glubb Pasha")
- Abdullah **2:**57
- dismissal **9:**388
- Hussein **8:**1131
GLUBOKOYE (tn., Belor.) **7:**624
- ghetto **13:**770
Gluck, Adolph **10:**739
GLUCK, ALMA **7:**625
Gluck, Bernard **7:**625
GLUCK, SANDOR **5:**1272
GLUCKMAN, HENRY **7:**625
Gluckman, Katie **15:**198
Gluckman, Lawrence **15:**303
Gluckman, Leon **15:**1060; **15:**209
GLUCKMAN, MAX **7:**626
GLUCKSMAN, HARRY L. **7:**626
GLUCKSTEIN (Eng. fam.) **7:**626
Gluckstein, Isidore **7:**626; **15:**1177
Gluckstein, Isidore Montague **7:**626
Gluckstein, Montague **7:**626
Gluckstein, Sir Louis Halle **7:**626
Gluckstein, Sir Samuel **7:**626
GLUECK, ABRAHAM ISAAC **7:**626
Glueck, Barbara Elisabeth **7:**449
Glueck, Maxwell H. **15:**311
GLUECK, NELSON **7:**627
- Transjordan **15:**1316
- *illus:*

- - text
- - Kennedy, John F., inauguration **10**:908
- - Synagogue Council celebration **15**:631
GLUECK, SHELDON **7**:628
Glueckberg, Alexander Mikhailovich, *see* CHERNY, SASHA
GLUECKEL OF HAMELN **7**:629
- autobiography **8**:560; **11**:352
- *The Memoirs of Glueckel von Hameln* **16**:805
- *illus:* text
GLUECKS, RICHARD **7**:630
Gluecksberg, Michael **12**:1456
Gluecksberg, Nathan **13**:1369
GLUECKSOHN, MOSHE **7**:630
- *Haaretz* **7**:1007
- Odessa **12**:1326
GLUECKSTADT (tn., Ger.) **7**:631
- shipbuilding **14**:1413
Glueckstadt, Emil **4**:177
GLUECKSTADT, ISAAC HARTVIG **7**:631
Glueck-Touroff, Eleanor **5**:1108; **7**:628
Glukhov (city, Ukr.) **5**:392
- pogroms **13**:699
Glusberg, Samuel, *see* ESPINOZA, ENRIQUE
GLUSK, ABRAHAM ABBA **7**:631
GLUSKA, ZEKHARYAH **7**:632
Glusker Maggid **7**:631
GLUSKIN, ZE'EV **7**:632
- General Zionists **7**:385
- *illus:*
- - Menuḥah ve-Naḥalah Society **9**:556
Glusman, Sara **5**:448
GLUSSK (tn., Belor.) **7**:632
Glustrom, S. **6**:734
Gmul (Histadrut investment company, Isr.), *see* Gemul
Gnaeus Pompeius Magnus, *see* POMPEY
GNAT (zool.) **7**:632
- Titus **15**:1170
Gneist, Rudolf von **16**:111
Gnesen (city, Pol.), *see* GNIEZNO
GNESIN, MIKHAIL FABIANOVICH **7**:633
Gnessin, Joshua Nathan **13**:665
GNESSIN, MENAHEM **7**:634
- cultural life in Israel **9**:1003
- Habimah **7**:1028
- *illus:*
- - original Habimah company **7**:1029
GNESSIN, URI NISSAN **7**:634
- Hebrew literature **8**:198
GNIEZNO (city, Pol.) **7**:636
GNOSTICISM **7**:637
- Abulafia, Todros **2**:194
- aeon doctrine and Kabbalah **10**:565ff
- antinomianism **3**:68
- *avodah zarah* **3**:981
- *birkat ha-minim* **4**:1035
- body and soul **4**:1165
- *gematria* **7**:369
- Jacob ben Jacob **9**:1219
- Jewish-Christian sects **10**:40
- Jewish mysticism **4**:433
- Jewish philosophy **13**:424
- Kabbalah **10**:493ff
- Kabbalah and *sefirot* **10**:392
- logos **11**:462
- Lurianic cosmogony **10**:600
- Lurianic Kabbalah **10**:547
- Merkabah mysticism **11**:1388
- *min* **12**:2
- Samael **14**:719
- Samaritan beliefs **14**:740
- *Shi'ur Komah* **3**:57; **14**:1418
- Worlds, the Four **16**:641
- *see also:* DUALISM
Gnu (gr., Ger.) **8**:491
GOA (city, dist., Ind.) **7**:638
- India **8**:1355
- Inquisition **8**:1391
- *illus:*
- - text
- - Inquisition procession **8**:1393
GOAT **7**:639
- dietary laws **6**:31
- sacrifice **14**:600
- *illus:*
- - text
- - *Worms Maḥzor* **11**:732
- *see also:* IBEX
Gobat, Samuel **6**:1153
Gobelsburg (vill., Aus.) **3**:890
Gobet, Aaron **15**:28
GOBINEAU, JOSEPH ARTHUR, COMTE DE **7**:641
Göcke (Nazi crim.), *see* Goecke
GOD **7**:641
- *Contents:*
- - Bible **7**:642
- - Hellenistic Literature **7**:652
- - Medieval Jewish Philosophy **7**:657
- - Kabbalah **7**:661
- - Modern Jewish Philosophy **7**:662
- - Attributes **7**:664
- - Justice and Mercy **7**:669
- - Conceptions **7**:670
- This entry is divided according to the following sub-divisions: (1) General (2) Attributes (3) Bible (4) Conceptions (5) Hellenistic Literature (6) Jewish Philosophy, Medieval (7) Jewish Philosophy, Modern (8) Kabbalah
(1) GENERAL
- Academy on High **2**:208
- ethics **6**:934f
- evil **7**:775ff
- free will **7**:125
- *kaddish* **10**:661
- logos **11**:462
- magic **11**:704ff
- medicine **11**:1179ff
- *menorah* **11**:1355
- Messiah **11**:1410
- mythology **12**:729ff
- oath **12**:1296
- prayer **13**:978ff
- Shabbetai Ẓevi **14**:1240
- sin **14**:1588ff
- *tefillin* **15**:901
- theology **15**:1103ff
- Titus' blasphemy **15**:1170
- truth **15**:1414
- Uriel **16**:7
- visions **16**:166ff
(2) ATTRIBUTES **7**:664; **7**:671
- General
- - Abraham **2**:119
- - *Addir bi-Melukhah* **2**:256
- - *Adonai, Adonai, El Raḥum ve-Ḥanun* **2**:294
- - Bible **4**:430
- - categories **5**:254ff
- - charity **5**:339
- - forgiveness **6**:1433ff
- - ḥasidic thought **7**:1403ff
- - Judaism **10**:385ff
- - Kalam **13**:429
- Existence
- - Aaron ben Elijah **2**:11,12
- - Albo's principles **2**:536; **6**:987
- - anthropomorphism **3**:56
- - Baḥya ibn Paquda **13**:435
- - Crescas, Ḥasdai **5**:1081ff; **13**:448ff
- - dogma **3**:654ff
- - Ibn Daud **8**:1161; **13**:440
- - Jewish Aristotelianism **3**:447
- - Kant, Immanuel **11**:95
- - Levi ben Gershom **11**:95
- - Maimonides **11**:771
- - Mendelssohn, Moses **11**:1330,1336
- - Moses ben Joseph ha-Levi **12**:422
- Father
- - Abba **2**:31
- - adoption **2**:300,301
- - *Avinu Malkenu* **3**:974
- - *Avinu she-ba-Shamayim* **3**:974
- - Israelites **9**:106ff
- - orphan **12**:1478
- Incorporeality
- - Crescas, Ḥasdai **5**:1081; **5**:1082
- - Maimonides **11**:760
- Justice and mercy **7**:673ff
- - Akiva's view **2**:492
- - Daniel B **5**:1279
- - exile **7**:283
- - forgiveness **6**:1433ff
- - free will **7**:125
- - Mendelssohn, Moses **11**:1330ff
- - mercy **11**:1383
- - providence **13**:1279
- - punishment **13**:1386ff
- - redemption **14**:2ff
- - repentance **14**:73
- - reward and punishment **14**:134ff
- - righteousness **14**:180
- - Rosh ha-Shanah **14**:307
- - suffering **9**:1159ff
- - vengeance **16**:93
- *see also:* GOOD AND EVIL
- King
- - *Avinu Malkenu* **3**:974
- - Israel **5**:1021
- - Rosh ha-Shanah **14**:307
- - throne **15**:1124
- Lover and Beloved
- - Akiva **2**:490
- - *Beraḥ Dodi* **4**:584
- - House of David **5**:1340
- - jealousy **9**:1305
- - Song of Songs **15**:146
- Omnipotence
- - Crescas, Ḥasdai **5**:1083
- - miracles **12**:74ff
- - philosophy, Jewish **13**:422
- Omniscience **7**:643ff
- - Akiva **2**:492
- - Crescas, Ḥasdai **5**:1083
- - Free Will **7**:125
- - Levi ben Gershom **11**:95ff
- - philosophy, Jewish **13**:422
- Transcendence
- - anthropomorphism **3**:52
- - creator **15**:1046
- - father image **3**:974
- - theology **15**:1109
- Unity
- - Aaron ben Elijah **2**:11ff
- - *Adon Olam* **2**:296
- - Crescas, Ḥasdai **5**:1081ff
- - exile **6**:882
- - Ḥasidism **7**:1404
- - heresy **8**:359
- - Jewish Aristotelianism **3**:447
- - Judaism **10**:387
- - poverty **9**:1230
- - *Shema* **14**:1372
- Will
- - Azriel of Gerona **3**:1013,1014
- - emanation **6**:694
- - Gabirol's theory **7**:240ff
- - Ibn Zaddik **13**:437
- - Kabbalah **10**:560ff
- - Latif, Isaac ben Abraham ibn **10**:1447ff
- - lots, casting of **11**:511
- - Mordecai Joseph Leiner of Izbica **9**:1159ff
- Wisdom
- - logos **11**:461ff
- - mysticism **10**:496
- - *Solomon, Wisdom of* **15**:120
- Views on
- - Aaron ben Elijah **2**:3
- - Albo's principles **2**:536ff
- - Asher ben David **3**:706
- - Crescas, Ḥasdai **5**:1084; **7**:668
- - Gabirol's theory **7**:244
- - Levi ben Gershom **7**:667; **11**:95; **13**:447
- - Maimonides **4**:436; **7**:666; **13**:441
- - Mendel of Kotsk **10**:1223
- - Moses ben Joseph ha-Levi **12**:422
- - Saadiah **13**:431
- - Ẓaddick, Joseph ben Jacob ibn **6**:1005; **16**:913
- *see also:* GOD, NAMES OF
(3) BIBLE **7**:642
- General
- - Commandments, the 613 **5**:783ff
- - consecrated property **8**:280
- - Host of Heaven **8**:1044
- - Jerusalem **9**:1550
- - Messiah **11**:1410,1412
- - Pentateuch **13**:233; **13**:258ff
- - plagues of Egypt **13**:605
- - Prophets and prophecy **13**:1150
- - sacrifice **13**:599ff
- - Satan **14**:896ff
- - signs **14**:1524
- - Sumer **15**:515
- - tabernacle **15**:686
- - theocracy **15**:1099
- Divine Creator
- - Angel of Death **2**:953
- - creation of world **5**:1059ff
- - labor **10**:1320
- Divine Lawgiver
- - Commandments, the 613 **5**:763f
- - Decalogue **5**:1435; **12**:120,123
- - law and morality **10**:1480
- - Torah **15**:1235
- Divine Personality **7**:650
- - Aaron ben Elijah **2**:12
- - anthropomorphism **3**:51ff
- - right hand **14**:178ff
- God and Israel **7**:646
- - beatitude **4**:359ff
- - co-suffering **4**:433
- - covenant **5**:1013ff
- - holiness **10**:866ff
- - Jeremiah **9**:1350ff
- - Jonah **10**:171
- - love **11**:524ff
- Man and God **7**:650
- - monarchy **10**:1012; **10**:1014
- - Moses **12**:374
- - nature of man **11**:846ff
- - marriage **11**:1028
- - revelation **14**:117
- - Twelve Tribes **15**:1383
- *see also under individual biblical figures and themes*
(4) CONCEPTIONS **7**:669ff
- Frankists **7**:60
- Genesis, Book of **7**:394; **7**:396
- gnostic beliefs **7**:637
- Herrera, Abraham Kohen de **8**:392
- Islam **9**:97
- Jewish-Hellenists **2**:590
- Karaites **10**:778
- monotheism **12**:260
- Moses ben Joseph ha-Levi **12**:421
- Muhammad **12**:508ff
- Neoplatonism **12**:958ff; **13**:433ff
- Nieto, David **12**:1152
- Orthodoxy **9**:764; **12**:1492ff
- pantheism **10**:601ff
- Pittsburgh Platform **13**:571
- Samaritans **14**:738
- *see also:* GOD, NAMES OF
(5) HELLENISTIC LITERATURE **7**:652
- Pharisees **13**:363ff
- Philo **13**:426ff
(6) JEWISH PHILOSOPHY, MEDIEVAL **7**:657; **13**:421;

- Nature of God 7:658
- - anthropomorphism 3:53
- - Arama 3:258
- - Ibn Ezra, Moses 8:1173
- - Ibn Zaddik 13:437
- - Maimonides 11:760; 11:771ff
- - *ru'aḥ ha-kodesh* 14:364,365
- - Saadiah Gaon 14:550
- - *Shekhinah* 14:1349
- - space and place 15:217ff
- - substance and accident 15:474ff
- - time 15:1142
(7) JEWISH PHILOSOPHY, MODERN 7:662
- Atlas, Samuel 3:829
- Buber, Martin 13:463
- Cohen, Hermann 13:460
- Fromm's views 7:207
- Kant, Immanuel 10:742ff
- Reconstructionism 13:1615
- Spinoza, Baruch 13:454; 15:279ff
(8) KABBALAH 7:661; 10:490ff
- *Adam Kadmon* 2:249
- *Bahir, Sefer ha-* 4:99
- emanation 6:694
- immediate cause 5:259
- Isaac the Blind 9:35
- Lurianic cosmogony 10:588ff
- Moses ben Joseph ha-Levi 12:422
- Pseudo-Baḥya 4:103
- *Sefirot* 14:1104
- *Shi'ur Komah* 14:1417
- *illus:*
- - Abel and Cain 2:58
- - Abraham, covenant with 5:1014,1016
- - appearing to the young Samuel 3:54
- - Bezalel inspired 4:787
- - creating the world 5:1066, *fcg.* 1067
- - creation 13:574
- - "Creation of Adam" (frsc., Michelangelo) 5:1068
- - creation of Eve 4:874
- - David praying to 4:321
- - Ezekiel's first vision 6:1084
- - "Garden of Delights" (paint., Hieronymus Bosch) 2:43
- - handing the Ten Commandments to Moses 5:1436,1438
- - Jacob's vision at Beth-El 3:52
- - ordering Jacob to go to Beth-El 4:730
- - Samuel called by 14:782
- - Satan cast down 2:970
- - *Shabbat ha-Gadol piyyut* 14:1217
- - Six Days of Creation 5:*fcg.* 1070
- - talking to Melchizedek 14:1266
- - thirteen *middot* 10:544
- *see also:* ANTHROPOMORPHISM; BELIEF; MONOTHEISM; PHILOSOPHY, JEWISH; REVELATION; THEOLOGY
God, Chariot of, *see* THRONE OF GOD
God, love and fear of, *see* LOVE
God, Mountain of (Bib.) 14:1597
GOD, NAMES OF 7:674
- General
- - abbreviations 2:50
- - acrostics 2:231
- - Adam *gematria* 2:248
- - Ahimaaz chronicle 8:666
- - amulets 2:909
- - anthropomorphism 3:55ff
- - astrology 3:792; 3:794
- - *ba'al shem* 4:5
- - Canaanite script 16:1335
- - creative power 7:754
- - *genizah* 16:1333,1335
- - Jahoel 11:1444
- - justice and mercy of God 7:669
- - Koran 10:1196
- - letters of 2:747
- - magic 11:711
- - oaths 12:1300
- - Samaritans 14:740
- - Shabbetai Ẓevi 14:1222
- - Talmud 8:1142; 14:1394
- - targums 7:655
- - tattoos 16:663
- - *tefillin* 15:900ff
- - Temple 15:976
- - *Temple Scroll* 15:996
- Specific Names
- - Abba 2:31
- - Ancient of Days 2:940
- - *Anna be-Kho'aḥ* 3:25
- - *Avinu she-ba-Shamayim* 3:974
- - *Makom* 7:672
- - Peace 13:197
- - Treasure 15:1361
- Bible
- - *avodah* 3:977
- - blasphemy 4:1074
- - creation 5:1060ff
- - Genesis, Book of 7:389ff
- - *paseq* rule 16:1459
- - patriarchal narratives 13:183
- - Pentateuch 13:234; 13:258ff
- - priestly blessing 13:1061
- - *qere perpetuum* 16:1421
- - revelation 12:374; 14:118
- - Urim and Thumim 16:8
- - Jonah, Book of 10:171
- - Torah 15:1241
- Kabbalah 7:662; 10:499; 10:501; 10:504ff
- - Christian 10:644
- - doctrine 10:565
- - Ein-Sof 6:535
- - exile 10:618
- - Lurianic cosmogony 10:591ff
- - prayer 10:628ff
- - *Sefer Yeẓirah* 16:785ff
- - *sefirot* 10:572
- - Torah 10:621ff
- Views on
- - Abraham ben Alexander of Cologne 2:134
- - Abulafia, Abraham ben Samuel 2:186
- - Alting's research 2:777
- - Asher ben David 3:706
- - Falk, Samuel 6:1159
- - Judah Halevi 10:363ff
- - Kaspi, Joseph ibn 10:810
- - Rav 13:1578
- - Reuchlin, Johannes 14:110
- - Rosenzweig, Franz 14:302
- *illus:*
- - text
- - amulets 2:907-914; 4:1051
- - Danish ducat (1645) 5:1538
- - forty-two-letter Holy Name 6:999
- - seventy-two-letter Holy Name 10:584
- - *Shivviti* plaques 13:44-45; 14:1420-1421
God, Throne of, *see* THRONE OF GOD
GODAL, ERIC 7:685
God Bless America (song) 4:658
Godchaux, Emile 11:520
GODDARD, PAULETTE 12:468
Goddel of Orenburg 4:1417
Godechau-Spire (print.) 11:1451
GODEFROI, MICHAEL HENRI 7:686
- Amsterdam 2:900
Goder Pereẓ (bk.), *see Minḥat Shai*
Godfather, *see* SANDAK
Godfrey of Bouillon
- Crusades 5:1135
- Jerusalem 9:267,271,1415ff
Godhead (conc.) 14:1223ff
- *see also:* EIN-SOF
GODIK, GIORA 15:1082
- Israel theater 9:1005
GODINER, SAMUEL NISSAN 7:686
GODINEZ, FELIPE 7:686
- Spanish literature 15:254
God-is-dead (theol. mvmt.) 13:1254
God of Abraham Praise (Prot. hymn.) 16:835
GODOWSKY, LEOPOLD (mus.) 7:687
Godowsky, Leopold (inv.) 7:687 12:699
Godwyn, Thomas 8:34
GOEBBELS, PAUL JOSEF 7:687
- history 8:737
- Nazi conference, 1938 7:688
Goecke (Nazi crim.) 11:389
Goeding (tn., Cz.), *see* HODONIN
Goelman, Elazar 7:861
GOERING, HERMANN WILHELM 7:688
- Holocaust 8:853; 8:855
- *illus:*
- - Nuremberg trial 16:290
GOERITZ, MATHIAS 3:601
GOERLITZ (tn., Ger.) 7:689
- Silesia 14:1536
Goes, Hugo van der 13:1490
- *illus:*
- - "meeting of Jacob and Rachel" (draw.) 13:1487
Goetel, Ferdynand 8:893
Goeth, Amon 16:295
GOETHE, JOHANN WOLFGANG VON 7:689
- Mendelssohn, Moses 11:1329
- Oppenheim, Moritz Daniel 12:1423
- Wandering Jew 16:261
- *illus:*
- - Mendelssohn, Felix, and 11:1327
GOETTINGEN (city, Ger.) 7:690
Goettingen, Eliezer 9:21
Goettingen, Eliezer Lipman 9:21
Goetz, Benjamin 11:409
Goetz, Meir ben Eliakim 10:1433
Goetz, William 12:449
Goez, Georg 8:34
GOFNAH (tn., Judea) 7:691
- Johanan ben Zakkai 9:241
Gog, J.L., *see* GINSBURG, JEKUTHIEL
Goga, Octavian 14:405
GOG AND MAGOG 7:691
- Crusades 9:271
- eschatology 6:868ff
- Gyges 11:621
- Islamic eschatology 6:885
- *illus:*
- - warrior 6:863
Gogol, Isaac 14:1127
Gogol, Nikolai 14:508; 15:1570
Gohl, J., *see* Golius, Jacob
Goi, see GENTILE
Goido, Isaac, *see* GORIN, BERNARD
GOIIM (Bib. term) 7:693
- chosen people 7:410
Goikhman, Boris 12:1377
Goitein (Hung. fam.) 10:1156
GOITEIN, BARUCH BENEDICT 7:693
GOITEIN, DENISE R. 1:30
Goitein, E. D. 15:205
Goitein, Jacob L. 16:1165
GOITEIN, SHLOMO DOV (Fritz) 7:694
- Cairo *genizah* 16:1340
- historiography 8:564
Goitein, Ẓevi Hirsch (Hermann) 7:693
Gojawiczyńska, Pola 13:801
Golah, see DIASPORA; GALUT
GOLAN (tn., Bashan) 7:694
- city of refuge 5:591
Golan, Menaḥem 12:462
- *illus:*
- - *Tevye and His Seven Daughters* 12:462
Golan, Shmuel 13:1340
Golan Heights (reg., Er. Isr.), *see* RAMAT HA-GOLAN
Golani Brigade (Isr. army)
- Haganah 7:1073
- historical survey 9:363
- War of Independence 16:309ff
Golant, Yevgeni Y. 6:464
Golb, N. 16:1336,1341
GOLCUV JENIKOV (tn., Bohem.) 7:695
Gold (met.) 11:1428; 11:1429ff
- alchemic theory 2:544ff
- goldsmiths 7:738
- jewelry 13:1012
- *Sefer Torah* letters 16:670
- Solomon 15:98
Gold, A. (Bib. trans.) 4:883
Gold, Arthur (mus.) 15:1369
GOLD, BENJAMIN 7:695
Gold, Bertram H. 11:503
Gold, E. S. 14:398
Gold, H. (poet) 16:822
GOLD, HENRY RAPHAEL 7:696
GOLD, HERBERT 7:696
- U.S. literature 15:1577
GOLD, HUGO 7:696
- press 13:1029
Gold, Ivan 15:1577
Gold, Joseph (physic.) 15:1218
Gold, Joseph (r.) 16:633
Gold, Leon 14:399; 16:1134
GOLD, MICHAEL 7:697
- New York City 12:1120
- U.S. literature 15:1571ff
Gold, Niusia 12:455
Gold, Thomas 3:807
GOLD, WOLF (Ze'ev) 7:697
- Declaration of Independence 5:1455
Golda, J. H. 7:92
Golda Jordanis 11:181
Goldberg (fam., U.S.) 3:450
Goldberg, A. (polit.) 16:1180
Goldberg, Aaron (polit., U.S.) 13:482
Goldberg, Aaron (stlr., U.S.) 13:482
Goldberg, Abraham 16:1142
- *illus:*
- - Hebrew Pen Club 12:1109
Goldberg, Adolph 13:482
GOLDBERG, ALEXANDER 7:698
- Technion 15:891
GOLDBERG, ARTHUR JOSEPH 7:698
- *illus:*
- - text
- - Synagogue Council of America celebration 15:631
Goldberg, B. Abbott 14:599
GOLDBERG, BAER (DOV) BEN ALEXANDER 7:700
- linguistic literature 16:1376
Goldberg, Benjamin (informer) 8:1369
GOLDBERG, BEN ZION 7:700
- *illus:*
- - Jewish Anti-Fascist Committee 3:63; 6:1203
GOLDBERG, BERTRAND 3:363
GOLDBERG, BORIS 7:701
- *illus:*
- - First Duma electors 14:445
Goldberg, Charles 13:482
Goldberg, David 13:482
Goldberg, Dov ben Alexander, *see* GOLDBERG, BAER BEN ALEXANDER
Goldberg, Elijah 6:831
Goldberg, Georges 3:359, 365
Goldberg, Gumpertz 12:266

Goldberg, H. (cmty. ldr.) **11:**498
Goldberg, Herman (law.) **16:**516
Goldberg, Hyman (stlr.) **13:**482
Goldberg, Hyman (polit.) **13:**482
Goldberg, Irving **15:**1036
GOLDBERG, ISAAC (au.) **7:**702
Goldberg, Isaac (stlr.) **13:**482
Goldberg, Isaac (Zion., S.A.) **15:**198
GOLDBERG, ISAAC LEIB **7:**702
- Appel, Judah Leib **3:**222
- *illus:*
- - First Duma electors **14:**445
- - F.Z.C. **16:**1165
Goldberg, Isaiah-Nissan Hakohen, *see* YAKNEHAZ
Goldberg, Isidore **15:**1479
GOLDBERG, J. B. **11:**1573
Goldberg, Joseph (lab. ldr.) **8:**1348
Goldberg, Joseph (judge) **16:**634
Goldberg, Joseph (film prod.) **12:**455
Goldberg, Joshua **14:**1509
GOLDBERG, LEA **7:**703
- drama **6:**207
- Hebrew literature **8:**201
Goldberg, Leo (stlr.) **13:**482
Goldberg, Leo (astron.) **3:**807
Goldberg, Marshall **15:**308
Goldberg, Menahem, *see* BORAISHA, MENAHEM
Goldberg, Milton M., *see* GORDON, MILTON M.
Goldberg, Morton **6:**1161; **15:**1206
GOLDBERG, MOSES WOLF **5:**382
Goldberg, N. (au.) **13:**133
Goldberg, Nathan **15:**68
GOLDBERG, OSCAR **7:**705
Goldberg, Rachel **7:**702
GOLDBERGER, IZIDOR **7:**706
- cartoons **5:**216
Goldberg, Samuel Leib **15:**817
Goldberg, Simon **11:**1167
Goldberg, William **5:**610
Goldberger, Daniel **5:**1545
GOLDBERGER, IZIDOR **7:**06
GOLDBERGER, JOSEPH **7:**706
Goldberger, Leo, *see* Buday, Leo
Goldberger, Samuel **15:**1040
Goldberger, Yozefa **16:**1004
Goldberger factory (Hung.) **4:**1450
Goldbert, B. Z. **14:**499
Goldblat, M. **10:**997; **15:**1075
Goldblatt, David (enc. ed.) **6:**731
Goldblatt, David (publ., S.A.) **13:**1049; **15:**193
Goldblatt, Emanuel **15:**303
Goldblatt, Harry **5:**606
Goldblatt, Jacob N. **7:**1239
Goldblatt, Mose **15:**310
Goldblatt, Sarah **15:**210
Goldblatt, Wilhelm **5:**1038
Goldbloom, Alton **11:**1202
GOLDBLOOM, JACOB KOPPEL **7:**706
- *illus:*
- - protest against Passfield White Paper **16:**1118
Goldbloom, Victor **12:**288; **13:**811
GOLDBLUM, ISRAEL ISSER (Isidore) **7:**707
Goldbogen, Avrom Hirsch, *see* TODD, MIKE
Goldburg, Ariel L. **14:**162
Golde, I. **16:**1181
GOLDEN, DAVID AARON **7:**707
- Canada **5:**112
GOLDEN, HARRY LEWIS **7:**707
- U.S. literature **15:**1579
GOLDEN, JOHN **15:**1082
Goldenaken (tn., Belg.), *see* Jodoigne
GOLDENBERG, BAERISH **7:**708
Goldenberg, Emanuel, *see* ROBINSON, EDWARD G.
Goldenberg, Grigori **15:**29
GOLDENBERG, H. CARL **7:**708
GOLDENBERG, LAZAR **7:**708
- Liebermann, Aaron Samuel **7:**1057
GOLDENBERG, SAMUEL LEIB **7:**709
Goldenblum, Aaron Isaac **7:**1232; **10:**1165
GOLDENBURG, SAMUEL **15:**1083
- Adler, Celia **2:**271
GOLDEN CALF **7:**709
- Aaron **2:**5
- Aaronides **2:**20
- ʿAglibol **15:**698
- Decalogue **5:**1442
- Exodus, Book of **6:**1061ff
- idolatry **8:**1228ff
- Islam **14:**757
- Jeroboam **8:**594; **9:**1047ff; **9:**1372
- kabbalistic view **10:**616
- Levites **11:**71; **13:**1082ff
- Moses **12:**376ff
- proscription **8:**346
- red heifer **14:**13
- Satan **14:**904
- tabernacle **15:**685; **15:**687
- tablets of the law **15:**691
Goldendach, David, *see* Riazanov, David
GOLDENE KEYT, DI (period.) **7:**713
Golden Gate (Jer.), *see* Gate of Mercy
GOLDEN HAGGADAH (illum. ms.) **7:**1099
- illuminated manuscripts **8:**1264
- *illus:* **4:**24,1059;**6:**238,980,1045; **7:**273,1084; **8:**1217; **10:**206; **11:**423,902; **12:***fcg.* 427; **13:**165,609; **14:**1550
Golden Haggadah, "Sister" to (illum. ms.)
- *illus.:* **2:**806;**7:***fcg.*1323
Golden Rule **8:**484
Goldenschmidt, Ludwig Henry **13:**820
GOLDENSON, SAMUEL HARRY **7:**713
- Albany **2:**524
- New York City **12:**1118
GOLDENTHAL, JACOB (orient.) **7:**713
Goldenthal, Jacob (maskil) **16:**1328
GOLDENWEISER, ALEXANDER ALEXANDROVICH **7:**714
- anthropology **3:**38
GOLDENWEISER, ALEXANDER SOLOMONOVICH **7:**714
GOLDENWEISER, EMANUEL ALEXANDROVICH **7:**714
Golder, Benjamin M. **13:**230; **16:**157
Golders Green (sub., London) **6:**449,762; **11:**478,479
- *illus:*
- - shift of population **11:**479
GOLDFADEN, ABRAHAM **7:**715
- *Akeydas Yitskhok* **2:**486
- history chart **8:**766-767
- theater **15:**1064ff
- Wandering Jew **16:**262
- *illus:* text
Goldfaden, Judel **10:**923
Goldfarb, S. (publ.) **13:**1376
Goldfarb, S. D. (enc. ed.) **6:**734
Goldfarb, William **13:**1339
Goldfein, M. **13:**1294
Goldfield (concen. camp, Est.) **7:**619
Goldfield (vill., Nev.) **12:**1017
Goldfish, Samuel, *see* GOLDWYN, SAMUEL
Goldflam, Samuel **11:**1198,1204
Goldfogle, Henry M. **12:**1104
- *illus:*
- - American Jewish Committee **2:**823
Goldhaft, Arthur **12:**1030; **16:**157
Goldhaft, Tevis **16:**158
Goldhahn, M., *see* Aurogallus, M.
GOLDHAMMER-SAHAWI, LEO **7:**717
GOLDHAR, PINCHAS **7:**717
Gold Hill (tn., Nev.) **12:**1017
Goldhurst, Herschel, *see* GOLDEN, HARRY LEWIS
GOLDIN, EZRA **7:**718
- Shalkovich, Abraham Leib **14:**1269
Goldin, Hyman **5:**452
GOLDIN, JUDAH **7:**718
Golding, Carl Ernest Louis **12:**911
GOLDING, LOUIS **7:**718
Goldkorn, Georges **13:**118
GOLDMAN (U.S. fam.) **7:**719
- Arizona **3:**450
- banking **4:**178
Goldman, A. (sol.) **11:**783
Goldman, Aaron **3:**421
GOLDMAN, BERNARD **7:**719
Goldman, Charley **15:**306
Goldman, Colonel **11:**1564
GOLDMAN, EDWIN FRANKO **7:**720
GOLDMAN, EMMA **7:**720
GOLDMAN, ERIC FREDERICK **7:**721
Goldman, Frank **4:**1147
Goldman, Gerald **13:**162
Goldman, Harry **15:**300
Goldman, Henry **7:**719
GOLDMAN, HETTY **7:**721
- archaeology **3:**302
Goldman, Hymen **16:**357
Goldman, Isaac **6:**731
Goldman, Jacob **7:**719
Goldman, J. D. **3:**459
Goldman, Julius **15:**304
Goldman, Leo **16:**338
Goldman, Marcus **7:**719
Goldman, Max **16:**1555
GOLDMAN, MAYER CLARENCE **7:**721
Goldman, Michael, *see* LIBER, MARC
Goldman, Moe **15:**303
Goldman, Mordecai **8:**206
GOLDMAN, MOSES HA-KOHEN **7:**722
- newspapers, Hebrew **12:**1052
Goldman, Moshe **2:**837
Goldman, Philip **6:**1364
Goldman, Richard Franko **7:**720
GOLDMAN, SOLOMON **7:**722
- *illus:*
- - protest against 1940 White Paper **15:**1632
Goldman, William **6:**785
GOLDMAN, YA'AKOV BEN ASHER **7:**722
GOLDMANN, EMIL **7:**723
Goldmann, Isidore, *see* ISOU ISIDORE
GOLDMANN, LUCIEN **7:**149
Goldmann, Marcus **4:**875
Goldmann, Max, *see* REINHARDT, MAX
GOLDMANN, NAHUM **7:**723
- COJO **16:**636
- Zionism **16:**1061ff; **16:**1176
- *illus:*
- - Ben-Gurion and Adenauer **2:**265
- - Biltmore Hotel Conference **15:**1633
- - German-Israel reparations agreement **7:**499; **14:**72
- - Hebrew Writers' Convention **8:**213
Goldmann, Sidney **15:**1376
Goldmann, Solomon Ẓevi **7:**723
Goldmann, Ze'ev, *see* BEN ḤAYYIM, ZE'EV
GOLDMARK (fam.) **7:**726
Goldmark, Henry **7:**726
Goldmark, Joseph **3:**894; **7:**726; **13:**809
GOLDMARK, KARL **7:**727
- family **7:**726
- stamps **15:**336
Goldmark, Pauline **7:**726
GOLDMARK, PETER CARL **8:**1431
Goldmark, Rubin **7:**726
Goldner, H. **13:**1369
Goldney, Edward **7:**1350
Goldovsky, Boris **12:**699
Goldreich, Arthur **15:**209
Goldreich, I. M. **4:**138
Goldreich, Samuel **15:**198; **16:**1140
Goldsboro (city, N. C.) **12:**1220
GOLDSCHEID, RUDOLF **7:**727
- sociology **15:**66
Goldscheider, Calvin **15:**68
Goldscheider, Isaac **7:**742
Goldscheider, Jacob **7:**742; **14:**381
Goldscheider, Ludwig **13:**1367
Goldschmidt (fam., Ger.) **5:**1010; **8:**435; **13:**1519
Goldschmidt, Abraham Meir **7:**728; **10:**1591; **16:**338
Goldschmidt, Adolf **3:**650
Goldschmidt, A. J. **11:**1472
Goldschmidt, Albert **13:**1366
Goldschmidt, Bendix (Benedict)
- banking **4:**173
- Court Jews **5:**1010
- Kassel **10:**812
GOLDSCHMIDT, ERNST DANIEL **7:**727
- *seliḥot* **14:**1134
GOLDSCHMIDT, GUIDO **7:**728
GOLDSCHMIDT, HANS **7:**728
GOLDSCHMIDT, HEINRICH JACOB **5:**382
- Goldschmidt, Victor Moritz **7:**732
GOLDSCHMIDT, HENRIETTE **7:**728
- education **6:**464
GOLDSCHMIDT, HERMANN (astron.) **7:**729
Goldschmidt, Hermann (cmty. ldr.) **2:**650; **4:**656; **10:**44
GOLDSCHMIDT, HUGO **12:**691
GOLDSCHMIDT, JAKOB **7:**729
- art collection **3:**648
Goldschmidt, Johanna **6:**464
GOLDSCHMIDT, LAZARUS **7:**729
- forgeries **6:**1431
- *Sefer Yeẓirah* **16:**788
GOLDSCHMIDT, LEVIN **7:**730
GOLDSCHMIDT, LUDWIG **7:**730
Goldschmidt, Max **13:**1049
GOLDSCHMIDT, MEIR ARON **7:**730
Goldschmidt, Meyer **5:**952
GOLDSCHMIDT, RICHARD BENEDICT **7:**731
GOLDSCHMIDT, RICHARD HELLMUTH **13:**1346
Goldschmidt, R. J. **10:**1121
Goldschmidt, S. H., *see* Goldschmidt, Hermann
Goldschmidt, Salomon **10:**1159; **16:**913
Goldschmidt, V. (bkseller) **4:**1239
GOLDSCHMIDT, VICTOR (sci.) **7:**732
GOLDSCHMIDT, VICTOR MORITZ (sci.) **7:**732
Goldschmied, Gabriel **15:**311
Goldschmied, Salvadore **15:**311
Goldshlak, Yehiel Mikhal ben Abraham **14:**1516
GOLDSMID (Eng. fam.) **7:**733
- Cohen, Benjamin **5:**666
- Falk, Samuel **6:**1160
- politics **13:**811
- *geneal. table:* **7:**735

Goldsmid, Aaron 7:733
Goldsmid, Abraham 4:174; 4:1289; 7:733
Goldsmid, Albert 7:733
GOLDSMID, ALBERT EDWARD WILLIAMSON 7:737
- *illus:*
- - El-Arish technical commission 6:565
Goldsmid, Anna Maria 7:734
Goldsmid, Asher 7:733; 12:198
Goldsmid, Benjamin 7:733
Goldsmid, Carmel 15:1092
Goldsmid, Sir Francis Henry 7:734
Goldsmid, Frederick David 7:734
Goldsmid, Sir Frederick John 7:734
Goldsmid, Sir Isaac Lyon 6:462; 7:733; 15:1166
- *illus:* 7:734
Goldsmid, Sir Julian 7:734; 13:317
Goldsmid, Lionel L. 13:1049
Goldsmid, Salomon 10:44
Goldsmith (fam.) 11:1302
Goldsmith, Georgiana 7:737
Goldsmith, Ike 10:738
Goldsmith, Jackie 15:303
GOLDSMITH, LEWIS 7:737
GOLDSMITH, MAURICE 1:30
Goldsmith, Minnie 16:357
Goldsmith, Oliver 10:305
Goldsmith, Raymond William 7:737
GOLDSMITH, SAMUEL ABRAHAM 7:737
GOLDSMITH, WILLIAM 8:1431
GOLDSMITHS AND SILVERSMITHS 7:738
- ceremonial objects 5:288f
- crafts 5:1041
- guilds 7:971ff
- Yemen 16:744
- *illus:*
- - text
- - alms boxes 5:342,347,353
- - book covers 4:244,1228,1230-1232
- - ceremonial objects 5:289-307; 10:975; 11:265-271; 15:1260-1261; 16:693
- - circumcision implements 5:567,569
- - *dreidel* (19th cent.) 7:1286
- - *etrog* silver container 15:*fcg.* 494
- - Hannukah lamps 4:1462; 5:301; 7:1300, 1307,1309,1313
- - *Havdalah* implements 3:529; 5:118,300; 7:*fcg.* 1259 and 1262, 1485-1488
- - marriage cup 11:*fcg. 1067*
- - *mezuzot* 11:1475
- - Purim noisemakers 13:1393
- - Sabbath lamps 5:299; 6:1383; 14:561
- - Sabbath table set 14:568
- - *seder* plate 11:1532
- - *tefillin* boxes 15:899
- - *tohorah* plate 15:1188
- - Torah breastplates 3:542; 4:1337-1345; 5:296
- - Torah crowns 3:640; 5:293; 14:1649; 15:1257
- - Torah scroll finials 3:530; 4:1527; 5:291,1444; 7:740; 12:725; 13:311
- - wedding rings 5:305; 11:*fcg.* 1067
- - Yemenite silversmith 5:1047; 16:750
Goldstein, Abe (sport.) 15:305
Goldstein, Abraham (journ.) 16:679
GOLDSTEIN, ABRAHAM SAMUEL 7:744
Goldstein, Alan 15:308
GOLDSTEIN, ALEXANDER 7:744
- *illus:*
- - Montevideo, Zionist Organization central committee 16:1126
- - *Razsvet* staff 13:1596
- - Ukrainian Provisional National Council 15:1515
GOLDSTEIN, ANGELO 7:745
- Židovská Strana 16:1018
Goldstein, B. (resist. ldr.) 4:1505
Goldstein, Bertha 7:747
Goldstein, Donald 15:303
Goldstein, Esther 15:306
GOLDSTEIN, EUGEN 7:745
GOLDSTEIN, FANNY 7:745
Goldstein, Harry (sport.) 15:310
Goldstein, Harry (police com.) 14:143
GOLDSTEIN, HERBERT S. 7:746
- Fischel, Harry 6:1317
Goldstein, Hyman 15:310
Goldstein, I. (comp.) 11:431
Goldstein, Isaac (resist. ldr.) 15:84
GOLDSTEIN, ISRAEL 7:747
- *illus:*
- - Biltmore Hotel conference 15:1633
- - protest against 1940 White Paper 15:1632
GOLDSTEIN, JENNIE 15:1083
Goldstein, Joe 13:1361
GOLDSTEIN, JOSEF 7:747
- music 12:651
GOLDSTEIN, JUDAH JAMISON 7:748
GOLDSTEIN, JULIUS 7:748
GOLDSTEIN, KURT 7:748
Goldstein, Leopold, *see* BALTAZAR, CAMIL
Goldstein, M. (Revisionist) 13:1598
Goldstein, Mateo (law.) 10:1502
Goldstein, Max 14:891
Goldstein, Mordecai 15:339
Goldstein, Nathaniel L. 12:1127
Goldstein, Pawel 11:1204
Goldstein, Perez 8:1104
Goldstein, Reuben 15:306
GOLDSTEIN, RICHARD FRANK 5:383
Goldstein, Robert 2:513
Goldstein, S.A. 3:839
GOLDSTEIN, SALWIAN 7:749
Goldstein, Samson M. 11:1553
Goldstein, Sholem, *see* GOLDENBURG, SAMUEL
GOLDSTEIN, SIDNEY (math.) 7:749
- Technion 15:890
GOLDSTEIN, SIDNEY EMANUEL (r.) 7:749
Goldstein, Simon 11:298
Goldstick, Isidore 11:482
Goldstine, Sidney 16:556
Goldston, Edward 13:1374
Goldstone, Barnard 11:1554
GOLDSTUECKER, EDUARD 7:750
- Czechoslovakia 5:1202
Goldszmidt, Henryk, *see* KORCZAK, JANUSZ
Gold Teachers' Seminary (Jer.), *see* Rabbi Gold Teachers' Seminary
Goldwasser (fam.), *see* GOLDWATER
Goldwasser, Edwin L. 7:751
Goldwasser, Israel (poet), *see* EMIOT, ISRAEL
GOLDWASSER, ISRAEL EDWIN 7:751
Goldwasser, J. 4:1480
GOLDWATER (fam.) 7:751
- Arizona 3:450
Goldwater, Baron 7:751
Goldwater, Barry M. 3:450; 7:751
Goldwater, Joseph 7:751; 13:481
Goldwater, Michael 3:450; 7:751; 13:481
Goldwater, Morris 3:450; 7:751
Goldwater, Samuel 5:1569
GOLDWATER, SIGMUND SCHULZ 7:751
- medicine 11:1202
- New York City 12:1093
GOLDWYN, SAMUEL 7:751
- Los Angeles 11:503
- motion pictures 12:447
GOLDZIHER, IGNAZ (Isaac Judah) 7:752
- Cairo *Genizah* 16:1339
- Heller, Bernát 8:307
Goleh (poet), *see* Fleischer, Ezra
GOLEM (homunculus) 7:753
- Abraham 2:122
- alchemy 2:545
- Ashkenazi, Zevi Hirsch 3:734
- folktales 6:1384
- Maharal mi-Prag 10:379
- *Sefer Yezirah* 10:508; 10:516
- Shabbateanism 10:586; 14:1241
Golf 15:308
Golgotha (loc., Jer.)
- Adam 2:225; 2:245
- Church of Holy Sepulcher 9:1406
- Gordon's identification 9:1544
GOLIATH (bib. fig.) 7:756
- Berbers 4:587
- David 5:1319, 1327
- Elhanan 6:611
- in the Arts 5:1334
- Orpah 12:1478
- warfare 16:271ff
- *illus:*
- - David with head of 5:1326
- - *Kaufmann Mishneh Torah* 7:*fcg.* 747
- - slain by David 4:1; 5:1330; 8:1283; 14:793
Goliger, Silviu, *see* SILVIU, GEORGE
GOLINKIN, MORDECAI 7:759
Golitsyn, A. 4:1129
GOLITSYN, COUNT NIKOLAI NIKOLAYEVICH 7:759
Golius, Jacob 8:34 3:998
Golke, Elfriede, *see* FISCHER, RUTH
Goll, Claire 7:760
GOLL, YVAN 7:759
GOLLANCZ, SIR HERMANN 7:760
GOLLANCZ, SIR ISRAEL 7:760
Gollancz, Samuel Marcus 7:760
Gollancz, Sir Victor 7:761
Gollanin, L. 12:660
GOLLER, IZAK 7:762
- English literature 6:784
- Psalms 13:1326
Gollubier, Emil 15:303
GOLLUF, ELEAZAR 7:762
Golluf, Isaac 7:762
Gollwitzer, Helmut 7:498
Golnitzki, Heshel 5:311
Golodetz (fam.) 14:1327
Golodetz, Hayyim 14:1327
GOLODNY, MIKHAIL 14:515
GOLOMB, ABRAHAM 7:763
GOLOMB, ELIYAHU 7:763
- Hagannah 9:683; 7:1065ff
- *illus:*
- - text
- - autograph 9:331
- - Haganah High Command 7:1070
- - Herzlia Gymnasium class 11:1448
- - Technion, protest against non-Hebrew teaching 9:331
Golomb, Eliyahu (refugee boat), *see* *Eliyahu Golomb*
Golombek, Harry 5:406
GOLOVANEVSK (tn., Rus.) 7:765
- self-defense 14:1127
Golphon, Joseph ben Mako 4:838
Golta (concen. camp, loc.) 12:1326; 13:326; 15:1333
Goltsch-Jenikau (tn., Bohem.), *see* GOLCUV JENIKOV
GOLUCHOWSKI, AGENOR, COUNT 7:765
Gomarus (Hebr.) 8:34
Gombault, Georges 13:109
GOMBERG, MOSES 7:765
Gomberg, Vladimir, *see* LIDIN, VLADIMIR GERMANOVICH
Gombin (tn., Pol.), *see* GABIN
GOMBINER, ABRAHAM ABELE BEN HAYYIM HA-LEVI 7:766
- on chess 5:403
- *illus:*
- - text
- - *Magen Avraham* 8:74
Gombiner, Jacob Isaac 7:766
Gombos, Sandor 12:1376
Gombrich, E. H. 3:651
GOMEL (city, Belor.) 7:767
- self-defense 14:1125
GOMEL, BLESSING OF 7:768
Gomelei hesed shel emet (burial socs.) 5:347
Gomelsky, Alexander 15:304
GOMER (bib. fig., people) 7:768
Gomer (Hosea's w.) 8:1010
Gomes d'Elvas, Luis 15:270
GOMEZ (fam., U.S.) 7:768
GÓMEZ, ANTONIO ENRÍQUEZ 7:769
- Amsterdam 2:896
- Babel, Tower of 4:26
- Enríquez Basurto, Diego 6:800
- Spanish literature 15:253
Gomez, Benjamin 7:769; 12:1074
Gomez, Daniel 7:769; 12:1067
Gomez, David 7:769
Gomez, Gabriel 5:1009
Gomez, Isaac 7:769
Gomez, Lewis Moses 7:768; 12:1125
Gomez, Maria 5:468; 15:1379
Gomez, Mordecai 7:769; 12:1067; 16:240
Gomez, Rachel 16:240
Gomez, Yolante 3:166
Gómez de León, Francisco 5:1146
Gomez de Mesquita, Moses, *see* Mesquita, Moses Gomez de
Gomez de Olivia, León 5:461
Gómez de Sossa, Abraham 7:770
Gómez de Sossa, Benito 7:770
GÓMEZ DE SOSSA, ISAAC 7:770
Gómez Frontera, Ruy, *see* Bueno, Joseph
Gómez Silveyra, Abraham 6:320
Gomorrah (bib. city), *see* SODOM AND GOMORRAH
GOMPERS, SAMUEL 7:770
- chronological chart 8:766-767
- tobacco workers 15:1177
Gomperts (fam.), *see* GOMPERZ
GOMPERTZ (fam., Eng.) 7:773
Gompertz, Benjamin 7:773; 8:1410
Gompertz, Ephraim 7:773
Gompertz, Isaac 7:773
Gompertz, Joseph 7:773
Gompertz, Lewis 7:773; 15:307
Gompertz, Richard 7:773
Gompertz, Solomon Barent 7:773
GOMPERZ (fam.) 7:773
- Auspitz family 3:875
- Court Jews 5:1009
- Netherlands 12:980
- *geneal. table:* text
Gomperz, Aaron Elias 7:1435; 7:774
Gomperz, Benedict Reuben, *see* WESEL, BARUCH BENDET BEN REUBEN
Gomperz, Elijah (17th cent.) 5:934; 7:773
Gomperz, Elijah (18th cent.) 7:774; 16:459
Gomperz, F. 14:295

Gomperz, Heinrich **7**:774; **7**:775
Gomperz, Julius von **4**:1384; **7**:774
Gomperz, Loeb ben Bendit (Leopold Benedict) Neumegen **7**:774
Gomperz, Max von **7**:774
Gomperz, Moses Levi **7**:774
Gomperz, Moses Salomon **7**:774
Gomperz, Phillip **7**:774
Gomperz, Reuben Elias **7**:773
GOMPERZ, THEODOR **7**:774
Gomplowicz, Ludwig **16**:1328
Gomulicki, Wiktor **13**:800
Gomulka, Władysław **3**:159; **13**:783ff
Gonçalves de Magalhães, Domingos José **15**:251
Gondar (tn., Eth.) **6**:1146ff
GONDOR, FERENC **10**:311
Gonen (kib., Isr.) **1**:place list
Gonen (sub., Jer.), *see* Katamon
Góngora, Luis de **15**:250
Gonick, Cy **11**:879 **15**:27
Gonorrhea (disease) **16**:941
Gonsalvo de Córdoba **2**:109; **8**:391
Gonta, Ivan **4**:413; **15**:1527
Gonzaga Dynasty (It.) **2**:215; **5**:600
Gonzague, Hyacinthe de, *see* DEUTZ, SIMON
Gonzala García de Santa María **13**:4
González, Alvar **5**:116
González, Pedro **5**:116
Gonzalo de Córdoba, *see* Gonsalvo de Córdoba
Good, Edward, *see* OVED, MOSHE
GOOD AND EVIL **7**:775
- General
- - *Azazel* ritual **3**:1002
- - knowledge **13**:77ff
- - Neoplatonism **12**:958
- - penal law **13**:222
- - Sodom **15**:70
- - *zaddik* **16**:910
- Related Concepts
- - Dualism **6**:242
- - ethics **6**:933
- - free will **7**:125
- - God, justice and mercy of **7**:669
- - justice **10**:477
- - man **11**:844
- - providence **13**:1279
- - repentance **14**:73
- - reward and punishment **14**:134
- - righteousness **14**:180
- - Satan **14**:902ff
- - sin **14**:1587
- - suffering **15**:485
- - vengeance **16**:93
- Ideologies
- - Dead Sea sect **5**:1409
- - Ḥasidei Ashkenaz **7**:1381
- - Ḥasidic thought **7**:1404; **7**:1408ff
- - Kabbalah **10**:531,579,583ff,596,608
- - Karaite Kalam **13**:433
- - Pharisees **13**:365
- Views on
- - Aaron ben Elijah **2**:12
- - Dov Baer of Mezhirech **6**:183
- - Elimelech of Lyzhansk **6**:662
- - Levi ben Gershom **11**:96
- - Luzzatto **10**:593
- - Maimonides **11**:774ff; **13**:442
- - Mendelssohn **11**:1329; **11**:1331ff
- - Saadiah Gaon **13**:432; **14**:552
- Literature
- - Dead Sea scrolls **7**:638
- - Genesis, Book of **7**:395
- - Job, the Book of **10**:121ff
- *illus:*
- - Michael and Gabriel amulet **11**:1488
Goode, Alexander **11**:1570
- *illus:*
- - memorial stamp **11**:1571
GOODENOUGH, ERWIN RAMSDELL **7**:778
GOODHART, ARTHUR LEHMAN **7**:779
Goodhart, Philip J. **7**:779
Goodman, Abram Vossen **2**:827
GOODMAN, BENNY **7**:779
Goodman, Edwin A. **15**:1264
Goodman, Harry **2**:423
Goodman, Isaac **11**:1114
Goodman, Joseph **12**:1017
Goodman, Martin **15**:1264
Goodman, Morris L. **11**:498
GOODMAN, NELSON **7**:780
GOODMAN, PAUL (Eng.) **7**:780
GOODMAN, PAUL (U.S.) **7**:781
- New York City **12**:1121
GOODMAN, PERCIVAL **7**:782
- synagogue **15**:625
- *illus:*
- - text
- - BethEl Synagogue, Springfield, Mass. **15**:318
- - B'nai Israel Synagogue, Millburn, N.J. **15**:625
- - Saint Paul, Minn., synagogue **12**:38
Goodman, Philip **4**:1220
Goodman, Romana **16**:593
- *illus:*
- - WIZO delegation to Twelfth Zionist Congress **16**:1101
Goodman, Samuel **15**:313
Goodman, Theodosia, *see* BARA, THEDA
GOODMAN, TOBIAS **7**:782
- Liverpool **11**:409
Goodspeed, E. J. **4**:870
Goodstein, Arnold **15**:213
GOOR, YEHUDAH **7**:783
- children's literature **5**:435
GOOSE **7**:784
- dietary laws **6**:34
- *kapparot* **10**:757
Goossens, Eugene **10**:461
Gopher (tree) **5**:1178; **16**:630
Gophna (toparchy, Er. Isr.), *see* GOFNAH
Gopner, Serafima **5**:794
Gora (cmty., Silesia), *see* Guhrau
GORA KALWARIA (tn., Pol.) **7**:784
Goral, *see* LOTS
Gorali, M., *see* Bronzaft, M.
Gorbato, Esther **11**:1167
GORDIMER, NADINE **7**:786
GORDIN, ABBA **7**:787
GORDIN, JACOB (plwrt.) **7**:787
- Entin, Joel **6**:801
- Shakespeare in Yiddish **14**:1264
- theater **15**:1066
- *illus:*
- - text
- - Lipzin, Keni, in *Mirele Efros* **15**:1068
Gordin, Jacob (Pol. commun.) **5**:803
Gordin, Judah Leib **15**:13
GORDIS, ROBERT **7**:789
Gordon (fam., Lith.) **16**:140
GORDON, ABRAHAM **7**:790
GORDON, AHARON DAVID **7**:790
- Deganyah **5**:1458
- Gordonia **7**:805
- history **8**:752
- kibbutz movement **10**:964
- nature **12**:891
- Zionist ideology **16**:1048
GORDON, ALBERT I. **7**:793
- Minneapolis-Saint Paul **12**:38
- sociology **15**:68
Gordon, Barukh (Bernard) **11**:1142
Gordon, Charles G. **9**:1459,1544
- *illus:*
- - Garden Tomb, Jerusalem **9**:1461
GORDON, CYRUS HERZL **7**:793
- archaeology **3**:302
Gordon, Daniel **12**:360
GORDON, DAVID **7**:794
- *Ha-Maggid* **7**:1221
GORDON, ELIEZER **7**:795
GORDON, LORD GEORGE **7**:795
- *illus:* text
Gordon, George (physic.) **12**:37
Gordon, Gerald **15**:209
GORDON, HAROLD **7**:796
GORDON, JACOB (r.) **7**:797
- Toronto **15**:1261; **15**:1262
GORDON, JEKUTHIEL BEN LEIB **7**:797
- Luzzatto, Moses **11**:601
GORDON, JUDAH LEIB **7**:797
- chronological chart **8**:766-767
- critic **5**:1118
- denouncement of **8**:1369
- Guenzburg, Mordecai **7**:964
- *Ha-Meliz* **7**:1233
- Haskalah, Russia **8**:187
- Jerusalem theme **9**:1565
- parody **13**:134
- promotion of culture **15**:58ff
- prosody **13**:1224,1226
- train poem **13**:1519
- *illus:*
- - autograph **3**:915
- - collected poems (1884) **8**:186
Gordon, Julius **16**:633
Gordon, Louis **15**:307, 308
GORDON, MAX **15**:1083
GORDON, MIKHEL **7**:803
GORDON, MILTON M. **7**:804
- sociology **15**:68
Gordon, Myron L. **11**:1589; **16**:556
Gordon, Nathan **5**:114
Gordon, Noah **14**:256
Gordon, Norman **15**:307
Gordon, Ruth **12**:469
GORDON, SAMUEL **6**:788
- children's literature **5**:450
- theater **15**:1092
GORDON, SAMUEL LEIB **7**:804
Gordon, Sidney **15**:301
- *illus:*
- - baseball **15**:300
Gordon Bennett, James, *see* Bennett, James Gordon
GORDONIA (mvmt.) **7**:805
Gordonyah (publ.) **1**:newsp. list
Gorelik, J. L. **3**:424
GORELIK, SHEMARYA **7**:807
- *illus:* text
Goren (mosh., Isr.) **1**:place list
Goren, A. A. **8**:568
GOREN, CHARLES HENRY **7**:807
Goren, L. **4**:138
Goren, Moshe **14**:1635
GOREN, NATAN **7**:808
GOREN, SHLOMO **7**:808
- Dead Sea *tefillin* **15**:904
- disinterment of soldiers **6**:73
- suicide, views **15**:490
- Temple Mount **15**:993
- transplant, views **15**:1339
- Zambrow **16**:923
Gorenćević, Ilko, *see* Grin, Lav
Goren Kiddon (journ.) **1**:newsp. list
Gorfinkiel, B. **14**:363
GORGIAS (Sel. comm.) **7**:809
Gorgorios (bk.) **6**:1151
GORIN, BERNARD **7**:809
Gorin, M. **16**:825
Goring (leg. conc.) **3**:986f **15**:1272ff
Goris, J. A. **15**:270
GORIZIA (city, It.) **7**:810
GORKI (city, Rus.) **7**:810
- pogroms **13**:696
GORKI, MAXIM **7**:810
- Litvinov, Maxim **11**:406
- views on Jewish matters **5**:796
- Wandering Jew **16**:262
GORLICE (tn., Pol.) **7**:811
- *illus:* text
GORNI (immigrants from Leghorn) **7**:813
- Algeria **2**:615
- Leghorn **10**:1572
Goro, Fritz **13**:484; **13**:485
Gorochov, Yedidyah, *see* ADMON, YEDDIDYAH
GORODENKA (city, Ukr.) **7**:813
- Shabbateanism **14**:1251
Gorodenka, Naḥman of, *see* NAḤMAN OF HORODENKA
GORODOK (city, Ukr.) **7**:814
- Maḥzikei Hadas **11**:731
GORODOK (tn., Belor.) **7**:815
Gorokhow (city, Pol.) **3**:842
Goron, Land of (Sov. Rep.), *see* GEORGIA
Górska, Halina **13**:801ff
Gort, Viscount, *see* Vereker, John Standish Surtees Prendergast
Gortyna (anc. tn., Crete) **7**:868
Gorz, André **7**:148
GORZOW WIELKOPOLSKI (tn., Pol.) **7**:815
Goses (dying man) **2**:291; **5**:1425
- *see also: Shekhiv Me'ra*
"Goset" (theat., Rus.), *see* Jewish State Theater (Moscow)
GOSHEN (reg., Egy.) **7**:816
- Bible history **8**:574; **8**:575
Goshen (city, Ind.) **8**:1361
Goshen-Gottstein, M. **12**:1461
Goskind, Itzhak **12**:454
Goskind, Shaul **12**:454
GOSLAR (city, Ger.) **7**:816
- Brunswick **4**:1421
- *illus:* text
GOSLAR, HANS **7**:817
GOSLAR, NAPHTALI HIRSCH BEN JACOB **7**:817
Goslar, Samuel **7**:818
Göslöw (city, Crimea), *see* YEVPATORIYA
Gospels, *see* NEW TESTAMENT
Gossip, *see* SLANDER
Gostick, Ron **5**:111
GOSTYNIN (tn., Pol.) **7**:818
GOTA, MOSES ZERAHIAH BEN SHNEUR **7**:818
GOTEBORG (Gothenburg; city, Swed.) **7**:819
- *illus:*
- - synagogue **15**:548
GOTHA (city, Ger.) **7**:819
Gotheim, Georg **16**:111
Gothia (mts., Rus.) **5**:1105
Goths (Germ. people) **7**:693
Gotkin, Hyman **15**:303
Gotko, Jacques **13**:117
GOTLIEB, ALLAN **7**:820
- Canada **5**:112
Gots, Mikhail **13**:819; **15**:29
GOTSFELD, BESSIE GOLDSTEIN **7**:820
Gotta, Salvatore **9**:1106
GOTTESFELD, CHONE **7**:820
GOTTESMAN (fam., U.S.) **7**:820
Gottesman, Benjamin **7**:821
Gottesman, David Samuel **7**:821
- Dead Sea scrolls **5**:1397
Gottesman, Esther **7**:821
Gottesman, Mendel **7**:820
Gottfried, Markus **12**:405
Gottfried von Eppstein **8**:942
GOTTHEIL, GUSTAV **7**:821
- Wise, Stephen **16**:566
GOTTHEIL, RICHARD JAMES HORATIO **7**:821
- Zionism **16**:1141ff
- Gottheimer, Albert, *see* GRANT, BARON ALBERT
Gotthelf, Bernhard **11**:1569
Gotthelf, Yehudah **5**:1316
Gotthoffer, Shikey **15**:303
Gottingen, Aaron **9**:21
Gottlieb, A. (schol.) **10**:648
GOTTLIEB, ADOLPH **7**:822

- *illus:*
- - text
- - Beth El Synagogue (Springfield, Mass.), valance **15:**319
Gottlieb, Allan, *see* GOTLIEB, ALLAN
GOTTLIEB, BERNHARD **7:**823
Gottlieb, Edward (pub. relations dir.) **13:**1360
Gottlieb, Edward (sport.) **15:**304
GOTTLIEB, FRANTISEK **7:**823
GOTTLIEB, HEINRICH **7:**823
GOTTLIEB, HINKO **7:**824
- literature **16:**874; **16:**889
- Zionism **16:**1151
GOTTLIEB, HIRSCH LEIB **7:**824
Gottlieb, J. (mer.) **5:**411
GOTTLIEB, JACOB **7:**825
GOTTLIEB, JEDIDIAH BEN ISRAEL **7:**825
Gottlieb, Leo **15:**303
Gottlieb, Leopold **3:**568; **7:**827
- *illus:*
- - "Artist's Mother" (paint.)**7:**826
GOTTLIEB, MAURYCY **7:**825
- *illus:*
- - text
- - "Jewish Wedding" (paint.) **3:**554
Gottlieb, Michael **5:**169
Gottlieb, Phyllis **5:**115
Gottlieb, Polly **14:**267
Gottlieb, Richard **8:**1052
Gottlieb, Wolf **7:**603
GOTTLIEB, YEHOSHUA **7:**827
Gottlieb, Yevgeni **15:**310
GOTTLOBER, ABRAHAM BAER **7:**827
- Ḥasidism **7:**1418
- Kovner, Abraham **10:**1231
- prosody **13:**1225
Gottsagen (fam., U.S.) **15:**790
GOTTSCHALK, ALBERT **3:**601
- Denmark **5:**1537
- *illus:*
- - "Winter Landscape near Copenhagen" **3:**623
Gottschalk, Joachim **12:**458
GOTTSCHALK, LOUIS REICHENTHAL **7:**829
Gottschalk, Marius **12:**1354
GOTTSCHALK, MAX **7:**830
Gottschalk, Michael **4:**653; **7:**94
Gottschalk of Bacharach, *see* Bacharach, Gottschalk of
Gottschalk of Kreuznach **10:**1260
Gottschalk von Recklinghausen, *see* Recklinghausen, Gottschalk von
GOTTSCHALL, MORTON **7:**831
Gottstein, Joseph **15:**311
Gouda (city, Neth.) **12:**976; **14:**350
Goudchaux (fam., Fr.) **12:**816
GOUDCHAUX, MICHEL **7:**831
GOUDSMIT, JOEL EMANUEL **7:**831
Goudsmit, L. **13:**707
GOUDSMIT, SAMUEL **6:**320; **6:**322
- children's literature **5:**453
Goudvis, Bertha **15:**209
Goudy, F.W. **15:**1488
GOUGENOT DES MOUSSEAUX, HENRI **7:**831
Goulburn (tn., Austr.) **3:**878
Gould, Barbara Ayrton **13:**812
Gould, Elliot **12:**451
- in *Move* **12:**466
Gould, Joseph **12:**1408
GOULD, MORTON **12:**691
Gould, Nathan J. **11:**1589
GOULD, SAMUEL BROOKNER **7:**831
Gould, T. **11:**1554
Gouldner, Alvin **15:**63
Gourary, Moishe, *see* GRAY, MORRIS ABRAHAM
GOURD (bot.) **7:**832
- plant list **13:**619
GOURI, HAIM **7:**832
- Hebrew literature **8:**205; **8:**207
Gourmont, A. **13:**109
Gourse, David L. **6:**1161
Gousset, Jacques **8:**34
GOVERNANCE IN ISRAEL **9:**598
- Va'ad Le'ummi **16:**49
- *illus:*
- - text
- - cabinets, 1949-1971 (table) **9:**669
- - finance, Palestine and Israel (tables) **9:**713, 734, 739-742, 750-759
- *map:* text
- *see also:* POLITICAL LIFE AND PARTIES IN ISRAEL
Government
- Israel **9:**598; **9:**610
- King David **5:**1323
- *see also:* DINA DE-MALKHUTA DINA
GOVERNMENT, PRAYER FOR THE **7:**834
- Shabbetai Ẓevi **14:**1230
- *illus:*
- - text
- - Mikveh Israel prayer for George Washington **15:**1595
Government House (Jer.) **9:**1473; **14:**1630
Government Institute for Technical Training (Isr.) **9:**881
Government of Israel Coin and Medals Corporation **5:**731
Government Printers (Isr.) **13:**1379
Gower, John **6:**776
Goy, *see* GENTILE
Goychmann, David **13:**117
Goyim (name of k.; gen. term "nations"), *see* GOIIM
GOZAN (anc. city, Assyr.) **7:**835
- Adrammelech cult **2:**304
- Lost Tribes **15:**1003
- Sambatyon **14:**763
GOZHANSKY, SAMUEL **7:**837
- socialism, Jewish **15:**41
GOZLAN, ELIE **7:**837
Gozlan, Jean **2:**617
Gozo (Maltese isl.) **11:**831
Gozolas (5th cent., Fr.) **12:**827
Graaff Reinet (tn., S.A.) **5:**135; **15:**185
- *illus:*
- - sale at trading station **15:**187
Graanboom, Aaron Moses Isaac **2:**900; **11:**450
Grabiner, Harry **15:**301
Grable, Betty **12:**694
Grabovski, Meir, *see* Argov, Meir
Grabowce (tn., Pol.) **4:**197
GRABSKI, STANISLAW **7:**837
Grabski, Wladyslaw **7:**837
- "Grabski *aliyah*" **8:**758; **9:**341; **9:**527
Grace, *see* LOVE
GRACE AFTER MEALS **7:**838
- Abraham **2:**116
- after bread **4:**1334
- after rice **14:**155
- *al ha-nissim* **2:**626
- Amen **2:**803
- *Barekhu* **4:**219
- *Berakhot* **4:**586
- blessing for the host **8:**1032
- bride and groom **11:**1040
- circumcision **5:**572
- Commandments, the 613 **5:**764
- David **5:**1327
- five species **6:**1333
- Gentile home **12:**24
- Jerusalem **9:**1561
- *niddui* and *ḥerem* **8:**351
- *piyyutim* **16:**1242
- priest **13:**1089
- *Shir ha-Ma'alot* **15:**1415
- washing hands before **12:**998
- wine blessing **16:**540
- *illus:*
- - text
- - *Al ha-Nissim* **7:**1282
- - *Seder Berakhot* **4:**486
- - *Seder Birkat ha-Mazon* **8:**1315; **9:**1562
- - *Shir ha-Ma'alot* **6:**1037
- - shortened forms **6:**387; **7:***fcg.* 846
- *see also:* GRACE BEFORE MEALS; MAYIM AḤARONIM
GRACE BEFORE MEALS **7:**841
- over bread **4:**1334
- washing of hands **12:**998
Grach, Rafael **12:**1377
GRACIAN, SHEALTIEL BEN SOLOMON **7:**841
GRACIAN, ZERAHIAH BEN ISAAC BEN SHEALTIEL **7:**842
- Aristotelianism **3:**446
- Avicenna, translated by **3:**959
- Themistius **15:**1099
- translator **15:**1321ff
Graciani, Abraham **14:**432
Grad, Gabriel **10:**461
GRADE, CHAIM **7:**843
- Musar movement **12:**537
- Yiddish literature **16:**820ff
- *illus:*
- - Yiddish writers, New York **16:**823
- - *Yung Vilne* group **16:**821
GRADE, SIR LEW **15:**1083
- television and radio **15:**930
Gradenwitz, Menahem Mendel **13:**1586
GRADENWITZ, PETER EMANUEL **12:**691
- music **12:**674
GRADIS (fam., Fr.) **7:**844
- slave trade **14:**1663
Gradis, Abraham **7:**844
Gradis, Benjamin (contr., Fr.) **5:**935
Gradis, Benjamin (pub. fig., Fr.) **7:**845
Gradis, David (mer., Fr.) **7:**844
Gradis, David (polit., writ., Fr.) **4:**1245; **7:**845; **11:**826
Gradis, Henri **7:**845
Gradis, Moses **7:**844
Gradner, Louis **5:**140
Gradner, Walter **5:**140
Gradner, Yisroel **4:**1391
Grady, Henry F. **13:**36; **16:**1090
GRAEBER, SCHEALTIEL EISIK **7:**845
- Appel, Judah Leib **3:**222
Graebner, Dr. **16:**111
GRAES, ORTWIN VAN DE **7:**845
- *De vita et moribus Judaeorum* **5:**158
Graetz (tn., Pol.), *see* GRODZISK WIELKOPOLSKI
GRAETZ, HEINRICH **7:**845
- *Contents:*
- - Career **7:**845
- - Visit to Ereẓ Israel **7:**846
- - Biblical Studies **7:**846
- - Controversy with Treitschke **7:**846
- - Popular History of the Jews **7:**847
- - The Historian **7:**847
- - The "History" **7:**848
- - The Historiographer **7:**848
- - Critics **7:**849
- - The "History": editions and translations **7:**849
- diacritical marks **16:**1429
- Hess, Moses **8:**727
- Hirsch, S.R. **8:**509
- history **8:**561
- history chart **8:**766-767
- Jewish scholarship **16:**579
- Judaism, views on **10:**385
- *Shi'ur Komah* **3:**57
- *illus:*
- - autograph **3:**915
- - portrait **8:**717
Graetz, Paul **15:**1056
GRAF, KARL HEINRICH **7:**850
- Christian Hebraists **8:**34
- Genesis criticism **7:**390
Graf, Moses ben Menahem, *see* MOSES BEN MENAHEM GRAF
Grafemus, Louise **11:**1568
Grafenwoerth (vill., Aus.) **3:**890
Graff, Robert F. de **13:**1373
Graffiti (inscriptions) **16:**663ff
Grafman, Elliot **11:**485
Grafstein, G., *see* Guria, Al
Grafting (agr.) **4:**1023; **12:**170ff
Graham, Katherine **11:**1463
Graham, Martha **4:**328
Grahamstown (tn., S.A.) **5:**135; **15:**185
Grain, *see* FIVE SPECIES
Grain offerings **5:**1159
Grain trade **2:**405
Grajal, Gaspar **8:**34
GRAJEWO (tn., Pol.) **7:**850
GRAJEWSKI, ARYEH LEIB **7:**850
GRAJEWSKI, ELIEZER ZALMAN **7:**851
Grajewski, Simeon Ḥayyim **7:**850
Grammar, Hebrew, *see* HEBREW GRAMMAR
Grammateus (cmty. offic.) **8:**647
Grammaticae Hebraeae libri duo (wk.) **3:**751
Gran (city, Hung.), *see* ESZTERGOM
GRANACH, ALEXANDER **7:**851
- theater **15:**1056; **15:**1070
GRANADA (city, Sp.) **7:**852
- history chart **8:**766-767
- Spain **15:**226
GRANADA, GABRIEL DE **7:**853
- Mexican Inquisition **8:**1392
Granada, Manuel de **7:**853
Granados, Jorge Garcia **7:**957; **10:**1456
- Palestine Inquiry Commission **13:**34
"Granas" (Js., Tun.) **14:**1442
Granat, A.N. **13:**1370
Granat, I.N. **13:**1370
Granat, Joseph Ẓevi, *see* RIMON, JOSEPH ẒEVI
Granberg, N. **8:**34
Grandchamp (16th cent., Fr. dipl.) **12:**838
Grand Forks (city, N.D.) **12:**1221
GRANDITSKY, PALLE **15:**1083
Grand Junction (city, Colo.) **5:**753
Grand Order Sons of Jacob (soc., Eng.) **7:**110
Grand Rapids (city, Mich.) **11:**1499
"Grand Sanhedrin des Israélites de France" (lith., E. Vernier) **8:**704
Grands Moulins flour mills (Er. Isr.) **9:**341
GRANDVAL, GILBERT YVES EDMOND **13:**827
Granich, Irwin, *see* GOLD, MICHAEL
GRANIN, DANIEL ALEKSANDROVICH **7:**853
Granite City (city, Ill.) **8:**1255
Granjeros Unidos (co-op., Arg.) **3:**432
GRANOTT, ABRAHAM (Granovsky) **7:**854
- *illus:* text
GRANOVSKY, ALEXANDER **7:**854
- Mikhoels, Solomon **11:**1530
- Yiddish theater **15:**1074
Granovsky, Samuel **13:**117

GRANT, BARON ALBERT 7:855
Grant, Madison 15:1651
Grant, Robert 6:755
- illus:
- - Jews dancing around statue of (caric.) 6:705
GRANT, ULYSSES SIMPSON 7:855
- anti-Jewish order 11:258; 15:1649
- history chart 8:766-767
- illus:
- - anti-Jewish General Order 15:1651
- - B'nai B'rith protest 15:1652
Grapefruit (bot.) 5:581
Grapes, see VINE
Grapo, Zach. (Grappius) 8:34
Graser, Conrad 8:34
Grasovski, Yehudah, see GOOR, YEHUDAH
Grass (bot.) 9:225
Grasse (dist., Fr.) 13:1259
GRASSHOPPER (zool.) 7:856
- see also: LOCUST
Grass pea 13:619
Grass Valley (city, Calif.) 5:56
GRATIAN (Franciscus Gratianus) 7:857
Gratius, Ortwin van de, see GRAES, ORTWIN VAN DE
GRATTENAUER, KARL WILHELM FRIEDRICH 7:858
- salons 14:709
Gratuity, slave's, see HA'ANAKAH
GRATZ (fam., U.S.) 7:858
- geneal. table: text
Gratz, Barnard 7:858; 14:1414
- illus: 7:859
Gratz, Benjamin 7:859; 10:1503
Gratz, Frances 7:860
Gratz, Hyman 7:859
Gratz, Jacob 7:859
Gratz, Joseph 7:860
Gratz, Michael 7:858; 14:1413; 16:162
- history chart 8:766-767
- illus: 7:859
Gratz, Rachel 7:860
- illus: text
Gratz, Rebecca 7:860; 10:219
- Scott's Ivanhoe heroine 14:1036
- illus: 7:859
Gratz, Richea 7:860
Gratz, Sara 10:219
Gratz, Simon 7:859; 15:1375
Gratzburg (tn.,N.Y.) 7:859
GRATZ COLLEGE (teachers' inst., U.S.) 7:860
- illus:
- - text
- - Samuel Netzky Adult Institute of Jewish Studies 13:374
Grau, Wilhelm 8:565; 14:37
Graubard, Judah Leib 11:811
Graubard, Moritz 12:1104
Graubart, David 5:415
GRAUBART, JUDAH LEIB 7:861
- Toronto 15:1261
GRAUMANN, SIR HARRY 7:862
- Johannesburg 10:155
Graur, A.L. 14:399
GRAUR, CONSTANTIN 7:862
Grave, Gravestones, see BURIAL; CEMETERY; EPITAPHS; TOMBS AND TOMBSTONES
Graven, Andreas 14:933
Gravenhage (city, Neth.), see HAGUE, THE
Graves, Robert 13:178
GRAY, HERBERT 7:862
GRAY, MORRIS ABRAHAM 7:862
- Winnipeg 11:880; 16:551
GRAYZEL, SOLOMON 7:863
- historiography 8:562
- Jewish Publication Society of America 10:81
- illus:
- - JPS Torah translation committee 10:80
GRAZ (city, Aus.) 7:863
- Austrian Jewry 3:897ff
- Klagenfurt Jews 10:1085
- Styria 15:465ff
- illus: text
Graziadio (Judah?) 4:1238
Graziani, A. 10:1498
Graziani, Colonel 11:1566
Graziano, Aaron 7:865
GRAZIANO, ABRAHAM JOSEPH SOLOMON BEN MORDECAI 7:865
- book collection 4:974
Great Academy, see SANHEDRIN
Great arenda, see ARENDA
Great Assembly, see SYNAGOGUE, THE GREAT
Great Bear (constellation), see Ursa Major
Great Britain, see ENGLAND; IRELAND; SCOTLAND; WALES
"Greater Israel" Movement, see Greater Land of Israel Movement
Greater Land of Israel Movement 9:413ff
- Alterman, Nathan 2:774
- Eldad, Israel 6:575
- Shamir, Moshe 14:1291
- Tamir, Shemuel 10:840
Greater Recording Company (U.S.) 13:1618
Great Falls (city, Mont.) 12:266
Great Gate (Temple) 15:969
Great German Synagogue (Ven.) 16:102
- illus: 3:453; 16:97
Great Maḥzor of Amsterdam (13/14 cent., ms., Ger.) 14:1443
Great Neck (dist., N.Y.) 12:551
GREAT POLAND (admin. unit, Pol.-Lith.) 7:865
- Haskalah 7:1441
- see also: POLAND
Great Rabbinic Bible 4:838
Great Revolt (2nd cent. C.E., N.Afr.) 2:331
Great Sanhedrin (Jer.), see SANHEDRIN
Great Synagogue (anc. assembly), see SYNAGOGUE, THE GREAT
Great Synagogue
- Amsterdam 2:903
- Bedzin 4:373
- - illus: 4:374
- Brussels
- - illus: 4:1424
- Chernovtsy 5:396
- - illus: 5:393
- Cluj 5:617
- - illus: 5:618
- Copenhagen
- - illus: 15:621
- Czestochowa 5:1212
- - illus: 5:1213
- Florence 5:1213
- - illus: 15:620-621
- Gabès
- - illus: 15:1438
- Johannesburg 10:56
- - illus: 10:156
- London 6:756; 8:520;
- - Adler, Nathan Marcus 2:285
- - Adler, Nathan Marcus 2:285
- - Falk, Samuel 6:1159
- - Schiff, David Tevele 14:959
- - Yigdal 11:229; 16:825
- - illus:
- - - interior 2:286; 11:474; 15:619
- - see also: UNITED SYNAGOGUE
- Manchester 11:858
- illus: 11:859
- Metz 11:1452
- - illus: 11:1451
- Moscow 12:366ff
- - illus:
- - - entrance 12:366
- - - Passover service 12:367
- Oshmyany 12:1497
- - illus: 12:1496
- Padua
- - illus: 15:613
- Paris 13:107
- - illus: 13:105
- Pinsk
- - illus: 13:539,540
- Piotrkow
- - illus: 13:556
- Plonsk
- - illus: 13:651
- Plunge
- - illus: 13:653
- Rome 14:253
- - illus:
- - - exterior 14:247
- - - interior 14:250
- Stockholm 15:407
- - illus: 15:408
- Sydney 3:880,881; 15:564,565
- - illus:
- - - exterior 3:881
- - - interior 15:563
- Tunis 15:1447,1448
- - illus: 15:615,1433
- Turin
- - illus: 15:1454
- Vilna
- - illus: 16:142
- Warsaw 16:352
- - illus: 16:337
- Zagreb
- - illus: 16:869,918
Greco-Roman Diaspora 6:8
GREECE 7:867
- Contents:
- - Second Temple Period 7:868
- - Early and Middle Byzantine Periods 7:870
- - - Forced Conversion 7:871
- - - Social and Economic Conditions 7:872
- - Fourth Crusade and Late Byzantine Period 7:874
- - - Jewish Immigrations 7:875
- - Ottoman (and Late Venetian) Rule 7:875
- - - Religious Culture 7:876
- - - Economic Situation 7:876
- - Greek Independence to World War II 7:876
- - - Civic and Cultural Conditions 7:877
- - Holocaust Period 7:878
- - - German Zone 7:878
- - - Other Districts under German Occupation 7:879
- - - Jewish Resistance 7:879
- - Contemporary Period 7:880
- - Relations with Israel 7:881
- - Musical Traditions (Greece and Balkans) 7:882
- General
- - anti-Semitism 3:817
- - archives 3:383
- - Benjamin of Tudela's travels 4:536
- - biblical history 9:1301
- - calendar 16:1262
- - communal organization 5:826
- - Corfu 5:970
- - Crete 5:1088
- - diaspora settlement 6:10; 8:640
- - Doenmeh sect 6:148
- - emancipation 6:709ff
- - history chart 8:766-767
- - Istrumsa, Ḥayyim Abraham 9:1100
- - Jewish agriculture 2:403
- - military service 11:1566
- - minority treaty 12:45
- - Nasi, Don Joseph 12:838
- - Rhodes 14:145
- - Salonika 14:699
- - Sephardim 14:1167ff; 14:700ff
- - U.N. on racial discrimination 15:1560
- Holocaust Period 8:851ff; 15:442
- - Arta 3:645
- - Athens 3:818ff
- - Church and Nazism 8:915
- - partisans 13:140
- - Salonika 14:704ff
- - Sephardim 14:1172
- - War Crimes Trials 16:289ff
- Jewish Culture
- - Jewish education 6:420
- - Judeo-Greek 10:426
- - Ladino press 13:1039
- - language 16:1415
- - Modern Greek literature 7:898ff
- - Romaniots 14:231
- - Sibylline oracles 14:1490ff
- - synagogues 1:syn. list
- illus:
- - text
- - Jewish badge decreed by Nazis 4:72
- - Salonika, memorial to victims of the Holocaust 14:701
- pop. tables:
- - text
- - Crete, major medieval communities 5:1089
- see also: BYZANTINE EMPIRE; OTTOMAN EMPIRE
Greed, see COVETOUSNESS
GREEK AND LATIN LANGUAGES, RABBINICAL KNOWLEDGE OF 7:884
- Contents:
- - Introduction 7:884
- - Languages in Contact 7:885
- - Greek as Prestige Language 7:886
- - Professional Expertise 7:886
- - Comparative Studies 7:887
- Greek
- - Aramaic borrowings 3:274
- - Dead Sea Scrolls 16:1589ff.
- - grammarians and Jewish sages 14:651
- - Hellenism 8:296
- - Hellenistic Jewish literature 8:303
- - influence on names 12:807ff
- - Judah ha-Nasi 10:370
- - Judeo-Greek 10:67,425
- - mishnaic Hebrew 16:1604
- - Murabba'at scrolls 12:529
- - parallels with Hebrew 8:295
- - Samaritans 14:752
- - Septuagint 4:851
- - used by Roman Jews 14:242
- Latin
- - Aramaic borrowings 3:274
- - Bible translations 4:856
- - Christian attitude 4:926
- - Dead Sea Scrolls 16:1589ff.
- - Hebrew translations 15:1320
- - influence on Hebrew syntax 8:20
- - influence on names 12:807ff
- - mishnaic Hebrew 16:1605
- - rabbinic attitude 14:243
- - source of Jewish languages 10:67
- see also: HEBREW LANGUAGE
Greek Colony (qtr., Jer.) 9:1516
Greek Literature (Jewish), see HELLENISTIC JEWISH LITERATURE
GREEK LITERATURE, ANCIENT 7:887
- concepts of God 7:652

- Greek debt to Jews **8**:300
- influence on Roman writers **14**:233
- *see also:* HELLENISTIC JEWISH LITERATURE
GREEK LITERATURE, MODERN **7**:898f
- *Contents:*
- - Influence of the Bible **7**:898
- - Figure of the Jew **7**:898
- - The Jewish Contribution **7**:980
Greek Mysticism **10**:490; **10**:504
Greek Octateuch (ms.), *see* Byzantine Octateuchs
Greek Orthodox Church (Isr.) **8**:935; **9**:296
- *illus:*
- - monk at Monastery of the Temptation **9**:913
- - patriarch enthroned **9**:912
Greek Philosophy **3**:55; **13**:423ff
Greek Rite (litur.), *see* Romanian Rite
Greeks
- *aggadah* **2**:579
- Jerusalem Christian community **9**:1459
- *illus:*
- - battle with Amazons **12**:1504
- *see also:* GREECE
Greek Writers on Jews, *see* GREEK LITERATURE, ANCIENT
Greeley (city, Colo.) **5**:753
Green, A. A. (prch., Eng.) **8**:957
GREEN, ABEL **7**:901
GREEN, ADOLPH **15**:1083
Green, Charley, *see* Rosenberg, Charley
GREEN, DAVID EZRA **5**:383
GREEN, GERALD **15**:1581
Green, Josef **12**:455
Green, Monroe **2**:318
Green, Nathan (mer., Holl., Can.) **11**:997
Green, Nathan (law., Can.) **11**:998
Green, Samuel **12**:1025
Green, S. Hart **11**:879
Green, Sydney **5**:112; **11**:879
- Socialism **15**:27
Green, William **8**:34
Green, William S. **12**:1025
GREENACRE, PHYLLIS **7**:901
GREENBAUM, EDWARD SAMUEL **7**:901
Greenbaum, Henry, *see* Greenebaum, Henry
Greenbaum, Samuel **7**:901
Greenbaum, Selina **7**:901
Green Bay (city, Wis.) **16**:555
Greenberg (r., Bess.) **10**:1068
Greenberg, Ben **12**:912
GREENBERG, DAVID MORRIS **7**:902
GREENBERG, ELIEZER **7**:902
Greenberg, Hank, *see* GREENBERG, HENRY BENJAMIN
Greenberg, Harry **14**:1511
GREENBERG, ḤAYYIM **7**:903
- *illus:*
- - protest against 1940 White Paper **15**:1632
GREENBERG, HENRY BENJAMIN **7**:904
- baseball **15**:301
GREENBERG, IRVING **7**:904
Greenberg, Ivan Marion **7**:905; **10**:42
Greenberg, Jack **10**:1505; **12**:934
Greenberg, Jacob Walter **13**:1371
GREENBERG, JOANNE **15**:1581
Greenberg, Joseph H. **3**:40
GREENBERG, LEOPOLD (judge, S.A.) **7**:904
- *illus:*
- - with Jan Smuts **15**:205
GREENBERG, LEOPOLD JACOB **7**:905
- *Jewish Chronicle* **10**:41
Greenberg, Meyer **16**:633
GREENBERG, MOSHE **1**:31
GREENBERG, NOAH **12**:692
GREENBERG, SAMUEL BERNARD **7**:905
GREENBERG, SIMON **7**:906
GREENBERG, URI ZEVI **7**:906
- Jerusalem theme **9**:1567
- Kurzweil, Baruch **8**:178; **8**:201; **10**:1303
- Revisionist press **4**:131
- *illus:*
- - Markish, Perez, and **11**:1006
Greenberg Teachers' Seminary, *see* Hayyim Greenberg Teachers' Seminary
Greenblatt, Milton **13**:1340
Greenboim, Mordecai ben Joshua **14**:1516
Greenburg (vill., Pa.) **13**:230
Greene, Graham **6**:781
GREENE, LORNE **15**:1083
GREENEBAUM (fam., U.S.) **7**:909
- California branch **5**:56
Greenebaum, Edgar N. **7**:910
Greenebaum, Elias **7**:909
Greenebaum, Hannah **7**:520
Greenebaum, Henry (cmty. ldr.) **5**:416; **7**:910
Greenebaum, Henry Everett **7**:910
Greenebaum, Jacob **7**:909
Greenbaum, James E. **7**:910
Greenebaum, Michael **7**:910
Greenebaum, Moses Ernst **7**:910
Greenebaum, Sarah **7**:520
GREENFIELD, ALBERT MONROE **7**:910
Greenfield, Alexander **16**:534
Greenfinch (ornith.) **6**:30
Greenhut, Adolph **6**:1364
Greenhut, Irving **6**:1364
Green River (tn., Wyo.) **16**:680
Greensboro (city, N.C.) **12**:1220
Greenson, Ralph **13**:1340
GREENSPOON, HENRY **3**:364
GREENSTEIN, HARRY **7**:911
Greenstein, Jesse L. (astron.) **3**:807
GREENSTEIN, JESSE PHILIP **5**:383
GREENSTONE, JULIUS HILLEL **7**:911
Greentree, Meyer **14**:210
Greenville (city, Miss.) **12**:156
Greenville (city, S.C.) **15**:211
GREENWALD, JEKUTHIEL JUDAH (Leopold) **7**:912
- transplants **15**:1338
Greenwald, Levi Isaac **7**:1399
Greenwald, Yekutiel, *see* GREENWALD, JEKUTHIEL JUDAH
Greenwood (city, Miss.) **12**:156
GREETINGS AND CONGRATULATIONS **7**:912
- Day of Atonement **5**:1381
- drinking toast **16**:540
- etiquette **6**:946
- letters **11**:62
- mourners **12**:490
- Rosh ha-Shanah **14**:309
- *illus:* text
- *see also:* ḤAZAK; SHALOM ALEIKHEM
Greeve, Egbert van, *see* Greve, Egbert van
Grego, A. **9**:1112
Grego, Isaac **13**:815
GREGOIRE, HENRI BAPTISTE **7**:917
- Alsace Jews **2**:755
- Ensheim, Moses **6**:801
- French Revolution **7**:152f
- history chart **8**:766-767
- *illus:* text
Gregore, Samuel **14**:423
Gregori, G. **8**:34
Gregorian reform (calendar) **5**:43
Gregorius (Bar Hebraeus), *see* BAR HEBRAEUS, JOHANAN
Gregorovius, Ferdinand **5**:1364
GREGORY I (the Great; pope) **7**:919
- attitude to Jews **13**:852; **14**:245
- Burchard of Worms **4**:1508
- conversion of Jews **2**:415; **8**:657ff
- history chart **8**:766-767
- protection of Jews **9**:1119
Gregory VII (pope) **13**:853
GREGORY IX (pope) **7**:919
- attitude to Jews **8**:689; **13**:854
- Church tithes **15**:1162
- Crusades **5**:1141
- history chart **8**:766-767
- papal bull **4**:1495
GREGORY X (pope) **7**:920
GREGORY XIII (pope) **7**:920
- attitude to Jews **13**:857
- calendar **16**:1266
- history chart **8**:766-767
- Jewish physicians **3**:196
- papal bull **4**:1496
Gregory XVI (pope) **13**:860
- Alatri, Samuel **2**:515
GREGORY, SIR THEODORE **7**:921
Gregory of Nyssa **5**:552
GREGORY OF TOURS **7**:921
- disputation with Priscus **6**:87ff
Greilsheimer, Julius **12**:356
Greiner, Andor, *see* GÁBOR, ANDOR
Greiser, Arthur **13**:754
Greissing, Bálint **8**:35
Grell, E. A. **12**:650
Grenfell, J. (writ.) **15**:209
Grenier, Pasquier **9**:1344
GRENOBLE (city, Fr.) **7**:922
- CDJC **5**:287; **14**:983
GRESSMAN, HUGO **7**:922
- Isaiah authorship **9**:45; **9**:63
Greve, Egbert van **8**:35
Grey, Sir Edward **4**:132ff; **9**:307
Grey, Lady Jane **8**:35
GREY, JOEL **15**:1083
Grey, Richard **8**:35
Greydinger, Froyim (flklr. char.) **6**:1381
Grey Matter (period.) **2**:317
Gries, Moses J. **5**:609,610
Griese, O. **16**:788
Griffin (myth. beast) **14**:1073
Griffo, Francesco **15**:1481
Griffon vulture (zool.) **16**:232
Grigori, Johann Gottfried **14**:507
Grigoriev (anti-Sem., Ukr.), *see* Grigoryev
Grigoriopol (tn., Rus.) **6**:257
Grigorovitch-Barsky, D.N. **4**:400
Grigoryev (anti-Sem., Ukr.) **2**:560
- pogroms **13**:699; **14**:1460
Griliches, Abraham **7**:923
GRILICHES, AVENIR **7**:922
Grillo (fam., Ger.) **7**:94
Grillparzer, Franz **7**:444
- Jewess of Toledo **10**:26
Grin, Lav **16**:888
Grin, Y. **16**:819
Grinberg, Abraham, *see* GRUNBERG, ABRAHAM
GRINBERG, ALEKSANDER ABRAMOVICH **7**:923
Grinberg, Svetlana **15**:314
Grinhaus, Nahum **12**:176
- *illus:*
- - Mizrachi conference, Lida **16**:1099
Grinhaut, David **10**:1118
Grininke Beymelekh (period.) **5**:459
GRINKER, ROY RICHARD SR. **7**:923
Grinstein, H. B. **8**:568
Grinszpan, Jehiel, *see* Grynszpan, Jehiel
GRISHABER, ISAAC **7**:924
Grishin (polit., Rus.), *see* KOPELSON, ZEMAH
Gritse (tn., Pol.), *see* GROJEC
GROB, DAVID **11**:1208
Grochow (sub., Warsaw) **8**:252
GROCK (clown, Switz.) **15**:1083
Groddeck, Gabr. **8**:35
Gródek Jagiellónski (city, Ukr.), *see* GORODOK
Grodner, Israel **15**:1064
Grodner Moment (newsp., Pol.) **13**:1042
GRODNO (city, Belor.) **7**:924
- *Contents:*
- - Early History **7**:924
- - Population Figures **7**:924
- - Occupations **7**:925
- - Rabbis and Authors **7**:925
- - Communal Institutions **7**:926
- - Labor and Socialist Movements **7**:926
- - Zionism **7**:926
- - Holocaust Period **7**:927
- - After World War II **7**:928
- agrarian rights **2**:403
- Altschul, Joseph **2**:782
- Epstein, Aryeh Leib ben Mordecai **6**:824
- ghetto **13**:769
- Lithuania **11**:361ff
- yeshivah **14**:1421
- *illus:*
- - text
- - He-Ḥalutz training farm **13**:747
Grodzieńska, Stefania **13**:802
Grodzinski (apos., Rus.) **16**:88
Grodzinski, Ḥanokh Zundel ben Jacob **13**:1383
GRODZINSKI, ḤAYYIM OZER **7**:928
- Dimanstein, Simon **6**:48
- *ḥiddushim* **8**:467
- Karelitz, Avraham Yeshayahu **10**:787
- *illus:*
- - first Duma electors **14**:445
Grodzinski, Solomon David **7**:928
GRODZISK MAZOWIECKI (tn., Pol.) **7**:929
GRODZISK WIELKOPOLSKI (tn., Pol.) **7**:929
- archives **3**:387
Groenewoud, Jacob Cornelis Swijghuisen **8**:35
GROJEC (tn., Pol.) **7**:929
Groll, Adolf **8**:35
Gromyko, Andrei **14**:493
- support of Jewish state **9**:359; **9**:428; **16**:1092
- *illus:*
- - speech at U.N., May 14,1947 **14**:493
Gronach, Isaiah, *see* GRANACH, ALEXANDER
Gronem, Elijah ben Samuel **13**:530
GRONEMANN, SAMUEL (Sami, Sammy) **7**:930
- plays **7**:441; **15**:1060
Gronemann, Selig **7**:930; **7**:1278; **13**:1255
Groner, I. D. **11**:1282
GRONINGEN (city, prov., Neth.) **7**:931
GROPER, JACOB ASHEL **7**:932
GROPPER, WILLIAM **7**:932
editorial cartoons **5**:220
- *illus:* text
Grosman, Haika **4**:809
Gross (fam., U.S.) **16**:633
GROSS, ADOLF **7**:933
GROSS, CHAIM **7**:933
- New York **12**:1122

- *illus:*
- - "My Friends" (paint.) **15:**217
GROSS, CHARLES **7:**933
Gross, Felix **15:**210
GROSS, HEINRICH (Henri) **7:**934
Gross, John Jacob **6:**785
Gross, Klara **11:**1567
Gross, Michael **3:**593
- *illus:*
- - "White House in the Desert" Pl. 17 **3**-ART
Gross, Milt **5:**216
GROSS, NACHUM **1:**31
GROSS, NAPHTALI **7:**935
- animal tales **3:**21
GROSS, NATHAN **7:**935
Gross, Wilhelm **16:**1165
Grossbard, Herz **11:**590; **15:**359
GROSSBERG, MENASSEH **7:**935
GROSSER, BRONISLAW **7:**936
Grosser, Maurice **13:**115
Grosseteste, Robert **13:**186
- Christian Hebraists **8:**13
Grossfeld, Abraham **15:**309
Grossi, Carlo **9:**1145
Grossinger, Harry **7:**936
GROSSINGER, JENNIE **7:**936
Grossman, Allan **12:**1408; **13:**811
Grossman, Arthur, *see* FREED, ARTHUR
Grossman, Gheorghe, *see* GASTON-MARIN, GHEORGHE
Grossman, H. **10:**89
GROSSMAN, LADISLAV **5:**1209
GROSSMAN, LEONID PETROVICH **14:**515
Grossman, Louis **5:**563
GROSSMAN, MEIR **7:**937
- Jewish Legion **10:**70
- Jewish State Party **10:**92ff
- Revisionists, Zionist **14:**129
GROSSMAN, MORTON IRVING **7:**938
Grossman, Reuven, *see* AVINOAM, REUVEN
Grossman, Robert **15:**300
Grossman, Rudolph **12:**1091
Grossman, Samuel S. **5:**451
GROSSMAN, VASILI SEMYONOVICH **7:**938
"Grossmanites," *see* JEWISH STATE PARTY
GROSSMANN, KURT RICHARD **7:**936
Grossmann, M. H. **11:**613
Grossmann-Rosanes, *see* Mann-Rosanes, Judith
Gross-Rosen (Ger. concen. camp) **5:**78
- gassing **16:**1332
Grosswardein (city, Rum.), *see* ORADEA
GROSS-ZIMMERMANN, MOSHE **7:**939
Grosz, George **12:**1122
Grotefend, Georg Friedrich **16:**1506
GROTIUS, HUGO **7:**939
- attitude to Jews **8:**701; **14:**20
- Christian Hebraists **8:**35
- Menasseh ben Israel **11:**856
Group of Jewish Social Democrats (Rus.) **4:**1499
Group of Jewish Socialists (Rus.) **16:**1230
"Group of Ten" (art assoc., Isr.) **3:**592
GROVES, SACRED **7:**940
Growas, Mordecai **13:**775
GROZNY (city, U.S.S.R.) **7:**940
- Mountain Jews **12:**480
Gruber, Mietek **11:**538; **13:**775
GRUBY, DAVID **7:**941
Grudberg, Itzhak, *see* Turkow, Itzhak
GRUEBER-HEINRICH **7:**942
GRUEN, ADOLF **5:**383
Gruen, Avigdor **4:**505
Gruen, David, *see* BEN-GURION, DAVID
Gruen, Edmund **5:**1209
Gruen, J. M. **10:**110
Gruen, Oscar **13:**1049
Gruen, Victor **3:**360
- *illus:*
- - Midtown Plaza, Rochester, N.Y. **3:**344
GRUENBAUM, ADOLF **7:**942
GRUENBAUM, HENRY **7:**942
GRUENBAUM, MAX **7:**942
Gruenbaum, Oskar **16:**127
GRUENBAUM, YIẒḤAK **7:**943
- Allonei Yiẓḥak **2:**657
- Jewish Agency **9:**873
- Reich dispute **13:**749
- Sejm **14:**1118
- Ugoda **15:**1508
- Warsaw **16:**337
- *illus:*
- - "Black Saturday" **9:**362
- - Jewish Agency Executive **10:**28
- - Kadimah **16:**338
Gruenberg, Abraham **13:**546
- *illus:*
- - Odessa Committee **12:**1329
Gruenberg, Carlos Moises **15:**255
GRUENBERG, KARL **7:**945
GRUENBERG, LOUIS **7:**945
Gruenberg, Mendel, *see* MILIAN, MAXIMIN
GRUENBERG, SAMUEL **7:**945
GRUENBERG, SIDONIE MATSNER **7:**946
Gruenblatt, Nathan, *see* GOREN, NATAN
Gruenebaum, Elias **10:**1384; **13:**22
Gruenewald, Matthias **9:**69
GRUENEWALD, MAX **7:**946
Gruenfeld, H. **15:**1042
GRUENFELD, JUDAH **7:**946
Gruenfeld, Simeon **7:**946
Gruenhut, Abraham **8:**802
GRUENHUT, DAVID BEN NATHAN **7:**946
GRUENHUT, ELEAZAR (Lazar) **7:**947
GRUENHUT, MAX **7:**947
GRUENING, ERNEST HENRY **7:**947
Grueninger, Johann **15:**424
Gruenschlag, Elijah **7:**864
Gruensfeld (tn., Ger.) **4:**59
Gruensfeld of Fuerth **7:**215
Gruenspan, Herschel, *see* GRYNSZPAN, HERSCHEL
GRUENSTEIN, NATHAN **5:**383
Gruenthal, Josef, *see* TAL, JOSEF
Gruenvald, Philipp *see* GRÜNVALD, PHILIP
Gruenwald, Jacob **10:**1220
Gruenwald, Judah *see* GRÜNWALD, JUDAH
Gruenwald, Malkiel **9:**396; **9:**670; **10:**816
Gruenwald, Menahem **15:**162
Gruenwald, Mordecai **4:**1485
GRUENWALD, MORITZ **7:**948
Gruman, Y. **7:**1036
Grumbach, Paul Emile **11:**1562
GRUMBACH, SALOMON **7:**948
GRUNBERG, ABRAHAM **7:**948
GRUNDMAN, ZWI **3:**601
Grundtvig, Nicolai Frederik Severin **14:**927
Grunebaum-Ballin, Paul **10:**1496
Gruner, Dov **8:**1468; **10:**1078
GRUNFELD, ISIDOR **7:**949
Grunfeld, Judith **7:**949
Grunhut, Karl Samuel **10:**1494
Gruntal, Robert, *see* NATHAN, ROBERT
GRÜNVALD, PHILIP (Fülop) **7:**949
GRÜNWALD, AMRAM **7:**949
Grünwald, Eliezer David **7:**950; **14:**908
GRÜNWALD, JUDAH **7:**950
- Satu-Mare **14:**908
Grunwald, Kurt **7:**951
GRUNWALD, MAX **7:**950
Grünwald, Moses **7:**950
Grunwall, Abraham **11:**1551
Grupo Hebraista (assoc., Chile) **16:**1125
Gruppe Revolutionaerer Pazifisten (Ger.) **8:**491
GRUSENBERG, OSCAR OSIPOVICH **7:**951
- Beilis case **4:**400
- Blondes case **4:**1114
Grusenberg, Samuel **7:**952
- *Voskhod* **16:**225
Gruzenberg, Michael Markovitsch, *see* BORODIN, MICHAEL MARKOVITSCH
Gruzinic (J. lang; Cauc.) **10:**68
Gruziya (Sov. Rep.), *see* GEORGIA
GRYDZEWSKI, MIECZYSLAW **13:**803,804
GRYNBERG, BERL **7:**953
GRYNBERG, HENRYK **13:**803,804
Grynberg, Menahem Mendel **16:**497
GRYNSZPAN, HERSCHEL **7:**953
- *illus:* text
- *see also:* KRISTALLNACHT
Grynszpan, Jehiel **11:**546; **13:**91; **13:**775
- *illus:*
- - Jewish partisans **13:**143
Gryphius, Andreas **15:**1055
Grytzhendler, Mieczyslaw, *see* GRYDZEWSKI, MIECZYSLAW
GUADALAJARA (city, Sp.) **7:**954
- Ferrer, Vicente **6:**1236
- *illus:* text
Guadalajara, Piedro de **15:**1480
GUADALUPE (tn., Sp.) **7:**955
- Inquisition **8:**1383
Gualtperius, Otto **8:**35
Gualves, Cristóbal **16:**57
Guanges, Jacob de **14:**353
Guarantee, *see* SURETYSHIP
Guard Force (Haganah unit, Er. Isr.) **7:**1070
Guardia Judaica (med. J. estate) **4:**792
Guardian, *see* APOTROPOS
Guardian Angel **2:**963
Guardians of the Faith (Orth. party, Hung.), *see* Shomrei Hadass Society
"Guardians of the Peace" (13th cent., Eng.) **8:**344
Guarin, Pierre **8:**35
Guarin, Th. **16:**1019
Guastali, Elisha, *see* Vestali, Elisha
Guastalla (tn., It.) **11:**895
GUASTALLA, ENRICO **7:**955
- military service **11:**1559
GUATEMALA (C. Am. rep.) **7:**956
- Inquisition **8:**1394
- Israel's relations with **9:**422
- Latin America **10:**1450ff
- synagogues **1:**syn. list
- UNSCOP **15:**1688
- *pop. table:* text
Guayaquil (city, Ec.) **6:**359
Gubbio, Bosone da **8:**1296
Gubelman, *see* YAROSLAVSKY, YEMELYAN
Gubner, Gary **15:**315
Gubow, Lawrence **5:**1572
Gucci, Giorgio **15:**1356
Guccio, Gionnino **10:**158
Guchkov, A. **12:**1318
Gudea (k., Sumer) **16:**1491
- Amana marble **2:**792
- Sumer **15:**512
Ğudezmo (lang.), *see* LADINO
Gudiel, Francisco de **5:**461
GUEBWILLER (tn., Fr.) **7:**957
Guedalla, David **7:**958
GUEDALLA, HAIM **7:**957
GUEDALLA, PHILIP **7:**958
GUEDEMANN, MORITZ **7:**958
- defense of Judaism **3:**199
- Herzl, Theodor **8:**409; **16:**1151
- history chart **8:**766-767
Guedj, Maurice **11:**1567
Guelders (prov., Holl.), *see* Gelderland
GUELMAN, JACOBO **7:**959
Guelph (tn., Can.) **12:**1408
Guenoun, Mas'ud **2:**623
Guens, Akiva Eger, *see* EGER, AKIVA BEN MOSES GUENS
Guensburg (fam. name), *see* GUENZBURG
Guenther, H.F.K. **5:**1533
Guenther, Rudolph **13:**1360
Guenz (fam. name), *see* GUENZBURG
Guenzberg (fam. name), *see also* GUENZBURG
Guenzberg, Jacob **11:**420
GUENZBURG (fam. name) **7:**959
GUENZBURG (fam., Rus.) **7:**960
- railroad building **8:**720
- Siberia **14:**1487
Guenzburg, Baron Alfred **11:**1439
- relief work **16:**734
Guenzburg, Behr **16:**1165
Guenzburg, Baron David **7:**962
- book collection **4:**975
- Katzenelson, Judah Leib **10:**832
- Romm press **14:**256
- *Yevreyskaya Entsiklopediya* **6:**732
Guenzburg, Gabriel Jacob **7:**960
Guenzburg, Baron Horace **7:**961; **4:**176
- history chart **8:**766-767
- petroleum industry **13:**345
GUENZBURG, ILYA YAKOVLEVICH **7:**963
Guenzburg, Baron Joseph Yozel (Yevsel) **7:**960
- history chart **8:**766-767
- Jewish Culture Society **15:**58
GUENZBURG, MORDECAI AARON **7:**964
- Haskalah **7:**1448
Guenzburg, Naphtali Herz, *see* Guenzburg, Baron Horace
Guenzburg, Pesaḥ, *see* Ginzburg, Pesaḥ
Guenzburg, Pierre **7:**963
Guenzburg, Shimon, *see* GINZBURG, SIMON
Guenzburg, Simeon (16th cent. Bav.) **7:**960
Guenzburg, Yvonne **7:**963
Guenzburg-Ulma, Jacob ben Eliezer **13:**583
Guenzhausen, Leah **5:**613
GUENZIG, EZRIEL (Azriel) **7:**964
GUENZLER, ABRAHAM **7:**965
Guérande (tn., Fr.) **4:**1383
Guer de Cordova, Abraham, *see* ESCUDERO, LORENZO
GUÉRIN, VICTOR **7:**965
Guernsey (Brit. isl.), *see* CHANNEL ISLANDS
Gueron, Yakir (Yaqir) **13:**18; **16:**1540
Guertler, Nic. **8:**35
Guèsde, Jules **6:**229
Guestrow (tn., Ger.) **11:**1163
Guessing (tn., Aus.) **4:**1511
Guete, Heinr. Ernst **8:**36
Guevas, Aloysaa Sigaea de **8:**35
Gufnah (tn. Er. Isr.), *see* GOFNAH

GUGGENHEIM (fam., U.S.) **7**:965
- *geneal. table:* text
- *illus:* text
Guggenhiem, Benjamin **7**:966
GUGGENHEIM, CAMILLE **10**:1508
Guggenheim, Daniel **2**:321; **7**:966
Guggenheim, Edwin **4**:1148
Guggenheim, Ernst **15**:464
Guggenheim, Froma **11**:1329
Guggenheim, Harry Frank **2**:321; **7**:967
- horse breeding **15**:311
Guggenheim, Isaac **7**:966
Guggenheim, Jacob **15**:1527
Guggenheim, Maharam, *see* Guggengeim, Meir
Guggenheim, Marguerite **7**:967
Guggenheim, Markus **4**:305
Guggengeim, Meir (r., Switz.) **6**:737
Guggenheim, Meyer (indus., U.S.) **7**:965
- metals and mining **11**:1439
Guggenheim, Murry **7**:966
GUGGENHEIM, PAUL **7**:968
Guggenheim, Peggy, *see* Guggenheim, Marguerite
Guggenheim, Simon **7**:967
Guggenheim, Solomon Robert **3**:649; **7**:966
Guggenheim, William **7**:967
Guggenheim, Willy (art., Switz.) *see* VARLIN
Guggenheimer (fam., Va.) **16**:163
Guggenheimer, Clarence M. **15**:312
GUGGENHEIM-GRUENBERG, FLORENCE **7**:969
Guggu (Lydian k.), *see* Gyges
Guglielmo (duke, It.) **3**:496
GUGLIELMO DA PESARO **7**:969
- Italian literature **9**:1108
- *illus:* text
Guglielmo Ebreo, *see* GUGLIELMO DA PESARO
Guglielmo Raimondo de Moncada, *see* MITHRIDATES, FLAVIUS
Guglielmus Siculus, *see* MITHRIDATES, FLAVIUS
Guhrau (tn., Ger.) **14**:1536
Gui, Bernard **15**:769
Guiana, Dutch, *see* SURINAM
Guibert of Nogent, *see* VIBERT OF NOGENT
GUIDACERIO, AGACIO **7**:970
- Christian Hebraists **8**:35
Guidacerius, Agathius, *see* GUIDACERIO, AGACIO
Guide of the Perplexed (wk., Maim.), *see* MAIMONIDES *(Guide of the Perplexed)*
Guidobaldo II della Rovere **13**:329
"Guild" cities (bib.) **5**:589
Guild of the Jews (orgn., Rum.) **9**:1293
GUILDS **7**:970
- *Contents:*
- - in Antiquity **7**:970
- - Middle Ages and Early Modern Era **7**:972
- General
- - Amsterdam **2**:896
- - anti-Semitism **3**:101
- - fines **6**:1289
- - Jews barred from **16**:1302
- - markets and fairs **11**:1002; **11**:1003
- - Nehemiah's chronicle **8**:621
- - organized by artisans **16**:1302
- - Rumania **14**:387
- - Second Temple era **16**:1275
- - tailoring **15**:704
- - Torah study **15**:459
- - vocational associations **8**:441
- - wine and liquor trade **16**:542
- Specific Guilds
- - Alexandrian seamen **16**:1276
- - Roman tailors **14**:248
- - Saragossa cobblers **16**:1287
- - Temple singers **13**:1316
- *illus:*
- - text
- - London Royal Exchange **11**:470
- - Prague **12**:546
- *see also:* ḤEREM HA-YISHUV
Guilhem, Felipe **4**:96
Guilhem Mancip, *see* Mancip, Guilhem
Guillaume of Bourges **4**:1275
Guilt, inherited **16**:978
Guilt offering, *see* Asham
Guinea (rep., Afr.) **9**:429; **9**:433; **9**:439
Guinea, Equatorial (rep., Afr.) **9**:439
Guinea-fowl **6**:34
GUINZBURG, HAROLD KLEINERT **7**:974
Guiscard, Robert **5**:252
Guise, William **8**:35
GUITERMAN, ARTHUR **15**:1581
Guizot, François **6**:1445
Gulack, George **12**:1376; **15**:309
GULAK, ASHER **7**:974
Guldenfenning (tax), *see* OPFERPFENNIG
Gulewski, Dov C. **15**:1339
Gulkowitsch, L. **15**:827
GULL (ornith.) **7**:974
- dietary laws **6**:34
Gumbel (goldsmith), *see* Gumpel, Mordechai
Gumbel, Eric **13**:1340
Gumberts (fam., U.S.) **8**:1361
Gumeldjina (tn., Turk) **13**:1395
Gumpel, Georges **3**:359
Gumpel, Mordecai (Heb. au.), *see* Levisohn, Marcus George
Gumpel, Mordechai (medal., Isr.) **7**:743; **11**:1167
Gumpel, Solomon ben Mordecai **7**:773
Gumpert (fam. name), *see also* GOMPERZ
Gumpert (cmty. ldr., Prus.) **13**:1453
GUMPERT, MARTIN **7**:975
Gumpert, Max (mayor, S.A.) **13**:909
Gumpertz (fam. name), *see also* GOMPERZ
Gumpertz, Aaron Solomon **11**:49
Gumpertz, Salman (Salomon) Emerich **7**:774
Gumpertz, Sydney G. **11**:1552
GUMPLOWICZ, LUDWIG **7**:975
- "anachronism" of Jews **15**:64ff
Gumprecht ben Abraham **2**:776
Gundashapur (city, Pers.), *see* Be Lapat
Gundbert (fam.), *see* GOMPERZ
Gundelfinger, Friedrich, *see* GUNDOLF, FRIEDRICH
Gundersheimer, Herman S. **3**:651
Gundersheimer, Nathan **5**:755
Gundisalvi, Dominicus **3**:948
- Christian Hebraists **8**:35
Gundissalinus (Gundisalvo), *see* Gundisalvi, Dominicus
GUNDOLF, FRIEDRICH **7**:977
Gungunum (k., Mesop.) **16**:1552
Guni (tribal clan) **12**:818
GUNKEL, HERMANN **7**:977
- form criticism **4**:907ff
Gunpowder **5**:375
GUNSBERG, ISIDOR **5**:408
Gunst, Sivert **14**:927
GUNZBERG, ARYEH LEIB BEN ASHER **7**:978
- *illus:* text
Gunzberg, Minda de **4**:1406
Gunzburg, Naphtali **13**:540
GUNZBURG, NIKO **7**:979
Gunzenhauser, Abraham **8**:1324
Gunzenhauser, Azriel **7**:980; **8**:1324
GUNZENHAUSER, JOSEPH BEN JACOB **7**:980
- incunabula **8**:1324
- *illus:*
- - Book of Psalms (1487) **8**:1329
- - Ibn Ezra's commentary on the Pentateuch **4**:894
- - Pentateuch (1488) **8**:1332
- - *Sha'ar ha-Gemul* (1490) **8**:1334
Gunzenheimer, Abraham **15**:635
Gur (tn., Pol.), *see* GORA KALWARIA
Gur, Mordekhai **14**:1630
Gur Aryeh Ha-Levy (Mahargah) **14**:1476
Gur dynasty (has.) **7**:784
- Agudat Israel **2**:423
- dynasties **1**:ḥas. table
- hasidic music **7**:1425; **13**:1617
Gurage (lang.) **14**:1153
GURA-HUMORULUI (tn., Buk.) **7**:980
Gurara (oasis, Alg.) **15**:1418
Gurarie, Morris, *see* GRAY, MORRIS ABRAHAM
Gur Aryeh (Fr. tos.), *see* JUDAH BEN ISAAC
Gurayev, General **12**:1234
Gurevich, Boris **12**:1376
Gurevich, M.O. (psych.) **13**:1340
GUREVICH, MOSHE (Bundist) **7**:980
Gurevicz (fam. name), *see also* HOROWITZ
Gurevitch, A. G., *see* Ḥoron, A. G.
Gurewich, E. **6**:268
Gurewicz, J.L. **11**:1281
Gurewitz, Yakov **12**:1514
Gurfinckel, Sorana, *see* GURIAN, SORANA
Guri, Israel **9**:863
Guria, Al **16**:822
GURIAN, SORANA **7**:981
Gurim (loc., Isr.) **9**:795
Gurji, Joseph **4**:89
Gurjim (Georgian Js.) **7**:423f
Gurk, Judah **7**:423
GURLAND, ḤAYYIM JONAH **7**:981
GURS (concen. camp) **7**:982
- art **3**:575
- Holocaust **7**:34; **8**:858
GURSHTEIN, AARON **7**:982
Guru (spiritual guide) **10**:631
Gurvich, Alexander Gavrilovich, *see* GURWITSCH, ALEXANDER GAVRILOVICH
Gurvich, Fyodor Ilyich, *see* DAN, FYODOR ILYICH
Gurvich, Larissa **15**:313
Gurvitch, Abraham **5**:407
GURVITCH, GEORGES **7**:983
Gurwicz (fam. name), *see also* HOROWITZ
Gurwicz, Leib **11**:492
GURWITSCH, AARON **7**:983
GURWITSCH, ALEXANDER GAVRILOVICH **7**:983
Gusdorfer, S.B. **7**:216
Gusen (concen. camp, Ger.) **5**:78; **11**:1137
Gusev, S. **5**:794
Gushen, Irving **15**:311
Gush Ezyon, *see* Ezyon bloc
Gush Ḥalav (city, Er. Isr.), *see* GISCALA
Gush Ḥalav, János, *see* GISZKALAY, JÁNOS
GUSIKOW, JOSEPH MICHAEL **7**:984
Gusman, Abraham Saul **16**:1099
GUSS, BENJAMIN **7**:984
Gusset, Jacques, *see* Gousset, Jacques
Gussing, Nils G. **15**:1561
Gustav Vasa Bible (Swed.) **4**:877
Gustloff, Wilhelm **7**:94
Gustman, Ze'ev **13**:148
GUSTON, PHILIP **3**:601
- *illus:*
- - "Dial" **3**:625
Gut, E. **5**:452
Guta of Ueberlingen **15**:1499
GUTENBERG, BENO **7**:985
Gutenberg, Johann **8**:1319
Guter, David **8**:828
GUTFREUND, OTTO **7**:985
Gutgeld, Mordekhai, *see* BENTOV, MORDEKHAI
GUTHE, HERMANN **7**:985
- Deutscher Palaestina-Verein **5**:1595
- Jerusalem **9**:1521
GUTHEIM, JAMES KOPPEL **7**:986
Guthman, Sidney **11**:485
Guthrie, Sir Tyrone **7**:1031
Gutians (anc. people) **16**:1491
Gut Khoydesh (Yid. greetings) **7**:916
Gutman (fam. name), *see also* Gutmann, Guttman, Guttmann
GUTMAN, ALEXANDER B. **7**:987
- medicine **11**:1202
Gutman, André **11**:1563
GUTMAN, CHAIM **7**:987
Gutman, Herbert **4**:175
Gutman, M., *see* Zelikovich, B.
GUTMAN, NAHUM **7**:987
- *illus:*
- - text
- - *Beatricha* **5**:439
- - *Be-Ereẓ Lobengulu Melekh Zulu* **5**:438
- - Bialik, and **4**:802
- - "Women on the Beach of Jaffa" (paint.) Fig. 90 **3**-ART
Gutman, Shemariah **8**:1450
Gutman, Tobias, *see* FEDER, TOBIAS
Gutman, Zygmunt **13**:776
Gutmann, David, Ritter von **7**:989
- metals and mining **11**:1440
GUTMANN, DAVID MEIR **7**:988
GUTMANN, EUGEN **7**:988
Gutmann, Jacob, *see* GUTTMANN, JACOB
Gutmann, Jean, *see* BABILEE, JEAN
GUTMANN, JOSEPH **7**:989
GUTMANN, JOSHUA **7**:989
Gutmann, Loeb **11**:61
Gutmann, Max **7**:990
Gutmann, Meta **16**:913
Gutmann, S. (prch., Gal.) **11**:612
Gutmann, Sarel **11**:61
Gutmann, Simḥa Alter, *see* BEN-ZION, S.
GUTMANN, WILHELM, RITTER VON **7**:989
Gut Morgen (newsp.) **11**:174
Gutnick, H. J. **11**:1284
Gutnick, S. **11**:1284
Gutsche, Thelma **15**:208
Gut Shabes (Yid. greeting) **7**:914
Gutstein, M. A. **8**:568
GUTT, CAMILLE **7**:990
Guttein (fam.) **10**:1156
Guttentag, J. **13**:1366
Guttentag-Tavyomi, Nahum Manasseh **14**:535
Gutterman, Jacob Aryeh **13**:1508
GUTTMACHER, ALAN F. **7**:990
GUTTMACHER, ELIJAH **7**:991
- *meḥiẓah* controversy **11**:1235
- Zionism in Poland **16**:1129
- *illus:* text
GUTTMACHER, MANFRED **7**:992
Guttman (fam., Hung.) **12**:766
Guttman, Eliahu, *see* GUTTMAN, LOUIS

GUTTMAN, LOUIS **7**:992
Guttmann, Adam **16**:1224
Guttmann, Alfred, *see* Hajos, Alfred
Guttmann, Bela **15**:299
Guttmann, I.M. **13**:1464
GUTTMANN, JACOB (r.) **7**:993
- Breslau Seminary **16**:577
- "Protestrabbiner" **13**:1255
Guttmann, Jacob (art.) **3**:566
- *illus:*
- - Chorin, Aaron (monument) **5**:495
GUTTMANN, JULIUS **7**:992
GUTTMANN, MICHAEL (Mihály) **7**:994
- Hertz Pentateuch **4**:884
GUTTMANN, ROBERT **7**:995
- *illus:* text
Gut Yontev (Yid. greeting) **7**:916
GUTZKOW, KARL FERDINAND **7**:996
- Wandering Jew theme **16**:262
GUY, PHILIP LANGSTAFFE ORD **7**:996
GUYANA (state, S. Am.) **7**:997
- Latin America **10**:1451
- *illus:* text
Guy de Lusignan **9**:268
- Jerusalem coin **9**:1579
Guyenne, Madame de **8**:36
Guzmán, Don Luis de **3**:498; **5**:39
- *illus:*
- - Arragel, Moses, presenting translation of the Bible **3**:498
Gvardeiskoye (vill., Ukr.), *see* Felshtin
Gvati, Hayyim **9**:676
Gwelo (city, Rhod.) **14**:148
Gwiazda (sports soc.), *see* Ha-Kokhav
Gyarmathi, Samuel **8**:36
Gyarmati, Dezso **12**:1376
Gyarmazi, István **8**:36
Gyges (Lydian k.) **11**:621
Gyles, J.F. **8**:36
Gyllembourg, Thomasine **14**:927
Gyllensten, Lars Johan Wictor **14**:930
GYMANSIUM (Gr. inst.) **7**:998
- Hellenism **8**:297
- sport in Hellenistic period **15**:291
Gymnastics **15**:309
- *illus:*
- - first Maccabiah **11**:663
GYONGYOS (city, Hung.) **7**:999
Gyöngyösi de Heteny, Paul **8**:36
GYŐR (city, Hung.) **7**:999
- *illus:* text
Gyór-Sziget (isl., Hung.) **7**:999
Gypsum (min.) **9**:813

H

H (bib. laws), *see* HOLINESS CODE
Ha-Abbir (r.), *see* Rosanes, Abraham ben Israel
Ha-Adamah (period.) **9:**1001
- statistics **1:**newsp. list
Ha-Aguddah ha-Ivrit ha-Sifrutit (soc., Iraq) **8:**1450
Ha-Aḥdut (journ.) **9:**1015
- cultural development **9:**330
- Hebrew newspapers **12:**1055
- Po'alei Zion **7:**1326
- statistics **1:**newsp. list
- Zerubavel, Jacob **16:**999
- *illus:*
- - editorial board **16:**999
Ha-Ahot be-Yisrael (journ.) **1:**newsp. list
Ha-Ai (city, Er. Isr.), *see* AI
Ha-Am (newsp., Isr.) **16:**407
- statistics **1:**newsp. list
Ha-Am (newsp., Rus.) **13:**1047
- Hebrew newspapers **12:**1051
- Shimoni, David **14:**1404
- statistics **1:**newsp. list
- *illus:*
- - masthead **12:**361
Ha-Am (journ. U.S.) **1:**newsp. list
Ha'amadah (diacritical mark) **16:**1453
Haan, Carolina Lea de, *see* BRUGGEN, CARRY VAN
HAAN, JACOB ISRAËL DE **7:**1001
- Agudat Israel **2:**424
- immigration to Israel **9:**341
- Sonnenfeld, Joseph **15:**156
- *illus:*
- - *Jerusalem* (1921) **6:**319
Haan, Jacob Meijer de, *see* DE HAAN, JACOB MEIJER
HA'ANAKAH (gratuity) **7:**1003
- *Contents:*
- - Scriptural References **7:**1003
- - Right to Gratuity **7:**1004
- - Substance of Gratuity Right **7:**1004
- - Severance Pay **7:**1005
- - State of Israel **7:**1006
- custom **12:**16; **12:**20
Ha-Aravah, Naḥal (wadi, Isr.), *see* Naḥal ha-Aravah
Haarbrucker, T. **8:**35
Haarburger, Ivan **4:**1112
HAARETZ (newsp.) **7:**1007
- Gluecksohn, Moshe **7:**630
- Hebrew newspapers **12:**1047; **12:**1056ff
- Jerusalem **9:**1473
- Ratosh, Yonathan **13:**1573
- statistics **1:**newsp. list
- *illus:* text
Haaretz Museum (Isr.) **12:**552
Haaretz Shellanu (weekly) **5:**458; **9:**1015
Ha-Arez (publ.) **1:**newsp. list
Ha-Arez ve-ha-Avodah (journ.) **1:**newsp. list
Ha-A-r-i, *see* LURIA, ISAAC BEN SOLOMON
Ha-Ari (syn. Isr.) **14:**630
Ha-Ari, Mount (Isr.) **9:**152; **9:**156
Ha-Ariel (newsp.) **9:**1014
- statistics **1:**newsp. list
Ha-Ari rite (litur.) **11:**400ff
Haarklou, J. **5:**1071
HAARLEM (city, Neth.) **7:**1008
Haas, Aaron **3:**825
Haas, Adolf **4:**610
Haas, Cyril **15:**303
Haas, de (name), *see* DE HAAS
HAAS, FRITZ **7:**1008
HAAS, GEORG **7:**1009
Haas, Hans **12:**1376
HAAS, HUGO **12:**468
- film director **13:**973
Haas, J. Gottfried **8:**35
Haas, Jacob **3:**824
Haas, Karl **5:**1572
HAAS, LEO **7:**1009
- *illus:*
- - "Loading a Transport . . ." (drg.) Fig. 81 **3**- ART
HAAS, LUDWIG **7:**1009
- *illus:*
- - Kohn, Pinchas, and **10:**1147
Haas, Peter **15:**435
Haas, Robert K. **13:**1372
HAAS, SOLOMON BEN JEKUTHIEL KAUFMANN **7:**1010
Haas, Walter A.Jr. **15:**435
Haas, Walter A.Sr. **15:**435
HAAS, WILLY **7:**1010
HAASE, HUGO **7:**1010
Ha-Ashuri (tal. schol.), *see* ḤEFEẒ BEN YAẒLI'AḤ
Ha-Asif (journ.) **1:**newsp. list
HA-ASIF (lit. annuals) **7:**1011
- Hebrew newspapers **12:**1050
- press **13:**1045
- statistics **1:**newsp. list
Ha'atakah (kab. concept) **7:**574
HAAVARA (orgn.) **7:**1012
- Arlosoroff, Chaim **3:**471
- German immigrants **9:**531ff
- refugees, Jewish **14:**29
Haaviv (period.) **5:**457
- Yugoslavia **16:**888
- Zionism **16:**1151
Ha'azinu (bib. song) **2:**179ff; **5:**783
- *illus:*
- - ms., Persia **4:**955
Hababou, Charles **2:**619
ḤABAD (ḥas. mvmt.) **7:**1013
- Aaron ben Moses **2:**17
- *aliyah* **9:**514
- Bacharach, Naphtali **4:**50
- Bobruisk **4:**1156
- dynasties **1:**ḥas. table
- Georgia Jews **7:**426
- Ḥasidic music **7:**1421,1426
- Hebron settlement **8:**232; **8:**234
- *ḥevra kaddisha* **8:**442
- in Israel **9:**899
- Kabbalah **10:**555
- Lawat, Abraham **10:**1485
- Lithuania **11:**362ff
- music, Jewish **12:**638
- prayer **13:**983
- publishing **13:**1376
- records **13:**1617
- righteous, wicked **14:**183
- Shneur Zalman of Lyady **14:**1432
- Vilna **16:**143
- yeshivot **16:**769; **16:**771
- *ẓimẓum* **7:**1403
- *illus:*
- - ḥasidic gathering **7:**1401
- - Hebron, emissary's credentials **8:**728
- - "*tefillin* campaign" **15:**900
- - traveling library **11:**195
- - Yod-Tet Kislev celebration **10:**883
- *scores:*
- - *Niggunim* **7:**1428,1430,1431,1432; **12:**639
- *see also:* SCHNEERSOHN (fam.)
Ḥabad, Motke **6:**1381
Ḥabad synagogue (Jer.) **9:**1459
Ha-Bahir, Sefer, *see* BAHIR, SEFER HA-
HABAKKUK (bib. fig.) **7:**1014
- articles of faith **10:**385
- Minor Prophets **12:**48
- *illus:*
- - text
- - *Pesher Habbakuk* **13:**332
- *see also: Pesher Habakkuk*
HABAKKUK, PROPHECY OF (apoc. wk.) **7:**1017
- *illus:* text
Habakkuk Commentary, *see Pesher Habakkuk*
HABAS, BRACHA **7:**1018
Ḥabash, *see* ETHIOPIA
Habash, George **9:**471
ḤABBĀN (tn., S. Arab.) **7:**1018
- *illus:*
- - text
- - immigrants rehearsing traditional dance **9:**1007
ḤABBAR, HABBAREI (gr., Babyl.) **7:**1020
HABE, HANS **7:**1021
Ha-Be'er (journ.) **1:**newsp. list
Habeler, Jakab **8:**35
HABER (fam.) **7:**1021
Haber, David **15:**311
HABER, FRITZ **7:**1021
- stamps **15:**335
- *illus:* text
Haber, Louis (Ludwig) **7:**1021
Haber, Moritz **7:**1021
Haber, Paul **15:**310
Haber, Salomon (Samuel) **7:**1021
Haber, Samuel (bnk., Ger.) **7:**1021
HABER, SAMUEL L. (pub. fig., U.S.) **7:**1022
HABER, SHAMAI **7:**1023
- *illus:*
- - text
- - "Le Mur" (sculp.) **14:**1068
Haber, Tobias **13:**117
Haber, William (econ.) **16:**556
Haber, Willliam (pres., Ort) **12:**1485
Haberfeld, Gustave **10:**1001
Haberfeld, J. **13:**60
Ha-Berit ha-Olamit shel Tenu'at Torah va-Avodah (rel. lab. orgn.) **7:**1321
Haberkasten, Kalonymus Kalman **12:**1513
Haberland (fam.) **5:**921
Haberland, Kurt **5:**921
Haberland, Solomon Georg **5:**921
HABERLANDT, GOTTLIEB **7:**1023
HABERMANN, ABRAHAM MEIR **1:**31; **7:**1024
- Cairo *genizah* **16:**1338
Habermann, Johannes **8:**35
Habern (tn., Bohem.), *see* Habry
Habert, Susanna **8:**35
ḤABIB, ḤAYYIM BEN MOSES BEN SHEM TOV **7:**1024
Ḥabib, ibn (name), *see also* Ibn Ḥabib
Habib, Levi Ben, *see* LEVI BEN ḤABIB
ḤABIB, MOSES BEN SOLOMON IBN **7:**1025
- Ephraim ben Jacob **6:**812
- *illus:* text
Habib, Shabbetai ben Abishai **13:**595
ḤABIBA, JOSEPH **7:**1026
- Jewish literature **11:**332
Habibi, Emil **5:**808
H-a-b-i-f, *see* PALACHE, ḤAYYIM
ḤABIL (place, Yem.) **7:**1026
HABILLO, DAVID **7:**1027
- *Sefer Yeẓirah* **16:**787
- Shabbetai Ẓevi **14:**1223
HABILLO, ELIJAH BEN JOSEPH **7:**1027
- translations **15:**1324

HABILLO, ELISHA **7:**1027
Habillo, Moses **15:**1359
HABIMAH (theat.) **7:**1028
- Brod, Max **4:**1387
- cultural life **9:**1004
- Gnessin, Menaḥem **7:**634
- history chart **8:**766-767
- Meskin, Aharon **11:**1405
- Stalin **15:**327
- Tel Aviv **15:**921; **15:**922
- *Yevsektsiya* **16:**780
- *illus:*
- - text
- - *Genesis* **15:**1063
- - *Dybbuk*, a scene **6:**19; **14:**356; **14:**465
- *see also:* THEATER
Habimah (drama circle, Ukr.) **12:**1160
Ha-Bimah ha-Ivrit (period.) **3:**424; **13:**1040
- statistics **1:**newsp. list
Ha-Binyan (journ.) **1:**newsp. list
HABIRU (anc. people) **7:**1033
- anthropology **3:**45
- Bible history **8:**574
- early agriculturalists **2:**387
- Egypt **6:**482
- identity **3:**305
- Megiddo **11:**1227
- slavery **12:**1289
- *illus:*
- - Seti I stele **8:**580
HA-BOKER (newsp., Pol.) **7:**1035
- Akavya, Avraham **2:**478
- *Haynt* **7:**1499
- statistics **1:**newsp. list
- *illus:* text
HA-BOKER (newsp., Isr.) **7:**1036
- Hebrew newspapers **12:**1056; **12:**1057
- Revisionists **14:**132
- statistics **1:**newsp. list
Ha-Boker Or (period.) **7:**828
- Braudes, Reuben **4:**1316
- Hebrew newspapers **12:**1049
- press **13:**1045
- statistics **1:**newsp. list
Ha-Boneh (pub.) **8:**1242
Ha-Boneh ha-Ḥofshi (journ.) **1:**newsp. list
HA-BONIM (mosh., Isr.) **7:**1036
- statistics **1:**place list
Habonim (youth mvmt.), *see* IḤUD HABONIM
Habonim-No'ar Ḥaluẓi **8:**1241
Habonim Tenu'ah Me'uḥedet (Isr.) **8:**1240
HABOR (riv., Mesop.) **7:**1036
Habor (reg., Assyr.) **4:**1470
- Ten Lost Tribes **15:**1003ff
Ḥabram (tn., Transj.), *see* Amrawa
Habry (tn., Bohem.) **7:**695
Habsburg Monarchy, *see* HAPSBURG MONARCHY
ḤABSHUSH, ḤAYYIM **7:**1037
- coppersmith **11:**1442
- Halévy, Joseph **7:**1185
- Messianic movement **16:**744
ḤABSHUSH, SHALOM BEN YAḤYA **7:**1037
Habu (site, Egy.), *see* Medinet Habu
Ḥabub (f., Ptolemy) **13:**1349
Ha-Bula'i ha-Ivri (journ.) **1:**newsp. list
Hacaliah (bib.fig.) **12:**936
Hachenburg, Max **10:**1497, 1509
Hachsharah (aliyah training) **8:**1241; **8:**254
- Australia **11:**1286
- *illus:*
- - Berdichev farm **14:**458
- - He-Ḥalutz training farm, Grodno **13:**747
- - pioneer group in Russia, 1919 **2:**406
- - Utena training farm **11:**367
HACKENBURG, WILLIAM BOWER **7:**1037
Hackensack (city, N.J.) **4:**612
Hacker, Leonard, *see* HACKETT, BUDDY
Hackerman, Norman **8:**1052
HACKETT, BUDDY **15:**1084
Hackspan, Theodoric **8:**35
Ha-Cohen, Aviasa **15:**1300
HACOHEN, DAVID **7:**1038
- Israel-China relations **5:**472
- *illus:*
- - "Black Saturday" **9:**362
- - Sharett, Moshe and **14:**1312
Hacohen, Eliahu **7:**1470
Ha-Cohen, Estenza, *see* Aragon, Estenza
Hacohen, Mordecai **11:**201
HACOHEN, MORDECAI BEN HILLEL **7:**1038
- Writers' Association **16:**652
HACOHEN, RAPHAEL ḤAYYIM **7:**1039
Ha-Cohen, Shalom **14:**978
Hadad (Edomite) **6:**374
- Siamun **14:**1416
- Solomon **15:**100
Hadad (s., Ishmael) **9:**89
HADAD (deity) **7:**1040
- Arameans **3:**256
- Rimmon **14:**186
- *illus:*
- - Hadad temple **3:**288
Hadad, Wassie **9:**471
Hadadezer (k., Aram), *see* BEN-HADAD II
Hadad-Rimmon **2:**762
- Rimmon **14:**186
Hadad son of Bedad (k., Edom) **6:**373
Hadamar, Ephraim **11:**1451
HADAMARD, JACQUES SALOMON **7:**1040
Hadar (k. Edom) **6:**373
Hadar (vill., Isr.), *see* HOD HA-SHARON
Hadar Am (stlmt., Isr.) **1:**place list
Hadar ha-Carmel (Haifa qtr.) **9:**341; **9:**563
Hadarniel (angel) **2:**973
Ha-Darom (journ.) **1:**newsp. list
Hadar-Ramatayim (vill., Isr.), *see* HOD HA-SHARON
Hadas (shrub), *see* MYRTLE
Hadas, Gershon **10:**740
HADAS, MOSES **7:**1041
- *illus:*
- - *Fables of a Jewish Aesop* **4:**597
Hadashot (journ.) **1:**newsp. list
Hadashot Aḥaronot (journ.) **1:**newsp. list
Hadashot Arkheologiyyot (journ.) **1:**newsp. list
Ḥadashot me-ha-Areẓ (weekly) **1:**newsp. list **4:**575
Hadassah (bib. fig.), *see* ESTHER
"Hadassah" (type) **15:**1488
HADASSAH, THE WOMEN'S ZIONIST ORGANIZATION OF AMERICA **7:**1041
- *Contents:*
- - Early history **7:**1041
- - Medical Organization in Israel **7:**1042
- - Youth Aliyah **7:**1044
- - U.S. activities **7:**1045
- Allonei Yiẓḥak **2:**657
- Epstein, Judith **6:**833
- Freund, Miriam **7:**167
- Ha-Shaḥar (youth orgn.) **16:**860
- health services **9:**982ff
- science and research **9:**966
- Seligsberg, Alice **14:**1133
- U.S.Zionism **16:**1142
- vocational training **7:**1044
- Youth Aliyah **16:**862
- Zionism **16:**1109ff
- *illus:*
- - text
- - typeface **15:**1486
Hadassah-Hebrew University Medical Center (Isr.) **7:**1043; **9:**1473; **9:**1479
- autopsies and dissection **3:**932
- health services **9:**982ff
- new site **9:**1493
- synagogue **15:**588
- *illus:*
- - Chagall's stained glass windows **4:**526; **5:**1258; **9:**1077
- - Mt. Scopus buildings **3:**350
- - nursing school **15:**667
- - Rachmilewitz, Moshe examining patient **9:**990
- - wounded soldier's arrival by helicopter **9:**990
- - Yassky, Haim, with nurses **16:**721
Hadassah Magazine (period.) **6:**833; **13:**1051
Hadassah Medical Organization (Isr.) **9:**985
HADASSI, JUDAH (ha-Avel) BEN ELIJAH **7:**1046
- articles of faith **3:**655
- Avelei Zion **3:**946
- Karaism **10:**766; **10:**770
- masorah **16:**1417
Hadassim (youth vill., Isr.) **6:**987
Hadayah, Ovadiah **10:**554
- responsa **14:**93
- *illus:*
- - Supreme Rabbinical Court **9:**641
Ha-Dayig ha-Yisraeli (journ.) **1:**newsp. list
Ha-Dayyan (Kar.) *see* ELIJAH BEN AARON BEN MOSES
ḤADDAD, EZRA **7:**1047
- author **8:**1452
Ḥaddād, Meir **9:**1041
Ḥaddād, Mīshīl **9:**1042
Ha-Degel (newsp.), *see Ha-Yehudi*
ḤADERAH (tn., Isr.) **7:**1047
- eucalyptus forest **9:**788
- Feinberg, Israel **6:**1209
- history chart **8:**766-767
- statistics **1:**place list
- synagogue **15:**620
- *illus:*
- - ossuaries **12:**1504
- - Volozhin Nes Ziona association **16:**214
Haderah River, *see* Naḥal Haderah
Haderech (mag., Eng.) **5:**460
Ha-Derekh (journ., Ger.-Switz.-Aus.) **1:**newsp. list
Ha-Derekh (journs., Isr.) **1:**newsp. list
Ha-Derekh (journ., Pol.) **1:**newsp. list
Ha-Deror (period.) **4:**1292
- Levias, Caspar **11:**88
- statistics **1:**newsp. list
Ha-Devir (journ.) **1:**newsp. list
Ha-Devorah (journ.) **1:**newsp. list
ḤAD GADYA (Hag. song) **7:**1048
- *illus:* text
- *scores:*
- - Piedmont **9:**1145
Ḥad Gadya (theat.) **4:**1392
Hadhramaut (reg., Arab.), *see* HADRAMAUT
Hadich (vill., Rus.) **14:**1434
HADID (tn., Er. Isr.) **7:**1050
Ḥadid (mosh., Isr.) **7:**1050
- statistics **1:**place list
Hadida (fam., Mor.) **15:**1030
Hadida, Judah **15:**791
Ḥadidah, Solomon **5:**34
ḤADITH (Isl. tradition) **7:**1051
- *see also:* ISLAM
Hadoar (weekly) **12:**1047, 1053; **16:**836
- statistics **1:**newsp. list
- *illus:*
- - first issue **15:**1627
Ha-Do'ar la-No'ar (weekly) **5:**457
- Persky, Daniel **13:**320
Ha-Dor (newsp., Isr.) **1:**newsp. list
Ha-Dor (period., Pol.) **13:**1375
- Akavya, Avraham Aryeh Leib **2:**478
- Frischmann, David **13:**1045
- Hebrew newspapers **12:**1051
- statistics **1:**newsp. list
Hadoram (bib. fig.), *see* ADONIRAM
Ha-Dover (newsp.) **4:**93; **13:**1041
HADRACH (city, Syr.) **7:**1052
- academy **15:**641
- Aramean state **3:**255
HADRAMAUT (Hadramawt; reg., Arab.) **7:**1053
Ḥaḍramautic (lang.) **14:**1152
HADRAN (cerem.) **7:**1053
- *siyyum* **14:**1642
- *illus:* text
HADRIAN I (pope) **7:**1056
HADRIAN, PUBLIUS AELIUS (Rom. emp.) **7:**1054
- Adrianople **2:**309
- Aquila **12:**1405
- attitude to Jews **14:**230
- Bar Kokhba **4:**232; **8:**646ff
- circumcision **5:**570
- Dio Cassius **6:**59
- Eleazar ben Parta **6:**595
- Ereẓ Israel **9:**245
- Gerizim shrine **7:**438
- history chart **8:**766-767
- Jerusalem **2:**319; **3:**936; **9:**1405
- Samaritans **14:**730
- Sibylline Oracles **14:**1491
- *illus:* text
Hadrianus Relandus, *see* RELAND, ADRIAN
Hadrumetum (loc., Tun.), *see* Sousse
Ḥadshot ha-Areẓ (newsp.) **7:**1007
- cultural life **9:**1015
- Hebrew newspapers **12:**1056
Ḥadshot ha-Erev (newsp.) **1:**newsp. list
Ḥadshot ha-Kalkalah ha-Ereẓ Yisre'elit (journ.) **1:**newsp. list
Ḥadshot ha-Neft (journ.) **1:**newsp. list
Ḥadshot ha-Sport (journ.) **12:**1058
- statistics **1:**newsp. list
Ḥadshot ha-Taḥburah (journ.) **1:**newsp. list
Ḥadshot ha-Yom (newsp.) **1:**newsp. list
Ḥadshot N.C.R. (journ.) **1:**newsp. list
Ḥadshot Pensiyyah u-Vittu'aḥ Soẓyali (journ.) **1:**newsp. list
Ḥadshot Sport ve-Toto (publ.) **1:**newsp. list
HADUTA BEN ABRAHAM **7:**1056
Hadyat al-Qārī (bk.) **16:**1471
Haecker, Emil **10:**89
Ha-Edah (newsp.) **1:**newsp. list
Ha-Edah ha-Ḥaredit (cmty., Jer.), *see* NETUREI KARTA
HA-EFRATI, JOSEPH **7:**1056
- drama, Hebrew **6:**195; **14:**916
- *illus:* text
Ha-Eitanim (period.) **1:**newsp. list
Ha-'Elohim (name of God) **7:**679
HA-EMET (period.) **7:**1057
- Hebrew newspapers **12:**1046; **12:**1050
- Liebermann, Aaron **11:**220
- statistics **1:**newsp. list
- Zionism **16:**1158
- *illus:* text
Ha-Emunah ha-Ramah (wk.) **8:**1161

Ha-Em ve-ha-Yeled (journ.) **1**:newsp. list
HAENDEL, IDA **12**:692
Haener, J. H. **8**:35
Ha-Enziklopedyah ha-Ivrit **6**:733
Ha-Enziklopedyah le-Ḥaklaut **6**:735
Ha-Esh (publ.) **1**:newsp. list
Ha-Eshkol (Heb. encyc.) **6**:731
- Friedberg, Abraham **7**:173
Ha-Eshkol (period.) **6**:1451; **7**:964
- statistics **1**:newsp. list
Haetzer, Ludwig **4**:873
HAETZYONI, YEHUDAH **7**:1058
Ha-Ezraḥ (journ.) **4**:575
- Dizengoff, Meir **6**:138
- statistics **1**:newsp. list
Haezrahi, M. **13**:839
Haezraḥi, Pepita **7**:1059
HAEZRAḤI, YEHUDA **7**:1059
Ḥafeẓ Ḥayyim (r.), *see* ISRAEL MEIR HA-KOHEN
ḤAFEẒ ḤAYYIM (kib., Isr.) **7**:1059
- statistics **1**:place list
- *illus:* text
Hafez Hayyim (tal. acad., N.Y.) **12**:1120
HAFFKINE, WALDEMAR MORDECAI **7**:1060
- self-defense **14**:1124ff
- stamps **15**:335
Haffkine Foundation (Lausanne) **7**:1061
Hafka'at kiddushin (marriage annulment) **12**:1445
HAFKA'AT SHE'ARIM (profiteering) **7**:1061
- *Contents:*
- - Profiteering and Overreaching **7**:1061
- - Price-Fixing and Control **7**:1061
- - In Ereẓ Israel **7**:1062
- - Measures to Prevent profiteering **7**:1062
- - In Israel **7**:1063
- supervision of prices **13**:796
- Theodosius' decree **16**:1277
- weights and measures **16**:390
- *see also:* ONA'AH
Hafla'ah (wk.) **8**:1000
HAFSIDS (Berber dyn.) **7**:1064
- Tunisia **15**:1437
Haft, Abraham **2**:456; **16**:1342
HAFTARAH (syn. reading) **16**:1342
- Karaites **10**:781; **10**:785
- liturgy **11**:394; **11**:402
- *maftir* **11**:685
- *minyan* **12**:67
- Neo-Aramaic **12**:951
- Reform Judaism **15**:1389
- Torah reading **15**:1248
- *illus:*
- - David ben Benayah's ms. **4**:471
- - Karaite cantillation **10**:784
- - Shabbatean edition **14**:1229
- - triennial cycle (chart) **15**:1387
- *see also:* CANTILLATION
Haga (vill., Swed.) **15**:549
Ha-Gadol mi-Minsk (tal.), *see* PERELMANN, JEROHMAN JUDAH LEIB BEN SOLOMON ZALMAN
Ha-Galgal (journ.) **1**:newsp. list
Ha-Galil (journ.) **1**:newsp. list
Ha-Galut ve-ha-Pedut (wk.) **8**:558
Ḥagam (orgn., Isr.) **7**:252; **9**:688
- Haganah **9**:688
Ha-Gan (period.) **7**:183
- statistics **1**:newsp. list
HAGANAH (mil. orgn., Isr.) **7**:1064
- *Contents:*
- - Initial Organization **7**:1064
- - During the '20's **7**:1065
- - 1931-1935 **7**:1066
- - Policy of Restraint **7**:1067
- - World War II **7**:1069
- - Policy of Resistance **7**:1071
- - War of Independence **7**:1073
- archives **3**:395
- Ben-Gurion, David **4**:508; **4**:509ff
- Ben-Zvi, Raḥel **4**:581
- Beriḥah **4**:632
- British White Paper **9**:687
- broadcasting **15**:930
- Dayan, Moshe **5**:1372
- Deedes, Sir Wyndham **5**:1456
- defense **8**:759ff; **16**:1089
- Defense Forces **9**:684
- Dori, Ya'akov **6**:173
- En-Harod **6**:792
- Golomb, Eliyahu **7**:763ff
- Histadrut **9**:856
- historical survey **9**:346ff
- history chart **8**:766-767
- Hungarian Jewry **8**:1104
- illegal immigration **8**:1249ff
- Irgun Ẓeva'i Le'ummi **8**:1466ff **9**:688ff
- Italy **16**:1123
- Jabotinsky **9**:1180
- Loḥamei Ḥerut Israel **9**:688ff; **11**:465
- Marcus, David **11**:945
- Poland **13**:786
- Reik, Ḥavivah **14**:54
- religious Jews' participation **9**:895
- Sadeh, Yiẓḥak **14**:623
- Sereni, Enzo **14**:1182
- settlement defense **9**:683f
- Sneh, Moshe **15**:16
- Sonneborn, Rudolf **15**:155
- Szenes, Hannah **15**:661
- Tel Aviv headquarters **15**:923
- U.S. help **16**:1144
- War of Independence **16**:306
- Wingate, Orde **16**:548
- Yadin, Yigael **16**:694
- *Yishuv* security **9**:341ff
- *illus:*
- - text
- - field squads unit **9**:685
- - Gesher ha-Ziv memorial **7**:526
- - *Haggadah* for soldiers (1948) **7**:1090
- - "illegal" immigrants **4**:626
- - Jabotinski, Vladimir, and group **9**:1182
- - Jewish Settlement Police member **9**:685
- - Katamon operation **16**:315
- - *kofer ha-yishuv* coupons **9**:355
- - Negev Brigade memorial **12**:931
- - Night Squads unit **9**:685
- - Palavir air unit **13**:47
- - Palmaḥ "German Squad" **13**:46
- - Piper Cub plane **9**:686
- - *Sea Lion*, Palmaḥ crew members **13**:45
- - Sedot Yam search **14**:1094
- - Ta'as, assembling hand grenades **9**:682
- - *Unafraid* "illegal" immigrants **9**:361
- *see also:* HA-SHOMER; JEWISH BRIGADE GROUP; PALMAḤ
HAGAR (bib. fig.) **7**:1074
- in the Arts: **2**:122
- Keturah **10**:934
- Sarah **14**:867; **14**:868
- *illus:* text
- - "Hagar in the Wilderness" (paint., J. B. C. Corot) **9**:81
- *see also:* ISHMAEL
Ḥagar (settlement) **7**:1530
"Hagar in the Wilderness" (paint., J. B. C. Corot) **9**:81
Ha-Gat (journ.) **1**:newsp. list
Hagbahah (legal term) **2**:218
HAGBAHAH, GELILAH (Torah rit.) **7**:1076
- children **5**:428
- Torah reading **15**:1254
Ha-Gedud (journ.) **1**:newsp. list
Hagege, Daniel, *see* HAJJĀJ, DANIEL
HAGEN (tn., Ger.) **7**:1078
HAGENBACH (vill., Germ.) **7**:1078
Hager (name, ḥas. dyn.), *see* VIZHNITZ
Hager, Baruch **16**:199
Hager, Baruch ben Menaḥem Mendel **16**:199
Hager, David **16**:902
Hager, Eliezer **16**:199
Hager, Ḥayyim **16**:199
Hager, Ḥayyim ben Israel **16**:199
Hager, Israel **16**:198
Hager, Israel ben Barukh **16**:199
Hager, Menaḥem Mendel ben Ḥayyim **14**:532; **16**:199
Hager, Phinehas **16**:199
Hagerup, Inger **14**:933
Ha-Gesher (journ.) **1**:newsp. list
Ha-Ge'ullah (newsp.) **10**:437; **13**:319
Ḥagga (amora), *see* HAGGAI
Haggadah (tal.), *see* AGGADAH
Haggadah, Amsterdam, see AMSTERDAM HAGGADOT
HAGGADAH, PASSOVER **7**:1079
- *Contents:*
- - Introduction **7**:1079
- - Component Parts **7**:1080
- - Ritual Acts **7**:1091
- - Textual Elaborations **7**:1092
- - Commentaries **7**:1092
- - Manuscripts and Editions **7**:1093
- - Illuminated Manuscripts **7**:1095
- - Printed Editions of Illustrated Haggadot **7**:1100
- - Musical Rendition **7**:1103
- Abudarham, David **2**:182
- *Addir bi-Melukhah* hymn **2**:256
- *Addir Hu* hymn **2**:258
- Afrikaans **15**:210
- antiquity of **11**:1292
- Apulian dialect **7**:884
- art **3**:536ff
- Ashkenazi **7**:1098
- Bedersi's parody **4**:370
- book illustrations **4**:1235
- *Eḥad Mi Yode'a* **6**:503
- Elijah Menahem ben Moses **6**:659
- first fruits offering text **6**:1314
- folklore **6**:1392
- *Ḥad Gadya* **7**:1050
- *Ha-Laḥma Anya* **7**:1155
- iconography **8**:1216ff
- illuminated mss. **8**:1263ff
- Italiener, Bruno **9**:1115
- kibbutz festivals **10**:959
- Kohen press **15**:1481
- *Mah Nishtannah* **11**:728
- Natronai **12**:887
- *Nishmat Kol Ḥai* **12**:1177
- number Four **3**:292
- plagues of Egypt **13**:611
- *Sarajevo Haggadah* **14**:871
- *Second Nuremberg Haggadah* **14**:775; **15**:110
- Trebitsch, Moses **15**:1363
- *Venetian Haggadah* **8**:1319
- Ya'ari's bibliography **16**:690
- *illus:*
- - text
- - *Amsterdam Haggadah* (1695) **3**:536; **7**:1089; **11**:927; **11**:972
- - *Az Rov Nissim* **3**:1014
- - *Barcelona Haggadah* (14th cent.) **2**:83; **7**:119,1081,1199; **11**:*fcg.* 1131; **12**:602; **13**:1544
- - *Bibliography of the Passover Haggadah* (A. Yaari) **4**:495
- - *Birds' Head Haggadah* (14th cent.) **2**:330, 480; **7**:*fcg.* 875, 1081,1543; **9**:1582; **12**:999; **13**:168
- - *Cincinnati Haggadah* (15th cent.) **4**:*fcg.* 364; **7**:1083
- - *Darmstadt Haggadah* (15th cent.) **3**:1014; **7**:*fcg.* 811, 1085
- - *Dayyeinu* **5**:*fcg.* 1387, 1391; **7**:*fcg.* 875, **7**:1083 *fcg.* 1451; **8**:1274; **10**:211
- - *Dragon Haggadah* (13th cent.) **4**:*fcg.* 1068
- - earliest print (c. 1482) **7**:954, 1087
- - *Eḥad Mi Yode'a* (illus., S. Raskin) **6**:504
- - *Erlangen Haggadah* (18th cent.) **8**:1031
- - *Erna Michael Haggadah* (15th cent.) **2**:554; **7**:*fcg.* 1067, 1229; **8**:1280
- - Ezekiel ben Sassoon Ezekiel Ya'uda's *Haggadah* (1868) **4**:87
- - Germany (14th cent.) **14**:1408
- - Gewitsch *Haggadah* (1730) **7**:534
- - *Golden Haggadah* (13th cent.) **4**:24, 1059; **6**:238,980,1045; **7**:273,1084; **8**:1217; **10**:206 **7**:273, 1084; **8**:1217; **10**:206; **11**:423,902; **12**:*fcg.* 427; **13**:165,609; **14**:1550
- - *Golden Haggadah*, "Sister" to (14th cent.) **2**:806; **7**:*fcg.* 1323
- - Ḥad Gadya **7**:1049,1050
- - *Ha Laḥma Anya* **3**:535; **5**:661 **7**:*fcg.* 1081,1085,1155
- - *Hallel* **7**:1199
- - *Hamilton Siddur* (13th cent.) **8**:*fcg.* 1079
- - *Hodu* **8**:*fcg.* 1079
- - Italy (1550) **14**:1193
- - *Joel ben Simeon Haggadah* (15th cent.) **3**:995; **7**:*fcg.* 1003; **10**:139
- - *Kaufmann Haggadah* (14th cent.) **6**:*fcg.* 1067; **7**:1086
- - *Leḥem Oni* (London, 1784) **11**:476
- - *Mantua Haggadah* (1560) **3**:538; **6**:863; **7**:1087
- - *Maror Zeh* **8**:1217
- - *Maẓẓah Zu* **11**:*fcg.* 1131,1157; **12**:602
- - *Mocatta Haggadah* (13th cent.) **2**:47; **5**:1391; **7**:*fcg.* 1451
- - Munich (15th cent.) **11**:1409
- - New York (1837) **12**:1073
- - *piyyut* **13**:599
- - *Pollak-Pratto Haggadah* (14th cent.) **3**:467; **7**:297
- - *Prague Haggadah* (1526) **3**:535; **7**:1088; **11**:729; **13**:360,567,1101
- - reading in synagogue to illiterates **2**:806
- - *Rylands Spanish Haggadah* (14th cent.) **5**:*fcg.* 1387
- - *Rylands Spanish Haggadah*, "Brother" to (14th cent.) **6**:*fcg.* 619; **7**:1083; **8**:1217; **11**:*fcg.* 939; **16**:858
- - *Sarajevo Haggadah* (14th cent.) **3**:456, 462, 530; **4**:1088; **5**:*fcg.* 1067; **7**:205, 1085, *fcg.* 1131, 1155,1346; **8**:1218,1272; **9**:1202,1285; **10**:204; **11**:885,1014,1157; **12**:379,1192; **13**:605,1602
- - Sasa edition **9**:908
- - *Sassoon Spanish Haggadah* (14th cent.) **7**:1084 *fcg.* 1387
- - *Schocken Haggadah* (15th cent.) **12**:83
- - *Second Nuremberg Haggadah* (15th cent.) **7**:*fcg.* 1195
- - *Sereni Haggadah* (15th cent.) **7**:1049
- - Sha'ar ha-Amakim edition **9**:908
- - *Shefokh Ḥamatkha al ha-Goyim* **6**:*fcg* 651, 863; **7**:*fcg.* 811; **8**:1280; **11**:1409
- - *Shir ha-Ma'alot* (illus., S. Raskin)

6:1037
- - Spain (14th cent.) **13**:164,167,607
- - Steinhardt's edition (1921) **13**:612
- - twelfth century ms. **2**:740
- - *Van Geldern Haggadah*, "Sister" to (18th cent.) **13**:172–173
- - *Venice Haggadah* (17th cent.) **2**:878; **3**:537; **7**:1088; **10**:211; **11**:1410
- - *Washington Haggadah* (15th cent.) **6**:*fcg.* 651; **7**:1086; **8**:1271
- - *Yahuda Haggadah* (15th cent.) **3**:*fcg.* 299; **14**:569
- - *yaknehaz* (15th cent.) **2**:49; **7**:1083
- - *Yehallelukha* **8**:*fcg.* 1079
- - *Zevaḥ Pesaḥ* (1545) **7**:1082
- *mus. notations:*
- - *Ḥad Gadya*, Piedmont **9**:1145
- *see also:* PASSOVER
Haggadah de-Rabbi Eliezer (wk.), *see* PIRKEI DE-RABBI ELIEZER
Haggadah le-Leil Shikkurim (bk.) **13**:132
Haggadah le-Shavuot, see MIDRASH ASERET HA-DIBBEROT
Haggadah le-Tishah be-Av (bk.) **13**:131
Haggadah shel ha-Bayit ha-Le'ummi (bk.) **13**:137
- *illus:*
- - title page (Tel Aviv, 1930) **13**:139
Haggadat Elleh Devarim Rabbah (Mid.), *see* DEUTERONOMY RABBAH
Haggahot (wk.), *see* Ha-Mappah
HAGGAHOT (corrections) **7**:1104
- Contents:
- - Correction of Errors **7**:1105
- - - Correction in the Content **7**:1105
- - - Correction of Stylistic or Graphic Errors **7**:1105
- - - Influence of Haggahot on Text **7**:1106
- - - Proofreaders **7**:1107
- - - Haggahot Literature **7**:1107
- - - Glosses on the codes **7**:1107
- - - Textual Notes and Emendations **7**:1109
Haggahot Asheri **9**:1071
HAGGAHOT MAIMUNIYYOT (hal. wk.) **7**:1110
HAGGAI (bib. fig.) **7**:1112
- eschatology **6**:869ff
- Minor Prophets **12**:48
- rebuilding of Temple **15**:956; **16**:1001
- Zechariah **16**:953
- *illus:*
- - Book of Haggai (ms.) **9**:1169; **10**:1
HAGGAI (amora) **7**:1114
Ḥaggai, Samuel, *see* Ḥagi, Samuel
Haggai ben Alzuk **6**:306
HAGGAI OF SEPPHORIS (amora) **7**:1115
Ḥaggim u-Zemannim Le-Sason (Heb. greeting) **7**:916
Haggith (w., K. David) **2**:294
Ḥag ha-Asif (Harvest Festival) **10**:962
Ḥag ha-Bikkurim (fest.), *see* SHAVUOT
Ḥag ha-Gez (Sheepshearing Festival) **6**:1405
- kibbutz festivals **10**:962
Ḥag ha-Keramim (Festival of the Vineyard) **6**:1405
- kibbutz festivals **10**:962
Ḥag ha-maẓẓot (fest.), *see* PASSOVER
Ḥag ha-Maẓẓot (Samar. fest.) **14**:742
Ḥag ha-Pesaḥ (fest.), *see*

PASSOVER
Ḥagi, Samuel **11**:795
Ha-Gibor (sports club, Prague) **15**:293
- *see also:* MACCABI WORLD UNION
Hagibor-Hamakabi (period.) **13**:1029
ḤAGIGAH (tract.) **7**:1115
Ḥagigat ha-Asif (kib. fest.), *see Ḥag ha-Asif*
Ḥagigat ha-Bikkurim (kib. fest.), *see* SHAVUOT
Ḥagigat ha-Gez (kib. fest.), *see Ḥag ha-Gez*
Ḥagigat ha-Keramim (kib. fest.), *see Ḥag ha-Keramim*
Hagin, Cok, *see* Cok Hagin son of Deulecresse
Ha-Ginnah (mag., Rus., Er. Isr.) **5**:435; **13**:1047
- statistics **1**:newsp. list
Hagin (son of Moses) of Lincoln **3**:398; **6**:659; **13**:1015
Hagiographa **4**:824
- General
- - as law source **12**:117
- - book arrangement **4**:829
- - Jewish literature **11**:309
- - Kabbalah, term for **10**:653
- - order **16**:1406
- - resurrection in **14**:97
- - Septuagint translation **4**:853ff
- - *teki'ata* **15**:915ff
- - Torah reading **15**:1248
- - wisdom literature **16**:559
- Commentaries
- - Abrabanel, Isaac **2**:105
- - Ibn Ezra, Abraham **8**:1166
- - Kimḥi, David **10**:1001
- - Levi ben Gershom **11**:92
- - Malbim, Meir **11**:821
- - *Meẓudat David; Meẓudat Zion* **2**:784
- - Naḥmanides **12**:774
- - Rashi **13**:1558
- - Sforno, Obadiah **14**:1210
- - Targums to **4**:848
- Books of
- - Chronicles, Book of **5**:517
- - Daniel, Book of **5**:1277
- - Ecclesiastes **6**:349
- - Esther, Scroll of **14**:1047
- - Ezra and Nehemiah **6**:1111
- - Job, Book of **10**:111
- - Lamentations, Book of **10**:1368
- - Nehemiah **12**:936
- - Proverbs **13**:1264
- - Psalms, Book of **13**:1303
- - Ruth, Book of **14**:522ff
- - Scrolls, the Five **14**:1057
- - Song of Songs **15**:144
- *illus:*
- - order of (table) **4**:829
- *see also:* BIBLE
HAGIOGRAPHY **7**:1116
- *Contents:*
- - Use of Biblical and Talmudic Material **7**:1117
- - Use of Contemporary Stories and Personages **7**:1117
- - - Ibn Ezra and Other Jewish Scholars **7**:1118
- - - Martyrologic Hagiography **7**:1118
- - - Hagiography and Kabbalah **7**:1119
- - - the Zohar and Later Kabbalistic Writings **7**:1119
- - - Isaac Luria and Other Sages of Safed **7**:1119
- - Modern Jewish Hagiography **7**:1120
- *aggadah* **2**:361
- biography **4**:1010
- folktale **6**:1380

- Israel Ba'al Shem Tov **9**:1056
- *Toledot ha-Ari* **15**:1207
- Yiddish **16**:804; **16**:809
- *see also:* FICTION, HEBREW; MA'ASEH BOOK
ḤAGIZ (fam., Mor.) **7**:1121
Ḥagiz, Abraham (16th cent.) **7**:1121
Ḥagiz, Abraham (17th cent.) **7**:1121
Ḥagiz, Jacob (Mor.) **7**:1121
ḤAGIZ, JACOB (Israel; Jer.) **7**:1121
- Jerusalem **9**:1438
- Shabbetai Ẓevi **14**:1225
ḤAGIZ, MOSES **7**:1122
- Alcorsono **2**:551
- Ashkenazi, Ẓevi **3**:734
- Bacharach, Naphtali **4**:50
- emissary **14**:1366
- Ḥayon, Nehemiah **7**:1502ff
- history chart **8**:766-767
- Luzzatto, Moses Ḥayyim **11**:599
- Malkhi, Ezra **11**:828
- Shabbateanism **14**:1249
Ḥagiz, Samuel (16th cent.) **7**:1121
Ḥagiz, Samuel (16/17th cent.) **7**:1121
Hagman, Saul **12**:844
Ha-Go'el ha-Malakh (tit.) **15**:1165
Hagor (mosh., Isr.) **1**:place list
Ha-Goren (journ., Ger.) **1**:newsp. list
Ha-Goren (journ., Rus.) **1**:newsp. list; **15**:1164
HA-GOSHERIM (kib., Isr.) **7**:1122
- statistics **1**:place list
HAGOZER, JACOB AND GERSHOM **7**:1123
H-a-g-r-a, *see* ELIJAH BEN SOLOMON ZALMAN
Hagrites (descendants of Hagar) **3**:194
HAGRONIA (tn., Mesop.) **7**:1123
Hag Same'aḥ (greeting) **7**:916
Hagshamah aẓmit (Zion. conc.) **9**:516
Hag Siyyum (rel. celebration), *see Se'udat Yitro u-Moshe*
Hagu, The Book of (law wk.) **5**:1248
HAGUE, THE (city, Neth.) **7**:1123
- Netherlands **12**:980ff
- *illus:*
- - text
- - Portuguese synagogue **13**:1061
- - Spinoza's house **15**:278
- - Spinoza's statue **15**:276
HAGUENAU (tn., Fr.) **7**:1126
Haguenau, Marc **7**:922
Haguenauer (r., Nancy) **12**:816
Hagut Z. S. (newsp.) **16**:1225
Ha-Ḥaklai (coop., Isr.) **14**:856
Ha-Harsa (journ.), *see Ha-Shemesh*
Ha-Ḥavaẓẓelet (period.), *see* ḤAVAẒẒELET
Ha-Ḥayyal ha-Ivri (publ.) **1**: newsp. list
Ha-Ḥayyal ha-Meshuḥrar (newsp.) **1**: newsp. list
Ha-Ḥayyim (period., Pers.) **10**:437; **13**:319
Ha-Ḥayyim (period., Isr.) **1**:newsp. list
Ha-Ḥayyim (journ., Vilna) **1**:newsp. list
Ha-Ḥayyim ha-Lalu (journ.) **1**:newsp. list
Ha-Ḥayyim ve-ha-Teva (children's weekly) **5**:457
Ha-Hed (monthly) **1**:newsp. list **13**:1458
Ha-Ḥerut (newsp.) **1**:newsp. list; **9**:329
- cultural life **9**:1015
- Elmaleh, Abraham **6**:681
- Hebrew newspapers **12**:1055
- *see also:* Ḥerut
Ha-Ḥevrah (period.) **1**:newsp. list;

16:407
Ha-Ḥibbur ha-Gadol (wk.) **16**:904
HA-ḤINNUKH (bk.) **7**:1126
- Jewish literature **11**:334
Ha-Ḥinnukh (journ.) **1**:newsp. list; **15**:888
Ha-Ḥinnukh ha-Gufani (period.) **1**: newsp. list
Ha-Ḥinnukh ha-Ivri (journ.) **1**: newsp. list
Ha-Ḥinnukh ha-Musikali (journ.) **1**: newsp. list
Hahiroth (tn., Egy.), *see* PI-HAHIROTH
Ha-Histadrut ha-Ḥakla'it ba-Galil u-vi-Yhudah (orgn.) **7**:1325
Ha-Histadrut ha-Kelalit shel ha-Ovedim be-Ereẓ Israel (lab. fed., Isr.), *see* HISTADRUT
Hahn, Aaron **5**:607
HAHN, ALBERT L. **7**:1127
Hahn, Gilbert Jr. **16**:356
Hahn, J. (Hung.) **11**:721
HAHN, JOSEPH BEN MOSES (Ger.) **7**:1128
- *illus:* text
HAHN, JOSEPH YUSPA BEN PHINEHAS SELIGMANN **7**:1128
Hahn, Kurt **6**:463
HAHN, MICHAEL **13**:827
HAHN, REYNALDO **12**:692
Ha-Ḥodesh, Shabbat, see Shabbat ha-Ḥodesh
Ha-Ḥoker (journ.) **1**: newsp. list
Ha-Ḥomah (publ.) **1**: newsp. list
Ha-Ḥoresh (assoc., Er. Isr.) **14**:1452
Ha-Ḥoterim (kib., Isr.) **1**: place list
Ha-Ḥozeh (journ.) **1**: newsp. list
Ha-Ḥozeh mi-Lublin (Ḥas. r., Pol.), *see* JACOB ISAAC HA-ḤOZEH MI-LUBLIN
Haiappa (bib. fig.) **15**:940
HAI BAR RAV DAVID GAON **7**:1129
- *Musar Haskel* **12**:534
- Yannai **16**:712
Ḥai ben Mekiẓ (poem) **8**:1166
HAI BEN NAHSHON (gaon) **7**:1129
- gaonate **7**:317
HAI BEN SHERIRA (gaon) **7**:1130
- Abraham ben Nathan **2**:153
- Abraham ben N . . . ha-Baghdadi **2**:154
- Albaradani, Nahum **2**:525
- Al-Bazak, Maẓli'aḥ **2**:527
- amulets **2**:911
- Asaph ha-Rofe **3**:674
- Bible exegesis **4**:892
- calendar, Jewish **5**:48
- gaonate **7**:315ff
- *hakkafot* **7**:1153
- Halakhot Gedolot **7**:1169
- Hebrew language **16**:1613
- history chart **8**:766-767
- Jerusalem Talmud **15**:775
- Kabbalah **10**:563
- linguistics **16**:1365; 1381
- mysticism, Jewish **10**:511
- philosophy, Jewish **13**:433
- responsa **14**:84
- seal **14**:1074
- Sherira ben Ḥanina **11**:59; **14**:1381
- talmudic commentary **15**:763
- *Targum Sheni* **15**:811
- tax **15**:850
- Tunisia **15**:1436
HAIDAMACKS (Ukr.) **7**:1132
- Balta Jews **4**:144
- Belaya Tserkov **4**:413
- Ḥasidism **7**:1391
- history chart **8**:766-767
- Podolia **13**:668
- Uman **15**:1527

- Volhynia **16:**209
Haidon (Haidar; concen. camp) **3:**818; **7:**879
HAIFA (city, Isr.) **7:**1133
- *Contents:*
- - Early History **7:**1133
- - Ottoman Rule **7:**1134
- - 18th-19th Centuries **7:**1135
- - Revival of Jewish Settlement **7:**1137
- - British Mandate Period **7:**1138
- - 1948-1970 **7:**1138
- broadcasting studios **15:**930
- Crusades 9:268; **9:**271
- dyeing center **6:**327
- harbor **9:**480,832
- Hebrew pronunciation **16:** 1586, 1595
- human geography of Israel **9:**572ff
- industrial zone **2:**226
- Jewish religious life **9:**891ff
- museum **12:**551
- Muslim community **9:**919
- oil refineries **9:**795
- Ottoman period **9:**287ff
- Palestine Economic Corporation **13:**39
- Plain **9:**126; **9:**128; **9:**147ff
- stamps **15:**330ff
- statistics **1:** place list
- Templars' settlement **15:**994; **15:**995
- Waley-Cohen, Sir Robert **5:**684
- *illus:*
- - Anglo-Palestine Bank **3:**348
- - Bahai Shrine **8:**933; **9:**924
- - emergency stamps **15:**334
- - *Exodus 1947* **9:**525
- - Grain Museum **12:**550
- - Kiryat Eliezer civic center **11:**893
- - Kishon River **10:**1069
- - loading Jaffa oranges **9:** 763
- - the market **6:**1428
- - night view **9:**573
- - Omna baby home **12:**211
- - Shemen Oil factory **9:**342
- - Technion
- - - buildings **3:**347,351; **15:**890,891
- - - Churchill Auditorium **9:**955
- - - student hostel room **9:**961
Haifa Bay area (reg., Isr.), *see* Zebulun Valley
HAIFA MUNICIPAL THEATER **7:**1140
Haifa Orchestra **9:**1008
Haifa University College **9:**924
Hai Gaon, *see* HAI BEN SHERIRA
Haigerloch (tn., Ger.) **8:**816
Ḥaikin, Simon Menahem **8:**234
Ha-Ikkar (newsp.) **1:**newsp. list; **11:**1220
Ha-Ikkar ha-Ẓa'ir (Zion. orgn.) **8:**254
Hail **13:**606
- *ʾelgavish* **13:**1011
- *illus:*
- - Moses and plagues of Egypt **13:**607
Haile Selassie (emp., Eth.) **6:**1145; **6:**944
- Wingate, Orde **16:**548
Hailey (city, Ida.) **8:**1222
Ḥā'im, Ibn al- **9:**1425
Ḥaim, Israel **14:**1168
Haimhausen, Cajetan of Berchem- **5:**485
Haimov, Vitali **4:**1489
Haimovich, Issachar **4:**630
Haimovitz, M. (Rum.) **11:**563
HAIMOWITZ, MORRIS JONAH (U.S.) **7:**1141
Hainaut (prov., Belg.) **4:**417
HAINDORF, ALEXANDER **7:**1141
- Muenster **12:**505
Hair
- folklore **6:**1400
- Lag ba-Omer **8:**495
- mourner **10:**1484
- Nabī Samwīl **14:**785
- Nazirite **12:**908
- priest's care **13:**1081
- Temple *mishmarot* **12:**91
- treatment of **5:**980
- *illus:*
- - Lag ba-Omer **6:**1407; **10:**1357
- - Nazirites **12:**906
- - plaits, Masada **11:**1090
Hairdressers **5:**982
- guilds **7:**972
Ha-Ishah (period.) **1:**newsp. list; **13:**1035
Ha-Ishah ba-Medinah (mag.) **1:**newsp. list
Ha-Ishah be-Yisrael (journ.) **1:**newsp. list
Ha-Israeli, Israel, *see* ISRAELI, ISRAEL
Haissin (tn., Podolia), *see* GAISIN
HAITI (isl., West Indies) **7:**1141
- Latin America **10:**1450ff
- West Indies **16:**473
Ha-Ittona'i ha-Yehudi (journ.) **1:**newsp. list
Ha-Itton ha-Rasmi (journ.) **1:**newsp. list
Ha-Ivri (paper, U.S.) **12:**1052
- Sarasohn, Kasriel **14:**873
- statistics **1:** newsp. list
Ha-Ivri (weekly, Mizrachi orgn.) **12:**177
- Bar-Ilan **4:**224
- Hebrew newspapers **12:**1051
Ha-Ivri (period., Gal.) **16:**1330
Ha-Ivri (journ., Ger.-U.S.) **1:**newsp. list; **14:**303
Ha-Ivri, David ben Jacob, *see* David ben Jacob ha-Ivri
Ha-Ivri he-Ḥadash (journ.) **1:**newsp. list
Hajar (city, Bahrein) **4:**102
Hajar Bin Humayd (site, Aden) **2:**539
HAJDU, MIKLÓS **7:**1142
Hajdu, Vavro **14:**1654
HAJEK, MARKUS **7:**1142
HAJJĀJ, DANIEL **7:**1143
- Tunisia **15:**1449
Hajj Muhammad Amīn al-Husseini, *see* HUSSEINI, HAJJ AMIN
Hajnówka (tn., Pol.) **10:**1123
Hajos, Alfred **12:**1373; **15:**299; **15:**313
Hajos-Guttmann, Henrik **12:**1375
Ha-Kabba'i ha-Mitnaddev (journ.) **1:**newsp. list
Ha-Kabbelan ve-ha-Boneh (journ.) **1:**newsp. list
Hakabessi, Abraham (gaon) **15:**1434
Ha-Kadosh Bârukh Hu *see* Holy One, Blessed Be He
Ha-Kala'i, *see* ALFASI, ISAAC BEN JACOB
Ha-Kalban (journ.) **1:** newsp. list
Ha-Kalkalah ha-Ereẓ-Yisre'elit (journ.) **1:** newsp. list
Ḥakam II, al- (caliph) **15:**225; **15:**1530
HA-KARMEL (period.) **7:**1143
- Hebrew newspapers **12:**1049
- press **13:**1044
- statistics **1:** newsp. list
- Vilna **16:**144
- *illus:* text
Ha-Karmel (period., Lvov) **11:**612
Hakashlari, Bonjudah Yeḥasel **7:**507
Ha-Kaspan (journ.) **1:** newsp. list
HAKDAMAH (bk. introduction) **7:**1144
- *see also:* COLOPHON; HASKAMAH
Hakdamah (wk.) **16:**1387
Hakdish (tax, Mor.) **14:**1344
Ha-Kedem (Hebr. pub.) **1:** newsp. list **10:**1398
Ha-Kehillah (period.) **12:**1035
Ha-Kenes ha-Madda'i ha-Meyuḥad (journ.) **1:** newsp. list
Ha-Kerem (journ., Pol.) **1:** newsp. list
Ha-Kerem (journ., Vilna) **1:**newsp. list
Ha-Kerem (journ., Ukr.) **1:** newsp. list
Ha-Kerem (journ., U.S.) **1:** newsp. list
Ha-Kesher (period.) **15:**245
Ha-Keshet (period.) **1:** newsp. list
Ḥakétia (Hakétie; lang.) **12:**332
- Tetuán **15:**1030
ḤAKHAM (rab. tit.) **7:**1145
- *dayyan* **13:**1449
- in Judaism **10:**388
- Kurdistan **10:**1298
- Meir **11:**1240
- semikhah **14:**1145
- title **15:**1165
Ḥakham, Al- (fam.), *see* AL-ḤAKAM
ḤAKHAM, SIMON **7:**1146
- Judeo-Persian literature **10:**436
ḤAKHAM BASHI (chief r.) **7:**1146
- Bardaki, Isaiah **4:**217
- Ereẓ Israel, Ottoman period **9:**299
- Jassy **9:**1293
- Jerusalem appointment **9:**1450ff
- office **13:**1451
- Ottoman Empire **16:**1540,1548
- role in Israel **9:**889ff
- San'a **14:**821
- Sephardim **14:**1175
- title **15:**1165
- Turkey **15:**1460
- *illus:*
- - traditional garb **12:**1182
- *see also:* MILLET
Ḥakham-Khane Niẓām Namesi (regulations, Ott. Emp.) **16:**1540
Ḥakham Rashum (tit.) **13:**1451
Ḥakham Vatik (tit.) **13:**1451
Ḥakham Ẓevi, *see* ASHKENAZI, ẒEVI HIRSCH BEN JACOB
HAKHEL (assembly) **7:**1148
- commandment of **15:**497
- sages **14:**642
- Torah reading **15:**1246
Ha-Khima'i be-Yisrael (journ.) **1:**newsp. list
Ḥakhmei ha-Shir (orgn., Turk.) **11:**485
- Zarco, Judah **16:**936
Ḥakhmei Lublin (yeshivah) **14:**532
- *illus:*
- - opening **16:**763
HAKHNASAT KALLAH (providing for bride) **7:**1149
- Sinzheim's responsa **14:**1617
- *see also:* CHARITY
Hakhnasat Kallah (bk.) **8:**202
Hakhnasat oreḥim (conc.), *see* HOSPITALITY
Hakhnasat Oreḥim (soc.) **5:**347
Hakhra'ot (wk.) **16:**1361
Hakhsharah (aliyah training), *see Hachsharah*
HA-KIBBUTZ HA-ARẒI HA-SHOMER HA-ẒA'IR (orgn.) **7:**1150
- Ha-Shomer ha-Ẓa'ir **7:**1374ff; **10:**964ff
- Ḥazan, Ya'acov **7:**1524
- labor economy of Israel **9:**852ff
- Yaari, Meir **16:**691
HA-KIBBUTZ HA-DATI (orgn.) **7:**1150
- Benei Akiva **4:**490
- bloc settlement **7:**1321
- Ha-Po'el ha-Mizrachi **10:**964; **10:**972ff
- National Religious Party **12:**882
HA-KIBBUTZ HA-ME'UḤAD (orgn.) **7:**1151
- Ha-Shomer ha-Ẓa'ir **7:**1374
- kibbutz movement **10:**970ff
- labor economy of Israel **9:**852ff
- Mapai **11:**913
Ha-Kibbutz ha-Meuḥad publications (Isr.) **13:**1378
Ḥakim, Eliahu **11:**464
Ḥakīm, Joseph (mer., Majorca), *see* Faquim, Jucef
Ḥakim, Joseph (r., Turk.) **13:**18
Ḥakim, Moses **7:**1151
Hakim, Samuel (r., Tun.) **15:**1439
ḤAKIM, SAMUEL BEN MOSES HA-LEVI IBN **7:**1151
Ḥakiman, Aaron, *see* AARON ḤAKIMAN
ḤĀKIM BI-AMR ALLAH, AL- (caliph) **7:**1152
- Druze **6:**492
- Ereẓ Israel **9:**262; **9:**265
- humiliation of Jews **8:**661
- persecutions **6:**1197
Ha-Kinnus ha-Arẓi la-Torah she-be-al Peh (publ.) **1:** newsp. list
Ha-Kinnus ha-Olami le-Madda'ei ha-Yahadut (publ.) **1:** newsp. list
Ha-Kiryah (govt. center, Jer.) **9:**1494
- Jerusalem topography **9:**1515
HAKKAFOT (cerem.) **7:**1153
- burial **4:**1521
- children's participation **5:**428
- Simḥat Torah **14:**1573
- Sukkot **15:**499; **15:**501
- *illus:* text
Hakkoz (fam.) **6:**1040; **8:**627; **13:**1086
Ḥakla'ut be-Yisrael (journ.) **1:**newsp. list
Ḥakmon, Moses **4:**503
Ha-Koaḥ (club, Aus.) **15:**293
- *see also:* MACCABI WORLD UNION
Ha-Kohelet (bk., hagiographa), *see* ECCLESIASTES
Ha-Kohen, *see also under first names*
Ha-Kohen, Abraham ben Moses, *see* ABRAHAM BEN MOSES HA-KOHEN HA-SEPHARDI
Ha-Kohen, Jacob, *see* MAZEH, JACOB
Ha-Kohen, Meshullam Solomon **16:**1232
Ha-Kohen, Shalom Ẓevi **16:**1007
Ha-Kohen, Solomon Judah **16:**1007
Ha-Kohen, Ẓevi Hirsch ben Simeon, *see* Ẓevi Hirsch ben Simeon ha-Kohen
Ha-Kokhav (sports soc.) **12:**1541
Ha-Kokhavim (journ.) **1:** newsp. list
Ha-Kokhavim be-Ḥodsham (journ.) **1:** newsp. list
Ha-Kol (newsp., Eur.) **12:**1050
Ha-Kol (newsp., Isr.) **9:**1016
- Hebrew newspapers **12:**1056
- statistics **1:** newsp. list
Ha-Kol (publ., Pol.) **1:** newsp. list
Ha-Kol (newsp., Prus.) **1:** newsp. list
Ha-Kol (newsp., U.S.) **1:** newsp. list
Ha-Konim (wk.), *see Ḥibbur ha-Konim*
Ha-Koẓer (immigrant gr.) **10:**887
Hakuk (loc., Isr.) **8:**1062
Ha-Kumkum (theat. co., Er. Isr.) **9:**1004
- Hameiri, Avigdor **7:**1231
Halabja (tn., Iraq) **15:**504
Halaf (site, Mesop.), *see* Tells (Halaf)
Ḥalaf (knife) **14:**1338
- *illus:* **14:**1339

Ḥalaf ibn Sargado, *see* AARON BEN JOSEPH HA-KOHEN SARGADO
ḤALAFTA (tan.) **7:**1154
ḤALAFTA BEN SAUL (amora) **7:**1154
Halah (city, Media), *see* Hulvan
HA LAḤMA ANYA (Hag.) **7:**1155
- Haggadah **7:**1080
- *illus:*
- - *Bird's Head Haggadah* **7:**1081
- - *Darmstadt Haggadah* **7:**1085
- - *Joel ben Simeon Haggadah* **7:***fcg.* 1003
- - *Prague Haggadah* **3:**535
- - *seder* plate (1654) **5:**661
HALAKHAH (J. law) **7:**1156
- *Contents:*
- - Definition **7:**1156
- - Dogmatics **7:**1157
- - Development **7:**1161
- - - Early Period **7:**1161
- - - Tannaitic Period **7:**1163
- - - Amoraic Period **7:**1163
- - - Codification **7:**1165
- - Authority **7:**1166
- General
- - Jewish identity **10:**23; **10:**53; **10:**57; **10:**59
- - law and morality **10:**1482
- - laws on proselytes **13:**1182ff
- - mathematics **11:**1121
- - *Middat Sedom* **15:**71
- - psychology **13:**1342
- - Red Heifer **14:**12
- - resistance value **8:**302
- - taxation **15:**842ff
- - technology **15:**892
- - woman's place **16:**624ff
- - writing **16:**669
- - writing of Bible **16:**1405
- History and Development
- - academies **2:**200,202
- - *amoraim* **2:**865ff
- - economic history **16:**1295
- - *geonim* **7:**316ff
- - *Halakhah le-Moshe mi-Sinai* **7:**1167
- - *hilkhata ke-vatra'ei* **3:**910ff; **5:**891
- - *kelal Israel* **10:**898
- - majority rule **11:**804
- - ordination **14:**1140
- - *pilpul* **13:**524
- - Provence **13:**1263
- - rabbinical authority **3:**907ff
- - Roman influence **14:**242
- - sages **14:**638ff
- - Sanhedrin **9:**243; **9:**252
- - *soferim* **15:**80
- - synagogues **15:**591
- - Talmud **15:**764
- - *tannaim* **15:**799
- - - Akiva **2:**490ff
- - - Bet Hillel and Bet Shammai **4:**737
- - - Ishmael ben Elisha **9:**84
- - - Johanan ben Zakkai **10:**150
- - - Joshua ben Hananiah **10:**280
- - - Joshua ben Korha **10:**282
- - - Meir **11:**1241
- - - Shammai **14:**1292
- - *tosafot* **15:**1278ff
- - *see also:* CODIFICATION OF LAW; MISHPAT IVRI; SHULḤAN ARUKH
- Admissibility as
- - *aggadah* **2:**354ff; **15:**455
- - antinomianism **3:**68ff
- - *bat kol* **4:**324
- - "because of appearances" **4:**1116
- - custom **12:**4
- - *gematria* **7:**371
- - interpretation **8:**1413
- - misrulings **13:**227
- - Prophets **13:**1176
- - *ru'aḥ ha-kodesh* **14:**366
- - *sevarah* **14:**1195
- - *takkanot ha-kahal* **15:**728
- - *see also:* ORAL LAW; TAKKANOT
- Literature **11:**314ff
- - *Midreshei Halakhah* **11:**1521
- - *minhagim* books **12:**26ff
- - Mishnah **12:**93
- - prayer books **13:**985ff
- - responsa **13:**1462; **14:**83ff
- Attitude Toward
- - Groups
- - - *anusim* **3:**169
- - - Ashkenazim **3:**720
- - - Christianity **5:**508
- - - Ḥasidei Ashkenaz **7:**1381
- - - Ḥasidism **7:**1417
- - - Haskalah **7:**1436
- - - Islam **9:**96; **10:**1197
- - - Israel politics **12:**881
- - - Kabbalah **10:**493; **10:**539; **10:**639
- - - Khazars **10:**948
- - - modern Judaism **10:**395
- - - Orthodoxy **12:**1486ff
- - - Pharisees **13:**364,365
- - - Pittsburgh Platform **13:**571
- - - Reform Judaism **12:**1442
- - - Samaritans **14:**740
- - - Sephardim **14:**1170
- - Individuals
- - - Aḥad Ha-Am **2:**447ff
- - - Allon, Gedalya **2:**654
- - - Buber, Martin **4:**1433
- - - Heller, Yom Tov Lipmann **8:**312
- - - Hirsch, S. R. **8:**512
- - - Horowitz, Pinḥas **8:**1000
- - - Johanan ben Nappaha **10:**146
- - - Krochmal, Nachman **10:**1272ff
- - - Levinsohn, Isaac **11:**117
- - - Mordecai of Izbica **9:**1159
- - - Naḥmanides **12:**778ff
- - - Philo **13:**412; **13:**426
- - - Rashi **13:**1564
- - - Rosenzweig **14:**301
- - - Saadiah Gaon **14:**547,548
- - - Samuel ben Meir **14:**810
- - - Schorr, Joshua **14:**997
- - - Soloveitchik, Joseph **15:**131
- *illus:*
- - codification of law, schematic representation **5:**635
HALAKHAH LE-MOSHE MI-SINAI **7:**1167
- Halakhah **7:**1158
- Maimonides **12:**114
- Mishnah **12:**97
- *Mi-Sinai Niggunim* **12:**152
- Moses **12:**394
- sages **14:**644
- scriptural reading **16:**1409
- tradition **15:**1309
- *zaken mamre* **16:**920
- *see also:* HALAKHAH
Halakhic Midrash, *see* MIDRESHEI HALAKHAH
Halakhic Miscellany (15th cent. ms), *see Hamburg Halakhah Miscellany*
HALAKHOT GEDOLOT (wk.) **7:**1167
- codification of law **5:**636
- Commandments, the 613 **5:**761
- Jewish literature **11:**330
- Maimonides **11:**766
- responsa **14:**86
- *She'iltot* **2:**450
Halakhot Ketannot (wk.) **5:**638; **11:**330
HALAKHOT KEẒUVOT (*Ketu'ot;* geonic wk.) **7:**1170
- codification of law **5:**636; **5:**637
HALAKHOT PESUKOT (geonic wk.) **7:**1171
- codification of law **5:**634
- Jewish literature **11:**330
- *She'iltot* **2:**450
- Yehudai ben Naḥman **16:**731
Halakhot Rabbati (bk., Alfasi), *see Sefer ha-Halakhot*
Ḥalāl (mt., Sinai), *see* Jebel al-Ḥalal
Ḥalama (demon k.) **5:**1531
Ha-Lamed-He (sols., War of Independence) **10:**880
Ḥalamish (city, Er. Isr.) **12:**897
Ha-Lapid (period.) **4:**261
Ha-Lavan, David ben Abraham, *see* DAVID BEN ABRAHAM HA-LAVAN
Halawa, Samuel **2:**613
Halaẓ, ibn (name), *see* Ibn Halaẓ
Halbersberg, Ḥayyim Isaiah ha-Kohen **7:**314
HALBERSTADT (city, Ger.) **7:**1172
- archives **3:**387
- seal **14:**1080
- *illus:* text
HALBERSTADT, ABRAHAM BEN MENAHEM MENKE **7:**1174
Halberstadt, Abraham Hirsch **4:**1448
Halberstadt, Meir **4:**1311
Halberstadt, Menahem Mendel **7:**1175
HALBERSTADT, MORDECAI **7:**1175
Halberstadt, Ẓevi Hirsch, *see* BIALEH, ẒEVI HIRSCH BEN NAPHTALI HERZ
HALBERSTAEDTER, LUDWIG **7:**1175
HALBERSTAM (ḥas. dyn.) **7:**1176
- dynasties **1:**Ḥas. table
- ḥasidic music **7:**142œ
- Nowy Sacz **12:**1246
- Sadgora conflict **14:**532
- *illus:* text
Halberstam, Aaron of Zanz **7:**1177
Halberstam, Baruch of Gorlice **7:**1177
Halberstam, Ben Zion **7:**1177
Halberstam, David of Kishinev **7:**1177
Halberstam, Ezekiel Schraga of Sieniawa **7:**1177
Halberstam, Ḥayyim ben Leibush **7:**1176
- responsa **14:**91
- Shapira family **14:**1295
HALBERSTAM, ISAAC BEN ḤAYYIM **7:**1177
Halberstam, Jacob Samson of Czchow **7:**1177
Halberstam, Jekuthiel Judah **7:**1177,1399; **9:**899
Halberstam, S. (polit., S.A.) **10:**1001
Halberstam, Solomon **7:**1177
Halberstam, Solomon ben Meyer Nathan of Bobova **7:**1177
HALBERSTAM, SOLOMON (Zalman) ḤAYYIM **7:**1178
Halberstzadt, Solomon (resist. ldr., Gal.) **4:**1399
Halbrajch, Benjamin **5:**1039
HALBWACHS, MAURICE **7:**1178
Halderman-Julius, Emanuel **13:**1372
Haldinstein (fam.) **12:**1227
Ha-Le'eh, *see* LIPSCHUETZ, HILLEL ARYEH LEIB BEN ZE'EV DOV
Halenius, Engelbert **8:**37
Ha-Le'om (period.) **1:**newsp. list; **7:**722; **8:**209
Ha-Le'ummi (period.) **1:**newsp. list
HA-LEVANON (newsp.) **7:**1178
- Brandes, R. A. **4:**1315
- Jerusalem **9:**1458
- newspapers **12:**1046; **12:**1050; **12:**1053ff
- statistics **1:**newsp. list
- *illus:*
- - text
- - Israel stamp **9:**844-845
Halevi (fam., Sp.) **15:**1201
Ha-Levi, Abraham **9:**1094
Halevi, Benjamin **6:**521
Halevi, Bezalel Sadi **13:**1038
Ha-Levi, David ben Samuel, *see* DAVID BEN SAMUEL HA-LEVI
Ha-Levi, Eliezer, *see* LOEWE, LOUIS
Ha-Levi, Elijah (15th cent., Turk.) **12:**182
Ha-Levi, Elijah (Mor.) **5:**161
HA-LEVI, EZEKIEL EZRA BEN JOSHUA **7:**1180
Halevi, Fabian S. **3:**423
Halevi, Ḥaim David **14:**94
Ha-Levi, Hirschel, *see* Marx, Heinrich
Ha-Levi, Isaac (tos.) **14:**1163
Ha-Levi, Isaac (Ukr.), *see* Isaac ha-Levi (16th cent.)
Ha-Levi, Isaac (Pol.), *see* Ḥarif ha-Levi, Isaac
Ha-Levi, Isaac (Lith.) **14:**1305
Ha-Levi, Jacob **13:**180
Ha-Levi, Don Joseph (15th cent.) **12:**289
HALEVI, JOSEPH ẒEVI BEN ABRAHAM **7:**1180
Halevi, Judah (11/12 cent.), *see* JUDAH HALEVI
Ha-Levi, Judah (Isr.), *see* LEVY, JUDAH BEN MENAHEM
Halevi, Meir A. (20th cent. bibl., Rum.) **14:**399
Ha-Levi, Meir Altar (19th cent.) **10:**1208
Ha-Levi, Moses (tos.) **14:**1163
Ha-Levi, Moses Uri (r., Neth.), *see* Moses Uri ha-Levi
Ha-Levi, Naphtali Herz **7:**1180
Halevi, Don Samuel (14/15 cent.) **5:**38; **14:**538
Ha-Levi, Samuel (r., Pol.) **14:**538
HA-LEVI, SASSON BEN ELIJAH BEN MOSES **7:**1181
Halevi, Saul **7:**1124
Halevi, Solomon, *see* PABLO DE SANTA MARÍA
Ha-Levi, Uri (Phoebus) ben Aaron, *see* URI (Phoebus) BEN AARON HA-LEVI
Ha-Levi, Yaḥya **14:**1344
Halevi, Yossef **3:**593
Ha-Levi Ish Horowitz (fam.), *see* HOROWITZ
HALÉVY (fam.) **7:**1181
Halévy, Daniel **7:**1182
HALÉVY, ÉLIE (philos.) **7:**1182
HALÉVY, ELIE HALFON (au.) **7:**1182
- Hebrew literature **8:**182
- *illus:* text
HALEVY, ISAAC **7:**1183
- Weiss, I. H. **16:**414
HALÉVY, JACQUES (François) FROMENTAL ÉLIE **7:**1184
- Jacques Offenbach **12:**1336
- *illus:* text
HALÉVY, JOSEPH **7:**1185
- Adrianople *haskalah* **2:**310
Halévy, Léon **7:**1181
Halévy, Ludovic **7:**1181
Halevy, Meir **10:**1090
HALEVY, MOSHE **7:**1186
- *illus:*
- - text

– – Habimah original company 7:1029
Haleywa, Judah **10**:543
Ḥalfan (fam.), *see* HALFANUS
ḤALFAN, ELIJAH MENAHEM **7**:1187
– family **7**:1188
– Kabbalah **10**:542
HALFANUS (fam.) **7**:1187
Halfanus, Abba Mari (15th cent., It.) **7**:1187
Halfanus, Abba Mari (16th cent., Prague) **7**:1188
Halfanus, Elias **7**:1188
Halfanus, Eliezer, *see* Wechsler, Eliezer ben Uri Shraga Phoebus
Halfanus, Uri Shraga Phoebus, *see* Wechsler, Uri Shraga Phoebus
Halff, Mayer **14**:823
Halff, Sol **14**:823
ḤALFON, ABRAHAM **7**:1188
Halfon, Judah **15**:1031
Ḥalfon, Raḥamim **7**:1188
Ḥalfon ben Madmūn ben Japheth **11**:681; **12**:763
ḤALFON BEN NETHANEL HA-LEVI ABU SAʿĪD (Dimyati) **7**:1188
– Aden **2**:260; **2**:261
– Cairo *genizah* **16**:1340
– economic history **16**:1280
– Judah Halevi **10**:356; **10**:357
Half-shekel tax **15**:980
HALHUL (anc. tn., Isr.) **7**:1188
– mount **9**:580
Halībrūy (tn., Iraq) **15**:504
Halicarnassus (city, As. M.) **6**:10
HALICZ (tn., Gal.) **7**:1189
Halicz (Halic; fam.) **7**:1189
– Istanbul **9**:1097
– typography **15**:1481
Halicz, Andreas, *see* Halicz, Samuel
Halicz, Asher **7**:1189; **3**:34
– Cracow press **5**:1037
Halicz, Elyakim **7**:1189
– Cracow press **5**:1037
Halicz, Ḥayyim **7**:1189
Halicz, Johannes, *see* Halicz, Elyakim
Halicz, Lukasz **7**:1190
Halicz, Paul, *see* Halicz, Asher
Halicz, Samuel **7**:1189
– Cracow press **5**:1037
– typography **15**:1482
HALIFAX (port, Can.) **7**:1191
– maritime provinces **11**:997
Halifin (mode of acquisition) **2**:219
Halikhot (publ.) **1**:newsp. list
– *see also Shanah be-Shanah*
Halikhot Sheva (wk.) **16**:1390
Ḥalil (wind instr.) **12**:563
Halimi, Alphonse **15**:305
Ha-Lishkah ha-Sheḥorah (anti-Zion. orgn., Rus.), *see* Lishkah Sheḥorah
Ha-Livni, David, *see* WEISS, DAVID
Ḥaliẓah (rit. cerem.), *see* LEVIRATE MARRIAGE AND ḤALIẒAH
HALKIN, ABRAHAM SOLOMON **1**:31; **7**:1191
HALKIN, HILLEL D. **1**:31
HALKIN, SHMUEL **7**:1191
– Shakespeare **14**:1265
– Yiddish literature **16**:818
– *illus:*
– – Jewish Anti-Fascist Committee **3**:63
HALKIN, SIMON **7**:1192
– Hebrew literature **8**:213
Hall, Jerome **10**:1505
HALL, OWEN **6**:788
– Frankau family **7**:77
ḤALLAH (bread) **7**:1193
– five species **6**:1333
– rice bread **14**:155
– Sabbath **6**:1422; **14**:566
– separation of **4**:1334
– *tevul yom* **15**:1032
– *illus:*
– – text
– – commandments incumbent on women **11**:1039
– – embroidered covers **6**:1385; **7**:*fcg.* 1262; **14**:572
– – traditional shapes **6**:1419
ḤALLAH (tract.) **7**:1195
– *illus:* text
Halldorf, Wolff Heinrich von **4**:647
HALLE (city, Ger.) **7**:1196
– Crusades **5**:1139
Halle, Aaron Wolfsohn **7**:1436
Halle, Israel ben Abraham **16**:263
HALLE, MORRIS **7**:1197
Halleck, Henry Wager **11**:258
HALLEGUA (fam.) **7**:1197
Hallegua, Ḥayyim Joseph **7**:1197
Hallegua, Joseph **7**:1197
Hallegua, Moses **7**:1197
Hallein (city, Aus.) **14**:717ff
Hallel (journ.) **1**:newsp. list
HALLEL (prayer) **7**:1197
– festivals **6**:1245
– *Haggadah* **7**:1103
– Mordecai **12**:309
– mourning **12**:491
– New Moon **12**:1040
– Passover **13**:362
– Psalms, Book of **13**:1322
– Rosh ha-Shanah **14**:310
– Sukkot **15**:499; **15**:501
– Temple service **15**:978
– *illus:* text
– *mus. notations:*
– – responsorial psalmody **12**:575
HALLELUJAH (litur. expression) **7**:1199
– influence of Judaism **10**:396
Hallelyah, Mahalalel ben Shabbetai, *see* MAHALALEL BEN SHABBETAI HALLELYAH
Hallenstein, Bendix **6**:274
Haller, Albrecht von **8**:37
Haller, Hermann **15**:1061
Haller, Józef **7**:1200
HALLER'S ARMY (Pol.) **7**:1200
Halley's Comet **3**:796
HALLGARTEN (fam.) **7**:1201
Hallgarten, Charles **7**:1201
Hallgarten, Julius **7**:1201
Hallgarten, Lazarus **7**:1201
Hallo, Gertrude, *see* Rubensohn, Gertrude
HALLO, RUDOLF **7**:1201
Hallo, Simon **7**:1201
Hallo, William W. **7**:1202; **16**:1508
HALMI, JOZSEF **10**:311
Halo **10**:637
Ha-Loḥem (newsp.), *see Ha-Ḥayyal ha-Meshuḥrar*
Haloxylon (bot.) **9**:225
Halper (r., U.S.) **15**:1206
HALPER, ALBERT **7**:1202
HALPER, BENZION **7**:1202
– Cairo *genizah* **16**:1336
Halperin (fam. name), *see also:* Galper(i)n; Halpern; Halprin; Heilperin; Heilpern; Heilprin; Helpern
Halperin, Daniel **13**:1049
Halperin, David **14**:532
Halperin, Dov Berish **12**:1475
Halperin, Falk **5**:440; **5**:459
Halperin, Hayyim (econ., Isr.) **8**:1226
Halperin, Ḥayyim Dov (ḥas. ldr.) **14**:532
Halperin, Isaac **10**:1503
Halperin, Jacob Joseph Solomon **14**:532
Halperin, M. (indus., Rus.) **15**:488
Halperin, Mikhl (pion., Er. Isr.), *see* HELPERN, MICHAEL
Halperin, Naḥman **4**:1362
Halperin, Robert **12**:1377; **15**:318
Halperin, S. (hist., U.S.) **8**:569
Halperin, Shalom (ḥas. ldr.) **14**:532
HALPERIN, YEḤIEL **7**:1203
– Abraham Avrunin **3**:990
Halperin, Uriel, *see* RATOSH, YONATHAN
Halperin, Vladimir **12**:1485
Halperin, Ze'ev **11**:1273
Halpern (fam. name), *see also:* Galper(i)n; Halperin; Halprin; Heilperin; Heilpern; Heilprin; Helpern
Halpern, Abraham **3**:895; **13**:809
HALPERN, BENJAMIN **7**:1203
– Zionism **16**:1148
Halpern, Esther Rachel, *see* Kaminska, Esther Rachel
HALPERN, GEORG GAD **7**:1204
Halpern, Harry **12**:1119
HALPERN, ISRAEL **7**:1204
HALPERN, JACK **5**:383
Halpern, Jacob Joseph **4**:590
Halpern, Joel ben Isaac **11**:588
Halpern, Joseph **5**:450
Halpern, Karl **15**:338
Halpern, Leivick, *see* LEIVICK, H.
HALPERN, LIPMAN **7**:1204
HALPERN, MOSHE LEIB **7**:1205
Halpern, Roberto **15**:309
Halpern, S. Alter **5**:450
Halpern, Yirmiyahu **4**:715
HALPHEN (fam.) **7**:1206
Halphen, Achille-Edmond **7**:1206
– *illus:* text
Halphen, Captain **11**:1561
Halphen, Fernand **7**:1206
Halphen, Georges-Henri **7**:1206
HALPHEN, LOUIS **7**:1206
Halprin (fam. name), *see also:* Galper(i)n; Halperin; Halpern; Heilperin; Heilpern; Heiprin; Helpern
HALPRIN, ANN **5**:1272
Halprin, Lawrence **3**:361
HALPRIN, ROSE LURIA **7**:1206
– Zionism **16**:1148
HALSMAN, PHILIPPE **7**:1207
Halter, G. Sydney **15**:308
Halter, Marek **13**:118
ḤALUKKAH (charity distribution) **7**:1207
– Eliezer ben-Yehuda **4**:566ff
– Ereẓ Israel history **9**:299
– *Ha-Levanon* **7**:1179
– Hebron **8**:232
– historical survey **9**:323
– income of Israel **8**:728
– Jacob Berdugo **4**:592
– Jewish community **9**:888ff
– Kalischer, Ẓevi **10**:708
– Lehren, Hirschel **10**:1584
– *yeshivot* **16**:771
– *illus:*
– – text
– – Altona receipt book **3**:379
– – Hebron, emissary's credentials **8**:728; **9**:288
– – Jerusalem, emissary's seal **14**:1359
– *see also:* KOLEL
Ḥalutzei Poale Zion (Zion. orgn.) **8**:254
Ḥalutzim, "the 105" (pion. gr.) **8**:251
Ḥalutziyyut (Zion. ideal) **9**:870
– *illus:*
– – Berdichev farm trainees **14**:458
– – *ḥalutzim* arriving in Jaffa (c. 1935) **9**:1258
– – Kletsk group **10**:1107
– – Russian ḥalutzim in Constantinople **14**:465
– – Utena training farm **11**:367
Ḥaluẓa (site, Er. Isr.), *see* ELUSA
Halys River (Mesop.) **16**:1497
HAM (bib. fig.) **7**:1216
– land of Gerar **7**:432
– Noah **12**:1191
– Semites **14**:1148
– *illus:*
– – the naked Noah **9**:1285; **12**:1196
HAM (bib. city, Transj.) **7**:1217
– Hamath **10**:1551
– Havvoth-Jair **7**:1494
– Transjordan **15**:1316
ḤAMA (of Nehardea; amora) **7**:1218
– Shapur II **14**:1307
Ha-Ma'ana (wk.), *see Sefer ha-Ma'aneh*
Ha-Ma'arav (publ.) **1**:newsp. list
Ha-Ma'aravi (Kar. au.), *see* SAMUEL BEN MOSES AL-MAGHRIBI
Ha-Ma'aravi, Joseph, *see* JOSEPH IBN TABŪL
Ha-Ma'as (period.) **1**:newsp. list
HAMA BAR BISA (2nd cent. C.E., Pal.) **7**:1218
– Oshaiah Rabbah **12**:1495
ḤAMA BAR ḤANINA (amora) **7**:1219
Hama bar Ukba (amora) **11**:75
Ha-Mabbit (journ.) **1**:newsp. list
Ḥama ben Tobiah **5**:143
Ha-M-a-b-i-t, *see* TRANI, MOSES BEN JOSEPH
Hamada (physiography, Isr.) **9**:135
HAMADAN (city, Iran) **7**:1219
– cultural center **13**:310
– Persia **13**:307
– Yudghan **16**:867
Ha-Madda ve-ha-Tekhnikah (journ.), *see Ha-Tekhna'i ha-Ẓa'ir*
ḤAMADYAH (kib., Isr.) **7**:1220
– statistics **1**:place list
– *illus:*
– – carpentry factory **10**:963
HA-MAGGID (newsp., Prus.) **7**:1221
– Eliezer Zuckermann **16**:1230
– Hebrew newspapers **12**:1046ff
– Ḥibbat Zion **16**:1038
– press **13**:1044
– statistics **1**:newsp. list
Ha-Maggid he-Ḥadash (period., Cracow) **5**:1036
– Fox, J. S. **6**:1451
Ha-Maḥanot ha-Olim (mvmt., Isr.) **9**:977; **9**:981
Ha-Mahar (publ.) **1**:newsp. list
Ha-Maḥnayim (period.) **8**:210
Ḥamai Gaon **10**:524
Hamaker, Hendrik Arent **8**:37
Ha-Makhtesh ha-Gadol (loc., Isr.) **9**:136; **9**:200ff; **9**:592; **12**:927
Ha-Makhtesh ha-Katan (loc., Isr.) **9**:200ff; **9**:592; **9**:810; **12**:927
Ha-Makkabbi (publ. Isr.) **1**:newsp. list
Ha-Makkabi (mag., Rus.) **1**:newsp. list **13**:1047
Ha-Makom (name of God) **7**:653
Ha-Makom Yenaḥem Ethem be-Tokh Avelei Ẓiyyon vi-Yrushalayim (consolation) **7**:916
Ha-Malakh (the Angel), *see* ABRAHAM BEN DOV OF MEZHIRECH
Hamam Lif (loc., Tun.), *see* Hammam-Lif
HAMAN (bib. fig.) **7**:1222
– Agagite **2**:341
– Amalek **2**:791
– Esther **6**:906

- Korah **10:**1193
- Mordecai **12:**308
- on Jewish dispersion **16:**1271
- parody **13:**126
- Purim **13:**1392
- Scroll of Esther **14:**1048ff
- *Targum Sheni* **15:**812
- *illus:*
- - Dura-Europos paintings **8:**649
- - genealogy **13:***fcg.* 1387
- - "Haman's ears" pastry **6:**1425
- - hanging of **10:**1313
- - hanging of ten sons **13:**64; **14:**1049
- - leading Mordecai on horse **6:**283; **12:**308; **13:**353
- - Purim rattle **13:**1343
- - twelfth cent. Bible **12:**733
Ha-Manhig (bk.) **12:**27
Hamantaschen (cakes) **13:**1392
Ha-Ma'or (bk.) **7:**509
Ha-Ma'or (journ.) **1:**newsp. list
HA-MA'PIL (kib., Isr.) **7:**1224
- statistics **1:**place list
Ha-Mappah (bk.) **5:**650; **9:**1083
Ha-Mappil (prayer), *see* NIGHT PRAYER
Ha-Mashbir (Kar. schol.), *see* JOSEPH BEN SAMUEL BEN ISAAC RODI
Ha-Mashbir (r., Mor.), *see* Berdugo, Moses
HAMASHBIR HAMERKAZI (coop.) **7:**1224
- cooperative movement **5:**946; **5:**948; **5:**950
- Histadrut **8:**539
- labor economy **9:**850ff
Hamashbir Hamerkazi le-Taasia (coop.) **5:**950
Ha-Mashkif (newsp.) **1:**newsp. list; **9:**1016; **12:**1056 **14:**132
Ha-Masoret ha-Gedolah (bk.), *see* OKHLAH VE-OKHLAH
Ha-Massad (bldg. co.) **8:**542
Hamata (anc. tn., Transj.), *see* AMMATHA
Ha-Matate (theat. co., Isr.) **9:**1004
Hamath (loc., Syr.-Isr.), *see* LEBO-HAMATH
Hamath-Tiberias, *see* HAMMATH
Ha-Matos (journ.) **1:**newsp. list
Ha-Mattarah (journ.) **1:**newsp. list
HA-MAVDIL (hymn) **7:**1224
Ha-Mavo li-Leshon ha-Kodesh (wk.), *see Mavo li-Leshon ha-Kodesh, ha-*
Ha-Ma'yan (journ.) **1:**newsp. list **7:**1242; **12:**820
Ha-Mazkir (suppl.) **1:**newsp. list
Hamborn (loc., Ger.) **6:**264
HAMBOURG, MARK **12:**692
Hambraeus, Jonas **8:**37
Hambro, Carl Joachim (bnk., Den.) **7:**1225
Hambro, Carl Joachim (polit., Nor.) **12:**1225
Hambro, Joachim **7:**1225
HAMBRO, JOSEPH **7:**1225
Hambro' Synagogue (Lond.) **11:**474; **12:**414
HAMBURG (city, state, Ger.) **7:**1225
- Abraham Teixeira de Sampaio **15:**912
- Ashkenazi, Ẓevi **3:**733
- banking **4:**172ff
- Bernays, Isaac **4:**673
- book art **3:**539
- Heine, Solomon **8:**275
- history chart (1649, 1811, 1818, 1841) **8:**766-767
- Purim Shpil **13:**1403
- Reform Judaism **14:**23
- seal **14:**1080
- Shabbateanism **14:**1234
- spice trade **15:**270
- sugar industry **15:**488
- synagogue **15:**620
- tobacco trade **15:**1176
- trade and commerce **15:**1302ff
- Vienna, Congress of **16:**132
- War Crimes Trials **16:**294
- *illus:*
- - New Jewish Hospital **8:**1037
- *see also:* ALTONA; WANDSBECK
HAMBURG, ABRAHAM BENJAMIN (Wolf) **7:**1229
- *illus:* text
Hamburger, B. **4:**1353
Hamburger, David A. **13:**1340
HAMBURGER, JACOB **7:**1230
Hamburger, Jean **11:**1202
Hamburger, Leopold **5:**310
HAMBURGER, MICHAEL **6:**785; **6:**788
Hamburger, Mordecai, *see* MOSES, MARCUS
Hamburg *Gebetbuch* (prayer bk.) **13:**989ff; **14:**23ff
Hamburg Halakhah Miscellany (15th cent. illum. ms., Padua) **4:**66; **8:**1270
Hamburg Miscellany (15th cent. illum. ms., Mainz?) **8:**1267
- *illus:* **7:**1271; **8:**671; **10:**457, *fcg.* 1335; **16:***fcg.* 615
Hamden (tn., Conn.) **5:**898
ḤAMDĪ, LEVI BEN YESHU'AH **7:**1231
Ha-Me'aggel, *see* ḤONI HA-ME'AGGEL
Ha-Me'ammer (collec.) **1:**newsp. list
Ha-Me'assef (period.), *see* ME'ASSEF
Ha-Meassef (J. theat.) **11:**1162
Ha-Me'assef ba-Areẓ ha-Ḥadashah (journ.) **1:** newsp. list
Ha-Me'assef li-Shenat ha-Sheloshim shel ha-Ẓefirah (journ.) **1:**newsp. list
Ha-Meir (journ.) **1:**newsp. list
Ha-Meiri (15/16 cent., r.), *see* ARAMA, MEIR BEN ISAAC
HAMEIRI, AVIGDOR **7:**1231
- translator **11:**422
- *illus:*
- - with *ḥalutzim* in Constantinople **14:**465
HAMEIRI, MOSHE **7:**1232
Ha-Mekiẓ (period.) **13:**494
Hamel, Jacob **4:**1238
Ha-Melaḥesh (bk.) **11:**353
Ha-Melakhah (journ.) **1:** newsp. list
Hamelin (city, Ger.), *see* HAMELN
HA-MELIẒ (newsp., Rus.) **7:**1232
- Friedberg, Abraham **7:**173
- *Ha-Yom* **7:**1500
- Hebrew journalism **12:**1046ff
- Ḥibbat Zion **16:**1038
- *Kol Mevasser* **10:**1165
- Kovner, Abraham **10:**1231ff
- press **13:**1044
- Slatkine, Menahem **14:**1655
- statistics **1:**newsp. list
- Zederbaum, Alexander **16:**964
- *illus:* text
Ha-Meliẓ (Samar. dict.) **14:**752; **14:**756
HAMELN (city, Ger.) **7:**1234
- *illus:* text
Ha-Melona'i (journ.) **1:**newsp. list
Ha-Melona'ut (journ.) **1:**newsp. list
Hamelsveld, Ysbrand van **8:**37; **4:**876
Hamenahel (mag.) **15:**1259
HAMENAḤEM, EZRA **7:**1234
- Jerusalem **9:**1568
Ha-Menorah Publishers (Isr.) **13:**1378
HA-ME'ORER (newsp., Eng.) **7:**1235
- Hebrew journalism **12:**1051
- statistics **1:**newsp. list
Ha-Me'orer (journ., Isr.) **1:**newsp. list
Ha-Merkaz ha-Ḥofshi (party, Isr.), *see* Free Center
HAMEROW, THEODORE STEPHEN **8:**546
Ha-Meshek ha-Ḥakla'i (journ.) **1:**newsp. list
Ha-Meshek ha-Shittufi (journ.) **1:**newsp. list
Ḥamesh Megillot, *see* SCROLLS, THE FIVE
Ha-Mesillah (journ., N.Y.) **1:**newsp. list
Ha-Mesillah (journ., Isr.) **1:**newsp. list
Ha-Mevakker ha-Penimi (journ.) **1:**newsp. list
Ha-Mevasser (journ., Gal.) **1:**newsp. list **12:**1049; **16:**1330
Ha-Mevasser (journ., Turk.) **1:**newsp. list
Ha-Mevatte'ah ha-Yisraeli (journ.) **1:**newsp. list
ḤAMEẒ (leavened bread) **7:**1235
- Commandments, the 613 **5:**777
- dietary laws **6:**40
- legal person **10:**1569
- mixture **6:**40
- Passover eve **12:**22
- sacrifice **14:**710
- *illus:*
- - searching for **13:**166
- *see also:* ḤAMEẒ, SALE OF; MAẒẒAH; PASSOVER
ḤAMEẒ, SALE OF **7:**1237
- rented property **10:**1534
- search **4:**372
Ḥameẓ, Operation (War of Indep.) **16:**310
Ha-Meẓayyer (poet), *see* MANNE, MORDECAI ẒEVI
Hamid, Abdul (sult.), *see* ʿAbd al-Ḥamīd II
Ha-Mifal (journ.) **1:** newsp. list
Ha-Mikhtam (bk.), *see Sefer ha-Mikhtam*
Hamilton (tn., Austr.) **11:**1286
HAMILTON (city, Can.) **7:**1238
- *illus:* text
Hamilton (city, Ohio) **12:**1344
Hamilton, Ian **10:**70
Hamilton, R. W. **9:**1531ff
Hamilton, Sir William Rowan **9:**1226
Hamilton siddur (13th cent., illum. ms.) **8:**1264
- *illus:* **8:** *fcg.* 1079
Ḥamin (stew), *see* CHOLENT
Ha-Minhal (journ.) **1:**newsp. list
Ha-Misderonah (journ.) **1:**newsp. list
Hamishah-Asar bi-Shevat (fest.), *see* TU BI-SHEVAT
Ḥamishah ha-Kunteresim (collec.) **1:**newsp. list
Ḥamishah Ḥomshei Torah, *see* PENTATEUCH
Ha-Misḥar (journ.) **1:**newsp. list
Ha-Misḥar ba-Amim u-ve-Yisrael (journ.) **1:**newsp. list
Ha-Mishmeret ha-Ze'irah (orgn., Mizrachi) **12:**180
Ha-Mishpat (journ.) **1:**newsp. list
Ha-Mishpat ha-Ivri (soc.) **12:**141
Ha-Mishpat ha-Ivri (journ., Isr.) **1:**newsp. list
Ha-Mishpat ha-Ivri (journ., Rus.) **12:**1051; **12:**141
- statistics **1:**newsp. list
Hamito-Semitic (lang. gr.) **14:**1149
Hamius, J. **8:**37
ḤAMIẒ, JOSEPH BEN JUDAH **7:**1239
- Zacuto **16:**907
HA-MIẒPEH (newsp., Cracow) **7:**1240
- Hebrew journalism **12:**1050
- statistics **1:** newsp. list
- *illus:* text
Ha-Miẓpeh (period., Warsaw) **1:** newsp. list **7:**1373
Ha-Mizpeh (journs., Isr., Rus., U.S.) **1:**newsp. list
Ha-Mizraḥ (journ., Isr.) **1:**newsp. list
Ha-Mizraḥ (period., Pol.) **12:**1051; **14:**59
- statistics **1:**newsp. list
Ha-Mizraḥ he-Ḥadash (journ.) **1:**newsp. list
Ha-Mizraḥi (weekly, Pol.) **1:**newsp. list; **12:**1051
Hamlyn, Paul **13:**1371
Ḥammah, El (site, Isr.), *see* ḤAMMAT-GADER
Ḥammām al-Shifā' Pool (Jer.) **9:**1539; **9:**1540
Hammam-Lif (loc., Tun.) **15:**1430
- *illus:*
- -synagogue mosaics **11:**268; **15:**572
Ḥamman (cult object) **2:**767
Hammarskjöld, Dag **15:**1548ff
- armistice **3:**482; **9:**426
- clashes **9:**1497
- settlement **9:**388ff
ḤAMMAT-GADER (Geder) **7:**1241
- frontier **9:**313
- Golan **13:**1532
- physiography **9:**171
- Solomon **15:**100
- synagogue **15:**598
- Syrian-Israel clash **15:**648
- Yarmuk **16:**718
- *illus:*
- - text
- - synagogue mosaics **7:**249,251
- - Yarmuk river **16:**719
- *see also:* GADARA
HAMMATH (Tiberias) **7:**1242
- baths **4:**321
- national parks **12:**879
- symbolism **15:**573
- synagogue **15:**597
- *illus:*
- - text
- - stone *menorah* **11:**1357
- - synagogue mosaic floor **3:**325; **15:**574,575
Ḥammath-Dor (bib. city, Er. Isr.) **7:**1242; **12:**820
Hammedatha (bib. fig.) **7:**1222
Hammel, Shimon **14:**1039
Hammer (fam.) **15:**790
Hammer (period., Aus.), *see Ha-Pattish*
Hammer, Philip **14:**843
Hammerschmidt, Andreas **14:**785
Hammerslough, Edward **8:**1255
Hammerslough, Julius **8:**1255
Hamerslough, Louis **8:**1255; **10:**739
HAMMERSTEIN (fam.) **7:**1244
Hammerstein, Arthur **7:**1244
Hammerstein, Oscar I **7:**1244
Hammerstein, Oscar II **7:**1244; **15:**1509
- *illus:*
- - Kern, Jerome and **15:**1060
Hammerstein, Wilhelm von **5:**906
Hammerstein, William **7:**1244
Hammolecheth (bib. fig.) **2:**73
Hammond, Sir E.L.L. **13:**32
Hammouda, Yehia **9:**469
HAMMURAPI (Hammurabi; k.) **7:**1245
- General
- - Amraphel **2:**894

– – Babel, Tower of **4**:23
– – Babylon **16**:1496ff
– – chronological chart **8**:766-767
– – Mari **11**:974; **11**:979
– – Sumer **15**:513
– – sun god **15**:517
– Code **16**:1496,
– – abduction **2**:55
– – abortion **2**:99
– – debt **6**:1008
– – moneylending **12**:245
– – virginity **16**:161
– *illus:* text
HAMNUNA (amora) **7**:1247
HAMNUNA SABA (amora) **7**:1247
HAMNUNA ZUTA (amora) **7**:1247
Ha-Modi'a (period., Rus.) **12**:1056; **13**:1046; **13**:839
– statistics **1**:newsp. list
Ha-Modi'a (newsp., Isr.) **12**:1056
– statistics **1**:newsp. list
Ha-Modi'a le-Ḥodashim (period., U.S.) **14**:275; **14**:293
– statistics **1**:newsp. list
Hamoj, Abraham **10**:641
HAMON (fam.) **7**:1248
HAMON, AARON BEN ISAAC **7**:1249
– music **12**:625
Hamon, Isaac (15th cent., physic.) **7**:1248
Hamon, Isaac (16/17 cent., physic.) **7**:1248
Hamon, Joseph (16th cent.) **7**:1248
Hamon, Joseph "the Elder" (15/16 cent.) **7**:1248
HAMON, LEO **7**:1249
Hamon, Moses **7**:1248
– chronological chart **8**:766-767
Hamo of Hereford **8**:344
HAMOR (bib. fig.) **7**:1249
– *illus:* text
Ha-Moreh (Bundist), *see* GOZHANSKY, SAMUEL
Ha-Moreh (mag., Rus.) **13**:1047
Ha-Moreh (journ., U.S.) **7**:722
– statistics **1**:newsp. list
Ha-Moriyyah (publ.) **1**:newsp. list
Ha-Mosad (immigration orgn.) **9**:687
Hamoy, Abraham **5**:479
Ha-Moẓah (place, Er. Isr.) *see* MOẒA
Ha-Moẓi, *see* GRACE BEFORE MEALS
Hampstead (sub., Montreal) **12**:287
Hampstead Garden Suburb (sub., London) **6**:449
Ḥamra (soil type, Isr.) **9**:126ff
Ḥamrah (mosh., Isr.) **1**:place list
Hamsa (talisman) **12**:965
Hamshakhah (kab. conc.) **10**:567
Ḥamsin (heat wave), *see Sharav*
Hamsun, Knut **14**:933
Hamta (anc. tn., Transj.), *see* AMMATHA
Hamul (bib. fig.) **13**:283
Ḥamūla (fam. group) **9**:1022ff
Ha-Musakh (journ.) **1**: newsp. list
Hamutal (bib. fig.) **9**:1316
Ḥana (gaon, Pumb.) **7**:318
Ḥ-a-n-a, *see* ABULAFIA, ḤAYYIM NISSIM BEN ISAAC
Hana (anc. kingdom) **16**:1497
Hana Bagdata'a (3rd cent. C.E., Bagh.) **8**:1445
ḤANA BAR ḤANILAI (amora) **7**:1250
ḤANA BEN BIZNA (amora) **7**:1251
"Ha-Nadiv ha-Yadu'a" *see* ROTHSCHILD, BARON EDMOND JAMES DE
Ḥanafi (school of Isl. law) **9**:918
Ḥanājra, Al- (Bedouin tribe) **9**:593
Hanamel (bib. fig.) **13**:1083
HANAMEL (Hananel; 1st cent. B.C.E., h. pr.) **7**:1251
– Alexandra's opposition **2**:587
– Alexandrians in Jerusalem **2**:590
– *aliyah* **9**:510
– Herod I **8**:380
Ḥanan (amora, Carthage) **15**:1430
Ḥanan (12th cent., Yem. cmty. ldr.) **6**:1032
Hananeel ben Paltiel **4**:500
Hananeel of Kairouan, *see* HANANEL BEN ḤUSHI'EL
HANAN THE EGYPTIAN (tan.) **7**:1251
– *aliyah* **9**:510
Hananel (1st cent. B.C.E., h. pr.), *see* HANAMEL
Hananel (amora) **13**:1441
– masorah **16**:1405
Hananel ben Amnon **13**:581
HANANEL BEN ḤUSHI'EL **7**:1252
– articles of faith **3**:655
– calendar **5**:49
– chronological chart **8**:766-767
– Jerusalem Talmud **15**:776
– ordination **13**:1453
– Talmud commentaries **11**:329
– *tosafot* **15**:1278
– Tunisia **15**:1434
HANANEL BEN SAMUEL **7**:1253
– Samuel ben Daniel **14**:805
Hananel ha-Bavli (h. pr.), *see* HANAMEL
Hanan ha-Miẓri (tan.), *see* HANAN THE EGYPTIAN
Hanan ha-Neḥba **15**:800
Hanani (Hananiah; br. Nehemiah, bib. fig.) **8**:622
Hanani (bib. fig., f. Jehu) **9**:1328
Hananiah (leg. fig.) **12**:1502
Hananiah (bib. fig.), *see* SHADRACH, MESHACH, ABED-NEGO
Hananiah (Samar. gov.) **14**:824
Hananiah (son of Onias, sol.), *see* ANANIAS AND HELKIAS
HANANIAH (Ḥanina; tan., nephew of Joshua ben Hananiah) **7**:1253
– Babylonian academy **2**:202
– Nehar Pekod **12**:936
Hananiah (amora), *see* ḤANINA (Hananiah, Comrade of the Rabbis)
Hananiah (art., syn. bldr.), *see* Ḥanina (art., Er. Isr.)
Hananiah ben Akbari (amora) **2**:487
Hananiah ben David (exil.) **10**:765
HANANIAH (Ḥanina) BEN ḤAKHINAI (tan.) **7**:1254
Hananiah ben Hezekiah ben Garon
– "Eighteen Rulings" **4**:738
– *Megillat Ta'anit* **11**:1230
Hananiah ben Judah (gaon) **7**:318
– Sherira ben Ḥanina Gaon **14**:1381
HANANIAH (Ḥanina) BEN TERADYON **7**:1254
– Beruriah, daughter **4**:701
– Eleazar ben Parta **6**:595
– execution **3**:218
– Yose ben Kisma **16**:855
– *illus:* text
Hananiah ben Yehudai (gaon, Pumb.), *see* Hananiah ben Judah
Hananiah ben Yose ha-Gelili (tan.), *see* Ḥanina ben Yose the Galilean
Hananiah of Ono (tan.), *see* Ḥanina of Ono
HANANIAH (Ḥanina) OF SEPPHORIS **7**:1256
HANANIAH SON OF AZZUR **7**:1256
– exile, Babylonian **6**:1037
Hananiah Yom Tov Lipa of Sighet, *see* Teitelbaum, Hananiah Yom Tov Lipa
Hananiyyah, Hill of (Er. Isr.) **9**:1515
Hanan of Iskiya **7**:318
Hanan son of Zaccur **15**:957
Hananya, Eliyahu **9**:1350ff; **13**:1039
HANAU (city, Ger.) **7**:1257
– Broda, Moses **4**:1390
– *illus:* text
Hanau, Samson ben Salman **8**:942
HANAU, SOLOMON ZALMAN BEN JUDAH LOEB HA-KOHEN **7**:1258
– *illus:* text
Hanauer, Alice, *see* Strauss, Alice
HANBURY, LILY **15**:1084
– Neilson, Julia **12**:945
Hănesti (tn., Bess.), *see* KOTOVSKOYE
Handali, Elijah **10**:991
Handali, Isaac **13**:583
HANDALI, JOSHUA BEN JOSEPH **7**:1259
Handali, Moses **2**:196, 625; **3**:800
Handasah ve-Adrikhalut (journ.) **1**:newsp. list
Handball **15**:310
Handbreadth (meas.), *see Tefaḥ*
Handel, George F.
– *Athalia* **3**:815
– *Israel in Egypt* **12**:409
– *Jephthah* **9**:1344
– *Saul* **14**:918
– *Solomon* **15**:110
– *Susanna* **15**:535
HANDELSMAN, MARCELI **7**:1259
Handful(s) (meas.), *see Ḥofen; Ḥofnayim; Komeẓ*
Handler, Mark **3**:810
HANDLER, MILTON **7**:1260
Handler, Miriam **7**:1260
HANDLER, PHILIP (chem.) **7**:1260
Handler, Philip ("Motsy"; sport.) **15**:308
Handler, Simon, *see* HEVESI, SIMON
Handlin, Mary, *see* Flug, Mary
HANDLIN, OSCAR **7**:1260
– U.S. literature **15**:1571
Handmaiden, *see* CONCUBINE
Hands
– *Ashrei*, recital of **3**:736
– right hand **14**:179; **14**:178
– symbolism **2**:911; **2**:912
– *ta'amei Torah* **16**:1413
– *illus:*
– – cosmic symbol **10**:514
– – Guidonian indication **12**:601
– – *Hamsa* **12**:965
– – washing of **12**:999
Hands, Washing of, *see* NETILAT YADAYIM
Handshake
– acquisition, mode of **2**:220
– admission **2**:290
– contract **5**:924; **5**:928
– obligation **15**:524ff
Handwriting, *see* CALLIGRAPHY AND WRITING MASTERS
Hanean nomads **16**:1497
– Mari **11**:982
Ha-Ne'eman (period.) **1**:newsp. list; **15**:938
Hanel, Melchior **8**:37
Hanen, Samuel **7**:883
Haner, György **8**:37
Hanes (city, Egy.) **5**:1253
Ha-Nesher (journ.) **1**:newsp. list
Hanewinkel, Gerhardus **8**:37
Haneẓ ha-Ḥammah ("daybreak") **5**:1376
HANFMANN, GEORGE MAXIM ANOSSOV **7**:1261
Hanft, Ben **13**:1363
HANGCHOW (city, China) **7**:1261
Hanging **5**:1133; **5**:142
Hanging Gardens (Babyl.) **4**:33
"Hanging Turkey" (paint., Soutine) **15**:214
Hanhagot Literature, *see* ETHICAL LITERATURE
Hanhagot Yesharot (bk.), *see* TOHOROT HA-KODESH
Hanhalat ha-Lashon (govt. lang. authority, Isr.) **9**:1001
ḤANĪF (Arab. term) **7**:1262
Hanigalbat (city, Mesop.) **16**:1498
Hanigun (choir) **16**:152
Ḥanin (pr. fam.), *see* ANAN BEN SETH
Ḥanin, Ezekiel ben Saliman **5**:41
Ḥanin, Judah ibn **5**:789
Ḥanina (amora, Pal.), *see* ḤUNYA OF BETH-HORON
ḤANINA (Ḥananiah, Comrade of the Rabbis; amora) **7**:1262
– *Sefer Yeẓirah* **16**:785
Ḥanina (4th cent. schol., Pers.) **4**:395
Ḥanina (art., Er. Isr.) **3**:508; **11**:990; **15**:599
– *illus:*
– – Bet Alpha mosaic **11**:989
Ḥanina (6/7 cent., gaon, Sura) **7**:318
Ḥanina, Mar (Babyl. head of acad.) **16**:1244
Ḥanina, Nephew of Joshua ben Hananiah (tan.), *see* HANANIAH (Ḥanina)
ḤANINA BAR ḤAMA **7**:1263
ḤANINA (Ḥinena) BAR-PAPA (Pappi) **7**:1264
ḤANINA BEN ABBAHU **7**:1264
ḤANINA BEN ANTIGONUS **7**:1265
ḤANINA BEN DOSA **7**:1265
– Araba, burial **3**:231
– bear and goat legend **4**:356
– ethics **6**:941
– Johanan ben Zakkai **10**:148
– piety **15**:454
ḤANINA BEN GAMALIEL **7**:1266
Ḥanina ben Ḥakhinai, *see* HANANIAH BEN ḤAKHINAI
Ḥanina ben Judah Gaon, *see* Hananiah ben Judah (Gaon)
Ḥanina ben Lezer (Eliezer) **10**:889
Ḥanina ben Teradyon, *see* HANANIAH BEN TERADYON
Ḥanina ben Yehudai, *see* Hananiah ben Judah (Gaon)
Ḥanina ben Yose the Galilean **16**:858
Ḥaninai (exil.) **4**:1537
Haninaiah bar Mesharsheya **7**:318
Haninai ben Huna, *see* ḤANINA KAHANA BEN HUNA
Haninai Kahana bar Abraham **7**:318
ḤANINA (Aḥonai) KAHANA BEN HUNA **7**:1266
– Yehudai ben Naḥman **16**:731
Ḥanina of Bei-Gihara **7**:318
Ḥanina of Caesarea, *see* ḤANINA BEN ABBAHU
Ḥanina of Nehar-Pekod **7**:318
Ḥanina (Hananiah) of Ono **15**:800
Ḥanina of Sepphoris, *see* HANANIAH OF SEPPHORIS
ḤANINA SEGAN HA-KOHANIM **7**:1266
Ha-Nir (Journ.) **1**:newsp. list
ḤANITAH (kib., Isr.) **7**:1267
– *illus:*
– – Harzfeld, Avraham, with first settlers **7**:1364
– – spraying fields with pesticide

9:781
HANKIN, YEHOSHUA **7:**1268
Ḥannā Abu Ḥannā, *see* Abu Ḥanna, Ḥanna
HANNAH (bib. fig.) **7:**1269
– *aggadah* **6:**613ff
– grave **14:**785
– in the Arts **14:**784
– Samuel **14:**780
– *illus:* text
HANNAH AND HER SEVEN SONS **7:**1270
– *Akedah* compared with **2:**481
– aggadic literature **2:**165
– in the Arts **7:**1457f; **10:**382
– *kiddush ha-Shem* **10:**982
– name of Maccabee **11:**656
– *illus:*
– – text
– – Hannah embracing her sons **5:**458
– – martyrdom **8:**671
– *see also:* MACCABEES, FOURTH BOOK OF
Hanna Szenes (ship) **8:**1250
HANNATHON (city, Er. Isr.) **7:**1272
– *see also:* ACHSHAPH
Hannaux, Emmanuel **11:**1165
Hanne(c)ken, Meno (Memnon) **8:**37
ḤANNELES, JUDAH LEIB BEN MEIR **7:**1272
HANNEMANN, PABLO **3:**601
Hannes, Edward **8:**37
Ḥanni'el (mosh., Isr.) **1:**place list
Hanno of Gaza **13:**1509
Hannover (city, Ger.), *see* HANOVER
HANNOVER, ADOLPH **7:**1273
HANNOVER, NATHAN NATA **7:**1273
– literature **11:**357
– Narol **12:**831
– social history **11:**1001
– Wiśniowiecki **16:**570
– *Yeven Meẓulah* **8:**560
– *illus:* text
HANNOVER, RAPHAEL LEVI **7:**1275
Hanoar (period.) **5:**457
Ha-No'ar ha-Dati ha-Oved (youth mvmt., Isr.) **7:**1321
– *illus:*
– – badge **9:**977
HA-NO'AR HA-IVRI—AKIBA (youth mvmt., Eur.) **7:**1275
– Glueckson, Moshe **7:**630
– kibbutz movement **10:**968
– origins **7:**385
– *see also:* HA-OVED HA-ẒIYYONI
Ha-No'ar ha-Musikali (journ.) **1:**newsp. list
Ha-No'ar ha-Oved (youth mvmt., Isr.) **9:**977
– Broides, Abraham **4:**1402
– *see also:* HA-NO'AR HA-OVED VE-HA-LOMED
Ha-No'ar Ha-Oved ha-Le'ummi (youth mvmt.) **9:**981
HA-NO'AR HA-OVED VE-HA-LOMED (youth mvmt.) **7:**1275
– *illus:*
– – badge **9:**977
Ha-No'ar ha-Oved ve-ha-Lomed ha-Leummi (youth mvmt.) **8:**542
Ha-No'ar ha-Ziyyoni (youth orgn.) **16:**1114
– *see also:* HA-NO'AR HA-IVRI—AKIBA
Ha-Noar ve-ha-Areẓ (period.) **1:**newsp. list
Ha-Noked (journ.) **1:**newsp. list
Ḥanokh, *see also under* Enoch
Ḥanokh, Gershon **12:**1518
Ḥanokh ben Ḥisdai ibn Shaprut **8:**533
ḤANOKH BEN MOSES **7:**1276
– "Four Captives" story **6:**1447ff
– gaonate **7:**318; **7:**324
– responsa **14:**86
– Umayyads **15:**1530
Ḥanokh Enoch ben Judah Leib ben Enoch Zundel **6:**799; **10:**374
ḤANOKH OF ALEKSANDROW **7:**1276
– joy, view of **10:**320
ḤANOKH ZUNDEL BEN JOSEPH **7:**1277
– *Oẓar ha-Tefillot* **13:**988
HANOVER (city, Ger.) **7:**1277
– Adler, Nathan Marcus **2:**285
– rabbinical office **13:**1453
– Vienna, Congress of **16:**132
– *illus:*
– – new synagogue **7:**501
HANRAY, LAWRENCE **15:**1084
Hansemann, David **4:**174
Hanshir-Juana (loc., Tun.) **15:**1431
Hanslick, Eduard **2:**277
HANSON, NORMAN LEONARD **7:**1279
Hansson, Christian Rasmus **14:**932
HANTKE, ARTHUR (Menaḥem) **7:**1280
– Auerbach, Israel **3:**847
HANUKKAH **7:**1280
– *Al ha-Nissim* **2:**626
– *Badḥan* **4:**74
– calendar **5:**47
– cloth donations **15:**1039
– cooking and food **6:**1426
– *"Dreydel"* top **7:**306
– festivities **7:**307
– folklore **12:**1392; **6:**1393
– Karaites **10:**779
– *Ma'oz Ẓur* **11:**910
– miracles **12:**75
– modern Israel **9:**903
– Modi'in torch **12:**206
– origin **14:**1216
– parody **13:**129
– Sabbath lights **14:**1356
– Samaritans **14:**742
– *Scroll of Antiochus* **14:**1045ff
– *Second Book of Maccabees* **11:**658
– *Shabbat Ḥanukkah* **14:**573
– torch relay run **15:**299
– *illus:*
– – *Al ha-Nissim* **2:**626
– – appeal to Jews of Egypt to observe the feast **7:**1
– – games and gambling **7:**306
– – "Hanukkah *gelt*" **14:**270
– – Modi'in torch **12:**207
– – *piyyut* **8:**671; fcg. 1335
– – U.S. army chaplain presenting gifts **11:**1553
– – Westerbork (concen. camp) celebration **16:**466
– *scores:*
– – *Hodu* **12:**635
– – *Maoz Ẓur* **11:**911
– – Ps. 30, Rome rite cantillation **9:**1143
– *see also:* ḤANUKKAH LAMP; HASMONEANS; MACCABEES, BOOK OF
ḤANUKKAH LAMP **7:**1288
– candles **5:**117
– electric *menorah* **14:**91
– folklore **6:**1393
– ritual art **3:**524; **15:**309
– talmudic plan **11:**1370
– *illus:*
– – text
– – Buenos Aires collection **4:**1462
– – Dutch (17th cent.) **12:**976
– – Galician **16:**1326
– – Italian, 16th century **10:**455; **11:**265
– – Libya, painted ceramic **2:**335
– – Lyons (14th cent.) **11:**624
– – Marrakesh (19th cent.) **11:**1016
– – Morocco (17th cent.) **12:**343
– – Persian (17th cent.) **13:**309
– – *Rothschild Miscellany* **2:**626
– – Sabbath candle-holders **14:**566
– – silver and enamel (18th cent.) **5:**301
– – Spain (15th cent.) **15:**232
– – Western Wall **9:**904
– – white tin (18th cent.) **6:**1395
Hanukkiyyah, see ḤANUKKAH LAMP
Hanun (Phil. chief) **13:**403
Hanun (bib. fig.) **16:**933
Hanun son of Nahash (Ammon. k.) **10:**107; **12:**770
Hanušovce (cmty., Slov.), *see* HUNCOVCE
Ha-Of (journ.) **1:**newsp. list
Ha-Ofek (journ.) **1:**newsp. list
HA-OGEN (kib., Isr.) **7:**1315
– statistics **1:**place list
– *illus:* text
– – elementary school class **9:**938
Ha-Ohalah (journ.) **1:**newsp. list
Ha-Ohel (journ.) **1:**newsp. list
Ha-Ohev Ammo ve-Ereẓ Moladeto (period.) **7:**845
HAOLAM (journ.) **7:**1315
– Druyanow, Alter **6:**242
– Russia **13:**1046
– statistics **1:**newsp. list
– Zionist journalism **12:**1051
Ha-Olam ha-Katan (wk.) **13:**437
Ha-Olam ha-Zeh **1:**newsp. list
Ha-Olam ha-Zeh—Ko'aḥ Ḥadash (polit. party, Isr.)
– Avnery's leadership **3:**976
– Histadrut elections **9:**861
– New Left **12:**1034
– periodical **3:**976
– place in politics **9:**680
Haoma (sacred drink) **7:**1222
Ha-Omer (period.) **4:**575
– Smilansky, Moshe **15:**3
– statistics **1:**newsp. list
HA-ON (kib., Isr.) **7:**1316
– statistics **1:**place list
– Syria **15:**648
Ha-Or (publ. house, Warsaw) **5:**434
Ha-Or (journ. Gal.) **1:**newsp. list
Ha-Or (pubs., Isr.) **1:**newsp. list
Ha-Or (newsp., Er. Isr.)
– Ben-Avi, Ithamar **4:**470
– Ben-Yehuda, Eliezer **4:**567
– Hebrew journalism **9:**1015; **12:**1054
– *see also: Ha-Ẓevi*
Ha-Or (monthly, Rum.) **14:**1533
Ha örl pin (city, China), *see* HARBIN
Ha-Otiyyot ha-Menuẓarim, *see Otiyyot menuẓẓarot*
Ha-Oved (journ.) **1:**newsp. list
Ha-Oved ha-Dati (journ.) **1:**newsp. list
Ha-Oved ha-Dati (polit. party, Isr.), *see* Religious Workers' List
Ha-Oved ha-Le'ummi (journ.) **1:**newsp. list
Ha-Oved ha-Ziyyoni (journ.) **1:**newsp. list
HA-OVED HA-ẒIYYONI (Isr. lab. orgn.) **7:**1317
– General Zionist **7:**386
– labor movement **9:**859
– *see also:* Ha-No'ar ha-Ẓiyyoni; GENERAL ZIONISTS; HISTADRUT
Ha-Oẓar (Heb. lexicon) **7:**213
Ha'palah, *see* ILLEGAL IMMIGRATION
Ha-Pardes (journ., Isr.) **1:**newsp. list
Ha-Pardes (journ., Pol.; U.S.) **1:**newsp. list
Ha-Pardes (annual, Rus.) **13:**1045
– statistics **1:**newsp. list
HA-PARNAS, SEFER (bk.) **7:**1317
– illus: text
Ha-Pattish (period.) **7:**1057
HAPAX LEGOMENA (Gr. "once said") **7:**1318
– linguistics **16:**1356
– *Masorah Gedolah* **16:**1425
Ha-Paytan, Abraham Motal **16:**872
Ha-Pedagog (period.) **1:**newsp. list
Ha-Peles (newsp.) **12:**1050; **13:**839
– statistics **1:**newsp. list
Ha-Peraḥ (journ.) **1:**newsp. list
Ha-Perahim (period.) **5:**457
Ha-Peraklit (journ.) **1:**newsp. list
Ha-Pe'ulah ha-Shemit ("Semitic Action"—Isr. polit. gr.)
– Avnery **3:**976
– Yellin-Mor **16:**738
HAPHARAIM (tn., Er. Isr.) **7:**1319
Hapiri (Hapiru; anc. people), *see* HABIRU
Ha-Pisgah (period.) **4:**146; **14:**1009; **16:**1141
– statistics **1:**newsp. list
HAPOEL (sports orgn., Isr.) **7:**1319
– *illus:*
– – text
– – stamp **9:**844-845
Ha-Po'el ha-Mizraḥi (journ.) **1:**newsp. list
HA-PO'EL HA-MIZRACHI (rel. lab. mvmt.) **7:**1320
– Agudat Israel **2:**425
– Benei Akiva **4:**490
– Elizur, sports organization **6:**674
– health insurance **9:**986
– Histadrut **9:**852
– Israel politics **9:**658ff
– kibbutz movement **10:**972
– merger with Mizrachi **12:**880
– *see also:* MIZRACHI
Ha-Po'el ha-Vatik (journ.) **1:**newsp. list
HA-PO'EL HA-ẒA'IR (lab. party, Er. Isr.) **7:**1324
– Aharonovitch, Yosef **2:**452
– Aḥdut ha-Avodah **2:**456; **2:**457
– aims of party **9:**657ff
– Baratz, Joseph **4:**203
– labor movement **9:**848ff
– labor problem **9:**329
– philosophy of labor **9:**519
– *illus:*
– – Aḥdut ha-Avodah, merger meeting **9:**660
– – Jaffa (1908) **9:**657
– *see also:* MAPAI
HA-PO'EL HA-ẒA'IR (newsp., Isr.) **7:**1326
– Hebrew journalism **12:**1047; **12:**1055; **12:**1056
– index **16:**1159
– statistics **1:**newsp. list
Ha-Posek (journ.) **1:**newsp. list
Happelius, Wigano **8:**37
Happiness, eternal, *see* BEATITUDE
Happizzez (fam., Er. Isr.) **12:**900
Ha-Problemai (journ.) **1:**newsp. list
HAPSBURG MONARCHY **7:**1327
– Austria **3:**887ff
– banking **4:**172
– Ereẓ Israel missions **9:**296
– history chart **8:**766-767
– Jewish descent **7:**1328
– *Kultusverein* **10:**1290
– Jewish self defense **14:**1124
– *see also:* CZECHOSLOVAKIA
Ḥaqīqat al-Amr (weekly) **9:**1041
Haquot (mdvl. Fr. J.) **14:**209

Ḥāra (J. qtr., Tun.) **15:**1441
Ḥāra al-Saghīra (loc., Djerba) **6:**139
- *illus:*
- Gharība synagogue **15:**1434
Ha-Rabbah (tn., Er. Isr.), *see* RABBAH
Ha-Rabbim (Qumran cmty.) **16:**699
Harafu (bib. fig.) **12:**1478
H-a-r-a-h (Sp. r.), *see* AARON BEN JOSEPH HA-LEVI
Ha-Raḥaman (name for God) **7:**684
Ha-Ramah, *see* RAMAH
Haram al-Sharīf (loc., Jer.) **8:**935
- ʿAbd al-Malik **9:**1423
- Hajj Muhammad Amin al-Husseini **9:**461
- Mamluk period **9:**1424
Ha-Ramatha (city, Er. Isr.) **13:**1529
Haran (bib. fig.)
- Abraham **2:**112
- Lot **11:**508
- Nahor **12:**790
Haran (tn., Er. Isr.), *see* BET(H)-HARAM
HARAN (city, Mesop.) **7:**1328
- Assyria **10:**292; **16:**1505
- astronomy **16?**1490
- Iraq **8:**1447
- Mari **11:**981
- moon cult **12:**290
- neo-Babylonians **16:**1505
- patriarchal background **8:**573
- Sargon II **14:**880
- Ur **16:**3
HARAN, MENAHEM **1:**31
- Isaiah **9:**62,64
HARARI (fam., Aleppo) **7:**1330
Harari, David **5:**1250
HARARI (Blumberg), ḤAYYIM **7:**1330
Harari, Ḥayyim Solomon **7:**1330; **12:**900
Harari, Isaac ben Moses **7:**1330
Harari, Izhar **7:**1330
Harari, Moses **7:**1330
Harari, Moses ben Isaac **7:**1330
Harari, Nissim ben Isaiah **7:**1330
Harari, Shalom (Selim) **7:**1330
HARARI, SIR VICTOR RAPHAEL **7:**1330
Harari, Yehudit **7:**1330
Harari (lang.) **14:**1153
Ha-Rashut ha-Mekomit (journ.) **1:**newsp. list
Harat (city, Afg.), *see* HERAT
Ḥārat al-yahūd (Jew. qtr.) **10:**84
Ha-Rav ha-Gadol (tit.) **13:**1451
Ha-Rav ha-Kolel (tit.) **13:**1450; **13:**1451
"*Ha-Rav ha-Magen*", *see* GALANTE, MOSES BEN JONATHAN
Ha-Rav ha-Manhig (tit.) **13:**1451
Ha-Rav ha-Rosh (tit.) **13:**1449
Ha-Rav Ḥemdat Yamim, *see* NATHAN OF GAZA
Harawi, Ali ben Abi Bakr Al-, *see* Ali ben Abi Bakr Al-Harawi
Harazi, Yahya ben Abraham **13:**597
Ḥarba (loc., Iraq) **8:**1447
HARBIN (city, China) **7:**1331
Ḥarbiyya (mil. ransom, Afg.) **2:**328
Harbors, Israel **9:**832
- Acre **2:**224
- Ashdod **3:**698
- Elath **6:**569
- Gaza **7:**341
- Haifa **7:**1139
- historical survey **9:**393ff
- Jaffa **9:**1254
- *illus:*
- - Acre **2:**227
- - Ashdod **3:**698; **9:**837
- - Haifa **7:**1135-1140
HARBURG, E.Y. (Edgar "Yip") **7:**1332
- theatre **15:**1059
HARBY, ISAAC **7:**1332
- historiography **8:**567
- U.S. literature **15:**1569
- *illus:* text
HARBY, LEVI MYERS **11:**1551; **11:**1573
HARDEN, MAXIMILIAN **7:**1333
- *Zukunft* **16:**1234
HARDENBERG, KARL AUGUST VON **7:**1335
- Bartholdy, Jacob **4:**264
- universities **15:**1677
Harding, John **8:**37
Harding, Stephen **8:**37
Har Di-Nur (pseud.), *see* FEUERBERG, MORDECAI ZE'EV
HARDMAN, JACOB BENJAMIN **7:**1335
- Bund **4:**1500
- socialism **15:**31
Hardt, Anthon Julius van der **3:**258; **7:**1050; **8:**37
HARE (zool.) **7:**1336
- dietary laws **6:**32
- fauna of Israel **9:**226
- *illus:* text
Hare, Francis **8:**37
Haredim, Sefer (kab. wk.) **10:**546
Ha-Refu'ah (journ.) **7:**190
- statistics **1:**newsp. list
HAREL (kib., Isr.) **7:**1337
Harel (altar section), *see* ARIEL
Har'el Brigade (Isr. Army) **7:**1073
- Jerusalem, defense of **9:**367
- Palmaḥ **13:**47
- War of Independence **16:**313
Har-El synagogue (Jer.) **9:**906
HARENDORF, SAMUEL JACOB **15:**1084
HA-REUBENI, EPHRAIM **7:**1337
Ha-Reubeni, Hannah **7:**1337
Har Gerizim (mt., Er. Isr.), *see* GERIZIM, MOUNT
Har ha-Karmel (Haifa qtr.) **9:**563
HAR HA-MELEKH (dist., Judea) **7:**1337
Har ha-Menuḥot (loc., Jer.) **9:**1515
- cemetery **9:**1496
Har ha-Zeitim (mt., Er. Isr.), *see* MOUNT OF OLIVES
Ḥari'a (dye plant), *see Koẓah*
ḤARIF (fam., Pol.) **7:**1338
Ḥarif, Ḥayyim ben Joseph **7:**1338
Ḥarif, Hirsch, *see* BIALEH, ẒEVI HIRSCH BEN NAPHTALI HERZ
Ḥarif, Isaac ben Joseph **7:**1338
Ḥarif, Israel (ben Moses) **7:**1338
Ḥarif, Israel **7:**1338
Ḥarif, Israel (kab., Gal.) **7:**373
Ḥarif, Jacob **7:**1338
Ḥarif, Jacob Isaac **7:**1338
Ḥarif, Joseph **7:**1338
Ḥarif, Judah Leib **7:**1338
Ḥarif, Moses Ḥayyim ben Eleazar **7:**1338
Ḥarif, Moses ha-Zaken ben Israel **7:**1338
Ḥarif, Moses Pinḥas **7:**1338
Ḥarif, Saul **7:**1338
Ḥarif, Ẓevi Hirsch **7:**1338
ḤARIF HA-LEVI (fam., Pol.) **7:**1338
Ḥarif Ha-Levi, Isaac **7:**1339
Ḥarif, Ha-Levi, Isaac Segal **7:**1338
Ḥarif Ha-Levi, Jekuthiel Zalman Segal **7:**1339
Ḥarif Ha-Levi, Joseph Segal **7:**1339
Ḥarif Ha-Levi, Moses Segal **7:**1338
Ḥarif Ha-Levi, Nathan Neta **7:**1339
Ḥarif Ha-Levi, Samuel Kamnitzer **7:**1338
Ḥarif Ha-Levi, Solomon ben Isaac Abraham **7:**1338
Ḥarif-Ullmann, Shalom **7:**112
Ha-Rikmah (wk., Isaac ha-Levy) **16:**1387
Ha-Rikmah (wk., Ibn Janaḥ), *see Kitab al-Lumaʿ*
Ha-Rikmah (wk., Tibbon), *see Sefer ha-Rikmah*
Harim (bib. fig.) **14:**45
Harim (pr. fam.) **9:**1322
- clan divisions **12:**89
ḤARIRI (fam., Kurd.) **7:**1339
- Kabbalah **10:**553
Hariri, Abraham ben Phinehas **7:**1339
Ḥarīrī, Al- , *see* Al-Ḥarīrī
Hariri, Ḥayyim **7:**1339
Hariri, Isaac (18th cent.) **7:**1339
Hariri, Isaac (19th cent.) **7:**1339
Hariri, Isaac ben Moses (17th cent.) **7:**1339; **14:**525
Hariri, Moses **7:**1339
Hariri, Phinehas **7:**1339; **14:**525
- Barazani **4:**204
Ḥārith, Al- **11:**971
Ḥarizi (paytan) **13:**581
ḤARIZI, ABU ISAAC ABRAHAM **7:**1339
- paytanim list **13:**577
Ḥarizi, Simḥah **7:**1339
Harkavah (wk.) **16:**1390
Harkavi, Yiẓḥak **16:**640
HARKAVY, ALBERT (Abraham Elijah) **7:**1339
- Cairo *genizah* **16:**1336
- promotion of culture **15:**58ff
HARKAVY, ALEXANDER **7:**1339; **14:**525
Harkavy, Deborah, *see* Romm, Deborah
HARKAVY, MINNA **3:**601
Harland, Henry **6:**780
- U.S. literature **15:**1573
Harlap, Eliezer **16:**836
ḤARLAP, JACOB MOSES BEN ZEBULUN **7:**1343
Ḥarlap, Zebulun **7:**1343
HARLAU (tn., Mold.) **7:**1344
- Rumania **14:**397
Harlech, Lord, see Ormsby-Gore, W.
Harlem (loc., N.Y.C.) **12:**1079f,1106
Harlingen (city, Tex.) **15:**1036
Harlotry, *see* PROSTITUTION
HARMAN (Herman), AVRAHAM **7:**1344
- COJO **16:**636
- *illus:*
- - Bonds dinner **12:**1113
Harman, Zena **7:**1345
- UNICEF **15:**1563
Harmatz, Willie **15:**310
Har Megiddo, *see* ARMAGEDDON
Harmelin, Marcus **7:**225
Har-Minni, *see* ARMENIA
Harmon (bib. loc.) **3:**473
Harmonie (orgn., N.Y.) **12:**1079
Har Moriah Hospital (N.Y.C.) **12:**1098
Har Nes (mt., Isr.) **9:**135
Harnick, Sheldon **15:**1060
Harnisch, Stanisław **9:**1165
HARO (city, Sp.) **7:**1345
Haro, Don Lope de **2:**157
Harod (loc., Isr.) **9:**147; **9:**575; **9:**590ff; **10:**102
Ḥarodona (loc., Er. Isr.), *see* BET ḤARODON
Ha-Ro'eh, Israel, *see* Israel ha-Ro'eh
Ha-Roeh u-Mevakker Sifrei Meḥabberei Zemannenu (journ.) **4:**1158
- statistics **1:**newsp. list
Ha-Rofe ba-Histadrut (journ.) **1:**newsp. list
Ha-Rofe ba-Mosad (journ.) **1:**newsp. list
Harofe ha-Ivri (journ.) **6:**533
- statistics **1:**newsp. list
Ha-Rokeaḥ, Sefer (wk.), *see Sefer ha-Rokeaḥ*
Ha-Roke'aḥ ha-Ivri (journ.) **1:**newsp. list
HAROSET (*seder* cerem.) **7:**1346
- *illus:*
- - text
- - distribution **3:**530
Ha-r-o-sh (r., Salonika), *see* SHALOM, ABRAHAM
HAROSHETH-GOIIM (Haroseth-Goiim; bib. loc.) **7:**1347
- Sisera **14:**1621
Ḥaroshet u-Melakhah (journ.) **1:**newsp. list
Harp (mus. inst.) **12:**1319
- *illus:*
- - David **14:**911
Harpania (city, Mesop.) **11:**1396
Har Ramon (mt., Isr.) **9:**135
Harran (city, Mesop.), *see* HARAN
Harris (r., U.S.) **15:**1207
Harris, C. M. **4:**1480
Harris, Dan, *see* Zev
HARRIS, SIR DAVID **7:**1347
Harris, David (phot.) **13:**487
Harris, D. Lou **16:**1111
Harris, Harry **15:**305
Harris, Henry **4:**138
HARRIS, JED **15:**1084
Harris, John **3:**877
Harris, Lewis **15:**313
HARRIS, MARK **15:**1581
Harris, Maurice H. **12:**1092
- *illus:*
- - J.W.B. committee **12:**873
HARRIS, MILTON **5:**383
HARRIS, SIR PERCY **13:**827
Harris, R. **16:**1508
HARRIS, SAM HENRY **15:**1059; **15:**1084
Harris, Sidney M. **5:**107
Harris, Sigmund **15:**307
Harris, Sol **4:**1112
HARRIS, ZELLIG SABBETAI **7:**1348
- linguistics **3:**40; **16:**1400
HARRISBURG (city, Pa.) **7:**1348
- Pennsylvania **13:**230
- *illus:* text
Harrison (vill., N.Y.) **16:**464
Harrison, Austen St. B. **3:**361; **14:**212
- *illus:*
- Rockefeller Museum, Jerusalem **3:**350; **14:**212
Harrison, Benjamin **15:**1658
Harrison, Earl G. **6:**76; **15:**1658
Harrison, Lester **15:**302
Harrison, Peter **12:**1043
Harrison, R.K. **4:**910
Harrison, S. B. **5:**311
Harrison, Thomas (16/17 cent.) **8:**37
Harrison, Thomas (18th cent.) **8:**37
Harrisonburg (city, Va.) **16:**163
Harrison Miscellany (illum ms.)
- *illus:* **3:**543; **5:**23,1421 **6:**56,211,534,808,859; **7:**1217; **9:**1552; **10:**223,1074,1316; **13:**574
HARRISSE, HENRY **7:**1349
Harrow (sub. Lond.) **11:**479
- *illus:*
- - population movement **11:**479
Harrwitz, David **5:**404
HARRY, MYRIAM **7:**1349
Harry Fischel Institute for Research in Jewish Law (Isr.) **7:**746
- endowment **6:**1317
- Isaac Herzog **8:**424
- research **15:**55
Harry Truman Peace Center (Jer.) **9:**1520

Har Shalom (au., Lith.), *see* FRIEDBERG, ABRAHAM SHALOM
Harster, Wilhelm **16:**296
Har Suggi (mt., Isr.) **9:**135
Harsusi (lang.) **14:**1153
HART (fam. Eng.) **7:**1350
Hart (fam., U.S.) **14:**143
Hart, Aaron (Uri Phoebus) **7:**1350
- *illus:*
- - London monument **11:**473
HART, AARON (pion., Can.) **7:**1351
- *illus:*
- - portrait **12:**285
Hart, Aaron Philip (sport.) **15:**310
HART, ABRAHAM **7:**1351
Hart, Alexander **16:**163
HART, BENJAMIN (sol., Can.) **7:**1352
- *illus:*
- - portrait **12:**285
Hart, Benjamin (Can. jur.) **5:**112
HART, BERNARD **7:**1353
Hart, Catherine, *see* Judah, Catherine
HART, CECIL M. **7:**1354
- sport **15:**316
HART, DANIEL **7:**1354
Hart, David **11:**1302; **15:**1008
Hart, Eli **12:**1075
HART, EMANUEL BERNARD **7:**1354
- Civil War **12:**1075
- *geneal. table:* text
HART, EPHRAIM **7:**1355
HART, ERNEST ABRAHAM **7:**1355
HART, EZEKIEL **7:**1356
- *illus:*
- - portrait **12:**285
Hart, Harry **15:**312
Hart, Henry **7:**1354
HART, HERBERT LIONEL ADOLPHUS **7:**1356
Hart, Hyman O. **11:**1286
HART, ISAAC **7:**1356
Hart, Sir Israel **10:**1589
HART, JACOB **7:**1356
HART, JOEL **7:**1357
- universities **15:**1677
Hart, John (Hebr.) **8:**37
Hart, John I. (cmty. fig.) **12:**1072
Hart, Lemon **13:**269
Hart, Lorenz **15:**1059
Hart, Moses (broker, Eng.) **7:**1350
- *illus:*
- - text
- - London monument **11:**473
Hart, Moses (bsmn., N.Y.) **12:**1067
HART, MOSS **7:**1357
- Kaufman, George S. **10:**841
- theatre **15:**1059
- *illus:* text
HART, MYER **7:**1358
- Pennsylvania **13:**229
HART, SAMUEL **7:**1358
Hart, Sarah **5:**162; **5:**1338
HART, SOLOMON ALEXANDER **7:**1358
- *illus:*
- - *Ivanhoe,* Rebecca (engr.) **6:**779
- - "Rejoicing of the Law . . ." (paint.) **3:**547
Hart, Uri Phoebus, *see* Hart, Aaron
Hartau, Ludwig **15:**1056
Harte, Bret **7:**1354
HARTFORD (city, Conn.) **7:**1358
- *illus:*
- - text
- - town record references (1659-1667) **5:**898
HARTGLAS, MAXIMILIAN MEIR APOLINARY **7:**1361
- *illus:*
- - Kadimah **16:**338
Harthausen (loc., Ger.) **15:**265
Hartheim (Nazi "euthanasia" center) **11:**1137
Hartjenstein, Fritz **12:**893
Hart Lion (Lyon; r., Eng.), *see* LEVIN, ZEVI HIRSCH BEN ARYEH LOEB
Hartlieb, Johann **12:**521
Hartman, Charles **12:**873
Hartman, F. **7:**93
Hartman, J. **7:**93
Hartmann, A. Theodor **8:**37
HARTMANN, HEINZ **7:**1361
Hartmann, J. Melchior **8:**37
Hartmann, J. P. **8:**37
Hartmann, Lavoslav (Leopold) **16:**888
- libraries **16:**918
- publishing **13:**1369
Hartmann, Ludo Moritz **7:**1362
HARTMANN, MORITZ **7:**1361
- *illus:* text
Hartmann, Olov **14:**930
Hartog, H. **6:**320
HARTOG, LEVIE DE **7:**1363
Hartog, Marion **5:**449; **6:**784
Hartog, Numa Edward **7:**1364
HARTOG, SIR PHILIP JOSEPH **7:**1363
Hartog, Salvador **6:**321
HARTOGENSIS, BENJAMIN HENRY **7:**1364
Hartogh, Abraham **13:**815
Hartstein, Jacob I. **15:**1679
Hartt, Maurice **13:**810
Hartuv (stlmt., Er. Isr.) **4:**774; **9:**583
Hartwig, Henriette **15:**1084
Hartwig, (Naphtali Hertz) Moses **7:**1350
Hartz, Sem. L. **15:**1479
Harun, Yahudi, *see* HAMON, AARON BEN ISAAC
Hārūn al-Rashīd (caliph, Iraq) **2:**42; **8:**1445
- Ramleh **13:**1540
- Samaritans **14:**732
- trade **15:**1297
Harun al-Yahudi (vizier, Mor.) *see* AARON BEN BATASH
Harussi, Emanuel **9:**1206
Ḥaruv (bot.), *see* CAROB
Ḥaruẓ (metal) **11:**1429
Ḥaruẓim (stlmt., Isr.) **1:**place list
Harvard University (U.S.) **15:**1654; **15:**1677; **15:**1681
Harvest, *see* AGRICULTURAL METHODS AND IMPLEMENTS IN ANCIENT EREẒ ISRAEL
Harvest Festival (kib. fest.), *see* Ḥag ha-Asif
HARVEY, LAURENCE **12:**468
Harvey, M. **9:**1537
Harz, Benjamin **13:**1374
HARZFELD, AVRAHAM **7:**1364
- *illus:* text
Ha-Sadeh (mag.) **10:**141
- statistics **1:**newsp. list
Ha-Sadeh la-Gan va-Nof (journ.), *see Gan va-Nof*
Ha-Sadeh la-No'ar (pub.) **1:**newsp. list **10:**141
Hasadiah Ben Hananeel **2:**850
Ha-Safah (journ.) **1:**newsp. list
Ha-Safran (journ.), *see Alim le-Bibliografyah u-le-Safranut*
Ha-Sallaḥ (poet, Sp.), *see* IBN EZRA, MOSES BEN JACOB
Hasan (7th cent.; son of Ali) **15:**1528
Hasan (k., Mor.) **2:**517
Hasan II (k., Mor.) **2:**517; **12:**346
ḤASAN, ABU ALI JEPHETH IBN BUNDĀR **7:**1365
Hasan, Ali al-Tabari Abul al-, *see* ALI IBN SAHL IBN RABBAN AL-TABARI
Ḥasan, David **3:**834
Ḥasan, Maḍmūn **7:**1365
Ḥasan ben Mar Ḥasan ha-Dayyan **7:**420
ḤASAN (Hussein) BEN MASHI'AḤ **7:**1365
Ha-Sanegor (period.) **1:**newsp. list
Hasan ibn al-Mufarrij **9:**262
Ḥasan ibn Ḥasan **3:**802
Ḥasan ibn Nu'man, *see* Ibn Nu'man Ḥasan
Ḥasā' River (Er. Isr.), *see* ZERED
Ha-Sar mi-Coucy (Fr. tosafists), *see* SAMSON BEN SAMSON OF COUCY
Hasba'ah ("satiation"; jur. term) **2:**291
Ḥaṣbayyā (bib. loc.) **4:**3
Ḥasbeya' (vill., Leb.) **15:**644
Hascama (cmty. statute), *see* TAKKANOT HA-KAHAL
Hasdâ, Augusto **13:**563
Ḥasdai (name), *see also* Ḥisdai
ḤASDAI BEN BARADOI **7:**1366
ḤASDAI BEN BUSTANAI **7:**1365
ḤASDAI BEN DAVID BEN HEZEKIAH **7:**1366
ḤASDAI BEN NATRONAI **7:**1366
Ḥasdai ha-Kohen Peraḥyah **4:**1270
Ḥasdai ibn Shaprut, *see* ḤISDAI IBN SHAPRUT
Hasdei David (Tosefta comment.), *see* PARDO, DAVID SAMUEL BEN JACOB
Hase, C. G. **8:**37
Ha-Sefer (bibl.) **1:**newsp. list
Ha-Sefer be-Yisrael (journ.) **1:**newsp. list
Ha-Segullah (journ.) **1:**newsp. list
Haselbacher, Karl **7:**528
Haselbauer, Franz **8:**37
Hasen, Irwin **5:**216
HASENCLEVER, WALTER **7:**1366
Ha-Seniri, Isaac ben Judah, *see* ISAAC BEN JUDAH HA-SENIRI
Ḥaser (masor. term), *see Male'* and *ḥaser*
"Ha-Sezon" (Haganah anti-I.Z.L. mission) **9:**688
Ḥasfiyah (vill., Er. Isr.), *see* Khasfīn
Ha-Sha'ar (journ.) **1:**newsp. list
Hashachar (mvmt.), *see* Ha-Shaḥar
HA-SHAḤAR (journ.) **7:**1366
- Braudes, Reuben Asher **4:**1316
- Smolenskin, Perez **15:**7
- statistics **1:**newsp. list
- Zionism **16:**1088
- Zuckermann, Eliezer **16:**1230
Ha-Shaḥar (youth orgn.) **7:**1046; **16:**860
Ha-Shaḥmat (newsp.), *see Shaḥmat*
Ha-Sharon (journ., Gal.) **1:**newsp. list
Ha-Sharon (journ., Pol.) **1:**newsp. list
Ha-Shavu'a (newsp.), *see* HA-MAGGID
Ha-Shavu'a ba-Kibbutz ha-Arẓi (journ.) **1:**newsp. list
Ha-Shavu'a la-Mishpaḥah (period.) **1:**newsp. list
Ha-Shayazi, Elijah **12:**420
Hashed-Ge'ullah (*aliyah* camp, Aden) **2:**263; **16:**751
Ha-Shelah ha-Kadosh (kab.), *see* HOROWITZ, ISAIAH BEN ABRAHAM HA-LEVI
Ha-Shem (name of God) **7:**680, 683
Ha-Shemesh (newsp.) **1:**newsp. list; **7:**824
Hashemite Kingdom of Jordan, *see* JORDAN, HASHEMITE KINGDOM OF
"Ha-Shetaḥ ha-Gadol" (tourist area, Isr.), *see* Jaffa Hill
Hashgaḥah peratit, *see* PROVIDENCE
Ḥashid-Geulah (camp, Aden), *see* Hashed-Ge'ullah
HA-SHILO'AH (newsp., Rus.) **7:**1368
- Aḥad Ha-Am **2:**441; **8:**191
- Klausner, Joseph **10:**1091
- publishing **13:**1375
- statistics **1:**newsp. list
- *illus:* text
Ha-Shilo'aḥ (annual) **13:**1045
Ha-Shilton ha-Mekomi be-Yisrael (journ.) **1:**newsp. list
Hashimoni, Eliezer **4:**1533
Hashish (bot.) **8:**323
Hashkafah (period.) **4:**567; **9:**1015; **12:**1054
Haskavah (prayer for the dead), *see* ASHKAVAH
HASHKIVENU (evening prayer) **7:**1370
- Satan **14:**904
Ḥashmal (bib. term) **11:**1436
"Hashoah" (sculp., B. Lishansky) **3:**633
Ha-Shofar (period., Bul.) **13:**652; **16:**1108
- *illus:*
- - masthead **16:**1109
Ha-Shofar (journ., Isr.) **1:**newsp. list
Ha-Shofar (journ., N.Z.) **12:**1129; **13:**1026
HA-SHOMER (assoc. of watchmen, Er. Isr.) **7:**1370
- Ben-Zvi, Iẓḥak **4:**579
- Dagestanis **9:**503
- defense forces **9:**681
- defense of settlements **8:**752ff; **16:**1051
- Giladi, Israel **7:**566
- Haganah **7:**1064ff
- history chart **8:**766-767
- Lishansky **11:**303
- Nadav, Ẓevi **12:**751
- *yishuv* security **9:**329
- Zeid, Alexander **16:**968ff
- *illus:*
- - text
- - early members **9:**682
- - guard **9:**682
- - mounted guards in Galilee **9:**517
- - Tel Ḥai cemetery **15:**932
Ha-Shomer (Gal. scout mvmt.) **7:**1372
- Scouting **14:**1037
Ha-Shomer ha-Dati (Zion. mvmt.) **7:**1321
Ha-Shomer ha-Le'ummi (youth mvmt.) **14:**1037
Ha-Shomer Hatẓair (pub., Mex.) **16:**1126
HA-SHOMER HA-ẒA'IR (Zion. youth mvmt.) **7:**1372
- *Contents:*
- - Educational Method **7:**1372
- - Personal Fulfillment **7:**1373
- - Beginnings in Ereẓ Israel **7:**1373
- - World Movement **7:**1374
- - Eve of World War II and Holocaust **7:**1374
- - Postwar Period **7:**1375
- - Israel **7:**1375
- - U.S.-Canada **7:**1375
- - Great Britain **7:**1376
- - South Africa **7:**1376
- - Australia **7:**1376
- - Neẓaḥ **7:**1376
- Anielewicz, Mordecai **3:**2
- Arab-Jewish scheme **9:**857
- Germany **7:**493
- Hebrew newspapers **12:**1052
- He-Ḥalutz in U.S. **8:**254
- Israel **9:**977

- Jewish-Arab relations **16:**1056
- kibbutz movement **10:**969
- Mapam **11:**914
- politics **9:**661ff
- scouting **14:**1037
- socialism, Jewish **15:**50
- Ya'ari, Meir **16:**691
- *yishuv* **9:**340
- Zionism **16:**1099*ff*
- *illus:*
- - Lag ba-Omer parade **16:**1131
- - Sarny camp **14:**885

Ha-Shomer ha-Za'ir (journ., Isr.) **1:**newsp. list
Ha-Shomer Ha-Za'ir (period., Warsaw) **7:**1372
- statistics **1:**newsp. list

Hashta'ah (jur. term) **2:**291
Ha-Shulamit (weekly) **4:**1375
Hashva'ah, ha- (wk.), *see Sefer ha-Hashva'ah*
Ḥasid (title) **15:**1164
Ḥasid, Ḥayyim **10:**1217
Ḥasid, Jacob Koppel **10:**1217
Ḥasid, Jacob Samson **10:**1217
Ḥasid, Jehiel Michael **11:**10
Ḥasid, Judah **14:**1247
Ḥasid, Menahem Mendel **10:**1217
Ḥasid, Michael (Mikhol) **4:**643
Ḥasid, Moses (kab., Cz.) **11:**819
- ethical wills **11:**346

Ḥasid, Moses (r., Kosov) **10:**1217
Ḥasidah (ornith.) **15:**416
Ha-Siddur ha-Shalem (prayer bk.) **13:**987
Hasideans (rel. sect, 4/3 cent., Er. Isr.), *see* HASSIDEANS
ḤASIDEI ASHKENAZ (rel. mvmt., 12/13 cent., Ger.) **7:**1377
- *Contents:*
- - Literature **7:**1377
- - Theology **7:**1379
- - Symbolism **7:**1380
- - Ethical Views **7:**1381
- - Social Doctrine **7:**1382
- conception of exile **7:**285ff
- Eleazar of Worms **6:**592
- ethical literature **6:**928
- *gematria* **7:**371ff
- Germany **7:**464
- history **8:**687ff
- history chart **8:**766-767
- homiletical literature **8:**954ff
- illuminated manuscripts **8:**1267
- Kabbalah, practical **10:**633
- literature **6:**1267
- *Ma'aseh Book* **16:**804
- magic **11:**710; **11:**712
- messianism **11:**1417
- mysticism **10:**508; **10:**514
- preaching **11:**698
- Samuel ben Kalonymus **14:**809
- *Sefer ha-Ḥayyim* **14:**1098
- self-punishment **13:**1389
- *Shi'ur Komah* **14:**1418
- *see also:* ḤASIDIM, SEFER

ḤASIDEI UMMOT HA-OLAM (righteous gentiles) **7:**1383
- Antoninus Pius **3:**165
- Job **10:**124
- *see also:* NOACHIDE LAWS; RIGHTEOUS OF THE NATIONS

Hasidic dynasties **1:**ḥas. table
ḤASIDIM ("pietists"; Tal. term) **7:**1383
- immersion duty **13:**1413
- law and morality **10:**1483
- mysticism **10:**494,512*ff*
- sages **14:**636ff
- torts **14:**652
- *yahrzeit* **16:**702
- *illus:* text
- *see also:* HASSIDEANS; ḤAVER, ḤAVERIM

Ḥasidim (rel. sect, 4/3 cent., Er. Isr.), *see* HASSIDEANS
Ḥasidim (12/13 cent., Ger), *see* ḤASIDEI ASHKENAZ
Ḥasidim (E. Eur. and mod. period), *see* ḤASIDISM
ḤASIDIM, SEFER (bk., Judah he-Ḥasid) **7:**1388
- Teachings
- - anti-legalism **10:**639
- - art **3:**522
- - chess **5:**403
- - ethical literature **6:**941; **11:**343
- - gentiles **7:**413
- - Messiah **11:**1414
- - mysticism **10:**514
- - visions **16:**168
- Miscellaneous
- - Abraham ben Moses ha-Kohen **2:**153
- - Abterode, David **2:**177
- - Alexander the Great **2:**580
- - exemplum **6:**1022
- - fiction, Hebrew **6:**1268
- - Ḥasidei Ashkenaz **7:**1377
- - history chart **8:**766-767
- - language **16:**1637
- - magic **11:**710ff
- - Samuel ben Kalonymus **14:**809
- *illus:* text

"Ḥasidim in a *Bet Midrash*" (paint., I. Kaufmann) **7:**1395
ḤASIDISM (mvmt., mod. period) **7:**1390
- *Contents:*
- - History **7:**1391
- - - Opposition to Ḥasidism **7:**1395
- - - Modern Period **7:**1397
- - - Ḥasidic Way of Life **7:**1400
- - Basic Ideas **7:**1403
- - Teachings of Ḥasidism **7:**1407
- - Ḥasidic Literature **7:**1413
- - Interpretations of Ḥasidism **7:**1416
- - Musical Tradition **7:**1421
- Teachings **7:**1403,1407
- - Ahijah the Shilonite **2:**460
- - *Akedah* interpretations **2:**483
- - *aliyah* **9:**293; **9:**297; **9:**514; **15:**1471
- - *am ha-areẓ* in **2:**836
- - Apocalypse in **3:**181
- - *Bet Hillel* and *Bet Shammai* **4:**741
- - Buber, Martin **7:**1490; **4:**1429; **4:**1433
- - *devekut* **5:**1599
- - dialogue with God **3:**974
- - divine forgiveness **6:**1435
- - function of rabbi **13:**1448
- - *gematriot* in **7:**373
- - homiletical literature **8:**955
- - imitation of God **8:**1293
- - joy **10:**320
- - Kabbalah **10:**555
- - *Lamed Vav Ẓaddikim* **10:**1367
- - liturgy **11:**400
- - messianism **11:**1426
- - prayer **13:**983
- - psychology **13:**1343
- - redemption **14:**6
- - repentance **14:**77
- - *shehitah* technique **14:**1343
- - *takkanot* **15:**737
- - theology **15:**1108
- - Torah study **15:**457
- - visions **16:**169
- - woman **16:**628
- - work praised **10:**793
- - Ẓaddikism **7:**1405; **9:**1228; **14:**183
- Leaders
- - Aaron of Chernobyl **15:**1471
- - Aaron Samuel ha-Kohen **2:**23
- - Abraham of Sochaczew **15:**24
- - Aryeh Judah Leib of Polonnoye **3:**667
- - David of Talna **5:**1363
- - Dov Baer of Mezhirech **6:**180
- - Elimelech of Lyzhansk **6:**661ff
- - Ḥanokh of Aleksandrow **7:**1276
- - Ḥayyim Ḥaikel of Amdur **7:**1510
- - Isaac Judah Jehiel Safrin **14:**635
- - Israel of Ruzhin **14:**526
- - Jacob Isaac of Lublin **9:**1228
- - Jacob Isaac of Przysucha (Pshiskhah) **13:**1300
- - Jacob Joseph of Polonnoye **9:**1228
- - Jacob Koppel of Mezhirech **9:**1231
- - Jehiel Michael (Michel) of Zloczow **9:**1314
- - Kozienice, Maggid of **10:**1234
- - Levi Isaac of Berdichev **11:**102
- - Ludomir, Maid of **11:**553
- - Meir ben Aaron Leib of Peremyshlyany **13:**277
- - Menahem Mendel of Peremyshlyany **11:**1309
- - Menahem Mendel of Vitebsk **11:**1310
- - Mordecai Dov of Hornistopol **15:**1472
- - Naḥman of Bratslav **12:**782
- - Naḥman of Kosov **12:**788
- - Naphtali Ropshitser **14:**259
- - Nathan Sternharz **15:**398
- - Samuel Shmelke of Nikolsburg **8:**1002
- - Shneur Zalman of Lyady **14:**1432
- - Simḥah Bunem of Pshiskhah **14:**1570
- - Uri ben Phinehas of Strelisk **15:**438
- Dynasties and Centers **1:**ḥas. table
- - Aleksandrow (Danziger) **2:**560
- - Amshinov **16:**304
- - Apta **3:**224
- - Baranovichi **4:**197
- - Belz **4:**452
- - Berdichev **4:**589ff
- - Chortkov **2:**368; **5:**497
- - David-Gorodok **5:**1361
- - Galicia **16:**1328
- - Gur (Ger) **7:**784
- - Hungary **8:**1092
- - Israel **9:**497ff; **9:**888ff
- - Izbica-Radzyn **9:**1159
- - Jerusalem **9:**1464
- - Karlin **10:**792
- - Koidanovo **10:**1152
- - Kosov **10:**1217
- - Kotsk **10:**1223
- - Kozienice **10:**1234
- - Kuzhmir (Modzhitz; Yabluna) **12:**207
- - Lachowicze **10:**1340
- - Lelov **11:**8
- - Lithuania **11:**362ff
- - Lubaczow **11:**628
- - Lubavich (Ḥabad) **7:**1013; **14:**1432; **14:**982
- - Modzhitz **12:**207
- - Moldavia **14:**398
- - Munkacs **14:**1295
- - Pinsk **13:**541
- - Podolia **13:**668
- - Przedborz **13:**1297
- - Przemysl **12:**1298
- - Przysucha (Pshiskhah) **13:**1300
- - Radoshits **13:**1504
- - Radzymin **13:**1508
- - Ropshits **14:**259
- - Ruzhin **14:**526
- - Rymanow **14:**534
- - Sadagora **7:**1176ff
- - Satmar **15:**909
- - Savran (Bendery) **14:**922
- - Slonim **14:**1671
- - Sochaczew **15:**24
- - Spinka **15:**275
- - Stolin **10:**792; **15:**412
- - Stretyn **15:**438
- - Subcarpathian Ruthenia **15:**470
- - Twersky (Chernobyl) **15:**1471
- - Vilna **16:**143
- - Vizhnitz **16:**199
- - Volhynia **16:**209ff
- - Warka **16:**303
- - Warsaw **16:**337
- - Zanz (Halberstam) **7:**1176
- - Zhidachov **16:**1008; **16:**1009
- - Zhitomir **16:**1012; **16:**968
- Opposition to Ḥasidism **7:**1395,1416
- - Avigdor ben Joseph Ḥayyim **3:**963ff
- - Brody Assembly (1772) **4:**1397
- - David of Makow **5:**1362ff
- - denunciations **8:**1369
- - dress **8:**1062
- - Elijah ben Solomon Zalman **6:**652ff
- - excommunication (Zelva) **16:**981
- - Haskalah **16:**809ff
- - imprisonment **8:**1302
- - *Kol Mevasser* **10:**1165
- - Levin, Menahem Mendel **11:**108
- - Levinsohn, Isaac Baer **11:**116ff
- - Loebel, Israel **11:**440
- - parodies **13:**132
- - Perl, Joseph **13:**291
- - polemics **13:**795
- - Segal, Israel ben Moses **14:**1107
- - *see also:* MITNAGGEDIM
- Musical Tradition **7:**1421
- - attitude to music **5:**487
- - dances **5:**1267
- - folksong **6:**1384
- - Modzhitz **12:**207
- - *niggunim* (melodies) **6:**744
- Miscellaneous
- - Adam Ba'al Shem **2:**247
- - *Admor* (title of ḥasidic rabbi) **2:**293
- - Agudat Israel **2:**423
- - Ashkenazic Hebrew **16:**1641
- - *ba'al shem;* title **4:**6
- - *Beriḥah* and Lubavich **4:**631
- - Chagall, Marc **5:**324
- - contemporary Judaism **10:**393; **10:**396
- - cooking and food **6:**1422ff
- - Dubnow's account **6:**256
- - fiction, Hebrew **6:**1271
- - hagiography **7:**1120
- - history **8:**723ff
- - leadership patterns **7:**1400
- - magic **11:**712
- - preaching **11:**699
- - Russian underground **7:**1402
- - Safed settlement **9:**1059
- - Shabbateanism **14:**1247
- - synagogue **15:**584
- - yeshivot **16:**770
- - Ysande, Torsten, views **16:**866
- *illus:*
- - text
- - Belz (Issachar Dov Roke'aḥ) **4:**452
- - Bojan (Fridman) **7:**1406
- - Gur (Israel Alter) **7:**784
- - Ḥabad
- - - Kefar Ḥabad, celebrations **10:**883
- - - Schneersohn, Menahem Mendel **7:**1401
- - - Shneur Zalman of Lyady **7:**1013
- - - *"Tefillin"* campaign **15:**900
- - Ḥasidim dancing **5:**1269,1270; **7:**1415,1419; **10:**320; **12:**672
- - "Ḥasidim in a *Bet Midrash*" (I. Kaufmann) **7:**1395
- - *ḥerem* imposed by Cracow rabbis

(1786) **5:**1037
- - Israel Ba'al Shem Tov's genealogical table **9:**1051
- - Kefar Ḥasidim **10:**885
- - Medzibezh, Israel Ba'al Shem Tov's *bet midrash* **9:**1053
- - Polish Ḥasid **6:***fcg.* 238
- - Ruzhin dynasty **14:**528
- - Satmar rebbe **14:**908; **15:**909
- - Twersky dynasty **14:**1472
- - Vizhnitz **16:**199
- *mus. notations:* **12:**637; **16:**987
- *see also:* ISRAEL BEN ELIEZER BA'AL SHEM TOV
"Ḥasid Studying" (paint., L. Krestin) **7:**1403
Ha-Sifrut (journ.) **1:**newsp. list
HASKALAH **7:**1433
- *Contents:*
- - Background **7:**1433
- - Linguistic Assimilation **7:**1437
- - Development of Hebrew **7:**1438
- - Education **7:**1439
- - Trends in Ideology **7:**1443
- - Haskalah in Russia **7:**1445
- Scope
- - Austria
- - - Beer, Peter **4:**379
- - - *Toleranzpatent* **3:**893
- - Ereẓ Israel **4:**115
- - Galicia **16:**1326ff
- - - Bolekhov **4:**1185
- - - Brody **4:**1398
- - - Buchner, Ze'ev Wolf **4:**1447
- - - Erter, Isaac **6:**847
- - - Hebrew literature, modern **8:**182
- - - Krochmal, Nachman **10:**1269ff
- - - Schorr, Joshua Heschel **14:**997
- - Germany
- - - Anhalt **3:**2
- - - Avigdor ben Simḥah ha-Levi **3:**964
- - - Berlin, Saul **4:**663
- - - early period **7:**476
- - - Hebrew literature, modern **8:**178
- - - Koenigsberg **10:**1129
- - - Lessing's influence **11:**49
- - - Mendlessohn **10:**393; **11:**1329ff
- - - Schiller's influence **14:**965
- - Italy
- - - Luzzatto's influence **11:**603
- - Lithuania **11:**369
- - - Hurwitz, Judah ben Mordecai ha-Levi **8:**1118
- - - Lebensohn, Abraham Dov **10:**1548ff
- - - Vilna **16:**143ff
- - Poland **13:**732
- - Rumania **4:**200
- - Russia **14:**439ff
- - - Braudes, Reuben Asher **4:**1316
- - - development **7:**1445
- - - Hebrew literature, modern **8:**185
- - - Hurwitz, Chaim **8:**1117
- - - *kazyonny ravvin* **10:**861
- - - *Kol Mevasser* **10:**1165
- - - Levinsohn, Isaac Baer **11:**116ff
- - - Lilienblum, Moses Leib **11:**240ff
- - - Mohilewer, Samuel **12:**217ff
- - - Smolenskin, Perez **15:**7
- - - Volhynia **16:**210
- - - Zhitomir **16:**1012
- - Turkey **2:**310
- Cultural Activity
- - apologetic literature **3:**197
- - Berr, Michel **4:**692
- - children's literature **5:**430
- - drama, Hebrew **6:**195
- - education **6:**423
- - encyclopedias, Hebrew **6:**730ff
- - fiction, Hebrew **6:**1271
- - Fuld, Aaron ben Moses **7:**217
- - *Ha-Meliẓ* **7:**1232
- - Homberg, Naphtali Herz **8:**940
- - Jewish studies **16:**571
- - *Kerem Ḥemed* **10:**912
- - language, Hebrew **16:**1641
- - letters **11:**60
- - literature, modern Hebrew **8:**178
- - *Me'aseff* **11:**1161
- - modern philosophy **13:**452
- - newspapers, Hebrew **12:**1045ff
- - parody **13:**131
- - Perl, Joseph **13:**290
- - prosody **13:**1199,1223ff
- - Weiss, I.H. **16:**414
- - Wessely, Naphtali Herz **16:**461
- - Yiddish literature **16:**799ff
- Opposition to Haskalah
- - Berdyczewski, Micha Josef **4:**593
- - Eliasberg, Mordecai and **6:**615
- - Ḥasidic reaction **7:**1397
- - Ḥasidim-Mitnaggedim controversy **7:**1396
- - Horowitz, Pinḥas ben Ẓevi Hirsch **8:**999
- - Landau, Ezekiel **10:**1390
- - Menaḥem Mendel of Lubavich **14:**1434
- - Ornstein, Jacob Meshullam **12:**1473
- - Orthodoxy **12:**1487
- - Sofer, Moses **15:**78
- Miscellaneous
- - autonomy, judicial **3:**931
- - *ba'alei shem,* attitude to **4:**7
- - communal autonomy **3:**921; **3:**926
- - denunciations **8:**1369
- - economic history **16:**1316
- - Frankists **7:**68
- - *haskamot,* forged **7:**1453
- - *ḥeder,* attitude to **8:**241
- - Ḥibbat Zion **16:**1038ff
- - history **8:**711ff
- - Jerusalem, attitudes to **9:**1564
- - Kabbalah **10:**556
- - Maimonidean controversy **11:**745
- - messianism **11:**1426
- - responsa **14:**91
- - Shakespeare's influence **14:**1262
- - socialism, Jewish **15:**38
- - Volozhin yeshivah **16:**216
- - woman **16:**628
- - *yeshivot* **16:**766; **16:**769
- - Zionism **16:**1158
- *illus:*
- - text
- - *Ha-Shaḥar* (1868) **7:**1367
- *see also:* EMANCIPATION
HASKAMAH (leg. and schol. term) **7:**1452
- censorship **8:**361
- *illus:* text
- *see also:* ASCAMA
HASKELL, ARNOLD LIONEL **7:**1454
HASKIL, CLARA **12:**692
Hasköy (dist., Turk.) **9:**1087; **15:**1462
Ḥāsbayya (loc., Leb.) **10:**1544
Hasmonaea (Zion. students' soc.) **10:**805; **13:**1043; **16:**1134; **16:**1135
HASMONEAN BET DIN **7:**1454
HASMONEANS (Maccabees) **7:**1455
- History
- - altar stones **2:**768
- - farmers and revolt **2:**393
- - Hassideans **7:**1468
- - Hellenism and Maccabees **8:**295
- - *Ḥever ha-Yehudim* **8:**438
- - Holofernes **8:**917
- - Jerusalem **9:**1392ff
- - Modi'in **12:**206
- - population **13:**870
- - Second Temple period **8:**629
- - Tobiads **15:**1178
- - *see also:* HASMONEAN BET DIN
- Dynastic Rule
- - Absalom **2:**176
- - administration **9:**120
- - Agrippa I **2:**415
- - Agrippa II **2:**417
- - Alexander (son of Aristobulus II) **7:**601
- - Alexander (son of Herod) **2:**567
- - Antigonus **3:**65
- - Antigonus II (Mattathias) **3:**65
- - Aristobulus I (Judah) **3:**440
- - Aristobulus II **3:**440
- - Aristobulus III **3:**441
- - Aristobulus (son of Herod) **3:**442
- - Aristobulus (grandson of Herod) **3:**443
- - Berenice (Agrippa's daughter) **4:**601
- - Eleazar the Hasmonean **6:**594
- - genealogy **7:**381
- - high priesthood **8:**473
- - Herod I **8:**376ff
- - Hyrcanus II **8:**1145
- - Jehoiarib, ancestor of **9:**1322
- - Johanan the Hasmonean **10:**155
- - John Hyrcanus **8:**1146
- - Jonathan the Hasmonean **10:**188
- - Judah Maccabee **10:**379
- - Mariamne **11:**989
- - Mattathias ben Simeon **11:**1129
- - Nabateans **12:**740
- - Ptolemy **8:**631
- - Salome Alexandra **14:**691
- - Seleucids, effect on **8:**292
- - Simeon the Hasmonean **14:**1565
- - Yannai, Alexander **16:**714
- Literature
- - Damascus document, date of **5:**1249ff
- - *First Book of Maccabees* **11:**656
- - Josephus **10:**263
- - *Moses, Assumption pf* **12:**411
- - *Scroll of Antiochus* **14:**1045ff
- - *Solomon, Psalms of* **15:**116
- Culture
- - archaeological evidence **3:**327
- - art in Ereẓ Israel **3:**506
- - calendar **16:**1264
- - coinage **5:**716
- - Jerusalem archaeology **9:**1526ff
- - Jews and European culture **6:**967
- - sages **14:**638
- Miscellaneous
- - messianism **11:**1420
- - name "Maccabee" **11:**656
- - tombstones **15:**1221
- - warfare **16:**278
- *geneal. table:* text
- *illus:*
- - text
- - coins **3:**322; **5:**699-701
- - Hezir tomb **15:**1219
- - Jaffa Gate Citadel fortifications **9:**1533
- - Jerusalem city wall **9:**1391
- - Jerusalem during Second Temple period (map) **9:**1395
- - Judah Maccabee **8:**1280; **10:**380,383
- - "Mattathias" (sculp., B. Schatz) **11:**1128
- - Mattathias slaying an idolater **6:**292
- - Zechariah's tomb **9:**1392
- *see also:* ḤANUKKAH
Ha-Soker (period.) **10:**1404; **11:**722
- Blau, Ludwig Lajos **4:**1076
- Loewinger, David Samuel **11:**454; **13:**1036
- statistics **1:**newsp. list
Ha-Solel (journ.) **1:**newsp. list
HA-SOLELIM (kib., Isr.) **7:**1459
- statistics **1:**place list
Ḥason, Aaron ibn **10:**701; **11:**83
Hason, Solomon ben Aaron **10:**1538; **14:**90
Ha-Sport (period.) **1:**newsp. list
- *see also: Sport ba-Olam*
Ha-Sport ha-Le'ummi (period.) **1:**newsp. list
Hassagah, ha- (wk.), *see Sefer ha-Hassagah*
HASSAGAT GEVUL (encroachment) **7:**1460
- *Contents:*
- - Encroachment on Land **7:**1460
- - Widening of the Concept **7:**1461
- - Trespass on Rights **7:**1461
- torts **15:**1272ff
- *see also:* LANDMARKS
Hassagat ha-Hassagah (wk.) **16:**1357
HASSAGOT (rabbinic wks.) **7:**1466
- Abraham ben David of Posquières **2:**136ff
- Naḥmanides **12:**781
Hassam, Hormuzd **16:**1507
Hassan (dey, Alg.) **4:**58
Hassan (crit., Rum.), *see* SANIELEVICI, HENRIC
HASSAN (Sp.-Mor. fam.) **7:**1467
Hassan (name), *see also under* Hasan
Haasan, Abraham, *see* HASSAN, SIR JOSHUA
Hassan, David **7:**1467
Hassan, Jacob of Murviedro **14:**1110
Hassan, Jahuda aben Haçen **7:**1467
HASSAN, SIR JOSHUA (Abraham) **7:**1467
Hassan, Raphael **7:**1467
- *illus:*
- - *Leḥem Oni* **11:**476
Hassan, Salvador **7:**1467
Hassan, Shemayyah **7:**1467
Hassan, Shem-Tob **7:**1467
Hassan, Solomon **7:**1467
ḤASSĀN IBN (Mar) ḤASSĀN **7:**1468
Hasse, J. Gottfried, *see* Haas J. Gottfried
Hassenfeld, Merrill L. **13:**1279
Ḥassid, David Kohn, *see* Kohn Ḥasid, David
HASSID, WILLIAM ZEV **4:**1032; **5:**383
HASSIDEANS (rel. sect, 4/3 cent., Er. Isr.) **7:**1468
- Alcimus **2:**549
- Essenes foreshadowed by **6:**901
- Judah ha-Nasi **9:**252
- Samaritan tradition **14:**730
- Seleucids and Hasmoneans **8:**629; **8:**632
- *see also:* ḤASIDIM; PHARISEES
Ḥassidim ("pietists"), *see* ḤASIDIM
Ḥassidim (rel. sect, 4/3 cent., Er. Isr.), *see* HASSIDEANS
Ḥassidim (rel. mvmt., 12/13 cent., Ger.), *see* ḤASIDEI ASHKENAZ
Ḥassidim (E. Eur. and mod. per.), *see* ḤASIDISM
Ḥassin, David ibn, *see* DAVID BEN AARON IBN ḤASSIN
Hassneh (insurance co., Isr.) **8:**539
Ḥasson, Aaron ibn, *see* Hason, Aaron ibn
Hasson, Solomon ibn **11:**64
Hassophereth, Sons of (bib. figs.) **14:**1042
HAST, MARCUS **7:**1547
Hat, Jewish, *see* BADGE, JEWISH
Ha-Ta'asiyyah (journ.) **1:**newsp. list
Ha'takah (leg. term.) **15:**1183ff
Hataklit (record co., Isr.) **13:**1618

Ha-Tamid, see Burnt offering
Ḥatam Sofer, *see* SOFER, MOSES
Ḥatan Bereshit (tit.), *see* BRIDEGROOMS OF THE LAW
Ha-Tanninim (riv., Isr.) **9**:144
Ḥatan Sofer, *see* EHRENFELD, SAMUEL BEN DAVID ẒEVI
Ḥatan Torah, see BRIDEGROOMS OF THE LAW
Ha-Tarbut ha-Yisraelit (journ.) **1**:newsp. list
Ha-Tashbeẓ (newsp.), *see Tashbeẓ*
HATCHWELL, SOL (Suleika) **7**:1469
Ha-Teḥiyya (soc., Warsaw) **16**:337
Ha-Teḥiyyah (period., U.S.) **14**:1009; **16**:578
Ha-Teḥiyyah (journ., Ger.) **1**:newsp. list
Ha-Tekhna'i be-Yisrael (journ.) **1**:newsp. list
Ha-Tekhna'i ha-Ẓa'ir (journ.) **1**:newsp. list
Ha-Tekhnion (journ.) **1**:newsp. list
HA-TEKUFAH (period.) **7**:1469
- Cahan, Ya'akov **5**:16
- Elisheva's poems **6**:671
- Hebrew press **13**:1047
- statistics **1**:newsp. list
- Tchernichowsky, Saul **15**:880
Ha-Tenu'ah le-Aḥdut ha-Avodah (polit. party, Er. Isr.) **9**:662; **9**:859
Ha-Tenu'ah le-Aḥdut ha-Avodah (journ.), *see Le-Aḥdut ha-Avodah*
Ha-Terumah (bk.) **11**:331
Ha-Te'ufah (journ. **1**:newsp. list)
Ha-Teva ve-ha-Areẓ (journ.) **1**:newsp. list
Hathor (deity, Egy.) **15**:1146
Hatikva (period., Rum.) **14**:399
- Zionism **16**:1134
Ha-Tikvah (qtr., Tel Aviv) **14**:1307
HA-TIKVAH (anthem) **7**:1470
- Imber, Naphtali Herz **8**:1290
- Jerusalem symbol **9**:1590
- *maqām* rendition **11**:938
- *Yigdal* melody **16**:835
Ha-Tikvah (period., It.) **9**:1140; **13**:1037
Ha-Tikvah (period., Nor.) **13**:1048
Ha-Tikvah (journ., U.S.) **1**:newsp. list
Ḥatimah (signature) **2**:230
Ḥatimah Tovah (Heb. greeting) **7**:916
Hatirah (crater, Isr.), *see* Ha-Makhtesh ha-Gadol
Hatirah River (Isr.) **9**:136
Hatlabba (Kurd. custom) **4**:756
Ha-To'eh be-Darkhei ha-Ḥayyim (bk.) **8**:188
Ha-Tor (period., Er. Isr.) **1**:newsp. list; **11**:741
Ha-Tor (period., Hung.) **7**:965
Ha-Torah ve-ha-Medinah (journ.) **1**:newsp. list
Ha-Toren (period.) **12**:1052
- Brainin, Reuben **4**:1292
- Shmarya Levin **11**:110
Hatra'ah, see warning
HATRED **7**:1473
Hattarat hora'ah (jur. authorization) **14**:1144
Hattarat nedarim, see Absolution from vows
Ḥattat, see Sin offering
Hatti, *see* HITTITES
Hattians **8**:787
Hatt-i-Hümayun (declaration, Turk.) **2**:54
Ḥattin (vill., Er. Isr.), *see* KEFAR ḤATTIN
Hatt-i-Sherif (declaration, Turk.) **2**:54
Hattu (Hatti-land; Syr.) **12**:913
Hattusas (anc. city, As. M.) **2**:496; **3**:369; **8**:787; **16**:275, 1497, 1507
Hattush (Shemaiah's son) **5**:1340
Hattush (pr. fam.) **8**:618
Hattusili(s) I (Hittite k.) **8**:788; **16**:1497
Hattusili III (Hittite k.) **8**:789
Ha-Tur ha-Shevi'i (newsp. column) **2**:774
Hatvany, Bertalan **7**:1475
Hatvany, Ferenc **7**:1475
Hatvany, Lajos **7**:1474
Hatvany, Lili **7**:1475
HATVANY-DEUTSCH (fam., Hung.) **7**:1474
- nobility **15**:1166
Hatvany-Deutsch, Antonia **7**:1475
Hatvany-Deutsch, József **7**:1475
Hatvany-Deutsch, Sándor **7**:1474
HAUBENSTOCK-RAMATI, ROMAN **12**:692
Haudebert, Lucien **9**:1344
Haude-und Spenser'sche Zeitung (period., Ger.) **4**:474
Haug, J. F. **4**:873
Hauge, Jens Christian **12**:1225
Haumadatha (Pers. sol., Elephantine) **7**:1222
Ha-Ummah (journs.) **1**:newsp. list
HAUPT, PAUL **7**:1475
- Adler, Cyrus **2**:273
Hauran (Hasm.), *see* ELEAZAR BEN MATTATHIAS
HAURAN (reg., Syr.) **7**:1476
- Druze **9**:927
- geology **9**:215; **9**:216
- Herod's kingdom **8**:635
- physiography **9**:181, 595
- Qaysites **9**:261
Haurina (Assyr. prov.), *see* HAURAN
HAURWITZ, BERNHARD **7**:1477
HAUSDORF, AZRIEL ZELIG **7**:1477
HAUSDORFF, FELIX (Paul Mongré) **7**:1478
Hause, Joseph Moses **15**:506
Hauseman, John, *see* HOUSEMAN, JOHN
HAUSER, EMIL **12**:692
- Conservatoire **12**:673
HAUSER, HENRI **7**:1478
HAUSER, PHILIP MORRIS **7**:1478
Hausieren, see PEDDLING
Hausman, Emanuel **13**:1378
Hausmann, Alexander **16**:1165
Hausmann, B. **15**:338
Hausmann, Ẓevi **15**:1488
HAUSNER, BERNARD **7**:1478
Hausner, Gideon **7**:1479
Haussa (lang.) **14**:1149
Hautecourt, H. Philipponeau de **8**:37
Hava'at ha-Omer (kib. litur.) **10**:960
Havana (city, Cuba) **5**:1148
Havaner Leben-Vida Habanera (newsp.) **5**:1149
HAVAS, GEZA **10**:311
HAVAZZELET (period.) **7**:1479
- Bak, Israel **4**:115
- Ben Yehuda **4**:566
- Frumkin **7**:210
- *Ha-Levanon* **7**:1179
- Jerusalem **9**:1458
Havaẓẓelet ha-Sharon (mosh., Isr.) **1**:place list
Havaẓẓelet ha-Sharon (bk.) **16**:1478
Havazzelet-Mevasseret Yerushalayim (period., Er. Isr.) **13**:1040
HAVDALAH (rit., close of Sabbath) **7**:1481
- *arvit* service **3**:666ff
- *Berakhot* **4**:586
- blessing of children **4**:1088
- folklore **6**:1378
- *Ha-Mavdil* hymn **7**:1224
- *Kiddush* recited with **10**:974
- myrtle **12**:729
- origin **15**:630
- *Pittum Ha-Ketoret* **13**:572
- Prometheus **6**:1378, 1391
- spice blessing **8**:1316
- spice-box **5**:309
- wine **16**:539
- *illus:*
- - goblets, candle holders, and spice boxes **3**:529; **5**:118, 300; **6**:1390; **7**:1260–1261
- *see also:* KIDDUSH; NESHAMAH YETERAH
Havdalah, Solomon **7**:1511
Havdalah de-Rabbi Akiva (wk.) **16**:43
Havemann, C. **8**:37
Havemann, Michael **8**:37
ḤAVER (fam.) **7**:1489
Haver (monthly, Arg.), *see Khaver*
ḤAVER, ḤAVERIM (name of gr., mish. period; tit.) **7**:1489
- *am ha-areẓ* **2**:834ff
- Anau, Phineas Ḥai **2**:935
- *Demai*, duties **5**:1486
- expulsion **13**:1389
- office, Erez Israel **13**:1448
- ritual purity **13**:88
- sages **14**:636ff
- tithing *hazakah* **7**:1522
- yeshivot usage **16**:768
- *see also:* ḤASIDIM; HASSIDEANS; HOLY CONGREGATION IN JERUSALEM
Ḥaver, Ḥayyim **7**:1489
Ḥaver, Isaac (r., Damascus) **7**:1489
Ḥaver, Isaac (r., Lith.) **14**:526
Ḥaver, Isaac Eisik (r., Pol.), *see* WILDMANN, ISAAC EISIK
Ḥaver, Isaac son of Ḥayyim (Damascus) **7**:1489
Ḥaver, Joshua **7**:1489
Ḥaver ba-Sanhedrin ha-Gedolah (tit., Er. Isr.) **13**:1449
Ḥaver Beit ha-Din (tit., Ott. Emp.) **13**:1450
Ḥaverenu (period.) **5**:459
Haverhill (city, Mass.) **11**:1113
Ḥaverim makshivim (kab. gr.) **3**:1008
ḤAVER IR (or *Ḥever Ir*; tal. conc.) **7**:1492
- *see also:* Seven Good Townsmen
Haverstraw (tn., N.Y.) **12**:1127
Ḥaver-Tov, Abraham **13**:1109
Ḥaver-Tov, Jacob **13**:1108
HAVILAH (bib. names) **7**:1493
- Eldad ha-Dani **6**:576
- metals and mining **11**:1429
Ḥavillo, David **4**:100
Havin, Reuben **13**:1025
Havinenu (prayer) **2**:845
Ḥaviv, Avshalom **8**:1469
Ḥaviva, Joseph ibn, *see* ḤABIBA, JOSEPH
ḤAVIV-LUBMAN, AVRAHAM DOV **7**:1494
Havlagah (Haganah policy) **9**:687; **7**:1068; **9**:351
Havlíček-Borovský, Karel **5**:1206
Havre (city, U.S.) **12**:266
HAVRE LE (city, Fr.) **7**:1494
Ḥavurah (membership assoc.), *see* ḤEVRAH, ḤAVURAH
Ḥavurah (term for Pal. amoraim) **7**:1491
Ḥavurah (body of schols., geonic period) **7**:322; **7**:1491
Ḥavurah (cmty. meals) **7**:840
Ḥavurah Kaddisha (cmty. orgn.), *see* ḤEVRA KADDISHA
Ḥavurat Shalom (U.S. gr.) **5**:906
Ḥavvat ha-Shomer (youth center, Isr.) **8**:1246
HAVVOTH-JAIR (loc., Er. Isr.) **7**:1494
- *see also:* JAIR
Ḥavvot Yair (bk.) **4**:48
HAWAII (U.S. state) **7**:1495
Ḥawaja Mussa, *see* SMILANSKY, MOSHE
Ḥawārith (wadi), *see* Wadi Ḥawārith
Hawatmah, Naif **9**:471
Hawizeh (loc., Iraq) **8**:1450
HAWK (ornith.) **7**:1496
- dietary laws **6**:34
Hawk missiles **10**:907; **15**:1666
Hawthorn (bot.) **9**:221 **15**:1118
Hawthorne, Nathaniel **16**:262
Hawzān (vill., Yem.) **11**:849
HÁY, GYULA (Julius) **8**:1085
HAY, JOHN MILTON **7**:1496
Ha-Ya'ar (journ.) **1**:newsp. list
Ha-Yad ha-Ḥazakah (code), *see* MAIMONIDES (*Mishneh Torah*)
Ha-Yahadut (period.) **1**: newsp. list
Ha-Yahalom (journ.) **1**: newsp. list
Haya'idna (name for Jews, Yem.) **7**:1496
Ha-Yam (journ.) **1**: newsp. list
Ha-Yama'i ha-Yisraeli (journ.) **1**: newsp. list
Ha-Yarden (period., Gal.) **15**:338
Ha-Yarden (newsp., Er. Isr.) **9**:1016; **12**:1056; **14**:132
- Netanyahu, Benzion **12**:970
Ha-Yarden (journ., Switz.-U.S.) **1**: newsp. list
Ha-Ya-re-a-h (r.) *see* Hazzan Joseph Raphael ben Hayyim Joseph
Ha-Yare'ah (journs.) **1**:newsp. list
Ha-Yarhon ha-Yisraeli le-Vula'ut (journ.) **1**: newsp. list
Hayatizade, Mustapha **14**:1237
Haycraft, Sir Thomas W. **13**:31
HAYDAN (tn., Yem.) **7**:1496
- migration to Erez Israel **16**:752
Haydani (fam., Yem.) **7**:1497
Hayden, Henri **13**:113
HAYDEN, MELISSA **7**:1497
Haydn, Joseph **15**:1186
Ha-Yedid ("The Friend"), *see* WINGATE, CHARLES ORDE
Ha-Yehudi (Heb. weekly, Cz.) **4**:1311
Ha-Yehudi (Heb. weekly, Eng.) **12**:1047, 1051; **15**:540
Ha-Yehudi (journ., U.S.) **1**: newsp. list
Ha-Yehudi ha-Kadosh (has. r., Pol.), *see* PRZYSUCHA, JACOB ISAAC BEN ASHER
Ha-Yehudi ha-Nizhi (journ.) **1**: newsp. list
Ha-Yekev (journ.) **1**: newsp. list
Hayem, Georges **11**:1198
Hayes, G. B. **9**:767
HAYES, ISAAC ISRAEL **7**:1497
Hayes, Judah **5**:109
HAYES, SAUL **7**:1498
Ha-Yesod (journ.) **1**: newsp. list
Ha-Yishuv (journ.) **1**: newsp. list
Ha-Yishuv he-Hadash (yeshivah) **2**:847; **16**:772
Ha-Yisraeli (journ.) **1**: newsp. list
Haykal, Yusuf **9**:1041
Hayman, Julius **5**:108; **5**:113
Hayman, Louis **15**:303, 308
HAYNT (newsp., Pol.) **7**:1498
- Warsaw press **16**:341
- Yiddish press **13**:1042
- Yinnon, Moshe **16**:836
- Zionism **16**:1132

Haynt (newsp., Urug.) **13:**1041; **16:**15
Ha-Yo'ez (period.) **13:**1043; **14:**398
Ha-Yogev (mosh., Isr.) **4:**731
- statistics **1:** place list
Ha-Yom (newsp., Isr.) **12:**1056; **14:**132
- statistics **1:** newsp. list
Ha-Yom (newsp., Pol.) **2:**478
- statistics **1:** newsp. list
HA-YOM (newsp., Rus.) **7:**1499
- Hebrew press **13:**1045
- Kantor, J. L. **10:**744; **11:**16
- statistics **1:** newsp. list
Ha-Yom (newsp., U.S.) **8:**209
- Goldman, Moses **7:**722ff
- statistics **1:** newsp. list
- Zivion **16:**1186
HAYON, NEHEMIAH HIYYA BEN MOSES **7:**1500
- Aaron ben Isaac **2:**12
- Alfandari, Hayyim **2:**598
- Amsterdam **2:**897
- Ashkenazi, Zevi Hirsch **3:**734
- Ayylon **3:**996ff
- Azubib's ban **3:**1015
- Benjamin Vitale **4:**532
- emissaries **14:**1366
- Ghiron, Johanan **7:**547
- *haskamah* forgery **7:**1453
- Nieto, David **12:**1152
- Shabbateanism **8:**233; 14:1248
- Skoplje **14:**1648
- *zimzum* **10:**593
Ha-Yonah (journ., Ger.) **1:** newsp. list
Ha-Yonah (journ., Rus.) **11:**741; **16:**578
Hayon ben ʿAmar **15:**1438
Ha-Yonim River (Isr.) **9:**151
HAYS (fam.) **7:**1503
Hays, Andrew **12:**284
HAYS, ARTHUR GARFIELD **7:**1503
Hays, Benjamin **7:**1503
HAYS, DANIEL PEIXOTTO **7:**1504
Hays, David **7:**1503
Hays, Isaac (d. 1765, stlr., U.S.) **7:**1503; **11:**939
Hays, Isaac (19th cent., stlr., U.S.) **5:**411
HAYS, ISAAC (physic., U.S.) **7:**1504
- medicine **11:**1198
Hays, Jacob (pion., U.S.) **7:**1503
Hays, Jacob (police of., U.S.) **7:**1503
Hays (Hayes), John Jacob **8:**1255; **8:**1361; **15:**1206
Hays, Joseph **5:**607
Hays, Judah **7:**1503; **11:**1550
Hays, Kaufman **5:**607; **5:**609
Hays, Michael (stlr., U.S.) **7:**1503
Hays, Michael (agr., U.S.) **7:**1503
Hays, Moses Judah **5:**112
Hays, Moses Michael **15:**1288
Hays, Richea, *see* Gratz, Richea
Hays, Solomon **7:**1503
Hayyah (kab. conc., "soul") **10:**611
Hayyat, Jacob **9:**1261
HAYYAT, JUDAH BEN JACOB **7:**1505
- Abulafia **2:**186
- Alcastiel **2:**542
- Kabbalah **10:**540, 541
Hayyat, Reuven, *see* TREBITSCH, ABRAHAM
Hayyei Adam (wk.) **5:**1298
Hayyeinu (monthly) **11:**205
Hayyei Olam (collec.) **1:** newsp. list
Hayyei Olam yeshivah (Jer.) **16:**771
Hayyei Sha'ah (journ.) **1:** newsp. list
Hayyei Yehudah (bk.) **4:**1012; **6:**1269
Hayyim (5th cent. knight, It.) **15:**1165
Hayyim (period.) **10:**919
Hayyim, Abraham ben Judah ibn, *see* IBN HAYYIM, ABRAHAM BEN JUDAH
Hayyim, Isaac Mor **13:**1608
Hayyim, Lipa **16:**923
Hayyim, Soliman (Sulaiman) **10:**919; **15:**906
Hayyim Abraham ben David **14:**1186
HAYYIM ABRAHAM RAPHAEL BEN ASHER **7:**1505
Hayyim Aharon ben David, *see* STRUCK, HERMANN
Hayyim Aryeh ha-Kohen **10:**681
Hayyim Baruch of Ostrava **8:**234
Hayyim Baruch of Skoplje **14:**1648
Hayyim ben Abraham **4:**277
HAYYIM BEN ABRAHAM HA-KOHEN (kab., Syr.) **7:**1506
- Kabbalah **10:**550
Hayyim ben Attar **6:**1382; **9:**1463
HAYYIM BEN BEZALEL **7:**1507
- Isserles, Moses **9:**1084
- Reformation **14:**22
Hayyim ben Bibas **9:**1300
Hayyim ben David (14th cent., copyist) **2:**793
Hayyim ben David ben Hayyim of Corfu (r., Turk.) **5:**1350
HAYYIM BEN HANANEL HA-KOHEN **7:**1508
- Eliezer of Metz **6:**628
Hayyim ben Hayyim the Martyr **4:**1422
Hayyim ben Hirsch of Wilhermsdorf **7:**216; **13:**1108
Hayyim ben Isaac ha-Kohen **9:**28
Hayyim ben Isaac ha-Levi Ashkenazi **8:**1324
Hayyim ben Isaac of Volozhin, *see* VOLOZHINER, HAYYIM BEN ISAAC
HAYYIM (Eliezer) BEN ISAAC "OR ZARU'A" **7:**1508
Hayyim ben Jacob **6:**320
Hayyim ben Jehiel (r., Ger.) **10:**1121
HAYYIM BEN JEHIEL HEFEZ ZAHAV (tal. schol., Ger.) **7:**1509
Hayyim ben Leib **16:**724
Hayyim ben Machir **13:**581
Hayyim ben Menahem Zanzer **9:**1229
Hayyim ben Moses ibn Habib, *see* HABIB, HAYYIM BEN MOSES BEN SHEM TOV
Hayyim ben Moses of Wiener-Neustadt **7:**1509
Hayyim ben Moses Tawil **2:**150
HAYYIM BEN SAMUEL BEN DAVID OF TUDELA **7:**1509
Hayyim (Abraham) ben Samuel Feivush (Phoebus) **6:**1159
Hayyim ben Samuel of Lerida **10:**536
Hayyim ben Shabbetai, *see* HAYYIM (Ben) SHABBETAI
Hayyim ben Solomon (Shab.), *see* MALAKH, HAYYIM BEN SOLOMON
Hayyim ben Solomon ben Baka **2:**41
HAYYIM BEN SOLOMON TYRER OF CZERNOWITZ **7:**1510
- hasidic thought **7:**1405
Hayyim ben Yihya ben Salim Alfityhi, *see* HABSHUSH, HAYYIM
Hayyim Brisker, *see* SOLOVEICHIK, HAYYIM
Hayyim Eleazar Wax of Piotrkow **13:**652
Hayyim fil' Moses of Lincoln, *see* Hagin (Hayyim) of Lincoln
Hayyim Friedlander of Lesko **16:**1004
Hayyim Greenberg Teachers' Seminary (Isr.) **10:**30
HAYYIM HAIKEL BEN SAMUEL OF AMDUR **7:**1510
Hayyim Ha-Kohen (tos.), *see* HAYYIM BEN HANANEL HA-KOHEN
Hayyim ha-Kohen (Prague) **4:**49
Hayyim ha-Kohen of Aleppo (kab.) **10:**552
- Bacharach, Naphtali **4:**50
- commandments **5:**791
Hayyim Hasid, *see* Hasid, Hayyim
Hayyim Heika ha-Levi **9:**1217
Hayyim ibn Vivas **3:**947
Hayyim Israel (trans.) **15:**1327
HAYYIM JUDAH BEN HAYYIM **7:**1511
Hayyim Meshullam ha-Kohen **13:**1384
Hayyim Mordecai ben Joseph **8:**1323
Hayyim of Blois **9:**36
Hayyim of Hameln **7:**629; **11:**225
Hayyim of Itinia, *see* Hager, Hayyim
Hayyim of Lincoln, *see* Hagin of Lincoln
Hayyim of Ostraha (Ostrog) **9:**1231
Hayyim of Vienne **12:**1292
Hayyim of Vilna **9:**293
HAYYIM PALTIEL BEN JACOB ("Tola'at") **7:**1511
HAYYIM (Ben) SHABBETAI (Maharhash) **7:**1512
- Escapa, Joseph ben Saul **6:**859
- Handali, Joshua **7:**1259
- Perahyah, Hasdai **13:**271
- responsa **14:**90
- Sarajevo **14:**871
- Skoplje **14:**1648
Hayyim Zevi (false mess.), *see* ALFANDARI, HAYYIM BEN ISAAC RAPHAEL
Hayyim Zevi of Sighet, *see* Teitelbaum, Hayyim Zevi
Hayyot (name of angels) **15:**1126
- *Sefer Yezirah* **16:**783ff
HAYYOT, MENAHEM MANISH BEN ISAAC **7:**1512
Hayyot, Zevi Hirsch **16:**1348
HAYYUJ, JUDAH (Jahah) BEN DAVID **7:**1513
- Bible exegesis **4:**892
- Dunash ben Labrat **6:**270
- Hebrew grammar **11:**324
- Ibn Janah, Jonah **8:**1182
- Judah ibn Daud **11:**1306
- Judeo-Arabic **10:**415
- linguistics **16:**1354
HAYYUN, ABRAHAM BEN NISSIM **7:**1514
HAYYUN, JOSEPH BEN ABRAHAM **7:**1514
- messianism **11:**1425
Hayyun, Samuel **4:**1270
HAZAEL (k., Aram) **7:**1515
- Ahaziah's war **2:**456
- Elisha **6:**665ff
Ha-Zafon (newsp.) **16:**407
- statistics **1:** newsp. list
HAZAI, SAMU **7:**1515
Hazail (k. of Arab.) **16:**1351
Ha-Ẓa'ir (journ., Isr.) **1:** newsp. list
Ha-Ẓa'ir (journ., Ukr.) **1:** newsp. list
ḤAZAK (salutation) **7:**1516
- *see also:* GREETINGS
Ḥazak, Abraham Isaac Fortis, *see* FORTIS, ABRAHAM ISAAC
Ḥazak, Jacob Raphael Hezekiah ben Abraham Israel, *see* FORTI, JACOB RAPHAEL HEZEKIAH BEN ABRAHAM ISRAEL
ḤAZAKAH (leg. term) **7:**1516
- *Contents:*
- - Proof of Ownership **7:**1516
- - - Immovable Property **7:**1516
- - - Movable Property **7:**1520
- - Legal-Factual Presumption **7:**1521
- - Middle Ages and Early Modern Times **7:**1522
- *arenda* **3:**404
- *Bava Batra* **4:**336
- *dina de-malkhuta dina* **6:**51
- endowments **8:**285
- Jewish Quarter **10:**83
- legal basis **14:**1197
- Ma'arufya **11:**640
- mode of acquisition **2:**218
- nuisance **12:**1246
- residence rights **8:**357
- servitudes **14:**1188
- status in *halakhah* **7:**1158
- Tunisian homes **15:**1442
- *illus:* text
- *see also:* EVIDENCE; LIMITATION OF ACTIONS; OWNERSHIP; PROPERTY
Ḥazak u-varukh (salutation) **7:**914, 1516
Ḥazak ve-emaẓ (salutation) **7:**914
Ḥazal (wk., Urbach) **16:**4
Ḥazan (fam. name), *see also:* Ḥazzan
Hazan, Fernand **13:**1368
ḤAZAN, YA'AKOV **7:**1523
Ḥazar, *see* KHAZARS
Hazar-Asam (loc., Er. Isr.) **16:**723
Hazard (leg. conc.) **3:**988ff
Ha-Zarefati (tos.), *see* BARUCH BEN ISAAC OF WORMS
Hazar-Enan (loc., Cana.) **5:**100
Hazar-Gaddah (tn., Er. Isr.) **7:**1530
Ḥaẓar Kinneret (city, Er. Isr.) **4:**778
Hazar-Shual (tn., Er. Isr.) **7:**1530
Ḥazas (pseud.), *see* SLONIMSKI, ḤAYYIM SELIG
Ḥaẓav (mosh., Isr.) **1:** place list
HAZAZ, ḤAYYIM **7:**1524
- drama, Hebrew **6:**201
- literature, Hebrew **8:**203
Hazazon-Tamar (loc., Er. Isr.), *see* TAMAR
Ḥaẓbani (riv.) **14:**1625; **15:**649
Ha-Ẓefirah (newsp., Pol.-Ger.) **1:** newsp. list
HA-ẒEFIRAH (period., Rus.) **7:**1529
- *Ha-Yom* **7:**1500
- Hebrew journalism **12:**1046
- Slonimski, Ḥayyim Selig **14:**1675
- statistics **1:** newsp. list
- Warsaw **16:**340
- *illus:* text
Ha-Zeman (lit. anth.) **7:**718
Ha-Zeman (*Ru'aḥ ha-Zeman;* period., Pol.) **4:**1316
Ha-Zeman (period., Vilna)
- children's literature **5:**434
- Hebrew journalism **12:**1050; **12:**1051
- Katz, Benzion **10:**822
- press **13:**1045
- statistics **1:** newsp. list
- Tawiow, Israel Ḥayyim **15:**836
- Vilna **16:**147
Ha-Zeman (newsp., Isr.) **1:** newsp. list
Ha-Zeman (journ., Rus.) **1:** newsp. list
- *illus:*
- - masthead (1903) **13:**1046
Ha-Zeman (journ., U.S.) **1:** newsp. list

ḤAẒER, ḤAẒERIM (bib. stlmts.) 7:1530
Ḥaẓerah (crater, Isr.), *see* Ha-Makhtesh ha-Katan
Ḥaẓerim (bib. tn., Er. Isr.) 13:1509
ḤAẒERIM (kib., Isr.) 7:1531
- statistics 1:place list
HAZEROTH (loc., Paran) 7:1531
ḤAẒEVAH (mosh., Isr.) 7:1531
- statistics 1:place list
Ḥaẓevah River (Isr.) 9:136
Ha-Ẓevi (fam.) 15:1488
- *illus:*
- - type face 15:1485
Ha-Ẓevi (newsp.) 9:326; 12:1054; 12:1055
- Ben-Avi 4:470
- Ben-Yehuda, Eliezer 4:567
- *Ḥavaẓẓelet* 7:1480
- statistics 1:place list
- *see also:* Ha-Or
Ha-Zibbul (journ.) 1:newsp. list
Ha-Zifroni, Israel, *see* ZIFRONI, ISRAEL BEN DANIEL
Ha-Zikhronot (wk.), *see Sefer ha-Zikhronot*
Ha-Ẓillum (journ.) 1:newsp. list
Ha-Ẓir (journ.) 1:newsp. list
Ḥazit Dor Benei Midbar (orgn., Lodz ghetto) 11:436
Ḥazit ha-Am (period.)
- Arlosoroff 3:471
- Hebrew journalism 9:1016
- Revisionism 14:132
- statistics 1:newsp. list
Ḥazit ha-Moledet (polit. gr., Er. Isr.) 6:574
Ḥazit ha-Oved (journ.) 1:newsp. list
Ha-Ẓiyyoni ha-Kelali (journ.) 1:newsp. list
Ha-Ẓiyyoni ha-Vatik (journ.) 1:newsp. list
Ha-Ẓiyyonut (journ.) 1:newsp. list
Ḥaziẓah (legal term) 2:82
HAZKARAT NESHAMOT (prayer) 7:1532
- *Ashkavah*, Sephardi 3:712
- Delos, evidence 5:1482
- *Yizkor* 16:842
- *illus:* text
- *see also:* EL MALE RAḤAMIM
Ḥazketto (It. r.), *see* FORTI, BARUCH UZZIEL BEN BARUCH
ḤAZKUNI, ABRAHAM 7:1533
Ḥazkuni, Jacob 7:1533
Hazleton (city, Pa.) 13:230
HA-ẒOFEH (newsp., Pol.) 7:1534
- Hebrew newspapers 12:1047, 1050
- statistics 1:newsp. list
HA-ẒOFEH (newsp., Isr.) 7:1534
- statistics 1:newsp. list
Ha-Ẓofeh (journ., Pol.) 1:newsp. list
Ha-Ẓofeh ba-Areẓ ha-Ḥadashah (period., U.S.) 8:209; 12:1052
- Bernstein, Z. H. 4:690
- statistics 1:newsp. list
Ha-Ẓofeh le-ha-Maggid (section of *Ha-Maggid*) 16:578
Ha-Ẓofeh le-Ḥokhmat Yisrael (journ., Hung.), *see Ha-Soker*
Ha-Ẓofeh le-Veit Yisrael (journ., Eng.) 1:newsp. list
Ha-Ẓofeh le-Veit Yisrael (journ., Pol.) 1:newsp. list
Ha-Ẓofeh me-Ereẓ Hagar (journ., Hung.), *see Ha-Soker*
Ha-Ẓohar, *see* REVISIONISTS, ZIONIST
"Hazomir" (U.S. choral soc.) 5:488
Ḥazon (mosh., Isr.) 1:place list
Ḥazon (journ.) 1:newsp. list
Ḥazon, *Shabbat* (special Sabbath), *see Shabbat Ḥazon*
Ḥazon Ish (tal. schol.), *see* KARELITZ, AVRAHAM YESHAYAHU
HAZOR (city, Er. Isr.) 7:1535
- Ahab's fortifications 2:437
- archaeology 3:306ff
- Baal-Hazor 4:4
- Bible history 8:584 8:578
- Jabin 9:1173
- Mari 11:980
- museum 3:997; 12:553
- pottery inscription 16:660
- proscription of 8:345
- Solomon 15:102ff
- temple 15:946
- Yadin, Yigael 16:695
- *illus:*
- - text
- - archaeological remains 2:386; 5:588, 1166
- - orthostat lion 11:263
ḤAẒOR (ha-Gelilit; tn., Isr.) 7:1539
- population 9:591
- statistics 1:place list
ḤAẒOR ASHDOD (kib., Isr.) 7:1540
- statistics 1:place list
HA-ZORE'A (kib., Isr.) 7:1540
- *illus:* text
HA-ZORE'IM (mosh., Isr.) 7:1541
- statistics 1:place list
Ḥaẓoẓerah (instru.), *see* Trumpet
Hazrak (city, Syr.), *see* HADRACH
Ḥāzrat al-Yahūd (qtr., Jer.) 9:1426
Ḥazut (journ.) 1:newsp. list
Ḥazut Kashah (wk.) 3:257
ḤAZZAN (Ḥazan; fam., Turk.) 7:1541
ḤAZZAN (syn. offic.) 7:1542
- age, minimum 13:1357
- Amsterdam contest 2:905
- choir 5:486
- confession 8:500
- dress 8:1140
- East Ashkenazi *ḥazzanut* 12:651
- *ḥazzan mata* 15:1164
- *maḥzor* 11:731; 11:735ff
- *Mi-Sinai niggunim* 12:151
- musical tradition 12:588
- musicians 12:678ff
- phonographic records 13:1617
- priestly blessing 13:1062
- purity 13:1413
- responsa on 16:1258
- salary 15:848
- *sheli'aḥ ẓibbur* 14:1355
- synagogue 15:583
- *tallit* 15:743
- tax exemption 15:857
- *illus:*
- - text
- - contract (Berdichev, 1861) 12:642
- - Dutch synagogue 12:617
- - *ḥazzan* and choir 5:487; 12:641
- - Kolo synagogue choir 10:1170
- - *Leipzig Maḥzor* 12:601
- - Leoni, Myer 11:30
- - Michael, Jehiel 12:629
- - reading the *Haggadah* in synagogue 7:*fcg.* 1323
- *mus. notations:*
- - Abrass' extension of E-flat 2:173
- - *Addir bi-Melukhah* 2:256
- - *Addir Hu* 2:257
- - *Adon Olam* 2:297
- - *Aleinu le-Shabbe'aḥ* 2:556
- - Algazi's *Avo el Mizbaḥ Elohim* 2:609
- - *Amen* 2:804
- - *Anim Zemirot* 3:22
- - *Avi Avi* 3:955
- - *Avinu Malkenu* 3:973
- - *Avodah* 3:978
- - dance-like melodies 12:631
- - *Eli Ẓiyyon ve-Areha* 6:672
- - *El Male Raḥamim* 6:682
- - Ḥanukkah *Hodu* 12:635
- - *Ḥazzan* and singer setting 12:643
- - *Kol Nidrei* 10:1168
- - Kwartin, two compositions 12:661
- - Mi-Sinai niggunim 12:151
- - ornamentation of single notes 12:589
- - Turkish style 12:623
- *see also:* CANTILLATION; LITURGY; MASORETIC ACCENTS
Hazzan, Abraham (kab., Sp.) 12:782
Hazzan, Abraham (r., Salonika) 11:76
Hazzan, Amram ben Moses 13:577
Ḥazzan, Bekhor Elijah 2:593; 7:1542
Ḥazzan, Ben-Zion 6:20
Ḥazzan, David (Kar.) 7:1189; 14:1360
Ḥazzan, David (print.) 3:727; 7:1541
Ḥazzan, Eliezer 7:1541
Ḥazzan, Elijah Raḥamim 7:1541
Ḥazzan, H. A. 5:434
Ḥazzan, Ḥayyim 7:1541
Ḥazzan, Ḥayyim David 7:1542
Ḥazzan, Ismael 15:1438
Ḥazzan, Israel
- Doenmeh 6:148
- Nathan of Gaza 12:865
- Shabbateanism 14:1241
ḤAZZAN, ISRAEL MOSES BEN ELIEZER 7:1552
Ḥazzan, Jacob (emis.) 7:1541
Ḥazzan, Jacob ben Judah, *see* JACOB BEN JUDAH OF LONDON
Ḥazzan, Joseph ben Elijah 7:1541; 9:1163
- *illus:*
- - *Ein Yosef* (1860) 9:1164
Ḥazzan, Joseph ben Nathan 13:585
Ḥazzan, Joseph Raphael ben Ḥayyim Joseph 3:58; 7:1541; 8:234
- *illus:*
- - *Sefer Ḥikrei Lev* 13:1109
Ḥazzan, Judah 7:1541
Ḥazzan, Moses Israel 2:593
Ḥazzan, Samuel ben Kalonymus 14:1416
Ḥazzan, Simḥah 6:47
Ḥazzan, Solomon 2:593; 7:1542
HE (Heb. let.) 8:1
HEAD, COVERING OF THE 8:1
- *Contents:*
- - Men 8:1
- - Women 8:6
- dress 6:222
- *ḥukkat ha-goi* 8:1062
- married woman 10:383
- Naḥman ben Isaac 12:772
- Ottoman Empire 16:1542
- Samaritans 14:741
- Solomon Luria 14:89
- *illus:*
- - *kaveze* 6:217
- - *kupke* 6:*fcg.* 238
- - scullcap, embroidered 5:1377; Pl. 11 6-DRESS
- - *shterntikhl* 6:*fcg.* 238
- - *shtreimel* 15:*fcg.* 491
- - women's headdresses 6:236–237
Head, Francis Bond 11:1343
Headdresses, Decorative, *see* CROWNS, DECORATIVE HEADDRESSES AND WREATHS
"Head of a Horse" (sculp., G. Ehrlich) 6:513
"Head of a Young Jew" (sculp., N. Altman) 2:778
Head Priest, *see* HIGH PRIEST
Healing 5:1134
- *see also:* MEDICINE
"Healing of the Blind" (etch., Rembrandt) 7:176
Health Insurance, Israel, *see* Kuppat Ḥolim
HEALTH SERVICES IN ISRAEL 9:982
- Arab, general survey 9:1023ff
- labor social services 9:868
- TOZ 15:1291
- WHO's assistance 15:1564
- *illus:*
- - Augusta Victoria Hospital 9:1475
- - Bikkur Ḥolim Hospital (Jer.) 9:983, 993
- - Central Jezreel Valley Hospital, Afulah 4:83
- - first Hadassah nurses' unit 7:1042
- - Hadassah Hospital (Jer.) 7:1043, 1044; 9:990
- - Hadassah Medical Center (Jer.) 3:350; 7:1043
- - Hadassah nurses 15:667; 16:721
- - Histadrut rest home, Nazareth 9:866
- - hygiene class in Arab school 9:1030
- - Israel stamps 9:844-845
- - Kuppat Ḥolim clinic (Jer.) 9:867,987
- - Malben institution 11:821
- - mobile medical unit (Gaza Strip) 9:987
- - Muslim community mortality and birth rates, 1927-39 (table) 9:701
- - Nathan Straus Health Center 15:429
- - Omna baby home, Haifa 12:211
- - Rothschild Hospital (Jer.) 9:1464
- - Sha'arei Zedek Hospital (Jer.) 9:991
- - Sinai, Israel doctor examining Bedouin child 9:1044
- - Tira medical center 9:990
- - welfare clinic (Rishon le-Zion) 9:987
- - WIZO's Jerusalem Baby Home 16:595
- - Zikhron Ya'akov rest home 13:1612
Heaps, A. A. 5:112
- Manitoba 11:879
- Winnipeg 16:551
Hearst, William Randolph 10:307
HEART 8:7
- responsa on transplants 14:94
- *Sefer Asaf ha-Rofe* 3:674
- sickness 14:1502
Heart, Lung, and Kidney diseases 11:1200
Heartfield, John 13:484
He-Arukh (wk., Ibn Dannan), *see Sefer He-Arukh*
He-Arukh (wk.), *see* NATHAN BEN JEHIEL OF ROME
He-Atid (journ., Ger.) 8:1119
- statistics 1:newsp. list
He-Atid (journ., pub., Isr.) 1:newsp. list
He-Atid (newsp., Pol.) 12:1049
- statistics 1:newsp. list
He-Avar (journ., Isr.) 1:newsp. list
He-Avar (journ., Rus.) 13:1047
- Hebrew newspapers 12:1051
- statistics 1:newsp. list
"Heaven" (name for God) 7:682
Heaven and Hell 14:100
Heavenly Academy, *see* ACADEMY ON HIGH
Heavenly Tablets 3:183; 3:185
Heavens, the Seven 4:273
Heave offering 14:604; 15:1023
Hebbel, Friedrich 10:459; 10:461
- Herod in drama 8:385
Hebelli, Servatius 5:34
Hebenstreit, J. C. 8:37
HEBER (bib. fig., s. of Beriah) 8:9

Heber (bib. fig.), *see* JETHRO
HEBER THE KENITE (bib. fig.) **8:**9
- Kenites **10:**907
- Sisera **14:**1622
Hebraeische Bibliographie (period.) **16:**578
Hebraeische Melodien (poems) **8:**274
Hebraeorum gens (papal bull) **4:**1496
Hebraeorum Supremus (tit.), *see* PRAEFECTUS JUDAEORUM
Hebraeus, Leo, *see* ABRABANEL, JUDAH
Hebrah Gemilut Hasadim (orgn., N.Y.) **12:**1072
Hebrah Gemilut Hesed (soc., N.Y.), *see* Hebrew Mutual Benefit Society
Hebrah Hesed Vaemet (orgn., N.Y.) **12:**1072
Hebraica, *see* SOCIEDAD HEBRAICA ARGENTINA
HEBRAISTS, CHRISTIAN **8:**9
- *Contents:*
- - Motivation **8:**9
- - Facilities for Scholarship **8:**11
- - Occasion **8:**11
- - 12th Century **8:**11
- - Rise of Mendicant Orders **8:**13
- - Jewish Scientific Writings **8:**15
- - Kabbalah, Italy, and Renaissance **8:**15
- - Reformation and Age of Printing **8:**16
- - Post-Reformation Catholic Hebraism **8:**17
- - Protestant Countries **8:**17
- - Nineteenth Century **8:**18
- - Tables **8:**21f
- Protestant universities **13:**1248
- *illus:*
- - text
- - Wagenseil's *Tela Ignea Satanea* **16:**239
- *see also:* LINGUISTIC LITERATURE, HEBREW; ORIENTALISTS
Hebreo, Dioquintio, *see* Rodriguez, Abrabao
Hebreo, León, *see* ABRABANEL, JUDAH
Hebrew **(period., U.S.) 13:**1052
Hebrew (term for J.) **10:**23; **12:**1289
- Yonathan Ratosh **13:**1574
Hebrew and Chaldaic Lexicon (bk.) **16:**37
Hebrew Authors Association, *see* WRITERS ASSOCIATION IN ISRAEL
Hebrew Benevolent Society (N.Y.) **5:**350; **12:**1072
HEBREW BOOK TITLES **8:**70
- *Contents:*
- - Bible **8:**71
- - Talmudic Era **8:**72
- - Middle Ages **8:**73
- - Modern Times **8:**77
- *illus:* text
- *see also:* BOOKS; PRINTING, HEBREW
Hebrew Christians (apos.) **13:**1252
Hebrew Committee for National Liberation **8:**1469
- U.S. Zionism **16:**1144
Hebrew Drama, *see* DRAMA, HEBREW
Hebrew Education (Isr.) **9:**929
Hebrew Education Society (U.S.) **5:**349
Hebrew Free Loan Society (N.Y.) **12:**1098
HEBREW GRAMMAR **8:**77
- *Contents:*
- - Phonology **8:**77
- - - Introduction **8:**77
- - - Phonology and Morphophonology **8:**80
- - Morphology **8:**102
- - - Introduction **8:**103
- - - Noun Formation **8:**108
- - - Verb Formation **8:**124
- - Syntax **8:**140
- - - Influence of Foreign Works **8:**140
- - - Parts of Speech **8:**141
- - - Sentence Types **8:**142
- - - Parts of the Sentence **8:**145
- - - Dependency within the Sentence **8:**162
- - - Links Beyond the Sentence **8:**169
- Abu al-Faraj **2:**178
- Almoli, Solomon **2:**664
- Archivolti, Samuel **3:**397
- Ben-Asher, Aaron **4:**467
- Ḥayyuj, Judah **7:**1513
- Ibn Janāḥ, Jonah **8:**1181ff
- Ibn Saruq (10th cent.) **11:**1305
- Isserles' responsum **14:**89
- Jewish literature **11:**323ff
- Judeo-Arabic literature **10:**414
- linguistics **16:**1352
- Monis, Judah **12:**257
- Rashi **13:**1562
- Saadiah Gaon **14:**552ff
- *Sefer ha-Shorashim* **2:**158
- Spain **15:**242
- Spinoza **15:**278
- Syntax **14:**140
- Yehudi ben Sheshet **16:**732
- *illus:*
- - *Binyan Shelomo* (1708) **7:**1259
- - *Cervera Bible* grammatical compendium **5:**313
- - *Compendium grammaticae ebraeo-chaldaicae* (1765) **8:**12
- - *Dickdook Leshon Gnebreet* (1735) **12:**257
- - Hebrew and Aramaic conjugations (tab.) **3:**263
- - *Maḥberet ha-Tigan* **16:***fcg.* 743
- - *Mikneh Avram* (1523) **4:**141
- - *Oraḥ Selulah le-Dikduk Sefat Ever* (1883) **4:**198
- - *Rudimenta Hebraica* (1520) **4:**1168
- - *Sefer Mikhlol* **4:**960; **5:***fcg.* 971; **10:**1002
- - *Si'aḥ Yiẓḥak* (1627) **9:**28
- - *Ta'amei Torah* (1822) **4:**216
- *see also:* HEBREW LANGUAGE; PRONUNCIATIONS OF HEBREW
Hebrew Institute (N.Y.), *see* Educational Alliance
Hebrew Intelligencer (period.) **13:**1031
Hebrew Journal (newsp.) **5:**113
HEBREW LANGUAGE **16:**1560
- *Contents:*
- - Pre-Biblical **16:**1560
- - - Nature of the Evidence **16:**1560
- - - Sources **16:**1561
- - - Phonology **16:**1562
- - - Morphology **16:**1566
- - Biblical **16:**1568
- - - The Names **16:**1569
- - - Ancient Evidence **16:**1569
- - - The Masoretic Text **16:**1570
- - - Consonants **16:**1572
- - - Vowels **16:**1573
- - - Stress **16:**1574
- - - Pronouns **16:**1575
- - - Tense System **16:**1576
- - - Verb Patterns **16:**1577
- - - Weak Verbs **16:**1579
- - - Substantives **16:**1581
- - - Adjectives **16:**1582
- - - Numerals **16:**1582
- - - Prepositions **16:**1582
- - - Clause Formation **16:**1583
- - - Vocabulary **16:**1583
- - Dead Sea Scrolls **16:**1583
- - - Discovery **16:**1583
- - - Main Elements of the Language **16:**1584
- - - Sources **16:**1585
- - - Language of the DSS **16:**1585
- - Mishnaic **16:**1590
- - - Types **16:**1591
- - - Geographical Provenance **16:**1591
- - - The Problem of Mishnaic Hebrew **16:**1592
- - - Problem of the Sources **16:**1593
- - - - Spelling **16:**1595
- - - - Phonetics **16:**1595
- - - - Morphology **16:**1596
- - - - Dialects **16:**1606
- - - - Palestinian Amoraim **16:**1607
- - - - Babylonian Amoraim **16:**1607
- - Medieval **16:**1608
- - - Introduction **16:**1608
- - - Early Piyyut **16:**1609
- - - Saadiah Gaon **16:**1612
- - - Secular Poetry **16:**1616
- - - Influence of Arabic **16:**1621
- - - The Components of Arab-Influenced Hebrew **16:**1625
- - - Italy **16:**1633
- - - The Karaites **16:**1634
- - - Provence and France **16:**1635
- - - Ashkenaz **16:**1636
- - Modern Period **16:**1642
- - - Period of Revival (1881–1918) **16:**1642
- - - The End of the Revival Period **16:**1644
- - - Linguistics Problems **16:**1645
- General
- - Austrian *Toleranzpatent* **3:**892
- - Cairo *genizah* **16:**1339
- - folklore **6:**1403
- - greetings and congratulations **7:**912
- - international trade **16:**1281
- - Italian pronunciation **9:**1142
- - Jewish law **12:**144
- - Jewish philosophy **13:**428ff
- - Kabbalah **16:**783ff
- - liturgy **11:**402
- - names **12:**803ff
- - Reformation **11:**585; **14:**19
- - Reform Judaism **14:**23
- - Samaritans **14:**752
- - Sephardi pronunciation **14:**1170
- - U.S.S.R. **11:**14; **14:**463
- Biblical Period
- - alphabetic script **2:**681
- - *hapax legomena* **7:**1318
- - Lachish ostraca **10:**1335
- - Pentateuch **13:**252
- - vocal commandments **15:**171
- Second Temple and After
- - Dead Sea scrolls **5:**1404
- - Hellenistic period **8:**293
- - history **8:**760ff
- - Judah ha-Nasi **10:**370
- - Mishnah **9:**253
- Revival
- - Agudat Israel **2:**422
- - Alkalai, Judah **2:**639
- - autonomism **3:**920
- - Ben-Avi **4:**470
- - Ben-Gurion, David **4:**505
- - Ben-Yehuda, Eliezer **4:**566ff
- - Haskalah **7:**1438ff
- - Hebrew Language Committee **2:**206
- - Hebrew schools **9:**327ff
- - Ivrit be-Ivrit **4:**393
- - language conflict **8:**752
- - Levinsohn, Isaac **11:**117
- - Mandate for Palestine **11:**862
- - radio broadcasts **15:**931
- - Sadan, Dov **14:**619ff
- - Satmar rebbe **15:**909
- - Society for the Promotion of Culture among Russian Jews **15:**59
- - Technion conflict **13:**137; **15:**890
- - U.S. Jewry **16:**1147
- - Wizen's researches **16:**592
- - Yellin, David **16:**737
- - Zionist forerunners **16:**1033
- In Israel
- - aim of Teachers' Association **15:**888
- - cultural life **9:**998
- - education **9:**929ff
- - population **9:**477
- - teaching **15:**888
- Languages
- - Arabic **3:**237ff
- - Aramaic **3:**263
- - Greek **8:**296
- - Ladino **10:**1345,1346
- - Mari West-Semitic dialect **11:**981
- - Neo-Aramaic **12:**951
- - related dialects **13:**473
- - Semitic languages **14:**1149
- - Yiddish **16:**790ff; **16:**799
- Literature
- - encyclopedias **6:**730
- - Hebrew literature, modern **8:**176
- - Hebrew newspapers **12:**1045ff
- - Jewish letters **11:**55; **11:**57
- - Jewish literature **11:**323ff
- - Koran **10:**1199
- - medieval translations **13:**443; **15:**1320
- - poetry **13:**671ff
- - U.S. literature **15:**1569
- *illus:*
- - Berit Ivrit Olamit, Third World Congress **4:**1382
- - Ereẓ Israel, Hebrew speaking population, 1914-1966 (table) **9:**475
- - Hebrew Book Month exhibition, Buenos Aires **4:**1464
- - Moscow, Hebrew teacher's advertisement (1970) **14:**504
- - *Moznei Leshon ha-Kodesh* (1546) **8:**1165
- - pronunciation (charts) **13:**1129,1139-1142
- - Russia, publications (1950's) **14:**489
- - Slutsk association **14:**1682
- - *Tappuḥei Zahav* (1618) **6:**162
- - Technion, protest against non-Hebrew teaching **9:**331, 1000
- - Yemen, pronunciations (map) **13:**1124
- *see also:* ALPHABET, HEBREW; HEBREW GRAMMAR; LINGUISTIC LITERATURE, HEBREW; PRINTING, HEBREW; PRONUNCIATIONS OF HEBREW; PROSODY, HEBREW
Hebrew Language Academy, *see* ACADEMY OF THE HEBREW LANGUAGE
Hebrew Language Committee **2:**205
Hebrew Leader (period.) **12:**1074
- Bondi, Jonas **4:**1203
- press **13:**1050
Hebrew linguistics, *see* LINGUISTIC LITERATURE, HEBREW
HEBREW LITERATURE, MODERN **8:**175
- *Contents:*
- - Definition and Scope **8:**176
- - Beginnings **8:**177
- - Periodization **8:**178
- - European Period **8:**178

- - - Haskalah (1781-1881) 8:178
- - - Modern Period (1881-1917) 8:188
- - Palestinian Period 8:197
- - - Ottoman Period (1905-1917) 8:197
- - - Mandate Period (1917-1948) 8:199
- - State of Israel Period 8:203
- - United States 8:208
- - - 1654-1870 8:208
- - - 1870-1918 8:209
- - - 1918-1970 8:211
- General
- - Canaanites' influence 5:102
- - cultural life 9:1001
- - David 5:1333
- - *Ha-Shilo'ah* 7:1369
- - Haskalah 7:1433
- - Haskalah in Russia 7:1445
- - *Mishlei Sindbad* 14:1608
- - *Moznayim* 12:495
- - Odessa 12:1324ff
- - Shakespeare 14:1262
- - Writers' Association in Israel 16:652ff
- - Yiddish literature 16:799; 16:809ff
- Types
- - allegory 2:641
- - children's literature 5:429ff
- - ethical literature 6:931
- - hagiography 7:1120
- - ḥasidic literature 7:1413
- - homiletic literature 8:957
- Personalities
- - Agnon, Shmuel Yosef 2:367
- - Ben-Yehuda, Eliezer 4:566
- - Ben-Zion, S. 4:575
- - Berdyczewski, Micha 4:592ff
- - Bialik 4:795
- - Fichmann, Jacob 6:1258
- - Gottlober, Abraham 7:828
- - Jabotinsky's contribution 9:1185
- - Klausner, Joseph 10:1093
- - Kurzweil, Baruch 10:1302
- - Lebensohn, Abraham 10:1549
- - Lichtenfeld, Gabriel 11:209
- - Luzzatto, Moses 11:603
- - Mapu's contribution 11:932
- - Mendele Mokher Seforim 11:1317
- - Peretz, Isaac Leib 13:279
- - Shimoni's technique 14:1406
- *illus:*
- - Writers' Association 16:653
- *see also:* CRITICISM, HEBREW LITERARY; FABLE; FICTION, HEBREW; HEBREW BOOK TITLES; HEBREW LANGUAGE; LITERATURE, JEWISH; POETRY; PROSODY, HEBREW

Hebrew Manuscripts, *see* MANUSCRIPTS, HEBREW
Hebrew Melodies (wk.) 4:1549
Hebrew Mutual Benefit Society (N.Y.) 12:1072
Hebrew National (newsp.) 13:1031
Hebrew National Orphan Home (N.Y.) 12:1098
Hebrew Newspapers, *see* NEWSPAPERS, HEBREW
Hebrew Observer (newsp., Eng.) 13:1031
- Benisch, Abraham 4:521

Hebrew Observer (U.S. newsp.) 5:608
Hebrew Observer (U.S. period.) 6:358
- press 13:1052

Hebrew Opera Company (S.A.) 15:1074
Hebrew Oriental Opera Company (S.A.) 15:1074
Hebrew Orphan Asylum (N.Y.) 12:1072; 12:1092
Hebrew Parody and Satire, *see* PARODY, HEBREW
Hebrew poetry, *see* POETRY
Hebrew prosody, *see* PROSODY, HEBREW
Hebrew Publishing Company (U.S.) 13:1376
Hebrew Review and Magazine of Rabbinical Literature (Eng.) 13:1031
Hebrews
- Bible history 8:574
- Eber 6:345
- Ḥabiru 7:1034
- Hyksos 8:1142
- Semites 14:1148
- *see also:* JEW

Hebrews, Land of 9:111
Hebrew script 14:1073
- *illus:*
- - comparative alphabets 2:683
- - cursive, 13th cent. (Eng.) 2:23
- - Gezer Calendar 2:386,679,684; 7:537
- - *Mikneh Avram* (1523) 4:141
- - Royal Steward inscription, Siloam 2:679; 6:819
- - script types 2:679-742
- *see also:* ALPHABET, HEBREW

Hebrew Sheltering and Guardian Society (U.S.) 5:350; 12:1092
Hebrew Sheltering and Immigrant Aid society, *see* UNITED HIAS SERVICE
Hebrew slaves, *see* SLAVERY
Hebrew Socialists Society (Lond.) 11:220
Hebrew Song Festival (Isr.) 8:1345
Hebrew Standard (newsp.) 13:1025
Hebrew Teachers' Association (Isr.) 9:327
- Hebrew pronunciation 16:1645

HEBREW TEACHERS COLLEGE (U.S.) 8:215
- *illus:* text

Hebrew Teachers' Seminary (Jer.) 16:737
Hebrew Theater of Palestine (Tel-Aviv) 15:1061
HEBREW THEOLOGICAL COLLEGE (U.S.) 8:216
- *illus:* text

Hebrew Theological College Museum (U.S.) 12:544
HEBREW UNION COLLEGE-JEWISH INSTITUTE OF RELIGION (U.S.) 8:216
- Glueck, Nelson 7:627
- history chart 8:766-767
- incunabula 8:1322
- libraries 11:192
- rabbinical seminaries 13:1465
- Reform Judaism 10:396
- Wise, Isaac Mayer 16:565
- Wise, Stephen Samuel 16:567
- *illus:*
- - text
- - a class 6:416
- - Jerusalem building 3:354

Hebrew Union College Annual (period.) 8:218
Hebrew Union College Biblical and Archaeological School (Jer.) 8:217; 9:1495
Hebrew Union College Monthly (period.) 8:219
Hebrew Union College School of Education and Sacred Music (U.S.) 8:217
Hebrew Union College synagogue (Isr.) 15:620
Hebrew Union Veterans Organization, *see* JEWISH WAR VETERANS OF THE UNITED STATES OF AMERICA
Hebrew University Bible Project 4:840
Hebrew University-Hadassah Medical Center, *see* Hadassah-Hebrew University Medical Center
HEBREW UNIVERSITY OF JERUSALEM 8:219
- adult education 9:964
- Arab terrorist attack 14:1638
- Assaf, Simḥa 3:757
- Brodetsky, Selig 4:1393
- higher education 9:952; 9:957
- Magnes, Judah 11:716
- Mount Scopus 12:484
- Nordau Institute 6:515
- science and research 9:966ff
- Sephardi cultural project 14:1176
- Terra Sancta 9:1494
- Thirteenth Zionist Congress 16:1172
- universities 15:1678
- Zionist commission 16:1163
- *illus:*
- - text
- - Aḥad Ha-Am's letter to Weizmann 2:445
- - Churchill, Winston, speaking on Mt. Scopus 9:1474
- - Givat Ram campus 3:351; 9:955
- - library, reading room 11:197
- - Mount Scopus campus 9:956
- - National Library, Mt. Scopus 3:349
- - "Opening of the Hebrew University of Jerusalem" (paint., Pilichowski) 13:519
- - Oppenheimer, J. Robert 12:1430
- - Philippine botany student 9:442
- - Schuster, Sir Arthur 14:1012
- - students attending lecture 9:958
- - students using an electron microscope 9:970
- - synagogue 13:1575
- - Terra Sancta College 9:1487
- - Wise Auditorium 3:354

Hebrew University synagogue 15:620
Hebrew Writers' Association, *see* WRITERS' ASSOCIATION IN ISRAEL
Hebrew Writers League (orgn.), *see* Aguddat Soferim Ivrim
Hebron (bib. fig.) 10:1135
HEBRON (city, Isr.) 8:226
- *Contents:*
- - Biblical Period 8:226
- - Post-Biblical Period 8:227
- - Arab Conquest 8:228
- - Crusader Rule 8:229
- - Mamluk Rule 8:229
- - Ottoman Rule 8:230
- - 1917-1948 8:235
- - After 1948 8:235
- Algazi, Yom Tov and Jacob 2:611
- Arab massacre 9:343,462
- as seal motif 14:1081
- Azulai, Abraham 3:1017
- Cairo *genizah* 16:1340
- emissaries 14:1359ff
- Epstein, Moses 6:835
- Eshkol and Mamre 2:950
- Ḥabad Ḥasidim 9:514; 14:1434
- holy places 8:921
- human geography 9:587ff
- Jewish religious life 9:890ff
- Judah territory 8:579
- Machpelah 11:670
- Mamluk provincial organization 9:277
- Mamre 11:670
- mountains 9:140
- oak of Abraham 12:1293
- Ottoman period 9:283ff
- proscription by Israel 8:345
- Roman military base 9:240; 9:248
- Six-Day War 14:1635
- special Purim 13:1398
- temple 13:1084
- tribal center 15:1383
- Ze'evi, Israel 3:1016
- *illus:*
- - Arab glassblowers 7:614
- - Arab riots, 1929 9:454
- - Cave of Machpelah mosque 8:923
- - letter of appointment of emissary 8:728
- - letter of recommendation for emissary (1811) 9:288
- - letter to Moses Montefiore (1886) 4:147
- - Machpelah, cave of 11:670
- - pilgrims setting out for Mecca 9:918
- - Sephardi community seal 9:888
- *see also:* ḤALUKKAH

Hebron Gate (Jer.), *see* Jaffa Gate
Hebron River (Judea), *see* Naḥal Ḥevron
Hebron Yeshivah (Isr.) 14:883
- *see also:* SLOBODKA YESHIVA

HECATAEUS OF ABDERA 8:236
- God 7:652
- Hellenistic-Jewish literature 8:304
- Jews, description of 7:888
- Moses 12:390
- priests 13:1086
- pseudo-Hecataeus 13:870

Hechal Shlomo (Jer.), *see* Heikhal Shelomo
Hechingen (tn., Ger.) 8:816
Hechinger, Fred M. 6:465
Hechinger, John 16:356
HECHLER, WILLIAM HENRY 8:237
- Zionism 16:1154

Hecht (fam., U.S.) 5:56
HECHT, BEN 8:239
- U.S. literature 15:1572

Hecht, George 13:1361
Hecht, Hermann 8:240
Hecht, I. A., *see* Candrea, I. A.
HECHT, JACOB 8:240
Hecht, Ladislav 15:314
Hecht, Reuben (Rudolf) 8:240
- numismatic collection 12:1272

HECHT, SELIG 8:240
Hecht, Sigmund 11:499
Hecht, Yosef 7:1065ff
Hechter, Josef, *see* SEBASTIAN, MIHAIL
HECKSCHER, ELI FILIP 8:240
Heckscher, Ephraim 2:780; 13:1106
Hed Arẓi (record co., Isr.) 13:1618
Heddernheim (cmty., W. Ger.) 12:841; 15:1481
HEDEGÅRD, OSKAR DAVID LEONARD 8:241
ḤEDER (school) 8:241
- Ben-Zion, S. 4:575
- education 6:409ff
- learning style 11:1103
- Levinsohn's criticism 11:117
- *illus:*
- - "Chaider" (drg., Epstein) 12:1090
- - Poland 13:741
- - Tunis, table of accents for Pentateuch 11:1103
- - Yemenite children, Jerusalem 9:897,942
- - *Yevsektsiya* Vitebsk trial 16:780

"Ḥeder" (paint., E. Brandon) 6:390
Ḥeder Metukkan (J. school) 8:241
- education 6:424ff

Hed ha-Am (pub.) 1: newsp. list
Hed ha-Defus (journ.) 1: newsp. list
Hed ha-Gan (period.) 1: newsp. list; 15:889
Hed ha-Ḥinukh (weekly, Isr.)

1:newsp. list; 15:889
Hed ha-Ḥinnukh (period., It.) 13:1037
Hed ha-Karmel (newsp.) 1:newsp. list
Hed ha-Kevuẓah (journ.) 1:newsp. list
Hed ha-Mizraḥ (period.) 1:newsp. list
Hed ha-Moreh (period.) 1:newsp. list
Hed ha-Sport (journ.) 1:newsp. list
Hed ha-Zeman (pub.), *see Ha-Zeman*
Hed ha-Ẓiyyoni ha-Vatik (pub.), *see ha-Ẓiyyoni ha-Vatik*
Hedim (journ.) 1:newsp. list
Hedim li-She'elot ha-Hevrah ha-Kibbutzit (journ.) 1:newsp. list
Hedin, Sven Anders 14:931
- Jerusalem 9:1577
Hedjaz (reg., Arab.), *see* HEJAZ
Hed Lita (journ.) 1:newsp. list; 16:833
Hedmann, C. 8:37
Ḥedvata (paytan), *see* HADUTA BEN ABRAHAM
Hed Yerushalayim (journ.) 1:newsp. list
Heemstede (vill., Neth.) 7:1008
Heeser, J. 8:37
HEFER, ḤAYIM 8:241
ḤEFER PLAIN (Isr.) 8:241
- human geography 9:572ff
- *illus:*
- - Jewish settlement 9:521
- - sand dunes 8:130
Hefetz, Moses, *see* Gentili, Moses ben Gershom
Ḥefez (It. fam.), *see* GENTILI
Ḥefez, Eliezer, *see* Gentili, Eliezer
ḤEFEẒ BEN YAẒLI'AḤ 8:242
- Cairo *genizah* 16:1336
- enumeration of *mitzvot* 5:783
- Judeo-Arabic literature 10:412
Ḥefez Zahav, *see* ḤAYYIM BEN JEHIEL ḤEFEẒ ZAHAV
HEFKER (ownerless property) 8:243
- acquisition 2:216
Hefker bet din hefker (leg. conc.) 3:214; 15:717
- *see also:* CONFISCATION, EXPROPRIATION, FORFEITURE
HEFTER, ALFRED (Hidalgo) 10:311
- Rumania 14:399
Heftman, Joseph H. 7:1036; 7:1530
ḤEFẒI BAH (kib., Isr.) 8:245
- statistics 1:place list
Hegedüs, Sándor 15:1156
Hegeh (newsp.) 5:1316
- cultural life 9:1017
- Hebrew newspapers 12:1057
- statistics 1:newsp. list.
HEGEL, GEORG WILHELM FRIEDRICH 8:245
- absolute religion 3:659
- Christian Kabbalah 10:646
- Commandments, reasons for 5:789
- Jewish philosophy 13:455
- Krochmal, Nachman 10:1269
- modern Jewish theology 15:1108
- Rosenzweig 13:461
Hegel und der Staat (bk.) 14:300ff
HEGENHEIM (tn., Fr.) 8:247
Heger, Col 4:885
Heger, Josef 4:885
Hegesippus (wk.) 10:263
Hegmon parnas, see EPISCOPUS JUDAEORUM
Hegyeshalom (tn., Hung.) 8:1104
Hegyon ha-Nefesh ha-Aẓuvah (wk.) 2:133
- homiletical literature 8:953
- philosophy 13:436
He-Hadar (journ.) 1:newsp. list
He-Ḥakham ha-Shalem (tit.) 13:1451
HE-ḤALUTZ (youth mvmt.) 8:247
- *Contents:*
- - Origin of the Movement 8:247
- - Russia 8:248
- - Poland 8:251
- - Lithuania 8:252
- - Latvia 8:253
- - Rumania 8:253
- - Central Europe 8:253
- - United States 8:253
- - Summary 8:254
- *aliyah* 9:340,519ff; 15:51
- Almog, Yehudah 2:661
- Barash, Ephraim 4:203
- Ben-Gurion 4:506; 4:507
- Dobkin, Eliyahu 6:143
- Germany 7:493
- Gilead, Zerubavel 7:572
- *hakhsharah* 11:436
- Ḥazan, Ya'akov 7:1524
- Hebrew newspapers 12:1052
- Holland 16:1120
- illegal immigration 8:1249
- Iraq 8:1453
- labor in Ereẓ Israel 9:854ff
- Luz, Kadish 11:593
- Podolia 13:669
- *shaḥariyah* 4:197
- Yevsektsiya 16:780
- youth movements 9:976
- *illus:*
- - farm near Kiev 15:1517
- - Grodno training farm 13:747
- - Tel Ḥai farm, Crimea 14:469
- - Zhmerinka branch 16:1013
HE-ḤALUTZ (period., C. Eur.) 8:255
- Galicia 16:1330
- Hebrew newspapers 12:1048
- Schorr, Joshua Heschel 14:997
- statistics 1:newsp. list
- *illus:* text
He-Ḥalutz (period., Rus.) 13:1047
He-Ḥalutz ha-Mizrachi (pion. orgn.) 9:520
He-Ḥalutz ha-Ẓa'ir (pub.) 1:newsp. list
He-Ḥasid (kab.), *see* ISAAC THE BLIND
He-Ḥasid (tos.), *see* JUDAH BEN ISAAC
HE-ḤAVER (orgn.) 8:255
- Dobkin, Eliyahu 6:143
He-Haver (news.) 5:434, 457
- newspapers 12:1051
- statistics 1:newsp. list
He-Ḥaver, Josiah ben Aaron, *see* JOSIAH BEN AARON HE-ḤAVER
He-Ḥazit (pub.) 1:newsp. list
Heiberg, Johan Ludvig 15:1084
- Scandinavian literature 14:927
HEIBERG, JOHANNE LUISE 15:1084
Heiberg, Peter Andreas 14:926
HEICHELHEIM, FRITZ MORITZ 8:256
Heida, Samuel ben Moses 10:552
Heidegger, J. H. 8:37
- Zurich 16:1242
HEIDELBERG (city, Ger.) 8:256
- Palatinate 13:21
- *illus:* text
Heidelberg, Israel of, *see* Israel of Heidelberg
Heidelberg, University of 15:1677
HEIDELBERGER, MICHAEL 8:257
- immunochemistry 11:1200
Heide-Lemberger, Abraham 13:977
Heidenberg, Johann, *see* TRITHEMIUS, JOHANNES
Heidenfeld, Wolfgang 5:407
HEIDENHAIN, RUDOLF 8:258
Heidenheim, M. 14:749
HEIDENHEIM, WOLF (Benjamin Ze'ev) 8:258
- angels 2:972
- masorah 16:1478
- prayer books 13:988
- typography 15:1487
- *illus:*
- - text
- - *Maḥzor Minhag Ashkenazi* 15:1485
Heidenreutergasse synagogue (Ger.) 15:618
HEIDINGSFELD (tn., Ger.) 8:259
- *illus:* text
Heifer, broken-necked, *see* EGLAH ARUFAH
Heifer, Red, *see* RED HEIFER
Heifer's Gangway (Temple mt.) 15:964
HEIFETZ, JASCHA 8:260
- *illus:* text
Heifitz, Yosif 12:456
Heigerlich, Moses 9:1081
Heightstown (N.J.) 8:254
Heigmans, S.E. 13:707
HEIJERMANS, HERMAN 8:261
- Dutch literature 6:320
- theater 15:1057
Heikhal (holy ark) 3:450
Ḥeikhal (Temple chamber) 15:948
Heikhal ha-Ivri (newsp.) 1:newsp. list
Heikhal ha-Tarbut, *see* Mann Auditorium
Heikhalot (kab. wk.) 10:498; 10:500ff
- angelic song 15:144
- Apocalypse 3:180
- Italian Jewish scholars 2:21
- magic 11:711ff
- visions 16:168
- Zohar 16:1195
Heikhalot Rabbati (wk.) 12:580
- Kabbalah 10:500ff
- Ten Martyrs 15:1007
- *see also:* MERKABAH MYSTICISM
Heikhalot Zutrati (wk.) 10:500
- *see also:* MERKABAH MYSTICISM
Heikhal Shelomo (Jer.) 9:1495
- library 11:195
- museum 12:552
- Wolfson, Isaac 16:619
- *illus:*
- - seat of Chief Rabbinate 9:1488
Heikhal YHWH, see Bet YHWH
HEILBORN, ERNST 8:262
HEILBRON, SIR IAN MORRIS 8:262
HEILBRON, ROSE 8:263
Heilbroner, Louis 15:300
HEILBRONN (city, Ger.) 8:263
- Talheim 15:740
- *illus:*
- - text
- - *Kristallnacht* 10:1265
Heilbronn, Anna 8:37
HEILBRONN, JACOB BEN ELHANAN 8:264
- translation 14:1670
HEILBRONN, JOSEPH BEN DAVID OF ESCHWEGE 8:265
- Worms, Asher 16:648
Heilbut, Abraham 11:1165
HEILBUT, ELEAZAR LAZI BEN JOSEPH BEN LAZI 8:265
Heilbut, Joseph ben Wolf 8:265
Heilbut, Moses 8:265
Ḥeil ha-Avir (journ.) 1:newsp. list
Ḥeil ha-Yam (journ.), *see Ma'arekhot Yam*
Heiligenbeil (concen. camp) 15:464
Ḥeil Nashim (women's army, Isr.), *see Ḥen*
Heilperin (fam. name), *see also:* Galper(i)n; Halperin: Halpern; Halprin; Heilpern; Heilprin; Helpern
Heilperin, Angelo 15:1350
HEILPERIN, FALK 8:265
Heilperin, Isaac Aizik ben Eliezer Lipman 15:1476
Heilperin, Jacob ben Elhanan 14:875
Heilperin, Joel ben Isaac Eisik 13:540
HEILPERIN, MICHAEL ANGELO 8:266
Heilpern (fam. name), *see also:* Galper(i)n; Halperin; Halpern; Halprin; Heilperin; Heilprin; Helpern
Heilpern, Edel 6:363
Heilpern, Moses Ashkenazi 6:363
HEILPERN (Raphael), YOM TOV LIPMAN BEN ISRAEL 8:266
- *illus:*
- - *Oneg Yom Tov* (1880) 8:267
Heilprin (fam. name), *see also:* Galper(i)n; Halperin; Halpern; Halprin; Heilperin; Heilpern; Helpern
HEILPRIN (fam., U.S.) 8:267
Heilprin, Abraham ben Ḥayyim, *see* ABRAHAM BEN ḤAYYIM
Heilprin, Elijah Joel 11:824
Heilprin, Jacob 2:233
HEILPRIN, JEHIEL BEN SOLOMON 8:268
- history chart 8:766-767
Heilprin, Louis 8:267
Heilprin, Michael 8:267
HEILPRIN, PHINEHAS MENAHEM 8:268
HEILPRIN, SAMUEL HELMANN BEN ISRAEL 8:269
Heilprin, Uri Shraga Phoebus 8:269
HEILPRUN, ELIEZER LEIZER BEN MORDECAI 8:269
Heiman, Isaac 8:1361
Heimann, Abraham 11:413
HEIMANN, MORITZ 8:269
Heimstaette (homestead) 4:307
HEIMWEHR (orgn., Aus.) 8:270
Heine (fam.) 5:1010
Heine, Amalie 8:271
Heine, Betty 8:271; 12:633
HEINE, HEINRICH 8:270
- *Contents:*
- - Life and Career 8:271
- - Poet in Exile 8:272
- - Heine the Jew 8:273
- - The Legacy 8:274
- Ben-Zion's Hebrew translation 4:575
- Boerne, Ludwig 4:1167
- *Der Rabbi von Bacharach* 4:45
- family descent 7:365
- German literature 7:441*f*
- history chart 8:766-67
- Judah Halevi 10:365
- Kulturverein 16:109
- *Magen David* 11:696
- Moses 12:405
- stamps 15:336
- Temple mourned 15:984
- *Two Grenadiers* parodied 13:133
- Weill, Alexandre 16:397
- Zunz, Leopold 16:1237
- *illus:*
- - text
- - autograph 3:915
- - portrait 8:709
- - Rabbi of Bacharach (wdct., J. Budko) 4:45
- - stamp 15:334
Heine, Isaak 11:285
Heine, Peira, *see* Heine, Betty
Heine, Samson 8:271
HEINE, SOLOMON 8:275
- *illus:* text
Heine, Therese 8:271

HEINE, THOMAS THEODOR 8:276
Heine-Geldern, Robert 3:39
HEINE-HEIMOWITZ, MORRIS 15:1084
Heineman, David E. 5:1569
Heineman, Emil S. 4:1541
HEINEMANN, FRITZ 8:276
Heinemann, Isaac, *see* HEINEMANN, YIZḤAK
HEINEMANN, JEREMIAH 8:277
HEINEMANN, JOSEPH 1:31
Heinemann, Wolf 12:1130
- Dunedin Zionist Society 6:273
HEINEMANN, YIZḤAK 8:277
Heinmann, Carl 7:819; 15:547
Heinrich, Pincas 16:1165
Heinsius, Dan (Heinzs) 8:37
- Hellenism and Jew 8:291
Heirut (Zion. gr.) 15:652
Heisenberg, Werner Carl 4:1099
Heisinovitch, Abba Shaul, *see* AḤIMEIR, ABBA
Heisler, Kalman 8:1434
Heit, Murray 12:1522
HEJAZ (reg., Arab.) 8:278
- Arabia 3:233ff
Hejaz Railway (Damascus-Mecca) 9:307ff
HEKDESH (consecrated property) 8:279
- *Contents:*
- - Consecration for Temple Needs 8:279
- - After Destruction of Temple 8:281
- - In State of Israel 8:286
- altar 2:764ff
- another's property 14:678
- bailment laws 14:1456
- begging 4:391
- Commandments, the 613 5:763,774
- communal amenities 2:806
- exempt from overreaching 12:1392,1393
- *ḥerem* 8:345ff
- impurity degrees 13:1407
- legal person 10:1568
- lien cancellation 11:230
- *Me'ilah*, tractate 11:1238
- *takkanot ha-kahal* 15:728
- tax-exempt 15:850
- trusteeship 3:218
- wills 16:524
- *illus:*
- - Barcelona, Hebrew inscription 4:211
- - profane use of a sacrifice 11:1238
- *see also:* CHARITY; ḤEVRAH, ḤAVURAH; POVERTY; PUBLIC AUTHORITY; SACRILEGE
Hekdesh (hostel) 8:1033ff
Hekhal, *see Heikhal*
Hekhim (r., Ger.), *see* HOECHHEIMER, MOSES BEN ḤAYYIM COHEN
HEKHSHER (licence) 8:287
- *illus:*
- - Mannheim seal 14:1077
Ḥekim Ja'qub (physic.) 2:310
Hekkesh (hermeneutical rule) 8:368
Ḥekmat, Shamsi 8:1440
Ḥel (place in Temple area) 2:200
- *illus:* 15:960
Hel (spice), *see Amomum*
Ḥelbo (amora) 8:287
- Avira 3:975
- Berechiah 4:596
Helbronner, Jacques 15:1535
Helcias Alexas (sol.) 2:595
- Silas 14:1532
HELD, ADOLPH 8:287
HELD, ANNA 15:1085
- Ziegfeld, Florenz 16:1018
Held, L. J. 10:795
Held, M. 16:1508
Heldai (bib. fig.) 16:955
- Temple 15:980
Heldai the Netophathite of Othniel (bib. fig.) 12:1521
Heldman, Julie 15:315
Helek (bib. fig.) 11:851
Ḥelek ha-Dikduk (bk.) 16:1478
Helen, Elhanan 10:663; 16:240
Helen, John 8:36
HELENA (1st cent. C.E., q., Adiabene) 8:288
- conversion of 2:924; 10:1296
- Talmud 12:905
- Temple 15:980
- Tomb of the Kings 9:1532
- *illus:* text
- *see also:* ADIABENE
Helena (Byz. q.) 8:922
- churches in Ereẓ Israel 9:255
- Ibn Shaprut 16:1339
- Jerusalem visit 9:1406
Helena (city, Mont.) 12:266
Helena Rubinstein Pavilion (Tel-Aviv) 12:552; 14:376
Helen of Troy (leg. fig.) 11:248
Heler, Mendel 15:1214
Ḥelev (part of offering) 5:1159
- dietary regulations 6:39
ḤELEẒ (oil site, mosh., Isr.) 8:289
- Beror Ḥayil oilfield 4:692
- oil explorations 9:393; 9:793
- statistics 1:place list
- *illus:*
- - oil well 9:380
Helfand, Ḥayyim Yankel, *see* LITWAK, A.
Helfeld, David 16:1555
HELFMAN, HESSIA MEYEROVNA 8:289
Helic (fam., Gal.), *see* HALICZ
Helic, Lukas 8:1136
Helicon (Hellen. apos.) 8:301
Helicz (fam., Gal.), *see* HALICZ
HELIODORUS (2nd cent. B.C.E., gov. offic.) 8:290
- Temple 15:958
Heliogabalus (Rom. emp.) 2:222
HELIOPOLIS (city, Egy.) 8:290
- Beth-Shemesh 4:774
- Onias 12:1404
- Per Atum (Pithom) 13:567
Heliopolis (tn., Leb.), *see* Baalbek
Helios (deity) 15:568ff
- Hammath synagogue 7:1243
- *illus:*
- - mosaic floor 15:574
Héliot of Vesoul 16:115; 16:1288
Heliotrope (bot.) 13:619
Helitz Brothers, *see* HALICZ (fam.)
Helkath (city, Er. Isr.) 3:701
Ḥelkat ha-Sadeh (bk.) 5:1587
Ḥelkat Yoav (comment.) 16:402
Helkias (2nd cent. B.C.E., gen.), *see* ANANIAS AND HELKIAS
Ḥelko shel Binyamin (bk.) 5:228
Hell 7:357
- Abraham and punishment 2:165
- Abrahamic legend 2:116
- Dante 5:1296
- *gilgul* 7:575ff
- Kabbalah 10:587
- Moses de Leon 10:603
- *Tofteh Arukh* 16:909
- *see also:* GARDEN OF EDEN; NETHERWORLD
Hellen, Elhanan ben Abraham, *see* Helen, Elhanan
HELLENISM 8:290
- *Contents:*
- - Introduction 8:290
- - Hellenism and Jews 8:295
- - Spiritual Resistance 8:301
- administration of Ereẓ Israel 9:119
- Alexandrian Jews 2:590
- allegorical exegesis 4:896
- Antiochus IV 3:74
- apologetics 3:189
- archaeological evidence 3:327
- architecture 13:522
- art in Ereẓ Israel 3:506
- assimilation 3:771
- Christianity 5:510
- circumcision 5:568
- Decapolis 5:1449
- diaspora 6:8
- dress 6:215
- Egypt 6:485ff
- Elisha ben Avuyah 6:669
- Ereẓ Israel (Second Temple period) 9:1292
- European culture and Jews 6:967
- Hadrian 9:246
- Hebrew illuminated mss. 8:1258
- Herod I 8:379ff
- Homer 8:944
- immortality in Judaism 10:389
- Ishmael ben Elisha 6:587
- Jerusalem 9:1389
- Jewish architecture 3:357
- Jewish folk narrative 6:1377
- Jewish identity 10:54
- Jewish philosophy 13:424
- Jewish symbolism 15:568
- Kabbalah 10:495
- *kiddush ha-Shem* 10:981
- *Letter of Aristeas* 3:439
- Menelaus 11:1351ff
- music, Jewish 12:566
- Philo 13:411
- Phoenicians 13:474; 13:478
- Platonism 13:628
- polygamy 12:259
- *Second Book of Maccabees* 11:658
- Septuagint 4:851
- sports 15:291
- Temple 15:958
- *illus:*
- - Ashkelon, architectural remains 3:716-717
- - Bet She'arim sarcophagus 15:568
- - Greek mythology subjects, Ereẓ Israel antiquities 3:513,518; 4:770; 12:1530
- - Mareshah, painting 11:953
- *see also:* GREEK AND LATIN LANGUAGES, RABBINICAL KNOWLEDGE OF; GYMNASIUM; HELLENISTIC JEWISH LITERATURE; HISTORY (Ereẓ Israel-Second Temple)
HELLENISTIC JEWISH LITERATURE 8:303
- Alexander Polyhistor 2:583
- Bible translations 11:312ff
- biblical anthropomorphisms 3:55
- Jewish literature 8:298ff; 11:311
- Josephus Flavius 10:258
- Moses 12:388ff
- *see also:* GREEK LITERATURE, ANCIENT
Heller (fam., Cz.) 13:1399
HELLER (fam., U.S.) 8:304
Heller, Aaron 7:1
Heller, Abraham 8:312
- Jerusalem Talmud 15:778
Heller, Anna, *see* Rosenthal, Anna
HELLER, ARYEH LEIB BEN JOSEPH HA-KOHEN OF STRY 8:306
- rabbinical authority 3:909
HELLER, BERNÁT 8:307
- Scheiber, Alexander 14:951
HELLER, BUNIM 8:307
Heller, David 8:306
HELLER, ḤAYYIM 8:308
Heller, Henry 11:1551
HELLER, HERMANN 8:308
Heller, Hirsch 8:306
Heller, Isidor 16:124
Heller, James Gutheim 5:563; 8:305
- *illus:* text
HELLER, JEHIEL BEN AARON 8:309
HELLER, JOSEPH 15:1577; 15:1581
Heller, Joseph Dov 8:306
HELLER, JOSEPH ELIJAH 8:309
HELLER, JOSHUA BEN AARON 8:309
HELLER, JUDAH 8:309
Heller, Levi 8:312
Heller, Ludvík 13:346
Heller, Maximilian 8:304
Heller, Moses 8:312
Heller, Moses ha-Levi 7:1
Heller, Otto 5:803
Heller, Samuel (17th cent.schol.) 8:312
Heller, Samuel (19th cent. r., Pol.) 13:1298
HELLER, SELIGMANN 8:310
HELLER, STEPHEN 8:310
HELLER, THEODOR 8:310
HELLER, YOM TOV LIPMANN BEN NATHAN HA-LEVI 8:311
- Bassevi of Treuenberg 4:317
- codification of law 5:653
- history chart 8:766-67
- Ibn Ezra 15:520
- Mishnah commentary 11:333
HELLER, ẒEVI HIRSCH 8:314
Hellerau Circle (lit. gr.) 2:286
Heller of Erfurt 15:1128
HELLINGER, MARK 10:311
Hellman (fam., U.S.) 5:56; 14:834
Hellman, Herman Wolf 8:315
Hellman, Irving 8:315
HELLMAN, ISAIAS WOLF 8:314
- banker 11:499; 11:501
HELLMAN, JACOB 8:315
- newspaper editor 14:175
HELLMAN, LILLIAN FLORENCE 8:315
Hellman, Marco 8:315
Hellman, Meyer 12:1373; 12:911
Hellman, Yehuda 5:871
- COJO 16:637
Hellmann, L. 8:36
Hellmuth, Isaac 11:482
Hellwitz, L. 15:75
Helm, Sir Knox 6:770
Helman, A. 8:36
Helman, Robert 13:117
Helman(n), Samuel 4:1390; 11:888
Helmets (mil. garb) 16:266
Helmond, M. 12:480
Helmont, Franciscus Mercurius van 10:1117
- Christian Kabbalah 10:646
Helmont, J. Baptist van 8:36
Helmstedt (tn., Ger.) 4:1421
Heln, Elhanan 16:804
Helner, Samuel 8:36
Héloïse (Eloise; nun) 2:60; 8:31
Helpern (fam. name), *see also:* Galper(i)n; Halperin; Halpern; Halprin; Heilperin; Heilpern; Heilprin
Helpern, Irma, *see* Helpern, Yermiyahu
HELPERN, MICHAEL 8:316
HELPERN, MILTON 8:317
Helpern, Yermiyahu 8:317
Helphand (Parvus), Alexander 15:1404
HELSINGFORS PROGRAM (Zion. ideol.) 8:318
- Bruck, Grigori 4:1413
- Goldstein, Alexander 7:744
- history chart 8:766-67
- Idelson, Abraham 8:1226
- Tschlenow, Jehiel 15:1415
- Zionism in Poland 16:1130
- Zionist program 16:1137
- *illus:*

- - members **16:**1137
Heltai, Gáspár **4:**882
- Christian Hebraists **8:**36
HELTAI, JENŐ **8:**319
Helvicus, Christophorus **8:**36
Helwig (Helvicus; Hebr.) **8:**36
HEMAN (bib. fig.) **8:**319
- Korah **10:**1191
- Psalms, Book of **13:**1318
Heman the Ezrahite (bib. fig.) **8:**320
Heman, Sons of (Bib.), *see* Sons of Heman
HEMAR, MARIAN **8:**320
Ḥemar River (Isr.) **9:**141
Hematology **11:**1199
Ḥemdah Genuzah (collec.) **1:**newsp. list
Ḥemdat Shelomo, see LIPSCHITZ, SOLOMON ZALMAN
ḤEMDAT YAMIM (bk.) **8:**320
- kabbalistic customs **10:**642
- Shabbateanism **14:**1251
Ḥemed(mosh., Isr.) **1:**place list
Hemerobaptists (sect) **14:**1087
- ablution **2:**82
- *see also:* Morning Bathers
Hemings, William **6:**778
- *illus:*
- - *The Jewes Tragedy* (1662) **6:**772
Hemistichs (poetic verses) **12:**572
HEMLOCK (plant) **8:**322
- plant list **13:**619
Hemolytic anemia (disease) **14:**1501
Hemophilia (disease) **11:**1184
HEMP (fibrous plant) **8:**323
- plant list **13:**619
- textiles **15:**1037
Hempel, Ernst Wilhelm **8:**36
Hemsi, A. **2:**608
Hen (zool.) **4:**1017; **6:**34
Ḥen (women's army, Isr.) **9:**692
- *illus:*
- - Meir, Golda, inspecting guard of honor **9:**695
Ḥ-e-n (abbrev.), *see Ḥokhmah Nistarah*
Ḥen, Abraham ibn **16:**936
Ḥen, Ḥayyim David Ẓevi **5:**391
Ḥen, Isaac Moses ben **16:**136
Hen, Józef **13:**803
Ḥen, Menahem Mendel **12:**1131
Ḥen, Nira **12:**670
Ḥen, Perez **5:**391
Ḥen, Shealtiel ben Solomon, *see* GRACIAN, SHEALTIEL BEN SOLOMON
Ḥen, Zerahiah ben Isaac ben Shealtiel, *see* GRACIAN, ZERAHIAH BEN ISAAC BEN SHEALTIEL
Hen, Zerahiah ben Shealtiel **11:**1189
Hena, Jacob **7:**1257
Hencry, Louis **12:**1021
Hendel, Helena, *see* HENDEL, NEHAMA
HENDEL, JUDITH **8:**323
HENDEL, NEHAMA **12:**693
- Moscow **12:**368
Henderson (city, Ky.) **10:**909
Henderson, Arthur **4:**1138
Hendersonville (city, N. C.) **12:**1220
Hendler, David **3:**612
Hendrick, Burton J. **15:**1651
HENDRICKS (fam., U.S.) **8:**323
- merchants **15:**1305
Hendricks, Edgar **8:**324
Hendricks, Harmon **8:**323
- metals and mining **11:**1439
- New York City **12:**1070
Hendricks, Henry **8:**323
Hendricks, Henry Harmon **8:**323
Hendricks, Henry S. **8:**324
Hendricks, Joshua **8:**323
Hendricks, Lilian, *see* Henry, Lilian
Hendricks, Montague **8:**323
Hendricks, Uriah (met.) **8:**323
Hendricks, Uriah (bsmn.) **8:**323
Henegouwen (Belg.), *see* Hainaut
Henessy, J. B. **9:**1531,1536
Hengel, M. **8:**291
HENGSTENBERG, ERNST WILHELM **8:**324
Henig, Sir Mark **10:**1589
Henigsman, Oscar **10:**1171
Henikh of Olesko **4:**453
Henikstein, Adam Albert, *see* Hoenig, Adam Albert
HENKIN, JOSEPH ELIJAH **8:**324
- rabbi **12:**1119
Henkin, Louis **8:**325
HENLE, ELKAN **8:**325
Henle, Friedrich Gustav, *see* HENLE, JACOB
HENLE, JACOB **8:**325
Henle, Jacob Buttenwies (en) **8:**325
HENLE, MORITZ **8:**325
HENNA (plant dye) **8:**326
- plant list **13:**619
- *illus:*
- - Yemenite wedding **11:**1046
- *see also:* COSMETICS
Henner, Artur **16:**724
Henoch, Edward **11:**1197
Henoch, Sol **8:**1361
HENOCHSBERG, EDGAR SAMUEL **8:**327
Henri de Valois (k., Fr.), *see* Henry III
HENRIQUES (Anglo-J. fam.) **8:**327
- Jamaica **9:**1274
Henriques (fam., Swed.) **15:**547
Henriques, Abraham Quixano **8:**327
Henriques, Sir Basil Lucas Quixano **8:**328
Henriques, Carlos **5:**463
Henriques, Cyril Quixano **8:**327,328
Henriques, Daniel Cohen, *see* Alvares, Duarte Henriques
Henriques, David **14:**1663
Henriques, David Quixano **8:**327
Henriques, Fernando Mendes **8:**1356
Henriques, Fini **5:**1537
Henriques, Gabriel **8:**1399
Henriques, Henry Straus Quixano **8:**327
Henriques, Isaac Nunes **10:**1381
Henriques, Isabel (Sp.), *see* ENRÍQUEZ, ISABEL
Henriques, Jacob **4:**172
Henriques, Jacob Cohen **12:**1063
Henriques, Jacob Quixano **8:**327
Henriques, Manuel **8:**1395
Henriques, Manuel Dias, *see* Aboab, Mattathias
Henriques, Moses **8:**327
Henriques, Nunes (fam., mer.) **15:**1303
Henriques, Robert David Quixano **8:**328
Henriques, Lady Rosa Louise **8:**328
Henriques, Rudolph Donald Cohen **8:**329
Henriques, Samuel Philip Cohen **8:**329
Henriques, Vernon Stanley **8:**329
Henriques de Castro (fam., Amst.), *see* CASTRO (fam.)
Henriquez (fam., U.S.) **14:**833
Henriquez, Philipe, *see* Senior, Jacob
Henríquez Basurto, Diego, *see* ENRÍQUEZ BASURTO, DIEGO
Henriquez Cutinho (fam., Curaçao) **5:**1012
Henry II (k., Cast.) **4:**1513
- Spain **15:**234
Henry II (k., Fr.) **4:**1244
Henry II (emp., Ger.) **6:**90
Henry III (k., Cast.) **15:**1204
Henry III (k., Eng.) **11:**470
- *Domus Conversorum* **6:**165
- Elias le Eveske **6:**618
- Hereford Jews **8:**344
- Jewish badge **4:**64
- Jewish community **6:**749
- Jewish Parliament **15:**838
- status of Jews **8:**677
- tax assessment **8:**1365
Henry III (k., Fr.) **3:**732
Henry IV (k., Cast.) **2:**606
Henry IV (k., Eng.) **15:**1356
HENRY IV (Ger., emp.) **8:**329
- autonomy, judicial **3:**929
- Crusades **5:**1137
- forced conversion victims **3:**170
- Speyer Jews' privilege **16:**1288
- Worms **16:**644
Henry VI (emp., Ger.) **8:**662
Henry VII (Holy Rom. emp.) **14:**247
- *illus:*
- - granting charter of privileges **7:**465
Henry VIII (k., Eng.) **7:**1187
- divorce issue **7:**1187; **11:**895
- Song of Songs **15:**151
HENRY, EMMA **6:**783; **6:**788
Henry, H.A. **14:**834
Henry, Hubert Joseph **6:**225
HENRY, JACOB (pub. fig.) **8:**329
- anti-Semitism **15:**1648
Henry, Jacob (stlr., Tex.) **15:**1034
HENRY, JULES **8:**330
Henry, Lilian **8:**324
HENRY, MICHAEL **6:**788; **10:**40
- journalist **10:**311
Henry, Walter **14:**158
Henry of Cossey **8:**13
Henry of Hessen **8:**36
Henry of Langenstein, *see* Henry of Hessen
Henry of Trastamara (k., Cast.), *see* Henry II
Henry VIII Psalter (bk.) **13:**1327
HENSCHEL, AUGUST **3:**602
Henschel, Elias **11:**1173
HENSCHEL, FRIEDRICH **3:**602
HENSCHEL, SIR GEORGE (Isidor Georg) **12:**693
HENSCHEL, MORITZ (art.) **3:**602
Henschel, Moritz (cmty. ldr.) **4:**648; **14:**51
HENSCHEL, WILHELM **3:**602
Henschel Brothers (art.) **3:**540; **3:**603
Henschke, Margarete **6:**464
Henschke, Ulrike **6:**464
HENSEL, KURT (math.) **11:**1125
Hensel, Kurt (dipl.) **11:**1326
Hensel, Sebastian **11:**1326
Henshel, Harry B. **8:**330
HENSHEL, HARRY D. **8:**330
- sport **15:**304
Henshir-Fouara (loc., Tunis) **15:**1431
Henstein, David **8:**1439
Henuk (13th cent., Slov.) **10:**1174
Henyekh, Hanokh, *see* Aleksandrow, Hanokh Henyekh
Hepatoscopy (divination method) **6:**114ff
Hepburn, (Jas.) Bonaventura **8:**36
HEP! HEP! (anti-J. rallying cry) **8:**330
- history **8:**713
- history chart **8:**766-767
- *illus:* text
Hepher (bib. fig.) **16:**979
HEPHER (city, Er. Isr.) **8:**332
- *see also:* ḤEFER PLAIN
Hephzibah (Apoc. fig.)
- Messiah **11:**1413
- *Zerubbabel, Book of* **16:**1002
Hepner, H. Sol **12:**266
HEPPNER, ARON **8:**333
Heppner, Henry **12:**1451
Heppner, John **14:**891
HERACLES (myth. Gr. hero) **8:**333
- Cleodemus **8:**300
- Jerusalem gymnasium **9:**1390
HERACLITUS (philos.) **7:**894
HERACLIUS (Byz. emp.) **8:**333
- Bedouin mercenaries **9:**259
- conversion decree **7:**871
- Ereẓ Israel **8:**655; **8:**658; **9:**259
- history chart **8:**766-767
- Jerusalem **9:**1407; **9:**1571
- population **13:**872
Heraklea (Gr. mart.) **5:**1482
HERALDRY **8:**334
- seals **14:**1079
- tombstones **15:**1233
- *illus:* General
- - Israel State emblem **11:**1366
- - tombstone decorations **15:**1226,1229
- *illus:* Coats of Arms
- - text
- - Abendana family **2:**65
- - Ames family **2:**833
- - Bassevi of Treuenberg, Jacob **4:**316
- - Brampton, Edward **4:**1293
- - Carmoly, Eliakim **5:**189
- - Corcos family **5:**691
- - David ibn abi Zimra **5:**1357
- - Foa family **6:**1370
- - Gallico family **7:**273
- - Hapsburg escutcheon **13:**1106
- - Leon, Castile and Aragon **4:**_fcg._ 876
- - Levi family (It.) **4:**1230
- - Lindo family **11:**259
- - Mendes, Isaac **4:**1222
- - Norsa (Norzi) family **8:**1284; **12:**1228
- - Rapa, Abraham ben Jacob ha-Kohen **13:**1553
- - Rothschild family **14:**335
- - Tedeschi family **14:**252
HERAT (city, Afg.) **8:**340
- *see also:* AFGHANISTAN
HERBERG, WILL **16:**1345
- messianism **11:**1416
Herbert, George **6:**778
Herbert of Bosham, *see* BOSHAM, HERBERT DE
Herbert of Cherbury, Lord **5:**1463
Herblock (cart.), *see* BLOCK, HERBERT LAWRENCE
HERBS, MEDICINAL **8:**341
- *illus:*
- blessing over spices **15:**265
Herbst, Joseph **4:**1493
HERBST, KARL **8:**342
- Zionism **16:**1108
- *illus:*
- F.Z.C. **16:**1165
HERBSTEIN, JOSEPH **8:**343
Herbstein, Morris Isaac **8:**343
Herculano de Carvalho E Araújo, Alexandre **15:**251
Hercules (myth. fig.), *see* HERACLES
Herczog, Jacob **2:**98
HERDAN, KURT LUCIAN **3:**602
HERDER, JOHANN GOTTFRIED **8:**343
- German literature **11:**1331
- *Hellenismus* **8:**291
- linguistics **16:**1395
Herder, Moses **2:**862; **16:**157
Hereafter, *see* AFTERLIFE
Heredia, Paul de **10:**643
Heredity **4:**1021ff
- *see also:* ANTHROPOLOGY, PHYSICAL; GENEALOGY; YUḤASIN
HEREFORD (tn., Eng.) **8:**344
ḤEREM (ban, proscription, dedication) **8:**344
- *Contents:*
- - Categories of Ḥerem **8:**344
- - Evolution of Term **8:**346

- - Deuteronomy's Reinterpretation of the Enemy Ḥerem **8**:348
- - In Later Jewish Law **8**:350
- - In Post-Talmudic Law **8**:353
- - Procedure of Pronouncing a Ḥerem **8**:355
- - In Later Centuries **8**:355
- Use of
- - assault **3**:760
- - banishment **4**:164
- - book copyright **7**:1464
- - conditional **10**:332
- - confession **5**:877
- - contempt of court **5**:922
- - covering of head **8**:2
- - damages enforcement measure **3**:987
- - debt dischargement **6**:1012; **6**:1019
- - gambling **7**:300
- - heresy **8**:361
- - informers **8**:1365ff
- - insult **8**:1409; **14**:1652
- - *ir ha-niddaḥat* **8**:1470
- - magic **11**:714
- - non-testimony **6**:996; **13**:956
- - oath **12**:1300
- - punishment **13**:1389
- - summons disregard **13**:954
- - synagogue **15**:584
- - tax evasion **15**:870
- History
- - Achan **2**:209
- - Amalekites **2**:789
- - autonomy, judicial **12**:127; **12**:140; **3**:929
- - Councils of the Lands **5**:999
- - Ḥasidim-Mitnaggedim **7**:1396
- - Inquisition, Spanish **8**:1383
- - Maimonidean controversy **13**:443; **15**:1203
- - Mari parallel **11**:987
- - Morocco **15**:791
- - Palestine gaonate **12**:483
- - sages **14**:639
- - Shabbateans **14**:1250
- - Spain **15**:233
- - Spinoza **15**:276
- - synods **15**:632
- - Temple **15**:972
- - Toledo **15**:1202
- Views
- - Abraham ben Moses **2**:151
- - Moses Mendelssohn **11**:1334; **11**:1336
- - Naḥmanides **12**:780
- *illus:*
- - Cracow, ban imposed on Ḥasidim (1786) **5**:1037
- - Konice community memorial book **3**:930
ḤEREM BET DIN (court legality ordinance) **8**:355
- shofar announcing **14**:1446
Ḥerem de-Rabbenu Gershom, see GERSHOM BEN JUDAH ME'OR HA-GOLAH
ḤEREM HA-IKKUL (ban on confiscation) **8**:356
ḤEREM HA-YISHUV (stlmt. ban) **8**:356
- Council of the Lands **5**:1002
- *ḥazakah* **7**:1520ff
- Rome **14**:249
- *see also:* DOMICILE
Herennius Philo, *see* PHILO OF BYBLOS
Herentals (tn., Belg.) **4**:417
Heres (city, Er. Isr.), *see* KIR HARESETH
Ḥeresh, see DEAF-MUTE
HERESY **8**:358
- *apikoros* **3**:177
- apostasy **3**:201
- Ḥasidism, early period **7**:1390
- homicide, justifiable **8**:945
- Inquisition **8**:1380ff
- Maimonidean controversy **11**:745
- mysticism **10**:498; **10**:526
- Ottoman Empire **16**:1550
- proselytes **13**:1185ff
- Shabbetai Ẓevi **14**:1219
- Sofer, Moses, on **14**:91
- *see also:* ARTICLES OF FAITH; BELIEF
Heretic, *see* MIN
Hereth, Forest of (bib.) **9**:787
ḤEREV LE-ET (mosh., Isr.) **8**:362
- statistics **1**:newsp. list
HERFORD, ROBERT TRAVERS **8**:362
Hering, Gottlieb **4**:455
HERLANDS, WILLIAM BERNARD **8**:363
Herlingen, Aaron Wolf **3**:539
Herlitz, Esther **8**:364
HERLITZ, GEORG **8**:363
Herliz, Eliakim **12**:1360
Herman, Abraham, *see* HARMAN, AVRAHAM
HERMAN, DAVID **8**:364
- theater **15**:1072
- Vilna Troupe **16**:151
Herman, Jerry **15**:1060
HERMAN, JOSEF **8**:364
- *illus:*
- - "Three Peasants" (drg.) **3**:557
Herman, L. **8**:563
Herman, Mildred, *see* HAYDEN, MELISSA
HERMAN, OSKAR **3**:602
- Zagreb **16**:918
- *illus:*
- - "Possession" (paint.) **3**:626
Herman, Samuel **4**:138; **11**:1285
Herman, Woody **12**:1122
Herman de Valenciennes **4**:880
HERMANN, GEORG (nov.) **8**:364
Hermann, George (sport.) **15**:313
HERMANN, LEO **8**:365
Hermann, Oscar, *see* HERMAN, OSKAR
Hermann Mestetz (tn., Bohem.), *see* HERMANUV MESTEC
Hermannstadt (city, Transyl.), *see* SIBIU
HERMANUS QUONDAM JUDAEUS (Herman of Scheda) **8**:365
HERMANUV MESTEC (tn., Bohem.) **8**:366
- *illus:* text
Hermaphrodite, *see* ANDROGYNOS
HERMENEUTICS (sci. of bib. interp.) **8**:366
- *Contents:*
- - The Thirteen Rules of R. Ishmael **8**:367
- - Other Rules **8**:370
- - R. Ishmael and R. Akiva **8**:371
- Sages **14**:644
- - Akiva ben Joseph **2**:491
- - Eliezer ben Hyrcanus **6**:621
- - Hillel **8**:482
- - Ishmael ben Elisha **9**:84
- - Jerusalem Talmud **15**:774
- - Neḥunya ben ha-Kanah **12**:941
- - *tannaim* **15**:800
- Use of
- - *Baraita of 32 Rules* **4**:194
- - Bible interpretation **4**:834; **8**:1417ff
- - *gematria* **7**:369
- - *halakhah* development **7**:1161
- - *kal va-ḥomer* exceptions **13**:222ff
- - *notarikon* **12**:1231
- Thought and Literature
- - apologetics **3**:195
- - Jewish philosophy **13**:422
- - logic and **11**:459
- - Philo **13**:426
- - *pilpul* **13**:524
- - revelation **14**:120
- - Stoic influence on **15**:410
- - tradition **15**:1309
- Movements
- - Ḥasidei Ashkenaz **8**:954
- - Islam **9**:96
- - Karaites **10**:777
- - Pharisees **13**:365
- Miscellaneous
- - perjury **13**:289ff
- - *zaken mamre* **16**:920
- *see also:* ORAL LAW
HERMER, MANFRED **3**:364
Hermes (deity), *see* MERCURY
Hermes-Thot (Gr. god) **8**:293
Hermes Trismegistos (Egy. deity) **3**:645; **8**:372ff
HERMETIC WRITINGS (rel., philos. texts) **8**:372
HERMIPPUS OF SMYRNA (writ.) **7**:894
HERMOGENES (hist.) **7**:894
Ḥermon (journ.) **1**:newsp. list
HERMON, MOUNT (mt. range, Leb., Syr., Isr.) **8**:373
- Fallen Angels **2**:966
- geology **9**:200
- human geography **9**:597ff
- physiography **9**:140
- *illus:*
- - foothills **9**:166
- - Jurassic limestone rocks **9**:217
- - Ma'sada village **9**:214
- - Sea of Galilee **7**:266
HERMON, ZVI **1**:31
Hermoni, Aaron **7**:1316; **7**:1534
Hermon River (Isr.) **9**:172; **9**:180
Hernandez, Diego **8**:1394
Hernando de Talavera **8**:1388
Hernisz, Stanislaus **13**:817
HEROD I (1st cent. B.C.E., k., Judea) **8**:375
- *Contents:*
- - Power Through Rome **8**:376
- - The Dynastic Murders **8**:380
- - Ereẓ Israel under Herod's Rule **8**:382
- - Relationship with Jewish Subjects **8**:383
- - In the Arts **8**:385
- - In Music **8**:386
- General
- - Arts **10**:263
- - gladiatorial contests **7**:598
- - historical chart **8**:766-767
- - hunting **8**:1111
- - Josephus Flavius on **10**:260
- - Macrobius, Ambrosius, on **14**:235
- - Nicholas of Damascus **12**:1140ff
- - Rhodes **14**:145
- - Roman Jews' attitude **14**:240
- Family
- - Alexander, son **2**:567
- - Alexandra **2**:587
- - Antipater **3**:77ff
- - Asinius Pollio **3**:749
- - Cypros, mother **5**:1179
- - Doris **6**:174
- - genealogy **7**:381
- - Glaphyra **7**:601
- - Herod Antipas **3**:75
- Rise to Power
- - Antigonus **3**:65ff
- - Caesar, Sextus Julius **5**:6
- - Cassius Longinus **5**:234
- - Hezekiah the Zealot **8**:455
- - Hyrcanus II **8**:1146
- - Jerusalem reconquest **9**:1393
- - Sosius, Gaius **15**:168
- - warfare **16**:279
- - Zenodorus **16**:992
- Rule
- - Agrippa, Marcus Vipsanius **2**:418
- - Ashdod **3**:696
- - Augustus **3**:852ff
- - Cleopatra **5**:604
- - consequences of death **3**:333ff
- - Costobar **5**:990
- - Edom **6**:377
- - Ereẓ Israel, Roman period **8**:635
- - Hellenism **8**:296
- - Nabateans **12**:742ff
- - organization of kingdom **9**:120
- - Samaritans **14**:730
- - Zamaris **16**:922
- Jewish Subjects
- - Avtalyon **3**:990ff
- - Bava ben Buta **4**:338
- - Herodians **8**:388
- - *Moses, Assumption of* **12**:411
- High Priesthood
- - Aristobulus III **3**:442
- - Boethus **14**:1554
- - Joshua ben Phabi **10**:285
- - manipulation **8**:474
- - priests **13**:1087
- - Simeon ben Boethus **4**:1169
- Cultural Heritage
- - Antipatris **3**:78
- - art, attitude to **3**:507ff
- - Athens **3**:815
- - building remains **3**:327
- - coinage **5**:717
- - Herodium **8**:388
- - Jerusalem **9**:1394,1525ff
- - Jewish architecture **3**:358
- - Masada **11**:1078
- - pillars **13**:522; **13**:523
- - sports stadia **15**:291
- - Temple **15**:961ff
- - Temple Mount architecture **9**:1398
- - tombs **15**:1217
- *geneal. table:* text
- *illus:*
- - text
- - Caesarea **5**:7-11
- - coins **5**:701-702
- - Herodium **8**:389
- - "Herod's Gate" (Jer.) **9**:1431
- - Mamre, remains **11**:839
- - Masada **8**:637; **11**:1079-1091
- - Phasael Tower **9**:1397, 1533
- - Samaria forum **14**:724
- - Temple (reconst.) **3**:511; **15**:960
- - Temple Mount, remains **3**:323; **9**:1399,1522,1534
- *maps:*
- - text
- - Jerusalem **9**:1395
- - kingdom borders **9**:118
HEROD (1st cent. B.C.E., s., Herod I) **8**:387
- Mariamne II **11**:990
- *geneal. table:* **8**:377
HEROD II (1st cent. C.E., Herodian k.) **8**:387
- Berenice **4**:601
- coinage **5**:718
- Silas **14**:1532
- *geneal. table:* **8**:377
Herod Agrippa II (Herodian k.), *see* AGRIPPA II
Herod Antipas (s., Herod I), *see* ANTIPAS, HEROD
Herodian Dynasty
- *geneal. table:* **8**:377
- *illus:*
- - coins **5**:701-705
HERODIANS (sect) **8**:388
- Boethusians **4**:1169
- Herod I **8**:383
- Josephus as drama source **10**:263
HERODIAS (granddau. Herod I) **8**:388
- Cypros **5**:1180
- Herod Antipas **3**:76
- John the Baptist **10**:160
- Salome **14**:689

- *geneal. table:* **8:**377
HERODIUM (Herodion; fort., Er. Isr.) **8:**388
- Bar Kokhba **4:**239
- Bassus' capture of **4:**317
- baths **4:**320
- Herod **3:**66; **8:**382; **8:**636
- *mikveh* **11:**1541
- pillars **13:**522
- synagogue **15:**595
- toparchy **9:**121
- *illus:*
- - stone missiles **4:**236
- - underground passage **4:**235
HERODOTUS (Gr. hist.) **7:**887; **7:**894
Herod Philip (s., Mariamne) **14:**689
HEROD PHILIP I (1st cent., ruler, Judea) **8:**390
- Augustus **3:**853
- coinage **5:**718
- Herod **8:**381
- history chart **8:**766-767
- *geneal. table:* **8:**377
- *illus:*
- - coin **5:**704
Herod's Gate (Jer.) **9:**1434
- settlement **9:**1459
- Six-Day War **9:**1501
- *illus:* **9:**1431
"Heroic Orpheus" (sculp., O Zadkine) **14:**1063
Herold, Jacques **13:**114
Herold, Sidney **11:**520
Heron (bird), *see* BITTERN
HERRERA, ABRAHAM KOHEN DE **8:**391
- Amsterdam **2:**896
- Kabbalah **10:**549,593
- pantheistic tendency **7:**662
Herrera, Alonso Nunez de, *see* HERRERA, ABRAHAM KOHEN DE
Herrera, Gabriel de **5:**222
Herrera, Isabel de **5:**221
Herrera, Maid of (conv. ldr.), *see* Inés of Herrera
HERRERA DE PISUEGRA (tn., Sp.) **8:**392
Herring (zool.) **6:**36
Herrman, Leo **14:**1120
HERRMANN, HUGO **8:**393
- Bar Kochba Association **4:**228
- Zionism **16:**1112
Hersch, Benzion **15:**198
HERSCH, PESACH LIEBMAN **8:**393
HERSCHBERG, ABRAHAM SAMUEL **8:**394
Herscheider, Samuel **5:**1007
Herschel (fam., Aus.) **5:**934
Herschel, Solomon, *see* HIRSCHEL, SOLOMON
Herschell, David **9:**1449
Herschell, Karl **14:**932; **14:**934
Herschengorn, Nehemiah **8:**394; **10:**1203
HERSCHMAN, MORDECHAI **8:**394
Herschmann, Bernard **15:**287
Herschmann, Otto **12:**1375
Hersey, John **15:**1579
HERSHELE (poet) **8:**395
Hershele Ostropoler, *see* OSTROPOLER, HERSHELE
Hershfield, Harry **5:**215
Hershfield, Reuben E. **10:**739
Hershkowitz, L. **8:**568
Hershkowitz, Victor **15:**310
HERSHMAN, ABRAHAM M. **8:**395
Hershowitz, (r., U.S.) **15:**1206
HERSKOVITS, MELVILLE JEAN **8:**395
Hersov, A.S. **11:**1441
Herstein, J. **4:**887
Herta (tn., Buk.), *see* GERTSA
Hertel, W.C. **8:**36
Hertz (name), *see also:* Herz
Hertz, A. (publ.) **14:**133
HERTZ, BENEDYKT **13:**802
Hertz, Daliah **6:**207
HERTZ, EMANUEL **8:**396
Hertz, Frances **15:**311
HERTZ, GUSTAV **8:**396
Hertz, Heinrich Rudolph (phys.) **8:**396
stamp **15:**335
HERTZ, HENRI (Fr.) **8:**396
HERTZ, HENRIK (Heyman; Den.) **8:**397
Hertz, Hyman (U.S.) **15:**1034
Hertz, John D. (bsmn.) **15:**311
Hertz, Joseph (stlr., U.S.) **15:**1034
HERTZ, JOSEPH HERMAN (r., Eng.) **8:**397
- calendar reform **5:**54
- England **6:**761ff
- Isaiah authorship **9:**46
- official garb **13:**1453
- Pentateuch **4:**872
- prayer book **13:**989
- Waley-Cohen, Sir Robert **5:**684
- *illus:*
- - Government House party (Jer.) **9:**339
- - Hebrew University opening ceremony **8:**221
Hertz, Paul **7:**500
HERTZBERG, ARTHUR **1:**31 **8:**398
- redemption **14:**9
Hertzberg, Sidney **15:**303
Hertzberg-Fraenkel, Leo, *see* HERZBERG-FRAENKEL, LEO
HERTZKA, EMIL **12:**693
HERTZKA, THEODOR **8:**399
Hertzog, J.B.M. **16:**1140
HERTZVELD, ESTELLA **6:**320; **6:**322
ḤERUT (mosh., Isr.) **8:**399
- statistics **1:**place list
Ḥerut (newsp.) **9:**1016; **12:**1056; **14:**132
- statistics **1:**newsp. list
ḤERUT MOVEMENT (party, Isr.) **8:**400
- Begin, Menaḥem **4:**392
- Betar **4:**715
- Gaḥal **7:**255
- Histadrut elections **9:**861ff
- Israel-German relations **9:**402
- Israel historical survey **9:**382; **9:**383; **9:**390
- Israel politics **9:**663ff
- Revisionists, Zionist **14:**131
- *illus:*
- - Central Committee meeting **9:**679
Ḥerutenu (period.) **13:**1035
Ḥeruti (pseud.), *see* SMILANSKY, MOSHE
HERXHEIMER, SALOMON **8:**401
Herz (name), *see also:* Hertz
Herz, Adolph (collec.) **16:**913
Herz, Elisa **7:**101; **10:**1354
Herz, Emil **13:**1367
HERZ, HENRI (Heinrich; mus.) **8:**401
HERZ, HENRIETTE **8:**402
- salons **14:**708
- *illus:* text
Herz, J. (plwrt.) **6:**910
Herz, Jacob (physic.) **6:**842
Herz, J.S. (print.) **11:**613
HERZ, LEOPOLD EDLER VON (Lippold) **8:**402
Herz, Lucyna **13:**775
HERZ, MARCUS **8:**403
- Boerne, Ludwig **4:**1166
- Kant **13:**417
- *illus:* text
Herz, Medicus **8:**475
Herz, Michael **4:**1249
Herz, Naphtali **11:**887
Herz, Salomon von **10:**1590
Herz, Susi **11:**1282
Herzberg (phys.) **13:**490
HERZBERG, ABEL JACOB **8:**404
- Netherlands **12:**983
- Zionism **16:**1119
Herzberg, Judith **6:**321
Herzberg, L. **4:**875
HERZBERG, WILHELM (Ze'ev) **8:**404
HERZBERG-FRAENKEL, LEO **8:**405
- Galicia **16:**1328
Herzberg-Fraenkel, Sigmund **8:**405
Herzen, A. **5:**131
Herzensohn, Aleksey Adolfovich **10:**1501
HERZENSTEIN, MIKHAIL YAKOVLEVICH **8:**405
HERZFELD, ERNST EMIL **8:**406
Herzfeld, Jacob **15:**1055
HERZFELD, LEVI **8:**406
- Brunswick **4:**1422
- historiography **8:**562
Herzfeld, Nat **15:**311
Herzl, Binyamin Ze'ev, *see* HERZL, THEODOR
Herzl, Hans **8:**408; **8:**421
- *illus:* **8:**411
Herzl, Hershel **8:**421
Herzl, Jacob **8:**420
- Zemun **16:**990
Herzl, Jeanette **8:**420
- *illus:* **8:**413
Herzl, Jenö, *see* HELTAI, JENÖ
Herzl, Julia **8:**408; **8:**421
Herzl, Margarete **8:**408; **8:**421
- *illus:* **8:**411
Herzl, Moshe **8:**421
Herzl, Mount (Jer.) **9:**1515
- Herzl's reinterment **9:**991
- national cemetery **9:**1495
- *illus:*
- - aerial view **9:**1493
- - Independence Day ceremony **8:**1345
- - military cemetery **9:**368,1493
Herzl, Pauline (sis., Herzl) **8:**407
Herzl, Pauline (dau., Herzl) **8:**408; **8:**421
- *illus:* **8:**411
Herzl, Simon Leib **8:**420
- Zemun **16:**990
HERZL, THEODOR **8:**407
- *Contents:*
- - Beginning of Zionist Activity **8:**408
- - Der Judenstaat **8:**410
- - Political Activities **8:**412
- - The Zionist Organization **8:**412
- - Negotiations with Great Britain **8:**414
- - The Uganda Scheme **8:**417
- - Activist and Thinker **8:**419
- - Herzl's Parents and Grandparents **8:**420
- - The End of Herzl's Family **8:**421
- Historical Role **8:**751ff
- - African problem **9:**433
- - archives **3:**389
- - Basle Program **4:**306
- - Dreyfus Affair **6:**229
- - flag **6:**1336
- - Hebrew language **12:**144
- - Hebrew University **8:**219
- - Hertzka's *Freiland* **8:**399
- - history chart **8:**766-767
- - Italy **16:**1122
- - Kharkov conference **10:**941ff
- - letters **11:**61
- - socialism, Jewish **15:**44
- - Turkish government **9:**327
- - Uganda Scheme **15:**1500ff
- - Vatican **16:**74
- - Vienna **16:**127
- - *Welt, Die* **16:**445
- - Zionism **16:**1032ff,1043,1151,1164,1170
- - Zionist Congresses **16:**1164ff
- Personalities
- - Aḥad Ha-Am **2:**441
- - Balfour, Arthur James **4:**130
- - Baruch, Joseph Marcou **4:**275
- - Ben-Yehuda, Eliezer **4:**568
- - Birnbaum, Nathan **4:**1040
- - Bliokh, Ivan **4:**1094
- - Bodenheimer, Max **4:**1160
- - Chamberlain, Joseph **5:**333
- - Cowen, Joseph **5:**1024
- - Farbstein, Joshua **6:**1181
- - Feiwel, Berthold **6:**1215
- - Frederick of Baden **7:**113
- - Gomperz, Theodor **7:**775
- - Greenberg, Leopold **7:**905
- - Guedemann, Moritz **7:**959
- - Hechler, William Henry **8:**238ff
- - Hess, Moses **8:**434
- - Mandelstamm, Max **11:**869
- - Marmorek, Alexander **11:**1013
- - Nordau, Max **12:**1212ff
- - Plehve, Vyacheslav von **16:**1137
- - Rabinowitz, Samuel Jacob **13:**1478
- - Reines, Isaac Jacob **14:**58
- - Trietsch, Davis **15:**1394
- - Warburg, Otto **16:**287ff
- - Werner, Siegmund **16:**453
- - Witte, Sergey **16:**591
- - Wolffsohn, David **16:**613
- - Zemun family **16:**990
- *geneal. table:* text
- *illus:*
- - text
- - autograph **3:**915
- - *Der Moment* **12:**235
- - design for a Jewish flag **6:**1335
- - diary extract **16:**1048
- - Donath, Adolph, essay on recollections of **6:**165
- - El-Arish investigation commission **16:**1072
- - F.Z.C. **16:**1165
- - Frederick I, grand duke of Baden **7:**112
- - *Haggadah shel ha-Bayit ha-Le'ummi* **13:**139
- - invitation to First Zionist Congress **16:**1045
- - Israel stamp **9:***fcg.* 843
- - leaving the Basle synagogue, 1903 **4:**305
- - Mandelstamm, and **11:**869
- - Moẓa, tree-planting **12:**495
- - Reḥovot visit **14:**45
- - remains received at Lydda airport **9:**376
- - Second Zionist Congress **16:**1169
- - tomb, Mt. Herzl **9:**1493
Herzl, Trude, *see* Herzl, Margarete
Herzliah (Hebrew acad., N.Y.) **6:**1213
Herzlia Hebrew Gymnasia (school, Isr.) **9:**929; **9:**329; **15:**916
- Metman-Cohen, Y. L. **11:**1448
- *illus:*
- - bas-relief of building **12:**370
- - first graduating class **9:**931; **11:**1448
- - original structure **15:**918
Herzl Institute (N.Y.) **13:**178
Herzlia High School (Isr.), *see* Herzlia Hebrew Gymnasia
HERZLIYYAH (tn., Isr.) **8:**421
- statistics **1:**place list
- synagogue **15:**620
Herzl-Moser Hospital (Eng.) **8:**1034
Herzl Museum (Isr.) **3:**389
Herzl Press (publ. firm, U.S.)

13:178; **13:**1376
HERZOG, AVIGDOR **1:**31
Herzog, Chaim **8:**424; **14:**1640
HERZOG, DAVID **8:**422
Herzog, Émile, *see* MAUROIS, ANDRÉ
HERZOG, GEORGE **12:**693
HERZOG, ISAAC (Isr.) **8:**422
- autopsies **3:**932
- Pius XII **8:**912
- religious life in Ereẓ Israel **9:**893
- responsa **14:**93
- *tekhelet* **15:**914
- Transnistria **15:**1336
- *illus:*
- - National Council meeting **9:**365
Herzog, Jacob **8:**424
- *illus:*
- - Jewish Theological Seminary (Jer.) **9:**907
Herzog, Joel **8:**422; **8:**424
HERZOG, REGINALD OLIVER **8:**425
Herzog, Sarah **8:**424
Herzog, Wilhelm **7:**446
Herzogenbusch (concen. camp, Holl.), *see* VUGHT
Herzowitch, Montgomery Moe **12:**1375
Hesban (tn., Jor.), *see* Ḥisbān
HESCHEL, ABRAHAM JOSHUA **8:**425
- Conservative Judaism **5:**905
- existentialism **6:**1042
- faith **4:**436
- free will **7:**131
- miracles **12:**80
- neo-Ḥasidism **7:**1399
- problem of evil **7:**778
- prophecy **13:**1180
- redemption **14:**7
- revelation **14:**125
- theology **15:**1109
- *illus:*
- - Bea (cardinal), and **4:**354
- - civil rights march (1965) **12:**932
HESCHEL, ABRAHAM JOSHUA BEN JACOB **8:**427
- Babad family **4:**14
Heschel, Abraham Joshua of Apta *see* ABRAHAM JOSHUA HESCHEL OF APTA
Heschel, Isaac Meir **2:**160
Heschel, Jacob **15:**472
Heschel, Meshullam Zussia **2:**160
Hescheles, Henryk **5:**558
Hescheles, Marian, *see* HEMAR, MARIAN
Ḥesed (sefirah), *see Gedullah*
Ḥesed ben Yashar, *see* Abū Naṣr Fadl
HESHBON (city, Transj.) **8:**428
- Bible history **8:**577
- Transjordan **15:**1317
- *see also:* SIHON
Heshbona'ut u-Missim (journ.) **1:**newsp. list
Heshbon River (Er. Isr.) **9:**178
Ḥeshek Shelomo (wk.) **10:**1347, 1349
Heshel ben Jacob **8:**487
Heshel ben Meir **5:**372
Heshels, Y. **16:**822
HESHIN, SHNEUR ZALMAN **8:**429
- *illus:*
- - Supreme Court bench **9:**637
Ḥeshvan (month), *see* MARḤESHVAN
Hesiod (Gr. poet) **3:**189
HESPED (eulogy) **8:**429
- ethical literature **6:**924
- *kinah* **10:**1009
- *Megillat Ta'anit* **11:**1230
- mourning **12:**487
- proverbs **13:**1287
- Samaritan burial service **14:**747
Hesperides (city, Libya), *see* BENGHAZI
Hess, David **5:**742
Hess, Ernst **9:**1361
Hess, Julius **11:**1201
HESS, MENDEL **8:**430
HESS, MICHAEL **8:**431
HESS, MOSES **8:**431
- Auerbach, Berthold **3:**845
- Damascus Affair **8:**727
- Duenner, Joseph Zevi **6:**261
- Graetz, Heinrich **7:**848
- Hirsch, S.R. **8:**514
- history chart **8:**766-767
- Jewish nationalism **16:**1035ff
- socialism **15:**25
- *illus:*
- - portrait **8:**708
HESS, DAME MYRA **8:**434
Hess, Rudolf **4:**1250
- *illus:*
- - Nuremberg Trial **16:**289
Hess, Simon **9:**1191
Hess, Solomon **8:**1438
Hess, Tevele of Mannheim **2:**24; **5:**613
HESSE (state, Ger.) **8:**434
- history chart **8:**766-767
- rabbinical office **13:**1453
Hesse, Anna Sophia von **8:**36
Hesse-Darmstadt (princip., Ger.) **8:**437
- *illus:*
- - register of assessment and taxes (1723-40) **6:**1281
Hesse-Homburg, *see* HOMBURG
Hesse-Kassel (princip., Ger.) **8:**434
Hesselberg, Edouard **12:**466
HESSEN, JOSEPH VLADIMIROVICH **8:**437
HESSEN, JULIUS ISIDOROVICH **8:**437
Hesse-Nassau (prov., Ger.) **12:**841
Hessenberg (loc., Ger.) **14:**113
Hesset (form of impurity) **16:**942
Hessiona (soc. Zion. gr.) **15:**652
HESTRIN, SHLOMO **8:**438
Hesychius (Bib. trans.) **4:**853
ḤET (Heb. let.) **8:**438
Het Beloofde Land (period.), *see Palestine*
Het Joodsche Weekblad (newsp.), *see Joodse Weekblad, Het*
Ḥet-kau-ptaḥ (city, Egy.) **12:**184
Hetter iskah (investment deed), *see* SHETAR
Hetzel, J.W.F. **8:**36
Heuman, Maurice **11:**1499
Heuser Trial (Nazi trial) **16:**299
Ḥevel (meas. instr.) **16:**378
Ḥevel middah (meas. instr.) **16:**378
Ḥever (vill., Er. Isr.) **15:**675
- statistics **1:**place list
Ḥever ha-Kevuẓot (kib. fed., Isr.) **10:**964ff, 968ff
ḤEVER HA-YEHUDIM (ruling body, Er. Isr.) **8:**438
Ḥever Ir (tal. conc.), *see* ḤAVER IR
Heves, K. **15:**669
Hevesi, András **8:**439
Hevesi, Eugene **11:**679
Hevesi, F. **11:**721; **15:**659
HEVESI, LAJOS (Ludwig) **8:** 1085
HEVESI, SÁNDOR **8:**439
HEVESI, SIMON **8:**439
HEVESY, GEORGE CHARLES DE **8:**439
Ḥevlei mashi'aḥ, *see* Messiah, Birthpangs of the
ḤEVRAH, ḤAVURAH (assoc.) **8:**440
- Afghanistan **2:**327
- communal organization **3:**925
- endowments **8:**285; **8:**286
- finances, autonomous **6:**1282
- fines imposition **6:**1289
- Ḥasidim **7:**1391
- legal person **10:**1569
- ransom of captives **5:**155
- Torah study **15:**458
- *illus:*
- - Ancona, *Takkanot* **15:**713
- - Florence, *Ḥevrat Mattir Asurim* **9:**1136
- *see also:* FRATERNAL SOCIETIES; ḤEVRA KADDISHA
Ḥevrah Ḥadashah (qtr., Tel Aviv) **15:**920
Ḥevrah Ḥesed ve-Emet (burial soc.) **8:**440
ḤEVRA (*Ḥavurah*) KADDISHA (assoc.) **8:**442
- Adar, the Seventh of **2:**253
- Altschul, Emil **2:**782
- ceremonial art **5:**310
- communal responsibility **4:**1518
- Ereẓ Israel **9:**889
- finances, autonomous **6:**1283
- gamblers **7:**300
- *gemilut ḥasadim* **7:**376
- glass beakers **7:**613
- *seliḥot* **14:**1134
- *illus:*
- - alms box (c. 1750) **5:**342
- - Amsterdam, community tokens **12:**977
- - *Ashkavah* recital **3:**713
- - body cleansing implements **4:**1521
- - Charleston, S.C., seal **7:**376
- - Cluj, minute book **15:**1343
- - decorated jug, and silver lid **4:**1519,1520
- - glass beakers **5:**308; **7:**609; **12:**185
- - *hakkafot* around a coffin **7:**1153
- - London, receipt for sixpence (1771) **5:**343
- - Mikulov, faience pitcher **12:**304
- *see also:* BURIAL; CHARITY; ḤEVRAH, ḤAVURAH
Ḥevra shas (study soc.) **15:**53
Ḥevrat Doreshei Leshon Ever (Heb. lang. soc.) **4:**642; **7:**1438; **15:**53
Ḥevrat ha-Ḥayyim (anti-Zion. gr.), *see* NETUREI KARTA
ḤEVRAT HA-OVEDIM (co-op. soc., Er. Isr.) **8:**446
- Histadrut **8:**538
- labor economy of Israel **9:**851ff
Ḥevrat Marbei ha-Haskalah, *see* SOCIETY FOR THE PROMOTION OF CULTURE AMONG THE JEWS OF RUSSIA
Ḥevrat No'ar (youth cmty., Isr.) **16:**864ff
Hevrat Olim (Zion. gr., Holl.) **16:**1120
Ḥevrat Shoḥarei Or ve-Haskalah (gr., Volhynia) **16:**210
Ḥevrat Terumat Kodesh (orgn.), *see* Officers, Overseers, and Treasurers of Ereẓ Israel
Ḥevrat Yishuv Ereẓ Israel al Yedei Avodat Adamah (soc., Rum.) **16:**1132
Ḥevron, Naḥal (wadi, Er. Isr.), *see* Naḥal Ḥevron
Ḥevrot tehillim (Psalm soc.) **13:**1325
Hexagram, *see* MAGEN DAVID
Hexapla (Bib. trans.) **4:**853ff
- Cairo *Genizah* **16:**1335
- Origen **12:**1467
- Peshitta **4:**859ff
Hexaplar, Syro- (Bib. trans.) **4:**860
Hexateuch (6 bks. of Bib.) **13:**233
HEXTER, JACK H. **8:**447
Hexter, Morris **9:**346
HEYD, URIEL **8:**447
HEYDEMANN, HEINRICH **8:**448
HEYDENFELDT, SOLOMON **8:**448
Heydius, Thomas, *see* HYDE, THOMAS
HEYDRICH, REINHARD TRISTAN **8:**448
- Gestapo **7:**527
- ghetto **7:**543
- Goering, Hermann **7:**688ff
- Himmler, Heinrich **8:**498
- Holocaust **8:**855ff
- Judenrat **10:**407
Heyeh Nakhon (publ.) **1:**newsp. list
Heyermans, Herman, *see* HEIJERMANS, HERMAN
Heyman, Arthur **15:**303
Heyman, Johannes **8:**36
Heyman, Mayer **13:**359
Heyman, Moses (court J.) **5:**1010
HEYMAN, MOSES DAVID (inv.) **8:**1431
Heyman, Seymour C. **12:**1353
Heymann, Carl **13:**1367
HEYMANN, FRITZ **8:**449
Heymann, Jules **11:**1562
Heymann, Lewis **12:**1234
HEYMANN, WALTER **8:**449
HEYMANS, GERARDUS F. **8:**449
Heymland (journ.) **10:**1304; **13:**1048
HEYSE, PAUL **8:**450
Ḥez (demon) **5:**1524
HEZEKIAH (bib. fig.) **8:**450
- chronological chart **8:**766-767
- copper serpent **5:**957ff
- Deuteronomy, Book of **5:**1575
- Eltekeh battle **6:**688
- high places **5:**1167
- history **8:**605ff
- Hosea **8:**1010
- in the Arts **9:**69
- Isaiah **9:**46
- Jerusalem **9:**1383
- Kings, Book of **10:**1028ff
- Manasseh **11:**853
- Messiah **11:**1411
- Micah **11:**1180ff
- musicians **13:**1316
- purity laws **13:**1414
- Sargon II **14:**881
- Sennacherib **16:**1509
- Shebnah, scribe **14:**1329
- Siloam tunnel **14:**1541
- Temple **15:**944
- war and warfare **16:**276
- water supply, Jerusalem **9:**1398; **9:**1538
- Zephania **16:**994
- *geneal. table:* **5:**1341
- *illus:*
- - text
- - Sennacherib's campaign **3:**319
- - Siloam Tunnel and inscription **3:**316; **8:**603
- - tribute to Sennacherib **12:**573
- - warned by Isaiah **9:**68
HEZEKIAH (the Zealot) **8:**455
HEZEKIAH (amora) **8:**455
- mother **10:**451
Hezekiah (13/14 cent., r.) **14:**1530
HEZEKIAH, THE HIGH PRIEST **8:**456
- Pseudo-Hecataeus **8:**237
Hezekiah, Pool of **9:**1398; **9:**1539; **9:**1541
- *illus:*
- - from the south side **9:**1460
Hezekiah, Tunnel of (Jer.) **9:**1540ff
- *illus:*
- - Jerusalem water supply **9:**1539
HEZEKIAH BEN DAVID (exil., gaon) **8:**456
- gaonate list **7:**318
Hezekiah ben David (exil.) **8:**457
- Baghdad academy **8:**1446
- David ben Hezekiah **5:**1350
HEZEKIAH BEN DAVID DA

SILVA (r., Jer.) **8:**457
- Abraham ben Mordecai **2:**150
- *illus:* text
Hezekiah ben Elchanan **10:**1046
HEZEKIAH BEN JACOB **8:**458
- Avigdor ben Elijah **3:**963
Hezekiah ben Judah **8:**456
HEZEKIAH BEN MANOAH **8:**459
- *illus:* text
Hezekiah ben Nedebeus **2:**923; **6:**585
Hezekiah ben Reuben **4:**1240
Hezekiah ha-Nagid **15:**264
Hezel, J.W.F., *see* Hetzel, J.W.F.
HEZIR (bib. fig.) **8:**460
Hezir, Tomb of sons of (Jer.) **9:**1393; **12:**484; **13:**522
- inscription **16:**669
- *illus:* **15:**1219
Ḥezkat arenda (lease rights), *see* ARENDA
Ḥezkat ha-kehillah (stlmt. rights), *see* ḤEREM HA-YISHUV
Hezkat ha-yishuv (residence rights), *see* ḤEREM HA-YISHUV
Ḥezkat ironut (residence rights), *see* ḤEREM HA-YISHUV
Hezron (bib. fig.) **13:**283
Hiamo, Amos **16:**112
Hiamo, Jacob **16:**112
Hiamo, Solomon **16:**112
HIAS (soc., N.Y.), *see* UNITED HIAS SERVICE
Hiatt Institute (Isr.) **14:**590
HIBAT ALLAH, ABU AL-BARAKĀT (NATHANEL) BEN ALI (ELI) AL-BAGHDĀDĪ **8:**461
- philosophy **13:**439
- space and place **15:**218
Ḥibat Allah ibn al-Ḥasan ben Ephraim **10:**421
ḤIBAT ALLAH, IBN JUMAY IBN ZAYN **8:**462
- David ben Solomon **5:**1356
ḤIBBAT ZION (mosh., Isr.) **8:**463
- statistics **1:**place list
ḤIBBAT ZION (mvmt.) **8:**463
- Abendanan, Saul **2:**68
- *aliyah and absorption* **9:**515ff
- Baltimore **4:**146
- Benei Moshe **4:**492ff
- Berlin, Naphtali **4:**662
- Eliasberg, Mordecai **6:**615ff
- Ephrati, David **6:**815
- Farbstein, Joshua **6:**1181
- Galicia **16:**1330
- Goldbloom, Jacob **7:**706
- *ḥalukkah* **7:**1215
- *Ha-Meliẓ* **7:**1233
- Ḥasidic opposition **7:**1397
- Hebrew newspapers **12:**1046ff
- Herzl **8:**411
- history chart **8:**766-767
- Jewish studies **16:**580
- Joseph Maman al-Maghribi **10:**245
- Kattowitz conference **10:**819ff
- letters **11:**61
- Levanda, Lev Osipovich **11:**66,67
- Lilienblum, Moses Leib **11:**240ff
- Mohilewer, Samuel **12:**218
- Odessa Committee **12:**1328
- philanthropy **13:**389
- Pinsker, Leon **13:**545
- Russia **14:**452
- U.S. **16:**1141
- Warsaw **16:**337
- Yugoslavia **16:**1148
- Zionism **16:**1037ff
- Zionist Congresses **16:**1164
- Zionist Organization **16:**1097
- *illus:*
- - Kattowitz Conference **10:**820
Hibbing (vill., Minn.) **12:**39
Ḥibbur ha-Konim (wk.) **16:**1387,1474
Ḥibbur Harsha'ot (bk.) **2:**138
Ḥibbur Yafeh me-ha-Yeshu'ah (bk.), *see Sefer ha-Ma'asiyyot*
ḤIBBUT HA-KEVER (conc., "beating in the grave") **8:**464
- *Tofteh Arukh* **16:**909
HICEM (emigration assoc.) **2:**830
- Hias Service **15:**1539
- philanthropy **13:**388
HICKL, MAX **8:**464
- press **13:**1027
Hickory (city, N. C.) **12:**1220
Ḥ-I-D-A, *see* AZULAI, ḤAYYIM JOSEPH DAVID
Ḥidah, see PARABLE
Hidalgo, Alfred, *see* HEFTER, ALFRED
Ḥiddushei Ha-Rashba le-Aggadot Ha-Shas (bk.) **2:**308
Ḥiddushei ha-Rim (bk.) **7:**785
ḤIDDUSHIM (novellae) **8:**464
- codification of law **5:**633
- development of law **12:**117; **12:**122; **12:**132
- Jewish literature **11:**332
- Maimonides **11:**754
- Naḥmanides **12:**778ff
- *illus:* text
Hidekel (river), *see* TIGRIS
ḤIDKA (tan.) **8:**467
Ḥidka's Meal (Sabbath) **8:**468
Hiegentlich, Jacob **6:**321
HIEL (bib. fig.) **8:**468
- Jericho **9:**1368
Hierakonpolis (anc. loc.) **16:**273
HIERAPOLIS (city, Syr.) **8:** 468
- guilds **7:**971
- Hadad and Atar'ata **7:**1040
Hieroglyphics **8:**790; **14:**1073, 1150
- *illus:*
- - Lachish seal **14:**1076
Hieronymus (ch.f.), *see* Jerome
Hieronymus de Sancta Fide, *see* LORKI, JOSHUA
Hieropolis (city, Egy.) **7:**816
Hierosolyma (Jerusalem) **9:**1379
Hierosolymitanische Kasse (inst.) **8:**468
HIEROSOLYMITANISCHE STIFTUNG (orgn.) **8:**468
Higgayon (Psalm term) **13:**1322
HIGGER, MICHAEL **8:**469
Higham, J. **8:**569
"High Commissioner" (paint., A. Aroch) Pl.12 **3**-ART
HIGH COMMISSIONER FOR PALESTINE **8:**470
- *illus:* **8:**471-472; **9:**1475; **14:**799
- *see also:* WHITE PAPERS
High Commission for Refugees from Germany **8:**905; **14:**32
High Commission for Revision of Jewish Legislature, *see* Pahlen Commission
"Higher criticism" (Bib.) **4:**905
HIGHER EDUCATION IN ISRAEL **9:**952
- Arabs in universities **9:**1029
- Bar Ilan University **4:**225
- Bezalel Academy **4:**788
- Haifa University **7:**1140
- Hebrew Union College **8:**217
- Hebrew University **8:**219
- historical survey **9:**396
- Rubin Academy of Music **5:**1271; **9:**1496 **12:**673
- Technion **15:**889
- Tel Aviv University **15:**925
- University of the Negev **4:**385
- Weizmann Institute **16:**438
- yeshivot **16:**771ff
- *illus:*
- - academic staff in academic institutions, 1948-69 (chart) **9:**953
- - Bar-Ilan University **9:**955, 963, 971
- - estimates of accumulated capital investments in univerisites (charts) **9:**959
- - Hebrew University **9:**955, 956, 958, 970
- - participation of public in budgets of universities (chart) **9:**959
- - protest poster against technion re language of instruction **9:**1000
- - students and recipients of degrees, 1948-69 (chart) **9:**953
- - Technion **9:**955,961,968; **15:**890,891
- - Tel Aviv University **9:**956; **15:**925
- - Weizmann Institute **9:**956,967; **16:**439ff
High Holidays, *see* DAY OF ATONEMENT; ROSH HA-SHANAH
Highland Park (city, Ill.) **5:**415; **8:**1256
High places (Bamot), *see* CULT PLACES, ISRAELITE
High Point (city, N.C.) **12:**1220
HIGH PRIEST **8:**470
- General
- - Aaronides **2:**18; **2:**20
- - *am ha-arez* **11:**840
- - Boethusians **4:**1169ff
- - Dorotheus **6:**176
- - Fadus, Cuspius **6:**1135
- - Herod **8:**379
- - Josephus' list **10:**262
- - Pentateuch **13:**241
- - sages **14:**640ff
- - Samaritans **14:**727ff
- - Second Temple period **8:**626ff; **9:**1389ff
- - *Yoma* tractate **16:**844
- - Zealots **16:**949
- Customs and Laws
- - abolition result **9:**238
- - altar encirclement **14:**179
- - anointing **3:**27ff
- - Ark of Covenant **3:**463
- - *Avodah* **3:**977ff
- - city of refuge **5:**593
- - Commandments, the 613 **5:**773
- - confession of sins **5:**878
- - *Hakhel* ceremony **7:**1149
- - Holy of the Holies **15:**989
- - incense **8:**1314
- - marriage **11:**1028
- - *met mitzvah* **15:**1185
- - prayers of **11:**392
- - priesthood **13:**1074
- - red heifer **14:**13
- - sacrifice **14:**600ff
- - sexual offenses **14:**1208
- - Temple **15:**959; **15:**973ff
- - trial of **4:**721
- - Urim and Thummim **3:**792
- - vestments of **13:**1064
- - virginity **16:**161
- - widow **16:**488ff
- List of
- - Aaron **2:**4
- - Ahimaaz **2:**20
- - Alcimus **2:**549
- - Amariah **2:**20
- - Anan ben Anan **10:**278
- - Ananias ben Nedebeus **2:**923
- - Ananus son of Seth **10:**277
- - Aristobulus I **3:**440
- - Aristobulus II **8:**1145
- - Aristobulus III **3:**441
- - Azariah **2:**20
- - Boethus **14:**1554
- - Eleazar **6:**583
- - Eleazar ben Harsom **6:**589
- - Eleazer son of Boethus **4:**1169
- - Eleazar son of Onias I **12:**1402
- - Eliakim Alkimos **9:**1392
- - Eliashib **6:**1118
- - Elionaeus ben Cantheras **4:**1169
- - Hilkiah **8:**481
- - Hyrcanus II **8:**1145
- - Hyrcanus, John **8:**1146
- - Ishmael ben Phiabi II **9:**86
- - Jaddua **6:**1118
- - Jason **9:**1390
- - Jehohanan **6:**1118
- - Jehoiada **2:**20
- - Jeshua **10:**1
- - Joezer son of Boethus **10:**139
- - Johanan **10:**144
- - Joiada **6:**1118
- - Joiakim **6:**1118
- - Jonathan **9:**1392
- - Jonathan Appus ben Mattathias **7:**1456
- - Joseph ben Elem **10:**227
- - Joseph ben Simeon **9:**86; **10:**1009
- - Joseph Caiaphas **10:**1009
- - Joseph son of Camei **8:**385
- - Joseph son of Kimḥit **10:**1009
- - Joshua ben Damnai **10:**278
- - Joshua ben Gamla **10:**278
- - Joshua ben Jehozadak **13:**1086
- - Joshua ben Phabi **10:**285
- - Joshua son of Seth **10:**277
- - Jozadek **6:**1118
- - Manasseh son of Onias I **12:**1402
- - Mattathias ben Anan **14:**1554
- - Mattathias ben Johanan **7:**1456
- - Mattathias son of Theophilus **15:**1111
- - Menelaus **11:**1351
- - Onias I **12:**1402
- - Onias II **12:**1402
- - Onias III **12:**1402
- - Onias IV (Egypt) **12:**1402
- - Phinehas **13:**466
- - Phinehas ben Samuel **13:**470
- - Seraiah **14:**1179
- - Simeon ben Boethus **4:**1169
- - Simeon ben Mattathias **7:**1456
- - Simeon Cantheras **4:**1169
- - Simeon the Just **14:**1566
- - Simeon son of Kimḥit **10:**1009
- - Simeon son of Onias I **14:**1565
- - Theophilus **15:**1110
- - Urijah **2:**20
- - Yeshovav **10:**1009
- - Zadok **3:**27
- *illus:*
- - administering ordeal **12:**1448
- - Alexander the Great paying homage to **2:**580
- - burning frankincense **7:**100
- - precious stones in breastpiece (chart) **13:**1007
- - Samaritan **14:**733
- - *Urim* and *Thummim* **6:**112
- - vestments **13:**1065
- - wearing the ephod **6:**805
- *see also:* PRIESTS AND PRIESTHOOD
"High Red" (paint., A. Arikha) PL. 14 **3:**ART
Hightstown (boro., N.J.) **12:**1030
High Ways to Perfection (bk.) **10:**513
Higier, Henry K. **11:**1204
Ḥigra (amora) **2:**32
Higyenah Ruḥanit (journ.) **1:**newsp. list
Higyenah u-Veri'ut (journ.) **1:**newsp. list
Hija, Don David de la, *see* David de la Hija
Hijackings **2:**620; **9:**416, 472; **15:**1564
HĪJAR (tn., Sp.) **8:**474
- Hebrew printing **8:**1321; **8:**1325
- *illus:*
- - Alantansi's printers' mark **13:**1093

Ḥijâz (reg., Arab.), *see* HEJAZ
Hijman, Levi **14:**349
Hijmans, Dorothea Salomea, *see* HERTZVELD, ESTELLA
Hikok (stlmt., Er. Isr.) **8:**1062
Ḥikrei Avodah (journ.) **1:**newsp. list
Hilah (amora), *see* ILAI
Hilai (gaon) **7:**316; **12:**886
Hilai bar Hanina (gaon) **7:**318
Hilai bar Natronai **7:**318
Hilai ha-Levi of Naresh **7:**318
Hilāl, Shihāb ibn, *see* Ibn Hilāl, Shihāb al-dīn Ahmad ben Muhammad ben Ibrāhim
Hilālī (sharif dyn.), *see* ALAWIDS
Hilālī, Abu Zayd al- (leg. hero) **9:**1038
Hilarová, Dagmar **5:**1208
Hilary (bp.) **3:**468
Hilberg, R. **8:**566
Hilborn, David **14:**696
HILDEBERT OF LAVARDIN **8:**475
HILDESHEIM (city, Ger.) **8:**475
- Eliakim Goetz ben Meir **6:**614
Hildesheim, Isaac, *see* Hiller, Justus
HILDESHEIMER, AZRIEL (Israel) **8:**476
- chronological chart **8:**766-767
- Falashas **6:**1153
- Israel settlement **16:**1039
- neo-Orthodoxy **12:**957
- rabbinical seminary **13:**1464
Hildesheimer, Hirsch
- Esra oganization **6:**895
- *Juedische Presse* **8:**477; **10:**462
- Zionism **16:**1033
HILDESHEIMER, MEIR **8:**478
Hildesheimer, Wolfgang **7:**453
HILDUIN (bp.) **8:**478
Ḥilfai (amora), *see* ILFA
HILFERDING, RUDOLF **8:**479
HILFSVEREIN DER DEUTSCHEN JUDEN (orgn.) **8:**479
- Auerbach, Israel **3:**847
- Cohn-Reiss, Ephraim **5:**693
- education in Israel **9:**330
- establishment of schools **8:**234
- Hildesheimer, Azriel **8:**477
- history chart **8:**766-767
- language of instruction **15:**888
- Nathan, Paul **12:**855
- philanthropy **13:**387
- Rivlin, Joseph **14:**201
- Technion **15:**889
Hilkhata ke-vatra'ei (hal. rule) **3:**910ff; **5:**891
Hilkhot Bekhorot (wk.) **12:**780
Hilkhot Ḥallah (wk.) **12:**780
Hilkhot Nedarim (wk.) **12:**780
Hilkhot Re'u (geonic wk.), *see* HALAKHOT PESUKOT
Hilkhot Yeẓirah (bk.) **16:**785
HILKIAH (bib. fig.) **8:**481
Hilkiah (2nd cent. B.C.E., sol.), *see* ANANIAS AND HELKIAS
Hill, G.F. **12:**1271
Hill, Sir John Grey **12:**484
ḤILLA (tn., Iraq) **8:**481
Ḥillazon (snail) **15:**913; **15:**914
Ḥillazon River (Isr.) **9:**152
Hill cultivation (Er. Isr.) **2:**389
Hillel (fam., Ḥabban) **7:**1018
"Hillel" (paint., Jack Levine) **11:**114
HILLEL (the Elder; tan.) **8:**482
- academies of Second Temple **2:**201
- Alexandrian *ketubbot* **8:**1425
- *aliyah* **9:**511
- Bible interpretation **8:**1417
- chronological chart **8:**766-767
- codification of law **5:**632
- conflict of opinion **5:**890
- ecology **4:**1028
- ethics **6:**933
- Judah ha-Nasi **10:**367
- Judaism **10:**384
- Paschal lamb **12:**12; **15:**1309
- *prosbul* **13:**1181
- reward and punishment **14:**134
- sages **14:**640ff
- Shammai **14:**1291ff
- Torah **15:**1239
- Torah interpretation **11:**315
- *see also:* BET HILLEL AND BET SHAMMAI
HILLEL (3rd cent. C.E.,) **8:**485
HILLEL (II; 4th cent., nasi) **8:**486
- calendar **5:**48
- chronological chart **8:**766-767
Hillel, the Babylonian, *see* HILLEL (the Elder)
Hillel, F. **11:**284
Hillel, Mount (Isr.) **9:**156
Hillel, school of, *see* BET HILLEL AND BET SHAMMAI
Hillel, Shelomo **9:**680
HILLEL BEN ELIAKIM **8:**487
Hillel Benjamin of Lask **11:**586
Hillel ben Moses **12:**763
HILLEL BEN NAPHTALI ẒEVI (Herz) **8:**487
Hillel ben Samuel (amora) **14:**813
HILLEL BEN SAMUEL (of Verona) **8:**488
- Averroes **3:**952
- Avicenna **3:**959
- beatitude **4:**362
- philosophy, Jewish **13:**444
- psychology **11:**340
- reward, punishment **14:**136
- translations **15:**1322; **15:**1326
Hillel ben Shakhar, *see* LANDAU, JUDAH LOEB
Hillel ben Valas (tan.) **10:**1576
Hillel the Elder (tan.), *see* HILLEL
Hillel the Elder (15th cent.), *see* HILLEL OF ERFURT
Hillel Foundation, *see* B'NAI B'RITH (Hillel Foundation)
HILLEL OF ERFURT **8:**490
Hillel of Greece, *see* HILLEL BEN ELIAKIM
HILLELS, SHELOMO (writ.) **8:**490
- *illus:*
- - Hebrew Pen Club **8:**211
- - Hebrew writers' convention **8:**213
- - Writers' Association in Israel **8:**205
HILLER, FERDINAND **8:**490
- Oppenheim's portrait **12:**1424
- Saul in art **14:**918
Hiller, Justus **8:**490
HILLER, KURT **8:**491
Hiller, M. **8:**36
Hillesum, Ettie **6:**321
HILLESUM, JEREMIAS **8:**491
Hilliger, J. W. **8:**36
Hillman, Archibald M. **16:**634
Hillman, David **8:**492
HILLMAN, SAMUEL ISAAC **8:**492
HILLMAN, SIDNEY **8:**493
Hill of the Heads (mon., Er. Isr.), *see* Tell al-Ru'ūs
HILLQUIT, MORRIS **8:**494
- New York City **12:**1105
Hillside (tn., N. J.) **15:**1534
Hillside Hospital (N.Y.C.) **12:**1116
Ḥilluk (hal. wk.) **14:**755
Ḥilluk (study method) **11:**333
HILLULA (festivity) **8:**495
HILLULA DE-RABBI SHIMON BAR YOḤAI **8:**495
Ḥillul ha-Shem, *see* KIDDUSH HA-SHEM AND ḤILLUL HA-SHEM
Ḥilo, Isaac **8:**230; **11:**351
Hilpert, J. **8:**36
Hilsner, Leopold **8:**496
HILSNER CASE (bld. lib.) **8:**496
- Allianz, Israelitische **2:**654
- history chart **8:**766-767
Hilvai, János **8:**36
HIM, GEORGE **3:**602
Himmalayas (mts.) **8:**1311
HIMMELFARB, GERTRUDE **8:**546
Himmelfarb, Meir **15:**1421
HIMMELSTEIN, LENA **8:**497
HIMMLER, HEINRICH **8:**497
- Amsterdam reprisal orders **2:**902
- Auschwitz **3:**854ff
- concentration camps **5:**77
- Gestapo **7:**527
- Hoess, Rudolf **8:**806
- Holocaust **8:**842; **8:**855ff
- Kersten **13:**1583
- Lodz Ghetto **13:**756
- Roman Jews **14:**252
- SS and SD **15:**322
- *illus:*
- - at Auschwitz camp **3:**861
Himnona (amora) **16:**1471
ḤIMYAR (tribe, Arab.) **8:**498
- Arabia **3:**232ff
- Yusuf 'As'ar **16:**897ff
Hin (meas.) **16:**377; **16:**380; **16:**388
Hin, Raphael ben Joseph, *see* Raphael Joseph
Hinatuna (city, Er. Isr.), *see* HANNATHON
Hincks, Edward **8:**36; **16:**1506
Hindemith, Paul **4:**411; **12:**700
Hindenburg (city), *see* ZABRZE
Hindes, M. **13:**1598
Hindiya (tn., Iraq) **8:**1450
HINDUS, MAURICE GERSCHON **8:**500
HINDUS, MILTON HENRY **1:**31
Hine, Edward **4:**1381
- *illus:*
- - *Forty-Seven Identifications . . .* **4:**1381
Ḥinena Bar-Papa (Pappi), *see* ḤANINA BAR PAPA
HINENI HE-ANI MI-MA'AS (litur.) **8:**500
Hinkelmann, A. **8:**36
Hinković, Hinko **16:**917
Hinlopen, Jelmer **8:**36
Ḥinna (amora) **15:**1430
Ḥinnah (cerem.) **11:**1044
Ḥinnatuni (city, Er. Isr.), *see* HANNATHON
Hinnom, Valley of, *see* GEHINNOM
Ḥinnukh (journ.) **1:**newsp. list
Ḥinnukh Aẓma'i (educ. system) **9:**899; **15:**167
Ḥinnukh Gufani Murhav (orgn.), *see* Ḥagam
Ḥinnukh Nearim (school, Ger.) **7:**1439
Hinnumah (bridal veil) **5:**1130; **11:**1033
Hinrichsen (fam., Court Js.) **5:**1010
HINRICHSEN (fam., mus.) **12:**693
Hinrichsen, Heinrich **12:**693
Hinrichsen, Max **12:**693
Hinrichsen, Michael (of Glueckstadt) **11:**1163; **15:**1176
Hinrichsen, M. R. **11:**1164
Hinrichsen, Ruben **5:**1010
Hinstin, Adolphe **11:**1562
Hipparchus (schol.) **8:**293
Hippo (Sidonian clny.) **14:**1506
Hippocrates (physic.) **3:**674; **13:**1337
Hippo-Diarrhytus (loc., Tun.), *see* Bizerta
Hippolytus of Rome **5:**551
Hippone (city, Alg.), *see* BÔNE
Hippopotamus (zool.) **3:**7; **4:**394; **6:**32; **9:**225
Hippos Regius (city, Alg.), *see* BÔNE
Hippos (city, Er. Isr.), *see* SUSITA
ḤIRA (city, Mesop.) **8:**500
HIRAM (k., Tyre) **8:**500
- David **5:**1322; **8:**589
- in Greek literature **7:**894ff
- metals and mining **11:**1429ff
- Phoenicians **13:**477
- sarcophagus **16:**665
- Solomon **8:**591ff; **15:**98,116
- Syriac translation of Bible **4:**858
- Temple **15:**943
- trade **15:**1295; **16:**1269
- widow's son **16:**490
- *illus:*
- - sarcophagus **13:**473
HIRAM (k., Zidonians) **8:**501
HIRAM (bib. crftn.) **8:**502
Ḥiram, Operation (War of Indep.) **16:**328
Hire, *see* LEASE AND HIRE
Ḥireq (vowel) **16:**1431,1459
Hirsch (cantor, Pol.) **9:**1091; **12:**628
Hirsch (partisan) **15:**1235
Hirsch (fam., Ger.) **7:**1173
Hirsch (stlmt., Can.) **2:**413; **3:**33; **14:**891
Hirsch, Aaron **8:**476
Hirsch, Adolph **3:**806
Hirsch, Alexander **14:**1585
Hirsch, Aron (bsmn.) **8:**502; **11:**1438
HIRSCH, ARON SIEGMUND (indust.) **8:**502
- mining **11:**1438
HIRSCH, AUGUST **8:**502
Hirsch, Clara de **8:**505
- *geneal. table:* **4:**1056
Hirsch, Dave (cart.) **5:**220
Hirsch, David (sol.) **11:**1554
Hirsch, Edward **8:**516
Hirsch, Emil **11:**1438
HIRSCH, EMIL GUSTAVE (r.) **8:**503
- football **15:**307
Hirsch, Harold **7:**429
Hirsch, J. (Bib. trans.) **4:**876
Hirsch, Jacob (maskil) **7:**1446; **12:**216
Hirsch, Jacob (pion., U.S.) **11:**1499
- Judaism, modern **13:**1345
Hirsch, Joseph (bsmn.) **11:**1438
HIRSCH, JOSEPH (art.) **3:**602
HIRSCH, JULIUS **8:**504
Hirsch, Luciende **8:**506
HIRSCH, MARKUS **8:**504
- *illus:* text
Hirsch, Maurice (U.S. philan.) **8:**1052
HIRSCH, BARON MAURICE DE **8:**505
- Alliance Israélite Universelle **2:**651
- Argentinian agricultural settlement **3:**428ff
- chronological chart **8:**766-767
- finance **8:**719
- Herzl **8:**408; **16:**1070ff
- horse racing **15:**310
- Jellinek, Adolf **9:**1338
- railroads **13:**1519
- *illus:*
- - autograph **3:**315
- - portrait **8:**710
- - Salonika hospital **14:**699
- *see also:* JEWISH COLONIZATION ASSOCIATION
Hirsch, Max **13:**814
Hirsch, Mayer **8:**517
HIRSCH, MENDEL **8:**507
Hirsch, Mordecai Amram, *see* HIRSCH, MARKUS
Hirsch, Mordecai ben Ẓevi **11:**53
HIRSCH, OTTO **8:**508
Hirsch, Paul **13:**814; **15:**26
HIRSCH, RACHEL **8:**508
Hirsch, Raphael **8:**508

HIRSCH, ROBERT PAUL **15:**1055,1085
HIRSCH, SAMSON (Ben) RAPHAEL **8:**508
- *Contents:*
- - Life **8:**508
- - Jewish Education **8:**510
- - Attitude to Reform **8:**510
- - Conception of Judaism **8:**512
- - On Commandments **8:**513
- - Bible Exegesis **8:**513
- - Jewish Nationalism **8:**514
- absolute religion **3:**660
- Adass Jeshurun synagogue **2:**255
- Bamberger, Seligmann **4:**155
- Bruell, Nehemiah **4:**1415
- education **6:**422
- Frankel, Zacharias **7:**81
- Graetz, Heinrich **7:**847
- Hildesheimer, Azriel **8:**477
- history chart **8:**766-767
- *Iggeret Ẓafon* **11:**60
- Jewish identity **10:**59
- Judaism, modern **10:**395
- Moses **12:**400
- Neo-Orthodoxy **12:**956
- Orthodoxy **12:**1488ff
- prophecy **13:**1180
- revelation **14:**125
- Sabbath **14:**566
- sacrifices **14:**613
- *sha'atnez* **14:**1214
- Torah study **15:**458
- *illus:* text
HIRSCH, SAMUEL **8:**515
- miracles **12:**79
- nature **12:**890
- philosophy **13:**457
- revelation **14:**124
HIRSCH, SOLOMON **8:**516
Hirsch, William **15:**1206
Hirsch, Y. F. **7:**1173
Hirschbein, Esther, *see* SHUMIATCHER-HIRSCH-BEIN, ESTHER
HIRSCHBEIN, PERETZ **8:**517
- Hebrew drama **6:**201; **6:**203
- Yiddish theater **15:**1069
Hirsch ben Ḥayyim **13:**1108
Hirschberg, Alfred **5:**1177; **13:**465
HIRSCHBERG, HAÏM Z'EW **1:**31; **8:**518
HIRSCHBERG, JULIUS **8:**519
Hirsch Darshan **8:**487
Hirschel, David, *see* Berliner, David
HIRSCHEL, LEVIE (Louis) **8:**519
Hirschel, Meyer, *see* HIRSHEL, MEYER
Hirschel, Moses **10:**1286
HIRSCHEL, SOLOMON **8:**520
- Alexander, Levy **2:**571
- Hort, Abraham **8:**1008
- portrait **3:**540
- *illus:*
- - portrait **3:**546
Hirschel of Zistersdorf **11:**1140
Hirschenberg, Helen, *see* Glicenstein, Helen
Hirschenhorn, Jacob **11:**544
HIRSCHENSOHN (fam.) **8:**521
Hirschensohn, Clara **16:**1165
Hirschensohn, Eve **8:**521
Hirschensohn, Ḥayyim **8:**521
Hirschensohn, Isaac **8:**521
Hirschensohn, Jacob Mordecai **8:**521
Hirschensohn, Jakob **16:**1165
HIRSCHENSOHN-LICHTEN-STEIN, JEHIEL ẒEVI HERMANN **8:**522
Hirschenstein, Jekuthiel **16:**1148
HIRSCHFELD, ALBERT **8:**523
- *illus:* text
HIRSCHFELD, EPHRAIM JOSEPH **8:**523
HIRSCHFELD, GEORG **8:**524
HIRSCHFELD, GUSTAV (arch.) **8:**525
HIRSCHFELD, HARTWIG **8:**525
- Cairo *genizah* **16:**1336,1337
- linguistics **16:**1392
HIRSCHFELD, HEINRICH OTTO **8:**526
- archaeology **3:**301
HIRSCHFELD, ISADOR **8:**527
Hirschfeld, Oscar **13:**1033
Hirschfeld, Pascal **8:**524
Hirschfield, Gus **13:**482
Hirsch Ḥarif, *see* BIALEH, ẒEVI HIRSCH BEN NAPHTALI HERZ
Hirschhorn, Fred **15:**1177
Hirschhorn, Henriette, *see* Hartwig, Henriette
HIRSCHHORN, SAMUEL **8:**527
HIRSCHKAHN, ẒEVI **8:**527
Hirschl, Nikolaus **12:**1376
Hirschl, Salomon **12:**1236
Hirschler, I. (Rhod.) **4:**1480
HIRSCHLER, IGNAC **8:**528
HIRSCHLER, PÁL **8:**528
HIRSCHLER, RENÉ **8:**528
- Alsace-Lorraine **2:**757
- Strasbourg community **15:**424; **15:**425
HIRSCHMAN, ALBERT OTTO **8:**528
Hirschmann, Ira A. **8:**907; **15:**369
Hirschmann, Lew **15:**473
Hirsch-Ollendorf, Gilbert Yves Edmond, *see* GRANDVAL, GILBERT YVES EDMOND
Hirschovitz, Shneur Zalman **11:**279
Hirschprung, Harold **11:**1198
Hirsch School (N.Y.C.) **12:**1119
Hirsh (cantor, Pol.), *see* Hirsch
Hirshberg, Samuel **11:**1590
HIRSHBERG, YEHUDAH **8:**529
Hirshel, Meyer (15th cent.) **3:**890
HIRSHEL, MEYER (17th cent.) **8:**529
- informers **8:**1368
HIRSHENBERG, SAMUEL **3:**602
- *illus:*
- - "Spinoza" (paint.) **8:**350
- - "Synagogue in Jerusalem" (paint.) **3:**627
HIRSHFIELD, MORRIS **3:**602
HIRSHHORN, JOSEPH HERMAN **8:**529
Hirsh Mesharet, *see* RYMANOWER, ẒEVI HIRSH
Hirszband, Napoleon, *see* Jellenta, Cezary
HIRSZFELD, LUDWIK **8:**530
HIRSZOWICZ, ABRAHAM **8:**530
Hirt, August **5:**85; **12:**893
Hirth, J. F. (Hirtius) **8:**36
Hirz ben Hirsch Wiener, *see* Lemon, Hartog de
Ḥisbān (tn., Jor.) **8:**429; **9:**596
Ḥisbān River (Er. Isr.), *see* Heshbon River
ḤISDA (amora) **8:**531
- Avimi **3:**970
- cantillation **16:**1412
- Ḥuẓal **8:**1137
- study method **15:**757
- use of mnemonics **12:**187
Hisdai (name), *see also* Ḥasdai
ḤISDAI IBN ḤISDAI, ABU AL-FAḌL **8:**532
- Islam **11:**754
HISDAI IBN SHAPRUT **8:**533
- Cairo *genizah* **16:**1339
- chronological chart **8:**766-767
- Dioscorides **7:**894
- Ibn Saruq **11:**1305ff
- Jewish history **11:**350
- Joseph, Khazar king **16:**870
- Khazars **10:**950; **11:**59; **16:**917
- poetry **13:**685
- *resh kallah* **14:**83
- Spain **8:**660; **8:**666; **15:**225
- translations **15:**1326
- Umayyads **15:**1530
- *illus:*
- - letter to Khazar king **10:** 949
Hisham II (caliph) **15:**1530
Hishām III (caliph) **15:**1531
Hisham Palace (Er. Isr.) **9:**1370
ḤISIN, ḤAYYIM **8:**534
HISO (Belg. orgn.) **3:**168
Hispania (Lat., Sp.) **14:**1164
Hispanic Society Bible (illum. ms.) **4:***fcg.* 876; **13:**923
Hispanic Society of America **8:**1265
Hispanus, John **3:**948
HISTADRUT (lab. fed., Isr.) **8:**534
- *Contents:*
- - Constitution **8:**535
- - Trade Unions **8:**536
- - Economic Activities **8:**538
- - Mutual Aid **8:**539
- - Educational and Cultural Activities **8:**540
- - Arab Workers **8:**540
- - International Affiliations **8:**540
- Aḥdut ha-Avodah **2:**458
- Arab workers **9:**1028; **9:**868
- Ben-Gurion **4:**507
- Ben-Zvi **4:**579
- Chizhik, Ḥannah **5:**480
- cooperatives **5:**947ff
- *Davar* **5:**1316
- fundraising **13:**390
- Haganah **7:**1064ff
- Ha-Mashbir le-Ẓarkhan **5:**1547; **7:**1224
- Ha-Oved ha-Ẓiyyoni **7:**1317ff
- Ha-Po'el ha-Mizrachi **7:**1321
- Ha-Shomer ha-Ẓa'ir **7:**1374ff
- health insurance **9:**985
- Ḥevrat ha-Ovedim **8:**446ff
- historical survey **9:**340; **9:**346
- history chart **8:**766-767
- housing **9:**564
- ILO **15:**1564
- industry **9:**821
- Israel's economic development **9:**716
- Jewish workers **9:**848ff
- Katznelson, Berl **10:**837
- library **11:**194
- Mo'eẓet ha-Po'alot **12:**211
- Po'alei Zion **13:**663
- political roots **9:**659
- Remez, Moshe David **14:**69
- Revisionists, Zionist **14:**129ff
- Socialism **15:**32
- Solel Boneh **15:**92
- Teacher's Association **15:**889
- Tel Aviv's development **15:**921
- U.S. Zionism **16:**1147
- *illus:*
- - election posters **9:**857
- - founding conference **9:**849
- - labor-affiliated cooperative sector (table) **5:**951
- - membership growth, 1920-1939 (table) **9:**717
- - rest home, Nazareth **9:**866
Histadrut Building (Jer.) **9:**1496
Histadrut ha-Morim be-Israel, *see* TEACHERS' ASSOCIATION IN ISRAEL
Histadrut ha-No'ar ha-Amamit ha-Halutzit Gordonia, *see* GORDONIA
HISTADRUT HA-OVEDIM HA-LEUMMIT (lab. fed., Isr.) **8:**541
- Betar **4:**714
- Histadrut **9:**346; **9:**854
Histadrut ha-Po'alim ha-Ḥaredit (lab. fed., Isr.) **13:**655
Histadrut ha-Po'alim ha-Ẓe'irim be-Ereẓ Israel (newsp., Isr.), *see* HA-PO'EL HA-ẒA'IR
Histadrut ha-Ẓofim be-Israel (scouts fed., Isr.) **14:**1040
HISTADRUT IVRIT OF AMERICA (orgn.) **8:**542
Histadrut Nashim Mizrachi (orgn.) **12:**179
Histadrut Seminary for Painting and Sculpture (Isr.) **3:**976
Histalkut (kab. conc.) **10:**547; **10:**590
HISTORIA AUGUSTA (Lat. biog.) **8:**542
- attitude towards Judaism **14:**234
Historia Judaica (period.), *see* REVUE DES ETUDES JUIVES
HISTORIANS **8:**543
- *see also:* HISTORIOGRAPHY
Historiarum adversum paganos libri septem (bks.) **12:**1477
Historia Universalis (wk.) **12:**1140
Historical and Ethnographic Society (orgn., Rus.) **14:**464
Historical Dictionary of the Hebrew Language **2:**207
Historical geography **11:**918
"Historical Judaism", *see* CONSERVATIVE JUDAISM
Historical Society of Israel **15:**55
HISTORICAL SURVEY, LAND OF ISRAEL (beginnings—1880)
- Beginning until Monarchy **8:**569
- - Abraham **2:**112ff
- - Adoni-Zedek **2:**296
- - alphabetic inscriptions **2:**677
- - anthropology **3:**41
- - architecture **3:**336
- - Baal-Berith worship **4:**1
- - coins and currency **5:**695
- - crafts **5:**1044ff
- - dress **6:**215
- - Genesis **7:**386ff
- - *ḥerem* and conquest **8:**348
- - Hittites **8:**789
- - human geography **9:**567ff
- - Hyksos **8:**1142
- - Jerusalem **9:**1379
- - Judges, Book of **10:**442
- - Land of Judah **10:**330
- - Samaritan origins **14:**727
- - Samson **14:**773
- - sanctity **2:**763; **2:**770
- - Sinai **14:**1595ff
- - social structure **8:**609ff
- - trade and commerce **15:**1293ff
- - urban culture **5:**584ff
- - war and warfare **16:**268ff
- - *see also:* CANAAN, LAND OF
- Kingdoms of Judah and Israel **8:**586; **9:**1047
- - Ahab **2:**435ff
- - Amaziah **2:**798
- - Amon **2:**862
- - Aram-Damascus **3:**287
- - Asa **3:**671
- - David **5:**1318
- - designation **9:**111
- - Edom **6:**374
- - Ezra **6:**1104
- - Hezekiah **8:**450
- - Jehoshaphat **9:**1325
- - Jehu **9:**1328
- - Jeremiah **9:**1345
- - Jeroboam **9:**1371
- - Jerusalem **9:**1383
- - kingship **10:**1014
- - Manasseh **11:**852
- - Nehemiah **12:**936
- - Omri **12:**1390
- - Prophets' influence **13:**1157ff
- - Samaritans **14:**728, 736
- - Samuel **14:**780, 789
- - Saul **14:**909
- - social structure **8:**613
- - Solomon **15:**97ff
- - Tribes, the Twelve **15:**1381

- - Uzziah **16:**43
- Hellenistic-Roman Period **8:**625
- - academies **2:**199ff
- - *agoranomos* **2:**372
- - Agrippa I **2:**216
- - Alexander the Great **2:**577
- - Anan son of Anan **2:**919
- - *angaria* **2:**950
- - anthropology **3:**47
- - Anthiochus **3:**73
- - architecture **3:**357
- - art **3:**506
- - Caesar **10:**470
- - Cassius Longinus **5:**234
- - circumcision **5:**568ff
- - Dead Sea Sect **5:**1408
- - Decapolis **5:**1449
- - emperor worship **6:**729
- - Essenes **6:**899
- - Gabinius Aulus **7:**235
- - Hasmoneans **7:**1455
- - Herod I **8:**375
- - Hezekiah the Zealot **8:**455
- - high priest **8:**470ff
- - historiography **8:**552
- - Jason **9:**1291
- - Jerusalem **9:**1384
- - Jesus **10:**10
- - Johannan ben Zakkai **10:**148
- - Josephus Flavius **10:**251
- - Julian the Apostate **10:**467
- - messianism **11:**1408
- - Nakdimon ben Guryon **12:**801
- - Nero **12:**964
- - Pharisees **13:**363
- - Pompey **13:**846
- - Pontius Pilate **13:**848
- - procurators **13:**1117
- - Ptolemy **13:**1347
- - Samaritans **14:**729ff
- - Sicarii **14:**1491
- - Sikarikon **14:**1529
- - Titus **15:**1168
- - Zealots **16:**947
- Destruction of Second Temple to Arab Conquest **8:**643; **9:**237
- - Abba Sikra **2:**43
- - academies **2:**201ff
- - Akiva **2:**489
- - *amoraim* **2:**868ff
- - *angaria* **2:**950
- - Antipatris **3:**78
- - Antoninus **3:**166
- - *archisynagogos* **3:**335
- - *arnona* **3:**488
- - *aurum coronarium* **3:**854
- - Bar Kochba revolt **4:**228
- - Cilician collections **5:**562
- - crucifixion **5:**1134
- - emperor worship **6:**729
- - Hadrian **7:**1054
- - Heraclius **8:**333
- - imperial estates **10:**367
- - Judah ha-Nasi **10:**367ff
- - Meir **11:**1241
- - Negev **12:**928ff
- - Roman emperors **14:**229
- - Samaritans **14:**731ff, 736
- - Simeon bar Yoḥai **14:**1551
- - tax gatherers **15:**873
- - Vespasian's campaign **16:**116
- Arab Period **9:**259
- - Aḥa of Shabḥa **2:**449
- - Apulian Jewry **3:**226
- - Fatimids **6:**1196
- - gaonate **7:**315; **7:**317
- - Jerusalem **9:**1423
- - Samaritans **14:**732, 737
- - Umayyads **15:**1528ff
- - Yehudai Gaon **16:**731
- Crusader Period **5:**1138; **9:**267
- - agriculture **2:**398
- - archaeology **3:**329
- - Ayyūbids **3:**998
- - Franciscan settlement **7:**47
- - Jerusalem **9:**1415ff
- - *nagid* **12:**763
- - Pethahiah of Regensburg **13:**340
- - Saladin **14:**669
- Mamluk Period **9:**274
- - Jerusalem **9:**1423
- - Mamluks **11:**834
- - Samaritans **14:**733,737
- Ottoman Period **9:**282
- - Abulafia, Hayyim Nissim **2:**188
- - Aḥad ha-Am **2:**442
- - Aliyah, First and Second **2:**633ff
- - Alliance Israélite Universelle **2:**652
- - Antebi, Albert **3:**36
- - Bilu **4:**998
- - capitulations **5:**150
- - coins and currency **5:**723
- - Hebrew literature **8:**197
- - Hildesheimer, Azriel **8:**477
- - Ibrahim Pasha **8:**1214
- - "illegal" immigration **8:**1248
- - Jerusalem **9:**1426
- - J.D.C. aid **2:**828
- - Jew's autonomy **3:**927
- - Montefiore **12:**271
- - Napoleon **12:**824
- - Nasi, Joseph **12:**838
- - Nili **12:**1162ff
- - Portuguese *anusim* **3:**174
- - Samaritans **14:**734,737
- - Shabbateanism **14:**1247
- - Yishuv **8:**757
- *illus:*
- - Caesarea, Crusader city wall **9:**276
- - Ḥittin, site of Crusader battle **9:**275
- - Masada **11:**1079-1091
- - Sennacherib's eighth campaign **14:**1162
- - *see also under individual subjects*
- *maps:*
- - Abraham's wanderings **2:**115
- - Alexander Yannai's kingdom **9:**118
- - Ammonite region and towns **2:**854
- - Amorite towns, Israelite conquest period **2:**876
- - Arab rule, 8th cent. **9:**260
- - Aramean regions and cities **3:**253
- - archaeological sites **3:**304
- - Asher, tribe territory **3:**700
- - Bar Kochba revolt **4:**232
- - Bashan area in ancient times **4:**291
- - Battle of Karkar **2:**436
- - Benjamin, tribe territory **4:**522
- - Canaan, borders **9:**112
- - Canaan, El-Amarna age **5:**99
- - Crusader kingdom of Jerusalem **9:**270
- - Dan, tribe territory **5:**1256
- - David, limits of kingdom **9:**115
- - David's wars and conquest **5:**1320-1323
- - Decapolis **5:**1450
- - Ephraim, tribe territory **6:**807
- - Exodus, routes from Egypt to Moab **6:**1043, 1048
- - Gad, tribe territory **7:**247
- - Hasmonean kingdom **7:**1455
- - Herod's kingdom **8:**375; **9:**118
- - Issachar, tribe territory **9:**1075
- - Jerusalem
- - - Byzantine period **9:**1403
- - - Crusader period **9:**1421
- - - First Temple Period **9:**1385
- - - Nehemiah's period **9:**1387
- - - Second Temple period **9:**1395
- - Judah, tribal territory **10:**327
- - Judah and Israel, divided kingdom **9:**116,117
- - Judges, period of, limits of Israelite control **9:**113
- - Levitical cities **11:**137
- - Mamluk rule, 14th cent. **9:**277
- - Manasseh, tribal territory **11:**852
- - Naphtali, tribal territory **12:**820
- - Ottoman rule period **9:**283
- - Reuben, tribal territory **14:**104
- - Saul, limits of kingdom **9:**114
- - Simeon, tribal territory **14:**1548
- - Solomon, limits of kingdom **9:**115
- - Yehud province **9:**119
- - Zebulun, tribal territory **16:**951
- - *see also:* ARCHAEOLOGY; OTTOMAN EMPIRE

HISTORICAL SURVEY OF ISRAEL (1880-1948) **9:**322
- Abdullah ibn Hussein **2:**56
- Agudat Israel **2:**424ff
- Allenby, Edmund **2:**647
- Arab National Movement **9:**453
- Attlee **3:**836
- Balfour Declaration **4:**131ff
- Beriḥah **4:**632
- Bevin's policy **4:**784
- Biltmore Program **4:**997
- cartoons, political **5:**178
- Churchill **5:**556
- Haganah **7:**1064
- Ḥājj Amīn al-Husseini **8:**1132
- Hebrew Language Committee **2:**206
- Hebrew literature **8:**199
- high commissioners **8:**470
- ICA **10:**47
- "illegal" immigration **8:**1248
- I.Z.L. **8:**1466
- Jewish Agency **10:**26ff
- Jewish Brigade Group **10:**35
- Jewish Legion **10:**69
- Jewish religious life **9:**887ff
- Jew's autonomy **3:**927
- land transfer regulations **4:**508
- League of Nations **10:**1521
- legislation to preserve forests **9:**789
- Lloyd George **11:**413ff
- Loḥamei Ḥerut Israel **11:**463
- Mandate for Palestine **11:**861
- Negev **12:**929ff
- Palmaḥ **13:**45
- Revisionists **14:**128
- Roosevelt **14:**257
- "Saison" **7:**1071; **9:**356
- Sinai **14:**1596
- Sokolow, Nahum **15:**85
- Stalin **15:**327
- Truman, Harry **15:**1409
- U.N. **15:**1543, 1688
- Va'ad Le'ummi **16:**49
- War of Independence **16:**306
- western anti-Semitism **3:**135
- White Papers **16:**482
- Zionist Congresses **16:**1176
- *illus:*
- - Balfour Declaration **4:**131
- - Biltmore Hotel conference **15:**1633
- - Bols' "delivery note" for Palestine **3:**392; **9:**336
- - Churchill's letter to Weizmann re Jewish Fighting Force (1944) **3:**394
- - disturbances of May, 1921, Commission of Inquiry report **9:**339
- - Gromyko's speech at U.N. (May, 1947) **14:**493
- - "illegal" immigration **8:**1251-1253
- - Israel Declaration of Independence, full text **5:**1453
- - Jewish Legion at El-Arish, 1918 **9:**335
- - King David Hotel explosion **8:**1469
- - London Round Table Conference **9:**353
- - *Managem*, yacht used for Nili information **12:**1164
- - Mauritius detainees at Haifa **11:**1134
- - Peel Commission, 1936 **9:**351
- - proclamation of the State of Israel **4:**513
- - resolution re establishment of State **10:**34
- - Samuel, Sir Herbert, letter of appointment **14:**799
- - Sharett testifying before UNSCOP **16:**1093
- - Turks surrender Jerusalem **9:**1471
- - U.S. Senate's endorsement of a Jewish national home in Palestine **3:**393
- - War of Independence **16:**307-330
- - Wauchope's letter re settlement in Transjordan **9:**342
- - Weizmann, Chaim, and Emir Faisal **9:**336
- - Zionist delegation to Palestine, 1918 **9:**336; **16:**1163
- - *see also under individual subjects*
- *maps:*
- - British Mandate, 1922 **9:**317
- - Franco-British agreements, 1920-23 **9:**316
- - Plan C, Woodhead Commission, 1938 **13:**38
- - Sykes-Picot agreement, 1916 **9:**315
- - Turco-British agreement, 1906 **9:**315
- - UNSCOP partition plan, 1947 **9:**317
- - Zionist Movement frontier proposals, 1919 **9:**316

HISTORICAL SURVEY OF ISRAEL (1948-1970) **9:**365
- al-Fatḥ **9:**1033; **9:**467
- Arab refugees **9:**446
- assimilation **3:**775ff
- Bernadotte **4:**669
- boycott against Israel **4:**1282
- Declaration of Independence **5:**1451
- defense forces **9:**689ff
- Eichmann Trial **6:**521
- *fedayeen* **9:**1034; **9:**387ff
- governance **9:**610
- Hussein **8:**1131ff
- Jerusalem foreign missions **9:**1495
- Lavon Affair **10:**1477
- Nasser **12:**841ff
- Palestinian identity **9:**470ff
- Sinai Campaign **14:**1600
- Six-Day War **14:**1624
- Vatican **16:**77
- Zionism **16:**1060ff
- *illus:*
- - *Altalena* burning **8:**1470
- - *Der Tog* (May 15, 1948) **12:**1111
- - Eilat, hoisting of the Israel flag, 1949 **6:**567
- - General Armistice Agreements with Arab states (1949) **3:**479-482
- - Israel flag hoisted at U.N. headquarters **14:**1312
- - Israel Liberata coin **11:**1169
- - Shertok's letter to Bernadotte offering peace talks with Arab states **3:**478
- - Weizmann addressing Knesset **16:**433
- - *see also under individual subjects*
- *maps:*
- - armistice demarcation lines, 1949 **9:**318
- - Jerusalem municipal borders before and after reunification **9:**1505
- - Six-Day War cease-fire lines **9:**318

HISTORIOGRAPHY **8:**551
- *contents:*
- - Bible **8:**551
- - Second Temple Period **8:**552
- - Chronicles of the Jews **8:**554
- - Systematic Histories **8:**560
- - United States **8:**567
- Allon, Gedalya **2:**655
- Crusades **5:**1144
- Dubnow, Simon **6:**255
- Eupolemus **6:**964
- Eusebius **6:**977
- Graetz, Heinrich **7:**847
- Hebrew fiction **6:**1265
- Hecataeus of Abdera **8:**236
- *Historia Augusta* **14:**234
- Ibn Daud **8:**1159
- Ibn Verga, Solomon **8:**1203
- Jewish literature **11:**314; **11:**348ff
- Jewish scholarship **16:**578
- Josephus, Flavius **10:**253ff
- *Josippon* **10:**296
- Krochmal **13:**458
- Nicholas of Damascus **12:**1140
- Philo (Pseudo-) **13:**408
- resistance literature **8:**302
- responsa as history **14:**87
- Roth, Cecil **14:**326
- Urbach **16:**4
- Wissenschaft des Judentums **16:**578
- Yiddish **16:**805
- Zacuto, Abraham **2:**455; **16:**904
- *illus:*
- - text
- - *Divrei ha-Yamim le-Arazot Rumanyah* **14:**388
- - Josephus Flavius
- - - compendium of history (1529) **10:**260
- - - Latin translation of works (1486) **10:**252
- - Mark's *Geshikhte fun Yidn in Poyln* **10:**52
- - *Shalshelet ha-Kabbalah* (1587) **8:**1209
- *see also:* CHRONOLOGY; HISTORIANS; HISTORY
Historische Kommission fuer Geschichte der Juden in Deutschland **3:**493; **8:**563; **15:**53
HISTORY **8:**569
- *Contents:*
- - Beginning until Monarchy **8:**571
- - - Patriarchs **8:**571
- - - Exodus and Wanderings **8:**575
- - - Conquest and Settlement **8:**577
- - - Judges **8:**583
- - Kingdoms of Judah and Israel **8:**586
- - - David **8:**588
- - - Solomon **8:**591
- - - Earliest Kings **8:**593
- - - Asa; Omride Dynasty **8:**595
- - - Jehu Dynasty **8:**599
- - - Last Days of Samaria **8:**602
- - Social structure of ancient Israel **8:**609
- - - Source **8:**609
- - - Methods **8:**609
- - - Society Prior to Conquest **8:**609
- - - Period of Settlement **8:**609
- - - Tribal Units **8:**610
- - - Institutions **8:**610
- - - Changes Among Settlers **8:**610
- - - Urbanization **8:**611
- - - Changes in Tribal System **8:**611
- - - Monarchy and Tribal System **8:**612
- - - National Class Structure **8:**613
- - - Landowning Class **8:**613
- - - Merchant Class **8:**614
- - - Artisan Class **8:**614
- - - Marginal Elements **8:**615
- - - Slaves **8:**615
- - Destruction to Alexander **8:**615
- - - Restoration **8:**615
- - - Ezra **8:**616
- - - Nehemiah **8:**620
- - Ereẓ Israel—Second Temple (Hellenistic-Roman Period) **8:**625
- - - Ptolemaic Rule **8:**625
- - - Seleucid Rule **8:**628
- - - Hasmonean Rule **8:**631
- - - Herod's Rule **8:**636
- - - Procurators **8:**639
- - - The Revolt (First Roman War) **8:**641
- - Diaspora—Second Temple Period **8:**642
- - Aftermath of the First Roman War **8:**643
- - - Revolts Against Trajan **8:**644
- - - Bar Kokhba War **8:**646
- - - Roman Empire **8:**647
- - - Babylonian Diaspora **8:**649
- - Fourth to Seventh Centuries **8:**651
- - - Reshaping of Forces and Circumstances **8:**651
- - Middle Ages **8:**658
- - - Formative Times (7/11 Centuries) **8:**658
- - - Crystallization of Jewish Medieval Culture (12/15 Centuries) **8:**668
- - - Transition to Modern Times (16/17 Centuries) **8:**692
- - Modern Times **8:**703
- - - Up to Completion of Emancipation (to 1880) **8:**703
- - - From 1880's to Present (1970) **8:**731
- *see also:* ARCHAEOLOGY; CHRONOLOGY; ECONOMIC HISTORY; HISTORICAL SURVEY, LAND OF ISRAEL; HISTORICAL SURVEY OF ISRAEL (1880-1948); HISTORICAL SURVEY OF ISRAEL (1948-1970); HISTORIOGRAPHY; *and under individual subjects*
History, economic, *see* ECONOMIC HISTORY
History of Daniel (Apoc. wk.) **5:**1277
History of Egypt (wk.) **3:**178
History of Jewish Literature (wk.) **16:**368
History of the Jewish People (bk.) **11:**1070
History of the Jews in Christian Spain (bk.) **4:**82 **8:**564
Hit (tn., Iraq) **8:**781
HITAḤDUT (lab. party) **8:**781
- Arlosoroff, Chaim **3:**470
- Bienenstock, Max **4:**984
- socialist parties **15:**50
Hitaḥadut ha-Ikkarim be-Yisrael, *see* FARMERS' FEDERATION OF ISRAEL
Hitaḥadut ha-Koremim (co-op., Er.Isr.) **9:**328
Hitaḥadut ha-Moshavot (fed., Er. Isr.) **15:**3
Hitaḥadut ha-Ẓofim ve-ha-Ẓofot be-Israel **14:**1040
Hitaḥdut Olei Germania ve-Austria (orgn., Isr.) **14:**271
Hitaḥdut Olei Merkaz Europa (orgn., Isr.) **10:**1415
Hitbonenut, *see* MEDITATION
Ḥitfa (Ḥit; vocalization sign) **16:**1443
Hithalfut (conc., exchange of souls) **7:**574
Hitlahavut (rel. ecstasy) **7:**1405
HITLER, ADOLF **8:**782
- *Contents:*
- - anti-Semitism Origins **8:**782
- - Myth of the Jews **8:**783
- - Prelude to "Final Solution" **8:**784
- - Extermination of European Jewry **8:**784
- Austrian Holocaust **3:**899
- Bormann **4:**1250
- camps, concentration **5:**77ff
- Euthanasia **16:**1332
- Germany **7:**488
- Gestapo **7:**527
- ghetto **7:**542
- Goering **7:**688ff
- Himmler **8:**497ff
- history **8:**737ff
- history chart **8:**766-767
- Holocaust **8:**832ff
- Mussolini **12:**719
- Nostradamus' prediction **12:**1231
- SS and SD **15:**322
- Wagner, Richard **16:**241
- *illus:*
- - Husseini, Hājj Amin al-,and **8:**1132
- - portrait **8:**831,852
- - Wannsee minutes **16:**264
- *see also:* NATIONAL SOCIALISM; RACE, THEORY OF
Hitler, The Blonde, *see* Loritz, Alfred
Hitna'arut (orgn., Isr.) **14:**131
Hitnaẓẓelut (apologetics) **3:**189
Hitnoẓeẓut (kab. conc.) *see Niẓoẓot*
Hitpashetut (kab. term) **10:**547; **10:**590
HITSCHMANN, EDWARD **8:**786
Hittin, Kefar (Ḥittayya; vill., Er. Isr.), *see* KEFAR HATTIN
HITTITES (anc. people) **8:**786
- *Contents*
- - History **8:**787
- - in the Bible **8:**789
- - Hieroglyphic Writing **8:**790
- anthropology **3:**42; **3:**46
- Bible history **8:**576; **8:**577
- cuneiform script **16:**661
- ethics **6:**940
- king, kingship **10:**1013; **10:**1014
- Lydians **11:**621
- Mesopotamia **16:**1497
- Que **13:**1421ff
- Solomon's concubines **15:**100
- sun worship **15:**516
- war and warfare **16:**268ff
- *illus:*
- - art **3:**503
- *map:* text
Hittitology **16:**1507
Hityashevut ha-Elef (stlmt. scheme, Er. Isr.) **9:**854
Hitzig, Elias Daniel **9:**1152
HITZIG, FERDINAND **8:**790
- Itzig family **9:**1152
Hitzig, Friedrich **8:**791
HITZIG, JULIUS EDUARD **8:**791
- Hitzig, Elias Daniel **9:**1152
- *geneal. table:* **9:**1151
Hitzkowski (print., Ger.) **13:**1111
Ḥivi al-Balkhī, *see* ḤIWI AL-BALKHĪ
HIVITES, THE (anc. people) **8:**791
- Benjamin tribe **8:**579
- Hurrians **8:**1116ff
ḤIWI AL-BALKHĪ **8:**792
- Balkh **4:**138
- Cairo *genizah* **16:**1336
Hiwis-Hilfswillige (police units, Ger.) **8:**869
Hiwwa (leg. fig.) **16:**43
Hiyya (leg. fig.) **16:**43
ḤIYYA (tan.-amora) **8:**793
- Aibu **2:**473
- exilarchs **6:**1025
- Judith **10:**451
- Rabbah bar Ḥanina **13:**1441
- Rav **13:**1576
- Tosefta **15:**1284
Ḥiyya Abraham ben Moses, *see* BOTON, ABRAHAM BEN MOSES DI
Hiyya al-Dayyan, *see* Dayyan, Hiyya al-
ḤIYYA BAR ABBA (amora) **8:**796
- Academy on High **2:**208; **2:**209
- alphabet of **7:**370
- Aurum Coronarium **3:**854
- *beraitot* of **4:**191ff
- Eleazar ben Pedat **6:**596
- Judah ha-Nasi **10:**370ff
- *sheluḥei Ereẓ Israel* **14:**1361
ḤIYYA BAR AVIN (amora) **8:**796
- Idi bar Avin **8:**1227
Hiyya Bar Ba (va), *see* HIYYA BAR ABBA
Ḥiyya Bar Bun, *see* ḤIYYA BAR AVIN
Ḥiyya bar Mattnah (3rd. cent. C.E.) **11:**1132
Hiyya ben Al-Daudi **13:**581
Ḥivva ben Joseph Dayvan, *see* Dayyan, Hiyya ben Joseph
Ḥiyya Meir ben David **7:**1107
Ḥiyya of Meshan **7:**318
ḤIYYA ROFE **8:**797
Ḥiyyon River (Isr.) **9:**135
- *illus:* **9:**165
Ḥizzuk Emunah (bk.) **6:**96 **15:**1403
Ḥizzunim (prayer bk.) **11:**402
ḤLADIK, ABRAHAM **8:**797
Hlinka, Andrej **15:**1428
Hlinka Guard (Slovak fascist units) **8:**869
"Hlinka"party (Cz.), *see* Slovak People's Party
HLOHOVEC (tn., Slov.) **8:**797
Hlusk (tn., Belor.), *see* GLUSSK
Hoarding **7:**1062
Hobab (bib. fig.) **9:**1247
- Numbers, Book of **12:**1253
- *see also:* JETHRO
Hobart (city, Austr.) **3:**878
- Tasmania **15:**830
Hoboken (city, N.J.) **8:**1057
HOBSBAWM, ERIC JOHN ERNEST **8:**546
HOBSON, LAURA Z. **15:**1581
Hoch, Max **13:**528
Hochberg, Aaron **7:**621
Hochberg, Julian **13:**1345
Hochberg, S. **16:**1076ff
HOCHEIMER, HENRY **8:**798
Hocheimer, Lewis **8:**798
Hochgelehrter, Jacob Isaac, *see* Harif, Jacob Isaac
HOCHHUTH, ROLF **8:**798
HOCHMAN, JULIUS **8:**798
Hochmeister (title) **13:**1447
Hochmuth, A. **16:**117
HOCHSCHILD, MAURICIO **8:**799
HOCHSCHULE FUER DIE WISSENSCHAFT DES JUDENTUMS **8:**799
- *Allgemeine Zeitung* **2:**648
- Frankl, Pinkus Fritz **7:**102
- history chart **8:**766-767
- library **11:**192
- rabbinical seminaries **13:**1464
- Wissenschaft des Judentums **16:**577
Hochstetter, Andreas Adam **8:**36
Hochwald, Sigmund **12:**1245
Hochward, L.F. **7:**205
Hock, Karl Ferdinand **16:**86
HOCK, SIMON (Sinai) **8:**801
- historiography **8:**564
Hod (sefirah) **10:**570ff
HOD (orgn.), *see* Holland Deutschland

Hod, Mordechai **13**:48
- Six-Day War; **14**:1629
Hoda'ah, see ADMISSION
Hodava, Eleazar **13**:579
Hodayah (Amidah ben.) **2**:841
Hodayah ben Jesse ha-Nasi **10**:295
- Joseph ben Gershom **6**:1033
Hodayot, see THANKSGIVING PSALMS
Hoddis, Jacob von **7**:450
Hoddu, see INDIA
Hodel (dau. Besht.), *see* ADEL
Hodes, Richard **15**:790
HODESS, JACOB **8**:802
HOD HA-SHARON (cmty., Isr.) **8**:802
Hodiyyah (mosh., Isr.) **1**:place list
Hod Melekh (wk.) **4**:1545
HODMEZOVASARHELY (city, Hung.) **8**:802
HODONIN (tn., Cz.) **8**:803
Hody, Humphrey **8**:36
HOECHHEIMER, MOSES BEN ḤAYYIM COHEN **8**:803
Hoeflich, Eugen, *see* BEN-GAVRIEL, MOSHE YA'AKOV
Hoellriegel, Arnold, *see* BERMANN, RICHARD ARNOLD
HOELSCHER, GUSTAV **8**:804
Hoemesz (newsp.) **15**:1453
Hoenig, Aaron Moses **8**:805
Hoenig, Adam Albert **8**:805
Hoenig, Enoch **8**:805
Hoenig, Israel **8**:804
Hoenig, Loebel (Leib, Loew) **8**:804
Hoenig, Leopold, *see* Hoenigsberg, Loew von
Hoenig, Marianne **8**:805
Hoenig, Maximilian **8**:804
HOENIGSBERG (fam.) **8**:804
- Frankists **7**:68
- Leidesdorfer family **10**:1590
Hoenigsberg, Franceska, *see* Dobruschka-Schoenfeld, Franceska
Hoenigsberg, Israel Hoenig Edler von, *see* Hoenig, Israel
Hoenigsberg, Loew von **7**:70; **8**:805
Hoenigsberg, Soliman von **8**:805
Hoenigstein, Von (fam.) **7**:68
HOENIGSWALD, RICHARD **8**:805
Hoerling, J. **7**:1173
Hoeschel, the Rebbe Reb, *see* JOSHUA HOESCHEL BEN JACOB
HOESCHEL (Joshua) BEN SAUL **8**:806
Hoeschel, the Rebbe Reb, *see* JOSHUA HOESCHEL BEN JACOB
Hoeschke, Reuben **10**:640
HOESS, RUDOLF FRANZ FERDINAND **8**:806
- Auschwitz trials **3**:873
- Eichmann **6**:520
- gassing **16**:1332
Hoexter (dist., Ger.) **13**:7
Hof (city, Ger.) **4**:352
Hofagent, see COURT JEWS
Ḥofen (meas.) **16**:379 **16**:388
HOFER, ANDREAS **8**:806
- Basevi, Gioacchino **4**:289
Hofer, Y. **16**:825
HOFF, HANS **8**:807
Hoff, Syd **5**:220
Hoffaktor, see COURT JEWS
Hoffberger, Jerold **15**:301
Hoffenberg, Zemach **7**:1359
Hoffer (vill., Sask.) **14**:892
Hoffer, Leopold **5**:401
Hoffer, Moses **14**:892
HOFFER, WILLI **8**:807
HOFFER, YEHIEL **8**:808
Hoffman (fam. name), *see also:* Hoffmann, Hofman(n)
Hoffman, Abby **12**:1031
Hoffman, Benzion, *see* ẒIVION
Hoffman, Bernard **13**:484
Hoffman, Chaim, *see* YAHIL, CHAIM
HOFFMAN, CHARLES ISAIAH **8**:808
Hoffman, Charles W. (sol.) **11**:1552
Hoffman, Eduard, *see* REMENYI, EDUARD
Hoffman, Isidore B. **8**:808
Hoffman, Josef (archit.) **15**:624
Hoffman, N.D. **13**:1049
Hoffman, Paul G. **14**:276
Hoffman, Philip E. **6**:904
- *illus:*
- - A.J.C. delegation to Pope Paul VI, 1964 **5**:543
Hoffman, Ronald **15**:311
Hoffman, Samuel D. **12**:1021
Hoffmann, (art., Yug.) **16**:918
Hoffmann, A.J. (bk. firm) **4**:1239
HOFFMANN, CAMILL **8**:808
Hoffmann, Christoph **15**:994
HOFFMANN, DAVID ẒEVI **8**:808
- Auerbach, Benjamin **3**:843
- Berliner's collaboration **4**:665
- history chart **8**:766-767
- *Midreshet Halakhah* **11**:1521
- Pentateuch **13**:263
- sacrifices **14**:613
- Wissenschaft des Judentums **16**:578
HOFFMANN, DUSTIN **12**:468
Hoffmann, Hannah **11**:1070
HOFFMANN, JACOB (Revisionist) **8**:810
Hoffman, Jacob (r.) **7**:89; **13**:1496
Hoffmann, J.G. (Hebr.) **8**:36
Hoffmann, Moses **4**:1355
Hoffmann, Norbert **11**:1371
Hoffmann, Poul **14**:926
Hoffmann, Sandor, *see* HEVESI, SÁNDOR
Hoffner, Dan H. **4**:788
Hofhalter, Raphael **16**:131
Hofi, Yitzḥak **13**:48
Ḥofit (rural stlmt., Isr.) **1**:place list
Hofjude, see COURT JEWS
Hofman (name), *see also* Hoffman(n)
Hofman, Henryk **11**:1558
Hofman, Lonek **4**:1249
Hofman, Zina **11**:1558
Hofmann, Alois (indus.) **4**:381
HOFMANN, ISAAC LOEW **8**:811
HOFMANNSTHAL, HUGO VON **8**:811
- Braun, Felix **4**:1318
- nobility **15**:1166
Ḥofnayim (meas.) **16**:379
Ḥofshi-Mendes, David, *see* FRANCO-MENDES, DAVID
HOFSTADTER, RICHARD **8**:812
HOFSTADTER, ROBERT **8**:813
HOFSTEIN, DAVID **8**:813
- Yiddish **16**:818
Hofstein, Israel **7**:785 **14**:1301
HOGA, STANISLAV **8**:814
Hoglah (Bib. fig.) **16**:979
ḤOGLAH (mosh., Isr.) **8**:814
- statistics **1**:place list
Hogras ben Levi (Temple mus.) **12**:566
Hoham (bib. fig.) **8**:226
HOHENAU (tn., Aus.) **8**:814
HOHENEMS (tn., Aus.) **8**:815
- Vorarlberg **16**:223
- *illus:* text
Hohensalza (city), *see* INOWROCLAW
Hohenstaufen, Manfred (k., Sicily) **8**:45
HOHENZOLLERN (prov., Ger.) **8**:816
Hoherman, Alice **13**:117
Ho'il Moshe (wk.) **4**:530
- Mat, Moses **15**:520
Ḥokhmah (sefirah) **10**:570ff; **15**:1237
- Torah **15**:1237
Hokhmah nistarah (kab.) **10**:494
Ḥokhmah penimit, see KABBALAH
Ḥokhmah Yevanit (study) **11**:747
Ḥokhmat Adam (wk.) **5**:1298
Ḥokhmat ha-Ḥizzayon (wk.) **2**:132
Ḥokhmat ha-ẓeruf (mystic practice), *see* Letter-combinations
Ḥokhmat Ḥokhmata (wk.) **4**:222
Ḥokhmat Shelomo (wk.) **11**:333
Hokianga (co., N.Z.) **12**:1128
Hokitika (boro., port, N.Z.) **12**:1128
Ḥok u-Mishpat (journ.) **1**:newsp. list
Hol (bird), *see* PHOENIX
HOLBACH, PAUL HENRI DIETRICH, BARON D' **8**:817
Holbein, Hans **14**:785
- *illus:*
- - "King Rehoboam" (drg.) **14**:43
Holberg, Ludvig **14**:926
Holberg, Waldemar **15**:306
Holche Yosher (society) **15**:1534
Holder, J. **14**:1523
HOLDHEIM, SAMUEL **8**:817
- history chart **8**:766-767
- Oral Law **12**:1443
- rabbinical conferences **13**:1460
- Reform Judaism **14**:25
- *illus:*
- - text
- - portrait **8**:717
Ḥolem (vowel) **16**:1431,1449
HOLESOV (tn., Morav.) **8**:819
- Kyjov **10**:1308
- Moravia **12**:301
- museums **12**:543
- *illus:*
- - text
- - Shabbetai ben Meir ha-Kohen's tombstone **14**:1218
Ḥol ha-Mo'ed (intermediate fest. day) **6**:1244
- court sessions **13**:952
- *Mo'ed Katan* **12**:209
- mourning **11**:239; **12**:490
- Samaritans **14**:743
- *tefillin* **15**:901
- *illus:*
- - tasks permitted **12**:209
Holič (vill., Slov.) **11**:441
- Slovakia **14**:1679
Holiday, Clifford **3**:361
Holidays, *see* FESTIVALS
Holiness, *see* KEDUSHAH
HOLINESS CODE (bib. laws) **8**:820
- *Contents:*
- - Characteristic Features **8**:820
- - Priestly Editing **8**:822
- - Content **8**:822
- - Date of Composition **8**:824
- Leviticus **11**:143
HOLITSCHER, ARTHUR **8**:825
Holkham Bible (14th cent. illum. ms.) **5**:1066; **10**:1365
HOLLAENDER (fam.) **8**:825
Hollaender, Felix **8**:825
Hollaender, Friedrich **8**:826
Hollaender, Gustav **8**:825
Hollaender, L. (trans.) **12**:886
HOLLAENDER, LUDWIG (law.) **8**:826
- *illus:* text
Hollaender, Markus **13**:1022
Hollaender, Victor **8**:826
Hollaenderski, Leon **11**:8; **13**:817
Holland, *see* NETHERLANDS, THE
HOLLAND, JOSHUA ZALMAN **8**:827
Holland, Leonard **14**:143
Holland, Thomas **8**:36
Holland Deutschland (orgn.) **9**:1456
Hollander, A. **7**:224
Hollander, F. C. (S.A.) **12**:845
HOLLANDER, FRANKLIN (physiol.) **11**:1208
HOLLANDER, ISAIAH BEN AARON **8**:827
HOLLANDER, JOHN **15**:1578,1581
Hollandersky, Abe **15**:306
Hollandse Schouwburg **2**:904
Hollandus, Isaac (alch.) **2**:547
Hollandus, John Isaac (physic., alch.) **2**:547
Hollenberg, W. **8**:36
Holleschau (tn., Morav.), *see* HOLESOV
HOLLIDAY, JUDY **12**:468
HOLLZER, HARRY AARON **8**:827
HOLMAN, NAT **8**:827
HOLOCAUST **8**:828
- *Contents:*
- - Introduction **8**:831
- - First Period (1933-39) **8**:832
- - - Nazi Accession **8**:828
- - - Geography **8**:837
- - - Nazi Policy **8**:838
- - - Influence in Other Countries **8**:839
- - - Attitudes of Germans **8**:839
- - - German Jewry **8**:840
- - - World Jewry **8**:841
- - Second Period (1939-45) **8**:842
- - - The Jewish Situation **8**:842
- - - Geography **8**:842
- - - The Extermination Policy **8**:853
- - - Territorial Solution **8**:854
- - - Secrecy and Deception **8**:854
- - - Nomadization **8**:857
- - - The Final Solution **8**:859
- - - Concentration Camps **8**:873
- - - German Churches **8**:874
- - - Churches Outside Germany **8**:875
- - - Local Population **8**:875
- - - Red Cross **8**:877
- - - Jewish Society **8**:877
- - - Jewish Attitudes **8**:878
- - - Jewish Councils **8**:879
- - - Jewish Police **8**:883
- - - Liberation of Europe **8**:884
- - - Number of Victims **8**:885
- - - Rescue Possibilities **8**:886
- - - Material Losses **8**:809
- - End of a Civilization **8**:889
- - - Estimates of Victims **8**:889
- - The Behavior of the Victims **8**:890
- - - Who can Judge? **8**:890
- - - Mass Behavior **8**:891
- - - Jewish Officials **8**:896
- - - Physical Resistance—Revolt **8**:900
- - - Post-War Trials **8**:901
- - - Conclusions **8**:902
- - Sources and Literature **8**:902
- - - Sources **8**:902
- - - Comprehensive Works **8**:903
- - - Bibliographies **8**:903
- - - Specialized Periodicals **8**:904
- - - Collections of Documents **8**:905
- General
- - history **8**:731ff
- - history chart **8**:766-767
- - Karaites **10**:776
- - Sephardi Jewry **14**:1172
- - socialism, Jewish **15**:49
- In Various Countries
- - Albania **2**:523
- - Algeria **2**:616
- - Alsace **2**:757
- - Austria **3**:898
- - Belgium **4**:415
- - Bulgaria **4**:1485

- - Crete **5:**1090
- - Czechoslovakia **5:**1195
- - Denmark **5:**1538
- - Estonia **6:**917
- - Finland **6:**1298
- - France **7:**32
- - Gdansk (Danzig) **7:**348
- - Germany **7:**488
- - Greece **7:**879
- - Hungary **8:**1096
- - Italy **9:**1132
- - Latvia **10:**1467
- - Libya **11:**202
- - Lithuania **11:**385
- - Luxembourg **11:**591
- - Morocco **12:**342
- - Netherlands **12:**984
- - Norway **12:**1224
- - Poland **13:**752
- - Portugal **13:**925
- - Rumania **13:**397
- - Spain **15:**244
- - Sweden **15:**547
- - Switzerland **15:**559
- - Tunisia **15:**1434
- - U.S.S.R. **14:**478ff
- - Yugoslavia **16:**868
- - *see also under individual towns and regions*
- Perpetration
- - Babi Yar **4:**27
- - Badge, Jewish **4:**71
- - *Der Stuermer* **15:**460
- - forced labor **6:**1429
- - Frank, Anne **7:**53
- - gassing **16:**1332
- - Gestapo **7:**527 **8:**1472
- - ghettos **7:**543
- - Iron Guard **8:**1471
- - Judenrat **10:**407
- - kapo **10:**754
- - Kristallnacht **10:**1263
- - legislation, anti-Jewish **10:**1573
- - Nazi-Deutsch **12:**904
- - Nazi emigration organization **14:**51
- - Nuremberg laws **12:**1281
- - refugees **14:**28
- - Reichsvertretung **14:**50
- - RSHA **14:**363
- - Schacht Plan **14:**937
- - SS and SD **15:**322
- - synagogues **15:**585
- - Union Générale des Israelites **15:**1534
- - *see also:* CAMPS (Concentration and Extermination); FINAL SOLUTION
- War Criminals
- - Antonescu, Ion **3:**163
- - Antonescu, Mihai **3:**163
- - Hitler **8:**782
- - Katzmann, Friedrich **10:**834
- - Laval, Pierre **10:**1475
- - Mengele, Josef **11:**1353
- - Mussolini **12:**719
- - Pohl, Oswald **13:**701
- - Rosenberg, Alfred **14:**275
- - Streicher, Julius **15:**436
- - Tiso, Josef **15:**1155
- - Wirth, Christian **16:**553
- - Wisliceny, Dieter **16:**569
- - *see also:* FINAL SOLUTION
- Protest and Resistance
- - American Jewish Congress **2:**825
- - Amsterdam **2:**902
- - Anielewicz, Mordecai **3:**2
- - Ascoli, Ettore **3:**691
- - Auschwitz **3:**856
- - Baum, Herbert **4:**332
- - Bernheim Petition **4:**681
- - Bialystok **4:**808
- - Galaction, Gala **7:**256
- - Gerstein, Kurt **7:**520
- - Grodno **7:**927
- - Grueber, Heinrich **7:**942
- - Grynszpan, Herschel **7:**953
- - Haganah **7:**1071
- - Ha-Shomer ha-Ẓa'ir **7:**1375
- - Lichtenberg, Bernhard **11:**208
- - Lvov **11:**615
- - Mir **12:**72
- - Paris **13:**110
- - partisans **13:**140
- - Piotrkow partisans **13:**557
- - Reik, Ḥavivah **14:**54
- - Reviczky, Imre **14:**1039; **14:**128
- - scout movement **14:**1039
- - self-defense **14:**1128
- - Sereni, Enzo Ḥayyim **14:**1182
- - Sobibor **15:**21
- - students' movements **15:**452
- - Szenes, Hannah **15:**661
- - Treblinka **15:**1369
- - Vilna Ghetto **16:**591
- - Warsaw Ghetto **16:**342
- - Weissmandel, Michael Dov **16:**418
- - Witenberg, Yiẓḥak **16:**591
- - Zolochev **16:**1218
- Aftermath
- - Ashkenazi Jewry **3:**721
- - Auschwitz trials **3:**873
- - *beriḥah* **4:**630
- - Conference on Claims **5:**872
- - Council of German Jews **5:**994
- - demographic changes **5:**1497; **13:**894
- - denazification **5:**1533
- - displaced persons **6:**75
- - Eichman trial **6:**520
- - European Jewry **6:**976
- - Genocide Convention **7:**409
- - Ḥasidism, effect on **7:**1399
- - Jewish Cultural Reconstruction **10:**49
- - Ladino **10:**1348
- - migrations and **16:**1522,1523ff
- - Protestants **13:**1250
- - reparations **14:**72
- - restitution **14:**95
- - Righteous of the Nations **14:**184
- - South Africa **15:**187
- - survivors **6:**75
- - tracing service **8:**1412
- - UNRRA **15:**1688
- - URO **15:**1567
- - vital statistics **16:**181ff
- - War Crimes Trials **16:**288
- Documentation
- - archives **3:**384
- - Auschwitz museum **3:**856
- - Centre de Documentation **5:**287; **15:**54
- - Ghetto Fighters' House **7:**546
- - International Tracing Service **8:**1412
- - Jewish research **8:**565
- - Warsaw institute **10:**52
- - Wiener Library **16:**503
- - Yad Vashem **16:**697
- Religious Aspects
- - *agunah* **2:**430
- - *Ani Ma'amin* **3:**5
- - conversion **3:**174
- - prayer books **13:**993
- - responsa **10:**979; **14:**92
- - theology **14:**138
- Art and Literature
- - art **3:**568ff
- - Ben-Zvi, Ze'ev **4:**582
- - cartoons **5:**178
- - children's literature **5:**446
- - *Deputy, The* **8:**798
- - Greenberg, Uri Zevi **7:**908
- - K. Zetnick **10:**1310
- - Lasansky's "Nazi Drawings" **10:**1431
- - memorial literature **6:**1247
- - motion pictures **12:**457ff
- - Munk, Kaj **12:**525
- - Schwarz-Bart, André **14:**1027
- - Sachs, Nelly **14:**595
- - Uris, Leon **16:**10
- - Weiss, Peter **16:**415
- - Wiesel, Élie **16:**507
- - Zuckmayer, Carl **16:**1231
- *illus:*
- - Alessandria, memorial **9:**1137
- - Amsterdam
- - - Jewish quarter **12:**984
- - - schoolchildren wearing yellow badge **12:**987
- - - statue for dockers' strike, 1942 **2:**904
- - Anielewicz memorial **3:**3
- - Bergen-Belsen, Nazi doctor **4:**610
- - Bergen-Belsen Trial **16:**295
- - Bialystok ghetto **4:**805
- - Bologna, memorial plaque **4:**1191
- - Bonn, plaque for destroyed synagogue **4:**1211
- - Brandt's negotiations with Eichmann, Hull's cable **8:**909
- - Breisach, memorial for destroyed synagogue **4:**1345
- - Brno synagogue ruins **5:**1196
- - Buban monument for Nis Jews **12:**1175
- - camp and ghetto artists' drawing Figs. 75-85 **3-**ART: **5:**95
- - concentration camp memorials, East German stamp **4:**1445
- - Constance synagogue ruins **5:**912
- - Czechoslovak commemorative stamp (1967) **5:**1198
- - Czestochowa, Great Synagogue ruins **5:**1213
- - deportation scenes **2:**902; **7:**31; **8:**763; **12:**990
- - deportations to Theresienstadt (map) **15:**1113
- - Dusseldorf, anti-Semitic slogan **7:**489
- - Eichmann trial **6:**519; **9:**405
- - encouragement slogan, Dutch underground **4:**71
- - forced labor **6:**1429
- - German soap factory **13:**761
- - Germany, major communities, 1933 and 1970 (map) **7:**487
- - Germany, *takkanot* for communities not having a *minyan* **15:**716
- - Gestapo telegrams re concentration camps and deportation **7:**528,529
- - Ghetto Fighters' House, Israel **7:**546
- - Haga, memorial to victims of Nazism **15:**459
- - Hanau synagogue, burning of **7:**1257
- - "Ha-Shoah" memorial at Neẓer Sereni **3:**633
- - herding of Jews into mass grave **8:**763
- - Himmler's visit to Auschwitz **3:**861
- - "Homage to Six Million" (sculp., L. Nevelson) **3:**635
- - identity card stamped "J" (Cologne, 1939) **5:**742
- - Insterburg, final entry in community book (1941) **5:**825
- - Jassy, Jews slaughtered by Rumanian and German soldiers **14:**400
- - Jewish badge, Cracow, order of November, 1939 **4:**69
- - Jewish badge, Dutch woman, 1942 **4:**70
- - Jewish badges for occupied countries of Europe **4:**72
- - Jews forced to ride each other **13:**757
- - Johannesburg memorial **10:**157
- - "Kaddish" (lith., A. Krol) **10:**662
- - *Khurbn Vilne* (1947) **10:**659
- - Klein, Bergen-Belsen Nazi doctor **4:**610
- - *"Kristallnacht"* **4:**651; **10:**1263-1265
- - Lodz ghetto **11:**427-436; **14:**428
- - Lodz ghetto coin **5:**726
- - Lublin, expulsion **11:**543
- - *Magen David* brand on Jews **13:**758
- - "Main Gate of Kaunas Ghetto" (drg., E. Lurie) **10:**849
- - Majdanek camp, commemorative stamp **11:**794
- - Mauthausen concentration camp **11:**1137, 1138
- - Memorial to the Unknown Jewish Martyr, Paris **13:**112
- - Mengele, survivors of experiments **3:**866
- - Minsk Mazowiecki Jews taken to forced labor **12:**60
- - Munich, Ohel Yakob synagogue **12:**523
- - Munich Central Synagogue after *Kristallnacht* **8:**738
- - Novi Sad memorial **12:**1236
- - Nuremberg Trial **16:**289,293
- - Olkusz Jews humiliated **12:**1368
- - Opava synagogue fire **12:**1412
- - Paris War Crimes Trial **16:**301
- - poison gas, delivery note and correspondence **3:**861-862
- - Poland, document describing conditions (1943) **13:**759
- - Prague, looted clocks **13:**975
- - Prague, Pinkas Synagogue memorial wall **13:**976
- - Riga ghetto **14:**175
- - "Ruins of Synagogue" (etch., A. Bogen) **3:**620
- - Sachsenhausen camp, roll call **8:**761
- - Salonika, memorials to Nazi victims **7:**882; **14:**701
- - "selection" of arrivals to camp **3:**863
- - Sobibor death camp plan **15:**22
- - Sombor, memorial to Nazi victims **15:**135
- - Stroop, Juergen, in Warsaw ghetto **15:**442
- - Stroop's report on liquidation of Warsaw ghetto **16:**346
- - Taylor's memo re Bermuda Conference **8:**906
- - Theresienstadt ghetto "bank note" **5:**726
- - Theresienstadt ghetto children drawings **5:**1203
- - Transnistria police memo **15:**1330
- - Treblinka camp model **15:**1368
- - Vilna Jews digging their own graves **16:**145
- - Wannsee Conference minutes **16:**264
- - Warsaw ghetto **7:**544; **16:**343-352
- - - children's choir **12:**657
- - - commemorative stamp **15:**336
- - - Jewish boy giving himself up **13:**757
- - - uprising memorial **16:**351
- - Westerbork camp **16:**466
- - women forced to undress prior to being shot **13:**757
- - Wuerzburg, deportation of Jews **7:**495
- - Yad Vashem (Jer.) Fig. 110 **3-**ART; **9:**1488; **16:**697
- - Yiddish writers, survivors **16:**821
- - Zamosc Jews waiting for

deportation **4**:454
- *see also:* NATIONAL SOCIALISM
HOLOCAUST, RESCUE FROM **8**:905
- American Jewish Committee **2**:824
- *beriḥah* **4**:629
- Bermuda Conference **4**:668
- Bernadotte, Folke **4**:669
- Brand, Joel **4**:1294
- China **5**:470
- Denmark **5**:1538
- Dunant, Jean Henry **6**:270
- Europa plan **6**:966
- Evian conference **6**:987
- Fleischmann, Gisi **6**:1343
- Haavara **7**:1012
- JDC ("Joint") **2**:830
- Kasztner, Rezső Rudolf **10**:815
- Komoly, Otto **10**:1176
- Reviczky, Imre **14**:128
- Wallenberg, Raoul **16**:255
- War Refugee Board **16**:332
- Westerweel, Joop **16**:472
- Youth Aliyah **16**:861ff
- *illus:*
- - text
- - Jewish refugees rowed to Sweden **5**:1539
- - refugees **14**:28,32
HOLOCAUST AND THE CHRISTIAN CHURCHES **8**:910f
- *Contents:*
- - The Catholic Church **8**:910
- - Protestant, Greek Orthodox **8**:914
- Holocaust **8**:874
Holocaust Chamber (Mt. Zion, Jer.) **16**:1031
Holocaust Museum (Isr.) **11**:463
- *illus:* **11**:463
HOLOCAUST REMEMBRANCE DAY **8**:916
- Yad Vashem **16**:697
HOLOFERNES (Apoc. fig.) **8**:917
- in the Arts **10**:459*f*
- *Judith, Book of* **10**:451
- *illus:*
- - text
- - decapitated by Judith **3**:1; **10**:453-458
HOLON (city, Judea) **8**:918
- *illus:*
- - ORT vocational high school **12**:1485
Holon (reg., Moab) **8**:918
ḤOLON (city, Isr.) **8**:918
- Samaritan center **14**:736
- statistics **1**: place list
- Tel Aviv **15**:924
Ḥolo shel mo'ed (intermediate fest. days), *see Ḥol ha-Mo'ed*
Holt, Kare **14**:934
Holten, Albert **8**:36
HOLTZ, AVRAHAM **1**:31
Holtzendorff, F. von **4**:873
Holtzer, Rachel **12**:454
Holub, D. **7**:1368
Holubek, Franz **3**:83; **14**:224
Ḥol va-Ru'aḥ (journ.) **1**:newsp. list
Holy Ark, *see* ARK
Holy Blossom (syn., Can.) **5**:103; **15**:1260-1261
- *illus:*
- - exterior **5**:106
- - interior **15**:1261
HOLY CONGREGATION IN JERUSALEM **8**:919
- Simeon ben Menasya **14**:1561
- *see also:* ḤAVER, ḤAVERIM
Holy Cross, Church of the (Jer.) **9**:1416
Holy Ghost (conc.) **14**:365; **14**:367
Holy Land, *see* ISRAEL
Holyland Hotel (Jer.) **9**:1496
Holy Names, *see* GOD, NAMES OF
Holy of Holies **15**:948ff
- ass worship **3**:784
- high priest **3**:977
- incense **8**:1314
- sacrifice **14**:600
- status in *halakhah* **15**:989
- Tabernacle **15**:680; **15**:681
- Temple rock **6**:985
- Titus **15**:1170
- Western Wall **16**:467
- Yaḥad belief **16**:699
Holyoke (city, Mass.) **11**:1113
Holy One, Blessed Be He (name of God) **10**:871
HOLY PLACES **8**:920
- *Contents:*
- - Jewish **8**:920
- - Christian **8**:922
- - Muslim **8**:935
- - Other Religions **8**:936
- - Political Aspect **8**:936
- Canaan **15**:1383
- Christian **9**:1502; **16**:73ff
- history chart (1852) **8**:766-767
- Israel's protection of **9**:427
- Jerusalem **9**:1516ff
- - Arab period **9**:1423ff
- - maps **9**:1544
- - superintendent **9**:1423
- Karlowitz, Treaty of **9**:299
- *kever avot* **10**:934
- law protecting **14**:616
- Muslim holy places **9**:919; **9**:921ff
- *shivviti* plaque **14**:1420
- Six-Day War **14**:635
- State of Israel **15**:1548; **15**:1549
- theophany **14**:117
- *illus:* text
- *illus:* Bahai
- - Temple, Haifa **9**:924
- *illus:* Christian
- - Basilica of the Agony **9**:1455
- - Basilica of the Annunciation **8**:929; **12**:901
- - Church of Jesus the Child **12**:903
- - Church of John the Baptist **10**:160
- - Church of the Multiplication **15**:689
- - Church of the Nativity **4**:300,742; **9**:912
- - Dormition Abbey **9**:1465
- - Garden Tomb (Jer.) **9**:916,1461
- - Gethsemane, Russian Church of **9**:1462
- - Grotto of the Nativity **4**:746
- - Holy Sepulcher **9**:913,914,1418,1439
- - Monastery of the Temptation **9**:913
- - Nazareth, "The Synagogue" **12**:900
- - Tomb of Mary **9**:1417
- - Via Dolorosa **9**:1401
- *illus:* Druze
- - Nabi Shu'ayb **10**:20,886
- *illus:* Jewish
- - Elijah's cave **6**:641
- - *Even ha-Shetiyyah* **9**:1557
- - Machpelah, Cave of **5**:58; **11**:670,671
- - Meir Ba'al ha-Nes tomb **9**:276; **15**:1132
- - Mount Zion **9**:1465
- - nineteenth cent. drawing **9**:*fcg.* 1531
- - Rachel's tomb **13**:1489
- - Simeon bar Yoḥai's tomb **14**:1552
- - Simeon the Just's tomb **14**:1567
- - Temple Mount **9**:1413; **15**:988,991
- - Western Wall **9**:901,1439,1467,1478,1499; **12**:672; **13**:1063; **16**:469,470
- *illus:* Muslim
- - Al-Aqṣā **9**:1413,1439
- - Dome of the Rock **9**:920,1413,1557
- - Machpelah, Cave of **5**:58; **11**:670, 671
- - Nebi Mūsā **9**:99
- - Temple Mount **15**:988,991
- *see also:* CULT PLACES, ISRAELITE; ITINERARIES OF EREẒ ISRAEL; PILGRIMAGE; *and individual places*
Holy Roman Empire
- Anselm ha-Levi **3**:33
- Crusades **5**:1135*ff*
- *Landjudenschaft* **10**:1405
- population **13**:876
- *see also individual emperors and countries*
Holy See, *see* VATICAN
Holy Sepulcher, Church of the (Jer.) **8**:922; **8**:936
- al-Ḥākim **9**:265
- Christian community **9**:910,1441
- Christianity **9**:1570ff
- Constantine **9**:1406
- Crusader times **9**:1416
- Jerusalem in Art **9**:1579
- Jerusalem second wall **9**:1526; **9**:1537
- maps **9**:1544
- 1953 fire **9**:1492
- topography **9**:1516
- *illus:*
- - aerial view **9**:1439
- - Copts receiving Patriarch **9**:913
- - entrance **9**:1418-1420
- - interior **8**:928
- - Syrian Orthodox rites **9**:914
Holy Society of Rabbi Judah Ḥasid **14**:1247
Holy sparks (kab. conc.), *see Niẓoẓot*
Holy Spirit, *see* RU'AH HA-KODESH
Holzbauer, Ignaz **10**:460
Holzberg, Feivel **15**:127
Holzberg, Isaac Raphael **15**:127,939
Holzberg, T. J. **15**:209
Holzer, Charlotte **4**:332
Holzer, Harry A. **11**:501
Holzer, Isaac **15**:821
Holzman, William **15**:304
Holzmann, S.Z. **10**:880
Holzstock-Holzstick, Meir Jehiel, *see* MEIR JEHIEL HA-LEVI OF OSTROWIEC
ḤOMA (w., Abbaye) **8**:940
"Homage to Hieronymus Bosch" (sculp., I. Tumarkin) Fig. 108 3-ART
"Homage to Six Million" (sculp., L. Nevelson) **3**:635
Ḥomah (newsp.) **7**:1071
Ḥomah u-Migdal, *see* STOCKADE AND WATCHTOWER
Homann (cartog.) **11**:927
Homberg, J.F. **8**:36
HOMBERG, NAPHTALI HERZ **8**:940
- assimilation **16**:1327
- Haskalah **7**:265; **8**:183
- history chart **8**:766-767
- homiletical literature **8**:956
- Tarnow school **15**:820
- Vienna **16**:124
HOMBURG (city, Ger.) **8**:942
Homburger, August **6**:464
Home, *see* FAMILY; PARENT AND CHILD; PARENTS, HONOR OF
Homel (tn., Belor.), *see* GOMEL
HOMEM, ANTONIO **8**:943
Homem, Francisco Nuñez, *see* Abendana, David
HOMER (poet) **8**:944
- Hellenism **8**:293
- Judaism **3**:189
Homer (meas.) **16**:379ff
HOMICIDE **8**:944
- abortion **2**:99; **2**:101
- autopsy **3**:932ff
- *avot nezikin* **3**:987
- banishment **4**:163
- blood-avenger **4**:1116
- bloodguilt **4**:1118
- city of refuge **5**:591ff
- Commandments, the 613 **5**:769,771,779
- complicity **13**:224
- compounding offences **5**:856
- death through flogging **6**:1350
- *eglah arufah* **6**:475
- expiation by elders **6**:578
- gentiles **12**:1189ff
- imprisonment **8**:1300
- impurity **13**:1406; **13**:1414
- informer **8**:1370
- *kiddush ha-Shem* **10**:978
- liability for killed agent **10**:1330
- *Makkot* **11**:808
- of condemned person **13**:961
- perjury **13**:289
- prosecution **13**:959
- public insult **8**:1408
- punishment **13**:224; **13**:1386
- Sanhedrin **14**:840
- sin **14**:1592
- transgression or death **14**:1196
- *illus:*
- - *eglah arufah* ceremony **6**:476
- *see also:* ASSAULT; CAPITAL PUNISHMENT; SUICIDE
HOMILETIC LITERATURE **8**:946
- *Contents:*
- - Middle Ages **8**:946
- - Structure of Sermon **8**:950
- - Aesthetics of Sermon **8**:951
- - History **8**:953
- - Modern Period **8**:955
- allegory **2**:643ff
- Bible exegesis **4**:890
- Ḥasidism **7**:1413
- Kabbalah **10**:490; **10**:642
- Kranz, Jacob ben Wolf **10**:1239
- *Leviticus Rabbah*, prototype **11**:149
- Midrash **11**:320ff
- Moscato, Judah **12**:358
- parody and satire **13**:125
- *Perek Shirah* **13**:274
- *peshat* **13**:329
- sages **14**:643
- *sevarah* **14**:1195
- *She'iltot* **2**:449ff
- *Tanḥuma Yelammedenu* **15**:794
- Targum Sheni **15**:811
- *Yalkut ha-Makhiri* **16**:706
- Yiddish **16**:801
- *Ze'enah u-Re'enah* **16**:967
- zodiac signs **16**:1192
- Zohar **16**:1194ff
- *illus:*
- - Baḥya ben Asher's commentary on the Pentateuch (1492) **4**:104
- - *Ein Yosef* (1860) **9**:1164
- - *Esh Dat* (1718) **2**:598
- - *Kedushat Yom Tov* (1843) **2**:611
- - *Kesef Nivḥar* (1605) **5**:1240
- - *Kohelet Ya'akov* (1578) **7**:260
- - *Korban Ḥagigah* (1704) **7**:259
- - *Malmad ha-Talmidim* (14th cent.) **2**:928
- - *Mattenot Kehunnah* (1595) **9**:1079
- - *Rei'aḥ Sadeh* (1738) **6**:326
- - *The Salvation of Israel* (1773) **5**:180
- - *Sefer Mareh Einayim* (1712) **4**:101
- *see also:* AGGADAH; DARSHAN; ETHICAL LITERATURE;

INTERPRETATION;
MAGGID; MIDRASH;
PREACHING
Homilies of the Monk James (Byz. miniature) **15:**150
Hominer, H. **2:**802
Homiyyah (tn., Belor.), *see* GOMEL
Hommel, Karl F. **8:**36
HOMOLKA, OSCAR **15:**1085
Homonna (tn., Cz.), *see* HUMENNE
HOMOSEXUALITY **8:**961
- Commandments, the 613 **5:**781
- ethics **6:**935
- sexual offences **14:**1207
- sodomy **15:**71
Homs (tn., Libya) **11:**202
Homs (tn., Syr.), *see* EMESA
Homunculus, *see* GOLEM
HOND, MEIJER DE **8:**962
- Dutch literature **6:**320
HONDURAS **8:**962
- Latin America **10:**1451
- military **11:**1551
Honegger, Arthur **10:**461
HONEIN (port) **8:**962
Honert, Taco Hajo van den **8:**36
Honesdale (boro.,Pa.) **13:**230
HONEY **8:**963
- beekeeping **2:**402
- food **6:**1416
- marriage custom **11:**1043
- Rosh ha-Shanah **14:**309
- sacrifice **14:**710
- *illus:*
- - sweetness of the Torah **6:**386
- *see also:* BEE
Honey badger (zool.) **9:**226
HONG KONG **8:**963
- Jewish Community **5:**470
- synagogues **1:**syn. list
HONI HA-ME'AGGEL (tal. fig.) **8:**964
- Adar, twentieth of **2:**252
- circle drawing **7:**1154
- Jeremiah **9:**1360
- magic **11:**707
- sages **14:**638
- Teacher of Righteousness **15:**888
Honig, Hugó, *see* CSERGŐ, HUGÓ
Honikman, Alfred **5:**140
HONOR (conc.) **8:**965
HONOR, LEO L. **8:**967
- Chicago College **5:**735
Honoratus de Bonafide, *see* DURAN, PROFIAT
Honorius (Hebr.) **8:**38
HONORIUS I (pope) **8:**967
HONORIUS III (pope) **8:**967
- Jewish envoys **16:**1291
- Jews **13:**854
- papal bull **4:**1495
- tithes, church **15:**1162
HONORIUS IV (pope) **8:**967
HONORIUS FLAVIUS (Rom. emp.) **8:**968
- Apulian Jewry **3:**226
- arbitration courts **3:**295
- Ereẓ Israel **9:**257
- Jews **14:**230
Honor of parents, *see* PARENTS, HONOR OF
Hood, J. D. L. **13:**34
HOOFIEN, ELIEZER SIEGFRIED **8:**968
- Zionism **16:**1119
Hooghe, Romeyn de **5:**247
- *illus:*
- - "Circumcision" (drg.) **14:**827
Hooght, Everardus van der **8:**17, 38
HOOGSTRAATEN, JACOB **8:**969
- Reuchlin, Johannes **14:**109
HOOK, SIDNEY (philos.) **8:**969
Hooke, S. H. (Bib. trans.) **4:**871; **4:**908
HOOPOE (bird) **8:**970
- Asmodeus **3:**755
- dietary laws **6:**34
- Queen of Sheba **13:**1424
- *illus:* text
Hoornbeck, J. **8:**38
Hoover, Herbert **2:**828
Hooykaas, I. **4:**876
Hopensztand, Dawid Jakub **13:**803
Hope of Israel, The (wk.), *see Esperança de Israel*
Hope-Simpson, Sir John **9:**344; **13:**32 **16:**483
Hopferman, Simson **5:**606
Hophni (Babyl. r.) **14:**807
HOPHNI AND PHINEHAS (sons of Eli) **8:**970
- ark **13:**1077
- Eli **6:**613
- Ichabod **8:**1215
- Phinehas **13:**466
HOPHRA (Egy. k.) **8:**971
Hopkins, E. M. **15:**1681
Hopkinsville (city, Ky.) **10:**909
Hoquiam (city, Wash.) **16:**356
HOR (mt., Er. Isr.) **8:**971
- Edom **6:**370
Hor (Egy. deity) **8:**972
Hora'at sha'ah (leg. meas.) **6:**1073
- halakhah **7:**1159
HORACE, QUINTUS HORATIUS FLACCUS **8:**972
- Jews **14:**232
HORAH (Er. Isr. folk dan.) **8:**972
- Israel dancing **5:**1270; **9:**1008
- *illus:*
- - text
- - Dutch Zionists dancing **16:**1119
- - German refugees dancing, 1939 **9:**526
- *mus. notation:* text
Horam (k., Gezer) **7:**535
Horayat ha-Kore (bk.) **16:**1474
HORAYOT (tract.) **8:**973
Horche, H. **8:**38
Horeb (mt.), *see* SINAI, MOUNT
Horeb (bk.), *see Choreb*
Horeb (period., U.S.) **5:**557
- statistics **1:**newsp. list
HORE-BELISHA, LESLIE LORD **8:**974
- family origins **4:**437
- *illus:* text
Horelik, M. **7:**807
Ḥoreshim (kib., Isr.) **1:**place list
Ḥorev (school network, Isr.) **6:**427ff
Horev, Amos **13:**48
Ḥorev, Operation (Isr. War of Indep.) **16:**329
- *map:* **16:**312
Hor-Haggidgad (bib. loc.) **10:**300
Horites (anc. people)
- Hurrians **8:**1116
- Judah, tribe of **8:**582
- Land of Israel **9:**108
- mice sacrifice **2:**210
- Seir **6:**369; **6:**379
- Transjordan **15:**1316
Horizonte (period.) **11:**1459
Horkheim (tn., Ger.) **15:**740
HORKHEIMER, MAX **8:**975
- Adorno, Theodor **2:**303
ḤORMAH (Cana. city) **8:**976
- derivation of term **3:**243
- proscription **8:**345; **8:**346
Hormiz (demon) **11:**246
Hormizd IV (Sassanid k.) **4:**43
HORMUZ (isl., Pers. Gulf) **8:**976
Horn (shofar) **14:**308
- *illus:*
- - ivory, Ugarit **12:**563
Horn (leg. conc.), *see Keren*
Horn, General von **15:**552
Horn, Eduard, *see* EINHORN, IGNAZ
Horn, Milton **4:**787; **5:**1445; **10:**368
HORNBOSTEL, ERICH MORITZ VON **8:**977
Hornbostel, Helene Marcus **8:**977
Horne, Robert **8:**38
HORNER, HENRY **8:**977
HORNET (zool.) **8:**978
Horns of Hittin (loc., Er. Isr.), *see* KEFAR ḤATTIN
Horodenka (city, Ukr.), *see* GORODENKA
Horodenka, Naḥman of, *see* NAḤMAN OF HORODENKA
HORODEZKY, SAMUEL ABBA **8:**978
- Kabbalah **10:**648
Horodisch, A. **15:**143
HORODISCHTSCH, LEON **8:**979
- *illus:*
- - F.Z.C. **16:**1165
Horodno (city, Rus.), *see* GRODNO
Ḥoron, A. G. **5:**102
HORONAIM (Moab. city) **8:**979
- Israel-Moab war **11:**1397
HORONTCHIK, SIMON **8:**980
Horovitz (name), *see also:* Gurvi(t)ch; Gurwicz; Gurwitsch; Horowitz; Horwitz; Hurvitz; Hurwich; Hurwitz
Horovitz, Ármin **14:**1489
Horovitz, Bela **13:**1367
Horovitz, Eliezer ben Jacob Ha-Levi of Tarnogrod, *see* ELIEZER BEN JACOB HA-LEVI OF TARNOGROD
Horovitz, Feiwel, *see* Horovitz, Paul
Horovitz, H. S. **14:**1520ff; **14:**1522
Horovitz, J. (r., Hung.) **15:**669
HOROVITZ, JACOB (r., Ger.) **8:**980
Horovitz, Jacob Joseph ha-Levi **12:**1243
Horovitz, Jonathan (Jenö) **6:**157
HOROVITZ, JOSEF **8:**980
Horovitz, Leo (medal.) **11:**1167
HOROVITZ, LEOPOLD (art.) **8:**981
HOROVITZ, MARCUS **8:**981
- Zionism **13:**1255
Horovitz, Paul **13:**16; **13:**60
HOROVITZ, SAUL **8:**982
HOROVITZ, VLADIMIR **8:**983
- *illus:* text
Horowitz (name), *see also:* Gurvi(t)ch; Gurwicz; Gurwitsch; Horovitz; Horwitz; Hurvitz; Hurwich; Hurwitz
HOROWITZ (fam.) **8:**983
- Joselman of Rosheim **10:**229
- ethical wills **16:**532
Horowitz, Aaron **5:**112; **12:**1408
HOROWITZ, AARON JUDAH LOEB (Leon) **8:**984
Horowitz, Aaron Meshullam Zalman **8:**984
HOROWITZ, ABRAHAM BEN ISAIAH **8:**985
HOROWITZ, ABRAHAM BEN SHABBETAI SHEFTEL **8:**985
- ethical will **11:**346; **16:**532
- family background **8:**984
Horowitz, Abraham Ḥayyim **13:**651
Horowitz, Akiva **8:**1003
HOROWITZ, ARYEH LEIB BEN ELEAZAR HA-LEVI **8:**986
HOROWITZ, ARYEH LEIB BEN ISAAC **8:**986
Horowitz, Aryeh Leib ben Israel **11:**280
Horowitz, Aryeh Leib ha-Levi (Belor.) **6:**325
Horowitz, Azriel **9:**1228
Horowitz, Ben (physic.) **5:**591
Horowitz, Benjamin Zeeb **10:**288
HOROWITZ, BER **8:**987
HOROWITZ, DAVID (econ.) **8:**988
- Bank of Israel **9:**826
- committee on wage increases **9:**864
Horowitz, David (journ.) **13:**1192
Horowitz, David ben Eleazar ha-Levi **8:**998
HOROWITZ, DAVID JOSHUA HOESCHEL BEN ẒEVI HIRSCH HA-LEVI **8:**988
Horowitz, Dov Baer **8:**1006
Horowitz, Edler von, *see* HOROWITZ, SAMUEL BEN ISAIAH ARYEH LEIB HA-LEVI
Horowitz, Eleazar **8:**997
Horowitz, Eleazar ben David Joshua Hoeschel, *see* HOROWITZ, LAZAR BEN DAVID JOSHUA HOESCHEL
Horowitz, Eliezer Moses **8:**1005
Horowitz, Ḥayyim Aryeh **5:**1034; **8:**998; **10:**1260
HOROWITZ, ḤAYYIM DOV **8:**989
Horowitz, Isaac (cmty. ldr.) **8:**999
Horowitz, Isaac (Gal. r.) **8:**997
HOROWITZ, ISAAC HA-LEVI BEN JACOB JOKEL **8:**989
HOROWITZ, ISAIAH BEN ABRAHAM HA-LEVI (r.) **8:**990
- *Akedah* **2:**484
- *Aleinu le-Shabbe'aḥ* **2:**558
- Hebrew language **16:**1641
- history chart **8:**766-67
- Jerusalem **9:**289, 1437
- *kiddush ha-Shem* **10:**979
- *Shenei Luḥot ha-Berit* **10:**642; **11:**347; **16:**531
- travels **15:**1353
HOROWITZ, ISAIAH BEN JACOB HA-LEVI **8:**994
- ethical wills **16:**531
Horowitz, Isaiah ben Moses ha-Levi (cmty. ldr.) **8:**984
HOROWITZ, ISAIAH BEN SHABBETAI SHEFTEL **8:**994
- family **8:**984
Horowitz, Israel (mart.) **8:**984
Horowitz, Israel (chess pl.) **5:**407
Horowitz, Israel Ze'ev (r., Hung.) **9:**515
HOROWITZ, ISRAEL ZE'EV (geog., Pal.) **8:**994
Horowitz, Jacob (r., Ger.) **10:**1252
Horowitz, Jacob (theat. prod.), *see* HARRIS, JED
HOROWITZ, JACOB BEN ABRAHAM **8:**995
- ethical wills **11:**346; **16:**532
HOROWITZ, JACOB JOKEL BEN MEIR HA-LEVI **8:**995
Horowitz, Jacob Yokel ben Meshullam Issachar **8:**998
Horowitz, Joseph **8:**998
Horowitz, Joseph of Nowogrodek **4:**1401; **10:**142
Horowitz, Joseph (r., Slov.) **8:**1076
Horowitz, Joseph B. (art collec.) **5:**311
Horowitz, Joseph Gershon (Er. Isr.) **8:**1002
HOROWITZ, LAZAR BEN DAVID JOSHUA HOESCHEL **8:**996
- *illus:* text
HOROWITZ, LOUIS J. **8:**997
Horowitz, M. **14:**830
Horowitz, Mary E. **8:**997
Horowitz, Meir (Pol.) **15:**815
Horowitz, Meir Halevy (Gal.) **8:**995
Horowitz, Meir Jacob (Ger.) **8:**1001; **8:**1006
HOROWITZ, MESHULLAM ISSACHAR BEN ARYEH LEIB HA-LEVI **8:**997
Horowitz, Miriam Bella **9:**1082
Horowitz, Mordecai **10:**1172
HOROWITZ, MOSES BEN

JUDAH **8:**998
Horowitz, N. (prod., Gal.) **9:**1295
Horowitz, Nahum (r., Pol.) **8:**999
Horowitz, Nathan (r., Rus.) **8:**998
Horowitz, Nathan (maskil) **15:**817
Horowitz, Nathan (trans.) **4:**1549
HOROWITZ, PHINEHAS BEN ISRAEL HA-LEVI **8:**998
- family **8:**984
HOROWITZ, PHINEHAS BEN ẒEVI HIRSCH HA-LEVI **8:**999
Horowitz, Phinehas Elijah **10:**555
Horowitz, Samuel (schol.) **8:**999
HOROWITZ, SAMUEL BEN ISAIAH ARYEH LEIB HA-LEVI **8:**1001
HOROWITZ, SAMUEL SHMELKE OF NIKOLSBURG **8:**1001
Horowitz, Saul (schol.) **16:**577
Horowitz, Saul (Gal. r.) **8:**997; **15:**1492
HOROWITZ, SAUL ḤAYYIM BEN ABRAHAM HA-LEVI **8:**1002
Horowitz, Shabbetai Sheftel (cmty. ldr.) **8:**984
HOROWITZ, SHABBETAI SHEFTEL BEN AKIVA (kab.) **8:**1003
- ethical wills **11:**346; **16:**532
- Kabbalah **10:**549
- *sefirot* doctrine **10:**578
- soul, views on **10:**604
- Torah study circles **15:**459
- *ẓimẓum* **10:**593
- *illus:*
- - *Shefa Tal* (1612) **10:**514,574
Horowitz, Shabbetai Sheftel ben Isaiah **8:**984, 990 **16:**123
Horowitz, Shemaiah **15:**1492
Horowitz, Shmelke ben Ẓevi Joshua **8:**1007
HOROWITZ, SHRAGA FEIVEL HA-LEVI **8:**1003
HOROWITZ, YA'AKOV **8:**1004
HOROWITZ, YEHOSHUA **1:**31
Horowitz, Ze'ev Wolf ha-Levi **8:**985
Horowitz, Ẓevi ha-Levi **12:**1516
HOROWITZ, ẒEVI HIRSCH BEN ḤAYYIM ARYEH LEIBUSH HA-LEVI **8:**1004
HOROWITZ, ẒEVI HIRSCH BEN JOSHUA MOSES AARON HA-LEVI **8:**1005
HOROWITZ, ZEVI HIRSCH BEN PHINEHAS HA-LEVI **8:**1006
- Horowitz, Phinehas **8:**1001
HOROWITZ, ẒEVI JOSHUA BEN SAMUEL SHMELKE **8:**1006
Horowitz Proposal (econ. plan) **8:**988
Ḥorpi, Yiẓḥak, *see* Chizhik, Yiẓḥak
HORSE (zool.) **8:**1007
- dietary laws **6:**32
- fauna of Israel **9:**225
- Solomon's trade **15:**98
- *illus:*
- - text
- - Bet She'arim necropolis **4:**769
Horse racing **15:**310
Horshat Tal (park, Isr.), *see* Ḥurshat Tal
Horst, August **13:**1583
HORT, ABRAHAM **8:**1008
- New Zealand **12:**1128
Hort, Abraham (jr.) **8:**1008; **12:**1128
Hort, Alfred **8:**1008
Horthy, Miklós von Nagybánya **3:**499
- Hitler, Adolf **8:**785
Horticulture **2:**468; **15:**106
Hortus Deliciarum (ms.) **12:**407; **15:**150
Ḥorvat Beer-Sheba (site, Isr.) **4:**386
Ḥorvat Korazin (site, Isr.) **5:**492
Ḥorvat Ma'on (site, Er. Isr.) **11:**908
Ḥorvat Masos (Isr.), *see* Khirbat al-Mashāsh
Horween, Arnold **15:**307, 308
Horween, Ralph **15:**307, 308
Horwicz (fam.), *see* HOROWITZ
Horwitz (name), *see also:* Gurvi(t)ch; Gurwicz; Horovitz; Horowitz; Hurvitz; Hurwich; Hurwitz
Horwitz, Aaron ben Moses ha-Levy of Starosielce, *see* AARON BEN MOSES HA-LEVI OF STAROSIELCE
Horwitz, Bernardt **5:**405
Horwitz, Edel J. **15:**193
Horwitz, Israel Louis **10:**1502
Horwitz, Jonas **8:**1008
Horwitz, Maximilian **5:**287
Horwitz, Milton **15:**312
HORWITZ, PHINEAS JONATHAN **8:**1008
HOS, DOV **8:**1009
- Haganah **9:**683
- *illus:*
- - autograph **9:**331
- - Herzlia Gymnasium class **11:**1448
- - Technion, protest against non-Hebrew teaching **9:**331
Hos, Dov (ship), *see Dov Hos*
Hos, Rivka **6:**176
Hos, Tirzah **6:**176
Hosah (bib. fig.) **8:**481
Hosannah (prayer), *see* HOSHANOT
HOSCHANDER, JACOB **8:**1009
HOSEA, BOOK OF (Bib.) **8:**1010
- *Contents:*
- - Chapters 1-3 **8:**1010
- - Chapters 4-14 **8:**1017
- - Deuteronomy **8:**1022
- - In the Aggadah **8:**1024
- - In the Arts **8:**1025
- eschatological writings **6:**863ff
- history chart **8:**766-67
- Micah, relation to **11:**1483
- minor prophets **12:**48
- poetry **13:**680
- *illus:* text
Hosea ben Nun (bib. fig.), *see* JOSHUA
Hosea Commentary (D.S. Scroll); *see Pesher Hosea*
HOSELITZ, BERTHOLD FRANK **8:**1025
HOSHAIAH, RAV (amora) **8:**1026
- *Sefer Yeẓirah* **16:**785
- Torah **15:**1236
- Tosefta **15:**1284
Hoshaiah Rabbah, *see* OSHAIAH RABBAH
Hoshaiahu, Son of Shobai **16:**723
HOSHANA RABBA (fest.) **8:**1026
- calendar **5:**44
- custom origin **12:**9
- cooking and food **6:**1426
- *hakkafot* **7:**1153
- Holy Ark **3:**457
- *kapparot* **10:**756
- Mountain Jews **12:**479
- Mount of Olives **12:**483
- night vigil **10:**642
- Sukkot **15:**501
- *illus:*
- - text
- - *ḥallah*, traditional shapes **6:**1419
- *mus. notations:*
- - Ps. 117,118 **13:**1331
- *see also:* HOSHANOT
HOSHANOT (prayers; willow branches) **8:**1028
- *hakkafot* **7:**1153
- *halakhah le-Moshe mi-Sinai* **7:**1167
- Hoshana Rabba **15:**501
- *piyyut* **13:**599
- prayer books **13:**986
- sages innovation **14:**642
- *illus:* text
Hoshaya of Tiriah, *see* ABBA OSHAYA OF TIRIAH
HOSHEA (k., Isr.) **8:**1029
- alchemic writing **2:**542
- history **8:**605
- history chart **8:**766-67
- King So **15:**18
- Pekah **13:**214
Ḥoshen Mishpat (breastplate) **4:**1335
- *illus:*
- - precious stones in (chart) **13:**1007
Ḥoshen Mishpat (code), *see* SHULḤAN ARUKH
Hoshiah Rabbah (amora), *see* OSHAIAH RABBAH
Hosiasson, Philippe **13:**115; **13:**117
Hospitalers (knight order), *see* St. John, Order of
HOSPITALITY **8:**1030
- *ḥerem ha-yishuv* **8:**357
- *pletten* **13:**645
- Sabbath **14:**566
- Sodomites **15:**70
- *illus:* text
- *see also:* CHARITY; GEMILUT ḤASADIM
HOSPITALS **8:**1033
- health services in Israel **9:**982ff
- *hekdesh* **8:**286
- inquisition **8:**1403
- Lodz **11:**430
- medicine **11:**1182ff
- *illus:*
- - text
- - Afulah hospital **4:**83
- - Bikkur Ḥolim, Jerusalem
- - - newborn infants' ward **9:**993
- - - Old City building **9:**983
- - Chicago, Ill., Michael Reese Hospital **14:**18
- - Hadassah Medical Center, Jerusalem **7:**1043-1044; **9:**990
- - Milwaukee, Wis., Mount Sinai Medical Center **11:**1590
- - New York, N.Y., Mt. Sinai Hospital appeal **12:**1076
- - Nowy Sacz **12:**1246
- - Ostrowiec **12:**1517
- - Rothschild Hospital, Jerusalem **9:**1464; **14:**346
- - Salonika, Maurice de Hirsch Hospital **14:**699
- - Sha'arei Zedek, Jerusalem **9:**991
- *see also:* SICK CARE, COMMUNAL
HOST, DESECRATION OF (charge) **8:**1040
- Abraham a Sancta Clara **2:**130
- Alguades, Meir **2:**625
- Barcelona Jews **4:**210
- Benedict XII **4:**482
- Breslau Jews **5:**141
- Brunswick Jews **4:**1421
- Enns libel (1420) **3:**889
- France **7:**15
- Gregory of Tours **7:**921
- Korneuburg (1306) **3:**888; **10:**1206
- Paris **13:**106
- Prague **10:**758
- Pulkau **2:**530; **13:**1383 **3:**888
- Reformation **14:**19
- Rindfleisch massacres **14:**188
- Salzburg and Hallein **14:**718
- Vienna (1420) **16:**503
- *illus:*
- - text
- - Pressburg, 1591 **8:**688
- - stealing of the Host **3:**103-106
- *see also:* BLOOD LIBEL
Hostages, *see* CAPTIVES, RANSOMING OF
HOST OF HEAVEN **8:**1044
- angels **2:**957
- *see also:* MOON; SUN
HOSTOVSKÝ, EGON **8:**1046
Hostrup, Jens Christian **14:**927
Hota (fam., Mor.) **6:**1257
Ḥotam (period., Isr.) **1:**newsp. list
Ḥotam Tokhnit (wk.) **16:**1360,1387
Ḥoter (punctuation sign), *see Maqqel*
Ḥoter ben Solomon, *see* DHAMĀRĪ, MANṢUR SULEIMAN
Hotin (tn., Bess.), *see* KHOTIN
Hot Springs (city, Ark.) **3:**458
Hottinger, J. H. II **8:**38
Hottinger, J. J. **8:**38
HOTTINGER, JOHANN HEINRICH **8:**1047
- Hebraists **8:**38
Hotz, L. **8:**563
Hotzenplotz (vill., Cz.), *see* OSOBLAHA
Houbigantius, C. F. **8:**38
HOUDINI, HARRY **8:**1047
Hour (time) **5:**43; **5:**1375ff
Houri (Isl. figs.) **6:**884
Houri, Ḥayyim **10:**619
Hours of Catherine of Cleves (illum. ms.) **2:**247
Hours of Turin (illum. ms.) **15:**109
HOURWITZ, ZALKIND **8:**1048
- *Apologie des Juifs* **7:**1443
Household (sub-tribal unit) **8:**610
HOUSEMAN, JOHN **15:**1085
Houseman, Julius **11:**1499
HOUSE OF THE FOREST OF LEBANON (Jer.) **8:**1049
House of Omri (kdm.), *see* ISRAEL, KINGDOM OF
House of Wisdom (research center, Bagh.) **15:**1675
Housing and Mortgage Bank Ltd. (Isr.) **9:**828
HOUSING IN ISRAEL **9:**562
- historical survey **9:**381
- *illus:*
- - Bat Yam project **3:**350
- - cooperative project, Tel Aviv **3:**349
- - "Ma'abarah" (paint., M. Janco) Fig. 97 3-ART
- - Ramot Eshkol, Jerusalem **2:**846; **9:**1510
- - Talpiyyot *ma'barah*, Jerusalem **11:**654
Housman, Laurence **6:**776
- Samuel **14:**784
HOUSTON (city, Tex.) **8:**1049
- Texas **15:**1034ff
- *illus:* text
Houting, Hendrik **8:**38
ḤOVAH (w., R. Huna) **8:**1052
Ḥovah (J. cmty., Syr.) **5:**1239
Hove (tn., Eng.) **4:**1374
Hoverei shamayim (astrol.) **6:**115
Hovevei ha-Bamah ha-Ivrit (thea. gr., Er. Isr.) **7:**1330
Ḥovevei Sefat Ever (orgn., Rus.) **7:**963; **14:**457
- *illus:*
- - Gordon, Judah Leib, poems (1884) **8:**186
Ḥovevei Zion (mvmt.), *see* ḤIBBAT ZION
Ḥovot ha-Levavot (bk.) **4:**105
- ethical literature **6:**923; **6:**926
- fiction, Hebrew **6:**1267
- Ladino **10:**1349
- literature, Jewish **11:**343
- mysticism, Jewish **10:**513
- philosophy **13:**435
- study of **15:**460
- translation **15:**1129
- *illus:*
- - colophon (1489) **5:**785
- - title page (1737) **4:**106
HOWARD, LESLIE **12:**468

Howard, Thomas, Earl of Berkshire 6:753
Howe, Ellis Paul 13:1370
HOWE, IRVING 8:1052
- United States 15:1578
Howells, William Dean 15:1570
Howitt, Arthur 5:310; 12:543
Hoysfraynd (period., Rus.) 13:1045
Hoẓa'ah Ivrit (pub. co.) 10:464
Ḥozeh, *see* CONTRACT
Ḥoẓevim, Mount (Isr.) 9:1515
Ḥoẓin, Moses ben Ẓedakah 8:1053
ḤOẒIN, ẒEDAKAH BEN SAADIAH 8:1053
HRABANUS MAURUS 8:1053
- Hebraist 8:11
Hrabski, János 8:38
Hradec Kralove (city, Cz.) 5:1199
HRANICE (tn., Morav.) 8:1053
Hraszansky, Joseph 11:1131; 16:131
Hronov (vill., Cz.) 12:749
HROZNETIN (tn., Bohem.) 8:1054
HRUBIESZOW (tn., Pol.) 8:1054
Huancavelica (city, Peru) 13:324
Huáncayo (city, Peru) 13:324
HUARTE DE SAN JUAN, JUAN 8:1055
Hubay, Kálmán 3:499
Hubbard, Adolph 7:1042
Hubbard Woods (sub., Chicago) 5:415
Huberband, Simon 15:585
HUBERMAN, BRONISLAW 8:1055
- *illus:* text
Hubmeier, Balthasar 14:36
Hübschmann, I. M. 8:38
H.U.C. (-J.I.R.), *see* HEBREW UNION COLLEGE-JEWISH INSTITUTE OF RELIGION
Huche (archive), *see* ARCHA
HŪD (term; myth. fig.) 8:1056
Hudal, A. 14:253
Hudida (city, Egy.) 14:15
Hudson (city, N.Y.) 12:1126
HUDSON, STEPHEN 6:783; 6:788
HUDSON COUNTY (N.J.) 8:1057
Ḥudūd (emanations) 10:20
HUEBSCH, ADOLPH 8:1057
- prayer books 13:991
- *illus:*
- - Reform prayer book 13:1113
Huebsch, Ben W. 8:1057; 13:1371
Huehner, Leon 2:827; 8:568
Huelgas, monastery of (Sp.) 6:261
Huepte (tn., Sp.), *see* HUETE
Huergai, Cipriano de la 8:38
Huerta, Vicente García de la 10:26
HUESCA (city, Sp.) 8:1058
- Host desecration 8:1043
- land cultivation 16:1286
- taxes 6:1284; 15:855
Huet, Pierre Daniel 8:38
HUETE (tn., Sp.) 8:1060
Huettig, Hans 12:893
Huff, Jacob 9:1191
Hufnagel, G. F. 8:38
Hugel, Friedrich, Baron von 12:268
HUGH OF LINCOLN 8:1061
- *illus:*
- - alleged tomb 4:1120
Hugh of Lincoln, Saint (Avalon) 8:1061; 11:256
Hugh of St. Cher 8:38
Hugh of St. Victor 2:948; 8:38
Ḥugim (mvmt., Er. Isr.) 4:569; 9:977
HUGÓ, KÁROLY 8:1081, 1085
Hugo, Victor Marie 7:141; 7:143; 9:68
Hugo Insulanus, T. 8:38
Huig de Groot, *see* GROTIUS, HUGO
Ḥujja, al- (wk.), *see Kitāb al-Ḥujja*
HUKKAT HA-GOI (customs) 8:1061
- head covering 8:5
- *kapparot* 10:756
Ḥukkei ha-Torah (rules of study) 6:409
Ḥukkim (statutes) 5:783ff; 14:12
HUKOK (city, Er. Isr.) 8:1062
- kibbutz 1:place list
- *illus:*
- - national Water Carrier pipeline 9:769
Hulaga Khan (Mongol ldr.) 15:641
Hullah Valley, *see* ḤULEH VALLEY
ḤULATAH (kib., Isr.) 8:1062
- statistics 1: place list
Hulatah swamps (Isr.) 9:172
HULDAH (bib. fig.) 8:1063
- Achbor ben Micaiah 2:210
- Ahikam 2:460
- Jerusalem grave 9:1553
- *illus:*
- - house of 13:513
Ḥuldah (kib., Isr.) 8:1063
- Arab attacks 9:344
- Chizhik, Efrayim 5:480
- statistics 1: place list
- *illus:*
- - Shavuot folkdance 5:1267
Huldah Gate (Temple mt.) 15:963
- *illus:*
- - street leading to 9:1399
Huldrich, J. J. 8:38
Huldschinsky, Eduard 3:648
HULEH (val., lake, Isr.) 8:1064
- frontier, Palestine 9:312
- papyrus 9:225; 16:658
- spices 8:1311
- Syria and drainage 15:648
- Syrian-Israel clash 15:1553
- *illus:*
- - Merom's photograph 13:487
- - papyrus 13:71
- *see also:* ḤULEH VALLEY
"Huleh" (phot., P. Merom) 13:487
Ḥuleh Nature Reserve (Isr.) 9:590
- *illus:*
- - papyrus growths 9:227
- - pelicans 9:235
HULEH VALLEY (Isr.) 8:1065
- formation of 9:171
- human geography 9:589ff
- Jordan 10:192
- *illus:*
- - carp ponds 9:786
- - Hurshat Tal park 9:172-173
- - Kiryat Shemonah 9:577
- *see also:* ḤULEH
Huleiqat (loc., Er. Isr.), *see* HELEẒ
Hulievca-Berezovca (concen. camp) 15:1330
HULL (city, Eng.) 8:1068
ḤULLIN (tract.) 8:1068
- sacrifice 14:599
- *illus:* text
Hulsius, Antonius 8:38; 2:67
Hulsius, Paul 8:38
Hulvan (city, Media) 12:936; 13:308; 15:1003
HUMAN GEOGRAPHY OF ISRAEL 9:567
- *illus:*
- - text
- - Negev (map) 12:926
- - Safed 14:627
Humanism (philos. conc.) 2:103; 2:104; 3:196; 12:615
Human race, *see* SON OF MAN
Humboldt, Alexander von 8:1071
- Herz, Henriette 8:402
- Jacobi, Karl 9:1226
HUMBOLDT, WILHELM VON 8:1071
- Herz, Henriette 8:402
- universities 15:1677
HUMENNE (tn., Cz.) 8:1071
- Kosice 10:1216
HUMILITY 8:1072
- Akiva 2:490
- cherub in Eden 5:397
- gentiles 12:1190
- Ḥasidic thought 7:1404
- impurity 13:1414
- Jewish philosophy 13:423
- Micah 11:1482; 11:1483
- Moses 12:394
- sacrificial offering 10:1484
- sages 14:649; 14:652
- veil 16:83
- *illus:*
- - Me'ah She'arim notice on modesty 9:1489
- - Olkusz Jews 12:1368
Humman (Elamite deity) 7:1222
ḤUMMASH (Pentateuch) 8:1073
- *see also:* BIBLE; PENTATEUCH; TORAH
Ḥummash ha-Pekudim, *see* NUMBERS, BOOK OF
Humor, *see* PARODY, HEBREW
ḤUMRA (leg. term) 8:1073
HUNA (amora) 8:1073
- Ḥisda 8:531
- history chart 8:766-767
- Isaac bar rav Judah 9:12
- Rav 13:1577
- Sura academy 11:319
Huna (gaon, Pumb.), *see* Ḥana
Huna (gaon, Sura) 7:318
HUNA BEN AVIN HA-KOHEN (amora) 8:1075
Huna ben Ḥanina (amora) 14:634
HUNA BEN JOSHUA (amora) 8:1075
- Idi bar Avin 8:1227
HUNA BEN NATHAN (amora) 8:1075
- Ashi 3:710
Huna ha-Levi bar Isaac (gaon) 7:318
Huna Mari (exil.) 4:42
Huna Mari bar Joseph (gaon) 7:318
HUNA OF SEPPHORIS (amora) 8:1076
HUNA RESH GALUTA (exil.) 8:1073
- history chart 8:766-767
Hunayn ibn Isḥāq (Bib. trans.) 2:579,581,628; 4:863; 11:1466
HUNCOVCE (vill., Cz.) 8:1076
- Slovakia 14:1679
Hundakas (tan.), *see* ḤIDKA
HUNDT-RADOWSKY, HARTWIG VON 8:1076
Hunfalu (vill., Cz.), *see* HUNCOVCE
Hungarian (lang.)
- Bible translations 4:883
- children's literature 5:454; 5:457
- Jewish encyclopedias 6:735
Hungarian Jewish Review (period.), *see* MAGYAR ZSIDÓ SZEMLE
Hungarian-Jewish Society for Literature, *see* IZRAELITA MAGYAR IRODALMI TÁRSULAT
HUNGARIAN LITERATURE 8:1077
- *Contents:*
- - Biblical Influences 8:1077
- - Figure of the Jew 8:1079
- - Jewish Contribution 8:1080
- - Capsules 8:1084
- journalism 10:304ff
- *Zsido Szemle* 4:326
HUNGARY 8:1088
- *Contents:*
- - Middle Ages 8:1088
- - Ottoman Conquest 8:1089
- - 18/19 Centuries 8:1089
- - Emancipation Period 8:1090
- - 19th Century Internal Life 8:1091
- - 1919–1939 8:1095
- - Holocaust Period 8:1096
- - Contemporary Period 8:1105
- - Relations with Israel 8:1108
- General
- - dress 6:222
- - Esztergom 6:920
- - Hebrew MSS 11:906
- - history chart 8:766-767
- - homiletic literature 8:956
- - Lajos Kossuth 10:1219ff
- - minority treaty 12:45
- - Ottoman conquest 16:1536
- - Slovakia 14:1678ff
- Organizations and Movements
- - Alliance Israélite Universelle 2:650
- - emancipation 6:708ff
- - Ḥasidism 7:1394
- - Haskalah 7:1438ff
- - neology 12:952
- - ORT 12:1482
- - Orthodoxy 12:1487ff
- - Po'alei Zion 13:657ff
- - socialism 15:26
- - Status Quo Ante 15:347ff
- - Zionism 16:1120ff
- Social and Communal Life
- - censorship 5:280
- - communal organization 5:825
- - communist period 5:805
- - crime among Jews 5:1091
- - divorce statistics 6:135
- - rabbinical seminary 13:1464
- - *shtetl* 14:1471
- - synagogues 1:syn. list
- - universities 15:1678
- Professions and Occupations
- - finance 4:169
- - glassmaking 7:613
- - law 10:1497
- - military service 11:1555
- - mintmasters 12:62
- - press 13:1035
- - publishing 13:1369
- - sugar industry 15:488ff
- - textiles 15:1040
- - trade and commerce 15:1298
- Anti-Semitism
- - Arrow Cross Party 3:499
- - Church 8:914; 8:915
- - Gestapo 7:530
- - Holocaust 8:840; 8:852ff
- - Nazi 4:1294; 4:605
- - ninteenth century 3:124
- - Numerus Clausus 10:1523; 12:1268
- - political parties 8:738
- - *sheḥitah ban* 14:1345
- - Szálasi, Ferenc 15:656
- - Sztójay, Döme 15:670
- - U.N. resolution 15:1560
- - War Crimes Trials 16:295
- - *see also:* ANTI-SEMITIC POLITICAL PARTIES AND ORGANIZATIONS
- Demography
- - *aliyah* 9:515; 9:538
- - emigration 16:1527
- - population 13:872ff
- *illus:*
- - anti-Semitic parties, 1882-1910 (tab.) 3:81
- - Jewish badge decreed by Nazis 4:72
- - Zamenhof stamp 16:925
- *pop. tables:*
- - Budapest, 1813-1967 4:1449
- - Jewish communities, 1910 and 1946 8:1093
- *see also:* AUSTRIA; BUDAPEST; SUBCARPATHIAN RUTHENIA
Ḥuniah ben Avin ha-Kohen, *see*

HUNA BEN AVIN HA-KOHEN
Hunsche, Otto **10:**1077
Hunsdorf (vill., Slov.), *see* HUNCOVCE
Hunt, Thomas **8:**38
Hunter, Sa **3:**652
Hunter-Salomon, Peter **14:**694
HUNTING **8:**1110
- dietary restrictions **7:**307
- economic history **16:**1268
- moral and legal considerations **3:**5
Huntington (city, W.Va.) **16:**475
Huntington, Bishop **4:**976
Huntington, Henry **11:**499
Huntzinger, Charles **11:**1562
HUNYA OF BETH-HORON (amora) **8:**1112
HUPFELD, HERMANN **8:**1112
- Hebraist **8:**38
Huppah (marriage ceremony) **11:**1032; **11:**1040; **11:**1047
- ceremonial art **5:**309
- Priestly Blessing **13:**1063
- Samaritans **14:**746
- *tallit* **15:**744
- *illus:*
- - Frankfort bridal procession **11:**1027
- - German wedding, 18th cent. **11:**1031
- - "Jewish Wedding" (paint., M. Gottlieb) **3:**554
- - *see also:* MARRIAGE
Ḥuppat Eliyahu (agg. Mid.), *see* AGGADAT BERESHIT
Hupper, Leopold **16:**1165
Huppim (bib. clan) **4:**523
HUR (bib. fig.) **8:**1113
- *illus:*
- - supporting hands of Moses **2:**788; **12:**382
- - watching battle **14:**1258
HUR (Midianite k.) **8:**1113
Ḥurbat Rabbi Yehudah he-Hasid, *see* Hurvah Synagogue
Huré, C. **8:**38
Hurewitz, Isaac S. **7:**1359
ḤURFAYSH (vill., Isr.) **8:**1113
- human geography **9:**589
Ḥurga, Eleazar ben Samuel **11:**550
Hurman (permit) **13:**1451
HUROK, SOLOMON **8:**1113
Huron (city, S.D.) **15:**213
Hurowic, Naphtali **14:**362
HURRIANS (anc. people) **8:**1114
- anthropology **3:**46
- Hittites **8:**788
- Hivites **8:**792
- Mesopotamia **16:**1491,1497,1498
- Nuzi tablets **12:**1287ff
- Patriarchs **8:**573; **13:**182
- Speiser, Ephraim **15:**259
- story of the flood **6:**1357
- *illus:*
- - text
- - Egyptian record of name **3:**313
- - Nuzi document **8:**575
- *see also:* Horites
Ḥurshat Tal (nat. park, Isr.) **7:**1122; **12:**879
- *illus:*
- - Tabor oaks **9:**172-173
HURST, FANNIE **8:**1117
Ḥuru (country) **9:**108
Ḥurūf al Ma'ānī (wk.), *see Kitāb Ḥurūf al-Ma'ānī*
Ḥurvah synagogue (Er. Isr.)
- Arab Legion destruction **9:**1486
- Ezekiel Ben Reuben Manasseh **6:**1101
- Ibrahim Pasha Ibra **8:**1215
- Jerusalem **9:**1448,1458
- seal motif **14:**1081
- synagogue **15:**587,624
- *illus:*
- - ruins **9:**1485
- - view and interior **9:**1445,1446
Hurvitz (name), *see also:* Gurvi(t)ch; Gurwicz; Gurwitsch ; Horovitz; Horowitz; Horwitz; Hurwich; Hurwitz
Hurvitz, Joseph B. **12:**38
Hurvitz, Ya'ir **8:**206
Hurvitz, Ẓiviah **16:**338
Hurwich (name), *see also:* Gurvi(t)ch; Gurwicz; Gurwitsch; Horovitz, Horowitz, Horwitz, Hurvitz, Hurwitz
HURWICH, LOUIS **8:**1117
Hurwitz (surname), *see also:* Gurvi(t)ch; Gurwicz; Gurwitsch; Horovitz, Horowitz, Horwitz, Hurvitz, Hurwich.
HURWITZ, ADOLF **8:**1117
HURWITZ, CHAIM (Haykl) **8:**1117
Hurwitz, E. L. (educ., Lith.) **7:**213
Hurwitz, Elimelech (ḥas. ldr.) **15:**657
Hurwitz, H. (r., Eng.) **16:**844
HURWITZ, HENRY (educ.) **8:**1118
Hurwitz, Hirsch (schol., Ukr.) **7:**1447; **15:**1528
Hurwitz, Isaac **15:**383
Hurwitz, Israel ha-Levi **15:**343
Hurwitz, Israel Zalman, *see* LIBIN, Z.
Hurwitz, Joseph Josel **12:**1237
HURWITZ, JUDAH BEN MORDECAI HA-LEVI **8:**1118
- Haskalah in Russia **7:**1445
Hurwitz, Louis **11:**1286
Hurwitz, Meir ha-Levi **15:**343
HURWITZ, PHINEHAS ELIJAH **8:**1119
- Haskalah **7:**1446
HURWITZ, SAMUEL JUSTIN **8:**547
HURWITZ, SAUL ISRAEL **8:**1119
Hurwitz, Shmuel, *see* LITVIN, A.
HURWITZ, STEPHAN **8:**1120
Hurwitz, Zalkind, *see* HOURWITZ, ZALKIND
Hurwitz, Ẓevi Dov, *see* Hurwitz, Hirsch
Hus, Jan, *see* Huss, John
Husayn (Isl. warrior) **3:**739
Ḥusayn-ʿali, Mīrzā, *see* Baha' Allāh
Husayn bin Ṭalāl, *see* HUSSEIN
Ḥusaynī (Musl. fam.), *see* Husseini, al-
Husaynī, Ibn al-Fātiḥ Aḥmad ibn **11:**936
Husban (tn., Jor.), *see* Ḥisbān
HUSBAND AND WIFE **8:**1120
- *Contents:*
- - General Rights and Duties **8:**1120
- - Wife's Rights **8:**1121
- - Husband's Rights **8:**1125
- - Contracting out of Law **8:**1126
- - In Israel **8:**1128
- absolution from vows **16:**227
- adultery **2:**313ff
- Asmodeus **3:**754
- chastity **5:**364
- civil marriage **5:**595
- concubine **5:**862
- cosmetics allowance **5:**980
- divorce and *niddui* **8:**354
- domicile of wife **6:**159
- dowry **6:**185
- etiquette **6:**947
- family **6:**1166ff; **16:**777
- female slave **14:**1662
- inheritance rights **15:**477ff
- *ketubbah* **10:**926
- *Ketubbot* (tractate) **10:**932
- liability **11:**184
- litigation **13:**953
- loans **11:**417
- maintenance **11:**783ff
- *niddah* **12:**1141ff
- peace between **13:**197; **14:**1356
- prohibited marriages **11:**1051
- property *ḥazakah* **7:**1518
- succession ordinance, 1923 **12:**143
- Talmud **12:**833
- waiver of rights **13:**634
- waiver of usufruct **11:**1232
- widow **16:**487
- wife as sister **12:**1288
- wills **16:**527ff
- woman **16:**623; **16:**627
- *illus:*
- - Andrychow tombstone **15:**1228
- - Chryzanow tombstone **15:**1225
- - *maror zeh* custom **11:***fcg.* 939
- *see also:* DIVORCE; MARRIAGE; PARENT AND CHILD
Husen, F. van **8:**38
Hūsha (loc., Er., Isr.), *see* USHA
HUSHAI THE ARCHITE (bib. fig.) **8:**1128
Ḥushai ha-Arki, *see* LEVONTIN, JEHIEL JOSEPH
HUSHI'EL BEN ELHANAN (of Kairouan) **8:**1129
- bridal veil **16:**84
- Cairo *genizah* **16:**1336
- four captives **6:**1447
- history chart **8:**766-767
- Nathan ben Abraham **15:**123
- rabbinical ordination **13:**1449
- Tunisia **15:**1434
HUSI (tn., Mold.) **8:**1130
Ḥusifah (anc. vill., Er. Isr.) **16:**20
HUSIK, ISAAC **8:**1130
Hushim (bib. fig.) **5:**1259
Huṣn ʿAjlūn (site, Er. Isr.) **13:**1543
Ḥusni, David **10:**785
- *mus. notations:*
- - *Karati be-Koli* **10:**784
Huss, John
- Bible translation **4:**884
- history chart **8:**766-767
- Hussites **8:**1134
- Kara's influence **10:**759
Hussein (name), *see also:* Husayn
HUSSEIN (k., Jor.) **8:**1131
- Jordanian civil war **9:**472
- Nasser **14:**1624
- Six-Day War **9:**498ff **14:**1626
Ḥussein ben Mashi'aḥ, *see* ḤASAN BEN MASHI'AḤ
Hussein, Rashīd **9:**1042
Husseini, ʿAbd al-Qādir al- **9:**360; **16:**309
Husseini, al- (fam.) **9:**459; **9:**461
HUSSEINI, ḤĀJJ (Muhammad) AMIN **8:**1132
- Abdullah ibn Hussein **2:**57
- *aliyah* **15:**1336
- Arab general survey **9:**1032ff
- Arab National Movement **9:**460ff
- Jerusalem **9:**1435; **9:**1474
- Muslim community in Ereẓ Israel **9:**919
- opposition to *yishuv* **9:**338
- Pavelic, Ante **13:**192
- Shaw Commission **13:**31
- Yugoslavia **16:**872
- Zionism **16:**1084
- *illus:*
- - text
- - Arab leaders **9:**460
Husseini, Isḥāq Mūsā al- **9:**1040ff
Husseini, Jamāl al- **14:**660 **16:**1085
Husseini, Kāmil al- **9:**461
Husseini, Musa Kazim al- **9:**457ff
Hussein ibn Ali (k. of Hejaz)
- Abdullah ibn Hussein **2:**56
- negotiations with McMahon **9:**309ff
Hussein Pasha **2:**513
HUSSERL, EDMUND GUSTAV ALBRECHT **8:**1133
Husserl, Malvine **8:**1134
Hussgen, Johannes, *see* Oecolampadius, Johannes
HUSSITES (Chr. ref. mvmt.) **8:**1134
- Albert V **2:**530
- attitude towards Jews **13:**966
- Jews' attitude towards **14:**21
- Vienna Jewry **16:**502
- *illus:* text
Husté (Huszt; city, Ukr.), *see* KHUST
Husyatin, Israel of, *see* Israel of Husyatin
Huszi, György **8:**38
Ḥuṭ (inst. for meas.) **16:**378
Hutcheson, J. C. **13:**33
- *illus:*
- - Anglo-American Committee of enquiry **16:**1089
Hutin, Marcel **10:**306
HUTNER, ISAAC **8:**1136
Hutrer, Oskar **15:**445
Hutten, Ulrich von **14:**109
Hutter, Elias **8:**38
Hutter, Elijah **12:**1279
Hutzler, Charles **14:**161
Hutzmann (bp., Ger.), *see* RUEDIGER
Ḥuyay ibn Akhṭab **10:**942
HUẒAL (of Benjamin; tn., Babyl.) **8:**1137
- Aḥai ben Josiah **2:**448
- Babylonian academies **4:**39
"Ḥuẓim" (Bohem. Jewry), *see* "Draussige"
Ḥuẓin, Joshua **4:**93
Ḥuẓin, Solomon Bekhor **4:**93
Ḥuẓ la-areẓ (hal. conc.), *see* ISRAEL, LAND OF (Religious Laws Appertaining to)
ḤUẒPIT HA-METURGEMAN (tan.) **8:**1137
- *amoraim* **2:**864,865
Hyacinth (gem) **13:**1011
Hyacinthe de Gonzague, *see* DEUTZ, SIMON
Hyams, Angel **15:**305
Hyams, Henry M. **11:**519; **12:**1041
HYAMSON, ALBERT MONTEFIORE **8:**1137
HYAMSON, MOSES **8:**1138
HYAMSON, NATHAN **8:**1138
Hyannis (vill., Mass.) **11:**1113
HYATT, ABRAHAM **2:**323
Hybrid, *see* MIXED SPECIES
Hyde, Orson **16:**1154
HYDE, THOMAS (Hydius) **8:**1139
- Hebraist **8:**38
Hydraulis, *see* ORGAN
Hydroponics **7:**1059
- *illus:*
- - Naḥal Yam **12:**767
HYENA (mammal) **8:**1139
- dietary laws **6:**32
- evolution **6:**1003
- fauna of Israel **9:**225
- *illus:* text
HYÈRES (tn., Fr.) **8:**1139
Hydeia (Rom. goddess) **9:**1406
HYGIENE **8:**1140
- bathing **4:**319
- biology **4:**1030
- dietary laws **6:**43
- medicine **11:**1184
- *mikveh* **11:**1534ff
- perfumes **8:**1310
- *pikku'aḥ nefesh* **13:**509
- rabbinical emphasis **10:**1484
- *Sefer Asaf ha-Rofe* **3:**675
- vital statistics **16:**179
HYKSOS (anc. people) **8:**1141
- anthropology **3:**36
- Anath **2:**925
- ancient Egypt **6:**480; **10:**205
- Beth-Shemesh **4:**773
- Bible history **3:**305; **8:**573ff

- history chart **8:**766-767
- Manetho **11:**872
- scarab seals **14:**1073
- war **16:**267

HYMAN, AARON **8:**1143
HYMAN, ARTHUR (philos.) **1:**31
Hyman, Arthur B. (Dov) **8:**1143
Hyman, Cecil **8:**1143
Hyman, Freda Clark **5:**451
HYMAN, HAROLD MELVIN **8:**547
Hyman, Henry **12:**1071
Hyman, Herbert **15:**68
HYMAN, JOSEPH C. **8:**1143
Hyman, Marcus **11:**880 **8:**1143
Hyman, Prue **15:**307
Hyman, William **5:**112
HYMANS, PAUL **8:**1144
- stamps **15:**335

Hymans, Solomon Louis **8:**1144
Hymns, Liturgical, *see* LITURGY
Hymns, Table, *see* ZEMIROT
Hyndman, H. M. **15:**25
Hyperbole **14:**651
HYPSICRATES OF AMISUS **7:**895
Hypsistarians (sect, As. M.) **14:**1087
HYRAX (mammal) **8:**1144
- dietary laws **6:32**

HYRCANIA (fort., Er. Isr.) **8:**1144
- history chart **8:**766-767

Hyrcanus I (h. pr.), *see* HYRCANUS, JOHN
HYRCANUS II (h. pr.) **8:**1145
- Alexandra **2:**587
- Aristobulus II **3:**441
- Aristobulus III **3:**442
- Avtalyon **3:**990
- Caesar, Sextus Julius **5:**6
- Coinage **5:**717
- Ethnarch **6:**945
- Hasmoneans **8:**632
- Herod **8:**375f
- history chart **8:**766-767
- Man of Lies **11:**234
- Nabateans **12:**741; **12:**742
- Pompey **13:**846
- Wicked Priest **16:**486
- *geneal, table:* **7:**1475
- *illus:*
- - coins **5:**700

Hyrcanus (Tobiad) **8:**295; **15:**1179; **15:**1490
Hyrcanus (s. of Herod of Chalcis) **4:**601
Hyrcanus (s. of Josephus Flavius) **10:**254
HYRCANUS, JOHN (Johanan; h. pr.) **8:**1146
- Alexander Yannai **16:**714
- Antiochus **3:**75
- Athenians **3:**816
- coinage **5:**716
- Hasmoneans **8:**630; **8:**631; **8:**632
- Hebron **8:**228
- history chart **8:**766-767
- *Maccabees, Book of* **11:**657f
- Parthians **4:**37
- Pharisees **13:**364
- Ptolemy **13:**1349
- sages **14:**638
- Samaritans **14:**729; **14:**730
- shrine on Mount Gerizim **7:**437
- *takkanot* **11:**652f
- visions **16:**167
- war **16:**279
- *geneal, table:* **7:**1457
- *illus:*
- - coin **3:**75

HYSSOP (plant) **8:**1148
- plant list **13:**619
- spices **15:**269

I

Iabu-šum (anc. name) 9:1308
IACOBESCU, D. 14:426
I.A.E.A., *see* International Atomic Energy Agency
Ialo (city, Er. Isr.), *see* AIJALON
Iamani (Phil. ldr.) 13:403
Iamhad (anc. kdm.) 11:978ff
Iamnia (city, Er. Isr.), *see* JABNEH
Iancovici, Dorel, *see* DORIAN, DOREL
I and Thou (bk.) 4:1432
Iao (deity) 15:572
Iaoel (angel) 2:126
I-a-sh-a-r, *see* REGGIO, ISACCO SAMUEL
Iasi (city, Rum.), *see* JASSY
Iasus (city, Syr.) 6:10
IBADIDS (Ibāḍiyya; Musl. sect) 8:1149
Ibal-pi-El (k., Eshnunna) 16:1496
Ibañez, Vincente Blasco 11:803
Ibbi-Sin (k., Mesop.) 15:513; 16:3, 1494
Ibbur ("impregnation" of souls) 7:574; 7:576ff
Ibbur ha-shanah, *see* CALENDAR
Ibelin, House of (Crus. fam.) 9:269
IBEX (wild goat) 8:1149
- dietary laws 6:31
- fauna of Israel 9:226
- *illus:*
- - En-Gedi hills 9:233
Ibillin (val., vill., Isr.), *see* AVELIM
Ibis (Egy. deity) 3:646
Ibis, Baldheaded (bird) 6:30
Ibiza (isl.) 12:41
IBLEAM (city, Er. Isr.) 8:1151
- Balaam's name 4:122
Ibn . . ., *see also under proper names*
Ibn Abbas (Almería) 2:661
Ibn Abbas, Ishmael ben Joseph (Navarre) 15:1425
Ibn Abbas, Judah (12th cent.), *see* ABBAS, JUDAH BEN SAMUEL IBN
IBN ABBAS, JUDAH BEN SAMUEL II (13th cent.) 8:1151
Ibn Abbas, Samuel, *see* SAMAU'AL BEN JUDAH IBN ABBAS
Ibn Abbasi, Jacob, *see* ABBASI, JACOB BEN MOSES IBN
IBN ABĪ AL ṢALT (physic., Tun.) 8:1152
Ibn Abī al-Ṣalt, Umayya (Isl. fig.), *see* UMAYYA IBN ABĪ AL-ṢALT
Ibn Abi Saʿīd al-Mawṣilī 3:445; 12:444; 15:218
Ibn-Abi Sufyān, Yazīd, *see* Yazīd ibn-Abi Sufyān
IBN ABITUR, JOSEPH BEN ISAAC 8:1152
- gaon 7:324
- Ḥanokh ben Moses 7:1276
- Spain 15:242
Ibn Abi Uṣaybiʿa
- Abraham Maimonides 2:152
- David ben Solomon 5:1356
- Saladin 14:669
Ibn Abi Zimra, David, *see* DAVID BEN SOLOMON IBN ABI ZIMRA
Ibn ʿĀdiyā, Al-Samaw'al, *see* SAMUEL IBN ʿADIYA
Ibn Adoniyahu, Jacob ben Ḥayyim 15:777ff
Ibn Adret, Moses, *see* ADRET, MOSES IBN
Ibn Adret, Solomon ben Abraham, *see* ADRET, SOLOMON BEN ABRAHAM
Ibn Aknin, Joseph, *see* AKNIN, JOSEPH BEN JUDAH BEN JACOB IBN
Ibn Ala'mani, Jacob ben Judah 13:583
Ibn al-Balia (fam., Sp.) 11:1385
IBN AL-BARQŪLĪ (fam.) 8:1153
Ibn al-Barqūli, Abu al-Ghaña'im 8:1153
Ibn al-Barqūlī, Ezra 8:1153
Ibn al-Barqūlī, Joseph (Bagh.) 8:1153
Ibn al-Barqūlī, Joseph (Wāsit) 8:1153; 16:361
Ibn al-Barqūlī, Mevorakh 8:1153
Ibn al-Barqūlī, Samuel (Baghdad) 8:1153
Ibn al-Barqūlī, Samuel (Wāsit) 8:1153; 16:361
Ibn Albene, Jacob 2:672; 13:583
Ibn al-Dastūr (gaon), *see* SAMUEL BEN ALI
IBN ALFAKHAR (fam.) 8:1153
Ibn Alfakhar, Abraham Abu Isḥak 8:1153, 1200; 10:346; 15:1201
Ibn Alfakhar, Joseph 8:1154; 15:1201
Ibn Alfakhar, Judah 2:190; 8:1154, 1179; 11:748, 1190; 15:1203
Ibn Alfakhar, Meir 8:1154
Ibn Alfakhar, Solomon 8:1154
Ibn al-Fara, Isaac, *see* Al-Fara, Isaac ibn
Ibn al-Fātiḥ Aḥmad ibn Ḥusaynī, *see* Husaynī, Ibn al-Fātiḥ Aḥmad ibn
Ibn al-Fawal, Menahem 14:859
Ibn al-Fawwāl, Joseph 15:1324
Ibn al-Firkāh, Burhān al-din Ibrāhīm 15:1358
Ibn al-Furat 16:1283
Ibn al-Gezzar 3:674
Ibn al-Ḥā'im, *see* Hā'im, Ibn al-
Ibn al-Ḥasan, Ḥibat Allah, *see* Ḥibat Allah ibn al-Ḥasan ben Ephraim
IBN AL-HĪTĪ, DAVID BEN SE'ADEL 8:1154
- Ḥasan ben Mashi'aḥ 7:1365
Ibn al-ʿIbrī, *see* BAR HEBRAEUS, JOHANAN
Ibn al-Jawzī, Abu al-Faraj, *see* Abu al-Faraj ibn al-Jawzī
Ibn Alkabeẓ, Moses ha-Levi 16:1533
Ibn al-Kash 10:278
Ibn ʿAllan al-Yehudi 16:1283
Ibn Almali, Nethanel 15:1324
Ibn Almani, Ẓadok ben Aaron 13:597
Ibn al-Muʿalim, *see* DHAMĀRI, MANSUR SULEIMAN
Ibn al-Muhadjir, Joseph ben Meir 13:585
Ibn al-Mukapah, Abdullah 10:705
IBN AL-RABĪB, ABRAHAM 8:1154
Ibn al-Saigh, *see* AVEMPACE
Ibn al-Sawdāʿ, *see* ABDALLAH IBN SABAʿ
Ibn al-Shami, Isaac 13:583
Ibn al-Shami, Joseph 13:587
Ibn Altabban, Jacob 8:1155
IBN ALTABBAN, LEVI BEN JACOB 8:1155
- linguistics 16:1358,1383
IBN AL-TAQANA, MOSES 8:1155
Ibn-al-Wālī, *see* ELIJAH BEN AARON BEN MOSES
Ibn al-Yatom (fam., Sp.) 14:1201
Ibn al-Yatom, Isaac 10:358
Ibn Arama, Abraham, *see* Abraham ibn Arama
IBN ARDUT, ḤAYYIM JOSEPH BEN AZRIEL HA-KOHEN 8:1155
Ibn Arieh (ps.-mess.) 5:964 11:1422
Ibn Arundi, Isaac, *see* ARUNDI, ISAAC
Ibn Arzarkāli 3:801
Ibn ʿAsākir, al-Qāsim 15:1358
Ibn Atar (Seph. fam.), *see* ATAR; Attar; Benatar; Ben Attar
Ibn Avitur (Sp. fam.) 11:1385
Ibn Ayyūb, Solomon ben Joseph 7:853; 15:1322
Ibn Azarchel, *see* Ibn Arzarkāli
Ibn Azhar, Abu al-Fatḥ Eleazar, *see* Abu al-Fatḥ Eleazar ibn Azhar
Ibn Azuz, Abraham 11:1212
Ibn Baḥya, Abraham, *see* Abraham ibn Baḥya
Ibn Bakoda, David, *see* IBN PAQUDA, DAVID BEN ELEAZAR
IBN BALʿAM, JUDAH BEN SAMUEL 8:1156
- Bible exegesis 4:892
- linguistics 16:1357,1383
IBN BARUN, ABU IBRAHIM ISAAC BEN JOSEPH IBN BENVENISTE 8:1157
- linguistics 16:1358,1383
IBN BARZEL, JOSEPH 8:1158
Ibn Baṭṭūṭa 7:1262; 15:1538
IBN BIKLĀRISH, JUNAS (Jonah) BEN ISAAC 8:1158
IBN BILIA, DAVID BEN YOM-TOV 8:1158
- Maimonides' "13 Principles" 3:656
Ibn Bundar, Abu Ali al-Hasan, *see* Japheth (Hasan) ben Bendar
Ibn Chordabeh 15:270, 1297; 16:1287
Ibn Cid, Yishak 15:1326
Ibn Crispin Cohen, Moses 10:420
Ibn Danan (fam.), *see* ABENDANAN
IBN DANAN, SAADIAH BEN MAIMUN 8:1158
- Abendanan family 2:68
- linguistics 16:1399
Ibn Danon, Moses 9:1310
Ibn Dartah, *see* Taviya ben Darta
Ibn Daud, Abraham (tal.), *see* ABRAHAM BEN DAVID OF POSQUIERES
IBN DAUD, ABRAHAM BEN DAVID HALEVI (philos.) 8:1159
- General
- - Albalia, Baruch 2:522
- - Avendauth 3:948
- - Avicenna 3:958
- - chronology 16:1265
- - historian 8:556
- - history chart 8:766-767
- - Jewish history 11:348
- - titles in chronicle 13:1446
- - Zacuto, Abraham 16:905
- Philosophy 11:339; 13:440
- - angels 2:976
- - Aristotelianism 3:445ff
- - astrology 3:791
- - evil 7:777
- - existence of God 7:658ff, 666
- - form and matter 6:1439
- - free will 7:127
- - nature 12:889
- - Neoplatonism 12:960; 12:961
- - providence 13:1284
- - reason for commandments 5:786
- - reward and punishment 14:137
- - sensory function in animals 4:1030
- - soul 15:173
- - soul, immortality of 15:178
- - space and place 15:218
- - substance and accident 15:474
- *illus:* text

Ibn Daud, Judah, *see* Judah ibn Daud
Ibn Dugi, Menahem ben Solomon (ps.-mess.), *see* ALROY, DAVID; Ibn Ruḥi, Menahem ben Solomon
Ibn Esqira, Elhanan ibn Abraham 10:536
Ibn Ezra (fam., Sp.) 15:1201
IBN EZRA, ABRAHAM (bib. comment.) 8:1163
- *Contents:*
- - Life 8:1163
- - Poetry 8:1165
- - Bible Commentaries 8:1166
- - Grammar 8:1168
- - Science 8:1168
- - Philosophy 8:1168
- General
- - Avicenna 3:957; 3:958
- - Béziers 4:793
- - Ezra of Montcontour 6:1124
- - history chart 8:766-767
- - in legend 7:1118
- - Joshua ben Elijah ha-Levi 10:278
- - Judah ha-Levi 10:357ff
- - Luzzatto, S.D. 11:605
- - Naḥmanides 12:777
- - *Rabbi ben Ezra* 4:1412
- - Spinoza 15:282
- - *tefillin* 15:898
- - travels 15:1349
- Bible commentary
- - allegorical exegesis 4:897
- - Bible exegesis 4:893; 11:324
- - introduction to 7:1145
- - Moses Kimḥi 10:1008
- - on *Akedah* 2:482
- - Supercommentators 15:520
- - - Asher Crescas 5:1078
- - - Bonfils, Joseph 4:1208
- - - Ezra ben Solomon 7:336
- - - Ibn Motot, Samuel 8:1190
- - - Moses of Kiev 12:421
- Philosophy 11:339; 13:437
- - angels 2:975
- - chess 5:402
- - evil 7:777
- - Kabbalah influenced by 10:515; 10:520
- - microcosm doctrine 11:1502
- - Moses 12:400
- - Neoplatonism 12:960ff
- - pantheistic tendency 7:672
- - providence 7:660
- - reasons for commandments 5:786
- - reward and punishment 14:137
- - *Sefer Yeẓirah* 16:787
- - *Shi'ur Komah* 14:1418
- - soul in Kabbalah 10:609
- - Torah 15:1237
- Language and Literature
- - Isaiah authorship 9:44
- - linguistics 16:1453
- - liturgical poets 16:1610
- - poetry 11:327; 13:688
- - satire 13:126
- - *Sefer ha-Ḥayyim* 14:1098
- - translations 15:1318
- - vocalization signs 16:1417
- Science
- - alchemy 2:543; 2:548
- - animal life 4:1030
- - astrolabe, treatise 3:787
- - astrology 3:790; 3:791ff
- - astronomy 3:803
- - calendar reckoning 5:47
- *illus:*
- - text
- - Exodus, commentary (1488) 8:1332
- - *Megillat Setarim* (1553) 8:1190
- - Pentateuch commentary (15th cent.) 4:894
- - *Reshit Ḥokhmah* (13th cent.) 2:738
Ibn Ezra, Abraham (r., Turk.), *see* Abraham Ibn Ezra
IBN EZRA, ISAAC (poet) 8:1170
- Hibat Allah 8:461
- Judah Halevi 10:357; 10:358
Ibn Ezra, Isaac ben Jacob (br. of Moses) 8:1171
IBN EZRA, JOSEPH BEN ISAAC 8:1170
- Medina, Samuel di 11:1212
- tax law 15:872
Ibn Ezra, Joseph ben Jacob 8:1171; 10:355; 10:359
Ibn Ezra, Judah 2:604; 4:170; 5:39 15:1201
IBN EZRA, MOSES BEN JACOB 8:1170
- Afghanistan community 2:326
- Albalia, Baruch 2:522
- Bible exegesis 4:892
- Cairo *genizah* 16:1336
- *El Nora Alilah* 6:685
- history chart 8:766-767
- Judah Halevi 10:355
- letter-writing 11:59
- linguistics 16:1384
- liturgical poetry 16:1611, 1618
- Neoplatonism 12:960ff
- philosophy 13:437
- poetry 13:681ff
- prosody 13:1215
- religious poems 11:327
IBN EZRA, SOLOMON BEN MOSES 8:1174
IBN FADANJ (Fadanq; fam.) 8:1174
Ibn Fadanj, Ibrahim 8:1174
Ibn Fadanj, Jacob 8:1174
Ibn Falaquera (name), *see* Falaquera
Ibn Falija (fam., Sp.) 13:16
Ibn Farukh, Muhammad, *see* Muhammad ibn Farukh
Ibn Fasad, Isaac ben Judah, *see* GERONDI, ISAAC BEN JUDAH
Ibn Ferrizuel, Solomon 10:356; 10:359
Ibn Gabbai, Meir 10:567
Ibn Gabir, Joseph 11:764
Ibn Gabirol, Solomon ben Judah, *see* GABIROL, SOLOMON BEN JUDAH IBN
IBN GAON, SHEM TOV BEN ABRAHAM 8:1174
- Abraham of Posquières 2:140
- Adret, Solomon 2:307
- *aliyah* 9:512
- Baruch 4:268
- Isaac the Blind 9:35
- Naḥmanides 15:520
Ibn Gasom 12:1183
Ibn Ghānim (Musl. fam.) 9:1425
IBN GHAYYAT (fam.) 8:1175
Ibn Ghayyat, Isaac ben Judah 8:1175
- Duran, Ẓemaḥ 6:298
- Ibn Ezra, Moses 8:1171
- liturgy 11:400ff
- *piyyut* 13:599
- *Sefer ha-Ner* 2:367
Ibn Ghayyat, Judah ben Isaac 8:1176
- Judah Halevi 10:358
Ibn Ghayyat, Solomon 13:395; 10:358; 8:1177
Ibn Ḥabib, Ḥayyim, *see* HABIB, ḤAYYIM BEN MOSES BEN SHEM TOV
Ibn Habib, Isaac ben Menahem 2:793
IBN ḤABIB, JACOB BEN SOLOMON 8:1176
- Albo, Joseph 2:535
- Bibago, Abraham 4:812
- history chart 8:766-767
- Ottoman Empire 16:1549
- *illus:*
- *Ein Ya'akov* (1546) 8:73
Ibn Ḥabib, Levi, *see* LEVI BEN ḤABIB
IBN ḤABIB, MOSES BEN SHEM TOV 8:1178
- incunabula 8:1324
- linguistics 16:1389
- translations 15:1328
Ibn Ḥabib, Moses ben Solomon, *see* ḤABIB, MOSES BEN SOLOMON IBN
Ibn Ḥakan ha-Levi, Samuel 16:1533,1535
Ibn Ḥalaẓ, Judah ben Shem-Tov 8:1325
Ibn Ḥalaẓ, Shem-Tov 8:1325
IBN ḤASAN, JEKUTHIEL BEN ISAAC 8:1178
- Saragossa 14:858
Ibn Ḥasdai (name), *see also* Ibn Ḥisdai
IBN ḤASDAI, ABRAHAM BEN SAMUEL HA-LEVI 8:1179
- *Ben Ha-Melekh ve-ha-Nazir* 4:518
- Israeli, Isaac 9:1063ff
- Jewish literature 11:352
- Neoplatonism 12:959
- translations 15:1323
- *illus:*
- - *Ben ha-Melekh ve-ha-Nazir* (15th cent.) 4:518
Ibn Ḥasdai, Joseph, *see* JOSEPH BEN AHMAD IBN ḤASDAI
Ibn Ḥasdai, Judah 8:1179
Ibn Ḥassin, David, *see* DAVID BEN AARON IBN ḤASSIN
IBN ḤAYYIM, AARON (ben Abraham; Mor.) 8:1179
IBN ḤAYYIM, AARON (Egy.) 8:1180
IBN HAYYIM, ABRAHAM BEN JUDAH 8:1180
- art 3:536
IBN HAYYIM, JOSEPH 8:1181
- *First Kennicott Bible* 4:960
- *illus:*
- - *Kennicott Bible* 3:525,787; 4:960; 5:*fcg.* 971,1336
Ibn Ḥazm, Aḥmad, *see* Aḥmad ibn Ḥazm
Ibn Ḥen, Abraham, *see* Ḥen, Abraham ibn
Ibn Hilāl, Shihāb al-dīn Ahmad ben Muhammad ben Ibrāhīm 15:1358
Ibn Hisām, ʿAbd al-Raḥmān, *see* ʿAbd al-Raḥmān ibn Hisām
Ibn Ḥisdai (name), *see also* Ibn Ḥasdai
Ibn Ḥisdai, Abraham 15:1322
Ibn Ḥisdai, Bon Senior 15:1327
Ibn Ḥisdai, Ḥisdai *see* ḤISDAI IBN ḤISDAI, ABU AL-FAḌL
Ibn Ḥisdai, Joseph 13:583; 8:532; 14:859
Ibn-Ibrāq (bib. city, Er. Isr.), *see* BENE-BERAK
Ibn Jabirol, *see* GABIROL, SOLOMON BEN JUDAH IBN
Ibn Jamaʿ (fam.) 7:234
Ibn Jamāʿa (Musl. fam.) 9:1425
IBN JAMIL, ISAAC NISSIM 8:1181
IBN JANAḤ, JONAH 8:1181
- *Contents:*
- - Life 8:1181
- - Works 8:1182
- - - Manuscripts 8:1183
- - - Sources 8:1184
- - Influence 8:1185
- - Personality 8:1185
- Bible exegesis 4:892
- chronological chart 8:766-767
- grammar 11:324
- linguistics 16:1356
- poetry 16:1618
- translations of 15:1129
IBN JAU, JACOB 8:1186
- Ibn Abitur 8:1152
- Manṣur, al- 11:894
- nagid 12:760
- silk industry 15:1038
- Umayyads 15:1530
Ibn Jau, Joseph 8:1186
- silk industry 15:1038
Ibn Job, *see* Solomon ben Joseph ibn Ayyub
Ibn Jubayr, Abu al-Husayn Muhammad 15:1358
Ibn Jumay, Ḥibat Allah, *see* ḤIBAT ALLAH IBN JUMAY IBN ZAYN
Ibn Kamaniel, Joseph 15:1201
IBN KAMMŪNA, SAʿD IBN MANṢUR 8:1186
Ibn Kamniel (fam., Sp.), *see* Kamniel, ibn
IBN KAPRON, ISAAC 8:1187
- Dunash ben Labrat 6:270; 7:563
- linguistics 16:1380
Ibn Kastar, Abu Ibrahim, *see* IBN YASHUSH, ISAAC ABU IBRAHIM
IBN KHALFUN, ISAAC 8:1187
- Gabirol, Solomon ibn 7:242
Ibn Khiḍer, Abdallah, *see* Abdallah ibn Khiḍer
Ibn Khurdadhbah (Kordabheh) *see* Ibn Chordabeh
IBN KILLIS, ABU AL-FARAJ YAʿQŪB IBN YŪSUF 8:1188
- Paltiel 13:49
- Syria 15:640
Ibn Labi, Solomon, *see* LABI, SOLOMON (IBN)
Ibn Lahīʿa 7:1051
Ibn Laḥmish, Solomon, *see* ALAMĪ, SOLOMON
Ibn Latif, Isaac, *see* LATIF, ISAAC BEN ABRAHAM IBN
Ibn Latimi, Joseph, *see* JOSEPH BEN SHESHET IBN LATIMI
Ibn Lavi (fam., Arag.), *see* CAVALLERIA, DE LA
Ibn Lev, Joseph, *see* LEV, JOSEPH BEN DAVID IBN
Ibn Mahdi, ʿAbd al-Nabīʾ, *see* ʿAbd al-Nabiʾ ibn Mahdī
Ibn Māja 7:1052
Ibn Makhir, Moses 16:1549
Ibn Malca (Mor. fam.), *see* MALCA
Ibn Malik, Menahem ben Abraham 4:957
- *illus:*
- - *Damascus Keter* 4:*fcg.* 844; 5:1238
IBN MAR SAUL, ISAAC BEN LEVI 8:1188
Ibn Marwān, ʿAbd al-Mālik, *see* ʿABD AL-MĀLIK IBN MARWĀN
Ibn Maskaran, Abu Ibrahim Isaac 13:577
Ibn Matkah, Judah, *see* MATKAH, JUDAH BEN SOLOMON HA-KOHEN
Ibn Matud (Matut), Samuel, *see* IBN MOTOT, SAMUEL BEN SAADIAH
Ibn Mazah, Joseph 10:524
Ibn Megas, *see* Ibn Migash
Ibn Migash, Abraham 6:95; 16:1152
- on Reformation 14:21
IBN MIGASH, JOSEPH BEN MEIR HA-LEVI 8:1188
- codification of law 5:639
- *ḥiddushim* 8:465
- informers' execution 8:1371
- Joseph ben Mamal 13:1449
- Judah Halevi 10:356; 10:358
- Spain 15:226; 15:242
- Toledo 15:1202
Ibn Migash, Meir 8:1189; 14:1201

IBN MOTOT, SAMUEL BEN SAADIAH **8:**1189
- *Sefer Yeẓirah* **16:**787
- translations **15:**1323
Ibn Mu'allim, Abū Ayyub Sulayman **2:**667; **12:**329; **14:**1201; **15:**225
Ibn Muhajir (fam., Sp.) **8:**1155; **14:**1201
IBN MUHAJIR, ABRAHAM BEN MEIR **8:**1191
Ibn Muhajir, Abu Sulayman, *see* DAVID IBN HAJJAR
Ibn Muhajir, Isaac **8:**1191
Ibn Muhajir, Joseph **8:**1191
Ibn Muhajir, Oheb **8:**1191
IBN MŪSĀ, ḤAYYIM BEN JUDAH **8:**1191
- disputations **6:**93ff
Ibn Mussa, Joseph ben Solomon **2:**527
Ibn Naḥish, Solomon, *see* ALAMI, SOLOMON
Ibn Naḥmias, Joseph **15:**1325
Ibn Na'im, Jacob **16:**1536
Ibn Nehemias, Jacob **5:**1479
Ibn Nehemias, Joshua ben Samuel **10:**540
Ibn Nūḥ, Joseph, *see* JOSEPH BEN NOAH
Ibn Nu'man, Hasan **15:**1432
Ibn Nunez, Jacob **12:**81; **16:**63
Ibn Paquda, Abu Isḥak **8:**1191
Ibn Paquda, Baḥya, *see* BAḤYA BEN JOSEPH IBN PAQUDA
IBN PAQUDA, DAVID BEN ELEAZAR **8:**1191
IBN PLAT, JOSEPH **8:**1192
- Abraham of Narbonne **2:**146
Ibn Pollegar, Isaac, *see* POLLEGAR, ISAAC BEN JOSEPH IBN
Ibn Qamni'el, Abraham (Qanbil; ling.) **16:**1283
Ibn Qamni'el, Abraham (physic.), *see* Kamni'el, Abu al Ḥasan Abraham ibn
Ibn Qayyim ibn al-Jawziya **9:**102
IBN QURAYSH, JUDAH **8:**1192
- linguistics **16:**1356
- *Sefer Asaf ha-Rofe* **3:**674
Ibn Rabbān, Sahl, *see* Tabarī, Sahl ibn Rabbān al-
Ibn Roshd (Rusd), *see* AVERROES
Ibn Rich, Ḥayyim **11:**917
Ibn Ruḥi, Menahem ben Solomon **10:**1297
- *see also*: ALROY, DAVID
Ibn Sabā', Abdallah, *see* ABDALLAH IBN SABĀ'
Ibn Saba, Abraham, *see* Abraham ibn Saba
Ibn Sahl, Abu-Amr, *see* IBN SAHL, JOSEPH BEN JACOB
Ibn Sahl, Abu-Ayyub **8:**1194
IBN SAHL, ABU ISḤAQ IBRAHIM **8:**1193
Ibn Sahl, Abu Naṣr, *see* Abū Naṣr Fadl
Ibn Sahl, Abū Sa'd, *see* ABU SA'D AL-TUSTARĪ
IBN SAHL, JOSEPH BEN JACOB **8:**1193
Ibn Sahula, Isaac, *see* SAHULA, ISAAC BEN SOLOMON ABI
Ibn Sahula, Meir, *see* SAHULA, MEIR BEN SOLOMON ABI
IBN SA'ID, ISAAC **8:**1194
- translation **15:**252
Ibn Sakatar, Abu Ibrahim, *see* IBN YASHUSH, ISAAC ABU IBRAHIM
Ibn Salām, Abdallah, *see* ABDALLAH IBN SALĀM
Ibn Samun **10:**346
IBN SĀQAWAYH (Sakuyah; Saqūyah) **8:**1194
Ibn Sargado, Ḥalaf, *see* AARON BEN JOSEPH HA-KOHEN SARGADO
Ibn Saruq, Menahem, *see* MENAHEM BEN JACOB IBN SARUQ
IBN SASSON, SAMUEL BEN JOSEPH **8:**1195
Ibn Saud, Abdul Aziz (k.) **9:**314
Ibn Sayyaḥ, Joseph **10:**577
Ibn Shadad (ps.-mess.) **4:**188
Ibn Shahin, Jacob, *see* JACOB BEN NISSIM IBN SHAHIN
Ibn Shahin, Ẓemaḥ **12:**1181; **14:**545
Ibn Shamun, Joseph ben Judah **11:**757; **11:**770ff; **13:**443
Ibn Shaprut, Ḥisdai, *see* ḤISDAI IBN SHAPRUT
Ibn Shaprut, Shem Tov, *see* Shem Tov Ben Isaac Ibn Shaprut
Ibn Shatanash, *see* IBN ABITUR, JOSEPH BEN ISAAC
IBN SHEM TOV, ISAAC BEN SHEM TOV **8:**1195
- Aristotelianism **3:**446
IBN SHEM TOV, JOSEPH BEN SHEM TOV **8:**1195
- allegorical exegesis **4:**899
- Averroes **3:**952
- *illus:* text
IBN SHEM TOV, SHEM TOV **8:**1198
- Albalag **2:**521
- commandments, reasons for **5:**788
- Kabbalah **10:**539
- philosophy **13:**449ff
- *ẓimẓum* **10:**588
IBN SHEM TOV, SHEM TOV BEN JOSEPH BEN SHEM TOV **8:**1199
- allegorical exegesis **4:**899
- philosophy **11:**343; **13:**450
Ibn Shim'on, Joseph, *see* SHIM'ON, JOSEPH BEN JUDAH IBN
Ibn Shortmeqas, *see* OHEV BEN MEIR HA-NASI
IBN SHOSHAN (fam.) **8:**1199
- Toledo **15:**1201
Ibn Shoshan, Abraham (13/14 cent.) **8:**1200
- Toledo **15:**1203
Ibn Shoshan, Abraham (15/16 cent.) **16:**1533,1535
Ibn Shoshan, Abu' Omar Joseph **8:**1200
- Toledo **15:**1199; **15:**1201
Ibn Shoshan, Abu Suleiman David **8:**1199
IBN SHOSHAN, DAVID **8:**1201
Ibn Shoshan, Ephraim **15:**1204
Ibn Shoshan, Jacob ben Joseph **8:**1200
Ibn Shoshan, Joseph **4:**169; **15:**607
Ibn Shoshan, Meir **4:**169; **8:**1200
Ibn Shoshan, Moses **15:**1204
Ibn Shoshan, Samuel ben Zadok **8:**1200
IBN SHUAIB, JOEL **8:**1201
- preaching **13:**1000
IBN SHUAIB, JOSHUA **8:**1201
- allegorical exegesis **4:**899
- Kabbalah **10:**536
- on Naḥmanides **15:**520
Ibn Shushan, Judah ha-Kohen **6:**1256; **12:**330
IBN SHUWAYK, ISAAC BEN ISRAEL **8:**1202
Ibn Sid, Isaac, *see* IBN SA'ID, ISAAC
Ibn Sighmar (fam., Tun.) **10:**698; **15:**1434
Ibn Sīnā, *see* AVICENNA
Ibn Soli *see* Ibn Suli, Joseph
Ibn Suleiman **8:**1445
Ibn Suli, Joseph **13:**585; **13:**689
Ibn Sunbal, Naḥman, *see* Sunbal, Nahman ibn
Ibn Sūsān (Mor. fam.), *see* BENSUSAN
Ibn Sūsān, Issachar, *see* SUSAN, ISSACHAR BEN MORDECAI
Ibn Sūsān, Judah **4:**554; **11:**755
Ibn Tabul Joseph, *see* JOSEPH IBN TABŪL
Ibn Tamim, Dunash, *see* DUNASH IBN TAMIM
Ibn Ṭāriq, Jacob **15:**1348
Ibn Tatef, Isaac **11:**347
Ibn Tava, Abraham ben Jacob **16:**1536
Ibn Teboul, Joseph **12:**335
Ibn Tibbon (fam.), *see* TIBBON, IBN
Ibn Tibbon, Samuel, *see* TIBBON, SAMUEL BEN JUDAH IBN
Ibn Tūmart, *see* Abu-'Abdullāh' Muhammad ibn Tūmart
Ibn 'Unnāba ('Ussaba), *see* MUBASHSHIR BEN NISSI HA-LEVI
Ibn Venisti, Raphael, *see* Venisti, Raphael Isaac Meir ibn
IBN VERGA, JOSEPH **8:**1202
- *Shevet Yehudah* **8:**556; **11:**349
Ibn Verga, Judah **8:**1203
- Ocana **12:**1316
- Seville **14:**1205
- *Shevet Yehudah* **8:**557; **11:**349
Ibn Verga, Meir **11:**28
IBN VERGA, SOLOMON **8:**1203
- Disputation of Tortosa **15:**1271
- Jewish-Gentile relations **8:**696
- Martin de Lucena **15:**1206
- meaning of exile **7:**289ff
- *Shevet Yehudah* **8:**557; **11:**349; **15:**1271
Ibn Vivas, Ḥayyim **15:**1323
Ibn Vives, Joseph, *see* Abenvives, Joseph
Ibn Wahb, Abdallah, *see* Abdallah ibn Wahb
IBN WAQAR (Sp. fam.) **8:**1205
Ibn Waqar, Abraham **8:**1205
Ibn Waqar, Isaac **8:**1205
- Alfonso X of Castile **6:**574
Ibn Waqar, Joseph (trans.) **8:**1205
Ibn Waqar, Joseph (physic.) **8:**1206
IBN WAQĀR, JOSEPH BEN ABRAHAM (philos.) **8:**1206
- Kabbalah and philosophy **10:**537
- Toledo **15:**1202
- Zohar **16:**1212
Ibn Waqar, Joseph ben Isaac ben Moses (astron.) **8:**1206; **15:**1235
Ibn Waqar, Judah **8:**1205
Ibn Waqar, Samuel **6:**356; **8:**1205
Ibn Yabajai, Gedaliah, *see* Yabajai, Gedaliah ibn
Ibn Yaḥya (name), *see also* Yaḥya
Ibn Yaḥya (Tam.), *see* TAM IBN YAḤYA
Ibn Yahya, Aaron **16:**55
Ibn Yahya, David (14th cent.) **5:**419
IBN YAḤYA, DAVID BEN JOSEPH (15/16 cent.) **8:**1207
IBN YAḤYA, DAVID BEN SOLOMON (15/16 cent.) **8:**1207
- Almoli, Solomon **2:**664
- linguistics **16:**1388
IBN YAḤYA, GEDALIAH BEN DAVID **8:**1208
- Jewish history **11:**349
IBN YAḤYA, GEDALIAH BEN JOSEPH **8:**1208
- chronological chart **8:**766-767
- Ibn Yaḥya, Joseph ben David **8:**1210
- *Shalshelet ha-Kabbalah* **8:**268, 556
IBN YAHYA, GEDALIAH BEN TAM **8:**1210
Ibn Yaḥya, Joseph (Port.) **11:**299
IBN YAḤYA, JOSEPH BEN DAVID (It.) **8:**1210
- Ibn Yaḥya, David ben Joseph **8:**1207
- *illus:* text
Ibn Yahya al-Magribi, Samuel, *see* SAMAU'AL BEN JUDAH IBN ABBAS
Ibn Yaish (fam. name), *see* Abenaes; Yaish
Ibn Yaqūb, Solomon **15:**1324; **15:**1327
IBN YASHUSH, ISAAC ABU IBRAHIM **8:**1211
- linguistics **16:**1357,1382
Ibn Zabara, Jacob ben Joseph **7:**264
IBN ZABARA, JOSEPH BEN MEIR **8:**1211
- Hebrew tales **11:**352
- *Sefer ha-Sha'shu'im* **11:**937
Ibn Zabara, Moses ben Jacob **4:**960; **8:**1181
- *illus:*
- - *Kennicott Bible* **3:**525,787; **4:**960; **5:***fcg.* 971,1336
IBN ZABARRA, JUDAH **8:**1212
Ibn Ẓaddik, Joseph, *see* ẒADDIK, JOSEPH BEN JACOB IBN
Ibn Zadok, Abbās Rabī'a Solomon, *see* IBN ZADOK, SOLOMON
Ibn Zadok, Isaac **2:**429; **8:**1212
- banking **4:**169
- salt concessions **14:**712
- Spain **15:**230
IBN ZADOK, SOLOMON **8:**1212
- Abulafia, Todros **2:**195
Ibn Zahav, Ari **14:**1265
IBN ZAKBEL, SOLOMON **8:**1212
- *maqama* **11:**937
Ibn Zara, Judah, *see* Abenzara, Judah
Ibn Zaytun, Shalom ben Saadiah **10:**540
Ibn Zimra (fam., Sp.) **14:**1203
Ibn Ziza, Judah **10:**524
Ibn Zughmār (fam.), *see* Ibn Sighmār
IBN ZUR, JACOB BEN REUBEN **8:**1213
Ibn Ẓur, Joseph **14:**1246
Ibn Zur, Solomon **11:**579
ibn Zuta **9:**1405
Ibrahim (14th cent., Pers.) **13:**1566
Ibrahim, Ḥannā **9:**1042
Ibrahim, Ibrahim Mūsā **9:**1041; **12:**1464
Ibrahim al-Awwal (ship) **14:**1603
Ibrāhīm al-Kabāsī **14:**756
Ibrāhīm ben Ishā ben Mārūth **14:**755
Ibrāhīm ben Ya'qūb al-'Ayya **2:**511; **14:**753; **14:**756
Ibrāhīm ibn al-Aghlab (Aghlabid emir) **2:**366
IBRĀHĪM IBN SAHL AL-ANDALUSI AL-ISRA'ILI (Abū Isḥāk) **8:**1213
IBRAHIM IBN YA'QŪB OF TORTOSA **8:**1214
- salt industry **14:**712
- slave trade **14:**1661
- trade and commerce **7:**223; **15:**1298
- travels **15:**1349
IBRAHIM PASHA **8:**1214
- Ereẓ Israel **9:**294
- Jaffa **9:**1255
- Jerusalem community **9:**1447; **9:**1454
- Middle East campaign **9:**305
- *illus*
- - Tiberias **15:**1133
Ibraila (city, Rum.), *see* BRAĪLA
'Ibri, Ibn-al, *see* BAR HEBRAEUS, JOḤANAN
Ibzan (judge) **14:**773
I.C.A., *see* JEWISH COLONIZATION ASSOCIATION
ICAO, *see* International Civil

Aviation Organization
Ice Hockey **15:**316
Icel (city, Cilicia), *see* MERSIN
Iceland **9:**445
ICELAND, REUBEN **8:**1215
Icelandic (lang.) **4:**877
ICHABOD (bib. fig.) **8:**1215
Ichenhausen (tn., Ger.) **15:**1481
Icina (loc., Afr.), *see* Locus Judaorum Augusti
Ickowich (indus., Azer.) **4:**119
Iconoclasm
- art, figurative **3:**505ff
- Jews in Byzantine Empire **4:**1553
ICONOGRAPHY **8:**1216
- illuminated manuscripts **8:**1261
- music **12:**557
- Solomon **15:**110
Iconolatry (image worship) **8:**1228
Icor (Am. orgn., Rus.) **4:**1047
IDAHO (U.S.) **8:**1222
- *pop. table:* text
Idan, David **6:**139
Iddan Ḥadash (journ.) **1:**newsp. list
Iddin-Dagan (k., Mesop.) **16:**1490
Iddiyyot (tract.), *see* EDUYYOT
Iddo (bib. fig.) **14:**1374; **16:**953
Ideal (pub.) **5:**747
Idelman, Max **16:**679
IDELOVITCH, DAVID **8:**1223
- children's literature **5:**435; **5:**457; **7:**783
IDELSOHN, ABRAHAM ẒVI (musicol.) **8:**1224
- Algazi, Léon **2:**610
- ḥasidic music **7:**1420
- Leoni's *Yigdal* **16:**835
- music, Jewish **12:**656
- musical recordings **13:**1618
- *illus:*
- - Pentateuch cantillation motives **11:**1101
IDELSON, ABRAHAM (Zion.) **8:**1225
- *illus:*
- - *Razsvet* staff **13:**1596
IDELSON, BEBA **8:**1226
Idelson, Israel, *see* BAR-YEHUDAH, ISRAEL
Identity, Jewish, *see* JEWISH IDENTITY
IDEOLOGY OF LABOR (Isr.) **9:**870ff
- labor philosophy **10:**1324
I.D.F., *see* DEFENSE FORCES OF ISRAEL
Idgeskom (orgn., Rus.) **16:**735
IDI (amora) **8:**1227
IDI BAR AVIN (amora) **8:**1227
Idiglat, Idigna (riv.), *see* TIGRIS
Idiot
- agency disqualification **2:**351
- gift **7:**562
- liability **3:**989; **11:**184
- torts **15:**1273
- *see also:* DEAF MUTE; Legal capacity; Minor
Idisches Folksteater-IFT (theat. gr., Arg.) **15:**1073
Idishe Folk (period.) **12:**1102
Idishe Gazetten (period.) **12:**1102
Idl, Judah **10:**1228
Idl, Moses **10:**1228
Idleness **10:**1320; **10:**1322
IDOLATRY **8:**1227
- *Contents:*
- - History **8:**1227
- - The Biblical Injunction against Idolatry **8:**1231
- - Idolatry in Near Eastern Religions **8:**1232
- - The View of Kaufmann **8:**1234
- - In the Talmud **8:**1235
- General
- - abomination **2:**97
- - adultery as metaphor for **2:**315
- - *akkum*, worshiper **8:**1061
- - art **3:**500ff
- - Diaspora **6:**13
- - dysphemism **6:**960ff
- - gentiles **7:**410ff
- - Ḥasidism viewed as **7:**1395
- - Hellenism **8:**293
- - Islam, Maimonides on **11:**766
- - Islam rejection **9:**99
- Examples
- - Ahab's worship **2:**438
- - Ahaz **2:**455
- - Ares **3:**407
- - Asa's purge **8:**595
- - emperor worship **6:**729
- - gold and silver idols **11:**1430
- - high places **15:**954
- - household gods **12:**1289
- - image-making **15:**573
- - magic **11:**705
- - Mercury **11:**1382
- - Moloch **12:**230
- - moon **12:**291
- - sun **15:**516
- - tattoo **15:**831
- - teraphim **15:**1015
- - wood and stone **16:**630
- - *see also:* ASHERAH; ASHTORETH; GOLDEN CALF
- *Halakhah*
- - *Avodah Zarah* **3:**980
- - Commandments, the 613 **5:**769,771f
- - false prophets **12:**73
- - gentiles warned against **12:**1189ff
- - harlot prohibition **14:**1208
- - *ḥerem* **8:**344ff
- - heresy **8:**359
- - *ḥukkat ha-goi* **8:**1061
- - impurity **13:**1406ff
- - *karet*, punishment for **10:**788
- - *kiddush ha-Shem* **10:**978
- - love of neighbor **11:**530
- - *sha'atnez* **14:**1214
- - wine **16:**540
- Views
- - *Aḥikar, Book of* **2:**461
- - apologists' denunciation **3:**190
- - Herberg, W. **16:**1345
- - Kaufmann, Y. **16:**1350
- - Krochmal **13:**458
- - Mendelssohn **11:**1338
- - polemics denouncing **6:**81ff
- - sages **14:**650
- - *Solomon, Wisdom of* **15:**120
- *illus:*
- - "Adoration of the Golden Calf" (paint., N. Poussin) **7:**709; **8:**1233
- - Elijah humiliating the prophets of Baal **6:**290
- - Mari goddess **11:**984
Idra de-Ha'azinu (kab. wk.), *see Idra Zuta*
Idra de-Naso (kab. wk.), *see Idra Rabba*
Idra de-vei Mashkena (kab. wk.) **16:**1195
Idra Rabba (kab. wk.)
- *Sefirot* doctrine **10:**569
- Zohar **16:**1194
Idra Zuta (kab. wk.)
- *Sefirot* doctrine **10:**569
- *Shi'ur Komah* **14:**1418
- Zohar **16:**1195
Idris (Egy. deity), *see* Hermes Trismegistos
Idrīsī, Al- (Arab geog.)
- Ammatha **2:**851
- Arnon **3:**487
- Falashas **6:**1152
- map **11:**925
Idrot (part of *Zohar*) **10:**547
Idumea (anc. people, country), *see* EDOM
Idunum (city, Aus.), *see* JUDENBURG
Ieşau (soc., Rum.), *see* WECHSLER, MAX
Iether (vill., Er. Isr.) **9:**1300
Iezer (bib. figs.; clan), *see* ABIEZER
Ifarkoris (stlmt., Syr.) **5:**1239
Ifra Hormizd (Pers. q.) **14:**1306
Ifran (cmty., Mor.), *see* OFRAN
Ifrīqiyā (loc., N. Afr.)
- Aghlabids **2:**366
- Tunisia **15:**1433
- Zirids **16:**1183
Igel, Eliezer Elijah **5:**394
I.G. Farben-Werke (Ger. cartel)
- Auschwitz factories **3:**855
- Auschwitz trials **3:**873
Iggeret Al Tehi ka-Avotekha (bk.), *see Al Tehi ke-Avotekha*
Iggeret Ba'alei Ḥayyim (bk. of fables) **6:**1130
Iggeret de-Rav Sherira Gaon (wk.) **11:**59; **14:**84,1381
Iggeret ha-Ḥarafot (epistle) **3:**195
Iggeret ha-Ḥaverim (*ha-Haverut*; wk.), *see Rasa'il al-Rifāq*
Iggeret ha-Keruv ve-ha-Yishuv (wk.), *see Risālat al-Taqrīb wa al-Tashīl*
IGGERET HA-KODESH (kab. bk.) **8:**1237
- Kabbalah **10:**642
Iggeret ha-Musar (bk.) **2:**509; **15:**1272
Iggeret ha-Neḥamah (wk.) **11:**755
Iggeret ha-Shemad (wk.) **11:**755
Iggeret ha-Tokhaḥah ve-ha-Emunah (bk.), *see Iggeret ha-Musar*
Iggeret kelalit (emis. letter) **14:**1358
Iggeret Kiddush ha-Shem (wk.), *see Iggeret ha-Shemad*
Iggeret la-Ḥaverim (journ.) **1:**newsp. list; **10:**969
Iggeret le-Ḥinnukh (journ.) **1:**newsp. list **10:**969
Iggeret li-Meḥannekhim (journ.) **1:**newsp. list
Iggeret li-nedivim (emis. letter) **14:**1358
Iggeret Musar (bk.), *see Iggeret ha-Musar*
Iggeret of R. Joshua ben Levi (wk.) **13:**84
Iggeret Rav Sherira Gaon (wk.), *see Iggeret de-Rav Sherira Gaon*
Iggeret Teiman (wk., Maim.) **11:**757ff; **16:**742
Iggeret Teiman (bk., Joseph Saphir) **16:**745
Iggeret Tesurah (epistle) **8:**664ff
Iggerot Shelomim (collec. Heb. lets.) **11:**59
Iggerot Ẓafon (bk.), *see Neunzehn Briefe ueber Judentum*
Iggud ha-Ẓeva'i ha-Yehudi (orgn.) **14:**1127
Iggud le-Ma'an Toẓeret ha-Areẓ (agr. assoc.) **9:**764
Iggud Ovedim Tekhelet-Lavan (lab. mvmt., Isr.), *see* Blue-White Workers' Association
Iglau (city, Morav.), *see* JIHLAVA
Iglesia de Dios (Prot. sect, Mex.) **11:**1460
Iglesia Israelita (Judaiz. sect, Chile) **5:**463; **10:**398
Ignace, Edouard **13:**813
Ignatev, S. D. **6:**145
Ignatius of Smolensk **15:**1356
IGNATOFF, DAVID (nov.) **8:**1238
- U.S. literature **15:**1578
IGNATYEV, COUNT NIKOLAI PAVLOVICH **8:**1239
- May Laws **11:**1147
IGNOTUS, HUGÓ **8:**1239
Ignotus, Pál **8:**1239
- Fejtö, Ferenc **6:**1216
I. Gordon Circle (theat. gr.) **15:**1071
IGRA, MESHULLAM (Moses) BEN SAMSON **8:**1240
IHNATOWICZ, JANUSZ ARTUR **4:**885
Iḥud (pub., Pol.) **13:**1043
Iḥud (soc., Er. Isr.) **4:**633
IḤUD HABONIM (youth mvmt.) **8:**1240
- *Contents:*
- - Germany **8:**1241
- - Canada and U.S. **8:**1241
- - Britain **8:**1243
- - Latin America **8:**1243
- - South Africa **8:**1243
- - Australia **8:**1243
- Great Britain **6:**449,768
- kibbutzim **10:**879,884
- U.S. Zionism **16:**1147
- *table:* text
IḤUD HA-KEVUẒOT VE-HA-KIBBUTZIM (Fed. of stlmts., Isr.) **8:**1243
- Kibbutz movement **10:**964; **10:**968ff
Iḥud ha-Kibbutzim (kib. fed., Isr.) **10:**968
Iḥud ha-No'ar ha-Ḥaluẓi (youth mvmt.) **8:**1240
Iḥud ha-Yeshivot (Isr.) **16:**772
Iḥud Olami (Zion. orgn.) **10:**1331; **16:**639ff
IJON (city, vill., Er. Isr.) **8:**1244
- Ha-Gosherim **7:**1123
- physiography **9:**172
Ijon River (Isr.) **9:**172,597
- *illus:*
- - Tannur waterfall **9:**150
Ijzim (vill., Er. Isr.) **5:**186
Ikausu (k., Ekron) **2:**210; **6:**560; **13:**402
Iken (ius), Conrad **8:**38
Ikhshidids (dyn., Egy.) **9:**262,1410
Ikhwān al-Ṣafā, *see* BRETHREN OF SINCERITY, EPISTLES OF
Ikkarei Yisrael (journs.) **1:**newsp. list
Ikkarim (principles), *see* ARTICLES OF FAITH
Ikkarim, Sefer ha- (Joseph Albo), *see Sefer ha-Ikkarim*
Ikkurim (cmty. offics.) **10:**1406
Ikkuv ha-keri'ah (*ikkuv ha-tefillah*), *see* BITTUL HA-TAMID
IKOR, ROGER **8:**1244
"Ikriti" (philos.), *see* SHEMARIAH BEN ELIJAH BEN JACOB
Ikshidids (dyn., Egy.) **9:**262,1410
Ikuf Bleter (newsp.) **4:**1441
Ikusu (k., Ekron), *see* Ikausu
Ila (Ilaa; amora), *see* ILAI
ILAI (tan.) **8:**1245
- *tanna* **15:**800ff
ILAI (amora) **8:**1245
ILAN (found., Isr.) **9:**985
Ilan, A. **6:**207
ILANIYYAH (mosh., Isr.) **8:**1245
- cooperatives **5:**946
- ICA's activity **10:**48
- statistics **1:**place list
- *illus:*
- - colonist **9:**522
Ilanshil-Polio (orgn., Isr.), *see* ILAN
Ilarion (writ.) **14:**506
Il Corriere israelitico (journ.) **13:**1036; **15:**1393; **16:**1122
Il Decamerone (bk.) **4:**1156
Ile-de-France (Fr. prov.) **7:**19
Ilerda (city, Sp.), *see* LERIDA
Ilert, Dr. **16:**646
ILF, ILYA **8:**1246
- Bagritski, Eduard **4:**95
Ilf, Levi **4:**641
ILFA (amora) **8:**1247
Ilfeld, Charles **12:**1037
Ilford (sub., Lond.) **6:**449,450;

11:479
- *illus:*
- - shift of population **11:**479
ILGEN, KARL DAVID **8:**1247
I.L.G.W.U., *see* International Ladies' Garment Workers' Union
ILIN, M. **14:**515
- children's literature **5:**454
- popular science **11:**1059
Ilina, Yelena **5:**454; **11:**1059
ILINTSY (tn., Ukr.) **8:**1248
Ilintsy, Gedaliah ben Isaac of, *see* LUNIETZ, GEDALIAH BEN ISAAC OF
Ilja (vill., Belor.), *see* ILYA
Il Judio (newsp.) **16:**70
Il-Khan (dyn.) **13:**312
Illafsky (fam.), *see* ILLOWY
Illai (tan.), *see* ILAI
Illawy (fam.), *see* ILLOWY
"ILLEGAL" IMMIGRATION (Er. Isr.) **8:**1248
- *Contents:*
- - Between World Wars **8:**1248
- - During World War II **8:**1249
- - After World War II **8:**1249
- aliyah and absorption **9:**527ff
- Arazi, Yehudah **3:**291
- Athlit detention camp **3:**822
- Ben-Gurion, David **4:**508; **4:**509
- Elizur **6:**674
- Haganah **9:**687; **7:**107ff
- history **8:**769; **9:**352
- Holocaust **8:**857; **8:**905
- Irgun Ẓeva'i Le'ummi **8:**1467
- Muslim countries **8:**771
- Palestine office and **13:**41
- Palmaḥ **13:**46
- partisan activity **13:**149
- Revisionists, Zionist **14:**131
- Sereni, Ada **14:**1182
- *illus:*
- - text
- - *Af Al Pi* refugee boat **8:**1467
- - Beriḥah **4:**623-628
- - captain of *Atrato* adressing passengers **9:**521
- - escape tunnel at Cyprus detention camp **9:**526
- - *Exodus 1947* arrival in Haifa **9:**525
- - immigrant wearing Nazis' Jewish badge **11:**694
- - Mauritius detainees at Haifa **11:**1134
- - *Shabbetai Luzinski* at Ashdod **9:**361
- - *Theodor Herzl* in Haifa port (April, 1947) **7:**1072; **8:**767
- - thirtieth anniversary medal **11:**1170
- - *Tiger Hill* off Tel Aviv (September, 1939) **2:**634
- - *Unafraid* immigrants **9:**361
- *see also:* ALIYAH; BERIḤAH; DISPLACED PERSONS; "PATRIA"
Illegal Press **12:**1057
Illegitimacy, *see* MAMZER
Illereichen-Altenstadt (vill., Bav.), *see* ALTENSTADT
ILLÉS, BÉLA **8:**1080,1085
ILLESCAS (tn., Cast.) **8:**1254
Ille-sur-la-Têt (tn., Fr.) **14:**353
Illiberis (tn., Sp.), *see* ELVIRA
Illinois (Ind. tribe, N. Am.) **13:**229
ILLINOIS (U.S.) **8:**1254
- *illus:* text
- *pop. table:* text
Illiteracy, *see* Literacy
Illness, *see* SICKNESS
Illovy, Rudolf **8:**1257
Illoway, Henry **8:**1257; **11:**1208
ILLOWY (Illovy; fam.) **8:**1256
ILLOWY, BERNARD **8:**1257
- barnacle goose **4:**247
- slavery defense **4:**148
Illowy, Jacob (mer.) **8:**1256
Illowy, Jacob (r.) **8:**1257
Illowy, Jacob Loeb **8:**1257
Illowy, Phinehas **8:**1257
Illowy, Samuel **8:**1256
Illowy, Solomon **8:**1257
Illui (punctuation sign) **16:**1457
Illu Finu (piyyut) **13:**600
ILLUMINATED MANUSCRIPTS, HEBREW **8:**1257
- *Contents:*
- - Hebrew Illumination in Hellenistic Times **8:**1258
- - Character of Hebrew Manuscript Illumination **8:**1259
- - Materials and Techniques **8:**1261
- - Oriental School **8:**1262
- - Spanish Illumination **8:**1264
- - French School **8:**1266
- - German School **8:**1267
- - Italian School **8:**1268
- - Post-Medieval Illumination **8:**1285
- *aggadah* **2:**365
- Bible **4:**950
- books **4:**1233
- Cairo *genizah* **16:**1341
- *Haggadot* **7:**1095
- Ibn Ḥayyim, Abraham **8:**1180
- Ibn Ḥayyim, Joseph **8:**1181
- iconography **8:**1216
- Italiener, Bruno **9:**1115
- Kaifeng Book of Esther **10:**697
- *ketubbot* **10:**930
- *maḥzor* **11:**731ff
- masorah **16:**1427
- *menorah* representations **11:**1369
- *minhagim* books **12:**30
- Moses **12:**407
- music, Jewish **12:**556
- Saul **14:**917
- Scroll of Esther **13:**1392
- Temple theme **15:**986ff
- Trebitsch, Moses **15:**1363
- *illus:*
- - text
- - Ashkenazi Bible (c. 1300, Ger.) **4:**966
- - Benaiah manuscript (1475, Yem.) **4:**963
- - *British Museum Miscellany* (13th cent., Fr.) **2:** 341,453,788; **3:**788; **5:**398,958,1130; **6:**907; **7:**757; **8:**1279; **14:**772
- - *Canon of Avicenna* (15th cent., Ferrara) **3:***fcg.* 955; **8:**1283; **11:**1192
- - eleventh cent. Bible, Cairo **3:***fcg.* 524
- - *Guide to the Perplexed* (14th cent., Sp.) **8:***fcg.* 1143
- - *Hamburg Halakhah Miscellany* (15th cent.) **4:**66, **16:***fcg.* 615
- - *Hamburg Miscellany* (15th cent., Mainz.?) **7:**1271; **8:**671; **8:***fcg.* 1335; **10:**457;
- - *Harrison Miscellany* (18th cent., It.) **3:**543; **5:**23,1421; **6:**56, 211, 534, 808, 859; **7:**1217; **9:**1552; **10:**223,1074, 1316; **13:**574
- - Isaac ben Elisha Ḥazzan's illum. Bible (1310, Brussels) **4:**1423
- - *Jerusalem Mishneh Torah* **8:**fcg. 1015
- - Judeo-Persian paraphrase of the Pentateuch (1686, Tabriz) **4:**932
- - Karaite Bible (10th cent., Pal.) **4:**953
- - *Kaufmann Mishneh Torah* (1295) **2:**242; **5:**630; **7:***fcg.* 747; **8:**1280
- - *Malmad ha-Talmidim*, opening page (14th cent., Bologna) **2:**928
- - *Mishneh Torah* **8:**fcg. 1207; **11:**761,762
- - Mordecai ben Hillel's Mishnah commentary **12:**313
- - Nahmanides' Pentateuch commentary **12:**775
- - *omer* chart **12:**1385
- - *Pesakim de-Rabbi Yeshayahu mi-Trani* (14th cent., Bologna) **5:**1235; **8:**1282
- - Proverbs, Book of (15th cent., It.) **13:**1269
- - *Rothschild Miscellany* (15th cent., Ferrara?) **2:**626; **3:**455; **4:**283; **5:**487; **8:**1029, 1282; **10:**fcg. 107; **10:**114, 456; **11:**1248,1474; **12:**486, 1177; **13:**1326; **14:**74,306,1043; **15:**71
- - Ruzhin *siddur* **11:***fcg.* 875
- - Scroll of Esther **3:**541,543; **14:**1049-1056
- - *Sefer Ibberonot* (17th cent., Ger.) **10:**1527
- - *Sefer Mitzvot Katan* (1395) **9:**21
- - *Tur* **4:***fcg.* 716; **11:***fcg.* 1003; **12:**602
- - Yemenite Bible (1469, San'a) **4:**962
- *see also:* CALLIGRAPHY AND WRITING MASTERS; MAḤZOR; MANUSCRIPTS, HEBREW
Illuyankas (myth. fig.) **12:**730
Il Messaggero Israelitico (period.) **5:**325
ILNA'E, ELIEZER ISAAC **8:**1288
ILO (inst., U.N.), *see* International Labor Organization
Ilok (vill., Croatia) **16:**873
I. L. Peretz Theater (Fr.) **15:**1071
Il Regime Fascista (newsp.), *see Cremona Nuova*
Il Romanziere israelitico (pub.) **13:**1036
Iltis, Rudolf
- community leader **5:**1200
- editor **13:**1030
Ilustrirte Literarishe Bleter (period.) **13:**1040
Il Vessillo Israelitico (pub.), *see* VESSILLO ISRAELITICO, IL
ILYA (vill., Belor.) **8:**1289
Ilyās, *see* ELIJAH
ʿImād al-Din Zengi, *see* Zengi, ʿImād al-Dīn
Image of God, *see* GOD
Images (idolatrous) **5:**771; **8:**1231
IMAGINATION **8:**1289
- dreams **6:**210
- Maimonides **11:**773
- *see also:* Senses
ʿImārat al-Khuraysha (mt., Er. Isr.) **8:**972
Imbecile, *see* Legal capacity
IMBER, NAPHTALI HERZ **8:**1290
- Hebrew literature **8:**210
- *illus:*
- - *Ha-Tikvah*, original manuscript **7:**1472
IMBER, SAMUEL JACOB **8:**1291
Imber, Shemaryahu **8:**1290; **8:**1291
IMBONATI, CARLO GIUSEPPE (Imbonatus) **8:**1292
- Hebraist **8:**17, 38
I.M.C., *see* International Missionary Council
Im Deutschen Reich (period.), *see* C. V. ZEITUNG
IMIT (soc.), *see* IZRAELITA MAGYAR IRODALMI TARSULAT
IMITATION OF GOD (theol. conc.) **8:**1292
- Commandments, the 613 **5:**764
- *devekut* **3:**55
- forgiveness **6:**1435
- holiness of God **7:**651; **8:**820
Imlah (bib. fig.) **11:**1484
Immahot Ovedot (working mothers) **12:**211
Immanuel (name), *see also* Emanuel; Emmanuel
IMMANUEL (name and statement) **8:**1293
Immanuel ben Jacob **15:**1329
Immanuel ben Joseph **13:**581
Immanuel of Benevento **16:**1212
IMMANUEL (ben Solomon) OF ROME **8:**1295
- Anav, Zedekiah **2:**940
- Ancona **2:**941
- Avicenna **3:**959
- Caro's censorship **5:**281
- chronological chart **8:**766-767
- Dante Alighieri **5:**1296ff
- Italian literature **9:**1107
- language **16:**1634
- linguistics **16:**1328
- Paradise and Hell **13:**84
- poetry **11:**328; **13:**691
- prosody **13:**1198,1222
- Roman scholarship **14:**246
- visions **16:**169
- *Yigdal* hymn **16:**835
- *illus:*
- - text
- - *Sefer ha-Maḥbarot* (1491) **4:**1235,1352; **16:**1192
Immanuel of Zamora **8:**1326
IMMA SHALOM (1/2 cent.) **8:**1298
Immer (priestly clan) **9:**1322; **12:**89
Immersion, *see* ABLUTION
Immigration, *see* MIGRATION
Immigration, "Illegal," *see* "ILLEGAL" IMMIGRATION
Immigration to Israel, *see* ALIYAH AND ABSORPTION IN ISRAEL
Immortality, *see* AFTERLIFE; DEATH; PARADISE; OLAM HA-BA
Immortality of soul, *see* SOUL, IMMORTALITY OF
Immovable property, *see* PROPERTY
Immunology **11:**1196ff
IMOLA (tn., It.) **8:**1298
IMPALEMENT (method of execution) **8:**1298
Imposta (J. tax) **14:**1662
Impotence, *see* BARRENNESS AND FERTILITY
Imprecation, *see* BLESSING AND CURSING
IMPRISONMENT **8:**1299
- *Contents:*
- - In the Bible **8:**1299
- - In the Talmudic Period **8:**1300
- - In the Post-Talmudic Period **8:**1300
- - - Arrest and Detention **8:**1301
- - - Imprisonment to Compel Compliance with the Court **8:**1301
- - - Contempt of Court **8:**1301
- - - Punitive Imprisonment **8:**1301
- - - The Pillory and House Arrest **8:**1303
- - - Treatment of Prisoners **8:**1303
- abduction **2:**55
- attempted suicide **15:**491
- before trial **13:**959
- blessing on release **7:**768
- contempt of court **5:**922ff
- *haliẓah* refusal **11:**129
- informers **8:**1372
- Inquisition **8:**1403
- tax unpaid **15:**868ff
- *see also:* IMPRISONMENT FOR DEBT; PUNISHMENT
IMPRISONMENT FOR DEBT **8:**1303
- *Contents:*

- - Prevalence in Other Legal Systems **8:**1303
- - Biblical and Talmudic Sources **8:**1304
- - Post-Talmud Period **8:**1304
- - Tax Debts **8:**1306
- - Takkanot ha-Kahal **8:**1306
- - In State of Israel **8:**1308
- bankruptcy and charity **10:**227
- tax **15:**868ff
- wife's maintenance **11:**788
- *see also:* IMPRISONMENT; PUNISHMENT
Impurity, ritual, *see* PURITY AND IMPURITY, RITUAL
IMRANI (poet) **8:**1309
- dialects **10:**432
Imrédy, Béla **16:**296
Imri, Rakhel, *see* FEYGENBERG, RAKHEL
I.M.T. (International Military Tribunal), *see* Nuremberg Trials; WAR CRIMES TRIALS
ʿImwās (anc. tn., Er. Isr.), *see* EMMAUS
'Imẓa' (vocalization sign), *see Miqpaẓ puma'*
Inanna Ishtar (deity, Sumer) **6:**837; **16:**1489,1490
Inaros, rebellion of **8:**766-767
INBAL DANCE THEATER (Isr.) **8:**1309
- Robbins, Jerome **14:**204
- Yemenite Jews **16:**756
- *illus*
- - text
- - performance **16:**747
INBER, VERA MIKHAILOVNA **8:**1310
Inca (tn., Majorca) **11:**800
Incantation, *see* MAGIC
Incarnation **10:**644; **14:**1245
Incense Altar **2:**765; **8:**1314; **14:**600ff
- *illus:*
- - altars **2:**762
- - Amaziah with burner **12:**1293
- - burning stands **4:**481,762; **5:**1156-1160
- - high priest burning incense **7:**100
INCENSE AND PERFUMES **8:**1310
- *Contents:*
- - Sources **8:**1311
- - Spice Route through Israel **8:**1312
- - Perfumes **8:**1313
- - Incense Offerings **8:**1313
- - Preparation of the Incense **8:**1315
- altar **2:**765
- Avtinas **3:**991
- cinnamon **5:**566
- Commandments, the 613 **5:**774
- consecration **8:**279
- *costus* **15:**267
- crafts **5:**1042ff
- cult use **5:**1162
- desecration of **5:**1560
- frankincense **7:**99
- *ḥukkat ha-goi* **8:**1061
- impurity **13:**1079
- lots, casting **11:**511
- *manna* **11:**8°6
- Mesopotamia **16:**1490
- *nataf* **4:**142
- sacrifices **14:**608ff
- spikenard **15:**274
- Talmud **15:**786
- tragacanth **15:**1311
- *illus:*
- - text
- - Arad altars **2:**762
- - cinnamon **5:**566
- - myrrh **12:**727
- - shovel **6:**821
- - tragacanth **15:**1312
- *see also:* COSMETICS; OILS; PITTUM HA-KETORET; SPICES
Incense offerings **5:**1162
INCEST **8:**1316
- artificial insemination **3:**661
- chastity **5:**363
- Commandments, the 613 **5:**781
- Karaites and catenary theory **10:**3; **10:**780
- *mamzer* **11:**840
- Pentateuch **13:**245
- punishment **10:**788
- sin **14:**1592
- source for prohibition validity **12:**120
- under duress **12:**1400
- validity of marriage **11:**1052
- *illus:* text
- *see also:* MARRIAGE; MARRIAGE, PROHIBITED; SEXUAL OFFENSES
INCLINATION, GOOD AND EVIL **8:**1318
- Angel of Death **2:**953
- free will **7:**125
- ḥasidic thought **7:**1404
- idolatry and immorality **8:**1235
- Kabbalah **10:**585
- marriage **11:**1028
- nature of man **11:**847f
- psychology **13:**1342
- sages **14:**653ff
- Satan **14:**904
- sex drive **14:**1206
- sin **14:**1592
- theology **15:**1105
- worldly evil **7:**776
- *see also:* GOOD AND EVIL; MUSAR MOVEMENT; REWARD AND PUNISHMENT; SIN
Income taxes in Israel **9:**749f
In commendam (leg. transaction) **13:**153
Incorporeality of God **5:**1081; **5:**1082; **11:**760; **13:**422
Incrimination, self-, *see* CONFESSION
Incubation (divine communion process) **6:**208
INCUNABULA **8:**1319
- *Contents:*
- - Introduction **8:**1319
- - Numbers of Incunabula **8:**1319
- - Size and Number of Leaves **8:**1320
- - Size of Editions, Appearance, Colophons **8:**1320
- - Printing Methods **8:**1320
- - Pagination, Signatures, Voweled Texts, Title Pages, Ornamentation **8:**1321
- - Type Production, Paper **8:**1321
- - Study of Incunabula **8:**1322
- - List of Printers **8:**1322
- - - Italy **8:**1323
- - - Spain and Portugal **8:**1325
- - - Constantinople **8:**1326
- Oesterreichische Nationalbibliothek **12:**1333
- publishing **13:**1364
- Rome **14:**252
- *illus:*
- - text
- - *Beḥinat ha-Olam* (1476-80) **15:**1483
- - *Maḥzor Minhag Roma* (1486) **15:**141
- - Mishnah, first edition **12:**98
- - Pentateuch (Bologna, 1482) **15:**1483
- - *Perush ha-Berakhot ve-ha-Tefillot* (Lisbon, 1489) **11:**301
- - Rashi's commentary colophon **14:**38
- - Rashi's Pentateuch commentary (1475) **15:**1483
- - *Seliḥot* edition (1475) **15:**1483
- *see also:* BIBLIOGRAPHY; PRINTING, HEBREW
Indelman, Elḥanan **5:**457
Indelman, Moshe, *see* YINNON, MOSHE
Indenbaum, Léon **13:**116
- *illus:*
- - portrait **13:**115
INDEPENDENCE DAY, ISRAEL **8:**1344
- *Contents:*
- - Official Ceremonies **8:**1344
- - Cultural Events, Sport, and Entertainments **8:**1345
- - Prayers **8:**1345
- calendar **5:**48
- commemorative coins **5:**730
- festivals **6:**1246
- Jerusalem parades **15:**1548
- prayer books **13:**993
- religious life **9:**903
- Samaritans **14:**742
- U.S. Jewry **16:**1147
- *illus:*
- - text
- - commemorative coins (1959, 1968) **5:**733
- - Gadna parade, Jerusalem **7:**252
- - "Gates of Jerusalem" stamps **15:**334
- - Israel stamps **9:**844-845
- - Jerusalem, 1968 parade **9:**696
- - President Shazar addressing diplomatic corps **14:**1327
- - tenth anniversary celebrations **9:**405
- *see also:* YOM HA-ZIKKARON
Independent education (educ. system), *see* Ḥinnukh Aẓma'i
INDEPENDENT JEWISH WORKERS PARTY (Rus.) **8:**1347
INDEPENDENT LIBERAL PARTY (Isr.) **8:**1349
- General Zionists **7:**385
- Ha-Oved ha-Ẓiyyoni **7:**1317
- Histadrut elections **9:**861
- Israel historical survey **9:**398ff
- Israel occupied territories **9:**413
Independent Order Brith Abraham (U.S.) **4:**1379
In der Medinas Yisroel in Yor 2000 (wk.) **16:**1152
Index Expurgatorius (Ch. bk. list) **5:**277
Index of Articles of Jewish Studies (wk.) **16:**1159
Index to Jewish Periodicals (wk.) **16:**1159
INDIA **8:**1349
- *Contents:*
- - Early Phase **8:**1349
- - Portuguese India **8:**1355
- - Dutch India **8:**1355
- - Mogul India **8:**1355
- - British India **8:**1356
- - Contemporary Period **8:**1357
- - Relations with Israel **8:**1359
- - Musical Traditions **8:**1359
- Aden Jews **2:**260ff
- *aliyah* **9:**505; **9:**512
- Bene Israel **4:**493
- Bombay **4:**1192
- Cairo *genizah* **16:**133, 1340
- Calcutta **5:**39
- Cochin **5:**621
- dress **6:**219
- Ernakulam **6:**845
- folklore **6:**1382
- Haffkine, Mordecai **7:**1060ff
- Isaacs, Rufus Daniel **13:**1600
- Israel's relations **9:**432
- military service **11:**1567
- ORT **12:**1485
- population **13:**872ff
- press **13:**1036
- Sanscrit **16:**1414
- spices **8:**1311
- synagogues **1:**syn. list
- Ten Lost Tribes **15:**1006
- UNSCOP **15:**1688
- War Crimes Trials **16:**291
- Zionism **16:**1127
- *illus:*
- - text
- - Cochin, "White Jewish" bridal pair **5:**626
- - Cochin synagogue stamp **15:**335
- - Goa, Inquisition procession **8:**1393
- *pop. table:* text
India and Israel (period.) **13:**1036
INDIANA (state, U.S.) **8:**1360
- intermarriage rate **12:**165
- *illus:* text
- *pop. table:* text
INDIANAPOLIS (city, U.S.) **8:**1362
- *illus:*
- - Beth El Zedeck synagogue **8:**1362
Indians, American
- anthropology **3:**38,40
- Boas' studies **4:**1152
- Brandão's "Israelites" **4:**1295
- Chilean Judaizers **5:**463
- dietary laws **12:**1218
- Fast's novel **6:**1188
- Hebrew literature in the U.S. **8:**211
- Jewish traders **7:**859; **14:**662; **15:**1589
- Lowie's field work among **11:**535
- Mexican Judaizers **11:**1458,1460
- Montezinos in Ecuador **12:**278
- Puritan view of **15:**1568
- Radin's studies **13:**1498
- Salvador, Francis **16:**715
- Sequoyah's Bible translation **4:**888
- Stiles, Ezra **15:**403
- Ten Lost Tribes **12:**278; **15:**1006,1350
- Torres, Luis de **15:**1266
- *illus:*
- - *Journey to Jerusalem* (1786) **15:**1004
- - Meyer, Julius, with Indian chiefs **12:**912
- *see also under names of individual tribes*
Indice (period.) **5:**1225
Indigo (dye) **15:**913
Indo-Arians **16:**1498
Indo-Israel Review (period.) **8:**1359; **13:**1036
INDONESIA **8:**1363
Indre-et-Loire (dept., Fr.), *see* TOURAINE
ʿIndūr (city, Er. Isr.) **6:**739
Indus River (Himalayas) **13:**78
INDUSTRIAL REMOVAL (U.S. mvmt.) **8:**1363
- B'nai B'rith **4:**1145
Industry, *see* ECONOMIC HISTORY; TRADE AND COMMERCE; *and under individual countries*
INDUSTRY IN ISRAEL **9:**815
- aircraft **9:**839
- ancient period **8:**614ff
- Arab industry **9:**1022
- building **9:**564
- chemicals **5:**377
- economic life **9:**707ff; **16:**1268
- glassmaking **7:**613
- historical survey **9:**354ff; **9:**393ff

- human geography **9:**575ff
- Jerusalem **9:**1423; **9:**1436
- kibbutz movement **10:**970
- medieval period **9:**263
- Negev **12:**930ff
- oil and gas **9:**795ff
- science and research **9:**970
- Steel City **2:**226; **7:**1139
- sugar **15:**488
- tailoring **15:**709
- textiles **15:**1042
- trade unions **9:**850ff
- wine **16:**547
- *illus:*
- - clothing exports (chart) **15:**710
- - Givat Brenner, industrial area **7:**597
- - Haifa, Shemen oil factory **9:**342
- - Ḥamadyah, carpentry (factory) **10:**963
- - Ha-Ogen, plastics factory **7:**1315
- - Ha-Zore'a furniture factory **7:**1540
- - Hebron, Arab glassblowers **7:**614
- - Levant Fair, 1934 **9:**347
- - mink farm, Jerusalem **7:**224
- - Naẓerat Illit, Ford automobile plant **12:**904
- - Palestine and Israel statistics (tables) **9:**701–703, 707-710, 721,728-732,761
- - small and medium enterprises in Israel (table) **5:**1057
- - Timna, copper works **15:**1147
- - Timna, sulfuric acid plant **9:**798

Inés of Herera **8:**393
"Infamous decree" (Napoleon), *see* Décret infâme
Infant baptism **4:**184ff
Infanticide **10:**983
Infantile Amaurotic Idiocy, *see* Tay-Sachs Disease
INFELD, LEOPOLD **8:**1364
Infeld, Zvi **16:**1140
Infidels **9:**1440
Infinite (kab. term), *see* EIN-SOF
Information Juive (period.) **2:**617
Information Processing Association of Israel **9:**975
INFORMERS **8:**1364
- *Contents:*
- - Talmudic Tradition **8:**1364
- - In Middle Ages **8:**1364
- - Categories of Slander **8:**1365
- - Spain **8:**1365
- - Regulations of Communities **8:**1367
- - Eastern, Central Europe **8:**1368
- - Russia **8:**1368
- - Jewish Law **8:**1370
- - Talmudic Law **8:**1370
- - Medieval Law **8:**1370
- *Birkat ha-Minim* **2:**841; **4:**1035
- Flavians **9:**242
- Ḥasidim and Mitnaggedim **7:**1396
- punishment **8:**1301; **8:**1303; **13:**1388
- Ruzhin, Israel of **14:**527
- Troyes synod **15:**633
- witnesses **16:**586ff
- *see also:* SLANDER

INGATHERING OF THE EXILES **8:**1373
- *Contents:*
- - Talmud **8:**1374
- - Liturgy **8:**1374
- - Apocalyptic Writings **8:**1374
- - Modern **8:**1375
- abolition of restrictions **9:**534ff
- Aḥad Ha-Am **2:**447
- *Amidah* benediction **2:**840
- Ben-Gurion **4:**511
- eschatology **6:**860
- Israel historical survey **9:**378ff
- Israel inter-communal problems **9:**505
- Muslim countries **8:**770
- sages on **14:**654
- *illus:*
- - Elijah heralding Messiah **6:**863; **11:**1409–1412
- - Messiah entering Jerusalem **11:**1410
- *see also:* OLAM HA-BA; REDEMPTION, Zion, Return to

Ingemann, Bernhard Severin **14:**927
In generali concilio (papal bull) **4:**1495
Ingenheim (cmty., Ger.) **13:**22
INGOLSTADT (city, Bav.) **8:**1375
INGWILLER (tn., Fr.) **8:**1375
Inheritance, *see* SUCCESSION
Inigo López de Leon **4:**1469
Initials, *see* ABBREVIATIONS
Injury
- assault **3:**758
- *avot nezikin* **3:**986
- damages **5:**1233; **15:**1272
- slavery **14:**1656

Ink **14:**1100; **16:**665f
INKELES, ALEX **8:**1375
Inman, Henry **12:**1074
"In the Market of Lemberg" (drg., Pennell) **11:**1001
Inmestar (loc., Syr.) **3:**72
INNOCENT II (pope) **8:**1376
INNOCENT III (pope) **8:**1376
- attitude toward Jews **8:**669ff
- Auxerre Jews **3:**934
- Crusaders **5:**1139,1141
- history chart **8:**766-767
- Jewish usurers **16:**1290
- Lateran Council, Fourth **10:**1446
- papal bull **4:**1495
- popes **13:**853
- tithes, church **15:**1162

INNOCENT IV (pope) **8:**1377
- history chart **8:**766-767
- nature of the Talmud **8:**689
- papal bull **4:**1496
- popes **13:**854
- Valréas **16:**65

INNOCENT VIII (pope) **8:**1378
- Inquisition **8:**1384

Innocent X (pope) **13:**858
Innocent XI (pope) **13:**858
INNSBRUCK (city, Aus.) **8:**1378
- Tyrol **15:**1491

INOWROCLAW (city, Pol.) **8:**1379
- Klodawa **10:**1109
- Zechariah Mendel ben David **5:**1353

Inquisidora, La, *see* Sanchez, Isabel
INQUISITION **8:**1380
- *Contents:*
- - Early Inquisition **8:**1381
- - Spain (until 1492) **8:**1381
- - From 1492 **8:**1385
- - End of (Peninsula) **8:**1389
- - Statistics **8:**1390
- - Portuguese Possessions **8:**1391
- - Spanish Colonies **8:**1392
- - Elsewhere in Europe **8:**1396
- - Procedure **8:**1400
- General
- - Abenatar Melo, David **2:**65
- - Alfonso de Espina **2:**605
- - Antuñes family **3:**166
- - *anusim* **3:**173
- - auto da fé **3:**911; **8:**1404
- - Church, Catholic **5:**536
- - Ferdinand and Isabella **6:**1228
- - history chart **8:**766-767
- - Jewish identity **10:**57
- - Jews and Conversos **8:**1367
- - John XXII **10:**159
- - *kiddush ha-Shem* **10:**984
- - La Guardia **10:**1359
- - Maldonado de Silva **11:**825
- - Marrano Diaspora **11:**1019
- - Naḥmanides **4:**215
- - New Christians **12:**1022
- - Sephardim **14:**1164
- - Talmud condemnation **15:**769
- - Torquemada, Tomás de **15:**1264
- - Vieira, Antonio **16:**121
- - Ximenes **16:**687
- Places
- - America **2:**808
- - Carcassone **5:**160
- - Goa **8:**1355
- - Latin America **10:**1448
- - Lisbon **11:**301
- - Llerena **11:**413
- - Majorca **11:**798
- - Mexico **11:**1454
- - Peru **13:**322
- - Portugal **13:**921ff
- - Saragossa **14:**864ff
- - Seville **14:**1205
- - Spain **15:**232ff
- - Tangier **15:**791
- - Tauste **15:**835
- - Venice **16:**97
- *illus:*
- - "Canto de Fe" (paint.) **3:**912
- - Goa, standard of the Inquisition **7:**639
- - Majorca, account of confiscated property **11:**796
- - Marranos procession **3:**171
- - victim wearing the *sanbenito* **15:**236
- *see also:* LIMPIEZA DE SANGRE

Inscriptions
- Arabian peninsula **3:**233
- Arabic **3:**237ff
- Arad temple **3:**249
- Avigad, Naḥman **3:**961
- epitaphs **6:**818
- Gezer calendar **7:**538
- Greek **4:**771; **8:**295; **8:**296ff
- Hebrew **2:**681; **16:** 1569
- Jerusalem **9:**1389
- Mtskheta **7:**423
- patriarchal history **8:**572
- Roman **5:**250; **9:**239; **14:**242
- seals **14:**1073
- Siloam **9:**1525
- stone **16:**656
- Temple Mount wall **9:**1537
- Tiberias commercial stations **9:**250
- Ugaritic **15:**1506
- weights and measures **16:**380
- writing **16:**665ff
- *illus:*
- - Arabic
- - - Jaffa Gate, Jerusalem **9:**288
- - - Suleiman I **9:**1428
- - Aramaic
- - - Bar-Rekub stele **2:**684
- - - Ben-Hadad stele **4:**516
- - - Beth She'arim, tombs **2:**687
- - - Zakir stele **16:**664
- - Cuneiform
- - - *Babylonian Chronicle* **12:**914
- - - Black Obelisk of Shalmaneser III **3:**320
- - - El-Amarna, clay tablet **3:**370
- - - Flood, Babylonian version **6:**1355
- - - Gilgamesh Epic tablet **6:**1355
- - - Mari, Yaḥdun-Lim **11:**986
- - - Nuzi document **8:**575
- - - Sargon stele **14:**881
- - - Sennacherib's clay prism **12:**573
- - - Sumerian kings list **3:**367
- - Greek
- - - Bet Alpha, mosaic **11:**989
- - - Cave of Nicanor ossuary **12:**1133
- - - Cyprus, record of synagogue reconstruction **5:**1183
- - - dedicatory stone, synagogue in Ophel **3:**335
- - - Delos, prayer for vengeance **5:**1482
- - - Hammath, synagogue mosaic **7:**1244; **15:**575
- - - Jerusalem, sarcophagus **12:**1505
- - - Stobi synagogue **12:**238
- - - Temple, prohibition of entry **9:**1555
- - - Tortosa, trilingual epitaph **15:**1270
- - Hebrew
- - - Arad seal **16:**660
- - - Ararat, N.Y., foundation stone **4:**1465
- - - Béziers, synagogue, foundation stone **4:**791
- - - Bingen, *Traustein* **11:**1041
- - - Brandys nad Labem, tombstone **4:**1307
- - - Calabria, tombstone **5:**33
- - - Cardozo, Abigail Aboab, tombstone **3:**527
- - - Chorazin, synagogue *bimah* **3:**326
- - - commemorative medal, Edward VI of England **6:**753
- - - Copper Scroll **5:**956
- - - flag presented to Abraham Lincoln **15:**1601; **3:**527
- - - German tombstone (1427) **3:**527
- - - Gezer calendar **2:**386,679, 683
- - - glass decanter (18th cent.) **7:**608
- - - glass goblet (18th cent.) **7:**611
- - - "Hebron" seal **8:**227
- - - Iron Age basalt weight **16:**391
- - - Jerusalem, Herodian stone **9:**1501
- - - Jerusalem, Karaite synagogue **10:**782
- - - Jerusalem, sarcophagus **12:**1505
- - - Jotham's seal **10:**302
- - - Judeo-Persian (8th cent.) **10:**430
- - - Kachanga synagogue dedication stone **5:**623
- - - key given to Ferdinand III by Seville Jews **14:**1203
- - - León tombstone **15:**225
- - - *le-veit ha-teki'ah* **12:**573
- - - Magna Graecia catacombs **2:**697
- - - Mainz epitaph (11th cent.) **2:**725
- - - Meisel, Mordecai ben Samuel, tombstone **11:**1262
- - - Meshullam ben Kalonymus tombstone **11:**1402
- - - mourner's pewter plate **12:**489
- - - Orléans, tombstone epitaph **12:**1469
- - - Plovdiv Yeshurun synagogue **13:**653
- - - Polish coins **12:**61; **13:**727
- - - Prague, tombstone (1786) **3:**528
- - - Regensburg, *kahal* seal **14:**35
- - - Rome, Monteverde catacomb **2:**723
- - - seals **2:**684; **3:**396,733; **4:**258; **5:**418; **7:**351,376; **10:**302,1421; **14:**1075-1078
- - - second century epitaph **2:**723
- - - Shabbetai ha-Parnes tombstone **3:**890
- - - *shekel* **14:**1348
- - - Siloam, lintel stone **15:**1219
- - - Siloam, royal steward inscr. **2:**679; **6:**819
- - - Siloam tunnel **2:**684; **3:**315
- - - Tarentum tombstone **9:**1123; **15:**807

- - - Tel Qasila, ostracon **16:**657
- - - *tohorah* plate **15:**1188
- - - tombstones **15:**1224-1232
- - - Tortosa Cathedral epitaph **2:**722; **15:**1270
- - - Uzziah, record of reburial **2:**712
- - - Vienna, boundary stone **11:**692
- - - Vilna, Elijah Gaon's tombstone **6:**654
Hieratic, execration text **8:**572
- - Hieroglyphic
- - - "Ashkelon" **3:**716
- - - Lachish, scarab seal **14:**1076
- - - Merneptah stele **3:**313
- - - Seti I stele **4:**761; **7:**580
- - Latin
- - - Narbonne, epitaph (688/9 C.E.) **12:**828
- - - Pontius Pilatus **3:**323
- - - Regensburg, synagogue **14:**36
- - - Roman Tenth Legion **4:**234
- - - Tortosa, trilingual epitaph **15:**1270
- - Moabite, Mesha stele **2:**684; **3:**319
- - Phoenician
- - - Aḥiram sarcophagus **2:**676,683
- - - Esmun'azar sarcophagus **2:**679,683
- - - seal **14:**1076
- - - Yeḥawmilk stele **13:**476
- - Proto-Canaanite
- - - Lachish **10:**1333
- - Samaritan **2:**679
- - Tamil, Cochin copper plate **8:**1351
- - Ugaritic, Baal's message **4:**11
- *see also:* TOMBS AND TOMBSTONES; WRITING, SCRIPTS, MATERIALS, AND INSCRIPTIONS
Insects **6:**27
- *table:* animals of the Bible and Talmud **3:**9-16
- *see also:* ANIMALS OF THE BIBLE AND TALMUD; FLORA AND FAUNA IN ISRAEL
Insel (anth.) **11:**877
Insemination **4:**1017
- *see also:* ARTIFICIAL INSEMINATION
In Shpan (journ.) **4:**609
Inshushinak (deity, Elam) **14:**1483
Insler, A. **5:**558
Inspector of Kashrut, *see* MASHGI'AḤ
Inspiration, Divine, *see* RU'AḤ HA-KODESH
Installation offering, *see* Ordination offering
Institute for the Dissemination of Music (Isr.) **9:**1006
Institute for Fibers and Forest Products (Isr.) **9:**970
Institute for Fisheries and Forest Products (Isr.) **9:**968
Institute for Israel Youth Leaders **9:**982
Institute for Mexican-Israel Cultural Relations (Mex.) **11:**1461
Institute for the Photography of Hebrew Manuscripts (Isr.) **11:**906
Institute for Proletarian Jewish Culture (Rus.) **15:**61
Institute for Religious and Social Studies (J. Theol. Seminary of Am.) **10:**96
INSTITUTE FOR THE RESEARCH OF MEDIEVAL HEBREW POETRY (Isr.) **8:**1407
Institute for Standardization and Control of Pharmaceuticals (Isr.) **9:**971
Institute of Contemporary Jewry **15:**56
Institute of Jewish Affairs (research inst., World J. Congress) **16:**638
- archives of **3:**385
- Robinson, Neḥemiah **14:**207
- statistics on **15:**347
- War Crimes Trials **16:**291ff
Institute of Jewish Studies (Eng.) **2:**779
Institute of Judaistic Sciences (Warsaw) **15:**351
Institute of Metals and Mechanical Testing Laboratory (Isr.) **9:**970
Institute of Microbiology (Parasitology; Jer.) **9:**991
Institute of Petroleum Research and Geophysics (Isr.) **9:**970
Institute of Science and Halakhah (Isr.) **15:**894
Institute of Sephardi Studies (Sp.) **15:**245
Institute on Ethics (J. Theol. Seminary of Am.) **10:**96
Institutions for the Care of Handicapped Immigrants, *see* MALBEN
Instituto Arias Montano de Estudios Hebraicos (Sp.) **3:**435; **15:**245
Instituto Chileno-Israelita de Cultura (Chile) **16:**1125
Instituto Convitto Rabbinico (It.), *see* COLLEGIO RABBINICO ITALIANO
Instituto Cultural Peru-Israel (Peru) **16:**1125
Instituto Cultural Venezuela-Israel (Venez.) **16:**1127
Instituto de Relaciones Culturales Méjico-Israel (Mex.) **16:**1126
Instituto Judío Argentino de Cultura e Información (Arg.) **3:**417; **3:**424
Institutum Judaicum (Berlin) **8:**1408
Institutum Judaicum (Halle) **8:**1408
INSTITUTUM JUDAICUM DELITZSCHIANUM (inst. for J. study and miss. wk.) **8:**1408
- Delitzsch, Franz **5:**1474
- Protestants **13:**1249
Institut zur Foerderung der Israelitischen Literatur (soc.) **2:**648; **15:**54; **16:**577
Instytut Nauk Judaistycznych, *see* Institute of Judaistic Sciences
"In the Sukkah" (paint., M. Oppenheim) **3:**547
INSULT **8:**1408
- punishment **8:**351,352; **13:**1389
- *see also:* SLANDER
INSURANCE **8:**1409
- craftsmen **7:**971
- legal person **10:**1569
- *illus:*
- - Workmen's Circle (N.Y.), charter **12:**1095
Insurance Business Law (Isr.) **9:**831
INSURANCE IN ISRAEL **9:**830
- health insurance **9:**985ff
- retirement insurance schemes **9:**884ff
- social security **9:**994
- *illus:*
- - monthly national insurance contributions (chart) **9:**995
"Integral Jewishness" (conc.) **7:**763
INTELLECT **8:**1410
- Alexander of Aphrodisias **2:**581
- Aristotelianism **13:**430
- Gersonides **13:**446
- Hillel ben Samuel **13:**444
- Ibn Daud **8:**1162
- Ibn Gabirol **7:**241
- Israeli, Isaac ben Solomon **9:**1064ff
- kabbalistic interpretation **10:**490
- Levi ben Gershom **11:**96
- Maimonides **11:**773
- Moses ben Joseph ha-Levi **12:**422
- Providence **13:**1285; **14:**137
- redemption **14:**5
- soul **15:**172
- Themistius **15:**1099
- Torah **15:**1237ff
Intention, *see* KAVVANAH
Inter-American Conference on Problems of War and Peace **10:**1450
Intercalation, *see* CALENDAR
Intercalation, Secrets of (baraita) **3:**797
Intercollegiate Menorah Association (U.S.) **15:**450
Intercollegiate Zionist Association (U.S.) **15:**450
Intercollegiate Zionist Federation of America (U.S.) **15:**451
Intercom (period.) **12:**1490
INTERCOMMUNAL PROBLEMS IN ISRAEL **9:**505ff
- Ashkenazi-Sephardi rift **14:**1175
- Bene Israel **4:**498
- psychological problem **9:**395ff
- Yemenite Jews **16:**754ff
- Zionism **16:**1064ff
Intercontinental Hotel (Jer.) **9:**1491
- *illus:*
- - aerial view **12:**481
Interest, *see* USURY
Inter-Governmental Committee for Refugees **6:**991; **14:**31
"Interior of a Synagogue at Safed" (paint., Y. Frenkel) FIG. 99 3-ART
Intermarriage, *see* MIXED MARRIAGE
Intermediary beings **13:**426
INTERNATIONAL AID AND COOPERATION, ISRAEL **9:**435ff
- Asia **2:**336; **9:**391ff
- defense forces **9:**693
- medical contributions **9:**991
- U.N. commissions **15:**1563
International Association of Conservative Rabbis **5:**903
International Atomic Energy Agency **15:**1565
International Bible Contest for Jewish Youth (Isr.) **8:**1345
- *illus:*
- - Jerusalem, 1969 **4:**921
International Center for Community Development (Isr.) **9:**436
International Children's Emergency Fund **15:**1563
International Civil Aviation Organization **15:**1564
International Commission of Jurists **14:**499ff
INTERNATIONAL CONFERENCE OF JEWISH COMMUNAL SERVICE **8:**1412
International Congress of Yiddish Culture **16:**788
International Consultative Committee of Organizations for Christian-Jewish Cooperation **13:**1252
International Council of Jewish Women **12:**870
International Emergency Conference of Jews and Christians **13:**1250
International Federation of Teachers' Associations **15:**889
International Fur Workers Union **7:**225
International Geographical Union **2:**849
International Jewish Colonization Society **15:**1021
International Labor Organization (U.N.) **6:**991; **14:**30; **15:**1564
International Ladies' Garment Workers' Union (U.S.) **4:**1357; **12:**1086
- history chart **8:**766-767
International League Against Anti-Semitism, *see* Ligue Internationale contre le Racisme et l'Antisémitisme
International Military Tribunal, *see* Nuremberg Trials
International Missionary Council **13:**1249; **13:**1251
International navigation, *see* Navigation
International Red Cross, *see* Red Cross, International
International Refugee Organization (IRO; U.N.)
- Adler-Rudel, Salomon **2:**289
- Inter-Governmental Committee **6:**991
- refugees **14:**31
- UNRRA **15:**1688
International Relations of Israel, *see* FOREIGN POLICY AND INTERNATIONAL RELATIONS OF ISRAEL
International Synagogue Museum (N.Y.C.) **12:**544
International Telecommunication Union **15:**1565
INTERNATIONAL TRACING SERVICE (for victims of Nazis) **8:**1412
- archives **3:**385
International Workers' Order **4:**368; **5:**804; **7:**110; **16:**788
International Workingmen's Association **11:**1073; **15:**26
Interpretatio (Rom. law term) **8:**1416
INTERPRETATION (hal.) **8:**1413
- *Contents:*
- - Definition of Terms **8:**1413
- - Bible Exegesis **8:**1414
- - Halakhah **8:**1413
- - Documents **8:**1424
- - Takkanot ha-Kahal **8:**1427
- *aggadah* **2:**354
- codification of law **5:**630
- *de-oraita* and *de-rabbanan* **12:**113
- hermeneutics **8:**366
- law and morality **10:**1482
- Mishnah **12:**95
- *Pesher* **13:**331
- preaching **13:**994
- reward and punishment **14:**134
- Septuagint **9:**243
- *sevarah* **14:**1195
- *takkanah* **15:**713
- *takkanot ha-kahal* **15:**734
- tax law **15:**866
- wills **16:**525
- Wolfson's view **16:**618
- *see also:* ORAL LAW; PENAL LAW
Interpreters **3:**837; **16:**1280
Interpreter's Dictionary of the Bible **6:**734
Interrogation **5:**877
Interruption of prayers, *see* BITTUL HA-TAMID
Inter-University Jewish Federation (Eng.) **6:**451; **15:**448
Intoxication, *see* DRUNKENNESS
Introductions and forewords, *see* HAKDAMAH
INVENTORS AND ENGINEERS **8:**1429
- *illus:* text
- *see also:* CONSTRUCTION
Inverness (tn., Scot.) **14:**1036
Invertebrates **3:**18; **6:**38
Investing (Tal. law) **16:**30
INVESTMENT POLICY OF ISRAEL **9:**823
- historical survey **9:**393ff
Invisible ink **16:**670
IN-ZIKH (mvmt., U.S.) **8:**1434
- Glanz-Leyeles, Aaron **7:**600
- Glatstein, Jacob **7:**614

– Katz, Aleph **10**:821
– Sutzkever, Abraham **15**:538
– Yehoash **16**:730
– Yiddish literature **16**:817
– *Yunge, Di* **16**:896
– *illus:* text
In-Zikh (period.) **4**:1136; **8**:1434
– *illus:*
– – first page (New York, 1920) **8**:1435
IOANNINA (tn. and reg., Gr.) **8**:1435
– Judeo-Greek dialect **10**:426
– *illus:* text
Iokhelman, I. **11**:961
IONESCO, EUGÈNE **8**:1436
Ionia (anc. reg., As. M.) **3**:747; **9**:1301
Ionice (Rom. woman) **9**:1405
Ioppe (port city, Er. Isr.), *see* JAFFA
Iosif, B. **5**:453
IOSIFESCU, SILVIAN **14**:423; **14**:426
I.O.U., *see* SHETAR
Iouda (Ioudaia; country) **9**:111
IOWA (U.S.) **8**:1437
– *illus:* text
– *pop. table:* text
I.P.A., *see* Information Processing Association of Israel
Ipsala (vill., Turk.) **14**:1239
IPSWICH (tn., Eng.) **8**:1439
Iqlīm, al- (tn., Er. Isr.) **9**:274
IRAN **8**:1439
– *contents:*
– – Education **8**:1440
– – Publications **8**:1440
– – Women **8**:1440
– – Economic Situation **8**:1441
– – Religion **8**:1441
– – Hygiene **8**:1441
– – Zionism **8**:1441
– – Community Organization **8**:1442
– – Relations with Non-Jews **8**:1442
– – Kurdish Jews **8**:1443
– – Relations with Israel **8**:1443
– Alliance Israélite Universelle **2**:652; **2**:653
– community in Israel **9**:501ff
– education **6**:460ff
– Israel oil imports **9**:795
– Israel's relations **9**:433
– Kurdistan **10**:1295
– mental illness **11**:1375
– ORT **12**:1485
– population **13**:871ff
– sickness **14**:1501
– synagogues **1**:syn. list
– UNSCOP **15**:1688
– Uzbekistan Jews **16**:40
– Zionism **16**:1128
– *illus:*
– – text
– – Alliance school in Hamadan **2**:649
– – *Shiwiti* plaques **14**:1420-1421
– *pop. table:* text
– *see also:* PERSIA; TEHERAN
Irānī, Mahmud Sayf al-Dīn al- **9**:1041
Ira the Jairite (bib. fig.) **13**:1071ff
IRAQ **8**:1444
– *Contents:*
– – History (634-1917) **8**:1444
– – Under British Mandate **8**:1449
– – Under Iraqi Rule **8**:1450
– – Community Life **8**:1451
– – From 1948 **8**:1452
– – After 1952 **8**:1455
– – Kurdish Jews **8**:1456
– – Israel Relations **8**:1456
– – Musical Traditions **8**:1458
– – Customs **8**:1461
– Aaron ben Amram **2**:9
– agriculture **2**:401
– Alliance Israélite Universelle **2**:652
– Arab League **3**:242ff
– armistice agreements **3**:479; **9**:377
– Battat, Reuben **4**:328
– Benjamin, Moses **4**:529
– Daniel, Menaḥem Salih **5**:1290
– David ben Zakkai **5**:1358
– demography **5**:1501
– discrimination **6**:71
– Elias, Joseph **6**:615
– goldsmiths **7**:740
– hanging of Jews **15**:1561
– Ḥanukkah lamps **7**:1292
– history chart **8**:766-767
– immigration to Ereẓ Israel **9**:499ff; **9**:536
– Israel War of Independence **9**:366ff; **16**:306ff
– Jewish Neo-Aramaic dialects **12**:948
– Kurdistan **10**:1295
– masoretic accents **11**:1109
– minority rights **12**:45ff
– Ottoman conquest **16**:1536
– politics **13**:816
– sickness **14**:1501ff
– Six-Day War **9**:408; **14**:1624
– synagogues **1**:syn. list
– U.N. **15**:1550
– Warburg's settlement plans **16**:287
– Yemen Jews **16**:741
– Zionism **16**:1127; **16**:1128
– *pop. tables:*
– – text
– – Kurdistan, 1920-1947 **10**:1296
– *see also:* BABYLONIA; BAGHDAD; MESOPOTAMIA
ʿIrāq al-Amīr (arch. site) **3**:327
– Tobiad center **15**:1178ff
– Tyre of the Tobiads **15**:1490
– *illus:*
– – Tobiad palace ruins **3**:338
ʿIRĀQĪ, ELEAZAR BEN AARON HA-KOHEN **8**:1461
– printing press **5**:40; **5**:41
IRAQI, SHALOM HA-KOHEN (al-Usta) **8**:1462
ʿIRĀQĪ SHALOM JOSEPH **8**:1462
ʿIrāq Ismāʿīn (loc., Isr.) **6**:920
Iraq-Suweidan (fort., Er. Isr.) **9**:371
Iraq Times (newsp.) **13**:1041
Irbid (tn., Jor.) **9**:179
– Arbel **3**:294
– Jordanian civil war **9**:472
– Northern Gilead **9**:597
IRBIL (Assyr. tn., Iraq) **8**:1462
Irby, Ann Sarah Huguenin **2**:572
IRC, *see* Red Cross, International
Ir David (wk.) **10**:1428
IRELAND **8**:1463
– *Contents:*
– – Modern Period **8**:1465
– – Relations with Israel **8**:1466
– – Northern Ireland **8**:1466
– Belfast synagogue **4**:415
– politics **13**:812
– relations with Israel **9**:431
– *sheḥitah* **14**:1341
– synagogues (Gt. Britain) **1**:syn. list
– textiles **15**:1042
– *pop. tables:*
– – text
– – postwar communities **5**:839
– *see also:* DUBLIN
Ir-Gannim (gr. of stlrs.) **13**:1530
Ir Gannim (sub., Jer.) **9**:1515
– Jerusalem development **9**:1496
Irgun, *see* IRGUN ẒEVA'I LE'UMMI
Irgun Bet (mvmt., Er. Isr.) **8**:759
Irgun Imahot Ovedot (organ., Isr.) **9**:869
Irgun Olej Merkaz Europa (orgn.) **10**:1399; **14**:271
Irgun Ovedei ha-Ẓohar u-Betar (lab. fed.), *see* HISTADRUT HA-OVEDIM HA-LE'UMMIT
Irgun Sanitari Ivri (orgn.), *see* OZE
IRGUN ẒEVA'I LE'UMMI (underground orgn.) **8**:1466
– Aḥimeir, Abba **2**:464
– *Altalena* affair **9**:368ff
– attacks on British **16**:1087
– Begin, Menaḥem **4**:392
– Ben-Gurion **4**:509ff
– Beriḥah **4**:632
– Betar **4**: 714ff
– Briscoe, Robert **4**:1378
– broadcasting **15**:931
– chronological chart **8**:766-767
– defense forces **9**:684f
– Golomb, Eliyahu **7**:764
– Haganah **7**:1066ff
– Hecht, Ben **8**:239
– Ḥerut movement **8**:400
– history **8**:759; **9**:352ff
– Jabotinsky **9**:1182
– Jerusalem attacks **9**:1476
– Jerusalem clashes **9**:1484
– Loḥamei Ḥerut Israel **11**:463ff
– Raziel, David **13**:1593ff
– Revisionists, Zionist **14**:131
– Tel Aviv headquarters **15**:923
– U.S. Zionism **16**:1144
– War of Independence **16**:306
– Yellin-Mor, Nathan **16**:738
– *illus:*
– – text
– – *Altalena* burning off Tel Aviv coast **16**:318
– – Feinstein suicide report, *Palestine Post* **11**:463
– – Goldschmidt House, attack on **9**:361
– – Jerusalem railway station explosion **9**:1479
– – Kenya detention camp **10**:910
– *see also:* STERN, AVRAHAM
Ir ha-Gefanim (city, Fr.), *see* AVIGNON
IR HA-NIDDAḤAT (subverted city) **8**:1470
– domicile **6**:159
– Bible exegesis **8**:1423
– Jerusalem **9**:1553
Irhuleni, King of Hamath **2**:437
Irijah (bib. fig.) **13**:1075
Irira, Abraham, *see* HERRERA, ABRAHAM KOHEN DE
Iris (bot.) **6**:1365
– plant list **13**:619
IRKUTSK (city, Rus.) **8**:1471
– Siberia **14**:1487ff
Ir Lavan (city, Bess.), *see* BELGOROD-DNESTROVSKI
Irmiyā (prophet), *see* JEREMIAH
IR-NAHASH (city, Er. Isr.) **8**:1471
Ir-Nahash (bib. fig.) **10**:906
IRO (U.N. agency), *see* International Refugee Organization
Irodalmi Ujság (period.) **6**:1162
– Ignotus, Pál **8**:1240
IRON (bib. city) **8**:1471
Iron (Cana. tn.) **3**:231
Iron (metal) **11**:1432ff
– folklore **6**:1399
IRON GUARD (anti-Sem. mvmt.) **8**:1472
– Antonescu, Ion **3**:162
– Archangel Michael League **14**:394ff
Iron Hills (Isr.) **9**:588
Iroquois (Ind. tribe, N. Am.) **3**:38; **7**:714
IRRIGATION IN ISRAEL **9**:767
– agriculture **9**:776
– Arabah **3**:232
– Besor, brook of **4**:703
– FAO **15**:1564
– Jordan River **10**:192
– Kinneret **10**:1034
– Kishon **10**:1069
– National Water Carrier **11**:1274
– Negev **12**:929
– physiography **9**:123
– Tahal **15**:701
– Yarkon **16**:717
– Yarmukh **16**:720
– *illus:*
– – Avedat Farm Project **2**:397,399
– – Caesarea aqueduct **5**:9
– – "Irrigation, Zionist Development, Palestine" (paint., David Bomberg) **4**:1196
– – water-wheel, primitive **2**:381
– *see also:* AGRICULTURAL METHODS AND IMPLEMENTS IN ANCIENT EREẒ ISRAEL
Ir-Shemesh (bib. city) **4**:772
IRSO (int. orgn.), *see* JEWISH SUCCESSOR ORGANIZATIONS (Germany)
Irusalem (Jerusalem) **9**:1380
IRVING, JULES **15**:1058,1085
Irwell, Henrietta **16**:593
– *illus:*
– – WIZO delegation to Twelfth Zionist Congress **16**:1101
Ir Yizre'el (tn., Isr.), *see* AFULAH
Is (city, Mesop.) **8**:781
ʿIsā, Ḥannā al- **9**:1040
ISAAC (bib. fig.) **9**:1
– *Contents:*
– – Life **9**:1
– – In The Aggadah **9**:4
– – In Christian Tradition **9**:5
– – In Islam **9**:6
– – In The Arts **9**:6
– Abimelech **2**:76ff
– Abraham **2**:113ff
– blessing of children **4**:1087
– God's revelation **14**:118
– in the Arts **2**:123,484; **9**:1202f
– kabbalistic view **10**:575
– *minḥah* (afternoon prayer) **12**:31
– Nuzi documents **16**:1510
– patriarchs **13**:181
– Rebekah **13**:1601
– sacrifice **14**:605
– Sarah **14**:867
– Tamar **15**:783
– *zekhut avot* **16**:976
– *illus:*
– – text
– – *Akedah* **2**:120,121,480-486; **3**:511,615; **4**:244,880,1231,1339; **6**:285; **8**:1272,1285,1286; **15**:673
– – *Ashburnham Pentateuch* **4**:943
– – asking Esau to go hunting **6**:855
– – blessing Esau **6**:856
– – blessing Jacob **6**:855; **13**:1602
– – deathbed **3**:515
– – reaping the hundredfold harvest **4**:486
– – Rebekah's marriage to **13**:1601
– *see also:* AKEDAH
ISAAC (tan.) **9**:8
Isaac (amora, Carthage) **15**:1430
Isaac (amora) **12**:774
– scriptural reading **16**:1409
Isaac (exil.) **4**:364
ISAAC (7th cent., gaon) **9**:8
– Iraq **8**:1444
ISAAC (8/9th cent., mer.) **9**:8
– interpreter **16**:1281
– trade and commerce **15**:1297
Isaac (11th cent., gaon) **7**:318; **15**:523
Isaac (12th cent., pros.) **13**:1188
ISAAC (12/13th cent., poet) **9**:8
Isaac (13th cent., paytan, Castile) **13**:581
Isaac (13th cent., r.) **14**:659
Isaac (13th cent., copyist) **7**:1098; **11**:734

Isaac (dayyan, Pal.) **2:**158
Isaac (au. of *Sefer ha-Menahel*) **10:**1160
ISAAC, AARON **9:**9
– Sweden **15:**407; **15:**545
– *illus:* text
Isaac, Abraham (court J.) **5:**1009
Isaac, Abraham (stlr., U.S.) **12:**1024
Isaac, Benjamin **12:**185
Isaac, Bernard **13:**60
Isaac, Ephraim **11:**681
Isaac, Heinrich **9:**1361
Isaac, Jacob **13:**1297
Isaac, Joseph **11:**285
ISAAC, JULES MARX **9:**10
– Christianity and the Holocaust **3:**200
Isaac, Moses (r., Gr.), *see* Moses Isaac ha-Levi
Isaac, Noah Samuel **5:**1010
– salt trade **14:**713
Isaac, Sacrifice of, *see* AKEDAH
Isaac, Saul **13:**811
Isaac, son of Joce (12th cent., Eng.) **16:**1285
ISAAC, TESTAMENT OF (bk.) **9:**10
Isaac, Yiḥya **2:**198
Isaac Abd al-Hakk **4:**1274
Isaac Aboab Synagogue (Isr.) **14:**630; **15:**610
Isaac al-Balagh, *see* Balagh, Isaac al-
Isaac Ashkenazi (kab.), *see* LURIA ISAAC BEN SOLOMON
Isaac Barceloni, *see* Barceloni, Isaac ben Judah
ISAAC BAR DORBELO **9:**11
Isaac bar Hananiah (gaon) **7:**318
ISAAC BAR ISRAEL IBN AL-SHUWAYK **9:**11
– governor **14:**618
ISAAC BAR JOSEPH (amora) **9:**12
Isaac Bar Mar Yishi (gaon), *see* Zadok bar Mar Yishi
ISAAC BAR RAV JUDAH (amora) **9:**12
Isaac bar Sheshet, *see* ISAAC BEN SHESHET PERFET
Isaac Baruch of Cairo **5:**31
Isaac Bekhor David **14:**90
Isaac ben Aaron (gaon) **7:**323
Isaac ben Aaron d'Este (print., It.) **8:**1323
Isaac ben Aaron of Karlin **9:**1213
Isaac ben Aaron of Prostitz **5:**1038
ISAAC BEN ABBA MARI OF MARSEILLES **9:**12
– Abba Mari ben Isaac of St. Gilles **2:**38
– codification of law **11:**331
– Ephraim ibn Avi Alragan **6:**814
– *illus:* text
ISAAC BEN ABRAHAM (tos.) **9:**14
Isaac ben Abraham (16th cent., landesrabbiner) **5:**1597
ISAAC BEN ABRAHAM DI MOLINA **9:**14
ISAAC BEN ABRAHAM HA-GORNI **9:**14
– troubadour **13:**689
Isaac ben Abraham ha-Kohen **2:**145
Isaac ben Abraham ha-Parnas **13:**581
Isaac ben Abraham Moses Israel **6:**958
ISAAC BEN ABRAHAM OF NARBONNE **9:**15
ISAAC BEN ABRAHAM OF POSEN **9:**15
Isaac ben Abraham Troki, *see* TROKI, ISAAC BEN ABRAHAM
Isaac ben Abun **10:**719
Isaac ben Ali **2:**631
Isaac ben Arroyo **3:**294
ISAAC BEN ASHER HA-LEVI (11/12th cent.) **9:**16
– trade **15:**1298
ISAAC BEN ASHER HA-LEVI (12th cent.) **9:**16
ISAAC BEN AVDIMI (amora) **9:**17
Isaac ben Avigdor **11:**566
Isaac ben Baruch ibn Abbatio **14:**554
ISAAC BEN BEZALEL OF VLADIMIR **9:**17
Isaac ben Bol Faraj **15:**1438
Isaac ben David of Marseilles **6:**24
Isaac ben Durbal **11:**737
ISAAC BEN ELEAZAR (2nd cent., amora) **9:**17
ISAAC BEN ELEAZAR (4th cent., amora) **9:**17
Isaac ben Eleazar ben Isaac (11th cent.) **10:**719
Isaac ben Eleazar ha-Levi (ling.), *see* Isaac ha-Levi ben Eleazar
ISAAC BEN ELIAKIM OF POSEN **9:**18
ISAAC BEN ELIEZER (11th cent.) **9:**18
Isaac ben Elisha Ḥazzan **4:**1422
– *illus:*
– – colophon **4:**1423
Isaac ben Fayun **13:**581
Isaac ben Ghayyat, *see* Ibn Ghayyat, Isaac ben Judah
Isaac ben Ḥayyim (Ger.) **2:**470
ISAAC BEN ḤAYYIM BEN ABRAHAM **9:**19
– Isaac ben Hunai (Ḥanina) **5:**1351
Isaac ben Isaac of Chinon **5:**475
Isaac ben Israel Ibn Shuwaykh, *see* ISAAC BAR ISRAEL IBN AL-SHUWAYK
ISAAC BEN JACOB HA-KOHEN **9:**19
– emanation doctrine **10:**564
ISAAC BEN JACOB HA-LAVAN OF PRAGUE **9:**20
ISAAC BEN JACOB MIN HA-LEVIYYIM **9:**20
Isaac ben Jacob of Husyatin, *see* Friedmann, Isaac ben Jacob
ISAAC BENJAMIN WOLF BEN ELIEZER LIPMAN **9:**21
Isaac benJehiel **13:**562; **16:**1291
Isaac ben Joseph **11:**754
Isaac ben Joseph ibn Pollegar, *see* POLLEGAR, ISAAC BEN JOSEPH IBN
Isaac ben Joseph Israeli, *see* ISRAELI, ISAAC BEN JOSEPH
ISAAC BEN JOSEPH OF CORBEIL (Semak) **9:**21
– codification of law **11:**334
– *illus:*
– – text
– – *Sefer Mitzvot Katan* (1379) **7:**593
– see also: *Sefer Mitzvot Katan*
Isaac ben Joshua ben Abun **10:**719
ISAAC BEN JUDAH (11th cent., paytan) **9:**22
Isaac ben Judah (cantor, Ger.), *see* OFFENBACH, ISAAC
Isaac ben Judah (trans.) **15:**1329
Isaac ben Judah ha-Kohen (r.), *see* RAPPAPORT, ISAAC BEN JUDAH HA-KOHEN
ISAAC BEN JUDAH HA-SENIRI **9:**22
Isaac ben Judah Leib (syn. art.) **15:**610
Isaac ben Judah Loebush (r., Pol.) **10:**288
Isaac ben Judah Loeb Yuedels (print.) **13:**1107ff
ISAAC BEN JUDAH OF MAINZ **9:**23
Isaac ben Kalonymus, *see* Isaac Nathan ben Kalonymus
Isaac ben Krispin **9:**9
ISAAC BEN MEIR (Ribam) **9:**23
Isaac ben Meir ben Isaac (mart.) **11:**1255
Isaac ben Meir Latif, *see* Latif, Isaac ben Meir
Isaac ben Meir of Dueren, *see* DUEREN, ISAAC BEN MEIR
ISAAC BEN MELCHIZEDEK OF SIPONTO **9:**24
ISAAC BEN MENAḤEM THE GREAT **9:**24
– Orleans **12:**1470
ISAAC BEN MERWAN HA-LEVI **9:**24
Isaac ben Meshullam of Lunel **11:**1400
ISAAC BEN MORDECAI (Ribam; tos.) **9:**25
– Joel ben Isaac ha-Levi **10:**137
Isaac ben Mordecai (physic.) **8:**488 **11:**1193; **12:**1137
Isaac ben Mordecai (philos.) **13:**854
Isaac ben Mordecai Gershon Treves, *see* GERSHON, ISAAC
Isaac ben Moses (11th cent., r.) **13:**1188
Isaac ben Moses ha-Levi, *see* DURAN, PROFIAT
Isaac ben Moses Hezekiah ha-Levi **13:**581
Isaac ben Moses ibn Sakrī, *see* Sakrī, Isaac ben Moses ibn
Isaac ben Moses of Beja (r.) **4:**1484
Isaac ben Moses of Mainz **15:**125
ISAAC BEN MOSES OF VIENNA **9:**25
– Amnon of Mainz **2:**861
– Avigdor ben Elijah ha-Kohen **3:**963
– barnacle goose **4:**247
– codification of law **11:**334
– sport **15:**292
– *illus:* text
Isaac ben Naḥman (3rd cent., Er. Isr.) **9:**1218
Isaac ben Naḥman (16th cent., mer.) **11:**609; **12:**747
Isaac ben Nathan of Cordova **15:**694
Isaac ben Netira **12:**1000
ISAAC BEN NOAH KOHEN SHAPIRA **9:**27
Isaac ben Perez of Northampton **9:**1220
Isaac ben Phoebus **4:**49
Isaac ben Redifa (amora) **10:**294
Isaac ben Reuben (schol.) **5:**1354
Isaac ben Reuben (trans.) **15:**1329
ISAAC BEN SAMSON HA-KOHEN **9:**27
Isaac ben Samuel **7:**1101
Isaac ben Samuel abu al-Khayr **3:**800
ISAAC BEN SAMUEL HA-LEVI **9:**28
– Jacob Koppel Sasslower **9:**1231
– *illus:* text
Isaac ben Samuel ha-Sephardi **2:**261
ISAAC BEN SAMUEL OF ACRE **9:**29
– Four Worlds **10:**581; **16:**642
– Kabbalah **10:**536; **10:**538
– Naḥmanides **15:**521
– practical Kabbalah **10:**635
– *Shi'ur Komah* **14:**1418
– Togarmi **4:**267
– visions **16:**169
– Zohar **16:**1209
ISAAC BEN SAMUEL OF DAMPIERRE **9:**31
– Baruch ben Isaac **4:**278
– Isaac ben Meir **9:**24
Isaac ben Samuel of Meiningen **11:**1300
Isaac ben Sasson **16:**1243
Isaac ben Shangi **2:**792
ISAAC BEN SHESHET PERFET (Ribash) **9:**32
– attorneys and advocates **3:**837
– Gracian, Shealtiel **7:**841
– history chart **8:**766-767
– imprisonment for debt **8:**1305
– Meir ben Baruch ha-Levi **11:**1247
– New Christians' status **12:**1023
– rabbinical office **13:**1447,1449
– responsa **11:**337; **14:**86
– Salamanca murder **14:**671
– Spain **15:**236
– *takkanot* **15:**735
– Tunisia **15:**1439
ISAAC BEN SOLOMON **9:**33
– *illus:* text
Isaac ben Solomon de Braga, *see* Braga, Isaac ben Don Solomon de
Isaac ben Solomon ibn Elhada **3:**802
ISAAC BEN TODROS (14th cent., physic.) **9:**34
ISAAC BEN TODROS OF BARCELONA **9:**34
Isaac ben Walid **15:**1030
ISAAC BEN YAKAR **9:**34
"Isaac Blessing Jacob" (drg., Rembrandt) **9:**6
ISAAC THE BLIND **9:**35
– Abraham ben Isaac **2:**144
– Asher ben David **3:**706
– *devekut* **10:**627
– *Ein-Sof* **10:**557ff
– history chart **8:**766-767
– Kabbalah **10:**523ff; **11:**347
– magic **11:**713
– *Sefer Yeẓirah* **16:**787
Isaac Cap of Barcelona **16:**1288
Isaac da Fonseca Aboab, *see* ABOAB DA FONSECA, ISAAC
Isaac de Leon **13:**583
Isaac de Melija **8:**1200
Isaac de Pinto **8:**766-767
Isaac Eisik ha-Kohen **7:**373
Isaac Eisik of Szydlowiec **4:**598
Isaac Eizik of Komarno **7:**1415
Isaac Eizik of Zhidachov **14:**635; **15:**275
– Kabbalah **10:**555
– Zhidachov **16:**1009
Isaac Elchanan Theological Seminary, *see* Rabbi Isaac Elchanan Theological Seminary
ISAAC FROM OURVILLE **9:**36
Isaac Gershon of Safed **13:**1102
Isaac Gershon of Venice **4:**538
Isaac the Great, *see* ISAAC BEN ABRAHAM OF POSEN
Isaac ha-Baḥur of Dampierre, *see* ISAAC BEN ABRAHAM
Isaac ha-Darshan **6:**958
Isaac ha-Ḥazzan ben Joseph **13:**583
Isaac ha-Kohen (12/13 cent., Fr.) **2:**137; **14:**106
Isaac ha-Kohen (17th cent., au.) **6:**649
Isaac ha-Kohen (r., Er. Isr.) **14:**377
Isaac ha-Kohen ben al-Furat (10/11th cent., physic.) **2:**144
Isaac ha-Kohen of Soria **10:**579
Isaac Ḥakola (amora), *see* ISAAC BEN ELEAZAR (2nd cent.)
Isaac ha-Levi (11/12 cent., ling.) **6:**624; **15:**1329; **16:**1358,1385
Isaac ha-Levi (16th cent. r.) **5:**1354
Isaac ha-Levi, Shalom (r., Fr. Isr.), *see* Yiḥye, Shalom Isaac ha-Levi
Isaac ha-Levi, Yiḥye (r., Yem.), *see* YIḤYE, ISSAC HA-LEVI
Isaac ha-Levi Asir ha-Tikvah (14th cent., Jer.) **9:**1426
Isaac ha-Levi ben Eleazar (13th cent., ling.) **16:**1387
Isaac ha-Nasi **7:**507
Isaac Ḥayyut ben Abraham **13:**1242
Isaac ha-Zaken ben Samuel **10:**345

Isaac Ḥilo of Larissa **8**:230
Isaac ibn al-Fara, *see* Al-Fara, Isaac ibn
Isaac ibn Ezra, *see* IBN EZRA, ISAAC
Isaac ibn Muhājir, *see* Ibn Muhājir, Isaac
Isaac ibn Sa'id, *see* IBN SA'ID, ISAAC
Isaac ibn Shaprut **11**:1305
Isaac Ibn Wakar, *see* Ibn Waqar, Isaac
Isaac ibn Zadok, *see* Ibn Zadok, Isaac
Isaac Iskoi ben Solomon (exil.) **15**:122
Isaac Jacobwicz Synagogue (Cracow) **15**:602,606
Isaac Jare ben David **13**:1108
Isaac the Jew (8th cent., trav.) **15**:1348
Isaac the Jew (9th-10th cents., trav.), *see* Isḥāq the Jew
Isaac Judaeus (Egy. philos.), *see* ISRAELI, ISAAC BEN SOLOMON
Isaac Judah Jehiel of Komarno **7**:1415
Isaac Katznelson Ghetto Fighters' Museum **3**:390
Isaacks, Jacob (inv.), *see* ISAACS, JACOB
Isaac Laquedem, *see* WANDERING JEW
Isaac Mar Saul **7**:563
Isaac Mayer Wise Temple (syn., O.), *see* B'nai Yeshurun
Isaac Nafuci, *see* NIFOCI, ISAAC
ISAAC NAPPAḤA (amora) **9**:37
Isaac Nathan ben Kalonymus **3**:469; **16**:1360, 1388
Isaac of Bendery, *see* Bendery, Isaac of
Isaac of Bohemia, (tos.), *see* ISAAC BEN JACOB HA-LAVAN OF PRAGUE
Isaac of Bohush, *see* Friedmann, Isaac
Isaac of Botosani **4**:43
Isaac of Buhusi, *see* Friedmann, Isaac
Isaac of Camerino **2**:936
Isaac of Carcassone **9**:15ff
ISAAC OF CHERNIGOV **9**:38
Isaac of Cracow **4**:14
ISAAC OF EVREUX **9**:38
Isaac of Ghazni **13**:310
Isaac of Grodno **6**:824
Isaac of Kaschau **8**:1088
Isaac of Lienz **15**:1491
Isaac of Norwich **10**:475; **13**:916
– *illus:*
– – caricature (1233) **5**:171
Isaac of Pinczow **3**:224
Isaac of Radzivilow **2**:160; **9**:1315
Isaac of Regensburg, *see* ISAAC BEN JACOB HA-LAVAN OF PRAGUE
Isaac (ben Ezekiel) of Russia, *see* ISAAC OF CHERNIGOV
Isaac of Rymanow, *see* Friedmann, Isaac
Isaac of Salzburg **14**:717
Isaac of Skvira **15**:1472
Isaac of Spain **5**:1028
Isaac of Tunis **15**:1439
Isaac of Valladolid **16**:926
Isaac of Verona **3**:963
Isaac of Vilna **11**:359
Isaac of Vorka, *see* Warka, Isaac of
Isaac of Worcester **8**:344
Isaac Or Zaru'a, *see* ISAAC BEN MOSES OF VIENNA
Isaac the Rich of Jena **15**:1128
Isaac Ruba (tan.) **7**:1105
ISAACS (fam., U.S.) **9**:38
Isaacs, A. (apos., Er. Isr.) **9**:1256
Isaacs, Abraham (U.S.) **12**:1067
Isaacs, Abraham (Eng.) **11**:997
Isaacs, Abram Samuel **9**:39
– American Jewish Historical Society **2**:826
Isaacs, Barnett, *see* BARNATO, BARNEY
Isaacs, David **4**:138; **8**:1008; **12**:1128
ISAACS, EDITH JULIET **15**:1085
– family **9**:39
Isaacs, Eva Violet, *see* Reading, Marchioness of
Isaacs, Gerald Rufus, *see* Reading, Second Marquess of
Isaacs, Harry **12**:1376
Isaacs, Henry **3**:840; **12**:1130
ISAACS, SIR ISAAC ALFRED **9**:40
– anti-Zionism **16**:1105
– Melbourne **11**:1281; **11**:1284
– *illus:*
– – portrait **3**:883
ISAACS, ISAIAH **9**:41
Isaacs, Israel **11**:997
ISAACS, JACOB (inv.) **9**:41
ISAACS, JACOB (lit. schol.) **6**:788
Isaacs, Jeremy **15**:930
ISAACS, JORGE **9**:41
ISAACS, JOSEPH **9**:41
Isaacs, Lazarus **7**:613
Isaacs, Lewis Montefiore **9**:39
Isaacs, Maurice **10**:1502
Isaacs, Myer Samuel **9**:39
– Baron de Hirsch fund **4**:255
– Civil War **12**:1075
– Vineland **16**:157
ISAACS, NATHAN **9**:42
ISAACS, NATHANIEL **9**:42
– travels **15**:1350
Isaacs, Rufus Daniel, *see* Reading, First Marquess of
Isaacs, Samuel Myer **9**:38
– New York City **12**:1071; **12**:1074
– Texas **15**:1034
Isaacs, Simon **10**:1492
Isaacs, Stanley Myer **9**:40
– New York **12**:1111
ISAACS, SUSAN SUTHERLAND **9**:43
Isaacs, Wilfred **15**:307
Isaac Saba **5**:194
Isaac Sagi Nahor, *see* ISAAC THE BLIND
Isaac Sar-Shalom **16**:361
Isaac Seckel Spitz of Nikolsburg **4**:1213
ISAACSOHN, SIEGFRIED **8**:547
Isaacson (fam., U.S.) **3**:450
Isaacson, David **14**:228
Isaacson, Israel **7**:1344
Isaacson, J.J. **15**:311
Isaacson, Leo **15**:1409
Isaacson, Michael (Niky) **5**:220
Isaacson, S. (pion., Austr.) **11**:1285
Isaacson, Solomon (r., Mold.) **14**:228
Isaacssohn, Joseph **14**:350
Isaac Tauroci, *see* ISAAC BEN TODROS
Isaak (court J., Aus.) **5**:1009
Isaak, Moses **15**:399
Isaakovich, Naḥman **12**:748
Isaaks, Jacob (inv.), *see* ISAACS, JACOB
Isabella of Castile, *see* FERDINAND AND ISABELLA
'Isā ben Nestorius **6**:1197
Isachko (15th cent., physic.) **5**:1028
Isaia, Adolfo **14**:917
ISAIAH (prophet) **9**:44
– alchemy **2**:544
– ancestry **15**:783
– arts **8**:454
– canon, place in **4**:828
– Cyrus **5**:1185ff
– Dead Sea Scrolls **16**:1585
– death **10**:1432; **11**:854
– dietary laws **6**:40
– eschatological writings **6**:864ff
– God's holiness **10**:867
– history chart **8**:766-767
– Lost Tribes **15**:1004
– Maher Shalal Hash Baz **11**:724
– Micah **11**:1481; **11**:1483ff
– morality **10**:1481
– peace **13**:196
– poetry **13**:676ff
– principles of faith **10**:385
– resurrection **14**:98
– Servant of the Lord **14**:1187
– *illus:*
– – Dead Sea Scroll **2**:711; **5**:1399,1415
– – fifteenth century ms. **4**:*fcg.* 972
– – *Hispanic Society Bible* **4**:*fcg.* 876
– – *Parma Bible* **9**:*fcg.* 43
ISAIAH, ASCENSION OF (Chr. apocalypse) **9**:71
– Hellenistic Jewish literature **8**:304
– *see also:* ISAIAH, MARTYRDOM OF
Isaiah, Deutero, *see* Deutero-Isaiah
ISAIAH, MARTYRDOM OF (wk.) **9**:71
Isaiah ben Abba Mari **11**:1247
ISAIAH BEN ABRAHAM **9**:72
ISAIAH BEN ELIJAH DI TRANI **9**:73
– Joshua Boaz **10**:285
Isaiah ben Joseph of Tabriz **10**:537
ISAIAH BEN MALI DI TRANI **9**:73
– *ḥiddushim* **8**:467
– tosafot Rid **15**:1281
– *illus:*
– – *Pesakim* **5**:1235; **8**:1282
ISAIAH BEN UZZIAH HA-KOHEN **9**:74
Isaiah ha-Kohen **3**:1018; **4**:1544
Isaiah ha-Levi **3**:668
Isaiah ha-Levi bar Mar Abba (gaon) **7**:318
ISAIAH ḤASID FROM ZBARAZH (17/18 cent.) **9**:74
– Shabbateanism **14**:1248
– Zbarazh **16**:944
ISAIAH MENAHEM BEN ISAAC **9**:75
– Vladimir Volynski **16**:200
Isaiah of Kalish **13**:1297
Isaiah of Przedborz **13**:1297
Isaiah of Salant **11**:280
Isaiah of Tarichae (tan.) **2**:38
Isaiah Religious Society (Hung.) **7**:1142
Isaiah Scroll (D.S. Scroll) **4**:835
– Isaiah authorship **9**:44
Isaiah son of Joel Ba'al Shem **11**:696
Isak, Aron, *see* ISAAC, AARON
Isakov, Amrami **12**:480
Isakov, Simcho **4**:1493
Isatis (dye plant) **6**:329
Isawites (J. sect) **10**:764
ISBAKH, ALEXANDER ABRAMOVICH **14**:515
ISCANDARI (fam.) **9**:75
Iscandari, Abba **16**:1535
Iscandari, Abraham ben Eleazar **9**:76
– Ottoman Empire **16**:1535
Iscandari, Eleazar ben Abraham **9**:76
– Ottoman empire **16**:1553
Iscandari, Joseph ha-Levi **9**:76
Iscariot, Judas (N.T. fig.), *see* Judas Iscariot
Isdud (Arab vill., Er. Isr.) **3**:696
– Egyptian army **9**:367
Isenberg, Conrad **16**:634
ISENSTEIN, KURT HARALD **3**:602
– *illus:*
– – Born, Max (lith.) **4**:1251
– – Melchior, Marcus (lith.) **11**:1287
ISER, JOSIF **9**:76
– Rumania **14**:414
– *illus:* text
ISFAHAN (city, Iran) **9**:77
– Persia **13**:308; **13**:315ff
– sickness **14**:1501
– *illus:*
– – text
– – synagogue **13**:305
– – Torah scroll niches **15**:620-621
Isfahanī, Isaac ben Jacob al-, *see* ABU 'ISÂ, ISAAC BEN JACOB AL-ISFAHÎNÎ
Isfahanians (J. sect) **2**:184
– Persia **13**:309
Isfiya (vill., Isr.), *see* 'USIFIYYA
Isḥak (12/13th cent., poet), *see* ISAAC
Isḥâq abu al-Khayr **15**:1325
Isḥâq ben Ibrâim al-Tadmuri, *see* Al-Tadmuri, Isḥâq ben Ibrâhim
Isḥâq the Jew (9/10 cent., trav.) **15**:1348
Ishbibenob (bib. fig.) **2**:80; **12**:1478
Ishbi-Irra (dyn. found., Mari) **11**:974
– Ibbi-Sin **16**:1494
Ishbili, Yom Tov ben Abraham, *see* YOM TOV BEN ABRAHAM ISHBILI
ISH-BOSHETH (k. Isr.) **9**:79
– Abner **2**:87
– Hebron **8**:226
– history **8**:588
– Palti **13**:49
– Rechab and Baanah **13**:1609
Ish Ger, *see* GRAZIANO, ABRAHAM JOSEPH SOLOMON BEN MORDECAI
Ishguza (anc. people), *see* Ashkuza
Ish ha-Kazav, *see* LIES, MAN OF
Ish-Horowitz, Samuel Joseph **7**:1420
Ishi-Benob, *see* Ishbibenob
ISH-KISHOR, EPHRAIM **9**:80
– Maccabeans, Ancient Order of **11**:656
– *illus:*
– – F.Z.C. **16**:1165
Ish-Kishor, Sulamith **5**:451
ISHMAEL (bib. fig.) **9**:80
– Abraham **2**:112; **2**:119ff
– *aggadah* **12**:808
– Isaac **9**:1ff
– Ishmaelites **9**:87
– Nabateans **12**:739
– Sarah **14**:868
– *illus:*
– – text
– – Islamic version of the *akedah* **2**:120
– – "Sacrifice of Ishmael" **2**:482
– – sent away by Abraham **7**:1075
– *see also:* HAGAR
ISHMAEL (mil. comm., Judea) **9**:83
Ishmael (tan.), *see* ISHMAEL BEN ELISHA
ISHMAEL BEN ABRAHAM ISAAC HA-KOHEN **9**:83
– moneylending **12**:253
Ishmael ben Eleazar (tan.) **15**:798
ISHMAEL BEN ELISHA (tan.) **9**:83
– *aggadah* **12**:920
– Akiva's hermeneutics **2**:491
– asceticism **3**:679
– Avelei Zion **3**:945
– *Baraita of 32 Rules* **4**:195
– Bible interpretation **8**:1417ff
– emissary **9**:243
– *halakhah* development **7**:1163
– halakhic midrashim **14**:1520
– hermeneutics, and Akiva **8**:371; **14**:1394
– *Mekhilta of R. Ishmael* **11**:1267

- *Midreshei Halakhah* **11:**1523
- mystical literature **11:**347
- mysticism **10:**499
- *Shi'ur Komah* **3:**56; **14:**1418
- Zohar **16:**1200
ISHMAEL BEN JOHANAN BEN BEROKA (tan.) **9:**86
ISHMAEL BEN PHIABI (PHABI) II (h. pr.) **9:**86
- Ananias ben Nedebeus **2:**923
- corrupt priesthood **14:**641
ISHMAEL BEN YOSE BEN ḤALAFTA (tan.) **9:**87
- Avdan **3:**941
- Samaritans criticized **13:**791
Ishmael Ḥanina of Valmontone **6:**1175
- *paytan* list **13:**583
ISHMAELITES (nomadic tribes) **9:**87
- Amalekites **2:**790
- connections with Kedemites **10:**865
- Genesis, Book of **7:**389
- *illus:* text
ISHMAEL OF 'UKBARA **9:**90
- Ukbarite **10:**765
Ishmaiah the Gibeonite (bib. fig.) **2:**794
Ishme-Dagan (k., Assyr.) **11:**978
Ish-Naomi, Elimelech **4:**703
Ishrûn Maqâlât (bk.) **13:**432
Ish Shalom, Meir, *see* FRIEDMANN, MEIR
Ish-Shalom, Mordekhai **9:**673
- Jerusalem affairs **9:**1498
Ishtar (Akk. deity) **3:**738
- Athena prototype **2:**927
- Chemosh **5:**390
- idolatry **8:**1228
- Nineveh temple **12:**1169
- prostitution **13:**1244
- Sabea **14:**588
- Scroll of Esther **14:**1052ff
- Sumerian pantheon **16:**1489
- *see also:* ASHTORETH
Ishum (Mesop. deity) **3:**711
Ish Vilna be-Kherson, *see* BEHAK, JUDAH
Ishwaʿ (vill., Er. Isr.) **6:**892
Ish Yehudi, *see* RABINOVICH, YEHUDAH LEIB
Isi ben Ḥanin (Ḥanan, Johanan; tan.), *see* ABBA YOSE BEN ḤANIN
Isi ben Judah (tan.) **11:**1229
ISIDOR, LAZARE **9:**90
ISIDORE OF SEVILLE **9:**91
- Christian Hebraist **8:**11
Isidoros, *see* LAMPON AND ISIDOROS
Isidorus Hispalensis, *see* ISIDORE OF SEVILLE
Isin (k., Mesop.) **16:**1486
- Ishbi-Irra **11:**974
Isin (city, Mesop.) **16:**1494ff
- Ibbi-Sin **15:**513
Isis (Egy. deity) **8:**293
Iskah (investment of partners), *see* SHETAR
Iskandari, Abraham, *see* Iscandari, Abraham
ISKENDERUN (tn., Turk.) **9:**91
Iskorasten (city, Ukr.), *see* KOROSTEN
Iskowitch, Isidor, *see* CANTOR, EDDIE
ISKOWITZ, GERSHON **9:**92
Iskoy II (exil.) **6:**1028
Iskra (partisan unit, Belor.) **11:**213
ISLAM **9:**92
- General
- - *Amen* in liturgy **2:**803
- - coinage **12:**64
- - Karaites **10:**765
- - Samaritans **14:**732ff
- - travelers, Muslim **15:**1358
- History
- - Abbasids **2:**42
- - Abdallah ibn Sabāʾ **2:**53
- - Algeria **2:**615
- - Almohads **2:**662
- - Ḥâkim bi-Amr Allah, Al- **7:**1152
- - Jerusalem **9:**1423f
Jihâd **10:**103
- - Kharaj and Jizya **10:**937
- - Muhammad **12:**508ff
- - Persia **13:**308
- - Seljuks **14:**1135
- - Umayyads **15:**1528
- Religion, Philosophy
- - *Ahl al-Kitab* **2:**468
- - ʿÂshūrfāʾ, fast day **3:**739
- - *Ḥadith* **7:**1051
- - Ḥibat Allah **8:**462
- - Jerusalem **9:**1575ff
- - Kaʿb al-Aḥbâr **10:**488
- - Koran **10:**1194
- - Neoplatonist influence **12:**960
- - pantheistic mysticism **10:**601
- - polygamy **12:**259
- - *Ruʾaḥ ha-Kodesh* **14:**367
- - Sufism **15:**486
- - usury **12:**248
- - *see also:* KALÂM; Shiʿism; Sunnites
- Bible **4:**927
- - Abrahamic stories **2:**119
- - Adamic legend **2:**241
- - *Akedah* **2:**481
- - David **5:**1332
- - Isaac **9:**6
- - Jacob **9:**1201
- - Job **10:**125
- - Joseph **10:**212
- - Moses **12:**402
- - Noah **12:**1195
- - Pharaoh **13:**362
- - Saul **14:**916
- Culture
- - Arabic language **16:**1414
- - Balkan music **7:**883
- - illuminated manuscripts **8:**1260ff
- - Jewish art **3:**521
- - Jewish music **12:**590
- Attitude to Jews
- - African Jews **2:**332
- - agriculture **2:**401
- - *dhimma* **5:**1604
- - disputations **6:**91
- - economic life **16:**1278
- - exile, Jews in **7:**282ff
- - forced conversion **3:**170; **3:**174
- - Jewish identity **10:**57,58
- - Jewish quarter **10:**84ff
- - Omar, Covenant of **12:**1378ff
- - Yahûd **16:**703
- Judaism and Attitude to **8:**658ff; **10:**387; **10:**396
- - *aggadah* **2:**364
- - apostasy **3:**203
- - *Guide of the Perplexed* **10:**809
- - Jerusalem Talmud **15:**775
- - Jewish influence **8:**656ff
- - Judah Halevi **10:**363ff
- - *Keshet u-Magen* **3:**194
- - *kiddush ha-Shem* **10:**982
- - Maimon ben Joseph **11:**744
- - Maimonides **8:**685; **11:**766
- - Noachide Laws **12:**1189
- - philosophy **13:**421; **13:**426; **13:**427
- - polemics **3:**193ff; **11:**310ff
- - rabbinate **13:**1448
- Israel, State of
- - Arab National Movement **9:**453
- - divorce **16:**629
- - holy places **8:**920ff
- - Israel community **9:**917ff
- - jurisdiction **9:**628ff
- *illus:*
- - Temple Mount mosques **9:**1413
- *pop. tables:*
- - postwar Jewish communities in Muslim countries **5:**837
- *see also:* Arabs; DEMOGRAPHY
Islamic Literature, *see* ORIENTAL LITERATURE
Islamic Museum (Jer.) **12:**552
Islands, Bay of (N.Z.) **12:**1128
Isler, M. **14:**168
ISLE-SUR-LA-SORGUE, L' (tn., Fr.) **9:**105
- *illus:* text
Isma'il (bib. fig.), *see* ISHMAEL
Ismail (13th cent., sult.) **9:**269
Ismaʿil (imam, Yem.) **16:**744
Ismail (sharif, Mor.) **2:**516
Ismail (gov., Acre) **9:**294
Ismail (city, Bess.), *see* IZMAIL
Ismâʿîl al-Rumayhî, *see* Yshmael Haramḥi
Ismâʿîl al-ʿUkbarî, *see* ISHMAEL OF ʿUKBARA
Ismail ibn Nagrel'a, *see* SAMUEL HA-NAGID
Ismailism (rel.-polit. mvmt.) **9:**924; **9:**928
Ismailiya (tn., Egy.)
- inscription **16:**661
- Sinai campaign **14:**1607
- Six-Day War **14:**1636
Ismâʿiliyya Movement (Isl.) **4:**1364
- Fatimids **6:**1196
Isnimit (Turk. port), *see* IZMIT
Isny (tn., Bav.)
- Fagius, Paulus **6:**1136
- Levita, Elijah **11:**133
- *illus:*
- - Fagius' printer's mark **13:**1094
Isolepis (zool.) **9:**226
ISOU, ISIDORE **7:**150
Ispalatro minhag (Seph. minhag) **14:**185
Isparagos (bot.) **5:**1
Ispir, Elie Vitte **5:**208
ISRAEL (name) **9:**106
- archangel **2:**966
- Genesis, Book of **7:**389
- Isaac **9:**4
- Jacob **9:**1195ff
- Jeshurun **10:**4
- Jew's name **10:**22
ISRAEL (LAND OF)
- this entry is divided according to the following sub-divisions: (1) Archaeology (2) Boundaries (3) Climate (4) Flora and Fauna (5) Geology (6) History (7) Names (8) Physiography (9) Religious Laws Appertaining to
(1) ARCHAEOLOGY **3:**302
- agricultural implements **2:**382
- Alphabet, Hebrew **2:**674
- anthropology **3:**40
- architecture **3:**336
- art **3:**499
- Bar Kokhba letters **4:**228
- Beth-Shean **4:**757
- Bet She'arim **4:**765
- catacombs **5:**249
- coins and currency **5:**695
- Dead Sea Scrolls **5:**1396
- dolmens **6:**156
- En-Gedi **6:**741
- epitaphs **6:**818
- Eusebius **6:**978
- Gezer Calendar **7:**538
- Ḥanukkah lamps **7:**1289
- Israel Exploration Society **9:**1060
- Jericho **9:**1365
- Jerusalem,**9:**1521
- Judean Desert Caves **10:**403
- Lachish **10:**1332
- Masada **11:**1079
- Megiddo **11:**1222
- *menorah* **11:**1355
- Mesha Stele **11:**1398
- Murabba'at Scrolls **12:**527
- ossuaries and sarcophagi **12:**1503
- ostraca **12:**1509
- pillars **13:**520
- pottery **13:**937ff
- Qumran **13:**1429
- Sinai **14:**1593
- Tell Arad **3:**244
- urbanization **5:**583
- *illus:*
- - text
- - agricultural implements and methods **2:**375-399; **6:**1417; **9:**133,205
- - archaeological sites in Ereẓ Israel (map) **3:**304
- - Bar Kokhba period antiquities **3:**325, 375; **4:**229-231,239,734,735; **5:**708-710; **6:**1448; **8:**645,647; **10:**405; **12:**569
- - biblical period remains **2:**438; **3:**316,320,1004; **4:**717,729; **5:**418,587,589,1259; **6:**327; **7:**351,551,557; **8:**591,594,603; **9:**1381-1384,1460,1523,1527; **11:**1222-1226; **12:**174,1413; **13:**1536; **14:**1332,1400
- - Byzantine period antiquities **9:**1536; **11:**677; **12:**929; **14:**1419
- - Canaanite period remains **2:**760, 761, 926; **3:**247,311,318,504,704; **5:**1163-1168; **7:**738; **16:**655
- - Christian antiquities **2:**181; **3:**329; **4:**746; **5:**1457; **8:**928,930; **9:**913-916,1401,1417-1420,1439, 1460–1461
- - coffins **13:**401
- - coins **3:**322,333,509; **4:**229-231; **5:**697-715; **6:**1448; **7:**1055; **8:**625,630; **9:**109-110; **11:**1169,1357; **12:**569; **13:**848; **14:**1348
- - Crusader castles **2:**419; **3:**188,327,328,330,821; **5:**1136-1145; **9:**172 **12:**880; **16:**728
- - cult objects **2:**761,762,766,767; **3:**318,501,504,696,704; **5:**1156-1160; **4:**481; **6:**743; **7:**1293; **8:**1313
- - Dead Sea Scrolls **3:**371,681; **5:**1396–1406, 1409, 1411, 1413–1418; **13:**332, 1433; **14:**1371; **15:**903,997; **16:**668
- - Early Israelite antiquities **2:**397; **3:**338,509; **5:**579,583,938,1163-1168; **7:**535-537; **8:**571,591; **11:**263,1223-1226; **12:**174; **13:**1536; **16:**377-386
- - glass objects **5:**1041; **7:**605,607
- - Hasmonean period antiquities **3:**321,340,509; **8:**460; **9:**1391,1533; **15:**1219-1221
- - Hellenistic and Roman antiquities **2:**394; **3:**321, 322, 323, 335, 337, 510, 518; **4:**234, 1286; **5:**658; **6:**62,177; **7:**433, *fcg.* 619; **8:**288; **9:**1401; **11:**953,1585; **12:**1504-1505,1530; **13:**341,1537; **14:**723; **15:**535,568
- - Herodian antiquities **3:**78,323,340,511; **4:**235-236,320; **5:**7-13; **8:**380,383,389,633,637,923; **9:**1397,1399,1501,1522,1531,1533, 1535; **11:**839, 1079–1091, 1358; **12:**672,1505; **14:**205,723-725; **15:**960; **16:**44,333,535,469-470
- - Hittite antiquities **3:**503
- - ivory objects **3:**315,337,504; **5:**397,979,1227; **8:**596; **9:**1154;

11:268,1222
- - Jerusalem excavations **9**:1382-1402,1522-1539
- - Jerusalem gates and city walls **9**:1382,1384,1391,1397,1401, 1427-1432, 1470, 1472, 1518, 1522, 1533, 1536
- - jewelry **7**:738,739; **11**:1363
- - Judean Desert caves **10**:405
- - Mamluk period remains **3**:78,330; **8**:923; **9**:275,1424; **11**:619,835
- - Masada **11**:1079-1091
- - Megiddo excavations **11**:1222-1226
- - Moabite antiquities **3**:319
- - museums **3**:350,354,631; **5**:1397; **6**:792; **9**:951,1010 *fcg.* 1534; **11**:1460; **12**:549; **14**:212
- - Nabatean antiquities **3**:943; **12**:739
- - ossuaries **3**:321,513,1012; **7**:1047; **12**:1133,1504
- - ostraca **2**:390,679,680,684; **3**:317,320,372,373; **6**:591; **11**:513; **12**:1509; **16**:657
- - Ottoman period remains **9**:1427-1434
- - Philistine antiquities **3**:314,696; **13**:401,404
- - pottery types and objects **3**:307-310,314; **4**:761,781; **5**:939,1156-1160,1522; **7**:1047,1293-1295; **8**:1313; **11**:1362; **12**:1348; **13**:404; **14**:559,1075; **15**:492; **16**:386,668
- - prehistoric remains **2**:383; **3**:41,43,501; **5**:187; **15**:1220
- - Qumran excavations **13**:1433
- - Samaria, Israelite remains **2**:438; **3**:315,337,372,503; **5**:397
- - seals **3**:509; **5**:418; **7**:351; **8**:227; **9**:110,1374; **10**:302; **13**:1537; **14**:1075; **16**:386,660
- - synagogues, ancient **3**:293,325,511,513,517; **4**:711; **5**:202; **6**:337,893; **7**:249,251,314,1243,1244; **9**:1370,1443; **10**:878; **11**:689,908,989,1085,1357,1391; **12**:569, 737,900; **13**:44,217,905,1532-1534; **15**:574,596-599
- - *see also under individual archaeological sites and subjects*

(2) BOUNDARIES **9**:112
- Acre **2**:223
- Asher **3**:700
- Beersheba **4**:384
- Benjamin **4**:523
- Dan **5**:1259
- Ephraim **6**:807
- Gad **7**:246
- Gerar, Land of **7**:432
- Issachar **9**:1075
- Judah **10**:330
- levitical cities **11**:136
- *Limes* Palestinae **9**:240
- Manasseh **11**:851
- Naphtali **12**:818
- Red Sea **14**:15
- Reuben **14**:103
- Saul **14**:912
- Simeon **14**:1547
- Solomon **15**:102ff
- Talmud **15**:1024
- Twelve Tribes **15**:1381
- Zebulun **16**:950ff
- *maps:*
- - text
- - Abraham ben Jacob's map (1695) **11**:927
- - Asher territory **3**:700
- - Benjamin territory **4**:522
- - British mandate, 1922 **9**:317
- - Dan territory **5**:1256
- - Ephraim territory **6**:807
- - Franco-British agreements, 1920-23 **9**:316
- - Gad territory **7**:247
- - Gaza Strip **7**:344
- - Herod's kingdom, division of **8**:375
- - Hittite empire **8**:788
- - Issachar territory **9**:1075
- - Jordan River **10**:191
- - Judah territory **10**:327
- - levitical cities **11**:137
- - Madaba map **11**:922
- - Manasseh territory **11**:852
- - Moab, time of Mesha **12**:193
- - Naphtali territory **12**:820
- - Near East, 3rd millenium B.C.E. **15**:513
- - Philistine Pentapolis **13**:400
- - pictorial map (12th cent.) **11**:923
- - Plan C, Woodhead Commission, 1938 **13**:38
- - Reuben territory **14**:104
- - Robert's map of Erez Israel (1750) **11**:929
- - Saul's kingdom **14**:910
- - Simeon territory **14**:1548
- - Solomon's kingdom **15**:97
- - Sykes-Picot agreement, 1916 **9**:315
- - Turco-British agreement, 1906 **9**:315
- - UNSCOP partition plan, 1947 **9**:317
- - Vesconte's map of Erez Israel (14th cent.) **11**:925
- - Zebulun territory **16**:951
- - Zionist movement frontier proposals, 1919 **9**:316

(3) CLIMATE **9**:181
- Ashbel's research **3**:695
- Bet Dagan Meteorological Station **4**:719
- Coastal Plain **9**:571
- Dew **5**:1600
- Jerusalem **9**:1514
- rain **2**:388; **13**:1520ff
- *illus:* text
- *maps* and *charts:*
- - dew nights
- - - annual number **9**:187
- - - average value **5**:1601
- - potential evaporation **9**:184
- - rainfall **9**:186; **13**:1521,1522
- - temperature
- - - annual means **9**:190
- - - January means **9**:192
- - - July means **9**:193
- - - Tel Aviv and Jerusalem means **9**:189

(4) FLORA AND FAUNA **9**:220
- afforestation **2**:387; **9**:787
- animals **3**:7
- early Israelite period **2**:388
- Estori ha-Parḥi **6**:918
- Jerusalem **9**:1515
- nature reserves **12**:891
- spice route **8**:1312
- *illus:*
- - text
- - afforestation in Galilee **10**:79
- - animals of the Bible and Talmud (list) **3**:9-16
- - Dan riverside vegetation **9**:231
- - Eilat Gulf coral fauna **9**:172-173
- - En-Gedi nature reserve **12**:892
- - flowers, shrubs and trees **6**:1388-1389
- - "Little Switzerland" vegetation **9**:235
- - Mount Gilboa vegetation **9**:231
- - plants and products of plants mentioned in the Bible and Mishnah (list) **13**:615-626
- - plants brought by Thutmose III from Palestine **2**:385
- - vegetation of Israel and adjacent areas (map) **9**:223
- - *see also:* Flora and Fauna

(5) GEOLOGY **9**:194
- Arabah **3**:231
- earthquake **6**:340
- human geography **9**:571ff
- Negev **12**:925
- oil and gas **9**:793
- *illus:*
- - text
- - Timna, schematic columnar section of area **9**:799

(6) HISTORY
- Beginning until the Monarchy **8**:569
- - Abraham **2**:112ff
- - Adoni-Zedek **2**:296
- - alphabetic inscriptions **2**:677
- - anthropology **3**:41
- - architecture **3**:336
- - Baal-Berith worship **4**:1
- - burial customs **15**:1216
- - coins and currency **5**:695
- - Commandments, the 613 **5**:774f
- - crafts **5**:1044ff
- - dress **6**:215
- - Genesis, Book of **7**:386
- - *ḥazer, ḥazerim* **7**:1530
- - *ḥerem* **8**:348
- - historical right **13**:257; **13**:237
- - Hittites **8**:789
- - human geography **9**:567
- - Hyksos **8**:1142
- - Jerusalem **9**:1379
- - Judah, Land of **10**:330
- - Judges, Book of **10**:442
- - oils **12**:1347ff
- - poetry **13**:671ff
- - providence **13**:1279
- - Samaritan origins **14**:727
- - Samson **14**:773
- - Sinai **14**:1595ff
- - social structure **8**:609ff
- - strangers' status **15**:419ff
- - textiles **15**:1037
- - trade and commerce **15**:1293ff
- - urban culture **5**:584ff
- - war and warfare **16**:268ff
- - weights and measures **16**:376
- - wisdom **16**:558ff
- - *see also:* CANAAN, LAND OF
- Monarchy and the Divided Kingdom **9**:1047; **8**:586
- - Ahab **2**:435ff
- - Amaziah **2**:798
- - Amon **2**:862
- - Aram-Damascus **3**:287
- - Asa **3**:671
- - David **5**:1318
- - designation **9**:111
- - Edom **6**:374
- - Ezra **6**:1104
- - Hezekiah **8**:450
- - Jehoshaphat **9**:1325
- - Jehu **9**:1328
- - Jeremiah **9**:1345
- - Jeroboam **9**:1371
- - Jerusalem **9**:1383
- - kingship **10**:1014
- - Manasseh **11**:852
- - Nehemiah **12**:936
- - Omri **12**:1390
- - Prophets' influence **13**:1157ff
- - Samaritans **14**:728; **14**:736
- - Samuel **14**:780; **14**:789
- - Saul **14**:909
- - social structure **8**:613
- - Solomon **15**:97ff
- - Twelve Tribes **15**:1381
- - Uzziah **16**:43
- Hellenistic-Roman period **8**:625
- - academies **2**:202
- - agoranomos **2**:372
- - Agrippa I **2**:416
- - Alexander the Great **2**:577
- - *aliyah* **9**:511
- - Anan, son of Anan **2**:919
- - angaria **2**:950
- - anthropology **3**:47
- - Antiochus **3**:73ff
- - architecture **3**:357
- - art **3**:506
- - Cassius Longinus **5**:234
- - circumcision **5**:568ff
- - Dead Sea sect **5**:1408
- - Decapolis **5**:1449
- - economic progress **16**:1272
- - Essenes **6**:899
- - Gabinius Aulus **7**:235
- - Hasmoneans **7**:1455
- - Herod I **8**:375
- - high priest **8**:470ff
- - historiography **8**:552
- - Jason **9**:1291
- - Jerusalem **9**:1384; **9**:1394
- - Jesus **10**:10
- - Johanan ben Zakkai **10**:148
- - Josephus Flavius **10**:251
- - Julius Caesar **10**:470
- - literature **8**:293
- - messianism **11**:1408
- - mysticism **10**:496
- - Nakdimon ben Guryon **12**:801
- - Nero **12**:964
- - Pharisees **13**:363
- - Pompey **13**:846
- - Pontius Pilate **13**:848
- - priesthood **13**:1085ff
- - procurators **13**:1117
- - Ptolemy **13**:1347
- - Samaritans **14**:729; **14**:730
- - Sicarii **14**:1491
- - Sikarikon **14**:1529
- - Titus **15**:1168
- - Tobiads **15**:1178
- - Zealots **16**:947
- - Zeno, papyri of **16**:992
- - Zion **16**:1030
- Destruction of the Second Temple until the Arab Conquest **9**:237
- - Abba Sikra **2**:43
- - academies **2**:201ff
- - aftermath of first Roman war **8**:643
- - Akiva's role in revolt **2**:489
- - *amoraim* **2**:868ff
- - angaria **2**:950
- - Antipatris **3**:78
- - Antoninus **3**:166
- - archisynagogos **3**:335
- - arnona **3**:488
- - Aurum Coronarium **3**:854
- - Bar Kokhba revolt **4**:228
- - Cilician collections **5**:562
- - crucifixion **5**:1134
- - emperor worship **6**:729
- - Hadrian **7**:1054
- - Heraclius **8**:333
- - Hezekiah the Zealot **8**:455
- - imperial estates **10**:367
- - Josephus Flavius **10**:251
- - Judah ha-Nasi **10**:367ff
- - Julian the Apostate **10**:467
- - Meir's views on settlement **11**:1241
- - mishnaic Hebrew **16**:1591
- - Negev **12**:928ff
- - ordination **14**:1142
- - Palmyra conquest **15**:697
- - proselytes **13**:1185
- - Roman emperors **14**:229
- - Samaritans **14**:731ff; **14**:736
- - Sanhedrin **14**:836
- - Simeon bar Yoḥai **14**:1551
- - tax gatherers **15**:873
- - Vespasian's campaign **16**:116
- - *see also:* JUDEA; PALESTINE
- Arab Period **9**:259
- - Aḥa of Shabḥa **2**:449
- - Apulian Jewry **3**:226

- - Carthaginians **5:**215
- - Fatimids **6:**1196
- - gaonate **7:**315; **7:**317; **7:**323
- - Jerusalem **9:**1423
- - Samaritans **14:**732; **14:**737
- - Umayyads **15:**1528; **15:**1529
- - Yehudai Gaon **16:**731
- Crusader Period **9:**267
- - agriculture **2:**398
- - archaeology **3:**329
- - Ayyūbids **3:**998
- - Crusades **5:**1137
- - emissaries **14:**1358ff
- - Franciscans **7:**47
- - Jerusalem **9:**1415ff
- - *nagid* **12:**763
- - Pethahiah of Regensburg **13:**339
- - Roman Jews **14:**245
- - Saladin **14:**669
- - travelers and travels **15:**1351ff
- Mamluk Period **9:**274
- - Jerusalem **9:**1423
- - Jewish life **13:**517ff
- - Mamluks **11:**834
- - Samaritans **14:**733; **14:**737
- Ottoman Period **9:**282; **16:**1534
- - Abdu-l-Hamid II **16:**1553
- - Abulafia, Ḥayyim Nissim **2:**188
- - Aḥad Ha-Am **2:**442
- - Aliyah, First and Second **2:**633ff
- - Alliance Israelite Universelle **2:**652
- - Antebi, Albert **3:**36
- - architecture **3:**336
- - Bilu **4:**998
- - blood libel **16:**1544
- - capitulations **5:**150
- - ḥasidic aliyah **7:**1392
- - Hebrew literature **8:**197
- - Hildesheimer, Azriel **8:**477
- - Ibrahim Pasha **8:**1214
- - "illegal" immigration **8:**1248
- - Jaffa **15:**918; **15:**920
- - J.D.C. aid **2:**828
- - Jerusalem **9:**1426
- - Jews' autonomy **3:**927
- - Kabbalah **10:**545
- - Montefiore, Sir Moses **12:**271
- - Napoleon Bonaparte **12:**824
- - Nasi, Joseph **12:**838
- - Nili **12:**1162ff
- - Portuguese *anusim* **3:**174
- - Samaritans **14:**734; **14:**737
- - settlement **16:**1037
- - Shabbateanism **14:**1247
- - Yishuv **8:**756
- *illus:*
- - text
- - Academies, *tannaim, amoraim* and *geonim* (charts) **2:**866,869-872; **7:**323
- - Anglo-American Commission of Enquiry **4:**511; **16:**1089
- - Antipatris fort **3:**78
- - Ashkelon, conquest by Ramses II **3:**715
- - Balfour Declaration **4:**131,135
- - Barazani and Feinstein suicide report **11:**463
- - "Ben Ya'ir" ostracon **6:**591
- - Bethar **4:**734-735
- - Biltmore Hotel Conference **15:**1633
- - Bols' "Delivery note" for Palestine **3:**392; **9:**336
- - British search for arms caches **14:**1094; **16:**698
- - Churchill's letter to Weizmann re Jewish fighting force (1944) **3:**394
- - Crusader castles **2:**181,419; **3:**188, 327-330, 821; **5:**1136-1145; **9:**172-173,207; **12:**880; **16:**728
- - Declaration of the Establishment of the State of Israel, full text **5:**1453
- - disturbances of May, 1921, Commission of Enquiry report **9:**339
- - Gromyko's speech at U.N., May, 1947 **14:**493
- - *ha'apalah* medal **11:**1170
- - Hasmoneans confronting Seleucid armies **7:**1457
- - Herodium **4:**235-236; **8:**389
- - "illegal" immigration **8:**1251-1253
- - Jemal Pasha and Turkish governor of Jerusalem **9:**332
- - Jewish and Transjordan Arab leaders, meeting (1933) **9:**346
- - Jewish Legion at El-Arish, 1918 **9:**335
- - Jewish soldiers in Turkish army **9:**335
- - King David Hotel explosion **8:**1469
- - king of Judah **3:**320
- - *Managem*, Yacht used for Nili information **12:**1164
- - Masada **4:**320; **8:**383; **11:**1079-1091
- - Mauritius detainees at Haifa **11:**1134
- - Megiddo **2:**760; **3:**316; **8:**591
- - Moabite stone record **3:**319
- - Peel Commission, 1936 **9:**351
- - proclamation of the State of Israel **4:**513
- - resolution re establishment of State **10:**34
- - riots of 1936, *Palestine Post's* reporting **9:**350
- - Rothschild, Edmond James de, in Ereẓ Israel **14:**344,345
- - Samuel, Herbert, letter of appointment **14:**799
- - Semitic clan in Egypt **3:**311
- - Sennacherib's campaign against Hezekiah **3:**319
- - Sennacherib's eighth campaign **14:**1162
- - Shalmaneser's victory over Jehu **3:**320
- - Sharett giving evidence before UNSCOP **16:**1093
- - Transjordan, declaration of independence **9:**339
- - Turkish army recruits in Palestine (1915) **11:**1568
- - Turkish surrender of Jerusalem **9:**1471
- - U.S. Senate's endorsement of a Jewish national home in Palestine **3:**393
- - War of Independence **16:**307-330
- - Wauchope's letter re settlement in Transjordan **9:**342
- - Weizmann, Chaim, and Emir Faisal **9:**336
- - World War I, Jewish refugees at Jaffa **9:**335
- - Zionist delegation to Palestine, 1918 **9:**336; **16:**1136
- - *see also:* Israel (land of) Archaeology; *and under individual subjects*
- *maps:*
- - text
- - Abraham's wanderings **2:**115
- - Academies **2:**203
- - Alexander Yannai's kingdom **9:**118
- - Ammonite region and towns **2:**854
- - Amorite towns **2:**876
- - Aramean regions and towns **3:**253
- - Bar Kokhba revolt **4:**232
- - Bashan area **4:**291
- - battle of Karkar **2:**436
- - British Mandate, 1922 **9:**317
- - Canaan **5:**99; **9:**112
- - David's kingdom **9:**115
- - David's wars and conquests **5:**1320-1323
- - Decapolis **5:**1450
- - Exodus, routes **6:**1043,1048
- - Franco-British agreements **9:**316
- - Gideon's war **7:**557
- - Hasmonean kingdom **7:**1455
- - Herod's kingdom, and division of **8:**375; **9:**118
- - Jerusalem
- - - Byzantine period **9:**1403
- - - Crusader period **9:**1421
- - - First Temple period **9:**1385
- - - Nehemiah's period **9:**1387
- - - Second Temple period **9:**1395
- - Judges, period of, limits of Israelite control **9:**113
- - Saul's kingdom **9:**114
- - Solomon's kingdom **9:**115
- - Sykes-Picot agreement, 1916 **9:**315
- - Turco-British agreement, 1906 **9:**315
- - UNSCOP partition plan, 1947 **9:**317
- - Woodhead Commission, Plan C, 1938 **13:**38
- - Yehud province **9:**119
- - Zionist movement frontier proposals, 1919 **9:**316
(7) NAMES **9:**108
- Amurru **2:**875
- Canaan **5:**98
- Merneptah inscription **6:**482
- Palestine **13:**29
- Phoenicia **13:**471
- *illus:*
- - Merneptah stele **3:**313; **6:**497
- - Yahud coins **3:**322; **5:**697-698
(8) PHYSIOGRAPHY **9:**123
- Arabah **3:**232
- Bible and Talmud **7:**415
- Estori ha-Parḥi **6:**918
- Galilee **7:**265
- Golan **7:**694
- Haduta's *kerovot* **7:**1056
- Ḥuleh **8:**1064
- human geography **9:**570ff
- Jerome **9:**1378
- Jezreel, Valley of **10:**101
- maps **11:**918
- Negev **12:**925
- Shephelah **14:**1380
- Sodom **15:**71ff
- travel books **11:**351ff
- Zohar **16:**1200
- *illus:*
- - text
- - Amudei Amram **9:**213
- - Bet Guvrin caves **4:**732
- - chalk formations **9:**203,205,208
- - columnar basalt **9:**213
- - Dead Sea caves **8:**645
- - Dead Sea Rift Valley **9:**217
- - flash flood **9:**185
- - Ḥuleh Valley **9:**207,212
- - Jordan River and Valley (map) **10:**191
- - Judean Desert **9:**99
- - Kidron Valley gorge **10:**987
- - Lashon formations **9:**205
- - Levona intermontane basin **9:**209
- - loess badlands **9:**203
- - loess soil in Naḥal Besor **9:**573
- - Ma'aleh Akrabbim rock formation **11:**635
- - Makhtesh Ramon **9:**209
- - Nubian sandstone formations **9:**207
- - Red Sea area **14:**15
- - Rift Valley, Northern part **9:**211
- - Sedom area, aerial view **15:**73
- - *Sefer Kaftor va-Feraḥ* (1549) **6:**919
- - Sorek Valley **15:**164
- - Tabor, mount **15:**692
- - terrace landscape **9:**205
- - Valley of Kinnarot **10:**1032
- - Wadi al-Murrah **12:**928
- - Yarmuk River **16:**719
(9) RELIGIOUS LAWS APPERTAINING TO
- child's custody **13:**98
- Commandments, the 613 **5:**777
- First Fruits **6:**1312
- *Ḥallah* **7:**1193
- *ḥibbut ha-kever* exemption **8:**464
- husband or wife's residence rights **8:**1121
- idolatry **8:**1227
- impurity **13:**1409; **13:**1407
- king, kingship **10:**1011
- Leket, Shikhhah, and Pe'ah **11:**3
- mixed species **12:**169
- nazirite laws **12:**909
- Omer **12:**1382
- pilgrimage festivals **13:**519
- sabbatical year **14:**574
- sacrifices **14:**599
- sanctity **2:**763; **2:**770
- slavery **14:**1659
- Syria **15:**639
- Temple **15:**942
- *terumah* **15:**1025
- tithes **15:**1156
- visitor and second festival day **6:**1245

ISRAEL (STATE OF; 1880-1970)
- this entry is divided according to the following sub-divisions: (1) General (2) Aliyah, Absorption and Settlement (3) Arab Population (4) Cultural Life (5) (5) Defense Forces (6) Economic Affairs (7) Education and Science (8) Governance (9) Health, Welfare and Social Security (10) Historical Survey (11) Human Geography (12) Labor (13) Legal and Judicial System (14) Political Life and Parties (15) Population (16) Religious Life and Communities
(1)GENERAL
- anti-Semitic cartoons **5:**178
- anti-Semitism **3:**136ff
- archives **3:**385,388
- Austrian Jews **3:**902
- autonomy **3:**922; **3:**923; **3:**927
- B'nai B'rith **4:**1147
- Bund **4:**1506
- Diaspora **6:**18; **7:**293ff
- flags and emblems **6:**1337; **12:**1365
- freemasons **7:**124
- French Jews **7:**39
- Hebrew mss **11:**906
- messianism **11:**1412
- Neo-Nazi attitude **12:**955
- *illus:*
- - Israel stamps **9:**844-845
- - State emblem **11:**1366
(2)ALIYAH, ABSORPTION AND SETTLEMENT
- Introduction **9:**508
- Aliyah and Absorption **9:**515
- - architecture **3:**361
- - Ashkenazim **9:**497ff
- - Ben-Gurion **4:**998
- - British regulations **16:**1086
- - Churchill, Winston **5:**556
- - Cochin Jews **5:**627
- - El Al's role **6:**560
- - *haavara* **7:**1012
- - historical survey **2:**633; **9:**323ff; **9:**378; **9:**393ff
- - "illegal" immigration **4:**632; **8:**1248
- - immigration and labor centers **9:**849
- - Indian Jews **8:**1357

-- Ingathering of the Exiles **8:**1375
-- Iraqi community **5:**1098
-- Jerusalem **9:**1437
-- Jewish Agency **10:**27ff
-- Keren Hayesod **10:**914
-- Kurdish Jews **10:**1298; **10:**1299
-- Law of Return **10:**1485
-- *ma'barah* **11:**654
-- migrations **16:**1522,1525ff
-- New Immigrants
--- defense forces **9:**689
--- health standards **9:**983ff
--- industry **9:**819
--- tax exemptions **9:**755
-- North African Jews **5:**1099
-- Palestine, Inquiry Commissions **13:**31ff
-- Palestine Office **13:**40
-- Persian Jews **13:**318
-- refugees **14:**28ff
-- Russian Zionists **16:**1138ff
-- Sephardim **9:**498ff; **14:**1176
-- Six-Day War effects **9:**412ff
-- South African Jews **16:**1140
-- White Papers **9:343; 16:**482
-- Yemenite community **5:**1099; **16:**743; **16:**751; **16:**752ff
-- Youth Aliyah **16:**861ff
-- Zionist movement **16:**1061ff
- Housing **9:**562
-- Amidar **2:**846
-- architecture **3:**336; **9:**1012
-- economic development **9:**709ff
-- historical survey **9:**381
-- new immigrants **9:**536
-- Office for Public Works and Building **9:**849
-- *ma'barah* **11:**654
- Land Ownership **9:**555
-- Arabs **9:**1021; **9:**628; **9:**918ff
-- I.C.A. **10:**47
-- J.N.F. **10:**77
-- P.I.C.A. **13:**495
-- Hope-Simpson report **13:**32
- Land Reclamation **9:**558
-- eucalyptus trees **9:**788
-- Huleh Valley **8:**1067
-- J.N.F. **10:**77
- Planning **9:**559
-- Adullam Region **2:**312
-- Jerusalem **9:**1517
-- regional councils **9:**621
- Settlement **9:**546
-- agriculture **9:**773
-- Aḥad Ha-Am **2:**441ff
-- Alkalai **2:**639
-- Auerbach, Meir ben Isaac **3:**848
-- Berlin, Naphtali Ẓevi Judah **4:**662
-- Berman, Simeon **4:**667
-- Bilu **4:**998
-- communal separatism **9:**495
-- cooperative movement **5:**944
-- economic development **9:**699ff
-- Eshkol, Levi **6:**888ff
-- Esra organization **6:**895
-- Gawler, George **7:**338
-- Gordon, Aharon David **7:**790
-- Hacohen, Mordecai **7:**1038
-- *Ha-Levanon* **7:**1179
-- Harzfeld, Avraham **7:**1364
-- Ḥibbat Zion **16:**1039ff
-- history **8:**751ff; **9:**381; **11:**862
-- human geography **9:**567
-- Jewish labor organization **9:**849ff
-- Keren Hayesod **10:**914
-- kibutz movement **10:**963
--- *Haggadot* **7:**1103
-- motives **9:**508ff
-- Naḥal **9:**691; **12:**766
-- Negev **12:**929ff
-- new immigrants **9:**538
-- Po'alei Zion **13:**656
-- Ruppin, Arthur **14:**431
-- Satmar Rebbe **15:**909
-- Templers **15:**996
-- Territorialism **15:**1021ff
-- Warburg, Otto **16:**287ff
-- Yemenite Jews **16:**752ff
-- Zionist congresses **16:**1164
- *illus:*
-- text
-- Aden immigrants **9:**502
-- Adullam region **9:**586
-- army sergeant teaching new immigrants **9:**964
-- craftsmen among immigrants to Israel, 1950-1968 (table) **5:**1055
-- displaced persons, demonstration **6:**77
-- East European immigrants **9:**498
-- Georgian Jews, letter to Israel Prime Minister, 1969 **7:**427
-- German refugee children **16:**682
-- Gerofit founder-members **9:**980
-- Ḥabbán immigrants **7:**1019, 1020
-- Ḥalutzim arriving in Jaffa **9:**1258
-- Hefer Valley settlement **9:**521
-- "illegal" immigration **2:**634; **8:**1251-1253
-- immigrant learning carpet weaving **5:**1049
-- immigrants from India **8:**1354
-- immigration figures (1919-1970) **9:**473; **16:**1127
-- Iraqi immigrant in *ma'barah* **8:**1448
-- Jezreel Valley **9:**585
-- Kurdistan immigrants **9:**504
-- Leningrad Jews telegram (1970) **14:**503
-- Magic Carpet operation 1949 **2:**264
-- metal craftsmen from Tripoli **5:**1051
-- Negev **12:**926
-- North African immigrants **9:**499
-- Operation Magic Carpet arrivals **16:**749
-- Polish refugee children **9:**496
-- Ramot Eshkol housing project, Jerusalem **9:**1510
-- refugees in Venice **14:**28
-- Rosh ha-Ayin transit camp **9:**379
-- Russian *ḥalutzim* in Constantinople **14:**465
-- Russian immigrants at Lydda airport **14:**503
-- Sharett visiting Aden transit camp **16:**750
-- Tel Aviv tent camp **15:**920
-- ulpan classroom **15:**1526
-- Volozhin Nes Ziona ass'n **16:**214
-- tower and stockade model **9:**550; **15:**405
-- Yemenite silversmith **5:**1047
-- Yemenite women doing embroidery work **5:**1046
- *pop. tables:*
-- text
-- Asian countries, main period of *Aliyah* **3:**746
-- growth of Jewish population, 1840-1966 **3:**745
-- Iran, emigration to Israel, 1948-1968 **8:**1441
-- settlements **9:**485,487,489,491,547,549
(3)ARAB POPULATION
- General Survey **9:**1021
-- agriculture **9:**780
-- Arab Higher Committee **9:**1475
-- banks **9:**1023
-- Berit Shalom **4:**632
-- cooperatives **5:**949
-- culture **9:**1038
-- economy **9:**698
-- education **9:**949
-- Gaza Strip **7:**343ff
-- geographical distribution **9:**569ff
-- governance **9:598ff**
-- health services **9:**992ff
-- Histadrut **8:**540
-- Jaffa **9:**1255ff
-- Jerusalem, reunited **9:**1504
-- Knesset **9:**854,868; **10:**1115
-- labor movement **9:**854ff
-- labor problems **9:**329ff
-- living standards **9:**397
-- Mapam **11:**914
-- national movement **9:**453
-- population **9:**486ff
-- Ramleh **13:**1541
-- refugees **9:**446
-- religious life **9:**917
-- Teachers' Association **15:**889
-- West Bank **9:**411ff
- Arabic Literature **9:**1040
-- Hebrew poetry **11:**325ff
-- modern literary Arabic **3:**241
- Bedouin **9:**1043
-- Defense Forces **9:**692
-- general survey **9:**1021
-- geographical distribution **9:**569ff, 593
-- health services **9:**991; **9:**992
-- land distribution **9:**338
- Popular Culture **9:**1038
-- general survey **9:**1029ff
-- radio broadcasts **15:**931
- *illus:*
-- Bedouin
--- children, Negev **12:**930
--- plowing **9:**782
--- settlement figures **9:**485
-- Bir al-Sheikh elementary school **9:**944
-- Manaḥat village **9:**581
-- schoolboys at Israel Museum workshop **9:**951
-- Shazar greeted by Nazareth school children **14:**1325
-- Tira medical center **9:**990
(4)CULTURAL LIFE **9:**996
- General
-- America-Israel Cultural Foundation **2:**817
-- architecture **3:**336; **9:**1012
-- army **9:**689
-- art **3:**576ff; **4:**788; **9:**1009
-- food and cooking **6:**1422ff
-- Histadrut **8:**540; **9:**853; **9:**868
-- historical survey **9:**329, 396
-- inter-communal relations **9:**506ff
-- kibbutz movement **10:**966; **10:**972ff
-- libraries **9:**1018; **11:**194ff
-- Mifal ha-Payis **11:**513
-- museums **9:**1013; **12:**551ff
-- sculpture **9:**1012; **14:**1069
-- sports **9:**1018ff; **11:**664; **15:**294
-- Yemenite Jews **16:**755ff
-- Zionism **16:**1064
- Broadcasting **9:**1017
-- radio and T.V. **15:**931
--- Arabic programs **9:**1029
--- Hebrew pronunciation **16:**1646
--- religious life **9:**901
- Hebrew Language **9:**998; **16:** 1642
-- Academy of Hebrew Language **2:**206
-- Ben-Gurion, David **4:**505
-- Ben-Yehuda, Eliezer **4:**566ff
-- education **9:**929ff
-- language conflict **8:**752; **13:**137; **15:**890
-- Sephardi pronunciation **14:**1170
-- Teachers' Association **15:**888
- Literature
-- children's literature **5:**434; **5:**457
-- folklore **6:**1403; **14:**1176
-- Hebrew **8:**203; **9:**715
-- prosody **13:**1200
-- Shenhar, Yitzhak **14:**1377
-- Shimoni's poetry **14:**1406
-- Writers' Association **16:**652ff
-- Yiddish **16:**824
- Music and Dance **5:**1270; **12:**668
-- Batsheva and Bat-Dor companies **4:**327
-- Inbal **8:**1309
-- Israel Philharmonic Orchestra **9:**1072
-- music and dance festival **9:**846
-- recording companies **13:**1618
- Press **9:**1014
-- advertising **2:**319
-- book bindings **4:**1232
-- Hebrew newspapers **12:**1053
-- Ladino press **13:**1041
-- newspapers, non-Hebrew **12:**1058
-- printing **13:**1114
-- publishing **13:**1377
-- typography **15:**1487
- Theater **9** 1003 **15:**1061, 1074
-- Cameri **5:**73
-- drama **6:**205
-- film industry **12:**460
-- Habimah **7:**1028
-- Haifa Municipal Theater **7:**1140
-- Millo, Josef **11:**1584
-- Ohel **12:**1342
- *illus:*
-- text
-- basketball, European Championship Games **15:**296
-- Binyanei ha-Ummah main auditorium **3:**353
-- Cameri production of *Saint Joan* **15:**1062
Chess Olympics medal **11:**1174
-- concert at Caesarea Roman theater **12:**673
-- Eliẓur basketball teams **6:**673
-- Four-Day March **15:**297
-- Ghetto Fighters' House, Loḥamei ha-Getta'ot **7:**546
-- Habimah production of *Genesis* **15:**1063
-- Ḥanukkah torch relay **7:**1286
-- Hapoel International Games, 1966 **7:**1319
-- International Paraplegic Olympics **15:**297
-- Israel Museum **3:**354; **11:**1460; **14:**1061-1068
-- Israel Philharmonic Orchestra **9:**1071
-- Jerusalem College for Women library **9:**899
-- Maccabiah **11:**663
-- Mishkan La-Ommanut Museum, En-Harod **6:**732
-- Modi'in torch **12:**207
-- Ohel theater
--- *Ammekha* **12:**1343
--- *A Streetcar Named Desire* **15:**1063
-- Rockefeller Museum **3:**350; **14:**212
-- sailing world championship **15:**317
-- Schocken Institute **14:**987
-- Shrine of the Book, Jerusalem **3:**631; **5:**1397
-- skiers on Mount Hermon **8:**374
-- soccer game, Israel-Australia **15:**298
-- swimming, annual crossing of Lake Kinneret **15:**297
-- Tel Aviv bulletin board **15:**921
-- Tel Aviv Museum **12:**224
-- Three-Day March **11:**694
-- Writers' Ass'n **16:**653
-- Yad Mordekhai museum **16:**696
-- Yad Vashem, Jerusalem Fig. 110 **3**-ART
-- *see also under individual activities and institutions*
(5)DEFENSE FORCES
- Ottoman and Mandatory Periods **9:**631
-- Haganah **7:**1064

-- historical survey 9:350ff
-- Irgun Ẓeva'i Le'ummi 8:1470
-- Jewish Brigade Group 10:35
-- Loḥamei Herut Israel 11:463
-- Maḥal 11:722
-- Palmaḥ 13:45
-- War of Independence 16:306
-- *yishuv* problems 9:328ff
- 1948-1970 9:689
-- adult education 9:964
-- Arab guerrilla clashes 9:469ff
-- archives 3:395
-- disinterment 6:73
-- Druze 9:927
-- Egyptian cease-fire violations 9:418ff
-- exhibitions 9:765
-- Gadna 7:252
-- Goren, Shlomo 7:808
-- historical survey 9:366, 385
-- Jerusalem clashes 9:1484
-- Jewish religious life 9:903
-- Kafr Qāsim case 10:674
-- *kasher* food law 12:147
-- ministry of defense 9:691
--- Ben-Gurion, David 4:505ff
--- Dayan, Moshe 5:1372
--- Eshkol, Levi 6:888
-- Naḥal 12:766
-- prayer book 14:1176
-- radio and television stations 12:671; 15:931
-- reprisal raids against Syria 15:648
-- science and research 9:971
-- Sinai Campaign 14:1605
-- Six-Day War 14:1624
-- sports events 15:297
-- travel prayer 15:1348
-- woman's role 16:628
-- Yadin, Yigael 16:695
-- *yeshivot* 16:772
- *illus:*
-- text
-- Ben-Gurion with soldiers 9:379
-- Cherbourg boats 9:431
-- Congolese paratroopers 9:443
-- Druze soldiers 9:927
-- girl soldier teacher 9:964
-- Ha-Shomer mounted guards 9:517
-- Hawk missiles 9:430
-- homemade armor 16:320
-- Israel stamps 9:844-845
-- Jerusalem fighting, 1948 9:366
-- military cemetery, Jerusalem 9:368,1493
-- Mt. Scopus convoy at Mandelbaum Gate 9:1490
-- paratroopers at Mitla Pass 9:379
-- Sinai Campaign 14:1601, 1603
-- Six-Day War 9:409; 14:1627ff
-- Suez Canal 9:420
-- Sukkot prayers in Negev trenches (1948) 16:323
-- Tampaler mortar 9:818
-- tanks in 10th Independence Day celebrations 9:405
-- Tel Ḥai cemetery 15:932
-- War of Independence map 9:373; 16:307-330
-- wounded soldier's arrival at Hadassah Hospital 9:990
(6) ECONOMIC AFFAIRS
- Agriculture (General) 9:773
-- Arab methods 9:1021ff
-- aviation 9:838
-- citrus 5:580
-- economic development 9:689ff
-- exhibitions 9:764
-- famine and drought 6:1172
-- Farmers' Federation 6:1186
-- Hibbat Zion 16:1039ff
-- historical survey 2:382ff; 9:345ff; 9:392ff
-- human geography 9:568ff
-- kibbutz movement 10:970
-- labor economy 9:849ff
-- methods and implements 2:374
-- Negev 12:930ff
-- olive growing 12:1365
-- pig-breeding 13:507
-- rain 13:1520
-- science and research 9:969
-- Tahal 15:701
-- taxation 9:749
-- tobacco 15:1178
-- Yemenite Jews 16:752ff
- Agriculture (Afforestation) 9:787
-- flora 9:225ff
-- J.N.F. 10:77
-- Tu bi-Shevat 15:1420
- Agriculture (Fisheries) 9:785ff
-- fish and fishing 6:1326
-- science and research 9:969
- Banking and Commerce
-- Banking (General) 9:824ff
--- Arab's role 9:1022
--- coins and medals 6:1309; 11:1173ff
--- currency 5:727ff
--- Hoofien, Eliezer Siegfried 8:969
--- Recanati 13:1607
-- Banking (Bank Hapoalim) 9:828
--- economic affairs 9:716
--- Histadrut 8:539
--- labor economy 9:850; 9:855
-- Banking (Bank Leumi le-Israel) 9:827
--- Jewish Colonial Trust 10:44
--- Levontin, Zalman 11:152
-- Banking (Bank of Israel) 9:825ff
--- currency 5:727
--- Horowitz, David 8:988
-- Banking (Israel Discount Bank) 9:828
-- Chambers of Commerce 9:828
-- Insurance 9:830
--- health schemes 9:985ff
--- retirement schemes 9:884ff
--- social security 9:994
-- Stock Exchange, Tel Aviv 9:829
- Communications
-- Postal Services 9:841
--- Arab States 15:1564
--- Turkish rule 9:1454
--- stamps 15:330ff
-- Telecommunications 9:840
--- Arab states and 15:1565
--- PBS broadcasting 15:931
-- Transportation 9:831
--- Acre harbor 2:224
--- Ashdod port 3:698
--- Dan 5:949; 5:951
--- economic development 9:711ff
--- Egged 6:473
--- El Al 6:560
--- Elath airport and port 6:569
--- Gaza harbor 7:341
--- Haifa port 7:1139
--- historical survey 9:306ff,323,392ff
--- I.C.A.O. 15:1564
--- Jaffa harbor 9:1256
--- Jerusalem 9:1461,1492ff
--- Lydda airport 11:620
--- maritime law 11:996
--- Tel Aviv 15:918
--- Zim 16:1023
- Economic Development 9:689
-- agriculture 9:773
-- Arab boycott 4:1282
-- Bonds 4:1204ff
-- exports 9:759
-- *Haavara* 7:1012
-- Histadrut 8:538
-- historical survey 9:392ff
-- immigrants, new 9:382ff; 9:538
-- industry 9:815ff
-- Jerusalem 9:1508ff
-- labor economy 9:849
-- Palestine Economic Corporation 13:39ff
-- philanthropy 13:386
-- reparations 14:72
-- science and research 9:970
-- tailoring 15:709
-- Tel Aviv 15:923
-- U.S. aid 9:430; 15:1665ff
-- War of Independence 9:370ff
-- Yemenite Jews 16:753ff
- Energy Sources
-- atomic energy 9:795
--- Dimonah atomic reactor 6:50
--- I.A.E.A. 15:1565
--- science and research 9:967; 9:969
--- Sorek reactor 15:93
--- Weizmann Institute 16:439
-- Electricity 9:790
--- historical survey 9:393ff
--- industry 9:821; 9:823
-- Oil and Gas 9:793
--- Elath pipeline 3:718; 6:569
--- historical survey 9:393
--- human geography 9:576
--- refineries 9:823
--- U.S. 15:1663
- Foreign Exchange Rates 9:758
-- banking 9:824
-- currency 5:723,727
-- industry 9:815
- Foreign Trade (General) 9:759
-- African trade 9:434
-- agricultural exports 9:774
-- Austria 3:904
-- Canada 16:1261
-- customs duties 9:749ff
-- economic development 9:710ff
-- Foreign Ministry 9:627
-- foreign relations 9:421
-- industrial exports 9:815ff
-- investment policy 9:823
-- Jaffa 9:1256
-- Japan 9:1283
-- oil and gas 9:795
-- Poland 13:788
-- Red Sea route 14:14
-- tailoring 15:709
-- Turkey 15:1463
-- West Bank 14:1638,1640
- Foreign Trade (Exhibitions) 9:764
-- art 3:591
- Industry (General) 9:815
-- aircraft 9:839
-- Arab boycott 4:1282
-- Arabs 9:1022
-- building 9:564ff
-- chemicals 5:377
-- diamonds 6:6
-- economic development 9:707ff
-- glassmaking 7:613
-- historical survey
--- ancient period 8:614ff
--- medieval period 9:263
--- 1880-1948 9:341; 9:345ff
--- 1948-1970 9:393ff
-- human geography 9:575ff
-- Jerusalem 9:1423; 9:1436; 9:1496
-- kibbutz movement 10:970
-- Negev 12:930ff
-- oil and gas 9:795ff
-- science and research 9:970
-- Steel City 2:226; 7:1139
-- sugar 15:488
-- tailoring 15:709
-- textiles 15:1042
-- tobacco 15:1178
-- trade unions 9:850ff
-- wine 16:546ff
- Industry (Investment Policy) 9:815; 9:823
-- historical survey 9:393ff
- Mineral Resources 9:797
-- Arabah 3:231
-- Dead Sea 5:1391; 16:1274
-- geology 9:194
-- Negev 12:927
-- Sodom 15:71ff
-- Timna mines 15:1145ff
- Taxation 9:749; 15:857ff
-- *arnona* 3:488
-- Sharef, Ze'ev 14:1308
- Tourism 9:845
-- archaeological sites 3:303
-- Egged 6:473
-- El Al 6:560
-- holy places 8:920ff
-- Jerusalem 9:1496; 9:1503
-- national parks 12:878
-- nature reserves 12:891
-- Tel Aviv 15:923
-- Zim 16:1023
- Water and Irrigation (General) 9:767
-- agriculture 9:776
-- Arabah 3:232
-- Besor, Brook of 4:703
-- electricity power 9:790
-- FAO 15:1564
-- Jerusalem 9:1380; 9:1471; 9:1480; 9:1537
-- Jordan River 10:192
--- Israel-Arab dispute 9:385; 9:403ff; 14:1625; 15:1553
-- Kinneret 10:1034
-- Kishon 10:1069
-- legislation 9:653
-- National Water Carrier
--- Eshkol, Levi 6:888ff
--- Mekorot Water Company 11:1274
-- Negev 12:929
-- physiography 9:123
-- Rutenberg, Pinḥas 14:516
-- Tahal 15:701
-- U.S. plans 15:1665
-- Yarkon 16:717
-- Yarmukh 16:720
- Water and Irrigation (Desalination) 9:771
-- Johnson-Eshkol agreement 9:400
-- Tahal 15:701
-- U.S.-Israel negotiations 9:430
- *illus:*
-- text
-- Acre fishermen 9:1029
-- Acre harbor 2:227
-- African agricultural student 9:439
-- Afulah-Nazareth road construction (1920) 9:517
-- agricultural workers 9:858; 10:1033
-- Arabah, intensive farming 9:*fcg.* 171
-- arts and crafts display, N.Y.C. 2:817
-- Ashdod port 3:698
-- Avedat experimental farm 12:739
-- Balfour Forest 9:585,586
-- Ben-Gurion opening Eilat road 9:380
-- chicken coop, Manarah 10:973
-- clothing exports (table) 15:710
-- coins and paper currency 5:723-724,728-733
-- cotton fields 10:966
-- cultivation of roses for export 9:781
-- diamonds, import and export, 1950-1969 (table) 6:5,7
-- El Al jet aircraft 6:560,561
-- Expo 1967 pavilion 14:1316
-- Ford automobile plant, Naẓerat Illit 12:904
-- Gaza Strip trade(table) 9:1037
-- Givat Ye'arim 9:577
-- Givat Yo'av vegetable harvest 9:578
-- grape harvesting 14:194
-- Haifa port 7:1135-1140

– – harvesting muskmelon 11:1294
– – Helez oil well 9:380
– – Hezekiah's tunnel 9:1539
– – industry (chart) 9:819
– – International Trade Fair (1970) 9:818
– – Israel Bonds dinner, N.Y.C. 12:1113
– – Jerusalem aqueduct 9:1538
– – Jerusalem public fountains 9:1433,1434
– – Jewish Agency finances, 1948-1970 10:913
– – Jordan River 9:153,157,235; 10:196,197
– – Judea and Samaria trade (table) 9:1037
– – Kinneret region 9:585
– – loading wheat at Gederah 9:517
– – Ma'agan Mikha'el fishponds 11:635
– – Mikveh Israel Agricultural School 11:1544,1545
– – minerals (chart) 9:813
– – National Water Carrier 11:1274
– – Negev Institute for Arid Zone Research 9:966
– – olive-oil press, Arab 9:1028
– – Palestine Potash Co. 15:73
– – plowing the fields at Tel Yosef 13:485
– – Protestants visiting Jerusalem Garden Tomb 9:916
– – ration books (1950-58) 9:375
– – salt formations, Dead Sea 14:710
– – Siloam Pool, Jerusalem 14:1400
– – terracing in Judean Mountains 9:133,205
– – Timna, Copper Works 15:1147
– – Timna, sulfuric acid plant 9:798
– – Tnuva central dairy 15:1175
– – Tnuva Export packing house 5:582
– – tomato growing 12:767
– – water ration card (1920) 9:1476
– – water rationing, Jerusalem 9:1482
– – Yarmuk River 16:719
– – Yotvatah vegetable fields 10:964
– – Zim freighter *Shiqma* 16:1023
– *maps:* text
– *tables:* text
(7) EDUCATION AND SCIENCE
– Adult Education 9:964
– – learned societies 15:55ff
– Education 9:928
– – Arabs 9:1023ff
– – Behar, Nissim 4:393
– – Belkind, Meir 4:438
– – Ben-Gurion, David 4:512
– – Cohn-Reiss, Ephraim 5:693
– – Defense Forces 9:689,693
– – Gadna 7:252
– – health services 9:988ff
– – Hebrew language 16:1642
– – Hebrew schools 9:326ff
– – Histadrut 8:540; 9:853,867
– – historical survey 9:384; 9:394
– – inter-communal integration 9:507
– – Jerusalem 9:1465
– – Jewish studies 16:583
– – Kibbutz movement 10:966ff
– – Mizrachi 12:178
– – musical 12:673ff
– – ORT 12:1484
– – population 9:477
– – religious education 9:888ff
– – scout movement 14:1040
– – sport 15:294; 15:296
– – Teachers' Association 15:888
– – Ulpan 15:1525
– – UNESCO 15:1565
– – vocational training 9:881
– – WIZO 16:595ff
– – *yishuv* education 9:345
– – Youth Aliyah 9:539ff
– Higher Education 9:952
– – Arabs 9:1029
– – Bar-Ilan University 4:225
– – Bezalel academy 4:788
– – Haifa University College 7:1140
– – Hebrew Union College 8:217
– – Hebrew University 8:219
– – historical survey 9:396
– – Rubin Academy of Music 5:1271; 12:673; 9:1496
– – Technion 15:889
– – Tel Aviv University 15:925
– – University of the Negev 4:385
– – Weizmann Institute 16:438
– – *yeshivot* 16:771ff
– Science and Research 9:965
– – chemicals 5:379
– – Hebrew University 8:219
– – medical research 9:989ff; 11:1203ff
– – physics 13:491
– – Technion 15:889
– – UNESCO aid 15:1565
– – Weizmann Institute 16:438
– Youth Movements 9:976
– – *Aliyah* and absorption 9:527ff
– – Benei Akiva 4:490
– – Betar 4:714
– – Ha-No'ar ha-Oved ve-ha-Lomed 7:1275
– – Ha-Shomer ha-Zair 7:1372
– – He-Halutz 8:247
– – Ihud Habonim 8:1240
– – kibbutz movement 10:969
– – labor movement 9:869
– – scouting 14:1037ff
– – students' movements 15:450ff
– *illus:*
– – text
– – Bar-Ilan University 4:225; 9:1003
– – Bedouin school class 9:1044
– – Bezalel Academy of Arts 4:789; 9:331,1487
– – Boys Town school, Jerusalem 9:900
– – Daliyat-al-Karmil school 9:926
– – Ez Hayyim yeshivah, Jerusalem 16:764
– – Gaza Strip, 1967-70 (table) 9:1037
– – girls' school, Jaffa 9:1253
– – Hebrew University 3:349,351,354; 8:222-226; 11:197; 13:1575
– – hygiene class in Arab school 9:1030
– – Jerusalem *heder* 9:897
– – Judea and Samaria (table) 9:1037
– – Kol Torah yeshivah, Jerusalem 16:766
– – Midreshet Sedeh Boker 14:1090
– – Mikveh Israel Agricultural School 11:1544,1545
– – music recorder lesson 12:671
– – nursery school children 9:907
– – ORT vocational high school 12:1485
– – Porat Yosef yeshivah, Jerusalem 16:765
– – scout camp, Jerusalem 14:1040
– – Technion, Haifa 3:347,351; 15:890-892
– – Tel Aviv University 3:351; 15:925
– – ulpan classroom 15:1526
– – University of the Negev 4:385
– – Weizmann Institute 3:352; 16:439ff
– – years of schooling (table) 9:479
– – Yemenite class, Siloam 16:749
– *tables:* text
(8) GOVERNANCE
– Ottoman and Mandatory Periods
– – Central Government 9:598
– – – high commissioners 8:470
– – – historical survey 9:322ff
– – – Jewish Agency 10:26ff
– – – Mandate for Palestine 11:861
– – Jewish Communal Organization 9:606
– – – communities 9:495
– – – I.C.A. 10:47
– – – Jewish Agency 10:26
– – – P.I.C.A. 13:495
– – – Va'ad Le'ummi 16:49
– – Local Government 9:603ff
– – – planning 9:559
– State of Israel (1948-1970)
– – Central Government
– – – historical survey 9:365ff
– – – immigrant absorption 10:33
– – – Jerusalem 9:1492
– – – Knesset 10:1112
– – – Kohn, Leo 10:1146
– – – legislation 9:650ff
– – – political life 9:656
– – – president 13:1020
– – Civil Service 9:623
– – – Palestine Civil Service 9:603
– – – governmental system 9:617ff
– – Foreign Service 9:627ff
– – – foreign trade 9:759
– – – international relations 9:421
– – – Jewish Agency 10:26
– – Local Government 9:620ff
– – – Arab local councils 9:1029
– – – Jerusalem 9:1497; 9:1504
– – State Comptroller 9:617ff
– – – governmental system 9:617ff
– *illus:*
– – text
– – cabinets, 1949-1971 (table) 9:669
– – finance, Palestine and Israel (tables) 9:713,734,739-742,750-759
– – Knesset 10:1112,1113
– – National Council meeting (May 14, 1948) 9:365
– – registration certificate of land 9:557
– – Va'ad Leu'mi meeting 16:50
– – Weizmann addressing Knesset 16:433
– *maps:* text
(9) HEALTH, WELFARE AND SOCIAL SECURITY
– Health Services 9:982
– – Arab population 9:1023ff
– – Histadrut 8:539
– – Histadrut ha-Ovdim ha-Leummit 8:541ff
– – labor social services 9:850ff,868
– – lifetime longevity 14:1499ff
– – *ma'barot* 9:537
– – Malben 11:821
– – medicine 11:1203
– – mental illness 11:1373ff
– – Montefiore's contribution 9:1455
– – science and research 9:970
– – Toz 15:1291
– – WHO's assistance 15:1564
– – WIZO 16:595ff
– Social Security and Welfare 9:993
– – care for aged 2:348
– – family allowances 9:865
– – ICA's activities 10:49
– – sociology 15:69
– *illus:*
– – text
– – Augusta Victoria Hospital, Jerusalem 9:1475
– – Central Jezreel Valley Hospital, Afulah 4:83
– – Hadassah Medical Organization
– – – first nurses unit 7:1042
– – – Hebrew University-Hadassah Medical Center 7:1043-1044
– – – hospital nurses 16:721
– – – nursing school graduates 15:667
– – – Rothschild Hospital, Jerusalem 9:1464
– – Histadrut rest home, Nazareth 9:866
– – hygiene class in Arab school 9:1030
– – Israel stamps series 9:844-845
– – Kuppat Holim laboratory, Jerusalem 9:867
– – Malben institution 11:821
– – Muslim community, mortality and birth rates, 1927-39 9:701
– – Omna Baby Home, Haifa 12:211
– – Sinai, Israel doctor examining Bedouin child 9:1044
– – Wizo Baby Home, Jerusalem 16:595
– – Zikhron Ya'akov rest home 13:1612
(10) HISTORICAL SURVEY
– Introduction 9:301
– The Land of Israel in International Affairs (1798-1923) 9:304
– – Balfour Declaration 4:131
– – Berlin, Congress of 4:656
– – *halukkah* 7:1207
– – Mandate for Palestine 11:861
– – Muhammad Ali 9:294; 9:298; 12:511
– – Sykes-Picot Treaty 15:565
– Frontiers 9:311
– – Armistice Agreements 3:478; 9:374ff
– – demarcation lines 9:423ff
– – Gaza Strip 7:343
– – Goldman, Nahum 7:724
– – international affairs 9:304
– – Mapai 11:913
– – Palestine, partition 13:34
– *illus:*
– – border police 9:695
– – Mandelbaum Gate 9:1490
Musrarah quarter, warning notice 9:1489
– *maps:*
– – Jerusalem boundaries before and after 1967 9:1505
– – Negev 12:926
– – partition under Sykes-Picot treaty 15:566
– – Sinai Peninsula 14:1594
– – *see also:* Boundaries of Israel
– 1880-1948 9:322
– – Abdullah ibn Hussein 2:56
– – Agudat Israel 2:424ff
– – *aliyah* 9:515
– – Allenby, Edmund Henry 2:647
– – anti-Semitism, Western 3:135
– – Arab National Movement 9:453
– – Attlee 3:836
– – Balfour Declaration 4:131
– – Berihah 4:632
– – Bevin's policy 4:784
– – Biltmore Program 4:997
– – cartoons, political 5:178
– – chief rabbinate 14:1175
– – Churchill, Winston 5:556
– – forestry law 9:789
– – governance 9:598
– – Haganah 7:1064
– – Hājj Amīn al-Husseini 8:1132
– – Hebrew language 16:1642
– – Hebrew Language Committee 2:206
– – Hebrew literature 8:199
– – Hebrew parody 13:137
– – high commissioners 8:470
– – human geography 9:567
– – "illegal" immigration 8:1248
– – international relations 9:304
– – I.Z.L. 8:1466
– – Jaffa riots 9:1257; 10:75; 15:921
– – Jewish Agency 10:26ff
– – Jewish Brigade group 10:35
– – Jewish Colonization Association 10:47

– – Jewish Legion **10:**69
– – Jewish religious life **9:**887ff
– – Jews' autonomy **3:**927
– – land transfer regulations **4:**508
– – League of Nations **10:**1521ff
– – legal system **9:**628; **12:**145
– – Lloyd George, David **11:**413ff
– – Loḥamei Ḥerut Israel **11:**463
– – Mandate for Palestine **11:**861
– – messianism **11:**1416
– – migrations **16:**1520
– – Negev **12:**929ff
– – Palestine, Inquiry Commissions **13:**30
– – Palmaḥ **13:**45
– – Persian aliyah **13:**318
– – Po'alei Zion **13:**659
– – Proclamation of State **16:**1096
– – Revisionists **14:**128
– – Roosevelt, Franklin D. **14:**257
– – St. James Conference **14:**660
– – "Saison" **7:**1071; **9:**356
– – Samuel, Herbert **14:**798
– – Sinai **14:**1596
– – socio-economic patterns **16:**1323
– – Sokolow, Nahum **15:**85
– – Stalin **15:**327
– – Tel Aviv's role **15:**918
– – Truman, Harry **15:**1409; **15:**1661
– – U.N. **15:**1543ff
– – UNSCOP **15:**1688
– – Va'ad Le'ummi **16:**49
– – War of Independence **16:**306
– – White Papers **16:**482
– – Yemenite *aliyah* **16:**751; **16:**752ff
– – Zionist commission **16:**1163
– – Zionist congresses **16:**1176
– – Zionist farming **16:**1317
– *illus:*
– – text
– – Anglo-American Committee of Enquiry **16:**1089
– – Barazani and Feinstein suicide report **11:**463
– – Biltmore Hotel Conference **15:**1633
– – British soldiers searching for arms **14:**1094; **16:**898
– – Gromyko's speech at U.N., May, 1947 **14:**493
– – *ha'apalah* medal **11:**1170
– – *Haggadah shel ha-Bayit ha-Le'ummi* **13:**139
– – *Managem*, yacht used for Nili information **12:**1164
– – Mauritius detainees at Haifa **11:**1134
– – Samuel, Herbert, letter of appointment **14:**799
– – Sharett giving evidence before UNSCOP **16:**1093
– – Turkish army recruits in Palestine (1915) **11:**1568
– – Turks surrender Jerusalem **9:**1471
– – War of Independence **16:**307-330
– – Weizmann and Emir Faisal **16:**428
– – Zionist Commission's arrival (1918) **16:**1163
– – *see also:* HISTORICAL SURVEY OF ISRAEL (1880-1948)
– *maps:* text
– 1948-1970 **9:**365
– – Al-Fatḥ **9:**1033; **9:**467
– – *aliyah* **9:**515
– – Arab refugees **9:**446
– – Arabs **9:**1021
– – assimilation **3:**775
– – Bernadotte **4:**669
– – boycott against Israel **4:**1277
– – Declaration of Independence **5:**1451
– – defense forces **9:**689
– – Eichmann Trial **6:**521
– – *fedayeen* **9:**1034; **9:**387ff
– – governance **9:**610
– – Hebrew language **16:**1642
– – human geography **9:**567
– – Hussein **8:**1131ff
– – Jerusalem foreign missions **9:**1495
– – Lavon Affair **10:**1478
– – legal system **9:**628
– – Nasser **12:**841ff
– – Palestinian identity **9:**470ff
– – politics **9:**656
– – Sinai Campaign **14:**1600
– – Six-Day War **14:**1624
– – Vatican relations **16:**77
– – War Crimes Trials **16:**299
– – Zionism **16:**1060ff
– *illus:*
– – text
– – Israel flag hoisted at U.N. headquarters **14:**1312
– – Israel Liberata coin **11:**1169
– – Jerusalem J.N.F. postal stamp (1948) **15:**333
– – Weizmann addressing Knesset **16:**433
– – *see also under individual subjects*
– *maps:*
– – text
– – Jerusalem municipal boundaries before and after 1967 **9:**1505
– Foreign Policy and International Relations **9:**421
– – General
– – – historical survey **9:**402ff
– – – Jerusalem foreign missions **9:**1495
– – – Vatican **16:**78
– – Countries
– – – Algeria **2:**619
– – – Argentina **3:**426ff
– – – Australia **3:**886
– – – Austria **3:**904ff
– – – Belgium **4:**424
– – – Bolivia **4:**1189
– – – Brazil **4:**1333
– – – Bulgaria **4:**1491
– – – Burma **4:**1527
– – – Canada **16:**1261
– – – Ceylon **5:**317
– – – Chile **5:**467
– – – China **5:**472
– – – Colombia **5:**747
– – – Costa Rica **5:**990
– – – Cuba **5:**1150
– – – Cyprus **5:**1182
– – – Czechoslovakia **5:**1202
– – – Denmark **5:**1541
– – – Dominican Republic **6:**161
– – – Ecuador **6:**361; **6:**500
– – – El Salvador **6:**687
– – – England **6:**770
– – – Ethiopia **6:**944ff
– – – Finland **6:**1298
– – – France **7:**40
– – – Germany **7:**501
– – – Greece **7:**881
– – – Guatemala **7:**957
– – – Guyana **7:**998
– – – Haiti **7:**1142
– – – Honduras **8:962**
– – – Hungary **8:**1108
– – – India **8:**1359
– – – Iran **8:**1443
– – – Iraq **8:**1456
– – – Ireland **8:**1466
– – – Italy **9:**1141
– – – Jamaica **9:**1274
– – – Japan **9:**1282
– – – Jordan **10:**198
– – – Kenya **10:**910
– – – Latin America **10:**1451; **10:**1455
– – – Lebanon **10:**1546
– – – Libya **11:**205
– – – Luxembourg **11:**591
– – – Madagascar **11:**677
– – – Malta **11:**831
– – – Mexico **11:**1460
– – – Morocco **12:**346
– – – Netherlands **12:**992
– – – New Zealand **12:**1130
– – – Nicaragua **12:**1135
– – – Norway **12:**1225
– – – Panama **13:**54
– – – Paraguay **13:**85
– – – Peru **13:**325
– – – Philippines **13:**395
– – – Poland **13:**785
– – – Portugal **13:**926
– – – Rumania **14:**411; **14:**415ff
– – – Russia **12:**366ff; **14:**487ff
– – – Singapore **14:**1609
– – – South Africa **15:**198ff
– – – Spain **15:**246
– – – Sweden **15:**552
– – – Switzerland **15:**554
– – – Syria **15:**646
– – – Thailand **15:**1044
– – – Tunisia **15:**1450
– – – Turkey **15:**1460ff
– – – Uruguay **16:**15
– – – U.S. **15:**1658ff
– – – Venezuela **16:**93
– – – Yemen **16:**752
– – – Yugoslavia **16:**883
– *illus:*
– – Barzilai, Israel, envoy to Poland **13:**781
– – Ben-Nathan, Asher, and German president **9:**406
– – German reparations agreement **14:**72
– – Israel diplomatic corps' visit to Auschwitz **13:**782
– – McDonald, J.G., presenting credentials **11:**666
– – Meir, Golda, ambassador to Russia **11:**1243
– – Moscow, welcome to Israel youth delegation **14:**490
– – Philippine ambassador **13:**396
– – Russian ambassador **14:**497
– – Shazar addressing diplomatic corps **14:**1327
– International Aid and Cooperation **9:**435ff
– – Africa and Asia **2:**336; **9:**391ff
– – Israel Defense Forces **9:**689
– – medical contributions **9:**991
– – moshav movement **12:**435
– – U.N. commissions **15:**1563
– Arab refugees **9:**446
– – absentee property **9:**1031ff
– – Arab National Movement **9:**466ff
– – employment and social conditions **9:**412ff
– – Gaza Strip **7:**344
– – Jerusalem camps **9:**1492ff
– – Lebanon **15:**1546
– – Palestine Conciliation Commission **9:**377ff
– – population **9:**490
– – Sidon **14:**1508
– – Six-Day War **14:**1625
– – U.N. **15:**1549
– – U.S.-Israel relations **9:**430; **15:**1666
– *illus:*
– – text
– Arab National Movement
– – Abdullah **2:**56
– – Agudat Israel **2:**424
– – Al-Fatḥ **3:**243ff
– – Alliance Israélite Universelle **2:**652
– – Arab boycott **4:**1282
– – Arabic language **3:**241
– – Arab League **3:**242
– – Arab Revolt **9:**348ff; **9:**460ff
– – armistice agreements **3:**482
– – China **5:**474ff
– – growth of movement **9:**330, 347ff
– – Ḥājj Amīn al-Husseini **8:**1132
– – Hussein **8:**1131
– – inquiry commissions **13:**31
– – Jaffa riots **9:**1257
– – Jewish immigration **9:**523ff
– – liberation fronts **2:**620; **9:**471; **10:**200
– – liberation organization **9:**404; **9:**414,1033; **16:**307
– – opposition to Jews **8:**757
– – partition plans **13:**34; **16:**1175
– – Palestinian Arabs rights **9:**355
– – Sykes-Picot treaty **15:**566
– – Syria **15:**647
– – terrorism (Lebanon) **15:**1546
– – Zionism **16:**1075ff
– *illus:*
– – Abdullah and Arab Legion **9:**352
– – *see also:* HISTORICAL SURVEY OF ISRAEL (1948–1970); *and under individual subjects*
(11) HUMAN GEOGRAPHY **9:**567
– Jerusalem **9:**1483; **9:**1504; **9:**1513
– physiography **9:**123
– population **9:**472
– Tel Aviv **15:**916
– *illus:*
– – text
– – Negev **12:**926
– – Safed **14:**627
(12) LABOR
– Employment **9:**885
– – Arab workers **8:**540; **9:**1028
– – building Ereẓ Israel **9:**519
– – economic development **9:**715ff
– – industry 9:815
– – labor economy **9:**853
– – labor exchanges **9:**874ff
– – labor philosophy **9:**870ff; **10:**1324
– – Levinsohn **11:**117
– – Lilienblum **11:**240ff
– – new immigrants **9:**394ff
– Jewish Labor Organizations **9:**848
– – archives **3:**395
– – Ben-Gurion, David **4:**505
– – Betar **4:**714
– – cooperatives **5:**945
– – courts **9:**639ff; **9:**883ff
– – Gordon, Aharon **7:**790
– – *Ha-Po'el ha-Ẓa'ir* **7:**1326
– – Hebrew newspapers **12:**1057
– – Histadrut ha-Ovdim Ha-Leummit **8:**541
– – Katznelson, Berl **10:**836
– – labor problems in *yishuv* **9:**328ff; **9:**347
– – labor unity **9:**568
– – legislation **9:**653; **9:**874ff
– – ministry of labor **9:**875
– – Po'alei Zion **13:**659
– – Revisionists **14:**129
– – socialism **15:**31ff
– Labor Relations **9:**872
– – Histadrut **8:**534
– *illus:* text
– *tables:*
– – text
– – growth of Jewish working class (1926-39) **9:**715
– – Histadrut membership (1920–39) **9:**717
– – industry **9:**819
– – non-Jewish employment (1969) **9:**1025
– – occupational distribution (1958-1969) **9:**724
– – unemployment among Jews (1938-1945) **9:**722
(13) LEGAL AND JUDICIAL SYSTEM
– Judiciary **9:**628

- *illus:*
- - text
- - Druze judge sworn in by President Shazar **9:**925
- - Eichmann trial **6:**519
- - Muslim religious judges,9:922
- Legislation **9:**645ff
- - abortion **2:**101
- - anti-profiteering laws **7:**1063
- - Assaf, Simḥa **3:**757
- - bailment laws **14:**1458
- - Bedouin **9:**1043ff
- - Ben-Gurion, David **4:**512
- - custody, maintenance **13:**99
- - Druze courts **9:**927
- - historical survey **9:**368ff; **9:**383
- - Holocaust law **8:**898
- - holy sites **14:**616
- - Jewish law **12:**142ff
- - Knesset **10:**1112
- - labor legislation **9:**874ff
- - law **10:**1506
- - Law of Return **10:**1485
- - legacy of property **16:**528
- - petroleum law **9:**793
- - rape **13:**1549
- - sale **14:**680
- - torts **15:**1277
- - trade laws **7:**1062
- - women's rights **16:**586; **16:**628
- - *see also under specific law articles*
- Police **9:**655
- - border force **9:**689
- - crime **5:**1096
- - Druze **9:**927
- - historical survey **9:**351ff
- *illus:*
- - Arab rioters in Jaffa (1936) **9:**464
- - Druze members of Border Police **9:**928
- Rabbinical Courts **9:**634ff
- - arbitration **3:**299
- - *bet din* **4:**727
- - Mishpat Ivri **12:**142
- - practice and procedure **13:**958
- - religious and judicial authority **9:**889; **9:**896

(14) POLITICAL LIFE AND PARTIES **9:**656
- General
- - Arab community **9:**1030ff
- - Central Government **9:**616ff
- - dual loyalty **13:**808
- - election broadcasts **15:**930
- - Goldmann, Nahum **7:**725
- - Histadrut elections **8:**535
- - historical survey **9:**372ff
- - Knesset **10:**1112
- - new immigrants' role **9:**394ff
- - Tel Aviv municipality **15:**917
- Parties
- - Agudat Israel **2:**425
- - Communists **5:**807
- - Gaḥal **7:**255
- - General Zionists **7:**384
- - Ha-Po'el ha-Ẓa'ir **7:**1324
- - Ha-Po'el ha-Mizrachi **7:**1323
- - Ḥerut movement **8:**400
- - Independent Liberal Party **8:**1349
- - Israel Labor Party **9:**1068
- - Mapai **11:**912
- - Mapam **11:**914
- - Mizrachi **12:**178
- - National Religious Party **12:**880
- - New Left **12:**1032
- - Po'alei Agudat Israel **13:**655
- - Po'alei Zion **13:**656
- - Rafi **13:**1512
- - religious parties **9:**895
- - Revisionists **14:**128
- Politicians
- - Allon, Yigal **2:**655
- - Almogi, Yosef **2:**662
- - Aranne, Zalman **3:**289
- - Avneri, Uri **3:**976
- - Bar-Yehudah, Israel **4:**285
- - Begin, Menahem **4:**392
- - Ben-Aharon, Yiẓhak **4:**457
- - Bentov, Mordekhai **4:**555
- - Burg, Yosef **4:**1510
- - Carmel, Moshe **5:**185
- - Dayan, Moshe **5:**1372
- - Dinur, Ben-Zion **6:**57
- - Eban, Abba **6:**343
- - Galili, Israel **7:**270
- - Gruenbaum, Yiẓhak **7:**943
- - Hazan, Ya'akov **7:**1523
- - Joseph, Dov **10:**220
- - Kahana, Kalman **10:**681
- - Kol, Moshe **10:**1158
- - Lavon, Pinḥas **10:**1477
- - Levin, Yiẓhak Meir **11:**111
- - Luz, Kadish **11:**593
- - Maimon, Judah Leib **11:**739
- - Minz, Benjamin **12:**68
- - Naftali, Perez **12:**756
- - Namir, Mordekhai **12:**815
- - Nir, Nahum **12:**1172
- - Peres, Shimon **13:**278
- - Pinkas, David Ẓevi **13:**537
- - Remez, Moshe David **14:**69
- - Rosen, Pinḥas 14:271
- - Sapir, Joseph **14:**856
- - Sapir, Pinḥas **14:**857
- - Sasson, Eliyahu **14:**895
- - Shapira, Ḥayyim Moshe **14:**1297
- - Sharef, Ze'ev **14:**1308
- - Shitreet, Beḥor **14:**1417
- - Sneh, Moshe **15:**16
- - Sprinzak, Joseph **15:**319
- - Warhaftig, Zeraḥ **16:**303
- - Weizmann, Ezer **16:**422
- - Ya'ari, Meir **16:**691
- Presidents
- - Ben-Zvi, Iẓhak **4:**577
- - Shazar, Shneur Zalman **14:**1323
- - Weizmann, Chaim **16:**423
- Prime Ministers
- - Ben-Gurion, David **4:**505; **4:**510
- - Eshkol, Levi **6:**887
- - Meir, Golda **11:**1244
- - Sharett, Moshe **14:**1309ff
- *illus:*
- - text
- - Arab and Druze districts, votes cast, 1949-69 (table) **9:**1031
- - Druze Knesset members **9:**925
- - Jewish and Arab voters, 1949-69 (table) **9:**1025
- - Neturei Karta monetary scrip **12:**1003
- - N.R.P. representation in Knesset (table) **12:**881
- - Weizmann addressing Knesset **16:**433

(15) POPULATION **9:**472; **13:**887ff
- General
- - Arab growth **9:**1023ff
- - Bahais **9:**923
- - Bedouin **9:**1043
- - census **9:**372
- - Christians **9:**909
- - demography **5:**1499; **5:**1516
- - Druze **9:**924
- - economic development **9:**699ff
- - first decade **9:**393
- - Galilee **7:**270
- - Gaza Strip **7:**344ff
- - health standards **9:**984ff
- - historical survey **8:**733ff; **9:**323
- - human geography **9:**569ff
- - Jerusalem **9:**1470; **9:**1436
- - Jewish communities **9:**497ff
- - Muslims **9:**917
- - Negev **12:**930ff
- - statistics **15:**344; **16:**182ff
- - Tel Aviv-Jaffa **15:**924
- Intercommunal Problems **9:**505ff
- - Ashkenazi-Sephardi rift **14:**1175
- - Bene Israel **4:**498
- - crime **5:**1096f
- - Jewish identity **10:**62ff
- - Karaites **10:**777
- - *mamzerim* **11:**842
- - psychological problem **9:**395ff
- - Samaritans **14:**735
- - Wadi-Salib riots 9:395ff; **9:**672
- - Yemenite Jews **16:**754ff
- - Zionism **16:**1064ff
- Jewish Communities **9:**495
- - Aramaic-speaking Jews **12:**949
- - Ashkenazim and Sephardim **3:**721; **14:**1174ff
- - Bukharan Jews **4:**1472
- - community tokens **5:**853
- - governance **9:**606
- - historical survey **9:**378ff
- - *landsmannschaften* **10:**1415
- - Neturei Karta **12:**1002
- - Yemenites **16:**752ff
- *illus:*
- - text
- - Druze **9:**925
- *pop. tables:*
- - text
- - Asian countries, main periods of *aliyah* **3:**746
- - growth and decrease of Jewish population in Asia, 1840-1966 **3:**745
- - increase of permanent population (1922-39) **9:**701
- - Jewish population **5:**1502; **9:**473-496, 533-545
- - major Jewish communities **13:**901
- - non-Jewish population **9:**1024,1025
- - towns with 100,000 or more Jews, 1967 **5:**1514
- - vital statistics **16:**180-188
- - *see also:* COMMUNITY; DEMOGRAPHY (Asia; Israel)

(16) RELIGIOUS LIFE AND COMMUNITIES
- Baha'is **9:**923
- - Acre **2:**226
- - Haifa **7:**1139
- - holy places **8:**936
- Christians **9:**909
- - Armenians **3:**475
- - Defense Forces **9:**692
- - geographical distribution **9:**569ff
- - institutions **9:**583
- - judiciary **9:**638ff
- - Protestants **13:**1251; **13:**1253ff
- - scouting **14:**1040ff
- - Six-Day War **13:**1253; **13:**1254
- - Vatican **16:**77
- *illus:*
- - Basilica of the Agony, Jerusalem **9:**1455
- - Basilica of the Annunciation **12:**901
- - Christian and Armenian quarters, Jerusalem **9:**1439
- - Church of Jesus the Child **12:**903
- - Church of St. Anne, Jerusalem **9:**1453
- - Eshkol, Levi, meeting with leaders after Six-Day War **9:**410
- - Garden Tomb, Jerusalem **9:**1461
- - Holy Sepulcher and Christian Quarter **9:**1460
- - Monastery of Notre-Dame de France, Jerusalem **9:**1463
- - Mount Zion **9:**1465
- - Russian Church of Gethsemane **9:**1462
- - Russian Church property **9:**1457
- *tables:* **9:**491
- Druze **9:**924
- - court jurisdiction **9:**641ff
- - Defense Forces **9:**692
- - Gadna **7:**253
- - Galilee **7:**269
- - general survey **9:**1026ff
- - geographical distribution **9:**569; **9:**597 **9:**570ff
- - health services **9:**992ff
- - historical survey **9:**397ff
- - holy places **8:**936
- - Knesset **10:**1116
- - scouting **14:**1040ff
- *tables:* **9:**491
- Jews **9:**887
- - chief rabbinate **14:**1175
- - chief rabbinate *takkanot* **15:**713
- - Conservative Judaism **5:**906
- - definition of Jew **10:**23
- - *halakhah* and technology **15:**893ff
- - Ḥasidism **7:**1399ff; **7:**1400; **7:**1426
- - historical survey **9:**323ff; **9:**399ff
- - holy places **8:**920ff
- - itineraries of Ereẓ Israel **9:**1148
- - Jerusalem **9:**1436
- - Jewish Cultural Reconstruction **10:**49
- - Jewish identity **3:**209; **10:**62ff
- - Jewish settlement **4:**434
- - Judaism, trends **10:**388,395
- - Kook, Abraham Isaac **10:**1187
- - Orthodoxy **12:**1488ff
- - proselytes **13:**1191
- - rabbinical office **13:**1448; **13:**1450
- - Reform Judaism **14:**26ff
- - responsa **14:**92
- - Satmar *rebbe* **15:**909ff
- - synagogues **1:**synagogue list; **15:**587,591
- - television controversy **15:**931
- - Torah-reading *minhag* **15:**1247
- - Torah study **15:**1243
- - Yemenites **16:**754ff
- *illus:*
- - text
- - Ashdod *mikveh* **11:**1541
- - Bukharan community celebrating Simḥat Torah **14:**1573
- - Cochin Jews wedding **11:**1049
- - Eshkol, Levi, meeting with leaders after Six-Day War **9:**410
- - Eẓ Ḥayyim yeshivah, Jerusalem **16:**764
- - first anniversary of reunification of Jerusalem **9:**410
- - Heikhal Shlomo, Jerusalem **9:**1488
- - Jerusalem children celebrating Shavuot **14:**1321
- - Jerusalem synagogues **9:**1443-1446
- - Kol Torah yeshivah, Jerusalem **16:**766
- - Maimuna celebration **11:**782
- - Meir Ba'al ha-Nes tomb **11:**1132
- - Mt. Zion **9:**1465
- - Mt. Zion wedding **11:**1048
- - Neturei Karta token currency **12:**1003
- - Porat Yosef yeshivah, Jerusalem **16:**765
- - Safed
- - - Ha-Ari synagogue **14:**629
- - - Isaac Aboab synagogue **14:**631
- - Simeon bar Yoḥai's tomb **14:**1552
- - Simeon the Just's tomb **14:**1567
- - *sukkot* in Battei Varsha quarter **15:**501
- - *tashlikh* ceremony **15:**829
- - Tu bi-Shevat celebration **15:**1420
- - wedding party at Western Wall **11:**1045
- - Western Wall **9:**1467
- - Yad Mordekhai, triple wedding **11:**1050
- - Yemenite bride and groom **11:**1047

-- Yemenite Torah scribe **14:**1045
-- Yemenite wedding **11:**1046
- Muslims **9:**917
-- Arab National Movement **9:**466
-- geographical distribution **9:**570ff
-- health services **9:**992ff
-- judiciary **9:**634ff
-- scouting **14:**1040ff
- *illus:*
-- Church of St. Anne, Jerusalem **9:**1453
-- Eshkol, Levi, meeting with leaders after Six-Day War **9:**410
-- Shari'a Court **9:**640
- *tables:* **9:**491
-- mortality and birth rates (1927-1939) **9:**701
- Samaritans **14:**738; **14:**736
-- geographical distribution **9:**569ff
-- holy places **8:**936
- *illus:*
-- betrothal ceremony **14:**745
-- Passover sacrifice **14:**743
-- Torah scroll **14:**737,739
- *see also:* HOLY PLACES; *and under individual subjects*
ISRAEL (fam.) **9:**1045
Israel (period., Arg.) **3:**424; **13:**1040
Israel (period., Den.) **13:**1049
Israël (period., Egy.) **5:**31; **6:**499; **13:**1041
Israël (period., Fr.) **12:**441
Israel (period., Gr.) **12:**223
Israel (period., Ind.) **10:**897
Israel (period., It.) **9:**1140
- *La Rassegna Mensile de Israel* **13:**1567
- Pacifici, Alfonso **13:**5
- press **13:**1037
- Rome **14:**253
- Viterbo, Carlo Alberto **16:**193
- Zionism **16:**1122
Israel, Abraham ben Moses **9:**1046; **14:**1366
Israel, Charles **14:**917
ISRAEL, DORMAN DANIEL **8:**1432
Israël, Edmond **11:**591
ISRAEL, EDWARD (astron.) **9:**1046
- Michigan **11:**1499
ISRAEL, EDWARD LEOPOLD (r., U.S.) **9:**1046
Israel, Elijah ben Moses **2:**593; **9:**1046
Israel, Ḥayyim Rafael **9:**1046
Israel, Heinz **3:**39
Israel, Jacob Ḥai (Vita) **13:**583
Israel, James **11:**1197
Israel, Jedidiah Solomon **2:**593; **9:**1046
Israel, Jeremias **11:**1163
Israel, John William **15:**830
Israel, Joseph (U.S. pion.) **11:**782
Israël, Joseph (writ.) **4:**1493
ISRAEL, KINGDOM OF **9:**1047
- Ahab **2:**435
- Amaziah **2:**798
- Aram-Damascus **3:**287
- Assyria **16:**1502
- Assyrian chronology **16:**1509
- Athaliah **3:**814
- history **8:**586
- history chart **8:**766-67
- Isaiah **9:**46ff
- Jehu **9:**1328
- Jeroboam **9:**1372; **9:**1374
- Jezreel, Valley of **10:**102
- kingship **10:**1011ff
- Messiah **11:**1407
- northern border **10:**1551
- population **13:**866ff
- Rechabites **13:**1610ff
- Samaritan tradition **14:**727
- Sargon II **14:**880
- social structure **8:**613
- social unrest **16:**1270
- warfare **16:**272
- Zimri **16:**1027
- *illus:*
-- Samaria ostracon **12:**1509
-- Saul's kingdom (map) **14:**910
- *pop. tables:*
-- 1000-586 B.C.E. **13:**869
- *see also:* SAMARIA
Israel, Mannes **11:**1499
Israel, Michael (stlr., Va.) **16:**162
Israel, Michael Boaz, *see* CRESSON, WARDER
Israel, Moses (Er. Isr.) **9:**1045
Israel, Moses (Egy.) **2:**593; **9:**1046
Israel, Moses (hal.) **7:**314
Israel, Nathan **9:**1048
Israel, New (Chr. term), *see* New Israel
Israel, People of (bib. term), *see* CONGREGATION
Israel, Pool of (Jer.), *see* Pool of Israel
Israel, Raḥamim Judah **14:**146
Israel, Richard **14:**143
Israel, Salomon (writ. master) **5:**63
Israel, Solomon (stlr., U.S.) **16:**162
Israel, Victor **13:**323
ISRAEL, WILFRID **9:**1048
ISRAEL, YOM TOV BEN ELIJAH **9:**1048
- Cairo **5:**31
Israel Aaron (Court J.) **4:**640
Israel Abraham of Chernyostrov **16:**1243
ISRAEL ACADEMY OF SCIENCES AND HUMANITIES **9:**1049
- Jerusalem building **9:**1495; **9:**1049
- science and research **9:**969
- societies, learned **15:**55
- *illus:*
-- aerial view **9:**1490
Israel Advertising Association **2:**319
Israel Aircraft Industries
- arms manufacture **9:**694
- historical survey **9:**400
- industry **9:**823
- Lydda **11:**620
- transportation **9:**839
- *illus:*
-- Beth-Shemesh turbo engines **9:**818
-- transport planes' overhaul **9:**817
Israel Air Force
- Sinai Campaign **14:**1606
- Six-Day War **9:**408; **14:**1629
- War of Independence **9:**367
- Weizmann, Ezer **16:**422
- *illus:*
-- Egyptian planes destroyed **14:**1631
Israel-American Industrial Development Bank Ltd. **9:**828 **8:**539
Israel Anti-Tuberculosis League **9:**985
Israel Archives Association **15:**56
Israel-Argentina Cultural Institute **3:**425; **3:**427
Israel Army, *see* DEFENSE FORCES OF ISRAEL
Israel Army Radio Station, *see* Gallei Ẓahal
Israel Astronautical Society **2:**79
Israel Atomic Energy Commission **9:**796
Israel Ba'al Shem Tov (found. of Ḥas.), *see* ISRAEL BEN ELIEZER BA'AL SHEM TOV
Israel bar Samuel bar Hophni (gaon), *see* ISRAEL BEN SAMUEL HA-KOHEN
Israel Basketball Association **15:**296
Israel ben Abraham (print.) **3:**1
Israel ben Abraham (pros.), *see* GORDON, LORD GEORGE
ISRAEL BEN BENJAMIN OF BELZEC **9:**1049
ISRAEL BEN ELIEZER BA'AL SHEM TOV **9:**1049
- Abraham Gershon of Kutow **2:**158
- Adam Ba'al Shem **2:**247
- Adel **2:**258
- Ahijah the Shilonite **2:**460
- *aliyah* **9:**514
- folklore **6:**1382
- Frankists **7:**65; **14:**359
- Ḥasidism **7:**1391ff; **7:**1400; **7:**1403
- history chart **8:**766-67
- Mendel of Kotsk **10:**1126
- music **12:**637
- Naḥman of Bratslav **12:**782
- psychiatry **13:**1337
- Shabbateanism **14:**1247; **16:**1223
- Tolstoy **15:**1212
- will **16:**531
- *geneal table:* text
- *illus:*
-- autograph **3:**913
Israel ben Ḥayyim Bruna, *see* BRUNA, ISRAEL BEN ḤAYYIM
Israel ben Isaac of Nuremberg **7:**471
Israel ben Ittamar **10:**1433
Israel Benjamin (r.), *see* BENJAMIN, ISRAEL
ISRAEL BEN JOEL (Susslin) **9:**1058
- Thuringia **15:**1128
ISRAEL BEN JONATHAN FROM LECZYCA **9:**1058
Israel ben Joseph ha-Levi **3:**967
Israel ben Meir (copyist) **7:**1099; **9:**1263
- *illus:*
-- *Darmstadt Haggadah* **3:**1014; **7:***fcg.* 811,1085
Israel ben Mordecai (art.) **15:**607
Israel ben Moses **7:**1196; **13:**1107ff
Israel ben Moses Najara, *see* NAJARA, ISRAEL BEN MOSES
ISRAEL BEN PEREZ OF POLOTSK **9:**1059
- Menaḥem Mendel of Vitebsk **11:**1311
Israel ben Samuel ha-Dayyan, *see* ISRAEL HA-DAYYAN HA-MA'ARAVI
ISRAEL BEN SAMUEL HA-KOHEN (gaon) **9:**1059
- gaonate families **7:**317
- Sura **15:**523
ISRAEL BEN SAMUEL OF SHKLOV **9:**1059
- *aliyah* **9:**293; **9:**514;
- Bardaki, Isaiah **4:**217
- Elijah ben Solomon Zalman **6:**657
Israel ben Samuel of Tarnopol **13:**540
Israel ben Shalom of Ruzhany **14:**525
Israel ben Shalom Shakhna **11:**580; **14:**1287
Israel ben Simḥa **4:**311
Israel Bond Organization **4:**1204; **16:**1146
Israel Broadcasting Authority **15:**930
- radio **15:**931
Israel Broadcasting Service, *see* Kol Israel
Israel Cabinet **9:**610ff; **9:**663ff
Israel Cancer Association **9:**985
Israel Chamber Ensemble **12:**669
Israel Communist Party **9:**660ff
- Arab community **9:**1030; **9:**466
- communism **5:**807
Israel Company for Fairs and Exhibitions **9:**767
Israel Corporation (investment corp.) **9:**836
Israel Declaration of Independence, *see* DECLARATION OF INDEPENDENCE, ISRAEL
Israel Defense Forces, *see* DEFENSE FORCES OF ISRAEL
Israel dei ragazzi (period.) **13:**1037
Israel Development and Mortgage Bank Ltd. **9:**828
Israel Diabetes Association **9:**985
Israel diplomatic and consular missions abroad **9:**918
Israel Discount Bank Ltd. **9:**826
Israel Dov Baer of Weledniki **15:**1471
Israel Education Fund **9:**401
Israel Eliakim, *see* BENJAMIN, ISRAEL
Israelewicz, Hersh Aaron **15:**1215
Israel Exploration Journal **14:**53
ISRAEL EXPLORATION SOCIETY **9:**1060
- archaeology **15:**55
Israel Festivals (music and drama) **9:**846
- *illus:*
-- concert at Caesarea's Roman theater **9:**1007
-- Daliyyah dance festival **9:**1010
-- Zimriyyah concert **9:**1010
Israel Film Art Archives **3:**390
Israel Folklore Society **15:**55
Israel Folk-Tale Archives **2:**328
Israel Football Association **15:**296
Israel Foreign Ministry **9:**627
Israel Foundation for Handicapped Children, *see* ILAN
Israel Frontier Guard **9:**656
Israel Fuel Corporation, *see* Delek
Israel Fund Raisers' Association **13:**386
Israel Government Coin and Medals Corporation **6:**1309
Israel Government Tourist Corporation **9:**845
Israel Gymnastic Club, *see* MACCABI WORLD UNION
Israel ha-Darshan, *see* Shapira, Israel ben Nathan
ISRAEL (ben Samuel?) HA-DAYYAN HA-MA'ARAVI **9:**1061
ISRAEL ḤARIF OF SATANOV **9:**1061
Israel ha-Ro'eh **14:**46
Israel ha-Ẓe'irah (youth mvmt.) **7:**385
Israel ha-Zifroni, *see* ZIFRONI, ISRAEL BEN DANIEL
Israel Ḥazzan of Castoria, *see* Hazzan, Israel,
Israel Historical Society **10:**49
ISRAELI, BENZION **9:**1062
ISRAELI, ISAAC BEN JOSEPH **9:**1062
- Asher ben Jehiel **3:**707
- astronomy **3:**803
ISRAELI, ISAAC BEN SOLOMON **9:**1063
- Albertus Magnus **2:**532
- atomism **3:**830
- beatitude **4:**359
- Creation **5:**1067ff
- Dunash ibn Tamim **6:**271
- emanation **6:**695
- imagination **8:**1289
- Maimonides **11:**769
- medicine **11:**1187
- microcosm **11:**1502
- nature **12:**889
- Neoplatonism **12:**960ff
- philosophy **13:**433
- revelation **14:**122
- soul **15:**172
- soul, immortality of **15:**176
- translations **15:**1323; **15:**1328

– Tunisia **15:**1434
– Zaddik, Joseph ben Jacob ibn **16:**912
Israeli, Isaac d', *see* D'ISRAELI, ISAAC
ISRAELI, ISRAEL **9:**1065
– *Mitzvot Zemanniyot* **14:**849
Israeli, Joseph ben Isaac **9:**1062
Israëlietische Nieuwsbode (newsp.) **14:**221
Israëlietisch Weekblad (newsp.) Holl.) **13:**1056
Israel Independence Day, *see* INDEPENDENCE DAY, ISRAEL
Israelino (mag.) **5:**457
Israel Institute for Biological Research **9:**969
Israel Institute for Meteorology **4:**719
Israel Institute of Applied Social Research **15:**69
Israelis (newsp.) **5:**1149
ISRAEL ISSERL BEN ISAAC SEGAL **9:**1066
– Broda, Abraham **4:**1390
Israel Isser ben Mordecai **16:**1014
ISRAELIT, DER (newsp., Ger.) **9:**1066
– Frankfort **7:**89
– *Ha-Levanon* **4:**1374
Israelit, Der (period., Gal.) **11:**612; **14:**1458; **16:**1330
Israelita (rel. gr., Mex.) **11:**1460
Israelita (newsp., Pol.) **13:**1045
ISRAELITE (Musl. lit.) **9:**1067
Israelite (term for Jew) **10:**23
Israelite, The (period.), *see* AMERICAN ISRAELITE
Israeliten (period., Swed.) **13:**1048
Israelite Press-Dos Yiddishe Vort (newsp., Can.), *see Yiddish Press*
Israelites, *see* CONGREGATION
Israelitische Allianz zu Wien, *see* ALLIANZ, ISRAELITISCHE, ZU WIEN
Israelitische Annalen (period.) **16:**576
Israelitische Presse (period., U.S.) **13:**1053
Israelitische Religionsgesellschaft (cmty., Ger.) **2:**255; **8:**510
Israelitischer Frauenverein (orgn., Pol.) **15:**1278
ISRAELITISCHES FAMILIENBLATT (period.) **9:**1067
– German press **7:**493; **13:**1032
Israelitisches Wochenblatt fuer die Schweiz/Revue Juive (newsp., Switz.) **13:**1049
Israelitisches Wochenblatt. Zentralorgan fuer die Israeliten in der Schweiz, Baden und Elsass-Lothringen (period., Switz.) **13:**1049
Israelitische Wochenschrift fuer die religioesen und sozialen Interessen des Judentums (period., Ger.) **13:**1032
ISRAELITISCH-THEOLOGISCHE LEHRANSTALT (instit., Aus.) **9:**1067
– Austria **3:**895
– rabbinical seminaries **13:**1464
Israelitisk Tidende (period., Den.) **13:**1048
Israelitisk Ugeblad for Norden (period., Den.) **13:**1048
Israelitul Român (Rum. period.) **4:**200; **13:**1043; **14:**398
Israel Jabotinsky Institute (Tel Aviv) **3:**391
Israel Jonah of Campana **11:**1492
Israel Jordanis (14/15 cent., Pol.) **11:**181
ISRAEL LABOR PARTY **9:**1068
– Aḥdut ha-Avodah **2:**456
– Dayan, Moshe **5:**1374
– government formation **9:**612ff
– *Ha-Po'el ha-Za'ir* **7:**1326
– Histadrut elections **9:**864
– occupied territories **9:**413
– place in politics **9:**678ff
– Po'alei Zion **13:**664
– Rafi **13:**1512
– Six-Day War **9:**413
– socialism **15:**33
– World Labor Zionist Movement **16:**639
– *see also:* MAPAI
Israel Land Authority **10:**79
Israel Library Association **11:**195
Israel Manufacturers' Association **9:**765
Israel Medical Association **9:**989
– *illus:*
– stamp **9:**844-845
Israel Meir (print.) **13:**1108
ISRAEL MEIR HA-KOHEN (Ḥafez Ḥayyim) **9:**1068
– Dyatlovo **6:**325
– righteousness **14:**181
– *illus:* text
Israel Ministry of Posts **9:**842
Israel Ministry of Religious Affairs **9:**896ff
ISRAEL MOSES BEN ARYEH LOEB **9:**1070
Israel Moses ben Jehiel Meir **9:**1313
Israel Museum (Jer.) **12:**551
– America-Israel Cultural Foundation **2:**817
– Billy Rose art garden **3:**649
– cultural life **9:**1013
– Jerusalem development **9:**1495
– library **11:**195
– *illus:*
– – Arab schoolboys in children's workshop **9:**951
– – Billy Rose Art Garden **14:**267
– – general view **3:**354
– – Mexican exhibits **11:**1460
– – opening of a Chagall exhibition **9:**1010
– – sculptures **14:**1061-1068
– – *shofarot* display **14:**1445
– – stamp **9:**844-845
Israel Music and Dance Festival, *see* Israel festivals
Israel Music Foundation (record co.) **13:**1618
Israel Nathan ben Samuel **4:**837
Israel National (petroleum co., Isr.) **9:**795
Israel National Opera **5:**1548
Israel National Parks Authority **12:**878ff
Israel Navy
– Sinai Campaign **14:**1606
– Six-Day War **14:**1630
– War of Independence **9:**367
Israel New Left (orgn.), *see* Semol Yisre'eli Ḥadash
Israel Numismatic Journal **12:**1271
Israel Numismatic Society **14:**53
ISRAEL OF BAMBERG **9:**1071
Israel of Belzec, *see* ISRAEL BEN BENJAMIN OF BELZEC
Israel of Campana, *see* Israel Jonah of Campana
Israel of Heidelberg **8:**257
Israel of Husyatin **14:**531
ISRAEL OF KREMS **9:**1071
– Krems **10:**1258
Israel of Leczyca, *see* ISRAEL BEN JONATHAN FROM LECZYCA
Israel of Modzhitz **12:**207
Israel of Nuremberg, *see* Israel ben Isaac of Nuremberg
Israel of Perugia **9:**280
Israel of Polotsk, *see* ISRAEL BEN PEREZ OF POLOTSK
Israel of Ruzhany, *see* Israel ben Shalom of Ruzhany
Israel of Ruzhin, *see* RUZHIN, ISRAEL
Israel of Satanov, *see* ISRAEL ḤARIF OF SATANOV
Israel of Shklov, *see* ISRAEL BEN SAMUEL OF SHKLOV
Israel of Tarnopol, *see* Israel ben Samuel of Tarnopol
Israel of Zamosc, *see* ZAMOSC, ISRAEL BEN MOSES HA-LEVI
Israel Olympic Committee **15:**296
Israel Philatelic Societies, Association of **9:**842
ISRAEL PHILHARMONIC ORCHESTRA **9:**1072
– cultural life in Israel **9:**1006
– German and Austrian Jews **9:**531
– *illus:*
– – text
– – Bernstein, Leonard **4:**687
– – Heifetz, Jascha **8:**261
– – Huberman, Bronislaw **8:**1056
– – Piatigorsky, Gregor, **8:**261
ISRAEL PROGRAM FOR SCIENTIFIC TRANSLATIONS **9:**1073
– publishing **13:**1379
Israel Provisional Government **9:**663
Israel Purchasing Mission in Germany **5:**873
Israel Renaissance Society, *see* Teḥiyyat Israel Society
Israel Rogosin Center for Ethics and Human Values (U.S.) **16:**761
Israëls, Isaac **9:**1074; **12:**984; **3:**566
– *illus:*
– – Fischer, Jean (paint.) **6:**1319
ISRAËLS, JOZEF **9:**1073
– art **3:**565; **14:**918
– *illus:*
– – "Aurivius Family" (paint.) **3:**550
Israel Seen from Within (journ.) **16:**641
Israel's Herald (period.) **4:**1535; **13:**1052
Israel shipyards **9:**837
Israel Sifroni, *see* ZIFRONI, ISRAEL BEN DANIEL
Israelski (law.) **10:**1180
Israel Society for Biblical Research **15:**55
Israel Society of Special Libraries and Information Center **9:**975
ISRAELSOHN, JACOB IZRAILEVICH **9:**1074
Israel Song Competition Festival **9:**1590
Israel son of Mohar of Brandenburg **9:**1263
Israel Sports Federation **15:**296
Israel Stela **11:**1389
Israel Technical Aid Program **9:**627
Israel Tenth Anniversary Exhibition **9:**765
Israel Today (newsp.), *see Jewish Times* (Scot.)
Israel Universities Press (publ. firm) **13:**1379
Israel Zifroni, *see* ZIFRONI, ISRAEL BEN DANIEL
Isrāfīl (Isl. angel) **6:**885
Isrā'īliyyāt (Musl. lit.), *see* ISRAELITE
ISRU ḤAG (day after festival) **9:**1075
ISSACHAR (bib. fig.) **9:**1075
– breastplate stone **13:**1008
– industriousness **10:**1321
– settlement **8:**579; **9:**115
– Twelve Tribes **15:**1382ff
ISSACHAR, SIMḤAH **9:**1077
Issachar, Testament of, see PATRIARCHS, TESTAMENT OF THE TWELVE
ISSACHAR BAER BEN SOLOMON ZALMAN (Klazki) **9:**1078
ISSACHAR BAER BEN TANHUM **9:**1078
Issachar Baer of Kremnitz **16:**1213
Issachar Baer of Lubavich **9:**1059
Issachar Baer of Radoszyce, *see* RADOSHITSER, ISSACHAR BAER
Issachar Baer of Sokal **4:**452
Issachar Berish **4:**14
ISSACHAR BERMAN BEN NAPHTALI HA-KOHEN **9:**1078
– *illus:* text
ISSACHAR DOV BAER BEN ARYEH LEIB OF ZLOCZOW **9:**1079
– Abraham Ḥayyim ben Gedaliah **2:**159
Issachar Dov of Belz (Gal.) **4:**453; **14:**325; **16:**325
– Munkac, Hayyim Eliezer of **14:**1296
Issachar Dov of Belz (Isr.) **4:**453
Issachar Leib of Zhidachov **16:**1009
Issakovitch, Eliash **10:**1261
ISSAR JUDAH BEN NEHEMIAH OF BRISK **9:**1079
'Issaron (meas.) **16:**380ff
Issawiya (vill., Isr.) **9:**1497
Isserlein, Israel ben Jehiel **6:**1302
ISSERLEIN, ISRAEL BEN PETHAHIAH **9:**1080
– Aaron of Neustadt **2:**22
– Austrian *yeshivot* **3:**889
– history chart **8:**766-767
– Israel of Krems **9:**1071
– responsa **11:**337
– seals **14:**1079
– taxation **15:**845ff
– *illus:* text
Isserles, Eliezer **9:**1082
Isserles, Isaac **9:**1082
Isserles, Joseph **9:**1082
Isserles, Judah Leib **9:**1082
Isserles, Meir **16:**907
Isserles, Miriam Bella, *see* Horowitz, Miriam Bella
ISSERLES, MOSES BEN ISRAEL (Rema) **9:**1081
– Ashkenazi usage **3:**721
– chess **5:**403
– codification of law **5:**650; **11:**335
– Cracow **5:**1029
– Falk, Joshua **6:**1158
– history chart **8:**766-67
– Luria dispute **13:**722
– Maimonides' philosophy **11:**760
– Meir ben Baruch of Rothenburg **11:**1251
– Prague **13:**976
– *Shulḥan Arukh* **14:**1475
– social problems **8:**698
– sport on Sabbath **15:**292
– Torah study **15:**457
– tradition **15:**1310
– *illus:*
– – text
– – autograph **3:**915
– – portrait **14:**1476
ISSERMAN, FERDINAND MYRON **9:**1085
– Toronto **15:**1261
Issi (amora), *see* ASSI
Issi ben Akavyah (tan.), *see* YOSE BEN AKAVYAH
Issi ben Gamaliel (tan.) **16:**851
Issi ben Gur Aryeh (tan.) **16:**851
Issi ben Judah (tan.) **16:**851
Issi ben Mahalalel (tan.) **16:**851
I.S.S.L.I.C., *see* Israel Society of Special Libraries and Information Center
Issues (period.) **2:**820
ISSUR GIYYORA (pros.) **9:**1085

- Mari ben Issur **11:**992
ISSUR VE-HETTER (hal. rulings) **9:**1085
- custom **12:**9ff
- *dina de-malkhuta* **6:**53
- eligible age for public duties **13:**1357
- imprisonment for debt **8:**1308
- *mishpat ivri* **12:**110ff
- *sevarah* **14:**1196
- witness **16:**585
Istambuli synagogue (Jer.) **9:**1447; **15:**610
- *illus:*
- - *bimah* and women's gallery **9:**1444
ISTANBUL (city, Turk.) **9:**1086
- Adrianople **2:**311
- Alliance Israélite **2:**653
- capitulations **5:**148
- Turkey **15:**1461
- *illus:*
- - Ahrida synagogue **15:**1460
- - Toferei Begadim synagogue **15:**1461
- - Yambol synagogue **14:**1169
- *see also:* CONSTANTINOPLE
Istanbul synagogue (Jer.), *see* Istambuli synagogue
Ištar (Akk. deity), *see* Ishtar
Istehar (leg. fig.) **2:**967; **16:**43
Istīfā', al- (wk.), *see Kitāb al-Istīfā'*
Istighnā', al- (wk.), *see Kitāb al-Istighnā'*
Istiqlāl (polit. party) **9:**347
Istituto Convitto Rabbinico, *see* COLLEGIO RABBINICO ITALIANO
ISTOCZY, GYÖZÖ **9:**1099
- Kaposvar **10:**756
- Tiszaeszlar **15:**1155
Istres (loc., Prov.) **9:**1099; **13:**1259
ISTRIA (penin.) **9:**1099
Istrumsa, Daniel, *see* ESTROSA, DANIEL
ISTRUMSA (ISTRUSA), ḤAYYIM ABRAHAM **9:**1100
Isunians (J. sect), *see* Isfahanians
Isvolsky (polit.) **16:**615
Itabyrion (mt., Er. Isr.), *see* TABOR, MOUNT
Itai, Avner **12:**672
ITALIA, SHALOM **9:**1100
- art **3:**538; **3:**539
- *Rotterdam Ketubbah* **10:**931
- Templo, Jacob Judah **15:**999
- *illus:*
- - Esther Scroll **9:**1101; **14:**1053
- - *ketubbah* **3:**541; Pl. 4 **10**-KETUBBAH
- - Templo, Leon (portrait) **15:**998
Italiaander, Isak **15:**1176
Italian Hospital (Jer.) **9:**1461
Italian language **16:** 1634
- Hebrew influences **9:**1102
- Judeo-Italian **10:**67,427
ITALIAN LITERATURE **9:**1101
- Bible translations **4:**878
- children's literature **5:**453; **5:**457
- *illus:*
- - text
- - poem for coronation of Leopold II (1791) **6:**1358
Italian mina (meas.), *see* Mina
Italian rite (litur.), *see* Roman rite
Italian Synagogue (Jer.) **5:**869; **15:**618
Italian Synagogue (Venice) **9:**1135; **15:**618; **16:**100
Italie, H. **16:**37
ITALIENER, BRUNO **9:**1115
Italkian (lang.), *see* JUDEO-ITALIAN
ITALY **9:**1115
- General
- - Alfasi's *Sefer ha-Halakhot* **2:**603
- - caricatures **5:**175
- - Provence **13:**1263
- - stamps **15:**330
- - wax inscriptions **16:**663
- History **8:**666ff
- - Crusades **5:**1143
- - early settlements **8:**640
- - French Revolution **7:**157
- - history chart **8:**766-67
- - Holocaust **8:**840; **8:**851ff
- - neo-Fascism **12:**951
- - partisans **13:**140; **13:**147
- - Sykes-Picot treaty **15:**565ff
- Demography
- - *aliyah* **9:**512
- - Israel community **9:**498
- - population **13:**870ff
- - statistics **15:**346
- Social and Economic Life
- - Apulian Jewry **3:**226ff
- - archives **3:**382
- - Assembly of Jewish Notables **3:**761; **3:**763
- - Avelei Zion **3:**946
- - communal organization **5:**824
- - Diaspora **6:**10
- - dress **6:**219
- - education **6:**405,416,420
- - emancipation **6:**704ff
- - ghetto **10:**82ff
- - Haskalah **7:**1435
- - hospitals **8:**1034
- - Jewish-Christian disputations **6:**94ff
- - market days and fairs **11:**1003
- - Marrano diaspora **11:**1022
- - *mikveh* **11:**1541
- - military service **11:**1559
- - Purim customs **13:**128
- - Sephardim **14:**1172
- - Shabbateanism **14:**1243; **14:**1245
- - student movements **15:**453
- - synagogues **15:**601, 613; **1:**syn.list
- - synagogue choirs **5:**486
- - synods **15:**634ff
- - *takkanot* **15:**726,736
- - taxation **15:**839ff
- - *yeshivot* **16:**764ff
- - Zionism **16:**1122
- Cultural Life
- - book illustrations **4:**1233
- - funerary art **3:**522
- - homiletical literature **8:**954ff
- - incunabula **8:**1319ff
- - Italian literature **9:**1101
- - Ladino language **10:**1343
- - libraries **11:**193
- - manuscripts, Hebrew **8:**1268; **11:**906
- - medieval Hebrew **16:** 1633ff
- - *piyyut* **13:**574
- - poetry **11:**328; **13:**690
- - press **13:**1036
- - prosody **13:**1199,1220
- - sculpture **14:**1060
- - *talmud torah* libraries **11:**190
- - theater **15:**1057
- - universities **15:**1675
- - Yiddish literature **16:**806
- Trades and Professions **15:**1297ff
- - agriculture **2:**402
- - banking **4:**168f,173
- - journalism **10:**304ff
- - law **10:**1491ff
- - letter-writing **11:**60
- - moneylending **12:**255
- - politics **13:**815
- - publishing **13:**1368
- - secondhand goods trade **14:**1085
- - typography **15:**1478,1487
- Anti-Semitism **3:**102
- - Benedict, popes **4:**481
- - forced conversions **3:**170
- - *sheḥitah* ban **14:**1341
- - Tuscany **15:**1468ff
- *illus:*
- - Assembly of Jewish Notables, map of delegations **3:**761
- - Bologna, memorial to deported Jews **4:**1191
- - bride's niello key casket **11:**1039
- - Brindisi, Via Giudea **4:**1376
- - *Casale Pilgrim* travelogue **13:**513
- - Ḥanukkah lamps **7:**1301–1304,1306
- - Jewish badge (15th cent.) **4:**67
- - Jewish bride and bridegroom **4:**66
- - Magna Graecia catacomb, epitaph **2:**698
- *pop. tables:*
- - text
- - Jewish population of S. Italy, 12th cent. **3:**226
- - *see also:* PIEDMONT; ROME
Itchele (writ.), *see* JUSTMAN, MOSHE BUNEM
ITELSON, GREGOR **9:**1147
Ithaca (tn., N.Y.) **12:**1127
Ithai (bib. fig.), *see* ITTAI
ITHAMAR (bib. fig.) **9:**1147
- Gershonites **7:**514
Ithiel (k.), *see* SOLOMON
Ithiel (r.) **10:**720
Ithra the Ishmaelite (Jesraelite; bib. fig.), *see* Jether the Ishmaelite
Itil (Khazar capital), *see* ATIL
ITIM (news agency), *see* Associated Israel Press
ITINERARIES OF EREẒ ISRAEL **9:**1148
- *Darkhei Ẓiyyon* **13:**904
- maps **11:**919
- Ruter **9:**280
- *illus:*
- - text
- - Benjamin of Tudela, map of travels **4:**535
- - *Casale Pilgrim* travelogue (1958) **4:**533
- - Litmanowitz's lithograph **9:**1587
- - *Shivḥei Yerushalayim* (1785) **4:**275
- *see also:* HOLY PLACES; TRAVELERS AND TRAVELS TO EREẒ ISRAEL
ITINERARIUM ANTONINI (bk.) **9:**1149
ITINERARIUM HIEROSOLYMITANUM or ITINERARIUM BURDIGALENSE (bk.) **9:**1149
Itkis, Mikhail **15:**313
ITO, see International Telecommunication Union
I.T.O. (orgn.), *see* Jewish Territorial Organization
"I to the Hills" (sculp., Schotz) **14:**1000
I.T.S., *see* INTERNATIONAL TRACING SERVICE
ITTAI (bib. fig.) **9:**1150
Iṭṭim (diviner) **6:**114
Ittim (period.) **1:**newsp. list
Ittinga, Aaron ha-Levi (schol.) **12:**1475
Ittinga, Isaac Aaron **14:**635
Ittinga, Mordecai Ze'ev ben Isaac Aaron Segal, *see* ETTINGER, MORDECAI ZE'EV BEN ISAAC AARON SEGAL
Ittonenu (period.) **5:**458; **6:**986
Ittonenu la-Ketannim (period.) **5:**458
Itton ha-Bonim (period.) **1:**newsp. list
Itton ha-Tenu'ah(period.) **16:**348
Itton le-Misḥar (period.) **1:**newsp. list
Itton Meyuḥad (newsp.) **1:**newsp. list
'Iṭṭur soferim (Bib.; textual omissions) **15:**80; **16:**1410
Ittur Soferim (bk.), *see Sefer ha-Ittur*
Itureans (people, Er. Isr.)
- Aristobulus I **3:**440 **7:**1456; **8:**631
- Pompey **8:**1064; **9:**120
Itzele of Volozhin, *see* VOLOZHINER, ISAAC BEN HAYYIM
Itzelle Peterburger, *see* BLASER, ISAAC
Itzhak Katzenelson Ghetto Fighters' House (Isr.), *see* GHETTO FIGHTERS' HOUSE
Itzig (fam.) **8:**791; **12:**64
Itzig, Bluemchen, *see* Friedlaender, Bluemchen
Itzig, Cecily, *see* Eskeles, Cecily
ITZIG, DANIEL **9:**1150
- Arnstein, Fanny **3:**490
- Behr, Issachar Falkensohn **4:**395
- *illus:*
- - text
- - medal by Abraham Abramson **3:**545
- - portrait **5:**1010
Itzig, Elias Daniel, *see* Hitzig, Elias Daniel
ITZIG, GEORG **3:**364
- *illus:*
- - Palazzo Revoltella, Trieste **3:**341
Itzig, Isaac Daniel **7:**178; **9:**1152
Itzig, Julius Eduard, *see* HITZIG, JULIUS EDUARD
Itzig, Moritz Jonathan **9:**1152
Itzkhakov, P., *see* PERLOV, YIẒḤAK
Itzkowski, H. **4:**654
Iudaea, *see* Provincia Judaea
IUDEX JUDAEORUM (mdvl. offic., Aus.) **9:**1152
Iudovich, Mikhail **5:**406
Iugatio (tax), *see* ARNONA
IUJF (Eng.), *see* Inter-University Jewish Federation
Iunu (city, Egy.), *see* HELIOPOLIS
Iussim, Henrique **5:**456; **13:**1370; **15:**255
Iussim Segal, Bat-Sheva **5:**456
IVANCICE (tn., Morav.) **9:**1153
Ivanhoe (bk.) **14:**1036
- *illus:*
- - Rebecca (S. A. Hart) **6:**779
Ivanici (vill., Rus.), *see* Iwanie
IVANJI, IVAN **16:**890
Ivanov Frankovsk (city, Ukr.), *see* STANISLAV
IVANOVO (tn., Belor.) **9:**1153
Ivan the Terrible (czar) **13:**837
"Ivan the Terrible" (sculp., Antokolski) **3:**556
IVANYI-GRUNWALD, BELA **3:**602
Ivireanu, Antim **4:**882
Ivomai (gaon) **7:**316
IVO (Ives) OF CHARTRES **9:**1154
- Burchard's *Decretum* **4:**1508
IVORY **9:**1154
- inscriptions **16:**662
- Solomon's trade **15:**98
- tusks **6:**603
- *illus:*
- - text
- - Ahab's house **3:**315,337,503; **5:**397,1227; **8:**596
- - Astarte (8th cent. B.C.E.) **3:**317
- - horn, Ugarit **12:**563
- - Joseph and brothers **10:**207
- - Megiddo box **11:**268
- - Megiddo tablets **11:**1222
- - perfume bottle **5:**979
- - relief illustrating Psalm 27 (c. 870) **13:**1304

Ivory Coast (rep., Afr.)
- Israel's relations **9:**440
Ivrea (tn., It.) **13:**1397
ʿIvri (conc.), *see* Hebrew
Ivriah (orgn., Chile) **16:**1125
Ivri Anokhi (period.)
- hostility to Ḥibbat Zion **12:**1046
- Schorr, Joshua Heschel **14:**997
- statistics **1:**newsp. list
- Werber, Baruch **16:**450
"Ivrit be-Ivrit" (Heb. teaching method) **7:**706
Ivriyyah (Heb. lang. mvmt.)
- Brit Ivrit Olamit **4:**1382
- Lewinsky, Elhanan Leib **11:**174
IVY (bot.) **9:**1155
- plant list **13:**619
IVYE (tn., Belor.) **9:**1155
Ivyer, Moses **9:**1155
Iwanie (vill., Rus.) **7:**59
Iwanski, Henryk **16:**349
Iwje (tn., Belor.), *see* IVYE
Ixar (tn., Sp.), *see* HÍJAR
IYOV of Minsk, *see* BRILL, JOSEPH
IYYAR (month) **9:**1156
- *illus:* text
- *see also:* CALENDAR
Iyyar, the 14th of, *see* PASSOVER, SECOND
Iyyar, the 18th of, *see* LAG BA-OMER
Iyyar, the 28th of **2:**221; **14:**785
Iyyim (period., Eng.) **1:**newsp. list
Iyyon (city; Jor. headstream), *see* IJON
Iyyon valley (Er. Isr.), *see* ʿAyūn valley
Iyyun (journ.) **1:**newsp. list
Iyyunim Beinle'ummiyyim (pub.) **1:**newsp. list
Iyyunim bi-Ve'ayot Ḥevrah (journ.) **1:**newsp. list
Iyyunim le-Vikkoret ha-Medinah (pub.) **1:**newsp. list
Izagayev, Zion **9:**1157; **12:**480
IZATES II (k., Adiabene) **9:**1157
- Abgar VII **6:**366
- Abgar's Peshitta **4:**858
- Adiabene **2:**267ff
- Ananias of Adiabene **2:**924
- Helena, mother of **8:**288
IZBAN, SHMUEL **9:**1158
IZBICA LUBELSKA (tn., Pol.) **9:**1158
IZBICA-RADZYN (ḥas. dyn.) **9:**1159
- dynasty **1:**ḥas. table
- *see also under:* Leiner
Izbitski, Joseph, *see* MIKHALEVICH, BENISH
Izdundad (Pers. prin.) **4:**1537; **8:**1444
Ize dil Pirlilo (writ.) **5:**446
IZFA (U.S.), *see* Intercollegiate Zionist Federation of America
Izhar (bib. fig.) **10:**1135
Izikzon, Joshua **4:**197
IZIS (phot.) **9:**1160
I.Ẓ.L. (resist. org.), *see* IRGUN ẒEVA'I LE'UMMI
IZMAIL (city, Bess.) **9:**1161
IZMIR (city, Turk.) **9:**1162
- capitulations **5:**148
- chief rabbinate **13:**1451
- dress **6:**216
- Shabbateanism **14:**1243
- Shabbetai Ẓevi **14:**1222ff
- Turkey **15:**1462
Izmirlis (Doenmeh sect) **6:**149ff
IZMIT (Turk. port.) **9:**1165
IZRAELITA (weekly) **9:**1165
IZRAELITA MAGYAR IRODALMI TÁRSULAT (IMIT; soc.) **9:**1166
- Acsády, Ignác **2:**232
Izraelskie Nowiny i Kurier (newsp.) **9:**1017
Izraelski Far (newsp.) **9:**1017
IZYASLAV (city, Ukr.) **9:**1166
- Aryeh Leib ben Elijah **3:**668
Izyaslav case, *see* Zaslavl case
ʿIzz al-Dawla (tit., Iraq) **8:**1186
Izzumin (tal. term), *see* ASMAKHTA

J

Jaarboek van de Nederlandse Zionistische Studentenorganisatie (period.) **16:**1120
Jaare-Oregim (bib. fig.) **6:**611
Jaareshiah ben Joseph **3:**1009
JAAZANIAH (bib. figs.) **9:**1169
Jabaʿ (vill., Er. Isr.) :349, 350
JABAL (bib. fig) **9:**1170
Jabal (mt.) *see also* Jabel, Jebel
Jabal al-Zevedani (mt., Syr.) **2:**792
Jabal Drūz (reg., Bashan) **9:**597
"Jabalī" (lang.) **5:**1461; **12:**949
Jabārāt, Al- (Bedouin tribe) **9:**593
Jaʿbarī, Muhammed Ali al- **8:**235
JABBOK (riv., Er. Isr.) **9:**1170
- geography of Israel **9:**595
- physiography **9:**168ff; **9:**177
- Transjordan **15:**1316
Jabel (mt.), *see also* Jabal, Jebel
Jabel Bishri (mt., Mesop.) **16:**1495
JABÊS, EDMOND **7:**150
- Oriental literature **12:**1465
JABESH-GILEAD (city, Er. Isr.) **9:**1171
- Benjamites **4:**525
- proscription of **8:**345; **8:**347
- Saul's body retrieved **14:**914
Jabesh River, *see* Yābis River
Jabez (bib. fig.) **12:**1521
JABEZ (Sp. fam.) **9:**1172
Jabez, Isaac ben Joseph (It.) **9:**1172 **10:**243
Jabez, Isaac ben Solomon **9:**1172
Jsbez, Joseph (print.) **2:**310; **9:**1097, 1172
JABEZ, JOSEPH BEN ḤAYYIM (prch.) **9:**1173
- articles of faith **3:**658
- Jabez family **9:**1172
- polemics **13:**793
- Spanish *yeshivot* **16:**763
Jabez, Solomon **2:**310; **9:**1097; **9:**1172
JABIN (Cana. k.) **9:**1173
- Benjamites **4:**525
- Bible history **8:**584
- Ḥazor **7:**1535
- Judges, Book of **10:**445
Jabir (alch.) **2:**545
Jābiya, al- (Arab camp, Golan) **9:**261
Jabiyya (city, Er. Isr.) **4:**292
JABLONEC NAD NISOU (city, Bohem.) **9:**1174
Jablonka (cmty., Pol.) **16:**923
JABLONNA (mil. camp, Pol.) **9:**1175
Jablonowska, Anna **14:**1512
Jablonski (-y), Daniel E. **4:**653; **11:**1110; **12:**558
JABNEEL (tn., vill., Er. Isr.) **9:**1175
- ICA's activity **10:**48
- statistics **1:**place list
- *see also:* JABNEH
JABNEH (city, Er. Isr.) **9:**1176
- academy proceedings **2:**202
- authority **3:**909
- *Bet Hillel* **4:**740ff
- Capito, Marcus Herennius **5:**147
- Gamaliel's academy **2:**202
- history **8:**630; **8:**638; **8:**643; **9:**240ff
- Johanan ben Zakkai **10:**152
- Song of Songs in canon **15:**147
- Usha, Synod of **16:**18
- *see also:* JABNEEL
Jabneh (tn., Isr.), *see* YAVNEH
Jabneh-Yamnia (Jabneh-Yam; tn., Er. Isr.) **9:**1176
Jabotinsky, Eri **9:**1186
- Betar **4:**715
JABOTINSKY, VLADIMIR (Ze'ev) **9:**1178
- Ben-Gurion, David **4:**508ff
- Betar **4:**714 **9:**855
- exiles to Alexandria **2:**593
- Golomb, Eliyahu **7:**764
- Grossman, Meir **7:**937
- Haganah **7:**1064
- Hebrew language **16:**1646
- Herut ideology **8:**400
- history **8:**756
- Jewish Legion **10:**69ff
- Jewish military units **16:**1050
- *Razsvet* **13:**1598
- reinterment **9:**398
- Samson novel **14:**775
- self-defense **14:**1123
- settlement defense **16:**681f
- 17th Zionist Congress **16:**1173
- Weizmann, Chaim **16:**427
- Zionism **16:**1055ff
- *illus:*
- - text
- - Jewish Legion soldiers **9:**682
- - Kovno youth movement **16:**1098
- - Patterson, John Henry, and **13:**187
- - *Razsvet* staff **13:**1596
- - Soskin, Selig Eugen, and **15:**169
- *see also:* REVISIONISTS, ZIONIST
JACA (city, Sp.) **9:**1186
Jacar, Samuel **8:**977
Jacchia, Luigi **3:**806
J'Accuse (Emile Zola) **6:**227; **16:**1216
Jachia, Samuel, *see* DENIS, ALBERTUS
JACHIN AND BOAZ (pillars, Temple) **9:**1186
- Temple **15:**950ff
- *illus:* text
Jachin ben Nethanel **6:**493
Jacie, Henry, *see* JESSEY, HENRY
Jacimus (ruler, Bathyra) **13:**394; **16:**922
JACKAL (zool.) **9:**1189
- dietary laws **6:**32
- fauna of Israel **9:**226
- *illus:* **9:**233
- *see also:* FOX
Jackan, Samuel Jacob **7:**1498
Jackson (city, Calif.) **5:**56
- *illus:*
- - synagogue **15:**1604
Jackson (city, Mich.) **11:**1499
Jackson (city, Miss.) **12:**155
- *illus:*
- - Beth Israel synagogue **12:**155
Jackson (city, Tenn.) **15:**1009
Jackson, Anne **15:**1092
Jackson, Daniel **12:**1072
Jackson, Hamlet **15:**1346
JACKSON, HARRY **15:**1086
Jackson, Joseph **10:**1495
JACKSON, SOLOMON HENRY **9:**1189
- New York **12:**1074
- press **13:**1050
- *illus:* text
Jackson, Willie **15:**306
JACKSONVILLE (city, Fla.) **9:**1190
- Florida **6:**1362ff
- *illus:* text
Jacksonville (city, Ill.) **8:**1256
Jacksonville (tn., N. C.) **12:**1220
Jacksonville (city, Oreg.) **13:**911
JACOB (bib. fig.) **9:**1191
- *Contents:*
- - The Birthright **9:**1191
- - His Flights **9:**1192
- - His Marriages **9:**1192
- - The Tribes **9:**1193
- - Jacob and Laban **9:**1193
- - The Return **9:**1194
- - The Rape of Dinah **9:**1195
- - Beth-El **9:**1195
- - Jacob and Joseph **9:**1196
- - The Other Biblical Traditions **9:**1196
- - The Name **9:**1196
- - In the Aggadah **9:**1197
- - In Islam **9:**1201
- - In the Arts **9:**1202
- *arvit* **3:**664
- Genesis, Book of **7:**389ff
- God's revelation **14:**118
- in the Arts **10:**213f.; **13:**1490
- Isaac **9:**4
- Joseph **10:**202*f*
- kabbalistic view **10:**575
- Laban **10:**1315
- marriages **8:**1316
- *Midrash va-Yissa'u* **11:**1520
- moon **12:**291
- patriarch **8:**573; **13:**183
- Rachel **13:**1486
- Rebekah **13:**1602ff
- sacrifice **14:**605
- sciatic nerve **6:**39
- sheep incident **4:**1024
- sun **15:**517
- Tamar **15:**783
- twelve tribes **15:**1381
- vow of **16:**227
- *zekhut avot* **16:**976
- *illus:*
- - text
- - at Isaac's deathbed **3:**515
- - at Rachel's deathbed **4:**523
- - Benjamin taken to Egypt **10:**329; **14:**105
- - birth **4:**943; **13:**1602
- - blessing Ephraim and Manasseh **6:**281, 809; **7:**1084; **14:**67
- - blessing his sons **6:**281; **9:**1208
- - blessing Pharaoh **7:**1084
- - death **5:**1423; **7:**1084
- - dream **3:**52,636; **4:**244; **6:**291; **8:**1286; **9:**1205; **13:**63
- - entrusting Benjamin to Judah **4:**524
- - Esau selling his birthright **4:**943; **6:**859
- - going down with sons to Egypt **7:**1001
- - "Isaac Blessing Jacob" (drg. Rembrandt) **9:**6
- - Joseph relating his Dreams **10:**204,215
- - Joseph's brothers **4:**944
- - Joseph's reunion with **13:**1103
- - journey to Beth-El **4:**730
- - Laban and **10:**1077,1316
- - Laban's flock (chart) **4:**1025
- - leading household across Jabbok river **9:**1171
- - Leah and her four sons **10:**1526
- - meeting Rachel **13:**1487
- - meeting with Esau **6:**854, 858
- - messengers to Esau **2:**956
- - mourning Joseph's death **10:**206
- - sons **9:**1202
- - various episodes **4:**949
- *see also:* ESAU; JACOB, BLESSING OF
Jacob(bnk., Babyl.) **16:**1271
Jacob (br. of Jesus), *see* James
Jacob (2nd cent., tan.), *see* JACOB BEN KORSHAI
JACOB (3/4 cent., amora) **9:**1206
Jacob (r., Er. Isr.) **10:**885
Jacob (poet, Er. Isr.) **13:**583

Jacob (mdvl. schol., Fr.) **6**:47
Jacob (13th cent., emis.) **14**:1362; **15**:1352
Jacob (13th cent., Sp. kab.) **12**:426
Jacob (13th cent., mintmaster, Pol.) **12**:61
Jacob (15th cent., poet, Prov.) **6**:1185
Jacob (16th cent., mer., Latv.) **14**:172
Jacob (fam., Can.) **5**:104
Jacob (fam., Ind.) **5**:40
JACOB, BENNO **9**:1206
JACOB, BERTHOLD **9**:1207
JACOB, BLESSING OF **9**:1207
- blessing of children **4**:1087
- right, left in blessing **14**:177
- *illus:* text
- *see also:* JACOB; MOSES, BLESSING OF
Jacob, Edmond **4**:909
JACOB, FRANÇOIS **9**:1210
JACOB, HEINRICH EDUARD **9**:1211
Jacob, Isaac **10**:1495
JACOB, MAX **9**:1211
- *illus:* text
JACOB, NAOMI ELLINGTON **6**:783; **6**:788
Jacob, Solomon **8**:1357
JACOB, TESTAMENT OF (Apoc. wk.) **9**:1213
Jacob Aben Nuñez **5**:976
Jacob Abu Ḥazirah, *see* Abi Ḥasirah, Jacob ben Masoud
Jacob the Alexandrian **5**:1479
Jacob Anatoli, *see* ANATOLI, JACOB BEN ABBA MARI BEN SAMSON
Jacob the Armenian **3**:474
Jacob Aryeh of Radzymin **11**:1492; **13**:1508
Jacob Ashkenazi, *see* TEMERLS, JACOB BEN ELIEZER
Jacob bar Jekuthiel, *see* Jacob ben Jekutiel of Rouen
Jacob bar Natronai (gaon) **7**:317
Jacob bar Samson (tos.), *see* JACOB BEN SAMSON
Jacob ben Aaron (polit., Iraq) **4**:311
Jacob ben Aaron(Samar. h. pr.), *see* Jacob ben Hārūn
JACOB BEN AARON OF KARLIN **9**:1213
Jacob ben Abba Mari Anatoli, *see* ANATOLI, JACOB BEN ABBA MARI BEN SAMSON
Jacob ben Abraham (poet, It.), *see* D'Ascoli, Jacob ben Abraham
Jacob ben Abraham (r., Prague) **9**:1214
Jacob ben Abraham (Kurd. schol.) **4**:204
Jacob ben Abraham (print., Pol.) **9**:1259
Jacob ben Abraham of Jasov, *see* Jasov, Jacob ben Abraham of
Jacob ben Abraham of Mezhirech (print.) **11**:649
- *illus:*
- - *Ayn Shoyn Mayse Bukh* (Basle, 1602) **11**:650
JACOB BEN ABRAHAM SOLOMON **9**:1213
JACOB BEN AḤA (4th cent., Pal. amora) **9**:1214
Jacob ben Aḥa (5th cent., Babyl.) **2**:440
Jacob ben Alexander **5**:1027
Jacob ben Amram of Mahdīyya **10**:699; **12**:760; **15**:123
JACOB BEN ASHER (Sp.) **9**:1214
- General
- - Ashkenazi usage **3**:721
- - chronological chart **8**:766-767
- - codification **5**:645; **7**:1165; **11**:335
- - ethical wills **11**:345
- - Naḥmanides' commentary **12**:778
- - Spain **15**:234
- *Tur Shulḥan Arukh*
- - Adret, Moses **2**:305
- - Ascandarani, Joseph **9**:75
- - Ashkenazi, Judah **3**:728
- - *Bayit Ḥadash* (Sirkes) **5**:647
- - *Beit Yisrael* (Falk) **5**:647
- - *Beit Yosef* (Caro) **5**:196; 648
- - *Darkhei Moshe* (Isserles) **5**:650
- - illuminated manuscript **8**:1270
- - Jewish literature **11**:336
- - subject restriction **12**:132
- - *Va-Yiggash Yehudah* **7**:1272
- *illus:*
- - text
- - *Arba'ah Turim* **3**:533; **8**:1333; **12**:602
- - *Tur Even ha-Ezer* **11**:*fcg.* 1003
- - *Tur Ḥoshen Mishpat* (15th cent.) **4**:*fcg.* 716
- - *Tur Oraḥ Ḥayyim* (1495) **4**:1234; **8**:1330
- - *Tur Yoreh De'ah* **14**:1339
Jacob ben Asher (Cz.) **13**:976
JACOB BEN BENJAMIN ZE'EV **9**:1216
- *aliyah* **9**:513
Jacob ben Crisp **15**:1202
Jacob ben David, *see* TAM IBN YAḤYA, JACOB BEN DAVID
Jacob ben David ben Yom Tov **3**:802; **13**:300
Jacob ben David Shapira **10**:1123
JACOB BEN DUNASH BEN AKIVA **9**:1216
JACOB BEN ELEAZAR **9**:1216
- *Kalila* and *Dimnah* **6**:1266
- linguistics **16**:1358, 1383
- translations **15**:1328
Jacob ben Eli (Pers.) **13**:310
Jacob ben Eli (Fr. schol.) **5**:160
Jacob ben Elijah (tal.) **10**:1462
Jacob ben Elijah (trans.) **15**:1325
Jacob ben Ephraim **10**:413
JACOB BEN EPHRAIM NAPHTALI HIRSCH OF LUBLIN **9**:1217
Jacob ben Ḥabib, *see* IBN ḤABIB, JACOB BEN SOLOMON
Jacob ben Hananel Sikili, *see* SIKILI, JACOB BEN HANANEL
Jacob ben Hārūn (Samar. h. pr.) **14**:735; **14**:754; **14**:755; **14**:757
- *illus:* **14**:733
Jacob ben Ḥayyim **7**:1507
JACOB BEN ḤAYYIM BEN ISAAC IBN ADONIJAH **9**:1217
- Bible edition **4**:838
- Hebraist **8**:16
- Masorah **11**:323 **16**:1427
- *Okhlah ve-Okhlah* **12**:1353
Jacob ben Ḥayyim of Tunis, *see* JACOB BEN ḤAYYIM BEN ISAAC IBN ADONIJAH
JACOB BEN ḤAYYIM TALMID **9**:1218
JACOB BEN IDI (amora) **9**:1218
Jacob ben Inaktur **15**:1321
Jacob ben Isaac **10**:421
Jacob ben Isaac ben Eliezer ha-Levi (Ya'veẓ) **9**:18; **15**:264
Jacob ben Isaac Luzzat of Posen **11**:599
Jacob ben Isaac Roman, *see* ROMAN, JACOB BEN ISAAC
Jacob ben Ishmael, *see* Yacob ben Yishma'el
Jacob ben Israel of Karlin, *see* Karlin, Jacob ben Israel of
JACOB BEN JACOB HA-KOHEN **9**:1219
- *Shiur Komah* **14**:1418
Jacob ben Jakar, *see* JACOB BEN YAKAR
Jacob ben Jekuthiel of Rouen **13**:1546; **14**:351
Jacob ben Joel of Gulkha **10**:466
Jacob ben Joseph (tos.) **16**:109
Jacob ben Joseph ben Jawb ha-Rofe **12**:899
JACOB BEN JUDAH (poet, Fr.) **9**:1220
- Troyes **15**:1407
Jacob ben Judah (writ., Prov.) **2**:565
Jacob ben Judah (14th cent., Ger.), *see* JAECKLIN, JUD
Jacob ben Judah de Lotra (poet, Fr.), *see* JACOB BEN JUDAH
Jacob ben Judah the Galilean (1st cent. C.E., Er. Isr.) **10**:355
- Zealots **16**:949
Jacob ben Judah Leib, *see* FRANK, JACOB, AND THE FRANKISTS
JACOB BEN JUDAH OF LONDON **9**:1220
- Addir bi-Melukhah **2**:256
JACOB BEN KORSHAI (Kodshai) **9**:1220
- Elisha ben Avuyah **6**:669
- views on afterlife **12**:1355; **12**:1356
Jacob ben Machir ibn Tibbon, *see* Tibbon, Jacob ben Machir ibn
Jacob ben Meir (13th cent., Fr.) **13**:1286
Jacob ben Meir Levi (paytan) **16**:788
Jacob ben Meir Tam (tos.), *see* TAM, JACOB BEN MEIR
Jacob ben Meir ben Isaac (mart., Ger.) **11**:1255
Jacob benMeshullam of Lunel **11**:566
- Jacob Nazir **9**:1232
- Meshullam ben Jacob **11**:1400
JACOB BEN MORDECAI OF SCHWERIN **9**:1221
Jacob ben Moses **4**:793
Jacob ben Moses Debalincia **13**:23
JACOB BEN MOSES OF BAGNOLS **9**:1221
Jacob ben Na'im **9**:1163
JACOB BEN NAPHTALI **9**:1222
Jacob ben Naphtali of Gazolo (Gazzuala) **13**:1101
- Mantua **11**:897
- Meir ben Ephraim **11**:1253
- Sabbioneta **14**:586
- *Yiḥus ha-Ẓaddikim* **9**:1148
Jacob ben Nathaniel-Daniel (Trier) **14**:1080
Jacob ben Nethanel (trav.) **15**:1352
JACOB BEN NETHANEL BEN (AL-) FAYYŪMĪ (Yem.) **9**:1222
- *Iggeret Teiman* **11**:758
- Maimonides **16**:742
JACOB BEN NISSIM IBN SHAHIN **9**:1222
- chronological chart **8**:766-767
- *ḥaver* **7**:1491
- Sherira ben Ḥanina **14**:1381
- Tunisia **15**:1434
Jacob ben Phinehas **5**:34
JACOB BEN REUBEN (Kar. schol.) **9**:1223
- *Sefer ha-Osher* **10**:770
Jacob ben Reuben (Fr.) **3**:194; **4**:898
JACOB BEN SAMSON (tos.) **9**:1223
- Masorah **16**:1433
Jacob ben Samson ben Anatoli (It.) **2**:929
Jacob ben Samuel **9**:1286
Jacob ben Saul of Lunel, *see* JACOB NAZIR
Jacob ben Sheshet Gerondi, *see* GERONDI, JACOB BEN SHESHET
JACOB BEN SIMEON (Kar. tr.. **9**:1223
Jacob ben Simeon (Fr.) **13**:104
Jacob ben Solomon Ibn Ḥabib, *see* IBN ḤABIB, JACOB BEN SOLOMON
JACOB BEN SOSAS (Susa) **9**:1224
- Roman War **6**:378
Jacob ben Tafirah (Tapiero) **3**:787
Jacob ben Uzzi ha-Kohen **14**:737
JACOB BEN YAKAR **9**:1224
- Eliezer ben Isaac **6**:623
JACOB BEN ẒEMAḤ BEN NISSIM **9**:1224
- Baghdad **4**:89
Jacob ben Ẓur (17th cent., r., Mor.) **16**:42
Jacob ben Ẓur (18th cent., r., Mor.) **14**:880
Jacob ben Zur (poet, Mor.) **10**:553
"Jacob Blessing the Sons of Joseph" (paint., Rembrandt) **14**:67
Jacob Bogaty **9**:1333
Jacob Bonacosa **13**:8
"Jacob by the Well" (paint., L. Lippi) **9**:1197
JACOB DAVID BEN ISRAEL ISSAR **9**:1225
Jacob David of Amshinov **16**:304
Jacob David of Warka **16**:304
Jacob de la Roque **5**:205
Jacob de Lunel, *see* LUNEL, JACOB DE
Jacob de Paz **2**:622
Jacob di Alemagna **15**:1380
Jacobellus of Stribro (Mies) **8**:1135
Jacob Francis of Mantua **10**:638
Jacob "Gaon" of Rome **14**:245
Jacob ha-Bachri, *see* BACHRACH, JACOB BEN MOSES
Jacob Hagozer, *see* HAGOZER, JACOB AND GERSHOM
JACOB HA-KATAN **9**:1225
- Averroes **3**:953
- Avicenna **3**:959
- medicine **11**:1189
- translations **15**:1328
- Jacob ha-Kohen (18th cent., Ger.) **11**:600
JACOB HA-KOHEN BAR MORDECAI (gaon) **9**:1225
- family **7**:316
- Ḥanina Kahana ben Huna **7**:1266
- visions **16**:169
Jacob ha-Kohen of Gazzuolo, *see* Jacob ben Naphtali of Gazolo (Gazzuala)
Jacob ha-Kohen of Nehar-Pekod (gaon) **7**:318
Jacob ha-Kohen the Pious **10**:720
Jacob ha-Lavan (tos.) **13**:339
Jacob ha-Levi (physic., Prov.) **2**:565
Jacob ha-Levi (r., Ger.) **12**:1279
Jacob ha-Levi he-Ḥasid of Marvege (tos.), *see* JACOB OF MARVEGE
Jacobi, Abraham (mer.) **11**:498
JACOBI, ABRAHAM (physic.) **9**:1225
- medicine **11**:1201
- United States **15**:1607
Jacobi, F.H. (schol., Ger.) **11**:1340
JACOBI, FREDERICK (comp.) **12**:693
- choirs **5**:487
- music **12**:663
- *mus. notation:*
- - composition for synagogue **12**:665
JACOBI, GEORG **12**:693
Jacobi, J.A. **8**:39

JACOBI, KARL GUSTAV JACOB **9:**1226
JACOBI, LOU **15:**1085
JACOBI, MORITZ (Moses) HERMANN **9:**1227
Jacobi, Roland **15:**314
Jacob ibn Albene **2:**672
Jacob ibn Jau (Jaww), *see* IBN JAU, JACOB
Jacob ibn Meir **16:**926
Jacobi Hospital (N.Y.) **12:**1116
Jacobins (Cath. order), *see* DOMINICANS
JACOB ISAAC BEN SHALOM **9:**1227
JACOB ISAAC HA-ḤOZEH MI-LUBLIN **9:**1227
- Apta, Meir **3:**224
- Eichenstein, Zevi **16:**1009
- Elimelech of Lizhansk **10:**1223
- Przysucha, Jacob Isaac **13:**1300
Jacob Isaac ha-Levi **5:**791
Jacob Isaac of Przysucha, *see* PRZYSUCHA, JACOB ISAAC BEN ASHER
Jacob Israel ben Benjamin of Belzec, *see* ISRAEL BEN BENJAMIN OF BELZEC
Jacob Israel of Cherkassy **15:**1472
Jacobite Christianity **13:**428
Jacobites (cmty., Jer.) **9:**1441
Jacobius, Henry, *see* Jacobs, Henry (Hebr., Eng.)
JACOB JOSEPH BEN ẒEVI HA-KOHEN KATZ OF POLONNOYE **9:**1228
- ḥasidic leader **7:**1392ff
- history chart **8:**766-767
- Israel Ba'al Shem Tov **9:**1054
- Naḥman of Kosov **12:**788
- *illus:*
- - *Toledot Ya'akov Yosef* **8:**960
JACOB JOSEPH OF OSTROG **9:**1230
Jacob Joseph of Vilna **12:**1094
Jacob Kaphanton **15:**1328
JACOB KOPPEL BEN AARON SASSLOWER **9:**1231
JACOB KOPPEL BEN MOSES OF MEZHIRECH **9:**1231
- Kabbalah **10:**552
- Shabbateanism **14:**1251
Jacob Koppel Ḥasid, *see* Ḥasid, Jacob Koppel
Jacob Leib of Trisk **15:**1472
Jacob Levi ben Israel **10:**1199
Jacob Levi of Tarascon **8:**1323
- *illus:*
- - *Beḥinat ha-Olam* **15:**1483
Jacob Manish ben Meir **13:**583
Jacob Meir, *see* MEIR, JACOB
JACOB NAZIR **9:**1232
- *Aẓilut* **3:**1009
- Kabbalah **10:**519
Jacob Obrechtlein Synagogue (Amst.) **15:**620
JACOB (Jakób) OF BELZYCE **9:**1232
Jacob of Castilia **13:**583
Jacob of Chinon (tos.) **5:**475
JACOB OF CORBEIL (tos.) **9:**1233
Jacob of Coucy **12:**418
Jacob of Courson (schol.) **14:**778
Jacob of Dubno, *see* KRANZ, JACOB BEN WOLF
Jacob (Jekel) of Eger, *see* JACOB OF VIENNA
Jacob of Fulda, *see* JACOB BEN MORDECAI OF SCHWERIN
Jacob of Juelich **10:**466
Jacob of Kefar Neburaya **10:**889
JACOB OF KEFAR SAKHNAYYA (Sama) **9:**1233
- Eleazar ben Damma **6:**588
- heretics **8:**1070
- Jesus **10:**15
- Postel's identification **13:**933
Jacob of Lissa, *see* LORBEERBAUM, JACOB BEN JACOB MOSES OF LISSA
Jacob of London (archpresbyter) **3:**398
- England **6:**748
- London **11:**470
- *Presbyter Judaeorum* **13:**1015
Jacob of Malitsch **14:**260
JACOB OF MARVEGE (tos.) **9:**1233
- Ezra of Montcontour **6:**1124
- maggid **11:**699
- reliance on dreams **6:**211
JACOB OF ORLEANS **9:**1234
Jacob of Oxford **12:**1534
Jacob of Paris **11:**351
JACOB OF PONT-SAINTE-MAXENCE **9:**1234
Jacob of Prague **6:**1345
Jacob of Provence **13:**1286
Jacob of Serugh (Sarug) **5:**553
Jacob of Triel **2:**538
Jacob of Triesh **15:**1376
Jacob of Venice **6:**91; **11:**355
JACOB OF VIENNA **9:**1234
- Aaron of Neustadt **2:**22
Jacob of Wuerzburg **2:**939
Jacob of Zhidachov **10:**958
Jacobovitch, Lou, *see* JACOBI, LOU
Jacobowicz, Isaac **15:**602; **15:**606
Jacobowitz, A. L. **7:**1498
JACOBOWSKI, LUDWIG **9:**1235
- Jewish rights **16:**111
Jacob the Parnas **3:**204
Jacob Pasha **16:**1552
Jacob Qerido, *see* QUERIDO, JACOB
Jacobs (Eng. fam.) **14:**1336
Jacobs (fam., U.S.) **14:**833
Jacobs, Abraham (mer., Ind.) **5:**39
Jacobs, Abraham (medal., Ger.) **11:**1165
Jacobs, Abraham (mer., U.S.) **5:**1543
JACOBS, ALETTA **13:**827
Jacobs, Arthur L. **13:**1462
Jacobs, Cecil Isidore **4:**1480
Jacobs, Clair S. **12:**1375
Jacobs, David (stlr., Que.) **13:**1423
Jacobs, David (act., Eng.) **15:**930
Jacobs, Elias **5:**247
Jacobs, Ethel **15:**310
Jacobs, Eugene **15:**310
Jacobs, Frances Wisebart **5:**1543
Jacobs, Hagman **5:**247
Jacobs, Henry (Hebr., Eng.) **8:**39
Jacobs, Henry (mayor, U.S.) **12:**266
Jacobs, Henry S. (r., U.S.) **16:**566
Jacobs, Herman **11:**1498
Jacobs, Hirsch **15:**310
Jacobs, Irving **15:**310
Jacobs, Isaac **7:**613; **9:**1236
Jacobs, James **15:**310
Jacobs, John **15:**930
JACOBS, JOSEPH **9:**1235
- *The American Hebrew* **2:**821
- historical sources **8:**563
- *illus:* text
JACOBS, LAZARUS **9:**1236
- glass **7:**613
Jacobs, Levy **14:**1664
Jacobs, Louis (mer., U.S.) **14:**954
JACOBS, LOUIS (r., Eng.) **9:**1236
- Bible criticism **13:**264
- "Jacobs affair", the **6:**766
- *Jewish Chronicle* **10:**41
- Jews' College **10:**99
- Maimonides **3:**660
Jacobs, Max **12:**1124
Jacobs, Melville **3:**40
Jacobs, Michael (18th cent.) **12:**1067
Jacobs, Mike (sport.) **12:**1124; **13:**1361; **15:**306
Jacobs, Monty **7:**451
Jacobs, Morris (19th cent., Austr.) **11:**1285
Jacobs, Morris (20th cent., Austr.) **11:**1285
Jacobs, Paul **15:**31
JACOBS, ROSE GELL **9:**1237
Jacobs, Samuel (mer., Can.) **15:**1305
Jacobs, Samuel (surv., U.S.) **8:**1438
Jacobs, Samuel W. (polit., Can.) **5:**112
Jacobs, Sidney **15:**310
JACOBS, SIMEON (law., S.A.) **10:**1509
Jacobs, Simon (stlr., U.S.) **15:**213
JACOBS, SOLOMON (U.S.) **9:**1237
- Richmond **14:**160
Jacobs, Solomon (Can.) **15:**1261; **15:**1262
Jacobs, Solomon (Austr.) **11:**1285
Jacobs, Walter F. **11:**1552
Jacobs, William **12:**1408
Jacob Samson Ḥasid, *see* Ḥasid, Jacob Samson
JACOB SAMSON OF SHEPETOVKA **9:**1238
"Jacob's Dream" (paint., S. Moskovitz) **3:**636
"Jacob's Dream" (paint., Ribera) **9:**1205
Jacobsen (19th cent., Ger.) **13:**989
JACOBSEN, ARNE EMIL **9:**1238
Jacobsen, Thorkild **16:**1508
Jacob the Small, *see* JACOB HA-KATAN
JACOBSON, KURT **5:**384
- Portugal **13:**926
Jacobsohn, P. B. **15:**1044
JACOBSOHN, SIEGFRIED **9:**1238
Jacobson, Avigdor, *see* JACOBSON, VICTOR
JACOBSON, DAN **9:**1239
- *illus:*
- - *The Zulu and the Zayda* **14:**1650
Jacobson, David **14:**823
JACOBSON, EDWARD (Eddie) **9:**1239
- Truman, Harry **15:**1408
- *illus:*
- - Truman, Harry, and **4:**1146
Jacobson, Harold G. (sci., U.S.) **11:**1201
Jacobson, Harry (act.), *see* JACKSON, HARRY
Jacobson, Hilda **12:**945
Jacobson, Howard **15:**310
JACOBSON, ISRAEL **9:**1240
- organ, used by **12:**1454
- Westphalia **16:**474
- Wolfenbuettel school **16:**609
- *illus:* text
JACOBSON, LUDVIG LEVIN **9:**1241
- *illus:* text
Jacobson, M. (prch.) **8:**958
Jacobson, Meir (Mayer; mer., Ger.) **9:**1240; **14:**1097
Jacobson, Mink Samson **9:**1240
Jacobson, M. L. **13:**707
Jacobson, N. **11:**1284
JACOBSON, PAUL HEINRICH **9:**1242
Jacobson, Samuel **15:**307, 308
JACOBSON, SYDNEY **9:**1242
JACOBSON, VICTOR **9:**1242
- Zionism **16:**1075ff
Jacobson, W. S. **8:**957
Jacobson de Jong, Moses **11:**1297
Jacobsson, Morris **4:**177
Jacob's staff (astron. instr.) **3:**804
- Levi ben Gershom **11:**98
- nautical aid **14:**1413
- *illus:* **8:**1430
Jacobsthal, E. **3:**359
JACOBSTHAL, GUSTAV **12:**694
JACOBSTHAL, PAUL FERDINAND **9:**1243
Jacob's Well (Er. Isr.) **14:**1492
JACOBUS APELLA VICEDOMINUS **9:**1244
"Jacob Wrestling with the Angel" (paint., Rembrandt) **9:**1199
Jacoby, Ḥanokh **12:**670
Jacoby, Hosea **16:**917
JACOBY, JOHANN **9:**1244
- *illus:* text
JACOBY, OSWALD **9:**1245
Jacoby, Philo **15:**313; **15:**315
Jacoby, Sigismund **11:**1286
Jacome de Mallorca, *see* Cresques, Judah
Jacotin (Fr. cartog.) **11:**928
Jacques, Heinrich **10:**1493
Jacques, M. E., *see* ZHERNENSKY, MOSHE ELIYAHU
Jacques Duèse (pope), *see* JOHN XXII
Jacubson, Gedaliah Samuel **4:**455
Jacur, Leone Romanin **13:**557
JADASSOHN, JOSEF **9:**1245
JADASSOHN, SALOMON **12:**694
JADDUA (Jaddus; h. pr.) **9:**1246
- Alexander the Great **2:**577
- history **8:**625
- Sanballat **14:**824
Jaddua the Babylonian (tan.) **15:**800
Jadid, Salaḥ **15:**649
JADĪD AL-ISLĀM (forced convs.) **9:**1246
- Abbas II **2:**39
- Persian Jews **3:**174; **13:**319
JADLOWKER, HERMANN **12:**694
Jadovno (concen. camp., Croatia) **16:**877
Jadwin, E. **12:**323
JAECKLIN, JUD **9:**1246
Jaeger, Karl **16:**41
JAEL (bib. fig.) **9:**1247
- arts **5:**1432
- *illus:*
- - text
- - killing Sisera **14:**1622
JAÉN (city, Sp.) **9:**1248
Ja'far (Ott. comm.) **9:**289
JAFFA (brs., U.S.) **9:**1248
JAFFA (city, Er. Isr.) **9:**1249
- *Contents:*
- - Early History **9:**1249
- - Hellenistic Period **9:**1250
- - Roman Period **9:**1250
- - Arab Period (636-1099) **9:**1251
- - Crusader Period (1099-1268) **9:**1252
- - Mamluk Period (1268-1517) **9:**1253
- - Ottoman Period (1517-1831) **9:**1254
- - Modern Period **9:**1254
- History
- - Crusades **5:**1139; **9:**267; **9:**269
- - Hasmoneans **8:**630; **8:**635
- - history chart (1906,1921) **8:**766-767
- - Mamluk destruction **9:**278
- - post-Jewish war **9:**237; **9:**245
- - Ẓāhir al-Omar **9:**291ff
- Community
- - Ashkenazi community **9:**497
- - Chelouche, Aharon **15:**919
- - early Zionist activity **15:**919
- - human geography **9:**571
- - Maghreb community **9:**499
- - religious life **9:**891ff
- - Rokach, Shimon **15:**919
- - Samaritans **14:**734
- - Tel Aviv **15:**916ff
- - Templers' settlement **15:**995
- Trade and Commerce **15:**1294
- - harbor **9:**832

- - post office **15:**330
- - shipping **14:**1412
- *illus:*
- - text
- - Arab rioters, (1936) **9:**464
- - clock tower, Turkish **3:**347
- - Herzlia Gymnasium class **11:**1448
- - Israel stamp **9:**844-845
- - "Women on the Beach of Jaffa" (paint., N. Gutman) Fig. 90 3-ART
Jaffa, Henry N. **9:**1248
Jaffa, Nathan **9:**1248
- mayor **12:**1038
Jaffa Gate (Jer.) **9:**1433
- *illus:*
- - Allenby entering Old City **9:**1472
- - area in front of (c. 1913) **9:**1469
- - general view **9:**1427
- - inscriptions **9:**288,1428
Jaffa Hill (tourist area, Isr.) **15:**924
Jaffa National Chamber of Commerce **9:**829
Jaffa orange **5:**581; **9:**571; **9:**707
Jaffa Sea (Er. Isr.) **9:**1249
JAFFE (fam., Pol.) **9:**1258
Jaffe (fam. name), *see also* Jaffee; Joffe; Yaffe; Yoffe; Yoffey
Jaffe, Aaron **9:**1261
JAFFE, ABRAHAM B. **9:**1259
Jaffe, Arthur **9:**1266
JAFFE, BENJAMIN **1:**32
- Jaffe, Leib **9:**1263
JAFFE, BEZALEL **9:**1260
- *geneal. table:* **9:**1259
Jaffe, Daniel (Ger.) **15:**1011
Jaffe, Daniel Joseph (Ire.) **4:**415; **9:**1265
Jaffe, E. (r., S.A.) **13:**1058
Jaffe, E. L. (plwrt.) **6:**198
Jaffe, Ernest (sci.) **11:**1200
Jaffe, Hannah **9:**1258
Jaffe, Ḥayyim **9:**1259
Jaffe, Israel (publ., Rus.) **9:**1057
JAFFE, ISRAEL BEN AARON (kab.) **9:**1261
Jaffe, Joseph (Const.) **9:**1266
Jaffe, Joseph (Pol.) **9:**1259
Jaffe, Joseph ben Moses (Rus.), *see* Yoffey, Joseph ben Moses
Jaffe, Kalonymus **9:**1258; **14:**1261
JAFFE, LEIB **9:**1262
- *geneal. table:* **9:**1259
- *illus:*
- - text
- - Keren Hayesod bldg. cornerstone ceremony **10:**916
- - Passfield protest **16:**1118
Jaffe, Leo **16:**1165
JAFFE, LEONARD **2:**322; **2:**323
Jaffe, M. (poet) **16:**822
Jaffe, Max (sci.) **10:**1129
JAFFE, MEIR OF ULM **9:**1263
- art **3:**523
- books **4:**1230
- *illus:*
- - Bible binding **4:**1228
- - *First Cincinnati Haggadah* **4:**fcg. 364; **7:**1083
JAFFE, MORDECAI BEN ABRAHAM **9:**1263
- *Anim Zemirot* **3:**22
- codification **11:**335 **5:**653
- cosmic cycles **10:**583
- *Shulḥan Arukh* **14:**1476
- *geneal. table:* **9:**1259
JAFFE, MORDECAI-GIMPEL **9:**1265
- Naḥmanides **15:**521
- *geneal. table:* **9:**1259
JAFFE, SIR OTTO **9:**1265
- mayor **4:**415
Jaffe, Philip **8:**543
Jaffe, Ruth **13:**1340
JAFFE, SAM **12:**468
JAFFE, SAMUEL BEN ISAAC ASHKENAZI **9:**1266
Jaffe, Sarah **9:**1259
Jaffe, Shlomo E. **12:**1094
Jaffe, Solomon Zalman **9:**1259
Jaffe, Ẓevi Hirsch **9:**1259
- *illus:*
- - *Kiddushin* (Lublin, 1618) **11:**544
Jaffee, Alan **5:**220
Jaffee, G. M. **15:**311
Jaffee, Irving **12:**1376; **15:**317
JAFFE-MARGOLIOT, ISRAEL DAVID **9:**1266
- astronomy **3:**806
JAGEL, ABRAHAM **9:**1267
- autobiography **4:**1011
JAGEL, ABRAHAM BEN HANANIAH DEI GALICCHI **9:**1268
- ten lost tribes **15:**1005
- identification **9:**1267
- visions **16:**169
- *illus:* text
Jagel, Camillo **9:**1269
Jahali (Assyr. offic.) **11:**511
JAHAZ, JAHAZA (city, Moab) **9:**1269
Jahbadh (coin tester) **14:**886
Jahbadhiyya (bnk.) **4:**167
Jahijan (loc., Iraq) **8:**1447
Jahn, Father **8:**330
Jahn, J. **8:**39
Jahoel (angel) **11:**1444
Jahon, Isaac **14:**708
Jahrbuch der Juedisch-Literarischen Gesellschaft (annual, Ger.) **10:**465
Jahrbuch fuer Israeliten (annual, Vienna) **10:**1172; **15:**657
Jahrbuecher fuer juedische Geschichte und Literatur (annual, Ger.) **4:**1415; **16:**106
Jahrzeit (anniversary of death), *see* YAHRZEIT
Jahshān, Adīb **9:**1039
Jahzah, *see* JAHAZ
Jahzeel (tribal clan) **12:**818
Jai Alai (sport) **15:**311
Jails, *see* IMPRISONMENT
Jaime Ribes, *see* Cresques, Judah
Jaim Zhitlowsky school (Urug.) **16:**14
JAIR (bib. fam., fig.) **9:**1269
Jair (bib. judge) **9:**1269
- Judges, Book of **10:**448
Jair, Isaac **5:**484
Jair ben Manasseh (bib. fig.) **9:**1270
Jaïs, Meyer **7:**1126
Jais, Roger **2:**617
Jajinci (vill., Yug.) **16:**874; **16:**875
Jakarta (city, Indon.) **8:**1363
Jakeh (k.), *see* SOLOMON
Jakim (h. pr.), *see* ALCIMUS
Jakim (anc. fam., Er. Isr.) **14:**626
Jakmak (sult., Egy.), *see* Jaqmaq, al-Ẓāhir Sayf-al-Dīn
Jakób of Belzyce, *see* JACOB OF BELZYCE
JAKOBOVITS, IMMANUEL **9:**1270
- autopsies **3:**933
- transplants **15:**1337ff
- United Synagogue **15:**1672
Jakobovits, Julius **9:**1270
JAKOBOVITS, TOBIAS **9:**1270
JAKOBSON, MAX **13:**827
JAKOBSON, ROMAN **9:**1271
- anthropology **3:**40
Jakobstadt (tn., Latv.), *see* JEKABPILS
Jaktorow (concen. camp, Pol.) **16:**1218
Jakubowicz (Lodz ghetto) **11:**436
Jalʿa (tn., Iraq) **8:**1450
Jal'aza (Assyr. satrapy) **7:**571
Jaljūliya (vill., Isr.) **7:**573
Jalomstein, M. **16:**833
Jama, Jacob ibn **9:**1271
JAMA, SAMUEL IBN **9:**1271
JAMAICA (W. Indies) **9:**1272
- America **2:**809
- Latin America **10:**1451
- slave trade **14:**1663
- sugar trade **15:**488
- synagogues **1:**syn. list
- tax **15:**840
- *illus:* text
JAMAL, SOLOMON (Suleiman) **9:**1274
Jamal Pasha **9:**333
- Aaronsohn, Aaron **2:**27
- Jewish expulsions **16:**1078
- Jewish Legion **10:**69
- *illus:*
- - governor of Jerusalem, and **9:**332
Jámbor, Ferenc **15:**1510
Jambres (leg. Egy. sorcerer), *see* JANNES AND JAMBRES
James (br. of Jesus) **10:**10ff
- Apostolic Council **3:**216
- Jacob of Kefar Sakhnayya **9:**1233
- Sanhedrin **14:**836
James (apostle) **15:**1005
James I (k., Aragon)
- Alconstantini, Baḥye and Solomon **2:**550
- Barcelona **4:**209; **4:**213
- censorship **5:**277
- informers **8:**1366
- Jewish badge **4:**66
- Naḥmanides **12:**775
- slave trade **14:**1661
- Spain **15:**231
- Vives ben Joseph **2:**70
James I (k., Eng.) **6:**1285
James II (k., Aragon)
- Bonsenyor, Judah **4:**1213
- Burriana **4:**1530
- Pastoureaux **5:**1141
- Spain **15:**234
James, Al **15:**306
JAMES, DAVID **15:**1086
JAMES, HARRY (mus.) **12:**694
James, Henry (au.) **15:**1571
JAMES, SIDNEY **12:**469
James Striar School of Jewish Studies (N.Y.) **16:**761
Jāmiʿ al-Alfāz (wk.), *see Kitāb Jāmiʿ al-Alfāz*
Jamin (bib. fig.) **14:**1549
Jamla (vill., Jor.) **7:**295
Jamma (tell, Isr.) **5:**1131; **11:**1428; **11:**1433; **13:**343
Jammāla (ruin, Er. Isr.) **10:**881
JAMMER, MOSHE **13:**492
Jamnia (tn., Er. Isr.), *see* JABNEH
Jamnia (toparchy, Er. Isr.) **9:**121
Jamnitz (tn., Cz.), *see* JEMNICE
JAMPEL, SIGMUND **9:**1275
Jamūsīn (vill., Isr.) **15:**923
Janah (city, Er. Isr.), *see* JANOAH
Janāḥ, Jonah ibn, *see* IBN JANĀḤ, JONAH
Jana Jasienskiego (print. firm) **16:**148
Jān-Birdi al-Ghazālī **9:**282
JANCO, MARCEL **9:**1275
- art **3:**592ff
- *illus:*
- - Baltazar, Camil (drg.) **4:**144
- - Fondane, Benjamin (caric.) **6:**1413
- - "Ma'abarah" (paint.) Fig. 97 3-ART
Janesville (city, Wis.) **16:**556
Janina (tn., reg., Gr.), *see* IOANNINA
Janissaries (sols., Ott. emp.) **2:**615; **16:**1538
Janissaries' Revolt (1330) **4:**563
JANKÉLÉVITCH, VLADIMIR **9:**1276
Janks, Mickey **15:**309
Jannaeus, Alexander, *see* YANNAI, ALEXANDER
JANNER, LORD BARNETT **9:**1276
- *illus:*
- - text
- - Board of Deputies celebration **6:**773
Janner, Greville Ewan **9:**1277
JANNES AND JAMBRES (leg. Egy. sorcerers) **9:**1277
- Golden Calf **7:**711
JANOAH, JANAH (cities, Er. Isr.) **9:**1277
Janovice (loc., Cz.) **10:**1087
Janovo (tn., Lith.), *see* JONAVA
JANOVSKY, SAUL JOSEPH **9:**1278
- socialism **15:**33
Janower, Joseph **15:**198
Janowicz, Yiẓḥak **13:**1294
Janowitz, Hans **12:**453
JANOWITZ, HENRY D. **11:**1208
JANOWITZ, MORRIS **9:**1278
JANOW LUBELSKI (tn., Pol.) **9:**1278
Janów Polski (tn., Belor.), *see* IVANOVO
Janowska Road Camp (Lvov, Ukr.) **11:**615
JANOWSKI, DAVID MARKELOVICH **5:**408
JANOWSKY, OSCAR ISAIAH **1:**32; **9:**1279
Janszon (cartog.) **11:**927
Janthur, Richard **11:**1237
Janua, Peter de **4:**213
JANUARIUS (leg. gen.) **9:**1280
January (month) **9:**1280
Janus (Rom. k.) **9:**1280
Janvier (Januarius), René **8:**39
JAPAN **9:**1280
- Anti-Semitism **14:**1161
- Israel **9:**433
- Judaizers **10:**398
- population **13:**887ff
- synagogues **1:**syn. list
- Ten Lost Tribes **15:**1006
- Tokyo **15:**1192
- *illus:* text
JAPHET, ISRAEL MEYER **9:**1284
Japhet, Ludwig **15:**306
Japhet, S. **4:**175
JAPHETH (bib. fig.) **9:**1284
- Canaan, curse of **5:**98
- in the Arts **12:**1197
- Noah **12:**1191
- *illus:*
- - text
- - covering the naked Noah **6:**238; **14:**1369
JAPHETH AL-BARQAMĀNĪ **9:**1285
Japheth ben Abraham **12:**64
Japheth ben Ali, *see* Japheth ben Elijah
JAPHETH BEN ALI HA-LEVI **9:**1286
- Karaites **10:**766
Japheth (Hasan) ben Bendar **2:**260; **12:**763; **16:**741
JAPHETH BEN DAVID IBN ṢAGHĪR **9:**1286
Japheth ben Elijah **2:**223; **11:**756; **11:**762
Japheth ben Manasseh of Corfu **8:**231
Japheth Printing Press (Isr.) **13:**1379
JAPHIA (city, Er. Isr.) **9:**1286
- synagogue **15:**598
Jaqmaq, al-Ẓāhir Sayf-al-Dīn
- Ereẓ Israel **9:**274
- Jerusalem **9:**1424
Jaquelot, Isaac **2:**947

Jaquete, Soliman **2:**622
Jar, Alexandru **14:**424
Jarash (tn., Transj.) **9:**596; **12:**181; **15:**1318
Jarawa (tribe, Alg.) **2:**612; **13:**1417; **15:**1432
Jarbā (loc., Transj.) **9:**264
JARBLUM, MARC **9:**1287
- Russia **14:**499
- Zionism **16:**1114
- *illus:* text
Jarcho, Saul **11:**1198
JARÈ (It. fam.) **9:**1287
Jarè, Berechiah Reuben **9:**1287
Jarè, Giuseppe di Graziadio **9:**1288
Jarè, Isaac **9:**1288
Jarè, Mordecai **9:**1288
Jarè, Moses **9:**1287
Jarè, Pethahiah **9:**1287
Jarecka, Gustawa **13:**802
Jarīd (J. center, N. Afr.) **8:**1149
Jargon (lang.), *see* YIDDISH
Jarkon (riv., Isr.), *see* YARKON
Jarmon (Jarmona; N. Afr. fam.), *see* DARMON
Jarman (Jarmūn; Rom. agent) **4:**17
JARMUTH (city, Er. Isr.) **9:**1288
- *see also:* RAMOTH
Jaroslavsky, Naum **13:**820
JAROSLAW (tn., Pol.) **9:**1288
- *illus:* text
Jaroslaw, Aaron **4:**875
Jaross, Andor **8:**1099
Jarrett, Thomas **8:**39
Jarring, Gunnar **15:**1552ff
- Middle East peace talks **9:**415
- Six-Day War **14:**1640
- Syria **15:**649
- *illus:*
- - Meir, Golda, and **9:**410
Jarvik, Murray **13:**1345
Jasenovac (vill., camp, Yug.) **8:**858; **14:872; 16:**877
- Split Jewry **15:**290
Jashar, Book of (anon. wk.), *see* SEFER HA-YASHAR
JASIEŃSKI, BRUNO **9:**1290
JASINOWSKI, ISRAEL ISIDORE **9:**1290
- Hovevei Zion **16:**337
- *illus:*
- - F.Z.C. **16:**1165
Jasius (philos.), *see* Gesius
JASLO (tn., Pol.) **9:**1290
Jasmin (bot.) **6:**1366; **8:**1311
JASNY, NAUM **9:**1291
JASON **9:**1291
- Antiochus IV **3:**74; **8:**628
- history chart **8:**766-767
- *Maccabees II* **11:**658ff
- Hellenism **8:**295; **9:**1390
- Jerusalem **13:**1086
- Tobiads **15:**1180
- war and warfare **16:**278
Jason, Tomb of (Jer.) **9:**1393
- inscriptions **2:**689; **16:**669
Jason ben Eleazar **14:**240
JASON OF CYRENE **9:**1292
- Cyrene **5:**1184
- history **8:**553
Jasov. Jacob ben Abraham of **5:**561
Jasper (gem)
- *bareqet* **13:**1009
- *'odem* **13:**1009
- *yashfeh* **13:**1011
Jassa, de (fam., Sp.) **15:**1300
JASSINOWSKY, PINCHAS **9:**1292
JASSY (city, Rum.) **9:**1293
- Rumania **14:**386, 388, 390, 391, 395, 397, 398
- *illus:*
- - Jews slaughtered **14:**400
- - *more judaico* (1886) **12:**1304
JASTROW (fam.) **9:**1296
Jastrow, Joseph **9:**1298; **13:**1344
Jastrow, Marcus Mordecai **8:**957 **9:**1296
Jastrow, Morris **9:**1297
- linguistic literature **16:**1390
JASTRUN, MIECZYSLAW **9:**1208
JÁSZI, OSZKÁR **9:**1299
Jataka (Ind. fables) **3:**20
JÁTIVA (city, Sp.) **9:**1299
Jatt (vill., Er. Isr.) **7:**335; **9:**589
JATTIR, JETHIRA (city, Er. Isr.) **9:**1300
Jau, Jacob Ibn, *see* IBN JAU, JACOB
Ja'ūna (stimt., Er. Isr.) **14:**311, 1002
JAUNJELGAVA (city, Latv.) **9:**1300
JAURÈS, JEAN LÉON **9:**1301
- Dreyfus Affair **6:**229
Java (Indon. isl.) **8:**1363
JAVAL (fam.) **9:**1301
Javal, Adolphe **9:**1301
Javal, Emile **9:**1301
Javal, Ernest **9:**1301
Javal, Jacques **9:**1301
Javal, Jean **9:**1301
Javal, Leopold **9:**1301
JAVAN (bib. fig.) **9:**1301
- Rhodians **14:**215
- Zechariah **16:**957
Javan (bib. loc.) **11:**1433
Javan (loc., S.E. Eur.) **11:**667
Javelin (weapon) **16:**266ff
JAVETZ, BARZILLAI BEN BARUCH **9:**1302
JAVID BEY **9:**1302
JAVITS, JACOB KOPPEL **9:**1302
Javorov (city, Ukr.), *see* YAVOROV
Jawālī (tax, Ott. Emp.), *see* KHARĀJ AND JIZYA
Jawhar, Al (mil. ldr.) **13:**49
Jawitz, Joseph, *see* JABEZ, JOSEPH BEN HAYYIM
JAWITZ, ZE'EV **9:**1303
- children's literature **5:**432
- Hebrew literature **8:**198
- history **8:**562
- travels **15:**1354
Jawnieli, Shemuel, *see* YAVNE'ELI, SHEMUEL
Jawno, Lionel **10:**1001
Jaworów (city, Ukr.), *see* YAVOROV
Jaww, Jacob Ibn, *see* IBN JAU, JACOB
Jawziya, Ibn Qayyim ibn al-, *see* Ibn Qayyim ibn al-Jawziya
Jay, Allan **12:**1377
Jazaniah (bib. figs.), *see* JAAZANIAH
JAZER (city, Jor.) **9:**1304
Jazīrat Far'ūn (isl., Gulf of Elath) **6:**1103; **15:**1146
- Jotabah **10:**300
JAZĪRAT IBN 'UMAR (tn., Iraq) **9:**1305
Jazzār, Abu al- **11:**1187
Jazzar, Al (msq., Isr.) **2:**226; **9:**919
Jazzār, Al- (school, Er. Isr.) **9:**919
J.B.O. (J. educ. found., Amst.), *see* Joods Bijzonder Onderwijs
J.C.R., *see* JEWISH CULTURAL RECONSTRUCTION
J.D.C., *see* AMERICAN JEWISH JOINT DISTRIBUTION COMMITTEE
J.D.L., *see* Jewish Defense League
JEALOUSY **9:**1305
- man and wife **15:**170
- ordeal **12:**1449
Jean ben Samuel of Falaise **6:**1140
Jean de Saint-Rémy **12:**1230
Jean François de Binans, *see* Binans, Jean François de
Jean-Javal, Lily **7:**148; **9:**1301
Jean le Roux **7:**14
Jeanne (q., Fr.) **13:**1260; **15:**807
Jeanneret, Charles Edouard, *see* Le Corbusier
J.E.A.S. (soc., Pol.) **14:**1533
Jebaltowsky, Morris, *see* Jeby, Ben
Jebel (fort., Er. Isr.), *see* DOK
Jebel (reg., Isr.), *see* SEIR, MOUNT
Jebel (mt.) . . ., *see also:* Jabal . . ., Jabel . . .
Jebel Abu Hasan (Egy.) **4:**13
Jebel 'Akkār (Leb.) **8:**972
Jebel al-Ahmar (Er. Isr.) **9:**176
Jebel al-'Aṣūr **4:**4
Jebel al-Dahī (bib. loc.), *see* Gibeath-Moreh
Jebel al-Halāl **6:**1049; **14:**1599
Jebel al-Hasā' **15:**1316
Jebel al-Rumayda **8:**226
Jebel al-Sheikh (al-Thalj), *see* HERMON, MOUNT
Jebel al-Sudūm **9:**159; **9:**164; **15:**70
- *illus:*
- - Dead Sea shore **9:**161
Jebel al-Ṭūr, *see* GERIZIM, MOUNT
Jebel Bāqir **9:**176
Jebel Barāsh (Yem.) **14:**820
Jebel el-Aqra' (As.) **4:**9
Jebel el-Druze **4:**293; **7:**1477; **9:**924; **9:**927
Jebel Fārān **13:**88
Jebel Fureidis **8:**389
Jebel Halāl, *see* Jebel al-Halāl
Jebel Hallet eṭ-Ṭūri **16:**669
Jebel Hārūn **8:**972
Jebeli (lang., Kurd.), *see* Jabali
Jebel Judi, *see* Ture Kardu
Jebel Katherina **6:**1049; **11:**931; **14:**1599
Jebel Libni **14:**1606
- *illus:*
- - Eshkol with soldiers (1967) **9:**409
Jebel Madra **8:**971
Jebel Maghāra **14:**1599
Jebel Makmal **8:**972
Jebel Musa **6:**1049; **14:**1594ff
Jebel Nafūsh (N. Afr.) **8:**1149
Jebel Qafza **12:**900
Jebel Qarantal (mt., Er. Isr.), *see* Mons Quarantana
Jebel Qiblī **9:**284
Jebel Rafayd **14:**80
Jebel Serbal, *see* Jebel Sirbāl
Jebel Shāmī **9:**284
Jebel Shayhān **12:**910
Jebel Shomar **14:**1599
Jebel Sīhān **15:**1316
Jebel Sinn-Bishr **6:**1049; **14:**1599
Jebel Sirbāl **6:**1049; **11:**931; **14:**1599
Jebel Ya'allaq **6:**1049
Jeberechiah (bib. fig.) **16:**958
JEBUS, JEBUSITE (bib. people) **9:**1307
- Araunah **3:**290
- Judah, tribe of **8:**579; **10:**329
- Uriah **16:**5
- Zion **16:**1030
- *illus:*
- - Jerusalem, city wall **9:**1382
- - Jerusalem, eastern ridge **9:**1381
- - Zion citadel **9:**1384
Jeby, Ben **15:**305
Jechoniah (Jeconiah; k., Judah), *see* JEHOIACHIN
JEDAIAH (bib. figs.) **9:**1308
- Jehoiarib **9:**1322
- Jeshua's lineage **10:**2
- priestly divisions **12:**89
- Ptolemaic period **8:**626
- Temple **15:**980
- Zechariah **16:**955
JEDAIAH BEN ABRAHAM BEDERSI (ha-Penini) **9:**1308
- Béziers yeshivah **16:**763
- didactic literature **11:**353
- Maimonidean controversy **11:**752
- *Mivhar ha-Peninim* **12:**164
- poetry **13:**689
Jedīd al-Islām (forced convs.), *see* JADID AL-ISLAM
Jedidiah, *see* SOLOMON
Jedidiah (ben Jesse) **14:**974
Jedidiah, Raphael **16:**1536
Jedidiah ben Aryeh Judah Leib ha-Kohen **3:**667
JEDIDIAH (AMADIO) BEN MOSES OF RECANATI (Rimini) **9:**1310
Jedidiah ben Zakkai **12:**835
Jedidiah of Melun **11:**1296
Jedidiah of Nuremberg **9:**1071
Jedidja (newsp.) **5:**456
Jedioth Hadashoth (newsp.) **9:**1017
JEDRZEJOW (tn., Pol.) **9:**1310
JEDUTHUN (bib. fig.) **9:**1311
- Asaphites **3:**672
- Psalms, Book of
Jeduthun ha-Levi **13:**583
Jefferson (city, Tex.) **15:**1035
JEFFERSON, THOMAS **9:**1311
- *illus:*
- - statue by M. Ezekiel **11:**521
Jefferson City (city, Mo.) **12:**158
Jeffroykin, Jules **16:**1115
Jegier, Samuel **11:**538; **13:**775
Jehezekiah bar Halafta **15:**1324
Jehezkel, David ben Ben Zion, *see* David ben Ben Zion Jehezkel
Jehiel (18th cent., r., Hung.) **15:**659
Jehiel bar Mattathias Beit-El, *see* Pisa, Vitale da
Jehiel ben Abraham **13:**585
Jehiel ben Asher **13:**585
Jehiel ben Isaac of Pisa, *see* Pisa, Vitale da
Jehiel ben Israel Luria **13:**585
Jehiel ben Jacob min ha-Anavim (Anav) **13:**585
Jehiel ben Jekuthiel ben Benjamin ha-Rofe **15:**776
Jehiel ben Jekuthiel of Rome **16:**531
Jehiel ben Joseph **13:**585
JEHIEL BEN JOSEPH OF PARIS (tos.) **9:**1312
- Acre *aliyah* **9:**274; **9:**511
- apologetics **11:**354
- Donin, Nicholas **6:**167
- history chart **8:**766-767
- Isaac ben Joseph of Corbeil **9:**21
- Paris disputation **6:**92
- yeshivah **16:**764
Jehiel ben Mattathias **13:**104
Jehiel ben Moses Saks, *see* Saks, Jehiel ben Moses
Jehiel da Pesaro, *see* Vitale de'Medici
JEHIEL MEIR (LIFSCHITS) OF GOSTYNIN **9:**1312
- Perlmutter, Abraham Zevi **13:**297
JEHIEL MICHAEL (Michel) BEN ABRAHAM MEIR OF CIFER **9:**1313
JEHIEL MICHAEL (Michel) BEN ELIEZER **9:**1313
JEHIEL MICHAEL (Michel) BEN JUDAH LEIB HE-HASID **9:**1314
Jehiel Michael of Michelisbok **13:**989
JEHIEL MICHAEL (Michel) OF ZLOCZOW **9:**1314
Jehiel Mikhal ben Uzziel **10:**552
Jehiel of Italy **16:**1360,1388
Jehiel of Paris (tos.), *see* JEHIEL BEN JOSEPH OF PARIS
Jehiel of Porto **7:**960
Jehiel of Rome **2:**568 **13:**853; **14:**246
Jehiel of Wuerzburg **12:**63
Jehiel Trabotto ben Azriel, *see* Trabot, Jehiel ben Azriel
Jehne, L. H. S. **8:**39

Jehoahaz (9th cent. B.C.E., k., Judah), *see* AHAZIAH
JEHOAHAZ (k., Isr.) **9:**1315
- history **8:**600ff
- history chart **8:**766-767
JEHOAHAZ (7th cent. B.C.E., k., Judah) **9:**1316
- anointing **3:**31
- history **8:**607
- history chart **8:**766-767
- kingship **10:**1013
- Neco **12:**919
Jehoash (835-793 B.C.E., k., Judah), *see* JOASH
JEHOASH (801-785 B.C.E., k., Isr.) **9:**1317
- Amaziah **2:**798; **4:**773
- history **8:**600ff
- history chart **8:**766-767
- Nergal-eseš stele **16:**1509
Jehohanan son of Eliashib (Temple offic.) **15:**957
Jehohanan son of Tobiah (bib. fig.) **15:**1179
JEHOIACHIN (k., Judah) **9:**1318
- Amel Marduk **16:**1270
- Exile, Babylonian **6:**1037
- history **8:**600
- history chart **8:**766-767
- in the Arts **9:**1360; **12:**917
- Shealtiel **14:**1328
- tomb **10:**1285
- Zedekiah **16:**961
- Zerubbabel **16:**1000; **16:**1001
- *geneal. table:* **5:**1341
JEHOIADA (h. pr.) **9:**1319
- Jerusalem revolt **8:**600
- Joash **10:**110
- priesthood **13:**1084
- Temple **15:**944
JEHOIAKIM (k., Judah) **9:**1321
- Baruch's scroll **4:**266
- Elnathan ben Achbor **6:**684
- Exile, Babylonian **6:**1037
- history **8:**607ff
- history chart **8:**766-767
- Neco **12:**919
- Rechabites **13:**1609
- Zebudah **16:**951
- Zephania **16:**994
- *geneal. table:* **5:**1341
JEHOIARIB (pr. clan) **9:**1322
- Jedaiah **9:**1308
- priestly divisions **12:**89; **12:**90
JEHORAM (k., Isr.) **9:**1323
- Edom **6:**375
- Elisha **6:**665
- history **8:**598
- history chart **8:**766-767
- Jehoram son of Jehoshaphat **9:**1324
- Jehoshaphat **9:**1325ff
- *illus:*
- - Moabite stone record **3:**319
JEHORAM (k., Judah) **9:**1324
- Ahab **2:**435
- Athaliah **3:**814
- history **8:**599ff
- history chart **8:**766-767
- *geneal. table:* **5:**1341
JEHOSEPH HA-NAGID **9:**1324
- Albalia, Isaac **2:**522
- Ali ben Amram **2:**631
- Daniel ben Azariah **5:**1291
- Muslim Spain **8:**666
- Samuel ha-Nagid **14:**816
- Zirids **16:**1184
Jehoshaphat (bib. fig.) **14:**789
JEHOSHAPHAT (k., Judah) **9:**1325
- Ahaziah **2:**456
- Asahel **3:**672
- Edom **6:**375
- history **8:**598ff
- history chart **8:**766-767
- merchant fleet **14:**1411
- trade and commerce **15:**1295
- Zedekiah **16:**964
- *geneal. table:* **5:**1341
- *illus:*
- - Moabite stone record **3:**319
Jehoshaphat (Kar.) **9:**266
Jehoshaphat, Tomb of (Jer.) **9:**1327; **9:**1398
JEHOSHAPHAT, VALLEY OF (Er. Isr.) **9:**1327
- Kidron Valley **10:**988
- *illus:*
- - Tomb of Miriam **9:**1417
Jehosheba (bib. fig.) **3:**814; **9:**1319; **10:**110
Jehosiphia the Proselyte, *see* JOSIPHIAH THE PROSELYTE
JÉHOUDA, JOSUÉ **7:**150
Jehovah (name of God) **7:**680
Jehozabad (bib. fig.) **10:**111
Jehozadak (pr.) **10:**1
JEHU (prophet) **9:**1328
- Baasha **4:**13
JEHU (k., Isr.) **9:**1328
- Ahaziah **2:**456
- anointing **3:**31
- Elisha **6:**665ff
- history **8:**599ff
- history chart **8:**766-767
- Israel, Kingdom of **9:**1047
- kingship **10:**1013
- Rechabites **13:**1609ff
- *illus:*
- - payment of tribute to Shalmaneser III **3:**220
Jeiel (bib. fig.) **10:**1063
JEITELES (fam.) **9:**1330
- *geneal. table:* text
- *illus:* text
Jeiteles, Aaron (apos.) **9:**1332
Jeiteles, Aaron ben Baer (tal.) **9:**1330
Jeiteles, Alois **9:**1332
Jeiteles, Andreas Ludwig Joseph Heinrich, *see* Jeiteles, Aaron
Jeiteles, Baruch (Benedict) **9:**1330
Jeiteles, Berl **9:**1330
Jeiteles, Berthold **9:**1333
Jeiteles, Bezalel (Gottlieb) **9:**1332
Jeiteles, Ḥayyim **12:**1419
Jeiteles, Ignaz (Isaac; writ.) **7:**523; **9:**1331
Jeiteles, Isaac (physic.) **9:**1332
Jeiteles, Isaac (nov.) **9:**1333
Jeiteles, Israel **9:**1330
Jeiteles, Issachar Baer (17th cent.), *see* Jeiteles, Berl
Jeiteles, Issashar Baer (19/20 cent.), *see* Jeiteles, Berthold
Jeiteles, Jonas **9:**1330
- *illus:* text
Jeiteles, Judah Loeb **7:**523; **9:**1332
Jeiteles, Leopold **9:**1332
Jeiteles, Loeb **9:**1330
Jeiteles, Mishel Loeb **9:**1330
Jeiteles, Moses ben Simeon **9:**1330
Jeiteles, Moses Wolf **9:**1330
Jeiteles, Richard **9:**1333
Jeiteles, Samuel **9:**1332
Jeiteles, Simon **9:**1330
Jeitteles (fam.), *see* JEITELES
JEKABPILS (tn., Latv.) **9:**1333
Jekele Bogaty, *see* Jacob Bogaty
JEKELES (fam.) **9:**1333
Jekeles, Isaac ben Jacob **9:**1334
Jekeles, Jutta **5:**34
Jekeles, Moses **5:**34
Jekeles, Moses ben Isaac **9:**1334
Jekeles, Moses ben Jacob **9:**1334
Jekelin of Strasbourg **4:**168
Jekel of Eiger, *see* JACOB OF VIENNA
Jekuthiel ben Isaac ha-Kohen **16:**1387
JEKUTHIEL BEN JUDAH HA-KOHEN **9:**1334
- *ga'yah* rules **16:**1450
- Masorah **16:**1476
Jekuthiel ben Moses ben Kalonymus **10:**720; **11:**326
Jekuthiel ben Solomon of Narbonne **15:**1328
Jekuthiel ha-Kohen, *see* Jekuthiel ben Isaac ha-Kohen
Jekuthiel Judah of Sighet, *see* Teitelbaum, Jekuthiel Judah
Jekuthiel Lazi ben Nahum Ashkenazi **9:**1231
Jekuthiel of Vilna **13:**585
Jekuthiel Shmelke of Sasov **12:**432
Jelenowicj, Hirsch **7:**742
JELEŃSKI, JAN **9:**1336
JELGAVA (city, Latv.) **9:**1336
Jelinek, Sydney **12:**1376
Jellenta, Cezary **13:**802
JELLIN, ARYEH LOEB BEN SHALOM SHAKHNA **9:**1337
Jellinek (fam.) **8:**1136
JELLINEK, ADOLF **9:**1337
- apologetics **3:**199
- history chart **8:**766-767
- Wise, Stephen **16:**568
- *illus:*
- - portrait **8:**708
JELLINEK, GEORG **10:**1491; **10:**1509
- Jellinek, Adolf **9:**1337
JELLINEK, HERMANN **9:**1339
- Jellinek, Adolf **9:**1337
JELLINEK, KARL **5:**384
Jellinek, Walter **10:**1509
Jellyfish (zool.) **6:**38
Jemal Pasha, *see* Jamal Pasha
Jemdat Nasr (arch. period) **16:**1485
Jemmeh (tell, Isr.) **11:**1428
JEMNICE (tn., Cz.) **9:**1339
- *illus:*
- - Jewish quarter **12:**300
Jemsel, Samuel ben David **14:**304
Jena (city, Ger.) **15:**1128
Jenei, György **8:**39
JENER, ABRAHAM NAPHTALI HIRSCH BEN MORDECAI **9:**1340
JENIN (tn., Samar.) **9:**1340
- En-Gannim **6:**741
- human geography **9:**587
- Mamluks **9:**274
- Six-Day War **14:**1630
JENKINSON, SIR HILARY **9:**1341
Jennikau, Aaron, *see* KORNFELD, AARON BEN MORDECAI BAER
Jennin (tn., Samar.), *see* JENIN
Jennings, David **8:**39
Jennis, Dennis, *see* ABOAB, ISAAC DE MATTATHIAS
Jephson, D. L. A. **15:**307
JEPHTHAH (bib. fig.) **9:**1341
- aggadic literature **6:**340
- Bible history **8:**586
- Judges, Book of **10:**448
- vow **16:**228
- *illus:* text
Jeqôn (angel) **2:**966
Jerablus (tn., Syr.) **5:**160
Jérada (tn., Mor.), *see* Djérada
Jerahmeel (bib. fig.) **14:**1549
JERAHMEEL BEN SOLOMON **9:**1345
- history **8:**555
Jeraka, Afda **13:**1110
Jeraka, Shabbetai **13:**1110
Jerash (tn., Transj.), *see* Jarash
Jerawa (tribe), *see* Jarawa
Jerba (isl., Tun.), *see* DJERBA
Jeremiad (lit. term) **10:**1375
JEREMIAH (prophet) **9:**1345
- Abiathar **2:**71
- Ahab, son of Kolaiah **2:**439
- Ahikam **2:**460
- Anathoth **2:**927
- Ark of Covenant legend **3:**464
- Balkh **4:**137
- Baruch **4:**270ff
- *Baruch, Book of* **4:**272
- *Baruch, Rest of the Words of* **4:**276
- *Ben Sira, Alphabet of* **4:**548
- Elnathan ben Achbor **6:**684
- eschatological writings **6:**867ff
- ethics **6:**934
- Exile, Babylonian **6:**1036ff
- Ezekiel **6:**1090; **6:**1093
- Haggai **16:**1001
- Hananiah, son of Azzur **7:**1256ff
- history chart **8:**766-767
- Hosea, Book of **8:**1016
- in the Arts **10:**1375
- Joseph ben Uzziel **10:**238
- Lamentations **10:**1370-1373
- letters **11:**55
- lost tribes **15:**1004
- messianism **6:**873ff
- Micah **11:**1481
- Obadiah **12:**1304
- poetry **13:**675ff
- Rechabites **13:**1609ff
- Septuagint **4:**852
- Tema **15:**940
- Zedekiah **16:**962ff
- *illus:*
- - text
- - Michelangelo (frsc.) **4:**940
- - mourning Jerusalem **13:**1417
- - Schatz, Boris (rlf.) Fig. 89 **3-ART**
- - thirteenth cent. manuscript **10:**1
Jeremiah (4th cent., B.C.E.) **9:**1362
Jeremiah (amora), *see* JEREMIAH BEN ABBA
"Jeremiah" (rlf., B. Schatz) Fig. 89 3-ART
Jeremiah, Chronicles of (apoc. bk.), *see* BARUCH, REST OF THE WORDS OF
JEREMIAH, EPISTLE OF (apoc. bk.) **9:**1361
- *Baruch, Rest of the Words of* **4:**276
Jeremiah bar Ḥiyya (amora) **8:**796
JEREMIAH BEN ABBA (amora) **9:**1362
- Isaac bar Joseph **9:**12
JEREMIAH BEN ISAAC (r.) **9:**1364
Jeremiah of Libnah (bib. fig.) **9:**1316
Jeremiah's Grotto (Jer.) **9:**1544
JEREMIAS, ALFRED **9:**1364
Jeremias, Karl **15:**1020
Jeremie (tn., Haiti) **7:**1142
Jeremiel (angel) **2:**962
Jeremy, Epistle of (apoc. bk.), *see* JEREMIAH, EPISTLE OF
JEREZ DE LA FRONTERA (city, Sp.) **9:**1364
JERICHO (tn., Er. Isr.) **9:**1365
- General
- - agriculture **2:**394
- - Arabah **3:**231
- - balsam **16:**1273
- - Crusaders **9:**267
- - human geography **9:**589
- - in the Arts **10:**268
- - palms and dates **13:**43
- - Six-Day War **14:**1635
- Archaeology
- - anthropological evidence **3:**45
- - fortifications **16:**273
- - Mesolithic art **3:**505
- - synagogues **15:**598ff
- - wooden objects **16:**630
- Bible
- - Achan **2:**209
- - Ahab **2:**437
- - city structure **5:**584
- - history **8:**578
- - *ir ha-niddaḥat* **8:**1470
- - proscription **8:**345ff
- *illus:*

- - text
- - Arab refugee camp 9:447
- - archaeological remains 3:41,501; 5:583
- - Bronze Age tomb 8:571
- - capture by Israelites 3:517
- - city walls 9:1148
- - collapse of the walls 10:264
- - *menorah* from synagogue 11:1360
- - plastered skull, Neolithic period 15:1219
- - synagogue mosaic 2:690
JEROBOAM (928-907 B.C.E., k., Isr.) 9:1371
- Abijah's war 2:75
- Ahijah the Shilonite 2:459
- anthropomorphism 3:53
- Baasha 4:13
- Beth-El shrine 4:729; 5:1164
- calendar 5:50
- golden calves 7:711; 7:738
- history 8:593; 8:593ff
- history chart 8:766-767
- in the Arts 15:109
- Israel, Kingdom of 9:1047ff
- Karaite schism 10:765
- Rehoboam 14:42
- sacrifice 14:606
- Shishak 14:1416
- Solomon 15:103
- Temple 15:944
- widow's son 16:490
- *illus:*
- - text
- - divided kingdom (map) 9:116
- - episodes 10:1028
JEROBOAM II (789-748 B.C.E., k., Isr.) 9:1374
- Amaziah 2:799
- history 8:601ff
- history chart 8:766-767
- Hosea 8:1010ff
- slander 10:1432
- *illus:*
- - text
- - divided kingdom (map) 9:117
Jeroham ben Joseph 3:1009
JEROHAM BEN MESHULLAM 9:1375
- codification of law 5:644
- Jewish literature 11:335
JEROME (Ch. F.) 9:1376
- Abrabanel, Isaac 2:106
- Alcuin 2:551
- Augustine 3:851
- Church Fathers 5:553
- Hebrew transcriptions 16:1569
- Jerusalem 9:1406
- map of Ereẓ Israel 11:919
- Septuagint 4:855
- Vulgate 4:857
Jerozolimski, Mendel Wolf ha-Kohen 11:430
Jerrawas (tribe), *see* Jarawa
Jerrmann, Eduard 15:1056
Jersey (isl.) 5:335
Jersey City (city, N.J.) 8:1057; 12:1028
Jerubaal (Jerubbesheth; bib. fig.), *see* GIDEON
Jerubaal (period.) 4:676
JERUSALEM 9:1378
- This entry is divided according to the following sub-divisions (1) Geography and Archaeology (2) History (3) Religions (4) The Arts
(1) GEOGRAPHY AND ARCHAEOLOGY
- Archaeological Survey 3:306ff; 9:1521
- - Avigad, N. 3:961
- - David's tomb 5:1329
- - Kidron Valley 10:987
- - Mazar, Benjamin 11:1150
- - *menorah* 11:1363ff
- - Olives, Mt. of 12:481
- - seal motif 14:1081
- - Temple Mount 15:988
- - Zion, Mt. 16:1030
- Cartography 9:1542
- - maps of world 11:920ff
- - Madaba map 11:677
- Geography 9:1513
- - Kidron Valley 10:987
- - mountains 9:140
- - Mount of Olives 12:481ff
- - Ophel 12:1413
- - Temple Mount 15:988
- - Western Wall 16:467
- Water Supply 9:1537
- - British Mandate Period 9:1471; 9:1480
- - Herod's palace 9:1394
- - Kidron 10:987
- - Mamluks 9:1424
- - Ottoman Rule 9:1457
- - Pontius Pilate 13:848
- - Siloam Pool 14:1399
- - Suleiman's fountains 9:1434
- *illus:*
- - text
- - Absalom's Tomb 3:340
- - Aelia Capitolina (plan) 2:319; 9:1401-1402
- - Antonia fortress (plan) 3:163
- - Avi-Yonah's model 8:633
- - Beth-Cherem citadel (plan) 4:717
- - Cave of Nicanor ossuary 12:1133
- - Damascus Gate 9:*fcg.* 174
- - David's tomb 8:924
- - Hasmonean city wall 9:1391
- - Herodian masonry, Temple esplanade 3:323
- - Herodian stone inscription 9:1501
- - Herod's city (model) 3:340
- - Herod's palace (reconst.) 8:380
- - Herod's Temple (reconst.) 3:511; 15:960
- - Hezekiah's pool 9:1460
- - Hezir family tomb 8:460; 15:1219
- - Jason's Tomb, restored 4:1518
- - Jebus, site and city wall 9:1381,1382
- - Kidron Valley monuments 3:509
- - Madaba map 11:677
- - Mamluk mausoleum 9:1424
- - Manaḥat village 9:581
- - Mount of Olives 12:481
- - Mount Scopus sarcophagus 12:1505
- - Old City gates 9:1427-1432
- - Ophel 12:1413
- - Ophel, dedicatory stone, 1st cent. synagogue 3:335
- - Ophel ostracon 12:1510
- - Phasael tower 9:1397
- - pictorial map, 12th cent. ms. 11:923
- - public fountains 9:1433,1434
- - Queen Helena's tomb 8:288
- - Robinson's Arch 14:205
- - Rockefeller Museum 14:212
- - Siloam graves 15:1220
- - Siloam pool 14:1400
- - Siloam Tunnel and inscription 3:316; 8:603
- - Talpiyyot *ma'barah* 11:653
- - Temple *menorah* 11:1358
- - Temple Mount 9:1399,1413
- - Tombs of the Sanhedrin 3:340; 6:171
- - Valley of Jehoshaphat 9:1328
- - Warren's shaft 16:333
- - Western Wall 8:923; 16:469-470
- - Wilson's Arch 16:535
- - Zechariah's Tomb 3:339; 9:1392; 15:1221
- - Zion, Jebusite citadel 9:1384
(2) HISTORY
- Name 9:1378
- - Shalem 14:1265
- Early History 9:1379
- - cultic center 5:1163ff
- - destruction, Babylonian 3:936ff; 10:1372
- - - in the Arts 10:1375
- - fortifications 16:276
- - Hezekiah 8:451
- - Hyksos 8:1142
- - Jebusites 9:1307
- - Jeroboam 9:1373
- - Nebuchadnezzar II 16:1505
- - population 13:868
- - priesthood 13:1084ff
- - Sennacherib 14:1162; 16:1504,1509
- Second Temple Period 9:1384
- - Adar, 16th of 2:252
- - Alexander the Great 2:578
- - Alexandrian community 2:590
- - *aliyah le-regel* 13:510
- - Antigonus II 3:66ff
- - Antiochus 3:73ff
- - Antonia 3:164
- - Costobar 5:990
- - Cyrene Jews 5:1184
- - economic distress 16:1272
- - eschatology 11:1410
- - *even ha-to'im* 6:985
- - Ezra and Nehemiah 6:1114ff; 8:619ff
- - goldsmiths and silversmiths 7:739
- - gymnasium 7:998
- - Hellenistic rule 8:626ff
- - Jason and Hellenism 8:295; 9:1292
- - population 13:871
- - Ptolemy Soter 13:1347
- - Samaritans 14:728
- - Sosius, Gaius 15:168
- - synagogues 15:582ff
- - Titus 15:1168
- - Tobiads 15:1179ff
- Herodian Period 9:1394
- Roman and Byzantine Period 9:1405
- - Aelia Capitolina 2:319
- - Bar Kokhba revolt 4:234
- - destruction of Temple (in the Arts) 10:263; 15:1170
- - Ereẓ Israel history 9:237ff
- - Holy Congregation 8:919
- - Jabneh 9:1176
- - Judah ha-Nasi 10:369
- - population 13:872
- Arab Period 9:1423
- - Avelei Zion 3:945
- - Ben-Meir, Aaron 4:539
- - Cairo *Genizah* 16:1339
- - Ereẓ Israel history 9:261ff
- - Fatimids 6:1197
- - gaonate 7:323ff
- - Karaite community 9:504ff; 10:769
- - Omar ibn al-Khattāb 12:1382
- - Persian Jewish community 9:501
- - Qūmisī, Daniel al- 5:1292
- - Solomon ben Judah 15:122
- - Umayyads 15:1528
- Crusader Period 9:1415
- - Crusades 5:1138
- - dyeing center 6:328
- - Ereẓ Israel history 9:267ff
- - Maghreb community 9:499ff
- Mamluk Period 9:1423
- - Ashkenazi community 9:497ff
- - Bertinoro, Obadiah 4:699; 11:351
- - Ereẓ Israel history 9:277ff
- - Sephardi community 9:498ff
- Ottoman Period 9:1426; 16:1549
- - A.J.A. Activities 2:977
- - *aliyah* 9:512
- - Armenians 3:475ff
- - Ashkenazim and Sephardim 3:722
- - Brill, Jehiel 7:1179
- - Bukharan community 9:502
- - emissaries 14:1359ff
- - Ereẓ Israel history 9:282ff; 9:325ff
- - Georgian community 9:501ff
- - governance 9:598ff
- - *ḥalukkah* 7:1207
- - Horowitz, Saul Ḥayyim 8:1002
- - Jewish housing 9:888
- - journalistic controversy 7:1479
- - Judeo-Persian Cultural Center 10:436
- - Kalischer, Ẓevi Hirsch 10:709
- - Kurds community 9:503
- - Palmerston 13:1250
- - Persian community 13:319
- - Shabbateanism 14:1247
- - Shabbetai Ẓevi 14:1223
- - Suleiman al-Qānūnī 16:1535
- - Templers 15:995
- - Turkish Jews 9:1092
- - Urfals 9:504
- - Yemenite community 9:500ff; 16:752
- 1918-1948 9:1469
- - Arab Legion 9:1032ff
- - Passover riots, 1920 9:683
- - PBS broadcasting 15:930
- - U.N. 15:1547
- - UNSCOP 15:1688
- - War of Independence 8:770; 9:367ff; 16:313ff
- 1948-1970 9:1483
- - Arab population 9:1032
- - Arab terrorist attack 14:1639
- - Armistice Agreements 3:481
- - bread and salt offering 14:711
- - broadcasting studios 15:931
- - frontiers 9:320
- - growth and planning 9:560; 9:1519
- - internationalization problem 9:378ff,424,1484; 15:1665ff
- - libraries 11:195
- - *Misgav Yerushalayim* center 14:1176
- - museums 12:551
- - plan for 9:560
- - Six-Day War 9:408ff; 14:1629
- - Tel Aviv and 15:918
- - Vatican relations 16:74; 16:76; 16:78
- - Zionist center 16:1098
- Reunification: Progress and Problems 9:1504
- - UNESCO resolution 15:1566
- *illus:*
- - text
- - Arab Legion position 16:317
- - Arch of Titus 15:1167
- - *Babylonian Chronicle* 12:914
- - Ben Yehudah Street bombing 9:362
- - British soldiers evacuation 9:362
- - David's conquest (map) 5:1320
- - I.Ẓ.L. attack on British officers club 9:361
- - Jemal Pasha and Turkish governor 9:332
- - "Jerusalem the Holy" (Hasmonean bronze shekel) 3:322
- - J.N.F. postal token (1948) 15:333
- - King David Hotel, 1946 explosion 8:1469
- - "King David's Entry into Jerusalem" (tpst., M. Chagall) 5:*fcg.* 334
- - pilgrims eating second tithe 11:653
- - public hanging, Ottoman regime 9:300

-- Sennacherib's eighth campaign **14:**1162
-- Shalem **14:**1266
-- Six-Day War
--- armoured forced advance **14:**1632
--- Dayan entering Jerusalem **9:**409
--- Lions' Gate **8:**777
-- Suleiman, Jaffa Gate inscription **9:**288
-- title deed for land, 1874 **9:**555
-- Twenty Third Zionist Congress **9:**379
-- War of Independence fighting **9:**366
(3) RELIGIONS
- Christianity **9:**1568
-- Adam's burial place **2:**240
-- Crusades **5:**1138
-- Ethiopian Church **6:**943
-- Jesus **10:**11
-- Ottomans **9:**1439ff
- Islam **9:**1575
-- eschatology **6:**885ff
-- *even shetiyyah* **6:**985
-- Ka'b al-Aḥbār **10:**488
-- Muhammad **12:**510
-- Temple Mount **15:**988
- Judaism
-- Aggadah **9:**1556
-- *even shetiyyah* **6:**985
-- Kamẓa and Bar Kamẓa **10:**732
-- Moriah **12:**324
- Bible **9:**1549
-- Adoni-Zedek **2:**296ff
-- David **5:**1323; **8:**588ff
-- Ezekiel **6:**1082f
-- history **8:**579; **8:**581
-- Isaiah **9:**44
-- Jeremiah **9:**1345
-- Joel **10:**131
-- lots **11:**510
-- Melchizedek **11:**1287
-- Micah **11:**1481
-- Psalms, Book of **13:**1303
-- righteousness **14:**181
-- sacrifices **14:**606
-- Solomon **15:**102ff
-- Temple **15:**943
-- Throne of God **15:**1124
-- Zechariah **16:**956
- Halakhah **9:**1553
-- bachelor *takkanah* **7:**1505
-- *eglah arufah* **6:**477
-- expansion rights **4:**722
-- horticulture regulations **4:**1029
-- husband or wife's residence rights **8:**1121
-- impurity prohibitions **13:**1410
-- *ir ha-niddaḥat* **8:**1470
-- legacy *takkanot* **16:**528
-- marriage custom **11:**1043
-- masoretic accents **16:**1405
-- *mikva'ot* **11:**1436ff, 1541ff
-- pilgrimages **13:**510ff; **13:**519
-- *tashlikh* **15:**829
-- Temple Mount **15:**989
-- tithes **15:**1025ff
-- *zaken mamre* **16:**920
- Kabbalah **9:**1563
-- eschatology **6:**868ff
- Liturgy **9:**1560
-- *Amidah* **2:**841ff
-- Av, Ninth of **3:**936
-- grace after meals **7:**838
-- *Kaddish* **10:**661
-- *kinot* **10:**1009
-- *Ya'aleh ve-Yavo* **16:**689
- Holy Places, *see* HOLY PLACES
- *illus:*
-- Al-Aqṣā mosque **8:**931
-- Basilica of the Agony **9:**1455
-- Church of the Dormition **8:**929
-- Church of St. Anne **9:**1453
-- desecrated graves in Mt. of Olives Jewish cemetery **9:**1485
-- Dome of the Rock **8:**931
-- emissary in Morocco **14:** 1363
-- emissary's seal **14:**1359
-- Ecce Homo arch **9:**1401
-- Eẓ Ḥayyim yeshivah **16:**764
-- Franciscans in the Via Dolorosa **9:**916
-- Garden Tomb **9:**916,1461
-- Hall of the Last Supper **8:**930
-- Ḥassidim in Me'ah She'arim **7:**1398
-- Holy Sepulcher **8:**928; **9:**913,914,1418,1420,1439
-- Ḥurvah Synagogue ruins **9:**1485
-- Jewish Legion *seder* **9:**1473
-- Jewish Quarter **9:**1480
-- Karaite synagogue, Old City **10:**782
-- Kurdish Jews celebrating Passover **13:**171
-- Monastery of Notre-Dame de France **9:**1463
-- Mount of Olives cemetery **5:**273
-- Mt. Zion wedding **11:**1048
-- Nabi Mūsā pilgrimage **9:**920
-- pilgrims in the Via Dolorosa **9:**916
-- Porat Yosef yeshivah **16:**767
-- Priestly Blessing at Western Wall **13:**1063
-- Ramadan prayers at Al-Aqṣā **9:**920
-- Russian Church of Gethsemane **9:**1462
-- Russian Church property **9:**1457
-- Russian Orthodox church **9:**914
-- Simḥat Torah procession **9:**907
-- *sukkot* in Battei Varsha quarter **15:**501
-- synagogues **9:**1443-1446
-- Temple Mount **9:**1413
-- Tomb of Miriam **9:**1417
-- Via Dolorosa **9:**1401
-- Western Wall **9:**901,1478
-- Yemenite Torah scribe **14:**1045
(4)THE ARTS
- Art **3:**507ff; **9:**1532,1578ff
-- Bar Kokhba coins **4:**234; **5:**719
-- stamps **15:**330ff
-- Temple **15:**945ff
- Literature **9:**1577
-- Blake, William **4:**1070
-- Salvador, Joseph **14:**716
-- Wiesel, Elie **16:**507
-- Zion **16:**1030
- Hebrew Literature **9:**1564
- Music **9:**1589
-- *Hatikvah* **7:**1470
-- musical activities **12:**672
-- *romancero* musical tradition **10:**1353
-- television and radio **15:**931
- *illus:*
-- text
-- Chagall's mosaic, Knesset building **5:**323
-- Chagall's stained glass windows **4:**526; **5:**1258; **9:**1077
-- Elijah riding into the city **7:**1086
-- festival pilgrimage (18th cent. engr.) **7:**1115
-- "Gates of Jerusalem" stamp series **15:**334
-- Golden Gate *(Mantua Haggadah)* **6:**863
-- Israel stamps **9:**844-845
-- Jeremiah mourning **13:**1417
-- "Jerusalem" (wtrcl., Y. Zaritsky) Pl.3 **3**-ART
-- "Jerusalem: Mount Scopus and Government House" (paint., D. Bomberg) **3:**555
-- "Jerusalem Hills" (drg., A. Ticho) Fig. 95 **3**-ART
-- "Jerusalem Landscape" (paint., L. Engelsberg) **3:**619
-- "King George Avenue in Jerusalem" (paint., H. Gliksberg) Pl.5 **3**-ART
-- Messiah **6:**863; **11:**1409,1410,1412
-- Mount of Olives (wdct.) **4:**115
-- pilgrims on their way to **13:**511
-- Solomon entering the city **10:**1024
-- "Street in Jerusalem" (wdct., J. Steinhardt) Fig. 93 **3**-ART
-- *sukkah* wall painting **15:***fcg.* 491
-- "Synagogue in Jerusalem" (S. Hirshenberg) **3:**627
-- Temple Mount (wdct.) **4:**115
-- "Toward Jerusalem" (paint., M. Ardon) Pl. 8 **3**-ART
-- "Western Wall" (paint., S. Alva) **2:**785
-- Western Wall (wdct.) **4:**115
- *illus:* General
-- Arab voting in municipal elections **9:**622
-- Bikkur Ḥolim Hospital in Old City **9:**983
-- Billy Rose Art Garden **14:**267
-- Binyenei ha-Ummah main auditorium **3:**353
-- Boys Town **9:**943
-- Egged bus station **6:**473
-- Hadassah Hospital **9:**990
-- Hadassah Hospital nurses **16:**721
-- Hadassah medical center, Ein Karem complex **7:**1043
-- Hadassah Medical Center, Mt. Scopus **3:**350; **7:**1043
-- Hebrew Union College building **3:**354
-- Hebrew University
--- Givat Ram campus **3:**351; **9:**955
--- Mount Scopus campus **9:**956
--- students at lecture **9:**958
--- synagogue **13:**1575
-- Heikhal Shlomo **9:**1488
-- Herzl's tomb **8:**421
-- Hungarian Quarter **3:**347
-- Independence Day parade **8:**1347; **9:**696
-- Ioannina Jews synagogue **8:**1436
-- Israel Museum **3:**354; **14:**1061-1068
-- Italian Rite synagogue **5:**869
-- Jeshurun Synagogue **15:**623
-- Jewish Agency building **3:**350
-- Jewish Hospital, 1855 **8:**1035
-- J.T.S. College **9:**907
-- Kennedy Memorial **3:**356
-- Kiryat Noar (Boys Town) **6:**436
-- Knesset building **3:**354; **5:**323; **10:**1112
-- Knesset *Menorah* **6:**675
-- Laemmel School **9:**929
-- Maimuna celebration **11:**782
-- Me'ah She'arim **9:**581
-- Mount Herzl cemetery **9:**368
-- Naḥalat Shivah alleyway **9:**563
-- Nathan and Lina Straus Health Centre, cornerstone ceremony **15:**429
-- National Library building, Mt. Scopus **3:**349
-- policeman on duty **9:**655
-- Ramot Eshkol housing project **2:**846
-- Rockefeller Museum **3:**350; **14:**212
-- scout camp **14:**1040
-- Sephardi community seal **14:**1078
-- Sha'arei Ẓedek Hospital **9:**991
-- Shrine of the Book **3:**631; **5:**1397
-- temperatures, mean (table) **9:**189
-- Temple Mount **15:**988
-- Twenty-Seventh Zionist Congress **16:**1175
-- water rationing **9:**1482
-- Wise Auditorium **3:**354
-- WIZO Baby Home **16:**695
-- Yad Vashem Memorial Hall Fig. 110 **3**-ART; **16:**697
Jerusalem (bk.) **11:**1333; **13:**455ff
"Jerusalem" (wtrcl., Y. Zaritsky) Pl. 3 **3**-ART
JERUSALEM, KARL WILHELM **9:**1593
Jerusalem, Kingdom of (Crus. state, Er. Isr.) **9:**268; **9:**269; **9:**1415
- *illus:*
-- 1187 C.E. (map) **9:**270
Jerusalem, Leopold **4:**1178
Jerusalem, Little (city, Fr.), *see* BÉZIERS
Jerusalem, Moses **4:**1178
"Jerusalem: Mount Scopus and Government House" (paint., D. Bomberg) **3:**555
Jerusalem, Mourners of (rel. gr.) **3:**946
Jerusalem, Solomon **4:**1178
JERUSALEM, WILHELM **9:**1593
Jerusalem Academic Press (Isr.) **13:**1379
Jerusalem Agricultural Museum **5:**479
Jerusalem airfield **9:**837
Jerusalem Artists' House **9:**1496
Jerusalem Brigade (Isr. army) **14:**1630
Jerusalem coins **5:**722
Jerusalem College for Women **9:**899
Jerusalem corridor (reg., Isr.) **9:**587
Jerusalem Economic Conference **9:**413
Jerusalem Electric and Public Services Corporation Ltd. **9:**1470; **9:**792
Jerusalem Emergency Committee **9:**1479
"Jerusalem et Suburbia Eius" (map) **9:**1542
Jerusalem Forest **9:**1495
Jerusalem gates **9:**1433ff
"Jerusalem Hills" (drg., A. Ticho) Fig. 95 **3**-ART
Jerusalemite Kingdom (Crus.), *see* Jerusalem, Kingdom of
Jerusalem itinerary (bk.), *see* ITINERARIUM HIEROSOLYMITANUM or ITINERARIUM BURDIGALENSE
"Jerusalem Landscape" (paint., L. Engelsberg) **3:**619
Jerusalem Mishneh Torah (illum. ms.) **8:**1269
- *illus:* **3:**455; **8:***fcg.* 1015
Jerusalem National Park **12:**879
Jerusalem of Lithuania, *see* VILNA
Jerusalem pine **9:**221 **9:**1515
JERUSALEM POST (newsp.) **9:**1594
- Agron, Gershon **2:**420
- Arab bomb attack **9:**363,1479
- Israel press **9:**1017
- Jerusalem **9:**1473
- *illus:*
-- Arab civil disobedience campaign, 1936 **9:**463
-- bomb explosion (1948) **9:**1481
-- establishment of the State report, May 16, 1948 **9:**364
-- front page (April, 1936) **7:**1067
-- Leḥi suicide report, April 22, 1947 **11:**463
-- reporting on 1936 riots **9:**350
Jerusalem Prize (lit.) **14:**1027; **15:**255
Jerusalem Program (Zion. mvmt.) **4:**308; **10:**30; **16:**1176; **16:**1177
Jerusalem School (art gr.) **3:**591

Jerusalem Talmud, *see* TALMUD, JERUSALEM
Jerusalem Theater **9:**1495
- *illus:*
- - aerial view **9:**1490
Jerusalem Walls **9:**1426ff
Jerusalem Windows (Hadassah hospital, Jer.) **5:**323
- *illus:* **4:**526; **5:**1258; **9:**1077
JERUSALIMSKI, MOSES NAHUM BEN BENJAMIN **9:**1594
Jerusha (bib. fig.) **10:**301
Jerwan (loc., Assyr.) **16:**1504
Jesau (concen. camp, Pol.) **15:**464
JESCHURUN (period.) **10:**1
- Hirsch, S. R. **8:**514
- press **13:**1056
- Wissenschaft **16:**578
- Wohlgemuth, J. **16:**600
- *illus:*
- - title page (1855) **8:**511
Jesenská, Milena **5:**1193; **10:**672
JESHUA (h. pr.) **10:**1
- Baghdad **4:**86
- Great Synagogue **15:**629
- history **8:**617
- Johanan **10:**144
- priestly house **8:**626; **13:**1086
- Second Temple **9:**1389
- Temple reconstruction **15:**955
- Zechariah **16:**954
- Zerubbabel **16:**1000
Jeshua ben Elijah ha-Levi, *see* JOSHUA BEN ELIJAH HA-LEVI
Jeshua ben Galgolah, *see* Joshua ben Galgula
JESHUA BEN JOSEPH HA-LEVI **10:**3
- Tlemcen **15:**1073
JESHUA BEN JUDAH **10:**3
- atomism **3:**830
- Bible translations **4:**863
- Commandments, reasons for **5:**785
- Judeo-Arabic literature **10:**414
- philosophy **13:**433
JESHURUN (name) **10:**4
Jeshurun Synagogue (Jer.), *see* Yeshurun Synagogue
JESI, SAMUEL **10:**5
Jeske-Choiński, Teodor **13:**800
JESSE (bib. fig.) **10:**5
- David **5:**1339
- *geneal. table* **5:**1341
Jesse, Benjamin **2:**547
JESSE BEN HEZEKIAH **10:**6
- Maimonidean controversy **15:**642
Jesse ben Mordecai **11:**1277
Jessel, Sir Charles James **10:**6
Jessel, Frederick Henry **10:**6
JESSEL, SIR GEORGE **10:**6
JESSEL, GEORGE ALBERT **10:**6
Jessel, Herbert Merton **10:**6
Jessel, Richard Frederick **10:**6
JESSELSON, LUDWIG **10:**7
- bibliophiles **4:**976
JESSEY, HENRY **10:**7
- *illus:* text
Jessica (Shakespearian fig.) **14:**1261
JESSNER, LEOPOLD **10:**8
- Kortner, Fritz **10:**1213
Jessnitz (city, Ger.) **3:**1
Jessurun (fam.), *see* JESURUN
Jessurun, Isaac, *see* JESURUN, ISAAC BEN ABRAHAM ḤAYYIM
Jessurun Rodrigues, Joseph, *see* Salvador, Joseph
Jester, *see* BADḤAN
JESUITS (Cath. order) **10:**8
- history chart **8:**766-767
Jesu Maria (tn., Calif.) **5:**56
JESURUN (fam.) **10:**9
- Split **15:**289
Jesurun, David **10:**9
Jesurun, Isaac **10:**9
JESURUN, ISAAC BEN ABRAHAM ḤAYYIM **10:**9
- family **10:**9
Jesurun, Joseph **10:**9
JESURUN, REUEL **10:**9
Jesurun, Sarah, *see* Abudiente, Sarah
JESUS **10:**10
- *Contents:*
- - The Gospels **10:**10
- - Name, Birth, and Death Date **10:**10
- - Family and Circle **10:**11
- - Arrest **10:**11
- - "Trial" and Crucifixion **10:**12
- - The Jewish Background **10:**12
- - As The Messiah **10:**13
- - Talmud and Midrash **10:**14
- General
- - *Aleinu le-Shabbe'aḥ* **2:**557
- - Ben Stada **4:**554
- - blood libel **4:**1121
- - chronological chart **8:**766-767
- - Druze religion **9:**928
- - golden calf **7:**712
- - Islamic eschatology **6:**884
- - Jewish Christian sects **10:**38ff
- - Judeo-Christians **9:**244
- - logos **16:**635
- - Satan **14:**904
- - "son of man" **15:**160
- - talmudic statements **3:**191
- - Vatican **16:**74
- - Wandering Jew **16:**259ff
- Life History
- - ablution, neglect of **2:**85
- - apostles **3:**215
- - Bethany **4:**733
- - Bethlehem **4:**742
- - Caiaphas, Joseph **5:**20
- - Christianity **5:**506ff
- - crucifixon **5:**1133
- - Davidic descent **5:**1331; **5:**1343
- - Greek language **8:**297
- - *haftarah* reading **16:**1343
- - Herodians **8:**388
- - Jacob of Kefar Sakhnayya **9:**1233
- - Jerusalem Garden Tomb **9:**1459
- - John the Baptist **10:**160
- - Joshua ben Peraḥyah **10:**285
- - lepers, curing of **11:**37
- - messianism **11:**1409,1410,1420
- - money-changers **15:**982; **16:**1273
- - Mount of Olives **12:**483
- - Nazareth **12:**899
- - Paul of Tarsus **13:**191
- - Pontius Pilate **13:**848
- - Sanhedrin **14:**836
- - Sidon **14:**1507
- - Siloam Pool **9:**1540
- - Temple **15:**983
- - Zealot **16:**949
- Literature
- - Hebrew literature **6:**1266
- - *Isaiah, Ascension of* **9:**71
- - New Testament **12:**1059
- - Song of Songs **15:**147
- - *Testament of the Patriarchs* **13:**185
- - *Toledot Yeshu* **15:**1208ff
- Typology
- - Aaron **2:**8
- - Abel **5:**23
- - Abraham **2:**119
- - Adam **2:**240
- - Balaam **4:**124
- - Elijah **6:**635
- - Isaac **9:**5
- - Joseph **10:**216
- - Joshua **10:**268
- - Melchizedek **11:**1289
- - Moses **12:**412
- - Noah **12:**1195
- - Samson **14:**776
- - Solomon **15:**108
- Views on
- - Akiva **16:**844
- - Christian Kabbalah **10:**644ff
- - Emden, Jacob **3:**198
- - Hirsch, Samuel **13:**457
- - Israel Ba'al Shem Tov **9:**1055
- - Josephus, Flavius **10:**261
- - Karaites **3:**192
- - Kaufmann, Y. **16:**1350
- - Klausner's studies **10:**1094
- - Lorki, Joshua **15:**1271
- - Naḥmanides **4:**214
- *illus:*
- - arguing with the sages **9:**1581
- - Basilica of the Agony mosaic **9:**1455
- - David, and **15:**1497
- - "Delivery of the Keys" (paint., Perugino) **9:**1585
- - entering Jerusalem **9:**1584
- - flagellation **8:**660
- - flanked by Ecclesia et Synagoga **6:**347
- - Garden Tomb **9:**1461
- - Grotto of the Nativity **4:**746
- - Holy Sepulcher frieze **9:**1419
- - Nazareth synagogue **12:**900
- - on the cross **13:**356
- - submitting to circumcision **8:**1135
Jesus, Son of Sapphas, *see* JOSHUA, SON OF SAPPHAS
Jesus, Son of Seth (h. pr.), *see* JOSHUA, SON OF SETH
Jesus, Son of Thebuthi, *see* Joshua, Son of Thebuthi
Jesus the Child, Church of (Nazareth) **12:**903
Jether (bib. fig.), *see* JETHRO
Jether the Ishmaelite (bib. fig.) **2:**74; **2:**793; **9:**89
Jethira (city, Er. Isr.), *see* JATTIR, JETHIRA
JETHRO (bib. fig.) **10:**17
- Druze religion **9:**928
- Exodus, Book of **6:**1055ff
- in the Arts **12:**404
- Moses **12:**373
- Nabī Shu'ayb **10:**886
- Putiel **13:**1415
- Zipporah **16:**1182
- *illus:*
- - text
- - Nabī Shuʿayb celebration **8:**933; **10:**886
Jetur (bib. fig.), *see* Jether the Ishmaelite
Jetzius, Paul **8:**39
Jeuel (bib. fig.), *see* Jeiel
Jeune Nation (neo-Fascist party) **12:**952
Jeuschsohn, B., *see* JUSTMAN, MOSHE BUNEM
JEVICKO (tn., Morav.) **10:**21
- *illus:* text
Jevrejska Tribuna (newsp., Yug.) **14:**871
Jevrejski Almanah (pub., Yug.) **2:**541; **16:**882,890
Jevrejski Glas (newsp., Yug.) **14:**871; **16:**1151
Jevrejski Glasnik (period., Yug.) **16:**888
Jevrejski Narodni Kalendar (period., Yug.) **16:**1151
Jevrejski Život (period., Yug.) **16:**1150
Jew (period., U.S.) **12:**1074; **13:**1050
- *illus:*
- - masthead (1823) **13:**1050
JEW **10:**21
- *Contents:*
- - Semantics **10:**21
- - Halakhic Definition **10:**23
- definition **3:**654; **9:**672; **10:**1486ff; **12:**111
- Gentile **7:**410ff
- original designation **12:**806
- physical anthropology **3:**40
- population **13:**885
- Ratosh, Yonathan **13:**1574
- *see also:* APOSTASY; JEWISH IDENTITY; JUDAISM
"Jew at Prayer" (drg., L. Segall) **14:**1108
Jewelry, *see* PRECIOUS STONES AND JEWELRY
JEWESS OF TOLEDO (leg. and lit. fig.) **10:**25
Jewish Academic House (Pol.) **15:**136
Jewish Advocate (period., Ind.) **13:**1036
Jewish Affairs (journ., S.A.) **13:**1049
Jewish Affairs, Committee for (Pol. senate) **16:**601
JEWISH AGENCY (Zion. orgn.) **10:**26
- *Contents:*
- - Early History **10:**27
- - Subsequent Developments **10:**28
- - Functions **10:**28
- - World War II and the Struggle for the State **10:**29
- - After 1948 **10:**30
- - Department in U.S. **10:**32
- - Finances **10:**33
- - New Directions **10:**33
- General
- - Abdullah ibn Hussein **2:**57
- - Agudat Israel **2:**424
- - Arab attacks **9:**1479
- - Beriḥah **4:**629
- - Biltmore Program **4:**998
- - Haganah **7:**1067ff; **9:**684f
- - Irgun Ẓeva'i Le'ummi **8:**1467
- - Israel historical survey **9:**370; **9:**381ff
- - Israel politics **9:**661ff
- - mandate for Palestine **11:**862; **16:**1053
- - Mapai **11:**912
- - U.N. **15:**1543
- - U.S. Zionism **16:**1143ff
- - Va'ad Le'ummi **16:**49
- - White Papers **16:**484ff
- - Zionist commission **16:**1164
- - Zionist Congress **16:**1172
- - Zionist policy **16:**1082ff,1103
- Housing and Immigration
- - absorption of immigrants **9:**527ff
- - Amidar corporation **2:**846
- - housing in Israel **9:**564
- - Inter-Governmental Committee for Refugees **6:**991
- - Youth Aliyah **16:**861ff
- Personalities
- - Arlosoroff, Chaim **3:**470
- - Ben-Gurion **4:**508; **4:**509
- - Dugdale, Blanche **6:**264
- - Eshkol, Levi **6:**888
- - Laski, Neville **10:**1438
- - Mond, Alfred **12:**242
- - Ruppin, Arthur **14:**431
- - Sharett, Moshe **14:**1309
- - Weizmann, Chaim **16:**431
- *illus:*
- - text
- - chief boatman greeting new immigrants **9:**522
- - Head Office building, Jerusalem **3:**350
Jewish Agency-American Section, Inc. (orgn., U.S.) **10:**32
Jewish Agency for Israel, Inc. (orgn., U.S.) **10:**32
JEWISH AGRICULTURAL SOCIETY (U.S.) **10:**35
- Nebraska **12:**912
- *illus:* text
Jewish Aid Committee for German Jews **16:**170

Jewish Algerian Committee for Social Studies **2:**616; **2:**617
Jewish Almanac (pub., Yug.), *see* *Jevrejski Almanah*
Jewish American (period.) **5:**1571
Jewish Anti-Fascist Committee (Rus.), *see* ANTI-FASCIST COMMITTEE, JEWISH
Jewish Antiquities (wk.) **8:**304; **8:**554; **10:**257ff
- *illus:*
- - fifteenth cent. illum. ms. **10:**256
- - twelfth cent. ms. **13:**1
Jewish-Arab relations, *see* Arabs (Arab-Jewish relations)
Jewish Art Theater (U.S.), *see* Yiddish Art Theater
Jewish Assocation for the Diffusion of Religious Knowledge (Eng.) **6:**447
"Jewish Autonomous Region" (Rus.), *see* BIROBIDZHAN
Jewish bagpipe band **14:**1038
Jewish-Bedouin alliance **12:**929
Jewish Berbers (N. Afr.) **4:**588
Jewish Blind Society (Lond.) **4:**1092
Jewish Board for Welfare Work in the United States Army and Navy **12:**872
Jewish Board of Guardians (Eng.) **2:**286; **6:**757
Jewish Book Annual (U.S.) **4:**973; **12:**878; **13:**1377
Jewish Book Council of America **7:**863
Jewish Braille Institute of America (N.Y.) **2:**744
JEWISH BRIGADE GROUP (mil. unit) **10:**35
- Beriḥah **4:**629ff
- Churchill, Winston **5:**556
- Haganah **9:**687
- Israel historical survey **9:**355
- Irgun Ẓeva'i Le'ummi **8:**1467
- World War II **16:**1058
- Youth Aliyah **16:**863
- Zionism in Italy **16:**1123
- - *illus:*
- - Benghazi, Hebrew school **4:**505
- - guarding German prisoners **9:**686
- - Sharett, Moshe, and **9:**359
Jewish Center (conc.) **15:**586
- National Jewish Welfare Board **12:**874
- rabbi's role **13:**1456
Jewish Central Information Office (Amst.), *see* WIENER LIBRARY
Jewish Chaplain (period.) **12:**878
Jewish Chautauqua Society **4:**634
Jewish Child (period.) **5:**457
Jewish Children's Theater (Rus.) **15:**1076
Jewish-Christian relations, *see* Christian-Jewish relations
Jewish-Christians, *see* JEWISH CHRISTIAN SECTS; Judeo-Christians
JEWISH CHRISTIAN SECTS **10:**38
- Children of Israel of the New Testament **13:**1473
- Christianity **5:**507
- Ishmael ben Elisha **9:**85
- Jewish identity **10:**56
- *min* **12:**2
- Paul of Tarsus **13:**191
- Protestantism **13:**1248
- *see also:* NEW TESTAMENT
JEWISH CHRONICLE (period.) **10:**40
- caricatures **5:**176
- Greenberg family **7:**905
- *Hebrew Observer* **4:**521
- historical chart **8:**766-767
- Leopold Kessler **10:**923
- Palestine colonization **6:**270; **13:**1031; **13:**1056
- press **13:**1031; **13:**1056
- *illus:* text
Jewish Civic Leader (newsp.) **16:**634
JEWISH COLONIAL TRUST (Zion. bnk.) **10:**42
- Cowen, Joseph **5:**1024
- Levontin, Zalman **11:**152
- Revisionists, Zionist **14:**128
- Zionism **16:**1097
- Zionist Congress (2nd)
- *illus:*
- - text
- - founders' share **3:**394
- - Jaffa, Anglo-Palestine Bank, 1903 **9:**1255
- *see also:* BANKING IN ISRAEL
JEWISH COLONIZATION ASSOCIATION (orgn.) **10:**44
- *Contents:*
- - Emigration **10:**44
- - Aid and Settlement **10:**44
- - - Eastern Europe **10:**44
- - - Argentina **10:**46
- - - Brazil **10:**46
- - - United States **10:**46
- - - Canada **10:**46
- - - Ereẓ Israel **10:**47
- - - Cyprus and Turkey **10:**48
- - World War II and After **10:**49
- General
- - Alliance Israélite Universelle **2:**651
- - Anglo-Jewish Association **2:**978
- - Ettinger, Akiva **6:**953
- - Hirsch, Baron Maurice de **8:**50ff
- - historical chart **8:**766-767
- - Israelitische Allianz **2:**654
- - Raffalovich, Isaiah **13:**1511
- - Rothschild, Edmond de **14:**343
- - Warburg, Otto **16:**287ff
- Aid
- - agricultural colonies **16:**1069
- - Argentina **3:**413ff
- - Belorussia **2:**408
- - Brazil **2:**414; **4:**1326
- - Canada **2:**413
- - cooperatives **5:**942
- - Israel **9:**325,773
- - Latin America **10:**1454
- - Mexico **11:**1456
- - Rumania **2:**411
- - Ukraine **2:**408
- - Uruguay **16:**11
- *illus:* text
- *see also:* Settlement and Colonization Schemes (pre-State)
Jewish Commissariat (Rus.) **16:**779
- *illus:*
- - order re closing of *kehillot* central office **14:**461
- - order re discontinuation of Hebrew teaching **14:**462
Jewish Committee (polit. orgn., Pol.) **13:**778
Jewish Committee for Relief Abroad **5:**285; **15:**1688
JEWISH COMMUNAL ORGANIZATION IN ISRAEL **9:**598
- Va'ad Le'ummi **16:**49
- Yemenites **16:**752*ff*
- *illus:*
- - Va'ad Le'ummi meeting **16:**50
JEWISH COMMUNITIES IN ISRAEL **9:**495
- historical survey **9:**378*ff*,395
- TV controversy **15:**931
- *illus:*
- - text
- - Ashdod *mikveh* **11:**1541
- - Bukharan Jews celebrating Simḥat Torah **14:**1573
- - Cochin Jews' wedding **11:**1049
- - Eẓ Ḥayyim Yeshivah, Jerusalem **16:**764
- - Heikhal Shlomo (Jer.) **9:**1488
- - Jerusalem children celebrating Shavuot **14:**1321
- - Jerusalem reunification, first anniversary **9:**1503
- - Jerusalem synagogues **9:**1442-1446
- - Kol Torah yeshivah, Jerusalem **16:**766
- - Kurdish Jews celebrating Passover **13:**171
- - Maimuna celebration **11:**782
- - Meir Ba'al ha-Nes tomb **15:**1132
- - Mt. Zion wedding **11:**1048
- - N eturei Karta monetary scrip **12:**1003
- - Porat Yosef yeshivah, Jerusalem **16:**765
- - priestly blessing at Western Wall **13:**1063
- - Safed, Ha-Ari Synagogue **14:**629
- - Safed, Isaac Aboab Synagogue **14:**631
- - Simeon bar Yoḥai's tomb **14:**1552
- - Simeon the Just's tomb **14:**1567
- - *sukkot* in Battei Varsha quarter, Jerusalem **15:**501
- - Sukkot prayers in trenches (1948) **16:**323
- - *Tashlikh* ceremony **15:**829
- - Tu bi-Shevat celebration **15:**1420
- - wedding party at the Western Wall **11:**1045
- - Western Wall **9:**1467
- - Yad Mordekhai, triple wedding **11:**1050
- - Yemenite bride and groom **11:**1047
- - Yemenite Torah scribe **14:**1045
- - Yemenite wedding **11:**1046
Jewish Company for the Settlement of the Holy Land **16:**1037
Jewish Congress Organization Committee (U.S.) **5:**876
Jewish Consumptives' Relief Society, *see* American Medical Center
Jewish Correspondence Bureau, *see* JEWISH TELEGRAPHIC AGENCY
Jewish Council for Russian War Relief (U.S.) **3:**62,687
- history chart **8:**766-767
Jewish Court, *see* BET DIN AND JUDGES
Jewish Cultural Association (Ger.), *see* JUEDISCHER KULTURBUND
Jewish Cultural League (Rus.), *see* Cultural League, Jewish
JEWISH CULTURAL RECONSTRUCTION **10:**49
- Jewish museums **12:**540
Jewish Daily Bulletin (newsp.) **13:**1024
JEWISH DAILY FORWARD (newsp.) **10:**49
- Americanization **15:**47
- Asch, Sholem **3:**687
- historical chart **8:**766-767
- Miller, Louis E. **11:**1581
- New York City **12:**1086; **12:**1101*ff*
- Schlesinger, Benjamin **14:**972
- Vinchevsky, Morris **16:**154
- Yiddish press **13:**1054
- Zionism **16:**1143
- *illus:* text
Jewish Daily Press (*World;* period., U.S.) **14:**213
JEWISH DAY (newsp.) **10:**51
- Bernstein, Herman **4:**685
- Boraisha, Menahem **4:**1241
- Glanz-Leyeles, Aaron **7:**600
- Hirschbein, Peretz **8:**519
- Zionism **16:**1143
- *illus:*
- - text
- - masthead (1948) **12:**1111
Jewish Defense League (U.S.) **12:**934; **14:**1128
- *illus:*
- - protest rally for Soviet Jewry **12:**1123
Jewish Democratic Committee (Rum.), *see* Comitetul Democrat Evreesc
"Jewish Doctor" (paint., Rembrandt) **13:**917
Jewish Dramatic Society (S.A.) **2:**273; **15:**1074
- history chart **8:**766-767
Jewish Eagle (newsp.), *see* KANADER ADLER
Jewish Echo (period.) **7:**603; **13:**1031
Jewish education, *see* EDUCATION
Jewish Education (period.) **6:**442
- Dushkin, Alexander **6:**312
Jewish Educational Aid Society (Eng.) **7:**521
Jewish Education Newsletter (period.) **2:**819
Jewish Emigrant Aid Society (Warsaw), *see* J.E.A.S.
Jewish Encyclopedia **6:**732
- Adler, Cyrus **2:**273
- historical chart **8:**766-767
- Singer, Isidore **14:**1611
- Wissenschaft des Judentums **16:**581
Jewish Examiner (period.) **2:**821
Jewish Exponent (period.) **8:**808; **13:**1051
Jewish Family (period.) **13:**1031
Jewish Family Services (U.S.) **5:**350; **12:**1092
Jewish Farmer (period.) **10:**35
Jewish Fellowship (orgn.) **8:**328
Jewish Fighting Organization (Pol.), *see* Z.O.B.
Jewish Floridian (period.) **6:**1363; **11:**1480
Jewish Folk Schools (U.S.) **6:**436; **10:**1331
Jewish Forum (period.) **12:**1490
Jewish Free School (Ger.), *see* JUEDISCHE FREISCHULE
Jewish Frontier (journ.) **16:**640
- press **13:**1051
- U.S. Zionism **16:**1142
Jewish Gazette (period.) **13:**1031
Jewish Graphic (period.) **13:**1031
Jewish Guardian (period.) **13:**1031
Jewish Health Organization (It.), *see* Organizzazione Sanitaria Ebraica
Jewish Herald (journ., S.A.) **13:**1049; **14:**131
Jewish Herald (newsp., U.S.) **8:**1050
Jewish Herald-Voice (newsp., U.S.) **8:**1052; **15:**1036
Jewish Historical Cultural Museum (Du.W. Indies) **12:**551
Jewish Historical-Ethnographical Society (Ger.) **12:**658
Jewish Historical General Archives (Isr.) **3:**385
JEWISH HISTORICAL INSTITUTE, WARSAW **10:**51
- archives **3:**380; **3:**386
- Holocaust research **15:**54
- *illus:* text
Jewish Historical Museum (Mex.) **12:**551
JEWISH HISTORICAL SOCIETY OF ENGLAND **10:**53
- Abrahams, Sir Lionel **2:**165
- Adler, Michael **2:**283
- Anglo-Jewish history **15:**54
- archives **3:**382
- historiography **8:**563; **8:**564
- museum **12:**540
"Jewish Holidays" (tpst., A.

Gottlieb) 7:822
Jewish Hospital for Chronic Diseases (N.Y.C.) 12:1116
Jewish Hospital of Brooklyn (U.S.) 8:1039
Jewish Hospital of Cincinnati (U.S.) 8:1034
JEWISH IDENTITY 10:53
- assimilationist redefinition 3:773
- Israel religious controversy 9:396
- Karl Marx 11:1074
- Law of Return 10:1486ff
- Lueger, Karl 11:557
- Mendelssohn 11:1334ff
- modern Jewish thought 13:453
- Mussolini, Benito 12:718
- State of Israel law 12:147
- Zohar on 10:610
- *see also:* JEW; WISSENSCHAFT DES JUDENTUMS
JEWISH IMMIGRANT AID SERVICES OF CANADA 10:65
- Caiserman, Hananiah M. 5:32
Jewish Information Society of America 13:1192
Jewish Institute for the Blind (Jer.) 2:744; 4:1092
Jewish Institute for the Blind (Aus.) 14:1612
Jewish Institute of Religion, *see* HEBREW UNION COLLEGE—JEWISH INSTITUTE OF RELIGION
Jewish Journal of Sociology 6:769; 15:67
JEWISH LABOR COMMITTEE (U.S.) 10:65
- anti-Nazi boycott 4:1281
JEWISH LABOR ORGANIZATIONS IN ISRAEL 9:848
- archives 3:395
- Ben-Gurion 4:505
- Betar 4:714
- cooperatives 5:945
- courts 9:639ff; 9:883ff
- Gordon, Aharon 7:790
- Ha-Po'el ha-Ẓa'ir 7:1326
- Hebrew newspapers 12:1057
- Histadrut ha-Ovedim 8:541
- Katznelson, Berl 10:836
- labor problems in the *yishuv* 9:328*ff*,346
- labor unity 9:656
- legislation 9:653; 9:874ff
- Ministry of Labor 9:875
- Po'alei Zion 13:659
- Revisionists, Zionist 14:129
- socialism 15:31ff
- *illus:*
- - Bet ha-Po'alim, Jerusalem, cornerstone laying 4:511
- - Histadrut, budget and unions, 1969 (chart) 8:536,537
Jewish Lads' Brigade (mvmt., Eng.) 14:1038
- *illus:* 14:1038
JEWISH LANGUAGES 10:66
- *Contents:*
- - History 10:66
- - Causes 10:68
- - Name 10:68
- - Hebrew and Aramaic Elements 10:68
- - Script 10:69
- Judeo-Alsatian 2:751
- Judeo-Arabic 10:409
- Judeo-Berber 10:410
- Judeo-Catalan 10:439
- Judeo-Corfiote 9:1146
- Judeo-French 10:423
- Judeo-Greek 10:425
- Judeo-Iranian 10:432
- Judeo-Italian 10:427
- Judeo-Persian 10:429
- Judeo-Portuguese 10:439
- Judeo-Provençal 10:439
- Judeo-Romance 4:865
- Judeo-Tajiki 10:432
- Judeo-Tāt 10:441
- Judeo-Tatar 4:865
- Ladino (Judeo-Spanish 10:1342
- Yiddish (Judeo-German) 16:789
Jewish Law, *see* MISHPAT IVRI
Jewish Lawyers Association (Isr.) 6:617
JEWISH LEGION 10:69
- *Contents:*
- - Zion Mule Corps 10:69
- - Royal Fusiliers 10:70
- - Palestinian Volunteers 10:72
- - American Volunteers 10:73
- - After the War 10:73
- - Demobilization 10:74
- - During 1920-21 Riots 10:75
- Aḥdut ha-Avodah 2:456
- defense forces 9:681
- Haganah 7:1064
- history 8:756
- Mountain Jews 12:479
- Negev 12:929
- Revisionists, Zionist 14:128
- role in Ereẓ Israel 9:337
- settlement defense 9:681,683
- Trumpeldor, Joseph 15:1412
- Zionism 16:1079ff
- Zionist movement 16:1050
- Zuckerman, Baruch 16:1229
- *illus:*
- - text
- - Ben-Gurion, David, in uniform 4:510
- - Ben-Zvi, Izhak, in uniform 4:577
- - El-Arish, 1918 9:335,518
- - Jabotinsky, Vladimir, and soldiers 9:682
- - Jabotinsky, Vladimir, in uniform 9:1181
- - *seder* in Jerusalem 9:1473
- - veterans protest against 1939 White Paper 9:357, 525
Jewish Life (period.) 12:1490
Jewish literature, *see* LITERATURE, JEWISH
Jewish Memorial Council (Eng.), *see* Jewish War Memorial
Jewish Memorial Hospital (N.Y.C.) 12:1116
JEWISH MESSENGER, THE (period.) 10:76
- Isaacs, Samuel Myer 9:38
- New York City 12:1071; 12:1072; 12:1074
- press 13:1051
Jewish Military League (Rus.), *see* Iggud ha-Ẓeva'i ha-Yehudi
Jewish Minorities Research (publ.) 14:499
"Jewish Mobile Theater" (Belor.) 15:1076
Jewish Monitor (period.) 2:505
Jewish Monthly (period.) 2:978
JEWISH MORNING JOURNAL 10:76
- Blum, Eliezer 4:1136
- Fishman, Jacob 6:1331
- New York City 12:1101ff
- Nissenson, Aaron 12:1180
- Yiddish press 13:1055
- *illus:* text
Jewish Municipal Guard (Warsaw) 16:335
Jewish Museum (N.Y.) 10:96
Jewish Museum of Temple Mishkan Tefila (Boston) 12:544
Jewish Music Council (U.S.) 12:877
Jewish Music Forum (N.Y.) 12:661
Jewish Music Journal (period.) 7:1546
Jewish-Muslim relations, *see* Arabs; ISLAM
Jewish mysticism, *see* KABBALAH
Jewish National and University Library (Jer.), *see* LIBRARY, JEWISH NATIONAL AND UNIVERSITY
Jewish National Council (Aus.), *see* NATIONALRAT
Jewish National Council (Cz.) 14:1613; 16:1017
Jewish National Council (Rus.) 5:876
JEWISH NATIONAL FUND 10:77
- Adullam region 2:312
- afforestation program 9:789
- Ettinger, Akiva 6:953
- Granott, Abraham 7:854
- Gross, Nathan 7:935
- Hadassah 7:1045
- historical chart 8:766-767
- immigrant employment 9:537
- Kremenetzky, Johann 10:1257
- land purchase 9:340*ff*
- Negev settlement 12:929
- Origen 16:1097
- philanthropy 13:390
- role in Israel 9:370
- Schapira, Hermann 14:941
- stamps 15:332
- stockade and watchtower settlements 15:404
- Tel Aviv 15:920
- Tsur, Jacob 15:1418
- Ussishkin, Menaḥem 16:26
- Zionism 16:1110
- Zionist Congress 16:1168
- *illus:*
- - Israel stamp 9:*fcg.* 843
- - Jerusalem stamp (1948) 15:333
- - Kiryat Gat afforestation project 9:786
- - registration certificate of land 9:557
- - Riga sport assembly 14:174
- - trees planted up to 1968 (map) 9:789
Jewish National Home 4:131,133
- Allenby, Edmund 2:647
- Amery, Leopold 2:833
- Arab National Movement 9:458
- Churchill, Sir Winston 5:556
- League of Nations 10:1521ff
- mandate for Palestine 11:861
- partition plans 13:35
- Peel Commission 13:32
- Vatican 16:75
- Zionist Commission 16:1163
- Zionist Congress 16:1175
- *illus:*
- - Balfour Declaration 4:131
- - U.S. Senate's endorsement 3:393
- *see also:* ISRAEL (HISTORICAL SURVEY); ZIONISM
Jewish Nationalism
- Aḥad Ha-Am 2:443ff
- *aliyah le-regel* 13:511
- autonomism 3:919
- communism 5:794ff
- definition of Jew 10:23
- Haskalah 7:1444
- Hirsch, S.R. 8:514
- in Judaism 10:387; 10:394
- Jewish law 12:124
- Kalischer, Ẓevi 10:708
- Lenin 11:13
- Mendelssohn, Moses 11:1335
- Montefiore, Claude 12:269
- prophets 13:1161
- race, theory of 13:1484
- Riesser, Gabriel 14:167
- self-defense 14:1124
- Smolenskin, Perez 15:11
- socialism, Jewish 15:39ff
- Stalin 15:327ff
- Zionist Congress 16:1167
- *see also:* ISRAEL (HISTORICAL SURVEY); MESSIAH; TORAH; ZIONISM
Jewish National Party (Aus.), *see* VOLKSPARTEI, JUEDISCHE
Jewish National Workers' Alliance 7:110; 16:1141
Jewish News (newsp.) 5:1571
Jewish oath, *see* OATH MORE JUDAICO
Jewish Observer (period., U.S.) 2:426
Jewish Observer and Middle East Review (period., Eng.) 13:1031
Jewish Palestine Exploration Society, *see* ISRAEL EXPLORATION SOCIETY
Jewish Parent (period.) 15:1259
Jewish parliamentary club (Rum.) 14:393,396
Jewish Party (Cz.), *see* ŽIDOVSKÁ STRANA
Jewish People 5:1493
- Amalek 2:787
- *Atta Eḥad* 3:833
- covenant with God 5:1013
- education 6:383
- exodus from Egypt 6:1042
God and 7:646ff,669
- Horowitz, Isaiah 8:992
- Judaism 10:387
- Moses 12:371
- sages on 14:653
- Torah 15:1238; 15:1239ff
- Transjordan 15:1316
- "treasure" 15:1361
- *see also:* ANTHROPOLOGY; ASSIMILATION; CHOSEN PEOPLE; DIASPORA; EMANCIPATION; GALUT; SOCIOLOGY; WANDERING JEW
Jewish People's Fraternal Order, *see* International Workers' Order
Jewish People's Party (Rus.) 6:255
Jewish People's University, Kiev 14:1533
Jewish Popular Socialism (pam.) 3:470
Jewish Popular University (Paris) 11:1013
Jewish Population Studies (period.) 15:343
Jewish Post (newsp.) 16:551
Jewish Protest Committee Against Pogroms (Lond.) 13:695
JEWISH PUBLICATION SOCIETY OF AMERICA 10:80
- Adler, Cyrus 2:273
- Grayzel, Solomon 7:863
- historical chart 8:766-767
- publishing 13:1376; 15:53
- *illus:*
- - text
- - *The Torah: The Five Books of Moses* (1962) 4:872
JEWISH QUARTER 10:81
- *Contents:*
- - Establishment of the Ghetto 10:82
- - In Muslim Countries 10:83
- Jerusalem 9:1516
- - Arab Legion destruction 9:1486
- - Arab period 9:1424
- - inscriptions 16:669
- - reconstruction 9:1502
- *Judenwinkel* 16:998
- Lvov 11:610
- Marrakesh 11:1015
- Ottoman Empire 16:1540,1542
- Paris 13:103ff
- San'a 14:820
- Tarragona 15:822
- Tudela 15:1424
- Venice 16:94
- *illus:*

- - text
- - Amsterdam **15:**499
- - Amsterdam, Nazi period **12:**984
- - Becov (Bohemia) **4:**1175
- - Brody **16:**1327
- - Chodorow **13:**727
- - Constantinople, medieval **5:**918
- - Dubrovnik **16:**871
- - Jemnice **12:**300
- - Jerusalem, aerial view **9:**1439
- - Jerusalem, Old City **9:**1446,1480
- - Kojetin **10:**1156
- - Kromeriz **10:**1274
- - Leeds **10:**1560
- - Lipnik nad Becvou **11:**283
- - London, Petticoat Lane **11:**1004
- - Madrid **11:**682
- - Majorca **11:**798
- - Meknes mellah **11:**1273
- - Morocco, Sabbath scene **12:**331
- - Mukachevo **12:**513
- - New York City **12:**1087,1099
- - Oxford (plan) **12:**1535
- - Paris (plan) **13:**104
- - Paris, Pletzel **13:**109
- - Prague **13:**965
- - Rhodes **14:**147
- - Seville **14:**1202
- - Trebic **15:**1362
- - Tripoli, Libya **15:**1398
- - Tudela **15:**1424
- - Vilna **16:**141,142
- *see also:* GHETTO; *and under individual cities and countries*
JEWISH QUARTERLY REVIEW **10:**88
- Adler, Cyrus **2:**273
- Dropsie College **6:**236
- historiography **8:**563
- Montefiore, Claude **12:**268
"Jewish Question" **8:**706; **8:**715
- socialism **15:**38
- Zionism **16:**74
"Jewish Rabbi" (paint., Rembrandt), *see* "Bearded Man in a Cap"
Jewish Record (period., Eng.) **13:**1031
Jewish Record (newsp., Eng.) **13:**1031
Jewish Record (period., U.S.) **3:**826
Jewish Reform Society (U.S.) **11:**1144
Jewish Refugees' Committee (Eng.) **5:**285
"Jewish Refugees from Russia . . ." (engr., C. J. Staniland) **12:**1084
Jewish Relief Committee for War Victims (Rus.), *see* YEKOPO
Jewish Religious Council (Pol.) **13:**778
Jewish Religious Education Board (Eng.) **6:**447
Jewish religious life in Israel, *see* JEWISH COMMUNITIES IN ISRAEL
Jewish Religious Music, Tel Aviv Institute of **7:**600
Jewish Religious Union (Eng.) **12:**265; **12:**268
- historical chart **8:**766-767
Jewish Reporter (newsp.) **5:**608
Jewish Research Institute of the Ukrainian Academy of Science, Kiev **2:**177
Jewish Resistance Movement (Er. Isr.) **9:**357*ff*
Jewish Restitution Successor Organization **10:**93
Jewish Review (period., Eng.) **13:**1031
Jewish Review (newsp., U.S.) **5:**608
Jewish Review (monthly, Yug.), *see Židovska Smotra*
Jewish Review and Observer (newsp., U.S.) **5:**608
Jewish-Roman war, *see* Jewish War
Jewish Sabbath Journal (Eng.) **5:**456; **13:**1031
Jewish School of Paris (art), *see* PARIS SCHOOL OF ART
Jewish Science Center (N.Y.) **11:**156
Jewish Secondary Schools Movement (Eng.) **6:**449
Jewish Sejm Club (Pol.), *see* Koło
Jewish Settlement Police (Er. Isr.) **7:**1068*ff*; **9:**351; **9:**684
JEWISH SOCIAL DEMOCRATIC PARTY (Gal.) **10:**89
Jewish Socialist Federation (U.S.) **10:**90
- Bund **4:**1500
- socialism **15:**31
Jewish Socialists (Rus.), *see* JEWISH SOCIALIST WORKERS' PARTY
Jewish Socialist Union (Rus.) **16:**1010
JEWISH SOCIALIST VERBAND (orgn.) **10:**90
JEWISH SOCIALIST WORKERS' PARTY (Rus.) **10:**90
- socialism **15:**45
- United Jewish Party **15:**1541
Jewish Social Service Quarterly (U.S.) **4:**366
Jewish Social Studies (period.) **5:**874; **15:**55; **15:**67
Jewish Society (newsp.) **13:**1031
JEWISH SOCIETY FOR HISTORY AND ETHNOGRAPHY (Rus.) **10:**92
Jewish Soldiers' Committees (Aus.-Hung.) **14:**1128
Jewish Spectator (journ.) **13:**1051; **16:**419
Jewish Standard (newsp., Can.) **5:**113
Jewish Standard (newsp., Eng.) **13:**1031; **14:**131
Jewish Standard (newsp., U.S.) **8:**1057
Jewish Star (period.) **14:**213
Jewish State (pub., Arg.) **16:**1123
JEWISH STATE PARTY (Zion.) **10:**92
- Grossman, Meir **7:**938
- Zionism **16:**1099; **16:**1131
Jewish State Theater (Moscow) **15:**1075
- Chagall, Marc **5:**318
- Granovsky, Alexander **7:**854
- Russia **12:**365; **14:**464
- *illus:*
- - *King Lear* production **12:**361
- - Mikhoels as King Lear **11:**1530
Jewish State Theater (Warsaw) **10:**730; **15:**1073
Jewish Statistical and Demographic Institute (Ger.) **12:**1230
Jewish Statute (1804, Rus.) **2:**569
Jewish Studies, *see* WISSENSCHAFT DES JUDENTUMS
JEWISH SUCCESSOR ORGANIZATIONS (in Germany) **10:**93
- Jewish Cultural Reconstruction **10:**49
Jewish Tax (Rom.), *see* FISCUS JUDAICUS
Jewish Teacher (journ.) **6:**312
Jewish Teachers' Association of the German Empire **5:**1595
Jewish Teachers' Seminary (Kiev) **6:**144
Jewish Teachers' Seminary (Smolensk) **15:**7
Jewish Teachers' Seminary (U.S.) **6:**801
JEWISH TELEGRAPHIC AGENCY **10:**95
- history chart **8:**766-767
- Katz, Aleph **10:**821
- press **13:**1051
- *illus:* text
Jewish Territorial Organization **15:**1019ff
Jewish Theater, Moscow, *see* Jewish State Theater
Jewish Theatrical Guild (U.S.) **5:**133
JEWISH THEOLOGICAL SEMINARY OF AMERICA, THE **10:**95
- Adler, Cyrus **2:**273
- Arzt, Max **3:**670
- Cairo *genizah* **16:**1334
- Concordance to the Jerusalem Talmud **9:**1049
- Conservative Judaism **5:**902; **9:**906; **10:**396
- Finkelstein, Louis **6:**1293
- Ginzberg, Louis **7:**584
- Greenberg, Simon **7:**906
- Hebrew incunabula **8:**1322
- Hebrew mss. **11:**906
- history chart (1886) **8:**766-767
- Lieberman, Saul **11:**218
- library **11:**192
- Morais, Sabato **12:**294
- New York City **12:**1119ff
- Rabbinical Assembly **13:**1460
- rabbinical seminaries **13:**1465
- Schechter, Solomon **14:**949
- television and radio **15:**929
- United States **15:**1620
- Wise, Isaac **16:**564
- *illus:*
- - text
- - Jerusalem branch **9:**907
Jewish Theological Seminary of Amsterdam **16:**238
Jewish Theological Seminary-Schocken Library (Jer.) **11:**195
Jewish Times (newsp.), *see Canadian Jewish Times*
Jewish Times (newsp., Eng.), *see* ZEIT, DIE
Jewish Times (period., N.Z.) **13:**1025
Jewish Times (period., U.S.) **6:**679
Jewish Times (Scot. newsp.) **7:**603
Jewish Topics (period.) **13:**1031
Jewish Tribune (period., Eng.) **13:**1031
Jewish Tribune (period., Ind.) **13:**1036
Jewish Trust Corporation (claims against Ger.) **10:**93
Jewish Unity (newsp.) **11:**1480
Jewish Vanguard (newsp.) **13:**1031; **16:**640
"Jewish Vizier," *see* SA'D AL-DAWLA AL-ṢAFĪ IBN HIBBATALLAH
Jewish War (66-70) **8:**641; **10:**251ff
- astrological augury **3:**789
- cause **9:**1405
- Damascus Jews **15:**639
- Dio Cassius **6:**58
- Edomites **6:**378
- Hellenistic states **8:**292
- Jerusalem **9:**1399
- Kamẓa legend **10:**732
- *Maccabees, Book of* **11:**656
- messianism **11:**1421
- piracy **14:**1412
- sages **14:**643
- *Sikarikon* **14:**1529
- Temple **15:**959
- Zealots **16:**947
- *illus:*
- - Ben Ya'ir ostracon **11:**513
- - coins, 1st-4th years **5:**705-707
- - Herodium fortress **4:**235
- - Israel stamp **9:***fcg.* 843
- - *Josippon* **8:**1331
- - *Judaea Capta* coin **9:**110
- - Masada **4:**320; **5:**981; **6:**591; **8:**383,637; **11:**1079-1091
- - Roman Tenth Legion, stamp **4:**234
- - *Shekel Yisrael* (68 C.E.) **9:**109; **14:**1348
Jewish War (wk., Josephus) **10:**253ff
- historiography **8:**554
- literary style **8:**304
Jewish War Memorial (educ. project, Eng.) **5:**684; **6:**448
JEWISH WAR VETERANS OF THE UNITED STATES OF AMERICA **10:**97
- anti-Nazi boycott **4:**1281
- Zionism **16:**1147
"Jewish Wedding" (paint., M. Gottlieb) **3:**554
"Jewish Wedding" (paint., Oppenheim) **11:***fcg.* 1067
Jewish Week (newsp., U.S.) **16:**359
Jewish Weekly (period., Eng.) **13:**1031
Jewish Weekly (newsp., Neth.) **12:**986
Jewish Welfare Board (Eng.) **6:**757; **13:**379
Jewish Western Bulletin (period.) **5:**113; **16:**67
Jewish Western News (newsp.) **16:**551
Jewish Woman (period.) **13:**1031
JEWISH WORLD (newsp., Eng.) **10:**98
- press **3:**1031
Jewish World (newsp., U.S.) **13:**1054
Jewish World News Agency (Eng.) **13:**1031
Jewish Year (period., U.S.) **11:**160
Jewish Year Book (Eng.) **7:**905
JEWNIN, ABRAHAM JONAH **10:**98
Jewnin, Bezalel **10:**98
Jewnin, Nathan **10:**98
Jewnin, Samuel **10:**98
Jew of Mantua (mus.) **3:**496
Jew of Pallughta (ps.-Mess.) **14:**1200
Jewry, *see* Jewish people
"Jews at the Wailing Wall" (drg., Pasternak) **16:**470
JEWS' COLLEGE (Eng.) **10:**98
- Adler, Hermann **2:**278
- Adler, Nathan **2:**286
- Buechler, Adolf **4:**1458
- education **6:**447ff
- Epstein, Isidore **6:**826
- ministers **13:**1453
- Orthodox Judaism **10:**396
- rabbinical seminaries **13:**1464
- *illus:* text
Jews' College Publications (Eng.) **10:**99
Jews' Free School (Eng.) **6:**447ff; **6:**759; **11:**477
- Van Oven, Joshua **16:**68
- *illus:*
- - cooking class **11:**475
- - science class **11:**478
Jews' General Literary and Scientific Institution (Eng.) **6:**447
Jews' Hospital (Eng.) **5:**349
Jews' Hospital (U.S.), *see* Mount Sinai Hospital
Jews in Egypt and in Palestine under the Fatimid Caliphs (wk.) **16:**1338
Jews' Infant Schools (Eng.) **16:**68
JEWS IN ISRAEL **9:**887
"Jews in Line for a Meal at Orzyglow" (paint., J. Fuks) Fig. 76 3-ART
Jews' Pennies (coins), *see* JUDENPFENNIGE
Jews' stone (med. material) **7:**894
Jew Suess, *see* OPPENHEIMER, JOSEPH BEN ISSACHAR SUESSKIND
Jezaniah (bib. fig.) **9:**1169

Jezdegerd (Pers. k.) **14:**750
JEZEBEL (bib. fig.) **10:**99
- Ahab **2:**438
- Ahaziah **2:**456
- Elijah **6:**633ff
- history **8:**597ff
- magic **11:**705
- Naboth **11:**55
- *illus:*
- - text
- - Naboth being stoned **12:**747
Jezer (tribal clan) **12:**818
Jezierski, Jacek **4:**1539
Jeziory (tn., Belor.), *see* OZERY
Jezīrat el-Farʿūn (loc., Elath gulf), *see* Jazīrat-Farʿun
Jezreel (bib. fig.) **8:**1010
JEZREEL (city, Er. Isr.) **10:**101
- dyeing center **6:**328
- Saladin **9:**268
- *see also:* JEZREEL, VALLEY OF
JEZREEL, VALLEY OF (Isr.) **10:**101
- cotton **9:**292
- geography **9:**589
- geology **9:**215
- Hankin, Yehoshua **7:**1268
- physiography **9:**147ff
- settlements **9:**340
- *illus:*
- - text
- - Alexander Zeid statue **16:**969
- - digging drainage ditches **9:**585
- - Gan ha-Sheloshah **12:**879
- - Gilboa slopes **9:**145
- - moshavim in Taanach regional settlement area **9:**578
- - view of Megiddo **11:**1225
- *see also:* JEZREEL
Jhirad, Joseph Ephraim **11:**1567
JIAS, *see* JEWISH IMMIGRANT AID SERVICES OF CANADA (JIAS)
Jib, Al- (vill., Er. Isr.) **4:**383; **7:**551; **16:**667
Jibāl, Al- (reg., Isr.), *see* SEIR, MOUNT
Jiblah (tn., Yem.) **14:**543
Jibneh (pub. house, Aus.) **12:**660
Jidoviţa (vill., Rum.), *see* Entràdàm
Jidyó (lang.), *see* LADINO
Jifna (Arab vill., Isr.) **7:**691
JIHĀD (Holy War, Isl.) **10:**103
- Koran **10:**1198
JIHLAVA (city, Cz.) **10:**104
- Albert V **2:**530
Jilīn (stlmt., Bashan) **9:**596; **13:**1534
Jiljiliya (vill., Er. Isr.) **9:**575
Jilovsky (fam.), *see* ILLOWY
Jilovsky, Georg **4:**1219
Jimenes de Cisneros, Francisco, *see* XIMENES DE CISNEROS, FRANCISCO
Jiménez Rueda, Julio **15:**255
"Jimmy Walker" (sculp., E. Glicenstein) **14:**1061
JINDRICHUV HRADEC (tn., Cz.) **10:**104
J.I.R., *see* HEBREW UNION COLLEGE—JEWISH INSTITUTE OF RELIGION
Jiradi, Al- (loc., Er. Isr.) **14:**1629
JIRKU, ANTON **10:**105
Jirwāh (vill., Yem.) **11:**849
Jishsh (vill., Isr.), *see* Gush Ḥalav
JITTA, DANIEL JOSEPHUS **10:**1500; **10:**1509
Jīzeh (loc., Egy.) **14:**762
Jizfān, Joseph **10:**105
JIZFĀN, JUDAH BEN JOSEPH **10:**105
Jizfān, Solomon **10:**105
Jizya (tax), *see* KHARAJ AND JIZYA
J. L. B. (mvmt., Eng), *see* Jewish Lads' Brigade
J. N. F., *see* JEWISH NATIONAL FUND
JOAB (bib. fig.) **10:**106
- Abishai **2:**79
- Abner **2:**87
- Absalom **2:**174
- Adonijah **2:**294
- Amasa **2:**794
- Jerusalem capture **9:**1381
- population **13:**868
- Solomon **15:**97
- *geneal. table:* **5:**1342
Joab (paytan) **13:**585
Joab ben Benjamin **13:**585
Joab ben Daniel **13:**585
Joab ben Jehiel **11:**903
- paytanim **13:**585
JOAB BEN JEREMIAH **10:**108
- Jeremiah ben Isaac **9:**1364
JOAB THE GREEK (Ha-Yevani) **10:**108
Joab of Camerino **2:**936
Joachim (1st cent. C.E.) **16:**132
Joachim II (elector of Brandenburg) **11:**288
JOACHIM, JOSEPH **10:**108
- Lord Byron **4:**1549
Joachim of Fiore **10:**644
JOACHIMSEN, PHILIP J. **10:**110
- soldier **11:**1551
Joachimsthal, J. L. **4:**1239; **13:**1365
Joah (bib. fig.) **3:**673
Joakim (apoc. fig.) **15:**532
Joanna (countess of Provence) **3:**964
Joanna I (14th cent., q. of Naples) **3:**228
Joanna II (14/15 cent., q. of Naples) **3:**228; **5:**253; **11:**1064
Joan of Arc
- history chart **8:**766–767
João II (k. of Port.), *see* JOHN II
JOASH (835–798, k. of Judah) **10:**110
- anointing **3:**31
- history **8:**600ff
- history chart **8:**766-67
- kingship **10:**1013
- *geneal. table:* **5:**1341
Joash (801–785, k. of Israel), *see* JEHOASH
Joazar (h. pr.), *see* JOEZER, SON OF BOETHUS
JOB, THE BOOK OF **10:**111
- *Contents:*
- - Introduction **10:**111
- - Critical Analysis **10:**112
- - Message and Meaning of **10:**121
- - In the Aggadah **10:**124
- - In Islam **10:**125
- - In the Arts **10:**125
- General
- - Abraham **2:**117
- - *Aḥikar, Book of* **2:**461
- - canonization **4:**824
- - Jethro **10:**19
- - Job, Testament of **10:**129
- - Masorah **16:**1441
- - Scandinavian literature **14:**930
- Content and Ideas
- - ethical teaching **6:**936
- - poetry **13:**676ff
- - resurrection **12:**1356; **14:**97
- - reward and punishment **14:**134
- - sacrifice **14:**605
- - Satan **14:**904
- - wisdom **16:**557; **16:**559
- Interpretations
- - Aristeas **3:**438
- - Maimonides **11:**774
- - Naḥmanides **12:**778
- - Sommo, Judah **15:**138
- - Spinoza **15:**283
- Translations
- - Aramaic **5:**280
- - Arnheim, Heymann **3:**485
- - Dead Sea *targum* **5:**1401
- - Judeo-Greek **10:**425
- - *targum* **4:**848
- *illus:*
- - text
- - *Rothschild Miscellany* **10:***fcg.* 107
- - Satan departing from the Lord **14:**903
- - sitting down among the ashes **6:**377
- - wife and friends **4:**934; **15:**1522
"Job" (lith., D. Bokros-Birman) **4:**1184
Job, Solomon ibn, *see* Solomon ben Joseph ibn Ayyub
JOB, TESTAMENT OF (Gr. pseudepig. bk.) **10:**129
- apocalypse **3:**180
"Job and Comforters" (tpst., Ullmann) **15:**1522
Joba (city, Egy.) **14:**15
Jobab (bib. fig.) **10:**129
"Job and his Wife" (paint., A. Duerer) **10:**128
"Job Cursing Day he Was Born" (engr., W. Blake) **10:**115
Job's Well (Isr.) **6:**800
JOCHEBED (bib. fig.) **10:**130
- in the Arts **12:**408
- Moses **11:**55; **12:**372
- Shiphrah **14:**1410
Jochebed (dau. of Rashi) **13:**1559
JOCHELSON, VLADIMIR (Waldemar) **10:**130
- ethnology **15:**1351
Jockisch, Matthaeus **4:**886
Jode, Gerard de **11:**917
Joden Savane (loc., Surinam) **2:**413; **15:**530ff
Jødisk Familieblad (period.) **13:**1049
Jødisk Tidsskrift (period.) **13:**1047
Jodoigne (tn., Belg.) **4:**416
Joede, Fritz **14:**1313
Joel (bib. fig., s. of Samuel) **10:**131; **14:**784
Joel (12th cent., trans.) **6:**1266; **10:**163; **13:**1188
Joel (art.) **11:**1173
JOEL (bib. bk.) **10:**131
- eschatological writings **6:**866ff
- Minor Prophets **12:**48
- *illus:*
- - text
- - *Stavordale Bible* **4:**64
"Joel" (frsc., Michelangelo) **10:**133
Joel, Alessandro **10:**135
Joel, Sir Asher **13:**820
Joel. Carl, *see* JOEL, RAPHAEL
JOEL, DAVID HEYMANN **10:**133
Joel, Ephraim Fischel **11:**556
Joel, George W. **13:**1371
Joel, Herman R. **10:**134
Joel, Issachar Bernhard **4:**973
- *illus:*
- - Bashevis Singer, Isaac and **4:**294
Joel, Jack **15:**311; **10:**136
JOEL, KARL **10:**134
JOEL, MANUEL **10:**134
- articles of faith **3:**659
- Tiktin, Gedaliah **15:**1140
Joel, Moses **6:**367
JOEL, OTTO J. **10:**135
JOEL, RAPHAEL **10:**135
JOEL, SOLOMON BARNATO ("Solly") **10:**136
- horse breeding **15:**311
- *illus:* text
Joel, Yale **13:**484
Joel Ba'al Shem I **4:**7
Joel Ba'al Shem of Zamosc **4:**6; **10:**635
Joel ben Abraham Shemariah of Vilna **11:**346
JOEL BEN ISAAC HA-LEVI **10:**137
- Baruch of Regensburg **4:**278
- Eliezer of Bonn **6:**625
- Ephraim of Bonn **6:**813
- Wuerzburg **16:**675
JOEL BEN MOSES GAD **10:**137
JOEL BEN SIMEON **10:**138
- illuminated *haggadah* **7:**1098
- illuminated *maḥzorim* **11:**734
- illuminated manuscripts **8:**1267
- *illus:*
- - text
- - *Joel ben Simeon Haggadah* **3:**995; **7:***fcg.* 1003; **10:**139
- - *Washington Haggadah* **6:***fcg.* 651; **8:**1271
Joel David, "the Vilner Baalebessel", *see* Strashunsky, Joel David
Joel of Bonn, *see* JOEL BEN ISAAC HA-LEVI
Joel of Gulkha **10:**466; **12:**1418
Joel of Wetzlar **16:**478
Joelson, Annette **15:**209
Joelson, Charles S. **13:**179
Joez ben Jacob **16:**114
JOEZER, SON OF BOETHUS (h. pr.) **10:**139
- Anan ben Seth **2:**922
- Boethusian **4:**1169
- Roman census **16:**947
- Simeon ben Boethus **14:**1554
Joezer of ha-Birah (tan.) **7:**296; **12:**1468
Joffe (fam. name), *see also* Jaffe, Yaffe, Yoffe(y)
JOFFE, ABRAHAM FEODOROVICH **10:**139
Joffe, Abram Moiseyevich, *see* DEBORIN, ABRAM MOISEYEVICH
JOFFE, ADOLPH ABRAMOVICH **10:**140
- communism **5:**794
JOFFE, ELIEZER LIPA (Isr.) **10:**140
- He-Ḥalutz **8:**254
- Moshav Ovedim **12:**435
JOFFE, HILLEL **10:**141
- *illus:*
- El-Arish technical commission **6:**565
Joffe, Joseph, *see* Yoffey, Joseph ben Moses
JOFFE, JUDAH ACHILLES **10:**141
Joffe, Shalom Elḥanan **8:**210
Joffe, W. G. **13:**1340
JOFFEN, ABRAHAM **10:**142
Jogbeha (bib. site, Er. Isr.) **14:**105
JOGICHES, LEON **10:**143
JOHANAN (bib. fig.) **10:**143
Johanan (f., Jesus) **15:**1209
Johanan ben Bag Bag (tan.) **4:**473
JOHANAN BEN BEROKA (tan.) **10:**143
JOHANAN BEN GUDGADA (tan.) **10:**143
- ritual purity **13:**1411
JOHANAN BEN HA-ḤORANIT (tan.) **10:**144
Johanan ben Isaac (r.) **8:**820
Johanan ben Israel of Karlin **10:**794
JOHANAN BEN JEHOIADA (h. pr.) **10:**144
- Temple **15:**982
JOHANAN BEN JOSHUA HA-KOHEN **10:**144
- Joshua **10:**270
Johanan ben Josiah **5:**1340; **9:**1316
Johanan ben Levi of Giscala, *see* JOHN OF GISCALA
JOHANAN BEN NAPPAḤA (amora) **10:**144
- Academy on High **2:**208
- *Akedah* **14:**603
- Babylonian Talmud **2:**873

- Bible cantillation **16:**1412
- diseases **4:**1030; **6:**1368
- forbidden food **14:**1197
- idols **15:**1132
- Jerusalem Talmud **15:**772ff
- Kahana **10:**677
- Kamẓa legend **10:**732
- *Megillat Yuhasin* **11:**1232
- Messianic era **12:**1355
- Nasi and Sanhedrin **9:**253
- Palmyra **9:**254
- pilgrimage tradition **15:**1309
- Rav **13:**1577
- *Seder Olam Rabbah* **14:**1093
- *Sefer Yuḥasin* **11:**1232
- taxes **15:**873
- Yose ben Zimra **16:**857

JOHANAN BEN NURI (tan.) **10:**147
- Temple incense formula **3:**991

Johanan ben Saadiah **16:**114
Johanan ben Saul **7:**1154
Johanan ben Simeon **11:**1127
JOHANAN BEN TORTA (tan.) **10:**148
JOHANAN BEN ZAKKAI (tan.) **10:**148
- *Contents:*
- - Johanan and the Temple **10:**149
- - As a Teacher **10:**150
- - The Period of the Destruction **10:**152
- - Johanan at Jabneh **10:**153
- Abba Sikra **2:**44
- academies **2:**201ff
- apologetics **3:**191
- *arba'ah minim* **15:**499
- disputations **6:**81
- fear of God **6:**1199
- fox fables **3:**20
- Hanina ben Dosa **15:**454
- Hillel's forecast **6:**961
- history chart **8:**766-767
- Jabneh **11:**315
- leadership **9:**240
- letters **11:**57
- mysticism **10:**498
- peace **13:**197
- Pharisees **13:**790
- sages **14:**643
- Tiberias tomb **15:**1135
- Vespasian **10:**253; **10:**254

Johanan ben Zakkai Synagogue (Jer.) **9:**1447; **9:**889
- *illus:*
- - interior **9:**1444

Johanan ben Zavda **3:**673; **3:**676; **11:**1186
Johanan the Essene, *see* JOHN THE ESSENE
JOHANAN HA-SANDELAR (tan.) **10:**154
- *illus:*
- - tomb **8:**926

JOHANAN THE HASMONEAN **10:**155
Johanan Hyrcanus, *see* HYRCANUS, JOHN
Johanan Mordecai Judah, *see* Alatrini, Angelo
Johanan of Lachowicze, *see* Lachowicze, Johanan of
Johanan of Rotmistrovka **15:**1472
Johanan son of Hakkoz **6:**964; **8:**627; **13:**1086
Johanan Taros **11:**1247
Johanan Trèves, *see* Trèves, Johanan
Johanes from Caesarea **15:**873
Johani (faith healer) **11:**707
Johann II (archbp.) **11:**1190
JOHANNESBURG (city, S.A.) **10:**155
- Alexander, Bernard **2:**573
- education **6:**455ff
- museum **12:**551
- South Africa **15:**186ff
- *illus:*
- - text
- - Park Synagogue **15:**191
- - President Street Synagogue **15:**194
- - Smuts, J. C. bust ceremony **15:**205

Johannes de Capua, *see* JOHN OF CAPUA
Johannesen, Georg **14:**934
Johannes Hispalenis, *see* AVENDAUTH
Johannes Luccae **8:**39
Johannes of Wurtzburg **15:**1355
Johannis (leg. sorcerer), *see* JANNES and JAMBRES
Johanniter Order hospice (Jer.) **9:**1455
Johannson, T. Carl **8:**39
John (pr.), *see* Johanan son of Hakkoẓ
John (4/5 cent., bp.) **9:**1406
John (11/12 cent., bp.) **15:**263
John (k., Bohem.) **16:**1289
John (k., Eng.) **11:**470
- history chart **8:**766-767

John (k., Sic.) **15:**1675
John I (k., Aragon)
- Barbastro Jews **4:**207
- Barcelona Jews **4:**211
- Cervera Jews **5:**314
- Cresques de Vivers **5:**1086
- Spain **15:**237

John I (k., Cast.) **3:**930
John I (k., Port.) **3:**498
JOHN II ("The Good"; k., Fr.) **10:**158
John II (k., León) **16:**926
JOHN II (k., Port.) **10:**158
- Aboab, Isaac **2:**93
- Abrabanel, Isaac **2:**109
- Abraham of Beja **2:**161

John II (k., Cast.) **15:**238; **15:**1204
JOHN III (k., Port.) **10:**158
- Azemmour Jews **3:**1004
- inquisition **8:**1385

John XVIII (pope) **7:**13
JOHN XXII (pope) **10:**159
- Pastoureaux **5:**1141
- Popes **13:**855

JOHN XXIII (pope) **10:**159
- Christian-Jewish relations **3:**137; **16:**78
- Holocaust **8:**875
- Israel **16:**78
- popes **13:**860
- rescue of Jews **8:**913

John, Father of Eupolemus, *see* Johanan son of Hakkoẓ
John, St. (Chr. apostle) **3:**215
JOHN THE BAPTIST **10:**160
- asceticism **3:**682
- Ein Karem **16:**1324
- Elijah **6:**635
- Essenes **6:**901
- Hemerobaptists **14:**1088
- Herod Antipas **3:**76
- in the Arts **14:**690
- Jesus **10:**11ff
- Salome **8:**388; **14:**689
- Samaria **14:**725
- Yaḥya ibn Zakariyyā **12:**917
- *illus:*
- - "Dance of Salome" (paint., Gozzoli) **14:**691
- - Salome with head of **6:**775

John ben Levi, *see* JOHN OF GISCALA
John ben Sosas **9:**1224
John Birch Society (mvmt., U.S.) **12:**952
JOHN CHRYSOSTOM **10:**161
- anti-Jewish sermons **8:**654
- church **5:**552

John de Sacrobosco **3:**800
JOHN THE ESSENE **10:**162
- Yaḥad **16:**701

John Hyrcanus, *see* HYRCANUS, JOHN
John of Brescia **3:**801
John of Bristol **8:**14
JOHN OF CAPUA **10:**163
John of the Cross, St. (poet) **15:**248
JOHN OF GISCALA **10:**163
- Anan, son of Anan **2:**919
- Ananias, son of Ẓadok **2:**924
- Eleazar ben Simeon **6:**598
- Josephus Flavius **10:**252
- Lion of Wrath **11:**276
- Man of Lies **11:**234
- Silas **14:**1533
- Temple **15:**959
- Titus **15:**1168; **15:**1169
- warfare **16:**280

John of Hollywood, *see* John de Sacrobosco
John of Mandeville **15:**1356
John of Nogaret **13:**393
John of Saint Just **13:**393
John of Seville, *see* Hispanus, John
John Scotus Erigena, *see* Erigena, Johannes Scotus
Johns Hopkins University (U.S.) **15:**1678
Johnson, Edgar Mayer **15:**300
Johnson, Edward Israel **14:**822
Johnson, Eyvind **14:**931
Johnson, H.G. **12:**323
Johnson, Joseph E. **9:**449; **15:**1550
JOHNSON, LYNDON BAINES **10:**164
- Eshkol, Levi **6:**889
- Israel desalinization project **9:**400
- Israel military aid **9:**418
- Israel-U.S. relations **9:**430ff
- *illus:*
- - text
- - Eshkol, and **9:**405
- - inauguration of John F. Kennedy **10:**908

Johnson, Meyer Albert **10:**308
Johnson, Philip **15:**626
Johnston, Eric **9:**385; **14:**649; **15:**1665
Johnstown (city, Pa.) **13:**230
John Zebedee **14:**836
Joiachin (k., Judah), *see* JEHOIACHIN
Joiakim (pr., s. of Jeshua) **13:**466
Joiarib (pr. clan), *see* JEHOIARIB
JOIGNY (tn., Fr.) **10:**165
"Joint", *see* AMERICAN JEWISH JOINT DISTRIBUTION COMMITTEE
Joint Anglo-American Committee of Inquiry **15:**1544
Joint Boycott Council (orgn., U.S.) **4:**1281; **10:**66
Joint Consultative Council (orgn., U.S.) **5:**665
Joint Diseases Hospital (N.Y.C) **12:**1116
Joint Distribution Committee, *see* AMERICAN JEWISH JOINT DISTRIBUTION COMMITTEE
Joint (conjoint) Foreign Committee (Eng.) **6:**757
Joint Foreign Committee (Eng.), *see* ANGLO-JEWISH ASSOCIATION
Joint Sheḥitah Board of the Ashkenazim, Perushim and Ḥasidim (Jer.) **6:**74
Joio, Norman dello **14:**918
JOKNEAM (Yokneam, city, mosh., Isr.) **10:**165
- statistics **1:**place list
- *illus:*
- - text
- - metal works **9:**818

JOKTAN (bib. fig.) **10:**166
Joktheel (tn., Edom) **2:**798; **6:**375
Jolek, Shelomo **16:**1218
Joliet (city,U.S.) **8:**1256
JOLLES, JACOB ẒEVI BEN NAPHTALI **10:**166
Jolles, Sussman **10:**167
JOLLES, ZECHARIAH ISAIAH **10:**167
- *illus:* text

JOLLES, ZVI ENRICO **10:**167
Jolowicz, H.T. **10:**1495
JOLSON, AL **10:**168
- *illus:*
- - text
- - *The Jazz Singer* **12:**451

Jolson, Julius, *see* STAHL, FRIEDRICH JULIUS
Jona (fam.) **5:**226
JONA, GIOVANNI BATTISTA **10:**168
- Bartolocci, Giulio **4:**265
- Morosino, Giulio **12:**347

Jona, Leon **16:**1105
Jonadab (bib. fig.) **13:**1609ff
Jonah (bib. fig.), *see* JONAH, BOOK OF
JONAH (amora) **10:**177
- Yose **16:**850

Jonah (12th cent., schol.) **2:**224
Jonah (Viennese mart.) **16:**503
JONAH, BOOK OF **10:**169
- *Contents:*
- - Outline of Contents **10:**169
- - Unity of the Book **10:**170
- - Motifs of the Book **10:**171
- - Teaching of the Book **10:**172
- - Date of Origin **10:**172
- - In the Aggadah **10:**173
- - In Christianity **10:**174
- - In Islam **10:**174
- - In the Arts **10:**175
- castor-oil plant **5:**241
- flight to Tarshish **15:**825
- Judeo-Greek **10:**425
- Minor Prophets **12:**48
- Nineveh **16:**1502
- tomb of **7:**336; **8:**333; **12:**1169
- *illus:*
- - text
- - beside the walls of Nineveh **12:**1169
- - ejected by the whale Pl. 9 **10:**-KETUBBAH
- - the great fish **5:**369; **15:**1
- - Latin Bible **15:**1
- - micrographic depiction **4:**966
- - Preaching to the Ninevites **4:**1043
- - swallowed by the great fish **11:**90

Jonah, Michael Solomon **15:**1455
JONAH, MOSES **10:**178
- Lurianic tradition **10:**591; **11:**575

Jonah, Psalm of **10:**170
Jonah, Shabbetai, *see* Shabbetai Jonah
JONAH BEN ABRAHAM GERONDI **10:**179
- Adret, Solomon **2:**305
- Asher ben David **3:**706
- ethical literature **11:**344
- judicial autonomy **3:**929
- Maimonidean controversy **11:**749
- Naḥmanides **12:**774
- *Sefer ha-Yashar* **14:**1099
- *illus:* text

Jonah ben Jacob of Zalocze **13:**1109
- *illus:*
- - *Ma'aseh Rav* (1736) **9:**1098

"Jonah beside the Walls of Nineveh" (drg., Rembrandt) **12:**1169
Jonah ibn Janāḥ, *see* IBN JANĀḤ, JONAH
"Jonah Preaching to the Ninevites" (lith., Birnbaum) **4:**1043
Jonas, Abraham **10:**181
Jonas, Benjamin Franklin **10:**181

Jonas, Deborah **4**:565; **4**:566
JONAS, EMILE **12**:694
JONAS, HANS **10**:181
JONAS, JOSEPH **10**:181
- Ohio **12**:1344
JONAS, NATHAN S. **10**:182
Jonas, Samuel Naphtali Herz **4**:564; **4**:567
JONATHAN (bib. fig., s. of Gershom) **10**:182
- Gershom **7**:511
- Micaiah **11**:1484
- priestly family **13**:1073
JONATHAN (bib. fig. s. of Shimea) **10**:182
JONATHAN (bib. fig., s. of Uzziah) **10**:182
JONATHAN (bib. fig., s. of Abiathar) **10**:182
JONATHAN (bib. fig., s. of Kareah) **10**:183
JONATHAN (bib. fig. s. of Jerahmeel) **10**:183
JONATHAN (bib. fig. f. of Ebed) **10**:183
JONATHAN (bib. fig., s. of Asahel) **10**:183
JONATHAN (bib. fig., f. of Zechariah) **10**:183
JONATHAN (bib. fig., s. of Joiada) **10**:183
JONATHAN (bib. fig., s. of Saul) **10**:183
- David **5**:1319ff
- Geba **7**:349
- in the Arts **5**:1337; **14**:917
- Saul **14**:911; **14**:913
Jonathan (h. pr.), *see* ARISTOBULUS III
Jonathan (2nd cent. C.E., schol.) **9**:86
Jonathan (13th cent., moneylender) **13**:106
Jonathan, Targum of *see* TARGUM
JONATHAN BEN ABRAHAM ISAAC **10**:185
JONATHAN BEN AMRAM **10**:185
JONATHAN BEN ANAN (h. pr.) **10**:185
- Felix **8**:639
- Sicarii **14**:1492
- Theophilus **15**:1111
Jonathan ben Bayahu **4**:231; **4**:238
JONATHAN BEN DAVID HA-KOHEN OF LUNEL **10**:186
- Abraham of Posquiéres **2**:137
- *aliyah* **9**:273
- Ephraim ibn Avi Alragan **6**:814
- Ibn Migash, Meir **8**:1189
- Maimonides **11**:760ff
JONATHAN BEN ELEAZAR (amora) **10**:186
Jonathan ben Harkinas **6**:178
Jonathan ben Isaac (13th cent.) **16**:675
Jonathan ben Isaac ha-Levi (18th cent.) **4**:1390
JONATHAN BEN JACOB (Hung.) **10**:187
Jonathan ben Jacob of Wielowies **6**:250
JONATHAN BEN JOSEPH OF RUZHANY **10**:187
- Ruzhany **14**:526
Jonathan ben Mattathias **13**:106
Jonathan ben Moses Jacob **12**:1244
Jonathan ben Nathan Nata, *see* EYBESCHUETZ, JONATHAN
JONATHAN BEN UZZIEL **10**:188
- Jewish literature **11**:313
- Theodotion **4**:855
- Zechariah **16**:958
Jonathan David Publishing Co. (U.S.) **13**:1377
Jonathan ha-Kohen, *see* JONATHAN BEN DAVID HA-KOHEN OF LUNEL
JONATHAN THE HASMONEAN **10**:188
- Acra **9**:1392
- Alexander Balas **2**:576
- Demetrius **5**:1489
- Hasmonean revolt **8**:629
- Hellenism **8**:296
- history chart **8**:766-767
- Jerusalem **14**:837
- *Scroll of Antiochus* **14**:1045
- war and warfare **16**:279
- Wicked Priest **16**:486
- *geneal. table* **7**:1457
Jonathan of Lunel, *see* JONATHAN BEN DAVID HA-KOHEN OF LUNEL
Jonathan of Ruzhany, *see* JONATHAN BEN JOSEPH OF RUZHANY
JONATHAN SON OF ABSALOM **10**:189
Jonathan the Weaver **11**:199
JONAVA (tn., Lith.) **10**:190
- *illus:*
- - a Jew **11**:380
- - timber punting **11**:383
Jones, Benjamin Franklin **11**:519
Jones, C.N. **9**:1524
Jones, Ernest **13**:1338
Jones, Henry **4**:1145; **12**:1072
Jones, Israel I. **2**:505; **14**:1664
Jones, William **8**:39
Jong, David de **6**:321
Jong, Dola de **6**:321
JONG, LOUIS DE **10**:190
Jong, P. de **8**:39
Jonge, Moses Jacobson de **13**:1287
Jonk (hymnbook) **2**:311
Jonker, Abraham H. **15**:208
Jonquières (vill., Fr.) **12**:1447
Jonsson, Steinn **4**:877
Joods Bijzonder Onderwijs (found., Amst.) **2**:904
Joodse Invalide, De (found., Amst.) **2**:904
Joodse Jeugdfederatie (orgn., Holl.) **16**:1119
Joodse Raad (council, Neth.) **2**:920ff
Joodse Weekblad, het (period.) **2**:903; **12**:986; **13**:1035
- *illus:*
- - first issue **12**:982
Joplin (city, Mo.) **12**:158
Joppah (port city, Er. Isr.), *see* JAFFA
Joram (bib. fig.), *see* JEHORAM
JORDAN (riv.) **10**:190
- Arab diversion plans **14**:1625
- Armistice Agreements **3**:481
- Bet Yeraḥ **4**:778
- course of **9**:113
- electric energy **9**:791
- frontier territory **9**:313ff
- geography **9**:589
- guerilla attacks **14**:1639
- source region **9**:171
- Syria and division of waters **15**:649
- Transjordan **15**:1316
- U.N. **15**:1553; **15**:1556
- U.S. plans **15**:1665
- valley **9**:167ff
- *illus:*
- - text
- - Ark of the Covenant carried across **3**:461
- - Ashdot Ya'acob **3**:699
- - Christian pilgrims **9**:326
- - delta **9**:157
- - Gesher Benot Ya'akov bridge **7**:525
- - Gilead mountains **7**:570
- - Madaba map **11**:677
- - meandering course **9**:153
- - Naaman's leprosy **11**:34
- - Naharayim electric power plant **9**:790
- - water buffaloes **9**:235
JORDAN, CHARLES HAROLD **10**:197
Jordan, Colin **12**:954
JORDAN, HASHEMITE KINGDOM OF **10**:198
- General
- - Abdullah ibn Hussein **2**:56
- - Arab general survey **9**:1021
- - history chart **8**:766-767
- - Jordan designation **9**:112
- - Palestine **13**:29ff
- - population **13**:870
- - Transjordan **15**:1315
- Internal Affairs
- - Arab guerrilla organizations **9**:469ff
- - Arab League **3**:242ff
- - Arab National Movement **9**:466ff
- - Arab refugees **9**:448ff; **9**:467ff
- - civil war (1970) **9**:472
- - joint Arab command **14**:1605
- Relationship with Israel
- - armistice agreements (1949) **3**:479
- - armistice talks **9**:377
- - clashes **9**:386ff; **9**:1497ff
- - frontier **9**:320
- - Jerusalem **9**:1487; **16**:77
- - Jerusalem demarcation line **9**:425ff
- - Samaritans **14**:736
- - Six-Day War **9**:404ff **14**:1624
- - U.N. **9**:415; **15**:1546ff
- - War of Independence **9**:366ff; **16**:306ff
- *illus:*
- - text
- - Arab Legion soldiers on Old City wall **9**:1483
- - Arab refugee camp (Jericho) **9**:447
- - Armistice Agreement, Rhodes **9**:375
- - convoy crossing Allenby Bridge **9**:410
- - Israel-Jordan General Armistice Agreement (1949) **3**:479,480
- - Six-Day War **14**:1633,1636
- *see also:* HUSSEIN
Jordán, Samuel Sandor (r.) **14**:908
Jordan Exploration Company **9**:793
Jordania (Zion. orgn.) **10**:805
Jordanis, Abraham, *see* Abraham Jordanis
Jordanis, Canaan, *see* Canaan Jordanis
Jordanis, Golda, *see* Golda Jordanis
Jordanis, Israel, *see* Israel Jordanis
Jordanis, Lewko, *see* LEWKO JORDANIS
Jordan Jordanis (14/15 cent.) **11**:180
Jordan Jordanis (15th cent.) **11**:181
Jordan of Poland (Jordanis) **13**:720
Jordan Project **15**:701
- *see also:* JORDAN
Jordan Valley (Er. Isr.) **9**:589ff
- ancient settlements **8**:580
- geology **9**:215ff
- Kinnarot Valley **10**:1032
- regional council **9**:621
- Transjordan **15**:1315
- *illus:*
- - Bet ha-Aravah **4**:716
- - Gilead Plateau **9**:169
- - Lashon formations **9**:205
- - Naḥal Gilgal **9**:585
- - view from Belvoir **12**:880
- *see also:* JORDAN
Jorge (fam.,) **15**:1301ff
Jornal Israelita (period.) **4**:1331
Josaphat, Israel Beer, *see* REUTER, PAUL JULIUS, BARON VON
Josce of Gloucester **7**:624
JOSCE OF YORK **10**:200
- Aaron of York **2**:22
Josce son of Isaac **3**:398; **6**:748
Jose (name), *see also* Yose
Jose ben Tanḥum **10**:887
Jose de la Rosa, *see* Rosa, Jose de la
Josefov (Josefstadt; J. dist. of Prague) **13**:969
Josefowicz (fam.), *see* JOZEFOWICZ
Josel ben Ze'ev Wolf ha-Levi, *see* JOSEPH BEN ZE'EV WOLF HA-LEVI
Joselein ben Moses, *see* JOSEPH BEN MOSES
Joselevich, Jacobo **16**:1123
JOSELEWICZ, BEREK **10**:201
- history chart **8**:766-767
- *illus:* text
Joselewicz, Berko **12**:1238
Joselmann of Rosheim, *see* JOSEPH BEN GERSHON OF ROSHEIM
Joselowitz, Joseph **11**:237
JOSEPH (bib. fig.) **10**:202
- *Contents:*
- - Joseph and His Brothers **10**:202
- - In Potiphar's House **10**:202
- - In Prison **10**:203
- - Pharaoh's Dreams **10**:203
- - Joseph's Elevation **10**:205
- - The Reconciliation **10**:206
- - The Migration to Egypt **10**:207
- - Joseph's Agrarian Measures **10**:208
- - Joseph's Last Days **10**:208
- - The Nature of the Narrative **10**:208
- - Joseph in the Rest of the Bible **10**:209
- - The Name **10**:209
- - In the Aggadah **10**:209
- - In Islam **10**:212
- - In the Arts **10**:213
- - In Music **10**:216
- abduction, and sale of **2**:56
- Benjamin **4**:522ff
- Bible history **8**:574ff
- breastplate stone **13**:1009
- Genesis, Book of **7**:389ff
- Hyksos **6**:481; **8**:1142
- Jacob **9**:1193ff
- *Joseph and Asenath* **10**:223
- kabbalistic view **10**:575; **14**:183
- Manasseh **11**:850
- Naḥmanides **12**:777
- *Naphtali, Testament of* **12**:821
- Pharaoh **13**:360ff
- Potiphar **13**:933
- Rachel **13**:1486
- Samaritans **14**:727
- tomb of **8**:921; **11**:673
- *illus:*
- - text
- - Asenath and **3**:693
- - binding of Simeon **14**:1550
- - brothers and **6**:281
- - Coptic story of **6**:944
- - cupbearer's and baker's dreams **5**:1172
- - in prison **2**:364
- - interpreting Pharoah's dream **13**:363
- - Islamic depiction **9**:1203
- - Jacob blessing sons **14**:67
- - Judeo-Persian ms. (15th cent.) **10**:434
- - Pharaoh's dream **6**:211; **8**:1218
- - Potiphar's wife Pl. 2 **10**:KETUBBAH; **13**:354,934
- - rescued by Ishmaelites **9**:88
- - reunion with Jacob **13**:1103
- - sheaves of wheat dream **6**:209
- - sold into slavery **13**:354
JOSEPH (br., Herod) **10**:217

- Antigonus II **3**:66
- Massada **8**:376
- *geneal. table* **8**:377
Joseph (f., Jesus) **10**: 10ff; **15**:1209
Joseph (f., R. Akiva) **13**:1186
Joseph (2nd cent. C.E., Rom. emp.) **4**:1480
Joseph (4th cent., amora), *see* JOSEPH BEN ḤIYYA
Joseph (4/5 cent., apos.) **9**:255; **10**:334
Joseph (savora), *see* Yose
Joseph (gaon) **7**:318
Joseph (f., Saadiah Gaon) **9**:1252
JOSEPH (k. of Khazars) **10**:218
- Ben Aaron **7**:420
- correspondence **10**:950
- Jewish history **11**:350
Joseph (Croatia), *see* Mar Joseph
Joseph (12th cent., pros.) **13**:1188
Joseph (12th cent., Iraq) **12**:444
Joseph (12th cent., York) **16**:848
Joseph (14th cent., scribe) **9**:*fcg.* 43
Joseph (15/16 cent., scribe) **4**:470
Joseph (schol., Lith.) **16**:140
JOSEPH II (Holy Rom. Emp.) **10**:218
- Austrian Jews **3**:892
- familiant laws **6**:1162
- Galicia **16**:1326
- Haskalah movement **7**:1441ff
- history chart **8**:766-767
- law **10**:1493
- medicine **11**:1195
- Theben, Jacob **15**:1093
- *Toleranzpatent* **8**:706; **15**:1209
- universities **15**:1677
- *illus:*
- - text
- - Hebrew poem for capture of Belgrade **4**:426
- - *Toleranzpatent* **15**:1210
JOSEPH (fam., Can.) **10**:219
JOSEPH (fam., Eng) **10**:220
Joseph (demon) **5**:1528
Joseph, Abraham **10**:219
- Quebec **13**:1422
Joseph, Anshel **15**:306
Joseph, Bernard, *see* JOSEPH, DOV
Joseph, David **5**:406
JOSEPH, DOV **10**:220
- Jerusalem **9**:1479; **9**:1484
- *illus:*
- - "Black Saturday" **9**:362; **10**:31
Joseph, Henry (mer., Can.) **10**:219
- Quebec **13**:1422
Joseph, Henry (sport.) **15**:307; **15**:311
JOSEPH, HENRY (r.) **10**:221
- Argentina **3**:410
Joseph, Jacob (r., Eng.) **15**:519
Joseph, Jacob (bsmn.) **11**:1285; **12**:853
JOSEPH, JACOB (r., U.S.) **10**:221
- history chart **8**:766-767
- New York City **12**:1094
Joseph, Jacob Henry (indus.) **10**:219
Joseph, Jesse **10**:219
- *illus:*
- - portrait **12**:285
Joseph, Josephus **4**:1380
Joseph, Sir Keith **10**:220
Joseph, Lazarus **10**:221; **12**:1113
Joseph, Lily Delissa **15**:118
Joseph, Michael **13**:1370
JOSEPH, MORRIS **10**:222
- peace **13**:199
Joseph, Rachel, *see* Solomons, Rachel
Joseph, Raphael, *see* Raphael Joseph
JOSEPH, SAMUEL (sociol.) **10**:222
Joseph, Sir Samuel George (polit.) **10**:220
Joseph, Sara, *see* Gratz, Sara
JOSEPH SAUL ABDALLAH **10**:222
Joseph, Testament of (pseudepig.), see PATRIARCHS, TESTAMENTS OF THE TWELVE
Joseph Amarkala the Levite **15**:1005
JOSEPH AND ASENATH (pseudepig. work) **10**:223
- *illus:* text
JOSEPH AND AZARIAH BEN ZECHARIAH **10**:224
- Gorgias **7**:809
Joseph the Babylonian (tan.) **16**:851
JOSEPH BAR ABBA (gaon) **10**:225
Joseph bar Ḥanina (amora), *see* YOSE BAR ḤANINA
JOSEPH BAR HIYYA (gaon) **10**:225
Joseph bar Jacob (gaon), *see* JOSEPH BEN JACOB BAR SATIA
JOSEPH BAR NISSAN **10**:225
Joseph bar Ravi (gaon) **7**:318
Joseph bar Shila (gaon) **7**:321
Joseph Baruch ben Jedidiah Zechariah of Urbino **13**:585
- *Dialoghi di Amore* **2**:110
Joseph Baruch of Neustadt, *see* Epstein, Joseph Baruch of Neustadt
Joseph Bekhor Shor, *see* BEKHOR SHOR, JOSEPH BEN ISAAC
Joseph ben Aaron ben Benjamin (k. of Khazars), *see* JOSEPH
Joseph ben Abdallah **16**:745
Joseph ben Abitur, *see* IBN ABITUR, JOSEPH BEN ISAAC
Joseph ben Abraham (14th cent.) **6**:300
Joseph ben Abraham al-Baṣīr, *see* BAṢIR, JOSEPH BEN ABRAHAM HA-KOHEN HA-RO'EH AL-
Joseph ben Abraham ben Seth **10**:232
Joseph ben Abraham Caravita, *see* Caravita, Joseph
Joseph ben Abraham ibn Ḥiyyun, *see* HAYYUN, JOSEPH BEN ABRAHAM
JOSEPH BEN AḤMAD IBN ḤASDAI **10**:225
Joseph ben al-ʿAysh **11**:1303
Joseph ben Amram **14**:1528
Joseph ben Ardict **9**:286; **16**:1535
JOSEPH BEN ASHER OF CHARTRES **10**:226
- Chartres **5**:362
- Josce of York **10**:200
JOSEPH BEN BARUCH OF CLISSON **10**:226
Joseph ben Berechiah **10**:348
Joseph ben David (15th cent.) **5**:915
Joseph ben David (17/18 cent.), *see* JOSEPH DAVID
Joseph ben David (18th cent.) **14**:1245
JOSEPH BEN DAVID HA-YEVANI **10**:226
- linguistics **16**:1388
Joseph ben David Ibn Lev, *see* LEV JOSEPH BEN DAVID IBN
Joseph ben David of Breslau **14**:61
JOSEPH BEN ELEM (h. pr.) **10**:227
Joseph ben Eli, *see* Joseph ha-Kohen ben Eli ben Aaron
Joseph ben Elijah (13th cent.) **15**:1290
JOSEPH BEN ELIJAH OF ZASLAW **10**:227
Joseph ben Ephraim ha-Levi ibn Shabbat, *see* ECIJA, JOSEPH DE
Joseph ben Ezron, *see* Joseph ha-Kohen ben Ezron
Joseph ben Gabir **11**:765
Joseph ben Gershon (r., Egy.) **10**:295
- Alexandrian community **2**:592
- Hodayah ben Jesse **6**:1033
JOSEPH BEN GERSHON OF ROSHEIM **10**:227
- Antonius Margarita **5**:356
- Calvin, John **5**:67
- Colmar Jews **5**:737
- history chart **8**:766-767
- Luria family **11**:569
- Luther, Martin **5**:737; **11**:585; **14**:19; **14**:21
- portrait **13**:916
- seal **14**:1080
- *shtadlanut* **14**:1463
- Strasbourg **15**:424
- *illus:*
- - the golden calf (16th cent. poster) **3**:140
Joseph ben Gorion ha-Kohen **10**:296ff
- *see also:* JOSEPHUS FLAVIUS
Joseph ben Ḥanina (amora), *see* YOSE BAR ḤANINA
JOSEPH BEN ḤIYYA (amora) **10**:229
- Babylonian Talmud **11**:319
- decisions in controversies **5**:891
- knowledge **15**:756
- Nathan de Ẓuẓita **12**:860
- parental honor **13**:101
Joseph ben Isaac (grandf. of Maim.) **11**:754
Joseph ben Isaac (cmty. ldr., Iraq) **5**:1461
Joseph ben Isaac Bekhor Shor, *see* BEKHOR SHOR, JOSEPH BEN ISAAC
JOSEPH BEN ISAAC HA-LEVI (philos.) **10**:230
Joseph ben Isaac ha-Sefardi, *see* IBN ABITUR, JOSEPH BEN ISAAC
Joseph ben Isaac ibn Ezra **4**:1482
Joseph ben Isaac Israeli of Toledo **10**:420
Joseph ben Isaac of Ashkelon **9**:1097
Joseph ben Isaac of Chinon **5**:475
Joseph ben Isaac of Orleans **4**:410
- *piyyut* **13**:585
JOSEPH BEN ISRAEL (poet) **10**:230
Joseph ben Israel (16th cent., Mar.), *see* Nuñes, Gaspar Rodrigues
Joseph ben Israel Issar of Vilkomir **13**:1465
JOSEPH BEN ISSACHAR BAER OF PRAGUE **10**:231
JOSEPH BEN JACOB (11th cent., poet) **10**:231
Joseph ben Jacob (12th cent., schol.) **11**:472
JOSEPH BEN JACOB BAR SATIA (gaon) **10**:231
- David ben Zakkai **5**:1359
- gaon **7**:317
- Saadiah **14**:547
Joseph ben Jacob ha-Levi **13**:585
Joseph ben Jacob of Pinczow **10**:1237
Joseph ben Jehiel **9**:1312
Joseph ben Joshua (3rd cent. C.E.) **10**:283
Joseph ben Joshua ha-Kohen (15/16 cent.) **11**:585
JOSEPH BEN JOSHUA MOSES OF FRANKFORT **10**:231
Joseph ben Judah (Fr.) **13**:1559
Joseph ben Judah (Bagh.) **14**:803
Joseph ben Judah (Rus.) **10**:1154; **10**:350
Joseph ben Judah ibn Shim'on, *see* SHIM'ON, JOSEPH BEN JUDAH IBN
Joseph ben Judah Leib **6**:250
Joseph ben Judah Loebush **10**:288
JOSEPH BEN JUSTU OF JAÉN **10**:232
JOSEPH BEN KALONYMUS HA-NAKDAN I **10**:232
- linguistics **16**:1387
Joseph ben Kalonymus ha-Nakdan II **10**:232
Joseph ben Kimḥit, *see* Joseph son of Kimḥit
Joseph ben Mamal **13**:1449
Joseph ben Mattathias (hist.), *see* JOSEPHUS FLAVIUS
Joseph ben Mattathias (paytan) **13**:585
Joseph ben Meir ben Ezra **13**:585
Joseph ben Merwan ha-Levi **9**:25
Joseph ben Meshullam (15th cent., It.) **10**:540
Joseph ben Meshullam of Lunel (12th cent.) **11**:1400
Joseph ben Meshullam Phoebus **11**:1404
Joseph ben Minir **5**:915
JOSEPH BEN MORDECAI GERSHON HA-KOHEN OF CRACOW **10**:233
- Ashkenazi, Eliezer **3**:726
- Cracow **5**:1029
- Isserles, Moses **9**:1081
JOSEPH BEN MORDECAI HA-KOHEN (Er. Isr.) **10**:233
Joseph ben Mordecai Ẓevi (Turk.) **14**:1222
Joseph ben Moses (s. of Naḥmanides) **12**:776
JOSEPH BEN MOSES (15th cent., Bav.) **10**:234
JOSEPH BEN MOSES (Ashkenazi), DARSHAN OF PRZEMYSLANY **10**:234
Joseph ben Moses Kilti **10**:226
JOSEPH BEN MOSES OF KREMENETS **10**:234
JOSEPH BEN MOSES OF TROYES **10**:234
- Caen **5**:5
Joseph ben Moses of Ulm **8**:1267
JOSEPH BEN MOSES PHINEHAS **10**:235
Joseph ben Moses Trani, *see* TRANI, JOSEPH BEN MOSES
Joseph ben Nathan of Etampes **10**:226
Joseph ben Nathan Official **3**:195; **10**:811; **14**:1163
Joseph ben Netira **12**:1000
Joseph ben Nissan of Shaveh Kiriathaim **13**:574; **16**:865
JOSEPH BEN NOAH **10**:235
- linguistics **16**:1380
Joseph ben Obadiah **11**:754
Joseph ben Paltoi **8**:1192
JOSEPH BEN PHINEHAS (10th cent.) **10**:235
- economic history **16**:1283
Joseph ben Phineḥas (18th cent.) **13**:294
Joseph ben Plat, *see* IBN PLAT, JOSEPH
Joseph ben Saadiah **12**:897
JOSEPH BEN SAMUEL BEN ISAAC RODI **10**:236
Joseph ben Samuel ha-Kohen **15**:1397
Joseph ben Samuel ha-Nagid, *see* JEHOSEPH HA-NAGID
Joseph ben Shabbetai, *see* Joseph of Raszkow
JOSEPH BEN SHALOM ASHKENAZI **10**:236
- Kabbalah **10**:536, 537, 567, 634
- *Sefer Yeẓirah* **10**:563; **16**:787
Joseph ben Shemtov, *see* IBN SHEM TOV, JOSEPH BEN SHEM TOV
JOSEPH BEN SHESHET IBN LATIMI **10**:237
- poetry **13**:689
Joseph ben Sidon **10**:935
Joseph ben Simeon (h. pr.), *see*

Joseph son of Simeon
Joseph ben Simeon (philos.) **11**:1257
Joseph ben Solomon (13th cent.) **6**:223
Joseph ben Solomon ha-Kohen (11th cent.) **6**:650
JOSEPH BEN SOLOMON OF CARCASSONNE **10**:237
JOSEPH BEN TANHUM YERUSHALMI **10**:237
Joseph ben Tobiah, *see* Joseph son of Tobiah
JOSEPH BEN UZZIEL (pseudepig. fig.) **10**:238
- *see also:* BEN SIRA, ALPHABET OF
Joseph ben Yakar **3**:850; **14**:1261
Joseph ben Yehudai (gaon) **7**:1171
JOSEPH BEN ZADDIK **10**:239
- Jewish history **11**:348
- microcosm doctrine **11**:339
Joseph ben Zechariah, *see* JOSEPH AND AZARIAH BEN ZECHARIAH
Joseph ben Zechariah Mendel **16**:960
JOSEPH BEN ZE'EV WOLF HA-LEVI **10**:239
Joseph ben Zevi ha-Kohen **13**:837
Joseph the Builder, *see* Yose ha-Banai
Joseph Darshan, *see* CALAHORA, JOSEPH BEN SOLOMON
JOSEPH DAVID (Salonika) **10**:239
- *illus:*
- - *Zemah David* (1785) **8**:1156
Joseph de Ávila **3**:968
Joseph de Cerui **14**:381
JOSEPH DELLA REINA **10**:240
- Poner's drama **6**:197
- practical Kabbalah **10**:544; **10**:635
Joseph de Montagna **9**:280; **15**:642
Joseph de Vesoul **11**:872
Joseph ha-Arokh, *see* JOSEPH BEN SHALOM ASHKENAZI
Joseph Haconstandini **16**:1386,1474
Joseph ha-Dayyan **7**:1510
Joseph ha-Efrati **14**:916
Joseph ha-Kohen (11th cent., r.) **15**:122
Joseph ha-Kohen (mintmaster), *see* Joseph of Kalisz
JOSEPH HA-KOHEN (hist.) **10**:241
- Avignon **3**:967
- historiography **8**:558
- history chart **8**:766-767
- Jerusalem walls **9**:1433
- Jewish history **8**:696,701
- Reformation **14**:22
- Talmud, burning of **15**:771
Joseph ha-Kohen (r., Leb.), *see* Joseph ben Samuel ha-Kohen
Joseph ha-Kohen ben Eli ben Aaron (writ., Iraq) **8**:1463
Joseph ha-Kohen ben Ezron (gaon) **7**:323
Joseph ha-Levi (prch., It.) **14**:1233
Joseph ha-Levi ben Ephraim, *see* ECIJA, JOSEPH DE
Joseph ha-Lorki **15**:1327
Joseph ha-Ma'aravi (kab.), *see* JOSEPH IBN TABUL
Joseph ha-Ma'aravi (emis., Er. Isr.), *see* JOSEPH MAMAN AL-MAGHRIBI
Joseph ha-Nagid, *see* JEHOSEPH HA-NAGID
Joseph ha-Qostandini, *see* Joseph Haconstandini
Joseph the Harif **4**:589
JOSEPH HAYYIM BEN ELIJAH AL-HAKAM **10**:242
- family **2**:626
JOSEPH HA-ZAREFATI **10**:243
- *illus:*
- - *Cervera Bible* **2**:642; **5**:313; **10**:1002; **16**:*fcg.* 935
- - colophon **4**:961
JOSEPH HAZZAN BEN JUDAH OF TROYES **10**:243
- Troyes **15**:1407
Joseph Hin, Raphael ben, *see* Raphael Joseph
Joseph ibn Abitur, *see* IBN ABITUR, JOSEPH BEN ISAAC
Joseph Ibn al-Barqūlī, *see* Ibn al-Barqūlī, Joseph
Joseph bin Hayyim (scribe), *see* IBN HAYYIM, JOSEPH
Joseph ibn Lev, *see* LEV, JOSEPH BEN DAVID IBN
Joseph ibn Migash, *see* IBN MIGASH, JOSEPH BEN MEIR HA-LEVI
Joseph ibn Nūḥ, *see* JOSEPH BEN NOAH
Joseph ibn Peso **8**:1324
- *illus:*
- - Mishnah (1492) **8**: 1328
Joseph ibn Samon **7**:1188
JOSEPH IBN SHRAGA **10**:243
JOSEPH IBN TABUL **10**:244
- Benjamin, Israel **4**:528
- Lurianic tradition **10**:549; **10**:589; **11**:575
- Ottoman Empire **16**:1549
Joseph ibn Zagyah **10**:583
JOSEPH ISSACHAR BAER BEN ELHANAN **10**:244
JOSEPH JOSKE BEN JUDAH JUDEL OF LUBLIN **10**:244
Joseph Landau of Litin, *see* Landau, Joseph
JOSEPH MAMAN AL-MAGHRIBI **10**:245
- Bukhara **4**:1473; **10**:436
Joseph Meir Weiss of Spinka, *see* SPINKA, JOSEPH MEIR WEISS OF
JOSEPH MOSES BEN JEKUTHIEL ZALMAN **10**:245
JOSEPH MOSES OF SALOSITZ **10**:245
Joseph of Arles **6**:25; **12**:226; **15**:1378
Joseph of Ashkelon, *see* Joseph ben Isaac of Ashkelon
Joseph of Bendery, *see* Bendery, Joseph of
Joseph of Carcassone, *see* JOSEPH BEN SOLOMON OF CARCASSONNE
Joseph of Chartres, *see* JOSEPH BEN ASHER OF CHARTRES
Joseph of Chinon, *see* Joseph ben Isaac of Chinon
Joseph of Clisson, *see* JOSEPH BEN BARUCH OF CLISSON
Joseph of Cracow, *see* JOSEPH BEN MORDECAI GERSHON HA-KOHEN OF CRACOW
Joseph of Etampes, *see* Joseph ben Nathan of Etampes
Joseph of Frankfort, *see* JOSEPH BEN JOSHUA MOSES OF FRANKFORT
JOSEPH OF GAMALA **10**:246
Joseph of Hamadan **7**:575; **10**:578
Joseph of Hormuz **8**:976
Joseph of Huzal **8**:1137; **16**:851
Joseph of Israel (Jerusalem), *see* JOSEPH BEN BARUCH OF CLISSON
Joseph of Jaén, *see* JOSEPH BEN JUSTU OF JAÉN
Joseph of Kalisz **12**:61; **13**:710
Joseph of Kremenets, *see* JOSEPH BEN MOSES OF KREMENETS
Joseph of Lincoln **9**:1220; **11**:256
Joseph of Litin, *see* Landau, Joseph
Joseph of Lublin, *see* JOSEPH JOSKE BEN JUDAH JUDEL OF LUBLIN
Joseph of Marseilles **13**:1264
Joseph of Nowogrodek, *see* Horowitz, Joseph
Joseph of Orleans, *see* Joseph ben Isaac of Orleans
Joseph of Orly, *see* Joseph of Arles
Joseph of Pinczow, *see* Joseph ben Jacob of Pinczow
Joseph of Prague, *see* JOSEPH BEN ISSACHAR BAER OF PRAGUE
Joseph of Przemyslany, *see* JOSEPH BEN MOSES, DARSHAN OF PRZEMYSLANY
Joseph of Radziwillow, *see* Radziwillow, Joseph of
Joseph of Raszkow **14**:1219
Joseph of Rosheim, *see* JOSEPH BEN GERSHON OF ROSHEIM
Joseph of Salositz, *see* JOSEPH MOSES OF SALOSITZ
Joseph of Shushan **10**:535; **13**:1608
Joseph of Spinka, *see* SPINKA, JOSEPH MEIR WEISS OF
Joseph of Tiberias **14**:1361
Joseph of Toledo, *see* Joseph ben Isaac Israeli of Toledo
Joseph of Tomar **15**:1213
Joseph of Tours **13**:285
Joseph of Troyes (tos.), *see* JOSEPH BEN MOSES OF TROYES
Joseph of Troyes (schol.), *see* JOSEPH HAZZAN BEN JUDAH OF TROYES
Joseph of Ulm, *see* Joseph ben Moses of Ulm
Joseph of Ventura **8**:1323
Joseph of Yampol **9**:1315
Joseph of Zaslaw, *see* JOSEPH BEN ELIJAH OF ZASLAW
Joseph Porat, *see* JOSEPH BEN MOSES OF TROYES
"Joseph the Righteous", *see* JOSEPH BEN MOSES PHINEHAS
JOSEPH ROSH HA-SEDER **10**:246
- Baruch of Aleppo **4**:277
Josephs, J. **12**:1075
Josephs, Joseph L. **12**:1075
Josephs, Moses (of Glueckstadt) **5**:1010
Joseph Samuel ben Abraham **3**:967
JOSEPH SAMUEL BEN ZEVI OF CRACOW **10**:246
Joseph Solomon of Eupatoria **4**:865
Joseph Solomon Rofe of Candia (philos.), *see* DELMEDIGO, JOSEPH SOLOMON
JOSEPH SOLOMON ZALMAN BEN MEIR **10**:247
JOSEPHSON (fam., Swed.) **10**:247
Josephson, Erland **10**:249
- Scandinavian literature **14**:931
Josephson, Ernst Abraham **10**:248
- *illus:*
- - "Spanish Smiths" (paint.) **3**:551
Josephson, Gunnar **10**:249
Josephson, Jacob Axel **10**:247
Josephson, Ludvig Oscar **10**:248
JOSEPHSON, MANUEL **10**:249
- Washington, George **16**:361
- *illus:*
- - text
- - Washington's letter **13**:369
JOSEPHSON, MATTHEW **10**:250
Josephson, Ragnar **10**:249
- Scandinavian literature **14**:931
Josephson, Salomon **10**:247
Joseph son of Kimḥit (h. pr.) **2**:923; **10**:1009
Joseph son of Simeon (h. pr.) **9**:86; **10**:1009
Joseph son of Tobiah **15**:1179
- Hellenistic period **8**:295
- history **8**:627
- Josephus **10**:259
- monogamy **12**:259
"Joseph Telling his Dreams" (etch., Rembrandt) **10**:215
JOSEPHTHAL, GIORA **10**:250
- *illus:*
- - German-Israel reparations agreement **7**:499; **14**:72
JOSEPHTAL, LOUIS MAURICE **11**:1573
Josephthal, Senta **10**:251
JOSEPHUS FLAVIUS **10**:251
- *Contents:*
- - Biography **10**:251
- - - Early Life **10**:251
- - - As Commander of Galilee During the Jewish War **10**:251
- - - "Prophecy" Regarding Vespasian **10**:253
- - - Exploitation of Circumstances Surrounding Nero's Death **10**:253
- - - In Jerusalem with Titus **10**:254
- - - Favored by Roman Rulers and Hated by Jews **10**:254
- - - Inauspicious Family Life **10**:254
- - Works **10**:254
- - - The Jewish War **10**:254
- - - Jewish Antiquities **10**:257
- - - The Life **10**:262
- - - Against Apion **10**:262
- - Evaluation of Josephus **10**:262
- - - As a Jew **10**:262
- - - As a Writer **10**:263
- - - As a Historian **10**:263
- - In the Arts **10**:263
- General
- - art **3**:507
- - astrology **3**:789
- - Hellenism **8**:298
- - history chart **8**:766-767
- - in the Arts **6**:200; **15**:1171
- - *Josippon* **10**:297ff
- - *karet* **10**:789
- - *kiddush ha-Shem* **10**:982
- - *Maccabees, fourth book of* **11**:661
- - population **13**:870
- - Porphyry **13**:905
- - synagogue **15**:582; **15**:592
- Biography
- - Cabul **5**:2
- - Gamala **7**:295
- - Jehoiarib **9**:1322
- - John of Giscala **10**:163
- - Joshua ben Gamala **10**:279
- - Justus of Tiberias **10**:479ff
- - lots **11**:512
- - Sanhedrin **14**:836ff
- - Silas **14**:1533
- - Vespasian **10**:152
- - Zealots **16**:947
- Writings and Sources
- - agriculture in Israel **2**:393ff
- - apologetics **3**:189
- - biblical history **8**:304
- - *Contra Apionem* **3**:178
- - Eupolemus **6**:965
- - *Ezra, Greek Book of* **6**:1110
- - folkloric material **6**:1376
- - history books **11**:314ff
- - law source **12**:117
- - letters **11**:56
- - lost tribes **15**:1004
- - Manetho's writings **11**:872
- - Moses **12**:389; **12**:392
- - Nicholas of Damascus **12**:1141
- - Sambatyon **14**:763
- - Sicarii **14**:1492
- - Titus **15**:1168ff
- - Torah **15**:1239,1244
- - warfare **16**:280

- - Zimri **16:**1027
- - *see also: Jewish War*
- Evaluations
- - Basnage, Jacques Christian **4:**309
- - economics **16:**1274
- - Ezra-Nehemiah, Book of **6:**1114ff
- - historiography **8:**553ff
- - *Maccabees, third book of* **11:**661
- - *Megillat Ta'anit* **11:**1230
- - Schulman's translation **14:**1006
- *illus:*
- - Antiquities of the Jews (12th cent. ms.) **13:**1
- - *Josippon, Sefer bin Guryon* **8:**1331
Joseph Uziel ben Abraham **16:**42
Joseph Yisre'eli **15:**1326
Joseph the Zealot, *see* OFFICIAL, NATHAN BEN JOSEPH and JOSEPH
Joseph zum goldenen Schwan (fin.) **4:**172
Joses (br. of Jesus) **10:**10ff
Jose Solomon Rofe of Candia, *see* DELMEDIGO, JOSEPH SOLOMON
Jose son of Levi **15:**596
JOSHUA (bib. fig.) **10:**265
- *Contents:*
- - Life **10:**265
- - In the Aggadah **10:**266
- - In Christianity **10:**267
- - In Islam **10:**267
- - In the Arts **10:**268
- *Aleinu le-Shabbe'aḥ* **2:**557
- Amalekites **2:**787
- chronological chart **8:**766-767
- Eglon **6:**477
- Gibeonites **7:**552
- *ḥerem* **8:**345ff
- Jeremiah **9:**1359
- king of Dor **6:**172
- legal traditions **15:**1311
- lots **13:**1078
- Moses **12:**377
- Moses comparison **12:**291
- Rahab **13:**1513
- Rephidim **14:**80
- Samaritan belief **14:**740
- sun's obedience **15:**517
- tabernacle **15:**685
- *takkanot* **15:**721
- war and warfare **16:**275
- *illus:*
- - text
- - capture of Jericho **3:**517; **10:**264
- - Mount Ebal altar **5:**1020
- - on Mount Sinai **5:**1438
- - putting up the twelve stones **4:**943
- - *Sarajevo Haggadah* **7:***fcg.* 1131
- *see also:* JOSHUA, BOOK OF
JOSHUA (s., Akiva, tan.) **10:**270
- Joshua ben Korḥa **10:**281
Joshua (amora) **8:**1227
JOSHUA (paytan) **10:**270
JOSHUA, BOOK OF **10:**271
- *Contents:*
- - The Composition of the Book **10:**271
- - The Content of the Book **10:**272
- - - Conquest of Canaan **10:**272
- - - Division of the Land **10:**274
- - - The Concluding Chapters (22-24) **10:**276
- Bible history **8:**577
- Hexateuch **13:**233
- Samaritan chronology **14:**754
- Spinoza **15:**283
- *illus:*
- - *Lisbon Bible* **8:**1278
- - Simon ben Samuel's Bible (1442) **5:**159
JOSHUA, SON OF SAPPHAS **10:**277
- Eleazar ben Ananias **6:**585
- Tiberias **15:**1132
JOSHUA, SON OF SETH (h. pr.) **10:**277
Joshua, son of Thebuthi **13:**468
JOSHUA BEN ABRAHAM MAIMUNI **10:**277
Joshua ben Abun **10:**719
Joshua ben Asayahu **11:**687
Joshua ben Bathyra (tan.) **4:**324
JOSHUA BEN DAMNAI (h. pr.) **10:**278
- Ananias ben Nedebeus **2:**923
JOSHUA BEN ELIJAH HA-LEVI **10:**278
Joshua ben Galgula **4:**231; **4:**237; **12:**528
JOSHUA BEN GAMLA (h. pr.) **10:**278
- education **6:**401ff
- Martha **11:**1062
Joshua ben Gamaliel (h. pr.) **10:**278
JOSHUA BEN HANANIAH (tan.) **10:**279
- Akiva **2:**488; **2:**489
- animal tales **3:**20
- apologetics **3:**191
- astronomy **3:**796
- Avelei Zion **3:**945
- dispute **15:**1024
- Eliezer ben Hyrcanus **6:**620ff
- Gamaliel, Rabban II **7:**296
- Ishmael ben Elisha **5:**154
- Johanan ben Zakkai **9:**242
- Mishnah **12:**98
- Peki'in academy **2:**202
- righteous gentiles **12:**1357
JOSHUA BEN HYRCANUS **10:**281
Joshua ben Jehozadak (h. pr.), *see* JESHUA
Joshua ben Joseph (16/17 cent.), *see* JOSHUA HOESCHEL BEN JOSEPH OF CRACOW
Joshua ben Joseph ha-Kohen (paytan, Egy.) **13:**587
Joshua ben Joseph ha-Levi (15th cent.), *see* JESHUA BEN JOSEPH HA-LEVI
Joshua ben Judah (Kar.), *see* JESHUA BEN JUDAH
Joshua ben Judah Loebush (Pol.) **10:**288
JOSHUA BEN KORḤA (tan.) **10:**281
- Joshua son of Akiva **10:**270
JOSHUA BEN LEVI (amora) **10:**282
- Angel of Death **2:**953
- tradition **15:**1309
Joshua ben Madmun **12:**763
JOSHUA BEN MORDECAI FALK HA-KOHEN **10:**284
Joshua ben Nachrim **6:**24
JOSHUA BEN PERAḤYAH (nasi) **10:**284
- Jesus **10:**15
JOSHUA BEN PHABI (h. pr.) **10:**285
- Ishmael ben Phiabi II **9:**86
Joshua ben Saul, *see* HOESCHEL BEN SAUL
JOSHUA BOAZ BEN SIMON BARUCH **10:**285
- *illus:*
- - *Kiẓẓur Mordekhai ve-Simanav* (1557) **5:**1078
JOSHUA HA-GARSI (tan.) **10:**286
- Gerasa **7:**434
Joshua ha-Kohen (paytan, Er. Isr.) **13:**587
Joshua he-Ḥaver ben Nathan **13:**587
JOSHUA HOESCHEL BEN JACOB **10:**286
- Aryeh Leib ben Samuel Ẓevi Hirsch **3:**668
JOSHUA HOESCHEL BEN JOSEPH OF CRACOW **10:**287
- Grodno **7:**925
Joshua Hoeschel of Jakow **11:**280
JOSHUA IBN NUN **10:**288
Joshua Isaac of Slonim **15:**778
Joshua Joseph ben David Levi, *see* LEVI, JOSHUA JOSEPH BEN DAVID
Joshua Lorki, *see* LORKI, JOSHUA
Joshua of Belz **4:**453
- assimilation **16:**1329
- *maḥzor* **11:**730
- Shomer Israel **14:**1459
Joshua of Bologna **15:**1328
Joshua of Kurnik, *see* JOSHUA BEN MORDECAI FALK HA-KOHEN
Joshua of Makow **5:**1363
Joshua of Mantua **2:**593
Joshua of Pristik **16:**787
Joshua of Sikhnin (amora) **13:**67
Joshua of Trier **15:**1390
Joshua Roll (illum. ms.) **3:**508
- *illus:* **3:**517; **4:**943; **10:**267, 269
Joshua son of Jehozadak (h. pr.), *see* JESHUA
Joshua the Stylite, Chronicle of **4:**402
JOSIAH (bib. fig.) **10:**288
- *Contents:*
- - Life **10:**288
- - The Reform **10:**290
- - Stages of the Reform **10:**291
- - Centralization of Cult **10:**292
- - Significance of the Reform **10:**292
- - Death of Josiah **10:**292
- - In the Aggadah **10:**293
- General
- - Amon **2:**862; **2:**863
- - anointing oil **8:**1313
- - Ark of Covenant **3:**465
- - chronological chart **8:**766-767
- - corvée workers **5:**977
- - Deuteronomy, Book of **5:**1575
- - Hilkiah **8:**481ff
- - history **8:**606ff
- - Neco **12:**919
- - priests **13:**1084ff
- - tablets of the Law **15:**691
- - Torah canon **4:**822
- - Yavneh-Yam fortress **16:**723
- - Zebulun **16:**951
- - Zechariah **16:**955
- - Zephaniah **16:**994
- Reforms
- - Arad temple **3:**249
- - archaeology **3:**306
- - destruction of cultic centers **5:**1164; **5:**1167
- - magic **11:**705
- - moon cult **12:**290
- - sun worship **15:**517
- - Temple **15:**945
- - *teraphim* **15:**1015
- *geneal. table:* **5:**1341
- *illus:* text
JOSIAH (tan.) **10:**293
- Huẓal **8:**1137
JOSIAH (amora) **10:**294
JOSIAH BEN AARON HE-ḤAVER (gaon) **10:**294
- Damietta **5:**1253
- geonim **7:**323
- history **9:**267
JOSIAH BEN JESSE **10:**295
Josiah ben Judah ben Aaron of Troki **2:**149; **15:**1402
JOSIAH BEN SAUL BEN ANAN **10:**295
- Karaite prayer **10:**765
Josiah (Ḥasan) ben Zakkai (exil.) **3:**999
- David ben Daniel **5:**1349
- David ben Zakkai II **5:**1359
- Dayyan family **5:**1389
- Saadiah Gaon **14:**546
Josiah the Great (tan.), *see* JOSIAH
Josiah of Usha (amora) **10:**294
JOSIPHIAH THE PROSELYTE **10:**295
JOSIPPON (bk.) **10:**296
- Azariah dei Rossi **14:**317
- chronological chart (953) **8:**766-767
- Eliezer of Beaugency **6:**631
- *Esther Rabbah* **6:**915
- fiction **6:**1262
- history **8:**555
- Jewish literature **11:**348
- Moskoni, Judah **12:**438
- *illus:*
- - text
- - colophon page (1475) **5:**861
- - incunabulum (Mantua) **8:**1331
Joske, Alexander **14:**823
JOSKO (15/16 cent., mer.) **10:**298
Joslin, Alfred H. **13:**1278; **14:**143
Josse bar Nissan, *see* JOSEPH BAR NISSAN
Jossel ben Joshua Moses of Frankfort, *see* JOSEPH BEN JOSHUA MOSES OF FRANKFORT
Josselsohn, Florrie **15:**309
Jossko, *see* JOSKO
Jost, Heinz **8:**869
JOST, ISAAC MARCUS **10:**298
- Anhalt Jewry **3:**2
- apologetics **3:**199
- chronological chart **8:**766-767
- historiography **8:**561
- history **8:**726
- Jewish scholarship **16:**572
- *illus:* text
JOTABAH (isl., Gulf of Elath) **10:**299
- *see also:* Jazīrat-Far'un
JOTAPATA (fort., Er. Isr.) **10:**300
- Josephus **10:**253
- lots, casting of **11:**512
JOTBATH, JOTHBATAH (bib. place) **10:**300
JOTHAM (s., Gideon) **10:**301
- bramble **15:**1119
JOTHAM (k., Judah) **10:**301
- chronological chart **8:**766-767
- history **8:**602ff
- Hosea **8:**1011
- kingship **10:**1016
- Micah **11:**1480; **11:**1482
- Tobiads **15:**1178
- *geneal. table:* **5:**1341
- *illus:* text
Jothbatah (bib. place), *see* JOTBATH, JOTHBATAH
Jouegati, Ezra Ḥayyim **2:**564
JOURNALISM **10:**303
- history **8:**714
- *illus:*
- - text
- - *Razsvet* staff **13:**1596
- *see also:* NEWSPAPERS, HEBREW; PRESS
Journal of Contemporary History (Eng.) **15:**54
Journal of Jewish Bibliography **4:**973
Journal of Jewish Communal Service (U.S.) **12:**869
Journal of Jewish Studies (Eng.) **2:**779; **6:**769
"Journey" (paint., B. Meninsky) **3:**635
Journey, prayer for, *see* TRAVEL, PRAYER FOR
Jousting (sport) **15:**292
Jovanović, Vitomir **16:**889
Jövő (newsp.) **10:**1175
Jowett, Benjamin **12:**268
JOY **10:**319
- Ba'al Shem Tov **9:**1051; **9:**1054
- ḥasidic view **7:**1402; **7:**1404ff

- Philo **13:**427
- reward and punishment **14:**135
- sages **14:**653ff
- *illus:*
- - salutations for family events (table) **7:**915
"Joy" (drg., Chagall) **14:**1467
Joyce, James **6:**249
Jozacar (s. of Shimeath) **10:**111
Jozadak (pr.), *see* Jehozadak
Józefowicz (fam. name), *see also* Ezofovich
JÓZEFOWICZ (fam.) **10:**321
József, Attila **7:**1475; **8:**1239
J.P.S., *see* JEWISH PUBLICATION SOCIETY OF AMERICA
J.Q.R., *see* JEWISH QUARTERLY REVIEW
J.R.C. (Eng.), *see* Jewish Refugees Committee
J.R.S.O., *see* Jewish Restitution Successor Organization
J.S. (Rus.), *see* JEWISH SOCIALIST WORKERS' PARTY
J.S.F., *see* Jewish Socialist Federation
J.S.P. (Er. Isr.), *see* Jewish Settlement Police
J.T.A. *see* JEWISH TELEGRAPHIC AGENCY
J.T.C. *see* Jewish Trust Corporation
J.T.S., *see* JEWISH THEOLOGICAL SEMINARY OF AMERICA, THE
Juan (k., Cast.), *see* John I
JUAN DE CIUDAD **10:**322
- Almosnino, Abraham **2:**667
Juan de Çolivera **8:**1384
JUAN DE ESPAÑA **10:**322
Juan de Lucena, *see* Lucena, Juan de
Juan de Marchena **8:**391
Juan de Oraña **10:**1359
Juan de San Martin **8:**1383
JUAN DE VALLADOLID **10:**322
- music **12:**596
- satirical poem **16:**62
Juan de Zamora **2:**606
Juan el Viejo, *see* JUAN DE ESPAÑA
Juan Espera en Dios, *see* WANDERING JEW
Juan Poeta, *see* JUAN DE VALLADOLID
Juan Sanchez de Calatayud, *see* Golluf, Isaac
Juarez, Pedro **13:**4
Juba II (k., Libya) **7:**601
Jubail (tn., Leb.). *see* JUBAYL
JUBAL (bib. fig.) **10:**323
- Adam **2:**233
JUBAR (vill., Syr.) **10:**323
JUBAYL (tn., Leb.) **10:**324
- Canaan **13:**474ff
- papyrus trade **16:**658
- Phoenician inscriptions **16:**665
- war and warfare **16:**267ff
- *illus:*
- - Yeḥawmilk stele **13:**476
Jubayr, Abu al-Husayn Muhammad ibn, *see* Ibn Jubayr, Abu al-Husayn Muhammad
Jubilee, *see* SABBATICAL YEAR AND JUBILEE
JUBILEES, BOOK OF **10:**324
- Albeck, Ḥanokh **2:**528
- Apocalyptic writing **3:**180
- astrology **3:**789
- calendar **5:**48,51
- Dead Sea Scrolls **5:**1402
- *Enoch, Book of* **6:**796
- Hellenistic Jewish literature **8:**304
- *Job, Testament of* **10:**129
- *Judah, Testament of* **13:**185
- *Levi, Testament of* **11:**88
- Mastema **11:**1119ff
- Philo **13:**408; **13:**409
- sages **14:**640
- Samaritan chronology **14:**751
Jud, Andres **15:**293
Jud. Leo **8:**39; **4:**870; **4:**873
JUDA, WALTER **8:**1432
Judaea (Rom. prov.), *see* JUDEA; Provincia Judaea
Juda Elias of Hanover **13:**1329
JUDAESAPTAN (leg. kdm.) **10:**326
- Austria **3:**887
JUDAH (bib. fig.; tribe) **10:**326
- *Contents:*
- - In the Pentateuch **10:**326
- - History of the Tribe **10:**328
- - Land of Judah **10:**330
- - In the Aggadah **10:**332
- The Man
- - Benjamin **4:**522
- - ecologist **4:**1028
- - Genesis, Book of **7:**394
- - levirate marriage **11:**122
- - *Naphtali, Testament of* **12:**821
- - suretyship **15:**524
- - Tamar **15:**782ff
- - term *Yehudi* **10:**21
- The Tribe
- - Bet-Shemesh, city **4:**772
- - breastplate stone **13:**1008
- - Calebites **2:**212; **5:**41
- - Jerusalem **9:**1380; **9:**1551
- - levites **11:**72
- - lion **11:**275ff
- - settlement **8:**579ff; **9:**115
- - Solomon's administration **15:**102
- - twelve tribes **15:**1382ff
- *geneal. table:* **5:**1342
- *illus:*
- - banner and emblem **4:**181
- - Jacob entrusting Benjamin to **4:**524
- - parents and brothers **10:**1526
Judah (br. of Jesus) **10:**10ff
Judah (Rebbi; tan.), *see* JUDAH HA-NASI
Judah (Rabbi Judah; tan.), *see* JUDAH BAR ILAI
JUDAH (Nesiah; amora) **10:**333
- chronological chart **8:**766-767
- Nasi and Sanhedrin **9:**253
- Yalta **16:**710
JUDAH III (Judah Nesiah II) **10:**333
- chronological chart **8:**766-767
JUDAH IV (4/5 cent., amora) **10:**334
- chronological chart **8:**766-767
Judah (gaon) **7:**318
Judah (9th cent., ambassador) **7:**10
Judah (paytan, 9/10 cent.) **13:**587
JUDAH (fam., U.S.) **10:**334
Judah, Abigail **10:**334
Judah, Baruch **10:**334
Judah, Baruch H. **10:**334
Judah, Benjamin S. **4:**1219; **10:**334; **12:**1071
Judah, Bernard S. **10:**335
Judah, Catherine **10:**335
Judah, Daniel, *see* OLIVER Y FULLANA, NICOLÁS DE
Judah, David **12:**1221
Judah, Dorothea Catherine **7:**1351
Judah, Emanuel **10:**335
Judah, Grace **10:**334; **11:**1008
Judah, Hillel **10:**334
Judah, Isaac (stlr.) **12:**284
Judah, Isaac H. (ḥazzan) **10:**334
Judah, Johanan, *see* Alatrini, Angelo
Judah, Joshua Abraham **15:**872
JUDAH, KINGDOM OF **8:**586
- Ahab **2:**435ff
- Amon **2:**862
- Aram-Damascus **3:**287
- Asa **3:**671
- Athaliah **3:**814
- chronological chart **8:**766-767
- Edom **15:**1317
- Gedaliah **7:**351
- Isaiah **9:**46ff
- Jeremiah **9:**1346ff
- Jerusalem **9:**1383
- Judah **10:**330
- king, kingship **10:**1014ff
- Manasseh **11:**852
- Messiah **11:**1408
- Nebuchadnezzar II **16:**1505
- population **13:**868ff
- pottery **13:**941
- Rehoboam **14:**42
- social structure **8:**613
- Uzziah **16:**43
- warfare **16:**272
- pop. tables (1000-586 B.C.E.) **13:**869
- *illus:*
- - Divided kingdom (map) **9:**116, 117
Judah, Manuel **10:**334
Judah, Michael (bsmn.) **10:**335
Judah, Michael (scribe, Neth.) **15:**1482
Judah, Naḥman **5:**376
Judah, Naphtali **10:**335; **12:**1071
Judah, Samuel (Can.) **10:**335; **12:**284
Judah, Samuel (mer., U.S.) **10:**334
Judah, Samuel (polit., U.S.) **10:**335
JUDAH, SAMUEL BENJAMIN HELBERT **10:**335
- family **10:**335
- U.S. literature **15:**1569
Judah, son of Ishmael **5:**492
Judah, son of Sariphaeus **4:**782
JUDAH, SON OF ẒIPPORAI **10:**336
Judah, Testament of (Pseudepig.). *see* PATRIARCHS, TESTAMENTS OF THE TWELVE
Judah, Uriah **10:**335; **12:**284
Judah, Walter Jonas **8:**209; **10:**334; **12:**1070
Judah Aaron of Chelm **5:**371
Judah Aristobulus (k., Judea), *see* ARISTOBULUS I
JUDAH ARYEH LEIB BEN DAVID **10:**336
JUDAH BAR EZEKIEL (amora) **10:**336
- Abba **2:**30
- history chart **8:**766-767
- Isaac bar Rav Judah **9:**12
- Pumbedita academy **11:**319
JUDAH BAR ILAI (tan.) **10:**337
- decisions **5:**891
- *Eruvin* **6:**850
- marriage dance **11:**1033
- vows **16:**228
- Yose ha-Gelili **16:**858
Judah bar Pazzi (amora), *see* JUDAH BAR SIMEON
Judah bar Samuel (gaon) **7:**318
Judah bar Samuel (13th cent., writ.) **11:**731
JUDAH BAR SHALOM (ha-Levi; amora) **10:**339
JUDAH BAR SIMEON **10:**339
- aggadist **2:**868
Judah the Believer (mart.), *see* VERA Y ALACRON, LOPE DE
Judah ben ʿAbbās, *see* ABBAS, JUDAH BEN SAMUEL IBN
Judah ben Abraham **12:**1165
Judah ben Agra (tan.) **10:**877
JUDAH BEN ASHER **10:**340
- ethical wills **11:**345; **16:**532
Judah ben Baruch **16:**644
JUDAH BEN BARZILLAI AL-BARGELONI **10:**341
- Abraham bar Ḥiyya **2:**131; **2:**132
- Al-Mukammiṣ **2:**671
- Asher of Lunel **3:**709
- Barcelona **4:**208
- rabbinical ordination **13:**1449
- *Sefer Yezirah* **10:**518; **16:**787
- *takkanot* **15:**735
- Torah **15:**1237
JUDAH BEN BATHYRA I (1st cent., tan.) **10:**342
- Babylonia **4:**39
- Bathyra, sons of **4:**324
- Nisibiṣ academy **2:**202; **12:**1178
- *illus:*
- - burial place **4:**323
JUDAH BEN BATHYRA II (2nd cent., tan.) **10:**343
JUDAH BEN BAVA (tan.) **10:**343
Judah ben Dama (tan.) **15:**800
Judah ben David (9th cent., exil.) **5:**1351
Judah ben David (10th cent., gram.), *see* Judah ibn Daud
Judah ben David (12th cent., apos.), *see* HERMANUS QUONDAM JUDAEUS
Judah ben David (14/15 cent., r.), *see* BONDAVIN BONJUDAS
Judah ben David of Melun **6:**167
JUDAH BEN DOSOTHEOS (tan.) **10:**344
Judah ben Eleazar (Isr.) **7:**691
Judah ben Eleazar (Vilna) **16:**138
JUDAH BEN ELI (Elan) **10:**344
Judah ben Eliezer (12/13 cent.) **15:**1407
JUDAH BEN ELIEZER (18th cent.) **10:**344
- Samuel ben Avigdor **14:**804
Judah ben Eliezer Lipman, *see* Kaẓin, Judah
Judah ben Enoch **6:**799
JUDAH BEN GERIM (tan.) **10:**345
Judah ben Hagra (tan.), *see* Judah ben Agra
Judah ben Hezekiah **6:**590
Judah ben Hillel ha-Levi **13:**587
JUDAH BEN ḤIYYA (amora) **10:**345
- Judith **10:**451
JUDAH BEN ISAAC (Sir Leon of Paris) **10:**345
- Baruch of Worms **4:**278
- parody **13:**127
- Samson of Coucy **14:**779
- title of nobility **15:**1165
JUDAH BEN ISAAC (musicol.) **10:**346
- *illus:*
- - Guidonian Hand **12:**601
JUDAH BEN ISAAC IBN SHABBETAI (poet) **10:**346
Judah ben Jacob (Shab.), *see* PROSSNITZ, JUDAH LEIB BEN JACOB HOLLESCHAU
JUDAH BEN JACOB HA-KOHEN (r.) **10:**347
Judah ben Jacob he-Arukh (hazzan) **9:**1220
Judah ben Jedidiah **15:**888
JUDAH BEN JEHIEL (Messer Leon) **10:**347
- Aristotelianism **3:**446
- Averroes **3:**952
- Colon, Joseph **5:**748
- Kabbalah and Platonism **10:**540
- linguistics **16:**1389
- philosophy **13:**450
- title of nobility **15:**1165
- Torah **15:**1241
Judah ben Joseph ha-Kohen **10:**680
JUDAH BEN JOSEPH OF KAIROUAN **10:**348
Judah ben Joseph Sijilmassi, *see* Sijilmassi, Judah ben Joseph
Judah ben Josiah **6:**1033
JUDAH BEN KALONYMUS BEN MEIR **10:**348
- Baruch of Mainz **4:**280
- Speyer **15:**264

JUDAH BEN KALONYMUS BEN MOSES OF MAINZ **10**:349
- Abraham he-Ḥasid **2**:155
- Eliezer of Bonn **6**:625
- Joel ben Isaac ha-Levi **10**:137
- Kalonymus family **10**:719; **10**:721
Judah ben Kardena **15**:1324
Judah ben Koreish **6**:646
Judah ben Lakish (tan.) **15**:800
Judah ben Makhir **14**:1413
Judah ben Manasseh **4**:238
JUDAH BEN MENAHEM OF ROME **10**:350
Judah ben Meremar **11**:1383; **11**:940
Judah ben Mordecai Gumpel **13**:1105
Judah ben Moses (12th cent., Egy.) **12**:424
Judah ben Moses (12th cent., poet), *see* LEONTE BEN MOSES
Judah ben Moses Cohen (13th cent., astron.) **8**:1194
JUDAH BEN MOSES HA-DARSHAN (11th cent.) **10**:350
- Isaac ben Merwan **9**:25
Judah ben Moses ha-Kohen (12/13 cent.) **2**:605; **11**:1248
Judah ben Moses of Arles **13**:1263
JUDAH BEN MOSES OF LUBLIN **10**:350
Judah ben Moses of Saltars **13**:587
JUDAH BEN NAḤAMANI (Naḥman; amora) **10**:350
- amoraim **2**:865; **2**:863
Judah ben Nakosa (tan.) **6**:80
JUDAH BEN NATHAN (tos.) **10**:351
Judah ben Nathan (14th cent., physic.) **15**:1321; **15**:1323
Judah ben Nethanel of Beaucaire **9**:22
JUDAH BEN NISSAN **10**:351
Judah ben Nissim ibn Malca, *see* MALKAH, JUDAH BEN NISSIM IBN
JUDAH BEN PEDAYA (Padah; amora) **10**:351
Judah ben Saadiah **12**:761
- Egypt **6**:492
- Fatimids **6**:1198
- Mevorakh ben Saadiah **11**:1453
Judah ben Samuel (gaon)
- Joseph bar Abba **10**:225
- Joseph ben Phinehas **10**:236
- Sherira ben Ḥanina **14**:1381
- Ukba, Mar **15**:1512
- wedding *takkanah* **15**:723
Judah ben Samuel ha-Levi of Estella **6**:906
Judah ben Samuel ha-Nagid **14**:816
JUDAH BEN SAMUEL HE-ḤASID **10**:352
- Abraham he-Ḥasid **2**:155
- *Anim Zemirot* **3**:21
- Ash, Joel ben Meir **3**:694
- barnacle goose **4**:247
- Eliezer of Bonn **6**:625
- ethical literature **11**:343
- hagiography **7**:1118
- *Ḥasidim, Sefer* **7**:1388
- history chart **8**:766-767
- Jewish mysticism **10**:514; **10**:516
- Judah ben Isaac **10**:346
- Kabbalah **10**:635
- Kalonymus family **10**:721; **10**:719
- Messiah **11**:1414
- Pethahiah of Regensburg **13**:339
- piety **13**:505
- *illus:*
- - *Anim Zemirot*, score **3**:22
Judah ben Samuel Shalom (trans.) **15**:1324
Judah ben Shalom (ps.-Mess., Yem.) **16**:745
JUDAH BEN SHAMMUA (tan.) **10**:353
Judah ben Shem-Tov ibn Ḥalaẓ, *see* Ibn Ḥalaẓ, Judah ben Shem-Tov
Judah ben Sheshet, *see* YEHUDI BEN SHESHET
Judah ben Simeon ben Pazzi, *see* JUDAH BAR SIMEON
Judah ben Solomon (Yem.) **16**:742
Judah ben Solomon ibn Matka, *see* MATKA, JUDAH BEN SOLOMON HA-KOHEN
Judah ben Solomon Nathan **3**:967
JUDAH BEN TABBAI (tan.) **10**:353
- Simeon ben Shetaḥ **14**:1563ff
JUDAH BEN TEMA (tan.) **10**:354
JUDAH BEN YAKAR **10**:354
- Gerona Kabbalah **10**:525
- Jerusalem Talmud **15**:776
- Naḥmanides **12**:774
Judah ben Yom Tov (tos.) **9**:23; **9**:31
Judah de Segura, *see* Segura, Judah de
Judah Eleazar (14th cent., Sp.) **16**:56
Judah Elias of Hanover (comp.) **12**:633,635
JUDAH THE GALILEAN **10**:354
- Hezekiah **8**:455
- messianism **11**:1420; **11**:1410
- Zealot party origin **16**:947ff
Judah Gaon, *see* Judah ben Samuel
Judah Hadassi, *see* HADASSI, JUDAH BEN ELIJAH
Judah ha-Kohen (11th cent., Ger.) **10**:720
- Eliezer of Worms **6**:623
Judah ha-Kohen (12th cent., Egy.) **4**:994
Judah ha-Kohen ben Eleazar he-Ḥasid (Syr.), *see* AL-MADARI, JUDAH HA-KOHEN BEN ELEAZAR HE-ḤASID
Judah ha-Kohen ibn Susan (Fez.) *see* Ibn Susan, Judah
Judah ha-Kohen of Prague **5**:1038
JUDAH HALEVI (poet, philos.) **10**:355
- *Contents:*
- - Biography **10**:355
- - Poetry **10**:358
- - Philosophy **10**:362
- - In Jewish Literature **10**:365
- General
- - Abendana, Jacob **2**:67
- - Alamani, Aaron **2**:509
- - Albalia, Baruch **2**:522
- - Al-Ghazālī **7**:539
- - Avicenna **3**:958
- - Cairo *Genizah* **16**:1340
- - history chart **8**:766-767
- - Ibn Ezra, Abraham **8**:1163
- - Ibn Ezra, Moses **8**:1171
- - Ibn Migash, Joseph **8**:1189
- - Khazars **10**:947
- - Luzzatto, S.D. **11**:606
- - Rosenzweig's translations **14**:302
- - Samuel ben Hanania **14**:807
- - travels **15**:1352
- Philosophy and Theology **11**:339; **13**:438
- - Adam **2**:239
- - alchemy **2**:548
- - angels **2**:976
- - apologetics **3**:193
- - astrology **3**:792ff
- - beatitude **4**:361
- - belief **4**:435
- - cause and effect **5**:260
- - Chosen People **5**:501; **8**:684
- - commandments **5**:786
- - eternity and creation **6**:100[illegible]
- - exile **7**:285
- - existence of God **7**:658ff
- - free will **7**:127
- - holiness **10**:873
- - Jewish humiliation **8**:684
- - microcosm doctrine **11**:1502
- - miracles **12**:77
- - Moses **12**:399
- - nature **12**:889
- - Neoplatonism **12**:961
- - polemical literature **11**:354
- - revelation **14**:123
- - reward and punishment **14**:136
- - *ru'aḥ ha-Kodesh* **14**:367
- - Sabbath **14**:565
- - *Shekhinah* **14**:1352
- - *shi'ur komah* **3**:57; **14**:1418
- - soul **15**:173
- - soul, immortality of **15**:177
- - substance and accident **5**:253; **15**:474
- - Throne of God **15**:1125
- - Torah **15**:1237; **15**:1240
- Poetry **11**:327; **13**:681
- - *Givat Sha'ul* **10**:222
- - Jerusalem as theme **9**:1562
- - Joshua ben Elijah ha-Levi **10**:278
- - Judeo-Arabic literature **10**:418
- *illus:*
- - Knesset *menorah* **8**:683
Judah ha-Levi (14th cent., tax farmer) **4**:170
JUDAH HA-LEVI BEI-RABBI HILLEL **10**:366
Judah ha-Levi of Gibraltar **4**:1200
Judah ha-Naḥtom (tan.) **15**:800
JUDAH HA-NASI (tan.) **10**:366
- *Contents:*
- - His Power in Ereẓ Israel and Relationship with Rome **10**:367
- - Judah's Bet Din **10**:369
- - Aristocracy of Learning **10**:370
- - Redaction of the Mishnah **10**:371
- aggadah on animals **3**:6
- Antoninus Pius **3**:165; **3**:166
- Ardavan **3**:399
- Bar-Kappara's fable **13**:125
- Bathyra, Sons of **4**:324
- Bet She'arim **2**:202; **4**:766
- calendar **5**:49
- codification of law **5**:631ff; **5**:891
- Damascus **5**:1239
- Greek **8**:296
- history **8**:648
- history chart **8**:766-767
- Ḥiyya **8**:793
- Jonathan ben Amram **10**:185
- labor commandment **10**:1321
- magic **11**:707
- Meir **2**:459; **11**:1241
- Messiah **11**:1411
- Mishnah redaction **11**:316; **12**:102ff
- Mishnah versions **15**:772
- presidency **9**:251
- *illus:* text
JUDAH HA-PARSI **10**:372
- Yudghan **16**:868
Judah ha-Sefardi **14**:1362
JUDAH ḤASID (Segal) HA-LEVI (Shab.) **10**:373
- *aliyah* **9**:513
- history chart **8**:766-767
- Jerusalem group **9**:1438
- Siemiatycze **14**:1514
- *illus:*
- - Ḥurvah synagogue **9**:1446
Judah ha-Yarḥoni **3**:673; **11**:1186
Judah he-Ḥasid, *see* JUDAH BEN SAMUEL HE-ḤASID
Judah he-Ḥasid Synagogue, *see* Ḥurvah Synagogue
Judah ibn Abbas, *see* ABBAS, JUDAH BEN SAMUEL IBN
Judah ibn Bal'am, *see* IBN BAL'AM, JUDAH BEN SAMUEL
Judah ibn Bulat **6**:730
Judah ibn Daud (gram.) **11**:1306; **14**:547; **16**:1380
Judah ibn Quraysh, *see* IBN QURAYSH, JUDAH
Judah ibn Shabbetai **11**:353
Judah Jonah of Safed, *see* JONA, GIOVANNI BATTISTA
JUDAH LEIB BEN BARUCH **10**:374
JUDAH LEIB BEN ENOCH ZUNDEL **10**:374
JUDAH LEIB BEN HILLEL OF SCHWERSENZ **10**:374
Judah Leib ben Ze'ev **14**:978
Judah Leib of Zelechow **2**:804; **12**:627
Judah Loeb ben Elijah **2**:142; **14**:349
Judah Loeb ben Ephraim Anschel ha-Kohen **11**:474
Judah Loeb ben Mordecai Gumpel, *see* Judah ben Mordecai Gumpel
Judah Loebush ben Isaac **10**:288
JUDAH LOEW BEN BEZALEL (Maharal) **10**:374
- alchemy **2**:548
- angels **2**:972
- *Anim Zemirot* **3**:21
- astrology **3**:793
- Azariah dei Rossi **14**:318
- Bak, Jacob **4**:113
- censorship **8**:697ff
- codification of law **5**:652
- education **8**:696
- exile **7**:291
- folktales **6**:1382
- *Haggadah* commentary **7**:1093
- Ḥasidism **14**:1437
- history chart **8**:766-767
- Moses **12**:400
- prayer against informers **8**:1368
- synagogue **15**:592
- Torah **15**:1238; **15**:1241
- *illus:* text
- *see also:* GOLEM
JUDAH MACCABEE **10**:379
- Ashtaroth temple **3**:737
- Bacchides **4**:44ff
- Ephron **6**:816
- Eupolemus **6**:964
- Gorgias **7**:809
- Hebron **8**:227
- history chart **8**:766-767
- in the Arts **7**:1457
- *Maccabees, Book of* **11**:658ff
- resurrection **14**:96
- Seleucids **8**:629
- Simeon the Hasmonean **14**:1565
- Spinoza on **15**:283
- Temple **15**:958
- war and warfare **16**:278
- *geneal. table:* **7**:1457
- *illus:*
- - text
- - *Kaufmann Mishneh Torah* **8**:1280
- *see also:* ḤANUKKAH; HASMONEANS
Judah Nesiah II (amora), *see* JUDAH III
Judah of Arles, *see* Judah ben Moses of Arles
Judah of Beaucaire, *see* Judah ben Nethanel of Beaucaire
Judah of Ciudad Rodrigo **5**:594
Judah of Corbeil (tos.) **5**:960; **9**:1233
Judah of Estella, *see* Judah ben Samuel ha-Levi of Estella
Judah of Fez, *see* ABBAS, JUDAH BEN SAMUEL IBN
Judah of Gibraltar, *see* Judah ha-Levi of Gibraltar
Judah of Kairouan, *see* JUDAH BEN JOSEPH OF KAIROUAN
Judah of Kfar Akko (tan.), *see* Judah

ben Agra
Judah of Lar **10:**1428
Judah of Lublin, *see* JUDAH BEN MOSES OF LUBLIN
Judah of Mainz, *see* JUDAH BEN KALONYMUS BEN MOSES OF MAINZ
Judah of Nuremberg **11:**736
Judah of Ofen **9:**513
Judah of Paris (tos.), *see* JUDAH BEN ISAAC
Judah of Prague (Maharal), *see* JUDAH LOEW BEN BEZALEL
Judah of Prague (print.), *see* Judah ha-Kohen of Prague
Judah of Regensburg, *see* JUDAH BEN SAMUEL HE-ḤASID
Judah of Rome, *see* JUDAH BEN MENAHEM OF ROME
Judah of Rozdol, *see* Judah Ẓevi of Rozdol
Judah of Salzburg **14:**718
Judah of Schwersenz, *see* JUDAH LEIB BEN HILLEL OF SCHWERSENZ
Judah of Sopron **15:**161
Judah of Stretyn, *see* STRETYN, JUDAH ẒEVI HIRSCH OF
Judah of Tivim **15:**1172
Judah of Vilna, *see* Judah Loeb ben Elijah
Judah of Zelechow, *see* Judah Leib of Zelechow
Judah Sir Leon le Blund **15:**1165
Judah Sir Leon of Paris (tos.), *see* JUDAH BEN ISAAC
Judah the Tiberian, *see* JUDAH BEN ELI
Judah Uziel ben Samuel, *see* Uziel, Judah ben Samuel
Judah Ẓevi Hirsch of Stretyn, *see* STRETYN, JUDAH ẒEVI HIRSCH OF
Judah Ẓevi of Rozdol **16:**1009
Judaica (sci.), *see* WISSENSCHAFT DES JUDENTUMS
Judaica (period., Cz.) **4:**777
Judaica Historical Philatelic Journal (U.S.) **15:**335
JUDAISM **10:**383
- *Contents:*
- - Definition **10:**383
- - - The Term "Torah" **10:**383
- - - Modern Distinctions Between "Judaism" and "Torah" **10:**384
- - Essence of Judaism **10:**384
- - - Talmudic Attempts to State Essence **10:**385
- - - Maimonides' 13 Principles **10:**385
- - - Reactions to Maimonides **10:**385
- - - Modern Trends **10:**386
- - - Concept of "Normative Judaism" **10:**386
- - - Recognition of Constant Ideas **10:**387
- - Development of Judaism **10:**387
- - - Biblical Period **10:**387
- - - Pre-Rabbinic Age **10:**389
- - - Rabbinic Period **10:**390
- - - Middle Ages **10:**391
- - - Period of Transition **10:**393
- - - Emancipation **10:**394
- - - Contemporary Judaism **10:**395
- - Influence of Judaism **10:**396
- General
- - censorship **5:**280
- - Crusades **5:**1143
- - festivals **6:**1237
- - holy places **8:**920ff
- - homiletical literature **8:**947ff
- - Jewish languages **10:**69
- - magic **11:**713
- - *menorah* as emblem **11:**1368
- - psychology **13:**1342
- - symbolism **15:**568
- - *takkanah* **15:**717ff
- Ideology **3:**654
- - afterlife **2:**336
- - belief **4:**429
- - cardinal offences **9:**243; **14:**1196
- - Commandments **5:**760; **5:**783
- - Divine command **12:**120
- - election of Israel **5:**498
- - eschatology **6:**860
- - ethical instruction **6:**940
- - evolution **6:**1000
- - free will **7:**125
- - God **7:**641
- - good and evil **7:**775
- - *hekdesh* **8:**281
- - heresy **8:**358
- - idolatry **8:**1235
- - *kedushah* **10:**866
- - *kelal Yisrael* **10:**898
- - Messiah **11:**1407
- - *minhag* **12:**4
- - monotheism **12:**262
- - Moses **12:**393
- - *olam ha-ba* **12:**1355
- - Oral Law **12:**1439
- - paradise **13:**77
- - providence **13:**1279
- - redemption **14:**1
- - repentance **14:**73
- - resurrection **14:**96
- - revelation **14:**117
- - reward and punishment **14:**134
- - sin **14:**1587
- - soul **15:**172
- - soul, immortality of **15:**174
- - study **15:**453; **16:**570
- - synagogue **15:**580
- - Torah **15:**1235
- - tradition **15:**1308
- Regional Practice
- - Diaspora **6:**8
- - *galut* **7:**275
- - Israel **9:**887
- - Jewish quarters **10:**82ff
- - Marrano Diaspora **11:**1019
- - Muslim states **5:**1604
- - *see also:* COMMUNITY; *and under individual countries*
- Movements
- - Conservative Judaism **5:**901
- - Ḥasidism **7:**1391
- - Haskalah **7:**1436; **7:**1445ff
- - Kabbalah **10:**638
- - Mitnaggedim **12:**161
- - Musar **12:**534
- - Neo-Orthodoxy **12:**956
- - Orthodoxy **12:**1486
- - Pharisees **13:**365; **13:**366
- - Reconstructionism **13:**1615
- - Reform and Liberal Judaism **13:**571; **14:**23
- - Zionism **16:**1031
- Groups and Sects
- - *anusim* **3:**169
- - Baḥuẓim **4:**102
- - Essenes **6:**899
- - Falashas **6:**1147
- - Frankists **7:**59
- - Judaizers **10:**397
- - Judeo-Christians **10:**38
- - Karaites **10:**761
- - New Christians **12:**1022
- - New Israel **12:**1026
- - Sadducees **14:**620
- - Samaritans **14:**725
- - Shabbateans **14:**1219
- Other Religions and Ideologies
- - Catholic Church **5:**536; **10:**159
- - Christianity **5:**505; **9:**244ff
- - communism **16:**779
- - Gentiles **7:**410
- - Hellenism **8:**294
- - Islam **9:**92ff; **10:**1196
- - Protestantism **13:**1247
- - Roman paganism **14:**241
- Views
- - Aḥad Ha-Am **2:**444ff; **8:**190
- - Buber, Martin **4:**1433
- - Dubnow, Simon **6:**255ff
- - Formstecher, Solomon **6:**1440ff
- - Geiger, Abraham **7:**358
- - Graetz, Heinrich **7:**847
- - Hirsch, S. R. **8:**512
- - Judah Halevi **10:**362ff
- - Justinian I **10:**478
- - Kant, Immanuel **10:**742
- - Kook, A. I. **10:**1186
- - Mendelssohn, Moses **11:**1332
- - Muhammad **12:**509ff
- - Nietzsche, F. **12:**1154
- - Philo **13:**411ff
- - Saadiah Gaon **14:**549
- - Schechter, Solomon **14:**949
- - Spinoza **15:**278
- - Tacitus **15:**695ff
- - Tillich, Paul **15:**1142
- - Zunz, Leopold **16:**1236
- *see also:* JEW; JEWISH IDENTITY; PHILOSOPHY; THEOLOGY
Judaism (period.) **2:**826; **11:**157
Judaism, Conservative, *see* CONSERVATIVE JUDAISM
Judaism, conversion from, *see* APOSTASY; BAPTISM FORCED; Conversion, forced
Judaism, conversion to, *see* PROSELYTES
Judaism, Liberal, *see* REFORM JUDAISM
Judaism, Orthodox, *see* NEO-ORTHODOXY; ORTHODOXY
Judaism, Positive Historical *see* CONSERVATIVE JUDAISM
Judaism, Reconstructionist, *see* RECONSTRUCTIONISM
Judaism, Reform, *see* NEOLOGY; REFORM JUDAISM
Judaism, Traditional, *see* NEO-ORTHODOXY; ORTHODOXY
Judaism and Modern Man (bk.) **16:**1345
Judaistica, *see* WISSENSCHAFT DES JUDENTUMS
Judaizare (usury) **4:**168
Judaized Berbers (J. tribe, N. Afr.), *see* BAḤUẒIM
JUDAIZERS (sects) **10:**397
- Abrahamites **2:**159
- Black Jews in America **4:**1068
- India **8:**1355
- Inquisition **8:**1383ff
- Latin America **10:**1448
- Muslim lands **13:**1187
- Peru **13:**322
- proselytism **13:**1189ff
- Russia **14:**434
- Spain **15:**222
- Tunisia **15:**1430
- *Turbato Corde* **4:**216
- *illus:*
- - auto da fé **8:**1401
- - Casa de Dios sect **11:**1459
- - Mexico, record of trial (1590) **8:**1397
- - U.S. Black Jew in Israel, 1970 **4:**1068
Judan (emis.) **14:**1361
JUDAS (Chr. writ.) **14:**235
Judas Iscariot **10:**12
- apostles' number **3:**216
- Christian attitude **10:**22
Judas tree (bot.) **9:**221
JUDE, DER (periods.) **10:**402
- apologetics **3:**199
- Juedischer Verlag **10:**464
- press **13:**1033
- Riesser, Gabriel **14:**167
- *illus:* text
JUDEA (prov., Er. Isr.) **10:**403
- Ancient Period to 66 C.E. **8:**625ff
- - Agrippa I **2:**416
- - *arnona* **3:**487
- - Cassius Longinus **5:**234
- - crucifixions **5:**1134
- - literature **8:**293
- - Pontius Pilate **13:**848
- - Tobiads **15:**1178
- - *see also:* Provincia Judaea
- 66 C.E. to Modern Period **9:**237
- - Arab population **9:**1035ff
- - Arab refugees **9:**451
- - Bar Kokhba revolt **4:**228
- - Crusader communities **9:**272
- - health services **9:**992ff
- - Jund-Filasṭīn **9:**261
- - mishnaic Hebrew **16:**1591
- Descriptions
- - designations **9:**111
- - geology **9:**200ff
- - human geography **9:**584ff
- - Zion **16:**1030
- *map:*
- - Alexander Yannai's kingdom **16:**715
- *see also:* Judean Desert; Judean Mountains; Judean Plain
Judean (Heb. lang.) **16:**1569
Judean Desert (reg., Er. Isr.) **9:**141
- *illus:*
- - En-Gedi **12:**892
- - Jordan River **10:**197
- - Nebi Mūsā **9:**99
JUDEAN DESERT CAVES (Er. Isr.) **10:**403
- documents **4:**237
- En-Gedi **6:**741
- Hebrew mss **11:**900
- *illus:*
- - text
- - Bar Kokhba period, objects **3:**326
Judean Desert Documents **4:**237
Judean Desert sect **10:**161; **14:**648
"Judean Hills" (drg., L. Krakauer) Fig. 96 **3**-ART
Judean Mountains (reg., Er. Isr.) **9:**139,1513
- *illus:*
- - Sorek Valley **9:**137; **15:**164
- - terracing **9:**133, 205
Judean Plain (reg., Er. Isr.) **9:**126; **9:**127ff
- human geography **9:**576
Judeans, First (army battalion) **8:**756; **9:**337; **10:**73
Judeis, Cornelius de **11:**918
Judeis, Gerard de, *see* Jode, Gerard de
Judeja (orgn., Yug.) **16:**1148
Judel Ben Moses of Lublin, *see* JUDAH BEN MOSES OF LUBLIN
Judenaeltester (head of Judenrat) **10:**407
Judenbach (vill., Ger.) **5:**619
Judenbischof (tit., Ger.) **15:**264
Judenbolleten (tax, Aus.) **10:**1589
JUDENBURG (city, Aus.) **10:**405
- *illus:* text
Judendorf (-Strassengel; tn., Aus.) **15:**465
Judenfrei (Nazi term), *see* JUDENREIN
Judenfreiheit (term) **15:**1524
Judengasse, *see* JEWISH QUARTER
Judengeleit (tax), *see* LEIBZOLL
Judengesetz (law; Switz.) **2:**3
Judenkaiser (tit.) **16:**457
Judenmeister (J. offic.) **10:**1409
Judenordnung (law, Ger.) **16:**677
- *illus:*

-- title page (1753) **3:**903
- *see also:* TAKKANOT HA-KAHAL
JUDENPFENNIGE (coins, Rhineland) **10:**406
JUDENRAT (J. council) **10:**407
- ghetto administration **7:**545ff
- Holocaust **8:**879,896
- Lublin **11:**545
- Lvov **11:**614
- Poland **13:**753
- Russia **14:**476
- Warsaw Ghetto **16:**347
Judenreferat (J. report, Gestapo) **3:**855
Juden Reglements (law, Prus.) **16:**334
JUDENREIN (Nazi term) **10:**408
- Germany **7:**489
- Holocaust **8:**838
- *see also:* RACE, THEORY OF
Judenrichter (J. judge, Morav.) **3:**875
Judenschlaeger (Ger. anti-Sems.) **3:**483
Judenstaat, Der (bk., Herzl) **4:**307; **16:**1044
"Judenstain" (Jewish stone) **12:**1275
Judenstern (lamp) **7:**1291
Judenstern (badge), *see* BADGE, JEWISH
Judenwinkel (J. qtr., Ger.) **16:**998
Judenzoll (tax), *see* LEIBZOLL
Judeo-Alsatian (J. lang.) **2:**751
JUDEO-ARABIC (J. lang) **10:**409
- Jewish languages **10:**67
- middle Arabic **3:**239ff
- *illus:* text
- *see also:* ARABIC LANGUAGE
JUDEO-ARABIC LITERATURE **10:**410
- *Contents:*
-- The East **10:**411
-- Karaites **10:**413
-- The West **10:**414
-- Religious Philosophy and Theology **10:**417
-- From the 13th Century **10:**420
- ʿAdanī, Saadiah **2:**250
- Bekache, Shalom **4:**407
- *see also:* Arabic Literature
Judeo-Berber (J. lang.) **10:**410
- Jewish languages **10:**67
Juedo-Catalan (J. lang.), *see* Catalanic
Judeo-Christians (sect) **10:**39
- after Temple destruction **9:**244
- antinomianism **3:**69
- heresy **8:**359
Judeo-Corfiote (J. lang.) **9:**1146
JUDEO-FRENCH (Old Fr. in J. usage) **10:**423
- *Complainte de Troyes* **15:**1407
- influence on Hebrew **16:**1635
- Jewish languages **10:**67
- Samuel ben Meir **14:**810
Judeo-German (J. lang.), *see* YIDDISH LANGUAGE
JUDEO-GREEK (J. lang.) **10:**425
- linguistic development **10:**67
- *illus:* text
- *see also:* GREEK AND LATIN LANGUAGES, RABBINICAL KNOWLEDGE OF
Judeo-Iranian (J. lang.) **10:**432
JUDEO-ITALIAN (J. langs.) **10:**427
- Del Monte's poetry **5:**1481
- Jewish languages **10:**67
- Roman Jews **14:**249
- *illus:*
-- prayer book (15th cent. ms.) **9:**1124
JUDEO-PERSIAN (J. lang.) **10:**429
- Jewish languages **10:**67
- *illus:* text
JUDEO-PERSIAN LITERATURE **10:**432
- *Contents:*
-- Hebrew Bible Translations **10:**433
-- Pioneers of Poetry **10:**434
-- Classical Poetry in Hebrew Transcription **10:**435
-- Literary Productivity (17/18 Centuries) **10:**435
-- Literary Productivity of Bukharan Jews **10:**435
-- Literary Revival in Jerusalem **10:**436
-- Literary Revival in Teheran **10:**437
-- European Investigation **10:**438
- Afghanistan Jews **2:**327
- Aklar, Mordecai **2:**501
- Bible translations **4:**864
- *illus:*
-- text
-- Shahin Shirazi's paraphrase of the Pentateuch **2:**733; **4:**932; **12:**395; **14:**1258; **16:**1027,1182
Judeo-Portuguese (J. lang.), *see* Portuguesic
JUDEO-PROVENÇAL (J. lang.) **10:**439
- Avignonese Hebrew **3:**967
- Jewish languages **10:**67
- *illus:* text
Judeo-Roman (J. lang.), *see* JUDEO-ITALIAN
Judeo-Romance (J. lang.) **4:**865
Judeo-Spanish (J. lang.), *see* LADINO
Judeo-Tajiki (J. lang.) **10:**432; **10:**435
- Bukharan Jews **4:**1473; **9:**502; **14:**760
JUDEO-TĀT (J. lang.) **10:**441
- Jewish languages **10:**67
- Judeo-Iranian **10:**432
- Mountain Jews **12:**478ff
Judeo-Tatar (J. lang.) **4:**865
Judería (J. qtr., Sp.) **4:**1513; **15:**233
Judeus, Tidericus **14:**712
Judezmo (J. lang.), *see* LADINO
Judge(s), *see* BET DIN AND JUDGES
Judgment, Day of, *see* DAY OF THE LORD
JUDGES, THE BOOK OF (bib. bk.) **10:**442
- *Contents:*
-- Completion of the Conquest **10:**443
-- Introduction to Careers of the Judges **10:**444
--- Othniel **10:**444
--- Ehud **10:**444
--- Shamgar **10:**445
--- Deborah and Barak **10:**445
--- Gideon **10:**446
--- Abimelech **10:**447
--- Tola and Jair **10:**448
-- Introduction to Later Judges **10:**448
--- Jephthah **10:**448
--- Samson **10:**449
-- Migration of Dan to the North and Benjamite War **10:**449
- Abdon **2:**55
- Abimelech **2:**77
- Balak **4:**127
- Bible history **8:**577; **8:**583
- Deborah **5:**1429
- Ehud **6:**515
- Gideon **7:**557
- Jair **9:**1269
- Jephthah **9:**1341
- Mari term **11:**986
- Othniel **12:**1520
- Samson **14:**773
- Shamgar **14:**1288
- Spinoza on **15:**283
- *illus:*
-- text
-- Israelite control (map) **9:**113
Judges, Tombs of the (Jer.), *see* Sanhedria
Judgment (legal), *see* PRACTICE AND PROCEDURE
Judgment, Divine, *see* DAY OF THE LORD
"Judgment of Solomon" (sculp.) **14:**1061
Judi ben Sheshet (Shishat), *see* YEHUDI BEN SHESHET
Judicial autonomy, *see* AUTONOMY, JUDICIAL
Judiciary
- Gentiles **12:**1189ff
- pleas **13:**631
- practice and procedure **13:**952
- proselytes **13:**1185
- verdicts **11:**804
- *see also:* BET DIN AND JUDGES
JUDICIARY IN ISRAEL **9:**628
- *illus:*
-- text
-- Druze judge sworn in by President Shazar **9:**925
-- Muslim religious judges **9:**922
-- Supreme Court **9:**637
Jūdīn (Crus. castle) **16:**728
JUDIN, SAMUEL **10:**451
- *illus:* text
Judíos francos (Sp.) **15:**235
Judisk Kronika (period., Fin.) **13:**1048
Judisk Kronika (period., Swed.) **4:**1369; **13:**1048
Judisk Tidskrift (period., Swed.) **13:**1048; **16:**59
JUDITH (w. of Ḥiyya) **10:**451
- Ḥiyya **8:**794
Judith (q., Eth.) **6:**1143; **6:**1144
JUDITH, BOOK OF **10:**451
- agricultural description **2:**392
- Hellenism **8:**298; **8:**302
- Hellenistic Jewish literature **8:**304
- Holofernes **8:**917
- Septuagint **4:**852
- *illus:*
-- ceremonial object motif **5:**296
-- eighteenth-cent. *ketubbah* Pl.2 **10**-KETUBBAH
-- Holofernes being decapitated **3:**1
-- "Judith and Holofernes" (sculp., Donatello) **10:**453
-- "Judith and Holofernes" (paint., A. Mantegna) **10:**454
-- "Judith with the Head of Holofernes" (Lucas Cranach the Elder) **8:**917
Judith Lady Montefiore College (Eng.) **6:**450; **11:**449; **12:**270
Judo (sport) **15:**311
Judovin, Solomon, *see* Yudubin, Shlomo
Jud Suess, *see* OPPENHEIMER, JOSEPH BEN ISSACHAR SUESSKIND
Jud Suess (bk.) **6:**1249
Judycz, Saul, *see* WAHL, SAUL BEN JUDAH
Juedels, Isaac, *see* Isaac ben Judah Loeb Yuedels
Juedische Arbeits- und Wanderfuersorge (period.) **2:**289
Juedische Colonial Bank, *see* JEWISH COLONIAL TRUST
JUEDISCHE FREISCHULE (Ger. school) **10:**461
- Ben David, Lazarus **4:**474
Juedische Hilfskommittee. Roter Halbmond fuer Palaestina (orgn., Ger.) **15:**1021
Juedische Hochschule (Berlin), *see* HOCHSCHULE FUER DIE WISSENSCHAFT DES JUDENTUMS
Juedische Jugendblaetter (period.) **4:**228
Juedische Jugendhilfe (orgn., Ger.) **16:**862
Juedische Kulturgemeinschaft (Arg. orgn.) **3:**416
Juedische-liberale Zeitung (period.) **7:**487; **16:**110
Juedische Litteratur seit Abschluss des Kanons (bk.) **16:**552
Juedische Monatshefte (period.) **10:**1147
Juedische Morgenpost (newsp), *see* *Yiddishe Morgenpost*
Juedische Partei (Aus.), *see* VOLKSPARTEI, JUEDISCHE
Juedische Post (journ.) **13:**1053
Juedische Presse (newsp., Aus.) **13:**1034
Juedische Presse (newsp., Cz.) **4:**777
JUEDISCHE PRESSE (period., Ger.) **10:**462
- press **13:**1032
Juedische Pressezentrale (newsp., Switz.) **13:**1049
Juedische Pressezentrale (agency, Switz.) **13:**1024
Juedischer Central-Verein (orgn., Ger.), *see* CENTRAL-VEREIN DEUTSCHER STAATSBUERGER JUEDISCHEN GLAUBENS
Juedische Revue (period.) **13:**1029
JUEDISCHER FRAUENBUND (orgn., Ger.) **10:**462
- Karminski, Hannah **10:**799
JUEDISCHER KULTURBUND (orgn., Ger.) **10:**462
- Berlin **4:**647
- Bab, Julius **4:**14
Juedischer Pressedienst (period.) **13:**1033
Juedischer Reformverein, *see* Jewish Reform Society
JUEDISCHE RUNDSCHAU (journ., Ger.) **10:**463
- Germany **7:**493
Juedische Rundschau Maccabi (period., Switz.) **4:**305; **13:**1049
JUEDISCHER VERLAG (publ. house) **10:**463
- Berlin **4:**653
- Feiwel, Berthold **6:**1215
- Germany **7:**500
- Kaznelson, Siegmund **10:**860
- Lilien, Ephraim **11:**240
Juedischer Volksfreund (newsp.) **4:**1320
Juedischer Volksverein (orgn.) **10:**1051
Juedisches Familienblatt (period.) **13:**1028
Juedisches Gemeindeblatt fuer die Britische Zone (journ.) **13:**1033
Juedisches Lexikon (encyc., Ger.) **6:**732; **8:**364
Juedisches Nachrichtenblatt (newsp.) **3:**900; **14:**51
Juedische Stimme (period.) **13:**1028
Juedisches Volksblatt (period., Ger.) **13:**1032
Juedisches Volksblatt (period., Yug.) **16:**1151
Juedisches Wochenblatt (period.) **7:**348
Juedische Turnerschaft (orgn.) **11:**664
Juedische Turnzeitung (journ.) **11:**664
Juedische Volkshochschule (J. college) **7:**488
Juedische Volkspartei (Aus.), *see* VOLKSPARTEI, JUEDISCHE
JUEDISCHE VOLKSPARTEI (Ger.) **10:**464

Juedische Volksstimme (journ., Aus.) **7**:696
Juedische Volksstimme (period., Cz.) **4**:1385; **5**:1191; **16**:1111
Juedische Volkszeitung (period., Cz.) **5**:1191; **13**:1028
Juedische Volkszeitung und Zentralorgan fuer die Israeliten in der Schweiz (period., Switz.), *see Israelitisches Wochenblatt. Zentralorgan fuer die Israeliten in der Schweiz, Baden und Elsass-Lotheringen*
Juedische Welt (newsp.) **13**:1034
Juedische Wochenschau (period.) **3**:424
Juedische Zeitschrift fuer Wissenschaft und Leben (period.) **13**:1056
Juedische Zeitung (period., Aus.) **2**:61; **4**:326; **13**:1033
- Stricker, Robert **15**:439
Juedische Zeitung (newsp., Cz.) **4**:777
Juedische Zeitung (period., U.S.) **13**:1053
Juedische Zeitung fuer Mittelsachsen (newsp., Ger.) **10**:795
JUEDISCH-LITERARISCHE GESELLSCHAFT (Ger.) **10**:464
- Auerbach, Moses **3**:844
- Isaac Halevy **7**:1184
Juedisch-Nationale (Aus.), *see* VOLKSPARTEI, JUEDISCHE
Juedisch-theologische Lehranstalt (rab. school) **16**:577
JUEDISCH-THEOLOGISCHES SEMINAR, BRESLAU **10**:465
- Frankel, Zacharias **7**:80
- library **11**:192
- rabbinical seminaries **13**:1464
- *illus:* text
JUELICH (duchy, tn., Ger.) **10**:466
- Berg community **4**:607
Juez Mayor (tit., Sp.) **13**:1468
Jugend (period.) **16**:896
Jugerum (Rom. meas.) **16**:381; **16**:390
Juhász, Péter Melius **4**:883
Juili, Elia **4**:503
Juiverie, see JEWISH QUARTER
Juiverie, La (vill., Fr.) **3**:23
JUJUBE (bot.) **10**:467
- flora of Israel **9**:222,225
- plant list **13**:619
- *illus:* text
Julia (early syn. donor) **15**:600
JULIAN THE APOSTATE (Rom. emp.) **10**:467
- Ammianus Marcellinus **2**:851
- Babylonia **4**:42
- Ereẓ Israel **9**:256
- *fiscus Judaicus* **3**:854; **6**:1326
- history chart **8**:766-767
- Jerusalem **9**:1406
- Judaism, attitude to **7**:891; **8**:653
Julia Neapolis (loc., Isr.), *see* NABLUS
Julianos ben Judah, *see* Luliana ben Judah
Julianus, *see* PAPPUS AND JULIANUS
Julianus, Flavius Claudius, *see* JULIAN THE APOSTATE
Julias (city, Er. Isr.), *see* BET(H)-HARAM; BETHSAIDA
Julio Levin (colony, Arg.) **3**:431
Julius II (pope) **8**:1398; **13**:856
JULIUS III (pope) **10**:469
- Amatus Lusitanus **2**:796
- Catechumens, House of **5**:253
- universities **15**:1676
Julius, Samuel **5**:934
JULIUS ARCHELAUS **10**:470
JULIUS CAESAR **10**:470
- Antigonus II **3**:65
- Aristobulus II **3**:441
- Augustus **3**:852
- Caesar, Sextus Julius **5**:6
- calendar **16**:1263
- Hyrcanus II **6**:945
- Malchus I **12**:742
- Roman Jews **14**:240
JULIUS FLORUS **14**:235
JULIUS SEVERUS **10**:471
- Bar Kokhba revolt **4**:233; **9**:247
JUN-BRODA, INA **10**:471
Junckkerot (Bib. trans.) **4**:873
Jund al-Urdun (Jor. prov.) **4**:292
Jund-Filasṭīn (Arab prov., Er. Isr.) **9**:267
Jundishapur, University of (Pers.) **15**:1675
Jung, C.G. **7**:162
Jung, Guido **13**:815
Jung, Julius **10**:471
JUNG, LEO **10**:471
Jung, Meir **10**:471
Jung, Moritz **15**:1509
Jung, Moses **10**:471
Jungbunzlau (tn., Cz.), *see* MLADA BOLESLAV
Jungfernhof (extermination camp) **8**:871
Junghof, Caspar **11**:1564
JUNGHOLZ (vill., Fr.) **10**:472
Jung Israel (orgn., Ger.) **11**:446
Jung-Israel (period.) **5**:456
Jung Juda (period.) **5**:456; **13**:1026
Jungman, Moshe, *see* YUNGMAN, MOSHE
Jungreis, Abraham ha-Levi **10**:472
JUNGREIS, ASHER ANSHEL **10**:472
Jungreis, Moses Nathan Nata ha-Levi **10**:472
Jungreis, Samuel David Segal **10**:473
Jungreis, Samuel Ze'ev ha-Levi **10**:472
Jungreisz (name), *see* Jungreis
Junior Chronicle (period.) **5**:460
Junior congregation, *see* CHILDREN'S SERVICES
Junior Hadassah (orgn.) **7**:1046
Junior Jewish Encyclopedia **6**:734
Junior Technical College (Isr.) **15**:891
JUNIPER (tree) **10**:473
- *berosh* **5**:1178
- *no'aẓuẓ* **15**:1119
- plant list **13**:619
Junius, François **8**:39
JUNOSZA, KLEMENS **10**:474
Junta (committee of J. cmty.) **15**:792
Jupiter (planet) **3**:798
Jupiter, Temple of (Jer.) **9**:1405
Jupiter Capitolinus (Rom. deity) **6**:15; **8**:293
- Aelia Capitolina **2**:319
- Fiscus Judaicus **6**:1325
- Vespasian's decree **9**:238
Jūra, Al-(vill., Isr.) **3**:717
Jurados (cmty. Idr.) **2**:259
Juramentum Judaeorum, see OATH MORE JUDAICO
Jurandot, Jerzy **13**:802
JURBARKAS (Jurburg; tn., Lith.) **10**:474
Jurieu, Pierre, **8**:39
Jurisdiction
- autonomy, judicial **3**:928ff
- community **5**:812
- Gerona **7**:505
- over gentiles **12**:1190ff
- practice and procedure **13**:952
- *see also:* BET DIN AND JUDGES; CONFLICT OF LAWS
JURNET OF NORWICH **10**:475
Jurowich, Isidor **5**:135
Jus gazaga (lease ordinance) **7**:1523
- *ḥerem ha-Yishuv* **8**:358
- Rome **14**:249
Jus Gladii (leg. term) **13**:1117
JUSTER, GEORGE **3**:603
JUSTER, JEAN **10**:475
- historiography **8**:562
JUSTICE **10**:476
- Commandments, the 613 **5**:769,779
- ethics **6**:933
- God **7**:669
- honor, reward of **8**:966
- Judaism **10**:388
- king, kingship **10**:1016
- Messiah, kingdom of **11**:1408
- Micah **11**:1482
- peace **13**:197
- sages' concept of **14**:652ff
- self-defense **14**:1124
- Sodom **15**:71
- *takkanot ha-kahal* **15**:733
- *see also:* BET DIN AND JUDGES: LAW AND MORALITY: PROVIDENCE
Justice and mercy of God, *see* GOD
Justices of the Jews (mdvl. govt. offic.) **6**:1007
JUSTIN (Lat. au.) **14**:235
JUSTINIAN I (emp.) **10**:477
- Bible translation**4**:855
- Ereẓ Israel **9**:258
- history chart **8**:766-767
- Jerusalem **9**:1407
- Jews **4**:1551; **8**:656ff
- rabbinic exegesis **16**:1338
- Samaritans **14**:732; **14**:736
- *Targum Sheni* **15**:813
- Tiberias community **9**:265
- Tunisian Jews **15**:1432
- *see also: Corpus Juris Civilis*
Justinianus, Augustus, *see* GIUSTINIANI, AGOSTINO
Justin Martyr **4**:924; **6**:83ff
Justinus, Marcus Junianius, *see* JUSTIN
JUSTMAN, JOSEPH **10**:479
JUSTMAN, MOSHE BUNEM **10**:479
Justus (s. of Josephus) **10**:254
Justus (s. of Paragonis) **12**:828
Justus Frey, *see* Jeiteles, Aaron
JUSTUS OF TIBERIAS **10**:479
- Greek **8**:298
- history **8**:553
- Jewish history **11**:314
- Josephus **10**:261
Jutrzenka (period.) **12**:1108; **13**:1045; **16**:341
Jutrznia (period., Warsaw ghetto) **16**:348
JUVENAL (Rom. writ.) **10**:481
- Judaism **14**:233
Juvenal (5th cent., bp.) **9**:1407
Juvenile delinquency **5**:1100
Juventud (journ.) **3**:424; **13**:1040; **15**:52
Juventud Israelita Argentina (orgn.) **15**:52
Juwal-Verlag (publ. house, Ger.) **15**:57
Juwwa (dist., Aden) **16**:741
Juynboll, Dietrich W. van **8**:39
Jūzjānī, Al- (hist., Afg.) **2**:327
J.W.B., *see* NATIONAL JEWISH WELFARE BOARD
J.W.B. Circle (period.) **12**:878
J.W.B. Year Book **12**:878
J.W.V., *see* JEWISH WAR VETERANS OF THE UNITED STATES OF AMERICA

K

Kaaba (shrine, Mecca), *see* Ka'ba
Kaaden (tn., Bohem.), *see* KADAN
Ka'at (bird) **12:**1530
– *see also:* PELICAN
KAATZ, SAUL **10:**485
Ka'ba (shrine, Mecca) **9:**92
– Abraham **2:**120
– Muhammad **12:**509
– *illus:*
– – Mecca and the Great Mosque **9:**93
Kababir (vill., Isr.) **9:**921
KABACHNIK, MARTIN IZRAILOVICH **5:**384
KABAK, AARON ABRAHAM **10:**485
KABAKOFF, JACOB **10:**487
KA'B AL-AḤBĀR (7th cent., apos.) **10:**488
– Jerusalem **9:**1575
– prayer on Temple Mount **15:**989
– Yemen **16:**740
KA'B AL-ASHRAF (7th cent., poet) **10:**488
Kabar, Isaac **11:**1558
Kabars, *see* KHAZARS
Kabbala Denudata (bk.) **10:**1117
– Kabbalah **10:**645
KABBALAH (J. mysticism) **10:**489
– *Contents:*
– – Introduction **10:**493
– – – General Notes **10:**493
– – – Terms used for Kabbalah **10:**494
– – Historical Development **10:**495
– – – Early Beginnings **10:**495
– – – Apocalyptic Esotericism and Merkabah Mysticism **10:**497
– – – Esoteric Literature **10:**500
– – – Jewish Gnosis and Sefer Yeẓirah **10:**506
– – – Geonic Period **10:**508
– – – Ḥasidic Movements **10:**512
– – – Provence **10:**518
– – – Gerona **10:**525
– – – Other Currents in 13th Century **10:**528
– – – 14th Century up to Expulsion **10:**535
– – – After Expulsion and in Safed **10:**540
– – – Later Times **10:**551
– – Basic Ideas of Kabbalah **10:**556
– – – God and Creation **10:**557
– – – – Will **10:**560
– – – – Thought **10:**561
– – – – Nothingness **10:**562
– – – – Three Lights **10:**563
– – – Emanation and Sefirot **10:**563
– – – Sefirot and their Symbolism **10:**570
– – – Worlds and Creative Cycles **10:**579
– – – Problem of Evil **10:**583
– – – Creation in Lurianic Kabbalah **10:**588ff
– – – – Ẓimẓum **10:**588
– – – – Breaking of the Vessels **10:**594ff
– – – – Tikkun **10:**596
– – – Kabbalah and Pantheism **10:**601
– – – Man and his Soul **10:**606ff
– – – Exile and Redemption **10:**617
– – – Torah and Significance **10:**619
– – – – As Mystical Name **10:**621
– – – – As Living Organism **10:**622
– – – – Divine Speech **10:**623
– – – The Mystic Way **10:**624
– – – – Devekut **10:**624
– – – – Prayer, Kavvanah, Meditation **10:**627
– – – – Ecstasy **10:**630
– – – Practical Kabbalah **10:**632
– – Influences and Scholarship **10:**638
– – – Influence on Judaism **10:**638
– – – Christian Kabbalah **10:**643ff
– – – Scholarship **10:**646
– General
– – Ashkenazi influence **3:**721
– – emissaries **14:**1365
– – Hellenized Jewish mysticism **15:**573ff
– – *maggid* **11:**699
– – organized societies **8:**441
– – Reformation **14:**19
– – yeshivah curriculum **16:**767
– Ideas and Practices **10:**556ff
– – *adam kadmon* **2:**248ff
– – *aggadah* **2:**361
– – Ahijah the Shilonite **2:**460
– – *Akedah*, interpretations **2:**483
– – *aliyah* **9:**513
– – allegory **2:**644
– – alphabet **2:**748
– – antinomianism **3:**69
– – astrology **3:**794
– – *ba'al shem* **4:**5ff
– – *Bet Hillel, Bet Shammai* **4:**741
– – Chosen People **5:**501
– – Commandments, reasons for **5:**789
– – covering of head **8:**2
– – David **5:**1331
– – *Ein-Sof* **6:**535
– – Emanation **6:**696
– – *gematria* **7:**372
– – *gilgul* **7:**574ff
– – *hakkafot* **7:**1154
– – *hibbut ha-kever* **8:**464
– – *Lamed Vav Ẓaddikim* **10:**1367
– – love **11:**527
– – mystical traditions **15:**1309
– – Omer, counting of **12:**1384; **12:**1387
– – Orchard of Holy Apples **3:**224
– – peace **13:**198
– – piety **13:**505
– – righteousness **14:**183
– – Sabbath **14:**567
– – sacrifices **14:**615
– – *Sefirot* **14:**1104
– – *sheḥitah* **14:**1342
– – *Shekhinah* **14:**1353ff
– – *tagin* **15:**700
– – *tefillin* **15:**900ff
– – Torah **15:**1237; **15:**1241ff
– – Torah reading **15:**1253
– – Torah study **15:**457
– – Tu bi-Shevat **15:**1419
– – woman **16:**627
– – Worlds, the Four **16:**641ff
– Philosophy and Theology
– – anthropomorphism **3:**56
– – Aristotelianism **3:**445
– – dualism **6:**244
– – gnosticism and theosophy **9:**1219
– – God **7:**661ff
– – Judaism **10:**392
– – Neoplatonism **12:**960ff
– – pantheism **7:**662; **7:**673
– – philosophy, attempt at reconciliation **8:**1206
– – philosophy, Jewish **13:**422
– – providence **13:**1282
– – redemption **14:**5
– – repentance **14:**76
– – soul, immortality of **15:**180
– – theology **15:**1107
– Prayers and Meditation **10:**627ff
– – *devekut* **5:**1598
– – *kavvanah* **10:**853
– – *Lekhah Dodi* **11:**4
– – liturgical commentaries **13:**988
– – meditation **11:**1217
– – *nusaḥ ha-Ari* **11:**400
– – prayer **13:**983
– Literature
– – Apocalypse **3:**180ff
– – *Aẓilut*, treatise on **3:**1009
– – *Beit Aharon* **2:**17
– – *Berit Menuḥah* **2:**145; **2:**146
– – *Emek ha-Melekh* **4:**50
– – English literature **6:**776
– – eschatology **6:**880ff
– – ethical literature **6:**930
– – fiction, Hebrew **6:**1268
– – hagiography **7:**1119
– – *Ḥemdat Yamim* **8:**321ff
– – *Hermetica* **8:**372
– – homiletical literature **8:**954
– – German literature **7:**440
– – *Keter Shem Tov* **2:**134
– – *Ma'arekhet ha-Elohut* **11:**637
– – *Ma'aseh Efod* **6:**301
– – *Me'ir la-Arez* **4:**992
– – *Mikdash Melekh* **4:**1545
– – *Mo'ed Katan* **7:**549
– – mystical literature **11:**346ff
– – *Perek Shirah* **13:**274
– – *Perush al Eser Atarot* **2:**135
– – polemics **13:**793ff
– – *Razim, Sefer ha-* **13:**1594
– – responsa **14:**93
– – *Sefer Yeẓirah* **16:**782
– – *Shi'ur Komah* **3:**57; **14:**1417
– – Talmud, burning of **15:**771
– – *Tefillah le-Moshe* **4:**530
– – *Temunah, The Book of* **15:**999
– – *Toledot ha-Ari* **15:**1207
– – *see also:* BAHIR, SEFER HA-; ZOHAR
– Persons and Views
– – Aaron Selig ben Moses **2:**24
– – Abelson, Joshua **2:**63
– – Abraham ben David **2:**140
– – Abraham ben Eliezer **2:**143
– – Abraham ben Simeon of Worms **2:**156
– – Abulafia, Abraham **2:**186ff
– – Abulafia, Todros **2:**194
– – Adam *Ba'al Shem* **2:**247
– – Akiva **2:**490
– – Alcastiel **2:**542
– – Alfandari, Ḥayyim **2:**597
– – Alkabez, Solomon **2:**635
– – Asher ben David **3:**706
– – Azikri, Eleazar **3:**1008
– – Azriel of Gerona **3:**1012
– – Bacharach, Jair Ḥayim **4:**48
– – Bacharach, Naphtali **4:**49
– – Bahya ben Asher **3:**104
– – Baruch of Kosov **4:**281
– – Benjamin ha-Cohen Vitale **4:**531
– – Cardozo, Abraham **5:**163
– – Caro, Joseph **5:**199
– – Cordovero, Moses **5:**967
– – Crescas, Ḥasdai **5:**1085
– – David ben Abraham **5:**1347
– – David ben Judah **5:**1351
– – David ibn Abi Zimra **5:**1358
– – Eleazar of Worms **6:**593
– – Emden, Jacob **6:**723
– – Eybeschuetz, J. **6:**1075
– – Ezra ben Solomon **6:**1123
– – Fano, Menahem Azariah da **6:**1175
– – Frank, Jacob **7:**55
– – Gabirol **7:**243
– – Gikatilla, Joseph **7:**564
– – Ḥayon, Nehemiah Ḥiyya **7:**1501
– – Herrera, Abraham Kohen de **8:**391
– – Horodezky, S. A. **8:**978
– – Ibn Waqar, Joseph **8:**1206
– – Isaac ben Jacob Ha-Kohen **9:**19
– – Isaac ben Sheshet Perfet **9:**33

- - Isaac the Blind 9:35ff
- - Israel Ba'al Shem Tov 9:1053
- - Isserles, M. 14:89
- - Jacob ben Jacob ha-Kohen 9:1220
- - Joel, David Heymann 10:133
- - Johanan ben Zakkai 10:151
- - Joseph ibn Tabul 10:244
- - Kafah, Yihye 10:670
- - Kook, A. I. 10:1184
- - Latif, Isaac ibn 10:1447
- - Luria, Isaac 11:572
- - Luzzatto, Moses Hayyim 11:601ff
- - Luzzatto, Samuel David 11:606
- - Maimon, Solomon 11:741
- - Malkah, Judah ibn 11:827
- - Moses de Leon 12:425
- - Nahmanides 12:78; 12:778; 12:782ff
- - Nathan of Gaza 12:861
- - Ostropoler, Samson 12:1516
- - Rashba 2:308
- - Recanati, Menahem 13:1608
- - Sarug, Israel 14:889
- - Scholem, Gershom 14:991
- - Shabbetai Zevi 14:1241ff
- - Sharabi, Solomon 14:1307
- - Simeon bar Yohai 14:1551
- - Spira, Nathan Nata 15:284
- - Taitazak, Joseph 15:712
- - Taku, Moses 15:737
- - Tam ibn Yahya 15:785
- - Tishby, Isaiah 15:1153
- - Vilna Gaon 6:656
- - Vital, Hayyim 16:171ff
- Practical Kabbalah 10:632ff
- - alchemy 2:544ff
- - amulets 2:911
- - chiromancy 5:477
- - *Dibbuk* 6:19
- - Golem 7:753
- - magic 11:712
- Angels and Angelology 2:972ff
- - Asmodeus 3:755
- - demons 5:1528
- - female demon 11:246
- - Metatron 11:1443
- - Raziel 13:1591
- - Samael 14:719
- - Sandalfon 14:828
- - Uriel 16:7
- Christian Kabbalah 10:643ff
- - Agrippa, H. Cornelius 15:1400
- - Egidio da Viterbo 6:475
- - Gaffarel, Jacques 7:253
- - Galatinus, P. Columna 7:262
- - Giorgio, Francesco 7:587
- - Giustiniani, Agostino 7:595
- - Knorr von Rosenroth 10:1117
- - Le Fèvre de la Boderie, Guy 10:1563
- - Lull, Raimon 2:545; 8:14
- - Martini, Raymond 11:1065
- - Molitor, Franz Joseph 12:227
- - Nigri, Petrus 12:1158
- - Pellicanus, Conrad 13:220
- - Pico della Mirandola 13:500
- - Pistorius, Johannes 13:566
- - Postel 13:932
- - Reuchlin, Johannes 14:108
- - Ricius, Paulus 14:163
- - Secret, François 13:933
- - Trithemius, Johannes 15:1400
- - Vigenère, Blaise de 16:134
- - Westcott, Wynn 16:787
- - *see also:* HEBRAISTS, CHRISTIAN
- Movements
- - Avelei Zion 3:945
- - Doenmeh 6:148
- - Frankists 7:55
- - Habad 7:1013
- - Hasidei Ashkenaz 7:1377
- - Hasidism 7:1391ff
- - Karaites 10:769
- - Shabbateanism 14:1220ff
- - Zhidachov Hasidism 16:1009
- Locations
- - Avila 3:968
- - Gerona 7:507
- - Jerusalem 9:1437; 9:1563ff
- - Provence 8:686ff
- - Safed 9:286
- - Spain 8:686ff; 15:233
- - Yemen 16:746
- *illus:*
- - *atbash* letter combinations 2:148
- - Bet El synagogue, Jerusalem 9:1564
- - chiromantic observations 5:477
- - *Ez ha-Hayyim* 16:173
- - *Kohelet Ya'akov* (1578) 7:260
- - *Magen David* 11:692
- - *Maggid Mesharim* (1646) 5:198
- - *Megalleh Amukot* (1795) 7:370
- - *menorah* 13:931
- - *Pardes Rimmonim* (1592) 5:968
- - *Sefer Berit Menuhah* (1807) 5:1527
- - *Sefer ha-Bahir* (1706) 4:97
- - *Sefirot* tree 14:1105
- - *Sha'arei Ziyyon* (1671) 7:1274
- - *Shivviti* plaque 14:*fcg.* 1422
- - *Tikkunei ha-Zohar* (1558) 5:280
- - *Tur Bareket* (1654) 7:1506
- *see also:* MERKABAH MYSTICISM; MESSIAH; THRONE OF GOD; VISIONS
KABBALAH ("tradition") 10:653
- as legal source 12:119
- Moses 12:400
- sages 14:639
- *see also:* TRADITION
KABBALAT SHABBAT (litur.) 10:654
- *Ba-Meh Madlikin* 4:158
- *Lekhah Dodi* 11:4
- *Mizmor Shir le-Yom ha-Shabbat* 12:173
- Song of Songs 14:1057
- *illus:* text
KA'B BEN ASAD 10:656
- Qurayza 13:1436
Kabiljo-Danilus, Daniel 14:871
Kabinettfaktor, see COURT JEWS
KABIR, ABRAHAM SĀLIH AL- 10:656
Kabir, Joseph al- 10:656
Kabold (tn., Aus.), *see* Kobersdorf
Kabos, Endre 12:1376
KABRI (kib., Isr.) 10:657
- statistics 1:place list
KABRITHA (vill., Er. Isr.) 10:657
Kābul (city, Afg.) 2:327ff; 10:958
Kabul (city, Er. Isr.), *see* CABUL
Kabunowski, D. 12:658
Kacew, Romain, *see* GARY, ROMAIN
Kaçiç, Isaac, *see* Kagig, Isaac
KACYZNE, ALTER 10:657
KACZÉR, ILLÉS 10:658
KACZERGINSKY, SHMERL 10:658
- Sutzkever, A. 15:538
- *illus:*
- - text
- - fellow Yiddish writers 7:616; 16:821
KADAN (tn., Bohem.) 10:659
KÁDAR, JÁN 12:469
KADARI, SHRAGA 10:659
KADDISH 10:660
- Abraham Maimonides 2:151
- Amen 2:803
- efficacy 13:84
- *hadran* 7:1054
- *kiddush ha-Shem* 10:981ff
- Maimonides mentioned 11:758
- *minyan* 12:67
- Samaritan custom 14:748
- variations in liturgy 11:398ff
- *yahrzeit* 16:702
- *Yekum Purkan* 16:736
- *illus:*
- - text
- - Russian transliteration (1950's) 14:489
- *mus. notations:*
- - text
- - *Mi-Sinai niggunim* 12:151
- - *Musaf* of *Yamim Nora'im* 12:647
- - Sabbath eve 12:625
"Kaddish" (lith., A. Kroll) 10:662
Kaddish, Day of 8:917
Kaddish, Solomon Kajjem 7:815
- Prussia 13:1288
Kaddish de-Rabbanan, see KADDISH
Kadduri (agr. school, Isr.), *see* KADOORIE
KADESH (loc., city) 10:664
- Gerar 7:432
- tribal center 15:1383
- war and warfare 16:268ff
- *illus:*
- - stele 2:926
- *see also:* Kedesh: REPHIDIM
Kadesh, Operation (1956), *see* SINAI CAMPAIGN
KADESH-BARNEA (bib. loc.) 10:664
- Aaron 2:6
- fortifications 16:276
- history 8:576,577
- Moses 12:386
Kadesh Naphtali (city, Er. Isr.), *see* KEDESH-NAPHTALI
Kadesky, Max 15:307
Kad ha-Kemah (bk.) 11:344
KADIMAH (stlmt., Isr.) 10:667
- statistics 1:place list
KADIMAH (assoc., Vienna) 10:665
- Austria 3:896
- history chart 8:766-767
- Zion 16:1107
- *illus:* text
Kadimah (Zion. mvmt., Belor.) 8:255
Kadimah (Zion. mvmt., Ger.) 8:1241
Kadimah (newsp., Paris) 12:441; 15:450
Kadimah (journ., Ukr.) 1:newsp. list
Kadimah (journ., U.S.) 1:newsp. list
Kadimah (pub., Yug.) 16:882
Kadischevitz (fam.) 10:1084
Kadischevitz-Klabin, Wolff 10:1085
Kadishman, Menashe 14:1070
- *illus:*
- - "Segments" (sculp.) Pl. 20 3-ART
- - "Suspense" (sculp.) 14:1065
Kadison, Leib 16:151
Kadkod (gem) 13:1011
KADMAN, GURIT 10:667
Kadman, L. (act., Pol.) 15:1072
Kadman, L. (numis., Isr.) 12:1271
- *illus:*
- - exhibit 12:549
Kadmi Cohen, Isaac, *see* COHEN, ISAAC KADMI
Kadmonites (bib. people) 10:906
Kadmoniyyot (period.) 1:newsp. list; 15:55
KADOORIE (fam.) 10:667
KADOORIE (agr. school, Isr.) 10:668
- Zemach, Shlomo
- statistics 1:place list; 16:982
Kadoorie, Sir Ellis 10:667, 1049
Kadoorie, Sir Elly Silas 4:89; 10:667
Kadoorie, Ezra 8:1450
Kadoorie, Horace 10:667
Kadoorie, Laura 10:667
Kadoorie, Lawrence 10:667
Kadoorie, Rima 4:92; 10:667
Kadoorie, Sālih 10:667
KADOORIE, SASSON 10:668
Kadoorie Synagogue (Port.) 12:1417
- *illus:*
- - cornerstone ceremony 13:924
Kadosh (title) 15:1165
KADUSHIN, MAX 10:668
Kaelter, Walli 11:485
KAEMPF, SAUL ISAAC 10:669
- Bible 4:875
Kaernten (prov., Aus.), *see* CARINTHIA
KAF (Heb. let.) 10:669
KAFAH, YIHYE BEN SOLOMON 10:670
- Kabbalah 10:556
- Yemen 16:746
KAFAH, YOSEF 10:671
- Yemenite community 16:746
Kaffa (port, Ukr.), *see* FEODOSIYA
Kaffa and Karasubazar *Siddur* (prayer bk.) 11:398
Kafih, Yihye ben Solomon, *see* KAFAH, YIHYE BEN SOLOMON
Kafih, Yosef, *see* KAFAH, YOSEF
Kafka (fam.) 8:1136
KAFKA, BRUNO ALEXANDER 10:672
- Czechoslovakia 5:1191
Kafka, Emil 13:974
KAFKA, FRANTIŠEK 5:1208,1209
KAFKA, FRANZ 10:672
- Baum, Oscar 4:332
- Brod, Max 4:1387
- Goldstuecker, Eduard 7:750
- Weltsch, Felix 16:446
- *illus:*
- - autograph 3:915
- - drawing by Bedrich Feigl 6:1207
Kafka, Vladimir 5:1208
Kafkafuni (demon) 5:1531
Kaf Nahat (bk.) 7:232
Kafra (loc., Er. Isr.) 13:468
Kafra, Phinehas ben Jacob ha-Kohen, *see* PHINEHAS BEN JACOB HA-KOHEN
Kafr ʿAnān (vill., Isr.) 10:884
Kafranjī River (Er. Isr.) 9:178
Kafr ʿAqab (vill., Er. Isr.) 9:1492
Kafr Bir'am (loc., Isr.), *see* KEFAR BARAM
Kafr Hārib (vill., Er. Isr.) 13:1533
Kafri (tn., Babyl.) 8:793
Kafrisin (bot.) 5:136
KAFR KAMĀ (vill., Isr.) 10:674
- Israel 9:921
- *illus:*
- - mosque 9:920
Kafr Kannā (vill., Er. Isr.), *see* KEFAR KANNA
Kafr Mandā (vill., Isr.), *see* KEFAR MANDI
Kafrmandi, Abraham, *see* Abraham ben David al-Kafrmandi
KAFR QĀSIM (vill., Isr.) 10:674
- Sinai Campaign incident 9:390
Kaftor va-Ferah (bk.) 2:398; 6:918
Kafusi, Hayyim 3:58; 5:30
Kagan (fam. name), *see also* Cohen; Cohn; Kahan; Kahn; Kohn
Kagan, Hayyah 8:1348
Kagan, Kh. 13:345
Kagan, Koppel, *see* KAHANA, KOPPEL
Kagan, N.S. 11:1558
Kagan, Rachel 5:1455; 16:594
KAGAN, SOLOMON ROBERT 10:674
KAGANOVICH, LAZAR MOISEYEVICH 10:675

KAGANOWSKI, EFRAIM 10:675
Kagig, Isaac 5:915
Kagul (city, Bess.) 4:705
Kahal, *see* COMMUNITY
Kahal (title) 15:1164
Kahal Kadosh shel Ba'alei Teshuvah (Salonika) 3:174
Kahan (fam. name), *see also* Cohen; Cohn; Kagan; Kahana; Kahane; Kahn; Kohn
Kahan, Abraham Isaac 14:326
KAHAN, BARUCH MORDECAI 10:676
Kahan, Jacob 8:1025
Kahan, José 10:676
Kahan, L. (r., Eng.) 7:334
Kahan, Lazar (cmty. ldr., Pol.), *see* Cohen, Lazar
KAHAN, LOUIS (art.) 10:676
Kahan, Marcus 16:1165
Kahan, Nissan 4:1058
KAHAN, SALOMON 10:676
Kahan, Samuel, *see* KURSKY, FRANZ
Kahan, Shimshon 16:897
- *illus:*
- *Yung Vilne* group 16:821
KAHANA (amora; pupil of Rav) 10:677
- autonomy of Babylonian Jews 4:40
KAHANA (amora, pupil of Huna) 10:677
KAHANA (amora, pupil of Rabbah) 10:677
KAHANA (amora, pupil of Rava) 10:677
KAHANA (amora, Pumb.) 10:677
Kahana (Pal. amora) 10:294
Kahana (name of amoraim), *see also:* PESIKTA DE RAV KAHANA
Kahana (fam. name), *see also* Cohen; Kagan; Kahan; Kahane; Kahn
KAHANA, ABRAHAM (hist., Er. Isr.) 10:678
- Bible exegesis 4:902ff
- historiography 8:564
KAHANA, ABRAHAM ARYEH LEIB BEN SHALOM SHAKHNA (r., Rus.) 10:678
KAHANA, AHARON 10:679
- *illus:*
- - mural fig. 100 3-ART
Kahana, Baruch (r., It.) 13:285
Kahana, Baruch (Zion., Rum.) 10:879
KAHANA, DAVID (schol., Rus.) 10:679
- Kabbalah studies 10:648
Kahana, David (r., Pol.) 11:1569
Kahana, Eliezer ben Reuben 9:1295
Kahana, Ḥayyim Aryeh 10:680
Kahana, Hermann, *see* KAHANA, AHARON
Kahana, Hillel 7:421
KAHANA, JACOB BEN ABRAHAM 10:680
Kahana, Jacob Gedaliah 10:680
KAHANA, JEHIEL ẒEVI BEN JOSEPH MORDECAI 10:680
Kahana, Joseph Mordecai 10:680
KAHANA, KALMAN 10:681
KAHANA, KOPPEL 10:681
Kahana, Loeb Scheines, *see* KAHANA, ABRAHAM ARYEH LEIB BEN SHALOM SHAKHNA
Kahana, Meir Michael 12:1497
Kahana, Moses Nehemiah 11:564
KAHANA, NAḤMAN 10:681
Kahana, Shalom Shakhna 10:678
Kahana, Shmuel Zanwil 10:682
KAHANA, SOLOMON DAVID 10:681
Kahana bar Ḥaninai (gaon) 7:318
Kahana bar Ḥiyya 8:796
Kahana bar Malkiya (amora) 4:750
KAHANE, ANNE 3:603
- *illus:*
- - "Broken Man 3" (sculp.) 3:616
KAHANE, ARTHUR 10:682
KAHANE, ISAAK (Yiẓhak Ze'ev) 10:682
- responsa studies 14:87
Kahane, Meir 14:1129
KAHANE, PENUEL PETER 1:32
KAHANEMAN, JOSEPH ("Ponevezer rav") 10:683
- *illus:*
- - months of *Kallah* 10:711
KAHANOV, MOSES NEHEMIAH 10:684
Kahanovich, Aaron 5:1554
Kahanovich, Pinkhes, *see* DER NISTER
Kahanovitch, Israel 16:550
Kahanstam, A. *see* KAHNSHTAM, AHARON
KAHINA (Berber q.) 10:685
- Africa 2:332
- Tunisia 15:1432
Kāhinān (name, Arab.) 13:1436
KAHLE, PAUL ERNST 10:685
- Cairo *genizah* 16:1366
- linguistics 16:1390
- Septuagint 4:854
Kahlenberg (r., Fr.) 11:1451
Kahler, Eugen von 13:115
Kahn (fam. name), *see also* Cohen; Cohn; Kahan; Kahana; Kahane
Kahn (fam.) 5:1229
KAHN, ALBERT 10:686
- synagogues 15:625
- *illus:*
- - Ford's Rouge Plant, Dearborn, Mich. 3:345
KAHN, ALEXANDER 10:687
- *illus:*
- - Joint Distribution Committee 2:829
KAHN, ALFRED JOSEPH 10:687
Kahn, Augustus 10:692
KAHN, BERNARD 10:687
Kahn, Boris 15:25
KAHN, DOROTHY C. 10:688
Kahn, Edwin 15:308
KAHN, ELY JACQUES 10:688
KAHN, ERICH ITOR 12:694
Kahn, Florence Prag 5:57
- Zionism 16:1113
KAHN, FRANZ (Zion. ldr.) 16:1345
Kahn, Franz (astron.) 3:807
KAHN, GUSTAVE 10:688
- *illus:* text
Kahn, Joseph 15:1391
KAHN, JULIUS 10:689
KAHN, LEON 10:690
KAHN, LOUIS (engin.) 10:690
KAHN, LOUIS I. (arch.) 10:690
- synagogue 15:624
- *illus:*
- - Yale University Art Gallery 3:346
Kahn, M. (r., Ger.) 11:1384
Kahn, Máximo José (writ., Arg.) 15:255
Kahn, Nathan Uri 10:795
KAHN, OTTO HERMANN 10:691
- New York 12:1122
KAHN, RICHARD FERDINAND, LORD 10:692
Kahn, Sam 13:820
Kahn, Solomon 12:1166
Kahn, Tom 15:31
KAHN, ZADOC 10:692
- chronological chart 8:766-767
- learned societies 15:54
- *illus:* text
Kahn, Zelda 15:20
Kahn-Freund, Otto 10:1495
KAHNSHTAM, AHARON 10:694
- Society for the Promotion of Culture among Russian Jews 15:61
Kahnweiler, Simon 12:1027; 15:1375
Kaidan (tn., Lith.), *see* KEDAINIAI
Kaidanover, Aaron Samuel, *see* KOIDANOVER, AARON SAMUEL BEN ISRAEL
Kaidanover, Ẓevi Hirsch, *see* KOIDANOVER, ẒEVI HIRSCH
Kaidanovo (tn., Rus.), *see* KOIDANOVO
KAIFENG (city, China) 10:695
- Jewish community 5:469
- Chao family 5:336
- *illus:*
- - text
- - Esther scroll 13:*fcg.* 1387
- - synagogue, Torah reading 5:471
Kaikjes (J. boatmen, Const.) 14:1414
Kain (bib. loc.) 10:907
Kainen, Jacob 13:486
Kainuka (tribe, Arab.), *see* QAYNUQA
KAIROUAN (tn., Tun.) 10:697
- Abraham ben Nathan 2:153
- Elhanan ben Ḥushiel 6:612
- Jewish quarter 10:86
- nagid 12:760
- *resh kallah* title 14:83
- Sura and Pumbedita 14:1381
- Tunisia 15:1432ff
- Ẓemaḥ bar Ḥayyim 7:317
- Zirids 16:1183
- *see also:* AGHLABIDS
Kaisan (tn., Er. Isr.) 9:251
KAISER, ALOIS 7:1548
Kaiser, Ephraim 4:148
Kaiser, Georg 10:459
KAISERSLAUTERN (city, Ger.) 10:699
- *illus:* text
Kaiserwald (concen. camp, Latv.) 10:1467; 14:175
KAISH, LUISE 3:603
- *illus:*
- - Ark of the Law (bronze) 3:627
KAISH, MORTON 3:603
Kāitbay (sult.), *see* Qā'itbāy
Kaizerman, Nathan 9:829
Kajamānu (Akk. deity) 14:1531
Kajar (dyn.) 13:316
Kajon, Daniel 14:871
KĀKHYA (govt. offic., Turk.) 10:700
- Ottoman Empire 16:1547
Kakungulu, Semei 10:398
Kal (angel) 2:969
Kalāb ibn Yūfannā (bib. fig.), *see* CALEB AND CALEBITES
Kaladei (vill., Bohem.) *see* KOLODEJE NAD LUZICI
Kalafri, Zeeb Wolf 13:931
Kalah (city, Assyr.), *see* Calah
Kalahora (fam.), *see* CALAHOR(R)A
Kalai, Baruch 10:701; 14:89
KALAI, JOSEPH BEN JACOB 10:700
KALAI, MORDECAI BEN SOLOMON 10:701
- Boton, Abraham 4:1269
Kalai, Raḥamim 13:593
KALAI, SAMUEL BEN JOSEPH 10:701
KALAI, SAMUEL BEN MOSES 10:701
Kalakh (Mish. term) 14:1539
KALĀM (Isl. theol.) 10:701
- Aaron ben Elijah 2:11
- Aaron ben Joseph ha-Rofe 2:15
- Aristotelianism 3:446; 3:447
- articles of faith 3:655
- atomism 3:830
- attributes of God 7:665
- beatitude 4:359
- Commandments, reasons for 5:784ff
- cosmology 5:984
- existence of God 7:658
- *gilgul* 10:510
- Jewish philosophy 13:429
- Karaism 10:769
- medieval Jewish theology 15:1106
- physics 13:488
- Saadiah Gaon 13:431; 14:549
- time 15:1142
- Ẓaddik, Joseph ibn 16:912ff
Kalamazoo (city, Mich.) 11:1499
Kalantur (cmty. ldr., Afgh.) 2:328
KALARASH (tn., Mold.) 10:703
Kalau, A., *see* Calov(-ius), A.
Kalba Savu'a, *see* BEN KALBA SAVUA
Kalckar, N.S. 10:214
Kalderon, Samuel Jacob 14:1648
Káldi, György 4:883
KALDOR, NICHOLAS 10:704
Kaleb 'Ella Aṣbaḥa (k., Eth.) 16:897ff
KALECKI, MICHAL 10:704
KALEF, YEHOSHUA 10:704
Kaleko, Masha 16:152
Kalendar und Jahrbuch fuer Israeliten (period.) 13:1052; 15:1533
Kalevi Liiva (camp, Est.) 6:917
Kalfo, Moses 12:859
Kalgoorlie (loc., Austr.) 3:878
Kalhu (city, Assyr.), *see* Calah
Kali, Mordecai *see* KALAI, MORDECAI BEN SOLOMON
Kal'i, Samuel (r., Turk.), *see* KALAI, SAMUEL BEN MOSES
KALICH, BERTHA 10:705
Kalich, Jacob 13:501
Kalichmacher, Meir 15:1214
KALILA AND DIMNA (cycle of fables) 10:705
- animal tales 3:21
- fiction 6:1266
- folklore 6:1379
- Hebrew translation 15:1321
- *illus:* text
Kalilan (indigo; dye plant) 6:330
Kalimani, Joshua, *see* Calimani, Joshua Abraham
Kalinin, Mikhail 4:1046; 16:779
KALININDORF (vill., Ukr.) 10:706
Kaliningrad (city), *see* KOENIGSBERG
Kalininskoye (vill., Ukr.), *see* KALININDORF
KALINKOVICHI (tn., Belor.) 10:707
Kalir, Leon 4:1398
Kalisch (city, Pol.), *see* KALISZ
KALISCH, DAVID 10:707
Kalisch, I. (au.) 16:787
Kalisch, Isidore (r., U.S.) 5:606; 11:1589
Kalisch, Ludwig 11:53
Kalisch, Samuel 10:1504
Kalischer, Abraham Moses 10:707
KALISCHER, JUDAH LEIB BEN MOSES 10:707
Kalischer, Ze'ev Wolf 10:709; 11:499
KALISCHER, ẒEVI HIRSCH 10:708
- chronological chart 8:766-767
- Jewish nationalism 16:1034; 16:1035
- S. R. Hirsch's criticism 8:514
- Zionism in Poland 16:1129
Kalischer Leben (newsp.) 16:1348
Kalischer Vokh, Die (period.) 16:1348
Kalish (city, Pol.), *see* KALISZ

Kalish (ḥas. dyn.), *see* WARKA
Kalish, Hirsch **6:**1160
Kalish, Leib, *see* JUDAH ARYEH LEIB BEN DAVID
Kalish, Max **5:**612
Kalish, Israel Jeḥiel **13:**493
Kalish, Simḥah Bunem **13:**493
Kalish, Sophie, *see* TUCKER, SOPHIE
KALISZ (city, Pol) **16:**1346
- *illus:*
- - statute of Kalisz (illum., A. Szyk) **3:**922
Kalkar, C.A.H. **4:**877
Kalkar, Simeon Isaac **15:**369; **16:**474
Kalkelan (journ.) **1:**newsp. list
Kalkreuth, Count Adolf **11:**742
KALLAH (tract.) **10:**709
- *Derekh Ereẓ* **5:**1552
- minor tractates **12:**49
KALLAH, MONTHS OF (study months) **10:**710
- adult education in Israel **9:**965
- Aḥa of Shabḥa's *She'iltot* **2:**449
- Babylonian sages **2:**204
- geonic responsa **14:**85
- Kahaneman, Joseph **10:**684
- *resh kallah* **14:**82; **15:**1164
- Talmud redaction **11:**319
Kallah Rabbati (tract.) **10:**709 **12:**49
Kallai, Kopis János **8:**39
Kállay, Miklós **8:**1098
Kallday (vill., Bohem.) *see* KOLODEJE NAD LUZICI
KALLEN, HORACE MEYER **10:**712
- Zionism **16:**1143
Kallet, A. Harry **15:**307
Kallia (loc., Er. Isr.) **5:**1395; **15:**71
Kallier, Meier, *see* KALLIR, MEIER
Kallir, Alexander Susskind **10:**716
KALLIR, ELEAZAR **10:**713
- calendar **5:**50
- Ephraim of Bonn **6:**813
- history chart **8:**766-767
- *hoshanot piyyutim* **8:**1029
- *kerovah* **13:**1205
- liturgical poetry **11:**326
- messianic age **11:**1414
- mysticism **10:**508
- piyyutim **15:**914
- *Sefer Yeẓirah* **16:**786
- *Shi'ur Komah* **3:**57; **14:**1418
- Tiberias **15:**1133
- Yannai **16:**712
- *yozerot* **16:**865
- *illus:*
- - *piyyut* (8th cent. ms.) **2:**715
KALLIR, ELEAZAR BEN ELEAZAR **10:**716
KALLIR, MEIER **10:**716
Kallir, Nathan von **10:**716
Kallirhoe (loc., Er. Isr.) **5:**1394
Kallison, Perry **14:**823
Kallman, Moritz **8:**263
KALLO, YIZḤAK ISAAC (of Taub) **10:**716
Kalman (crftn., Pol.) **5:**1051
Kálmán, Charles **10:**717
KÁLMÁN, EMMERICH (Imre) **10:**717
Kálmán, Karoly **4:**883
Kalmankes, Solomon Zalman, *see* Jaffe, Solomon Zalman
Kalmanks, Abraham **10:**549
KALMAN OF WORMS **10:**717
KALMANOVITCH, ZELIG **10:**717
- *illus:*
- - Yiddish writers, Vilna **16:**813
KALMANOWITZ, ABRAHAM **10:**718
Kalmansohn, Jacques **7:**1418
Kalmár, György **8:**39
Kalmyk (Mongol nomads, Rus.) **14:**1486
KALNITSKY, GEORGE **5:**384
Kalomiti (fam.) **5:**329
Kalomiti, David **5:**329
Kalon ha-Romi **13:**589
Kalonya (vill., Isr.), *see* Qālūnya
Kalonymus (mish. period schol.) **10:**718
Kalonymus (12/13 cent., Ger.) **6:**90
Kalonymus (kab., Pol.) **11:**572
KALONYMUS (fam., Ger.) **10:**718
- Ḥasidei Ashkenaz **7:**1377
- liturgical poetry **11:**326
- Lucca yeshivah **16:**764
- *Megillat Aḥimaaz* **2:**21
- Weinheim martyrs **16:**402
- *illus:*
- - house, Mainz **7:**459; **11:**789
Kalonymus ben David ben Todros **4:**141; **15:**1323
Kalonymus ben Eliezer ha-Nakdan **6:**838
Kalonymus ben Gershon **10:**721
Kalonymus ben Isaac ha-Zaken **10:**719; **10:**721; **15:**264
Kalonymus ben Judah (9/10 cent., It.) **10:**719
Kalonymus ben Judah ha-Baḥur (11/12 cent.) **10:**721
Kalonymus ben Kalonymus ben Meir (Ha-Nasi) **10:**721
- Avignon **3:**967
- chess condemned **5:**403
- Galen **7:**264
- medicine **11:**1193
- parodies and satires **11:**353ff; **13:**127ff
- poetry **13:**689
- translations **15:**1321
Kalonymus ben Meir **11:**1122
Kalonymus ben Meshullam ha-Parnas **10:**721
- Crusades **5:**1137
- Mainz **11:**789
Kalonymus ben Meshullam of Mainz **10:**721
- Amnon of Mainz legend **2:**861
- Jewish literature **11:**326
- *U-Netanneh Tokef* **15:**1531
- *illus:*
- - tombstone, Mainz **10:**719
Kalonymus ben Moses ben Judah **10:**719
Kalonymus ben Moses ben Kalonymus **10:**719; **10:**720
- Jewish literature **11:**326
Kalonymus ben Moses of Lucca **10:**721
Kalonymus ben Shabbetai **6:**920
Kalonymus ben Shabbetai of Rome **16:**644
- paytanim **13:**589
Kalonymus ben Todros **8:**334
Kalonymus ha-Nasi of Beaucaire **10:**721
Kalonymus ha-Zaken **13:**589
Kalonymus of Lucca **10:**721
- gaon, title **7:**324
Kalov (ḥas. dyn.) **7:**1425
- *score:*
- - *niggun* **7:**1428
Kaloyannis, Vassos **7:**887; **7:**898
Kalpei (urn) **11:**512
Kals, J. H. **8:**39
Kalsman, Pincus **13:**482
KALTENBRUNNER, ERNST **10:**722
- Holocaust **8:**859
- *illus:*
- - Nuremberg Trial **16:**289
Kalthoff, J. A. **8:**39
KALUSH (city, Ukr.) **10:**722
KALUSZYN (tn., Pol.) **10:**723
Kal va-ḥomer (hermeneutical rule) **8:**367
KALVARIJA (tn., Lith.) **10:**723
Kalvaryski, Haim, *see* MARGOLIS KALVARYSKI, HAIM
Kamai, Abraham Ẓevi **12:**71
Kamai, Elijah Baruch **6:**1290
Kamaiky, Leon **12:**1102
- *illus:*
- - A. J. C. delegation **2:**823
Kamāl al-Dīn ibn Abi Sharīf, *see* Din ibn Abi Sharīf, Kamāl al-
Kamarási, Pál **8:**39
Kame'a, see AMULET
KAMELHAR, JEKUTIEL ARYEH BEN GERSHON **10:**724
Kamelhar, Moses **10:**724
Kamen, Martin **4:**1032
KAMENETS-PODOLSKI (city, Ukr.) **10:**725
- Podolia **13:**668f
KAMENETZKY, ABRAHAM SHALOM **10:**726
KAMENETZKY (Kamenecki), JACOB **10:**726
- Torah Umesorah **15:**1259
- Union of Orthodox Rabbis **15:**1538
KAMENEV, LEV BORISOVICH **10:**726
- Trotsky **15:**1405
Kamenitzer Maggid, *see* MACCOBY, ḤAYYIM ZUNDEL
KAMENKA, ẒEVI HIRSCH OF **10:**727
KAMENKA-BUGSKAYA (Strumilovskaya; city, Ukr.) **10:**727
Kamenker, Moses Meir **9:**74
Kamhi, Leon **12:**239
- Zionism **16:**1149
Kami'a, see AMULET
Kamieniecki, Isaac **12:**1242
Kamienna (tn., Pol.), *see* SKARZYSKO-KAMIENNA
Kamiensk (vill., Pol.) **13:**557
Kāmil (13th. cent., sultan) **3:**998; **9:**269
Kamīl, al- (wk.) **16:**1358
Kāmil al-Husseini, *see* Husseini, Kāmil al-
KAMINER, ISAAC **10:**728
Kaminer, Nadezhda, *see* Axelrod, Nadezhda
KAMINETSKY, JOSEPH **10:**729
- Torah Umesorah **15:**1259
KAMINKA, ARMAND (Aaron) **10:**729
- Zionism **16:**1148
- *illus:*
- - F.Z.C. **16:**1165
Kaminker, Simone, *see* SIGNORET, SIMONE
Kaminska (fam.), *see* KAMINSKI
Kaminska, Esther Rachel **10:**730
Kaminska, Ida **10:**730
- Yiddish theater **15:**1073
KAMINSKI (fam.) **10:**730
Kaminski, Abraham Isaac **10:**730
Kaminski, Daniel, *see* KAYE, DANNY
Kaminski, Jacob **10:**853
Kaminski, Joseph **10:**730
- music **12:**670
Kaminski, Moses Meir **16:**1014
Kaminski Theater, Warsaw **10:**730
Kaminsky, Robert (Rick) **15:**303
Kamionka (tn., Pol.) **11:**538
Kamionka Strumiowa (city, Ukr.), *see* KAMENKA-BUGSKAYA
Kamionski, M., *see* Kamyonski, M.
Kam lei bi-derabba minei (leg. conc.) **15:**1095
Kamm, Josephine **5:**450
Kamma (s. of Rabbah) **13:**1443
Kammah (journ.) **1:**newsp. list
Kammelhar, Israel **4:**1013
Kammerknechtschaft (royal servants), *see* SERVI CAMERAE REGIS
Kammon (spice), *see* CUMIN
Kammona (Cana. city), *see* JOKNEAM
Kamniel, Abu al-Ḥasan Abraham ibn **14:**1201; **15:**226
KAMNIEL, ABU AL-HASAN MEIR IBN **10:**731
- Almoravides **2:**667
Kamniel, Ibn (fam., Sp.) **14:**1201
Kamnitzer, Samuel, *see* Ḥarif Ha-Levi, Samuel Kamnitzer
Kámory, Samuel **4:**883
Kampala (tn., Uganda) **9:**442
Kampaneli, Jacob **7:**887
Kampanietz, Aba **15:**1072
KAMPEL, STEWART **1:**32
Kampen, Jan van, *see* CAMPEN(-SIS) JOHANNES VAN
Kampf, Abraham **3:**652
KAMSON, YA'AKOV (Jacob) DAVID **10:**731
Kamusch, Jacob **15:**1177
Kamyonski, M. **7:**1058; **10:**993
KAMẒA AND BAR KAMẒA (tal. figs.) **10:**732
- Jerusalem destruction **9:**1557
Kan, Ilya **5:**405
KANADER ADLER (newsp.) **10:**732
- Canada **5:**113
- Roback, A. A. **14:**204
KANAH (city, riv., Er. Isr.) **10:**733
- *see also:* KEFAR KANNA
KANAH, BOOK OF (kab. work) **10:**733
- Kabbalah **10:**539
- visions **16:**169
Kanah ibn Gedor (leg. fig.) **10:**734
Kanal, Israel **16:**351
Kana'na, M. 'Abd al-Qādir **9:**1043
Kanatha (city, Ḥauran), *see* KENATH
Kandahar (city, Afgh.) **2:**327; **10:**958
Kandalanu (ruler, Babyl.) **16:**1504
KANDEL, ISAAC LEON **10:**734
- education **6:**465
Kandinski, Vasili **13:**115
KANE, IRVING **10:**735
KANEE, SOL **10:**735
Kaneh ("reed"; meas.) **16:**378ff
KANEV (city, Ukr.) **10:**735
Kanfer, Moses **12:**1245
Kaniel, Yehoshua **9:**893
Kaniewski, Julian, *see* Ajzenman-Kaniewski, Julian
Kanin, Garson **12:**451; **12:**469
Kaniš (city, As. M.), *see* Kultepe
Kanīsat Mūsā (syn., Dumuh) **6:**268
Kanitz (tn., Morav.), *see* DOLNI KOUNICE
Kanjiža (vill., Serb.) **16:**873
Kanka, Gejsa **5:**1196
Kankakee (city, Ill.) **8:**1256
Kann (fam.) **4:**1151; **7:**87
Kann, Beer Loeb Isaac **10:**737
KANN, JACOBUS HENRICUS **10:**736
- Zionism **16:**1076; **16:**1118
KANN, MOSES **10:**737
Kann, Sacki **4:**656
Kanna'im (loc., Isr.) **9:**794
Kanna'im (1st cent. C.E. sect), *see* ZEALOTS
Kannegiesser, Karl Ludwig **9:**1343
KANNER, LEO **10:**737
Kannot (vill., Isr.) **7:**354
- statistics **1:**place list
Kanof, Abram **2:**827
KANSAS **10:**738

- *pop. tables:* text
KANSAS CITY **10**:739
- Kansas **10**:739
- museum **12**:551
- *illus:* text
Kansk (city, Sib.) **14**:1486
KANT, IMMANUEL **10**:741
- autonomy **6**:323
- Bendavid, Lazarus **4**:474; **4**:475
- Cohen, Hermann **5**:673ff
- duty **6**:323
- Herz, Markus **8**:403ff
- Jewish philosophy **13**:455
- Jews **13**:417
- Maimon, Solomon **11**:742ff
- Mendelssohn **3**:659; **11**:1329; **11**:1331ff
- modern Jewish theology **15**:1108
- nature **12**:890
- post-Kantian philosophy **13**:417ff
- universities **15**:1677
Kantara (loc., Sinai), *see* Qantara
Kanter, Anita **15**:315
Kanter, Edward **5**:1567
KANTOR, JACOB ROBERT **10**:744
KANTOR, JUDAH LEIB **10**:744
- *illus:*
- - first Duma electors **14**:445
KANTOR, MORRIS **3**:603
Kantorberg, Friedrich, *see* TORBERG, FRIEDRICH
Kantorovich, Lea **11**:1567
KANTOROWICH, ROY **10**:745
KANTOROWICZ, ERNST HARTWIG **10**:745
KANTOROWICZ, HERMANN **10**:746
Kantorowicz, Yasha **12**:1238
Kantrovich, W. **10**:908
KANTROWITZ, ADRIAN **10**:746
KANTROWITZ, ARTHUR **10**:746
Kantrowitz-General Electric Pacemaker **10**:746
Kaolin (min.) **9**:813
Kapai, *see* Erez Israel Workers' Fund
Kapanjilar (sect), *see* Izmirlis
Kapara (Aram. K.) **2**:304
Kaparot (rite), *see* KAPPAROT
"Kaparot" (paint., J.D. Kirszenbaum) **10**:1053
Kapeller, Pedro Jack **13**:1370
Kapiluto, Jacob **3**:722
KAPITZA, PETER LEONIDOVICH **10**:747
Kaplan (phys.) **13**:490
KAPLAN, ABRAHAM **10**:747
KAPLAN, ALEXANDER SENDER BEN ZERAH HA-KOHEN **10**:747
KAPLAN, ANATOLI LVOVICH **10**:748
- *illus:* text
Kaplan, Bert **13**:1340
Kaplan, Cecil **15**:315
Kaplan, E. E. (Pol.) **13**:1375
- *illus:*
- - Menuhah ve-Nahalah Society **9**:556
KAPLAN, ELIEZER (Er. Isr.) **10**:749
- *illus:*
- - proclamation of the State of Israel **4**:513
- - Thirteenth Zionist Congress **16**:1173
Kaplan, Elijah (r.) **12**:1490
Kaplan, Fanya **11**:14
Kaplan, George **12**:38
Kaplan, Hayyim **6**:425
KAPLAN, ISAAC **10**:750
- Argentina **3**:432
Kaplan, Israel L. **9**:1190
KAPLAN, JACOB **10**:750
- chaplaincy **11**:1569
- France and Israel **7**:39
Kaplan, Jeremiah **13**:1372
Kaplan, Josef (Warsaw ghetto) **16**:349
KAPLAN, JOSEPH (phys. U.S.) **10**:750
Kaplan, Julio **5**:407
Kaplan, Louis "Kid" (sport.) **15**:305
- *illus:*
- - boxing **15**:306
KAPLAN, LOUIS LIONEL (educ.) **10**:751
KAPLAN, MORDECAI MENAHEM **10**:751
- concept of God **7**:664
- Conservative Judaism **5**:904
- creation, theory of **5**:1070
- faith **4**:436
- free will **7**:131
- Jewish community center **12**:875
- messianism **11**:1416
- miracles **12**:80
- problem of evil **7**:778
- prophecy **13**:1180
- redemption **14**:8
- sociology **15**:68
- synagogue **15**:586
- Torah **15**:1243
- Zionism **16**:1145
- *illus:*
- - Greenberg, Simon, and **7**:906
- *see also:* RECONSTRUCTIONISM
KAPLAN, MORDECHAI (MAX) **1**:32
Kaplan, Pavel **2**:862
KAPLAN, PESAH **10**:753
Kaplan, Robert **15**:1264
Kaplan, Y. (Yid. au.) **16**:819; **16**:825
Kaplan, Y. (arch.) **3**:303
Kaplan, Yakov (Judenrat ldr., Ostrog) **12**:1514
KAPLANSKY, KALMAN **10**:753
KAPLANSKY, SHELOMO **10**:754
- Ben-Gurion **4**:507
- Gross, Nathan **7**:935
- Tenth Zionist Congress **16**:1170
Kapler, V. **15**:327
Kaplinski, Elias **7**:70
Kaplinski, Hirsch **13**:146
Kaplowitz, Daniel **15**:303
KAPO (camp guard) **10**:754
- concentration camps **5**:86; **5**:88
Kapon, Abraham **16**:888
KAPOSI, MORITZ **10**:755
Kaposi, Samuel **8**:39
KAPOSVAR (city, Hung.) **10**:755
Kapp (fam.) *see* HOENIGSBERG
KAPP, EDMOND **3**:603
- *illus:*
- - "Underground Shelter in Mile End" (drg.) **3**:629
KAPPAROT (propitiatory rite) **10**:756
- Al-Harizi's parody **13**:126
- *illus:*
- - *Kirchliche Verfassung der heutigen Juden* **5**:1385
Kappel, Alexander, *see* MUKDONI, A.
KAPPER, SIEGFRIED (Vítězslav) **10**:757
- Yugoslavia **16**:874
- Yugoslav literature **16**:888
- Zagreb **16**:917
Kappler, H. **14**:252
Kapporet (Ark cover) **3**:460
- Tabernacle **15**:682
- Torah ornaments **15**:1256
- *illus:*
- - Kassel synagogue **15**:1256
Kapulia (tn., Belor.), *see* Kopyl
KAPUZATO, MOSES HA-YEVANI **10**:758
Kara (Bib. comment.), *see* MENAHEM BEN HELBO
KARA, AVIGDOR BEN ISAAC **10**:758
Kara, Dober ben Samuel **14**:631
Kara, Isaac **10**:758
KARA, JOSEPH **10**:759
- Bible exegesis **4**:893
KARA, MENAHEM BEN JACOB **10**:760
- Avigdor ben Isaac **10**:759
Kara, Simeon **10**:759
- *Yalkut Shimoni* **11**:322; **16**:706
Kara, Zevi **4**:1436
Karabchevsky, N. P. **4**:400
Karachais (ethnic gr.) **10**:953
Karachi (city, Pak.) **13**:14
- illus:
- - Magen Shalom Synagogue **13**:15
KARÁCSONY, BENÖ **8**:1085
KARACZEWSKI, HANINA **10**:761
Karada (vill., Kurd.) **10**:1297
Karaferia (city, Gr.), *see* VEROIA
Karaffa-Krevtenkraft, Colonel **11**:1564
Kara'im, *see* KARAITES
Karaimskaya Zhizn (Kar. monthly) **10**:776
Karaimskoye Slovo (Kar. period.) **10**:776
KARAITES **10**:761
- *Contents:*
- - Name; Relation to Biblical Tradition **10**:761
- - Karaism and the Dead Sea Scrolls **10**:762
- - Historical Development **10**:763
- - Karaite Doctrine **10**:777
- - Attempts at Karaite/Rabbanite Reconciliation **10**:781
- - Karaite Printing **10**:781
- - Musical Tradition **10**:783
- General
- - Abu Imrān Al-Tiflīsī **2**:183
- - Cairo *genizah* **16**:1333
- - Mazli'ah (moshav) **11**:1153
- - printers **13**:1110ff
- Doctrine and Practice
- - abortion **2**:99
- - angelology **2**:974
- - articles of faith **3**:655
- - Av, the Tenth **3**:936
- - Bible exegesis **4**:891
- - Bible study **4**:920
- - calendar **5**:51
- - commandments, reasons for **5**:785ff
- - Day of Atonement **5**:1382
- - *gilgul* **10**:510
Haggadah edition **7**:1095
- - homiletics **13**:999
- - Jewish identity **10**:56
- - *karet* **10**:789
- - legal system **15**:1183ff
- - marriage **10**:3
- - *mazzah* **11**:1158
- - messianic movements **11**:1417
- - *mezuzah* **11**:1476
- - *niddah* laws **12**:1145; **12**:1147
- - *omer* **12**:1383
- - principles **7**:549; **9**:33
- - Sabbath **14**:566
- - Samaritan beliefs **14**:741
- - special Purim **13**:1399
- - synagogue **15**:588
- Centers
- - Aden **2**:261
- - Adrianople **2**:310
- - Alexandria **2**:593
- - Azerbaijan **3**:1005
- - Bakhchisarai **4**:116
- - Byzantine Empire **4**:1554
- - Cairo **5**:26ff
- - Crimea **5**:1104
- - Erez Israel **9**:266ff; **9**:504ff; **9**:509; **9**:511
- - Greece **7**:873
- - Halicz community **7**:1189
- - Jerusalem **14**:1360; **14**:1364
- - Nabī-Samwīl **14**:785
- - Ottoman Empire **16**:1547
- - Persia **13**:309
- - Troki **15**:1401ff
- - Turkey **15**:1462
- - Yevpatoriya **16**:778
- Languages **10**:68
- - Hebrew language **16**:1634ff
- - Judeo-Arabic **10**:413
- - Judeo-Greek **10**:426
- - linguistics **16**:1353
- Karaism and Rabbanism
- - apologists **3**:192
- - Avelei Zion **3**:946
- - codification of law **5**:637; **5**:641
- - geonic way of life **8**:664ff
- - *halakhah*, effect on **15**:735ff
- - *Halakhot Gedolot* **7**:1168
- - *mamzer* **11**:841
- - masorah controversy **16**:1417
- - nagid and **12**:761
- - Palestine gaonate and bans on **12**:483
- - philosophy, Jewish **13**:433ff
- - "Rabbanites" **13**:1446
- - Rabbanites, relations with **4**:391
- - rabbinical literature **13**:1463
- - rabbinical tradition **15**:1310
- - *Seder Olam Zuta* **14**:1093
- - *Shi'ur Komah* **3**:57; **14**:1418
- Karaites and Rabbanites
- - Aaron ben Elijah **2**:10
- - Abraham Yerushalmi **2**:150
- - Aha of Shabha **2**:450
- - Anan ben David **2**:920f
- - Bashyazi family **4**:297
- - Basir, Joseph al- **4**:301
- - Ben Meir, Aaron **4**:539
- - Daniel al-Qūmīsī **5**:1292
- - David ben Joshua **5**:1351ff
- - David ibn Abi Zimra **5**:1356
- - Delmedigo, Joseph Solomon **5**:1479ff
- - Hadassi, Judah **7**:1046
- - Hai ben Nahshon **7**:1129
- - Hakim, Samuel ha-Levi **7**:1152
- - Ibn al-Hītī, David **8**:1154
- - Ibn Daud **8**:1159
- - Ibn Kammūna, Sa'd **8**:1187
- - Judah Halevi **10**:363
- - Kimhi, Solomon **9**:1095; **10**:1009
- - Kirkisānī **10**:1047
- - Maimonides **11**:756ff
- - Mizrahi, Elijah **12**:183
- - Nahawandi, Benjamin al- **12**:771ff
- - Natronai bar Hilai **12**:887
- - Ramlites **11**:826
- - Saadiah Gaon **14**:552
- - Saul ben Anan **14**:918
- - Solomon ben Judah **15**:122
- - Tam ibn Yahya, Jacob **15**:785
- - Yehudai Gaon **16**:731
- Studies on
- - Ankori, Zevi **16**:1260
- - Firkovich **6**:1305ff
- - Frankl, P. F. **7**:102
- - Harkavy, Albert **7**:1340
- - Poznański, S.A. **13**:929
- *illus:*
- - text
- - bill of divorcement (8th cent.) **6**:124
- - cemetery in Crimea **5**:1105
- - *Emunah Omen* (1846) **13**:1111
- - Firkovich, Abraham **6**:1305
- - Istanbul synagogue **9**:1092
- - Pentateuch, 10th cent. **8**:665
- - prayer book (16th cent.) **2**:742
- - script types **2**:701,742
- *scores:*
- - text
Karaïto-Arvic (Kar. lang., Egy.)

10:68
Karaïto-Yevanic (Kar. lang., Byz.) **10:**68
Karak, Al- (tn., Transj.), *see* KIR HARESETH
Karak, Al- (vill., Jor.) **10:**911
Karakashlar (sect), *see* Konyosos
Karama (tn., Jor.) **9:**416; **14:**1639; **15:**1559
Karasick, Joseph **15:**1537
Karaso, Josef **13:**1039
KARASU, ALBERT **10:**311
KARASUBAZAR (city, U.S.S.R.) **10:**785
Karatepe inscription **16:**666
Karay (Kar. lang., Lith., Pol.) **10:**68
Karben, Victor von, *see* CARBEN, VICTOR VON
Karczew (concen. camp, Pol.) **12:**1526
KARDINER, ABRAM **10:**786
- anthropology **3:**39
KARDOS, ALBERT **8:**1085
KARDOS, LÁSZLÓ **10:**786
Kar-duniash (anc. kdm.), *see* BABYLONIA
Kareh, Joseph **10:**787
KAREH, SOLOMON **10:**787
KAREL, RUDOLF **12:**694
KARELITZ, AVRAHAM YESHAYAHU (Ḥazon Ish) **10:**787
- *ḥiddushim* **8:**467
- Sabbatical year **14:**585
- *illus:*
- - *prosbul* **13:**1182
Kareski, G. **10:**464
KARET (punishment) **10:**788
- banishment **4:**163
- children of sinner **5:**426
- Commandments, the 613 **5:**766
- false measures **16:**391
- *ḥamez* **7:**1236; **14:**155
- hunting **8:**1111
- imprisonment **8:**1300
- *niddah* **12:**1142
- non-circumcision **5:**567
- *see also:* DIVINE PUNISHMENT
KARFUNKEL, AARON BEN JUDAH LEIB HA-KOHEN **10:**789
Karga (tax) **6:**1027
KARGAU, MENAHEM MENDEL BEN NAPHTALI HIRSCH **10:**790
Karger, Gus J. **13:**1360
Karger, S. **13:**1367
Karigal, Raphael Ḥayyim Isaac, *see* CARIGAL, RAPHAEL ḤAYYIM ISAAC
Karimi (fam.) **15:**1302
KARIV, AVRAHAM YIZḤAK **10:**790
- as critic **5:**1123
- Litvin, A. **11:**405
Kariv, Yiẓḥak **9:**1498
KARIYAH, AL- (J. sect, Egy.) **10:**791
Karka (J. agr. stlmt.) **15:**13
Karkabī, Qayṣar **9:**1042
Karkamiš (city, Syr.), *see* CARCHEMISH
Karka'ot (real estate), *see* PROPERTY
KARKAR (city, Hamath) **10:**791
- Ahab's battle **2:**437; **16:**1502,1509
- map of battle **2:**436
Karkemisha (metal), *see* Lead
Karkur (mosh., Isr.), *see* PARDES ḤANNAH-KARKUR
Karl, Max H. **11:**1589
Karlfelt, Erik Axel **14:**930
Karlin (tn., Belor.) **13:**541
KARLIN (ḥas. dyn.) **10:**792
- dynasties **1:**ḥas. table
- ḥasidic music **7:**1426
- *mus. notations*
- - *niggunim* **7:**1430,1432
Karlin, Aaron ben Jacob of **6:**181; **10:**792
- Eliezer of Pinsk **6:**626
- *takkanot* **15:**737
Karlin, Aaron the Second of **10:**793
- Lachowicze Ḥasidim **10:**1340
Karlin, Abraham Elimelech of **10:**794
Karlin, Asher ben Aaron of **10:**793
Karlin, Asher the Second of **10:**794
Karlin, Israel ben Asher of **10:**794
Karlin, Jacob ben Israel of **10:**794
Karlin, Solomon ben Meir ha-Levi of **10:**793; **10:**794
KARLINER, BARUCH **7:**1548
Karl Ludwig (Ger. Elector) **7:**474
Karlskrona (city, Swed.) **15:**546
KARL-MARX-STADT (Chemnitz city, Ger.) **10:**794
- *illus:*
- - Schocken department store **11:**1323
Karlovy Vary (tn., Cz.), *see* CARLSBAD
Karlsbad (tn, Cz.), *see* CARLSBAD;
Karlsburg, *see* ALBA IULIA
Karlsburg, Judah, *see* Carlburg, Judah Loeb
KARLSRUHE (city, Ger.) **10:**795
Karlweis, C., *see* Weiss, Karl
Karm al-Sheikh (area, Jer.) **9:**1459
KÁRMÁN, MÓR **10:**796
KÁRMÁN, THEODORE VON **10:**797
Karmasin, Franz **5:**1195
Karmel (mag.), *see* HA-KARMEL
Karmelit (period.) **1:**newsp. list
KARMI (Crémieux; fam.) **10:**797
- Aix en-Provence **2:**476
Karmi (newsp.) **2:**310; **13:**1039
- statistics **1:**newsp. list
Karmī, 'Abd al-Karīm al- **9:**1040
Karmi, Abraham **5:**205; **10:**797
Karmi, David, *see* Carmi, David ben Joseph
KARMI, DOV **10:**798
- Israel architecture **3:**362
- *illus:*
- - Knesset building **3:**354; **10:**1112
- - Wise Auditorium **3:**354
Karmi, Jacob Israel, *see* Carmi, Jacob Israel
Karmi, Mordecai **10:**797
Karmi, Moses **2:**476; **10:**797
Karmi, Ram **3:**364
Karmi, Solomon Hayyim **10:**798
KARMI'EL (tn., Isr.) **10:**799
- statistics **1:**place list
- *illus:* text
KARMINSKI, HANNAH **10:**799
KARMINSKI, SIR SEYMOUR EDWARD **10:**800
Karmi Sheli (journ.) **1:**newsp. list
KARMIYYAH (kib., Isr.) **10:**800
- statistics **1:**place list
Karm Jabali (site of Tel Aviv) **15:**920
Karmon, Alexander **6:**204; **6:**205
Karmon, Jonathan **5:**1271
Karna (amora) **2:**866; **13:**1577
Karnaia (vill., Arab.) **10:**800
KARNAIM (city, Bashan) **10:**800
- *see also:* ASHTAROTH, ASHTEROTH-KARNAIM, KARNAIM
Karnei Hittin (volcano, Isr.) **9:**151
Karneinu (journ., Jer.) **1:**newsp. list
Karnenu (pub., It.) **13:**1037; **14:**253
Karni (publ. firm, Isr.) **13:**1378
KARNI, YEHUDA **10:**801
- Jerusalem theme **9:**1566
- *illus:*
- - with fellow Hebrew writers **4:**499
Karnik, Moses ben Akiva, *see* KRONIK, MOSES BEN AKIVA
KARNIOL, ALTER YEHIEL **10:**801
Karnovsky, Herman **5:**1547
Karo, Simeon, *see* Kara, Simeon
Karoli, Miriam **11:**1167
Károlyi, Gáspár **4:**883
- Hebraists **8:**39
KARP, ABRAHAM J. **10:**802
- historiography **8:**568
KARP, MAX **15:**1086
KARP, SOPHIE (Sarah) **15:**1086
Karpathos (isl., Gr.) **5:**141
Karpati, Gyorgy **13:**1376
Karpati, Karoly **13:**1376
KARPEL, HERMAN **10:**802
KARPELES, GUSTAV (Gershon) **10:**802
- *Allgemeine Zeitung* **2:**648
Karpeles, Jiři, *see* KARS, JIŘI
Karpeles, Leopold **11:**1551; **15:**318
Karpeles, Moses **9:**1153
KARPF, MAURICE JOSEPH **10:**803
Karpf, Samuel **15:**305
KARPINOWITCH, ABRAHAM **10:**803
Karpinowitz, S. **16:**825
KARPLUS, HEINRICH **5:**1112
Karpman, Ben **5:**1110
Karpov, V.D. **12:**945
Karregal, Ḥayyim, *see* CAREGAL, ḤAYYIM MOSES BEN ABRAHAM
Karregal, Raphael Ḥayyim Isaac, *see* CARIGAL, RAPHAEL ḤAYYIM ISAAC
KARS, JIRI **10:**803
- Paris school **13:**115
KARSEN, FRITZ **10:**804
Kartan (anc. city, Isr.) **12:**820
KARTELL-CONVENT DER VERBINDUNGEN DEUTSCHER STUDENTEN JUEDISCHEN GLAUBENS **10:**804
KARTELL JUEDISCHER VERBINDUNGEN (orgn., Ger.) **10:**805
- German students **7:**486; **10:**804
- Rosen, Pinḥas **14:**271
- students' movements **15:**448
Kartell Zionistischer Verbindungen (orgn.) **10:**805
Karter (4th cent., Pers.) **13:**308
Kartha (city, Er. Isr.) **3:**821
Kartin, Pinkus **16:**349
Kartir (3rd cent. C.E., Babyl.) **4:**41
Kartusskaya Bereza (tn., Rus.), *see* BEREZA
KARU, BARUCH **10:**805
- encyclopedia **6:**735
KASABI, JOSEPH BEN NISSIM **10:**806
Kasabi, Moses **10:**806
Kasani, Moses ben Samuel **3:**731
Kaschau (city, Cz.), *see* KOSICE
Kasdan, H. S. **16:**838
Kasdim (ethnic gr.), *see* Kesed
KASEJOVICE (tn., Bohem.) **10:**806
Kaser, Arthur Leroy **15:**1058
KASHAN (city, Iran) **10:**806
- Persia **13:**318
Kashani, Eliezer **8:**1468
KASHDAN, ISAAC **5:**408
KASHER **10:**806
- dietary laws **6:**40
- *hekhsher* **8:**287
- *mashgi'aḥ* **11:**1094
- *nevelah* **12:**1020
- *sheḥitah* **14:**1337
- *terefah* **15:**1016
- *illus:*
- - Mannheim, *kashrut* seal for meat **14:**1077
KASHER, MENAHEM **10:**807
- Messiah **11:**1416
Kasher, Shimon **10:**808
Kashering of meat **6:**28
- *see also:* MEAT; SHEḤITAH
Kashfi, Jamshid **8:**1443
Kashisha ("the elder"), *see* ABBAYE KASHISHA
Kashkīl, Moses ibn **2:**223
KASHMIR (reg., As.) **10:**808
- India **8:**1356
Kashrut, *see* DIETARY LAWS; KASHER
Kashrut, overseer of, *see* MASHGI'AḤ
Kashtan, Solomon, *see* WEINTRAUB, SOLOMON
Kashti, David ben Elijah **6:**623; **9:**1097
Kasila (site, Isr.), *see* Tells (Qasīla)
Kasim Pasha **14:**1237
KASKEL (fam.) **10:**808
Kaskel, Cesar **11:**258
Kaskel, Karl **10:**809
Kaskel, Michael **10:**808
Kaskele (fam.), *see* KASKEL
Kaskele, Jacob **10:**808
Kaslari, Israel **15:**1328
Kasovsky, Abraham Abele **10:**809
Kasovsky, Benjamin **10:**809
KASOVSKY, CHAYIM YEHOSHUA **10:**809
Kasovsky, Moshe **10:**809
Kaspare Cohn (fam.) **5:**56
KASPI, JOSEPH BEN ABBA MARI IBN **10:**809
- Aristotelianism **3:**446; **3:**448
- ethical wills **11:**345
- Hebrew grammar **11:**324
- Ibn Ezra **15:**520
- Jewish philosophy **11:**340; **13:**444
- linguistics **16:**1360,1388
- Messiah **11:**1419
- *Sefer ha-Musar* **16:**532
KASPI, NETHANEL BEN NEHEMIAH **10:**811
Kasprowicz, Jan **13:**798
Kaṣr ibn Hubayrah (tn., Babyl.), *see* QAṢR IBN HUBAYRAH
Kasrilevke Cycle (wk.) **14:**1282
Kassa (city, Cz.), *see* KOSICE
KASSEL (city, Ger.) **10:**811
- consistory **9:**1240
- experimental school **16:**474
- Hessen **8:**437
- history chart **8:**766-767
- museums **12:**538
- synod **13:**1461
- *illus:*
- - text
- - synagogue *parokhet* **15:**1256
KASSEL, DAVID **10:**813
Kasselowitz (tn., Bohem.), *see* KASEJOVICE
Kassem, Abdul Karim **14:**1624
KASSIL, LEV ABRAMOVICH **10:**813
Kassitera, Kassiteron (metals), *see* Tin
Kassites (anc. people) **16:**3, 1497
- Nimrod **12:**1166
Kassowitz, Max **11:**1197
Kaštarita (k., Media) **11:**1177
KASTEIN, JOSEPH **10:**814
- German literature **7:**452
Kastel (vill., Er. Isr.), *see* Qastal, al
Kastenberg, Jacob **11:**426
Kastilaẓ, Simeon **16:**1535
Kaštiliaš (k., Babyl.) **5:**1020
Kastina (vill., Isr.), *see* Qastīna
Kastor, Isador **16:**679
Kastor, Shirley **16:**679
KASTORIA (tn., Gr.) **10:**814
- Greece **7:**876
- Shabbateanism **14:**1239
Kasvan, Avner **16:**1133
Kaszaniczky, Ádám (de Nagy Selmecz) **8:**39

KASZTNER, REZSŐ RUDOLF 10:814
- Eichmann 8:1102
- Gruenwald's accusations 9:396
- history chart 8:766-767
- Judenrat 8:883
- Komoly 4:1294
- trial 9:670
- Zionism 16:1122
Kataf (bot.), *see* BALSAM
Katamon (qtr., Jer.) 9:1517
- Jerusalem development 9:1496
- Jerusalem topography 9:1515
- Jerusalem under Turks 9:1459
- *illus:*
- - Haganah soldiers capturing house 16:315
- - view from Holyland Hotel 9:1491
Katamon Tet (qtr., Jer.) 9:1504
Katan (Chr. fam.) 9:1435
Katan, see Minor
Katančić, Matia Petar 4:885; 16:885
Katav, Shalom, *see* Kātib, S. al-
Katayev, Valentin 14:512
Katbughā (13th cent., sultan) 9:1424
Katchalski, Aharon, *see* KATZIR, AHARON
KATCHALSKI, EPHRAIM 10:816
Katelman, Joe 8:1439
Katem (metal) 11:1429
Katherine (tn., Gr.) 7:879
Kathros (pr. fam.) 14:1554; 16:669
Kātib, S. al- 9:1041
- Oriental literature 8:1452; 12:1465
Katie, Amanda 8:1290
Katif (journ.) 1:newsp. list
KATKOV, MIKHAIL NIKIFOROVICH 10:817
Katmandu (city, Nepal) 9:445
Katona, George 13:1344
Katona Gelei, István 8:41
Katorzo, Isaac ben Judah 12:823
KATOWICE (city, Pol.) 10:817
- archives 3:387
- *illus:*
- - Kattowitz Conference 10:820
Katowice Conference, *see* KATTOWITZ CONFERENCE
Katros (pr. fam.), *see* Kathros
KATSH, ABRAHAM ISAAC 10:818
Katsisne, A. 16:819
Kattan, H. 16:1092
KATTAN, NAÏM 10:819
- Canada 5:112
KATTINA, JACOB 10:819
Kattowitz (city, Pol.), *see* KATOWICE
KATTOWITZ CONFERENCE (Zion. mvmt.) 10:819
- Ḥibbat Zion 16:1040
- history chart 8:766-767
- Mohilewer, Samuel 12:218
- *illus:* text
KATUNIN, ILYA BORISOVICH 11:1574
Katute, Al-(sub., Petra) 13:342
Katz, Aaron 10:827
Katz, Abraham Isaac, *see* KATSH, ABRAHAM ISAAC
Katz, Abraham Samson, *see* Abraham Samson ha-Kohen Katz
KATZ, ALBERT 10:821
- *Allgemeine Zeitung* 2:648
KATZ, ALEPH 10:821
KATZ, ALEX 3:603
Katz, A. Martin 8:1362
Katz, A. Raymond 4:1219
KATZ, BENZION (journ.) 10:822
- illus:
- - *Ha-Zeman,* first issue 13:1046
KATZ (Benshalom), BENZION (lit. crit.) 10:822
Katz, Benjamin 10:1256
KATZ, SIR BERNARD 10:823
Katz, Bezalel 10:826
Katz, Daniel 13:1346
KATZ, DAVID 10:823
Katz, Elias (r., Cz.) 4:1312; 12:1187
Katz, Elias (sport, Fin.) 12:1376
Katz, Emanuel, *see* MANÉ-KATZ
Katz, Ephraim 10:1153
Katz, Gabriel ben Jacob of Szamotuly 6:746
Katz, Geronim, *see* Kohen, Gronem
Katz, Gershom ben Solomon Kohen, *see* Kohen, Gershom ben Solomon Ha-
Katz, Hannah 11:359
Katz, Illés, *see* KACZÉR, ILLÉS
Katz, Isaac (r., Prague) 4:49
Katz, Isaac (ha-Kohen; r., Rus.) 10:826
Katz, Isaac bar Judah Yudeh (print.) 15:507
Katz, Isaac ben Samson (schol.) 11:1518
KATZ, ISRAEL (engin., U.S.) 10:824
Katz, Israel (cmty. ldr., U.S.) 16:634
Katz, Israel J. (mus.) 10:1352
- *Romancero* research 10:1353
Katz, Izidor 10:1216
KATZ, JACOB 10:824
- historiography 8:565
- *illus:*
- - Parkes, James, and 13:121
Katz, Jacob Joseph ben Ẓevi Ha-Kohen,, *see* JACOB JOSEPH BEN ẒEVI HA-KOHEN KATZ OF POLONNOYE
Katz, Jake 12:1352
Katz, Joseph (r., Pol.), *see* JOSEPH BEN MORDECAI GERSHON HA-KOHEN OF CRACOW
Katz, Joseph (educ., Can.) 6:464
KATZ, JOSEPH BEN ELIJAH 10:824
Katz, Joseph ha-Levi 7:624
Katz, Karl 3:652
Katz, Katriel 16:697
KATZ, LABEL A. 10:824
- COJO 16:637
Katz, Louis 11:1200
KATZ, MENAHEM 10:825
Katz, Mickey 15:1083
KATZ, MINDRU 12:694
Katz, Morris Abraham, *see* KATZ, ALEPH
Katz, Morris C. 14:162
Katz, Moses (print., Prague), *see* Kohen, Moses (17th cent.)
KATZ, MOSES (journ.) 10:825
- children's literature 5:458
Katz, Moses Ḥayyim (maskil, Tarnopol) 15:817
Katz, Moses Menaḥem (print.) 13:1108
Katz, Moshe (writ.) 12:1160
KATZ, NAPHTALI BEN ISAAC (ha-Kohen) 10:826
- Ashkenazi, Ẓevi 3:734
- Ḥayon, Nehemiah Hiyya 7:1501
Katz, Nehemiah 15:1207
Katz, Nina, *see* Cassian, Nina
Katz, Otto, *see* SIMONE, ANDRÉ
Katz, Philip C. 11:1552
Katz, Reuben Hoeshke, *see* REUBEN HOESHKE BEN HOESHKE KATZ
KATZ, REUVEN 10:826
Katz, Rudolf 14:974
Katz, Samuel ben Abraham 6:330
KATZ, SHOLOM 7:1548
Katz, Simeon 10:827
KATZ, SIMḤA 1:32
Katz, Solomon (Rum. writ.), *see* GHEREA-DOBROGEANU, CONSTANTIN
KATZ, SOLOMON (hist.) 10:827
Katz, Solomon (r., N. Z.) 3:839
Katz, Zalman 16:395
KATZBURG, DAVID ẒEVI 10:827
- Silberstein, D. 14:1535
Katzen, David 15:305
Katzenelbogen, Benjamin ben Saul 10:1280
Katzenelbogen-Wahl, Meir, *see* Kaẓin Elin Bogen, Meyer
Katzenelbogen, Abraham ben David 4:1362; 10:828
Katzenelenbogen, Phinehas 10:555
Katzenellbogen, Naphtali Hirsch ben Eliezer 10:826
Katzenellenbogen (name), *see also* Katzenelson, Katznelson
KATZENELLENBOGEN (fam.) 10:828
KATZENELLENBOGEN, DAVID TEVEL 10:828
Katzenellenbogen, Eliezer (Lazarus Riesser) 10:828
- Cleves-*get* 9:614
- Kohen, Raphael 10:1140
- Riesser, Gabriel 14:169
Katzenellenbogen, Ezekiel ben Abraham 10:828
Katzenellenbogen, Hirsch of Pfalz 5:614
Katzenellenbogen, Jacob Phinehas 12:1334
Katzenellenbogen, Joel (Ashkenazi) 10:828
KATZENELLENBOGEN, MEIR BEN ISAAC 10:829
- Alashkar, Moses 2:512
- Ibn Yaḥya, David 8:1207
- responsa 11:337
Katzenellenbogen, Naphtali Hirsch ben Moses 10:828
Katzenellenbogen, Samuel Judah 10:828
- Wahl, Saul 16:242
Katzenellenbogen, Saul 8:269
KATZENELLENBOGEN, ẒEVI HIRSH (Naphtali) 10:830
Katzenellenbogen-Sulzbach, Hirsch 4:1355
Katzenellenbogen-Sulzbach, Loebel 4:1355
Katzenelsohn, P. 16:1165
Katzenelson (name), *see also* Katzenellenbogen, Katznelson
KATZENELSON, BARUCH 10:830
Katzenelson, H. Y. 10:862
KATZENELSON, ITZHAK 10:830
- drama 6:198
- Ghetto Fighters' House 7:546
- Yiddish literature 16:800; 16:820
Katzenelson, Jacob Benjamin 10:830; 16:1007
KATZENELSON, JUDAH LEIB BENJAMIN 10:832
KATZENELSON, NISSAN 10:833
KATZENELSON, YOSEF 10:833
Katzenstein, Ernst 10:93
Katzenstein, H. J. 14:987
Katzenstein, Julius, *see* KASTEIN, JOSEPH
Katzigin (fam.), *see* Clava
KATZIR, AHARON 10:834
Katzizne, Alter, *see* KACYZNE, ALTER
KATZMAN, HERBERT 3:603
Katzman, Larry 5:220
KATZMAN, SAM 12:469
KATZMANN, FRIEDRICH (Fritz) 10:834
- Lvov 11:614
Katznelson, *see also* Katzenellenbogen, Katzenelson
Katznelson, Avraham, *see* NISSAN, AVRAHAM
KATZNELSON, BERL (Beeri) 10:834
- Aḥdut ha-Avodah 2:456
- Ben-Gurion 4:507ff
- Golomb, Eliyahu 7:763
- Histadrut leadership 9:856
Katznelson, Berl (boat), *see Berl Katznelson*
Katznelson, Jacob Benjamin 10:382
KATZNELSON, RAḤEL 10:839
- *illus:*
KATZNELSON, REUBEN 10:839
Katznelson, Siegfried 14:1120
Katz-Simone, André 14:1653
KATZ-SUCHY, JULIUSZ 10:840
Kauder, Moses 10:840
KAUDER, SAMUEL JUDAH BEN DAVID 10:840
Kauen (city, Lith.), *see* KAUNAS
Kauff, Benjamin Michael 15:301
Kauffman, Mildred 2:321
Kauffmann, Felix 10:841
Kauffmann, Ignatz 10:841
KAUFFMANN, ISAAC 10:840
Kauffmann, J. 4:973; 4:1239; 7:92; 10:840
Kaufman (fam.) 15:1426
Kaufman, A. (cmty ldr.) 11:886
Kaufman, A. H. (govt. offic., U.S.) 14:162
Kaufman, Al (cart.) 5:220
KAUFMAN, BEL 15:1581
Kaufman, Bela 15:1426
Kaufman, Benjamin (sport.) 15:312
Kaufman, Benjamin (sol.) 11:1552
Kaufman, Bessie, *see* Thomashefsky, Bessie
KAUFMAN, BORIS 12:469
Kaufman, Charles L. 12:1216
Kaufman, David 15:1036
Kaufman, David S. 15:1034
Kaufman, Denis, *see* VERTOV, DZIGA
Kaufman, Elias 3:360
KAUFMAN, GEORGE SIMON 10:841
- Ferber's collaboration 6:1225
Kaufman, Irving R. 14:280
Kaufman, Jay 16:637
Kaufman, Louis 12:266
Kaufman, Michael 12:475
Kaufman, M. Ralph 13:1340
Kaufman, Paul J. 16:476
Kaufman, Reuben 16:35
Kaufmann (fam.) 14:834
KAUFMANN, ARTHUR 3:603
KAUFMANN, DAVID 10:842
- book collection 4:975
- Budapest seminary 4:1108
- history 8:563
- history chart 8:766-767
- Jewish art 3:593
Kaufmann, Edmund 16:1143
KAUFMANN, FELIX 10:843
KAUFMANN, FRITZ (philos.) 10:844
KAUFMAN, FRITZ MORDECAI 10:844
Kaufmann, Gurit, *see* KADMAN, GURIT
KAUFMANN, HANNE 14:934; 14:928
Kaufmann, Hugo 11:1167
KAUFMANN, ISIDOR 10:844
- *illus:*
- - text
- - "Blessing over the Candles" (paint.) 4:487
- - "Bride" (paint.) 11:*fcg.* 1070
- - "Chess Players" (paint.) 5:403
- - "Descendant of the High Priest" (paint.) 15:*fcg.* 491
- - "Ḥasidim in a *Bet Midrash*" (paint.) 7:1395
- - "Teacher and Young Pupil" (paint.) 3:553
Kaufmann, Judah, *see* EVEN SHEMUEL, JUDAH

Kaufmann, Marco **10:**1503
Kaufmann, Moses Jekuthiel **10:**1280
Kaufmann, M. W. (book firm) **4:**1239; **13:**1373
KAUFMANN, OSKAR **3:**364
Kaufmann, Philip **10:**845
KAUFMANN, RICHARD **10:**845
- Israel architecture **9:**559
- Kefar Yehoshu'a **10:**896
- *illus:*
- - Moledet plan **9:**560
Kaufmann, Rosa **13:**175
KAUFMANN, WALTER **10:**845
KAUFMANN, YEHEZKEL **16:**1349
- Bible exegesis **4:**903
- idolatry, views on **8:**1234ff
- Isaiah **9:**62
- Pentateuch **13:**239
KAUFMANN HAGGADAH (illum. ms.) **7:**1099
- illuminated mss. **8:**1265
- *illus:* **6:***fcg.* 1067; **7:**1086
Kaufmann Mishneh Torah (13th cent., illum. ms., Ger.) **8:**1267
- *illus:* **2:**242; **5:**630; **7:***fcg.* 747; **8:**1280
Kaukab al-Hawa (site, Isr.), *see* AGRIPPINA
Kaukji, Fawzi al- **16:**720
- War of Independence **9:**348; **16:**307ff
- *illus:*
- - "Kaukji's Irregulars" **9:**465
KAULLA (fam.) **10:**846
- banking **4:**173
Kaulla, Albert Von **10:**846
Kaulla, Chaila (Caroline) Raphael **10:**846
Kaulla, Jacob Raphael **10:**846
Kaulla, Joseph Wolf **10:**846
KAUNAS (city, Lith.) **10:**846
- Diskin, Moses **6:**74
- ghetto art **3:**575
- Holocaust **8:**899 **2:**100
- special Purim **13:**1397
- Spektor, Isaac Elhanan **15:**259
- *illus:*
- - text
- - "Children in Kovno Ghetto School" (drg., Lifschitz) Fig. 77 **3:**ART
- - ḥasidic synagogue **11:**383
- - Hilfsverein children's home **8:**480
- - Maccabi soccer team **11:**377
- - ORT school **12:**1482
- - OSE nursing course **12:**1538
- - Volozhin Nes Ziona Association **16:**214
- - "Wooden Bridge in the Kovno Ghetto" (drg., Lurie) Fig. 78 3-ART
Kausch, Hans Joachim **13:**771
KAUSHANY (vill., Bess.) **10:**850
KAUTZSCH, EMIL FRIEDRICH **10:**850
- *Deutscher Palaestina-Verein* **5:**1595
KAUVAR, CHARLES ELIEZER HILLEL **10:**851
Kav (journ.) **1:**newsp. list
Kavadh I (Sassanian k.) **6:**1027
Kavaja (tn., Alb.) **2:**523
KAVALLA (city, Gr.) **10:**851
- Greece **7:**875
KAVERIN, BENJAMIN ALEKSANDROVICH **10:**851
Kav(qav) ha-middah (measuring line) **16:**378
Kav ha-Middah (kab. wk.) **16:**1196
Kav ha-Yashar (bk.) **11:**344
Kavod (divine glory) **10:**515; **10:**516ff
KAVVANAH (devotional intent) **10:**852
- Alexander Susskind of Grodno **2:**586
- *Amidah* **2:**839
- *devekut* **5:**1598
- *Berakhot* **4:**585
- *Gematria* and mysticism **10:**510; **10:**519; **10:**538
- ḥasidic teachings **7:**1409; **7:**1417
- Ḥayyim of Volozhin **7:**1417
- Kabbalah **10:**627ff
- Lurianic Kabbalah **10:**548; **10:**553
- *mikveh* **2:**83; **11:**1535
- prayer **13:**981
- *Sefer Torah,* writing **14:**1100
- *Shema,* reading of **14:**1372
- *see also:* MEDITATION
Kavvanah (leg. conc.; "intention") **2:**217; **12:**906
Kavveret (journ.) **1:**newsp. list
Kawkab al-Hawā (site, Isr.), *see* AGRIPPINA
Kawkabān (tn., Yem.) *see* SHIBĀM AND KAWKABĀN
KAYE, DANNY **10:**853
- *illus:* text
Kaye, M. **5:**450
KAYE, NORA **10:**854
- *illus:* text
Kayser, Jacques **10:**306
KAYSER, RUDOLF **10:**855
Kayser, Stephen S. **3:**652; **12:**544
KAYSERLING, MEYER (Moritz) **10:**855
- Baer, Yitzḥak **8:**564
Kaysersberg (vill., Fr.) **2:**752
Kayyara, Simeon **4:**310
- Adler family **2:**268
- *Halakhot Gedolot* **7:**1169; **11:**330
- history chart **8:**766-767
KAZ, NATHANIEL **3:**603
- *illus:*
- - "The Offering" (sculp.) **3:**629
KAZAKEVICH, EMMANUIL GENRIKHOVICH **10:**856
Kazakov (sol., Rus.) **13:**699
KAZAN (city, U.S.S.R.) **10:**857
Kazanlik (city, Bulg.) **4:**1483
Kazantzakis, Nikos **7:**887; **7:**898
KAZARNOVSKI, ISAAC ABRAMOVICH **10:**857
KAZATIN (city, Ukr.) **10:**857
Kazav, Avigdor Ashkenazi **14:**252
KAZAZ, ELIJAH **10:**857
- cantors' school **16:**778
Kazcerginsky, S. **16:**147
KAZDAN, ḤAYYIM SOLOMON **10:**858
Kazem (Musl. fam.) **9:**1454
Kazerun (city, Pers.) **13:**309
Ka-Zetnick (poet), *see* K. ZETNICK
Kazimierz (sub., Cracow) **15:**606
- *see also:* CRACOW
KAZIMIERZ (Ḥas. dyn.) **10:**858
- synasties **1:**ḥas. table
Kāzimiyya (tn., Iraq) **8:**1449
KAZIN, ALFRED **10:**859
- U.S. literature **15:**1578
Kaẓin, Judah (Ger.) **9:**21
KAZIN, JUDAH BEN YOM TOV (Aleppo) **10:**859
- Laniado, opposed by **10:**1423
Kaẓin, Meir **11:**1246
Kazin, Moses **13:**556
KAZIN, RAPHAEL BEN ELIJAH **10:**859
- Baghdad **4:**89
Kaẓin Elin Bogen, Meyer **10:**828
- Wahl, Saul **16:**243
Kaẓin ve-Rosh (tit.) **13:**1450
Kaẓir (journs.) **1:**newsp. list
Kazis, Abraham **16:**633
Kazmarin, Boris **16:**1165
KAZNELSON, SIEGMUND **10:**860
Kazrin (site, Isr.), *see* Kefar Kazrin
KAZVIN (city, Iran) **10:**860
KAZYONNY RAVVIN (Rus. "official rabbi") **10:**860
- history **8:**724
Kazzaz, al- (name), *see* Qazzaz
K-C, *see* KARTELL-CONVENT DER VERBINDUNGEN DEUTSCHER STUDENTEN JUEDISCHEN GLAUBENS
Keats, John **14:**523
Kebra Negast (Eth. chron.) **6:**943
KECSKEMET (city, Hung.) **10:**862
- *illus:* text
KECSKEMÉTI, ÁRMIN **10:**863
KECSKEMÉTI, GYÖRGY **10:**311
KECSKEMÉTI, LIPÓT **10:**864
- literature **8:**1079
Kedainiai (dist. Lith.) **14:**768
KEDAINIAI (tn., Lith.) **10:**864
- *illus:*
- - text
- - scouts **14:**1037
Kedar (bib. fig.) **9:**89
KEDAR (anc. people) **16:**1351
- Arabs **3:**194
- Jeremiah **9:**1354
Kedem (journ.) **1:**newsp. list
KEDEMITES (anc. peoples) **10:**865
- Edom **6:**369
- Ishmaelites and **9:**89
KEDEMOTH (city, Er. Isr.) **10:**865
Kedesh (city, Er. Isr.)
- Aharoni's excavations **2:**451
- city of refuge **5:**591
- Huleh **8:**1064
- Kadesh **10:**664
- Naphtali **12:**820
- physiography **9:**155
- *illus:*
- - polje **9:**169
Kedesh-Naphtali (city, Er. Isr.) **10:**665
Kedeshah (cult prostitute) **6:**935; **16:**625
Kedmah (bib. fig.) **9:**89
Kedmah (stlmt., Isr.) **1:**place list
Kedmah (journ.) **1:**newsp. list
Kedmah (ship) **16:**1024
Kedoshei Kahir (Martyrs of Cairo) **11:**1078
Kedron (tn., Er. Isr.) **7:**354
KEDUSHAH (holiness) **10:**866
- *Contents:*
- - General Considerations **10:**866
- - Holiness of God **10:**867
- - Fire as Symbol of God's Holiness **10:**868
- - Transitive Effects of God's Holiness **10:**868
- - Polarity of Holiness **10:**869
- - Holiness and Glory **10:**869
- - Comparative Considerations **10:**869
- - In Rabbinic Literature **10:**871
- - In Jewish Philosophy **10:**872
- - - Maimonides **10:**873
- - - Judah Halevi **10:**873
- - - Nachman Krochmal **10:**874
- - - Moritz Lazarus **10:**874
- - - Hermann Cohen **10:**874
- - - Franz Rosenzweig **10:**874
- Buber's view **7:**1419
- degrees of **8:**920
- dietary laws and **11:**142
- divine **7:**651
- ethics **6:**941
- ḥasidic doctrine **7:**1405
- hygiene and **8:**1140
- imitation of God **8:**1292
- Judaism **10:**388
- Kook, A. I. **10:**1185
- Otto's conception of **12:**1523
- priesthood **13:**1080ff
- purity **13:**1414
- *Ru'aḥ ha-Kodesh* **14:**365
- sacrilege **14:**616
- *Sefer Torah* **14:**1103
- speech **13:**1119
- Tabernacle **15:**686
- Temple Mount **15:**989
- throne **15:**1124
KEDUSHAH (ben., Amidah) **10:**875
- *Amidah* **2:**840
- angelic song **15:**144
- *kedushta* **13:**1204-5
- *kerovah* **10:**920
- *kiddush ha-Shem* **10:**981
- liturgy **11:**398ff
- *Minyan* **12:**67
- *mystic hymns* **10:**501; **10:**506ff
- priestly blessing **13:**1062
- *yozerot* **16:**866
Kedushata (piyyut), *see Kedushta*
Kedushat ha-Shem (ben., Amidah), *see* KEDUSHAH
Kedushta (piyyut) **13:**598, 1204
Keeley, Mary Anne Goward **15:**1054
Keeley, Robert **15:**1054
Keene (city, N.H.) **12:**1024
Keeney brothers **15:**1177
Keepers of the Jews (mdvl. Eng. govt. ofs.) **6:**1007
KEESING, ISAAC **10:**877
Kefar Agun (Agin; vill., Er. Isr.) **4:**782; **5:**1459; **15:**797
Kefar Aharon (stlmt.) **4:**491
Kefar Aḥim (mosh., Isr.) **1:**place list
Kefar Akavyah (vill., Isr.) **13:**1532
KEFAR AKKO (vill., Isr.) **10:**877
Kefar Ata (tn.), *see* KIRYAT ATA
Kefar Aviv **1:**place list
Kefar Avodah (vill. type) **9:**381
Kefar Avodah (mosh., Isr.), *see* PORIYYAH
Kefar Avodah (educ. inst., Isr.) **1:**place list
Kefar Avraham (loc., Isr.) **13:**338
Kefar Avraham (cmty., Syr.) **5:**1239
KEFAR AZAR (mosh., Isr.) **10:**877
- statistics **1:**place list
Kefar Aziz (vill., Isr.) **9:**84; **9:**244
Kefar Azzah (kib., Isr.) **1:**place list
KEFAR BARAM (vill., Isr.) **10:**877
- Crusader period **2:**398; **9:**272
- synagogue **13:**523ff; **15:**596
- *illus:*
- - text
- - archaeological remains **3:**517
KEFAR BARUKH (mosh., Isr.) **10:**878
- statistics **1:**place list
KEFAR BIALIK (mosh., Isr.) **10:**879
- statistics **1:**place list
KEFAR BILU (mosh., Isr.) **10:**879
- statistics **1:**place list
Kefar Bin Nun (mosh., Isr.) **1:**place list
Kefar Bish (vill., Isr.) **7:**1337
KEFAR BLUM (kib., Isr.) **10:**879
- statistics **1:**place list
Kefar Dagon (bib. city), *see* BET(H)-DAGON
Kefar Dan (vill., Isr.) **5:**1260
Kefar Dani'el (mosh., Isr.) **1:**place list
KEFAR DAROM (vill., kib., Isr.) **10:**879
- Deir al-Balaḥ **5:**1463
- statistics **1:**place list
- war **7:**1322; **16:**315
- *illus:* text
Kefar Etam (vill., Isr.) **6:**920
KEFAR EẒYON (kib., Isr.) **10:**880
- Ha-Po'el ha-Mizrachi **7:**1322
- statistics **1:**place list
- *illus:* text
Kefar Gallim (agr. school, Isr.) **1:**place list
KEFAR GAMALA (vill., Isr.) **10:**881
- Beit Jimāl **4:**405

Kefar Gannim (loc., Isr.) **13:**338
Kefar Gevirol ha-Nagid (loc., Isr.) **7:**1497
KEFAR GIDEON (mosh., Isr.) **10:**881
- statistics **1:**place list
KEFAR GILADI (kib., Isr.) **10:**881
- library **11:**194
- statistics **1:**place list
- *illus:* text
KEFAR GLICKSON (kib.,Isr.) **10:**882
- statistics **1:**place list
Kefar Gun, *see* Kefar Agun
KEFAR ḤABAD (vill., Isr.) **10:**882
- statistics **1:**place list
- *illus:*
- - text
- - annual bar mitzvah celebration **9:**904
- - Simḥat Torah dancing **5:**1269
KEFAR HA-ḤORESH (kib., Isr.) **10:**883
- Galilee **7:**268
- statistics **1:**place list
KEFAR HA-MACCABI (kib., Isr.) **10:**884
- statistics **1:**place list
Kefar ha-Nagid (mosh., Isr.) **1:**place list
KEFAR ḤANANYAH (vill., Isr.) **10:**884
- Crusader period **9:**272
- Ottoman period **9:**285
KEFAR HA-NASI (kib., Isr.) **10:**884
- statistics **1:**place list
Kefar ha-Noar (agr. school, Isr.), *see* NIẒẒANIM
Kefar ha-No'ar ha-Dati (rel. agr. school) **3:**954; **10:**885
- statistics **1:**place list
Kefar ha-Rif (mosh., Isr.) **1:**place list
KEFAR HA-RO'EH (mosh., Isr.) **10:**884
- statistics **1:**place list
- yeshivah **16:**772
Kefar Ḥaruba, *see* Kafr Ḥārib
Kefar ha-Shiloaḥ, *see* SHILOAḤ, SILOAM
KEFAR ḤASIDIM (mosh., Isr.) **10:**885
- Ezekiel of Yablonov **10:**858
- Ḥasidim **7:**1398; **7:**1403
- statistics **1:**place list
- *illus:* text
- *see also:* REKHASIM
KEFAR ḤATTIN (vill., Isr.) **10:**885
- Battle of Ḥattin **9:**268
- Jethro and Druzes **9:**928; **10:**20
- Madon **11:**681
- *illus:*
- - text
- - Eshkol inspecting Druze honor guard **9:**927
- - site of Crusader battle **9:**275
- - tomb of Nabi Shu'ayb **10:**20
KEFAR ḤAYYIM (mosh., Isr.) **10:**886
- Arlosoroff, Chaim **3:**471
- statistics **1:**place list
KEFAR HESS (mosh., Isr.) **10:**886
- statistics **1:**place list
Kefar Hittaya, *see* KEFAR ḤATTIN
KEFAR ḤITTIM (mosh., Isr.) **10:**886
- statistics **1:**place list
Kefar Hittin, *see* KEFAR ḤATTIN
KEFAR JAWITZ (mosh., Isr.) **10:**887
- statistics **1:**place list
KEFAR KANNA (Kenna; vill., Isr.) **10:**887
- holy places **8:**935; **9:**583
- Kanah, identified with **10:**733
- Mamluk period **9:**280
- Ottoman period **9:**285
- *illus:* text
Kefar Karinos (J. cmty., Syr.) **5:**1239
Kefar Karzum (Karnayim; tn., Transj.) **7:**1223
Kefar Kazrin (site, Isr.) **13:**1533
KEFAR KISCH (mosh., Isr.) **10:**888
- statistics **1:**place list
Kefar Maimon (stlmt., Isr.) **10:**48
- statistics **1:**place list
KEFAR MALAL (mosh., Isr.) **10:**888
- statistics **1:**place list
KEFAR MANDI (vill., Isr.) **10:**888
Kefar Marmorek (stlmt., Isr.) **14:**1307
KEFAR MASARYK (kib., Isr.) **10:**888
- statistics **1:**place list
KEFAR MENAḤEM (kib., Isr.) **10:**889
- statistics **1:**place list
KEFAR MONASH (mosh., Isr.) **10:**889
- statistics **1:**place list
KEFAR MORDEKHAI (mosh., Isr.) **10:**889
- statistics **1:**place list
Kefar Moshe Sharett (kib., Isr.), *see* Senir
Kefar Naḥum, *see* CAPERNAUM
Kefar Nathan Laski, *see* BET ZERA
KEFAR NEBURAYA (vill., Isr.) **10:**889
KEFAR NETTER (mosh., Isr.) **10:**890
- statistics **1:**place list
Kefar Ono, *see* KIRYAT ONO
KEFAR OTNAY (vill., Isr.) **10:**890
- Roman Legion **9:**246; **10:**103; **10:**1573
Kefar Philadelphia (vill., Isr.) **2:**226
KEFAR PINES (mosh., Isr.) **10:**890
- statistics **1:**place list
Kefar Rosenwald (mosh., Isr.) **1:**place list
KEFAR ROSH HA-NIKRAH (kib., Isr.) **10:**890
- statistics **1:**place list
KEFAR RUPPIN (kib., Isr.) **10:**891
- statistics **1:**place list
KEFAR SAVA (tn., Isr.) **10:**891
- statistics **1:**place list
- *illus:*
- - text
Kefar Shalem (vill., Isr.) **7:**1020
Kefar Shalma (sub., Jer.) **9:**1515
Kefar Shammai (mosh., Isr.) **1:**place list
Kefar Shaul (sub., Jer.) **9:**1496; **9:**1515
- *see also:* Deir Yasin
KEFAR SHEMARYAHU (stlmt., Isr.) **10:**892
- statistics **1:**place list
Kefar Shemu'el (mosh., Isr.) **1:**place list
Kefar Shiḥin (city), *see* SHIḤIN
KEFAR SHIḤLAYIM (vill., Idumea) **10:**892
- Har ha-Melekh **7:**1337
Kefar Silver (agr. school, Isr.) **1:**place list
Kefar Sitrin, *see* Bet Zevi
KEFAR SYRKIN (mosh., Isr.) **10:**893
- statistics **1:**place list
KEFAR SZOLD (kib., Isr.) **10:**893
- statistics **1:**place list
- *illus:* text
Kefar Tanḥum (stlmt., Isr.) **9:**272
KEFAR TAVOR (mosh., Isr.) **10:**893
- Jewish colonization **10:**48
- statistics **1:**place list
- *illus:* text
KEFAR TRUMAN (mosh., Isr.) **10:**894
- statistics **1:**place list
KEFAR URIYYAH (mosh., Isr.) **10:**894
- statistics **1:**place list
KEFAR VITKIN (mosh. Isr.) **10:**894
- statistics **1:**place list
KEFAR WARBURG (mosh. Isr.) **10:**895
- Emica **10:**48
- statistics **1:**place list
Kefar Ya'beẓ, *see* KEFAR JAWITZ
Kefar Yamma (tn., Isr.) **9:**1175
KEFAR YASIF (vill., Isr.) **10:**895
- Ottoman period **9:**285
KEFAR YEḤEZKEL (mosh., Isr.) **10:**896
- statistics **1:**place list
- *illus:*
- - general view **12:**436
KEFAR YEHOSHU'A (mosh., Isr.) **10:**896
- statistics **1:**place list
KEFAR YONAH (stlmt., Isr.) **10:**896
- statistics **1:**place list
Kefar Zarit, *see* Kefar Rosenwald
Kefar Zeitim (mosh., Isr.) **1:**place list
Kefir, Mount (Isr.) **9:**152
Kefirhe-Ḥaron, *see* LION OF WRATH
Keftiu (people) **5:**141
Ke-gufo (leg. conc.) **3:**989
Kehal Medinah, *see* LANDJUDENSCHAFT
Kehe, G. J. **8:**41
Kehilatenou (journ.) **13:**1026
Kehillah (orgn., N.Y.), *see* New York Kehillah
Kehillah (conc.), *see* COMMUNITY
Kehilla Kaddisha de-bi-Yrushalayim (2nd cent. C.E.), *see* HOLY CONGREGATION IN JERUSALEM
Kehilliyyatenu (journ.) **1:**newsp. list
KEHIMKAR, ḤAYIM SAMUEL **10:**897
Keidaner, Isaac **16:**1014
Keidany (tn., Lith.), *see* KEDAINIAI
Keil (fam., U.S.) **16:**534
KEIL, KARL FRIEDRICH **10:**897
KEILAH (city, Er. Isr.) **10:**897
- Bethleptepha **4:**747
Keilil (3rd cent. C.E, fig.) **2:**44
Keimann (writ.) **14:**785
Keini (nomadic clans), *see* KENITE
Keissariyyon (city, Er. Isr.), *see* BANIAS
Kekkermannus, B. **8:**41
Kelaḥim (mosh., Isr.) **1:**place list
Kelaḥ Pitḥei Ḥokhmah (bk.) **11:**601
Kelal (publ. house) **8:**1119
Kelal Kaẓer mi-Kol ha-Rashum bi-Khetav (encyc.) **6:**730
Kelalei ha-Nikkud... (wk.) **16:**1385
Kelal u-ferat (hermeneutical rule) **8:**369
KELAL YISRAEL (J. cmty. as a whole) **10:**898
- *see also:* KENESET YISRAEL
Kelbasin (concen. camp) **13:**770; **15:**84
Keleman, Adolf **6:**1135
KELEN, IMRE **10:**898
- Versailles **5:**219
- *illus:* text
KELETI, AGNES **10:**899
- Olympic games **12:**1376
KELIM (mish. tract.) **10:**899
- *illus:* text
Kelimat ha-Goyim (tract.) **6:**299
Kelin, Samuel ben Nathan ha-Levi, *see* KOLIN, SAMUEL BEN NATHAN HA-LEVI
Kelippot (kab. conc.)
- Israel Ba'al Shem Tov **9:**1054
- Kabbalah **10:**547; **10:**551; **10:**585ff,596
- Naḥman of Bratslav **12:**785,786
- Shabbetai Ẓevi **14:**1238
- Worlds, the Four **16:**642
Kelitah, *see* ALIYAH AND ABSORPTION IN ISRAEL
Keller, G. W. **8:**41
Keller, Melvin **12:**671
KELLER, MORTON **8:**547
KELLERMANN, BENZION **10:**900
Kellert (fam.) **5:**104
Kellert, H. **12:**1408
Kellgren, Johan Henric **14:**929
KELLNER, LEON **10:**900
KELMAN, WOLFE **10:**901
KELME (tn., Lith.) **10:**902
Kelmer, Samuel ben Jacob, *see* SAMUEL BEN JACOB OF KELMY
Kelmer Maggid, *see* MOSES ISAAC
Kelniker, Aaron **8:**428
Kelp, Márton **8:**41
KELSEN, HANS **10:**902
"Kelulot" (kibb. litur.) **10:**961
Kemal Atatürk (states.) **6:**151
Ke-mamono (leg. conc.) **3:**989
KEMELMAN, HARRY **15:**1579; **15:**1581
Kemény, Ferenc **6:**463
KEMÉNY, SIMON **8:**1086
Kemény, Zsigmond **15:**140
Kemink, H. H. **8:**41
Kemmel, János **8:**41
Kemoi, Mar Rav **10:**225
Kemosh (Moab. deity), *see* CHEMOSH
KEMPEN (tn., Ger.) **10:**903
KEMPF, FRANZ MOSHE **10:**903
- *illus:* text
Kempinski, David **12:**1518
Kempner, Alfred, *see* KERR, ALFRED
KEMPNER, HARRIS **10:**904
Kempner, Isaac Herbert **10:**904
KEMPNER, ROBERT MAX WASILII **10:**904
- War Crimes Trials **16:**294
Kempner, Ruth Lydia **10:**905
Kemuel ben Naḥor (bib. fig.) **10:**1317
Kemuel ben Shiphtan (bib. fig.) **6:**576
Kena'ani (mer.) **16:**1269
KENAANI, DAVID **10:**905
Kena'anim (mvmt., Isr.), *see* CANAANITES
Kenan, Mount (Isr.) **9:**156
KENATH (city, Ḥauran) **10:**905
- Bashan **4:**292
- coins **5:**720
- *Provincia Judaea* **9:**239
- *see also:* DECAPOLIS
Kenaz (bib. fig.) **12:**1520
Kendler, Howard **13:**1345
Keneder Adler (newsp.), *see* KANADER ADLER
Keneset (lit. anths.) **1:**newsp. list **5:**16; **10:**1338
Keneset Beit Yiẓḥak yeshivah (Lith.) **10:**848; **14:**1668
Keneset Eliyahu synagogue (Jer.), *see* Ḥabad synagogue
Keneset ha-Gedolah (bk.) **4:**560
Keneset ha-Gedolah (journ.) **1:**newsp. list
Keneseth Israel Jewish Museum (U.S.) **12:**544

Keneset Israel (orgn.) **7:**795; **7:**928
Keneset Israel Yeshivah (Lith.), *see* SLOBODKA YESHIVAH
KENESET YISRAEL (conc. and orgn.) **10:**906
- Concept
- - Kabbalah **10:**507,509,519; **10:**575; **10:**613
- - Kelal Yisrael **10:**898
- Organization
- - Agudat Israel **2:**424
- - Ashkenazi community **9:**889; **9:**892
- - autonomy **3:**927
- - historical survey **9:**343
- - Va'ad Le'ummi **16:**49ff
Keneset Yisrael (ship) **8:**1250
Keneset Yisrael (journs.) **1:**newsp. list; **10:**906; **12:**1050; **13:**1045
Keneset Yisrael (lexicon) **7:**213
Kenesiyyah ha-Gedolah (Agudat Israel inst.) **2:**423
Keni (bib. fig.), *see* JETHRO
Kenigsberg, D. **16:**819
Kenilworth (sub., Chicago) **5:**415
KENITE (nomadic clans) **10:**906
- Amalekites **2:**790
- Arad **3:**243; **3:**244
- mining **11:**1431
- Rechabites **13:**1610
- Timna **15:**1146ff
- *illus:*
- - Arad antiquities **3:**245
Kenizzites (bib. people)
- Caleb **5:**42
- Kenites **10:**906
KENNEDY, JOHN FITZGERALD **10:**907
- Ben-Gurion, David **4:**512
- chronological chart **8:**766-767
- Israel **9:**402; **9:**430
- Ribicoff, Abraham **14:**152
- *illus:*
- - text
- - Kennedy Memorial **3:**356
Kennedy, Thomas **11:**1077
Kennedy (John F.) Memorial (Isr.) **2:**853
Kennicott, Benjamin **8:**41; **4:**976
Kennicott Bible (15th cent. illum. ms., Sp.) **4:**960; **8:**1260; **8:**1265
- art **3:**522
- Corunna **5:**976
- Ibn Ḥayyim, Joseph **8:**1181
- *illus:*
- - text
- - **3:**525,787; **5:***fcg.* 971,1336; **10:**171
Kenosha (city, Wis.) **16:**556
"Kensington Gardens" (paint., J. Oppenheimer) **3:**638
Kent County (R.I.) **14:**143
KENTRIDGE, MORRIS **10:**908
- memoirs **15:**210
KENTUCKY **10:**909
- *pop. table:* text
KENYA **10:**910
- synagogues **1:**syn. list
- Zionism **16:**1140
- *illus:* text
Kenyatta, Jomo **10:**910
Ken Yehi Raẓon (litur.) **2:**803
KENYON, KATHLEEN MARY **10:**911
- Jerusalem **9:**1523ff
- *illus:*
- - Jerusalem excavations **9:**1523
Kepno (tn., Pol.) **8:**487
Kerak (tn., Transj.), *see* KIR-HARESETH
KERAK OR CHARAX (site, Er. Isr.) **10:**911
Kera Satan (acrostic) **3:**25
Kerazim (tn., Transj.), *see* Kefar Karzum
KERCH (city, Crimea) **10:**911
- Bosphorus **4:**1263
- Crimea **5:**1103
Kerem Avraham (qtr., Jer.) **9:**1472; **9:**563
Kerem Ben Zimrah (mosh., Isr.) **1:**place list
Kerem be-Yavneh Yeshivah (Isr.) **10:**31
- statistics **1:**place list
Kerem ha-Teimanim (J. qtr., Jaffa) **15:**919
KEREM ḤEMED (annual) **10:**912
- Bick, J. S. **4:**977
- Goldenberg, S. L. **7:**709
- Haskalah, Galician **8:**183
- Hebrew newspapers **12:**1048
- letter form **11:**60
- statistics **1:**newsp. list
Kerem Maharal (stlmt., Er. Isr.) **5:**187
- statistics **1:**place list
Kerem Shalom (kib., Isr.) **1:**place list
Kerem Sheli (newsp.) **2:**310
Kerem Yavneh, *see* Kerem be-Yavneh Yeshivah
Keren (ram's horn), *see* SHOFAR
Keren (tort category) **3:**986ff; **15:**1273
Keren ha-Karmel (site, Isr.) **9:**588
KEREN HAYESOD (Pal. Found. Fund) **10:**914
- Farbstein, J. H. **6:**1181
- Goldstein, A. **7:**745
- Hantke, A. **7:**1280
- history chart **8:**766-767
- philanthropy **13:**390
- Zlatopolsky, H. **16:**1188
- Zionism **16:**1082; **16:**1143
- *illus:*
- - text
- - Montevideo appeal **16:**1126
- *see also:* JEWISH AGENCY
Keren ha-Yovel (ram's horn), *see* SHOFAR
Keren Kayemet le-Israel, *see* JEWISH NATIONAL FUND
Keren mu'edet (tort conc.) **3:**987
Keren Nekhut (orgn., Isr.) **8:**539
Keren Or (journ.) **1:**newsp. list
Kerensky, A. **6:**268
Keren tammah (tort conc.) **3:**987
Keren Yaldenu (orgn., Isr.) **9:**896
Kerényi, Károly **4:**884
Keresztes, József **8:**41
Kereszetesi, Pál **8:**41
Keresztúr (tn., Aus.), *see* DEUTSCHKREUTZ
Kereszturi, Bálint **8:**41
Keret (k., Sidon) **14:**1505
Keri (Bib. text form), *see Keri* and *ketiv*
KERI'AH (rending of the garments) **10:**916
- ruins of the Temple **15:**994
- *see also:* BURIAL; MOURNING
Keri and *ketiv* (Bib. text form)
- biblical Hebrew **16:**1571
- masorah **16:**1410,1419,1420
- Pentateuch **13:**263
Keri'at Shema, see SHEMA, READING OF
Keri'at Shema al ha-Mittah, see NIGHT PRAYER
Kerin, Nora **12:**945
Kerith (brook, Er. Isr.), *see* CHERITH
KERITOT (Mish. tract.) **10:**917
- *illus:* text
Kerker (sing., Cana.) **16:**662
Kerkha (riv., Mesop.) **16:**1490
Kerler, Y. **16:**826
KERMANSHAH (city, Iran) **10:**918
Kermanyan (trans., Iran) **15:**906
Kermatistes (N.T. fig.) **12:**244
Kermes (dyestuff) **16:**1285
Kermes oak **9:**1515
KERN, JEROME DAVID **10:**919
- theater **15:**1059
- *illus:*
- - Hammerstein, Oscar, and **15:**1060
Kern, Mihály **8:**41
Kerner, Benjamin **15:**304
Kerosine (oil) **9:**795
Kerosites (fam.) **16:**667
KEROVAH (litur.) **10:**920
- Haduta **7:**1056
- *piyyut* **13:**598
- prayer books **13:**986
- prosody **13:**1204,1205,1206
- variations **11:**398
- Yannai **16:**713
Kerpen (tn., Ger.) **5:**1137
KERR, ALFRED **10:**920
- *illus:* text
KERSH, GERALD **6:**788
Kerssenbroich, Hermanus **8:**41
Kerstein, Lincoln **12:**1122
Kerstein, Solomon **13:**1376
Kersten, Felix **8:**907; **10:**922; **15:**549
Kertesz, Alice **12:**1377; **15:**309
Keruspedai (tan.) **14:**307
Keruv (bot.), *see* CABBAGE
Kerzner, Jerome **16:**515
Kesafim u-Misḥar (journ.) **1:**newsp. list
Kesalon (mosh., Isr.) **1:**place list
Kesed (bib. fig.) **5:**330
Kesef (metal), *see* Silver
Kesef Mishneh (hal. wk.), *see* CARO, JOSEPH BEN EPHRAIM
Kesherim (cmty. members) **13:**948
Kesher ve-Elektronikah (journ.) **1:**newsp. list
Keshet (period.) **1:**newsp. list **2:**848; **5:**102; **13:**1378
Keshet (zodiac sign), *see* Sagittarius
KESHET, YESHURUN **10:**921
Keshet Neḥushah (bk.) **2:**951
Kesiṭah (weight) **16:**381
Kesler, J. Conrad **8:**41
Kessel, Dmitri **13:**484
KESSEL, JOSEPH **10:**922
- *illus:* text
Kessel, Leon **15:**312
Kesselman, Joseph **16:**1013
Kesselman, Rachel **16:**1013
KESSLER, DAVID **10:**923
Kessler, David Francis **10:**923
KESSLER, LEOPOLD **10:**923
- *illus:*
- - El-Arish technical commission **6:**565
Kessler, S. **12:**505
Kest (support for groom) **6:**186
Kestelmann, Jehiel **4:**89
KESTEN, HERMANN **10:**923
KESTENBERG, LEO **10:**924
Kestner, René, *see* REHFISCH, HANS JOSÉ
Kestrel (zool.) **6:**34
KESZI, IMRE **8:**1080; **8:**1086
KESZLER, JÓZSEF **8:**1086
Ketav Ashuri (square script) **14:**1101
Ketav harsha'ah, see Attorney, Power of
Ketavim (journ.) **1:**newsp. list **9:**779
Ketav Livonai (kab. letters) **2:**912
Ketav Masmikh (ordination writ) **13:**1449
Ketav Minnuy (appointment writ) **13:**1449
Ketav Rabbanut (rab. writ) **13:**1448
Ketav Sofer (r., Hung.), *see* Sofer, Abraham Samuel Benjamin Wolf
Keter (Bib. ms.), *see Keter Aram Ẓova*
Keter (crown) **5:**1130ff; **15:**1256
Keter (kab. conc.) **10:**570ff,589
Keter Aram Ẓova (Bib. ms.) **4:**465; **11:**900
- *illus:*
- - ms., 10th cent. **11:**901
Keter Elyon (kab. conc.) **10:**561
Keter Kehunnah (enc.) **10:**1428
Keter Malkhut (hymn)
- astronomy **3:**803
- Gabirol, Ibn **7:**243
- literature, Jewish **11:**327
- prosody **13:**1218
Keter Publications (Isr.) **13:**1379
Keter Shem Tov (bk.) **2:**134; **10:**527
Ketev (demon) **5:**1524
Ketev Meriri (demon) **5:**1528
Ketev Yashud Ẓohoraim (demon) **5:**1528
KETI'A BAR SHALOM **10:**925
- *see also:* FLAVIUS CLEMENS
Ketiv (Bib. text form), *see Keri* and *ketiv*
Ketivah Tovah (Heb. greeting) **7:**916
Ketling, Szemley (Cesary) **16:**350
Ketonet Yosef (lexicon) **4:**592
Ketoret, see INCENSE AND PERFUMES
Ketterisch, K. **4:**1312
Ketterisch, O. **4:**1312
KETUBBAH (leg. doc.) **10:**926
- *Contents:*
- - The Concept **10:**926
- - The "Main" Ketubbah and its Increment **10:**927
- - Dowry **10:**928
- - Custom Concerning Consolidation of all Ketubbah Amounts **10:**928
- - Ketubbah Conditions **10:**929
- - Loss of Ketubbah Deed **10:**929
- - In State of Israel **10:**929
- - Conservative and Reform **10:**929
- - Illuminated Ketubbot **10:**930
- *agunah* **2:**432
- art **3:**538ff; **8:**1262; **9:**1589
- childlessness **6:**127
- civil marriage **5:**596
- concubine **5:**864
- conflict of laws **5:**883ff
- counter claims **11:**787
- inheritance rights **13:**97; **15:**477ff
- *lashon hediot* **8:**1425
- levir **11:**124
- lien rights **11:**227ff
- limitation of action **11:**252
- maintenance **11:**785; **11:**787
- marriage **11:**1033ff
- monogamy clause **4:**987
- orphan **12:**1479
- rabbinical law **12:**114
- recovery from *zibburit* **12:**1311
- Samaritans **14:**746
- Simeon ben Shetaḥ **14:**1564
- suretyship **15:**527
- *takkanah,* gaonic **2:**399; **15:**723
- *takkanah,* 1944 **12:**143; **15:**728
- *tena'im* stipulation **4:**756
- virginity **16:**162
- widow **16:**491ff
- *illus:*
- - Ancona (1784) **8:**1285
- - Cochin (1774) **5:**624
- - Corfu (1781) **5:**971
- - Damascus (1848) **5:**1243
- - Ferrara (1755) **6:**1234
- - Gibraltar (1872) **7:**555
- - Herat (1875) **8:**341
- - illuminated **10:***fcg.* 939
- - Isfahan (1874) **9:**78
- - Jerusalem, as ornamentation **9:**1587
- - Karaite (1833) **10:**772
- - Krems (1392) **3:**543
- - Meshed (1898) **11:**1399
- - Pesaro (1735) **6:**1375
- - Rotterdam (1648) **3:**541
- *see also:* DOWRY; HUSBAND AND WIFE; KETUBBOT; SHETAR

KETUBBOT (tract.) **10**:932
- *illus:* text
- *see also:* KETUBBAH
KETURAH (bib. fig.) **10**:934
- Abraham **2**:113
- Hagar **7**:1076
- Heracles myth **8**:333
Ketuvim, *see* BIBLE
Ketuvim (mag.) **8**:200; **12**:495
- statistics **1**:newsp. list
- Steinman, Eliezer **15**:372
Ketuvim Aḥaronim (Apoc. in Heb. trans.) **7**:5
Keut (journ.), *see* HARDEN, MAXIMILIAN
Keveh (anc. place), *see* QUE
KEVER AVOT (parents' grave) **10**:934
- *see also:* ZEKHUT AVOT
Kevi (animal), *see* KOI
Kevi'ah (calendar term) **5**:44
Kevish ha-Gevurah (highway, Er. Isr.) **9**:584
Kevod ha-Levanon (newsp.) **7**:1179
Kevuẓah (Isr.), *see* KIBBUTZ MOVEMENT
Kevuẓat Hakhamim (journ.) **1**:newsp. list
Kevuẓat Schiller (kib., Isr.), *see* GAN SHELOMO
Kevuẓat Yavneh (kib., Isr.) *see* YAVNEH
Kewall, Benjamin **10**:268
Key, Ted **5**:216
Keymakh, David **12**:55
Keyser, Ephraim, *see* Kaiser, Ephraim
KEYSERLING, LEON H. **10**:935
Keysor, Leonard **11**:1554
Keyworth, Thomas **8**:41
Keẓah (bot.), *see* FENNEL
Ke-zayit (meas.) **16**:389
KEẒAẒAH (leg. term) **10**:935
Keẓ ha-Yamim, *see* ESCHATOLOGY
Keziah (spice) **5**:565; **5**:566
Kežmarok (tn., Slov.) **10**:1216; **14**:1680
Khabarovsk (terr., Sib.) **14**:1488
Khabur (riv., Mesop.) **16**:1498
Khadīja (w. of Muhammad) **12**:508
Khaḍr, Al (area, Er. Isr.) **9**:1542
- inscription **16**:665
Khaibar (tn., Saud. Arab.), *see* KHAYBAR
Khairbeg (Egy. pasha) **5**:244
Khalameyzer (teacher, Rus.) **11**:1058
KHALAẒ, JUDAH BEN ABRAHAM (r., Sp.) **10**:935
Khalaẓ, Judah ben Abraham ha-Kohen (schol.) **10**:936
Khalaẓ, Moses ben Eleazar **10**:936
Khalfon, Abraham, *see* ḤALFON, ABRAHAM
Khalfon, Isaac **4**:503
Khalfon, Joseph **11**:303
KHALIASTRE (gr. of poets) **10**:936
Khaliastre (lit. anth.) **10**:936
Khalid ben Jasikhi **2**:547
Khālidī (Musl. fam.) **9**:1435
Khālidī, Muhammad Rūḥī al- **9**:1040
Khālidī, Ṣāliḥ al- **9**:1041
Khalīfa al-Kabīr, *see* Khalīfa ben Ḥayun ben Waqqāṣa
Khalīfa al-Ṣaghīr **16**:265
Khalīfa ben Ḥayun ben Waqqāṣa **16**:265
Khalifa ben Malca, *see* Malca, Khalifa ben
Khalil (sult., Egy.), *see* Ashraf, Malik al-
Khalil al-Raḥmān (city, Er. Isr.) **8**:228
Khalisioi, *see* KHAZARS
Khallas (fam., Alg.) **15**:1173
Khallas, Judah II **2**:623
Khāmjird (Uzbek reg.; person) **10**:955
Khamlīkh (Khazar tn.), *see* ATIL
KHANAQIN (tn., Iraq) **10**:936
- Diyala **6**:137
Khanbaligh (Khazar tn.), *see* ATIL
Khan-Bandaq (site, Er. Isr.) **13**:1532
Khangiri (Uzbek reg.; person), *see* Khāmjird
Khanikin (Khaniqin; tn., Iraq), *see* KHANAQIN
Khan Theater (Jer.) **9**:1496
Khanush, Moses **10**:399
KHĀN YŪNIS (tn., Er. Isr.) **10**:937
- Sinai Campaign **14**:1607
- Six-Day War **14**:1629
Khapers (kidnappers, Rus.) **5**:131; **14**:438
KHARAJ AND JIZYA (taxes) **10**:937
- *Ahl al-Kitāb* **2**:468
- Almoravides **2**:667
- Ibrahim Pasha **8**:1215
- Jewish farmers **2**:401
- Ottoman Empire **16**:1530,1540
- taxation **15**:838
- Tunisia **15**:1433
- Umayyads **15**:1530
KHARASCH, MORRIS SELIG **5**:384
Kharats, Meir **5**:396; **16**:819
Kharg (isl., Pers. Gulf) **4**:1535
KHARIK, IZI (Itzhak) **10**:939
- Minsk Group **10**:1289
KHARKOV (city, Ukr.) **10**:939
- synagogue **15**:590
- War Crimes Trials **16**:291
KHARKOV CONFERENCE (Zion.) **10**:940
- Uganda **15**:1501
Khartoum Arab Summit Conference (1967) **9**:414; **14**:1639
Khasfīn (Ḥasfiyah; vill., Golan) **13**:1533
Khashchevatsky, M. **10**:936
Khatīb (Musl. fam.) **9**:1435
Khatūsh, Ibn al- (fam.) **5**:1534
Khaver (monthly) **5**:459
Khavkin, M. **4**:1047
KHAYBAR (tn., Saud. Arab.) **10**:942
- Arabia **3**:235
- *dhimma*, *dhimmi* **5**:1606
- Muhammad **12**:511
- Ten Lost Tribes **15**:1005
Khaybarites (people), *see* KHAYBAR
Khayml, *see* SIEMIATYCKI, CHAIM
KHAZARS **10**:944
- *Contents:*
- - Origins **10**:944
- - Consolidation of State **10**:944
- - Relations with Byzantium and the Arabs **10**:945
- - Double Kingship **10**:946
- - Date of Conversion to Judaism **10**:947
- - Empire **10**:947
- - Extent of Khazar Judaism **10**:948
- - Downfall of Khazaria **10**:949
- - Khazar Correspondence **10**:950
- - After Fall of Kingdom **10**:952
- Armenia **3**:472
- Britain **4**:1478
- Cairo *genizah* **16**:1336
- Correspondence **8**:533; **10**:950
- Crimea **5**:1103ff
- Harkavy, Albert **7**:1340
- history **8**:667ff
- history chart **8**:766-767
- Karaites **6**:1305
- Khorezm **10**:955ff
- *Kuzari* **10**:363; **13**:438
- Obadiah **12**:1304
- Uzbekistan Jews **16**:40
- *illus:* text
- *see also:* JOSEPH (k. of Khazars)
Khāzin, Ibn **5**:1534
Khazna, Al- (bldg., Petra) **13**:343
- *illus:*
- - façade **13**:342
Khazraj (tribe, Arab.) **12**:509
KHERSON (prov., city, Ukr.) **10**:953
Kheziv (city, Er. Isr.), *see* ACHZIB
Khilāf al-Irshād (Samar. wk.), *see Ḥillūk*
Khill, Yusuf al- **9**:1039
Khirbat (ruin, Er. Isr.) . . .
- ʿAbbād **15**:69
- Abu al-Shabaʿ **4**:386
- Adasa, *see* ADASA
- ʿAjlan (Agla) **6**:477
- al-ʿAmrī **14**:41
- al-Ashraf **11**:793
- al-Athala **7**:573
- al-Baṣal **12**:317
- al-Bīra (vill.) **4**:375
- al-Bitar **2**:382
- al-Dilba **5**:1025
- al-Farriyya **7**:1319
- al-Ḥarbaj **2**:213; **7**:1272; **7**:1347
- al-Ḥūḥ **6**:920
- ʿAlīn (vill., Judea) **8**:918
- al-Ishshī **6**:566
- al-Jūl **13**:1529
- al-Kadīsh **10**:665
- al-Kafrayn (Jor.) **2**:62
- al-Karak **4**:778; **14**:1161
- al-Kawm (Er. Isr.) **16**:663
- al-Lūza **7**:438
- al-Mafjar **7**:573
- al-Maʿīn, *see* Maon
- al-Makhna **11**:724
- al-Mashāsh **8**:976
- al-Mird **8**:1145
- Almit **2**:665
- al-Muqana **6**:560; **6**:688
- al-Mushayrifa **12**:154
- al-Muyayyit (Jor.) **12**:911
- al-Nabratayn **10**:889
- al-Nāṭif **4**:752
- al-Rabba **13**:1439
- al-Riḥab **14**:44
- al-Rūma **14**:386
- al-Rumayl **10**:866
- al-Ṣafṣāfa **6**:739
- al-Ṣār (city, Jor.) **9**:1305
- al-Ṣira (city, Jor.) **9**:1305
- al-Tibnā **15**:1147
- al-Tubayka, *see* BET(H)-ZUR
- al-ʿUrayma **7**:579
- al-ʿUrma **14**:386
- al-Waṭan **12**:225
- al-Yahūd **4**:733
- al-Yānūn **9**:1277
- al-Yarmūk **9**:1288
- al-Zurra **7**:336
- ʿAnab al-Ṣaghīra **2**:916
- Arabah **11**:1483
- Arair **3**:492
- Arara **3**:492
- ʿAttarus **3**:814
- ʿAttīr, *see* JATTIR JETHIRA
- Awja al-Taḥtā **3**:333
- Badd Faluḥ (vill.), *see* NETOPHAH
- Baydūs, *see* NARBATA
- Bayūḍāt **14**:1158
- Beit Baṣṣa **4**:736
- Beit-Lay **16**:667
- Beit Mizza **12**:494
- Beit Zakarya **4**:782
- Bir al-Ḥilū **13**:1439
- Burj al-Ṣur, *see* BET(H)-ZUR
- Deleilat esh-Sherqiyeh (Moab. city) **2**:667
- el-Ḥanūttiyya (Jor.) **12**:40
- el-Jadīra **7**:354
- el-Maḥalib (Leb.) **2**:467
- el-Oreimeh, *see* Tells (Kinrot)
- et-Tabaik **16**:273
- Faḥil **13**:219
- Fassāil **13**:367
- Faynān **13**:1390
- Fuṭays, *see* PHOTIS
- Ḥaiyan **2**:472
- Ḥanūtā **7**:1268
- Ḥarazān **4**:736
- Ḥarithiyya **7**:349
- Ibzīq **4**:790
- Irbid, *see* ARBEL
- Iskandar (Jor.) **9**:1269
- Jadīra **7**:354
- Jadūr **7**:355
- Jalʿad **12**:174
- (Bayt) Jann **6**:741
- Jaʿtūn **7**:229
- Jifat **10**:300
- Kānif **13**:1532
- - *illus:*
- - - synagogue **13**:1532
- Kannā **10**:733
- Karmil **5**:185
- Kerazeh **5**:492
- Khaybar **10**:943
- Kurdani **3**:177
- Madīn **11**:681
- Majdal **11**:1528
- Maʿṣūb **11**:1158
- Mird **5**:1404
- Miyāmās **11**:793
- Naḥās **10**:906
- Nīḥā **9**:1278
- Qabārṣa **10**:657
- Qarqur (Hamath), *see* KARKAR
- Qīlā **10**:897
- Qumran, *see* QUMRAN
- Qunayṭira **15**:1131
- Rābūḍ **5**:1429
- Sa'ad **12**:317
- Salamiyya, *see* Selemia
- Ṣaliḥ, *see* RAMAT RAḤEL
- Shaḥla **10**:893
- Sheikh al-Shamsāwī **4**:774
- Shuwayka **15**:69
- Shuwaykat al-Ra's **15**:70
- Sīmūniyya **14**:1407
- Summāqa **12**:181
- Surayk, *see* SOREK, VALLEY OF
- Taqu' **15**:916
- Tawfīq (Syr.) **14**:1625
- Tibna **15**:1148
- Umm al-Ramāmīn **6**:799
- Umm-Jubayl **3**:1011
- ʿUyūn Mūsā (Jor.) **12**:911
- Uzzah **16**:276
- Yamma **9**:1175
- Zanūʿ **16**:93?
- *see also:* Tells
Khīva (Uzbek reg.), *see* KHOREZM
Khlysty (Rus. sect) **16**:866
KHMELNIK (tn., Ukr.) **10**:954
Khmelnitski, Bogdan, *see* CHMIELNICKI, BOGDAN
KHODASEVICH, VLADISLAV FELITSIANOVICH **10**:955
- Brafman, Jacob **4**:1288
Khoi (tn., Iran) **3**:1005
Khomenko, Ivan **4**:887
Khorasan (prov., Pers.), *see* KHURASAN
Khorazin (tn., Er. Isr.), *see* CHORAZIN
KHOREZM (Uzbek reg.) **10**:955
- Transoxiana **15**:1336
KHOROL (reg., Ukr.) **10**:956
Khorsabad (city, Assyr.)
- archives **3**:369
- excavations **16**:1506
- *gematria* **7**:369
Khosroes I (k., Pers.) **6**:1027

Khosroes II (k., Pers.) **9:**1407; **9:**1571 **14:**876
– Babylonia **4:**43
Khotan (tn., China) **5:**468
KHOTIN (tn., Bess.) **10:**956
– Bessarabia **4:**706
KHOUSHI, ABBA **10:**957
Khovanski, Count **16:**87
Khoza Kokos **5:**1105; **6:**411
Khronika Yevreyskoy Zhizni (period.) **13:**1047; **13:**1597
Khrushchev, Nikita Sergeyevich
– anti-Semitism **3:**150
– Birobidzhan failure **4:**1049
– discrimination **6:**69; **14:**484, 498
– Zionism **16:**1139
Khudayr, Abdallah **6:**1097
Khuftīdhkān (Khuftiyān; place, Iraq) **8:**1447
Khuli, Jacob, *see* CULI, JACOB
Khumesh mahl (festive meal) **14:**1195
Khunrat, Heinrich **10:**646
KHURASAN (prov., Pers.) **10:**958
– *see also:* AFGHANISTAN
Khushqadam (sult.) **11:**837
– Jerusalem **9:**1424
Khusro (k., Pers.), *see* Khosroes
KHUST (city, Ukr.) **10:**958
– *illus:* text
Khuzistan (reg., Pers.) **2:**470; **13:**303
Khvolson, Daniel Avraamovich, *see* CHWOLSON, DANIEL
Khwarizm (Uzbek reg.), *see* KHOREZM
Khwarizms (mercenary army) **9:**1418
Kiabrig (city, Mesop.) **16:**1490
Kiaer, Alice Damrosch Wolf **15:**317
Kiāhya (govt. offic., Turk.), *see* KĀKHYA
Kibarty (tn., Lith.), *see* KYBARTAI
Kibbud av va-em, see PARENTS, HONOR OF
Kibbush (training farm, Lith.) **8:**252
Kibbush ha-avodah (Zion. conc.) **7:**1324ff; **9:**870
Kibbutz Buchenwald (pion. gr.) **12:**1131
KIBBUTZ FESTIVALS **10:**959
– *illus:*
– – Daliyyah dance festival **5:**1229; **9**·1010
– – *Haggadah*, Deganyah Bet **7:**1093
– – Sasa *Haggadah* **9:**908
– – Sha'ar ha-Amakim *Haggadah* **9:**908
– – Shavuot celebrations, Gan-Shemuel **6:**1314; **7:**314
– – Shavuot folkdance, Ḥuldah **5:**1267
– *see also: Ḥagigat...*
Kibbutz *Haggadah* (Isr.) **7:**1104
Kibbutz Ḥerut (pion. gr.) **8:**1241
KIBBUTZ MOVEMENT (Isr.) **10:**963
– *Contents:*
– – Character **10:**964
– – Organization **10:**965
– – Social and Educational Aspects **10:**966
– – Iḥud ha-Kevuẓot ve-ha-Kibbutzim **10:**968
– – Ha-Kibbutz ha-Arẓi—Ha-Shomer ha-Ẓa'ir **10:**969
– – Ha-Kibbutz ha-Me'uḥad **10:**970
– – Ha-Kibbutz ha-Dati **10:**972
– Ben-Gurion **4:**507
– care for the aged **2:**348
– cooperatives **5:**950
– economy **9:**852ff
– festival observance **9:**905
– Ha-Kibbutz ha-Arẓi—Ha-Shomer ha-Ẓa'ir **7:**1150
– Ha-Kibbutz ha-Dati **7:**1150
– Ha-Kibbutz ha-Me'uḥad **7:**1151
– history **8:**752ff; **9:**381ff
– Iḥud ha-Kevuẓot ve-ha-Kibbutzim **8:**1243
– mental illness **11:**1376
– Ya'ari, Meir **16:**691
– *illus:*
– – text
– – Yad Mordekhai, triple wedding **11:**1050
– – Yavneh, reading Purim *megillah* **13:**1395
– *see also:* MOSHAV SHITTUFI
Kibbuẓ galuyyot, see INGATHERING OF THE EXILES
Kibbuẓ Niddeḥei Israel (assoc., Belor.) **12:**52
KIBEL, WOLF **10:**974
Kiber, David, *see* Kyber, David
Kichko, Trofim, *see* Kychko, Trofim
KIDD, MICHAEL **5:**1272
Kiddah (spice) **5:**565; **5:**566
KIDDUSH **10:**974
– *Arvit* **3:**666
– *Berakhot* **4:**586; **4:**737
– bread **4:**1335
– cup in art **14:**571
– folklore **6:**1391
– grape juice **12:**1444
– *onen* **3:**23
– origin **15:**630
– Sabbath **14:**564
– synagogue **15:**583
– wine **16:**539
– *illus:*
– – text
– – Bohemian glass cup **4:**1181
– – Dead Sea stone cup **6:**1387
– – *ḥallah* cover, embroidered **6:**1385; **7:***fcg.* 1262
– – Passover **3:**531
– – pewter plate **13:**353
– – silver gilt cup **5:***fcg.* 302
– *see also:* HAVDALAH
Kiddush ha-Shem (wk.) **16:**151
KIDDUSH HA-SHEM AND ḤILLUL HA-SHEM (sanctification and desecration of Divine Name) **10:**977
– *Contents:*
– – In the Bible **10:**977
– – Rabbinic Literature **10:**978
– – Kiddush ha-Shem: Historical Aspects **10:**981
– General
– – *Akedah* **2:**480ff
– – asceticism **3:**678
– – *Av ha-Raḥamim* **3:**953
– – *Barukh Shem Kevod . . .* **4:**285
– – "building an altar" **2:**770
– – Gentiles, relations with **7:**412; **7:**413
– – hagiography **7:**1116ff
– – Horowitz, Isaiah **8:**992
– – Israel, People of **9:**106
– – love of God **11:**528
– – *Memorbuch* reading **11:**1299
– – miracles **12:**76
– – *Sefer ha-Kuzari* **3:**193
– – *talmid ḥakham* **15:**749
– Historical Instances
– – Akiva **2:**488; **2:**489
– – Antiochus IV Epiphanes **8:**628
– – Bamberg Jews **4:**149
– – Barcelona Jews **4:**211
– – Basle Jews **4:**303
– – Black Death **4:**1067
– – Crusades **5:**1137, 1142
– – Germany **7:**461ff
– – Hadrianic persecutions **9:**248
– – Hannah **7:**1270ff
– – Ḥasidei Ashkenaz **7:**1377; **7:**1380
– – Holocaust **8:**879
– – Inquisition **8:**1404ff
– – martyrologies **8:**555ff
– – Masada **11:**1079
– – Ten Martyrs **15:**1006
– – Troyes martyrs **15:**1407
– – York Jews **16:**849
– Laws Concerning
– – cardinal offenses **10:**385; **12:**1398; **13:**224; **14:**1196
– – Commandments, the 613 **5:**763
– – desecration of God's Name **5:**1559
– – gentile martyrdom **12:**1189
– – *Ḥukkat ha-Goi* **8:**1061
– – idolatry **8:**1235
– – *kaddish* **10:**981ff
– – *niddui* **8:**351, 353
– – proselytes **13:**1189
– – sages **14:**648ff
– – *Shema* **14:**1373
– – suicide **15:**489
– *illus:*
– – Antiochus Epiphanes, martyrdom scenes **8:**675
– – burning of Jewish martyrs **7:**466; **8:**675
– – Dornhan *Memorbuch* **3:**380
– – Frankfort *Memorbuch* **11:**1300
– – Inquisition torture bed **8:**1399
– – Munich martyrs of 1285, ms. record **12:**522
– – Prague blood libel (1694) **8:**700
– – torture of the Jews of Trent **7:**467
– – York, Clifford's tower **16:**849
Kiddushin, see BETROTHAL
KIDDUSHIN (tal. tract.) **10:**986
– *illus:*
– – text
– – title page (Lublin, 1618) **11:**544; (Venice, 1520) **15:**757
Kiddush Levanah (prayer), *see* MOON, BLESSING OF THE
Kid Lewis, *see* LEWIS, TED
Kidnapping, *see* ABDUCTION
Kidod (loc., Isr.) **9:**794
KIDRON (val., Er. Isr.) **10:**987
– burial **5:**272
– Jehoshaphat **9:**1327
– necropolis **9:**1393; **9:**1398
– Shiloah waters **14:**1400ff
– Temple **15:**963
– *illus:*
– – text
– – Absalom's Tomb **3:**340
– – Hezir tomb **15:**1219
– – Jehoshaphat Valley **9:**1328
– – Miriam, Tomb of **9:**1417
– – monuments, Second Temple period **3:**509
– – Shiloah graves **15:**1220
– – view from Temple Mount **9:**1522
– – Zechariah's Tomb **3:**339; **9:**1392; **15:**1221
– *see also:* Kidron, Naḥal; SHILOAH, SILOAM
Kidron (mosh., Isr.) **1:**place list
Kidron, Naḥal (riv., Er. Isr.)
– Jerusalem topography **9:**1515
– Jerusalem water supply **9:**1537
– tombs **15:**1217
– *see also:* KIDRON
KIEL (city, Ger.) **10:**988
– Schleswig-Holstein **14:**974
– *illus:* text
KIELCE (city, Pol.) **10:**989
– ghetto **13:**767
– pogrom **4:**630
Kielland, Alexander Lange **14:**932
Kielland, Axel **14:**933
Kiepert (Ger. cartog.) **11:**930
KIERA (16th cent., Turk.) **10:**990
Kierkegaard, Sören Aabye **2:**119, 484; **15:**1109
– Mendel of Kotsk **10:**1223
– Wandering Jew **16:**262
Kiesler, Adolph **5:**1545
KIESLER, FREDERICK JOHN **3:**604
– Shrine of the Book **12:**552
– *illus:*
– – Shrine of the Book, Jerusalem **3:**631
KIEV (city, Ukr.) **10:**991
– *Contents:*
– – Jewish Community before 1667 **10:**991
– – From 1793 **10:**992
– – Holocaust Period **10:**995
– – After World War II **10:**996
– Aronson, Solomon **3:**496
– Babi Yar **4:**27
– history chart (1910) **8:**766-767
– Hofstein, David **8:**813
– Holocaust **14:**476
– museums **12:**540
– promotion of culture **15:**61
– self-defense **14:**1125
– synagogue **15:**589
– trade routes **15:**1297ff
– *illus:*
– – Ukrainian Jewish Council **15:**1515
KIEVAL, HERMAN **10:**998
Kiev Group (Yid.) **12:**233
Kiev Jewish Municipal Theater (Rus.) **15:**1076
Kiev Jewish Teachers' Seminary, *see* Jewish Teachers' Seminary (Kiev)
Kifayat al-ʿAbidin (bk.), *see High Ways to Perfection*
Kifl, Al- (tn., Iraq) **8:**1450
Kifra (sub., Tiberias) **15:**1134
Kifri (tn., Iraq) **8:**1449; **8:**1450
Kigali (tn., Rwanda) **9:**441
Kihn, H. **8:**41
Kik (bird), *see* PELICAN
Kikayon, *see* CASTOR-OIL PLANT
Kikeriki (period.) **5:**219
– *illus:*
– – Jew as vampire (cart.) **3:**153
Kikkar (meas.), *see* Talent
Kikkar ha-Yarden (val., Er. Isr.) **9:**167, 589
Kiklar (genre of poem) **13:**1205
KIKOINE, MICHEL **10:**998
– Paris **13:**116
Kikyon Yonah (journ.) **1:**newsp. list
Kilamuwa inscription (Turk.) **16:**666
Kilamuwa son of Hayya **16:**661
KILAYIM (tract.) **10:**999
– *illus:* text
Kilayim (Bib. prohibition), *see* MIXED SPECIES
Kilbye, Richard **8:**41
Kilgore (city, Tex.) **15:**1036
KILIYA (city, Bess.) **10:**1001
Kilkis, Nathan ben Moses **10:**537
Killer, *see* HOMICIDE
Kilshon, Operation (War of Indep.) **16:**314
KIMBERLEY (city, S. Afr.) **10:**1001
– *illus:*
– – synagogue **15:**199
Kimche, David (journ.) **10:**312
KIMCHE, JON **10:**312
Kimḥa de-Avishuna (comment.) **15:**1378
Kimḥi (fam., Turk.) **9:**1094
Kimḥi, Abraham **10:**1008
KIMḤI, DAVID **10:**1001
– Abrabanel, Isaac **2:**106
– Bible exegesis **4:**893; **11:**325
– burning of Talmud **15:**769
– chronological chart **8:**766-767
– grammar **11:**324
– Kimḥi, Mordecai **10:**1007
– linguistics **16:**1355
– Maimonidean controversy **11:**748
– meaning of exile **7:**287ff
– peace **13:**198
– usury **12:**249

- *illus:*
- - text
- - Bible commentary (1494) 4:895
- - Book of Psalms, commentary (1487) 8:1329
- - Former Prophets, commentary (1495) 8:1334
- - *Sefer Mikhlol* (15th cent.) 4:960; 5:*fcg.* 971
KIMḤI, DOV 10:1004
- Jerusalem books 9:1568
Kimḥi, Ḥayyim 9:1094
Kimḥi, Isaac 10:1007
KIMḤI, JACOB BEN SAMUEL 10:1005
KIMḤI, JOSEPH 10:1006
- apologetics 3:194
- cult of angels 2:972
- Dunash-Menahem 6:270
- linguistics 16:1358, 1359, 1373, 1385
- polemical literature 11:354
KIMḤI, MORDECAI 10:1007
KIMḤI, MOSES 10:1007
- linguistics 16:1359, 1373, 1386
- *illus:*
- - *Rudimenta Hebraica* (1520) 4:1168
Kimḥi, Nissim Joseph David 10:1008
KIMḤI, RAPHAEL ISRAEL BEN JOSEPH 10:1008
Kimḥi, Samuel 10:1005
KIMḤI, SOLOMON BEN NISSIM JOSEPH DAVID 10:1008
- Abraham de Camondo 16:1501
- Istanbul 9:1094; 9:1095
Kimḥit (mo., h. pr.) 8:6; 10:1009
KIMḤIT (fam., h.pr.) 10:1009
Kimoi bar Aḥai (gaon) 7:318
Kimoi bar Ashi (gaon) 7:317; 12:432
Kimpet-Tsetl (amulet) 2:906; 6:1400
- *illus:*
- - papercuts 13:44-45
Kimpulung (tn., Rum.), *see* CAMPULUNG MOLDOVENESC
Kinah (bib. loc.) 10:907
KINAH (poem) 10:1009
- Anav 2:938
- Av, the Ninth 3:938
- Bible 13:678
- liturgy 11:398ff
- Jerusalem 9:1561
- prayer books 13:987
- Psalms, Book of 13:1314
- *mus. notations:*
- - *Avi Avi* refrain 3:955
- - *Eli Ẓiyyon ve-Areha* 6:672
- - oriental, Amsterdam 12:627
- *see also:* LAMENTATIONS, BOOK OF; MUSIC; MOURNING
Kinderfreund, Aleksander, *see* Konar, Alfred Aleksander
KINDERFREUND, ARYEH LEIB 10:1010
Kinder Journal (period.) 5:445; 5:459; 14:1584
Kinder Zeitung (period.) 5:445; 5:459
KINDĪ, AL-ABU YŪSUF YA'QŪB IBN IṢHAQ 10:1010
- Israeli, Isaac ben Solomon 9:1063ff
- soul 15:173
KINDLER, ARIE 1:32
- numismatics 12:1271
Kine (animal) 6:31
Kine'at ha-Shem Ẓevaot (wk.) 11:603
King, Geoffrey 8:41
King, H. C. 13:30
KING, KINGSHIP 10:1011
- *Contents:*
- - In the Bible 10:1011
- - - Concept of Monarchy 10:1011
- - - Origins in Israel 10:1011
- - In Rabbinic Literature 10:1020
- Abrabanel 2:108
- adoption 2:300
- Alexander Yannai 7:1456
- anointment 3:27; 8:1312
- Austrian Jews 3:898
- Canaan 13:474
- chieftain 5:420ff
- Commandments, the 613 5:770,781
- David 5:1318
- education 6:389ff
- elders 6:579
- ethnarchy 6:945
- expropriatory powers 5:881
- firstborn succession 6:1307
- Gideon and Abimelech 8:585
- *hakhel* ceremony 7:1149
- Hasmoneans 8:632
- Hellenism 8:294
- Jewish-Christian sects 10:39
- Judah and Israel list 8:766-767
- king parables 13:74
- law, force of 6:51ff; 12:136
- lots 11:510
- *mamzer* 11:840
- Mesopotamia 16:1485
- Messiah 11:1407
- *nasi* 12:834
- New Year 12:1061
- non-Jewish laws 6:51ff
- priests 13:1083ff
- prophecy 13:1157ff
- proselytes 13:1185
- queen mother 6:1167
- Rehoboam 14:42
- sages 14:654
- Samuel 14:781
- Samuel, Book of 14:789
- *Sanhedrin* 14:840
- Saul 14:909ff
- social structure 8:612ff
- Solomon 15:96
- Temple 15:954
- Temple Scroll 15:997
- throne 15:1124
- Urim and Thummim 16:9
- woman's eligibility 13:1358
- *illus:*
- - Israel stamp 9:844-845
- - "King Judah" (paint., J. Levine) 10:331
- - king of Judah (pottery) 3:320
King, Martin Luther 12:933
King, Phil 15:307
King, Prayer for, *see* GOVERNMENT, PRAYER FOR THE
King Artus (leg. stories), *see* ARTHURIAN LEGENDS
King-Crane Commission 13:30
King David Hotel (Jer.) 9:358; 9:1473; 9:1477; 16:1090
- *illus:*
- - I.Z.L. bomb explosion 8:1469
King David School (S.A.) 10:156; 15:196
"King David's Entry into Jerusalem" (tpst., M. Chagall) 5:*fcg.* 334
Kingdom of David (Crus.), *see* Jerusalem, Kingdom of
Kingdom of Israel, *see* ISRAEL, KINGDOM OF
Kingdom of Jerusalem (Crus.), *see* Jerusalem, Kingdom of
Kingdom of Judah, *see* JUDAH, KINGDOM OF
Kingdom of Samaria (Isr.), *see* ISRAEL, KINGDOM OF
Kingdoms, the Four 4:356
King Features Syndicate (comic strips) 5:215
"King George Avenue in Jerusalem" (paint., Ḥ. Gliksberg) Pl. 5 3-ART
King James Version 4:870
"King Jehoshaphat" (r.), *see* GALANTE, MOSES BEN JONATHAN
"King Judah" (paint, J. Levine) 10:331
Kinglake, Alexander William 6:782
Kingly Crown (poem), *see Keter Malkhut*
"King of Abyssinia" (hist.), *see* MARKUS, LUDWIG
"King Rehoboam" (drg., Holbein) 14:43
KINGS, BOOK OF 10:1021
- *Contents:*
- - First Part 10:1022
- - Second Part 10:1026
- - Third Part 10:1028
- - Compilation and Redaction 10:1030
- - Aims and Purposes 10:1030
- Chronicles 5:518
- chronicles of the kings 4:1236
- Spinoza 15:283
- taxation 15:840
- *illus:*
- - text
- - *Hispanic Society Bible* 4:*fcg.* 876
Kings Highway (loc., Er. Isr.)
- agriculture 2:387
- alphabet 2:686
- Edom 6:374
- history 8:589ff
- human geography 9:595
- Solomon's kingdom 15:97
Kingship, *see* KING, KINGSHIP
Kings Hotel (Jer.) 9:1496
Kingsley, Charles 6:779
KINGSLEY, SIDNEY 10:1031
KING'S LYNN (city, Eng.) 10:1032
- Crusades 5:1140
Kingsmill, T. R. 8:41
Kingston (city, Jam.) 3:699; 13:883
- *illus:*
- - synagogue 9:1273
Kingston (city, N.Y.) 12:1125
Kingston (vill., R. I.) 14:143
Kingston (co., Ont.) 12:1407
Kinnamon (spice), *see* CINNAMON
KINNAROT, VALLEY OF (loc., Er. Isr.) 10:1032
- tribes 8:580
- *illus:*
- - text
- - Kibbutz Ginnosar 9:582
Kinneman Besem (spice), *see* CINNAMON
KINNERET (moshavah, Isr.) 10:1033
- Chizhik family 5:479
- statistics 1:place list
- *illus:*
- - text
- - early settlers 9:554
KINNERET (kib., Isr.) 10:1033
- statistics 1:place list
- *illus:* text
Kinneret (gr., Peru) 16:1125
Kinneret (journ.) 13:1049
"Kinneret" (paint., A. Giladi) Fig. 98 3-ART
KINNERET, LAKE (Isr.) 10:1034
- Bet Yeraḥ 4:778
- fishing 9:785
- French rule 9:309
- frontier 9:319ff
- Habas' story 7:1018
- human geography 9:589ff
- political status 15:648
- power station 9:791
- regional physiography 9:168
- Sennabris 14:1161
- spices 8:1312
- *illus:*
- - text
- - aerial view 15:1131
- - annual crossing 15:297
- - Church of Beatitudes 8:927
- - wooded shore 9:170
KINNIM (tract.) 10:1036
- *illus:* text
Kinnor (instr.), *see* Harp
Kino-Teater-Radio (pub., Pol.) 13:1043
KINROSS, ALBERT 10:313
Kinsbrunner, Max 15:303
Kinshasa (city, Congo) 5:893; 9:438
- *illus:*
- - Ben-Zvi, Izhak and Raḥel, state visit 4:579
Kinship, *see* FAMILY
Kinsky, Countess, *see* Suttner, Bertha, Baroness von
KINSKY, GEORG LUDWIG 12:695
Kinukos (cynic) 5:1178
Kinyan (leg. conc.), *see* ACQUISITION
Kinyan Torah (acquisition of Torah) 3:984
Kiov (city, Ukr.), *see* KIEV
Kipen, Miguel 3:432
Kipling, Rudyard 6:760; 16:262
KIPNIS, ALEXANDER 12:695
Kipnis, Igor 12:695
KIPNIS, ITZIK 10:1037
- *Khaliastre* 10:936
KIPNIS, LEVIN 10:1038
- children's literature 5:435
KIPNIS, MENAḤEM 10:1038
- Gebirtig, Mordecai 7:350
- Justman, Moshe 10:479
- *illus:* 12:660
Kipnis, Zimra, *see* Seligsfeld, Zimra
Kippat ha-Yarden (incense) 8:1316
KIPPER (bib. conc.) 10:1039
- *Contents:*
- - Etymology 10:1039
- - As "Cover" 10:1039
- - As "Purge" 10:1039
- - The Theology 10:1040
- - Remaining Cases 10:1040
- - As "To Represent" or "to Transfer" 10:1040
- - As "To Expiate" 10:1041
- - *Kipper* Blood 10:1041
- - Ritual Atonement without *Kipper* 10:1041
- - Non-Ritual *Kipper* for Sin 10:1042
- - Forgiveness 10:1042
Kipper, M. 16:779
Kippod (zool.) 12:1531
Kippurim (tract.), *see* YOMA
Kir (bib. loc.) 2:883
Kira (16th cent., Turk.), *see* KIERA
Kircher, Athanasius 8:41; 10:645; 12:558
Kirchhan, Elhanan Hendel 11:358; 12:558
- *mus. notation: Ma'oz ẓur* 11:911
KIRCHHEIM, RAPHAEL 10:1044
KIRCHHEIMER, OTTO 10:1045
Kirchhof, David 7:63
Kirchmayer, K. 7:1103
KIR HARESETH (city, Er. Isr.) 10:1045
- boundaries 9:122
- Crac du Désert 9:268; 9:596
- human geography 9:596
- Israel-Moab war 11:1397
- Mamluks 9:277
- Moab 12:191
- physiography 9:178
- Transjordan 15:1317
Kiriath Ahab (city, Transj.) 15:1316
Kiriathaim (bib. site, Er. Isr.) 14:105
Kiriath-Arba (bib. city, Er. Isr.) 8:226
KIRIATH-JEARIM (city, Er. Isr.) 10:1045
- ark 14:792
- Baalah 4:1

– Benjamin tribe **8:**579
– Judah boundary **10:**330
– *see also:* ABU GHOSH
Kiriath-Sannah (Kiriath-Sepher; city, Gilead), *see* DEBIR
Kiriath Sepher (period.), *see* KIRJATH SEPHER
KIRIMI, ABRAHAM **10:**1046
Kirjath Sepher (publ. firm, Isr.) **13:**1378
KIRJATH SEPHER (period.) **10:**1046
– bibliography **4:**972
– Festschriften **6:**1247
– publishing **13:**1379
– statistics **1:**newsp. list
– Ya'ari, Abraham **16:**691
– Zionism **16:**1157
KIRKISĀNĪ, JACOB AL- **10:**1047
– Abu Imrān **2:**183
– Al-Mukammas **3:**193
– Karaites **10:**769
– Munajja ben Sadaqa **14:**755
– Philonic influence on **10:**496; **10:**510
– Samaritan calendar **14:**749
– Zadokite document **16:**1335
Kirkisiya (tn., Syr.) **5:**161; **8:**1447
Kirkland Lake (tn., Ont.) **12:**1408
KIRKPATRICK, ALEXANDER FRANCIS **10:**1048
KIRKUK (tn., Iraq) **10:**1048
– Kurdish Jews **8:**1456
Kirman, Y. **16:**819
Kirmisin (city, Iran), *see* KERMANSHAH
Kir of Moab (city, Er. Isr.), *see* KIR-HARESETH
Kirovabad (city, Rus.) **3:**1005
KIROVOGRAD (Kirovo; city, Ukr.) **10:**1049
– Jewish self-defense **14:**1123
– *illus:*
– – He-Ḥalutz group, 1918 **8:**248
KIRSANOV, SEMYON ISAAKOVICH **10:**1049
Kirsch, Olga **15:**210
KIRSCHBAUM, ELIEZER SINAI **10:**1050
KIRSCHBRAUN, ELIJAH **10:**1050
Kirschen, Bernard **13:**110
Kirschner, Bruno **6:**732; **8:**364
Kirschner, Conrad, *see* PELLICANUS, CONRAD
KIRSCHNER, EMANUEL **10:**1051
Kirschner, Nicolai **15:**198; **16:**1140
Kirschner, Sidney, *see* KINGSLEY, SIDNEY
KIRSCHSTEIN, MORITZ **10:**1051
– translation **4:**876
KIRSCHSTEIN, SALLI **10:**1051
– ceremonial objects **5:**310
– museums **12:**539,544
KIRSHBLUM, MORDECAI **10:**1052
Kirshenbaum, David **11:**482
KIRSHON, VLADIMIR MIKHAILOVICH **10:**1052
Kirshrot, Jan **16:**337
Kirsner, Joseph **11:**1200
KIRSTEIN, LINCOLN **10:**1052
KIRSTEIN, LOUIS EDWARD **10:**1053
KIRSZENBAUM, JESEKIEL DAVID **10:**1053
– Paris **13:**120
Kirszenstein, Irena **12:**1377
Kiryanos (city, Bashan), *see* KARNAIM
KIRYAT ANAVIM (kib., Isr.) **10:**1054
– Ettinger, Akiva **6:**953
– statistics **1:**place list
KIRYAT ATA (tn., Isr.) **10:**1054
– Ḥasidim **7:**1398
– statistics **1:**place list
KIRYAT BIALIK (tn., Isr.) **10:**1054
– Haifa **7:**1138
– Israel **9:**580
– statistics **1:**place list
KIRYAT EKRON (tn., Isr.) **10:**1055
– Ḥaydānī family **7:**1497
– statistics **1:**place list
– *see also:* MAZKERET BATYAH
Kiryat Eliezer (dist., Isr.) **7:**1139
– *illus:*
– – civic and commercial center **11:**893
KIRYAT GAT (tn., Isr.) **10:**1055
– statistics **1:**place list
– sugar industry **15:**488
– *illus:*
– – afforestation project **9:**786
– – Lachish district planning diagram **9:**562
– – textile factory **9:**817
– – view from west **9:**574
KIRYAT-ḤAROSHET (vill., Isr.) **10:**1056
– statistics **1:**place list
Kiryat ha-Yovel (sub., Jer.)
– development **9:**1496
– Hadassah Community Center **9:**985
– topography **9:**1515
Kiryat Ḥayyim (tn., Isr.)
– Chaim Arlosoroff **3:**471
– Haifa **7:**1138
– historical survey **9:**345
– housing **9:**563
– human geography **9:**580
Kiryati Brigade (mil. unit) **9:**363
– Haganah **7:**1073
– War of Independence **16:**310
KIRYAT MAL'AKHI (tn., Isr.) **10:**1056
– religious controversy **9:**399
– statistics **1:**place list
Kiryat Mattersdorf (sub., Jer.) **9:**1495; **9:**899
Kiryat Menaḥem (sub., Jer.) **9:**1496
Kiryat Moshe (sub., Jer.) **9:**1472; **9:**1519
KIRYAT MOTZKIN (tn., Isr.) **10:**1056
– Haifa **7:**1138
– housing **9:**563
– Israel **9:**580
– statistics **1:**place list
KIRYAT ONO (tn., Isr.) **10:**1056
– statistics **1:**place list
Kiryat Satia (vill., Er. Isr.) **12:**317
Kiryat Sefer (vill., Isr.), *see* BEN SHEMEN
Kiryat Sefer (period.), *see* KIRJATH SEPHER
Kiryat Sefer (bk., Meiri) **16:**1476
Kiryat Sefer (bibl., Bartolocci) **4:**265
Kiryat Sefer, Bibliotheca Hebraica Post-Mendelssohniana (bk.) **4:**972
KIRYAT SHEMONAH (tn., Isr.) **10:**1057
– statistics **1:**place list
– *illus:*
– – text
– – general view **9:**577
Kiryat Shemuel (qtr., Tiberias) **15:**1133
– *illus:* **14:**39
Kiryat Shemuel (qtr., Jer.) **9:**1472
KIRYAT TIV'ON (tn., Isr.) **10:**1057
– statistics **1:**place list
– *see also:* TIVON
Kiryat Tsanz (tn., Isr.), *see* Kiryat Zanz
KIRYAT YAM (tn., Isr.) **10:**1058
– Haifa **7:**1138
– Israel **9:**580
– statistics **1:**place list
Kiryat Ye'arim (educ. center, Isr.) **16:**864
Kiryat Yismaḥ Moshe (tn., Isr.) **9:**899
Kiryat Yovel (Jer. sub.), *see* Kiryat ha-Yovel
Kiryat Zanz (tn., Isr.) **9:**542; **9:**899
KIRZHNITZ, ABRAHAM **10:**1058
Kiš, Danilo **16:**890
Kisā'ī, Al- (11th cent., writ.) **4:**931
KISCH (fam., Br.) **10:**1059
KISCH (fam., Prague) **10:**1059
Kisch, Abraham **10:**1059; **11:**1329
KISCH, ALEXANDER **10:**1060
KISCH, BRUNO ZECHARIAS **10:**1060
Kisch, Cecil **10:**1059
Kisch, Daniel Montagu **10:**1059; **13:**1058; **15:**1340
KISCH, EGON ERWIN **10:**1061
Kisch, Enoch Heinrich **10:**1059
KISCH, FREDERICK HERMANN **10:**1061
– Zionist Congress **16:**1172
– Zionist executive **16:**1082ff
– *illus:*
– – Amery, Leopold **2:**833
KISCH, GUIDO **10:**1062
Kisch, Hermann Michael **10:**1059
Kisch, Joseph **10:**1059
Kisel, Dovid, *see* KASSEL, DAVID
KISH (bib. fig.) **10:**1063
– Saul **14:**909
Kish (city, Mesop.) **13:**312; **16:**1340,1485ff
KISHINEV (city, Mold.) **10:**1063
– *Contents:*
– – Persecutions and Pogroms **10:**1064
– – 1914-1939 **10:**1066
– – Holocaust Period **10:**1068
– – Contemporary Period **10:**1068
– history chart **8:**766-767
– Krushevan, Pavolaki **10:**1281
– Plehve, Vyacheslav von **13:**644
– pogroms **8:**735; **13:**697
– self-defense **14:**1124
– *illus:*
– – text
– – some of the pogrom victims **8:**735
– *see also:* BESSARABIA
Kishinev Program (Zion. platform) **16:**971
Kishkis (fam., Lith.) **10:**864
KISHON (riv., Isr.) **10:**1069
– Haifa **7:**1139
– physiography **9:**128; **9:**148
– port **9:**580
– *illus:*
– – text
– – fishing vessels **9:**786
KISHON, EPHRAIM **10:**1070
– *illus:*
– – *Sallah Shabbati* **12:**457
Kishon Valley **9:**215
Kishont, Ferenc (writ.), *see* KISHON, EPHRAIM
Kishu'im (*Kishut*), *see* CUCUMBER
Kis Lap (newsp.) **2:**342
KISLEV (Heb. month) **10:**1070
– *illus:* text
– *see also:* CALENDAR
Kislev, Fifteenth of (minor fest.) **8:**444
Kislev, Nineteenth of (minor fest.) **10:**883
– ḥasidic holiday **14:**1433ff
Kislev, Twentieth of (minor fest.) **8:**444
KISLING, MOISE **10:**1071
– *illus:* text
Kismarjai Weszelin, Pál **8:**41
Kismarton (city, Aus.), *see* EISENSTADT
Kiss, Arnold **4:**1449; **16:**117
– homiletic literature **8:**957
– translations **4:**884
Kiss, Gershon **13:**136
KISS, JÓZSEF **10:**1072
– Hungarian literature **8:**1081
– Kóbor, Tamás **10:**1122
KISS AND KISSING **10:**1073
– *mezuzah* **11:**1477
– *illus:* text
Kisse ha-Kavod, *see* THRONE OF GOD
Kisselhoff, Sussman **15:**57
Kisse Melekh (bk.) **4:**1545
Kisse shel Eliyahu, *see* ELIJAH, CHAIR OF
Kisse ve-Ippodromin shel Shelomo ha-Melekh (wk.) **16:**1517
Kissin, Y. **16:**822
KISSINGEN (tn., Ger.) **10:**1075
– *illus:* text
KISSINGER, HENRY ALFRED **10:**1076
– politics **13:**822
Kissman, J. **10:**89
Kiss of God, *see Mitah bi-neshikah*
KISSUFIM (kib., Isr.) **10:**1076
– statistics **1:**place list
KISTARCSA (transit camp, Hung.) **10:**1076
Kistemaeckers, Henry Hubert **7:**147
Kister, M. J. **12:**1461
KISVARDA (tn., Hung.) **10:**1077
– *illus:* text
Kitāb al-Af'āl al-Mushtaqqa min al-Asmā' (wk.) **16:**1358,1383
Kitāb al-Af'āl Dhawāt al-Mithlayn (wk.) **16:**1356,1381
Kitāb al-Af'āl Dhawāt Ḥuruf al-Līn (wk.) **16:**1356,1381
Kitāb al-Amānāt wa-al-I'tqādāt (wk.), *see Emunot ve-Deot*
Kitab al-Bayan (wk.) **15:**797
Kitāb al-Ḥaqā'iq (bk.) **16:**745
Kitāb al-Ḥāwī (wk.) **16:**1365,1381
Kitāb al-Ḥujja (wk., Samuel ha-Nagid) **16:**1357,1382
Kitābal-Hujja wa-al-Dalīl fī Nasr al-Dīn al Dhalil (wk., Judah Halevi), *see Kuzari*
Kitāb al-Ḥulf (bk.) **16:**1472ff
Kitāb al-Ishārāt (wk.) **4:**222
Kitabal-Isrā'īliyyāt (wk.) **16:**242
Kitāb al-Istīfā' (wk.) **16:**1357,1382
Kitāb al-Istighnā' (wk.) **16:**1357,1382
Kitāb al-Kāfī fi-al-Lugha al-'Ibrāniyya (wk.) **16:**1381
Kitāb al-Luma' (wk.) **16:**1357
Kitāb al-Mirāth (wk.) **14:**741
Kitāb al-Muḥaḍara wa-al-Mudhākara (wk.) **8:**1171; **16:**1362
Kitāb al-Mushtamil 'alā . . . (wk.) **16:**1365,1381
Kitāb al-Mustalḥaq (wk.) **16:**1357ff
Kitāb al-Muwāzana bayn . . . (wk.) **16:**1358,1383
Kitāb al-Qawanīn li Irshād al-Muta'illimīn (wk.) **16:**1386
Kitab al-Sab'īn Lafẓa al-Mufrada (wk.) **16:**1356,1379
Kitāb al-Sumūm wa-al-Mutaharriz min al-Ádwiya al-Qitala (wk.) **11:**779
Kitāb al-Ṭabbākh (wk.) **2:**179; **14:**749; **14:**754; **14:**755
Kitāb al-Tadhkīr wa al-Ta'nīth (wk.) **16:**1357,1383
Kitāb al-Tajnīs (wk.) **16:**1358,1382
Kitāb al-Tanqīḥ (wk., Ibn Janaḥ) **16:**1357,1382
Kitāb al-Tanqīṭ (wk., Ḥayyuj) **16:**1381
Kitab al-Ta'rīkh (wk.) **14:**754
Kitāb al-Tasārīf (wk.) **16:**1357,1382
Kitāb al-Tashwīr (wk.) **16:**1357,1381
Kitāb al-Taswi'a (wk.) **16:**1357,1381

Kitāb al-Tawṭi'a (wk.) **16:** 1384
Kitāb al-ʿUqūd fī . . . (wk.) **16:** 1381
Kitāb al-Uṣūl (wk., Ibn Janaḥ) **16:** 1357ff, 1382
Kitāb al-Uṣūl wa al-Fusūl fi al-Lugha al-ʿIbrāniyya (wk., Abu al-Faraj) **16:** 1364
Kitāb Faṣīḥ lughat al-ʿIbrāniyyīn (wk.) **16:** 1431
Kitāb Ḥurūf al-Maʿānī (wk.) **16:** 1358, 1383
Kitāb Jāmiʿ al-Alfāz (wk.) **2:** 600; **16:** 1356, 1380
Kitāb Maʿānī al-Nafs (wk.) **4:** 103
Kitāb Uṣūl al-Shiʿr al-ʿIbrānī (wk.), *see Sefer ha-Agron*
Kitchener, Lord **11:** 931
Kitchener-Waterloo (tn., Ont.) **12:** 1408
KITE (bird) **10:** 1078
- dietary laws **6:** 34
KITEL (litur. garment) **10:** 1079
- dew **5:** 1603
- folklore **6:** 1392
- marriage **11:** 1036
- rain **13:** 1524
- *illus:*
- - belt buckle for (1821) **5:** 1381
Kitev (tn., Rus.), *see* KUTY
Kition (city, Cyprus) **10:** 1080; **14:** 1506
Kitniyyot, *see* LEGUMES
Kitor (city, Sheba) **13:** 1424
Kitover, Gershon, *see* ABRAHAM GERSHON OF KUTOW
Kitover, Yakar ben Abraham Gershon **4:** 1523
KITSEE, ISADOR **8:** 1432
KITTEL, RUDOLPH **10:** 1079
Kitti (city, Cyprus), *see* Kition
KITTIM (loc., people) **10:** 1080
- Arad temple **3:** 249
- Phoenicia **13:** 478
- Qumran texts **13:** 332
- Yaḥad community **16:** 702
Kittsee (tn., Aus.) **4:** 1511; **7:** 112
KITTSEE, ḤAYYIM BEN ISAAC **10:** 1082
- Alberti-Irsa **2:** 532
KITTSEE, JEHIEL MICHAEL BEN SAMUEL **10:** 1082
Kitvei ha-Universitah (journ.) **1:** newsp. list
Kitwe (tn., Zambia) **16:** 922
Kitz, Leonard **7:** 1191; **11:** 998
KITZINGEN (city, Ger.) **10:** 1083
Kitzler, N. **5:** 453
Kiviat, Abel **12:** 1375; **15:** 316
Kivrat ereẓ (meas.) **16:** 378
Kivyakhol (rab. term) **3:** 55
Kiyum Publishing House (Arg.) **10:** 658
Kiyyum (period.) **16:** 727
Kiẓẓur Or Zaru'a (bk.) **7:** 1509
Kiẓẓur Shulḥan Arukh (bk.) **7:** 314
Kizzuwatna (anc. kdm.) **16:** 1498
Kjellgren, Josef **14:** 931
K. J. V. (orgn., Ger.), *see* KARTELL JUEDISCHER VERBINDUNGEN
K. K. L., *see* JEWISH NATIONAL FUND
Klaar, Alfred **7:** 451
KLABIN (fam., Braz.) **10:** 1084
Klabin, Berta **10:** 1085
Klabin, Jenny **14:** 1108
Klabin, Mauricio **10:** 1084
KLACZKO, JULIAN (Judah) **10:** 1085
Klaczko, Mordecai, *see* KLATZKO, MORDECAI BEN ASHER
Klaczko, P. G. **5:** 454
Klaermann, Bernát, *see* KARACSONY, BENÖ
KLAGENFURT (city, Aus.) **10:** 1085
Klagsbald, Victor **5:** 311
Klai, J., *see* Clajus, Johannes
KLAIDMAN, STEPHEN **1:** 32
Klaipeda (tn., Lith.), *see* MEMEL
Klajn, Hugo **16:** 889
Klaksbald, A. **12:** 1272
Klamath (Ind. tribe, N. Am.) **15:** 66
KLANG, HEINRICH **10:** 1086
Klaperman, Lilly M. **5:** 451
KLAPPER, PAUL **10:** 1086
KLAR, BENJAMIN MENAḤEM **10:** 1087
- linguistic literature **16:** 1377
Klarman, Yosef **16:** 863
KLARWEIN, JOSEPH **3:** 364
- *illus:*
- Knesset building **3:** 354; **10:** 1112
Klatchkin, Raphael, *see* Klatzkin, Raphael
KLATOVY (Klattau; tn., Cz.) **10:** 1087
- Holocaust **5:** 1199
KLATZKIN, ELIJAH BEN NAPHTALI HERZ **10:** 1088
Klatzkin, Israel Issar **10:** 1088
KLATZKIN, JACOB **10:** 1088
- redemption **14:** 9
Klatzkin, Joshua Mordecai **10:** 1088
Klatzkin, Raphael **16:** 212
- *illus:*
- - in *Genesis* **15:** 1063
KLATZKO, MORDECAI BEN ASHER **10:** 1090
Klauber, Isaac, of Posen **10:** 375
Klaus, Kloyz (ḥas. prayer house) **15:** 584; **15:** 606
- Kabbalah **10:** 554
- yeshivot **16:** 766
- *see also:* BET (HA)-MIDRASH
Klaus, Philip W. **14:** 162
Klausenburg (city, Rum.), *see* CLUJ
Klausenburger Rebbe, *see* Halberstam, Yekuthiel Judah
Klausenburg-Sandz Ḥasidim **7:** 1399
KLAUSNER, ABRAHAM **10:** 1090
- Aaron of Neustadt **2:** 22
- Israel of Krems **9:** 1071
- *minhagim* books **12:** 28
KLAUSNER, ISRAEL **10:** 1091
Klausner, Jacob **10:** 1096
KLAUSNER, JOSEPH GEDALIAH **10:** 1091
- *Contents:*
- - Life **10:** 1091
- - Literary Criticism and Philology **10:** 1092
- - Literary History **10:** 1093
- - Revival of Hebrew **10:** 1094
- - History of Christianity **10:** 1094
- - As a Historian **10:** 1095
- - As a Zionist **10:** 1095
- Berdyczewski, Micha **4:** 594
- critic **5:** 1120
- *Ha-Shilo'ah* **7:** 1368
- Hebrew literature **8:** 178
- historiography **8:** 562
- *illus:*
- - F.Z.C. **16:** 1165
- - Hebrew writers with **8:** 193
Klausner, M. A. **4:** 876
Klausner, Mordecai Isaac **10:** 1096
Klausner, Ze'ev Wolf **10:** 1096
KLAUSNER, ẒEVI HIRSCH **10:** 1096
Klaus Synagogue (Prague) **13:** 969
- *illus:*
- - exhibition of Jewish ritual objects **13:** 973
- - interior **15:** 605
Klavan, Hillel **16:** 357
KLAVAN, ISRAEL **10:** 1096
- Rabbinical Council **13:** 1462
- *illus:*
- - Rabbinical Council of America **13:** 1462
Klazki, Issachar Baer, *see* ISSACHAR BAER BEN SOLOMON ZALMAN
Klebanov, Y. **13:** 1597
Kleck (tn., Belor.), *see* KLETSK
KLEE, ALFRED **10:** 1096
- Auerbach, Israel **3:** 847
- Juedische Volkspartei **10:** 464
Klee, Hans **13:** 1049
Klee, Paul **13:** 115
KLEEREKOPER, ASSER BENJAMIN **10:** 1097
- Holland **6:** 320
Kleerekoper, Isaiah **10:** 1097
Kleiber, Erich **12:** 685
Kleiman, Abraham **14:** 891
KLEIN, ABRAHAM MOSES **10:** 1097
Klein, Agnes, *see* KELETI, ÁGNES
KLEIN, ALBERTO **8:** 1432
Klein, Benjamin **15:** 445
Klein, Ed (bsmn.) **8:** 1050
KLEIN, EDWARD E. (r.) **10:** 1098
Klein, E. F. (judge) **11:** 1334
Klein, Ernest (chess pl.) **5:** 406
Klein, Esther **13:** 375
Klein, Franjo (Francis) **16:** 917
Klein, Franz **12:** 1122
KLEIN, GOTTLIEB **10:** 1099
- Sweden **15:** 547
Klein, Henry, *see* AVIDOV, ZVI
KLEIN, HYMAN **10:** 1099
KLEIN, ISAAC **10:** 1100
Klein, Jacob **10:** 1103
Klein, Joseph (Hung.) **4:** 112
Klein, Joseph (U.S.) **16:** 633
KLEIN, JULIUS (sol.) **10:** 1100
KLEIN, JULIUS LEOPOLD (plwrt.) **10:** 1100
Klein, J. W. (r.) **8:** 957
Klein, K. **4:** 1428
Klein, Martin **16:** 1022
KLEIN, MELANIE REIZES **10:** 1101
Klein, Milton **13:** 810
Klein, Mordechai, *see* Klein, Martin
KLEIN, MORITZ **10:** 1101
- Zrenjanin **16:** 1224
Klein, Moses **10:** 1103
KLEIN, PHILIP (r.) **10:** 1101
KLEIN, PHILIP (soc. wkr.) **10:** 1102
Klein, Phinehas Ḥayyim **10:** 1103
Klein, Robert **13:** 972
KLEIN, SALOMON WOLF **10:** 1102
- Alsace **2:** 756
KLEIN, SAMUEL (hist.) **10:** 1102
- Mesopotamia **16:** 1509
KLEIN, SAMUEL SHMELKA (r.) **10:** 1103
- Weiss, Joseph **16:** 414
Klein, Samy **2:** 757; **15:** 425
Klein, Shalom **10:** 1103
Klein, Stanislaus **11:** 1204
KLEIN, WILHELM **10:** 1103
- archaeology **3:** 301
Klein, William **13:** 484
Kleinbaum, Moshe, *see* SNEH, MOSHE
Kleinberg, Eleazar **11:** 120
Kleiner, Juliusz **13:** 803
Kleinman, Mór, *see* KÁRMÁN, MÓR
KLEINMANN, MOSHE **10:** 1104
- *illus:*
- - with ḥalutzim in Constantinople **14:** 465
Kleinwardein (tn., Hung.), *see* KISVARDA
Klemm, J. C. **8:** 41
Klemm, J. F. **8:** 41
KLEMPERER, GUTMANN (Gumper) **10:** 1104
KLEMPERER, OTTO **10:** 1105
KLEMPERER, PAUL **10:** 1105
Klemperer, Victor **7:** 451
Klenbart, Hanan J., *see* AYALTI, HANAN J.
Klepetar, Otto **13:** 973
Klepfish, Motele **10:** 1106
KLEPFISH, SAMUEL ZANVIL **10:** 1106
- Kahana, Solomon **10:** 681
Klerksdorp (tn., Transvaal) **15:** 1340
Klesmer, Asaph, *see* COHEN, FRANCIS LYON
KLETSK (tn., Belor.) **10:** 1106
- *illus:*
- - text
- - Ha-Shomer ha-Ẓa'ir Lag ba-Omer parade **16:** 1131
KLETZKI, PAUL **12:** 695
Kletzkin, Buris **16:** 148
KLEY, EDUARD (Israel) **10:** 1108
- homiletic literature **8:** 956
Klezmerim (music) **12:** 631, 678ff
- *mus. notations:*
- - characteristics of early music **12:** 633
- - international dance tunes **12:** 597, 599
KLIBANSKY, RAYMOND **10:** 1108
Kligier, M. **11:** 435; **11:** 436
KLIGLER, ISRAEL JACOB **10:** 1108
- health services **9:** 991
- medicine **11:** 1203
Klineberg, Otto **13:** 1345
Klingenfuss (Nazi crim.) **12:** 956
Klinger, Aaron **10:** 287
Klinov, Y. **13:** 1598
KLINTSY (city, Rus.) **10:** 1109
Klober, Isaac **11:** 580
KLODAWA (tn. Pol.) **10:** 1109
Kloetzel, C. Z. **5:** 452
Kloiz, *see* BET (HA-)MIDRASH
Klonowicz, Sebastian Fabian **13:** 799
Klooga (concen. camp) **6:** 917
Klopfer, Bruno **13:** 1345
Klopfer, Donald **5:** 312; **13:** 1371
Kloppenburgh, J. **8:** 41
Klopper (fam.) **10:** 1104
KLOSTERNEUBURG (tn. Aus.) **10:** 1110
KLOTZ, LOUIS-LUCIEN **10:** 1110
Kluger, Abraham Benjamin **10:** 1111
KLUGER, SOLOMON BEN JUDAH AARON **10:** 1110
- Aryeh Leib ben Elijah **3:** 668
- Nathanson, Joseph **12:** 867
Klugman, N. **16:** 1165
KLUMEL, MEIR **10:** 1111
KLUTZNICK, PHILIP MORRIS **10:** 1111
Klutznick Exhibit Hall (Wash., D.C.) **16:** 358
Knaanic (J. lang.) **16:** 795
Knafo, Masʿud **12:** 213; **12:** 340
Knapheys, M. **16:** 819
Knappertsbusch, Hans **4:** 517
Knasmal (engagement meal) **4:** 756
KNEFLER, FREDERICK **11:** 1551; **11:** 1574
- Indianapolis **8:** 1362
Kner, Imre **13:** 1369
Kner, Izidor **13:** 1369
Knesset Tifereth Israel Synagogue (N.Y.) **15:** 626
KNESSET (Parliament, Isr.) **10:** 1112
- *Contents:*
- - Elections **10:** 1113
- - Organization **10:** 1114
- - Knesset and the Government **10:** 1115
- - Legislative Process **10:** 1115
- - Members and their Prerogatives **10:** 1116
- - Building **10:** 1116
- Arab members **9:** 1030ff

- Chagall 5:323
- Defense Forces 9:690
- first elections 9:372
- history chart 8:766–767
- Jerusalem 9:1484; 9:1492
- legislature 9:650ff
- library 11:195
- Luz, Kadish 11:593
- *menorah* 11:1370
- place in governmental system 9:614ff
- religious parties 9:895
- women 16:628
- *illus:*
- - Druze members 9:925
- - gobelin tapestry by M. Chagall 5:*fcg.* 334
- - Meir, Golda, declaration of allegiance 9:618
- - mosaic wall by M. Chagall 5:323
- - night view of building 3:354
- - Prime Minister's Conference of Jewish Leaders 9:405
- - Weizmann addressing 16:433
- *tables:*
- - Agudat Israel representation 2:425
- - N.R.P. representation 12:881
- - results of elections, 1949–69 9:667
- *see also:* POLITICAL LIFE AND PARTIES IN ISRAEL

Knesset ha-Gedolah (anc. assembly), *see* SYNAGOGUE, THE GREAT
Knesset Yisrael (annual), *see Keneset Yisrael*
KNIEZA, EMIL 5:1210
Knights of Mary Phagan (anti-Sem. orgn.) 7:74
Knights of Zion (U.S.) 16:1141
Knipe, Thomas 8:41
Knoblauch (tn., Ger.) 8:1043
Knoblauch, Joseph ben Moses 16:504
Knobloch, Johann 15:424
Knochen, Helmuth 13:110; 16:296
- *illus:*
- - Paris war crimes trial 16:301

Knock, Dr., *see* DORIAN, EMIL
Knollys, Manserd 8:41
Knoodweed (bot.) 13:619
KNOPF, ALFRED A. 10:1116
Knopf, Alfred A., Jr. 10:1117
Knopf, Blanche Wolf 10:1117
KNORR VON ROSENROTH, CHRISTIAN 10:1117
- alchemic writings 2:545; 2:546
- Christian Kabbalah 10:645
- Hebraist 8:41
- Zohar translation 16:1214
- *illus:*
- - Kabbala Denudata (17th cent.) 10:558

Knowledge
- man's use 11:845
- Philo 13:427
- providence 13:1284, 1285
- Saadiah Gaon 14:549
- Spinoza 15:280
- Torah 15:1240ff
- wisdom literature 16:561
- *see also:* STUDY

Knowlles, Richard 8:41
Knox, Ronald A. 4:871
Knoxville (city, Tenn.) 15:1009
Knucklebones (game) 7:300
Ko'ah Hadash (journ.) 1:newsp. list
Kobak, Joseph 4:149; 16:1328
- *Jeschurun* 8:557; 10:1

KOBAYASHI, MASAYUKI 10:1118
KOBE (city, Jap.) 10:1118
- Japan 9:1281

KOBER, ADOLF 10:1119
KOBER, ARTHUR 15:1582
Koberger Bible (15th cent. illum. print., Nuremberg) 4:787, 874; 8:473
Kobersdorf (tn., Aus.) 4:1511
KOBIELSKI, FRANCISZEK ANTONI 10:1119
KOBLENZ (city, Ger.) 10:1120
- slave trade 14:1662

KOBLER, FRANZ 10:1122
- anthologies of letters 11:62

Kobo, David Isaac 5:627
KOBOR, TAMAS 10:1122
KOBRIN (city, Belor.) 10:1122
Kobrin, Aaron of 10:1125
Kobrin, David Solomon of 10:1125
KOBRIN, LEON 10:1124
- Shakespearean elements 14:1265
- theater 15:1069

Kobrin, Moses Aaron of 10:1125
KOBRIN, MOSES BEN ISRAEL POLIER OF 10:1124
Kobrin, Noah Naphtali of 10:1125
Kobrin, R. M. 15:778
KOBRIN, SOLOMON 5:1110; 5:1112
Kobryń (city, Pol.), *see* KOBRIN
Koc, Adam 12:1540
Koch, Erich 4:807
Koch, Ernst 5:85
Koch, F. C. 8:41
Koch, Hal 5:1539
Koch, Hirsch 16:515
Koch, Johannes, *see* COCCEIUS, JOHANNES
Koch, Karl 4:1442; 11:794
KOCH, KENNETH 15:1578; 15:1582
- New York City 12:1121

Koch, Richard 14:301
Koch, Robert 8:325
Koch, Simon 14:928
Kochanowski, Jan 4:885; 10:1375; 13:798
Kocherginski, S., *see* KACZERGINSKY, SHMERL
Kochhaff, David, *see* Chytraeus, David
Kochowski, Wespazjan 13:798
Kochubiyevski, Boris 10:998
KOCK (Kotsk; tn., Pol.) 10:1125
- Hasidism 7:1400

Kock, Menahem Mendel of, *see* KOTSK, MENAHEM MENDEL OF
Kocsi Csergo, Istvan 8:40
Kocsi, Major, Ferenc 8:40
Kocsi Sebestyén, István 8:40
Koczan, Mor, *see* Kovacs, Mor
Kodály, Zoltán 12:699
KODASHIM (Mish. order) 10:1126
- *illus:* text

"Kodashim" (mural, H. Lerner) 10:1126
Kodashim kalim (sacrifices) 14:608
KODER, SAMUEL SHABDAI 10:1127
Koder, Shabdai Samuel 10:1127
Kodesh ha-Kodashim, see Holy of Holies
Kodícek, Josef 5:1209; 13:1026
Kodshei kodashim (sacrifices) 14:608
KOEBNER, RICHARD 10:1127
Koecher, H. F. 8:40
Koegel, Max 11:794; 13:1583
Koehler, Ludwig 16:1400
Koellner, Johann 7:91
Koeln (city, Ger.), *see* COLOGNE
Koenig, Abraham 10:1502
KOENIG, GHISHA 3:604
- *illus:*
- - "Fettling Shop I" (rlf.) 3:634

Koenig, Julian 2:318
KOENIG, LEO 10:1128
Koenig, Marie-Pierre 7:42
Koenig, Rafael 12:85
Koenig, Samuel S. 12:1111; 13:822
KOENIGSBERG (city, Rus.) 10:1128
- archives 3:387
- committee for refugees 2:650
- Epstein, Aryeh Leib 6:825
- Prussia 13:1287
- university 15:1677

KOENIGSBERG, DAVID 10:1130
KOENIGSBERG, MOSES 10:1130
- King Features Syndicate 5:215

Koenigsberg, Solomon 6:330
Koenigsberger (bnk.) 4:176
KOENIGSBERGER, BERNHARD (Barukh) 10:1130
Koenigsberger, L. 15:669
Koenigsdorf, Richard H. 10:741
Koenigswart (tn., Cz.) 15:607
KOENIGSWARTER (fam.) 10:1131
- nobility 15:1166

Koenigswarter, Heinrich 10:1131
Koenigswarter, Hermann Freiherr von 10:1131
Koenigswarter, Jonas Freiherr von 10:1131
Koenigswarter, Jonas Hirsch 10:1131
Koenigswarter, Josephine 10:1131
Koenigswarter, Karl Wilhelm 10:1131
Koenigswarter, Leopold 10:1131; 13:1518
Koenigswarter, Louis Jean 10:1131
Koenigswarter, Marcus 10:1131
Koenigswarter, Maximilian 10:1131
Koenigswarter, Moritz 10:1131
Koenigswarter, Moritz, Baron von 10:1131
Koenigswarter, Simon 10:1131
Koepfel, Wolfgang Fabricius, *see* CAPITO, WOLFGANG FABRICIUS
Koepniwsky, David 15:408
Koeppen, N. 8:40
KOERNER, MOSES BEN ELIEZER PHOEBUS 10:1132
- Breslau 4:1355

KOESTLER, ARTHUR 10:1132
- Sperber, Manès 15:261

Koethen (city, Ger.) 3:1
KOF (Heb. let.) 10:1133
- masorah 16:1409

Kofer, see RANSOM
Kofer be-ikkar, see HERESY
Kofer ha-Yishuv (tax, Er. Isr.) 5:854; 7:1069; 9:352
- *illus:*
- - coupons 9:355

KOFFKA, KURT 10:1133
Koffler, Camilla 13:485
Kofler, Leo 15:64
Kofler, Solomon 5:119
KOGAN, ABRAHAM 10:1134
Kogan, David, *see* KAHANA, DAVID
Kogan, Elizabeth 10:1135
Kogan, L. (polit.) 11:385
KOGAN, LEONID BORISSOVICH (mus.) 10:1134
KOGAN, MOYSE 10:1135
- Parisian art 13:117
- *illus:* text

Kogan, Pavel 10:1135
Kohanim (Kohanites), *see* AARONIDES
KOHATH AND KOHATHITES (bib. figs.) 10:1135
- Ark 10:1137
- Elkanah 6:676
- Gibbethon 7:549
- Korahites 10:1191ff

Kohelet (bk., hagiographa), *see* ECCLESIASTES
Kohelet (journ.) 1:newsp. list
KOHELETH MUSSAR (period.) 10:1137
- Hebrew newspapers 12:1045; 12:1047
- statistics 1:newsp. list

Kohelet Rabbah (agg. Midrash), *see* ECCLESIASTES RABBAH
Kohelet Zuta (wk.) 16:1515
Kohen, see PRIESTS AND PRIESTHOOD
Kohen (fam. name), *see also* Cohen, Cohn; Kagan; Kahan; Kahana; Kahn; Katz; Kohn
KOHEN (fam. print.) 10:1138
- printing 13:1095

Kohen, Aaron (Prague) 10:1139
Koehn, Aaron bet Elijah (Ger.) 13:1106
Kohen, Abraham (r., Lvov) 11:612
Kohen, Abraham Hayyim (kab.) 11:696
KOHEN, ALBERT 10:313
Kohen, Benjamin (r., It.) 14:1245
Kohen, Benjamin (publ.) 4:864
Kohen, Bezalel 10:1138
Kohen, David 10:11391
KOHEN, ELEAZAR BEN ZE'EV WOLF 10:1139
Kohen, Elijah 14:1495
Kohen, Gershom ben Bezalel 13:976
Kohen, Gershom ben Solomon ha- 10:1138
- books 4:1235
- Gersonides 13:967; 13:976
- *haggadah* 2:258; 7:1079
- Shahor family 14:1260
- typography 15:1481
- *illus:*
- - *Prague Haggadah* (1526) 3:535; 13:1101

Kohen, Gronem (Jerome) 4:1235; 7:1101; 10:1138
- *illus:*
- - *Prague Haggadah* (1526) 13:1101

Kohen, Herman, *see* Kohen, Gershom ben Solomon ha-
Kohen, Isaiah, see PYRRHUS, DIDACUS
Kohen, Israel 10:1139
Kohen, Jacob ben Jacob 10:613
Kohen, Jeremiah 14:1495
Kohen, Joseph Daniel 5:627
Kohen, Joshua 10:1139
Kohen, Judah 10:1138
Kohen, Leo 4:1493
Kohen, Michael 11:1566
Kohen, Mordecai 10:1138
Kohen, Moses (16th cent.) 10:1138
Kohen, Moses (16/17th cent.) 10:1139; 13:976
Kohen, Moses (17th cent.) 10:1139
Kohen, Moses (r., Fr.) 12:831
Kohen, Moses (r., Isr.) 13:1092
Kohen, Moses Judah ben Kalonymus (Leib Harif) 11:450
KOHEN, RAPHAEL BEN JEKUTHIEL SUESSKIND 10:1139
- Berlin, Saul 4:663
- *haskamah* 7:1454

Kohen, Sami 10:313
Kohen, Solomon 10:1138
Kohen, Zevi Hirsch 10:1140
Kohen ha-Resha, see WICKED PRIEST
Kohen ha-Rosh (chief pr.) 9:1320
Kohen-Solal (fam.), *see* SOLAL
Kohen-Solal, Abraham 15:92
Kohen-Solal, David 15:91
Kohen-Solal, Hayyim 15:92
Kohen-Solal, Nathan, 15:92
Kohen-Solal, Nathan ben Hayyim 15:92
Kohen-Solal, Moses ben Isaac 15:92
Kohen-Solal, Nissim 15:92
KOHEN-ZEDEK, JOSEPH 10:1140
Kohen Zedek, Moses 5:739
Kohen-Zedek, Solomon 10:437;

15:906
KOHEN-ZEDEK BAR IVOMAI (bar Ikhumai gaon) 10:1141
- gaonate families 7:322
KOHEN ZEDEK OF PUMBEDITA (bar Joseph: gaon) 10:1141
- gaonate 7:317
- Musbashir 12:497
- Saadiah Gaon 14:545ff
Kohl, Max 11:1589
KOHLBACH, BERTALAN 10:1141
KOHLER, KAUFMANN 10:1142
- Abba title 2:31
- anti-Zionism 16:1144
- Einhorn, David 6:532
- Oral Law 12:1443
- prophecy 13:1179
- *ru'ah ha-kodesh* 14:368
KOHLER, MAX JAMES 10:1143
- historiography 8:568
Kohler, Wolfgang 10:1134
Kohn (fam. name), *see also* Cohen; Cohn; Kagan; Kahan; Kahana; Kahn; Katz; Kohen
Kohn, A. (Educ.) 7:334
Kohn, Aaron (medal.) 11:1165
KOHN, ABRAHAM (r.) 10:1144
- Bernstein, Jacob 4:686
Kohn, Abraham (polit.) 5:416 13:207
- *illus:*
- - Abraham Lincoln presentation 15:1601
Kohn, David 15:135
KOHN, EUGENE 10:1144
Kohn, Feibel 11:559
Kohn, Gustav 10:1591
KOHN, HANS 10:1144
- Bar-Kochba Association 4:228
KOHN, JACOB 10:1145
KOHN, JINDRICH 10:1145
Kohn, Josef (Bav.) 12:1279
Kohn, Joseph (Gal.) 14:1458
Kohn, Judah 11:1113
KOHN, LEO 10:1146
KOHN, MAIER 10:1146
Kohn, Moriz, *see* KAPOSI, MORITZ
Kohn, Oskar 11:426
Kohn, Otto, *see* KOMOLY, OTTO
KOHN, PINCHAS 10:1146
- Agudat Israel 2:424
- Ansbach 3:32
Kohn, Rudolph 5:1189
KOHN, SALOMON 10:1147
KOHN, SAMUEL 10:1147
- *illus:* text
Kohn, Schwerin Goetz 4:112
Kohn, Siegmund 16:1165
Kohn, S. Joshua 16:35
Kohn, Sol 10:739
KOHN, THEODOR 10:1148
Kohn, Yehudah Pinhas, *see* KOHN, LEO
Kohn, Zsigmond, *see* KUNFI, ZSIGMOND
Kohner, Adolf 15:1040
Kohner, Falk 13:665
Kohner, Heinrich 15:1040
Kohn Ḥasid, David 15:1373
Kohn-Kostelhore, Samuel 13:665
KOHS, SAMUEL CALMIN 10:1148
KOHUT (fam.) 10:1149
Kohut, Adolf 10:1151
Kohut, Alexander 10:1149
- Conservative Judaism 5:902ff
- Wise, Stephen 10:566
Kohut, George Alexander 10:1151
Kohut, Rebecca 4:776; 10:1150
KOI (animal) 10:1152
- buffalo 4:1467
KOIDANOV (ḥas. dynasty) 10:1152
- Dynasties 1:ḥas. table
Koidanov, Aaron 10:1152
Koidanov, Abraham Aaron, of Pukhovichi 10:1152
Koidanov, Baruch Mordecai 10:1152
Koidanov, Joseph 10:1153
Koidanov, Nehemiah 10:1153
Koidanov, Noah 10:1152
Koidanov, Shalom (Belor.) 10:1153; 10:1340
Koidanov, Shalom Alter (Pol.) 10:1153
Koidanov, Solomon Ḥayyim of 10:1152; 10:1340
Koidanovo (ḥas. dynasty), *see* KOIDANOV
KOIDANOVO (tn., Belor.) 10:1153
- Baranovichi 4:197
KOIDONOVER, AARON SAMUEL BEN ISRAEL 10:1153
- Ephraim ha-Kohen 6:812
- responsa 14:806
KOIDONOVER, ZEVI HIRSCH 10:1154
- ethical literature 11:345
- kabbalah 10:552
KOIGEN, DAVID 10:1155
Koine (Gr. dialect) 8:294
Koi-Sanjaq (vill., Kurd.) 10:1297
Kojeteiner (fam.) 10:1156
KOJETIN (Kojetein; tn. Morav.) 10:1155
- *illus:* text
KOJEVE, ALEXANDRE 10:1156
KOKAND (city, U.S.S.R.) 10:1156
- *see also:* BUKHARA
Kokas, Abraham 11:612
Kokas, Jacob 11:612
Kokashvili, Georgi 7:427
KOKESCH, OZER 10:1156
- Zionism 16:1107
Kokhaw (Zion., Belor.), *see* MAZEH, JACOB
Kokhav (loc., Isr.) 9:794
Kokhav (deity) 2:884
Kokhav ha-Yarden (site, Isr.), *see* AGRIPPINA
KOKHAVI, DAVID BEN SAMUEL 10:1157
- articles of faith 3:656
Kokhav Mikha'el (mosh., Isr.) 1:place list
Kokheva (J. cmty., Syr.) 5:1239
Kokhevei Yiẓhak (period.) 4:993
- Hebrew newspapers 12:1048
- statistics 1:newsp. list
- Sterc, Max Emanuel 15:390
Kokina (loc., Ukr.) 15:1330
Kokizow (Kar. fam.), *see* KUKIZOW
Kokoschka, Oskar 14:918
- *illus:*
- - Kestenberg, Leo (portrait) 10:925
- - portraits 5:580
KOKOVTSOV, PAUL KONSTANTINOVICH 10:1157
- linguistic literature 16:1376
Kokut, Joseph 10:1383
KOL, MOSHE 10:1158
Kolaba (tn., Ind.) 14:898
Kolaiah (bib. fig.) 16:964; 2:439
Kol Ami Museum (U.S.) 12:544
Kolár, Josef Jiří 5:1206
Kolar, Victor 5:1572
KOLAROVGRAD (tn., Bul.) 10:1158
Kolatch, Alfred J. 13:1377
Kolatkar, Haskelji Israel 11:1567
Kol Aẓmotai (poem) 13:600
Kolbasin (concen. camp), *see* Kelbasin
KOLBERG (city, Pol.) 10:1158
Kol-Bo (prayer bk. type) 13:987
KOL BO (hal. wk.) 10:1159
- *Orḥot Ḥayyim* 2:13
- *illus:* text
Kolbon (fee) 12:244
Kolchak, Admiral 13:700
Kölcsey, Ferenc 9:1360
Koldewey, R. 4:33
KOLDYCHEVO (Koldyczewo) CAMP (Nazi labor camp) 10:1160
KOLEL 10:1161
- *halukkah* 7:1209; 9:888ff
- in Israel 9:299; 9:898
- *yeshivot* 16:769; 16:771
- *illus:*
- - emissary, letter of appointment 7:1211-1214; 8:728
Kolel Perushim (Kovno) 16:769
Koleséri, Samuel 8:40
Kolet, Elizer 5:1346
Kol ha-Am (newsp.) 9:1016
- communism 5:808
Kol ha-No'ar (journ.) 1:newsp. list
Kol ha-Remez (wk.) 16:906
Kolhari, Isaac Aaron 5:34
Kol ha-Shabbat (journ.) 1:newsp. list
KOLIN (city, Bohem.) 10:1161
- Holocaust period 5:1199
KOLIN, SAMUEL BEN NATHAN HA-LEVI 10:1162
- Boskowitz, Benjamin 4:1263
KOLISCH, IGNAZ VON 5:408
KOLISCH, RUDOLF 12:695
KOLISCHER, HEINRICH 10:1163
Kol Israel (radio, Isr.) 15:931; 9:1017
Kol Israel Ḥaverim, *see* ALLIANCE ISRAÉLITE UNIVERSELLE
Kol Israel Orchestra (Isr.) 9:397; 15:930
Kolkhozes, Jewish 2:409
- *illus:*
- - Emes farm members 14:470
- - Soviet Jewish farmers 2:407-410
- - vine growers in Crimea 5:1107
Kol la-Am (period.) 16:1235
Kollam (port, Ind.), *see* Quilon
Kollek, Tamar 14:1023
KOLLEK, THEODORE (Teddy) 10:1163
- Jerusalem development 9:1496; 9:1498
- *illus:*
- - Kessel, Joseph, and 10:922
Kollenscher, M. 10:464
KOLLER, CARL 10:1164
KOLLONITSCH, LEOPOLD 10:1164
- Austrian Jews 3:890
Kollybistès (N.T. term) 12:244
Kol Maḥazikei ha-Dat (period.) 7:965
KOLMAN, ARNOŠT (Ernest) 10:1164
KOLMAR, GERTRUD 10:1165
KOL MEVASSER (period.) 10:1165
- Lifshits, Shiye-Mordkhe 11:237
- Zederbaum, Alexander 16:964
- *illus:* text
Kolmodin, Olaf 14:928
Kol Nekhei Milḥamah (journ.) 1:newsp. list
KOL NIDREI (litur.) 10:1166
- Academy on High 2:208
- *Aleinu le-Shabbe'aḥ* 2:559
- Hai ben Naḥshon 7:1129
- Hirsch, S. R. 8:511
- Meir of Ramerupt 11:1255
- Naḥmanides 12:780
- Naḥshon bar Zadok 12:793
- *mus. notations:*
- - text
- - *Mi-Sinai niggunim* 12:151
KOLNIK, ARTHUR 10:1169
- Parisian school 13:120
- *illus:* text
Kolno'a (journ.) 1:newsp. list
KOLO (tn., Pol.) 10:1169
- *illus:* text
Kolo (J. club) 13:749; 15:1508
KOLODEJE NAD LUZICI (vill., Cz.) 10:1170
- *illus:* text
Koloman (k., Hung.) 8:1104
KOLOMYYA (Kolomea; Kolomyja; city, Ukr.) 10:1171
- ghetto 13:768
Kolonikos (Mish. schol.), *see* Kalonymus
Kolonisations-Verein fuer Palaestina (orgn., Ger.) 11:493
Kolonist Kooperator (period.) 3:423
Kolonymus (name), *see* Kalonymus
Kolos-Vari, *see* Kolozsvari, Zsigmund
Kolosya (period.) 5:456
Kolot (period., Isr.) 16:401
Kolot (journ., Pol.) 1:newsp. list; 15:372
Kolozsvár (city, Rum.), *see* CLUJ
Kolozsvari, Zsigmund 13:117
Kol Sinai (journ.) 1:newsp. list
Kolsy, Mordecai 2:40
KOLTANOWSKI, GEORGE 10:1172
KOLTHOFF, IZAAK MAURITS 10:1172
Kol Torah Yeshivah (Jer.) 16:771
- *illus:*
- - *bet ha-midrash* 16:766
Kol Torah (journ.) 1:newsp. list
Kolvirt-Emes (period.) 10:706
Kol Ya'akov (journ.) 1:newsp. list
Kol Yisrael (journ.) 1:newsp. list
Kol Yisrael Ḥaverim, *see* ALLIANCE ISRAÉLITE UNIVERSELLE
Kol Ẓiyyon la-Golah (radio, Isr.) 9:1018; 15:930
Koma, Herz, *see* COMA, HERZ
Komai, Elijah Baruch 10:718
Komar, Julian 13:776
KOMARNO (tn., Slov.) 10:1174
KOMARNO (tn., Ukr.) 10:1173
Komárom, Woelfel of, *see* Woelfel of Komárom
KOMÁROMI CSIPKÉS, GYÖRGY 10:1174
- Hebraist 8:40
KOMAROVSKY, MIRRA 10:1175
Kombund (orgn., Rus.) 5:799; 15:48
Komedant, Avraham 12:1514
Komemiyyut (mosh., Isr.) 1:place list
Komemiyyut (wk.) 16:1152
Komemiyyut (journ.) 1:newsp. list
Komez (meas.) 16:379; 16:388
Komion al-Arab, Al- (mvmt.) 9:471ff
Komjadi, Bela 15:314
KOMLOS, ALADAR 10:1175
Komlós, O. Y. 15:659
Kommerziendirektor (Kommerzienrat), *see* COURT JEWS
KOMOLY, OTTÓ 10:1176
- Va'adat Ezrah ve-Haẓẓalah 4:1294
- Zionism 16:1122
KOMOR, ANDRÁS 8:1080; 8:1086
Komor, Paul 14:1293
Komorau (loc., Cz.) 12:1412
Komorn (tn., Slov.) *see* KOMARNO
Komotau (city, Cz.), *see* CHOMUTOV
Komotine (Komotini; city, Gr.) 7:879
- Istrumsa, Ḥayyim 9:1100
- special Purim 13:1397
KOMPERT, LEOPOLD 10:1177
- Austrian Jewry 3:887; 3:895
- Oesterreichisches Central-Organ 12:1333

KOMROFF, MANUEL 15:1582
- children's literature 5:451
Komzet (orgn., Rus.), *see* Commission for Jewish Settlement
KON, FELIKS 10:1178
Kon, Geca 13:1369; 16:888
Kon, Leib 16:496
Konar, Alfred Aleksander 13:802
Konev, I. S. 6:144
KONFINO, ŽAK 10:1178
- Yugoslav literature 16:887
Kongelige Bibliotek (library, Den.) 8:1322
Kongregacja (orgn., Pol.), *see* Jewish Religious Council
Kongressdeutsch (Zion.) 16:1167
Konice (tn., Morav.) 3:387; 8:1368
- *illus:*
- - memorial book *ḥerem* text 3:930
König, G. 8:40
Konig, Imre 5:407
König, S. 8:40
Konigsberg, Allen Stewart, *see* Allen, Woody
Konikov, Caesar 11:1558
Konim, ha- (wk.), *see Ḥibbur ha-Konim*
KONIN (tn., Pol.) 10:1179
- Auerbach, Ẓevi 3:843
Konir, Mordecai, *see* MEISEL, MORDECAI BEN SAMUEL
Konishchuk (part. ldr.) 13:146
KONITZ (tn., Pol.) 10:1180
- history chart (1900) 8:766-767
Konopnicka, Maria 13:798; 13:800
KONOTOP (city, Ukr.) 10:1180
KONSKIE (Konsk; tn., Pol.) 10:1181
KONSKOWOLA (tn., Pol.) 10:1181
Konstam, Kenneth 5:169
Konstantinis, Raphael 7:887
Konstanz (city, Ger.), *see* CONSTANCE
Konti, Isidore 11:1167
KONVITZ, MILTON RIDVAS 1:32; 10:1182
Konyosos (Doenmeh sect) 6:149ff
Koogan, Abrahão 13:1370
KOOK, ABRAHAM ISAAC 10:1182
- *Contents:*
- - Life 10:1182
- - Mysticism 10:1184
- - Modern Challenges to Judaism 10:1184
- - Social Philosophy 10:1185
- - The Sacred and the Profane 10:1185
- - Science 10:1186
- - Universalism and Nationalism 10:1186
- - Works 10:1187
- Agudat Israel 2:424
- autopsies and dissection 3:932
- courts, rabbinical 12:142
- evolution 6:1002ff
- Harlap, Jacob 7:1343
- *ḥiddushim* 8:467
- kabbalistic influence 10:643
- *Kiddush ha-Shem* 10:979
- messianism 11:1416
- nature 12:891
- Orthodox Judaism 12:1492
- peace 13:199
- philosophy 13:463
- prophecy 13:1180
- redemption 14:9
- religious life 9:890; 9:891ff
- repentance 14:77
- responsa 14:93
- revelation 14:125
- Sonnenfeld, Joseph 15:156
- soul, immortality of 15:180
- Torah and Israel 15:1243
- *geneal. table:* 9:1259
- *illus:*
- - Ḥafeẓ Ḥayyim's letter re Radun yeshivah 9:1069
- - Hebrew University, opening ceremony 8:221
- - *semikhah* granted by 14:1141
Kook, Hillel 9:1186; 16:1144
KOOK, SAUL ḤONE BEN SOLOMON ZALMAN 10:1187
- *geneal. table:* 9:1259
KOOK, ẒEVI JUDAH BEN ABRAHAM ISAAC HA-KOHEN 10:1187
Koolhaas, J. C. 8:40
Koolhaas, Willem 8:40
Ko'operaẓyah (journ.) 1:newsp. list
Koor (indus. concern) 9:862 8:540
Koordynacja (orgn., Pol.) *see* Coordination
Köpcsény (tn., Aus.), *see* Kittsee
KOPE (orgn., Rus.) 16:735
Kopel brothers (underground ldrs.) 12:1518
Kopelev, Lev 14:513
Kopelevich, Levi 4:630
Kopeliovitz, Yehudah, *see* ALMOG, YEHUDA
Kopell, Ralph 13:485
Kopelman, Leo G. 16:476
Kopelowitz, Naum 16:1165
KOPELSON, ẒEMAḤ 10:1188
KOPF, MAXIM 10:1188
Köpfel, Wolfgang Fabricius, *see* CAPITO, WOLFGANG FABRICIUS
Kophinas, Moshe 16:1243
Kopinski, Leon 5:1212
Koplewitz, Jacob, *see* KESHET, YESHURUN
KOPLIK, HENRY 10:1189
KOPMAN, BENJAMIN 3:604
- *illus:*
- - "Self Portrait" (paint.) 3:632
Kopnivski, David 13:1048
Kopp, Joseph 11:1465
Koppe, J. B. 9:45
Koppe, Wilhelm 7:637; 8:1380
Koppel, Valdemar 14:928
KOPPELMAN, JACOB BEN SAMUEL BUNIM 10:1189
Köppen, N. 8:40
Kopperl, Moritz 15:1035
Koppitt, Arthur 15:1578
KOPPLEMANN, HERMAN PAUL 10:1189
- Connecticut 5:899
Köprülü, Ahmed 14:1231
KOPS, BERNARD 10:1190
Kopsteyn, Brakhe 16:822
Kopyl (tn., Belor) 11:1317; 12:52; 14:477
Kopys (tn., Rus.) 14:477, 1436
Kor (meas.) 16:377; 16:379ff
KORAH (bib. fig.) 10:1190
- Aaron 2:6
- Aaronide-Levite struggle 2:19
- *apikoros* 3:177
- Asaph 3:673
- dispute 5:890
- Heman 8:319ff
- in the Arts 12:405f
- Moses 12:377
- priesthood 13:1082
- *illus:*
- - swallowed up by the earth 5:1311
KORAḤ, AMRAM IBN YAḤYĀ 10:1193
KORAḤ, ḤAYYIM BEN JOSEPH 10:1194
KORAḤ, SHALOM BEN YAḤYA 10:1194
KORAḤ, YAḤYA BEN SHALOM 10:1194
Korahites (Psalms) 13:1318
KORAN 10:1194
- *Contents:*
- - Literary Form 10:1195
- - Influence of Judaism on Islam 10:1196
- - Eschatology 10:1196
- - Names of God 10:1196
- - Prophetic and Narrative Material 10:1197
- - Five Pillars of Islam, Ritual Commandments, and Legal Prohibitions 10:1197
- - In Jewish Literature and the Hebrew Language 10:1199
- Adamic legend 2:241
- Arabic 3:238
- Aramaic 3:282
- Bible tales 4:929ff
- eschatology 6:883ff
- Jerusalem holiness 9:1575
- Jethro 10:20
- Kalam 13:429
- language 16:1415
- Muhammad 12:508ff
- Pharaoh 13:362
- poetry 13:682
- Queen of Sheba 13:1424
- *Yahūd* 16:703
- *illus:* text
- *see also:* ISLAM
Koranis (tn.) 7:1223
Korányi, Markus 15:1373
Korazim (tn., Er. Isr.), *see* CHORAZIN
Korban Netanel (bk.) 16:396
Korban Todah (bk.) 7:1037
KORCHNOY, VIKTOR LVOVICH 5:408
Korčula (isl., Adriatic.) 16:880
KORCZAK, JANUSZ 10:1200
- children's literature 5:455
- *Nasz Przeglad* 12:844
- Warsaw ghetto 16:348
- *illus:* text
KORDA, SIR ALEXANDER 10:1201
- Biro, Lajos 4:1044
- Cluj 15:1343
- motion pictures 12:452
Korda, Zoltan 12:452
Korea (North), People's Republic of 9:444
Korea (South), Republic of 9:444; 9:991
KOREFF, DAVID FERDINAND 10:1202
- *illus:* text
Kore ha-Dorot (bk. Cohen) 5:685
Kore ha-Dorot (bk., Conforte) 5:892; 11:349
- *illus:*
- - title page (1846) 5:892
Koren (publ. firm, Isr.) 13:1378
"Koren" (type let.) 15:1488
- *illus:*
- - Hebrew type face 15:1486
KORENE, VERA 15:1086
KORETS (tn., Ukr.) 10:1202
- *illus:* text
KORETS, PHINEHAS BEN ABRAHAM ABBA SHAPIRO OF 10:1204
- ḥasidic leader 7:1392ff
Koretz, Ẓevi 7:879; 14:705
Koritsa (city, Alb.) 2:523
Korkes, N. 10:90
KORKIS, ABRAHAM ADOLF 10:1204
- *illus:*
- - F.Z.C. 16:1165
Korman, N. D. (poet) 5:1149
Korman, N. I. (typographer) 15:1480
Korman, Samuel 15:1002
KÖRMENDI, FERENC 10:1205
Kormis, F. J. 11:1167
KORN, ARTHUR 8:1430; 8:1432
KORN, BERTRAM WALLACE 10:1205
- historical society 2:827
KORN, RACHEL 10:1205
Korn, Yiẓḥak 16:640
Kornaros (writ.) 7:887
KORNBERG, ARTHUR 10:1206
- biology 4:1032
Kornberg, F. 3:361
- *illus:*
- - National Library, Jerusalem 3:349
KORNBERG, HANS LEO 5:384
Kornbluht, Moritz 16:1165
Kornbluht, Wilhelmina 16:1165
KORNEUBURG (tn., Aus.) 10:1206
- Austrian anti-Semitism 3:888
- Host desecration 8:1043
- *illus:* text
KORNFELD, AARON BEN MORDECAI BAER 10:1207
KORNFELD, JOSEPH SAUL 10:1208
KORNFELD, PAUL 10:1208
KORNFELD, ZSIGMOND 10:1208
- bankers 4:176
- Kornfeld, Aaron 10:1208
KORNGOLD, ERICH WOLFGANG 10:1209
Korngold, Julius 10:1209
Korngold, Liber 7:6
Korngold, Z. 15:1488
Kornhaber, Adolph 11:1556
KORNIK (tn., Pol.) 10:1209
KORNIK, MEIR BEN MOSES 10:1210
Kornik, Moses ben Akiva, *see* KRONIK, MOSES BEN AKIVA
Kornitzer (r., Pol.) 5:1038
KORNITZER, LEON 10:1210
Kornjude (medal, Ger.) 11:1168
KOROBKA (tax) 10:1211
- Council of Four Lands 5:1000
- *sheḥitah* 14:1343
- *see also:* CANDLE TAX; TAXATION
Korobkoff, Hillel 16:1165
KOROLENKO, VLADIMIR GALAKTIONOVICH 10:1212
- Josephus 10:264
- Poltava 13:839
Koromla, Joseph Schey von 10:1493
KORONE (port, Gr.) 10:1213
Kororareka (loc., N. Z.) 12:1128
- *illus:*
- - view of bay 13:706
Körösi, Mihaly 8:40
Körösi, Uri Janos 8:40
KOROSTEN (city, Ukr.) 10:1213
Korot (journ.) 1:newsp. list
Korot ha-Ittim (wk.) 14:1365
Korot ha-Ittim (period.) 9:1295
Korschule (syn. Vilna) 16:146
Korsokh (period.) 12:479
KORSUN-SHEVCHENKOVSKI (city, Ukr.) 10:1213
- Haidamacks 7:1132
Kortabi, Abraham, *see* Kurtabi, Abraham
KORTNER, FRITZ 10:1213
- Germany 7:500
- theater 15:1057
Korvin, Sándor 14:673
Korzec (tn., Ukr.), *see* KORETS
Korzeń, Nathan 13:648
Korzeniowski, Józef 13:800
KOS (isl.) 10:1214
Kos (owl) 12:1530
Koš, Erih 16:889
Kosaki (concen. camp.) 16:1218
Kōsar (deity), *see* Kōshar
Kosch, Raphael 11:53
KOŚCIUSZKO, TADEUSZ 10:1214
- Joselewicz, Berek 10:201

- Polish partition **8:**715
Kosdini, Aaron ben Judah, *see* AARON BEN JUDAH KUSDINI
Kosegarten, J. G. L. **8:**40
Koshar (deity) **4:**10ff; **5:**141
Kosher, *see* KASHER
Koshland (fam.) **5:**56
Koshnitzki, Gerald **5:**407
Kosht Imrei Emet (bk.) **3:**996
Kosiba coins **5:**722
KOSICE (city, Cz.) **10:**1215
KOSICE, GYULA **10:**1216
Kosidowski (writ.) **13:**799
Kosiowicz, Solomon **11:**538
Koslov (city, Crimea), *see* YEVPATORIYA
Koslowsky, Pinḥas, *see* SAPIR PINḤAS
Kosman, Joseph **7:**1129
Kosmas Indikopleustes (ms.) **9:**1360
- *illus:* **6:**184,793,1303; **9:**68; **11:**72; **12:**376
Kosor, Josip **16:**887
KOSOV (tn., Ukr.) **10:**1216
- dynasties **1:**ḥas table
- Naḥman of Kosov **12:**788
- *illus:* text
KOSOVÁ HORA (tn., Bohem.) **10:**1218
Kosover, Barukh (kab.) **10:**593
Kosover Shtime (period.) **10:**1217
Kosovsky, Isaac **9:**1156
Kosów (tn., Ukr.), *see* KOSOV
Kosow, Sophia, *see* SIDNEY, SYLVIA
Kossakowski, Moliwda (Ignacy) **7:**61
Kosseir (loc., Egy.) **13:**1009
Kossmann, Jonah **11:**1271
Kossmann, Juspa **5:**1597
KOSSOFF, DAVID **15:**1054; **15:**1086
- television **15:**929
KOSSOFF, LEON **3:**604
- *illus:*
- - "Self Portrait" (drg.) **3:**631
KOSSOVSKI, VLADIMIR **10:**1218
Kossowitz (tn., Bohem.), *see* KASEJOVICE
Kossowsky, Isaac **10:**156
Kossowsky, Michel **10:**156
KOSSUTH, LAJOS **10:**1219
KOSTELANETZ, ANDRE **12:**695
Kosters, W. H. **4:**876
Kostić, Boris **5:**405
Kostić, Laza **16:**885
KOSTOMAROV, NIKOLAI IVANOVICH **10:**1219
- Ukraine **15:**1517
Kostov Trial (Bul.) **14:**1654
Kos Yeshu'ah u-Neḥamah (bk.) **7:**184
Kosygin, Aleksei **3:**158; **15:**1557
KŐSZEG (tn., Hung.) **10:**1220
KOTARBIŃSKA, JANINA **10:**1220
Kotel Ma'aravi, see WESTERN WALL
Kotevet (meas.) **16:**389
Kothar (deity), *see* Koshar
KOTIK, YEḤEZKEL (Ezekiel) **10:**1221
KOTLER, AARON **10:**1221
- Agudat Israel **2:**426
Kotler, Oded **7:**1141; **9:**1006; **12:**462
- *illus:*
- - *Three Days and a Child* **12:**460
Kotlier, Abraham **13:**136
Kotlyar, Leonti **11:**1558
Kotovsk (tn., Rus.), *see* BIRZULA
KOTOVSKOYE (tn., Bess.) **10:**1222
Kotsishvili, Joseph **7:**427
Kotsk (tn., Pol.), *see* KOCK
KOTSK, MENAHEM MENDEL OF **10:**1126
- Abraham of Sochaczew **15:**24
- dynasties **1:**ḥas. table
- Isaac of Warka **16:**304
KOTSUJI, SETSUZO (Abraham) **10:**1224
- *illus:* text
Kott, Jan **13:**803
Kottataj, H. **13:**732
Kottek, Heymann **10:**464
Kottendorf (stlmt., Aus.), *see* Gattendorf
Kottler, Miriam, *see* FREUND, MIRIAM KOTTLER
Kottler, Mischa **5:**1572
KOTTLER, MOSES **10:**1224
- *illus:*
- - text
- - Michaelis, Sir Max (bust) **11:**1492
- - Smuts, Jan Christiaan (bust) **15:**205
Kotvanim, see SCRIBE
Kotzk (tn., Pol.), *see* KOCK
KOUFAX, SANFORD (Sandy) **10:**1225
- baseball **15:**301
Koussevitzky, Alexander **10:**1227
Koussevitzky, David **10:**1227
Koussevitzky, Jacob **10:**1226
KOUSSEVITZKY, MOSHE **10:**1226
- music **12:**661
KOUSSEVITZKY, SERGE **10:**1227
Koussevitzky, Simcha **10:**1227
Kovačica **14:**872
Kovacs, Mor **12:**1375
Kovad I (k., Babyl.) **4:**42
Kovarsky, Anatole **5:**220
KOVEL (tn., Ukr.) **10:**1228
- *illus:* text
Kovesim, Mishlei (fable), *see Mishlei Kovesim*
Kovez al Yad (*Jad;* journ.) **1:**newsp. list
Kovez "B" le-Yom ha-Zikkaron, "Ha-Sho'ah ve-ha-Mered" (kib. fest. anth.) **10:**960
Kovez Ḥag ha-Gez (kib. litur.) **10:**960
Kovez ha-Hevrah le-Hakirat Erez Yisrael (journ.) **1:**newsp. list
Kovez Harza'ot ha-Ḥevrah ha-Historit (journ.) **1:**newsp. list
Kovez Harza'ot shel ha-Iggud ha-Yisra'eli le-Ibbud Informazyah (journ.) **1:**newsp. list
Kovez ha-Tammim (journ.) **1:**newsp. list
Kovez ha-Tosafot, Ozar Neḥmad (wk.) **6:**734
Kovez li-Be'ayot ha-Ḥinnukh ha-Gufani (journ.) **1:**newsp. list
Kovez Ma'amarim le-Divrei Yemei ha-Ittonut ha-Ivrit be-Erez Yisrael (journ.) **1:**newsp. list
Kovez Meḥkarim (period.) **16:**698
Kovez Schocken le-Divrei Sifrut (journ.) **1:**newsp. list
Kovez Sifruti (journ.) **1:**newsp. list
KOVNER, ABBA **10:**1229
- Beriḥah **4:**629ff
- Hebrew literature **8:**206
- partisan brigade **13:**145
- *illus:*
- - text
- - Jewish partisan group, Vilna **13:**144
KOVNER, ABRAHAM URI **10:**1230
- critic **5:**1117
- Hebrew literature **8:**188
- Paperna **13:**66
- Zederbaum, Alexander **8:**1369
- *illus:* text
Kovner Emes (newsp.) **10:**848; **16:**833
Kovno (city, Lith.), *see* KAUNAS
Kovo, Asher **16:**1539
Kovo, Elijah **14:**702
Kovo, Jacob **14:**703
Kovo, Juda **16:**1538
KOWALSKY, JUDAH LEIB **10:**1232
Kowalsky, Sholem B. **13:**1462
Kowno (city, Lith.), *see* KAUNAS
KOYRE, ALEXANDRE **10:**1233
Kozah (dye plant) **6:**329
KOZAKOV, MIKHAIL EMMANUILOVICH **10:**1233
Középvisó (vill., Rum.) **16:**165
KOZIENICE (Kozenitsy; tn., Pol.) **10:**1233
KOZIENICE, ISRAEL BEN SHABBETAI HAPSTEIN **10:**1234
Kozinets, Isay Pavlovich **12:**55
Kozirynek (tn., Pol.), *see* RADZYN
KOZLE (tn., Pol.) **10:**1235
Kozma, Sándor **15:**1155
Kozminka (vill., Pol.) **16:**1348
Koznitz, the Maggid of, *see* KOZIENICE, ISRAEL BEN SHABBETAI HAPSTEIN
Kozyr-Zyrko (Cossack) **12:**1529; **13:**699
KRACAUER, ISADOR **10:**1235
KRACAUER, SIEGFRIED **10:**1235
Kraehhaus, A. **4:**867
Krafft, Karl **8:**40
KRAFT, LOUIS **10:**1235
- National Jewish Welfare Board **12:**873
Kraft, Werner **7:**451
Krain (city, Aus.), *see* LJUBLJANA
Kraiserbard, David **10:**1502
Kraj (period.) **16:**367
KRAKAUER, LEOPOLD **10:**1236
- Israeli architecture **3:**361
- *illus:*
- - "Judean Hills" (drg.) Fig. 96 3—ART
Krakauer-Wolf, Grete **10:**1236
Krakover, Isaac **4:**1398
Kraków (city, Pol.), *see* CRACOW
Krakow (tn., Ger.) **11:**1163
Krakowitzer, Ernst **15:**1607
Krakowski, Joseph **13:**776
Kraljevica (vill., Croatia) **16:**880
Kramer, Barry **15:**303
Kramer, Ben **15:**303
Kramer, Danny **15:**306
Kramer, Imre, *see* KESZI, IMRE
KRAMER, JACOB **10:**1236
- Gertler, Mark **7:**521
- *illus:* text
Kramer, Josef **4:**610,611; **12:**893; **16:**294
- *illus:*
- - Bergen-Belsen trial **16:**295
Kramer, Leopold **13:**973
Kramer, Louis **15:**300
Kramer, Max **10:**1236
KRAMER, MOSES BEN DAVID, OF VILNA **10:**1237
- Elijah Ḥasid **14:**199
Kramer, N. **14:**1041
Kramer, Naḥum (Shadmi) **7:**1072
KRAMER, SAMUEL NOAH **10:**1238
- archaeology **3:**302
- Sumerian literature **16:**1508
Kramer, Sheftel **14:**379
Kramer, Sidney **8:**1361
Kramer, Simon **5:**416; **8:**216
KRAMER, STANLEY E. **10:**1238
KRAMER, THEODOR **10:**1238
KRAMM, JOSEPH **15:**1582
Kramsztyk, Isaac **16:**338
Kramsztyk, Roman **3:**575
- *illus:*
- - "Old Jew with Children" (drg.) Fig. 75 3-ART
Kran, Shimeon, *see* Kron, Shimeon
Kranjčerić, Silvije Strahimir **16:**885
KRANTZ, PHILIP **10:**1239
- press **13:**1053
- socialism **15:**35
Krantz, Samuel **7:**603
Kranz, Isaac **10:**1239
KRANZ, JACOB BEN WOLF (Maggid of Dubno) **10:**1239
- Dyatlovo **6:**325
- fables **6:**1131
- Kluger, Solomon **10:**1110
- *maggid* **11:**699
Kranzler, G. **8:**568
Krasiński, Gabriel **13:**799
Krasiński, Jan Kazimierz **15:**89
Krasiński, Josef **12:**1455
Krasiński, Zygmunt **13:**798,799
KRASLAVA (tn., Latv.) **10:**1240
KRASNA, NORMAN **12:**469
KRASNER, LEE **3:**604
- *illus:*
- - "Transition" (paint.) **3:**634
KRASNIK (tn., Pol.) **10:**1241
- *illus:* text
Krasno (tn., Cz.) **14:**533
KRASNODAR (city, Rus.) **10:**1242
- War Crimes Trials **16:**291
Krasnopolski, Horace **10:**1494
Krasnostav (tn., Pol), *see* KRASNYSTAW
Krasnostawski, Moshe **10:**1203
Krasnoyarsk (reg., Sib.) **14:**1488
KRASNOYE (vill., Ukr.) **10:**1242
Krasny Ostrov (vill., Ukr.), *see* Kukizov
KRASNYSTAW (tn., Pol.) **10:**1242
Krasucki, Israel **5:**1036
Kratzenstein (r.) **11:**591
KRAUS, ADOLF **10:**1243
KRAUS, FRANTIŠEK R. **5:**1208,1210
KRAUS, GERTRUD **5:**1272
- Israeli dance **9:**1008
Kraus, Hans-Joachim **4:**909
Kraus, Irka (ghetto child art.) **5:**1203
KRAUS, KARL **10:**1243
- *illus:* text
KRAUS, MICHAEL **8:**547
KRAUS, OSKAR **10:**1244
Kraus, Ota B. **5:**1208
KRAUS, PAUL ELIEZER **10:**1245
Kraus, William **15:**1206
KRAUSE, ELIYAHU **10:**1246
Krause, Judith **10:**1246
Krause, Robert **8:**1438
Kraushar, Aleksander, *see* Alkar
KRAUSKOPF, JOSEPH **10:**1246
- Berkowitz, Henry **4:**634
- chaplaincy, Jewish **11:**1570
KRAUSS, FRIEDRICH SALAMO **10:**1247
KRAUSS, JUDAH HA-KOHEN **10:**1248
Krauss, Lehman **15:**1206
KRAUSS, SAMUEL **10:**1248
- *Toledot Yeshu* **15:**1208
- translations **4:**884
Krausz, Moses Aaron **4:**108
KRAUSZ, ZSIGMOND **10:**1250
Kraut, Paul **8:**40
Krautheimer, Richard **3:**650
Kravar, Pavel **8:**1135
KRAVETS, LYUDMILA **11:**1567; **11:**1574
Kravetz, Marc **7:**39; **12:**1034
KRAYN, HUGO **10:**1250
KREBS, SIR HANS ADOLF **10:**1250
Krech, David **13:**1345
Kredens, Aladaār, *see* KOMLÓS, ALADĀR
Kreeger, David Lloyd **16:**358
KREFELD (city, Ger.) **10:**1251
- Belgian Jewry **4:**417

- *illus:* text
KREIN, ALEXANDER ABRAMOVICH **10:**1252
Krein, Grigori **10:**1252
Krein, Julian **10:**1252
KREININ, MEIR **10:**1253
Kreis, James **15:**313
KREISEL, HENRY **10:**1253
- Canada **5:**115; **5:**116
KREISER, JACOB GRIGORYEVICH **10:**1253
- anti-fascist **3:**62
- military **11:**1558
- Russia **14:**479
KREISKY, BRUNO **10:**1254
- Austrian anti-Semitism **3:**903
Krelenboim, Yosef Aharon, *see* ALMOGI, YOSEF AHARON
Krell, Wilhelm **13:**1034
Krémègne, Pinkus **13:**116
KREMENCHUG (city, Ukr.) **10:**1254
- Poltava **13:**840
- Slobodka yeshivah **14:**1669
KREMENETS (tn., Ukr.) **10:**1255
- *illus:* text
Kremenetzki, Paulus, *see* MEYER, PAULUS
KREMENETZKY, JOHANN **10:**1256
- Zionism **16:**1107
Kremenitser Lebn (period.) **10:**1256
KREMER, ARKADI (Aaron, Alexander) **10:**1257
- socialism **15:**41
- *illus:*
- - Bundists **4:**1499
Kremer, Pati **10:**1258
Kremnitz, Issachar Baer of, *see* Issachar Baer of Kremnitz
KREMNITZER, JOHANAN BEN MEIR **10:**1258
KREMS (city, Aus.) **10:**1258
- Albert II **2:**530
- *illus:*
- - text
- - *ketubbah* (14th cent.) **10:**930
Krems, Israel of, *see* ISRAEL OF KREMS
Kremsier (tn., Morav.), *see* KROMERIZ
Křenek, Ernst **10:**1376
KRENGEL, MENAHEM MENDEL **10:**1259
Krepkina, Vera **12:**1377
Kreslavka (tn., Latv.), *see* KRASLAVA
Krespia (gram.) **4:**597
Krespin, Joshua Abraham, *see* KRISPIN, JOSHUA ABRAHAM
KRESSEL, GETZEL **1:**32; **10:**1260
Kressin, Miriam **12:**455
KRESTIN, LAZAR **3:**604
- *illus:*
- - "Ḥasid Studying" (paint.) **7:**1403
Krestovski, Vsevolod **14:**508
KRETINGA (tn., Lith.) **10:**1260
Kretōwce (vill., Pol.) **16:**944
Kretsch (polit.) **12:**1353
Kreutner, S.Y. **10:**916
Kreuzberger, Max **12:**1369
Kreuzburg (tn., Latv.), *see* KRUSTPILS
KREUZNACH (city, Ger.) **10:**1260
Kreuznach, Abraham von **4:**168
Krever, David Michel **13:**117
KREYMBORG, ALFRED **15:**1582
Kri (bib. text form), *see Keri* and *ketiv*
Krichefski, W.H. **5:**335
KRICHEV (tn., Belor.) **10:**1261
Kriegel, František **5:**1202
Kriegel-Valrimont, Annie Besse **13:**828
KRIEGEL-VALRIMONT, MAURICE **13:**828
Krieger, J. A. **12:**1244; **16:**372
KRIEGER, LEONARD **8:**547
Krieger, Solly **15:**305
Krim (penin., Rus.) *see* CRIMEA
Krimchak (people, lang.; Rus.) **10:**68
- Bakhchisarai **4:**116
- Crimea **5:**1104ff
- immigration to Israel **9:**503
- Jewish languages **10:**68
- Sevastopol **14:**1198
KRINITZI, AVRAHAM **10:**1261
- *illus:* text
Krinki (tn., Pol.), *see* KRYNKI
Krinki, Joseph **16:**768
Krinkin, Yaffah **5:**437
Krinski, J. **14:**526
Krinski, Judah Leib **15:**520
KRIPS, JOSEF **12:**695
KRIS, ERNST **10:**1262
Kris, Marianne **10:**1262
- psychiatry **13:**1339
Krisa, Leib ben Nathan **7:**63
Krishaber, B. **13:**336
Krishaber, Isaac **13:**16
Krisiloff, Steve **15:**300
Krisokata, Georgios **3:**801
Krispin, Aaron **10:**1262
Krispin, Isaac **10:**1262
KRISPIN, JOSHUA ABRAHAM **10:**1262
Kriss, Gregory **12:**1377
Krisse, Leib **11:**610
KRISTALLNACHT (Nazi pogrom) **10:**1263
- Austrian Jews **3:**899; **3:**900
- Heydrich, Reinhard **8:**448
- history chart **8:**766-767
- Holocaust **8:**839
- *illus:*
- - text
- - Baden-Baden **8:**845
- - Berlin synagogue **4:**651
- - Landau in der Pfalz **8:**849
- - Magdeburg **8:**849
- - Munich Central Synagogue **8:**738
- - Munich Ohel Yakob synagogue **12:**523
Kristeller, Franz **3:**650
KRISTELLER, PAUL OSKAR **10:**1266
KRISTELLER, SAMUEL **10:**1266
KRISTIANPOLLER (fam.) **10:**1266
Kristianpoller, Alexander **10:**1266
Kristianpoller, Jehiel Michael **10:**1266
Kristianpoller, Meir **10:**1266
Kristianpoller, Meir ben Ẓevi Hirsh **10:**1266
Kristol, Gertrude, *see* HIMMELFARB, GERTRUDE
Krivine, Alain **7:**39; **12:**1034
KRIVOI ROG (city, Ukr.) **10:**1267
Krivoshein, Semyon **11:**1557; **14:**479
KRIVOYE OZERO (vill., Ukr.) **10:**1267
- Balta **4:**144
- Podolia **13:**668
Krize, Yehiel **3:**592
- *illus:*
- - "Slaughterhouse" (paint.) Fig. 101 **3**—ART
Krleža, Miroslav **16:**885
Kro, Ẓevi Hirsch **16:**243
KROCH, JACOB LEIB BEN SHEMAIAH **10:**1267
Kroch, Shemaiah **10:**1267
KROCHMAL, ABRAHAM **10:**1268
Krochmal, Aryeh Judah Loeb **10:**1269
Krochmal, Ḥayyim **10:**246
KROCHMAL, MENAHEM MENDEL BEN ABRAHAM **10:**1268
- anti-profiteering **7:**1063
- codification of law **5:**655
- Moravia **12:**301
- responsa **14:**90
KROCHMAL, NACHMAN **10:**1269
- *Contents:*
- - Philosophy **10:**1270
- - Philosophy of History **10:**1271
- - Contribution to the "Science of Judaism" **10:**1272
- - Halakhah **10:**1272
- - Aggadah **10:**1272
- God **7:**663
- history chart **8:**766-767
- holiness **10:**874
- Lag ba-Omer **12:**1388
- Levinsohn **11:**116
- miracles **12:**80
- *Moreh Nevukhei ha-Zeman* **8:**183
- nature **12:**890
- philosophy **13:**457
- *Shekhinah* **14:**1353
- revelation **14:**124
- Torah **15:**1238; **15:**1242
- Weiss, I.H. **16:**414
- Wissenschaft des Judentums **16:**574
- *illus:* text
Krochmalnik, Shalom **10:**1269
KROCK, ARTHUR **10:**1273
Krohn, Abraham **13:**482
KROJANKER, GUSTAV **10:**1273
- Agnon, Shmuel **2:**371
Krok, Helge **14:**933
Krol, A., *see* Gruenhut, Abraham
Krol, Abram **13:**118
- *illus:*
- - *"Kaddish"* (lith.) **10:**662
Krol, Ḥayyim **11:**431
Krol, M. (stlr., Sib.) **14:**1487
Kromayer, J. **8:**40
KROMERIZ (tn., Morav.) **10:**1274
- Aboab, Samuel **2:**94
- prayer against informers **8:**1368
- seal **14:**1080
- *illus:*
- - text
- - Frankl-Gruen, Adolf Abraham **7:**103
Kromolow (tn., Pol.) **16:**942
Kron, Shimeon **14:**536
Kronberger, Lily **15:**317
Kroneburg, Benjamin Solomon **13:**1107
KRONECKER, HUGO **10:**1275
KRONECKER, LEOPOLD **10:**1275
KRONENBERG (fam.) **10:**1275
Kronenberg, Julius **10:**1276
Kronenberg, Leopold (Leibel) **10:**1275; **13:**1519; **15:**1177
Kronenberg, Samuel Leizer **10:**1275
Kronenberg, Stanislaw **10:**1276
Kronenberg, Wladyslaw **10:**1276
KRONENBERGER, LOUIS **10:**1276
Kroner, H. **12:**1461
KRONER, RICHARD **10:**1277
KRONER, THEODOR **10:**1277
Kronfeld, Robert **2:**321
Kronick, Sam **15:**1263
KRONIK, MOSES BEN AKIVA **10:**1277
Kronish, Leon **11:**1478
Kronstadt (city, Transyl.), *see* BRASOV
Kroonstad (tn., S.A.) **12:**1448
KROSHNER, MIKHAIL YEFIMOVICH **12:**696
KROSNO (tn., Pol.) **10:**1278
KROSS, ANNA **10:**1278
Krotoschin, Benjamin, *see* Benjamin Beinish ha-Kohen of Krotoszyn
KROTOSZYN (tn., Pol.) **10:**1279
- archives **3:**387
- sick, care of **14:**1498
- tailors **15:**705
Krottingen (tn., Lith.), *see* KRETINGA
Krouch, Erna **12:**1354
Krouch, Julius **12:**1354
Krouch, Max **12:**1354
Krueger, Bernhard **5:**727; **14:**597
Krueger, Wilhelm **13:**764
Krug, Marx M. **6:**465
KRUG, WILHELM TRAUGOTT **10:**1280
Kruger, Claus **8:**566
Kruger, Paul **4:**248; **10:**156; **15:**189
- *illus:*
- - Marks, Samuel, letter **13:**1058
- - synagogue consecration **15:**191
Kruger, Stephanus Johannes **2:**539
Krugersdorp (tn., Transvaal) **15:**1340
Kruh, Shmuel **5:**497
Kruk, J. **15:**1542
KRULEWITCH, MELVIN LEVIN **11:**1574
Krumey, Hermann **8:**1099; **10:**1077
Krupp (fam.) **3:**873
Krusenstjerna, Agnes von **14:**931
KRUSHEVAN, PAVOLAKI **10:**1281
- Dashewski **5:**1310
Kruskal, H.N. **14:**288
KRUSTPILS (tn., Latv.) **10:**1281
Kruzhki (orgn., Eur.) **15:**39
Krym (penin., Rus.), *see* CRIMEA
KRYMOV, YURI **14:**515
KRYNKI (tn., Pol.) **10:**1281
Krzemieniec, *see* KREMENETS
KRZEPICE (tn., Pol.) **10:**1283
Krzepicki, Maurycy **5:**1034
Krzywicka, Irena **13:**803
Ktav Publishing House (U.S.) **13:**1377
Ktiv (bib. text), *see Keri* and *Ketiv*
KUBA (city, Azer.) **10:**1283
- Azerbaijan **3:**1005*ff*
Kubashi, Saadiah **5:**1455
Ku-Bau (q., Mesop.) **16:**1489
Kube (Nazi crim.) **12:**55
Kubelsky, Benny, *see* BENNY, JACK
Kubie, Lawrence S. **13:**1340
Kubinsky, Ephraim **6:**157
KUBLIN, HYMAN **1:**32; **10:**1283
KUBOVY (Kubowitzki), ARYEH LEON **10:**1284
- Poland **13:**786
- Slánský trials **14:**1654
KUBRICK, STANLEY **12:**469
Ku Bukh (collec. of fables) **16:**804
Kudish, Leib **16:**201
KUENEN, ABRAHAM **10:**1284
Kuenstlinger, Georg **13:**1034
Kuersner, Conrad, *see* PELLICANUS, CONRAD
Kuestendje (city, Rum.), *see* CONSTANTA
KUFA (tn., Iraq) **10:**1285
Kufri (place, Iraq) **8:**1447
Kugel (fam.) **5:**311
KUGEL, ḤAYYIM **10:**1285
Kuh (fam.) **15:**213
KUH, DAVID **10:**1285
Kuh, Emil **7:**451
KUH, EPHRAIM MOSES **10:**1286
Kuh, Moritz **16:**124
KUḤAYL, SHUKR SĀLIM **10:**1286
Kūhīn, Raḥmīn **12:**1463
Kūhīn, Salīm Zakī **12:**1463
Kūhīn, Zakī, of Beirut **12:**1463
Kuhn (phys.) **13:**490
Kuhn, Abraham (bnk.) **8:**1361;

10:1287
Kuhn, Abraham (pion., Iowa) **8:**1438
Kuhn, Heinrich **11:**664
Kuhn, Isaac **8:**1438
Kuhn, Joseph **8:**1438
Kuhn, K.G. **5:**955
KUHN, THOMAS S. **10:**1287
KUHN-LOEB (fam.) **10:**1287
- railroads **13:**1519
KUIBYSHEV (city, Rus.) **10:**1287
- Siberia **14:**1486
Kuk, Abraham Isaac, *see* KOOK, ABRAHAM ISAAC
Kukizov (vill., Ukr.) **15:**1402
KUKIZOW (fam.) **10:**1288
Kukizow, David ben Mordecai **10:**1288
Kukizow, Judah **10:**1288
Kukizow, Mordecai ben Nisan **10:**1288
Kukizow, Nisan **10:**236
Ku Klux Klan (orgn., U.S.) **12:**952; **15:**1626; **15:**1653
Kulania (loc., Syr.) **5:**65
Kulantur (cmty. ldr., Rus.) **14:**759
KULBAK, MOSHE **10:**1288
- Yiddish literature **16:**817
Kulcar, Shlomo **13:**1340
Kuli, Jacob, *see* CULI, JACOB
Kulik, Cyril **7:**1103
Kulischer, Zigmund **16:**124
Kulish, P. **4:**887
KULISHER (fam.) **10:**1289
Kulisher, Alexander **10:**1290
Kulisher, Eugene **10:**1290
Kulisher, Joseph **10:**1290
Kulisher, Michael **10:**1289
Kulisher, Moses **10:**1289
Kulisher, Reuben **10:**1289
Kulke, Eduard **5:**452
Kulla (leg. term) **8:**1073
Kullani (loc., Syr.) **5:**65
Kulm (vill., Cz.), *see* Chlumec
Kulmbach (city, Ger.) **4:**352
Kulmhof (extermination camp), *see* CHELMNO
Kulp, David Meyer **10:**737
Kultepe (loc., Turk.) **2:**495
Kultur Fareyn (orgn., Cuba) **5:**1147
Kulturgeschichtliche Bibliothek Warburg (library, Eng.) **3:**301
Kultur-Gezelshaftlekher Farband fun di Yidn in Poylen (orgn., Pol.), *see* Cultural-Social Association of the Jews in Poland
Kultur Kongres (orgn.) **3:**423
Kultur Lige (orgn.) **16:**780
Kultur un Leben (period.) **13:**1056
Kulturverein (soc.), see VEREIN FUER KULTUR UND WISSENSCHAFT DES JUDENTUMS
Kultusgemeinde (cmty. orgn.) **13:**832
KULTUSVEREIN (cmty. orgn.) **10:**1290
- Austria **3:**895
- learned societies **15:**54
Kumkum (theat., Tel Aviv) **2:**774; **15:**1061; **15:**921
Kümmel, Caspar **8:**40
Kumos (bot.) **8:**1312
KUN, BÉLA **10:**1290
Kun, L. **16:**117
Kunat, Jacob **13:**584
Kuneitra (tn., Golan), *see* QUNAYTIRA, AL-
KUNFI, ZSIGMOND **10:**1291
'Kunig Armleder,' *see* Zimberlin, John
Kunikos (cynic), *see Kinukos*
Kunikov (vill., Rus.) **11:**1558
Kunin, Laser **16:**1165
Kunitz, Loeb **11:**298
KUNITZ, STANLEY JASSPON **10:**1292
Kunitzer, Moses **4:**1449
Kuniz (tn., Morav.), *see* DOLNI KOUNICE
Kunjar-Kari (loc., Ind.) **8:**1355
Kunmadaras (tn., Hung.) **8:**1105
Kunreuther, Ignatz **5:**411
Kunschak, Leopold **3:**903
Kunstadt, Eliezer Lipmann **13:**1496
KUNSTADT, ISAAC (Ignāz) BEN ELIEZER LIPMAN **10:**1292
- Abony **2:**98
Kunstadt, Jacob Koppel, *see* Altenkundstadt, Jacob Koppel
Kunstler, William **10:**1505; **12:**934
Kunstmann, W. **14:**1414
KUNTERES (bk., collec.) **10:**1292
Kunteres (period. Er. Isr.) **10:**837; **14:**1326
Kunteres (journ., Pol.) **1:**newsp. list
Kunteres Bibliografi (journ., Isr.) **1:**newsp. list
Kunteres Elleh Shemot (bibl.) **7:**1413
Kunteres ha-Sefer ha-Torani, see Ha-Sefer
Kunteresim (journ.) **1:**newsp. list
Kunteres Magenza (bk.) **12:**27
Kunteres Shemot ha-Gittin (bk.) **6:**919
Kuntilla, El- (loc., Sinai) **9:**388; **14:**1605,1636
Kunya (Arab name) **2:**178
KUNZ, JOSEF LAURENZ **10:**1293
Kunzelmann, Dieter **12:**1034
Kuomintang (Chin. polit. party) **4:**1258
Kupari (loc., Yug.) **16:**880
Kupat-Am Bank Ltd. (Isr.) **9:**824
Kupat Milveh la-Oleh (bank, Isr.) **9:**827
Kupchik, Abraham **5:**407
Kuper, Emil Albertovich, *see* COOPER, EMIL ALBERTOVICH
Kuper, G., *see* SINGER, ISRAEL JOSHUA
KUPER, SIMON MEYER **10:**1293
- law **10:**1502
Kuperman, Hassia **16:**822
KUPERNIK, ABRAHAM **10:**1293
Kupernik, Lev **10:**1294
Kupferberg, Alfred **9:**1067
KUPISKIS (Kupiškiai; Kupishki; tn., Lith.) **10:**1294
Kuppah (charity fund) **4:**388
Kuppat Ḥolim (med. insurance fund, Isr.) **9:**982; **9:**985ff
- East Jerusalem branch **9:**869
- Histadrut **8:**539
- labor social services **9:**866
- medical aid for workers **9:**850ff
- *illus:*
- - dental clinic **9:**987
- - laboratory **9:**867
- *see also:* HEALTH SERVICES IN ISRAEL
Kuppat Ḥolim Ammamit **9:**986
Kuppat Ḥolim le-Ovedim Le'ummiyyim **8:**541; **9:**986
Kuppat Ḥolim Maccabi **9:**986
Kuppat Po'alei Ereẓ Yisrael, *see* Ereẓ Israel Workers' Fund
Kuppat Sefer (period.) **5:**435
Kuprill, Ahmed, *see* Köprülü, Ahmed
Kuprin, Alexander Ivanovich **14:**507
Kuranda (fam.) **8:**1136
KURANDA, IGNAZ **10:**1294
Kurdish (lang.) **10:**1298
- Kurds **9:**503
- Neo-Aramaic **12:**950
KURDISTAN (reg., Middle E.) **10:**1295
- *Contents:*
- - History **10:**1296
- - Economic Conditions **10:**1297
- - Instability of Living Conditions **10:**1297
- - Organization of the Communities **10:**1298
- - Kurdish Language **10:**1298
- - Aliyyot to Palestine **10:**1299
- - Musical Tradition **10:**1299
- *aliyah* **9:**503; **9:**515
- Alroy, David **2:**750
- Barazani, Samuel **4:**205
- Iran **8:**1443
- Iraq **8:**1456ff
- marriage custom **11:**1043; **11:**1044
- Neo-Aramaic dialect **12:**948
- Shabbateanism **14:**1234; **14:**1243
- sickness **14:**1501ff
- Targum **15:**811
- Ten Lost Tribes **15:**1006
- *illus:*
- - immigrants to Israel **9:**504
- - Passover *seder* **13:**171
Kurek, Jalu **13:**801
Kurigalzu I (k., Mesop.) **16:**3, 1499
Kurkar (rock type) **9:**125ff
Kurkeyah (bird), *see* CRANE
Kurland (ghetto ldr.) **15:**1370
Kurlander (fam.) **5:**40
Kurlano, Abraham **12:**1376
Kurnik, (tn., Pol.), *see* KORNIK
Kurnik, Meir ben Moses, *see* KORNIK, MEIR BEN MOSES
Kurnub (site, Isr.) **13:**48
- Israel War of Independence **9:**371
- *see also:* MAMPSIS
Kurowski, Stefan **10:**1500
Kurrein, Adolf **15:**1363
KURREIN, MAX **8:**1432
Kurrein, Viktor **11:**262
Kursheedt, E. Isaac **12:**1041
Kursheedt, Gershom **12:**1041; **15:**1289
KURSHEEDT, ISRAEL BAER **10:**1301
- New York City **12:**1072
Kursiner, Conrad, *see* PELLICANUS, CONRAD
KURSK (oblast, Rus.) **10:**1301
KURSKY, FRANZ **10:**1302
Kursner, Conrad, *see* PELLICANUS, CONRAD
Kurtabi, Abraham **13:**577
Kurtemei (dye plant), *see Koẓah*
KURTH, ERNST **12:**696
Kurti (phys.) **13:**490
Kurtov (meas.) **16:**388
KURTZ, AARON **10:**1302
Kurtz, Louis **14:**214
Kurtzman, David H. **6:**465
Kuruc massacre (Morav.) **15:**1509
Kūruš (k., Pers.), *see* CYRUS
Kuryer Polski (newsp.) **16:**367
Kurz, Otto **3:**651
Kurzbeck, Joseph Elder von **16:**131
KURZWEIL, BARUCH (Benedict) **10:**1302
- Agnon, Shmuel **2:**371
- critic **5:**1123
- Hebrew literature **8:**178
Kusayla (Berber ldr.) **15:**1432
Kusbar (*Kusbarta*; bot.), *see* CORIANDER
Kuschke, A. **5:**1595
Kusdini, Aaron ben Judah, *see* AARON BEN JUDAH KUSDINI
Kuseima (loc., Sinai), *see* Quseima
Kusel, R. **4:**61
Kusevitsky, Moshe, *see* KOUSSEVITZKY, MOSHE
Kush (anc. kdm.; s. of Ham), *see* CUSH
Kushman, Joseph **7:**1129
Kushner, Chaim Nachman **16:**551
Kushnir, Shlomo **10:**1161
KUSHNIROV, AARON **10:**1303
Kushta (city, Turk.), *see* ISTANBUL
Kushta, Israel **5:**431
Kushu (anc. tribes) **11:**1506
Kuššar (anc. tn., As. M.) **8:**787
Kustantina (city, Turk.), *see* ISTANBUL
Kustendil (tn., Bulg.) **4:**1486; **4:**1489
Kutais (Kutaisi; city, rus.) **4:**1130; **7:**425; **14:**442
Kut al-Ḥayy (tn., Iraq) **8:**1450
Kutchuk Kainarji Treaty **9:**306
Kuti, see MIN
Kutim (people) **7:**350
Kutim (tract.) **12:**49
KUTNO (tn., Pol.) **10:**1304
- Shapira, Joshua **14:**1299
Kutow (tn., Rus.), *see* KUTY
KUTSCHER, EDWARD YECHEZKEL **10:**1305
Kuttenplan (tn., Bohem.), *see* CHODOVA PLANA
Kuttna, S. **10:**756
Kutub al-Lugha (wk.), *see Kitāb Faṣīh lughat al-Ibrāniyyīn*
KUTY (tn., Rus.) **10:**1305
- Naḥman of Kosov **12:**788
Kutz, Milton **16:**534
Kuwait (Arab state) **3:**237
- Arab League **3:**242
- Arab refugees **9:**449
- Israel's relations **9:**444
- Six-Day War **9:**408; **14:**1626
Kuzari (wk.) **10:**357; **10:**363ff
- apologetic literature **3:**193
- Jewish literature **11:**339
- Kabbalah **10:**520
- revelation **14:**123
- translation **15:**1129
- *illus:*
- - title page (Venice, 1547) **10:**356
Kuzārīm, *see* KHAZARS
Kuzhmir (ḥas. dyn.), *see* KAZIMIERZ
KUZNETS, SIMON **10:**1306
- trade and commerce **15:**1304
Kuznetsov, Anatoli **4:**30; **14:**511
- Babi Yar massacre **10:**995
- Holocaust **8:**893
Kvam, Ragnar **14:**933
Kvater (godfather), *see* SANDAK
Kvaternik, Eugen **13:**192
Kvazimodo, Stevan **16:**890
Kvesim, Mishlei (fable), *see Mishlei Kovesim*
Kviatkovsky-Pinhasik, Rivka **5:**448
KVITKO, LEIB **10:**1307
- Hofstein, David **8:**813
Kvitl (ḥas. term) **7:**1400
Kwakiutl (Ind. tribe, N. Am.) **4:**1152
Kwartalnik Poświecony Badiniu Zydów w Polsce (period.) **3:**750
KWARTIN, ZAVEL (Zevulun) **10:**1307
- *mus:* **12:**661
Kwaśniewski, Moshe **5:**485
Kwasnik, Oskar K., *see* RABINOWICZ, OSKAR K.
Kwint, Gershon **14:**1673
KYBARTAI (tn., Lith.) **10:**1308
Kyber, David **8:**40
Kychko, Trofim **3:**150; **14:**488; **15:**1519; **15:**1562
- *illus:*
- - *Judaism Without Embellishments* **14:**491
KYJOV (tn., Morav.) **10:**1308
- Duschak, Mordecai **6:**311
- Uhersky Brod **15:**1510
Kylashi (tn., Rus.) **7:**428
Kynil (pr., Bul.) **8:**915
Kypke, Georg David **8:**40
Kyra (16th cent., fig.), *see* KIERA
KYUSTENDIL (tn., Bul.) **10:**1309
K. ZETNICK (writ.) **10:**1309
- *illus:*
- - Auschwitz camp **3:**857

L

La (amora), *see* ILAI
Laa (tn., Aus.) **8:** 1043
La Aguila (newsp.) **13:** 1039
La Alborada (newsp.) **4:** 1485; **14:** 871
La-Am (publ. house, Er. Isr.) **7:** 1326
La America (newsp.) **12:** 1102; **13:** 1039
LA'AZ (trans.) **10:** 1313
- early glosses **15:** 764
- Gruenwald's study **7:** 948
- Judeo-French **10:** 424
- Yiddish language **16:** 795
- *illus:*
- - Karaite Pentateuch **8:** 665
Lab, Joseph ben David ibn, *see* LEV, JOSEPH BEN DAVID IBN
LABAN (bib. fig.) **10:** 1315
- genealogy **12:** 790
- in the Arts **9:** 1204; **13:** 1490
- Jacob **9:** 1192ff
- Rachel **13:** 1486
- *illus:*
- - text
- - crossbreeding of the flock by Jacob (chart) **4:** 1025
- - embracing Jacob **10:** 1074
- - various episodes **4:** 949
Laban (site, Er. Isr.), *see* LIBNAH
LABAND, PAUL **10:** 1317
LABANOWSKI (fam.) **10:** 1318
Labanowski, Abraham ben Samuel (17th cent.) **10:** 1318
Labanowski, Abraham ben Samuel (18th cent.) **10:** 1318
Labanowski, Samuel (17/18 cent.) **10:** 1318
Labanowski, Samuel (18th cent.) **10:** 1318
Labarna (Hittite k.) **8:** 787
Labat, A.S. **14:** 834
Labatt, Abraham **15:** 1034
Labatt, Samuel **11:** 498
Labaya (Labayu; k., Shechem)
- Hannathon **7:** 1272
- Megiddo **11:** 1227
- Shechem **14:** 1331
La Benevolencia (soc., Yug.) **14:** 872
LABI, SIMEON **10:** 1318
- alchemy **2:** 544
- Kabbalah **10:** 542
- Zohar **16:** 1212
LABI, SOLOMON (IBN) **10:** 1319
La Boderie, Guy Le Fevre de, *see* LEFEVRE DE LA BODERIE, GUY
LA BOÊTIE, ETIENNE DE **10:** 1319
- philosophy **13:** 416
LABOR **10:** 1320
- *Contents:*
- - In the Bible and Apocrypha **10:** 1320
- - In the Talmud **10:** 1321
- - Laborers and Employers **10:** 1323
- - Later Rabbinic Writings and Modern Trends **10:** 1323
- - Labor Ideology in Europe **10:** 1323
- - In the United States **10:** 1324
- economic history **16:** 1298ff
- severance pay **7:** 1005ff
- women's rights **16:** 629
- *see also:* LABOR LAW
Labor, General Federation of, *see* HISTADRUT
LABOR, IDEOLOGY OF (Isr.) **9:** 870ff
- building Ereẓ Israel **9:** 515ff
- labor philosophy **10:** 1324
- Lilienblum's views **11:** 240ff
Labor Archives (and Museum; Isr.) **3:** 395
Labor Camps (Nazi Ger.), *see* CAMPS (Concentration and Extermination)
Labor councils in Israel **9:** 875
Labor Courts (Isr.) **9:** 639ff; **9:** 883ff
LABOR EMPLOYMENT IN ISRAEL **9:** 885
- Arab workers **8:** 540; **9:** 1028
- economic development **9:** 715ff
- industry **9:** 815
- labor economy **9:** 853
- labor exchanges **9:** 874ff
- new immigrants **9:** 394ff
- *illus:*
- - text
- - road construction workers, 1914 **9:** 328
- *tables:*
- - text
- - growth of Jewish working class, 1926-1939 **9:** 715
- - Histadrut membership, 1920-1939 **9:** 717
- - industry **9:** 819
- - non-Jewish employment (1969) **9:** 724
- - occupational distribution, 1958-1969 **9:** 726
- - unemployment among Jews, 1938-1945 **9:** 722
Laborer **10:** 1325
Labor Friends of Israel (Zion. orgn.) **16:** 640
LABOR LAW **10:** 1325
- *Contents:*
- - In Scripture **10:** 1325
- - Hired Servant and Independent Contractor **10:** 1325
- - Contractof Hired Service **10:** 1325
- - Personal Nature of Service Contract **10:** 1326
- - Remuneration **10:** 1326
- - Obligations of the Parties **10:** 1326
- - Period of Service **10:** 1327
- - Withdrawal by the Master **10:** 1328
- - Compensation on Dismissal **10:** 1328
- - Withdrawal by the Servant **10:** 1328
- - Servant's Liability to his Master **10:** 1329
- - Master's Liability to the Servant **10:** 1329
- - In State of Israel **10:** 1330
- Bible **10:** 1320
- conflict of laws **5:** 885
- debt discharge **6:** 1010
- eating of field produce **4:** 341
- *ha'anakah* and severance pay **7:** 1003
- Jewish workers preferred **16:** 1294
- oaths **12:** 1299
- public authority **13:** 1354
- Sabbath **14:** 563
- sharecropping **10:** 1534ff
- specific performance **5:** 932
- working hours **12:** 14
Labor legislation (Isr.) **9:** 653; **9:** 874ff
Labor Movement, Jewish
- Israel **9:** 773; **9:** 871
- U.S. **15:** 1616
- Yiddish literature **16:** 811
- Zionism **16:** 1110; **16:** 1131
- *see also:* BUND
Labor Movement in Israel, *see* JEWISH LABOR ORGANIZATIONS IN ISRAEL
Labor Movements and Socialism, *see* SOCIALISM
Labor Palestine Committee **9:** 853
LABOR RELATIONS IN ISRAEL **9:** 872
- Histadrut **8:** 534
Labor Unions in Israel, *see* HISTADRUT
LABOR ZIONIST ORGANIZATION OF AMERICA **10:** 1331
- Zionism **16:** 1110
- Zuckerman, Baruch **16:** 1228
- *see also:* PO'ALEI ZION
La Boz del Pueblo (journ.), *see La Epoca de New York*
Labu (anc. city) **10:** 1551
Labūdā (bib. fig.) **5:** 23
La Buenca Esperanza (newsp.) **9:** 1165
Labwa (vill., Leb.) **10:** 1551
Lac des Juifs (place, Fr.) **14:** 921
LA CHAUX-DE-FONDS (tn., Switz.) **10:** 1332
Lachine (city, Can.) **12:** 286
LACHISH (city, Er. Isr.) **10:** 1332
- anthropological evidence **3:** 46ff
- architecture **3:** 357
- fortifications **16:** 276
- Gedaliah's seal **7:** 352
- graffiti **16:** 663
- inscriptions **16:** 667
- letters **11:** 56
- pictographic scripts **16:** 654
- military archive **3:** 374
- ostraca **2:** 682
- temple **14:** 607
- *illus:*
- - archaeological remains **3:** 337; **5:** 589
- - captive lyre players **12:** 586
- - dagger **16:** 655
- - jar handle seal **16:** 386
- - limestone scarab seal **14:** 1076
- - Sennacherib's siege **3:** 337; **5:** 213,590
- - weights, Israelite **16:** 379
Lachish (mosh., Isr.) **1:** place list
LACHISH OSTRACA **10:** 1334
- alphabet **2:** 682
- Elnathan ben Achbor **6:** 684
- historical evidence **8:** 608
- numerals **12:** 1255
- Old-Hebrew **16:** 1569
- ostraca **16:** 667ff
- *illus:* **3:** 373
- - cursive script **2:** 679
- - Hebrew script **2:** 684
- *see also:* OSTRACA
LACHISH REGION (Isr.) **10:** 1335
- Adullam Region **2:** 312
- ancient history **10:** 1334
- Emica **10:** 48
- Kiryat Gat **10:** 1055
- *illus:*
- - Kiryat Gat **9:** 574
- - planning diagram **9:** 562
- *map:* text
Lachman (fam.) **5:** 56
Lachman, Charles **14:** 133
Lachman, Emil **7:** 210
LACHMAN, FREDERICK RICHARD **1:** 32
Lachman-Mosse, Hans **12:** 441
Lachmann, Hedwig **10:** 1400
LACHMANN, ISAAK **7:** 1548
LACHMANN, ROBERT **10:** 1336
Lachower, P. **13:** 1375
LACHOWER, YERUḤAM FISHEL **10:** 1338
- Hebrew literature **8:** 178
- *illus:*
- - Writers' Ass'n in Israel **8:** 205
Lachowicze (city, Belor.), *see* LYAKHOVICHI

Lachowicze, Aaron of **10:**1340
Lachowicze, Johanan of **10:**1340
LACHOWICZE, MORDECAI BEN NOAH OF **10:**1340
Lachowicze, Mordecai of **10:**1340
Lachowicze, Noah of (18/19 cent.) **10:**1340
Lachowicze, Noah of (20th cent.) **10:**1340
Lachrymabilem Judaeorum (papal bull) **4:**1496
LACHS, MANFRED **10:**1340
- law **10:**1500
LACHVA (Lachwa; tn., Belor.) **10:**1341
Lackenbach (tn., Burgenland) **4:**1511
Lackie Wielkie (lab. camp) **16:**1218
La Commission Française des Archives Juives **3:**382
Laconia (city, N.H.) **12:**1024
La Coruña (city, Sp.), *see* CORUNNA
LACRETELLE, JACQUES DE **10:**1342
Lacretelle, Pierre Louis **7:**22; **11:**1451; **15:**1118
La Crosse (city, Wis.) **16:**556
Lacrosse (sport) **15:**311
Lactantius Firmianus **14:**1199
L'Action Française (anti-Sem. mvmt.), *see* ACTION FRANÇAISE
L'Action française (newsp.), *see Action Française, L'*
Lacus Asphaltitis, *see* DEAD SEA
Lacus Balneorum (Jer.), *see* Pool of Towers
Lacus Germani (Jer.), *see* Snake Pool
Lacus Legerii (pool, Jer.) **9:**1541
Lada'at (journ.) **1:**newsp. list
Ladan (bib. fig.), *see* Libni
Laden, Leo **6:**342
Ladenberg (bnk., U.S.) **4:**178
LADENBURG (fam.) **10:**1342
LADENBURG, ALBERT **10:**1342
Ladenburg, Hayum Moses Hirsch **10:**1342
Ladenburg, Karl **10:**1342
Ladenburg, Mayer **10:**1342
Ladenburg, Moses Hirschel **10:**1342
Ladenburg, Wolf Hayum **10:**1342
Laderman, Manuel **5:**1545
Ladi, Shneur Zalman of, *see* SHNEUR ZALMAN OF (LIOZNA) LYADY
LADINO (lang.) **10:**1342
- *Contents:*
- - Origins **10:**1343
- - Togography **10:**1343
- - Literature **10:**1348
- - Musical Tradition **10:**1351
- Language
- - Bible translations **4:**865
- - Gruenbaum's chrestomathy **7:**942
- - Gruenwald's study **7:**948
- - *Haggadah* **7:**1103
- - Jewish languages **10:**67
- - Judeo-Provençal **10:**439
- - linguistic development **10:**67
- - Morocco **12:**332
- - music **12:**657
- - Ottoman Empire **16:**1550
- - Sephardim **14:**1168
- - Turkey **15:**1461
- - Ya'ari, Abraham **16:**690
- Literature
- - children's literature **5:**445
- - Culi, Jacob **5:**1155
- - Istanbul **9:**1094
- - Jewish literature **11:**358
- - *Me'am Lo'ez* **11:**1158
- - Ottoman Empire **16:**1550
- - press **13:**1037ff; **14:**1174
- - Yugoslavia **16:**888
- *illus:*
- - text
- - *Akedah* ballad **12:**597
- - *Gazeta de Amsterdam* (1675) **13:**1024
- - *Me'am Lo'ez* **13:**1108
- *see also:* SPANISH AND PORTUGUESE LITERATURE
Ladislas (k., Naples) **3:**228
Ladislas II (VI; k., Hung.) **2:**160; **8:**1088
Ladmir (city, Ukr.), *see* VLADIMIR VOLYNSKI
Lador Publishing House (N.Y.) **5:**438
L'Advocat, Jean Baptiste **8:**42
Lady Desart, *see* Bischoffsheim, Ellen Odette
Laehn (tn., Silesia) **14:**1536
Laemel, Leopold von **10:**1354
LAEMEL, SIMON VON **10:**1353
- *illus:* text
Laemel School (Jer.) **7:**100ff; **9:**928
- *illus:* **9:**929
LAEMMLE, CARL **10:**1355
- Los Angeles **11:**503
La Epoca (journ.) **13:**1038
La Epoca de New York (journ.) **13:**1040
La Esperansa (pub.) **13:**1039
LAETUS (Laïtos; trans.) **7:**895
La Famille De Jacob (period.) **3:**967
Lafayette (city, Ind.) **8:**1361
Lafayette (city, La.) **11:** 517
Lafayette, Marquis de **11:**1451
Lafer (fam.) **10:**1084
LAFER, HORACIO **10:**1355
Lafer, Miguel **10:**1085
La France Juive (bk.) **6:**236; **7:**29
LAGARDE, PAUL ANTON DE **10:**1356
- humanitarianism **8:**853
- Madagascar Plan **11:**678
Lagash (city, Mesop.) **16:**1488
- archaeological finds **16:**1507
- Sumer **15:**512
La Gata (journ.) **13:**1039
La Gazette d'Israël (period.) **15:**1449
LAG BA-OMER (minor fest.) **10:**1356
- *ḥevra kaddisha* celebration **8:**444
- *Hillula* celebration **8:**495
- *Hillula de-Rabbi Shimon bar Yoḥai* **8:**495
- Israel **9:**903
- *omer* **12:**1386ff
- Tlemcen **15:**1173
- *yom tov* **6:**1246
- *illus:*
- - text
- - hair-cutting **6:**1407
- - Ha-Shomer ha-Ẓa'ir parade **16:**1131
- - Ḥasidim dancing at Meron **5:**1270; **7:**1419
- - Warsaw ghetto children's choir **12:**657
Lagedi (concen. camp, Est.) **6:**917
Lagergeld (concen. camp money) **5:**725
Lagerkvist, Fabian **14:**930
Lagerlöf, Selma **9:**1577; **14:**929
La-Gever (journ.) **1:**newsp. list
LAGOS (city, Port.) **10:**1358
Lagos (tn., Nig.) **9:**440
- *illus:*
- City Hall **15:**93
La Goulette (loc., Tun.) **15:**1442
Lagovier, Nahum Osipovich **10:**1501
Lagu, Pedro **16:**10
LA GUARDIA, FIORELLO HENRY **10:**1358
- New York City **12:**111
- *illus:*
- - Soviet Anti-Fascist delegation **12:**1110
LA GUARDIA, HOLY CHILD OF (bld. lib.) **10:**1359
- Ávila **3:**969
- historical chart **8:**766-767
LAGUNA, DANIEL ISRAEL LOPEZ **10:**1360
Lagunilla (tn., Mex.) **11:**1457
Lagus (anc. fig., Egy.) **13:**1347
LAHARANNE, ERNEST **10:**1361
- Zionism **16:**1070
Lahav (kib., Isr.) **1:**place list
LAHAVOT HA-BASHAN (kib., Isr.) **10:**1361
- statistics **1:**place list
Lahavot Ḥavivah (kib., Isr.) **1:**place list; **14:**54
La-ḥayyal (journ.), *see Ha-Ḥayyal ha-Ivri*
Lahazan Bakha, *see* ASHRIKI, MORDECAI
Lahmi (bib. fig.) **6:**611
Lahmias, Moses **13:**1483
Lahore (city, Mogul Ind.) **8:**1356
- *illus:* **16:**104
LAHR, BERT (Irving Lahrheim) **15:**1086
Laibach (city, Yug.), *see* LJUBLJANA
Laicstein (cartog.), *see* Laiksteen, Pieter
La Idea-Sionista (period.) **16:**1124
Laiksteen, Pieter **9:**1543
Lainez, Diego **3:**204; **13:**416
Laínez, Pedro **14:**1178
Laish (bib. fig.) **13:**49
Laish (bib. city), *see* DAN
La-Ishah (journ.) **1:**newsp. list
Laïtos (trans.), *see* LAETUS
Lajjun, Al- (vill., Er. Isr.) **10:**103; **10:**1573
La Juive (opera) **7:**1184
La Justice (newsp.) **13:**1041; **15:**1449
Lakatos, Géza **8:**1103
LAKATOS, LÁSZLÓ **10:**1362
Lake Charles (city, La.) **11:** 517
Lakemacher, Johann Gottfried **8:**40
Lakeman, Stephen **11:**1567
Lake Mead (U.S.) **12:**1018
Lake Placid (tn., N.Y.) **12:**1127
Lake Tahoe (U.S.) **12:**1018
Lakewood (city, N.J.) **2:**412; **10:**1222; **12:**1030
- *illus:*
- - Sons of Israel Synagogue **4:**1005
Lakhish (mosh., Isr.), *see* Lachish
Lakner, Yehoshua **12:**670
Lakompak (tn., Burgenland), *see* Lackenbach
La-Kore ha-Za'ir (journ.) **1:**newsp. list
Lalande, Michel-Richard de **10:**1376
La Libre Parole (newsp.) **7:**29
- *illus:*
- - Jew and the Angel of Death (cartoon, 1893) **3:**152
La Loi Divine (period.) **3:**967
La Luz (period., Arg.) **3:**424; **13:**1039
La Luz (period., Bul.) **13:**1039
La Luz del Sábado (pub.) *see El Sábado Secreto*
La Mancha (reg., Sp.) **5:**594
La Manta (Inquis. list., Sp.) **15:**1426
Lamartine, Alphonse de **7:**141
Lamashtu (Lamaštu; demon) **5:**1420,1522
La Matatja (lab. union) **14:**871
La-Matḥil (journ.) **1:**newsp. list
Lamb, *see* SHEEP
Lamb, Charles **6:**779
Lamballe (tn., Fr.) **4:**1383
LAMBERT, AIMÉ **10:**1362
LAMBERT, MAYER **10:**1362
Lambert, Phyllis **4:**1407
LAMBERT, RAYMOND RAOUL **10:**1362
Lambert of Luettich **15:**1391
Lambesc (loc., Prov.) **13:**1259
Lambeth Bible (12th cent.) **14:**915
Lamdan (tal. schol.) **10:**395
LAMDAN, YIẒḤAK **10:**1363
- Hebrew literature **8:**200
- Writers' Association **16:**653
- *illus:*
- - Writers' Ass'n in Israel **8:**205; **16:**653
LAMECH (bib. fig.) **10:**1365
- Adah **2:**233
- *Lamech, Book of* **10:**1367
- Noah **12:**1191
- song **13:**679
- *illus:*
- - killing Cain **5:**25
LAMECH, BOOK OF (Apoc.) **10:**1367
Lamech Scroll (D. S. Scroll)
- Aramaic **3:**268
- ink **16:**665
- Lot narrative **11:**508
- *illus:*
- - unrolling of scroll **5:**1402-1403
- *see also:* DEAD SEA SCROLLS
LAMED (Heb. let.) **10:**1367
- masorah **16:**1409
- *see also:* ALPHABET, HEBREW
Lamed, Louis and Esther (fund, U.S.) **5:**1571
LAMED, MEIR **1:**32
"Lamed" project (housing estate, Tel Aviv) **15:**924
LAMED VAV ẒADDIKIM (righteous men) **10:**1367
- folktale **6:**1380
- Jehiel Meir of Gostynin **9:**1313
- Schwarz-Bart's novel **14:**1027
LAMEGO (fam.) **10:**1368
Lamego (tn., Port.) **16:**135
Lamego, Isaac **10:**1368
Lamego, Moses **10:**1368; **15:**310
Lameira (fam.) **14:**209
La-Menaẓẓe'aḥ (Psalm superscription) **13:**1319
La Menorah (period.) **6:**502
Lament, Lamentation (lit. form), *see* KINAH
LAMENTATIONS, BOOK OF **10:**1368
- *Contents:*
- - Style **10:**1370
- - Contents and Ideology **10:**1371
- - Authorship and Date **10:**1373
- - Relation to Mesopotamian Lamentations **10:**1375
- - In the Arts **10:**1375
- - In Music **10:**1375
- Av, The Ninth **3:**938
- Greek canon **4:**825
- musical rendition **14:**1059
- Scrolls, The Five **14:**1057
- *illus:*
- - text
- - Latin, 13th cent. ms. **13:**1417
LAMENTATIONS RABBAH (agg. Mid.) **10:**1376
- Talmud **15:**762
- Ten Martyrs **15:**1007
- *illus:* text
- *see also:* MIDRASH
La-Merḥav (youth mvmt., Isr.) **10:**969
La-Merḥav (newsp.) **2:**458; **5:**186; **9:**1016; **12:**1056
- statistics **1:**newsp. list
Lamgi-Mari (k., Mari) **11:**972
La-Mifneh (polit. orgn., Isr.) **7:**1323; **10:**973; **12:**882
La Migresse, Sarah **11:**1190
Lamina (orgn., Rum.) **15:**29
La-Mishpaḥah (journ.) **1:**newsp. list

Lamlum (tn., Iraq) **8:**1450
Lamm, Aaron Levi **15:**407
Lamm, Herman Fredrik **10:**1378
Lamm, Louis **3:**388; **4:**1239; **13:**1373
LAMM, MARTIN **10:**1378
LAMM, NORMAN **10:**1378
LAMM, PAVEL ALEKSANDROVICH **10:**1379
Lammlin, Asher, *see* LEMLEIN, ASHER
La-Mo'ed (journ.) **1:**newsp. list
La-Motte-du-Caire (loc., Fr.) **14:**1623
Lamp, Eternal, *see* NER TAMID
Lámpel, R. **13:**1369
LAMPON AND ISIDOROS (Gr. ldrs., Egy.) **10:**1379
Lamport, Nathan **12:**1085; **16:**112
LAMPRONTI, ISAAC HEZEKIAH BEN SAMUEL **10:**1379
- abortion **2:**100
- Anau, Phinehas **2:**935*f*
- chess **5:**403
- hunting, views on **8:**1111
- Morpurgo, Samson **12:**350
- talmudic methodology **11:**338
- *illus:*
- - Anau, Phinehas, rabbinical ordination certificate **2:**935
Lampronti, Solomon **14:**37
Lamps, *see* POTTERY
Lampstand, *see* MENORAH
La Mutua Agrícola (co-op., Arg.) **3:**432
Lamy, Bernhard **8:**40
La Nation Française (newsp.) **2:**232
LANCASTER (city, Pa.) **10:**1381
Lancaster (tn., Ont.) **12:**1408
LANCUT (tn., Pol.) **10:**1381
- *illus:*
- - synagogue **15:**607
LÁNCZY, GYULA **10:**1383
- Lánczy, Leó **10:**1383
LÁNCZY, LEÓ **10:**1383
Land, *see* Land ownership; PROPERTY
Land, Aaron ben Gershon **3:**727
LAND, EDWIN H. **10:**1384
Landa, Abraham Isaac (au.) **13:**133
LANDA, ABRAM (polit.) **10:**1384
Landa, Gertrude **5:**450
Landa, Ḥayyim Segal **13:**667
Landa, Jacob **12:**840
Landa, Joseph **15:**1035
Landa, Liva **12:**66
LANDA, MYER JACK **6:**784; **6:**789
LANDAU (city, Ger.) **10:**1384
- *illus:* text
Landau, Abraham (proofreader) **10:**1393
Landau, Abraham ben Raphael (r.), *see* CIECHANOW, ABRAHAM BEN RAPHAEL LANDAU OF
LANDAU, ADOLPH **10:**1385
- Leskov, N.S. **11:**46
- press **13:**1045
- *Voskhod* **16:**225
LANDAU, ALFRED **10:**1386
Landau, Anastaszy **11:**1204
Landau, Benjamin Ẓe'ev Wolf ben Ezekiel **15:**820
Landau, Cyril, *see* Popper-Bozian, Cyril
Landau, Dan **5:**561
Landau, David **6:**211
LANDAU, EDMUND **10:**1387
Landau, Edward **16:**634
Landau, Eleazar **10:**1388
LANDAU, ELEAZAR BEN ISRAEL **10:**1387
- Landau, Ezekiel **10:**1391
- Teomim, Aryeh Leib **15:**1010
Landau, Eliezer **10:**1397
Landau, Elijah, *see* LANDAU, ISAAC ELIJAH BEN SAMUEL
Landau, Elimelech Menahem Mendel **15:**447
LANDAU, EUGEN **10:**1388
LANDAU, EZEKIEL BEN JUDAH **10:**1388
- autopsies and dissection **3:**931; **3:**932
- Brill, Azriel **4:**1374
- gentile courts **12:**140
- Ḥasidism **7:**1405
- *haskamah* **7:**1454
- *ḥiddushim* **8:**467
- history chart **8:**766-767
- hunting, views on **3:**7; **8:**1112
- Modai, Ḥayyim **12:**200
- Orthodoxy **12:**1487
- responsa **11:**333
- *Toleranzpatent* **15:**1210
- Wessely, N.H. **16:**463
LANDAU, GREGORY ADOLFOVICH **10:**1391
Landau, Ḥayyim **9:**680
Landau, Ḥayyim ben Abraham **10:**1392
Landau, Isaac **15:**157
LANDAU, ISAAC ELIJAH BEN SAMUEL **10:**1392
- prayer books **13:**988
Landau, Israel **10:**1391
LANDAU, ISRAEL JONAH BEN JOSEPH HA-LEVI **10:**1392
Landau, J. (hist.) **8:**563
LANDAU, JACOB (Ger.) **10:**1393
- *Agur haskamah* **7:**1452
- codification of law **5:**646
- incunabula **8:**1324
- *illus:*
- - Bible incunabulum (1487) **8:**1329
Landau, Jacob (Gal.) **10:**1390
Landau, Jacob (engin.) **10:**1466
LANDAU, JACOB (journ.) **10:**1394
Landau, Jacob ben Isaac (Pol.) **15:**816
Landau, Jekuthiel Zalman **16:**191
Landau, Joseph **9:**1294
Landau, Joseph Samuel **10:**1392
Landau, Judah **10:**1393
LANDAU, JUDAH LOEB (Leo) **10:**1394
- drama **6:**196,201
Landau, L. (polit.) **10:**89
LANDAU, LEIB (law.) **10:**1509
- Steiger trial **15:**349
LANDAU, LEIBUSH MENDEL (r.) **10:**1395
LANDAU, LEOPOLD **10:**1395
LANDAU, LEV DAVIDOVICH **10:**1396
Landau, Ludwik **16:**353
Landau, M. (law.) **10:**1067
Landau, Marcus (hist.) **4:**1398; **16:**1328
Landau, Mark Aleksandrovich, *see* ALDANOV, MARK
Landau, Menahem Mendel Ḥayyim **12:**1244
Landau, M.J. **4:**875
Landau, M.M.H. **13:**989
LANDAU, MOSES (print.) **10:**1397
- Prague **13:**977
Landau, Moses Israel (bib. schol.) **4:**875
Landau, Moses Issachar (maskil) **10:**1394
LANDAU, MOSHE (educ.) **1:**32
Landau, Moshe (judge) **6:**521
- *illus:*
- - Fortas, Abe, and **6:**1441
Landau, Naḥman **4:**1363
LANDAU, NATHAN (r.) **10:**1397
Landau, Nathan (Zion.) **16:**1149
Landau, Raphael **5:**1037
Landau, Salo **5:**406
Landau, Samuel ben Ezekiel **10:**1388; **10:**1390
Landau, Samuel Isaac **15:**24
Landau, Saul (r.) **5:**1034
LANDAU, SAUL RAPHAEL (journ.) **10:**1397
- Basle Program **4:**306
- *Die Welt* **16:**445
- Po'alei Zion **13:**658
- Zionism **16:**1107
- *illus:*
- - F.Z.C. **16:**1165
LANDAU, SHEMUEL ḤAYYIM **10:**1398
Landau, Solomon Segal **6:**1155
Landau, Theodor **10:**1395
Landau, W. (Bib. schol.) **4:**875
Landau, Wolf (r.) **6:**212; **9:**1296
Landau, Ya'akov **13:**655
Landau, Ze'ev Wolf **15:**447
LANDAU, ZISHE **10:**1398
- Yiddish literature **16:**815
Landau, Zygmund **13:**116
LANDAUER, GEORG **10:**1399
LANDAUER, GUSTAV **10:**1399
- socialism **15:**34
Landauer, Hedwig, *see* Lachmann, Hedwig
LANDAUER, MEYER HEINRICH HIRSCH **10:**1401
LANDAUER, SAMUEL **10:**1402
Landauer, Wilhelm **4:**176
Land Betterment Tax Objection Committee (Isr.) **9:**640
Land courts (Isr.) **9:**632ff
Lande, Harold **5:**114
Landed property, *see* PROPERTY
LANDES, DAVID SAUL **10:**1402
Landes, M. **15:**1456
LANDES, RUTH **10:**1403
Landes, Zdenek **13:**1028
Landeshut (loc., Silesia) **15:**1042
LANDESJUDENSCHAFT, BOEHMISCHE (orgn.) **10:**1403
- Moravia **12:**300
Landesjudensollicitator (cmty. offic.) **4:**1384
Landesman, A. F. **8:**568
Landesmann, Heinrich, *see* LORM, HIERONYMUS
Landesrabbiner (rab. office), *see* LANDRABBINER
LANDESRABBINERSCHULE (rab. seminary, Hung.) **10:**1404
- Hildesheimer, Azriel **8:**476
- Wissenschaft **16:**577
LANDJUDENSCHAFT (cmty. inst.) **10:**1405
- *illus:* text
Land legislation in Israel **9:**654
LANDMAN, ISAAC **10:**1408
- *American Hebrew, The* **2:**821
Landman, Samuel **16:**426
Landmann, Arthur **2:**321
LANDMARKS **10:**1408
Land of Gazelle Nose (reg.) **6:**479
Land of Israel, *see* ISRAEL (Land of)
LAND OF ISRAEL IN INTERNATIONAL AFFAIRS **9:**304
- Balfour Declaration **4:**131
- Berlin, Congress of **4:**656
- *ḥalukkah* **7:**1207
- Mandate for Palestine **11:**861
- Muhammad Ali **9:**294; **9:**298; **9:**298; **12:**511
- Sykes-Picot Treaty **15:**565
"Land of Israel" Movement, *see* Greater Land of Israel Movement
Landolfo VI (prin.) **4:**500
Landor, Robert Eyres **6:**774
Land Ownership
- Alsace Jews **2:**753
- Barcelona Jews **15:**228ff
- Christian confiscations **16:**1284
- Church tithes **15:**1162
- Ereẓ Israel history **8:**613ff; **9:**237ff; **9:**265
- legal aspects **12:**1532; **12:**1533
- legislation **12:**248
- Mesopotamia **16:**1490
- *illus:*
- - Austria, "the Jew Zlomus" (deed, 1204) **3:**89
- - Lucca, land transfer deed (11th cent.) **14:**1389
LAND OWNERSHIP IN ISRAEL **9:**555
- Arab farmers **9:**1021; **9:**628; **9:**918ff
- Hope-Simpson report **13:**32
- I.C.A. **10:**47
- J.N.F. **10:**77
- P.I.C.A. **13:**495
- *illus:*
- - Volozhin, Nes Ziona Association **16:**214
LANDOWSKA, WANDA **10:**1408
LANDRABBINER (rab. office) **10:**1409
- Moravia **12:**300ff
- state law **13:**1453
LAND RECLAMATION IN ISRAEL **9:**558
- eucalyptus **9:**788
- Huleh Valley **8:**1067
- J.N.F. **10:**77
- *illus:*
- - Jezreel Valley **9:**585
Landriani, Ignazio **8:**40
Lands, Gentile, *see* *Huẓ la-areẓ*
Landsberg, A. **15:**1215
Landsberg, Aaron Isaac **12:**1438
Landsberg, Benjamin **10:**1256
Landsberg, Gershon ben Jehiel **7:**929
Landsberg, Max **14:**210
Landsberg, Mordecai **4:**653; **13:**1107
Landsberg, Moses **13:**1107
LANDSBERG, OTTO **10:**1410
Landsberg, Wolf **4:**664
Landsberg, Yiẓḥah, *see* SADEH, YIZḤAK
Landsberg an der Warthe (tn., Pol.), *see* GORZOW WIELKOPOLSKI
LANDSBERGER, ARTHUR **10:**1410
LANDSBERGER, BENNO **10:**1411
- Assyriology **16:**1508
Landsberger, Franz **3:**651; **8:**218
Landsberger, Julius **12:**1389
"Landscape" (paint., A. Feder) **13:**118
LANDSHUT (city, Ger.) **10:**1412
- *illus:* text
LANDSHUT, SIEGFRIED **10:**1412
- sociology **15:**64
LANDSHUTH, ELIEZER (Leser) **10:**1413
- liturgy **13:**988
LANDSMANNSCHAFTEN (orgn.) **10:**1414
- Argentina **3:**423
- Bund **4:**1499
- *ḥevrah kaddisha* **3:**921
- *see also:* FRATERNAL SOCIETIES; KOLEL
LANDSOFER, JONAH BEN ELIJAH **10:**1415
- Broda, Abraham **4:**1390
LANDSTEINER, KARL **10:**1416
- *illus:*
- - Austrian stamp **12:**1203
Land un Lebn (period.) **13:**1043
Landynski, N. **7:**334
Lane, Frederic **15:**312

LANG, FRITZ **10:**1416
- motion pictures **12:**453
- *illus:* text
Lang, Kristóf **8:**40
Lang, Pearl **5:**1270
Lang, Sylvan **14:**823
LANGALLERIE, PHILIPPE GENTIL DE **10:**1417
LANGDON, DAVID **10:**1418
- *illus:* text
Langdon, Samuel **14:**20
Lange, Gerson **10:**464
Lange, Halvard **12:**1225
Lange, Herbert **5:**374
Lange, Jacob **15:**464
Lange, J. Christian **8:**40
Lange, Johann **4:**886
Lange, Kurt **11:**1200
Lange, Sven **14:**926ff
Lange, W. **8:**40
Langenbuch, Isaac **7:**91
Langenes, H. **8:**40
Langenhoven, C.J. **15:**210
Langenlois (tn., Aus.) **3:**890
Langenstein von, *see* Henry of Hessen
LANGER, FRANTIŠEK **10:**1418
Langer, Georg **10:**673
Langer, Isidor **15:**287
Langer, Jerry **15:**312
LANGER, JIŘI MORDECHAI **10:**1419
- Czechoslovak literature **5:**1208
LANGERMANN, MAX **10:**1420
Langfuhr (sub., Gdansk) **7:**347
LANGFUS, ANNA **10:**1420
Langgaesser, Elisabeth **7:**454
Langier, J. **8:**40
Langius, W., *see* Lange, W.
Langland, William **6:**776
Langmuir, Irving **6:**313
LANGNER, LAWRENCE **15:**1087
Langner, Thomas **11:**1375
Langton, Stephen **8:**13
Language
- assimilation **3:**772
- *derekh ereẓ* **5:**1551
- etiquette **6:**946
- euphemisms **6:**959ff
- folk music **12:**669
- *lashon ha-ra* **10:**1432ff
- Midrash **12:**886
- mysticism **10:**523; **10:**547
- profanity **13:**1119ff
- Rosenzweig's views **14:**302
- *tables:*
- - Jewish world population, by language of country of residence, 1931 and 1967 **5:**1505
- *see also:* ETHICS; INFORMERS; INSULT; JEWISH LANGUAGES; SLANDER; *and under individual languages*
Language, Canaan, *see* CANAAN, LAND OF (Language and Script)
Language, Samaritan, *see* SAMARITANS (Language and Literature)
Language Conflict (Er. Isr.) **7:**693; **9:**930; **9:**999
Language of Judaism (enc.) **6:**734
LANGUEDOC (prov., Fr.) **10:**1421
- French Jewry **7:**19ff
- *illus:* text
Laniado (fam., Syr.) **15:**645
LANIADO, ABRAHAM BEN ISAAC **10:**1422
Laniado, Abraham ben Samuel **10:**1423
Laniado, M. (journ.) **7:**325
Laniado, Moses (paytan) **2:**565
LANIADO, RAPHAEL SOLOMON BEN SAMUEL **10:**1423
Laniado, Samuel **10:**1423
LANIADO, SAMUEL BEN ABRAHAM **10:**1423
Laniado, Saul **14:**887
LANIADO, SOLOMON BEN ABRAHAM **10:**1423
- Shabbetai Ẓevi **14:**1227
La Nostra Bandiera (newsp.) **15:**1455
Lansdowne, Lord Henry Charles **4:**130
Lansing (city, Mich.) **11:**1499
L'Antologia ebraica (journ.) **13:**1037
Lantz, Michael **11:**1167
Lanu, *see* GOZHANSKY, SAMUEL
LAODICEA (city, As. M.) **10:**1424
- Asia Minor **3:**746
- Diaspora **6:**10
- Phrygia **13:**487
Laos (kdm., As.) **9:**444
La Paix, revue religieuse, morale et littéraire (period.) **5:**1072
La Palestine Nouvelle (pub.) **16:**1114
La Pampa (prov., Arg.) **10:**46
LAPAPA, AARON BEN ISAAC **10:**1424
- Algazi, Solomon **2:**610
- Shabbetai Ẓevi **14:**1229
La Paz (city, Bol.) **4:**1188ff
La Paz (tn., Ariz.) **3:**449
LA PEYRÈRE, ISAAC **10:**1425
- philosophy **13:**417
- *illus:* text
Lapide, Cornelius à **8:**40
LAPIDOT, ALEXANDER MOSES **10:**1426
Lapidoth (bib. fig.) **5:**1432
Lapidoth Israel Oil Prospecting Co. **9:**793; **9:**795
LAPIDUS, MORRIS **3:**364
LAPIN, BERL **10:**1427
- Shakespeare **14:**1265
Lapin, Beẓalel **10:**1427
LAPIN, ISRAEL MOSES FISCHEL **10:**1427
- *geneal. table:* **9:**1259
Lapin, Joshua **10:**1427
Lapis lazuli (gem) **13:**1010
- *illus:*
- - bead **11:**976
Lapkovski, Beinush **5:**1549
Lapp, Ephraim Dov of Jaroslav **15:**778
Lapp, P.W. **7:**549
LAPSON, DVORA **5:**1272
La Puerta del Oriente (journ.) **13:**1038
Lapuseanu, Alexander **12:**838
Lapwing (zool.), *see* HOOPOE
Laquedem, Isaac (leg. fig.), *see* WANDERING JEW
LAQUEUR, WALTER ZE'EV **10:**1428
LAR (tn., Iran) **10:**1428
Lara, Abraham Cohen de **10:**1429
LARA, DAVID BEN ISAAC COHEN DE **10:**1428
LARA, ḤIYYA KOHEN DE **10:**1429
- Marrakesh **11:**1016
LARA, ISAAC COHEN DE **10:**1429
Lara, Johann **4:**886
Lara, Manrique de **12:**338
Lara, R. de **12:**284
Larache (city, Mor.) **12:**338
Larak (city, Mesop.) **16:**1485
Laramie (city, Wyo.) **16:**680
Laramie County (Wyo.) **16:**679
Larceny, *see* THEFT AND ROBBERY
L'Arche (journ.) **13:**1032
L'Arche de Noé (mag.) **5:**460
Larchmont (vill., N.Y.) **16:**464
Laredo (city, Tex.) **15:**1036
Larédo, Abraham **15:**792
Larédo, Isaac **15:**792
La Renaissance Juive (newsp.) **13:**1041
La Revue Juive (period.) **5:**664
Lari, Yahuda **10:**435
LARIN, YURI **10:**1430
Larindorf (dist., Rus.) **5:**1107; **14:**468
LARISSA (city., Gr.) **10:**1430
- Greece **7:**875
La Rivista Israelitica (journ.) **13:**1037
Lark (zool.) **9:**226
Larnaka (city, Cyp.) **13:**478
Laroche, Sophia **8:**402
La Rochelle (city, Fr.), *see* ROCHELLE, LA
"La Ronde" (paint., G. Michanze) **13:**116
Laroque, Raymond **11:**1562
Larsa (anc. kdm.) **16:**1495,1496
Larsson, Zenia **14:**932
LASANSKY, MAURICIO **10:**1430
- *illus:* text
Las Cruces (tn., New Mex.) **12:**1037
LASDUN, DENYS **3:**364
La Señora, *see* NASI, GRACIA
Laser, Simon Menahem **7:**1222; **7:**1240
La Serena (city, Chile) **5:**466
LASERSON, MAX **10:**1431
La Settimana Israelitica (journ.) **13:**1037
Lash (tn., Bohem.), *see* HROZNETIN
Lashkowitz, Herschel **12:**1221
LASHON HA-RA (evil speech) **10:**1432
- Eleazar ben Parta **6:**595
- flogging **6:**1349
- snake venom **15:**14
- *see also:* SLANDER
Lashon Lake (reg., Er. Isr.) **9:**156
Lashon Nekiyyah, *see* EUPHEMISM
Lashon Peninsula (Er. Isr.) **5:**1394; **9:**164; **9:**589
illus:
- - Jordan and Amaẓyahu rivers **9:**153
LASK (tn., Pol.) **10:**1433
LASK, EMIL **10:**1434
Lask, I.M. **5:**451
Laska, Moses **12:**186
Laskai, Matko János **8:**40
LASKER (fam.) **10:**1434
Lasker, Albert Davis **2:**316; **10:**1434
Lasker, Berthold **10:**1437
LASKER, EDUARD (polit.) **10:**1436
- Orthodox/Reform secession **8:**512
Lasker, Edward (chess pl.) **5:**405
- *illus:*
- - Reshevsky, Samuel, and **14:**82
LASKER, EMANUEL **10:**1436
- chess **5:**405; **5:**407
- *illus:* text
Lasker, Etta, *see* ROSENSOHN, ETTA LASKER
Lasker, Florina **10:**1435
Lasker, Henry **15:**318
Lasker, Isaac, *see* LASKER, EDUARD
Lasker, Loula Davis **10:**1435
Lasker, Morris **10:**1434; **15:**1035
LASKER-SCHUELER, ELSE **10:**1437
- German literature **7:**450
LASKI (fam.) **10:**1438
LASKI, HAROLD JOSEPH **10:**1438
- *illus:* text
Laski, Jan **2:**581
Laski, Marghanita **10:**1438
Laski, Nathan **10:**1438
Laski, Neville Jonas **10:**1438
Laski, Sarah **10:**1438
LASKIN, BORA **10:**1439
- Canada **5:**112
Laskin, Saul **12:**1408
LASKOV, ḤAYYIM **10:**1440
Lasky, Jesse Jr. **10:**1441
LASKY, JESSE L. **10:**1441
- United States **15:**1628
La Sociedad de Beneficencia Israelita de 1870 (cmty., Peru) **13:**323
La Solidaridad Ouvradera (journ.), *see Avante*
Las Palmas (city, Can. Is.) **8:**1396
Lassal, Heyman (Chayim) **10:**1441
LASSALLE (LASSAL), FERDINAND **10:**1441
- socialism **15:**26
- *illus:*
- - text
- - portrait **8:**709
LASSAR, OSCAR **10:**1444
Lassar-Cohn, *see* COHN, LASSAR
LASSAW, IBRAM **10:**1445
- *illus:* text
Lasso, Orlando di **15:**534
LASSON, ADOLF **10:**1445
Lasson, Georg **10:**1445
Laster, Max O. **14:**161
Last Judgment, *see* DAY OF THE LORD
Last of the Just, The (bk.) **14:**1027
Last Supper, Church of the (Jer.) **9:**1424; **9:**1441; **16:**1030
- *illus:*
- - Mount Zion **9:**1465
"Last things", *see* ESCHATOLOGY
Las Vegas (city, Nev.) **12:**1017ff
Las Vegas (city, New Mex.) **12:**1037
Laszczower, Joshua **4:**1397
LASZLO, PHILIP ALEXIUS DE LOMBOS **3:**604
- portraits **13:**917
Latas, Elijah de **11:**1168
Latas, Rica de **11:**1171
LATERAN COUNCILS III, IV **10:**1445
- anti-Jewish canons **3:**102; **8:**1377
- badge enforced by **4:**64
- Christians and Jews **5:**546; **8:**673ff
- Crusaders **5:**1145
- Jewish landowners' tithes **16:**1285
- popes **13:**853
- tithes, church **15:**1162
- Toledo **15:**1202
La Terre Retrouvée (newsp.) **16:**1114; **16:**640
Latgale (prov., Latv.) **14:**174
LATIF, ISAAC BEN ABRAHAM IBN **10:**1446
- Gabirol and Kabbalah **10:**561
- Kabbalah **10:**528ff
Latif, Isaac ben Meir (r.) **9:**1426
Latif, Samuel **11:**897; **13:**1100
LATIN AMERICA **10:**1448
- *Contents:*
- - Colonial Period **10:**1448
- - Jewish Emancipation **10:**1449
- - Jewish Immigration **10:**1450
- - Economic and Social Status **10:**1451
- - Patterns of Jewish Organization **10:**1452
- - Ties with Israel **10:**1455
- General
- - *aliyah* to Israel **9:**539ff
- - America **2:**813
- - American Jewish Committee **2:**824
- - Evian Conference **6:**988
- - Israel relations **9:**432
- - Marrano Diaspora **11:**1024
- - socialism **15:**33
- - U.N. decisions **15:**1549ff
- - War Crimes Trials **16:**297ff
- Countries
- - Argentina **3:**408
- - Barbados **4:**205

- - Bolivia **4:**1187
- - Brazil **4:**1322
- - Chile **5:**461
- - Colombia **5:**744
- - Costa Rica **5:**988
- - Cuba **5:**1146
- - Dominican Republic **6:**160
- - Ecuador **6:**359
- - El Salvador **6:**687
- - Guatemala **7:**956
- - Guyana **7:**997
- - Haiti **7:**1141
- - Honduras **8:**962
- - Jamaica **9:**1272
- - Mexico **11:**1453
- - Nicaragua **12:**1135
- - Panama **13:**53
- - Paraguay **13:**85
- - Peru **13:**322
- - Surinam **15:**529
- - Uruguay **16:**10
- - Venezuela **16:**90
- Communal Life
- - assimilation **3:**779
- - communal organization **5:**843
- - Habonim **8:**1243
- - *landsmannschaften* **10:**1414
- - ORT **12:**1485
- - refugees, Jewish **14:**30
- - Sephardi immigration **14:**1173
- - vital statistics **16:**178
- - Yiddish education **6:**437
- - Zionism **16:**1123; **16:**1127
- Cultural Life
- - press **13:**1040
- - television and radio **15:**929
- - theater **15:**1073
- Trades and Professions
- - agriculture **2:**413ff
- - law **10:**1502
- - medicine **11:**1202
- - politics **13:**820ff
- - publishing **13:**1370
- - trade and commerce **15:**1301
- *illus:*
- - new immigrants arriving in Haifa **9:**53
- *pop. tables:*
- - text
- - Jewish population, 1900-1968 **2:**809-816
- *see also:* JEWISH COLONIZATION ASSOCIATION

Latin Kingdom of Jerusalem, *see* Jerusalem, Kingdom of
Latin Language, *see* GREEK AND LATIN LANGUAGES, RABBINICAL KNOWLEDGE OF
Latino, *see* JUDEO-ITALIAN; LADINO
Latins (Chr. cmty., Isr.) **9:**912
Latman, Barry **15:**301
Latouche, Auguste **8:** 40
La Tribune Juive (period.) **5:**31; **6:**499; **13:**1041
LATRUN (site, Er. Isr.) **10:**1457
- frontier, Israel-Jordanian **9:**320
- Six-Day War **14:**1630
- War of Independence **16:**318
- *illus:* text
Latrun (immigrant ship) **8:**1250
LATTEINER, JOSEPH **10:**1459
- theater **15:**1066
Latteiner-Mogulesco Troupe **10:**1459
LATTES (It. fam.) **10:**1460
- *illus:* text
Lattes, A. (law.) **10:**1498
Lattes, Aaron Elijah **10:**1460; **15:**1455
LATTES, ABRAHAM BEN ISAAC **10:**1460
Lattes, Aldo **16:**116
LATTES, BONET **10:**1461
- astrolabe **3:**788
- popes **13:**856
- Reuchlin, Johannes **14:**109
LATTES, DANTE **10:**1461
- family **10:**1460
- Padua **13:**12
- Zionism **16:**1122
Lattes, Elia **10:**1460
Lattes, Elijah ben Isaac **10:**1460
Lattes, Elijah de, *see* Latas, Elijah de
Lattes, Emmanuel ben Isaac **14:**170
Lattes, Giuseppe **15:**1455
Lattes, Guglielmo **9:**1111; **16:**116
Lattes, Isaac (schol.) **5:**862
LATTES, ISAAC BEN JACOB **10:**1461
- Abba Mari ben Eligdor **2:**37
- *Zohar* **10:**543
Lattes, Isaac ben Judah **10:**1460
Lattes, Isaac Emanuel de **5:**324; **14:**1338
LATTES, ISAAC JOSHUA **10:**1461
- responsa **14:**89
Lattes, Jacob **10:**1462
Lattes, Jacob ben Emanuel, *see* LATTES, BONET
LATTES, JUDAH **10:**1462
Lattes, Moses **10:**1460
Lattes, Simone **10:**1460; **13:**1368
LATVIA **10:**1462
- *Contents:*
- - Jewish Population **10:**1463
- - Economic Life **10:**1464
- - Public and Political Life **10:**1465
- - Culture and Education **10:**1466
- - Holocaust Period **10:**1467
- - After the Liberation **10:**1469
- Betar **4:**714
- emancipation **6:**717
- Holocaust **8:**840
- minority rights **12:**45ff
- ORT **12:**1484
- population statistics **14:**483
- South Africa **15:**186
- *pop. tables:* text
LATZKY-BERTHOLDI, JACOB ZE'EV WOLF (Wilhelm) **10:**1469
- *illus:*
- - Ukrainian Provisional National Council **15:**1511
Lau, Joseph **10:**1172
Laub, Philip Alexius de Lombos, *see* LASZLO, PHILIP ALEXIUS DE LOMBOS
Laub, William **15:**302
Laucheimer, Charles **11:**1552
Laud, William **13:**665
Lauda (tn., Ger.) **4:**59; **10:**232
LAUDANUM (spice) **10:**1470
- plant list **13:**621
- source **8:**1311
Laud Maḥzor (illum. ms.) **11:**732ff
- *illus:* **11:***fcg.* 811
Lauenburg (tn., Pol.), *see* LEBORK
Lauer, James **14:**1041
LAUFBAHN, YITSHAK **10:**1470
LAUFER, B. **12:**1462
LAUINGEN (tn., Bav.) **10:**1471
Laun (tn., Bohem.), *see* LOUNY
Launceston (city, Austr.) **3:**878; **15:**830
Laundering **5:**1046ff
Laurel (bot.) **13:**621
Laurence, Richard **8:**40
LAURENCE, WILLIAM L. **10:**313
Laurentius Andraeas **14:**928
LAURENTS, ARTHUR **15:**1582
Laurie, Joe, Jr. **7:**901
Laurin, A. **5:**1251
L'Aurore (period.) **5:**31; **6:**499; **13:**1041
LAUSANNE (city, Switz.) **10:**1471
- Switzerland **15:**558
- treaty of **15:**1456
- *illus:* text
Lausitz (reg., Ger., Pol.) **12:**63
LAUTERBACH, ASHER ZELIG **10:**1473
LAUTERBACH, EDWARD H. **10:**1473
- New York City **12:**1103
LAUTERBACH, JACOB ZALLEL **10:**1473
- American Academy for Jewish Research **2:**818
LAUTERPACHT, SIR HERSCH **10:**1474
- War Crimes Trials **16:**291
La'uyeh (site, Er. Isr.) **13:**1532
Lav, Joseph ben David Ibn, *see* LEV, JOSEPH BEN DAVID IBN
Lavadores (corpse washers) **8:**444
LAVAL, PIERRE **10:**1475
La Vara (newsp.) **13:**1039
Lavat, Abraham David **2:**17
Lavater, Johann Casper **6:**97ff **11:**1332ff; **13:**455
- *illus:*
- - Mendelssohn, Moses, and **11:**1331
Lavender (perfume) **15:**269
- plant list **13:**621
Laver (Tabernacle vessel) **15:**683
- *illus:*
- - Padua synagogue **13:**11
- - Tedeschi family **14:**252
La Vera Luz (period.) **15:**1461
La Verdad (journ.) **13:**1040
La Vérité Israélite (period.) **5:**680
Lavi (fam.) **13:**690
LAVI (kib., Isr.) **10:**1475
- proselytes **13:**1192
- statistics **1:**place list
- *illus:* text
Lavi, Elijah **4:**503
Lavi, Joseph ben **13:**690
LAVI, SHELOMO **10:**1476
LAVI, THEODOR **1:**33; **10:**1477
- Rumania **14:**399
Lavi, Vidal Joseph ben *see* Benveniste, Vidal Joseph
Lavi, Yoḥanan, *see* LOEWENSON, JEAN
Lavie, Raffi **3:**593
- *illus:*
- - "Composition in Brown" (paint.) Fig. 106 **3**-ART
LAVIEL (angel), *see* RAPHAEL
Lavi (Leon) ha-Levi **13:**129
Lavlar, see SCRIBE
Lavnin (loc., Er. Isr.), *see* Tells (al-Baydā)
La Voie Nouvelle (period.) **14:**131
La Voix Juive (period.) **15:**1499
LAVON, PINḤAS **10:**1477
- Ben-Gurion, David **4:**511ff
- Dayan, Moshe **5:**1373
- Eshkol, Levi **6:**889ff
- Israel politics **9:**387; **9:**398; **9:**665
- Mapai **11:**913ff; **13:**1512
La Voz Sionista (pub.) **16:**1126
Lavrov, P. **11:**220; **15:**25, 39
LAVRY, MARC **10:**1479
Lavuzov, Y. **16:**1327
Law, *see* TORAH
Law, Ceremonial
- circumcision **5:**570
- dietary laws **6:**26
- festivals **6:**1237
- firstborn, redemption of **6:**1308
- *havdalah* **7:**1481
- Judaism **10:**388
- Karaites **10:**778
- *kiddush* **10:**974
- *mezuzah* **11:**1474
- Reform Judaism **14:**25ff
- Sabbath **14:**557
- *tallit* **15:**743
- *tefillin* **15:**898
- *ẓiẓit* **16:**1187
- *see also under individual ceremonies*
Law, Civil, *see Dinei Mammonot*
Law, Codification of, *see* CODIFICATION OF LAW
Law, Commercial, *see Dinei Mammonot*
Law, Conventional **2:**536
Law, Criminal, *see* PENAL LAW
Law, Divine, *see* DIVINE PUNISHMENT
Law, Jewish, *see* MISHPAT IVRI
Law, Labor, *see* LABOR LAW
Law, M. C. **13:**1022
Law, Monetary, *see Dinei Mammonot*
Law, Moral, *see* ETHICS
Law, Natural **2:**12; **2:**536; **12:**74; **12:**78ff; **13:**1248
Law, Oral, *see* ORAL LAW
Law, Private International, *see* CONFLICT OF LAWS
Law, Reading of, *see* TORAH, READING OF
Law, Ritual, *see* ISSUR VE-HETTER
Law, Roman **2:**349; **3:**295
Law, Written, *see* BIBLE; TORAH
Law and Administration Ordinance (Isr.) **9:**649ff
LAW AND MORALITY **10:**1480
- *Contents:*
- - In the Bible **10:**1480
- - Talmudic Period **10:**1481
- *Bava Kamma* **4:**340
- custom and equity **12:**24
- ethics **6:**34f
- favoritism in court **13:**955
- homosexuality **8:**961
- kissing **10:**1074
- love of neighbor **11:**529
- man, nature of **11:**844
- *mishpat ivri* **12:**113
- Noachide laws **12:**1189
- prostitution **14:**1243
- protection of poor **13:**633ff
- *takkanot ha-kahal* **15:**733
- talion **15:**741
- Torah **15:**1239ff
- usury **16:**28ff
- *see also:* SIN; UNJUST ENRICHMENT
LAWANI, DA'UD **10:**1484
LAWAT, ABRAHAM DAVID BEN JUDAH LEIB **10:**1484
LAWE, JOHN **11:**1498; **16:**555
Lawn Bowls (sport) **15:**312
Law of Determinability (philos. conc.) **11:**743
Law of Moses and Israel **5:**595; **11:**1047
LAW OF RETURN **10:**1485
- aliyah and absorption **5:**534
- apostates **3:**209
- Brother Daniel case **3:**209; **10:**63
- Christianity **5:**507
- historical survey **9:**378
- Israel constitution **16:**1065
- Jewish identity **10:**24; **10:**63
- non-Jewish relatives **10:**24
- proselytes **13:**1192
- Samaritans **14:**736
Lawrence (city, Mass.) **11:**1113
LAWRENCE, DAVID **10:**1487
Lawrence, D. H. **6:**775; **6:**781; **14:**784, 918
LAWRENCE, GERALD **15:**1086
LAWRENCE, THOMAS EDWARD **10:**1488
- Akaba **2:**477
- Sinai expedition **16:**632
- *illus:* text
Laws, Conflict of, *see* CONFLICT OF LAWS
Laws of the State, *see* DINA DE-MALKHUTA DINA
LAWSON (fam.) **10:**1489
LAWSON, JOHN HOWARD

15:1582
LAWTON, SAMUEL T. **11:**1574
LAWYERS **10:**1490
Laxon (tn., Fr.) **11:**496; **12:**815
La-Ya'aran (journ.) **1:** newsp. list
Layfield, John **8:**42
Laying on of hands, *see* SEMIKHAH
La-Yogev (journ.) **1:**newsp. list
LAYTON, IRVING **10:**1512
Layzer, David **3:**806
Laza (fig., Ger.) **9:**1221
Lazar, David **12:**1245
LAZAR, MOSHE **1:**33
Lazar, Nathan **15:**303
LAZAR, SAMSON **14:**426
Lazar, Simeon Menahem **5:**1036; **12:**1050
Lazar ben Pedat, *see* ELEAZAR BEN PEDAT
LAZARD (fam.) **10:**1513
Lazard, Alexandre **10:**1513
Lazard, Elie **10:**1513
Lazard, Frederic **5:**407
Lazard, S. (cmty, Isr., U.S.) **11:**498
Lazard Fréres (bnk. house, U.S.) **4:**178
Lazard Speyer-Elissen K.a.A. (bnk. house, Ger.) **4:**174
LAZARE, BERNARD **10:**1514
- Dreyfus Affair **6:**226
- Pèguy, Charles-Pierre **13:**212
Lazare, Isidore, *see* Leizerowicz, J. A.
LAZAREANU, BARBU **10:**1514
- Jewish milieu **14:**414
Lazareff, Pierre **10:**306; **13:**109
Lazari (fam.) **12:**493
Lazaro de Frigeis, *see* FRIGEIS, LAZARO DE
LAZARON, MORRIS SAMUEL **10:**1515
Lazarov, Lydia **15:**297; **15:**317
Lazarovici, Baruch, *see* LAZAREANU, BARBU
Lazarovitch, Irving, *see* LAYTON, IRVING
LAZARSFELD, PAUL F. **10:**1515
Lazarus (N. T. fig.) **4:**733
- *illus:*
- - Epstein's sculpture **6:**829
- - Holy Sepulcher frieze **9:**1420
LAZARUS (fam.) **10:**1516
- Cincinnati **5:**565
"Lazarus" (sculp., J. Epstein) **6:**829
Lazarus, David **6:**342
LAZARUS, EMMA **10:**1516
- U.S. literature **15:**1570, 1607
- *geneal. table* **12:**849
- *illus:*
- - sonnet on base of Statue of Liberty **15:**1608
Lazarus, Fred **10:**1516
Lazarus, Fred Jr. **5:**565; **10:**1516
Lazarus, Gerald N. **15:**193
Lazarus, Harry **15:**305
Lazarus, Henry A. **11:**520
Lazarus, I. **16:**1165
Lazarus, Israel **15:**305
Lazarus, Jeffrey **10:**1516; **16:**534
Lazarus, Johnny **15:**305
Lazarus, L. (schol., Ger.) **10:**465
Lazarus, L. (r. Lith.) **11:**1297
Lazarus, Mark **15:**299
Lazarus, Mel **5:**216
Lazarus, Michael **5:**359
LAZARUS, MORITZ **10:**1517
- ethics **6:**323, 940; **10:**743
- history chart **8:**766–767
- holiness, views on **10:**874
- philosophy **13:**460
- soul, immortality of **15:**179
- Torah **15:**1242
LAZARUS, NAHIDA RUTH **10:**1519
Lazarus, Ralph (19 th cent.) **10:**15
Lazarus, Ralph (20th cent.) **10:**151
Lazarus, Robert **10:**1516
Lazarus, Simon (19th cent., mer.) **10:**1516
Lazarus, Simon (r.) **5:**755
Lazarus, Simon (20th cent. bsmn.) **10:**1516
Lazarus, Solomon, *see* LEE, SIR SIDNEY
Lazarus of Sobota **10:**1556
Lazarussohn, Aaron, *see* LASSON, ADOLF
Lazebnik, M. **14:**917
LAZEROWITZ, MORRIS **10:**1519
Lazerwitz, Bernard **15:**68
LAZNE KYNZVART (tn., Bohem.) **10:**1519
LAZURICK, ROBERT **10:**1520
Lazzarelli, Lodovico **8:**42
Lazzaro da Pavia **6:**1135
Lazzaro da Viterbo, *see* Eliezer of Viterbo
LEA, HENRY CHARLES **10:**1521
Lead (metal) **11:**1434
LEAF, HAYIM **10:**1521
LEAF, REUBEN **4:**1219; **15:**148(
League V (anti-Fascist com.) **3:**62
League for the Abolition of Religious Coercion **9:**399
League for Equal Rights for Jews **12:**44
League for Jewish-Arab Understanding (Er. Isr.) **4:**633; **14:**1577
League for the Rights of Man **13:**85
League for the Seventh Dominion **16:**371
League of Anti-Semites (Ger.), *see* Anti-Semitic League
League of Cambrai **5:**153
League of the Communists (League of the Just) **11:**1072
League of Czecho Jews, *see* CECHU-ZIDU, SVAZ
League of National Christian Defense (Rum.) **5:**1177; **14:**394
- *illus:*
- - campaign poster **14:**395
LEAGUE OF NATIONS **10:**1521
- Arlosoroff, Chaim **3:**470
- Basle Program **4:**307
- holy places in Erez Israel **8:**939
- mandate for Palestine **11:**861ff
- minority rights **12:**43ff
- *numerus clausus* in Hungary **12:**1268
- refugees, Jewish **14:**29
- Thirteenth Zionist Congress **16:**1172
- White Papers **16:**484
- *see also:* COMITE DES DELEGATIONS JUIVES
LEAH (bib. fig.) **10:**1525
- in the Arts **9:**1204; **13:**1490
- Jacob **9:**1192ff
- Laban **10:**1315
- matriarch **13:**181
- Rachel **13:**1487
- tribes **15:**1384
- *illus:*
- - given in marriage to Jacob **4:**949
Le-Aḥdut ha-Avodah (journ.) **1:**newsp. list; **2:**457
Leakey, L. S. B. **3:**39; **15:**1181
Leal, Josi **11:**1215
Lealtad (fam.) **2:**614
Leander of Seville (archbp.) **9:**91
Le'anot (psalm) **13:**1321
LEAO, GASPAR DE **10:**1527
LEAP YEAR **10:**1527
- calendar **5:**43
- Samaritans **14:**748
- *illus:*
- - calendars (14th cent.) **5:**48, 52
Lear, Edward **9:**1580
- *illus:*
- - Jerusalem from the Mount of Olives (wtrcl.) **9:**1585
Learning, Torah *see* STUDY
Learsi, Rufus **8:**562
LEASE AND HIRE **10:**1528
- acquisition **2:**216
- *arenda* **3:**402
- competition restrictions **7:**1463
- custom in transaction **12:**21
- *ḥazakah* **7:**1518ff
- possession **12:**1532; **12:**1533
- servant and labor law **10:**1325
- waiver **11:**1232
- wine and liquor trade **16:**543
- *illus:*
- - land lease deed (2nd cent.) **4:**237
- *see also* SALE; SHOMERIM
LEATHER INDUSTRY AND TRADE **10:**1536
- crafts **5:**1044ff
- Lublin **11:**543
- textiles **15:**1036ff
- writing on **16:**659
- *illus:*
- - tanners, Strykow **15:**446
Leaven, *see* ḤAMEẒ
Leavenworth (city, Kan.) **10:**738
LEAVITT, MOSES A. **10:**1542
Leb. Joseph ben David ibn, *see* LEV, JOSEPH BEN DAVID IBN
LEBANON **10:**1542
- Alliance Israélite **2:**652
- Arab League **3:**242
- Arab refugees **9:**448ff
- armistice agreements **3:**479 **9:**377
- Beirut **4:**402
- civil war **14:**1624
- Druze community **9:**924ff
- frontier (Palestine, Israel) **9:**320
- Galilee rule **9:**309
- history chart **8:**766–767
- Palestinian guerrillas **9:**416
- Solomon's corvée **15:**102
- synagogues **1:**syn. list
- U.N. **15:**1546, 1558, 1561
- War of Independence **9:**366; **16:**306ff
- *illus:*
- - text
- - Cedars of Lebanon **5:**268
- - Druze population (map) **9:**926
- - Franco-British frontier agreements, 1920–23 (map) **9:**316
- - Israel-Lebanon General Armistice Agreements, 1949 **3:**481
Lebanon, Forest of **9:**787
LE BE, GUILLAUME **10:**1547
- typography **15:**1482
Lebeau, Samuel S., *see* LEIBOWITZ, SAMUEL SIMON
LEBEDEFF, AARON **15:**1086
- recordings **13:**1617
Lebel, Joannis **15:**745
Lebenhart, Filip **13:**1026
LEBENSOHN, ABRAHAM DOV **10:**1548
- Gordon, Mikhel **7:**803
- *Haskalah* **8:**185
- Loewisohn, Solomon **11:**455
- Pappenheim, Solomon **13:**69
- prosody **13:**1277
LEBENSOHN, MICAH JOSEPH **10:**1549
- *Haskalah* **8:**186
- Jerusalem theme **9:**1565
- Pappenheim, Solomon **13:**69
- prosody **13:**1226
- Schulman, Kalman **14:**1003
- *illus:* text
LEBENSOLD, FRED **3:**364
- *illus:*
- - Queen Elizabeth Theater, Vancouver, B.C. **3:**355
LEBERT, SIGMUND **12:**696
Lebhar (fam.), *see* DELMAR
Lebhar, Jacob **5:**1476
Lebns Fragn (journ.) **4:**1502; **4:**1503; **11:**1176
Lebn un Visnshaft (period.) **11:**405
LEBO-HAMATH (loc. Er. Isr.) **10:**1551
- Israel border **9:**116
- Kadesh **10:**665
- Nebuchadnezzar **12:**913
LEBORK (tn., Pol.) **10:**1552
LEBOVIC, DJORDJE **10:**1552
- Yugoslav literature **16:**889
Lebovich, Markus **4:**536
Lebovitch, Jeroham **12:**536
LEBRECHT, FUERCHTEGOTT **10:**1552
Lebrowitz, Barney, *see* Levinsky, Barney
Lebrun, Charles **9:**1344
Le Brun of London (mdvl. fig.) **2:**22
LEC, STANISLAW JERZY **10:**1553
- Polish literature **13:**801
LECACHE, BERNARD **10:**1553
Lecanomancy (divination) **6:**114
LECCA, RADU **10:**1553
- Rumania **14:**407
LECCE (city, It.) **10:**1554
- anti-Jewish riots (1463) **3:**228 **16:**1172
L'Echo Sioniste (journ.) **16:**1114
Leclef (Belg. pr.) **4:**422
Le Clerc, David, *see* Clericus, David
Le Clerc, Jean, *see* Clerc, Jean-Thomas
Le Coat, G. **4:**888
Le Corbusier **2:**167
L'Eco Sionista d'Italia (period.) **16:**1122
Le Cri du Citoyen Contre Les Juifs (wk.) **4:**381
Lectisternium (rel. rite) **7:**249
Lecture Bureau (U.S. agency) **12:**877
LECZNA (tn., Pol.) **10:**1554
LECZYCA (tn., Pol.) **10:**1555
Leczyca, Israel ben Jonathan of, *see* ISRAEL BEN JONATHAN FROM LECZYCA
LEDA, EDUARD **10:**1557
Le Defenseur (period.) **15:**1449
LEDERBERG, JOSHUA **10:**1557
- genetics **4:**1031
LEDEEN, HYMAN **8:**1432
Lederer (fam.) **11:**1499
LEDERER, ABRAHAM **10:**1558
Lederer, Eduard, *see* LEDA, EDUARD
LEDERER, FRANCIS **15:**1086
- Prague **13:**973
Lederer, Ignác, *see* GABOR, IGNAC
LEDERER, JEROME F. **10:**1558
Lederlin, J. H. **8:**42
Lederman, David **13:**1025
L'Educatore Israelita (journ.), *see* VESSILLO ISRAELITICO, IL
Lee, Edward **8:**42
Lee, Elizabeth **10:**1559
Lee, Joseph de **11:**1201
LEE, MALKE **10:**1559
Lee, Samuel (17th cent.) **8:**42
Lee, Samuel (18/19 cent.) **8:**42
Lee, Sydney (sport.) **15:**304
LEE, SIR SIDNEY (lit. hist.) **10:**1559
LEECH (zool.) **10:**1559
- dietary laws **6:**38
LEEDS (city, Eng.) **10:**1560
- Burton, Sir Montague **4:**1533
- England **6:**757ff
- tailoring **15:**707
- *illus:* text
LEEK (bot.) **10:**1561
- plant list **13:**621
Leek, Wild **13:**621

Leers, Johannes von **12:**956
LEES, LESTER **2:**323
LEESER, ISAAC **10:**1561
- Board of Delegates of American Israelites **4:**1149
- Conservative Judaism **5:**901
- Jewish Publication Society **10:**80
- Philadelphia **13:**372
- St. Louis **14:**663
- *illus:* text
LEEUW, AVRAHAM DE **8:**1432
LEEUW, JACOB BEN HAYYIM (Heymann) DE **10:**1562
Leeuw, Oscar **12:**1159
Leeward Islands **11:**1019
Le-Ezrat ha-Am (newsp.) **13:**1035
LE FÈVRE DE LA BODERIE, GUY **10:**1563
- Antwerp Polyglot Bible **13:**614
- Giorgio, Francesco **7:**588
- Hebraists **8:**42
- Levita, Elijah **11:**134
- Postel **13:**933
- Psalms **5:**1335; **13:**1326
- *illus:* text
Le Fèvre de la Boderie, Nicolas **10:**1563
- Hebraists **8:**42
- Vigenère, Blaise de **16:**134
Lefèvre d'Etaples, Jacques **4:**881
- Hebraists **8:**42
- Pellicanus **13:**220
Leff, Moe **5:**216
Leff, Moses **11:**482
Leff, Sam **5:**216
Lefin, Menahem Mendel, *see* LEVIN, MENAHEM MENDEL
Lefi Sha'ah (journ., Isr.) **1:** newsp. list
Lefkowitch, Henry **13:**1618
Lefkowitz, Louis J. **12:**1127
Lefkowitz, Sidney M. **9:**1191
Lefmann, Salomon **8:**402
Le Foyer Israélite (period.) **5:**456
LEFRAK, SAMUEL J. **10:**1564
LEFSCHETZ, SOLOMON **11:**1125
Left (direction), *see* RIGHT AND LEFT
Left Po'alei Zion (polit. party) **9:**854ff
- Comintern **15:**49
- Zionism **16:**639
LEFTWICH, JOSEPH **10:**1564
Legacy **16:**519ff
Legal capacity
- *agunah* **2:**429
- *apotropos'* responsibility **3:**218,221
- court representation **13:**952; **13:**956
- embryo **6:**720
- liability **11:**184; **11:**185
- marriage **11:**1049
- minor, definition **8:**1424
- orphan **12:**1479
- ownership, loss of **12:**1533
- penal law **13:**222
- public office **13:**1357
- sale **14:**677
- suicide **15:**489ff
- testimony **16:**586
- theft **15:**1095,1097
- usury **16:**30ff
- waiver **11:**1234
- wills **16:**523
- see also: CONTRACT; DEAF-MUTE; Idiot; Minor
Legal Codes, *see* CODIFICATION OF LAW
Legal error **13:**227; **13:**957ff
Legal fiction
- *eruv* **6:**849
- *hetter iska* **14:**1388; **16:**1283
- nonexistence of condemned person **13:**961
- *prosbul* **13:**1181
"Legalists," *see* INDEPENDENT JEWISH WORKERS PARTY
LEGAL MAXIMS **10:**1564
- *Contents:*
- - Historical Periods **10:**1564
- - The Mishnaic Kelal **10:**1565
- - Compilations **10:**1567
LEGAL PERSON (corp. leg. body) **10:**1567
- *Contents:*
- - Talmudic and Post-Talmudic Law **10:**1567
- - Modern Rabbinic Law **10:**1569
- hired service contract **10:**1325
- taxation in Israel **9:**755
- *see also:* HEKDESH; PARTNERSHIP; TAKKANOT HA-KAHAL
Legal precedent, *see* MA'ASEH
Legal Procedure, *see* PRACTICE AND PROCEDURE
Legal system, Jewish, *see* MISHPAT IVRI
Legend, *see* AGGADAH; FABLE; FICTION, HEBREW; HAGIOGRAPHY; MIDRASH
Leggett, F. **13:**33
LEGHORN (port, It.) **10:**1570
- *Halukkah* **7:**1208
- museum **12:**544
- Shabbateanism **14:**1245
- special Purim **13:**1397
- synagogue **15:**618; **15:**627
- Tunisia **15:**1442
- *illus:*
- - text
- - ancient Synagogue, Rejoicing of the Law (paint., A. Hart) **3:**547
- - Jewish community gift **9:**1129
- - synagogues **9:**1139; **15:**627
- *see also:* TUSCANY
LEGIO (city, Er. Isr.) **10:**1573
- Jezreel, Valley of **10:**103
- *see also:* KEFAR OTNAY
Legion, Jewish, *see* JEWISH LEGION
Legion, Sixth Roman (Ferrata) **9:**246; **10:**1573
Legion, Tenth Roman (Fretensis)
- Herod's towers **9:**1405
- Jerusalem archaeology **9:**1535
- Judean garrison **9:**239; **9:**251
- transfer to Elath **9:**1406
- *illus:*
- - seal **13:**1537
Legion of Archangel Michael (orgn., Rum.) **8:**1472
Legislation, *see* CODIFICATION OF LAW; HALAKHAH; MISHPAT IVRI; TAKKANOT; TAKKANOT HA-KAHAL
Legislation, anti-Jewish (general)
- migrations **16:**1522
- *numerus clausus* **12:**1263
- Paris **13:**103ff
- Prussia **13:**1289ff
- socialism **15:**36
- South Africa **15:**187ff
- Spain **15:**222ff,226
- Toledo **15:**1198,1201
- Tortosa **15:**1269
- *illus:*
- - Prague, Maria Theresa's expulsion edict **11:**991
- *see also:* ANTI-SEMITISM; MINORITY RIGHTS
LEGISLATION, ANTI-JEWISH, IN THE NAZI PERIOD **10:**1573
- Nuremberg laws **12:**1281
- War Crimes Trials **16:**289ff
- *illus:*
- - Nuremberg Laws **12:**1281
- *see also:* HOLOCAUST
Legislation, Subordinate, *see* Subordinate Legislation
LEGISLATION IN ISRAEL **9:**645ff
- historical survey **9:**368ff,383ff
- labor legislation **9:**874ff
- Petroleum Law **9:**793
Legislature (Israel), *see* KNESSET
LEGNICA (tn., Pol.) **10:**1574
- Silesia **14:**1536ff
Le Goglu (pam.) **5:**110
Le Grand Gerin (site, Er. Isr.), *see* JENIN
Legrel, Florin, *see* MUGUR, FLORIN
LEGUMES **10:**1575
- *kapparot* **10:**756
- mixed species prohibition **12:**170
- prickly plants **15:**1120
- *see also:* VEGETABLES
Le-Ḥag Mizmor (kibb. fest. cantata) **10:**961
Le-Hasi Betulah (charitable assoc.) **14:**355
Lehavah, Joseph, *see* Fiametta, Joseph
Le-Ḥayyim (Heb. greeting) **7:**916
- wine **16:**540
Le-Ḥayyim Tovim u-le-Shalom (Heb. greeting) **7:**916
Le-hazkir (Psalm superscription) **13:**1320
Leḥem ha-panim, *see* SHEWBREAD
Leḥem Mishneh (bk.) **4:**1269
Leḥem oni ("bread of affliction"), *see* MAẒẒAH
Leḥem Oni (wk.) **7:**1467
- *illus:*
- - title page (1784) **11:**476
Leḥem Rav (bk.) **4:**1269
Lehi (bib. place) **14:**772
Leḥi (underground orgn., Pal.), *see* LOḤAMEI ḤERUT ISRAEL
Lehli (Turk. "Palestine") **15:**1462
LEHMAN (fam.) **10:**1576
- *illus:* text
Lehman, Allan S. **10:**1577
Lehman, Arthur **10:**1577
- *illus:*
- - Joint Distribution Committee **2:**829
Lehman, Emanuel **10:**1576
- welfare society **2:**505
LEHMAN, ERNEST **12:**470
Lehman, Helen **4:**1540
Lehman, Henry **10:**1576
LEHMAN, HERBERT HENRY **10:**1577
- New York **12:**1127
- *illus:*
- - Mikoyan, Anastas, and **12:**1112
LEHMAN, IRVING **10:**1579
- National Jewish Welfare Board **12:**872ff
- New York **12:**1127
Lehman, Mayer **10:**1576
Lehman, Philip **10:**1577
Lehman, Robert **10:**1577
- horse breeding **15:**311; **15:**312
LEHMANN, BEHREND **10:**1579
Lehmann, Charles **11:**1562
Lehmann, Else **15:**1056
LEHMANN, EMIL **10:**1580
Lehmann, Felix **13:**1366
Lehmann, G. **8:**42
LEHMANN, JOSEPH (Fr. r.) **10:**1581
Lehmann, Joseph (pub.) **13:**1366
Lehmann, Julian **9:**1067
LEHMANN, KARL **10:**1581
LEHMANN, LÉONCE **10:**1582
- law **10:**1495
LEHMANN, MARCUS **10:**1582
- *Der Israelit* **9:**1066
- *illus:* text
Lehmann, Oskar **9:**1066
LEHMANN, SIEGRIED **10:**1583
LEHMANN-HAUPT, CARL FRIEDRICH **10:**1583
Lehmans, Moses **2:**900
Lehmbruck, Wilhelm **13:**115
- *illus:*
- - "Young Girl" (sculp.) **13:**117
Lehranstalt fuer die Wissenschaft des Judentums, *see* HOCHSCHULE FUER DIE WISSENSCHAFT DES JUDENTUMS
Lehrberger, M. **10:**841; **13:**1112; **14:**220
LEHREN (fam.) **10:**1584
- philanthrophy **2:**900
Lehren, Akiva **10:**1584
- *illus:* text
Lehren, H. **13:**1095
Lehren, Jacob Meir **10:**1585
Lehren, Moses **10:**1584
Lehren, Ẓevi Hirsch **10:**1584
- emissaries **14:**1363
- Ereẓ Israel hospital **9:**300
LEHRER, LEIBUSH **10:**1585
- education **6:**444
Lehrer, Mayer, *see* MAYER, LEOPOLD
Lehrer, Reuben **12:**968
Lehrman, Daniel **13:**1345
LEHRMAN, IRVING **10:**1585
Lehrman, Simon Maurice **5:**450
- homiletic literature **8:**957
Lehrmann, Cuno **11:**591
Lehrs, Max **3:**650
Leib, Chilian **8:**42
Leib, Mani, *see* MANI-LEIB
Leib ben Ozer **13:**1241
Leibel ben Mordecai **10:**1279ff
Leibele Prossnitz, *see* PROSSNITZ, JUDAH LEIB BEN JACOB HOLLESCHAU
Leib Ḥarif, *see* Kohen, Moses Judah ben Kalonymus
LEIBL, DANIEL **10:**1585
- *illus:*
- - Markish, Peretz, and **11:**1006
Leibler, I. J. **11:**1284
- Russian Jewry **14:**499
Leibmauth (body tax), *see* LEIBZOLL
Leibniz, Gottfried Wilhelm von **10:**1118
Leib of Szydlowiec, *see* Judah Loebush ben Isaac
Leibov, Baruch **11:**14
Leibovich, Adolfo **3:**432
Leibovich, Fannie **10:**1503
Leibovich, Jeroham **13:**56
Leibovici, A., *see* BARANGA, AUREL
Leibovitz, Dov, *see* ARIEL, DOV
Leibowici, Arthur, *see* Arsene, Maria
LEIBOWITZ, BARUCH BER **10:**1586
- Slobodka **14:**1669
Leibowitz, Hershel **13:**1345
LEIBOWITZ, JOSHUA O. **10:**1586
Leibowitz, Nehama(h) **10:**1588
LEIBOWITZ, RENE **12:**696
LEIBOWITZ, SAMUEL SIMON **10:**1587
- law **10:**1505
LEIBOWITZ, YESHAYAHU **10:**1587
- religious life in Israel **9:**899
- Torah and Jewish nationalism **10:**1382; **15:**1243
Leibush, Aryeh **10:**1382
Leibush, Joseph Azriel **2:**159
LEIBZOLL ("body tax") **10:**1588
- Alsace Jews **2:**754; **2:**756
- Charles William Ferdinand **4:**1421
- history chart **8:**766-767
- Joseph II **10:**218
LEICESTER (tn., Eng.) **10:**1589
Leicester (tn., Mass.) **11:**1113; **16:**633
LEICHTENTRITT, HUGO **12:**696
Leidesdorf (fam.), *see*

LEIDESDORFER
Leidesdorf, Aaron **10**:1590
Leidesdorf, August **10**:1590
Leidesdorf, Babetta (Bela) **10**:1590
Leidesdorf, Ignaz **10**:1590
Leidesdorf, Markus **10**:1590
Leidesdorf, Menachem Mendel **10**:1590
LEIDESDORF, SAMUEL DAVID **10**:1589
LEIDESDORFER (fam.) **10**:1589
Leidesdorfer, Ḥayyim, *see* Leidesdorfer, Joachim
Leidesdorfer, Isaac **10**:1589
Leidesdorfer, Joachim **10**:1590
Leidesdorfer, Judith **10**:1590
Leidesdorfer, Loeb **10**:1589
Leidesdorfer, Moses **10**:1590
Leidesdorfer, Samuel **10**:1589
L'E.I.F. (journ., Fr.) **14**:1039
Leigh, Edward **8**:42
Leigheb, Claudio **15**:1057
LEIMDOERFER, DAVID **10**:1590
Leiner, Benjamin, *see* LEONARD, BENNY
Leiner, Gershon Henikh **9**:1160
- *tekhelet* **15**:914
Leiner, Jacob **9**:1160
Leiner, Mordecai Joseph Eleazar **9**:1160
Leiner, Mordecai Joseph of Izbica, *see* Mordecai Joseph Leiner of Izbica
Leiner, Samuel Solomon **9**:1160; **13**:1509
Leininger, Harald, *see* MUNK, KAJ
LEINSDORF, ERICH **12**:696
Leipnik (tn, Morav.), *see* LIPNIK NAD BECVOU
Leipnik, Joseph ben David **8**:1287
Leipniker, Abraham Broda **16**:20
LEIPZIG (city, Ger.) **10**:1590
- fairs **11**:1004ff
- fur trade **7**:223ff
- history chart (1869) **8**:766-767
- synod **13**:1461
- *illus:* text
LEIPZIGER, EMIL WILLIAM **10**:1592
LEIPZIGER, HENRY M. **10**:1592
Leipzig Maḥzor (14th cent. illum. ms.) **11**:732ff
- illuminated manuscripts **8**:1261
- *illus:* **2**:118; **4**:394; **5**:1441; **6**:386; **8**:1218; **11**:734; **12**:601,916,944
LEIRIA (city, Port.) **10**:1593
LEISERSON, WILLIAM MORRIS **10**:1593
Leist, Hans **5**:169
Leites (indus. Azer.) **4**:119
Leitmeritz, (Bohem.), *see* LITOMERICE
Leivik (fam.) **14**:833
LEIVICK, H. **10**:1594
- *illus:*
- - text
- - Hebrew writers' convention, 1943 **8**:213
- - Yiddish writers, New York **16**:823
Leizerl of Kalisz, *see* Auerbach, Eliezer ben Ḥayyim
Leizerowicz, J. A. **7**:1498
Lejbman, Leib **15**:539
Lejtman, Shelomo **12**:55
Le Juge (newsp.) **4**:275
Lekaḥ Tov (mid.), *see* MIDRASH LEKAḤ TOV
Lekar, Isaac, *see* Rofe, Isaac
LEKERT, HIRSCH **11**:1
- Vilna **16**:144
LEKET, SHIKHHAH, AND PE'AH (form of charity) **11**:3
- ethical commandments **6**:938
- *Pe'ah* laws **13**:200
- Pentateuch **13**:250
- *illus:*
- - poor man gleaning wheat **13**:200
- - Ruth gleaning in the fields of Boaz **4**:1154
- *see also:* CHARITY; POOR, PROVISION FOR THE; POVERTY
Leket Omarim (journ., Rus.) **1**: newsp. list
LEKHAH DODI (litur.) **11**:4
- Alkabez, Solomon **2**:637
- Hahn, Joseph Yuspa **7**:1129
- Jerusalem **9**:1561
- kabbalistic influence **10**:642
- mourning melody **6**:672
- Sabbath service **10**:654
- *illus:*
- - wall plaque **10**:655
LEKHNO, DAVID **11**:7
Leksikon fun der Yidisher Literatur, Prese un Filologi **14**:63
Leksikon Judaizma i Kršćanstva (bk.) **6**:735
Leksikon Mikra'i (bk.) **6**:734
Le-lammed (Psalm superscription) **13**:1321
LELEWEL, JOACHIM (Ignacy) **11**:7
- Polish literature **13**:799
Lelio della Torre **5**:1297
Lellever, Heinrich **11**:665
Lellouche, Jules **13**:118
Le Long, J. **8**:42
LELOUCH, CLAUDE **12**:470
- *illus:*
- - *A Man and A Woman* **12**:459
LELOV (Lelow; ḥas. dyn.) **11**:8
- dynasties **1**:ḥas. table
- Karlin Ḥasidim **10**:794
Lelov (Lelow), David of **16**:303; **11**:8
LELOW (vill., Pol.) **11**:9
Lelower, Isaac **5**:35
LELYVELD, ARTHUR JOSEPH **11**:9
Le-ma'alah (gram. term) **16**:1431
Le-ma'alan (gram. term) **16**:1431
Le-Ma'an ha-Yeled ve-ha-No'ar (journ., Isr.) **1**: newsp. list
Lema'an Yisrael-Pro Israel (period.) **13**:1039
Le Maistre, Louis Isaac **4**:881
Lemaître, Jules **7**:1349
Le Mans (city, Fr.), *see* MANS, LE
LEMANS, MOSES **11**:10
- *illus:* text
Lemansky, P., *see* HERSCH, PESACH LIEBMAN
Le-matah (gram. term) **16**:1431
Le-matan (gram. term) **16**:1431
Lemberg (city, Gal.), *see* LVOV
Lemberg, Disputation of, *see* Lvov, Disputation of
Lemberg, Jakub **16**:947
LEMBERGER, MOSES BEN AARON **11**:10
Lemberger Togblat (newsp.) **11**:613
Lemberger Zeitung (newsp.) **16**:250
Lemel, Asher **5**:1028; **6**:1329; **13**:834
Lemel, Hendel, *see* Fishel, Hendel
Lemkau, Paul **13**:1340
LEMKIN, RAPHAEL **11**:11
- genocide **7**:409
- War Crimes Trials **16**:291
Lemle, H. **5**:456
LEMLEIN, ASHER **11**:11
- Kabbalah **10**:544
- messianism **11**:1425
Lemoine, Henry **8**:42
Lemon (bot.) **5**:580
Lemon, Hartog de **2**:889,900
Le Monde Juif: la Revue du C.D.J.C. (period.) **5**:288; **15**:54
Lemonick, Bernard **15**:308
L'EMPEREUR, CONSTANTIN **11**:11
- Hebraists **8**:42
Lempereur, Jean **9**:1442
LEMUEL (k., Proverbs) **11**:12
- *see also:* SOLOMON
"Le Mur" (sculp., S. Haber) **14**:1068
Lemuria (funeral rites) **12**:1389
Lenartowicz, Aleksander Teofil **13**:799
Lenchitsa (tn., Pol.), *see* LECZYCA
Lenchna (tn., Pol.), *see* LECZNA
Lendinara (tn., It.) **14**:354
LENDVAI, ERWIN **12**:696
Lenel, Otto **7**:133
Lengnau (vill., Switz.), *see* ENDINGEN AND LENGNAU
LENGYEL, EMIL **10**:313
LENGYEL, JÓZSEF **11**:12
LENGYEL, MENYHÉRT (Melchior) **11**:12
Lenigo, Isaac **13**:1095
LENIN, VLADIMIR ILYICH **11**:13
- attitude to Jews **16**:779
- communism **5**:792ff
- Esther (M. Lifschitz) **6**:913
- history chart **8**:766-767
- Jewish socialism **15**:41
- Kamenev, Lev Borisovich **10**:726
- Litvinov, Maxim **11**:406
- Martov, Julius **11**:1068
- Stalin **15**:327
- Trotski, Lev Davidovich **15**:1404ff
LENINGRAD (city, Rus.) **11**:14
- Chwolson, Daniel **5**:559
- libraries **11**:193
- museums **12**:540
- Society for the Promotion of Culture **15**:58ff
- synagogue **15**:589; **15**:620
- *illus:*
- - text
- - Ha-Teḥiyyah members **16**:1137
Leningrad (ship) **14**:1640
Leningrad Bible, First (illum. ms.) **9**:1579
- Aaron ben Asher **16**:1472
- Masorah versions **16**:1423
Leningrad Bible, Second (ms.) **8**:1261; **8**:1262ff
- Lamentations, Book of **10**:1371
- Psalms, Book of **13**:1306
- *illus:* **5**:*fcg.* 43; **8**:1273; **11**:904
Leningrad Trial (1970/1) **9**:429; **14**:493
LENKEI, HENRIK **8**:1079; **8**:1086
Lenkowich, A. **5**:1038
Lenormant, F. **4**:881
LENSKI, ḤAYYIM **11**:20
- Siberia **14**:1488
Lent, Ā **8**:42
LENTIL (bot.) **11**:21
- food **6**:1416
- plant list **13**:621
- *illus:*
- - mourner's pewter plate **12**:489
Lentshits (tn., Pol.), *see* LECZYCA
Lentzen (Nazi crim.) **11**:389
Lenya, Lotte **16**:398
Lenz, J. L. **8**:42
Lenz, Sidney **5**:169
Lenzer, B. **4**:138
Lenzer, Jacob **11**:1277
Lenzi, Mariano **2**:110
Leo (zodiac sign) **16**:1191
- *illus:*
- - Bet Alfa mosaic **3**:935
- - Worms *Maḥzor* **16**:1191
LEO III (the Isaurian; Byz. emp.) **11**:23
- Bulgaria **4**:1480
- forced conversions **3**:170
- Greece **7**:871
LEO VI, THE WISE (Byz. emp.) **11**:23
- *Vision of Daniel* **5**:1290
- Jews in Byzantine Empire **4**:1553
Leo I (the Great; pope) **5**:553; **13**:852
LEO VII (pope) **11**:22
- attitude to Jews **13**:852
LEO X (pope) **11**:22
- attitude to Jews **13**:856
- Reuchlin, Johannes **14**:109ff
Leo XII (pope) **5**:1597
- popes **13**:859
LEO XIII (pope) **11**:22
- *Civiltà Cattolica, La* **5**:599
- popes **13**:860
Leo, Christopher **8**:42
Leo Baeck College (Eng.) **6**:450
Leo Baeck Institute (U.S.) **2**:820
- archives **3**:384
LEO BAECK INSTITUTE (Isr.) **11**:23
- historical research **15**:55
- library of **11**:191
- *illus:* text
Leoben (city, Aus.) **15**:465
Leobschuetz (fam.), *see* LIPSCHUETZ
Leo Hebraeus, *see* ABRABANEL, JUDAH
Leominster (city, Mass.) **11**:1115
Leon . . ., *see also* De Leon
LEON (fam.) **11**:25
LEON (city, Sp.) **11**:24
- Spain **15**:227
- *illus:*
- - tombstone inscription **15**:225
Leon, Aaron **11**:28
Leon, Abraham David **4**:351
Leon, Abraham de (paytan) **11**:26
Leon, Abraham de (stlr., U.S.) **11**:26
Leon, Abraham Judah **11**:26
Léon, Adrien **4**:1246
León, Andrés, *see* Zamora, Andreas de León
Leon, Asher **4**:376
Leon, David de **11**:1551
Leon, Elijah de **11**:26
LEON, HARRY JOSHUA **11**:26
Leon, H.C., *see* CECIL, HENRY
Leon, Isaac ben Eliezer de (It.) **11**:26
LEON, ISAAC DE (Sp.) **11**:27
- Cavalleria, Alfonso de la **5**:265
Leon, Isaac de (Turk.) **11**:26
Leon, Jacob de **11**:26
Leon, Jacob Judah **15**:985
Leon, Jacob Rodriguez de **11**:26
Leon, Joseph de (Er. Isr.) **11**:26
Leon, Joseph de (It.) **11**:26
Leon, Joshua de **11**:26
Leon, Judah (emis.) **14**:251, 1366
Leon, Judah Ḥayyim (r., Ger.) **11**:26
LEON, LUIS DE **11**:27
- Hebraists **8**:42
- Spanish literature **15**:247
Leon, Manuel de **11**:26
Leon, Meir de **11**:26
LEON, MESSER DAVID BEN JUDAH **11**:27
- Kabbalah **10**:542
- ordination dispute **13**:1449
- *Sefirot* doctrine **10**:567
- Valona **16**:63
Leon, Messer Judah ben Jehiel, *see* JUDAH BEN JEHIEL
Leon, Morris J. **11**:26
Leon, Moses (U.S.) **11**:26
Leon, Moses P. de **11**:26
Leon, Pedro de **11**:26
Leon, Samuel **10**:1492
Leon, Samuel de **11**:26
Leon, R.N. **12**:845
Leon, Sigmund **15**:1073
LÉON, XAVIER **11**:28
LEONARD, BENNY **11**:28
LEONARD, LOTTE **12**:696
Leon ben Elhanan **14**:1617
Leon ben Michael ha-Parnas **13**:589
León Bible (1162, illum. ms., Sp.) **2**:175; **3**:461; **5**:1328, 1426, 1436;

6:633,636,666; **9**:1349,1369; **10**:1024; **12**:386
Leon De Ser Daniel, *see* ROMANO, JUDAH BEN MOSES BEN DANIEL
LEONE, LEON (Judah) DI **11**:29
Leone, Pietro di **13**:503
Leone de Modena, *see* MODENA, LEONE
Leone Ebreo, *see* ABRABANEL, JUDAH
LEONHARD, RUDOLF **11**:29
León Hebreo, *see* ABRABANEL, JUDAH
LEONI, MYER **11**:29
- Braham, Meir **4**:1289
- theater **15**:1052
- *Yigdal* **16**:835
- *mus. notations:*
- - *Yigdal* **16**:834
Leonid, *see* BERMAN, LEONID
Leon Joseph **5**:160; **15**:1328
Léon-Lévy, Lily, *see* Jean-Javal, Lily
Leon of Paris, Sir, *see* JUDAH BEN ISAAC
Leonovich (fam.) **7**:1189
Leonovich, Abraham **7**:1189
Leon Pinelo, Antonio (law., S. Am.) **10**:1502
Leon, Pinelo, Antonio de (bibl., Sp.) **3**:409; **15**:254
Leon Pinelo, Diego **10**:1502
Leonte ben Abraham **13**:589
LEONTE (Judah) BEN MOSES **11**:30
Leontes Valley (Leb.), *see* Litani Valley
LEONTOPOLIS (loc., Egy.) **11**:31
- history chart **8**:766-767
- Zealot revolt **16**:949
- Ptolemy **13**:1348
- *see also:* Onias, Temple of
LEONTOVICH, EUGENIE **15**:1087
LEONTOVICH, FEDOR **11**:31
LEOPARD (zool.) **11**:31
- dietary laws **6**:32
Leopardi, Giacomo **9**:1105
LEOPOLD I (Holy Rom. Emp.) **11**:32
- Vienna expulsion **16**:123
- Wertheimer, Samson **16**:457
Leopold I (duke, Tuscany), *see* Leopold II
Leopold II (Holy Rom. Emp.) **15**:1468
- Jewish rights **16**:1327
- illus:
- - Leghorn community gift **9**:1129
- - poem in honor of coronation **6**:1358
Leopold III (duke) **2**:530
- Austrian Jews **3**:888
Leopold, E. **8**:42
Leopold, Isaiah Edwin, *see* WYNN, ED
Leopold, Nathan Freudenthal **11**:441
Leopold brothers **5**:1567
Leopold-Rappaport, Malke, *see* LEE, MALKE
Leopoldstadt (dist., Vienna) **13**:1465
Leopoldville (city, Congo), *see* Kinshasa
Leopolita, Jan **4**:885
Leovigild (k., Sp.) **13**:1608
LEOVO (Leova; tn., Bess.) **11**:32
Lepanto (tn., Gr.), *see* NAUPAKTOS
Le Pays (period) **5**:680
Lepecki, M. **11**:679
LEPEL (city, Belor.) **11**:33
Leper, *see* LEPROSY
Leper Hospital (Jer.) **9**:1460
Leper Knights (order), *see* St. Lazarus, Order of
Le Petit Gerin (site., Er. Isr.), *see* JEZREEL
Le Peuple Juif (journ.), *see L'Echo Sioniste*
Lepkofer, Bernard **15**:311
LEPROSY **11**:33
- *Contents:*
- - Laws of Leviticus 13-14 **11**:34
- - Role of Priest **11**:34
- - Ritual **11**:35
- - In Second Temple and Talmud **11**:37
- - In the Aggadah **11**:38
- *bet ḥofshit* **8**:1033
- Commandments, the 613 **5**:765
- covering of head **8**:2
- divorce **6**:126; **6**:129
- *eglah arufah* **6**:476
- euphemism for **6**:961
- impurity **11**:143; **13**:1405ff
- medicine **11**:1180
- Naaman **12**:733
- *Nega'im* **12**:923
- oils **12**:1349
- priestly cure **13**:1079
- red heifer **14**:10
- rehabilitation anointment **3**:27; **3**:28
- sacrifice **14**:601ff
- synagogue **15**:593
- veil **16**:84
- *illus:*
- - text
- - Pharaoh bathing in Hebrew infants' blood **13**:360
- - priests inspecting suspects **12**:924
Lepton (coin) **5**:716
Lepusculus, Sebastian **8**:42
LERER, YEHIEL **11**:39
Le Réveil de Maroc (newsp.) **5**:680
- Tangier **15**:792
Le Réveil Juif (period.) **15**:1449
Lerfler, Wilhelm **2**:745
LÉRIDA (city, Sp.) **11**:39
- Agramunt **2**:373
Lerma, Judah **7**:165; **11**:41; **14**:871
LERMA, JUDAH BEN SAMUEL **11**:41
Lerma, Samuel **7**:1106; **11**:41
Lerman, Elijah **13**:1381
Lerman, I. **5**:437
Lermontov, Mikhail **14**:508
Lerner (ling.) **16**:1378
LERNER, ABBA PETACHJA **11**:41
LERNER, ALAN JAY **11**:42
Lerner, Daniel **13**:1340
Lerner, Hannah **10**:1126
LERNER, ḤAYYIM ẒEVI BEN TODROS **11**:42
Lerner, I. Michael **4**:1031
Lerner, J. B. **11**:558
LERNER, JOSEPH JUDAH **11**:43
LERNER, MAX **11**:43
LERNER, MAYER BEN MORDECAI OF ALTONA **11**:44
Lerner, Yosl **5**:396
LE ROITH, HAROLD HIRSCH **11**:44
Leroux, Etienne **15**:208
Le Roux, Jean (duke, Brittany) **4**:1383
Leroux, Pierre-Henri **10**:125
LE ROY, MERVYN (film prod., U.S.) **12**:470
LERT, ERNST **12**:697
Le Safran (tn., Er. Isr.), *see* SHEPHARAM
Les Archives Israélites de France (journ.), *see Archives Israelites de France*
Lesbianism **8**:961; **14**:1208
Leschetizky, Theodor **12**:683
Le Sephorie (city, Er, Isr.), *see* SEPPHORIS
"Les Français chez les dames juives à Alger" (wtrcl., E. Delacroix) **6**:217
Le-Shabbat (journ., Isr.) **1**:newsp. list
Le-Shanah Tovah Tikkatevu (ve-Teḥatemu) (Heb. greeting) **7**:916
Leshem (city, Er. Isr.), *see* DAN
Leshem (gem) **13**:1010
Le-shem Yiḥud . . . (rit. formula) **7**:1405
Leshishit (dye plant) **6**:330
LESHNEV (tn., Ukr.) **11**:45
- *illus:* text
Leshonenu (journ.) **2**:207; **15**:55
- Hebrew spelling **16**:1646
- Tur-Sinai **15**:1466
Leshonenu la-Am (period.) **2**:207
Leshon Limmudim (wk., Ibn Yaḥya) **16**:1389
Leshon Limmudim (wk., Moses ben Isaac ben ha-Nesiah) **16**:1387
Leshon Limmudim (wk., Solomon ben Abba Mari Yarḥi) **16**:1388
Lesinsky, Charles **3**:450
Lesinsky, Harry **3**:450
LESKO (tn., Pol.) **11**:45
- *illus:*
- - tombstone **15**:1231
LESKOV, NIKOLAY SEMYONOVICH **11**:46
LESLAU, WOLF **11**:46
- historiography **8**:562
LESLIE, ROBERT L. **11**:47
- typography **15**:1480
Les Loges (riv., Er. Isr.), *see* YARKON
Lesman, Boleslaw, *see* LESMIAN, BOLESLAW
Lesman, Jan Wiktor, *see* BRZECHWA, JAN
LEŚMIAN, BOLESLAW **11**:47
Les Milles (detention camp, Fr.) **7**:34
Lesotho (state, Afr.) **9**:440
Les Ponts-de-Cé (tn., France) **3**:23
LESS, EMIL **11**:47
Lesser (art.) **11**:1174
LESSER POLAND (dist.) **11**:48
- *see also:* POLAND
"Lesser YHWH" (Metatron name) **11**:1444
LESSING, GOTTHOLD EPHRAIM **11**:49
- apologetics **3**:198
- Jews in plays **7**:443
- Moses Mendelssohn **11**:1329ff
- theater **15**:1055
- toleration of Jews **8**:711
- *illus:*
- - Mendelssohn, Moses, and **11**:1331
Lessing, Julius **3**:650
LESSING, THEODOR **11**:50
- Calé's suicide **5**:41
Lessman, Leo **13**:1033
Lessmann, May **9**:1067; **13**:1033
Lestai (pat.), *see* SICARII
LESTER, RICHARD **12**:470
LESTSCHINSKY, JACOB **11**:50
- historiography **8**:562
LESTCHINSKY, JOSEPH **11**:52
Leszniów (tn.), *see* LESHNEV
LESZNO (tn., Pol.) **11**:52
- Behrend Lehmann **10**:1580
- guilds **8**:441
- sick care **14**:1498
- tailors **15**:705
- *illus:* text
Le Tartrier, Adrien **8**:42
Letekh (meas.) **16**:377; **16**:380ff
Leterman (fam.) **16**:163
Lethenyei, János **8**:42
LETICHEV (tn., Rus.) **11**:53
Le Toron aux Fontaines Sourdes (castle, Er. Isr.) **3**:78
Le Toron des Chevaliers (Crus. fort., Er. Isr.) **10**:1458
Letste Nayes (newsp., Isr.) **9**:1017
Letste Nayes (newsp., Pol.), *see Der Tog*
Lette, G. J. **8**:42
Letteratura (journ.) **5**:1428
Letter-combinations (Kab.), *see* Letter mysticism
Letteris (fam.) **13**:1111; **16**:1015
Letteris, Gershon **16**:6
LETTERIS, MEIR (Max) **11**:54
- Bush, Isidor **4**:1534
- drama **6**:196
- Galicia **16**:1328
- literature, Hebrew **8**:184
- Luzzatto **11**:606
- *illus:* text
Letteris, W. **11**:613
Letter mysticism (kab. technique)
- Ba'al Shem Tov **9**:1054ff
- kabbalistic combinations **10**:494; **10**:507ff
Letters, Hebrew alphabet, *see* ALPHABET, HEBREW, *and under individual letters*
LETTERS AND LETTER-WRITERS **11**:55
- *Contents:*
- - Biblical Period **11**:55
- - Persian and Greek Periods **11**:56
- - New Testament: Bar Kokhba Letters **11**:56
- - Talmudic Literature **11**:56
- - Medieval Hebrew Literature **11**:57
- - Modern Period **11**:57
- - Enlightenment and Wissenschaft des Judentums **11**:60
- - Jewish-Christian Correspondence **11**:61
- - Women Letter Writers **11**:61
- - Collections of Letters **11**:61
- - Formulas and Style **11**:62
- Bertinoro, Obadiah **4**:699
- Cairo *genizah* **16**:1336
- Maimonides **11**:760
- papyrus **16**:658ff
- responsa **14**:83ff
- Tell el-Amarna **15**:933*ff*
- Ya'ari's anthology **16**:690
- *illus:*
- - forms of greeting (table) **7**:915-918
- - Ibn Shaprut to king of Khazars **10**:949
- - Judeo-Persian (8th cent.) **10**:431
Lettland (state, N.E. Eur.), *see* LATVIA
LETTUCE **11**:62
- plant list **13**:621
- *illus:* **11**:1014
Lettuce, wild **13**:621
Leuccio **14**:247
Leucht, Isaac **11**:519
Leucos Limen (anc. Seaport), *see* Minet el-Beida
Leukemia (disease) **14**:1503
LEUSDEN, JOHANN **11**:63
- Hebraist **8**:42; **8**:17
- Lightfoot, John **11**:238
- Utrecht **16**:37
- *illus:* text
Leuvielle, Gabriel-Maximilien, *see* LINDER, MAX
LEV, ABRAHAM **11**:64
Lev, David ben Joseph ibn **11**:64
LEV (Lab; Leb), JOSEPH BEN DAVID IBN (Maharival) **11**:64
- bibliography **4**:973
- exporting **10**:1538
- *Ḥiddushim* **8**:467
- Istanbul **9**:1090
- Monastir **12**:239
- Pope Paul IV **8**:699
- responsa **14**:89

Lev, Moses ben Joseph ibn **11**:64
Lev, R. R. **3**:395
Levadi, Solomon S. **4**:1219
– *illus:*
– – bookplate for Abraham Levinson **4**:1222
LEVAILLANT, ISAÏE **11**:65
LEVANDA, LEV (Leo; Yehudah Leib) OSIPOVICH **11**:65
– Fuenn, Samuel Joseph **7**:213
– promotion of culture **15**:58ff
– Vilna **16**:144
Levanda, Vitali Osipovich **11**:67
Levanon (Wessely; wk.), *see Gan Na'ul*
LEVANON, MORDECAI **11**:68
– *illus:*
– – "Synagogue in Safed" (paint.) Pl. 9 3-ART
LEVANT, OSCAR **12**:697
Levantadores (syn. term) **7**:1078
Levant Fairs (Er. Isr.) **9**:345; **9**:765
– *illus:*
– – Tel-Avivi 1934 and 1936 **9**:347,766
Levantine Synagogue (Ven.) **15**: 618
– *illus:*
– – reader's desk **16**:99
Levaton, Mordecai **2**:565
Levee, Marian, *see* GODDARD, PAULETTE
LEVEEN, JACOB **11**:68
LEVEN, NARCISSE **11**:68
– Alliance Israélite **2**:650
– *illus:*
– – letter re settlement in Sinai (1903) **10**:47
LEVENBERG, SCHNEIER ZALMAN **1**:33
Levendall (police chief, Kishinev) **10**:1065
Levend Joods Gelo (period.) **13**:1056
Levene, Harry **15**:306
Levene, Israel **15**:307,308
LEVENE, PHOEBUS AARON THEODOR **11**:69
LEVENE, SAM **15**:1087
LEVENFISH, GRIGORI YAKELOVICH **5**:407
LEVENSON, JOSEPH RICHMOND **8**:547
LEVENSON, SAM(-UEL) **15**:1087
Levent, Isaac **4**:653
Leventhal, Albert R. **13**:1373
Leventman, Seymour **15**:68
Lever, Leslie **11**:69
LEVER, NORMAN HAROLD **11**:69
LEVERSON, ADA **11**:70
Leverson, Ernest **11**:70
LEVERTIN, OSCAR IVAR **11**:70
– Scandinavian literature **14**:931
LEVERTOFF, PAUL PHILIP **11**:71
Levertov, Denise **15**:1578
Levetus, Celia (Moss) **6**:784
– children's literature **5**:449
– Moss, Marion **7**:1363
LEVEY, BARNETT **15**:1087
Levey, James **15**:301
Lev Hadash (journ., Isr.) **1**:newsp. list
Levi (name), *see also* Levy
LEVI (bib. fig. tribe) **11**:71
– *Contents:*
– – The Man **11**:71
– – The Tribe **11**:71
– – In the Aggadah **11**:74
– History
– – Aaron **2**:6
– – Aaronides **2**:18ff
– – Asaph family **3**:672
– – David's integration **8**: 590ff
– – firstborn **6**:1307ff
– – Genesis, Book of **7**:393
– – Gershon **7**:513
– – Golden Calf **7**:710ff
– – Josiah **10**:292
– – *Jubilees, Book of* **10**:325
– – Moses **12**:376
– – Pentateuch **13**:252
– – Samaritan's **14**:728; **14**:734
– – *Testament of Naphtali* **12**:821
– – Tribes, the Twelve **11**:850ff; **15**:1383
– Levites' functions
– – age restrictions **2**:345
– – Commandments, the 613 **5**:763,770f
– – court of Levites **4**:722
– – judges **3**:908
– – music **12**:580ff
– – priests' ablution **2**:85
– – sacrifices **14**:608
– – Tabernacle **15**:683
– – Temple **15**:953,955*ff*
– – Temple divisions **12**:89; **12**:91
– – Temple Mount **15**:989
– – Temple singers **12**:559
– – Torah reading **15**:1247; **15**:1253
– – wood offerings **16**:630
– Miscellaneous
– – *aggadah* **15**:1385
– – breastplate stone **13**:1008
– – modern functions of Levites **13**:1089
– – seals **14**:1080
– – tax exemption **15**:841
– – tithe **15**:1159*ff*
– – tribal laws **11**:138
– *illus:*
– – text
– – parents and brothers **10**:1526
– – slaying Hamor and Shechem **7**:1250
– *see also:* LEVITICAL CITIES; PRIESTS AND PRIESTHOOD
Levi (2nd cent. C.E., Samar.) **14**:731
LEVI (amora) **11**:75
– *Megillat Yuhasin* **11**:1231
LEVI (fam., Salonika) **11**:75
Levi, Aaron, *see* MONTEZINOS, ANTONIO DE
Levi, Abraham, *see* ARPA, ABRAMO DALL'
LEVI, ABRAHAM BEN JOSEPH **11**:76
– family **11**:76
Levi, A.D. (Zion., Yug.) **16**:1149
Levi, Adolphus **12**:1021
Levi, Alexander **8**:1437
Levi, Asher **11**:1550
Levi, Baruch Isaac, *see* LEVI, BENEDETTO
Levi, Baruch Joseph **5**:623
LEVI, BEHREND **11**:77
Levi, Bendit Axelrod **12**:300
LEVI, BENEDETTO **11**:77
Levi, Benjamin **3**:539; **4**:1219
– Hart, Moses **7**:1350
– Waley family **16**:251
– *illus:*
– – coat of arms for Isaac Mendes **4**:1222
Levi, Benjamin Wolf **14**:1018
Levi, Camille Baruch **11**:1562
LEVI, CARLO **11**:77
– Italian literature **9**:1113
– *illus:* text
Levi, David, *see* LAWĀNI, DA'UD
LEVI, DAVID (Hebr.) **11**:78
– Bible translation **4**:871
– *illus:* text
Levi, David (It.) **5**:422
LEVI, DORO **11**:79
LEVI, EDWARD H. **11**:79
Levi, Eliezer **12**:1388
Levi, Eliphas **10**:648
Levi, Ernst Josef Maria, *see* LERT, ERNST
LEVI, EUGENIO **11**:79
– Italian literature **9**:1114
Levi, Gerd **10**:1591; **12**:64; **14**:924
Levi, Gerson B. **11**:79
LEVI, GIORGIO RENATO **11**:80
LEVI, GIULIO AUGUSTO **11**:80
Levi, Giuseppe (r., journ.) **13**:1036; **14**:197; **16**:107
LEVI, GIUSEPPE (biol.) **11**:80
– Ginzburg, Natalia **7**:586
LEVI, GRAZIADIO DAVID **11**:81
– Italian literature **9**:1110
Levi, Harris L. **12**:912
Levi, Harry **4**:1265
Levi, Henry **3**:824
Levi, Herman (Kielce) **10**:990
LEVI, HERMANN (Ger.) **11**:81
Levi, I. M. (r., Pers.) **13**:318
Levi, Isaac (Mor.) **14**:626
Levi, Isaac (Gr.) **11**:76
Levi, Isaac (Belor.) **13**:541
Levi, Isaac (Eng.) **4**:1219
LEVI (Bet ha-Levi), ISAAC BEN SOLOMON **11**:82
– family **11**:76
LÉVI, ISRAEL **11**:82
Levi, Jacob (Gr.) **11**:76
Levi, Jacob (Eng.) **16**:251
Levi, Jacob (U.S.) **15**:635
LEVI, JACOB BEN ISRAEL **11**:83
– Salonika **11**:76
Levi, Jacob ben Moses, *see* MOELLIN, JACOB BEN MOSES
Levi, James **4**:1239
Levi, Joel ben Lipman **3**:539; **11**:1173
Levi, Joseph (Cochin) **5**:623
Levi (Bet ha-Levi), Joseph (cmty. ldr., Gr.) **11**: 76
Levi, Joseph (Gr.) **11**:76
Levi, Joseph (schol., Gr.) **11**:76
– Constantinople yeshivah **16**:1549
– Salonika yeshivah **16**:1549
Levi, Joseph (Ger.) **10**:1252
LEVI, JOSHUA JOSEPH BEN DAVID **11**:83
Levi, Juan de **15**:1425
Levi, Judah (Gr.) **11**:76
Levi, Judah (Mor.) **14**:626
Levi, Lazzaro di Graziano **16**:22
LEVI, LEO **12**:697
Levi, Leo N. **2**:826
– Texas **15**:1035
Levi, Levin Hirsch **15**:407
Lévi, Lucien **11**:1562
LEVI, MARIO GIACOMO **11**:83
Levi, Menahem **7**:1220
Levi, Mirtzel **5**:737
Levi, Moritz **14**:871
Levi, Naphtali Herz, *see* Naphtali Herz of Emden
Levi, Nathan **15**:209
Levi, Nathaniel **11**:1285; **13**:808
Levi, Nini **5**:1009; **12**:505
Levi, Nissim **11**:76
Levi, Norman **4**:1380
LEVI, PAOLO **11**:84
LEVI, PAUL **11**:84
Levi, Philip **15**:310
Levi, Pinthus **15**:1041
LEVI, PRIMO **11**:85
– Italian literature **9**:1113
Levi, R. (publ., Ger.) **13**:1366
LEVI, RINO **3**:365
Levi, Rofe Johanan **4**:1238
LEVI, SAID BEN SHALOM **11**:85
Levi, Salomon **11**:77
Levi, Samuele **10**:461
Levi, Sara **12**:633
LEVI, SHABBETAI **11**:85
Levi, Sigmund, *see* LEBERT, SIGMUND
Levi, Solomon (Gr.) **11**:75
Levi, Solomon (Ger.) **13**:7
LEVI, SOLOMON BEN ISAAC **11**:85
– family **11**:76
LEVI (Bet ha-Levi), SOLOMON BEN ISAAC (Gr.) **11**:87
LÉVI, SYLVAIN **11**:87
– Alliance Israélite **2**:650; **2**:653
– Zionism **16**:1114
– *illus:*
– – Zionist delegation to Palestine, 1918 **9**:336
LEVI, TESTAMENT OF (pseudepig.) **11**:88
– Greek Testament of Levi **13**:184
– *see also:* PATRIARCHS, TESTAMENT OF THE TWELVE
Levi, Yoseph **12**:769
Levi (al-Levi) Abulafia (fam.) **2**:184
LEVIANT, CURT **1**:33
LEVIAS, CASPAR **11**:88
Leviash, Ruth **12**:705
LEVIATHAN (bib. animal) **11**:89
– Anath **2**:926
– crocodile **5**:1125
– iconography **8**:1222
– mythology **12**:730ff
– resurrection **14**:100
– *illus:*
– – *Ambrosian Bible* **4**:360, *fcg.* 907
– – fight with Behemoth **4**:394
– – "Shevousl", paper-cut **13**:65
– – *Shivviti* plaque **14**:*fcg.* 1422
– – *see also:* BEHEMOTH
LEVI BEN ABRAHAM BEN HAYYIM **11**:91
– allegorical exegesis **4**:898
– Aristotelianism **3**:446
– Roussillon **14**:353
LEVI BEN GERSHOM (Ralbag) **11**:92
– *Contents:*
– – Scientific Works **11**:92
– – Talmudic and Liturgical Works **11**:93
– – Commentaries on Aristotle and Averroes **11**:93
– – Biblical Commentaries **11**:94
– – Sefer Milhamot Adonai **11**:94
– – Philosophy **11**:95
– – Views on **11**:97
– – Astronomy **11**:98
– Philosophy **11**:341; **13**:446ff
– – Aristotelianism **3**:446ff
– – astronomy **3**:803
– – atomism opposed **3**:830
– – attributes of God **7**:667
– – beatitude **4**:362
– – Bible exegesis **11**:325; **15**:1240
– – – allegorical **4**:898
– – commandments, reasons for **5**:787
– – creation **5**:1069ff
– – deistic tendency **7**:673
– – emanation **6**:695
– – existence of God **7**:658ff
– – free will **7**:128
– – logic **11**:460
– – nature **12**:890
– – providence **13**:1286; **14**:137
– – revelation and reason **4**:436
– – soul **15**:173
– – substance and accident **15**:475
– Philosophers
– – Abrabanel, Isaac **2**:106
– – Averroes **3**:951
– – Avicenna **3**:958
– – Duns Scotus, John **6**:274
– – Themistius **15**:1099
– Miscellaneous
– – astrology **3**:793
– – history chart **8**:766-767
– – "Jacob's staff" (quadrant) **14**:1413
– – loans to aliens **12**:250
– – Purim parodies **13**:129
– *illus:*
– – text

- - Bible commentary (1494) **4**:895
- - Deuteronomy commentary (1546) **5**:1580
- - Exodus commentary (1546) **6**:1065
- - Former Prophets, commentary (1495) **8**:1334
- - "Jacob's staff" **8**:1430
LEVI BEN HABIB (Ralbaḥ) **11**:98
- Alashkar, Moses **2**:512
- Jacob ibn Ḥabib **8**:1178
- Jerusalem community **9**:265; **9**:286; **9**:1436
- Ottoman Empire **16**:1549
- *illus:* text
Levi ben Ḥama (amora), *see* Levi ben Laḥma
Levi ben Isaac Hijo Caro **8**:*fcg.* 1143
Levi ben Isaac ibn Mar Saul **8**:1188; **15**:1268
LEVI BEN JAPHETH **11**:99
- linguistics **16**:1380
Levi ben Laḥma (amora) **3**:237; **11**:75
Levi ben Shem Tov **14**:865
LEVI BEN SISI (amora) **11**:100
LEVI-BIANCHINI, ANGELO **11**:101
- Zionism **16**:1082; **16**:1122
- *illus:*
- - Zionist delegation to Palestine, 1918 **9**:336
LEVI-CIVITA, TULLIO **11**:102
LEVI DELLA VIDA, GIORGIO **11**:102
Levi de Veali (fam.) **2**:567
Levi de Veali, Matassia ben Moses Zacut **2**:567
Levie, Werner **10**:463
Levien, Benjamin Goldsmid **11**:1285
Levien, J. F. **13**:808
Levi ibn Mar Saul (paytan), *see* Levi ben Isaac ibn Mar Saul
LEVI ISAAC BEN MEIR OF BERDICHEV **11**:102
- Hasidism **7**:1394; **7**:1397
- *Kaddish* **10**:663
- Naḥman of Bratslav and **12**:783
- *illus:*
- - text
- - autograph **3**:916
Levi-Lissner, Hinda **5**:449
Levi-Monsino, Yosif (Joseph) **14**:871
Levin (name), *see also* Levine
LEVIN, ALTER ISAAC **11**:105
Levin, Charles **5**:1572
Levin, D. (plwrt., Isr.) **6**:207
Levin, Dan **5**:612
LEVIN, EMANUEL **11**:105
Levin, Gershon **7**:1499; **15**:1582
LEVIN, HARRY (crit., U.S.) **15**:1582
Levin, Harry (judge, U.S.) **16**:158
Levin, Heshel **15**:428
Levin, Hirschel, *see* LEVIN, ZEVI HIRSCH BEN ARYEH LOEB
Levin, Issachar **15**:1375
Levin, Jacob **14**:1664
LEVIN, JUDAH LEIB (poet) **11**:105
Levin, Judah Leib (U.S.) **5**:1568
Levin, J. Z. **5**:433
LEVIN, LEWIS CHARLES **11**:106
- Pennsylvania **13**:230
Levin, Ludwig, *see* ROBERT, LUDWIG
LEVIN, MAKSIM GRIGORYEVICH **11**:106
- anthropology **3**:39
LEVIN (Lefin), MENAHEM MENDEL **11**:107
- Bick, Jacob Samuel **4**:977
- Haskalah, Russian **7**:1433
- prose style **8**:183
- Leningrad **11**:14
Levin, Menahem Mendel, *see* LEVIN, EMANUEL
LEVIN, MEYER **11**:108
- U.S. literature **15**:1572
Levin, Morris J. **16**:112
Levin, Moshe **16**:987
illus:
- *Yung Vilne* group **16**:821
LEVIN, NATHANIEL WILLIAM **11**:109
LEVIN, POUL THEODOR **14**:935
Levin, Rahel, *see* VARNHAGEN, RAHEL
Levin, Sander **5**:1571
Levin, Saul **11**:113
Levin, Saul ben Moses of Karlin **13**:541
LEVIN, SHMARYA **11**:109
- rabbinate **10**:862
- *illus:*
- - text
- - first Duma electors **14**:445
- - thirteenth Zionist Congress **16**:1173
Levin, Solomon I. **12**:38
LEVIN, THEODORE **11**:111
Levin, William Hort **11**:109
Levin, Y. **4**:1047
LEVIN, YIZḤAK MEIR **11**:111
- Agudat Israel **2**:425
LEVIN, ZEVI HIRSCH (-el) BEN ARYEH LOEB **11**:112
- David Tevele of Lissa **5**:1353
- Moses Mendelssohn **11**:1333
- *illus:* text
LEVINAS, EMMANUEL **11**:113
- Torah **15**:1243
Levine (name), *see also* Levin
Levine, Charles A. **2**:321
- *illus:*
- - *N. Y. Times's* announcement of flight **2**:323
Levine, Dan **15**:306
Levine, David **5**:220
Levine, E. (r., Eng.) **8**:957
LEVINE, EUGENE (journ.) **11**:113
LEVINE, JACK **11**:114
- U.S. art **12**:1122
- *illus:*
- - text
- - etching **3**:562
- - "King Judah" (paint.) **10**:331
LEVINE, JOSEPH E. **12**:470
LEVINE, LES **3**:604
LEVINE, PHILIP **11**:115
- Landsteiner, Karl **10**:1416
Levine, Rachmiel **11**:1200
Levine, Robert **16**:556
Levine, Samuel **7**:1239
Levinger, Elma, *see* Ehrlich, Elma
Levinger, Elmer C. **15**:1058
LEVINGER, LEE JOSEPH **11**:115
LEVIN-SHATZKES, YIZḤAK **11**:115
Levinsky, Barney **15**:305
Levinsky, Elhanan Leib **16**:1151
Levinsky Women Teachers' Seminary (Er. Isr.), *see* Lewinsky Teachers' Seminary
Levinsohn, Abba **10**:185
LEVINSOHN, ISAAC BAER **11**:116
- apologetics **3**:200
- Haskalah, Russia **8**:185
- *illus:*
- - text
- - *Te'udah be-Yisrael, haskamah (1828)* **7**:1453
Levinsohn, Jacob Israel **11**:118
Levinsohn, Nahum Mendel, *see* KOSSOVSKI, VLADIMIR
Levinsohn, Solomon **16**:1390
Levinson (fam., Can.) **5**:104
Levinson (fam., U.S.) **16**:465
LEVINSON, ABRAHAM **11**:119
- *illus:*
- - bookplate **4**:1222
Levinson, Alan **15**:318
Levinson, Albert **13**:40
LEVINSON, ANDRE **11**:119
Levinson, Benjamin **2**:319
Levinson, Boris **13**:1345
Levinson, Harry **15**:318
Levinson, N. P. **4**:61
LEVINSON, SALMON OLIVER **11**:120
LEVINSTEIN, HERBERT **5**:385
Levinstein, Kurt **6**:464
Levinstein, Meir David **5**:1455
LEVINTHAL (fam.) **11**:120
Levinthal, Bernard Louis **11**:120
Levinthal, Elias **11**:499
Levinthal, Israel Herbert **11**:121
- homiletic literature **8**:959
Levinthal, Louis Edward **11**:121
- *illus:*
- - Biltmore Hotel Conference **15**:1633
- - JPS Torah translation committee **10**:80
Levi of Zhitomir **2**:23
LEVI-PEROTTI, GIUSTINA **11**:121
LÉVI-PROVENÇAL, EVARISTE **11**:121
LEVIRATE MARRIAGE AND HALIẒAH **11**:121
- *Contents:*
- - Definition **11**:122
- - In the Bible **11**:122
- - In the Talmud **11**:123
- - Duty of Ḥaliẓah **11**:125
- - Priority Between Levirate Marriage and Ḥaliẓah **11**:125
- - Order of Ḥaliẓah **11**:126
- - Post-Talmudic Period **11**:127
- - Problems of Leivrate Marriage—The Apostate Levir **11**:127
- - Problems of Ḥaliẓah **11**:128
- - Takkanah of Chief Rabbinate of Ereẓ Israel **11**:128
- - In State of Israel **11**:129
- - Ceremony of Ḥaliẓah **11**:130
- Halakhah
- - adoption **2**:300
- - children **5**:426
- - Commandments, the 613 **5**:769,781
- - custom effectiveness **12**:14
- - divorce, conditional **2**:432; **6**:133
- - documents **14**:1388
- - elders of city **6**:578
- - *gilgul* and *ḥaliẓah* **7**:574
- - identification of participants **6**:996
- - Israel *takkanah* **15**:728
- - laws, origin **12**:7
- - maintenance *takkanah*, 1944 **12**:143
- - *mamzer* **11**:840
- - polygamy **12**:259
- - right foot **14**:179
- - woman **16**:629
- - *Yevamot* **16**:776
- Bible and History
- - Chinese Jews **5**:470
- - Christological symbolism **3**:192
- - Onan and Tamar **12**:1396
- - Ruth and Boaz **14**:518
- - Samaritans **14**:741
- - Tamar and Judah **10**:332; **16**:490
- *illus:*
- - *ḥaliẓah* ceremony **11**:123; **16**:776
Leviseur, Moritz **4**:1112; **13**:820
Leviseur, Sophie **4**:1112
Levisky, Fernando **15**:255
Levisohn, Marcus George **7**:1436
Levisohn, Robert Frank, *see* Arnold, Robert F.
Levisohn, Solomon **14**:1262; **16**:572
Levison (fam.) **5**:56
Levison, Gumperz (Georg) **11**:1195
Levison, J. B. (bsmn.) **14**:834
LEVISON, WILHELM **11**:131
Levisson brothers (prints.) **13**:1143
LEVI-STRAUSS, CLAUDE **11**:131
Levit, Jacob **15**:1487
- *illus:*
- - "Haim" type face example **15**:1485
LEVITA, ELIJAH (Baḥur) **11**:132
- *Bove-Bukh* **4**:1276
- Drusius on works of **6**:241
- Fagius, Paul **15**:424
- Hebrew grammar **11**:324
- history chart **8**:766-767
- *keri* notations **16**:1421
- linguistics **16**:1389,1391
- masorah **16**:1476
- Muenster, Sebastian **12**:505
- prosody **13**:1223
- romances **11**:359
- Scaliger, Joseph Justus **14**:925
- *Sefer ha-Baḥur, haskamah* **7**:1452
- universities **15**:1675
- Yiddish literature **16**:806
- *illus:*
- - *Buovo d'Antona* (1541) **4**:1276
- - *Sefer ha-Dikduk* (1525) **8**:19
Levita, Joseph Naphtali Hirz, *see* HIRSHEL, MEYER
Levita, Leon **16**:1131
LEVITAN, ISAAC ILITCH **11**:135
- stamps **15**:336
- *illus:*
- - landscape (paint.) **3**:553
Levitan, M. **16**:779
Levitan, Rita **15**:309
LEVITAN, SOLOMON **11**:135
Levitan, Zevi **10**:847; **14**:1668
LEVI-TANNAI, SARA **5**:1272
- choreography **8**:1309; **16**:756
- music **12**:670; **14**:1191
LEVITATS, ISAAC **1**:33
Levitch, Joseph, *see* LEWIS, JERRY
Levites, *see* LEVI
LEVITICAL CITIES **11**:136
- David **9**:116
- function and character **5**:588
- Israelite kingdom **8**:591
- Joshua, Book of **10**:276
- Kohathite cities **10**:1136
- Pentateuch **13**:250
- refuge for manslayer **5**:593
- tribe of Levi **11**:73
- *map:* text
LEVITICUS, BOOK OF **11**:138
- *Contents:*
- - Contents
- - - Chapters 1-7 **11**:139
- - - Chapters 8-10 **11**:141
- - - Chapters 11-16 **11**:142
- - - Chapters 17-26 **11**:143
- - - Chapter 27 **11**:147
- Holiness Code **8**:820
- Hurrian customs **12**:1290
- Pentateuch **13**:232ff
- *Sifra* **14**:1517
- *tokheḥah* **15**:1192
- *illus:*
- - text
- - opening page (1290) **4**:966
- - tenth cent. ms. **16**:1478
LEVITICUS RABBAH (midrash) **11**:147
- *illus:*
- - opening page (Venice, 1545) **13**:1096
- *see also:* MIDRASH
Levitsky, Dmitri **12**:42
LEVITSKY, JACOB **11**:150
LEVITSKY, LOUIS MOSES

11:150
LEVITSKY, MISCHA 12:697
Levitski, Sarah, *see* Adler, Sarah
LEVITT (fam.) 11:150
Levitt, Abraham 11:150
Levitt, Alfred S. 11:151
Levitt, Andrew 11:151
Levitt, Arthur 12:1127
Levitt, Ezekiel 5:438
Levitt, Joel 15:319
Levitt, John 11:151
Levitt, V. 11:1558
Levitt, William Jaird 11:150
Levitt, William Jaird Jr. 11:151
Levitte, Simon 16:1115
Levittown (tn., Pa.) 13:230; 13:374
Lévi-Valensi, André 2:616
Levkovitz, Shelomo, *see* LAVI, SHELOMO
Levkovski, M. 10:90
– Vozrozhdeniye 16:229
LEVNER, ISRAEL BENJAMIN 11:151
– *illus:* text
Levoca (tn., Cz.) 8:1076
Levonah Valley (Er. Isr.) 9:587
– *illus:*
– – intermontane basin 9:209
LEVONTIN, JEHIEL JOSEPH 11:151
– *illus:*
– – Benei Zion meeting 12:359
LEVONTIN, ZALMAN DAVID 11:152
– Feinberg, Yosef 6:1209
– Gaza settlement 12:929
Levontin, Ẓevi 11:152
Levovitz, Pesach Z. 13:1462
Lev Tov (wk.) 9:18; 16:804
Levush ha-Orah (wk.) 15:520
Levush Malkhut (wk.) 9:1263
– codification of law 5:653; 11:335; 14:1476
Levy (name), *see also* Levi
Levy (bnk., Pol.) 4:176
LEVY (fam., Fr.) 11:153
LEVY (fam., Mor.) 11:153
Levy (fam., Philippines) 13:395
Levy (fam., Tex.) 15:1035
Levy (fam., U.S.) 14:143
LEVY, AARON (mer., U.S.) 11:154
LEVY, AARON (sol., U.S.) 11:154
– military activity 11:1551
Levy, Aaron (r., Eng.) 3:878
Levy, Aaron J. (polit., N.Y.C.) 12:1104
Levy, Abraham (pion., Austr.) 11:1285
Levy, Abraham (r., S.A.) 13:909
Lévy, Abraham (sol., Fr.) 11:1561
LEVY, ABRAHAM EUGENE (sol., Fr.) 11:1561; 11:1574
Levy, Abraham R. (U.S.) 5:414
Levy, Adrian F. 15:1035
Levy, Albert (ed., U.S.) 13:1039
Lévy, Albert (pres., UGIF) 15:1535
LEVY, SIR ALBERT 11:154
Lévy, Alexandre-Nathan 11:154; 13:1368
LEVY, ALFRED 11:154
– homiletic literature 8:957
– *illus:* text
Lévy, Alvarez 11:1562
LEVY, AMY 11:155
Levy, Andrew 13:568
Lévy, Antoine 4:1440
Levy, A. R. 5:438
Levy, Armand (Fr. offic.) 11:1501
Levy, Armand (soc., It.) 15:26
Levy, Arnie 15:312
LÉVY, ARTHUR (hist.) 8:548
Levy, Arthur (philos.), *see* LIEBERT, ARTHUR
LEVY, ASSER 11:156
– banking 4:178
– New Amsterdam 12:1063ff
Levy, Barnard 15:303
Levy, Barnett 3:880
Levy, Benjamin (r., Eng.) 11:156
LEVY, BENJAMIN (cmty. ldr., Eng.) 11:156
– Adolphus, Moses 2:293
– *illus:*
– – tombstone, London 11:473
Levy, Benjamin (crftn., N.Z.) 12:1128
Levy, Benjamin (sol., U.S.) 11:1551
LEVY, BENN WOLFE 6:783; 6:789
Lévy, Benoît 11:1561
Lévy, Calmann 11:154; 13:1368
Levy, Chabib 15:906
LEVY, CHAPMAN 11:156
LEVY, CLIFTON HARBY 11:156
LEVY, SIR DANIEL 10:1510
– politics 13:809
Levy, David (poet, It.) 15:1455
Levy, David (psych., U.S.) 13:1339
Levy, David (polit., U.S.), *see* YULEE, DAVID LEVY
Levy, David (pion., U.S.) 14:1083
Levy, Derrick 15:312
Levy, Edward Lawrence 15:316
Levy, Eleazer 13:1423
Levy, Elias (cmty. ldr., Eng.) 11:156
– *illus:*
– – London monument 11:473
Levy, Elias (apos., U.S.) 11:162
Levy, Emanuel 15:830
LEVY, FELIX ALEXANDER 11:157
Levy, Gaston 11:154
Levy, George Morton 15:311
Lévy, Georges 11:154
Levy, Gershon 11:1498; 15:114
Levy, Harold 13:1361
LEVY, HAYMAN 11:157
Levy, Henry, *see* RUSSELL, HENRY
LEVY, HYMAN 11:157
Levy, Irma, *see* LINDHEIM, IRMA LEVY
Levy, Isaac (polit., Mor.) 11:153
Levy, Isaac (mer., Am.) 11:162
– New York 12:1067
– Philadelphia 13:368
Levy, Isaac (mer., Can.) 7:1191
Levy, Isaac (r., Pol.) 11:158
LÉVY, ISAAC (Fr. r.) 11:157
Levy, Isaac (judge, Tex.) 15:1035
LÉVY, ISIDORE 11:157
Levy, Israel 16:577
LEVY, JACOB (r., lexicog., Pol.) 11:158
– dictionary 3:278; 16:579
Levy, Jacob (U.S. pion.) 11:1499
Lévy, Jacques-Victor, *see* Vehel, J.
Lévy, Jean-Pierre 13:148
LEVY, JEFFERSON MONROE 11:158
Levy, J. Leonard 11:1570
Levy, Jonas (U.S. law.) 3:459
LEVY, JONAS PHILLIPS (nav. of., U.S.) 11:158
– military career 11:1551
– Washington 16:356
Levy, Joseph (16th cent., interp.) 11:153
Levy, Joseph (stlr., U.S.) 12:1024
Levy, Joseph (cmty. ldr., U.S.) 12:36
LEVY, JOSEPH LANGLEY 10:308; 10:313
LEVY, JOSEPH LEONARD 11:159
Levy, Joseph Moses 10:1489
– *illus:*
– – cartoon 10:316
Levy, Judah (mer., Mor.) 11:153
LEVY, JUDAH BEN MENAHEM (r., Er. Isr.) 11:159
– pilgrims 9:1257
Levy, Judith, *see* Zbitkower, Judith
Levy, Julius, *see* RODENBERG, JULIUS
Levy, Kurt 12:1461
Levy, Lazare (soc., Fr.) 15:26
LÉVY, LAZARE (mus.) 12:697
Levy, Leon (mer., U.S.) 12:1021
Levy, Leon (pub. fig., U.S.) 15:1376
Levy, Leon (exec., U.S.) 15:311
LEVY, LEONARD WILLIAMS 11:159
Lévy, Léopold 13:113
LEVY, LOUIS (poet, Den.) 14:935
Levy, Louis (cmty. ldr., U.S.) 11:499
LEVY, LOUIS EDWARD 11:160
LEVY, LUCIEN 11:160
Levy, M. (cmty. ldr., Austr.) 4:138
LEVY, MARION JOSEPH, JR. 11:160
Levy, Marvin 15:308
Lévy, Maurice 11:591
Levy, Max (cmty. ldr., U.S.) 3:459
Levy, Max (inv.) 15:1479
Levy, Mercado, *see* LEVY, JUDAH BEN MENAHEM
Levy, Meyer 11:153
Levy, Michel (publ., Fr.) 11:153
Levy, Michel (physic., Fr.) 11:1198
Levy, Milton 15:307
Levy, Moise 13:1039
Levy, Moritz 5:1537
Levy, Morris 8:1050
Levy, Moses (fin., Mor.) 11:153
LEVY, MOSES (U.S. mer.) 11:161
– *illus:* text
LEVY, MOSES (judge, U.S.) 11:161
– universities 15:1677
Levy, Moses (pion., Tex.) 15:1034
Levy, Moses (r., Congo) 5:893
Levy, Moses Albert 14:822
LEVY, MOSES ELIAS 11:162
– agricultural community 2:411
– Florida 6:1361
LEVY, NATHAN 11:162
– Philadelphia 13:368; 13:369
– trade 15:1305
Levy, Neville 12:1042
LÉVY, PAUL (Fr. hist.) 11:162
– anthropology 3:39
Levy, Paul (Fr. math.) 11:160
Lévy, Paul (publ., Fr.) 11:154
LÉVY, RAPHAËL (bld. lib. vict., Fr.) 11:162
– Simon, Richard 7:142; 14:1583
Lévy, Raphaël (Tun. au.), *see* RYVEL
Levy, Raphael (adv., U.S.) 13:1363
LEVY, REUBEN 11:163
Levy, Robert 15:311
Levy, Roland Alexis Manuel, *see* ROLAND-MANUEL
LEVY, RUDOLF 11:163
– *illus:* text
LEVY, SAM SAADI 11:164
Levy, Samson, Jr. 10:1503
LÉVY, SAMUEL (r., fin., Fr.) 11:164
– fiscal affairs 11:568
Levy, Samuel (Mer., U.S.) 11:161
Levy, Samuel Zanvill 8:209
Levy, Sigmund, *see* LEBERT, SIGMUND
Levy, Simha 15:1449
Levy, Simon 12:284
Levy, Solomon (trader, N.Z.) 12:1127
Levy, Solomon (crftn., N.Z.) 12:1128
Levy, Solomon (U.S. mfr.) 2:524
Levy, Stuart 15:311
LEVY, URIAH PHILLIPS 11:164
– anti-Semitism 15:1648
– military service 11:1551
– *illus:* text
Levy, Victor 10:1351
Levy, W. (prch.) 8:958
Levy, William (soc., Alg.) 2:618
Levy, William Mallory (law., U.S.) 10:1504
Levy-Agronsky, Ḥasyah 5:1271
LEVY-BACRAT, ABRAHAM BEN SOLOMON 11:166
– Tlemcen 15:1173
– Tunisia 15:1441
Levy-Bensheton (fam.) 3:399
Levy Bensusan (fam.), *see* BENSUSAN
Lévy-Bensusan, Joshua 4:555
Levy-Bram (mer., Alg.) 12:1446
Lévy-Bruhl, Henri 11:166
LÉVY-BRUHL, LUCIEN 11:166
Lévy-Dreyfus, Robert 16:1114
Lévy Frères, Michel (publ. firm) 13:1368
Levy-Lawson (fam.), *see* LAWSON
Levy-Lawson, Sir Edward, First Baron Burnham 10:1489
– *illus:*
– – caricature (Spy) 10:1490
Levy-Lawson, Sir Harry Lawson Webster, Viscount Burnham 10:1489
Levy of Arles 3:469
Levytski, I.S. 4:887
Levy-Yuly (Mor. fam.), *see* YULY
Lew, Henry 10:1408
Lewald, August 11:167
LEWALD, FANNY 11:167
LEWANDOWSKI, LOUIS 11:167
– *scores:*
– – *Addir Hu* 2:257
– – *Aleinu Leshabbe'aḥ* 2:556
Lewartowski, Aron 5:803; 16:349
Lewek, Jordanis, *see* LEWKO, JORDANIS
Lewensohn, Joel David, *see* LOEWENSTEIN-STRASCHUNSKY, JOEL DAVID
Lewenstein, Tobias 5:1538
Lewental, S. 13:1369
LEWI, MAURICE J. 11:168
LEWIN, AARON BEN NATHAN OF RZESZOW 11:168
Lewin, Abraham 6:330
LEWIN, ADOLF 11:169
LEWIN, BENJAMIN MANASSEH 11:169
– *geonim* 7:318
Lewin, Boleslao 8:563
Lewin, Eliezer Shemuel 11:171
Lewin, Georg, *see* WALDEN, HERWARTH
LEWIN, GERSHON 11:170
– medicine 11:1204
Lewin, Hirschel, *see* LEVIN, ẒEVI HIRSCH BEN ARYEH LOEB
LEWIN, JOSHUA HESHEL BEN ELIJAH ZE'EV HA-LEVI 11:170
LEWIN, JUDAH LEIB 11:171
LEWIN, KURT ZADEK 11:172
LEWIN, LOUIS 11:173
– Eliezer Landshuth 10:1413
Lewin, R. (prch.) 8:958
Lewin, Rachel, *see* VARNHAGEN, RAHEL
Lewin, Reinhold 4:1355
Lewin, Samson 10:988
LEWIN-EPSTEIN, ELIAHU ZE'EV 11:173
– *illus:*
– – Menuḥah ve-Naḥalah Society 9:556
– – Odessa Committee convention 12:1329
Lewin-Epstein Printers (Isr.) 13:1379
Lewinsky, A. 8:476
LEWINSKY, ELHANAN LEIB 11:173
– publishing 12:325
Lewinsky, L. 3:494
LEWINSKY, YOM TOV 11:174
Lewinsky Teachers' Seminary (Isr.)

11:174; 15:920
Lewinsohn, Richard 15:210
LEWINSTEIN, JOSEPH BEN ABRAHAM ABUSH 11:175
Lewinstein, Y. B. 11:612
Lewis, Arthur D. 7:781
Lewis, Mrs. A. S. 16:1334
LEWIS, SIR AUBREY JULIAN 11:175
LEWIS, BERNARD 11:176
LEWIS, DAVID (Can. law.) 11:176
- politics 13:811; 15:1264
Lewis, David (Eng. mer.) 5:661
LEWIS, SIR GEORGE 10:1510
- law 10:1495
Lewis, Godfrey 10:1502
Lewis, Harry 15:306
Lewis, H. Myron 16:35
LEWIS, HYMAN 6:789
Lewis, Isaac (S.A.) 15:204
Lewis, Isaac (Wyom.) 16:679
LEWIS, JERRY 12:470
LEWIS, LEOPOLD DAVIS 6:789
LEWIS, OSCAR 11:176
Lewis, Robert 15:303
Lewis, Samuel 13:1370
Lewis, Stephen 12:1408
LEWIS, TED (Kid) 11:177
Lewis, Thomas 8:42
Lewis, Wyndham 6:781
Lewis brothers (S.A.) 11:1008
LEWISOHN (fam.) 11:177
Lewisohn, Adolph 11:177
- *The American Hebrew* 2:821
Lewisohn, Frederick 11:177
Lewisohn, Irene 15:1078
Lewisohn, James 11:179
Lewisohn, Julius 11:177
Lewisohn, Leibush 9:1343
Lewisohn, Leonard 11:177
LEWISOHN, LUDWIG 11:178
- U.S. literature 15:1572ff
Lewisohn, Margaret, *see* Seligman, Margaret
Lewisohn, Sam Adolph 11:177
Lewisohn, Samuel 11:177
Lewisohn, Solomon 5:1115
Lewiston-Auburn (cities, U.S.) 11:782ff
Lewit, Tonya, *see* Soloveitchik, Tonya
LEWITE, LEON 11:179
LEWKO JORDANIS (court bnk.) 11:180
- *arenda* 3:402
Lewkowicz, Fishel 16:200
LEWKOWITSCH, JULIUS 5:385
LEWKOWITZ, ALBERT 11:181
Lewsen, Phyllis 15:210
Lewy (Hung. print.) 4:1312
Lewy, Adolf 10:1180
Lewy, Hans, *see* LEWY, YOḤANAN
LEWY, ISRAEL 11:181
LEWY, JULIUS 11:182
Lewy, Moritz 10:1180
LEWY, YOḤANAN 11:182
- Hellenism 8:291
LEWYSOHN, ABRAHAM 11:183
LEWYSOHN, YEHUDI LEIB LOUIS 11:183
Lex (Lat.: "the law") 15:1238
Lex Dei (bk.), *see* COLLATIO LEGUM MOSAICARUM ET ROMANARUM
Lexica, Lexicography
- *Al Murshid al-Kafi* 15:797
- auxiliary law literature 12:118
- Elmaleh, Abraham (Israel) 6:681
- *Em la-Binah* (Teomim) 15:1012
- English-Yiddish Encyclopedic Dictionary (1915) 16:1186
- Gesenius 16:1396
- *Hebrew and Chaldiac lexicon* (Scheidius) 16:37
- Jewish literature 11:323
- *Ketonet Yosef* 4:591
- Ladino-Spanish 10:1348
- *Lexicon Chaldaicum Talmudicum* 4:1543
- *Lexicon Hebraicum et Chaldaicum* 4:1543
- *Lexikon des Judentums* 6:734
- linguistics 16:1353
- *Millon* (Ben Yehuda) 16:583
- *see also:* Concordances; Dictionaries; ENCYCLOPEDIAS
Lexington (city, Ky.) 10:909
Lexington (tn., Mass.) 11:1112
Lex talionis (leg. conc.), *see* TALION
Ley, J. 13:676
Le-Yad ha-Hegeh (journ.) 1:newsp. list
Leyda (city, Sp.), *see* LÉRIDA
Leydekker (Leid-), Melchior 8:42
Leyden (city, Neth.) 11:193
Leyden, Lucas van, *see* Lucas van Leyden
Leyeles, A., *see* GLANZ-LEYELES, AARON
Leyon, Avram 15:1461
LEZAJSK (tn., Pol.) 11:184
Lezard, Adèle 15:210
Lezhnev, Abram Zakharovich 14:513
LHEVINNE, JOSEF 12:697
Lhévinne, Rosina 12:697
LIABILITY (leg. term) 11:184
- *avot nezikin* 3:986ff
- contract, breach of 5:932
- labor law 10:1328ff
- lien 11:227
- maintenance 11:784
- non-Jewish court rulings 6:54
- torts 15:1273ff
- transfer of 3:768
- *see also:* GERAMA AND GARME; LOAN; OBLIGATIONS, LAW OF
LIACHO, LÁZARO 11:185
Liachovitzky, Jacobo Simon 11:185; 15:255
Liadov, M. 5:794
Liaison (mag.) 13:1049
Liana (writ.), *see* Ascoli, Emilia
Libanius (Rom., Antioch) 7:892; 8:655; 11:57
Libanon (period.) 12:802; 16:1226
Libation offering 14:603
- place in cult 5:1161
- priests 13:1077
- *see also:* SACRIFICE; Water drawing, feast of
Libau (Libava; city, Latv.), *see* LIEPAJA
LIBEDINSKI, YURI NIKOLAYEVICH 11:185
Libel, *see* SLANDER
Libels, Anti-Semitic, *see* ANTI-SEMITISM; BLOOD LIBEL; ELDERS OF ZION, PROTOCOLS OF THE LEARNED; Well Poisoning libel
Liber, Akim, *see* Liber, Leon
Liber, Boris Gorev 11:186
Liber,Isaac 11:186
Liber, Julia 11:186
Liber, Leon 11:186
LIBER, MARC 11:186
- politics 13:819
LIBER, MAURICE 11:187
Liber, Olga 11:186
Liberalism (polit. ideology) 13:824
Liberal Judaism, *see* REFORM JUDAISM
Liberal Labor Movement (Isr.) 8:1349
Liberal Party (Isr.)
- Bernstein, Perez 4:688
- Gaḥal established 7:255
- General Zionist Party 7:385
- historical survey 9:398ff
- Sapir, Joseph 14:856
- *see also:* INDEPENDENT LIBERAL PARTY; Progressive Party
Liber Antiquitatum Biblicarum (chronicle), *see* PHILO (Pseudo-)
Liberberg, Joseph 4:1046; 10:995
Liber contra Judaeos (wk.) 2:915
Liber de Pomo (bk.) 3:446
LIBEREC (city, Bohem.) 11:187
- textiles 15:1041
Liberia (rep., Afr.)
- Black Jews 4:1069
- Israel medical training 9:991
- Israel's relations with 9:440
- *illus:*
- - Ben-Zvi, visit 9:436
Liberman, Alex 13:484
Liberman, Hyman 5:140
LIBERMAN, YEVSEY GRIGORYEVICH 11:188
- *illus:* text
Liber Profetiae Mosis (Apoc. wk.) 12:412
Libertà, La (newsp.) 3:294
Libertas (student assoc., Aus.) 15:447
Liberty (tn., N.Y.) 12:1127
Liberty, *see* FREEDOM
Libgold, L. Leo 12:455
Libien, Moses 16:515
LIBIN, Z. 11:189
- *illus:* text
Libman, Isaac, *see* LIPMAN, LEVI
LIBNAH (bib. site, Er. Isr.) 11:190
Libnah (Cana. city-state) 11:190
- proscription by Israel 8:345
Libni (bib. fig.) 7:513
Libo (anc. loc.) 10:1551
LIBOWITZ, SAMUEL NEHEMIAH 11:190
Libra (zodiac sign) 16:1191
- *illus:*
- - Bet Alfa mosaic 15:1154
- - *Dresden Maḥzor* 6:690
LIBRARIES 11:190
- *Contents:*
- - Communal Libraries 11:190
- - Public Libraries 11:191
- - Nazi Persecution 11:192
- - In Israel 11:194
- - Catalogs 11:195
- Berlin Rabbinical Seminary 13:1459
- Bibliotheca Judaica Simonseniana (Copenhagen) 5:953
- Bibliotheca Rosenthaliana (Amst.) 2:903
- Bibliothèque Nationale (Paris) 4:976
- Bodleian Library (Oxford) 4:1163
- Breslau Seminary 4:1355
- British Museum Hebraica 5:989
- Cambridge University 5:70
- Centre de Documentation Juive Contemporaine (Paris) 5:287
- Dropsie University 6:236
- Frankfort 7:89
- H.U.C.-J.I.R. (Cincinnati) 8:218
- Israel 9:1003
- Jewish National Library (Jer.) 9:1003
- Jewish Theological Seminary of America (N.Y.C.) 10:96
- Jews' College (Lond.) 10:99
- Leningrad (St. Petersburg) 11:17
- Leo Baeck Institute (N.Y.C.) 11:23
- New York Public Library 12:1120
- Nineveh 12:1170; 16:1504
- Palatina Library (Parma) 13:123
- Strashun Library (Vilna) 15:426
- Vatican MSS. collection 11:907
- Vienna Seminary 9:1068
- Wiener Library (Lond.) 16:503
- Yad Vashem (Jer.) 16:697
- YIVO (Vilna, N.Y.C.) 16:838
- *illus:*
- - Bar-Ilan University 9:963,1003
- - Ez Ḥayyim, Amsterdam 2:903; 12:279
- - Jerusalem College for Women 9:899
- - National Library building, Mt. Scopus 3:349
- - Strashun Library, Vilna 16:141
- - Tel Aviv University Library 3:351; 9:956
- *see also:* ARCHIVES; BIBLIOPHILES; BOOK TRADE; INCUNABULA; MANUSCRIPTS, HEBREW
LIBRARY, JEWISH NATIONAL AND UNIVERSITY (Jer.) 11:197
- archives 3:392
- Chasanowich, Joseph 5:362
- Hebrew incunabula 8:1322
- Hebrew mss 11:906
- Jerusalem development 9:1473
- *Kirjath Sepher* 10:1046
- libraries 11:194
- Wormann, Curt 16:643
- *illus:*
- - Mount Scopus building 3:349
Library of Congress (U.S.) 14:943
Libretti (mus. term) 12:557
Libreville (tn., Gabon) 9:439
LIBSCHITZ, BARUCH MORDECAI BEN JACOB 11:198
Libschuetz (fam.), *see* LIPSCHUETZ
Libshey (ḥas. dyn.), *see* LYUBESHOV
Libusch, Moses 12:414
LIBYA 11:198
- *Contents:*
- - Early History 11:198
- - Arab Period 11:201
- - Italian Rule 11:202
- - Holocaust Period 11:202
- - British Occupation 11:202
- - Contemporary Period 11:203
- - Social, Economic, and Religious-Cultural Conditions 11:204
- - Zionist Activity 11:204
- - Attitude Toward Israel 11:205
- ancient 13:1415
- Arab League 3:242
- demography 5:1504
- discrimination 6:71
- emigration to Israel 9:499ff
- Jews in metalwork 11:1442
- Jews' migration to Rome 14:253
- marriage customs 11:1043; 11:1044
- sickness 14:1501
- synagogues 1:syn. list
- Tunisia 15:1430
- U.N. on racial discrimination 15:1560
- war with Israel 16:306ff
- Zionism 16:1127; 16:1128ff
- *illus:*
- - Ḥanukkah lamp, ceramic (19th cent.) 2:335
- *see also:* BENGHAZI; CYRENE; TRIPOLI
L.I.C.A., *see* Ligue Internationale contre le Racisme et l'Antisémitisme
Lice (pest) 13:604
- *illus:*
- - Plagues of Egypt 13:609
Lichenstein, B. 6:273
LICHINE, DAVID 11:206
LICHT, ALEXANDER 11:206
- Zionism 16:1149; 16:917
Licht, D. 15:1072
LICHT, FRANK 11:207
Licht, Herman 16:1149
LICHT, MICHAEL 11:208

LICHTENBAUM, JOSEPH **11**:208
Lichtenbaum, Maksymilian (Marek) **11**:1261; **16**:349
LICHTENBERG, BERNHARD **11**:208
Lichtenburg (concen. camp) **5**:77; **13**:1583
LICHTENFELD, GABRIEL JUDAH **11**:209
Lichtenhein, Samuel **15**:316
Lichtenstadt (tn., Bohem.), *see* HROZNETIN
LICHTENSTADT, ABRAHAM AARON **11**:209
LICHTENSTADT, BENJAMIN WOLF BEN JUDAH **11**:209
Lichtenstadt, Jacob Aaron **10**:1403
Lichtenstadt, Solomon **11**:209
Lichtenstein (fam., Latv.) **15**:1428
Lichtenstein (r., U.S.) **15**:1206
Lichtenstein, David, *see* LICHINE, DAVID
Lichtenstein, E. (Cz.) **16**:1022
Lichtenstein, Eliezer (Belor.) **10**:1341
Lichtenstein, Erich **13**:1367
Lichtenstein, Ḥaya, *see* Weizmann, Ḥaya
Lichtenstein, Hermann, *see* HIRSCHENSOHN-LICHTENSTEIN, JEHIEL ZEVI HERMANN
LICHTENSTEIN, HILLEL BEN BARUCH **11**:210
- Plaut, H.F. **13**:630
Lichtenstein, Isaac **4**:1219
LICHTENSTEIN, WALTER **11**:210
Lichtensztain, Moses **12**:186
Lichtheim, George **11**:211; **15**:64
Lichtheim, Ludwig **10**:1129
LICHTHEIM, RICHARD **11**:210
- Revisionism **14**:129
LICHTMACHER, LAZAR **11**:1574
LICHTSTEIN, ABRAHAM BEN ELIEZER LIPMAN **11**:212
LICHTSTEIN, ABRAHAM JEKUTHIEL ZALMAN BEN MOSES JOSEPH **11**:212
- Vilna printing **16**:148
Lichtstein, Moses **11**:212
Lichtstein, Solomon **11**:212
Lichtwitz, Hans **13**:1026; **14**:1120
Licoricia (13th cent., fin.) **16**:537
Lictera (city, Er. Isr.), *see* ḤADERAH
Lid (type of poem) **16**:804
LIDA (tn., Belor.) **11**:212
- ghetto **13**:770
- yeshivah **16**:770
Lida, David **7**:1507; **14**:198
Lida, Pethahiah ben David **9**:1294
Lidarti, Cristiano Giuseppe **5**:127
L'Idea Sionista (It. period.) **12**:201; **13**:1037; **16**:1122
L'Idea Sionistica (Revisionist period., It.) **5**:208; **16**:1123
Lider, Elinke, *see* Schick, Elijah
LIDIN, VLADIMIR GERMANOVICH **11**:213
Lidové Noviny (newsp.) **13**:1026
Lidz, Theodore **13**:1340
LIDZBARSKI, MARK (Abraham Mordechai) **11**:214
Lidzki, J. **13**:1375
Lie, Haaron **12**:1225
Lie, Trygve Halvdan **3**:480, **12**:1225
Liebehenschel, Arthur **11**:794
Lieben (fam.) **3**:875
Lieben (vill., Cz.) **13**:968
LIEBEN, ADOLPH **11**:214
- *illus*: text
LIEBEN, KOPPELMANN **11**:215
LIEBEN, ROBERT VON **11**:215
- stamps **15**:335
- - *illus*: text
LIEBEN, SALOMON (physic.) **11**:215
LIEBEN, SALOMON HUGO (hist.) **11**:216
- museum **12**:538
Liebenfels, Joerg Lans von **8**:782
Liebentanz, M. **8**:42
Lieber, Akiva Ha-Kohen **7**:1177
Lieber "the Great" (r., Ukr.) **4**:589
Lieberman, Archie **13**:484
LIEBERMAN, CHAIM **11**:216
Lieberman, Chenoch (art.) **10**:320
LIEBERMAN, ELIAS **11**:217
Lieberman, Ella **8**:881
LIEBERMAN, HERMAN (polit.) **11**:217
- P.P.S. **13**:951
- *illus*: text
Lieberman, Herman (crit.), *see* LIEBERMAN, CHAIM
Lieberman, Judith **11**:220
LIEBERMAN, MYRON **11**:218
Lieberman, Samuel **6**:369
LIEBERMAN, SAUL **11**:218
- anthropomorphism **3**:57
- *Baraita of 32 Rules* **4**:195
- Hellenism **8**:291
- Jerusalem Talmud **4**:340; **7**:1107; **15**:773ff
- *ketubbah* formula **10**:929
- marriage **5**:905
- *illus*:
- - Finkelstein, Louis, and **2**:819
- - Greenberg, Simon, and **7**:906
LIEBERMANN, AARON SAMUEL **11**:220
- *Ha-Emet* **7**:1057
- socialism, Jewish **2**:420; **15**:39ff
LIEBERMANN, CARL THEODOR **11**:221
Liebermann, Eliezer Dov **11**:220
LIEBERMANN, FELIX **11**:222
Liebermann, H. **4**:1428
LIEBERMANN, MAX **11**:223
- letters **11**:61
- *illus*:
- - Cohen, Hermann (portrait) **5**:674
- - "The Spinners" (paint.) **3**:551
LIEBERMANN, ROLF **12**:697
Liebermann, Solomon **10**:233
LIEBERSON, GODDARD **12**:697
LIEBERT, ARTHUR **11**:224
Liebert, Julius **11**:485
Liebes (fam., El Salvador) **6**:687
Liebes (fam, U.S.) **14**:834
Liebeschitz (fam.), *see* LIPSCHUETZ
Liebesgaben (Nazi-confiscated goods) **2**:903
Liebeshutz, Solomon **16**:1123
Liebeskind, Adolf (Dolek) **5**:1039
Liebknecht, Karl **11**:592
Liebknecht, William **15**:26
Lieblein, Abraham **15**:521
Liebler, Naḥman **13**:987
Liebling, Jerome **13**:485
Liebman, Charles S. **8**:568; **15**:68
LIEBMAN, JOSHUA LOTH **11**:224
- *illus*: text
Liebman, Max **15**:1058
Liebman, P., *see* HERSCH, PESACH LIEBMAN
Liebman, S.B. **8**:563
Liebmann, Babetta (Bela), *see* Leidesdorf, Babetta
Liebmann, Benjamin Wolff **7**:815
Liebmann, Esther **12**:64
Liebmann, Irene **5**:449
Liebmann, Isaac **11**:225
Liebmann, Israel (Ignaz) **10**:1590
LIEBMANN, JOST **11**:225
- Aaron ben Isaac Benjamin **2**:12
- Isaac Benjamin **9**:21
Liebmann, Malka **11**:225
LIEBMANN, OTTO **11**:226
"Liebman of Creutzonach" **10**:1260
Liebow, Averile **11**:1202
Liebschuetz (name), *see* Lifschitz; Lifshitz; Lipschitz; Lipschuetz; Lipschutz; Lipshitz; Lipszyc
Liebster, Alfred **15**:314
Liechtenstein, P. **4**:1196
Lieder, Reb Noaḥ, *see* Zaludkowski, Noah
Lieff, Abraham **10**:1494
Liefman, Robert **7**:133
LIÉGE (city, Belg.) **11**:226
Liegnitz (tn., Pol.), *see* LEGNICA
LIEN (leg. term) **11**:227
- *Contents*:
- - The Concept **11**:227
- - Import of the Term Aḥarayut Nekhasim **11**:227
- - Substance of the Creditor's Right in the Debtor's Property **11**:227
- - Recovery of the Debt out of Encumbered Assets **11**:227
- - Creation of the Debt **11**:228
- contractual obligation **5**:927
- document **14**:1388
- firstborn inheritance **6**:1312
- non-Jewish court rulings **6**:54
- property redemption **10**:1482
- property subject to **13**:1146ff
- waiver **11**:1232
- wills **16**:522
- *see also*: EXECUTION; LOAN; OBLIGATIONS, LAW OF; PLEDGE; SHI'BUDA DE-RABBI NATHAN; SURETYSHIP
Lienz (cmty., Aus.) **15**:1491
LIEPAJA (city, Latv.) **11**:232
Liepmannssohn, S.L. **8**:958
LIES, MAN OF **11**:233
- Prophet of Lies **11**:234
- Teacher of Righteousness **15**:887
LIES, PROPHET OF **11**:234
- Man of Lies **11**:234
LIESSIN, ABRAHAM **11**:235
Lietuva, *see* LITHUANIA
Lietzmann, Hans **11**:1239
Life (bk.) **10**:262
LIFE AND DEATH **11**:235
- death **5**:1422
- medical transplant **15**:1337
- netherworld **12**:996
- righteous and wicked **14**:182
- theology **15**:1105
- two worlds **10**:391
- *Ẓaddik* **7**:1406
- *see also*: AFTERLIFE; ESCHATOLOGY
Life, Book of, *see* BOOK OF LIFE
Life, danger to, *see* PIKKU'AḤ NEFESH
Life in the World to Come, *see* AFTERLIFE; OLAM HA-BA
Life of Adam and Eve (wk.), *see* ADAM AND EVE, BOOK OF THE LIFE OF
Lifnim mi-shurat ha-din (leg. term) **6**:941; **12**:113; **14**:652
Lifschits, Jehiel Meir, *see* JEHIEL MEIR OF GOSTYNIN
Lifschitz (name), *see also*: Lifshitz; Lipschitz; Lipschuetz; Lipschutz; Lipshitz; Lipszyc
Lifschitz, Jacob **3**:575
- *illus*:
- - "Children in Kovno Ghetto School" (drg.) Fig. 77 **3**-ART
Lifschitz, Joachim **4**:653
Lifschitz, Malkah, *see* ESTHER (commun.)
Lifschitz, Uri **3**:593
- *illus*:
- - "Dancing Clown" (paint.) PL. 153 **3**-ART
Lifschutz, E. **8**:569
Lifshits (fam.), *see* LIPSCHUETZ
LIFSHITS, SHIYE-MORDKHE **11**:237
Lifshitz (name), *see also*: Lifschitz; Lipschitz; Lipschutz; Lipshitz; Lipszyc
LIFSHITZ, DAVID **11**:237
Lifshitz, Hayim, *see* LEAF, HAYIM
LIFSHITZ, NEHAMAH **11**:238
- *illus*: text
Lifshyts (name), *see* Lifschitz; Lifshitz; Lipschitz; Lipschuetz; Lipschutz; Lipshitz; Lipszyc
Lifson, Sol **13**:1361
Lift, David **15**:1074
Lifta (vill., Er. Isr.), *see* Mei-Neftoaḥ
Liga pro-Palestina Obrera (Mex.) **16**:1125
Light **6**:1304
- *Havdalah blessing* **7**:1481
- *Shekhinah* **14**:1350
Light (journ., Rum.), *see Likht*
Light, Solomon **15**:635
LIGHTFOOT, JOHN **11**:238
- Hebraists **8**:42
- linguistics **16**:1399
"Lighting of the Ḥanukkah Candles" (paint., M. Oppenheim) **7**:1281
"Lighting the Sabbath Candles" (drg., I. Szigeti) **14**:567
Lightning, *see* THUNDER AND LIGHTNING
Lights, Ḥanukkah, *see* ḤANUKKAH
Lignitzer, Jacob **15**:293
Ligonier (city, Ind.) **8**:1361
Ligue des Amis du Sionisme (Fr.) **16**:1114
Ligue des Droits de l'Homme, *see* League for the Rights of Man
Ligue Franco-Sioniste (Fr.) **16**:1114
Ligue Internationale contre le Racisme et l'Antisémitisme **10**:1553; **13**:85
- anti-Nazi boycott **4**:1281
Lihyānic (lang.) **14**:1152
Liḥyānite (ling.) **3**:237
Li-Kerat (journ.) **1**:newsp. list
Likht (period.) **4**:1272; **9**:1295; **13**:1043
LIKKUT AẒAMOT ("gathering of the bones") **11**:238
- *see also*: BURIAL; DISINTERMENT; MOURNING; OSSUARIES and SARCOPHAGI
Likkutei Amarim (wk.), *see Tanya*
Likkutei Yekarim (anth. of sermons), *see* JEHIEL MICHAEL OF ZLOCZOW
Likkutim Shonim mi-Sefer de-Vei Eliyahu (bk.) **5**:153
Liknaitz, David **11**:501
Li-La-Lo (theat., Isr.) **12**:687
Lilenfeld, L. **13**:667
Lilenthal (fam.) **16**:546
Liliana, Lili **12**:455
LILIEN, EPHRAIM MOSES **11**:239
- bookplates **4**:1219
- *illus*:
- - text
- - "Abraham looking at the Stars" (drg.) Fig. 86 **3**-ART
- - bookplate **4**:1224
- - Drogobych marketplace (etch.) **6**:233
- - Jewish beggar and child (etch.) **4**:389
- - Kishinev pogrom, dedication page **10**:1065
- - "Yemenite Torah scribe" (etch.)

14:1044
LILIENBLUM, MOSES LEIB 11:240
- critic 5:1117
- Guenzburg, Mordecai 7:964
- Hebrew literature 8:189; 8:190
- history chart 8:766-767
- Kefar Malal 10:888
- political Zionism 16:1042ff
- *illus:*
- - Odessa Committee convention 12:1329
- - with Hebrew writers 8:193
Lilienthal (fam.) 5:56
Lilienthal, Andre Amolodovich 5:406
LILIENTHAL, DAVID ELI 11:243
Lilienthal, Gustav 11:245
LILIENTHAL, MAX (Menahem) 11:243
- Cincinnati 5:563
- Eliasberg, Mordecai 6:615
- Guenzburg, Mordecai 7:964
- Riga 14:173
- Russia 14:439
- Uvarov, Sergey 16:38
- Wise, Isaac Mayer 16:563
LILIENTHAL, OTTO 11:245
- stamps 15:335
Lilit (ornith.) 12:1531
LILITH (demon) 11:245
- Adam 2:238
- Agrat bat Mahalath 2:374
- amulet 2:911
- Angel of Death 2:955
- childbirth charms 4:1051
- circumcision 5:576
- demon 5:1523
- Elijah inscription 6:645
- folklore 6:1400
- Samael 14:721
- *illus:*
- - amulet 5:1525
- - protective prayer against 4:1050
LILLE (city, Fr.) 11:249
Lille, de (cartog.) 11:927
Lily (bot.) 8:1312; 13:621
Lima (city, Ohio) 12:1345
LIMA (city, Peru) 11:250
- Inquisition 8:1394
- Peru 13:322ff
- *illus:*
- - text
- - community marriage register 3:386; 13:324
Lima, de (fam.) 5:1009
Lima, Joseph Suasso de 15:210
LIMA, MOSES BEN ISAAC JUDAH 11:251
Lima, Raphael ben Moses 11:251
Liman (mosh., Isr.) 1:place list
Limburg (prov., Neth.) 12:974
LIMBURG, JOSEPH 13:828
Limburg on the Lahn (tn., Ger.) 12:841
LIMERICK (city, Ire.) 11:251
Limes (Lat. "fenced in"), *see Ḥagar*
Limes Palestinae (Rom. frontier) 9:240; 9:251
"Limestone Head" (sculp., A. Modigliani) 14:1061
LIMITATION OF ACTIONS (leg. term.) 11:251
- *Contents:*
- - Concept and its Substance 11:251
- - Talmudic Period 11:252
- - Roman Law 11:252
- - Post-Talmudic Period 11:253
- - In State of Israel 11:254
- *ḥazakah* 7:1521
- maintenance arrears 11:787
LIMOGES (city, Fr.) 11:254
Limousin (prov., Fr.) 3:23
LIMOUX (tn., Fr.) 11:254
LIMPIEZA DE SANGRE (Inq. term) 11:255
- *anusim* 3:173
- Cervantes 5:313
- New Christians 3:108; 12:1002
LINCOLN (tn., Eng.) 11:256
- Crusades 5:1140
- history chart 8:766-767
- *illus:* text
Lincoln (city, Neb.) 12:912
LINCOLN, ABRAHAM 11:257
- Lincolnia collection 8:978
- *illus:*
- - B'nai B'rith protest against Grant's anti-Semitic Order 15:1652
- - flag with Hebrew inscription 15:1601
- - letter "About Jews" 15:1603
- - revocation of Grant's General Order 15:1651
Lincoln, Ignatius Timothy, *see* TREBITSCH-LINCOLN, IGNATIUS TIMOTHY
Lind, Jakov 7:454
Linda, Baruch, *see* Lindau, Baruch
LINDAU (tn., Bav.) 11:258
Lindau, Baruch 7:421; 7:1436
Lindberg, J. Christian 4:877; 8:42
Lindberg, Leopold 7:1031
Lindbergh, Charles A. 15:1655
Lindemann, Gustav 15:1057
Linden (city, N.J.) 15:1533
Linden (bot.) 9:1515
Linden, A., *see* MOTZKIN, LEO
Linden mastic (bot.) 9:1515
Lindenthal, I.L. 15:91
Linder, Jakub 4:1399
LINDER, MAX 12:453; 12:470
Lindheim, Herman 12:1038
LINDHEIM, IRMA LEVY 11:258
Lindheimer, Benjamin F. 15:308, 311
LINDO (fam.) 11:259
- *illus:* text
Lindo, Abigail 11:260
Lindo, Abraham Alexander 11:259
Lindo, Alexandre 14:1663
Lindo, David Abarbanel 11:260
Lindo, Elias Hayyim 11:260
Lindo, Elijah 7:1291
- *illus:*
- - Ḥanukkah lamp 7:1300
Lindo, Isaac 5:117; 11:259
Lindo, Lorenzo, *see* Lindo, Isaac
LINDO, MARK PRAGER 6:320; 6:322
Lindo, Moses 11:259; 13:1360; 15:211
Lindsay, John 12:1113
Lindsey, Mortver 15:305
- *illus:*
- - bowls 15:304
Linen 15:1036ff
- economic history 16:1274
- *sha'atnez* 14:1213
Line of flax (meas.), *see Petil Pishtim*
LINETZKY, ISAAC JOEL 11:260
Linfield, H.S. 15:346
L'Information (newsp.) 9:1017
LINGUISTIC LITERATURE, HEBREW 16:1352
- Alting 2:776
- Avrunin, Abraham 3:990
- Biesenthal 4:985
- Drusius 6:241
- Fuen 7:213
- Midrash 12:886
- sages and foreign loan-words 14:651ff
- Wessely 16:462
- *see also:* HEBRAISTS, CHRISTIAN; HEBREW GRAMMAR; HEBREW LANGUAGE; MASORAH; ORIENTALISTS; PRONUNCIATIONS OF HEBREW
Lingvistisher Zamelbukh (period.) 13:1048
Link, Joseph 8:1379; 15:1492
Link, P. 6:735
Linkov, G.M. ("Uncle Batya") 12:55
Linksz, Isaac 10:1220
Linn, Louis 14:1024
Linnaeus (Linné, Carl von) 14:929
Linnaeusstraat Synagogue (Amst.) 15:620
LINOWITZ, SOL MYRON 11:261
Linshes, Barbara *see* WEISBERGER, BARBARA
Lintel, *see* DOOR AND DOORPOST
Linton, J. Ralph 13:1340
LINZ (city, Aus.) 11:261
Linz-Auerbach (fam.), *see* AUERBACH
Linz Program (Aus.) 14:989
LION (zool.) 11:262
- dietary laws 6:32
- Hai Gaon 14:1074
- Jewish symbolism 15:571
- symbol of strength 14:1527
- synagogue art 15:597ff
- *illus:*
- - text
- - ceremonial object motif 15:1260-1261
- - Chryzanow tombstone 15:1226
- - Dagon temple, bronze head 11:976
- - emblem of Judah 12:*fcg.* 1259
- - Hammat Geder mosaic 7:251; 15:575
- - Horb synagogue paintings 15:*fcg.* 622
- - Iron Age basalt weight 16:391
- - Kefar Birim head 3:517
- - laver 14:252
- - Lesko tombstone decoration 15:1231
- - Lions' Gate (Jer.) 9:1432
- - Porta Leone seal 13:908
- - Samson rending 14:772
- - *Shivviti* plaque 14:1420-1421
- - Torah ornaments 15:1260-1261
Li On (Isr.) 1:place list; 2:312
Lion, Ascher 11:167
Lion, Hart, *see* LEVIN, ẒEVI HIRSCH BEN ARYEH LOEB
Lion, Kalman 12:36
LION, LEON M. 15:1054,1087
Lionaes, Aase 12:1225
Lion of Judah 11:275
LION OF WRATH (D. S. scrolls) 11:276
Lions Gate (Jer.) 9:1434; 9:1516; 14:1635
- *illus:*
- - general view 9:1431,1432
- - Dayan entering Jerusalem, Six-Day War 9:409
- - Six-Day War fighting 14:1632
Liozna, Shneur Zalman of, *see* SHNEUR ZALMAN OF LYADY
LIOZNO (tn., Belor.) 11:277
Lipa (r., Lith.) 7:798
Lipcani (tn., Belor.), *see* LIPKANY
LIPCHITZ, JACQUES (Chaim Jacob) 11:277
- *illus:*
- - text
- - "Mother and Child" (sculp.) 14:1064
- - "Theseus" (sculp.) 3:559
Lipets, D. 4:590
LIPINER, SIEGFRIED 11:278
Lipinski, Bernard 6:308
LIPKANY (tn., Belor.) 11:278
Lipke, Jan 10:1469
Lipkin, Emmanuel 6:342
Lipkin, Isaac 11:280
LIPKIN (Salanter), ISRAEL BEN ZE'EV WOLF 11:279
- ethics 6:941
- *kolel* system 10:1161
- Musar movement 12:534ff
- Salant, Joseph 14:673
- *ẓaddik* 14:183
LIPKIN, YOM TOV LIPMAN 11:280
- *illus:* text
Lipman, B. 8:957
LIPMAN, EUGENE JAY 11:281
LIPMAN, JACOB GOODALE 11:281
- Vineland 16:157
Lipman, Leib 15:539
LIPMAN, LEVI 11:282
Lipman, Moshe 12:455; 15:1072
LIPMANN, FRITZ ALBERT 11:282
LIPMANN, OTTO 11:283
Lipmann, Yom Tov 4:1310
Lipmann Berlin, *see* SONNENFELS, ALOYS VON
Lipmann-Muelhausen, Yom Tov, *see* MUELHAUSEN, YOM TOV LIPMANN
Lipna, Dinah 2:270
LIPNIK NAD BECVOU (tn., Cz.) 11:283
LIPNO (tn., Pol.) 11:284
LIPOVETS (tn., Ukr.) 11:284
Lipovska, Esther 12:454
Lipovski, Nahum 12:454
Lipp, Joseph J. 15:308
Lippard, George 15:1569
Lippay, Count 16:74
LIPPE (-Detmold; state, Ger.) 11:285
LIPPE, KARPEL 11:285
- Zionism 16:1133
- *illus:*
- - F.Z.C. 16:1165
Lippe, Wolf 7:999
Lippiano (loc. It.) 15:1468
Lippman ("Roli"; medal.) 11:1167
Lippmann (fin., Rus.) 11:14
Lippmann, Alexandre 12:1375
Lippmann, Benjamin 11:249
LIPPMANN, EDMUND OSKAR VON 11:286
LIPPMANN, EDUARD 11:286
Lippmann, Friedrich 3:566; 3:650
LIPPMANN, GABRIEL 11:286
- *illus:*
- - Swedish stamp 12:1203
Lippmann, Leo 7:1228
Lippmann, Moses Eliezer 16:1232
LIPPMANN, WALTER (U.S.) 11:287
Lippman, W.M. 11:1284
Lippmann, Yeruḥam, *see* Dembowski, Andreas
Lippmann-Muelhausen, Yom Tov, *see* MUELHAUSEN, YOM TOV LIPMANN
LIPPOLD (court J.) 11:288
Lippomani, Marco 8:43
Lippomano, Luigi 8:1386
Lippstadt (dis., Ger.) 13:7
Lip-reading 2:744
Lipschitz (name), *see also* Lifschitz; Lifshitz; Lipchitz; Lipschuetz; Lipshitz; Lipschutz, Lipszyc
Lipschitz, Baruch Mordecai, *see* LIBSCHITZ, BARUCH MORDECAI BEN JACOB
LIPSCHITZ, JACOB HA-LEVI 11:288
Lipschitz, Jacob Zalman 11:198
Lipschitz, Jacques, *see* LIPCHITZ, JACQUES
Lipschitz, Judah Loew ben Isaac 15:1499

Lipschitz, Meir Ezekiel **11**:198
Lipschitz, Nathan Nata **11**:289
LIPSCHITZ, RUDOLF OTTO SIGISMUND **11**:289
LIPSCHITZ, SOLOMON BEN MOSES **7**:1549
- music **12**:557
LIPSCHITZ, SOLOMON ZALMAN **11**:289
Lipschuetz (name), *see also* Lifschitz; Lifshitz; Lipschitz; Lipshitz; Lipshutz; Lipszyc
LIPSCHUETZ (fam.) **11**:290
Lipschuetz, Alejandro **5**:467
LIPSCHUETZ, BARUCH ISAAC BEN ISRAEL **11**:290
- *Tiferet Yisrael* **11**:293,294
Lipschuetz, Benjamin Benush **11**:290
Lipschuetz, Eliezer (r.) **11**:292
LIPSCHUETZ, ELIEZER MEIR (educ.) **11**:291
Lipschuetz, Elijah **11**:290
Lipschuetz, Ezekiel **11**:292; **16**:1348
Lipschuetz, Gedaliah ben Israel **11**:290; **11**:292
LIPSCHUETZ, GEDALIAH BEN SOLOMON ZALMAN **11**:292
Lipschuetz, Ḥayyim ben Isaac **11**:290
LIPSCHUETZ, HILLEL ARYEH LEIB BEN ZE'EV DOV **11**:292
Lipschuetz, Isaac **11**:290
LIPSCHUETZ, ISRAEL BEN ELIEZER **11**:292
- Cleves get **5**:613
- David Tevele of Lissa **5**:1353
Lipschuetz, Israel Mordecai ben Elijah **11**:290
Lipschuetz, Jacob **11**:292
Lipschuetz, Jehiel Meir, *see* JEHIEL MEIR OF GOSTYNIN
Lipschuetz, Jeremiah Meir **7**:818
Lipschuetz, M. (publ., Fr.) **4**:1239; **13**:1374
Lipschuetz, Moses ben Enoch **11**:290
Lipschuetz, Moses ben Isaac **11**:290
Lipschuetz, Moses ben Noah Isaac **11**:290
Lipschutz (name), *see also* Lifschitz; Lifshitz; Lipschitz; Lipschuetz; Lipshitz; Lipszyc
Lipschutz, Abraham **4**:1356; **11**:295
LIPSCHUTZ, ARYEH LEIB **11**:293
LIPSCHUTZ, ELIEZER BEN SOLOMON **11**:293
- Oppenheim, David **12**:1421
- Ostrowiec **12**:1517
LIPSCHUTZ, ISRAEL BEN GEDALIAH **11**:293
Lipschutz, Judah **11**:295
LIPSCHUTZ, SHABBETAI BEN JACOB ISAAC **11**:294
LIPSCHUTZ, SOLOMON BEN MORDECAI **11**:294
LIPSET, SEYMOUR MARTIN **11**:295
- sociology **15**:68
Lipshitz (name), *see also* Lifschitz; Lifshitz; Lipschitz; Lipschuetz; Lipschutz; Lipszyc
Lipshitz, Abraham **6**:1161
LIPSHITZ, ISRAEL LIPPY **11**:295
Lipshitz, Jacob **10**:1179
Lipshitz, Moses **11**:430
Lipshitz, Sam **15**:1263
Lipsitt, William **7**:1349
LIPSKI, ABRAHAM **11**:295
Lipsky, Eleazar **11**:296
Lipsky, Joel **11**:296
LIPSKY, LOUIS **11**:296
- U.S. Zionism **16**:1143
- *illus:*
- - Biltmore Hotel Conference **15**:1633
- - Thirteenth Zionist Congress **16**:1173
Lipsner, Benjamin B. **2**:321
Lipson, Daniel **11**:297
LIPSON, EPHRAIM **11**:297
Lipson, I.J. **13**:482
LIPSON, MORDEKHAI **11**:297
- *illus:*
- - Histadruth Ivrith of America **13**:371
Lipszyc (name), *see also* Lifschitz; Lifshitz; Lipschitz; Lipschuetz; Lipschutz; Lipshitz
Lipszyc, Henryk **16**:349
Lipton (vill., Can.) **2**:413; **14**:891
LIPTON, MAURICE **11**:297
LIPTON, SEYMOUR **11**:297
- *illus:* text
LIPTOVSKY MIKULAS (Liptószentmiklós; tn., Slov.) **11**:298
- Loew, Eleazar **11**:442
- Slovakia **14**:1679
LIPTZIN, SOL **1**:33; **11**:299
LIPZIN, KENI **15**:1088
- *illus:*
- - as Mirele Efros **15**:1068
Lipzin, V. **15**:1088
Liqā' (journ.), *see Mifgash-Liqā'*
Liquor trade, *see* WINE AND LIQUOR TRADE
Lira (Isr. currency), *see* Pound
Lis, K. **16**:819
Lisān Peninsula (Er. Isr.), *see* Lashon Peninsula
LISBON (city, Port.) **11**:299
- *Contents:*
- - Middle Ages **11**:299
- - Persecutions and Expulsions **11**:300
- - The Inquisition **11**:301
- - The Renewed Community **11**:302
- - Scholars **11**:303
- - Hebrew Printing **11**:303
- Abrabanel, Isaac **2**:103
- Abrabanel, Judah **2**:109
- *Arraby Moor* **3**:498
- history chart (1506) **8**:766-767
- Host desecration charge **8**:1043
- Inquisition **8**:1387
- Portugal **13**:919ff
- *illus:*
- - Vasco da Gama and Abraham Zacuto **16**:905
Lisbon Bible (15th cent. illum. ms.) **4**:838; **8**:1261; **8**:1265
- *illus:* **4**:541; **5**:519,762; **8**:1278; **11**:*fcg.* 299
Lischka, Kurt **14**:52
Lischovini, János **8**:43
Lisenheim, Moses **7**:602
LISHANSKY, BATYA **3**:605
- Chizhik statue **8**:1064
- sculpture **14**:1070
- *illus:*
- - Bat-Miriam, Yokheved (bust) **4**:326
- - Ben-Zvi, Izhak (head) **4**:578
- - "Ha-Sho'ah" memorial **3**:633
- - Ḥuldah defenders memorial **8**:1063
LISHANSKY, YOSEF **11**:303
- Feinberg, Avshalom **6**:1209
- Ha-Shomer **7**:1371
- Nili **12**:1162ff
Lishkah Sheḥorah (orgn., Lith.) **16**:1136
- Rabinowitz, S. J. **13**:1478
Lishkat ha-Gazit, *see* Chamber of Hewn Stone
Lisicky, K. **13**:34
LISITZKY, EPHRAIM E. **11**:304
- Hebrew literature **8**:212
Lisk (Lisko; tn., Pol.), *see* LESKO
Lisky, I.A. **13**:1031
LISMANN, HERMANN **11**:305
Lispector, Clarice **15**:255
L'Israelita (pub.) **13**:1036
L'Israélite Algérien (newsp.) **13**:1041
L'Israélite Français (period.) **7**:1182
Lissa (tn., Pol.), *see* LESZNO
Lissa, Abraham Abush, *see* ABRAHAM ABUSH BEN ẒEVI HIRSCH
LISSA, ZOFIA **12**:698
Lissa and Kann (bnk., Holl.) **4**:177
Lissabonna, Samuel **12**:862
LISSAUER, ERNST **11**:305
- German literature **7**:450
LISSER, JOSHUA FALK **11**:305
LISSITZKY, EL (Lazar) **11**:306
- *illus:*
- - color lithograph **3**:563
- - *Siḥat Ḥulin* **4**:1392
Lissner, Meyer **5**:57
List, Albert A. **6**:1161
LIST, EMANUEL **12**:698
List, O. **5**:406
Lisznyai, K. Pál **8**:43
LIT (fam.) **11**:307
Lit, Etta **11**:307
Lit, Jacob D. **11**:307
Lit, Jonker **11**:307
Lit, Juliet **11**:307
Lit, Rachel P. **11**:307
Lit, Samuel D. **11**:307
Lita, *see* LITHUANIA
Litai, Aaron **7**:1316
LITANI-LITTMAN, DORA **1**:33
Litani Valley (Leb.) **9**:597
LITAUER, JAN JAKUB **10**:1510
Li-Tekufot ha-Yamim (bk.) **13**:1478
Literacy **9**:477; **16**:586ff; **16**:751
- *illus:*
- - *Haggadah* read to illiterates **2**:806
- - Israel illiterates, 1931-1969 (table) **9**:480
Literarishe Bleter (period.) **11**:1149; **13**:1042
Literarishe Monatshriften (period.) **12**:1155; **16**:814
"Literary Club" (Arab polit soc.) **9**:457
LITERATURE, JEWISH **11**:307
- *Contents:*
- - Early Beginnings to the Medieval Period **11**:308
- - - Biblical Literature **11**:308
- - - Apocryphal Works **11**:310
- - - Apocalyptic Literature **11**:311
- - - Hellenistic Literature **11**:311
- - - Bible Translations **11**:312
- - - Exegesis **11**:313
- - - Philosophy **11**:313
- - - History **11**:314
- - - Halakhah and Aggadah **11**:314
- - Medieval Period (500–1750) **11**:322
- - - Grammar and Lexicography **11**:323
- - - Bible Exegesis **11**:324
- - - Poetry **11**:325
- - - Rabbinic Literature (500–1250) **11**:328
- - - Rabbinic Literature (1250–1750) **11**:332
- - - Philosophy and Theology **11**:338
- - - Ethics **11**:343
- - - Ethical Wills **11**:345
- - - Philosophic Exegesis **11**:346
- - - Mystical Literature **11**:346
- - - Prose Literature **11**:348
- - - Polemical and Apologetic Literature **11**:354
- - - Yiddish Literature **11**:356
- - - Ladino Literature **11**:360
- allegory **2**:643
- children's **5**:429
- Falasha **6**:1150
- folk **6**:1376
- Frankist **7**:69
- hagiographic **7**:1116
- *hakdamah* **7**:1144
- *haskamah* **7**:1452
- *ḥiddushim* **8**:464
- historiographic **8**:551
- homiletic **8**:949ff
- letters **11**:55
- linguistic **16**:1352
- liturgical **11**:392; **13**:573
- modern **8**:77
- parable **13**:72
- parody and satire **13**:124
- philosophical **13**:421ff
- poetic **13**:670
- polemic **13**:790
- rabbinical **13**:1462
- responsa **14**:83ff
- Zionist **16**:1155
- *illus:*
- - *Ben ha-Melekh ve-ha-Nazir* **4**:518
- - *Eẓ ha-Ḥayyim* **16**:173
- - Judeo-Greek Purim poem (18th cent.) **10**:426
- - *Kuzari* (Venice, 1547) **10**:356
- - *Meshal ha-Kadmoni* **3**:19,534,791; **5**:430; **6**:1128; **14**:657
- - *Mishlei Shu'alim* **4**:597; **5**:431
- - *Orḥot Ẓaddikim* **12**:1458
- - *Sefer ha-Maḥbarot* (15th cent.) **4**:1235,1352; **16**:1192
- *see also:* NEWSPAPERS, HEBREW; PRESS; *and under individual languages*
Literatur un Lebn (anth.) **13**:549
Lithology of Israel, *see* PHYSIOGRAPHY OF ISRAEL
LITHUANIA **11**:361
- *Contents:*
- - Character and Influence on the Diaspora **11**:361
- - Spiritual Trends and Leaders **11**:362
- - Haskalah **11**:369
- - Ḥibbat Zion and Zionism **11**:370
- - Jewish Socialist Movement **11**:371
- - In Belorussian S.S.R. **11**:372
- - In Poland **11**:373
- - In Independent Lithuania **11**:373
- - Soviet Rule in Lithuania, 1940–41 **11**:385
- - German Occupation, 1941–44 **11**:386
- - War Crimes Trials **11**:389
- - Liberation **11**:389
- - After the War **11**:390
- General
- - *arenda* system **2**:403; **3**:402ff
- - Ashkenaz **3**:721
- - autonomy **3**:924; **3**:930
- - banishment **4**:165
- - *Sefer ha-Maḥbarot* (15th cent.)
- - banking **4**:169
- - Bund **4**:1497ff
- - candle tax **5**:119
- - Chmielnicki massacres **5**:482f
- - communal organization **5**:820
- - cooperatives **5**:942
- - dress **6**:221
- - economic life **8**:692ff; **16**:1303
- - Great Poland **7**:865
- - guilds **7**:972ff
- - history chart **8**:766-767
- - Holocaust **8**:840
- - Jewish agriculture **2**:403
- - legal status of Jews **13**:716ff
- - livestock, trade in **11**:410
- - minority rights **12**:44; **12**:45ff
- - ORT **12**:1484
- - partisans **13**:140
- - population **13**:883ff; **14**:483
- - socialism **15**:29; **15**:39
- - South Africa **15**:186

- - Troki **15:**1401ff
- - War Crimes Trials **16:**301
- Religious and Cultural Life
- - Ashkenazi culture **3:**719
- - education **6:**425ff
- - emancipation **6:**717
- - Ḥasidism **7:**1391ff; **10:**792
- - Haskalah **7:**1399
- - Judaism, pattern of **10:**395
- - *Maggid* **11:**699
- - medieval cultural life **8:**687
- - *Mitnaggedim* **12:**161
- - Mizrachi **12:**176; **14:**58ff
- - Musar movement **12:**534
- - Orthodoxy **12:**1490
- - rabbinical office **13:**1447
- - Shabbateanism **14:**1243
- - *takkanot* **15:**725; **15:**737
- - Vilna Gaon **6:**651
- - *yeshivot* **16:**765ff
- *illus:*
- - text
- - Council of the Four Lands (map) **5:**997
- - dress **6:***fcg.* 238
- - Jewish badge decreed by the Nazis **4:**72
- - Kedainai, scouts **14:**1037
- - mass execution of Jews by Nazis **8:**861
- *pop. tables:* text
- *see also:* COUNCILS OF THE LANDS; POLAND; VILNA
Lithuania, Council of (1650) **5:**483
"Lithuanian Stock Exchange" (engr., Bisson) **4:**1404
LITIN (tn., Ukr.) **11:**390
- pogrom (1919) **13:**669
Litinski (fam.) **7:**700
LITINSKI, GENRIKH ILYICH **12:**698
Litinski, Gershon **7:**700
Litishevsky, Joseph **13:**1049
Litman, Archie **15:**306
LITMAN, SAMUEL **8:**1432
Litmanowicz, S. **11:**918
LITOMERICE (tn., Bohem.) **11:**391
LITON, ANYA **15:**1074, 1087
- motion pictures **12:**455
Litovich, B. I. **10:**739
LITTAUER, LUCIUS NATHAN **11:**391
- sports **15:**307; **15:**312
Littauer, William **15:**311; **15:**312
Little Bear (constellation), *see* Ursa Minor
Little Caesarea (city, Er. Isr.), *see* BANIAS
Little Genesis (pseudepig. wk.), *see* JUBILEES, BOOK OF
Little Jerusalem (tn., Fr.), *see* BÉZIERS
Little Saint Hugh, *see* HUGH OF LINCOLN
Little Triangle (area Isr.) **9:**1026
Littman (r., Pol.) **16:**1348
Littman, D. **12:**1272
Littman, Martin **13:**1049
Liturgical music, *see* Ḥazzan; MUSIC
Liturgische Zeitschrift (period., Ger.) **7:**1547
LITURGY **11:**392
- *Contents:*
- - Bible and Second Temple Period **11:**392
- - Talmudic Period **11:**393
- - Geonic Period **11:**395
- - Liturgical Rites **11:**397
- - Palestinian Group **11:**398
- - - Romanian Rite **11:**398
- - - Roman Rite **11:**398
- - - Northern France and Ashkenazi Rites **11:**399
- - Babylonian Group **11:**400
- - - Sephardi Rite **11:**400
- - - Provençal Rite **11:**401
- - - Yemenite Rite **11:**401
- - Other Rites **11:**401
- - Reform **11:**402
- General
- - Amram ben Sheshna **2:**892
- - Baer's cantorial manual **4:**79
- - Cairo *genizah* **16:**1337
- - choir **5:**486
- - folklore **6:**1384
- - greetings **7:**912
- - *hagbahah* **7:**1076
- - Hahn, Joseph Yuspa **7:**1129
- - *ḥazzan* **7:**1542
- - Hebrew pronunciation **13:**1121
- - illuminated manuscripts **8:**1263ff
- - Maimonides on **11:**760
- - *maqāma* **11:**937ff
- - miracles, thanksgiving prayers **12:**76
- - mourning **12:**491
- - Obadiah the Norman Proselyte **12:**1307
- - organ **12:**1453ff
- - poetry **11:**325ff; **13:**678
- - proselytes **13:**1184
- - Psalms compilation **13:**1302
- - reformation of **12:**644
- - Saadiah Gaon **14:**553
- - *sheli'aḥ ẓibbur* **14:**1355
- - *Targum* **4:**841ff
- - *Targum Sheni* **15:**813
- - tombstone consecration **15:**1222
- - traditions **15:**1310
- - translation into Malayalam **5:**626
- - Yiddish **16:**802
- - *see also:* CANTILLATION; MUSIC; NUSAḤ
- Main Components
- - *Adon Olam* **2:**296
- - *Akedah* **2:**481
- - *Aleinu le-Shabbe'aḥ* **2:**557
- - Amen **2:**803
- - *Amidah* **2:**838
- - *Ani Ma'amin* **3:**4
- - *Anna be-Kho'aḥ* **3:**25
- - *Arvit* **3:**664f
- - *Ashrei* **3:**736
- - *Avinu she-ba-Shamayim* **3:**974
- - *bakkashah* **4:**116
- - *Barekhu* **4:**218
- - *barukh* pattern in benediction **4:**283
- - *Barukh Shem Kevod* **4:**285
- - benedictions **4:**484
- - *Ein k-Elohenu* **6:**534
- - *haftarah* **16:**1342
- - *hallelujah* **7:**1199
- - *Hashkivenu* **7:**1370
- - *Kaddish* **10:**660
- - *Kedushah* **10:**875
- - *kerovah* **10:**920
- - *kinah* **10:**1009
- - *Minḥah* **12:**31
- - *Musaf* **12:**532ff
- - *Perek Shirah* **13:**274
- - *Pesukei de-Zimra* **13:**336
- - *Pittum ha-Ketoret* **13:**572
- - prayer for the government **7:**834
- - priestly blessing **13:**1060
- - Psalms, Book of **13:**1309; **13:**1319; **13:**1323
- - Sea, Song of the **14:**1071
- - *seliḥot* **14:**1133
- - *Shaḥarit* **14:**1257
- - *Shema* **14:**1370ff
- - Torah reading **15:**1246ff
- - *Yigdal* hymn **16:**834
- - *Yishtabbaḥ* **16:**837
- - *yoẓerot* **16:**865
- Sabbath **14:**566
- - *An'im Zemirot* **3:**23
- - *Attah Eḥad* **3:**833
- - *Havdalah* **7:**1481
- - *Lekhah Dodi* **11:**4
- - *Mizmor Shir le-Yom ha-Shabbat* **12:**173
- - New Moon announcement **12:**1040
- - *Nishmat Kol Ḥai* **12:**1176
- - *Yekum Purkan* **16:**735ff
- Rosh ha-Shanah and Day of Atonement **5:**1378; **14:**307
- - *Adonai, Adonai, El Raḥum ve-Ḥanun* **2:**294
- - *Aḥot Ketannah* **2:**469
- - *Al Ḥet* **2:**629
- - *Anna be-Korenu* **3:**26
- - *Ashamnu* **3:**694
- - *Attah Zokher* **3:**833
- - *Avinu Malkenu* **3:**974
- - *Avodah* **3:**977
- - *Hineni he-Ani mi-Ma'as* **8:**500
- - Holy Ark, opening of **3:**457
- - *Kol Nidrei* **10:**1167
- - *seliḥot* **14:**1133ff
- - *Shir ha-Yiḥud* **14:**1415
- - *Shofarot* **14:**1447
- - *teki'ata* **15:**914
- - Ten Days of Penitence **15:**1001
- - *U-Netanneh Tokef* **2:**861
- - *Yizkor* **16:**842
- Festivals **6:**1245
- - *Adonai, Adonai, El Raḥum ve-Ḥanun* **2:**294
- - *Akdamut millin* **2:**479
- - *Attah Horeta Lada'at* **3:**833
- - dew, prayer for **5:**1602
- - *Hallel* **7:**1197
- - *Havdalah* **7:**1481
- - *ma'aravot* **11:**637
- - Passover **13:**169
- - Scrolls, the Five **14:**1047
- - *seder* **14:**1091
- - Shavuot **14:**1321
- - Simḥat Torah **14:**1573
- - Sukkot **15:**499ff
- - *Yizkor* **16:**842
- Minor Festivals
- - Av, Ninth of **3:**938
- - Ḥanukkah **7:**1287
- - Israel Independence Day **8:**1345
- - Purim **13:**1390
- - Rosh Ḥodesh **12:**1040ff
- - - Hallel **7:**1197
- Themes
- - Bible **4:**918
- - David **5:**1329
- - Decalogue **5:**1446
- - Ingathering of Exiles **8:**1374
- - Inquisition **8:**1406
- - Jerusalem **9:**1555; **9:**1560ff
- - Kabbalah **10:**628ff, 641
- - *kiddush* and *ḥillul ha-Shem* **10:**980ff
- - peace **13:**197
- - Raphael **13:**1549
- - resistance **8:**302
- - resurrection **14:**98
- - sacrifices **14:**608ff
- - Satan **14:**904
- - sin **14:**1591
- - Western Wall **16:**468
- Forms
- - acrostics **2:**230
- - angelic song **15:**144
- - "chariot" hymns **10:**501, 510
- - *piyyut* **13:**573
- - *shtayger* **14:**1463ff
- - Yannai's *piyyutim* **16:**713
- Rite, Palestinian
- - Ashkenazi **3:**721; **13:**985ff
- - - Alsatian **2:**753
- - - "Apam" **3:**174, 785
- - - Frankfort on the Main **7:**92
- - - French **3:**785
- - - Ḥasidei Ashkenaz **7:**1380; **10:**517
- - - Judeo-French **10:**424
- - - *Maḥzor Vitry* **11:**736
- - - *Memorbuch* reading **11:**1299
- - - Wuerzburg **16:**676
- - Balkans **7:**882ff
- - Greece **7:**882ff
- - Roman **14:**245
- - Tiberias **9:**265
- Rite, Babylonian
- - Aḥa of Shabḥa **2:**449
- - Kurdistan **4:**205
- - Nehardea **12:**935
- - Provençal
- - - Avignon **3:**967
- - - Carpentras **5:**208
- - Sephardi **7:**1391; **13:**987; **14:**1170
- - - Cochin **5:**625
- - - Ispalatro **14:**185
- - - "Portuguese" (U.S.) **14:**1173
- Other Rites
- - Aram-Zobah **2:**565
- - Conservative **5:**901; **13:**1063
- - Falasha **6:**1147
- - Ḥabad **10:**1485
- - Karaite **2:**12; **10:**780
- - *Nusaḥ Aḥid* **14:**1176
- - *Nusaḥ ha-Ari* **7:**1401ff; **10:**549
- - Qumran **15:**1047
- - Reform **12:**1487; **14:**23; **15:**287
- - Romaniots **14:**231
- - Samaritan **14:**753
- - Yemenite **14:**542; **16:**757ff
- - - Alsheikh's commentary **2:**758
- *illus:*
- - *Aleinu le-Shabbe'aḥ*, censored versions **2:**558, 892
- - *Attah Nigleita* **2:**736
- - *Attah Noten Yad la-Poshe'im* **2:**725, 738
- - *Attah Zokher* **3:**834
- - Day of Atonement **11:**735
- - *Ein k-Elohenu* **6:**543
- - *Ha-Yom Harat Olam* **5:**1523
- - *Kaddish* and *Barekhu* **10:**663
- - Karaite Hymns **10:**783-784
- - *Kol Nidrei* **10:**1168
- - *Lekhah Dodi* **11:**5–8
- - *Maḥzor Minhag Roma (1485-86)* **8:**1327
- - *Musaf* **14:**306
- - *Ne'ilah* **12:**944
- - *Nishmat Kol Ḥai* **8:**1282
- - *Perush ha-Berakhot ve-ha-Tefillot* **11:**301
- - *piyyut* **14:**1320
- - prayer for government **7:**834-836
- - raising of the Torah scroll **7:**1077
- - Rosh ha-Shanah **11:**734
- - *Shabbat ha-Gadol piyyut* **14:**1217
- - Sukkot **11:**735
- - *Worms Maḥzor* **8:**1219
- *mus. notations:*
- - *Adon Olam* **2:**297
- - Ashkenazi melodies, High Holy Days **12:**585
- - Ashkenazi *shtayger* scales **12:**609
- - cantillation, choir tune development **12:**663
- - dance-like cantorial melodies **12:**631
- - *Hallel* **12:**575
- - *ḥazzan* and singer setting **12:**643
- - improvisatory variation **12:**591
- - introduction to Confession **12:**651
- - melodic extension **12:**605
- - *Mi-Sinai niggunim* **12:**151
- - modal pattern variations **12:**587
- - modern compositions **12:**665
- - modern psalmody **12:**667
- - *Musaf Kaddish* **12:**647
- - mutations of a *nusaḥ* pattern **12:**611
- - *nusaḥ* of Sabbath morning prayer

12:1283
- - old European scales 12:609
- - oriental singing, Amsterdam synagogue 12:627
- - ornamentation of single notes 12:589
- - poetry meters 12:593
- - prayer mode structures 12:581
- - priestly blessing 12:621
- - Psalm 19 12:571
- - psalmody, basic formula 12:571
- - psalmody tunes 13:1329-1332
- - Sabbath eve *Kaddish* 12:625
- - San'a group singing 16:747
- - *seliḥah* 14:1134
- - setting for *ḥazzan* and singer soli 12:653
- - *shofar* blowing 14:1443
- - *shtayger* melodies 14:1464-1466
- - traditional melody adaptations 12:645
- - variative development 12:591
- - Western Sephardi chromaticism 12:611
- - *Yigdal* 16:834,835
- *see also:* PRAYER; PRAYER BOOKS; MAḤZOR
Liturgy, Christian 5:510; 16:835
Liturgy, Midnight, *see* TIKKUN ḤAẒOT
Litvak (Lith. J.) 11:361
LITVAK, ANATOLE (Michael) 12:470
Litvak, Lila 11:1558
LITVAKOV, MOSHE 11:404
- *illus:*
- - Ukrainian Council 15:1515
LITVIN, A. 11:405
Litvinoff, Barnet 11:406
LITVINOFF, EMANUEL 11:405
Litvinov, Ivy, *see* Low, Ivy
Litvinov, L. M. 15:1075
LITVINOV, MAXIM MAXIMOVICH 11:406
LITVINOVSKY, PINḤAS 11:407
- *illus:*
- - text
- - "Arab with Flower" (paint.) Pl. 2 3-ART
- - Farkas, Ladislaus (portrait) 6:1186
- - Granott, Abraham (portrait) 7:854
Litwa, *see* LITHUANIA
Litwack, Harry 15:303
LITWAK, A. 11:408
"Litwak, David" (fig., Herzl's *Altneuland*) 16:613
Litzmannstadt (Ger. name for Lodz) 11:432
LIUZZI, FERNANDO 12:698
LIUZZI, GIORGIO 11:1574
LIUZZI, GUIDO 11:408
- military service 11:1574
Li Vaux Moyse (crus. Petra) 13:342
Livchitz, Georges 4:422
Lively, Edward 8:43
Liver 6:28; 11:974
Liver Cirrhosis (disease) 14:1503
Liveright (fam.) 6:1344
LIVERIGHT, HORACE BRISBIN 11:408
- publishing 13:1371
Li-Veri'ut (greeting) 7:914
LIVERPOOL (city, Eng.) 11:409
- Benas family 4:465
- Cohen family 5:661
- England 6:754f
- Goller, Izak 7:762
- Manchester's early settlers 11:858
- Rabinowitz, Samuel Jacob 13:1478
- *illus:*
- - text
- - Princes Road synagogue 6:765
Liverpool (tn., Can.) 7:1191,1358
Liverpool Hebrew Higher Grade School 6:448; 11:409; 12:351
- Fox, Jacob Samuel 6:1451
Liverpool Jewish Gazette (period.) 11:410
LIVESTOCK, TRADE IN 11:410
Livia (w. of Augustus) 3:696
Livias (tn., Er. Isr.) 3:76; 4:736
"Living Quarters in the Theresienstadt Ghetto" (paint., O. Ungar) Fig. 83 3-ART
Livingston (fam.) 15:213
Livingston (sub., N.J.) 6:904
Livingston (city, Mont.) 12:266
Livingstone (loc., Zambia) 16:922ff
Livingstone, Mary 15:1078
Livland (reg., Eur.), *see* Livonia
Livnat ha-Sappir (wk.) 16:1389
Livni, David ha-, *see* WEISS, DAVID
Livonia (reg., Eur.) 10:1462
Livorno (port, It.), *see* LEGHORN
Livshitz, M. 12:1516
LIVY (Rom. hist.) 14:232; 14:235
Livyat Ḥen (journ., Pol.) 1:newsp. list
Liwa of Ferrara 12:68
Lixheim (loc., Fr.) 11:497
LIZARD (zool.) 11:412
- dietary laws 6:36
Lizel, G. 8:43
LJUBLJANA (city, Yug.) 11:412
Llama (zool.) 6:32
Llandudno (tn., Wales) 16:251
Llanelly (tn., Wales) 16:251
LLERENA (city, Sp.) 11:413
Lloyd, Henry 8:43
LLOYD GEORGE, DAVID 11:413
- Balfour Declaration 4:132ff
- Christian Zionism 16:1153
"Loading a Transport of Old People . . ." (drg., L. Haas) Fig. 81 3-ART
Lo-Ammi (bib. fig.) 8:1011
LOAN 11:414
- *Contents:*
- - Oral Loan and Loan in Writing 11:414
- - Mitzvah of Lending 11:415
- - Nature of Repayment Obligation 11:415
- - Halva'ah and She'elah 11:415
- - Establishment of Loan 11:416
- - Repayment Date 11:416
- - Acceptance of Payment 11:417
- - Place of Payment 11:417
- - Method and Means of Payment 11:417
- - Fluctuation in Currency Values 11:418
- - Plea of Repayment 11:418
- - Multiple Loans 11:418
- - Conversion into Loan or Other Contractual Obligations 11:419
- - Minor as Party to a Loan 11:419
- - Measures to Prevent "Bolting the Door" to Borrowers 11:419
- admission 2:291
- antichresis applied 3:59
- Commandments, the 613 5:777
- debt assignment 3:768ff
- deceased 15:479ff
- documents 14:1385
- firstborn inheritance 6:1312
- forcible 15:1095
- *ḥazakah* on articles 7:1520
- Jacob of Orleans 9:1234
- legal person, interest 10:1569
- lien 11:227
- maintenance claim 11:252
- maintenance repayment 11:785ff
- *niddui* 8:352
- obligations 12:1311; 12:1313
- orphans' interest 12:12
- payment by third party 15:1685
- pleas 13:631
- pledge 13:636
- possession 12:1532
- promissory note 11:838
- Rabbi Nathan's lien 14:1397
- release of liability 3:769
- repayment procedure 13:632ff
- sabbatical year, Jubilee 14:574
- State of Israel 9:757
- surety 15:524
- trustees 14:1267
- usury 16:27
- waiver 11:1232
- *illus:*
- - impounding of pledge, written complaint (7th cent. B.C.E. ostracon) 3:317
- *see also:* EXECUTION (Civil); MONEYLENDING; SHOMERIM; USURY
Loan Bank Ltd. (Pal.) 13:39ff
Loan-banks, Jewish 4:1410; 12:251
Loans, Jacob ben Jehiel 6:462; 10:227; 14:110
LOANZ, ELIJAH BEN MOSES 11:420
- Broughton, Hugh 4:1410
LOBATO (fam.) 11:420
Lobato, Abraham Cohen 11:420
Lobato, Diego Gomez, *see* Lobato, Abraham Cohen
Lobato, Isaac Cohen 11:420
Lobato, Rehuel (math.) 11:421
Lobato, Reuel Cohen (trans.) 11:420
Loborgrad (concen. camp, Croatia) 14:872
Lobositz, (tn., Bohem.), *see* Lovosice
LOCAL GOVERNMENT IN ISRAEL 9:603-606
- Arab local councils 9:1029
- Jerusalem, Ottoman rule 9:1435
- State of Israel 9:620
- *illus:* text
- see also: JEWISH COMMUNAL ORGANIZATION IN ISRAEL
Loch, V. 4:881
Loches (tn., Fr.) 15:1288
Lock (door) 6:171
Locke, John 5:1464; 8:701; 11:1329,1336
LOCKER, BERL 11:421
- Zionist Congress (23rd) 16:1176
- *illus:*
- - Keren Hayesod bld'g cornerstone ceremony 10:916
LOCKER, MALKE 11:421
Lockhart (city, Tex.) 15:1036
Lockhart, Robert Hamilton Bruce 11:406
LOCKSPEISER, SIR BEN 11:422
- aeronautics 2:322
Lockspeiser, Eduard 11:422
Locus Judaeorum Augusti (loc., Afr.) 15:1442
LOCUST 11:422
- dietary laws 6:38
- plagues of Egypt 13:606
- *see also:* GRASSHOPPER
Lod (tn., Isr.), *see* LYDDA
Lodar (tn., S. Arab.) 2:263
LO-DEBAR (city, Er. Isr.) 11:424
LODÈVE (tn., Fr.) 11:424
LODI (tn., It.) 11:424
Lodmer (Lodomeria, Lodomira, Ludomir; city, Ukr.), *see* VLADIMIR VOLYNSKI
LODS, ADOLPHE 11:425
LODZ (city, Pol.) 11:425
- *Contents:*
- - Early History 11:425
- - Social Life and Culture 11:429
- - Holocaust Period 11:432
- - Contemporary Period 11:437
- Aescoly's history 2:325
- archives 3:380
- ghetto 7:544ff
- ghetto art 3:568
- Jews in 1914 8:732
- Poland 13:755ff
- Rumkowski, C. M. 14:428
- textiles 15:1040
- theater 15:1072
- *illus:*
- - text
- - children taken to extermination camp 8:873
- - *Geto Tsaytung* (1941) 13:1044
- - ghetto 14:428
- - ghetto coin (1943) 5:726
- - hanging of Jews by Nazis 8:865
- - "Market of the Lodz Ghetto" (paint., S. Szerman) Fig. 79 3-ART
- - Nazi ghetto gate 8:871
- *pop. tables:*
- - text
- - growth, 1793-1910 13:736
Lodzer Tageblat (newsp.), *see Lodzher Togblat*
Lodzher Folksblatt (newsp.) 11:432
Lodzher Morgnblat (newsp.) 11:432
Lodzher Togblat (newsp.) 11:431; 11:432; 13:1042
Loeb (bank., U.S.) 4:178
Loeb, Carl M. 15:303
Loeb, David 15:308
LOEB, ISIDORE 11:438
- Alliance Israélite 2:653
- learned societies 15:54
- *Revue des Etudes Juives* 14:133
- *illus:* text
LOEB, JACQUES 11:438
- Loeb, Leo 11:439
LOEB, JAMES 11:439
Loeb, Jules 12:1522
LOEB, LEO 11:439
Loeb, Louis 5:612
LOEB, MORRIS 11:440
Loeb, Nina 16:281
Loeb, Richard 11:441
Loeb, Rose 12:1036
Loeb, Solomon 10:1287
Loeb, William 14:259
Loeb ben Ozer 12:939
Loebel, Hirsh, *see* LEVIN, ẒEVI HIRSCH BEN ARYEH LOEB
LOEBEL, ISRAEL 11:440
LOEBL, EUGEN 11:441
- Slánský trials 14:1654
Loebl, Yehoshua, *see* ARIELI, YEHOSHUA
LOEB-LEOPOLD CASE (U.S.) 11:441
Loebstein, Heinrich 15:311
Loehner, Fritz, *see* BEDA
Loening, Edgar 10:1497
Loening, Karl, *see* Loewenthal, Karl
Loening, Richard 10:1497
Loerke, Oskar 6:1323
Loescher, Valentin Ernst 8:43
Loeser, Margaret Sybilla, *see* Einsiedel, M. Sybilla
Loeser, Meir 11:1165
Loeser, Nathan 11:1165
Loeserer, Bernhard 6:521
Loesser, Arthur 12:698
LOESSER, FRANK 12:698
LOEVENSTEIN, FEDOR 3:605
Loew (fam.) 15:658ff
Loew, Asher 10:795; 12:1334
Loew, Benjamin Wolf 7:1010
LOEW, ELEAZAR (18/19 cent.) 11:442
- *illus:* text
Loew, Eleazar (19th cent.) 14:907
LOEW, IMMANUEL 11:442
- Jewish Agency 16:1121
Loew, Israel 13:203
Loew, Jeremiah 8:956; 8:957; 14:906
Loew, Leo 7:1550
LOEW, LEOPOLD (Lipot) 11:444
- articles of faith 3:660
- Schwab, Löw 14:1015

Loew, Louis **10:**1495
LOEW, MARCUS **12:**470
- Los Angeles **11:**503
Loew, Max Anton **11:**557
LOEW, MORITZ **11:**445
Loew, W. **15:**659
LOEW-BEER (fam.) **11:**445
- Brno **4:**1384
Loew-Beer, Aaron **11:**445
Loew-Beer, Ignaz **11:**445
Loew-Beer, Jacob **11:**445
Loew-Beer, Jonas **11:**445
Loew-Beer, Max **11:**445
Loew-Beer, Moses **11:**445
Loew-Beer, Samuel **11:**445
LOEWE, FREDERICK **12:**698
LOEWE, FRITZ PHILIPP **11:**445
LOEWE, HEINRICH (Eliakim) **11:**446
- Juedische Volkspartei **10:**464
- physical education **15:**294
- *illus:*
- F.Z.C. **16:**1165
LOEWE, HERBERT MARTIN JAMES **11:**447
- Cambridge **5:**70
Loewe, Isidor, *see* LOEWE, LUDWIG and ISIDOR
LOEWE, JOEL (BRILL) **11:**447
- Bible **4:**875
LOEWE, LOUIS (orient.) **11:**448
- Munk, Solomon **12:**526
- travels **15:**1354
- *illus:* text
LOEWE, LUDWIG and ISIDOR **11:**449
Loewe, Maximilian **11:**532
LOEWE, RAPHAEL **1:**33; **11:**44
LOEWE, VICTOR **8:**548
Loewenbach, J.W. **11:**1167
- *illus:*
- - Munich synagogue medal **11:**1166
Loewenberg, Jacob **7:**449
Loewenfeld, Erwin, *see* LENDVAI, ERWIN
Loewenfeld, Theodor **10:**1496
Loewenfisch, G. Y., *see* LEVENFISH, GRIGORI YAKELOVICH
Loewenger, D.S. **11:**722
Loewenherz, Josef **16:**127
Loewenkopf, K. **12:**1481
LOEWENSON, JEAN (Hans) **11:**449
Loewenson, P. **9:**1290
Loewenstadt (tn., Pol.), *see* BRZEZINY
LOEWENSTAMM (fam.) **11:**450
Loewenstamm, Aryeh Loeb **11:**450
- Amsterdam **2:**899
LOEWENSTAMM, AYALA **1:**33
Loewenstamm, Jacob Moses **11:**450
- Amsterdam **2:**899
Loewenstamm, Jehiel Aryeh Loeb **11:**450
Loewenstamm, Kurt **15:**255
Loewenstamm, Moses, *see* Loewenstamm, Jacob Moses
Loewenstamm, Saul (Pol.) **11:**450
Loewenstamm, Saul (Neth.) **11:**450
- Amsterdam **2:**899
Loewenstamm, S.E. **16:**1508
LOEWENSTEIN, BERNHARD **11:**451
- Nathanson, J. S. **12:**867
Loewenstein, Herbert, *see* AVENARY, HANOCH
Loewenstein, Issachar Ber, *see* LOEWENSTEIN, BERNHARD
LOEWENSTEIN, KARL **11:**451
Loewenstein, Kurt **10:**463
Loewenstein, Leo **14:**49
LOEWENSTEIN, LEOPOLD **11:**451
Loewenstein, L.H. **4:**875
LOEWENSTEIN, NATHAN **11:**452
Loewenstein, Rudolf (poet) **10:**305
LOEWENSTEIN, RUDOLPH MAURICE (psych.) **11:**452
Loewenstein, Theodor, *see* LAVI, THEODOR
Loewenstein, Ẓevi Hirsch **11:**453
LOEWENSTEIN-STRASHUNSKY, JOEL DAVID **11:**453
LOEWENTHAL, EDUARD **11:**453
LOEWENTHAL, JOHANN JAKOB **5:**408
Loewenthal, Kaethe, *see* GERSHON, KAREN
Loewenthal, Karl (Zacharias) **13:**1343
LOEWENTHAL, RUDOLF **1:**33
Loewenthal, Wilhelm **3:**427; **3:**428
LOEWENTHAL, ZDENKO **1:**33
LOEWI, OTTO **11:**453
- biologist **4:**1032
- Froehlich, Alfred **7:**205
LOEWINGER, DAVID SAMUEL **11:**454
- Bible **4:**884
LOEWINSON-LESSING, FRANZ YULYEVICH **11:**455
LOEWISOHN, SOLOMON **11:**455
- history **8:**560
- literature **8:**181
Loewit, Isidor **4:**331
LOEWITH, KARL **11:**456
Loewitt, R. **13:**1374
Loewner (fam.) **16:**163
Loewy, Albert **4:**521
Loewy, Bernát **11:**457
Loewy, D. **12:**1016
LOEWY, EMANUEL **11:**456
Loewy, Ferenc **15:**814
Loewy, Francisco **3:**432
LOEWY, ISAAC (indus.) **11:**457
Loewy, Isaac (act.) **10:**673
LOEWY, JACOB EZEKIEL BEN JOSEPH **11:**457
Loewy, Joachim **11:**457
LOEWY, MAURICE **11:**458
Loft-Dove (bird) **6:**184; **16:**381
16:390
Log (meas.) **16:**380ff
Logansport (city, U.S.) **8:**1361
LOGGEM, MANUEL VAN **11:**458
LOGIC **11:**459
- Jewish philosophy **13:**421
- Palágyi's works **13:**20
- translations **15:**1321
- *see also:* ARISTOTLE; CATEGORIES; Reason; SEVARAH
LOGOS **11:**460
- *Contents:*
- - Greek Philosophy **11:**461
- - Bible **11:**461
- - Jewish Hellenistic Literature **11:**461
- - Philo **11:**461
- - Gospel of John **11:**462
- creation **5:**1066
- mysticism **10:**496; **10:**520; **10:**528ff
- Neoplatonism **13:**429
- Philo **13:**413; **13:**426ff
- *Ru'aḥ ha-Kodesh* **14:**366
- space and place **15:**217
- stoicism **15:**409
- Torah **15:**1236
- word **16:**635
LOḤAMEI HA-GETTA'OT (kib., Isr.) **11:**462
- statistics **1:**place list
- *illus:*
- - Ghetto Fighters' House **7:**546
LOḤAMEI ḤERUT ISRAEL (Leḥi, orgn., Pal.) **11:**463
- Ben-Gurion, David **4:**509ff
- Beriḥah **4:**632
- broadcasting **15:**930
- Eldad, Israel **6:**574
- Golomb, Eliyahu **7:**764
- history **8:**759; **9:**356ff
- history chart **8:**766-767
- Irgun Ẓeva'i Le'ummi **8:**1467; **8:**1468
- Jerusalem attacks **9:**1477; **9:**1484
- Tel Aviv headquarters **15:**923
- *Tenu'at ha-Meri* **9:**688
- War of Independence **16:**306
- Yellin-Mor, Nathan **16:**738
- *illus:*
- - text
- - escape from Acre prison **8:**1469
- - Kenya detention camp **10:**910
- - "Wanted" poster **8:**1468
- *see also:* STERN, AVRAHAM
Lohse, Geinrich **8:**856; **11:**385
Lohsing, Ernst **10:**1494
Loisel, P., *see* Ouseel, P.
LOISY, ALFRED FIRMIN **11:**465
Lollard Bible **4:**868
Lolly, Eudi **13:**12
Lom, Benny **15:**307
LOM, HERBERT **12:**471
Lomazzo, Giovanni Paolo **3:**496
LOMBARDY (reg., It.) **11:**466
- banking **4:**169
Lombroso, Abraham **15:**1446
LOMBROSO, CESARE **11:**467
- apologetics **3:**199
- psychiatry **13:**1337
Lombroso, Isaac **15:**1444
Lombroso, Jacob **15:**1443
Lombroso, Raphael **15:**1443
Lomé (city, Togo) **9:**442
Lomser, Ḥayyim, *see* WASSERZUG, ḤAYYIM
LOMZA (Lomzha, Lomzhe; tn., Pol.) **11:**468
- *illus:*
- - text
- - Yeshivah **16:**762
Lomza Yeshivah (Isr.), *see* YESHIVOT (Lomza)
Lomzer, Ḥayyim, *see* WASSERZUG, ḤAYYIM
Lomzher Lebn (newsp.) **11:**469
Lomzher Shtime (newsp.) **11:**469
Lomzher Veker (newsp.) **11:**469
Londin, Jack **15:**310
LONDON (city, Eng.) **11:**469
- *Contents:*
- - Medieval Period **11:**469
- - Middle Period **11:**472
- - Resettlement Period **11:**473
- - Contemporary Period **11:**478
- - Hebrew Printing **11:**481
- archives **3:**382
- banking **4:**172ff
- Castilian **10:**1343
- diamond trade **6:**4
- education **6:**446ff
- England **6:**747f
- history chart **8:**766-767
- Jews in 1914 **8:**732
- Kook, Abraham Isaac **10:**1182
- libraries **11:**192ff
- museum **12:**538,543; **14:**368
- secondhand goods trade **14:**1086
- Sephardi community **14:**1171
- socialism, Jewish **15:**46
- stock exchange **15:**406
- sugar trade **15:**488
- tailors **15:**705
- theater **15:**1070
- trade **15:**1303
- United Synagogue **15:**1672
- Zionism **16:**1097
- *illus:*
- - text
- - Benedict, Sir Julius, house and commemorative plaque **4:**483
- - Bevis Marks Synagogue **14:**1167; **15:**615,620-621
- - Fonseca, Alvaro de, declaration re purchase of land **6:**1413
- - Great Synagogue **15:**619
- - Great Synagogue, Jews at prayer (caric.) **3:**141
- - Houndsditch, a scene **6:**764
- - Jewish Museum **12:**548
- - *Jewish Standard* (1888) **13:**1029
- - Jew's College **10:**99
- - Jews' Hospital *Neveh Ẓedek* **8:**1036
- - Marx, Karl, grave **11:**1073
- - New Synagogue **15:**619
- - Passfield protest **16:**1118
- - Petticoat Lane **5:**769; **11:**1004
- - readmission, plaque commemorating site of first synagogue **6:**754
- - St. Albans Place Synagogue, consecration **6:**757
- - Sephardi home for the aged, plaque **8:**1035
- - Spitalfields Jewish soup kitchen **5:**346
- - *takkanot* of Westminster Congregation **15:**714
- - U.S. congregations (map) **15:**1617
- - *Voice of Jacob, The* (1841) **13:**1027
- - Workmen's Circle leader **12:**1095
- *map:* text
LONDON (city, Can.) **11:**482
- Ontario **12:**1407
LONDON, ARTUR **11:**482
- Slánský trials **14:**1653
London, Dr. (physic., Jer.) **11:**194
LONDON, FRITZ **11:**483
London, George **10:**306
LONDON, JACOB BEN MOSES JUDAH **11:**483
LONDON, MEYER **11:**483
- New York **12:**1105
London, Perry **13:**1344
LONDON, SOLOMON ZALMAN BEN MOSES RAPHAEL **11:**484
London, University of **15:**1677
London Agreement (post-W.W. II) **16:**291
London Board of Jewish Religious Education (Eng.) **6:**449ff
London Conference (1920) **9:**523
London Conference (1939), *see* ST. JAMES CONFERENCE
Londonderry (county boro., Ire.) **8:**1464
London Diocesan Council for Work amongst the Jews (miss. soc.) **11:**71
Londoner, Wolfe **5:**1544
Londoner Israelit (newsp.) **13:**1031
Londoner Yiddish-Deitche Zeitung (newsp.) **13:**1031
London Express Newspaper Company **4:**1141
London Group (artists) **4:**1197
London Jewish Deaf and Dumb Home **16:**68
London Jewish Hospital **8:**1034
London Jews' Society (Bib. soc.) **4:**970; **13:**1248
London Polyglot (Bib.) **4:**841
London Program (Herzl) **4:**306
London Society for Promoting Christianity among Jews, *see* London Jew's Society
London Society for the Study of Religion **12:**268
London Spanish-Portuguese Board of Guardians (Eng.) **5:**350
Long, Martin **16:**515
LONG BEACH (city, Calif.) **11:**485

Long Branch (city, N.J.) **12:**1030
Longfellow, Henry Wadsworth **15:**1569
Longhena, Baldassare **15:**618
Longimanus (Pers. k.), *see* ARTAXERXES I
Longinus, Pseudo- (Gr. au.), *see* PSEUDO-LONGINUS
Long Island (N.Y.) **12:**1126
Long Island Jewish Hospital (N.Y.) **12:**1116
Longmeadow (sub., Mass.) **15:**319
LONGO, SAADIAH **11:**485
Longview (city, Tex.) **15:**1036
Lonisade, Aldo **5:**417
Lonsky, Chaikal **12:**539
LONS-LE-SAUNIER (tn., Fr.) **11:**486
LONZANO, ABRAHAM BEN RAPHAEL DE **11:**486
LONZANO, MENAHEM BEN JUDAH DE **11:**486
- Eliezer of Worms **6:**624
- *ga'yot* **16:**1451
- masorah **16:**1477
- *Midrash Agur* **16:**1515
- music, Jewish **12:**613
Lonzoda, Hannah **12:**1021
Looking Ahead (bk.) **16:**1152
Looking Backward 1887-2000 (wk.) **16:**1152
LOOKSTEIN, JOSEPH HYMAN **11:**487
- Bar-Ilan University **4:**225
Lop, Solomon ibn **12:**530
Lopatin, Dov **10:**1341
Lopatyn (tn., Ukr.) **15:**84
Lope de Vega **10:**25; **15:**250
Lope de Vera y Alarcon, *see* VERA Y ALARCON, LOPE DE
LOPES (fam.) **11:**488
- coat of arms **8:**339
- Franco, Ralph **7:**50
Lopes, Alves **11:**472
Lopes, Sir Henry Charles **11:**488
Lopes, Joao **13:**858
Lopes, Sir Lopes Massey **11:**488
Lopes, Manasseh **11:**488
Lopes, Manasseh Masseh (Massey) **11:**488
Lopes, Mordecai Rodrigues **11:**488
Lopes, Sir Ralph **11:**488
Lopès-Dubec, Camille **4:**1246
Lopès-Dubec, Salomon **4:**1245
Lopez (fam., U.S.) **11:**1113; **14:**143
LOPEZ, AARON **11:**488
- Leicester **16:**633
- slave trade **14:**1663
- trade **15:**1305 **15:**1302
- *illus:* text
Lopez, Alonso **11:**803
Lopez, Diego **8:**1399
Lopez, Isaac **4:**1264
Lopez, Maria **14:**865
Lopez, Michael **5:**63
LOPEZ, ROBERT SABATINO **11:**489
LOPEZ, RODERIGO **11:**489
- Antonio **3:**166
- medicine **11:**1191
- Shylock **14:**1262
- *illus:* text
LOPEZ, SABATINO **11:**490
- literature **9:**1111
Lopez da Fonseca, Jacob **12:**993
López de Ayala, Pedro **15:**249
Lopez de Mendizabal, Bernardo **12:**1037
López de Villanova, Ursula, *see* Perez, Ursula
López Fonseca, Salomón, *see* Fonseca, Salomón López
López-Penha, Abraham **15:**255
LOPEZ ROSA (fam.) **11:**491
Lopez Rosa, Duarte **11:**491
Lopez Rosa, Moses (Duarte) **11:**491
Lopez Rosa, Simon **2:**896; **11:**491
Lopian, Eliezer **11:**492
LOPIAN, ELIJAH **11:**491
Lopian, Ḥayyim Shemu'el **11:**492
Lopian, Leib **11:**492
Lo' qeri (masorah), *see Keri* and *ketiv*
LORBEERBAUM, JACOB BEN JACOB MOSES OF LISSA **11:**492
"Lord of Hosts" **8:**1044
- *illus:*
- - Joshua bowing to captain of **10:**267
Lord's Temple (mosque, Jer.), *see* Al-Aqṣā
Lorenz, Jonah **15:**424
Lorenzo de Sepúlveda **10:**25
LORGE, IRVING **11:**493
Loria (name), *see also:* Luria
LORIA, ACHILLE **11:**493
Loria, Lamberto **15:**1351
Loritz, Alfred **12:**954
LORJE, CHAIM **11:**493
- Ereẓ Israel settlement **16:**1037
Lorki, Joseph ben Joshua **3:**959
- paytanim **13:**585
LORKI, JOSHUA **11:**494
- Abner of Burgos **2:**89
- Astruc ha-Levi **3:**810
- Pablo de Santa María **13:**4
- Spain **15:**238
- Tortosa disputation **15:**1271ff
LORM, HIERONYMUS **11:**495
- *illus:* text
Loronha, Fernão, *see* NORONHA, FERNÃO DE
LORRAINE (reg., Fr.) **11:**496
- Crusades **5:**1135
- France **7:**20ff
- gaonate **7:**324
- *see also:* ALSACE
LORRE, PETER **12:**471
- *illus:*
- - in *M.* **10:**1417
Lorsch, Julius **9:**1066
Lo-Ruhamah (bib. fig.) **8:**1010
Losa, Isabella **8:**43
Los Alamos (cmty., N. Mex.) **12:**1037
LOS ANGELES (city, Calif.) **11:**497
- *Contents:*
- - Beginnings **11:**497
- - Population Growth and Communal Development **11:**500
- - Religious Developments **11:**501
- demography **5:**1513
- historical chart (1849) **8:**766-767
- Rosenblatt, H. **14:**281
- trade **15:**1306
- *illus:* text
Loscan, J. F. **8:**43
Loschitz (vill., Morav.), *see* LOSTICE
Loshinsky, Mikhail **15:**298
Loshn un Lebn (period.) **13:**1031; **15:**379
LOSICE (Lositsy; tn., Pol.) **11:**504
Losinsky, M. **16:**1165
Losius, J. Justus **8:**43
Losonc (tn., Slov.), *see* LUCENEC
Losontzi Hányoki, István **8:**43
Losow, Isaac **3:**430
"Lost Horizon" (wtrcl., L. Schatz) Pl. 16 **3**-ART
LOSTICE (vill., Morav.) **11:**504
LOST PROPERTY **11:**504
- *Contents:*
- - Basis of the Law **11:**504
- - Avedah with Retention of Ownership **11:**505
- - Restoration **11:**505
- - Avedah with Loss of Ownership **11:**506
- broker liability **2:**352
- Commandments, the 613 **5:**770
- Even ha-To'im **6:**985
- gentile **7:**412
- *hefker* **8:**243; **8:**244
- minor **8:**1424
- parent and child **13:**95
- premises ownership **12:**1533
- return by expropriation **5:**880
- sacrifice **14:**601
- theft **15:**1097
- wife's finds **8:**1126
- *ye'ush* **16:**774ff
- *see also:* PROPERTY; SHOMERIM
LOT (bib. fig.) **11:**507
- Abraham **2:**122ff
- in the Arts **15:**73
- Moab **12:**190
- Sodom **15:**70
- virginity **16:**161
- *illus:*
- - being made drunk by his daughters **6:**240; **14:**67
- - men of Sodom **4:**943
- - taken into captivity **5:**370
Lot, Operation (War of Indep.) **5:**1395; **15:**72
LOTAN, GIORA **11:**509
Lothar (Merovingian k.), *see* CLOTHAIRE II
LOTHAR, ERNST **11:**509
LOTHAR, RUDOLF **11:**510
Lotharingia (reg., Fr.), *see* LORRAINE
"Lot's Wife" (rock formation, Dead Sea, Isr.) **9:**167
LOTS **11:**510
- *Contents:*
- - Biblical Data **11:**510
- - Second Temple Period **11:**511
- - Post-Talmudic Times **11:**512
- bride dowry **14:**1617
- Day of Atonement *Avodah* **3:**977
- divination **6:**119
- gambling **7:**301
- ostraca **16:**660
- priestly lot **13:**1078
- Purim **13:**1390
- Saul **14:**910
- urim and thumim **16:**8
Lotta Continua (New Left orgn., It.) **12:**1034
Lotter, F.W. **10:**795
Lottery, *see* LOTS
Lotti, A. **9:**1344
Lotus Jujube (bot.) **9:**222
Łotwa (Baltic state), *see* LATVIA
Louchheim, Stuart F. **6:**1344
Loud, G. **11:**1222
Loudun (tn., Fr.) **13:**704
Louhans (tn., Fr.) **4:**1358
Louis I (duke of Anjou) **5:**356
LOUIS I (the Pious; Holy Rom. Emp.) **11:**513
- Abraham of Saragossa **2:**161
- Agobard **2:**372
- Jews **7:**10; **8:**662
- slave trade **14:**1661
Louis IV (Ger. emp.) **8:**942
LOUIS VI (k., Fr.) **11:**514
LOUIS VII (the Young; k., Fr.) **11:**514
- Jews **7:**13
- Vitry **16:**195
LOUIS VIII (k., Fr.) **11:**514
- seals **14:**1079
LOUIS IX (k., Fr.) **11:**515
- badge, Jewish **4:**65
- Caesarea **5:**12
- Christiani, Pablo **5:**505
- France **7:**14
- history **8:**677
LOUIS X (the Quarreler; k., Fr.) **11:**516
- historical chart **8:**766-767
LOUIS XI (k., Fr.) **11:**516
- Aix-en-Provence **2:**475
LOUIS XII (k., Fr.) **11:**516
- Bergamo Jews **4:**608
LOUIS XIII (k., Fr.) **11:**516
Louis XIV (k., Fr.) **2:**70
Louis XV (k., Fr.) **3:**809
- *illus:*
- - Metz Jews' petition **11:**1450
LOUIS XVI (k., Fr.) **11:**517
- Jews **7:**22
- *illus:*
- - Letters Patent re Portuguese Jews in France (1776) **3:**926
Louis, Lionel **6:**760
LOUIS, MORRIS **3:**605
- *illus:*
- - "Saraband" (paint.) **3:**635
Louis, Nathan **8:**1438
Louis Claude de St. Martin **10:**646
Louis de Valois of Alais **8:**43
Louise Amoena **8:**43
Louis Ginzberg Microfilm Collection (U.S.) **11:**906
LOUISIANA (U.S.) **11:**517
- *Contents:*
- - Early New Orleans **11:**517
- - Civil War and After **11:**519
- - Jewish Life **11:**519
- slave trade **14:**1663
Louisiana (city, Mo.) **8:**766-767; **12:**157
Louis Napoleon (Fr. emp.), *see* Napoleon III
Louis Napoleon (k., Holl.), *see* Bonaparte, Louis
Louis of Nice **14:**922
LOUISVILLE (city, Ky.) **11:**520
Loule (tn., Port.) **10:**1358
LOUNY (tn., Bohem.) **11:**522
Lourie (fam.), *see also* LURIA
LOURIE, ARTHUR (dipl.) **11:**522
LOURIÉ, ARTHUR (Vincent; comp.) **12:**698
Lourie, Grégoire **16:**1165
Lourie, Isadore **15:**213
Lourie, Norman (S.A.) **8:**1243
LOURIE, NORMAN VICTOR (U.S.) **11:**523
Lourie, Reginald **13:**1339
Lousada (fam.) **2:**614
Lousada, Duke **15:**1166
Lousada, Isaac de **8:**334; **15:**1166
LOUSE (insect) **11:**523
- *see also:* Lice (pest)
Louth, Robert, *see* LOWTH, ROBERT
Louvain (city, Belg.) **4:**416
LOUVISH, MISHA **1:**33
Lovasbereny (tn., Hung.) **7:**212
LOVE **11:**523
- *Contents:*
- - In the Bible **11:**523
- - Post-Biblical **11:**527
- - - Love and Fear of God **11:**528
- - - Love of Neighbor **11:**529
- Bible **7:**650ff
- cherubim **5:**399
- Commandments, the 613 **5:**763,770
- Crescas **13:**449
- *devekut* **5:**1598
- *Dialoghi di Amore* **2:**110ff
- ethics **6:**933f
- fear of God's holiness **10:**867
- God's love for Israel **7:**669
- Ḥasidei Ashkenaz **10:**514
- ḥasidic thought **7:**1404; **7:**1405ff
- imitation of God **8:**1292
- Jewish philosophy **13:**423
- Judaism **10:**388
- Kabbalah **10:**624
- piety **13:**504ff
- Rosenzweig on **14:**301
- Torah **15:**1238
- *illus:*
- - Scroll of the Law, hugging of **8:**fcg. 1015
- *see also:* FEAR OF GOD; Love of

neighbor
Love, afflictions of, *see* Afflictions of love
Love grass **9:**222
- plant list **13:**621
LOVELL, LEOPOLD SOLOMON **11:**530
Lovenstein, William **14:**162
Love of neighbor
- Commandments, the 613 **5:**770
- ethics **6:**933f
- gentiles warned on **12:**1190
- hatred **7:**1473
- love **11:**529
- rebuke and reproof **13:**1605
- Torah **15:**1241
- *see also:* COMPASSION
Love songs **15:**144ff
LOVESTONE, JAY **11:**531
Lovich (tn., Pol.), *see* LOWICZ
Lovosice (tn., Bohem.) **11:**391
LOVY, ISRAEL **11:**531
LOW (fam.) **11:**532
Low, Edith **11:**532
- WIZO **16:**593
- *illus:*
- - WIZO delegation to Twelfth Zionist Congress **16:**1101
- - WIZO executive **16:**594
Löw, Immanuel, *see* LOEW, IMMANUEL
Low, Ivy **11:**533
Low, Leo **14:**1620
Löw, Leopold, *see* LOEW, LEOPOLD
Low, Sir Maurice **11:**532
Low, Sir Sidney James Mark **11:**532
Low, Tibor **10:**1498
Lowan Shire (tn., Austr.) **11:**1286
Lowdermilk, Walter B. **9:**767
LOWE, ADOLPH **11:**533
Lowe, Johann M. S. **4:**1219
Lowe, Karl **9:**1344
Lowell (city, Mass.) **11:**1113
Lowell, A. Lawrence **15:**1654; **15:**1681
Lowenberg (cmty., Silesia) **14:**1536
Lowenberg, David **12:**1216
Lowengard, Leon **7:**1348
Lowenstamm, Abraham **4:**1356
Lowenstamm, Ḥayyim **4:**1357
Lowenstamm, Menahem Mendel **4:**1357
Lowenstein, Alexander **11:**1285
Lowenstein, Beatrice **11:**717
Lowenstein, Benjamin **12:**1037
Lowenstein, Jake **15:**310
Lowenstein, Mose **15:**310
LOWENSTEIN, SOLOMON **11:**533
Lowenthal, Adolph **15:**307
Lowenthal, Fred **15:**308
Lowenthal, Israel Ber **13:**1384
LOWENTHAL, MARVIN **11:**533
Lowentritt, Aaron **5:**606
"Lower criticism" (Bib.) **4:**905
Lower East Side (loc., N.Y.) **12:**1077ff
- *illus:*
- - ritual articles store **12:**1101
- - street scene **12:**1099
Lower Galilee (reg., Er. Isr.), *see* GALILEE
LOWICZ (tn., Pol.) **11:**534
LOWIE, ROBERT HARRY **11:**535
- anthropology **3:**38
LOWINSKY, EDWARD **12:**699
LOWN, PHILIP W. **11:**535
- education **2:**819; **6:**444
Lowndes, I. **8:**43
Lown School of Near Eastern and Judaic Studies (Brandeis Univ., U.S.) **11:**535
LOWTH, ROBERT **11:**535
- Hebraists **8:**43
- poetry **13:**672ff
Lowy, Israel, *see* LOVY, ISRAEL
Lowy, Jacob **4:**976
Loyalty, Double **3:**763
Loyev, Elimelech **14:**1273
Loyev, Olga **14:**1273
Loyola, Ignatius of **10:**8; **13:**323
Loyola y Haro, Juan de **13:**323
Loytsker, E. **15:**1076
Loz, Mt. (Isr.) **12:**927
Lozada (fam.) **11:**1504
Lozada, Aaron **12:**1027
Lozada, Jacob **12:**1027
Lozano, Abigail **15:**255
Lozère (reg., Fr.), *see* GÉVAUDAN
LOZINSKI, SAMUEL **11:**536
Lozinsky, Kadish, *see* LUZ, KADISH
Lozniany (tn., Belor.), *see* LIOZNO
LOZOVSKI, SOLOMON ABRAMOVICH (Dridzo) **11:**536
Lozovsky, A. **5:**794
Lu'aḥ, *see* CALENDAR
Lu'aḥ Aḥi'asaf (annual) **12:**1051
- statistics **1:** newsp. list
Lu'aḥ Aḥi'ever (journ.) **1:** newsp. list
Lu'aḥ Ereẓ Yisrael (annual) **12:**1055
- statistics **1:** newsp. list
Lu'aḥ ha-Ammim (geog. table) **7:**415
Lu'aḥ ha-Areẓ (journ.) **1:** newsp. list
Lu'aḥ ha-Em ve-ha-Yeled (journ.), *see Ha-Em ve-ha-Yeled*
Lu'aḥ ha-Me'orer (journ.) **1:** newsp. list
Lu'aḥ Keren Kayemet (journ.), *see Moladti*
Lu'aḥ Ko'operativi (journ.) **1:** newsp. list
Lu'aḥ Sha'ashu'im (journ.) **1:** newsp. list
Lu'aḥ Yerushalayim (journ.) **1:** newsp. list
Luanshya (Zambia) **16:**922
LUBACZOW (tn., Pol.) **11:**537
- *illus:*
- - tombstone **15:**1229,1230
Luban (tn., Lower Silesia) **3:**756
Luban, Chaim Selig **12:**1213
Lubanov (r., Rus.) **11:**18
Lubar, Mount (unidentified) **3:**290
LUBARSKY, ABRAHAM ELIJAH **11:**537
- *illus:*
- - F.Z.C. **16:**1165
- - Odessa Committee **12:**1329
Lubart (fort., Ukr.) **11:**589
LUBARTOW (tn., Pol.) **11:**537
LUBAVICH (tn., Rus.) **11:**538
- Shneur Zalman of Lyady **14:**1432
- yeshivah **16:**769
- *illus:*
- - Shneur Zalman of Lyady **7:**1013
Lubavich (ḥas. trend), *see* ḤABAD
Lubavich (tal. acad., N.Y.C.) **12:**1120
Lubavich Yeshivah College (Austr.) **11:**1282
- *illus:* **11:**1285
Lubavich Youth Organization **14:**1435
Lubbock (city, Tex.) **15:**1036
Lubchansky, Morris **12:**1035
Lubel, Samaya **5:**419
LUBETKIN, ẒIVIA **11:**538
- Warsaw **16:**351
Lubetzki, I. E. **5:**1120
LUBETZKY, JUDAH **11:**539
Lubianiker, Pinḥas, *see* LAVON, PINḤAS
Lubicz-Milosz, Oscar Venceslas de, *see* MILOSZ, OSCAR
Lubieszów (ḥas. dyn.), *see* LYUBESHOV
Lubin, David **16:**409
LUBIN, ISADOR **11:**540
Lubin, Sigmund **12:**446
LUBIN, SIMON JULIUS **11:**540
Lubinski, Georg, *see* LOTAN, GIORA
Lubitch, Joseph **13:**116
LUBITSCH, ERNST **11:**541
LUBLIN (city, Pol.) **11:**541
- *Contents:*
- - Early History **11:**541
- - Hebrew Printing **11:**544
- - Holocaust Period **11:**544
- - Contemporary Period **11:**546
- Poland **13:**764
- "reservation" **8:**854
- *illus:*
- - tombstones **14:**1287; **15:**1229
- - Yeshivat Ḥakhmei Lublin **16:**763
Lublin, Gedaliah **11:**547
LUBLIN, MEIR BEN GEDALIAH **11:**546
- Case, Joseph **5:**227
- chronological chart **8:**766-767
- codification of law **5:**653
- *ḥiddushim* **8:**467; **11:**333
- markets and fairs **11:**1002
- Rymanow **14:**533
Lublin, Seer of, *see* JACOB ISAAC HA-ḤOZEH MI-LUBLIN
Lubliner, Ludwig (Joshua; Ozeasz) **11:**8; **13:**817
Lubliner Tageblatt (newsp.) **13:**1042
LUBLINSKI, SAMUEL **11:**548
Lubman, Avraham Dov, *see* ḤAVIV-LUBMAN, AVRAHAM DOV
Lubman, Mordekhai **7:**1494
LUBNY (city, Ukr.) **11:**548
Lubny (dist., Ukr.) **13:**841
Lubofsky, R. **11:**1284
Lubomirski, Oscar von **8:**1379
Lubomirsky (fam.) **14:**537
Luboml (city, Ukr.), *see* LYUBOML
LUBOSHITZKI, AARON **11:**549
LUBOSHUTZ (fam.) **12:**699
Luboshutz, Anna **12:**699
LUBOSHUTZ, LEA **12:**699
Luboshutz, Pierre **12:**699
Lubotzky, Binyamin, *see* Eliav, Binyamin
LUBRANIEC (tn., Pol.) **11:**549
Lubumbashi (city, Cong Kinshasa) **5:**893
Luca, A., *see* AXELRAD, AVRAM
LUCA, B. **14:**422; **14:**426
LUCAN (Marcus Annaeus Lucanus) **14:**235
Lucas, Alice, **6:**784; **16:**835
Lucas, Louis Arthur **15:**1350
Lucas van Leyden **9:**1344; **14:**917
- *illus:*
- - "Potiphar's Wife Accusing Joseph" (engr.) **10:**217
LUCCA (city, It.) **11:**549
- yeshivah **16:**764
- *see also:* TUSCANY
Lucca, John of, *see* Johannes Luccae
LUCCA, PAULINE **12:**699
LUCENA (tn., Sp.) **11:**550
- Jews **10:**88
- Natronai bar Hilai **12:**886
- Spain **15:**224; **15:**226
- *yeshivot* **16:**763
Lucena, Abraham de **12:**1062
Lucena, Jacob de **2:**524; **12:**1125
Lucena, James **10:**1503
Lucena, Juan de **8:**1325
- publishing **13:**1364
- Seville **14:**1205
- Toledo **15:**1206
Lucena, Martin de **15:**1206
LUCENEC (tn., Slov.) **11:**551
Lucerna (fam.), *see* MA'OR KATAN
LUCERNE (city, Switz.) **11:**551
Lucero, Diego Rodríguez **8:**1387
Luchins, Abraham **13:**1344
Lucian (Bib. trans.) **4:**853
Lucienville (clny., Arg.) **3:**431
"Lucifer" (sculp., J. Epstein) **6:**829
Lucius, J. **5:**742
Lucius, Reuben, *see* GOLDBERG, RUBE
Lucius Annaeus Seneca, *see* SENECA THE YOUNGER
Lucius Caecilius Firmianus Lactantius, *see* Lactantius Firmianus
Lucius Quietus, *see* QUIETUS, LUSIUS
Lucius Septimius Severus, *see* SEVERUS, SEPTIMIUS
Luck (tn., Bohem.), *see* LUKA
Luck (city, Ukr.), *see* LUTSK
Luck, see *Mazzal*
Lucka, Koppelman **12:**699
Lucki (fam. name), *see under* Luzki
Lucki, Joseph Solomon, *see* LUZKI, JOSEPH SOLOMON BEN MOSES
Lucki, Simḥah Isaac, *see* LUZKI, SIMḤAH ISAAC BEN MOSES
LUCKMAN, SIDNEY **11:**552
- sport **15:**308
Lucrecius, *see* WIDMANSTETTER, JOHANN ALBRECHT
LUCUAS (J. "king," Cyrene) **11:**552
- Cyrene **5:**1184
- Libya **11:**200
Lud (Luddu), *see* LYDIA, LYDIANS
Ludlow, Baron, *see* Lopes, Sir Henry Charles
Ludmir (city, Ukr.), *see* VLADIMIR VOLYNSKI
LUDO, ISAC IACOVITZ **11:**553
- press **13:**1043; **14:**399
Ludolf, Susanna Magdalena **8:**43
Ludolf of Suchem **15:**1355
Ludomir (Lodmer, Lodomeria, Lodomira; city, Ukr.), *see* VLADIMIR VOLYNSKI
LUDOMIR, MAID OF **11:**553
Ludovici (Ludovicus), C.L., *see* Ludwig, C. L.
Ludovicus Sancti Francisci, *see* São Francisco, Luiz de
Ludus (vill., Transyl.) **8:**1103
LUDVIPOL, ABRAHAM **11:**554
- *illus:*
- - F.Z.C. **16:**1165
Ludwig, C. L. **8:**43
LUDWIG, EMIL **11:**554
Ludwig, Jack **5:**115; **16:**551
Ludwig, Maximilian **15:**1056
LUDWIG, REUBEN **11:**555
Ludwig IV of Bavaria (H.Rom. Emp.)
- Armleder bands **3:**484
- Austrian Fredericianum **3:**888
Ludwigsburg (city, Ger.) **16:**298; **16:**674
Ludwigshafen (cmty., Ger.) **13:**22
LUDZA (tn., Latv.) **11:**555
LUEBECK (city, Ger.) **11:**555
- Vienna, Congress of **16:**132
LUEGER, KARL **11:**556
- Abraham a Sancta Clara **2:**130
- anti-Semitism **3:**84,896; **16:**1044
- Hitler, Adolf **8:**782
LUENEBURG, (city, Ger.) **11:**557
- War Crimes Trials **16:**294
- *illus:*
- - text
- - Bergen-Belsen guards on trial **16:**295
Lueth, Erich **7:**1229; **7:**498
Luettich (city, Belg.), *see* LIÈGE
Luft, Anda **15:**339
Luft, Samuel **16:**351
Luftevir (Luftbehr), Abrahm **11:**1261; **16:**986

Luftglas, Markus 10:1574
Luftmenshen (Yid. term) 10:1323
Luftspring, Sammy 15:305
Lugalbanda (k., Mesop.) 16:1487
Lugal-zagge-si (k., Mesop.)
- Mari 11:974
- Mesopotamia 16:1489
- Ur 16:3
LUGANSK (city, Rus.) 11:558
Lugha, al- (wk.), *see Kitāb Faṣīḥ Lughat al-ʿIbrāniyyīn*
LUGO (tn., It.) 11:558
LUGOJ (Lugos; city, Rum.) 11:558
Luḥot Genuzim (poem) 14:1431
Luḥot Temidim (wk.), *see Ha-Ḥibbur ha-Gadol*
LUIDOR, JOSEPH 11:559
Luigi Einaudi Library 16:1004
Luik (city, Belg.), *see* LIEGE
Luis de Alcalá, *see* Alcalá, Luis de
Luis Henry of Conde 11:1190
Luiz, Thomás, *see* CASTRO TARTAS, ISAAC DE
LUKA (tn., Bohem.) 11:559
Luka (city, Ukr.), *see* LUTSK
LUKÁCS, GEORG (György) 11:560
LUKAS, PAUL 12:471
Lukaszkiewicz, Zdzistaw 15:1366
Luke (gospel) 10:10
- "apostle" term 3:216
Luke, H. C. 13:31
LUKOW (tn., Pol.) 11:560
Lukuas (J. "king"), *see* LUCUAS
LULAV (bot.) 11:561
- Bet Alfa mosaics 4:713
- *hakkafot* 7:1153
- Ḥanukkah 7:1284
- *hoshanot* 8:1029
- kibbutz and ownership 10:1570
- right hand 14:180
- Sabbath 7:1159
- Sephardi custom 14:1170
- Sukkot 15:501; 15:502
- synagogue art 15:597
- Temple destruction 9:241
- *illus:*
- - text
- - Bet She'arim tombstone 6:821
- - bone carving (4th-7th cent.) 6:948
- - Dura-Europos wall paint. 6:285
- - ḥasidic boy with 15:*fcg.* 491
- - oil lamp 12:1349
- - Ostia, synagogue relief 12:1508
- - Sukkot prayers in trenches of Kibbutz Sa'ad (1948) 16:323
Luliana (Julianos) ben Judah 10:889
Lulianus (tal. fig.), *see* PAPPUS AND JULIANUS
Luling (city, Tex.) 15:1036
Lull (-y, -ius), Raimon (Raymond)
- alchemy 2:545
- Hebraists 8:43; 8:14
Lullo (8th cent., It.) 13:192
Lullubean mountaineers (Mesop.) 16:1491
Lumaʿ, al- (wk.), *see Kitab al-Lumaʿ*
Lumberton (tn., N. C.) 12:1220
LUMBROSO (fam.) 11:561
Lumbroso, Abram 11:562
Lumbroso, Achille 11:563
Lumbroso, Alberto Emmanuele 11:563
Lumbroso, Daniel 11:561
Lumbroso, David 11:563
Lumbroso, Giacomo (mer.) 11:562
Lumbroso, Baron Giacomo (schol.) 11:563
Lumbroso, Isaac ben Jacob 11:561
Lumbroso, Isaac Vita 11:562
Lumbroso, Jacob 11:561
Lumbroso, Raphael 11:561
Lumbrozo, Jacob 11:1076; 15:1648
Lumbrozo de Mattos, Abraham, *see* Mocatta, Abraham
Lumbrozo de Mattos, Moses 12:198
Lumbrozo de Mattos, Rebecca 12:198
Lumet, Sidney 12:471
LUMINA (Rum. soc. party) 11:563
- Gelerter, L. L. 7:365
Luna, Doña Beatrice de, *see* NASI, GRACIA
Luna, Peter de (antipope), *see* BENEDICT XIII
Lunacharski, Anatoli 7:1029
Lunar cycle, *see* CALENDAR; MOON
LUNCZ, ABRAHAM MOSES 11:564
- Jerusalem 9:1466
- newspapers 12:1055
Lund, David 8:43
Lund, John 8:43
Lundenburg (tn., Cz.), *see* BRECLAV
LUNEL (tn., Fr.) 11:565
- Meshullam ben Jacob 11:1400
- scholars of 10:186
- yeshivah 16:763
LUNEL, ARMAND 11:566
LUNEL, JACOB DE 11:567
Lunenfeld, Bruno 11:1204
LUNÉVILLE (tn., Fr.) 11:567
- *illus:* text
LUNGE, GEORG 5:385
LUNIETZ, GEDALIAH BEN ISAAC OF 11:568
L'Univers Israélite (period.), *see* UNIVERS ISRAÉLITE
Lunski, Khaykel 15:427
LUNTS, LEV NATANOVICH 11:568
Luntschitz, Abraham Isaac 10:1556
Luntschitz, Ephraim Solomon ben Aaron, *see* EPHRAIM SOLOMON BEN AARON OF LUNTSHITS
Luntshits (tn., Pol.), *see* LECZYCA
Lunzano, Menahem ben Judah di, *see* LONZANO, MENAHEM BEN JUDAH DE
Lupin, Henry 12:266
Lupine (bot.) 13:621
Lupis, Isaac 11:355
LURIA (fam.) 11:568
Luria, Aaron (15th cent.) 11:569
Luria, Aaron (16/17 cent.) 11:569
Luria, Abraham 5:438; 8:210
LURIA, ALEXANDER ROMANOVICH 11:570
- education 6:465
Luria, Aryeh 16:147
LURIA, DAVID BEN JACOB AARON 11:570
LURIA, DAVID BEN JUDAH 11:571
Luria, Gabriel 4:1238
Luria, Gershom Loeb 16:147
LURIA, ISAAC BEN SOLOMON (Ha-Ari) 11:572
- Abulafia, Jacob 2:189
- *Adam Kadmon* 2:248
- alchemy 2:545
- *Berit Menuḥah* 2:146
- Caro, Joseph 5:195
- hagiography 7:1119
- Ḥasidism 7:1391; 7:1403ff
- history chart 8:766-67
- Jonah, Moses 10:178
- Joshua ibn Nun 10:288
- Kabbalah 10:546f,588,610,640; 11:347
- *kapparot* 10:756
- messianism 11:426
- prayer books 13:987
- *Toledot ha-Ari* 15:1207
- Vital, Ḥayyim 16:172ff
- woman 16:627
- Worlds, the Four 16:642
- Zhidachov Ḥasidim 16:1009
- *illus:*
- - text
- - *Ein-Sof* and *Sefirot* 10:558
- - Ha-Ari Synagogue 14:629
- - thirteen *middot* 10:544
Luria, Jacques 10:1351
Luria, Jehiel 11:569
Luria, Jehiel ben Aaron 4:1361; 9:1081; 11:570
LURIA, JEHIEL BEN ISRAEL ASHKENAZI 11:579
Luria, Johanan 11:569
- Alsace 2:753
- *shtadlanut* 14:1463
Luria, Joshua Moses 11:569
Luria, Moses 14:1305
LURIA, NOAH 11:579
Luria, Phinehas 8:1071
LURIA, SALVADOR EDWARD 11:579
Luria, Shemariah of Mohilev 7:190; 9:514
Luria, Solomon (r.) 11:569
Luria, Solomon (physic.) 11:542; 11:570
LURIA, SOLOMON BEN JEHIEL (Maharshal) 11:580
- *Anim Zemirot* 3:22
- Benjamin Ze'ev of Arta 4:538
- Brest-Litovsk 4:1361
- codification 5:652
- history chart 8:766-67
- Isserles, Moses 9:1082; 13:722
- proselytizing 13:1190ff
- responsa 14:89
- *Shulḥan Arukh* 14:1476
- Talmud commentary 8:467; 11:333
- *illus:*
- - text
- - Lublin, Maharshal Shul 11:545
Luria, Solomon Zalman 10:1430; 10:862; 10:994
Lurianic Kabbalah
- Bacharach, Naphtali 4:49ff
- Kabbalah 10:559; 10:614ff
- Vital, Ḥayyim 16:172ff
- Worlds, the Four 16:642
Lurie, B. 6:734
Lurie, Esther 3:575
- *illus:*
- - "Main Gate of Kaunas Ghetto" (drg.) 10:849
- - "Wooden Bridge in the Kovno Ghetto" (drg.) fig. 78 3-ART
LURIE, HARRY LAWRENCE 11:582
LURIE, JOSEPH 11:582
Lurie, Raanan 5:219
LURIE, TED 10:313
- *Jerusalem Post* 9:1594
LURIE, ẔVI 11:583
Luristan (prov., Iran) 13:78
Lurja (Lurje; fam.), *see* LURIA
Lury, J. 16:1165
Lurye, Mikhail Alexandrovich, *see* LARIN, YURI
Lurye, Noyekh, *see* LURIA, NOAH
Lusaka (tn., Zambia) 9:443; 16:922
Lusça (vill., Rum.) 13:1605
LUSCHAN, FELIX VON 11:583
Lusignan (vill., Fr.) 13:704
Lusitano, Salusque, *see* USQUE, SOLOMON
Lusitanus, Amatus, *see* AMATUS LUSITANUS
Lusitanus, Pyrrhus, *see* PYRRHUS, DIDACUS
Luska, Sidney, *see* Harland, Henry
Lustig, Alvin 15:1480
LUSTIG, ARNOŠT 11:584
Lustig, Emil, *see* DORIAN, EMIL
LUSTIG, MOSES 10:313
Lustig, Oliver 14:424
Lustig, Walter 7:495
Lustration, Water of (mei niddah) 14:10
Lūṭ (bib. fig.), *see* LOT
LUTHER, MARTIN 11:584
- alchemy, Jewish 2:546
- antinomianism 3:68
- Bible translation 4:873ff; 7:439
- Brunswick riots 4:1421
- German Jews 7:472
- Hebraists 8:43
- history chart 8:766-67
- Joselman of Rosheim 15:424
- Kabbalistic apocalypse 10:545
- Melanchthon, Philipp 11:1276
- messianism 11:1426
- Reformation 14:18ff
- status of Jews 8:692ff
- *Tobit, Book of* 15:1186
- *illus:*
- - *Von den Jüden und jren Lügen* (1543) 3:105
- *see also:* PROTESTANTS
Luther, Martin (Nazi offic.) 5:1539; 8:860
Lutheran Church
- anti-Semitism 3:108
- Luther, Martin 11:584
- Nazism 8:915
- Protestant-Jewish relations 13:1251
- *see also:* PROTESTANTS
LUTOMIERSK (tn., sub., Pol.) 11:586
LUTOSTANSKI, HYPPOLITE 11:587
Lutowski, Jerzy 13:802
LUTSK (city, Ukr.) 11:587
- Carlsbad 5:184
- *illus:* text
Lutz, Charles 8:1104; 8:907
Lutzerner (Aus. fam.), *see* MA'OR KATAN
Lutziner, Itzele 11:555
Lutzki (fam. name), *see also under* LUZKI
Lutzki, M. 7:1105
LUTZKY, A. 11:589
- *illus:*
- - writers' group 16:823
Lux, Lilian 4:1531
LUX, STEFAN 11:590
LUXEMBOURG 11:590
- synagogues 1:syn. list
- War Crimes Trials 16:289ff
- *illus:*
- - Israel-German reparations agreement 7:499; 14:72
LUXEMBURG, ROSA 11:592
- German politics 8:737
- Jogiches, Leon 10:143ff
- sociology 15:63
- stamps 15:336
- *illus:* text
Luxury, *see* SUMPTUARY LAWS
LUZ (city, Er. Isr.) 11:593
- Beth-El 4:728; 9:1195
- luz of the spine 11:596
- *tekhelet* 15:913
LUZ, KADISH 11:593
Luzada, Jacob 15:1443
Luzern (city, Switz.), *see* LUCERNE
Luzerner (Aus. fam.), *see* MA'OR KATAN
Luzit (mosh., Isr.) 1: place list
LUZKI, ABRAHAM BEN JOSEPH SOLOMON 11:594
LUZKI, JOSEPH SOLOMON BEN MOSES 11:594
LUZKI, SIMḤAH ISAAC BEN MOSES 11:595
LUZ OF THE SPINE (spinal bone) 11:595
Luzzara (tn., It.) 11:895
Luzzatti (fam.), *see* LUZZATTO
LUZZATTI, LUIGI 11:596
- history chart 8:766-767
LUZZATTO (fam.) 11:597

- banking **14:**829
- *illus:*
- - San Daniele del Friuli Ark **15:**1255
Luzzatto, Abraham **11:**597
Luzzatto, Angelo, *see* LUZZATTO, EPHRAIM
Luzzatto, Baruch **9:**1109
Luzzatto, Benedetto **13:**12; **11:**597
LUZZATTO, EPHRAIM **11:**597
- Hebrew literature **8:**181; **8:**182
- Italian literature **9:**1109
Luzzatto, Federico **11:**597
Luzzatto, Filosseno **13:**12; **11:**597; **11:**605
- Falashas **6:**1149
LUZZATTO, GINO **11:**598
Luzzatto, Hezekiah **11:**597; **11:**604
LUZZATTO, ISAAC **11:**598
- Italian literature **9:**1109
LUZZATTO, JACOB BEN ISAAC **11:**598
Luzzatto, Marco **11:**597
LUZZATTO, MOSES ḤAYYIM (Ramḥal) **11:**599
- *Contents:*
- - Life **11:**599
- - Messianic Doctrine **11:**600
- - Kabbalistic Writings **11:**601
- - Ethical Works **11:**602
- - Poetry and Letters **11:**603
- Bacharach's influence **4:**50
- Basilea, supporter **4:**299
- Benjamin of Reggio **4:**532
- drama **6:**194
- Ginzburg, Simon **7:**587
- Hebrew literature **8:**178
- history chart **8:**766-67
- Kabbalah **10:**552; **10:**606
- *Le-El Elim* **2:**905
- literary criticism **5:**1115
- *maggid* **11:**701
- magic **11:**714
- prosody **13:**1223
- Shabbateanism **14:**1251
- Valle, Moses David **16:**63
- *illus:* text
Luzzatto, Nehemiah **8:**264
Luzzatto, Ohev Ger, *see* Luzzatto, Filosseno
Luzzatto, Philoxenus, *see* Luzzatto, Filosseno
LUZZATTO, SAMUEL DAVID **11:**604
- Bible exegesis **4:**901
- Haskalah, Galician **8:**184; **8:**185
- history chart **8:**766-67
- linguistics **16:**1399
- liturgy **11:**399
- masorah **16:**1418
- *Mekiẓei Nirdamim* **11:**1271ff
- philosophy **13:**459
- scholarship **16:**573
- Schorr, Joshua Heschel **14:**997
- Toledo **15:**1200
- Torah **15:**1242
- Zohar critique **16:**1214
- *illus:*
- - text
- - autograph **3:**916
LUZZATTO, SIMONE BEN ISAAC SIMḤAH **11:**607
- apologetics **3:**198; **8:**700
- history chart **8:**766-67
- Italian literature **9:**1109
Luzzatto, Tamar **11:**598
Luzzi, G. **4:**878
LVOV (Lemberg; city, Ukr.) **11:**608
- *Contents:*
- - Early Settlements **11:**608
- - Community and its Institutions **11:**609
- - 1684-1772 **11:**610
- - 1772-1914 **11:**611
- - 1914-1939 **11:**612
- - Hebrew Printing **11:**613
- - Holocaust Period **11:**613
- - Contemporary Period **11:**613
- history chart **8:**766-767
- museums **12:**539
- Nachmanovich family **12:**747
- *illus:*
- - text
- - "In the Market of Lemberg" (drg.; J. Pennell) **11:**1001
- - synagogue plan **15:**608
Lvov, Disputation of **7:**61 **4:**1037
LVOVICH, DAVID **11:**616
Lvov, Leo (Pesaḥ) **15:**57
LWOFF, ANDRÉ MICHEL **11:**617
Lwów (city, Ukr.), *see* LVOV
Lwowek Slaski (cmty., Silesia), *see* Lowenberg
LYADY (tn., Rus.) **11:**617
- *illus:*
- - Shneur Zalman of Lyady **7:**1013
Lyady, Shneur Zalman of, *see* SHNEUR ZALMAN OF LYADY
LYAKHOVICHI (city, Belor.) **11:**618
Lyakhovichi, Mordecai ben Noah of, *see* LACHOWICZE, MORDECAI BEN NOAH OF
Lyaschevski, Valaam **4:**886
Lycaonia (reg., As. M.) **3:**747
Lycia (reg., As. M.) **3:**746ff
LYCK (tn., Pol.) **11:**618
LYDDA (Lod; tn., Isr.) **11:**619
- academy **2:**202
- airport **9:**837
- Akiva **2:**488; **2:**489
- Arab capital **9:**261
- Crusader period **9:**268ff
- dyeing center **6:**327
- Jerusalem Talmud **15:**773
- Mamluk period **9:**277; **9:**279
- olive cultivation **12:**1365
- Ottoman period **9:**283; **9:**285; **9:**291
- Roman, Byzantine period **9:**244ff
- *Sifrei Zuta* **14:**1522
- statistics **1:**place list
- War of Independence **16:**323
- *illus:*
- - text
- - Academy, principal *Amoraim* (table) **2:**871
- - El Al Boeing 707 **9:**838
- - Israel Aircraft Industries' hangar **9:**817
- - loading fresh gladioli **9:**763
- - three millionth citizen arriving at **9:**529
- *see also:* Diospolis
LYDIA, LYDIANS (As. M.) **11:**620
- Asia Minor **3:**746ff
- Jewish colonists **10:**259
- Ludim and **12:**883
- Put **13:**1415
- Semites **14:**1148
- *illus:*
- - coin **5:**697
Lyebed (sub., Kiev) **10:**993
Lymphoma (disease) **14:**1503
Lynch, Hubert **11:**998
Lynchburg (city, Va.) **16:**163
Lynkeus (philos.), *see* POPPER, JOSEF
Lynn (city, Eng.), *see* KING'S LYNN
LYNN (city, Mass.) **11:**622
Lynnfield (tn., Mass.) **11:**622
Lynx (zool.) **9:**226
- fauna of Israel **9:**226
Lyon, Abraham de **7:**429; **14:**919
Lyon, Annabella **5:**1269
Lyon, Barnet **12:**284
Lyon, Benjamin **11:**1498
- Solomon, Ezekiel **15:**114
Lyon, Emma, *see* HENRY, EMMA
Lyon, George Lewis **10:**98
Lyon, Hart, *see* LEVIN, ẒEVI HIRSCH BEN ARYEH LOEB
Lyon, Morton Sahl, *see* SAHL, MORT
Lyon, Robert **12:**1074; **13:**1050
Lyon, Solomon **6:**447
LYON-CAEN, CHARLES LÉON **11:**623
LYONS (city, Fr.) **11:**623
- Alsace-Lorraine Jews **2:**756
- archives **3:**382
- history chart **8:**766-67
- slave trade **14:**1661
- stock exchanges **15:**406
- *illus:*
- - Ḥanukkah lamp (14th cent.) **7:**1296
LYONS, ALBERT MICHAEL NEIL **6:**789
Lyons, Cecil **15:**193
LYONS, EUGENE **10:**313
Lyons, Henry **5:**56; **14:**834
LYONS, ISRAEL (Hebr.) **11:**625
Lyons, Israel (sci.) **11:**626; **15:**1350
Lyons, Jacob **15:**1034
LYONS, JACQUES JUDAH **11:**626
- New York **12:**1071
- *illus:* text
LYONS, SIR JOSEPH **11:**626
- Gluckstein, Isidore **7:**626
Lyons, Keely **15:**305
LYONS, LEONARD **10:**307,313
Lyre (mus. instr.) **13:**1319
- *illus:*
- - Bar Kokhba coins **4:**230; **12:**569
- - David playing **4:**1,947; **7:**341
- - lyre players **12:**567,568
Lyre (Lyra; Lyranus), Nicholas de, *see* NICHOLAS DE LYRE
LYSANIAS (k., Chalcis) **11:**627
- Ptolemy **13:**1349
LYSIAS (Syr. sol.) **11:**627
- *Book of Maccabees II* **11:**658ff
- Hasmonean revolt **8:**629
- Judah Maccabee **10:**379
Lysias (fort., Leb.) **14:**1532
Lysimachus (s., Ptolemy of Jer.; schol.) **14:**1055
Lysimachus (2nd cent. B.C.E., pr., Jer.) **9:**1391
Lysimachus (cmty. ldr., Egy.), *see* ALEXANDER LYSIMACHUS
LYSIMACHUS OF ALEXANDRIA **11:**627
- anti-Jewish Greek literature **7:**889
- Esther, Book of **6:**914
Lysyanka (tn., Rus.) **7:**1133
Lytton, Robert Arthur (3rd Earl of) **4:**131
Lyubartov (tn. Pol.), *see* LUBARTOW
LYUBESHOV (ḥas. dyn.) **11:**628
LYUBOML (city, Ukr.) **11:**628
- *illus:*
- - synagogue **13:**727
Lyubranets (tn., Pol.), *see* LUBRANIEC
Lyutsin (tn., Latv.), *see* LUDZA
Lzhansk (tn. Pol.), *see* LEZAJSK

M

"Ma'abarah" (paint., M. Janco) Fig. 97 3-ART
MAACAH (bib. fig.) **11:**633
– Absalom **2:**174
– *geneal. table:* **5:**1341
Maacah (Phil. k.) **2:**211
Maacah (anc. city, Er. Isr.) **8:**1064
– *see also:* ABEL-BETH-MAACAH
Maacah (reg., Er. Isr.), *see* Bet(h)-Maacah
Ma'agan (kib., Isr.) **1:**place list
MA'AGAN MIKHA'EL (kib., Isr.) **11:**634
– statistics **1:**place list
– *illus:* text
MA'ALEH AKRABBIM (loc., Isr.) **11:**635
– Arab attack **9:**386
– *illus:* text
Ma'aleh Gilboa (kib., Isr.) **9:**588
– statistics **1:**place list
MA'ALEH HA-ḤAMISHAH (kib., Isr.) **11:**636
– Six-Day War **14:**1630
– statistics **1:**place list
Ma'aleh ha-Luḥit (reg., Er. Isr.) **4:**239
MA'ALOT TARSHĪḤĀ (urban cmty., Isr.) **11:**636
– statistics **1:**place list
MA'AMAD (Mahamad; Seph. council) **11:**637
– expulsion punishment **13:**1389
Ma'amadot (ḥas. dues) **15:**1471
– introduced among Ḥasidim **9:**1059
Ma'amadot (pr. divs.), *see* MISHMAROT AND MA'AMADOT
Ma'amad sheloshtan (three-sided agreement) **3:**768f
Ma'amar al Ishma'el (bk.) **3:**194
Ma'amar al Seder ha-Dorot (bk.) **2:**551
Maamar Elohi (bk.) **12:**422
Ma'amar ha-'Ibbur (bk.) **11:**754
Ma'amar Mufla al ha-Tanninim (bk.) **2:**542
Ma'amarot, the ten, *see* SEFIROT
Ma'amar Peloni Almoni (bk.) **2:**134
Ma'amar Teḥiyyat ha-Metim (wk.) **11:**757f
Ma'aminim ("believers") **14:**1228
Ma'an (Druze fam.) **9:**287
Maan (tn., Transj.) **9:**596; **15:**1318
Ma'aneh (meas.) **16:**390
Ma'aneh, Ha-(wk.), *see Sefer ha-Ma'aneh*
MA'ANIT (kib., Isr.) **11:**637
– statistics **1:**place list
Ma'anit (journ.) **7:**1321; **1:**newsp. list
Ma'arakh (polit. orgn.), *see* Alignment
Ma'arakhot (period.) **7:**1071; **1:**newsp. list
MA'ARAVOT (piyyutim) **11:**637
– prayer books **13:**986
MA'AREKHET HA-ELOHUT (kab. wk.) **11:**637
– *Ein-Sof* **10:**557f
– Kabbalah **10:**533
– mystical literature **11:**347
Ma'arekhet Sifrei Kodesh (wk.) **6:**730
Ma'arekhot Himmush (journ.) **1:**newsp. list
Ma'arekhot Yam (journ.) **1:**newsp. list
Ma'ariv (evening prayer), *see* ARVIT
MAARIV (newsp.). **11:**639
– Ben-Ami, Oved **4:**460
– Carlebach, Ezriel **5:**182
– Hebrew newspapers **12:**1057; **12:**1058
– Israel **9:**1016
– statistics **1:**newsp. list
Ma'arivim (piyyutim), *see* MA'ARAVOT
Ma'ariyyah (loc., Er. Isr.) **11:**702
Maarsen, Isaac **11:**640
– Naḥmanides **15:**521
Maarsen, Josef **6:**320
Maarssen (vill., Holl.) **12:**977; **16:**36
MA'ARUFYA (leg. conc.) **11:**640
– encroachment **7:**1463
– *ḥazakah* **7:**1523
Maas (fam.) **15:**790
MA'AS (mosh., Isr.) **11:**641
Maas, Nathan ben Solomon **5:**615; **8:**999
MA'ASEH (leg. conc.) **11:**641
– *contents:*
– – Substance of Ma'aseh **11:**641
– – An Act of Deciding the Law **11:**642
– – Conduct of a Halakhic Scholar **11:**643
– – Distinguishing Ma'aseh **11:**643
– – In Post-Talmudic Times **11:**645
– – Responsa Literature **11:**645
– – Jewish Law and Binding Precedent **11:**646
– codification of law **5:**630
– law source **12:**119
– rabbinic utilization of **3:**910
– *soferim* and Bible interpretation **8:**1417
– study and action **9:**243
– tax **15:**845
– *see also:* SEVARAH; TAKKANOT
Ma'aseh (ḥas. tale) **7:**1402
Ma'aseh Avraham Avinu (leg.) **6:**1262
Ma'aseh be-Rabbi Eliezer (Hag.) **7:**1080
Ma'aseh Bereshit (myst. conc.) **5:**1063
– Ishmael ben Elisha **9:**86
– Jewish philosophy **13:**424
– Maimonides **11:**770; **15:**1126
– mystical speculation **10:**494; **10:**498ff
– Naḥmanides **12:**782
– *see also:* CREATION AND COSMOGONY; MERKABAH MYSTICISM
Ma'aseh Beri'ah ve-Zimrah (bk.) **11:**359
MA'ASEH BOOK (Yid. anth.) **11:**649
– Jewish literature **11:**359
– Yiddish literature **16:**804
– *illus:* text
Ma'aseh Efod (wk.) **16:**1360,1373,1387
Ma'aseh ha-Ge'onim (wk.) **11:**669
Ma'aseh Merkavah, see MERKABAH MYSTICISM
Ma'aseh Nissim (wk.) **16:**804
Ma'aseh Rav (bk.) **4:**529
Ma'aseh Shimshon (play) **11:**603
Ma'aseh Torah (wk.), *see Midrash Sheloshah ve-Arba'ah*
Ma'aseh Tuviyyah (bk.) **4:**119; **6:**731
Ma'aseh yadeha (wife's earnings) **11:**784
Ma'aseh Yerushalmi (fairy tale) **2:**152; **6:**1266
Ma'asei Adonai (bk.) **2:**493
Maaseiah son of Shallum (bib. fig.) **13:**1075
Ma'aser (tithe), *see* TERUMOT AND MAASEROT; TITHE
MA'ASEROT (tract.) **11:**651
– *illus:* text
MA'ASER SHENI (tract.) **11:**652
– *illus:* text
Maastricht (tn., Neth.) **12:**974
– *illus:*
– – synagogue **12:**979
– – synagogue medal **11:**1166
Maatschappij tot Nut der Israëlieten in Nederland (Du. assoc.) **13:**554
Ma'avak (period.) **12:**1056
– statistics **1:**newsp. list
Ma'ayani, Ami **12:**671
Maaz (bib. fig.), *see* AHIMAAZ
Maaze, Ida **5:**445
Maaziah (priestly clan) **12:**89
MA'BARAH (immigrant center) **11:**654
– absorption **9:**537ff
– Beth-Shemesh **4:**774
– housing problems **9:**563
– new immigrant **9:**381
– *illus:*
– – text
– – Rosh ha-Ayin **9:**379
– – Tiberias **9:**530
MA'BAROT (kib., Isr.) **11:**655
– statistics **1:**place list
Ma'abarot (period.) **7:**1326; **9:**1001
– statistics **1:**newsp. list
Mabartha (vill., Er. Isr.) **7:**438; **12:**744
M-a-b-a-sh, *see* CHAJES, GERSHON BEN ABRAHAM
Mabasser; the Jewish Gazette (period.) **13:**1036
Mabbat Hadash (journ.) **1:** newsp. list
Mabbu'a (journ., Isr.) **1:**newsp. list
Mabbu'a (journ., U.S.) **1:**newsp. list
Mabbu'im (rural center, Isr.) **1:**place list
Mabinjan (period.) **13:**1035
Mabkhūsh, Evariste (Fr. orient.), *see* LÉVI-PROVENÇAL, EVARISTE
Mabovitch, Golda, *see* MEIR, GOLDA
Mabug (amora) **8:**468
Mabug (city, Syr.), *see* HIERAPOLIS
MAC (U.N., com.), *see* Mixed Armistice Commissions
MACALISTER, ROBERT ALEXANDER STEWART **11:**655
– excavations **3:**46; **4:**1095
– Jerusalem **9:**1522
McAllen (city, Tex.) **15:**1036
Macarius (bp., Jer.) **9:**1406,1570
MACAULAY, THOMAS BABINGTON **11:**655
– Jews, attitude to **8:**715
– Jews, defense of **3:**198
Maccabean, The (period.)
– Amram, D. W. **2:**891
– Lipsky, Louis **11:**296
– U.S. Zionism **16:**1141; **16:**1178
Maccabean Land Company, (Er. Isr.) **11:**656
MACCABEANS, ORDER OF ANCIENT (soc., Eng.) **11:**656
– fraternal societies **7:**110
Maccabee (orgn., Gr.) **14:**703
MACCABEE (name given to Judah ben Mattathias) **11:**656
– in the Arts **7:**1457
– sages **14:**638ff
– *see also:* HASMONEANS; JUDAH MACCABEE; MATTATHIAS
Maccabee, Judah, *see* JUDAH

MACCABEE
Maccabee, Operation (Isr. War of Indep.), *see* Makkabi, Operation
MACCABEES, FIRST BOOK OF **11**:656
- Abomination of Desolation **2**:98
- historiography **8**:553
- history chart **8**:766-67
- literary style **8**:304
- *Megillat Ta'anit* **11**:1230
- Septuagint **4**:853
MACCABEES, SECOND BOOK OF **11**:658
- historiography **8**:553
- Jason of Cyrene **9**:1292
- Jewish philosophy **13**:425
- literary style **8**:304
- magic **11**:705
- Septuagint **4**:853
- *illus:*
- - text
- - Hannah and her seven sons **7**:1271
MACCABEES, THIRD BOOK OF **11**:660
- Hellenism **8**:299
- Septuagint **4**:853
MACCABEES, FOURTH BOOK OF **11**:661
- commandments, reasons for **5**:784
- Greek influence **8**:300
- Jewish philosophy **13**:425
- *kiddush ha-Shem* **10**:982
- Septuagint **4**:853
- visions **16**:167
Maccabi (period.) **8**:1359; **13**:1036
Maccabi, Ḥayyim Zundel, *see* MACCOBY, ḤAYYIM ZUNDEL
MACCABIAH (int. games, Isr.) **11**:662
- Israel **9**:1020
- Maccabi World Union **11**:665
- sport **15**:295 .
- *illus:*
- - text
- - Israel stamp **9**:844-850
Maccabi ha-Ẓair (youth mvmt.) **7**:806; **9**:981
MACCABI WORLD UNION (sports orgn.) **11**:664
- *illus:*
- - soccer team at Mazeikiai **15**:294
McCaul, Alexander **8**:43 **2**:574
Macchiero (fam., Bosnia) **15**:289
McClelland, Roswell **8**:907
MACCOBY, ḤAYYIM ZUNDEL **11**:665
McCoy, Al, *see* Rudolph, Albert
McDONALD, JAMES GROVER **11**:666
- Palestine, Inquiry Commission **13**:33
- *illus:*
- - Anglo-American Committee **16**:1084
MacDonald, Malcolm **9**:343 **16**:484
MacDonald, Ramsay$**9**:344; **16**:484
MacDonald Letter **16**:1078
- history chart **8**:766-67
MacDonald White Paper **16**:484
- history chart **8**:766-67
Mace (weapon) **16**:266
MACEDONIA **11**:667
- Greece **7**:868
- Hellenistic states **8**:292
- Kittim **10**:1081
- Samaritans **8**:625; **8**:626
- Yugoslavia **16**:868ff
Macelama,Macelarama, *see* MASHĀ'ALLAH B. ATHAN
Mach, Alexander **16**:295
Mach, Saño **5**:1195
Macha, J. **8**:43
Macha Allah al Mesri, *see* MASHĀ'ALLAH B. ATHAN
Machabea, Judah **5**:63
MACHABEY, ARMAND **12**:699
MACHADO (fam.) **11**:667
Machado, Aaron **11**:667; **12**:1067
Machado, Antonio **11**:667
Machado, David Mendez **11**:667
Machado, Isabel **11**:667
Machado, Raquel **10**:1429
Machado, Rebecca, *see* Phillips, Rebecca Machado
Machado, Zipporah Nuñez **11**:667; **12**:1274
MACHAERUS (fort., Transj.) **11**:667
- Bassus **4**:317
- Herod **8**:636
MACHAUT, DENIS DE **11**:668
- Paris Jews **13**:106
MACHIR (bib. fig.) **11**:668
- Manasseh **11**:851
MACHIR BEN JUDAH **11**:669
- Charlemagne **12**:828
MACHLUP, FRITZ **11**:669
Machma (city, Er. Isr.), *see* MICHMASH
Machol, Michaelis **5**:607
Machon Gold, *see* Rabbi Gold Teachers' Seminary
Machover, Jona **10**:92
MACHPELAH, CAVE OF **11**:670
- access to Jews **13**:517
- Hebron Shrine **8**:921
- patriarchs **13**:182
- pillars **13**:523
- seal motif **14**:1081
- *illus:*
- - text
- - folkloristic embroidery **6**:1385
- - Hebron Sephardi community seal **9**:888
- - mosque **8**:923
- *plan:* text
- *see also:* HEBRON
MACHT, DAVID **11**:674
MACHTA, LESTER **11**:674
Machtenberg, Meyer **5**:487
Machzike Hadath (orgn.), *see* MAHZIKE HADAS
MACIAS, ENRICO **15**:1088
Maciejowski, Ignacy **13**:800
Maciejowski Psalter, see Morgan Picture Bible
MACK, JULIAN WILLIAM **11**:674
- American Jewish Committee **2**:823
- Brandeis, Louis,**4**:1298n
- Szold, Henrietta **15**:666
- Young Men's Hebrew Association **12**:874
Mack, Raymond **15**:68
McKeesport (city, Pa.) **13**:230
Mackerras, Catherine **12**:853
Mackerras, Charles **12**:853
Macklott, M. **10**:795
- Job **10**:126
McMahon, Sir Henry **9**:309ff
MacMichael, Sir Harold **8**:470; **9**:353f,601
- *illus:* **8**:471
Macmillan Bible Atlas **2**:452
MACNIN (fam.) **11**:675
Macnin, Masʿūd **11**:675
Macnin, Meir **11**:675
MÂCON (city, Fr.) **11**:675
Macon (city, Ga.) **7**:429
MACROBIUS, AMBROSIUS **14**:235
MACS (U.N. com.), *see* Mixed Armistice Commissions
McWilliams, Joseph E. **12**:1114
Macy, George **13**:1372
Macznik, Jacob **13**:117
MADABA, MEDEBA (Moab. city) **11**:676
- human geography **9**:596
- John Hyrcanus **8**:631
- Moabite revolt **11**:1397
- Nabateans **12**:740
- Omri **12**:1390
- Transjordan **15**:1317
- *illus:* text
Madaba Map **11**:676
- cartography **11**:918
- Jerusalem in art **9**:1579
- Jerusalem topography **9**:1543ff
- *illus:*
- - Ashdod **3**:697
- - full view **11**:677
- - Ashkelon **3**:715
- - Gilgal **7**:572
- - Jerusalem **9**:1543
- - Palmer and Guthe's reproduction **11**:921
MADAGASCAR **11**:677
- settlement plan **11**:679
MADAGASCAR PLAN (J. stlmt.) **11**:678
- Holocaust **8**:854
Madai (bib. fig.) **11**:1176
Madai (anc. people), *see* MEDES AND MEDIA
Madā'in Ṣāliḥ (tn., Arab.), *see* Al-Ḥijr
Madame Kaulla, *see* Kaulla, Chaila Raphael
Madariaga, Salvador de **15**:250
Madatankil (loc., Cochin), *see* Muttam
Madaus, Gerhard **5**:85
Madda (journ.) **1**:newsp.itist
Madd'ei ha-Yahadut (journ.) **1**:newsp. list
Madden, F. W. **12**:1271
Madder (bot.), *see Pu'ah*
Madeira (isl.) **15**:487
Madeyevski, Abraham **10**:956
Madhmār (vill., Yem.) **11**:849
Mádi, János **8**:45
Maʿdi Karib Yaʿfur (k., S. Arab.) **16**:898
Madīna (city, Arab.), *see* MEDINA
MADISON, JAMES **11**:679
- Mordecai Noah **15**:1445
Maḍmun (nagid, Yem.) **12**:763
Maḍmūn ben David **2**:261
- Yemenite Jews **16**:742
MAḌMŪN BEN JAPHETH BEN BUNDĀR **11**:680
- Aden **2**:260; **16**:741
- *nagid* **12**:763
Madoba (tn., Transj.), *see* MADABA, MEDEBA
MADON (Cana. city) **11**:681
Madpis, H. D. **11**:613
MADRAS (city, Ind.) **11**:681
- Abendana, Isaac Sardo **2**:66
- India **8**:1356
Madrasa (Musl. theol. coll.) **9**:919; **14**:1136
MADRID (city, Sp.) **11**:682
- *Contents:*
- - Community's Status **11**:682
- - Persecutions and Expulsion **11**:682
- - Conversos **11**:683
- - Reestablished Community **11**:684
- archives **3**:376
- Spain **15**:245
- *illus:* text
Madrid, Congress of, *see* Congress of Madrid
Madrigal, Alfonso Tostado, *see* Tostado, Alfonso de Madrigal
Madrikh li-Mekomot Avodah Me'urganim (journ.) **1**:newsp. list
Madruzzo, Cristoforo **14**:196
Maduro, Moses Salomo Levy **12**:993
Maehren (reg., Cz.), *see* MORAVIA
Maehrisch-Aussee (tn., Morav.), *see* USOV
Maehrisch-Budwitz (tn., Morav.), *see* MORAVSKE BUDEJOVICE
Maehrisch-Kromau (tn., Cz.), *see* MORAVSKY KRUMLOV
Maehrisch-Ostrau (tn., Morav.), *see* OSTRAVA
Maehrisch-Weisskirchen (tn., Morav.), *see* HRANICE
Maerkisch-Friedland (tn., Ger.), *see* Miroslawiec
Maerlant, Jacob van **12**:975
MAES, ANDREAS **11**:684
- Hebraists **8**:44
Maestre Boninfante **12**:267
Maestre Bonjua, *see* BONDAVIN, BONJUDAS
Maestre Geronimo De Santa Fé (Megadef), *see* LORKI, JOSHUA
Maestre Leo de Bagnols, *see* LEVI BEN GERSHOM
Maestre Petit de Nions, *see* Kimḥi, Isaac
Maestre Vidal Bellsom, *see* MOSES BEN JOSHUA OF NARBONNE
Maestro, Jacob **14**:871
Maestro Calo, *see* Kalonymos ben Meir
Maestro David de Caslari, *see* Caslari, David ben Abraham
Maestro Gaio, *see* Isaac ben Mordecai
Maestro Manoel, *see* HABILLO, ELIJAH BEN JOSEPH
Maeterlinck, Maurice **8**:517; **15**:538
Mafdal (Isr. polit. party), *see* NATIONAL RELIGIOUS PARTY
Mafraq (mil. outpost, Jor.) **9**:597
Mafte'aḥ (wk.), *see Sefer ha-Mafte'aḥ*
MAFTIR (Torah reading) **11**:685
- *see also:* HAFTARAH
Maftirim Choral Society (Turk.) **2**:311; **12**:615
Maftir keneset (tit., Babyl.) **15**:1164
Magadan (city, Er. Isr.), *see* MAGDALA
Magalif (law., Pol.) **12**:967
Ma'gallum (rural center, Isr.) **1**:place list
Magaza of Cappadocia (city), *see* CAESAREA IN CAPPADOCIA
Magazin fuer die Wissenschaft des Judentums **4**:665; **16**:578
MAGDALA (city, Er. Isr.) **11**:685
- *Provincia Judaea* **9**:239
MAGDEBURG (city, Ger.) **11**:685
- *illus:*
- - *Kristallnacht* **8**:849
Magdeburg, Council of (1370) **5**:548
MAGDEBURG LAW **11**:687
- Polish Jewry **13**:711
Magdi'el (vill., Isr.), *see* HOD HA-SHARON
Magdola (tn., Egy.) **6**:9
Maged, A. **6**:735
Magen (kib., Isr.) **1**:place list
Magen Avot (bk., Bikayam) **4**:992
Magen Avot (wk., Me'iri) **12**:781
Magen Avraham (bk.) **7**:766
- *illus:*
- - title page (Amsterdam, 1732) **8**:74
MAGEN DAVID (Shield of David) **11**:687
- amulet **2**:911
- flag **6**:1336ff
- Jewish badge **4**:72
- Jewish Legion insignia **10**:73
- philosopher's stone **2**:546
- seals **14**:1080
- *Shivviti* plaque **14**:1420

- synagogue art **15:**597
- *illus:*
- - text
- - amulets **2:**913; **4:**1051
- - Bilu stamp **4:**1000
- - Jerusalem seal **14:**1078
- - Jewish Badge **4:**70,72
- - Jews branded with, Poland **13:**758
- - Nazi ghetto coins and paper currency **5:**726
- - Purim noisemaker **13:**1393
Magen David (wk., David ben Samuel) **5:**1355
Magen David (wk., Elisha ben Abraham) **16:**1361, 1389
Magen David (period.) **16:**348
MAGEN DAVID ADOM (Isr. first aid soc.) **11:**697
- health services **9:**984
- philanthropy **13:**390
Magen Gibborim (bk.) **6:**919
Magen Shalom synagogue (Karachi) **13:**14
- *illus:*
- - entrance **13:**15
Magerit (city, Sp.), *see* MADRID
Maggal (kib., Isr.) **1:**place list
MAGGID **11:**698
- Contents:
- - As Preacher **11:**698
- - In Kabbalah **11:**699
- Taitazak's influence **15:**712
- titles,**15:**1164
- *see also:* DARSHAN
MAGGID, DAVID **11:**701
Maggid, Pinehas **11:**702
Maggid Devarav le-Ya'akov **7:**1413
Maggidim (kab. conc.) **10:**545
Maggid Meisharim (period.) **5:**41; **13:**1036
Maggid Meisharim of Yampol, *see* JEHIEL MICHAEL OF ZLOCZOW
Maggid Mesharim (wk.) **5:**200 **10:**545
Maggid Mishneh (wk.) **5:**198; **16:**119
Maggid Mishneh (journ.) **1:**newsp. list
Maggid of Brody, *see* KLUGER, SOLOMON BEN JUDAH AARON
Maggid of Deretschin, *see* EZEKIEL FEIVEL BEN ZE'EV WOLF
Maggid of Dubno, *see* KRANZ, JACOB BEN WOLF
Maggid of Kamenets, *see* MACCOBY, HAYYIM ZUNDEL
Maggid of Kelme, *see* MOSES ISAAC (Darshan)
Maggid of Mezhirech, *see* DOV BAER OF MEZHIRECH
Maggid of Posvoler, *see* Posvoler Maggid
MAGGID-STEINSCHNEIDER, HILLEL NOAH **11:**702
Maggishei Minhah (bk.), *see Sefer ha-Maggid*
Maggot, *see* WORM
MAGHĀR, AL- (vill., Isr.) **11:**702
Magharriya, Al- (J. sect)
- angelology **2:**974
- Karaite literature **10:**762
- sects **14:**1088
Maghili, al- (Musl. prch.) **15:**1418
MAGHREBI-MA'ARAVI (N. Afr. Js.) **11:**702
- communal organization **5:**814
- community in Ereẓ Israel **9:**499ff
- goldsmiths **7:**740
- Judeo-Arabic, Judeo-Berber **10:**409
Maghrebim (N. Afr. cmty., Cairo) **5:**29
Maghribi, Al-Samaw'al, *see* SAMAU'AL BEN JUDAH IBN ABBAS
MAGIC **11:**703
- *Contents:*
- - In the Bible **11:**703
- - In the Apocrypha **11:**705
- - Talmudic Period **11:**706
- - Medieval Hebrew Literature **11:**707
- General
- - abomination **2:**97
- - anointing **3:**27
- - divination **6:**111
- - medicine **11:**1179
- - microcosm **11:**1502
- - papal bull **4:**1496
- - seals **14:**1074
- - sorcery **15:**163
- Angels
- - Angel of Death **2:**954
- - demons, demonology **5:**1521
- - Lilith **11:**246ff
- - Raziel **13:**1592
- Judaism
- - amulets **2:**906
- - *ba'al shem* **4:**6
- - biblical prohibition **7:**649
- - Falashas **6:**1152
- - Gentiles **12:**1189
- - Kabbalah **10:**493; **10:**500ff
- - Magen David **11:**687ff
- - Maimonides **11:**761
- - Moses **12:**393
- - Pentateuch **13:**249
- - plagues of Egypt **13:**605
- - practical Kabbalah **10:**632ff
- - prayer **13:**980
- - purity ritual **13:**1414
- - sages **14:**650
- - Yose ben Zimra **16:**857
- Literature
- - Hermetic literature **8:**372
- - *Sefer ha-Razim* **2:**965; **13:**159
- - *Sefer Yeẓirah* **16:**784ff
- - *Solomon, Testament of* **15:**118
- *illus:*
- - amulets **2:**907-914
- - execration text, Egyptian **8:**572
- - incantation bowls **2:**694; **5:**1522
- *see also:* ABRACADABRA; BLESSING AND CURSING; FOLKLORE; GOLEM
Magic Carpet, Operation (Yem. aliyah) **2:**263; **9:**501; **9:**534; **16:**751
- *illus:*
- - Aden and Yemen refugees **2:**264
- - arriving in Israel **16:**749
- - Yemenites on way to Israel **9:**529
MAGIDOV, JACOB **11:**716
Magidsohn, Joseph **15:**301; **15:**307
Magino, Gabriel **11:**496; **12:**815; **15:**1391
MAGINO, MEIR **11:**716
Magister Benjamin of Cambridge, *see* BENJAMIN OF CAMBRIDGE
Magister Judaeorum (offic., Fr.) **7:**10
Magister Leo Hebraeus, *see* LEVI BEN GERSHOM
Magister Mosseus, *see* MOSES BEN YOM-TOV
Magistrates' Courts (Isr.) **9:**632
Magna Carta (Eng.) **6:**748
- history chart **8:**766-767
Magna Graecia (clny., It.) **2:**704ff
Magnasco, Alessandro **5:**171
MAGNES, JUDAH LEON **11:**716
- archives **3:**387
- New York City **12:**1086
- Zionism **16:**1141
- *illus:*
- - Hadassah Hospital **16:**721
- - Schuster, Sir Arthur **14:**1012
Magnes, L. E. **4:**177
Magnesia (city, As. M.) **3:**1017; **11:**878
Magnes Press (Isr.) **8:**224; **13:**1379
Magnin (fam.) **5:**56
MAGNIN, EDGAR FOGEL **11:**718
- Los Angeles **11:**501
Magnin, I. **14:**834
Magnin, J. **14:**834
MAGNUS (fam., Eng.) **11:**719
Magnus, David **15:**312
MAGNUS, EDUARD (art., Ger.) **11:**719
Magnus, Edward (bnk., Swed.) **4:**177
Magnus, György **8:**45
MAGNUS, HEINRICH GUSTAV **11:**720
Magnus, Katie **11:**719
Magnus, Laurie **11:**719
Magnus, Lazarus Simon **5:**365
MAGNUS, MARCUS **11:**720
- Aaron Wolf **2:**12
Magnus, Meyer **11:**720
MAGNUS, PAUL WILHELM **11:**720
Magnus, Sir Philip (pub. fig., Eng.) **11:**719
Magnus, Sir Philip Montefiore (biog., Eng.) **11:**719
MAGNUS, RUDOLPH **11:**721
MAGNUS, SOLOMON WOLFF **10:**1510
Magnus-Allcroft, Sir Philip, *see* Magnus, Sir Philip Montefiore
Magrabi, Joseph, *see* JOSEPH IBN TABUL
Magrefah (Temple instr.) **12:**1453ff; **12:**566
Magribi, Samaw'al, *see* SAMAU'AL BEN JUDAH IBN ABBAS
Magriso, Isaac ben Moses **11:**1159
- *illus:*
- - *Me-Am Lo'ez* (1751) **5:**1154
Magrizo, Isaac **14:**1169
Magshimim (mosh., Isr.) **1:**place list
Magus, Simon, *see* Simon Magus
Magyar Israelita (journ.) **11:**1472
Magyar Izraeliták Országos Képviselete (orgn.) **8:**1106
Magyar Zsidó (period.) **10:**1250
Magyar Zsidók Pro Palestina Szóvetsége (assoc.) **13:**178
Magyar Zsidó Lexikon (enc.) **6:**735; **8:**1082
Magyar-zsidó oklevéltár (archiv.) **8:**563
MAGYAR ZSIDÓ SZEMLE (period.) **11:**721
- Blau, Ludwig Lajos **4:**1076
- Landesrabbinerschule **10:**1404
- Loewinger, David Samuel **11:**454
Magyar Zsinagóga (journ.) **13:**1035
MAHAL (volunteers, Isr.) **11:**722
Mahalakh Shevilei ha-Da'at (wk.) **16:**1359,1373,1386
Mahalalel (pseud.), *see* GOTTLOBER, ABRAHAM BAER
MAHALALEL BEN SHABBETAI HALLELYAH **11:**723
Mahalath (w., Esau) **6:**857
Mahalath (m., demons) **5:**1530; **11:**246; **11:**247
- identity **2:**374
Mahalla, see JEWISH QUARTER
MAHALLA AL-KUBRA (tn., Egy.) **11:**723
Mahallat al-Yahūd, see JEWISH QUARTER
Mahalliba (Cana. city), *see* AHLAB
Mahaloket, see CONFLICT OF OPINION
Mahalol (loc., Er. Isr.) **12:**768
Mahamad (Seph. cmty. council), *see* MA'AMAD
MAHANAIM (loc., Er. Isr.) **11:**724
- Solomon **15:**1317
MAHANAYIM (kib., Isr.) **11:**724
- statistics **1:**place list
- *illus:*
- - Israel-Syria negotiations **3:**481
Mahanayim (qtr., Jer.) **9:**1472
Mahanayim (journ.) **1:**newsp. list
Mahaneh Yehudah (stlmt., Er. Isr.) **9:**572
- Petah Tikvah **13:**338
Mahaneh Yehudah (qtr., Jer.) **9:**1459,1460,1515
- *illus:*
- - market **9:**1489
Mahaneh Yisrael (stlmt., Isr.) **1:**place list
- *illus:*
- - Malben institutions **11:**821
Mahaneh Yisrael (qtr., Jer.) **9:**1457
Mahaneh Yosef (qtr., Jaffa) **15:**919
Mahanot (journ.) **1:**newsp. list
Mahanot Olim (youth mvmt.), *see* Hugim
M-a-h-a-r-a-d-a-kh, *see* DAVID BEN HAYYIM OF CORFU
M-a-h-a-r-a-f (tos.), *see* PEREZ BEN ELIJAH OF CORBEIL
M-a-h-a-r-a-l Mi-Prag, *see* JUDAH LOEW BEN BEZALEL
M-a-h-a-r-a-m, *see* MEIR BEN BARUCH OF ROTHENBURG
M-a-h-a-r-a-m (r., Pol.), *see* LUBLIN, MEIR BEN GEDALIAH
M-a-h-a-r-a-m A-sh (Esh; 17/18 cent.), *see* EISENSTADT, MEIR
M-a-h-a-r-a-m E-sh (19th cent.), *see* EISENSTADTER, MEIR BEN JUDAH LEIB
M-a-h-a-r-a-m of Padua, *see* KATZENELLENBOGEN, MEIR BEN ISAAC
M-a-h-a-r-a-m Shick, *see* SHICK, MOSES BEN JOSEPH
M-a-h-a-r-a-m Schiff, *see* SCHIFF, MEIR BEN JACOB HA-KOHEN
M-a-h-a-r-a-n-a-h, *see* ELIJAH BEN HAYYIM
M-a-h-a-r-a-sh-d-a-m, *see* MEDINA, SAMUEL BEN MOSES DE
M-a-h-a-r-g-ah, *see* Gur Aryeh Ha-Levy
M-a-h-a-rh-a-sh, see HAYYIM (ben) SHABBETAI
M-a-h-a-r-h-a-t, *see* Toledano, Hayyim ben Moses ben Baruch
M-a-h-a-r-i-k (15th cent.), *see* COLON, JOSEPH BEN SOLOMON
M-a-h-a-r-i-k (16th cent.), *see* CORCOS, JOSEPH
M-a-h-a-r-i-k-a-s, *see* CASTRO, JACOB BEN ABRAHAM
M-a-h-a-r-i-l, *see* MOELLIN, JACOB BEN MOSES
M-a-h-a-r-i-ṣ, *see* ṢALIH, YAHYA BEN JOSEPH
M-a-h-a-r-i Se-ga-l, *see* MOELLIN, JACOB BEN MOSES
M-a-h-a-r-i-t, *see* TRANI, JOSEPH BEN MOSES
M-a-h-a-r-i-t, *see* Toledano, Jacob
M-a-h-a-r-i-v, *see* WANNEH, ISAAC BEN ABRAHAM
M-a-h-a-r-i-v-a-l, *see* LEV, JOSEPH BEN DAVID IBN
M-a-h-a-r-i-ẓ, *see* ṢĀLIH, YAHYA BEN JOSEPH
M-a-h-a-r-l-a-h, *see* HANNELES, JUDAH LEIB BEN MEIR
M-a-h-a-r-sh-a, *see* EDELS, SAMUEL ELIEZER BEN

JUDAH HA-LEVI
M-a-h-a-r-sh-a (Turk.), *see* ALFANDARI, SOLOMON ELIEZER BEN JACOB
M-a-h-a-r-sh-a-k (Gal.), *see* KLUGER, SOLOMON BEN JUDAH AARON
M-a-h-a-r-sh-a-kh (Gr.), *see* Cohen, Solomon
M-a-h-a-r-sh-a-l, *see* LURIA, SOLOMON BEN JEHIEL
M-a-h-a-r-sh-a-m, *see* SHVADRON, SHALOM MORDECAI BEN MOSES
M-a-h-a-r-s-h-a-t, *see* Toledano, Solomon ben Eliezer
Maḥaseyah (stlmt., Isr.) **1**:place list
Maḥazikei ha-Dat (period.) **7**:965
-statistics **1**:newsp. list
Maḥazor ha-Levanah (lunar cycle) **5**:43
Maḥazor Katan (lunar cycle) **5**:43
Maḥbarot (bk.) **11**:328
- Immanuel of Rome **8**:1295
- *illus:*
- - first page (1491) **8**:1297
- - Zodiac signs **16**:1192
Maḥbarot le-Marxizm (journ.) **1**:newsp. list
Maḥbarot le-Sifrut (journ.) **1**:newsp. list
Maḥbarot le-Sozyologyah (journ.) **1**:newsp. list
Maḥberet (rhymed prose) **11**:936
Maḥberet (wk.) **11**:1305; **16**:1356,1380
Maḥberet (journ.) **1**:newsp. list
Maḥberet Ben-Asher (bk.), *see Sefer Dikdukei ha-Te'amim*
Maḥberet ha-Tene (bk.) **2**:467
Maḥberet ha-Tijan (bk.) **16**:1474
Maḥberet he-Arukh (wk.) **16**:1358,1385
Mahdī, Al-(caliph) **9**:1426
Mahdī, ʿAbd al-Nabīʾ ibn, *see* ʿAbd al-Nabīʾ ibn Mahdī
Mahdiyya (loc., Tun.) **13**:1449; **15**:1434
MAHER SHALAL HASH BAZ (bib. fig.) **11**:724
- Isaiah **9**:44
- Zechariah **16**:953
Mahlah (bib. fig.) **2**:73; **16**:979
Mahlat (m., demons), *see* Mahalath
MAHLER, ARTHUR **11**:725
- politics **13**:809
Mahler, Baruch **5**:609
MAHLER, EDUARD **11**:725
MAHLER, GUSTAV **11**:726
- Bekker, Paul **4**:411
- stamps **15**:336
- Walter, Bruno **16**:258
- *illus:* text
- *mus. notations:* **12**:655
MAHLER, MARGARET **11**:727
Mahler, Menahem Eliezer **7**:6
MAHLER; RAPHAEL **11**:727
- historiography **8**:565
Mahler-Kalkstein, Menahem, *see* AVIDOM, MENAHEM
MAHLON AND CHILION (bib. figs.) **11**:728
- Ruth, Book of **14**:518ff
- *see also:* ORPAH
Mahlul law (Isr.) **9**:555
Mahmud II (sult., Turk.) **9**:294
- Gabbai Ezekiel **16**:1537
Mahmud IV (sult., Turk.), *see* Mehmed IV
Maḥmūdiyya (mt., Egy.), *see* BAAL-ZEPHON
MAH NISHTANNAH (Hag.) **11**:728
- children's recitation **5**:428
- *Haggadah* **7**:1080
- *illus:*
- - Prague Haggadah **11**:729
MAḤOZA (tn., Babyl.) **11**:729
- Julian the Apostate **4**:42
- Mar bar Rav Ashi **11**:940
- prison **8**:1300
- *table:* principal *Amoraim* **2**:869
Mahpakh (cantillation sign) **16**:1455
Mahr al-Qalb (loc., Assyr.) **16**:656
Mahri (lang.) **14**:1153
Mahrt, Haakon B. **14**:932
Mahseiah (bib. fig.) **14**:1179
MAH TOVU (bib., litur. pass.) **11**:730
MAḤZIKE HADAS (orgn., Gal.) **11**:730
- Orthodoxy **12**:1491
MAḤZOR (fest. prayer bk.) **11**:731
- *Contents:*
- - Maḥzorim, Illuminated **11**:731
- - Leipzig Maḥzor **11**:734
- - Worms Maḥzor **11**:735
- General
- - illuminated manuscripts **8**:1268; **11**:731
- - prayer books **13**:985
- Individual Compilations
- - Aleppo **7**:1339
- - Apam **11**:399
- - Aram-Ẓova **11**:402
- - Avignon **11**:401
- - *Bilti Noda* **11**:400
- - Carpentras **11**:401
- - Constantine **11**:400
- - *ke-fi Minhag Italiani* **11**:399
- - Leipzig (Lipsiae) **7**:1098; **8**:1261
- - *mi-kol ha-Shanah* **12**:1074
- - Rabbi Friedman of Ruzhin **11**:733
- - Roma **15**:142
- - Romania **4**:533; **11**:398
- - Rothschild **8**:1270
- - Sephardi **11**:400
- - *Siftei Renanot* **11**:400
- - Soncino-Casalmaggiore **11**:399
- - Tripartite **15**:110
- - Tripoli **11**:400ff
- *illus:*
- - text
- - Apam rite (18th cent.) **3**:175
- - Ashkenazi rite **11**:397
- - *Bak Maḥzor* (1680) **4**:114; **5**:753
- - Carpentras (1739) **11**:403
- - *Dresden Maḥzor* (14th cent.) **2**:251; **6**:690
- - Germany (13th cent.) **14**:1444
- - *Great Maḥzor of Amsterdam* **14**:1443
- - handwritten (1803) **5**:359
- - *Laud Maḥzor* **11**:*fcg.* 811
- - *Leipzig Maḥzor* (14th cent.) **2**:118; **4**:394; **5**:1441; **6**:386; **8**:1218; **11**:734; **12**:601,916,944
- - *Maḥzor Minhag Ashkenazi* **15**:1485
- - *Maḥzor Minhag Roma* (1485) **8**:1327; **15**:141,1483
- - *Maḥzor Pesaro* (1480) **5**:750; **11**:735
- - *Nuremberg Maḥzor* **11**:*fcg.* 747
- - *Rothschild Maḥzor* (15th cent.) **3**:*fcg.* 907; **8**:1284; **15**:99
- - *Schocken Italian Maḥzor* **14**:*fcg.* 11
- - silver binding (1726) **4**:1231
- - *Tripartite Maḥzor* (14th cent.) **2**:*fcg* 11, 355; **4**:1154; **11**:*fcg.* 683
- - *Worms Maḥzor* (13th cent.) **8**:1219; **11**:732,*fcg.* 619; **14**:1217, 1320; **16**:1191
Maḥzor de-Rav Amram (prayer bk.), *see Seder Rav Amram*
Maḥzor ha-Gadol (prayer bk. type) **13**:987
Maḥzor ha-Shanah (prayer bk. type) **13**:987
Maḥzor Pesaro (illum. ms.) **5**:750
MAḤZOR VITRY (prayer bk.) **11**:736
- Avelei Zion **3**:946
- cantillation signs **16**:1417
- Jewish literature **11**:331
- prayer books **13**:986ff
- Samuel ben Meir **14**:812
- Shemaiah of Troyes **14**:1375
- Simḥah ben Samuel **16**:195
Mai, Johann Heinrich (jun.) **8**:45
Maiblum, Dr. **16**:1218
Maidanek (concen. camp), *see* MAJDANEK
Maida Vale (dist., Lond.) **6**:762
Maiden, *see* VIRGIN, VIRGINITY
MAIER, JOSEPH (U.S. sociol.) **11**:738
Maier, Joseph (r., Ger.) **15**:462
Maierzuk, Hanna, *see* MERON, HANNA
MAILER, NORMAN **11**:738
- U.S. literature **15**:1577
Maillol, Aristide **10**:1135
Maimana (city, Afg.) **2**:327
Maimaran, Abraham **3**:812; **13**:816
Maimaran, David **5**:627
MAIMI, SIMON **11**:739
- Arraby Moor **3**:498
- Lisbon **11**:300
Maimin, Abraham **13**:577; **10**:549
Maiming by order of court **4**:1092; **5**:620; **8**:1366; **13**:1389
Maimon (fam., Lith.) **13**:1399
MAIMON, ADA **11**:739
Maimon, Bonet (of Perpignan) **13**:300
Maimon, Jacob **2**:746
MAIMON, JUDAH LEIB **11**:739
- religious life in Ereẓ Israel **9**:892
- *illus:*
- - Jewish Agency Executive **10**:28
- - Mizrachi conference **16**:1099
- - proclamation of the State of Israel **4**:513
MAIMON, SOLOMON (philos.) **11**:741
- autobiography **4**:1013; **8**:182
- chronological chart **8**:766-767
- Ibn Ezra **15**:520
- Kant critique **13**:418
- *illus:* text
Maimon, Solomon (r., U.S.) **14**:1083
MAIMON BEN JOSEPH **11**:744
- *aliyah* **9**:511
- Ibn Migash, Joseph **8**:1189
- Maimonides **11**:754ff
- Maimuna festivity **11**:781
- meditation on exile **7**:286ff
Maimon ben Nono **15**:1438
Maimon the Black (demon) **5**:1531
- Lilith **11**:249
MAIMONIDEAN CONTROVERSY **11**:745
- *Contents:*
- - First Clash **11**:745
- - First Stage in Europe **11**:747
- - Renewed Outbreak **11**:751
- - Aftermath of Controversy **11**:753
- Abraham Maimuni **2**:151
- Abulafia, Meir **2**:192
- Aix-en-Provence Jews **2**:476
- Astruc, Abba Mari **3**:807
- Daniel ben Saadiah ha-Bavli **5**:1294
- Falaquera, Shem Tov **6**:1141
- French rabbis' views **14**:777
- Hillel ben Samuel **8**:488
- history chart **8**:766-767
- Jewish philosophy **13**:443ff
- Jonah ben Abraham Gerondi **10**:179
- Jonathan ha-Kohen of Lunel **10**:186ff
- kabbalists' position **10**:527
- Naḥmanides **12**:774ff
- Solomon of Montpellier, **15**:121
- Spain **15**:229; **15**:233
- Toledo **15**:1203
- *see also:* MAIMONIDES *(Guide of the Perplexed; Mishneh Torah)*
MAIMONIDES, MOSES **11**:754
- *Contents:*
- - Biography **11**:754
- - Influence **11**:760
- - As Halakhist **11**:764
- - Philosophy **11**:768
- - As Physician **11**:777
- - Astronomy **11**:779
- - Translations **11**:780
- General
- - descendants **11**:837
- - economic history **16**:1292
- - geonic hierarchy **8**:678
- - hero of folktales **6**:1382
- - history chart **8**:766-767
- - Inquisition **15**:769
- - Saadiah Gaon **14**:549; **14**:554
- - Samuel ben Ali **14**:803
- - stamps **15**:335
- - Tiberias tomb **15**:1133
- *Mishneh Torah* **11**:766ff
- - General
- - - Bashuysen translation **4**:296
- - - burning of **4**:215
- - - codification of law **5**:639; **11**:330
- - - economics **16**:1292
- - - illuminated manuscripts **8**:1265ff
- - - Jerusalem in art **9**:1580
- - - Jewish literature **11**:336
- - - *Midrash ha-Gadol* **11**:1515
- - - *Sefer Mitzvot Gadol* **12**:419
- - - subjects **12**:132; **12**:136
- - - Tanḥum's lexicon **15**:797
- - - "Yad" **16**:693
- - Commentators and Critics
- - - Abraham ben David of Posquieres **2**:139; **5**:641,651 Abulafia, Meir **2**:192
- - - ʿAdanī, David **2**:250
- - - ʿAdanī, Saadiah **2**:250
- - - Adret, Moses ibn **2**:305
- - - Albotini *(Yesod Mishneh Torah)* **2**:538
- - - Algazi *(Sha'ar Yehudah)* **2**:608
- - - Ardit *(Marpeh Lashon)* **3**:400
- - - Ascandarani, Joseph,**9**:75
- - - Berab, Jacob **4**:584
- - - Bordjel *(Migdanot Natan)* **4**:1247
- - - Boton, Abraham de *(Lehem Mishneh)* **5**:642
- - - Caro *(Kesef Mishneh)* **5**:196*ff*,642
- - - Casès *(Ḥelko shel Binyamin)* **5**:228
- - - David ibn Abi Zimra *(Yekar Tiferet)* **5**:642,1358
- - - *Haggahot Maimoniyyot* **5**:642; **7**:1110
- - - Ibn Gaon *(Migdal Oz)* **5**:642; **8**:1175
- - - Landau *(Yad ha-Melekh)* **10**:1387
- - - Manoah of Narbonne **11**:892
- - - Rakaḥ, Masud Ḥai **13**:1527
- - - Rosanes *(Mishneh le-Melekh)* **5**:642; **14**:262
- - - Samson of Sens **14**:777
- - - Vidal, Yom Tov *(Maggid Mishneh)* **5**:642; **16**:119
- *Guide of the Perplexed* **11**:757*ff*,768*ff*
- - General
- - - Copenhagen manuscript **8**:1261ff
- - - denounced and burned **15**:769
- - - illuminated mss **8**:1266
- - - Islam, allusions to **3**:194

- - - Jewish literature **11:**339
- - - kabbalistic interpretation **10:**538
- - - Toledo *herem* **15:**1203
- - Commentators and Critics
- - - Abrabanel, Isaac **2:**105*ff*,107*ff*
- - - Abulafia, Abraham **2:**185; **10:**529
- - - Abulafia, Joseph **2:**189*ff*
- - - Albo, Joseph **2:**535
- - - Alexander of Hales **2:**583
- - - Alḥarizi, Judah **5:**1078
- - - Ashkenazi, Joseph **3:**727
- - - Crescas, Asher **5:**1078
- - - Crescas, Ḥasdai **5:**1081ff
- - - Emden, Jacob **6:**724
- - - Ergas, Joseph **6:**841
- - - Ibn Shem Tov, Shem Tov **8:**1199; **13:**450
- - - Judah Loew of Prague **10:**376
- - - Kaspi, Joseph ibn **10:**809
- - - Luzzatto, Samuel David **11:**605
- - - Moses ben Joshua of Narbonne **12:**423
- - - Samuel abu Rabīʿa ha-Kohen **14:**805
- - - Shalom, Abraham **14:**1270
- - - Tabrizi, Mahomet **15:**694
- - - YomTov Ishbili **16:**847
- *Halakhah* **11:**764
- - calendar reckoning **5:**47
- - chess **5:**402
- - codification of law **5:**630ff
- - Commandments, the 613 **5:**783f
- - Fast of Esther **6:**914
- - Gentiles **7:**413
- - Islam, codification of law of **9:**103
- - Jerusalem Talmud **15:**773
- - Karaites **15:**736
- - New Christians' status **12:**1022
- - responsa **14:**86
- - Samaritans **14:**741
- - Sanhedrin **4:**583
- - *takkanot* **15:**715
- - Talmud **15:**765
- - talmudic *halakhah* **7:**1163ff
- - Torah study **15:**456
- - *ye'ush* **16:**774ff
- Philosophy and Theology **11:**768
- - anthropomorphism **3:**56
- - apologetics **11:**354
- - articles of faith **3:**654ff
- - atomism **3:**830
- - beatitude **4:**361ff
- - belief **4:**434ff
- - categories **5:**254
- - Christian thought influenced by **13:**451
- - commandments, reasons for **5:**787ff
- - creation **5:**1067ff
- - death **11:**236
- - dualism **6:**245
- - election of Jewish people **8:**684ff; **10:**392
- - eternity of the universe **6:**1001
- - ethics **6:**940f
- - evil, problem of **7:**777ff
- - exile, meaning of **7:**286ff
- - form and matter **6:**1439
- - free will **7:**128
- - God, attributes of **7:**666; **10:**392
- - God, existence of **7:**658ff
- - God as "first cause" **5:**259; **5:**260
- - holiness **10:**873
- - imagination **8:**1290
- - *imitatio dei* **8:**1292
- - *Kalām* **10:**703
- - logic **11:**459ff
- - Mendelssohn's philosophy and **11:**1336
- - messiah, views on **11:**1414,1419*ff*
- - metaphysics and love of God **4:**436
- - microcosm doctrine **11:**1503
- - miracles **12:**77
- - monotheism **12:**262; **12:**263
- - nature **12:**889
- - Neoplatonism **12:**961ff
- - philosophical exegesis **4:**897
- - philosophy **11:**339; **13:**440ff
- - prayer **13:**982
- - prophecy **13:**1178
- - providence **7:**660; **13:**1285
- - rationalism **4:**436
- - redemption **14:**5
- - repentance **14:**76
- - resurrection **2:**338; **12:**1357; **14:**101
- - revelation **14:**123
- - reward and punishment **14:**137
- - righteousness **14:**182
- - *Ru'aḥ ha-Kodesh* **14:**367
- - *Shekhinah* **14:**1352
- - soul **15:**173
- - soul, immortality of **15:**178
- - space and place **15:**218
- - Spinoza and **15:**280
- - substance and accident **15:**474
- - suffering **15:**485
- - theology **15:**1106
- - throne of God **15:**1125ff
- - time **15:**1142
- - Torah **15:**1237; **15:**1240,1244
- - truth **15:**1414
- - *Yigdal* hymn **16:**835
- Views and Attitudes
- - Adam **2:**239
- - *Akedah* **2:**483
- - amulets **2:**911
- - angels **2:**972f
- - *apikoros*, definition **3:**177
- - art **3:**521
- - astrology **3:**792ff
- - astronomy **3:**803
- - charity **5:**343
- - conduct of scholars **5:**1551
- - divination **6:**117
- - hunting **8:**1112
- - Job **10:**121
- - *karet* **10:**789
- - love **11:**527ff
- - magic **11:**714
- - *mikveh* **11:**1434*ff*
- - Moses **12:**399
- - peace **13:**198
- - piety **13:**505
- - proselytes **13:**1183ff; **13:**1188
- - rabbinate **13:**1449
- - rabbinical tradition **15:**1310
- - righteous Gentiles **7:**1383
- - Sabbath **14:**565
- - sacrifice **14:**613
- - *sha'atnez* **14:**1214
- - *sheḥitah* **14:**1339
- - *tagin* **15:**700
- - taxation **15:**856
- - Temple Mount **15:**990
- - woman **16:**627
- Medicine **11:**1188; **11:**777
- - Galen **13:**628
- - Meyerhof, Max **11:**1467
- - psychiatry **13:**1337
- - psychology **13:**1342ff
- Kabbalah **10:**520; **10:**538
- - as kabbalist **12:**500
- - emanation **6:**695
- - Kabbalah on messianic era **6:**882
- - *ma'aseh bereshit* **13:**424
- - *Shi'ur Komah* **10:**502; **14:**1418
- - Zohar **10:**609; **16:**1202
- Literature and studies
- - "alchemic writings" **2:**548
- - Baneth's studies **4:**161
- - correspondence **11:**59
- - *hakdamot* **7:**1145ff
- - ethical literature **6:**927; **11:**344
- - Goldberg, Oscar on **7:**705
- - Hebrew language **16:**1632
- - Hebrew mss. **11:**904*ff*
- - Jewish literature **11:**329
- - Judeo-Arabic literature **10:**416
- - Munk's studies **12:**526
- - Pococke's translation **13:**666
- - *Sefer ha-Mitzvot* **5:**783; **12:**781
- - Tibbon family **15:**1130ff
- - translation of works **15:**1320; **15:**1324
- Places
- - Córdoba **5:**965
- - Spain **15:**242
- - Toledo **15:**1203
- - Tunisia **15:**1437ff
- - Yemen and **16:**742
- Influences
- - Aaron ben Elijah **2:**11
- - Albertus Magnus **2:**532
- - Alconstantini, Enoch **2:**550
- - Alexander of Aphrodisias **2:**581
- - Al-Farabi **6:**1176
- - Al-Ghazali **7:**539
- - Aquinas **3:**230
- - Aristotle **3:**445ff
- - Avempace **3:**947
- - Averroes **3:**950ff
- - Avicenna **3:**957; **3:**958ff
- - Ben-Asher, Aaron **4:**466
- - Cusa, Nicholas of **5:**1173
- - Dioscorides **7:**894
- - Duns Scotus **6:**274
- - Eckhart **6:**357
- - Gibbor, Judah ben Elijah **7:**549
- - Ḥefeẓ ben Yaẓli'aḥ **8:**242
- - Ibn Biklarish, Junas **8:**1158
- - Ibn Migash **8:**465ff
- - Shim'on, Joseph ibn **14:**1403
- - William of Auvergne **16:**517
- *illus:*
- - autograph **3:**916
- - Commandments, the 613 (list) **5:**763-782
- - Cordoba
- - - Plazuela de Maimonides **5:**965
- - - Rambam Synagogue **5:**964
- - *Guide to the Perplexed*
- - - Levi ben Isaac Hijo Caro's ms. **8:***fcg.* 1143
- - - title page (Warsaw, 1872) **11:**763
- - Knesset menorah **8:**683
- - *Millot ha-Higgayon* (1865) **5:**860
- - Mishnah, commentary (1942) **8:**1328
- - *Mishneh Torah*
- - - *Frankfort Mishneh Torah* (15th cent.) **3:** *fcg.* 988
- - - incunabulum (1475) **8:**1328
- - - *Jerusalem Mishneh Torah* (c. 1400) **3:**455; **8:***fcg.* 1015
- - - *Kaufmann Mishneh Torah* (13th cent.) **2:**242; **5:**630; **7:** *fcg.* 747; **8:**1280
- - - manuscripts **11:**761,762
- - - Shelomo 'n Alzuk's ms. **8:***fcg* 1207
- - - Spanish-Italian illuminated manuscript (14th cent.) **4:**357
- - portrait **14:**1476
- - Temple plans **15:**970
- *see also:* MAIMONIDEAN CONTROVERSY

Maimonides, Abraham ben Moses *see* ABRAHAM BEN MOSES BEN MAIMON

Maimonides College (U.S.), *see* JEWISH THEOLOGICAL SEMINARY OF AMERICA

Maimonides Hospital (U.S.) **8:**1039

Maimonides Jewish Day School (Can.) **6:**453ff

Maimonides Library Association (N.Y.) **12:**1073

Maimon of Montpellier **3:**800

Maimora (fam.), *see* MAYMERAN

MAIMUNA (Mor. fest.) **11:**781
- carnival **7:**308
- music **16:**1259
- *illus:* text

Maʿīn (vill., Transj.) **4:**5

MAINE (U.S.) **11:**782

"Main Gate of Kaunas Ghetto" (drg., E. Lurie) **10:**849

MAINTENANCE (leg. term) **11:**783
- *Contents:*
- - Scope of Maintenance Obligation **11:**784
- - Separated Parties **11:**785
- - Claim for Maintenance Cannot be Assigned or Set Off **11:**787
- - Arrear Maintenance **11:**787
- - Nonpayment of Maintenance: Consequences **11:**787
- - In the State of Israel **11:**788
- betrothal **11:**1048; **11:**1050
- children (early *halakhah*) **8:**1424
- civil marriage **5:**598
- concubine **5:**865
- conflict of laws **5:**883
- cosmetics **5:**980
- debtor's obligations to wife **6:**1011; **6:**1015
- deceased brother's wife **11:**124ff
- divorce **6:**128ff
- imprisonment in State of Israel **8:**1309
- inheritance **15:**478ff
- intermarriage **12:**168
- *ketubbah* **10:**929
- lien liability **11:**229
- parent and child **12:**111; **13:**95ff
- prohibited marriage **11:**1054ff
- *takkanot*, 1944 **12:**143
- time limitation **11:**252
- widow **16:**493
- *see also:* DOWRY; HUSBAND AND WIFE

MAINZ (city, Ger.) **11:**788
- *Contents:*
- - Medieval Settlements **11:**788
- - Community in Middle Ages **11:**789
- - Resettlement and Modern Community **11:**791
- - Holocaust and Contemporary Periods **11:**791
- archives **3:**387
- banking **4:**168
- Crusades **5:**1135*ff*
- gaonate **7:**324
- history chart (1012,1473) **8:**766-767
- informers **8:**1367
- museum **12:**538
- Rudolf I of Habsburg **14:**380
- synod **15:**633ff
- trade routes **15:**1297ff
- Worms **16:**644ff
- *illus:*
- - text
- - Hebrew epitaph (11th cent.) **2:**725
- - Jewish museum **12:**541
- - Kalonymos family, remains of house **7:**459
- - Meshullam ben Kalonymus tombstone **10:**719
- - *Schutzjuden* list **14:**1014
- *see also:* SHUM

MAIORESCU, GEORGE TOMA **14:**423; **14:**426

MAIROVICH, ZVI **3:**605
- *illus:*
- - "Desert-Summer Vision" (paint.) Pl. 11 3-ART

MAISEL, ELIJAH ḤAYYIM **11:**792

MAISELS, ISRAEL AARON **11:**792

Maisels, Jeffery **15:**315

MAISELS, MOSES ḤAYYIM (Misha) **11**:793
- *illus:*
- - Hebrew Pen Club **8**:211; **12**:1109
- - Hebrew writers' convention, 1943 **8**:213
Maisel-Shoḥat, Hannah **10**:1033; **12**:769
Maisler, Benjamin, *see* MAZAR, BENJAMIN
Maistre Petit, *see* KIMḤI, DAVID; KIMḤI, JOSEPH
Maitland (tn., Austr.) **3**:878
MAIUMAS (anc. feast) **11**:793
MAIUMAS (locs., Er. Isr.) **11**:793
- Gaza harbor **7**:341
Majali (polit., Jord.) **14**:1624
Majdal (anc. city, Er. Isr.), *see* MAGDALA
Majdal (tn., Isr.) **3**:717; **9**:285
- *illus:*
- - Egyptian plane downed **16**:328
MAJDAL AL-SHAMS (vill., Golan) **11**:793
MAJD AL-KURŪM (vill., Isr.) **11**:794
Majdal Yābā (site, Er. Isr.) **6**:344
MAJDANEK (concen. camp, Pol.) **11**:794
- gassing **16**:1332
Majdanek Tatarski (ghetto, Pol.) **13**:765
Majjani (fam.) **10**:698; **15**:1435
Majolica (pottery)
- Azulai family **3**:1016
- Cohen family **5**:661
- *Seder* plates **13**:172
- *illus:*
- - Sabbath plate **3**:1016
- - *Seder* plates **3**:531; **5**:661
- - *see also:* POTTERY
MAJOR, ERVIN **12**:699
Major, József **8**:45
MAJOR, JULIUS (Gyula, Jacob) **12**:699
MAJORCA (Balearic Isl.) **11**:795
- *Contents:*
- - Beginning of Aragonese Rule **11**:795
- - From Alphonso III (1285-95) Until Pedro IV (1343) **11**:797
- - - Organization and Administration of Community **11**:799
- - From Pedro IV (1343-87) Until the End of the Jewish Settlement **11**:800
- - 1391 Persecutions **11**:801
- - Fate of Conversos **11**:802
- history chart **8**:766-767
- illuminated mss. **8**:1264
- Inquisition **8**:1388ff
- *limpieza de sangre* **11**:255
- nautical instruments **14**:1413
- Perpignan **13**:299
- refugees in Algeria **4**:1274
- slave trade **14**:1661
- Spain **15**:231; **15**:235; **15**:237
- *takkanot* **15**:735
- *see also:* CHUETAS
Majorca (tn., Austr.) **11**:1285
MAJORITY RULE (leg. conc.) **11**:804
- Akiva **2**:490
- arbitration courts **3**:299
- basis **7**:1522
- election to public post **13**:1356
- *niddui* **8**:352
- practice and procedure **13**:961
- rabbinical authority **3**:908
- source **14**:1197
- status in *halakhah* **7**:1158
- *takkanot ha-kahal* **15**:730
Majrovitz, Meir Jehuda **5**:1465
Majtek, Michael **6**:334
Majzels, Ẓevi Aryeh Judah **10**:1433
MAKAI, EMIL **11**:806
Makai, Gergely **8**:45
MAKAROV (tn., Ukr.) **11**:807
Makeda (Q. of Sheba) **13**:1424
Makhachkala (tn., Rus.) **12**:480
Makhir, Moses ibn, *see* ibn Makhir, Moses
Makhir ben Abba Mari **16**:706
Makhno, Nestor **8**:735
- pogroms **13**:700
- socialism **15**:34
Makhon le-Hokhmat Yisrael, *see* Makhon le-Madda'ei ha-Yahadut
Makhon Le-Madda'ei ha-Yahadut (r. seminary) **13**:1465; **16**:341
MAKHSHIRIN (tract., Mish.) **11**:807
- *illus:* text
Makhtesh (bib. qtr., Jer.) **10**:289
Makhtesh ha-Gadol (Er. Isr.), *see* Ha-Makhtesh ha-Gadol
Makhtesh ha-Katan (Er. Isr.), *see* Ha-Makhtesh ha-Katan
Makhtesh Ramon (reg., Er. Isr.), *see* Ramon
Maki (Isr. Commun. Party) **5**:807
- Arab community **9**:1030
- historical survey **9**:398
- Israel politics **9**:677
Makkabbi (journs.), *see* *Ha-Makkabbi*
Makkabbi ha-Ẓa'ir (youth mvmt., Ger.) **7**:493
Makkabea (orgn., Hung.) **16**:1121
"Makkabi" Operation (War of Indep.) **10**:1054; **12**:441; **16**:314
Makkabit (protected city, Er. Isr.), **12**:207
MAKKEDAH (Cana. city) **11**:808
- Maqueda **11**:938
- proscription by Israel **8**:345
MAKKOT (tract.) **11**:808
- *Sanhedrin* **14**:839
- *illus:* text
Maklakov, Vassily **4**:400
MAKLEFF (fam.) **11**:810
Makleff, Aryeh Leib **11**:810
Makleff, Avraham **11**:810
Makleff, Batyah Ḥayyah **11**:810
Makleff, Minnah **11**:810
Makleff, Mordechai **11**:810
- *illus:*
- - Israel-Syria General Armistice Agreement, 1949 **3**:482
- - Israel-Syria negotiations, 1949 **3**:481
Makleff, Rivkah **11**:810
Makmish (loc., Er. Isr.) **16**:668
MAKO (tn., Hung.) **11**:811
Makom ("place"; philos. term), *see* SPACE AND PLACE
Makom (cultic installation) **5**:1167
Makor, ha- (wk.), *see Sefer ha-Makor*
Makor Library (Isr.) **16**:653
Makov (tn., Pol.), *see* MAKOW MAZOWIECKI
Makower, Hermann **10**:1496
MAKOW MAZOWIECKI (tn., Pol.) **11**:811
Makre me-Dardekei (wk.) **16**:1383
- Trabot, Perez **15**:1292
Makrokheir (Pers. k.), *see* ARTAXERXES I
Maktū (Isl. form of payment) **10**:938
Malaatha (city, Er. Isr.) **12**:225
Malabaila, Damiano, *see* LEVI, PRIMO
Malabar (dist., Ind.) **5**:624; **8**:1350ff
- Benjamin of Tudela **11**:350
- Jews **13**:272
Malabari (lang., Cochin), *see* Malayalam
MALACH, LEIB **11**:812
Malachi, A. R. **8**:211,213
MALACHI, BOOK OF **11**:812
- eschatology **6**:869ff
- Minor Prophets **12**:48
- Mordecai **12**:309
- Temple cult **15**:958
MALACHI, ELIEZER RAPHAEL **11**:816
MALACHI BEN JACOB HA-KOHEN **11**:817
- Ergas, Joseph ben Emanuel **6**:841
- Pinheiro, Moses **13**:537
- talmudic methodology **11**:338
Malachite (gem) **13**:1009
MALACHY, YONA **1**:33
Malack, Leib **15**:1073
MÁLAGA (city, Sp.) **11**:817
- *illus:*
- - Solomon ibn Gabirol (statue) **7**:244
MALAKH, ḤAYYIM BEN SOLOMON **11**:818
- Jerusalem group **9**:1438
- Joshua Heshel Ẓoref **16**:1223
- Shabbateanism **14**:1247
Malakh ha-Mavet, *see* ANGEL OF DEATH
Malakhi, Abraham **5**:207
Malakhovka (tn., Rus.) **3**:157; **12**:366ff; **14**:488
- synagogue **15**:589
Malaki, Solomon al-, *see* Al-Malaki
Malamina, Caesar **8**:45
MALAMUD, BERNARD **11**:819
- literature **12**:1121; **15**:1576
- *illus:*
- - *The Angel Levine* **12**:464
Malan, Daniel François **15**:190ff
Malaparte, Curzio **9**:1107
Malaria (disease) **9**:844-845
Malaria Research Station (Isr.) **9**:991
Malashkin, Sergey **14**:511
Malatha (city, Er. Isr.) **12**:225
Malavsky (fam.) **7**:1549
MALAVSKY, SAMUEL **7**:1549
Malawi (state, Afr.) **9**:440; **9**:992
Malayalam (lang.) **5**:626; **9**:505
MALAYSIA (state) **11**:820
MALBEN (orgn.) **11**:821
- Beckelman, Moses W. **4**:367
- health services **9**:984
- J.D.C. **2**:831
- Jordan, Charles Harold **10**:198
MALBIM, MEIR LOEB BEN JEHIEL MICHAEL **11**:821
- Bible exegesis **4**:901
- Bucharest **4**:1439
- chronological chart **8**:766-767
- Mogilev **12**:215
Malbush (kab. conc.) **10**:591
MALCA (fam.) **11**:824
Malca, Jacob ben Joseph ben **11**:824
Malca, Judah ibn, *see* MALKAH, JUDAH BEN NISSIM IBN
Malca, Khalifa ben **11**:824,1343
Malca, Nissim ibn **11**:824
Malcam (deity) **8**:349
- *see also:* Milcom; Molech
Malchi, Esperanza **11**:61
Malchijah (bib. fig.) **4**:717
- Rechabites **13**:1611
Malchijah (Temple crftn.) **15**:956
Malchijah (pr. clan) **12**:89
Malchin (tn., Ger.) **11**:1163
Malchus I (Nabatean k.) **12**:742
Malcolm, Sir Neill **14**:33
Malden (city, Mass.) **4**:1265; **11**:1112
Maldive Islands (Ind. O.) **9**:444
Maldonado, Juan de **8**:45
MALDONADO DE SILVA, FRANCISCO **11**:825
- Lima Inquisition **3**:409
- Treviño de Sobremonte **15**:1380
Maleakh, Ḥayyim **9**:513
Male' and *Ḥaser* (masor.) **16**:1421
Malediction, *see* BLESSING AND CURSING
Maleh, Jacques **6**:502
Maleha, Don Çag de la, *see* Ibn Zadok, Isaac
MALESHERBES, CHRETIEN GUILLAUME DE LA-MOIGNON DE **11**:825
Malḥa (sub., Jer.) **9**:1496
- *illus:* **9**:581
Malḥa, Lake (Isr.) **8**:1064
Malḥata (loc., Er. Isr.) **3**:249
Malherbe, Daniel François **14**:784
Mali (rep., Afr.) **9**:440
Mali, Malasha **16**:825
Mali, Nahum **5**:485
Malichus **2**:584; **8**:1146
Malik (Isl. angel) **6**:885
Malik, al-Adil I, al-, *see* Adil I, al-Malik al-
Malik al-Ashraf Barsbay, al, *see* Ashraf Barsbay, al-Malik al-
Malik al-Ashraf Khalīl, al, *see* Ashraf Khalīl, al-Malik al-
Malik al-Mu'ayyad Shaikh, al-, *see* Mu'ayyad Shaikh, al-Malik al-
MALIK AL-RAMLĪ **11**:826
- Karaite sect **10**:766
Mālik ibn Anas **7**:1051
Malikites (J. sect), *see* Ramlites
Malik Shāh the Seljuk **3**:998
Malin, I. **15**:1575
Malina, Judith **12**:1121
- literature **15**:1578
MALINES (tn., concen. camp) **11**:826
- Belgium **4**:416
- camp **3**:168; **4**:1423
MALINOVSKI, JOSEPH BEN MORDECAI **11**:827
- Troki, Isaac **15**:1403
Malinovski, Zephaniah **10**:772
Malitsch, Jacob of, *see* Jacob of Malitsch
MALKAH, JUDAH BEN NISSIM IBN **11**:827
- family **11**:824
- Kabbalah **10**:537
Malkele the Triskerin **16**:628
Malkha (gaon) **7**:318
Malkha bar Aḥa (gaon) **7**:318
MALKHI, EZRA BEN RAPHAEL MORDECAI **11**:828
- emissaries **14**:1367
- Greece **7**:876
- Malkhi, Moses **11**:828
- messianism **9**:509
- Moses ibn Adret **2**:305
MALKHI, MOSES **11**:828
- Newport **12**:1043
MALKHI, MOSES BEN RAPHAEL MORDECAI **11**:828
- Malkhi, Ezra **11**:828
- *aliyah* **9**:292
Malkhut (kab. conc.) **10**:570ff
- Oral Law **15**:1237
- *Shekhinah* **14**:1353
MALKHUYYOT (litur.) **11**:829
- *Aleinu* prayer **2**:555
- Rosh ha-Shanah **14**:307
- *see also:* TEKI'ATA; ZIKHRONOT
Malki, Ezra, *see* MALKHI, EZRA BEN RAPHAEL MORDECAI
Malkī, Sa'd Litto **12**:1464
MALKIEL, YAKOV **11**:829
Malkiel ben Meir **13**:589
Malkiyyah (kib., Isr.) **1**: place list
Mall, Sebastian **8**:45
Mallard (bird) **6**:30
MALLER, JULIUS BERNARD **11**:829
Mallorca, *see* MAJORCA
Mallove, Harvey **12**:1035

MALLOW (bot.) **11**:830
- *illus:* text
Mallūl, Nissim **12**:1464
- Farḥi, Hillel **6**:1183
MALMÖ (city, Swed.) **11**:831
Malot, Charles **8**:560
Małpolska (reg. Pol.), *see* LESSER POLAND
Malraux, Andre **15**:262
Malshinim, see INFORMERS
Malsin, Albert **8**:497
MALTA **11**:831
- catacombs **5**:251
- Inquisition **8**:1397
- Maltese **14**:1152
- synagogues **1**:syn. list
- *illus:* text
MALTER, HENRY **11**:832
- American Academy for Jewish Research **2**:818
- Cairo *genizah* **16**:1336
- Steinschneider **15**:374
Maltese (lang.) **14**:1152
Malthace (w., Herod) **3**:75, 333; **8**:381
Malti, Aaron ben Moses **13**:575
Maltinski, Ḥayyim **4**:1048
MALTZ, ALBERT **11**:833
Maltzan, Heinrich von **2**:262
Maluenda (fam.) **15**:1300
Maʿlūl (vill., Isr.) **12**:768
Maʿlūla dialects **12**:948
MALVANO, GIACOMO **11**:833
Maly Przeglad (mag.) **5**:457; **12**:844
Maly Trostinec (loc., concen. camp) **8**:871; **12**:55
Malzan, Isaac **13**:988
MALZBERG, BENJAMIN **11**:833
- mental illness **11**:1373ff
Maman (fam.) **12**:337
- Meknes **11**:1272
Mamaroneck (tn., N.Y.) **12**:1127; **16**:464
Mamelok, A. **16**:1348
Mamelukes (Musl. sults.), *see* MAMLUKS
Mamillah Pool (Jer.) **9**:1539; **9**:1541
Mamistabolob, Abraham **7**:428
Mamlakat al-Karak (prov., Transj.) **15**:1318
Mamlakat Dimashq (prov., Transj.) **15**:1318
MAMLUKS (Muslim sults.) **11**:834
- Crusader kingdom **9**:271
- dynasty **3**:998
- Egyptian Jews **6**:494
- Ereẓ Israel **9**:121; **9**:274
- Hebron **8**:229
- Jerusalem **9**:1423ff
- Ottomans **16**:1534
- Samaritans **14**:733; **14**:737
- Syrian Jews **15**:641
- Transjordan **15**:1318
- *illus:*
- - Antipatris fort **3**:78
- - Gaza, Caravanserai **9**:275
- - Ibrahim Tushtumur Mausolem, Jer. **9**:1424
- - land of Israel under the Mamluks (map) **9**:277
- - Lydda bridge **9**:280; **11**:619
- - Ramleh tower **3**:330
Mammals **3**:8; **6**:31
Mammoth (zool.) **4**:394
MAMPSIS (city, Er. Isr.) **11**:837
- Negev **12**:929
MAMRAM (promissory note) **11**:838
- assignment of debt **3**:770
- moneylending **12**:255
- Polish Jews **13**:729
Mamre (bib. fig.), *see* ANER, ESHKOL, AND MAMRE
MAMRE (loc., Er. Isr.) **11**:839
- burial place **13**:184
- Butnah **4**:1538
- Genesis, Book of **7**:390
- *illus:* text
- *see also:* HEBRON
Mamroth, L. **16**:1347
Mamsa (tn., Mor.) **2**:261
Mamshit (site, Er. Isr.), *see* MAMPSIS
Ma'mūn, al- (caliph) **2**:42
- Iraq **8**:1445
- Jerusalem **9**:1426
- Samaritans **14**: 732
Ma'mūn, al- (caliph, Sp.) **2**:663
MAMZER (personal status) **11**:840
- *Contents:*
- - Definition **11**:840
- - Consequences of the State of Mamzerut **11**:840
- - Asufi ("a Foundling") **11**:841
- - Shetuki ("Undisclosed") **11**:841
- - Karaites **11**:841
- abortion **2**:101
- *Agunah* and marriage **2**:430
- artificial insemination **3**:660
- Commandments, the 613 **5**:781
- Daniel Ḥayyata on **5**:1295
- determination of **16**:892ff
- family purity **15**:703
- firstborn rights **6**:1311
- Hillel the Elder **8**:1425
- honor of parents **13**:95
- *karet* **10**:788
- marriage **13**:1185
- *shomeret yavam* **11**:124
- Simeon ha-Timni's ruling **14**:1566
- slavery **14**:1659
- *takkanah* for prevention **15**:723
- vital statistics **16**:189
MAN, THE NATURE OF **11**:842
- *Contents:*
- - In the Bible **11**:842
- - - Names of Man **11**:842
- - - Psychological Terms **11**:843
- - - Man's Origin **11**:843
- - - Image of God **11**:844
- - - Free Will **11**:844
- - - Afterlife **11**:845
- - - End of Days **11**:845
- - In Rabbinic Thought **11**:846
- - - Physical Natures of Man **11**:846
- - - Character **11**:846
- - - Man and Woman **11**:847
- - - Destiny **11**:848
- - - Significance **11**:848
- Albo, Joseph **2**:536
- anthropomorphism **3**:51
- creation of **5**:1060ff
- ethics **6**:933f
- Genesis, concept of **7**:395
- God's relationship **7**:650ff
- illuminated manuscripts **8**:1260
- kabbalistic doctrine **10**:606ff
- Kook, Abraham Isaac **10**:1184
- longevity **14**:1499
- Maimonides **11**:774ff
- microcosm **11**:1502
- mythology **12**:729
- philosophy **13**:423
- Pittsburgh Platform **13**:571
- prayer **13**:978
- prehistoric man **9**:225
- providence **14**:137
- repentance **14**:73
- Saadiah Gaon **13**:432; **14**:551
- suffering **15**:486
- torts **15**:1272ff
- woman **16**:624
- *illus:*
- - *Tikkun Middot ha-Nefesh* **7**:238
- *see also:* FREE WILL
Man, Herman de **6**:321
Man, Primordial (Kab. conc.), *see* ADAM KADMON
Mana (tan.) **11**:653
Mana (amora) **11**:875
Mana ben Jonah (amora), *see* MANI
Manāfi al-Hayawān (Pers. illum. ms., 13th cent.) **4**:941; **5**:21
Managem (yacht) **12**:1164
Managua (city, Nicaragua) **12**:1135
Manaḥat (sub., Jer.), *see* Malḥa
MANĀKHA (tn., Yem.) **11**:849
- Yemen **16**:746
Manama (tn., Bahrein) **4**:102
MANARAH (kib., Isr.) **11**:849
- iron ore **9**:200
- statistics **1**:place list
- *illus:*
- - babies' house **10**:967
- - chicken coop **10**:973
MANASSEH (bib. fig., tribe) **11**:850
- Ashtaroth **3**:737
- Bible history **8**:579ff
- Ephraim **6**:806ff
- Genesis, Book of **7**:393
- Jacob's hands **14**:177
- Joseph **10**:206
- Machir **11**:668
- "right" border **14**:178
- Samaritans **14**:727
- settlement **9**:115
- Simeon **14**:1550
- Transjordan **15**:1317
- tribes **15**:1383
- *illus:*
- - birth **6**:808
- - blessed by Jacob **6**:281, 809; **7**:1084
- *map:* text
MANASSEH (k., Judah) **11**:852
- Apocryphal psalm **11**:854
- chornological chart **8**:766-767
- destruction of Temple **10**:1371
- Deuteronomy, Book of **5**:1577
- history **8**:606ff
- Isaiah's death **9**:44
- Lamentations, Book of **10**:1369
- magic **11**:705
- moon cult **12**:290
- sun worship **15**:517
- transgressions **2**:862; **2**:863
- *geneal. table* **5**:1341
- *see also:* MANASSEH, PRAYER OF
Manasseh (4th cent. B.C.E.) **8**:624
- Sanballat **14**:729; **14**:824
Manasseh, Ezekiel ben Reuben **4**:89
MANASSEH, PRAYER OF (Apoc. psalm) **11**:854
- Hellenistic Jewish literature **8**:304
Manasseh bar Mar Joseph (gaon), *see* Manasseh ben Joseph of Ba'quba
MANASSEH BEN ISRAEL **11**:855
- apologetics **3**:197
- Buxtorf, Johannis II **4**:1543
- Christian slander **2**:557
- chronological chart **8**:766-767
- cosmic cycles **10**:582
- Cromwell, Oliver **5**:1126
- *galut* **7**:292ff; **8**:1375
- *Heroica Historia* **8**:560
- history **8**:701
- Jessey, Henry **10**:7
- letters **11**:61
- Lost Tribes **15**:1006
- Montezinos, Antonio de **12**:278
- Pococke, Thomas **13**:666
- printers' marks **13**:1095
- printing **2**:896; **13**:1104; **15**:1482
- Rembrandt **13**:917
- Sambatyon **14**:764
- soul, views on **10**:604
- travelers **15**:1350
- usury **12**:252
- *illus:*
- - text
- - autograph **3**:916
- - *Conciliador* (1651) **4**:1325
- - petition to Oliver Cromwell re. religious services **5**:1127
- - printers' mark **13**:1093
Manasseh ben Joseph of Ba'qúba **2**:399; **4**:188
MANASSEH BEN JOSEPH OF ILYA **11**:857
Manasseh Forest (Isr.), *see* Menasheh Forest
Manasseh ibn Ibrahim al-Qazzāz **5**:1241
Manasseh of Hotzenplotz **12**:63
Manasseh of Rome **8**:1323
Manasseh region (Er. Isr.) **9**:143
Manasseh Son of Onias I (h. pr.) **12**:1402; **14**:1568
Manasses, Hirsch **11**:1384
MANCHESTER (city, Eng.) **11**:858
- Altmann, Alexander **2**:779
- Asher, Joseph Michael **3**:703
- England **6**:754ff.
- Golding's "Doomington" **7**:718
- Laski, Nathan **10**:1438
- Rothschild, Nathan Meyer **14**:337
- Schiller-Szinessy, Solomon **14**:966
- Sieff, Israel **14**:1510
- Slotki family **15**:1677
- tailoring **15**:707
- Weizmann, Chaim **16**:425
- Yoffey family **16**:844
Manchester (city, N.H.) **12**:1024
MANCHURIA (reg., China) **11**:860
- Japanese rule **9**:1281
- *see also:* MONGOLIA
Mancip, Guilhem **5**:158
MANCROFT (fam.) **11**:861
Mancroft, Arthur Michael Samuel **11**:861
Mancroft, Stormont **11**:861
Mandaeans (gnostic sect) **2**:468; **10**:161
Mandaic (Aram. dialect) **3**:277
- mysticism **10**:498; **10**:504; **10**:506
Mandalī (tn., Iraq) **8**:1450
MANDATE FOR PALESTINE **11**:861
- Hebrew language **16**: 1642
- history chart **8**:766-767
- Inquiry Commissions **13**:30
- Jewish Agency **10**:26ff
- Jewish defense **9**:681ff.
- League of Nations **10**:1521
- maps of Ereẓ Israel **11**:931
- partition **13**:34
- parodies **13**:137ff
- U.N. **15**:1543
- Va'ad Le'ummi **16**:49
- Vatican **16**:76
- White Papers **16**:482ff
- Zionist Congress (13th) **16**:1172
- Zionist leaders **16**:1081
- *illus:*
- - Biltmore Conference **15**:1633
- - British civil administration stamp **15**:332
- - Kibbutz Yagur, arms search **16**:698
- - New York protest **16**:1059
- - pictorial stamps **15**:332
- - Samuel, Sir Hebert **14**:799
- - Sedot Yam, arms search **14**:1094
- - Sharett testifying before UNSCOP **16**:1093
- - U.N. session (May 14, 1948) **15**:1544
- *map:*
- - administrative division, 1939 **9**:600
- *see also:* ISRAEL (Historical Survey); PALESTINE
Mandel (tn., Wyo.), *see* Sheridan
Mandel, Abraham **15**:705
MANDEL, ARNOLD **11**:863
MANDEL, ELI **5**:115; **5**:116
Mandel, Fritz **8**:270
MANDEL, GEORGES **11**:863
Mandel, Harry **16**:679
Mandel, Isaac **13**:1243
MANDEL, MARVIN **11**:864

Mandel, Mayer **13:**1243; **15:**705
Mandel, Menashe **10:**1306
Mandel, Mordekhai, *see* AVI-SHAUL, MORDEKHAI
Mandel, Moses **15:**705
MANDELBAUM, BERNARD **16:**1401
MANDELBAUM, DAVID GOODMAN **11:**864
Mandelbaum, Ephraim **13:**117
Mandelbaum Gate (Jer.) **9:**1483; **16:**324
- *illus:*
- - Mt. Scopus convoy **9:**1490
MANDELBERG, AVIGDOR (Victor) **11:**864
- Siberia **14:**1488
Mandelberg, N. **16:**229
Mandelkern, Julius **10:**307
MANDELKERN, SOLOMON **11:**865
- *illus:*
- - F.Z.C. **16:**1165
Mandell, Mike **12:**1038
MANDELSHTAM, LEONID ISAAKOVICH **11:**866
Mandelshtam, M., *see* Liadov, M.
MANDELSHTAM, OSIP EMILYEVICH **11:**866
Mandelstamm, Aryeh Loeb, *see* MANDELSTAMM, LEON
MANDELSTAMM, BENJAMIN **11:**867
Mandelstamm, Ezekiel **11:**868
MANDELSTAMM, LEON **11:**868
- Bible translation **4:**876
MANDELSTAMM, MAX EMMANUEL **11:**868
- Baratz, Hermann **4:**203
- territorialism **15:**1020
- *illus:*
- F.Z.C. **16:**1165
Mandeville, Sir John **6:**782
- *illus:*
- - setting out for the Holy Land **6:**783
Mandic, O. **6:**735
Mandīl ("tallit") **2:**264
Mandil, Jovan **16:**888
Mandl, Ignaz **11:**556
Mandl, Jacob Koppel, *see* THEBEN, JACOB KOPPEL
Mandler, Arnošt **5:**1209
MANDRAKE (bot.) **11:**870
- biblical aphrodisiac **4:**258
- evolution **6:**1002
- folklore **6:**1402
- plant list **13:**621
- *illus:*
- - text
- - eighteenth cent. engraving **4:**257
Manduzion, Donato **14:**843
Manea, Norman **14:**423
Maneh (coin) **5:**696; **14:**1347; **16:**388
MANÉ-KATZ **11:**870
- *illus:*
- - text
- - "Epicier" (paint.) **13:**119
Manes (rel. ldr.) **14:**1306
Manesse Codex (14th cent. ms.) **15:**484
MANESSIER DE VESOUL **11:**871
- Treves, Johanan **15:**1378
- Vesoul **16:**115
MANETHO (hist.) **11:**872
- anti-Jewish Greek literature **7:**888
- Apion **3:**178
- Mesopotamia **16:**1486
- Moses **12:**390
MANETTI, GIANNOZZO **11:**873
- Hebraists **8:**16,45
Mangan (wadi, Isr.) **15:**1145
MANGER, ITZIK **11:**873
- Hershele Ostropoler **12:**1516
- Yiddish literature **16:**820
- *illus:*
- - fellow Yiddish writers **7:**616; **16:**821
Manger, Samuel Hendrik **8:**45
Mangup (tn., Crimea), *see* Doros
Manhattan (boro., N.Y.C.) **12:**1077ff
- *illus:* **12:**1080,1099,1101,1065
Manhig (tit.) **13:**1447; **15:**1164
Manhig Olam (bk.) **2:**154; **2:**181
Mani (rel. ldr.), *see* Manes
MANI (amora) **11:**874
- Avin **3:**971
- Hanuniah **7:**1256
- Judah IV **10:**334
- Yose **16:**850
- Yudan **16:**867
Mani (comp.) **5:**126
MANI (fam.) **11:**875
Mani, Abraham **8:**1452; **11:**876
Mani, Elijah ben Suleiman **8:**234; **11:**875
Mani, Elijah Moses **11:**876
Mani, Isaac Malchiel **11:**876
Mani, Israel **11:**876
Mani, Mazal (Mathilda), *see* Mosseri, Mazal
Mani, Shalom Ezekiel **11:**876
Mani, Suleiman Menahem **8:**1452; **11:**876
MANICHAEISM **11:**876
Manichaeus (rel. ldr.), *see* Manes
Manila (city, Philippines) **13:**395
MANI-LEIB (Brahinsky; poet) **11:**876
- children's literature **5:**445

MANIN, DANIELE **11:**877
- *illus:* text
"Man in Open Air" (sculp., Nadelman) **14:**1062
MANISCHEWITZ, HIRSCH **11:**877
Manish ben Meir **13:**583
MANISSA (tn., Turk.) **11:**878
MANITOBA (prov., Can.) **11:**879
- ICA **10:**46
Manitov (educ.), *see* Askenazi, Léon
Manitowoc (city, Wis.) **16:**556
Manjacoria, Nicholas **8:**45
Manker, Moses **15:**1527
Mankiewicz, Frank **13:**1362
MANKIEWICZ, JOSEPH LEO **12:**471
Mankin, Valentin **15:**318
MANKOWITZ, WOLF **11:**880
"Man Like Me Won't Flee" (wdct., Budko) Fig. 87 **3**-ART
MANN, ABRAHAM AARON OF POSNAN **11:**880
MANN, DANIEL **12:**451; **12:**471
- *illus:*
- - *The Last Angry Man* **12:**455
MANN, DELBERT **12:**451; **12:**471
Mann, Erika **11:**883
Mann, Frederick **10:**1495
MANN, FREDERIC RAND **11:**880
- Cultural Foundation **2:**817
Mann, Heinrich **11:**882
MANN, JACOB **11:**881
- Cairo *genizah* **16:**1338
- historiography **8:**564
- H.U.C. **8:**218
Mann, Klaus **11:**883
MANN, MENDEL **11:**882
- Yiddish literature **16:**826
MANN, THOMAS **11:**882
MANNA (bib. food) **11:**883
- bdellium **4:**354
- Bodenheimer's theories **4:**1159
- coriander **5:**972
- Exodus, Book of **6:**1055
- folklore **6:**1407
- Sabbath **14:**558
- Sabbath loaves **4:**1335
- *illus:*
- - *Birds' Head Haggadah* **7:***fcg.* 875
- - jar kept in Tabernacle **3:** *fcg. 524*
Mannai (anc. tribe) **14:**880
Mannassee, Joseph **14:**829
Mann Auditorium (Isr.) **10:**799
- *illus:*
- - Israel Philharmonic Orchestra **9:**1071
- - Zimriyyah concert **9:**1010
MANNE, MORDECAI ẒEVI **11:**886
Mannerheim, Baron von **6:**1298
MANNES (fam.) **12:**699
Mannes, Clara Damrosch **12:**699
Mannes, David **11:**887; **12:**699
MANNES, LEOPOLD **11:**887; **12:**699
MANNHEIM (city, Ger.) **11:**887
- Palatinate **13:**21
- Shabbateanism **14:**1248
- *illus:*
- - *kashrut* seals **14:**1077,1342
- - *Kristallnacht* **10:**1265
- - synagogue **10:**1264
Mannheim, David **12:**1017
MANNHEIM, HERMANN **11:**888
Mannheim, József **4:**884
MANNHEIM, KARL **11:**889
MANNHEIM, LUCIE **15:**1087
Mannheimer, D. **11:**1240
MANNHEIMER, ISAAC NOAH **11:**890
- commandments, reasons for **5:**789
- history chart **8:**766-767
- homiletic literature **8:**956
- Sulzer, Salomon **15:**510
- Vienna **16:**124
MANNHEIMER, THEODOR **11:**891
Manningham-Buller, R. E. **13:**33
- *illus:*
- - Anglo-American committee **16:**1089
Mann-Rosanes, Judith **11:**613; **13:**1111
Mannstein, Elizabeth **10:**1151
Manoah (bib. fig.) **13:**1070; **14:**118; **14:**771
Manoah Handil ben Shemaryah **3:**801
Manoah of Béziers **8:**459
MANOAH OF NARBONNE **11:**892
- *Mishneh Torah* **11:**566
Manoel Dias Soeiro, *see* MANASSEH BEN ISRAEL
Manoello Giudeo, *see* IMMANUEL (Ben Solomon) OF ROME
Manoel Lopes de Carvalho **8:**1392
MANOSQUE (tn., Fr.) **11:**892
MANS, LE (city, Fr.) **11:**892
Mansbach, J. **12:**505
Mansch, Filip **14:**1458
Mansfeld (fam.) **3:**450
MANSFELD, ALFRED **11:**893
- *illus:*
- - Israel Museum **3:**354
Manshiyeh (qtr., Jaffa) **15:**919
Mansky, Mordechai **6:**904
Manslaughter, *see* HOMICIDE
MANSO, LEO **3:**607
Mansohn, Dov Baer **14:**532
Mansohn, Ḥayyim David **14:**532
Mansohn, Israel **14:**532
Mansohn, Joseph **14:**532
Mansohn, Levi Isaac **14:**532
Mansperger, Joseph Julian **8:**45
Manstealing, *see* ABDUCTION
MANSUR (al-) **11:**893
Manṣūr (Abbasid caliph) **2:**42; **9:**1426
Manṣūr, Abu Yusuf Ya'qūb al- (caliph, Sp.) **2:**663
Mansur, ʿAtā Allāh **9:**1042
MANSURA (tn., Egy.) **11:**894
Mansura (loc., Golan) **14:**1638
MANSURAH, SA'ADIAH BEN JUDAH **11:**894
MANSURAH, SHALOM BEN JUDAH **11:**895
Manṣūr al-Ḍamārī **16:**745
Manṣur al-Yahūdī, al-, *see* AL-MANṢUR AL-YAHŪDI
Mansuriya (vill., Mor.) **6:**190
Mansuriya, Al- (tn., Iraq) **8:**1450
Mantegna, Andrea **10:**460
- *illus:*
- - David with head of Goliath **5:**1326
- - "Judith and Holofernes" (paint.) **10:**454
- - Samson and Delilah **5:**1473
Mantic (seer) **6:**112
Manticore (leg. beast) **9:**1360
Mantinband, Charles **12:**156
Mantinga, Hector, *see* MOK, MAURITS
MANTINO, JACOB BEN SAMUEL **11:**895
- Aristotle's works **2:**928
- Paul III **14:**248
MANTUA (Mantova; city, It.) **11:**895
- *Contents:*
- - History **11:**895
- - Cultural Life **11:**897
- archives **3:**383
- Arpa family **3:**496
- Basilea, Solomon **4:**299
- book art **3:**537
- Ghetto disaster (1776) **2:**187
- Giovanni, Maria **7:**588
- Inquisition **8:**1400
- *illus:*
- - text
- - Basilica di Sant' Andrea **13:**916
- - prayer for Francis II **7:**836
Mantua Haggadah (1560, printed) **9:**1580; **7:**1101
- *illus:* **3:**538; **6:**863; **7:**1087
Mantuirea (newsp.) **13:**1043; **14:**399
Manual Enciclopédico Judio (Arg.) **6:**735
Manual of Discipline, *see* DISCIPLINE, MANUAL OF
MANUEL I (k., Port.) **11:**899
- forced conversion **3:**173
- Inquisition **8:**1385
- Zacuto, Abraham **16:**904
Manuel, Don Juan **15:**249
Manuel, Eugène **2:**649
MANUEL, FRANK EDWARD **8:**548
Manuel Abreu de Campo **8:**1392
MANUEL I COMNENUS **11:**899
Manuel du Lecteur (bk.), *see* *Maḥberet ha-Tijan*
Manuel Gil de la Guardia **8:**1394
Manuelo of San Miniato **11:**873
Manufacturers' Association (Isr.) **4:**406; **9:**858ff; **15:**1564
Manumission (slave) **6:**51; **16:**1275
MANUSCRIPTS, HEBREW **11:**899
- *Contents:*
- - 500 B.C.E.-500 C.E. **11:**900
- - 500-1500 **11:**900
- - 1500-1970 **11:**904
- - Owners and Other Lists **11:**905
- - - Collection of the Material **11:**906
- - - Austria **11:**906
- - - Denmark **11:**906
- - - England **11:**906
- - - France **11:**906
- - - Germany **11:**906
- - - Hungary **11:**906
- - - Italy **11:**906
- - - Israel **11:**906
- - - Netherlands **11:**907
- - - Poland **11:**907

– – – Switzerland 11:907
– – – U.S.A. 11:907
– – – U.S.S.R. 11:907
– – – Vatican 11:907
– General
– – autographs 3:912
– – music 12:558
– – *qeri* notations 16:1420
– – Samaritan Pentateuch 13:267
– – Tiberian masorah 16:1461ff
– – Yemenite Jews 16:756
– Catalogs, Collections
– – Adler, Elkan Nathan 2:275
– – Assemani 3:761
– – Giovanni de' Rossi 5:1557
– – Jewish National Library 11:197
– – Sassoon 14:899
– – Steinschneider 15:374
– – Vatican Library 3:760
– *illus:*
– – text
– – abecedary, 10th cent. 8:658
– – "Apam" *mahzor* (1702) 3:175
– – Arthurian legends (1279) 3:653
– – Asaph ha-Rofe's oath 3:675
– – Ben-Asher, Aaron, masoretic lists (10th cent.) 4:466
– – Ben-Asher, Moses, manuscript of the Prophets (896) 4:468
– – *Ben ha-Melekh ve-ha-Nazir* (1423) 4:518
– – Dornhan *Memorbuch* 3:380
– – *Genizah* of Cairo, fragment 3:376
– – *haftarot*, David ben Benayah (15th cent.) 4:471
– – Jerusalem Talmud (13th cent.) 2:937
– – Judeo-Italian prayer book (15th cent.) 9:1124
– – *Kaufmann Mishnah* 12:94
– – *mahzor* (1816) 4:219
– – script types 2:689-742
– – *Sefer Mareh Einayim* (1712) 4:101
– – twelfth-century Judeo-Arabic ms. 10:409
– *see also:* BOOKS; BOOK TRADE; COLOPHON; ILLUMINATED MANUSCRIPTS, HEBREW; PAPYRI
Manutius (Manuzio), Aldus, *see* ALDO MANUZIO
Manvel, Esther, *see* Grafemus, Louise
Manzoni, A. 9:1105
Manzurah, Shalom 16:836
Maoch (Phil. k.) 2:210
MA'ON (city, Er. Isr.) 11:907
– *mikveh* 11:1541
Maon (site, Er. Isr.) 11:908
– *illus:* text 15:598ff
Maon Basin (reg., Transj.) 9:176ff
Maonites (tribe, Er. Isr.) 11:908
Ma'or (mosh., Isr.) 1:place list
MA'OR KATAN (fam.) 11:909
Ma'or Katan, Aaron 11:909
Ma'or Katan, Judah Leib 11:909
Ma'or Katan, Moses ben Loeb 11:909
Ma'ot hittim (Passover charity), *see* ME'OT HITTIM
MA'OZ HAYYIM (kib. Isr.) 11:909
– statistics 1:place list
Ma'oz Zion (Isr. stlmt.) 11:1453
MA'OZ ZUR (hymn) 11:910
– Zerubbabel 16:1001
– *scores:* text
MAPAI 11:912
– Ahdut ha-Avodah 2:457
– Ahdut ha-Avodah-Po'alei Zion 2:458
– Alignment 9:676ff
– Ben-Gurion 4:508ff
– Dayan, Moshe 5:1372
– Eshkol, Levi 6:889
– *Ha-Po'el ha-Za'ir* 7:1326
– Israel politics 9:660ff
– kibbutz movement 10:971
– labor activities 9:854ff
– *Min ha-Yesod* 14:325
– Rafi 13:1512
– religious parties 9:383
– socialism 15:33
– Zionist Labor 16:639
– *illus:*
– – Arab and Druze districts, votes cast, 1949-69 (table) 9:1031
– – merging meetings, (1930, 1968) 9:660, 677
– *see also:* ISRAEL LABOR PARTY
MAPAM (party, Isr.) 11:914
– Eisenhower Doctrine 9:391
– Israel Arabs 9:1030; 9:466
– Israel politics 9:662ff
– kibbutz movement 10:971
– labor movement 9:860ff
– occupied territories 9:413
– Palmah 9:371
– Po'alei Zion 13:664
Ma'pilim ("illegal" immigrants) 9:532
MAP MAKERS 11:917
– *illus:*
– – text
– – Cresques' Catalan Atlas 5:1086; 8:681; 11:915
– – Simon von Geldern's drawing of the globe 7:365
– – Tobias Cohn's map of the world 7:416
– *see also:* GEOGRAPHY; JERUSALEM (Cartography); MAPS OF EREZ ISRAEL
Mappah (flag) 6:1334
Mappah (bk.), *see Ha-Mappah*
Mappiq (gram. sign) 16:1450
Maps (city, Er. Isr.), *see* MAMPSIS
MAPS OF EREZ ISRAEL 11:918
– *Contents:*
– – Ancient Cartography 11:918
– – Middle Ages 11:919
– – Arab Cartography of Middle Ages 11:925
– – Modern Times 11:926
– – 18th and 19th Centuries 11:928
– itineraries 9:1148
– *Itinerarium Antonini* 9:1149
– *Itinerarium Hierosolymitanum* 9:1149
– Jerusalem cartography 9:1542
– Macmillan Bible Atlas 2:452
– P.E.F. 13:40
– Wilson 16:535
– *illus:*
– – Abraham ben Jacob's map 11:927
– – Cresques, Abraham and Judah, map 5:1086
– – French map (1713) 5:1392
– – Fuller's map of Paran Desert 13:89
– – Jerusalem, 18th cent. etching 9:1547
– – Jerusalem and Erez Israel, pictorial map (12th. cent.) 11:923
– – "Jerusalem et Suburbia Eius" 9:1542
– – Jerusalem map by Buenting 9:1547
– – Jerusalem map by Reuwich 9:1545
– – Madaba map 3:697, 715; 7:572; 9:1543
– – Robert's map (1750) 11:929
– – Vesconte's map (14th cent.) 11:925
MAPU, ABRAHAM 11:932
– children's literature 5:431
– Haskalah 8:187
– history chart 8:766-767
– Isaiah theme 9:68
– Jerusalem theme 9:1565
– Schur, Zev Wolf 14:1009
– *illus:*
– – *Ahavat Ziyyon* (1853) 8:189
– – autograph 3:916
Mapug (city, Syr.), *see* HIERAPOLIS
Maqala (game) 9:1038
Maqāla fi al-Rabw (wk.) 11:779
MAQAM (mus. term) 11:936
MAQAMA (lit. genre) 11:937
– allegory 2:644
– exemplum 6:1021
– poetry 13:687ff
– Zarco, Judah 16:936
Maqdisī, Al- 9:1426
Maqnā (port, Gulf of Elath) 9:264
Maqqaf (punctuation sign) 16:1459ff
Maqqel (punctuation sign) 16:1459
MAQUEDA (tn., Sp.) 11:938
– Calatrava, Order of 5:39
Maquis (partisans) 13:148; 14:1039
MAR (tit.) 11:939
– *amoraim* 2:873
– title 15:1164
Mar (amora), *see* SAMUEL
Mar (Mohar), Jehiel 12:220
Mara, William de (la) 8:45
Maracaibo (city, Venez.) 16:91
Maracay (city, Venez.) 16:91
Mara de-atra (tit.) 13:1447; 15:1164
M-a-r-a-f, *see* PEREZ BEN ELIJAH OF CORBEIL
Maragha (Maragheh; tn., Iran) 3:1005; 13:302
Marām (bib. fig.), *see* MIRIAM
Maram, *see* Mo'ezet ha-Rabbanim ha-Mitkaddemim
Máramaros (reg., Transyl.), *see* Máramures
Máramarossziget (tn., Rum.), *see* SIGHET
Máramarossziget (period.) 14:1523
Mar Amram (r.) 16:870
Máramures (has. syn.), *see* Marmarosh
Máramures (reg., Transyl.) 14:1523; 15:1344; 15:470ff
Maran (Seph. name for J. Caro) 14:1170
Maran Beit Yosef (syn., Bul.) 12:1160
Marani, Paolo 11:1559
Maran le-Even ha-Ezer (bk.) 4:349
Marathi (Ind. lang.)
– Bene Israel 8:1358; 9:505; 12:1465 13:14
– homiletic literature 8:957
– Rajpurkar's translations 13:1526
– *illus:*
– – *Haggadah* (Poona, 1874) 4:495
Maravel (tn., Ind.) 8:1355
Maravelidhou, Ioanna Dhriva 7:898
Mar bar Ameimar (amora) 2:802
Mar bar Huna (gaon) 7:318
MAR BAR RAV ASHI (amora) 11:939
MAR BAR RAVINA (amora) 11:940
– marriage ceremony 11:1033
Marbeh Ezah (bk.) 14:1299
Marbeh raglayim (centipede) 5:283
Marbeh-Tevunah (bk.) 14:1299
Mar Berei de-Ravina (amora), *see* MAR BAR RAVINA
Marbit (leg. term) 16:27
Marbiz Torah (title) 13:1450; 15:1165
Marble 13:1010
Marblehead (tn., Mass.) 11:622
MARBURG (city, Ger.) 11:941
– *illus:* text
Marburg (city, Yug.), *see* MARIBOR
Marburg, Israel, *see* ISSERLEIN, ISRAEL BEN PETHAHIAH
Marburger (fam.) 12:348
Marburger, Jacob 4:172
Marburger, Moses 4:172
Marcaria, Jacob 13:1102; 13:1365
– Riva 14:196
MARCEAU, MARCEL 11:941
– *illus:* text
Marcellius, Publius 9:247; 10:471
Marcello, Benedetto 9:1146
– music 12:558
– Psalms 13:1329
– *scores:*
– – *Ma'oz Zur* 11:911
Marcellus (1st cent. C.E., Rom. gov.) 13:848
Marcellus (2nd cent. C.E., Rom. gov.), *see* Marcellius, Publius
Marcellus II (pope) 13:856
Marcellus Empiricus 11:1183
Marchegg (vill., Aus.) 3:889; 3:890; 13:352
Marches, Samuel ben Solomon 13:1143
Marchina, Maria 8:45
Marcin Czechowic 9:1232
Marcion (Chr. heretic)
– Old Testament 4:925
– *Shi'ur Komah* 3:57
– views on Judaism 5:508
Marck, J. van 8:45
MARCK, SIEGFRIED 11:942
MARCKWALD, WILLY 11:942
Marcoff, Cella, *see* SERGHI, CELLA
Marcolin (mart., Ger.) 10:227
Marco Polo 5:469; 7:424
MARCOSSON, ISAAC 10:314
MARCOUSSIS (Marcous), LOUIS 11:943
– Paris 13:113
– *illus:*
– – text
– – "Portrait of Guillaume Apollinaire" (lith.) 13:114
Marcquefoy, Alexandre 11:1560
MARCULESTI (J. clny., Bess.) 11:943
Marcus (s., Alexander Lysimachus) 4:601
Marcus, A. 16:1118
MARCUS, AARON 11:944
– *illus:*
– – F.Z.C. 16:1165
Marcus, Ben 16:556
Marcus, Bertha 16:1165
Marcus, David (r., Turk.) 15:1461; 15:1462
MARCUS, DAVID DANIEL (U.S. sol.) 11:945
Marcus, Eduard, *see* VORONCA, ILARIE
Marcus, Eli 12:505
MARCUS, ERNST 11:946
MARCUS, FRANK 6:789
Marcus, Jacob (collec.) 15:1573
MARCUS, JACOB RADER (hist.) 11:946
– American Jewish Archives 2:822
– Historical Society 2:827
– historiography 8:564; 8:568
– Jewish Publication Society 10:80
Marcus, Jerry 5:216
Marcus, Joseph (cmty. ldr., Ger.) 4:1355
MARCUS, JOSEPH (schol., Rus.) 11:946
Marcus, Leon 15:303
Marcus, Louis 16:33
Marcus, Ludwig 7:448
Marcus, Mickey, *see* MARCUS,

DAVID DANIEL
Marcus, Moses (Eng. apos.) **12:**414
Marcus, Moses (schol., U.S.) **11:**947
MARCUS, RALPH **11:**947
- Job **10:**123
Marcus, Rixi **5:**169
Marcus, Samuel **5:**1568
MARCUS, SIEGFRIED **11:**948
MARCUS, SIMON **1:**34
Marcus, Stanley **5:**1232
Marcus, Tobias **18:**1165
Marcus, William **5:**220
Marcus Agrippa **15:**979
Marcus Annaeus Lucanus, *see* LUCAN
Marcus Antonius, *see* Antony
Marcus Aurelius Alexander Severus, *see* SEVERUS, ALEXANDER
MARCUS AURELIUS ANTONINUS (2nd cent. C.E., Rom. emp.) **11:**948
- attitude to Jews **9:**249
- history chart **8:**766-767
- Jerusalem coins **9:**1406
- Judah ha-Nasi **10:**367
Marcus Aurelius Antoninus (3rd cent. C.E., Rom. emp.), *see* CARACALLA, MARCUS AURELIUS ANTONINUS
Marcus ben Binah, *see* HIRSCHFELD, EPHRAIM JOSEPH
Marcus Cocceius Nerva (Rom. emp.), *see* NERVA
Marcus Julius Alexander **2:**581
Marcuse, Adolf **3:**806
MARCUSE, HERBERT **11:**948
- New Left **12:**1033
- sociology **15:**63
MARCUSE, LUDWIG **11:**950
MARCUSE, MOSES **11:**950
Marcus Julius (k., Chalcis), *see* AGRIPPA II
MARCZALI, HENRIK **11:**950
Marder, John I. **15:**307
Mardia, Micer Sancho **8:**1398
MARDIN (tn., Kurd.) **11:**951
Mardoché Joseph **15:**1299
MARDUK (deity) **11:**951
- Babel, Tower of **4:**23
- Babylon **16:**1497
- Nebuchadnezzar I **16:**1502
- New Year enthronement **14:**307
- rise of cult **7:**1247
- Scroll of Esther **14:**1052ff
- temple in Babylon **4:**33
- Tiglath-Pileser III **16:**1503
- *illus:*
- - Babylon temple **4:**31
Marduk-balaṭsu-ikbi (Babyl. k.) **5:**331
Mardush (r., Pol.) **10:**234
Mare, William de (la), *see* Mara, William de (la)
Mareh Einayim (bk.) **4:**101
Mareh ha-Panim (bk.) **11:**963
MAREK, PESACH (Piotr) **11:**954
- *illus:*
- - Benei Zion meeting **12:**359
Maremar (amora) **11:**940
Marenof, Martha **5:**451
MARESHAH (city, Er. Isr.) **11:**954
- anthropological evidence **3:**48
- battle, Asa and Zerah **3:**671
- Hellenistic-Roman period **8:**626; **8:**631; **8:**633
- tomb pillar **13:**522
- *illus:*
- - Hellenistic burial cave **3:**321
- - Hellenistic town quarter (plan) **3:**337
- *plan:* text
Margaliot (name), *see also* Margalioth, Margalit, Margolies, Margolio(u)th, Margolis, Margul(i)es
Margaliot, Alexander ben Ẓevi **14:**905
MARGALIOT, MORDECAI **11:**956
- Assaf, Simḥa **3:**757
Margaliot, Rachel **11:**957
MARGALIOT, REUBEN **11:**957
Margalioth (name), *see also* Margaliot, Margalit, Margolies, Margolio(u)th, Margolis, Margul(i)es
Margalioth, Ḥayyim David Zilber **10:**1170
Margalioth, Saul **10:**1173
Margalit (name), *see also* Margaliot(h), Margolies, Margolio(u)th, Margolis, Margul(i)es
Margalit, David **11:**1204
Margalit, Isaac **4:**1536
Margalit, Meir **12:**1342
Margalita, Anton, *see* MARGARITA, ANTON
Margalita, Moses, *see* MARGOLIOUTH, MOSES
Margaliyyot (mosh., Isr.) **1:**place list
Margaliyyot, Enẓiklopedyah li-Yladim (enc.) **6:**735
Margalya (star) **11:**249
Margaret of Brabant, *see* Aleyde of Brabant
Margaretten (tn., Transyl.), *see* MARGHITA
Margaret Theresa (emp., Ger.) **11:**32
MARGARITA, ANTON **11:**958
- Joseph of Rosheim, disputation **5:**356; **10:**228
- Luther, Martin **11:**585
- *illus:* text
Margelan (city, Rus.), *see* BUKHARA
MARGET, ARTHUR W. **11:**959
MARGHITA (Margit(t)a; tn., Transyl.) **11:**959
MARGO, BORIS **3:**605
Margolies (name), *see also* Margaliot(h), Margalit, Margolio(u)th, Margolis, Margul(i)es
MARGOLIES, ISAAC BEN ELIJAH **11:**959
Margolies, Morris S. **4:**1266
Margolies, Moses (r., Lith.) **15:**778
MARGOLIES, MOSES SEBULUN (r., U.S.) **11:**960
Margolies, Naḥman Idl **12:**1528
Margolies, Naphtali Herz **7:**6
Margolies-Schlesinger-Jaffe, Israel David ben Mordecai, *see* JAFFE-MARGOLIOT, ISRAEL DAVID
Margolin, Anna **16:**822
MARGOLIN, ARNOLD **11:**960
Margolin, David S. **14:**1414
MARGOLIN, ELIEZER **11:**961
- Jewish Legion **10:**71
MARGOLIN, MOSES **11:**962
Margolin, Sonia, *see* RABBINOWITZ, SARAH
Margoliot, Isaac Meir **10:**724
MARGOLIOT, MOSES BEN SIMEON **11:**963
MARGOLIOTH (fam. name) **11:**964
Margolioth (name), *see also* Margaliot(h), Margalit, Margolies, Margolio(u)th, Margolis, Margul(i)es
Margolioth, David Solomon **12:**1518
MARGOLIOTH, EPHRAIM ZALMAN BEN MENAHEM MANNES **11:**964
- anti-Shabbateanism **16:**1224
- Ḥarif ha-Levi **7:**1338
- *Shulḥan Arukh* **14:**1477
Margolioth, Ḥayyim Mordecai **14:**1477
Margolioth, Isaac Eizik **11:**965
Margolioth, Jacob (15th cent.) **11:**965
MARGOLIOTH, JACOB (15/16 cent.) **11:**965
- matchmaker **14:**1254
Margolioth, Joseph **5:**1036
MARGOLIOTH, JUDAH LOEB **11:**965
- Haskalah **7:**1445
Margolioth, Mendel **11:**964
Margolioth, Mordecai **11:**964
Margolioth, Moses (r., Cracow) **11:**964
Margolioth, Naphtali **11:**964
Margolioth, Samuel (cmty. ldr., Pol.) **11:**964, 965
Margolioth, Shalom Shakhna **11:**965
Margolioth, Zelig Isaac **13:**647
Margoliouth (name), *see also* Margaliot(h), Margalit, Margolies, Margolioth, Margolis, Margul(i)es
MARGOLIOUTH, DAVID SAMUEL **11:**966
Margoliouth, Ezekiel **11:**966
Margoliouth, George **11:**966; **16:**1339
MARGOLIOUTH, MEIR OF OSTRAHA (Ostrog) **11:**966
MARGOLIOUTH, MOSES **11:**966
Margolis (name), *see also* Margaliot(h), Margalit, Margolies, Margolio(u)th, Margul(i)es
Margolis, Berl, *see* BRODER, BERL
Margolis, David **15:**310
Margolis, Gabriel **4:**1266
Margolis, H. (print., Ukr.) **12:**1243
Margolis, Harry S. **12:**38
Margolis, Isaac **13:**833
Margolis, Jacob **13:**833
Margolis, Jacob of Regensburg **12:**68
MARGOLIS, MAX LEOPOLD **11:**967
- Bible edition **10:**678
- historiography **8:**562
Margolis, Samuel **5:**609
Margolis, Solomon **12:**1419
MARGOLIS-KALVARYSKI, HAIM **11:**968
Margolius, Rudolf **14:**1653
MARGOSHES, SAMUEL **11:**969
MARGOULIES, BERTHA **3:**605
Margovski, Jacob Samuel, *see* MOROGOWSKI, JACOB SAMUEL
Margovski, Sejdel, *see* MOROGOWSKI, JACOB SAMUEL
Margules (name), *see also* Margaliot(h), Margalit, Margolies, Margolio(u)th, Margolis, Margulies
MARGULES, MAX **11:**969
Margulies (name), *see also* Margaliot(h), Margalit, Margolies, Margolio(u)th, Margolis, Margules
MARGULIES, EMIL **11:**970
- Bernheim Petition **4:**681
Margulies, Ephraim Zalman, *see* MARGOLIOTH, EPHRAIM ZALMAN BEN MENAHEM MANNES
Margulies, Israel **4:**809
Margulies, Jacob **5:**487
Margulies, Meyer **3:**843
Margulies, Mordecai (fin., Aus.), *see* Schlesinger, Marx
Margulies, Mordecai (Isr., U.S.), *see* MARGALIOT, MORDECAI
Margulies, Moses **11:**964
MARGULIES, SAMUEL HIRSCH **11:**970
- *Rivista Israelitica* **14:**197
Margulies-Joffe, Rabbi **10:**1590
Margulies Rabbinical School (Turin, It.), *see* S. H. Margulies Rabbinical School
Margulois, David, *see* Merrick, David
Marḥa, Al- (Markha; reg., Sinai) **14:**1594
MARḤAB AL-YAHUDI IBN AL-ḤĀRITH **11:**971
Marhah (Samar. paytan) **14:**753
Mar Ḥanina, *see* Ḥanina, Mar
Mar-Ḥayyim, Isaac **10:**540
- kabbalistic pantheism **10:**602
MARḤESHVAN (month) **11:**971
- *see also:* CALENDAR
MARI (city, Mesop.) **11:**972
- *Contents:*
- - Excavations and Discoveries **11:**973
- - Under West Semitic Rule **11:**977
- - Bible **11:**981
- archives **3:**368
- Benjamin (name), **4:**522
- census documents **16:**1510
- excavations **16:**1508
- Hazor **7:**1535
- language **14:**1151
- patriarchal history **8:**573
- prophecy **13:**1159
- West-Semites **8:**609ff
- *illus:* text
Mari, son of Samuel's daughter (amora), *see* MARI BEN ISSUR
Maria (q., Arag.) **16:**1286
Maria, Eugenio, *see* ZOLLER, ISRAEL
Maria, Paolo **4:**563
Maria Christina (q., Sp.) **8:**1390
Maria Dorothea (archduchess, Aus.) **8:**996
Maria Eleonore **8:**45
Maria Elizabeth **8:**45
Maria Hebraea, *see* "Mary the Jewess"
Mariama (sis., Jehezkiah), *see* Miriam
MARIAMNE (Hasm. q.) **11:**989
- Alexandra **2:**587
- Aristobulus III **3:**442
- Cypros **5:**1179
- Herod I **8:**376ff
- Parthians **3:**66
- *geneal. table:* **8:**377
- *illus:*
- - Miriam tower (model) **3:**340
Mariamne (dau., Simeon b. Boethus) **10:**285; **11:**990
- Herod **8:**381
- identification **14:**1554
- Martha **11:**1062
- *geneal. table:* **8:**377
Mariamne (dau., Herod) **4:**1169
Mariamne (dau., Agrippa I) **5:**1179
Mariampol (city, Lith.), *see* MARIJAMPOLE
Mariana, Juan **13:**878
- Hebraists **8:**45
MARIANOS (art.) **11:**990
- art in Ereẓ Israel **3:**508
- Bet Alfa mosaics **4:**710
- Beth-Shean **15:**599
- *illus:* text
Mariánskē Lázně (tn., Bohem.), *see* MARIENBAD
Maria Prophetissa, Moysis Soror, *see* "Mary the Jewess"
MARIA THERESA **11:**991
- Austrian Jews **3:**891
- history chart **8:**766-767

- Horowitz, Samuel Shmelke 8:1002
- Rocamora 14:209
- *illus:*
- - text
- - Juden-Ordnung 3:903
Maria-Theresiopol (tn., Yug.), *see* SUBOTICA
Mari ben Dimi (gaon) 7:318
MARI BEN ISSUR (amora) 11:992
Mari ben Rachel, *see* MARI BEN ISSUR
MARIBOR (city, Yug.) 11:992
- museums 12:538
- Yugoslavia 16:870
Marie Aline de Sion 9:1526
MARIE-BENOIT 11:993
- Donati, Angelo 6:166
"Marie Henry with her Daughter Lea" (paint., M. de Haan) 3:549
MARIENBAD (tn., Cz.) 11:993
- Agudat Israel 2:423; 2:424
- contemporary period 5:1200
- *illus:* text
Marienwerder (tn., Prus.) 13:1287
Marignola, Giovanni de 15:1356
Mari ha-Levi bar Mesharsheya (gaon) 7:318
MARIJAMPOLE (city, Lith.) 11:994
Mari Kohen of Nehar Pekod (gaon) 7:318
MARIL, HERMAN 3:605
Marinette (city, Wis.) 16:556
Marini (fam.) 16:114
Marini, Marco 3:397
- Hebraists 8:45
Marini, Salomon 13:12
Marini, Shabbetai ben Isaac 13:12
MARINI, SHABBETHAI ḤAYYIM (Vita) 11:994
MARINOFF, JACOB 11:995
Marinus (philos.) 6:164; 7:893
Marinus (gram.), *see* IBN JANĀḤ, JONAH
Marissa (city, Er. Isr.), *see* MARESHA
MARITAIN, JACQUES and RAÏSSA 11:995
Maritime Court (Isr.) 9:638
MARITIME LAW 11:996
Maritime League (Isr.) 9:1019
Maritime Museum (Isr.) 12:553
MARITIME (ATLANTIC) PROVINCES (Can.) 11:997
Mariupol (city, Ukr.), *see* ZHDANOV
MARIX, ADOLPH 11:1551; 11:1574
- *illus:*
- - portrait 11:1552
Marix, Henry 11:1574
Marj Bani ʿĀmir 9:284
Marj Lubban (reg., Er. Isr.), *see* Levonah Valley
Marjoram, Syrian (bot.) 13:621
Mar Joseph (savora) 14:920
Mar Joseph (Croatia) 16:870; 16:917
- Khazars 10:950
Marj Sānūr (reg., Er. Isr.) 9:588
Mark, Aaron 12:36
Mark, Abraham 5:395
MARK, BERNARD (Berl) 11:998
- societies, learned 15:54
- *illus:*
- - *Di Geshikhte fun Yidn in Poyln* 10:52
Mark, Gospel of (N.T.) 3:216; 10:10
Mark, Julius 12:1118
MARK, YUDEL 11:998
MARKAH (Samar.) 11:999
- circumcision ceremony 14:744
- translations 13:268
- *see also: Meimar Markah*
Mark Antony, *see* Antony
MARKEL, LESTER 11:1000
Markel, S. 16:474
MARKET DAYS AND FAIRS 11:1000
- book trade 4:1238
- Breslau 4:1353
- brokers 4:1403
- commerce 15:1298ff
- Jews' role 16:1288
- Lublin 11:541
- *maggidim* 11:698
- Mir 12:70
- synods 15:632
- Zelva 16:981
- *illus:*
- - text
- - Jews in Tartar market 14:437
- - Noerdlingen fair permit 12:1205
"Market of the Lodz Ghetto" (paint., S. Szerman) Fig. 79 3-ART
"Market Place in Town" (paint., Budko) 14:1470
Markfeld, Wallace 15:1577
Markfield, Mark 12:1121
Markiewicz, Henryk 13:803
MARKISH, PEREZ 11:1005
- Halkin, Shmuel 7:1191
- Hofstein, David 8:813
- *"Khaliastre"* leader 10:936
- Yiddish literature 16:816; 16:818
- *illus:*
- - text
- - Jewish Anti-Fascist Committee 3:63
- - *Literarishe Bleter* board 16:818
Markl (informer) 8:1369
MARKON, ISAAC DOV BER 11:1006
Markon, J. 16:229
Markos (gnostic) 14:1418
Markov, Mark 15:1071
MARKOVA, ALICIA 11:1007
- *illus:* text
MARKOVITS, RODION (Jakab) 8:1086
Markowitz (r., U.S.) 13:569
Markowitz, Arthur 15:209
Marks, A. (stlr., Ill.) 8:1255
Marks, Alfred (act., Eng.) 15:1054
Marks, Alexander (stlr., Jap.) 9:1280
Marks, Barnett E. 13:482
Marks, Bruce 5:1269
Marks, B. S. 5:161
Marks, David 8:1255
Marks, David Woolf 10:314; 13:990
- homiletical literature 8:957
Marks, Grace, *see* Judah, Grace
MARKS, HARRY HANANEL 10:314
MARKS, HAYMAN 11:1008
Marks, Hertha, *see* AYRTON, HERTHA
Marks, Jacob 14:829
Marks, Lewis 12:1071
Marks, Dame Lilian Alicia, *see* MARKOVA, ALICIA
MARKS, MARCUS M. 11:1008
Marks, Mark 5:161
Marks, Michael 11:1009
Marks, Milton 14:834
Marks, S. (polit., S.A.) 15:1340
Marks, Sadye, *see* Livingstone, Mary
MARKS, SAMUEL 11:1008
- *illus:*
- - letter to Paul Kruger 13:1058
MARKS, SIMON, LORD 11:1009
- *illus:* text
Marks, Sol 15:1480
Marks and Spencer (dept. store) 5:1546; 5:1547
MARKSON, AARON DAVID 11:1010
Markson, Harry 13:1361; 15:306
Marktbreit (tn., Bav.) 4:657
Markus, Aaron 5:1036
Markus, Dezso 10:1498
MARKUS, LUDWIG 11:1010
Markuse, Hermann 4:174
Markuse, Moses 7:1447
Marlborough, Duke of, *see* Churchill, John
MARLÉ, ARNOLD 15:1088
MARLI, SAMUEL (RAPHAEL) BEN MAẒLI'AḤ 11:1010
Marlorat du Pasquer, Augustin 8:45
MARLOWE, CHRISTOPHER 11:1011
Mármaros (dist., Rum.) *see* Máramures
Marmarosh (ḥas. dyn.) 7:1425
Marmochini, G. 9:1101
MARMOR, KALMAN 11:1012
MARMOREK, ALEXANDER 11:1012
Marmorek, Isidor 11:1013; 16:1113; 16:445
Marmorek, Oscar 11:1013; 16:1113
- *illus:*
- - F.Z.C. 16:1165
Marmorosh-Blank (bnk., Rum.) 14:398
MARMORSTEIN, ARTHUR 11:1013
Marmoutier (vill., Fr.) 2:752; 2:754
Marnas (deity) 7:340
Maron, Hanna, *see* MERON, HANNA
Maron, John 10:1543
Maroni (bp.) 9:289
Maronites (Chr. sect.) 10:1543
- blood libel 15:645
- Druze 9:927
- Gush Ḥalav 7:589
MAROR ("bitter herb") 11:1014
- *Haggadah*, Passover 7:1079
- *illus:* text
- *see also:* LETTUCE
Maroschick, Sheila 15:310
Marosszentkirály (vill., Transyl.) 15:813
Marosvásárhely (tn., Transyl), *see* TARGU-MURES
Mar'ot ha-Kalkalah be-Yisrael (journ.) 1: newsp. list
Marovitz, Abraham L. 5:416
Mar Paḥra (Paḥda; exil.) 16:1244
Marpe Lashon (wk.) 16: 1389
Marperger, Bernhard W. 8:45
Marpurger (fam.), *see* Marburger
Marquand (Ger.) 15:6
Marquet, Judith, *see* Krause, Judith
Marquis d'Argens, *see* ARGENS, JEAN BAPTISTE DE BOYER
Marr, Heinrich 15:1056
MARR, WILHELM 11:1015
Marrache, Isaac 5:224
MARRAKESH (city, Mor.) 11:1015
- Abendanan, Saul 2:68
- Aẓancot family 3:998
- Cabessa, Abraham 5:1
- Jewish quarter 10:87
- Yūsuf ibn Tāshifīn 2:667
- *illus:*
- - text
- - copper craftsman 12:335
- - house interior 12:326
- - Jewish women in festive dress 12:340
MARRANO ("New Christian") 11:1018
- history chart 8:766-767
- *see also:* NEW CHRISTIANS
MARRANO DIASPORA 11:1019
- *Contents:*
- - Muslim Countries 11:1020
- - Protestant Countries 11:1020
- - Other Catholic Countries 11:1021
- - Other Territories 11:1023
- - Activities of the Marranos 11:1024
- Activities
- - literature of 10:1348
- - maritime commerce 14:1413
- - slave trade 14:1662
- - synagogues 15:612
- - tobacco trade 15:1176
- Distribution
- - Amsterdam 2:895ff
- - Ancona 2:942
- - Antwerp 3:167
- - Bordeaux 4:1244
- - Brittany 4:1383
- - Brussels 4:1422
- - Dublin 6:248
- - Ereẓ Israel 9:280
- - Ferrara 6:1232
- - France 7:20
- - Hamburg 7:1225
- - India 8:1355
- - Languedoc 10:1422
- - New World 2:808
- - Rouen 14:351
- - Salonika 14:700
- - Texas 15:1034
- *illus:*
- - text
- - *Exemplar Humanae Vitae* (1687) 5:987
- - prayer book (1687) 8:1406
Mar-Rava (gaon), *see* RABBAH
Mar Rav Aaron 14:546
Mar Rav Netira 14:546
MARRIAGE 11:1025
- *Contents:*
- - The Concept 11:1026
- - - In the Bible 11:1026
- - - In Sectarian Teaching 11:1027
- - - In Rabbinic Literature 11:1028
- - - In Medieval and Modern Times 11:1031
- - Marriage Ceremony 11:1032
- - - In the Bible 11:1032
- - - In the Talmud 11:1032
- - - Post-Talmudic Period 11:1035
- - Legal Aspects 11:1045
- - - Modes of Effecting Kiddushin 11:1045
- - - Nissu'in 11:1047
- - - Legal Consequences 11:1048
- - - Manner of Celebrating Kiddushin and Nissu'in 11:1048
- - - Legal Capacity of the Parties 11:1049
- - - In the State of Israel 11:1050
- General
- - Angel of Death legends 2:954ff
- - ceremonial art 5:309ff
- - folktale, romantic 6:1380
- - population 13:887
- - vital statistics 16:177ff
- History
- - Alsace-Lorraine 2:753; 2:755
- - Beror Ḥayil 4:692
- - Bet Hillel, Bet Shammai 14:647
- - Elephantine 6:606
- - Emancipation era 12:140
- - Familiants laws 6:1163ff
- - French Sanhedrin on 3:763; 14:841
- - license 15:838
- - markets, fairs 11:1002
- - Palatinate 13:21
- - rabbinic office 13:1446
- Groups, Countries
- - Aden 2:264
- - Ancient Israel 6:1168ff
- - Ashkenazim-Sephardim 9:507
- - Bulgarian Romaniots 4:1482
- - Conservative Judaism 5:904ff
- - Doenmeh 6:151
- - Falashas 6:1146
- - Hurrians 12:1288ff
- - Iraq 8:1461
- - Karaites 10:3ff; 10:780; 11:842

-- Marranos **12:**1023
-- Mesopotamia **10:**1316
-- Morocco **16:**1258
-- mountain Jews **12:**479
-- Poland **13:**721
-- Samaritans **14:**745
-- Sumerians **15:**787
-- Yaḥad community **16:**700
-- Yemenites **16:**754
- Halakhah
-- adultery **2:**313
-- agency **2:**349
-- *agunah* **2:**429
-- annulment, retroactive **2:**432
-- apostates **3:**212
-- bigamy, polygamy **4:**985
-- child marriage **5:**423
-- civil marriage **5:**595
-- Commandments, the 613 **5:**770,774ff
-- concubine **5:**864
-- conflict of laws **5:**883
-- contracts **10:**932
-- dowry **6:**185
-- duress **12:**1398
-- *ḥazakah* **7:**1522
-- intermarriage **12:**164
-- *ketubbah* **10:**926
-- *keẓaẓah* **10:**935
-- *kiddushin* **10:**986
-- levirate marriage **11:**122
-- maintenance **11:**783
-- *mamzer* **11:**840
-- money *kinyan* **7:**1162
-- monogamy **12:**258
-- *niddah* **12:**1142ff
-- *niddui* **8:**353
-- offspring **16:**892
-- pledge **13:**640
-- priests **13:**1081ff,1090
-- proselytes **13:**1184
-- stipulations **8:**1127; **11:**539
-- waiver affecting mode of **11:**1234
- Rabbis' Attitude
-- celibacy **5:**268
-- chastity **5:**363
-- gamblers **7:**300
-- *hakhnasat kallah* **7:**1150
-- music **7:**470
-- peace in **14:**1356
-- ring **15:**735
-- Rozin's responsum **14:**93
-- secret marriage **8:**1302
-- *takkanot* **15:**718; **15:**722ff
-- *talmid ḥakham* **15:**748
-- *yiḥus* **16:**836
- Customs
-- astrology **3:**795
-- *aufrufen* **3:**849
-- *badḥan* **4:**74
-- *bedeken* **4:**74
-- blessing of children **4:**1087
-- candles, torches **6:**1397; **6:**1404
-- choirs **5:**488
-- dances **5:**1264ff
-- festivals **6:**1244
-- glass breaking **11:**940
-- grace after meals **7:**840
-- *hakkafot* **7:**1154
-- head covering **8:**6
-- henna **8:**327
-- *kitel* **10:**1079
-- matchmakers **14:**1254
-- music **12:**579
-- *Omer* period **12:**1386
-- perfumes **5:**980
-- priestly blessing **13:**1063
-- synagogue facilities **15:**585
-- *tallit* **15:**744
-- Three Weeks **15:**1124
-- veil, bridal **16:**84
-- virgin **16:**162
- Israel
-- common law **12:**147
-- population **9:**478
-- religious courts **9:**896ff
- *illus:*
-- text
-- Arab village wedding **9:**1027
-- *badḥan* **4:**74
-- benedictions **4:**283
-- betrothal ceremony (18th cent.) **4:**754
-- betrothal ceremony, Samaritan **14:**745
-- bride, groom, and musicians **11:***fcg.* 1003
-- Bukharan wedding party **4:**1474
-- child bride, North Africa **5:**424
-- *ḥallah,* traditional shape **6:**1419
-- *Hamburg Halakhah Miscellany* **16:***fcg.* 615
-- Italian bride and bridegroom **4:**66
-- "Jewish Wedding" (paint., M. Gottlieb) **3:**554
-- "Jewish Wedding" (paint., M. Oppenheim) **11:***fcg.* 1067
-- *ketubbot,* illuminated **3:**541, 543; **5:**624,971,1243; **6:**1234,1375; **7:**555; **8:**341,1285; **9:**78; **10:**772,930; *fcg.* 939f; **11:**1399
-- levirate marriage certificate (1735) **11:**129
-- Lima community register **3:**386; **13:**324
-- marriage deeds **2:**692,736
-- "Mitzva Tanz" (paint., S. S. Alva) **5:**1265
-- Moroccan bride **6:**1378
-- Rothschild family **14:**339,341
-- *Traustein* (marriage stone) **11:**693, *fcg.* 1067
-- vital statistics (tables) **16:**183,186
-- wedding ceremony **5:**291; **10:**986; **12:**602,622
-- "Wedding in Shtetl" (paint., Raskin) **14:**1467
-- wedding melodies, Yemenite (mus.) **16:**748
-- wedding pageant, Urbino **15:**1051
-- wedding plate **6:**887
-- wedding procession at kibbutz Sa'ad **10:**972
-- wedding rings **5:**305; **11:***fcg.* 1067; **16:**458
-- woman receiving a *ketubbah* **10:**933
-- *see also:* BARRENNESS AND FERTILITY; BETROTHAL; BIGAMY and POLYGAMY; CHASTITY; DIVORCE; MONOGAMY; SEX
Marriage, mixed, *see* MIXED MARRIAGE, INTERMARRIAGE
MARRIAGE, PROHIBITED **11:**1051
- *Contents:*
-- Prohibited and Void **11:**1052
-- Prohibited but Valid **11:**1052
-- Legal Consequences **11:**1053
-- In the State of Israel **11:**1054
- agency **2:**350
- Anan ben David **2:**921
- Commandments, the 613 **5:**781
- concubine **5:**864
- consanguinity **6:**1166
- Damascus document **5:**1247
- divorce coercion **6:**130
- firstborn **6:**1311
- Gentiles **7:**410
- heretics **8:**361
- high priest **16:**491
- imprisonment **8:**1301
- incest **8:**1316
- inheritance rights **8:**1126; **15:**477ff
- intermarriage **12:**168
- Karaites **11:**842
- Koran **10:**1198
- levirate marriage **11:**124ff
- *mamzer* **11:**840ff
- offspring **16:**893ff
- *Yevamot* **16:**775
- *see also:* CHASTITY; SEXUAL OFFENSES
"Marriage Ceremony of Portuguese Jews" (drg., B. Picart) **11:**1030
Marron (city, Er. Isr.) **11:**681
Marron, Hanna, *see* MERON, HANNA
Mars (planet) **3:**798
Marsa (loc., Tunisia) **15:**1430
Mar Saba (monastery, Er. Isr.) **10:**988
MARSALA (tn., Sic.) **11:**1055
Mar Samuel (amora), *see* SAMUEL
Mar Saul **16:**870; **16:**917
- Khazars **10:**950
MARSCHAK, JACOB **11:**1055
Marseilili, Samuel, *see* Samuel ben Judah of Marseilles
MARSEILLES (city, Fr.) **11:**1055
- archives **3:**382
- Clermont-Ferrand Jews **3:**170
- inscriptions **16:**668
- shipping **14:**1413
Marsh, Wilson Filson **9:**299
Marshak, Ilya Yakovlevich, *see* ILIN, M.
MARSHAK, SAMUEL YAKOVLEVICH **11:**1058
Marshalkovitch, Zadok **10:**1392
Marshall (city, Tex.) **15:**1036
Marshall, Armina **15:**1086
MARSHALL, DAVID SAUL **11:**1059
Marshall, George **11:**1062
Marshall, Jack **5:**112; **11:**997
Marshall, James **11:**1062
MARSHALL, LOUIS **11:**1060
- A.J.C. **2:**822; **2:**823
- J.D.C. **2:**827
- Jewish Agency **10:**27
- Schechter, Solomon **14:**949
- U.S. immigration **15:**1652
- Zionism **16:**1055; **16:**1143
- *illus:*
-- text
-- American Jewish Committee **2:**823
-- J.W.B. **12:**873
Marshall, Robert **11:**1062
Marsham, John **8:**45
Marshelik (ent.), *see* BADḤAN
Marshutz, S. G. **11:**501
Marsik, Ẓevi **15:**1003
Marsilius Ficinus, *see* Ficino, Marsilio
MARSUS, C. VIBIUS **11:**1062
Marteau, Henri **12:**680
Martel, Julian, *see* Miró, José María
Marten, Alexander **12:**454ff
MARTHA (dau. of Boethus) **11:**1062
Martha's Vineyard (isl., Mass.) **11:**1113
Marti, Benedictus, *see* Aretius, Benedictus
MARTI, KARL **11:**1063
MARTIAL (Rom. au.) **11:**1063
Martin I (k., Arag.) **6:**24
- Agrigento Jews **2:**415
- Barcelona Jews **4:**212
- Cavalleria, Judah **5:**262
MARTIN IV (pope) **11:**1063
MARTIN V (pope) **11:**1063
- *aliyah* prohibition **9:**512
- Aquila Jews **3:**228
- history chart **8:**766-76
- Jews, attitude to **13:**855
- Roman Jews **14:**247
- *Wiener Gesera* **16:**503
- *illus:*
-- Jewish delegation at Constance **5:**913
Martin, A. Levy **4:**177
Martin, Alvin Morris, *see* MARTIN, TONY
Martin, D. (Bib. trans.) **4:**881
Martin, Daniel (sport.) **15:**305
MARTIN, DAVID (au.) **11:**1064
Martin, Frank **3:**815
Martin, Manuel Joseph **6:**910
Martin, Sylvia Wene **15:**305
MARTIN, TONY **15:**1087
Martin du Gard, Roger **7:**144
Martine (Gr. mart.) **5:**1482
Martinet, A. **8:**45
MARTÎNEZ, FERRANT **11:**1064
- Seville **14:**1204
- Spain **15:**236
Martinez, Martinus **8:**45
Martinez Cantalapiedra, Martin **8:**45
MARTÎNEZ DE OVIEDO, GONZALO **11:**1065
- Spain **15:**233
Martínez de Villagómez, Leonor **15:**1379
Martinez Dormido, Manuel, *see* DORMIDO, DAVID ABRABANEL
Martini, Antonio **4:**878
Martini, C. S. **8:**45
Martini, G. (Bib. trans) **9:**1101
Martini, Giovanni Battista (comp.) **10:**460; **12:**558
Martini, J. Benjamin **8:**45
MARTINI, RAYMOND **11:**1065
- Abner of Burgos **2:**88; **2:**89
- Arnaldo of Villanova **3:**484
- Barcelona disputation **4:**213ff
- Hebraists **8:**45
- Rashba **2:**307
- *illus:*
-- *Pugio Fidei* (1687) **4:**214,215
Martinique (isl.) **13:**883
- sugar trade **15:**488
- West Indies **16:**473
Martinsburg (city, W.Va.) **16:**475
Martinu, Bohuslav **9:**70
Martinius, Petrus **8:**44
Martinus, Dirck (Theodoricus) Martens **8:**44
Marton, A. (journ.) **15:**1510
Márton, Áron (bp.) **8:**1102
MARTON, ERNŐ JECHEZKEL **11:**1067
- Zionism **16:**1122
Marton, Gisela **15:**1511
Marton, Michael **15:**1511
MARTON, YEHOUDA **1:**34
Mártonfalvi, Tóth György **8:**44
MARTOV, JULIUS **11:**1067
- Abramowitz, Raphael **2:**170
- Dan, Fyodor Ilyich **5:**1261
- socialism, Jewish **15:**41
Martyr, Peter **8:**44
Martyrdom, *see* KIDDUSH HA-SHEM AND ḤILLUL HA-SHEM
Martyrdom of Isaiah (Apoc.) **9:**71
"Martyrdom of Simon of Trent" (paint.) **15:**1374
Martyrion (tomb, Jer.) **9:**1416
Martyrs, Alexandrian, Acts of, see ALEXANDRIAN MARTYRS, ACTS OF
Martyrs, the Ten, *see* TEN MARTYRS, THE
Martyrs' and Heroes' Remembrance Authority, *see* YAD VASHEM
Mar Ukba (exil.), *see* UKBA, MAR
Mar Ukva (amora), *see* UKBA
Marulić, Marko **10:**459; **16:**885
Marum, L. **4:**61
Marwan (gram.), *see* IBN JANAḤ JONAH
Marwān II (caliph) **9:**1425
MARWICK, LAWRENCE **11:** 1069
MARX, ADOLF BERNHARD (musicol.) **11:**1069
Marx, Adolph (ent.), *see* Marx,

Harpo
MARX, ALEXANDER **11:**1070
- American Academy for Jewish Research **2:**819
- historiography **8:**562
- *Seder Olam Rabbah* **14:**1093
- Steinschneider **15:**374
Marx, Alfred **15:**463
Marx, Arthur, *see* Marx, Harpo
Marx, Asher **12:**1071
Marx, Assur **5:**1010
Marx, Benjamin **4:**177
Marx, Chico **11:**1075
Marx, David **3:**825
Marx, D.R. **10:**795
Marx, Edmond **11:**591
Marx, Eleanor **11:**1075; **15:**25
Marx, Esther **11:**1070
Marx, G.A., *see* DALMAN, GUSTAF HERMANN
Marx, Groucho **11:**1075
Marx, Guido **15:**1206
Marx, Gummo **11:**1075
Marx, Harpo **11:**1075
Marx, Heinrich (f. of Karl Marx) **11:**1071
Marx, Heinrich (J. offic., Prus.) **13:**1291
Marx, Henrietta **11:**1071
Marx, Henry **7:**148
Marx, Herbert, *see* Marx, Zeppo
Marx, Julius, *see* Marx, Groucho
MARX, KARL (Ger. publ.) **10:**314
- rehabilitation of German Jews **7:**500
MARX, KARL HEINRICH (commun. philos.) **11:**1071
- Deutsch, Simon **5:**1593
- Duehrung, Karl **6:**260ff
- Hess, Moses **8:**432
- Jews, attitude to **8:**714
- Jews in sociology **15:**62
- kibbutz ideology **10:**965
- Lassalle, Ferdinand **10:**1442
- socialism **15:**26
- stamps **15:**336
- *illus:*
- - text
- - *Neue Rheinische Zeitung* **10:**304
- - portrait **8:**709
- - stamp **15:**335
Marx, Leonard, *see* Marx, Chico
Marx, Manfred **13:**1049
Marx, Melvin **13:**1344
Marx, Milton, *see* Marx, Gummo
Marx, Minnie **11:**1075
Marx, Mordecai **15:**1391
Marx, Moses (r.) **10:**464
Marx, Moses (libn.) **11:**1070
Marx, Roger **3:**566
Marx, Zeppo **11:**1075
MARX BROTHERS (ents.) **11:**1075
- *illus:* text
Marxhall (tn., Tex.) **15:**1035
Marxism
- Gordon, Aharon David **7:**792
- Marx, Karl **11:**1071
- socialism, Jewish **15:**39ff
- *see also:* COMMUNISM
Mary (m. of Jesus) **10:**10ff
- Ein Karem **16:**1324
- Eve compared with **6:**983
- Israel holy places **8:**935; **9:**1540
- *Toledot Yeshu* **15:**1209
- tomb **9:**1575
- *illus:*
- - Dormition Abbey **9:**1465
- - Holy Sepulcher frieze **9:**1419
- - tomb **9:**1417
- - washing Jesus' feet **9:**1420
Mary, Church of (Temple Mount) **9:**1425
Maryam (bib. fig.), *see* MIRIAM
MARYAN (art.) **3:**605
- Paris school **13:**118
Mar Yanka (gaon), *see* Ravya
Maryborough (tn. Austr.) **11:**1285
Maryina Roshcha (tn., Rus.) **12:**366
"Mary the Jewess" **2:**546; **8:**1430
MARYLAND **11:**1076
- history chart (1826, 1828) **8:**766-767
- *pop. tables:* text
Marysville (city, Calif.) **5:**56
Mar Zadok (gaon), *see* Zadok bar Mar Yishi
Marzevah (reg., Er. Isr.) **9:**127
MARZOUK, MOSHE **11:**1077
- history chart **8:**766-767
Marzuk ben Tāwa **15:**1172
Mar Zutra I **16:**1244
Mar Zutra II **16:**1244
Mar Zutra III **16:**1245
- archipherecites **3:**335
- history chart **8:**766-767
Mar Zutra ben Mari (amora) **11:**992; **16:**1245
Mar Zutra ben R. Naḥman (amora) **16:**1245
MASADA (fort., Isr.) **11:**1078
- *Contents:*
- - History **11:**1078
- - History of Exploration **11:**1079
- - Early Settlements **11:**1080
- - Herodian Period **11:**1084
- - Period of the Zealots **11:**1088
- - Roman Siege **11:**1090
- - Byzantine Period **11:**1090
- ancient baths **4:**320
- aniconism at **3:**327
- Antigonus' war with Herod **3:**66ff
- *Ben Sira, Wisdom of* **4:**553
- Dead Sea Scrolls' date **5:**1398
- history chart **8:**766-767
- inscriptions **16:**669
- lots, casting of **11:**512; **16:**661
- martyrdom **10:**982
- Menahem, son of Judah **11:**1313
- *mikveh* **11:**1541
- pillars **13:**522
- suicide **15:**489
- synagogue **15:**595
- warfare **16:**280
- Yadin, Yigael **16:**695
- *illus:*
- - text
- - aerial view **8:** 637
- - bar mitzvah service **5:**460
- - bathhouse **4:**320
- - cosmetic objects **5:**981
- - "Ben Ya'ir ostracon" **6:**591; **11:**513
- - Dead Sea shore cliffs **9:**161
- - Herod's palace **8:**383
- - *mikveh* **11:**1535
- - museum **12:**250
- *see also:* ELEAZAR BEN JAIR
Masada (sport orgn.) **14:**129
Masada airfield (Isr.) **9:**838
Masakh (journ.) **1:**newsp. list
Masalla (8/9 cent., astron.), *see* MASHĀ' ALLAH
Māsarjuwayh of Basra **4:**310; **11:**1187
MASARYK, JAN GARRIGUE **11:**1091
- Beriḥah **4:**631
- *illus:* text
MASARYK, THOMAS GARRIGUE **11:**1092
- Hilsner case **8:**496
- Kefar Masaryk **10:**889
Masat Binyamin (wk.) **5:**227
Masbata, see JEWISH QUARTER
Masbelah ben Simeon **4:**231; **4:**238
Mascarenhas, João Rodriguez **11:**300
Maschke, Maurice **5:**611
Masci, Girolamo (pope), *see* NICHOLAS IV
Masclefius, F. **8:**44
Masconi, Leon **15:**91
Masefield, John **6:**775
Masel, Alec **11:**1281
MASHĀ'ALLAH B. ATHAN (8/9 cent. astron.) **11:**1093
- astrolabe treatise **3:**786
- astrological treatises **3:**790
- Basra **4:**310
- mathematics **11:**1122
- translations **15:**1325
Mashabbei Sadeh (kib., Isr.) **9:**772
- statistics **1:** place list
MASHĀ'IRI, AL-(fam.) **11:**1093
Mashā'iri, Eleazar al- **11:**1093
Mashā'iri, Eleazar Amīn Abu Manṣur Ibn al- **11:**1094
Mashā'iri, Eliezer al- **11:**1094
Mashā'iri, Ezekiel al- **11:**1094
Mashā'iri, Isaac al- **11:**1094
Mashā'iri, Isaac Muhadhdhib al-Dawla Ibn-al **11:**1093
Mashāiri, Mahadhdhib al-Dawla Naṣar Ibn **11:**1094
Mashā'iri, Obadiah al- **11:**1094
Mashā'iri, Yeshuah al- **11:**1094
Mashait script **2:**729
- *illus:*
- - script types **2:**731-742
Mashal, see ALLEGORY; FABLE; PARABLE; PROVERB
Mashal ha-Kadmoni (bk.), *see Meshal ha-Kadmoni*
Mashallah (astron.), *see* MASHĀ'ALLAH
Mashash, Yosef **9:**894
Mashbir, Eliezer **14:**1124
Mashen (mosh., Isr.) **1:** place list
MASHGI'AḤ (inspector) **11:**1094
- *see also:* KASHER
Mashhad (city, Iran), *see* MESHED
'Mashi'aḥ (r.), *see* Antibi, Ḥayyim Judah Shabbetai Raphael
MASHIV HA-RU'AḤ (rain prayer) **11:**1094
Mashkim (tract., Mish.), *see* MAKHSIRIN
Mashkin (tract., Mish.), *see* MO'ED KATAN
Mashkon (leg.term), *see* PLEDGE
Mashkoni, Judah Leon ben Moses, *see* MOSKONI, JUDAH LEON BEN MOSES
Mashnim (teachers of Mishnah) **15:**80
Mashvah Nephesh (soc., Eng.), *see* Bread, Meat, and Coal Society
M-a-sh-y-a, *see* ABBAS, MOSES JUDAH BEN MEIR
MASIE, AARON MEIR **11:**1095
- Tchernichowsky, Saul **15:**881
- Va'ad ha-Lashon **16:**1653
Masius, Andreas, *see* MAES, ANDREAS
"Masked Ball" (engr.) **13:**1394
MASKIL (mus. term) **11:**1095
- Psalms **13:**1319
Maskil (tit. for schol.) **13:**1451
Maskil ("intellectual"), *see* HASKALAH
Maskileison, Aaron ben Abraham **11:**1096
MASKILEISON, ABRAHAM BEN JUDAH LEIB **11:**1096
Maskileison, Abraham Isaac **11:**1096
Maskileison, Moses Nisan **11:**1096
Maskileison, Naphtali ben Abraham **11:**1096; **13:**1505
Maskilim ("intellectuals"), *see* HASKALAH
Maskil le-David (wk.) **15:**20
Maskil le-Eitan, Abraham, *see* MASKILEISON, ABRAHAM BEN JUDAH LEIB
Maskit (co., Isr.) **5:**1371
- *illus:*
- - oriental gown **9:**822
Maslakh, al- (qtr., Jer.) **9:**1580
Masliah (fam.) **5:**40
Masli'aḥ, Nissim **8:**1452; **11:**1096
MAṢLI'AḤ ṢĀLIḤ **11:**1096
Maṣli'aḥ ha-Kohen **16:**741
MASLIANSKY, ZVI HIRSCH **11:**1097
MASLOW, ABRAHAM H. **11:**1097
- psychology **13:**1344
MASLOW, SOPHIE **5:**1273
Maslul (mosh., Isr.) **1:**place list
Maslul (journ.) **1:**newsp. list
MASNUT, SAMUEL BEN NISSIM **11:**1097
Masok (aviation co., Isr.) **9:**839
Mason, Harry **15:**306
Masonry (craft) **5:**1042ff
Masons, *see* FREEMASONS
MASORAH **16:**1401
- *Contents:*
- - Transmission of the Bible **16:**1404
- - - The Soferim **16:**1405
- - - Written Transmission **16:**1405
- - - Oral Transmission **16:**1409
- - Beginnings of Grammar **16:**1414
- - - General **16:**1414
- - - Among the Jews **16:**1416
- - The Written Masorah **16:**1418
- - - Masorah Qetannah **16:**1419
- - - Masorah Gedolah **16:**1424
- - - Targum Onkelos **16:**1428
- - - Independent Masorah **16:**1428
- - Diacritical Marks **16:**1429
- - - Graetz's Theory **16:**1429
- - - Mille'el and Millera' **16:**1431
- - - Relative Notation **16:**1432
- - Vocalization and Cantillation **16:**1433
- - - Palestinian System **16:**1433
- - - Babylonian System **16:**1441
- - - Tiberian System **16:**1447
- - - Tiberian Non-Conventional System **16:**1461
- - - Mixing of the Systems **16:**1466
- - - Samaritan System **16:**1468
- - Masoretes and Grammarians **16:**1471
- - - First Masoretes **16:**1471
- - - Aaron ben Asher **16:**1472
- - - Anonymous Codification **16:**1473
- - - Continuators of the Masorah **16:**1475
- *al tikrei* **2:**776
- Aptowitzer's studies **3:**225
- Baer, S.I., studies **4:**80
- Ben-Asher, Aaron **4:**465
- Ben-Asher, Moses **4:**467
- Ben -Naphtali, Moses **4:**540
- Bible exegesis **4:**891
- Bible redaction **4:**835ff
- biblical Hebrew **16:**1570ff
- Buxtorf, Johannes **4:**1543
- Cairo *genizah* **16:**1336
- cantillation, Yemenite **16:**756
- Dead Sea Scrolls **5:**1401
- Great Synagogue **15:**630
- Isaiah text in DSS **16:**1585ff
- Jewish literature **11:**323ff
- Levita, Elijah **11:**132
- linguistics **16:**1353ff, 1392
- *Okhlah ve-Okhlah* **12:**1353
- Psalms, Book of **13:**1307
- Samaritans **14:**740
- Samuel, Book of **14:**789
- Tagin **15:**700
- *tikkun soferim* **15:**1139
- *illus:*
- - text
- - Ben-Asher and Ben -Naphtali, list of masoretic differences **4:**541,959,967
- - *Damascus Keter* **4:***fcg.* 844

-- Esther scroll with *tagin* **15:**700
-- micrographic writing **11:**689
-- outline for illustrations **4:**966
-- Second Leningrad Bible **11:**904
-- Yemenite ms. (1496) **11:**903; **16:** *fcg.* 743
- *see also:* CANTILLATION; HEBREW GRAMMAR; HEBREW LANGUAGE; MASORETIC ACCENTS; MUSIC; PRONUNCIATIONS OF HEBREW; TRADITION
Masorah Emẓa'it (collec.) **16:**1427
Masorah Gedolah **16:**1424ff, 1427
Masorah Ketannah **16:**1419ff
Masorah Me'arekhit (wk.) **16:**1427
Masorah Ravta (collec.), *see Masorah Gedolah*
Masorat ha-Masorah (wk.) **16:**1390
- Masorah **16:**1476
Masoret, see MASORAH; TRADITION
Masoretes **16:**1471ff
Masoret ha-Gedolah (wk.), *see* OKHLAH VE-OKHLAH
Masoret ha-Shas (tal. comment.) **4:**659
MASORETIC ACCENTS (MUSICAL RENDITION) **11:**1098
- masorah **16:**1418ff
- music **12:**578
- Scrolls, The Five **14:**1058
- Talmud melody **15:**753
- Torah reading **15:**1254
- *mus. notations:* text
- *see also:* CANTILLATION
Masoretic Cantillation, *see* CANTILLATION; MUSIC
Masoretic dots **16:**1407ff
Masoret Seyag la-Torah (bk.) **2:**191; **16:**1476ff
Masrekah (tn., Edom) **6:**370
Masrūq (pros. k.), *see* YŪSUF 'AS'AR YATH'AR DHU NUWĀS
Mass, Reuben **13:**1373; **13:**1378
Massa (s., Ishmael) **9:**89
- Tema **15:**940
Massa (period.) **8:**188; **14:**1289
- statistics **1:**newsp. list
Massachusetts (Ind. tribe, N. Am.) **4:**888
MASSACHUSETTS **11:**1111
- *illus:* text
- *pop. tables:* text
Massacres, *see* POGROMS
Massad (journ., Isr.) **1:**newsp. list
Massad (journ., U.S.) **1:**newsp. list
MASSADAH (kib., Isr.) **11:**1115
- statistics (kib., Isr.) **1:** place list
- *illus:* text
Massadah (training farm, Rum.) **8:**253
Massadah (encyc.) **2:**478
Massah and Meribah (bib. loc.), *see* REPHIDIM
Massa Ḥayyim (wk.) **15:**872
Massa le-Ereẓ-Yisrael bi-Shenat Tat (wk.) **16:**1151
Massa Melekh (wk.) **15:**872
Massarani, Isaiah **14:**170
Massarani, Ria **14:**170
Massarani, Simone **9:**1108
MASSARANI, TULLO **11:**1116
- Mantua **11:**899
Massarano, Abraham ben Isaac **8:**558; **11:**1117
MASSARANO, JACCHINO or ISACCHINO **11:**1117
MASSARY, FRITZI (Friedrike Massarik) **15:**1056 **15:**1088
MASSEKHET (tract.) **11:**1117
- *see also:* MISHNAH; TALMUD
Massekhet (journ., Isr.) **1:**newsp. list
Massekhet Aniyyut (parody) **13:**135
Massekhet Azilut (kab. wk.) **11:**347
Massekhet Ḥanukkah (parody) **13:**129ff
Massekhet ha-Omer (kib. litur.) **10:**960
Massekhet ha-Sho'ah ve-ha-Gevurah (kib. fest. anth.) **10:**960
Massekhet Prohibishon (bk.) **13:**136
Massekhet Purim (parody) **11:**353; **13:**127
- *illus:*
-- title page (Hanover, 1844) **13:**125
Massekhet Soḥarim (parody) **13:**135
Massel, J. **10:**382; **14:**774
- *illus:*
-- F.Z.C. **16:**1165
MASSELL, SAM JR. **11:**1117
- Atlanta **3:**825
Massena (tn., N.Y.) **12:**1127
MASSERMAN, JULES HOMAN **11:**1118
Massis, Mount (Turk.) **3:**290
Mass Murder, *see* CAMPS; GENOCIDE CONVENTION; HOLOCAUST
Massorah, *see* MASORAH
Massuot (kib., Er. Isr.), *see* MASSU'OT YIẒHAK
Massu'ot (annual) **13:**1047
- statistics **1:**newsp. list
MASSU'OT YIẒHAK (mosh., Isr.) **11:**1118
- Hapoel ha-Mizrachi **7:**1322
- statistics **1:**place list
- *illus:* text
MASTBAUM, JOEL **11:**1119
- *illus:* text
Mastbaum, Jules E. **11:**307
MASTEMA (devil) **11:**1119
- demonology **5:**1525
- *see also:* JUBILEES, BOOK OF; SATAN
MASTER, ARTHUR M. **11:**1120
Master Aaron (r., It.), *see* AARON OF BAGHDAD
Master Gabriel (ps. prophet) **11:**301
Master Gaio (13/14 cent., It.), *see* Isaac ben Mordecai (physic.)
Mastermann, E.W.G. **9:**1525
MASTIC (bot.) **11:**1120
- Jerusalem flora **9:**1515
- plant list **13:**621
Mastodon (zool.) **9:**225
Mas'ud Hai Rakah, *see* RAKAH, MAS'UD HAI BEN AARON
Mas'ūd ha-Kohen al-Ḥaddād **10:**244
Mas'ūd *Ma'aravi, see* AZULAI, MAS'UD
Mas'ūd *Saggi-Nahor, see* AZULAI, MAS'UD
Masu'ot (journ.) **12:**1051
Masur, Norbert **13:**1583
Mat, Abraham (16th cent., mart.) **11:**1120
Mat, Abraham (16/17 cent., Pol.) **11:**1121
MAT, MOSES **11:**1120
Matalon (fam., (Isr.) **15:**919
Matalon (fam., Jam.) **9:**1274
Matalon, Abraham **11:**1566
Matalon, Mordecai **14:**894
MATA MEḤASYA (tn., Babyl.) **11:**1121
- academy **11:**940
Matanot Publishing House (U.S.) **5:**445
Matanzas (prov., Cuba) **5:**1148
Matarasco, M. **13:**1039
Matarasso, J. **7:**887
Matas, Roy **16:**551
Matate (theat., Er. Isr.), *see* Kumkum
Matatron, *see* METATRON
Match, Pincus **15:**303
"Maternity" (paint., M. de Haan) **3:**549
Maternity Insurance, Israel **9:**995
Mateusz Józef, *see* BIRNBOIM, MOSES JOSEPH
Matfre d'Ermengaud **11:**695
MATHEMATICS **11:**1121
- Abraham bar Ḥiyya **2:**132
- Israel **16:**439
- Jewish contributions **8:**743
- translations **15:**1324
- *see also:* NUMBERS, TYPICAL AND IMPORTANT
Mathieu le Juif **7:**146
Matif ha-Kazav, see LIES, PROPHET OF
Matisse, Henri **13:**113
Matitiah, Joseph **16:**64
MATKAH, JUDAH BEN SOLOMON HA-KOHEN **11:**1126
- Abulafia, Meir **2:**192
- alchemy **2:**548
- encyclopedia **6:**730
- Joseph ben David ha-Yevani **10:**226
Matlies, Itshe, *see* PERLOV, YIẒḤAK
Matlin, David A. **15:**316
Matlin, Moses **16:**760
Matmor, Yoram **6:**206
Matnan (reg., Er. Isr.), *see* BASHAN
Matnitin ve-Tosefta (kab. wk.) **16:**1196
Matos, Francisca de **5:**221
Matred (bib. fig.) **6:**373
Matres lectionis (gram. term) **16:**1413ff
Matriarchs **13:**183
Matrikel-Gesetz (anti-J. law) **3:**838; **4:**109
Matrimony, *see* MARRIAGE
Matrona (d. of Paragonis) **12:**828
Matrona (kab. conc.) **10:**575
Matsas, Joseph **7:**887
MATSAS, NESTORAS **11:**1127
Matta (mosh., Isr.) **1:**place list
Mattan (Baal pr.) **3:**814
Mattanah Hamazri (Samar. litur., Egy.) **14:**753
Mattaniah (k. Judah), *see* ZEDEKIAH
Mattan Torah, see REVELATION
Mattapan (sub., Boston) **4:**1265; **11:**1112
MATTATHIAS (Hasm. ldr.) **11:**1127
- *First Book of Maccabees* **11:**657
- in the Arts **7:**1457
- Modi'in **12:**206
- revolt against Antiochus **8:**629
- sons **12:**808
- *geneal. table:* **7:**1457
- *see also:* ḤANUKKAH; HASMONEANS
Mattathias (Hasm.k.), *see* ANTIGONUS II
MATTATHIAS (Heb. poet) **11:**1129
"Mattathias" (sculp., B. Schatz) **11:**1128
Mattathias bar Mar Ravi (gaon) **7:**318
Mattathias ben Absalom **10:**190
Mattathias ben Anan (h. pr.), *see* Matthias ben Anan
Mattathias ben Benjamin Ze'ev **4:**538
Mattathias ben Ḥeresh (tanna), *see* MATTIAH BEN ḤERESH
Mattathias ben Isaac **5:**475
Mattathias ben Joseph **15:**1376; **15:**1378 **16:**764
MATTATHIAS BEN SIMEON **11:**1129
MATTATHIAS HA-YIẒHARI **11:**1129
- Tortosa disputation **14:**862; **15:**1271ff
Mattathias Gaon **13:**104
Matteh Moshe (bk.) **4:**530
Mattekhet (jounr.) **1:**newsp. list
Mattenat bari (type of legacy) **16:**519ff
Mattenat shekhiv me-ra (type of legacy) **16:**519
Matteo da Reggio **8:**1398
Matteo di Girgenti **14:**1184
Matteo di Ser Cambio **13:**325
- *illus:*
-- *Jerusalem Mishneh Torah* **8:***fcg.* 1015
Matter, *see* FORM AND MATTER
Matter, J. **8:**291
MATTERSDORF (Mattersburg; tn., Aus.) **11:**1130
Mattersdorf (sub., Jer.), *see* Kiryat Mattersdorf
MATTERSDORF, JEREMIAH BEN ISAAC **11:**1131
Mattersdorf, Joab **11:**1131
Matthew (apostle) **3:**216; **10:**15
Matthew, Gospel of (N.T.) **10:**10
- Muenster's Hebrew version **4:**1069; **12:**506
Matthew, Wentworth A. **4:**1069
Matthew Paris (chronicler) **16:**260
Matthias I (k., Hung.) **2:**493; **13:**963
Matthias, Elias Germanus **8:**44
Matthias Aquarius **8:**44
Matthias ben Anan **2:**922; **10:**185; **14:**1554
MATTHIAS BEN THEOPHILUS **11:**1131
- Theophilus **15:**1111
Matthias of Janov **8:**1135
Matthias von Rammung **15:**265
Matthioli (physic.) **2:**797
MATTIAH BEN ḤERESH **11:**1132
- Rome academy **2:**202
Mattithiah ha-Kadosh, *see* Serero, Mattathias
Mattityahu ben Ḥeresh (tan.), *see* MATTIAH BEN ḤERESH (tan.)
MATTNAH (3rd cent., amora) **11:**1132
Mattnah (4th cent., amora) **11:**1132
Mattoon (city, Ill.) **8:**1256
MATTUCK, ISRAEL ISIDOR **11:**1132
Ma'ṭūf (fam. div., Arab.) **7:**1018
Ma'tuk, Judah ben Jacob **11:**1133
MA'TUK, SULAYMAN BEN DAVID **11:**1133
Maturity, age of, *see* PUBERTY
Maturity, Religious and Legal, *see* BAR MITZVAH, BAT MITZVAH
Matya of Dobrath (amora) **6:**143
Matywiecki, Menashe **13:**775; **16:**353
MATZ, ISRAEL **11:**1133
Matz, Solomon **15:**1632
Matzah, see MAẒẒAH
Mauclerc, Pierre **4:**1383
Maudsley, H. **9:**1526
Mauer, Johann **3:**903
Mauer, Wilhelm (Nazi crim.) **3:**903; **16:**300
Mauhub ha-Ḥazzan ben Aaron ha-Ḥazzan **2:**592
Maundrell, Henry **6:**782
Maupassant, Guy de **10:**675
Maurer, Emil **3:**904
Maurer, F.J.V.D. **8:**44
Mauriac, François **6:**1279
Maurice de Hirsch Hospital (Salonika) **14:**704
Maurice Spertus Museum (Chicago) **12:**544
Mauricia (tn., Braz.) **2:**429; **4:**1324; **14:**1662
Mauricio (clny., Arg.) **3:**432
- *illus:*

- - colonists and gauchos **3**:431
Maurier, George du **6**:780
Mauritania (rep., Afr.) **9**:440
MAURITIUS (isl.) **11**:1133
- "illegal" immigrants **8**:1249
- *illus:* text
Maurogonato, Isaac **13**:815
MAUROIS, ANDRÉ **11**:1134
- Bloch, Jean-Richard **4**:1102
MAURRAS, CHARLES **11**:1135
- *L'Action française* **2**:232
Maušel, Mordecai ben Samuel, *see* MEISEL, MORDECAI BEN SAMUEL
Mauss, Ch. **9**:1537
MAUSS, MARCEL **11**:1136
- sociology **3**:37
MAUTHAUSEN (concen. camp., Aus.) **11**:1136
- Austria **3**:901
- concentration camps **5**:86
- Dutch Jews **2**:902
- *illus:* text
MAUTHNER, FRITZ **11**:1138
Mautner, Isaac **12**:749
Mavet (demon) **5**:1523
Mavki'im (mosh., Isr.) **1**:place list
Mavo ha-Dikduk (wk.) **16**:1388
Mavo li-Leshon ha-Kodesh, ha- (wk.) **16**:1387
Ma-Wara-n-Nahr (reg., As.), *see* TRANSOXIANA
Mawjib, al- (riv., Transj.), *see* ARNON
Mawṣili, ibn Abi Saʿīd al-, *see* Ibn Abi Saʿīd al-Mawṣili
MAWZAʿ (reg., Arab.) **11**:1139
- Yemen Jews' exile **16**:743
Max, Edouard Alexander de **15**:1055
Max, Sol **12**:1522
Maxač-Kala (tn., Cauc.) **10**:442
Maximianupolis (city, Er. Isr.), *see* LEGIO
MAXIMILIAN I (H. Rom. emp.) **11**:1140
- Austrian Jews **3**:889
MAXIMILIAN II (H. Rom. emp.) **11**:1140
- *illus:*
- - decree of privileges **3**:923
Maximilian Henry (elector, Ger.) **8**:475
MAXIMON (Maximowski), SHALOM DOV BER **11**:1140
Maxims, Legal, *see* LEGAL MAXIMS
MAXIMUS, MAGNUS CLEMENS **11**:1141
- Rome synagogue rebuilt **2**:801
Maximus of Turin (Ch. F.) **5**:553
Maximus the Usurper, *see* MAXIMUS, MAGNUS CLEMENS
Maxwell Abbel Research Institute in Rabbinics (N.Y.C.) **10**:97
Maxwell, General **10**:70
Maxwell, Robert **13**:1371
MAXY, MAX HERMAN **3**:606
May, Alfred A. **5**:1572
May, Henry John, *see* Schlosberg, Herzl J.
May, J. (bnk.) **4**:177
May, Jacques Meyer (sci.) **7**:422
May, Kurt **15**:1568
May, Lewis **12**:1075
May, M.L. (print., Pol.) **6**:330
May, Moses (print., Fr.) **11**:1451
Mayaguez (city, Puerto Rico) **16**:1555
Mayakovski, Vladimir **14**:510
Ma'yan (Zion gr.) **5**:1107; **8**:250
MA'YAN BARUKH (kib., Isr.) **11**:1141
- statistics **1**:place list
Ma'yan ha-Ḥasidut (journ.) **1**:newsp. list
- *see also: Ha-Ma'yan*
Ma'yan Ḥarod (nat. park, Isr.) **12**:879
Ma'yanot (journ.) **1**:newsp. list
MA'YAN ẒEVI (kib., Isr.) **11**:1142
MAYBAUM, IGNAZ **11**:1142
MAYBAUM, SIGMUND **11**:1142
- homiletic literature **8**:956
- "Protest rabbiner" **13**:1255
Maydān (area, Jer.) **9**:1456
Mayence (city, Ger.), *see* MAINZ
Mayenowa, Maria Renata **13**:803
Mayer (fam.) **5**:934
Mayer, Albert (archit., U.S.) **3**:360
Mayer, Albert (polit., Gdr.) **15**:1525
MAYER, ARNO JOSEPH **8**:548
Mayer, Astorre **11**:1146
Mayer, Carl **12**:453
MAYER, DANIEL **11**:1143
- politics **13**:813
- *illus:*
- - Jarblum, Marc **9**:1287
Mayer, David **3**:824; **3**:825
Mayer, Erskine **15**:301
Mayer, George Toma, *see* MAIORESCU, GEORGE TOMA
Mayer, Grace **13**:486
MAYER, GUSTAV **11**:1143
Mayer, Helene **12**:1376
Mayer, H. H. (sci.) **7**:205
Mayer, Henry **5**:219
Mayer, Isaac (mintmaster), *see* Meir, Isaac
Mayer, Isaac (r.) **7**:1359
Mayer, J.F., *see* Meyer, J.F.
Mayer, Johann Simon, *see* Mayr, Johann Simon
Mayer, Jonas **6**:211
MAYER, LEO ARY **11**:1144
- Eshtemoa **6**:892
- numismatics **12**:1271
MAYER, LEOPOLD **11**:1144
- Denver **5**:1543
MAYER, LEVY **11**:1145
MAYER, LOUIS BURT **11**:1145
- Hollywood **11**:503
Mayer, Montagu **15**:307
MAYER, RENÉ **11**:1146
MAYER, SALLY **11**:1146
- J. D. C. **2**:830; **6**:966; **8**:907
Mayer, Samuel Harum **15**:1426
Mayer, Wolf **4**:875
Mayerberg, Samuel S. **10**:740; **10**:741
Mayerchik, Hanna, *see* MERON, HANNA
Mayer-Gross, W. **13**:1340
Mayerhofer, A.J.L. **16**:1015
Mayerowitz, Benjamin **11**:1302
Mayers, M. **8**:560
Mayfaʿī (fam. div., Arab.) **7**:1018
Mayflower (petroleum co., Isr.) **9**:795
MAYIM AḤARONIM (hand washing) **11**:1147
- reasons **14**:711
MAYKAPAR, SAMUIL MOYSEYEVICH **12**:700
MAY LAWS (Rus.) **11**:1147
- effect on Jews **13**:26
- history chart **8**:766-767
- Podolia **13**:668
- *see also:* ANTI-SEMITISM (Russia)
Maymaran (r., Sp.) **11**:938
MAYMERAN (fam.) **11**:1148
Maymeran, Abraham **11**:1149; **11**:1272; **15**:1194
Maymeran, Joseph **2**:516; **4**:1461; **11**:1149; **11**:1272
Maymeran, Meir **11**:1148
Maymeran, Moïse **11**:1149
Maymeran, Samuel **11**:1149
Maymo, Asher Bonnim **8**:1260
Mayne, Seymour **5**:115
Mayne Zikhroynes (bk.) **10**:1221
Mayo, Isaac di **9**:1163
Mayo, Raphael Isaac **3**:728
Mayo, Raphael Jacob de **11**:828
Mayques (fam.) **12**:1446
Mayr, George **8**:44
Mayr, Simon **3**:815; **14**:785
Mayse Bikhlekh (Yid. lit.), *see* CHAPBOOKS
Mayzel, Maurycy **5**:1210
MAYZEL, NACHMAN **11**:1149
- *illus:* **16**:818
Mazaca (Mazaga; city, As. M.), *see* CAESAREA IN CAPPADOCIA
Mazagan (city, Mor.) **3**:1004; **12**:344
Mazal, Joseph **11**:857
Mazanderan (reg., Iran), *see* Tabaristan
Mazanik, E.G. **12**:55
Mazār (vill., Isr.) **11**:1392
MAZAR, BENJAMIN **11**:1150
- archaeology **3**:302ff
- Bet She'arim excavations **3**:331; **4**:766
- historiography **8**:562
- Jerusalem archaeology **9**:1525ff
- Tobiads **15**:1178
- *illus:*
- Temple Mount excavations **9**:1533,1535,1538
Mazdaism, *see* Zoroastrianism
Mazdak, Mazdakites (fig., tribe, Babyl.) **4**:42; **6**:1027
MAZE, IDA **11**:1150
MAZEH, JACOB **11**:1151
- *illus:*
- - Benei Zion meeting **12**:359
- - Tarbut kindergarten **14**:447
MAZER (fam.) **11**:1152
Mazer, Abraham **11**:1152
Mazer, Jacob **11**:1152
Mazer, Joseph M. **11**:1152
Mazer, William **2**:817; **11**:1152
Maziah (pr. mishmeret) **7**:1242
Mazie, Aharon, *see* MASIE, AARON MEIR
Mazin, Jack **13**:1374
Mazin, Max **11**:684
Mazin, R. **4**:1239; **13**:1374
MAZKERET BATYAH (mosh., Isr.) **11**:1152
- Hameiri, Moshe **7**:1232
- statistics **1**:place list
- *illus:* text
- *see also:* KIRYAT EKRON
Mazkeret Moshe (qtr., Jer.) **9**:1460
Mazkeret Moshe be-Erez ha-Kodesh (orgn.) **16**:1040
Mazkir (bib. hist.) **8**:552
Mazkir (prayer), *see* HAZKARAT NESHAMOT
Mazle Dina (agg. fig.) **15**:71
MAẒLI'AḤ (mosh., Isr.) **11**:1153
- statistics **1**:place list
Maẓliaḥ, Moses ben Joseph **5**:627
Mazliah, Nissim, *see* Maṣli'aḥ, Nissim
Maẓliaḥ, Ṣāliḥ, *see* MAṢLI'AḤ, ṢĀLIḤ
Maẓli'aḥ ben Japheth **5**:1349
MAẒLI'AḤ BEN SOLOMON HA-KOHEN **11**:1153
- Aden Jewry **2**:260
- *geonim* **7**:323; **7**:324
- Maḍmūn ben Japhet **11**:680
Mazo, Mordecai **15**:1072; **16**:151
Mazor (mosh., Isr.) **1**: place list
Mazovsher Vokhenblat (period.) **11**:534
Mazowiecki (tn., Pol.), *see* GRODZISK MAZOWIECKI
Maẓpen (New Left mvmt., Isr.) **12**:1034
Maẓpen (journs.) **1**:newsp. list
Mazra'a, al- (vill., Er. Isr.) **9**:575
MAẒRANUT (leg. term) **11**:1153
- *niddui* for disregard **8**:351
- *takkanot* **15**:721
MAZUR, ELIYAHU **11**:1154
Mazur, Zelik **5**:445; **5**:459
Mazur, Ẓevi Meir **11**:1154
Mazūrān (tn., Iraq) **15**:504
Mazure, Maurice M. **16**:633
Mazya, Frida **5**:448
MAẒẒAH (unleavened bread) **11**:1155
- barley **4**:242
- blood libel **4**:1124
- Commandments, the 613 **5**:764,767
- grain types **6**:1333
- *Haggadah* **7**:1079ff
- *Ha Laḥma Anya* **7**:1155
- Passover customs **6**:1424
- St. Petersburg prohibition **11**:18
- women's obligation **10**:1566
- *illus:*
- - text
- - baking **12**:26
- - Bene Israel baking *maẓẓah* **4**:495
- - distribution **3**:530
- - father distributing **13**:165
- - *kahal maẓẓah*, holder **11**:693
- - Moscow bakery **12**:365
- - N.Y. sale **15**:1607
- - Ostia oven **12**:1508
- *see also:* ḤAMEẒ; PASSOVER
Mazzal (luck; fate) **3**:789; **3**:790; **14**:137; **14**:137; **14**:178
Mazzal Tov (greeting) **7**:916
Mazzal Tov, Elijah ben David **13**:579
Mazzal-Tov, Elisha **13**:613
Mazzal Tov ben David **13**:589
Maẓẓevah (tombstone) **15**:1218
Maẓẓevah (cult) **3**:244; **3**:705; **8**:1228
Mazzikim (demons) **5**:1526; **11**:245
Mazzini, Giuseppe **9**:1106; **14**:251; **14**:314
Maẓẓiv (orgn., Isr.) **8**:539
Mazzochi, J. **14**:252
MAẒẒUVAH (kib., Isr.) **11**:1158
- statistics **1**: place list
M. Cocceius Nerva (Rom. emp.), *see* NERVA
Meadow, Franklin **15**:308
Meadow Pipit (fauna), *see* Pipit
Me'ah (weight) **16**:388
Me'ah Berakhot (prayer bk.) **16**:1417
Me'ah She'arim (qtr., Jer.) **9**:1517
- Auerbach, Meir **3**:848
- housing **9**:563
- municipal affairs **9**:1498
- Turks **9**:1459
- *illus:*
- - byway **9**:581
- - Ḥasidim **7**:1398
- - market **9**:1489
Meal, *see* SE'UDAH
Meal offering, *see Minḥah* (offering)
Meals, Community, *see Ḥavurah*
Meals, Grace after, *see* GRACE AFTER MEALS
ME-AM LO'EZ (bib. comment.) **11**:1158
- Ladino literature **10**:1349
- Ssphardi literature **14**:1169
- *illus:*
- - title page (1751) **5**:1154; (1764) **13**:1108
Me'arot (site, Er. Isr.) **11**:702
Mears, Abraham **7**:299
MEARS, OTTO **11**:1160
- *illus:*
- - text
- - Colorado Utes chief **5**:754
Me'assef (journ. Isr.) **1**: newsp. list
ME'ASSEF (period., Rus.) **11**:1161
- Ben Ze'ev, Judah Leib **4**:573
- critical reviews **5**:1116

- Haskalah **7:**1438ff
- Hebrew literature **8:**180ff
- Hebrew newspapers **12:**1048; **13:**1056
- Koenigsberg **10:**1129
- societies, learned **15:**55
- *Sulamith* **15:**502
- statistics **1:**newsp. list
- *illus:*
- - title page (1788) **7:**1435; **8:**181
Me'assefim Madda'iyyim shel ha-Tekhnion (journ.) **1:**newsp. list
Me'assef Soferei Ereẓ-Yisrael (journs.) **1:**newsp. list
Measures, *see* WEIGHTS AND MEASURES
Measuring line, *see Ḥevel middah; Kav (qav) ha-middah*
Measuring reed, *see Qene ha-middah*
MEAT **11:**1162
- Abu ʿImrān al-Tiflisī **10:**766; **10:**780
- dietary laws **6:**27,39 **4:**1027
- economic life **16:**1268ff
- *ḥazakah* **7:**1521
- *Ḥullin* **8:**1069
- kashering **6:**27
- laws **11:**142
- *onen* **3:**23
- philosophers **3:**7
- *sheḥitah* **14:**1338
- tax **15:**850
- Temple destruction **9:**238
- *illus:*
- - clean and unclean animals (table) **6:**29-38
- - seals **14:**1077,1342
- - *sheḥitah* and *bedikah* rules (1804) **6:**41,43,45
- - *sheḥitah* scene **14:**1339
- - *Ẓinah David* (1750) **6:**39
- *see also:* BLOOD
Meati, Ha- (fam.) **9:**1121
Me'at me-Harbeh (journ.) **1:**newsp. list
Meat tax, *see* KOROBKA
Meaux-Paris, Council of (9th cent.) **2:**915; **5:**547
Mebaragesi (ruler, Mesop.) **16:**1487
Mecca (city, Saud. Arab.) **3:**232ff
- Arab National Movement **9:**455
- Islam **9:**92
- Jewish prohibition **10:**87
- Muhammad **12:**508ff
- Muslim prayer **10:**1198
- *illus:*
- - Catalan Atlas **11:**915
- - Great Mosque and Ka'ba **9:**93
- - Hebron pilgrims setting out for **9:**918
Mechanicus, Philip **6:**321
Mechelen (tn., concen. camp, Belg.), *see* MALINES
Mechelin, Leo **6:**1297
Mechlin (tn., Belg.), *see* MALINES
Mechlovitz, Zoltan **15:**314
MECKLENBURG (duchy, Ger.) **11:**1163
- first settlers **15:**1176
Mecklenburg, Jacob Z. **10:**1129
Mecklenburg-Schwerin (Ger.) **6:**531
Medaba (tn., Transj.), *see* MADABA, MEDEBA
Medad (bib. fig.), *see* ELDAD AND MEDAD
MEDALIE, GEORGE ZERDIN **11:**1164
MEDALISTS **11:**1165
- *illus:* text
MEDALS **11:**1168
- Friedenberg, Samuel **7:**175
- portraits of Jews **13:**917
- symbolism **15:**571ff
- *illus:*
- - Abensur, Daniel, and Sara de Castro **2:**69
- - Amsterdam Jewish Orphanage **11:**1165,1166
- - Astruc, Elie-Aristide **3:**808
- - Balfour Declaration jubilee **16:**155
- - Bergson, Henri Louis **4:**621
- - B'nai B'rith lodge in Frankfort **4:**1147
- - Cologne synagogue **16:**498
- - Crémieux, Isaac Adolphe **5:**1074,1250
- - Damascus Affair **5:**1250
- - Edward VI of England **6:** 753
- - Ehrlich, Paul **6:**514
- - England, tercentenary of resettlement **6:**772
- - Franco-Prussian war victims **15:**91
- - Friedenberg, Samuel **7:** 175
- - Hesse Jews to Caroline Henriette **8:**435
- - Itzig, Daniel **3:**545
- - Joseph II's *Toleranzpatent* **10:**218
- - Lattes, Elia and Rica de **10:** 1460
- - Lindo family **11:**259
- - Maastricht Synagogue **11:**1166
- - Mahler, Gustav **11:**726
- - Maria Theresa **11:**991
- - Montefiore, Sir Moses **5:**1250
- - Munich Synagogue **11:**1166
- - Napoleon's Sanhedrin **12:**823
- - Nasi, Gracia **12:**836
- - Neuburger, Max **12:**1006
- - Olympic Games (table) **12:**1373,1375ff
- - Oppenheimer, Joseph Suess ("Jew Suess") **5:**1011
- - Peter III ruble (S. Judin) **10:**451
- - Philanthropin centenary **7:**88
- - Righteous of the Nations **14:**184
- - "Santina" (Zadikow) **16:**913
- - Second Zionist Congress **4:**380
- - Seixas, Gershom Mendes **7:**221
- - *Toleranzpatent* **15:**1210
- - Westphalian Jews **16:**474
- - Wildenstein, Georges **16:**511
- *see also:* COINS AND CURRENCY; MINTMASTERS AND MONEYERS; NUMISMATICS
Medan (bib. fig.) **9:**89
MEDAN, MEIR **1:**34
Medanites (bib. nation) **9:**89
Médanos (clny., Arg.) **3:**430
Médéa (tn., Alg.) **2:**613
Medeba (Moab. city), *see* MADABA, MEDEBA
Medeba Map, *see* Madaba Map
Medek, Rudolf **5:**1207
Medellín (city, Colom.) **5:**745
Medem, Alexander **9:**1448
MEDEM, VLADIMIR **11:**1175
MEDES AND MEDIA **11:**1176
- Babylonia **4:**34
- diaspora **6:**11
- Nehavend **12:**936
- Persia **13:**302ff,312
- Sargon II **14:**880
Medgyesi, Pál **8:**44
Medical Association of Ereẓ Israel **4:**691
Medical ethics **3:**676
Medical services in Israel, *see* HEALTH SERVICES IN ISRAEL
Medicare (U.S.) **8:**1040; **14:**152
Medici (fam.) **10:**1571
Medici, Cosimo I de' **3:**408; **6:**1359ff; **15:**1467
Medici, Cosimo III de' **15:**1468
Medici, Ferdinand I de' **11:**1194
Medici, Giovanni de' (pope), *see* LEO X
Medici, Marie de **11:**1194
Medici, Paolo Sebastiano **5:**963; **15:**1468
- *illus:*
- - *Conversione di Sabbato Nachamu* (1735) **3:**208
Medici, Vitale de', *see* Vitale de'Medici
MEDICINE **11:**1178
- *Contents:*
- - In the Bible **11:**1178
- - The Talmudic Era **11:**1181
- - The Middle Period **11:**1185
- - 19th-20th Centuries **11:**1195
- - Capsules **11:**1205
- amulets **2:**910; **2:**911
- discrimination in U.S. **15:**1654
- dissection **3:**931ff
- folklore **6:**1405
- *halakhah* **15:**895
- Ibn Biklarish, Junas **8:**1158
- Jewish tradition **8:**714
- lavender **15:**269
- leprosy **11:**33
- Macht's studies **11:**674ff
- magic **11:**710
- Maimonides **11:**777
- medicinal plants **16:**1490
- microcosm **11:**1502
- Ottoman Empire **16:**1540,1552
- Physician's Oath **3:**676
- purity ritual **13:**1407
- sages **14:**650
- sickness **14:**1499
- TOZ's activities **15:**1291
- transplant **15:**1337
- universities **15:**1675ff
- *illus:*
- - text
- - Asaph ha-Rofe's oath (ms.) **3:**675
- - *Cambridge Medical Miscellany* (15th cent.) **14:***fcg.* 1515
- - *Canon of Avicenna* **3:***fcg.* 956; **8:**1283
- - *De Ratione Victus* (1559) **4:**1414
- - Gregory XIII's bull re Jewish physicians **4:**1495
- - Hadassah Medical Center **7:**1043-1044
- - *In Dioscoridis enarrationes* (1553) **2:**795
- - "Jewish Doctor" (paint., Rembrandt) **13:**917
- - *Sefer Eẓ ha-Sadeh* **4:**1016
- - twelfth-century Judeo-Arabic ms. **10:**409
- *see also:* ANATOMY; HERBS, MEDICINAL; HOSPITALS; MENTAL ILLNESS
Medicus Herz, *see* Herz, Medicus
Medieval Hebrew, *see* HEBREW LANGUAGE
Medina (fam.) **11:**877
MEDINA (city, Arab.) **11:**1211
- Abdallah Ibn Salām **2:**54
- Arabia **3:**232ff
- Babylonians **16:**1505
- goldsmiths and silversmiths **7:**740
- Islam **9:**92
- Jewish prohibition **10:**87
- Muhammad **12:**509ff
Medina, Abraham **14:**304
Medina, David di **10:**554
Medina, Joseph de **12:**977
Medina, Judah **11:**1214
Medina, Moses **11:**1214
MEDINA, SAMUEL BEN MOSES DE **11:**1212
- Boton, Abraham **4:**1269
- chief rabbinate **13:**1451
- Ottoman Empire **16:**1549
- Sephardi prayer rites **8:**699
Medina, Shemaiah **11:**1214
MEDINA, SIR SOLOMON DE **11:**1214
- ennobled **15:**1166
MEDINACELI (tn., Sp.) **11:**1214
MEDINA DEL CAMPO (tn., Sp.) **11:**1215
MEDINA DE POMAR (tn., Sp.) **11:**1215
MEDINAH (Heb. term) **11:**1215
Medina Iwrit-Judenstaat (period.) **13:**1029
Medinat Zamet (reg., Lith.), *see* SAMOGITIA
Medinet Habu (site, Egy.) **13:**399; **16:**271
Medinḥa'i (masorah version) **16:**1423,1442
MEDINI, ḤAYYIM HEZEKIAH BEN RAPHAEL ELIJAH **11:**1216
- *Sedeh Ḥemed* **6:**734
MEDITATION **11:**1217
- Ḥasidism **14:**1437
- Isaac the Blind **10:**523
- Kabbalah **10:**538; **10:**627ff
- Worlds, the Four **16:**643
- *see also:* KAVVANAH
MEDVEDEV, MIKHAIL **12:**700
Medvedevka (loc., Rus.) **12:**782ff
MEDZIBEZH (Medzibozh; tn., Ukr.) **11:**1220
- Podolia **13:**667
- special Purim **13:**1397
- *illus:*
- - Israel Ba'al Shem Tov's *Bet ha-midrash* **9:**1053
Meelführer, J. M. **8:**44
MEEROVITCH, MENACHÉ **11:**1220
- *illus:*
- - Amery, Leopold **2:**833
Meersohn, Abraham **10:**1502
"Meeting of Jacob and Rachel" (drg., Hugo Van der Goes) **13:**1487
Me-Et le-Et (journs., Lith.; U.S.) **1:**newsp. list
Meetkerke, Edward **8:**44
Mefallesim (kib., Isr.) **1:**place list
Mefareshim (bib. and tal. comment.) **13:**927
Mefkure (refugee ship) **8:**857; **14:**404
Megaddef, *see* LORKI, JOSHUA
Megadim (mosh., Isr.) **1:**place list
Megalith (prehist. stone structure) **6:**156
Megalleh Amukkot (bk.) **15:**284
Megalleh Temirin (bk.) **8:**184; **11:**116
Megammot (journ.) **1:**newsp. list
MEGASTHENES **7:**895
Meged (vill., Er. Isr.), *see* PARDES ḤANNAH-KARKUR
MEGED, AHARON **11:**1221
- *illus:*
- - *Genesis* production **15:**1063
Meged, Matti **11:**1221
Meged Geresh Yeraḥim (period.) **1:**newsp. list; **12:**1333
Meged Yeraḥim (period., Gal.) **1:**newsp. list; **16:**1330
Megerlin, David F. **8:**44
MEGIDDO (site, Er. Isr.) **11:**1222
- Ahab **2:**437
- anthropological evidence **3:**45ff
- architecture **3:**357
- Armageddon **3:**472; **16:**1499
- battle (history chart) **8:**766-767
- ivory inscription **16:**662
- ivory vessels **6:**603
- museum **11:**553
- pictographic scripts **16:**654
- pillars **13:**521,522
- pottery **13:**938
- pre-Israelite *bamah* **5:**1166
- settlement of Israel tribes **8:**581
- Solomon **15:**102
- Song of Deborah **8:**585

- Taanach **15**:674
- temple **15**:951
- war and warfare **16**:269ff
- *illus:*
- - text
- - Canaanite temple **2**:760
- - fortress gates **3**:316
- - horned altar **2**:766
- - ivory carved box **11**:268
Megiddo (kib., Isr.) **11**:1227
- statistics **1**:place list
Megiddo, Valley of (Isr.) **7**:1040
Megiles Vintz (poem), *see Megillat Vinz*
MEGILLAH (scroll) **11**:1228
- art **3**:538
- scribe **14**:1044
- *see also:* SCROLL OF ESTHER; SCROLLS, THE FIVE
MEGILLAH (tract.) **11**:1228
- Purim **13**:1392
- *Mishloah Manot* **2**:17
- synagogue service **15**:583
- *illus:* text
Megillat Ahimaaz (bk.), *see Ahimaaz, Scroll of*
Megillat Eikhah (agg. Mid.), *see* LAMENTATIONS RABBAH
Megillat Ester, see SCROLL OF ESTHER
Megillat ha-Megalleh (wk.) **2**:133; **11**:1414; **13**:436
Megillat Sefer (bk.) **5**:227
MEGILLAT SETARIM (concealed scroll) **11**:1229
- *see also:* MIDRASH
Megillat Setarim (wk., ibn Motot) **15**:520
Megillat Setarim (wk., Levi ben Gershon) **11**:353; **13**:129
Megillat Setarim (wk., Nissim ben Jacob) **12**:1183
MEGILLAT TA'ANIT (tan. wk.) **11**:1230
- calendar **5**:47,48
- law source **12**:117
- Talmud **11**:1229
- *see also:* MIDRASH
Megillat Vinz (poem) **13**:1220; **16**:804
MEGILLAT YUHASIN (geneal. bk.) **11**:1231
Megillat Yuhasin (chronicle), *see Ahimaaz, Scroll of*
Megillot (journ.) **1**:newsp. list
Meginnei Erez (hal. comment.) **14**:1476
Meginnei ha-Histadrut (orgn.) **16**:338
Megizah of Cappadocia, *see* CAESAREA IN CAPPADOCIA
Megorashim (cmty., Mor.) **2**:669; **14**:1083
Me-Hag le-Hag (journ.) **1**:newsp. list
Mehallekhim (journ.) **1**:newsp. list
Mehamat mitah (mortis causa) **16**:521
Me-Havayot ha-Zeman (journ.) **1**:newsp. list
Me-Havvenu (period.) **7**:356
Meheimanuta de Kholla (bk.) **3**:996; **14**:1249
Meheleb (Cana. city), *see* AHLAB
Mehemet Ali, *see* MUHAMMAD ALI
Mehetabel (q., Edom) **2**:543; **6**:373
Me-Hevel (Cana. city), *see* AHLAB
MEHILAH (waiver) **11**:1232
MEHIZAH **11**:1234
- synagogue **15**:584; **15**:588; **15**:595; **15**:602ff
- *illus:*
- - Siena synagogue **14**:1514
- - Spanish synagogue, Venice **15**:618
- - Worms synagogue **15**:603
Mehkarim ba-Geografyah shel Erez-Yisrael (journ.) **1**:newsp. list
Mehler, Judah (r., Ger.) **5**:1597; **5**:613
Mehler, Judah ben Samuel (au., Ger.) **7**:218
- *illus:*
- - *Sefer Ibberonot* **10**:1527
Mehlman, Israel **4**:976
MEHLSACK, ELIAKIM BEN JUDAH HA-MILZAHGI **11**:1236
- Kabbalah **10**:648
Mehmed II (sult., Turk.), *see* Mahmud II
Mehmed IV (sult., Turk.) **14**:1237
Meholah (mosh., Isr.) **1**:place list
Meholat ha-Mahanayim (bk.) **9**:1266
Mehoza (tn., Baby.), *see* MAHOZA
Mehr (tn., Ger.) **5**:1137
Mehr, Hjalmar **15**:551
Mehri (lang.), *see* Mahri
MEHRING, WALTER **11**:1236
MEI AMMI (kib., Isr.) **11**:1236
- statistics **1**:place list
Meidner, Elsa **11**:1237
MEIDNER, LUDWIG **11**:1237
Meier (r., U.S.) **15**:1207
Meier, Adolph **11**:520
Meier, Ernst H. **8**:44
Meier, J., *see* Meyer, J.
MEIER, JULIUS **11**:1237
Meier of Sobota **10**:1556
Meijer, J. **6**:734
Meijler, Isaac **15**:520
ME'ILAH (tract.) **11**:1238
- agency **2**:350
- *illus:* text
Meilhac, Henri **12**:1337
Meimar Markah (mid. wk.) **11**:1000
Mei Neftoah (vill., Er. Isr.) **9**:1496; **9**:1515
MEINERTZHAGEN, RICHARD HENRY **11**:1239
Meinhardt, Gustav, *see* HERZBERG, WILHELM
Meinhardt of Goerz **11**:1252
Meinhart, G. F. **8**:44
Meinhof, Ulrike **12**:1034
MEINHOLD, JOHANNES FRIEDRICH **11**:1239
Meinigius, C. G. **8**:44
MEININGEN (city, Ger.) **11**:1239
Mein Kampf (bk.) **8**:784; **8**:832; **8**:853
Meinsters, Moses **12**:1516
Meinstril, Solomon Shlomil **15**:1352
MEIR (tan.) **11**:1240
- Beruriah **4**:701
- decisions in controversies **5**:891
- fox fables **3**:20
- Hammath **7**:1242,1244
- Holy Congregation in Jerusalem **8**:919
- Judah bar Ilai **10**:338
- labor and study **10**:1322
- Lost Tribes **15**:1005
- masorah **16**:1405
- Meir Ba'al ha-Nes **11**:1246
- Mishnah compilation **11**:316
- Oenomaus **12**:1332
- proselyte descent **13**:1186
- Satan **14**:903
- Torah study **15**:455
- vows **16**:228
- *see also:* AHERIM
Meir (gaon) **7**:323
Meir (r., Egy.) **2**:158
Meir (r., Ukr.) **13**:277
Meir (r., Pol.) **14**:1509
MEIR, GOLDA **11**:1242
- chronological chart **8**:766-767
- Israel-Africa relations **9**:433
- Israel-Arab negotiations **9**:418
- Mapai **11**:913
- politics **9**:664ff
- Rafi party **13**:1512
- *illus:*
- - text
- - autograph **3**:916
- - Ben Zvi, Yizhak and Rahel **4**:580
- - Bonds Drive function, Montreal **5**:110
- - Bonds-U.J.A. dinner **15**:1668
- - Central Conference of American Rabbis **5**:286
- - Dropsie College doctorate **10**:818
- - inspecting a Hen guard of honor **9**:695
- - Jarring, Gunnar, and **9**:410
- - Knesset, declaration of allegiance **9**:618
- - Knesset session **10**:1113
- - Lindsay, John, and **12**:1118
- - Nixon, Richard, and **15**:1670
- - Soviet immigrants **8**:779
Meir, Isaac **12**:63
Meir, Israel, *see* Israel Meir
MEIR, JACOB (Er. Isr.) **11**:1245
- Israel religious life **9**:889; **9**:892
- *illus:*
- - firman of appointment **7**:1148
- - Hebrew University opening ceremony **8**:221
- - Straus center ceremony **15**:429
Meir, Jacob (r., Als.) **14**:1617
Meir, Joseph **16**:674
Meir, Samuel **5**:432
Meir, Ya'akov, *see* MEIR, JACOB
Me'irat Einayim (wk., Eliakim Goetz) **6**:615
Me'irat Einayim (wk., Isaac ben Samuel) **9**:30; **10**:536
Meirav (vill., Er. Isr.) **15**:673
MEIR BA'AL HA-NES, TOMB OF **11**:1245
- Tiberias tomb **15**:1135
- *illus:*
- - text
- - tomb **9**:172-173,276; **15**:1132
Me'ir Bat Ayin (wk.) **4**:992
Meir ben Aaron Leib, *see* PEREMYSHLYANY, MEIR BEN AARON LEIB OF
Meir ben Abraham **13**:589
MEIR BEN BARUCH HA-LEVI **11**:1247
- Treves, Johanan **15**:1378
- rabbinate **13**:1447
MEIR BEN BARUCH OF ROTHENBURG (Maharam) **11**:1247
- Avigdor ben Elijah **3**:963
- Bamberg, Samuel **4**:150
- chronological chart **8**:766-767
- Germany **7**:468
- *hiddushim* **8**:467
- hunting, views on **8**:1111
- *kinyan* and public authority **13**:1353
- *minhagim* literature **12**:28
- Nicholas IV **12**:1137
- responsa **11**:337; **14**:86
- Rudolf I of Hapsburg **14**:381
- seals **14**:1079
- Spain **15**:233
- taxation **15**:845ff; **16**:1285
- trade and commerce **15**:1299
- *illus:* text
Meir ben David **16**:1357, 1387
Meir ben Eleazar **2**:550
Meir ben Eliakim Goetz, *see* Goetz, Meier ben Eliakim
MEIR BEN ELIJAH **11**:1252
MEIR BEN ELIJAH OF NORWICH **11**:1253
MEIR BEN EPHRAIM OF PADUA **11**:1253
Meir ben Gedaliah of Lublin, *see* LUBLIN, MEIR BEN GEDALIAH
MEIR BEN HIYYA ROFE **11**:1254
- Shabbateanism **8**:233
Meir ben Isaac (paytan) **12**:1470
Meir ben Isaac Ashkenazi (r.) **13**:1242
MEIR BEN ISAAC OF TRINQUETAILLE **11**:1254
- Nahmanides **12**:774
MEIR BEN ISAAC SHELI'AH ZIBBUR **11**:1255
- *Akdamut Millin* **2**:479
- Avelei Zion **3**:946
- Meir Ba'al ha-Nes **11**:1246
Meir ben Isaiah **11**:566
Meir ben Jacob **11**:1246
Meir ben Joseph ben Merwan Levi **12**:421; **12**:829
Meir ben Judah Loeb, *see* LEONI, MYER
Meir ben Judah of Norwich **13**:692
Meir ben Kalonymus **10**:349; **15**:264
Meir ben Menahem ha-Kohen **10**:1556
Meir ben Moses of Rome **2**:936; **2**:938
MEIR BEN SAMUEL OF RAMERUPT **11**:1255
MEIR BEN SAMUEL OF SHCHEBRESHIN **11**:1256
- prosody **13**:1220
MEIR BEN SIMEON HA-ME'ILI **11**:1256
- Asher ben David **3**:706
- *Bahir, Sefer ha-* **4**:100
- defense of Jews **3**:194
- Kabbalah **10**:540
- moneylending **12**:249
- usury **16**:1295
Meir Dan of Ostrova Plotzki, *see* PLOTZKI, MEIR DAN OF OSTROVA
Me'ir Einayim (journ.) **1**:newsp. list
Me'ir Einei Hakhamim (tal. comment.) **11**:547
Meir Eliezer ben Pinhas **4**:534
Meir Etoile, *see* Etoile, Meir
Meir ha-Kohen (10/11 cent., r.) **10**:720
Meir ha-Kohen (13th cent., tal.) **7**:1108; **7**:1110
Meir Harif, *see* EPSTEIN, ABRAHAM MEIR BEN ARYEH LEIB
MEIRI, MENAHEM BEN SOLOMON **11**:1257
- attorney **3**:838
- chess **5**:403
- Gentiles **7**:413
- Hebrew language **16**: 1635
- *hiddushim* **8**:466
- Jewish history **11**:348
- Kabbalah **10**:540
- Maimonidean controversy **11**:752
- masorah **16**:1476
- *minhagim* books **12**:27
- money transactions **12**:248
- Nahmanides **12**:781
- Talmud commentaries **11**:332
Meir ibn Bibas **14**:545
MEIR JEHIEL HA-LEVI OF OSTROWIEC **11**:1260
Meir Kazin, *see* Kazin, Meir
Me'ir la-Arez (wk.) **4**:992
Me'ir Nativ (Bib. concordance) **12**:854
Me'ir Nativ (wk.; Isaac ben Kalonymus) **16**:1360,1388
Meir of England, *see* MEIR BEN ELIJAH OF NORWICH
Meir of Kastoria **10**:814
Meir of Segovia **11**:817
Meir of Shebsh **13**:277

Meir of Sopron **15:**161
Meir of Tannhauser **7:**1272
Meirov, Shaul, *see* AVIGUR, SHAUL
Meirovitch, Menashe, *see* MEEROVITCH, MENASHÉ
Meirovitz, M. **16:**226
Meirovitz, Zvi **8:**323
Meir Shebseir **13:**277
ME'IR SHEFEYAH (agr. school, Isr.) **11:**1260
– statistics **1:**place list
MEIR SIMḤAH HA-KOHEN OF DVINSK **11:**1260
– *ḥiddushim* **8:**467
– self-defense **14:**1126
Meir the Vocalizer **9:***fcg.* 43
Meisel, Elijah Ḥayyim **11:**431
Meisel, Eve **11:**1262
Meisel, Frumet **11:**1263
MEISEL, MAURICI **11:**1261
MEISEL, MORDECAI (MARCUS, MARX) BEN SAMUEL **11:**1262
– synagogue **15:**604; **15:**620
– *illus:* text
Meisel, Mordechai (r.) **6:**1336
MEISEL, MOSES BEN MORDECAI **11:**1263
MEISEL, NOAH **11:**1263
Meisel, Sara **11:**1567
Meisel, W. A. **15:**400
Meisels, Abraham Nathan Neta **3:**668
Meisels, Aryeh Judah Jacob **11:**1264; **14:**92
Meisels, Czerna **5:**1038
MEISELS, DAVID DOV **11:**1264
MEISELS, DOV BERUSH **11:**1264
– politics **13:**817
Meisels, Dresel **9:**1082
Meisels, I. A. (Zion. ldr.) **16:**1140
Meisels, Isaac (ḥas. ldr.) **11:**1264
Meisels, Israel (r.) **11:**1265; **14:**1509
Meisels, Jacob **11:**1264
Meisels, Joseph **13:**1300
Meisels, Judah **5:**1038
Meisels, M. (ed., U.S.) **8:**213
Meisels, Menahem Nahum (print.) **5:**1038; **13:**1109
Meisels, Moses Ẓevi Hirsch, *see* Meizlisch, Moses Ẓevi Hirsch
Meisels, Pinḥas Elijah **11:**1264
Meisels, Simḥah Bunim **9:**1082
MEISELS, UZIEL BEN ẒEVI HIRSCH **11:**1265
Meisels, Ze'ev Wolf **11:**1264
Meisenbach, Georg **15:**1479
Meiser (journ.) **9:**1266
Meishar (mosh., Isr.) **1:**place list
MEISL, JOSEPH **11:**1266
Meisl, Mordecai ben Samuel, *see* MEISEL, MORDECAI BEN SAMUEL
Meislisch, Alexander **6:**269
Meiss, Léon **15:**1536
MEISSEN (city, Ger.) **11:**1266
Meister Eckhert, see ECKHART, MEISTER
Meitner, Eva
– *illus:*
– – "Seder" (drg.) Fig. 85 **3-**ART
MEITNER, LISE **11:**1267
MEITUS, ELIAHU **11:**1267
Meizlisch, Moses Ẓevi Hirsch **10:**1382
Mejelle (Ott. law) **9:**646ff; **9:**872
Mekhawenim (kab.) **10:**853
Mekhel (mer.) **16:**159
Mekhes ve-Ta'avurah (journ.) **1:**newsp. list
Mekhilta (mid.) **11:**316
– *Exodus Rabbah* **6:**1068
– *Sifrei* **14:**1519; **14:**1520
– *see also:* MIDRASH
Mekhilta de-Ereẓ Yisrael, *see* MEKHILTA OF R. ISHMAEL
Mekhilta de-Sanya, *see* MEKHILTA OF R. SIMEON BEN YOḤAI
MEKHILTA OF R. ISHMAEL **11:**1267
– De-Bei R. Ishmael **9:**84
– *Midrash ha-Gadol* **11:**1515
– moneylending **12:**246
– *tannaim* **15:**799
MEKHILTA OF R. SIMEON BEN YOḤAI **11:**1269
– Hezekiah **8:**455
– *Midrash ha-Gadol* **11:**1515
– *Midreshei Halakhah* **11:**1522
– Simeon bar Yoḥai **14:**1553
– *tannaim* **15:**799
– *see also:* ZOHAR
Mekhilta ve-Elleh Shemot, *see* MEKHILTA OF R. ISHMAEL
Mekhiltin de-R. Akiva, *see* MEKHILTA OF R. SIMEON BEN YOḤAI
Mekhirat Ḥamez, *see* ḤAMEẒ, SALE OF
MEKHLIS, LEV ZAKHAROVICH **11:**1270
Mekhon ha-Tekanim (journ.) **1:**newsp. list
MEKIẒE NIRDAMIM (soc.) **11:**1270
– Berliner, Abraham **4:**665
– publishing **15:**53
MEKLENBURG, JACOB ẒEVI **11:**1271
Mekler, Eliezer, *see* WOLF, LEIZER
Mekler, I. L. **6:**198
MEKNÈS (tn., Mor.) **11:**1272
– community leaders **3:**737
– Ibn Ẓur, Jacob **8:**1213
– Jewish quarter **10:**87
– *illus:* text
Mekor Barukh (qtr., Jer.) **9:**1472
Mekor ha-Shemot (wk.), *see Shorshei ha-Shemot*
Mekor Ḥayyim (sub., Jer.) **9:**1472; **9:**1516
Mekor Ḥayyim (bk., Gabirol) **7:**240ff; **11:**339
– Neoplatonism **12:**960
– philosophy **13:**434
Mekor Ḥayyim (wk.; Ḥayyim ha-Kohen) **10:**550
Mekor Ḥayyim (wk., Yaḥyā Ṣāliḥ ben Jacob) **7:**1037
Mekor Ḥayyim (wk., Zarza) **16:**939
MEKOROT WATER COMPANY **11:**1274
– Eshkol, Levi **6:**888
– labor movement **9:**860
– water and irrigation in Israel **9:**767
– *illus:* text
– *see also:* TAHAL
Meksikaner Yidish Lebn (newsp.) **11:**1459; **13:**1040
Melacha (soc., Yug.) **14:**871
Melafefon, *see* CUCUMBER
Melakim (vowels) **16:**1448
Melamed, A. (writ.) **5:**396
Melamed, Abraham **15:**314
Melamed, Abraham Shelomo **13:**135ff
MELAMED, EZRA ZION **11:**1275
– *Tarbiz* **15:**809
Melamed, Hirsch **10:**215
Melamed, Jacques, *see* Asenov, Dragomir
MELAMED, MEIR **11:**1275
Melamed, Meir ben Shem-Tov **8:**1170
Melamed, Nissan Cohen, *see* Cohen Melamed, Nissan
MELAMED, RAḤAMIM REUVEN **11:**1275
MELAMED, SIMAN TOV **11:**1276
Melammed (teacher) **6:**404ff; **8:**241
Melammed, Meir **9:**1164
Melammed, Shem Tov ben Jacob **13:**180
Melancholy **7:**1404
MELANCHTHON, PHILIPP **11:**1276
– Hebraist **8:**44
– Reuchlin, Johannes **14:**110
Melania (Rom. philan.) **9:**1407
Melas, Spyros **7:**887
MELAVVEH MALKAH (post-Sabbath festivities) **11:**1276
MELBOURNE (city, Austr.) **11:**1277
– library **11:**191
– *illus:*
– – text
– – Beth Rivkeh Ladies College **3:**886
– – B'nai B'rith House **3:**885
– – Israel exhibition **16:** 1105
– – Monash University **3:**883
– – Mount Scopus College library **11:**194
– – Mount Scopus War Memorial College **3:**884
– *pop. tables:* text
– *see also:* AUSTRALIA
Melcer, Wanda **13:**801
Melchett (fam.), *see* MOND
MELCHIOR (fam., Den.) **11:**1286
– Melchior, A. W. **8:**44
Melchior, Bent **5:**1538; **11:**1287
MELCHIOR, CARL **11:**1286
Melchior, Carl Henriques **11:**1286
Melchior, Fred **2:**321
Melchior, Gerson **11:**1286
Melchior, Harald Raphael **11:**1286
Melchior, J. **8:**44
MELCHIOR, MARCUS **11:**1287
– press **13:**1049
Melchior, Moritz Gerson **11:**1286
Melchior, Moses (1736–1817) **11:**1286
Melchior, Moses (1825-1912) **11:**1286
Melchior, Nathan Gerson **11:**1286
Melchites **4:**2859ff; **9:**915, 1441
– *illus:*
– – Nazareth chapel **12:**900
MELCHIZEDEK (bib. fig.) **11:**1287
– the arts **2:**122
– *Enoch, Slavonic Book of* **6:**797
– Jerusalem **9:**1380
– Shem **14:**1369
– son of man **15:**160
– *illus:*
– – God talking to **14:**1266
– – meeting Abraham **2:**122; **9:**1552
Melczer, Joe **13:**482
MELDOLA (fam.) **11:**1289
Meldola, David **11:**1290; **14:**1186
Meldola, Jacob **11:**1289
Meldola, Moses Hezekiah **11:**1290
Meldola, Raphael (Fr.) **4:**351
MELDOLA, RAPHAEL (r., Eng.) **11:**1290
– *illus:*
– – text
– – portrait **4:**243
MELDOLA, RAPHAEL (chem., Eng.) **11:**1290
Meldola, Samuel **11:**1289
Meldola de Sola, Aaron David **12:**285
MELEAGER OF GADARA **7:**890; **7:**895
– Gadara **7:**251
Mele'ah (vill., Er. Isr.) **15:**675
– statistics **1:**place list
Melekhet ha-Dikduk ha-Shalem (wk.) **16:**1360,1390
Melekhet Shelomoh (wk.) **2:**265
Meles of Marseilles, *see* Samuel ben Judah ben Meshullam
Melilah (journ.) **1:**newsp. list
Melilot (mosh., Isr.) **1:**place list
Melin, H. M. **4:**878
Méline, Felix Jules **6:**226
Melisande (q., Er. Isr.) **9:**1370
MELITO OF SARDIS **11:**1291
MELITOPOL (city, Ukr.) **11:**1292
– Hebrew Language Association **6:**1214
Melitz, Samuel **5:**900
Melitzer, Samuel **15:**302, 303
Melius, Juhász Péter **8:**44
Meliz Eḥad Minni (journ.) **1:**newsp. list
Melkman, Joseph, *see* MICHMAN, JOZEPH
Mellah, *see* JEWISH QUARTER
Meller, Berish, *see* KIMḤI, DOV
Melli, Jehiel **16:**121
Melli, Samuel **6:**1231
Méllili, Hayyim **15:**1439
Mellish, William **16:**137
Mellissander, Casparus **8:**44
Mello, Antonio Rodriguez, *see* ABENATAR MELO, DAVID
Mello, Sebastian José de Carvalho de, *see* Pombal, Sebastião José de Carvalho e Mello, Marquês de
Melman, Meir **10:**730
Melnick, Joseph **8:**1052
– *illus:*
– – F.Z.C. **16:**1165
MELNIKOFF, AVRAHAM **3:**606; **14:**1069; **15:**1413
– *illus:*
– – portrait Pl. 1 **3-**ART
– – Tel Ḥai Memorial **3:**633
Melnikoff, Pamela **5:**450
Melo, Diego Henriques **2:**65
Melo, Francisco Manuel de **15:**251
Melodies from Mt. Sinai, *see* MI-SINAI NIGGUNIM
MELOKHIM BUKH (wk.) **11:**1292
– *see also:* SHMUEL BUKH; YIDDISH LITERATURE
MELON (fruit) **11:**1293
– evolution **6:**1003
– food **6:**1416
– plant list **13:**621
– *see also:* CUCUMBER
Melon, chate (bot.) **13:**621
Melos (Gr. Isl.) **6:**10; **6:**12
Melqart (deity) **4:**515; **16:**666
– *illus:*
– – Ben-Hadad stele **4:**516
Melrose Park (sub., Chicago) **5:**415
Melting pot (sociol. conc.) **3:**777
MELTON, SAMUEL MENDEL **11:**1295
MELTZER, ISSER ZALMAN **11:**1295
– Broida, Simḥah **4:**1401
– Ḥiddushim **8:**467
– Kotler, Aaron **10:**1221
– Slobodka Yeshivah **14:**1668
– *illus:*
– – Talmud lesson **16:**764
MELTZER, SHIMSHON **11:**1296
Melukhat Sha'ul (wk.) **7:**1056
MELUN (city, Fr.) **11:**1296
Melun, Ordinance of **11:**515
Melville, Herman **15:**1572
MELVILLE, LEWIS **6:**783; **6:**789
Melzer, Marcus **10:**1503
Melzer, Mordecai ben Asher, *see* KLATZKO, MORDECAI BEN ASHER
Melzer, Shimshon, *see* MELTZER, SHIMSHON
MEM (heb. let.) **11:**1297
Memar Markah (Samar. Targum) **14:**738ff
MEMEL (tn., Lith.) **11:**1297

- He-Ḥalutz training farm **8**:252
MEMMI, ALBERT **11**:1298
- Prix de Carthage **15**:1449
MEMMINGEN (city, Ger.) **11**:1299
Memoirs (wk.) **7**:629; **16**:805
Memoram (negotiable deed), *see* MAMRAM
Memora Technica, *see* MNEMONICS
MEMORBUCH (memorial list) **11**:1299
- archives **3**:387
- *Hazkarat Neshamot* **7**:1533
- *kiddush ha-Shem* **10**:984
- *illus:*
- - text
- - Dornham (18th cent.) **3**:380
- - Halberstadt (1695) **7**:1174
- - Koblenz, *Yizkor* for Rhineland communities **10**:1120
- - Nuremberg **12**:522
Memorial, *see* YAD
"Memorial" (paint., M. Feuerring) **3**:623
Memorial Day (Isr.), *see* YOM HA-ZIKKARON
Memorial Foundation for Jewish Culture **5**:873; **10**:66
- history chart **8**:766-767
MEMORIAL LIGHT **11**:1301
- *see also:* YAHRZEIT
Memorial Prayer, *see* HAZKARAT NESHAMOT
Memorial to the Unknown Jewish Martyr (Paris) **13**:110
- *illus:* **13**:112
MEMPHIS (city, Egy.) **11**:1301
- Dumuh **6**:268
- *Ḥet-kau-ptaḥ* **12**:184
MEMPHIS (city, Tenn.) **11**:1301
- Tennessee **15**:1009
Memra (amoraic statement) **4**:190ff; **11**:461ff; **16**:635
Memshalah, *see* Israel cabinet
Memunnim (cmty. offics.) **2**:805
Mena, Juan de **15**:253
Mena'ane'im (mus. instr.) **12**:564
Menachovsky, Moshe **5**:113
MENAHEM (k., Isr.) **11**:1302
- Assyrian tax **14**:736
- chronological chart **8**:766-767
- history **8**:602ff
- Hosea, Book of **8**:1017
Menahem (minter) **12**:61
Menahem (r., Sp.) **16**:60
Menahem (alchem.) **11**:800
Menahem (scribe) **11**:734
- *illus:*
- - *Birds' Head Haggadah* **2**:330,480; **7**:*fcg.* 875,1081,1543
Menahem Azariah of Fano, *see* FANO, MENAHEM AZARIAH
Menahem bar Joseph bar Ḥiyya **7**:318
Menahem ben Aaron (paytan) **13**:589
MENAHEM BEN AARON IBN ZERAḤ **11**:1303
- Abrabanel, Samuel **2**:102
- codification of law **5**:647
- parody **13**:126
- Toledo **15**:1200
Menahem ben Aaron of Volterra **4**:974
Menahem ben Abraham, *see* BONAFOS, MENAHEM BEN ABRAHAM
Menahem ben Ḥayyim ha-Arokh **14**:671
MENAHEM BEN ḤELBO **11**:1304
- Bible exegesis **4**:893
- Judeo-French glosses **10**:424
Menahem ben Hezekiah **11**:1411
MENAHEM BEN JACOB **11**:1305
MENAHEM BEN JACOB IBN SARUQ **11**:1305
- Bible exegesis **4**:892
- chronological chart **8**:766-767
- Dunash ben Labrat **6**:270
- Hayyuj, Judah **7**:1513
- Hebrew grammar **11**:324
- Hisdai ibn Shaprut **8**:666
- letters **11**:59
- linguistics **16**:1356,1379
- poetry **13**:683ff
- Samuel ben Meir **14**:811
- Spain **15**:225
Menahem ben Jacob of Lutra **11**:1305
Menahem ben Joseph Ḥazzan **10**:243; **15**:1407
Menahem ben Judah (Rome) **10**:350
Menahem ben Judah de Lonzano, *see* LONZANO, MENAHEM BEN JUDAH DE
Menahem ben Judah the Galilean, *see* MENAHEM SON OF JUDAH
MENAHEM BEN MICHAEL BEN JOSEPH **11**:1306
MENAHEM BEN MOSES HA-BAVLI **11**:1307
Menahem ben Nathan **14**:186
Menahem ben Nethanel **15**:1329
Menahem ben Simeon of Posquières **10**:1006
MENAHEM BEN SOLOMON **11**:1307
- linguistics **16**:1367
- liturgical traditions **14**:246
Menahem ben Solomon ha-Me'iri, *see* MEIRI, MENAHEM BEN SOLOMON
Menahem ben Solomon ibn Duji, *see* ALROY, DAVID
Menaḥem ben Yose **11**:1228
Menahem ben Zerah, *see* MENAHEM BEN AARON IBN ZERAH
Menahem David ben Isaac **15**:1476
Menahem de Vardimas **6**:223
MENAHEM THE ESSENE **11**:1308
- Hillel **8**:483
Menahem the Gaul **9**:510
Menahem ha-Kohen **14**:1617
Menahem ibn Dugi, *see* ALROY, DAVID
Menahem ibn Saruq, *see* MENAHEM BEN JACOB IBN SARUQ
Menahem Isaiah ben Isaac, *see* ISAIAH MENAHEM BEN ISAAC
Menahemites (sect) **2**:751
MENAḤEMIYYA (mosh., Isr.) **11**:1308
Menahem Mann ben Solomon **13**:707
Menahem Mendel (folk type) **6**:1382
MENAHEM MENDEL BEN ISAAC **11**:1308
Menahem Mendel ben Jacob **11**:45
Menaḥem Mendel ben Ẓevi Hirsh **16**:1189
Menahem Mendel Ḥasid, *see* Ḥasid, Menahem Mendel
Menahem Mendel of Buhusi, *see* Friedmann, Menahem Mendel
Menahem Mendel of Kamieniec **15**:1353
Menahem Mendel of Kotsk, *see* KOTSK, MENAHEM MENDEL OF
Menahem Mendel of Lubavitch, *see* Schneersohn, Menaḥem Mendel
MENAHEM MENDEL OF PEREMYSHLANY **11**:1309
- *aliyah* **9**:514
- Simḥah ben Joshua **14**:1569
- travels **15**:1353
Menahem Mendel of Rymanow, *see* RYMANOWER, MENAHEM MENDEL
MENAHEM MENDEL OF SHKLOV **11**:1310
- *aliyah* **9**:514
- Israel ben Samuel **9**:1060
- Jerusalem **9**:1463
Menahem Mendel of Tysmenitsa **15**:1492
MENAHEM MENDEL OF VITEBSK **11**:1310
- Abraham of Kalisk **2**:133
- *aliyah* **9**:514
- chronological chart **8**:766-767
- Ḥasidism **7**:1392; **7**:1396ff
- Vilna Gaon **14**:1432
Menahem Mendel of Warka **16**:304
Menahem-Mendel Avigdors, *see* ISAIAH MENAHEM BEN ISAAC
Menahem Nahum ben Israel **13**:647
Menahem Nahum ben Ẓevi of Chernobyl, *see* Nahum of Chernobyl
Menahem Nahum of Czernowitz, *see* Friedmann, Menahem Nahum
Menahem Nahum of Husyatin, *see* Friedmann, Menahem Nahum
Menahem Nahum of Itzkani, *see* Friedmann, Menahem Nahum
Menahem Nahum of Stefanesti, *see* Friedmann, Menahem Nahum
Menahem of Amshinov **16**:304
MENAHEM OF MERSEBURG **11**:1312
Menahem of Worms, *see* MENAHEM BEN JACOB
MENAHEM SON OF JUDAH **11**:1313
- Absalom **2**:176
- Ananias ben Nedebeus **2**:923
- Eleazar ben Ananias **6**:585
- Hezekiah, the Zealot **8**:455
- Jewish War **16**:949
- Masada **11**:1079
- messianism **11**:1410, 1421
- revolt against Rome **8**:639
- Teacher of Righteousness **15**:887
Menahem Ẓevi Hirsh of Hanipoli **16**:1243
MENAḤEM ẒIYYONI **11**:1313
- magic **11**:714
- practical Kabbalah **10**:634
Menahem Ẓiyyon Synagogue (Jer.) **9**:1448
MENAḤOT (tract.) **11**:1314
- *illus:* text
Menaker, Abraham, *see* MOREWSKI, ABRAHAM
Menaker, Hirsch **15**:1363
Menakhem Mendl (wk.) **14**:1280
MENANDER OF EPHESUS **7**:895
MENANDER OF LAODICEA **7**:895
Menander of Pergamum **7**:895
Menasce, Alfred de **11**:1316
Menasce, Bakhor de **11**:1316
MENASCE, DE (fam.) **11**:1316
Menasce, Felix de **11**:1316
Menasce, George de **11**:1316
Menasce, Jacob David de **11**:1316
Menasce, Jacques de **11**:1316
Menasce, Jean de **11**:1316
Menasché, Marcelo **15**:255
Menase, Israel **9**:1096
Menashe, A. **4**:1480
Menashe ben al-Farrar *see* QAZZAZ, MANASSEH BEN ABRAHAM IBN
Menashe, Boaz, *see* Effendi, Boaz
Menashe, Moses **14**:146
Menasheh Forest (Isr.) **12**:88 **9**:588
Menasheh hills (Isr.) **9**:588
Menassah, Ezekiel **11**:820
Menasseh ben Israel, *see* MANASSEH BEN ISRAEL
Mencken, H. L. **2**:978; **15**:1571
MENDA, ELIEZER **10**:314; **15**:1461
MENDEL (fam.) **11**:1316
MENDEL, ARTHUR **12**:700
Mendel, David, *see* NEANDER, AUGUST
Mendel, Emmanuel **13**:1249
MENDEL, HERMAN **12**:700
Mendel, I. (Ger.) **11**:1164
Mendel, Isaac **11**:1316
Mendel, Israel **11**:1316
Mendel, Jacob **11**:1316
Mendel, Judah **11**:1316
MENDEL, LAFAYETTE BENEDICT **5**:385
Mendel, Mendel Schwartz **11**:1316
Mendel, Vera **15**:1479
Mendel (Menahem) Avigdors, *see* ISAIAH MENAHEM BEN ISAAC
Mendelbaum, Benjamin Ze'ev **14**:908
MENDELE MOKHER SEFORIM **11**:1317
- Berdyczewski, Micha Josef **4**:594
- Bialik **4**:799
- Feitelson, Menahem Mendel **6**:1214
- Hebrew literature **8**:191
- Kovner, Abraham Uri **10**:1231
- Lifshits, Shiye-Mordkhe **11**:237
- museums **12**:540
- Society for the Promotion of Culture among the Jews of Russia **15**:58ff
- Yiddish literature **16**:810
- *illus:*
- - fellow writers **8**:193; **16**:809, 813
- - Odessa Museum **12**:542
Mendel of Cekinowka **11**:1309
Mendeloff, Gershon, *see* LEWIS, TED
Mendel of Novy Bydzov **12**:1241
Mendel of Satanov, *see* LEVIN, EMANUEL
Mendelovici-Meron, I. **5**:453
Mendelowicz, Samuel **14**:537
MENDELS, MAURITS **13**:829
Mendels, Moses, *see* BACHRACH, MOSES BEN ISAIAH MENAHEM
Mendelsohn, Alfred **14**:415
MENDELSOHN, ERIC **11**:1323
- Hadassah Hospital **3**:361
- synagogues **15**:625
- *illus:*
- - text
- - Einstein Tower, Potsdam **3**:342
- - Hadassah Medical Center, Mt. Scopus **3**:350
- - Schocken Institute **14**:987
MENDELSOHN, FRANKFURT MOSES **11**:1324
- Hebrew literature **8**:182
Mendelsohn, Herbert **15**:312
Mendelsohn, Jack **5**:220
Mendelsohn, Meyer **10**:1001
Mendelsohn, Robert **14**:834
MENDELSOHN, SHELOMO **11**:1324
Mendelson, Mendel **13**:648
MENDELSON, YOSE (José) **11**:1324
MENDELSSOHN (fam.) **11**:1324
- railroads **13**:1518
- *geneal. table:* text
Mendelssohn, Abraham **11**:1325; **11**:1326
Mendelssohn, Alexander **11**:1330
Mendelssohn, Arnold (physic.) **11**:1326
MENDELSSOHN, ARNOLD (comp.) **12**:700
Mendelssohn, Dorothea (Brendel), *see* SCHLEGEL, DOROTHEA

VON
Mendelssohn, Ernst **11:**1326
Mendelssohn, Fanny **11:**1326
MENDELSSOHN, FELIX (Jakob Ludwig Felix) **11:**1326
- Bartholdy, Jacob **4:**264
- family **11:**1325
- stamps **15:**336
- *geneal. table* **9:**1151; **11:**1325
- *illus:* text
Mendelssohn, Franz **11:**1326
Mendelssohn, Fromet **11:**1324
Mendelssohn, Georg Benjamin **11:**1325
Mendelssohn, Henriette (Sorel) **11:**1326
Mendelssohn, Joseph **4:**174; **11:**1324; **11:**1330
- *illus:*
- - portrait **11:**1325
MENDELSSOHN, KURT ALFRED GEORG **13:**492
Mendelssohn, Lea **11:**1326
Mendelssohn, Maria, *see* Mendelssohn, Henriette
MENDELSSOHN, MOSES **11:**1328
- *Contents:*
- - Philosophy **11:**1329
- - Critic of German Literature **11:**1331
- - Dispute with Lavater **11:**1332
- - Civic Status of Jews **11:**1333
- - *Jerusalem* **11:**1335
- - State and Church **11:**1336
- - Attitude to Christianity **11:**1338
- - Jewish Culture **11:**1338
- - Mendelssohn, Lessing, Spinoza **11:**1339
- - Appreciation and Influence **11:**1340
- General
- - apologetics **3:**198
- - chess **5:**404
- - heresy **8:**362
- - history **8:**711
- - history chart **8:**766-767
- - medal **11:**1173
- - model for *Nathan der Weise* **11:**49
- - seal **14:**1080
- Contemporaries
- - Eybeschuetz, Jonathan **6:**1075
- - Guenzburg, Mordecai Aaron **7:**964
- - Herz, Markus **8:**403; **8:**404
- - Horowitz, Phinehas **8:**999
- - Lavater, Johan Caspar **6:**97ff
- - Lessing, Gotthold Ephraim **11:**49
- - Levin, Zevi Hirsch **11:**112
- - Margolioth, Judah Loeb **11:**965
- - Sonnefels, Joseph **15:**158
- - Wessely, N.H. **16:**462
- Jewish Culture
- - Berlin **4:**642
- - Bible exegesis **4:**899ff
- - Bible translations **4:**875ff
- - ethics **6:**940
- - Haskalah **7:**1433; **7:**1445
- - Hebrew literature **8:**179
- - homiletical literature **8:**956
- - linguistics **16:**1399
- - literary criticism **5:**1115
- Judaism **10:**393
- - articles of faith **3:**659
- - commandments, reasons for **5:**789
- - *haskamot* **7:**1454
- - prophecy, view on **13:**1179
- - Torah **15:**1241
- Philosophy **13:**417; **13:**452; **13:**454ff
- - God, concept of **7:**662; **7:**668; **7:**673
- - hell **13:**85
- - miracles **12:**79
- - revelation **14:**124
- - soul, immortality of **15:**179
- *geneal. table:* **11:**1325
- *illus:*
- - autograph **3:**916
- - Bible translation, manuscript page **7:**1434
- - *Lesebuch fuer Juedische Kinder* (1779) **5:**433
Mendelssohn, Paul **11:**1326
Mendelssohn, Sidney **15:**210
Mendelssohn-Bartholdy, Albrecht **10:**1497; **11:**1326
Mendelssohn-Bartholdy, Carl **11:**1326
Mendelvich, Nathan, *see* BOGORAZ, VLADIMIR GERMANOVICH
Menderson, Nathan **15:**300
MENDES (fam., Eng.) **11:**1342
MENDES (fam., N. Afr.) **11:**1343
MENDES (fam., U.S.) **11:**1343
Mendes (Mar. fam.) **4:**1422; **12:**817
Mendes (Seph. fam.), *see* ABENDANA
Mendes, Abraham Pereira **11:**1343; **12:**1043
Mendes, Alvaro, *see* ABENAES, SOLOMON
Mendes, Anthony, *see* Costa, Anthony da
Mendes, Antonio Fernando **5:**694; **11:**1342
Mendes, Beatrice de Luna, *see* NASI, GRACIA
Mendes, Catherine, *see* COSTA, DA, CATHERINE
MENDÈS, CATULLE **11:**1344
- *illus:* text
Mendes, Deborah **11:**825
MENDES, DIOGO **11:**1345
- Nasi, Gracia **12:**836
- spice trade **15:**270
- trade and commerce **15:**1300
Mendes, Fernando **3:**598 **8:**339; **11:**1342
- *illus:*
- - portrait **11:**1342
Mendes, Francisco **11:**1345
- Marrano trade **11:**1024
- Nasi, Gracia **12:**836
- spice trade **15:**270
- trade and commerce **15:**1300
Mendes, Francisco (schol.), *see* Abenaes, Jacob
Mendes, Frederic de Sola **11:**1343
Mendes, Gideon **11:**1343
Mendes, Heitor **15:**270; **15:**1301
Mendes, Henry Pereira **11:**1343; **16:**1152
Mendes, Isaac **11:**1343
- *illus:*
- - bookplate with coat of arms **4:**1222
Mendes, Jacob **11:**1343
Mendes, Joseph **11:**1343
Mendes, Joshua **11:**1343
Mendes, Lewis **8:**1410
Mendes, Moses **11:**1343
- English literature **6:**783
Mendes, Rachel, *see* COSTA, DA, CATHERINE
Mendes, Raphael **5:**935
Mendes, Reyna **12:**836
Mendes, Rui **4:**172; **15:**270; **15:**1300
Mendes, Solomon **11:**1343
Mendes da Costa (fam), *see* COSTA
Mendes dos Remedios **8:**563
MENDÈS-FRANCE, PIERRE **11:**1345
- history chart **8:**766-767
- students' movements **15:**449
Mendez (fam.), *see* MENDES
Mendez, Alvaro, *see* ABENAES, SOLOMON
Mendez, Antonio **5:**1146
Mendicancy, *see* BEGGING AND BEGGARS
Mendiz (fam., N. Afr.), *see* MENDES
MENDLOWITZ, SHRAGA FEIVEL **11:**1346
- Torah Umesorah **15:**1259
Mendola, David, *see* Meldola, David
Mendòla, Samuel, *see* Meldola, Samuel
MENDOZA (prov., city, Arg.) **11:**1347
- *illus:* text
Mendoza, Aaron **15:**305
MENDOZA, DANIEL **11:**1348
- boxing **15:**305, 306
- *illus:* text
Mendoza, Duarte Furtado de, *see* Furtado de Mendoza, Duarte
MENE, MENE, TEKEL, U-FARSIN (bib.) **11:**1348
- *illus:* text
Meneghetti, Egidio **9:**1107
MENELAUS (h. pr.) **11:**1351
- Hellenism **8:**295
- history chart **8:**766-767
- Jerusalem **9:**1391
- Seleucids and Judea **8:**628; **8:**629
- Tobiads **15:**1180
- Wicked Priest **16:**486
Menelik (bib. fig.) **6:**1143; **13:**1424
Menell, S.G. **11:**1441
Menéndez Pidal **14:**1170
Menendez y Pelayo, M. **14:**1170
MENES, ABRAM **11:**1352
Menge, Hermann **4:**874
MENGELE, JOSEF **11:**1353
- Argentinian sanctuary **12:**956
- *illus:*
- - survivors of experiments **3:**866
Mengs, Anton Raphael **3:**540
Meni (deity) **7:**249
Me Niddah see Lustration, Water of
MENINSKY, BERNARD **3:**606; **7:**521
- *illus:*
- - "The Journey" (paint.) **3:**635
Menippus (writ., Transj.) **7:**251; **8:**298; **14:**145
Menir, Hayyim ben Shem Tov **15:**1425
MENKEN (fam.) **11:**1353
MENKEN, ADAH ISAACS **11:**1353
- U.S. literature **15:**1569
Menken, Alexander Isaac **11:**1354
Menken, Jacob Stanwood **11:**1353
Menken, Jules **11:**1353
Menken, Nathan Davis **11:**1353
Menken, Solomon **11:**1353
Menken, S. Stanwood **11:**1353
MENKES, ZYGMUNT **11:**1354
- *illus:* text
Menlin of Ueberlingen, *see* Ueberlingen, Menlin of
Menmaʿrē-ʿSety, *see* SETI I
Menocchio, Giovanni Stefano **8:**44
Men of the Great Synagogue, *see* SYNAGOGUE, THE GREAT
Menois (loc., Er. Isr.) **9:**240; **11:**908
Menophilus (1st cent., act.) **15:**1050
Menora (period.) **5:**747
MENORAH **11:**1355
- *Contents:*
- - Tabernacle **11:**1355
- - First Temple **11:**1357
- - Second Temple **11:**1359
- - Arch of Titus **11:**1363
- - Reproductions (Temple) **11:**1366
- - Later History **11:**1366
- - In Kabbalah **11:**1367
- - In Art **11:**1368
- amulet **2:**911, 912
- Avigad's excavations **9:**1532
- Bet Alfa mosaics **4:**713
- Bet She'arim catacombs **4:**771
- Bet Yeraḥ ruins **4:**780
- catacombs of Rome **5:**250
- Hasmoneans **7:**1283
- in the Arts **9:**1578ff; **15:**984, 1167
- Le Fèvre de la Boderie **10:**1563
- metals **11:**1435ff
- *ner tamid* **12:**965
- pagan symbols **15:**569
- Pellicanus **13:**220
- Postel **13:**932
- *shivviti* plaque **14:**1420
- State emblem **6:**1338
- synagogue **15:**588; **15:**597ff
- Tabernacle **15:**682ff
- Talmud **11:**1315
- *see also:* ḤANUKKAH LAMP
- *illus:*
- - text
- - amulet **2:**913
- - Antigonus II *Perutah* **3:**66
- - architectural motif **3:**227,716,947; **4:**768; **6:**675, 821,1226; **8:**1466
- - Beth-Shean synagogue mosaic **13:**905
- - Bet She'arim bas-relief **4:**768
- - *Bibliothèque Nationale Pentateuch* **11:***fcg.* 1355
- - *British Museum Miscellany* **8:***fcg.* 1271
- - ceremonial object motif **3:**452; **4:**244,763,1340; **5:**296, 1035; **6:**948; **7:***fcg.* 619 and 622
- - Dura-Europos **6:**277,285
- - Elkan, Benno (sculp.) **6:**675; **12:**382
- - En-Gedi excavations **6:**743
- - Ferber, Herbert (sculp.) **6:**1226
- - Galicia (18th cent.) **16:**1326
- - Gross, Chaim (sculp.) **7:**934
- - illuminated manuscript motif **2:**642; **3:***fcg.* 524; **4:**977 **8:**1274,1275
- - Israel stamp **9:**844-845
- - kabbalistic **13:**932
- - *mizraḥ* paper-cuts **13:**44-45, 61
- - Naarah synagogue mosaics (plan) **12:**737
- - Narbonne, epitaph (688/9 C.E.) **12:**828
- - oil lamp **12:**1348, 1349
- - Ostia, synagogue relief **12:**1508
- - Postel's kabbalistic **10:**625-626; **13:**932
- - Sabbath oil lamp **14:**559
- - *Sefirot* **10:**625
- - *Shivviti* paper cut **13:**63
- - *Shivviti* plaques **14:**1420-1421
- - Tarrytown, Temple Beth Abraham **16:**465
- - tomb, Malta **11:**831
- - Villa Torlonia catacomb **15:**569
- - Zechariah's vision **16:***fcg.* 935
MENORAH (period., Aus.) **11:**1370
MENORAH ASSOCIATION AND MENORAH JOURNAL **11:**1371
- press **13:**1051
- statistics **1:**newsp. list
- student journal **15:**450
- United States **15:**1628
- *illus:*
- - text
- - first collected volume **4:**1144
Menorah Hospital (U.S.) **8:**1039
Menorah Journal, see MENORAH ASSOCIATION AND MENORAH JOURNAL
Menorah Monthly **6:**679
Menorah Records (co.) **13:**1618
Menorah Review (period.) **10:**689
Menorah Society, *see* MENORAH ASSOCIATION AND MENORAH JOURNAL
Menorat ha-Ma'or (bk.; Isaac

Aboab) **2:**90ff; **11:**344
- Ladino **10:**1349
Menorat ha-Ma'or (bk.; Israel al-Nakawa) **2:**92; **2:**672ff; **10:**539; **11:**344
Menorat ha-Ma'or (wk.; Joseph ha-Yevani) **16:**1388
Menschel, Menahem **13:**1376
Menschen, Gerhard, *see* Meuschen, Gerhard
Mensheviks (Rus. polit. party) **5:**1260; **5:**794ff
Menshevism **4:**1502; **11:**1067
Menssier de Vezou, *see* MANESSIER DE VESOUL
Menstruation, *see* NIDDAH
Mental capacity, *see* Legal capacity
MENTAL ILLNESS **11:**1372
- *ba'al shem* **4:**7
- Shabbetai Ẓevi **14:**1222
- *see also:* PSYCHOLOGY
Mentel, Johann **4:**873
Mentsch, Jacob **12:**219
Menuḥah (mosh., Isr.) **1:**place list
Menuḥah ve-Naḥalah (Zion. gr., Pol.) **7:**632; **14:**44; **16:**337
- *illus:*
- - leaders **9:**556
Menuhin, Hephzibah **11:**1379
Menuhin, Jeremy **11:**1379
Menuhin, Yalta **11:**1379
MENUHIN, YEHUDI **11:**1378
Menzel, Wolfgang **8:**272; **14:**168
Me'onah (mosh., Isr.) **1:**place list
Me'onen (soothsayer) **6:**114
Me'or Einayim (bk.) **8:**557; **11:**350; **14:**315
Me'orei Or (bk.) **4:**992
Me'orerei Yeshenim (antiq. soc.) **6:**1277
ME'OT ḤITTIM (Passover charity) **11:**1379
- tax **15:**841
- *see also:* CHARITY; PASSOVER
Mephaath (site., Er. Isr.) **14:**105
MEPHIBOSHETH (bib. fig.) **11:**1379
- Rizpah **14:**203
- Ziba **16:**1016
Me-Puga (riv., Er. Isr.), *see* YARKON
MER, GIDEON **11:**1380
MERAB (bib. fig.) **11:**1380
MERANO (tn., It.) **11:**1381
- Italy **9:**1136
- Tyrol **15:**1491
- *illus:* text
Merari (Merarites; bib. clan)
- Jahaz **9:**1269
- Jokneam **10:**165
- Levites **11:**71
- Tabernacle **15:**684
Merari (f., Judith) **10:**452
Merari, Mose **11:**83
MÉRAY, TIBOR **8:**1086
Mercado (tal.), *see* ALFANDARI, SOLOMON ELIEZER BEN JACOB
Mercado (r., Sarajevo), *see* HABILLO, ELISHA
Mercado, Abraham de **4:**205; **13:**1613
Mercado, Caleb **11:**1245
Mercado, Ḥayyim de **2:**215; **4:**351
Mercado, Luis **11:**1191
- *illus:*
- - portrait **11:**1193
Mercanti (Merchants) **3:**173
Mercantile Bank of Israel **9:**828
Mercantilist absolutism **8:**705ff
Mercator (cartog.) **11:**927
Merced (city, Calif.) **5:**56
Mercedes (cmty., Urug.) **16:**13
Mercerus, Joannes, *see* MERCIER, JEAN
Merchant, Vivien **13:**551
Merchant of Venice, The (play) **7:**443; **14:**1261ff
- *illus:*
- - Shylock and Jessica **14:**1262
Merchants, *see* BROKERS; CRAFTS; ECONOMIC HISTORY; GUILDS; TRADE AND COMMERCE
MERCIER, JEAN **11:**1381
- Hebraists **8:**44
MERCURY (deity) **11:**1382
- Hermes-Thot **8:**293
- Jerusalem gymnasium **9:**1390
Mercury (met.) **2:**545ff; **3:**798
MERCY **11:**1382
- God **7:**669
- imitation of God **8:**1292
- Luzzatto, S.D. **13:**459
- Micah **11:**1482; **11:**1483
- *see also:* COMPASSION
Mercy, Gate of (Jer.), *see* Gate of Mercy
Mercy Killing, *see* EUTHANASIA
Meredith, George **6:**780
MEREMAR (amora) **11:**1383
Meremoth (pr. clan) **3:**249; **13:**466; **16:**667
Merenids, *see* MERINIDS
Merenos (Pal. schol.) **12:**1496
Meretsky, Aaron **16:**537
Meretsky, Jacob **16:**537
Meretsky, Mike **16:**537
Merezhin, A. **16:**779
Mergenthaler, Ottmar **15:**1478
MERGENTHEIM (city, Ger.) **11:**1383
Merhavia, H. **5:**1297
Merḥavim (stlmt., reg., Isr.) **9:**594; **12:**930
MERḤAVYAH (kib. mosh., Isr.) **11:**1384
- Gross, Nathan **7:**935
- Nadav, Ẓevi **12:**752
- statistics **1:**place list
- *illus:*
- - text
- - first permanent building **9:**554
Meri (s., Ukba) **15:**1512
Meri (zool.), *see* BUFFALO
Meribaal (bib. fig.), *see* MEPHIBOSHETH
Meribah, Waters of (bib. place), *see* KADESH-BARNEA; REPHIDIM
Merib-Baal (bib. fig.), *see* MEPHIBOSHETH
MÉRIDA (city, Sp.) **11:**1385
Meridi, *see* IBN ABITUR, JOSEPH BEN ISAAC
Meridina (city, Miss.) **12:**156
Merin, Moshe **13:**763
MERINIDS (Berber dyn.) **11:**1385
- Sijilmassa **14:**1529
- Waqqāṣa family **16:**265
Merirut (bitterness) **7:**1404
Merism (deviation) **14:**179
Merit of the fathers, *see* ZEKHUT AVOT
Merj Bani Amir (Er. Isr.), *see* JEZREEL, VALLEY OF
Merka' (cantillation sign) **16:**1440,1455
MERKABAH MYSTICISM **11:**1386
- alchemy **2:**546
- *Aleinu le-Shabbe'aḥ* **2:**557
- anthropomorphism **3:**56
- Apocalypse **3:**180
- Eleazar ben Arakh **6:**585
- *haftarah* **16:**1343
- Hermetic writings **8:**372
- Ishmael ben Elisha **9:**86
- Italy **2:**21
- Jewish literature **11:**347
- kabbalistic cosmology **10:**580
- magic **11:**711ff
- Maimonides **11:**770; **15:**1126
- meditation **11:**1217
- origin and development **10:**497ff
- *Perek Shirah* **13:**274
- philosophy **13:**424
- *Sefer Raza Rabba* **13:**1591
- visions **16:**168
- Worlds, the Four **16:**642
- *illus:*
- - chiromantic observations **5:**477
- *see also:* KABBALAH; SHI'UR KOMAH; THRONE OF GOD
Merka' kefulah (cantillation sign) **16:**1455
Merkaz (publ. firm, Pol.) **13:**1375
Merkaz Ba'alei Melakhah (qtr., Tel Aviv) **15:**920
Merkaz ha-Avodah (bldg. co.) **8:**542
Merkaz ha-Rav (yeshivah, Jer.) **10:**1183; **10:**1187
Merkaz La-Golah (refugee center) **4:**629
Merkaz Shapira (rural center, Isr.), *see* Deganim
Merkel, Georg **13:**115
Merkevet ha-Mishneh (kab. conc.) **10:**580
Merkil, Mordecai **4:**277
Merkin, Zalman, *see* ERIK, MAX
Merkos l'Inyonei Chinuch (publ. firm, U.S.) **13:**1376
Mermnadae (Lydian dyn.) **14:**876
MERNEPTAH (k., Egy.) **11:**1389
- Bible history **8:**576
- history chart **8:**766-767
- stele **3:**305
- *illus:*
- - stele **3:**313; **9:**109
MERODACH (deity) **11:**1389
MERODACH-BALADAN (bib. fig.) **11:**1389
- Babylon **4:**32; **16:**1502
- Hezekiah letters **16:**1512
- Nebuchadnezzar **12:**915
- Sargon II **14:**880; **16:**1504
Meröe (city, Sud.) **7:**329
Merom (vill., Isr.), *see* MERON
Merom (aviation co., Isr.) **9:**839
Merom, Peter **13:**487
- *illus:*
- - "The Ḥuleh" (phot.) **13:**487
Merom Golan (kib., Isr.) **13:**1436; **13:**1534
- statistics **1:**place list
- *illus:*
- - children's shelter during Syrian artillery attack **9:**419
Merom Zion Yeshivah (Jer.) **9:**1495
Meron (mosh., Isr.) **1:**place list
MERON (vill., Isr.) **11:**1390
- Azmon **3:**1011
- Crusader period **9:**272
- *Hillula de-Rabbi Shimon bar Yoḥai* **8:**495
- human geography **9:**580
- Lag ba-Omer **10:**1357
- Madon **11:**681
- physiography **9:**156
- pilgrimage center **8:**921
- synagogue **1:**syn. list
- *illus:*
- - text
- - Benjamin ben Japheth's burial place **4:**533
- - Lag ba-Omer dancing **5:**1270; **7:**1419
- - tombs of Johanan ha-Sandelar and Simeon bar Yoḥai **8:**926; **14:**1552
MERON, HANNA **11:**1391
- *illus:*
- - *He Walked in the Fields* **5:**74
- - in *Hello Dolly* **15:**1063
"Meron" Tune (Ḥas. mus.) **7:**1425
MEROZ (bib. loc.) **11:**1392
Merrick, David **12:**1121
MERRICK, LEONARD **11:**1392
Merritt, Robert **15:**310
MERSEBURG (city, Ger.) **11:**1392
Merseyside Jewish Representative Council (orgn., Eng.) **4:**465; **11:**410
MERSIN (city, Cilicia) **11:**1393
Merthyr Tydfil (tn., Wales) **16:**251
MERTON (fam.) **11:**1393
Merton, Henry R. **11:**1394; **11:**1439
Merton, Ralph **11:**1393
MERTON, ROBERT KING **11:**1394
Merton, William **11:**1394
Merunowicz, Teofil **3:**84
MERV (city, Rus.) **11:**1395
Mervis, Joel **10:**308
Merwan, Moses ben Joseph **9:**24; **10:**186
Merzbach, Henryk **11:**8 **13:**800
MERZBACHER (fam.) **11:**1395
Merzbacher, Abraham **3:**32; **11:**1395; **13:**1466
Merzbacher, Eugen **11:**1395
MERZBACHER, GOTTFRIED **11:**1395
- travels **15:**1351
MERZBACHER, LEO **11:**1396
- New York City **12:**1071
- prayer books **13:**990
Mesa (city, Ariz.) **3:**450
Mesa, Juan Rodríguez **5:**744
Mesalati, Isaac **12:**731
Mesannepada (dyn. founder, Ur) **11:**973
- *illus:*
- - inscription **11:**976
Meśaret (cantillation sign) **16:**1440
Mescallath, *see* MASHA'ALLAH
MESENE (terr., Mesop.) **11:**1396
Meritz, Samuel **4:**149
Mesgid (syn. of Falashas) **6:**1147
MESHA (k., Moab) **11:**1397
- Ahab **2:**437
- Ahaziah **2:**456
- Aroer **3:**492
- Baal-Meon **4:**5
- Edom **6:**375
- history **8:**597
- inscription **14:**1151; **16:**665
- Mesha stele **11:**1398
- proscription **8:**348
- *illus:*
- - Moab (map) **12:**193
- - Moabite stone **3:**319
Mesha (tan.), *see* MEIR
Meshach (bib. fig.), *see* SHADRACH, MESHACH, ABED-NEGO
Meshah (mosh., Isr.), *see* KEFAR TAVOR
Mesh'al, Judah **14:**304
Meshal ha-Kadmoni (wk.) **6:**1129; **11:**352; **14:**656
- *illus:* **3:**19,534,791; **5:**430; **6:**1128; **8:**1268; **14:**657
Meshalim, *see* PROVERB
Meshalma ben Murjān **14:**756
Meshammesh (cmty. offic.) **7:**1400
Meshān (Charax, city, Mesop.) **11:**1396
Mesharet, Hirsch **14:**534
Meshariyya, Rav **2:**440
Mesharsheya bar Taḥlifa (gaon), *see* Sheshna
Mesharsheya Kahana bar Jacob (gaon), *see* MOSES KAHANA BEN JACOB
Meshash, Moses **2:**623
MESHA STELE **11:**1398
- Arnon **3:**487
- Clermont-Ganneau, Charles **5:**605
- Horonaim **8:**979
- Moab **12:**192
- script **2:**685
- *illus:*
- - text

- - Moabite script **2**:684
- - record of victories **3**:319
- *see also:* MESHA
MESHECH (nat., As.M.) **11**:1399
MESHED (city, Iran) **11**:1399
- *anusim* **2**:327; **3**:174
- history chart **8**:766-767
- Israel community **9**:501
- *ketubbot* **10**:931
- *illus:* text
Meshek ha-Bakar ve-ha-Ḥalav (journ.) **1**:newsp. list
Meshek ha-Ofot (journ.) **1**:newsp. list
Meshi (fabric) **14**:1539; **15**:1036
Meshikhah (leg. term) **2**:218
Meshorer, Y. **12**:1271
Meshorerim (mus.) **2**:173; **2**:659; **12**:663
- *illus:*
- - Dutch synagogue **12**:617
- - *Leipzig Maḥzor* **12**:601
- - synagogue choir **12**:641
Meshuḥrar (student tit.) **16**:768
Meshuḥrarim (gr., Ind.) **5**:621
Meshullam (bib. fig.) **14**:1042
Meshullam (r., Egy.) **11**:765; **15**:777
- Meshullam, Vita **13**:9
Meshullam ben Benzion ha-Levi **12**:972
Meshullam ben Gershom, *see* Samuel ben Gershom
MESHULLAM BEN JACOB OF LUNEL **11**:1400
Meshullam ben Joab of Pisa **14**:586
Meshullam ben Jonah **15**:1327
MESHULLAM BEN KALONYMUS **11**:1401
- *Amiẓ Ko'ah* **3**:978
- *Beraḥ Dodi* **4**:585
- liturgical poetry **11**:326
- title **7**:324
- *illus:* text
Meshullam ben Machir **11**:566
Meshullam ben Menahem **11**:351
MESHULLAM BEN MOSES **11**:1402
Meshullam ben Moses of Mainz **13**:589; **6**:651
MESHULLAM BEN NATHAN OF MELUN **11**:1403
Meshullam Cusi Rafa ben Moses Jacob, *see* Cusi, Meshullam
Meshullam da Pierra, *see* DA PIERA, MESHULLAM BEN SOLOMON
Meshullam di Farra **16**:1619
Meshullam Ha-Sofer **13**:589
Meshullam Igra of Presburg **8**:306
Meshullam of Volterra **2**:593; **9**:1426; **15**:1352
MESHULLAM PHOEBUS BEN ISRAEL SAMUEL **11**:1404
Meshullam son of Berechiah **15**:1179; **15**:956
MESHULLAM ZALMAN HA-KOHEN **11**:1404
Meshullam Zusya of Hanipoli, *see* ZUSYA OF HANIPOLI
Meshullemeth of Jotbah (bib. fig.) **16**:951
Meshummadim, see APOSTASY
MESHWI AL-'UKBARI **11**:1404
- Ishmael of Ukbara **9**:90
- Karaites **10**:766
- 'Ukbarā **15**:1512
Mesibbah (journ.) **1**:newsp. list
Mesillah Ḥadashah (agr. center, Turk.) **10**:49
Mesillat Yesharim (wk.) **6**:941, **10**:643
- *illus:*
- - title page (Amsterdam, 1740) **11**:600 **11**:602
MESILLAT ZION (mosh., Isr.) **11**:1405
- statistics **1**:place list
MESILLOT (kib., Isr.) **11**:1405
- statistics **1**:place list
Mesillot (journ.) **1**:newsp. list
Mesirah (leg. term) **2**:218
MESKIN, AHARON **11**:1405
- *illus:*
- - *Be-Arvot ha-Negev* **6**:200
- - head, by Ze'ev Ben-Zvi (sculp.) Fig. 92 **3**:-ART
Mesnick, Charles **11**:503
MESOPOTAMIA **16**:1483
- General
- - *aliyah* **9**:512
- - calendar **16**:1262
- - dress **6**:213
- - ethics **6**:939
- - history chart **8**:766-767
- - king, kingship **10**:1011ff
- - Nineveh **12**:1170
- - origin of the Jews **3**:41ff
- - Paddan-Aram **13**:6
- - seals **14**:1072
- - stone monuments **16**:656
- - trade and commerce **15**:1293ff
- - war and warfare **16**:266
- - weights and measures **16**:376
- History
- - Assyrians **9**:1047ff
- - Bible history **8**:572,584
- - Genesis, Book of **7**:393
- - Israelite exiles **6**:1035
- - Mari **11**:972
- - Micah, prophecies of **11**:1481
- - Solomon's kingdom **15**:101
- - Trajan **15**:1312
- Language and Literature
- - Akkadian **2**:494
- - Book of Covenant laws **4**:1214
- - clay inscriptions **16**:661
- - Flood Stories **6**:1352ff
- - lamentations **10**:1375
- - patriarchal narratives **13**:182
- - poetry **13**:676
- - Semitic languages **14**:1151
- - wisdom literature **16**:559
- *illus:*
- - Babylonian palaces (reconst.) **4**:31-33
- - cylinder seal **14**:1077
- - Hammurapi stele **7**:1246
- - Ziggurat of Ur **16**:1
- *maps:*
- - Akkad and Sumer **2**:494
- - Aramean regions and cities **3**:253
- - Mari Age **11**:973
- - *see also:* ASSUR; BABYLON; BABYLONIA; IRAQ; SHINAR; SUMER, SUMERIANS
Mesorah Gedolah, see Masorah Gedolah
Mesorot, see MASORAH
MESQUITA (fam.) **11**:1406
- New York **12**:1069
- *see also:* BUENO
Mesquita, Abraham Bueno de **11**:1406
Mesquita, Benjamin Bueno de **4**:1461; **11**:1406
Mesquita, Daniel de **4**:1461
Mesquita, Francisco de **5**:695
Mesquita, Joseph Bueno de **11**:1406
Mesquita, Luis de **11**:1406
Mesquita, Moses Gomes de **11**:1406 **3**:1007
- *illus:*
- - portrait **11**:1406
Messa-Banin (fam.), *see* Banin (Benjamin), Messa
Messalahach (astron.), *see* MASHĀ'ALLAH
Messalamus, *see* ANDRONICUS SON OF MESHULLAM
MESSEL (fam.) **11**:1407
Messel, Aaron **11**:1407
MESSEL, ALFRED **3**:365
- family **11**:1407
- *illus:*
- - Wertheim department store **16**:454
Messel, Oliver **11**:1407
Messel, Rudolph **11**:1407
Messel, Simon Benjamin **11**:1407
MESSERER, ASAF MIKHAILOVICH **11**:1407
Messerer, Sulamith **11**:1407
Messer Leon, David ben Judah, *see* LEON, MESSER DAVID BEN JUDAH
Messer Leon, Judah ben Jehiel, *see* JUDAH BEN JEHIEL
MESSIAH **11**:1407
- *Contents:*
- - Term **11**:1407
- - Second Temple Period **11**:1408
- - Rabbinic Thought **11**:1410
- - Middle Ages **11**:1412
- - Modern Thought **11**:1415
- General
- - ancestry **15**:782
- - Bar Kokhba **4**:228ff
- - Falashas **6**:1148ff
- - Frankists **7**:64
- - *gematria* **14**:1243
- - Haskalah movement **7**:1443
- - philosophy **13**:421; **13**:453
- - Sabbath **14**:562
- - Samaritan belief **14**:738; **14**:751
- - Tortosa disputation **15**:1271
- - Ẓaddik **6**:662
- Conception and Nature of
- - Academy on High **2**:209
- - *adam kadmon* **2**:249
- - *aggadah* **2**:362
- - *Aleinu le-Shabbe'aḥ* **2**:558
- - anointed one **3**:27
- - Antichrist **3**:60
- - antinomianism **3**:68ff
- - Armilus **3**:476
- - ass **3**:756
- - autonomy **3**:921
- - Avelei Zion **3**:945
- - David **5**:1331
- - *devekut* **5**:1598
- - Elijah **6**:635ff
- - exile **7**:282
- - Gog and Magog **7**:692ff
- - heresy **8**:359
- - Ingathering of the Exiles **8**:1374ff
- - intertestamental eschtatology **6**:873
- - justice **10**:476
- - logos **11**:460,462
- - *olam ha-ba* **12**:1355
- - Paradise **13**:83; **13**:84
- - peace **13**:197
- - redemption **14**:3ff
- - resurrection **14**:96
- - Samson **14**:773
- - Seth **14**:1192
- - "son of man" **15**:159
- - Tribes, Twelve **15**:1386
- - Zerubbabel **16**:1001
- Dead Sea sects **5**:1411
- - Dead Sea Scrolls **6**:877ff; **15**:1046
- - Pesher document **13**:332
- - Teacher of Righteousness **15**:886
- - Yaḥad community beliefs **16**:701
- Judaism **10**:388; **10**:390; **10**:394
- - article of faith **3**:655ff
- - controversies to be decided **5**:890
- - Reform Judaism **8**:726
- Kabbalah **10**:611,618
- - eschatology **6**:881
- - Jewish gnosis **10**:506ff
- - Lurianic Kabbalah **10**:548; **11**:578
- - Shabbatean Kabbalah **10**:551
- - Zohar **16**:1208
- Literature
- - *Baruch, Apocalypse of* **4**:271
- - *Enoch, Ethiopic Book of* **6**:795
- - fiction, Hebrew **6**:1261ff
- - pseudepigrapha **3**:184
- - rabbinical literature **13**:1463
- Views on
- - Abdallah ibn Sabā **2**:53
- - Abrabanel, Isaac **2**:105; **2**:109
- - Abraham ben Eliezer ha-Levi **2**:140ff
- - Abu 'Isā **2**:183
- - Aḥad Ha-Am **2**:445
- - Albo's dogma **2**:536
- - Bendavid, Lazarus **4**:475
- - Buber, Martin **4**:1433
- - Christianity **5**:506ff
- - Cohen, Hermann **13**:461
- - Israel Ba'al Shem Tov **9**:1053
- - Judah ha-Levi **10**:357
- - Judah ha-Nasi **10**:367
- - Judah Loew ben Bezalel of Prague **10**:378
- - Klausner, Joseph Gedaliah **10**:1094
- - Levi ben Gershom **11**:97
- - Luzzatto, Moses Hayyim **11**:600ff
- - Maimonides **11**:764; **11**:776ff; **13**:443
- - Mendelssohn, Moses **11**:1334ff
- - Mordecai Joseph Leiner of Izbica **9**:1159
- - Naḥman ben Simḥah of Bratslav **12**:783
- - Naḥmanides **4**:214
- - Philo **13**:427
- - Saadiah **13**:432
- - sages **14**:654ff
- *illus:*
- - text
- - Elijah heralding the **6**:683
- *see also:* AFTERLIFE; MESSIANIC MOVEMENTS
Messiah, Birthpangs of the **11**:1418
Messiah ben David **11**:1411,1413
Messiah ben Joseph **11**:1411,1413
- Abraham Zalman **14**:1228
- oldest record of **14**:1199
- Prossnitz, Judah Leib **13**:1241
- Safrin, Isaac Judah Jehiel **14**:635
Messiah of Setūbal, *see* DIAS, LUIS
Messianic banquet **6**:879
MESSIANIC MOVEMENTS **11**:1417
- *Contents:*
- - Basic Elements **11**:1417
- - Movements **11**:1420
- - Early Middle Ages **11**:1421
- - Later Middle Ages **11**:1422
- - Spain and Marranos **11**:1424
- - 16th-18th Centuries **11**:1425
- - Modern Period **11**:1426
- General
- - emigration to Ereẓ Israel **9**:509
- - folktales **6**:1382
- - Ḥasidism **7**:1391ff
- - Hebrew parodies **13**:130ff
- - *Iggeret Teiman* **11**:758
- - Isaiah **9**:47
- - Kabbalah **10**:541; **10**:544
- - Lurianic Kabbalah **10**:548
- - prophecy **13**:1176
- - Shabbateanism **14**:1219ff
- - Umayyads **15**:1529
- - Yudghanites **16**:867
- - *Zerubbabel, Book of* **16**:1002
- - Zionism **16**:1033ff
- Countries
- - Ereẓ Israel **9**:285; **9**:286
- - Germany **7**:459
- - Spain **13**:24; **15**:243
- - Yemen **16**:741; **16**:744ff
- History
- - Bar Kokhba revolt **9**:247
- - Crusades **9**:271,273
- Pseudo-Messiahs

-- Abu ʿĪsā of Isfahan **2**:55
-- Abulafia, Abraham ben Samuel **2**:185
-- Alfandari, Ḥayyim **2**:598
-- Alroy, David **2**:750
-- Avila prophet **3**:970
-- Botarel, Moses **4**:1268
-- Dias, Luis **6**:7
-- Dusitheos **6**:313
-- Ezra of Montcontour **10**:515
-- Frank, Jacob **7**:55
-- Ibn Arieh **5**:964
-- Kuhayl, Shukr ibn Sālim **10**:1286
-- Lemlein, Asher **11**:11
-- Molcho, Solomon **12**:225
-- Moses of Crete **5**:1088
-- Nathan of Gaza **12**:861
-- Reuveni, David **14**:114
-- Shabbetai Ẓevi **14**:1219
- *illus:*
-- Frank, Jacob **7**:55
-- Shabbetai Ẓevi **8**:691
- *see also:* MESSIAH
MESSINA (city, Sic.) **11**:1427
Messing, H. **6**:735
Mestechko (township), *see* SHTETL
MESTEL, JACOB **11**:1428
- *illus:* text
Mestel, Leon **3**:807
Mestitz, Johann **11**:1556
Mestre (tn., It.) **16**:95ff
Mesurah (meas.) **16**:388
Mészáros, Zs. **5**:454
Metabolism and Endocrinology **11**:1200
Metaethical **6**:941
METALS AND MINING **11**:1428
- *Contents:*
-- In the Bible **11**:1428
-- In Rabbinic Literature **11**:1434
-- Jews as Metalworkers and Miners **11**:1437
- alchemy **2**:542ff
- art **3**:536
- crafts **5**:1042ff
- inscriptions **16**:661ff
- Kenites **10**:906
- Mesopotamia **16**:1490
- ritual impurity **14**:1565
- secondhand goods trade **14**:1086
- Sidon **14**:1506
- Solomon's trade **15**:99
- Timna **15**:1146ff
- war and warfare **16**:266ff
- *illus:*
-- metal craftsmen from Tripoli **5**:1051
-- Timna **15**:1145,1147
METAPHYSICS (philos.) **11**:1442
- Alexander, Samuel **2**:576
- philosophy **13**:421; **13**:430; **13**:452
- providence **14**:137
Metastasio, Pietro **9**:1103; **10**:460; **10**:460
METATRON (angel) **11**:1443
- Academy of Heaven **2**:208
- amulet **2**:911; **2**:912
- celestial hierarchy **2**:968
- dualism **6**:244
- Enoch **6**:794
- Magen David **11**:695
- magic **11**:711
- mystical speculation **10**:504; **10**:506ff
- *Shi'ur Komah* **14**:1418
- spiritual mentor **10**:631
- visions **16**:168; **16**:169
- Worlds, the Four **16**:642
Metayers (agr.) **7**:1518
Metcalfe, Robert **8**:44
METCHNIKOFF, ELIE **11**:1446
- Haffkine, Mordecai **7**:1060
- *illus:*
-- stamp **12**:1204
Meteg (diacritical mark) **16**:1451
Metempsychosis, *see* GILGUL
Meteorology, *see* Weather
Meteorologyah be-Yisrael (journ.) **1**:newsp. list
Metheg-Ammah (place, Er. Isr.) **7**:335
Methodius (monk) **4**:1481; **4**:884; **16**:885
Methodology, Talmudic **5**:121; **11**:338
Methone (city, Gr.), *see* MODON
Methusael (bib. fig.) **11**:1448
METHUSELAH (bib.fig.) **11**:1447
- *Enoch, Slavonic Book of* **6**:797
Metigah (punctuation mark) **16**:1461
Metivta (Babyl. acad. lecture) **2**:449
Metivta de Mata Romi (yeshivah, Rome) **14**:245
Metivta de-Raki'a, see ACADEMY ON HIGH
Metivta Rabba (acad.) **2**:199
Metman-Cohen, Fania **11**:1449
METMAN-COHEN, YEHUDAH LEIB **11**:1448
- *illus:* text
Met mitzvah (unclaimed corpse) **4**:1517; **15**:1185
Metoposcopy (mantic art) **5**:478
Metrology, *see* WEIGHTS AND MEASURES
Metro Music Shop (N.Y.) **13**:1618
METTERNICH, PRINCE KLEMENS WENZEL VON **11**:1449
- Ottoman Empire Jews **16**:1078
Metuchen (boro., N.J.) **11**:1504
METULLAH (Metulah; vill., Isr.) **11**:1449
- frontier **9**:312ff
- statistics **1**:place list
Meturgeman (tit.) **2**:203; **2**:863;
Meturgeman (wk.) **16**:1360,1390
METZ (city, Fr.) **11**:1449
- archives **3**:382; **3**:387
- Be'er-Bing, Isaiah **4**:381
- Broda, Abraham **4**:1390
- Brussels **4**:1423
- Crusades **5**:1138
- history chart (1670 and 1824) **8**:766-767
- *illus:* text
Metz, Isaac **12**:1421
Metz, Loecki **11**:1167
Metz, Moses, *see* ENSHEIM, MOSES
METZGER, ARNOLD **11**:1452
Metzger, Kurt **10**:1385
Metzger, Léon **16**:1114
METZGER, OTTILIE (Metzger-Latterman) **12**:700
Metzlar (Hebr.) **8**:44
Metzlein-Auerbach (fam.), *see* AUERBACH
Me'un (marriage refusal declaration) **5**:425; **13**:833
Meunim (tribe) **7**:432; **11**:908
MEUNITES (Arab tribe) **11**:1452
Meurthe, Yvonne de la, *see* Guenzburg, Yvonne
Meurthe-et-Moselle (prov., Fr.) **12**:815
Meuschen, Gerhard **8**:44
Mevakker, see GORDON, JUDAH LEIB
Mevakker (cmty. offic.) **16**:700
Mevakkeshei Derekh (Jer. cong.) **9**:909
Mevarekhin, Shabbat, see NEW MOON, ANNOUNCEMENT OF
Mevasser (period.) **5**:41
Mevasseret Yerushalayim (stlmt., Isr.) **11**:1453
- *illus:*
-- new immigrants at **9**:529
MEVASSERET ZION (stlmt., Isr.) **11**:1453
- immigrant absorption center **9**:1504
- statistics **1**:place list
Mevasseret Ẓiyyon (period.) **4**:566; **7**:1479; **9**:1014
- statistics **1**:newsp. list
Mevasser Kahana ben Kimoi (gaon) **2**:14
- gaonate **7**:318
- *hassagot* **7**:1466
- Judeo-Arabic literature **10**:412
- Kohen Ẓedek of Pumbedita **10**:1141
Mevasser Tov (bk.) **4**:407
Mevo Beitar (mosh., Isr.) **1**:place list
Mevo Ḥammat (kib., Golan) **7**:1242; **13**:1534
- statistics **1**:place list
Mevo Ḥoron (loc., Isr.) **1**:place list
Mevo Modi'im (kib., Isr.) **1**:place list
Mevo'ot (period.) **15**:690
- statistics **1**:newsp. list
Mevorach, Moshe **14**:34
MEVORAH, BARUCH **1**:34
Mevorakh, Solomon **12**:614
Mevorakh ben David **13**:589
Mevorakh ben Moses **12**:424
Mevorakh ben Nathan **13**:589
MEVORAKH BEN SAADIAH **11**:1453
MEVORAKH HA-BAVLI **11**:1453
Mevorakh Ibn al-Barqūlī, *see* Ibn al-Barqūlī, Mevorakh
Mexican Cultural Museum **11**:1461
MEXICO **11**:1453
- Antuñes family **3**:167
- education **6**:458ff
- Indian Jews **10**:398
- Inquisition **8**:1392ff
- Latin America **10**:1449ff
- Marranos **2**:808
- press **13**:1040
- synagogues **1**:syn. list
- Treviño de Sobremonte, Tomás **15**:1379
- Wise, George **16**:563
- Zionism **16**:1125
- *illus:*
-- Inquisition torture bed **8**:1399
-- Judaizer, record of trial (1590) **8**:1397
- *pop. tables:* text
Mexico City (Mex.) **8**:1392
Me-Yarkon (riv., Isr.), *see* YARKON
Meyer, Adolf **14**:964
Meyer, Alfred **11**:1462
Meyer, Alvah T. **12**:1375
Meyer, André **10**:1513
MEYER, ANNIE NATHAN **11**:1461
- *geneal. table:* **12**:849
Meyer, Arthur **10**:306
Meyer, Baron de Hirsch **11**:1478; **11**:1479
Meyer, Ben R. **11**:501
Meyer, Sir Carl **4**:175
MEYER, EDUARD **11**:1462
- historiography **8**:562
Meyer, Elias (sol., U.S.) **5**:1566
Meyer, Elias (cmty. ldr., Ind.) **5**:40
MEYER, ERNST HERMAN **12**:700
MEYER, EUGENE **11**:1462
Meyer, Fred **12**:1375
Meyer, H. (print.) **7**:1173
Meyer, Hank (Henry) **6**:1364; **13**:1361
MEYER, HANS JOHANNES LEOPOLD **5**:385
Meyer, Herrmann **15**:143
Meyer, Hirschel, *see* HIRSHEL, MEYER
Meyer, I.S. **8**:568
Meyer, Isaac **5**:934
Meyer, J. **8**:44
Meyer, J. F. **8**:44; **16**:787
Meyer, Jonas **5**:1009; **14**:924
MEYER, JONAS DANIEL **11**:1463
- Amsterdam **2**:900
Meyer, Julius (mer., U.S.) **12**:1374; **12**:911
Meyer, Julius (cmty. ldr., Ger.) **4**:651
Meyer, L. A. **15**:1488
- *illus:*
-- Hebrew typeface **15**:1485
Meyer, Leo **12**:1353
MEYER, LEON **11**:1464
Meyer, Lipmann **11**:1173
Meyer, Louis **15**:277
MEYER, LUDWIG BEATUS **14**:935
Meyer, Sir Manasseh **14**:1608
Meyer, Marshall **3**:422
MEYER, MARTIN ABRAHAM **11**:1464
Meyer, Max **16**:679
Meyer, Moritz **11**:1566
Meyer, Nathan **12**:1215
MEYER, PAULUS (Pawly) **11**:1464
Meyer, Richard Emil **11**:1465
MEYER, RICHARD JOSEPH **5**:385
MEYER, RICHARD MORITZ **11**:1465
Meyer, Samuel **11**:1563
MEYER, TORBEN LOUIS **10**:314
- press **13**:1049
MEYER, VICTOR **11**:1465
Meyerbeer, Carola, *see* Richter, Carola
MEYERBEER, GIACOMO **11**:1465
- Berlijn, Anton **4**:639
MEYERHOF, MAX **11**:1466
MEYERHOF, OTTO **11**:1467
Meyerhofer (publ., Pol.) **13**:1111
MEYERHOFF, HANS **11**:1467
MEYERHOFF, JOSEPH **11**:1468
- P.E.C. **13**:40
Meyerlein, Juden von Ulm, *see* JAFFE, MEIR OF ULM
MEYER-LÉVY, CLAUDE **3**:365
- synagogues **15**:627
MEYEROWITZ, HERBERT VLADIMIR **3**:606
Meyerowitz, Jan **6**:912
Meyers (fam.) **14**:833
Meyers (Jost), Benedict **2**:571
- *illus:*
-- Hebrew-English prayer book (1770) **3**:5
MEYERS, EDUARD MAURITS **11**:1468
Meyers, Isadore **11**:501
Meyers, Joseph **13**:1373
Meyers, Mrs. William **16**:679
Meyers, William **16**:679
MEYERSON, EMILE **11**:1468
- *illus:* text
Meyerson, Golda, *see* MEIR, GOLDA
Meyerson, Martin **15**:1679
MEYERSTEIN, EDWARD HARRY WILLIAM **11**:1469
MEYERSTEIN, EDWARD WILLIAM **11**:1470
Meynell, Francis **15**:1479
Meynert, T.H. **7**:161
Meysels, W.A. **4**:1451
Meyshan, J. **12**:1272
Meysl, Mordecai ben Samuel, *see* MEISEL, MORDECAI BEN SAMUEL
Meyuḥas (paytan) **13**:589
Meyuḥas (fam.) **13**:1399
MEYUḤAS, ABRAHAM BEN SAMUEL **11**:1470
Meyuḥas, Benjamin Moses **11**:1470
Meyuḥas, Joseph Jacob **11**:1470

Meyuḥas, Margalit 11:1471
MEYUḤAS, MOSES JOSEPH MORDECAI BEN RAPHAEL MEYUḤAS 11:1470
MEYUḤAS, RAPHAEL MEYUḤAS BEN SAMUEL 11:1470
- Azulai, Isaac Zerahiah 3:1017
Meyuḥas, R. 8:1462
MEYUḤAS, YOSEF BARAN 11:1471
- Va'ad ha-Lashon 16:1653
Meẓad Ḥashavyahu (fort., Isr.) 2:682; 16:723
Meẓad Ḥasidin (fort., Er. Isr.) 12:528
MEZAḤ (SEGAL), JOSHUA HA-LEVI 11:1471
Me-zahab (bib. fig.) 2:543ff; 6:373
Meẓallin (sect), *see* Mossalians
Mezammerei Barukh she-Amar (frat. orgn.) 12:615
Mezan, Saul, *see* Oram ben Ner
Mezei, Ernö 11:1472
MEZEI, MÓR 11:1472
Meẓer (kib., Isr.) 1:place list
MEZEY, FERENC 11:1472
- *Magyar Zsidó Szemle* 11:721
Mezhibezh (tn., Ukr.), *see* MEDZIBEZH
MEZHIRECH (Mezhirichi; tn., Ukr.) 11:1473
Mezhirech (tn., Pol.), *see* MIEDZYRZEC PODLASKI
Mezigah of Cappadocia, *see* CAESAREA IN CAPPADOCIA
Meẓillot (metal instr.) 12:564
Meẓiltayim (mus. instr.), *see* Cymbals
Mezo, Ferenc 12:1373
MEZŐFI, VILMOS 11:1473
Mezonot, *see* MAINTENANCE
Mezordi, Moses 5:1479
Mezostikhon (lit. style) 2:230
Mezrich (tn., Pol.), *see* MIEDZYRZEC PODLASKI
Mezrits Gadol (tn., Ukr.), *see* MEZHIRECH
Meẓudah (journ.) 1:newsp. list
Meẓudat David (wk.) 2:784
Meẓudat Ẓion (wk.) 2:784
MEZUZAH 11:1474
- amulet 2:906
- ceremonial art 5:310
- Commandments, the 613 5:763
- folklore 6:1394
- gentile 7:592
- Karaites 10:781
- kissing of 10:1074
- Korah 10:1192
- Magen David 11:688
- Monobaz 2:268
- *niddui* 8:353
- position of 7:1289
- scribe 14:1043
- *shema* 14:1372
- *tagin* 15:700
- Talmud 11:1315
- tannery 10:1537
- writing 16:670
- *illus:*
- - silver case (1873) 5:307
Mezuzah (tract.) 12:49
MEZZROW, MILTON (Mess) 12:700
Mhamid (vill., Mor.) 6:190
Mi Al Har Ḥorev (piyyut) 12:1307
MIAMI (loc., Fla.) 11:1477
- Florida 6:1363ff
- history chart (1896) 8:766-767
Miami Beach (city, Fla.) 11:1477ff
- Florida 6:1363
Miasteczko, *see* SHTETL
Mibashan, *see* BRAUNSTEIN, MENAHEM MENDEL
Mibashán, Abrahám (publ., Arg.) 13:1370
Mi-Bayit (journ.) 1:newsp. list
Mi-Bet El (De Synagoga; fam.) 2:934
Mi-Bifnim (period.) 10:972 7:572;
- statistics 1:newsp. list
Mibsam (bib. fig.) 9:89; 14:1549
MICA (Micah; bib. fig.; s. of Mephibosheth) 11:1480
MICAH (prophet) 11:1480
- articles of faith 10:385
- eschatological writings 6:866ff
- Minor Prophets 12:48
- morality 10:1481
- poetry 13:680
Micah Commentary (D. S. scroll), *see Pesher Micah*
Micah of Trier 15:1390
MICAIAH (Micah; bk. of Judges) 11:1483
- bread 4:1335
- golden calf 7:712
- idol of silver 7:738
- Zedekiah's prophecy 16:964
MICAIAH (Micah; Ephramite) 11:1484
Micaiah, daughter of Uriel (bib. fig.) 11:633
Micas, Agostinho (Samuel) 12:838
Micas, João, *see* NASI, JOSEPH
MICHAEL II (Byz. emp.) 11:1485
Michael III (Byz. emp.) 4:1481
- *Vision of Daniel* 5:1290
MICHAEL VIII (Palaeologus; Byz. emp.) 11:1485
Michael, David 15:544
MICHAEL, HEIMANN JOSEPH ḤAYYIM 11:1486
- book collection 4:974
- *illus:* text
MICHAEL, JAKOB 11:1486
Michael, Jehiel 12:627
MICHAEL, M. (educ.) 5:459
MICHAEL, MOSES 11:1487
Michael, Simon 3:891
MICHAEL AND GABRIEL (angels) 11:1487
- Abraham 2:129
- angels 2:958; 2:962
- dreams of the righteous 6:210
- Islamic eschatology 6:885
- Jerusalem Talmud 15:775
- Kabbalah 10:504
- *Ru'aḥ ha-Kodesh* 14:367
- Samael 14:719; 14:720ff
- *Solomon, Testament of* 15:118
- Tamar 15:783
- Uriel 16:7
- *illus:*
- - watching over Shadrach, Meshach, and Abed-nego 2:960
Michael ben Caleb 13:589
Michael ha-Kohen (exeg.) 6:649
Michaelis, Sir Archie 3:880; 13:809
Michaelis, Ch. B. 11:1490
Michaelis, Hannie 6:321
MICHAELIS, JOHANN DAVID 11:1490
- Hebraist 8:44
- linguistics 16:1395
- Moses Mendelssohn 11:1334
Michaelis, J. H. 8:46, 4:839; 7:1196
MICHAELIS, LEONOR 11:1491
MICHAELIS, SIR MAX 11:1491
- *illus:* text
Michael Reese Hospital (U.S.) 8:1039; 14:18
Michaels, Frances 12:285
Michaels, Levy 12:284
Michaels, Morris 11:498
Michaels, Moses, *see* MICHAEL, MOSES
Michaels, Myer 12:284
Michael Solomon Jonah, *see* Jonah, Michael Solomon
MICHAELSON, EZEKIEL ẒEVI BEN ABRAHAM ḤAYYIM 11:1491
MICHAELSON, ISAAC CHESAR 11:1492
MICHAL (bib. fig.) 11:1493
- art 14:917
- Palti 13:49
- *tefillin* 15:899
- teraphim 15:1014
- *illus:*
- - *Bohum Psalter* 14:541
Michal (au.), *see* PINES, YEḤIEL MICHAEL
MICHALI, BINYAMIN YIẒḤAK 11:1494
Michall, Moses, *see* MICHAEL, MOSES
MICHALOVCE (tn., Cz.) 11:1494
- Kosice 10:1216
Michel, Georges-Ephraïm, *see* MIKHAEL, EPHRAIM
MICHEL, JUD 11:1495
Michel, Merle 11:1495
Michelangelo Buonarroti
- Isaiah 9:69
- Jeremiah 9:1360
- Judith 10:460
- Moses 12:406
- *illus:*
- - "Creation of Adam" (frsc.) 5:1068
- - "Deluge" (frsc.) 6:1353
- - Isaiah (frsc.) 9:45
- - Jeremiah (frsc.) 4:940
- - Joel (frsc.) 10:133
- - Zechariah (frsc.) 16:954
Michel de Nostre-Dame, *see* NOSTRADAMUS
Michelet, Jules 5:1593
Michel Ḥasid, *see* JEHIEL MICHAEL BEN JUDAH LEIB HE-ḤASID
Michel-Levy, Albert Victor 11:1496
MICHEL-LEVY, AUGUSTE 11:1495
Michelsbergstrasse synagogue (Wiesbaden) 16:506
MICHELSON, ALBERT ABRAHAM 11:1496
- *illus:*
- - stamp 12:1204
MICHELSON, CHARLES 11:1497
Michelson, Selig 13:482
MICHELSTAEDTER, CARLO 11:1497
- Debenedetti 5:1428
- Italian literature 9:1112
Michener, James 15:1573
MICHIGAN 11:1498
Michigan Daily (newsp.) 4:1541
MICHMAN JOZEPH 1:34
- Dutch literature 6:332
MICHMASH (Michmas; city, Er. Isr.) 11:1500
- Geba, war with 7:349
- Hasmoneans 8:629
Michonze, Grégoire 13:114
Michtam, Meir 10:1138
MICKIEWICZ, ADAM 11:1500
- Polish Jews 13:737
MICROCOSM (philos. conc.) 11:1501
- Kabbalah 10:607ff
- Moses ibn Ezra 13:437
- Neoplatonism 13:429
- Temple 15:984
Micrography and figurated script 8:1261ff
- *illus:*
- - Book of Jonah (1891) 10:176
- - *Damascus Keter* 4:*fcg.* 844
- - decorative patterns 11:689
- - eighteenth cent. *ketubbah* Pl. 11
10-KETUBBAH
- - eleventh century Bible (Cairo) 3:*fcg.* 523
- - Esther, Book of 14:1055
- - German Bible (13th cent.) 4:966
- - German Pentateuch (14th cent.) 5:1575
- - *Lisbon Bible* 11:*fcg.* 299
- - masorah 11:272; 16: 1479
- - *omer* chart 12:1385
- - *Reuchlin Bible* 8:1271
- - *Second Leningrad Bible* 5:*fcg.* 43; 8:1273; 11:904
- - *Shivviti* plaques 14:1420-1421
- - Shneur Zalman of Lyady's portrait 7:1013
- - Spektor, Isaac Elhanan, portrait 15:260
- - thirteenth cent. Pentateuch 11:145
- - "Wailing Wall and its Surroundings" (drg., S. Schulmann) 9:*fcg.* 1531
- - Yemenite Bible (15th cent.) 4:962; 16:*fcg.* 743
Microphone 14:93
Microscopy 11:1196ff
Micu, Samuil 4:882
MICZYŃSKI, SEBASTIAN 11:1503
- Popper-Bozian, Wolf 13:865
Midanik, J. Sydney 15:1264
Middelburg (tn., Transvaal) 15:1340
Middle Atlas (reg., Mor.), *see* Fazāz
Middle-Aramaic (dialect) 12:948
MIDDLESEX COUNTY, NEW JERSEY 11:1504
Middletown (tn., R. I.) 14:143
MIDDOT (tract.) 11:1504
- Eliezer ben Jacob 6:624
- *illus:*
- - Temple plan 15:970
Mide, Adolf 15:1073
Midhorp, J. 8:46
Midi (reg.) 5:1141
Midian (bib. fig.) 9:89
MIDIAN, MIDIANITES (bib. loc. and people) 11:1505
- Place
- - Gideon period history 8:585
- - Jethro 10:17
- - modern settlement scheme 7:193
- - Moses 12:373
- People
- - Genesis, Book of 7:389
- - Ishmaelites 9:89
- - Judge, The Book of 10:447
- - language 14:1152f
- - mining 11:1432
- - proscription 8:346
- - Timna 15:1146ff
- - warfare 16:271
- *illus:*
- - Gideon's war against (map) 7:557
Midler, Mark 12:1377
Midrakh Oz (mosh., Isr.) 1:place list
Midras (form of impurity) 16:941
MIDRASH 11:1507
- General
- - alchemy 2:548
- - Dead Sea sect 5:1417
- - Dura-Europos 6:294
- - folklore 6:1376
- - history 8:656
- - illuminated manuscripts 8:1261
- - Jewish law 12:119,121,130
- - Jewish literature 11:320ff
- - Neo-Aramaic 12:951
- - Rashi 13:1560
- - resistance literature 8:302
- - sages 14:638
- - source for sermons 13:996
- - Yannai 16:714
- - *Zohar* 10:533
- - *see also under individual*

midrashim
- Themes
- - Abba Kolon **2**:36
- - *Akedah* **2**:481,482
- - allegory **2**:643
- - animal tales **3**:20
- - apologetics **3**:190ff
- - astrology **3**:789
- - astronomy **3**:796
- - circuses and theaters **5**:577
- - Jesus **10**:14
- - metals **11**:1435ff
- - proselytes **13**:1185
- - revelation **14**:119
- - Satan **14**:904
- - *Shekhinah* **14**:1350
- - the story **6**:1261
- Exegesis
- - allegorical exegesis **4**:895
- - Bible exegesis **4**:890
- - exegesis and homiletics **8**:948ff
- - legal maxims **10**:1565
- - rabbinical utilization of **3**:910
- - *see also:* HERMENEUTICS; INTERPRETATION
- Influences
- - Apocalypse **3**:181
- - Muslim **9**:1424
- - Philo **13**:409
- - Stoic **15**:409
- *illus:*
- - Leviticus (8th cent. ms.) **2**:717
- - *Pirkei de-Rabbi Eliezer* (1567) **13**:559
- *see also:* AGGADAH; BARAITA, BERAITOT; HOMILETIC LITERATURE

Midrash Abarbanel ve-Ginzei Yosef (library, Jer.) **4**:1148; **9**:325
Midrash Abba Guryon (bk.) **2**:35; **16**:1515
- *Esther Rabbah* **6**:915
- *Targum Sheni* **15**:813
Midrash Abi Manshi (rab. acad., Bagh.), *see* Bet Zikha
Midrash Aggadah (wk.) **2**:489ff; **2**:865; **16**:1517
Midrash Agur (wk.) **16**:1515
Midrash Ahasuerus (agg.), *see* ESTHER RABBAH
MIDRASH ASERET HA-DIBBEROT **11**:1514
- fiction **6**:1264
Midrashat Sedeh Boker (school), *see* Midreshet Sedeh Boker
Midrash Avkir (wk.) **16**:1516
Midrash Bereshit Rabbah (wk.) **15**:1100
Midrash de-Simeon ben Yoḥai (wk.), *see* ZOHAR
Midrash Eser Galuyyot (wk.) **16**:1516
Midrash Esfah (wk.) **16**:1516
Midrash Et La'asot, *see* MIDRASH SAMUEL
Midrash ha-Be'ur (wk.) **5**:1604
MIDRASH HA-GADOL (wk.) **11**:1515
- Richietti, Joseph **14**:159
- Yemenite Jews **16**:742; **16**:745
Midrash ha-Gadol de Parisi (yeshivah, Er. Isr.) **9**:512
Midrash ha-Ḥokhmah (bk.) **6**:730; **10**:226
Midrash Hallel (wk.) **16**:1516
Midrash ha-Ne'elam (wk.) **16**:1196
- Hellenism **10**:496
- Kabbalah **10**:533
- Zohar **16**:1196
Midrash Ḥaserot vi-Yterot (wk.) **7**:371; **16**:1516
- *matres lectionis* **16**:1414
Midrash Ḥazita (agg.), *see* SONG OF SONGS RABBAH
Midrash ha-Zohar (wk.), *see* ZOHAR
Midrash ha-Zohar: Die Religionsphilosophie des Sohar und ihr Verhaeltnis zur allgemeinen jüedischen Theologie **10**:133
MIDRASHIM, SMALLER **16**:1515
Midrashiyyat Ruppin (research center, Isr.) **8**:242
Midrash Kinot (agg.), *see* LAMENTATIONS RABBAH
Midrash Kohelet (agg.), *see* ECCLESIASTES RABBAH
Midrash Konen (wk.) **13**:84; **16**:1516
MIDRASH LEKAḤ TOV (wk.) **11**:1516
Midrash Mah Rabbu (wk.), *see Pesikta Ḥadta*
Midrash Megillat Esther (agg.) *see* ESTHER RABBAH
Midrash Megillat Ruth be-Panim Aḥerim (wk.), *see Ruth Zuta*
Midrash Mishnat Rabbi Eliezer (wk.) **4**:195
Midrash Panim Aḥerim, *see* SIFREI ZUTA
Midrash Panim Aḥerim le-Ester, Nosaḥ Alef (wk.) **16**:1515
- *Esther Rabbah* **6**:915
- *Targum Sheni* **15**:813
Midrash Petirat Moshe Rabbenu (wk.) **12**:413
MIDRASH PROVERBS **11**:1517
- Jewish literature **11**:321
Midrash Psalms, *see* MIDRASH TEHILLIM
Midrash Rabbah (wk.) **11**:320ff
- Arḥa, Eliezer **3**:434
- *Deuteronomy Rabbah* **5**:1584
- early edition **3**:702
- *Ecclesiastes Rabbah* **6**:355
- *Esther Rabbah* **6**:915
- *Exodus Rabbah* **6**:1067
- *Genesis Rabbah* **7**:399
- Jaffe, Samuel **9**:1266
- *Lamentations Rabbah* **10**:1376
- *Leviticus Rabbah* **11**:147
- *Numbers Rabbah* **12**:1261
- *Pi Shenayim* **2**:492
- *Ruth Rabbah* **14**:524
- *Song of Songs Rabbah* **15**:152
- Strashun, Samuel **15**:428
- *illus:*
- - *Deuteronomy Rabbah* (1566) **5**:1584
- - *Exodus Rabbah* (1545) **6**:1068
- - *Genesis Rabbah* **2**:737; **7**:400
- - *Lamentations Rabbah* (1545) **10**:1377
- - *Leviticus Rabbah* (1545) **13**:1096
- - *Mattenot Kehunnah* (1595) **9**:1079
- - *Midrash Ḥamesh Megillot* **11**:1507
- - *Numbers Rabbah* **12**:1262
- - *Song of Songs Rabbah* **15**:153
Midrash Rabbi Neḥunya (bk.), *see* BAHIR, SEFER HA-
"Midrash Ruth" (agg. wk.), *see* RUTH RABBAH
MIDRASH SAMUEL (*Shemuel;* wk.) **11**:1517
- Jewish literature **11**:321
Midrash Sheloshah ve-Arba'ah, *see* AGGADAT BERESHIT
Midrash Sheloshim u-Shetayim Middot (wk.), *see Midrash Agur*
Midrash shel Shavuot, *see* MIDRASH ASERET HA-DIBBEROT
Midrash Sheni be-Fanim Aḥerim, *see* SIFREI ZUTA
Midrash Shir ha-Shirim (smaller midrash) **16**:1515
Midrash Shir ha-Shirim (agg.), *see* SONG OF SONGS RABBAH
Midrash Shoḥer Tov, *see* MIDRASH PROVERBS
Midrash Soferim (bk.) **13**:138
Midrash Tadshe (wk.) **16**:1517
Midrash Talpiyyot (bk.) **10**:552
Midrash Tanḥuma, *see* TANḤUMA YELAMMEDENU
MIDRASH TANNAIM **11**:1518
- *tannaim* **15**:799
- *see also:* MIDRESHEI HALAKHAH
MIDRASH TEHILLIM **11**:1519
- Jewish literature **11**:321
- Psalms, Book of **13**:1323
Midrash Temurah (wk.) **16**:1518
MIDRASH VA-YISSA'U (wk.) **11**:1520
- apocalypse **3**:181
- fiction **6**:1262
- *Testament of Judah* **13**:185
Midrash va-Yekhullu (*Rabbati;* wk.) **16**:1517
Midrash va-Yosha (wk.) **16**:1517
Midrash Yehi Or (wk.), *see* ZOHAR
Midrash Yelammedenu, *see* TANḤUMA YELAMMEDENU
Midrash Yonah (wk.) **11**:1515
Midreshei Ge'ullah (bk.) **10**:508
MIDRESHEI HALAKHAH **11**:1521
- Akiva's systematization **2**:489ff
- *amoraim* **2**:865
- Hebrew mss. **11**:903f
- *Mekhilta of R. Ishmael* **11**:1269
- *Mekhilta of R. Simeon ben Yohai* **11**:1267
- *Midrash Tannaim* **11**:1518
- mishnaic Hebrew **16**:1591
- *Sifra* **14**:1517
- *Sifrei* **14**:1519
- *Sifrei Zuta* **14**:1522
- *tannaim* **15**:799
- *see also:* MIDRASH
Midreshei Ḥanukkah (wk.) **16**:1518
Midreshei ha-Peli'ah **10**:552
Midreshet Ruppin (seminary, Isr.) **1**:place list
Midreshet Sedeh Boker **14**:1089
MIDSTREAM (period.) **11**:1523
Midya, Al- (vill., Er. Isr.) **12**:206
Miedzyborz (tn., Ukr.), *see* MEDZIBEZH
Miedzyrzec (tn., Ukr.), *see* MEZHIRECH
MIEDZYRZEC PODLASKI (tn., Pol.) **11**:1523
- ghetto **13**:765
Mieg, J. F. **8**:46
MIELEC (tn., Pol.) **11**:1525
MIELZINER, MOSES **11**:1526
Mielziner, Saul **15**:308
Mieroslawski, Ludwik **13**:800
Miesel, Hugo **15**:299
Meisel, Willy **15**:299
MIESES, FABIUS **11**:1526
Mieses, Isaac **16**:1328
Mieses, J. (r., Pol.) **4**:885; **11**:1569
MIESES, JACQUES (Jacob) **5**:408
MIESES, MATTHIAS **11**:1526
Mieses, Meir Jerahmeel **11**:612
MIESIS, JUDAH LEIB **11**:1527
- *illus:* text
Mieszko III (k., Pol.) **12**:61
Mieszko the Younger (k., Pol.) **12**:61
Mifal ha-Payis (Isr. lottery) **9**:435; **11**:513
Mifgash-Liqā' (journ.) **9**:1042
Miflagah Datit Le'ummit, *see* HA-POEL HA-MIZRACHI; MIZRACHI; NATIONAL RELIGIOUS PARTY
Miflagah Komunistit Yisre'elit (Isr. commun. party), *see* Maki
Mifleget ha-Avoduh ha-Yisre'elit, *see* ISRAEL LABOR PARTY
Mifleget ha-Avodah ha-Ẓiyyonit (polit. party, Isr.), *see* HITAHDUT
Mifleget ha-Po'alim ha-Me'uḥedet (Isr. soc. party), *see* MAPAM
Mifleget Po'alei Ereẓ Israel (lab. party), *see* MAPAI
Mifleget Poalim Soẓialistim (polit. party, Isr.) **5**:807; **9**:659; **14**:133
Mifshata (vill., Er. Isr.) **6**:1188
Miftaḥ puma (vocalization sign) **16**:1443
Migas, Ibn (name), *see under* Ibn Migash
MIGDAL (mosh., Isr.) **11**:1527
- statistics **1**:place list
- Tschlenow, Jehiel **15**:1416
Migdal Aphek (loc., Isr.) **3**:176
Migdal-Ashkelon (tn., Isr.), *see* ASHKELON
Migdal Baal-Zephon (anc. loc.) **4**:13
Migdal David (loc., Jer.), *see* David, Tower of
Migdal-Eder (anc. site, Er. Isr.) **14**:105
Migdal-Gad (bib. loc.) **7**:249
MIGDAL HA-EMEK (tn., Isr.) **11**:1528
- Bet She'arim **9**:538
- inter-communal conflict **9**:395f
- statistics **1**:place list
Migdal Nunaiya (city, Er. Isr.), *see* MAGDALA
Migdal Or (inst. for blind) **4**:1092
Migdal Oz (bk., Ibn Gaon) **8**:1175
Migdal Oz (play, Luzzatto) **11**:603
Migdal Senaah (loc., Er. Isr.), *see* SENAAH
Migdal Shalom (bldg., Tel Aviv) **15**:917
- *illus:* **9**:573; **15**:923
Migdal Ẓevaya (Zevd'aya; Zobaiya; bib. loc.) **2**:199; **6**:327; **11**:685
MIGDOL (Cana. city) **11**:1528
Migdol (anc. Egy. city) **11**:1528
Miggo (leg. conc.) **13**:635; **14**:1197
Mignard, Pierre **9**:1344
MIGRATIONS **16**:1518
- General
- - Ashkenazi Jewry **3**:721ff
- - communities, Jewish **5**:833
- - economic history **16**:1298
- - Elimelech of Lyzhansk **6**:661
- - Ḥasidim **7**:1398ff
- - Holocaust **8**:838; **8**:840; **8**:884ff
- - Orthodoxy influenced by **12**:1489
- - population **13**:880ff
- - socialism, Jewish **15**:47
- - statistics **15**:344
- - Syrkin, Nachman **15**:653ff
- - territorial settlement **15**:1021ff
- - U. S. literature **15**:1570ff
- Emigration
- - Austria **3**:899ff
- - Belgium **3**:168
- - East Europe **16**:1320
- - Greece **7**:880
- - India **8**:1357
- - Nazi Germany **7**:491
- - Pale of Settlement **13**:27
- - Rome **14**:251
- - Rumania **14**:390ff
- - Spain **15**:227ff
- Immigration
- - France **7**:31ff
- - Greece **7**:875
- - Israel **9**:473f
- - Latin America **10**:1449ff
- - Ottoman Empire **16**:1532
- - Palestine **13**:40
Siberia **14**:1486ff
- - South Africa **15**:186ff
- - Uruguay **16**:11ff
- - U.S. **15**:1408; **15**:1629; **15**:1650
- Organizations, Movements and Plans
- - Alliance Universelle **2**:650
- - Beriḥah **4**:622f

– – Evian conference **6**:987
– – Galveston movement **7**:294
– – I.C.A. **10**:44
– – J.D.C. **2**:830ff
– – Nazi **14**:52
– – Revisionists, Zionist **14**:128; **14**:130
– – United Hias Service **15**:1539ff
– – White Papers **16**:483ff
– – Youth Aliyah **16**:862ff
– – Zionist Socialist Workers Party **16**:1180
– *illus:*
– – emigrants at Ellis Island **15**:1609
– – emigrants on their way to U.S.A. **8**:739
– *pop. tables:*
– – Asia, dispersion of Jews from the 1700s to 1945 **3**:741
– – Asian countries, main periods of *aliyah* **3**:746
– – Europe, waves of Ashkenazi emigration 18th-20th cent. **3**:719
– – expulsions, 1000 to 1500 C.E. **8**:689
– – Germany, emigration of Jews, 1933-1939 **7**:491
– – intercontinental, 1881-1914 **8**:729
– – intercontinental, 1915-30 and 1931-39 **8**:753
– – Iran, emigration to Israel, 1948–1968 **8**:1441
– – Israel, growth of Jewish population, and decrease in other parts of Asia 1840-1966 **3**:745
– – Israel, immigration from Arab countries till 1948 **16**:1127
– – Russia, inter-regional **14**:471–472
– *see also:* ALIYAH; DEMOGRAPHY; REFUGEES; VITAL STATISTICS
Miguel de Castanhoso **6**:1152
Miguel de Morillo **8**:1383
Míguez, João, *see* NASI, JOSEPH
MIHAILENI (tn., Rum.) **11**:1528
– Rumania **14**:397
MI'ILYA (vill., Isr.) **11**:1529
Mijamin (pr. clan) **12**:89
Mījana (poetry) **9**:1038
Mikal (deity) **14**:81
Mikardo, Ian **13**:812; **15**:27
Mikdash (cult place) **5**:1164ff
Mikdash Me'at (bk.) **14**:171
Mikdash Melekh (wk.) **4**:1545
MIKÉFE, *see* Society for the Promotion of Handicrafts and Agriculture among Hungarian Jews
Mi-Keren Zavit (journ.) **1**:newsp. list
MIKES, GEORGE **6**:789
– Langdon, David **10**:1418
Mikhael, Albert **4**:1493
MIKHAEL, EPHRAIM **7**:150
Mikhael, Murād **8**:1452
Mikhaelashvili, Shalom **7**:428
Mikhaelowitz, Moses **10**:1078
MĪKHĀ'ĪL, MURĀD **12**:1466
Mikhailishker, Abraham Dov, *see* LEBENSOHN, ABRAHAM DOV
Mikhal, *see* LEBENSOHN, MICAH JOSEPH
MIKHALEVICH, BEINISH **11**:1529
Mikhelson, Mordecai Mottel **10**:723
Mikhlol (wk.) **10**:1002; **16**:1355,1359,1373,1386
Mikhlol, Enziklopedyah la-No'ar (enc.) **6**:735
Mikhemtat Valley (Er. Isr.) **9**:588
MIKHMORET (mosh., Isr.) **11**:1530
– statistics **1**:place list
MIKHOELS, SOLOMON **11**:1530
– anti-Fascism **3**:62ff
– Moscow **12**:365
– motion pictures **12**:456
– Shakespeare **14**:1265
– Yiddish theater **15**:1075
– *illus:*
– – text
– – in *King Lear* **12**:361
Jewish Anti-Fascist Committee **3**:63
– – La Guardia, Fiorello, and **12**:1110
– – portrait **14**:492
Mikhtam (Psalm superscription) **13**:1320
Mikhtav Ḥozer (journ.) **1**:newsp. list
Mikhtav le-David (wk.) **5**:1353
Mikhtav li-Yhudei Teiman (wk.) **11**:331
Mikkun Ḥakla'i (journ.) **1**:newsp. list
Miklat (period.) **1**:newsp. list; **8**:213
Miklishansky, Abba Ḥayyim **10**:1106
Miklós, Andor **13**:1369
Mikneh Avram (wk.) **16**:1360,1374,1390
Mikra, *see* HUMMASH
Mikra Kodesh (soc., Ukr.) **11**:612
Mikra'ot Gedolot (Bib.) **16**:1427,1476
– history chart **8**:766-767
– *illus:* **2**:783
Mikra soferim ("scribal reading") **15**:80; **16**:1409
MIKULOV (tn., Morav.) **11**:1531
– anti-profiteering enactment **7**:1063
– archives **3**:387
– imprisonment *takkanot* **8**:1307
– museums **12**:543
– tailors **15**:705
– *illus:* text
Mikulski (pr., Pol.) **7**:62
MIKVA'OT (tract.) **11**:1533
– *illus:* text
– *see also:* BATH, BATHING; MIKVEH
MIKVEH (rit. bath) **11**:1534
– ablution **2**:82
– communal amenities **2**:805
– *halakhah le-Moshe mi-Sinai* **7**:1167
– Karaites **11**:760
– Masada **11**:1089
– *niddah* **12**:1142ff
– scribe **14**:1044
– synagogue **15**:592
– *taharat ha-mishpaḥah* **15**:703
– Talmud **11**:1533
– tax for **15**:848
– washing dead **15**:1189
– *illus:*
– – text
– – Andernach, 14th cent. **2**:946
– – *Hamburg Miscellany* **8**:*fcg.* 1335
– – immersion in a natural pool **11**:1534
– – Masada **11**:1087
– – Plock **13**:648
– – Speyer **15**:263
– – woman immersing herself (15th cent. ms.) **2**:85
– *see also:* BATH, BATHING
Mikveh Israel (syn., Pa.) **12**:1069; **15**:624
– Philadelphia **13**:369f
– *illus:*
– – Cherry St. synagogue **13**:371
– – dedication service **15**:1595
– – *Rimmonim* **12**:725
– – Washington's letter **13**:369
MIKVEH ISRAEL (school, Isr.) **11**:1544
– Alkalai **2**:639
– Alliance Universelle **2**:652
– Bilu settlers **4**:1000ff
– history chart **8**:766-767
– Netter, Charles **12**:1001
– statistics **1**:place list
– *illus:*
– – text
– – entrance **2**:400
Mil (meas.) **16**:389
Mil (Pal. currency) **5**:723
MILAN (city, It.) **11**:1545
– Borromeo, Carlo **4**:1258
– history chart (1597) **8**:766-767
– Inquisition **8**:1398
– library **11**:193
– Vitale, Simone **2**:566
– *illus:* text
Milan, Edict of **8**:652
Milan, Gabriel **16**:164
Milanesi, Guido **9**:1106
MILANO, ATTILIO **1**:34; **11**:1547
Mila' pum (vowel) **16**:1449
MILBAUER, JOSEPH **11**:1547
Milcah (Bib. fig.) **16**:979
Milch, Klara **12**:1375
Milchig, *see* MILK
Milcom (deity) **9**:1342
– dysphemism **6**:960
– Judges, the Book of **10**:449
Miler, Buzi **4**:1048
Miles City (city, Mont.) **12**:266
MILETUS (anc. city, As. M.) **11**:1547
– Diaspora **6**:10
– synagogue **15**:599
MILEYKOWSKY, NATHAN (Netanyahu) **11**:1548
Milgrom, Felix **11**:1200
Milgroym (journ.) **4**:609 **16**:555
Milḥamot Adonai (bk., Levi ben Gershom) **11**:94; **11**:341; **13**:446
Milḥamot Adonai (wk.; Naḥmanides) **12**:781f
Milḥamot Adonai (wk.; Solomon ben Jeroḥam) **11**:58
Milḥamot Benei Ya'akov (wk.), *see* MIDRASH VA-YISSA'U
Milḥamtenu (journ.), *see Be-Terem*
Milḥemet ha-Ḥokhmah ve-ha-Osher (bk.) **11**:353
Milḥas (zool.), *see* Ziz
Milhau, Moïse **12**:283
Milhaud (fam.) **2**:476
MILHAUD, DARIUS **11**:1548
– Aix-en-Provence **2**:476
Milḥemet Mitzvah (bk.) **11**:1256
MILIAN, MAXIMIN **10**:314
– Rumania **14**:399
Miliana (tn., Alg.) **2**:613; **15**:1439
MILICH, ADOLPHE **11**:1549
– Paris school **13**:116
– *illus:* text
Milik, J.T. **4**:239; **9**:1535; **9**:1537
Military College of Education (Isr.) **9**:693
Military Courts (Isr.) **9**:633
– *illus:*
– – al-Fatḥ terrorists trial **9**:639
Military Government (Isr.) **9**:397; **9**:411; **9**:1031
MILITARY SERVICE **11**:1550
– *Contents:*
– – U.S.A. **11**:1550
– – Great Britain **11**:1552
– – British Commonwealth **11**:1554
– – Czarist Russia **11**:1554
– – Austro-Hungary **11**:1555
– – U.S.S.R. **11**:1556
– – Italy **11**:1559
– – Germany **11**:1559
– – France **11**:1560
– – Poland **11**:1563
– – Rumania **11**:1565
– – Bulgaria **11**:1565
– – Greece **11**:1566
– – Switzerland **11**:1566
– – Holland **11**:1566
– – Other Countries **11**:1567
– – Women **11**:1567
– – Conclusion **11**:1568
– – Jewish Chaplaincy **11**:1568
– – Capsules **11**:1572
– Diaspora **6**:13
– education **6**:388
– Elephantine **6**:604ff
– French Revolution **7**:155
– history chart (1842) **8**:766-767
– Numbers, Book of **12**:1249ff
– Samuel Ha-Nagid **14**:816
– self-defense **14**:1123
– Sofer, Moses **14**:91
– South Africa **15**:202
– World War I **8**:755
– *illus:*
– – American Civil War casualty list **15**:1602
– – burial of Russian Jewish soldier **14**:445
– – cantonist's oath **14**:439
– – France, memorial to Jewish soldiers **7**:41
– – *Haggadah*, German army, World War I **7**:1090
– – *Haggadah* for U.S. soldiers, World War II **7**:1089
– – Jamaica, exemption re arms on Sabbath **9**:1272
– – Jewish Brigade **9**:359; **10**:36, 37
– – Jewish Municipal Guard, Warsaw **16**:335
– – Monash, Sir John **3**:882
– – Montefiore, Moses **12**:271
– – Mount Herzl military cemetery (Jer.) **9**:368
– – Palestinian volunteers for British army **9**:358
– – Saigon, U.S. servicemen *seder* **12**:876
– – Schomberg, Alexander **14**:993
– – Schwarzbard, Shalom **14**:1027
– – Trumpeldor, Joseph **15**:1411
– – Turkey, Jewish soldiers **9**:335
– – Willesden Jewish cemetery, memorial, London **11**:476
– – Zion Mule Corps **10**:70
– *see also:* JEWISH BRIGADE GROUP; JEWISH LEGION; Zion Mule Corps
MILK **11**:1577
– dietary laws **6**:40
– food **6**:1417
– milking on Sabbath **15**:896
Milkilu (k., Gezer) **7**:535
Milko, Isidor **15**:473
MILKWEED (bot.) **11**:1577
Milky Way (galaxy) **3**:799
Mill, David **8**:46
Mill, J. **8**:46
MILL, JOSEPH SOLOMON (John) **11**:1577
– Bund **16**:338
Mill, William Hodge **8**:46
Millan, Francisco **8**:1392
Millão, Anrique Dias **2**:70
Millão, Paul de, *see* Abensur, Moses (mer., Ger.)
Millas (tn., Fr.) **14**:353
Millás Vallicrosa, Francisca Vendrell **11**:1578
MILLÁS VALLICROSA, JOSÉ MARIA **11**:1578
Millbank, Joseph Duveen, Lord *see* DUVEEN, JOSEPH, LORD
Millburn (tn., N. J.) **15**:625
Mille'eil (gram. term) **16**:1422,1429
Millenarians (sect, Isr.) **9**:296; **14**:1233; **16**:1153
Miller, Abe W. **6**:369
MILLER, ARTHUR **11**:1579
– U.S. literature **15**:1578
Miller, Betty **11**:1580
Miller, David **5**:612
MILLER, EMANUEL **11**:1580
– psychiatry **13**:1340
Miller, Henry **10**:739

MILLER, IRVING **11:**1580
MILLER, ISRAEL **11:**1581
- *illus:*
- - Rabbinical Council of America convention **13:**1462
Miller, Jonathan **11:**1580
Miller, Joseph **11:**485
Miller, J. S. **10:**74
MILLER, LOUIS **1:**34; **11:**1581
MILLER, LOUIS E. **11:**1581
- socialism **15:**34
MILLER, MARTIN RUDOLF **15:**1088
Miller, Michael **5:**1546
Miller, Norman **15:**301
Miller, Ray **15:**306
Miller, Ruth **15:**209
Miller, Samuel **10:**1502; **12:**845
MILLER, SAMUEL AARON **1:**34
Miller, Saul **11:**879
- Minister of Youth **5:**112
- socialism **15:**207
- Winnipeg **16:**551
MILLER, SHAYE **11:**1582
Miller, Stanley **8:**1361
Miller, T. Z. **4:**1537
Miller, Walter **15:**309
Millera' (gram. term) **16:**1422,1429
Milles (refugee camp, Fr.) **2:**476
MILLET (rel. cmty., Ott. Emp.) **11:**1582
- 'Abd al-Majīd **2:**54
- *ḥakham bashi* **7:**1146
- Ottoman Empire **16:**1539,1548
- Turkey **9:**1087
MILLET (bot.) **11:**1583
- plant list **13:**621
- poppy **15:**269
- rice **14:**156
- *see also:* SORGHUM
Millhiser, Gustavus **14:**161
MILLIN, PHILIP **11:**1583
MILLIN, SARAH GERTRUDE **11:**1584
- South African literature **15:**209
Millman, Daniel **15:**309
MILLMAN, JACOB **8:**1433
Millo (fort., Jer.) **9:**1383
- *illus:*
- - site **9:**1384
MILLO, JOSEF **11:**1584
Millo, Yemima **5:**74
Millon Ḥadash u-Meẓuyyar-Menukkad (wk.) **6:**986
Millot ha-Higgayon (wk.) **11:**459; **11:**754
MILLSTONE **11:**1585
Millstream (period.) **8:**219
Mill Street Synagogue (N.Y.), *see* Shearith Israel Congregation
Millu'im, *see* Ordination offering
Milman, Henry Hart **6:**782; **8:**560
Milner, Lord **4:**133
Milner, John **8:**46
MILNER, MOSES MICHAEL **11:**1586
MILOSZ, OSCAR **11:**1586
Milsahagi, Elyakim, *see* MEHLSACK, ELIAKIM
MILSTEIN, NATHAN **11:**1587
- Auer, Leopold **3:**840
Miltenberg-on-Main (loc.) **15:**603
MILTON, ERNEST **15:**1088
MILTON, JOHN **11:**1587
- English literature **6:**774,778
- Hebraists **8:**46
- Lebensohn, Micah **10:**1550
- *Samson Agonistes* **14:**774
MILWAUKEE (city, Wis.) **11:**1588
- Friedman, Herbert A. **7:**186
- *illus:*
- - Temple Emanu-El **16:**556
Milwidsky, Hanoch **11:**1204
Milyukhin (prch.) **10:**400
Mi-Mizraḥ u-mi-Ma'arav (period.) **4:**1291
- statistics **1:**newsp. list
Mimram (promissory note), *see* MAMRAM
Mimran (fam.), *see* MAYMERAN
MIN (heretic; sectarian) **12:**1
- apologetics **3:**192
- *Birkat ha-Minim* **4:**1035
- censorship **5:**280
- Christianity **5:**511
- Damascus document **5:**1246ff
- definition **13:**790ff
- Doenmeh **6:**149
- dualism **6:**243
- Elisha ben Avuyah **6:**669
- heresy **8:**359ff
- Jewish Christian sects **10:**38
- mishnaic attitude **3:**654
- mystical tendencies **10:**498
- term for Christian **7:**411
- *see also:* APIKOROS; GNOSTICISM; SIFREI HA-MINIM
Mina (weight, coin) **5:**696ff; **16:**378; **16:**381ff,387
Mina, Al- (vill., Er. Isr.) **11:**793
Minaea (anc. kdm., Arab.) **14:**587
Minas Gerais (state, Braz.) **4:**1330
Mīnat al-Qal'a (loc.) **3:**696
Min Bet-El (fam.), *see* Min ha-Kenesset
Minc, A. **5:**803
MINC, HILARY **12:**3
MINCO, MARGA **12:**4
Minda, Albert G. **12:**38
Mindel, Nissan **5:**452
MINDEN (tn., Ger.) **12:**4
MINDLIN, HENRIQUE **3:**365
Minean (lang.) **14:**1152
MINERAL RESOURCES IN ISRAEL **9:**797
- Dead Sea region **16:**1274
- Negev **12:**927
- Sodom **15:**71ff
- Timna mines **15:**1145ff
- *illus:*
- - Dead Sea Works **5:**376-377
- - Palestine Potash Co. **15:**73
- - salt formations at Dead Sea **14:**710
- - Timna copper mines **5:**378; **9:**172-173; **15:**1147
Minet el-Beida (anc. seaport) **15:**1501
Min ha-Adummim (fam.) **14:**315
MINHAG (custom) **12:**4
- *Contents:*
- - Definition **12:**5
- - General **12:**5
- - In Jewish Law **12:**7
- - - As a Source of Law **12:**7
- - - Elucidation of Terms **12:**9
- - - Scriptural Support for the Validity of Minhag as a Legal Source **12:**10
- - - Functions and Categories **12:**10
- - - As Deciding the Halakhah **12:**11
- - - As Adding to Existing Halakhah **12:**12
- - - "Custom Overrides the Law" **12:**13
- - - Proof of the Existence of a Custom **12:**19
- - - Custom and Usage **12:**20
- - - General and Local Custom **12:**22
- - - Minhag and the Conflict of Laws **12:**23
- - - Control over Minhag by the Halakhic Scholars **12:**23
- General
- - Abraham ben Nathan ha-Yarḥi **2:**154
- - Ben Baboi **7:**317
- - Ben Sira **4:**552
- - *doreshin lashon hedyot* **8:**1425
- - Falashas **6:**1146ff
- - Isserles, Moses **9:**1084
- - kabbalistic influence **10:**641ff
- - Mountain Jews **12:**479
- - Palestinian **11:**147
- - Sephardim **14:**1170
- - *yeshivot* **16:**767
- Legal Practice
- - acquisition, modes of **2:**220; **14:**1390
- - contractual obligation **5:**928
- - endowment witnesses **8:**285
- - limitation of actions **11:**253
- - maintenance **11:**784
- - partnership **13:**150
- - sales **14:**675ff
- - servant's liability **10:**1329
- - tax **15:**845ff
- - transgression or death **9:**243
- Ritual Practice
- - Day of Atonement **5:**1379
- - dew, prayer for **5:**1603
- - Jerusalem **9:**1554
- - marriage in Poland **13:**721
- - masoretic accents **11:**1098
- - music **12:**605
- - Sabbath **14:**566
- - *Sefer Torah* **14:**1103
- Legal Theory
- - codification of law **5:**630
- - conflict of laws **5:**883ff
- - *dat Yehudit* **10:**383
- - halakhic category **7:**1160
- - *ḥerem bet din* **8:**356
- - Jewish law **12:**119ff
- - non-Jewish law **6:** 52ff
- - offenses **10:**1408
- - overriding *halakhah* **16:**778
- - rabbinical utilization **3:**910
- - responsa **14:**88
- - status in *halakhah* **7:**1157; **14:**647
- - *takkanah* **15:**714
- - *takkanot ha-kahal* **15:**728
- - tradition **15:**1309
- *illus:*
- - *Amsterdam Minhagim Book* (1662) **12:**30; **13:**1401
- - *Traustein* ("marriage stone") **11:**693,1031,1041
- - *Venice Minhagim Book* **12:**26; **13:**1402
- *see also:* FOLKLORE; MINHAGIM BOOKS; SEVARAH
Minhag (rite), *see* LITURGY
Minhag America (prayerbook) **16:**564ff
Minhagei Ereẓ Yisrael (bk.) **12:**30
Minhagei Spira (bk.) **12:**27
Minhag Elzos (Als. rite) **2:**753
Minhag ha-Lo'azim (Romi; litur.), *see* Roman rite
Minhagim (illus. bk., Venice) **12:**30
MINHAGIM BOOKS **12:**26
- *Contents:*
- - Introduction **12:**26
- - Middle Ages **12:**27
- - Modern Period **12:**29
- - Illustrations **12:**30
- illuminated manuscripts **8:**1261
- illustrations **4:**1234
- Sefer ha-Mangig **2:**154
- Tyrnau, Isaac **15:**1491
- *illus:*
- - *Amsterdam Minhagim Book* (1707) **13:**1402
- - *Venice Minhagim Book* (1601) **13:**1401
Minhagot (wk.) **2:**182
Minhag Oystraikh (*Peihem; Polin;* litur.), *see* Polish rite
Minhag Rainus (litur.), *see* Rhine rite
Minhag Shinkali (litur.) **5:**625
Minhag Teiman (litur.), *see* Yemenites
MINḤAH (prayer service) **12:**31
- Isaac **9:**5
- Leviticus **11:**140
- liturgy **11:**393ff
- priestly blessing **13:**1061
- Samaritan Sabbath **14:**741
- *see also:* AMIDAH
Minḥah (grain offering) **5:**1159
- *bikkurim* **6:**1313
- *ḥallah* **7:**1194
- incense **8:**1314
- sacrifice **14:**599; **14:**602ff
- *illus:*
- - preparation of **11:**1315
Minḥah (journ.) **1:**newsp. list
Min ha-Kenesset (fam.) **2:**934; **15:**1467
Min ha-Ne'arim (fam.) **4:**1190
Min ha-Tappuḥim, David, *see* Pomis, David de
Minḥat Ḥinnukh (wk.) **4:**15
Minḥat Shai (bk.) **16:**1477
Minḥat Yehudah (wk., Judah Gibbor) **7:**549
Minḥat Yehudah (wk., Judah ben Eliezer) **15:**520
Min ha-Yesod (polit. faction, Isr.) **9:**676; **10:**1478; **14:**325
Min ha-Yesod (journ.) **1:**newsp. list
Min ha-Zekenim (name), *see* Del Vecchio
Minhelet ha-Am (nat. exec., Isr.) **9:**663
MINIS (fam.) **12:**32
Minis, Abigail **12:**32
Minis, Abraham **12:**32
- Georgia **7:**429; **14:**919
Minis, Esther **12:**32
Minis, Leah **12:**32
Minis, Philip (18th cent.) **12:**32
Minis, Philip (18/19 cent.) **7:**429
Minis, Simon **12:**32
Ministry of Defense Publishing House (Isr.), *see* Misrad ha-Bittaḥon Hoẓa'ah la-Or
MINKIN, JACOB SAMUEL **12:**32
MINKOFF, NAḤUM BARUCH **12:**33
- Glanz-Leyeles **7:**600
- Licht, Michael **11:**208
MINKOWSKI, EUGÈNE **12:**33
Minkowski, Françoise **12:**34
MINKOWSKI, HERMANN **12:**34
Minkowski, Maurice **12:**551
- *illus:*
- - "Water-Carrier at the Town Well" (paint.) **8:**755
Minkowski, Mieczyslaw **12:**34
Minkowski, Oskar **11:**1200
MINKOWSKI, PINCHAS **12:**35
Minkowsky, Mordecai **14:**830
MINNEAPOLIS-SAINT PAUL **12:**35
MINNESOTA (state, U.S.) **12:**39
- *pop. tables:* text
Minnim (mus. instr.) **12:**564
MINNITH (loc., Er. Isr.) **12:**40
- agriculture **2:**391; **16:**480
Minoan civilization **8:**295
Minocchi, S. **4:**878
Minor (leg. conc.) **13:**1350
- action time limitation **11:**254
- agency **2:**351
- child marriage **5:**423
- definition in Talmud **8:**1424
- father's maintenance duty **12:**111
- gift **7:**562
- *haftarah* reading **16:**1344
- *ḥaliẓah* **11:**128
- inheritance rights **15:**480
- levir **11:**123
- liability **11:**184
- loans **11:**419
- *minyan* **12:**23
- rape **13:**1548

- sale **12:**1392
- torts **15:**1273
- waiver **11:**1234
- wills **16:**523
- *see also:* BAR MITZVAH, BAT MITZVAH; DEAF-MUTE; Legal capacity; PARENT AND CHILD
Minor, Clorinda **16:**1154
MINOR, OSIP S. (Joseph) **12:**40
MINOR, SOLOMON ZALMAN (Zalkind) **12:**40
- *kazyonny ravvin* **10:**862
- Moscow **12:**364
MINORCA (isl., Medit.) **12:**41
- Inquisition **8:**1388ff
- refugees **4:**1274
Minority, *see* MAJORITY RULE
MINORITY BLOC (Pol.) **12:**41
MINORITY RIGHTS **12:**43
- *Contents:*
- - Development of the Idea **12:**43
- - Popular Movement **12:**44
- - At the Peace Conference **12:**45
- - Minority Treaties **12:**45
- - Implementation of Treaty Provisions **12:**45
- - Treatment of Jews by Countries **12:**46
- - After World War II **12:**48
- Alliance Israélite **2:**650
- autonomy **3:**921; **3:**926
- Austrian Jews **3:**896
- communist theory **5:**795ff
- discriminatory taxes **16:**1312
- Greece **7:**877
- Gruenbaum, Yizḥak **7:**944
- history **8:**756
- Holocaust **8:**841
- Homberg, Naphtali Herz **8:**941
- Jewish identity **10:**60
- Jewish socialism **15:**41; **15:**49; **15:**50
- League of Nations **10:**1523
- millet **11:**1582
- Negro civil rights **12:**932ff
- Ottoman **16:**1538
- Politische Gemeinde **13:**832
- Riesser, Gabriel **14:**167
- Russia **15:**56; **15:**1678
- Schutzjuden **14:**1013
- self-defense **14:**1124
- Seljuks **14:**1136
- *shtadlan* **14:**1463
- Spain **15:**220ff
- *Toleranzpatent* **15:**1209
- Turkey **15:**1456; **15:**1458
- Umayyads **15:**1529; **15:**1530
- U.N. **15:**1561
- Vienna, Congress of **16:**131
- *illus:*
- - Cracow, agreement limiting Jewish commercial rights (1485) **5:**1029
- - England, petition to Oliver Cromwell re religious services **5:**1127
- *see also:* AUTONOMISM; AUTONOMY; EMANCIPATION
Minority Treaties **12:**45
MINOR PROPHETS **12:**48
- Murabba'at scrolls **12:**528
MINOR TRACTATES **12:**49
- Talmud **15:**763
MINOW, NEWTON NORMAN **12:**51
MINSK (city, Belor.) **12:**51
- *Contents:*
- - Early History **12:**51
- - Hebrew Printing **12:**53
- - The Minsk Province **12:**53
- - Holocaust Period **12:**53
- - Resistance **12:**55
- - Contemporary Jewry **12:**56
- Assaf, Simḥa **3:**756
- museums **12:**540
- self-defense unit **14:**1124
- synagogue **15:**590
- *illus:* text
MINSK CONFERENCE **12:**58
- Zionism **16:**1136
- *illus:* text
Minsker, Sender, *see* POLACHEK, SENDER
Minsk Group (Yid. au.) **10:**1289; **12:**59
MINSKI, NIKOLAI MAXIMOVICH **12:**59
MINSK MAZOWIECKI (tn., Pol.) **12:**59
- *illus:*
- - text
- - Jews humiliated by Nazis **13:**757
MINSKY, LOUIS **10:**314
Minstrels, Jewish **14:**1426
- *illus:*
- - Suesskind von Trimberg **15:**484
- *see also:* MUSIC
Mint (bot.) **15:**269
- plant list **13:**621
Mintchine, Abraham **13:**116
MINTMASTERS AND MONEYERS **12:**60
- economic history **16:**1281
- Poland **13:**710
- *illus:*
- - text
- - Polish coins, 13th cent. **13:**727
- *see also:* COINS AND CURRENCY; MEDALISTS; NUMISMATICS
Mintoff, Dom **11:**831
Mînturea (period.)
Mintz (stlr., Can.) **16:**537
Mintz, Alexander
- *illus:*
- - F.Z.C. (Vienna) **16:**1165
Mintz, Herman **12:**1295
Mintz, Isaac **12:**66
Mintz, Meir **16:**1328
Mintz, Michael **13:**1053; **15:**1088
Mintz, Minlan **12:**66
MINTZ, MOSES BEN ISAAC **12:**65
- Bamberg **4:**149
MINTZ, PAUL **12:**66
Mintz, Rachel **5:**449
Mintz, Siegmund **4:**306
Mintzberg, Israel Ze'ev **14:**93
MINYAN (prayer quorum) **12:**67
- *Amidah* **2:**838
- children **5:**428
- *Kedushah* **10:**875
- marriage **11:**1040; **11:**1048
- minor **12:**23
- *niddui* and *ḥerem* **8:**351
- priestly blessing **13:**1062
- *illus:*
- - Cape Town, written record (1841) **15:**185
- - Germany, Orthodox rabbinate's *takkanot* for communities without **15:**716
Minyan shetarot (Sel. era) **14:**1092
MINYAT ZIFTA (tn., Egy.) **12:**67
MINZ, ABRAHAM BEN JUDAH HA-LEVI **12:**68
- Abraham Ha-Sephardi **2:**153
- Pollack, Jacob ben Joseph **13:**834
MINZ, BENJAMIN **12:**68
- Po'alei Agudat Israel **13:**655
Minz, Joseph ben Abraham **12:**69
MINZ, JUDAH BEN ELIEZER HA-LEVI **12:**69
- Capsali, Elijah **5:**152
- responsa **11:**337
Minz, Moses ben Isaac ha-Levi, *see* MUENZ, MOSES BEN ISAAC HA-LEVI
Minzberg, Leib **11:**430
Miqdash, *see* TABERNACLE
Miqpaẓ puma' (vocalization sign) **16:**1443
Miqra'ot Gedolot (Bib.), *see Mikra'ot Gedolot*
Miqra' soferim (scriptural reading), *see Mikra Soferim*
Miques, João, *see* NASI, JOSEPH
MIR (tn., Belor.) **12:**70
- *illus:* text
Mir (yeshivah) **12:**71ff
- Japan **9:**1282
- New York **12:**1120
- Tiktinski family **15:**1141
MIRABEAU, HONORÉ GABRIEL RIQUETI, COMTE DE **12:**73
- Alsace Jews **2:**755
- French Revolution **7:**152
MIRACLE **12:**73
- *Contents:*
- - In the Bible **12:**73
- - In the Talmud **12:**74
- - In Medieval Jewish Philosophy **12:**76
- - Neoplatonism **12:**76
- - The Challenge of Aristotelianism **12:**77
- - Maimonides **12:**77
- - Naḥmanides **12:**78
- - Ḥasdai Crescas **12:**78
- - In Later Jewish Thought **12:**79
- - Contemporary Views **12:**80
- Arama's explanations **3:**257
- Ark of Covenant **3:**463
- cause and effect **5:**260
- divination **6:**116
- Eliezer of Beaugency **6:**631
- Ḥasidism **7:**1395ff
- Hirsch, Samuel **13:**457
- Israel Ba'al Shem Tov **9:**1050
- Jerusalem **9:**1556
- Jewish Aristotelianism **3:**447
- Judah Loew ben Bezalel **10:**377
- Kaspi, Joseph ibn **10:**810
- Levi ben Gershom **11:**97
- magic **7:**649; **11:**704
- Maimonidean controversy **11:**750
- Mendelssohn **11:**1336ff
- Messiah **11:**1419
- Moses **12:**374
- nature **12:**888; **12:**890
- prophets and prophecy **13:**1158ff
- sages **14:**638
- signs **14:**1524
- *Solomon, Wisdom of* **15:**119
- Yose ben Zimra **16:**857
- *illus:*
- - Aaron performing with his rod **12:**379
- *see also:* PLAGUES OF EGYPT
Mira de Amescua, Antonio **15:**250
Miranda, Abraham Enriques **4:**991; **14:**1245
Miranda, George **13:**229
Miranda, Isaacs **10:**1381; **10:**1503; **13:**229
Miranda, Joseph Enriques **4:**991
MIRANDA, SALOMON RODRIGUES DE **12:**81
MIRANDA DE EBRO (city., Sp.) **12:**81
Mirandola, Giovanni Pico della, *see* PICO DELLA MIRANDOLA, GIOVANNI
Mirat, Eugène **8:**272
Mirawa (vill., Kurd.) **10:**1297
- *Mirele Efros* (wk.) **14:**1264
- *illus:*
- - Lipzin, Keni, as Mirele Efros **15:**1068
Mireles (print.) **4:**653
MIRELMAN (fam.) **12:**82
Mirelman, Jacob **12:**82
Mirelman, Joseph **12:**82; **13:**1370
Mirelman, Leon **12:**82
Mirelman, Robert **12:**82
Mirelman, Simon **12:**82
Mirels (fam.) **7:**1
MIRÈS, JULES ISAAC **12:**82
- railroads **13:**1518
Mirezo, Bartholomeo Marques **16:**105
MIRIAM (bib. fig.) **12:**82
- Arts **12:**408
- Hazeroth **7:**1531
- leprosy **11:**38
- Moses **12:**372
- Sea, Song of the **14:**1072
- *illus:*
- - text
- - dancing with a drum **13:**166
Miriam (w. of Herod), *see* MARIAMNE
Miriam (m. Jesus), *see* Mary
Miriam (apos.) **3:**201; **15:**495
Miriam (dau. of Rashi) **10:**351; **13:**1559
Miriam (dau. of S. Spira) **11:**569
Miriam (15/16 cent., scribe) **4:**470
Miriam and Her Seven Sons, *see* HANNAH AND HER SEVEN SONS
Miriam Hospital (U.S.) **8:**1039
MIRISCH, HAROLD **12:**472
MIRISCH, MARVIN **12:**472
MIRISCH, WALTER **12:**472
Mirkevet ha-Mishneh (wk.) **3:**34; **11:**357; **16:**800
Mirkin, Joseph
- *illus:*
- - F.Z.C. (Montpellier) **16:**1165
Mirkish, Solomon Zalman **12:**70
Mirkowski, Rudolph **3:**807
Mirles, David, *see* FRAENKEL, DAVID BEN NAPHTALI HIRSCH
Miro, Heinrich **4:**1355
Miró, Jose Maria **3:**413
MIRODAN, ALEXANDRU **14:**423; **14:**426
Miron, Dan **5:**74
MIRON, ISSACHAR **12:**701
Mironov, P. G. **4:**1114
Mirorgrad (dist., Rus.) **13:**840
MIROSLAV (tn., Morav.) **12:**84
Miroslawiec (tn., Pomerania) **6:**469
Mirov, Nenad **16:**889
Mirsim (site, Er. Isr.), *see* Tells (Beit Mirsim)
Mirski, Canonicus Joseph **16:**148
MIRSKY, AARON **12:**85
Mirski, B. **10:**997
Mirsky, Jacob **12:**1521
MIRSKY, SAMUEL KALMAN **12:**85
Mir Viln Lebn (period.) **5:**806
Mirvish, Edwin **15:**1264
Mirvish, M. Ch. **15:**191
Mīrwa (tn., Iraq) **15:**504
Mīrzā Ali Muhammad **8:**936
- *illus:*
- - burial shrine **8:**933
Mīrzá Yaḥyá **9:**923
Miṣbāḥ, al- (journ.) **14:**1318
Miscarriage **6:**1309
- *illus:*
- - amulet **2:**909
- *see also:* BARRENNESS AND FERTILITY; BIRTH
Miscegenation **3:**44
Miscellanies (period.) **15:**54
Miscellany (collec. of mss.)
- *British Museum Miscellany* **8:**1266
- *Halakhic Miscellany* **8:**1270
- *Hamburg Miscellany* **8:**1267
- *Rothschild Miscellany* **8:**1270
- *illus:*
- - medical and philosophical treatises (15th cent.) **11:**1195
- - *see also:* ILLUMINATED MANUSCRIPTS, HEBREW
Mischakoff, Mischa **5:**1572
Mischlinge (part-Jew) **16:**667; **12:**1281

Mi-Sefer ha-Zikhronot shel Rav Littai (wk.) **14:**1655
Mises, Judah Leib **7:**1418
MISES, LUDWIG EDLER VON **12:**86
MISGAV AM (kib., Isr.) **12:**86
- statistics **1:**place list
Misgav Dov (mosh., Isr.) **1:**place list
Misgav Yerushalayim (inst., Jdr.) **14:**1176
Misha ben Abra, *see* MASHĀ'ALLAH
Mishael (bib. fig.), *see* SHADRACH, MESHACH, ABED-NEGO
Mishael ben Uzziel **13:**1305; **16:**1437,1472
Mishal (city, Er. Isr.) **3:**701
Mishan (orgn., Isr.) **8:**539
Mishan, Isaac **15:**1397
Mishan, Judah **11:**577
Mishar ha-Makkolet (journ.) **1:**newsp. list
Mishar ve-Ta'asiyyah (journ.) **1:**newsp. list
Mishawayh al-ʿUkbarī, *see* MESHWI AL-ʿUKBARĪ
Mishawayhites (sect.) **11:**1404
Mishbeẓet Tarshish (bk.) **10:**222
MI SHE-BERAKH (prayer) **12:**86
- Amen **2:**803
Misheiker, Betty **5:**450; **15:**210
Mishkan, *see* TABERNACLE
Mishkenot Sha'ananim (Jer.) **9:**1516; **9:**563; **9:**1457
- *illus:*
- - apartments **9:**1451
- - Montefiore Foundation seal **9:**1451
Mishkinski, Ḥayyim Jacob **15:**543
MISHKINSKY, MOSHE **1:**34
Mishle (*Mishlei*), *see* PROVERBS, BOOK OF
Mishlei Agur (wk.) **5:**685
Mishlei Arav (wk.) **9:**8
Mishlei Irasto (wk.) **6:**1131
Mishlei Kovesim (Kvesim; fable) **3:**20; **6:**1127
Mishlei Musar (wk.), *see Mishlei Arav*
Mishlei Shu'alim (fables) **3:**21; **6:**1129; **11:**353
Mishlei Sindbad (Sindabar) **6:**1130; **14:**1608
Mishlei Ysopeto (fables) **3:**21
Mishlo'aḥ manot (custom, Purim) **13:**1392
- *illus:*
- - silver plate **13:**1393
Mishma (s. of Ishmael) **9:**89; **14:**1549
Mishmar (orgn., Crimea) **5:**1107; **8:**250
Mishmar (newsp.) **9:**1016; **12:**1056
Mishmar Ayyalon (mosh., Isr.) **1:**place list
Mishmar David (kib., Isr.) **1:**place list
MISHMAR HA-EMEK (kib., Isr.) **12:**87
- battle **16:**720
- statistics **1:**place list
MISHMAR HA-NEGEV (kib., Isr.) **12:**88
- statistics **1:**place list
MISHMAR HA-SHARON (kib., Isr.) **12:**88
- statistics **1:**place list
Mishmar ha-Sheloshah (mosh., Isr.) **9:**1175
Mishmar ha-Shivah (mosh., Isr.) **1:**place list
MISHMAR HA-YARDEN (mosh., Isr.) **12:**88
- ICA **10:**47
- statistics **1:**place list
Mishmar li-Yladim (period.) **5:**458
MISHMAROT (kib., Isr.) **12:**89
- statistics **1:**place list
MISHMAROT AND MA'AMADOT (Temple watches) **12:**89
- *Contents:*
- - Historical **12:**89
- - Talmudic Data **12:**90
- - Activities **12:**91
- - History **12:**92
- Dead Sea Scrolls **5:**1403
- Haduta **7:**1056
- liturgy **11:**393
- lots, casting of **11:**512
- priests **13:**1085
- red heifer ashes **13:**1413
- synagogue **15:**583
- *Ta'anit* (tract.) **15:**675
- Temple service **15:**970ff
Mishmarot Eliẓur (coast guards) **6:**674
Mishmeret (mosh., Isr.) **1:**place list
Mishmeret ha-Bayit (bk.) **2:**308
MISHNAH **12:**93
- *Contents:*
- - Sources **12:**93
- - Production and Arrangement **12:**97
- - Judah ha-Nasi's Redaction **12:**102
- - The Question of Committing the Mishnah to Writing **12:**105
- - Division of **12:**105
- - Text **12:**106
- - Printed Editions **12:**107
- - Commentaries **12:**107
- - Translations **12:**108
- General
- - Abendana, Jacob **2:**67
- - Akiva's collection **2:**491
- - Cairo *genizah* **16:**1337
- - Gamaliel, Rabban **7:**297
- - Gershom ben Judah **7:**513
- - Hebrew mss. **11:**903
- - history chart **8:**766-767
- - Jewish literature **11:**316ff
- - Justinian's prohibition **8:**656ff
- - Kasovsky's concordance **10:**809
- - language **16:**1362,1591
- - Mishnah of Meir **11:**1241
- - mnemonics **12:**189
- - mysticism **10:**498
- - plants and plant products (list) **13:**615-626
- - Samaritans **14:**740
- - study **15:**456,459
- - traditional pronunciation **13:**1121
- Redaction and Exegesis **12:**102ff
- - *Amoraim* **2:**863; **2:**865ff
- - Babylonian Talmud **15:**755
- - Bar Kappara **4:**227
- - editing of text **9:**252
- - Eleazar ben Pedat **6:**597
- - Jerusalem Talmud **15:**772ff
- - Judah ha-Nasi **10:**366
- - Simeon ben Judah ha-Nasi **14:**1558
- Division Of **12:**105ff
- - *Zeraim* **16:**997
- - *Moed* **12:**208
- - *Nashim* **12:**833
- - *Nezikin* **12:**1132
- - *Kodashim* **10:**1126
- - *Tohorot* **15:**1189
- - order of tractates and subject matter (chart) **15:**751
massekhet **11:**1117
- Development as Law
- - codification **5:**631ff
- - conflict of opinion **5:**891
- - general rules **10:**1565
- - *haggahah* **7:**1106
- - *halakhah* **7:**1156
- - *halakhic* exegesis **8:**1419
- - law source **12:**117; **12:**121; **12:**136
- - morality **10:**1481
- - Oral Law **12:**1439
- Commentators **12:**107
- - Abraham of Posquieres **2:**138
- - Adani, David **2:**250
- - Adeni, Solomon **2:**265
- - Adret, Moses ibn **2:**305
- - Asher ben Jehiel **3:**708
- - Ashkenazi, Joseph **3:**727; **3:**728
- - Azulai, Abraham **3:**1019
- - Bertinoro, Obadiah **4:**698; **4:**699
- - Elijah Menahem ben Moses **6:**659
- - Fraenkel-Teomim **7:**6
- - Heller, Yom Tov **8:**312
- - Isaac of Siponto **9:**24
- - Isaac ben Solomon Gabbai **7:**232
- - Lipschutz, Israel **11:**293
- - Luria, David **11:**571
- - Maimonides **11:**754ff
- - Nathan ben Abraham **12:**857
- - Vilna Gaon **6:**657
- - Zacuto, M. **16:**907
- *illus:*
- - text
- - incunabulum (1492) **8:**1328
- - *"Kodashim"* (mural, H. Lerner) **10:**1125
- - manuscript (12/14 cent.) **11:**902
- - Mordecai ben Hillel ha-Kohen's commentary **12:**313
- *see also:* BARAITA, BERAITOT; TANNA, TANNAIM; TOSEFTA; *and under individual tractates*
Mishnah Berurah (bk.) **9:**1070
Mishnah of Abba Saul **2:**40
MISHNAT HA-MIDDOT (bk.) **12:**109
- *see also:* MIDRASH
Mishnat Ḥasidim (code) **14:**652
Mishnat Melekhet ha-Mishkan, see BARAITA DE-MELEKHET HA-MISHKAN
Mishnat R. Eliezer (wk.), *see Midrash Agur*
Mishneh (qtr., Jeru.) **10:**289
Mishneh le-Melekh (bk.) **14:**262
Mishneh Torah (Bib. bk.), *see* DEUTERONOMY
Mishneh Torah (wk., Maim.), *see* MAIMONIDES
Mishpat ha-Shalom ha-Ivri (judicial inst., Er. Isr.) **12:**142
Mishpat ha-Shalom ha-Ivri (journ.) **1:**newsp. list
Mishpatim (ordinances) **5:**783ff
MISHPAT IVRI **12:**109
- *Contents:*
- - Definition and Terminology **12:**109
- - "Religious" Halakhah and "Legal" Halakhah **12:**110
- - Law and Morals **12:**113
- - *De-Oraita* and *De-Rabbanan* **12:**113
- - The Basic Norm and Sources of Jewish Law **12:**115
- - Different Periods of Jewish Law **12:**121
- - Jewish Law—A Law of Life and Practice **12:**123
- - Evolution of Jewish Law **12:**129
- - Evolution of Jewish Law Reflected in its Literary Sources **12:**131
- - Different Branches of Jewish Law **12:**132
- - Public Jewish Leadership in the Development of Jewish Law **12:**136
- - Relationship Between Jewish Law and Foreign Law **12:**137
- - Era of Emancipation **12:**139
- - Period of Jewish National Awakening **12:**141
- - In the State of Israel **12:**145
- General
- - Commandments, reasons for **5:**783
- - conceptual meaning **8:**286
- - *dat Yehudit* **10:**383
- - *Din Torah* **6:**929
- - penal law **13:**222
- - talion **15:**741
- - torts **15:**1272ff
- Development
- - authority, rabbinical **3:**907ff
- - autonomy, judicial **3:**928ff
- - codification **5:**628
- - commandments **5:**760
- - *halakhah* **7:**1156
- - *halakhah le-Moshe mi-Sinai* **7:**1167
- - halakhic midrash **8:**1415
- - law of Moses and Israel **5:**595; **11:**1047
- - legal maxims **10:**1564
- - Mesopotamian law **16:**1492
- - *minhag* **12:**4
- - Mishnah redaction **9:**253
- - *sevarah* **14:**1196
- - *takkanot* **15:**712
- - *takkanot ha-kahal* **15:**728
- Procedure
- - bailees **14:**1455
- - bet din and judges **4:**719
- - conflict of laws **5:**882
- - extension **7:**1466
- - jurisdiction over gentiles **7:**411; **12:**1190ff
- - law and morality **10:**1480
- - oaths **12:**1298
- - practice **13:**952
- - Sanhedrin **14:**836
- - witness **16:**584
- *illus:*
- - Jerusalem *bet din* **4:**727
- - *see also under individual subjects*
Mishpat ve-Khalkalah (journ.) **1:**newsp. list
Mishpetei ha-Ḥerem (wk.) **12:**780
Mishpetei ha-Te'amim (bk.) **16:**1478
Mishpetei Shevuot (wk.) **5:**1354
MI-SINAI NIGGUNIM (Melodies) **12:**151
- *Aleinu le-Shabbe'aḥ* **2:**559
- *Amidah* **2:**845
- *Avodah* **3:**979
- *mus. notations:* text
Miska, Mordecai ben Samuel, *see* MEISEL, MORDECAI BEN SAMUEL
MISKOLC (city, Hung.) **12:**153
Miṣlawim (Mosul Jews) **10:**1295
Mison (loc., Fr.) **14:**1623
Misrad ha-Bittaḥon Hoẓa'ah la-Or (publ. firm, Isr.) **13:**1379
Misrai (fam., Yug.) **15:**289
Misraki (fam. name), *see* Mizraḥi
MISREPHOTH-MAIM (loc., Er. Isr.) **12:**154
Missionaries (non-J.)
- Anselm **3:**33
- Christianity **5:**511
- Israel **9:**295; **9:**296; **9:**299; **9:**1450; **9:**1573ff
- Luther, Martin **11:**584
- Paul of Tarsus **13:**190
- Protestants **13:**1248ff; **14:**18ff
- Spain **15:**237ff
- *illus:*
- - *The Jew* (1823) **13:**1050
Mission of Israel **5:**498
MISSISSIPPI (state, U.S.) **12:**154
- *illus:* text
- *pop. table:* text
Misslitz (tn., Morav.), *see* MIROSLAV
Missoula (city, U.S.) **12:**266

MISSOURI (state, U.S.) **12:**156
- *illus:* text
- - *pop. table:* text
MISTAKE (legal term) **12:**158
- custom **12:**23
- public body **13:**1354
- sale **14:**676ff
- waiver **11:**1234
- *see also:* ASMAKHTA
Misteczkin, Sh. **3:**361
"Mr. Rubin, farmer from Metullah" (phot., M. Bar-Am) **13:**483
Mistra (anc. city state), *see* SPARTA
Mistral, Frédéric **4:**882
Misztótfalusi, Kis Miklós **8:**46
Mitah bi-neshikah (death kiss) **10:**1074
Mitah Yafah, see EUTHANASIA
Mitanni (anc. kdm., people) **8:**1114ff; **16:**1498
- anthropology **3:**42
- settlement in Canaan **9:**122
Mitassekim (burial wkrs.) **8:**442
Mitau (Mitava; city, Latv.), *see* JELGAVA
Mitchell (city, S.D.) **15:**213
Mitchell, Hyman **3:**458
Mitchell, Jacob **3:**458
Mitchell, Joseph **10:**40
Mitchell, Julius **5:**1543
Mitchell, Louis **3:**458
Mitchell, Matthew **11:**1285
Mitchell, Maurice B. **15:**1679
Mitchell, Roland M. **12:**1072
MITCHELL, YVONNE **15:**1054,1088
- motion pictures **12:**453
Mitchell Hall (Jer.) **9:**1496
Mi-Teiman le-Ẓiyyon (journ.) **1:**newsp. list
Mi-Tekufat ha-Even (journ.) **1:**newsp. list
MITHREDATH (Pers. name) **12:**159
Mithridates (1st cent. C.E., gov.) **3:**4
MITHRIDATES, FLAVIUS **12:**160
- Allemand, Johanan **2:**646
- Christian Kabbalah **10:**643
- Reuchlin, Johannes **14:**108
- *illus:* text
Mithridates VI Eupator **8:**292; **11:**1183
- Kittim **10:**1082
MITIN, MARK BORISOVICH **12:**160
Mitla Pass (loc., Sinai) **9:**389; **14:**1606,1636
- *illus:*
- - paratroopers, Sinai Campaign **9:**379
- - Six-Day War **14:**1632
Mitnaddevei Ḥuẓ la-Areẓ, see MAḤAL
MITNAGGEDIM **12:**161
- denunciations by **8:**1369
- ethical literature **6:**931
- history **8:**724ff
- Loebel, Israel **11:**440
- *Maggidim* **11:**699
- Musar Movement **12:**534
- polemics **13:**795
- rabbinical office **13:**1448
- Shneur Zalman of Lyady **14:**1432
- Vilna **16:**143
- Vilna Gaon **6:**654
- *see also:* ḤASIDISM
Mitrani, Joseph Moses **10:**1538
Mit Riheina (vill., Egy.) **11:**1301
Mitteilungen (period.) **15:**1533
Mitteilungsblatt fuer die juedischen Gemeinden der Nordrheinprovinz (journ.) **13:**1033
Mittelberg (tn., Aus.) **8:**1043
Mittelstelle fuer Juedische Erwachsenenbildung (orgn.) **4:**1431
Mitternacht, J. S. **8:**46
MITTWOCH, EUGEN **12:**161
MITZVAH (rel. precept) **12:**162
- General
- - art **3:**500ff
- - ceremonial objects **5:**288
- - duty **6:**323
- - wisdom literature **16:**560
- Observance of
- - angels **10:**324
- - Conservative Judaism **5:**903ff
- - Dead Sea Sect **5:**1412
- - Essenes **6:**899ff
- - Falashas **6:**1146ff
- - home and family **6:**1172
- - Jewish Christian sects **10:**39
- - joy **10:**319
- - *kavvanah* **10:**853
- - love and fear of God **11:**528
- - *niddui* **8:**352
- - parental honor **13:**101
- - Pharisees **13:**365
- - piety from **13:**504ff
- - proselytes **13:**1184
- - reward and punishment **14:**134
- - slaves **14:**1656
- - strangers and gentiles **12:**1189; **15:**419ff
- - study **15:**454
- - *takkanah* not to perform **15:**717
- - Temple destruction **9:**238
- - Temple Scroll **15:**996ff
- - transgression or death **9:**243; **10:**385
- - women **10:**1566
- Views on
- - Akiva **2:**491
- - apologists **3:**190
- - Buber, Martin **13:**463
- - Halevi, Judah **13:**439
- - Ḥanokh of Aleksandrow **7:**1277
- - Ḥasidism **7:**1405ff
- - Haskalah **7:**1436ff
- - Johanan ben Zakkai **10:**151
- - Kabbalah **10:**617
- - Korets, Phinehas **10:**1204
- - Maimonides **13:**442
- - Menahem Mendel of Vitebsk **11:**1312
- - Mendelssohn, Moses **11:**1337ff; **13:**455
- - Philo **13:**412
- - Rosenzweig, Franz **13:**462; **14:**301
- - Shabbetai Ẓevi **14:**1223
- - *Zohar* **10:**533
- *tables:*
- - Commandments, the 613 **5:**761
- - mandatory commandments and prohibitions, Maimonides' list **5:**763-782
- - *see also:* COMMANDMENTS, REASONS FOR; COMMANDMENTS, THE 613
"Mitzva Tanz" (paint., S. S. Alva) **5:**1265
Mitzvot, *see* MITZVAH
Mitzvot ha-Nashim (manual) **11:**358
Mitzvot ha-teluyot ba-areẓ (commandments peculiar to Isr.)
- child's custody **13:**98
- Commandments, the 613 **5:**777
- first fruits **6:**1312
- *ḥallah* **7:**1193
- *ḥibbut ha-kever* **8:**464
- husband's or wife's residence rights **8:**1121
- idolatry **8:**1227
- impurity **13:**1409
- king, kingship **10:**1011
- *leket, shikhhah* and *peah* **11:**3
- mixed species **12:**169
- nazarite laws **12:**909
- *omer* **12:**1382
- pilgrimage festivals **13:**519
- sabbatical year **14:**574
- sacrifices **14:**599
- sanctity **2:**763, 770
- slavery **14:**1659
- Syria **15:**639
- Temple **15:**942
- *terumah* **15:**1025
- tithes **15:**1156
Mitzvot Zemanniyyot (wk.) **14:**849
Miudji (vill., Rus.) **3:**1005; **3:**1006
Miudji-Aftaran (vill., Rus.) **3:**1005
Mi'ut hermeneutical rule **8:**370
MIVḤAR HA-PENINIM (bk.) **12:**163
- ethical wills **16:**531
- Jewish literature **11:**353
- *illus:*
- - incunabulum (1484) **8:**1332
Mivrak (period.) **1:**newsp. list; **2:**848
Mivtaḥim (mosh., Isr.) **1:**place list
Mivtaḥim (fund, Isr.) **8:**539; **9:**866
Mivẓar Dan (loc., Isr.), *see* BANIAS
Mivẓar Yisrael (encyc.) **6:**735
Mix, Ronald **15:**308
Mixed Armistice Commissions **3:**480; **9:**377; **15:**1546ff
Mixed courts, *see* Courts, Mixed
MIXED MARRIAGE, INTERMARRIAGE **12:**164
- *Contents:*
- - Problems of Measurement **12:**164
- - Extent of Jewish Intermarriage **12:**164
- - Social Factors Related to Intermarriage **12:**164
- - Size of the Jewish Community **12:**165
- - Prevention of Intermarriage **12:**167
- - Legal Aspects **12:**168
- - The State of Israel **12:**168
- - Reform and Conservative Practice **12:**169
- General
- - anthropology **3:**50
- - Assembly of Jewish Notables **3:**763; **3:**764
- - Ḥasidim **7:**1396
- - Malachi on **11:**813ff
- - Mussolini on **12:**718
- - Philo on **8:**301
- - population changes **13:**889
- - vital statistics **16:**182ff
- *Halakhah*
- - child's custody **13:**99
- - Gentiles **7:**410
- - *gerim* **15:**421
- - inheritance rights **15:**476
- - *mamzer* **11:**840
- - non-Jewish bread **4:**1335
- - proselytes **13:**1190ff
- History
- - Amsterdam **2:**901
- - British Columbia **4:**1380
- - Canaanites **8:**347
- - community **5:**846
- - Constantius II (chart, 339) **8:**766-767
- - deportation **2:**903; **3:**901
- - Ezra **8:**618ff
- - Israel **9:**478; **16:**893
- - Italy **9:**1119
- - Nazi euthanasia **16:**1332
- - North America **15:**1590
- - Phoenicians **13:**476
- - Prague **13:**971
- - Samaritans **14:**735; **14:**738; **14:**746
- - statistics **8:**731ff
- - Spain **3:**173; **15:**220
- *tables:*
- - text
- - Bohemia, percentage of mixed marriages, 1881-1930 **4:**1179
- - vital statistics **16:**184
- *see also:* MARRIAGE, PROHIBITED
MIXED SPECIES (bib. prohibition) **12:**169
- *Contents:*
- - Mixing of Seeds **12:**170
- - Mixing of Trees **12:**170
- - Mixing in the Vineyard **12:**171
- - Mixing of Cattle **12:**171
- - Plowing and Driving with Two Species **12:**171
- - Problems of Definition **12:**171
- - Reasons for Precept **12:**172
- Commandments, the 613 **5:**778
- evolution **6:**1003
- gentiles **12:**1189ff
- grain types **6:**1333
- heredity **4:**1023
- *kilayim* **10:**999
- Pentateuch **13:**248
- *sha'atnez* **14:**1214
- tares and wheat **15:**810
Mi-Yamim Rishonim (journ.) **1:**newsp. list; **4:**1538
Mi-Yrushalayim (journ.) **1:**newsp. list
Miẓaf puma (vocalization sign), *see Miqpaẓ puma'*
Mizbeaḥ, see ALTAR
Mi-Ẓiyyon (journ.) **1:**newsp. list
Mizler, Harry **15:**306
Mizleta (10th cent., moneyer) **12:**60
MIZMOR LE-DAVID (psalms) **12:**172
- Psalms, Book of **13:**1319
MIZMOR SHIR LE-YOM HA-SHABBAT (litur.) **12:**173
Miznak (ship) **14:**1604
Mizolo, Guglielmo, *see* Portaleone, Benjamin ben Mordecai
MIẒPAH (mosh., Isr.) **12:**173
- *illus:*
- - general view **9:**574
Mizpeh (rural stlmt., Isr.) **1:**place list
Mizpeh (publ. firm, Pal.) **13:**1378
MIZPEH; MIZPAH (bib. locs.) **12:**173
- Badè's excavations **4:**59
- Saul **14:**910
- synagogue **15:**581
- *illus:* text
MIẒPEH RAMON (tn., Isr.) **12:**174
- astronomical observatory **15:**927
- statistics **1:**place list
Mizpeh Shalem (Isr.) **1:**place list
Mizpeh Shemuel (loc., Er. Isr.), *see* Nabī Samuīl
Miẓ puma (vocalization sign), *see Miqpaẓ puma'*
MIZRA (kib., Isr.) **12:**175
- statistics **1:**place list
- *illus:*
- - chicken house **5:**946
- - cultivation of roses for export **9:**781
- - *menorah* **11:**1365
MIZRACHI (mvmt.) **12:**175
- *Contents:*
- - Beginnings **12:**175
- - From Crisis to Expansion **12:**176
- - In Ereẓ Israel **12:**177
- - Educational Work **12:**178
- - Structure of World Movement **12:**179
- - Projects and Achievements **12:**179
- - In the United States **12:**180
- Agudat Israel **2:**421; **2:**425
- Amiel, Moshe Avigdor **2:**846
- archives **3:**392
- Bar-Ilan, Meir **4:**224
- educational network **6:**428ff
- Hameiri, Moshe **7:**1232
- *Ha-Miẓpeh* **7:**1240
- ḥasidism **7:**1398
- *Ha-Ẓofeh* **7:**1534
- history chart **8:**766-767
- Jawitz, Ze'ev **9:**1304

- Judaism trend 10:396
- Kook, Rabbi, and 10:1183
- Maimon, Y. L. 11:740
- Mohilewer's "Spiritual Center" 12:218
- Nobel, Nehemiah Anton 12:1200
- Orthodoxy 12:1488
- Pick, Hermann 13:499
- Poland 16:1130
- politics 9:658ff
- Rabinowitz, Samuel Jacob 13:1478
- Reines, Isaac 14:58
- religious education 9:894
- Struck, Hermann 15:443
- Torah va-Avodah 15:1259
- Zionism 16:1052,1099ff,1142
- illus:
- - Lida conference (1903) 16:1099
- see also: HA-PO'EL HA-MIZRACHI; NATIONAL RELIGIOUS PARTY
Mizrachi, David ben Solomon 14:91
Mizrachi, Yahya ben David 14:91
Mizrachi Bank Ltd. (Isr.) 9:824
Mizrachie (period.) 16:1120
Mizrachi-Ha-Po'el ha-Mizrachi Organization of Canada 16:1110
Mizrachi ha-Ẓa'ir (mvmt.) 16:1146
Mizrachi Leben (pub.) 16:1126
Mizrachi Pioneers (mvmt.) 10:972ff
Mizrachi World Organization (mvmt.), see MIZRACHI
MIZRAḤ (east) 12:180
- paper-cuts 13:61
- tablets 9:1589
- illus:
- - paper cuts 11:271; 12:fcg. 173; 13:44-45,61,64
- see also: SHIVVITI
Mizraḥi (fam.) 10:1298
Mizrahi (fam., Yug.), see Misrai
Mizraḥi, Alfred 13:1040
Mizraḥi, Barukh ben Samuel 10:1298
MIZRAḤI, DAVID BEN SHALOM 12:182
MIZRAḤI, ELIJAH 12:182
- community leader 11:1582
- Comtino, Mordecai 5:859
- Elijah ha-Levi 6:647
- history chart 8:766-767
- Ibn Yaḥya, David 8:1207
- Istanbul 9:1088; 9:1089
- Naḥmanides on Rashi 12:781
- on Rashi 15:520
- Ottoman Empire 16:1547
- rabbinical ordination 13:1449
- responsa 11:337
- Tam ibn Yaḥya, Jacob 15:785
Mizraḥi, Ephraim 3:800
Mizraḥi, Faraj Ḥayyim 2:594
Mizraḥi, Gershon ben Elijah 12:183
Mizraḥi, Ḥanina 15:906
Mizraḥi, Israel ben Elijah 12:183
Mizraḥi, Jacob ben Judah 16:1537
Mizraḥi, Moses Baruch 4:93; 13:1041
Mizraḥi, Mullah Ḥayyim Elijah 15:906
Mizraḥi, Reuben ben Elijah 12:183
Mizraḥi, Samuel ben Jacob ben Judah 16:1537
Mizraḥi, Simon 10:1503
Mizraḥi, Simon ben Jonah 10:1298
Mizraḥi, Yiḥya 12:182; 14:91
Mizraḥi Teachers' Seminary (Er. Isr.) 11:291
Mizrah-u-Ma'arav (period.) 1:newsp. list; 6:682
Mizrayim (period.) 5:31; 6:499
- illus:
- - masthead (1904) 13:1042
MIẒRAYIM (Heb. place name) 12:184
Miẓvah (commandment), see MITZVAH
MKBY (name) 11:695
MLADA BOLESLAV (tn., Cz.) 12:184
- Holocaust 5:1199
- illus: text
Mlauer Lebn, Dos (period.), see Dos Mlaver Lebn
MLAWA (Mlwa; Mlava; tn., Pol.) 12:185
Mlinarsky, Emil 14:374
Mlinow (tn., Ukr.) 10:794
Mlodetsky, Meir 15:28
Młyniewo (concen. camp) 16:672
M. Mizrachi (publ. firm, Isr.) 13:1378
MNASEAS OF PATARA 7:895
- ass worship 3:784
Mnēmōn (k., Pers.), see ARTAXERXES II
MNEMONICS 12:187
- acrostics 2:230
- asmakhta 3:751
- avot 3:984
- Masorah Gedolah 16:1424ff
- tannaim 15:799
- illus:
- - hand movements for masoretic accents 11:1099
- - order of seder ceremony 2:47
- - yaknehaz 2:49
- see also: ABBREVIATIONS
MOAB (anc., kdm., people) 12:190
- Contents:
- - People and Country 12:190
- - History and its Relation with Israel 12:192
- - Under Assyrian and Babylonian Rule and the End of their Kingdom 12:195
- Land of
- - Arnon, boundary 3:486
- - human geography of Israel 9:596ff
- - inscriptions script 2:685
- - Mesha's conquests 8:348; 11:1397ff
- - Nabateans 12:740
- - physiography 9:177
- - prehistoric agricultural settlements 2:382
- - revelation 14:121
- - Transjordan 15:1316ff
- People of
- - Ammon 2:856ff
- - Bible history 8:576ff
- - Commandments, the 613 5:773
- - David's wars 5:1320
- - history 8:587ff
- - in the Aggadah 11:1506
- - Jephthah 9:1342
- - Jeremiah 9:1354
- - language 14:1150; 16:1398
- - Lot's deed 11:508
- - proselytisation 8:1423
- - Solomon's concubines 15:100
- illus:
- - comparative alphabets 2:683
- - David's wars against (map) 5:1322
- - Dead Sea and Plateau 9:172-173
- map: text
Moab (tn., Er. Isr.), see RABBAH
Moabites, see MOAB
Moabite Stone, see MESHA STELE
Mo'adim (prayer bk. type) 13:987
Mo'adim le-Simḥah (Heb. greeting) 7:916
Mo'adon Mekhoniyyot ve-Sayyarut be-Yisrael (journ.) 1:newsp. list
Moatti, Aaron 2:622; 2:623
Moatti, Isaac 15:1173
Mobile (city, Ala.) 2:505ff
Mobiloil Petroleum Company, see Sonol
MOCATTA (fam., Eng.) 12:197
- library 10:53; 11:192
- illus:
- - coat of arms 8:336
Mocatta, Abraham (18th cent.) 12:198
Mocatta, Abraham (18/19 cent.) 12:198
Mocatta, Sir Alan Abraham 12:198
Mocatta, David 12:198
- illus:
- - design for a railway station, England 3:342
Mocatta, Frederick David 12:198
Mocatta, Isaac Lindo 12:198
Mocatta, Jacob 13:1613
Mocatta, Moses (17th cent.) 12:197
Mocatta, Moses (18/19 cent.) 12:198; 15:1403
Mocatta, Rachel 12:198; 12:275
Mocatta Haggadah (13th cent. illum. ms., Sp.) 2:47; 5:1391; 7:fcg. 1451
Mocatta Library (Eng.) 10:53; 11:192
MOCH, JULES (sol., Fr.) 11:1561; 11:1574
MOCH, JULES SALVADOR (polit., Fr.) 12:199
MOCHA (tn., Yem.) 12:199
Mockery 13:124
Moczar, Mieczysław 3:159
Moda'ah (notification) 12:1399
MODAI, ḤAYYIM 12:200
- Adler, Nathan 2:284
Modai, Nissim Ḥayyim 12:200
MODEH ANI (prayer) 12:200
Modeh be-Mikẓat, see Partial Admission
Model (fam.) 3:32; 12:201
Model, Calman 11:1384
MODEL, MARX 12:201
Model, Mordecai 13:1108
Model, Simon 5:1009
Modell, Arthur B. 15:308
MODENA (city, Lt.) 12:201
- archives 3:387
- educational regulations 6:417ff
- Graziano, Abraham 7:865
- library 11:193
- Shabbateanism 14:1245
- illus:
- - text
- - synagogue ark 3:451
Modena, Aaron Berakhiah, see AARON BERECHIAH BEN MOSES OF MODENA
MODENA, ANGELO 11:1575
MODENA, AVTALYON (da) 12:202
Modena, Gustavo 15:1057
Modena, Isaac 12:202
MODENA, LEONE (Judah Aryeh) 12:202
- Alatrini, Angelo 2:515
- alchemy 2:548ff
- apologetics 3:196
- Archivolti, Samuel de 3:397
- Ashkenazi, Naphtali 3:730
- autobiography 4:1012; 8:560; 11:352
- chess 5:402
- fiction 6:1269
- founder of choir 5:486
- history chart 8:766-767
- Italian literature 9:1109; 16:22
- Italy 9:1145
- Kabbalah 10:550
- on gambling 5:168
- portraits of Jews 13:917
- Zohar critique 16:1214
Modena, Mordecai da 15:1165
Modena, Samuel, see MEDINA, SAMUEL BENMOSES DE
MODERN, JUDAH 12:204
Modern Review (period.) 2:170
Modern Times (weekly), see NEUZEIT, DIE
Modestus (7th cent., patr.) 9:1407
Modesty, see HUMILITY
Modi (meas.) 16:388
Modigliana (tn., It.) 15:1468
MODIGLIANI, AMEDEO 12:205
- Kisling, Moise 10:1071
- Pevsner, Anton 13:350
- stamps 15:336
- illus:
- - text
- - "Limestone Head" (sculp.) 14:1061
- - "Portrait of Leon Inderbaum" (paint.) 13:115
Modigliani, Elio 15:1351
Modigliani, Ettore 3:651
MODIGLIANI, VITTORIO EMANUELE 12:206
Modigliano, Joseph Samuel (Giuseppe) 11:828; 12:205
Modigliano, Samuel Isaac 9:1163
MODI'IN (Modi'im; vill., Er. Isr.) 12:206
- Hasmoneans 7:1456; 11:1127
- illus: text
MODON (city, Gr.) 12:207
Modon, Isaac Cohen 13:172
Modon, Samson Kohen 13:593
MODZHITZ (ḥas. dyn.) 12:207
- music 7:1425; 13:1617
- dynasties 1:ḥas. table
- scores:
- - niggun 7:1429
Modzhitz, Israel of, see Israel of Modzhitz
Moe, Finn 12:1225
MO'ED (order of Mish.) 12:208
- Ḥullin 8:1069
MO'ED KATAN (tract.) 12:208
- illus: text
Mo'ed Katan (minor fest.), see PURIMS, SPECIAL
Moeller, Nathan Nata 15:387
MOELLIN, JACOB BEN MOSES (Maharil) 12:210
- Aaron of Neustadt 2:22
- ḥerem impositions 8:354
- history chart 8:766-767
- matchmaker 14:1254
- memorbuch reading 11:1299
- Runkel, Solomon 14:429
- seals 14:1079
- tombstones 15:1222
- Worms 16:646
- illus:
- - portrait 14:1476
Moerne, Arvid 14:931
Mo'eẓet Gedolei ha-Torah (Orth. orgn.) 2:422
- Bloch, Elijah Meyer 4:1097
Mo'eẓet ha-Am (council, Isr.) 9:663ff
MO'EẒET HA-PO'ALOT (Council of Women Workers) 12:211
- Chizhik, Ḥannah 5:480
- woman 16:628
- illus: text
Mo'eẓet ha-Rabbanim ha-Mitkaddemim (council of Ref. rabbis) 9:906
Mo'eẓet Po'alim, see Labor councils in Israel
Moffatt, J. 4:870
MOGADOR (port, Mor.) 12:212
- Abenatar, Abraham 3:813
- Abendanan, Saul 2:68
- Agadir Jews 2:340
- A.J.A. 2:977
- Jewish quarter 10:87
- illus:
- - text
- - Auguste Baumier School 12:332
Mogens, Victor 14:934

Moghrabi Quarter (Jer.) **16:**467,468
Mogi (city, Braz.) **4:**1327
MOGILEV (city, Belor.) **12:**214
- *illus:* text
MOGILEV-PODOLSKI (tn., Ukr.) **12:**216
- Podolia **13:**668,669
- Transnistria **15:**1330ff
Mograbi (dialect), *see* JUDEO-ARABIC
MOGULESKO, SIGMUND (Zelig) **15:**1088
- Sandler, Jacob **14:**830
MOHÁCSI, JENŐ **12:**217
Mohammad (Mohammed), *see* MUHAMMAD
Mohar (bride price), *see* DOWRY
Mohar, Jehiel, *see* Mar, Jehiel
Mohar betulot, see DOWRY
Mohariel (r., Egy.) **11:**572
Moḥeh (masor.) **16:**1471
Mohel (circumciser) **5:**570
Mohelever, Aryeh **5:**406
Mohelnice (tn., Morav.) **12:**296
Mohilewer, Joseph **12:**219
- *illus:*
- - F.Z.C. **16:**1165
MOHILEWER, SAMUEL **12:**217
- history chart **8:**766-767
- Mizrachi **12:**175
- *illus:*
- - Kattowitz Conference **10:**820
- - Odessa Committee convention **12:**1329
MOHR, ABRAHAM MENAHEM MENDEL **12:**219
MOHR, MEIR **12:**220
- *illus:*
- - Persky, Daniel, and **13:**321
Mohr, Sigismund **13:**1422
MOINESTI (tn., Rum.) **12:**220
MOÏSE, ABRAHAM **12:**220
Moise, Columbus **12:**1038
MOÏSE, PENINA **12:**221
MOISE, THEODORE SYDNEY **12:**221
- *illus:* text
MOISEIWITSCH, BENNO **12:**222
Moiseiwitsch, Tanya **12:**222
Moises, Irwin Stern **12:**1039
Moisésville (tn., Arg.) **3:**421; **10:**46
- *illus:*
- - deed of sale of the land **3:**427
- - milk depot **3:**428
- - Mutua Agricola cooperative **5:**945
Moisésville Teachers' Seminary (Arg.) **6:**456
Moisling (vill., Ger.) **11:**556
Moissac (tn., Fr.) **2:**750
MOISSAN, HENRI **12:**222
- *illus:*
- - Swedish stamp **12:**1204
MOISSIS, ASHER **12:**223
Mojajon, Elijah **14:**1245
MOJECKI, PRZECLAW **12:**223
MOK, MAURITS **12:**224
MOKADY, MOSHE **12:**224
- *illus:*
- - "Still Life" (paint.) Pl. 6 3—ART
Mokelumne Hill (vill., Calif.) **5:**56
Mokhesim (tax farmers) **15:**873
Mokhi'aḥ (prch., Hung.), *see* MORDECAI (Mokhiaḥ) BEN ḤAYYIM OF EISENSTADT
Mokhi'aḥ (ḥas. exegete), *see* ARYEH JUDAH LEIB OF POLONNOYE
Mokhi'aḥ, Isaiah **13:**1241
Molad (journ.) **1:**newsp. list
Molad (new moon) **5:**43
- *see also:* NEW MOON
MOLADAH (city, Er. Isr.) **12:**225
Moladti (journ.) **1:**newsp. list
Molcho (fam.) **14:**707
MOLCHO, DAVID EFFENDI ISAAC PASHA **11:**1567; **11:**1575
MOLCHO, SOLOMON **12:**225
- Ancona **2:**941
- autobiography **4:**1012
- Charles V **5:**356
- Clement VII **5:**601
- flag **6:**1336
- Glanz-Leyeles **7:**600
- history chart **8:**766-767
- Kabbalah **5:**199; **10:**544; **10:**553
- messianism **9:**285; **11:**1426
- Reuveni, David **14:**115
- seal **14:**1080
- Taitaẓak, Joseph **15:**712
- Venice **16:**98
- *illus:*
- - autograph **3:**916
Molco (fam.) **2:**614
Moldau (mus. comp., Smetana) **16:**835
Moldautein (tn., Bohem.), *see* Tyn nad Vltavou
Moldavia, *see* RUMANIA
MOLE (rodent) **12:**227
Molech (deity), *see* MOLOCH
MOLEDET (mosh., Isr.) **12:**227
- statistics **1:**place list
- *illus:*
- - plan **9:**560
Moledet (annual) **5:**450
Molho, M. **8:**563
Molina (city, Sp.) **15:**478
Molinaea, Maria **8:**46
Molinari, Bernardino **7:**1472
Moline (city, Ill.) **8:**1255
Molitor, C. **8:**46
MOLITOR, FRANZ JOSEPH **12:**227
- Christian Kabbalah **10:**646
Molkho, Isaac **2:**310
Molkhov, Yakov **4:**1494
Mollā Hizqiyā **10:**432
Moller, Daniel **8:**46
MOLLER, ERICH **12:**228
MOLLER, HANS **12:**228
Moller, Helena Sybilla Wagenseil **8:**46
Mollet, Guy **3:**982; **9:**389
Mollusks (zool.) **6:**38
MOLNAR, AKOS **8:**1806
Molnár, E. **5:**457
MOLNÁR, FERENC **12:**229
- Hungarian literature **8:**1082
Molnar, János **8:**46
MOLOCH, CULT OF **12:**230
- Ahaz **2:**455
- Commandments, the 613 **5:**771
- dysphemism **6:**960
- idolatry **8:**1227
- *Solomon, Testament of* **15:**118
- *illus:*
- - human sacrifice **8:**1237
Molodaya Iudeya (mvmt., Rus.) **11:**1059
Molodaya Iudeya (journ.) **11:**1058
MOLODECHNO (tn., Belor.) **12:**233
MOLODOWSKY, KADIA **12:**233
- *illus:*
- - *Pitḥu et ha-Sha'ar* **5:**440
Molokan Sabbath Observers (sect, Rus.) **10:**400; **10:**401
Molotov, Vyacheslav **9:**388; **16:**289
Molsheim (tn., Fr.) **2:**752
Molza-Porrino, Tarquinia **8:**46
MOMBERT, ALFRED **12:**234
MOMENT, DER (newsp.) **12:**235
- Zeitlin, Hillel **10:**936
- Zionism **16:**1132; **16:**1152
- *illus:* text
MOMIGLIANO, ARNALDO DANTE **12:**235
MOMIGLIANO, ATTILIO **12:**236
- Italian literature **9:**1114
MOMIGLIANO, FELICE **8:**548
MOMMSEN, THEODOR **12:**236
- Dessau, Hermann **5:**1563
- Hirschfeld, Heinrich **8:**526
- Taeubler **15:**699
Monarchy, *see* KING, KINGSHIP
Monasch, B.L. **13:**1373
Monasch of Krotoszyn **13:**930
- *illus:*
- - *Talmud Yerushalmi* **10:**1279
MONASH, SIR JOHN **12:**237
- Australian army **11:**1554
- Melbourne **11:**1281; **11:**1284
- Zionist Federation **16:**1105
- *illus:*
- - autograph **3:**916
- - bust **3:**882
- - Monash University, Melbourne **3:**883
Monastero (tn., It.) **2:**216
Monastery of the Cross (Jer.) **8:**935; **9:**1417,1455
Monastery of Notre-Dame de France (Jer.), *see* Notre-Dame de France
Monastery of Saint Catherine (Sinai), *see* St. Catherine's Monastery
Monastery of the Temptation (Er. Isr.) **9:**1371
- *illus:*
- - Greek Orthodox monk **9:**913
Monasterzyska (city, Ukr.), *see* MONASTYRISKA
MONASTIR (tn., Yug.) **12:**238
- Yugoslavia **16:**872ff
- Zionism **16:**1149
- *illus:* text
Monastiriota Synagogue (Salonika) **14:**703
Monastritsh Ẓaddik (ḥas. r.) **7:**1399
MONASTYRISKA (city, Ukr.) **12:**239
Monatsblaetter des Kulturbundes deutscher Juden (journ.) **10:**463
Monatsblaetter zur Belehrung ueber das Judentum (period.) **13:**1032
MONATSSCHRIFT FUER GESCHICHTE UND WISSENSCHAFT DES JUDENTUMS (period.) **12:**240
- Frankl, Pinkus **7:**102
- learned societies **15:**54
MONCALVO (tn., It.) **12:**240
- *see also:* APAM
Moncontour (vill., Fr.) **13:**704
MONCORVO (tn., Port.) **12:**241
Moncton (city, Can.) **11:**997
MOND (fam.) **12:**241
Mond, Alfred Moritz **4:**1298; **12:**241
MOND, BERNHARD STANISLAW **12:**242
Mond, Eva Violet, *see* Isaacs, Eva Violet
Mond, Henry **12:**242
Mond, Julian Edward Alfred **12:**242
Mond, Ludwig **12:**241
- art collection **3:**648
Mond, Sir Robert Ludwig **12:**241
MONDA, VIRGILIU **14:**427
MONDAY AND THURSDAY **12:**243
- fastdays **6:**1193,1195
- *seliḥot* **14:**1134
- *illus:*
- - *Mi she-Berakh* **12:**87
MONDOLFO, RODOLFO **12:**243
Mond-Turner Agreement (lab.) **12:**242
MONDZAIN, SIMON **3:**606
Money
- acquisition **2:**219
- acquisition of *ḥekdesh* **8:**280
- courts of three **14:**840
- *kapparot* **10:**757
- marriage **11:**1045
- *see also:* BANKING AND BANKERS; COINS AND CURRENCY; MINTMASTER AND MONEYERS; MONEY CHANGERS; MONEYLENDING; USURY
MONEY CHANGERS **12:**243
- Temple **15:**965
- *see also:* BANKING AND BANKERS
Moneyers, *see* MINTMASTERS AND MONEYERS
MONEYLENDING **12:**244
- *Contents:*
- - Religious Context **12:**244
- - - Biblical Period **12:**244
- - - Talmudic Period **12:**246
- - - Geonic Period **12:**247
- - - Early Rabbinic Period **12:**248
- - - Late Rabbinic Period **12:**250
- - - From Otherhood to Brotherhood **12:**252
- - historical context **12:**253
- General
- - Calvin, John **5:**66
- - caricatures **5:**171
- - crafts **5:**1050ff
- - economic doctrines **16:**1294
- - execution (civil) **6:**1007
- - *gemilut ḥasadim* **7:**376
- - legal fictions **16:**1282
- - secondhand goods **14:**1085ff
- History **3:**812
- - autonomy, medieval **3:**921
- - Crusades **5:**1144
- - France **7:**18,24
- - Germany **7:**461ff
- - goldsmithery replaced **7:**743
- - Islamic lands **16:**1282
- - Jewish economic pattern **8:**674ff
- - *ma'arufya* **11:**640
- - Majorca **11:**796
- - monti di pietà **12:**279
- - Nuremberg **12:**1278
- - Paris **13:**106
- - Poland **13:**717
- - Poznan **13:**949
- - Regensburg **14:**35
- - Roman Jews **14:**249
- - Spain **15:**232
- - Toledo **15:**1203
- - Tuscany **15:**1467
- Regulations
- - apostate **10:**24
- - Catholic Church **5:**538
- - *ḥerem ha-yishuv* **8:**358
- - Louis IX **11:**515
- - Montpellier **12:**282
- - Philip II **13:**392
- *illus:*
- - Aaron of Lincoln, Latin receipt **2:**21
- - Aaron of York, Hebrew statement **2:**23
- - anti-Semitic caricatures **3:**139-146
- - edict re Jewish deceit in monetary matters (Berlin, 1726) **7:**479
- - Hartford, Conn., town records (1660) **5:**898
- - impounding of pledge, written complaint (7th cent. B.C.E.) **3:**317
- - Jewish moneylenders **4:**171; **7:**462; **8:**674
- - Jewish pawnbroker **4:**173
- *see also:* BANKING AND BANKERS; MONEY CHANGERS; STOCK EXCHANGES; USURY
Monforte (tn., Sp.) **12:**1452
MONGOLIA (region, As.) **12:**256
Mongols **9:**271; **9:**1423; **15:**641
Mongré, Paul, *see* HAUSDORFF, FELIX
MONIS, JUDAH **12:**256
- Hebrew literature **8:**209

- *illus:* text
Monism (philos. conc.) **6:**182
MONITOR (reptile) **12:**258
- dietary laws **6:**36
- *illus:* text
Monk, Abraham **3:**421
Monk, Henry Wentworth **16:**1154
Monnickendam, Martin **12:**984
MONOBAZ I (k., Adiabene) **12:**258
- Adiabene **2:**267
- Helena **8:**288
- Temple **15:**980
MONOBAZ II (k., Adiabene) **12:**258
- conversion of **2:**924; **10:**1296
- munificence and piety **2:**267,268
MONOGAMY **12:**258
- Ashkenaz **3:**721; **8:**667
- biblical ideal **11:**844
- family **6:**1169
- Gershom ben Judah **7:**512
- *takkanah* **5:**1251
- *see also:* BIGAMY AND POLYGAMY
Monolatry (henotheism) **12:**260
Monophysite monks **9:**1407
Monoszon, Elye I. **6:**465
MONOTHEISM **12:**260
- Aḥad Ha-Am **2:**445,446
- Akhenaton **2:**487
- angelology **2:**961
- demons, demonology **5:**1521
- dualism **6:**243ff
- idolatry **8:**1234
- Islam **9:**93
- Jewish Hellenistic literature **8:**302
- Jewish philosophy **13:**422
- Judaism **10:**387
- Julian the Apostate **10:**468
- Kabbalah **10:**526
- Kaufmann's views **16:**1350
- Maimonides on Islam **11:**766
- Neoplatonism **12:**958ff
- Pentateuch **13:**234
- prophecy **13:**1164
- theology **15:**1104
- *see also:* GOD
Monroe (city, La.) **11:**517
Monroe, James **15:**1648
Monroe, Marilyn **11:**1579; **12:**451,465
- *illus:*
- - Miller, Arthur, and **11:**1579
Monroe Doctrine **8:**766-767
Monrovia (city, Liberia) **9:**440; **9:**991
Mons (tn., Belg.) **4:**417ff
Monsano, Judah **12:**336
Monsanto (fam.) **11:**518
- slave trade **14:**1663
Monsanto, Isaac Rodriguez **12:**1041
Mons Casius (mt., Syr.), *see* BAAL-ZEPHON
Mons Gaudii (loc., Isr.), *see* Nabi Samwīl
Monsi, Benjamin delli **13:**690
MONSKY, HENRY **12:**263
- *illus:*
- - Eisenhower, Dwight D., and **6:**544
Monsky, Leroy **15:**308
Monson, (city, Sp.), *see* MONZÓN
Mons Quarantana (mt., Er. Isr.) **6:**153; **9:**1371
- *illus:*
- - Monastery of the Temptation **9:**913
Montabaur (tn., Ger.) **12:**841
Montagnana, Joseph de, *see* Joseph de Montagna
Montagnana, Petrus **8:**46
MONTAGU (fam.) **12:**264
Montagu, Edwin Samuel **12:**265
- Balfour Declaration **4:**134
- Zionist opposition **16:**1068; **16:**1080
Montagu, Ewen **6:**766; **12:**264
Montagu, Gladys **12:**264
Montagu, Ivor **15:**314
Montagu, Lilian Helen **12:**265
Montagu, Louis Samuel **12:**264
MONTAGU, MONTAGUE FRANCIS ASHLEY **12:**266
- anthropology **3:**40
Montagu, Samuel (First Baron Swaythling) **12:**264
- chronological chart **8:**766-767
Montaigne, Michel Eyquem de **7:**146; **13:**416
Montakhab, Enayatollah **15:**906
Montalban, Alvaro de **15:**1206
Montalcino, Cornelio da **14:**248
Montaldi, J. **8:**46
Montale, Eugenio **9:**1107
Montalto, Elijah **3:**197
- Marrano Diaspora **11:**1024
- medicine **11:**1194
- Morteira, Saul Levi **12:**355
Montalto, Moses **11:**542
Montalto, Philotheus Eliajus, *see* Montalto, Elijah
Montalván, Juan Pérez de **15:**254
MONTANA (state, U.S.) **12:**266
- *pop. tables:* text
Montano, Bentio Arias, *see* ARIAS MONTANO, BENITO
Montaureanu, Virgil **13:**1369
MONTCLUS (tn., Sp.) **12:**267
Monte, Andrea del, *see* Sarfati, Joseph (apos.)
Monte di pietà (bnk. type), *see* MONTI DI PIETÀ
Montefiore (clny., Arg.) **3:**430
Montefiore, Abraham **12:**271; **12:**275
MONTEFIORE, CLAUDE JOSEPH GOLDSMID **12:**268
- Anglo-Jewish Association **2:**978
- Balfour Declaration **2:**978
- Loewe, Herbert **11:**447
- Schechter, Solomon **14:**948
- Zionism **16:**1117
Montefiore, Eliezer Levi **2:**259
Montefiore, Henrietta, *see* Rothschild, Henrietta
Montefiore, Hugh **3:**210; **12:**276
Montefiore, Jacob **12:**270; **12:**275; **13:**808
- *illus:*
- - portrait **3:**879
Montefiore, Joseph **12:**275
MONTEFIORE, JOSEPH BARROW **12:**269
- Adelaide community **2:**259
- New Zealand **12:**1128
- Sydney **15:**564
Montefiore, Joseph Elias **12:**275
Montefiore, Joseph Mayer **12:**275
MONTEFIORE, JOSHUA **12:**270
- family **12:**275
- Vermont **16:**112
Montefiore, Judah Leone **8:**339
MONTEFIORE, JUDITH **12:**270
- Cohen family **5:**658
- travels **15:**1354
- *illus:*
- - Montefiore Foundation seal **9:**1451
Montefiore, Leonard **10:**44
MONTEFIORE, SIR MOSES **12:**270
- Antibi, Jacob **3:**58
- Bleichroeder **4:**1081
- Board of Deputies **4:**1151
- chronological chart **8:**766-767
- coat of arms **8:**339
- Cohen, Levi-Abraham **5:**680
- Crémieux, Isaac **5:**1075
- Damascus Affair **5:**1251
- Dunant **6:**270
- Ereẓ Israel **9:**298,299ff
- Friedland, Natan **7:**184
- Gawler, George **7:**339
- *Ḥavaẓẓelet* **7:**1479
- Hebron **8:**234; **16:**1576
- Isaac of Warka **16:**304
- Jaffa **9:**571
- Jerusalem **9:**1455*ff*
- Kalischer's request **16:**1035
- Loewe, Louis **11:**448
- Montefiore, Joseph Barrow **12:**269
- Montefiore, Judith **12:**270
- Mortara Case **12:**354
- Persian Jews **13:**316
- Rachel's tomb **13:**1490
- title **15:**1166
- travels **13:**514; **15:**1354
- Uvarov, Sergey **16:**38
- Western Wall **16:**471
- *geneal. table:* text
- *illus:*
- - text
- - autograph **3:**917
- - Bikkur Ḥolim hospital **9:**983
- - coat of arms **8:**337
- - Damascus Affair, commemorative medal **5:**1250
- - Hebron community letter **4:**147
- - *Kiddush* cup **10:**976
- - letter to Abraham Corcos **5:**962
- - letter to Kadimah ass'n **10:**666
- - *Megillat Setarim* **5:**1462
- - Mishkenot Sha'ananim apartments **9:**1451
- - Montefiore Foundation seal **9:**1451
- - portrait **8:**718
- - Sultan of Morocco, reception **12:**329
- - Yemin Moshe **9:**1451
Montefiore, Moses Vita **12:**275
Montefiore, Nathaniel **12:**275
Montefiore, Rachel, *see* Mocatta, Rachel
Montefiore, Sarah **12:**275; **14:**1084
MONTEFIORE, SEBAG-MONTEFIORE (fam.) **12:**275
- military service **11:**1553
Montefiore Clinic for Chronic Invalids (N.Y.) **5:**349
Montefiore College (Eng.), *see* Judith Lady Montefiore College
Montefiore Hospital (N.Y.C.) **12:**1116
Montefiore Society (N.Y.) **12:**1072
Montefiore's windmill (Jer.) **9:**1456
- *illus:*
- - Montefiore Foundation seal **9:**1451
Montego Bay (city, Jam.) **9:**1273
Monteiro, Manoel **15:**251
MONTÉLIMAR (tn., Fr.) **12:**276
Montemayor, Jorge de **15:**253
Montenegro (rep., Yug.) **16:**874
Montepulciano (tn., It.) **15:**1467ff
MONTEREAU (tn., Fr.) **12:**276
Montesa, Jaime de **14:**865
Monte San Savino (tn., It.) **15:**1468ff
Montes Pietatis, *see* MONTI DI PIETÀ
MONTESQUIEU, CHARLES LOUIS DE SECONDAT, BARON DE LA BRÈDE ET DE **12:**276
- on Jews **7:**142
Montessori, Maria **12:**896
MONTEUX, PIERRE **12:**277
- *illus:* text
Monteux, Saul ben Joseph **5:**208
MONTEVIDEO (city, Urug.) **12:**278
- education **6:**457ff
- Uruguay **16:**11*ff*
- *illus:*
- - Sholem Aleichem School **16:**12
- - Zionist Organization central committee **16:**1126
MONTEZINOS, ANTONIO DE **12:**278
- Ten Lost Tribes **15:**1006
- travels **15:**1350
MONTEZINOS, DAVID **12:**279
- book collection **4:**975
Montezinos, Raphael **12:**279
Montfalcon (-ius), B. de **8:**46
Montferrat (dist., It.) **13:**501
Montfort (Crus. cas., Isr.)
- archaeology **3:**329
- Israel **9:**269
- Mi'ilya **11:**1529
- *illus:*
- - ruins **5:**1136; **9:**172-173
Montfort, Marquis de, *see* Solis, Francisco da Silva
Montfort, Simon de, *see* Simon de Montfort
Montgisard (Crus. fort.) **9:**268
Montgomery (city, Ala.) **2:**505; **2:**506
- *illus:*
- - civil rights march (1965) **12:**931
- - Lehman, Durr and Co. offices **10:**1577
Montgomery (co., Md.) **11:**1077; **16:**358
Montgomery (co., Pa.) **13:**368
Month, *see* CALENDAR; YEAR
Monthope (loc., Isr.) **16:**1154
Monticelli d'Ongina (tn., It.) **13:**493
Monticello (tn., N.Y.) **12:**1127
MONTI DI PIETÀ (bnk. type) **12:**279
- Bernardino da Feltre **4:**672
- Franciscans **7:**47
- interest on loans **12:**251,252
- Italian economic life **16:**1290
- Piacenza Jews **13:**492
MONTIEL (tn., Sp.) **12:**280
Montisson (city, Sp.), *see* MONZÓN
Montjoie (loc., Isr.), *see* Nabi Samwīl
Montmélian (cmty., Fr.) **14:**921
Montmorillon (tn., Fr.) **13:**704
MONTOR, HENRY **12:**281
- public relations **13:**1363
MONTORO, ANTÓN DE **12:**281
- Cota de Maguaque **5:**991
- Spanish literature **15:**253
Montpelier (city, Vt.) **16:**112
MONTPELLIER (city, Fr.) **12:**282
- dyeing center **6:**328
- university **11:**1190; **15:**1675
MONTREAL (city, Can.) **12:**283
- Abramowitz, Herman **2:**169
- Becker, Lavy Mordecai **4:**368
- Canada **5:**103ff
- de Sola family **5:**1562
- education **6:**453
- Richter's tales **14:**159
- *illus:*
- - Israel pavilion at Expo 1967 **14:**1316
- - Zionist Organization of Canada, convention delegates (1950) **16:**1110
Montreal (loc., Transj.), *see* Shawbak
Montreux (resort, Switz.) **10:**1472
Montro, Hezekiah **8:**1323
Montrose, Dave **15:**306
Monzalavi, Eleazar **4:**528
MONZÓN (city, Sp.) **12:**288
MONZON, ABRAHAM (16/17 cent.) **12:**289
MONZON, ABRAHAM (18th cent.) **12:**289
Moody, Ron **12:**461
MOON **12:**290
- *Sefirot* **10:**575
- sun **15:**517
- worship **16:**1505
- year **16:**724

– *illus:*
– – text
– – Abraham bar Hiyya's illustration of lunar eclipse **3:**797
– *see also:* ASTRONOMY; CALENDAR; DAY AND NIGHT; MOON, BLESSING OF THE; NEW MOON; NEW MOON, ANNOUNCEMENT OF
MOON, BLESSING OF THE (prayer) **12:**291
– *illus:*
– – text
– – benediction, *Seder Berakhot* (1687) **4:**486
Moonen, Arnold **8:**46
Moor, I. D. **11:**520
Moore, Cecil **15:**625
Moore, George (nov.) **6:**782
MOORE, GEORGE FOOT (theol.) **12:**293
Moore, Thomas Sturge **6:**775; **10:**459
Moor Gate (Jer.), *see* Dung Gate
Moos, L. **15:**1525
Moose Jaw (city, Can.) **14:**892
Moosomin (tn., Can.) **2:**412; **14:**891
MOPP (art.) **12:**294
– *illus:*
– – text
– – Altenberg, Peter (drg.) **2:**772
Mopsim (polit. party, Isr.), *see* Mifleget Po'alim Sozialistim
Morag, Shelomo **16:**1337,1440
Morais, H. S. **4:**1014
MORAIS, SABATO **12:**294
– Conservative Judaism **5:**902ff
– J.T.S. **10:**96
– paradigm **13:**1456
Morales, C. **10:**1376
Morales, Diego de **10:**1448
Moralia (wk.) **4:**1508
Morals, *see* ETHICS
Moram (Seph. name for M. Isserles) **14:**1170
Morasha (qtr., Jer.), *see* Musrara
Moravchik, Moses **6:**413ff
MORAVIA (Morava; reg., Cz.) **12:**295
– Aguilar, Diego d' **2:**427
– Ashkenaz **3:**721
– banking **4:**168
– council **8:**1307
– Familiants Laws **6:**1162
– Frankists **7:**55
– gold-and silversmithery **7:**742
– guilds **7:**972ff
– Haskalah **7:**1441
– Holocaust **5:**1198
– illuminated manuscripts **8:**1287
– peddling **13:**205
– Politische Gemeinde **13:**832
– Shabbateanism **14:**1248
– *takkanot* **15:**736
– textiles **15:**1040ff
– tobacco industry **15:**1177
– *illus:*
– – text
– – Jemnice, street in old Jewish quarter **9:**1340
– – Jevicko, Jewish quarter **10:**21
– – Jewish badge decreed by the Nazis **4:**72
– – Pinkas Synagogue memorial wall, Prague **13:**976
– *pop. tables:* text
MORAVIA, ALBERTO **12:**305
– Italian literature **9:**1113
Moravska Ostrava (tn., Morav.), *see* OSTRAVA
MORAVSKE BUDEJOVICE (tn., Morav.) **12:**306
Moravsky, Michael **13:**1095
MORAVSKY KRUMLOV (tn., Cz.) **12:**307
MORAWITZ, KARL RITTER VON **12:**307
Morawitz, Richard **15:**1041
Morbidity **14:**1499ff; **15:**489ff
Morchenstern (tn., Bohem.), *see* Smrzovka
Morcinek, Gustaw **13:**801
MORDECAI (Bib. figs.) **12:**307
– adoption **2:**300
– alleged tomb **7:**1220
– Babylonian exile **6:**1040
– Esther **6:**906
– feast of Purim **13:**1390
– great synagogue **15:**629
– Haman **7:**1222
– Malachi **11:**816
– Scroll of Esther **14:**1048ff
– Shimei **14:**1403
– *Targum Sheni* **15:**812
– *illus:*
– – Dura-Europos painting **8:**649
– – led by Haman **6:**283; **7:**1223; **13:**353
– – Purim rattle **13:**139
– – triumph **12:**994
Mordecai (savora) **14:**920
Mordecai (alch.) **2:**546; **2:**548
Mordecai (fam., Jam.) **9:**1274
Mordecai (wk.), *see Mordekhai*
Mordecai, Abram **2:**505
MORDECAI, ALFRED (19th cent.) **12:**310
– Washington D.C. **16:**356
– *illus:* text
Mordecai, Alfred (19/20 cent.) **12:**310
Mordecai, B. **14:**1664
Mordecai, George Washington **12:**1218
MORDECAI, JACOB **12:**310
– *illus:* text
Mordecai, Moses (Belor.) **12:**52
Mordecai, Moses (Eng.) **4:**1219
Mordecai, Moses (U.S.) **16:**162
Mordecai bar Jacob of Cieplice **5:**1029
Mordecai ben Azriel **14:**1302
Mordecai ben Berechiah Jare **13:**589
Mordecai ben David **10:**348
MORDECAI (Mokhiaḥ) BEN ḤAYYIM OF EISENSTADT **12:**311
– Shabbateanism **14:**1246ff
Mordecai ben Hillel (Zion.) **15:**1354
– *illus:*
– – Odessa Committee **12:**1329
MORDECAI BEN HILLEL HA-KOHEN **12:**311
– Banet, Mordecai **4:**159
– codification of law **5:**643; **11:**334
– *haggahot* **7:**1108
– linguistics **16:**1387
– *meḥiẓah* custom **11:**1235
– Wuerzburg **16:**675
– *illus:*
– – text
Mordecai ben Isaac (It.), *see* Angelo di Gaio
Mordecai (Marcus) ben Isaac (Pol.) **12:**748
Mordecai ben Jacob (Fr.) **5:**208
Mordecai ben Jacob (Pol.) **5:**1027
Mordecai ben Jacob (Prague) **8:**1003
Mordecai ben Joseph (Worms) **13:**589
Mordecai ben Joseph of Avignon **3:**967; **5:**505
MORDECAI BEN JUDAH HA-LEVI **12:**314
Mordecai ben Leibush of Zolkiew **14:**995
Mordecai ben Manlin Dessau, *see* MAGNUS, MARCUS
Mordecai ben Moses of Hamburg, *see* MOSES, MARCUS
MORDECAI BEN NAPHTALI HIRSCH OF KREMSIER **12:**314
Mordecai ben Nathan, *see* Luzzatto, Marco
MORDECAI BEN NISAN **12:**314
– Luzki, Simḥah **11:**595
Mordecai ben Noah of Lachowicze, *see* LACHOWICZE, MORDECAI BEN NOAH OF
Mordecai ben Yaish **5:**627
Mordecai Bilshan (bib. fig.), *see* Bilshan
Mordecai da Modena, *see* Modena, Mordecai da
Mordecai Dov of Hornistopol **15:**1472
Mordecai ha-Levi Model of Schwabach **8:**1006
Mordecai Joseph Leiner of Izbica **9:**1159
– Eger, Judah Leib **6:**471
– Menahem Mendel of Kotsk **10:**1223
Mordecai of Avignon, *see* Mordecai ben Joseph of Avignon
Mordecai of Chernobyl **14:**526 **15:**1471
Mordecai of Cieplice, *see* Mordecai bar Jacob of Cieplice
Mordecai of Duesseldorf, *see* HALBERSTADT, MORDECAI
Mordecai of Hamburg, *see* MOSES, MARCUS
Mordecai of Hornistopol, *see* Mordecai Dov of Hornistopol
Mordecai of Izbica, *see* Mordecai Joseph Leiner of Izbica
Mordecai of Kremenets **9:**1315
Mordecai of Kremsier, *see* MORDECAI BEN NAPHTALI HIRSCH OF KREMSIER
Mordecai of Lachowicze, *see* LACHOWICZE, MORDECAI BEN NOAH OF
MORDECAI OF NESKHIZ **12:**315
Mordecai of Orange **12:**1447
Mordecai of Schwabach, *see* Mordecai ha-Levi Model of Schwabach
Mordecai of Trisk **15:**1472
Mordecai of Troki **10:**783
Mordecai of Tykocin **15:**1476
Mordecai of Zolkiew, *see* Mordecai ben Leibush of Zolkiew
Mordecai Sheraga of Husyatin, *see* Friedmann, Mordecai Shraga
Mordecai Ẓevi (mer., Turk.) **14:**1222
Mordekhai (bk.) **7:**1108; **11:**334; **12:**311
MORDELL, LOUIS JOEL **12:**315
MORDELL, PHINEḤAS **12:**315
Mordkin, Abrami **13:**117
Mordkowski, Shmuel **11:**618
MORDOVTSEV, DANIIL LUKICH **12:**316
MORDVINOV, NICOLAI SEMIONOVICH **12:**316
– Velizh **16:**88
More, Alexander **8:**46
Moré, Eugène **8:**46
More, Hannah **6:**774
More, Henry **8:**46 **6:**776; **10:**1117
More, Mullah Elijah Ḥayyim **10:**437; **15:**906
Moreau, J. B. **3:**815
Mored (rebellious husband) **8:**1122
Moredet (rebellious wife) **8:**1121ff
MOREEL, BEN **11:**1568; **11:**1575
MOREH, SHMUEL **9:**1041; **12:**1466
Moreh Horaah (tit.) **13:**1450
Moreh Nevukhei ha-Zeman (bk.) **8:**183; **10:**1270ff; **16:**574
Moreh Nevukhim (bk.), *see* MAIMONIDES
Moreh Nevukhim, Copenhagen (ms.) **8:**1264
Moreh Ẓedek (tit.) **13:**1450; **15:**1164
Moreh Ẓedek (rel. ldr., Qumran), *see* TEACHER OF RIGHTEOUSNESS
More Judaico, Oath, *see* OATH MORE JUDAICO
Morell, Thomas **9:**1344
Moreno, Jacob L. **12:**316
Morenu (tit.) **14:**1145; **15:**1164; **16:**768
Morenzi, Isaiah **4:**1485
Moresco (fam.) **5:**1537
Moresco, Moses **2:**900
MORESHET (inst., Isr.) **12:**317
– Ha-Kibbutz ha-Arẓi **10:**970
Moreshet (journ.) **7:**1321
MORESHETH-GATH (tn., Er. Isr.) **12:**317
– identification **7:**335
– Micah **11:**1482
Moretti, Marino **9:**1107
MOREWSKI, ABRAHAM **15:**1072, 1088
– Kacyzne, Alter **10:**658
– motion pictures **12:**454; **12:**455
– Shakespeare **14:**1265
Morgan, Robert **8:**46
Morgan, Thomas **5:**1464
Morgan, William **8:**46 **4:**888
Morgan City (La.) **11:**517
Morgan Picture Bible (13th cent. illum. ms., Fr.) **2:**860; **3:**30 **7:**567; **9:**1342; **10:**184; **11:**1493; **12:**736,818; **14:**781
Morgantown (city, W. Va.) **16:**475
Morgenfray (period.) **16:**348
Morgen Journal, *see* JEWISH MORNING JOURNAL
Morgenstern, Clara **6:**464
Morgenstern, David **7:**215
Morgenstern, Ḥayyim Israel **13:**1381
Morgenstern, Isaac Zelig **15:**90
Morgenstern, Joseph **10:**1126
MORGENSTERN, JULIAN **12:**317
MORGENSTERN, LINA **12:**319
– Arendt, Otto **3:**406
Morgenstern, Mendel **16:**373
Morgenstern, Michael **16:**1347
Morgenstern, Mihály **11:**950
MORGENSTERN, OSKAR **12:**319
Morgenstern, Theodor **12:**319
Morgenstunden (wk.) **11:**1330
Morgensztern, David Shelomo **16:**680
Morgensztern, Hershele **11:**561
Morgensztern, Jacob Aryeh **16:**680
Morgensztern, Moses Baruch **16:**598
MORGENTHAU (fam.) **12:**320
MORGENTHAU, HANS JOACHIM **12:**322
Morgenthau, Henry Sr. **12:**320; **12:**322
Morgenthau, Henry Jr. **12:**321
– Jewish Agricultural Society **10:**35
– U.S. war policy **15:**1634
Morgenthau, Robert Morris **12:**322
MORGENTHAU COMMISSION **12:**322
Morgentoi, Leib **5:**449
Morgentsaytung (newsp., Arg.) **3:**423
Morgentsaytung (newsp., Urug.) **16:**15
Morgen-Zhurnal, *see* JEWISH MORNING JOURNAL
MORGULIS, MANASSEH (Mikhail) **12:**323
MORHANGE (tn., Fr.) **12:**324
Morhange, Charles Henri-Valentin, *see* ALKAN, CHARLES HENRI-VALENTIN
MORHANGE, PIERRE **7:**150
Mōrī (tit.) **13:**1452
MORIAH (bib. loc.) **12:**324
– *Akedah* **2:**481

- holiness **9:**1559
- Temple Mount **15:**943,988
- topography **9:**1516
MORIAH (pub. house) **12:**325
- children's literature **5:**434
- Rawnitzky, Hana **13:**1588
Moriah (period.) **11:**721
Moriah (school network) **6:**428
Moriah (orgn.) **5:**1587
Moriah (syn., Warsaw) **16:**337
Morijah (soc., Ger.) **11:**44
Morika (dye plant), *see Kozah*
Morin, Jean **8:**46
Morini, Stephanus **8:**46
Moriscos (Arab-speaking Js.) **6:**540
Moritz, Louis **11:**1463
Moritz, Ricardo **10:**459
Moriyyah (newsp.) **1:**newsp. list; **9:**1015; **12:**1055
Morley, Edward Williams **11:**1497
Mormons (rel. sect) **6:**794; **16:**33; **16:**1154
Mornay, Philippe de **8:**46 **11:**1382
Morning Bathers **2:**82; **13:**1412; **14:**1087
MORNING BENEDICTIONS **12:**325
- variations in liturgy **11:**396; **11:**403
- *see also:* BENEDICTIONS
MORNING FREIHEIT (newsp.) **12:**326
- Epstein, Melech **6:**835
- Feinberg, Leon **6:**1212
Morning Journal, see JEWISH MORNING JOURNAL
Morning Service, *see* SHAHARIT
"Mornington Crescent with Statue of Sickert's Father-in-law III" (paint., F. Auerbach) **3:**618
Moro, Joseph, *see* Filippo
MOROCCO **12:**326
- *Contents:*
- - Early History **12:**327
- - Arab Conquest and Rule **12:**328
- - - Almoravides and Almohads **12:**329
- - - Merinids and Wattasids **12:**330
- - - Allawids **12:**336
- - - Beginnings of European Intervention **12:**337
- - French Protectorate **12:**341
- - Holocaust Period **12:**342
- - Contemporary Period **12:**342
- - Attitude to Israel **12:**346
- Alliance **2:**650ff
- Arab League **3:**242
- capitulations **5:**149
- communal organization **5:**815; **5:**828
- demography **5:**1499ff.; **13:**870ff
- divorce statistics **6:**136
- dress **6:**219
- Hanukkah lamps **7:**1292
- history chart (1954-55) **8:**766-767
- I.C.A. **10:**49
- immigration to Israel **9:**499ff; **9:**538
- Jewish quarters **10:**87ff
- marriage custom **11:**1044
- mining **11:**1442
- music **16:**1257
- Omar, Covenant of **12:**1378
- ORT **12:**1485
- politics **13:**816
- rabbi, rabbinate **13:**1451
- *romancero* musical tradition **10:**1353
- Shabbateanism **14:**1236; **14:**1243
- special Purim **13:**1397
- synagogues **1:**syn. list
- trade and commerce **15:**1301
- Tunisia **15:**1439ff
- Zionism **16:**1127ff
- *illus:*
- - text
- - Aroumiath synagogue **6:**395
- - bridal costume Pl. 6 6-DRESS; **11:**1044
- - Debdou Jewish woman **5:**1427
- - Dra Jewish women **6:**190
- - Hanukkah lamps **7:**1294-1298, 1312
- - J.D.C. school, Casablanca **2:**831
- - Jerusalem emissary **14:**1363
- - Jewish artisan **5:**1043
- - Jewish Berbers **4:**588
- - Jewish woman cooking **5:**940
- - Meknès mellah **11:**1273
- - *mezuzah* cover **11:**1475
- - Muhammad XVII, letter of protection **5:**961
- - *Shivviti* plaque **14:***fcg.* 1419
- - Talouet villagers dancing the *Ahwash* **5:**1271
- - wedding **11:**1037
- *pop. tables:* text
MOROGOWSKI, JACOB SAMUEL **12:**347
MOROSINI, GIULIO **12:**347
- Segrè's polemic **14:**1114
Morphology (Heb. gram.) **8:**102ff
- Arabic **3:**238 **16:**1682ff
- Dead Sea Scrolls **16:**1586
- mishnaic Hebrew **16:**1596ff
Morphophonology (Heb. gram.) **8:**80
MORPURGO (fam.) **12:**348
- nobility **15:**1166
- split **15:**289
Morpurgo, Abram Vita **12:**348
Morpurgo, Benedetto **12:**348
Morpurgo, David **2:**942
Morpurgo, Edgardo (physic.) **12:**348
Morpurgo, Edgardo Uri (Zion.) **12:**348
Morpurgo, Elijah **12:**348
Morpurgo, Emilio **12:**348
Morpurgo, Ezekiel **2:**942
Morpurgo, Gino **12:**348
Morpurgo, Giulio **12:**348
MORPURGO, GIUSEPPE **12:**349
- Italian literature **9:**1111
Morpurgo, Baron Hubert de **15:**314
Morpurgo, Luciano **12:**348; **13:**1368
Morpurgo, Marco **12:**348
Morpurgo, Mosé **4:**559; **12:**348
MORPURGO, RACHEL **12:**349
MORPURGO, SALOMONE **12:**349
MORPURGO, SAMSON BEN JOSHUA MOSES **12:**350
- Hayon, Nehemiah **7:**1502
- hunting, views on **8:**1111
- Papo, Samuel **13:**67
- *illus:* text
Morpurgo, Vittorio **12:**348
Morris, Charles W. **11:**522
Morris, Frederick **11:**1554
MORRIS, HENRY HARRIS **12:**351
- Zionism **16:**1140
Morris, Hyman **12:**351
Morris, Ira Nelson **12:**352
Morris, Judah **15:**1177
Morris, Lewis **15:**310
Morris, Moses **12:**266
MORRIS, NATHAN **12:**351
MORRIS, NELSON **12:**352
Morris, Noah **7:**603
Morris, R. H. (polit.) **13:**31
MORRIS, RICHARD BRANDON **12:**352
Morris, Robert **14:**695; **15:**1591
- *illus:*
- - Benjamin Levy's letter **15:**1590
Morrison, Lord Herbert **13:**33; **13:**36; **16:**1090
Morrison-Grady Plan (Er. Isr.) **9:**359
- Bevin, Ernest **4:**784
- palestine partition **13:**34; **13:**36
- Zionist Congress **16:**1176
MORSE, DAVID ABNER **12:**352
Morse, Jacob **15:**300
MORSE, LEOPOLD **12:**353
Morse, Ralph **13:**484
Mortality
- eternity of God **6:**1346
- Israel **9:**483ff; **9:**984
- sickness **14:**1499ff
- vital statistics **16:**177ff
Mortara, Edgardo, *see* MORTARA CASE
MORTARA, LODOVICO **12:**353
MORTARA, MARCO **12:**353
- *illus:* text
MORTARA CASE **12:**354
- Alliance Universelle **2:**649
- Cahen, Isidore **5:**17
- Delegates of American Israelites **4:**1149
- history chart **8:**766-767
- *illus:* text
MORTEIRA, SAUL LEVI **12:**355
- Aboab da Fonseca **2:**95
- Amsterdam Talmud Torah **2:**896
- Spinoza, Baruch **15:**281
Mortgage, *see* PLEDGE; PROPERTY
Mortkowicz, J. **13:**1369
Mortkowicz-Olczakowa, Hanna **13:**803
MORTON, LOUIS C. **8:**548
Morton Grove (sub., Chicago) **5:**415
MORWITZ, EDWARD **12:**355
Mosad Bialik (publ. firm, Isr.) **13:**1378
Mosad ha-Rav Kook (publ. house, Isr.) **3:**390; **11:**195, 740; **13:**1378
- *illus:*
- - library **11:**196
Mosad Le-Aliyah Bet (orgn.) **4:**630ff; **8:**1249; **9:**532ff
Mosaic (mag.) **5:**460
Mosaic faith (term for Jud.) **3:**773
Mosaics
- Bet Alfa synagogue **4:**710
- Medeba map **11:**918
- pillars **13:**523
- synagogue **15:**598
- synagogue symbolism **15:**572ff
- *illus:*
- - Abraham's separation from Lot **11:**507
- - Abraham's visitation by the three angels **4:**938; **14:**867
- - Basilica of the Agony, Jer. **9:**1455
- - Bet Alfa synagogue **3:**511, 513; **4:**711; **8:**651; **11:**268,990
- - Bet Guvrin, Byzantine church (6th cent.) **5:**1457
- - Bet-Shean, Byzantine church (5th-6th cent.) **4:**764
- - Beth-Shean synagogue **13:**905
- - "Call of the Shofar" (B. Shahn) **14:**1259
- - Church of the Multiplication **15:**689
- - Church of the Nativity (4th cent.) **4:**745
- - Creation (13th cent., Venice) **5:**1062
- - Esau and Jacob story (12th cent.) **6:**855
- - expulsion from Paradise (12th cent., Palermo) **6:**981
- - Gaza synagogue **7:**340-341
- - Gerasa synagogue **7:**434
- - Hamam Lif synagogue (c. 4th cent.) **3:**519; **11:**268; **15:**572
- - Hammat Gader synagogue **7:**249, 251
- - Hammath synagogue **3:**325; **7:**1244; **15:**574,575
- - Jericho synagogue **2:**690; **9:**1370; **11:**1360
- - Knesset building, wall by M. Chagall **5:**323
- - Lamech killing Cain (12th cent., Monreale) **5:**25
- - Madaba map **3:**697, 715; **7:**572; **9:**1543; **11:**677,921
- - Ma'on synagogue **6:**604; **11:**908
- - Masada **11:**1083
- - Naarah synagogue **12:**737
- - Ostia synagogue **12:**1507
- - Tower of Babel (13th cent., Venice) **4:**23
Mosaisk Samfund (period.) **13:**1048
Mosaism (ideology) **4:**379
- Auerbach, Berthold **3:**845
MOSBACH (city, Ger.) **12:**356
MOSBACHER, EMIL JR. **12:**356
- sports **15:**317
Mosbacher, Robert **15:**317
Mosberg, Samuel **12:**1375
MOSCATI, SABATINO **12:**357
MOSCATO, JUDAH BEN JOSEPH **12:**357
- Italian literature **9:**1109
- Rieti family **14:**170
MOSCHELES, IGNAZ **12:**358
- *illus:* text
Moschos (3rd cent. B.C.E., slave) **7:**868
Mościska (city, Rus.), *see* MOSTISKA
Mosconi, Judah Leon, *see* MOSKONI, JUDAH LEON BEN MOSES
Moscovici, A., *see* TOMA, A.
Moscovici, Virgiliu, *see* MONDA, VIRGILIU
MOSCOVITCH, MAURICE **15:**1088
Moscovitch, M. E. **2:**531
MOSCOW (city, Rus.) **12:**359
- expulsion of Jews **8:**735
- history chart (1891) **8:**766-767
- Judaizers **10:**400
- libraries **11:**193
- Mazeh, Jacob **11:**1151
- synagogues **15:**589
- *illus:*
- - text
- - Israel at eighth European Championship Games **15:**295
- - Israel youth delegation **14:**490
- - Trotsky in Red Square **15:**1404
Moscow (city, U.S.) **8:**1223
Moscow Chamber State Jewish Theater, *see* Jewish State Theater
Moscow Declaration (war crimes) **16:**290
Mosedot le-Tippul be-Olim Nehshalim (orgn.), *see* MALBEN
Mosellanus (physic.) **11:**1186
Moselle (reg., Fr.) **3:**382; **11:**1452
MOSENTHAL (fam.) **12:**369
Mosenthal, Adolph **12:**369
- *illus:*
- - Graaff Reinet trading station **15:**187
Mosenthal, Harry **12:**369
Mosenthal, Joseph **12:**369; **13:**820
- *illus:*
- - portrait **12:**369
Mosenthal, Julius **12:**369; **13:**820
MOSENTHAL, SALOMON HERMANN **12:**370
- Oppenheim's illustrations **12:**1424
Mosenthal, William **12:**369
MOSER, JACOB **12:**370
- Bradford **4:**1287
- *illus:* text
MOSER, MOSES **12:**371
- Gans **7:**311
- German history **7:**448
Moser, P. N. **8:**46
Moserah (mt., Er. Isr.), *see* Jebel Madra
Moserim, see INFORMERS

MOSES **12:**371
- *Contents:*
- - Biblical View **12:**372
- - - Biography **12:**372
- - - Critical Assessment **12:**378
- - In Hellenistic Literature **12:**388
- - - Inventor and Civilizer, Lawgiver and Philosopher **12:**388
- - - Anti-Semitic Attacks on Moses **12:**390
- - Rabbinic View **12:**393
- - - In the Aggadah **12:**395
- - In Medieval Jewish Thought **12:**399
- - Modern Interpretations **12:**401
- - In Christian Tradition **12:**402
- - In Islam **12:**402
- - In the Arts **12:**404
- - - Literary Works by 20th Century Non-Jewish Writers **12:**405
- - - 20th Century Jewish Writers **12:**405
- - - In Art **12:**405
- - - In Music **12:**405
- Bible History **8:**576
- - Aaron **2:**4
- - Aaronides **2:**20
- - Ark of Moses **3:**466
- - Balaam **4:**123
- - Decalogue **5:**1435ff
- - Exodus, Book of **6:**1051ff
- - God's revelation **14:**118,119ff
- - Golden Calf **7:**710
- - jealousy **9:**1306
- - Jethro **10:**17
- - Joshua **10:**265
- - Kenites **10:**906
- - Kiss of Death **5:**1427
- - Korah **10:**1190ff
- - lots, casting of **11:**512
- - Miriam **12:**82
- - Moses, Blessing of **12:**412; **13:**1082
- - new moon sanctification **12:**291
- - Numbers, Book of **12:**1253
- - ordination **14:**1144
- - Patriarchs **13:**183
- - Pentateuch **13:**260
- - plagues of Egypt **13:**605
- - priestly *mishmarot* **12:**92
- - prophet **13:**1152ff
- - Rephidim **14:**80
- - Tabernacle **15:**683; **15:**687
- - Tablets of the Law **15:**690
- - veil **16:**84
- - Zelophehad's daughters **16:**979
- - Zipporah **16:**1182
- in Judaism
- - Albo's dogma **2:**536
- - articles of faith **3:**655ff; **8:**359
- - fear of God **6:**1199
- - *halakhah* **7:**1156
- - *halakhah le-Moshe mi-Sinai* **7:**1167
- - justice **10:**477; **13:**197
- - legal traditions **15:**1309; **15:**1311
- - messianism **6:**862,873
- - *takkanot* **15:**721
- - Torah **15:**1237; **15:**1240
- - Torah reading **11:**394
- in Aggadah
- - Adar, seventh of **2:**252
- - Akiva ben Joseph **7:**1163
- - Angel of Death **2:**953
- - angels **11:**1489
- - Elijah **6:**637
- - fitness for leadership **3:**6
- - Og and Sihon **12:**1314
- - Oral Law **12:**1440
- - rod of Moses **14:**219
- - tribe of descendants **6:**577
- - war on Midian **11:**1506
- Literature
- - *al-Asāṭīr* **2:**510
- - alchemic writings **2:**542
- - *Assumption of Moses* **12:**412
- - *Chronicles of Moses* **12:**413
- - Greek literature **7:**888ff
- - Hellenistic literature **8:**298; **8:**300
- - illuminated *maḥzorim* **11:**733
- - magic book **11:**706
- - Psalms, Book of **13:**1318
- - *Ra'aya Meheimna* **16:**1197; **16:**1208
- - rabbinic literature **13:**360ff
- Views on
- - Artapanus **3:**645ff
- - Astruc, Jean **3:**809
- - Druze **9:**928
- - Freud **7:**163
- - Hecataeus of Abdera **8:**236
- - Islam **6:**885; **13:**362
- - Jewish Christian tradition **10:**40
- - kabbalistic **10:**575; **10:**616
- - Karaites **10:**778
- - Luzzatto, M. H. **11:**601
- - Maimonides **11:**773ff
- - Manetho **11:**872
- - philosophical **13:**421
- - Samaritans **14:**738ff
- - Spinoza **15:**282
- - Tacitus **15:**695
- *illus:*
- - text
- - Aaron and Hur supporting hands **2:**788
- - *Ambrosian Bible* **8:**1279
- - assembling the leaders **10:**266
- - *Birds' Head Haggadah* **7:***fcg.* 875
- - blessing Children of Israel **12:**386
- - blessing Phinehas **13:**467
- - brought by Bithiah before Pharaoh **4:**1059
- - burning bush **4:**1529; **6:**282
- - ceremonial object motif **3:**542; **4:**244,1232,1339
- - chosen by the hand of God **10:**1191
- - death **5:**1426
- - Dura-Europos wall paint. **6:**283
- - episodes **12:***fcg.* 427
- - folk-art portrait **8:**1286
- - found by Pharaoh's daughter **6:**285
- - hail, seventh plague of Egypt **13:**607
- - hand of God giving the Ten Commandments to **5:**1437
- - in the bulrushes,**4:**932
- - Joshua and **10:**266
- - *Kaufmann Haggadah* **8:**1275
- - *ketubbah* (19th cent.) Pl. 5 **10**-KETUBBAH
- - Korah, Dathan and Abiram **5:**1311
- - leading the Israelites out of Egypt **7:**1086
- - led by angel to Mt. Sinai **2:**965
- - Mount Sinai **5:**1438
- - ordering the sea to part **6:**1045
- - pleading with Pharaoh **13:**605
- - pointing at the Torah **4:**1161
- - reading the Torah **6:**286
- - receiving the Tablets of the Law - - **2:***fcg.* 11; **3:***fcg.* 907; **4:**430, 787; **5:**1436,1441; **8:**1218; **14:**1597
- - *Regensburg Pentateuch* **14:***fcg.* **1323**
- - *Sarajevo Haggadah* **7:***fcg.* 1131
- - slaying the Egyptian **8:**1
- - speaking to the Israelites **4:**857
- - teaching the Ten Commandments **12:**1
- - Theresienstadt ghetto "bank note" **5:**726
- - watching battle with Amalek **14:**1258
- - with Aaron before Pharaoh **2:**952

"Moses" (sculp., G. Pisano) **12:**406
Moses (paytan) **13:**589
Moses(9th cent., gaon) **7:**323
Moses (13th cent., Anjou) **3:**23
Moses (14th cent., kab.) **12:**426
Moses, Aaron (N.H.) **12:**1024
Moses, Aaron (N.C.) **12:**1217
Moses, Aaron (Pol.) **10:**1159
Moses, Abraham Lyons **11:**1393
Moses, Adolph **11:**522
Moses, Albert Lurie **12:**1218
Moses, Alexander **14:**1414
Moses, Alfred (r.) **5:**514
Moses, Alfred (govt. offic.) **14:**162
MOSES, ASSUMPTION OF (apoc. wk.) **12:**411
- *Abraham, Testament of* **2:**129
- apocalyptic writing **3:**180
- Hellenistic Jewish literature **8:**304
- Herod's rule **8:**384
- Moses **12:**392ff
- salvation **11:**1408
MOSES, BLESSING OF **12:**412
- blessing Children of Israel **12:**386
- *see also:* JACOB, BLESSING OF
Moses, *Chin-Shih, see* Chao Ying-Ch'eng
MOSES, CHRONICLES OF **12:**413
Moses, David **13:**1504
Moses, E. **4:**498
Moses, Five Books of, *see* BIBLE; PENTATEUCH
Moses, Gedaliah **11:**890
Moses, Isaac **11:**154
Moses, Mrs. Isaac **12:**1071
MOSES, ISAAC S. **12:**413
- Meyers, Moses **12:**725
- prayer books **13:**991
Moses, Jacob (cmty. offic.) **13:**1290
Moses, Jacob (nav. of.) **15:**1181
Moses, Levy **8:**1356
Moses, Lionel **15:**312
Moses, Loebel (Levy) **11:**156
MOSES, MARCUS **12:**414
- London **11:**474
- Nathan, Abraham **12:**849
Moses, Maurice **4:**370
Moses, Michael **7:**858
Moses, Mordecai **4:**1219
Moses, Moritz **16:**1165
Moses, Moses **5:**606
MOSES, MYER **12:**414
Moses, Rachel, *see* Gratz, Rachel
MOSES, RAPHAEL J. **12:**414
MOSES, ROBERT **12:**415
MOSES, SIEGFRIED **12:**415
Moses, Song of, *see* SEA, SONG OF THE
Moses, Sons of **6:**577
Moses, Testament of (apoc. wk.) **12:**412
Moses Aaron Taub of Nowy Dwor **10:**858
Moses ben Abraham (Pol. r.) **7:**925
Moses ben Abraham (print., Ger.) **7:**1196; **13:**1107
Moses ben Abraham Maimuni **10:**277
Moses ben Abraham of Nîmes **3:**801
MOSES BEN ABRAHAM OF PONTOISE (tos.) **12:**416
Moses ben Abraham of Przemysl, *see* MAT, MOSES
Moses ben Adonin ha-Levi **13:**589
Moses ben Asher **11:**900; **16:**1472
Moses ben Attar, *see* Abenatar, Moses
Moses ben Benjamin Sofer **13:**589
MOSES BEN DANIEL OF ROHATYN **12:**416
- Bashuysen **4:**296
Moses ben David of Lelov **11:**9
Moses ben Eleazar **10:**721
Moses ben Eleazar ha-Kohen (13th cent.) **10:**1121
Moses ben Eleazar ha-Kohen (14/15 cent.) **6:**928
Moses ben Elias Pobian **4:**887
Moses ben Eliezer Rafael **8:**1323
Moses ben Elijah **15:**1353
Moses ben Elijah the Greek **3:**799
MOSES BEN HA-NESI'AH **12:**416
- linguistics **16:**1359,1387
MOSES BEN ḤANOKH **12:**417
- four captives story **6:**1447ff
- responsa **14:**86
- Spain **15:**225
- title **7:**324
Moses ben Ḥayyim **12:**899
Moses ben Ḥayyim Shabbetai **7:**1512
Moses ben Hillel **8:**487
Moses ben Ḥiyya **13:**591
Moses ben Isaac (11th cent.), *see* IBN AL-TAQANA, MOSES
Moses ben Isaac (paytan, Tyre) **13:**591
Moses ben Isaac (15th cent.) **4:**1220; **8:**1321
Moses ben Isaac ben ha-Nesi'ah, *see* MOSES BEN HA-NESI'AH
Moses ben Isaac ben Jacob **13:**591
MOSES BEN ISAIAH KATZ **12:**418
Moses ben Isaiah Menahem **9:**75
Moses ben Israel al Ṭabib al-Kūfī, *see* Mūsā ibn Isrā'īl al Ṭabib al-Kūfī
Moses ben Israel of Stolin **10:**794
Moses ben Jacob ibn Ezra, *see* IBN EZRA, MOSES BEN JACOB
MOSES BEN JACOB OF COUCY **12:**418
- attitude towards Gentiles **7:**413
- codification of law **5:**643; **11:**334
- French *yeshivot* **16:**764
- Heschel, Abraham **8:**428
- seals **14:**1079
- significance of exile **7:**285ff
- *tefillin* **15:**899
- *illus:*
- - *Sefer Mitzvot Gadol* (1488) **8:**1333; **9:**1125
MOSES BEN JACOB OF KIEV **12:**420
- Bayshyazi, Elijah **4:**298
Moses ben Japheth al Raḥbi **13:**1516
Moses ben Jekuthiel **15:**263
Moses ben Jekuthiel Zalman **14:**154
MOSES BEN JOAB **12:**421
Moses ben Joel (12th cent., r.) **9:**25
- Joel ben Isaac **10:**137
Moses ben Joel (16th cent., mart.) **8:**984
Moses ben Joseph (11th cent.) **2:**631
Moses ben Joseph (paytan) **13:**591
Moses ben Joseph Abi Zardil **2:**198
MOSES BEN JOSEPH BEN MERWAN LEVI **12:**421
- Abraham of Posquières **2:**136
Moses ben Joseph ben Moses of Lucena **6:**272; **14:**549
MOSES BEN JOSEPH HA-LEVI **12:**421
- Aristotelianism **3:**446
Moses ben Joseph Trani, *see* TRANI, MOSES BEN JOSEPH
MOSES BEN JOSHUA OF NARBONNE **12:**422
- Abner of Burgos **2:**88
- Aristotelianism **3:**446
- Avempace **3:**947
- Averroes **3:**951ff
- Jewish philosophy **13:**446
- Kabbalah **10:**537
- *Shiur Komah* **14:**1418
- soul **15:**173
- Themistius **15:**1099
- translations **15:**1322
Moses ben Joske **12:**1475
Moses ben Judah **10:**350; **11:**588
Moses ben Judah ben Kalonymus

10:719
Moses ben Judah he-Ḥasid 7:1388
- Judah he-Ḥasid 10:352
Moses ben Judah of Béziers 11:566,1402; 12:1165
Moses ben Kalonymus ben Judah 10:719; 10:720ff
- German mysticism 10:510
- Jewish literature 11:326
Moses ben Kefa 4:858
MOSES BEN LEVI 12:424
Moses ben Maimon, *see* MAIMONIDES
Moses ben Makhir 6:540; 11:6
Moses ben Mazliaḥ 13:1231
Moses ben Meir 6:1231
Moses ben Menahem (philos.), *see* MENDELSSOHN, MOSES
Moses ben Menahem (print.) 16:147
MOSES BEN MENAHEM GRAF 12:424
Moses ben Mendel Frankfurt, *see* MENDELSOHN, FRANKFURT MOSES
Moses ben Meshullam of Lucca 10:721
MOSES BEN MEVORAKH 12:424
Moses ben Mordecai 4:653
Moses ben Mordecai of Mantua (Brescia) 4:866; 4:867
Moses ben Musa 5:38
Moses ben Naḥman, *see* NAḤMANIDES
Moses ben Nethanel (12th cent.) 7:1188
- gaon 7:324
Moses ben Nethanel (14th cent.), *see* MOSES NATHAN
Moses ben Raphael Mordecai, *see* MALKHI, MOSES
Moses ben Samuel ben Absalom 13:591
MOSES BEN SAMUEL OF DAMASCUS 12:425
- Mecca pilgrimage 15:642
Moses ben Sason 2:593
Moses ben Schne'or, *see* MOSES OF EVREUX
Moses ben Shabbetai 13:591
Moses ben Shemaiah of Troyes 14:1375
MOSES BEN SHEM TOV DE LEON 12:425
- Abulafia, Joseph 2:194; 2:195
- alchemy 2:545
- Basilea 4:299
- history chart 8:766-767
- Kabbalah 10:532; 10:602; 10:612
- Worlds, the Four 16:641
- Zohar 11:347; 16:1209ff
Moses ben Shem Tov ibn Ḥabib, *see* IBN ḤABIB, MOSES BEN SHEM TOV
MOSES BEN SOLOMON BEN SIMEON OF BURGOS 12:427
- Kabbalah,10:530; 10:567
Moses ben Solomon ha-Kohen of Mainz 4:280
Moses ben Solomon of Beaucaire 4:363
Moses ben Solomon of Salerno 2:929; 6:1180
Moses ben Solomon of Salon, *see* Salon, Moses de
Moses ben Todros ha-Nasi 9:25
Moses ben Yiẓḥak Eisik 10:1382
MOSES BEN YOM-TOV 12:427
- Jacob ben Judah 9:1220
- linguistics 16:1386
- Oxford 12:1534
Moses ben Ẓadkah 5:1241
Moses ben Zakar 15:1172
Moses ben Ẓevi of Ujhely, *see* Teitelbaum, Moses ben Ẓevi
Moses ben Zur 13:591
Moses da Rosa, *see* PROVENÇAL, MOSES BEN ABRAHAM
Moses David of Podhajce 6:1159
Moses de Salon, *see* Salon, Moses de
Moses de Toledo, *see* TOLEDO, MOSES DE
Moses di Trani, *see* TRANI, MOSES BEN JOSEPH
Moses the Elder 11:1401
Moses el-Ḥazzan 14:1495
MOSES ESRIM VE-ARBA 12:428
- Balbo 4:129
- Kabbalah 10:540
- *Shmuel Bukh* 14:1427
Moses Gerondi, *see* NAḤMANIDES
Moses Gikatilla, *see* GIKATILLA, MOSES BEN SAMUEL HA-KOHEN
Moses the Greek, *see* Moses ben Elijah the Greek
MOSES HA-DARSHAN (11th cent.) 12:429
- *Genesis Rabbati* 7:401
Moses ha-Darshan (tos.), *see* MOSES BEN JACOB OF COUCY
Moses ha-Darshan (14th cent.) 16:675
Moses ha-Dayyan 9:75
Moses ha-Goleh, *see* MOSES BEN JACOB OF KIEV
Moses ha-Kohen (gaon), *see* MOSES KAHANA BEN JACOB
Moses ha-Kohen (11th cent.) 16:685
MOSES HA-KOHEN OF TORDESILLAS 12:429
- apologetics 3:195
Moses ha-Levi ben Nethanel, *see* Moses ben Nethanel
Moses ha-Levi ha-Katan 10:783
Moses ha-Nakdan 16:1387,1476
Moses Hanoch of Prague 11:358
Moses ha-Parnas 8:1365
Moses Ḥasid (r., Kosov), *see* Ḥasid, Moses
Moses Ḥasid of Ropshitz 10:1387
Moses ha-Yevani Capuzato, *see* Capuzato, Moses ha-Yevani
MOSES ḤAYYIM EPHRAIM OF SUDYLKOW 12:430
- *geneal. table:* 9:1051
Moses Hillel of Zolkiew 2:24
Moses ibn Crispin Cohen, *see* Ibn Crispin Cohen, Moses
Moses ibn Ezra, *see* IBN EZRA, MOSES BEN JACOB
Moses ibn Forma 3:523
Moses ibn Ḥabib, *see* IBN ḤABIB, MOSES BEN SHEM TOV
Moses ibn Makhir, *see* Moses ben Makhir
Moses ibn Shealtiel 8:1325
MOSES ISAAC (Darshan; Kelmer Maggid) 12:430
- Kelm 10:902
Moses Isaac ha-Levi (r., Gr.) 10:814
Moses Jekubel Kaufmann, *see* Kaufmann, Moses Jekubel
Moses Judah Leib 10:1106
MOSES KAHANA BEN JACOB (gaon) 12:432
- gaon 7:316
MOSES LEIB OF SASOV 12:432
Moses Meir ben Ephraim of Padua, *see* MEIR BEN EPHRAIM OF PADUA
Moses Meir of Kamenka 14:1249
Moses Mendels, *see* BACHRACH, MOSES BEN ISAIAH MENAHEM
Moses Mevorakh 13:591
Moses Nakdan of London, *see* Moses ha-Nakdan
MOSES NATHAN 12:432
Moses Nisan Leib 11:1096
Moses of Alexandria 2:542
Moses of Arles 3:469; 13:1263
Moses of Beaucaire, *see* Moses ben Solomon of Beaucaire
Moses of Bristol 4:1378; 4:483
Moses of Burgos, *see* MOSES BEN SOLOMON BEN SIMEON OF BURGOS
Moses of Chorene 7:423; 13:307
Moses of Coucy, *see* MOSES BEN JACOB OF COUCY
Moses of Cracow, *see* Friedmann, Moses
Moses of Damascus, *see* MOSES BEN SAMUEL OF DAMASCUS
Moses of Desseau, *see* MENDELSSOHN, MOSES
Moses of Dolina, *see* MOSES SHOHAM BEN DAN OF DOLINA
MOSES OF EVREUX 12:433
- Jonah Gerondi 10:179
Moses of Grodno, *see* MOSES ZE'EV BEN ELIEZER OF GRODNO
Moses of Kamenka, *see* Moses Meir of Kamenka
MOSES OF KIEV (12th cent.) 12:433
Moses of Kiev (15/16 cent.), *see* MOSES BEN JACOB OF KIEV
Moses of Korostyshev 15:1472
Moses of Lelov, *see* Moses ben David of Lelov
Moses of Lincoln 13:1015
Moses of London (elder), *see* MOSES BEN YOM TOV
Moses of London (younger), *see* MOSES BEN HA-NESI'AH
Moses of Lucca, *see* Moses ben Meshullam of Lucca
Moses of Mainz, *see* Moses ben Solomon ha-Kohen of Mainz
Moses of Mantua, *see* Moses ben Mordecai of Mantua
Moses of Narbonne (12th cent.), *see* MOSES BEN JOSEPH BEN MERWAN LEVI
Moses of Narbone (14th cent.), *see* MOSES BEN JOSHUA OF NARBONNE
Moses of Nîmes, *see* Moses ben Abraham of Nîmes
Moses of Nowy Dwor, *see* Moses Aaron Taub of Nowy Dwor
Moses of Oxford, *see* MOSES OF BRISTOL
Moses of Padua, *see* MEIR BEN EPHRAIM OF PADUA
MOSES OF PALERMO 12:433
MOSES OF PAVIA 12:434
- Amittai 2:850
Moses of Podhajce, *see* Moses David of Podhajce
Moses of Pontoise, *see* MOSES BEN ABRAHAM OF PONTOISE
Moses of Prague (15th cent.) 7:342
Moses of Prague (17th cent.), *see* Moses Hanoch of Prague
Moses of Przemysl (15th cent.) 5:1028
Moses of Przemysl (16/17 cent.), *see* Moses ben Abraham of Przemysl
Moses of Przeworsk 14:535
Moses of Rohatyn, *see* MOSES BEN DANIEL OFN ROHATYN
Moses of Ropshitz, *see* Moses Ḥasid of Ropshitz
Moses of Russia 12:433
Moses of Salerno, *see* Moses ben Solomon of Salerno
Moses of Salon, *see* Salon, Moses de
Moses of Sambor 14:635; 16:1009ff
Moses of Sasov, *see* MOSES LEIB OF SASOV
Moses of Satanov 7:1396; 7:1416
Moses of Siemiatycze 7:353
Moses of Speyer 15:140
Moses of Stolin, *see* Moses ben Israel of Stolin
Moses of Sudylkow, *see* MOSES ḤAYYIM EPHRAIM OF SUDYLKOW
Moses of Tordesillas, *see* MOSES HA-KOHEN OF TORDESILLAS
Moses of Trani, *see* TRANI, MOSES BEN JOSEPH
Moses of Troyes, *see* Moses ben Shemaiah of Troyes
Moses of Tunis 15:1439
Moses of Ujhely, *see* Teitelbaum, Moses ben Ẓevi
Moses of Vladimir-Volynski 9:1315
Moses of Znaim 9:1071; 10:1090
Moses of Zolkiew, *see* Moses Hillel of Zolkiew
Moses of Zurich 7:1108; 9:22; 15:556; 16:1241
Moses Parnes 12:28
Moses Praeger, *see* MOSES BEN MENAHEM GRAF
Moses (al-) Roti 16:1388
MOSES SHOHAM BEN DAN OF DOLINA 12:434
Mosessohn, Aaron 13:1290
Moses Uri ha-Levi 2:895; 16:6
MOSES ZE'EV BEN ELIEZER OF GRODNO 12:434
Moses Zevi Savran, *see* Savran, Moses Ẓevi
Moshal, Solomon 6:308
MOSHAV (Moshav Ovedim; stlmts.) 12:435
- cooperatives 5:950
- geographical distribution 9:570ff
- history 8:752ff; 9:381ff
- Jewish labor 9:854ff
- Yemenite Jews 16:753
- *illus:*
- - text
- - Nahalal 12:768
- *see also:* MOSHAV SHITTUFI
Moshavah (type of vill.) 9:604
Moshav Bareket (Isr.) 7:1020
Moshav Ovedim, *see* MOSHAV
MOSHAV SHITTUFI (stlmts.) 12:438
- cooperatives 5:950
Moshav Zekenim (old age home) 2:345ff
Moshe bar Jehiel, *see* MICHAEL, MOSES
Moshe ben Gershon 11:811
Mosheim, Grete 16:1056
Mosheim, J. Lorenz von 8:46
Moshel ba-Elyonim Attah Yadata (litur.) 4:56
Moshe Moḥeh (masor.) 16:1423,1471
Moshe Rabbenu, *see* MOSES
Moshevitsky, Ephraim 16:1099
Moshi, Salmān 8:1461
Moshides, Tobias 8:469
Mosk, Stanley 5:56; 14:834
MOSKONI, JUDAH LEON BEN MOSES 12:438
- book collection 4:974
MOSKOVITZ, SHALOM 3:606
- *illus:*
- - "Jacob's Dream" (paint.) 3:636
Moskowitz, Belle Linder Israels 12:439
MOSKOWITZ, HENRY 12:439
- New York City 12:1104
Moskva (city, Rus.), *see* MOSCOW
Moskva (Rus. ship) 14:1640
Moslem Religious Courts, *see* Sharia Courts
Moslems, *see* ISLAM
Mosler, A. 10:89
MOSLER, HENRY 12:439

Mosley, Sir Oswald **6**:763
- London **11**:478
- neo-Fascism **12**:952
- pro-Nazi **8**:741
- Wesker's play **16**:460
Mosque of the Mughrabis (Jer.) **9**:1459
Mosque of Omar (Jer.), *see* Dome of the Rock
Mosque of Peace (Nazareth) **9**:921
Mosquera (loc., Navarre) **15**:1424
Moss, Asher **15**:305
Moss, Celia, *see* Levetus, Celia
MOSS, JOHN **12**:439
Moss, Marion, *see* Hartog, Marion
Moss, Matthew **13**:809
Mossalians (sect) **14**:1087
MOSSE (fam.) **12**:440
Mosse, Albert **10**:1497; **12**:440
Mossé, B. **4**:882
Mosse, Emil **12**:440
MOSSE, GEORGE L. **12**:441
Mosse, Hans Lachman, *see* Lachman-Mosse, Hans
Mosse, Markus **12**:440
Mosse, Maximus **12**:440
Mosse, Paul **12**:440
Mosse, Rudolf **12**:440
Mosse, Rudolf S. **4**:647
Mosse, Salomon **12**:440
MOSSERI (fam.) **12**:441
Mosseri, Albert **12**:441
Mosseri, Eli **12**:441
Mosseri, Jacques **12**:441
Mosseri, Joseph **12**:441
Mosseri, Maccabee **12**:441
Mosseri, Maurice **12**:441
Mosseri, Mazal Mathilda **12**:441
- family **11**:876
Mosseri, Nissim **12**:441
Mosseri, Victor **12**:441
MOSSINSOHN, YIGAL **12**:442
- *illus:*
- - *Be-Arvot ha-Negev* in Habimah **6**:200
MOSSINSON, BENZION **12**:442
- Boger, Ḥayyim **4**:1170
MOSSNER, WALTHER VON **12**:443
MOST (city, Cz.) **12**:443
Mostaganem (city, Alg.) **2**:613
Mostar (city, Yug.) **16**:877; **16**:880
MOSTEL, ZERO **12**:443
- *illus:*
- - in *The Angel Levine* **12**:464
MOSTISKA (city, Rus.) **12**:444
Mostny, Grete **5**:467
Mosty Wielkie (city, Ukr.) **15**:84
MOSUL (city, Iraq) **12**:444
- Alroy, David **2**:750
- Barazani **4**:204,205
- David ben Zakkai **5**:1359
- Jewish community **10**:1295
- Kurdish Jews **8**:1456
- Sura **15**:523
Moszkowicz, Daniel **4**:809
Moszkowski, Alexander **12**:701
MOSZKOWSKI, MORITZ **12**:701
Mot (deity) **4**:10
- Anath **2**:926
Mota, Anrique da **15**:251
Mota, Nehemias **5**:626
Mota Aron (bk.) **6**:1151
MOTAL, ABRAHAM BEN JACOB **12**:445
Motal, Gershon ben Abraham **6**:919
Mota Musye (bk.) **6**:1151
MOTH (insect) **12**:445
Mother, *see* PARENT AND CHILD
"Mother and Child" (sculp., M. Kottler) **10**:1225
"Mother and Child" (sculp., J. Lipschitz) **14**:1064
Mother-and-child care centers (Isr.) **9**:986
- *illus:*
- - Rishon le-Zion clinic **9**:987
"Mother Russia" (paint., M. Chagall) **5**:319
MOTION PICTURES **12**:446
- *Contents:*
- - United States **12**:446
- - Britain **12**:451
- - France **12**:453
- - Germany **12**:453
- - Poland **12**:454
- - U.S.S.R. **12**:455
- - Other European Countries **12**:456
- - Films on Jewish Themes **12**:456
- - Israel **12**:460
- - Capsules **12**:463
- *illus:*
- - text
- - Douglas, Kirk, in *Cast a Giant Shadow* **6**:180
- - Kaye, Danny, in *Me and the Colonel* **10**:854
- - Lorre, Peter, in *M.* **10**:1417
- - Marx Brothers **11**:1076
- - Meron, Hanna, in *M.* **10**:1417
- - Mestel, Jacob, in *Uncle Moses* **11**:1428
- - the four Warner brothers **16**:305
Motl Peyse dem Khazns (bk.) **14**:1283
Motorboating **15**:312
Motorcycling **15**:312
Motot, Samuel ibn, *see* IBN MOTOT, SAMUEL BEN SAADIAH
Mott, John **8**:47
Motta (fam., Jam.) **9**:1274
Motta, Jacob de la **14**:919
MOTTL, FELIX JOSEF **12**:476
Motzi (blessing before meals), *see* GRACE BEFORE MEALS
MOTZKIN, LEO (Aryeh Leib) **12**:476
- archives **3**:388
- Basle program **4**:307
- Bernheim Petition **4**:681
- Zionist Congress **16**:1167
- *illus:*
- - text
- - membership card, first Zionist Congress **3**:388
- - Zionist Congresses **16**:1165,1173
Moudrá, Paula **5**:1193
Moulay, Muhammad **2**:516
Moulay-Idris (tn., Mor.) **10**:88
Moulay Ismail **11**:1149
Moulay Yusuf **2**:517
Moulins, Guiard des **4**:881
Moulins Bible (12th-cent. illum. ms., Fr.) **10**:1313
MOUNTAIN JEWS (tribe) **12**:478
- Judeo-Tat **10**:441
- *see also:* CAUCASUS
Mountbatten, Earl, of Burma **5**:230
Mountbatten, Edwina, Lady **5**:230
Mount Canaan (Er. Isr.) **14**:630
Mount Carmel (Isr.), *see* CARMEL, MOUNT
Mount Carmel (boro., Pa.) **13**:230
Mount Clemens (city, Mich.) **11**:1235; **11**:1500
Mount Gerizim (Isr.), *see* GERIZIM, MOUNT
Mount ha-Menuḥot (Isr.), see Har Ha-Menuḥot
Mount Hope (clny., Er. Isr.) **9**:1256
- Jaffa **9**:1256
Mount Horeb, *see* SINAI, MOUNT
Mount Kisco (tn., N.Y.) **16**:464
Mount Meron (Isr.), *see* MERON
Mount Nisir (Mesop.), *see* Nisir Mount
Mount of Beatitudes (Isr.), *see* Beatitudes, Mount of
Mount of the Forty (Er. Isr.), *see* Mons Quarantana
MOUNT OF OLIVES (Jer.) **12**:481
- Arab Legion **9**:1487
- Christianity **9**:1571
- Hoshana Rabba **8**:1027
- illuminated mss. **15**:986
- Islamic eschatology **6**:884
- Jerusalem boundary **9**:1515
- olives **12**:1364
- pilgrimage center **8**:921
- tombs **9**:1525; **9**:1532ff; **9**:889
- War of Independence **9**:1480
- Western Wall **16**:468
- *illus:*
- - text
- - desecrated Jewish graves,**9**:1485
- - Jewish cemetery **5**:273
- - ossuaries **12**:1504
- - pilgrims guide (16th cent.) **13**:513
- - primitivist depiction **4**:115
- - Rabinovich, Joseph **13**:1472
- - tombstones used for Arab Legion barracks **9**:1485
- - view from Temple Mount **9**:1522
Mount Paran, *see* Paran, Mount
Mount Perazim, (Er. Isr.), *see* BAAL-PERAZIM
Mount Prospect (sub., Chicago) **5**:415
Mount Royal (sub., Montreal) **12**:287
Mount Scopus (Isr.), *see* Scopus, Mount
Mount Scopus College (Austr.) **11**:1281ff
Mount Sinai, *see* SINAI, MOUNT
Mount Sinai, Melodies from, *see* MI-SINAI NIGGUNIM
Mount Sinai Hospital (U.S.) **5**:349; **8**:1034,1039; **12**:1072; **12**:1075; **12**:1092
- *illus:*
- - appeal (1845) **12**:1076
Mount Vernon (city, U.S.) **16**:464
Mount Zion, *see* ZION
Mount Zion, Church of (Jer.) **9**:1407
Mount Zion Temple and Community Center (Minn.) **15**:625
Mourner's *Kaddish* **10**:660
Mourners of Jerusalem (rel. gr.), *see* Jerusalem, Mourners of
Mourners of Zion (mvmt.), *see* AVELEI ZION
MOURNING **12**:485
- *Contents:*
- - Introduction **12**:485
- - Lamentations **12**:487
- - Talmudic and Medieval Periods **12**:487
- - Modern Practice **12**:490
- - Prayers in the Home and Changes in the Liturgy **12**:491
- General
- - Angel of Death **2**:955
- - *Duda'ei ha-Sadeh* **5**:1587
- - *gemilut hasadim* **7**:375
- - musical expression **12**:560
- - Olper, Samuel **15**:1455
- - Samaritans **14**:747
- - soul **15**:175
- - synagogue **15**:584
- - women wailers **8**:1461
- In *Halakhah*
- - halakhic decisions **7**:1164
- - *ḥazakah* **7**:1519
- - *Mo'ed Katan* **12**:209
- - rabbinical emphasis **10**:1484
- Private Practice
- - abstention from meat **11**:1163ff
- - apostates **3**:214
- - cosmetics **5**:980
- - covering of head **8**:1
- - eggs **6**:474
- - greetings **7**:915
- - *ḥalizah* **11**:126
- - *Kaddish* **10**:662
- - marriage **11**:1034ff
- - *niddui* and *ḥerem* **8**:351
- - priestly blessing **13**:1062
- - priests **13**:1081
- - shaving **4**:356
- - *sheloshim* **14**:1357
- - suicide **15**:489
- - Torah study **15**:456
- - wine **16**:539
- - *yahrzeit* **16**:702
- - *see also:* ANINUT; KERI'AH
- Public Practice
- - Av, the Ninth **3**:936ff
- - fasting **6**:1190; **6**:1193
- - Grace After Meals **7**:840
- - Jerusalem destruction **9**:1555
- - *kever avot* **10**:934
- - Nine Days period **12**:1168
- - *omer* period **12**:1385
- - *see also:* KINAH
- Burial Procedure **4**:1515
- - disinterment **6**:73
- - *hakkafot* **7**:1154
- - *ḥevra kaddisha* **8**:442
- - reinterment **11**:239
- - tombstones **15**:1222
- *illus:*
- - text
- - condolence formula (table) **7**:915
- - Tisha be-Av scenes **3**:937
- *see also:* HESPED
MOUSE (rodent) **12**:493
- dietary laws **6**:32
- evolution **6**:1002
- fauna of Israel **9**:226
Mousha, Isaac **15**:305
Moustiers-Sainte-Marie (loc., Provence) **13**:1259
Moutier-Grandval Bible (9th cent. illum. ms., Tours) **10**:266
Mouvement contre le Racisme, L'Antisémitisme et pour la Paix (orgn.) **13**:85
Mouvement des Jeunesses Sionistes (Fr.) **7**:35; **16**:1115
Mouvement National Contre le Racisme (Fr.) **7**:36
Mouyal, Andre **12**:1377
Movement for Torah Judaism (Isr.) **9**:900
Movement for an Undivided Ereẓ Israel, *see* Greater Land of Israel Movement
Movies, *see* MOTION PICTURES
Movimento Sociale Italiano (Neo-Fascist party) **12**:951
Movimiento Universitario Peruano Israelita (orgn.) **16**:1125
MOWINCKEL, SIGMUND OLAF PLYTT **12**:493
- Bible **4**:908
Moyal (fam.) **14**:682; **15**:919
Moyal, Abdallah Nadīm **12**:1464
Moyal, Avraham, *see* MUYAL, AVRAHAM
MOYAL, ESTHER **12**:493
Moyal, Simon **12**:1464; **12**:494
Moyne, Lord **9**:356
Moyne, Étienne le **8**:47
Moyses, Nathan **14**:713
Moyshe Kapoyr (folk type) **6**:1382
Moyzeszowa, Raszka *see* Fishel, Rachel
MOZA, (HA-) MOZAH (loc., Er. Isr.) **12**:494
- Moẓa Illit. **1**:place list; **12**:494
- Moẓa Taḥtit **1**:place list
- Roman colony **9**:239
- *illus:* text
Mozart, Wolfgang Amadeus **5**:1300; **10**:461; **15**:1171
Mozley, Charles **11**:409
MOZNAYIM (period.) **12**:495

- Lachower, Yeruḥam **10:**1338
- statistics **1:**newsp. list
- Steinberg, Jacob **15:**361
Moznayim (wk., Ibn Ezra), *see Sefer Moznayim*
MOZYR (city, Belor.) **12:**496
M.R.A.P. (Fr. orgn.), *see* Mouvement contre le Racisme, l'Antisémitisme et pour la Paix
MSI (Neo-Fascist party), *see* Movimento Sociale Italiano
MSTISLAVL (city, Belor.) **12:**496
Mtskheta (tn., Georgia) **7:**423
Mu'ad (leg. conc.) **3:**987ff; **15:**1274ff
Mu'allim, Abu Ayub Sulayman ibn, *see* Ibn Mu'allim, Abu Ayyub Sulayman
Mu'allim Moses **11:**951
Mu'ammar, Tawfiq **9:**1042ff
Mu'atti, Aaron **5:**814
Muʿâwiya (Umayyad caliph) **9:**261; **9:**264
- Jerusalem **9:**1425
- Umayyads **15:**1528
Mu'âwiya II **15:**1529
Mu'ayyad Shaikh, al-Malik al- **11:**836
Mu'aẓẓamiyya madrasa, Al- **9:**1425
Mu'azzam Tūrān Shāh, Al- **3:**998
Mubashshir ben Ephraim he-Haver **13:**591
MUBASHSHIR BEN NISSI HA-LEVI **12:**497
MUBASHSHIR BEN RAV KIMOI HA-KOHEN **12:**497
Mucaddam (Bene Isr. ldr.) **4:**498
Muchacho, Zebulun Maẓliaḥ **14:**871
MUCIANUS, CAIUS LICINIUS **12:**497
Muckrakers (mvmt.) **12:**723
Mudaliar (cmty. ldr.) **5:**1059; **5:**623; **8:**1355
Mudah (bot.) **13:**621
Mudge, Zachary **8:**47
Muehldorf (vill., Aus.) **14:**717
MUEHLHAUSEN (city, E. Ger.) **12:**498
MUEHSAM, ERICH **12:**498
- *illus:* text
Muelhausen (city, Als.), *see* MULHOUSE
MUELHAUSEN, YOM TOV LIPMANN **12:**499
- *Aleinu le-Shabbe'aḥ* **2:**557
- angels **2:**972
- apologetics **3:**197
- disputations with Christians **6:**94
- *Orḥot Zaddikim* **12:**1458
- polemical literature **11:**355
- *illus:*
- - *Sefer Nizzaḥon* **2:**737
Mueller, Anton von, *see* BIENENFELD, FRANZ RUDOLF
MUELLER, DAVID HEINRICH **12:**502
MUELLER, ERNST **12:**503
- Kabbalah studies **10:**648
- Zohar anthology **16:**1214
Mueller, Ernst Lothar, *see* LOTHAR, ERNST
MUELLER, HEINRICH **12:**503
- Gestapo **7:**527
- Holocaust **8:**859
Mueller, Hermann **16:**94
Mueller, Ignatius **11:**522
MUELLER, JOEL **12:**503
Mueller, Johannes **8:**325
Mueller, Moritz **3:**575
MUELLER-COHEN, ANITA **12:**504
Muenchhause, Boerries Freiherr von **11:**240
Muenchner Judische Nachrichten (period.) **13:**1033
Muenden, Christian **8:**47
MUENSTER (city, Ger.) **12:**504
- Warendorf **16:**302
- Westphalia **16:**475
MUENSTER, SEBASTIAN **12:**505
- cosmography maps **11:**928
- Hebraists **8:**47
- Jerusalem in art **9:**1580
- Levita, Elijah **11:**132
- linguistics **16:**1360,1390
- typography **15:**1482
- *illus:*
- - Levita's *Sefer ha-Dikduk* **8:**19
MUENSTERBERG, HUGO **12:**506
- psychology **13:**1344
MUENZ, ELEAZAR BEN ARYEH LEIB **12:**507
Muenz, Joseph Isaac **12:**508
MUENZ, MOSES BEN ISAAC HA-LEVI **12:**507
- Brill, Azriel **4:**1374
- homiletical literature **8:**956
- Landau **10:**1384
Muenzjuden ("mint Jew") **12:**63ff
Mufarrij ibn Danfal ibn al-Jarrāḥ, al **9:**262
Mufti of Jerusalem, *see* HUSSEINI, HĀJJ AMIN
Mufulira (tn., Zambia) **16:**922
Muggia (tn., Istria) **9:**1099
Muggia, Mose Levi **11:**83
Mughār (ridge, Isr.) **4:**1
Mughrebis (cmty., Jer.) **9:**1465
MUGUR, FLORIN **14:**423,427
Muḥāḍara, al- . . . (wk.), *see Kitāb al-Muḥāḍara wa al-Mudhākara*
Muhadd'ab Abu-l-Hasan ben al-Muwafak, Al- **5:**1348
Muhadhdhib al-Dawla Naṣr, *see* Mashāʿīrī, Mahadhdib al-Dawla Naṣir ibn
MUHAMMAD **12:**508
- General
- - Kaufmann, Y., on **16:**1350
- - *Yahūd* **16:**703
- History
- - Abdallah ibn Saba **2:**53
- - chart **8:**766-767
- - Jerusalem **9:**1425
- - Jews' economic status **16:**1278
- - Naḍīr **12:**754
- - Najran **12:**800
- - Qaynuqāʿ **13:**1419
- - Qurayẓa **13:**1436
- - Transjordan Jews **9:**259
- - Umayyads **15:**1528
- - Umayya ibn Abī al-Ṣalt **15:**1531
- Thought and Literature
- - *Ahl al-Kitāb* **2:**467
- - Druze religion **9:**928
- - eschatological views **6:**883ff
- - Jerusalem **9:**1575
- - *Ḥadith* **7:**1051
- - *jihād* **10:**103
- - Koran **10:**1194
- Judaism
- - Abrahamic stories **2:**119ff
- - *aggadah* **2:**364
- - *Aleinu le-Shabbe'aḥ* **2:**557
- - apologetics **3:**192,193
- - Bible **4:**928ff
- - Jacob **9:**1201
- - Jewish influence **8:**656ff
- - Maimon ben Joseph **11:**744
- - Noah **12:**1195
- *see also:* ISLAM
Muhammad (ruler, Tun.) **15:**1446
Muhammad I (Ott. sult.) **16:**1531
Muhammad II (Ott. sult.) **16:**1531
Muhammad III (Ott. sult.) **9:**287
Muhammad V (Ott., sult.) **16:**1074
Muhammad V (k., Mor.) **2:**517
Muhammad I, Al-Malik alNāṣir **9:**274; **9:**1424
Muhammad II, al-Malik al-Nasir **6:**269
Muhammad Abū Nabūt **9:**1254
MUHAMMAD ALI **12:**511
- Ereẓ Israel **9:**294; **9:**298; **16:**1035
- history chart **8:**766-767
- Middle East campaign **9:**305ff
- *illus:*
- - Montefiore, Moses, and **12:**271
Muhammad ibn Abdallah **2:**516; **3:**737
Muhammad ibn Farukh **9:**289
- Jerusalem **15:**1207
- Karaite community **5:**1351
- persecutions **9:**1437; **9:**513
Muhammad ibn Isḥāq **10:**489
Muhammad ibn Maslama **10:**488
Muhammad ibn Tāhir **6:**367
Muhammad ibn Tūmart, *see* Abu-Abdullāh Muhammad ibn Tūmart
Muḥammad Shaiṭan **5:**244
Muhajir, Abu Sulayman ibn, *see* DAVID IBN HAJJAR
Muhajir, ibn (fam.), *see* Ibn Muhajir
Muḥannawiyya (tn. Iraq) **8:**1450
Muḥarakh (piyyut) **13:**600
Muhl, J. **8:**47
Muhle (Muhlius), H. **8:**47
Muhlhauser, Frederic **5:**608; **5:**609
MUHR, ABRAHAM **12:**512
- rabbinical office **13:**1453
Muhr, Joseph **12:**513
Muis, Simon Marotte de **8:**47
Muʿizz, Al- (Egy.) **6:**1197
Muʿizz, Al- (Tun.) **2:**153
Mujīr al-Dīn al-ʿUlaymī **9:**278
- Umayyads **15:**1529
Mukachevo (ḥas. dyn.), *see* SHAPIRA
MUKACHEVO (city, Ukr.) **12:**513
- *illus:*
- - text
- - Jewish boy **8:**1107
Mukachevo, Samuel Ẓevi of **15:**275
Mukden (city, China) **11:**860
MUKDONI, A. **12:**514
Mukhā (tn., Yem.), *see* MOCHA
Mukhliṣ, Abdallah **9:**1040
Mukhmās (vill., Isr.), *see* MICHMASH
Mukhtaṣar al-Tawti'a (wk.) **16:**1390
Mukin-zeri (Assyr. ldr.), *see* Nabu-mukin-zeri
Mukish (anc. kdm.) **16:**1498
MUKẒEH (hal. term) **12:**515
- *amoraim* **2:**867
- festivals **6:**1243
Mulabbis (vill., Er. Isr.) **13:**337
Mulaynishmaep (k., Mor.) **3:**812
Mulay Muhammad (sult., Mor.) **12:**339f
- *illus:*
- - receiving Sir Moses Montefiore **12:**329
Mulay Sheikh (k., Mor.) **16:**365
MULBERRY (bot.) **12:**515
- Italy **2:**402
- plant list **13:**621
MULDER, SAMUEL ISRAEL **12:**516
- *illus:* text
MULE **12:**516
- dietary laws **6:**32
- evolution **6:**1003
Mule Corps (W.W.I.), *see* Zion Mule Corps
Mulfingen (tn., Ger.) **12:**1150
Mulheim (city, Ger.) **6:**264
MULHOUSE (city, Fr.) **12:**517
- Alsace **2:**752ff
- Armleder massacre **3:**483
MULISCH, HARRY **12:**518
Mulla Murad, *see* AKLAR, MORDECAI BEN RAPHAEL
Mulla Or Shrage (cmty. ldr.) **16:**782
Muller, August **8:**47
Muller, F. (book firm) **4:**1239
Muller, Frederick (publ.) **13:**1370
MULLER, HERMAN JOSEPH **12:**518
- Central Europe federation **2:**820
Muller, J.M. **8:**47
Muller, L. Christian **8:**47
MULLER, ROBERT **6:**789
MULT ÉS JÖVŐ (journ.) **12:**519
- Zionism **16:**1121
MULŪK AL-TĀWĀIF (dyn., Sp.) **12:**519
Mumar, *see* HERESY
Mummification, *see* EMBALMING
Munaḥ (cantillation sign) **16:**1455
Munaḥ legarme (cantillation sign) **16:**1440,1455
Munajja ben Ṣadaqa **14:**754
Munch, Andreas **14:**932
Munchik, Eliahu **8:**247
Munday, Anthony **9:**1343
Mundi, I. **6:**207
Mundo Israelita (newsp.) **3:**424; **13:**1040; **16:**640
Mung, Leo **4:**1481
MUNI, PAUL **12:**520
- *illus:*
- - text
- - in *The Last Angry Man* **12:**455
MUNICH (city, Bav.) **12:**521
- Aub, Hirsch **3:**838
- history chart (1285-1938) **8:**766-767
- museums **12:**538
- synagogue **15:**619
- *illus:*
- - text
- - Central Synagogue after *Kristallnacht* **8:**738
- - new synagogue medal **11:**1166
Municipal Courts (Isr.) **9:**633
Municipal unions (govt. legis., Isr.) **9:**622ff
Municipalities, *see* LOCAL GOVERNMENT IN ISRAEL
Muninkhuizen, J. H. **7:**1124
Munis, Isaac Michael **15:**817
MUNK (fam.) **12:**524
- *see also:* HOROWITZ; Theomim
Munk, Alois **16:**1165
Munk, Eli (r., Br.) **12:**524
Munk, Elias (r., Ger.) **12:**524
Munk, Elie (r., Fr.) **12:**524
Munk, Ezra **12:**524
MUNK, HERMANN **12:**524
Munk, Immanuel **12:**525
MUNK, KAJ **12:**525
Munk, Leo **12:**525
Munk, Michael **12:**524
MUNK, SOLOMON **12:**525
- Alliance Israélite **2:**650
- Antibi, Jacob **3:**58
- Damascus Affair **5:**1251
- history chart **8:**766-767
- Jewish scholarship **16:**575
- linguistic literature **16:**1391
Munk, Zevi Hirsch **13:**647
Munka (fam.), *see* HOROWITZ
Munka, Zalman **8:**984
Munkacz (ḥas. dyn.), *see* SHAPIRA
Munkács (city, Ukr.), *see* MUKACHEVO
MUNKÁCSI, BERNÁT **12:**526
MUNKÁCSI, ERNŐ **12:**527
Munster (tn., Fr.) **2:**752
Munsterus, *see* MUENSTER, SEBASTIAN
Munthe, Axel **8:**251
Muntinge, Herman **8:**47
MUNTNER, SUESSMANN **1:**34
Munweis, Paula, *see* Ben Gurion, Paula

MUQADDIM (tit.) **12:**527
- community **5:**815
- Spain **15:**230
Muqays (vill., Transj.) **7:**251; **9:**597
Muqdadiya (tn., Iraq) **8:**1450
Muqtadi, Al- **14:**1136
Muqtadir, Al- **2:**42
- exilarchate **6:**1029
- employment restrictions **14:**886
MURABBA'AT SCROLLS **12:**527
- deeds of sale **2:**396
- letters **11:**56
- papyrus **16:**658
- *illus*
- - *Shema* fragment **14:**1371
- *see also:* DEAD SEA SCROLLS
Murad II **16:**1531
Murad III **16:**1538
- Abenaes, Solomon **9:**287
Murad IV **16:**1537-8
- Ereẓ Israel **9:**287
Murad, Arieh **8:**1443; **15:**906
Murād, Mikhael **9:**1041
Murad Bey **8:**231
Muradov, Gershon **12:**479
MURASHU'S SONS (fam.) **12:**529
- banking **16:**1271
Muraviev, Kosta **4:**1488
Muraviev, Nikita **5:**1451
MURCIA (city, Sp.) **12:**530
Murda of Ginzburg **11:**358
Murder, *see* HOMICIDE
Murer, Franz **16:**300
- Neo-Nazism **12:**956
Murex (zool.) **13:**472
Muristan market (Jer.) **9:**1426
MURMELSTEIN, BENJAMIN **12:**531
Murner, Beatus **7:**1101
Murner, Thomas **8:**47
- *haggadah*, illustrated **7:**1101
Murphy, Robert **2:**617
Murrār, Mustafa **9:**1042
Murray, A.A. **15:**208
Murshid al-Kāfī, al- (wk.) **16:**1359,1387
Muršili I (Hittite k.) **8:**788; **16:**1497
Muršili II (Hittite k.) **8:**788
Murtaji, General **9:**408
MURVIEDRO (city, Sp.) **12:**531
Mūsā al-ʿAlamī **9:**1033; **9:**1371
Musa ben Eleazer **6:**1197; **13:**50
Musaeus (myth. seer) **3:**645
MUSAF (litur.) **12:**532
- *Adon Olam* **2:**296
- festivals **6:**1238ff
- liturgical variations **11:**393ff
- priestly blessing **13:**1061
- sacrifice **14:**610
- Temple **15:**974
- *illus:*
- - Rosh Ha-Shanah **14:**306
- *mus. notations:*
- - *mi-Sinai niggunim* **12:**151
- *see also:* AMIDAH
Mūsā ibn Isrāīl al Tabib al-Kūfī **10:**1285
Musa Kazim al-Husseini, *see* Husseini, Musa Kazim al-
Musaphia, Jacob **10:**988
MUSAR HASKEL (poem) **12:**534
Musar Literature, *see* ETHICAL LITERATURE
MUSAR MOVEMENT **12:**534
- Concepts
- - ethics **6:**941
- - repentance **14:**77
- - righteousness **14:**183
- Personalities
- - Blaser, Isaac **4:**1072
- - Dessler, Elijah Eliezer **5:**1564
- - Finkel, Nathan Zevi **6:**1291
- - Joffen, Abraham **10:**142
- - Moses Isaac **12:**430
- - Salant, Joseph Sundel **14:**673
- - Salanter, Israel **11:**279
- - Shabbateanism **14:**1248
- - Slobodka **14:**1668; **16:**769
- - Volozhiner, Ḥayyim **16:**218
- *see also:* MAGGID
Musayyab, Al- (tn., Iraq) **8:**1450
Muscatine (city, Ia.) **8:**1437
Musculus, Gerhard, *see* Meuschen, Gerhard
Musée d'Art Juif (Paris) **12:**543
Muṣeiri, Nissim **14:**1186
Muselevitsh, Iser, *see* TOLUSH
MUSELMANN (Nazi term) **12:**537
Musetto (fam.) **16:**118
Musetto, Salomon **14:**354
Museu Luso-Hebraico Abraham Zacuto (Port.) **15:**1213
Museum of Jewish Ceremonial Objects (N.Y.) **5:**905; **10:**96
Museum of Man and his Work (Tel Aviv) **12:**553
Museum of Musical Instruments (Jer.) **12:**551
Museum of Natural History (Jer.) **2:**451; **12:**552
Museum of the Temple (U.S.) **12:**544
MUSEUMS **12:**538
- *Contents:*
- - Introduction **12:**538
- - In Eastern Europe **12:**539
- - After the Holocaust **12:**540
- - In Western Europe **12:**543
- - In North and South America **12:**544
- - In Israel **12:**551
- Babylon **16:**1505
- folklore **6:**1396
- Israel **9:**1013
- Lieben, Salomon Hugo **11:**216
- Nazis **13:**974
- taxation **15:**872
- Toledo **15:**1206
- Tomar **15:**1213
- *illus:*
- - text
- - Amsterdam, Anne Frank House **7:**53
- - Eisenstadt, Wolf Museum **6:**547
- - En-Harod, Mishkan la-Ommanut **6:**792
- - Jerusalem
- - - Israel Museum **3:**354; **9:**951,1010; **11:**1460; **14:**267, 1061-1068, 1445
- - - Rockefeller Museum **3:**350; **9:***fcg.* 1534; **14:**212
- - - Shrine of the Book **3:**631; **5:**1397
- - - Yad Vashem Memorial Hall Fig. 110 3-ART
- - Loḥamei ha-Getta'ot, Ghetto Fighters' House **7:**546; **11:**463
- - Prague **13:**973
- - Tel-Aviv, Mokady exhibition **12:**224
- - Yad Mordekhai **16:**696
- - Zenica synagogue **16:**882
- *see also:* SCULPTURE
Mushāʿ (vill. ownership, Er. Isr.) **9:**1021
Mushnanov, Nikola **4:**1486; **11:**1566
Musher, Sidney **5:**385
Mushezib-Marduk **5:**331
Mushkanites (sect) **16:**868
Mushka of Qum (sect. ldr.) **11:**1422; **13:**309
Mushkin, Ilya **12:**54; **12:**56
MUSROOMS (bot.) **12:**553
- plant list **13:**621
Mushtamil, al- . . . (wk.) *see Kitāb al-Mushtamil ʿalā* . . .
MUSIC **12:**554
- *Contents:*
- - Introduction **12:**555
- - - Written Sources of Direct and Circumstantial Evidence **12:**556
- - - Material Relics and Iconography **12:**557
- - - Notated Sources **12:**557
- - - Oral Tradition **12:**558
- - History **12:**559
- - - Biblical Period **12:**559
- - - Second Temple Period **12:**565
- - - The Emergence of Synagogue Song **12:**566
- - - The Roots of Synagogue Song in the Near Eastern Communities **12:**571
- - - Music of the Medieval Diaspora (c. 950-1500) **12:**590
- - - The Formation of Concepts of Jewish Music (12th-14th Centuries) **12:**598
- - - The Consolidationn of Regional Styles **12:**606
- - - Migration and Blending of Musical Styles (c. 1500-1750/1800) **12:**612
- - - Modern Times **12:**636
- - Folk Music **12:**664
- - Music in Modern Ereẓ Israel **12:**668
- General
- - Cantatas, Choral Works **5:**123
- - folklore **6:**1384
- - Folk Music society **15:**57
- - Israel Philharmonic Orchestra **9:**1072
- - Moscato, Judah **12:**357
- - phonograph records **13:**1617
- - Profiat Duran **6:**300
- Locations
- - Adrianople **2:**311
- - Amsterdam **2:**904
- - Balkans **7:**882
- - India **8:**1359
- - Iraq **8:**1458
- - Israel **9:**1006; **9:**1008
- - Italy **9:**1142ff
- - Kurdistan **10:**1299
- - North Africa **16:**1257
- Communal Traditions
- - Ḥasidism **7:**1402ff
- - Ladino **10:**1351
- - Karaite **10:**783
- - Kazimierz dynasty **10:**858
- - Yemenites **16:**756ff
- Themes
- - *Akedah* **2:**486
- - Book of Lamentations **10:**1375
- - Jerusalem **9:**1589; **9:**1590
- - Psalms, Book of **13:**1327; **13:**1329
- - *see also individual biblical figures, themes*
- Religious and Liturgical
- - Algazi's collection **2:**610
- - Al-Ḥarizi's writings **2:**628
- - cantillation **5:**128
- - choir **5:**486
- - *ḥazzanut* **7:**1543
- - Idelsohn, Abraham Zvi **8:**1224
- - Lewandowski, Louis **11:**167
- - *mi-Sinai niggunim* **12:**151
- - *maqāma* **11:**937
- - masoretic accents **11:**1098
- - *nusaḥ* **12:**1283
- - Obadiah the Norman Proselyte **12:**1307
- - Shmuel Bukh **14:**1426
- - *shtayger* **14:**1463ff
- - Talmud melody **15:**753
- Liturgical Melodies
- - *Aleinu le-Shabbe'aḥ* **2:**559ff
- - Amen **2:**804
- - *Amidah* **2:**845ff
- - *Haggadah* **7:**1103
- - *Kaddish* **10:**662
- - *Kedushah* **10:**876
- - *Kol Nidrei* **10:**1167
- - *Lekhah Dodi* **11:**6ff
- - *Ma'oz Ẓur* **11:**909
- - *Yigdal* **16:**835
- Ancient Period
- - Bible **4:**937
- - Korahites in Temple **10:**1191
- - levites **15:**952
- - poetry, biblical **13:**671ff
- - prophets **13:**1158
- - psalmody **13:**1316
- - sacrifice **14:**610
- - Temple **15:**978
- *Halakhah*
- - Maimonides **11:**763
- - mourning **15:**1124
- - *Omer* period **12:**1386
- - Rabbinic attitude **12:**598
- *illus:*
- - text
- - concert at Caesarea's Roman theater **9:**1007
- - David inspired by the muse Melodia **4:**947
- - David playing harp **14:**911
- - first orchestra in Ereẓ Israel **9:**1007
- - Israel Philharmonic Orchestra **9:**1071
- - J.L.B. pipers and drummers **14:**1038
- - King Solomon and minstrel **15:**99
- - Mendelssohn playing for Goethe **11:**1327
- - Molodechno school orchestra **12:**233
- - Moscow Jewish folk music society, minute book **3:**380
- - Persian bridegroom playing a *tar* **11:**1036
- - *Porta Accentuum* (1715) **5:**128,129
- - Purim jesters **13:**1402
- - Rubinstein, Artur **14:**374
- - Warshawski's *Yudishe Folkslider* **16:**354
- - Zimriyyah concert **9:**1010
- *mus. notations;*
- - text
- - Ḥasidic *niggunim* **7:**1427-1432
- - *Ha-Tikvah* anthem **7:**1471
- - *Ma oz Ẓur* **11:**911
- - "March of the Jewish National Guard in Warsaw" **13:**733
- - *Pirkei Avot* **15:**753
- - psalmody
- - - Djerba tradition **13:**1329
- - - Frankfort tradition **13:**1329
- - - Psalm 95 **13:**1331
- - - Psalms, chanting rites **9:**1143-1145
- - Sabbath and *Havdalah zemirot* **16:** 987-988
- - Sabbath morning prayers **12:**1283
- - Salome de' Rossi's *Madrigaletti* **14:**319
- - Song of the Sea **14:**1070
- - Yemenite melodies **16:** 749-750
Music, Cantorial, *see* ḤAZZAN
Music, Liturgical, *see* ḤAZZAN
MUSICIANS **12:**678
- levites **13:**1088
- *illus:*
- - Ashurbanipal feasting **12:**1169
- - *Barcelona Haggadah* **11:***fcg.* 1131; **12:**602
- - Ben Sira on **12:**574
- - Bernstein, Leonard, conducting the Israel Philharmonic Orchestra **4:**687
- - double pipe player **12:**567
- - embroidered *sukkah* hanging **15:***fcg.* 494
- - Frankfort bridal procession

11:1027
-- Gallichi, Volunio, cantata (1786) **5:**123,125
-- Hezekiah's tribute to Sennacherib **12:**573
-- incense stand, Ashdod **12:**568
-- Israel stamps **9:**844-845
-- Jubal **10:**323
-- Lyre players, Nineveh **12:**568
-- marriage scene **11:***fcg.* 1003; **12:**622
-- *Vatican Arba'ah Turim* **12:**602
-- Wieniawski brothers **16:**505
Musicology, *see* MUSIC
Musicology, International Society of **2:**278
MUSIL, ALOIS **12:**715
Musk (bot.) **8:**1311
Muskegon (city, Mich.) **11:**1500
Muskmelon (bot.) **11:**1243
- *illus:*
-- harvesting in the Arabah **12:**1294
Muskogee (city, Okla.) **12:**1354
Muslim (Musl. writ.) **7:**1051
Muslim ben Murjān (Samar. writ.), *see* Meshalma ben Murjān
Muslim Brotherhood (soc.) **9:**919
Muslim-Christian Society (soc.) **9:**457
Muslim Higher Council **9:**919
Muslim Quarter (Jer.) **9:**1516
Muslims, *see* Arabs; ISLAM
Muslims, New, *see* JADID AL-ISLAM
Muslims in Israel **9:**917
- geographical distribution **9:**570ff
- health services **9:**992ff
- *illus:*
-- Church of St. Anne, Jer. **9:**1453
-- Eshkol, Levi, meeting with leaders after Six-Day War **9:**410
-- Hebron pilgrims setting out for Mecca **9:**918
-- holy places **8:**923,931
-- Kafr Kamā mosque **9:**920
-- Nabi Mūsā pilgrimage **9:**920
-- Shari'a Court **9:**640
- *tables:* **9:**491
-- mortality and birth rates, 1927-39 **9:**701
-- population figures, 1922-1936 **9:**717
MUSOLINO, BENEDETTO **12:**716
- Zionism **16:**1155
Musrara (qtr., Jer.) **9:**1459,1495
- *illus:*
-- warning notice of Jordanian border **9:**1489
Muṣri River, *see* EGYPT, BROOK OF
Mussafia, Abraham Ḥai **12:**717
MUSSAFIA, ADOLFO **12:**716
MUSSAFIA, BENJAMIN BEN IMMANUEL **12:**717
MUSSAFIA, ḤAYYIM ISAAC **12:**717
Mussafiah, Jacob **5:**1010; **12:**64, 1359
MUSSERT, ANTON ADRIAAN **12:**717
Musset, Alfred de **13:**1492
MUSSOLINI, BENITO **12:**718
- Al-Aqṣā Mosque **9:**1473
- fascism **6:**1187
- Italy **9:**1132
- Jews **8:**741
Mussolini, Edda **12:**718
Mustafa I (Ott. sult.) **9:**287
Mustafa II (Ott. sult.) **9:**290
Mustafa III (Ott. sult.) **16:**1538
Mustafī, Al- (Abbasid caliph) **2:**43
Mustalḥaq, Al- (wk.), *see Kitāb al-Mustalḥaq*
Mutanṣir, Al- (11th cent., caliph) **15:**1302
Mustanṣir, Al- (13th cent., caliph) **2:**43; **5:**61
MUSTAʿRAB, MUSTAʿRABS (J. cmty.) **12:**719
- Cairo **5:**29
- Israel community **9:**504
MUSTARD (bot.) **12:**720
- plant list **13:**621
- spices **15:**269
Mustaṣim, Al- (Abbasid caliph) **2:**43; **5:**61
Musu Garsas (journ.) **16:**833
Muṣur River, *see* EGYPT, BROOK OF
Musy, Jean-Marie **8:**907
MUSZKAT, MARION (Max) **12:**720
Muʿtadhid, Al- **16:**1279
Mutahhar, Al- **16:**742
Muʿtamid, al, *see* Abbad III
Muʿtaṣim (Abbasid caliph) **14:**732
Mutawakkil, Al- (9th cent.) **2:**42; **6:**216; **8:**1445
Mutawakkil, Al (15/16th cent.) **2:**43
Muʿtazilites (Isl. gr.) **10:**702ff
- *see also:* KALAM
MUTER (Mutermilch), MELA **12:**720
Mutilation (of corpse) **3:**931
MUTNIK, ABRAHAM **12:**721
- *illus:*
-- fellow Bundists **4:**1499
Muttam (tn., Ind.) **5:**624
Mutua Agricola (coop.) **3:**431
Mutual Aid Societies, *see* FRATERNAL SOCIETIES
Mutualista Israelita del Uruguay (orgn.) **16:**12
Mutzig (tn., Fr.) **2:**754
Muwatalli (Hittite k.) **8:**788
Muwāzana, Al- . . . (wk.), *see Kitāb al-Muwāzana Bayn* . . .
MUYAL, AVRAHAM **12:**721
Muze'on ha-Areẓ (journ.) **1:**newsp. list
Muzikalisher Pinkas (journ.) **12:**658
Mycenae (tn., anc. Gr.) **13:**940
Mycology (sci.) **7:**941
Myer, Elkan B. **12:**722
Myer, Harry **16:**973
Myer, Jacob **16:**162
Myer, Lawrence **15:**316
MYER, MORRIS **12:**721
- *Zeit, Die* **16:**973
MYER, SIDNEY BAERSKI **12:**722
Myerlin, David F. **8:**47
Myers, Abraham C. **6:**1361
MYERS, SIR ARTHUR MELZINER **12:**722
MYERS, ASHER ISAAC **10:**314
Myers, Bernard **12:**1130
MYERS, CHARLES SAMUEL **12:**722
- psychology **13:**1344
Myers, Edmund **11:**1554
MYERS, GUSTAVUS (hist.) **12:**723
Myers, Gustavus Adolphus (polit.) **12:**726; **14:**160
Myers, Herman **14:**920
Myers, Hyman **13:**1422
Myers, J. (writ.) **5:**450
Myers, J. E. (r., N.Z.) **12:**1128
Myers, John (mer.) **12:**725
Myers, Joseph (freemason) **7:**124; **16:**162
Myers, Julius (Eng.) **6:**342
MYERS, LAWRENCE E. (Lon) **12:**723
MYERS, SIR MICHAEL **12:**724
MYERS, MORDECAI **12:**724
- Buffalo Jewry **4:**1465
- *illus:* text
MYERS, MOSES (mer.) **12:**724
- Norfolk **12:**1215
- *illus:*
-- text
-- Norfolk home **12:**1216
Myers, Moses (r.) **11:**474
MYERS, MYER (artisan) **12:**725
- New York City **12:**1067
- *illus:*
-- text
-- silver tankard **7:**741
Myers, Myer (stlr., Can.) **12:**284
MYERS, SAMUEL **12:**726
- Richmond **14:**160
- Virginia **16:**163
- *illus:* text
Myers, Stanley C. **11:**1478
Myers Cohen, Abraham, *see* Cohen, Abraham Myers
Myerson, Golda, *see* MEIR, GOLDA
Myerson, Michael **12:**1032
"My Friends" (paint., Soyer) **15:**217
Mylitta (deity) **13:**1244
Mylius, Andreas **8:**47
MYRRH (bot.) **12:**727
- balsam **4:**143
- incense and perfumes **8:**1311ff
- plant list **13:**621
- *illus:* text
- *see also:* LAUDANUM
MYRTLE (bot.) **12:**728
- *havdalah* ceremony **7:**1482
- *hoshanot* **8:**1029
- plant list **13:**621
- *see also:* FOUR SPECIES
MYSH, MICHAEL **12:**729
Mysia (reg., As. M.) **3:**747
Myśl Karaimska (period) **10:**776
Mysticism
- anthropomorphism **3:**56
- antinomianism **3:**68
- Maimonidean controversy **11:**747ff
- music **12:**580
- Neoplatonism **12:**960
- sages **14:**650
- study circles **15:**457
- *see also:* KABBALAH; MERKABAH MYSTICISM
Mysticism, Muslim **9:**97,1576
Myszkinski, Hezekiah Joseph **10:**1282
MYTH, MYTHOLOGY **12:**729
- *aggadah* **2:**356
- Anath **2:**926
- demons, demonology **5:**1521
- fiction, Hebrew **6:**1268
- Flood, the **6:**1351
- folklore **6:**1377
- idolatry **8:**1234
- Kabbalah **10:**556
- Kaufman's views **16:**1350/
- Paradise **13:**80
- Samson narratives **14:**773
- seal patterns **14:**1073
- biblical ethics **6:**935
- Sumerian literature **16:**1490
Mytilene, Duke of, *see* ABENAES, SOLOMON
MZAB (oases, Alg.) **2:**614; **3:**49ff **12:**730

N

NAAMAH (dau., Lamech) **12:**733
- Tubal-Cain **15:**1418
NAAMAH (w., Solomon) **12:**733
Naamah (demon) **5:**1530; **11:**247
NAAMAN (bib. fig.) **12:**733
- *illus:*
- - bathing in the Jordan **11:**34
- - Elisha and **10:**1021
Na'aman (riv., Isr.) **2:**223; **9:**128
Naaman, Lionel **7:**148
NA'AN (kib., Isr.) **12:**734
- statistics **1:**place list
Naar (fam.) **15:**1534
NAAR, DAVID **12:**735
- Trenton **15:**1375
- *illus:* text
NAARAH (Naaran; tn., Er. Isr.) **12:**735
- art **3:**521
- *mizraḥ* **12:**181
- synagogues **15:**598ff
- statistics **1:**place list
- *illus:* text
Naarden (tn., Neth.) **3:**167
Naʿari, Moses ben Judah, *see* NAGARI, MOSES BEN JUDAH
Na'aseh ve-Nishma (journ.) **5:**219
Naasenes (sect) **7:**638
Nāb (vill., Golan) **13:**1533
Nabaiāte (tribe, Er. Isr.), *see* NEBAIOTH
NABAL (bib. fig.) **12:**736
- Abigail **2:**73; **2:**74
- Carmel **5:**184
- in the arts **5:**1334
- *illus:* text
NABATEANS (anc. people) **12:**739
- *Contents:*
- - Nabateans and the Jews of the Second Temple **12:**740
- - Nabateans and Herod and his House **12:**742
- agriculture **2:**397
- Alexander Yannai **16:**715
- Antipater II **3:**77ff
- archaeology **3:**328
- Avedat **3:**942
- Herod **8:**635
- Nebaioth **12:**910
- Negev **12:**929
- Petra **13:**342
- Pompey's settlement **9:**120
- script **2:**686
- *illus:*
- - text
- - Avedat (plan) **3:**943
- - irrigation methods **2:**397,399
Nabi Danyal (tomb, Iran) **14:**1483
Nabigha al-Dhubyani, al, *see* Dhubyani, al-Nabigha al
Nabī Mūsā (tomb, Er. Isr.) **8:**935; **9:**919
- *illus.*
- - general view **9:**99
- - Jerusalem pilgrimage **9:**920
Nabi Musa (Arab. fest.), *see* Nebi Musa
Nabī Rūbīn (tomb, Er. Isr.) **8:**935
Nabī Sabālan (tomb, Er. Isr.) **8:**936
Nabī Ṣaliḥ (Musl. prophet) **9:**922
Nabi Samuīl (loc., Er. Isr.) **14:**785
- Beeroth **4:**383
- Estori ha-Parḥi **9:**279
- Six-Day War **14:**1629
Nabī Shuʿayb (loc., Er. Isr.) **8:**936; **10:**886
- *illus:*
- - Druze celebration **8:**933; **10:**886
- - Eshkol inspecting Druze honor guard **9:**927
- - tomb of Jethro **10:**20
Nabi Yūshaʿ, al- (fort., Er. Isr.) **15:**1316; **16:**309
Nabla (string instru.), *see Nevel*
NABLUS (city, Er. Isr.) **12:**744
- Crusader period **9:**267; **9:**268; **9:**272
- Fatimid period **9:**264
- Gerizim shrine **7:**438
- Greek literature **7:**893
- human geography **9:**587ff
- Mamluk period **9:**278
- Ottoman period **9:**283ff
- Roman city **9:**239
- Samaritans **5:**1140; **14:**731ff
- soap industry **9:**707
- *illus:*
- - text
- - Caracalla coin **5:**157
- - general view **9:**578
- *see also:* SHECHEM
Nabonassar (k., Babyl.), *see* Nabunasir
NABONIDUS (k., Babyl.) **12:**745
- Arabia **3:**233
- Cyrus **5:**1184
- Mesopotamia **16:**1505
- Tema **15:**940
- Ur **16:**2, 3
- *see also:* NEBUCHADNEZZAR
Nabonidus, Prayer of (Dead Sea text), *see Prayer of Nabonidus*
Nabopolassar (k., Babyl.) **5:**331; **12:**912; **16:**1504
NABOTH (bib. fig.) **12:**746
- Ahab **4:**13; **5:**881
- Jezebel **10:**100
- vineyard **2:**391; **10:**101
- *illus:* text
Nabulsi, Suleiman al- **9:**1033
Nabulusī, ʿAbd al-Ghanī ben Ismā'il al-, *see* ʿAbd al-Ghanī ben Ismā'il al-Nabulusī
Nabu-mukin-zeri (Assyr. ldr.) **16:**1503
Nabu-nadin-zer (k., Babyl.) **11:**1389
Nabunasir (k., Babyl.) **16:**1503*ff*
Naçan, Moses, *see* MOSES NATHAN
Nacan del Gabay, *see* Falaquera, Nathan ben
Nácar Fuster, E. **4:**879
Nachemson, Joseph **15:**329
NACHÉZ, TIVADAR **12:**701
Nachimowicz, F. **16:**1219
Nachlas, Sidney **15:**316
Nachlas, Wolf, *see* ALEXEYEV, ALEXANDER
Nachman ben Nathan **11:**811
NACHMANOVICH (Nachmanowicz; fam.) **12:**747
Nachmanovich, Chwalka **12:**748
Nachmanovich, Isaac (younger) **12:**748
Nachmanovich, Mordecai **12:**748
Nachmanowicz, Isaac (elder) **15:**606
Nachmansohn, David **4:**1032
NACHOD (tn., Cz.) **12:**749
NACHOD, JACOB **12:**749
NACHOD, OSKAR **8:**549
Nacht, I. **14:**392
Nacht, Jacob **6:**1371; **13:**1496; **14:**392
Nacht, Józef, *see* Prutkowski, Józef
Nacht und Nebel (Nazi terror campaign), *see* "Night and Fog"
Nacogdoches (city, Tex.) **15:**1034
Nacub (moneyer) **12:**60
NADAB (bib. fig., pr.) **12:**750
- fire offering **6:**1304
- Gibbethon **7:**549
- intoxication **6:**238
- mourning rites **13:**1081
- sacrificial procedure **11:**142
- *illus:* text
NADAB (bib. fig., k.) **12:**751
- Baasha **4:**13
- chronological chart **8:**766-767
- history **8:**595
Nadab (Nadan; s. of Ahikar) **2:**460; **2:**461
NADAF, ABRAHAM ḤAYYIM **12:**751
Nadas, Alexander **11:**1201
NADAV, ẒEVI **12:**751
Naddal (zool.) **5:**283
NADEL, ARNO **12:**752
Nadel, M.J. **15:**827
NADEL, SIEGFRED FREDERICK **12:**753
NADELMAN, ELIE **12:**753
- *illus:*
- - text
- - "Man in Open Air" (sculp.) **14:**1062
Nadi, M. **12:**854
NADIR (tribe, Arab.) **12:**754
- Arabia **3:**234; **3:**235
- Khaybar **10:**942
- Muhammad **12:**510ff
- Qurayza **13:**1436
NADIR, MOSHE **12:**755
NĀDIR SHAH (k., Pers.) **12:**755
Nadjar (fam.), *see* NAJAR
NADLER, MARCUS **12:**756
Nadn, see DOWRY
NADSON, SEMYON YAKOVLEVICH **14:**516
NADVORNAYA (Nadwórna; city, Ukr.) **12:**756
- Shabbateanism **14:**1251
Naegelsbach, Carl W.E. **8:**47
NAEH, BARUKH BEN MENAHEM **12:**1466
Nafah (Nafat; bibl. term) **6:**172
Nafari (fam.), *see* Najari
Nafis ben Daud al-Tabrizi **15:**693
Nafnes (r.) **2:**594
NAFTALI, PEREZ (Fritz) **12:**756
- *illus:*
- - proclamation of the State of Israel **4:**513
Naftalin, Arthur **12:**37
Naftulski, Noah **9:**1062
Nafusi (r.) **2:**594
Nafusi, Isaac (Nafuci; astron.), *see* NIFOCI, ISAAC
Nafusid (tribe, N. Afr.) **8:**1149
Nagara (city, Sp.), *see* NÁJERA
NAGARI, MOSES BEN JUDAH **12:**757
NAGASAKI (city, Jap.) **12:**757
- Japan **9:**1280
NAGEL, ERNEST **12:**757
Nagel, J. A. M. **8:**47
Nagel, Moritz **3:**575
NAGID (Isl. cmty, head) **12:**758
- *Contents:*
- - History of the Institution **12:**758
- - Spain **12:**759
- - Kairouan **12:**760
- - Egypt **12:**760
- - Yemen **12:**763
- - North Africa **12:**763
- autonomy **3:**923
- Egypt **5:**814; **6:**492ff
- Mamluk rule **11:**837
- Ottoman Empire **16:**1534
- Samaritans in Egypt **14:**734
- title **15:**1164
NAGIN, HARRY S. **8:**1433
Nagler, Alexander **14:**694
NAGLER, ISADORE **12:**764
Nagler, Shmuel **13:**1340
Nagrin, Daniel **15:**787
Naguib, Mohammad **9:**387; **12:**842
NAGY, ENDRE **8:**1086
Nagy, János **8:**47

Nagy, László Moholy **14:**1069
NAGYBACZONI-NAGY, VILMOS **12:**764
Nagybánya (tn., Transyl.), *see* BAIA-MARE
Nagybecskerek (city, Yug.), *see* ZRENJANIN
Nagykallo (tn., Hung.) **12:**1291
NAGYKANIZSA (city, Hung.) **12:**765
- *illus:* text
Nagykároly (tn., Transyl.), *see* CAREI
Nagymarton (tn., Aus.), *see* MATTERSDORF
Nagymihály (tn., Cz.), *see* MICHALOVCE
Nagysurany (tn., Hung.) **13:**630
Nagyszalonta (tn., Rum.), *see* SALONTA
Nagyszeben (city, Transyl.), *see* SIBIU
Nagyszöllös (tn., Ukr.), *see* Vinogradov
Nagyszombat (city, Cz.), *see* TRNAVA
Nagytapolcsány (tn., Cz.), *see* TOPOLCANY
Nagyvárad (city, Transyl.), *see* ORADEA
NAḤAL (orgn., Isr.) **12:**766
- defense forces **9:**691,692
- I.L.O. **15:**1564
- Jewish National Fund **10:**79
- youth movements **9:**980
- *illus:*
- - text
- - Gerofit founder-members **9:**980
- - Givat Yo'av **9:**578
- - group of soldiers **8:**775
- - Naḥal Gilgal **9:**585
- - Naḥal Snir settlers **9:**554
Nahal . . . (riv.), *see also Wadi*
Naḥalah (mosh., Isr.) **1:**place list
Naḥalah (death anniversary), *see* YAHRZEIT
NAHALAL (mosh., Er. Isr.) **12:**768
- statistics **1:**place list
- *illus:* text
NAHALAL (tn., Er. Isr.) **12:**768
- *nahalolim* **15:**1119
Naḥal Ammud (stream, Isr.) **7:**579; **10:**1032
- human geography **9:**588; **12:**758
- physiography **9:**151; **9:**156
- vine **16:**157
Naḥal Arbel, *see* Arbel River
Naḥal Arugot **6:**741
Naḥalat Israel Ramah (orgn., Er. Isr.) **14:**786
Naḥalat Jabotinsky (mosh., Isr.) **4:**1009; **9:**1186
Naḥalat Shivah (qtr., Jer.)
- foundation **9:**1454
- housing **9:**563
- Jerusalem **9:**1516
- Turks **9:**1457
- Yehoshua Yellin **16:**736
- *illus:*
- - aerial view **9:**1452
- - alleyway **9:**563
Nahalat Yehoshu'a (wk.) **14:**1299
NAḤALAT YEHUDAH (stlmt., Isr.) **12:**769
- human geography **9:**572
- statistics **1:**place list
Naḥalat Yosef (wk.) **2:**251
Naḥal Avivim **9:**165
Naḥal Be'er Sheva (stream, Isr.) **9:**139; **12:**927
Naḥal ben -Hinnom (val., Er. Isr.), *see* GEHINNOM
Naḥal Besor, *see* BESOR, BROOK OF
Naḥal Boker **9:**185
Naḥal Dan, *see* Dan River
Nahal David (stream, Er. Isr.) **6:**743
Naḥal Diklah (mosh., Isr.) **1:**place list
Naḥal Egozim (val., Er. Isr.) **10:**987
- Jerusalem development **9:**1491
- Jerusalem settlement **9:**1459
- Six-Day War **9:**1501
- topography **9:**1515
Naḥal Gerar (stream, Isr.) **12:**927
Naḥal Geshur (stlmt., Golan) **1:**place list; **13:**1534
Naḥal Gilgal (kib., Isr.) **1:**place list
- *illus:*
- - general view **9:**585
Naḥal Golan (stlmt., Golan) **1:**place list; **13:**1534
Naḥal ha-Aravah (val., Isr.) **12:**927
Naḥal Ḥaderah (stream, Isr.) **7:**1048
Naḥal Harod, *see* Harod
Naḥal Hermon, *see* Naḥal Sion
Naḥal Ḥever (loc., Isr.) **2:**689; **5:**1401; **11:**56
- *illus:*
- - Bar Kokhba papyrus **8:**647
Naḥal Ḥevron (val.) **9:**140; **12:**927
Naḥali'el (mosh., Isr.) **9:**548; **9:**572
Naḥali'el (journ.) **1:**newsp. list
Naḥal Iron (loc. Isr.) **2:**387
Naḥal Kalliah (stlmt., Isr.) **1:**place list; **4:**716
Naḥal Lachish (stream, Isr.) **9:**575ff
Naḥal Mangan, *see* Mangan
Naḥal Massu'ah (mosh., Isr.) **1:**place list
Nahal Mishmar (val., Er. Isr.) **3:**505
Naḥal Neḥushtan, *see* Neḥushtan
Nahalol (loc., Er. Isr.), *see* NAHALAL
NAḤAL OZ (kib., Isr.) **12:**769
- statistics **1:**place list
Naḥal Paran (Isr.), *see* Paran, Nahal
Naḥal Senir (stream, Er. Isr.) **10:**192
Naḥal Shikmah (riv., Isr.) **15:**1564
Naḥal Sinai (kib., Isr.) **1:**place list
Naḥal Sion (stream, Er. Isr.) **10:**192,197
Naḥal Sorek (val., Isr.), *see* SOREK, VALLEY OF
Naḥal Sorek Nuclear Center (Isr.) **9:**967
- *illus:*
- - atomic reactor **9:**796
Naḥal Tanninim (stream, Isr.) **9:**579
Naḥal Timna, *see* TIMNA
Nahal Yam (kib., Isr.) **1:**place list
- *illus:*
- - tomato growing **12:**767
Naḥal Zalmon (stream, Isr.) **7:**579
Naḥal Zered (Transj.) **9:**595
Naḥal Ẓofar (kib., Isr.) **1:**place list
Naḥam (mosh., Isr.) **1:**place list
Naḥamani, *see* NAḤMANIDES
Naḥamu, Shabbat, see Shabbat Naḥamu
Nahant (tn., U.S.) **11:**1112; **11:**622
Nahara u-Feshateh (wk.) **4:**1388
Naharay ben Nissim **7:**223
Naharayim (loc., Isr.) **10:**196
- *illus:*
- - electric power plant **9:**790
NAHARIYYAH (city, Isr.) **12:**769
- human geography **9:**580
- statistics **1:**place list
- *illus:*
- - emergency stamps (1948) **15:**334
NAHASH (bib. fig.) **12:**770
- Abigail **2:**74
- Twelve Tribes' war **15:**1384
Naḥash (divination) **6:**116
Nahavand (tn., Iran), *see* NEHAVEND
Nahawendi, Anan ben Moses **10:**1048
NAH'ĀWENDĪ, BENJAMIN BEN MOSES AL- **12:**771
- Baṣīr, al-, Joseph **4:**301
- Karaite doctrine **10:**767
Naḥem (litur.) **3:**939; **9:**1033
Naḥḥālīn (loc., Jor.) **9:**1033
Naḥlat Aḥim (sub., Jer.) **9:**1472; **9:**1525
Naḥlat Binyamin (qtr., Tel Aviv) **15:**920
Naḥlat Shivah (qtr., Jer.), *see* Naḥalat Shivah
Naḥli'el (mosh., Er. Isr.), *see* Naḥali'el
NAḤMAN BAR RAV HUNA (amora) **12:**772
NAḤMAN BEN ISAAC (amora) **12:**772
- *resh kallah* **14:**83
Naḥman ben Isaac (Pol. mer.), *see* Isaakovich, Naḥman
NAḤMAN BEN JACOB (amora) **12:**773
- controversies **5:**891
- Kiss of Death **5:**1427
Naḥman ben Moses **11:**345; **12:**776
Naḥman ben Samuel (amora) **14:**813
Naḥman ben Samuel of Busk **4:**1536
Naḥman ben Simḥah of Bratslav, *see* NAḤMAN OF BRATSLAV
Naḥmani (amora), *see* ABBAYE
Naḥman ibn Sunbal, *see* Sunbal, Naḥman ibn
NAḤMANIDES **12:**774
- *Contents:*
- - Life **12:**774
- - Works **12:**776
- - As Bible Commentator **12:**777
- - As Halakhist **12:**778
- - In Kabbalah **12:**782
- General
- - Ashkenazi system **3:**721
- - Barcelona disputation **4:**213; **11:**354
- - Christiani, Pablo **5:**505
- - Clement IV **5:**601; **6:**92ff
- - ethical wills **11:**345
- - *hiddushim* **8:**467
- - history chart **8:**766-767
- - Maimonidean controversy **11:**749; **13:**793
- - Raymond de Peñaforte **8:**1329
- - responsa **14:**86
- - *Sefer ha-Bahir* **4:**97
- - *Sefer Yeẓirah* **16:**787
- - Spain **15:**232
- - supercommentaries on **15:**520
- - Talmud commentaries **11:**332
- - travels **9:**273,509,512,1423; **15:**1352
- Scholars
- - Abraham of Posquières **2:**137
- - Adret, Solomon **2:**305,307; **2:**308
- - Al-Bargeloni, Isaac **2:**525
- - Al-Bargeloni, Judah **10:**341
- - Asher ben David **3:**706
- - Ephraim ibn Avi Alragan **6:**814
- - Gerondi, Moses **7:**508
- - Ibn Gaon, Shem Tov **8:**1174
- - Maimonides **11:**766
- - Moses ha-Levi **12:**421
- - Yom Tov Ishbili **16:**847
- Theology and Views
- - *Akedah* **2:**483
- - amulets **2:**911
- - asceticism **3:**683
- - Bible exegesis **4:**893; **11:**325
- - *creatio ex nihilo* **10:**562
- - demons, demonology **5:**1529
- - *devekut* **10:**627
- - eschatology **6:**880ff
- - exile, significance of **7:**287ff
- - Kabbalah **10:**526ff
- - *karet* **10:**789
- - lost property **16:**775
- - messianism **11:**1418
- - miracles **12:**78
- - Moses **12:**400
- - resurrection **14:**102
- - Sambatyon **14:**763
- - *sha'atnez* **14:**1214
- - space and place **15:**219
- - *ẓimẓum* **10:**589
- *illus:*
- - text
- - *Ḥiddushei ha-Torah* **4:**898; **8:**1329
- - Ramban Synagogue, Jerusalem **9:**1443
- - *Sha'ar ha-Gemul* (1490) **8:**1334
NAḤMAN OF BRATSLAV **12:**782
- *Contents:*
- - Life **12:**782
- - As a Spiritual Figure **12:**783
- - Works **12:**784
- - Bratslav Ḥasidism **12:**785
- - Teachings **12:**785
- Aryeh Leib of Shpola **3:**669
- death commemoration **5:**1268
- forgiveness **6:**1435
- grave **15:**1527
- ḥasidic music **7:**1423
- Katz, Aleph **10:**821
- peace **13:**199
- pilgrimage **13:**514
- Savran, Moses Ẓevi **14:**922
- Steinman, Eliezer, on **15:**372
- Sternharz, Nathan **15:**398ff
- stories **16:**809
- travels **15:**1353
- *geneal. table:* **9:**1051
Naḥman of Busk, *see* Naḥman ben Samuel of Busk
NAḤMAN OF HORODENKA **12:**787
- ḥasidic teachings **7:**1407
- Naḥman of Bratslav **12:**782
- Simḥah of Zalozhtsy **14:**1569
- travels **15:**1353
- *geneal. table:* **9:**1051
NAḤMAN OF KOSOV **12:**788
- ḥasidic teachings **7:**1407
Naḥman of Krzywicze **7:**63
Naḥman of Tulchin **12:**785
Nahmias (fam.), *see* ABENDANA
Nahmias, David ibn **8:**1326; **12:**788
Naḥmias, Eliezer Raphael **2:**792
NAHMIAS, IBN (fam.) **12:**788
- Istanbul **9:**1097
NAHMIAS, JOSEPH BEN JOSEPH **12:**789
Nahmias, Samuel ibn (elder) **8:**1326; **12:**788
Nahmias, Samuel ibn (younger) **12:**788
Naḥmias, Don Shem Tov ibn **16:**194
NAHMIJAS, DANILO **16:**891
Naḥmoli, Joseph (18th cent.) **2:**187
Naḥmuli, Joseph (19th cent.) **5:**972
NAHON (fam.) **12:**789
Nahon, Benjamin **12:**789
Nahon, Isaac **12:**789
Nahon, Isaac ben Joseph **12:**789
Nahon, Jonas Benasuli **12:**789
Nahon, Joseph **12:**789
Nahon, Moses (Moise) **12:**789
Nahon, Samuel **11:**803
Nahon, Solomon, of Tetuan **11:**803
NAHOR (bib. fig.; anc. city, Turk.) **12:**789
- Abraham **2:**112
- Mari **11:**981
- Nahur **15:**1014
- patriarchs **13:**182
Nahorites (anc. people) **6:**372
NAHOUM, ḤAIM **12:**791
- Egypt **6:**501
Nahr Abu Fuṭrus (riv., Er. Isr.), *see* YARKON
NAHRAI BEN NISSIM **12:**792
- book trade **4:**1237
Nahr al-ʿAllān (riv., Syr.) **7:**694

Nahr al-ʿAwjā (riv., Isr.) **16:**717ff
Nahr al-Muqattaʿ (riv., Isr.), *see* KISHON
Nahr al-Yahūd (riv., Iraq) **4:**310
Nahr al-Zarqāʾ (riv., Isr.), *see* JABBOK
NAHRAWĀN (tn., Iraq) **12:**792
Nahrays (fam.) **15:**1435
Nahr Barada (Syr. riv.), *see* Amanah
Naḥsholim (kib., Isr.) **1:**place list
NAHSHON (bib. fig.) **12:**792
- *geneal. table;* **5:**1347
Naḥshon (kib., Isr.) **1:**place list
Naḥshon, Operation (War of Indep.) **7:**1073; **9:**363; **9:**689; **16:**308
NAHSHON BAR ZADOK (gaon) **12:**793
- eschatological writings **6:**867
- gaonate families **7:**317
- history chart **8:**766-767
Naḥshonim (kib., Isr.) **1:**place list
NAHUM (bib. fig.) **12:**793
- Minor Prophets **12:**48
- tomb **5:**1268
Nahum (paytan) **13:**591
NAHUM, AARON SASSON BEN ELIJAH **12:**795
NAHUM, ELIEZER BEN JACOB **12:**795
- Azulai, Isaac **3:**1017
Nahum, Ḥayyim **6:**1145
Naḥumai (amora), *see* REḤUMEI
Nahum ben Kanah ibn Gedor (leg. fig.) **10:**734
Nahum ben Moses **13:**714
Nahum ben Simai (amora) **10:**871
Nahum ben Uzziel **7:**926
Nahumck, Nadia, *see* CHILKOVSKY, NADIA
Nahum Commentary (D. S. Scroll), *see Pesher Nahum*
Nahum ha-Ma'aravi **6:**272; **15:**1324
NAHUM THE MEDE **12:**795
Nahum of Chernobyl **5:**393; **6:**182
- Abraham of Ovruch **2:**157
- Savran dynasty **14:**922
- Twersky dynasty **15:**1471
NAHUM OF GIMZO (tan.) **12:**796
- Akiva **2:**488
- Bible interpretation **8:**1417
Nahum of Makarov **15:**1472
Nahum of Stefanesti **7:**305
Nahum of Trisk **15:**1472
Nahumowicz, Isaiah **12:**1480
Naḥutei (schols.), *see* NEḤUTEI
Naian (city, Er. Isr.), *see* AI
Naidich, Judah **12:**1119
NAIDITSCH, ISAAC ASHER **12:**796
- *illus:*
- - Benei Zion meeting **12:**359
- - Biltmore Hotel Conference **15:**1633
Naidus, L. **16:**815
Naiera (city, Sp.), *see* NÁJERA
Nails, Cutting of **8:**1140; **12:**998
Naim (terr., Er. Isr.) **10:**103
- En-Dor **6:**739
Naim, Aziz ben Jonah **10:**437; **13:**319; **15:**906
Naimovich, Isak **4:**1493
Naimovich, Maxim **4:**1494
NAIN (vill., Er. Isr.) **12:**796
Nairobi (city, Ken.) **10:**910
NAJAR (fam.) **12:**797
- Bougie **4:**1274
Najar, David **12:**797
Najar, Judah ben Jacob **12:**797
Najar, Maimon **5:**915 **12:**796
Najar, Mordecai **12:**797
Najar, Nathan ben Maimon **12:**797
NAJARA (fam.) **12:**797
Najara (city, Sp.), *see* NÁJERA
NAJARA, ISRAEL BEN MOSES **12:**798
- Altaras, Joseph **2:**772
- *maqāmāt* **11:**938
- music, Jewish **12:**614
- prosody **13:**1220
- religious poetry **11:**328
- *Yah Ribbon Olam* **16:**702
- *mus. notations:*
- - *Kumi Yonah Yekushah* **12:**623
- - refrain of a *pizmon* **12:**623
Najara, Jacob **12:**798; **14:**1224
Najara, Judah **12:**798
Najara, Levi **12:**797
Najara, Moses (16th cent.) **12:**797
Najara, Moses (17th cent.) **12:**798
Najara, Moses (18th cent.) **12:**798
Najari (fam., Sp.) **15:**1022
NAJDORF, MIKHAIL (Miguel) **12:**799
NAJDUS, LEIB **12:**799
NÁJERA (city, Sp.) **12:**799
NAJĪB AL-DAWLA **12:**800
Najjār, Judah **15:**1172
Najjār, Saadiah **15:**1172
Najm al-Dawla (tit., Iraq) **8:**1186
NAJMAN, JULIJA **16:**889; **16:**891
NAJRAN (tn., Yem.) **12:**800
- Jewish community **16:**741
- Yusuf ʿAs'ar **16:**897ff
Nakai (disciple of Jesus) **10:**15
Nakar, Meir **8:**1469
NAKDIMON BEN GURYON **12:**801
- daughter's perfume basket **5:**980
Nakhl (loc., Sinai) **14:**1605; **14:**1636
Naksh-i Rustam (loc., Mesop.) **16:**669
Nalchik (city, Rus.) **12:**480
NAME, CHANGE OF **12:**802
- Academy on High **2:**208
- folklore **6:**1401
NAMENYI, ERNEST (Erno) **12:**802
NAMES **12:**803
- *Contents:*
- - In the Bible **12:**803
- - In the Talmud **12:**807
- - Medieval Period and Establishment of Surnames **12:**809
- - Modern Times **2:**50; **12:**811
- Alsace-Lorraine Jews **2:**755
- Babylonian influence **16:**1000
- change of **12:**802
- Egypt **6:**487
- Ezra, Yemenite Jews **3:**235
- giving of **4:**1052
- Hellenization **8:**627; **8:**633
- man **11:**842
- Omar, Covenant of **12:**1379
- Torah reading **15:**1253
- *illus:*
- - text
- - Mainz, register of name changes (1808) **7:**484
- - Napoleon's decree re adoption of surnames (1808) **7:**27
Names of God, *see* GOD, NAMES OF
NAMES OF THE LAND OF ISRAEL **9:**108
- *see also:* AMORITES; CANAAN, LAND OF; PHOENICIA
NAMIAS, JEROME **12:**813
Namier, Julia **12:**813
NAMIER, SIR LEWIS **12:**813
NAMIR, MORDEKHAI **12:**815
- *illus:*
- - Eilat road, opening of **9:**380
Namrūd (Namrūdh; leg. fig.), *see* NIMROD
Nanah (Samar. paytan) **14:**753
Nánási, Lovász József **8:**47
NANCY (tn., Fr.) **12:**815
- archives **3:**387
- museums **12:**544
- Ullmann, Salmon **15:**1523
Nanna (deity) **16:**1492
Nansen, Fridtjof **12:**1225
Nansen, Odd **12:**1225
Nansen, Peter **14:**928
Nansen office (immigration agency) **14:**29
NANTES (city, Fr.) **12:**817
- Brittany **4:**1383
Nantua, Simon **14:**829
NAOMI (bib. fig.) **12:**817
- adoption **2:**300
- in the Arts **14:**524
- Ruth, Book of **14:**518ff
- *illus:*
- - in the field of Boaz **4:**1154
- - ninth cent. Bible **9:**1
Naon, Avram, *see* NOM, IBRAHIM
Naor, Uri, *see* Lichtwitz, Hans
Naphish (bib. fig.) **9:**89
NAPHTALI (bib. fig.) **12:**818
- Beth-Shemesh **4:**773
- deer **5:**1457
- Ginnosar plain **7:**579
- Kurdish Jews **10:**1296
- settlement **8:**580; **9:**115
- *illus:*
- - banner and emblem **8:**335
NAPHTALI, TESTAMENT OF **12:**821
- Greek Testament **13:**184
- *see also:* PATRIARCHS, TESTAMENTS OF THE TWELVE
Naphtali ben Abraham **6:**1135
Naphtali ben Azriel of Vilna **3:**727
Naphtali ben Isaac ha-Kohen, *see* KATZ, NAPHTALI BEN ISAAC
Naphtali ben Mansur **16:**1553
Naphtali ha-Kohen **4:**49
Naphtali Herz of Emden **13:**1105
- *illus:*
- - *Sefer ha-Tashbeẓ* (1741) **12:**978
Naphtali Herz of Shargorod **14:**1314
Naphtali Hirz Oettingen of Przemysl **11:**209
Naphtali Range (Er. Isr.) **9:**148
- *illus:*
- - Huleh Valley **9:**207
Naphtali Zevi Ropshitser, *see* ROPSHITSER, NAPHTALI ZEVI
Naphtha (petroleum co., Isr.) **9:**795
Napierski, Stefan **13:**802
Napir-Asu (q., Elam) **14:**1483
Naples (city, Er. Isr.) **12:**745
NAPLES (city, It.) **12:**822
- Abrabanel, Judah **2:**109
- Apulian Jews **3:**227ff
- Gaeta community **7:**253
- history chart (1541) **8:**766-767
- Ibn Yaḥya, David **8:**1207
- Inquisition **8:**1398
- Jewish defense **8:**657
Naples Bible **4:**837; **13:**1306
NAPOLEON BONAPARTE **12:**823
- Acre **2:**224
- Alexandrian community **2:**593
- Alsace-Lorraine Jews **2:**755
- Broglie, Victor-Claude **4:**1401
- consistory organization **5:**907
- freedom of Jews **8:**712ff
- French Jewry **7:**23
- French Revolution **7:**156
- ḥasidic traditions **7:**1397
- hero of folktales **6:**1383
- history chart **8:**766-767
- influence on Heine **8:**271
- Jacob Isaac of Lublin **9:**1228
- Jewish music **12:**640
- Kargau's hymn **10:**790
- maps of Ereẓ Israel **11:**928
- Middle East campaign **9:**304
- Ottoman empire **9:**291
- Sanhedrin, French **14:**840
- Westphalia **16:**474
- *illus:*
- - text
- - Consistory letter re special synagogue service **5:**909
- - decree re adoption of surnames **7:**27; **12:**811
- - medal for emancipation of Westphalian Jews **16:**474
Napoleon III (emp., Fr.)
- Alliance Israélite **2:**649
- Ennery, Jonas d' **6:**792
- Fould, Achille **6:**1445
- Friedland, Natan **7:**184
- Mortara Case **12:**354
"Napoleonchiks" (Isr. Army artillery) **16:**322
Napoleonic Wars (1800-1813) **11:**1555
- *illus:*
- - Jew as a fighter (caric.) **11:**1554
Naqad, see Masoretic dots
NAQUET, ALFRED JOSEPH **12:**825
Naquet, David **5:**206
Naquet-Laroque (sol., Fr.) **11:**1562
NARA (orgn., Pol.) **12:**826
Narâm-Sin (k., Mesop.) **2:**493; **11:**974; **14:**1482; **16:**1490
NARBATA (loc., Er. Isr.) **12:**826
- *see also:* ARBATTA; MA'ANIT
NARBONI (fam.) **12:**827
Narboni, Allal ben Sidun ben Joshua **12:**827
Narboni, André **12:**827
Narboni, David ben Joseph, *see* David ben Joseph of Narbonne
Narboni, Elie **12:**827
Narboni, Georges **12:**827
Narboni, Mordecai **12:**827
Narboni, Moses ben Joshua, *see* MOSES BEN JOSHUA OF NARBONNE
Narboni, Shalom **12:**827
NARBONNE (tn., Fr.) **12:**827
- Abraham ben Isaac **2:**147
- anti-Moor expeditions **5:**1135
- gaonate **7:**324
- Moses ben Joseph ha-Levi **12:**421
- Spanish expulsion **15:**221
- special Purim **13:**1397
Narbutt, Ignacy, *see* Robb-Rosenfarb, Ignacy
Narcisse Levin (clny., Arg.) **3:**430; **3:**431
Narcissus (2/3 cent., bp.) **9:**1406
Narcissus (bot.) **6:**1365
- perfumes **8:**1311
- plant list **13:**623
Nard (spice), *see* SPIKENARD
NARDI, NAHUM **12:**830
Nardi, Shulamit **5:**451
NARESH (tn., Mesop.) **12:**830
- *table;* principal *amoraim* **2:**869
NARKISS, BEZALEL **1:**34
- illuminated manuscripts **3:**652
NARKISS, MORDECHAI **12:**831
- numismatics **12:**1271
- *illus:*
- - Schatz, Boris, and **14:**945
Narkiss, Uzi **13:**48; **14:**1630
- *illus:*
- - Six-Day War, entering Jerusalem **9:**409
Narkiss, Zvi **11:**1167; **15:**1488
Naro (loc., Tun.) **15:**1430; **15:**600
Narodietzky, Nahum, *see* NARDI, NAHUM
Narodnaya Volya (rev. orgn., Rus.) **11:**1148; **16:**1230
Narodna Židovska Svijest (newsp.) **14:**871
Narodniki (gr., Rus.) **3:**124
Národní Rada Židovská (Cz. orgn.), *see* Jewish National Council
Narodowa Demokracja (party, Pol.), *see* ENDECJA
NAROL (tn., Pol.) **12:**831
NAROT, JOSEPH **12:**832

Narragansett (tn., R.I.) **14**:143
Narrative, Hebrew, *see* FICTION, HEBREW
Narseh (3/4 cent., k.) **4**:41
Narses (5th cent.) **15**:1337
Naru Kabaru (riv., Babyl.) **4**:34
Narva (city, Est.) **6**:916ff
NASA, *see* National Aeronautics and Space Administration
Nasā'ī, Al- (9/10 cent., writ.) **7**:1052
NASATIR, ABRAHAM PHINEAS **12**:832
NASAUD (tn., Rum.) **12**:832
Naṣba (site, Er. Isr.), *see* Tells (al-Naṣb)
Naschauer, Julia, *see* Herzl, Julia
Naschitz, Theodor, *see* NACHÉZ, TIVADAR
Nash, Thomas **6**:776
Nash, William M. **15**:301
Nash, W. L. (arch.) **12**:833
Nashāshībī (fam.) **9**:1435; **9**:459; **9**:1474; **9**:1476
Nashāshībī, Is'āf al- **9**:1040
Nashāshībī, Rāghib Bey al-, *see* Rāghib Bey al-Nashāshībī
NASHIM (tal. order) **12**:833
Nashim Ẓadkaniyyot (soc., Ger.) **5**:347
NASH PAPYRUS **12**:833
- Decalogue **5**:1438
- Hellenism **8**:297
- *illus:* text
Nashua (city, N.H.) **12**:1024
Nashville (city, Tenn.) **15**:1009
NASI (tit.; ldr.) **12**:833
- Academy continuation **9**:273
- archisynagogos **3**:336
- Babylonian community **5**:814
- Barcelona documents **4**:209ff
- Bathyra, Sons of **4**:324
- emissaries **14**:1361
- Ferruziel **15**:1201
- Gamaliel ha-Zaken **7**:295
- history 1st-7th century **9**:240ff
- Iraq **8**:1451
- Nagid **12**:758
- Ottoman period **16**:1537
- sages **14**:636; **14**:643
- *ṣarrāf* **14**:887
- Simeon ben Gamaliel II **14**:1556
- title **15**:1164
- Umāyyads **15**:1530
- Usha, Synod of **16**:18
- *zugot* **16**:1233
- *see also:* CHIEFTAIN
Nasi, Beatrice, *see* Nasi, Gracia II
Nasi, Bernardo, *see* Nasi, Samuel
NASI, GRACIA (elder) **12**:836
- boycott of Ancona **2**:942
- conflict of laws dipute **5**:884
- Ibn Lev, Joseph **11**:64; **14**:89
- Istanbul **9**:1090
- medals **11**:1168
- Nasi, Joseph **12**:838ff
- spice trade **15**:270
- Tiberias revival **9**:260
- Trani's responsa **11**:338
- Usque, Abraham **16**:21
- Venice **16**:98
- *illus:* text
Nasi, Gracia II (younger) **12**:836
Nasi, Joseph (15th cent.) **11**:1215
NASI, JOSEPH (16th cent.) **12**:837
- Almosnino, Moses **2**:670
- history chart **8**:766-767
- Ibn Lev, Joseph **11**:64
- Istanbul **9**:1090; **9**:1098
- Nasi, Gracia **12**:836ff
- Ottoman Empire **16**:1535,1552
- Tiberias revival **9**:286
- title **15**:1166
- *geneal. table:* text **12**:838
Nasi, Reyna **12**:837,838
- Istanbul **9**:1090
- printing **2**:951; **13**:1104
Nasi, Samuel **12**:836
Nasi, Sen Boniac **9**:1221
Nasibov, Nikolai **15**:310
NASIELSK (tn., Pol.) **12**:839
- *illus:* text
Nasif el-Yāzijī **4**:864
Nāṣir, al-(12/13 cent., caliph) **2**:43
Nāṣir al-dīn Muhammad ben Khiḍr al-Rūmī al-Jalālī **15**:1359
Nasir-i Khosrau **15**:1358
Nasiriya (tn., Iraq) **8**:1450
Nāṣir Muhammad, al-Malik al-, *see* Muhammad I, Al-Malik al-Nāṣir
NASNA (vill., Rum.) **12**:840
- Targu-Mures **15**:813
Nasrâni (name for Christians), *see* Nazarenes
Nasr-el-Din (shah, Pers.) **13**:316ff
- *illus:*
- - Polak, Jacob **13**:708
Nass (fam.), *see* LEIDESDORFER
Nassau (city, Bahamas) **16**:473
NASSAU (-Usingen; duchy, Ger.) **12**:841
Nassau County (sub., N.Y.C.) **12**:1108
NASSAUER, RUDOLF **6**:785; **6**:790
NASSER, GAMAL ABDUL **12**:841
- Alexandrian Jews **2**:593
- Baghdad Pact **15**:1664
- Ben-Gurion **4**:511
- Hussein **8**:1131; **8**:1132; **14**:1624
- Israel-Egyptian relations **9**:387; **9**:403ff
- Poland's support **13**:787
- Six-Day War **14**:1626ff
- *illus:* text
Nassi, David, *see* Nuñez de Fonseca, Joseph
NASSY, DAVID DE ISAAC COHEN **12**:843
Nasyelsk (tn., Pol.), *see* NASIELSK
Nasz Glos (newsp.) **10**:1172
Nasz Kurjer (period.) **12**:844; **16**:342
Naszod (tn., Rum.), *see* NASAUD
NASZ PRZEGLAD (newsp.) **12**:844
- press **13**:1042
- Zionism **16**:1132
Nata (ẓaddik) **5**:372
Nata ben Menahem Mendel of Shklov, *see* Nathan Nata ben Menahem Mendel of Shklov
Nataf (spice), *see* BALSAM
Natal (city, Braz.) **4**:1327
NATAL (prov., S. A.) **12**:844
- South Africa **15**:184ff
Natan, Zhak **4**:1489
Natanson, Henryk **12**:1455
NATANSON, LUDWIK **12**:845
Natanson, Marc **15**:28
Natanson, Wolf Zelig **12**:845
Natchez (city, Miss.) **12**:154
Natchitoches (city, La.) **11**:517
NATHAN (bib. fig., prophet) **12**:846
- Samuel **14**:784
- Solomon **15**:96ff
- *illus:*
- - text
- - David and **14**:541
- - David and Bath-Sheba **11**:633
Nathan (bib. fig., s. of Bath-Sheba) **4**:321
Nathan (2nd cent. C.E. schol.) **4**:39
Nathan (gaon) **14**:545
Nathan (13th cent., Morav.) **12**:296
Nathan (Ḥas.) **12**:785
NATHAN (fam., Eng.) **12**:847
NATHAN (fam., U.S.) **12**:848
- *geneal. table:* text
NATHAN, ABRAHAM **12**:848
Nathan, Annie, *see* MEYER, ANNIE NATHAN
Nathan, Benjamin **12**:1075
NATHAN, DAVID **12**:849
- Auckland **3**:839
- *illus:*
- - portrait **3**:839
Nathan, Emile **13**:820
NATHAN, ERNESTO **12**:851
- Pius X **13**:572
Nathan, Fernand **13**:1368
Nathan, Sir Frederic Lewis **12**:847
NATHAN, GEORGE JEAN **12**:851
Nathan, Giannetta **14**:314
Nathan, Harry Alfred **12**:853
NATHAN, HARRY LOUIS, BARON **12**:851
NATHAN, HENRY **12**:852
- Canada **5**:111
Nathan, Isaac (physic.), *see* NATHAN, MOREDECAI
NATHAN, ISAAC (comp.) **12**:852
- Braham, John **4**:1290
- Byron **4**:1549
- *illus:* text
Nathan, Isaac Mendes, *see* Nathan, Seixas
Nathan, J. (U.S.) **12**:1218
Nathan, Jacob (Eng.) **11**:858
Nathan, Jonah (mfr., Eng.) **12**:847
NATHAN, JOSEPH EDWARD (N.Z.) **12**:853
- New Zealand **12**:1130
Nathan, Josephine **12**:848
Nathan, L.D. **12**:1130
Nathan, Lemon **11**:858
Nathan, Levi **5**:1597
Nathan, Louis Edward **5**:504
NATHAN, MANFRED **12**:853
Nathan, Sir Matthew **12**:848
Nathan, Maud **12**:848
Nathan, Max H. **8**:1051
Nathan, Meyer (Michael) **12**:847
NATHAN, MORDECAI **12**:854
Nathan, Moses, *see* MOSES NATHAN
Nathan, Moses, of Hamburg **12**:848
NATHAN, MULLA IBRAHIM **12**:854
Nathan, Musa **12**:854
Nathan, Sir Nathaniel **12**:847
NATHAN, PAUL **12**:855
Nathan, Philip **4**:1423
Nathan, Sir Robert (govt. offic.) **12**:848
NATHAN, ROBERT (nov.) **12**:856
- U.S. literature **15**:1573
- *geneal. table* **12**:849
NATHAN, ROBERT ROY (econ.) **12**:856
Nathan, Seixas **12**:848
Nathan, Simon (early stlr., U.S.) **12**:848
Nathan, Simon (Colo. mer.) **5**:1543
"Nathan Admonishing David" (drg., Rembrandt) **12**:846
Nathan bar Ukba (tal. fig.) **15**:1512
NATHAN BEN ABRAHAM I **12**:857
- Solomon ben Judah **15**:123
NATHAN BEN ABRAHAM II **12**:857
- commentator **12**:107
Nathan ben Eliezer Ha-Me'ati, *see* Nathan Ha-Me'ati
Nathan ben Ephraim **6**:819
NATHAN BEN ISAAC HA-KOHEN HA-BAVLI **12**:858
NATHAN BEN JEHIEL OF ROME **12**:859
- Al-Bazak, Maẓli'aḥ **2**:527
- Anau, Jehiel **2**:934
- Hebrew poetry **14**:245
- history chart **8**:766-767
- Jama, Samuel ibn **9**:1271
- Kohut, A. **3**:278
- linguistics **16**:1362
- talmudic lexicography **11**:330; **15**:764
Nathan ben Joseph Official, *see* OFFICIAL, NATHAN BEN JOSEPH AND JOSEPH
Nathan ben Machir ben Menahem of Ancona **16**:1442
Nathan ben Meshullam (tan.) **16**:856
Nathan ben Meshullam of Melun **6**:920; **11**:1403
Nathan ben Mordecai **10**:1423
Nathan ben Naharai **5**:1534
Nathan ben Samuel he-Ḥaver **13**:591
Nathan ben Simeon **14**:1569
Nathan David of Parczew **14**:1295
Nathan der Weise (play) **7**:443
NATHAN DE-ẒUẒITA RESH GALUTA **12**:860
Nathanel (fam.) **2**:151
NATHAN HA-BAVLI (tan.) **12**:861
- *Avot de-Rabbi Nathan* **3**:985
- decisions **5**:891
- lien **14**:1397
- Meir **11**:1240
- Nasi **9**:250
- Simeon ben Gamaliel **6**:1024; **14**:1556
- *Yarḥei Kallah* **2**:204; **10**:711
- Yose ha-Gelili **16**:858
Nathan ha-Me'ati **9**:1121
- Avicenna **3**:959
- Galen, Claudius **7**:264
- Gracian, Zerahiah **7**:842
- translations **15**:1326
Nathan ha-Parnas **8**:263; **16**:673
Nathaniel of Chinon (tos.), *see* NETHANEL OF CHINON
Nathan Nata ben Jacob **15**:815
Nathan Nata ben Menahem Mendel of Shklov **11**:1310
- *aliyah* **9**:514
Nathan Nata ben Solomon Spira **7**:373
Nathan Nata Selig of Cracow **9**:1153
Nathan Note of Shklov, *see* NOTKIN, NATA
Nathan of Churt, Baron, *see* NATHAN, HARRY LOUIS, BARON
NATHAN OF GAZA **12**:861
- Aboab, Samuel **2**:95
- Abulafia, Hayyim ben Jacob **2**:187
- evil, doctrine of **10**:586
- Gediliah, Abraham **7**:355
- *Ḥemdat Yamim* **8**:321
- history **8**:693
- history chart **8**:766-767
- Pinheiro, Moses **13**:536
- Sambatyon **14**:764
- Shabbetai Ẓevi **14**:1224ff
- Syria **15**:644
- tomb **16**:872
- *Tu bi-Shevat* **15**:1419
- *Zerubbabel, Book of* **16**:1002
- *ẓimẓum* **10**:593
- *illus:* text
Nathan of Montpellier **6**:1140
Nathan of Salo **8**:1323
Nathan of Trinquetaille **11**:1254
Nathan-Ra'anan, Shalom **10**:1188
Nathans, Nathan (mer., Can.) **7**:1191
Nathans, Nathan (law., U.S.) **10**:1503
NATHANSEN, HENRI **12**:866
Nathansen, Moritz **10**:306
Nathan Shklover, *see* NOTKIN, NATA
Nathanson (fam.) **4**:176
Nathanson, Aryeh Leibush **12**:866
NATHANSON, BERNHARD (Dov Baer) **12**:866
NATHANSON, JOSEPH SAUL **12**:866

- Arye Leib ben Elijah **3:**668
- Heilprin, Jehiel **8:**268
- Lvov **11:**612
NATHANSON, MENDEL LEVIN **12:**868
Nathanson, Sarah Idel, *see* Ettinger, Sarah Idel
Nathanson, Zalman **9:**829
Nathan Sternherz (Sternhartz) of Nemirov, *see* NAHMAN OF BRATSLAV
Nathan Straus Health Center (Jer.) **9:**1473; **9:**989; **15:**430
Natick (tn., Mass.) **11:**1112
Nation (orgn., Fr.) **4:**1244
National Advisory Council for Aeronautics **2:**322
National Advocate (period.) **12:**1074
National Aeronautics and Space Administration **2:**322
National and University Library, Jerusalem, *see* LIBRARY, JEWISH NATIONAL AND UNIVERSITY
National Association of Synagogue Administrators (U.S.) **15:**1674
National Bible Society of Scotland **4:**969
National Community Relations Advisory Council, *see* NATIONAL JEWISH COMMUNITY RELATIONS ADVISORY COUNCIL
NATIONAL CONFERENCE OF JEWISH COMMUNAL SERVICE **12:**869
National Council for Jewish Education (U.S.) **15:**55
National Council for Research and Development **9:**967ff
National Council of the Churches of Christ in the United States **13:**1250
NATIONAL COUNCIL OF JEWISH WOMEN (U.S.) **12:**869
- American, Sadie **2:**817
- Zionism **16:**1147
National Council of Jews (Cz.) **4:**1387
National Council of Young Israel, *see* YOUNG ISRAEL, THE NATIONAL COUNCIL OF
National Defense Party (Arab gr.) **9:**1474
National Democratic Party (Ger.) **12:**955
National Desertion Bureau, *see* Family Location Service
National Farm School (U.S.) **2:**412; **10:**1247
National Federation of Jewish Men's Clubs (U.S.) **15:**1674
NATIONAL FOUNDATION FOR JEWISH CULTURE **12:**871
National Front (fascist orgn., It.) **12:**952
National Gallery (Eng.) **4:**359
National Home, Jewish, *see* Jewish National Home
National Hungarian Jewish Cultural Association, *see* O.M.I.K.E.
National Insurance Institute (Isr.) **9:**865; **9:**877ff
National Interfaith Committee (Can.) **4:**368
Nationalism, Arab, *see* Arabs
Nationalism, Jewish, *see* Jewish Nationalism
NATIONAL JEWISH COMMUNITY RELATIONS ADVISORY COUNCIL (U.S.) **12:**871
- Jewish Labor Committee **10:**66
- Zionism **16:**1147
NATIONAL JEWISH HOSPITAL (U.S.) **12:**872
National Jewish Ledger (newsp.), *see* *Jewish Week*
National Jewish Monthly (period.) **13:**1051
NATIONAL JEWISH WELFARE BOARD (U.S.) **12:**872
- *Contents:*
- - World War I **12:**872
- - World War II **12:**873
- - Postwar Period **12:**873
- - Jewish Center Movement **12:**874
- - Development of Movement **12:**875
- - Program **12:**875
- - Survey Report: Aims **12:**875
- - Centers in 1960s **12:**877
- chaplaincy **11:**1570
- *illus:*
- - text
- - *Haggadah* for U.S. soldiers **7:**1089
Nationaljuedische Vereingung (Zion. orgn.) **4:**306; **16:**1115
National Labor Court (Isr.) **9:**640
National Labor Federation (Isr.), *see* HISTADRUT HA-OVDIM HA-LE'UMMIT
National Liberal Immigration League, American **4:**393
National List (polit. party, Isr.) **4:**513; **9:**679ff; **13:**1512
NATIONAL PARKS IN ISRAEL **12:**878
- *illus:*
- - text
- - Ashkelon Antiquities Park **3:**717
- - Ḥurshat Tal **9:**172-173
- - Ramat Gan **13:**1530
National Physical Laboratory (Isr.) **9:**967
"National Radical Camp" (orgn., Pol.) *see* NARA
NATIONALRAT (Council, Aus.) **12:**879
National Refugee Service (U.S.) **15:**1629
NATIONAL RELIGIOUS PARTY (Isr.) **12:**880
- boundaries of Israel **9:**413ff
- Burg, Yosef **4:**1510
- Ha-Kibbutz ha-Dati **10:**972ff
- Ha-Po'el ha-Mizrachi **7:**1322
- *Ha-Ẓofeh* **2:**963; **7:**1534
- Jewish registration **9:**396
- Mizrachi **12:**179
- rabbinate **13:**1456
- religious life **9:**895
- Shapira, Ḥayyim Moshe **14:**1298
- *tables:* text
National Religious Women's Movement in Ereẓ Israel **12:**179
National Resources Planning Board (U.S.) **2:**778
National Revival Society (Er. Isr.), *see* Teḥiyyat Israel Society
National Secular Society (Eng.) **5:**668
NATIONAL SOCIALISM (Nazism) **12:**882
- General
- - Abraham a Sancta Clara **2:**130
- - Arab National Movement **9:**464ff
- - art and anti-Semitism **3:**567
- - boycott, anti-Nazi **4:**1280
- - churches **8:**910
- - German Jews **7:**488
- - influence of Reformation **14:**23
- - Judenrat **10:**407
- - Juedischer Kulturbund **10:**462
- - partisans **13:**140ff
- - race theory **16:**1332
- - racism **8:**737
- - self-defense **14:**1128
- - Templers **15:**996
- - U.S. Jews **15:**1628
- Leaders
- - Bormann **4:**1250
- - Eichmann **6:**517ff
- - Frank, Hans **7:**54
- - Goebbels **7:**687
- - Goering **7:**688
- - Hess **4:**1250
- - Heydrich **8:**448ff
- - Himmler **8:**497ff
- - Hitler **8:**782ff
Mussolini, and **12:**719
- - Ribbentrop **14:**150
- - Rosenberg **14:**275
- - Seyss-Inquart **14:**1209ff
- - Streicher **15:**436ff
- - Wisliceny, Dieter **6:**966
- Anti-Jewish Measures **3:**136
- - blood libel **4:**1128
- - censorship **5:**279
- - concentration camps **5:**77ff
- - extermination **8:**765
- - forced labor **6:**1429
- - Gestapo **7:**527ff
- - ghetto **7:**543
- - Jewish badge **4:**71ff
- - Jewish libraries **11:**192
- - legislation **10:**1573
- - Nuremberg laws **12:**1281
- - propaganda **5:**176; **6:**581
- - RSHA **14:**363
- - SS and SD **15:**322
- *illus:*
- - Amsterdam Jewish quarter **12:**984
- - anti-Jewish boycott posters **4:**1278-1280
- - Berlin, Nazi mass rallies **7:**490; **8:**761, 829
- - burning of books **8:**841
- - Gestapo telegrams re. concentration camp and deportation **7:**528,529
- - *Het Joodsche Weekblad* **12:**982
- - Hitler youth forcing Jews to scrub streets **8:**847
- - humiliation of Polish Jews by S.S. men **8:**855-860
- - "Jew bending to Nazi boot" (Russian cartoon, 1963) **3:**155
- - major camps in Europe (map) **5:**95
- - march of the "New Order" **8:**853
- - mass execution of Jews, Poland and Lithuania **8:**861-866
- - Nazi persecution and extermination in Europe, 1939-45 (map) **8:**843
- - Nazi pickets outside Jewish shops **4:**1278; **8:**837
- - Nazism vying with Inquisition (Russian cartoon) **8:**850
- - Nuremberg, Nazi mass rally, 1933 **8:**829
- - Nuremberg Laws **12:**1281
- - Nuremberg Trial **16:**289,293
- - Olkusz, Jews humiliated **12:**1368
- - Opava, synagogue being burned **12:**1412
- - Wannsee Conference minutes **16:**264
- - Warsaw Ghetto, General Juergen Stroop in **15:**442
- *see also:* HOLOCAUST; NEO-NAZISM
National Socialist Labor Front (trade union), *see* Deutsche Arbeitsfront
National Society for Hebrew Day Schools, *see* TORAH UMESORAH
Nationalsozialistische Deutsche Arbeiterpartei, *see* NATIONAL SOCIALISM
National Tribunal of Bratislava **15:**1155
National Union of Hebrew Teachers (Eng.) **6:**451
National Union of Israel Students **9:**962; **15:**452
National Water Carrier (Isr.) **9:**576; **15:**648
- *illus:*
- - open section in W. Galilee **11:**1274
National Women's League of the United Synagogue of America **15:**1674
"Nations" (gen. term), *see* GOIIM
Nations, David **15:**316
NATIONS, THE SEVENTY **12:**882
- geography **7:**415
- Jesus' disciples **3:**216
- mnemonic device **16:**1424
- national angels **2:**969
- *maps:* text
Nativ (journ.) **1:**newsp. list
Nativity, Church of the (Isr.) **8:**922; **8:**935
- *illus:*
- - Armenians celebrating Christmas **9:**914
- - Greek Orthodox patriarch enthroned **9:**912
- - Greek Orthodox procession **8:**927
Natkin, Nathan Nata **14:**673
Natko (15th cent., fin.) **13:**718
Naton, Avraham **3:**592
NATONEK, JOSEPH **12:**886
Natorei Karta (anti-Zion. gr.), *see* NETUREI KARTA
Natra, Sergiu **12:**671
Natreih Raḥamana u-Varkhei (greeting) **7:**918
NATRONAI BAR HILAI **12:**886
- female slaves **16:**1281
- gaonate families **7:**322
- history chart **8:**766-767
- masorah **16:**1417ff
- population **13:**874
NATRONAI BAR NEHEMIAH (gaon) **12:**887
- gaonate list **7:**318
NATRONAI BEN ḤAVIVAI (Zavinai) **12:**887
- Kairouan **10:**697
Natronai Kahana (gaon) **2:**449 **7:**315
Natronai Nasi bar Hakhinai **16:**731
Natufian culture **2:**382; **3:**45; **16:**237
- *illus:*
- - agricultural implements **2:**383
Natural Law, *see* Law, Natural
NATURE **12:**888
- *Contents:*
- - In Rabbinic Literature **12:**888
- - In Hellenistic and Medieval Jewish Philosophy **12:**888
- - Modern Period **12:**890
- Aristotelianism **3:**447; **13:**430
- Cohen, Hermann **13:**461
- kabbalistic emanation **10:**564
- Lurianic cosmogony **10:**589
- microcosm **11:**1501
- miracles **12:**74ff
- parables **13:**75
- Philo **13:**426
- philosophy **13:**424
- plagues of Egypt **13:**605
- sages **14:**653
- soul **15:**172
- Spinoza **15:**279; **15:**282ff
- Torah **15:**1239
Nature of God, *see* GOD
Nature Preservation Society (Isr.) **9:**965
NATURE RESERVES IN ISRAEL **12:**891
- *illus:*
- - text
- - Ḥuleh, papyrus growths **9:**227
NATZWEILER-STRUTHOF (concen. camp) **12:**892

- *illus:* text
Nauavi, Isaac **14:**304
Nauavi, Shabbetai **14:**304
NAUHEIM (tn., Ger.) **12:**893
Nauheim, Sigmund **5:**311; **12:**538
Naumann, Erich **8:**869; **12:**955
Naumann, Max **4:**646; **16:**106
NAUMBOURG, SAMUEL **12:**894
- *illus:* text
- *mus. notations:*
- - *Musaf Kaddish* **12:**647
NAUMBURG (fam.) **12:**895
Naumburg, Elkan **12:**895
Naumburg, Elsie Margaret Binger **12:**895
Naumburg, George Washington **12:**895
Naumburg, Jacob **14:**1139
NAUMBURG, MARGARET **12:**895
Naumburg, Robert Elkan **12:**895
Naumburg, Walter Wehle **12:**895
NAUPAKTOS (tn., Gr.) **12:**896
- Greece **7:**873
Nā'ūra, Al (vill., Er. Isr.) **2:**917
Nautical geography **7:**422
"Naval Officer" (paint., Hogarth) **14:**993
Navarra, Menahem **4:**315; **16:**114
NAVARRO (fam.) **12:**896
NAVARRO, ABRAHAM **12:**897
Navarro, Bekhor Isaac **4:**1200
Navarro, Judah **12:**896
Navarro, Moses (14th cent.) **11:**299; **12:**896
Navarro, Moses (14/15 cent.) **12:**896
Navarro, Solomon **6:**670; **10:**240
NAVEH (city, Er. Isr.) **12:**897
Naveh, J. **16:**723
Navel of the world (Gk. conc.), *see* *Tabbur ha-areẓ*
Navi, ha- (title) **15:**1164
Navigation **3:**788
- Jews **4:**546; **10:**690ff
- U.S. support for Israel **15:**1665
Navon (tit.) **13:**1451
Navon (fam.) **9:**1094
Navon, Aryeh (cart.) **5:**219
Navon, Aryeh Judah (schol.) **12:**898
NAVON, BENJAMIN MORDECAI BEN EPHRAIM **12:**897
Navon, Eliahu **12:**899
NAVON, EPHRAIM BEN AARON **12:**897
NAVON, ISAAC ELIYAHU **12:**898
NAVON, JONAH BEN HANUN **12:**898
- Azulai, Ḥayyim **3:**1019
NAVON, JONAH MOSES BEN BENJAMIN **12:**898
NAVON, JOSEPH **12:**899
Navon, Joseph Saadiah **12:**898
Navon, Judah **2:**611
Navon, Mordecai **12:**898
Navon, Yiẓḥak **9:**1568
Navon, Zeev **13:**139
Nawā (vill., Isr.) **12:**897
Nawardok yeshivah **12:**537
NAWI (fam., Iraq) **12:**899
Nawi, Manasseh Salomon **12:**899
Nawi, Reuben ben David **12:**899
Nawi, Solomon Reuben **12:**899
Naxos, Duke of, *see* NASI, JOSEPH
Naye Folkstsaytung (newsp.) **4:**1504; **13:**1042
Naye Land (period.) **13:**1055
Naye Leben (newsp., Pol.), *see* *Dos Naye Lebn*
Naye Lebn (journ., U.S.) **13:**1055
Naye Post (period.) **12:**1102
Naye Prese (daily) **5:**806
Nayer Folksblat (newsp.) **11:**432; **13:**1042
Nayes (daily) **12:**514
Naye Tsayt (newsp., Rus.) **13:**1047; **15:**1543
Naye Tsayt (period., U.S.) **13:**1053
Naye Yidishe Presse (period., Gal.) **16:**1330
Naye Yidishe Tsaytung (period., Ger.) **13:**1033
Naysants (city, Pol.), *see* NOWY SACZ
Nay Zlatopol (stlmt., Rus.) **14:**468
Nazan, Moses, *see* MOSES NATHAN
Nazar (disciple of Jesus) **10:**15
Nazar, Hak **13:**316
Nazarenes (J. Chr. sect) **3:**69; **10:**39; **12:**900
Nazarenism (conc.) **8:**274
NAZARETH (tn., Er. Isr.) **12:**899
- Arab survey **9:**1028
- Crusades **9:**269
- Fatimid period **9:**264
- holy places **8:**935
- Jesus **10:**11
- Joseph the Apostate **9:**255
- Mamluk provincial organization **9:**274
- nineteenth century **9:**293
- *illus:*
- - text
- - automobile assembly plant **9:**822
- - Basilica of the Annunciation **8:**929
- - Histadrut rest home **9:**866
- - Shazar, Zalman **14:**1325
- - telephone exchange **9:**841
Nazareth Democratic List (polit. party, Isr.) **9:**374; **9:**664
Nazarites (sect) **3:**69
Naẓerat Illit (tn., Isr.) **12:**903
- statistics **1:**place list
- *illus:*
- - Ford automobile plant **12:**904
- - ulpan classroom **15:**1526
NAZI-DEUTSCH (lang.) **12:**904
- history **8:**766
Nazi legislation, anti-Jewish, *see* LEGISLATION, ANTI-JEWISH IN THE NAZI PERIOD
NAZIMOVA, ALLA **12:**472
Nazi Party, *see* NATIONAL SOCIALISM
NAZIR (tract.) **12:**905
- *illus:* text
Nazir, Joseph **12:**907
NAZIR, MOSES HA-LEVI **12:**907
NAZIRITE **12:**907
- Commandments, the 613 **5:**765, 777
- impurity **13:**1410
- legitimate desecration of **5:**1559
- *met mitzvah* **15:**1185
- sacrifice **14:**601ff
- Samson **14:**771
- *illus:*
- - cutting of hair **12:**906
- *see also:* ASCETICISM
Nazirites Chamber (Temple) **15:**966
Nazism, *see* NATIONAL SOCIALISM
Náznánfalva (vill., Rum.), *see* NASNA
Nazor, Vladimir **16:**886
N.C.J.C.S., *see* NATIONAL CONFERENCE OF JEWISH COMMUNAL SERVICE
N.C.R.D., *see* National Council for Research and Development
Ndola (municipality, Zambia) **16:**922
Nea, Church of the (Jer.) **9:**1407
Néa Evropi (newsp.) **14:**704
Neale, John Mason **9:**1577
Neale, Thomas **8:**47
NEANDER, AUGUST **12:**910
- Protestantism **13:**1249
Neander, Conradus Burgens **8:**47
Neapolis (loc., Isr.), *see* NABLUS
Neapolitanus (1st cent. C.E., Rom.) **5:**315
Neara (tn., Jor. Val.), *see* NAARAH
Ne'arim (fam.) **12:**757
Nebaioth (s. of Ishmael) **9:**89
NEBAIOTH (tribe, Er. Isr.) **12:**910
- Arabs **3:**194
- Nabateans **12:**739
Nebat (bib. fig.) **9:**1371
Nebe, Artur **8:**869
Nebel, Abraham Isaac **14:**709
Nebellat (vill., Er. Isr.) **4:**752
Nebenzahl, Yiẓḥak **9:**620
Nebeský, Václav Bolemir **5:**1205
Nebi Musa (Arab fest.) **12:**410
Nebi Samuīl (Samwil; Er. Isr.), *see* Nabi Samuīl
Nebi Yunus (mound, Mesop.) **16:**1507
- Jonah's tomb **12:**1168
NEBO (loc., Transj.) **12:**910
- Ark concealed **3:**464
- Babel, Tower of **4:**23
- Borsippa temple **4:**1259
- Moabite revolt **11:**1397
- Moses **12:**387
- Transjordan **15:**1316
NEBRASKA (state, U.S.) **12:**911
- *illus:* text
- *pop. tables:* text
Nebrija, Antonio de **8:**47; **10:**1043
Nebrzydowski, Colonel **13:**775
NEBUCHADNEZZAR (Nebuchadrezzer; bib. fig.) **12:**912
- Contents:
- - Life **12:**912
- - In the Aggadah **12:**914
- - In Islam **12:**916
- - In the Arts **12:**917
- Balkh **4:**137
- campaign against Judah **6:**1090ff
- Daniel **5:**1277ff
- exile, Babylonian **6:**1037
- history **8:**607ff
- Jehoiachin's exile **9:**1318
- Jeremiah **9:**1351
- Jerusalem **16:**1513
- *Judith, Book of* **10:**451
- Mesopotamia **16:**1505
- Nabonidus **12:**746
- Neco defeated **12:**919
- palaces in Babylon **4:**33
- Rechabites **13:**1609
- Solomon's throne **15:**812
- Temple **15:**945
- Ur **16:**3
- Vashti, granddaughter **16:**72
- Watchers **16:**365
- writing on the wall **11:**1351
- *illus:*
- - text
- - Temple attacked **15:**985
Nebuchadnezzar I (k., Babyl.) **16:**1502
Nebuchadnezzar II (k., Babyl.), *see* NEBUCHADNEZZAR
"Nebuchadnezzar" (wtrcl., W. Blake) **12:**918
Nebushazban (bib. fig.) **13:**1481
NEBUZARADAN (bib. fig.) **12:**918
- Jerusalem **9:**1384; **16:**1513
- Necheles, Heinrich **11:**1200
- Zechariah **16:**952
Neckam, Alexander **8:**47
Neckarsulm (tn., Ger.) **15:**1348
NECO (k., Egypt) **12:**919
- Assyria **16:**1505
- history **8:**606ff
Necromancy, *see* DIVINATION; MAGIC
Necropolis **9:**1525; **9:**1532
- Bet She'arim **4:**766
- *menorah* **11:**1368
- *see also:* CEMETERY
NEDARIM (tract.) **12:**920
- vows and vowing **16:**227
- *illus:* text
Nedavah, *see* Free will offering
Nedebo, Nissim **5:**1246
Nedelnaya khronika Voskhoda (period.) **16:**225
Neder, *see* Votive Offering; VOWS AND VOWING
Nederlands Vak-Verbond, *see* Dutch Labor Federation
Nederlandse Zionistenbond (Zion. orgn.) **16:**1118
Nedivot, Isaac **6:**1256
Nedivot, Samuel **6:**1256
Nedreaas, Torborg **14:**934
Nedunyah, *see* DOWRY
Ne'eman (tit.) **7:**1489; **15:**1164
Ne'eman, Amitai **9:**1345; **12:**670
Ne'eman, P. **6:**734
Ne'eman, Samuel **11:**594
NE'EMAN, YEHOSHUA LEIB **7:**1549
Ne'eman, Yinon **9:**1590
NE'EMAN, YUVAL **12:**922
Ne'emanim (offics. Sp.) **4:**209ff
- *see also:* Fideles
Ne'emanut, *see* Credibility
Nefertiti (w. of Akhenaton) **2:**487
Nefesh (soul)
- Kabbalah **10:**609ff
- Man, the nature of **11:**843
- *see also:* SOUL
Nefesh (tombstone) **15:**1221
Nefesh Books (Isr.) **16:**653
Nefesh David (bk.) **5:**1353
Nefesh ha-Ḥayyim (bk.) **7:**1417
Nefilat appayim (prayer), *see* TAḤANUN
Nefilim (giants) **3:**789
Nefūsa (anc. people) **15:**1431
NEGA'IM (tract.) **12:**923
- leprosy **11:**37
- *illus:* text
NEGBAH (kib., Isr.) **12:**924
- Lachish **10:**1336
- oil exploration **9:**794
- statistics **1:**place list
- *illus:* text
Neged ha-Zerem (period.) **3:**3; **16:**348
NEGEV (Isr.) **12:**925
- *Contents:*
- - Geography **12:**925
- - History **12:**928
- Armistice Agreements **3:**478
- Bedouin **9:**1043ff
- biblical times **8:**573; **8:**579
- Byzantine agriculture **9:**258
- Crusader frontier **9:**268
- forest **9:**787
- geography **12:**925ff
- geology **9:**200ff
- *ḥaẓer, ḥaẓerim* **7:**1530
- highlands **9:**132ff
- history **12:**928ff
- human geography **9:**592ff
- Muslim rule **9:**261; **9:**263
- Palestine partition plans **15:**1546
- Philistines **10:**329
- plains **9:**126ff
- *illus:*
- - text
- - Arad **3:**245-248; **9:**577
- - Avedat (plan) **3:**943
- - Avedat experimental farm **12:**739
- - Bedouin plowing **9:**782
- - Be'er Orah, Gadna training camp **4:**382
- - flash flood **9:**185
- - Heleẓ oil well **9:**380
- - Ma'aleh Akrabbim rock

formation **11**:635
– – Nahal Amaẓyah **3**:231
– – phosphorite composition (chart) **9**:808
– – tamarisk **9**:230
– – Tel Yeruḥam dam **9**:769
– – terebinth **9**:234; **15**:1016
– – Yotvatah **16**:859
– *maps:* text
Negev Brigade (Palmaḥ) **7**:1073; **16**:315
– Palmaḥ **13**:47
– *illus:*
– – memorial **12**:931
Negev Coastal Plain (Isr.) **12**:925
– human geography **9**:575ff
Negev Hills (Isr.) **12**:925ff
Negev Institute for Arid Zone Research (Isr.) **9**:968
– Beersheba **4**:385
– desalination **9**:772
– *illus:*
– – pilot plant for water desalination **9**:966
Negev Nuclear Research Center (Isr.) **9**:975
"Negev Sheep" (sculp., Y. Danziger) **5**:1298
Negidim, *see* NAGID
Neginot (Psalm superscription) **13**:1320
Negligence
– liability **11**:184
– torts **15**:1273ff
– Yavneh-Yam finds **16**:723
– *see also:* PENAL LAW
Negre, Astruc de Sen, *see* ABBA MARI BEN ELIGDOR
Negri, Ada **9**:1107
Negrin, Solomon **5**:1250
Negro, Solomon **12**:896
Negro-Jewish relations in South Africa **15**:202
NEGRO-JEWISH RELATIONS IN THE U.S. **12**:932
– *Contents:*
– – Early Defense of Civil Liberties **12**:932
– – 1954 and After **12**:933
– – Relations in the Northern Urban Community **12**:933
– – The Legal Battle **12**:934
– Alabama **2**:506
– American Jewish Committee **2**:824
– anti-Semitism **3**:136
– Birmingham **4**:1038
– New York City **12**:1114
– self-defense **14**:1128
– Spingarn brothers **15**:274
– universities **15**:1681
– U.S. **15**:1656
– Zionism **16**:1063
– *see also:* BLACK JEWS IN AMERICA; NEW LEFT
Negro Jews, *see* BLACK JEWS IN AMERICA
Negropont (Gr. port), *see* CHALCIS
Neḥaisi, Elijah **11**:204
NEḤALIM (mosh., Isr.) **12**:934
– Ha-Gosherim **7**:1122
– statistics **1**:place list
Nehama, J. **8**:563
NEHARDEA (tn., Babyl.) **12**:934
– Abba ben Abba ha-Kohen **2**:34
– academy **2**:204
– Anilaeus and Asinaeus **3**:4
– destruction **8**:650
– diaspora **6**:11
– Dimi of Nehardea **6**:49
– history chart **8**:766-767
– Samuel **14**:786
– *table:* principal *amoraim* **2**:869
Neharim (bib. sea moster) **11**:89
Nehar Papa (canal, Babyl.) **13**:1384
NEHAR PEKOD (tn., Babyl.) **12**:936
NEHAVEND (tn., Iran) **12**:936
NEHEMIAH (bib. fig.) **12**:936
– Artaxerxes I **3**:647
– Ashdod **3**:696
– Day of Atonement **5**:1387
– economic hardships **16**:1317
– Great Synagogue **15**:629
– history chart **8**:766-767
– Jerusalem **8**:620ff; **9**:1389
– Jews in Babylonia **4**:35
– Johanan, supporter **10**:144
– Persian conquest **9**:1407
– priestly divisions **12**:90
– priests **13**:1085
– Samaritans **14**:728
– Teacher of Righteousness **15**:887
– Temple **15**:957
– Tobiads **15**:1178
– Tobiah **8**:627
– usury **16**:28
– war and warfare **16**:278
– Zerubbabel **16**:1001
– *illus:*
– – text
– – Jerusalem boundaries (map) **9**:1387
– *see also:* EXILE, BABYLONIAN; EZRA AND NEHEMIAH, BOOK OF
NEHEMIAH (tan.) **12**:937
– Akiva **2**:489
– Judah bar Ilai **10**:339
– *Mishnat ha-Middot* **12**:109
– Tosefta **15**:1284
Nehemiah (ruler, Jer.) **9**:1407
Nehemiah, Book of, *see* EZRA AND NEHEMIAH, BOOK OF
Nehemiah, Moses **16**:162
Nehemiah bar Ḥiyya **8**:796
NEHEMIAH BAR KOHEN ZEDEK (gaon) **12**:938
– gaonate families **7**:317
– Sherira Gaon **14**:1381
Nehemiah ben Amshel **16**:1027,1182
Nehemiah ben Arakh (tan.), *see* NEHORAI
Nehemiah ben Ḥushiel **9**:259
– warfare **16**:281
– *see also:* MESSIAH
Nehemiah ben Solomon ben Heiman ha-Nasi **13**:591
NEHEMIAH HA-KOHEN (kab., Pol.) **12**:939
– Shabbetai Ẓevi **14**:1236ff
Nehemiah ha-Kohen (schol., It.) **2**:935
Nehemiah ha-Navi **10**:514
Nehemiah of Bet Deli (tan.)
– Gamaliel the Elder **2**:201; **7**:296
Nehemiah son of Azbuk (bib. fig.) **12**:936
Neher, Albert **12**:939
NEHER, ANDRÉ **1**:34; **12**:939
– *illus:* text
Neher, Richard **12**:939
Neher-Bernheim, Renée **5**:452; **12**:940
NEHORAH (vill., Isr.) **12**:940
– statistics **1**:place list
NEHORAI (tan.) **12**:940
– Akhbarei **2**:487
– Torah study **10**:1322
Nehorai (tan. 2nd cent.), *see* MEIR
Nehorai (11th cent., Ger.), *see* MEIR BEN ISAAC SHELI'AḤ ẒIBBUR
Nehorai (12th cent., Er. Isr.) **9**:1232
Neḥoshet (metal), *see* Copper
Neḥuna ben Elinathan of Kefar ha-Bavli (tan.) **12**:941
Neḥunia (amora), *see* ḤUNYA OF BETH-HORON
Neḥuniah ben Abin ha-Kohen, *see* HUNA BEN AVIN HA-KOHEN
NEḤUNYA BEN HA-KANAH (tan.) **12**:941
– *Annah be-Kho'aḥ* **3**:25
– Bible exegesis **8**:1417
– circuses **5**:577
– *Kanah, Book of* **10**:734
Nehushta (royal fig., Judah) **9**:1318
Neḥushtan (wadi, Isr.) **15**:1145
NEHUSHTAN (copper serpent) **12**:942
– *see also:* COPPER SERPENT, THE
Nehushtan, Alfred, *see* Kupferberg, Alfred
NEHUTEI (travelling schols.) **12**:942
– *Amoraim* **2**:868
– Avin **3**:971
– *Beẓah* **4**:786
– Isaac bar Joseph **9**:12
Neiberg, Eliezer of Mannheim **5**:613
Neiberg, Isaac (Itzik) **5**:613
Neier, Aryeh **10**:1505
Neie Zeit (journ.) **11**:51
Neiger, Ḥayyim **15**:821
Neighbor, love of, *see* Love of neighbor
NE'ILAH (litur.) **12**:943
– *mus. notations:*
– – *Mi-Sinai niggunim* **12**:151
– *see also:* DAY OF ATONEMENT
Neilson, Adelaide **15**:1054
Neilson, Alexander Ritchie **12**:944
NEILSON, JULIA **12**:944
Neilson-Terry, Dennis **12**:945
Neilson-Terry, Phyllis **12**:945
Neiman, Jack (Nibs) **15**:303
Neiman-Pick's Disease **14**:1501
NEIPRIS, JOSEPH **1**:34
Neirab (loc., Syr.) **16**:667
Neisse (cmty., Silesia) **14**:1536
NEISSER, HANS PHILIPP **12**:945
Nei-Zlatopol (J. autonomous reg., Ukr.) **16**:935
Nekamah ("revenge"; J. gr.) **13**:145; **13**:774
Nekel, Marek **12**:1367
Nekevah (gram. term) **16**:1422
NEKLYUDOV, NICOLAI ADRIANOVICH **12**:945
Nekrasov, Nikolai **14**:508
Nelhans, Erich **4**:650
Nelson (city, N.Z.) **12**:1128
– *illus:*
– – synagogue **12**:1130
NELSON, BENJAMIN **12**:945
– sociology **15**:68
Nelson, George **15**:310
Nelson, Horatio **7**:733
NELSON, LEONHARD **12**:945
NELSON, LOUIS **12**:946
Nelus, Thomas, *see* Neale, Thomas
Nemenoff, Genia **12**:699
Neményi, Endre **4**:884
Nemer, Jerry **15**:303
NEMEROV, HOWARD **15**:1578; **15**:1583
Nemes, Béla **6**:165
Nemesis (deity) **9**:1406
NÉMETH, ANDOR **8**:1086
Németkeresztúr (tn., Aus.), *see* DEUTSCHKREUTZ
Nemetz, Nathan **10**:1494
– Vancouver **16**:67
NEMIROV (tn., Ukr.) **12**:946
– Chmielnicki massacre **5**:482
– Podolia **13**:668
Nemirovsky, Leon **3**:431
Nemirovsky, Mordekhai, *see* NAMIR, MORDEKHAI
NÉMIROWSKY, IRÈNE **7**:150
Nemon, Oscar **12**:1499
NEMOY, LEON **1**:34; **12**:947
NEMȚEANU, BARBU **12**:948
NEO-ARAMAIC **12**:948
– *Contents:*
– – Phonology **12**:949
– – Morphology **12**:950
– – Writing **12**:951
– *see also:* ARAMAIC
NEO-FASCISM **12**:951
Neofiti (converts)
– Amalfi **2**:792
– Apulian *anusim* **3**:227
– Catechumens, House of **5**:253
– Trani **15**:1313
– *see also:* CRYPTO-JEWS
Neo-Ḥasidism **7**:1420
– *see also:* ḤASIDISM
NEOLOGY (Neologism; Ref. cmties., Hung.) **12**:952
– Transylvania **15**:1342ff
– *see also:* REFORM JUDAISM
NEO-NAZISM **12**:954
– Germany **7**:499
NEO-ORTHODOXY **12**:956
– Adass Jeshurun, Adass Jisroel **2**:254
– Agudat Israel **2**:421ff
– Hildesheimer, Azriel **8**:477
– Jewish identity **10**:59
– modern Jewish thought **13**:453
– modern Judaism **10**:395
– rabbinical office **13**:1448
– *yeshivot* **16**:771
– *see also:* HIRSCH, SAMSON (BEN) RAPHAEL; ORTHODOXY
Neopathetisches Cabarett (gr., Ger.) **8**:491
NEOPLATONISM **12**:958
– Abrabanel, Judah **2**:110ff
– Aristotelian approach to religion **3**:446
– Aristotelian physical concepts **13**:488
– beatitude **4**:359ff
– cosmology **5**:983
– dualism **6**:242
– form and matter **6**:1438ff
– Gabirol, Solomon ibn **7**:240ff
– God **7**:665ff
– Ibn Ezra, Abraham **8**:1168
– Israeli, Isaac **9**:1063ff
– Jewish mysticism **10**:513; **10**:520; **10**:547
– Jewish philosophy **13**:429; **13**:433
– Kabbalah **10**:556
– kabbalistic psychology **10**:609
– medieval Jewish theology **15**:1106
– microcosm **11**:1502
– miracles **12**:76
– nature **12**:889
– pantheism and Kabbalah **10**:602
– revelation **14**:122ff
– soul **15**:173
– Worlds, the Four **16**:641
Neo-Punic (lang.) **14**:1149
Ne'ot Golan (mosh., Isr.) **13**:1534
– statistics **1**: place list
Ne'ot ha-Kikkar (mosh., Isr.) **1**:place list
NE'OT MORDEKHAI (kib., Isr.) **12**:962
– statistics **1**: place list
Nepal
– Israel's relations **9**:444
– spices **8**:1311
NEPHILIM (giants, Cana.) **12**:962
– Ahiman, Sheshai, Talmai **2**:463
– Uriel **16**:7
– *see also:* ANAK, ANAKIM
NEPPI, HANANEL (Grazziadio) **12**:963
Nepünk (newsp.) **12**:1438
Nequam, Alexander, *see* Neckam, Alexander
Ner (bib. fig.) **10**:1063
Ner (agg. fig.), *see* Abiel
Ner (period.) **4**:633
– statistics **1**: newsp. list
Nergal (deity)
– Chemosh **5**:390

- Cuth **5:**1175
- Resheph **14:**81
Nergal-eses̆ stele (Mesop.) **16:**1509
Nergal-Sar-Uṣur (k., Babyl.), *see* NERGAL-SHAREZER
NERGAL-SHAREZER (k., Babyl.) **12:**964
- Evil-Merodach **6:**1000
- Rab-Saris **13:**1481
Ner ha-Ma'arav (bk.) **15:**1197
Ner ha-Ma'aravi (period.) **1:** newsp. list
Neriah (bib. fig.) **14:**1179
Neriah, Moshe Ẓevi **7:**1321
Neriglissar (k., Babyl.), *see* NERGAL-SHAREZER
Ner Israel Rabbinical College (U.S.) **4:**146; **14:**379
Ner Israel Yeshiva (Can.) **15:**1262
Nerium oleander (bot.), *see* OLEANDER
Ner Ma'aravi (period.) **8:**209
- statistics **1:** newsp. list
Ner Neshamah ("lamp of the soul"), *see* MEMORIAL LIGHT
NERO (Rom. emp.) **12:**964
- Festus, Porcius **6:**1247
- *Isaiah, Ascension of* **9:**71
- Sabina Poppaea **13:**861
- Titus, Flavius Vespasianus **15:**1168
- *illus:*
- - bust (coin) **2:** 223
Neronias (city, Er. Isr.), *see* BANIAS
Nerot Shabbat (journ.) **1:** newsp. list
Nerrelter, David **8:**47
NER TAMID (eternal lamp) **12:**965
- art **5:**309
- Bet Alfa mosaics **4:**713
- Holy Ark **3:**457
- priestly care of **13:**1077
- Torah ornaments **15:**1255
- *illus:*
- - text
- - Istanbul, Yambol Synagogue **14:**1169
- - Jerusalem, Yad Vashem memorial shrine **16:**697
Ner Tamid (publ. house, Ger.) **7:**500
Neruda, Jan **5:**1206
NERVA (Rom. emp.) **12:**965
- Fiscus Judaicus **6:**1325
- history chart **8:**766-767
- tax of Jews **8:**644
- *illus:*
- - coin commemorating abolition of Jewish tax **6:**1325
Nerve, sciatic, *see Gid ha-nasheh*
Nes (flag) **6:**1335
Nes, *see* MIRACLE
Nesa (city, As. M.) **8:**787
Nesekh, *see* Libation offering
Neshamah (kab. conc., "soul") **10:**609ff
NESHAMAH YETERAH ("additional soul") **12:**966
- body and soul **4:**1165
Nes Harim (mosh., Isr.) **1:** place list
Neshei Agudat Israel (women's mvmt.) **2:**421
Neshekh (leg. term) **16:**27
NESHER (urb. cmty., Isr.) **12:**966
- statistics **1:** place list
Nesher (period.) **16:**1330
Nesher Cement Factory (Isr.) **8:**538; **9:**341
- *illus:*
- - export chart **9:**814
Nesi'im (Sp. cmty. ldrs.), *see Nasi*
Neskhiz, Mordecai of, *see* MORDECAI OF NEZKHIS
Nessanah (tn., Isr.), *see* NIZZANAH
Nessiat kappayim, *see* PRIESTLY BLESSING
Nessimi, Hodja **12:**65
Nesterov (city, Gal.), *see* ZHOLKVA
Nestorians (Chr.) **4:**859; **9:**1441; **13:**428
NESVIZH (tn., Belor.) **12:**966
- Minsk **12:**53
NES ZIYYONAH (tn., Isr.) **12:**968
- ICA's aid **10:**47
- statistics **1:** place list
- *illus:* text
NES ẒIYYONAH (Zion. soc., Rus.) **12:**969
- *illus:*
- - Volozhin executive committee **16:**214
NETA'IM (mosh., Isr.) **12:**969
NETANYAH (city, Isr.) **12:**969
- Ben-Ami, Oved **4:**460
- oil exploration **9:**795
- statistics **1:** place list
- *illus:*
- - text
- - diamond cutting **9:**817
NETANYAHU, BENZION **12:**970
- historiography **8:**562
Neta Revai (fourth year crop) **6:**1314
- tithes **12:**13
Nethanel (1st cent., C.E.) **6:**176
Nethanel (3rd cent. C.E., Samar. h. pr.) **4:**17
Nethanel (cmty. ldr., Yem.) **14:**617
Nethanel (14/15 cent., Luria fam.) **11:**569
NETHANEL BEN AL-FAYYUMI **12:**971
- linguistics **16:**1360; 1383
- philosophy **13:**440
Nethanel ben Eleazar ha-Kohen **2:**592
NETHANEL BEN ISAIAH **12:**971
Nethanel ben Joseph of Chinon (tos.) **12:**973
NETHANEL BEN MESHULLAM HA-LEVI **12:**972
- translations **15:**1329
NETHANEL BEN MOSES HA-LEVI (gaon) **12:**972
- gaonate **7:**324
- Nethanel ben Al-Fayyumi **12:**971
Nethanel ben Naaman **13:**591
Nethanel ben Shabbetai ha-Dani **15:**1455
NETHANEL OF CHINON **12:**972
- Chinon **5:**475
NETHERLANDS, THE **12:**973
- *Contents:*
- - Middle Ages **12:**973
- - Marranos and Early Communities **12:**975
- - Economic Expansion **12:**977
- - Cultural Activities of the Portuguese Community **12:**978
- - Ashkenazim **12:**980
- - Emancipation **12:**980
- - The Twentieth Century **12:**983
- - Holocaust Period **12:**984
- - Contemporary Period **12:**989
- - Relations with Israel **12:**992
- General
- - crime **5:**1092ff
- - dress **6:**220
- - Dutch literature **6:**316ff
- - history chart **8:**766-767
- - population **13:**880ff
- - South Africa **15:**189
- - statistics **15:**346
- - theater **15:**1057
- - UNSCOP **15:**1688
- Communal and Religious Life
- - Barrios, Daniel Levi de **4:**259
- - communal organization **5:**824
- - Duenner, Joseph **6:**261
- - education **6:**422ff
- - Ḥanukkah lamps **7:**1292
- - Hebrew mss. **11:**907
- - Manasseh ben Israel **11:**855
- - Morteira, Saul Levi **12:**355
- - Orthodoxy **12:**1489
- - Protestant-Jewish relations **13:**1251
- - Sasportas, Jacob **14:**893
- - synagogue **1:** syn. list
- - Zionism **16:**1118ff
- Commerce and Professions
- - journalism **10:**304ff
- - law **10:**1491ff
- - military service **11:**1566
- - peddling **13:**207
- - politics **13:**814
- - press **13:**1034ff
- - publishing **13:**1365
- - secondhand goods trade **14:**1085
- - trade **15:**1299ff
- - typography **15:**1482
- History
- - *aliyah* **9:**515
- - Amsterdam **2:**896; **2:**900ff
- - Antwerp Jews **3:**167
- - Anusim community **8:**693
- - archives **3:**383,385
- - Arnhem **3:**486
- - court Jews **5:**1007ff
- - emancipation **6:**703ff
- - French Revolution **7:**156
- - Haskalah **7:**1437
- - history, modern **8:**706ff
- - J.D.C. **2:**828
- - Napoleonic occupation **3:**766
- - Reformation **14:**20
- - Shabbateanism **14:**1233
- - Spinoza **15:**275ff
- Holocaust **8:**842,891ff
- - Church and Nazism **8:**914; **8:**915
- - Committee for Jewish Affairs **2:**902
- - Jewish badge **4:**73
- - refugees, Jewish **14:**30
- - Sephardim, fate of **14:**1172
- - "special" cases **2:**903
- - War Crimes Trials **16:**289ff
- - Westerbork **16:**466
- *illus:*
- - text
- - dress **6:** *fcg.* 238
- - Dutch Jewish quarter **10:**87
- - Dutch underground, pro-Jewish badge (1942) **4:**71
- - Ḥanukkah lamp (18th cent.) **7:**1297
- - Jewish badge decreed by the Nazis **4:**70,72
- - Westerbork, Nazi camp **16:**466
- - *pop. tables:* text
- *see also:* HAGUE, THE
NETHERLANDS ANTILLES **12:**993
- *Contents:*
- - Aruba **12:**993
- - Curaçao **12:**993
- - St. Eustatius **12:**995
- - St. Martin **12:**995
- *illus:* text
NETHERWORLD **12:**996
- death in Bible **11:**845
- hell **13:**83
- resurrection **14:**100
- Sumer **15:**515
- Uriel **16:**7
- world to come **12:**1356
- *see also:* GEHINNOM; Hell
Nethinim (pariah gr.), *see* GIBEONITES AND NETHINIM
NETILAT YADAYIM (hand washing) **12:**998
- ablution **2:**84ff
- hygiene **8:**1140ff
- impurity **13:**1409; **13:**1412
- priests **13:**1080
- *illus:*
- - text
- - *Yadayim* illustration **16:**693
- *see also:* ABLUTION; MAYIM AḤARONIM
Netira (fam.) **2:**154
NETIRA (9/10 cent., Bagh.) **12:**999
- economic history **16:**1279
- Iraq **8:**1446
Netivah (journ.) **7:**1321
- statistics **1:** newsp. list
Netivei Irgun (journ.) **1:** newsp. list
NETIV HA-LAMED-HE (kib., Isr.) **12:**1000
- Adullam Region **2:**312
- statistics **1:** place list
Netiv ha-Shayyarah (mosh., Isr.) **1:** place list
Netiv Meir Yeshivah (Jer.) **9:**1495
NETIVOT (tn., Isr.) **12:**1000
- Shalkovich, A. L. **14:**1269
- statistics **1:** place list
Netivot (journ., Isr.) **1:** newsp. list
Netivot (journ., Pol.) **1:** newsp. list
Netivot Olam (wk.) **11:**118
NETOPHAH (vill., Er. Isr.) **12:**1001
NETTER, CHARLES **12:**1001
- afforestation **9:**788
- Alliance Israélite **2:**649ff
- Benisch **4:**521
- history chart **8:**766-767
- Mikveh Israel **11:**1544
- *illus:* text
Netter, Claude **12:**1376
Netter, Solomon Zalman **15:**520
Netter, Yiẓḥak, *see* NETTER, CHARLES
Nettl, Bruno **12:**701
NETTL, PAUL **12:**701
Nettles (bot.) **15:**1120
- plant list **13:**623
Netu'ah (vill., Er. Isr.) **7:**270
- statistics **1:** place list
NETUREI KARTA (anti-Zion. gr., Isr.) **12:**1002
- Agudat Israel **2:**425
- Blau, Amram **4:**1074
- *ḥalukkah* **7:**1210
- Hungarian community **8:**1095
- Israel, State of **10:**395
- Orthodoxy **12:**1488
- Teitelbaum, Joel **15:**909
- *illus:*
- - text
- - *ḥerem* on owner of television set **8:**354
Netzler, Iosef, *see* TRIVALE, ION
NEUBAUER, ADOLF (Abraham) **12:**1003
- Cairo *Genizah* **16:**1335
- historiography **8:**564
- history chart **8:**766-767
- linguistic literature **16:**1390
- *Megillat Yuḥasin* **2:**463
NEUBAUER, JACOB (Jekuthiel) **12:**1005
Neubauer, Peter B. **13:**1339
Neuberg, Assia **16:**1157
NEUBERG, GUSTAV EMBDEN CARL **12:**1005
NEUBERGER, ALBERT **12:**1005
Neuberger, H. Maurine (Brown) **12:**1006
Neuberger, Josef **7:**500; **10:**1497; **13:**814
Neuberger, Leah Thall **15:**314
NEUBERGER, RICHARD LEWIS **12:**1006
- Oregon **12:**1451
Neubitschow (tn., Cz.), *see* NOVY BYDZOV
Neuburger, Gabriel Loew **3:**688
NEUBURGER, MAX **12:**1006
- medicine **11:**1198
- *illus:* text
NEUCHÂTEL (canton, city, Switz.) **12:**1007

Neuda, Aaron Moses **12:**1007
NEUDA, ABRAHAM **12:**1007
Neuda, Fanny **12:**1008
Neue Deutsche Rundschau (period.) **4:**1290
Neue Freie Presse (newsp.)
- Bacher, Eduard **4:**50
- Herzl, Theodor **8:**408
- Vienna **16:**127
Neue Israelitische Zeitung (period.) **10:**1060; **13:**1049
Neue Juedische Korrespondenz (J. news agency, Ger.) **13:**1024
Neue Juedische Presse (period.), *see* ISRAELITISCHES FAMILIENBLATT
Neue Nationalzeitung (newsp.) **10:**1398
Neue Reichsvereinigung (board of Js., Ger.) **4:**649
Neues Pester Journal (newsp.) **4:**1401
Neue Welt (newsp.) **13:**1034; **14:**131
Neue Zeitung (Yid. period.) **4:**1041
Neufchâteau (tn., Fr.) **11:**496
Neufeld (tn., Aus.) **4:**1511
NEUFELD, DANIEL **12:**1008
- Orgelbrand, S. **12:**1455
Neufeld, Joseph **3:**361
- Israel architecture **3:**361
Neufeld, Judah Reuben **12:**1244
NEUGEBAUER, OTTO **12:**1009
NEUGROESCHEL, MENDEL **12:**1009
Neuhardthof (clny., Er. Isr.) **9:**571
Neuhaus (tn., Bohem.), *see* JINDRICHUV HRADEC
Neukollin (city, Bohem.), *see* KOLIN
Neuman, A. (r., Rus.) **11:**16; **15:**59
NEUMAN, ABRAHAM AARON (r., U.S.) **12:**1009
Neuman, Elias **10:**1503
Neumann, Abraham (art., Pol.) **5:**1038
NEUMANN, ALFRED **12:**1010
Neumann, Angelo **13:**973
Neumann, Anshel **16:**51
Neumann, Ede **12:**802
NEUMANN, EMANUEL **12:**1011
- Farbstein, J. H. **6:**1181
- U.S. Zionism **16:**1143
- *illus:*
- - Keren Hayesod bldg., cornerstone ceremony **10:**916
- - Transjordan Arab leaders and **9:**346
NEUMANN, ERICH **12:**1012
Neumann, Ernest, *see* NAMENYI, ERNEST
Neumann, Ferenc, *see* MOLNÁR, FERENC
Neumann, Heinrich **16:**127
NEUMANN, HENRY **12:**1012
Neumann, Isador **11:**1196
Neumann, Israel **4:**875
NEUMANN, JOHANN (Johnny) LUDWIG VON **12:**1012
Neumann, Joseph **4:**1384; **13:**1110
Neumann, Moses Samuel **7:**421; **9:**1343
- children's literature **5:**431
Neumann, Oskar **5:**1201; **13:**1028
Neumann, Paul **12:**1375; **15:**313
NEUMANN, ROBERT **12:**1013
Neumann, Salomon **4:**656
Neumann, Stephan Theodor **8:**421
NEUMANN, YEḤESKEL MOSHE **12:**1014
Neumark (tn., Ger.) **4:**1301
NEUMARK, DAVID **12:**1014
- *illus:*
- - F.Z.C. **16:**1165
NEUMARK, EPHRAIM **12:**1015
Neumark, Hirsch **12:**1334
Neumark, Judah Loeb **4:**653; **13:**1107
Neumark, Nathan **4:**653 **13:**1107
Neumark-Mirels, Meshullam Zalman **3:**733
Neumarkt (tn., Transyl.), *see* TARGU-MURES
NEUMEYER, KARL **12:**1015
Neunzehn Briefe ueber Judentum (bk.) **8:**509ff
- letters **11:**60
Neu Oderberg (tn., Morav.), *see* NOVY BOHUMIN
Ne'urim (vill., Isr.) **4:** 548
- statistics **1:** place list
Neurology **11:**1201
- Edinger's studies **6:**368
Neurosis **11:**1372,1375
Neu Sandec (city, Pol.), *see* NOWY SACZ
Neusatz (city, Yug.), *see* NOVI SAD
Neuschul, A.M. **16:**1165
Neu-Sedlitz (tn., Morav.), *see* AUSTERLITZ
NEUSNER, JACOB **12:**1015
Neusner, Samuel **7:**1359
Neusohl (tn., Slov.), *see* BANSKA BYSTRICA
Neuss (tn., Ger.) **5:**1137; **16:**685
Neustadt (tn., Ger.) **13:**22
Neustadt (city, Morav.) **12:**299
Neustadt (tn., Pol.), *see* Nowe Miasto
Neustadt, David, *see* AYALON, DAVID
Neustadt, Isaac Eli **8:**1362
Neustadt, Israel, *see* ISSERLEIN, ISRAEL BEN PETHAHIAH
Neustadt, Melech **16:**640
Neustadt an der Aisch (tn., Ger.) **4:**352
Neustadter (fam.) **5:**56; **14:**834
Neustadtl, Isaac **11:**1588
Neutitschein (tn., Cz.), *see* NOVY JICIN
Neutra (tn., Cz.), *see* NITRA
NEUTRA, RICHARD JOSEPH **12:**1016
- synagogue **15:**624
Neuwall, Albert Von **10:**1590
Neuwert, Adolf, *see* NOWACZYNSKI, ADOLF
Neuwied (tn., Ger.) **3:**844
Neuzedlisch (tn., Cz.) **15:**607
NEUZEIT, DIE (weekly) **12:**1016
- Jellinek, A. **9:**1338
- press **13:**1033
- Szanto, Simon **15:**657
NEVADA (U.S.) **12:**1017
Nevada City (Calif.) **5:**56
NEVAKHOVICH, JUDAH LEIB **12:**1018
- Haskalah **7:**1447
- Peretz, Abraham **13:**279
- *illus:*
- - *Kol Shavat Bat Yehudah* (1803) **7:**1446
NEVATIM (mosh., Isr.) **12:**1019
- statistics **1:**place list
Neveh Afekah (qtr., Tel Aviv) **15:**924
Neveh Ammi'el (vill., Isr.) **14:**1091
Neveh Avot (inst., Isr.) **1:**place list
Neveh Efrayim (stlmt., Isr.) **1:**place list; **16:**731
NEVEH EITAN (kib., Isr.) **12:**1019
- statistics **1:**place list
Neveh Hadassah (kib., Isr.), *see* TEL YIẒḤAK
Neveh Ilan (stlmt., Er. Isr.) **1:**place list **9:**584
Neveh Mivtaḥ (mosh., Isr.) **1:**place list
Neveh Monosson (stlmt., Isr.), *see* Neveh Efrayim
Neveh Oved (housing co., Er. Isr.) **9:**564
Neveh Oved (stlmt., Isr.), *see* PORIYYAH
Neveh Sha'anan (qtr., Tel Aviv) **15:**921
Neveh Shalom (qtr., Jaffa) **9:**1257 **9:**326; **15:**919
Neve Shalom Berit Avraham (yesh., Er. Isr.) **2:**609; **6:**137
Neveh Sharett (qtr., Tel Aviv) **15:**924
Neveh Ur (kib., Isr.) **1:**place list
- *illus:*
- - cotton fields **10:**966
Neveh Ya'akov (vill., Er. Isr.) **9:**583
- Jerusalem development **9:**1473
Neveh Ya'ir (kib., Isr.), *see* EIN HA-SHELOSHAH
NEVEH YAM (kib., Isr.) **12:**1019
- statistics **1:** place list
Neveh Yamin (mosh., Isr.) **1:**place list
Neveh Yarak (mosh., Isr.) **16:**718
- statistics **1:**place list
Neveh Ẓedek (qtr., Jaffa) **9:**1257 **9:**326; **15:**919
Nevel (lyre) **12:**564
Nevel (meas.) **16:**381
NEVELAH (carcass) **12:**1019
- dietary laws **6:**39
- eggs **6:**474
- hunting **8:**1112
- impurity laws **11:**143
- Pentateuch **13:**247
NEVELSON, LOUISE **3:**606
- *illus:*
- - "Homage to Six Million" (sculp.) **3:**635
- - "Night Zag VI" (sculp.) **14:**1063
"Never again" (slogan, J.D.L.) **14:**1128
- *illus:*
- - J.D.L. protest rally for Soviet Jewry **12:**1123
NEVERS (tn., Fr.) **12:**1020
Nevi'im ("prophets") **11:**309
- Ahab **2:**439
- as law source **12:**117
- education of **6:**396ff
- Greek canon **4:**825
- *haftarah* **16:**1342
- order of books **16:**1406
- *teki'ata* **15:**915ff
- *illus:*
- - Latter Books, order of (table) **4:**828
- - manuscript, 895 C.E. **11:**900
- *see also:* MINOR PROPHETS; *and under individual prophets*
Nevis (isl., W. Indies) **16:**473
Nevlinski, Michael **8:**412
NEVU'AT HA-YELED (Heb. story) **12:**1020
- fiction **6:**1270
New Age, The (period.) **14:**218
New Amsterdam (early name for N.Y.) **12:**1062ff; **15:**1586,1589
- history chart **8:**766-767
Newark (city, N.J.) **6:**902
- *illus:*
- - Temple B'nai Abraham **12:**1029
New Babylon (stlmt., Aus.) **4:**1185
NEW BEDFORD (tn., Mass.) **12:**1021
- Massachusetts **11:**1112
New Bern (city, N.C.) **12:**1220
NEW BRUNSWICK (city, N.J.) **12:**1021
- Middlesex County **11:**1504
- New Jersey **12:**1028
New Brunswick (prov., Can.) **5:**105; **11:**997
Newburger, Morris **10:**80
Newburgh (city, N.Y.) **12:**1125
New Castle (tn., N.H.) **12:**1024
New Castle (city, Pa.) **13:**230
NEWCASTLE-UPON-TYNE (tn., Eng.) **12:**1022
- *see also:* GATESHEAD ON TYNE
New Catholic Encyclopedia **6:**733
New Central Synagogue (Eng.) **15:**627
NEW CHRISTIANS **12:**1022
- General
- - auto da fé **3:**912
- - ennobled **15:**1165
- - Host desecration charge **8:**1043
- - Kayserling's studies **10:**856
- - La Guardia, Holy Child of, trial **10:**1360
- - martyrs (Ancona) **2:**942
- - medicine **11:**1191
- - Order of Calatrava **5:**39
- - philosophy **13:**416
- - Sephardim **14:**1164ff
- - spice trade **15:**270
- - trade and commerce **15:**1300ff
- Judaism and
- - apologetics **3:**197
- - attitude of Jews toward **3:**204; **3:**212
- - conflict of laws **5:**884; **5:**889
- - Jewish identity **10:**57
- - messianism **11:**1424
- - *Thesouro dos Dinim* **11:**856
- Individual Personalities
- - Aboab, Immanuel **2:**90
- - Alfonso de Oropesa **2:**606
- - Barros Basto, Arturo **4:**261
- - Benjamin Ze'ev of Arta **4:**538
- - Caceres, Simon **5:**4
- - Cervantes **5:**312f
- - Costa, Uriel da **5:**988
- - Ferrer, Vicente **6:**1235
- - Ibn Shuaib, Joel **8:**1201
- - Isaac ben Sheshet Perfet **9:**32
- - Maldonado de Silva, Francisco **11:**825
- - Molcho, Solomon **12:**225ff
- - Nasi, Gracia **12:**836
- - Reuveni, David, and **14:**114
- - Schwarz, Samuel, rediscovered **14:**1025
- - Torquemada, Tomás de **15:**1264
- - Ximenes, Francisco **16:**688
- Centers
- - Badajoz **4:**59
- - Barbastro **4:**207
- - Bordeaux **4:**1244
- - Brazil **2:**413; **4:**1322
- - Burriana **4:**1531
- - Córdoba **5:**965
- - France **7:20**
- - India **8:**1355
- - Latin America **10:**1448
- - Lisbon **11:**300ff
- - Madrid **11:**683
- - Mexico **11:**1453ff
- - Peru **13:**322
- - Portugal **13:**921ff
- - São Paulo **14:**850
- - Saragossa **14:**862
- - Seville **14:**1205ff
- - Spain **15:**237ff,240
- - Toledo **15:**1205
- - Tortosa **15:**1269
- - Valencia **16:**57
- - Valladolid **16:**62
- - Vila Real **16:**134
- *illus:*
- - Portugal, Oporto synagogue **13:**924
- - Spain, Jewish and Converso communities, 1474 (map) **15:**223
- *see also:* ALBORAYCOS; ANUSIM; BAPTISM, FORCED; CHUETAS; CONVERSOS; CRYPTO-JEWS; INQUISITION; LIMPIEZA DE SANGRE; MARRANO; MARRANO DIASPORA; SPANISH AND PORTUGUESE

LITERATURE
New Chronicle (wk.), *see Chronicles, Samaritan*
Newcombe (surveyor) **11**:931
Newcome, Henry **8**:47
New Communist List (commun. party, Isr.), *see* Rakaḥ
New Concise Jewish Encyclopedia **6**:734
New Daily (period.), *see* NOWY DZIENNIK
New Deal (U.S. policy) **15**:1630
- Cardozo, Benjamin **5**:167
- Horner, Henry **8**:978
- Roosevelt **14**:257ff
New English Bible **4**:871
New Era (mag.) **14**:158
Newfield, Morris **4**:1037
Newfoundland (prov., Can.) **5**:105; **11**:997; **13**:1423; **13**:1424
New France (Fr. colony), *see* QUEBEC
New Gate (Jer.) **9**:1434
- *illus:*
- - general view **9**:1432
New Granada (Colom.) **8**:1395; **10**:1448
NEW HAMPSHIRE (U.S.) **12**:1024
- *pop. tables:* text
New Hanover (co., N.C.) **12**:1218
NEW HAVEN (port, Conn.) **12**:1025
- Connecticut **5**:898
New Horizons (art gr., Isr.) **3**:592ff
NEWHOUSE, SAMUEL IRVING **12**:1026
New Iberia (city, Louis.) **11**:517
NEW ISRAEL (rel. sect) **12**:1026
New Israel (Chr. term) **5**:537
NEW JERSEY (U.S.) **12**:1027
- *illus:*
- - text
- - Woodbine, Baron de Hirsch Agricultural School **16**:158
- *pop. tables:* text
New Jerusalem (stlmt., Can.) **14**:891
New Jerusalem (Chr. term) **9**:1569ff
New Jewish Encyclopedia **6**:734
New Jewish Version (Bib.) **4**:871
New Kensington (city, Pa.) **13**:230
NEW LEFT (rad. orgn.) **12**:1031
- *Contents:*
- - In the United States **12**:1031
- - In Western Europe **12**:1033
- - In Israel **12**:1034
- assimilation **3**:778
- Marcuse, Herbert **11**:949
- Negro-Jewish relations (U.S.) **12**:933
- Paris **13**:111
- socialism **15**:32
- student movements **15**:451
- United States **8**:743
- U.S. Zionism **15**:1647; **16**:1147
- *see also:* COMMUNISM
NEWLINSKI, PHILIPP MICHAEL **12**:1034
NEW LONDON (city, Conn.) **12**:1035
New Lots (section, N.Y.C.) **12**:1081
Newman, Alfred (cmty. ldr., Eng.) **10**:53
Newman, Alfred (comp., U.S.) **12**:451
NEWMAN, ARNOLD **12**:1035
Newman, Emanuel **15**:302
Newman, Harry **15**:308
NEWMAN, ISIDORE **12**:1035
Newman, Jacob **8**:957
Newman, James R. **12**:758
Newman, Leopold C. **11**:1551
NEWMAN, LOUIS ISRAEL **12**:1036
Newman, Mike **13**:1361
Newman, Mordecai **13**:1378
NEWMAN, PAUL **12**:472
NEWMARK (fam.) **12**:1036
- California **5**:56
- *illus:* text
Newmark, David **15**:302
Newmark, Harris **12**:1036
Newmark, Joseph **12**:1036
- Iowa **8**:1438
- Los Angeles **11**:498; **11**:499
Newmark, Marco Ross **12**:1036
Newmark, Maurice Harris **12**:1037
- Los Angeles **11**:501
Newmark Loeb, Estelle **12**:1036
Newmark Newmark, Sarah **12**:1036
NEW MEXICO (U.S.) **12**:1037
- *illus:* text
- *pop. tables:* text
NEW MOON **12**:1039
- additional prayer **12**:532ff
- after Temple destruction **9**:241; **9**:250
- *Barekhi Nafshi* **4**:218
- Cohn, B., studies **5**:688
- customs **12**:5
- fasting **6**:1193
- festival, second day **6**:1244
- Jerusalem in liturgy **9**:1561
- Judaism **10**:388
- Karaite calendar **10**:778
- Mount of Olives **12**:483
- Saadiah Gaon against Aaron ben Meir **14**:544
- sacrifice **5**:763; **14**:600ff
- *Shabbat Mevarekhin* **14**:572
- *Shabbat Rosh Ḥodesh* **14**:572
- women **12**:24
- *see also:* CALENDAR; FESTIVALS; MOON; MOON, BLESSING OF THE; NEW MOON, ANNOUNCEMENT OF
NEW MOON, ANNOUNCEMENT OF **12**:1040
- Great Academy **2**:202
- Judah ha-Nasi **10**:367; **10**:369
- laws of **14**:311
- *illus:*
- - *Harrison Miscellany* **3**:553
- - priests lighting fire to announce **14**:310
- *see also:* CALENDAR; MOON, BLESSING OF THE; NEW MOON
New Moon, blessing of, *see* MOON, BLESSING OF THE
New Muslims, *see* JĀDID AL-ISLĀM
NEWMYER, ARTHUR GROVER **10**:315
New Netherland (prov., N. Am.) **15**:1586
New Odessa (stlmt., U.S.) **2**:862
NEW ORLEANS (city, La.) **12**:1041
- Behrman, Martin **4**:396
- history chart (1826) **8**:766-767
- *illus:* text
New Palestine, The (mag.), *see Maccabean, The*
Newport (city, Ky.) **10**:909
NEWPORT (city, R.I.) **12**:1042
- Rhode Island **14**:143
- *illus:*
- - text
- - deed of sale for Jewish cemetery **15**:1587
- - *mazzah* board (18th cent.) **11**:1157
- - Seixas' address to George Washington **14**:144
- - Touro Synagogue, Ark **3**:454
- - Washington's letter to Hebrew Congregation **16**:359
Newport News (city, Va.) **16**:163
New Provinces (anth.) **10**:1097
New Rochelle (city, N.Y.) **12**:1125; **16**:464
News From Israel (period.) **8**:1359; **13**:1036
Newsletter (period.) **13**:1026
New South Wales, *see* AUSTRALIA
New Spain (Latin Am.) **10**:1448
NEWSPAPERS, HEBREW **12**:1044
- *Contents:*
- - Spread of the Hebrew Press **12**:1045
- - Main Stages of Development **12**:1045
- - Duration of Hebrew Periodicals **12**:1047
- - Leading Periodicals and Newspapers in Europe **12**:1047
- - Hebrew Press in North America **12**:1052
- - Erez Israel Press **12**:1053
- - Press in the State of Israel **12**:1058
- *illus:*
- - children's Hebrew and Yiddish newspapers, 1893-1969 (table) **5**:441-444
- - children's Hebrew and Yiddish newspapers, mastheads (1901-1958) **5**:448-458
- - *Davar* (first issue) **5**:1317
- - *Do'ar ha-Yom* (1935) **6**:142
- - *Ha-Aḥdut*, editorial board **16**:999
- - *Ha-Am* (1917) **12**:361
- - *Ha-Asif* (1884) **7**:1011
- - *Ha-Boker* (Warsaw, 1909) **7**:1035
- - *Hadashot Haaretz* (1919) **7**:1007
- - *Hadoar*, first issue **15**:1627
- - *Ha-Emet* (Vienna, 1877) **7**:1058
- - *Ha-Karmel* (Vilna, 1860) **7**:1144
- - *Ha-Maggid* (Lyck, 1856) **7**:1221
- - *Ha-Me'assef* (Koenigsberg and Berlin, 1788) **7**:1435
- - *Ha-Meliz* (1861) **7**:1233
- - *Ha-Mizpeh* (Cracow, 1917) **7**:1241
- - *Ha-Shaḥar* (Vienna, 1868) **7**:1367
- - *Ha-Shilo'aḥ* (Berlin, 1897) **7**:1369
- - *Ha-Shofar* **16**:1109
- - *Ha-Tekufah* (Moscow, 1918) **7**:1470
- - *Ḥavazzelet* (Jerusalem, 1870) **7**:1480
- - *Ha-Yom* (St. Petersburg, 1886) **7**:1500
- - *Ha-Ẓefirah* (Berlin, 1874) **7**:1530
- - *Ha-Zeman*, first issue **13**:1046
- - *Jeschurun* (Frankfort, 1855) **8**:511
- - *Kevod ha-Levanon* (1873) **7**:1179
- - *Mevasser* (*Maebussaer;* 1873) **5**:40
- - *Pirḥei Ẓafon* (Vilna, 1841) **7**:1448
- *see also:* PRESS
New Square (vill., N.Y.) **14**:214,1651
- Ḥasidim **7**:1400
New Standard Jewish Encyclopedia, The **6**:734
New Synagogue (Lond.) **15**:619
Newt (zool.) **6**:36
NEW TESTAMENT **12**:1059
- *Contents:*
- - Composition and Acceptance of Various Writings **12**:1059
- - Canonization **12**:1060
- - Language **12**:1060
- - Ethic of **12**:1061
- Amen in **2**:803
- anti-Semitism in **3**:96
- Aramaic language **16**:1591
- belief **4**:429
- Bethany **4**:733
- Delitzsch **5**:1474
- demons **5**:1526
- Epistles **11**:56
- Feast of Booths in **15**:498
- folkloric material in **6**:1376
- *haftarah* reading **16**:1343
- Herod in **8**:386
- Isaiah **9**:44
- Jesus, identified as Davidic Messiah **11**:1410
- "Jew" and "Israel" in **10**:22
- marriage **11**:1027
- Noachide laws **12**:1190
- Passover **13**:171
- Paul **13**:190
- Pharisees **13**:366; **14**:648
- resurrection **14**:97
- Satan **14**:903; **14**:905
- synagogue **15**:582
- *tefillin* **15**:899
- term **4**:817
- word **16**:635
- *illus:*
- - *Ecclesia et Synagoga* (13th cent. ms.) **3**:92
- - Mary Magdalene and the apostles **3**:217
- *see also:* CHRISTIANITY; CHURCH, CATHOLIC; JESUS; JEWISH-CHRISTIAN SECTS
Newton (city, Mass.) **11**:1112
- Boston **4**:1265
Newton, Francis, *see* HOBSBAWM, ERIC JOHN ERNEST
Newton, James William **8**:47
New Waterford (tn., Can.) **11**:998
NEW YEAR **12**:1061
- calendar **5**:48
- *Jubilees, Book of* **10**:325
- Sukkot **15**:497
- *see also:* ROSH HA-SHANAH
New Year for Trees, *see* TU BI-SHEVAT
New York Association for New Americans **5**:877
New York Board of Rabbis **6**:693; **12**:1119
NEW YORK CITY **12**:1062
- *Contents:*
- - 1654-1870 **12**:1062
- - 1870-1920 **12**:1075
- - 1920-1970 **12**:1105
- Barsimon, Jacob **4**:262
- demography **5**:1513ff
- early settlement **2**:809
- education, Jewish **6**:437ff
- history chart (1730) **8**:766-767
- Jewish Theological Seminary **10**:95
- Levantine community **14**:1174
- Levy, Asser **11**:156
- mental illness **11**:1373
- mortality rate **14**:1499
- museums **12**:538ff,544
- population in 1914 **8**:732
- press **12**:1052; **13**:1050
- Public Library **11**:193
- Rockland County **14**:214
- Sephardim **14**:1173ff
- slave trade **14**:1664
- universitites **15**:1680
- U.S. **15**:1586ff
- Westchester County **16**:465
- Yeshiva University **16**:760
- *illus:*
- - A.J.C. anti-Nazi demonstration **15**:1629
- - America-Israel Culture House **2**:817
- - announcement of five Yiddish plays **15**:1067
- - Beth Israel Medical Center **8**:1038
- - Biltmore Hotel Conference **15**:1633
- - boycott of Nazi goods **15**:1631
- - Bronx, pupils of Sholem Aleichem School **6**:434
- - Crown Heights, night patrol by Jewish volunteer organization **15**:1646
- - Ellis Island, immigrants at **15**:1609
- - *Forward*, advertisement page **15**:1619
- - garment workers' strike

15:1616,1617
– – *Hadoar*, first issue **15:**1627
– – Israel arts and crafts display **2:**817
– – Israel Bonds-U.J.A. dinner **15:**1668
– – Jewish craftsmen, 1890 (table) **5:**1054
– – Jewish Museum **12:**550
– – Jewish Theological Seminary **10:**97
– – Leo Baeck Institute **11:**24
– – Magnes, Judah L., letter re community debts **6:**1284
– – *mazzah* machine (19th cent.) **11:**1157
– – *mazzot* sale **15:**1607
– – Mount Sinai Hospital **8:**1037
– – *New Yorker Juedische Zeitung*, first issue **13:**1054
– – protest against Palestine policy (1947) **16:**1059
– – Purim fête poster **13:**1391
– – rally for a Jewish Palestine **15:**1659
– – rally opposing U.S. Palestine policy **15:**1663
– – Rosenberg demonstration **14:**280
– – Shearith Israel congregation, constitution (1805) **5:**830
– – Shearith Israel synagogue **14:**1175
– – shoelace seller (1896) **13:**207
– – Temple Emanu-El (old building) **3:**344
– – *The Jew* (1823) **13:**1050
– – Triangle Shirtwaist fire **15:**1615
– – U.J.A. National Conference **15:**1541
– – Yeshiva University **16:**760,767
– – Yiddish writers' group **16:**823
– – YIVO publications **16:**838
– – Z.O.A. Convention (1939) **16:**1177
– *maps:* text
– *pop. tables:* text
– *see also:* NEW YORK STATE
New Yorker (mag.) **5:**220
New Yorker Israelite (period.) **13:**1053
New Yorker Yidisher Folkstsaytung (period.) **13:**1053
New Yorker Yidishe Tsaytung (period.) **13:**1053
– *illus:*
– – masthead (1870) **13:**1054
New York Guild for the Jewish Blind **4:**1092
New York Kehillah (orgn.) **11:**716; **12:**1095ff
New York Post (newsp.) **4:**57
NEW YORK STATE **12:**1125
– *see also:* NEW YORK CITY
New York Times (newsp.) **2:**318; **15:**509
– *illus:*
– – protest against anti-Semitic propaganda in the U.S. (1921) **15:**1654
New York Yiddish Art Theater, *see* Yiddish Art Theater
NEW ZEALAND **12:**1127
– Israel's relations **9:**432
– mental illness **11:**1373ff
– Polack, Joel **13:**706
– population **13:**887ff
– press **13:**1025
– Six-Day War **9:**543
– synagogues **1:** syn. list
– U.N. **15:**1553
– Vogel, Sir Julius **16:**203
– War Crimes Trials **16:**291
– Zionism **16:**1105
– *illus:* text
– *pop. tables:*
– – text
– – 19/20 centuries **13:**893,898
– – postwar communities **5:**839
New Zealand Jewish Chronicle (period.) **12:**1129; **13:**1026
New Zealand Jewish Times (period.) **12:**1129
New Zionist Organization **16:**1098
– *see also:* REVISIONISTS, ZIONIST
Nexon (camp, Fr.) **7:**34
Neyhus, David K., *see* NILES, DAVID K.
NEYRAC, PIERRE **7:**150
Neẓaḥ (Zion. gr.) **7:**1376
Neẓaḥ (kab. conc.) **10:**570ff
Neẓaḥ Israel (soc., Rus.) **12:**969
Neẓaḥ Yisra'el (educ. network, Er. Isr.) **11:**169
Nezchies, Mordecai of, *see* MORDECAI OF NEZKHIS
Nezed ha-Dema (bk.) **14:**1107
Nezer (headdress) **5:**1130
NEẒER SERENI (kib., Isr.) **12:**1131
– Givat Brenner **7:**597
– statistics **1:**place list
– *illus:*
– – text
– – "Hashoah" memorial (B. Lishansky) **3:**633
Nezhdanov, Andrey, *see* SOBOL, ANDREY MIKHAILOVICH
NEZHIN (city, Ukr.) **12:**1131
Nezifah (reprimand) **8:**351; **8:**354
Nezikin (leg. conc.), *see* TORTS
NEZIKIN (order, Mish.) **12:**1132
– Jerusalem Talmud **15:**773
– minor tractates **12:**49
– piety **14:**652
Nezirut Shimshon (bk.) **4:**1110
N-e-ẓ-i-v, *see* BERLIN, NAPHTALI ẒEVI JUDAH
Nezivim (anc. city, Mesop.) **7:**1036
Neznažov (vill., Bohem.) **10:**1171
Niagara Falls (city, Ont.) **12:**1408
Niamey (city, Niger) **9:**440
Nicaea, Council of (325) **5:**546
Nicaea, Empire of **7:**874
NICANOR (Syr. of.) **12:**1132
– Alexandrians in Jerusalem **2:**590
– history chart **8:**766-767
– Judah Maccabee **2:**549; **10:**381
– *Scroll of Antiochus* **14:**1045; **14:**1046
– war and warfare **16:**278
Nicanor Day (fest.) **2:**252; **12:**1132
Nicanor of Alexandria **2:**590; **12:**1133ff; **15:**980; **16:**1272
– *illus:*
– – Cave of Nicanor ossuary **12:**1133
NICANOR'S GATE (Temple) **12:**1133
– Temple **15:**966
– *illus:* text
NICARAGUA **12:**1135
– Latin America **10:**1451
– synagogues **1:** syn. list
NICARCHUS (au.) **7:**896
NICE (city, Fr.) **12:**1135
– *illus:* text
Nicholas I (pope) **6:**216; **13:**852
NICHOLAS I (czar) **12:**1137
– constitution for Jews **8:**721ff
– Decembrists **5:**1451
– Pale of Settlement **13:**25
– Russian Jews **14:**436
– Talmud, translation of **5:**410
– Velizh **16:**87
– *illus:*
– – text
– – Montefiore, Moses, and **12:**271
NICHOLAS II (czar) **12:**1138
– Russian Jews **14:**446
– Union of the Russian People **15:**1538
NICHOLAS III (pope) **12:**1136
– Abulafia, Abraham **2:**185
– papal bull **4:**1496
– popes **13:**854
NICHOLAS IV (pope) **12:**1137
– popes **13:**855
NICHOLAS V (pope) **12:**1137
– popes **13:**856
– Roman Jews **14:**248
NICHOLAS, EDWARD **12:**1139
NICHOLAS DE LYRE **12:**1139
– Hebrew studies **8:**49
– Luther **11:**586
– Rashi **13:**1563
Nicholas of Cusa, *see* CUSA, NICHOLAS OF
NICHOLAS OF DAMASCUS **12:**1140
– history **8:**553
– Jews, description of **7:**890
– Josephus **8:**455; **10:**259
Nicholas of Hereford **4:**868
Nicholas of Manjacoria, *see* Manjacoria, Nicholas
"Nicholas Soldiers" (descendants of Cantonists) **13:**26
NICHOLS, JACK **3:**606
NICHOLS, MIKE **12:**1141
Nicholson, I. **8:**49
Nicodemus (4/5 cent., Er. Isr.) **9:**1376
Nicodemus (pr., Rum.) **8:**915
Nicolai, Friedrich **11:**1331
Nicolai, J.F. **8:**49
Nicomedia (Turk. port), *see* IZMIT
Nicopolis (city, Bul.), *see* NIKOPOL
Nicopolis -Emmaus (city, Er.Isr.) **5:**720; **9:**252
Nicosia (city, Cyp.) **5:**1182
NIDDAH ('menstruant woman') **12:**1141
– *Contents:*
– – In the Bible **12:**1142
– – In the Talmud **12:**1142
– – Woman after Childbirth **12:**1146
– – Non-Jewesses **12:**1147
– ablution **2:**82
– Akiva's ruling **2:**491
– *Baraita de-Niddah* **4:**194
– chastity **5:**363
– childbirth **4:**1050
– Commandments, the 613 **5:**765,781
– concubine **5:**864
– cosmetics **2:**491
– Falashas **6:**1148
– impurity **13:**1405ff
– Karaite use of bath **11:**760
– kissing forbidden **10:**1074
– *mikveh* **11:**1534ff
– Samaritans **14:**744
– synagogue **15:**593
– *illus:*
– – commandments incumbent on women **11:**1039
– – woman showing menstrual stain **12:**1148
– *see also:* MIKVEH; NIDDAH (tract.); TAHARAT HA-MISHPAḤAH
NIDDAH (tract.) **12:**1148
– laws of *niddah* **12:**1141ff
Niddui (ban), *see* ḤEREM
Niderschlezis Yiddish Theater (Pol.) **15:**1072
NIEBUHR, KARSTEN **12:**1149
– Persepolis inscriptions **16:**1506
NIEBUHR, REINHOLD **12:**1149
– missions to Jews **13:**1252
Niederhagen (Ger. concen. camp) **5:**78
Niederhagenthal (loc., Als.) **2:**754
Niederhoffer, Victor **15:**315
Niedermann, Maurice **16:**1224
Niedernai (loc., Als.) **2:**754
NIEDERSTETTEN (city, Ger.) **12:**1150
NIEGO, JOSEPH **12:**1150
Nielsen, Carl **14:**918
Nielson, Haraldur **4:**877
Niemcewicz, Julian Ursyn **13:**799
Niemeyer, Oscar **2:**167; **3:**362ff; **7:**1140
Niemirów (tn., Ukr.), *see* NEMIROV
NIEMIROWER, JACOB ISAAC **12:**1151
– Rumania **14:**392, 396, 397
Niemojewski, Andrzej **13:**801
Nierler, Meir **14:**1643
NIERMAN, LEONARDO **3:**607
Nierop, Ahasverus Samuel van **12:**1151
Nierop, Frederik Samuel van **12:**1152
Nierop, Hendrik Abraham van **12:**1152
NIEROP, VAN (fam.) **12:**1151
Nieśwież (tn., Belor.), *see* NESVIZH
Nieśwież Bible (Pol.) **13:**798
Nieto, Abraham Ḥayyim **12:**1153
NIETO, DAVID **12:**1152
– Ashkenazi, Ẓevi **3:**734
– history chart **8:**766-767
– portrait **3:**539
– Shabbateanism **14:**1249
– Vieira, Antonio **16:**122
NIETO, ISAAC **12:**1153
– Azevedo **3:**1007
Nieto, Phinehas **12:**1153
Nietzsche, Elizabeth, *see* Foerster, Elizabeth
NIETZSCHE, FRIEDRICH WILHELM **12:**1153
– anti-Semitism **7:**445
– Berg and doctrines of **4:**607
Nieuw Israëlietisch Weekblad (period.)
– Amsterdam **2:**904
– Netherlands **12:**991
– press **13:**1035
– publishing **13:**1365
Nieuw-Middleburgh (stlmt., Guyana) **7:**997
Nieuwsblad voor Israelieten (newsp.) **13:**1035
Nievo, Ippolito **9:**1105
Niezabitowski, Wacław **9:**1360
Niezwicki, A. **15:**57
Nifanius, Christian **8:**49
NIFOCI, ISAAC **12:**1154
– astrolabist **3:**787
– Bougie **4:**1274
– Majorca **11:**801
– Tunisia **15:**1438
Nifoci, Joseph **12:**1154
Nigel (tn., S.A.) **15:**1340
Niger (rep., Afr.) **9:**440
Niger, Pescennius (Rom. gov.), *see* Pescennius Niger
Niger, Peter, *see* NIGRI, PETRUS
Niger, Radulphus **8:**49
NIGER, SAMUEL **12:**1154
– *illus:*
– – Yiddish writers group, New York **16:**823
Nigeria (rep., Afr.) **9:**440; **12:**1156
– *illus:*
– – Solel Boneh's Lagos City Hall **15:**93
NIGER OF PEREA **12:**1156
Niggun (tune)
– folksong **6:**1384
– ḥasidic music **7:**1390
– Naḥman of Bratslav **12:**787
Niggun Akedah (*Akedah* tune) **2:**486
Niggunim mi-Sinai (melodies), *see* MI-SINAI NIGGUNIM
'Night and Fog' (Nazi terror campaign) **12:**893
NIGHTINGALE (bird) **12:**1156
Nightmare **11:**708

'Night of the Bridges' (Pal.) **9:**688
"Night over Vitebsk" (paint., M. Chagall) **16:**191
NIGHT PRAYER **12:**1157
- *Adon Olam* **2:**296
- *Shema* **14:**1371
"Night Zag VI" (sculp., L. Nevelson) **14:**1063
Nigra (masor. term) **16:**1432
NIGRI, PETRUS **12:**1158
- Hebraists **8:**56
NIJMEGEN (tn., Neth.) **12:**1158
Nikaso (bib. fig.) **8:**625
Nikbatah de-Iyun (city, Er. Isr.), *see* IJON
Nikel, J. **4:**875
NIKEL, LEA **12:**1159
- art **3:**592
- *illus:* **16:**1509
- - painting Pl. 13 **3:**ART
NIKITIN, VICTOR **12:**1159
Nikkal (deity) **15:**1507
Nikkud, ha- (wk.), *see Sefer ha-Nikkud*
Nikkur, see Porging
Nikodem, Theophil, *see* BEER, PETER
NIKOLAYEV (city, Ukr.) **12:**1159
- *illus:* text
Nikolsburg (tn., Morav.), *see* MIKULOV
Nikon (monk, Gr.) **7:**872
NIKOPOL (Nikopolis; city, Bul.) **12:**1160
- *illus:* text
NIKOVA, RINA **5:**1273
- Israel, cultural life **9:**1008
- *illus:*
- - in *Swan Lake* **5:**1264
"Niky," *see* Isaacson, Michael
Nīl, Al- (loc., Iraq) **8:**1447
NILE (riv., Afr.) **12:**1161
- Gihon river and **13:**78
- plagues of **13:**608
NILES, DAVID K. **12:**1161
Niles Township (Ill.) **8:**1255
Niles' Weekly Register (period.) **15:**1648
NILI (spying orgn.,Pal.) **12:**1162
- Aaronsohn family **2:**24; **2:**28
- Athlit, center **3:**822
- Belkind, Na'aman **4:**440
- Feinberg, Avshalom **6:**1209
- Lishansky, Yosef **11:**303
- Nadav, Ẓevi **12:**752
- *yishuv* attitude **9:**334
- *illus:*
- - text
- - Aaronsohn, Aaron **2:**25
- - Aaronsohn, Alexander **2:**25
- - Aaronsohn, Sarah **2:** 25,29
- - Belkind, Na'aman **4:**440
- - Feinberg, Avshalom **6:**1210
Niloe, J. **8:**49
NÎMES (city, Fr.) **12:**1165
Nimim (period.) **1:** newsp. list
Nimmukei Yosef (bk.) **8:**466
Nimmukim (wk.) **16:**1390
Nimrah (loc., Er. Isr.), *see* BET(H)-NIMRAH
Nimrīn (riv., Transj.) **15:**1316
NIMROD (bib. fig.) **12:**1166
- Abraham **2:**115
- Al-Raḥbah **13:**1515
- Tukulti-Ninurta I **16:**1501
- *illus:*
- - text
- - Abraham cast into fire **2:**118; **8:**1217
Nimrover (ling. schol.) **16:**1392
Nimrud (city, Mesop.), *see* Calah
NIMZOVITCH, AARON **12:**1168
NINE DAYS (mourning period) **12:**1168
- cooking and food **6:**1424
- *Shabbat Ḥazon* **14:**573
- *see also:* AV, THE NINTH OF; THREE WEEKS
"19 de Abril" (J. stlmt., Urug.) **16:**13
Nineteen Letters of Ben Uziel (bk.), *see Neunzehn Briefe ueber Judentum*
NINEVEH (city, Assyr.) **12:**1168
- *Contents:*
- - History **12:**1169
- - In the Bible **12:**1170
- - In the Aggadah **12:**1171
- Babylonia **4:**34
- Babylonian Chronicle **16:**1509
- history chart **8:**766-767
- Jonah, Book of **10:**169ff
- Mosul **12:**444
- Nahum's prophecy **12:**794ff
- Ninos **16:**1501
- Sennacherib **14:**1162
- *illus:*
- - text
- - "Jonah Preaching to the Ninevites" (lith., U. Birnbaum) **4:**1043
- - Sennacherib's palace **3:**319
Ningirsu (deity) **13:**260
NINGPO (city, China) **12:**1171
NINGSIA (city, China) **12:**1171
Ningursag (-a; deity)
- Elam **14:**1483
- Enki and **6:**979
- Sumer **15:**514
- *see also:* Ea; Enki; Ninlil
Ninio, Avraham **7:**1033
Ninlil (Ninmah; deity) **16:**1492
Niño (fam.) **5:**966
Ninos (myth. k.) **16:**1501
Ninos (anc. city), *see* NINEVEH
Ninth German Bible (15th cent., illum. print, Nuremberg), *see Koberger Bible*
Ninth of Av (fast day), *see* AV, THE NINTH OF
Ninurta (deity) **14:**1531
Ninurta I, Tikulti- (Mesop. k.,), *see* Tikulti-Ninurta I
Niort (tn., Fr.) **13:**704
Nipolis (city, Er. Isr.), *see* NABLUS
Nippur (city, Mesop.)
- archaeological finds **16:**1507
- Jewish exiles' community **16:**1270
- Sumer-league **16:**1486
Niqmaddu II (k., Ugarit) **15:**1503
Niqmepa (k., Ugarit) **15:**1503
Nir (lit. fig.) **6:**797
Nir (period., Isr.) **1:** newsp. list
- *see also: Ha-Nir*
Nir (period., U.S.) **1:**newsp. list
Nir (soc., Isr.) **9:**851ff
NIR, NAHUM **12:**1172
Nirah (mosh., Isr.) **4:**781; **14:**1213
Nir Akiva (mosh., Isr.) **1:** place list
NIR AM (kib., Isr.) **12:**1172
- Negev water supply **12:**929
- statistics **1:** place list
Nir Banim (stlmt., Er.Isr.) **10:**48
- statistics **1:** place list
NIR DAVID (kib., Isr.) **12:**1172
- statistics **1:** place list
Nir Eliyahu (kib., Isr.) **1:**place list
NIRENBERG, MARSHALL WARREN **12:**1173
NIR EẒYON (mosh.,Isr.) **12:**1174
- statistics **1:** place list
- *illus:* text
Nir Gallim (mosh., Isr.) **1:**place list
Nir Ḥen (mosh.,Isr.) **12:**940
- statistics **1:** place list
NIRIM (kib.,Isr.) **12:**1174
- pillar motif **13:**523
- statistics **1:**place list
Nir Ltd. (co., Isr.) **9:**828
Nir Moshe (mosh., Isr.) **1:** place list
Nir Oz (kib., Isr.) **1:** place list
Nirschi, F. **4:**1312
Nirschi, S. **4:**1312
Nir Yafeh (vill., Er.Isr.) **15:**675
- statistics **1:** place list
Nir Yisrael (mosh., Isr.) **1:** place list
Nir Yiẓḥak (kib., Isr.) **1:** place list
Nir Ẓevi (mosh., Isr.) **1:** place list
NIS (tn., Serb.) **12:**1175
- *illus:* text
Nisá (Turkmenistan) ostraca **2:**686; **3:**267
NISAN (month) **12:**1175
- Karaites **10:**779
- kings and festivals **12:**1061
- Samaritans **14:**748
- *Shabbat ha-Ḥodesh* **14:**573
- Sodom destroyed **15:**71
- Torah reading **15:**1386
- Twentyseventh of **12:**1389
- year **16:**725
- *illus:*
- - *tekufat* Nisan (Bet Alfa mosaics) **5:**45
- *see also:* CALENDAR
Nisan (period., Er. Isr.) **1:** newsp. list
Nisan (period., Pol.) **1:** newsp. list
Nisan Bak synagogue (Jer.), *see* Tiferet Yisrael synagogue
Nisan ben Azriel **16:**140
Nisanov, Ezekiel **12:**479
Nish (tn., Serb.), *see* NIS
NISHAPUR (tn., Pers.) **12:**1176
- lost tribes **15:**1005
Nishmat (piyyut) **13:**600
NISHMAT KOL ḤAI (prayer) **12:**1176
- Harari, Aryeh Judah **3:**667
- Peter (Simeon Caiaphas) **13:**348
- *illus:* text
Nishmit, Sarah **5:**448
Nishri, Ẓevi **15:**294
NISIBIS (tn., Anatolia) **12:**1178
- Diaspora **6:**11
- Judah ben Bathyra **2:**202
- Nimrod **6:**367
- trade route **7:**1036
- *illus:*
- - Judah ben Bathyra's burial place **4:** 323
Nisir, Mount (Mesop.) **3:**290; **6:**1356
Nisko (concen. camp Pol.) **6:**365; **8:**854; **8:**857; **12:**1512
NISSAN, AVRAHAM **12:**1179
Nissan Bek synagogue (Jer.), *see* Tiferet Yisrael synagogue
NISSELOVICH, LEOPOLD (Eliezer) **12:**1179
Nissen, Henry **15:**306
NISSENBAUM, ISAAC **12:**1179
- Lag ba-Omer **12:**1388
- Moriah synagogue **16:**337
NISSENSON, AARON **12:**1180
Nissi Belzer, *see* SPIVAK, NISSAN
NISSI BEN BERECHIAH AL-NAHRAWANI **12:**1181
- *piyyut* **13:**574
NISSI (Nissim) BEN NOAH **12:**1181
- cantillation **16:**1441
Nissim (poet, Babyl.) **11:**1096
NISSIM, ABRAHAM ḤAYYIM **12:**1181
Nissim, Hodja, *see* Nessimi, Hodja
NISSIM, ISAAC **12:**1182
- autopsies **3:**933
- religious life in Israel **9:**896
- *illus:*
- - Six-Day War, meeting religious leaders **9:**410
Nissim, Jacob Ẓemaḥ **5:**40
Nissim, Mu'allim **14:**525
Nissim, Paolo **13:**12
Nissim ben Abraham, *see* AVILA, PROPHET OF
Nissim ben Berechiah al-Nahrawani, *see* NISSI BEN BERECHIAH AL-NAHRAWANI
Nissim ben Jacob **10:**1199; **12:**1183
NISSIM BEN JACOB BEN NISSIM IBN SHAHIN **12:**1183
- Abramson, Shraga, on **2:**172
- ethical literature **6:**926
- history chart **8:**766-767
- Jerusalem Talmud **15:**776
- Jewish philosophy **13:**433
- ordination **13:**1449
- Talmud commentaries **11:**329
- Tunisia **15:**1434
- use of *suftaja* **16:**1282
Nissim ben Mordecai Dayyan, *see* Nathan ben Mordecai
NISSIM BEN MOSES OF MARSEILLES **12:**1185
NISSIM BEN REUBEN GERONDI **12:**1185
- Barcelona *yeshivah* **4:**210
- *Derashot ha-Ran* **5:**1549
- *ḥiddushim* **8:**466; **8:**467
- history chart **8:**766-767
- Jewish literature **11:**332
- title **7:**324
- *illus.* text
Nissim ben Solomon **15:**1323
Nissim Camondo Museum (Paris) **5:**76
Nissim Gaon, *see* NISSIM BEN JACOB BEN NISSIM IBN SHAHIN
Nissim of Damascus **11:**765
Nissim-Oglu, Ilya Sherbatovich, *see* ANISIMOV, ILYA SHERBATOVICH
Nissu'in (marriage) **11:**1032; **11:**1047; **14:**745
Nister, Der (writ.), *see* DER NISTER
Niterói (city, Braz.) **14:**190; **14:**191
Nitikman, Israel **16:**551
NITRA (tn., Cz.) **12:**1186
- Czechoslovakia **5:**1195; **5:**1200
- *illus:* text
Nitrae (tn., Egy.) **6:**9
NITTAI OF ARBELA (tan.) **12:**1187
Nitzana (loc., Er.Isr.), *see* NIẒẒANAH
Nitzanim (annual) **5:**450
Niv (period.) **10:**1521
- statistics **1:**newsp. list;
Niv ha-Kevuẓah (period.) **10:**969
- statistics **1:** newsp. list
Niv ha-Midrashiyyah (period., Isr.) **1:**newsp. list
Niv ha-Moreh (period.) **1:** newsp. list
Niv ha-Rofe (period.) **1:** newsp. list
N.I.W. (weekly), *see Nieuw Israëlietisch Weekblad*
Nixon, Richard **9:**421; **11:**1244
- *illus:*
- - Fisher, Max, and **6:**1331
- - Meir, Golda, and **11:**1244,1670
Nizak ben Vidal Yom Tov of Tolosa **2:**549; **16:**120
Nizām al-Dīn (trav.) **15:**1358
Nizan, Paul **7:**145
NIZER, LOUIS **12:**1187
Niẓḥana (loc., Er. Isr.) **13:**270
Nizhneudinsk (city, Sib.) **14:**1486
Nizhni Novgorod (city, Rus.), *see* GORKI
Niẓoẓ (period.) **1:** newsp. list
Niẓoẓot (kab. conc.)
- *gilgul* **7:**576ff
- ḥasidic theory of **7:**1405; **7:**1408ff
- Israel Ba'al Shem Tov **9:**1053; **9:**1054
- Jewish gnosis **10:**507
- Lurianic cosmogony **10:**596
- Naḥman of Bratslav **12:**786
- *illus:*

– – *ẓimẓum* **10**:574; 597
Nizza, Solomon **13**:12
Niẓẓaḥon (polem. manual) **6**:90
Niẓẓan, S. **5**:458
NIẒẒANAH (tn., Er. Isr.) **12**:1188
– Negev **12**:929
– Six-Day War **14**:1629
– War of Independence **9**:372; **9**:388ff
Niẓẓanei Oz (mosh., Isr.) **1**: place list
NIẒẒANIM (kib. youth vill.,Isr.) **12**:1188
– desalination plant **9**:772
– statistics **1**: place list
Niẓẓanim (period.) **11**:205
Njegoš, Petar Petrović **16**:885
Nkruma, Kwame (states., Ghana) **9**:439
No (city, Egy.), *see* THEBES
Noach, Laws of the Sons of, *see* NOACHIDE LAWS
NOACHIDE LAWS **12**:1189
– animals, cruelty to **3**:6; **6**:987
– *Avodah Zarah* tosefta **3**:981
– castration **5**:243
– Christian observance **11**:118
– incest **8**:1316
– *Kiddush ha-Shem* **10**:979
– non-Jewish law **6**:52
– non-Jews **7**:412ff
– righteous gentiles **7**:1383
– strangers and gentiles **15**:421
Noadiah (prophetess) **8**:622
NOAH (bib. fig.) **12**:1191
– *Contents:*
– – Life **12**:1191
– – In the Aggadah **12**:1194
– – In Christianity **12**:1195
– – In Islam **12**:1195
– – In the Arts **12**:1196
– angelology **2**:961
– angel Raziel **13**:1592
– blessing of children **4**:1087
– flood **6**:1351ff
– folklore **6**:1378
– Genesis, Book of **7**:395; **7**:396
– Ham **7**:1216ff
– kabbalistic view of **10**:616
– Lot story **11**:507
– Og's promise **12**:1341
– sacrifice **14**:605
– Shem **14**:1368
– Sibyl **14**:1490
– Uriel **16**:7
– *illus:*
– – text
– – drunk **6**:238; **7**:1217; **9**:1285; **14**:1369
– – leaving the ark **6**:980
– – 'Noah and the Ark' (paint., J David) **5**:1346
– – rainbow **13**:1525
– – the returning dove **6**:184
– *geneal. table:*
– – "table of nations" **12**:885
– *see also:* ARK OF NOAH
Noah (dau. of Zelophehad) **16**:979
NOAH, BOOKS OF **12**:1198
– *Enoch, Ethiopic Book of* **6**:796
– Lamech, Book of **10**:1367
Noah, Harold J. **6**:465
Noah, Jacob J. **12**:37; **12**:39
Noah, Joel **14**:834
Noah, Laws of the Sons of, *see* NOACHIDE LAWS
Noah, Manuel **12**:1198
NOAH, MORDECAI MANUEL **12**:1198
– Adams, John **2**:249
– anti-Semitism **15**:1648
– historiography **8**:567
– history chart **8**:766-767
– Jewish colony **2**:411; **4**:1465
– Jewish state **8**:728; **16**:1036
– journalism **10**:306
– literature **15**:1569,1575
– New York City **12**:1070; **12**:1074
– satire of **10**:335
– Tunisia **15**:1445
– *illus:*
– – text
– – Ararat, foundation stone **4**:1465
– – portrait **8**:707
Noah, Samuel **6**:1362; **15**:1034
'Noah and the Ark' (paint., J. David) **5**:1346
Noahian Laws, *see* NOACHIDE LAWS
Noah of Lachowicze (ḥas. r.), *see* Lachowicze, Noah of
Noah's ark, *see* ARK OF NOAH
No'am (mosh., Isr.) **1**: place list
No'am (youth orgn., Mizrachi), *see* Noar Mizrachi
No'am (hal. pub.) **10**:808
– statistics **1**:newsp. list
No-Amon (city, Egy.), *see* THEBES
No'am Yerushalmi (bk.) **14**:1299
No'aran (city, Judea) **3**:270
No'ar Ḥaluẓi Loḥem (Mil. Pion. Youth, Isr.), *see* NAḤAL
No'ar Mizrachi (youth orgn.) **9**:895; **12**:180
No'ar Oved (youth mvmt., Isr.) **8**:1240
NOB (bib. tn.) **12**:1200
– Abiathar **2**:71
– Nebo and **12**:911
– priests **8**:1216
– Saul's murder of priests **14**:913
Nob (vill., Golan), *see* Nāb
Nobah (bib. fig.) **10**:905; **11**:669
Nobel, Israel **12**:1201
Nobel, Joseph **12**:1200
NOBEL, NEHEMIAH ANTON **12**:1200
– homiletic literature **8**:957
– Rosenzweig **14**:301
– *illus:* text
NOBEL PRIZES **12**:1201
– *illus:* text
Nobility **16**:1305
Nobility, Jews in, *see* TITLES OF NOBILITY
Noble, James **8**:49
Noble, Luis **5**:461
Noc (moneyer, Bohem.) **12**:60
"Noce juive dans le Maroc" (paint., E. Delacroix) **11**:1037
Nochumowicz, Zimel **12**:1539
Nocturnal emission offspring (kab.) **10**:642
Noda bi-Yehudah (hal. au.), *see* LANDAU, EZEKIEL BEN JUDAH
Nodel, Sol **8**:1287
NOELDEKE, THEODOR **12**:1202
NOERDLINGEN (city, Ger.) **12**:1202
– *illus:* text
– *see also:* SWABIAN LEAGUE
NOETHER (fam.) **12**:1205
Noether, Emmy (Amalie) **12**:1205
Noether, Fritz **12**:1205
Noether, Max **12**:1205
Nofekh (stlmt., Isr.) **1**:place list
Nofekh (gem) **13**:1009
Nofet Ẓufim (wk.) **16**:1389
Nogah (mosh., Isr.) **12**:940
– statistics **1**:place list
Nogah ha-Yare'aḥ (journ.) **7**:708
– statistics **1**:newsp. list
Nogaret, John of, *see* John of Nogaret
Nogent, Guibert de **15**:83
Noginsk (city, Rus.), *see* Bogorodsk
Noḥumke, *see* Nahum ben Uzziel
Noise **6**:1399
NOLA, ELIJAH BEN MENAHEM DA **12**:1206
Nolad (hal. term) **12**:515
– festival, second day **6**:1245
Nolde, Christian **8**:49
NOM, IBRAHIM **12**:1466
NOMADISM **12**:1206
– fields plundered **2**:389
– Jabal, originator **9**:1170
– Rechabites **13**:1611
– Simeonites **14**:1549
– wilderness **16**:513
Nomberg, Ezekiel **11**:430
NOMBERG, HERSH DAVID **12**:1209
– *illus:* **16**:814
Nomos (Gr.: "law") **15**:1238
Non-Chalcedonians (Chr. cmty., Isr.) **9**:911
NONES, BENJAMIN **12**:1210
– Jews in military **11**:1551
Nones, Joseph B. **12**:1211
Nonius, Petrus, *see* Nunez, Pedro
Non-Jew, *see* GENTILE
Non-Sectarian Anti-Nazi League to Champion Human Rights (U.S. assoc.) **4**:1281
Noorath (tn., Jor. Val.), *see* NAARAH
Nootka (Ind. tribe, N. Am.) **14**:855
Norberg, Olav **8**:49
Norcia (tn., It.) **12**:1227
Norcia, da (fam.), *see* NORZI
Norcia, Manuele da **12**:1227
NORDAU, MAX **12**:1211
– Aḥad Ha-Am **2**:441
– Maccabi World Union **11**:664
– physical fitness **15**:293
– Zionism **16**:1055ff
– Zionist Congress (7) **16**:1168; **16**:1170
– *illus:*
– – F.Z.C. **16**:1165
Nordau, Maxa **12**:1213
NORDEN (fam.) **12**:1214
Norden, Benjamin **12**:1214
Norden, Harry **12**:1214
Norden, Joshua Davis **12**:1214
Norden, Marcus **12**:1214
Norden, Moses, *see* Nathan Moses
Norden, Samuel **12**:1214
Nordenflycht, Hedvig Charlotta **14**:929
NORDHAUSEN (city, Ger.) **12**:1214
– *kiddush ha-Shem* **10**:984
Nordheim, Lion **16**:1119
Nordheimer (fam.) **5**:103; **12**:1408
Nordheimer, Abraham **15**:1260
Nordheimer, Isaac **8**:209
Nordia (sport orgn.) **14**:129
Nordiska Rikspartiet (anti-Sem. party, Swed.) **12**:951
Nordiyah (qtr., Tel Aviv) **15**:921
Nordiyyah (mosh., Isr.) **1**: place list
Nordlingen, Joseph Yuspa ben Phinehas Seligmann, *see* HAHN, JOSEPH YUSPA BEN PHINEHAS SELIGMANN
Nordlyset (period.) **13**:1048
Nordman, A. **11**:1566
Nordman, Jean **11**:1566
Nordström, C. O. **2**:365
"Nord-Vest" (poet), *see* MINSKI, NIKOLAI MAXIMOVICH
NORFOLK (city, Va.) **12**:1215
– United States **15**:1596
– Virginia **16**:163
– *illus:* text
Norma (place, N.J.) **16**:157
NORMAN, EDWARD ALBERT **12**:1216
Norman, Norman B. **2**:317
Norman, Stephan Theodor, *see* Neumann, Stephan Theodor
Norman, Yiẓḥak **8**:200
Normandy (prov., Fr.) **7**:20
"Norman Fund", *see* AMERICA-ISRAEL CULTURAL FOUNDATION
Normative behaviour, *see* ETHICS
NORONHA, FERNÃO DE **12**:1216
– trade and commerce **15**:1301
Norrellius, A. **8**:49
Norristown (boro., Pa.) **13**:230; **13**:374
Norrköping (city, Swed.) **15**:545ff
– *illus:*
– – synagogue **15**:547
Norsa (fam.) **4**:173
– *illus:*
– – coat of arms **8**:1284
– *see also:* NORZI
Norṣa, da (fam.), *see* NORZI
Norsa, Daniel da **13**:916
– *illus:*
– – family portrait **4**:67; **13**:916
NORSA, HANNAH **15**:1052; **15**:1088
Norsa, (Abramo) Immanuel, *see* Norzi, Immanuel di
Norsa, Isaac (print.) **11**:898
Norsa, Isaac ben Moses (r.) **12**:1229
Norsa, Noah-Manuel **15**:1165
Norsa, Paolo **12**:1229
Norsa, Samuel **11**:898
Norsa, Solomon **11**:898
Norsa, Umberto **12**:1229
NORTHAMPTON (tn., Eng.) **12**:1217
– Colchester **5**:734
Northampton Donum (1194; tax) **12**:1217
– Amiot of Exeter **6**:1022
– Canterbury Jews **5**:127
– Hereford Jews **8**:344
North-Arabic, *see* ARABIC LANGUAGE
North Battleford (city, Can.) **14**:892
North Bay (city, Can.) **12**:1408
NORTH CAROLINA (U.S.) **12**:1217
– *Contents:*
– – Early History **12**:1217
– – Jewish Immigration **12**:1218
– – Contemporary Jewry **12**:1220
– Henry, Jacob **8**:329; **15**:1648
– *illus:*
– – text
– – Jacob Henry's speech **15**:1649
– *pop. tables:* text
NORTH DAKOTA (U.S.) **12**:1221
– *illus:* text
– *pop. tables:* text
Northern Kingdom (of Isr.), *see* ISRAEL, KINGDOM OF
North Italian Book of Psalms (15th cent.) **13**:1327
North Lawndale (sub., Chicago) **5**:414
North Miami Beach (city, Fla.) **11**:1478
North-West Semitic alphabet **2**:674
– *illus:*
– – script types **2**:675–688
Norton, Isaac **11**:501
Norton, John Lewis **6**:342
Norvid, M. **15**:1076
NORWALK (tn., Conn.) **12**:1221
NORWAY **12**:1222
– *Contents:*
– – Early History **12**:1222
– – The First Communities **12**:1224
– – Holocaust Period **12**:1224
– – Contemporary Period **12**:1225
– – Relations with Israel **12**:1225
– Church and Nazism **8**:915
– emancipation **6**:702
– Holocaust **8**:842; **8**:907
– literature **14**:932
– press **13**:1048
– *sheḥitah,* banned **14**:1341
– synagogues **1**:syn. list
– War Crimes Trials **16**:289ff

- Wergeland, Henrik **16:**452
- *illus:*
- - Oslo synagogue coupon **12:**1500
- *pop. tables:* text
- *see also:* DENMARK
Norwegian (lang.) **4:**877
NORWICH (tn., Eng.) **12:**1226
- archives
- chronological chart **8:**766-767
- massacre **5:**1140
- *illus:* text
Norwich, William (=G. N.) **8:**49
"Norwich Cattle Fair" (paint., Ch. Towne) **3:**545
Norwid, Cyprian Kamil **13:**798,799
NORZI (fam.) **12:**1227
- *illus:*
- - portrait **13:**916
Norzi, Benjamin ben Immanuel **12:**1227
Norzi, Eliezer ben David **12:**1228
Norzi, Ḥayyim ben Jehiel **12:**1228
Norzi, I. (print.) **16:**1019
Norzi, Immanuel di **2:**153; **6:**1301; **11:**1168
Norzi, Isaac ben Daniel **12:**1227
NORZI, JEDIDIAH SOLOMON RAPHAEL BEN ABRAHAM **12:**1229
- linguistics **16:**1394
- masorah **16:**1477
Norzi, Jehiel Vidal ben Jedidiah Solomon **12:**1228
Norzi, Moses ben Jedidiah **12:**1228
Norzi, Nathan **12:**1227
Norzi, Raphael ben Gabriel **12:**1227
Norzi, S. **16:**1019
Nosaḥ (litur. term), *see* NUSAḤ
Nose, Jewish **3:**49
Nose-ring (jewelry) **13:**1013
Nosotros (monthly) **13:**325
NOSSIG, ALFRED **12:**1229
- territorialism **15:**1020
Nostra aetate (Ch. declaration) **10:**159
NOSTRADAMUS (Michel de Nostre-Dame) **12:**1230
- *illus:* text
NOTARIKON (lit. device) **12:**1231
- Adam, David, Messiah **6:**881
- *aggadah* **2:**356
- *Baraita of 32 Rules* **4:**195
- Baruch Togarmi **4:**267
- *see also:* ABBREVIATIONS
Notation, Musical *see* CANTILLATION; MUSIC
Notenquetscher, Anton, *see* Moszkowski, Alexander
NOTH, MARTIN **12:**1232
- Deutscher Palaestina-Verein **5:**1595
Nothingness (kab. conc.) **10:**562
Notker Labeo (monk) **4:**872
Notkin, Anne Sybill **10:**308
NOTKIN, NATA **12:**1233
NOTOVICH, OSIP KONSTANTINOVICH **12:**1233
Notre-Dame de France (Fr. hostel, Jer.) **9:**1460
- *illus:*
- - façade **9:**1463
NOTTINGHAM (city, Eng.) **12:**1234
Nouă Suliţa (tn., Ukr.), *see* NOVOSELITSA
Nouns (Heb. gram.) **8:**108
- Arabic influence **16:**1628ff
- mishnaic Hebrew **16:**1601
- Semitic languages **14:**1154
- *tables:*
- - patterns of formation **8:**109
- - pronomial suffixes **8:**119
Noureddin (sult.), *see* Nur-al-Din
Nouzenus, Sebastianus, *see* Sebastianus, A. Nouzanus
Novak, Franz **10:**1077; **12:**956; **16:**300
Novak, Grigori **12:**1376
Novakhovichi, Benzion, *see* VINCHEVSKY, MORRIS
Novakovski, J. **10:**90; **16:**229
Novaky (lab. camp, Slov.) **13:**147
Novaredok (city, Belor.), *see* NOVOGRUDOK
Novarini, Aloysius **8:**49
NOVA SCOTIA (prov., Can.) **11:**997
- Canada **5:**105
- Quebec **13:**1423
Novatian (Ch. F.) **5:**552
Novation, *see* ASSIGNMENT (OF DEBT)
Nova Trajana Bostra (city, Er. Isr.), *see* BOZRAH (Bashan)
Novaya Aleksandriya (tn., Pol.), *see* PULAWY
NOVAYA USHITSA (tn., Ukr.) **12:**1234
Novel, the, *see* FICTION, HEBREW
Novellae, *see* ḤIDDUSHIM
Novello, Sebastian **15:**1380
Novelot Ḥokhmah **10:**549
November Pogrom (Nazi), *see* KRISTALLNACHT
NOVE MESTO NAD VAHOM (tn., Cz.) **12:**1234
Novenianus, P. **8:**49
Nové Sedlice (tn., Morav.), *see* AUSTERLITZ
Nove-Sedliste (tn., Cz.), *see* Neuzedlisch
NOVE ZAMKY (tn., Cz.) **12:**1235
NOVGOROD-SEVERSK (city, Ukr.) **12:**1235
- Judaizers **10:**399
NOVI SAD (city, Yug.) **12:**1236
- Hungary **8:**1097
- Zionism **16:**1151
- *illus:* text
Novi voshkod (newsp.) **13:**1046
Novoaleksandrovsk (city, Lith.), *see* ZARASAI
Novogrodski, Emmanuel **4:**1506
NOVOGRUDOK (city, Belor.) **12:**1237
- Belorussia **4:**444
- ghetto **13:**770
NOVOMEYSKY, MOSHE **12:**1239
Novomisky, Moses Joseph, *see* OLGIN, MOSHE J.
NOVOSELITSA (tn., Ukr.) **12:**1240
Novosibirsk (city, Sib.) **14:**1488
Novosibirsk (reg., Sib.) **14:**1488
NOVOSILTSEV, NICOLAI NIKOLAYEVICH **12:**1240
Novotný, Antonin **3:**159; **5:**1203
Novoye Vremya (newsp.) **14:**442
NOVOZYBKOV (tn., Rus.) **12:**1240
NOVY, JIM **12:**1241
NOVY BOHUMIN (tn., Morav.) **12:**1241
NOVY BYDZOV (tn., Cz.) **12:**1241
- Abrahamites **2:**159
NOVY DVOR (tn., Belor.) **12:**1242
Novy Izrail (rel. sect), *see* NEW ISRAEL
NOVY JICIN (tn., Cz.) **12:**1242
NOVY OLEKSINIEC (tn., Ukr.) **12:**1243
NOWACK, WILHELM GUSTAV HERMANN **12:**1243
NOWACZYŃSKI, ADOLF **13:**804
NOWAKOWSKI, DAVID **12:**1243
Nowa Wieś (tn., Pol.) **13:**556
Nowe Miasto (tn., Pol.) **5:**561
Nowogródek (city, Belor.), *see* NOVOGRUDOK
Nowokrzepice (J. qtr., Krzepice) **10:**1283
Nowy Czas (newsp.) **13:**1042
NOWY DWOR MAZOWIECKI (tn., Pol.) **12:**1244
NOWY DZIENNIK (daily) **12:**1245
- press **13:**1042
- Schwarzbart, Isaac **14:**1028
- Zionism **16:**1132
NOWY SACZ (city, Pol.) **12:**1245
- *illus:* text
Noy, Baruch Ẓevi **16:**1014
NOY, DOV **1:**35
Noy, Melech, *see* Neustadt, Melech
Noyer Leben, Das (newsp.) **16:**1348
Noyers, Pierre des **10:**1556
Noẓeri (name for Christians), *see* Nazarenes
Nozière, Fernand **7:**147
Noẓrat (tn., Er. Isr.), *see* NAZARETH
N.P.D. (Neo-Nazi party, Ger.), *see* National Democratic Party
N.S.D.A.P., *see* NATIONAL SOCIALISM
N'shei Poalei Agudath Israel (U.S.) **13:**656
Nuba (mus. form) **16:**1259
Nubia (anc. kdm., Afr.) **5:**1174
Nuclear Research Centers in Israel, *see* ATOMIC ENERGY IN ISRAEL
NUDELMAN, SANTIAGO I. **13:**820; **13:**829
Nuernberg (city, Ger.), *see* NUREMBERG
Nuernberger, Kalman **15:**1509
Nueva Sion (period.) **16:**1123
Nuevo, Castel **15:**1446
Nūḥ, *see* NOAH
Nūḥ, Joseph ibn, *see* Joseph ibn Nūḥ
NUISANCE (leg. conc.) **12:**1246
- servitudes **14:**1188
Nukba de-ze'eir (kab. conc.) **10:**599
Nu'man, Hasan ibn, *see* Ibn Nu'man, Hasan
Nuʿmān ibn abi al-Riḍā' **10:**421
NUMBERS, BOOK OF **12:**1249
- *Contents:*
- - Contents and Sequence **12:**1249
- - Critical View **12:**1252
- - Dating and Historical Value **12:**1253
- - Religious Values **12:**1253
- Levites **11:**138
- Pentateuch **13:**232ff
- *Sifrei* **14:**1519
- *Sifrei Zuta* **14:**1522
- *illus:*
- - *Duke of Sussex Pentateuch* **12:***fcg.* 1259
- - eleventh century manuscript **4:**954
- - Naḥmanides commentary **12:**775
- - *Shelah Lekha* portion (1106) **4:***fcg.* 812
NUMBERS, TYPICAL AND IMPORTANT **12:**1254
- *Contents:*
- - Biblical Arithmetic **12:**1254
- - Method of Expression **12:**1255
- - Symbolic and Rhetorical Use **12:**1255
- - Accuracy **12:**1259
- - Ascending and Descending Numbers **12:**1259
- - Numerical Harmony **12:**1260
- - Graded Numbers **12:**1260
- biblical Hebrew **16:**1582
- four **3:**292
- Hebrew alphabet **2:**743
- Hebrew grammar **8:**122
- Kabbalah **10:**493,507ff,529
- *illus:*
- - letters as numerical signs **2:**743
- *see also:* GEMATRIA
NUMBERS RABBAH (agg. Mid.) **12:**1261
- *Tanḥuma* **15:**794
- *illus:* text
- *see also:* MIDRASH
NUMENIUS (2nd cent. B.C.E., s. of Antiochus) **12:**1263
NUMENIUS OF APAMEA (Gr. philos.) **7:**896
Numerals, numerology, *see* NUMBERS, TYPICAL AND IMPORTANT
NUMERUS CLAUSUS **12:**1263
- *Contents:*
- - Introduction **12:**1263
- - In Czarist Russia **12:**1264
- - In the Soviet Union **12:**1265
- - In Poland **12:**1266
- - In Rumania **12:**1268
- - In Hungary **12:**1268
- - In the United States **12:**1269
- England **6:**71
- Hungary **10:**1523
- League of Nations **10:**1523
- Rumania **14:**394ff
- Russia **6:**69; **8:**734; **14:**444
- students' movements **15:**448ff
- United States **6:**70
- universities **15:**1678
- *see also:* BOYCOTT, ANTI-JEWISH; Legislation, Anti-Jewish
Numerus Nullus (anti-Sem., Rum.) **12:**1268
Numidia (loc., Tun.) **15:**1431
NUMISMATICS **12:**1270
- Estori ha-Parḥi **6:**918
- Kisch, Bruno Zecharias **10:**1060
- Merzbacher family **11:**1395
- *see also:* COINS AND CURRENCY; MEDALS; MINTMASTERS AND MONEYERS
Numquam dubitavimus (papal bull) **4:**1496
NUN (Heb. let.) **12:**1272
- *Ashrei, nun* verse **3:**736
- reversed **16:**1408
NUNBERG, HERMAN **12:**1272
Nunechius (bp.) **4:**1383
Nuñes, Augusto **5:**367
Nunes, Francisco de Bejar, *see* Bejar, Francisco Nunes de
Nunes, Franco **11:**1559
Nuñes, Gaspar Rodrigues **11:**855
Nunes, Isaac Cordoza, *see* Cordoza Nunes, Isaac
Nuñes, Isaac Israel, *see* Alvarez, Isaac
Nunes, João **15:**1301
Nunes, Samuel, *see* Nunez, Samuel
Nuñes, Zipporah, *see* Machado,Zipporah Nuñez
Nunes Carvalho, Naomi **12:**405
Nunes Henriques (fam.), *see* Henriques, Nunes
NUNES VAIS (fam.) **12:**1272
Nunes Vais, Abraham Joseph **12:**1273
Nunes Vais, Isaac Joseph **12:**1272
Nunes-Vais, Italo **12:**1273
Nunes Vais, Jacob **12:**1272
NUÑEZ (fam.) **12:**1273
Nuñez, Beatrice **12:**1273
Nuñez, Clara **12:**1273
Nunez, Daniel (N.J.) **12:**1021; **12:**1027
Nuñez, Daniel (Ga.) **12:**1274
NUÑEZ, HECTOR **12:**1274
Nuñez, Helen **12:**1273
Nuñez, Henrique (16th cent.) **12:**1273
Nunez, Henriques (18th cent.), *see* Nunez Ricus, Isaac
Nuñez, Isabel, *see* Alvarez, Isabel Nuñez
Nuñez, Jacob ibn, *see* Ibn Nuñez, Jacob
Nunez, Leonara Freire **12:**1274

Nuñez, Maria **12:** 1273
Nuñez, Moses **12:** 1274
Nuñez, Pedro **8:** 1407; **12:** 1273
Nuñez, Robert **12:** 1274
Nunez, Samuel (Ribeiro) **7:** 428; **12:** 1274; **14:** 920
Nuñez, Violante **12:** 1273
Nuñez, Zipporah, *see* Machado, Zipporah Nuñez
Nuñez Coronel, Fernando, *see* SENEOR, ABRAHAM
Nuñez da Costa (fam.), *see* CURIEL
Nuñez da Costa, Duarte, *see* Curiel, Jacob
Nuñez da Costa, Jeronimo, *see* Curiel, Moses
Nuñez da Costa, Manoel, *see* Curiel, Solomon
Nuñez de Fonseca, Joseph **15:** 529
Nuñez de Silva, Diego **11:** 825
Nunezes (fam.) **13:** 5
Nunez Ricus, Isaac **13:** 229
Nuñez-Torres, David **12:** 1273
Nunez-Vaez (fam.), *see* NUNES VAIS
Nunim menuzarot (Torah signs), *see Otiyyot menuzarot*
Nuqayb (loc., Syr.) **15:** 648
Nuqra, al- (val., Bashan) **7:** 1476; **9:** 597
Nur-al-Din (Nureddin; sult.) **7:** 525; **14:** 669
NUREMBERG (city, Ger.) **12:** 1274
- history chart (1499) **8:** 766-767
- Host desecration **8:** 1043
- judicial autonomy **3:** 929
- synod **15:** 633
- *illus:*
- - Jewish peddler **13:** 204
- - *Memorbuch* **12:** 522
- - Nazi Party mass rally, 1933 **8:** 829
- - Reform synagogue **15:** 622
Nuremberg, Israel of, *see* Israel ben Isaac of Nuremberg
Nuremberg Haggadah
- biblical illustrations **7:** 1097; **7:** 1098
- Samson in **14:** 775
- Samuel in **14:** 784
- Solomon in **15:** 110
- *illus:* **7:** *fcg.* 1195
NUREMBERG LAWS **12:** 1281
- Austrian Jewry **3:** 899
- chronological chart **8:** 766-767
- definition of Jew **7:** 489
- Hitler, Adolf **8:** 784
- Holocaust **8:** 839
- Reichsvereinigung **14:** 51
- *illus:* text
- *see also:* LEGISLATION, ANTI-JEWISH IN THE NAZI PERIOD
Nuremberg Mahzor (illum. ms.) **11:** 733
- *illus:* **11:** *fcg.* 747
Nuremberg Trials
- Abram, Morris Berthold **2:** 167
- Genocide Convention **7:** 409
- *illus:*
- - indictment page **16:** 293
- - session **16:** 289
- *see also:* WAR CRIMES TRIALS
Nurenberger, Meyer J. **5:** 113
Nurick, Gilbert **7:** 1348
Nuriel (angel) **16:** 7
Nur match factory (Er. Isr.) **9:** 341
Nurock, Aaron **11:** 233
NUROCK, MORDECHAI **12:** 1282
Nurock, Ẓevi Hirsch **9:** 1336; **12:** 1282
Nurshirwan the Just (k., Pers.) **15:** 1675
Nursia, Daniele de **12:** 1227
Nursia, de (fam.), *see also* NORZI
Nursia, Leone de **12:** 1227
NUSAḤ (litur.) **12:** 1283
- *mus. notations:* text
- *see also:* CANTILLATION; LITURGY
Nussbaum, Heniek **5:** 497
Nussbaum, Judah **5:** 755
Nussbaum, Mundek **5:** 497
NUSINOV, ISAAC **12:** 1284
Nussah, *see* NUSAḤ
NUSSBAUM, ARTHUR **12:** 1285
NUSSBAUM, HILARY (Hillel) **12:** 1285
NUSSBAUM, MAX **12:** 1285
Nussbaum, Perry E. **12:** 156
Nussbaum, Simon **12:** 1037
Nussenbaum, Yiẓḥak, *see* BEN-AHARON, YIẒḤAK
NUSSENBLATH, TULO **12:** 1286
NUT (bot.) **12:** 1286
- food **6:** 1416
- Rosh ha-Shanah **14:** 309
- wood offering **16:** 630
Nutkis, Benjamin Ẓevi **11:** 611
Nutt (schol.) **16:** 1341
NUZI (Nūz, Nuzu; anc. city, Iraq) **12:** 1287
- *Contents:*
- - Analogues to Patriarchal Narratives **12:** 1287
- - Analogues to the Book of the Covenant **12:** 1289
- - Analogues to Laws in Leviticus **12:** 1290
- - Analogues to Deuteronomy and Prophetic Literature **12:** 1290
- archaeological evidence **13:** 471
- archives **16:** 1498
- documents **16:** 1510
- Havvoth-Jair **7:** 1495
- Jacob story **9:** 1192ff
- marriage contract **2:** 298
- patriarchal history **8:** 573
- Sarah **14:** 866
- *teraphim* **15:** 1014
- *illus:*
- - a document **8:** 575
N.V.V., *see* Dutch Labor Federation
NYIREGYHAZA (tn., Hung.) **12:** 1291
- *illus:* text
Nyitra (tn., Cz.), *see* NITRA
Nympheum (pub. fountain, Jer.) **9:** 1406
NYONS (tn., Fr.) **12:** 1292
Nysa-Scythopolis (city, Er. Isr.) **5:** 720
Nyugat (period.) **7:** 1474; **8:** 1082; **8:** 1239
N.Z.O., *see* New Zionist Organization
Nzp (weight) **16:** 386
- *illus:*
- - dome-shaped units **16:** 377

O

O'ah (zool.), *see* OWL
OAK 12:1293
- afforestation in Israel 9:221
- Jerusalem flora 9:1515
- plant list 13:623
- *illus:*
- - Ḥurshat Tal Tabor oaks 9:172-173
- - "Little Switzerland" 9:235
- - maquis, Wadi al-Nimr 9:229
Oakes, John B. 12:1317
OAKLAND (city, Calif.) 12:1294
- museum 12:544
Oak Park (sub., Chicago) 5:415; 8:1256
Oak Ridge (loc., Tenn.) 15:1009
O.A.S., *see* Organisation Armée Secrète
OATH 12:1295
- *Contents:*
- - In the Bible 12:1295
- - - Definition and Form 12:1295
- - - The Use of Oaths in Ancient Israel 12:1296
- - - Sanctions 12:1297
- - - Appreciation of Oaths 12:1297
- - Talmudic Law 12:1298
- - - General Rules 12:1298
- - - Classes of Oaths 12:1299
- - - Administration of Oaths 12:1300
- - - Sanctions 12:1301
- - Post-Talmudic Law 12:1301
- - - Juramentum Judaeorum 12:1301
- General
- - *Amen* response 2:803
- - Commandments, the 613 5:771,774
- - crucifix 16:86
- - curses 4:1084ff
- - desecration 5:1560
- - euphemism 6:959
- - informers 8:1370
- - *shevu'ot* 14:1392
- - trial by ordeal 12:1449
- Legal aspects
- - admission 2:290ff
- - agency inapplicable 2:351
- - attorney 3:837
- - compromise 5:858
- - consecrated property 8:280
- - debt recovery 6:1012ff
- - duress 12:1400
- - flogging 6:1349
- - gambling 7:300
- - inheritance 15:480
- - Israel law 12:148
- - land dispute 13:1146
- - man and wife 14:1356
- - *niddui* 8:351
- - tax asset 15:844ff
- - vows 16:227
- - wage payment 10:1327
- - witness 16:585
- - worker's breakages 10:1329
- *illus:*
- - administration 14:1393
- - Landshut *Stadtbuch* (1361) 10:1412
- *see also:* OATH MORE JUDAICO; PLEAS
Oath, Physician's 3:676
OATH MORE JUDAICO (J. oath) 12:1302
- Austria 3:894
- Brunswick Jews 4:1422
- Crémieux, Isaac Adolphe 5:1075
- France 7:25
- Isidor, Lazare 9:90
- Majorca 11:801
- Manuel I Commenus 11:899
- Mendelssohn, Moses 11:1334
- Niemirower, Jacob Isaac 12:1151
- oaths 12:1301
- Rumania 12:1151
- Spain 15:229
- *illus:* text
- *see also:* AUTONOMY, JUDICIAL
Oath of Citizenship (Fr.) 4:1401
Oats, *see* FIVE SPECIES
Obadiah (bib. fig.) 12:1304
Obadiah (Pers. J. sect.), *see* ABU ῙSĀ, ISAAC BEN JACOB AL-ISFAHĪNĪ
OBADIAH (k. of Khazars) 12:1304
- Khazars 10:951
OBADIAH, BOOK OF (Bib.) 12:1304
- Minor Prophets 12:48
Obadiah, Elijah 2:847
Obadiah, Isaac, of Patras 7:876
Obadiah, Meyer 12:345; 13:816
OBADIAH, THE NORMAN PROSELYTE (11th cent.) 12:1306
- Baruch ben Isaac 4:277
- Cairo *genizah* 16:1339,1340
- Crusader period 9:272
- messianism 11:1422
- Moses *piyyut* 12:409
- music 12:589
- Muslim taxation of Jews 16:1279
- proselyte 13:1187
- *illus:* text
Obadiah, the Proselyte (12th cent.) 11:766
Obadiah ben Abraham Maimonides 10:513
Obadiah ben Baruch of Poland, *see* BERLIN, SAUL BEN ẒEVI HIRSCH LEVIN
Obadiah ben Moses 8:1323
- *illus:*
- - *Mishneh Torah* (1475) 8:1328
Obadiah ben Petaḥiah, *see* PERL, JOSEPH
Obadiah ben Solomon 11:754
Obadiah ben 'Ulah 12:763
Obadiah ha-Ger, *see* OBADIAH, THE NORMAN PROSELYTE
Obadiah ha-Sefardi 16:1359,1386
Obadiah of Bertinoro, *see* BERTINORO, OBADIAH BEN ABRAHAM YARE
Obadiah of Rome, *see* Obadiah ben Moses
OBADYA, ABRAHAM 12:1466
OBED (bib. fig.) 12:1308
- *geneal. table:* 5:1341
OBEDAS I (Arab. k.) 12:1308
- Alexander Yannai 16:715
- Nabateans 12:741
- warfare 16:279
OBEDAS II (Arab. k.) 12:1308
- Nabateans 12:742
Obedas III (Arab. k.) 12:742
OBED-EDOM (bib. figs.) 12:1309
- ark 13:1077
Obeid, El' (vill., Mesop.), *see* Ubaid
Oberammergau (vill., Ger.) 7:443
Oberdorfer, Moses 15:635
Oberehnheim (tn., Fr.), *see* OBERNAI
Oberg, Karl 16:296
- *illus:*
- - Paris war crimes trial 16:301
Oberhagenthal (loc., Als.) 2:754
Oberhoffaktor (tit.), *see* COURT JEWS
Oberkapo 10:755
Oberleitner, Franz Xavier 8:49
OBERMANN, JULIAN JOEL 12:1309
Obermayer, Leon J. 2:827
OBERMEYER, JACOB 12:1309
- Joseph Ḥayyim ben Elijah al-Hakam 10:242
Obermilizfaktor (tit.), *see* COURT JEWS
OBERNAI (tn., Fr.) 12:1310
- Alsace 2:751; 2:757
OBERNIK, JUDAH 12:1310
Obernik, Meir 14:978
Oberparnass (cmty.offic.) 10:1406
Oberwesel (tn., Ger.) 14:381
Obil the Ishmaelite (bib. fig.) 9:89
Obizoth (demon) 11:246
Oblations, *see* SACRIFICE
OBLIGATIONS, LAW OF 12:1310
- *Contents:*
- - Creation of the Obligation 12:1311
- - Fines 12:1311
- - Imperfect Obligations 12:1312
- - Personal and Proprietary Aspects of Obligation in Jewish Law 12:1312
- - Recovering Payment out of "Encumbered and Alienated" Assets 12:1313
- - Verbal and Written Obligations 12:1314
- - Parties to an Obligation 12:1314
- - Plurality of Creditors and Debtors 12:1315
- - Extinction of Obligation 12:1315
- - In the State of Israel 12:1315
- acquisition 2:221
- custom 12:17
- documents 14:1385
- *halakhah* 12:111; 12:133
- imprisonment for debt 8:1304
- joint liabilities 13:953
- lease and hire 10:1528
- limitations of action 11:251
- loans 11:414
- maintenance 11:784
- *prosbul* 13:1181
- Rabbi Nathan's lien 14:1397
- suretyship 15:524
- unjust enrichment 15:1683
- *see also:* ASMAKHTA; CONDITIONS; CONTRACT; EXECUTION (CIVIL); LIABILITY; LIEN
Oboda (city, Negev), *see* AVEDAT
Obodas I (k.), *see* OBEDAS I
Obodovka (vill., Ukr.) 14:1119
Obol (coin) 5:715
Obóz Narodowo-Radykalny (orgn., Pol.), *see* NARA
Obóz Zjednoczenia Narodowego (orgn., Pol.), *see* OZON
Obranski, David 11:1551
Obrister der Juedischkeit, see PRAEFECTUS JUDAEORUM
Obros (Heb.-Prov. songs) 10:441
Obscenity, *see* PROFANITY
Obscurantists (reactionary schol.) 14:108ff
Observances, *see* MITZVAH
Obshchestvo Rasprostraneniya Truda sredi Yevreyev, *see* ORT
Obshchestvo Zdravookhraneniya Yevreyev, *see* OZE
Óbuda (tn., Hung.) 4:1450; 15:619
O'byrne (Chr. Hebr.) 8:49
Ocala (city, Fla.) 6:1362
OCAÑA (tn., Sp.) 12:1316
Occident (newsp.) 10:1562; 13:1050
Occident (fascist orgn.) 12:952
Occitanus, Andreas Real, *see* Real(is) Occitanus, Andreas
Occult sciences 5:771
Occupations

– *derekh ereẓ* **5:**1551
– Greco-Roman Diaspora **6:**11
– handicrafts in Israel **9:**1012
– intermarriage **12:**166
– minstrel **12:**596
– seals **14:**1080
– *see also:* Professions, Free
OCHBERG, ISAAC **12:**1316
Ochrana, see Russian Secret Police
OCHRIDA (tn., Yug.) **12:**1316
OCHS (fam.) **12:**1317
Ochs, Adolph Simon **10:**307,315; **12:**1317; **15:**1009
– *illus:*
– – leading article **10:**312
Ochs, David **10:**1591
Ochs, George Washington **12:**1317
Ochs, Jacques **12:**1375
Ochs, Julius **12:**1317; **15:**1009
Ochs, Milton B. **12:**1317
OCHS, SIEGFRIED **12:**701
Ochsenmann, Karl **5:**453
Ochsman, Isaac **14:**527
Ochs-Oakes, George, *see* Ochs, George Washington
Ochus (Pers. k.), *see* ARTAXERXES III
Ockley, Simon **8:**49
Ocneanu, Emanuel **13:**1369
O'Connor, William Ulick **4:**1057
Octateuch (Bib.) **2:**365; **4:**861
Octavianus, Caius Julius Caesar, *see* AUGUSTUS
OCTOBRISTS (pol. party, Rus.) **12:**1318
Odaita (leg. conc.) **2:**291; **16:**521
"Odds or evens" (game) **7:**300
Oded (Zion. gr.) **16:**1115
Oded brigade (Isr. army) **9:**366; **16:**321
'Odem (precious stone) **13:**1009
ODENATHUS AND ZENOBIA **12:**1318
– Babylonian Jews **4:**41
– Ereẓ Israel Jews **9:**254
Odenburg (city, Hung.), *see* SOPRON
Odes of Solomon (Bib.) **4:**853
ODESSA (city, Ukr.) **12:**1319
– *Contents:*
– – Beginnings of Community **12:**1319
– – Growth of Jewish Population **12:**1320
– – Economic Status **12:**1320
– – Cultural Trends **12:**1322
– – Educational and Communal Institutions **12:**1322
– – Social and Political Activities **12:**1323
– – Pogroms **12:**1323
– – Zionist and Literary Center **12:**1324
– – Holocaust Period **12:**1325
– – Contemporary Period **12:**1327
– history chart (1871 and 1890) **8:**766-767
– massacre **3:**163
– museums **12:**540
– pogroms **13:**696ff
– self-defense movement **14:**1124ff
– Society for the Promotion of Culture among Russian Jews **15:**59ff
– synagogue **15:**589
– *illus:*
– – text
– – Museum of Jewish Art **12:**542
– – pogrom victim's funeral **13:**698
– – self-defense group **14:**445
ODESSA COMMITTEE (Zion. orgn.) **12:**1328
– Ereẓ Israel settlements **16:**1041
– *illus:* text
Odesser, Bezalel, *see* SHULSINGER, BEZALEL
Odesskaya Gazetta (newsp.) **14:**1677
ODETS, CLIFFORD **12:**1329
– New York City **12:**1121
Odhelius, L. **8:**49
Odita (leg. conc.), *see Odaita*
Odobesti (tn., Rum.) **14:**387
ODO OF CAMBRAI **12:**1331
ODO OF CHÂTEAUROUX **12:**1331
ODO OF SULLY **12:**1331
Odorico de Pordenone, *see* Pordenone, Odorico de
Oea (city, Libya), *see* TRIPOLI
Oecolampadius (Hussgen), Johannes **8:**49
Oef, Solomon, *see* Ohev, Solomon
Oeglin, Erhard **3:**850
Oehlenschlaeger, Adam Gottlob **14:**926
Oels (tn., Ger.), *see* OLESNICA
Oelschlaeger, Gothofred, *see* Olearius, Gothofred
Oelschlaeger, Johannes, *see* Olearius, Johannes
OENOMAUS OF GADARA **12:**1331
– Gadara **7:**251
– Jewish philosophy **13:**423
– Meir's disputations **5:**1178
OESTERLEY, WILLIAM OSCAR EMIL **12:**1332
Oesterlind (art.) **10:**248
OESTERREICHER, TOBIAS VON **11:**1575
Oesterreicher, Vojtěch, *see* RAKOUS, VOJTĚCH
OESTERREICHISCHE NATIONALBIBLIOTHEK **12:**1332
OESTERREICHISCHES CENTRAL-ORGAN FUER GLAUBENSFREIHEIT, CULTUR, GESCHICHTE UND LITERATUR DER JUDEN (period.) **12:**1333
Oesterreichische Wochenschrift (newsp.) **13:**1033
Oesterreichisch-Israelitische Union, *see* UNION, OESTERREICHISCH-ISRAELITISCHE
Oesterreichisch-Ungarische Kantoren-Zeitung (period.) **4:**331
Oetinger, F.C. **10:**646
OETTINGEN (tn., Bav.) **12:**1333
Oettingen, Joseph Levi **15:**506
Oettinger, Jacob Joseph **10:**1413
Oeuvre de Secour aux Enfants, *see* OZE
OFAKIM (tn., Isr.) **12:**1334
– statistics **1:**place list
Ofakim (journ., Isr.) **1:**newsp. list
Ofakim (journ., Pol.) **1:**newsp. list
Ofanim (angels) **2:**964
Ofek (journ.) **1:**newsp. list
OFEK, URIEL **12:**1334
– *illus:*
– – *Ha-Yom ha-Shemesh Meḥayyekhet* **5:**447
Ofen (tn., Hung.), *see* BUDAPEST
Ofer (mosh., Isr.) **1:**place list
Oferet (metal), *see* Lead
OFFENBACH (city, Ger.) **12:**1335
– archives **3:**387
– Frankists **7:**67; **14:**1253
– Hesse **8:**437
– *illus:* text
OFFENBACH, ISAAC **12:**1336
– Esther, Book of **6:**912
OFFENBACH, JACQUES **12:**1336
– Offenbach, Isaac **12:**1336
– *illus:* text
Offenbach, Judah **5:**742
OFFENBURG (tn., Ger.) **12:**1338
– Baden **4:**60
Offenses, Cardinal
– duress **13:**224
– homicide **8:**944
– idolatry **8:**1235
– incest **8:**1318
– Lydda assembly **9:**243
– martyrdom **10:**978
– Sabbath desecration **14:**557
– *sevara* **14:**1196
– sexual offenses **14:**1207
– sin **14:**1587
Offerhaus, Christian Gerhard **8:**49
"Offering" (sculp., N. Kaz) **3:**629
Offerings, *see* SACRIFICE
Office, public, *see* PUBLIC AUTHORITY
Officers, Overseers, and Treasurers of Ereẓ Israel (orgn.), *see Pekidim* and *Amarkalim*
OFFICIAL, NATHAN BEN JOSEPH and JOSEPH **12:**1338
– Cluny disputation **5:**619
– moneylenders **12:**249
Official, Nathan ben Meshullam, *see* Nathan ben Meshullam of Melun
Offredus, Ludovica Saracena **8:**49
OFNER, JULIUS **12:**1339
– *illus:* text
OFRAN (loc., Mor.) **12:**1340
– *illus:* text
OG (k., Bashan) **12:**1341
– Ashtaroth **3:**737
– descent **12:**962
– Eliezer **6:**619
– Israelite battle **12:**377
– proscription **8:**345ff
– *see also:* SIHON
Ogden (city, Utah) **16:**33
Ogdensburg (city, N.Y.) **12:**1126
Oglethorpe, James **7:**428
Ohad (mosh., Isr.) **1:**place list
Oḥana, Soliman **7:**1106
Ohanah, Nissim **9:**894
OHEL (theat. co.) **12:**1342
– Israel cultural life **9:**1004
– *illus:*
– – text
– – *Streetcar Named Desire* **15:**1063
Ohel (cemetery bldg.) **4:**1521
Ohel (journ.) **1:**newsp. list
– *see also: Ha-Ohel*
Ohel Mo'ed, see TABERNACLE
Ohel Mo'ed (wk.; Samuel Gerondi) **7:**509
Ohel Mo'ed (wk.; Solomon me'Urbino) **16:**1360,1389
Ohel Mo'ed (journs.) **1:**newsp. list
Ohel Moshe (qtr., Jaffa) **15:**919
Ohel Moshe (qtr., Jer.) **9:**1460
Ohel Moshe (syn., Warsaw) **16:**337
Ohel Moshe vi-Yhudit (yeshivah, Eng.), *see* Judith Lady Montefiore College
Ohel Torah (journ.) **1:**newsp. list
Ohel Yizḥak (yeshivah, Lith.) **13:**56
O.Henry, *see* Porter, William Sydney
Ohev, Solomon **2:**10
OHEV BEN MEIR HA-NASI **12:**1343
Ohev Ger (bk.) **11:**605
Ohienko, John **4:**887
OHIO **12:**1343
– *illus:* text
– *pop. tables:* text
Ohio State University **15:**1680
Ohlendorf, Otto **8:**869; **15:**1330
Oholah (bib. fig.) **2:**642; **9:**1563
Oholei Gadna (journ.) **1:** newsp. list
Oholei Shem (assoc., Rum.) **4:**1320; **9:**1294
Oholei Tam (bk.) **15:**785
OHOLIAB (bib. fig.) **12:**1346
– art **3:**506
– goldsmith **7:**738
– Tabernacle **15:**683
– tomb **14:**1508
– *illus:*
– – building the Tabernacle **4:**787
Oholibah (bib. fig.) **2:**642; **9:**1563
Oholo (cult. center, Isr.) **4:**780; **10:**1034
OHOLOT (mish. tract.) **12:**1346
– *Nega'im* **12:**924
OHRBACH (fam.) **12:**1346
Ohrbach, Jerome Kane **12:**1346
Ohrbach, Nathan M. **12:**1346
Ohrenstein, Aaron **7:**499
Ohrenstein, Alexander **11:**1554
Ohrenstein, Jiří, *see* ORTEN, JIŘÍ
Oifn Shvel (period.) **11:**1459
OIL IN ISRAEL **9:**793
– Heleẓ-Beror Ḥayil **9:**576
– Israel-Arab conflict **15:**1663
– wells **9:**393
– *illus:*
– – guarding pipeline to Haifa **7:**1069
– – Ḥelez, oil drilling **8:**289; **9:**380
– tables: text
OIL OF LIFE **12:**1347
– *illus:*
– – Adam on his deathbed **2:**247
OILS **12:**1347
– Augustus' ruling **16:**1276
– Babylonia **2:**400
– consecration to Temple **8:**279
– cosmetics **5:**978ff
– cult **5:**1161
– edible oil **6:**1418ff
– perfumes **8:**1312; **8:**1316
– safflower **15:**269
– seal **14:**1072
– Solomon's trade **15:**99
– *illus:*
– – text
– – Arab olive-oil press **9:**1028
– – olive press, ancient **6:**1417
– – Sabbath lamps **14:**559-563
– – Shemen vegetable oil factory **9:**342
– – Zechariah's vision **16:***fcg.* 935
– *see also:* ANOINTING; OLIVE
Oil tree **16:**630
Oisel, P., *see* Ouseel, P.
OISTRAKH, DAVID FEDOROVICH **12:**1352
Oistrakh, Igor **12:**1352
O.J.C. (partisan gr.), *see* Organisation Juive de Combat
Ojczyzna (newsp.) **2:**426; **11:**612
Okapi (zool.) **6:**31
Okashi, Avshalom **3:**592
– *illus:*
– – "Oriental Interior" (paint.) Fig. 102 **3**-ART
OKHLAH VE-OKHLAH (bk.) **12:**1353
– Bible **4:**839
– Dosa ben Eleazar **16:**1471
– masorah **16:**1428
Okker, Tom **15:**314
OKLAHOMA **12:**1353
– *illus:* text
– *pop. tables:* text
Oklahoma City **12:**1353
– *illus:*
– – Temple B'nai Israel **12:**1354
OKO, ADOLPH S. **12:**1355
Oktiaberl (mag.) **5:**459
Oktyabr (newsp.) **4:**447; **12:**53; **13:**1048; **14:**464; **16:**780
Olah, see Burnt offering
Olamenu (publ. house, Isr.) **7:**696
Olamenu (period.) **13:**1047
– statistics **1:**newsp. list
Olam ha-Asiyah (kab. conc.) **10:**580
Olam ha-Aẓilut (kab. conc.) **10:**580
OLAM HA-BA **12:**1355
– General
– – article of faith **3:**655ff
– – *Ashrei* recital **3:**736
– – death **5:**1423
– – eschatology **6:**874ff

- - evil **7**:776
- - Gentiles **4**:434
- - God welcomed **12**:291
- - *ḥuppah* for pious **11**:1041
- - Judaism **10**:391
- - kingdom of Israel **9**:1047ff
- - prophets **13**:1176
- - resurrection **14**:99
- - reward and punishment **14**:135ff
- - righteous Gentiles **7**:1383
- - Sabbath **14**:566
- - sin **14**:1592
- - soul, immortality of **15**:178
- - theology **15**:1105
- Exclusions
- - Ahab **2**:439
- - Ahithophel **2**:466
- - *apikoros* **3**:177; **14**:120
- - Doeg **6**:147
- - Gehazi **7**:357
- - informer **8**:1370
- - Jeroboam **9**:1047
- - Manasseh **11**:854
- - suicide **12**:1355
- - usurers **16**:31
- Views on
- - Aboab, Isaac **2**:92
- - Maimonides **11**:776
- - Naḥmanides **10**:527
- - Saadiah **13**:432
- *see also:* ACADEMY ON HIGH; AFTERLIFE; BEATITUDE; NETHERWORLD; PARADISE; REDEMPTION
Olam ha-Beriah (kab. conc.) **10**:580
Olam Ḥadash (period.) **5**:457
Olam ha-Defus (journ.) **13**:1379
Olam ha-Elektronikah (journ.) **1**:newsp. list
Olam ha-Ishah (journ.) **1**:newsp. list
Olam ha-Kolno'a (journ.) **1**:newsp. list
Olam ha-Mistorin (journ.) **1**:newsp. list
Olam ha-Sefer (journ.) **1**:newsp. list
Olam ha-Yeladim (period., Er. Isr.) **5**:458
Olam ha-Yeladim (period., U.S.) **15**:96
Olam ha-Yeẓirah (kab. conc.) **10**:580
Olam ha-Ẓillum (journ.) **1**:newsp. list
Olam katan (philos. conc.), *see* MICROCOSM
Olam Katan (period., Er. Isr.) **5**:457; **8**:1223
Olam Katan (period., Pol.) **5**:433,457; **12**:1051; **14**:1269
Olam Katon (publ. house, Rus.) **5**:432
Olamot Aḥerim (journ.) **1**:newsp. list
Olan, Levi A. **16**:633
'Olat tamid, see Burnt offering
OLBRACHT, IVAN **12**:1357
Old Arabic, *see* ARABIC LANGUAGE
Old Christians **15**:240
Old clothes, *see* SECONDHAND GOODS AND OLD CLOTHES, TRADE IN; TAILORING
OLDENBURG (city, Ger.) **12**:1358
Oldenburg, U. **4**:911
Oldendorf, Menaḥem **13**:692
Old French, *see* JUDEO-FRENCH
Old Hebrew Congregation (syn., Liverpool, Eng.) **10**:222; **11**:409
Old Konstantin (city, Ukr.), *see* STARO-KONSTANTINOV
Old Orchard Beach (tn., Me.) **11**:782
"Old Jewish Pedlar" (paint., G. Salomon) **3**:639
"Old Jew with Children" (drg., R. Kramsztyk) Fig. 75 **3**-ART
Old Paths (bk.) **11**:117
"Old" Synagogue (S.A.) **15**:192
"Old Synagogue" (wdct., S. Judovin) **14**:1469
Old Testament, *see* BIBLE
Old Town (city, Me.) **11**:782
"Old Tree and Old People" (paint., W. Gropper) **7**:932
Old *Yishuv* (Er. Isr.), *see Yishuv*
Old York Road Suburb (section, Pa.) **13**:374
Olean (city, N.Y.) **12**:1126
OLEANDER (bot.) **12**:1359
- flora of Israel **9**:225
- plant list **13**:623
Olearius, Gothofred **8**:49
Olearius, Johannes **8**:49
Oleh (*olim;* immigrant to Isr.) **9**:527; **9**:534
'Oleh ve-yored (cantillation sign) **16**:1457
Olelot ("gleanings") **11**:3; **13**:201
Olesh (mosh., Isr.) **1**:place list
OLESKO (tn., Ukr.) **12**:1359
OLESNICA (tn., Silesia) **12**:1360
- Hebrew press **15**:1481
OLESNICKI, ZBIGNIEW **12**:1360
- Polish Jews **13**:714
OLEVSKI, BUZI **12**:1361
OLGIN, MOSHE J. **12**:1361
OLGOPOL (tn., Ukr.) **12**:1361
Olin, Bob **15**:305
Olin, Irving **15**:303
Olinda (city, Braz.) **13**:1613
OLIPHANT, LAURENCE **12**:1362
- Bilu **4**:1000
- Ereẓ Israel **9**:299; **9**:324
- Zionism **16**:1154
OLITSKI, JULES **3**:607
OLITZKI, ARYEH LEO **12**:1363
OLITZKY (fam.) **12**:1363
Olitzky, Baruch **12**:1363ff; **16**:819
Olitzky, Leib **12**:1363ff; **16**:819; **16**:825
Olitzky, Mattes **12**:1363; **12**:1364; **16**:819
OLIVE **12**:1364
- biblical period **6**:1418
- commandments **11**:3
- cosmetics **5**:980
- economic history **16**:1276
- oils **12**:1347ff
- Pentateuch **13**:250
- plant list **13**:623
- tree of life **12**:1347
- wood **16**:630
- *illus:*
- - Arab olive-oil press **9**:1028
- - Tree in Garden of Gethsemane **9**:1514
- - Zechariah's vision **16**:fcg 935
Oliveira, Jacob de **4**:1461
Oliver (motion picture) **6**:787; **15**:1060
- *illus:*
- - Moody, Ron, as Faigin **12**:461
Olivers, Thomas **16**:835
Oliver Twist (bk.) **6**:22; **15**:1053
- *illus:*
- - "Mr. Fagin and Morris Bolter..." (illus., G. Cruikshank) **6**:781
OLIVER Y FULLANA, NICOLÁS DE **12**:1366
Olives, Mount of (Er. Isr.), *see* MOUNT OF OLIVES
Olivétan, Pierre Robert **4**:881
OLIVETTI (fam.) **12**:1366
Olivetti, Adolfo **11**:1559
Olivetti, Adriano **12**:1366
Olivetti, Camillo **12**:1366
OLIVEYRA, SOLOMON BEN DAVID DE **12**:1366
Olivier, Marcel **11**:679
OLKUSZ (tn., Pol.) **12**:1367
- *illus:*
- - text
- - mass execution of Jews by Nazis **8**:863
Ollendorf, Paul **13**:1368
Ollendorff, Fanny **12**:1369
OLLENDORFF, FRANZ **12**:1368
OLLENDORFF, FRIEDRICH **12**:1368
Olligoyen, Peter **7**:47; **16**:1151
OLMEDO (tn., Sp.) **12**:1369
OLMO, JACOB DANIEL BEN ABRAHAM **12**:1369
- poetry **13**:691
- Zacuto, M. **16**:909
Olomeinu (period.) **15**:1259
OLOMOUC (Olmuetz; city, Morav.) **12**:1370
- Holocaust **5**:1199
- Moravia **12**:296ff
Olper, Samuel Solomon **13**:502; **15**:1455
Olschki, Leo S. **13**:1368
OLSCHWANGER, ISAAC WOLF **12**:1370
- homiletic literature **8**:957
OLSHAN, ISAAC **12**:1371
- *illus:*
- - Eichmann trial **6**:519
- - Supreme Court bench **9**:637
Olshanski, Yosif **12**:456
OLSHAUSEN, JUSTUS **12**:1371
- Christian Hebraists **8**:49
- linguistics **16**:1391
Olson, B. E. **13**:1251
OLSVANGER, IMMANUEL **12**:1372
Olszanski, Abraham **5**:1361
Olszański, Teofil **15**:349
Oltramar, H. **4**:881
Olviopol (city., Rus.) **13**:326
OLYKA (tn., Rus.) **12**:1372
- *illus:* text
Olympia (city, Wash.) **16**:355
OLYMPIC GAMES **12**:1373
- *tables:* text
- *see also:* SPORTS
Olympios, Takis **7**:887
OMAHA (city, Neb.) **12**:1373
- *illus:* text
Omanut (publ. firm. Isr.) **5**:435; **13**:319; **13**:1374
Omanut (period.) **16**:1151; **16**:888; **16**:918
- statistics **1**:newsp. list
OMAR, COVENANT OF **12**:1378
- attitude to infidels **8**:661
- Dhimma, Dhimmi **5**:1604ff
- Fatimids' policy **6**:1197
- Ottoman Empire **16**:1540,1542
- Seljuks **14**:1136
- Umayyads **15**:1529
- Yemenite Jews **16**:744
Omar, Mosque of, *see* Dome of the Rock
Omar ibn ʿAbd al-ʿAzīz
- badge, origin of **4**:62
- Ereẓ Israel **9**:264
- intolerance **8**:1445
- Omar, Covenant of **12**:1378
- Umayyads **15**:1529
OMAR IBN AL-KHATTĀB **12**:1382
- Arabian Jews **3**:235
- Bustanai as exilarch **4**:1537
- caliphs **5**:61
- conquest of Jerusalem **9**:1408; **9**:1571
- Hebron **8**:228
- Mount of Olives **12**:483
- Omar, Covenant of **12**:1378
- seals **14**:1074
- Temple Mount **15**:989
Omayyads (dyn.), *see* UMAYYADS
Ombres, Rossana **9**:1107
Omen (vill., Er. Isr.) **15**:675
- statistics **1**:place list
Omen, *see* DIVINATION
Omepezoa, Pedro de **5**:461
Omer (stlmt., Isr.) **1**:place list
OMER (offering) **12**:1382
- *Contents:*
- - The Offering **12**:1382
- - Counting the Omer **12**:1384
- - A Time of Mourning **12**:1385
- - Lag ba-Omer **12**:1387
- - Other Explanations **12**:1388
- - Later Events During the Omer **12**:1389
- Sacrifice **14**:611
- - barley **4**:242
- - Commandments, the 613 **5**:778
- - festivals **6**:1241
- - five species **6**:1333
- - measures **16**:379; **16**:380ff
- - *Menahot* **11**:1314
- - modern ceremony of **14**:1355
- - Pentateuch **13**:249
- Counting of **12**:1384ff
- - ceremonial art **5**:309
- - Crusader massacres **5**:1142
- - kibbutz festivals **10**:959
- - Lag ba-Omer **10**:1356
- - Samaritans **6**:313; **14**:742
- Calendaric factors **5**:52; **10**:1528
- *illus:*
- - text
- - bringing first fruits to Jerusalem **6**:1313
- - papercut calendar **13**:44-45
- - symbolic reaping at Ramat Yoḥanan **10**:961
- *see also:* SHELOSHET YEMEI HAGBALAH
Omer (newsp.) **5**:1316; **8**:540; **9**:1017; **12**:1057
- statistics **1**:newsp. list
- *see also: Ha-Omer*
Omer (period.) **12**:1055
Omer, Devorah **5**:437
OMER, HILLEL **12**:1389
Omerei Bakkashot (sayers of supplications) **4**:116
Omer ha-Sadeh (wk.) **5**:1587
Omeriz (moneyer, Bohem.) **12**:60
Omez (mosh., Isr.) **1**:place list
O.M.I.K.E. (Hung. cult. assoc.) **4**:182; **8**:439
Ommanut (period.), *see Omanut*
Ommanut ha-Kolno'a (journ.) **1**:newsp. list
OMNAM KEN (piyyut) **12**:1390
Omnipotence (Divine) **5**:1083; **12**:74ff; **13**:422
Omniscience (Divine) **7**:643ff
- Akiva **2**:492
- Crescas, Ḥasdai **5**:1083
- free will **7**:125
- Jewish philosophy **13**:422
- Levi ben Gershom **11**:95ff
Omorka (primordial woman) **6**:339
OMRI (k., Isr.) **12**:1390
- General
- - Ahab **2**:435
- - archaeological evidence **3**:306
- - history **8**:596ff
- - history chart **8**:766-767
- - Israel, kingdom **9**:1047ff
- - Jerusalem trade routes **9**:1383
- - Moab **11**:1397ff
- - Tibni **15**:1135
- - trade and commerce **15**:1296
- - Zimri **16**:1028
- House of
- - Ḥazor rebuilt **7**:1538
- - Jonadab **13**:1610
- - Judah **2**:456
OMSK (tn., Sib.) **12**:1391
- Siberian Jews **14**:1486ff
OMZSA (relief orgn.) **10**:1215
On (city, Egy.), *see* HELIOPOLIS
"Ona" (paint., W. Barnet) **3**:617
ONA'AH (leg. conc.) **12**:1391
- economic history **16**:1294
- *hekdesh* **8**:280
- leasing and hire **10**:1529
- waiver **11**:1233

- *see also:* FRAUD; HAFKA'AT SHE'ARIM
ONAGER (zool.) **12:**1395
- dietary laws **6:**32
- *illus:* text
- *see also:* ASS
ONAN (bib. fig.) **12:**1395
- Tamar **15:**782
ONANISM **12:**1396
- *see also:* BIRTH CONTROL
Onderliczka, János **8:**49
ONDERWIJZER, ABRAHAM BEN SAMSON HA-KOHEN **12:**1397
Oneg Shabbat (soc., Pol.) **16:**348
Oneg Shabbat Archives (Pol.) **3:**385; **14:**190
One Hundred and One Unit (Isr. army), *see* Unit One Hundred and One
Onen (bereaved person), *see* ANINUT
'Onen (soothsayer), *see Me'onen*
ONES (leg. conc.) **12:**1397
- bailees **14:**1455ff
- divorce **6:**133
- loan cases **11:**419
- sale under duress **14:**676
- suicide **15:**490
- torts **15:**1273ff
- waiver **11:**1234
- work contract **10:**1328; **10:**1329
Onfang (newsp.) **13:**660
Onganía, Juan Carlos **3:**416; **3:**420
On Guard (orgn., Pol.), *see* Al ha-Mishmar
Onias (gen., Egy.) **13:**1348
ONIAS I (h. pr.) **12:**1402
- Areios I's letter **3:**402
- Sparta treaty **8:**296
ONIAS II (h. pr.) **12:**1402
- Tobiah **15:**1179
ONIAS III (h. pr.) **12:**1403
- Hellenism **9:**1390
- history chart **8:**766-767
- Simeon the Just and **14:**1567
- Teacher of Righteousness **15:**887
ONIAS IV (h. pr.) **12:**1403
- diaspora **6:**12
- Egypt **5:**603
- Onias, Temple of **12:**1404
- Zealots **16:**949
ONIAS, TEMPLE OF (Egy.) **12:**1404
- *Menahot* tractate **11:**1314
- Onias IV **12:**1403
- priests' disqualification **15:**970
Onias the rain-maker, *see* HONI HA-ME'AGGEL
ONION (bot.) **12:**1405
- food **6:**1416
- plant list **13:**623
Oniyyot u-Sefinot (shipping co.) **16:**1024
On the Jews (Samar. epic) **15:**1102
ONKELOS AND AQUILA (bib. trans.) **12:**1405
- anthropomorphisms **3:**53
- Cairo *genizah* **16:**1337
- Jesus **10:**15
- Targum **4:**842ff; **11:**313; **15:**811
- - Akiva **2:**490
- - Aramaic **3:**267
- - Berliner's edition **4:**664
- - Hebrew linguistics **16:**1393
- - Kasovsky's concordance **10:**809
- - masoretic notes **16:**1428
- - Rashi **13:**1561
- - Titus **15:**1170
- *illus:*
- - Targum to Pentateuch **15:**1483
Onkeneira, Isaac **12:**839
ONO (anc. tn., Judea) **12:**1406
ONÓDY, GÉZA **12:**1407
Onolzbach (city, Ger.), *see* ANSBACH
Onomasticon of Eusebius **6:**978
ONR (orgn., Pol.), *see* NARA
ONTARIO (prov., Can.) **12:**1407
Ontological argument (philos.) **7:**657; **10:**742
"On the Way to Jerusalem" (drg., A. Ticho) **15:**1136
ONYCHA (incense) **12:**1409
- incense and perfumes **8:**1311ff
Onyx (gem) **13:**1010
- *illus:*
- - priestly vestment **13:**1065
Oort, H. **4:**876
Oostende (tn., Belg.), *see* Ostend
Opal (gem) **13:**1010
Opatija (tn., Croatia), *see* Abbazia
Opatoshu, David **12:**1410
OPATOSHU, JOSEPH (Joseph Meyer Opatovsky) **12:**1409
- *illus:*
- - text
- - *Literarishe Bleter* editorial board **16:**818
- - Yiddish writers group, New York **16:**823
Opatov, Judah **11:**933
OPATOW (tn., Pol.) **12:**1410
Opatowski, Feibush **16:**946
OPAVA (city, Cz.) **12:**1411
- *illus:* text
Opelousas (city, La.) **11:**517
"Opening of the Hebrew University of Jerusalem" (paint., L. Pilichowski) **13:**519
Operation Atonement (Ger.), *see* Aktion Suehnezeichen
Operation Ezra and Nehemiah (Iraqi *aliyah*), *see* Ezra and Nehemiah, Operation
Operation Kadesh, *see* SINAI CAMPAIGN
Operation Magic Carpet (Yem. *aliyah*), *see* Magic Carpet, Operation
Operation Nahshon, *see* Nahshon, Operation
Operations, War of Independence, *see* WAR OF INDEPENDENCE
Opfergeld, F. **8:**49
OPFERPFENNIG (poll tax) **12:**1412
- Fiscus Judaicus **6:**1325
- taxation **15:**838
OPHEL (loc., Er. Isr.) **12:**1413
- Guthe, Herman **7:**985
- Jerusalem **9:**1521
- ostracon **16:**667
- Warren, Sir Charles **16:**332
- *illus:*
- - text
- - Jebusite and Israelite wall **9:**1382
- - ostracon **12:**1510
- - synagogue dedicatory stone **3:**335
- - Warren's dig at Temple Mount **9:**1522
OPHIR (bib. loc.) **12:**1413
- metals and mining **11:**1429ff
- Phoenician-Israelite expedition **16:**1269
- Solomon's trade **15:**98
- trade and commerce **15:**1295ff
Ophites (J. sect) **10:**498 **14:**719
OPHRAH (bib. locs.) **12:**1414
- Abiezrites **2:**73
- Gideon and kingship **8:**585
- Hapharaim **7:**1319
OPHUELS, MAX **12:**472
Opinia (newsp.) **11:**613
Opitius, Paul F., *see* Opitz, Paul F.
Opitz, H. **8:**49
Opitz, Joshua H. **8:**49
Opitz, Paul F. **8:**48
Opium **15:**269
OPLER, MARVIN KAUFMANN **12:**1415
- anthropology **3:**40
OPLER, MORRIS EDWARD **12:**1415
- anthropology **3:**40
Opnaim, Meyer, *see* Oppenheim, Meyer
OPOCZNO (tn.,Pol.) **12:**1415
Opoka, Nathan Lowenstein von, *see* LOEWENSTEIN, NATHAN
OPOLE LUBELSKIE (tn., Pol.) **12:**1416
- *illus:* text
OPORTO (city, Port.) **12:**1416
- Portugal **13:**919ff
- *illus:*
- - Kadoorie synagogue **12:**1417; **13:**924
- - Marrano meeting (1932) **11:**1021
Oppenhausen, Zalman Zevi **11:**355
OPPENHEIM (fam., Ger.) **12:**1418
OPPENHEIM (fam. Ger. bnks.) **12:**1418
- trade and commerce **15:**1303
OPPENHEIM (tn., Ger.) **12:**1417
Oppenheim, Abraham **4:**174; **12:**1418
Oppenheim, Beer (r., Cz.) **9:**1153
OPPENHEIM, BEER BEN ISAAC (r., Ger.) **12:**1419
Oppenheim, David (court J.) **12:**1334
Oppenheim, David (r.,Aus.) **12:**1423
Oppenheim, David (r., Serb.) **16:**1224
OPPENHEIM, DAVID (Heb. schol.) **12:**1419
OPPENHEIM, DAVID BEN ABRAHAM (r., Ger.) **12:**1419
- Ashkenazi, Zevi Hirsch **3:**734
- book collection **4:**974
- history chart **8:**766-767
- Jerusalem Talmud **15:**778
- Reischer, Jacob **14:**61
- *illus:* text
Oppenheim, David Joshua **16:**646
Oppenheim, Dagobert (David) **12:**1418
Oppenheim, Dov Baer **12:**1423
Oppenheim, Friedrich Carl **12:**1418
Oppenheim, Genendl **12:**1419
Oppenheim, George **7:**974
Oppenheim, H. (medal., Ger.) **11:**1167,1173
OPPENHEIM, HAYYIM (Heb. schol.) **12:**1422
Oppenheim, Hayyim (r.), *see* OPPENHEIM, JOACHIM
OPPENHEIM, HERMANN **12:**1422
Oppenheim, Hirsch **12:**1421
Oppenheim, Isaac **12:**1417
OPPENHEIM, JACQUES **12:**1422
OPPENHEIM, JAMES **15:**1583
Oppenheim, J.M. **7:**224
OPPENHEIM, JOACHIM **12:**1423
Oppenheim, Joel **12:**1418
Oppenheim, Joseph **4:**177
OPPENHEIM, LASSA FRANCIS LAWRENCE **12:**1423
Oppenheim, Max **3:**302; **12:**1418
Oppenheim, Meret **13:**114
Oppenheim, Meyer **4:**1038; **7:**613
OPPENHEIM, MORITZ DANIEL **12:**1423
- art **3:**565
- *illus:*
- - text
- - "Bar Mitzvah Speech" (paint.) **4:**245
- - Boerne, Ludwig (portrait) **4:**1167
- - "Child Entering the Covenant" (paint.) **5:**573
- - "Conclusion of the Sabbath" (paint.) **7:**1483
- - "Examination" (paint.) **6:**393
- - Heine, Heinrich (portrait) **8:**271
- - "In the Sukkah" (paint.) **3:**547
- - "Jewish Wedding" (paint.) **11:***fcg.* 1067
- - kidnaping of Edgardo Mortara (drg.) **12:**354
- - "Lighting of the Hanukkah Candles" (paint.) **7:**1281
- - "Passover Meal" (paint.) **10:**1079
- - "Purim at Home" (paint.) **13:**1403
- - "Rabbi's Blessing" (paint.) **4:**1087
- - "Return of Tobias" (paint.) **15:**1185
- - "Return of the Volunteer" (paint.) **11:**1561
- - "Shavuot" (paint.) **6:**1368
- - "Ushering in the Sabbath" (paint.) **14:**560
- - "*Yahrzeit* at the Front" **11:**1563
OPPENHEIM, PAUL LEO **12:**1424
Oppenheim, S. (hist., U.S.) **8:**568
Oppenheim, Sally **13:**812
Oppenheim, Seligmann, *see* Bing, Seligmann
Oppenheim, Shifra **12:**1420
Oppenheim, Simeon Wolff **16:**646
Oppenheim, Simon **12:**1418
Oppenheim, Solomon Jr. **12:**1418
Oppenheim, Waldemar **12:**1418
Oppenheimer (fam.), *see* OPPENHEIM
Oppenheimer (stlr., Ill.) **8:**1255
Oppenheimer, Anton **14:**823; **15:**1035
OPPENHEIMER, CARL **12:**1424
Oppenheimer, Charles **16:**66
Oppenheimer, Dan **14:**823; **15:**1035
Oppenheimer, David (r.), *see* OPPENHEIM, DAVID BEN ABRAHAM
Oppenheimer, David (mayor, Can.) **4:**1380; **5:**112; **16:**66
Oppenheimer, Emanuel **12:**1433
OPPENHEIMER, SIR ERNEST **12:**1425
- Kimberley **10:**1001
OPPENHEIMER, FRANZ **12:**1426
- Hertzka, Theodor **8:**399
- Nelson's socialism **12:**946
- Sixth Zionist Congress **16:**1168
- sociology **15:**65
- *illus:* text
Oppenheimer, Frederick **14:**823
OPPENHEIMER, FRITZ E. **12:**1427
Oppenheimer, Gabriel **16:**132
Oppenheimer, Godfrey **16:**66
Oppenheimer, Harry Frederick **12:**1425
Oppenheimer, Henry **3:**648
OPPENHEIMER, HILLEL (Heinz) REINHARD **12:**1427
Oppenheimer, Isaac **4:**1380; **16:**66
Oppenheimer, J.F. (ed.,Ger.) **6:**734
OPPENHEIMER, JOSEPH **3:**607
- *illus:*
- - "Kensington Gardens" (paint.) **3:**638
- - Levin, Shmarya (portrait) **11:**110
OPPENHEIMER, JOSEPH BEN ISSACHAR SUESSKIND **12:**1428
- history chart **8:**766-767
- medals, anti-Semitic **11:**1168
- *illus:*
- - text
- - medal **5:**1011
OPPENHEIMER, J. ROBERT **12:**1430
- *illus:* text
OPPENHEIMER, KARL **12:**1431
Oppenheimer, Max (art.), *see* MOPP
Oppenheimer, Meyer **16:**66
Oppenheimer, Nathan **16:**457

OPPENHEIMER, SAMUEL **12:**1431
- history chart **8:**766-767
- Kollonitsch, Leopold **10:**164
- Vienna **16:**123
- Worms **16:**646
- *illus:*
- - text
- - portrait **5:**1007
Oppenheimer, Sandela **12:**1432
Oppenheimer, Wolf **12:**201; **12:**1432
OPPENHEJM, RALPH GERSON **14:**928; **14:**935
Opper, Adolf, *see* BLOWITZ, HENRI GEORGES STEPHANE ADOLPHE OPPER DE
Opper, Bernard **15:**303
OPPER, FREDERICK BURR **12:**1433
- comic strips **5:**215
OPPERT, GUSTAV SALOMON **12:**1434
OPPERT, JULES JULIUS **12:**1434
- cuneiform **16:**1506
Oppman, Artur **13:**801
OPPRESSION (leg. conc.) **12:**1435
- ethics **6:**933,936
Oppyck, Constantin van, *see* L'EMPEREUR, CONSTANTIN
Ophthalmology **11:**1185
Optimism and pessimism **7:**1404
Oqome (masor. term) **16:**1432
ORABUENA (fam.) **12:**1436
Orabuena, Ishmael **12:**1436
Orabuena, Joseph (13th cent.) **12:**1436
Orabuena, Joseph (14th cent.) **12:**1436
- Pablo de Santa María **13:**4
- Tudela **15:**1425
ORACH (shrub) **12:**1436
Oracle, *see* DIVINATION; EPHOD; PROPHETS AND PROPHECY
ORADEA (Oradea Mare; city, Rum.) **12:**1437
- Fuchs, Moses Ẓevi **7:**212
- Transylvania **15:**1342ff
- *illus:* text
Or Adonai (wk.) **5:**1081ff
- Jewish literature **11:**341
Orah (Mosh., Isr.) **1:**place list
Orah (period.) **13:**1026; **16:**1110
Oraḥ Ḥayyim (Turim), *see* JACOB BEN ASHER
Oraḥ Ḥayyim (wk., Caro), *see* SHULḤAN ARUKH
OR AKIVA (tn., Isr.) **12:**1438
- statistics **1:**place list
ORAL LAW **12:**1439
- General
- - Eleazar ben Pedat **6:**597
- - heresy **8:**359
- - folklore **6:**1376
- - Maimonides **11:**766
- - Tablets of Law **15:**691
- - yeshivah curriculum **16:**767
- Development
- - *amoraim* **2:**865
- - codification of law **5:**628
- - conflict of opinion **5:**890
- - custom **12:**8
- - *halakhah* **7:**1156
- - *halakhah le-Moshe mi-Sinai* **7:**1167
- - halakhic midrash **8:**1414
- - hermeneutics **8:**366
- - masorah **16:**1409
- - Mishnah redaction **9:**252
- - *mishpat ivri* **12:**110; **12:**113; **12:**121
- - Moses **12:**394
- - pilpul **3:**524
- - *posekim* **13:**927
- - rabbinical authority **3:**907ff
- - *rishonim* **14:**192
- - sages **14:**639ff
- - Sanhedrin **4:**722
- - *soferim* **15:**80
- - *tannaim* **15:**798
- Literary Development
- - *aggadah* **2:**354
- - Alfasi code **2:**600
- - Asher, Rabbenu **3:**706
- - *baraita* **4:**189
- - *haggahot* **7:**1104
- - *hassagot* **7:**1466
- - *ḥiddushim* **8:**464
- - Midrash **11:**1507
- - Mishnah **12:**93
- - *Mishneh Torah* **11:**754
- - rabbinical literature **13:**1462
- - responsa **14:**83
- - *Shulḥan Arukh* **14:**1475
- - Talmud **15:**750
- - *Tosafot* **15:**1278
- - Tosefta **15:**1283
- - *Turim* **9:**1214
- Movements
- - Conservative Judaism **5:**901
- - Falashas **6:**1143
- - Ḥasidism **7:**1390
- - Kabbalah **10:**493; **10:**575
- - Karaites **10:**761; **15:**1183ff
- - Orthodoxy **12:**1486
- - Pharisees **13:**364-5
- - Reconstructionism **13:**1615
- - Reform Judaism **14:**23
- - Sadducees **14:**620
- *see also:* AUTHORITY, RABBINICAL; BIBLE (Exegesis): CODIFICATION OF LAW; HALAKHAH; HERMENEUTICS; TALMUD; TALMUD, BABYLONIAN; TALMUD, JERUSALEM
Oram ben Ner (poet) **4:**1485; **4:**1493; **9:**1578
ORAN (port, Alg.) **12:**1446
- Chouraqui, Isaac **5:**503
- special Purim **13:**1397
ORANGE (tn.,Fr.) **12:**1447
Orange (fruit) **5:**581
Orange, House of (Dyn., Neth.) **2:**900
Orange, trifoliate **13:**623
Orange County (Calif.) **11:**503
Orange County (N.Y.) **12:**1127
ORANGE FREE STATE (prov., S.A.) **12:**1447
- South Africa **15:**184ff
- *illus:* text
Oranienburg (concen. camp. Ger.) **5:**77
- Hoess, Rudolf **8:**806
Oranienburgerstrasse Synagogue (Ger.) **15:**620
- *illus:*
- - exterior **15:**621
Oranim (kib. seminary, Isr.) **1:**place list
Orano, Pietro **9:**1133
Oraşul Stalin (city, Transyl.), *see* BRAŞOV
Orazza, Cesare **11:**1559
Orbach, Abraham David **5:**484
Orbach, Hayyim ben Jacob **9:**18
Orban, Arpad **15:**299
Orchanski, Moses **16:**1165
Orchell, Francisco **8:**48
Orchid (bot.) **6:**1365
- plant list **13:**623
ORDEAL **12:**1448
- Akiva **2:**489
- autonomy, judicial **3:**929
- Inquisition **8:**1401
- ordeal of jealousy **12:**1449ff
- priests **13:**1078
- *illus:*
- - text
- - Moses' ordeal by fire **12:**395
- *see also:* DIVINATION
ORDEAL OF JEALOUSY **12:**1449
- adulteress **2:**314
- ceremony, abolition of **9:**240
- Commandments, the 613 **5:**774
- in the Arts **15:**984
- laws of writing **16:**670
- scroll and **4:**1226
- Temple **15:**966
- *illus:*
- - adulterous woman who has drunk the "bitter water" **15:**171
- - high priest administering **12:**1448
- *see also* : SOTAH
Order of the Indian Empire **7:**1060
Order of St. Gregory the Great **16:**78
Ordinance, *see* TAKKANOT
Ordination (rab.), *see* SEMIKHAH
Ordination offering **14:**605
Ordine Nuovo (polit. party, It.) **12:**952
Ordman, Jeanette **4:**328
Ordnungsdienst (J. militia) **11:**435; **16:**342
Ordo fratrum praedicatorum, *see* DOMINICANS
Ordon, Wladislaw **13:**802
Ordre Nouveau (Fascist orgn.) **12:**952
Ordronaux, John **11:**1551; **14:**1414
ORDZHONIKIDZE (city, Rus.) **12:**1450
Ore'aḥ Nata Lalun (bk.) **2:**370; **8:**202
OREB AND ZEEB (bib. figs.) **12:**1450
- Judges, Book of **10:**447
Orefice, G. **12:**1494
OREGON **12:**1451
- *pop. tables:* text
OREL (city, Rus.) **12:**1452
Oren (bot.) **4:**353
Oren, Baruch **5:**437
Oren, Menaḥem **5:**406
Oren, Mordekhai **11:**914; **14:**1654
Orena, Bernard de **14:**353
Oren River (Isr.) **9:**147
ORENSE (city, Sp.) **12:**1452
Orenstein (name), *see also* ORNSTEIN
ORENSTEIN, ALEXANDER JEREMIAH **12:**1452
Orenstein, A.N. (ed.) **6:**735
Orenstein, Joshua **13:**1378
Orenstein, Shimon **14:**1654
Orenstein, Ẓevi Hirsch **10:**1144; **11:**612
Orfali, P. G. **9:**1537
Orgad, Ben Ẓion **12:**671
ORGAN **12:**1452
- French synagogues **15:**1523
- *ḥukkat ha-goi* **8:**1062
- Italian communities **9:**1145
- Moses Sofer **14:**91
- synagogue service **12:**650; **14:**23ff; **15:**626
Organisation Armée Secrète **2:**618; **12:**952
Organisation Juive de Combat (Fr.) **7:**35
- French activities **13:**148; **15:**1287
Organización Israelita Argentina **3:**416
Organization para la Salud y Enseñanz, *see* OZE
Organización Sionista Sefardí (Mex.) **16:**1125
Organización Sionista Territorial (Urug.) **16:**1126
Organization, Jewish , *see* COMMUNITY
Organization for Hebrew Language and Culture **2:**206
Organization for the Support of Polish Trade and Industry (orgn., Pol.), *see* ROZWÓJ
Organization of Survivors from the British Zone, Bergen-Belsen **4:**612
Organization Sioniste de France **16:**1114
Organizzazione Sanitaria Ebraica *see* OZE
Orgelbrand, Hipolit **12:**1455
Orgelbrand, Maurycy **12:**1456
Orgelbrand, Mieczyslaw **12:**1455
ORGELBRAND, SAMUEL **12:**1455
- publishing **13:**1369
ORGEYEV (Orhei; city, Bess.) **12:**1456
- *illus:* text
Orgler, Alfred **10:**1497
Orgoños, Rodrigo de **5:**461
Or ha-Ganuz (wk.) **4:**100
Orhai (city, As. M.) **6:**366; **12:**1502
Or ha-Mizraḥ (journ.) **1:**newsp. list
OR HA-NER (kib., Isr.) **12:**1457
- statistics **1:**place list
Or Ḥayyim Yeshivah (Lith.) **10:**847
ORḤOT ḤAYYIM (eth. bk.) **12:**1457
- Aaron of Lunel **2:**12ff
- David of Narbonne **5:**1352
- Eliezer of Worms **6:**624
- ethical wills **16:**531
- *Kol Bo* **10:**1159ff
- Moses de Leon **12:**425
- Zohar **16:**1207
ORḤOT ẒADDIKIM (wk.) **12:**1458
- ethical literature **11:**344
- righteousness **14:**182
- *illus:* text
ORIA (tn., It.) **12:**1460
- Ahimaaz ben Paltiel **2:**463
- Amittai ben Shephatiah **2:**850
- Apulia **3:**226
- *illus:*
- - Piazza Shabbetai Donolo **6:**169
Orient (period.) **7:**214; **8:**477
"Oriental Interior" (paint., Okashi) Fig. 102 3—ART
ORIENTALISTS **12:**1460
Oriental Jews, *see* SEPHARDIM
ORIENTAL LITERATURE **12:**1462
Oriental manuscripts (Heb.) **8:**1262
Orient Colonising Company (Eng.) **15:**1021
Oriente (prov., Cuba) **5:**1148; **5:**1150
Orient Shipping Line **9:**835
ORIGEN (Origines; Ch.F.) **12:**1467
- Aquila translation of Bible **16:**1335
- Celsus **5:**270
- Church Fathers **5:**551
- Hebrew transcriptions **16:**1569
- magic **11:**706
- name of God **16:**1335
- Old Testament **4:**925ff
- Oshaiah Rabbah **12:**1496
- Song of Songs **3:**57
- translation, Bible **4:**853
Original sin
- Bar Ḥiyya **13:**436
- Buber, Martin **7:**778
- Crescas **5:**787
- death **5:**1424
- gnosticism **7:**637
- kabbalistic doctrine **10:**548,608,616
- Mendelssohn **3:**659
- redemption **14:**5
ORIHUELA (city, Sp.) **12:**1467
Orine (toparchy, Er. Isr.) **7:**1337; **9:**121
Orinin (tn., Podolia) **13:**669
Orinovsky, A. **8:**386
Orion (constellation) **3:**796
Orion, Ezra **14:**1070
Orkuta (vill., Slov.) **15:**1093
Orlah (foreskin) **5:**568

ORLAH (tract.) **12:**1467
- Caper **5:**135
- Commandments, the 613 **5:**778
- origin of prohibition **12:**9
- Talmud **11:**652ff
- Tu bi-Shevat **15:**1419
- *illus:* text
ORLAN, HAYYIM **12:**1468
ORLAND, HERSHL **12:**1468
ORLAND, YAAKOV **12:**1469
Orlando (city, Fla.) **6:**1363
Orlando di Lasso, *see* Lasso, Orlando di
ORLÉANS (tn., Fr.) **12:**1469
Orleska, Miriam **15:**1072; **16:**151
Orliffe, Herbert **15:**1264
ORLIK, EMIL **12:**1470
ORLIKOW, DAVID **12:**1471
- Canada **5:**112
- Manitoba **11:**879
- Winnipeg **16:**551
ORLINSKY, HARRY MEYER **12:**1471
- Hebrew **8:**218
- *illus:*
- - JPS Torah translation committee **10:**80
ORLOFF, CHANA **12:**1472
- *illus:*
- - text
- - Fleg, Edmond (bust) **6:**1341
- - mother and child (statue) **6:**528
Orloff, Zevi, *see* Nishri, Zevi
Orloff-Arieli, L. A. **6:**203
Orlogin (journ.) **1:**newsp. list
Orlovitz, N., *see* Resnick, N.
Orman, H. **10:**1047
ORMANDY, EUGENE **12:**702
Örmènyes, Lipót Hirsch de **13:**1369
Ormizd IV (k.), *see* Hormizd IV
ORMODY, BERTALAN **8:**1079; **8:**1086
Ormsby-Gore, W. **16:**1163
- White Papers **16:**484
- *illus:*
- - letter regarding Rivkah Aaronsohn **2:**27
- - Zionist Commission arriving in Palestine (1918) **16:**1163
Ormuz (isl., Pers. gulf), *see* HORMUZ
Ormuzd (demon), *see* Hormiz
Orna, Adolphe **7:**148; **14:**423
ORNAN, UZZI **1:**35
ORNEST, OTA **15:**1089
ORNI, EFRAIM **1:**35
Ornias (demon) **15:**118
Orinin (tn., Ukr.) **13:**669
Or Nerot ha-Menorah (wk.) **13:**932; **16:**89
ORNITZ, SAMUEL BADISCH **12:**1472
- New York City **12:**1121
- U.S. literature **15:**1574
Ornstein (name), *see also* Orenstein
ORNSTEIN, ABRAHAM FREDERICK **12:**1473
- Cape Town **5:**139
ORNSTEIN, JACOB MESHULLAM BEN MORDECAI ZE'EV **12:**1473
- Erter **6:**847
- family **12:**1475
- Lvov **11:**612
ORNSTEIN, LEO **12:**702
ORNSTEIN, LEONARD SALOMON **12:**1475
Ornstein, Mordecai Ze'ev ben Jacob Meshullam **12:**1473
ORNSTEIN, MORDECAI ZE'EV BEN MOSES **12:**1475
Ornstein, Moses Joshua Hoeschel **12:**1475
- Tarnograd **15:**815
Ornstein, O., *see* ORNEST, OTA
Ornstein, Samson **16:**1348
Ornstein, Zevi Hirsch **12:**1474
OROBIO DE CASTRO, ISAAC (Balthazar) **12:**1475
- Amsterdam **2:**897
- medicine **11:**1192
- Philipp van Limborch **6:**96
- philosophy **13:**417
- translation **2:**428
- *illus:*
- - text
- - *De Veritate Religionis Christianae* **6:**90
Orofernes (Apoc. fig.), *see* HOLOFERNES
Orofino (city, Ida.) **8:**1222
Oron (site, Isr.) **9:**595
- mineral resources **9:**808
- Negev **12:**930
- *illus:*
- - phosphate plant **9:**805
Oron, Zevi **3:**388
Oropesa, Alfonso de, *see* ALFONSO DE OROPESA
Oroshkes, Zevi *see* Oron, Zevi
OROSIUS, PAULUS **12:**1477
Or-Ot, Artur, *see* Oppman, Artur
OROT (mosh., Isr.) **12:**1477
- statistics **1:** place list
Orot (journs.) **1:** newsp. list
Oroville (city, Calif.) **5:**56
Orowan (phys.) **13:**490
Oroya, La (tn., Peru) **13:**324
ORPAH (bib. fig.) **12:**1477
- in the Arts **14:**524
- Ruth, Book of **14:**518ff
"Orpah the Moabite" (paint., Abel Pann) Fig. 88 **3**-ART
ORPHAN **12:**1478
- Ethical Aspects **6:**933, 936
- - Commandments, the 613 **5:**779
- - dowry **6:**185
- - fraud against **7:**111
- - *hakhnasat kallah* **7:**1150
- - insults **8:**1409
- - Yemenite Jews **16:**744
- Legal Aspects
- - *apotropos* **3:**219
- - compromise rights **5:**858
- - custody **13:**99
- - embryo **6:**720
- - endowment funds **8:**284
- - firstborn **6:**1309
- - Moellin's usury ruling **12:**12
- - property appraisement **6:**1013
- - property disposition **5:**880
- - surety payment **5:**888
Orpheus (myth. fig.) **15:**570ff
Orphism (Gr. philos.) **11:**843
Orrhoene (dist., Mesop.), *see* OSROENE
Or Same'ah (wk.) **11:**1260
ORSHA (city, Belor.) **12:**1479
ORSHANSKI, ILYA (Elijah) GRIGORYEVICH **12:**1480
- journalism **13:**1597
- *illus:* text
Orsini, Giovanni Gaetano (pope), *see* NICHOLAS III
ORSOVA (tn., Rum.) **12:**1481
Országos Magyar Izraelita Kozmüvelödési Egyesület, *see* O.M.I.K.E.
Országos Rabbikepzö Intézet (sem., Hung.), *see* LANDESRABBINERSCHULE
ORT (orgn.) **12:**1481
- *Contents:*
- - 1880-1920 **12:**1482
- - 1920-1945 **12:**1482
- - 1945-1960 **12:**1484
- - From 1960 **12:**1485
- agriculture **2:**408
- Alliance Israélite Universelle **2:**652
- cooperatives **5:**944
- Cullman, Howard **5:**1155
- Dreyfus-Brodsky **6:**224
- philanthropy **13:**387
- Poland **13:**779
- Silberfarb, Moses **14:**1533
- vocational training **9:**881
- *Yevsektsiya* takeover **16:**780
- *illus:*
- - Central Institutes, Geneva **15:**560
- - crafts specialization, 1950-1970 (table) **5:**1057
- - France, vocational training for refugees **6:**402
ORTA, GARCIA DE **12:**1486
- Bombay **4:**1192
- medicine **11:**1192
Ortaköy (loc., Turk.) **9:**1087
- *illus:*
- - Ez Hayyim synagogue **9:**1091
Ortas, Abraham de **8:**1326
- *illus:*
- - Former Prophets (1495) **8:**1334
- - *Tur Orah Hayyim* (1495) **4:**1234; **8:**1330
Ortas, Samuel de **8:**1326; **16:**82
Ortelius, Abraham **11:**918; **11:**927
ORTEN, JIŘÍ **12:**1486
Orthodox Church **5:**514; **9:**910
Orthodoxer Rabbinerverband (org.) **13:**1455
Orthodox Melchites, *see* Melchites
ORTHODOXY **12:**1486
- Attitudes
- - article of faith **3:**660
- - *halakhah* **7:**1166; **10:**395
- - Hasidism **7:**1395
- - Haskalah **7:**1440f
- - interfaith contacts **13:**1253
- - *mehizah* **11:**1235
- - Messiah **11:**1416
- - Neo-Orthodoxy **12:**957
- - organ in synagogue **12:**1454ff
- - proselytes **13:**1191ff
- - rabbinical conferences **13:**1460
- - rabbinical office **13:**1448
- - revelation **14:**125
- - synagogue **15:**584
- - tradition **15:**1311
- - *yeshivot* **16:**770
- Development
- - Adass Jeshurun, Adass Jisroel **2:**254
- - Adler, Nathan Marcus **2:**286
- - autonomy **3:**927
- - Banet, Mordecai **4:**159
- - Bernays, Isaac **4:**673
- - breaches within the community **8:**723
- - Breuer family **4:**1364f
- - Chorin's attack on **5:**495
- - Eger, Akiva **6:**469
- - Frankel, Zacharias **7:**80
- - Geiger's campaign against **7:**358
- - Grodzinski, Hayyim Ozer **7:**928
- - *herem* **8:**355
- - Hildesheimer, Azriel **8:**476
- - Hirsch, S.R. **7:**81; **8:**508f
- - influence of Reformation **14:**23
- - Leeser, Isaac **10:**1561
- - Maharam Schick **14:**958
- - parodies **13:**132
- Pharisee origins **13:**366
- - Rice, Abraham Joseph **14:**156
- - Sachs, Michael **14:**595
- - Sofer, Moses **15:**77
- - Tiktin, Solomon **15:**1140
- - Weyl, Meir **16:**479
- Modern Period
- - Agudat Israel **2:**421ff
- - England **6:**758f
- - Germany **7:**478f
- - Ha-Poel Ha-Mizrachi **7:**1320f
- - Holocaust **8:**878f
- - Israel (Religious Life) **9:**887f
- - Jacobs Affair **6:**766; **9:**1236
- - Jews' College **10:**98
- - Mahzike Hadas **11:**730
- - Maimon, Y.L. **11:**740
- - Mizrachi **12:**175f
- - newspapers **12:**1046f
- - New York City **12:**1094ff
- - Po'alei Agudat Israel **13:**655
- - Rabbiner Seminar **13:**1459
- - R.C.A. **13:**1461
- - Reich, Koppel **14:**46
- - Revel, Bernard **14:**116
- - Rosenheim, Jacob **14:**288
- - Silver, Eliezer **14:**1544
- - Soloveitchik, Joseph Dov **15:**132
- - South Africa **15:**193ff
- - United Synagogue **6:**757f **15:**1672
- - U.O.J.C.A. **15:**1537
- - U.S. **15:**1642ff
- - Yeshiva University **16:**760
- - Young Israel **16:**859
- - Zionism **16:**1145
- *see also:* CONSERVATIVE JUDAISM; NEOLOGY; NEO-ORTHODOXY; REFORM JUDAISM
Orthodoxy, German, *see* NEO-ORTHODOXY
Orthography **10:**424; **16:**1348
Ortigas (fam.) **15:**1300
Ortiz, Diego de Fuñez **5:**116
Ortolan Bunting (bird) **6:**30
Ortona, Abraham **16:**115
Or Torah (bk.) **16:**1477
Or Torah (journ., Er. Isr.) **1:** newsp. list
Or Torah (journ., Gal., Ger.) **1:** newsp. list
Oruba (tn., Surinam) **11:**1567
Oruro (city, Bol.) **4:**1188
ORVIETO (tn., It.) **12:**1493
Orvieto, Adolfo (ed.) **10:**306; **12:**1493
Orvieto, Alberto (r.) **4:**1191
- *illus:*
- - Bologna, memorial plaque **4:**1191
ORVIETO, ANGIOLO **12:**1493
- Italian literature **9:**1111
Orvieto, Laura Cantoni **12:**1494
OR YEHUDAH (cmty., Isr.) **12:**1494
- statistics **1:** place list
Or Yehudah Agricultural School (Turk.) **10:**48; **10:**1246
Or Yisrael (period.) **9:**1095
Or Yisrael (wk.) **5:**1353
Oryx (zool.) **3:**7
"Or Zaru'a" (13th cent., r.), *see* HAYYIM BEN ISAAC "OR ZARU'A"
Or Zaru'a, Isaac (12/13 cent., r.), *see* ISAAC BEN MOSES OF VIENNA
ORZESKOWA (Orzesko), ELIZA **12:**1494
- *Voskhod* **16:**226
Osachki, Enrique Oltuski **5:**1150
Osarsiph (pr.) **7:**888; **11:**872
OSBORN, MAX **3:**607
Osborn, William **8:**48
Osca (city, Sp.), *see* HUESCA
OSCHINSKY, LAWRENCE **12:**1495
OSE (health orgn.), *see* OZE
Oshaiah, Rav (3/4 cent., amora), *see* HOSHAIAH, RAV
OSHAIAH RABBAH (2nd cent. C.E, amora) **12:**1495
- *beraitot* **4:**191ff
- *Genesis Rabbah* **7:**399
- Hama bar Bisa **7:**1218
Oshawa (city, Ont.) **12:**1408
Oshaya ben Shammai (amora) **9:**18
Oshayah of Tiria **13:**217
Oshek (property offense), *see* OPPRESSION

Osherov, Shai **12:**460
OSHEROWITCH, MENDL **12:**1496
Oshins, Louis **15:**306
Oshkosh (city, Wis.) **16:**556
OSHMYANY (city, Belor.) **12:**1496
- ghetto **13:**770
- *illus:* text
Oshry, Ephraim **2:**100; **14:**94
Oshyot (journ.) **1:** newsp. list
Oshyanski, Abel-Aaron Itskovich, *see* ASHANSKI, ABEL-AARON ITSKOVICH
OSIANDER, ANDREAS **12:**1498
- Luther, Martin **11:**585
- Pezinok blood libel **13:**352
- Reformation **14:**19
- toleration of Jews **8:**701
Osiander, Luc **8:**48
Osiier, Ivan **12:**1375
OSIJEK (Eszek; tn., Yug.) **12:**1498
- Yugoslavia **16:**870ff
Osimo, Leone **13:**12
Osimo, Marco **13:**12
OSIPOVICH, NAHUM **12:**1499
Osiris (Egy. deity) **8:**293
OSIRIS, DANIEL ILLFA **12:**1499
- *illus:* text
OSLO (city, Nor.) **12:**1499
- Norway **12:**1224
- *illus:* text
Osman Baba (sect. ldr.), *see* Russo, Baruchiah
OSNABRUECK (city, W. Ger.) **12:**1500
- *illus:* text
OSOBLAHA (vill., Cz.) **12:**1502
Osofsky, Simḥa, *see* ASSAF, SIMḤA
Osorio (fam.), *see* ABENDANA
Osorkon I (k., Egypt) **16:**996
Osovitzky, Yehoshua, *see* OSSOWETZKY, O. YEHOSUA
Osowa (concen. camp, Pol.) **13:**765
Os Resurrectionis (bk.) **3:**675
OSROENE (dist., Mesop.) **12:**1502
Ossado, Ricardo **11:**1455
Ossining (city, N.Y.) **12:**1127; **16:**465
Ossipee (tn., N.H.) **12:**1024
OSSOWETZKY, O. YEHOSHUA **12:**1503
- Feinberg, Yosef **6:**1209
OSSUARIES and SARCOPHAGI **12:**1503
- abbreviations **2:**51
- art in Ereẓ Israel **3:**507ff
- Azor **3:**1011
- funerary inscriptions **16:**657
- funerary reliefs **8:**653
- Greco-Roman **15:**568ff
- Greek inscriptions **8:**296
- tombs **15:**1216
- Tomb of the Kings **9:**1532
- *illus:*
- - text
- - Bet She'arim sarcophagi **4:**769-770; **15:**568
- - Cave of Nicanor **12:**1133
- - Chalcolithic **7:**1047
- - clay **3:**1012
- - Eshmunezer's sarcophagus **13:**480
- - Hiram's sarcophagus **13:**473
- - king of Tyre sarcophagus **15:**1124
- - Second Temple period **3:**321,513
- - stone **4:**1517
- - Vigna Randanini, Rome **11:**1361
- *see also:* BURIAL; LIKKUT AẒAMOT
Ossuna, Moses Mendès **15:**1443
Ostara (period.) **8:**782
Ostend (tn., Belg.) **4:**423
Osterbroeck, Aggaeus **8:**48
Osterman, Joseph **15:**1034
Ostermann, Helmut, *see* AVNERI, URI
Ostervald, J.F. **4:**881
OSTIA (city, It.) **12:**1506
- synagogue **3:**521; **15:**582; **15:**600
- *illus:* text
Ostiano (tn., It.) **11:**895
Ostiglia, Jonah **3:**524
Ostjuedische Zeitung (newsp.) **6:**345
Ostmark (reg.), *see* AUSTRIA
OSTRACA (Ostracon, Ostrakon, Ostraka; inscribed potsherds) **12:**1509
- Hazeroth **7:**1531
- Hebrew inscriptions **2:**682
- inscriptions **16:**660
- Lachish letters **11:**56
- measures **16:**381; **16:**384
- Tell Arad **3:**249
- Yavneh-Yam potsherd **16:**723
- *illus:*
- - text
- - Arad **2:**390, 680
- - "Ben Ya'ir" (Masada) **6:**591; **11:**513
- - impounding of pledge, written complaint **3:**317
- - king of Judah (6th cent. B.C.E.) **3:**320
- - Lachish (6th cent. B.C.E.) **2:**679
- - Meẓad Ḥashavyahu (7th cent. B.C.E.) **2:**684; **3:**317
- - Samaria **3:**372
- - Tel Qasila **16:**657
- *see also:* PAPYRI
Ostracism **16:**660
Ostraha (tn., Rus.), *see* OSTROG
OSTRAVA (tn., Morav.) **12:**1511
- Holocaust period **5:**1199
- Moravia **12:**302ff
Ostrer, Moses ben Hillel **10:**554
OSTRICH (bird) **12:**1512
- dietary laws **6:**34
Ostroff, Eugene **13:**486
OSTROG (Ostraha; city, Rus.) **12:**1513
- Aaron Samuel ha-Kohen **2:**23
- special Purim **13:**1397
OSTROGORSKI, MOSES **12:**1514
OSTROLEKA (Ostrolenka; tn., Pol. **12:**1515
OSTROLENK, BERNHARD **12:**1515
OSTROPOLER, HERSHELE **12:**1516
- Baruch of Medzibozh **4:**279
OSTROPOLER, SAMSON BEN PESAḤ **12:**1516
- Kabbalah **10:**551
- Polonnoye **13:**836
Ostrovsky, Miriam, *see* Baratz, Miriam
Ostrovsky, Moshe, *see* HAMEIRI, MOSHE
OSTROWER, FEYGA **3:**607
OSTROWIEC (Ostrowiec Świętokrzyski; tn., Pol.) **12:**1517
- *illus:* text
OSTROW MAZOWIECKA (tn., Pol.) **12:**1518
- Auerbach, Menahem **3:**843
Ostry, Bernard **5:**112
Ostry, Sylvia **5:**112
OSTRYNA (tn., Belor.) **12:**1519
Ost und West (period.) **13:**1056
OSVÁT, ERNŐ **8:**1087
OSWIECIM (Auschwitz; tn., Pol.) **12:**1520
- *see also:* AUSCHWITZ
Oszmiana (city, Belor.) *see* OSHMYANY
Ot (journ.) **1:** newsp. list
Otaci (vill., Bess.), *see* ATAKI
Otago Daily Times (newsp.) **6:**1185
Other World, *see* AFTERLIFE; OLAM HA-BA
Othman (caliph, sult.), *see* ʿUthmān
OTHNIEL (bib. fig.) **12:**1520
- Achsah, wife **2:**212
- Bible history **8:**583
- Judges, Book of **10:**444
Otho (Otto), J.H. **8:**48
Otiyyot de-Avraham Avinu (bk.) **16:**786
Otiyyot de-Rabbi Akiva (wk.) **2:**748; **15:**1515
- Bartolocci, Giulio **4:**265
- Gan Eden and Gehinnom **13:**84
- mystical literature **11:**347
- *Sefer Yeẓirah* **16:**786
Otiyyot ha-ʿInyanim (wk.), *see Kitāb Ḥurūf al-Maʿānī*
Otiyyot ha-No'aḥ (wk.), *see Sefer Otiyyot ha-No'aḥ*
Otiyyot menuzzarot (Bib. signs) **16:**1407
Otiyyot teluyot (suspended letters; Bib.) **16:**1408
Otot (flags) **6:**1335
"Otot Mashi'aḥ" ("Signs of the Mess. age") **11:**1413
Otot u-Mo'adim (wk.) **4:**1388
OTRANTO (tn., It.) **12:**1521
Otrokócsi, Fóris Ferenc **8:**48
Ott (sport., Aus.) **15:**293
OTTA, FRANCISCO **3:**607
- Chile **5:**467
OTTAWA (city, Can.) **12:**1521
Otte, Johann Baptist **5:**278
OTTENSOSSER, DAVID **12:**1522
- history **8:**560
Otterstadt (vill., Ger.) **15:**265
Ottho, J.H. **7:**404
OTTINGER, ALBERT **12:**1522
Otto I (k., Gr.) **3:**817
Otto, Gottlieb **8:**48
Otto, J.H., *see* Otho, J.H.
Otto, Julius Conrad, *see* Margolioth, Naphtali
OTTO, RUDOLPH **12:**1523
OTTOLENGHI (fam.) **12:**1523
- Acqui **2:**216
Ottolenghi, Abraham Azariah **2:**216; **12:**1523
Ottolenghi, Adolfo **12:**1524
Ottolenghi, Bonaiuto, *see* Ottolenghi, Abraham Azariah
Ottolenghi, Carlos Alberti **6:**361
Ottolenghi, Donato (cmty. fig.), *see* Ottolenghi, Nathan
Ottolenghi, Donato (med. schol.) **12:**1524
Ottolenghi, Eleazar **12:**1523
Ottolenghi, Emilio **12:**1524
OTTOLENGHI, GIUSEPPE **12:**1524
Ottolenghi, Joseph (apos.) **6:**1023
OTTOLENGHI, JOSEPH BEN NATHAN (16th cent., r.) **12:**1525
Ottolenghi, Joshua **12:**1524
Ottolenghi, Lazzaro, *see* Ottolenghi, Eleazar
Ottolenghi, Mario **12:**1524
Ottolenghi, Michael **12:**1524
OTTOLENGHI, MOSES JACOB **12:**1525
Ottolenghi, Nathan **12:**1523
Ottolenghi, Raffaele **12:**1524
- *Rivista Israelitica* **14:**197
Ottolenghi, Salvatore, *see* Ottolenghi, Joshua
Ottolenghi, Solomon **2:**594
Ottolengo (fam.), *see also under* Ottolenghi
Ottolengo, Nathan **5:**869
OTTOLENGO, SAMUEL DAVID BEN JEHIEL **12:**1525
OTTOMAN EMPIRE **16:**1529
- Countries
- - Egypt **6:**496ff
- - Ereẓ Israel **2:**398; **9:**259
- - Greece **7:**875
- - Syria **15:**643
- - Transjordan **15:**1318
- - Tunisia **15:**1441
- - Turkey **15:**1457
- - Yemen **16:**742
- Political Life
- - Arab national movement **9:**454ff
- - capitulations **5:**148
- - communal organization **5:**815,818; **14:**1
- - Ereẓ Israel history **9:**282
- - Ereẓ Israel migration **16:**1039
- - millet **11:**1582
- - minority rights **12:**44
- - Omar, Covenant of **12:**1378
- - Po'alei Zion **13:**660
- - Sykes-Picot Treaty **15:**565ff
- - taxes **10:**938
- Miscellaneous
- - history chart **8:**766-767
- - Ladino **10:**1350
- - Marrano Diaspora **11:**1020
- - rabbinate **13:**1450
- - Samaritans **14:**734; **14:**737
- - Sambari's studies **14:**762
- - Sephardi immigration **14:**1174
- - slave trade **14:**1662
- - spice trade **15:**270
- - textiles **15:**1038
- - Tlemcen **15:**1173
- *illus:*
- - Ereẓ Israel administrative division (map) **9:**599
- - Jemal Pasha and Turkish governor of Jerusalem **9:**332
- - Jerusalem surrender **9:**1471
- - Land of Israel under Ottoman rule (map) **9:**283
- - Templers coins **15:**995
- *pop. tables:* text
- *see also:* BYZANTINE EMPIRE; ISRAEL (Land of, History, Ottoman Period); TURKEY
Ottoman Society of Union and Congress **16:**1553
Ottumwa (city, Iowa) **8:**1437
Otway, Thomas **6:**774
OTWOCK (tn., Pol.) **12:**1525
Ouagadougou (city, Upper Volta) **9:**442
Ouaknin, David **5:**224
Ouaknine, Jacques **11:**249
Ouatablé, Franciscus, *see* Vatable, François
Oudaios (leg. hero) **7:**893
Ouderkerk (vill. Neth.) **3:**58; **15:**1224
OUDTSHOORN (tn., S.A.) **12:**1526
ʾOuggāl (tit., Yem.) **14:**821
Oujda (Oudjda; tn., Mor.) **12:**344
Oulatha (val., Er. Isr.) **8:**1064
OULIF, CHARLES NARCISSE **12:**1526
Oultre Jourdain (princip., Transj.) **15:**1318
Oumansoff, Raïssa *see* MARITAIN, JACQUES AND RAÏSSA
Oungre (vill., Can.) **14:**892
Our Age (*Dorenu;* period.) **5:**460
Our People (newsp.), *see Nepünk*
Our Review (newsp.) *Our Voice, see* NASZ PRZEGLAD, **6:**1363
Our World (period.) **5:**460
Ouseel (Oisel, Loisel), P. **8:**48
Outhuijs, Gerrit **8:**48
"Out of Bondage" (paint., A. Bayefsky) **3:**613
Outram, William **8:**48
Outrein, J. d' **8:**48
Outremont (sub., Montreal) **12:**287
Ouzāl (bib. fig.) **14:**820
OUZIEL, BEN-ZION MEIR ḤAI **12:**1527
- abortion **2:**100; **2:**101
- autopsies and dissection **3:**933
- religious life **9:**891; **9:**893ff
- responsa **14:**93

- severance pay **7:**1005; **12:**20
- *illus:*
- - National Council meeting **9:**365
Ouziel, Joseph Raphael **12:**1527
Ov (diviner) **6:**114
Ovadiah (12th cent., sage) **10:**984
Ovadiah (14th cent., trans.) **15:**1329
Ovadya, Avraham **9:**1041
Ovalle (tn., Chile) **5:**466
Ovazza, Ettore **15:**1455
OVCHINSKI, LEVI **12:**1528
Ovdat, *see* AVEDAT
Ovdei kokhavim u-mazalot (idolators), *see* AKKUM
OVED, MOSHE **12:**1528
- *illus:* text
Oved avodah zarah (idolators), *see* AKKUM
Ovelim (vall., vill., Er. Isr.), *see* AVELIM
Overall, John **8:**48
Overcharging, *see* ONA'AH
Overijssel (prov., Neth.) **12:**974
Overreaching, *see* ONA'AH
OVID (1st cent., au.) **14:**232; **14:**235
Ovid Press (publ. house) **14:**218
Oviedo (loc., Sp.) **15:**227
Oviedo, Gonzalo Martinez de **6:**356
Ovnayim (journ.) **1:**newsp. list
Ovodovski, M., *see* OSHEROWITCH, MENDL
OVRUCH (city, Ukr.) **12:**1529
OVSAY, JOSHUA **12:**1529
Owen, Robert **15:**25
Owen Sound (tn., Ont.) **12:**1408
OWL (bird) **12:**1529
- dietary laws **6:**34
- *illus:* text
Owmann, M.J. **8:**48
OWNERSHIP **12:**1531
- *Bava Batra* **4:**336ff
- bought stolen property **12:**10
- consecration and endowment **8:**279
- debt obligation **12:**1313
- first-fruit offering **4:**993
- *hefker* **8:**243
- joint **13:**154
- lease and hire **10:**1528
- legal person **10:**1567ff
- lien dependent on **11:**229
- *mazranut* **11:**1153
- nature of man and **11:**847
- non-Jewish law **6:**51ff
- pledge **13:**640
- property and **13:**1146ff
- sealing **14:**1074
- servitudes **14:**1188
- synagogue **15:**594
- theft, robbery **15:**1094
- *ye'ush* **16:**774
- *see also:* ḤAZAKAH; LOST PROPERTY; SALE
Owtram, William, *see* Outram William
Ox (leg. conc.) **3:**986; **3:**987; **15:**1272ff
- cattle **5:**256
- *illus:*
- - *Bava Kamma* **4:**338
Ox, Wild (mammal) **6:**31
Ox, Wild (agg. animal), *see* WILD BULL
OXFORD (Eng.) **12:**1534
- Church Council **8:**766-767; **6:**749
Oxford, University of **15:**1677
Oxyrhyncus (vill., Egy.) **6:**9, 15
Oybervisha (vill., Rum.), *see* VISEUL DE SUS
Oyf dem Veg tsu der Nayer Shul (period.) **13:**1048
Oyf der Shvel (publ.) **14:**1326
Oyfgang (newsp., Cuba) **5:**1149
Oyfgang (publ., Rus.) **4:**609
Oyfn Shaydveg (period.) **15:**876
- Yefroykin, Israel **16:**727
Oyf'n Shprakh Front (period.) **13:**1048
Oyfn Shvel (period.) **15:**1022
Oyf'n Wisenshaftlikhen Front (period.) **13:**1048
OYSHER, MOISHE **7:**1549
- recordings **13:**1617
Oyshits Incident (trial) **12:**1234
Oyster **6:**38
Oz, Amos **8:**207; **9:**1568
Oẓar Genazim (journ.) **1:**newsp. list
Oẓar ha-Ge'onim (wk.) **11:**169
Oẓar ha-Hayyim (encyc.) **6:**730
- bloodletting **4:**1119
Oẓar ha-Hayyim (journ.) **1:**newsp. list
Oẓar ha-Ḥokhma (enc.) **6:**731
Oẓar ha-Ḥokhma ve-ha-Madda (journ.) **1:**newsp. list
Oẓar ha-Ḥokhmot (enc.) **6:**730
Oẓar ha-Moreh (publ. house) **15:**889
Oẓar ha-Posekim (wk.) **14:**1477
Oẓar ha-Ra'yonot ve-ha-Pitgamim (wk.) **14:**944
Oẓar ha-Sefarim (wk.) **4:**521; **4:**971
Oẓar ha-Shemot asher be-Kitvei ha-Kodesh (wk.) **6:**734
Oẓar ha-Shorashim (wk., Judah Leib ben Ze'ev) **4:**573
Oẓar ha-Shorashim (wk., Bialoblotzky) **4:**804
Oẓar ha-Sifrut (period.) **4:**1316; **7:**845
- statistics **1:**newsp. list
Oẓar ha-Targum (wk.) **10:**809
OZAR HATORAH (educ. soc., Medit.) **12:**1537
- Persian Jews **13:**318
- *illus:*
- - Shiraz, child learning Hebrew **6:**430
- - Tunis ghetto child in school **6:**428
Oẓar ha-Yahadut (enc.) **6:**732
Oẓar Ḥayyim (bk.) **9:**30
Oẓar Hityashvut ha-Yehudim, *see* JEWISH COLONIAL TRUST
Oẓar Ḥokhmah (period.) **16:**1330
- statistics **1:**newsp. list
Oẓar le-Ḥakla'ut (bank, Isr.), *see* Ya'ad Agricultural Development Bank
Oẓar Leshon ha-Mishnah (wk.) **10:**809
Oẓar Leshon ha-Tosefta (wk.) **10:**809
Oẓar le-Ta'asiyyah (bank, Isr.) **9:**827
Oẓar Neḥmad (period.) **11:**60
- Hebrew newspapers **12:**1048
- statistics **1:**newsp. list
- Vienna **16:**131
- Wissenschaft **16:**578
Oẓar Tov (journ.) **1:**newsp. list
Oẓar Yehudei Sefarad (journ.) **1:**newsp. list
Oźarów (ḥas. dynasty) **3:**668
Oẓar Razei (wk.) **4:**222
Oẓar Tov (Heb. suppl.) **4:**665
Oẓar Yisrael (enc.) **6:**732
- Eisenstein, J.D. **6:**553
OZE (OSE; orgn.) **12:**1537
- Cantoni, Raffaelle **5:**130
- philanthropy **13:**387
- Poland **13:**779
- Toz **15:**1291
Oẓem (mosh., Isr.) **12:**940
- statistics **1:**place list
Ozer Dalim (journ.) **5:**219
Ozer of Cracow **13:**722
OZERY (tn., Belor.) **12:**1539
Ozet (orgn., Rus.), *see* Society for the Promotion of Jewish Settlement
Ozhor (tn., Belor), *see* OZERY
Oz le-Elohim (bk.), *see* *Meheimanuta de-Kholla*
Ozmo, Daniel **14:**871
OZON (anti-Sem. orgn.) **12:**1540
OZORKOW (tn., Pol.) **12:**1540
Ozundzhovo (loc., Bul.) **4:**1482
Ozyuba, Ivan **15:**1519

P

Pa'amei Tashaz (mosh., Isr.) **1**:place list
Pa'amon (bell) **12**:564
PABIANICE (city, Pol.) **13**:1
Pablo Christiani, *see* CHRISTIANI, PABLO
PABLO DE SANTA MARIA (el Burguense) **13**:3
- Abner of Burgos **2**:89
- Bonjorn's conversion **3**:196
- Ferrer, Vicente **6**:1235
- hebraist **8**:14
- Lorki, Joshua **11**:494
- Spanish converts **15**:237
Pablo de Santa-Maria, *see* Benzamero, Moses
Pabyanitse (city, Pol.), *see* PABIANICE
Paçagon, Mayer (of Calatayud) **7**:146
Pacanowska, Felicia **13**:118
Pacelli, Eugenio Maria Giuseppe Giovanni (pope), *see* PIUS XII
PACHECO, RODRIGO BENJAMIN MENDES **13**:5
- New York City **12**:1067ff
PACHT, ISAAC **13**:5
PACIFICI, ALFONSO **13**:5
Pacifici, Isaac **16**:99
PACIFICI, RICCARDO **13**:5
- Genoa **7**:408
PACIFICO, DAVID **13**:6
- Athens **3**:817
Pacifico, Solomon **12**:1446
PACKMAN, JAMES JOSEPH **10**:315
Packter, M. **4**:1239
Pacovsky (fam.) **8**:1136
PADDAN-ARAM (bib. loc.) **13**:6
- Genesis, Book of **7**:390
PADERBORN (tn., Ger.) **13**:6
Paderewski, Ignace **12**:323
Padi (bib. fig.) **6**:560; **13**:403
Padova (city, It.) *see* PADUA
Padova, Zechariah **5**:175
Padovan, Giuseppe, *see* LUZZATTO, GINO
Padre Benedetto, *see* MARIE-BENOÎT
PADUA (city, Prov., It.) **13**:8
- Abrabanel, Isaac **2**:105
- archives **3**:387
- Archivolti, Samuel de **3**:397
- special Purim **13**:1397
- taxes **15**:839
- universities **15**:1676
Padua, Moïse **16**:1165
Paducah (city, Ky.) **10**:909
PADWAY, JOSEPH ARTHUR **13**:13
Paetges, Christian Heinrich **15**:1084
Paetges, Johanne Luise **14**:927
Paganism
- Hellenistic art **8**:301
- Hellenisic literature **8**:304
- Jewish philosophy **13**:425 **13**:456; **13**:457
- Jews and Christians **8**:625ff
- Julian the Apostate **10**:468ff
- monotheism **12**:260ff
- Neoplatonism **12**:958
- Reform Judaism and ritualism **12**:1443
- Rosenzweig, F. **14**:300
- slave trade **14**:1660
- symbolism, Jewish **15**:569ff
- synagogues **15**:595
- - *see also:* GENTILE; IDOLATRY
Pagan Martyrs, Acts of, see ALEXANDRIAN MARTYRS, ACTS OF
Pagel, Bernard **3**:807
PAGEL, JULIUS LEOPOLD **13**:13
Pagel, Walter **13**:13
Paggi, Allessandro **4**:456; **13**:1368
Paggi, Angiolo **8**:48
Paggi, Felice **4**:456; **13**:1368
Pagis, Dan **8**:206
PAGNINI, SANTES (Xanthus Pagninus) **13**:13
- Christian Hebraists **8**:48; **8**:17
- Kimhi, David **10**:1003
Paḥad (demon) **5**:1524
Paḥad Yiẓḥak (divine name) **9**:4
Paḥad Yiẓḥak (wk., Cantarini) **8**:558
Paḥad Yiẓḥak (wk., Lampronti) **10**:1380; **11**:338
Paḥal (city, Transj.) *see* PELLA
Pahath-Moab (fam.) **6**:1040
Pahlen Commission **11**:1148; **16**:71
Pahlevi (dyn., Pers.) **13**:319
Pahlevi, Riza Khān **13**:319
P.A.I. (party, Isr.) *see* PO'ALEI AGUDAT ISRAEL
Paicovitch, Reuven Yosef **2**:655
Paicovitch, Yigal, *see* ALLON, YIGAL
Paiewonsky, Ralph **16**:165
Paikin, Harold **12**:1408
PAILES, ISAAC (Jacques) **3**:607 **13**:113
Pain **2**:100; **3**:5
Paine, Thomas **11**:78
Painted Woods (clny., N.D.) **12**:39
"Pairs" (sages), *see* ZUGOT
Paiva, Alfonso de **15**:1349
PAIVA, JACQUES **13**:14
PAI Views (period.) **13**:656
Pak (fam.), *see* BAK
Pakid (cmty, offic.) **16**:700
PAKISTAN **13**:14
- Israel relations **9**:445
- synagogues **1**:syn. list
Pakku'at sadeh (pakku'ot), see CUCUMBER
Pakrojus (tn., Lith.) **14**:769
PAKS (tn., Hung.) **13**:15
PALACHE (fam.) **13**:16
- Safi **14**:633
- trade **15**:1302
Palache, Abraham (fin.) **13**:17
Palache, Abraham (r.) **13**:17; **13**:18
Palache, David **13**:17
PALACHE, ḤAYYIM **13**:17
- Ashkenazi, Nissim **3**:731
- tax law **15**:872
Palache, Isaac (16th cent., r.) **13**:16
Palache, Isaac (19/20 cent., r.) **13**:17; **13**:19
Palache, Isaac ben Joseph **13**:17
Palache, Isaac ben Samuel **13**:16
Palache, Jacob-Carlos **13**:16
Palache, Joseph **13**:16
Palache, Joshua **13**:17
PALACHE, JUDAH LION **13**:19
Palache, Moses **13**:17
Palache, Samuel (dipl.) **2**:895; **13**:16; **13**:814
Palache, Samuel (mer.) **13**:17
Palacio (fam.), *see* PALACHE
Palaeologus (Byz., emp.) *see* Andronicus II
Palaestina (Rom. prov., Er. Isr.) **9**:121
- designation **9**:111
Palaestina Prima (prov., Er. Isr.)
- Arab conquest **9**:267
- Caesarea **5**:11
- Diocletian **9**:254
Palaestina Secunda (prov., Er. Isr.)
- Arab conquest **9**:261
- Beth-Shean **4**:758
- Diocletian **9**:254
Palaestina Tertia (prov. Er. Isr.)
- Diocletian **9**:254
- Petra **13**:342
Palaestina Treuhandstelle zur Beratung Deutscher Juden (trust co., Ger.) **7**:1012
Palaestina Verein (Er. Isr., assoc.) **8**:477
Palaggi (fam.), *see* PALACHE
Palaggi, Ḥayyim ben Jacob, *see* PALACHE, ḤAYYIM
PALAGYI, LAJOS **13**:19
- Palágyi, Menyhért **13**:20
PALAGYI, MENYHERT (Melchior) **13**:20
PALANGA(tn., Rus.) **13**:20
Palas, al- (fam.), *see* PALACHE
Palas, Moses al- **13**:16
Palasios, Raphael ben Joshua de **13**:1143
PALATINATE (reg., Ger.) **13**:21
- *see also:* BADEN
Palatine (sub., Chicago) **5**:415
Palatio, de (fam.), *see* PALACHE
Palatucci, Giovanni **14**:185
Palcos, Alberto **15**:255
PALDI, ISRAEL **13**:23
Paleche, Samuel *see* Palache, Samuel
PALENCIA (city, Sp.) **13**:23
Palencia, Gonzalez **15**:1202
PALE OF SETTLEMENT (Rus.) **13**:24
- Astrakhan **3**:786
- economic history **16**:1320
- history **8**:716ff
- history chart **8**:766–767
- labor ideology **10**:1324
- self-defense **14**:1124
- *shtetl* economy **8**:720
- Siberia **14**:1486ff
- socialism **15**:38
- *illus:*
- - Jewish crafts structure **5**:1053
- *see also:* RUSSIA
Paleography **5**:749; **6**:262
- *see also:* ARCHAEOLOGY
PALERMO (city, Sicily) **13**:28
- informers **8**:1370
- Jewish Parliament **15**:839
- metals and mining **11**:1441
PALESTINE **13**:29
- designation **9**:111
- frontiers **9**:311
- identity **9**:470ff
- origin of name **13**:399
- Truman, Harry **15**:1408

- Vatican **16:**74, 76
- Zionist Congress (15) **16:**1172
- *see also:* ISRAEL (Historical Survey); JORDAN, HASHEMITE KINGDOM OF; MANDATE FOR PALESTINE

Palestine (journ., Eng.) **14:**1510
Palestine (period., Holl.) **13:**1035
PALESTINE, INQUIRY COMMISSIONS **13:**30
- U.N. **15:**1544ff
- UNSCOP **15:**1688
- Va'ad Le'ummi **16:**50
- *illus:*
- - Anglo-American Committee **16:**1089
- - Peel Commisssion, 1936 **9:**351
- *see also:* WHITE PAPERS

PALESTINE, PARTITION AND PARTITION PLANS **13:**34
- *Contents:*
- - Introduction **13:**34
- - Palestine Royal Commission **13:**35
- - Palestine Partition Commission **13:**35
- - Morrison-Grady Scheme **13:**36
- - UNSCOP **13:**37
- Arab countries **9:**1031
- Arab National Movement **9:**463; **9:**465
- Ha-Po'el ha-Mizrachi **7:**1323
- Israel frontiers **9:**314
- Israel political parties **9:**662
- Latin America's influence **10:**1455
- League of Nations **10:**1521ff
- Morrison-Grady Plan **9:**359
- Peel commission **9:**349ff **16:**1084
- Revisionists **14:**130
- socialism **15:**37ff
- Syria **15:**647
- U.N. **15:**1543
- UNSCOP **15:**1688; **16:**1093
- Vatican **16:**76
- White Papers **16:**484
- Zionist Congress (21) **16:**1175
- *illus:*
- - voting chart of U.N. on partition of Palestine 1947 **9:**423
- *maps*
- - Sykes-Picot Treaty **15:**566
- - UNSCOP partition plans 1947 **9:**317
- *see also:* ST. JAMES CONFERENCE

Palestine Amateur Sports Federation **15:**295
Palestine and Zionism (wk.) **16:**1159
Palestine Arab National Movement, *see* Arabs (Nationalism)
Palestine Archaeological Museum, *see* ROCKEFELLER MUSEUM
Palestine Broadcasting Service, *see* Palestine Government Broadcasting Service
Palestine Colonization Society (Eng.) **16:**1155
Palestine Commission **10:**48
- *illus:*
- - U.N. session **15:**1544

Palestine Communist Party **5:**807; **9:**660ff
Palestine Conciliation Commission
- Arab Refugees **9:**447
- Armistice Agreements **3:**482
- Israel-Arab negotiations **9:**377
- U.N. **15:**1549ff

Palestine Conferences (Arab)
- 1920 **9:**457
- 1928 **9:**459ff
- 1964 **9:**467
- 1968 **9:**469

Palestine Constitution **9:**458
Palestine Cooperative Company, Inc. (U.S.) **13:**39
Palestine Corporation Ltd. (bank) **9:**824
PALESTINE ECONOMIC CORPORATION (U.S.) **13:**39
- Brandeis, Louis **4:**1298
- Cohen, Sir Robert **5:**684
- Joint Distribution Committee **2:**829
- U.S. Zionism **16:**1143

Palestine Electric Corporation **9:**342, 791; **14:**217
Palestine Endowment Funds **15:**668
Palestine Executive Committee **9:**457ff
PALESTINE EXPLORATION FUND **13:**40
- Bliss' excavations **4:**1095
- Crowfoot, John Winter **5:**1129
- Deutscher Palaestina Verein **5:**1595
- survey maps **11:**931
- Zionism **16:**1154

Palestine Exploration Fund Quarterly **5:**936
Palestine Football Association **15:**295
Palestine Foundation Fund, *see* KEREN HAYESOD
Palestine Government Broadcasting Service **9:**1473; **15:**930
Palestine Historical and Ethnographical Society, *see* Historical Society of Israel
Palestine Industrial Exhibition (Cairo) **9:**765
Palestine Jewish Colonization Association, *see* PICA
Palestine Journal of Botany **14:**48ff
Palestine Labor League **9:**853; **9:**868
Palestine Labor Party, *see* MAPAI
Palestine Land Development Company **15:**1123; **16:**287
Palestine Liberation Organization (Arab)
- Ahmad Shukeiri **9:**1033
- Arab League **3:**243
- Arab National Movement **9:**467ff
- Chinese recognition **5:**474ff
- Hussein **8:**1131
- Israel historical survey **9:**404; **9:**414
- terrorist activities **14:**1639
- *see also:* Fatah, Al

Palestine linden (bot.) **9:**1515
Palestine Mandate, *see* MANDATE FOR PALESTINE
Palestine Maritime League **9:**835
Palestine Maritime Lloyd (shipping line) **9:**835
Palestine Mortgage and Credit Bank Ltd. **13:**39
Palestine National-Socialist Party **15:**996
Palestine oak (bot.) **9:**1515
PALESTINE OFFICE **13:**40
- immigration to Erez Israel **9:**523
- labor movement **9:**329
- Zionist Congress (8) **16:**1169

Palestine Orchestra, *see* ISRAEL PHILHARMONIC ORCHESTRA
Palestine Order-in-Council **9:**633ff
Palestine Partition Commission, *see* Woodhead Commission
Palestine Police **9:**340
Palestine Post (newsp.), *see* JERUSALEM POST
Palestine Potash Company **5:**1395; **9:**345; **15:**71
- *illus:*
- - aerial view **15:**73

Palestine Psychoanalytical Society **6:**559
Palestine Royal Commission, *see* PEEL COMMISSION
Palestine Symphony Orchestra, *see* ISRAEL PHILHARMONIC ORCHESTRA
Palestine Telegram Service (period., Den.) *see Israel*
Palestine Water Company Ltd. **13:**39ff
Palestine Weekly (newsp.) **4:**470
Palestine White Papers, *see* WHITE PAPERS
Palestine Workers' Fund, *see* Erez Israel Workers' Fund
Palestinian Arabs
- Arab general survey **9:**1032
- Israel's attitude to **9:**413
- under Israel rule **9:**468ff

Palestinian Christian Aramaic (lang.) **3:**274
Palestinian Jewry (Egy.) **16:**1333
Palestinian Masorah **16:**1571, 1423, 1426
Palestinian Olympiad **15:**292
Palestinian Po'alei Zion (polit. party, Rus.) **15:**45
Palestinian pronunciation **13:**1125
Palestinian rites (litur.) **11:**394ff **16:**1333
Palestinian Sports Federation **9:**1019
Palestinian Talmud, *see* TALMUD, JERUSALEM
Palestinian Targum, *see* Targum (Yerushalmi)
Palewski, Gaston **13:**109
Paley, Johann (John) **5:**988; **14:**873; **16:**833
PALEY, WILLIAM SAMUEL **13:**41
Palga (demon) **5:**1527
Palgi, Phyllis **13:**1340
Palgi, Yoel **4:**166
PALGRAVE (fam.) **13:**42
Palgrave, Sir Francis **6:**783; **13:**42
Palgrave, Sir Francis Turner **13:**42
Palgrave, Sir Reginald Francis Douce **13:**42
Palgrave, Sir Robert Harry Inglis **13:**42
Palgrave, William Gifford **13:**42; **15:**1350
Palhedrin (Chamber in Temple) **3:**977
Palkovic, Georg **8:**48
Palkovič, J. **4:**885
Pallache (Pallas; fam.), *see* PALACHE
PALLENBERG, MAX **15:**1089
Palley, Clare **10:**1495
PALLIÈRE, AIMÉ **13:**43
PALM (bot.) **13:**43
- plant list **13:**623
- reproduction **4:**1019
- synagogue art **15:**597
- *illus:*
- - Bar Kokhba coins **4:**229
- - branching variety **9:**236
- *see also:* FOUR SPECIES; LULAV

Palm, J.H. van der **4:**876; **8:**48
Palma (Can. Is.) **5:**117
PALMA, LA (city, Sp.) **13:**45
Palma de Mallorca (city, Majorca) **11:**798ff
- *illus:*
- - Chueta district **5:**535
- - *rimmonim* **3:**530

PALMAH (mil. orgn., Er. Isr.) **13:**45
- Allon, Yigal **2:**655
- attacks on British posts **16:**1090
- Ben-Gurion, David **4:**509; **4:**510
- command problem **9:**371
- Golomb, Eliyahu **7:**764
- Haganah **7:**1071ff; **9:**688,689
- history **8:**760
- Palestine Scheme **9:**354
- Sadeh, Yizhak **14:**623
- War of Independence **16:**306
- Wingate, Orde **16:**548
- youth movements **9:**980
- *illus:*
- - text
- - attacking Arab irregulars **9:**686
- - Negev Brigade memorial **12:**931

Palmah (journ.), *see Alon ha-Palmah*
Palmahim (kib., Isr.) **1:**place list
Palmas, Las (city, Can. Is.), *see* Las Palmas
Palm Dove (zool.) **6:**34
Palmeira, Baron de, *see* Goldsmid, Sir Isaac Lyon
PALMER, EDWARD HENRY **13:**48
- Avedat **3:**942

Palmer, Leonard **15:**303
Palmers Green (sub., Lond.) **11:**479
- *illus:*
- - shift of population **11:**479

Palmerston, Henry, Viscount **13:**6; **13:**1250; **16:**1070
Palmira (tn., Arg.) **11:**1347
Palmistry, *see* CHIROMANCY
Palmroot, J. **8:**48
Palm Tales (fables) **6:**1127
Palm-trees, the language of the **6:**117
Palmyra (city, Syr.), *see* TADMOR
Paloma, La (song), *see* AVI, AVI
Paloma bat Abraham **2:**153
PALOMBO, DAVID **13:**48
- *illus:*
- - sculpture **14:**1068
- - Yad Vashem Memorial Hall, Jerusalem Fig. 110 3—ART

Palota, Aaron **16:**917
Palquera (fam.), *see* FALAQUERA
Palquera, Shem Tov Ben Joseph, *see* FALAQUERA, SHEM TOV BEN JOSEPH
PALTI (Paltiel; bib. fig.) **13:**49
- Michal **11:**1494

PALTIEL (10th cent., physic.) **13:**49
- Fatimid **6:**1197
- *Megillat Yuhasin* **2:**463

Paltiel, Zevi **11:**1260
Paltiel ben Samuel **5:**156
Paltit (bib. fig.) **15:**71
PALTOI BAR ABBAYE (gaon) **13:**50
- codification of law **5:**637; **5:**638
- gaonite list **7:**318
- gentile courts **12:**126
- Sabbath arrest **8:**1301

P.A.L.T.R.E.U. (trust co., Ger.), *see* Palaestina Treuhandstelle zur Beratung Deutscher Juden
Paludan-Mueller, Frederik **14:**926
Palur (tn., Ind.) **5:**624
Palyah (fam.), *see* PALACHE
PAM, HUGO **13:**50
Pam, Max **13:**50
Pamalyah (journ.) **1:**newsp. list
PAMIERS (tn., Fr.) **13:**50
Pampa, La (prov., Arg.), *see* La Pampa
Pampeluna (city, Sp.), *see* PAMPLONA
Pamphilius (law.), *see* RODE, WALTHER
PAMPHYLIA (reg., As. M.) **13:**51
- Asia **3:**746

PAMPLONA (city, Sp.) **13:**51
- archives **3:**376
- goldsmiths **7:**741

Pan (deity) **4:**162
- *illus:*
- - Banias grotto **4:**162

Pan, Toybi **11:**359
PANĂ, SAȘA **13:**52
Panadas (Sp. food) **14:**1167
Panagoria (anc. tn., Bosphorus)

4:1263
PANAMA (rep., C. Am.) 13:53
- Latin America 10:1450ff
- politics 13:821
- synagogues 1: syn. list
- Zionism 16:1127
Panama (city, Pan.) 13:53
Pan-Arab movement
- Arabic language 3:241
- Arab National Movement 9:464
- Nasser, Gamal Abdul 12:841
Pančevo (city, Serb.) 16:873
- *illus:*
- - synagogue 16:875
Panchatantra (Ind. fables) 3:20
Pancho (ship) 9:532
Panciu (tn., Rum.) 14:397
Pancosmosophia (wk.) 2:800
Pan Crescent (ship) 8:1254
Pandeleon (Sp. food) 14:1167
Pandira (tal. fig.) 4:554; 10:15
Pandre, Noah 14:1430
Paneas (city, Er. Isr.), *see* BANIAS
Panentheism 6:182, 7:1404; 10:542; 10:589ff
Paneriai (loc., Lith.), *see* PONARY
Panet (fam. name), *see also:* Banet; Baneth; Paneth
PANET, EZEKIEL BEN JOSEPH 13:54
Paneth (fam. name), *see also:* Banet; Baneth; Panet
Paneth, Ezekiel ben Jacob, *see* BANETH, EZEKIEL BEN JACOB
PANETH, FRIEDRICH ADOLF 13:54
Paneth, Joseph 13:54
Panets (r.) 10:996
PANEVEZYS (Panevezhis; city, Lith.) 13:55
- *illus:*
- - text
- - Karaite synagogue 11:366
Panias (city, Er. Isr.), *see* BANIAS
PANIGEL, ELIYAHU MOSHE 13:56
- religious life in Israel 9:889
PANIGEL, RAPHAEL MEIR BEN JUDAH 13:56
- Cochin 5:621
- Feinstein, Ḥayyim 6:1213
- religious life in Israel 9:889
Panim Aḥerim le-Esther Nosaḥ Bet (wk.) 16:1515
Panim el Panim (journ.) 1:newsp. list
Panini (Ind. gram.) 16:1414
PANKEN, JACOB 13:57
PANN, ABEL 3:607
- *illus:*
- - "Cossacks are Coming" (drg.) 8:736
- - "Orpah the Moabite" (paint.) Fig. 88 3—ART
Pannartz, Arnold 8:1319; 8:1323
Pannonia (Rom. prov.) 8:1088; 16:868
Pannonia (period.) 4:1401
Panofsky, Dora 13:57
PANOFSKY, ERWIN 13:57
- archaeology 3:301
Pan-religiosity (theol. conc.) 3:88
Pantheism 7:672
- emanation 6:694
- ḥasidic thought 7:1404
- Ibn Ezra, Abraham 8:1168; 13:438
- Kabbalah 7:662; 7:673ff; 10:564; 10:601ff
- Kook, A. I. 12:891
- Krochmal, N. 13:458
- nature 12:890; 12:891
- Spinoza, Baruch 13:453; 15:279ff
Panther, Peter, *see* TUCHOLSKY, KURT
Panticapaeum (anc. city), *see* KERCH
Pantira (tal. fig.) 4:554; 10:15
Pan York (ship) 8:1254
Panzer, Mitchell E. 7:861
Panzini, Alfredo 9:1106
Paoli, Betty, *see* Glueck, Barbara Elisabeth
Paolo (Chr. Hebr.), *see* Paul
PAOVLOTZKY, RAUL 3:607
PAP, ARTHUR 13:58
PAP, KÁROLY 13:58
PAPA (amora) 13:58
- *Hadran* prayer 7:1054
PAPA (tn., Hung.), 13:59
Papa ben Nazer 8:650; 12:1318
Papacy, *see* CHURCH, CATHOLIC; Papal States; POPES
Papadhaki, Sophia Mavroïdhi 7:887
Papageorgios (ling.) 10:426
Papal States
- bull of 1569 4:1496
- history chart (1569) 8:766-767
- Inquisition 8:1398
- Pesaro Jews 13:329
- Roman Jews 14:245
- *see also:* CHURCH, CATHOLIC; ITALY
Papapanayiotou, Kosta 7:898
Papareschi, Gregorio (pope), *see* INNOCENT II
Paper 8:1320; 13:71
Paper, Eliezer 10:954
PAPER, HERBERT HARRY 1:35
Paper, Lewis 12:38
PAPER-CUTS (folkart) 13:60
- *illus:*
- - text
- - horah (M. Gur-Arie) 8:973
- - *Kimpetbriefel* 13:44-45
- - *mizraḥ* 11:271; 12:*fcg.* 173; 13:44-45
- - *Omer* counting chart 13:44-45
- - Shavuot window decoration 6:1394
- - *Shivviti* plaques 13:44-45; 14:1420-1421
- - *ushpizin* decoration 13:44-45
PAPERNA, ABRAHAM BARUCH 13:65
PAPERNA, ABRAHAM JACOB 13:65
- critic 5:1117
Papert, Frederic S. 2:318
Paphlagonia (reg., As. M.) 3:747
PAPI (Babyl. amora) 13:66
PAPI (Pal. amora) 13:67
PAPIERNIKOV, JOSEPH 13:67
Papineau, Louis Joseph 5:103
Papini, Giovanni 9:1106
Paplug, A. 5:803
Papo, Abraham David 13:67
Papo, Eliezer Jichac 16:888
Papo, Eliezer Shem Tov 2:638; 14:871; 16:888
Papo, Isaac 14:871
PAPO, SAMUEL SHEMAIAH 13:67
Pappa (amora), *see* PAPA
Pappa ben Nazir, *see* Papa ben Nazer
PAPPENHEIM, BERTHA 13:68
- *illus:* text
Pappenheim, Eugen 6:464
PAPPENHEIM, SOLOMON 13:68
- Ash, Abraham 3:694
Pappias (savora) 14:920
PAPPUS AND JULIANUS (tal. figs.) 13:69
- Bar Kokhba War 8:646
PAPPUS BEN JUDAH (tan.) 13:69
- Akiva 2:491
- Ben Stada 4:554
Papus (Fr. trans.) 10:648; 16:788
PAPYRI 13:70
- Hellenism 8:291ff
- law source 12:117
- Oesterreichische Nationalbibliothek 12:1333
- *illus:*
- - Aramaic script 2:711
- - Bar Kokhba document 8:647
- - Egyptian cursive script, Hebrew 2:692
- - Elephantine 2:684; 6:607; 8:617
- - land-lease deed 4:237
- - Nash Papyrus 12:834
- - Saqqara 2:684
- *see also:* MANUSCRIPTS, HEBREW; PAPYRUS
PAPYRUS (bot.) 13:71
- books 4:1220
- Cairo *genizah* 16:1334
- economic history 16:1273
- plant list 13:623
- flora of Israel 9:225
- seals 14:1072
- writing material 16:658
- *illus:*
- - text
- - Ḥuleh Nature Reserve 9:227
- *see also:* PAPYRI
Pa-qa-ha (k., Isr.), *see* PEKAH
Paquda, Baḥya ibn, *see* BAḤYA BEN JOSEPH IBN PAQUDA
Pará (state, Braz.) 4:1328
PARABLE 13:72
- *Contents:*
- - Introduction 13:72
- - In the Talmud and Midrash 13:73
- - - King Parables 13:74
- - - Animal Parables 13:75
- - - Parables from Nature 13:75
- - Post-Talmudic Period 13:76
- Bible 13:1264
- sages' use of 14:651
- wisdom literature 16:561
- Yiddish literature 16:804
- *see also:* AGGADAH
Paracelsus (philos.) 2:544; 15:1400
Parachutists (Haganah) 9:688
- Holocuast 8:907
- Reik, Havivah 14:54
- Sereni, Enzo Ḥayyim 14:1182
- Szenes, Hannah 15:661
- *see also:* HAGANAH
Paradesi (J. gr., Ind.) 5:621
Paradis, Viola 13:1361
PARADISE 13:77
- *Contents:*
- - Contents of the Narrative 13:77
- - Specific Problems 13:78
- - - Location of the Garden 13:78
- - - Trees of Life and Knowledge 13:78
- - - The Serpent 13:80
- - - Mythological Features 13:80
- - Literary Composition 13:80
- - Literary and Folkloristic Affinities 13:81
- - Paradise and Hell in Later Jewish Thought 13:82
- - Apocalyptic Literature 13:83
- - Rabbinic Literature 13:83
- - - Gehinnom 13:83
- - - Gan Eden 13:84
- - Medieval Literature 13:84
- - Modern Period 13:85
- Academy on High 2:208
- eschatology 6:876ff
- in the Arts 2:242
- maps of world 11:919
- Mari fresco 11:975
- Muhammad's views 6:884
- mysticism and 10:499; 10:503ff
- Samaritans 14:738; 14:740
- soul 15:180
- soul in Kabbalah 10:611; 10:612
- Sumer 15:515
- *illus:*
- - "Adam and Eve in Paradise" (paint., Rubens and Jan Brueghel the Elder) 4:941
- - Herzl-Balfour parody 13:139
- - the righteous 4:360, *fcg.* 908
- *see also:* AFTERLIFE; GARDEN OF EDEN; OLAM HA-BA
"Paradise" (paint., Jan Brueghel the Elder) 7:325
Paradise Lost (wk.) 2:243; 11:1587
Parà donation (tax, Turk.) 9:1093
PARAF, PIERRE 13:85
Paragonis (s. of Sapandus) 12:828
PARAGUAY 13:85
- Latin America 10:1449ff
- synagogues 1:syn. list
- Zionism 16:1125
- *illus:* text
PARAH (tract.) 13:87
- *illus:* text
- *see also:* RED HEIFER
PARAH, PERATH (tn., Er. Isr.) 13:88
Parah, Shabbat, see Shabbat Parah
Parah adumah, see RED HEIFER
Paraiba (city, Braz.) 4:1323
Parakletos Jesu ben Pandera (invocation) 10:638
Paralia (reg., Er. Isr.) 9:120
Paralipomena Jeremiae (bk.), *see* BARUCH, REST OF THE WORDS OF
Paralipomenon, see CHRONICLES, THE BOOK OF
Paramaribo (city, Surinam) 15:530ff
PARAN (des., Sinai) 13:88
- human geography 9:595
- Negev 12:925ff
- Plateau 9:135ff
- *illus:* text
Paran, Mount (bib.) 14:1597
Paran, Naḥal (wadi, Isr.) 9:135; 12:927
- *illus:*
- - desert tamarisk 9:234
Paraná (city, Arg.) 6:802
Paranà (state, Braz.) 4:1330
Paranoia 11:1374
PARAPET 13:89
Parasang (meas.) 16:389
Parashah petuḥah (Torah div.) 16:1407ff
Parashah setumah (Torah div.) 16:1407ff
Parashat Shelaḥ Lekha (illum. ms.) 8:1263
- *illus:*
- - opening and closing pages 4:*fcg.* 811
Parashiyyot (commandments) 5:761
Parashot ha-shavu'a (Torah div.) 15:1247ff; 16:1407ff
Parasitology 7:941
"Parchemin Rouge" (paint., M. Castel) 5:236
Parchim (tn., Ger.) 11:1163
Parchment
- Cairo *genizah* 16:1334
- *sefer torah* 14:1100; 16:670
- writing 16:659
PARCZEW (tn., Pol.) 13:90
Pardes (co-op, Er. Isr.) 5:946; 5:948; 9:328
- Sapir, Joseph 14:856
Pardes (publ. firm, U.S.) 13:1376
Pardes (journ.) 1:newsp. list
- *see also: Ha-Pardes*
PARDES (mnemonic) 13:91
- Kabbalah 10:623
PARDES ḤANNAH-KARKUR (cmty., Isr.) 13:91
- statistics 1:place list
PARDESIYYAH (vill., Isr.) 13:92
- statistics 1:place list
Pardes Rimmonim (wk.) 5:968
- *illus:*
- - harmonic unity of *Sefirot* 10:614
- - *Sefirot* diagram 10:502
- - seventy-two-lettered Holy Name

10:584
- - title page (Cracow, 1592) **5:**968
PARDO (fam.) **13:**92
- *aliyah* **9:**513
- Split **15:**289
Pardo, Abraham **13:**93
Pardo, David (publ.) **13:**94
Pardo, David (r., Surinam) **13:**93
Pardo, David ben Joseph (r., Neth.) **13:**92
PARDO, DAVID SAMUEL BEN JACOB **13:**93
- Habillo, Elisha **7:**1027
- Sarajevo **14:**871
Pardo, Elijah **9:**1098
Pardo, Isaac **13:**93; **14:**871; **16:**888
Pardo, Jacob **13:**93
- Pardo, David Samuel **13:**93
- Sarajevo **14:**871
PARDO, JOSEPH (r., It.) **13:**94
- Amsterdam **2:**896
Pardo, Joseph (cant., Eng.) **13:**94
Pardo, Josiah **12:**993; **13:**92; **14:**349
PARDO, MOSES BEN RAPHAEL **13:**94
Pardo, Saul, *see* BROWN, SAUL PARDO
Pardon, *see* FORGIVENESS
Pardo-Roques (cmty. ldr., It.) **13:**563
Pardubice (city, Cz.) **5:**1199
Pareau, J. H. **8:**48
Pareira, Solomon **13:**1277
Parental Blessing, *see* BLESSING OF CHILDREN
PARENT AND CHILD **13:**95
- *Contents:*
- - Status of the Child **13:**95
- - Parental Rights **13:**95
- - Parental Obligations **13:**95
- - - Maintenance **13:**95
- - - Custody of Children **13:**98
- - Agreements between Parents Concerning their Children **13:**99
- - Children of Parents Who Are Not Both Jewish **13:**99
- - In the State of Israel **13:**100
- General
- - blessing of children **4:**1087
- - embryo **6:**719
- - family **6:**1166ff
- - fastdays **6:**1193; **6:**1195
- - firstborn **6:**1306
- - health services in Israel **9:**986ff
- - husband and wife **8:**1125
- - kibbutz movement **10:**967
- - nature of man **11:**846
- - virgin **16:**160ff
- - *zekhut avot* **16:**976ff
- Legal Aspects
- - abortion **2:**98; **2:**99
- - absolution from vows **16:**227
- - adoption **2:**301
- - *apotropos* **3:**218
- - assault **3:**758
- - child maintenance **8:**1424; **11:**784
- - Commandments, the 613 **5:**770
- - father's maintenance duty **12:**111
- - gentiles **12:**1190
- - *ḥazakah* **7:**1518ff
- - honor of parents **13:**100; **16:**778
- - Jewish law, 20th century **12:**143ff
- - levirate marriage **11:**123
- - marriage **11:**1028
- - marriage in nursing period **11:**1053ff
- - rebellious son **13:**1603
- - slavery **14:**1655
- - succession of inheritance **15:**475
- - tort liability **11:**184
- - witnesses **16:**587
- *see also:* BARRENNESS AND FERTILITY; CHILDREN
PARENTS, HONOR OF **13:**100
- domestic peace **14:**1357
- Esau, example of **6:**857
- teacher, honor of **10:**917
- *Yahrzeit* **16:**702
- *see also:* PARENT AND CHILD
Parentucelli, Tommaso (15th cent., pope), *see* NICHOLAS V
PARENZO (fam.) **13:**101
- *illus:* text
Parenzo (vill., Istria) **9:**1099
Parenzo, Asher **6:**46; **13:**102
Parenzo, Gershon **13:**102
Parenzo, Jacob **13:**101
Parenzo, Meir **13:**101
- typography **15:**1482
Parenzo, Moses **13:**102
Parev (neutral food), *see* PARVEH
Pargod (journ.) **1:**newsp. list
Pargod (kab. conc.) **10:**503; **10:**531
Parhedrin (chamber in Temple), *see* *Palhedrin*
Parḥi, Estori ha- (geog.), *see* ESTORI HA-PARHI
PARḤON, SALOMON BEN ABRAHAM IBN **13:**102
PARIENTE (fam.) **13:**102
Pariente, Abraham **13:**103
Pariente, Abraham de José **13:**924
Pariente, Jacob (cmty. ldr.) **13:**102
Pariente, Jacob (mer.) **13:**103
Pariente, Joseph **13:**103
Pariente, Judah ben Abraham **13:**103
Pariente, Samuel **13:**103
Pariente, Solomon **13:**103
- Tangier **15:**791
PARIS (city, Fr.) **13:**103
- *Contents:*
- - Early History **13:**103
- - Middle Ages **13:**104
- - Hebrew Printing **13:**109
- - Holocaust Period **13:**109
- - Contemporary Period **13:**110
- archives **3:**386,387
- burning of the Talmud **2:**939; **15:**769
- Comité de Bienfaisance **5:**350
- Consistoire **5:**907
- Council of 1213 **5:**548
- demography **5:**1513
- France **7:**9,22ff
- history chart **8:**766-767
- Host desecration charge **8:**1043
- Jewry **7:**22
- *meẓiẓah* abolished **5:**572
- museums **12:**538ff
- Sanhedrin, French **14:**840
- secondhand goods **14:**1086
- stock exchanges **15:**406
- synagogues **15:**619
- Zionism **16:**1113
- *illus:*
- - text
- - community seal (1207) **14:**1077
- - Don Isaac Abrabanel synagogue **3:**341
- - French Sanhedrin session (1807) **14:**841
- - Grande Synagogue, Rue de la Victoire **15:**620-621
- - Montmartre, Jewish Community Center **6:**406
- - Rothschild mansion **7:**39
- - War Crimes Trial **16:**301
- *map:* text
Paris, Disputation of **6:**92
- Abraham of Dreux **2:**155
- Nicholas Donin **6:**167
Paris, Matthew **11:**923
Paris, Treaty of (1229) **2:**534
Pariser Yiddisher Arbeiter Theater (Fr.), *see* PIAT
Parish-Alvars, Eli **2:**786
Parisi, Mordechai **11:**1566
Paris Opera **5:**323
Paris Psalter (illum. ms.), **4:**947; **5:**1263,1330; **8:**451
PARIS SCHOOL OF ART **13:**112
- *Contents:*
- - Jewish School **13:**112
- - Fauvist School **13:**113
- - The Cubists **13:**113
- - The Surrealists **13:**114
- - Montparnasse and La Ruche **13:**115
- - Victims of Nazism **13:**117
- - After World War II **13:**117
- - Traditionalists and Individualists **13:**120
- art **3:**567
- *illus:* text
Paris un Viene (bk.) **11:**359; **16:**807
PARKER, DOROTHY **13:**120
Parker, Horatio W. **9:**1589
Parker, M. **9:**1522ff
Parker, Margaret **2:**540
Parkersburg (city, W. Va.) **16:**475
Parker's Memorial (loc., Sinai) **14:**1605
PARKES, JAMES WILLIAM **13:**121
- historiography **8:**562
- missions to Jews opposed by **13:**1252
Park Forest (sub., Chicago) **5:**415; **8:**1256
Parkhurst, J. **8:**48
Park Ridge (sub., Chicago) **5:**415
Park Ridge (boro., N.J.) **4:**612
Park Synagogue (Ohio) **15:**625
Park Synagogue (S.A.) **10:**156
- *illus:*
- - consecration ceremony **15:**191
PARLAMENTSKLUB, JUEDISCHER ("Jewish caucus"; Aus.) **13:**121
Parliament of Jews (Eng.) **6:**749
- history chart **8:**766-767 **16:**632
- taxation **15:**838ff
PARMA (city, It.) **13:**122
- library **11:**193
- *illus:* text
Parma Bible (14th cent., illum. ms.) **9:***fcg.* 43
PARNAS (tit., cmty. head) **13:**123
- Council of the Four Lands **5:**1003; **5:**996
- *gabbai* **7:**230
- muqaddim **12:**527
- public and **13:**1351
- title **15:**1164
PARNAS, ḤAYYIM NAḤMAN **13:**124
- Barit, Jacob **4:**226
Parnas, Moses (14th cent.) **7:**1317
Parnas, Moses (17th cent.) **5:**373
Parnas, Moses ben Eliezer (16th cent., print.) **9:**1097
- Soncino **15:**142
PARNAS, YAKUB KAROL **5:**386
Parnasei Medinah (elders) **10:**1406
Parnes, Joseph **11:**614
Parnu (city, Est.) **6:**916
Parod (kib., Isr.) **1:**place list
PARODY, HEBREW **13:**124
- *Contents:*
- - Early Hebrew Literature **13:**124
- - Since the 12th century **13:**126
- - Early Haskalah **13:**131
- - Modern Times **13:**134
- Jewish literature **11:**353ff
- poetry, biblical **13:**687
- realistic folktale **6:**1381
- *illus:* text
Parokhet (Ark curtain) **3:**457; **5:**309
- synagogue **15:**594
- Torah ornaments **15:**1255
- *illus:*
- - Glogau, 18th cent. **15:***fcg.* 1259
- - Kassel synagogue **15:**1256
- - needlework **3:**531; **5:**297,961; **9:**1187; **11:**273; **12:**549
- - Prague, Altneuschul **15:***fcg.* 587, *fcg.* 619
Paros (Gr. isl.) **6:**10
Parosh, *see* FLEA
PARROT, ANDRÉ **13:**140
Parry, Hubert **14:**918
Parsah (meas.) **16:**389
Parsch, Pius **4:**875
Parschitius, Daniel **8:**48
Parshanut (Torah study) **8:**1414
Parsic (lang.), *see* JUDEO-PERSIAN
Parsley (bot.) **16:**83
Partenit (Parthenita; tn., Crimea) **5:**1103
Parthia, Parthians
- Antigonus II **3:**66ff
- exilarch **6:**1023ff
- Nabateans **12:**742
- Persia **13:**307
- Second Temple period **8:**631; **8:**635
Partial Admission **2:**290
Particles (Heb. gram.) **8:**122ff
- mishnaic Hebrew **16:**1602
Participle (Heb. lang.) **16:**1559
Particularism, Jewish **10:**388ff
- *see also:* CHOSEN PEOPLE
PARTISANS **13:**140
- Éclaireurs Israélites **14:**1039
- gassing **16:**1332
- Poland **13:**774ff
- Pushkin unit **16:**599
- *illus:*
- - text
- - Warsaw Ghetto **16:**346
- *map:* text
- *see also:* SELF-DEFENSE
Partition (syn.), *see* MEḤIẒAH
Partition plans for Palestine, *see* PALESTINE, PARTITION AND PARTITION PLANS
Partizanim-Ḥayyalim-Ḥalutzim (partisan orgn.) **13:**149
PARTNERSHIP **13:**149
- *Contents:*
- - Formation **13:**149
- - Distribution of Profits and Losses **13:**150
- - Powers and Duties **13:**151
- - Representation by One of its Members **13:**152
- - Dissolution of Partnership **13:**153
- - Iska ("In Commendam" Transactions) **13:**153
- - Joint Ownership **13:**154
- - A Legal Persona **13:**154
- - In the State of Israel **13:**155
- community **15:**844
- conflict of laws **5:**886
- contract **5:**928
- *ḥazakah* of property **7:**1518
- hired property **10:**1531ff
- legal rights **13:**953
- moneylending **12:**253
- oral formation of **12:**18
- subject to overreaching **12:**1394
- surety **15:**528
- trustee **14:**1267
- usury in **16:**30ff
- *see also:* LEGAL PERSON
PARTOS, OEDOEN **13:**155
PARTRIDGE (bird) **13:**156
- dietary laws **6:**30,34
- fauna of Israel **9:**226
Partridge, Red Legged (bird) **6:**30
Partsaver, Joseph ben Judah Leib **13:**1380
Parturition, *see* BIRTH
Parur (city, Ind.) **5:**621; **5:**624; **8:**1355
PARVAIM (bib. reg.) **13:**156
- metals and mining **11:**1429
PARVEH **13:**157
- dietary laws **6:**40

- *see also:* MEAT; MILK
Parys (tn., S. Afr.) **12:**1448
Parzel (*parzela;* metal), *see* Iron
Parẓuf, parẓufim (kab. conc.)
- Kabbalah **10:**547
- Lurianic Kabbalah **10:**599
- Worlds, the Four **16:**642
- *illus:*
- - thirteen *middot* **10:**544
Pasadena (tn., Tex.) **15:**1036
Pasatiempo (period., Yug.) **16:**888
Pascal, André (plwrt.), *see* Rothschild, Henri
PASCAL, BLAISE **13:**157
- French literature **7:**140
Pascal, Dave **5:**220
PASCANI (tn., Rum.) **13:**158
Paschal lamb (sacrifice) **13:**163ff
- Commandments, the 613 **5:**776
- Exodus **12:**375
- *Haggadah* **7:**1079
- Hillel's decision **3:**990; **12:**12
- Passover eve **12:**22
- place in cult **5:**1157
- sacrifice **14:**611
- sages on **14:**641
- Samaritan history **14:**734, 742
- slaughter of **15:**1309
- tractate *Pesaḥim* **13:**327
- *illus:*
- - preparation of **13:**165
- - Samaritan's sacrifice **13:**169
PASCHELES, WOLF **13:**158
PASCIN, JULES **13:**159
- *illus:* text
Pasenko, George **11:**1556; **14:**479
Paseq (punctuation sign) **16:**1459
Pasewalk (tn., Pomerania) **13:**842
PASHHUR (bib. pr.) **13:**159
- inscription **16:**667
- Jeremiah's arrest **9:**1358
- office **13:**1075
Pashhur (anc. fam., Er. Isr.) **14:**626
- Arad temple ostraca **3:**249
- Jehoiarib **9:**1322
- priestly divisions **12:**89
- *illus:*
- - Arad ostracon **3:**248
Pashkovsky, Leib **11:**1203
Pashman, Morris **13:**162
Pashta' (cantillation sign) **16:**1413, 1440, 1454
Pasini (-nus), Giuseppe Luca **8:**48
PASMANIK, DANIEL **13:**160
- *illus:* text
Pasor, Matthias **8:**48
Pasqually, Martines de **10:**646
Pasquato, Lorenzo **13:**12
Pasquier, Etienne Denis de **3:**762
Pass, De (fam.), *see* DE PASS
Pass, Frank Alexander De (sol.), *see* De Pass, Frank Alexander
Passagi (Chr. sect), *see* ALBIGENSES
PASSAIC-CLIFTON (twin cities, N.J.) **13:**161
- Paterson **13:**179
Passarowitz Peace Treaty **3:**891
PASSAU (city, W. Ger.) **13:**162
- Host desecration **8:**1043
Passfield, Lord (states., Eng.), *see* Webb, Sidney James
Passfield White Paper **16:**483
- *illus:*
- - London protest rally **16:**1118
PASSI, DAVID **13:**163
- Benveniste, Moses **4:**563
Passion, *see* LOVE
Passion plays
- anti-Semitism **3:**107
- *Exagoge* **6:**1103
- Germany **7:**442
- image of Jew **8:**669
PASSOVER **13:**163
- *Contents:*
- - Names and History **13:**163
- - The Seder **13:**166
- - The Laws and Customs of Passover **13:**169
- - Critical View **13:**169
- - - Feast of the Unleavened Bread **13:**171
- - Passover in the New Testament **13:**171
- - Passover Cookery **13:**172
- - In Art **13:**172
- General
- - history **12:**375
- - moon **12:**290
- - *Shabbat ha-Gadol* **14:**1217
- - year **16:**725
- Laws and Customs
- - *aẓeret* **3:**1006
- - Commandments, the 613 **5:**763–767f
- - firstborn fast **6:**1310
- - kibbutz festivals **10:**959
- - Maimuna **11:**781
- - *niddui* **8:**351
- - *Omer* **12:**1382ff
- - Pentateuch **13:**256ff
- - pilgrimage **13:**510ff
- - sacrifice **14:**600ff
- - Sephardi customs **14:**1170
- - work on eve of **12:**22
- - *see also:* Paschal lamb
- Bread: Leavened and Unleavened
- - *bedikat ḥameẓ* **4:**372
- - cooking and food **6:**1423
- - *ḥameẓ* **7:**1235
- - *hekhsher* **8:**287
- - *kotevet* **16:**389
- - legal person and *ḥameẓ* **10:**1569
- - *maẓẓah* **11:**1155
- - punishment for *ḥameẓ* **10:**788
- - rice **14:**155
- - sale of *ḥameẓ* **7:**1237
- *Seder*
- - *Addir bi-Melukhah* **2:**256
- - *afikoman* **2:**329
- - *Arba Kosot* **3:**292
- - Azulai family majolica **3:**1016
- - egg **6:**474
- - *Eḥad Mi Yode'a* **6:**503
- - Elijah, cup of **6:**645
- - *Ḥad Gadya* **7:**1048
- - *Haggadah* **7:**1079
- - *ḥaroset* **7:**1346
- - *kitel* **10:**1079
- - *Mah Nistannah* **11:**728
- - *maror* **11:**1014
- - *maẓẓah* **11:**1155
- - Mountain Jews **12:**479
- - plagues of Egypt **13:**611
- - resistance symbol **8:**302
- Liturgy
- - dew, prayer for **5:**1602
- - *Haggadah* **7:**1079
- - night prayers **12:**1158
- - Sea, Song of the **14:**1071
- - seventh day vigil **10:**642
- - Song of Songs **14:**1057; **15:**148; **15:**150; **15:**151
- - *Yagur Passover Service* **14:**1313ff
- In Literature and Art
- - Exodus, Book of **6:**1053ff
- - folklore **6:**1376
- - in illuminated *maḥzorim* **11:**732; **11:**735
- - *seder* plate **5:**309
- - tractate *Pesaḥim* **13:**327
- Sectarian Forms
Falashas **6:**1148
- - Karaites **10:**779
- - Mount Gerizim **7:**438
- - Samaritans **14:**734; **14:**741ff
- Christianity
- - blood libels **4:**1120
- - Catholic Church **5:**537
- - Easter **11:**1291
- - Justinian I **10:**478
- - Last Supper **10:**12
- *illus:*
- - text
- - abbreviations for order of *seder* procedure **2:**47; **7:**1081
- - Bucharest, *talmud torah* pupils' *seder* **14:**415
- - *Darmstadt Haggadah* **7:***fcg.* 811
- - Dutch family *seder* **6:**1165
- - Elijah coming on Passover Eve **6:***fcg.* 651
- - *Erna Michael Haggadah* **7:***fcg.* 1067
- - *ḥaroset* and *maẓẓot (Sarajevo Haggadah)* **3:**530
- - *ḥaroset* container **7:**1346
- - hiding the *afikoman* **2:**330
- - Jewish legion in Jerusalem **9:**1473
- - *Joel ben Simeon Haggadah* **7:***fcg.* 1003
- - *Kiddush* **3:**531; **10:**139
- - Kurdish immigrants' *seder* **10:**1296
- - lifting of the wine **3:***fcg.* 299
- - *Mah Nishtannah* **11:**729
- - *Maror* **11:**1014
- - master of the house presiding at *seder* **4:**3
- - *maẓẓah* baking **11:**1155-1157; **12:**26
- - Moscow Great Synagogue service **12:**367
- - *Omer* counting chart, papercut **13:**44-45
- - Passover Meal (paint., M. Oppenheim) **10:**1079
- - Saigon, U.S. servicemen *seder* **12:**876
- - Samaritan sacrifice **14:**743
- - search for leaven **4:***fcg.* 364,371
- - "Seder" (drg., E. Meitner) Fig. 85 **3**-ART
- - *seder* at Bet ha-Shittah **10:**961
- - *seder* in Dallas, Texas **15:**1611
- - *seder* plates **3:**531; **5:**304,661; **6:**1391; **7:**1049; **11:**1532; **13:**353
- - *Sefer Pesaḥ Me'ubin* (1692) **4:**560
- - *se'udah* **14:**1193
- - Warsaw *seder* (1960) **13:**781
- - washing of hands for *seder* **2:**83; **8:**1286
- *scores:*
- - *Addir bi-Melukhah* **2:**256
- - *Addir Hu* **2:**257
- *see also:* FESTIVALS; PASSOVER, SECOND; PILGRIM FESTIVALS
PASSOVER, ALEXANDER **13:**173
PASSOVER, SECOND **13:**173
- *Hillula* celebration **8:**495
- Meir Ba'al ha-Nes **11:**1246
- Passover **13:**163,170
"Passover Meal" (paint., M. Oppenheim) **10:**1079
PASSOW, AARON HARRY **13:**174
Pašta (cantillation sign), *see Pashta*
Past and Future (journ., Hung.), *see* MULT ÉS JÖVŐ
Pastel (Sp. food) **14:**1167
PASTERNAK, BORIS LEONIDOVICH **13:**174
- apostasy **3:**207
- *illus:* text
PASTERNAK, JOSEPH **12:**449; **12:**472
Pasternak, Leon **13:**801,802
PASTERNAK, LEONID OSIPOVICH **13:**175
- *illus:*
- - text
- - cover for *Shirei Yeladim* **12:**659
- - "Jews at the Wailing Wall" (drg.) **16:**470
- - Pasternak, Boris (sketch) **13:**174
- - Samuel, Herbert (drg.) **14:**798
- - Tchernichowsky, Saul (port.) **15:**878
Pastor, Judah Leib **11:**611
PASTOUREAUX (mvmt.) **13:**176
- Agen Jews **2:**349
- Crusades **5:**1141
- history chart **8:**766-767
- John XXII **10:**159
- Philip V **13:**394
- Tudela Jews **15:**1425
Pastritius, J. **8:**48
Pasvalys (cmty., Lith.) **14:**769
PAT, JACOB **13:**177
- Haganah **7:**1066
- *illus:*
- - Ha-Shomer group **7:**1371
Patai, Edith **8:**1080; **13:**178
PATAI, JÓZSEF **13:**177
- Zionism **16:**1121
PATAI, RAPHAEL **13:**178
- anthropology **3:**40
Patai, Shaul **13:**178
Pataki, István **8:**48
Patatzis, Sotiris **7:**887
Pateg, Gherardo **9:**1101
Patent of Tolerance (Aus.) **15:**1677
PATERSON (city, U.S.) **13:**179
- *illus:*
- - Barnert, Nathan, statue **4:**249
Pathaḥ (gram. term.) **16:**1422,1432
Pathaḥ (vowel) **16:**1430,1449
Pathaḥ gadol (vowel) **16:**1449
Pathaḥ qaṭan (vowel) **16:**1449
Pathology **11:**1183; **11:**1202
- autopsies **3:**932ff
- *Sefer Asaf ha-Rofe* **3:**675
PATHROS (reg., Egy.) **13:**180
PATINKIN, DON **13:**180
Patkin, A. L. **11:**1284
Patkin, Benzion **11:**1284
Paton, Alan **15:**208
PATRAS (city, Gr.) **13:**180
- Alashkar's yeshivah **2:**511
- Greece **7:**873ff
PATRIA (ship) **13:**181
- Haganah sabotage **9:**353
- illegal immigration **8:**1249
- Tel-Aviv **15:**923
- *illus:*
- - passengers brought ashore **8:**1252
Patriarchate (nesi'ut) **8:**648ff
- history chart **8:**766-767
- ordination, and **14:**1141
- *see also:* JUDAH HA-NASI; NASI
PATRIARCHS, THE **13:**181
- *Contents:*
- - History and Use of the Term **13:**181
- - Chronological Background **13:**181
- - Mesopotamian Background **13:**181
- - The Onomasticon **13:**182
- - Patriarchal Society **13:**182
- - Religion of the Patriarchs **13:**182
- - In the Aggadah **13:**183
- Abraham **2:**111
- agriculture **2:**387
- anthropology **3:**42
- Arameans **3:**253
- burial customs **15:**1216
- chieftain **5:**420ff
- family in the Bible **6:**1166
- history **8:**571
- Isaac **9:**1
- Jacob **9:**1191
- kabbalistic view of **10:**574
- Machpelah cave **11:**670
- Mari **11:**981
- Naḥmanides on **12:**777ff

- Nuzi documents **16:**1510
- Pentateuch **13:**258
- Philo on **13:**414
- sacrifice **14:**605
- statutory prayers **13:**981
- *takkanot* attributed to **15:**721
- Ur **16:**3
- *zekhut avot* **16:**976ff
- *illus: see* ART (Biblical Themes)
PATRIARCHS, TESTAMENTS OF THE TWELVE (pseudepig. wk.) **13:**184
- Apocalyptic writings **3:**180ff
- Greek influence **8:**298
- Hellenistic Jewish literature **8:**304
- Issachar **9:**1076
- Jewish literature **11:**311
- *Job, Testament of* **10:**129
- *Joseph and Asenath* **10:**223
- *Levi, Testament of* **11:**88
- *Naphtali, Testament of* **12:**821
Patricius (patriot ldr.) **9:**256; **16:**281
Patronka (concen. camp) **4:**1312
Patsanovski, Joseph **15:**521
Pattern poems **13:**1204,1206
PATTERSON, DAVID **13:**186
PATTERSON, JOHN HENRY **13:**186
- Jewish Legion **10:**70
Pattish (mosh., Isr.) **1:**place list
Paty de Clam, du (com. of J. affairs), *see* Du Paty de Clam
Patzschius, H. D. **8:**48
Pau (tn., Edom) **6:**370
PAUKER, ANA **13:**187
- *illus:* text
Pauker, Marcel **13:**187
Paul (Paolo; Chr. Hebr.) **8:**48
PAUL I (emp., Rus.) **13:**188
Paul III (pope) **13:**857
- Ancona Jews **2:**941
- Catechumens, House of **5:**253
- Mantino, Jacob **14:**248
PAUL IV (pope) **13:**188
- agriculture **2:**404
- Ancona *anusim* **8:**699
- anti-Jewish legislation **3:**196
- Ascoli Piceno Jews **3:**692
- Benevento Jews **4:**500
- censorship **5:**277
- Conversos **8:**1399
- history chart **8:**766-767
- Ibn Lev **14:**89
- Jewish badge **4:**68
- oppression of Jews **9:**1124; **13:**857
- papal bull **4:**1496
- Roman Jews **14:**249
- Tuscany Jews **15:**1467
PAUL VI (pope) **13:**189
- Israel **16:**78,79
- Jerusalem visit **9:**1492
- Second Vatican Council **13:**860
- Six-Day War **16:**78
- *illus:*
- - A.J.C. leaders, and **5:**543
- - praying in the Hall of the Last Supper **8:**930
Paul, Gabriel H. **15:**301
Paul, Gus **12:**1354
PAUL, SHALOM MORTON **1:**35
Paula (4/5 cent., trav.) **9:**1376
Pauler, Tivadar **15:**1155
PAULI, JOHANNES **13:**189
- Pellicanus, Conrad **13:**220
Paulinus, Simon **8:**48
Paulli, Holger (Oliger) **14:**926; **15:**219
Paulo de Pina, *see* JESURUN, REUEL
Paul of Burgos, *see* PABLO DE SANTA MARIA
PAUL OF TARSUS (apostle) **13:**190
- academy pupil **2:**201
- antinomianism **3:**68; **8:**299
- apostle's authority **3:**216
- Christianity **5:**508
- dualism **6:**243
- Duran on **11:**355
- Epistles **11:**56
- Festus, Porcius **6:**1247
- Gamaliel, Rabban **7:**296
- *haftarah* reading **16:**1343
- Jewish Christian sects **10:**39
- Jew of Tarsus **5:**562
- kabbalistic eschatology **6:**881
- Lost Tribes **15:**1005
- *min* **12:**1
- *Nishmat Kol Ḥai* **12:**1177
- Pharisees **13:**366
- Old Testament views **4:**924ff
- Remnant of Israel **14:**70
- Samuel Hirsch on **13:**457
- Sanhedrin **14:**836
- synagogue **15:**592
- Veroia **16:**112
- Wicked Priest **16:**486
Paul of Tella **4:**860
Paul Pfeddersheimer, *see* PAULI, JOHANNES
Paulsen, John **14:**932
Paulus, Heinrich Eberhard Gottlob **3:**199
- Riesser, Gabriel **14:**167
Paulus Aemilius **4:**867
Paulus Israelita, *see* RICIUS, PAULUS
Paulus of Aegina **11:**1183
Paulus of Sancta Maria, *see* PABLO DE SANTA MARIA
Paulus Pragensis (16th cent., apos.), *see* ELHANAN
Paulus von Eitzen **16:**260
Pauly, Jean de **16:**1214
PAUSANIAS (2nd cent. C.E., Au.) **7:**896
Pause, Jean de la, *see* PLANTAVIT DE LA PAUSE, JEAN
Pauw, Adriaan **12:**976
PAVELIĆ, ANTE **13:**192
- Zagreb **16:**918
Pavese, Cesare **9:**1113
PAVIA (city, It.) **13:**192
- disputation **2:**551
PAVLOGRAD (city, Ukr.) **13:**193
Pavlova, Anna **5:**1269
PAVOLOCH (vill., Ukr.) **13:**193
- Haidamacks **7:**1132
PAWLIKOWSKI, JOZEF **13:**193
Pawnbroking **16:**1286
Pawnees (Ind. tribe, Am.) **12:**911
Pawtucket (tn., R.I.) **14:**143
Pax super Israel (Cath. pub.) **13:**572
Payis, see LOTS
Paykel, M. **6:**1331
"Paysage Ombres Rouges" (paint., P. Haisiasson) **13:**119
Paysandú (city, Urug.) **16:**11
Paz (metal) **11:**1429
Paz (petroleum co., Isr.) **9:**795
PAZ, DUARTE DE **13:**194
- Portugal Jews aided by **13:**922
Paz, Enrique Enríquez de (poet), *see* GÓMEZ, ANTONIO ENRÍQUEZ
Paz, Israel da **13:**1109
Paz, La (tn., Ariz.), *see* La Paz
Paz, La (city, Bol.), *see* La Paz
Paz, Samuel de (dipl., Mor.) **15:**791
Paz, Samuel de (Shab., It.) **14:**1245
Pazer (cantillation sign) **16:**1440,1454
Pazer gadol (cantillation sign), *see Qarnei parah*
Pazi (tal. fig.) **8:**794; **10:**451
Paziza (pseud.), *see* ARICHA, YOSEF
Paznicul (newsp.) **6:**1371
P.B.S., *see* Palestine Government Broadcasting Service
P.C.C., *see* Palestine Conciliation Commission
P.D.P. (co.), *see* Petroleum Development of Palestine
PE (Heb. let.) **13:**194
- *parashah petuḥah* **16:**1407
Pea, Enrico **9:**1107
Peabody (city, Mass.) **11:**622
PEACE **13:**194
- *Contents:*
- - In the Bible **13:**196
- - In the Talmud **13:**196
- - In Post-Talmudic Jewish Thought **13:**198
- - Modern Jewish Thought **13:**199
- Aaron **2:**7
- angels of **2:**964
- domestic **14:**1356
- law and morality **10:**1481
- *Leviticus Rabbah* **11:**148
- olive leaf **12:**1365
- righteousness **14:**180
- *takkanot* **15:**716
Peace Congress (Zion.) **16:**1170
Peace Dale (vill., R.I.) **14:**143
Peace offering **11:**140; **14:**603ff
Peace with Israel (mvmt., Ger.) **7:**498
PEACH (bot.) **13:**199
- plant list **13:**623
PEACOCK (zool.) **13:**200
- dietary laws **6:**30,34
- Solomon's trade **15:**98
- *illus:*
- - Hammam Lif synagogue mosaic **15:**572
Péage corporel (body tax), *see* LEIBZOLL
PE'AH (tract.) **13:**200
- *Demai* **5:**1486
- *illus:* text
Pe'ah (conc.), *see* LEKET, SHIKHḤAH, AND PE'AH
PEAR (bot.) **13:**201
- plant list **13:**623
Pearl (gem) **13:**1010; **13:**1012
- *peninim* **5:**959
Pearle, Y. **16:**820
PEARLSTEIN, PHILIP **3:**607
Pearson, Lester **9:**444
Peas, *see* LEGUMES
Peasants **16:**1305
Pecci, Vincenzo Gioacchino, *see* LEO XIII
Pecherski, Gedaliah **11:**18
PECHERSKY, ALEXANDER **13:**201
PÉCHI, SIMON **13:**202
- Bible translations **4:**883
- Hebraists **8:**50
- Somrei Sabat **15:**139
PECHINA (vill., Sp.) **13:**202
Pechora (concen. camp, Rus.) **15:**1335,1428
Pechter, Salomon **16:**1105
PEC (U.S.), *see* PALESTINE ECONOMIC CORPORATION
Peckelman, Henry, *see* FURTUNĂ, ENRIC
Peckelsheim (tn., Ger.) **13:**7
Pecker, Jean-Claude **3:**807
PECS (tn., Hung.) **13:**203
- *illus:* text
Peczara (concen. camp), *see* Pechora
Pedagogic Reporter (period.) **2:**819
Pedagogy, *see* EDUCATION
Pedaiah (bib. fig.) **16:**1000
- Temple **15:**957
Pedat (amora) **2:**864
- Eleazar ben Pedat **6:**597
Pedayah (mosh., Isr.) **1:**place list
PEDDLING **13:**203
- caricatures **5:**171
- economic enterprise **16:**1301
- Israel **9:**880
- secondhand goods **14:**1085ff
- silver purveying **12:**63
- U.S. **15:**1597; **15:**1615
- Wandering Jew **16:**260
- *illus:*
- - text
- - David the Jew **5:**898
- - Jewish peddlers **6:**761; **8:**1097
- - Nuremberg hawker **12:**1277
- - "Old Jewish Pedlar" (paint., G. Salomon) **3:**639
Pedersen, Christiern **4:**876
PEDERSEN, JOHANNES **13:**210
Pediatrics **11:**1201
Pedro III (k., Aragon) **3:**929
- Jewish traders **16:**1288
- Teruel **15:**1022
Pedro IV (k., Arag.) **15:**235
- informers **8:**1366
- Tárrega **15:**824
Pedro (apos.) **15:**1204
Pedro, Dom **8:**50
Pedro the Cruel (k., Cast.) **15:**234
- Abulafia, Samuel **2:**193
- Toledo **15:**1203
Pedro de Cartagena **13:**4
Pedro de Santa Fé **11:**495
Peduyim (mosh., Isr.) **1:**place list
Peekskill (tn., N.Y.) **12:**1127; **16:**464
PEEL COMMISSION **13:**211
- Agudat Israel **2:**425
- Arab National Movement **9:**463
- Arab national strike **16:**1084
- immigration **9:**531
- inquiry commissions **13:**32
- Israel history **9:**349
- Israel politics **9:**662
- Jerusalem Mandate **9:**1475
- League of Nations **10:**1521
- Mapai **11:**913
- Palestine disturbances **13:**32
- partition plan **9:**314; **13:**34,35
- White Papers **16:**484ff
- Zionism **16:**1057; **16:**1174
- *illus:*
- - Lord Peel reading address **9:**351
Peele, George **6:**774
PEERCE, JAN **13:**211
Pegai (riv., Er. Isr.), *see* YARKON
Pegasus (myth. horse) **5:**397
Pegau (tn., Saxony) **12:**63
Pegnitz (tn., Ger.) **4:**352
PÉGUY, CHARLES-PIERRE **13:**211
Pehel (tn., Transj.), *see* PELLA
Peierls, Ronald Frank **13:**212
PEIERLS, SIR RUDOLF ERNST **13:**212
Peikinia (concen. camp) **14:**538
Peilisher Yidel (newsp. Eng.), *see Die Zukunft*
Peimer, Joseph **14:**1682
PEIPER, TADEUSZ **13:**212
Peitholaus (sol.) **2:**584
PEIXOTTO (fam.) **13:**213
Peixotto, Benjamin Franklin **13:**213; **14:**390; **15:**16
Peixotto, Daniel Levi Maduro **8:**209; **13:**213
- Trenton **15:**1375
Peixotto, David Levi Maduro **15:**1677
Peixotto, George da Maduro **13:**214
Peixotto, Moses Levi Maduro **13:**213
PEKAH (k., Isr.) **13:**214
- history **8:**603
- history chart **8:**766-767
- Menahem **11:**1303
- Rezin **14:**140
- Tabeel **15:**676ff
PEKAHIAH (k., Isr.) **13:**215
- history chart **8:**766-767
- Pekah **8:**603
PEKELIS, ALEXANDER HAIM **13:**215
- AJC **2:**826

Peker, Josef **11:**618
PEKERIS, CHAIM LEIB **13:**216
- *illus:*
- - Oppenheimer, J. Robert **12:**1430
Pekić, Borislav **16:**886
Pekid Ereẓ Israel (tit.), *see Gabbai Ereẓ Israel*
Pekidim and *Amarkalim* (soc.) **2:**900; **10:**1584; **14:**1363
- Prins, Abraham **13:**1095
PEKI'IN (vill., Isr.) **13:**216
- ḥasidic settlement **7:**1392
- Joshua's academy **2:**202
- Ottoman period **9:**285; **9:**292
- *illus:*
- - text
- - synagogue, stone frieze **5:**202
Peki'in ha-Hadashah (mosh., Isr.) **13:**218; **1:**place list
PEKING (city, China) **13:**218
PEKOD (tribe) **13:**218
Pekudat Elazar (bk.) **4:**101
Pelc, Moshe **10:**990
Peled, El'ad **13:**48
- Six-Day War **14:**1638
Peled, Mattityahu **13:**48
Peled, Nathan **9:**680
- *illus:*
- - Tserulnikov, Nathan, and **9:**529
Peleg (bib. fig., place) **13:**182
Pelethites (bib. people) **13:**402ff
- Solomon **15:**96
Peli (pseud.), *see* HEILPRIN, PHINEHAS MENAHEM
Peli, Berakhah **13:**1378
Peli, Meir **13:**1378
PELICAN (zool.) **13:**219
- *illus:*
- - Ḥuleh Nature Reserve **9:**235
- *see also: Ka'at*
Peli Printing Works (Isr.) **13:**1379
PELLA (city, Transj.) **13:**219
- Arab conquest **9:**261
- Christian community **9:**1394
- Transjordan **15:**1316
- *see also:* DECAPOLIS
Pella (tn., Judea), *see* BETHLEPTEPHA
PELLEG, FRANK **13:**220
Pellegrim, S.J. **9:**1344
PELLICANUS (Rubeaquensis), CONRAD **13:**220
- Hebraists **8:**50
- linguistics **16:**1391
- Muenster, Sebastian **12:**505
PELTIN, SAMUEL HIRSH **13:**221
Pelty, Barney **15:**301
Peltz, Betty Bental **15:**309
PELTZ, ISAC **13:**221
Pelugat Yam ha-Melaḥ (pion. gr., Er. Isr.) **5:**1395
Peluggot Sadeh (defense force) **9:**684
Pelugta, *see* CONFLICT OF OPINION
Pelusium (city, Egy.), *see* Sin
Pembroke (tn., Ont.) **12:**1408
Pen (writing) **16:**664
Pen, S. **12:**1324
Pen, Y. **16:**192
Peña, Ḥayyim **14:**1228
Peñaforte, Raymundo **8:**50
- Barcelona disputation **4:**213
PENAL LAW **13:**222
- *Contents:*
- - Principles of Legality **13:**222
- - Parties to Offenses **13:**222
- - Attempts and Inchoate Offenses **13:**224
- - Criminal Responsibility **13:**224
- admission **2:**291
- age, adjudication **13:**1357
- agency **2:**350
- autonomy, judicial **3:**928ff
- bailees **14:**1455
- definition **12:**110; **12:**135
- development **12:**134
- majority rule **11:**805
- practice and procedure **13:**958
- proselyte as judge **13:**1185
- *Sanhedrin* tractate **14:**840
- weights, measures **16:**390
- witness **16:**584
- *see also* PUNISHMENT; *and under indiviudal crimes*
Penalty, *see* FINES; PUNISHMENT
Pen case **16:**665
- *illus:*
- - Qumran **16:**668
PEN Club, Yiddish (U.S.) **6:**1212
Penei Aryeh (bk.) **5:**1353
Penei Melekh (bk.) **4:**1545
Penei Yehoshu'a (bk.) **11:**333
- Falk, Jacob Joshua **6:**1155ff
Penha, De la (fam., Neth.) **14:**349
Penha, Jacob Gutiérrez **8:**1400
Peniel (site, Er. Isr.), *see* PENUEL
Peninim (pearls) **5:**959
PENINNAH (bib. fig.) **13:**228
- *illus:*
- - Elkanah and Hannah **7:**1270
Penitence, *see* REPENTANCE
Penitence, Ten Days of, *see* TEN DAYS OF PENITENCE
Penitential Prayers, *see* SELIḤOT
Penížek, Josef **13:**1026
Penkar, Shalom Moses **11:**1567
Penker, David Joseph, *see* DAVID, JOSEPH
P.E.N. Klub Nayes of Vilna (period.) **13:**1043
PENN, ALEXANDER **13:**228
Penn, Irving **13:**484
PENN, JACK **11:**1203,1209
PENNE, JACOBUS **8:**50
Penn State University **15:**1680
PENNSYLVANIA (state, U.S.) **13:**229
- German proselytes **13:**1192
- *pop. tables:* text
Pennsylvania, University of **15:**1677
Pensacola (city, Fla.) **6:**1363
Pensions (Isr.) **9:**884ff,994
Penso (fam., Yug.) **15:**289
Penso, Joseph, *see* PENSO DE LA VEGA, JOSEPH
Penso, Moses **12:**994
PENSO DE LA VEGA, JOSEPH **13:**230
- Amsterdam **2:**898
- drama **6:**194
- Split **15:**289
- Venice **15:**289
Penso Felix, Isaac **13:**230
Pentacle, *see* "Star of Solomon"
PENTATEUCH **13:**231
- *Contents:*
- - Name **13:**232
- - Canonization **13:**232
- - The Critical View **13:**232
- - - Extent and Nature of the Corpus **13:**232
- - - Date and Composition **13:**233
- - - P and D—Theological Outlines **13:**243
- - - Laws Common to P and D **13:**248
- - - P and D—Comparison of Tradition and Style **13:**252
- - - Relation of P to JE **13:**253
- - - Relation of D to JE **13:**254
- - - The Tradition Underlying the Sources—Form Criticism **13:**257
- - The Traditional View **13:**261
- General
- - Jewish literature **11:**308
- - Judaism **10:**389
- - Samaritans **14:**738ff
- - *Sefer Torah* **14:**1100
- - Spinoza **15:**279
- - *teki'ata* **15:**915ff
- - term, origin of **4:**820
- - Torah reading **15:**1246
- - triennial cycle **15:**1386
- - Wellhausen **16:**443
- Books of
- - Genesis **7:**386ff
- - Exodus **6:**1050
- - Leviticus **11:** 38ff
- - Numbers **12:**1249
- - Deuteronomy **5:**1573
- Themes
- - Decalogue **5:**1435
- - Nazirite **12:**907
- - revelation **14:**117
- - *tokheḥah* **15:**1192
- Commentaries
- - Ibn Tibbon, Moses **15:**1130
- - *Imrei Yosef* **15:**275
- - *Mekor Ḥayyim* **16:**939
- - *Oznayim la-Torah* **15:**167
- - Spira, Nathan **15:**284
- - supercommentaries **15:**520
- - Toledano, Jacob **15:**1195
- - Vivanti, David Abraham **16:**197
- *illus:*
- - Bologna edition (1482) **15:**1483
- - Naḥmanides' commentary **12:**775
- - Rashi's commentary **14:**38; **15:**1483
- - *Sefer Sharḥ Shāhīn al ha-Torah* **14:**1258; **16:**1027,1182
- - Yemenite **16:***fcg.* 743
- - Karaite, 10th cent. **8:**665
- *mus. notations:*
- - cantillation signs **11:**1100
- - Comparative table of cantillation motives **11:**1101
- - tables of Accents **11:**1103,1105
- - *tevir* complex of masoretic accents **11:**1107
- *see also:* BIBLE
PENTATEUCH, SAMARITAN **13:**264
- Bible translations **4:**863
- *see also:* SAMARITANS (Language and Literature)
Pentecost, *see* SHAVUOT
Pentosuria (disease) **14:**1501
PENUEL (site, Er. Isr.) **13:**268
- Jacob **9:**1171
- proscription **8:**347
- tribal center **15:**1383
PENUELI, SHEMUEL YESHAYAHU **13:**269
PENZANCE (tn., Eng.) **13:**269
- archives **3:**382
People of the Land (bib.), *see* AM HA-AREẒ
People's Guard (orgn.) **16:**350
People's Party of Hlinka, *see* Slovak People's Party
People's Relief Committee (U.S.) **2:**827; **6:**801
- Zuckerman, Baruch **16:**1229
Peor (diety) **8:**1236
Peoria (city, Ill.) **8:**1255
PE'OT (sidelocks) **13:**269
- shaving prohibition **4:**356
- *illus:*
- - Spanish-Italian illuminated manuscript (14th cent.) **4:**357
Pepercorne, James Watts **8:**50
PEPPER (bot.) **13:**270
- food **6:**1417
- plant list **13:**623
- spices **15:**269
PEPPER, JOSEPH **13:**270
Pe'ra (qtr., Const.) **4:**1554
PERACHIM, JULES **3:**608
Peraea (reg., Transj.), *see* Perea
Peraḥim (newsp.) **11:**558
Peraḥ Shoshan (wk.) **16:**1389
PERAḤYAH, AARON BEN ḤAYYIM ABRAHAM HA-KOHEN **13:**271
- Salonika **14:**702
Peraḥyah, Benjamin **13:**577
PERAḤYAH, ḤASDAI BEN SAMUEL HA-KOHEN **13:**271
Peraḥyah, Isaac **11:**1159
Peraḥyah ben Joseph **11:**723
PERAHYAH BEN NISSIM **13:**271
Perakim (journ.) **1:**newsp. list
Perath (tn., Er. Isr.), *see* PARAH, PERATH
Per Atum (city, Egy.), *see* PITHOM
Perazon (vill., Er. Isr.) **1:**place list; **15:**675
Percival (pseud.), *see* Raphael John N.
Percy, Thomas **6:**774; **9:**1343
Perdicas (trav.) **15:**1355
Perdurabo, Frater **10:**648
Perea (reg., Transj.) **15:**1317
- administration regions **9:**120ff
- Ammon **2:**859
- Palaestina Prima **9:**254
- Provinćia Judaea **9:**239
Perec, Arieh **8:**1055
PEREFERKOVICH, NEHEMIAH **13:**271
Peregrine, *see* DEUTSCHER, ISAAC
Peregrino, Abraham Israel, *see* ESCUDERO, LORENZO
Pereira, Abraham
- Hebron Yeshivah **8:**233; **11:**1254
- Or Torah academy **4:**1461
- Shabbateanism **14:**1235
- sugar **15:**487
Pereira, Abraham Lopez, *see* Pereira, Gaspar Lopez
Pereira, Duarte Coelho **15:**487
Pereira, Ephraim Lopez **2:**427
Pereira, Francisco Lopes **6:**248
Pereira, Francisco Nuñez, *see* Abendana, David
Pereira, Gaspar de, *see* LEÃO, GASPAR DE
Pereira, Gaspar Lopez **11:**301
Pereira, Heinrich **3:**490
Pereira, Isaac (Amst.) **15:**487
Pereira, Isaac (Ire.) **8:**1463
Pereira, Jacob **3:**1017
Pereira, Juan Antonio **8:**1395
Pereira, Manuel Lopes **6:**248
Pereira, Moses (r., Sarajevo) **14:**870
Pereira, Moses Lopez, *see* AGUILAR, DIEGO D'
Pereira Coutinho, Fernando (Abraham) **2:**65
Pereira Coutinho, Manoel (Lisbon) **2:**66
Pereira Coutinho, Manoel (Hamburg) **2:**65
PEREIRA DE PAIVA, MOSES **13:**272
Pereire (fam.) **4:**608
PÉREIRE, EMILE (Jacob) and ISAAC **13:**272
- banking **4:**175; **8:**719
- railroads **13:**1517ff
- Saint-Simonism **14:**667
- socialism **15:**25
- *illus:* text
Pereire, Eugene **13:**273
Pereire, J. **5:**616
PÉREIRE, JACOB RODRIGUES **13:**273
- education **6:**462
- medicine **11:**1192
Pereiri, Justa, *see* Abendana, Abigail
PEREK SHIRAH (hymns) **13:**273
- *Beit Aharon* **2:**18
Perele (dau., Israel of Kozienice) **16:**628
PERELMAN, CHAIM **13:**275
- justice **10:**476
Perelman, Eliezer Yiẓḥak, *see* BEN-YEHUDA, ELIEZER

Perelman, Isaac **16:**112
Perelman, Joseph, *see* DYMOV, OSSIP
Perelman, Mikhail **15:**309
- olympics **12:**1376
PERELMAN, SIDNEY JOSEPH **13:**275
PERELMANN, JEROHMAN JUDAH LEIB BEN SOLOMON ZALMAN **13:**276
Perelmuth, Jacob Pincus, *see* PEERCE, JAN
PEREMYSHLYANY (tn., Gal.) **13:**276
- ḥasidic dynasty **13:**277
PEREMYSHLYANY, MEIR BEN AARON LEIB OF **13:**277
- Lipkany **11:**278
Perera-Molié, Isidore **15:**290
Peres (weight) **16:**383
Peres, Hardwig **11:**1302
Peres, Israel **11:**1302
Peres, Jacob J. **11:**1302
PERES, SHIMON **13:**278
- Ben-Gurion **4:**513
- Lavon's accusation **9:**674
- Mapai **11:**913
- Rafi party **13:**1512
- *illus:*
- - Labor parties merging meeting **9:**677
Pères Blancs monastery (Jer.), *see* White Fathers monastery
Peresh (bib. fig.) **11:**668
Pereszlényi, Pál **8:**50
Peretz (fam.) **12:**1018
PERETZ, ABRAHAM **13:**279
- Haskalah **7:**1447
Peretz, Alexander **13:**279
Peretz, Gregory (Hirsch) **13:**279
Peretz, Helena **13:**280
PERETZ, ISAAC LEIB **13:**279
- chronological chart **8:**766-767
- drama **6:**203
- Hebrew literature **8:**193
- Ladino **10:**1351
- neo-Ḥasidism **7:**1399
- socialism, Jewish **15:**42
- Warsaw **16:**340
- Yiddish literature **16:**812
- *illus:*
- - text
- - Asch, Sholem, and **16:**814
Peretz, Lev **13:**279
Peretz, Vladimir **13:**279
Peretz, Yegor **13:**279
PEREYASLAV-KHMELNITSKI (city, Ukr.) **13:**283
- *illus:* text
Pereyra, Juan Albano **5:**463
PEREZ (bib. fig.) **13:**283
- David **14:**518; **15:**782
- *geneal. table:* **5:**1342
Perez (fam.) **15:**270
Perez, Ḥayyim **6:**498
Perez, João of Covilhão **2:**161
- travelers **15:**1349
Perez, Juan, *see* SENIOR, SOLOMON
PEREZ, JUDAH BEN JOSEPH **13:**284
Perez, Luis **11:**1168
Perez, Manuel Batista **8:**1395
- Latin America **10:**1449
- Peru **13:**322
Perez, Marcus (Martin) **12:**975
- medals **11:**1168
Perez, Miguel **5:**38
Perez, Pasqual de Almaçan, *see* Almaçan, Pasqual Perez de
Perez, Ursula **11:**1168
Perez, Victor **15:**305
PEREZ BAYER, FRANCISCO **13:**284
- Hebraists **8:**50
PEREZ BEN ELIJAH OF CORBEIL (tos.) **13:**284
- Corbeil **5:**960
- Isaac ben Joseph **9:**22
- Kimḥi, Mordecai **10:**1007
- woman's status **8:**680
Perez ben Isaac ha-Kohen **15:**1376
- Isaac ben Sheshet **9:**32
PEREẒ BEN MOSES OF BRODY **13:**285
Pérez Galdos, Benito **15:**250
Perezhitoe (journ.) **13:**1047
Perez Uzzah (bib. loc.) **16:**43
Perfect de Pratis, *see* BENVENISTE, SHESHET BEN ISAAC BEN JOSEPH
Perfection, *see* MAN, THE NATURE OF; *Tikkun*
Perfet, Isaac ben Sheshet, *see* ISAAC BEN SHESHET PERFET
Perfit, Martin **15:**311
Perfumes, *see* INCENSE AND PERFUMES
PERGAMENT, MOSES **12:**702
PERGAMENT, OSIP YAKOVLEVICH **13:**286
Pergamenter, Solomon **4:**992
PERGAMUM (city, As. M.) **13:**286
- Asia Minor **3:**746
- diaspora **6:**10
- Hellenistic period **8:**292ff
PERGOLA, RAPHAEL DE LA **13:**286
- Alexandria **2:**593
PERI, HIRAM (Heinz) **13:**287
PERI-EẒ-ḤAYYIM (period.) **13:**287
- press **13:**1056
- statistics **1:**newsp. list
Perigors (Fr. schol.) **2:**522
Peri Ḥadash (bk.) **8:**457
Peri Megadim (bk.) **15:**1011
Peringer, Gustav **8:**50
Periodicals, *see* PRESS
"Period of Grace" (Inq.) **8:**1383; **8:**1400
Peripatos (philos.), *see* ARISTOTLE
Peri To'elet (journ.) **1:**newsp. list
Peritz, Curt **15:**1415
Peritz, Ismar **8:**50
PERIZZITES (anc. people) **13:**288
- Genesis, Book of **7:**389
PERJURY **13:**288
- evidence **16:**586ff
- punishment **13:**222; **13:**224; **13:**1387
- warning **13:**222
Pērkonkaists **10:**1467
Perl, David **6:**250
Perl, Feliks **13:**951
PERL, JOSEPH **13:**290
- Galicia **16:**1328
- Ḥasidism **7:**1418
- Haskalah **8:**184; **16:**1325
- parody **13:**132
- Tarnopol **15:**817
Perl, Moshe **10:**1229
PERLA, JEROHAM FISCHEL BEN ARYEH ẒEVI **13:**292
PERLBACH, MAX **13:**292
PERLE, JOSHUA **13:**293
Perlen, Richard **15:**464
PERLES (fam.) **13:**293
Perles (fam.), *see* ALTSCHUL(ER)
Perles (fam., Rus.) **4:**1397
Perles, Aaron ben Moses Meir **2:**781; **13:**295
Perles, Abraham ben Isaac **2:**781
Perles, Abraham Ẓevi **13:**294
Perles, Eleazar ben Abraham Ḥanokh **2:**780
Perles, Felix **13:**294
- Kahana, Abraham **10:**678
Perles, Isaac ben Eleazar **2:**781
PERLES, ISAAC MOSES **13:**294
- Bonyhad **4:**1213
Perles, Joseph **13:**293
- homiletic literature **8:**956
Perles, Max **13:**294
Perles, Meir **13:**294
Perles, Moritz **13:**1366
Perles, Moses **13:**295
PERLES, MOSES MEIR BEN ELEAZAR **13:**294
- Altschuler family **2:**781
Perles, Rosalie **13:**294
Perlhefter (fam.) **6:**222
Perlhefter, Baer **11:**700; **16:**907
- Shabbateanism **14:**1246ff
Perlhefter, Bella **13:**295
PERLHEFTER, ISSACHAR BEHR BEN JUDAH MOSES **13:**295
Perlhefter, Jacob **13:**295
Perlhefter, R. **12:**311
Perlin, Ḥayyim Lipmann, *see* SONNENFELS, ALOYS VON
Perlis, A. (jr.)
- *illus:*
- - F.Z.C. **16:**1165
PERLMAN, ALFRED EDWARD **13:**295
Perlman, Eliezer **14:**363
PERLMAN, HELEN HARRIS **13:**295
PERLMAN, JACOB **13:**296
Perlman, Max **15:**1074
PERLMAN, SAMUEL **13:**296
Perlman, Samuel J. **15:**311
PERLMAN, SELIG **13:**296
PERLMANN, MOSHE **13:**297
PERLMUTTER, ABRAHAM ẒEVI **13:**297
PERLMUTTER, IZSÁK **3:**608
Perlmutter, Yeḥiel, *see* YESHURUN, AVOT
Perlov, David **12:**462
Perlov, Jacob **12:**59
PERLOV, YIẒHAK **13:**297
Perlow, Israel **15:**412
Perlow, Moses **15:**412
Perlow, Solomon Ḥayyim, *see* Koidanov, Solomon Ḥayyim of
Perlow of Koidanov, *see* Koidanov, Shalom
Perlrott-Csaba, Vilmos **13:**113
Perls, A. **8:**957; **13:**203
Perls, Isaac Moses, *see* PERLES, ISAAC MOSES
Perls, M. **15:**347
Perlstein, J. **3:**362
Perlstein, Leah **15:**84
PERLSTEIN, MEYER A. **13:**298
Perlsticker (fam.) **6:**222
Perluss, Irving **14:**599
PERLZWEIG, MAURICE L. **13:**298
- *illus:*
- - London, Zionist rally **16:**1118
PERLZWEIG, WILLIAM ALEXANDRE **5:**386
Permanent Commission for Better Understanding Between Protestants, Catholics and Jews (U.S.) **10:**1408
Permanent Court of Arbitration, the Hague **3:**766
Pernambuco (city, Braz.), *see* RECIFE
PERNERSTORFER, ENGELBERT **13:**298
Perón, Juan Domingo **3:**416
- neo-Nazism **12:**956
Peroutka, Ferdinand **5:**1194
Pērōz (Sassanian k.) **6:**1027
Perozedor (journ.) **1:**newsp. list; **15:**1110
PERPIGNAN (city, Fr.) **13:**299
- Agde Jews **2:**343
- charitable associations **5:**346
- notarial archives **3:**376
- Roussillon **14:**353
- sick care **14:**1498
- *illus:* text
Perpignan Bible (13th cent. illum. ms.) **4:**977; **13:**300
Per-Ramses (city, Egy.) **8:**575
Perrault, Emile, *see* HARRY, MYRIAM
PERREAU, PIETRO **13:**301
Perrineville (stlmt., N.J.) **12:**1030
PERROT, JEAN **13:**302
Perry (city, Okla.) **12:**1353
Perryville (city, Mo.) **12:**157
Persecutions, *see* ANTI-SEMITISM
Persepolis (city, Pers.) **4:**34
- inscriptions **16:**1506
PERSIA **13:**302
- *Contents:*
- - Pre-Islamic Persia **13:**306
- - The First Six Centuries Under the Caliphate (642-1258) **13:**308
- - Under the Il-Khan Dynasty (1258-1336) **13:**312
- - Under the Safawid Dynasty (1502-1736) **13:**312
- - Under the Kajar Dynasty (1794-1925) **13:**316
- - Under the Pahlevi Dynasty (1925-) **13:**319
- General
- - *aliyah* to Israel **8:**771; **9:**501ff; **9:**512
- - calendar **16:**1264
- - history chart **8:**766-767
- - Judaism **10:**389
- - spices **8:**1311
- - ten lost tribes **15:**1006
- History
- - Abbas I **2:**38
- - Ereẓ Israel **9:**256; **9:**258
- - Ezra-Nehemiah **6:**1114ff
- - Holofernes **8:**917
- - Jerusalem conquest **9:**1407
- - Satrap **14:**907
- Language and Literature
- - Dead Sea Scrolls **16:**1589
- - Judeo-Persian **10:**67, 429
- - Mandean **12:**948
- - mishnaic Hebrew **16:**1604
- - Neo-Aramaic **12:**948
- - writing **16:**659
- Jewish Life
- - cooking and food **6:**1422ff
- - diaspora **6:**11
- - dress **6:**215
- - fiscal exploitation **16:**1278
- - goldsmiths **7:**740
- - Ḥanukkah lamps **7:**1289; **7:**1292
- - Jewish quarter **10:**86
- - liturgy **11:**401
- - marriage custom **11:**1044
- - tax **15:**841,842
- *illus:*
- - text
- - bride and bridegroom **11:**1035
- - mercantile document, c. 800 C.E. **11:**905
- - Parsic script types **2:**695, 717, 737, 733
- - YHD coins **5:**697-698
- *pop. tables:* text
- *see also:* BABYLON; BABYLONIA; ELAM; IRAN
Persian apple (peach) **13:**199
Persis (anc. kdm.) **5:**1284
PERSITZ, ALEXANDRE **3:**365
- *illus:*
- - Don Isaac Abrabanel Synagogue, Paris **3:**341
Persitz, Rafi **5:**406
PERSITZ, SHOSHANAH **13:**319
- *illus:*
- - Tarbut kindergarten **14:**447
Persitz, Y. **12:**364
PERSIUS (Rom. au.) **14:**233; **14:**235

Perski, Benjamin **10:**1260
PERSKI, JOEL DOV BAER **13:**320
PERSKY, DANIEL **13:**320
- Hebrew literature **8:**213
- *illus:*
- - text
- - Hebrew Pen Club, N.Y. **8:**211; **12:**1109
- - Hebrew writers' convention, 1943 **8:**213
- - Histadruth ivrit of America **13:**371
Persky, Shimon, *see* PERES, SHIMON
PERSOFF, NEHEMIAH **15:**1089
Personal status
- child marriage **5:**423
- civil marriage **5:**595
- concubine **5:**864ff
- conflict of laws **5:**882
- debtor **6:**1010
- divorce **6:**122
- embryo **6:**719
- intermarriage **12:**168
- liberty deprivation **8:**1304
- *mamzer* **11:**840
- marriage **11:**1048
- rabbinical courts **12:**143; **12:**145
- State of Israel **12:**145ff
- *see also:* Legal capacity
PERSOV, SHMUEL **13:**321
PERTH (city, Austr.) **13:**321
- *illus:* text
Perth Amboy (city, N.J.) **11:**1504; **12:**1027
Pertsch, W.H.F. **8:**50
Pertuis (loc., Prov.) **13:**1259
PERU **13:**322
- *Contents:*
- - Colonial Period **13:**322
- - Contemporary Period **13:**323
- - Peru-Israel Relations **13:**325
- Inquisition **8:**1394
- Israelitas **10:**398
- Latin America **10:**1448ff
- synagogues **1:**syn. list
- UNSCOP **15:**1688
- Zionism
- *illus:* text
Peru (city, Ind.) **8:**1361
Perugia (fam.) **11:**898; **13:**1108
PERUGIA (city, It.) **13:**325
Perugia, Israel of, *see* Israel of Perugia
Perugino (art.) **9:**69
Perush ha-Berakhot ve-ha-Tefillot (wk.) **8:**1340
- *illus:*
- - opening page (Lisbon, 1849) **11:**301
Perush ha-Sodot shel ha-RABE al ha-Torah (wk.) **15:**520
Perushim, see PHARISEES
Perushim (ascetics) **3:**945
- *see also:* ASCETICISM
Perushim (Gaon's disciples)
- *aliyah* **9:**293; **9:**514
- community life **9:**497ff
- Jerusalem synagogue **9:**1448
- religious life **9:**888
Perutah (coin) **5:**716; **5:**729ff; **14:**1348
- *illus:*
- - Antigonus II coin **3:**66
- - Archelaus coins **3:**333
PERUTZ, LEO **13:**326
PERUTZ, MAX FERDINAND **13:**326
Peruz-Shavur (tn., Babyl.) **13:**1384
PERVOMAISK (city, Ukr.) **13:**326
Pesaḥ (apos., Ger.), *see* Peter
Pesaḥ (fest.), *see* PASSOVER
Pesaḥ ben Abraham ha-Kohen **13:**593; **7:**218
PESAḤIM (tract.) **13:**327
- *illus:* text
Pesahovich, Nahum **13:**539
Pesaḥ Sheni, *see* PASSOVER, SECOND
PESAḤSON, ISAAC MORDECAI **13:**328
Pesakim de-Rabbi Yeshayahu mi-Trani (14th cent. illum. ms., Bologna) **5:**1235; **8:**1282
PESANTE, MOSES BEN ḤAYYIM BEN SHEM TOV **13:**328
PESARO (tn., It.) **13:**329
- special Purim **13:**1397
- synagogue **15:**614
- *illus:*
- - text
- - *ketubbah* (18th cent.) **6:**1375
- - synagogue **15:**617
PESARO, ABRAMO **13:**329
Pesaro, Duke of **8:**699ff
Pesaro, Isaac **9:**1129
Pesaro Maḥzor (ms.) **11:**734
- *illus:* **11:**735
Pescarol, Zanvil **5:**1077; **13:**1102
Pescennius Niger (Rom. gov.) **9:**251
Pesch, Sybille, of Aachen **8:**432
Peschiera, Baruch da **11:**897
Peschkowsky, Michael Igor, *see* NICHOLS, MIKE
Pescia (tn., It.) **15:**1467
Peseles, Elijah **6:**652
PESHAT (exegesis) **13:**329
- *Derash* **5:**1549
- Kabbalah **10:**623ff
- Samuel ben Meir **14:**810
Peshawar (city, Pak.) **13:**14
PESHER (Qumran term) **13:**331
Pesher Habakkuk **13:**332
- date **13:**846
- Kittim **10:**1081
- Lies, Prophet of **11:**234; **11:**235
- Teacher of Righteousness **15:**887
- War of the Kittim **10:**1081
- *illus:*
- - Dead Sea Scroll **13:**332
- *see also:* DEAD SEA SCROLLS
Pesher Hosea (D. S. Scroll) **11:**276
- *see also:* DEAD SEA SCROLLS
Pesher Micah (D. S. Scroll) **13:**333
- Lies, Prophet of **11:**234
- Teacher of Righteousness **15:**886
- *see also:* DEAD SEA SCROLLS
Pesher Nahum (D. S. Scroll) **10:**1081; **11:**276
- *see also:* DEAD SEA SCROLLS
Peshev, Dimiter **4:**1486; **4:**1487
Peshitta (Bib. trans.) **4:**858
- Lamentations, Book of **10:**1371
- Masorah **16:**1415
Peshitte (coin) **5:**722
Peshkov, Aleksey Maksimovich, *see* GORKI, MAXIM
Peshkova, Ekaterina **7:**811; **16:**1225
PESIKTA DE-RAV KAHANA (Mid.) **13:**333
- Jewish literature **11:**321
- *Leviticus Rabbah* **11:**149
- *see also:* MIDRASH
Pesikta Ḥadta (wk.) **16:**1518
PESIKTA RABBATI (Mid.) **13:**335
- Avelei Zion **3:**946
- Jewish literature **11:**321
- *see also:* MIDRASH
Pesikta Zutarta, see MIDRASH LEKAḤ TOV
Pesi'ot (journ.) **1:**newsp. list
Pesiq (cantillation sign), *see Paseq*
Peso, Joseph ibn, *see* Joseph ibn Peso
Pessaḥ, Moses **7:**880
Pessimism, *see* Optimism and pessimism
Pest (tn., Hung.) **4:**1450
Pestel, Pavel **5:**1451
Pester Juedische Zeitung (newsp.), *see Allgemeine Juedische Zeitung*
Pester Lloyd (newsp.) **6:**1159
Pestilence
- Black Death **4:**1063
- plagues of Egypt **13:**606
- Resheph **14:**81
- *illus:*
- - Plagues of Egypt **13:**609
PESTSZENTERZSEBET (tn., Hung.) **13:**336
PESUKEI DE-ZIMRA (litur.) **13:**336
- *Ashrei* **3:**736
- *Barukh she-Amar* **4:**283
- *Nishmat Kol Ḥay* **12:**1176
- Psalms **13:**1323
- variations in liturgy **11:**396ff
- *zemirot* **16:**987
Petaḥ (journ.) **1:**newsp. list
Petaḥ Devarai (wk.) **16:**1386
Petaḥim (journ.) **15:**1110
- statistics **1:**newsp. list
PETAḤ TIKVAH (city, Isr.) **13:**336
- Diskin, M. **6:**75
- eucalyptus forest **9:**788
- Gawler plan **7:**339
- history chart **8:**766-767
- library **11:**194
- Stampfer, Jehoshua **15:**329
- stamps **15:**332
- statistics **1:**place list **7:**339
- Tel Aviv **15:**924
- *illus:* text
Petaḥyah (mosh., Isr.) **1:**place list
Petaluma (city, Calif.) **5:**56
Peter (apostle)
- gentiles **3:**216
- Jewish Christian sects **10:**39
- popes **13:**851
- Sanhedrin **14:**836
- *illus:*
- - "Delivery of the Keys" (paint; Perugino) **9:**1585
Peter I (Czar, Rus.) **2:**215
- history chart **8:**766-767
Peter (Pesaḥ; apos., Ger.) **2:**557; **3:**197
Peter ben Moses of Regensburg **14:**1079
Peterborough (city, Ont.) **12:**1408
Peter the Cruel, *see* Pedro the Cruel
Peter de Luna, *see* BENEDICT XIII
Peter the Digester **8:**13
Peter the Hermit
- Bernard of Clairvaux **4:**672
- Crusades **9:**267; **15:**1137
- Trier **15:**1390
Peter the Lame **4:**563
Petermann, H. **8:**50
Peter Niger, *see* NIGRI, PETRUS
Peter of Alexandria **8:**50
PETER OF BLOIS **13:**338
PETER OF CLUNY **13:**339
- Bernard of Clairvaux **4:**672
- Cluny abbey **5:**619
- *illus:*
- - *Liber Contra Judaeos* **6:**82
Peter of Pisa **13:**192
Peter of St. Omer **8:**50
Peters, Roberta **12:**1122
Petersburg (city, Va.) **16:**163
Petersburg manuscript **16:**1467
Peter the Venerable, *see* PETER OF CLUNY
Peteul, Pierre, *see* MARIE-BENOIT
Pethahiah (emis., Er. Isr.) **8:**1463
Pethahiah, Leib (r., Belor.) **11:**213
PETHAHIAH OF REGENSBURG **13:**339
- commerce **15:**1298
- David ben Zakkai II **5:**1359
- population **13:**873ff
- Sambatyon **14:**763
- travel book **11:**351
- travels **15:**1349; **15:**1351
Pethor (bib. loc.) **4:**122
PETIḤAH (cerem.) **13:**340
Petil pishtim (meas.) **16:**378
Petit, David **4:**1245
Petit, Jacob **6:**1414
Petit, Jean Charles Henri, *see* DANIEL-ROPS, HENRI
Petit, Pietro Giovanni de **8:**50
Petit, S. (Chr. Hebr.) **8:**50
Petit, Solomon (r., Er. Isr.), *see* Solomon ben Samuel (Petit)
Petite Grammaire hébraïque provenant de Yemen (bk.) **16:**1474
Petitjean (tn., Mor.) **12:**344
PETLYURA, SIMON **13:**340
- Balta occupation **4:**144
- Schwarzbard, Shalom **14:**1027ff
PETRA (site, Edom) **13:**341
- Albright's excavations **2:**538
- geology **9:**199ff
- human geography **9:**596
- Kadesh **7:**432
- Palaestina Tertia **9:**121
- physiography **9:**177
- Pompey and Scaurus **12:**742
- Transjordan **15:**1317
- *illus:*
- - al-Siq gorge **9:**166
- - ruins **9:**207
- *see also:* Sela
Petra, Cardinal **13:**859
Petraeus, N. **8:**50
Petraeus, Severus **8:**50
Petrarch, Francesco **5:**75; **16:**22
Petri, Laurentius **4:**877
Petri, Olaus **14:**928
PETRIE, SIR WILLIAM MATTHEW FLINDERS **13:**343
- Sarābīt al-Khādim **2:**674
Petrikau (Petrokow; tn., Pol.), *see* PIOTRKOW
Petrograd (city, Rus.), *see* LENINGRAD
PETROGRAD CONFERENCE (Zion.) **13:**344
PETROLEUM AND OIL PRODUCTS **13:**344
- in Israel **9:**793
Petroleum Development of Palestine (co.) **9:**793
Petroleum refineries (Isr.) **9:**823
PETRONIUS, PUBLIUS **13:**346
- Caligula's image **8:**638
PETRONIUS ARBITER, GAIUS **13:**347
Petrópolis (city, Braz.) **14:**190; **14:**192
Petrov, Valleri **4:**1494
Petroveanu, Mihail **14:**423
Petrovgrad (city, Yug.), *see* ZRENJANIN
Petrovic, Joso **12:**238
Petrus Abaelardus, *see* ABELARD, PETER
PETRUS ALFONSI **13:**347
- chess **5:**402
- folktales **6:**1379
Petrus Canisius Society (Holl.) **4:**876
Petrus Damiani, *see* DAMIAN, PETER
Petrushka, Simcha **5:**113; **6:**730
Petrus Venerabilis, *see* PETER OF CLUNY
Petržalka (concen. camp) **4:**1312
Petschau (tn., Bohem.), *see* Becov
Petschau, Joseph **7:**216
Petschau, Mendel Beer **7:**216
Petschauer, Attila **12:**1376
PETSCHEK (fam.) **13:**347
Petschek, Ignaz **13:**347
Petschek, Isidore **13:**347
Petschek, Julius **13:**347
Petschek, Karl **13:**348
Petschek, Moses ben Israel **13:**347
Pettau (vill., Sloven.) **14:**717
PETTER BEN JOSEPH **13:**348
Pettersson, J. **8:**50
Petticoat Lane (engr., 19th cent.)

11:1004
Pettigrew, Samuel **13:**568
PETUCHOWSKI, JAKOB JOSEF **13:**349
Peutinger Table (geog. chart) **11:**919
- Jerusalem **9:**1542
PEVSNER, ANTON and NAUM NEHEMIA (Gabo) **13:**350
- sculpture **14:**1069
- *illus:*
- - text
- - "Construction in space . . ." (sculp.) **3:**564
Pevsner, J. **6:**734
PEVSNER, SIR NIKOLAUS **13:**350
PEVZNER, SAMUEL JOSEPH **13:**350
- *illus:*
- - F.Z.C. **16:**1165
PEWTER PLATES **13:**351
- *illus:*
- - text
- - mourner's plate **12:**489
PEYREHORADE (tn., Fr.) **13:**352
- Acosta, Isaac **2:**215
Peyrolles-en-Provence (loc., Fr.) **13:**1259
Peyser, Jefferson **14:**834
Peza'el (mosh., Isr.) **1:**place list
Peza'el valley (Isr.) **9:**589
PEZINOK (tn., Slov.) **13:**352
Pfaffman, Carl **13:**1345
Pfalz (reg., W. Ger.), *see* PALATINATE
Pfalz, Elisabeth of, *see* Elisabeth, Abbess of Pfalz
Pfeddersheimer, Paul, *see* PAULI, JOHANNES
PFEFFER, LEO **13:**355
PFEFFERKORN, JOHANNES (Joseph) **13:**355
- apostasy **3:**205
- history chart **8:**766-767
- Hoogstraaten, Jacob **8:**969
- Luther, Martin **11:**584
- Reuchlin, Johannes **14:**108
- *illus:* text
Pfefferkorn, Meir **13:**355; **13:**833
Pfeffermann, Abel, *see* PANN, ABEL
Pfeiffer, A. F. **8:**50
Pfeiffer, Augustus **8:**50
PFEIFFER, ROBERT HENRY **13:**357
Pflaum (fam.) **12:**37
Pflaum, Heinz, *see* PERI, HIRAM
P.F.L.P., *see* Popular Front for the Liberation of Palestine
PFORZHEIM (city, Ger.) **13:**358
- Reuchlin **14:**108ff
- *illus:* text
PFORZHEIMER, CARL HOWARD **13:**359
Phabi (pr. fam.), *see* Phiabi
Phaedon (wk.) **4:**381; **11:**1330;
Phainon (city, Edom), *see* PUNON
PHALSBOURG (vill., Fr.) **13:**359
Phanagoria (tn., Crimea), *see* Sennaya
Phantom Host (myth) **8:**1046
Phanuel (angel) **2:**963
PHARAOH **13:**359
- *Contents:*
- General **13:**359
- - In the Aggadah **13:**360
- - In Islam **13:**362
- Aaron **2:**4
- Arts **12:**404f
- Bible history **8:**575
- crocodile **5:**1125
- Exodus **6:**1047
- Exodus, Book of **6:**1051ff
- Moses **12:**372
- plagues of Egypt **13:**606
- Solomon **15:**100
- throne **15:**1124
- *illus:*
- - text
- - Aaron performing miracle with rod **12:**379
- - blessed by Jacob **7:**1084
- - entreating Moses and Aaron **13:**605
- - expelling the Israelites from Egypt **2:**952
- - infant Moses brought before **4:**1059
- - Moses and Aaron **12:***fcg.* 427
- - Moses challenging **12:**395
- - Moses pleading with **13:**605
- *see also:* MERNEPTAH
Pharaoh's Daughter, Tomb of (Jer.) **12:**484
- *illus:* **9:**1526
Pharaonic law **6:**1164; **13:**355
Pharar, Abraham **12:**978
Pharar, Abraham "El viejo" **12:**978
Pharar, David **12:**978ff
PHARISEES **13:**363
- History
- - Agrippa I **2:**416
- - Alexander Yannai **16:**715; **16:**716
- - Essenes **6:**900
- - Hellenism **8:**295; **8:**296
- - Herod I **8:**384
- - Herodians **8:**388
- - Hyrcanus, John **8:**1147
- - Jesus **10:**12ff
- - religious politics **11:**315
- - Sadducees **14:**621ff
- - sages **14:**636; **14:**639ff
- - Samaritan chronicle **14:**730
- - Second Temple period **8:**632
- - Simeon ben Shetaḥ **14:**1563ff
- - Zealots **16:**948
- Views and Philosophy of
- - ablution **2:**82
- - *am ha-areẓ* **2:**834ff
- - art **3:**507ff
- - ban **8:**350; **8:**361
- - Bible interpretation **8:**1417
- - free will **7:**129
- - gentiles and Judeo-Christians **9:**244
- - high priesthood **8:**474ff
- - immersion **13:**1412
- - law **3:**68
- - mystical tendencies **10:**496
- - oral law **10:**389
- - priests **13:**1087
- - Providence **13:**1281
- - red heifer **14:**12
- - resurrection **14:**98
- - Temple **15:**974
- In Literature
- - Damascus document **5:**1247; **5:**1249
- - Lies, Prophet of **11:**234
- - New Testament **13:**1445
- - polemic literature **2:**811; **13:**790; **15:**283
- Talmud, self-criticism **14:**648
- *see also:* HASSIDEANS; ḤAVER, ḤAVERIM
Pharmacists guilds **7:**972
Pharmacology **3:**675
PHAROS (isl., Egy.) **13:**366
PHASAEL (br., Herod) **13:**367
- Herod **8:**376ff
- Jerusalem governor **8:**636
- *geneal. table:* **8:**377
Phasael, Tower of (Jer.) **9:**1394
- *illus:*
- - citadel entrance **9:**1397
- - Johns' excavations **9:**1533
- - model **3:**340
- *see also:* David, Tower of
PHASAELIS (city, Er. Isr.) **13:**367
- fortress **8:**636
Phasael valley (Isr.), *see* Peza'el valley
Phasgo (loc., Transj.), *see* NEBO
Phasis (interval of time) **5:**45
Phatir (6th cent., conv.) **13:**1117
PHEASANT (bird) **13:**376
- dietary laws **6:**30,34
Pheibush (fam.), *see* PHILLIPS
Phenomenology (philos.)
- Husserl, Edmond **8:**1133
- Jewish contribution **13:**419
- Reinach, Adolf **14:**57
Phenylketonuria (disease) **14:**1501
PHERORAS (gov., Transj.) **13:**368
- *geneal. table:* **8:**377
P.H.H. (partisan orgn.), *see* Partizanim-Ḥayyalim-Ḥalutzim
Phiabi (pr. fam.) **6:**18
- Alexandria **2:**590
- high priest **8:**474
- Ishmael ben Phiabi **9:**86
- Joshua ben Phabi **10:**285
- priests **13:**1087
Philadelphia (tn., Egy.) **6:**9
Philadelphia (anc. city, Transj.) **5:**720; **13:**1348
- *see also:* RABBATH-AMMON
Philadelphia (county, Pa.) **13:**368
PHILADELPHIA (city, U.S.) **13:**368
- *Contents:*
- - Origins of the Jewish Community **13:**368
- - Revolutionary Period **13:**369
- - Early Nineteenth Century **13:**370
- - National Influence **13:**372
- - Mass Immigration and Communal Chaos **13:**373
- - Post-World War I **13:**373
- - 1970 **13:**374
- demography **5:**1513ff
- early settlement **2:**811
- history chart **8:**766-767
- Jewish popuation in 1914 **8:**732
- Liberty Bell **14:**1443
- museum **12:**551
- slave trade **14:**1664
- *illus:*
- - text
- - Beth Shalom synagogue **15:**625
- - Gratz College **7:**861
- - Lincoln's letter **11:**257
- - Mikveh Israel synagogue **10:**691; **15:**1595
PHILADELPHIA, JACOB **13:**376
- *illus:* text
Philadelphia Hebrew Sunday School Society (U.S.) **5:**349
Philadelphia Rabbinical Conference (1869) **6:**532
- history chart **8:**766-767
Philanthropin (school, Ger.) **10:**462; **14:**1080
- *illus:*
- - centenary medal **7:**88
PHILANTHROPY **13:**376
- *Contents:*
- - State Taxation for Jewish Communal Services **13:**377
- - Voluntary Associations or Benevolent Societies **13:**377
- - Fund Collectors on the Local Communal Level **13:**378
- - France **13:**378
- - England **13:**379
- - Germany **13:**379
- - Russia **13:**380
- - United States **13:**381
- - Canada **13:**385
- - Argentina **13:**386
- - Israel **13:**386
- - Fund Raising by International Organizations **13:**386
- - Old Type Fund Collection for Ereẓ Israel **13:**388
- - Zionist and Modern Israel Fund Raising **13:**389
- - The Modern Campaigns and Their Goals **13:**391
- associations **8:**441
- communal organization **3:**926
- Council of Jewsh Federations (U.S.) **5:**993
- Ereẓ Israel **10:**1161
- ORT **12:**1481
- South Africa **15:**195ff
- United Jewish Appeal **15:**1540
- U.S. Jews' activities **16:**1301
- U.S. Zionism **16:**1145
- *tables:* text
Philaster (bp., It.) **9:**1119
Philatelic Services in Israel **9:**842
- *illus:*
- - Stamp Day issues **9:**843,844
- - *see also:* STAMPS (Israel)
Philately, *see* STAMPS
Philharmonic Orchestra (Isr.), *see* ISRAEL PHILHARMONIC ORCHESTRA
Philhellene (tit.) **3:**440
Philip (ruler, Judea), *see* HEROD PHILIP I
Philip (br., Alexander the Great) **14:**729
PHILIP II (k., Fr.) **13:**392
- Bray-sur-Seine Jews **4:**1322
- French Jewry **7:**13
- Jewish badge **4:**65
- Paris Jews **13:**104
- seals **14:**1079
Philip II (k., Port.) **15:**270
Philip II (k., Sp.)
- Inquisition **8:**1388; **8:**1392
- Plantin, Christophe **13:**614
- *illus:*
- - Mercado, Luis, and **11:**1193
PHILIP III (k., Fr.) **13:**393
Philip III (k., Sp.) **8:**1388
PHILIP IV (k., Fr.) **13:**393
- Beaucaire Jews **4:**363
- Châlons-sur-Marne Jews **5:**331
- French Jewry **7:**15
- Troyes martyrs **15:**1407
- *illus:*
- - breviary **14:**793
Philip IV (k., Sp.) **8:**1388
PHILIP V (k., Fr.) **13:**394
- Troyes Jews **15:**1407
Philip V (k., Sp.) **8:**1388
Philip, Duke of Edinburgh **6:**463,765; **15:**1672
- *illus:*
- - Janner, Barnett, and **9:**1276
Philip Augustus (k., Fr.), *see* PHILIP II
Philip the Bold (k., Fr.), *see* PHILIP III
Philip the Fair (k., Fr.), *see* PHILIP IV
PHILIP OF BATHYRA (sol.) **13:**394
- Agrippa **16:**922
Philip of Hesse (landsgrave) **11:**585
Philipopolis (anc. city, Bul.), *see* PLOVDIV
Philipp, Aharon **9:**905
Philippe, E. **8:**50
Philippe, Edis de (opera dir.), *see* DE PHILIPPE, EDIS
Philippi (city, Gr.) **6:**10
PHILIPPINES **13:**395
- Inquisition **8:**1393
- Israel's relations with **9:**432
- Jerusalem issue **15:**1548
- synagogues **1:**syn. list
- *illus:*
- - text
- - student at Hebrew University **9:**442
Philippion (s., Ptolemy) **2:**588; **13:**1349
Philipp Lang von Langenfels **14:**381
Philipps, E. P. **7:**603

Philipps, W. T. **8:**50
Philippsohn (physic., Sic.) **13:**29
Philippson (name), *see also* Philipson; Phillipson
PHILIPPSON (Ger. fam.) **13:**396
- *illus:* text
Philippson (agr. stlmt., Braz.) **4:**1326ff
Philippson, Alfred **13:**397
Philippson, Franz M. **13:**398
- bank **4:**177
Philippson, Jules **13:**398
Philippson, Ludwig **13:**396
- Bible **4:**875
- children's literature **5:**432; **5:**452
- history chart **8:**766-767
- homiletic literature **8:**956
- press **2:**648
- rabbinical conferences **13:**1460
- *illus:*
- - *Allgemeine Zeitung des Judenthums (1837)* **2:**648
Philippson, Martin **13:**397
Philippson, Maurice **13:**398
Philippson, Moses **13:**396
- Bible **4:**875
Philippson, Paul **13:**398
Philippson, Paula **13:**398
Philippson, Phoebus **13:**398
- Bible **4:**875
Philippsthal (physic., Ger.) **4:**647
Philips (name), *see also* Phillips
Philips, Coleman **12:**1130
Philips, Jacob **4:**1112; **13:**909
PHILIPS, MARIANNE **6:**321; **6:**322
Philips, Namie **15:**193
Philips, Philip A. **3:**840; **12:**1130
Philips, Sir Thomas Williams **4:**976
Philipsburg (city, Mont.) **12:**267
PHILIPSEN, THEODOR **3:**608
- Denmark **5:**1537
Philipson (name), *see also* Philippson; Phillipson
Philipson (fam.) **12:**157
PHILIPSON, DAVID **13:**398
- Reform **5:**563
Philipson, Ivar **15:**549
Philipson, Joseph **14:**662
Philip the Tall (k., Fr.), *see* PHILIP V
PHILISTINES **13:**399
- agriculture **2:**390
- Aphek, stronghold **3:**176
- archaeological evidence **3:**306
- Benjamites **4:**525
- Beth-Shemesh **4:**772
- Cult of Dagon **5:**1223
- David's wars **5:**1320ff
- Ekron **6:**559
- Geba **7:**349
- Genesis, Book of **7:**389; **7:**394
- Gerar, Land of **7:**432
- Gibbethon **7:**549
- history **8:**586ff
- history chart **8:**766-767
- Israel settlement history **8:**584; **8:**585
- Judah, tribe of **10:**329
- pottery **1:**pottery chart; **13:**941
- Samson **14:**771
- Saul **14:**911ff
- sea peoples **16:**1501
- war and warfare **16:**271
- *illus:*
- - Ark carried into battle against **14:**781
- - clay jug **3:**314
- - David fighting **11:**1493
- - David's wars against (map) **5:**1320
- - female deity figurine **3:**696
- - Jonathan fighting the **4:**879
- - returning the Ark of the Covenant **3:**461
- - Samson in battle against **14:**775
- - Saul and sons dead on Mount Gilboa **7:**567
- - sea battle with Ramses III **8:**587
Phillipo (Ger. spy) **13:**149
Phillips (name), *see also* Philips
PHILLIPS (fam.) **13:**405
Phillips, Al **15:**306
Phillips, Edis, *see* DE PHILIPPE, EDIS
Phillips, Henry M. **13:**230
Phillips, J.B. (Bib. trans., Eng.) **4:**870
Phillips, Jonas (bsmn.) **13:**405
- Albany **2:**524
- petitions **13:**370
- *illus:*
- - portrait
Phillips, Jonas B. (law, plwrt.) **10:**1503; **15:**1569
Phillips, Joseph **8:**1255
PHILLIPS, LAZARUS **13:**406
- Canada **5:**112
- Montreal **12:**288
PHILLIPS, SIR LIONEL **13:**406
- politics **13:**820
Phillips, Louis **12:**1129
Phillips, Manuel **13:**405
Phillips, Marion **13:**812
Phillips, Naphtali **12:**1199; **13:**405
PHILLIPS, NATHAN **13:**829
- Canada **5:**112
- Ontario **12:**1408
- Toronto **15:**1263
Phillips, Pharez **10:**1492; **11:**1286
PHILLIPS, PHILIP (U.S. polit.) **13:**407
Phillips, Sir Phillip (law., Austr.) **10:**1492
Phillips, Rebecca Machado **11:**667
Phillips, Sydney, *see* REHFISCH, HANS JOSÉ
Phillips, W. **13:**33
- *illus:*
- - Anglo-American Committee **16:**1089
Phillips, Zalegman **13:**406
Phillipson (name), *see also* Philippson; Philipson
PHILLIPSON, IRVING JOSEPH **11:**1575
PHILO (The Elder; Gr. poet) **13:**407
- apologetics **3:**189
- Greek influence on **8:**300
- Hellenistic Jewish literature **8:**304
PHILO (Pseudo-; early J. chronicle) **13:**408
- Hellenism **8:**298; **8:**302
Philo-Atlas; Handbuch fuer die juedische Auswanderung (wk.) **6:**734
PHILODEMUS (2/1 cent., philos., Er. Isr.) **7:**896
- Hellenism **8:**298
PHILO JUDAEUS (phil.) **13:**409
- *Contents:*
- - Writings **13:**410
- - Philosophy **13:**411
- - Influence **13:**415
- General
- - folkloric material **6:**1376
- - synagogue **15:**582
- - Wolfson's studies **16:**618
- Life and Influence
- - Clement of Alexandria **5:**602
- - history **8:**553
- - letter to the emperor **11:**56
- - Maghāriya sect **14:**1088
- Hellenism **8:**297; **8:**298; **8:**300
- - Alexandria **2:**590
- - apologetics **3:**189
- - Hellenistic influences **15:**573
- - Jewish literature **8:**304
- Bible and Commandments
- - abortion, penalty **2:**99
- - *Akedah* **2:**482; **2:**483
- - allegorical exegesis **4:**896
- - Bible exegesis **11:**313
- - circumcision **5:**572
- - commandments **5:**784ff
- - creation of Adam **2:**238
- - *karet* **10:**789
- - Moses **12:**389; **12:**392
- - prophecy **13:**1176
- - sacrifice **14:**613
- - Torah **10:**622; **15:**1236ff
- - usury **12:**246
- - writings as law source **12:**117
- Philosophy **11:**313; **13:**425ff
- - angels and demons **2:**973f
- - anthropomorphism avoided **3:**55
- - antinomianism **3:**69
- - articles of faith **3:**654
- - creation, theory of **5:**1065
- - cynic *chriae* **5:**1177
- - dogmas of Judaism **4:**432
- - dualism **6:**243
- - evil, problem of **7:**776
- - free will **7:**125
- - God **7:**653ff
- - imitation of God **8:**1292
- - immortality **11:**236
- - justice, mercy of God **7:**669
- - logos **11:**460ff
- - Messiah **11:**1410
- - microcosm doctrine **11:**1502
- - music **12:**566
- - mysticism **10:**495ff
- - nature **12:**889
- - Platonism **13:**628
- - revelation **14:**122
- - *ru'aḥ ha-Kodesh* **14:**366
- - soul, immortality of **15:**176
- - space and place **15:**217
- - word **16:**635
Philo-Lexikon; Handbuch des juedischen Wissens (wk.) **6:**734
Philology
- halakhic exegesis **14:**651ff
- *diagrams:*
- - Akkadian, Assyrian and Babylonian, lines of development **2:**495
- *see also:* LINGUISTIC LITERATURE, HEBREW
Philo of Alexandria (phil.) *see* PHILO JUDAEUS
PHILO OF BYBLOS (Gr. hist.) **7:**896
- Hecataeus' writings **8:**237
Philoponus, John **15:**1099
Philosoph, Jacob, *see* QUERIDO, JACOB
Philosoph, Joseph **6:**148
Philosopher's Stone **2:**542ff
PHILOSOPHY **13:**416
- *Contents:*
- - 14th to 17th centuries **13:**416
- - 18th to 19th centuries **13:**417
- - 20th century **13:**418
- Jewish contributions **8:**743
- *see also:* PHILOSOPHY, JEWISH
PHILOSOPHY, JEWISH **13:**421
- *Contents*
- - Biblical and Rabbinic Antecedents **13:**421
- - - Bible **13:**422
- - Hellenistic Jewish philosophy **13:**424
- - - Philo **13:**424
- - Medieval Period **13:**427
- - - Sources and Translations **13:**428ff
- - - Main Schools **13:**429
- - - Saadiah **13:**431
- - - Rabbanite Followers of the Kalam **13:**432
- - - Karaites **13:**433
- - - Israeli, Isaac **13:**433
- - - Ibn Gabirol **13:**434
- - - Baḥya **13:**435
- - - Abraham bar Ḥiyya **13:**436
- - - Ibn Ezra **13:**437
- - - Judah Halevi **13:**438
- - - Hibat Allah **13:**439
- - - Nethanel al-Fayyumi **13:**440
- - - Abraham ibn Daud **13:**440
- - - Maimonides **13:**440
- - - Hebrew Translators (13th cent.) **13:**443
- - - Maimonidean Controversy **13:**443
- - - Hillel ben Samuel **13:**444
- - - Isaac Albalag **13:**445
- - - Abner of Burgos **13:**445
- - - Moses of Narbonne **13:**446
- - - Levi ben Gershom **13:**446
- - - Ḥasdai Crescas **13:**447
- - - Simon ben Ẓemaḥ Duran **13:**449
- - - Joseph Albo **13:**449
- - - Shem Tov family **13:**449
- - - Abrabanel **13:**450
- - - Delmedigo, Elijah **13:**450
- - - Delmedigo, Joseph **13:**450
- - - Christian Thought **13:**451
- - - Christian Influences **13:**451
- - Modern Period
- - - Introduction **13:**452
- - - Spinoza **13:**453
- - - Mendelssohn **13:**454
- - - Kant **13:**455
- - - Formstecher **13:**456
- - - Samuel Hirsch **13:**457
- - - Krochmal **13:**457
- - - S.D. Luzzatto **13:**459
- - - Steinheim, S.L. **13:**459
- - - Lazarus **13:**460
- - - Hermann Cohen **13:**460
- - - Rosenzweig **13:**461
- - - Buber **13:**462
- Ancient
- - Alexandrian Jews **2:**590
- - Aristotelianism **3:**445ff
- - Hellenistic period **8:**293
- - Philo **13:**409
- - Stoicism **15:**410
- Medieval
- - Aaron ben Elijah **2:**10
- - Abner of Burgos **2:**88
- - Abrabanel, Isaac **2:**103
- - Abrabanel, Judah **2:**109
- - Abraham bar Ḥiyya **2:**130
- - Abraham ben Moses **2:**150
- - Aknin, Joseph **2:**501
- - Albalag, Isaac **2:**520
- - Albo, Joseph **2:**535
- - Al-Mukammis, David **2:**671
- - Anatoli, Jacob **2:**927
- - Baḥya ibn Paquda **4:**105
- - Baṣīr, Joseph **4:**301
- - Crescas, Ḥasdai **5:**1079
- - Delmedigo, Elijah **5:**1477
- - Delmedigo, Joseph **5:**1478
- - Duran, Profiat **6:**301
- - Duran, Simeon **6:**302
- - Falaquera, Shem Tov **6:**1140
- - Gabirol, Solomon ibn **7:**235
- - Gerundi, Nissim **5:**1549
- - Hibat Allah **8:**461
- - Hillel ben Samuel **8:**488
- - Ibn Daud, Abraham **8:**1159
- - Ibn Ezra, Abraham **8:**1163
- - Ibn Ezra, Moses **8:**1170
- - Ibn Waqar, Joseph **8:**1206
- - Israeli, Isaac **9:**1063
- - Judah Halevi **10:**362ff
- - Kaspi, Joseph ibn **10:**810
- - Latif, Isaac **10:**1447
- - Levi ben Gershom **11:**92
- - Maimonides **11:**768ff
- - Moses ben Joshua **12:**422
- - Neoplatonism **12:**958ff
- - Nethanel ben al-Fayyūmī **12:**971
- - Pollegar, Isaac **13:**835
- - Portugal **13:**416
- - Rossi, Azariah de **14:**315
- - Saadiah Gaon **14:**548
- - skeptics and skepticism **14:**1644
- - Spain, **13:**416; **15:**243

- - Zaddik, Joseph ibn **16**:911
- Islamic influences **9**:104
- - Al-Farabi **6**:1177
- - al-Ghazālī **7**:539
- - Avempace **3**:947
- - Averroes **3**:950ff
- - Avicenna **3**:957ff
- - *Brethren of Sincerity* **4**:1364
- - Kalām **10**:702ff
- - Sufism **15**:486
- Modern
- - Bendavid, Lazarus **4**:474
- - Bergson, Henri **4**:619
- - Blau, Joseph Leon **4**:1075
- - Buber, Martin **4**:1432ff
- - Cohen, Hermann **5**:673
- - Enlightenment Period **3**:111
- - existentialism **6**:1041
- - Formstecher, Solomon **6**:1439
- - God **7**:662; **7**:668
- - Goodman, Nelson **7**:780
- - Gordon, Aharon David **7**:791ff
- - Hegel's influence on **8**:246
- - Herz, Markus **8**:403
- - Heschel, Abraham Joshua **8**:425ff
- - Hirsch, Samuel **8**:515
- - Kook, Abraham Isaac **10**:1182
- - Krochmal, Nachman **10**:1269
- - Lazarus, Moritz **10**:1517
- - Luzzatto, Samuel David **11**:604
- - Maimon, Solomon **11**:741
- - Mendelssohn, Moses **11**:1330
- - Orobio de Castro **12**:1475
- - Pinto, Isaac de **13**:552
- - psychology **13**:1343
- - Rosenzweig, Franz **14**:299
- - Sanches, Francisco **14**:825
- - Simon, Akiva Ernst **14**:1577
- - Spinoza **15**:275ff
- - Steinheim, Solomon Ludwig **15**:370
- Opposition to Philosophy
- - Asher ben Jehiel **3**:707
- - Ashkenazi, Joseph **3**:727
- - ban and heresy **8**:360
- - Benveniste, Abraham **4**:559
- - Duran, Simeon **6**:303ff
- - Ibn Abi Zimra **5**:1357
- - Ibn Shem Tov, Joseph **8**:1195
- - Ibn Shem Tov, Shem Tov **8**:1198
- - Isserles' defense **14**:89
- - Jacob ibn Ḥabib **8**:1178
- - Maimonidean controversy **11**:745
- - Moscato, Judah **12**:357
- - Torah study **15**:456
- Bible and
- - allegorical exegesis **4**:897ff
- - Ecclesiastes **6**:352
- - Frankists **7**:59
- - Greek philosophy **3**:444ff
- - Ḥasidism **7**:1402
- - homiletics **8**:953ff
- - Judaism and **10**:391; **10**:392
- - Kabbalah **10**:490; **10**:513; **10**:527; **10**:537; **10**:556
- - Karaism **10**:778
- - Moses **12**:398
- Concepts and Ideas
- - *Akedah* **2**:484
- - allegory **2**:643; **2**:644
- - articles of faith **3**:655
- - categories **5**:253
- - cosmology **5**:982
- - duty of speculation **3**:656
- - emotions **6**:727
- - evil, problem of **7**:776
- - faith and reason **7**:657
- - form and matter **6**:1438ff
- - free will **7**:125
- - God **7**:657; **7**:657ff
- - holiness **10**:872
- - Judaism and Christianity **5**:514
- - Messiah **11**:1414
- - metaphysics **11**:1442
- - microcosm theory **11**:1501
- - music **12**:600
- - physics **13**:488
- - prophecy **13**:1177
- - providence **13**:1284
- - redemption **14**:4
- - repentance **14**:76
- - resurrection **14**:101
- - revelation **14**:122ff
- - reward and punishment **14**:136
- - *ru'aḥ ha-kodesh* **14**:366
- - Sabbath **14**:565
- - *Shekhinah* **14**:1352ff
- - soul **15**:172
- - soul, immortality of **15**:176ff
- - space and place **15**:217ff
- - substance and accident **15**:473
- - suffering **15**:485
- - time and eternity **15**:1142ff
- - Torah **15**:1235
- Literature **6**:1267
- - English **6**:776
- - ethical **6**:925
- - Hebrew translations **15**:1321ff
- - Jewish **11**:313; **11**:338
- - Judeo-Arabic **10**:417
- *see also:* BIBLE (Philosophical Interpretations):: CAUSE AND EFFECT; ETHICAL LITERATURE; ETHICS; INTELLECT; KABBALAH; MUSAR MOVEMENT; PHILOSOPHY; THEOLOGY

Philosophy of religion **13**:421; **13**:426
PHILOSTRATUS (Gr. au.) **7**:896
Philoteria (city, Er. Isr.) **4**:780; **10**:1036; **13**:1348
PHILO VERLAG (publ. house, Ger.) **13**:465
Philoxenus (bp.) **4**:860
Phinehas (name), *see also* Pineḥas, Pinḥas
PHINEHAS (s. of Eleazar) **13**:465
- Samaritan calendar **14**:749
- Samaritan priesthood **14**:727; **14**:734
- vow of Jephthah **16**:228
- zeal, exemplified by **9**:1306; **16**:947
- Zimri **16**:1026
- *illus:*
- - text
- - Zimri and Cozbi **16**:1027

Phinehas (son of Eli), *see* HOPHNI AND PHINEHAS
PHINEHAS (1st cent. C.E., Temple offic.) **13**:468
- Temple **15**:966

Phinehas bar Meir (mart.) **15**:1214
Phinehas ben Clusoth **9**:1224
PHINEHAS BEN ḤAMA HA-KOHEN (amora) **13**:468
PHINEHAS BEN JACOB HA-KOHEN (Kafra) **13**:468
- *kerovot* **10**:920
- Yannai **16**:712

PHINEHAS BEN JAIR (tan.) **13**:469
- captives, ransom of **5**:154
- *Demai* **5**:1487
- Judah ha-Nasi **9**:252
- piety **13**:505
- Zohar **16**:1200

Phinehas ben Joseph (Samar. h. pr.) **2**:179; **14**:733; **14**:753; **14**:757
PHINEHAS BEN JOSEPH HA-LEVI (paytan, Sp.) **13**:470
Phinehas ben Meshullam **2**:592
Phinehas ben Pazzi **5**:577
PHINEHAS BEN SAMUEL **13**:470
Phinehas ben Yusuf (Samar. h. pr.), *see* Phinehas ben Joseph
Phinehas ha-Kohen (11th cent., Babyl.) **13**:513
Phinehas ha-Kohen of Lutomirsk **7**:1276
Phinehas Hananiah Argosi de Silva, *see* Jeiteles, Baruch
Phinehas of Borsa, *see* Hager, Phinehas
Phinehas of Boskowitz **14**:1105
Phinehas of Wlodawa **11**:45
PHLORINA (city, Gr.) **13**:471
- Greece **7**:876

Phobian, Moses ben Eliezer **10**:425
Phocas (7th cent., emp.)
- Antiochian Jews **3**:72
- Jerusalem Jews **9**:1571

Phocas, Johannes **15**:1355
Phocylides (Gr. poet) **13**:1335
Phoebus ben Aaron ha-Levi, *see* URI BEN AARON HA-LEVI
PHOENICIA, PHOENICIANS **13**:471
- *Contents*
- - Names **13**:471
- - The Land **13**:471
- - People and Language **13**:472
- - History to 1200 B.C.E. **13**:473
- - Internal Development to 1200 B.C.E. **13**:474
- - The Transition **13**:475
- - 1200-1000 B.C.E. **13**:475
- - Emergence-First Contacts with Israel **13**:475
- - Height and Decline 1000-750 B.C.E. **13**:477
- - 750-538 B.C.E. **13**:477
- - 538-64 B.C.E. **13**:478
- - Phoenician Colonization **13**:478
- - Religion **13**:479
- - Language and Literature-Later Period **13**:480
- General
- - African Jews **2**:331
- - Ahab **2**:435ff
- - assimilation **3**:771
- - Carthage **5**:214ff
- - coinage **14**:1347
- - David's relations with **5**:1322
- - Hellenism **8**:626
- - Jerusalem tomb style **9**:1525
- - Semites **14**:1148
- - Sidon **14**:1506
- - Tammuz, god of **15**:788
- - *tekhelet* **15**:914
- Commerce
- - merchant proselytes **16**:1277
- - overseas commerce **16**:1269
- - ships and sailing **14**:1411
- - trade and commerce **15**:1293ff
- Language and Script
- - Hebrew language **16**:1395,1560
- - inscriptions **16**:661; **16**:665
- - script **2**:674ff; **4**:773; **16**:654
- - seals **14**:1073
- - Semitic languages **14**:1149
- - Ugaritic **15**:1507
- *illus:*
- - text
- - Ahiram sarcophagus **2**:676, 683
- - comparative alphabets **2**:683
- - Eshmun-Azar sarcophagus **2**:680
- - seal (9/8 cent.) **14**:1076
- *see also:* AMORITES; CANAAN, LAND OF

Phoenicia glass factory (Isr.) **7**:613; **8**:538
PHOENIX (city, Ariz.) **13**:481
- Arizona **3**:449; **3**:450

PHOENIX (bird) **13**:482
- *illus:* text

Phologombos, Terentius, *see* JUDAH, SAMUEL BENJAMIN HELBERT
Phonetics
- Arabic and Hebrew **3**:238
- DSS language **16**:1586
- linguistics **16**:1400
- mishnaic Hebrew **16**:1595
- origins of vowels **16**:1432

Phonograph records, *see* RECORDS, PHONOGRAPH
PHONOLOGY **16**:1560
- biblical Hebrew **16**:1562

Phorcensis, *see* REUCHLIN, JOHANNES
Phosphates (Isr.) **9**:807; **12**:930
- *illus:*
- - Oron plant **9**:805

PHOTIS (vill., Er. Isr.) **13**:483
PHOTOGRAPHY **13**:483
- *illus:*
- - text
- - "Synagogue Court" (R. Vishniac) **16**:166

Phraortes (k., Media), *see* Kaštarita
PHRYGIA (dist., As. M.) **13**:487
- Asia Minor **3**:746ff
- Jewish colonists **10**:259

Phybes of Hanover **12**:63
Phylacteries, *see* TEFILLIN
Physicians, *see* MEDICINE
PHYSICS **13**:488
- *Contents:*
- - In Medieval Philosophy **13**:488
- - In Modern Times **13**:489
- - Research in Israel **13**:491
- Aristotelianism **13**:430
- Jewish contributions **8**:743
- research in Israel **16**:440
- translations **15**:1321

Physiognomy **10**:500
- Jewish nose **3**:49

PHYSIOGRAPHY OF ISRAEL **9**:123
- human geography **9**:570ff
- Negev **12**:925
- Sodom **15**:71ff
- *illus:*
- - Amazyahu River, Canyon **9**:153
- - Amudei Amram, Eilat region **9**:213
- - Arabah Valley near Ein Ḥazevah **9**:145
- - Bet Guvrin caves **4**:732
- - Birkat-Rām **9**:167
- - Chalk cliffs, Rosh ha-Nikrah **9**:205
- - Chalk formations, Arabah Valley **9**:203
- - chalk formations, Safed region **9**:208
- - columnar basalt, Golan Heights **9**:213
- - Dead Sea caves **8**:645
- - Dead Sea cliffs **9**:161
- - Dead Sea Rift Valley **9**:217
- - Eilat Mountains, canyon **9**:149
- - flash flood in the Negev **9**:185
- - Gilboa Mountains **9**:145
- - Gilead Plateau **9**:167
- - Hermon Massif foot hills **9**:166
- - Ḥuleh Valley **9**:207,212
- - Jezreel Valley **9**:145
- - Jordan, delta **9**:157
- - Jordan, flood plain **9**:153
- - Jordan River and Valley (map) **10**:191
- - Judean Desert **9**:99
- - Kadesh Naphtali polje **9**:169
- - Kidron Valley gorge **10**:987
- - Lake Kinneret **9**:168
- - Lashon formations, Jordan Valley **9**:205
- - Levonah intermontane basin **9**:209
- - loess badlands **9**:573
- - loess soil in Naḥal Besor **9**:573
- - Ma'aleh Akrabbim rock formation **11**:635
- - Makhtesh Ramon **9**:133,209
- - Mount Sodom **9**:162
- - Mount Tabor **9**:149
- - Naḥal Avivim geological pillars **9**:165
- - Nubian sandstone formations

9:133,207
- - Petra basin, al-Siq gorge 9:166
- - Red Sea area 14:15
- - Rift Valley, Ḥiyyon River exit 9:165
- - Rift Valley from Poriyyah Heights 9:211
- - sand dunes, Ḥefer Plain 9:130
- - sandlands, Arabah 9:165
- - seashore, abrasion platform 9:129
- - Sedom area, aerial view 15:73
- - *Sefer Kaftor va-Feraḥ* (1549) 6:919
- - Senir Valley 9:168
- - Shelomo Massif, aerial view 9:129
- - Sorek Valley 9:137, 15:164
- - Tabor, Mount 15:692
- - Tannur waterfall 9:150
- - terrace landscape, Judean Hills 9:133,205
- - Valley of Kinnarot 10:1032
- - Wadi al-Murrah 12:928
- - Yarmuk 9:157; 16:719
PIACENZA (city, It.) 13:492
Piameta, Joseph, *see* Fiametta, Joseph
PIASECZNO (tn., Pol.) 13:493
Piaski (city, Ukr.) 10:1229
Piaski (ghetto, Pol.) 13:765
Piast (leg. fig., Pol.) 13:1119; 15:1071
PIAT (theat., Fr.) 15:1071
PIATIGORSKY, GREGOR 13:493
- *illus:*
- - Israel Philharmonic Orchestra 8:261
PIATRA-NEAMT (Piatra; tn., Rum.) 13:493
PIATTOLI, SCIPIONE 13:495
PICA (Colonization Assoc.) 13:495
- afforestation 9:789
- Alummot site 2:784
- Ashdot Ya'akov 3:698
PICARD, EDMOND 13:496
PICARD, JACOB 13:496
PICARD, LEO 1:35; 13:496
PICART, BERNARD 13:497
- *illus:*
- - text
- - Amsterdam Sephardi synagogue (engr.) 2:898
- - Amsterdam marriage ceremony (engr.) 11:1029
- - burial scene (engr.) 8:443
- - circumcision scene (drg.) 5:573
- - Day of Atonement in a Dutch synagogue (drg.) 3:831
- - Dutch family *seder* (drg.) 6:1165
- - *hakkafot* around a coffin (engr.) 7:1153
- - Hoshana Rabba in synagogue (engr.) 8:1026
- - "Marriage Ceremony of Portuguese Jews" (drg.) 11:1030
- - priestly blessing (drg.) 13:106
- - raising of the Torah scroll (drg.) 7:1077
- - "Redemption of the Firstborn" (engr.) 6:1309
- - search for leaven (drg.) 4:371
- - "*Simhat Torah* in the Synagogue" (drg.) 14:1571
- - *sukkah* meal 15:496
Picasso, Pablo 5:318
- *illus:*
- - Jacob, Max (portrait) 9:1212
- - Stein, Gertrude (portrait) 15:352
PICCIOTTO (fam.) 13:498
- politics 13:816
Picciotto, Elijah 13:498
Picciotto, Ezra 13:498
Picciotto, Haim Moses H. 13:498
Picciotto, Ḥai Moses 13:498
Picciotto, Hillel 13:498
Picciotto, Hillel Ḥayyim 13:498
Picciotto, Isaac Levi 5:1250
Picciotto, James 13:498
Picciotto, Joseph 13:498; 13:816
Picciotto, Moses ben Ezra 13:498
Picciotto, Raphael 13:498
Picho, Azariah, *see* FIGO, AZARIAH
PICHO (Pichon), JOSEPH 13:498
- Spain 15:234
Picinello, Felipe 8:50
Pick, Adolf 6:462
PICK, ALOIS 13:499
Pick, Behrendt 3:301
Pick, David 15:1012
PICK, ERNST PETER 13:499
Pick, Friedrick 11:1556
PICK, ḤAYYIM HERMANN 13:499
Pick, Isaiah, *see* BERLIN, ISAIAH BEN JUDAH LOEB
Pick, Otto 5:1209
Pick, Wolf 4:659
Pickthall, Marmaduke William 6:782
PICO DELLA MIRANDOLA, GIOVANNI 13:500
- Abrabanel, Judah 2:109
- Crescas, Ḥasdai 5:1085
- Hebrew studies 8:46; 8:15ff
- Kabbalah 2:545; 2:548; 10:643ff
PICON, MOLLY 13:501
- recordings 13:1617
- *illus:*
- - in *The Circus Girl* 15:1068
Picot, Georges 15:565
Picquart, Georges 6:226ff
Picques, L. 8:50
Picquigny, Baron of *see* CALMER, MOSES ELIEZER LIEFMANN
Picture Dictionary of Jewish Life 6:734
Piczenik, A. 13:930
Pidal, Ramón Menéndez 12:658; 12:1353
- *romancero* traditions 10:1353
Pidyon (has. term) 7:1400
Pidyon ha-Ben (firstborn redemption) 6:1308ff
- priestly function 13:1088ff
- Samaritans 14:744
- *see also:* CHILDREN
Pidyon shevuyim, *see* CAPTIVES, RANSOMING OF
PIEDMONT (reg., It.) 13:501
- history chart (1723 and 1848) 8:766-767
Piedro de Guadalajara, *see* Guadalajara, Piedro de
Piek, Arnold 13:973
Piena (vill., Rus.) 14:1434
P'ien-liang (city, China), *see* KAIFENG
Piera, Solomon da, *see* Da Piera, Solomon ben Immanuel; DA PIERA, SOLOMON BEN MESHULLAM
PIERCE, SYDNEY DAVID 13:503
PIERLEONI (fam.) 13:503
- Anacletus II 2:916
- *illus:*
- - Pierleone tower, Rome 2:917
Pierleoni, Baruch 2:916; 13:503
Pierleoni, Leo 2:916; 13:503
Pierleoni, Pietro, *see* ANACLETUS II, PETER PIERLEONE
Pierpont Morgan Picture Bible, *see Morgan Picture Bible*
Pierre de Nostra-Donna 12:1230
PIESTANY (tn., Cz.) 13:503
Piestanyer, Judah Leib 7:1407
Pietermaritzburg (city, S.Afr.) 12:844ff
Pietersburg (tn., Transvaal) 15:1340
Pietralewicze (tn., Belor.) 14:1673
Pietrasza (loc., Pol.) 4:807
Pietro della Valle 16:1506
Pietro Martire Vermigli, *see* Martyr, Peter
PIETY AND THE PIOUS 13:504
- Ḥasidei Ashkenaz 7:464
- Ḥasidim 7:1383
- Job 10:113
- Judah Halevi 13:421
- sages 14:652ff
- wisdom psalms 16:562
- *see also:* RIGHTEOUSNESS; ZADDIK
Pietzash, M. 14:1426
Pieve-Santo-Stefano (tn., It.) 15:1468
Piexotto, Daniel L. M. 12:1344
PIG 13:506
- Babylon 13:1407
- dietary laws 6:32
- Edom 6:379
- euphemism 6:961
- Israel law, 1962 12:147
- prohibition 6:43
- Rabbi Judah 4:1030
Pigeon, *see* DOVE
Pigeon fanciers 16:1274
Piggul, *see* ABOMINATION
Pigit, Samuel 10:775
PI-HAHIROTH (tn., Egy.) 13:508
Pijade, Bukić 16:888
Pijade, David 16:888
PIJADE, MOŠA 13:508
PIKE, LIPMAN E. (Lip) 13:508
- sport 15:300, 315
Pike, Samuel 8:50
PIKKU'AḤ NEFESH (danger to life) 13:509
- abortion 2:99; 2:100
- autopsies 3:931ff
- euthanasia 6:979ff
- government decrees 15:842
- heretics 8:360
- *kiddush ha-Shem* 10:979
- medicine 11:1181
- payment 15:1684
- preservation of life 11:235
- religious life in Israel 9:903
- Sabbath 14:563
- transplants 15:1337
- *see also:* HYGIENE
Pilarik, András 8:50
Pilarik, Esaias 8:50
Pilarik, István 8:51
Pilate, Pontius, *see* PONTIUS PILATE
PILCH, JUDAH 1:35
PILCHIK, ELY E. 13:510
Pilderwasser, Joshua, *see* WEISSER, JOSHUA
PILGRIMAGE 13:510
- *Contents:*
- - Second Temple Period 13:510
- - The Pilgrimage 13:512
- - The Rituals 13:512
- - The Stay in Jerusalem 13:512
- - Post-Temple Period 13:513
- - Christian Pilgrimages 13:514
- - Information on the Jews 13:517
- Holy Land
- - ancient economic life 16:1272
- - Canaan sites 15:1383
- - Commandments, the 613 5:764
- - holy places in Israel 8:920ff
- - itineraries of Israel 9:1148
- - Jerusalem map 9:1544
- - maps of Ereẓ Israel 11:919ff
- - Mount Zion 16:1031
- Jewish
- - diaspora 6:18
- - Estori ha-Parḥi 9:279; 9:280
- - ḥasidic 7:1400
- - Mount of Olives 12:483; 12:484
- - obligation of blind 4:1091
- Non-Jewish
- - Christian 9:1570ff
- - Jerusalem in Crusader period 9:1415
- - Jerusalem in Mamluk period 9:1423
- - Muslim 10:1198
- *illus:*
- - text
- - Hebronites setting out for Mecca 9:918
- - Japan's Original Gospel Tabernacle group 9:1284
- - Sir John Mandeville setting out to the Holy Land 6:783
- - Nabi Mūsa 9:920
- - Russian pilgrims on the Jordan 9:326; 10:194
- - Simeon the Just's tomb 14:1567
- - Via Dolorosa on Good Friday 9:916
- *see also:* TRAVELERS AND TRAVELS TO EREẒ ISRAEL
PILGRIM FESTIVALS 13:519
- additional prayer 12:532
- Jeroboam 9:1373; 9:1553; 9:1555
- Jerusalem 9:1553
- laws in *Ḥagigah* 7:1116
- path purity 13:1409
- Passover 13:163
- Ptolemy II 14:730
- sacrifice 14:610
- Samaritans 14:741ff
- Shavuoth 14:1319
- Sukkot 15:495
- tanners 10:1537
- Temple 15:952
- *illus:*
- - pilgrims eating second tithe 11:653
- - pilgrims going up to Jerusalem 7:11
Pilica (tn., Pol.) 2:166; 11:442
PILICHOWSKI, LEOPOLD 13:520
- *illus:*
- - text
- - Achron, Joseph (sketch) 2:211
PILLAR 13:520
- *illus:*
- - Hezir, Tomb of the Sons of 15:1219
- - Jerusalem, Maḥaneh Yehudah find 15:965
- - Lancut synagogue *bimah* 15:607
- - Ostia synagogue 12:1508
- - *Shivviti* plaques 14:1420-1421
- - Wolpa synagogue 15:610
- - Zholkva synagogue 16:1014
Pillar of Absalom (tomb), *see* Yad Avshalom
PILLAR OF CLOUD AND PILLAR OF FIRE 13:523
- revelation 14:118
Pillitz, D. 15:659
Pillory 8:1303
PILPUL 13:524
- Augsburg *ḥillukim* 3:849
- Ḥayyim of Volozhin 16:769
- Kabbalah 10:490
- Lara, David 10:1429
- source of word 13:270
- Volozhin yeshivah 16:214
- *see also:* HOMILETIC LITERATURE
Pilpul al Zeman, Zemannim, Zemanneihem (bk.) 13:130
PILSEN (city, Cz.) 13:527
- Czechoslovakia 5:1200
- *illus:* text
PILSUDSKI, JÓZEF 13:528
Piltene (reg., city, Latv.) 5:1005
Pim (weight) 16:381; 16:386;
- *illus:*
- - dome-shaped units 16:377
Pimental, Aaron 12:848
Pimentel, Manuel 8:339
Pimetiela, Joseph 15:739
Pimienta, Abraham 15:792
Pimienta, Jose Dias 8:1396

PIMSLEUR, SALOMON **12:**702
Pina, Abigail de **13:**529; **14:**66
PINA, JACOB (Manuel) DE **13:**529
Pina, Paulo de **6:**320
PINANSKI, ABRAHAM **13:**529
Pinar del Río (prov., Cuba) **5:**1148
Pinch, Abraham **16:**536
Pinchasoff, Solomon Babajan **10:**437
Pincherle (fam.) **16:**114
Pincherle, Alberto, *see* MORAVIA, ALBERTO
Pincherle, Joseph **4:**172
Pincherle, Leone **9:**1129; **13:**815
PINCHERLE, MARC **12:**702
Pinchev (Pinchov; tn., Pol.), *see* PINCZOW
PINCHIK, PIERRE **7:**1549
Pinck, Bernard D. **13:**162
PINCUS, GREGORY GOODWIN **13:**529
Pincus, Jacob **15:**310
Pincus, Jules, *see* PASCIN, JULES
PINCUS, LOUIS ARIEH (Louis Abraham) **13:**530
- Jewish Agency **10:**33
- Twenty-seventh Zionist Congress **16:**1178
- Zionist Executive **16:**1103
PINCZOW (tn., Pol.) **13:**530
PINE (bot.) **13:**530
- Bethar *ḥuppah* **11:**1040
- flora of Israel **9:**221
- plant list **13:**623
- *illus:*
- - text
- - Aleppo pine **9:**236; **13:**623
Pine, Samson **7:**446; **12:**597
Pine, stone (bot.) **13:**623
Pineau, Christian **9:**389
Pine Brook (loc., N.J.) **12:**1030
PINEDA, JUAN DE **13:**532
- Baena, Juan Alfonso de **4:**79
- Toledo **15:**1206
Pinehas (name), *see also* Phinehas; Pinḥas
Pinehas ben Meshullam **5:**631
Pinel, Duarte, *see* USQUE, ABRAHAM
Pinel, Phillipe **13:**1337
PINELES, HIRSCH MENDEL BEN SOLOMON (Shalosh) **13:**532
Pineles, Naḥman **15:**817
PINELES, SAMUEL **13:**533
- Zionism **16:**1133ff
- *illus:*
- - F.Z.C. **16:**1165
Pineles, Shemuel Yeshayahu, *see* PENUELI, SHEMUEL YESHAYAHU
Pinelo, Antonio de León, *see* León Pinelo, Antonio
Pinelo, Diego León, *see* León Pinelo, Diego
Pinero, Arthur Wing **6:**783
Pines, Dan **12:**1057
Pines, Eliezer **7:**713
Pines, Heineman **12:**284
Pines, I.A. **5:**1149
Pines, Jehiel Michael, *see* PINES, YEHIEL MICHAEL
PINES, MEYER ISSER **13:**533
Pines, Ned L. **13:**1373
PINES, NOAH **13:**534
PINES, SHLOMO (Solomon) **13:**534
Pines, Shneur Zalman **10:**1221
PINES, YEḤIEL MICHAEL (Michal) **13:**535
- Bilu **9:**515
- travels **15:**1354
Ping Pong, *see* Table Tennis
Pinḥas (fam.) **3:**539
Pinḥas (name), *see also* Phinehas; Pinehas
Pinḥas al ha-Malbush **13:**468
Pinḥas ben Isaac (Yisḥak) Hakohen **14:**753,755,757
Pinḥas ben Yūsaf (Samar, h. pr.), *see* Phinehas ben Joseph
Pinḥas Rosh ha-Yeshivah (masor.) **11:**324; **16:**1416,1471
PINHEIRO, MOSES **13:**536
- Cardoza, Abraham Miguel **5:**164
- Shabbateanism **14:**1245
Pinheiros (fam.) **12:**1069
Pinhel, Duarte, *see* USQUE, ABRAHAM
Pinia, Ḥayim Solomon **9:**1589; **11:**918
PINKAS (record book) **13:**537
- archives **3:**377
- Councils of the Lands **5:**996
- legal activity **12:**123
- *illus:*
- - Altona, donations to Erez Israel **3:**379
- - Altona, *Pinkas ha-Takkanot* (1726) **5:**821
Arnswalde *Memorbuch, prayers* **7:**113
- - Berlin community minute book (1723), **4:**664
- - Bordeaux, *Registre des délibérations de la nation portugaise* **4:**1243
- - Buttenheim, register of community members (1768-70) **5:**822
- - Cracow, Yiddish statute book (1595) **5:**1031
- - Dornhan *Memorbuch* **3:**380
- - Dublin, *Takkanot u-Minhagim* (1839) **6:**248
- - Ferrara, regulations re taxes (1782) **6:**1233
- - Finale, *ḥevrat gemilut ḥasadim* minute and account book **5:**349
- - Hesse-Darmstadt, register of assessment and taxes (1723-40) **6:**1281
- - Insterburg, final entry (1941) **5:**825
- - Konice community, *ḥerem* **3:**930
- - Lima marriage register **3:**386
- - London marriage register **3:**386
- - London *bet din*, minute book (1830) **3:**880
- - New York, constitution of Shearith Israel congregation (1805) **5:**830
- - Poznan community register **3:**381
- - Venice region register of circumcisions **3:**383
- - Worms, register of financial transactions (1657-58) **6:**1280
Pinkas (journ.) **1:**newsp. list
PINKAS, DAVID ẒVI **13:**537
- Israel Declaration of Independence **5:**1452
Pinkas, Herman **11:**1201
Pinkas, Israel (indus.) **11:**586
Pinkas ha-Sheliḥut (emis. letter) **14:**1358
Pinkas Histadrut ha-Ovedim (journ.) **1:**newsp. list
Pinkas le-Inyenei ha-Pekidim (journ.), *see Shurot*
Pinkas-Schul (syn., Prague) **13:**966,969,974; **15:**604
- *illus:*
- - Holocaust memorial wall **13:**976
- - interior **15:**605
PINKEL, BENJAMIN **2:**323
- aeronautics **2:**322
Pinkerfeld, Anda, *see* AMIR, ANDA
Pinkerfeld, J. **9:**1536
Pinkus, Israel (poet) **8:**206
Pinkuss, Fritz **14:**851
Pinna, David de **11:**1110
PINNER, ADOLF **5:**386
Pinner, Albert **10:**1497
PINNER, EPHRAIM MOSES BEN ALEXANDER SUSSKIND **13:**537
- Talmud in German **15:**768
PINNER, FELIX **13:**538
PINNER, MORITZ **13:**538
Pinon (pr., Edom) **13:**1390
Pinon (loc., Isr.) **11:**1437
Pinso (isl., Cuba) **5:**1146
PINS, JACOB **3:**608
- *illus:*
- - "Bull" (wdct.) **3:**636
PINSK (city, Belor.) **13:**538
- *Contents:*
- - History **13:**538
- - Under Russian Rule **13:**541
- - In Independent Poland **13:**542
- - Holocaust and Postwar Periods **13:**543
- *illus:*
- - text
- - synagogue **15:**609
PINSKER, LEON (Judah Leib) **13:**545
- anti-Semitism **16:**1042ff
- chronological chart **8:**766-767
- Ḥibbat Zion **16:**1039ff
- Judaism **8:**751
- Kattowitz Conference **10:**819ff
- Levanda, Lev **11:**66-7
- medicine **11:**1206
- Ruelf, Isaac **14:**384
- Society for the Promotion of Culture among Russian Jews **15:**58ff
- *illus:*
- - Kattowitz Conference **10:**820
- - Odessa Committee convention **12:**1329
PINSKER, SIMḤAH **13:**548
- Wissenschaft **16:**579
- *illus:* text
Pinsker Sztyme (newsp., Belor.) **13:**543
PINSKI, DAVID **13:**549
- Hirschbein **8:**517; **16:**262
- Wandering Jew **16:**262
Pinski, Kalman **11:**492
PINSON, KOPPEL S. **13:**551
Pintadura, Culema **15:**739
PINTER, HAROLD (plwrt.) **13:**551
Pinthus, Kurt **7:**451
PINTO (fams.) **13:**552
Pinto (fam., U.S.) **12:**1025
Pinto, Aaron Adolf de **13:**554
Pinto, Abraham (r., Mor.) **13:**552
Pinto, Abraham (stlr., U.S.) **5:**898
Pinto, Abraham ben Reuben **13:**552
Pinto, Abraham de (jur.) **13:**554
Pinto, Daniel **2:**925; **14:**1228
Pinto, David **13:**94
PINTO, DE (fam.) **13:**554
- Rotterdam **14:**349
Pinto, Ḥayyim **6:**1382 **13:**552
PINTO, ISAAC (mer.) **13:**552
PINTO, ISAAC DE (philos.) **13:**552
- Amsterdam Jews **2:**898
- philosophy **13:**417
- Voltaire **16:**220
Pinto, Jacob (r.) **3:**1018; **4:**1544; **13:**552
Pinto, Jacob (stlr., U.S.) **5:**898
Pinto, Joseph **14:**1116
PINTO, JOSIAH BEN JOSEPH **13:**553
- *illus:*
- - *Kesef Nivḥar* (1605) **5:**1240
Pinto, Manuel Alvarez **8:**339
Pinto, Raphael **15:**1359
Pinto, Solomon (U.S.) **5:**898
Pinto, Solomon M. (Mor.) **15:**792
PINTO, VIVIAN DE SOLA **6:**784; **6:**790
Pinto Delgado, Gonçalo **14:**351
PINTO DELGADO, JOÃO (Mosseh) **13:**554
Pioche (vill. Nev.) **12:**1018
Pioneering (lab. ideal), *see Ḥalutziyyut*
Pioneers of the Popular War of Independence (Arab orgn.), see Sa'ikah, Al-
PIONEER WOMEN (orgn.) **13:**555
- U.S. Zionism **16:**1147
Pioneras (orgn., Mex.) **16:**1125
PIOTRKOW (Piotrkow-Trybunalski; tn., Pol.) **13:**555
- *illus:* text
PIOVE DI SACCO (tn., It.) **13:**557
- Colon, Joseph **5:**748
- typography **15:**1480
Pipano, David **4:**1485
Piperno, Ugo **15:**1057
PIPERNO BEER, SERGIO **13:**558
PIPES, RICHARD EDGAR **13:**558
"Pipe Smoker" (paint., M. Kisling) **10:**1072
Pipifax (period.) **5:**219; **13:**1031
Pipit (zool.) **9:**226
Piqua (city, O.) **12:**1344
Piracy **5:**154; **6:**1446; **14:**1413; **16:**1274
Pirandello, Luigi **5:**1428; **9:**1106; **14:**60
- *illus:*
- - Reinhardt's direction of play **14:**60
Pirani, Fred **12:**1130
Piratin, Phil **13:**812
Pir Bakran (site, Pers.) **13:**315
Pirbright, Baron, *see* Worms, Baron Henry de
Pires, Diogo (ps.-Mess.), *see* MOLCHO, SOLOMON
Pires, Diogo (poet), *see* PYRRHUS, DIDACUS
Pirez, Sancho **2:**469
Pirḥei Ḥavaẓẓelet (period.) **7:**1479
Pirḥei Ẓafon (period.)
- Fuenn **7:**213
- Haskalah **7:**1448
- Hebrew newspapers **12:**1049; **13:**1044
- Katzenellenbogen **10:**830
- statistics **1:**newsp. list
- *illus:*
- - title page (Vilna, 1841) **7:**1448
Pirkei Avot (trac.), *see* AVOT
Pirkei Bessarabyah (journ.) **1:**newsp. list
PIRKEI DE-RABBI ELIEZER (wk.) **13:**558
- Apocalypse **3:**181
- Apocrypha **3:**186
- calendric data **5:**49
- Eliezer ben Hyrcanus **6:**623
- Islam **3:**193
- Jewish literature **11:**321
- *meḥiẓah* **11:**1234
- midrash **11:**1507
- *Targum Sheni* **15:**813
- *illus:* text
Pirkei Eliyahu (wk.) **16:**1390
Pirkei Moshe **11:**778
Pirkei Rabbenu ha-Kadosh (wk.), *see* AGGADAT BERESHIT
PIRKOI BEN BABOI **13:**560
- geonic influence **7:**317
- Hebrew language **16:**1613
Pirlilo, Ize de, *see* Ize dil Pirlilo
Pirmansens (city, Ger.) **13:**22
Pirnitz (tn. Morav.), *see* Pyrnice
PIROGOV, NIKOLAI **13:**561
Pīr Omar Gudrun (mt.) **3:**290
Pirsumei ha-Iggud ha-Yisre'eli le-Ibbud Informaẓyah (journ.)

1: newsp. list
Piruz Shapur (tn., Babyl.) **4**:42
PIRYATIN (city, Ukr.) **13**:561
PISA (city, It.) **13**:561
- archives **3**:387
- banking **4**:169
- *see also:* TUSCANY
Pisa, Abraham ben Isaac da **13**:575
PISA, DA (fam.) **13**:563
- Anau family **2**:934
- Arezzo bankers **3**:408
Pisa, Daniel D. C. **13**:564
Pisa, Isaac da **13**:563
Pisa, Isaac di Manuele Da, *see* Rimini, Isaac di Manuele Da
Pisa, Samuel da (Simone; 15th cent.) **6**:1301; **13**:563
Pisa, Samuel da (Simone; 16th cent.) **13**:564
Pisa, Vitale da (Jehiel) **11**:733; **13**:563
Pisa, Vitale da (Jehiel ben Isaac) **2**:104, 645; **6**:1360; **13**:563
Pisa, Vitale da (Jehiel Nissim) **13**:564
Pisa *Maḥzor* (illum. ms.) **11**:733
Pisanovich, Israel, *see* Fisanovich, Israel
Piscator, Erwin **4**:703; **14**:1584
Piscator J., **8**:51
Piscator Bible **4**:873
Pisces (Zodiac sign) **16**:1191
- *illus:* **2**:251
Pişculescu, Grigore, *see* GALACTION, GALA
PISEMSKI, ALEXEY **14**:508
PISGAH (mt., Transj.) **13**:564
- *see also:* NEBO
Pi Shenayim (wk.) **2**:492
Pishon (riv.) **13**:78
Pisidia (reg., As. M.) **3**:747
Pisiris (k., Syr.) **5**:161
PISK, PAUL AMADEUS **12**:702
Piskei Ḥallah (wk.) **2**:308
Piskei ha-Rosh (wk.) **5**:643; **11**:334
Pisko, Oskar **10**:1494
Pisqa'ot (Torah div.) **16**:1407
PISSARRO, CAMILLE **13**:564
- *illus:*
- - "Place du Théâtre Français . . ." (paint.) **3**:549
Pissaro, Felix **13**:565
Pissaro, Georges **13**:565
Pissaro, Lucien **13**:565; **15**:1478
Pissaro, Ludovik-Rudolphe **13**:565
Pissaro, Paul-Emile **13**:565
Pissuk (Bib., textual dv.) **16**:1410ff
PISTACHIO (bot.) **13**:566
- fruit **6**:1416
- graft result **12**:171
- heredity **4**:1023
- Israel **9**:788
- plant list **13**:623
- terebinth **15**:1016
Pister, Hermann **4**:1445
Pistiner, J. **10**:90
Pistis Sophia (wk.) **10**:500; **10**:503; **10**:531
Pistoia (prov., It.) **15**:1467
PISTORIUS (de Nida), JOHANNES **13**:566
- Christian Hebraists **8**:51
Pistrak, Moses M. **6**:464
Pistus (1st cent. C.E. sol.) **10**:163
Pit (leg. conc.), *see Bor*
Pita, Jan **2**:159
Pitdah (precious stone) **13**:1009
Pite, Sam **15**:303
Pitha (*Pit;* vocalization sign), *see Miftaḥ Puma*
Pithana (Hittire k.) **8**:787
Pithei Teshuvah (wk.) **6**:549
Pithiviers (concen. camp, Fr.) **7**:35
PITHOM (city, Egy.) **13**:566
- Bible history **8**:575
- Goshen **7**:816
- *illus:* **13**:1544
- *see also:* RAMSES
Pitigliano (tn., It.) **9**:1142; **13**:1397; **15**:1468
- *illus:*
- - synagogue **15**:1469
PITIGRILLI (au.) **13**:567
- Italian literature **9**:1112
Pitka'ot (shards) **11**:512
Pitkowsky, I. **12**:1129
Pitler, Jacob A. **15**:301
Pitler, Jake **15**:301
Pitron Sefer ha-Emunah (wk.) **14**:548
Pitron Shivim Millim (wk.) **14**:552
Pitshe Odesser (Ḥazzan), *see* ABRASS, OSIAS
Pitt, Thomas **2**:63
PITTSBURGH (city, U.S.) **13**:568
- *illus:* text
PITTSBURGH PLATFORM (Ref. Jud.) **13**:570
- chronological chart **8**:766-767
- Messiah **11**:1415
- Oral Law **12**:1443
- Reform Judaism **14**:26
- resurrection **14**:102
- synods **13**:1461
Pittsfield (city, Mass.) **11**:1113
PITTUM HA-KETORET (litur.) **13**:572
- incense offering **8**:1315
Pity, *see* CHARITY; COMPASSION; MERCY
Piura (city, Peru) **13**:324
Pius II (pope) **13**:856
Pius IV **13**:857
- medicine **11**:1194
- universities **15**:1675
Pius V **13**:857
- exclusion of Jews **14**:249
- papal bull **4**:1496
- Spoleto **15**:290
- Tuscany Jews **15**:1467
Pius VI **13**:859
- chronological chart **8**:766-767
- *illus:*
- - edict re baptism of children (1776) **3**:213
Pius VII **13**:859
Pius VIII **5**:1597; **13**:859
Pius IX **13**:860
- Alatiri, Samuel **2**:515
- homage ceremony **5**:191
- Mortara Case **12**:354
PIUS X **13**:572
- attitude toward Jews **13**:860
- Herzl, Theodor **16**:1073; **16**:74
PIUS XI **13**:572
- attitude toward Jews **13**:860
- Nazism **8**:910
PIUS XII **13**:573
- attitude toward Jews **3**:137; **13**:860
- Hochhuth **8**:798
- Holocaust **8**:911
- Israel **16**:77
Pivnick, Edwin J. **15**:1264
PIYYUT (litur.) **13**:573
- *Contents:*
- - History **13**:574
- - *Paytanim* **13**:576
- - Types of *Piyyut* **13**:598
- - Language and Style **13**:601
- - Rhyme and Meter **13**:601
- - Signatures **13**:602
- - Collections **13**:602
- General
- - acrostics **2**:230
- - *gematriot* **7**:371
- - Hebrew language **16**:1362, 1609
- - *sefirah* **12**:1389
- - vowel signs **16**:1438
- - Zodiac signs **16**:1192
- Literature **11**:326ff
- - *aggadah* **2**:360
- - Bonfils, Joseph **4**:1208
- - Cairo *genizah* **16**:1338
- - Gabirol, Solomon ibn **7**:238
- - Haduta **7**:1056
- - Judah Halevi **10**:359
- - Kallir, Eleazar **10**:713
- - liturgical hymns **12**:588
- - liturgy **11**:394ff
- - Maimonides **11**:763
- - prayer books **13**:985ff
- - prosody **13**:1199, 1200ff
- - Saadiah Gaon **14**:553; **16**:1615
- - Yannai **16**:712
- - Josiphiah the proselyte **13**:1188
- Themes
- - *Akedah* **2**:481
- - angels **2**:971
- - Crusader massacres **5**:1142
- - Day of Atonement **5**:1379
- - Jerusalem **9**:1561ff
- - *teki'ata* **15**:914
- Types
- - *Amidah* **2**:840
- - *azharot* **3**:1007
- - *bakkashah* **4**:116
- - evening service **11**:637
- - *kerovah* **10**:920
- - *kinah* **10**:1009
- - *maqāma* **11**:937ff
- - *mishmarot* **12**:92
- - *pizmon* **13**:602
- - *seliḥot* **14**:1133
- - *yoẓerot* **16**:865
- Traditions
- - cantor's permission **14**:83
- - *ḥazzan* **7**:1542
- - Iraqi **8**:1452
- - Judeo-Persian **2**:327
- - Karaite **10**:784
- - Samaritan **14**:748
- - Sephardi **14**:1170
- Commentators on
- - Ephraim of Bonn **6**:813
- - Kara, Joseph **10**:760
- - Menahem ben Helbo **11**:1305
- *illus:*
- - *Adon Ḥasdekha* **10**:362
- - *Adon Imnani* **11**:*fcg.* 811
- - *Ahallela* **2**:231
- - *Akhtir Dar Tehillah* **4**:394
- - *Az Rov Nissim* **3**:1014
- - Cavaillon prayer book, special Purim **7**:15
- - *Dayyeinu* **5**:*fcg.* 1387, 1391; **7**:*fcg.* 875, 1083, *fcg.* 1451 **8**:1274; **10**:211
- - *Eitan Hikkir Emunatekha* **2**:118
- - *El Mitnasse...* **11**:*fcg.* 619
- - Ḥannukah **8**:671, *fcg.* 1335
- - *Hoshana* **8**:1029, 1327
- - *Itti mi-Levanon Kallah* **6**:348
- - Kallir, Eleazar (ms.) **2**:715
- - *Leil Shimmurim* **11**:*fcg.* 875
- - *Lekhah Dodi* **10**:655; **11**:5
- - *Melekh Azur Gevurah* **11**:734
- - *Mi Al Har Ḥorev* **12**:1307
- - *Mo'ohav ve-Yaḥid le-Immo* **2**:118
- - *Nifla'im Ma'asekha* **8**:1284
- - *Om Asher Bakh Devukah* **14**:*fcg.* 11
- - *Or ve-Yesha* **11**:*fcg.* 747
- - *Parashat Zakhor* **11**:397
- - *reshut for Avodah* **2**:733
- - *Shabbat ha-Gadol* **14**:1217
- - Shavuot **14**:1320
- - twelfth century manuscript **2**:740
- *mus. notations:*
- - *Addir bi-Melukhah* **2**:256
- - *Addir Hu* **2**:257
- - *Anim Zemirot* **3**:22
- - *Avo el Mizbaḥ Elohim* **2**:609
- - Karaite Hymns **10**:783-784
- - *Lekhah Dodi* **11**:5-8
- - *Maoz Ẓur* **11**:911
- - *Mi Al Har Ḥorev* **12**:1307
- - *Selihah* **14**:1134
- *see also:* PARODY, HEBREW; POETRY; *and under individual piyyutim*
P.I.Z., *see* Portuguese Jewish Hospital, Amsterdam
Piza, David **12**:285
PIZMON (litur. poem) **13**:602
- *see also:* PIYYUT
Piznai (demon) **11**:246
Pizzighettone, David
- Bomberg, David **4**:1196
- Finzi-Norsa controversy **6**:1302
- Jacob ben Hayyim **9**:1218
P.K.P., *see* Palestine Communist Party
Place (philos. term), *see* SPACE AND PLACE
Place, Victor **16**:1507
"Place du Théâtre Français, Soleil d'Après-midi en Hiver" (paint., C. Pissarro) **3**:549
Plácel, Václáv **8**:1136
Placerville (city, Calif.) **5**:56
Placus, Andreas **8**:51
PLACZEK, ABRAHAM **13**:603
Placzek, Baruch Jacob **4**:1384; **13**:604
Plague, *see* Diseases and remedies
PLAGUES OF EGYPT **13**:604
- *Contents:*
- - Accounts **13**:604
- - Function **13**:605
- - Structure of the Narrative **13**:606
- - Hardening Pharaoh's Heart **13**:608
- - Interpretations of the Plagues **13**:608
- - The Variant Versions **13**:608
- - Midrashic Embellishment **13**:611
- Aaron **2**:4
- Arts **12**:404ff
- Exodus, Book of **6**:1053ff
- first-born **6**:1308; **13**:362
- frogs **7**:206
- locust **11**:422
- Moses **12**:375
- *Solomon, Wisdom of* **15**:119
- *illus:*
- - text
- - Blood **7**:205
- - Death of the Firstborn **2**:952; **6**:1045; **11**:1
- - Flies **6**:1369
- - Frogs **7**:205
- - *Kaufmann Haggadah* **8**:1276
- - Locusts **11**:423
Plahm, Baer **10**:1239
Plainfield (city, N. J.) **15**:1533
Plain of Exaloth (Isr.) **10**:103
Plain of the Bean (Isr.), *see* JEZREEL, VALLEY OF
Plamadon Libel Case (Can.) **2**:169
Planck, Max **2**:128; **6**:536
Planek, Benno, *see* Placzek, Baruch Jacob
Planet of Birth **3**:790
PLANE TREE (bot.) **13**:613
- flora of Israel **9**:225
- plant list **13**:623
PLANNING IN ISRAEL **9**:559
- Adullam Region **2**:312
- Jerusalem **9**:1517
- *illus:*
- - text
- - Adullam region **9**:586
PLANTAVIT DE LA PAUSE, JEAN **13**:613
- Christian Hebraists **8**:51
PLANTIN, CHRISTOPHE **13**:613
- Le Bé, Guillaume **10**:1547
- Polyglot Bible **3**:434; **10**:1563; **11**:684
- Postel **13**:933
- printing **13**:1099; **15**:1482
Plantin-Moretus Museum (print. house) **13**:614
PLANTS **13**:614
Contents:
- - In the Bible **13**:614

-- In Talmudic Literature **13:**614
-- Table **13:**615f
- economic importance **16:**1273
- mixed species **12:**170ff
- *see also* Flora and Fauna; FLORA AND FAUNA IN ISRAEL; and *under individual plants*
Plaović, Rasa **16:**886
Plaquemine (tn., Louis.) **11:**520
PLASENCIA (city, Sp.) **13:**627
Plaskov, Hirsh **11:**1557; **14:**479
PLASZOW (concen. camp, Pol.) **13:**627
- Poland **13:**766
- Rymanow **14:**534
- Zmigrod Nowy **16:**1189
Platanus orientalis (bot.), see PLANE TREE
Platau, Edward **11:**1204
Platea Judaeorum, see JEWISH QUARTER
Platen, August Graf von **8:**272
Plates, Seder **5:**661 **13:**172
Platho, Julius **4:**656
Platkes, Elijah, *see* Riveles, Elijah
PLATO AND PLATONISM **13:**628
- *androgynos* **2:**949
- body-soul dichotomy **11:**843
- Christian Kabbalah **10:**643
- commandment reasons **5:**784ff
- Cherniss **5:**392
- dualism **6:**242
- Hellenistic literature **8:**304
- Hellenistic period **8:**293
- imitation of God **8:**1292
- influence of Bible **3:**444
- influence of Judaism **3:**189
- influence on rabbis **8:**298
- Jewish Aristotelianism **13:**430
- logos **11:**462
- Lurianic cosmogony **10:**591
- Maimonides **11:**769
- Neoplatonism **12:**959
- Philo **13:**426ff; **14:**122
- *Sefirot* doctrine **10:**566
- soul **15:**172
Plato of Tivoli (Tiburtinus) **8:**51
Platt, Samuel **12:**1017
Plattsburg (city, N.Y.) **12:**1126
Plauen (city, Ger.) **14:**923
PLAUT, HEZEKIAH FEIVEL **13:**630
- Katzburg, David **10:**827
PLAUT, HUGO CARL **13:**630
Plaut, Jacob **12:**1215
Plaut, Max **7:**1228
Plaut, Walter H. **13:**631
PLAUT, W. GUNTHER **13:**631
- historiography **8:**568
- Minnesota **12:**38
Plavnik, Samuil Yefimovich, *see* BYADULYA-YASAKAR, ZMITROK
"Player" (sculp., E. Glicenstein) **7:**618
PLEAS (leg.) **13:**631
- *Contents:*
-- Nature of Pleas **13:**631
-- The Plaintiff **13:**631
-- The Defendant **13:**632
-- Repayment **13:**632
-- Insolvency **13:**633
-- Counterclaim **13:**633
-- Identical Pleas **13:**633
-- Pleas of Law **13:**634
-- Weight of Pleas **13:**534
-- Rejection of Pleas **13:**635
-- Suggestion of Pleas **13:**636
- claims proof **14:**1196
- debtors **11:**415ff
- denial of obligation **12:**1314
- limitation of actions **11:**251
- methods of submitting **13:**955ff
- oath **12:**1298
- orphan **12:**1479
- surety **15:**525ff
- tax appeal **15:**863
Pleasure, *see* JOY
PLEDGE **13:**636
- *Contents:*
-- The Concept **13:**636
-- After Establishment of the Debt **13:**637
-- When the Debt is Established **13:**639
-- Modes of Establishing a Pledge **13:**639
-- Ownership and Responsibility **13:**640
-- Use of the Pledge **13:**640
-- Recovery of Payment **13:**640
-- Usufruct **13:**641
-- In the State of Israel **13:**643
- antichresis **3:**59
- debt repayment **6:**1011
- firstborn inheritance **6:**1312
- maintenance claim validity **11:**252
- ownership **12:**1533
- tax **15:**865
- transfer of **3:**768
- usury **16:**29
- waiver of debt **11:**1234
- *illus:*
-- impounding of, written complaint (16th cent. B.C.E. ostracon) **3:**317
- *see also:* LIEN
PLEHVE, VYACHESLAV KONSTANTINOVICH VON **13:**644
- Herzl **8:**418; **16:**1072; **16:**1137
Pleistocene Age **9:**225
PLESSNER, MARTIN (Meir) **13:**644
Plessner, Solomon **8:**956; **6:**470; **12:**956
PLETTEN (meal tickets) **13:**645
PLEVEN (Plevna; city, Bul.) **13:**645
Plieksnas, Jānis, *see* Rainis, J.
Plew (concen. camp) **16:**1218
PLINY THE ELDER **13:**645
- agriculture **2:**394
- anti-Jewish accusations **3:**190
- Apion **3:**178
- balsam **16:**1273
- Essenes **13:**1430
- papyrus writing material **16:**658
- Sambatyon **14:**763
PLISETSKAYA, MAYA **13:**646
Plissa (vill., Rus.) **7:**624
PLOCK (city, Pol.) **13:**647
- *illus:* text
PLOESTI (city, Rum.) **13:**649
Płomienie (period.) **16:**348
PLONSK (tn. Pol.) **13:**650
- *illus:* text
Plotina (emp., Parthia) **15:**1312
Plotinus (philos.) **12:**958ff
Plotkin, Gershon **5:**74
Plotkin, Michael **11:**1558; **14:**479
- *illus:*
-- portrait **11:**1556
Plotnicka, Frumka **4:**374
Plotnicki, Shamai **14:**1513
Plotsk (city, Pol.), *see* PLOCK
PLOTZKI, MEIR DAN OF OSTROVA **13:**652
Plough, Abe **11:**1302
PLOVDIV (city, Bul.) **13:**652
- *illus:* text
Plover, Golden (zool.) **6:**30
Plowing **2:**374f; **12:**171
"Plowing the Fields at Tel Yosef in the Jezreel Valley" (phot., S. J. Schweig) **13:**485
Pludermacher, Shalom **15:**427
PLUM (bot.) **13:**653
Plumer, Lord Herbert Onslow **8:**470; **9:**340; **9:**601
- *illus:*
-- Straus Health Center cornerstone ceremony **15:**429
Plumer, Joseph **11:**498
Plummer, Beatrice **13:**812
Plum Street Temple (O.) **15:**620
PLUNGE (city, Lith.) **13:**653
- *illus:*
-- text
-- Jewish fire brigade **11:**379
PLUNGIAN (Plungiansky), MORDECAI **13:**654
Plungyany (city, Lith.), *see* PLUNGE
Pluralism, cultural, *see* Cultural pluralism
PLUTARCH **13:**654
- ass worship **3:**784
- Greek literature **7:**890
Plutzik, Hyam **15:**1578
Plutus (journ.) **4:**676
PLYMOUTH (city, Eng.) **13:**654
- *illus:*
-- congregation seal **14:**1075
Plymouth (tn., Mass.) **11:**1113
Plymouth Brethren (sect., Eng.) **16:**1153
Plyukfelder, Rudolf **12:**1377
Plzen (city, Cz.) *see* PILSEN
Pnei Moshe (wk.) **11:**963
Pniower, Otto **7:**451
Pnompenh (city, Cambodia) **9:**444
PO'ALEI AGUDAT ISRAEL (rel. party, Isr.) **13:**655
- Agudat Israel **2:**421ff
- America **13:**656
- Ḥafez Ḥayyim **7:**1059
- health insurance **9:**986
- Israel religious life **9:**895ff
- Kahana, Kalman **10:**681
Poalei Ẓedek (J. lab. union, Rus.) **10:**1281
- Nesvizh **12:**967
PO'ALEI ZION (mvmt.) **13:**656
- *Contents:*
-- History **13:**656
-- In Russia **13:**656
-- In the Austro-Hungarian Empire **13:**657
-- In the United States **13:**658
-- In Ereẓ Israel **13:**659
-- The World Union **13:**660
-- During World War I **13:**660
-- Postwar Developments **13:**661
- Beginnings and Development
-- Aḥdut ha-Avodah **2:**456
-- Argentina **3:**414
-- Gross, Nathan **7:**935
-- history chart **8:**766-767
-- Independent Jewish Workers' Party **8:**1348
-- Jewish Socialist Workers' Party **10:**90
-- Mapai **11:**912
-- Poland **13:**750; **16:**1130; **16:**1131
-- self-defense **14:**1125
-- Shazar, Shneur Zalman **14:**1323
-- U.S.founding convention **4:**146
-- U.S. Zionism **16:**1141
-- Warsaw **16:**338
-- Zionism **16:**639
-- Zionist Socialist Workers' Party **16:**1179
-- Zuckerman, Baruch **16:**1228
- Ideology
-- aims of Israel party **9:**657ff
-- Bernstein, Eduard **4:**684
-- Bolsheviks **14:**463
-- Jewish labor problem **9:**329
-- relations with Communists **5:**799ff
-- socialism **15:**26,44ff
-- socialist-Zionist philosophy **9:**519ff
-- Syrkin, Nachman **15:**652ff
-- Vozrozhdeniye **16:**229ff
-- Yevsektsiya **16:**780
-- Židovská Strana **16:**1017
-- Zionism **16:**1099ff
- *illus:*
-- group of members **4:**581
-- Plonsk group **4:**505
POBEDONOSTSEV, KONSTANTIN PETROVICH **13:**664
POBEZOVICE NA SUMAVE (vill., Bohem.) **13:**665
- Klatovy **10:**1087
Pobian, Moses ben Eliezer, *see* Phobian, Moses ben Eliezer
Pocatello (city, Ida.) **8:**1223
POCHEP (city, Rus.) **13:**665
POCOCKE, EDWARD **13:**665
- Bible scholarship **4:**976
Pococke, Edward (jr.) **13:**666
- Hebraic studies **8:**51; **8:**18; **13:**666
Pococke, Thomas **13:**666
Podēbrady (tn., Cz.) **5:**1200
PODGAITSY (city, Ukr.) **13:**666
- Shabbateanism **14:**1251
Podhajce (tn., Podolia), *see* Podgaitsy
Podgorny, Nikolai **14:**1638
Podheizer, Moses David **14:**1251
PODHORETZ, NORMAN **13:**667
Podivi (13/14 cent., city found.) **5:**920
PODKAMEN (tn., Ukr.) **13:**667
Podol (suburb, Kiev) **10:**993
PODOLIA (reg., Ukr.) **13:**667
- antinomianism **14:**1248
- Balta **4:**144
- Ḥasidism **7:**1391ff
Podoloff, Maurice **15:**304
Podolski, Ignac **13:**775
Podolyer, Menakhem, *see* OSHEROWITCH, MENDL
PODVOLOCHISK (Podwloczyska; tn., Ukr.) **13:**670
Poel, Jacob, *see* Bonet, Jacob
Poema de Yocef (wk.) **10:**1349
Poema de Yucuf (wk.) **10:**1349
Poemenia (Rom. philan.) **9:**1407
Poesing (tn., Slov.), *see* PEZINOK
Poeta, Juan, of Valladolid, *see* JUAN DE VALLADOLID
POETRY **13:**670
- *Contents:*
-- Biblical Poetry **13:**671
--- The Hebrew Language and Poetry **13:**671
--- History of Interpretation **13:**671
--- Parallelismus Membrorum **13:**672
--- Strophe **13:**675
--- Meter **13:**676
--- Genre **13:**677
--- Style **13:**679
--- Medieval Hebrew Secular Poetry **13:**681
--- Spain and Provence **13:**681
--- Italy **13:**690
--- France and Germany **13:**692
--- England **13:**692
- Ancient
-- biblical songs **12:**565
-- Book of Jashar **4:**1217
-- David **5:**1327
-- Samuel, Book of **14:**790
-- Song of Songs **15:**144
- Medieval
-- allegory **2:**644
-- Cairo *genizah* **16:**1337ff
-- Dunash ben Labrat **6:**271
-- Gabirol, Solomon ibn **7:**245
-- Joseph, Saul Abdallah **10:**222
-- Judah Halevi **10:**358
-- Judeo-Arabic **10:**409
-- *piyyut* **13:**573
-- Samuel ha-Nagid **14:**816
-- Spain **15:**242
- Modern

- - Carmi, T. 5:188
- - Iraq 8:1452
- - Lebensohn, Micah Joseph 10:1549
- - Loewisohn, Solomon 11:455
- - Luzzatto, Moses Ḥayyim 11:603
- - poetry for children 5:436; 5:437
- - Schirmann's studies 14:969
- - Yemen 14:969,1215
- - Yiddish literature 11:359ff; 16:803; 16:804; 16:816ff
- Miscellaneous
- - Hebrew language 16:1116
- - Jewish literature 11:325ff
- - Jews of Rome 14:245
- - Kabbalah 10:549
- - music manuscripts 12:557
- *see also:* CRITICISM, HEBREW LITERARY; HEBREW LITERATURE, MODERN; PROSODY, HEBREW
Pofcher, Elias 16:634
Poggetti, Jacob ben Mordecai 16:121
Poggibonsi, Niccolo da 15:1355
Poggibonzi, Solomon da 11:60
POGREBISHCHENSKI (Pogrebishche; tn., Ukr. S.S.R.) 13:694
- Haidamacks 7:1132
- *illus:* text
POGROMS 13:694
- *Contents:*
- - Introduction 13:694
- - In the 1880s 13:695
- - 1903 to 1906 13:697
- - 1917 to 1921 13:698
- Incidence
- - Austria, Nazi rule period 3:898ff
- - Belaya Tserkov 4:413
- - Black Death 4:1064ff
- - "Black Hundreds" 4:399ff; 15:1538
- - Chmielnicki, Bogdan 5:481
- - *Gezerot tatnav* (1096) 7:461
- - Hep! Hep! 8:330
- - Kishinev 10:1064ff
- - Odessa 12:1323
- - Pale of Settlement 13:27
- - Paris 13:106
- - Przytyk 13:1301
- - Rome 14:244ff
- - Russia 5:1535; 8:735ff; 14:444 16:1520
- - "White Terror, The" 8:1095
- - *Wiener Gesera* 16:502ff
- Miscellaneous
- - Bilu reaction 4:998
- - history chart 8:766-767
- - Jewish literature 6:1254
- - Russian Civil Rights Society 15:56
- - self-defense 14:1123ff
- - Sixth Zionist Congress 16:1168
- - socialism, Jewish 15:44ff
- - Tcherikower, E., on 15:876
- *illus:*
- - Armleder massacres (map) 3:483
- - Asch, Sholem, report (1919) 3:685
- - Bialystok community notice (1906) 4:810
- - Chmielnicki, Bogdan (statue) 5:481
- - "Cossacks are Coming" (drg., A. Pann) 8:736
- - Duermenach riots, 1848 2:753
- - Frankfort 6:1248; 7:85,472
- - Hep! Hep! riots, 1819 (map) 8:331
- - Kishinev, Lilien's dedication page 10:1065
- - Kishinev, some of the victims 8:735; 10:1066
- - Kishinev, victims awaiting burial 10:1067
- - Lvov, Great Synagogue 11:611
- - Minsk, self-defense convention 14:448
- - Proskurov, victims 14:449
- - Yekaterinoslav, victims 14:445
- *see also:* EXPULSIONS
Pohl, Baruch, *see* POLLINI, BERNHARD
Pohl, Max 15:1056
POHL, OSWALD 13:701
Pohorbishch (tn., Ukr.), *see* POGREBISHCHENSKI
POHORELICE (Pohrlitz; vill., Cz.) 13:701
Pohorille, Marcus 10:1382
Pohoryles, Karol 15:818
Pohovitzer, Judah Leib 10:554
Pohrlitz (vill., Cz.), *see* POHORELICE
Pointer (cerem. object), *see* YAD
Point of View (journ.) 10:66
Point Pleasant (boro., N.J.) 12:1030
POISON 13:702
- *illus:*
- - Lopez, Roderigo, plot to poison Queen Elizabeth 11:489
POITIERS (city, Fr.) 13:704
POITOU (reg., Fr.) 13:704
- Jewish population 7:14
POKI, JUDAH BEN ELIEZER CHELEBI 13:705
Pol (bot.), *see* BEANS
Pola (loc., It.) 9:1118
POLACCO, VITTORIO 13:705
- universities 15:1679
POLÁČEK, KAREL 13:705
- press 13:1026
Polacheck, S. H. 12:1119
POLACHEK, SENDER 7:1550
POLACHEK, SOLOMON 13:705
POLACHEK, VICTOR HENRY 10:315
Polack, Elisabeth 6:911
Polack, Isaac 6:220
POLACK, JOEL SAMUEL 13:706
- *illus:* text
Polack, Solomon 13:706
POLAK (fam.) 13:707
Polak, Arthur 5:311
Polak, A. S. 4:1219
Polak, Carel H. F. 13:707
POLAK, GABRIEL ISAAC 13:707
- Amsterdam, Tongeleth Society 2:900
Polak, Grigori 4:119
POLAK, HENRI 13:707
POLAK, JACOB EDUARD 13:708
- *illus:* text
Polak, Jacques A. 13:707
Polak, Joseph 11:48
POLAK, LEONARD 13:708
Polak, Moritz 13:707
Polak, M. S. 13:707
Polak, Michael 4:119
Polak, Nico J. 13:707
Polak, Saveli (Shevaḥ) 4:119
Polakevich, Mattityahu Moshe, *see* SHOHAM, MATTITYAHU MOSHE
Polanco, Alfonso de 10:8
POLAND 13:709
- *Contents:*
- - Early Settlements 13:709
- - Jewish Legal Status 13:712
- - Economic Activity 11:863
- - Cultural and Social Life 13:718
- - 1569-1648: Ukraine Colonization 13:723
- - Internal Jewish Life 13:726 From Chmielnicki to the First Partition 13:730
- - After Partition 13:732
- - Independent Poland 13:738
- - Holocaust Period 13:752
- - - Reichsgau Wartheland 13:754
- - - Reichsgau Danzig-Westpreussen 13:756
- - - Regierungsbezirk Zichenau 13:756
- - - Regierungsbezirk Kattowitz 13:756
- - - General Gouvernement 13:763
- - - Bezirk Bialystok 13:768
- - - Generalbezirk Litauen und Weissrussland 13:770
- - - Generalbezirk Wolhynien-Podolien 13:771
- - - Demography 13:771
- - - Jewish Resistance 13:771
- - - Jewish-Polish Relations During the War 13:776
- - - Rescue of Jewish Children 13:777
- - After World War II 13:778
- - - Cultural, Religious and Economic Life 13:779
- - - The Flight from Poland 13:780
- - - Anti-Jewish Excesses 13:780
- - - The Soviet Example 13:783
- - - 1956-1967 13:784
- - - Final Liquidation 13:785
- - Relations with Israel 13:785
- - - The Change of 1950 13:786
- - - Improved Relations in 1956 13:786
- - The Six-Day War 13:787
- - - Emigration to Israel 13:787
- - - Trade Relations 13:788
- General
- - crime among Jews 5:1094ff
- - demography 5:1499
- - divorce statistics 6:135
- - dress 6:220
- - emigration 16:1527
- - migration to Ereẓ Israel 9:538; 9:546
- - population
- - Prussia 13:1290
- - relations with Israel 9:428
- - South Africa 15:186
- - Youth Aliyah 16:862
- Communal Life 5:820; 5:826
- - autonomy 3:924
- - autonomy, judicial 3:930
- - finances, autonomous 6:1281
- - hospitals 8:1034
- - Joint Distribution Committee 2:828; 2:829ff
- - *shtetl* 14:1466
- - *takkanot ha-kahal* 15:736
- Cultural Life 8:687
- - Alliance Israélite Universelle 2:650
- - education 6:423ff
- - Hebrew language 16:1636
- - Hebrew mss. 11:907
- - Hebrew newspapers 12:1045ff
- - Jewish literature 11:333
- - museums 12:539
- - press 13:1042
- - Prohovnik, Abraham, legend 13:1119
- - theater 15:1071
- - universities 15:1676ff 16:1282
- - Yiddish education 6:434
- - Yiddish literature 16:818
- Religious Life
- - Frankists 7:55
- - Ḥasidism 7:1391ff
- - homiletic literature 8:955
- - Orthodoxy 12:1488
- - rabbinical office 13:1447
- - rabbinical seminaries 13:1465
- - Shabbateanism 14:1235; 14:1243
- - synagogues 1:syn. list; 15:600; 15:604
- - *takkanot* 15:725
- - Torah study ideal 10:393
- - *yeshivot* 16:765ff
- Economic Life and Employment 8:692ff; 16:1303
- - agriculture 2:403ff
- - *arenda* 3:402
- - banking 4:168
- - cooperatives 5:942
- - gold- and silversmiths 7:742
- - grain trade 2:405
- - guilds 7:972ff
- - Hebrew on coins 16:1282
- - ICA 10:45; 11:877
- - law 10:1491
- - livestock trade 11:410
- - markets and fairs 11:1001ff
- - medicine 11:1204
- - mining 11:1439
- - mintmasters and moneyers in 12:61
- - ORT 12:1484ff
- - peddling 13:206
- - publishing 13:1369
- - salt trade 14:712
- - secondhand trade 14:1086
- - sugar trade 15:488
- - tailoring 15:705
- - textiles 15:1039ff
- - trade and commerce 15:1299ff
- - wine and liquor trade 16:542ff
- Political Life
- - Agudat Israel in Sejm 2:423
- - Berman, Jakob 4:666
- - Bund 4:1497ff
- - communism 5:803
- - Gruenbaum, Yiẓḥak 7:943
- - Ha-No'ar ha-Ivri—Akiba 7:1275
- - Jewish participation 13:817ff
- - Jewish socialism 15:29ff; 15:39; 15:49
- - minority bloc 12:41
- - Mizrachi 12:176
- - P.P.S. party 13:951
- - Revisionism 14:131
- - Sejm 14:1117
- - student movements 15:448ff
- - Zionism 16:1129
- - Zionist socialists 16:1180
- Status of Jews
- - aid to Haganah 7:1069
- - anti-Semitism 3:159
- - Butrymowicz, Mateusz 4:1539
- - censorship of literature 5:279
- - court Jews 5:1007ff
- - discrimination 6:68
- - emancipation 6:711ff
- - Endecja 6:735
- - Great Poland 7:865
- - Korobka 10:1211
- - military service 11:1563
- - minority rights 12:44ff
- - *numerus clausus* 12:1266ff
- - Pale of Settlement 13:25
- - partitions 8:715
- - refuge for European Jews 3:107
- - Ugoda 15:1508
- Nazi Period
- - Church attitudes 8:914
- - collaboration in extermination 8:768
- - Frank, Hans Michael 7:54
- - Gestapo 7:529
- - Heydrich, Reinhard 8:448
- - Holocaust 8:840; 8:842ff
- - Ozon 12:1540
- - partisans 13:140ff
- - Piotrkow ghetto 13:557
- - Samuel Commission 14:815
- - Sauckel, Fritz 14:909
- - Treblinka 15:1367
- - War Crimes Trials 16:289ff
- - Warsaw Ghetto 8:879; 8:892ff
- *illus:*
- - text
- - anti-Semitic parties, 1881-1911 (table) 3:81
- - Barzilai, Israel, ambassador 9:425
- - children's dresses, 19th cent.

6: *fcg* 238
- - coins with Hebrew inscriptions 12:61
- - Council of the Four Lands (map) 5:997
- - Cracow, agreement re commercial rights (1485) 5:1029
- - Ḥanukkah lamps 7:1298,1305,1311,1313
- - ḥasidic couple 6: *fcg.* 238
- - history chart 8:766-767
- - Jewish badge decreed by the Nazis 4:72
- - Jewish merchants in Cracow marketplace 5:1039
- - Jewish Protest Committee Against Pogroms, announcement 13:695
- - Lublin, a street 11:541
- - Majdanek death camp stamp 11:794
- - Mark's *Geshikhte fun Yidn in Poyln* 10:52
- - mass execution of Jewish women and children by Nazis 8:861
- - partisan units and armed uprisings, 1941-44 (map) 13:141
- - refugee children arriving in Israel 9:496,526
- - Warsaw ghetto stamp 15:336
- - *see also under individual cities*
- *pop. tables:*
- - text
- - Bialystok, 1765-1948 4:811
- - Cracow, 1900-1955 5:1027
- - Lodz, 1820-1931 11:425
- *see also:* ANTI-SEMITIC POLITICAL PARTIES AND ORGANIZATIONS; BELORUSSIA; CASIMIR III; COUNCILS OF THE LANDS; GALICIA; GREAT POLAND; LESSER POLAND; LITHUANIA; POMERANIA; UKRAINE; *and under individual cities.*
Poland, Great, *see* GREAT POLAND
Poland-Lithuania 13:709
Polangen (tn., Rus.), *see* PALANGA
POLANSKI, ROMAN 12:472
- *illus:*
- - *Repulsion* 12:458
POLÁNYI, KARL 13:789
POLANYI, MICHAEL 13:789
Po(o)le, Matthew 8:51
POLEMICS AND POLEMICAL LITERATURE 13:790
- *Contents:*
- - Talmudic Period 13:790
- - Geonic Period 13:791
- - Middle Ages 13:791
- General
- - *aggadah* 2:363
- - Islam
- - Jewish literature 11:310ff
- - Jewish philosophy 13:425
- - letters 11:58
- - linguistics 16:1361
- Persons and Writings
- - Abner of Burgos 2:88
- - Abraham the Proselyte of Augsburg 13:1206
- - Briel, Judah ben Eliezer 4:1372
- - Church Fathers 5:551ff
- - Crescas, Ḥasdai 5:1079
- - David, Levi 11:78
- - *De vita et moribus Judaeorum* 5:158
- - Duran, Profiat 6:299
- - *Entdektes Judenthum* 6:545; 8:1186
- - Jacob ben Solomon ibn Ḥabib 8:1178
- - Jesus' messianic claims 10:16
- - Kara, Avigdor ben Isaac 10:758
- - L'Empereur, Constantin 11:11
- - Martini, Raymond 11:1066ff
- - Mendelssohn 13:455
- - *Mishmeret ha-Bayit* 2:308
- - Muelhausen, Yom Tov Lipmann 12:499
- - Petrus Alfonsi 13:347
- - Pollegar, Isaac ben Joseph ibn 13:835
- - Saadiah Gaon 14:549
- - *Tanqīḥ al-Abḥāth lil-Milal al-Thalāth* 8:1186
- *illus:*
- - *Colloquium Heptaplomeres* (1857) 4:1162 11:895
- - *Ḥazut Kashah* (1552) 3:258
- - Wagenseil's *Tela ignea Satanea* 16:239
- *see also:* DISPUTATIONS AND POLEMICS; HEBREW LITERATURE, MODERN; PARODY, HEBREW
Polemon, Julius (k., Pontus) 13:795
POLEMON II (k., Cilicia) 13:795
POLEMON OF ILIUM 7:896
Polesine (dist., It.) 14:354ff
POLGAR, ALFRED 13:795
Polgar, Isaac 10:540
Poli, Umberto, *see* SABA, UMBERTO
Poliakoff (fam.) *see* POLYAKOV
POLIAKOV, LÉON 1:35; 13:796
Policar, Isaac ben Joseph ibn, *see* POLLEGAR, ISAAC BEN JOSEPH IBN
Policar, Jack (U.S.) 14:1083
Police 13:959
- *illus:*
- - Warsaw ghetto 16:343
POLICE IN ISRAEL 9:351ff; 9:655
- *illus:*
- - Arab rioters in Jaffa, 1936 9:464
- - Druze members of Border Police 9:928
- *see also:* CRIME
Police nad Metuji (tn., Cz.) 12:749
POLICE OFFENSES 13:796
Police School (Jer.) 9:1501
- Six-Day War 14:1630
Polier, Justine Wise 16:566
Polier, Moses ben Israel of Kobrin, *see* KOBRIN, MOSES BEN ISRAEL POLIER OF
Polis (city-state)
- Ereẓ Israel in Second Temple Period 8:626ff
- Jewish War casualties 9:237
- Jerusalem 9:1390
- Maccabees 8:295
Polish (lang.)
- Bible translations 4:885
- children's literature 11:899
POLISH, DAVID 13:797
POLISH LITERATURE 13:797
- *Contents:*
- - Biblical and Hebraic Influences 13:797
- - Image of the Jew 13:799
- - Jewish Contribution 13:802
- - Capsules 13:803
Polish rite (litur.) 11:399
Polishuk, Samuel 14:830
Politeuma (Hellen. cmty. orgn.) 3:921; 6:16
Politi, Maurice 7:148
POLITICAL LIFE AND PARTIES IN ISRAEL 9:656
- Arab community 9:1030ff
- central government 9:616ff
- election broadcasts 15:930
- historical survey 9:372ff
- new immigrants 9:394ff
- *illus:*
- - Arab and Druze districts, votes cast, 1949-69 (table) 9:1031
- - Druze Knesset members 9:925
- - N.R.P. representation in Knesset 12:881
- - Weizmann addressing the Knesset 16:433
Political Zionism, *see* ZIONISM
POLITICS 13:805
- *Contents:*
- - Introduction 13:805
- - Australia 13:808
- - Austria 13:809
- - Canada 13:810
- - England 13:811
- - France 13:812
- - Germany 13:813
- - Holland 13:814
- - Italy 13:815
- - Muslim States 13:815
- - Poland 13:817
- - Russia 13:818
- - South Africa 13:819
- - South America 13:820
- - United States 13:821
- - Capsules 13:825
- General
- - Orthodoxy's influence 12:1490
- - Riesser, Gabriel 14:168
- - Sarajevo 14:871
- - Sejm 14:1117
- - Slovakian Jews 14:1680ff
- - South Africa 14:257; 15:187ff; 15:200; 15:1630
- - U.S. Jews 14:257; 15:1630
- - Zionist socialists 15:45
- Theory
- - Abrabanel 2:103; 13:450; 14:532
- - history 8:714ff
- - Philo 13:427ff
- - Prophets 13:1157
- - theocracy 15:1099
- *illus:*
- - Bucharest, Jewish Parliamentary Club 14:393
- - House of Commons, Lionel Rothschild taking seat 14:340
- - North Carolina, Jacob Henry's speech in House of Commons 15:1649
- - Rumania, League of National Christian Defense, campaign poster 14:395
- - Solomon, Saul, in political cartoon 15:112
- *see also:* PARLAMENTSKLUB, JUEDISCHER; *and under individual ideologies*
POLITISCHE GEMEINDE (Morav.) 13:832
- Dolni Kounice 6:157
POLITZER, ADAM 13:832
Poljokan, Raphael 16:1149
Poll, S. 8:568
POLLACK, EGON 12:703
Pollack, F. W. 13:1036
POLLACK, JACOB BEN JOSEPH 13:833
- responsa 14:89
- talmudic studies 11:333
Pollack, Leslie 12:1425
Pollack, Maurice 13:1423
Pollack, Michael Solomon, *see* ALEXANDER, MICHAEL SOLOMON
POLLACK, PETER 1:35
Pollaiuolo, Antonio 15:1186
- *illus:*
- - "Tobit and the Angel Raphael" (paint.) 15:1184
Pollak, Esther, *see* Fishel, Esther
Pollak, Frank, *see* PELLEG, FRANK
Pollak, Ḥayyim Joseph 6:266
Pollak, Hillel 14:40
Pollak, Jacob (print.), *see* Jacob ben Abraham of Mezhirech
Pollák, Károly, *see* PAP, KÁROLY
Pollak, M. (stlr., Hung.) 15:658; 16:1001
Pollak, Matilda 15:27
Pollak, Mikha'el 11:635
POLLAK, MIKSA 13:834
Pollak, Moritz 16:124
POLLAK, MOSES HA-LEVI 13:834
- Bonyhad 4:1213
Pollak, Oscar 15:26
Pollak, Sh. F. 16:51
POLLAK, WALTER HEILPRIN 13:835
Pollak-Pratto Haggadah (illum. ms.) 3:467; 7:297
POLLEGAR, ISAAC BEN JOSEPH IBN 13:835
- Abner of Burgos 2:88
- Albalag 2:521
- apologetic literature 3:195
- Jewish philosophy 13:445ff
POLLINI, BERNHARD 12:703
Pollio, Gaius Asinius, *see* ASINIUS POLLIO, GAIUS
Pollio (Pollion) the Pharisee 3:749; 3:990
Pollock (fam.) 14:143
Poll tax, *see* TAXATION
POLNA (tn., Cz.) 13:836
Polna Case, *see* HILSNER CASE
Polo (sport) 15:312
Polo, Water (sport), *see* Water Polo
Polock, Isaac 16:356
Polock, Isabella 14:271
Polock, Moses 14:272
Polok, Solomon 15:412
Polonetzky, Sam 8:1439
Polonier Talmud Torah (N.Y.) 6:437ff
POLONNOYE (tn., Ukr.) 13:836
- Aryeh Judah Leib (Ha-Mokhi'aḥ) 3:667
- Kahana, Abraham Aryeh Leib 10:679
POLOTSK (city, Belor.) 11:918
Polotsk, Israel ben Pereẓ of, *see* ISRAEL BEN PEREẒ OF POLOTSK
Polotsk, Phinehas ben Judah 16:147
Polotski, Semyon 14:507
POLOTSKY, HANS JACOB 13:837
Polska Partia Socjalistyczna (Pol.), *see* P.P.S.
POLTAVA (city, Ukr.) 13:839
- self-defense 14:1127
- - *illus:* text
Poltoratsk (city, Rus.), *see* ASHKHABAD
Polyak, G. 8:187; 14:1414
Polyak, Mikhail 13:345
Polyak, Saveli 13:345
Polyakevich, *see* KOPELSON, ẒEMAḤ
Polyakov (name), *see also* Poliakov
POLYAKOV (fam.) 13:841
- Israelsohn, Jacob 9:1074
Polyakov, Eliezer 13:841
Polyakov, Jacob 13:841
Polyakov, Samuel 8:720; 13:841; 13:1518
Polyandry 12:258
Polyanker, Hirsh 10:994
POLYBIUS OF MEGALOPOLIS 7:896
Polycarp (Chr. trans.) 4:860
Polycharmos, Claudius Tiberius 12:238
Polycythemia Vera (disease) 14:1503
Polygamy, *see* BIGAMY AND POLYGAMY; MONOGAMY
Polygraphia (wk.) 15:1400
Polygyny, *see* BIGAMY AND

POLYGAMY; MONOGAMY
Polyteuma (Hellen. cmty. orgn.), *see* Politeuma
Polytheism
- demonology **5:**1521
- Greco-Roman period **15:**568ff
- Jewish philosophy **13:**425
- monotheism **12:**260ff
- polemics denouncing **6:**81ff
Pomar, Joseph, *see* Joseph ben Ardict
Pombal, Sebastião José de Carvalho e Mello, Marquês de **8:**1389 **13:**924
POMEGRANATE (bot.) **13:**841
- plant list **13:**623
- *illus:*
- - Hammath stone *menorah* **11:**1357
- - Hasmonean shekel **3:**322
POMERANIA (duchy) **13:**842
POMERANTZ, BERL **13:**843
Pomerantz, Gershon **5:**113
POMERANTZ, SIDNEY IRVING **8:**549
Pomeranus (Chr. ref.), *see* BUGENHAGEN, JOHANN
Pomianowski, Jerzy **12:**1245; **13:**803
Pomiechowek (concen. camp, Pol.) **12:**1245
POMI(S), DE' (fam.) **13:**844
- *illus:* text
Pomi(s), Elijah de' **13:**844
- Boniface VIII **13:**854
Pomis, David de' **13:**844
- Hull **8:**1068
- Spoleto **15:**290
- views on moneylending **12:**252
- *illus:*
- - *Ẓemaḥ David* (1587) **13:**845
Pomis, Isaac de **13:**844
POMMER, ERICH **12:**453; **12:**472
Pomoshch (period.) **16:**733
Pompeii (anc. city, It.) **9:**1117
Pompeius (Rom. gen.), *see* POMPEY
POMPEIUS TROGUS **13:**845
- Hellenism **8:**292
- Judaism **14:**232
POMPEY (Gnaeus Pompeius Magnus) **13:**846
- Aristobulus II **3:**441
- Ashdod **3:**696
- chronological chart **8:**766-767
- Decapolis **5:**1449
- Ereẓ Israel **8:**633
- Nabateans **12:**742
- settlement in Ereẓ Israel **9:**120
- Solomon, Psalms of **15:**115ff
- Temple **9:**1393; **15:**959
- Transjordan **15:**1317
Pompianski, A. A. **10:**862
- Riga **14:**174
Pomplona (city, Sp.), *see* PAMPLONA
POMPONIUS MELA (Rom. geog.) **14:**236
PONARY (Paneriai; loc., Lith.) **13:**847
Ponca (Ind. tribe, Am.) **12:**1374
Ponce (city, Puerto Rico) **16:**1555
Ponce Feugerons, *see* Feugerons, Ponce
Poner, Meir **6:**197
Ponevezh (city, Lith.), *see* PANEVEZYS
Ponevezher Rav, *see* KAHANEMAN, JOSEPH
Ponholzer, Bartholomaeus **10:**451
Poniatowa (concen. camp) **8:**874
Ponidi (fam.), *see* BONDI
Pontack (Hebr.) **8:**51
Pontack(ous), Arnold **8:**51
Ponta Delgada (city, Azores) **3:**1012
- *illus:*
- - synagogue **13:**925
Pont-à-Mousson (tn., Fr.) **11:**496
Pont-de-Vaux (vill., Fr.) **4:**1358
Pont-de-Veyle (vill., Fr.) **4:**1358
Ponte, Lorenzo da, *see* DA PONTE, LORENZO
PONTECORVO, BRUNO **13:**847
Pontiac (city, Mich.) **11:**1500
Pontifical (Jesuit) Biblical Institute (Jer.) **9:**1473; **12:**552
PONTIUS PILATE **13:**848
- chronological chart **8:**766-767
- Jerusalem aqueduct **9:**1394; **9:**1540
- Jesus **10:**12
- Samaritans **7:**437
- *illus:*
- - coins, Judean **5:**712
- - Tiberius Caesar, inscription **3:**323
Ponto Delgado, *see* Ponta Delgada
PONTOISE (tn., Fr.) **13:**848
- *illus:* text
Pontoppidan, Henrik **14:**927
Pontremoli (sol., It.) **11:**1559
Pontremoli, Abraham **5:**446
Pontremoli, Aldo **2:**321
- exploration **15:**1350
PONTREMOLI, EMMANUEL **3:**365
Pontremoli, Esdra **16:**107
- press **13:**1036
Pontremoli, Gabriel **15:**1455
Pontremoli, Raphael Ḥiyya **11:**1159
Pontus de Tyard (Chr. Hebr.), *see* Tyard, Pontus de
Pontypridd (tn., Wales) **16:**251
POOL, DAVID DE SOLA **13:**849
- historiography **8:**564
- *illus:*
- - J.W.B. committee **12:**873
Pool, Tamar de Sola **13:**849
- *illus:*
- - Biltmore Conference **15:**1633
Poole, Matthew, *see* Po(o)le, Matthew
Po'olei ha-Kefel (wk., A. Ibn Ezra), *see Sefer Po'olei ha-Kefel*
Po'olei ha-Kefel (wk., Gikatilla), *see Sefer Po'olei ha-Kefel*
Pool of Baths (Jer.), *see* Hezekiah, Pool of
Pool of Bethesda (Jer.), *see* Bethesda Pool
Pool of Hezekiah (Jer.), *see* Hezekiah, Pool of
Pool of Israel (Jer.) **9:**1539
Pool of Siloam (Jer.), *see* SHILOAH, SILOAM
Pool of Towers (Jer.), *see* Hezekiah, Pool of
POONA (city, Ind.) **13:**850
- *Haggadah* **7:**1103
- Sassoon, David **14:**897
POOR, PROVISION FOR THE **13:**850
- Akiva's interest **2:**489
- charity **5:**338
- Commandments, the 613 **5:**770,777
- communal assistance **2:**805
- ethics **6:**933
- *leket, shikhḥah,* and *pe'ah* **11:**3
- Leviticus Rabbah **11:**148
- *ma'aser ani* **5:**1486
- *Pe'ah* **13:**200
- *prosbul* **13:**1181
- protection in court **13:**633
- tax exemption **15:**854
- tithe **15:**1022
- widow **16:**489ff
- *see also:* CHARITY; GEMILUT ḤASADIM; POVERTY
Popatov, L. P. **3:**39
Pope, Marvin **4:**913
POPES **13:**851
- Anacletus II, legends **2:**917
- *Civiltà Cattolica, La* **5:**599
- Deutz, Simon **5:**1597
- Giovanni, Maria **7:**588
- history chart **8:**766-767
- kabbalistic eschatology **6:**882
- Zionism **16:**73ff
- *illus:*
- - prayer for **11:**403
- *see also:* BULLS, PAPAL; CHURCH, CATHOLIC; CHURCH COUNCILS; VATICAN; *and under individual popes*
Popiele (lab. camp, Ukr.) **4:**1249
Popkin, Louis **13:**1362
POPKIN, RICHARD H. **1:**35
Popkin, Zelda Feinberg **13:**1362
- U.S. literature **15:**1573
POPLAR (tree) **13:**861
- flora of Israel **9:**225
- willow and **16:**517
POPPAEA, SABINA **13:**861
- Gessius Florus **7:**526
- Josephus Flavius **10:**251
- Nero **12:**964
Poppel, A. **11:**382
Poppelauer, M. **4:**1239; **13:**1373
POPPER (fam.) **13:**861
POPPER, DAVID **12:**703
Popper, Hans **11:**1202
Popper, Ḥayyim (Joachim Edler von) **6:**144; **13:**862
POPPER, JOSEF (Lynkeus; philos.) **13:**862
- aviation **2:**320
Popper, Joseph (soc. wkr.) **5:**1192; **15:**350
POPPER, JULIUS **13:**863
POPPER, SIR KARL RAIMUND **13:**863
POPPER, SIEGFRIED **11:**1575
POPPER, WILLIAM **13:**864
Popper, Wolf **13:**861
Popper-Bozian, Cyril **13:**864
Popper-Bozian, Israel Gershon ha-Kohen **13:**864
POPPER-BOZIAN, WOLF **13:**864
Popper brothers (Morav.) **15:**1041
POPPERS, JACOB BEN BENJAMIN HA-KOHEN **13:**865
POPPERS, MEIR BEN JUDAH LOEB HA-KOHEN **13:**865
- *Bahir, Sefer ha-* **4:**100
- Benjamin, Israel (I) **4:**528
- Lurianic doctrine **10:**581
- Vital, Ḥayyim **16:**174
Poppert, S. **13:**1106
Poppy (bot.) **6:**1365
Poppyseed (bot.) **15:**269
Poprad (tn., Slov.) **8:**1076
Pops, Friedrich **16:**881; **16:**1151
Populaire, Le (period.) **4:**1109
Popular Dictionary of Judaism **6:**734
Popular Front for the Liberation of Palestine (Arab terrorist orgn.) **9:**471
- attacks on El Al planes **2:**620; **9:**416
- terrorist activities **14:**1639
Popular Theater (Arab., Isr.) **9:**1039
POPULATION **13:**866
- *Contents:*
- - Methodological Uncertainties **13:**866
- - Ancient Israel **13:**867
- - Second Commonwealth **13:**870
- - Medieval Islam and Byzantium **13:**872
- - Medieval West **13:**875
- - 1500-1800 **13:**879
- - 1800-1939 **13:**884
- - 1940-1971 **13:**894
- census in Bible **5:**281
- communities, Jewish **5:**833
- growth among Jews **8:**721ff
- human geography of Israel **9:**569ff
- Israel **9:**472
- Jewish communities in Israel **9:**497ff
- vital statistics **16:**179-188
- *see also:* DEMOGRAPHY; DIASPORA; POPULATION OF ISRAEL; STATISTICS; VITAL STATISTICS; *and under individual countries and cities*
POPULATION OF ISRAEL **9:**472
- Arab, general survey **9:**1023ff
- Ashkenazi community **9:**497ff
- first decade **9:**393
- health standards in Israel **9:**984ff
- Jerusalem **9:**1470
- Jerusalem, Ottoman period **9:**1436
- Negev **12:**930ff
- Sephardi community **9:**497ff
- War of Independence **9:**372
- Yemenite community **9:**501; **16:**752ff
- *illus:* text
- *maps:*
- - Druze **9:**925
- *pop. tables:*
- - text
- - increase of permanent population, 1922-39 **9:**701
- - Jewish population **9:**473-496, 533-545
- - major Jewish communities **13:**901
- - non-Jewish population **9:**1024,1025
- - vital statistics **16:**180-188
Populists (polit. mvmt.) **15:**39
Popuna (tn., Babyl.) **11:**1132
Por, Bertalan **13:**113
Porada, Arnold von, *see* Rapoport, Arnold
Porat (mosh., Isr.) **1:**place list
Porat, Joseph, *see* JOSEPH BEN MOSES OF TROYES
PORAT, ORNA **15:**1089
- Cameri **5:**74
- *illus:*
- - *Saint Joan* **15:**1062
Porath, Israel **5:**610
Porath, Joseph **5:**406
Porat Yosef (Bib. comment.) **15:**711
Porat Yosef Yeshivah (Jer.) **9:**1495; **16:**771
- *illus:* **16:**765
Porcelain **2:**261
PORCHETUS SALVAGUS **13:**903
Pordenone, Odorico de **15:**1356
Pordes, H. **13:**1371
Porecki, Leon, *see* Perec, Arieh
Porges (fam.) **13:**969
PORGES, HEINRICH **12:**703
Porges, Leopold **15:**1041
Porges, Moses (mfr., Prague) **7:**70; **15:**1041
PORGES, MOSES BEN ISRAEL NAPHTALI **13:**904
PORGES, NATHAN **13:**904
- Leipzig **10:**1591
Porging **6:**39
PORIYYAH (places, Isr.) **13:**904
- St. Louis settlers **14:**665
- statistics **1:**place list
- Tiberias **15:**1134
PORPHYRY (philos.) **13:**905
- Jerome **9:**1377
- Neoplatonism **12:**958
Porr, H. J. **15:**827
Portage La Prairie (tn., Man.) **11:**879
PORTAL (archit.) **13:**905
- *illus:*
- - text
- - Portaleone seal **13:**908
- - Qaṣrayn synagogue **13:**1534
PORTALEONE (fam.) **13:**907

- Sommo, Judah **15:**137
Portaleone, Abraham ben Benjamin **13:**908
PORTALEONE, ABRAHAM BEN DAVID II **13:**908
- alchemy **2:**548
- Sommo, Judah **15:**137
Portaleone, Abraham ben Eleazar **13:**907
Portaleone, Angelo, *see* Portaleone, Mordecai
Portaleone, Benjamin ben David **13:**908
Portaleone, Benjamin ben Elhanan **13:**907
Portaleone, Benjamin ben Mordecai (d.c. 1432) **13:**907
Portaleone, Benjamin ben Mordecai (1420-1500) **13:**907
Portaleone, David ben Abraham **13:**907
- *illus:*
- - seal **13:**908
Portaleone, David ben Eleazar **13:**907
Portaleone, Eleazar ben Benjamin **13:**907
Portaleone, Elhanan ben Menahem **13:**907
Portaleone, Eliezer ben Abraham **13:**907
Portaleone, Judah **13:**907
Portaleone, Judah ben Abraham (Mantua) **13:**907
Portaleone, Judah ben Abraham (Sermide) **13:**907
Portaleone, Leone de Sommi, *see* SOMMO, JUDAH LEONE BEN ISAAC
Portaleone, Meir **13:**907
Portaleone, Mordecai (Angelo) ben Benjamin **13:**907
Portaleone, Mordecai (Angelo) ben Menahem **13:**907
Portaleone, Samuel ben Elisha Sha'ar Aryeh **7:**1150; **10:**548; **16:**787
Portaleone, Solomon (physic.) **13:**908
Portaleone, Solomon ben Abraham **13:**907
Portales, Diego **5:**461
Portalis, Joseph Marie **3:**762
Port Arthur (city, Tex.) **15:**1035
Port Chester (vill., N.Y.) **16:**464
Port Colborne (tn., Ont.) **12:**1408
Porteira, David **6:**1187
Porteira, Samuel **6:**1187; **8:**1325
PORT ELIZABETH (city, S.A.) **13:**909
- *illus:* text
PORTELLA, DE (fam.) **13:**910
Portella, Ishmael de **13:**910; **15:**808
Portella, Muca de **13:**910; **15:**808
PORTEN, BEZALEL **1:**35
Porter, J. **8:**51
Porter, John Scott **8:**51
Porter, Maurice **15:**193
Porter, William Sydney **16:**262
Port Gibson (tn., Miss.) **12:**156
Porthcawl (tn., Wales) **16:**251
Portheim, Moses von, *see* Porges, Moses
Portico d'Ottavia (journ.) **14:**253
Portland (city, Me.) **11:**782ff
PORTLAND (city, Oreg.) **13:**910
- Oregon **12:**1451
Port Natal (city, S.A.), *see* DURBAN
Portnoy, Antonia **15:**255
PORTNOY, JEKUTHIEL (Noah; Yuzef) **13:**912
Portnoy, Vladimir **12:**1377; **15:**308
Porto (fam. name), *see also:* Porto-Rafa; Rapaport; Rapoport; Rappaport; Rappoport
PORTO (fam.) **13:**912
Porto (port, It.) **9:**1117
Porto, Abraham **13:**912
Porto, Abraham de, *see* Alvarez, Fernando
PORTO, ABRAHAM MENAHEM BEN JACOB HA-KOHEN **13:**913
- Porto-Rafa, Moses **13:**915
- Rapoport family **13:**1552
- *illus:*
- - escutcheon **13:**1553
Porto, Abraham Menahem ben Jehiel ha-Kohen **13:**915
Porto, Domingo do **6:**1413; **11:**681
Porto, Gershon **13:**913
Porto, Isaac ben David **13:**913
Porto, Isaac do **11:**681
Porto, Jehiel **13:**913
Porto, Menahem Zion (Emmanuel) **13:**913
Porto, Pedro Pereira Antonio do **8:**1356
Porto, Simḥah **13:**913
Porto, Zechariah ben Ephraim Mahalalel **13:**913
Porto, Ẓemaḥ ben Isaac **13:**913
PÔRTO ALEGRE (city, Braz.) **13:**914
- *see also:* BRAZIL
Port of Spain (city, Trinidad) **16:**1126
Porto-Rafa (fam. name), *see also:* Porto; Rapaport; Rapoport; Rappaport; Rappoport
PORTO-RAFA, MOSES BEN JEHIEL HA-KOHEN **13:**914
PORTO-RICHE, GEORGES DE **13:**915
- *illus:* text
"Portrait of Guillaume Appollinaire" (lith., L. Marcousis) **13:**114
"Portrait of Leon Indenbaum" (paint., A. Modigliani) **13:**114
"Portrait of Winston Churchill" (sculp., Epstein) **14:**1062
"Portrait of the Young Girl Elvira" (paint., A. Modigliani) **12:**205
PORTRAITS OF JEWS **13:**915
- *illus:*
- - text
- - "Aaron, son of the Devil" (1277) **3:**93; **4:**63
- - Aboab da Fonseca, Isaac (A. Naghtagael) **2:**96
- - Abraham ben Shabbetai ha-Kohen (self-portrait) **2:**155
- - Abrahams, Harriet **15:**1054
- - Abramson, Abraham (S. Rosenberg) **2:**171
- - Achron, Joseph (L. Pilichowsky) **2:**211
- - Adler, Alfred (S. Bril) **2:**272
- - Adler, Hermann (Spy) **2:**279
- - Adler, Jankel (self-portrait) **2:**280
- - Adolphus, John **2:**293
- - Aguilar, Ephraim Lopez Pereira d' **2:**427
- - Alexander, Abraham, Sr. (L. Sully) **2:**572
- - Alexander, Morris (J. H. Amshewitz) **2:**574
- - Alexander, Samuel (J. Epstein) **2:**576
- - Almosnino, Solomon **2:**668
- - Altenberg, Peter (Mopp) **2:**772
- - Amatus Lusitanus **2:**796
- - Arikha, Avigdor (self-portrait) **3:**436
- - Arnstein, Fanny von **3:**491
- - Arnstein, Nathan Adam **3:**490
- - "Artist's Mother" (M. Gertler) **7:**521
- - "Artist's Mother" (L. Gottlieb) **7:**826
- - Artom, Benjamin **3:**662
- - Asch, Sholem **3:**684
- - Ascheim, Isidor (self-portrait) **3:**689
- - Ascoli, Graziadio Isaia **3:**691
- - Ashkenazi, Ẓevi Hirsch **7:**478
- - Astruc, Elie-Aristide (Ch. Weiner) **3:**808
- - Aub, Max (J. Madrid) **3:**839
- - Ayllon, Solomon ben Jacob **3:**996
- - Azulai, Ḥayyim Joseph David **8:**227
- - Ba'al Shem of London (J. Copley) **6:**1160
- - Babel, Isaac **4:**20
- - Baeyer, Adolf von **4:**85
- - Ballin, Albert **4:**139
- - Baltazar, Camil (M. Janco) **4:**144
- - Barasch, Julius **4:**199
- - Barnay, Ludwig **4:**248
- - Barrios, Daniel de, and family (A. De Chaves) **4:**259
- - Barth, Jacob (H. Struck) **4:**262
- - Baruh, Bora (self-portrait) **3:**618
- - Baruk, Henri (B. Benn) **4:**282
- - Basevi Cervetto, Jacob (J. Zoffany) **4:**290
- - Beer, Aaron (B. H. Bendix) **4:**376
- - Beer, Michael (anon.) **4:**378
- - Bendemann, Eduard (C. Eppelin) **4:**475
- - Benedikt, Moritz **4:**489
- - Benjamin, Harry M. **11:**1589
- - Bennett, Solomon (self-portrait) **3:**545; **4:**543
- - Berdyczewski, Micha Josef (M. Aryeh) **4:**593
- - Berény, Róbert (self-portrait) **4:**604
- - Bergson, Henri **8:**750
- - Bernhard, Georg (G. Sax-Bernhard) **4:**677
- - Bernhardt, Sarah **4:**678
- - Bernheimer, Charles L. (L. Betts) **4:**680
- - Bernstein, Samuel **6:**218
- - Bialik, Ḥayyim Naḥman **4:**796
- - Birnbaum, Nathan (J. Budko) **4:**1040
- - Blecher, Marcel (self-portrait) **4:**1080
- - Bloch, Marcus Eliezer (A. Graff) **4:**1107
- - Blowitz, Henri Georges (A. Werner) **4:**1134
- - Blumenthal, George (A. Deckenaud) **4:**1142
- - Boerne, Ludwig (M. Oppenheim) **4:**1167; **8:**709
- - Born, Max (H. Isenstein **4:**1251
- - Braham, John (R. Dighton) **4:**1289
- - Brainin, Reuben (H. Struck) **4:**1292
- - Braun, Felix (Stumpp) **4:**1319
- - Buber, Solomon **4:**1434
- - Bueno, Ephraim Hezekiah **12:**975
- - Călugăru, Ion (self-portrait) **5:**65
- - Carigal, Raphael (S. King) **5:**179
- - Cassel, Sir Ernest Joseph (Spy) **5:**230
- - Castro Sarmento, Jacob de **5:**247
- - Cohen, Hermann **5:**674; **8:**749
- - Cohn, Albert **5:**687
- - Cohn, Tobias ben Moses **5:**693
- - Cologna, Abraham Vita **5:**738
- - Cone, Moses H. **5:**868
- - Cordova, Jacob de **8:**1050
- - Costa, John da (C. da Costa) **5:**985
- - Crémieux, Isaac Adolphe **5:**1074,1075; **8:**710
- - Da Ponte, Lorenzo **5:**1301
- - Darmesteter, Arsène (A. Waltmér) **5:**1305
- - David, David **12:**285
- - David, Ferdinand **5:**1345
- - D'Avigdor-Goldsmid, Sir Osmond **5:**1367
- - De Leon, David Camden **5:**1471
- - Delmedigo, Joseph **5:**1479
- - De Sola, Aaron David Meldola **12:**285
- - De Sola, Abraham **12:**285
- - De Sola, David Aaron (N. Raphael) **5:**1562
- - Deutsch, Israel **5:**1591
- - Deutsch de la Meurthe, Émile **5:**1593
- - Deutz, Emanuel **7:**30
- - Disraeli, Benjamin **6:**104-108; **8:**707
- - D'Israeli, Isaac (J. B. Hunt) **6:**110
- - Dreyfus, Isaac **6:**224
- - Dropsie, Moses Aaron **6:**234
- - Dubno, Solomon ben Joel **6:**251
- - Duveen, Joseph (E. Fuchs) **6:**324
- - Edrehi, Moses ben Isaac (J. C. Hunter) **6:**380
- - Eger, Akiva ben Moses Guens (Constalt) **6:**470
- - Ehrlich, Paul (Goetz) **6:**514
- - Eichenbaum, Jacob **6:**516
- - Einhorn, David **6:**531
- - Einstein, Albert (H. Struck) **8:**749
- - Elijah ben Solomon Zalman ("Vilna Gaon") **6:**652; **8:**717
- - Elkan, Benno (Stumpp) **6:**674
- - Elyashar, Jacob Saul ben Eliezer Jeroham **6:**692
- - Engel, József **6:**746
- - Erlanger, Michel **6:**843
- - Erter, Isaac **6:**847
- - Etting, Solomon (W. Jarvis) **6:**952
- - Ettinger, Solomon **6:**955
- - Ettlinger, Jacob **6:**956
- - Eybeschuetz, Jonathan **6;**1075; **7:**475
- - Falk, Samuel Jacob Ḥayyim (J. Copley) **6:**1160
- - Farkas, Ladislaus (P. Litvinovsky) **6:**1186
- - Feivel, Berthold (L. A. Rubitschek) **6:**1215
- - Feuchtwanger, Lion (S. Carvallo-Schvelein) **6:**1249
- - Fima (self-portrait) **6:**1278
- - Firkovich, Abraham **6:**1305
- - Fischel, Harry **6:**1316
- - Fischer, Jean (I. Israels) **6:**1319
- - Fischhoff, Adolf **6:**1324; **8:**707
- - Fondane, Benjamin (M. Janco) **6:**1413
- - Frank, Jacob **7:**55
- - Frankl, Ludwig August (C. Kotterba) **7:**101
- - Franks, David Salisbury **7:**107; **12:**1064
- - Franks, Jacob (anon.) **7:**108; **12:**285
- - Freehof, Solomon Benett (J. Margulies) **7:**121
- - Friedlaender, David **7:**178
- - Frischmann, David (H. Struck) **7:**202
- - Furtado, Abraham (A. Maurin) **7:**222
- - Gans, Eduard **7:**312
- - Gaster, Moses **7:**333
- - Geiger, Abraham **7:**358; **8:**718
- - Gentili, Moses **7:**414
- - Gerchunoff, Alberto (A. Sirio) **7:**435
- - Gernsheim, Friedrich (H. Struck) **7:**504
- - Gherea-Dobrogeanu, Constantin

7:541
-- Glueckel of Hameln 7:629
-- Goldmark, Karl 7:727
-- Goldsmid, Abraham (Ridley) 7:734
-- Goldsmid, Sir Isaac Lyon (R. Dighton) 7:734
-- Golomb, Eliyahu 7:764
-- Gorelik, Shemarya (H. Struck) 7:807
-- Gottlieb, Maurycy (self-portrait) 7:826
-- Graetz, Heinrich 8:717
-- Granott, Abraham (P. Litvinovsky) 7:854
-- Gratz, Barnard (Ch. P. Polk) 7:859
-- Gratz, Michael (Th. Sully) 7:859
-- Gratz, Rebecca (Th. Sully) 7:859
-- Grynszpan, Herschel 7:953
-- Guttmacher, Elijah (H. Struck) 7:991
-- Guttmann, Robert (self-portrait) 7:996
-- Haber, Fritz (A. Bursch) 7:1022
-- Haffkine, Waldemar 7:1061
-- Hager, Menaḥem Mendel 16:199
-- Hahn, Joseph ben Moses 7:1128
-- Halévy, Jacques 7:1185
-- Halevy, Moshe (R. Rubin) 7:1187
-- Hamburg, Abraham 7:1230
-- Hannover, Adolph 7:1273
-- Hart, Aaron 7:1351; 12:285
-- Hart, Benjamin 12:285
-- Hart, Bernard 7:1354
-- Hart, Ezekiel 12:285
-- Hart, Moses 7:1350
-- Hartmann, Moritz (A. Weger) 7:1362
-- Heidenheim, Wolf 8:259
-- Heine, Heinrich 8:271,709
-- Heine, Solomon 8:276
-- Hendriks, Harmon (J. W. Jarvis) 8:324
-- Herz, Henriette 8:402
-- Herz, Marcus 8:403
-- Hess, Michael 8:431
-- Hess, Moses 8:708
-- Hillman, Samuel Isaac (D. Hillman) 8:492
-- Hirsch, Emil Gustave (J. L. Butensky) 8:503
-- Hirsch, Lazare 5:911
-- Hirsch, Markus 8:505
-- Hirsch, Maurice, Baron de 8:710
-- Hirsch, Solomon 8:516
-- Hirschel, Solomon 3:546; 8:520
-- Hirschfeld, Georg (H. Struck) 8:525
-- Hoffmann, David Ẓevi (etch., H. Struck) 8:809
-- Hofmannsthal, Hugo von (sculp.) 8:812
-- Holdheim, Samuel 8:717, 818
-- Hollaender, Ludwig (Wolfsfeld) 8:826
-- Horner, Henry 8:977
-- Horovitz, Vladimir (E. Spiro) 8:983
-- Horowitz, Lazar (Eleazar) 8:996
-- Huberman, Bronislaw (E. Spiro) 8:1056
-- Indenbaum, Leon (paint., A. Modigliani) 13:115
-- Isaac (Isak), Aaron (Aron) 9:9
-- Isaacs, Jorge (bust) 9:42
-- Isserles, Moses ben Israel 9:1082
-- Itzig, Daniel 3:545; 5:1010
-- Itzig, Isaac Daniel (A. Graff) 9:1152
-- Jacob, Max (Picasso) 9:1212
-- Jacobowski, Ludwig 9:1235
-- Jacobs, Joseph (J. D. Blatter) 9:1236
-- Jacobson, Israel 9:1241
-- Jacobson, Ludwig Levin 9:1241
-- Jacoby, Johann 9:1244
-- Jaffe, Leib (Robitschek) 9:1262
-- Jeiteles, Jonas 9:1331
-- Jellinek, Adolf 8:708; 9:1338
-- Joel, Solomon Barnato 10:136
-- Jolles, Zechariah Isaac 10:167
-- Josephson, Manuel 10:250
-- Jost, Isaac Marcus 10:299
-- Kafka, Franz (B. Feigl) 6:1207
-- Kahn, Gustave (drg., A. Bass) 10:689
-- Kahn, Zadoc 10:693
-- Kaposi, Moritz 10:755
-- Kerr, Alfred (lith., Stumpp) 10:921
-- Kestenberg, Leo (paint., O. Kokoschka) 10:925
-- Kimḥi, Jacob ben Samuel (drg., Humphry) 10:1005
-- Kohn, Samuel (sculp.) 10:1148
-- Kopman, Benjamin (self-portrait) 3:632
-- Koreff, David Ferdinand 10:1202
-- Kossoff, Leon (self-portrait) 3:631
-- Kovner, Abba (drg., M. Simon) 10:1230
-- Kraus, Karl (lith., Stumpp) 10:1244
-- Krinitzi, Avraham (sculp., N. Rapaport) 10:1261
-- Kursheedt, Israel Baer (paint., Thompson) 10:1301
-- Laemel, Simon von 10:1354
-- Landau, Ezekiel ben Judah (engr., Klauber) 10:1389
-- Laski, Harold Joseph 10:1439
-- Lassalle, Ferdinand 8:709, 10:1442
-- Lattes, Elia de (medal) 10:1460
-- Lattes, Rica 10:1460
-- Lazarus, Emma (engr., Johnson) 10:1516
-- Lebensohn, Micah Joseph (drg., N. Matz) 10:1549
-- Leeser, Isaac 10:1562
-- Lehmann, Marcus 10:1582
-- Lehren, Akiva 10:1584
-- Leivick, H. (drg., Glicenstein) 10:1594
-- Lemans, Moses 11:10
-- Letteris, Meir 11:54
-- Levanon, Mordecai (paint., self portrait) 11:68
-- Levi, David 11:78
-- Levin, Shmarya (paint., J. Oppenheimer) 11:110
-- Levin, Zevi Ḥirsch (-el) ben Aryeh Loeb 11:112
-- Levinsohn, Isaac Baer 11:116
-- Levinthal, Bernard Louis (paint., Suzanne) 11:120
-- Lévy, Alfred 11:155
-- Levy, Moses 11:161
-- Levy, Rudolf (self-portrait) 11:163
-- Lewald, Fanny 11:167
-- Liberman, Yevsey Grigoryevich 11:189
-- Libin, Z. (drg., B. Gussow) 11:189
-- Lieben, Adolph (sculp.) 11:214
-- Lieben, Robert von 11:215
-- Lieberman, Herman 11:217
-- Liebermann, Felix (J.P. Veth) 11:222
-- Liebermann, Max (self-portrait) 11:223
-- Lifshitz, Nehamah 11:238
-- Lipkin, Yom Tov Lipman 11:281
-- Lissitzky, El (self-portrait) 11:306
-- Loeb, Isidore 11:438
-- Loew, Eleazar 11:442
-- Loew, Leopold 11:444
-- Loewe, Louis 11:448
-- Loewy, Isaac 11:457
-- Lopez, Aaron 11:489
-- Lorm, Hieronymus 11:495
-- Lublin, Meir ben Gedaliah 11:547
-- Luzzatto, Samuel David (lith.) 11:605
-- Lyons, Jacques Judah (J.H. Lazarus) 11:626
-- Maimon, Solomon 11:741
-- Maimonides 11:755
-- Manasseh ben Israel (etch.) 11:855
-- Manger, Itzik (drg., Alva) 11:873
-- Mannheimer, Isaac Noah 11:890
-- Mapu, Abraham 11:933
-- Marix, Adolph 11:1552
-- Marshall, Louis (etch., H. Struck) 11:1060
-- Marx, Adolf Bernhard 11:1069
-- Marx, Karl 8:709
-- Mears, Otto 11:1160
-- Meidner, Ludwig 11:1237
-- Meisels, Dov Berush 11:1264
-- Melchior, Marcus 11:1287
-- Meldola, Raphael 4:243
-- Melnikoff, Avraham (R. Rubin) Pl.1 3-ART
-- Mendelssohn, Felix 11:1327
-- Mendelssohn, Joseph 11:1325
-- Mendelssohn, Moses 11:1328
-- Mendes, Fernando 11:1342
-- Mercado, Luis 11:1193
-- Mesquita, Moses Gomez de 11:1406
-- Meyer, Jonas Daniel 11:1463
-- Meyerbeer, Giacomo 11:1466
-- Meyerson, Emile 11:1469
-- Michael, Heimann Joseph Ḥayyim 11:1486
-- Michael, Jehiel 12:629
-- Michaelis, Sir Max 11:1492
-- Michaels, Frances 12:285
-- Miesis, Judah Leib 11:1527
-- Mikhoels, Solomon (drg.) 14:492
-- Mithridates, Flavius 12:160
-- Mocatta, Abraham Lumbrozo de Mattos 12:198
-- Montefiore, Moses 8:718
-- Monteux, Pierre 12:277
-- Mopp (self-portrait) 12:294
-- Mordecai, Alfred 12:310
-- Mordecai, Jacob 12:311
-- Morpurgo, Samson ben Joshua Moses 12:350
-- Mortara, Marco 12:354
-- Moscheles, Ignaz 12:359
-- Mosenthal, Joseph 12:369
-- Moses, Rachel (E.G. Malbone) 7:860
-- Muehsam, Erich 12:499
-- Mulder, Samuel Israel (lith., M. Calish) 12:516
-- Munk, Solomon 12:525
-- Myers, Mordecai 12:724
-- Myers, Moses 12:725
-- Myers, Samuel 12:726
-- Naar, David 12:735
-- Nathan of Gaza 12:862
-- Naumbourg, Samuel 12:894
-- Netter, Charles 12:1001
-- Neumann, Alfred 12:1010
-- Nieto, David (engr.) 12:1152
-- Noah, Mordecai Manuel 8:707; 12:1199
-- Nobel, Nehemiah Anton 12:1200
-- Norsa, Hannah 15:1053
-- Offenbach, Jacques 12:1337
-- Oppenheim, David ben Abraham 12:1420
-- Oppenheim, Moritz Daniel (self-portrait) 12:1424
-- Oppenheimer, Joseph Suess 5:1011; 12:1429
-- Oppenheimer, Samuel 5:1007
-- Orlik, Emil (self-portrait) 12:1470
-- Orobio de Castro, Isaac (J. Groenwolt) 12:1476
-- Orshanski, Ilya Grigoryevich 12:1480
-- Osiris, Daniel Illfa 12:1499
-- Palgrave, Francis 13:42
-- Pasmanik, Daniel (drg., N. Altman) 13:160
-- Pasternak, Boris Leonidovich 13:174
-- Pasternak, Leonid Osipovich 13:175
-- Péreire, Emily 13:272
-- Péreire, Isaac 13:273
-- Peretz, Isaac Leib 13:280
-- Philadelphia, Jacob 13:376
-- Phillips, Jonas 13:405
-- Pinsker, Simḥah 13:549
-- Pissarro, Camille 13:564
-- Porto-Riche, Georges de 13:915
-- Prague Jew (caric.) 5:172
-- Rabinovitch, Joseph 13:1472
-- Rachel (actress) 13:1492
-- Raḥel 13:1516
-- Rapoport, Solomon Judah Leib 13:1555
-- Rathenau, Walther 13:1569
-- Regelson, Abraham 14:34
-- Reggio, Isacco Samuel 14:38
-- Reines, Isaac Jacob 14:58
-- Reuter, Paul Julius 8:707
-- Revere, Giuseppe Prospero (sculp.) 14:126
-- Ricardo, David 14:153
-- Rice, Abraham Joseph 14:156
-- Riesser, Gabriel 14:167
-- Rivera, Jacob Rodriguez 14:197
-- Roda Roda, Alexander 14:215
-- Rodin, Elisha 14:217
-- Rose, Ernestine Potovsky 14:267
-- Rosenberg, Isaac (self-portrait) 14:278
-- Rosenfeld, Morris (drg., J. Epstein) 14:285
-- Roth, Cecil (sculp., H. Wald) 14:327
-- Rothenstein, Sir William (self-portrait) 14:333
-- Rothschild, Baron Edmond de 8:750
-- Rothschild, Lionel de 8:710
-- Rubin, Reuven (self-portrait) 14:371
-- Salten, Felix 14:712
-- Samuel, Herbert (drg., L. Pasternak) 14:798
-- Samuel ben Avigdor 14:804
-- Saphir, Jacob 14:852
-- Saphir, Moritz Gottlieb 14:854
-- Sasportas, Jacob 14:893
-- Sassoon, Abdulla 14:896
-- Sassoon, David S. 14:896
-- Sassoon, Siegfried Lorraine 14:902
-- Schechter, Solomon 14:949
-- Schiff, David Tevele 14:960
-- Schiller-Szinessy, Solomon Mayer 14:966
-- Schlegel, Dorothea von 14:970
-- Schneerson, Menahem Mendel 14:1433
-- Schoenberg, Arnold (self-portrait) 14:988
-- Schomberg, Alexander 14:993
-- Schomberg, Ralph 14:993
-- Schulman, Kalman 14:1005
-- Schuster, Felix (Spy) 14:1011
-- Schwarz, Yehoseph 14:1026
-- Schwerin-Goetz, Eliakim ha-Kohen 14:1033
-- Segal, Arthur (self-portrait) 3:641
-- Seixas, Gershom Mendes (M. Furst) 7:221; 14:116

- - Shabbetai Zevi 9:691; 14:1221, 1225
- - Shazar, Shneur Zalman 4:1332
- - Sheftall, Mordecai 14:1336
- - Shimoni, David (drg., L. Schwerin) 14:1405
- - Shneour, Zalman (lith., H. Struck) 14:1429
- - Shneur Zalman of Lyady (H. Ḥazan) 7:1013
- - Sinzheim, Joseph David 14:1616
- - Sneersohn, Ḥayyim Ẓevi 15:16
- - Sofer, Moses 15:78
- - Soloveichik, Ḥayyim 15:129
- - Sonnenthal, Adolf Ritter von 15:158
- - Sonnino, Sidney 15:159
- - Soutine, Chaim (self-portrait) 8:749
- - Spektor, Isaac Elhanan 15:260
- - Spielman, Marion Harry Alexander 15:273
- - Spinoza, Baruch 8:694; 15:276
- - Spiro, Eugen (self-portrait) 3:642
- - Stein, Gertrude (paint., Picasso) 15:352
- - Steinheim, Salomon Ludwig 15:370
- - Steinitz, Wilhelm 15:371
- - Stern, Abraham Jacob 15:381
- - Straus, Oscar 15:432
- - Stricker, Robert 15:439
- - Suasso, Antonio Lopez (sculp.) 15:467
- - Sulzer, Solomon 15:510
- - Tchernichowsky, Saul (L. Pasternak) 15:878
- - Templo, Leon (engr., S. Italia) 15:998
- - Tiktin, Abraham 15:1141
- - Tiktin, Solomon 15:1141
- - Toller, Ernst (lith., Stumpp) 15:1211
- - Touro, Judah 15:1289
- - Tzara, Tristan (drg., F. Léger) 15:1494
- - Ussishkin, Abraham Menahem Mendel (etch., H. Struck) 16:23
- - Valentin, Gabriel Gustav 16:59
- - Van Oven, Joshua 16:67
- - Wassermann, August von 16:362
- - Wessely, Naphtali Herz 16:461
- - Wieniawski, Henri and Joseph 16:505
- - Wolff, Bernhard 8:707
- - Wolfskehl, Karl (drg., R. Grossman) 16:616
- - Wormser, Seckel 16:649
- - Young Jewish woman (paint., I. Kaufmann) 10:845
- - Yulee, David Levy (paint., G.P.A. Healy) 16:894
- - Zacutus Lusitanus 16:910
- - Zunz, Leopold 8:717
- - Zweig, Arnold (etch., H. Struck) 16:1247
- - *see also:* HISTORY (text illustrations); SCULPTURE
Port Royal (tn., Jam.) 9:1273
Ports, Israel, *see* Harbors, Israel
PORT SAID (city, Egy.) 13:918
PORTSMOUTH (port, Eng.) 13:918
Portsmouth (city, N.H.) 12:1024
Portsmouth (city, O.) 12:1344
Portsmouth (tn., R.I.) 14:143
Port Sudan (city, Egy.) 14:15
PORTUGAL 13:919
- *Contents:*
- - Early History 13:919
- - Resettlement 13:924
- - Holocaust Period 13:925
- - Contemporary Period 13:925
- - Relations with Israel 13:926
- General
- - Abulafia, Samuel 2:193
- - Arraby Moor 3:497
- - history chart 8:766-767
- - Holocaust rescue 8:906
- - Israel relations 9:431
- - Ottoman Empire 16:1532, 1547
- - population 13:878ff
- - rabbinate 13:1447
- - seals 14:1079
- - synagogues 1:syn. list; 15:609
- Language and Literature 15:247
- - Bible translations 4:879
- - children's literature 5:456
- - encyclopedias 6:735
- - illuminated mss. 8:1265
- - Sephardim 14:1167ff
- Persecutions
- - Amsterdam Jewish merchants 2:897
- - Ankara community 3:24
- - Apulian communities 3:228
- - Aragão, Fernão Ximenes da 3:251
- - Azemmour 3:1004
- - Inquisition 8:1385ff
- - John (kings) 10:158
- - *limpieza de sangre* 11:255
- - Manuel I 11:899
- - Marrano Diaspora 11:1019
- - New Christians 12:1022
- Trades and Professions
- - banking 4:171
- - Hebrew printing 8:1325
- - journalism 10:304
- - publishing 13:1364
- - trade and commerce 15:1299ff
- *illus:*
- - text
- - Fonseca, Miguel Henriques, Inquisition sentence 8:1389
- - Goa, Inquisition procession 8:1393
- - Inquisition's request re converts 8:1385
- - Marrano meeting, Oporto, 1932 11:1021
- *pop. tables:* text
Portugali, Mendel 7:1370
PORTUGALOV, BENJAMIN OSIPOVICH 13:926
Portugal-Yaḥya (cmty., Salonika) 6:919
Portugees Israëlietisch Ziekenhuis, *see* Portuguese Jewish Hospital, Amsterdam
Portugies, Michael, *see* Hinrichsen, Michael
Portuguese (lang.), *see* PORTUGAL (Language and Literature)
Portuguese Jewish Hospital, Amsterdam 2:904
Portuguese literature, *see* SPANISH AND PORTUGUESE LITERATURE
Portuguese Minhag (litur., U.S.) 14:1173
Portuguesic (lang.) 10:67,439
Portulani maps 11:920
PORUMBACU, VERONICA 13:927
- Rumanian literature 14:414
Porumbák (Porumbacul de Sus; vill., Transyl.) 6:1135
Porush, I. 15:565
Poryat, Moses 9:1437
Porzer, Julius 11:557
Porzó (pseud.), *see* ÁGAI, ADOLF
Poseidon (ship) 8:1249
Poseidonius of Apamea, *see* POSIDONIUS
POSEKIM (rab. decisors) 13:927
- yeshivah curriculum 16:767
- *see also:* CODIFICATION OF LAW; RISHONIM; SHULḤAN ARUKH
Posen (city, Pol.), *see* POZNAN
Posen, Isaac ben Abraham of, *see* ISAAC BEN ABRAHAM OF POSEN
Posen, S. (r.) 15:162
Posen, Samuel (gram.) 3:846
Posener (fam. name), *see also* Posner, Pozner
POSENER, GEORGES HENRI 13:928
POSENER, SOLOMON 13:928
POSIDONIUS (philos.) 13:928
- ass worship 3:784
- Greek literature 7:890
- Moses 12:390
- Philo 13:426
Poslednive Izvestia (newsp.) 13:1045
Posnack, Max 15:303
POSNANSKI (fam. Pol.) 13:929
Posnanski, Adolf 13:929
- Jerusalem 9:1573
Posner (fam.) 5:34
Posner (fam. name), *see also* Posener, Pozner
Posner, Abraham 6:811
POSNER, AKIVA BARUKH (Arthur) 13:930
- Kiel 10:988
Posner, Aryeh Leib 13:931
POSNER, DAVID BEN NAPHTALI 13:931
Posner, David Tevele 13:931
Posner, Elijah 13:931
Posner, Moses 13:931
Posner, Rachel 13:930
POSNER, RONALD 1:35
Posner, Solomon (r.,Ger.) 5:991
Posner, Solomon (sol., Pol.) 13:651
Posner, Solomon Zalman, *see* LIPSCHITZ, SOLOMON ZALMAN
POSNER, SOLOMON ZALMAN BEN JOSEPH 13:931
- Calahora family 5:34
- Plock 13:647
Posner, Stanislaw 5:35
POSQUIÈRES (tn.,Fr.) 13:931
- Abraham ben David 2:136; 14:101
- yeshivah 16:763
Poss (r.), *see* ASHKENAZI, GERSHON
"Possession" (paint., O. Herman) 3:626
Possession (leg.), *see* ḤAZAKAH; OWNERSHIP
Possner, Lou 15:303
Post, *see* PILLAR
Post, Di (newsp.), *see Di Post*
POSTAL, BERNARD 1:35
POSTAL SERVICES IN EREẒ ISRAEL 9:841
- angaria 2:950
- Arab states 15:1564
- statistics 9:845
- Turkish rule 9:1458
- *illus:*
- - Benei Akiva emblem 4:491
- *see also:* STAMPS
POSTAN, MICHAEL MOISSEY 13:931
Postawy (vill., Rus.) 7:624
POSTEL, GUILLAUME 13:932
- Christian Hebraists 8:51
- Christian Kabbalah 10:645
- Jerusalem 9:1568
- Levita, Elijah 11:132
- Maes, Andreas 11:684
- Muenster, Sebastian 12:506
- *Sefer Yeẓirah* 16:787
- Widmanstetter 16:487
- Zohar translation 16:1214
- *illus.*
- - *Or Nerot ha-Menorah* (1548) 10:625
Postemus (tal. fig.), *see* APOSTOMOS
Posthumius (Syr. Procurator) 3:218
Postman, Leo 13:1345
Post miserabile (papal bull) 4:1495
Post-Mortem, *see* AUTOPSIES AND DISSECTION
POSTOLSKY, SHALOM 12:703
Postrelko, Avraham, *see* HARZFELD, AVRAHAM
Posts, Israel Ministry of, *see* Israel Ministry of Posts
Pöstyén (tn., Cz.), *see* PIESTANY
Posvoler Maggid (prch.) 4:804
Poswoler, Abele, *see* ABRAHAM ABELE BEN ABRAHAM SOLOMON
Potash (min.) 5:1395; 9:801ff; 15:18,72
- *illus:*
- - Dead Sea works 5:1394; 9:805
Potash, Rekuda 16:825
'Potato Vendor at Bershad Camp' (drg., A. Daghani) Fig.80 3-ART
Potchefstroom (tn., Transvaal) 15:1340
Poterium thorn (bot.) 9:221
POTIPHAR (bib.fig.) 13:933
- homosexuality 8:961
- in the Arts 10:213f
- rabbinic literature 13:360
- *illus:*
- - text
- - Joseph and Potiphar's wife 13:354
'Potiphar's Wife Accusing Joseph' (engr., Lucas van Leyden) 10:217
POTI-PHERA (bib. fig.) 13:934
- Potiphar 13:933
- Putiel 13:1415
Potkin, Johann 5:741
POTOCKI, VALENTINE 13:934
POTOFSKY, JACOB SAMUEL 13:935
POTOK, CHAIM 15:1579; 15:1583
- J.P.S. 10:81
Potosí (city, Bol.) 4:1188
Potovsky, Ernestine, *see* ROSE, ERNESTINE POTOVSKY
Potresov, Alexander 11:1068
POTTERY 13:936
- *Contents:*
- - Pottery Manufacture 13:936
- - Neolithic Period 13:937
- - Chalcolithic Period 13:938
- - Early Bronze Age 13:938
- - Middle Bronze Age 13:938
- - Late Bronze Age 13:939
- - Iron Age 13:940
- - Persian Period 13:942
- - Hellenistic Period 13:942
- - Roman Period 13:942
- - Byzantine Period 13:942
- Amiran, Ruth 2:849
- archaeology 3:304ff
- Beth-Shemesh 4:773
- crafts 5:1041
- Crowfoot, Grace Mary 5:1129
- inscriptions 2:682; 16:660ff
- Israel, ancient 16:1268
- *menorah* design 11:1369
- Mesopotamia 16:1483
- ostraca 12:1509
- Samarian 2:437
- seals 14:1072; 14:1073
- Syria 6:11
- types 1:pottery chart
- *illus:*
- - anthropomorphic vessel 4:759
- - bowl 4:781
- - ceramic lamp decorated with a *menorah* 11:1362
- - clay oven 5:939
- - coffin lid, anthropoid 3:314; 4:761
- - Dead Sea Scroll jars 3:371; 15:492

- - ewer, Lachish 10:1333
- - Grain Museum, Haifa 12:550
- - *hevra kaddisha* pitcher 12:304
- - incantation bowls 2:694; 5:1522
- - incense burning stands 4:481,762; 5:1156-1160; 8:1313; 12:567
- - jar handles 14:1075; 16:386
- - Masada finds 11:1091
- - oil lamps 12:1348; 14:1559
- - ossuaries 3:1012; 7:1047
- - ostraca 12:1509, 1510; 16:657
- - peddler 13:108
- - pen-cases (Qumran) 16:668
- - Philistine clay jug 3:314
- - Philistine female deity 3:696
- - plates 11:*fcg.* 1070; 13:172-173; 14:308,788; 15:1419
- - pottery types (table) 3:307-310
- - rattles 12:561
- - reconstruction work 3:312
- - Sennacherib's prism 14:1162
- - YHD stamp, jar handle 9:110
- *see also:* Majolica
Pottsville (city, Pa.) 13:230
Pougatchov, Emanuel *see* AMIRAN, EMANUEL
Poughkeepsie (city, N.Y.) 8:254; 12:1126
Poujade, Pierre 12:952
Poultney (tn., Vt.) 16:112
Poultry 11:1163
- *see also:* CHICKEN
Pound (Isr. currency) 5:727
POUND, EZRA LOOMIS 13:943
- U.S. literature 15:1585
POUPKO, BERNARD 13:944
Poupko, Israel Meir, *see* ISRAEL MEIR HA-KOHEN
Poussin, Nicolas 12:407; 14:524
- *illus:*
- - "Adoration of the Golden Calf" (paint.) 7:709; 8:1233
POVERTY 13:944
- closeness to God 9:1230
- criterion 5:341
- debts 6:1008ff
- moneylending 12:246ff
- Pentateuch 13:250
- slavery 14:1655ff
- *see also:* POOR, PROVISION FOR THE
Powecki, Piotr, *see* SKARGA, PIOTR
Powell, David 12:1522
Powell, Raphael 10:1495
Power of Attorney, *see* Attorney, Power of
Powidzki (fam.) 6:1329
Powidzki, Stephan, *see* Fishel, Stephan
Powis Smith, J.W. 4:870
Poylishe Yidl (period.) 15:46
Pozarevac (Pozharevats; tn., Yug.) 16:869
POZNAN (city, Pol.) 13:946
- *Contents:*
- - Organization of Community (16-18 centuries) 13:948
- - Holocaust Period 13:950
- - Postwar Period 13:950
- archives 3:387
- Brandys Nad Labem Jews 4:1307
- crafts 5:1052ff
- Great Poland 7:865
- history chart (1399; 1687) 8:766-767
- imprisonment for debt *takkanot* 8:1307
- informers 8:1368
- Prussia 13:1291
- special Purim 13:1397
- tailors 15:705
- *takkanot* 15:736
- textiles 15:1039
- *illus:*
- - community register (1651) 3:381
Poznanski (fam.), *see* POSNANSKI
Poznański (indus.) 11:426; 11:432
Poznański, Edward (Isaac Jacob) 13:930
Poznański, Israel 11:430; 13:736
Poznański, Samuel Abraham 8:957; 13:929; 16:1339
POZNANSKY, MENAHEM 13:951
- *illus:* 16:653
Pozner (fam. name), *see also* Posener, Posner
Pozner, Nahum 14:917
Pozner, Solomon, *see* POSENER, SOLOMON
Pozsony (Slov. city), see BRATISLAVA
Pozzi, Angiolo, *see* Burgonovo, Archangelus de
Pozzuoli (tn., It.) 9:1117
P.P.S. (polit. party) 13:951
Praag, Joe Van 14:148
PRAAG, SIEGFRIED EMANUEL VAN 13:952
Prache, Hilaric 8:51
Practical Kabbalah, *see* KABBALAH (Practical)
PRACTICE AND PROCEDURE 13:952
- *Contents:*
- - Civil 13:952
- - - Court Sessions 13:952
- - - Parties 13:952
- - - Venue 13:953
- - - Summonses 13:953
- - - Default Procedure 13:954
- - - Subject Matter 13:954
- - - Settlement 13:954
- - - Court Decorum 13:954
- - - Equality of Parties 13:955
- - - Pleadings 15:955
- - - Evidence 13:956
- - - Deliberations 13:956
- - - Judgment 13:957
- - - Revision 13:957
- - - Modern Law 13:958
- - Penal 13:958
- - - Court Sessions 13:958
- - - Duplicity of Trials 13:959
- - - Arrest 13:959
- - - Bail 13:959
- - - Default Proceedings 13:959
- - - Prosecution 13:959
- - - Defense 13:960
- - - Evidence 13:960
- - - Deliberations 13:960
- - - Judgment 13:957
- General
- - arbitration 3:294
- - attorney 3:837
- - bet din 4:719
- - compromise 5:857
- - Erez Israel rabbinical courts 12:143
- - extra-legal dispensation 6:1073
- - orphan 12:1479
- - partnership 13:153
- - penal law 13:222
- - role of scribe 14:1041
- - Talmud 14:1394
- Judgment and Execution
- - capital punishment 5:142
- - execution 6:1007
- - *herem* bet-din 8:355
- - imprisonment 8:1303
- Evidence 6:991
- - confession 5:877
- - documents 14:1385
- - *kallah* months 10:710
- - oath 12:1295
- - pleas 13:631
- - witness 16:584
- *illus:*
- - Sanhedrin 14:839
Prades (tn., Fr.) 14:353
Prado, Abraham 11:1552
PRADO, JUAN (Daniel) DE 13:962
- philosophy 13:417
- Spinoza 15:276
Prado, L. Ramirez de 8:51
PRAEFECTUS JUDAEORUM (ldr.,Hung.J.) 13:963
Praeger, Moses, *see* MOSES BEN MENAHEM GRAF
Praescription (property rental rights) 7:1523
Praetorius, Abdias 8:51
Prag, Isaac 9:1464
Praga (sub., Warsaw) 16:944
Prager (fam.) 16:360
Prager, George 4:463; 8:1356
Prager, Jacob 14:959
Prager, Lyon 4:463; 8:1356
Prager, Regina 13:1617
PRAGER, RICHARD 13:963
Prager, R. L. (publ.) 13:1366
Prager Tagblatt (newsp.) 4:1387; 13:1026
Prag Kahn, Florence, *see* Kahn, Florence Prag
PRAGUE (city, Cz.) 13:964
- *Contents:*
- - History 13:964
- - Holocaust Period 13:973
- - Contemporary Period 13:975
- - Hebrew Printing 13:976
- archives 3:380
- book-art 3:537
- Crusades 5:1138
- Frankists 7:70
- guilds 7:972
- Hart, Moses 7:1350
- history chart (1389; 1541; 1745) 8:766-767
- Host desecration 8:1043
- Jesuits 5:279
- Jewish goldsmiths 7:742
- Kafka 10:672
- Kohen family 10:1138ff
- Magen David 11:695
- museum 12:538ff
- nationalism and Jews 8:726
- seal 14:1080
- Shabbateanism 14:1249; 14:1251
- slave trade 14:1661
- special Purim 13:1397
- stock exchange 15:406
- synagogue 15:590
- tailoring guild 15:705
- textiles 15:1041
- Torah study groups 15:459
- trade and commerce 15:1298
- typography 15:1481
- yeshivah 16:764
- *illus:*
- - text
- - Altneuschul
- - - Ark of the Law 15:*fcg.* 619
- - - *bimah* 4:1004
- - - plan 15:603
- - banner of the Jewish community (16th cent.) 6:1334
- - blood libel broadsheet (1694) 8:700
- - cemetery 5:273
- - Delmedigo's tombstone 5:1480
- - 18th Zionist Congress 16:1097
- - Gans, David ben Solomon, tombstone 7:311
- - Ghetto, Three Fountain Place 5:1191
- - Jewish quarter, 17th cent. (plan) 10:84
- - Klaus Synagogue 15:605
- - Maharal's statue 10:376
- - Meisel's tombstone 11:1262
- - pharmacist's tombstone 7:973
- - Pinkas Schul 15:605
- - revocation of expulsion medal 11:991
- - stamps, commemorative 5;1197
- - State Jewish Museum 12:546
- - Zalman Hayat tombstone 7:971
- *see also:* BOHEMIA; CZECHOSLOVAKIA
Prague Circle (lit.gr.) 13:972
PRAGUE HAGGADAH 7:1101
- *illus:* 3:535; 7:1088; 11:729; 13:360,567,1101
Praguer, Moshe 5:448
Praha (city, Cz.), *see* PRAGUE
Prahran (tn., Austr.) 11:1285
Pranaitis, Justin 4:1130; 4:400
Prat, J.M. 4:879
Pratensis, Felix, *see* Prato, Felice da
Prathet Thai (kdm.), *see* THAILAND
Prato (tn., It.) 15:1476ff
PRATO, DAVID 13:977
Prato, Felice da 4:1195; 4:838; 16:101
Prausnitz(tn., Pol.) 3:841
Praust (concen. camp) 15:464
Pravda (newsp.) 10:726
PRAWER, JOSHUA 13:978
Praxis (period.) 1:newsp. list
PRAYER 13:978
- *Contents:*
- - In the Bible 13:978
- - - Terminology 13:978
- - - The Character of Prayer 13:979
- - - Accessories of Prayer 13:980
- - - Answer to Prayer 13:980
- - In the Apocryphal Literature 13:981
- - In Rabbinic Thought 13:981
- - - The Value of Prayer and Concentration in Prayer 13:981
- - - Proper Forms of Prayer 13:982
- - - The Addressing of Prayers Directly to God 13:982
- - In Medieval Thought 13:982
- - - Maimonides 13:982
- - - The Kabbalists 13:983
- - The Hasidim 13:983
- - - Swaying in Prayer 13:984
- - In Modern Thought 13:984
- General
- - *Berakhot* 4:585
- - calendar 5:43
- - evening, duty or optional 14:83
- - *gematria* 7:371
- - hospitality 8:1032
- - impurity 13:1411; 13:1413
- - *Kiddush Ha-Shem* 10:980ff
- - Muslim 9:1423; 10:1197
- - *piyyut* 13:573
- - plague of flies 6:1368
- - poetry 13:671
- - preaching 13:997
- - Psalms 13:1323
- - Samaritan Sabbath 14:741
- - *see also:* BENEDICTIONS; BLESSING AND CURSING
- Ideological Background
- - answered by God 3:657
- - asceticism 3:679
- - beliefs expressed in 3:654
- - Providence 13:1280
- - *Shekhinah* 14:1351
- - sin 14:1590
- - tradition 15:1310
- - *zekhut avot* 16:976
- Manner of
- - agency 12:111
- - children's service 5:460
- - covering of head 8:5
- - dancing 5:1268
- - *devekut* 5:1598
- - direction 12:180
- - drunkenness 6:239
- - Hebrew language 16:1591
- - kabbalistic *tikkun* 10:617; 10:627ff
- - *kavvanah* 10:852
- - *minyan* 12:67
- - musical expression 12:571;

12:605ff
– – mystical *kavvanot* **10:**510; **10:**519
– – sacrifice **5:**1155; **14:**614
– – *sheli'ah zibbur* **14:**1355
– – silent worship **16:**304
– – *tefillin* **15:**898
– – vernacular in **16:**479
– – washing of hands **12:**998
– Setting of
– – altar **2:**764
– – ark **3:**450
– – *bet midrash* **4:**751
– – *bimah* **4:**1002
– – ceremonial objects **5:**288
– – synagogue **15:**580ff
– – Temple **15:**953ff
– – Western Wall **16:**468
– Attitudes Toward
– – Abraham ben Moses **2:**151
– – Ba'al Shem Tov **9:**1050; **9:**1054
– – Bratslav ḥasidim **12:**784,786
– – Da Fano **14:**89
– – Gamaliel II **9:**243
– – Geiger, Abraham **7:**358ff
– – Ḥasidism **7:**1391ff; **15:**457
– – kabbalistic doctrine **10:**561
– – Karaites **10:**781
– – Korets, Phinehas **10:**1204
– – Lurianic Kabbalah **10:**548
– – Meir **11:**1242
– – Moses Sofer **14:**91
– – Pharisees **13:**364; **13:**366
– – Prophets **13:**1161
– – Sadducees **14:**622
– – United Synagogue of America **15:**1674
– *illus:*
– – Austrian Jewish soldiers at Western Wall **11:**1565
– – classroom wall chart (1590, Ferrara) **6:**387
– – *El Male Raḥamim* **6:**682
– – for George Washington **15:**1595
– – *Havdalah* **14:**569
– – Leningrad synagogue **11:**16
– – *Nishmat* **12:**1177
– – *Or Olam* **14:**74
– – Poznan community register **3:**381
– – travel **15:**1348
– – Tripoli Jews' public prayer **11:**203
– *see also:* LITURGY; PRAYER BOOKS; WORSHIP
Prayer Book Press (publ. firm, U.S.) **13:**1377
PRAYER BOOKS **13:**985
– *Contents:*
– – Siddur and Maḥzor **13:**985
– – Early Siddurim **13:**985
– – – Seder Rav Amram Gaon **13:**985
– – – Siddur Saadiah Gaon **13:**985
– – – Maḥzor Vitry **13:**986
– – – Manuscripts from Other rites **13:**986
– – Printed Prayer Books **13:**987
– – Types of Prayer Books **13:**987
– – Textual Editions **13:**987
– – Critical Editions **13:**988
– – Commentaries **13:**988
– – Ḥasidic Siddurim **13:**989
– – Modern Prayer Books (English editions) **13:**989
– – Reform Prayer Books **13:**989
– – Conservative and Reconstructionist Prayer Books **13:**991
– – Reform **13:**992
– – Prayers for Contemporary Events **13:**993
– General
– – ancient period **2:**803
– – Baer, Seligman **4:**80
– – Hannover, Nathan **7:**1274
– – inconography **8:**1221
– – kabbalistic influence **10:**641
– – Kohen-Ẓedek **10:**1141
– – poetry **11:**325
– – Psalm 67 **11:**1368
– *Siddurim*
– – Alnakar **2:**672
– – *Defter* (Samaritan) **14:**741; **14:**753
– – *Eẓ Ḥayyim Siddur* **11:**399
– – Kaffa and Karasubazar *Siddur* **11:**398
– – *maḥzor* **11:**731
– – *Maḥzor Vitry* **11:**736
– – *Me'ah Berakhot* **16:**1417
– – Reconstructionist *Sabbath Prayer Book* **13:**1616
– – Russian **14:**976
– – *Seder ha-Tefilla* **11:**397,401
– – *Seder Rav Amram* **2:**892ff; **11:**396ff
– – *Siddur ha-Ari* **7:**1401; **10:**630ff
– – *Siddur Maharid* **14:**1434
– – *siddur* of the Rabbi of Ruzhin **8:**1267
– – *siddur* of Saadiah Gaon **11:**397,401; **14:**553
– – *siddur* of Solomon ben Nathan **11:**397
– – *Siddur Rashi* **11:**397
– – *Siddur Troyes* **11:**399
– – Singer **11:**402; **14:**1614
– – *see also under Siddur . . .*
– Commentaries and Translations
– – Arnheim, Heymann **3:**485
– – *Avodat ha-Bore* **2:**492
– – Gamaliel ben Pedahzur **7:**299
– – *Iyyun Tefillah* **11:**1272
– – *Kimḥa de-Avishuna* **15:**1378
– – Marathi **13:**1526
– – Wagenaar, Lion **16:**238
– – Yiddish **11:**357ff
– *illus:*
– – *Arvit* prayer, North Italian *siddur* **3:**666
– – Austria (1751) **15:**268
– – *Avodat Yisrael* (1868) **4:**81
– – Ben Porat's (1490) **8:**1327
– – Cochin rite **11:**401
– – *Derekh Yesharah* (1967) **6:**833
– – *Hamilton Siddur* (13th cent.) **8:***fcg.* 1079
– – Hebrew-Russian (1950s) **14:**489
– – Huebsch's **13:**113
– – Jackson's Hebrew-English edition (1826) **9:**1190
– – Judeo-Italian (15th cent.) **9:**1124
– – Judeo-Provençal (14th cent.) **10:**440
– – *Kenaf Renanim* (1626) **5:**188
– – Marrano (1687) **8:**1406
– – *Maḥzor Romania* (1586) **11:**393
– – *Mi she-Berakh* **12:**87
– – *Orden de Bendiciones* (1687) **11:**1019
– – Roman rite **11:**395
– – *Rothschild Siddur* (15th cent., illum. ms., It.), *see Rothschild Mahzor*
– – *Seder ha-Kunteres* (1765) **3:**965
– – *Seder Rav Amram* **2:**892
– – *Seder Tikkunei Shabbat* (1715) **11:**5
– – *Siddur of the Rabbi of Ruzhin* **8:**281; **11:***fcg.* 875
– – silver binding (17th cent., It.) **4:**1230
– – Thirteen Articles of Faith **3:**5
– *see also:* LITURGY
Prayer for the Government, *see* GOVERNMENT, PRAYER FOR THE
Prayer of Azariah, *see* SONG OF THE THREE CHILDREN AND THE PRAYER OF AZARIAH
Prayer of Nabonidus (Dead Sea text) **5:**1277
Prayer shawl, *see* TALLIT
PREACHING **13:**994
– *Contents:*
– – In the Talmudic Period **13:**994
– – – Nature and Purpose of the Sermon **13:**994
– – – The Sermon and the Audience **13:**994
– – – Forms of the Sermon **13:**996
– – – Homilies in the Midrashim **13:**998
– – Medieval Period **13:**998
– – – The Preacher **13:**998
– – – Contents **13:**998
– – – Structure and Style **13:**1000
– – – Social Impact **13:**1001
– – 18th-to early 19th century **13:**1002
– – In Modern Times **13:**1002
– – – The Modern Sermon **13:**1002
– – – Preaching Techniques **13:**1004
– – – Issues of the Day in Preaching **13:**1005
– *Aggadah* **2:**358
– *darshan* **5:**1309
– *derashah* **5:**1549
– *Derashot ha-Ran* **5:**1549
– emissaries **14:**1365
– Ḥasidism **7:**1400
– Hirsch, S.R. **8:**510
– homiletics **8:**946ff
– Kranz, Jacob **10:**1239
– *maggid* **11:**698
– Maharam Schick **14:**958
– Midrash **11:**320ff
– Moscato, Judah **12:**358
– Moses of Coucy **12:**418
– rabbinic office **13:**1446,1452
Pre-biblical Hebrew, *see* HEBREW LANGUAGE
Precedent, legal, *see* MA'ASEH
Precepts, *see* COMMANDMENTS, THE 613; MITZVAH
PRECIOUS STONES AND JEWELRY **13:**1007
– *Contents:*
– – In the Bible **13:**1007
– – Rabbinical Literature **13:**1011
– gold **11:**1430
– scarab seals **14:**1073
– Solomon's trade **15:**98
– taxation **15:**850
– Yemenite Jews **16:**756
– *illus:*
– – *Brusttuch* **11:***fcg.* 1070
– – glass pendant (Tyre) **7:**606
– – Lodz ghetto **11:**435
– – Ofran woman and child **12:**1340
– – ring (3/4 cent.) **11:**1363
– – *sterntichl* **6:***fcg.* 238
– – Torah breastplate **15:***fcg.* 1262
– – wedding ring of Samson Wertheimer **16:**458
– – wedding rings **5:**305; **11:***fcg.* 1067
– – Yemenite necklaces **6:***fcg.* 235
– – Yemenite silversmith **5:**1047
Predestination, *see* PROVIDENCE
Prediction **13:**1150
– *see also:* DIVINATION
Predski, Artur **13:**802
Preemption, *see* MAZRANUT
PREGER, JACOB **13:**1013
Pregnancy
– abortion **2:**98; **2:**99ff
– divorce **11:**1053ff
– remarriage **6:**720
– women's rights **16:**629
– *see also:* ARTIFICIAL INSEMINATION; BARRENNESS AND FERTILITY; BIRTH; PARENT AND CHILD
Pregulman, Mervin **15:**308
PREIL, GABRIEL JOSHUA **13:**1013
– Hebrew literature **8:**214
Preis, Liya Yakovlevna, *see* Ilina, Yelena
Preiskel, Abram **13:**162
Preiswerk, S. **8:**51
Prejudice, *see* ANTI-SEMITISM; DISCRIMINATION; NEGRO-JEWISH RELATIONS; NUMERUS CLAUSUS
PREMINGER, OTTO LUDWIG **13:**1014
– *illus:*
– – *Exodus* scene **12:**456
PŘEMYSL OTTOKAR II **13:**1014
– Moravia **12:**296
Prenn, Daniel **15:**314
Prensa Israelita (period.) **11:**1459; **13:**1041
Prenzlau (tn., Pomerania) **13:**842
Prepositions (bib. Heb.) **16:**1582
Prero, Amram **14:**823
PRESBYTER JUDAEORUM **13:**1014
– *see also:* ARCHPRESBYTER
Preschel, Johanan Moses **12:**69
Prescott (city, Ariz.) **3:**450
Prescription, extinctive, *see* LIMITATION OF ACTIONS
PRESENCE, DIVINE **13:**1015
– *Contents:*
– – The Corporeal Notion **13:**1015
– – The Abstract Notion **13:**1017
– Pentateuch **13:**243
– Tabernacle **15:**684
– Temple **15:**947
– *see also:* SHEKHINAH
Prešéren, France **16:**887
President Hotel (Jer.) **9:**1496
PRESIDENT OF ISRAEL **13:**1020
– role **9:**617ff
– *illus:*
– – Ben Zvi, Izhak
– – – Africa tour, return from **4:**580
– – – autograph **3:**913
– – – bust (B. Lishansky) **4:**578
– – – Leopoldville, state visit **4:**579
– – – Liberia, state visit **9:**436
– – – Tsedaka, Japheth ben Abraham, and **14:**735
– – president's residence (Jer.) **9:**1490
– – Shazar, Shneur Zalman
– – – addressing diplomatic corps **14:**1327
– – – autograph **3:**917
– – – Brazilian stamp **4:**1332
– – – Druze judge sworn in **9:**925
– – – Eshkol, Levi, and **6:**891
– – – First German ambassador and **7:**502
– – – I.D.F. generals with **14:**1634
– – – Philippine ambassador and **13:**396
– – – Yod-Tet Kislev celebration **10:**383
– – Weizmann, Chaim
– – – addressing the Knesset (1949) **16:**433
– – – autograph **3:**918
– – – inaugural speech **9:**615
– – – military ceremony (1949) **6:**173
– – – presenting Torah scroll to Harry S. Truman **15:**1409
– – – Russian ambassador and **14:**497
– – – taking the oath **9:**370
– – *see also under names of individual presidents*
Presidents' Conference (U.S.), *see* CONFERENCE OF PRESIDENTS OF MAJOR AMERICAN JEWISH ORGANIZATIONS
President Street Synagogue (Johannesburg) **15:**194

PRESOV (tn., Cz.) **13:**1022
- Kosice **10:**1216
- *illus:* text
PRESS **13:**1023
- *Contents:*
- - History **13:**1023
- - Australia and New Zealand **13:**1025
- - Canada **13:**1026
- - Belgium **13:**1026
- - Czechoslovakia **13:**1026
- - England **13:**1029
- - France **13:**1029
- - Germany and Austria **13:**1031
- - Holland **13:**1033
- - Hungary **13:**1035
- - India **13:**1036
- - Italy **13:**1036
- - Ladino Press **13:**1037
- - Latin America **13:**1040
- - Middle East and North Africa **13:**1041
- - Poland **13:**1043
- - Rumania **13:**1044
- - Russia **13:**1044
- - - U.S.S.R. (1917-1970) **13:**1047
- - Scandinavia **13:**1049
- - South Africa **13:**1050
- - Switzerland **13:**1051
- - United States **13:**1051
- advertising **2:**319
- children's magazines **5:**456; **5:**457; **5:**458
- Israel **9:**1014; **9:**1017
- Zionism **16:**1157
- *illus:*
- - text
- - *Allgemeine Zeitung des Judenthums* (first issue, 1837) **2:**648
- - *Archives Israélites de France* (1st volume, 1840) **5:**18
- - Bundist papers and pamphlets **15:**40
- - *Chwila* (Lvov, 1939) **11:**615
- - *Council Woman* **12:**870
- - *Day, the* (U.S.) **10:**51
- - *Der Birobidzhaner Shtern* **14:**491
- - *Der Jude* (Berlin, 1927) **10:**402
- - *Der Moment* (1914) **12:**235
- - *Der Tog* (May 15, 1948) **12:**1111
- - *Die Palme* (Pest, 1871) **8:**1100
- - *Die Welt* first issue **16:**445
- - *El Tresoro* (Rushchuk, 1894) **4:**1487
- - *Forward* (New York, 1920) **10:**50; **15:**1619
- - *Gazeta Jurnal* (Harbin, 1931) **7:**1331
- - *Gazeta Lomzynska* **11:**469
- - *Ha-Aḥdut* editorial board **16:**999
- - *Ha-Am* (1917) **12:**361
- - *Hadoar*, first issue **15:**1627
- - *Ha-Me'assef* (1788) **8:**181
- - *Ha-Shofar* **16:**1109
- - *Ḥavazzelet* (Jerusalem, 1870) **9:**327
- - *Haynt* **7:**1499
- - *Het Joodsche Weekblad* **12:**982
- - *In-Zikh* (1920) **8:**1435
- - *Israelite, The* (1854) **2:**821
- - *Jewish Chronicle* (first issue) **10:**41
- - *Jewish Morning Journal, The* (N.Y., 1906) **10:**77
- - *Jewish Record* (Dec. 13, 1862) **15:**1602
- - *JTA'S Jewish Daily Bulletin* (first issue) **10:**95
- - *Kol Mevasser* (Odessa, 1st issue) **10:**1166
- - *L'E.I.F.*, cover page **14:**1039
- - *Literarishe Bleter* editorial board **16:**818
- - *Lomzer Shtime* **11:**469
- - *Lomzer Veker* **11:**469
- - *Lomzer Vort* **11:**469
- - *Lomzer Arbeiter Tribune* **11:**469
- - *Lomzer Leben* **11:**469
- - *Lomzer Letzte Najes* **11:**469
- - *Maariv* (Tel Aviv, 1948) **11:**639
- - *Menorah Journal, The* **11:**1371
- - *Nosotros* (1963) **11:**250
- - *Palestine Post* (Jerusalem, 1936) **7:**1067; **9:**350; **9:**364
- - *Pinsker Sztyme* **13:**542
- - *Przegläd Lomżyński* **11:**469
- - *Razsvet* staff **13:**1596
- - *Sinai* (Baltimore, 1858) **15:**1600
- - *Sovietisch Heymland* **14:**491; **15:**216
- - *Sulamith* (1806) **15:**503
- - *Uj Kelet*, first issue **15:**1510
- - *Unzer Vort* **11:**469
- - *Weekly Gleaner, The* (1857) **5:**57
- - *Yiddish Lomze* **11:**469
- - YIVO publications **16:**838
- - *Zeichen der Zeit* (Chicago, 1869) **5:**411
- *see also:* NEWSPAPERS, HEBREW; PUBLISHING; *and under individual places and languages*
Press, Anti-Semitic, *see* Anti-Semitic Press
PRESS, FRANK **13:**1056
PRESS, YESHAYAHU **13:**1057
- physical education **15:**294
Pressburg, (city, Cz.), *see* BRATISLAVA
Pressburg, Henrietta, *see* Marx, Henrietta
Pressburger, Abraham **2:**532
Pressburger, Aron **4:**1214
Pressburger, Gabriel Isaac **10:**247
Pressburger, Samuel **10:**247
Presser, Deborah **13:**1057
PRESSER, JACOB **13:**1057
PRESSMAN, DAVID **5:**386
PRESSMAN, LEE **13:**1057
PRESSMANE, JOSEPH **3:**608
- Paris **13:**116
Press Survey (agency, Gt. Brit.) **13:**1031
Prester John **3:**475; **15:**1005
Prestwich (tn., Eng.) **11:**859
PRETORIA (city, S.A.) **13:**1058
- *illus:* text
Pretorius, Paul **4:**885
PREUSS, HUGO **13:**1058
PREUSS, JULIUS **13:**1059
PREUSSEN, *see* PRUSSIA
Preussischer Landesverband juedischer Gemeinden (assoc., Prus.) **4:**646; **5:**1595; **13:**1293
Prevelakyis, Pantlis Georgiou **7:**887
Prevesa (city, Gr.) **10:**426
Preysing, Bishop (of Berlin) **8:**911
PREZIOSI, GIOVANNI **13:**1059
- Holocaust **8:**851
Pribram, Aaron **4:**1178
PRIBRAM, ALFRED FRANCIS **13:**1060
PRIBRAM, KARL **13:**1060
Pribram, Solomon **4:**1178
Price, Jacob **15:**310
Price, Richard **8:**715
Price control, *see* HAFKA'AT SHE'ARIM
Pride, *see* ETHICS; HUMILITY
Prideaux, Humphrey **8:**51
Priene (anc. tn., Ionia) **12:**181; **15:**599
- *illus:*
- - *Menorah* **11:**1361
Priest, High, *see* HIGH PRIEST
Priestley, Joseph **11:**78
PRIESTLY BLESSING **13:**1060
- *Contents:*
- - Introduction **13:**1060
- - In the Halakhah **13:**1061
- General
- - Amen **2:**803
- - amulet **2:**909
- - *Birkat ha-Shalom* **2:**841
- - blessing of children **4:**1087
- - *dukhan* **6:**267
- - folklore **6:**1402
- - Johanan ben Zakkai **9:**242
- - peace **13:**196
- - priest **13:**1076
- - *Ta'anit* **15:**675
- - Talmud **15:**786
- - Temple **15:**972
- - variations in liturgy **11:**393, 402
- Requirements
- - ablution **2:**85
- - covering of head **8:**5
- - disqualifications **4:**1083
- - marriage **11:**1038
- - *minḥah* **12:**11
- - *minyan* **12:**67
- - mourning **12:**491
- - *tallit* **15:**744
- *illus:*
- - text
- - amulets **2:**908-910
- - hands as cosmic symbol **10:**514
- - lavers **2:**86; **6:**1402
- - Lubaczow tombstone decoration **15:**1230
- - Padua synagogue laver **13:**11
- - Prague tombstone (1786) **3:**528
- - Torah crown **15:**1260-1261
- - Wlodawa synagogue decoration **16:**598
- *mus. notations:*
- - *Amen* **2:**804
- - Italian rite **12:**621
"Priestly Blessing" (paint., Adler) **3:**558
Priestly Code **5:**1579; **5:**1581; **11:**138; **13:**231
PRIESTLY VESTMENTS **13:**1063
- dress **6:**212
- mixed species **14:**1213
- Torah symbol **4:**1335
- *Urim* and *Thummim* **16:**8
- *illus:*
- - text
- - high priest's breastpiece (chart) **13:**1007
PRIESTS AND PRIESTHOOD **13:**1069
- *Contents:*
- - Definition of Priesthood **13:**1069
- - Right to Serve **13:**1076
- - Levels Within the Priesthood **13:**1073
- - Functions **13:**1076
- - Holiness of the Priesthood **13:**1080
- - History **13:**1082
- - From the Hellenistic Era to the Destruction of the Temple **13:**1086
- - In the Halakhah **13:**1088
- - In Modern Times **13:**1089
- General
- - Abraham **2:**115
- - education **6:**396ff
- - Falashas **6:**1147
- - Melchizedek **11:**1287
- - messianism **11:**1409
- - Qumran community **6:**66
- - sages **14:**640ff
- - Samaritans **14:**740; **14:**741
- - seals **14:**1080
- - theocracy **15:**1099
- - Tunisia legend **15:**1430
- History
- - Aaronides **2:**18
- - Ananias **16:**1274
- - court of priests **4:**722
- - Jehoiada's institutions **9:**1320
- - Jerusalem, Hellenistic period **9:**1389ff
- - Judah ha-Nasi **10:**372
- - Judaism **10:**388
- - king, kingship **10:**1017
- - prophet **13:**1150
- - Reform Judaism **14:**24
- - Sadducees **14:**621
- - Second Temple period **8:**627ff
- Genealogy **7:**379
- - Aaron **2:**4
- - Aaronides **2:**18
- - altar service **2:**769
- - care of tables **11:**1231
- - family purity **6:**1170
- Law
- - cemeteries **5:**272
- - desecration of **5:**1559
- - disqualifications **13:**1062
- - Johanan ben Zakkai **9:**242; **10:**150
- - leprosy **11:**35
- - levitical cities **11:**136
- - marriage laws **16:**892
- - - divorce bills **6:**132; **6:**134
- - - levirate marriage **11:**125; **16:**776
- - - marriage with a proselyte **13:**1184
- - - prohibited marriages **11:**1052ff
- - - prostitutes **13:**1244
- - - raped wife **13:**1548
- - - sexual offenses **14:**1208
- - nazirite **12:**907
- - *niddui* and dues **8:**351
- - ritual impurity **13:**1405ff
- - Temple Mount **15:**989
- Duties and Customs
- - ablution **2:**82; **2:**85
- - anointment **3:**27
- - atonement **10:**1039ff
- - blessing **13:**1060
- - decisions **3:**908
- - lot casting **11:**511
- - *mishmarot* and *ma'amadot* **12:**89
- - *Omer* ceremony **12:**1382ff
- - red heifer **14:**10
- - sacrifice **14:**608ff
- - Temple **15:**953ff
- - *Urim* and *Thummim* **16:**9
- - wood offerings **16:**630
- Privileges
- - firstborn **6:**1308
- - first fruits **6:**1313; **6:**1315
- - *ḥallah* **7:**1195
- - ḥerem property **8:**345
- - tax-exemption **15:**842
- - tithes **5:**1486; **15:**1025
- - Torah-reading **15:**1247; **15:**1253
- Literature
- - Commandments, the 613 **5:**763f,773f
- - Leviticus **11:**138ff
- - *Leviticus Rabbah* **11:**148
- - Numbers, Book of **12:**1244
- - *Parah* **13:**87
- - Pentateuch **13:**251
- *geneal. table* **2:**19
- *illus:*
- - Aaron (Dura-Europos paint.) **6:**278
- - Amaziah **12:**1293
- - Ark of the Covenant carried across the Jordan **3:**461
- - capture of Jericho **3:**517
- - cutting hair of Nazirites **12:**906
- - ephod **6:** 805
- - high priest **8:**473
- - inspecting leprosy **12:**924
- - lighting fire to signal new moon **14:**310
- - performing the sacrifice **3:**fcg. 988
- - receiving dough-offering **7:**1196
- - vestments **4:**786; **6:**805; **13:**1066
- *see also:* HIGH PRIEST
Prigoff, James **15:**315
Prijs, Bernard **13:**1091
PRIJS, JOSEPH **13:**1091

Prijs, Leo **13:**1091
Priluk, Aryeh Loew **12:**1517
Priluker, Jacob **12:**1027
PRILUKI (tn., Ukr.) **13:**1091
Primakoff, Henry **5:**692
Prime Minister of Israel **9:**614ff
Primera Sociedad Agrícola Israelita (coop., Arg.) **3:**431
Primitivism (art) **5:**324
PRIMO, SAMUEL (Judah) **13:**1091
- Alfandari, Hayyim **2:**598
- Shabbetai Ẓevi **14:**1225; **14:**1235; **14:**1244
Primogeniture, *see* FIRSTBORN
Primordial man (kab. conc.), *see* ADAM KADMON
Prince Albert (city, Can.) **14:**892
Prince and the Hermit, The (wk.), *see* BEN HA-MELEKH VE-HA-NAZIR
Prince des Juifs (ldr. Hung.), *see* PRAEFECTUS JUDAEORUM
Prince Edward Island (prov., Can.) **11:**997
- Quebec **13:**1423; **13:**1424
Prince Georges (co., Md.) **11:**1077; **16:**358
Prince of Light (angelic fig.) **2:**962
Princes of the Peoples (angels) **2:**963
Princes Road Synagogue (Liverpool, Eng.), *see* Old Hebrew Congregation
Princeton (city, W. Va.) **16:**475
Príncipe (isl.) **15:**487
Principles of Faith, *see* ARTICLES OF FAITH
Pringle, Edward **5:**1544
Pringsheim, Fritz **7:**133
PRINGSHEIM, HANS **5:**386
PRINS, ABRAHAM **13:**1095
- Proops family **13:**1143
Prins, Izak M. **13:**1035
PRINS, LIEPMAN PHILIP **13:**1095
Prins, Sonja **6:**321
Prinstein, Myer **15:**316 **12:**1375;
Printed Editions of the Hebrew Bible **4:**836
PRINTERS' MARKS **13:**1095
- *menorah* design **11:**1369
- Ya'ari's work **16:**690
- *illus:*
- - Bak, Israel **4:**115
- - Cavalli, Georgio di **5:**1584
- - Fagius, Paulus **6:**1136
- - Foa family **6:**1370
- - Frankfort a/O **7:**93
- - *Magen David* **11:**691
- - Mordecai ben Gershon ha-Kohen's sons **9:**1586
- - Parenzo brothers **13:**101
- - Prague **5:**1197
- - Soncino, Gershom ben Moses **15:**140
- - Yaari's collection **13:**1093
- *see also:* HERALDRY
PRINTING, HEBREW **13:**1096
- *Contents:*
- - Introduction **13:**1096
- - Signature and Pagination **13:**1099
- - Title Pages and Decoration **13:**1099
- - 1500-1550 **13:**1100
- - 1550-1627 **13:**1100
- - The 17th and 18th Centuries **13:**1104
- - Modern Period **13:**1110
- - In Ereẓ Israel **13:**1114
- General
- - book trade **4:**1238
- - colophon **5:**752
- - *haskamot* **7:**1452ff
- - history chart **8:**766–767
- - Kabbalah **10:**543
- - Karaites **10:**781; **16:**778
- - Marrano Diaspora **11:**1024
- Locations
- - Aden **2:**262
- - Aleppo **2:**564
- - Algeria **2:**615
- - Altona **2:**780
- - Amsterdam **2:**901ff
- - Basle **4:**304
- - Bologna **4:**1191
- - Bombay **4:**1193ff
- - Cairo **5:**31
- - Calcutta **5:**41
- - Cochin **5:**626
- - Cologne **5:**741
- - Cracow **5:**1037
- - Cremona **5:**1077
- - Damascus **5:**1242
- - Djerba **6:**139
- - Dyhernfurth **6:**330
- - Ereẓ Israel **9:**298
- - Europe **6:**971
- - Fano **6:**1174
- - Ferrara **6:**1234
- - Fez **6:**1256ff
- - Frankfort on the Main **7:**89
- - Frankfort on the Oder **7:**93ff
- - Fuerth **7:**216ff
- - Halberstadt **7:**1173
- - Halle **7:**1196
- - Hanau **7:**1257
- - Homburg **8:**942
- - Instanbul **9:**1097
- - Izmir **9:**1165
- - Jerusalem **9:**1454
- - Karlsruhe **10:**795
- - Korets **10:**1202
- - Leipzig **10:**1592
- - Leiria **10:**1593
- - Lisbon **11:**303
- - Lithuania **11:**369
- - London **11:**481
- - Lublin **11:**544
- - Lvov **11:**613
- - Lyck **11:**618
- - Metz **11:**1451
- - Minsk **12:**53
- - Naples **12:**823
- - Nowy Dwor Mazowiecki **12:**1244
- - Nuremberg **12:**1279
- - Olesnica **12:**1360
- - Padua **13:**12
- - Paris **13:**109
- - Piovi Di Sacco **13:**557
- - Polonnoye **13:**836
- - Prague **13:**967
- - Roedelheim **14:**219
- - Rome **14:**252ff
- - Russia **14:**463
- - Sabbioneta **14:**586ff
- - Safed **14:**628ff
- - Salonika **14:**707
- - Seini **14:**1115
- - Shklov **14:**1420
- - Slavuta **14:**1665
- - Strasbourg **15:**424
- - Sulzbach **15:**507
- - Tarnopol **15:**817
- - Utrecht **16:**37
- - Venice **16:**101ff
- - Vilna **16:**147
- - Viseul de Sus **16:**165
- - Wandsbeck **16:**263
- - Warsaw **16:**342
- - Zhitomir **16:**1012
- - Zholkva **16:**1014
- - Zurich **16:**1242
- Families and Individuals
- - Abraham ben Carton **2:**142
- - Abraham the Dyer **2:**143
- - Adelkind, Israel **2:**259
- - Altaras **2:**771
- - Bass, Shabbetai **4:**313ff
- - Bomberg, David **4:**1195
- - Bueno, Ephraim **4:**1460
- - Dangoor, Ezra **5:**1274
- - Foa **6:**1369
- - ʿIrāqī, Eleazar **8:**1462
- - Jabez **9:**1172
- - Jaffe **9:**1258
- - Kohen **10:**1138
- - Le Bé, Guillaume **10:**1547
- - Manasseh ben Israel **11:**855
- - Margolis, H. **12:**1243
- - Plantin, Christophe **13:**613
- - Proops **13:**1143ff
- - Prostiz, Isaac **13:**1247
- - Romm **14:**255
- - Shaḥor **14:**1260ff
- - Soncino **15:**140ff
- - Uri Phoebus ha-Levi **16:**6
- - Uzan **16:**39
- - Zifroni, Israel **16:**1019
- Works
- - Bible editions **4:**836
- - book-art **3:**536
- - *Haggadah* **7:**1100
- - Hebrew Fiction **6:**1270
- - illuminated manuscripts **8:**1259, 1285
- - incunabula **8:**1319ff
- - *kunteres* **10:**1292
- - Mishnah **12:**107
- - prayer books **13:**987
- - *Shulḥan Arukh* **7:**1166
- - Talmud **15:**765
- *illus:* Amsterdam
- - *Amsterdam Haggadah* (1965) **3:**536; **7:**1089
- - *Amsterdam Minhagim Book* **12:**30; **13:**1402
- - Bible (1661) **15:**1484
- - Carpentras *Maḥzor* (1739) **11:**403
- - *Emek ha-Melekh* (1648) **10:**597
- - *Esperanca de Israel* **11:**856
- - *haftarot,* Shabbatean edition (1666) **14:**1229
- - *Hovot ha-Levavot* (1737) **4:**106
- - *Josippon,* Yiddish translation (1771) **10:**296
- - *Magen Avraham* (1732) **8:**74
- - *Marrano prayer book* (1687) **8:**1406
- - *Mesillat Yesharim* (1740) **11:**600
- - Mishnah, Hebrew-Latin (1700–1704), 58 frontispiece illustrations, *see* MISHNAH
- - *Or ha-Yashar* (1769) **5:**614
- - *Pa'amon ve-Rimmon* (1708) **10:**491
- - *Peri Ḥadash* (1692) **8:**458
- - protective prayer for women in childbirth (17th cent.) **4:**1050
- - *Raziel ha-Malakh* (1701) **13:**1593
- - *Seder Berakhot* (1687) **4:**486
- - *Sefer Elim* (1629) **3:**801
- - *Sefer ha-Tashbeẓ* (1741) **12:**978
- - *Sefer Yemin Moshe* (1718) **5:**170
- - *Sha'arei Ziyyon* (1671) **7:**1274
- - *Shevet Musar* (1734) **8:**959
- - *Shitah Mekubbezet* (1721) **8:**465
- - *Tikkun Keri'ah* (1666) **14:**1225
- - *Tur Bareket* (1654) **7:**1506
- *illus:* Antwerp
- - *L'Encyclie des secrets de l'eternite* (1571) **10:**1563
- *illus:* Augsburg
- - *Portae Lucis* (1516) **10:**635
- *illus:* Avigon
- - *Seder ha-Kunteres* (1765) **3:**965
- *illus:* Baghdad
- - *Megillat Paras* (1906) **4:**312
- *illus:* Basle
- - *Ammudei Shelomo* (1600) **11:**580
- - *Ayn Shoyn Mayse Bukh* (1602) **11:**650
- - *De arcanis catholicae veritatis* (1550) **7:**261
- - *Sefer ha-Dikduk* (1525) **8:**19
- - *Si'aḥ Yiẓhak* (1627) **9:**28
- - *Zurat ha-Arez* . . . (1546) **3:**786, 797, 800; **4:**303
- *illus:* Berdichev
- - *Birat Migdal Oz* (1836) **6:**723
- - *Sefer Berit Menuḥah* (1807) **5:**1527
- *illus:* Berlin
- - *Baal (ei) ha-Nefesh* (1762) **2:**137
- - *Ketina Kol-Bo* (1923) **5:**434
- - *Mishlei Shu'alim* (1756) **4:**597
- - *Sefer ha-Bahir* (1706) **4:**97
- - *Yesod Yosef* (1739) **5:**35
- *illus:* Bologna
- - Pentateuch, first edition with Targum Onkelos and Rashi's commentary (1482) **4:**1190; **15:**1483
- *illus:* Brescia
- - *Meshal ha-Kadmoni* (1491) **3:**534; **14:**657
- - *Sefer ha-Mahbarot* (1491) **4:**1352; **8:**1297; **16:**1192
- *illus:* Brody
- - *Beit Aharon* (1875) **10:**793
- *illus:* Cambridge, Mass.
- - *Dickdook Leshon Gnebreet* (1735) **12:**257
- *illus:* Constantinople
- - *Arba'ah Turim* (1493) **8:**1333
- - *Esh Dat* (1718) **2:**598
- - *Get Pashut* (1719) **7:**1025
- - *Ma'aseh Rav* (1736) **9:**1098
- - *Me-Am Lo'ez* (1751) **5:**1154
- - *Rei'ah Sadeh* (1738) **6:**326
- - *Sefer Meshivat Nefesh* (1748) **10:**1347
- - *illus:* Cracow
- - *Aguddah* (1571) **2:**585
- - *Pardes Rimmonim* (1592) **5:**968 **10:**502, 584, 614
- - *Sha'arei Teshuvah* (1595) **10:**179
- *illus:* Cremona
- - *Hizzekuni* (1559) **8:**459
- - *Kizzur Mordekhai ve-Simanav* (1557) **5:**1078
- - *Sefer Zori ha-Yagon* (1557) **6:**1141
- *illus:* Damascus
- - *Kesef Nivhar* (1605) **5:**1240
- *illus:*Dessau
- - *Zayit Ra'anan* (1704) **7:**766
- *illus:*Faro
- - Gacon's Pentateuch (1487) **8:**1331
- *illus:* Ferrara
- - classroom wall chart (1590) **6:**387
- - *Hassagot* (Moses Alashkar) (1556) **2:**512
- - *Kevod Elohim* (1556) **8:**1196
- - *Or Adonai* (1555) **5:**1079
- *illus:* Frankfort on the Main
- - *Bayit Hadash* (1697) **14:**1619
- - *Binyan Shelomo* (1708) **7:**1259
- - *Compendium Grammaticae Ebraeo-Chaldaicae* (1765) **8:**12
- - *Havvat Yair* (1699) **4:**47
- - *Hulin* (1719) **8:**1069
- - *Yad Kol Bo* (1727) **8:**75
- *illus:* Frankfort on the Oder
- - *Derekh Yesharah* (1697) **6:**833
- - *Ir Binyamin* (1698) **3:**52
- - *Sha'agat Aryeh* (1755) **7:**979
- *illus:* Fuerth
- - *Zinah David* (1750) **6:**39
- *illus:* Genoa
- - Polyglot Psalter (1516) **7:**408
- *illus* Guadalajara
- - calendar (c. 1482) **5:**52
- - *Haggadah,* earliest print (c. 1482) **7:**954, 1087

- illus: Hanau
- - *Shefa Tal* (1612) **10:**514,574
- illus: Hanover
- - *Massekhet Purim* (1844) **13:**125
- illus: Hijar
- - Alantansi's Bible (1487) **8:**1330
- - Pentateuch with Targum Onkelos and Rashi's commentary (1490) **4:**837
- illus: Isny
- - *Buovo d'Antona* (1541) **4:**1276
- illus: Izmir
- - *Ein Yosef* (1860) **9:**1164
- illus: Jassy
- - *Divrei ha Yamim le-Arazot Rumanyah* (1872) **14:**388
- illus: Jerusalem
- - *Avodat ha-Kodesh* (1841) **9:**1449
- - *Kedushat Yom Tov* (1843) **2:**611
- - *Ma'aseh ha-Ez* (1925) **5:**435
- - *Ma'aseh Nissim* (1930) **4:**75
- illus: Jessnitz
- - *Ma'aseh Tuviyyah* (1721) **5:**983; **7:**416, 419
- illus: Koretz
- - *Toledot Ya'akov Yosef* (1780) **8:**960
- illus: Kozlov
- - *Keter Torah* (19th cent.) **2:**10
- - *Sefer ha-Mivhar ve-Tov ha-Mishar (1835)* **10:**767
- illus: Krotoszyn
- - *Talmud Yerushalmi* (1866/67) **10:**1279
- illus: Leghorn
- - *Shivhei Yerushalayim* (1785) **4:**275
- - *Tur Piteda* (1655) **7:**232
- - *Zivhei Kohen* (1832) **6:**29
- illus: Leipzig
- - *Midrash Elleh Ezkera* (1853) **7:**1117
- illus: Leiria
- - Bible with Targum Jonathan and commentaries of Radak and Ralbag (1494) **4:**895
- - D'Ortas' Former Prophets (1495) **8:**1334
- - *Tur Orah Hayyim* (1495) **4:**1234; **8:**1330
- illus: Lemberg
- - chessboard layout (1809) **5:**401
- - *Megalleh Amukot* (1795) **7:**370
- - *Mikra'ot Gedolot* (1808) **2:**783
- - *Minhat Hinnukh* (1889) **4:**15
- - *Tiferet Zevi* (1816) **4:**288
- illus: Lisbon
- - *Hiddushei ha-Torah* (1489) **4:**898; **8:**1328
- - Pentateuch with Targum Onkelos (15th cent.) **4:**843
- - *Perush ha-Berakhot ve-ha-Tefillot* (1489) **11:**301
- illus: Lodz
- - *Yismah Yisrael* (1911) **2:**560
- illus: London
- - Hebrew-English prayer book (1770) **3:**5
- - *Kinat Yeshurun* (1817) **12:**641
- - *Lehem Oni* (1784) **11:**476
- - *Takkanot u-Minhagim* of the Dublin Hebrew Congregation (1839) **6:**248
- - *Tokhahat Megulla* and *Ha-Zad Nahash* (1715) **8:**840
- illus: Lublin
- - *Kiddushin* (1618) **11:**544
- - *Maggid Mesharim* (1646) **5:**198
- - *Yoreh De'ah* (1635) **9:**1215
- illus: Mantua
- - *Behinat ha-Olam* (1476-80) **15:**1483
- - *Josippon, Sefer bin Guryon* (c. 1480) **8:**1331
- - *Mantua Haggadah* (1560) **3:**538; **6:**863; **7:**1087
- - *Me'or Einayim* (1574) **8:**567
- - *Mishlei Shu'alim* (1557) **5:**431
- - *Orah Hayyim* (1772) **14:**1476
- - Poem in honor of Joseph II (1789) **4:**426
- - prayer for health (18th cent.) **11:**1196
- - *Seder Olam Rabbah* (1514) **8:**559
- - *Sefer ha-Kabbalah* (1514) **8:**1160
- - *Sefer Josippon* (1475) **5:**861
- - *Tikkunei ha-Zohar* (1558) **5:**280
- illus: Mikulov
- - *Seder Birkat ha-Mazon* (1728) **8:**1315
- illus: Moscow
- - Hebrew-Russian dictionary (1963) **14:**490
- - *Sihat Hulin* (1917) **4:**1392
- illus: Mukachevo
- - *Mahashevet Mordekhai* (1902) **4:**160
- illus: Naples
- - Ben Porat prayer book (1490) **8:**1327
- - Book of Psalms (1487) **8:**1329
- - Gunzenhauser's Pentateuch (1488) **8:**1332
- - *Hovot ha-Levavot* (1489) **5:**785
- - *Kol Bo*, first edition (1485?) **10:**1159
- - Mishnah (1492) **8:**1328; **12:**98
- - Pentateuch, Abraham ibn Ezra's commentary (1488) **4:**894
- - Pentateuch, Bahya ben Asher's commentary (1492) **4:**104
- - *Sha'ar ha-Gemul* (1490) **8:**1334
- - *Soncino Bible* (15th cent.) **4:**840
- - Song of Songs, with Rashi's commentary (1487) **4:**891
- illus: Newark
- - *Sefer ha-Ployderzakh* (1892) **13:**130
- illus: New York
- - *Haggadah* (1837) **12:**1073
- - *Ha-Yehudi ha-Kadosh* (c. 1930) **5:**436
- - Hebrew-English Sephardi prayer book (1826) **9:**1190
- - *Khurbn Vilne* (1947) **10:**659
- - *The Living Talmud* **4:**1143
- - *Megillat Setarim* (E. Deinard; 1928) **5:**1462
- illus: Offenbach
- - *Sefer Zurat ha-Arez* (1720) **7:**422
- illus: Ortona
- - *De arcanis catholicae veritatis* (1518) **8:**10
- illus: Padova
- - *Nezem Zahav* (1858) **2:**660
- illus: Paris
- - Estienne's (Stephanus') Bible edition (1544-46) **15:**1484
- illus: Piove di Sacco
- - *Selihot* (1475) **15:**1483
- illus: Prague
- - *Ga'on Zevi* (1737) **8:**1005
- - *Hiddushei Hilkhot Maharam Barby* (1792) **4:**208
- - *Orhot Zaddikim* (1581) **12:**1458
- - *Prague Haggadah* (1526) **3:**535; **7:**1088; **11:**729
- - *Toledot Yisrael* (1796) **7:**1440
- illus: Pressburg
- - *Gewitsch Haggadah* (1730) **7:**534
- illus: Reggio di Calabria
- - Rashi's Pentateuch commentary (1475) **14:**38; **15:**1483
- illus: Riva di Trento
- - *Sefer Milhamot ha-Shem* (1560) **11:**93
- - *Tikkun Middot ha-Nefesh* (1562) **6:**933
- illus: Roedelheim
- - *Avodat Yisrael* prayer book (1868) **4:**81
- - *Mahzor Minhag Ashkenazi* (1800-1807) **15:**1485
- illus: Rome
- - *Mishneh Torah* (1475) **8:**1328
- - *She'elot u-Teshuvot*, Nissim Gerondi (1546) **12:**1184
- illus: Sabbioneta
- - *Hazut Kashah* (1552) **3:**258
- - *Pirkei de-Rabbi Eliezer* (1567) **13:**559
- - *Sefer Ya'ir Nativ* (1533) **4:**586
- - *She'elot u-Tshuvot*, Moses ben Isaac Alashkar (1553) **8:**72
- illus: Safed
- - *Kohelet Ya'akov* (1578) **7:**260
- illus: St. Petersburg
- - Gordon, Judah Leib, collected poems (1884) **8:**186
- illus: Salonika
- - *Be'ur Luhot* (1568) **5:**53
- - *Genesis Rabbah* (1593) **7:**400
- - *Mattenot Kehunnah* (1595) **9:**1079
- - *Zemah David* (1785) **8:**1156
- illus: Shklov
- - *Kol Shavat Bat Yehudah* (1803) **7:**1446
- illus: Slavuta
- - *Tanya* (1796) **7:**1418
- illus: Soncino
- - *Arba'ah Turim*, first page (c. 1490) **3:**533
- - *Mahzor Minhag Roma* (1485-86) **8:**1327; **15:**141
- - *Mivhar ha-Peninim* (1484) **8:**1332
- - *Sefer ha-Ikkarim* (1485) **5:**788
- - *Sefer Mitzvot Gadol* (1488) **8:**1333; **9:**1125
- illus: Sulzbach
- - *Sefer Hasidim* (1685) **7:**1389
- illus: Tel Aviv
- - *Ba-Halomi* (1926) **5:**446
- - *Beatricha* (1942) **5:**439
- - *Be-Erez Lobengulu Melekh Zulu* (1938) **5:**438
- - *Haggadah shel ha-Bayit ha-Le'ummi* (1930) **13:**137
- - *Ha-Yom ha-Shemesh Mehayyekhet* (1967) **5:**447
- - Koran, Hebrew translation (1963) **10:**1195
- - *Pithu et ha-Sha'ar* (1945) **5:**440
- illus: Turin
- - *Rane Falet* (1797) **5:**422
- illus: Ungvar
- - *Peri he-Hag* (1871) **4:**1389
- illus: Venice
- - *Aggadat Shemu'el* (1576) **3:**438
- - *Baraita de-Melekhet ha-Mishkan* (1602) **4:**193
- - *Be'ur al ha-Torah* (1544) **5:**751
- - *Be'ur Sefer Kohelet* (1578) **7:**274
- - *Bikkurei Kezir Talmud Torah shel Kehillah Kedoshah Ferrara* (1715) **10:**1380
- - Deuteronomy, Isaac Arama's commentary (1546) **5:**1583
- - Deuteronomy, Levi ben Gershom's commentary (1546) **5:**1580
- - *Deuteronomy Rabbah* (1566) **5:**1584
- - *Ein Ya'akov* (1546) **8:**73
- - Exodus, Gersonides' commentary (1546) **6:**1065
- - *Exodus Rabbah* (1545) **6:**1068
- - *Halakhot Gedolot* (1548) **7:**1168
- - *Kenaf Rananim* (1626) **5:**188
- - *Kiddushin* (1520-23) **15:**757
- - *Korban Hagigah* (1704) **7:**259
- - *Kuzari* (1547) **10:**356
- - *Lamentations Rabbah* (1545) **10:**1377
- - *Lehem Shelomo* (1597) **5:**279
- - *Lev Aharon* (1609) **8:**1180
- - *Ma'aseh Tuviyyah* (1707-8) **3:**804
- - *Maḥzor Romania* (1586) **11:**393
- - *Megillat Setarim* (1553) **8:**1190
- - *Melekhet Maḥashevet* (1710) **7:**414
- - *Meshal ha-Kadmoni* (16th cent.) **5:**430
- - *Midrash Ḥamesh Megillot* (1545) **11:**1507
- - *Mi Khamokha* (1586) **10:**362
- - *Mikneh Avram* (1523) **4:**141
- - *Millei de-Avot* (1606) **7:**1514
- - *Moznei Leshon ha-Kodesh* (1546) **8:**1165
- - *Or Nerot ha-Menorah* (1548) **10:**625
- - *Perush ha-Torah* (1579) **5:**1131
- - *Pitron Ḥalomot* (1623) **2:**664
- - *Sefer Einei Moshe* (1601) **7:**514
- - *Sefer ha-Ittur* (1608) **9:**13
- - *Sefer Kaftor va-Ferah* (1549) **6:**919
- - *Sefer Pesaḥ Me'ubin* (1692) **4:**560
- - *Sha'arei Dimah* (1586) **2:**529
- - *Sha'ar ha-Shamayim* (1547) **7:**516
- - *Shalshelet ha-Kabbalah* (1587) **8:**1209
- - *She'elot ha-Rav Sha'ul ha-Kohen* (1574) **3:**732
- - *She'elot u-Teshuvot*, Bezalel Ashkenazi (1595) **3:**724
- - *She'elot u-Teshuvot*, Levi ben Ḥabib (1565) **11:**99
- - *Shulḥan Arukh* (1594) **5:**195
- - *Song of Songs Rabbah* (1545) **15:**15
- - *Terumat ha-Deshen* (1546) **9:**1081
- - *Torat ha-Bayit* (1607) **8:**76
- - *Venice Haggadah* (1604) **2:**878; **3:**537; **7:**1088; **10:**211
- - *Venice Minhagim Book* (1601) **12:**26; **13:**140
- - *Ẓemaḥ David* (1587) **13:**845
- - *Zevaḥ Pesaḥ* (1545) **7:**1082
- illus: Verona
- - *Midrash Tanḥuma* (1595) **4:**113
- illus: Vienna
- - *Melukhat Sha'ul* (1829) **7:**1057
- illus: Vilna
- - *Ahavat Ẓiyyon* (1853) **8:**189
- - *Massekhet Amerika* (1894) **13:**127
- - *Mishlei Yehudah* (1859) **7:**800
- - *Oneg Yom Tov* (1880) **8:**267
- - *Oraḥ Selulah le-Dikduk Sefat Ever* (1883) **4:**198
- - *Sefer ha-Parnas* (1891) **7:**1317
- - *Shabbat* (1859) **14:**255
- - *Ta'amei Torah* (1882) **4:**216
- illus: Warsaw
- - *Kol Neḥi* (1798) **6:**1201
- - *Millot ha-Higgayon* (1865) **5:**860
- - *More Nevukhim* (1872) **11:**763
- illus: Weckelsdorf
- - *Maḥzor* (1680) **4:**114; **5:**753; **11:**397
- illus: Zhitomir

- - *Or ha-Levanah* (1872) **9**:33
- - *Or Zaru'a* (1862) **9**:27
- *illus:* Zolkiew
- - *Olelot Efrayim* (1765) **8**:960
- *illus:* not specified
- - Josephus' history, a compendium (1529) **10**:260
- - *Shloyshe Sheorim* (1838) **4**:318
- *illus:* Printer's marks **13**:1093
- - Bak, Israel **4**:115
- - Cavalli, Georgio di **5**:1584
- - Fagius, Paulus **6**:1136
- - Foa family **6**:1370
- - Frankfort on the Oder **7**:93
- - *Magen David* **11**:691
- - Mordecai ben Gershon ha-Kohen's sons **9**:1586
- - Parenzo, Meir **10**:356
- - Parenzo brothers **13**:101
- - Prague **5**:1197
- - Soncino, Gershom ben Moses **15**:140
- *illus:* Script types
- - Ashkenazic mashait script (16th cent.) **2**:742
- - Ashkenazic square script (15th cent.) **2**:727
- - Hebrew type faces **15**:1486
- - incunabula **8**:1327-1334
- - Italkian mashait script (1476) **2**:739
- - Italkian square script (1482) **2**:726
- - Sephardic mashait script (18th cent.) **2**:736
- *see also:* BOOKS; PRESS; PUBLISHING; TYPOGRAPHERS; TYPOGRAPHY
Prinz, E. L. **13**:930
PRINZ, JOACHIM **13**:1116
Prior of Crato (pretender, Port.), *see* ANTONIO
Prisco, Moses **16**:1549
PRISCUS (6th cent.) **13**:1116
- Gregory of Tours **6**:87ff; **8**:658
Prison, *see* IMPRISONMENT
Prisoners of war **15**:1655
Pritzwalk (tn., Brandenburg) **4**:1301
Privateering, *see* Piracy
Private International Law, *see* CONFLICT OF LAWS
Priver, Aharon **14**:1070
Privileges **3**:929ff; **12**:124
- *illus:*
- - Charles V's charter to Jews of Worms (1552) **7**:470
- - Cochin copper plate **8**:1351
- - Conigliano family, charter re Jewish badge **9**:1132
- - Fredericianum (1244) **3**:892
- - Henry VII granting charter to Jews **7**:465
- - Kalonymos family house **7**:459
- - Louis XVI's Letters Patent re Portuguese Jews in France (1776) **3**:926
- - Maria Theresa's Juden-Ordnung (1753) **3**:903
- - Maximilian II's decree (1566) **3**:923
- - Maximilian of Bavaria's charter to Samuel Wertheimer (1765) **7**:482
- - Rudolf of Hapsburg's confirmation of the Fredericianum (1277) **3**:893
- - Statute of Kalish **3**:922
- - Venice, carrying of arms by Jews (1718) **3**:925
- *see also:* CAPITULATIONS; *and under individual countries, towns and rulers*
Probatike bath (Jer.), *see* Sheep's Pool
Problemai (journ.), *see Ha-Problemai*
Problemot (period.) **7**:787
- statistics **1**:newsp. list
PROBST, MENAHEM MENDEL **13**:1117
PROBST-KRAID, RIZA **3**:608
Prochownik, Abraham **13**:710
Proclus Diadochus (philos.) **6**:164
- Neoplatonism **12**:958ff
Procopiou, Anghelos Georgios **7**:887
Procor (Arg. soc.) **4**:1047
Procreation
- barrenness and fertility **4**:256
- Ben Azzai on **16**:777
- birth **4**:1050
- celibacy **5**:268
- laws of **16**:776
- women **10**:1566
- *see also:* SEX
PROCURATOR (Rom. tit.) **13**:1117
- Jerusalem **9**:1394
- *illus:*
- - coins **5**:711-714
Profacius Judaeus, *see* Tibbon, Jacob ben Machir ibn
PROFANITY **13**:1119
Professions, Free (Jews in) **16**:1316
- Amsterdam survey **2**:902
- Molé's questions on **3**:763
Profiat, Don Vidal **13**:470
Profiat, Duran, of Perpignan **6**:299
Profiat de Umos **6**:299
Profiat Duran (14/15 cent. schol.), *see* DURAN, PROFIAT
Profit **12**:249; **13**:150
Profiteering, *see* HAFKA'AT SHE'ARIM
Prognosis (med.) **3**:675
Progres (publ. firm, Pol.) **13**:1375
Progressive Judaism, *see* REFORM JUDAISM
Progressive Party (party, Isr.) **8**:1349
- Allonei Yiẓḥak **2**:657
- Berligne, Eliyahu **4**:639
- Foerder, Yeshayah **6**:1374
- General Zionists **7**:384; **7**:385ff
- Granott, Abraham **7**:854
- Ha-Oved ha-Ẓiyyoni **7**:1317
- place in politics **9**:663ff
- Rosen, Pinḥas **14**:271
Prohibited marriages, *see* MARRIAGE, PROHIBITED
Prohibitions (neg. commandment), *see* COMMANDMENTS, THE 613
PROHOVNIK, ABRAHAM (leg. J. fig., Pol.) **13**:1119
Pro-Jerusalem Society **9**:1470; **15**:417
Prokezz, Anton **8**:1430
Prokupets, Naum **12**:1377; **15**:307
Prolet (period.) **13**:1048
Proletariat, Jewish
- Second Temple period **16**:1275
- Second Zionist Congress **16**:1167
- - socialism, Jewish **15**:38ff
Proletarishe Emes (newsp.) **16**:159
Proletarisher Fon (newsp.) **13**:1048
Proletpen (writers orgn., U.S.) **16**:821
Promiscuity, *see* SEX; SEXUAL OFFENSES
Promise, Breach of **4**:755
Promissory note, *see* MAMRAM
Pronicheva, Dina (Vera) Mironovna **10**:995
Pronouns (Heb. gram.) **8**:119ff
- biblical Hebrew **16**:1575
- Dead Sea Scrolls **16**:1586
- mishnaic Hebrew **16**:1596
- *tables:*
- - pronominal suffixes **8**:119
PRONUNCIATIONS OF HEBREW **13**:1120
- Avignon **3**:967
- Galilee **15**:774
- linguistics and study of **16**:1400
- masorah **16**:1417
- mishnaic Hebrew **16**:1595
- modern Hebrew **16**:1645ff
- Semitic languages **14**:1153
- vocalization and cantillation **16**:1433
- *charts:* text
- *see also:* HEBREW GRAMMAR
PROOPS (fam.) **16**:1554
- Amsterdam printing **2**:896
- books **4**:1238
- Hebrew printing **15**:1487
Proops, Abraham **16**:1555
Proops, David **16**:1555
Proops, Jacob **16**:1555
Proops, Joseph **16**:1555
- Prins, Abraham **13**:1095
Proops, Solomon **16**:1555
Proops, Solomon ben Joseph **16**:1554
Propaganda, Anti-Semitic **5**:171ff; **8**:837ff
Pro-Palestine Federation (U.S.) **16**:1155
Pro-Palestine Labor League (Chile) **16**:1125
PROPERTY **13**:1146
- *Contents:*
- - Classification **13**:1146
- - Acquisition and Transfer of Proprietary Rights **13**:1148
- - Extinction of Ownership **13**:1149
- - In the State of Israel **13**:1149
- General
- - Church tithes **15**:1162
- - economic history **16**:1293ff
- - informers **8**:1370
- - Inquisition **8**:1403
- - Israel Arabs' attitude **9**:1031ff
- - Jewish Cultural Reconstruction **10**:49
- - lots, casting of **11**:510
- - Omar, Covenant of **12**:1379
- - taxation in Israel **9**:749
- - Women's Equal Rights Law (1951) **12**:109
- - Yaḥad rules **16**:699
- Halakhic aspects
- - acquisition **2**:216ff
- - agricultural arenda **3**:403
- - *apotropos* **3**:220
- - bailment laws **14**:1455
- - *Bava Batra* **4**:336ff
- - civil marriage **5**:598
- - conflict of laws **5**:890
- - consecration and endowment **8**:279ff
- - debt recovery **12**:15; **12**:17
- - debt repayment **6**:1011ff
- - despair of **16**:774
- - dowry **6**:185
- - encroachment **7**:1460
- - expropriation **5**:880
- - gentiles, sale and lease to **3**:980
- - *ḥazakah* **7**:1516
- - *hefker* **8**:243
- - *ḥerem* **8**:346ff
- - husband and wife **8**:1126ff
- - *keẓaẓah* **10**:935
- - lease and hire **10**:1528
- - levites **11**:136ff
- - lien **11**:227
- - lost property **4**:341; **11**:504
- - *mazranut* **11**:1153
- - non-Jewish law **6**:51ff
- - nuisance **12**:1246
- - oaths **12**:1298
- - overreaching **12**:1392ff
- - ownership **12**:1531
- - redemption **10**:1482
- - sabbatical year, Jubilee **14**:575ff
- - servitudes **14**:1188
- - slaves **14**:1657
- - tax **15**:848ff
- - torts **15**:1273ff
- - unstealable types **15**:1095
- - widow **16**:492ff
- - wills **16**:519ff
- *illus:*
- - land transference deed, Lucca (11th cent.) **14**:1389
- - Majorcan Jews, account of confiscations **11**:796
- *see also:* SALE
Property, Lost, *see* LOST PROPERTY
Prophatius Judaeus, *see* Tibbon, Jacob ben Machir ibn
"Prophet at Night" (paint., Ben-Zion) **4**:574
Prophets (Bib. div.), *see Nevi'im*
Prophets, false **5**:771; **6**:1450
- *see also:* MESSIANIC MOVEMENTS
PROPHETS, LIVES OF THE (wk.) **13**:1149
PROPHETS AND PROPHECY **13**:1150
- *Contents:*
- - In the Bible **13**:1151
- - - Classifications **13**:1151
- - - Nature of Prophecy **13**:1151
- - - Preclassical Prophets **13**:1154
- - - Comparison of Preclassical and Classical Prophets **13**:160
- - - Classical Prophecy **13**:1164
- - History **13**:1171
- - - Universalism and Election **13**:1171
- - - Supremacy of Morality **13**:1172
- - - Attitude Toward Ritual **13**:1172
- - - Morality and Destiny **13**:1173
- - - Repentance **13**:1173
- - - New Covenant **13**:1174
- - - Future of Israel **13**:1174
- - In the Talmud **13**:1175
- - Philo **13**:1176
- - Medieval Jewish Philosophy **13**:1177
- - - Saadiah **13**:1177
- - - Judah Halevi **13**:1177
- - - Maimonides **13**:1178
- - - Joseph Albo **13**:1179
- - Modern Jewish Thought **13**:1179
- General
- - ancient Egypt **6**:484
- - cessation **4**:823
- - Mari parallels **11**:987
- - Moses **12**:387
- - Providence **13**:1279
- - Saul **14**:910
- Themes of
- - adultery **2**:314
- - beatitude **4**:361; **4**:362
- - Day of the Lord **5**:1387
- - dietary laws **6**:40
- - ecstasy **6**:358ff
- - eschatology **6**:861ff
- - eternity of Torah **15**:1244
- - ethics **6**:933*f*
- - intercession **6**:1434
- - law and morals **10**:1480
- - Messiah **11**:1409ff, 1419
- - miracles **9**:30; **12**:73; **12**:77
- - monotheism **12**:260
- - repentance **14**:73
- - Sabbath **14**:559
- - sacrifice **14**:607
- - Tabernacle **15**:687
- - Temple reconstruction **15**:954
- - wisdom **16**:558
- Method and Workings of
- - *devekut* **5**:1599; **10**:627
- - divination **6**:112ff
- - dreams **6**:209
- - imagination **8**:1290
- - kabbalistic meditation **10**:631ff
- - parable **13**:73ff

-- prayer **13:**979
-- *Ru'ah ha-Kodesh* **14:**364ff
-- symbolic acts **14:**1525
-- word **16:**634
- Legal Aspects
-- article of faith **3:**655ff
-- Commandments, the 613 **5:**69,771
-- denial of **8:**359
-- *halakhah* **3:**908ff; **12:**119; **12:**1441
-- Judaism **10:**388
-- legal innovation **12:**1441
-- *takkanot* **15:**721
-- Torah **4:**431
-- tradition **15:**1309; **15:**1311
- Comparisons
-- ephod **6:**804
-- priest **11:**141
- Literature
-- Abulafia, Abraham **2:**186ff
-- Apocalypse **3:**179
-- Apocryphal beliefs **3:**185
-- Balaam in *Aggadah* **4:**123
-- Pentateuch **13:**262
- Views on
-- Abrabanel, Isaac **2:**105
-- Arama **3:**257
-- Crescas, Hasdai **5:**1083
-- Ibn Daud **8:**1162
-- Ibn Ezra, Abraham **8:**1169
-- Isaac of Acre **9:**30
-- Islam **9:**99
-- Israeli, Isaac **9:**1065; **13:**434
-- Judah Halevi **10:**363ff; **13:**438
-- Karaite **10:**778
-- Krochmal **13:**458
-- Levi ben Gershom **11:**97; **13:**446
-- Maimonides **11:**773ff; **13:**442
-- Naḥmanides **12:**777
-- Philo **13:**415; **13:**427ff
-- philosophy, Jewish **13:**421
-- sages **14:**638; **14:**654
- *illus:*
-- Amos **2:**880
-- Elisha **10:**1021
-- Elisha, punishment of the mocking boys **6:**666
-- Ezekiel **4:**945
-- Ezra **5:**1304; **6:**286,384,1105; **8:**1149
-- Habakkuk **7:**1015
-- Haggai prophesying **7:**1113
-- Hosea **8:**1013
-- Isaiah **9:**45
-- Jeremiah **4:**940; **9:**1349–1358
-- Joel **4:**64; **10:**133
-- Jonah **4:**966; **10:**170–177
-- "Jonah Preaching to the Ninevites" (lith., U. Birnbaum) **4:**1043
-- Malachi **11:**814
-- Nehemiah **12:**937
-- "Prophet at Night" (paint., Ben-Zion) **4:**574
-- Samuel **2:**341; **3:**28,54
-- Zechariah (paint., Michelangelo) **16:**954
- *see also: Nevi'im;* REVELATION; VISIONS
PROSBUL (leg. enactment) **13:**1181
- Hillel **8:**484
- literature **11:**315
- *takkanah* **15:**717
- *see also:* SABBATICAL YEAR AND JUBILEE
Prose, rhymed **13:**1218
Proscription, *see* ḤEREM
PROSELYTES **13:**1182
- *Contents:*
-- Laws of Conversion **13:**1182
-- Appreciation of the Proselyte **13:**1185
-- In the Middle Ages **13:**1186
-- In Modern Times **13:**1190
-- Recent Trends **13:**1191
-- In the U.S. **13:**1192
-- Non-Orthodox Views **13:**1193
- General
-- anthropology **3:**45
-- assimilation to Judaism **3:**771
-- Diaspora **13:**1182
-- *ger* **15:**421
-- pedigree **16:**893
-- priest and **13:**1089
-- Roman literature **14:**233
- History
-- Abraham **2:**116
-- Africa **2:**332
-- after Temple's destruction **9:**242; **9:**250
-- Bar Kokhba War **8:**647
-- Berbers **4:**587
-- Bezidul Nou **4:**791
-- Cairo *genizah* **16:**1341
-- Catholic Church **5:**537ff
-- converts of lions **11:**275
-- Crusades **9:**272
-- Dio Cassius **6:**59
-- Hasmonean era **16:**1350
-- Hypsistarians **14:**1087
-- Jewish identity **10:**54; **10:**55
-- Judaizers **10:**397
-- Kalmyk women **14:**1486
-- Khazars **10:**947
-- Kingdom of Adiabene **10:**1296
-- Palmyra **15:**698
-- Phoenician and Carthaginian traders **16:**1277
-- rabbinic period **10:**390
-- Rahab **13:**1515
-- Roman Empire **3:**48
-- Ruth as prototype **14:**518
-- San Nicandro **14:**843
-- Somrei Sabat **15:**139
- Law
-- ablution **2:**82
-- Argentinian rabbinical prohibition **3:**421
-- change of name **12:**810
-- circumcision **5:**569
-- Commandments, the 613 **5:**770
-- firstborn rights **6:**1311
-- first fruits **4:**993; **6:**1315
-- halakhic definition of Jew **10:**23ff
-- inheritance **8:**243; **15:**479
-- insults **8:**1409
-- legal attitudes to **16:**775
-- *mamzer* **11:**840
-- *mikveh* **11:**1534
-- Minor Tractates **12:**49
-- Pentateuch **13:**249
-- redemption **14:**3
-- remarriage **12:**168
-- slaves **14:**1661
-- wills **16:**523
- Attitudes Toward
-- Hillel **8:**484
-- Joshua ben Hananiah **10:**280
-- Maimonides **8:**684; **11:**766
-- Philo **13:**411
-- Rabbinic period **10:**390
-- Reform Judaism **12:**1443
-- sages **14:**640; **14:**654
-- Shammai **10:**13
-- *tannaim* **2:**362
- Famous Proselytes
-- Aquila **12:**1405
-- Assumpção Diogo da **3:**783
-- Bodo **4:**1164
-- Būlān of Khazaria **4:**1478
-- Cresson, Warder **5:**1087
-- Escudero, Lorenzo **6:**886
-- Flavius, Clemens **6:**1338
-- Fulvia **7:**220
-- Gordon, Lord George **7:**795
-- Helena of Adiabene **8:**288
-- Issur Giyyora **9:**1085
-- Izates II **9:**1157
-- Jackson, Hamlet **15:**1346
-- Josiphiah the Poet **10:**295
-- Kāhina the Berber **10:**685
-- Keti'a bar Shalom **10:**925
-- Kotsuji, Setsuzo **10:**1224
-- Lazarus, Nahida Ruth **10:**1519
-- Monobaz II **12:**258
-- Obadiah the Norman **12:**1306
-- Onkelos **12:**1405
-- Pallière, Aimé **13:**43
-- Potocki, Count Valentine **13:**934
-- Ruth **14:**518ff
-- Spaeth, Johann Peter **15:**219
-- Veray Alarcon, Lope de **16:**105
-- Voznitsyn, Alexander **16:**229
-- Weigel, Catherine **16:**376
-- Yūsuf Dhu Nuwās of Himyar **16:**897
PROSKAUER, JOSEPH MEYER **13:**1193
- Zionism **16:**1145
Proskowski, Hans Christolph von **16:**1231
PROSKUROV (city, Ukr.) **13:**1194
- Podolia **13:**668
- *illus:*
-- pogrom victims **14:**449
PROSODY, HEBREW **13:**1195
- *Contents:*
-- Introduction **13:**1196
-- Some Principles of Biblical Verse **13:**1200
-- The Classical Piyyut **13:**1203
-- Medieval Hebrew Poetry in Spain **13:**1211
-- Hebrew Poetry in Italy **13:**1220
-- Haskalah **13:**1224
-- The Modern Period **13:**1228
-- Summary **13:**1237
- *piyyut* **13:**573
- *see also:* HEBREW LITERATURE, MODERN; LITERATURE, JEWISH; POETRY
Prosser, James **8:**51
Prossnitz (city, Morav., Cz.), *see* PROSTEJOV
Prossnitz, Daniel, *see* PROSSTITZ, DANIEL
PROSSNITZ, JUDAH LEIB BEN JACOB HOLLESCHAU **13:**1240
- Shabbateanism **14:**1248
Prossnitz, Leibele, *see* PROSSNITZ, JUDAH LEIB BEN JACOB HOLLESCHAU
Prossnitz, Menahem, *see* KATZ, MENAHEM
PROSSTITZ, DANIEL **13:**1242
PROSTEJOV (city, Morav.) **13:**1242
- archives **3:**386
- Shabbateanism **14:**1248
- tailors **15:**705
PROSTITUTION **13:**1243
- *Contents:*
-- General **13:**1243
-- Post-Biblical **13:**1244
-- In Talmud and Halakhah **13:**1244
-- Post-Talmudic **13:**1245
- Argentinian Jews **3:**415ff
- banishment **4:**165
- Commandments, the 613 **5:**781
- concubine **5:**363; **5:**864
- ethics **6:**935
- imprisonment **8:**1302
- Jerusalem Christians **9:**1440
- marriage acquisition mode **11:**1046
- perfumes **8:**1312
- priestly restrictions **13:**1081
- Rahab **13:**1514
- sexual offenses **14:**1208
- woman **16:**625
Prostitz, Aaron **13:**1247
PROSTITZ, ISAAC BEN AARON **13:**1247
Prostitz, Issachar **13:**1247
Prostration
- *Aleinu le-Shabbe'aḥ* **2:**557
- sacrifices **11:**393
- *Taḥanun* **15:**702
- *see also:* PRAYER
Prostration Prayer, *see* TAḤANUN
Protection of Cultural Property (U.N. convention) **15:**1565
Protection of Holy Places Law **16:**78
Protectorate of Bohemia-Moravia, *see* MORAVIA
PROTESTANTS **13:**1247
- *Contents:*
-- Up to World War II **13:**1247
--- Missionary Activities **13:**1248
--- Converts in Academic Life **13:**1249
--- Jewish Return to Land of Israel **13:**1250
-- From 1945 **13:**1250
--- Declarations against Anti-Semitism **13:**1250
--- Liquidation of Theological Anti-Semitism **13:**1251
--- Church Committees for Relations with Jews **13:**1251
--- The Protestant Mission **13:**1252
--- Interfaith Movement **13:**1252
--- In the U.S. **13:**1253
- Calvin, John **5:**66
- England **6:**752,774
- Israel, activities in **9:**296; **9:**917
- Jesuits **10:**8
- Ladino literature **10:**1351
- Luther, Martin **11:**584
- Psalms **13:**1327
- United States **15:**1589
- Zionism **16:**1153
- *illus:*
-- Garden Tomb (Jer.) **9:**916,1461
- *see also:* CHRISTIANITY; Lutheran Church; REFORMATION
PROTESTRABBINER (term, Ger.) **13:**1255
Proti (cmty. ldrs., Sic.) **14:**1494
Proto-Arabic (lang.) **14:**1152
Proto-Canaanite script **2:**677ff
- inscriptions **16:**665
- writing systems **16:**654ff
- *illus:*
-- Lachish dagger inscription **16:**655
-- line of development (diagram) **2:**678
-- script type **2:**675
Protocols of the Learned Elders of Zion, see ELDERS OF ZION, PROTOCOLS OF THE LEARNED
Proto-Semitic (hypothetical lang.) **16:**1396
Proto-Sinaitic script **2:**674
- inscriptions **16:**665
- writing systems **16:**654
- *illus:*
-- script type **2:**675
Protozoa **6:**38
PROUDHON, PIERRE JOSEPH **13:**1255
- Deutsch, Simon **5:**1593
- Marx, Karl **11:**1072
- socialism **15:**26
Proust, Adrien **13:**1256
Proust, Jeanne **13:**1256
PROUST, MARCEL **13:**1256
- Debenedetti **5:**1428
Provençal (lang.) **4:**882
Provençal (Provenzale; fam.) **11:**905; **13:**1258
PROVENÇAL, ABRAHAM BEN DAVID **13:**1257
- universities **15:**1675
PROVENÇAL, DAVID BEN ABRAHAM **13:**1257
- education **6:**418
- Mantua **11:**898
- Provenzale, Moses **13:**1258

- Sommo, Judah **15:**137
- universities **15:**1675
PROVENÇAL, JACOB BEN DAVID **13:**1258
- sciences **11:**28
Provençal, Judah **11:**898
PROVENÇAL, MOSES BEN ABRAHAM **13:**1258
- Azariah dei Rossi **14:**317
- Mantua **11:**898
- Provençal, David **13:**1257
Provençal, Manoah **2:**943; **10:**1379
Provençal, Samuel ben David **3:**709
Provençale, Eliashib Joshua **13:**579
Provençal language **10:**67, 439
Provençal rite (litur.) **11:**401
PROVENCE (Fr.) **13:**1259
- Avignon **3:**964
- education **6:**407ff
- French Jewry **7:**17ff
- hawking **15:**292
- Hebrew language **16:**1635ff
- Hebrew manuscripts **8:**1264; **8:**1266
- history **8:**666ff,686
- Jewish literature **11:**330
- Kabbalah **10:**518
- Naḥmanides and school of **12:**779
- poetry **13:**681
- *pop. tables:* text
- *see also:* JUDEO-PROVENÇAL
Provenzale (fam. name), *see* Provençal
PROVERB **13:**1264
- folklore **6:**1374
- *see also:* AGGADAH; PARABLE
Proverbios Morales (wk.) **14:**849
PROVERBS, BOOK OF **13:**1268
- *Contents:*
- - Title **13:**1268
- - Wisdom Tradition **13:**1269
- - International Wisdom **13:**1269
- - Precepts and Proverbs **13:**1270
- - Structural Outline of the Book **13:**1271
- - Ethical and Religious Teachings **13:**1273
- *Aḥikar, Book of* **2:**461
- canonization **4:**824
- cantillation signs **16:**1441ff
- educational qualities **6:**395ff
- Egyptian parallels **6:**484
- ethical teaching **6:**936
- ethical wills **16:**530
- poetry in **13:**674ff
- punctuation marks **16:**1461
- Septuagint **4:**855
- Solomon **15:**105
- Spinoza on **15:**283
- wisdom **16:**557; **16:**558ff
- *illus:*
- - text
- - opening page (15th cent.) **4:**968
PROVERBS, TALMUDIC **13:**1273
Proviantlieferant, *see* COURT JEWS
PROVIDENCE (city, R.I.) **13:**1276
- *illus:* text
PROVIDENCE (conc.) **13:**1279
- *Contents:*
- - In the Bible **13:**1279
- - In the Apocrypha **13:**1280
- - In the Talmud **13:**1281
- - In the Kabbalah **13:**1282
- - In Medieval Jewish Philosophy **13:**1284
- General
- - anthropomorphism **3:**51
- - article of faith **3:**654ff
- - Dead Sea Scrolls **15:**1046
- - denial of **8:**359
- - emanation **6:**965
- - fear of God **6:**1199
- - free will **7:**125
- - good and evil **7:**775
- - history **7:**645
- - lots **11:**511
- - miracles **12:**76ff
- - stoicism **15:**409
- Views on
- - Aaron ben Elijah **13:**433
- - Aboab, Isaac **2:**92
- - Abrabanel, Isaac **2:**103; **2:**108
- - Aristotelianism **3:**447
- - Baruch of Kosov **4:**281
- - Crescas, Ḥasdai **5:**1083; **13:**448
- - ḥasidic thought **7:**1404ff
- - Ibn Ezra, Abraham **8:**1169
- - Jewish philosophy **13:**424
- - Levi ben Gershom **11:**95ff; **13:**447
- - Maimonides **11:**774; **13:**442
- - medieval philosophy **7:**660ff
- - Moses ben Joseph **12:**422
- *see also:* REWARD AND PUNISHMENT
Providence County (R.I.) **14:**143
Provincia Arabia (Rom. prov.) **9:**121; **13:**342
Provincia Africa (Rom. prov.) **15:**1430
Provincia Judaea (Rom. prov.) **9:**239; **14:**1491
- history chart **8:**766-767
- *illus:*
- - coins **5:**713-714; **9:**110
PROVINS (tn., Fr.) **13:**1286
Provisional Committee for General Zionist Affairs (U.S.) **16:**1143
Provisional State Council (Isr.) **10:**1112
- *illus:*
- - members **9:**611
Provocateur (Rus.) **8:**1370
Provocatio (term, Rom. law) **13:**1117
Proxy, *see* Attorney, Power of
Pruckner, A. **8:**51
PRUEWAR, JULIUS **12:**703
Prufer, K. E. **8:**51
Prunk, Michail, *see* DORIAN, EMIL
Prus, Bolesław **13:**800
Prusa (city, Turkey), *see* BURSA
Prusice (tn., Pol.), *see* Prausnitz
Pruslin, M. **12:**56
PRUSSIA **13:**1287
- *Contents:*
- - 1300-1740 **13:**1287
- - From Frederick II to Emancipation **13:**1289
- - Prussia Within the German Empire **13:**1292
- emancipation **6:**705ff
- Ereẓ Israel missions **9:**296
- freemasons **7:**123
- French Revolution and the Jews **7:**158
- Haskalah **7:**1441
- history chart (1812, 1847) **8:**766-767
- Jewish equality **16:**132
- Middle East interests **9:**306
- mintmasters and purveyors in **12:**64
- peddling **13:**206
- Poznan **13:**947ff
- rabbinical office **13:**1453
- status of Jews **8:**705ff
- stock exchanges **15:**406
- *illus:*
- - text
- - edict of emancipation (1812) **3:**927; **13:**1303
- - Frederick II, prayer for **7:**113
- - Jews in the army (caric.) **11:**1557
- *pop. tables:* text
- *see also:* GERMANY
Prutkowski, Józef **13:**802
Prużana (city, Belor.), *see* PRUZHANY
Pruzhansky, Yaakov **16:**1111
PRUZHANY (city, Belor.) **13:**1293
PRYLUCKI, NOAH **13:**1294
- Folkspartei **6:**1408
- Shabad, Ẓemaḥ **14:**1214
- *illus:* text
PRYLUCKI, ẒEVI HIRSCH **13:**1295
PRYNNE, WILLIAM **13:**1295
Prystor, Alexander **13:**1296
PRYSTOR, JANINA **13:**1296
Prytz, Carl Frederik **14:**934
Prywes, Moshe **11:**1204
PRZEDBORZ (tn., Pol.) **13:**1296
- *illus:*
- - text
- - synagogue **11:**693
PRZEDBORZ (Ḥas. dynasty) **13:**1297
- dynasties **1:**ḥas. table
Przeglad Codzienny (newsp.) **5:**1370
PRZEMYSL (city, Pol.) **13:**1297
- crafts **5:**1051ff
- dynasties **1:**ḥas. table
- ghetto **13:**766
- Rzeszow **14:**537
- Wolf, Simeon **3:**840
- *illus:* text
Przemyslany (tn., Ukr.), *see* PEREMYSHLYANY
Przemyslany, Meir **7:**906
PRZEWORSK (tn., Pol.) **13:**1299
Przeworski, J. **13:**1369
Przeworski, Stefan **3:**302
Przybyslawas, Isaac, *see* EULENBURG, ISAAC BEN ABRAHAM MOSES ISRAEL
PRZYSUCHA (city, Pol.) **13:**1299
- dynasties **1:**ḥas. table
Przysucha, Abraham Moses of, *see* Abraham Moses of Przysucha
PRZYSUCHA, JACOB ISAAC BEN ASHER **13:**1300
- Apta, Meir **3:**224
- Jacob Isaac of Lublin **9:**1228
- split with "Seer" **10:**1223
Przysucha, Simḥah Bunem of, *see* SIMḤAH BUNEM OF PRZYSUCHA
Przyszłość (period.) **16:**1330
- Lvov **11:**612
- Salz, Abraham **14:**717
- Zipper, Gershon **16:**1181
PRZYTYK (tn., Pol.) **13:**1301
- history chart **8:**766-767
Psalmody, *see* MUSIC
Psalm of Jonah (Bib.), *see* Jonah, Psalm of
PSALMS, APOCRYPHAL **13:**1302
PSALMS, BOOK OF **13:**1303
- *Contents:*
- - Title **13:**1304
- - Place in the Canon **13:**1305
- - Number of Psalms **13:**1306
- - Verse Division **13:**1307
- - Division into Books **13:**1307
- - Composition of the Psalter **13:**1309
- - Date of the Psalter **13:**1311
- - Ascription to David **13:**1313
- - Types of Psalms **13:**1314
- - Psalms and the Cult **13:**1315
- - The Text **13:**1317
- - Superscriptions and Technical Terms **13:**1317
- - In the Talmud and Midrash **13:**1322
- - In the Liturgy **13:**1323
- - In the Arts **13:**1325
- - Musical Rendition in Jewish Tradition **13:**1328
- General
- - arts **5:**1334
- - music **12:**571
- - Scandinavian literature **14:**928
- - wisdom literature **16:**557,559,561
- Composition
- - Albright, W. F. **2:**539
- - canonization **4:**824
- - dating **4:**913
- - David **5:**1327
- - Septuagint **4:**855
- - Spinoza **15:**283
- Text
- - *Asaph* **3:**673
- - *Ashrei* **3:**736
- - cantillation signs **16:**1441ff
- - *maqām* **11:**937
- - *Maskil* **11:**1095
- - *Mizmor le-David* **12:**172
- - *Shir ha-Ma'alot* **14:**1415
- - term *Tehillim* **3:**736
- - *see also under individual Psalms*
- Contents
- - ethical teachings **6:**936
- - magic **11:**711
- - poetry **13:**674ff
- - prayer **13:**980
- Commentaries on
- - Judeo-Persian dialect **2:**327
- - *Midrash Tehillim* **11:**1519
- - Targum **4:**849
- Use of
- - *ḥevrah* **8:**441
- - king's coronation **10:**1011
- - Kurdistan Jews **10:**1300
- - liturgy, ancient **11:**394
- - resistance literature **8:**302
- Temple **15:**786; **15:**952ff
- - Thanksgiving Psalms **15:**1047; **15:**1048
- *illus:*
- - text
- - *Angoulême Psalter* (13th cent.) **6:**1
- - *Bohum Psalter* (14th cent.) **14:**541
- - classroom wall chart (1590) **6:**387
- - *English Psalter* (13th cent.) **15:**103
- - *Extracts from Gregory the Great* **4:**1
- - *First Gaster Bible* **8:***fcg.* 951
- - incunabulum (1487) **8:**1329
- - *Ki le-Olam Ḥasdo* **2:**878
- - opening page (15th cent.) **5:**1558
- - *Paris Psalter* (10th cent.) **4:**947; **5:**1263, 1330
- - Persian amulet **11:**1364
- - polyglot Psalter (1516) **5:**757; **7:**408
- - Psalm 121 on amulet **11:**691
- - Psalm 137 **12:**621
- - *Psalter of King Wenceslas of Hungary and Bohemia* (13th cent.) **4:**949
- - *Psalter of York* (12th cent.) **11:**633
- - *Queen Mary Psalter* (14th cent.) **2:**970; **4:**880; **5:**22; **8:**1317
- - *St. Albans Psalter* (12th cent.) **3:**217; **15:**1497
- - *St. Louis Psalter* (13th cent.) **4:**321
- - *Stuttgart Psalter* (9th cent.) **10:**193
- - *Theodore Psalter* (11th cent.) **12:**1351
- - Yiddish version (16th cent.) **2:**702
- *mus. notations:*
- - text
- - chanting rites **9:**1143-1145
- - Psalm 19 **12:**571
Psalms of Solomon (pseudepig. wk.) *see* SOLOMON, PSALMS OF
Psalms Scroll (D. S. Scroll) **13:**1302
- *Ashrei, nun* verse **3:**736
Psalter, *see* PSALMS, BOOK OF
Psalter of King Wenceslas of Hungary

and Bohemia (illum. ms.) **4**:949
Psalter of York (12th cent., illum. ms.) **11**:633
Psammetichus I (k., Egy.) **3**:695
Psammetichus II (k., Egy.) **12**:920
Psammetichus III (k., Egy.) **5**:70
PSANTIR, JACOB **13**:1334
- Rumania **14**:399
- *illus:* **14**:388
Psenyris (tn., Egy.) **6**:9
Psephinus Tower (Jer.) **9**:1398
Pseudepigrapha, *see* APOCRYPHA AND PSEUDEPIGRAPHA
Pseudo-Baḥya, *see* BAḤYA
Pseudo-Epiphanius (wk.), *see* PROPHETS, LIVES OF THE
Pseudo-Eupolemus **6**:964
Pseudo-Hecataeus, *see* HECATAEUS OF ABDERA
Pseudo-Jonathan (Bib. trans.), *see* TARGUM (Jonathan)
PSEUDO-LONGINUS (Gr. au.) **7**:896
Pseudo-Messiahs, *see* MESSIANIC MOVEMENTS
Pseudo-Philo **8**:304
- Moses **12**:392
- *see also:* PHILO
PSEUDO-PHOCYLIDES (poet) **13**:1335
- Hellenistic Jewish literature **8**:304
PSEUDO-SCYLAX (Gr. au.) **13**:1336
Pshiskha, Abraham Moses of, *see* Abraham Moses of Przysucha
Pshiskha, Jacob Isaac ben Asher, *see* PRZYSUCHA, JACOB ISAAC BEN ASHER
Pshiskha, Simḥah Bunem of, *see* SIMHAH BUNEM OF PRZYSUCHA
Pskov (city, Rus.) **14**:434
PSYCHIATRY **13**:1336
- *Contents:*
- - The Biblical Period **13**:1336
- - In the Talmud **13**:1336
- - The Medieval Period **13**:1337
- - The Modern Period **13**:1337
- *see also* PSYCHOLOGY
Psychoanalytical Institute (Pal.) **6**:559
Psychologische Forschung (journ.) **10**:1134
PSYCHOLOGY **13**:1341
- *Contents:*
- - In the Bible **13**:1341
- - Post Biblical and Talmudic Period **13**:1341
- - Medieval Period **13**:1342
- - Responsa Literature **13**:1343f
- - Ḥasidism **13**:1343
- - Modern Period **13**:1343
- - Contemporary Period **13**:1344
- - Capsules **13**:1345
- Jewish literature **11**:340
- kabbalistic views **10**:606ff
Psychosis **11**:1372; **11**:1376
Ptah (deity) **16**:662
Ptolemaeus, Claudius, *see* PTOLEMY THE GEOGRAPHER
Ptolemais (city, Er. Isr.), *see* ACRE
Ptolemais (loc., Egy.) **15**:581
PTOLEMY (dyn., Egy.) **13**:1347
- Africa and Ereẓ Israel **2**:331
- Ereẓ Israel history **8**:625ff
- state organization **8**:294
- Transjordan **15**:1317
Ptolemy I (Soter; k., Egy.) **13**:1347
- Cyrene **5**:1184
- Egypt **6**:485
- history chart **8**:766-767
- Jerusalem **9**:1389
Ptolemy II (Philadelphus) **13**:1347
- Aristeas, Letter of **3**:439
- Egypt **6**:485
- history chart **8**:766-767
- Samaritan tradition **14**:729
- Septuagint **4**:852
- *illus:*
- - Letter of Aristeas **3**:439
Ptolemy III (Euergetes) **13**:1348
- Egypt **6**:485
- history chart **8**:766-767
- Joseph son of Tobiah **15**:1179
Ptolemy IV (Philopator) **13**:1348
- Egypt **6**:485
- history chart **8**:766-767
- *Maccabees, Third Book of* **11**:660
Ptolemy V (Epiphanes) **13**:1348
- Antiochus III **5**:603
Ptolemy VI (Philometor) **13**:1348
- Alexander Balas **2**:577
- Alexandria disputation **2**:949
- Cleopatra **5**:603ff
- Egypt **6**:485
- history chart **8**:766-767
- *illus:*
- - sacking the Temple **10**:256
Ptolemy VII (Euergetes II) **13**:1348
- Cleopatra **5**:603ff
- history chart **8**:766-767
Ptolemy VIII (Lathyrus, Soter II) **13**:1349
- Cleopatra **5**:603
- history chart **8**:766-767
- Yannai, Alexander **16**:279; **16**:715ff
Ptolemy IX (Alexander I) **13**:1349
- Cleopatra **5**:603
- history chart **8**:766-767
PTOLEMY (s., Ḥabub) **13**:1349
- Seleucids and Judea **8**:631
- Simeon the Hasmonean **14**:1566
PTOLEMY (s. of Mennaeus; k., Chalcis) **13**:1349
- Alexandra **2**:588
- Aretas III **12**:742
PTOLEMY THE BIOGRAPHER (Herodian court.) **7**:897
PTOLEMY THE GEOGRAPHER **7**:897
- *Almagest* **3**:799
- astrological treatises **3**:791
- maps of Ereẓ Israel **11**:919ff
PTOLEMY MACRON (Sel. gen.) **13**:1350
PTOLEMY OF CHENNOS (Gr. au.) **7**:897
PTOLEMY OF MENDE (Egy. pr.) **7**:897
Ptolemy son of Dorymenes **13**:1350
Ptuj (vill., Sloven.), *see* Pettau
Puah (s., Issachar), *see* Puvah
Puah (bib. fig.) **12**:83
- Pharaoh **12**:372
- *illus:*
- - before Pharaoh **6**:285
Pu'ah (bot.) **6**:329; **13**:621
PUBERTY **13**:1350
Publicani, *see* TAX GATHERERS
Publications of the American Jewish Historical Society, *see American Jewish Historical Society Quarterly*
PUBLIC AUTHORITY **13**:1351
- *Contents:*
- - Qualifications, Duties, and Standing of Communal leaders **13**:1351
- - Election of Public Office holders **13**:1356
- - In the State of Israel **13**:1356
- administrative law **12**:133
- Jews' economic role **16**:1291
- *takkanot* **15**:713
- *see also:* TAKKANOT HA-KAHAL; TAXATION
Public Buildings Ltd. (co., Isr.) **9**:838
Public Health **11**:1202
Publicker (fam.) **16**:546
Public Law **12**:135ff
- communal obligations, rights **4**:336ff
- confiscation, expropriation, forfeiture **5**:880
- *dina de-malkhuta dina* **6**:51
- *hekdesh* **8**:279
- public authority **13**:1351
- *takkanot* **15**:712
- *takkanot ha-kahal* **15**:728
- taxation **15**:837
- Zionist Congress (3rd) **16**:1167
- *see also:* AUTONOMY; AUTONOMY, JUDICIAL; KING, KINGSHIP
Public office, *see* PUBLIC AUTHORITY
PUBLIC RELATIONS **13**:1360
- *Contents:*
- - In Entertainment and Sport **13**:1361
- - In Politics and Public Affairs **13**:1361
- - In the Jewish Community **13**:1362
PUBLISHING **13**:1364
- *Contents:*
- - General Publishing **13**:1364
- - - The "Dutch Jerusalem" **13**:1365
- - - In Germany and Austria **13**:1366
- - - In Scandinavia **13**:1368
- - - In Italy **13**:1368
- - - In France **13**:1368
- - - In Czechoslovakia **13**:1368
- - - In Yugoslavia **13**:1369
- - - In Rumania **13**:1369
- - - In Hungary **13**:1369
- - - In Poland **13**:1369
- - - In Russia **13**:1370
- - - In Spain and Latin America **13**:1370
- - - In Great Britain **13**:1370
- - - In the United States **13**:1371
- - Book Clubs, Reprints, and Children's Literature **13**:1372
- - Publishing of Hebraica and Judaica **13**:1373
- - - Central and Western Europe **13**:1373
- - - In Great Britain **13**:1374
- - - Eastern Europe **13**:1375
- - - United States **13**:1376
- - In Israel **13**:1377
- - - New Developments **13**:1378
- book trade **4**:1238ff
- children's books (Er. Isr.) **5**:435
- culture promotion society **15**:59ff
- Ha-Shomer ha-Ẓa'ir **7**:1373
- learned societies **15**:53
- Pesaro **13**:329
- *see also:* BOOKS; PRESS; PRINTING, HEBREW
Publius Marcellius, *see* Marcellius, Publius
Puccini, Mario **9**:1106
- *illus:*
- - *Ebrei* (1931) **9**:1108
Puchowitzer, Judah Leib, *see* PUKHOVITSER, JUDAH LEIB
Puck (journ.) **5**:219; **5**:176
Pueblo (Ind. tribe, N. Am.) **12**:1038
Pueblo (co., Col.) **5**:753
Puerto Cabello (city, Venez.) **16**:90
Puertocarrero, Don Luis de **13**:45
Puerto del Cielo (bk.), *see Sha'ar ha-Shamayim*
PUERTO RICO (Carib. isl.) **16**:1555
- West Indies **16**:473
Pugghiesi (It. cmty.), *see* Pugliese congregations
Pugio Fidei (polem. wk.) **11**:1066
- Adret, Solomon **2**:307
- Barcelona dispute **4**:215
- forgeries **6**:1431
- *illus:*
- - title page and frontispiece (1687) **4**:214, 215
PUGLIESE, EMANUELE **13**:1380
Pugliese, Umberto **11**:1559
Pugliese congregations **3**:228
- Greece **7**:875,883
Puhakka, Antti **6**:1297
Puigcervez, Francisco Rivas **11**:1456
Pukh (metal), *see* Antimony
PUKHACHEWSKY, MICHAEL ZALMAN **13**:1380
Pukhachewsky, Neḥamah **13**:1380
Pukhovichi, Abraham Aaron of, *see* Koidanov, Abraham Aaron of Pukhovichi
PUKHOVITSER, JUDAH LEIB **13**:1380
Puklice (tn., Morav.) **10**:104
Pul (Assyr. k.), *see* Tiglath-Pileser III
PULAWY (tn., Pol.) **13**:1381
Pulgar, Isaac ben Joseph ibn, *see* POLLEGAR, ISAAC BEN JOSEPH IBN
Pulice (tn., Morav.) **10**:104
PULITZER, JOSEPH **13**:1382
- journalism **10**:307; **10**:315
- *illus:* text
PULKAU (tn., Aus.) **13**:1383
- Albert II **2**:530
- Host desecration **8**:1043
Pullitz, Gershon **12**:301
PULTUSK (tn., Pol.) **13**:1383
Pulu (Assyr. k.), *see* Tiglath-Pileser III
Puluj, J. **4**:887
Pulver, Isaac **5**:139
PULVERMACHER, OSCAR **10**:315
PUMBEDITA (tn., Babyl.) **13**:1384
- academies **2**:204
- *amoraim* **2**:867
- gaonate **7**:315ff
- *ha-rav ha-rosh* **13**:1449
- history chart (259 C.E.) **8**:766-767
- Iraq **8**:1446; **8**:1447
- Judah bar Ezekiel **10**:342
- Nehardea **12**:935
- Passover *Haggadah* **7**:1091
- *illus:*
- - principal *amoraim* **2**:869
- *see also:* SURA
Pumpenai (cmty., Lith.) **14**:769
Pumpian (tn., Lith.) **6**:616
Punch (journ.) **5**:175; **5**:219
Punic (lang.) **14**:1149; **16**:1398
PUNISHMENT **13**:1386
- General
- - Inquisition **8**:1402ff
- - Lamentations, Book of **10**:1370
- - leprosy **11**:38
- - ransom **13**:1546
- - vengeance **16**:93
- In Law
- - compounding offenses **5**:856
- - extraordinary remedies **6**:1071
- - law and morals **10**:1480; **10**:1484
- - non-Jewish law **6**:51
- - *takkanot* **15**:718
- - talion **15**:741
- - *see also:* PENAL LAW
- Forms of
- - banishment **4**:163
- - capital punishment **5**:142
- - confiscation **5**:880ff
- - divine punishment **6**:120
- - fasting **6**:1190
- - fines **6**:1287
- - flogging **6**:1348
- - *ḥerem* **8**:346ff
- - imprisonment **8**:1299ff
- - ordeal **12**:1448
- Crimes and Transgressions
- - Coca adulteress **5**:620
- - custom **12**:6; **12**:9
- - forgery **6**:1432

- - measures, false **16:**391
- - oaths, false **12:**1297
- *illus:*
- - flogging **6:**1349; **11:**809
- *see also:* REWARD AND PUNISHMENT
PUNON (city, Edom) **13:**1390
Purchase and Sale, *see* SALE
Purgation **5:**1384ff
Purgatory **10:**612
- *see also:* AFTERLIFE
Purification offering, *see* Sin offering
PURIM **13:**1390
- General
- - *Al ha-Nissim* **2:**626
- - calendar **5:**47
- - folklore **6:**1389; **6:**1393
- - plays in Yiddish **16:**802
- - scroll cases **5:**309
- - Scroll of Esther **14:**1047ff
- - Scrolls, the Five **14:**1058
- - *Shabbat Zakhor, Parah* **14:**573
- - *Targum Sheni* **15:**812
- Origin and History
- - Esther **6:**906
- - Fast of Esther **6:**914
- - Great Synagogue **15:**630
- - Haman **7:**1222
- - miracles **12:**75
- - Mordecai **12:**307
- - Purim Katan **13:**1396
- - Talmud **11:**1228
- - Theodosian Code **15:**1101
- Sects
- - Falashas **6:**1148
- - Karaites **10:**779
- - Samaritans **14:**742
- Celebration
- - Adloyada **2:**289
- - *badhan* **4:**74
- - cooking and food **6:**1427
- - drunkenness **6:**239
- - festivities **7:**304
- - Israel **9:**903
- - masquerade **12:**69
- - parodies **11:**353; **13:**126ff
- - *Purim shpil* **13:**1396
- *illus:*
- - text
- - actors and musicians **12:**618
- - *Adloyada* carnival **2:**290; **9:**907
- - *Al ha-Nissim* **2:**626
- - Dura-Europos paintings **8:**649
- - Elizabeth, N.J., program **15:**1533
- - embroidered towel **13:**1388-1389
- - Esther Scrolls **13:**1388-1389; **14:**1049-1056
- - jesters **13:**1402
- - Judeo-Greek poem (18th cent.) **10:**426
- - kindergarten party **11:**365
- - masked Purim players **13:**1401
- - *Massekhet Purim* **13:**125
- - merrymakers **12:**28
- - New York ball **12:**1081
- - Pereyaslav-Khmelnitski kindergarten **13:**283
- - pewter plate **13:**353
- - Scroll of Esther, reading of **11:**1229
- - *Shivviti* plaque **13:***fcg.* 1390
- - three-cornered pastry **6:**1425
- *mus. notations:*
- - songs **12:**633
- *see also:* PURIMS, SPECIAL
"Purim at Home" (paint., M. Oppenheim) **13:**1403
PURIM KATAN (fest.) **13:**1396
Purimon (journ.) **5:**219
PURIMS, SPECIAL **13:**1396
- Algiers **2:**622; **3:**1015; **4:**459
- Altschul **2:**780
- Ancona **2:**943
- Avignon **3:**967
- Cairo's *Purim Mizrayim* **5:**30,244
- Candia **5:**1090; **5:**152
- Chios **7:**876
- Fez **6:**1256; **6:**1257
- Fossano **6:**1444
- Frankfort on the Main **6:**1248; **7:**86; **7:**92; **10:**663
- Lepanto **12:**896
- Libya **11:**201
- *Maccabees, Third Book of* **11:**660
- Oran **12:**1446
- Ostrog **12:**1513
- Padua **13:**10
- *Povidl Purim* **12:**184
- Rovigo **14:**355
- Saragossa **14:**863
- Syracuse **15:**635
- Tangier **15:**792
- Vidin **16:**121
- *illus:*
- - Basra: *Megillat Paras* (1906) **4:**312
- - Cavaillon: *piyyutim* **7:**15
- - Chieri: *Rane Falet* (1797) **5:**422
- - Ferrara; *megillah* for a private Purim (1758) **6:**1232
- - Frankfort: execution of Vincent Fettmilch and followers **6:**1248
- - *Ma'aseh Nissim* (1930) **4:**75
- - Saragossa scroll **14:**803
PURIM-SHPIL (Purim play) **13:**1396
- Jewish literature **11:**359
- satires **13:**125
- Usque, Salomon **16:**22
- Yiddish dramas **16:**802
- *illus:*
- - actors and musicians **12:**618
"Purim-Shpil" (paint., J. Adler) **13:**1404
Purishkevich, V. N. **15:**1538
Puritanism **10:**398
- Zionism **16:**1153
PURITY AND IMPURITY, RITUAL **13:**1405
- *Contents:*
- - In the Bible **13:**1405
- - Purity Ritual **13:**1406
- - General **13:**1406
- - In Halakhah **13:**1407
- - Purification **13:**1412
- - Impurity and Purity at the Present Time **13:**1412
- - Reasons for Purity and Impurity **13:**1414
- General
- - baths and bathing **4:**319
- - euphemisms and dysphemisms **6:**961
- - evolution **6:**1002
- - hygiene **8:**1140
- - rituals, ancient **10:**1039
- - sages **14:**641
- - scribes **14:**1044
- - sealing **14:**1074
- Concept of Purity
- - atonement **3:**830
- - holiness **10:**869
- - *kitel* **10:**1079
- - sin **14:**1590
- In Bible
- - Commandments, the 613 **5:**765f,773f
- - fire **6:**1303
- - Pentateuch **13:**244
- - priests' role **13:**1078ff
- - red heifer **14:**9
- In Halakhah
- - ablution **2:**81
- - *adne ha-sadeh* **6:**1002
- - *am ha-arez* **2:**834
- - Commandments, the 613 **5:**765
- - food **11:**807
- - *halakhah le-Moshe mi-Sinai* **7:**1167
- - Jerusalem laws **9:**1553
- - leprosy **11:**35
- - *mikveh* **11:**1544
- - *nevelah* **12:**1019
- - *niddah* **12:**1142ff
- - *taharat ha-mishpahah* **15:**703
- - Temple **15:**972ff
- - Temple Mount **15:**989
- - *tevul yom* **15:**1032
- - tombstones **15:**1221
- - transplants **15:**1338
- - vessels **10:**899; **14:**1563
- - witness for **16:**585
- - woman **16:**625
- - wooden articles **16:**630
- - *zavim* **16:**941
- Literature
- - *Baraita de-Niddah* **4:**194
- - Leviticus **11:**142ff
- - *Parah* tractate **13:**87
- - rabbinical literature **13:**1463
- - Talmud **11:**1533
- - *Tohorot* **15:**1189; **15:**1190
- Sects
- - Bana'im **14:**1087
- - Dead Sea sect **5:**1412
- - Essenes **6:**899
- - Falashas **6:**1148
- - *haver* **7:**1489
- - Karaites **10:**780
- - Samaritans **14:**744; **14:**747
- - Temple Scroll **15:**997
- - War Scroll **16:**1559
- - *Yahad* community **16:**700
- *illus:*
- - amulet against nocturnal pollution **2:**908
- - *Hilkhot Niddah* **16:***fcg.* 0000
- - immersion before sunset **15:**1033
- - immersion in a natural pool **11:**1534
- - *Makhshirin* **11:**807
- - Masada *mikveh* **11:**1087
- - *mikveh* **11:**1535-1542
- - priests inspecting leprosy **12:**924
- - red heifer, burning of **13:**87
- - *tohorah* plate **15:**1188
- - *Ukzin* **15:**1520
- - washing of the hands **12:**999; **16:**693
Purity of Blood, *see* LIMPIEZA DE SANGRE
Purple worm (dye), *see* CRIMSON WORM
Purslane (bot.) **13:**623; **16:**83
Purvey, John **4:**868
Pusey, E. Bouverie **8:**51
- Oxford **12:**1537
Pushkin, Alexander **14:**507
Pustkow (lab. camp, Pol.) **14:**259
PUT (bib. fig; people) **13:**1414
Puteoli (It. tn.) **6:**12
Puteus, Archangelus Burgonovo, *see* Burgonovo, Archangelus de
PUTIEL (bib. fig.) **13:**1415
- *see also:* JETHRO
Puttelange (tn., Saar) **11:**496
PUTTERMAN, DAVID **13:**1415
Puvah (bib. fig.) **6:**329
PUY (-EN -VELAY), LE (tn., Fr.) **13:**1415
Puzur-Inshushinak (gov., Elam) **14:**1482
Puzur-Nirah (ruler, Mesop.) **16:**1583
PYE, JAEL HENRIETTA **6:**783
Pym (weight), *see Pim*
Pyrex (glass) **14:**93
Pyrnice (tn., Morav.) **10:**104
Pyrope (mineral) **13:**1009
PYRRHUS, DIDACUS **13:**1416
- Yugoslav literature **16:**887
PYTHAGORAS **13:**1416
- Bible **3:**444
- Jews **7:**888; **7:**894; **13:**905
Pythagoreanism
- Essenes **8:**299
- Hellenistic period **8:**293
- Jewish customs **15:**1024
- Kabbalah **10:**507
- Kabbalah, Christian **10:**643
- Neoplatonism **12:**959
- Pharisaic parallel **7:**1490
Pytheas (philos.) **8:**293
PZC, *see* Provisional Committee for General Zionist Affairs

Q

Qāʿ-al-Simʿ (Qāʿ al-Yhūd; J. qt., Sanʿa) **14:**820
Qāʿat al-Yahūd, see JEWISH QUARTER
Qabāṭiyya (loc., Er. Isr.) **14:**1635
Qabbalah, *see* KABBALAH
Qābīl (name), *see* CAIN
Qābis (tn., Tun.), *see* GABÈS
Qābisi, Abraham al- (gaon) **7:**234
Qaʿda, Al- (loc., Mt. of Olives) **12:**484
Qaddafi, Muammar, al- **11:**206
Qadi (Musl. judge) **9:**643ff; **15:**1441
Qadi madhhab (Druze judge) **9:**643
Qadma' (cantillation sign), *see 'Azla'*
Qa'īd (tit., Tun.), *see Zaken ha-Yehudim*
Qā'itbāy (15th cent., sultan) **11:**837; **9:**1424
Qalaʿat (city, Assyr.), *see* Kalah
Qalaʿat Sharkat (site, Assyr.) **16:**1507
Qal'a-e-Shush (bib. site, Iran), *see* SHUSHAN
Qalandiya (vill., Er. Isr.) **9:**1515
– *see also:* ATAROT
Qalansawa (vill., Er. Isr.) **9:**575
Qalʿat al Ḥuṣn (site, Isr.) **15:**536
Qalʿat al-Qurayn (Crus. castle), *see* Montfort
Qalʿat al-Shaqīf (Crus. castle), *see* Beaufort
Qal'at as Subayba (Crus. castle) **4:**163
QAL'AT ḤAMMĀD (city, Alg.) **13:**1417
– rabbinical office **13:**1449
Qalʿat Ilyās (mt., Transj.) **15:**1316
Qalʿat Mahdī ben Tawala (tn., Mor.) **14:**1528
Qalʿat-Ṣāliḥ (tn., Iraq) **8:**1450
Qalʿat Sharqāt (city, Assyr.), *see* ASSUR
Qalā'ūn (13th cent., sultan) **9:**1424
Qalqīlya (Qalqīliya; tn., Er. Isr.) **14:**1605,1635
Qālūnya (vill. Isr.) **12:**494; **12:**495; **16:**736
Qalyub (cmty., Egy.) **12:**424
Qameṣ (vowel)
– masorah **16:**1422
– *mille'eil* and *millera'* **16:**1430
– mnemonic device **16:**1423
– Tiberian masorah **16:**1449
Qameṣ (masor. term) **16:**1432
Qameṣ gadol (vowel) **16:**1430
Qameṣ-pum (vowel) **16:**1449
Qameṣ Qaṭan (vowel) **16:**1430,1449
Qamishli (tn., Syr.) **15:**646
Qamni'el, Abraham ibn, *see* Ibn Qamni'el, Abraham
Qana (city), *see* KENATH
Qanawāt, Al- (tn., Syr.) **10:**906
Qanbil, Abraham ibn, *see* Ibn Qamni'el, Abraham
Qaneh ("reed"; meas.), *see Kaneh*
Qantara (tn., Sinai) **14:**1607,1636
– *illus:*
– – Israel soldier observing Egyptian side **9:**420
Qantir (site, Egy.) **13:**1545
Qanu (city), *see* KENATH
Qānūnī, Suleiman al- (16th cent., sultan), *see* SULEIMAN I
Qaqqaru (city, Hamath), *see* KARKAR
Qāqūn (tn., Er. Isr.) **9:**274; **9:**284
Qarā, Abdallah al- **9:**1039
Qarā-Aymid (tn., Iraq), *see* Diyarbakir
Qarāfī (Arab polem.) **9:**102
Qarā'nyūn, *see* KARAITES
Qarantal (site), *see* Monastery of the Temptation
Qarat al-ʿUyūn (Loc., Er. Isr.), *see* IJON
Qarʿiyya, al- (J. sect, Egy.), *see* KARIYAH, AL-
Qarmatians (Arab sect) **9:**262
Qarnei Parah (cantillation sign) **16:**1454
Qarnini (Assyr. dist.) **10:**800
Qarn Sarṭaba (peak, Isr.) **14:**889
Qarqar (city, Hamath), *see* KARKAR
Qarqashandi, Al- (Musl. fam.) **9:**1425
Qārūn, (bib. fig.), *see* KORAH
Qaryat al-Inab (vill., Er. Isr.), *see* ABU GHOSH
Qasbat al-Makhzan (vill., Mor.) **6:**190
Qaṣīda (type of song) **16:**1258
Qasīla (site, Er. Isr.), *see* Tells (Qasila)
Qasim, Abd al-Karīm **8:**1455
Qāsim, ʿIzz al-Dīn al- **9:**348,462
Qāsim, Samīḥ al- **9:**1042
Qasimiyya River **9:**155
Qasimiyya Valley **9:**152
Qaṣr al-ʿAbd (anc. loc.) **15:**1178
Qaṣr al-ʿAsal (fort, Isr.) **5:**1394
Qaṣr al-Juhayniyya (Isr.) **15:**783
Qaṣr al-Zaʿfarān (tell, Isr.) **10:**866
Qaṣr ʿAntar (peak, Isr.) **8:**373
Qaṣrayn (loc., Er. Isr.) **13:**1534
– *illus:*
– – synagogue portal **13:**1534
QAṢR IBN HUBAYRAH (tn., Babyl.) **13:**1417
Qassām, 'Izz al-Dīn al-, *see* Qāsim, 'Izz al-Dīn al-
Qastal, Al- (vill., Er. Isr.) **9:**1493; **11:**1453; **16:**308
Qastīna (vill., Isr.) **4:**386; **6:**1154
Qataban, Kingdom of (Arab.) **4:**349; **14:**587ff
Qāṭāya (hist., Egy.), *see* SAMBARI, JOSEPH BEN ISAAC
Qatīfa, Al- (Qatif; tn., Bahr.) **4:**102; **13:**312
Qatna (city, Syr.) **11:**979; **16:**1496
Qatra (vill., Isr.) **4:**1; **7:**354
Qav (meas.) **16:**380ff
Qaʿwār, Jamāl **9:**1042
Qaʿwār, Najwā **9:**1042ff
Qāwuqjī, Fawzī al-, *see* Kaukji, Fawzi al-
QAYNUQĀʿ (J. tribes) **13:**1419
– Abdallah ibn Salām **2:**54
– Arabia **3:**234; **3:**235
– Muhammad **12:**510ff
Qays (city, Bahr.) **4:**102
Qazzaz, Adiyah ben Manasseh ibn (Al-) **13:**1419
Qazzaz, Ishmael ben Adiyah ibn (Al-) **13:**1419
QAZZAZ, MANASSEH BEN ABRAHAM IBN (AL-) **13:**1418
– Fatimids **6:**1197
Qazzaz, Samuel ben Adiyah ibn (Al-) **13:**1419
Qen (city), *see* KENATH
Qene ha-middah (meas. instr.) **16:**378ff
Qēni (nomadic clans), *see* KENITE
Qénizal, Jacob **12:**332
Qere perpetuum (masor. note) **16:**1421
Qeresh (Tabernacle component) **15:**681
Qeri (Bib. text form), *see Keri* and *ketiv*
Qibbuṣ (vowel) **16:**1450
Qibla (dir., Musl. prayer)
– *Even Shetiyyah* **9:**1423
– Jerusalem **9:**1575
– Muhammad **12:**510ff
Qibya (vill., Jord.) **9:**1033; **9:**386; **15:**1553
Qinot, see LAMENTATIONS, BOOK OF
Qinu (k., Qedar) **16:**661
Qirqisānī, al- (10th cent., Kar.), *see* KIRKISĀNĪ, JACOB AL-
Qirqīsiyya (tn., Syr.), *see* Kirkisiya
Qirqyer (Qirqer; tn., Crimea), *see* CHUFUT-KALE
Qishla (q); (fort., Jer.) **9:**1435
Qissa (poetry type) **10:**410
Qiṭfīr (bib. fig.), *see* POTIPHAR
Qīzil-Ribāṭ (loc., Iraq) **8:**1450
Qodesh ha-Qodashim, see Holy of Holies
Qof (Heb. let.), *see* KOF
Qom, El- (site, Er. Isr.) **16:**667
Qomeẓ (meas.), *see Komeẓ*
Qos (deity) **6:**377
Qosgabri (k., Edom) **6:**376
Qosmalaku (k., Edom) **6:**376
Qrê (Bib. text form), *see Keri* and *ketiv*
Quadrans Judaicus (astron. instr.) **15:**1130
– nautical aid **14:**1413
QUADRATUS, UMMIDIUS CAIUS **13:**1419
– Ananias ben Nedebeus **2:**923
– Nebuchadnezzar **12:**915
– zealots **5:**1134
Quadros, Diego (Didacus) de **8:**53
QUAIL (bird) **13:**1420
– dietary laws **6:**30,34
– *manna* **11:**883
– *illus:*
– – *Birds' Head Haggadah* **7:**fcg. 875
Quamvis perfidiam (papal bull) **4:**1496
Quara (reg., Eth.) **6:**1147
QUARESMIUS, FRANCISCUS **13:**1420
Quartz (mineral) **13:**1011
Quasimodo, Salvatore **9:**1107
QUASTEL, JUDAH HIRSCH **13:**1420
Quatro Irmãos (loc., Braz.) **4:**1326ff
Qubbat al-Ṣakhra (mosque), *see* Dome of the Rock
Quds, Al- (El-; Jer.), *see* Al-Quds
Quōsu (deity) **2:**926
– *see also:* ASHERAH
QUE (Cilicia; place) **13:**1421
– Solomon's imports **15:**98
– trade **15:**1295
Quebach, Meir **16:**1348
QUEBEC (prov., Can.) **13:**1422
– Jewish education **6:**452
QUEBEC (city, Can.) **13:**1423
Queen Mary Psalter (14th cent. illum. ms.)
– Moses **12:**407
– Ruth **14:**524
– Samuel **14:**784
– *illus:* **2:**970; **4:**880; **5:**22; **8:**1317
QUEEN OF SHEBA (bib. fig.) **13:**1424
– alchemy **2:**543
– balsam **4:**142
– in the Arts **15:**109ff
– Solomon **15:**98ff
– *illus:*
– – text
– – Catalan Atlas **11:**915
– – visit to Solomon **15:**103
Queens (boro, N.Y.C.) **12:**1077ff
Queenscliff (tn., Austr.) **11:**1286
Queen Sophia Bible **13:**797

Queensland, *see* AUSTRALIA
Quenstedt, J. Andreas **8:**53
Que Que (city, Rhod.) **14:**148
Querido, Aaron **14:**681
Querido, Emanuel **6:**320; **13:**1365,1424
QUERIDO, ISRAËL **13:**1424
- Amsterdam **2:**901
- *illus:*
- - *Saul en David* (1914) **6:**318
QUERIDO, JACOB **13:**1425
- Shabbateanism **6:**148; **14:**1244
QUETSCH, SOLOMON **13:**1427
Quevedo y Villegos, Francisco Gómez de **10:**1375; **15:**249
Quezon Y Molina, Manuel **13:**395
Quf (Heb. let.), *see* KOF
"Quiet Scene" (paint., E. Baizerman) **4:**111
QUIETUS, LUSIUS **13:**1427
- Apostomos **3:**218
- ban on Greek **8:**296
- Edessa **6:**366
- history chart **8:**766-767
- Jewish revolts **8:**645
- Trajan **15:**1312
- war of **9:**245
Quiller-Couch, A. T. **16:**262
Quilmes (city, Arg.) **3:**421
Quilon (port, Ind.) **8:**1355
Quimperlé (tn., Fr.) **4:**1383
QUINCE (bot.) **13:**1427
- hawthorn **15:**1119
- plant list **13:**623
Quincy (city, Ill.) **8:**1256
Quine, William van Orman **7:**780; **14:**1335
Quinet, Edgar **16:**261
Quinquarboreus, Johannes **8:**53
- Mercier, Jean **11:**1382
QUINTILIAN (Marcus Fabius Quintilianus) **14:**236
QUINTILIUS VARUS **13:**1427
- crucifixion of Jews **5:**1134
Quintus Septimus Florens Tertullianus, *see* Tertullian
Quiqui, Abraham ben **2:**516
QUIRINIUS, P. SULPICIUS **13:**1428
- Anan ben Seth **2:**922
- Zealot revolt **16:**947
Quirino, Carlo **13:**101
Quirinus, Laurus **8:**53
Quiroga, Prof. **11:**1202
QUISLING, VIDKUN ABRAHAM LAURITZ **13:**1429
- Norway **12:**1224
Quistrop, J. **8:**53
Quito (city, Ec.) **6:**359
Quittungen (ghetto money) **5:**725
Quiver **16:**266ff
Quixano, Abigail **8:**328
Quixano-Henriques (fam.), *see* HENRIQUES
Qūmisī, Daniel ben Moses al-, *see* DANIEL BEN MOSES AL-QŪMISĪ
QUMRAN (reg., Isr.) **13:**1429
- *Contents:*
- - Occupation of Khirbet Qumran **13:**1429
- - Description of Khirbet Qumran **13:**1430
- - Chronology of Khirbet Qumran **13:**1432
- The Sect
- - ablution **2:**82
- - Apostles' number **3:**216
- - asceticism **3:**216
- - calendar **5:**48
- - eschatology **6:**877ff
- - fastday **6:**1194
- - interpretation of prophecies **13:**331
- - marriage **11:**1027
- - *mezuzah* **11:**1476
- - New Oil festival **15:**997
- - *tefillin* **15:**903
- - treasures **15:**1361
- - zealots **16:**949
- Writings
- - angelic liturgy **15:**144
- - Bible texts **4:**832ff
- - *Copper Scroll* **5:**955
- - *Discipline, Manual of* **6:**63ff
- - *Job, Testament of* **10:**129
- - *Jubilees, Book of* **10:**325
- - Pentateuch, Samaritan **13:**267
- - Psalms, Apocryphal **13:**1302
- - Psalms, Book of **13:**1305
- - Pseudepigrapha **3:**185
- - Samuel, Book of **14:**789
- *illus:*
- - text
- - *Copper Scroll* **5:**956
- - excavations **3:**681
- - Khirbat Qumran **5:**1409
- - pen-cases **16:**668
- - scriptorium **5:**1411
- - *tefillin* **15:**903
- *see also:* DEAD SEA SCROLLS; DEAD SEA SECT
QUNAYTIRA, AL- (tn., Isr.) **13:**1435
- frontier **9:**312ff
- human geography **9:**597
- Khirbat Qunatira **15:**1131
- Six-Day War **9:**411; **14:**1638
- *illus:* text
Quodvultdeus (Ch. F.) **5:**553
Quorum, *see* MINYAN
Quota System **6:**68ff
Qur'ān, see KORAN
QURAYẒA (tribe, Arab) **13:**1436
- Arabic literature **16:**1415
Qurayẓa (tribe, Arab.) **13:**1436
- Arabia **3:**234; **3:**235
- Muhammad **12:**510
- *see also:* KA'B BEN ASAD
Qurna, al- (tn., Iraq) **8:**1450
Qusan (loc., Iraq) **8:**1447
Quseima (El-; loc. Sinai)
- Sinai Campaign **14:**1605
- Six-Day War **14:**1635
- *illus:*
- - Sinai Campaign **14:**1603
Qusṭanṭīniyya (city, Turk.), *see* ISTANBUL
Quṭayfar (bib. fig.), *see* POTIPHAR
Quyunjiq (loc., Iraq) **12:**1168
Qvitel (Ḥas. term) **7:**1400
Qyrym (city, Crimea), *see* Stary Krym

R

Raab (city, Hung.), *see* GYÖR
Raab (isl., Adriatic) **13:**147
Raab, Esther **13:**1437
RAAB, JUDAH **13:**1437
Raabe, Wilhelm **7:**444
Ra'ah (zool.), *see* BUZZARD
Raalte, Frits van **6:**320
Raama (Raamah; bib. fig.) **12:**883
Raamses (city, Egy.), *see* RAMSES
Raanan, Yoav **15:**314
RA'ANANNAH (tn., Isr.) **13:**1438
– statistics **1:**place list
Ra'aya Meheimna (wk.) **3:**70; **10:**534; **10:**541; **16:**1197
Rab (Isl., Adriatic) **16:**880
R-a-b-a-d, *see* ABRAHAM BEN DAVID OF POSQUIÈRES
R-a-b-a-d I, *see* IBN DAUD, ABRAHAM BEN DAVID HALEVI
Rab Akčesi (tax), *see Rab-Aqchesi*
R-a-b-a-n, *see* ELIEZER BEN NATHAN OF MAINZ
Raban, Ze'ev **4:**1220; **8:**1287; **15:**151
– *illus:*
– – bookplate for Batya and Shlomo Greenberg **4:**1223
– – Golden Book, Jewish National Fund **7:**744
Rabanus Maurux, *see* HRABANUS MAURUS
Rab-Aqchesi (tax) **5:**818; **13:**1451; **16:**1532,1547
Rabat (tn., Mor.), *see* SALÉ-RABAT
Rabat-Tinzulin (vill., Mor.) **6:**190
RABB, MAXWELL MILTON **13:**1438
Rabb, M. G. **16:**923
Rabb, Saul **8:**1361
Rabb, Theodore K. **13:**1476
Rabba, Elijah **13:**1439
RABBA, MENAHEM **13:**1439
RABBA BEN MATNAH (4/5 cent., amora) **13:**1439
Rabbah (2nd cent., tan.-amora), *see* ḤIYYA
Rabbah (3/4 cent., amora), *see* RABBAH BAR NAHAMANI
RABBAH (gaon) **13:**1440
– gaonate list **7:**318
Rabbah (8th cent.), *see* ABBA
RABBAH (tn., Er. Isr.) **13:**1439
– Ares **3:**407
– Transjordan **15:**1317
Rabbah bar Ammi (gaon), *see* Abba bar Ammi
RABBAH BAR BAR ḤANA (amora) **13:**1440
– Benjamin, Moses **4:**530
– Rabbah bar Ḥanna **13:**1441
Rabbah bar Dodai (gaon) **7:**318
RABBAH BAR ḤANA (amora) **13:**1441
RABBAH BAR HUNA (amora) **13:**1441
– Huna **8:**1074
Rabbah bar Meryon (amora) **10:**152
RABBAH BAR NAHAMANI (amora) **13:**1442
– Abba bar Marta **2:**32
– Abbaye **2:**44
– Academy on High **2:**208
– Babylonian Talmud **11:**319
– debate with God **2:**208
– decisions in controversies **5:**891
– history chart **8:**766-767
– Isaac bar Rav Judah **9:**12
– tax evasion **10:**710
RABBAH BEN AVUHA (amora) **13:**1443
RABBAH BEN SHILAH **13:**1444
Rabbah of Rov (savora) **14:**920
RABBAH TOSFA'AH (amora) **13:**1444
– Mar bar Rav Ashi **11:**940
Rabban (tit.) **2:**873; **15:**1163
Rabban, Joseph **5:**1059
Rabban, Ze'ev, *see* Raban, Ze'ev
Rabbana (amora), *see* ASHI
Rabbana (tit.), *see* Rabban
Rabbana Simeon, *see* SIMEON BAR ISAAC
RABBANITES **13:**1444
– Al-Tarās **2:**772
– Anan ben David **2:**920
– Bashyazi, Elijah **4:**298
– Ibn Kammūna **8:**1187
– Karaites **4:**391; **8:**665ff; **10:**761; **15:**735ff
– masorah controversy **16:**1417
– nazirites **12:**909
– rabbinical literature **13:**1463
– term origin **13:**1446
– Troki **15:**1401ff
– Turkey **15:**1462
Rabbat Ashlag potash works (Er. Isr.) **5:**1395; **9:**591
RABBATH-AMMON (city, Transj.) **13:**1444
– Ammon **2:**854
– battle of **16:**277
– human geography **9:**596
– Transjordan **15:**1317
– *see also:* DECAPOLIS; Philadelphia
Rabbath-Moab (city, Er. Isr.), *see* RABBAH
Rabbenu Asaph, *see* ASAPH HA-ROFE
Rabbenu Ephraim, *see* EPHRAIM IBN AVI ALRAGAN
Rabbenu Gershom, *see* GERSHOM BEN JUDAH ME'OR HA-GOLA
Rabbenu ha-Kadosh, *see* JUDAH HA-NASI
Rabbenu Moses Gerondi, *see* NAḤMANIDES
Rabbenu Nissim, *see* NISSIM BEN JACOB BEN NISSIM IBN SHAHIN
Rabbenu Tam, *see* TAM, JACOB BEN MEIR
"Rabbi," *see* JUDAH HA-NASI
"Rabbi" (paint., P. Litvinosky) **11:**407
RABBI, RABBINATE **13:**1445
– *Contents:*
– – Middle Ages **13:**1445
– – In the Muslim East **13:**1448
– – Modern Period **13:**1452
– – Functions of the Rabbi **13:**1452
– – Germany **13:**1453
– – United States **13:**1455
– – Israel **13:**1456
– *amoraim,* Palestinian **2:**873
– arbitrator **3:**296
– chief rabbi **5:**418
– communal autonomy **16:**1309
– community official **5:**812
– dress **6:**220
– encroachment safeguards **7:**1463
– *Ḥakham* **7:**1145
– Hakham Bashi **7:**1146
– Hebrew encyclopedias **6:**734
– Istanbul **9:**1094
– *Landrabbiner* **10:**409
– ordination **14:**1140ff
– Ottoman Empire **16:**1540
– presumptive right **16:**395
– Russia **10:**860
– synagogue **15:**583
– tax **15:**856
– title in Talmud **15:**1163
– *tokheḥah* **15:**1192
– *illus:*
– – *semikhah* **14:**1141
– – *takkanot* **15:**716
– – Warsaw conference **16:**341
– – White House delegation **15:**1663
– *see also:* RABBINICAL SEMINARIES; YESHIVOT
Rabbi ben Ezra (poem) **4:**1411
RABBI BINYAMIN (Heb. au.) **13:**1458
Rabbi Gold Teachers' Seminary (Isr.) **10:**31
Rabbi Isaac Elchanan Theological Seminary (N.Y.) **13:**1465; **16:**760
Rabbi Judah Leib Zlotnik Seminary (S.A.) **6:**455ff
Rabbi Kar (pseud.), *see* LEWINSKY, ELHANAN LEIB
Rabbi Kook Foundation, *see* Mosad ha-Rav Kook
Rabbi Mór (tit., Port.), *see* ARRABY MOOR
Rabbin Délégué (tit.) **13:**1451
Rabbiner, Ẓemaḥ **4:**1485
RABBINER-SEMINAR FUER DAS ORTHODOXE JUDENTUM (Ger.) **13:**1459
– Hildesheimer, Azriel **8:**476
– library **11:**192
– rabbinical seminaries **13:**1464
RABBINICAL ALLIANCE OF AMERICA **13:**1459
RABBINICAL ASSEMBLY **13:**1460
– Artz, Max **3:**670
– Conservative Judaism **5:**903
– United Synagogue of America **15:**1674
– Zionism **16:**1145
Rabbinical Authority, *see* AUTHORITY, RABBINICAL
RABBINICAL CONFERENCES **13:**1460
– Germany **7:**475; **13:**1454
– history chart **8:**766-767
– *see also:* SYNODS
Rabbinical Council (Isr.) **9:**609
RABBINICAL COUNCIL OF AMERICA **13:**1461
– *illus:* text
Rabbinical Courts, *see* BET DIN AND JUDGES; JUDICIARY IN ISRAEL
Rabbinical disputes, *see* CONFLICT OF OPINION
RABBINICAL LITERATURE **13:**1462
– codification of law **5:**628
– *ḥiddushim* **8:**464
– Jewish literature **11:**328ff
– Judaism **10:**390
– Talmud, Babylonian **15:**755
– Talmud, Jerusalem **15:**772ff
– *Tanḥuma Yelammedenu* **15:**794
– Urbach's studies **16:**4
– *see also:* HEBREW BOOK TITLES; MINHAGIM BOOKS
RABBINICAL SEMINARIES **13:**1463
– General
– – education **6:**421
– – history chart **8:**766-767
– – ordination **14:**1146
– – training **13:**1452; **13:**1454; **13:**1456
– – Wissenschaft des Judentums **16:**576
– Countries

-- Algeria
--- Ecole Rabbinique d'Algerie **2:**617
-- Austria
--- Vienna **3:**895; **6:**423; **16:**124
-- England
--- Jew's College **6:**450; **10:**98
--- Leo Baeck College **6:**450
-- France
--- Ecole Rabbinique **6:**421; **11:**192; **11:**1451; **13:**108; **14:**1147
--- Strasbourg **15:**424
-- Germany
--- Hochschule fuer die Wissenschaft des Judentums **6:**423; **8:**799; **16:**577
--- Juedisch-Theologisches Seminar **4:**1355; **6:**422
--- Kassel (1810) **16:**474
--- Rabbiner Seminar fuer das Orthodoxe Judentum **6:**423; **11:**192; **13:**1459
-- Hungary
--- Budapest **4:**1452; **6:**423
-- Iraq
--- Bet Zilkha **6:**1101; **8:**1451
-- Israel
--- Harry Fischel Institute **8:**424; **15:**55
-- Italy
--- Collegio Rabbinico Italiano **5:**736; **11:**192
-- Netherlands
--- Amsterdam **6:**422
--- Ez-Hayyim **13:**19
-- Poland
--- Bet ha-Midrash de-Parnas **2:**143
--- Warsaw **16:**336
-- South Africa
--- Rabbi Judah Leib Zlotnik Seminary **6:**455ff
-- Turkey
--- Alliance **2:**653
-- U.S.
--- Hebrew Theological College **8:**216
--- Hebrew Union College **6:**439; **8:**216
--- Jewish Theological Seminary **6:**439; **10:**95
--- Rabbi Isaac Elhanan Theological Seminary **6:**439 **16:**760
--- Reconstructionist Rabbinical College **13:**1616
--- University of Judaism **10:**96
- *illus:*
-- Berlin, Hochschule fuer die Wissenschaft des Judentums **8:**800
-- Breslau, Juedisch-Theologisches Seminar **10:**465
-- Cincinnati, Ohio, Hebrew UnionCollege **8:**217
-- Padua, regulations (1827) **7:**1442
-- Yeshivah University **16:**760,767
- *see also:* YESHIVOT
Rabbinical Seminary for Orthodox Judaism (Ger.), *see* RABBINER SEMINAR FUER DAS ORTHODOXE JUDENTUM
Rabbinical Supreme Court of Appeal (Er. Isr.), *see* Court of Appeal, Rabbinical Supreme
Rabbinism, *see* RABBANITES
Rabbino, Jedidiah **14:**154
Rabbinovicz (fam. name), *see also:* Rabbinowicz; Rabbinowitz; Rabinovich; Rabinovitch; Rabinovitz; Rabinowicz; Rabinowitz
RABBINOVICZ, RAPHAEL NATHAN NATA **13:**1465
- bibliography **4:**973
- *haggahot* **7:**1107
- Merzbacher, Abraham **11:**1395
- Talmud **15:**766
- Wissenschaft **16:**579
Rabbinowicz (fam. name), *see also:* Rabbinovicz; Rabbinowitz; Rabinovich; Rabinovitch; Rabinovitz; Rabinowicz; Rabinowitz
RABBINOWICZ, ISRAEL MICHEL **13:**1466
- Talmud in French **15:**768
Rabbinowicz, Joshua Jacob **13:**1466
Rabbinowitz (fam. name), *see also:* Rabbinovicz; Rabbinowicz; Rabinovich; Rabinovitch; Rabinovitz; Rabinowicz; Rabinowitz
RABBINOWITZ, SARAH **13:**1467
RABBINOWITZ, SAUL PHINEHAS **13:**1467
- Fuenn's *Ha-Oẓar* **7:**213
- Kattowitz conference **10:**820; **10:**821
- translation of Graetz **8:**561
- Wissenschaft **16:**578
- *illus:*
-- F.Z.C. **16:**1165
Rabbi of Apta, *see* ABRAHAM JOSHUA HESCHEL OF APTA
Rabbi of Bacharach (wdct., J. Budko) **4:**45
Rabbi's Prayer (ref. rite) **8:**500
"Rabbi with Torah" (paint., Mane-Katz) **11:**871
Rabchik, Josef **10:**321
RAB DE LA CORTE (offic.) **13:**1468
- Benveniste, Abraham **4:**559
- Spain **15:**230; **15:**239
Rabe, J. J. **8:**53
Rabel I (1st cent. B.C.E., k.) **12:**741
R-a-b-h, *see* Al-Nakawa, Ephraim
Rabi (writ.) **7:**148
RABI, ISIDOR ISAAC **13:**1469
R-a-b-i-a-h, *see* ELIEZER BEN JOEL HA-LEVI OF BONN
RABĪʿ IBN ABĪ AL-ḤUQAYQ **13:**1470
Rabin (amora), *see* AVIN
RABIN (fam.) **13:**1470
RABIN, CHAIM MENACHEM **1:**35; **13:**1470
Rabin, Israel Abraham **13:**1470
Rabin, Michael Oser **13:**1471
Rabin, Phil **15:**303
Rabin, S. (sport.) **12:**1376
Rabin, Solomon **11:**190
RABIN, YIẒḤAK **13:**1471
- *illus:*
-- Six-Day War, entering Jerusalem **9:**409
-- U.J.A. conference **15:**1541
Rabinkovich (fam.), *see* Josefowicz
RABINOFF, GEORGE W. **13:**1471
Rabinovich (fam. name), *see also* Rabbinovicz; Rabbinowicz; Rabbinowitz; Rabinovitch; Rabinovitz; Rabinowicz; Rabinowitz
Rabinovich, Abraham **5:**406
Rabinovich, D. B. **11:**431
Rabinovich, Ernestina **4:**635
Rabinovich, Ilya **5:**406
Rabinovich, Isaac (r.) **12:**1319
Rabinovich, Isaac (Zion. ldr.) **16:**1139
RABINOVICH, ISAAK MOSEYEVICH **8:**1433
RABINOVICH, ISAIAH **13:**1472
- Canada **5:**113
- Hebrew literature **8:**214
RABINOVICH, JOSEPH **13:**1472
Rabinovich, L. (Duma repr.) **6:**268
RABINOVICH, OSIP ARONOVICH **13:**1473
RABINOVICH, YEHUDAH LEIB (Leon) **13:**1474
RABINOVICH, ZALMAN KHAIMOVICH **11:**1575
Rabinovici, Benjamin **16:**73
Rabinovici, Motty **9:**1295
Rabinovitch (fam. name), *see also* Rabbinovicz; Rabbinowicz; Rabbinowitz; Rabinovich; Rabinovitz; Rabinowicz; Rabinowitz
Rabinovitch, Wladimir, *see* Rabi
RABINOVITZ, ALEXANDER SISKIND **13:**1474
- Kefar Azar **10:**877
- linguistics
- *illus:*
-- F.Z.C. **16:**1165, 1378
Rabinovitz, Esther **5:**437
Rabinovitz, Menahem Nahum **14:**1272
Rabinovitz, Misha **14:**1277
Rabinovitz, Olga, *see* Loyev, Olga
Rabinovitz, Raphael, *see* RABBINOVITZ, RAPHAEL NATHAN NATA
Rabinovitz, Shalom, *see* SHALOM ALEICHEM
Rabinovitz, Yitzhak Isaac **12:**967
Rabinowich, E. A. **16:**1136
Rabinowich, Solomon ha-Kohen, *see* RADOMSKO, SOLOMON HA-KOHEN RABINOWICH OF
Rabinowicz (fam.) **4:**1397
Rabinowicz, Joshua Jerahmeel **14:**1296
Rabinowicz, Meir Shalom **10:**723
Rabinowicz, Mordecai, *see* BEN-AMMI, MORDECAI
RABINOWICZ, OSKAR K. **1:**36; **13:**1475
Rabinowicz, Shalom **3:**735
Rabinowicz, Solomon **11:**944
Rabinowicz, Yehoshah Asher **3:**735
Rabinowicz, Zalman **11:**618
RABINOWITCH, EUGENE **13:**1476
Rabinowitz (fam. name), *see also* Rabbinovicz; Rabbinowicz; Rabbinowitz; Rabinovich;Rabinovitch; Rabinovitz; Rabinowicz
Rabinowitz, Azriel **15:**939
Rabinowitz, Baruch **12:**514
Rabinowitz, Benjamin **13:**1479
Rabinowitz, B. M. **4:**1239
RABINOWITZ, ELIAHU WOLF **13:**1476
Rabinowitz, Eliezer **10:**718
Rabinowitz, Ḥayyim **15:**938
Rabinowitz, Isaac, *see* HALEVY, ISAAC
Rabinowitz, Israel **5:**113
Rabinowitz, Jacob, *see* RABINOWITZ, YAAKOV
Rabinowitz, Jay A. **2:**514
Rabinowitz, Jerome, *see* ROBBINS, JEROME
RABINOWITZ, JOEL **13:**1476
RABINOWITZ, LOUIS ISAAC **1:**36, **13:**1477
RABINOWITZ, LOUIS MAYER **13:**1477
Rabinowitz, Mayer (publ.) **8:**210
Rabinowitz, Phil, *see* Rabin, Phil
Rabinowitz, Raphael, *see* RABBINOVICZ, RAPHAEL NATHAN NATA
RABINOWITZ, SAMUEL JACOB **13:**1478
- Liverpool **11:**409
Rabinowitz, Stanley **16:**357
RABINOWITZ, YAAKOV **13:**1478
- Barash, Asher **4:**201
- Shlonsky, Abraham **14:**1422
- *illus:*
-- Writers' Association **16:**653
RABINOWITZ, ZEVI HA-COHEN **13:**1479
RABINOWITZ, ZINA **13:**1479
- *illus:*
-- Hebrew writers' convention, 1943 **8:**213
RABINOWITZ-TEOMIM, ELIJAH DAVID BEN BENJAMIN **13:**1479
- Kaplan, A. S. **10:**748
- *geneal. table:* **9:**1259
Rabinowitz-Teomim, Ẓevi Judah **13:**1479
Rabinsohn, Ana, *see* PAUKER, ANA
Rabinsohn, Joseph Zundel **13:**1505
Rabinsohn, Joshua Ẓevi **13:**1505
Rabinsohn, Mordecai **4:**1156; **10:**862; **13:**1505
Rab-mag (Babyl. title), *see* RAB-SARIS
RABON, ISRAEL **13:**1481
- Yiddish literature **16:**819
RABOY, ISAAC **13:**1481
RAB-SARIS AND RAB-MAG (Babyl. title) **13:**1481
RAB-SHAKEH (tit., Babyl.) **13:**1482
- cup bearer **5:**1172
- Manasseh **11:**853
- olive **12:**1364
Raby, Naphtali Eliahu, *see* RAHABI, NAPHTALI ELIAHU
Răcăciuni, Isaia **14:**422
RACAH, GIULIO (Yoel) **13:**1482
Raccah, Isaac **13:**1482
RACCAH, MAS'UD BEN AARON **13:**1482
Raccah, Solomon **13:**1482
RACE, THEORY OF **13:**1483
- anthropology, physical **3:**43ff
- anti-Semitism **8:**737ff
- Arndt, Ernst Moritz **3:**485
- Black Death **4:**1068
- Chamberlain, Houston **5:**332
- concentration camps **5:**77
- gassing **16:**1332
- Hess, Moses **8:**433
- history **8:**737
- Holocaust **8:**835ff
- intermarriage **12:**164
- Jewish support **12:**933ff
- *limpieza de sangre* **11:**255
- Luschan, Felix von **11:**583ff
- Mussolini, Benito **12:**719
- Nazi Germany **7:**491
- Nuremberg Laws **12:**1281
- Pius XI **8:**911
- Rosenberg, Alfred **14:**275
- Semites **14:**1148
- Voltaire **16:**220
- *illus:*
-- *Der Stürmer* cartoon (1929) **8:**833
-- "Deutschland" (poster, 1920) **3:**154
-- "For Aryans only," park bench in Berlin, 1938 **6:**654
-- identity card stamped "J" (Cologne, 1939) **5:**742
-- Jew and Christian servant maid (cartoon, 1926, Ger.) **3:**133
-- Nazi anthropological juxtapositions **8:**737, 835
-- "Otto Mayer, the Nuremberg Jew" (Nazi cartoon) **3:**134
RACHEL (bib. fig.) **13:**1486
- *Contents:*
-- In the Aggadah **13:**1488
-- Tomb of Rachel **13:**1489
-- In the Arts **13:**1490
-- In Music **13:**1491

-- adoption **2:**298
- Arts **9:**1203f
- Bethlehem tomb **8:**921
- concubinage **12:**1288; **12:**1289
- envy **9:**1306
- Genesis **7:**389
- Jacob **9:**1192ff
- Laban **10:**1315
- matriarch **13:**181
- *teraphim* **15:**1014
- tribes **15:**1384
- *illus:*
-- given in marriage to Jacob **4:**949
-- Jacob at the deathbed of **4:**523
-- Nice portrayal **12:**1135
-- tomb **8:**925
-- tomb depicted on Palestine stamp **15:**332
- *see also:* LEAH
RACHEL (w., Akiva) **13:**1491
- Akiva **2:**488
- Ben Kalba Savu'a **4:**539
Rachel (dau., Mar Samuel) **11:**992
RACHEL (act.) **13:**1492
- stamps **15:**336
- *illus:* text
Rachel, Tomb of, *see* RACHEL
Rachelius, J. **8:**53
Rachlin, Carl **12:**934
RACHMILEWITZ, MOSHE **13:**1493
- *illus:*
-- medical students and **9:**990
Rachmilewitz, Naḥman **11:**376; **11:**382; **16:**212
Racial persecution, *see* RACE, THEORY OF
Racial Preservation Society (orgn., Eng.) **12:**952
Racine (city, Wis.) **16:**556
RACINE, JEAN **13:**1493
- Athaliah **3:**815
- Esther **6:**909
- Titus **15:**1170
Racism, *see* RACE, THEORY OF
RACKMAN, EMANUEL **13:**1494
Ráczböszörményi, János **8:**53
Raczkiewicz, Wladislaw **8:**911
RAD, GERHARD VON **13:**1494
- Bible **4:**909
Rada, Emanuel **5:**1193
R-a-d-a-k, *see* KIMḤI, DAVID
RADANIYA (Radanites; J. mers.) **13:**1495
- fur trade **7:**223
- routes to the East **16:**1281
- trade and commerce **15:**1297
- travels **15:**1348
RADAUTI (Radautz; city, Rum.) **13:**1495
R-a-d-b-a-z, *see* DAVID BEN SOLOMON IBN ABI ZIMRA
Radday, Y. T. **9:**45
RADEK, KARL **13:**1496
RADEMACHER, FRANZ **13:**1497
- Argentinian sanctuary **12:**956
- Belgrade **16:**875
Radhanites (J. mer.), *see* RADANIYA
Radical Zionist Alliance (U.S.) **16:**1147
Radimin (tn., Pol.), *see* RADZYMIN
Radin (tn., Pol.), *see* RADZYN
Radin (vill., Belor.), *see* RADUN
RADIN, ADOLPH MOSES **13:**1497
Radin, Asher **7:**421
Radin, Herman **13:**1498
RADIN, MAX **13:**1498
RADIN, PAUL **13:**1498
- anthropology **3:**38
Radio (journ.) **1:**newsp. list
Radio and television, *see* TELEVISION AND RADIO
Radiocarbon dating **16:**1262
Radiology **11:**1201
Radio ve-Elektronikah (journ.) **1:**newsp. list
Radio Yerushalayim (journ.) **1:**newsp. list
RADISH (bot.) **13:**1499
- plant list **13:**623
Radkinson (schol.) **11:**190
Radler-Feldmann, Yehoshua, *see* RABBI BINYAMIN
Radnice (J. tn. hall, Prague) **13:**969
- *illus:*
-- clock tower **13:**969
-- general view **13:**966
RADNÓTI, MIKLÓS **13:**1499
RADÓ, ANTAL **10:**315
Rado, Charles **13:**484
RADO, SANDOR **13:**1500
RADOM (city, Pol.) **13:**1500
- Perlmutter, Abraham Ẓevi **13:**297
- Poland **13:**766; **13:**767
- *illus:* text
Radomer Lebn (period.) **13:**1500
Radomer Shtime (period.) **13:**1500
Radomsk, Solomon Ha-Kohen Rabinowich of, *see* RADOMSKO, SOLOMON HA-KOHEN RABINOWICH OF
RADOMSKO (tn., Pol.) **13:**1502
- concentration camp **5:**1213
Radomsko, Abraham Issachar Ha-Kohen of **13:**1504
Radomsko, Ezekiel Ha-Kohen of **13:**1504
Radomsko, Solomon Enoch Ha-Kohen of **13:**1504
RADOMSKO, SOLOMON HA-KOHEN RABINOWICH OF **13:**1503
RADOMYSHL (city, Ukr.) **13:**1504
Radomyslski, Grigory Yevseyevich, *see* ZINOVIEV, GRIGORI YEVSEYEVICH
Radoner, Baruch, *see* Buchbinder, Baruch
RADOSHITSER, ISSACHAR BAER **13:**1504
RADOSHKOVICHI (Radoszkowice; tn., Belor.) **13:**1504
Radoszyce, Issachar Baer of, *see* RADOSHITSER, ISSACHAR BAER
Radovsky, David H. **6:**1161
Radovsky, H. William **6:**1161
Radowitzky, Simon **3:**414
Radu, Vasile **4:**882
Rădulescu, Ion Eliade **4:**882; **14:**417
Radulph (monk) **5:**1139
RADUN (vill., Belor.) **13:**1505
- *illus:*
-- yeshivah, Ḥafeẓ Ḥayyim's appeal for aid **9:**1069
Radvanyi, Netty, *see* SEGHERS, ANNA
Raḍwān (angel) **6:**885
Raḍwān, Suhayl **9:**1039
RADYMNO (tn., Pol.) **13:**1506
- *illus:* text
Radziechow (city, Rus.) **10:**728; **15:**84
RADZINOWICZ, SIR LEON **13:**1506
Radziwill (prin.) **11:**1194; **14:**1253
Radziwill Bible, *see* Brześć Bible
RADZIWILLOW (tn., Ukr.) **13:**1507
Radziwillow, Joseph of **14:**922
RADZYMIN (tn., Pol.) **13:**1508
RADZYMIN (ḥas., dyn.) **13:**1508
RADZYN (Radzýn-Podlaski; tn., Pol.) **13:**1508
Radzyn, Gershon Enoch of, *see* Gershon Enoch of Radzyn
Raedt, Al(h)art de **8:**53
R-a-f, *see* PEREZ BEN ELIJAH OF CORBEIL
Rafa (fam.) **13:**912
RAFA (Rafaḥ; tn., Er. Isr.) **13:**1509
- battle of **8:**626
- Crusader refugees **9:**272
- Dionysus **6:**62
- eleventh century **9:**264
- frontier line **9:**311ff
- Ḥaẓerim **7:**1531
- Ptolemy IV **13:**1348
- Sinai Campaign **9:**390; **14:**1606
- Six-Day War **14:**1629
Rafa, Jonah ha-Kohen **13:**130
Rafael, Al **15:**1072
Rafalkes, Nahum, *see* NIR, NAHUM
Rafalsky, M. **15:**1075
Rafa-Rapaport, Abraham Menahem ben Jacob ha-Kohen, *see* PORTO, ABRAHAM MENACHEM BEN JACOB HA-KOHEN
Rafeh (gram. sign) **16:**1422,1451
RAFES, MOSES **13:**1510
Raffaeli, S. (numis.), *see* Refaeli, Samuel
RAFFALOVICH, ARTHUR GERMANOVICH **13:**1511
RAFFALOVICH, ISAIAH **13:**1511
- Brazil **4:**1329
Raffelstetten (tn., Aus.) **14:**1661
RAFI (polit. party) **13:**1512
- Aḥdut ha-Avodah **2:**457
- Ben-Gurion, David **4:**512
- Dayan, Moshe **5:**1374
- Histadrut elections **9:**861ff
- historical survey **9:**398ff
- Israel Labor Party **9:**1068
- *illus:*
-- labor parties merging meeting **9:**677
Rafiaḥ (tn., Er. Isr.), *see* RAFA
Rafīd, A- (vill., Er. Isr.) **9:**597
Rafoul, *see* Harari, Nissim ben Isaiah
Rafram (2 *amoraim*, Pumb.) **2:**870; **14:**46
Ragendorf (tn., Hung.), *see* Rajka
Rāghib Bey al-Nashāshībī **9:**459
Ragia (coin) **5:**721
RAGOLER, ABRAHAM BEN SOLOMON **13:**1512
RAGOLER, ELIJAH BEN JACOB **13:**1512
Rag trade, *see* SECONDHAND GOODS AND OLD CLOTHES, TRADE IN
Raguel (angel) **2:**962; **15:**1184
Ragusa (port, Yug.), *see* DUBROVNIK
RAHAB (bib. fig.) **13:**1513
- Arts **10:**268
- Jeremiah **9:**1359
- Joshua **10:**267
Rahab (myth. fig.) **2:**966; **5:**1530; **11:**89; **12:**730
Rahabi, David **5:**626; **6:**111
Rahabi, Elias **5:**626
RAHABI, EZEKIEL **13:**1515
- Cochin **5:**624ff
RAHABI, NAPHTALI ELIAHU **13:**1515
- Cochin **5:**627
Raḥamim (conc.), *see* MERCY
Raḥamim (kab. conc.), *see* *Tiferet*
Raḥamim (newsp.) **10:**437; **15:**828
Raḥamim, Joseph Franco **11:**875
Raḥamim ben Reuben **4:**93
Raḥamim ha-Kohen **2:**188
Rahamūn, Salāma ibn **11:**1188
Rahav (Isr. submarine) **9:**696
RAḤBAH, AL- (Raḥbat Mālik ibn Tauq; tn., Babyl.) **13:**1515
- Iraq **8:**1447
RAḤEL (poet) **13:**1516
- Hebrew literature **8:**198
- prosody **13:**1232,1234
- *illus:* text
Raḥiyanu (k., Aram.), *see* REZIN
Rahm, Karl **15:**1115
Rahman, A. **13:**34
Raḥmani, L. Y. **9:**1535
RAHV, PHILIP **15:**1578; **15:**1583
- New York City **12:**1120
Rahway (city, N.J.) **15:**1533
Rai (tn., Iran) **13:**303
Raicu, Lucian **14:**423
Raikh, Zinaida **15:**1058
RAILROADS **13:**1517
- Israel **9:**831
- Todesco, Hermann **15:**1188
- *illus:*
-- Palestine, first locomotive **9:**835
- *maps:*
-- Israel network **9:**833
Raimundus Lullus, *see* RAMÓN LULL
RAIN **13:**1520
- agriculture **2:**388
- *'elgavish* stones **13:**1011
- Flood, the **6:**1351
- *mikveh* **11:**1538ff
- *see also:* THUNDER AND LIGHTNING
RAIN, PRAYER FOR **13:**1523
- Holy Ark **3:**457
- Ḥoni ha-Me'agel **8:**964
- Hoshana Rabba **8:**1028
- illustrations **4:**1234
- *Mashiv Ha-Ru'aḥ* **11:**1094
- rainfall (Israel) **9:**181ff; **9:**1514; **9:**1540
- Yemenite Jews **16:**757
- *illus:*
-- text
-- *Shevet Yehudah*, *piyyut* (mus. notation) **16:**749
RAINBOW **13:**1524
- Flood, the **6:**1352
- sign of the covenant **14:**1525
- *illus:* text
RAINER, LUISE **12:**473
- theater **15:**1056
Rainey, A. P. **16:**1509
Rainfall in Israel **9:**181ff; **9:**1514; **9:**1540
- *maps:*
-- annual means, 1921-60 **9:**186
Rainis, J. **10:**215
Rainolds, John **8:**53
Ra'īs al-Yahūd (tit.), *see* NAGID
Raisin (food) **6:**1416
Raisin, A. **16:**814; **16:**821
RAISIN, JACOB ZALMAN **13:**1525
RAISIN, MAX **13:**1525
RAISMAN, SIR ABRAHAM JEREMY **13:**1526
Rais of Syracuse **6:**24
RAISZ, ERWIN J. **13:**1526
Raizman, Juli **12:**456
Raj, T. **15:**659
Rajakowitsch, Erich Raja **12:**956; **16:**300
Rājib River (Er. Isr.) **9:**178
Rajk, László **16:**1122
Rajka (tn., Hung.) **10:**825
Rajk Trial (Hung.) **14:**1654
RAJPURKAR, JOSEPH EZEKIEL **13:**1526
Rajwān, Reuben Michael **8:**1461
Rajzman, Shmuel **15:**1370
Rakaḥ (party, Isr.) **9:**398; **9:**413
- communist list **5:**807
- general survey **9:**1030
- politics in Israel **9:**677
Rakaḥ, Masud Hai ben Aaron, *see* RACCAH, MAS'UD BEN AARON
Rakhmaelovich, Afrash, *see* Ephraim ben Jerahmeel

Rakishik (city, Lith.), *see* ROKISKIS
Rakita, Mark **12:**1377
Rakkath (city, Er. Isr.) **7:**1242; **10:**1035; **15:**1131
RÁKOSI, MÁTYÁS **13:**1527
- stamps **15:**336
RAKOUS, VOJTĚCH **13:**1527
Rakov (tn., Belor.) **10:**718
Rakov, Joseph **9:**1153
Rakovski, Khristian **16:**371
Rakovsky, Pua **6:**425
Rakowski, A. A. **5:**432
Rakowski, Gutman **5:**1032
R-a-l-b-a-g, *see* LEVI BEN GERSHOM
R-a-l-b-a-ḥ, *see* LEVI BEN ḤABIB
Raleigh (city, N.C.) **12:**1220
RALL, YISRAEL **13:**1528
Ralph, Nathan **5:**115
Ram (bib. fig.) **14:**1549
Ram (leg. fam.) **10:**734
Ram, *see* SHEEP
Ram, Al- (vill., Er. Isr.) **13:**1529; **13:**1543
RAM, MOSHE **8:**1433
RĀMA, AL- (vill., Isr.) **13:**1528
Ramadan (Musl. fast) **9:**93; **10:**1198
- *illus:*
- - prayers in Al-Aqṣā courtyard **9:**920
Ramādī (tn., Iraq) **8:**1450
RAMAH (locs., Er. Isr.) **13:**1528
Ramah (journ.) **1:**newsp. list
R-a-m-a-k, *see* CORDOVERO, MOSES BEN JACOB
RAMALLAH (tn., Er. Isr.) **13:**1529
- human geography **9:**587ff
- PBS broadcasting **15:**930
- Six-Day War **14:**1635
- television and radio **15:**930
Ramapo (dist., N.Y.) **14:**214
Rāmat al-Khalīl (site, Isr.)
- Butnah **4:**1539
- Mamre **11:**839
Ramat Aviv (sub., Tel Aviv) **15:**917
Ramatayim (vill., Isr.), *see* HOD HA-SHARON
Ramat Banias (kib., Isr.), *see* Senir
RAMAT DAVID (kib., Isr.) **13:**1529
- statistics **1:**place list
Ramat Efal (stlmt., Isr.) **1:**place list
- statistics **1:**place list
RAMAT GAN (city, Isr.) **13:**1530
- Tel Aviv **15:**924
- *illus:*
- - text
- - Bar-Ilan University **4:**225; **9:**955,963,971,1003
Ramat Gan Chamber Orchestra (Isr.) **9:**1008
Ramat Hadar (vill., Isr.), *see* HOD HA-SHARON
Ramat Hadassah (educ. center, Isr.) **16:**864
RAMAT HA-GOLAN (reg., Er. Isr.) **13:**1531
- Arab population **9:**1037ff
- Druzes **9:**924
- frontier, Palestine, Israel **9:**312ff
- human geography **9:**595ff
- physiography **9:**171; **9:**179
- political status **15:**647
- Qaysites **9:**261
- Six-Day War **14:**1637
- Syrian forces **15:**647
- *illus:*
- - text
- - Al-Quanayṭira **13:**1435
- - Birkat-Rām **9:**169
- - columnar basalt Hameshushim pool **9:**213
- - Druze population (map) **9:**925
- - Givat Yo'av **9:**578
- - Israel tanks, Six-Day War **9:**409
- - Nahal Snir **9:**554
- - Six-Day War fighting **14:**1633
Ramathaim-Zophim (bib. loc.) **13:**1529
- Elkanah **6:**676
- Ramleh **13:**1540; **14:**785
- *see also:* RAMAH
RAMAT HA-KOVESH (kib., Isr.) **13:**1534
- resistance to British **9:**356
- statistics **1:**place list
Ramat ha-Nadiv (loc., Isr.) **14:**345
RAMAT HA-SHARON (tn., Isr.)
- statistics **1:**place list
- Tel Aviv **15:**924
RAMAT HA-SHOFET (kib., Isr.) **13:**1535
- statistics **1:**place list
Ramath-Hazor (bib. loc., Er. Isr.), *see* BAAL-HAZOR
Ramath-Mizpeh (loc., Er. Isr.) **12:**174
Ramath-Negeb (city, Er. Isr.) **16:**667
Ramat Magshimim (stlmt., Golan) **1:**place list; **13:**1534
Ramat Pinkas (stlmt., Isr.) **1:**place list
RAMAT RAḤEL (site, kib., Isr.) **13:**1535
- archaeology **3:**306ff
- Beth-Cherem **4:**718
- development **9:**1473
- fortifications **16:**276
- Jordanian clash **9:**1497
- Netophah **12:**1001
- stamp seals **16:**668
- statistics **1:**place list
- topography **9:**1515
- *illus:*
- - antiquities **3:**317,320,338
- - jar handle seal **14:**1075
RAMAT RAZIEL (mosh., Isr.) **13:**1538
- statistics **1:**place list
Ramat Shalom (recreation center, Isr.) **8:**375
Ramat Tiomkin (stlmt., Isr.) **15:**1149
RAMAT YISHAI (stlmt., Isr.) **13:**1538
- statistics **1:**place list
RAMAT YOḤANAN (kib., Isr.) **13:**1538
- kibbutz festivals **10:**963
- statistics **1:** place list
- *illus:*
- - *omer* festival **10:**961
RAMAT ẒEVI (mosh., Isr.) **13:**1539
Rambach, Miriam, *see* RAMBERT, DAME MARIE
R-a-m-b-a-m, *see* MAIMONIDES
Rambam Library (Isr.) **11:**195
R-a-m-b-a-m of Fez, *see* Abendanan, Moses ben Maimon
R-a-m-b-a-n, *see* NAḤMANIDES
Ramban synagogue (Jer.) **9:**1437
- *illus:*
- - interior **9:**1443
R-a-m-b-e-m-a-n, *see* MENDELSSOHN, MOSES
RAMBERT, DAME MARIE **13:**1539
Ramenofsky, Marilyn **12:**1377
RAMERUPT (vill., Fr.) **13:**1539
Rames (tn., Isr.), *see* RAMLEH
Rameses (ks., Egy.), *see* RAMSES
Rameses (anc. city, Egy.), *see* RAMSES
R-a-m-ḥ-a-l, *see* LUZZATTO, MOSES ḤAYYIM
Rami bar Ezekiel (amora) **10:**342
Rami bar Ḥama (amora) **8:**531; **9:**12
Ramires, Lopo **15:**1303
Ramirez, Alfonso Francisco **10:**1455
Ramirez, Baltazar Laureano **11:**1460
Ramirez, Laureano **11:**1460
Rāmiyā (loc., Leb.) **13:**1529
RAMLEH (Ramla; city, Isr.) **13:**1540
- Arab period **9:**262ff
- capitulations **5:**148
- Crusades **5:**1139; **9:**267ff
- Malik al-Ramlī **11:**826
- Mamluk period **9:**277
- Ottoman period **9:**283ff
- Samuel's tomb **14:**785
- statistics **1:**place list
- *illus:*
- - text
- - Mamluk tower **3:**330
- - old city **9:**275
- - surrender of (July 12, 1948) **16:**319
Ramler, Karl Wilhelm **10:**1286
Ramlites (sect, Er. Isr.) **11:**826
Ram On (mosh., Isr.) **1:**place list
Ramon (reg., Er. Isr.) **9:**135
- crater **9:**592
- geology **9:**200ff
- mountain **9:**580
- Negev **12:**927
- *illus:*
- - Makhtesh Ramon **9:**133,209
Ramón Berenguer IV (ruler, Sp.) **15:**229
RAMÓN LULL **13:**1542
Ramot (mosh., Golan) **13:**1534
- statistics **1:**place list
Ra'mot (gem) **13:**1011
Ramot Eshkol (qtr., Jer.) **9:**1502; **9:**1507
- *illus:*
- - Jews and Arabs working on housing project **9:**1510
RAMOTH (city, Er. Isr.) **13:**1542
- city of refuge **5:**591
- *see also:* JARMUTH
RAMOT HA-SHAVIM (mosh., Isr.) **13:**1543
- statistics **1:**place list
RAMOTH-GILEAD (city, Er. Isr.) **13:**1543
- Mizpeh **12:**174
- Solomon **15:**1317
- Zedekiah **16:**964
Ramot Me'ir (mosh., Isr.) **1:**place list
RAMOT MENASHEH (kib., Isr.) **13:**1543
- statistics **1:**place list
RAMOT NAFTALI (mosh., Isr.) **13:**1544
- statistics **1:**place list
RAMSES I (k., Egy.) **13:**1545
RAMSES II (k., Egy.) **13:**1545
- Bible history **8:**575; **8:**577
- Canaan **9:**114
- Dor **6:**172
- Egypt **6:**482
- history chart **8:**766-767
- seals **14:**1073
- Transjordan **15:**1316
- *illus:*
- - Ashkelon, conquest of **3:**715
RAMSES III (k., Egy.) **13:**1545
- Edomites **6:**372
- *illus:*
- - sea battle with Philistines **8:**587
- - statue (Beth-Shean) **4:**760
RAMSES (anc. city, Egy.) **13:**1544
- Bible history **8:**575
- *illus:*
- - text
- - *Prague Haggadah* **13:**567
Ramsgate (tn., Eng.) **6:**450; **12:**270; **12:**271
Ramshak chronicle (forged ms.) **6:**1318; **11:**216
Ram's Head Books (publ. firm, U.S.) **13:**1377
Ram's horn, *see* SHOFAR
Ramukh (fam.), *see* BENREMOKH
Ramzor (period.) **1:**newsp. list
R-a-n, *see* NISSIM BEN REUBEN GERONDI
Ran and Nama (sings.), *see* HENDEL, NEHAMA
Rand, I.C. **13:**34
Rand, Nathan **15:**349
Randers, Gunnar **12:**1225
Randfontein (tn., Transvaal) **15:**1340
Random House Publishing Company **5:**312
Rangoon (city, Burma) **4:**1526
Rank, Beata **13:**1339
RANK, OTTO **13:**1545
Rannen (mosh., Isr.) **1:**place list
RANSCHBURG, BEZALEL BEN JOEL **13:**1546
Ranschburg, Gusztáv **13:**1369
Ranschburg, Joel **13:**665
Ranschburg, S. **7:**999
Ranschburg, Viktor **13:**1369
Ranschoff (fam.) **14:**834
RANSOM **13:**1546
- compounding offenses **5:**856
- damages **5:**856
- *ḥerem* **8:**345
- of wife **8:**1124
- *see also:* REDEMPTION
Ransom, Marius **2:**524
Ransom, Samuel **8:**53
Ransoming of captives, *see* CAPTIVES, RANSOMING OF
Rantis (loc., Er. Isr.), *see* Arimathea
Ranunculus (bot.) **6:**1365
Raoul (12th cent., monk) **8:**668ff
RAOUL GLABER **13:**1546
Rapa (fam.), *see* RAPOPORT
Rapacki, Adam **13:**787
Rapallo, Treaty of **11:**406
Rapaport (fam. name), *see also* Porto; Porto-Rafa; Rapoport; Rappaport; Rappoport
RAPAPORT, DAVID (psych.) **13:**1547
RAPAPORT, DAVID HA-KOHEN (r., Jer.) **13:**1547
- family **13:**1552
Rapaport, I. **11:**1284
Rapaport, Jacob **13:**1547
RAPAPORT, NATHAN **3:**608
- *illus:*
- - Anielewicz, Mordecai (memorial) **3:**3
- - Krinitzi, Avraham (bust) **10:**1261
- - sculpture at Weizmann Institute **16:**440
- - Warsaw Ghetto uprising memorial **16:**351
Rapaport, Samuel I. **15:**191
Rapaport, S. B. **5:**742
Rapaport, Simon **13:**1553
Rape (bot.) **16:**83
- plant list **13:**623
RAPE **13:**1548
- degrees of duress **12:**1400
- law of adultery **2:**314
- manslaughter **6:**1071
- punishment for **13:**224; **13:**227
- sexual offenses **14:**1207; **14:**1208
- virgin **16:**160
- *illus:*
- - Amnon and Tamar **2:**860
- - concubine of Gibeah **5:**863
RAPHAEL (angel) **13:**1549
- archangel **2:**962
- *Tobit, Book of* **15:**1184
- Uriel **16:**7
- *illus:*
- - Tobit and **15:**1184
Raphael (art.) **9:**69; **15:**1185
RAPHAEL, ALEXANDER

13:1550
Raphael, Benjamin I. 4:1219
RAPHAEL, CHAIM 6:785; 6:790
Raphael, David 4:205
Raphael, David Daiches 7:603
RAPHAEL, FREDERIC 13:1550
Raphael, John E. (sport.) 15:307; 15:313
Raphael, John N. (au.) 6:790
- journalism 10:98
Raphael, Michael 8:1438
RAPHAEL, RALPH ALEXANDER 13:1550
RAPHAEL, WILLIAM 3:608
RAPHAEL, YIẒḤAK 13:1550
Raphael, Yom Tov Lipman ben Israel, *see* HEILPERN, YOM TOV LIPMAN BEN ISRAEL
Raphael ben David of Makow 5:1363
Raphael ben Isaac de-Faenza 13:593
Raphael ha-Levi of Hanover 3:806
Raphael Jacob ben Abraham Manasseh 14:92
Raphael Joseph 6:498
- Abulafia, Ḥayyim ben Jacob 2:187
- Elisha Ḥayyim ben Jacob 6:670
- mintmasters 12:65
- Ottoman Empire 16:1535
- Shabbetai Ẓevi 14:1223ff
- Vital, Samuel 16:176
Raphael Kohen, *see* KOHEN, RAPHAEL BEN JEKUTHIEL SUESSKIND
RAPHAEL OF BERSHAD 13:1551
Raphaels, *see* KELLNER, LEON
Raphaelson, Samson 12:451
Raphaely, Siegfried 15:193
RAPHALL, MORRIS JACOB 13:1551
- Birmingham 4:1038
- David Aaron de Sola 15:91
Raphana (city, Er. Isr.) 4:292
- Decapolis 5:1449
Raphelengius, Franciscus 8:53
Raphia (tn., Er. Isr.), *see* RAFA
Rapid City (city, S.D.) 15:213
Rapke, Trevor 3:886
RAPKINE, LOUIS 13:1552
Rapoport (fam. name), *see also* Porto; Porto-Rafa; Rapaport; Rappaport; Rappoport
RAPOPORT (fam.) 13:1552
- *illus:* text
Rapoport, Abraham 13:1554
RAPOPORT, ABRAHAM BEN ISRAEL JEHIEL HA-KOHEN 13:1553
Rapoport, Alexander 13:1553
Rapoport, Arnold 5:1035; 13:1553
Rapoport, Benjamin ben Simḥah ha-Kohen 13:1552
RAPOPORT, BENJAMIN ZE'EV WOLF HA-KOHEN BEN ISAAC 13:1554
- family 13:1553
Rapoport, Ḥayyim ben Simḥah ha-Kohen 13:1552
- Birkenthal, Dov Baer 4:1037
- blood libel 6:97
- Frank, Jacob 7:63
- Israel Ba'al Shem Tov 9:1055
- Lvov 11:610
Rapoport, Isaac 13:1554
Rapoport, Moritz 12:405; 16:1328
Rapoport, Moshe 9:1590
Rapoport, Naḥman 7:925
RAPOPORT, SAMUEL 13:1555
- Port Elizabeth 13:909
Rapoport, Solomon ben Naḥman ha-Kohen 13:1552
RAPOPORT, SOLOMON JUDAH LEIB 13:1555
- Adler, Hermann 2:278
- biographical sketch 4:1013
- family 13:1553
- Hebrew literature 8:184
- history chart 8:766-767
- Levinsohn 11:116
- Mehlsack 11:1236
- Ornstein, Jacob 12:1473
- Wessely, W. 16:464
- Wissenschaft des Judentums 16:573
- illus: text
Rapoport, Solomon Zainwil, *see* AN-SKI, S.
Rappaport (fam. name), *see also* Porto; Porto-Rafa; Rapaport; Rapoport; Rappoport
Rappaport (r., Cracow) 5:1038
RAPPAPORT, ARMIN H. 8:549
Rappaport, Ben-Zion 16:500
RAPPAPORT, HENRY 11:1209
RAPPAPORT, ISAAC BEN JUDAH HA-KOHEN 13:1556
- Azulai, Ḥayyim 3:1019
- Bikayam, Meir 4:991
- family 13:1552
- Hezekiah da Silva 8:458
- Raccah, Mas'ūd 13:1482
- Turkey 13:1548
Rappaport, Reuben Kohen 4:16
Rappeduni ba-Tappuḥim (wk.) 6:615
Rappoch, A. L. 12:952
Rappoltsweiler (tn., Fr.), *see* RIBEAUVILLÉ
Rappoport (fam. name), *see also* Porto; Porto-Rafa; Rapaport; Rapoport; Rappaport
RAPPOPORT, CHARLES 13:1557
- family 13:1553
Rappoport, Mordecai ha-Kohen 12:1243
Rappoport, Nicolai 16:1165
Rāqilī, Abū Zakariyyā Yaḥyā al-, *see* Abū Zakariyyā Yaḥyā al-Rāqilī
RAQQA (Al-; city, Syr.) 13:1557
- Iraq 8:1447
Raruwski, Abraham 12:1238
Rās Abu Ḥumayd (Ḥamīd; loc., Isr.) 7:335
R-a-s-a-g, *see* SAADIAH GAON
Rasā'il al-Rifāq (wk.) 16:1357
Ra's al-'Amūd (loc., Isr.)
- mountain peak 12:482; 12:483
- village 9:1491
Ra's al-'Ayn (loc., Isr.), *see* ROSH HA-AYIN
Ra's al-'Ayn (loc., Iraq) 8:1447
Ra's al-Fashkha (loc. Er. Isr.) 10:988
Ra's al-Mushārif (mt., Er. Isr.), *see* ẒOFIM
Ra's al-Naqab (loc., Sinai) 14:607
Ra's al-Nibā' (peak, Jor.) 12:910
Ra's al-Shaqqa (frontier) 8:972
Ra'ṣ al-Shayyāḥ (monastery) 4:733
Ra'ṣ al-Siyāgha (mt. Transj.) 12:910; 13:564
Ra's al-Ṭāhūna (mt., Isr.) 16:986
Ra's al-Tamīm (loc., Isr.) 4:102
Ra's al-Zemara (mt., Isr.) 16:986
Rasaritul (period.) 9:1295
Râscani (tn., Mold.), *see* RYSHKANY
Rasch, Otto 8:869
Raschkow, Suesskind 4:1355
- children's literature 5:431
- Joseph 10:214
- Samson 14:774
Ra's el-Mesharref (loc., Er. Isr.), *see* ẒOFIM
RASEINIAI (city, Lith.) 13:1558
R-a-sh-a-l, *see* LURIA, SOLOMON BEN JEHIEL
R-a-sh-b-a, *see* ADRET, SOLOMON BEN ABRAHAM
Rashba Bible 8:1264
R-a-sh-b-a-d, *see* SAMUEL BEN DAVID
R-a-sh-b-a-m, *see* SAMUEL BEN MEIR
R-a-sh-b-a-sh (15th cent.), *see* DURAN, SOLOMON BEN SIMEON
R-a-sh-b-a-sh (15/16 cent.), *see* DURAN, SIMEON BEN SOLOMON
R-a-sh-b-a-ẓ, *see* DURAN, SIMEON BEN ẒEMAḤ
Rashei ha-perek (court heads, Isr.) 9:258
Rashei tevot, *see* ABBREVIATIONS
Rashgolski, Hillel, *see* BAVLI, HILLEL
RASHI (Solomon ben Isaac) 13:1558
- *Contents:*
- - His Life 13:1558
- - Biblical Exegesis 13:1559
- - Main Characteristics of His Commentary 13:1560
- - As Grammarian 13:1562
- - Other Characteristic Aspects of Rashi's Commentary 13:1563
- - Commentary to the Babylonian Talmud 13:1564
- - As a Halakhist 13:1564
- General
- - Ashkenaz term 3:720
- - folktales 6:1382
- - Gruenwald's study 7:948
- - history chart 8:766-767
- - Jerusalem Talmud 15:776
- - Naḥmanides 12:777
- - Shum 14:1480
- - Troyes 15:1406ff
- - Worms 16:644
- - yeshivah proceedings 2:203
- Genealogy and Circle
- - genealogy 7:382
- - Isaac ben Eliezer 9:18
- - Isaac ben Meir 9:23
- - Isaac ben Menahem 9:24
- - Jacob ben Samson 9:1223
- - Jacob ben Yakar 9:1224
- - Samuel ben Meir 14:809
- - Shemaiah of Troyes 14:1374
- - Tam, Jacob ben Meir 15:779
- - *Tosafot* 15:1278ff
- Works
- - Bible exegesis 4:893; 11:324; 13:331
- - Christian Hebraists and 8:11
- - Hebrew language 16:1635
- - *ḥiddushim* 8:465ff
- - Inquisition and 15:769
- - Judeo-French *la'azim* 10:1313; 10:424
- - *kunteres* 10:1293
- - Mashait script 2:741
- - on Talmud 11:329
- - printing 15:1480
- - responsa 14:86
- Views
- - abortion 2:100
- - art 3:522
- - Christological interpretations 3:195
- - Dunash-Menahem argument 6:270
- - exile 7:284ff
- - *tefillin* 15:900ff
- - trees 4:1029
- - usury 16:31
- - *yahrzeit* 16:702
- Supercommentaries on 15:520
- - *Be'er Mayim Ḥayyim* 7:1508
- - *Be'er Reḥovot* 3:847
- - Casès, Benjamin 5:227
- - *Divrei David* 5:1355
- - Dosa the Greek 4:1482
- - *Ḥeshek Shlomo* 10:798
- - *Ḥizzekuni* 8:459
- - *Ho'il Moshe* 11:1121
- - Leon, Isaac de 11:27
- - *Maskil le-Eitan* 12:717
- - *Meginnei Shelomo* 15:1196
- - Mizraḥi, Elijah 12:183
- *Perushim le-Rashi* 2:197
- - *Sefer ha-Zikkaron* 11:166
- - *Shem Efrayim* 11:964
- - *To'afot Re'em* 4:592
- - *Yosef Da'at* 10:231
- Critical Editions and Translations
- - Berliner, Abraham 4:664
- - Orlinsky, Harry 12:1471
- - Rosenbaum, Morris 14:273
- *geneal. table:* text
- *illus:*
- - *Kiddushin* commentary 15:757
- - Pentateuch, first edition with (1482) 4:1190
- - Pentateuch commentary 15:1483
- - Pentateuch commentary colophon 14:38
- - portrait 14:1476
- - Song of Songs (15th cent.) 4:891
- - Worms chapel 16:644
Rashi Community Center (Fr.) 15:1408
Rashid (tn., Egy.), *see* ROSETTA
Rashid, al-(sharif, Mor.) 2:516
Rashīd, Harun Hāshim 9:1041
RASHĪD AL-DAWLA (al-Dīn) 13:1566
Rashīd al-Dīn al-Ḥakīm, Khawāja 4:138
Rashid Effendi, *see* VAMBERY ARMINIUS
Rashid Moulai 6:572
Rashish, Pinḥas 4:629; 10:674
Rashkes, M. 15:1541; 16:1179
Rashkov (tn., Mold.), *see* VAD RASHKOV
Raskas, Bernard S. 12:38
Ras Kasrun (loc., Egy.) 4:13
Raskin, Ben Zion 16:338
Raskin, Max 11:1589
RASKIN, SAUL 13:1566
- *illus:*
- - *Eḥad Mi Yode'a* 6:504
- - *Shir ha-Ma'alot* 6:1037
- - Song of Songs 15:149
- - "Wedding in Shtetl" 14:1467
Raskowitz, Moses 4:1361
Ra's Maqābir (vill., Er. Isr.) 9:1487,1494
RASMINKSY, LOUIS 13:1566
- Canada 5:112
Ra's Nusrānī (loc., Sinai) 14:1605; 14:1607
Raspberry (bot.) 13:623
Rassam, H. 16:1507
Rassco (housing co., Isr.) 6:1373; 9:564
Rassco Quarter (Jer.) 9:1496
RASSEGNA MENSILE DI ISRAEL, LA (period.) 13:1567
- Italy 9:1140
- Padua 13:12
- Tedeschi, Gad 15:897
Rassern, Johann 15:1055
- *illus:*
- - *Ein Schoen Christlich neu Spil von Kinderzucht* 15:1056
Ra's Shamra (loc., Ugarit) 15:1501; 16:665
Ras Siyāgha (mt., Transj.), *see* Ras al-Siyāgha
Ras Sudar (loc., Sinai) 14:1607,1636
Raṣyān (8th cent. B.C.E., k.), *see* REZIN
RAT (rodent) 13:1567
- dietary laws 6:32
Ratbaum, Leah 15:1072
Ratenbildung (period.) 13:1048
Rath, Ernst vom 6:263; 7:954; 10:1263
RATH, MESHULLAM 13:1567
Rathaus (J. tn. hall, Prague), *see* Radnice
RATHAUS, KAROL 13:1568
RATHENAU, EMIL 13:1568
- *illus:* text

RATHENAU, WALTHER **13:**1569
- German politics **8:**737
- history chart **8:**766-767
- stamps **15:**335
- *illus:* text
Ratherius (bp.) **16:**113
Rathke and Schroth (print. house, Danzig) **7:**348
Rathom, Abraham **5:**126
Rationalism
- geonic writings **8:**665ff
- Ibn Da'ud **8:**1161
- intellect **8:**1410ff
- Kabbalah **10:**490
- Karaite Kalam **13:**433
- Maimonides **11:**761
- Moses Mendelssohn **11:**1329; **11:**1332
- *see also:* Reason
Rational soul **15:**173
Ration books (Isr.) **9:**382
- *illus:*
- - food and textile coupons **9:**375
- - water ration card (1920) **9:**1476
Ratisbon (city, Ger.), *see* REGENSBURG
Ratisbon monastery (Jer.) **9:**1459
Ratisbonne, Alphonse (Marie) **13:**1571
Ratisbonne, Théodore (Marie) **13:**1571
RATISBONNE BROTHERS **13:**1570
Ratner (fam.) **5:**612
RATNER, DOV BAER **13:**1572
- Friedlaender, Solomon **7:**183
- Kalvarija **10:**724
- *Seder Olam Rabbah* **14:**1093
RATNER, LEONARD **13:**1572
RATNER, MARC BORISOVICH **13:**1572
RATNER, SIDNEY **8:**549
RATNER, YOḤANAN **13:**1573
- Israel **3:**361
- *illus:*
- - Jewish Agency building, Jerusalem **3:**350
Ratnik (orgn., Bul.) **4:**414; **4:**1484
Ratoff, Gregory **15:**1087
RATOSH, YONATHAN **13:**1573
- Canaanites leader **5:**101
- Hebrew literature **8:**202
RATSHESKY, ABRAHAM CAPTAIN **13:**1574
Ratsionalistishe Gezelshaft (orgn., Arg.) **3:**423
Rattazzi, Urbano **5:**130
Ratti, F. V. **9:**1107
Ratti-Menton (dipl.) **5:**1250
Rattle, Purim **13:**1392
- *illus:*
- - wooden and silver **13:**1393
RATTNER, ABRAHAM **3:**608
- *illus:*
- - "Shekhina-Amalek" (paint.) **3:**637
Rattner, Sarah (Sonia) **6:**75
Ratukot ha-Kesef (wk.) **16:**1360, 1388
Rau, Christian **8:**53
RAU, HEINZ **13:**1575
- synagogues **15:**620
- *illus:*
- - text
- - Hebrew Union College building, Jerusalem **3:**354; **8:**219
Rau, J. J. **8:**53
Rau, Seebald **8:**53
Rau, Seebald Fulco J. **8:**53
Raubach (court J.), *see* MAGNUS, MARCUS
Rauch, Joseph **11:**522
Raudnitz an der Elbe (tn., Cz.), *see* ROUDNICE NAD LABEM
RAUH, FRÉDÉRIC **13:**1575
RAUH, JOSEPH L. **13:**1575
RAUTER, HANNS ALBIN **13:**1576
RAV (amora) **13:**1576
- afterlife **12:**1356
- *agoranomos* **2:**372
- Aibu **2:**473
- *Aleinu le-Shabbe'aḥ* **2:**557
- Babylonian Talmud **11:**319
- calendar **5:**49
- conflict of opinion **5:**891; **5:**891ff
- ecologist **4:**1027
- exilarchic relationship **6:**1025
- history chart **8:**766-767
- history of Babylonia **8:**650
- Jerusalem Talmud **15:**772
- Kahana **10:**676
- magic **11:**707
- New Year liturgy **15:**915
- Rav Assi **3:**767
- Samuel **14:**787
- Shela **14:**1354
- Sura **2:**204; **15:**521
- synagogues **15:**592
Rav (tit.), *see* RABBI, RABBINATE
Rav, school of **10:**1483
RAVA (amora) **13:**1579
- Abbaye **2:**44
- Academy on High **2:**208
- decision in controversies **5:**891
- Dimi of Nehardea **6:**49
- educational ordinances **6:**401ff
- polygamy **12:**259
- righteousness **14:**181
- sages **14:**646
- *ye'ush* **16:**775
Rava (8th cent., r.), *see* ABBA
RAVA, MAURIZIO **13:**1581
Rava, Menahem, of Padua **10:**549
Ravad (tit.), *see* AV BET DIN
Rav Ada, *see* AVILA, ELIEZER BEN SAMUEL BEN MOSES DE
Ravai (gaon) **7:**315
Ravalia (fam.), *see* RAVAYA
Rav Aqchesi (J. tax), *see* *Rab-Aqchesi*
Rav Assi (amora), *see* ASSI, RAV
RAVAYA (Ravaylla; fam.) **13:**1581
Ravaya, Astrug **13:**1581
Ravaya, Joseph **13:**1581
Ravaya, Moses **13:**1581
Rav ben Yohai **12:**857
Ravdin, Isidor **11:**1201
Raveh, Yiẓḥak **6:**521
Ravel, Maurice **12:**153; **14:**376
Ravel, Vincent **6:**687
Ravelingen, François van, *see* Raphelengius, Franciscus
RAVEN (bird) **13:**1581
- reproduction **4:**1018
RAVENNA (city, It.) **13:**1582
Ravenna, Calimano **14:**355
Ravenna, Felix **16:**1122
Ravenna, Joseph ben Michael **15:**1455
RAVENSBRUECK (concen. camp) **13:**1583
RAVENSBURG (tn., Ger.) **13:**1583
Ravetch, Shalom **11:**485
RAVIKOVITCH, DALIA **13:**1584
Ravikovitch, Levi **13:**1584
Ravin (amora), *see* AVIN
RAVINA I (amora) **13:**1584
- Aḥa bar Rav **2:**440
- Ashi **3:**709
- Avira **3:**975
- calendar **5:**49
RAVINA II (bar Huna; amora) **13:**1585
- history chart **8:**766-767
- Talmud redaction **15:**760
RAVINA, MENASHE **12:**670,703
- choir festival **9:**1006
- Society for Jewish Music **15:**58
Ravis, Christian, *see* Rau, Christian
RAVITCH, MELECH **13:**1585
- *illus:*
- - *Literarishe Bleter* board **16:**818
Ravitz, Melvin **5:**1571
RAVITZ, SHELOMO **13:**1586
Ravius, Christian, *see* Rau, Christian
Rav Metivta (wk.) **16:**1195
Ravnitzky, Yehoshua, *see* RAWNITZKI, YEHOSHUA ḤANA
Rav Pe'alim (wk.) **16:**1388
Rav rashi (tit.) **15:**1165
Rav Shisha, *see* Abitbol, Saul Jeshua ben Isaac
Ravya (gaon) **7:**318
Ravyah (wk.) **6:**625
Rav Yenuka (gaon), *see* NATRONAI BAR NEHEMIAH
Rav Ẓa'ir, *see* TCHERNOWITZ, CHAIM
Rawāfa Dam (loc., Sinai) **14:**1606
Rawanduz (tn., Kurd.), *see* RUWANDIZ
RAWICZ (Rawitsch; tn., Pol.) **13:**1586
- archives **3:**387
RAWIDOWICZ, SIMON **13:**1587
Rawlins (city, Wyo.) **16:**680
Rawlinson, Sir Henry Creswicke **-16:**1506
RAWNITZKI, YEHOSHUA ḤANA **13:**1588
- Ben-Zion **4:**575
- Bialik **4:**797ff
- *Sefer ha-Aggadah* **2:**364
- *illus:*
- - Bialik and **4:**802
- - fellow Hebrew writers **8:**193
- - Mendele Mokher Seforim and **11:**1322
Ray (zool.) **6:**36
RAY, MAN **13:**1589
Raya Meheimna (wk.), *see* *Raaya Meheimna*
Raʿyān (8th cent. B.C.E., k.), *see* REZIN
Rayhāna (slave, Arab.) **13:**1436
RAYKIN, ARKADI ISAAKOVICH **15:**1058,1089
Raymond V (prin. of Orange) **12:**1447
Raymond, Henry **15:**210
Raymond, Lew **15:**306
RAYMOND DE PENAFORTE **13:**1589
- Jewish disabilities **15:**231
Raymond Martini, *see* MARTINI, RAYMOND
Raymond of St. Gilles **9:**267; **9:**1415
- Abba Mari of St. Gilles **2:**37
Rayna, Al- (vill., Er. Isr.) **2:**59
RAYNAL, DAVID **13:**1590
Raynaud (duke of Sens) **13:**1547
RAYNER, ISIDOR **13:**1590
- Baltimore **4:**148
Rayner, John D. **6:**44
RAYSS, TSCHARNA **13:**1590
Raz (term) **13:**331
Raz, A. **6:**207
Raza de-Razin (wk.) **16:**1195
Raza de-Yiḥuda (bk.) **14:**1249
Raza di-Meheimanuta (bk.) **14:**1240; **14:**1249
R-a-z-a-h, *see* ZECHARIAH BEN SOLOMON ROFE
RAZA RABBA, SEFER **13:**1591
- *Bahir, Sefer ha-* **4:**100
- Jewish gnosis **10:**506; **10:**509
Razei torah (Kab.) **10:**494
Razhabi (publ.) **16:**1376
Rāzi, Muhammad al-, *see* Rhazes
RAZIEL (angel) **13:**1591
- encounter with man **2:**973
RAZIEL, BOOK OF **13:**1592
- circumcision ceremonial **5:**576
- Mehlsack, Eliakim **11:**1236
- *illus:* text
- *see also:* RAZIM, SEFER HA-
RAZIEL, DAVID **13:**1593
- Jabotinsky **9:**1182
- Stern, Avraham **15:**382
RAZIM, SEFER HA- (bk.) **13:**1594
- magic **11:**712
- Noah, Books of **12:**1198
Razinsky, Boris **12:**1377; **15:**298
RAZOVSKY, CECILIA **13:**1595
RAZSVET (periods., Rus.) **13:**1595
- Dubnow, Simon **6:**256
- Ḥibbat Zion **16:**1039
- Leningrad **11:**16
- Levanda, Lev **11:**66
- Marshak, Samuil **11:**1058
- press **13:**1045
- Revisionism **14:**128
- *illus:* text
Razsvet (weekly, Bul.) **16:**1108
RAZUMNI, EPHRAIM ZALMAN (Solomon) **13:**1598
- Alman, Samuel **2:**659
- *mus. notations:* **12:**627
Rbt (city, Er. Isr.) **13:**1439
Re (deity) **2:**487ff
- Beth-Shemesh **4:**774
Reade, Charles **6:**780
Reader, *see* SHELI'AH ẒIBBUR
READING (fam.) **13:**1598
Reading (city, Pa.) **13:**229
Reading, First Marquess of **13:**1598
- law **10:**1495
- nobility titles **15:**1166
Reading, Marchioness of **13:**1600
Reading, Second Marquess of **13:**1600
Reading D (power station, Tel Aviv) **15:**917
Reading of the law, *see* TORAH, READING OF
Ready-Reference Jewish Encyclopedia **6:**734
Re'aḥ niḥo'aḥ (odor) **14:**601
Reale, Shulamit **10:**658
Real-Encyclopaedie fuer Bibel und Talmud **6:**731
Real estate, *see* PROPERTY
Real(is) Occitanus, Andreas **8:**53
Reason
- Aristotelianism **3:**446; **3:**447
- articles of faith **3:**657ff
- Kaspi, Joseph ibn **10:**810
- logic **11:**459
- Mendelssohn **11:**1330; **11:**1330ff
- miracles **12:**76ff
- modern Jewish thought **13:**452
- philosophy, Jewish **13:**421
- revelation **10:**392; **10:**393
- Saadiah Gaon **14:**549
- Torah **15:**1240ff
- *see also:* BELIEF; LOGOS; Rationalism; REVELATION
REBEKAH (bib. fig.) **13:**1601
- Abimelech **2:**76
- Genesis **7:**389
- Hurrian customs **12:**1288
- in the Arts **9:**7
- Isaac **9:**2ff
- Jacob **9:**1191ff
- matriarch **13:**181
- Nuzi documents **16:**1510
- *illus:*
- - text
- - Esau and Jacob story **6:**855
- - espied by Abimelech **9:**3
- - "Rebekah and Eliezer" (paint., Murillo) **6:**619
- - tomb in Cave of Machpelah **11:**670
- - various episodes **4:**943
Rebellious elder, *see* ZAKEN

MAMRE
REBELLIOUS SON **13:**1603
- Bible exegesis **8:**1423
- Hurrian custom **12:**1290
- punishment purpose **13:**1387; **13:**1388
Rebenstein, A. *see* BERNSTEIN, ARON DAVID
Rebhan, Jacob **13:**1298
Rebhun, Paul **15:**534
Rebi, Josef, *see* Rabchik, Josef
Rebichkovich (fam.), *see* JÓZEFOWICZ
REBREANU (vill., Rum.) **13:**1605
Rebreanu, Liviu **14:**420
REBUKE AND REPROOF **13:**1605
- *nezifah* **8:**351; **8:**354
- sage **14:**649
Reburial, *see* DISINTERMENT
RECANATI (fam.) **13:**1607
- tobacco trade **15:**1178
RECANATI (tn., It.) **13:**1606
Recanati, Abraham **13:**1039
Recanati, Amadeo (Jedidiah) **10:**428; **13:**1607
Recanati, Daniel **13:**1608
Recanati, Emanuele **13:**1607
Recanati, Harry Rafael **13:**1608
Recanati, Jacob Ḥayyim **13:**1607ff
Recanati, Judah Ḥayyim **13:**1607
Recanati, Leon **9:**828; **14:**707
Recanati, Menahem (r.) **13:**1607
Recanati, Menahem (physic.), *see* Recanati, Emanuele
RECANATI, MENAHEM BEN BENJAMIN **13:**1608
- *menorah* symbol **11:**1367
- Rabad of Posquières **2:**140
- *Sefirot* **10:**567
- Zohar **16:**1211
Recanati, Moses **13:**1607
Recanati, Shabbetai Elhanan **13:**1607ff
Recanati, Yehudah Leib **13:**1607
RECCARED (Visigoth, Sp.)
- Spain **15:**220
Recceswinth (Visigoth, Sp.) **15:**221
- *anusim* **3:**170
Rechab (f., Rechabites) **13:**1609
RECHAB AND BAANAH (bib. figs.) **13:**1609
- Ish-Bosheth **9:**80
RECHABITES (bib. sect) **13:**1609
- asceticism **3:**677
- Kenites **10:**906
- nomadism **12:**1208
- wilderness **16:**513
RECHITSA (city, Belor.) **13:**1612
- Shneur Zalman of Lyady **14:**1436
Rechnitz (tn., Aus.) **4:**1511
RECHTER (fam.) **13:**1612
Rechter, Ya'akov **13:**1612
Rechter, Ze'ev **13:**1612
- Israel architecture **3:**361
- Karmi, Dov **10:**799
- *illus:*
- - Binyanei ha-Ummah main auditorium **3:**353
RECIFE (city, Braz.) **13:**1613
- Aboab da Fonseca **2:**95
- America **2:**809
- Dutch period **2:**809
- Inquisition **8:**1391
- New York **12:**1062
- slave tax **14:**1662
- *see also:* BRAZIL
Reckendorf, Hermann (Ḥayyim Ẓvi) **13:**1614
- Koran **10:**1199
RECKENDORF, HERMANN SOLOMON **13:**1614
Reckless, Walter C. **5:**1110
RECKLINGHAUSEN (tn., Ger.) **13:**1614
Recklinghausen, Christian Gerson von **15:**755
Recklinghausen, Gottschalk von **4:**168; **13:**1614
"Reclining Woman" (paint., J. Iser) **9:**77
"Reclining Woman" (paint., Y. Streichman) **3:**641
Reconstruction Foundation (philan. orgn.), *see* American Joint Reconstruction Foundation
RECONSTRUCTIONISM (mvmt.) **13:**1615
- Chosen People **5:**502
- Conservative Judaism **5:**904
- prayer books **13:**991
- publishing **13:**1376
- resurrection **14:**103
- ritual **13:**1461
- Zionism **16:**1145
Reconstructionist, The (period.) **5:**904; **13:**1051; **13:**1616
Reconstructionist Foundation (rel. orgn., U.S.) **13:**1616
Reconstructionist Press (publ. firm, U.S.) **13:**1376
Reconstructionist Rabbinical College (U.S.) **5:**905
Recorder, *see* SCRIBE
RECORDS, PHONOGRAPH **13:**1617
Red Cross, International (I.R.C.)
- Bergen-Belsen **4:**611
- Bernadotte, Folke **4:**669
- Dunant, Jean Henri **6:**270
- Holocaust **8:**877,907
- International Tracing Service **8:**1412
- Magen David Adom **11:**698
- "rescue train" **4:**629
- Theresienstadt ghetto **15:**1116ff
"Red Danny," *see* Cohn-Bendit, Daniel
Redeemer (Mess.), *see* MESSIAH
Redem (tn., Pol.), *see* RADYMNO
REDEMPTION **14:**1
- *Contents:*
- - General **14:**1
- - Dead Sea Sect **14:**3
- - In the Talmud **14:**3
- - Medieval Philosophy **14:**4
- - In the Kabbalah **14:**5
- - Modern Jewish Thought **14:**7
- Personal
- - choice **14:**138
- - man's nature **11:**844
- - repentance **2:**362
- Eschatology
- - Apocalypse **3:**179
- - exile termination **7:**282ff
- - messianic movement **11:**1417
- - paradise **13:**84
- - resurrection **14:**99
- - Zechariah **16:**956
- - *see also:* ESCHATOLOGY; MESSIAH
- Doctrines
- - Adam's sin **10:**608
- - *aggadot* on **15:**153
- - exile **10:**617ff
- - Haskalah **7:**1443ff
- - Kabbalah **10:**541,608,617ff.
- - Karaites **10:**778
- - Samaritans **14:**738
- - Shabbateanism **3:**70
- - Zohar **3:**70; **16:**1208
- Views on
- - Abrabanel, Isaac **2:**105
- - Alkalai, Judah **2:**638
- - Ba'al Shem Tov **9:**1053
- - Elimelech of Lyzhansk **6:**662
- - Friedland, Nathan **7:**184
- - Judah Halevi **10:**359
- - Kalischer, Ẓ. H. **10:**708
- - Luzzatto, M. Ḥ. **11:**600ff
- - Maharal **10:**378
- - Malbim **11:**823
- - Naḥman of Bratslav **12:**786
- - Nathan of Gaza **12:**863
- - Rosenzweig **13:**462; **14:**300; **14:**303
- - Saadiah Gaon **13:**432
- - Safrin, Isaac **14:**635
- - Shapira, Ḥ. E. **14:**1296
Redemption (legal) **8:**345
Redemption of the Firstborn, *see* *Pidyon ha-Ben*
"Redemption of the Firstborn" (eng., B. Picart) **6:**1309
REDER, BERNARD **3:**608
- *illus:*
- - "Wounded Woman" (sculp.) **3:**637
Red Guard (Vienna) **10:**1061
RED HEIFER **14:**9
- ablution **2:**82
- Commandments, the 613 **5:**765
- hyssop **8:**1148
- Ishmael ben Phiabi **9:**87
- *kipper* **10:**1040
- Mount of Olives **12:**483
- *Parah* tractate **13:**87
- purity ritual **13:**1406; **13:**1412; **13:**1413
- Temple **15:**964
- *illus:*
- - burning of **13:**87
- - *Schocken Italian Maḥzor* **14:***fcg.* 11
Red Indians **15:**1006
REDL, FRITZ **14:**13
"Red Letters" (Frankists) **7:**69; **7:**70ff
REDLICH, FREDERICK C. **14:**13
REDLICH, HANS FERDINAND **12:**703
- psychiatry **13:**1340
REDLICH, JOSEPH **14:**13
Redner, Eliasz **15:**1174
Redress **6:**1071ff
Red Russia (E. Gal.) **15:**1514
RED SEA **14:**14
- Baal-Zephon **4:**13
- Bible history **8:**576
- Exodus, Book of **6:**1054ff
- Exodus route **6:**1049ff
- Moses **12:**375
- Portolano maps **11:**920
- Sinai Campaign **14:**1607
- Solomon's trade **15:**98
- stone corals **5:**959
- *illus:*
- - major theories on site of (map) **6:**1043
- - Moses ordering the return of the waters **6:**1045
Red Shield of David, *see* MAGEN DAVID ADOM
Redstart (bird) **6:**30
RÉE, HARTVIG PHILIP **14:**17
REED (bot.) **14:**17
- flora of Israel **9:**225
- plant list **13:**623
Reed (meas.), *see* *Kaneh*
Re'em (zool.), *see* ANTELOPE
Rees (fam.) **12:**37
Reese, James Hymie **15:**301
REESE, MICHAEL **14:**18
REEVE, ADA **15:**1090
Refaeli, Samuel **13:**1511
- numismatics **12:**1271
Refah (fam.), *see* Rafa
Refa'im (suburb, Jer.), *see* German Colony
Refa'im Valley (Er. Isr.) **9:**1515; **15:**1156
REFORMATION **14:**18
- anti-Semitism **3:**107
- Antwerp Marranos **3:**167
- attitude to Jews **5:**512
- Bucer, Martin **4:**1435
- Budny, Szymon **4:**1456
- Calvin, John **5:**66
- Capito, Wolfgang **5:**147
- Christian Hebrew studies **8:**17; **16:**1591
- Judaizers **10:**399
- Luther, Martin **11:**584
- Melanchthon, Philipp **11:**1276
- Muenster, Sebastian **12:**505
- "New Jerusalem" **9:**1573
- position of Jews **8:**692ff
- Tyndale, William **15:**1477
- *see also:* PROTESTANTS
REFORM JUDAISM **14:**23
- *Contents:*
- - Introduction **14:**23
- - Aesthetic Reforms **14:**23
- - Ideological Developments **14:**24
- - - Geiger **14:**25
- - - Holdheim **14:**25
- - - American Reform **14:**26
- - - Recent American Developments **14:**27
- - Organizational Developments **14:**27
- General
- - autonomy **3:**924; **3:**928
- - economic history **16:**1319
- - forgeries **6:**1431
- - homiletical literature **8:**956ff
- - Jewish-Christian understanding **13:**1253; **13:**1254
- - newspapers **12:**1046; **12:**1048
- - Reformation **14:**23
- - synagogues **15:**584
- Theology and Philosophy
- - antinomianism **3:**69
- - Baeck, Leo **4:**77
- - *halakhah*, attitude to **7:**1166
- - Hirsch, Samuel **8:**516
- - Jewish identity **10:**59
- - Kantianism **10:**742
- - Mendelssohn, Moses **3:**659
- - messianism **11:**1415
- - modern Jewish thought **13:**453
- - nationalism **16:**1037
- - Neumark, David **12:**1014
- - Oral Law **12:**1442
- - Protestantism **5:**514
- - resurrection **14:**102
- - reward, punishment **14:**138
- - sacrifices **14:**614
- - theology **15:**1108
- - tradition **15:**1246; **15:**1310
- Relationship to Other Movements **10:**394ff
- - assimilation **3:**773
- - Conservative Judaism **5:**902ff
- - Haskalah **7:**1444
- - Neology **12:**952
- - Neo-Orthodoxy **12:**956
- - Orthodoxy **8:**723ff; **12:**1486ff
- - *see also:* RECONSTRUCTIONISM
- Synagogue Practice
- - choral music **5:**488
- - I. N. Mannheimer's ritual **11:**890
- - liturgy **11:**402
- - *minyan* **12:**67
- - *musaf* prayer **12:**534
- - organ **12:**1454ff
- - prayer books **13:**989ff
- - rabbinical office **13:**1446; **13:**1448
- - *tallit* **15:**744
- *Halakhah*
- - ablution **2:**83
- - Av, The Ninth **3:**939
- - circumcision **5:**570
- - dietary laws **6:**44
- - *ḥukkat ha-goi* **8:**1062
- - *ketubbah* **10:**930
- - *kohen* and divorcee **13:**1090
- - *niddah* laws **12:**1147
- - proselytes **13:**1192; **13:**1192ff
- - responsa literature **14:**95
- - *sukkah* **15:**501
- - Torah reading **15:**1253; **15:**1389
- In Australia **3:**884

- In England 6:758; 10:396
- - Joseph, Morris 10:222
- - Mattuck, Israel 11:1132
- - Montagu, Lilian Helen 12:265
- - Montefiore, Claude 12:268
- - Schiller-Szinessy, Solomon 14:966
- In Galicia
- - Kohn, Abraham 10:1144
- In Germany 7:477
- - Bendavid, Lazarus 4:475
- - Berlin 4:645
- - Bresselau, Meyer Israel 4:1358
- - Brunswick 4:1422
- - Einhorn, David 6:531
- - Frankfort on the Main 7:87ff
- - Frederick William III 7:116
- - Friedlander, David 7:177
- - Geiger, Abraham 7:357
- - Hamburg 7:1227
- - Holdheim, Samuel 8:817
- - Jacobson, Israel 9:1240
- - rabbinical conferences 13:1460ff
- - Riesser, Gabriel 14:168
- - synods 15:634
- - Union for Liberal Judaism 16:110
- - Westphalia 16:474
- - Wissenschaft Hochschule 8:799
- - Zunz, Leopold 16:1236
- In Hungary 8:1092
- - Chorin, Aron 5:496ff
- - Einhorn, Ignaz 6:533
- - Loew, Leopold 11:444
- In Israel 9:906ff
- In the Netherlands 2:900; 2:904
- In South Africa 15:193ff
- In the United States 2:811; 2:813; 15:1599; 15:1604; 15:1621; 15:1642ff
- - American Council for Judaism 2:819; 2:820
- - Central Conference of American Rabbis 5:285
- - Einhorn, David 6:531
- - Hebrew Union College 8:216
- - Kohler, Kaufmann 10:1142
- - Lauterbach, Jacob Zallel 10:1473
- - Morgenstern, Julian 12:317
- - New York City 12:1091ff
- - Pittsburgh Platform 13:570
- - Reformed Society of the Israelites 7:1333
- - Union of American Hebrew Congregations 15:1536
- - U.S. Zionism 16:1144
- - Wise, Isaac Mayer 16:563
- Critics and Opponents
- - Aḥad Ha-Am 2:447
- - Banet, Mordecai 4:159
- - Bernays, Isaac 4:673
- - Cohen, Shalom ben Jacob 5:685
- - Eger, Solomon ben Akiva 6:473
- - Frankel, Zacharias 7:80
- - Hamburg, Abraham Benjamin 7:1229
- - Heine, Heinrich 8:274
- - Hildesheimer, Azriel 8:477
- - Hirsch, Samuel Raphael 8:510ff
- - Kohut, Alexander 10:1150
- - Leeser, Isaac 10:1562
- - Montefiore, Sir Moses 12:271
- - Sachs, Michael 14:595
- - Schick, Maharam 14:958
- - Sofer, Moses 15:77
- - Tiktin, Solomon 15:1140
- *illus:*
- - *Kol Kore Bammidbar* (1859) 5:410
- - Montagu, Lilian, delivering sermon 12:265
- - *Zeichen der Zeit* (1869) 5:411
Reformed Society of the Israelites (U.S.) 7:1333
Reform-Zeitung, Die (period.) 4:682
Refu'ah Shelemah (greeting) 7:914
Refu'ah Veterinarit (journ.) 1:newsp. list
Refu'at ha-Shinnayim (journ.) 1:newsp. list
Refugees (pre-1933)
- Middle Ages
- - community autonomy 3:925
- - Ottoman Empire 16:1532
- - Spanish exile 15:241ff
- - Wandering Jew 16:259
- World War I
- - Austria 3:896
- - HIAS 15:1539
- - JDC 2:828
- - League of Nations 10:1524
- - Zentralstelle der Fuersorge fuer Kriegsfluechtlinge 16:993
- *illus:*
- - Riga Committee 14:173
- - Russian refugees passing Statue of Liberty 12:1084
- - Tarbut kindergarten 14:447
- *see also:* DEMOGRAPHY; EXPULSIONS; MIGRATION
REFUGEES (1933–1949) 14:28
- *Contents:*
- - General 14:28
- - The Refugee Movement and its Proportions 14:30
- - International Refugee Organizations (IRO) 14:31
- - High Commissioner for Refugees from Germany 14:32
- AJC 2:824
- Austria 3:902
- Beriḥah 4:622
- Bermuda Conference 4:668
- Eclaireurs Israélites 14:1038
- Evian Conference 6:987ff
- Haganah 9:688
- HIAS 15:1539
- Holocaust 8:841; 8:891ff
- immigration to Ereẓ Israel 9:356
- JDC 2:830
- Kasztner, Rezső Rudolf 10:815
- Macdonald, James Grover 11:666
- Nazi Germany 7:491ff
- Roosevelt, Franklin D. 14:257
- Sweden 15:407
- *illus:*
- - text
- - appeal for allowing refugees into Palestine (1943) 8:766
- - Berlin, waiting for Passover supplies, 1946 7:498
- - British Guiana, White Paper on settlement (1939) 7:997
- - Evian Conference documents 6:988-990
- - German refugees dancing *hora,* 1939 9:526
- - learning secretarial skills at an ORT school in France 6:402
- - Polish refugee children 9:496,526
- - United HIAS Service 15:1539
- - Youth Aliyah group 16:862
- *tables:* text
- *see also:* HOLOCAUST (Rescue); Red Cross, International
Refugees, Palestinian, *see* ARAB REFUGEES
Regards (journ.) 13:1026
REGAVIM (kib., Isr.) 14:33
- statistics 1:place list
REGBAH (mosh., Isr.) 14:33
- statistics 1:place list
Regel (leg. conc.) 3:986ff
- torts 15:1273
REGELSON, ABRAHAM 14:34
- *illus:* text
REGEM-MELECH (bib. name) 14:34
Regenheim, Asher Lemmle 9:74
Regensberg (fam.) 15:790
Regensberg, David C. 5:415
Regensberg, Dov Menahem 16:923
REGENSBURG (city, Ger.) 14:35
- archives 3:387
- Baruch ben Isaac 4:278
- history chart (1519) 8:766-67
- informers 8:1367
- seal 14:1079
- *shtadlanut* 14:1463
- synagogue 15:603
- trade routes 15:129ff
- *illus:* text
Regensburg, Judah ben Israel 2:783
Regensburg Pentateuch (c. 1300, illum. ms.) 3:754; 4:67,963; 14:*fcg.* 1323
Regesty i Nadpisi (pub.) 8:563
REGGIO, ABRAHAM BEN EZRIEL 14:37
REGGIO, ISACCO SAMUEL 14:38
- Bible translations 4:878
- Bush, Isidor 4:1534
- history chart 8:766-67
- *illus:* text
REGGIO DI CALABRIA (city, It.) 14:38
- typography 15:1480
- *illus:* text
REGGIO EMILIA (city, It.) 14:39
- archives 3:383
- Jewish bankers 14:40; 16:1290
- *illus:* text
REGHIN (Reghinul Săsesc; tn., Rum.) 14:40
REGINA (city, Can.) 14:40
Regional Enteritis (disease) 14:1503
Régis, Max 2:616; 3:85
Régné, Jean 8:563
Regnis, *see* Singer, Bernard
Regressus, Divine 10:560
Regulations, Communal, *see* TAKKANOT HA-KAHAL
Regulations, Legal, *see* TAKKANOT
Rehabiah ben Judah 13:593
Reḥaviah (qtr., Jer.) 9:345,563
- Jerusalem development 9:1472
- *illus:*
- - view from Valley of the Cross 9:1489
REHFISCH, HANS JOSÉ 14:41
REHINE, ZALMA 14:41
Rehitim, see Pattern Poems
Rehmer, Ernst 12:954
REHOB (tn., Er. Isr.) 14:41
- levitical city 3:701
- statistics 1:place list
REHOBOAM (k., Judah) 14:42
- Abijah 2:75
- Ammonite mother 2:860
- Hebron 8:227
- history 8:593ff
- history chart 8:766–67
- Jeroboam 9:1372
- kingship 10:1014
- revolt 15:841
- Shemaiah 14:1374
- Shishak 14:1416
- Tamar 15:783
- *geneal. table;* 5:1341
- *illus:*
- - text
- - divided kingdom (map) 9:116
REHOBOTH (site, Er. Isr.) 14:44
- Gerar 7:432
Rehoboth by the River (tn.), *see* Rehoboth ha-Nahar
Rehoboth ha-Nahar (tn., Er. Isr.) 14:44
- Al-Raḥbah 13:1515
- Edom 6:370
REḤOVOT (city, Isr.) 14:44
- history chart (1890) 8:766-67
- Lewin-Epstein, Eliahu Ze'ev 11:173
- statistics 1:place list
- *illus:*
- - text
- - desalination, reverse osmosis unit 9:769
- - plowing a vineyard 9:781
- - Weizmann Institute of Science 3:352; 9:956,967; 16:439ff
Reḥovot (qtr., Jer.), *see* Bukharan Quarter
REHUM (bib. fig.) 14:45
Rehum (Samar. offic.) 8:619
REḤUMEI (4th cent., amora) 14:45
REḤUMEI (5th cent., amora) 14:46
REḤUMEI (savora) 14:46
Reich, Abraham Ezekiel 14:46
Reich, A. H. 16:445
Reich, Dov Ber 14:362
REICH, IGNÁC 14:46
Reich, Karl (print., Ger.) 14:220
Reich, Karl (U.S. biol.) 4:1032
REICH, KOPPEL (Jacob) 14:46
REICH, LEON 14:46
- Gruenbaum dispute 13:749
- Sejm 14:1118
Reich, Mendel (Jaroslaw) 9:1289
Reich, Mendel (Buchach, Gal.) 4:1436
Reich, W. 4:62
REICH, WILHELM (psych.) 14:47
REICHARD, PIROSKA 8:1087
Reich Citizenship Law (1935, Ger.) 12:1281
Reichenau, Walter von 14:475
Reichenbach (city., Silesia) 14:1538
REICHENBACH, HANS 14:48
Reichenbach, Harry 13:1361
Reichenberg (city, Bohem.), *see* LIBEREC
Reichenberg, Suzanne 15:1055
Reichenberger, Philip 14:37
REICHER, EMANUEL 15:1056,1090
Reicher, Jacob 11:253
REICHERSON, MOSES 14:49
REICHERT, ISRAEL 14:49
REICHINSTEIN, DAVID 5:386
Reichler, Joe 13:1361
Reichler, Moses 16:35
Reichlin, Seymour 11:1200
Reichman, Avram, *see* DOMINIC, ALEXANDRU
Reichman, Hananiah 6:1132
Reichmann, Hans 15:1567
REICHSBUND JUEDISCHER FRONTSOLDATEN (orgn.) 14:49
Reich Security Head Office, *see* R.S.H.A.
Reichsfront (orgn.) 12:955
Reichsinstitut fuer Geschichte des Neuen Deutschlands 8:565
Reichssicherheitshauptamt (orgn.), *see* R.S.H.A.
REICHSTEIN, TADEUS 14:50
REICHSVEREINIGUNG (orgn.) 14:50
- Germany 7:491; 7:494ff
- journal 9:1067
REICHSZENTRALE FUER JUEDISCHE AUSWANDERUNG (orgn.) 14:51
Reicin, Bedřich 14:1653
REIFENBERG, ADOLF 14:52
- Eshtemoa 6:892
- numismatics 12:1271; 12:1272
REIFMANN, JACOB 14:53
REIK, ḤAVIVAH (Emma) 14:54
REIK, THEODOR 14:54
- anthropology 3:39
Reiling, Netty, *see* SEGHERS, ANNA
Reilly, Sidney, *see* ROSENBLUM, SIGMUND GEORGIEVICH
Re'im (kib., Isr.) 1:place list
Reimann, J.F. 8:53

Reimarus, Hermann Samuel **13:**1248
Rein, Raphael, *see* ABRAMOWITZ, RAPHAEL
Reina, Cassiodoro de **4:**879
– Hebraists **8:**53
REINACH (fam.) **14:**55
REINACH, ADOLF **14:**57
Reinach, Enrico **15:**1057
Reinach, Baron Jacques **15:**406
Reinach, Joseph **6:**46; **14:**55
Reinach, Solomon **14:**56
– archaeology **3:**302
– Goldmann, Nahum **7:**723
Reinach, Théodore **14:**56
– archaeology **3:**302
– history chart **8:** 766–767
– learned societies **15:**54
– numismatics **12:**1271
Reincarnation, *see* GILGUL
Reine, Eliahu **9:**894
Reineccius, C. **8:**53
Reiner, E. **16:**1508
REINER, FRITZ **12:**704
Reiner, Imre **15:**1479
REINER, MARKUS **14:**57
REINES, ISAAC JACOB **14:**58
– history chart **8:**766–767
– Lida yeshivah **16:**770
– Mizrachi **12:**175
– Rabinowitz, Samuel Jacob **13:**1478
– *illus:*
– – text
– – Mizrachi conference, Lida (1903) **16:**1099
Reinfeld, Fred **5:**407
Reinganum, Lemle Moses **13:**21
– salt **14:**713
Reingold (physic., Rus.) **11:**1558
REINHARDT, MAX **14:**59
– Theater **15:**1056
– *illus:* text
Reinhart, Arthur J. **12:**1025
Reinitz (fams.) **8:**1054
Reinitz, Joshua Baruch **10:**473
Reinitz, M.L. **4:**1358
Reinke, Laurent **8:**53
REINMANN, SALOMON **14:**60
– Burma **4:**1526
– Calcutta **5:**40
Reinterment **6:**72ff
Reinus, M. **16:**1165
Reis, *see* AUERBACH, ISAAC EISIG BEN ISAIAH
Reis, Herz **13:**1107
Reis, Isaac, *see* NADIR, MOSHE
Reis, Seligman ben Hirz **8:**942
– printing **13:**1107
REISCHER, JACOB BEN JOSEPH **14:**61
Reischer, Simeon **14:**61
Reischl, W. **4:**875
Reisen (tn., Pol.), *see* Rydzyna
REISEN, ABRAHAM **14:**62
– Asch, Sholem **3:**684
– Reizen, Zalman **14:**63
– *illus:*
– – Peretz, Isaac Leib, and **16:**814
– – Yiddish writers, New York **16:**823
Reisen, Kalman **14:**62
Reisen, Sarah **14:**62
Reisen, Zalman, *see* REJZEN, ZALMAN
Reisha bei Rabbanan (tit.) **16:**762
Reishei Kallah (tit.) **2:**203
Reish Mata (tit.) **13:**1451
Reiske, Johann **8:**53
Reiske, J. Jacob **8:**53
Reisler, Jerzy, *see* SAWICKI, JERZY
Reisman, Simon **5:**112
Reiss (educ., U.S.) **14:**665
Reiss, Abraham Joseph, *see* RICE, ABRAHAM JOSEPH
Reiss, Anselm **16:**1132; **16:**639
Reiss, Erich **13:**1367
Reiss, Jacob **13:**972
REISS, LIONEL **3:**609
– *illus:*
– – "Talmudists" (etch.) **3:**639
Reiss, Naḥman, *see* AVIGAD, NAḤMAN
Reissmann, August **12:**700
Reisz, Julius **5:**1191
Reiter, Max **14:**823
Reiter, Virginia **15:**1057
Reitler (physic.) **5:**627
Reitlinger, Frederick **10:**1496
Reitlinger, Gerald **8:**566
Reitman, Allan **13:**1362
Re'iyyah (tract), *see* ḤAGIGAH
Reizenstein, Elmer Leopold, *see* RICE, ELMER LEOPOLD
REIẒES (Reiẓeles; brs.) **14:**63
Reiẓes, Hayyim ben Isaac ha-Levi **14:**63
Reiẓes, Joshua **14:**63
Reizin, Jacob Zalman **12:**967
Reizin, Mordecai Ze'ev **12:**967
Rej, Mikolaj **13:**798
REJZEN, ZALMAN **14:**63
– Vilna **16:**148
– Yung Vilne **16:**896
"Rejoicing of the Law. . . ".(paint., S. A. Hart) **3:**547
Rekem (tn., Edom), *see* PETRA
REKHASIM (stlmt., Isr.) **14:**64
– statistics **1:**place list
– *see also:* KEFAR ḤASIDIM
Rekhesh (Isr. arms purchase) **9:**694
Rekhmire tomb (Egy.) **3:**305
RELAND, ADRIAN (Hadrian) **14:**64
– *Analecta Rabbinica* **16:**37
– Hebraists **8:**53
Relationships, Forbidden, *see* MARRIAGE, PROHIBITED
Relativity, Theory of **6:**535
RELGIS, EUGEN **14:**64
Religion
– General
– – anthropomorphism **3:**51
– – communal organization **3:**926
– – dualism **6:**242
– – Gnosticism **7:**637
– – idolatry **8:**1227
– – purity **13:**1405; **13:**1414
– – religious tale **6:**1379
– Trends
– – Christianity **5:**505
– – Falashas **6:**1147
– – Islam **9:**92
– – Judaism **10:**383
– – Manichaeism **11:**876
– – Reconstructionism **13:**1615
– – Samaritans **14:**738
– Views On
– – Al-Fārābī **6:**1177
– – Formstecher **13:**456
– – Gordon, Aharon David **7:**791ff
– – Krochmal **13:**458
– – Steinheim **13:**459
– Countries
– – Israel **9:**887ff
– – U.S. **15:**1598ff
– *illus:*
– – *De Republica Hebraeorum* (1631) **5:**1171
– – *see also:* ISRAEL, STATE OF (Religious Life and Communities); THEOLOGY; *and under various religions*
Religion of Reason **11:**1330; **11:**1330ff
Religion in Geschichte und Gegenwart (enc.) **6:**733
Religionsgeschichte (Bib. research) **4:**907; **4:**908
Religious Coercion, League for the Abolition of, *see* League for the Abolition of Religious Coercion
Religious councils in Israel **9:**897ff
Religious education **6:**385ff
– in Israel **9:**894
RELIGIOUS IMPACT OF THE BIBLE **4:**915
"Religious Liberty" (statue, M. Ezekiel) **3:**556
Religious Music Institute, *see* Jewish Religious Music, Tel Aviv Institute of
Religious observances, *see* COMMANDMENTS, THE 613; MITZVAH
Religious Scientists, Association of, *see* Association of Religious Scientists
Religious Workers' list (party, Isr.) **9:**679
– education **9:**897
– *see also:* HA-OVED HA-ẒIYYONI
Religious Zionism, *see* HA-PO'EL HA-MIZRACHI; MIZRACHI
Religious Zionists of America **16:**1146
Rellach, Johann **4:**873
R-e-m-a, *see* ISSERLES, MOSES BEN ISRAEL
R-e-m-a-k, *see* KIMḤI, MOSES
REMAK (fam.) **14:**65
Remak, Ernst Julius **14:**65
Remak, Robert **14:**65
Remaliah (bib. fig.) **15:**676
Remalt, E. S. **16:**1509
REMBRANDT VAN RIJN **14:**66
– Joseph **10:**216
– Manasseh Ben Israel **11:**856
– Moses **12:**408ff
– portraits of Jews **13:**917
– Samuel **14:**784
– Saul **14:**917
– Temple theme **15:**986
– Tobit **15:**1186
– view on Jews **14:**20
– *illus:*
– – text
– – "Abraham and Isaac" (etch.) **9:**3
– – Abraham sending Hagar away (drg.) **7:**1076
– – "Abraham's Sacrifice" (etch.) **2:**485
– – "Belshazzar's Feast" (paint.) **4:**449
– – "Daniel's Vision" (paint.) **5:**1287
– – "David playing the Harp before Saul" (paint.) **14:**911
– – "Healing of the Blind" (etch.) **7:**176
– – "Isaac Blessing Jacob" (drg.) **9:**6
– – "Jacob Wrestling with the Angel" (paint.) **9:**1199
– – Jael slaying Sisera (drg.) **9:**1247
– – "Jewish Doctor" (paint.) **13:**917
– – "Jonah beside the Walls of Nineveh" (drg.) **12:**1169
– – "Joseph Telling His Dreams" (etch.) **10:**215
– – Manasseh Ben Israel (etch.) **11:**855
– – Mordecai on the king's horse (etch.) **12:**308
– – "Nathan admonishing David" (drg.) **12:**846
Remény (journ.) **5:**457
REMÉNYI, EDUARD **12:**704
Remeth (city, Er. Isr.), *see* RAMOTH
Remez (exegesis form) **10:**623ff
Remez, Aharon **14:**70
REMEZ, MOSHE DAVID **14:**69
– religious education **9:**897
– Va'ad Le'ummi **16:**51
– *illus:*
– – National Council meeting **9:**365
– – proclamation of the State of Israel **4:**513
– – Va'ad Le'ummi meeting **16:**50
REMNANT OF ISRAEL **14:**70
– Isaiah **9:**47
– term **6:**883
Remoch (fam.), *see* BENREMOKH
Remos, Moses **14:**70
REMOS, MOSES BEN ISAAC **14:**70
Remphthis (loc., Er. Isr.), *see* RAMAH
Renaissance
– apologetic literature **3:**196
– European Jewry **6:**971
– fiction, Hebrew **6:**1269
– Italian literature **9:**1107
– music, Jewish **12:**615
Renaissance (journ.) **16:**640
Renaissance, Jewish **16:**1037
RENAN, ERNEST **14:**71
– Clermont-Ganneau **5:**605
Renasterea Noastră (period.) **13:**1043
– Rumania **14:**395,399
– Zionism **16:**1134; **16:**1135
Rending of garments, *see* KERI'AH
Rendsburg (tn., Ger.) **14:**973
Rendtorf, J. **8:**53
René of Anjou (k., Naples)
– Abraham of Saint Maximin **2:**156
– Aix-en-Provence Jews **2:**475
– Provence **13:**1261
Reneia (isl., Gr.) **5:**1482
Renick, Joseph and Samuel William **15:**310
Rennes (tn., Fr.) **4:**1383
Reno (city, Nev.) **12:**1017ff
Rent, *see* LEASE AND HIRE
Rentchnick, Pierre **11:**1202
Rentlen, Adrian von **11:**386
Renunciation of Gifts **16:**526
Reparation-offering, *see* ʾAsham; Sin offering
REPARATIONS, GERMAN **14:**72
– Adenauer, Konrad **2:**264
– American Federation of Jews from Central Europe **2:**820
– Austria **3:**902
– Barou, Noah **4:**256
– Ben-Gurion, David **4:**510
– Goldmann, Nahum **7:**724
– Greece **7:**880
– historical survey **9:**382ff
– Holocaust **8:**885
– Israel industry **9:**815ff
– Israel negotiations **9:**666
– Templers' property **15:**995
– *illus:*
– – text
– – signing of the agreement with Israel **7:**499
– *see also:* RESTITUTION AND INDEMNIFICATION
REPENTANCE **14:**73
– *Contents:*
– – Introduction **14:**73
– – Rabbinic Views **14:**74
– – In Jewish Philosophy **14:**76
– – Post-Medieval Period **14:**76
– – Modern Developments **14:**77
– General
– – Inquisition **8:**1401ff
– – marital relations **5:**364
– – mystical interpretation of **10:**493
– – prophecy **13:**1173
– – redemption **14:**3
– In Judaism
– – acceptable to God **3:**657
– – asceticism **3:**679
– – false measures **16:**391
– – fasting **6:**1190ff
– – forgiveness **6:**1433ff
– – *karet* **10:**788
– – *nezifah* **8:**351

- - Shofar **14:**308
- - Ten Penitence days **15:**1001
- - *see also* CONFESSION OF SINS; DAY OF ATONEMENT
- In Literature
- - *Adam, Apocalypse of* **2:**245
- - Apocalypse **3:**179
- - Nineveh **10:**169
- Views on
- - Alkalai, Judah **2:**638ff
- - Cohen, Hermann **13:**461
- - Ḥasidei Ashkenaz **7:**1381
- - Jacob ben Korshai **9:**1221
- - Kalischer, Ẓevi Hirsch **10:**708
- - Nathan of Gaza **14:**1225; **14:**1234
- - Rosenzweig **14:**299
- - Saadiah **13:**432
- *illus:* text
Repetur, Berl **5:**1455
Rephaiah ben Judah Kohen **13:**593
REPHAIM (bib. term) **14:**79
- Zamzummim **16:**929
REPHIDIM (bib. loc.) **14:**80
- Amalekites **2:**787
Reproof, *see* REBUKE AND REPROOF
Reptiles
- dietary laws **6:**34
- impurity **13:**1406; **13:**1411
- reproduction **4:**1017
- *table:* Animals of the Bible and Talmud **3:**9-16
- *see also:* ANIMALS OF THE BIBLE AND TALMUD; FLORA AND FAUNA IN ISRAEL
Republican Constitution (Sp., 1868) **15:**244
Republican Party (U.S.) **13:**821
Republic of Ireland, *see* IRELAND
Requisition, *see* CONFISCATION, EXPROPRIATION, FORFEITURE
Rescue Committee, *see* Va'ad ha-Hazalah
Rescue of Jews in World War II, *see* HOLOCAUST (Rescue); REFUGEES
"Rescue Train" (D.P. restlmt.) **4:**629
Research Council of Israel **2:**849; **14:**767
RESEN (bib. city) **14:**80
- Ctesiphon **5:**1146
Resen, H. P. **4:**877
Resende (city, Brazil) **4:**1327
Resende, García de **15:**251
RESH (Heb. alphabet) **14:**80
Reshafim (kib., Isr.) **1:**place list
Reshafim (period.) **1:**newsp. list
RESHEPH (deity) **14:**81
- demon **5:**1524
Reshet Dati (educ. trend, Isr.) **9:**897*ff*
Reshetnikov, Feodor **14:**508
RESHEVSKY, SAMUEL HERMAN **14:**82
- chess **5:**405
- *illus:* text
Resh Galuta, *see* EXILARCH
Reshimah Komunistit Ḥadashah (party, Isr.), *see* Rakaḥ
Reshimah Mamlakhtit (party, Isr.), *see* National List
Reshimat Ma'amarim be-Madda'ei ha-Yahadut (period.) **1:**newsp. list
Reshimat Pirsumei ha-Memshalah (period.) **1:**newsp. list
Reshimat Poalei Israel, *see* RAFI
Reshimu (kab. conc.) **10:**589ff
Reshit (journ.) **16:**401
- statistics **1:**newsp. list
Reshit (kab. conc.) **10:**560
Reshith (period.) **8:**219
Reshit ha-Lekaḥ (wk.) **16:**1390
Reshit Ḥokhmah (wk.) **16:**120
- Kabbalah **10:**546; **10:**642
RESH KALLAH (tit.) **14:**82
- academies **2:**203
- *alluf* **2:**657
- gaonate **7:**316
- titles **15:**1164
Resh Lakish (amora), *see* SIMEON BEN LAKISH
Resh Metivta (tit.), *see* GAON
Resh Pirka (tit.) **3:**335
Resh Sidra (tit.) **15:**1164
Reshummot (gazette, Isr.) **9:**650ff
- statistics **1:**newsp. list
Reshumot (journ., Rus.) **13:**1047
- statistics **1:**newsp. list
RESHUT (authority, domain, optional duty) **14:**83
- *eruv* **6:**849
- *see also:* OWNERSHIP
Reshut (hazzan's prayer) **14:**904
Reshut ha-Shiddur, *see* Israel Broadcasting Authority
Residence, *see* DOMICILE
Residence rights, *see* ḤEREM HA-YISHUV
Resident Aliens, *see* STRANGERS AND GENTILES
Resistance, *see* HOLOCAUST (Resistance); PARTISANS
Resničeк, Emil von **10:**461
Resnick, Louis **13:**1361
Resnick, N. **5:**448
Resnick, Salomón **15:**255
Reso, Harry **15:**1061
RESPONSA **14:**83
- *Contents:*
- - Introduction **14:**83
- - Geonic Period **14:**84
- - The Rishonim **14:**85
- - Historical Significance **14:**87
- - From the 16th Century **14:**88
- - The 20th Century **14:**92
- archives **3:**375
- Cairo *genizah* **16:**1336
- codification of law **5:**633
- Conservative Judaism **12:**1445
- Ets-Hayyim yeshivah **16:**767
- geonim **8:**664ff
- halakhic responsa **11:**58
- *ḥiddushim* **8:**465
- Jewish law development **12:**118; **12:**122; **12:**132
- Jewish literature **11:**331ff
- judicial autonomy **12:**125; **12:**141
- Maimonides **11:**765ff
- Meir of Rothenburg **11:**1247
- psychology **13:**1343
- rabbinic office **13:**1447
- technology **15:**892
- tradition **15:**1310
- *illus:*
- - Maimonides, manuscript **11:**758
- - Nissim ben Reuben Gerondi **12:**1184
- - *Sefer ha-Tashbeẓ* **12:**978
- - *Sefer Hikrei Lev* **13:**1109
- - *She'elot ha-Rav Sha'ul ha-Kohen* (1574) **3:**732
- - *She'elot u-Teshuvot*, Bezalel Ashkenazi (1595) **3:**724
- - *She'elot u-Teshuvot*, Levi ben Ḥabib (1565) **11:**99
- - *She'elot u-Teshuvot*, Moses ben Isaac Alashkar (1553) **8:**72
- - *see also:* PRINTING, HEBREW
- *see also:* KUNTERES; POLEMICS AND POLEMICAL LITERATURE
Responsibility, criminal **13:**223
Responsorial Psalmody, *see* MUSIC
Ress, Joseph W. **13:**1278
RESSLER, BENJAMIN **14:**95
Ressner, Franz, *see* ROESSLER, CARL
"Resting at the Bazaar" (paint., M. Sterne) **15:**397
Restitution (of theft) **15:**1095
RESTITUTION AND INDEMNIFICATION **14:**95
- Adenauer, Konrad **2:**264
- Austria **3:**902
- claims conference **5:**872
- cultural reconstruction **10:**49
- *see also:* REPARATIONS, GERMAN
Rest of the Words of Baruch, *see* BARUCH, REST OF THE WORDS OF
Restoration Movement (Chr. mvmt.) **16:**1153
Restraint (Yishuv policy), *see* *Havlagah*
Restrictions, Anti-Jewish, *see* ANTI-SEMITISM (legislation)
Restrictive Trade Board (Isr.) **9:**640
RESURRECTION **14:**96
- *Contents:*
- - Introduction **14:**96
- - In the Bible **14:**97
- - Rabbinic Period **14:**98
- - Medieval Jewish Philosophy **14:**101
- - Modern Period **14:**102
- Theology
- - article of faith **3:**655ff
- - body and soul **4:**1165
- - heresy **8:**359
- - human body **11:**846
- - intertestamental eschatology **6:**875
- - kabbalistic eschatology **6:**882
- - man's nature **11:**845
- - soul's immortality **15:**175
- - source of belief **10:**389
- - Torah mention **14:**840
- - world to come **12:**1356ff
- In Literature
- - *Apocalypse of Isaiah* **6:**870
- - Bible **5:**1422
- - *Ma'amar Teḥiyyat ha-Metim* **11:**759
- In Legend
- - golem legends **7:**755
- - *luz* of the spine **11:**595
- - Mount of Olives **8:**579; **8:**582; **12:**484
- - ossuary use **3:**327
- - valley of Jehoshaphat **10:**988
- Sectarian Doctrines
- - Boethusians **4:**1169
- - Dead Sea Scrolls **15:**1046
- - Essenes **6:**900
- - Falashas **6:**1149
- - Karaites **10:**778
- - Pharisee ideology **13:**365
- - Sadducees **14:**621
- - Samaritans **14:**738; **14:**739
- Views on
- - Aaron ben Elijah **2:**12
- - Abraham Bar Ḥiyya **2:**131
- - Albo, Joseph **2:**536
- - Levi ben Gershom **11:**97
- - Maimonides **11:**747; **13:**443
- - Muhammad **6:**883ff
- - Saadiah **13:**432
- *illus:*
- - Ezekiel's vision **3:**515; **4:**945; **6:**291,1093,1096
- - Lazarus **9:**1420
- *see also* AFTERLIFE; NETHERWORLD; PARADISE; REDEMPTION; REWARD AND PUNISHMENT
Resurrection, Church of the (Jer.), *see* Anastasis, Church of the
Retenu, Land of **9:**108
- Thutmose III **16:**1499
Reth, Alfred **13:**113
RETHYMNON (tn., Crete) **14:**103
RÉTI, RICHARD **14:**103
Retimo (tn., Crete), *see* RETHYMNON
Retribution, Divine, *see* REWARD AND PUNISHMENT
Retty, Leopold **3:**32
"Return" (paint., N. Bezem) **3:**1618
Return of the Craftsmen and the Smiths Society, *see* Shivat ha-Ḥarash ve-ha-Masger Society
"Return of the Volunteer" (paint., M. Oppenheim) **11:**1561
"Return of Tobias" (paint., M. Oppenheim) **15:**1185
Return to Zion (6th cent. B.C.E.), *see* Zion, Return to
REUBEN (bib. fig.) **14:**103
- Biblical Figure
- - breastplate stone **13:**1008
- - confession of **10:**332
- - Genesis, Book of **7:**393
- - grave **8:**935
- Tribe
- - *aggadah* **15:**1385
- - conditions prototype **5:**866
- - settlement **8:**579; **8:**582; **9:**115
- - Transjordan **15:**1317
- - tribal leadership **15:**1384
- *illus:*
- - text
- - banner and emblem **4:**181
- - parents and brothers **10:**1526
Reuben, Abraham **13:**14
Reuben, Flora (Farha) **4:**380
Reuben, Mordecai **10:**1110
Reuben, Testament of (Pseudepig.), *see* PATRIARCHS, TESTAMENTS OF THE TWELVE
Reuben ben Abraham **16:**872
Reuben ben Eliakim of Mayence **13:**1105
REUBEN BEN ḤAYYIM **14:**106
REUBEN BEN STROBILUS **14:**107
Reuben ha-Kohen Ḥazzan **13:**593
Reuben ha-Levi of Dziengowice **3:**668
REUBEN HOESHKE BEN HOESHKE KATZ **14:**107
- Kabbalah **10:**552
Reubeni, David, *see* REUVENI, DAVID
Reuben Shiloah Center for Middle Eastern and African Studies (Isr.) **15:**926
Reuchlin, Antonius **8:**53
REUCHLIN, JOHANNES **14:**108
- *Contents:*
- - General **14:**108
- - "Battle of the Books" **14:**108
- - Kabbalah **14:**110
- Christian Kabbalah **2:**545; **10:**644ff
- German Jews **7:**472
- Hebraists **8:**52
- history chart **8:**766-767
- linguistics **16:**1360,1389,1391
- Luther, Martin **11:**584
- Melanchthon, Philipp **11:**1276
- Pfefferkorn, Johannes **13:**356
- Pforzheim Jews **13:**358
- Talmud defense **15:**770
- *illus:* text
Reuchlin Bible (13th cent. illum. ms., Ger.) **8:**1261
- *illus:* **8:**1271
Reudenius, A. **8:**52
Reuel (s., Esau) **16:**996
Reuel (bib. fig.), *see* JETHRO
Reuel (Apoc. fig.), *see* Raguel
Reumah (bib. fig.) **12:**790
REUSS, EDUARD **14:**111
- Bible criticism **16:**79
- Bible translations **4:**873; **4:**881
Reuter, Herbert **14:**113
REUTER, PAUL JULIUS, BARON VON **14:**112
- history **8:**714
- *illus:*

- - text
- - cartoon **10:**305
- - portrait **8:**707
Reuthe-Fink, Cécil von **5:**1539
REUTLINGEN (city, W. Ger.) **14:**113
Reutlinger (fam.) **4:**173
Reutter, Georg **10:**460
Reutter, Hermann **14:**909
REUVENI, AHARON **14:**113
REUVENI, DAVID **14:**114
- autobiography **4:**1011
- Azemmour community **3:**1004
- Badajoz **4:**59
- Beirut **4:**402
- Castro, Abraham **5:**244
- Charles V **5:**356
- chronological chart **8:**766-767
- Clement VII **5:**601
- flag **6:**1336
- Glanz-Leyeles' drama on **7:**600
- Kabbalah **10:**544
- Llerena **11:**413
- messianism **11:**1426
- Molcho, Solomon **12:**225ff
- Ten Lost Tribes **15:**1005
- travel book **11:**351
- Venice **16:**98
Reuwich, Erhard **9:**1543; **9:**1580
- *illus:*
- - Jerusalem map **9:**1545
REVADIM (kib., Isr.) **14:**116
- statistics **1:**place list
REVAH, ISRAEL SALVATOR **14:**116
Revaḥah (mosh., Isr.) **1:**place list
Révai, Leó **13:**1369
Révai, Miklós **8:**52
Révai, Sámuel **13:**1369
Revayah (mosh., Isr.) **1:**place list
Revel (city, Est.), *see* TALLINN
REVEL, BERNARD (Dov) **14:**116
- universities **15:**1679
REVELATION **14:**117
- *Contents:*
- - General **14:**117
- - In Talmudic Literature **14:**119
- - Ancient and Medieval Jewish Philosophy **14:**122
- - Modern Jewish Philosophy **14:**124
- General
- - dreams **6:**208
- - *maḥzorim,* illuminated **11:**733
- - *Shekhinah* **14:**1351
- - Torah reading **15:**1253
- Bible
- - Exodus, Book of **6:**1056ff
- - in the Arts **12:**404*f*
- - Mt. Sinai **14:**1598
- - Pentateuch **13:**256,262
- - pillar of cloud **13:**524
- - Temple **15:**953
- - Torah **15:**1239
- - wilderness **16:**513
- - *see also:* DECALOGUE; PROPHETS AND PROPHECY
- In Judaism
- - articles of faith **3:**654ff
- - asceticism **3:**679
- - creation in Kabbalah **10:**620
- - denial **8:**359
- - fasting **6:**1191
- - gentile's obligation **12:**1190ff
- - Jewish Aristotelianism **3:**447
- - Kabbalah as **10:**490,493
- - law and morality **10:**1480
- - man's nature **11:**845
- - miracles **12:**76; **12:**77ff
- - necessity and purpose of **4:**431
- - Neoplatonism **12:**958; **12:**959
- - philosophy, Jewish **13:**421; **13:**422ff
- - providence **13:**1279
- - reason **10:**392; **10:**393
- - *Ru'aḥ ha-Kodesh* **14:**364ff
- - theology **15:**1107
- *Halakhah*
- - as law source **12:**120; **12:**123
- - *Halakhah le-Moshe mi-Sinai* **7:**1167
- - *halakhah's* relation to **4:**433
- - Written Law **7:**1157
- Movements, Conceptions of
- - Haskalah **7:**1436
- - Karaite Kalam **13:**433
- - Karaites **10:**778
- - Orthodoxy **12:**1489
- - Qumran community **13:**331
- - Reform Judaism **14:**25
- - Samaritan tradition **14:**743
- Views on
- - Albo, Joseph **2:**536
- - Buber, Martin **4:**1432ff; **13:**463
- - Formstecher **13:**456
- - Hirsch, S. R. **8:**512
- - Ibn Daud **8:**1161
- - Judah Halevi **10:**364ff
- - Levi ben Gershom **4:**436
- - Mendelssohn **11:**1336ff; **13:**455
- - Rosenzweig **13:**462; **14:**299; **14:**301
- - Saadiah Gaon **14:**549
- - Spinoza **15:**278; **15:**281ff
- - Steinheim **13:**459
Revelation (post-prophetic lit.), *see* APOCALYPSE
Revelation, Book of (N.T.) **3:**179
- angelic song **15:**144
Revere (city, Mass.) **11:**1112
Revere (vill., It.) **11:**895
REVERE, GIUSEPPE PROSPERO **14:**126
- Italian literature **9:**1111
- *illus:* text
Reverend (r. tit., Eng.) **13:**1453
REVESZ, BÉLA **14:**127
REVESZ, GEZA **14:**127
Revi'a (cantillation sign) **16:**1440,1454
REVICZKY, IMRE **14:**127
- Baia-Mare camp **4:**108
Revi'it (meas.) **16:**388; **16:**389
Revised Standard Version (Bib.) **4:**871
Revised Version (Bib.) **4:**870
REVISIONISTS, ZIONIST (party) **14:**128
- Activities
- - Histadrut **8:**541; **9:**854ff
- - immigration **8:**1249; **9:**527
- - Israel politics **9:**382; **9:**660ff
- - Italy **16:**1123
- - labor **9:**346
- - Palestine, partition **13:**34
- - Va'ad Le'ummi **16:**50
- - Warsaw ghetto **13:**774; **16:**349*ff*
- - Zionist Congress (7th) **16:**1173; **16:**1175
- - Zionist split **16:**1098
- Organizations
- - Betar **4:**714
- - Ḥerut **8:**400
- - I.Z.L. **8:**1467
- - Jewish Legion **10:**75
- - students' movements **15:**448
- Personalities
- - Ben-Gurion **4:**508
- - Greenberg, Ivan Marion **7:**905
- - Grossman, Meir **7:**937ff
- - Hecht, Ben **8:**239
- - Jabotinsky, Vladimir **9:**1180
- - Netanyahu, Benzion **12:**970
- *illus:*
Jabotinsky presenting flag to Kovno unit of youth movement **16:**1098
REVISTA CULTULUI MOZAIC (period.) **14:**132
- Bucharest **4:**1441
- Rumania **13:**1043; **14:**1029; **14:**413
Revista Israelită (period., Rum.) **13:**1043; **14:**1029
Revista Israelita de México (period.) **11:**1459
Revista Israelitica (It.) **13:**1036
REVIV, HANOCH **1:**36
REVIVIM (kib., Isr.) **14:**132
- Negev **12:**929
- statistics **1:**place list
Revivim (journ.) **1:**newsp. list
Revivim-Lahav (loc., Isr.) **9:**795
Revolt, The Great, *see* Jewish War
"Revolving Figures" (wdct., L. Schanker) **3:**639
REVSON, CHARLES HASKELL **14:**133
Revson, Joseph **14:**133
Revson, Peter **15:**300
Revue de droit international et de législation comparée **3:**766
REVUE DES ETUDES JUIVES (period.) **14:**133
- historiography **8:**563
- societies, learned **15:**54
REVUSKY, ABRAHAM **14:**133
REWARD AND PUNISHMENT **14:**134
- *Contents:*
- - General **14:**134
- - In Medieval Jewish Philosophy **14:**136
- - Modern Jewish Thought **14:**138
- General
- - duress **12:**1397
- - *karet* **10:**789
- - netherworld **12:**996
- - Rosh ha-Shanah **14:**307
- Theology and Philosophy
- - article of faith **3:**655ff
- - Aristotelianism **3:**448
- - eschatology **6:**874ff
- - ethics **6:**934
- - God's justice and mercy **7:**669
- - *kelippot* doctrine **10:**596
- - man's nature **11:**844
- - paradise and hell **13:**82ff
- - resurrection **14:**97; **14:**98
- - suffering **15:**486
- - *zekhut avot* **16:**976
- Literature
- - Daniel, Book of **5:**1279
- - Job, Book of **10:**121ff
- - religious tale **6:**1380
- - *Solomon, Wisdom of* **15:**119ff;
- Groups, Communities
- - Dead Sea Scrolls **6:**876*ff*
- - Islam **9:**100
- - Karaites **10:**778
- - Pharisees **13:**365
- - Sumer **15:**515
- Views on
- - Aaron ben Elijah **2:**12
- - Albo, Joseph **2:**536
- - Antigonus of Sokho **3:**67
- - Hillel ben Samuel **8:**489
- - Jacob ben Korshai **9:**1221
- - Maimonidean controversy **11:**748
- - Mendelssohn, Moses **11:**1331; **11:**1340
- - Naḥmanides **12:**781
- - Philo **13:**427
- - Saadiah Gaon **13:**432; **14:**551
- *see also:* BEATITUDE; GOOD AND EVIL; OLAM HA-BA; PROVIDENCE; REDEMPTION; SIN
REXINGEN (vill., Ger.) **14:**139
- Shavei Zion **16:**674
Reyes de Taifas (dyn.), *see* MULŪK AL-TAWĀ IF
Reyher, C. **8:**52
Reymont, Wladislaw Stanislaw **13:**800
Reyna, Joseph Della, *see* JOSEPH DELLA REINA
Reynolds, Debbie **15:**1082
Reynolds, John, *see* Rainolds, John
Reynolds, Sir Joshua **14:**785
Reyos Catolicos, *see* FERDINAND AND ISABELLA
Rezchik, *see* GORDON, ABRAHAM
REZEKNE (Rezhitsa; city, Latv.) **14:**140
REZIN (k., Aram) **14:**140
- chronological chart **8:**766-767
- Judah **15:**676
- Pekah **8:**603ff; **13:**214
REZINA (Rezinz; city, Mold.) **14:**140
REZNIK, DAVID **3:**365
- *illus:*
- - Hebrew University synagogue **13:**1575
- - Kennedy Memorial **3:**356
REZNIK, LIPE **14:**141
REZNIKOFF, CHARLES **14:**141
- U.S. literature **15:**1573ff
Rezon (bib. fig.) **3:**287; **15:**102
- chronological chart **8:**766-767
Rezzonius, F. **8:**52
Rhages (tn., Iran), *see* Rai
Rhamnus (flora) **9:**221
Rhazes (physic.) **11:**1187
- Ali ibn Sahl **2:**632
- Asaph ha-Rofe **3:**674
RHEIMS (city, Fr.) **14:**142
Rheinbayern (reg., Ger.) **13:**22
Rheinfelden (tn., Switz.) **15:**554
Rheinganum, Lemle Moses, *see* Reinganum, Lemle Moses
Rheinland-Pfalz (fed. state) **13:**22
Rhein-Mainische Volkszeitung und Handelsblatt (journ.) **5:**1564
Rhenferd, J. **8:**52
Rhenish Bavaria (reg., Ger.) *see* Rheinbayern
Rhenish Jewish Diet (orgn., Ger.) **16:**685
Rhenish Palatinate (reg., W. Ger.) *see* PALATINATE
Rhetoric **2:**868; **8:**947ff; **14:**651
Rhijn, H. van **4:**876
Rhineland **5:**1135ff
- *illus:*
- - *Monumenta Judaica* exhibition **5:**743
- - *Yizkor* prayer for destroyed communities **10:**1120
Rhine Rite (litur.) **11:**399
RHINEWINE, ABRAHAM **14:**142
Rhinoceros (zool.) **9:**225
Rhinokoroura (tn., Sinai), *see* EL-ARISH
RHODE ISLAND **14:**143
- *illus:* text
- *pop. tables:* text
RHODES (city, isl., Gr.) **14:**145
- armistice talks **3:**479; **9:**374ff; **15:**1546
- lead scroll **16:**662
- rabbinical seminary **13:**1464
- Rodanim **14:**215
- Seattle community **14:**1083
- Sephardim in Africa **14:**1172
- special Purim **13:**1397
- *illus:*
- - text
- - Israel-Jordan General Armistice Agreement, April 1949 **3:**479; **9:**375
Rhodes, Cecil John **4:**248; **4:**404; **5:**1368; **6:**6
Rhodes, Irving R. **11:**1589
RHODESIA **14:**148
- African Jews **2:**335
- Beit, Sir Alfred **4:**404
- Bulawayo **4:**1480
- Israel **9:**434
- synagogues **1:**syn. list
- Zambia **16:**922ff

- Zionism **16:**1140
- *illus:* text
- *pop. tables:*
- - text
- - postwar communities **5:**839
Rhodesia, Northern, *see* ZAMBIA
R-i (tos.), *see* ISAAC BEN SAMUEL OF DAMPIERRE
Riad, General **14:**1626
Riad, Mahmud **9:**418
R-i-a-z, *see* ISAIAH BEN ELIJAH DI TRANI
Riazanov, David **5:**794
R-i-b-a (Fr. tos.), *see* ISAAC BEN ABRAHAM
R-i-b-a (Ger. tos.), *see* ISAAC BEN ASHER HA-LEVI
R-i-b-a II (Ger. tal.) **9:**16
R-i-b-a ha-Baḥur **9:**16
R-i-b-a-l, *see* LEVINSOHN, ISAAC BAER
Ribalow, Harold Uriel **14:**150
RIBALOW, MENACHEM **14:**149
- *illus:*
- - Hebrew Pen Club N.Y. **8:**211; **12:**1109
- - Hebrew writers' convention, 1943 **8:**213
R-i-b-a-m (tos.), *see* ISAAC BEN MEIR
R-i-b-a-m (Ger. tos.), *see* ISAAC BEN MORDECAI
Ribas, de (fam.) **15:**1300
R-i-b-a-sh (Sp.), *see* ISAAC BEN SHESHET PERFET
R-i-b-a-sh (Morav.), *see* HOROWITZ, ẒEVI JOSHUA BEN SAMUEL SHMELKE
RIBBENTROP, JOACHIM VON **14:**150
- *illus:*
- - Nuremberg Trial **16:**289
Ribbono Shel Olam (name for God) **7:**683
Ribbui (hermeneutical rule) **8:**370
RIBEAUVILLE (tn., Fr.) **14:**150
- Alsace **2:**752; **2:**754
- Armleder massacre **3:**484
RIBEIRO, BERNARDIM **14:**151
Ribeiro, Tomás **15:**251
RIBEIRO SANCHEZ, ANTONIO **14:**151
Ribera, Daniel de **15:**276
Ribera, Francisco de **8:**52
Ribes, A. **16:**826
Ribes de Majorca, Jaime, *see* Cresques, Judah
RIBICOFF, ABRAHAM A. **14:**152
- Connecticut **5:**899
RIBLAH (anc. Syr. tn.) **14:**152
- Kadesh on Orontes **10:**665
Ribner, Herbert **16:**633
Ricardo (fam.) **16:**90
Ricardo, Abraham **14:**153
RICARDO, DAVID **14:**153
- *illus:* text
Ricaut, Paul **6:**753
RICCHI, RAPHAEL IMMANUEL BEN ABRAHAM ḤAI **14:**154
- *ẓimẓum* **10:**593
Ricci, Matteo **2:**475
Ricci, Paul, *see* RICIUS, PAULUS
Ricciotti, G. **4:**878
RICE **14:**155
- grain species **6:**1333
- plant list **13:**623
RICE, ABRAHAM JOSEPH **14:**156
- Baltimore **4:**145
- *illus:* text
RICE, ELMER LEOPOLD **14:**156
Rice, Isaac **16:**551
RICE, ISAAC LEOPOLD **14:**157
RICE, JAMES P. **14:**157
RICE, JOSEPH MAYER **14:**157
RICH (fam.) **14:**158
Rich, Daniel **14:**158
Rich, Emanuel **14:**158
Rich, Herbert **15:**308
Rich, J. M. **15:**193
Rich, Morris **14:**158
Rich, Silven **12:**454
Rich, William **14:**158
Richard I (Coeur de Lion; k., Eng.)
- anti-Jewish riots **6:**748
- Azor **3:**1011
- Crusade results **9:**268
- Hereford Jews **8:**344
- Jewish property **16:**1285
- Jews of England **5:**1140
- Josce of York **10:**200
- Maimonides **11:**757
Richard, Earl of Cornwall **6:**618
Richard of St. Victor (Hebr.) **8:**52
RICHARDS, BERNARD GERSON **14:**158
Richardson, John **8:**52
Richart (Hebr.) **8:**52
RICHIETTI, JOSEPH SHALLIT BEN ELIEZER **14:**159
Richland (vill., Wash.) **16:**356
RICHLER, MORDECAI **14:**159
- Canada **5:**115; **5:**116
RICHMAN, JULIA **14:**159
Richman, Ruben **15:**304
Richmond (boro., N.Y.C.) **12:**1077ff
RICHMOND (city, Va.) **14:**160
- Virginia **16:**162
- *illus:*
- - synagogue **16:**164
Richter, Carola **14:**163
Richter, F. **10:**93
Richter, Gustav (19th cent., Ger. art.) **14:**163
Richter, Gustav (Nazi, Rum.) **3:**164; **10:**1554; **16:**1135; **14:**401, 403
RICHTER, HANS **14:**162
Richter, K. **15:**400
Richter, Mischa **5:**220
Richter, Moses **12:**1220
RICHTER, RAOUL **14:**163
RICHTMANN, MÓZES **14:**163
RICIUS, PAULUS (Rici) **14:**163
- Christian Kabbalah **10:**644
- Reuchlin, Johannes **14:**109
- *illus:*
- - *Portae Lucis* (1516) **10:**635
Rickert, Heinrich **16:**111
RICKOVER, HYMAN GEORGE **14:**164
Ricqulès, Samuel Heyman **11:**624
Ricus, Isaac Nunez, *see* Nunez Ricus, Isaac
R-i-d-b-a-z, *see* WILLOWSKI, JACOB DAVID BEN ZE'EV
Riddles
- folk **6:**1389
- games **7:**307
- parable **13:**72
Ridgefield Park (vill., N. J.) **4:**612
Rie, Marianne, *see* Kris, Marianne
Rieder (publ. firm, Fr.) **13:**1368
Riefmann, Jacob **11:**637
RIEGELMAN, HAROLD **14:**165
RIEGER, ELIEZER **14:**165
RIEGER, PAUL **14:**166
- history **8:**563
- Rieti **14:**170
Riegl, A. (arch.) **3:**301
Riegler, G. **8:**52
Riegner, Gerhart **8:**916
Ries, Abraham **13:**1288
Ries, D. C. **8:**52
RIESMAN, DAVID **14:**166
Riess (fam.) **15:**406
Riess, Abraham **4:**640
RIESS, LUDWIG **14:**166
RIESSER, GABRIEL **14:**166
- apologetics **3:**199
- chronological list **8:**766-767
- emancipation **6:**706ff
- Oppenheim's portrait **12:**1424
- *illus:* text
Riesser, J. (Hebr.) **8:**52
RIESSER, JACOB **14:**169
Riesser, Lazarus, *see* Katzenellenbogen, Eliezer
Riessler, P. **4:**875
RIETI (fam.) **14:**169
Rieti, Angelo **14:**170
Rieti, Arturo **14:**170
Rieti, Asael Raphael **14:**170
Rieti, C. **4:**878
Rieti, David Naphtali **14:**170
Rieti, Elḥanan **14:**170
Rieti, Eliezer ben Isaac **14:**170
Rieti, Elijah Isaac **14:**170
Rieti, Ezechia da, *see* Rieti, Ḥezekiah
Rieti, Hananiah Eliakim **14:**170
Rieti, Ḥezekiah **9:**1102; **14:**170
Rieti, Isaac **14:**169
Rieti, Ishmael **15:**1378
Rieti, Joseph **14:**170
Rieti, Laudadio Ishmael **14:**169
Rieti, Maestro Gaio, *see* Rieti, Isaac
Rieti, Maestro Gaio da, *see* RIETI, MOSES BEN ISAAC DA
Rieti, Malkah **14:**170
Rieti, Michael **14:**169
Rieti, Mordecai **14:**170
RIETI, MOSES BEN ISAAC DA **14:**171
- family **14:**170
- Italian literature **9:**1109
- Kabbalah **10:**540
- prosody **13:**1222
Rieti, Moses da **14:**170
Rieti, Serena **14:**170
Rieti, Simone **14:**170
Rieti, Solomon Moses di **14:**170
Rieti, Vittorio (It.) **14:**170
RIETI, VITTORIO (U.S.) **12:**704
R.I.E.T.S., *see* Rabbi Isaac Elchanan Theological Seminary
Rietti (fam.), *see* RIETI
Rif, F. I. **7:**1331
R-i-f, *see* ALFASI, ISAAC BEN JACOB
Rifāʿī, ʿAbd al Munʿim al- **9:**1040
Riff, Naftoli H. **5:**71
RIFKIND, SIMON HIRSCH **14:**172
- Beriḥah **4:**630
- Zionist program **4:**308
Rift Valley (geog. reg., Er. Isr.) **9:**123; **9:**156ff; **9:**589
- *illus:*
- - Dead Sea Valley, Pleistocene formations **9:**217
- - Ein Ḥaẓevah, canyon exit **9:**145
- - Ḥiyyon River exit **9:**165
- - Ḥuleh Valley **9:**207,212
- - Jordan Valley and Lake Kinneret **9:**211
RIGA (city, port, Latv.) **14:**172
- *Contents:*
- - History **14:**172
- - Holocaust Period **14:**175
- - Contemporary Period **14:**176
- promotion of culture **15:**59ff
- synagogue **15:**589
- War Crimes Trials **16:**297
- *illus:*
- - Ẓe'irei Zion group **10:**1466
Rigelet, G. **8:**52
Rigg, J. M. **10:**53
RIGHT AND LEFT (in Bib. and Tal.) **14:**177
- *Contents:*
- - Right as Opposed to Left **14:**177
- - Direction (Cardinal Points) **14:**177
- - Strength and Weakness **14:**178
- - Merism **14:**179
- - In Talmudic Literature **14:**179
- angel Michael **11:**1490
Righteous Gentiles, *see* ḤASIDEI UMMOT HA-OLAM; RIGHTEOUS OF THE NATIONS
RIGHTEOUSNESS **14:**180
- ethics **6:**934f
- God **7:**669
- Judaism **10:**388
- piety **13:**504
- suffering **14:**135
- *ẓedakah* **16:**961
- *zekhut avot* **16:**976
- *see also:* ZADDIK
RIGHTEOUS OF THE NATIONS **14:**184
- Lithuania **11:**389
- Reviczky, Imre **14:**128
- Yad Vashem **16:**697
- *illus:*
- - text
- *see also:* ḤASIDEI UMMOT HA-OLAM
Right Po'alei Zion (polit. faction) **15:**49
RIGLER, LEO GEORGE **14:**184
- medicine **11:**1202
RĪḤĀNIYYA, AL- (vill., Isr.) **14:**185
- communities **9:**921
Rihut ve-Dekoraẓyah (journ.) **1:**newsp. list
RIJEKA (city, Croatia) **14:**185
Rijk, Esther de Boer van, *see* Boer van Rijk, Esther de
Rijkinstituut voor Oorlogsdocumentatie (archiv., Neth.) **3:**385
Rijl al-ʿAmūd (place, Er. Isr.) **7:**438
Rijswijk (tn., Neth.) **7:**1125
R-i-k-a-m, *see* KIMḤI, JOSEPH
Rikhpah (bot.) **6:**329
Rikhye, General (UNEF comm.) **9:**407
- *illus:*
- - Gaza Strip evacuation **9:**406
RIKLIS, MESHULAM **14:**186
Rikmah, ha- (wk., Ibn Janaḥ), *see Kitāb al-Lumaʿ*
Rikmah, Ha- (wk., Isaac ha-Levi), *see Ha-Rikmah*
Rikmah, ha- (wk., Tibbon), *see Sefer ha-Rikmah*
Riley, William E. **3:**480; **9:**385; **9:**386
- *illus:*
- - Rhodes, April 1949 **3:**479
Riley-Day's Disease, *see* Familial Disautonomia
Rimalt, Elimelekh **8:**1379; **9:**680; **15:**1492
Rimer, Irving **13:**1361
RIMINI (city, It.) **14:**186
- disputation (1447) **11:**873
Rimini, Isaac di Manuele Da **13:**563
Rimmon (bib. fig.) **13:**1609
Rimmon (tn., Er. Isr.), *see* EN-RIMMON
Rimmon (journ., Arg.) **1:**newsp. list
Rimmon (newsp., Isr.) **1:**newsp. list
RIMMON (deity) **14:**186
- Hadad **7:**1040
Rimmon, Valley of (Er. Isr.) **11:**1240ff
Rimmonim (Torah. orn.), *see* Finials
RIMMON-PEREZ (encampment) **14:**186
Rimoc (Rimokh; Mor. fam.), see BENREMOKH
RIMOCH, ASTRUC **14:**187
Rimon (period.) **16:**555
RIMON, JACOB **14:**187
RIMON, JOSEPH ẒEVI **14:**187
Rimon Verlag (publ.) **5:**434; **16:**555
Rīm-Sin (k. Larsa) **16:**1496
Rimsky-Korsakov **12:**659
Rimush (K. Akkad) **2:**493
Rinat Israel Chamber Choir (Isr.)

9:1008
Rināwī Brothers, The 9:1038
RINDFLEISCH (13th cent., knight, Ger.) 14:188
- chronological chart 8:766-767
- massacres 2:800; 4:149
Rindskopf, Joseph Jacob, *see* Ruetten, Joseph Jacob
Ring 11:1041ff
- jewelry 13:1012
- Samaritan marriage 14:746; 14:747
- seal 14:1073
- wedding 15:735
- *illus:*
- - *menorah* on 11:1363
- - wedding rings 5:305; 11:*fcg.* 1067; 16:458
Ring, J. 14:1523
RINGEL, MICHAEL 14:189
RINGELBLUM, EMANUEL (Menahem) 14:189
- Warsaw ghetto 16:348
- synagogue 15:585
Ringelblum Kultur-Tsenter (orgn., Arg.) 3:423
Ringelheim, Helena, *see* Peretz, Helena
Ringer, Benjamin F. 15:68
Ringworm infection (disease) 14:1502
Rinn (loc., Ger.) 2:948
Rinnatyah (mosh., Isr.) 1:place list
Rintel, Moses 11:1277
Riobamba (city, Ec.) 6:359
RIO DE JANEIRO (state, city, Braz.) 14:190
- *see also:* BRAZIL
Rio Grande do Norte (state, Braz.) 4:1327
Rio Grande do Sul (state, Braz.) 2:414; 4:1326ff; 10:46
Riohacha (tn., Colom.) 5:745ff
Riots, anti-Jewish, *see* POGROMS
Ris (meas.) 16:389
Risāla (wk.) 16:1356,1376;
Risālat al-Tanbīh (wk.) 16:1357, 1382
Risālat al-Taqrīb wa al-Tashil (wk.) 16:1357,1382
RISCHIN, MOSES 14:192
Rīsha (qtr., Jer.) 9:1436
Risha (city, Pol.), *see* RZESZOW
RISHONIM (hal. auth.) 14:192
- definition 7:1166
- *ḥiddushim* 8:466ff
- Jewish law periods 12:122
- rabbinical authority 3:910
- responsa 14:85ff
- tosafists 15:1278ff
- *see also:* GAON; POSEKIM
RISHON LE-ZION (city, Isr.) 14:194
- Bilu settlers 4:1001
- Ḥaviv, Avraham Dov 7:1494
- history chart (1882) 8:766-767
- stamps 15:332
- statistics 1:place list
- *illus:*
- - text
- - Bilu veterans 4:1001
- - first orchestra in Er. Isr. 9:1007
- - Mother-and-Child Welfare Clinic 9:987
RISHON LE-ZION (r. tit., Isr.) 14:193
- rabbinate 13:1451
- Sephardim 14:1175
Rishon le-Zion Club (sports orgn., Pal.) 15:294
Rishpe (demon) 5:1528
RISHPON (mosh., Isr.) 14:195
- statistics 1:place list
- *see also:* APOLLONIA
R-i-t-b-a, *see* YOM TOV BEN ABRAHAM ISHBILI
Rite, *see* LITURGY
Ritmeier, C. H. 8:52
Ritova (tn., Lith.) 13:1397
Ritschl, Albrecht 15:1108
RITTENBERG, DAVID 14:195
Rittenberg, Louis 15:318
Ritter, Bernhard Loebel 7:182; 14:350
RITTER, IMMANUEL HEINRICH 14:196
Ritterman, Ignatius 12:1072
Rittermann, Alexander 15:338
Rittner, Edward 10:1500
Ritual bath, *see* MIKVEH
Ritual impurity, *see* PURITY AND IMPURITY, RITUAL
Ritual murder, *see* BLOOD LIBEL
Ritual purity, *see* PURITY AND IMPURITY, RITUAL
Ritual slaughter, *see* SHEḤITAH
Ritual uncleannes, *see* PURITY AND IMPURITY, RITUAL
Ritvo, Samuel 13:1340
Ritz, Al 12:473
Ritz, Harry 12:473
Ritz, Jimmy 12:473
RITZ BROTHERS (comedians) 12:473
Riv'a (coin) 5:721
RIVA (di Trento; tn., It.) 14:196
Rivadabia (tn., Sp.) 12:1452
R-i-v-a-n (tos.), *see* JUDAH BEN NATHAN
Rivarol (weekly) 2:232
Riveles, Benjamin, *see* Rivlin, Benjamin
Riveles, Elijah 14:199
Riveles, Solomon Zalman 14:199
Rivera (fam.) 14:143
Rivera (tn., Arg.) 3:431; 3:432
RIVERA, JACOB RODRIGUEZ 14:196
- slave trade 14:1663
- United States 15:1587
- *illus:* text
Rivera, Maria de 7:853
River Forest (sub., Chicago) 5:415
RIVERS, LARRY 3:609
- *illus:*
- - "Dutch Masters President's Relief" (paint.) 3:638
Riverso, Luis de 5:461
Rivesaltes (internment camp, Fr.) 8:858
Rivet, André 8:52
Rivinus, Tileman Andreas 8:52
RIVISTA ISRAELITICA (period.) 14:197
- Collegio Rabbinico Italiano 5:736
- history 8:563
- Parma 13:122
Rivka'i-Rubin, Israel 13:1505
RIVKES, MOSES BEN NAPHTALI HIRSCH 14:197
- Rivlin family 14:199
Rivkes, Pethaḥiah 14:198
RIVKIN, BORUCH 14:198
RIVKIN, ELLIS 14:198
Rivkin, Mina Borda 14:198
RIVKIND, ISAAC 14:199
- *illus:*
- - Hebrew Pen Club, N.Y. 8:211
- - Hebrew writers' convention, 1943 8:213
- - Histadruth Ivrith of America 13:371
RIVLIN (fam.) 14:199
Rivlin, Benjamin (18/19 cent.) 14:199; 14:200
RIVLIN, ELIEZER 14:200
Rivlin, Elijah Joseph 14:200
RIVLIN, HARRY N. 14:200
Rivlin, Hillel 9:514; 14:200
Rivlin, Isaac Eisik 14:200
RIVLIN, JOSEPH JOEL 14:201
- Koran 10:1199
- Neo-Aramaic studies 12:951
- Zakho 16:921
- *illus:*
- - Koran, Hebrew translation (1963) 10:1195
Rivlin, Moses 14:200
Rivlin, Reuven 14:201
Rivlin, Samuel Moses 14:200
RIVLIN, SHELOMO ZALMAN (19/20 cent.) 14:202
Rivlin, Solomon Zalman (18/19 cent.) 14:199
RIVLIN, YOSEF YIẒḤAK 14:202
Rivlin, Zalman (of Shklov) 7:190
Riv'on ha-Aguddah ha-Zo'otekhnit (period.) 1:newsp. list
Riv'on Handasat Betiḥut (period.) 1:newsp. list
Riv'on Katan (journ.) 1:newsp. list
Riv'on le-Banka'ut (journ.) 1:newsp. list
Riv'on le-Inyenei Missim (journ.) 1:newsp. list
Riv'on le-Khalkalah (journ.) 1:newsp. list
Riv'on le-Matematikah (journ.) 1:newsp. list
Riv'on Merkaz ha-Beniyah ha-Yisre'eli (journ.) 1:newsp. list
Riv'on Mishteret Yisrael (journ.) 1:newsp. list
Riwkin, J.A. 16:1165
Rixheim (tn., Fr.) 2:754
RIZAIEH (tn., Iran) 14:202
- Azerbaijan 3:1005
R-i-ẓ-b-a (tos.), *see* ISAAC BEN ABRAHAM
Rizhinashvili, Itzko (Abraham Isaac) 4:13
Rizius, Paul, *see* RICIUS, PAULUS
RIZPAH (bib. fig.) 14:203
- Abner and 2:87
- concubinage 5:862
- in the Arts 14:917
Rizzi, Paulus, *see* RICIUS, PAULUS
RJF (orgn.), *see* REICHSBUND JUEDISCHER FRONTSOLDATEN
R-m-a (Sp. r.), *see* ARAMA, MEIR BEN ISAAC
Roadacher, R. M. 12:1072
Road networks in Israel
- historical survey 9:377
- Jerusalem highways 9:1493ff
- *illus:*
- - Haifa-Tel Aviv highway 9:836
Road of Valor (Er. Isr.) 9:1493
Roales, Robert, *see* Rolle, Robert
Roan, Anna Princess of 8:52
Roanoke (city, Va.) 16:163
Roash, Hal 12:449
ROBACK, ABRAHAM AARON 14:203
Robbery, *see* THEFT AND ROBBERY
ROBBINS, JEROME 14:204
- theater 15:1060
Robb-Rosenfarb (Narbutt), Ignacy 13:775; 16:353
ROBERT, LUDWIG 14:204
Robert, Rahel, *see* VARNHAGEN, RAHEL
Robert le Frison 9:1572
Robert of Anjou 2:475; 3:227; 13:1260
ROBERT OF READING 14:205
- proselytization 13:1189
Robert of Soest 15:74
Robert II the Pious (k., Fr.) 7:13
Roberts, David 9:1580
Robertson, F. 14:749
Robertson, James 8:52
Robertson, William 8:52
Robes, Abraham 15:305
Robespierre, Maximilien François Marie Isidore de 2:755
Robin (zool.) 6:30
Robinson (city, Ill.,) 8:1256
Robinson, Albert 6:308
Robinson, Benjamin 5:114
Robinson, Charles Phineas 6:308; 12:845; 13:820
Robinson, D. M. 3:840; 12:1130
ROBINSON, EDWARD (orient.) 14:205
- Jerusalem survey 9:1521ff
- maps of Erez Israel 11:930
- *illus:* text
ROBINSON, EDWARD G. (act.) 14:205
ROBINSON, JACOB 1:36; 14:207
ROBINSON, NEHEMIAH 14:207
Robinson, T. H. 12:1332
Robinson, Victor 11:1198
Robinson's Arch (bridge remains, Jer.) 15:964
- *illus:*
- - front view 9:1531
- - Mazar's excavations 9:1534
- - view from the South 14:205
ROBISON, SOPHIA 14:208
Robitschek, L. A. 6:1215; 9:1262
Robitshek (fam.) 12:37
ROBLES, ANTONIO RODRIGUES 14:208
Robles, Jacob 12:995
Robles Case (Eng.) 14:208
Roblik, Elias 8:52
Roborough, Baron, *see* LOPES
Robot, Alexandru 14:422
Robota, Rosa 5:561
Robson, Jeremy 6:785
ROBSON, WILLIAM ALEXANDER 14:208
Robustellus, J. W. 8:52
Roby, Naphtali Eliahu, *see* RAHABI, NAPHTALI ELIAHU
ROCAMORA, ISAAC DE 14:209
Rocamora, Solomon 14:209
Rocamora, Vincente de, *see* ROCAMORA, ISAAC DE
Rocca, Moses Della, *see* Basola, Moses (schol., 16th cent.)
Rocca, Solomon 16:907
ROCHBERG, GEORGE 12:704
ROCHELLE, LA (city, Fr.) 14:209
ROCHESTER (tn., Eng.) 14:209
Rochester (city, Minn.) 12:39
ROCHESTER (city, N.Y.) 14:209
- museum 12:551
- United States 15:1596
- *illus:*
- - text
- - Temple B'rith Kodesh, Ark 3:627
ROCHMAN, LEIB 14:211
- *illus:*
- - fellow Yiddish writers 7:616; 16:821
Rock, Irvin 13:1344
Rockaway (loc., N.Y.) 12:1108
Rock Bunting (zool.) 6:30
Rockefeller, John D., Jr. 14:212
ROCKEFELLER MUSEUM (Jer.) 14:212
- Jerusalem 9:1473
- Six-Day War 14:1630
- *illus:*
- - text
- - aerial view 9:*fcg.* 1534
- - general view 3:350
ROCKER (fam.) 14:213
Rocker, Henry A. 14:213
ROCKER, RUDOLF 14:213
- socialism 15:34
- Toronto 15:1262
Rocker, Samuel 14:213
ROCKET (bot.) 14:213
- plant list 13:623
- *illus:* text
Rockford (city, Ill.) 8:1256

Rock Island (city, Ill.) **8:**1255
Rockland (city, Me.) **11:**782
ROCKLAND COUNTY (N.Y.) **14:**214
Rock of Ages (hymn), *see* MA'OZ ẒUR
Rock Springs (city, Wyo.) **16:**680
Rockville (tn., Md.) **16:**358
- *illus:*
- - community foundation complex **16:**357
Rockwell, Lincoln **12:**954
Rocky Mount (city, N.C.) **12:**1220
Rodal, Leon **10:**990; **16:**351
RODANIM (inhabitants, Rhodes) **14:**215
- Javan **9:**1301
RODA RODA, ALEXANDER **14:**215
- *illus:* text
Rodblat, Josef **8:**1289
Rode, Leif S. **14:**934
RODE, WALTHER **14:**216
Rodef Shalom (syn., Pa.) **13:**371; **15:**620
- *illus:*
- - interior **15:**622
RODELL, FRED M. **14:**216
- law **10:**1505
Rodenberg, J. (Eng.) **14:**1576
RODENBERG, JULIUS (Ger.) **14:**216
Rodensky, Shmuel **12:**462
Rodeph Shalom (syn., N.Y.) **12:**1071*ff*
Rodeph Shalom (syn., Pa.), *see* Rodef Shalom
Rodericus, Joannus, *see* AMATUS LUSITANUS
RODGERS, RICHARD **14:**216
- theater **15:**1059
Rodin, Auguste (sculp.) **14:**267
- *illus:*
- - "Adam" **14:**267
RODIN, ELISHA **14:**217
- *illus:* text
RODKER, JOHN **14:**218
RODKINSON, MICHAEL LEVI **14:**218
- Talmud in English **15:**768
Rodobrana (Fascist orgn., Cz.) **15:**1427
ROD OF AARON **14:**218
- inscription **16:**662
- *illus:*
- - Aaron performing miracle **12:**379
- *see also:* AARON
ROD OF MOSES **14:**219
- Artapanus **12:**391
- Moses **12:**374
Rodosto (loc., Turk.) **14:**1244
Rodrigo (archbp., Sp.) **15:**1202
Rodrigo (astron., Port.) **3:**788
Rodrigo de Marcardo **15:**1205
Rodrigues (fam.) **3:**1004
Rodrigues (fam. name), *see also* Rodriguez
Rodrigues, Abraham (Fr.) **4:**1245
Rodrigues, Abraham Ḥayyim Raphael **11:**817; **13:**1483
RODRIGUES, BARTHOLOMEW **14:**219
- India **8:**1356
Rodrigues, Benjamin Olinde **14:**667,716; **15:**25
RODRIGUES, DIONISIUS (Diniz) **14:**219
- Brudo, Manuel **4:**1414
Rodrigues, Enrique, *see* Cohen, Samuel
Rodrigues, Felipo, *see* Montalto, Elijah
Rodrigues, Gomez **14:**219
Rodrigues, Isaac **4:**1245
Rodrigues, Joseph **4:**1246
Rodrigues, Lorenço, *see* Lindo, Isaac
Rodrigues d'Evora (fam.) **4:**172; **15:**270; **15:**1301ff
Rodrigues Pereira, S. **11:**1569
Rodrigues Vega, Manuel, *see* Vega, Manuel Rodrigues
Rodriguez (fam.) **12:**817
Rodriguez (fam. name), *see also* Rodrigues
Rodriguez, Abrabao **8:**1392
Rodriguez, Abraham (r., It.), *see* Rodrigues, Abraham Ḥayyim Raphael
Rodriguez, Abraham (Mor.) **14:**682
Rodriguez, Daniel **15:**289
Rodriguez, Diogo Rois, *see* Rodriguez, Abrabao
Rodriguez, Dionysius, *see* RODRIGUES, DIONISIUS
Rodriguez, Domingo **8:**1394; **13:**395
Rodriguez, Eugène **14:**667
Rodriguez, Francisco **8:**1395
Rodriguez, Jorge **8:**1394; **13:**395; **15:**270
Rodríguez, Luis **5:**1146
Rodriguez, Miguel **12:**1273
Rodriguez, Raphael Gil **8:**1393; **8:**1394; **11:**1455
Rodriguez, Ricardo **11:**1202
Rodriguez de Castro, José **8:**52
Rodriguez Solis (fam.), *see* Solis, Rodrigues
Rodriguez Solis, Jorge, *see* Rodriguez, Jorge
Rodulphus, Glaber, *see* RAOUL GLABER
RODZINSKY, ARTUR **12:**704
ROEDELHEIM (tn., Ger.) **14:**219
- Homburg press **8:**943
- Pentateuch **4:**839
Roedelsheim, Eliezer Zussman **2:**802
ROEDERER, COUNT PIERRE LOUIS **14:**220
Ro'eh ha-Ḥeshbon (journ.) **1:**newsp. list
ROEHRICHT, REINHOLD **14:**221
Ro'eh Yisrael Ezon Enkat Ẓonekha (piyyut) **2:**295
Roeker, Samuel **5:**609
ROESSLER, CARL **14:**221
ROEST, MAYER **14:**221
- *haskamot* **7:**1453
Roest, Rust, *see* ELKAN, SOPHIE
Roettingen (tn., Ger.) **8:**1043
Roey, Joseph van **4:**421
Roeytenberg, Effraim, *see* FIMA
Rofe, Hertz Levi, *see* Lemon, Hartog de
Rofe, Isaac **11:**1262
Rofe, Meir **14:**1245
Rofe, Samuel **7:**310
Rofeh, Aaron ben Moses **13:**1107
ROGACHEV (city, Belor.) **14:**221
Rogachover, The, *see* ROZIN, JOSEPH
Rogaler, Elijah **16:**1348
Rogasen (tn., Pol.), *see* Rogozno
ROGATIN (city, Ukr.) **14:**222
- Shabbateanism **14:**1251
Rogel, Spring of (Jer.), *see* EN ROGEL
Roger II (Norman ldr.) **15:**1436
Roger, E. (trav.) **9:**1441
Roger of Wendover **16:**259
ROGERS, BERNARD **12:**704
- Isaiah cantata **9:**70
Rogers, Clara Kathleen **12:**682
ROGERS, ERNESTO **3:**365
Rogers, Henry C. **13:**1361
Rogers, John (Chr. Hebr.) **8:**52
Rogers, William **9:**418ff; **14:**1640
ROGINSKI, SIMON ZALMANOVICH **14:**222
Roglit (mosh., Isr.) **1:**place list; **2:**312
ROGOFF, HARRY (Hillel) **14:**223
Rogoff Institute for Medical Research (Isr.) **15:**926
Rogosz, Józef **13:**800
Rogovin, Saul **15:**301
Rogovsky, Eduardo **3:**421
Rogoznizki, Gedalya, *see* ALLON, GEDALYA
Rogozno (tn., Pol.) **15:**705
Rohaček, J. **4:**885
Rohan, Anna Princess of, *see* Roan, Anna Princess of
Rohan, Michael **9:**412
- *illus:*
- - trial **9:**638
Rohatiner, Judah **11:**451
Rohatyn (city, Ukr.), *see* ROGATIN
RÓHEIM, GÉZA **14:**223
- anthropology **3:**39
ROHLING, AUGUST **14:**224
- anti-Jewish accusations **3:**199
- Catholic anti-Semitism **5:**540
- chronological chart **8:**766-767
- Delitzsch, Franz **5:**1475
Rohrbacher, René F. **8:**52
Rohrlich, Radu, *see* COSAȘU, RADU
Roht, Eberhard Rudolf **8:**52
Roir, Irving, *see* Roth, Irving
ROITMAN, DAVID **7:**1550
- music **12:**661
Roiyo, Abraham **15:**1353
ROJAS, FERNANDO DE **14:**224
- Toledo **15:**1206
Rojse of Lvov **12:**748
Rojzenfeld, Michal **16:**351
Rokach (fam. name), *see also under* Roke'aḥ
ROKACH, ELEAZAR **14:**225
- Rumania **14:**399
- Zionism **16:**1132
Rokach, Isaac **14:**226
Rokach, Israel **14:**226
- *illus:*
- - Muni, Paul, and **12:**520
- - Va'ad Le'ummi meeting **16:**50
ROKACH, SHIMON **14:**226
- Tel Aviv-Jaffa **15:**919
Rokeach, Milton **13:**1345
Roke'aḥ (bk.), *see Sefer ha-Roke'aḥ*
Roke'aḥ, Aaron, *see* Aaron of Belz
ROKEAḤ, DAVID **14:**226
Roke'aḥ, Eleazar, *see* ROKACH, ELEAZAR
Rokeaḥ, Eleazar (of Amsterdam) **4:**452; **9:**513
Roke'aḥ, Eleazar ben Aryeh Loeb **5:**1587
Roke'ah, Eleazar ben Judah, *see* ELEAZAR BEN JUDAH OF WORMS
Roke'aḥ, Issachar Dov, *see* Issachar Dov of Belz
Roke'aḥ, Joshua, *see* Joshua of Belz
Roke'aḥ, Mas'ud **13:**93
Roke'aḥ, Shalom of Belz **4:**452; **16:**1328
ROKISKIS (city, Lith.) **14:**226
Rokovsky, Abraham Abba **13:**135
Rol, P., *see* ROSENTHAL, PAVEL
Rola (newsp.) **9:**1336
Roland, Ida **5:**993
ROLAND-MANUEL **12:**704
Rolandus, Hadrianus, *see* RELAND, HADRIAN
Rolduc (loc., Neth.) **12:**973
Roli (medal.), *see* Lippman
Rolland, Romain **7:**144
Rolle, Robert **8:**52
Roller, Ḥayyim Mordechai **15:**1151
ROLNICK, JOSEPH **14:**227
Roloff, Bernard **13:**1361
Rom (J. cmty.) **5:**1239
Romaine, William **8:**54
Roma (deity) **9:**1406
Romaine, Isaac **15:**411
ROMAN (tn., Mold.) **14:**227
Rumania **14:**387
ROMAN, JACOB BEN ISAAC **14:**228
- linguistics **16:**1382
Roman Catholic Church (Isr.) **9:**296; **9:**912ff
Romance (lang.), *see* LADINO
Romance (lit.) **11:**358
Romancero (lit.) **10:**1350; **14:**1169; **14:**1176
- *scores:*
- - Eastern and Western traditions **10:**1352,1353
Roman de Renart **3:**21
ROMANELLI, SAMUEL AARON **14:**228
- Italian literature **9:**1110
- travels **15:**1350
ROMAN EMPERORS **14:**229
- sages' evidence **14:**651
Roman Empire
- General
- - anti-Semitism **3:**89
- - apocalyptic writings **3:**180
- - codex, use of **16:**1416
- - condition of Jews **14:**244
- - Hellenism **8:**292ff
- - history chart **8:**766-767
- - Jewish calendar **5:**49
- - magic **11:**706
- - Meir's views on **11:**1241
- - moneylending **12:**253
- - population **13:**870
- - resistance literature **8:**301
- - taxation **15:**838ff
- History **8:**643ff; **8:**652
- - African Jews **2:**331
- - Alexandrian martyrs **2:**594
- - Augustus' policies **3:**852
- - Babylonians **16:**1512
- - Bar Kokhba Revolt **4:**228; **4:**231
- - Bethar **4:**733
- - Egyptian Jews **6:**488ff
- - Ereẓ Israel **2:**394ff; **9:**237ff
- - Herod I **8:**375ff
- - Hyrcanus, John **8:**1147
- - Jerusalem **9:**1393
- - Jesus **10:**12
- - Josephus Flavius **10:**251
- - Judah ha-Nasi **10:**367ff
- - procurator **13:**1117
- - Syria **15:**639
- - Titus **15:**1168ff
- - warfare **16:**280
- - zealots **16:**947
- Identifications
- - Amalek **2:**791
- - Armilus **3:**476
- - Edom **6:**378ff
- - Esau **6:**858
- - Kittim **10:**1081; **13:**332
- - swine **13:**507
- *illus:*
- - Diaspora (map) **8:**643
- - Masada camps **11:**1088
- - Masada siege ramp **11:**1079
Romania (Js., Byz. Emp.), *see* ROMANIOTS
Romania (rep.), *see* RUMANIA
Romanian rite (litur.) **11:**398; **13:**987
Romanin, Aaron **13:**12
ROMANIN, SAMUELE **14:**230
ROMANIN JACUR, LEONE **14:**231
ROMANIOTS (Js., Byz. Emp.) **14:**231
- Chalcis **5:**329
- masoretic accents **11:**1110
- ordination disputes **13:**1449
- Ottoman Empire **16:**1530
Roman Law, *see* Law, Roman
ROMAN LITERATURE **14:**232
Romano, Albert (Egy.) **5:**32
Romano, Alberto (Bul.) **16:**1108
Romano, Emanuel **7:**619

Romano, Isaac Fresco **12:**625
Romano, Joseph, *see* Eliano, Vittorio
Romano, Judah **4:**1238; **13:**666
ROMANO, JUDAH BEN MOSES BEN DANIEL **14:**237
- translations **15:**1322
ROMANO, MARCO **14:**237
Romano, Menahem ben Abraham **14:**872; **16:**883
Romano, Mercado **11:**875
ROMANO, SAMUEL **14:**238
- children's literature **5:**457
- Yugoslav literature **16:**889
Romano, Solomon, *see* ELIANO, GIOVANNI BATTISTA
Romanoff, P. **12:**544
ROMANOS MELODOS **14:**238
- Byzantine hymnology **4:**1553
Romanowski, Mieczyslaw **13:**799
Roman Pomaria (city, Alg.), *see* TLEMCEN
Roman Rite (litur.)
- liturgy **11:**398ff
- *maḥzor* **11:**731
- prayer books **13:**987
- Rome **14:**245
- *illus:*
- - masoretic accents **9:**1099
- - Sabbath evening service **11:**395
ROMAN-RONETTI, MOÏSE **14:**238
Romans, *see* Roman Empire
ROMANUS I LECAPENUS (Byz. emp.) **14:**239
- Apulian Jewry **3:**226
- Greece **7:**872
- Otranto **12:**1521
- *Vision of Daniel* **5:**1290
Roman War (Er. Isr.), *see* Jewish War
ROMBERG, MORITZ HEINRICH **14:**239
Romberg, Rachel, *see* Berdyczewski, Rachel
ROMBERG, SIGMUND **14:**240
- *illus:*
- - *Rosalie* rehearsal **16:**1018
Rombro, Jacob, *see* KRANTZ, PHILIP
ROME (city, It.) **14:**240
- *Contents:*
- - The Classical Period **14:**240
- - In Talmudic Literature **14:**242
- - The Christian Empire **14:**244
- - Scholarship **14:**245
- - Papal Legislation **14:**246
- - The Renaissance Community **14:**248
- - The Counter-Reformation and the Ghetto period **14:**248
- - Freedom, Reaction, and Emancipation **14:**251
- - Hebrew Printing **14:**252
- - Holocaust Period **14:**252
- - Contemporary Period **14:**253
- General
- - calendar **16:**1262
- - emperor list **8:**766-767
- - Ereẓ Israel fruit imports **16:**1273
- - Greek inscriptions **8:**297
- - history chart (1793) **8:**766-767
- - Song of Songs **15:**147
- - Sibylline Books **14:**1490
- Anti-Semitism **3:**95f; **8:**911
- - annual races **2:**569
- - Benedict VIII **4:**481
- - expulsions **6:**1069
- - Inquisition **8:**1399
- - papal bulls **4:**1496
- - Talmud, burning of **15:**770
- Cultural life
- - archives **3:**383; **3:**387
- - art **3:**521; **5:**249
- - libraries **11:**193
- - Matya ben Heresh academy **2:**202
- - museums **12:**544
- Jewish community
- - *archisynagogos* **3:**335
- - Babylonian Jewry **6:**1023
- - Cappadocian Jews **5:**151
- - debt, laws of **6:**1008
- - Diaspora settlement **6:**10; **6:**13ff; **8:**640
- - fiscus judaicus **6:**1325
- - Judaizers **10:**397
- - medieval period **9:**1120
- - *menorah* **11:**1369
- - Nathan of Gaza **14:**1239
- - special Purim **13:**1399
- - synagogue **15:**582
- - taxes **15:**838ff
- - Tunisian trade **15:**1432
- Trades and Professions **16:**1287
- - banking **4:**173
- - glass industry **7:**607ff
- - Hebrew printing **8:**1320ff
- *illus:*
- - Arch of Titus **11:**1355; **15:**1167
- - ghetto **10:**83
- - Jewish cemetery **5:**271
- - Jewish Museum **12:**548
- - Monteverde Catacomb epitaph **2:**723
- - Patacca **9:**1106
- - Pierleone tower **2:**917
- - Via Appia catacomb **5:**249-252
- - Vigna Randanini sarcophagus **11:**1361
- - Villa Torlonia catacombs **9:**1582; **11:**1361; **15:**569
Rome (city, Ga.) **7:**429
ROME, DAVID **14:**254
Rome, Harold **15:**1059
Rome, Howard P. **13:**1340
Rome and Jerusalem (bk.) **8:**432ff
Rome-Babylon (leg. city) **2:**36
Romemah (dist., Haifa) **7:**1139
Romemah (qtr., Jer.) **9:**1472
- early settlers **9:**328
- Jerusalem topography **9:**1515; **12:**482
Römer, Maria Barbara Lehmann, von **8:**54
ROMM (fam.) **14:**255
- Abele Poswoler **2:**129
- copyright dispute **7:**1465
- Vilna **16:**148
Romm, Baruch ben Joseph **14:**255; **16:**148
Romm, David **14:**255; **16:**148
Romm, Deborah **14:**255; **16:**148
Romm, Ḥayyim Jacob **16:**148
Romm, Joseph Reuben **14:**255
- *illus:*
- - *Shabbat*, title page **14:**255
Romm, Menahem Mannes **14:**255; **16:**148
Romm, Mikhail **12:**456; **15:**299
Romm, Moses **15:**210
ROMNY (city, Ukr.) **14:**256
Romulus (leg. fig.) **3:**476
Romulus (Lat. writ.) **3:**21
Ron, J. **8:**54
RONA, PETER **14:**256
RÓNAI, JÁNOS **14:**257
- Zionism **16:**1120
- *illus:*
- - First Zionist Congress **16:**1165
Ronald, Sir Landon **14:**432
RONALL, JOACHIM O. **1:**36
Roncalli, Angelo Giuseppe (pope), *see* JOHN XXIII
Ronetti-Roman, Moïse, *see* ROMAN-RONETTI, MOÏSE
Ronkel, Zalman **16:**395
Ronli-Riklis, Shalom **12:**669
Ronnow, M. **8:**54
Ronsburg, Bezalel **2:**782; **7:**80
Ronsperg (vill., Bohem.), *see* POBEZOVICE NA SUMAVE
Roobot (tn., Er. Isr.), *see* REHOBOTH
Roodepoort (tn., Trans.) **15:**1340
Rooles, Robert, *see* Rolle, Robert
Room, Abraham **12:**456
Roorda, Taco **8:**54
Roos (U.S. fam.) **14:**834
Roos (schol., Holl.) **16:**37
Roos, S. H. de **15:**1479
Roos, Lawrence **14:**666
Roosevelt, Anna Eleanor **14:**258; **16:**865
- *illus:*
- - Ben-Gurion, and **14:**258
ROOSEVELT, FRANKLIN DELANO **14:**257
- Abelson, Paul **2:**63
- Brandeis, Louis Dembitz **4:**1296
- chronological chart **8:**766-767
- Cremieux Decree **2:**617
- Evian conference **6:**987
- Holocaust **8:**888
- Litvinov, Maxim Maximovich **11:**406
- New Deal **8:**741
- refugees, Jewish **14:**29
- U.S. **15:**1629ff
- Zionism **16:**1088
- *illus:*
- - Lehman, Herbert H., and **10:**1578
ROOSEVELT, THEODORE **14:**258
Root (Heb. gram.) **8:**103
ROPCZYCE (Ropshits; tn., Pol.) **14:**259
Rope (meas. instr.), *see Ḥevel*
ROPSHITSER, NAPHTALI ẒEVI **14:**259
- dynasties **1:**ḥas. table
Ropshitz, Moses Ḥasid of, *see* Moses Ḥasid of Ropshitz
Rosa, Dela (fam., Alg.) **2:**614
Rosa, Ḥayyim della **10:**553
Rosa, Jose de la **5:**222
Rosa, Moses da, *see* PROVENÇAL, MOSES BEN ABRAHAM
Rosa, Rahamim de la **14:**1367
Rosa, Salvator **14:**785
Rosales (fam.), *see* ROSANES
ROSALÈS, JACOB **14:**260
- family **14:**261
ROSALES, JACOB HEBRAEUS (Immanuel Bocarro Frances) **14:**260
Rosalis (fam.) **14:**1080
ROSANES (fam.) **14:**261
- *aliyah* **9:**513
Rosanes, Abraham **13:**1109
Rosanes, Abraham Abele **14:**261
Rosanes, Abraham ben Ḥayyim **14:**261
Rosanes, Abraham ben Israel **14:**262
Rosanes, Abraham ben Joseph **14:**261
Rosanes, Abraham ben Meir **14:**261; **14:**262
Rosanes, Isaac ben David **14:**261
Rosanes, Isaac ben Ḥayyim **14:**261
Rosanes, Jacob **14:**261
Rosanes, Judah **14:**263
ROSANES, JUDAH BEN SAMUEL **14:**262
- family **14:**261
Rosanes, Judith **14:**263
Rosanes, Mordecai **14:**262
ROSANES, SOLOMON ABRAHAM **14:**263
- family **14:**262
ROSANES, ẒEVI HIRSCH BEN ISSACHAR BERISH **14:**263
Rosani, Rita **15:**1393
Rosanove, Joan **10:**1493
Rosarier Lebn (period.) **14:**264
ROSARIO (city, Arg.) **14:**263
- Argentine **3:**414ff
Rosbrow, James M. **16:**534
Roschewski, Kurt **13:**1049
Rose (U.S. fam.) **12:**36
ROSE (bot.) **14:**265
- flowers **6:**1366
- oil **12:**1352
- plant list **13:**623
- *illus:*
- - Mizra, cultivation for export **9:**781
ROSE, ALEX **14:**266
ROSÉ, ARNOLD JOSEF **12:**705
ROSE, ARNOLD MARSHALL **14:**266
ROSE, BILLY **14:**266
Rose, Carl **5:**220
Rose, Emanuel **13:**911
ROSE, ERNESTINE POTOVSKY **14:**267
- *illus:* text
ROSE, HERMAN **3:**609
Rose, Louis **14:**829
Rose, Mauri **15:**300
ROSE, MAURICE **14:**268
- military **11:**1552
Rose, Max **12:**1526; **15:**205
Rose, Peter **15:**68
Rose, Seymour **12:**1295
Rose, William **14:**267
Rose Garden (Jer.) **9:**1554; **14:**265
Rose Gottlieb, Polly **14:**267
Roselle (tn., N.J.) **15:**1534
Roseman, James **15:**301
Rosemberg (r., It.) **15:**897
ROSEN, ABRAHAM **14:**268
Rosen, Abraham Aryeh **14:**270
Rosen, Albert **15:**301
Rosen, Goodwin **15:**301
ROSEN, JOSEPH A. (U.S.) **14:**269
ROSEN, JOSEPH BEN ISAAC (Rus.) **14:**269
Rosen, Kopul **6:**450
ROSEN, MATHIAS **14:**270
- Warsaw **16:**338
ROSEN, MOSES **14:**270
- *illus:*
- - text
- - Choir Synagogue, Bucharest **14:**411
ROSEN, PINḤAS **14:**271
- Declaration of Independence **5:**1452
- *illus:*
- - proclamation of the State of Israel **4:**513
ROSENAK, LEOPOLD **14:**271
Rosenau, Helen **3:**650
Rosenau, Milton J. **11:**1202
ROSENBACH, ABRAHAM SIMON WOLF **14:**271
- American Jewish Historical Society **2:**827
Rosenbach, Hesel **15:**635
Rosenbach, Meier **14:**272
Rosenbach, Ottomar **11:**1197
Rosenbach, Philip **14:**272
Rosenbaum, Abraham **5:**606
Rosenbaum, Borge, *see* BORGE, VICTOR
Rosenbaum, Daniel, *see* RANSCHBURG, BEZALEL BEN JOEL
Rosenbaum, Daniel **15:**790
Rosenbaum, Gershon **14:**273
Rosenbaum, Hercel, *see* DRZEWIECKI, HENRYK
Rosenbaum, Jeremiah ben Isaac, *see* MATTERSDORF, JEREMIAH BEN ISAAC
Rosenbaum, Judith, *see* Grunfeld, Judith
Rosenbaum, Mendel **15:**29
Rosenbaum, Milton **13:**1340
ROSENBAUM, MORRIS **14:**272
ROSENBAUM, MOSES HAYYIM

LITS **14:**273
Rosenbaum, Pinḥas **14:**273
Rosenbaum, Samuel **14:**273
ROSENBAUM, SEMYON (Shimshon) **14:**273
Rosenbaum, William **15:**314
Rosenberg (U.S. fam.) **5:**411
Rosenberg, Aaron **15:**307
ROSENBERG, ABRAHAM (lab. ldr.) **14:**274
ROSENBERG, ABRAHAM ḤAYYIM (writ.) **14:**274
- encyclopaedia **6:**734
Rosenberg, Adam **16:**1165
Rosenberg, Adolf **15:**1012
ROSENBERG, ALFRED **14:**275
- euthanasia **16:** 1332
- Nazi ideology **8:**737
- *illus:*
- - Nuremberg Trial **16:**289
Rosenberg, Allen P. **15:**312
ROSENBERG, ANNA M. **14:**276
ROSENBERG, ARTHUR **14:**276
Rosenberg, Benjamin (art.), *see* BENN, BEN
Rosenberg, Benjamin (pub. fig., Austr.) **11:**1285
Rosenberg, Bernard **15:**68
Rosenberg, Charley **15:305**
Rosenberg, Dave **15:**306
Rosenberg, Ethel **14:**280
ROSENBERG, EUGENE **14:**277
Rosenberg, Harris **16:**112
ROSENBERG, ISAAC (poet) **14:**277
- Gertler, Mark **7:**521
Rosenberg, Isaac (orgn. ldr., N.Y.) **12:**1072
ROSENBERG, ISRAEL (r.) **14:**278
Rosenberg, Jack **15:**635
Rosenberg, Jacob **3:**650
ROSENBERG, JAMES NAUMBURG **14:**278
Rosenberg, Julius **14:**280
Rosenberg, Lev Samuilovich, *see* BAKST, LEON
ROSENBERG, LOUIS **14:**279
ROSENBERG, LUDWIG **14:**279
- trade unions **7:**500
Rosenberg, Maurice **10:**1502
Rosenberg, Miles **16:**35
Rosenberg, Phil, *see* Rosenberg, Charley
Rosenberg, Ryuwen **5:**497
Rosenberg, S. (18/19th cent., art.) **2:**171
Rosenberg, Samuel (art.) **13:**570
Rosenberg, Sámuel (publ.), *see* Révai, Sámuel
Rosenberg, Siegmund **4:**306
ROSENBERG, STUART E. **1:**36; **14:**279
- historiography **8:**568
Rosenberg, William Samuel, *see* ROSE, BILLY
ROSENBERG CASE (U.S.) **14:**280
- *illus:* text
Rosenberger, Erwin **16:**445
Rosenbergius (Chr. Hebr.) **8:**54
ROSENBLATT, BERNARD ABRAHAM **14:**281
ROSENBLATT, H. **14:**281
Rosenblatt, John (polit.) **12:**1378
Rosenblatt, John J. (r.) **16:**633
ROSENBLATT, JOSEF (ḥazzan) **14:**282
Rosenblatt, Joseph (jur.) **5:**1035
ROSENBLATT, MORDECAI BEN MENAHEM **14:**282
ROSENBLATT, SAMUEL **14:**282
ROSENBLATT, SOL ARIEH **14:**283
Rosenblatt, Uri **11:**429
Rosenblatt, Yossele, *see* ROSENBLATT, JOSEF
Rosenblatt, Ẓevi **3:**471; **9:**1181
Rosenbloom, Celia Neumark **14:**283
Rosenbloom, Charles **14:**283
Rosenbloom, J.R. **12:**1274
Rosenbloom, Maxie **15:**305
Rosenbloom, Paul C. **6:**465
ROSENBLOOM, SOLOMON **14:**283
Rosenblueth, Felix, *see* ROSEN, PINḤAS
Rosenblueth, Ḥayyim, *see* ROSENBLATT, H.
Rosenblum, Jacob **15:**329
Rosenblum, Max **15:**635
Rosenblum, Naphtali Herzl **5:**1455; **10:**92; **16:**727
Rosenblum, Noah **15:**166
ROSENBLUM, SIGMUND GEORGIEVICH **14:**283
Rosenbluth, Len **15:**303
ROSENBUSCH, KARL HARRY FERDINAND **14:**284
Rosenbusch, Maximilian **15:**821
ROSENDALE, SIMON WOLFE **14:**284
Rosenfeld (U.S. fam.) **5:**411
Rosenfeld, Abraham **14:**1134
ROSENFELD, AHARON **14:**284
Rosenfeld, Albert A. **15:**313
Rosenfeld, Fanny **12:**1367; **15:**316
Rosenfeld, Henry **3:**39
Rosenfeld, Isaac **15:**1577
Rosenfeld, Joseph Eleazar **8:**798
Rosenfeld, Lev Borisovich, *see* KAMENEV, LEV BORISOVICH
ROSENFELD, MORRIS (poet) **14:**285
- socialism **15:**34
- *illus:* text
Rosenfeld, Morris (phot.) **13:**484
Rosenfeld, N.K. **12:**1073
Rosenfeld, Otto, *see* RANK, OTTO
ROSENFELD, PAUL **14:**286
ROSENFELD, SAMUEL **14:**286
Rosenfeld, Sándor Friedrich, *see* RODA RODA, ALEXANDER
ROSENFELD, YONA **14:**286
Rosenfield, Isadore **3:**361
Rosenhayn (vill., N.J.) **12:**1029; **16:**157
ROSENHEAD, LOUIS **14:**287
Rosenheck, S. **16:**1165
ROSENHEIM, ARTHUR **5:**387
ROSENHEIM, JACOB **14:**287
- Agudat Israel **2:**423
- Hirsch, S.R. **8:**514
ROSENHEIM, MAX (Leonard), BARON **14:**288
ROSENHEIM, OTTO **14:**288
Rosenkilde, Adolph **14:**932
Rosenkranz, Abraham Ẓevi **13:**1111; **16:**148
ROSENMAN, SAMUEL IRVING **14:**288
Rosenmann (r., Pol.) **4:**807
Rosenmann, Moses **4:**1556
ROSENMUELLER, ERNST FRIEDRICH KARL **14:**289
- Hebraists **8:**54
- Isaiah authorship **9:**45
Rosenn, Max **16:**516
ROSENNE, SHABTAI **14:**289
- *illus:*
- - Armistice Agreements, 1949 **3:**481-482; **9:**375
- - Rhodes, April 1949 **3:**479
Rosenroth, C. Knorr von, *see* KNORR VON ROSENROTH, CHRISTIAN
ROSENSAFT, JOSEF **14:**290
- Bergen-Belsen **4:**611
ROSENSOHN, ETTA LASKER **14:**290
- Lasker family **10:**1435
Rosenstein, Chaim David **6:**986
Rosenstein, Sami, *see* TZARA, TRISTAN
Rosenstiel, Lewis **4:**1301
Rosenstock (fam.) **14:**834
Rosenstock, Anthony **16:**163
Rosenstock, Joseph **10:**463
Rosenstock, M. (hist.) **8:**569
Rosenstock, Moritz (educ.) **14:**290
Rosenstock, Samuel **5:**56
ROSENSTOCK-HUESSY, EUGEN **14:**290
- Rosenzweig disputation **6:**98ff; **14:**299ff
- sociology **15:**65
Rosenthal, Aaron **12:**1521
Rosenthal, Albert **14:**295
Rosenthal, Anna **14:**296
Rosenthal, Arthur J. **13:**1372
Rosenthal, Sir Charles **11:**1554
Rosenthal, Elaine V. **15:**308
Rosenthal, Eliezer, *see* ROSENTHAL, LESER
Rosenthal, Elijah **14:**295
ROSENTHAL, ERICH **14:**292
ROSENTHAL, ERWIN **14:**292
Rosenthal, E.S. **14:**987
ROSENTHAL, FERDINAND **14:**292
ROSENTHAL, FRANZ **14:**292
Rosenthal, Baron Georg **4:**975; **14:**294
Rosenthal, Gyula, *see* Rozsavolgyi, Gyula
ROSENTHAL, HERMAN **14:**293
Rosenthal, Hershel **4:**809
Rosenthal, Isaac Jacob, *see* ROSENTHAL, ERWIN
Rosenthal, Jean **15:**1059
Rosenthal, Joe **13:**484
ROSENTHAL, JUDAH **14:**293
ROSENTHAL, LEON (Judah Leib) **14:**293
- Society for the Promotion of Culture among Russian Jews **15:**58ff
ROSENTHAL, LESER **14:**294
- book collection **4:**1239; **4:**973; **4:**975
Rosenthal, Litmann **16:**1165
Rosenthal, Louis **4:**148
ROSENTHAL, LUDWIG A. **14:**294
Rosenthal, M. (r., Aust.) **4:**138
ROSENTHAL, MANUEL (Emmanuel) **12:**705
Rosenthal, Mark Mordecai, *see* ROZSAVOLGYI, MARK
ROSENTHAL, MAX (art.) **14:**295
Rosenthal, Max (indus., Ger.) **14:**297
Rosenthal, Medem **4:**1501
Rosenthal, Mór **4:**884
Rosenthal, Moritz **8:**1081
Rosenthal, Moses (r., U.S.) **11:**501
Rosenthal, Moses (maskil, Rus.) **14:**293
ROSENTHAL, NAPHTALI **14:**295
Rosenthal, Newman H. **3:**886; **11:**1283
ROSENTHAL, PAVEL (Pinḥas) **14:**296
ROSENTHAL, PHILIPP **14:**297
Rosenthal, Rudolph **5:**610
Rosenthal, Samuel (chess pl.) **5:**405
Rosenthal, Samuel (polit., Can.) **12:**1522
Rosenthal, Toby **14:**834
Rosenthal, Z. **4:**697
Rosenthaliana library (Amst.), *see* Bibliotheca Rosenthaliana
Rosenveldt, Frederik Adrianus **15:**1057
Rosenveldt, Frederik Johannes **15:**1057
ROSENWALD (fam., U.S.) **14:**297
- department stores **5:**1546
Rosenwald, Julius **12:**932; **14:**297; **16:**1069
Rosenwald, Lessing Julius **14:**298
- American Council for Judaism **2:**820
- anti-Zionism **16:**1145
- art collection **3:**648
Rosenwald, William **14:**298
ROSENWILLER (Rosenweiler; tn., Fr.) **14:**299
Rosenzweig, A., *see* AGAI, ADOLF
Rosenzweig, Abraham, *see* ROSEN, ABRAHAM
Rosenzweig, Artur **5:**1038; **8:**883
ROSENZWEIG, FRANZ **14:**299
- apologetics **3:**200
- commandments **5:**789
- creation **5:**1070
- ethical and metaethical **6:**942
- existentialism **6:**1042
- God **7:**664
- Hallo, Rudolf **7:**1202
- holiness **10:**874
- Kantian ethics **6:**323
- miracles **12:**80
- philosophy **13:**461
- prophecy **13:**1180
- redemption **14:**7
- Reform Judaism **14:**27
- religious belief **4:**436
- repentance **14:**77
- revelation **14:**125
- Rosenstock-Huessy, Eugen **6:**98ff; **14:**291ff
- *Shekhinah* **14:**1353
- Torah **15:**1238; **15:**1242; **15:**1243
ROSENZWEIG, GERSON **14:**303
- Hebrew literature **8:**210
- satire **13:**136
- *illus:*
- - *Massekhet Amerika* **13:**127
Rosenzweig, Isaac **13:**482
Rosenzweig, J. **14:**1514
Rosenzweig, Leon **14:**216
Rosenzweig, Saul **13:**1344
Rosenzweig, Solomon **14:**523
Rosenzweig, Walther, *see* RODE, WALTHER
Rose oil, *see* ROSE
Röser, Jakab **8:**54
ROSETTA (tn., Egy.) **14:**304
ROSEWATER, EDWARD **14:**304
- Nebraska **12:**912
- Omaha **12:**1373
Rosewater, Victor **14:**304
Rosh (tit.) **15:**1164
R-o-sh, *see* ASHER BEN JEHIEL
Rosh, Alexander **12:**551
Rosh Amanah (bk.) **3:**659
ROSHEIM (tn., Fr.) **14:**305
- Alsace **2:**751; **2:**754
ROSH HA-AYIN (tn., Isr.) **14:**305
- Antipatris **3:**78
- Aphek **3:**176
- Arethusa **3:**407
- Jerusalem water supply **9:**1472; **9:**1480; **9:**1542
- statistics **1:**place list
- Yemenite Jews **16:**754
- *illus:*
- - new immigrants from Yemen and Aden **9:**379
Rosh ha-Keneset (cmty, ldr.), *see* ARCHISYNAGOGOS
Rosh ha-memshalah, *see* Prime minister of Israel
Rosh ha-Nikrah (kib., Isr.), *see* KEFAR ROSH HA-NIKRAH
Rosh ha-Nikrah (reg., Er. Isr.), *see* TYRE, LADDER OF
Rosh ha-Seder (tit.) **16:**762
ROSH HA-SHANAH (fest.) **14:**305
- *Contents:*
- - In the Bible **14:**305
- - In Rabbinic Literature **14:**307
- - The Shofar **14:**308

- - Laws and Customs **14:**309
- General
- - Adam **2:**236
- - Commandments, the 613 **5:**763-767f
- - illuminated *maḥzorim* **11:**733
- - sacrifice **14:**600ff
- Calendar **5:**44ff
- - Elul **6:**689ff
- - Ten Days of Penitence **15:**1001
- Customs
- - cooking and food **6:**1425
- - dancing **5:**1268
- - greetings **7:**915
- - *kapparot* **10:**756
- - *shofar* **6:**1392; **9:**238; **9:**241; **14:**1442; **14:**904
- - *tashlikh* **15:**829
- Sectarian Observance
- - Falashas **6:**1148
- - Karaites **10:**779
- - Samaritans **14:**742; **14:**743
- Liturgy, *see* LITURGY (Rosh Hashanah and Day of Atonement)
- *illus:*
- - text
- - blowing the *shofar* **3:**834; **11:**734
- - commentary on the liturgy **2:**739
- - *ḥallah*, traditional shapes **6:**1419
- - Riga (1967) **14:**176
- - "Rosh ha-Shanah in the Synagogue" (drg., B. Picart) **13:**497
- - salutations (table) **7:**915
- - *tashlikh* **15:**829
- *mus. notations:*
- - *Yigdal* **16:**835
- *see also:* FESTIVALS
ROSH HA-SHANAH (tal. tract.) **14:**310
- *illus:* text
"Rosh ha-Shanah" (paint., Y. Agam) Pl. 19 **3**-ART
"Rosh ha-Shanah in the Synagogue" (drg., B. Picart) **13:**497
Rosh Ḥavurah (tit.) **7:**322
Rosh Ḥodesh, *see* NEW MOON
Rosh Keneset (cmty. ldr.), *see* ARCHISYNAGOGOS
R-o-sh of Lunel, *see* ASHER BEN MESHULAM HA-KOHEN OF LUNEL
ROSH PINNAH (mosh., Isr.) **14:**311
- airfield **9:**837
- Safed **14:**629
- statistics **1:**place list
- *illus:*
- - text
- - Ben-Yosef, Shelomo, monument **4:**571
Rosh Pinnah sill (Isr.) **9:**591
Rosh Yeshivah shel Golah (tit.) **2:**203ff; **7:**321; **15:**1164
Rosh Yeshivat Ge'on Ya'akov (tit.), *see* GAON
Rosh Ẓurim (kib., Isr.) **6:**541
- statistics **1:**place list
Rosières-aux-Salines (vill., Fr.) **11:**496
Rosin, Abraham, *see* BEN-ADIR
ROSIN, DAVID **14:**312
- Samuel ben Meir **14:**810
Rosin, Heinrich (jur.) **14:**313
Rosin, Heinrich (med. schol.) **7:**133; **14:**313
Rositz, Baruch ben Menahem, *see* Veit, Benedict
Roskin, J.S. **12:**660
Rosmarin, Trude Weiss, *see* WEISS-ROSMARIN, TRUDE
ROSMARYN, HENRYK **14:**313
Rosner, Johny **15:**306
Rosner, Leopold **13:**1366
Rosner, Saidye **4:**1406
Rosner, S. B. **14:**917
Rosofsky, Barnet David, *see* ROSS, BARNEY
Rosowsky, Baruch Leib **14:**313
ROSOWSKY, SOLOMON **14:**313
Ross, Al, *see* Roth, Al
ROSS, BARNEY **14:**313
- New York City **12:**1124
Ross, Edward A. **15:**1651
ROSS, HERBERT **5:**1273
Ross, J. **4:**1220
Ross, Leonard Q., *see* ROSTEN, LEO CALVIN
Ross, Victor R. **15:**312
ROSSELLI (fam., It.) **14:**314
Rosselli, Carlo **14:**314
Rosselli, Nello **14:**314
Rosselli, Pellegrino **14:**314
Rosselius, Paul **8:**54
ROSSEN, ROBERT **12:**473
ROSSENA, DANIEL BEN SAMUEL OF **14:**315
Rossetti, Dante Gabriel **6:**775
Rossi (fam.) **14:**318
Rossi, Angelo de' **11:**898; **14:**319
Rossi, Anselmo de' **12:**619; **14:**315; **14:**319
ROSSI, AZARIAH (Bonaiuto) BEN MOSES DEI **14:**315
- Amatus Lusitanus **2:**797
- astrology **3:**794
- biography **4:**1011
- historiography **8:**693; **11:**350
- history chart **8:**766-767
- *Me'or Einayim* **8:**557
- Philo **13:**427; **13:**628
- poetry **13:**671
- Porto, Abraham Menachem **13:**913
- *illus:*
- - *Me'or Einayim* (1574) **8:**567
Rossi, Bonaiuto de' (f., Salamone) **14:**318
Rossi, Bonaiuto de' (s., Madama Europa) **14:**319
Rossi, Bonaiuto de' (s., Angelo) **14:**319
Rossi, David de **5:**314; **9:**286; **15:**1352
Rossi, Francesco de' **16:**115
- *illus:*
- - Siena print **14:**1515
Rossi, Giovanni Bernardo de', *see* DE' ROSSI, GIOVANNI BERNARDO
Rossi, Giuseppe de' **12:**619; **14:**319
Rossi, Moses ben Jekuthiel de **2:**467
ROSSI, SALAMONE DE' **14:**318
- *Adon Olam* **2:**298
- choral music **5:**487
- Italy **9:**1145
- liturgical chants **5:**124
- *illus:* text
Rossi, Solomon ben Moses de, *see* De Rossi, Solomon ben Moses
Rossillo, Mordecai ben Jacob **10:**542
ROSSIN, SAMUEL **14:**320
Rossini, Gioacchino **12:**409
Rossiter, C. **10:**1182
Rosskam, Edwin **13:**484
Rossman, I., *see* DAN, SERGIU
Rossmann, J. **4:**1384
ROSTEN, LEO CALVIN **14:**321
Rostock (tn., Ger.) **11:**1163
ROSTOV (city, Rus.) **14:**321
ROSTOW, EUGENE VICTOR **14:**322
ROSTOW, WALT WHITMAN **14:**322
Rostworowski, Karol Hubert **13:**799
Roswell (city, N. Mex.) **12:**1037
Rota, Orazio **8:**54
Rotary Yisrael (journ.) **1:** newsp. list
ROTBAUM, JACOB **15:**1072; **15:**1089
Rotberg, Meir **10:**837
Rotblum, David **5:**1036
ROTE (fam.) **14:**323
Rote, Abraham (15/16 cent.) **14:**323
Rote, Abraham (16/17 cent.) **14:**324
Rote, Abraham (17/18 cent.) **14:**324
Rote, Isaac ben Jacob **14:**324
Rote, Jacob (16th cent.) **14:**323; **16:**366
Rote, Jacob (16/17 cent.) **14:**324
Rote, Jacob (17/18 cent.) **14:**324
Rote, Moses **14:**323
Rotem, Ẓevi **12:**1057
Rotenberg, David **15:**1264
Rotenberg, M.H. **4:**591
ROTENBURG (fam., Ind.) **14:**324
Rotenburg, Joseph **14:**324
Rotenburg, Naphtali **14:**324
Rotenburg, Simon Samson **14:**324
ROTENSTREICH, FISCHEL **14:**324
- *Nasz Przeglad* **12:**844
- *illus:*
- - Jewish Agency Executive **10:**28
ROTENSTREICH, NATHAN **14:**324
ROTH, AARON **14:**325
Roth, Abraham Ḥayyim **14:**326
Roth, Al **5:**220
Roth, Alvin S. **2:**524
Roth, A. Sidney **15:**308
Roth, Ben (cart.) **5:**220
Roth, Benjamin (engin.) **2:**321
ROTH, CECIL **1:**36; **14:**326
- Anglo-Jewish letters **11:**62
- encyclopedias **6:**734
- historiography **8:**562
- *illus:* text
Roth, E. **7:**999
Roth, Ḥayyim Judah, *see* ROTH, LEON
ROTH, HENRY **14:**328
- New York City **12:**1121
- U.S. literature **15:**1574
Roth, Irving **5:**220
ROTH, JOSEPH **14:**328
ROTH, KLAUS FRIEDRICH **11:**1125
ROTH, LEON **14:**329
Roth, Lester W. **11:**501
ROTH, PHILIP MILTON **14:**330
- U.S.literature **15:**1577
Roth, Salo **5:**220
ROTHBERG, SAMUEL **14:**331
- *illus:*
- - U.J.A.dinner **15:**1668
Rothblatt, Chaim **16:**368
Rothchild, Jeroboam, *see* MANDEL, GEORGES
Rothenberg, B. **11:**1432; **15:**1145
Rothenberg, Isaac Meir, *see* Alter, Isaac Meir of Gur
Rothenberg, Israel **4:**590; **7:**1447
Rothenberg, Martin **12:**1295
ROTHENBERG, MORRIS **14:**331
- Zionism **16:**1143
Rothenburg, Moses **3:**734
ROTHENBURG OB DER TAUBER (city, Ger.) **14:**332
- expulsion **16:**458
Rothenstein, Albert Daniel **4:**1287; **14:**334; **15:**1479
Rothenstein, Sir John **14:**334
ROTHENSTEIN, SIR WILLIAM **14:**333
- Gertler, Mark **7:**521
- *illus:* text
Rother, Martin **4:**873
Rothfeld, Adolf **5:**558
ROTHKO, MARK **14:**334
- New York City **12:**1122
Rothman, Stephen **11:**1201
ROTHMUELLER, AARON MARKO **12:**705
ROTHSCHILD (fam.) **14:**334
- *Contents:*
- - The Founding Branch **14:**334
- - The French Branch **14:**339
- - The English Branch **14:**340
- art collection **3:**648
- banking **4:**173; **8:**719
- Bleichroeder, Samuel **4:**1081
- coat of arms **8:**340
- Ecuador **6:**361
- Hep! Hep! riots **8:**331
- Herzl, Theodor **8:**409
- Israel TV **15:**931
- Knesset building **9:**1495
- military service **11:**1553
- Moravia **12:**302
- nobility **15:**1166
- Oppenheim **12:**1423
- philanthropy **13:**379
- railroads **13:**1517ff
- stock exchange **15:**406
- *geneal. table:* text
- *illus:*
- - advertisement in the *Jewish Chronicle* **4:**180
- - coat of arms **8:**338
- - French caricature, 1898 **3:**143
- - Paris, Avenue Foch mansion **7:**39
Rothschild (medal.,Isr.) **11:**1167
Rothschild, Adelaide **7:**596; **14:**342
- *illus:*
- - at Shefeyah **14:**345
Rothschild, Adolf Karl **14:**338
Rothschild, Alain **14:**340
Rothschild, Alfred **14:**341
Rothschild, Aline Caroline **14:**901
Rothschild, Alphonse **14:**340
Rothschild, Alphonse Mayer **14:**338
Rothschild, Amschel Mayer **4:**174; **14:**339
- Kalischer, Ẓevi Hirsch **16:**1035
Rothschild, Amschel Moses **14:**334
Rothschild, Annie **14:**341
Rothschild, Anselm Salomon **14:**338
- *illus:*
- - marriage portrait **14:**339
Rothschild, Sir Anthony **14:**341
Rothschild, Anthony Gustav **14:**341
Rothschild, Batsheva (Bethsabée) **4:**327; **14:**340
Rothschild, Batsheva de, Foundation for the Advancement of Science in Israel **9:**976
Rothschild, Betty **14:**340
Rothschild, Charles **3:**817
Rothschild, Charlotte **8:**958 **14:**341
- *illus:*
- - marriage portrait **14:**339
Rothschild, Constance **14:**341
Rothschild, Dorothy **14:**1255
Rothschild, Edmond **14:**340
ROTHSCHILD, BARON EDMOND JAMES DE **14:**342
- agriculture in Ereẓ Israel **9:**773
- Athlit **3:**821
- Bashan holdings **9:**596
- chronological chart **8:**766-767
- Ereẓ Israel settlements **8:**751; **9:**324ff; **9:**516ff; **16:**1040
- family **14:**340
- Feinberg, Yosef **6:**1209
- Givat Ada **7:**596
- Gluskin, Ze'ev **7:**632
- Ḥaviv, Avraham Dov **7:**1494
- Herzl, Theodor **16:**1070ff
- synagogue **15:**587
- Western Wall **16:**471
- wine industry **16:**546
- yachting **15:**318
- Zionism **16:**1113
- *geneal, table* **14:**335
- *illus:*
- - text
- - portrait **8:**750
Rothschild, Edmund Leopold **14:**341
Rothschild, Edouard **14:**340; **15:**311; **15:**312
Rothschild, Elie **15:**312

Rothschild, Evelina **14:**341; **15:**311, 312
Rotschild, Ferdinand James **14:**341
ROTHSCHILD, FRIEDRICH SALOMON **14:**345
Rothschild, Gustave **14:**340
Rothschild, Guy **14:**340; **15:**311
Rothschild, Hannah **5:**658; **14:**337
Rothschild, Henri **7:**147
Rothschild, Henrietta **12:**275
Rothschild, Isaac Elhanan **14:**334
ROTSCHILD, JACOB M. **14:**346
- Atlanta **3:**825
Rothschild, James (Jacob; Fr.) **14:**339
ROTHSCHILD, JAMES ARMAND DE **14:**346
- Ashdot Ya'akov **3:**699
- Brandeis, Louis **4:**1298
- family **14:**340, 342, 344
- horsebreeding **15:**311
- railroads **13:**1517ff
- Zionist commission **16:**1163
- *geneal. table:* **14:**335
- *illus:*
- - text
- - Allenby, and **2:**647
- - at Government House, Jerusalem **2:**57
- - Zionist Commission arriving in Palestine (1918) **16:**1163
Rothschild, James Meyer **4:**174
Rothschild, Jeanette von **16:**648
Rothschild, Karl Mayer **4:**174; **14:**338; **14:**341
- *illus:*
- - caricature **14:**338
Rothschild, Leopold **14:**341; **15:**310
- *illus:*
- - marriage to Marie Perugia **14:**341
Rothschild, Lionel Nathan (1808-1879) **14:**340
- Disraeli, Benjamin **6:**105
- Jewish emancipation **8:**715
- politics **13:**811
- sports **15:**312
- *illus:*
- - portrait **8:**710
- - Rothschild marriage portrait **14:**339
- - taking seat in House of Commons **14:**340
Rothschild, Lionel Nathan (1882-1942) **14:**341
Rothschild, Lionel Walter **14:**341
- *illus:*
- - Balfour Declaration **4:**131
- - reply to Balfour's Declaration **4:**135
Rothschild, Louis **14:**338; **15:**312
Rothschild, Maurice **15:**311
Rothschild, Max **3:**817
Rotschild, Mayer Amschel **14:**334
- banking **4:**174
- chronological chart **8:**766-767
Rothschild, Mayer Karl **14:**339
Rothschild, Nathaniel (Natty) Mayer (fin.) **14:**341
- Herzl, Theodor **8:**415
- history chart **8:**766-767
- museums **12:**543
- nobility **15:**1166
ROTHSCHILD, NATHANIEL MAYER VICTOR, LORD **14:**347
Rothschild, Nathan Mayer **14:**337; **14:**339
- banking **4:**174
- Gompertz, Benjamin **7:**773
- railroads **13:**1517ff
- stock exchange **15:**405
- textiles **15:**1042
- *illus:*
- - Rothschild marriage portrait **14:**339
Rothschild, Peter **15:**312
Rothschild, Philippe **15:**318
Rothschild, Robert **14:**340; **15:**312; **15:**317
ROTHSCHILD, ROBERT PHINIAS **11:**1554; **11:**1575
Rothschild, Sally, *see* ROTHSCHILD, FRIEDRICH SALOMON
Rothschild, Salomon Albert **14:**338
Rothschild, Salomon Mayer **4:**174; **13:**1717; **14:**338
- *illus:*
- - Rothschild marriage portrait **14:**339
Rothschild, Simon F. **2:**125
ROTHSCHILD, WALTER N. **14:**347
- Abraham and Straus store **2:**125
- yachting **15:**318
Rothschild, Walter N., Jr. **2:**125; **14:**348
Rothschild, Wilhelm Karl **14:**339,342
Rothschild Freres (bnk., Fr.) **14:**339
Rothschild-Hadassah University Hospital (Isr.) **9:**1455; **9:**1461
- *illus:*
- - Rothschild, James de **14:**346
- - ward **9:**1464
- *see also:* Hadassah-Hebrew University Medical Center
Rothschild Hospital (Aus.) **16:**127
Rothschild Maḥzor (illum. ms.) **8:**1270; **11:**734
- *illus:* **3:***fig.* 907; **4:**430; **6:**350; **8:**1284; **15:**99
Rothschild Miscellany (illum. ms.) **3:**458; **7:**1098; **8:**1270; **11:**734; **12:**1177; **14:**74,306,1043; **15:**71
- *illus:* **2:**626; **3:**455; **4:**283; **5:**487; **8:**1029,1282; **10:***fcg.* 107; **10:**114,456; **11:**1248,1474; **12:**486; **13:**1326
Rothschild Museum (Ger.) **3:**651
Rothschild Siddur (illum. ms.), *see* *Rothschild Maḥzor*
Rothstein, Andrew **15:**25
ROTHSTEIN, ARNOLD **14:**348
Rothstein, Arthur **13:**484
ROTHSTEIN, IRMA **3:**609
- *illus:*
- - Broch, Hermann (bust)**4:**1385
Rothstein, Theodor **15:**25
Roti (fam.), *see* ROTE
Roti, Moses al-, *see* Moses (al-) Roti
Rotkin, Charles **13:**484
Rotman, Alter, *see* Robot, Alexandru
Rott, Konrad **15:**270
Rott, Moritz **15:**1056
Rotta, Angelo **8:**875
ROTTEMBOURG, HENRI **14:**348
ROTTERDAM (city, Neth.) **14:**349
- Netherlands **12:**980ff
- *illus:*
- - text
- - *ketubbah* (17th cent.) **3:**541
Rottman, Leon **12:**1377; **15:**307
ROUDNICE NAD LABEM (tn., Cz.) **14:**350
ROUEN (city, Fr.) **14:**351
- Crusades **5:**1135
ROUFFACH (tn., Fr.) **14:**352
- Alsace **2:**752
- Armleder massacre **3:**483
Roukhomovsky, Israel **7:**743
- *illus:* text
Round-Table Conference, *see* ST. JAMES CONFERENCE
Rousettus aegyptiacus (zool.) **4:**318
Rousseau, Alexandre-Samuel **9:**1344
ROUSSEAU, JEAN JACQUES **14:**352
- chronological chart **8:**766-767
- Hurwitz, Judah **8:**1118
- Lamentations, Book of **10:**1376
ROUSSILLON (reg., prov., Fr.) **14:**353
- French Jewry **7:**20
Roussillon, Abraham ben David de **14:**353
Routledge, George **13:**1375
ROUTTENBERG, MAX JONAH **14:**354
Rouvroy, Claude Henry de, *see* Saint-Simon, Henry
Rovere, Francesco della (pope), *see* SIXTUS IV
Rovighi, Cesare **10:**306; **11:**1559; **13:**1036
ROVIGO (tn., It.) **14:**354
- archives **3:**387
- Italy **9:**1142
- *illus:* text
ROVIGO, ABRAHAM BEN MICHAEL **14:**355
- *aliyah* **9:**513
- Benjamin ben Eliezer ha-Cohen Vitale **4:**532
- Bonafoux, Daniel **4:**1199
- *maggid* **11:**700
- Shabbateanism **14:**1245
- Zacuto, Moses **16:**907
ROVINA, HANNA **14:**356
- *illus:*
- - text
- - Bar-Yehudah, Israel, and Zalman Aranne **4:**285
- - Gnessin, Menahem, and Nahum Zemach **7:**634
- - Habimah original company**7:**1029
- - 'Hannah Rovina as Medea' (wdct., Miron Sima) **3:**644
- - in *Dybbuk* (wdct., Miron Sima) **6:**19
- - laying the Habimah Theater cornerstone **7:**1028
Rovner, Sejdel (Zaydel), *see* MOROGOWSKI, JACOB SAMUEL
ROVNO (city, Ukr.) **14:**357
Row, John **8:**54
Rowanduz (tn., Kurd.), *see* RUWANDIZ
ROWE, LEO STANTON **14:**358
- Iowa **8:**1438
Rowing (sport) **15:**312
Rowley, Alexander **8:**54
ROWLEY, HAROLD HENRY **14:**358
Równe (city, Ukr.), *see* ROVNO
Rowson, Sefton, *see* ROSENNE, SHABTAI
Rowson, Susanna Haswell **15:**1569
Roxbury (dist., Mass.) **4:**1265; **11:**1112
Roxelana (sult.) **9:**1434
Roy (Chr. Hebr.) **8:**54
Royal City **5:**589
Royal College of Surgery (Eng.) **15:**1677
Royal Commission on Palestine, *see* PEEL COMMISSION
Royal Dutch Petroleum Company **4:**358; **5:**684
Royal Exchange (London) **11:**474
- *illus:*
- - plan, 1760 **11:**470
Royal Fusiliers (Br. army) **10:**70
Royal Opera House (Eng.) **4:**95
Royal Portico (Temple) **15:**965
Royal Theater (Amst.) **4:**639
Royalty, Prayer for, *see* GOVERNMENT, PRAYER FOR THE
Royz, Olesh, *see* ROSE, ALEX
Rózana (tn., Belor.), *see* RUZHANY
Rozanes, Abraham, *see* Rosanes, Abraham ben Meir
Rozanes, Judah ben Samuel, *see* ROSANES, JUDAH BEN SAMUEL
ROZDOL (tn., Ukr.) **14:**359
- *illus:* text
ROZEANU, ANGELICA **14:**360
- sport **15:**314
Rozenak (ling.) **16:**1392
Rozenberg, Zwi Hirsh **4:**1363
Rozenberga, Elza **14:**523
Rozencvajg, Alfred, *see* Mirov, Nenad
Rozencvajg, Viktor, *see* Jovanović, Vitomir
Rozenshteyn, L. M. **13:**1340
RÓŻEWICZ, TADEUSZ **13:**804
Rozgony (Rožhanovce; tn., Slov.) **10:**1215
Rozhanoy (Rozhinoy; tn., Belor.), *see* RUZHANY
ROZIN (Rosen), JOSEPH **14:**360
- *ḥiddushim* **8:**467
- responsa **14:**93
Rozmirovich, Helena **5:**794; **5:**797
ROZOVSKI, PINḤAS **14:**361
Rozovsky, Mordecai **12:**962
Rozprze, Abraham Moses of, *see* Abraham Moses of Rozprze
Rózsavölgyi, Gyula **13:**1369; **14:**362
ROZSAVOLGYI, MARK **14:**362
- publishing **13:**1369
Rozvoj (period., Cz.) **5:**267; **13:**1026
ROZWADOW (tn., Pol.) **14:**362
ROZWÓJ (anti-Sem. orgn.) **14:**363
RSHA (Nazi orgn.) **14:**363
- Auschwitz **3:**855
- Eichmann, Adolf **6:**517
- Final Solution **6:**1278
- Heydrich, Reinhard **8:**448
- Holocaust **8:**859ff
- Kaltenbrunner, Ernst **10:**722
- Mueller, Heinrich **12:**503
- Pohl, Oswald **13:**701
- SS and SD **15:**322
Rtnw (name, Er. Isr.-Syr.), *see* Retenu
Ruad (Phoen. city), *see* ARADUS
Ru'aḥ (kab. conc.) **10:**609*ff*; **11:**843
RU'AḤ HA-KODESH ('holy spirit') **14:**364
- *Contents:*
- - General **14:**364
- - In Jewish Philosophy **14:**366
- - The Modern Period **14:**367
- Cohen, Hermann **5:**676; **13:**461
- Philo **13:**427
- *Shem ha-Kotev* **2:**190
- *see also:* GOD; REVELATION; SHEKHINAH
Ru'aḥ ha-Zeman (period.), *see* *Ha-Zeman*
Ru'aḥ Ḥen (compendium) **3:**959; **14:**1107
Rubanovich, Ilya **15:**36
Rubashov (tn., Pol.), *see* HRUBIESZOW
Rubashov, Shneur Zalman, *see* SHAZAR, SHNEUR ZALMAN
Rubber Research Association (Isr.) **9:**970
Rubbra, Edmund **10:**1376
Ruben, Samuel **4:**1032
RUBENOVITZ, HERMAN H. **14:**368
Rubenovitz, Mignon **14:**368
Rubens (paint., Neth.) **10:**460
- *illus:*
- - 'Adam and Eve in Paradise'

(paint.) 4:941
- - 'Bath-Sheba at the Fountain' (paint.) 4:322
- - 'Daniel in the Lions' Den' (paint.) 5:1283
RUBENS, ALFRED 14:368
Rubens, Bernice 6:785
Rubens, M.B. 13:707
RUBENS, PAUL ALFRED 6:790
Rubens, S. 10:1584
Rubensohn, Gertrude 7:1202
RUBENSON, ROBERT 14:368
Rubenstein, Abraham 15:317
RUBENSTEIN, LOUIS 14:369
- sport 15:316
Rubenstein, Moses 15:317
Rubenstein, Rachel 15:317
RUBENSTEIN, RICHARD LOWELL 14:369
- Divine justice 7:670
- faith 4:436
- Holocaust 14:138
Rubenstein, S. B. 16:1165
Rubianus, Crotus 14:109
Rubi Gotsce, *see* Joseph ben Jacob
Rubin, A.D. 6:734
Rubin, Albert 6:1161
Rubin, Arthur 15:304
Rubin, David 8:1289
RUBIN, EDGAR 14:369
Rubin, Eliahu 12:514
Rubin, George 8:1361
RUBIN, HADASSAH 14:370
- Yiddish literature 16:826
Rubin, Hyman 15:213
Rubin, Isidor 11:1201
Rubin, Israel, *see* RABON, ISRAEL
Rubin, Jerry 12:1031
Rubin, Joseph 5:97
Rubin, Lawrence A. 11:1498
Rubin, Leslie 13:820
Rubin, Markus 4:177; 5:1537
RUBIN, MORTON JOSEPH 14:370
RUBIN, REUVEN 14:370
- Kolnik, Arthur 10:1169
- *illus:*
- - text
- - Halevy, Moshe (drg.) 7:1187
- - Melnikoff, Avraham (portrait) Pl. 13:—ART
- - Pauker, Ana, and 13:188
Rubin, Roy 15:303
RUBIN, RUTH 12:705
Rubin, Samuel 2:817
Rubin, Saul J. 14:162
Rubin, Sol 5:1110
RUBIN, SOLOMON 14:371
- Kabbalah 10:648
- Peremyshlyany, Meir ben Aaron Leib of 13:277
Rubin Academy of Music (Jer.) 5:1271; 9:1496; 12:673
RUBINER, LUDWIG 14:372
Rubinfeld, Febus 16:1015
Rubinfeld, Zevi 13:1299
Rubinger, David 13:487
RUBINOW, ISAAC MAX 14:372
- New York City 12:1085
- Szold, Henrietta 15:667
Rubinowicz, David 5:448
Rubinowitz, Ephraim, *see* HA-REUBENI, EPHRAIM
RUBINSTEIN, AKIVA 14:373
RUBINSTEIN, ANTON GRIGORYEVICH 14:373
- *Babel, Tower of* 4:27
- Davydov, Karl Yulyevich 5:1370
- stamps 15:335
RUBINSTEIN, ARTHUR 14:374
RUBINSTEIN, AVRAHAM 1:36
Rubinstein, Chaim Zvi 8:216
RUBINSTEIN, HAROLD FREDERICK 6:790
RUBINSTEIN, HELENA 14:375
RUBINSTEIN, IDA 14:376
RUBINSTEIN, ISAAC 14:376
- Grodzinski, Ḥayyim Ozer 7:928
Rubinstein, Jehiel 13:2
RUBINSTEIN, JOSEPH 14:377
Rubinstein, M. (print.) 16:1015
Rubinstein, Michael 13:648
Rubinstein, Nikolay Grigoryevich 14:374
Rubinstein, O. 13:1025
Rubinstein, P.M. 8:1471
Rubinstein, R. 16:833
RUBINSTEIN, SERGEY LEONIDOVICH 14:377
Rubio, Abraham 14:378
RUBIO, MORDECAI 14:377
Rubitscek, Richard 15:317
Rublee, George 6:991; 14:937
Rubo (pub. fig., Prus.) 13:1453
Rubutu (city, Er. Isr.) 13:1439
RUBY, JACK 14:378
Ruckersfelder 8:54
RUDAVSKY, DAVID 14:378
Rudbeck, Olaus 14:928
Rudd, Irving 13:1361
Rudd, Mark 12:1031
Rudel (Ger. pilot) 12:956
Rudé Právo (newsp.) 14:1584
RUDERMAN, JACOB ISAAC 14:379
Ruderman, Jacob I. 4:146
Ruderman, Samuel 6:1161
RUDICH, MAYER 14:379
Rudimenta linguae hebraicae (wk.) 16:1360,1389
RUDIN, JACOB PHILIP 14:379
RUDINOW, MOSHE 12:705
Rudki (city, Ukr.) 10:1173
Rudman, Abraham H. 11:783
RUDNICKI, ADOLF 14:380
RUDOLPH (monk, Ger.) 14:380
RUDOLPH I (of Hapsburg, Holy Rom. emp.) 14:380
- Austrian Fredericianum 3:888
- Meir ben Baruch of Rothenburg 11:1251
- Or Zaru'a's responsa 7:1509
- illus:
- - decree confirming the 'Fredericianum' 3:893
RUDOLPH II (of Hapsburg; Holy Rom. emp.) 14:381
Rudolph IV (duke, Aus.) 3:888
Rudolph, Albert 15:305
Rudolph, B.G. 8:568
Rudolph, Harry 15:304
Rudolph, Jack 12:1222
Rudolph, Mendy 15:304
Rudy, Zvi 15:69
Rue (spice) 13:625 15:269
RUEBNER, TUVIA 14:382
Rueckert, F. 4:874
RUEDENBERG, REINHOLD 8:1433
RUEDIGER (Hutzmann; bp., Ger.) 14:382
- autonomy, judicial 3:929
- Speyer 15:262
RUEF, ABRAHAM 14:382
RUEFF, JACQUES 14:382
Ruehl (graphic art.) 15:1487
RUEHS, CHRISTIAN FRIEDRICH 14:383
- Hep! Hep! riots 8:330
Rue-Juif (hamlet, Fr.) 3:23
RUELF, ISAAC 14:383
Ruetten, Joseph Jacob 13:1366
Rufach (tn., Fr.), *see* ROUFFACH
RUFEISEN, JOSEPH 14:384
- Zionism 16:1112
Rufeisen, Oswald (Shemuel) 5:507
- apostasy 3:209
- Jewish identity issue 10:63
- Mir resistance 12:72
Ruff, Karl 15:996
Ruffinelli, T. 16:1019
Rufina (2/3 cent., Turk.) 9:1162
Rufinus (Rom. writ.) 10:263
Rufus (bld. lib. vict.) 8:797
Rufus of Ephesus 3:674; 14:385
RUFUS OF SAMARIA 14:385
- medicine 11:1183
Rufus Tinneius, *see* TINNEIUS RUFUS
Rugby (sport) 15:313
- *illus:*
- - Geffin, Aaron 15:312
Ruha, Al- (city, As.), *see* EDESSA
RUḤAMAH (kib., Isr.) 14:385
- statistics 1:place list
Ruḥamah (qtr., Jer.) 9:1462
Ruhe (demon) 5:1528
Ruheibah (loc., Er. Isr.) 7:432
Ruḥi, Menahem ben Solomon ibn, *see* ALROY, DAVID
"Ruins of Synagogue" (etch., A. Bogen) 3:620
Ruiz, Juan 15:249
Rujm al-Numayra, *see* Bet Nimrim
RUKEYSER, MERRYLE STANLEY 10:315
RUKEYSER, MURIEL 15:1577; 15:1583
RUMAH or ARUMAH (tns., Er. Isr.) 14:386
- Manasseh 11:851
RUMANIA 14:386
- *Contents:*
- - General 14:386
- - Emerging Rumania 14:387
- - Communal Institutions 14:387
- - Independent Rumania 14:388
- - Internal Organization 14:390
- - The Struggle for Naturalization 14:393
- - Increasing Anti-Semitism 14:394
- - Jewish Political Life 14:396
- General
- - Berlin, Congress of 4:655
- - Bucharest 4:1439
- - cooperatives 5:942
- - demography 5:1509ff
- - history chart 8:766-767
- - Israel relations 9:428
- - League of Nations 10:1524
- - minority treaty 12:45ff
- - population 13:872ff
- - socialism 15:29
- - Transylvania 15:1341
- Anti-Semitism 3:86; 3:124
- - Codreanu, Cornelius Zelea 5:656
- - Fourth Zionist Congress 16:1168
- - Iron Guard 8:1472
- - *numerus clausus* 12:1268
- - universities 15:1678
- Cultural Life
- - press 13:1043
- - Rumanian Literature 14:416
- - television and radio 15:929
- - theater 15:1071
- Holocaust 8:840; 8:851ff
- - Antonescu, Ion 3:162
- - Church and Nazism 8:915
- - Lecca, Radú 10:1554
- - Transnistria 15:1330
- Jewish Community
- - Alliance Israélite Universelle 2:650ff
- - demography 5:1509ff
- - emancipation 6:710ff
- - Ereẓ Israel settlement 16:1039ff
- - Jewish Colonization Association 10:45
- - Jews, status of 5:805; 8:722ff
- - migrations 9:538; 16:1520
- - military service 11:1565
- - organizations 5:827
- - ORT 12:1482
- - synagogues 1:syn. list
- - Zionism 16:1132ff
- Trades and Professions
- - agriculture 2:411
- - journalism 10:304
- - publishing 13:1369
- *illus:*
- - text
- - anti-Semitic parties, 1881-1911 (table) 3:81
- - oath *more judaico* 12:1304
- *pop. tables*
- - text
- - Bucharest, 1800-1969 4:1438
- *see also:* BESSARABIA
Rumanian Committee 2:977
RUMANIAN LITERATURE 14:416
- *Contents:*
- - Biblical and Hebraic Influences 14:416
- - Early Writings 14:417
- - Later Influences 14:417
- - Image of the Jew 14:418
- - Treatment by Jewish Writers 14:420
- - Jewish Contribution 14:421
- - Literature of the Holocaust 14:423
- - Capsules 14:425
- - Holocaust Period 14:399
- - During the War 14:401
- - Jewish Resistance 14:405
- - Contemporary Period 14:410
- - Israel-Rumania Relations 14:415
- Bible translations 4:882
- children's literature 5:453; 5:457
Rumayḥī, Ismāʿīl al- 2:511
Rumbold, Sir H. G. M. 13:32
Rumelinus, G. Burchard 8:54
Rumford Falls (vill., Me.) 11:782
Rumilly (tn., Fr.) 14:921
RUMKOWSKI, CHAIM MORDECHAI 14:428
- Lodz 11:432ff
- *illus:*
- - text
- - Lodz ghetto stamp 11:431
Rumma, Wadi er-, *see* Wadi er-Rumma
RUMPLER, EDUARD 14:429
- aviation 2:320
- *illus:* text
Rumsaniyya (Rumthāniyya; vill., Golan) 9:596; 13:1534
Rumshinsky, Joseph 13:1617
Rumyantsev, Count (Belor.) 7:767
Rundo, Hershel 12:1456
Rundt, Arthur 4:668 7:452
Runenberg (educ., fin.) 6:1297
Runes, D. D. 6:734
RUNITSCH, OSSIP 15:1058,1090
RUNKEL, SOLOMON ZALMAN (15th cent.) 14:429
Runkel, Solomon Zalman (16th cent.) 14:429
Runyon, Damon 15:1571
- Winchell, Walter 16:536
RUPPIN, ARTHUR 14:430
- Auster's assistance 3:875
- Eighth Zionist Congress 16:1169; 16:1171; 16:1172
- Mishpat ha-Shalom ha-Ivri 12:142
- sociological studies 11:1377
- *illus:*
- - Chancellor, John, and 8:471
- - Daniel Sieff Research Institute 16:439
- - Jewish Agency Executive 10:28
- - Kefar Ruppin 10:891
Ruppin, Shulamith 14:1313
Ruppin Institute (Isr.) 9:436
Ruqqād stream (Transj.) 9:180; 9:597
Ruqqāsa (fam.), *see* WAQQASA
Rural and Suburban Settlement Co. (Er. Isr.), *see* Rassco
Rus, Johann Reichard 8:54
Ruschat, A. 8:54
Ruschi, Francesco 3:524
RUSE (city, Bul.) 14:432

Rushi, Benjamin ben Moses **9:**1096
Rushnai (newsp.) **10:**437
Ruskolekier, Ajzyk **9:**1360
Ruslen, J. **7:**1291
- *illus.*
- - Ḥanukkah lamp (silver, 1709) **7:**1300
Russe (city, Bul.), *see* RUSE
Russell, Bertrand **7:**780
Russell, Charles Edward **16:**1155
RUSSELL (Levy), HENRY (comp.) **14:**432
Russell, Henry (theat. dir.) **14:**432
Russell, Landon Ronald, *see* Ronald, Sir Landon
Russell, Moses **16:**163
Russell, Philip Moses **16:**163,360
Russell, William Clark **14:**432
RUSSIA **14:**433
- *Contents:*
- - Until 1772
- - - Origins **14:**433
- - - From the 14th Century **14:**434
- - - Principality of Moscow **14:**434
- - 1772-1881 **14:**435
- - - Crystallization of Policy Toward the Jews **14:**435
- - - Nicholas I **14:**436
- - - Alexander II **14:**441
- - - Population Growth **14:**442
- - - Economic Position **14:**442
- - - Haskalah in Russia **14:**443
- - 1881-1917 **14:**444
- - - Jewish Population at the Close of the 19th Century **14:**450
- - - Economic Structure **14:**451
- - - Ideological Trends **14:**451
- - - Cultural Developments **14:**455
- - - World War I **14:**455
- - - The February Revolution **14:**456
- - - The Civil War **14:**458
- - The Soviet Regime **14:**459
- - - "Jewish Proletarian Culture" **14:**464
- - - Economic Reshuffle **14:**467
- - - Agrictultural Projects **14:**468
- - - Absorption into the Soviet Structure **14:**471
- - 1939-1945 **14:**472
- - - Soviet Annexation of Territories **14:**473
- - - German Invasion **14:**474
- - - Annihilation of the Jews **14:**475
- - - Jewish Resistance **14:**476
- - - Participation in the Partisan Movement **14:**477
- - - Jews in the Soviet Army **14:**478
- - - Position of Jews Behind the Front **14:**480
- - - Destruction of Yiddish Culture **14:**480
- - Contemporary Period **14:**481
- - - Stalin's Persecutions **14:**481
- - - After Stalin's Death **14:**481
- - - The Censuses of 1959 and 1970 **14:**482
- - - Repression of Jewish Culture **14:**487
- - - Pressure for Emigration to Israel **14:**488
- - Relations with Israel
- - - Soviet Support **14:**493
- - - Soviet Policy in the Middle East **14:**494
- - - 1947-1949 **14:**494
- - The Struggle for Soviet Jewry **14:**496
- - - Participation of Israel **14:**501
- - - From 1969 **14:**502
- General
- - Alexander I, II, and III **2:**569; **8:**721
- - Catherine II **5:**254
- - Caucasus **5:**257
- - history chart **8:**766-767
- - Iraq relations **14:**1624
- - Lenin, Vladimir Ilyich **11:**13
- - Moldavia and Walachia **14:**387
- - Moscow **12:**359
- - Nasser, Gamal Abdul **12:**842ff
- - Nicholas I and II **12:**1137ff
- - Siberia **14:**1486ff
- - Stalin's leadership **15:**327ff
- - Sykes-Picot treaty **15:**565ff
- - Trotski, Lev Davidovich **15:**1405
- - UNEF **15:**1554
- Anti-Semitism **3:**86; **3:**107; **3:**147ff
- - anti-cosmopolitan campaigns **5:**984; **5:**985
- - blood libel **4:**1128
- - cantonists **5:**130
- - cartoons **5:**178
- - censorship **5:**279
- - discrimination **6:**68; **6:**69ff; **8:**677ff; **15:**1560
- - Doctors' Plot **6:**144ff
- - Jewish self-defense **14:**1123; **14:**1124; **14:**1128
- - Korobka **10:**1211
- - May Laws **11:**1147
- - Mountain Jews **12:**479
- - *numerus clausus* **12:**1264ff
- - pogroms **8:**735ff; **13:**694
- - U.N. **15:**1543ff
- - UNESCO conference **15:**1565
- - Union of the Russian People **15:**1538
- - universities **15:**1678
- - *Yevsektsiya* activists **16:**781
- Culture
- - archives **3:**380
- - dress **6:**221
- - education **6:**423ff
- - Haskalah movement **7:**1434,1445
- - Hebrew mss **11:**907
- - Hebrew newspapers **12:**1045ff
- - Hebrew parody **13:**137ff
- - homiletic literature **8:**956f
- - Jewish studies **16:**582
- - Levinsohn, Isaac Baer **11:**117
- - Lilienthal, Max **11:**243
- - museums **12:**540
- - ORT **12:**1481ff
- - press **13:**1044ff
- Russian literature **14:**506
- - Society for the Promotion of Culture among Russian Jews **15:**58ff
- - stamps **15:**330
- - television and radio **15:**929
- - theater **15:**1058,1074
- - Yiddish education **6:**433
- - Yiddishists **8:**765
- - Yiddish Literature **16:**817
- Holocaust **8:**858ff
- - Babi Yar **4:**27
- - Berdichev **4:**591
- - Bolekhov **4:**1186
- - Grossman's *Black Book* **7:**939
- - Jewish anti-Fascist Committee **3:**62; **3:**63
- - partisans **13:**144ff
- - rescue **8:**907ff
- - Vatican attitude to **8:**912
- - War Crimes Trials **16:**289ff
- Israel relations **9:**407ff,428
- - Arab armies after 1967 war **9:**414
- - Egypt arms deal **9:**387ff
- - Egyptian defense system **14:**1639
- - Ereẓ Israel protection rights **9:**296; **9:**298
- - historical survey **9:**387; **9:**403
- - Jerusalem diplomatic representation **9:**1448
- - Middle East interests **9:**305ff
- - Sinai Campaign **14:**1602
- - Six-Day War **14:**1626
- - U.N. and Jewish State **16:**1092
- - U.S. and Israel-Arab conflict **15:**1663ff
- Jewish community
- - apostasy **3:**207
- - *arenda* **3:**403
- - assimilation **3:**780
- - autonomy **3:**926
- - autonomy, judicial **3:**931ff; **4:**727
- - cooperatives **5:**941
- - crime **5:**1091ff
- - demography **5:**1497ff
- - Deputies of the Jewish People **5:**1548
- - divorce statistics **6:**135
- - economic situation **16:**1321
- - emanicipation **6:**713ff
- - Ḥasidism **7:**1398ff
- - *ḥezkat ha-yishuv* **8:**358
- - J.D.C. **2:**828ff
- - Jewish Colonization Association **10:**44ff
- - Jewish identity **10:**64
- - Judaizers **10:**398
- - *kazyonny ravvin* **10:**860
- - migrations **8:**720; **9:**546; **16:**1520
- - military service **11:**1554,1556ff
- - minority rights **12:**43ff
- - organizations **5:**826; **5:**850
- - Pale of Settlement **13:**24
- - philanthropy **13:**380
- - population **8:**732ff; **13:**866ff
- - rabbinical seminaries **13:**1465
- - Shabbateanism **14:**1235
- - *shtetl* **14:**1471
- - Simḥat Torah **14:**1573
- - statistics **15:**344
- - status of Jews **8:**716ff
- - students' movements **15:**448,452
- - synagogues **1:**syn. list; **15:**588
- - U.N. **15:**1562ff
- - *yeshivot* **16:**768
- Politics **13:**818ff
- - Bund **4:**1497ff
- - capitulations **5:**150
- - communism **5:**792ff
- - Duma **6:**267
- - socialism **15:**26ff; **15:**38,48
- - *Yevsektsiya* **16:**779
- - Zionist Socialist Workers' Party **16:**1180ff
- Trades and Professions
- - agriculture **2:**406
- - banking **4:**176
- - journalism **10:**304ff
- - law **10:**1491ff
- - medicine **11:**1195ff
- - peddling **13:**206
- - petroleum and oil products **13:**345
- - publishing **13:**1370
- - railroads **13:**1518
- - sugar trade **15:**488ff
- - trade and commerce **15:**1304
- - typography **15:**1479
- - wine and liquor trade **16:**543ff
- Zionism **16:**1063; **16:**1069ff
- - Ha-Shomer Ha-Ẓa'ir **7:**1376
- - Ḥibbat Zion **8:**463; **16:**1038ff
- - kibbutz movement **10:**963
- - Mizrachi **12:**176
- - Po'alei Zion **13:**656
- - Revisionists **14:**128ff
- *illus:*
- - text
- - anti-Semitic parties, 1881-1911 (table) **3:**81
- - Baku Zionist conference, 1917 **4:**119
- - Berdichev, a Jewish house **4:**590
- - Birobidzhan region **4:**1045-1049
- - Chmielnicki, Bogdan (statue, Kiev) **5:**481
- - Crimea, election time in a Jewish kolkhoz **5:**1107
- - Israel demonstration of solidarity with Soviet Jewry **9:**434
- - J.D.L. protest for Soviet Jewry **12:**1123
- - Jerusalem Church property **9:**1457
- - *Maariv* report, September 1948 **11:**639
- - Meir, Golda, presenting credentials **11:**1243
- - Nicholas I extracting money from Jews (cartoon) **12:**1138
- - order closing all Zionist organizations (1919) **16:** 1138
- - Pale of Settlement (map) **13:**25
- - pioneer group, 1919 **2:**406
- - refugees passing Statue of Liberty **12:**1084
- - Russian Orthodox Church **9:**914,1457
- - "Russian Village" (paint., I. I. Levitan) **11:**135
- - Shalom Aleichem stamp **15:**335
- - Soviet Jewish farmers **2:**407-410
- - *Yevsektsiya* Vitebsk *ḥeder* trial **16:**780
- - Zionist exiles in Siberia **16:** 1139
- *pop. tables:*
- - text
- - Bessarabia, centers of Jewish settlement, 1897 **4:**707
- - Bialystok, 1765-1948 **4:**811
- - Birobidzhan, 1928-59 **4:**1049
- - Crimea, 1970 **5:**1104
- - Estonia, 1918-1940 **6:**917
- - Georgia **7:**424
- - Pale of Settlement **13:**25
- - Soviet Union Republics, 1959 **5:**1510
- - towns with 100,000 or more Jews, 1967 **5:**1514
- *see also under individual cities and regions*
Russian Civil War (1919-1920) **4:**413
Russian Compound (area, Jer.) **9:**1471,1516
- *see also:* Assyrian Camp
Russian Flag (newsp.), *see Russkoye Znamya*
Russian Imperial Library **16:**1334
Russian Jewish Congress **5:**876
Russian Jewish Encyclopedia, *see Yevreyskaya Entsiklopediya*
Russian Jewish Historical Ethnographic Society **15:**54
Russian-Jewish Scientific Society **12:**476; **16:**1115
RUSSIAN LITERATURE **14:**506
- *Contents:*
- - Biblical and Hebraic Influences **14:**506
- - The Image of the Jew **14:**507
- - The Soviet Position **14:**509
- - The Jewish Contribution **14:**512
- - Capsules **14:**514
- Bible translations **4:**886
- children's literature **5:**454; **5:**456
- Jewish encyclopedias **6:**732
- *illus:*
- - *Babi Yar*, English translation **4:**28
Russian Mendelssohn, the, *see* LEVINSOHN, ISAAC BAER
Russian Orthodox Church (Isr.) **9:**911
- *illus:*
- - priests procession **9:**914
Russian Revolution
- Ḥasidism **7:**1398
- influence on Jews' situation **3:**124
- Martov, Julius **11:**1067
- Pale of Settlement **13:**27
- Po'alei Zion **13:**661
- self-defense **14:**1125
- socialism, Jewish **15:**48
- Volhynia Jews **16:**211
Russian Secret Police **4:**1172

Russian Social Democratic Party **5**:792; **5**:794ff; **15**:41
Russian thistle (bot.) **9**:222
"Russian Village" (paint., M. Chagall) **5**:*fcg.* 334
Russische Korrespondenz (period., Ger.) **8**:480
Russki Evrei (Yevrey; newsp.) **10**:744; **13**:1045; **14**:444
Russkii (newsp.) **4**:668
Russkoye Znamya (newsp.) **15**:1538
Russo, Abraham Isaac **2**:518
Russo, Baruchiah **6**:149; **7**:56; **11**:818; **14**:1245
Russo-American treaty (1832) **2**:823
Russo-Jewish Committee for Relief of Jewish Refugees (Eng.) **2**:977; **13**:387
Russo-Turkish war (1877) **2**:654
Rustchuk (city, Bul.), *see* RUSE
Rusten, Allen **16**:534
Rutberg, Meir **7**:1066
Rutchick, Sol **15**:310
Rute (fam.), *see* ROTE
RUTENBERG, PINḤAS (Piotr) **14**:516
- Jewish Legion **16**:1079ff
- Va'ad Le'ummi **16**:51
- *illus:*
- - Naharayim electric power plant **9**:790
Rutgers, Antonie **8**:54
Rutgers University **15**:1680
Ruth (bib. fig.)
- Ammonites **2**:860
- Davidic ancestry **5**:1339
- levirate marriage **11**:122
- Mahlon and Chilion **11**:728
- Naomi **12**:818
- Ruth, Book of **14**:518ff
- *geneal. table:* **5**:1342
- *illus:*
- - gleaning in the fields of Boaz **4**:1154
- - Naomi and **12**:818
RUTH, BOOK OF **14**:518
- *Contents:*
- - Contents **14**:518
- - Aim of the Book **14**:518
- - Theology **14**:520
- - Date of Composition **14**:521
- - Ruth in the Canon **14**:522
- - In the Aggadah **14**:522
- - In the Arts **14**:523
- agriculture, Hebrew **2**:389
- Greek canon **4**:825
- musical rendition **14**:1058
- Scrolls, The Five **14**:1057
- *illus:*
- - text
- - ninth cent. Bible **9**:1
- - "Orpah the Moabite" (paint., Abel Pann) Fig. 88 **3**:ART
- - *Tripartite Maḥzor* **4**:1154
Ruthenia (reg., Ukr.), *see* SUBCARPATHIAN RUTHENIA
Rutherston, Albert Daniel, *see* Rothenstein, Albert Daniel
RUTH RABBAH (Mid.) **14**:524
- *see also:* MIDRASH
Ruth Zuta (wk.) **16**:1515
Ruti (fam.), *see* ROTE
RUTILIUS NAMATIANUS **14**:525
Rutland (city, Vt.) **16**:112
Rutland Psalter (13th cent., Eng.) **13**:1327
Ruttenberg of Berdichev **16**:210
Rutty (fam.), *see* ROTE
RUWANDIZ (tn., Kurd.) **14**:525
Rūz, Al- (site, Isr.) **11**:1392
RUZHANY (tn., Belor.) **14**:525
- Bojan **4**:1183
- Ḥasidism **7**:1392ff
Ruzhany, Israel ben Shalom of, *see* Israel ben Shalom of Ruzhany
Ruzhin (ḥas. dyn.) **1**:ḥas table
RUZHIN, ISRAEL **14**:526
- Abraham ben Dov of Mezhirich **2**:140
- Galicia **16**:1328
- Sadgora **14**:625
- *geneal. table:* text
- *illus:*
- - Sadgora synagogue **14**:625
Ruzhin, Siddur of the Rabbi of **8**:1267
Ruzhyn (tn., Belor.), *see* RUZHANY
Ružomberok (tn., Cz.) **5**:1200
Rwanda (rep., Afr.) **9**:441
Ryan, Carrol **5**:113
RYBACK, ISSACHAR **14**:532
- art **3**:576
- *illus:* text
Rybczykowicz, Michael **4**:1360
Rybiński, Maciej **4**:885
Rydberg, Abraham Viktor **14**:929ff
Rydzyna (tn., Pol.) **14**:1433
Rye (tn., N.Y.) **16**:464
Rye, *see* FIVE SPECIES
Rylands Spanish Haggadah (14th cent. illum. ms., Sp.) **7**:1097
- illuminated manuscripts **8**:1265
- *illus:* **5**:*fcg.* 1387
Rylands Spanish Haggadah, "Brother" to (14th cent., illum. ms., Sp.) **6**:*fcg.* 619; **7**:1083; **8**:1217; **11**:*fcg.* 939; **16**:858
Rylsky, Yakov **12**:1377
Rymanow (ḥas. dyn.) **1**:ḥas. table
RYMANOW (tn., Pol.) **14**:533
Rymanower, Joseph ha-Kohen **14**:535
RYMANOWER, MENAHEM MENDEL **14**:534
RYMANOWER, ẒEVI HIRSH **14**:535
RYPIN (tn., Pol.) **14**:535
Rypins, Isaac L. **12**:38
RYSHKANY (tn., Mold.) **14**:536
Ryskind, Morrie **15**:1059
RYSSEL, VICTOR **14**:536
RYVEL (au., Tun.) **14**:536
- Oriental literature **12**:1465
Ryvkin, Miron (Meyer) Davidovich **14**:513
Ryzhey, Peter Lvovich, *see* TUR BROTHERS
Ryzhyn, Israel of, *see* RUZHIN, ISRAEL
RZESZOW (city, Pol.) **14**:537
- ghetto **13**:766
Rzymowski, W. **12**:844

S

S.A. (Sturmabteilungen) **7:**527
- concentration camps **5:**77
- Himmler, Heinrich **8:**498
SA-2 (Rus. missile) **14:**1640
SA-3 (Rus. missile) **14:**1640
Sa, Manoel de **8:**54
SA'AD (kib., Isr.) **14:**541
- school for proselytes **13:**1192
- statistics **1:**place list
- *illus:*
- - Sukkot prayers in trenches (1948) **16:**323
- - wedding procession **10:**972
Sa'ad (journ.) **1:**newsp. list
SAʿADI, JUDAH BEN SOLOMON **14:**541
SA'ADI, SAʿID BEN SOLOMON **14:**542
- Yemen history **16:**743
SAADIAH (poet, Yem.) **14:**543
Saadiah (Zion. ldr., Belor.), *see* MAZEH, JACOB
Saadiah, Moses ben Mevorakh **6:**492
Saadiah al-Fayyumi (gaon), *see* SAADIAH GAON
Saadiah bar Joseph (gaon), *see* SAADIAH GAON
Saadiah ben Berakhot **11:**766
Saadiah ben Daud al-ʿAdeni, *see* ADANI, SAADIAH BEN DAVID
Saadiah ben Ephraim **7:**1491
Saadiah ben Isaac **14:**1528
SAADIAH BEN JOSEPH HA-LEVI (r., Yem.) **14:**543
Saadiah ben Nathan Nata **9:**1078
- aliyah **9:**514
SAADIAH (Ben Joseph) GAON **14:**543
- *Contents:*
- - General **14:**543
- - As Halakhist **14:**547
- - Saadiah's Philosophy **14:**548
- - As Grammarian **14:**552
- - Saadiah's Translation of the Bible **14:**553
- - As Liturgist and Paytan **14:**553
- - Saadiah's Influence **14:**554
- General
- - calendar **5:**50
- - enumeration of *mitzvot* **5:**783
- - Faiyum **6:**1139
- - gaonate **7:**315ff
- - history chart **8:**766-767
- - music **12:**591
- - psychology and **13:**1343
- - rabbinical tradition **15:**1310
- Literature and Language
- - Abudarham's use of *siddur* **2:**181
- - alchemic pamphlet **2:**548
- - Al-Mukammas' tractates **3:**193
- - Arabic Bible translation **4:**863
- - *azharot* **3:**1007
- - Bible exegesis **4:**892; **4:**897; **11:**324
- - biography **4:**1010
- - Cairo *genizah* **16:**1336
- - ethical literature **6:**925
- - *Hapax Legomena* **7:**1318
- - Hebrew grammar **11:**324
- - Hebrew language **16:**1612
- - Judeo-Arabic literature **10:**411
- - letter of moral instruction **8:**664
- - linguistics **16:**1353
- - *Mishpetei Shevuot* **5:**1354
- - prosody **13:**1211
- - rabbinical literature **13:**1463
- - *Sefer Yeẓirah* **16:**786
- - *Shi'ur Komah* **14:**1418
- - translations **15:**1323
- - vowel theory **16:**1431
- - *Zerubbabel, Book of* **16:**1002
- Views and Polemics
- - angels **2:**974f
- - anthropomorphism **3:**56
- - astrology **3:**791
- - atomism **3:**830
- - attributes of God **7:**665
- - autonomy **3:**922
- - beatitude **4:**359ff
- - belief **4:**435ff
- - categories **5:**254
- - commandments, reasons for **5:**784ff
- - creation **5:**1067ff
- - dualism **6:**245; **7:**671
- - exile **7:**282ff
- - existence of God **7:**658
- - free will **7:**126
- - Islam **3:**193
- - Jewish mysticism **10:**511
- - Jewish philosophy **11:**338; **13:**431ff
- - Kalām **10:**702ff
- - Karaites **8:**665; **10:**768
- - logic **11:**459
- - Messiah **11:**1414; **13:**198
- - microcosm doctrine **11:**1502
- - miracles **12:**76
- - nature **12:**889
- - polemics **11:**354; **13:**791ff
- - problem of evil **7:**777
- - providence **13:**1284
- - redemption **14:**4
- - repentance, concept of **14:**76
- - resurrection **12:**1357; **14:**101
- - revelation **14:**122
- - reward, punishment **14:**136
- - *Shekhinah* **14:**1352
- - skepticism **14:**1645
- - soul **15:**172ff
- - soul, immortality of **15:**176
- - space and place **15:**218
- - substance and accident **15:**474
- - Throne of God **15:**1125ff
- - Torah **15:**1237; **15:**1244
- - Yudghanites **16:**868
- Personalities
- - Aaron ben Amram **2:**9
- - Aaron Sargado **2:**13
- - Ben-Asher, Aaron **4:**465
- - Ben Meir, Aaron **4:**540
- - David ben Zakkai **5:**1359
- - Ḥasan ben Mashi'aḥ **7:**1365
- - Hiwi al-Balkhi **8:**793
- - Kohen Ẓedek of Pumbedita **10:**1141
- - Mubashir **12:**497
- - Salmon ben Jeroham **14:**689
- - Yannai **16:**712
Saadiah of Worms **11:**1194
Saadun, Eliezer **6:**1371
SAALSCHUETZ, JOSEPH LEWIN **14:**555
Saalschuetz, Louis **14:**555
Sa'ar (kib., Isr.) **1:**place list
Sa'arat Teiman (bk.) **10:**1193
SAARBRUECKEN (city, Ger.) **14:**555
Saaz (tn., Bohem.), *see* ZATEC
Saba, Abraham ibn, *see* Abraham ibn Saba
SABA, ABRAHAM BEN JACOB **14:**555
Saba, Saul **16:**926
SABA, UMBERTO **14:**556
- Debenedetti **5:**1428
- Italian literature **9:**1112
Sabac (tn., Serb.) **16:**869ff
- Zionism **16:**1148
Sabac (camp) **8:**858
Sabaean (lang.) **14:**1152
Sabalski, Yitzḥak **13:**1031
Saban, Raphael **9:**1096; **15:**1460
SABATH, ADOLF JOACHIM **14:**557
Sabato, Eliadi **6:**957
Sabato, Matassia di **13:**563
Sabatowski, Ḥayyim **13:**1503
Sabatowski, Herzke **13:**1503
Sabatowski, Mordekhai **13:**1503
Sabba, Al- (Masada, Isr.) **11:**1079
Sabba, Isaac **16:**907
Sabbadini, S. **5:**1297
Sabbaeus (2nd cent., Samar.) **2:**949
Sabba of Kelme, *see* BROIDA, SIMḤAH ZISSEL BEN ISRAEL
Sabbas (archbp.) **15:**1355
Sabbatarians **4:**790ff
Sabbateanism, *see* SHABBETAI ẒEVI
SABBATH **14:**557
- *Contents:*
- - In the Bible **14:**558
- - In the Apocrypha **14:**562
- - In Rabbinic Literature **14:**562
In Jewish Thought **14:**564
- - Laws and Customs **14:**566
- - In Kabbalah **14:**567
- - In Art **14:**570
- General
- - calendar **5:**43
- - Divine example **7:**645; **8:**1292
- - dress **6:**215
- - Egypt, ancient **6:**491
- - folklore **6:**1391
- - greetings **7:**914
- - hairstyle **5:**982
- - industrial labor **16:**1314
- - Judaism **10:**388; **10:**391
- - *manna* **11:**883
- - netherworld **12:**998
- - Phlorina **13:**471
- - *reshei kallah* **14:**83
- - Sambatyon **14:**763ff
- - *Sefirot* doctrine **10:**572
- - source for dogma **3:**658
- - symbol of joy **10:**321
- - Tablets of Law **15:**691
- - twilight and duration of **15:**1474
- - work on weekdays **10:**1321
- Laws and Customs
- - ablutions on eve of **2:**83
- - Anan ben David on **2:**921
- - animals **3:**5
- - *aninut* **3:**23
- - arrest **8:**1301
- - books printed on **5:**281
- - candles **14:**1356; **15:**735
- - carrying **6:**849
- - chess **5:**403
- - Commandments, the 613 **5:**764f,781
- - contract, illegal **5:**930
- - cooking and food **6:**1422
- - cooking on festivals for **6:**849
- - court action on **13:**958; **13:**959
- - dances **5:**1266
- - death **5:**1425ff
- - distributing books **7:**1151
- - eating of fish **6:**1327
- - *eruv* **6:**849
- - fastdays **6:**1193ff
- - festivals **6:**1237ff
- - fire prohibition **6:**1304
- - *gerogeret* **16:**389
- - *ḥallah* **7:**1195
- - hunting prohibited **8:**1111
- - Israel **9:**902ff
- - Israel law (1948) **12:**147
- - Jacob Moellin's ruling **7:**470
- - Jewish badge **4:**65
- - *karet* punishment **10:**788
- - Karaite practise **10:**779
- - laws **14:**1215
- - legal person **10:**1569
- - Meir Ba'al ha-Nes **11:**1246

- - milking **3**:6
- - mintmasters, work on **12**:63
- - mourning **12**:488ff
- - *mukẓeh* **12**:515
- - New Moon, announced on **12**:1040
- - Paschal slaughter knife **12**:12
- - Pentateuch **13**:241; **13**:245
- - *pikku'aḥ nefesh* **13**:509
- - *reshut* **14**:83
- - Sabbath *goi* **9**:1234
- - sacrifice **14**:610
- - *Sefer Torah,* rescue of, on **14**:1103
- - *shofar* on Rosh ha-Shanah **9**:241; **14**:1446ff
- - sick, visiting on **14**:1497
- - *sifrei ha-minim* **14**:1521
- - signet rings **14**:1074
- - *Targum Sheni,* in **15**:812
- - technology **15**:893ff
- - *tefillin* **15**:901
- - telegrams **14**:91
- - tennis **14**:875
- - violators' evidence ruling (1946) **12**:144
- - walking **6**:849
- - woman's work after **12**:24
- - writing prohibition **16**:670ff
- Liturgy and Services
- - *Amidah* **2**:843ff
- - *Arvit* **3**:665
- - *Atta Eḥad* **3**:833
- - *Avot* **3**:984
- - *Ba-Meh Madlikin* **4**:158
- - bridegroom's Torah reading **11**:1042; **11**:1043; **11**:1044
- - *Eshet Ḥayil* **6**:887
- - *haftarah* **16**:1342
- - *havdalah* **7**:1481ff
- - *hoshanot* **8**:1029
- - *Kabbalat Shabbat* **10**:654
- - Kiddush **10**:974
- - *Lekhah Dodi* **11**:4
- - *Melavveh Malkah* **11**:1276
- - *Musaf* **12**:532
- - Sabbaths of Affliction **15**:1124
- - sermons **13**:994
- - *seudah shelishit* **14**:1195
- - seven benedictions **11**:1040
- - *Shir ha-Yiḥud* **14**:1416
- - Song of Songs **13**:1057; **15**:150
- - special Sabbaths **14**:572
- - synagogue **15**:580
- - Temple service **15**:977
- - Torah reading **15**:1246ff
- - *Yozerot* **16**:866
- Movements and Views
- - Church Fathers **5**:537
- - Conservative Judaism **5**:901; **12**:1445
- - Dionysus, Cult of **6**:62
- - Falashas **6**:1147
- - Islam **10**:1198
- - *Jubilees, Book of* **10**:325
- - Judaizers **10**:397
- - Karaites **4**:297; **10**:779
- - Korets, Phinehas of **10**:1204
- - Naḥmanides **12**:777
- - Nehemiah's rebuke **8**:624
- - Reform Judaism **12**:1443; **14**:24ff
- - Sabbatarians **4**:790ff
- - Samaritans **14**:741ff
- - transfer to Sunday **8**:515
- - William Prynne's views **13**:1296
- *illus:*
- - text
- - "Blessing over the Candles" (piant., I. Kaufmann) **4**:487
- - Bombay, "For Jews Only" tram coupon **8**:1353
- - candlesticks **5**:*fcg.* 299; **11**:269
- - cholent pot (16th cent., Ger.) **5**:489
- - "Conclusion of the Sabbath" (paint., M. Oppenheim) **7**:1483
- - *Eruv Tavshillin* tablet **7**:*fcg.* 843
- - *ḥallah* cover, embroidered **6**:1385
- - *ḥallah* platter **7**:1194
- - *ḥallah* shapes **6**:1419
- - *havdalah* ceremony articles **3**:529; **5**:118,300; **6**:1390; **7**:1485–1488
- - Jamaica, exemption from carrying arms **9**:1272
- - Jews going to pray **14**:1216
- - lamps **4**:90; **5**:299; **6**:1383
- - *Lekhah Dodi* wall plaque **10**:655
- - Morocco, Jewish quarter **12**:331
- - Mukachevo, Jewish street **12**:513
- - Sabbath plate (majolica, 16th cent.) **3**:1016
- - salutations (table) **7**:913
- - scriptural readings chart **15**:1249
- - Second Temple inscription **12**:573
- - "Shabbat in Safed" (paint., M. Castel) Pl. 7. 3-ART
- - Western Wall on Sabbath cloth **16**:469
- - woman blessing lights **11**:1039
- *mus. notations:*
- - *nusaḥ* of morning prayers **12**:1283
- - psalmody, Ps. 95 **13**:1331
- *see also:* DAY AND NIGHT; NESHAMAH YETERAH
Sabbath, Albert **15**:311
Sabbath, Council for the (Isr.), *see* Council for the Sabbath
Sabbath, Reception of, *see* KABBALAT SHABBAT
Sabbath and Evening Schools **6**:433ff
Sabbath lamp **7**:1292
Sabbath League (int. orgn.) **5**:181
Sabbath Leaves (newsp.) **13**:1031
Sabbath Observance Council (Isr.) **9**:896
Sabbath Observers, *see* Subbotniki
SABBATHS, SPECIAL **14**:572
- *Contents:*
- - *Shabbat Mevarekhin* **14**:572
- - *Shabbat Rosh Hodesh* **14**:572
- - *Shabbat Shuvah* **14**:572
- - *Shabbat Hol ha-Mo'ed* **14**:573
- - *Shabbat Ḥanukkah* **14**:573
- - *Shabbat Shirah* **14**:573
- - *Shabbat Shekalim* **14**:573
- - *Shabbat Zakhor* **14**:573
- - *Shabbat Parah* **14**:573
- - *Shabbat ha-Hodesh* **14**:573
- - *Shabbat Ḥazon* **14**:573
- - *Shabbat Naḥamu* **14**:574
- Adar **2**:252
- *haftarah* reading **16**:1344
- illuminated *maḥzorim* **11**:735
- *Shabbat Shirah* **14**:1071
- *illus:*
- - *Adon Ḥasdekha* piyyut **10**:362
- - *maḥzor* for *Parshat Zakhor* **11**:397
- - *Parashat Parah, piyyut* **14**:*fcg.* 11
- - *Shabbat ha-Gadol, piyyut* **14**:1217
- - *Shabbat Shuvah, Or Olam* prayer **14**:74
- - *Worms Maḥzor* **11**:*fcg.* 619
- *see also:* SHABBAT BERESHIT; SHABBAT HA-GADOL
Sabbath Visitor (period.) **5**:564
- children's literature **5**:456
- Lilienthal, Max **11**:245
- press **13**:1052
SABBATICAL YEAR AND JUBILEE **14**:574
- *Contents:*
- - General **14**:574
- - Ancient Near Eastern Legal Background **14**:577
- - Post-Biblical **14**:578
- - Jubilee in the Second Temple Period **14**:578
- - - Halakhah and Development **14**:578
- - - The Calculation of the Jubilee **14**:579
- - - The Jubilee in History **14**:580
- - - The Jubilee in the Aggadah **14**:581
- - Sabbatical Year in Post-Biblical Times **14**:582
- - Observance
- - - Post-Biblical Period **14**:583
- - - Modern Period **14**:584
- General
- - eschatology **6**:883
- - famine **6**:1173ff
- - kabbalistic doctrine **10**:536; **10**:575; **10**:579; **10**:581ff
- - Roman land taxes **9**:250
- - Samaritan chronology **14**:748; **14**:751
- - *Shevi'it* (tract.) **14**:1391
- - Syria **15**:639
- Laws and Customs
- - *Arnona* exemption **3**:487ff
- - Commandments, the 613 **5**:767,778
- - gifts to poor **13**:850
- - *Hakhel* ceremony **7**:1148
- - hydroponics, use of **7**:1059
- - levitical property **11**:136; **13**:1077
- - Leviticus, Book of **11**:147
- - *ma'aser ani* **5**:1486
- - ownership of land **12**:1532; **12**:1533
- - Pentateuch **13**:245; **13**:254
- - pledge **13**:638
- - property return **14**:675
- - *prosbul* **13**:1181
- - religious life in Israel **9**:891ff
- - slavery **14**:1656
- - *takkanah* **15**:717
- Views and Controversies
- - Berlin, Naphtali Ẓevi **4**:662
- - Diskin, Moses Joshua **6**:74
- - Eliasberg, Mordecai **6**:616
- - Elyashar, Jacob Saul **6**:692
- - Engel, Joseph **6**:745
- - Judah ha-Nasi **9**:252; **10**:369
- - Karelitz, Avraham Y. **10**:788
- - Klepfish, S. Z. **10**:1106
- - Kook, A. I. **10**:1185
- - Mohilewer, Samuel **12**:218
- - 16th century controversy **9**:1426
- - Trunk, Israel Joshua **15**:1413
- *illus:*
- - hydroponics at Kibbutz Ḥafez Ḥayyim **7**:1059
- - *Shevi'it* **14**:1391
Sabbatyon (leg. riv.), *see* SAMBATYON
SABBIONETA (tn., It.) **14**:586
- *illus:* text
SABEA (anc. reg., S. Arab.) **14**:587
- *Ahl al-Kitāb* **2**:467
SABIN, ALBERT BRUCE **14**:588
Sabina Poppaea (w. of Nero), *see* POPPAEA, SABINA
Sab'īn Lafẓa al-Mufrada, al- (wk.), *see Kitāb al-Sab'īn Lafẓa al-Mufrada*
SABINUS (Rom. offic.) **14**:589
- Quintilius **13**:1428
Sabkhat al-Ṭāba (marsh, Isr.) **10**:300
Sabra (native Israeli) **9**:402
- *illus:*
- - group of youths **9**:505
Sabra Books (publ. firm, Isr.) **13**:1379
Sabshin, Melvin **13**:1340
SABSOVICH, H. L. **14**:589
- Vineland **16**:157
Sabta (Sabtah; bib. fig.) **12**:883
Sabteca (bib. fig.) **12**:883
Sabtūna' (anc. Syr. tn.), *see* RIBLAH
Sab'uni, Aaron ha-, *see* Aaron ha-Sab'uni of Salé
Sacchetti, Franco **9**:1104
Sacco, Pieve di **4**:1233
"Sacco and Vanzetti" (drg., Ben Shahn) **3**:561
Sacco-Vanzetti (murder case) **7**:95; **14**:589
SACERDOTE, DAVID **14**:589
Sacerdote, Leone **14**:590
Sacerdote, R.A. **5**:736
SACERDOTI, ANGELO-RAPHAEL CHAIM **14**:590
Sacerdoti, Eugenio Cohen **13**:12
SACHAR, ABRAM LEON **14**:590
- historiography **8**:562
Sachar, Howard Morley **14**:591
Sachar, Kreine Sonia, *see* LIPZIN, KENI
SACHER, HARRY **14**:591
Sacher, Michael **14**:592
Sacher, Miriam **14**:592
- *illus:*
- - Wizo delegation, 12th Zionist Congress **16**:1101
- - Wizo executive **16**:594
Sacher-Masoch, Leopold Ritter von **7**:445
SACHS (fam.) **14**:592
Sachs (bnk., U.S.) **4**:178
Sachs, A. (Zion.) **16**:1165
Sachs, Abraham (15th cent.) **10**:1393
SACHS, BERNARD (sci., U.S.) **14**:592
Sachs, Bernard (writ., S.A.) **15**:210
Sachs, Bonaventura **5**:1009
SACHS, CURT **14**:592
Sachs, Ernest **14**:592
Sachs, George **15**:210
SACHS, HANNS **14**:593
- psychiatry **13**:1338
Sachs, Harry **7**:719; **14**:592
Sachs, Howard Joseph **7**:719
Sachs, Joseph (r., U.S.) **14**:592
Sachs, Joseph (writ., S.A.) **15**:210
SACHS, JULIUS (bot.) **14**:594
- botany **4**:1030
SACHS, JULIUS (educ., U.S.) **14**:594
- family **14**:592
SACHS, LEONARD (Br. act.) **15**:1054; **15**:1089
Sachs, Leonard (sport., U.S.) **15**:303, 304, 308
Sachs, Leonie, *see* SACHS, NELLY
Sachs, Leopold **11**:1440
Sachs, Lippman **14**:834
Sachs, M. (indus., Rus.) **15**:488
Sachs, Mary **7**:1348
SACHS, MAURICE (au., Fr.) **14**:594
Sachs, Mavro (Maurice; physic., Yug.) **16**:918
SACHS, MICHAEL **14**:595
- chronological chart **8**:766-767
- commandments, reasons for **5**:789
- Steinschneider, Moritz **15**:374
- Veit, Moritz **16**:86
SACHS, NELLY **14**:595
- chronological chart **8**:766-767
- contribution to literature **8**:743
Sachs, Paul **3**:650; **14**:592
Sachs, Samuel (bnk., U.S.) **7**:719; **14**:592
Sachs, Samuel (r., Can.) **15**:1261
SACHS, SENIOR **14**:597
- Lebensohn, Micah Joseph **10**:1550
Sachs, S.J. **16**:1165
Sachs, Walter Edward **7**:719; **14**:592
Sachs, Wolf (stlr., U.S.) **13**:482
Sachs, Wolf (psych., S.Afr.) **13**:1340; **15**:210
Sachs Collegiate Institute (N.Y.) **14**:594
Sachse, Heinrich, *see* LOEWE,

HEINRICH
Sachsen (state, E. Ger.), *see* SAXONY
Sachsenburg (camp, Ger.) **5**:77
SACHSENHAUSEN ORANIENBURG (concen. camp, Ger.) **14**:597
- artists **3**:568
- forging foreign currency **5**:727
- Hoess, Rudolf **8**:806
- *illus:*
- - roll call **8**:761
Sachsenspiegel (law code, Ger.) **14**:923
SACK, BENJAMIN G. **10**:308; **10**:315
Sack, Jacob (Jack) **15**:308
Sack, J. J. **13**:1519
Sack, Martin, Sr. **9**:1191
Sack, Menahem Mendel **14**:174
Sack, Saul **6**:465
Sackheim, Maxwell B. **2**:318; **13**:1372
SACKLER, HARRY **14**:598
- drama **6**:198
- Hebrew literature **8**:212
Sacks, Leon **13**:230
Sacks, Moses **9**:514
SACKUR, OTTO **5**:387
Sacramentary of Gellone (8th cent. illum. ms., Fr.) **6**:337
SACRAMENTO (city, Calif.) **14**:598
Sacred music, *see* MUSIC
Sacred places, *see* HOLY PLACES
Sacred property, misuse of, *see* ME'ILAH
Sacred sites, *see* CULT PLACES, ISRAELITE
SACRIFICE **14**:599
- *Contents:*
- - In the Bible **14**:599
- - - Propitiatory Offerings **14**:600
- - - Dedicatory Offerings **14**:601
- - - Burnt Offerings **14**:601
- - - Meal Offerings **14**:602
- - - Libation Offerings **14**:603
- - - Fellowship Offerings **14**:603
- - - Peace Offerings **14**:603
- - - Wave Offerings **14**:604
- - - Votive Offerings **14**:604
- - - Freewill Offerings **14**:605
- - - Ordination Offerings **14**:605
- - In Biblical Tradition and History **14**:605
- - - Age of the Patriarchs **14**:605
- - - From Moses to Samuel **14**:606
- - - The Monarchy **14**:606
- - - The Return to Zion **14**:606
- - - The Prophetic and Wisdom Literature **14**:607
- - Second Temple Period **14**:607
- - - Daily Service **14**:608
- - - Sabbath Service **14**:610
- - - The Pilgrim Festivals **14**:610
- - - New Year **14**:612
- - - Sacrifices from Non-Jews **14**:612
- - - Cessation of Sacrifice **14**:612
- - Later Interpretations **14**:613
- - - Symbolic **14**:613
- - - Juridical **14**:613
- - - Rational **14**:613
- - - Kabbalah **14**:615
- General
- - Diaspora **6**:13
- - pillar of fire **13**:524
- - Saul **14**:913
- - sin **14**:1590ff
- - Solomon **15**:104
- - Uriel **16**:7
- Types and Contents
- - *Avodah* **3**:977ff
- - cattle **16**:1273
- - cult **5**:1155
- - Day of Atonement **5**:1384
- - doves **6**:184
- - *eglah arufah* **6**:475
- - fire **6**:1303
- - firstborn **6**:1308ff
- - first fruits **6**:1313
- - guilt and sin offerings **10**:917
- - guilt offering (Hurrian) **12**:1290
- - incense **8**:1310ff
- - *kipper* **10**:1039
- - leper **11**:35
- - New Moon **12**:1040; **12**:290
- - oils **12**:1348
- - ordeal of jealousy **12**:1449
- - post impurity **13**:1405
- - proselytes **13**:1183
- - red heifer **14**:9
- - right side **14**:177
- - Sabbath **14**:558
- - salt **14**:710
- - Samaritan paschal lamb **14**:734; **14**:742
- - *semikhah* **14**:1140
- - water libation **15**:499
- - wood offerings **16**:630
- - *zavah* and *niddah* **12**:1142; **12**:1146
- Laws and Customs
- - Aden customs **2**:264
- - agency applied to **2**:349
- - alien **6**:585
- - atonement **3**:830
- - Commandments, the 613 **5**:763,773
- - consecration **8**:279
- - desecration **5**:1559
- - disqualifying blemishes **4**:1082ff
- - forgiveness **6**:1433
- - Leviticus **11**:139
- - liturgy **11**:393; **11**:404
- - lots, casting of **11**:511
- - *mishmarot* **12**:91ff
- - *niddui* **8**:351
- - prayer as replacement **12**:532
- - proselyte **9**:242
- - Rhodes **14**:147
- Temple **15**:952ff
- - pilgrims **13**:510
- - Tabernacle **15**:683
- - Temple Mount **15**:993
- Synagogue **15**:580; **15**:594
- - prayer **13**:979
- Talmudic Literature
- - *Kinnim* **10**:1036
- - *Kodashim* **10**:1126
- - *Menaḥot* **11**:1314ff
- - *Pesaḥim* **13**:327
- - *Tamid* **15**:785
- - *Zevaḥim* **16**:1002
- Views and Attitudes
- - Amos **2**:888
- - antinomians **3**:69
- - Eleazar ben Hananiah **8**:639
- - Falashas **6**:1147
- - folklore **6**:1400
- - Isaiah **9**:47
- - Jewish Christian sects **10**:39
- - Judah Halevi **4**:435
- - Kalischer, Ẓevi Hirsch **10**:708
- - Maimonides **11**:776
- - Meshwi al-'Ukbarī **11**:1405
- - Nehemiah ben Ḥushiel **9**:259
- - Pharisee attitude **13**:366
- - prophets **13**:1161ff
- - sages **14**:645
- - *Yaḥad* **16**:699
- *illus:*
- - animals brought for **16**:1003
- - birds **10**:1037
- - Cain and Abel **2**:58
- - *eglah arufah* ceremony **6**:476
- - Mari wall painting **11**:979
- - Noah's offering **12**:885
- - preparation of **15**:786
- - priests performing the sacrifice **3**:*fcg.* 988
- - profane use of **11**:1238
- - sacrifices brought to the Temple **13**:327
- - sacrificial animals **6**:277
- - Samaritan paschal offering **8**:934; **13**:169; **14**:743
- - Temple service, Day of Atonement **16**:845
- *see also:* ALTAR; PRIESTS AND PRIESTHOOD
Sacrifice, human **2**:918, 304
- *Akedah* **2**:480; **2**:482
- Moloch **12**:230
- *illus:*
- - Jephthah sacrificing his daughter **9**:1342
- - Moloch **8**:1237
"Sacrifice of Isaac" (paint., D. Aronson) **3**:615
SACRILEGE **14**:616
- lots **11**:510
- *me'ilah* **8**:281
SACY, ANTOINE ISAAC SILVESTRE DE **14**:617
- Hebraist **8**:54
- Samaritan calendar **14**:749
Sacy, De (bib. trans.), *see* Le Maistre, Louis Isaac
Sadagura (vill., Ukr.), *see* SADGORA
ṢA'DAH (tn., Yem.) **14**:617
- Aden **2**:260
- Haydan **7**:1496
- Najran **12**:801
- Zaydis **16**:741
Sadai, Yiẓḥak **12**:671
SA'D AL-DAWLA AL-ṢAFĪ IBN HIBBATALLAH **14**:618
SADAN, DOV **14**:618
- Agnon, Shmuel Yosef **2**:371
- critic **5**:1123
- Israel **9**:900
Sadaqa ben Munajja al-Ḥakīm **14**:755
Sadat, Anwar **9**:421
- Egyptian-Israel cease fire **14**:1640
- Nazi sympathies **16**:1087
Sadboon, Joseph **10**:554
Saddan (journ.) **1**:newsp. list
Saddik el Mahdi **9**:441
Saddler (tn., Ill.) **8**:1256
Saddler, Morris **8**:1256
Saddlery **5**:1048
SADDUCEES **14**:620
- *Contents:*
- - Origin of the Name **14**:620
- - Beliefs and Doctrines **14**:621
- - Attitude toward Prayer and Sacrifice **14**:622
- - Fate **14**:622
- - New Testament **14**:622
- History
- - Aristobulus II **3**:440
- - civil affairs **11**:315
- - Hellenism **8**:296
- - Hyrcanus, John **8**:1147
- - Jesus **10**:12
- - Johanan ben Zakkai **9**:240; **10**:150
- - Karaites **10**:764
- - priests **13**:1087
- - Samaritan tradition **14**:730
- - Temple **15**:974
- - Zadok **3**:67
- Views and Attitudes
- - afterlife **3**:67
- - Bible **8**:1417
- - calendar **5**:50
- - free will **7**:129
- - *haftarah* **16**:1343
- - law **10**:389; **12**:1441
- - providence **13**:281
- - red heifer **14**:12
- - resurrection **14**:96
- - Sabbath carrying **6**:851
- - Sukkot **15**:499ff
- - tradition **15**:1310
- Pharisaic Judaism
- - *apikorsim* **8**:359
- - *birkat ha-minim* **4**:1035
- - defeat celebrated **14**:1563
- - menstruation **12**:1148
- - *min* **12**:2
- - polemic literature **13**:790ff
- - sages **14**:639ff
- - term for Christian **7**:411
- *see also:* BOETHUSIANS; PHARISEES
Sadduk (1st cent., Er. Isr.) **16**:916
Saddukiyya (J. sect) **16**:1335
ṢADE (Heb. letter) **14**:622
SADEH, PINḤAS **14**:623
- Hebrew literature **8**:207
SADEH, YIẒḤAK **14**:623
- Defense Forces **9**:684
- Palmaḥ **13**:45
- *illus:*
- - Dayan and Allon (1938) **7**:1070
- - Haganah High Command (1942) **7**:1070
SADGORA (vill., Ukr.) **14**:624
- Ruzhin, Israel of **14**:527
- *illus:* text
Sadgora (ḥas. dynasty) **15**:417
- dynasties **1**:ḥas. table
- Ḥasidism **7**:1422
- Ruzhin, Israel of **14**:527
Sa'd ibn Kammūna **10**:781
Sa'd ibn-Mu'ādh **12**:510
- Qurayza **13**:1436
Ṣadīd al-Dawla **8**:1447
Ṣadīq, Yehudah **8**:1453
SA'DIS (dyn. sharifs, Mor.) **14**:625
Sadler, John **6**:752
- British Israelites **4**:1381
- Hebraists **8**:54
Sadot (journ.) **1**:newsp. list
Sadoveanu, Mihail **14**:419
- *illus:*
- - Pauker, Ana, and **13**:188
Sadowsky, Reuben **12**:1083
Saechsisch-Regen (tn., Rum.), *see* REGHIN
Sá e Mesquita, Francisco de **4**:405
Saemundarson, Nicolaeus **15**:1355
Saenger, J. **7**:173
Saenger, Max **13**:973
Saertel, Moses **4**:867
Saewulf (Chr. trav.) **15**:1355
Safah Berurah (Heb. lang.mvmt.) **2**:205; **8**:521
- Israel **9**:999
Safah Berurah (dict.) **7**:1273; **11**:357
Safah Berurah (wk., Ibn Ezra) **16**:1358,1385
Ṣafāitic (ling. div.) **3**:237
- Semitic languages **14**:1152
Safarī, 'Īsā al- **9**:1041
Šafaríkovo (tn., Slov.) **10**:1216
Safawid (dyn.) **13**:312
Safd el-Batikh (site, Isr.) **4**:713
SAFDIE, MOSHE **3**:365
- *illus:*
- - "Habitat" **3**:356
SAFED (Safad; tn., Isr.) **14**:626
- *Contents:*
- - General **14**:626
- - Modern Period **14**:629
- - Historic Buildings and Archaeological Restorations **14**:630
- - Hebrew Printing **14**:631
- Arab attacks **9**:344
- Ashkenazi community **9**:497ff
- Berab, Jacob **4**:583
- Caro, Joseph **5**:194
- Crusader period **9**:269; **9**:272
- economy **8**:694; **8**:695
- emissaries from **14**:1359ff
- goldsmithery **7**:742
- ḥasidic settlement **7**:1392; **9**:1059
- Hebrew language **16**:1641
- Hebron and **8**:232
- history chart (1837) **8**:766-767

- homiletics **8**:954
- immigrants **9**:512
- Israel **9**:890ff
- Kabbalah **10**:541ff
- Luria, Isaac **11**:573
- Mamluk period **9**:274; **9**:279
- massacre (1929) **9**:462
- music, Jewish **12**:609
- Ottoman period **9**:283ff; **16**:1536,1549
- pilgrimage **8**:922
- seal motif **14**:1081
- Sephardi scholars **14**:1175
- stamps **15**:332
- statistics **1**:place list
- textiles **15**:1039
- Trani, Moses **15**:1315
- *illus:*
- - Ha-Ari synagogue **11**:572
- - "Interior of a Synagogue at Safed" (paint., M. Castel) Pl.7 3-ART
- - "Synagogue in Safed" (paint., N. Gutman) **7**:988
- - "Synagogue in Safed" (paint., M. Levanon) Pl.9 3-ART
- - "View of Safed" (paint., M. Shem) Pl.4 3-ART
- *see also:* ḤALUKKAH
Safed Museum of the Printing Arts **4**:1220
Safety, *see* PEACE
Safety and Hygiene Institute (Isr.) **9**:877
Safflower (bot.) **13**:625 **15**:269
SAFFRON (bot.) **14**:632
- flowers **6**:1365
- spices **15**:269
SAFI (tn., Mor.) **14**:633
Ṣafiyeh (16th cent., Turk.) **10**:991
Safiyya (w. of Muhammad) **2**:8; **10**:942
Safov (vill., Morav.) **12**:306
- Banet, Naphtali **4**:160
SAFRA (amora) **14**:634
Safra, Jacob Levi **15**:1214
Safra, Y. **6**:735
Safra Benayah ben Sa'adiah, *see* BENAYAH (fam.)
Safrah bank (Syr.) **15**:646
SAFRAN, ALEXANDER **14**:634
- Rumania **14**:406ff
SAFRAN, BEZALEL ZE'EV **14**:635
Safran, Hanoch Henikh **14**:635
Safran, Hillel **16**:1249
Safran, Joseph **14**:635
Safran, Menahem **13**:650; **14**:635
Safrin (ḥas. dyn.) **10**:1173
Safrin, Baruch **10**:1173
Safrin, Benjamin **16**:1165
Safrin, Isaac Eizik **16**:1212
SAFRIN, ISAAC JUDAH JEHIEL **14**:635
Safrin, Jacob Moses **16**:1212
Safrut (Mikra; publ., Warsaw) **5**:434
Sagalyn, Raphael **15**:318
Sagan, Szachna **16**:349
Sagar, William **10**:1001
SAGES **14**:636
- *Contents:*
- - Introduction **14**:636
- - Typology **14**:637
- - - As Jurist **14**:637
- - - As "Judge" **14**:638
- - - As "Prophet" **14**:638
- - - Sages and Sadducees **14**:639
- - Attitude to Oral Law **14**:639
- - Sages and Priests **14**:640
- - - Temple Ritual **14**:641
- - *Haverim* and the *Am ha-Areẓ* **14**:642
- - Organization of the Sages **14**:643
- - - Bet Hillel and Bet Shammai **14**:643
- - - The *Nesi'im* **14**:643
- - - Akiva **14**:644
- - Maintenance of the Sages **14**:644
- - Study versus Public Affairs **14**:645
- - The Dayyan **14**:646
- - *Halakhah* **14**:646
- - Relations between Teacher and Student **14**:647
- - The Donor **14**:648
- - The Conduct of the Sage **14**:648
- - Relations between the Sages and Other Classes **14**:649
- - General Knowledge **14**:649
- - The Influence of Non-Jewish Cultures **14**:650
- - The Concepts of Justice and Piety **14**:652
- - - The Ideal Sage and his Ideals **14**:652
- - - Asceticism and its Opponents **14**:652
- - The Jewish People and Its History **14**:653
- asceticism **3**:678
- conflict of opinion **5**:891
- emissaries **14**:1361
- Greek and Latin **7**:884
- Judaism **10**:388
- *Leviticus Rabbah* on **11**:148
- majority decisions **4**:433
- *mamzer* **11**:840
- Mordecai **12**:309
- right of rabbinic enactments **4**:433
- *soferim* **15**:80
- *talmid ḥakham* **15**:746
- Temple **15**:983
- title "rabbi" **13**:1445
- unlearned and **10**:370
- vengeance **16**:94
- *see also:* AMORAIM; ḤAKHAM; TANNA, TANNAIM
Sagi, Mt. (Isr.) **12**:927
Sagi Nahor (kab.), *see* ISAAC THE BLIND
Saginaw (city, Mich.) **11**:1500
SAGIS (fam.) **14**:655
Sagis, Jonathan **14**:655
Sagis, Joseph **14**:655
- Alexandria **2**:593
Sagis, Solomon ben Moses **14**:655
Sagittarius (Zodiac sign) **16**:1191
- *illus:* **10**:1071
"Saggittarius" (paint., H. Frankenthaler) **3**:621
Sagner, Stanley **15**:311
Sagunto (city, Sp.), *see* MURVIEDRO
Ṣaḥāba **7**:1051
SAHAGÚN (tn., Sp.) **14**:655
- Burgos community **4**:1512
Sahagún, Don Cag Merdohay of **6**:261
Sahagūn, David **6**:261
Sahagūn, Shem Tob **6**:261
Ṣāḥib al shurṭa (Arab. tit.), *see* IBN EZRA, MOSES BEN JACOB
Sahadic (dialect) **4**:861
Sahira, Plain of (Isr.) **9**:1434
SAHL, MORT **15**:1090
- U.S. literature **15**:1577
SAHLĀN BEN ABRAHAM **14**:656
Sahl ben Maẓli'aḥ **6**:88
- *Aliyah* **9**:511
- Avelei Zion **3**:946
- calendar **4**:540
- Hebrew language **16**:1634
- visiting graves **8**:922
Sahl ben Netira **12**:1000; **14**:545
Sahl ibn Bishr **3**:790; **15**:1326
SAHL IBN FADL **14**:656
Sahl ibn Rabban al-Tabarī, *see* Tabarī, Sahl ibn Rabban al-
SAHULA, ISAAC BEN SOLOMON ABI **14**:656
- Jewish literature **11**:352
- Kabbalah **10**:530; **10**:532
- *maqāma* **11**:937
- Zohar **16**:1209
- *illus:*
- - text
- - *Meshal ha-Kadmoni,* **3**:19,534,791; **5**:430; **6**:1128
SAHULA, MEIR BEN SOLOMON ABI **14**:657
- Ibn Shuaib, Joshua **8**:1202
- on Naḥmanides **15**:521
- *Sefer ha-Bahir* **4**:100
- *Sefer Yeẓirah* **16**:787
Sa'īd (poet, Yem.), *see* SAADIAH
Sa'id, Nuri **14**:1624
Sa'īd ben Abraham **16**:741
Sa'id ben Babshad ha-Kohen **13**:593
SA'ID IBN HASAN **14**:658
- Islam **9**:102
Sa'īdiyin (loc., Isr.) **12**:927
Saigon (city, S. Vietnam) **12**:876
Sa'ikah, Al- (Arab guerilla orgn.) **9**:471
- Lebanon **10**:1547
Sailors
- guilds **7**:971
- *mishmarot* **12**:92
SAINEANU, LAZAR **14**:658
- Rumanian **14**:399
St. Agathe des Monts (tn., Can.) **13**:1423
St. Albans (city, Vt.) **16**:112
St. Albans Psalter (12th cent. illum. ms., Eng.) **3**:217
- *illus:* **3**:217; **8**:660; **11**:1; **15**:1497
St. Andrew's Church (Jer.) **9**:1473
St. Anne, Church of (Jer.) **9**:1416
- renovations **9**:1455
- *illus:*
- - east aisle **9**:1453
St.-Avold (tn., Fr.) **11**:497
St. Basil (4th cent. C.E.) **11**:1183
- *illus:*
- - Ephraim the physician and **11**:1182
St. Brochardus **5**:186
St. Catharines (city, Ont.) **12**:1408
St. Catherine of Alexandria **14**:1599
- *illus:*
- - Brought for burial by angels **14**:1599
St. Catherine's Monastery (Sinai) **3**:239; **9**:1579
- *illus:*
- - "burning bush" **4**:1529
- - Jebel Mūsā **14**:1597
St.-Chef, Abbey Church of **9**:1580
St. Claire's convent (Jer.) **9**:1459
St.-Cyprien (Fr. concen. camp) **7**:982
- France **7**:34
SAINT-DENIS (city, Fr.) **14**:659
St.-Dié (tn., Fr.) **11**:496
St. Elias (Isr.) **5**:186
SAINTES (tn., Fr.) **14**:659
St. Etienne, Church of (Jer.) **9**:1461
St. Eustatius (isl., Antilles) **12**:995
St. Fons-Vénissieux (Fr.) **11**:625
St. Francisville (tn., Louis.) **11**:520
St. Francis Xavier (Ind.) **8**:1391
SAINT GALL (city, Switz.) **14**:660
- Hohenems' Jews **16**:223
Saint-Genix (cmty., Fr.) **14**:921
St. George's Church (Jer.) **9**:1462
St. George's Jewish Settlement (Lon.) **8**:328
St. Germain, Treaty of (1919) **3**:896
SAINT-GILES (tn., Fr.) **14**:660
Saint Gilles, Abraham de **11**:1190
Saint Gilles, Sara de **11**:1190
St. Helena, Pool of (Isr.), *see* 'Unayziyya cistern
St. Helier (Jersey isl.) **5**:335
St.-Hippolyte (vill., Fr.) **11**:496
St. James, Church of (Jer.) **9**:1407
St. James, Tomb of, *see* Ḥezir, Tomb of sons of
SAINT JAMES CONFERENCE (Lon., 1939) **14**:660
- Agudat Israel **2**:423
- Ben-Gurion **4**:508
- White Papers **16**:484
- *illus:*
- - Jewish and Arab delegates **9**:353
St. James Conference (war crimes) **16**:289ff
St. Jean d'Acre (city, Er. Isr.), *see* ACRE
SAINT-JEAN-DE-LUZ (tn., Fr.) **14**:661
Saint John (city, Can.) **11**:997
St. John, Church of (Jer.) **9**:1459
St. John, Order of **9**:1416
- *illus:*
- - Abu Ghosh church **2**:181
St. John Hospital (Jer.) **9**:1491
St. Johnsbury (tn., Ver.) **16**:112
St. Joseph (city, Mo.) **12**:158
St. Joseph monastery (Jer.) **9**:1461
St. Joseph of Arimathea (1st cent. C.E.) **4**:1381
St. Just, John of (14th cent., Fr.), *see* John of Saint Just
St. Kilda (sub., Austr.) **11**:1277
St. Laurent (sub., Montreal) **12**:287
St. Lazarus, Order of (knighthood order) **9**:1416
SAINT-LEON, ARTHUR MICHEL **14**:661
- dance **5**:1268
St.-Louis (tn., Fr.) **2**:757
SAINT LOUIS (city, Mo.) **14**:662
- *Contents:*
- - Introduction **14**:662
- - Early Community **14**:662
- - Eastern European Immigrants **14**:664
- - Charitable Institutions **14**:664
- - Zionism **14**:664
- - Other Communal Organizations **14**:665
- U.S. **15**:1596
- *illus:*
- - text
- - U.H.C. Synagogue **12**:157
St. Louis hospital (Jer.) **9**:1460
St. Louis Psalter (13th cent. illum. ms.) **9**:1344
- Lot's wife **15**:73
- Moses **12**:407
- Samuel **14**:784
- *illus:* **4**:321
St. Mark's Church (Venice) **12**:407
St. Martin (isl., Antilles) **12**:995
St. Mary of the Spasm Church (Jer.) **9**:1460
St. Mary's pool (Jer.) **9**:1541
Saint-Maximin (loc., Prov.) **13**:1259
Saintonge (reg., Fr.) **2**:750
St. Ottilien (D.P. camp, Ger.) **6**:77
Saint Paul (Minn.), *see* MINNEAPOLIS-SAINT PAUL
St. Paul's Hospice (Jer.) **9**:1462
SAINT-PAUL-TROIS CHÂTEAUX (tn., Fr.) **14**:666
St. Paul-Without-the-Walls Bible **15**:109
St. Peter Gallicantu Church (Jer.) **9**:1474
St. Petersburg (city, Fla.) **6**:1363
St. Petersburg (city, Rus.), *see* LENINGRAD
St. Petersburg Conservatory of Music **5**:1370
Saint Petersburg University (Rus.) **15**:1678
St. Peter's fish, *see* Tilapia
St. Poelton (loc.) **8**:1043; **13**:1383
St. Pudenziana, Church of (Rome) **9**:1579
SAINT-RÉMY-DE-PROVENCE

(tn., Fr.) **14**:667
St.-Servan (tn., Fr.) **4**:1383
Saint-Simon, Henry Claude de Rouvroy de **15**:25
- Saint-Simonism **14**:667
SAINT-SIMONISM (soc. philos.) **14**:667
St. Simon monastery (Jer.) **9**:1459
St. Sophia, Church of (Jer.) **9**:1407
St. Stephen, Church of (Jer.) **9**:1407
St. Stephen's Gate (Jer.), *see* Lions Gate
SAINT-SYMPHORIEN-D'OZON (vill., Fr.) **14**:668
St. Thomas Island **16**:165
- *illus:*
- - Sephardi synagogue **16**:164
St. Veit (tn., Aus.) **5**:181
St. Vincent de Paul monastery (Jer.) **9**:1459
St. Wendel (vill., Ger.) **14**:555
Sa'ir (owl) **12**:1531
"Saison" (anti-underground action, Er. Isr.) **9**:356
- Haganah **7**:1071
- I.Z.L. **8**:1467
SAJAROFF, MIGUEL **14**:668
- Kaplan, Isaac **10**:750
Sajet, Ben **13**:815
Sajmiste (camp) **8**:876
- Split Jews **15**:290
Sak, Jacob **3**:733
- Shabbateanism **4**:1449
Sak, Josef **16**:349
Sakākīnī, Khalīl al **9**:1040; **9**:1041
SAKEL, MANFRED JOSHUA **14**:668
Sak el-Farwein (loc., Arab.) **13**:156
SAKHAROFF, ALEXANDER **5**:1273
Sakharov, Andrei D. **6**:68
Sakhm al-Jawlān (vill., Syr.) **7**:694
Sakhneh (nat. park, Isr.), *see* Gan ha-Sheloshah
Sakhnīn (vill., Isr.) **14**:1530
Sakhnīn Basin (Isr.) **9**:152
Sakhra, al- (site, Er. Isr.) **7**:438
Sakhuta (J. cmty., Iraq) **5**:1239
SAKIAI (Shakyai, Shakay; city, Lith.) **14**:669
Sakis Adass (Aeg. isl.), *see* CHIOS
Sakkai, Joseph **5**:626
Sakowitz, Simon **8**:1052
Sakrī, Isaac ben Moses ibn **4**:86
- gaonate **7**:321
Saks, Jehiel ben Moses **5**:237
- Adel **2**:258
Saktsier, M. **16**:819
Sala (tn., Mor.), *see* SALÉ-RABAT
Sala, Eli **15**:1346; **15**:1440
Sala, Samuel **15**:1346; **15**:1440
SALADIN **14**:669
- Ayyūbid dynasty **3**:998
- banking, Jewish **4**:167
- Crusades **9**:268 ,273ff
- David ben Solomon **5**:1356
- history chart **8**:766-767
- Jerusalem **9**:1417
- Transjordan **15**:1318
- *illus:*
- - Ḥittin, site of battle **9**:275
Saladin, Louis **5**:126
Salah, Ephraim **5**:626
Ṣalāḥ al-Din, Yûsuf ibn Ayyûb (sult., Egy.), *see* SALADIN
Salahiya (tn., Iraq), *see* Kifri
Ṣalaḥiyya Madrasa, Al- (Musl. coll., Jer.), *see* Madrasa al Ṣalaḥiyya
Salām, Abdallah ibn, *see* ABDALLAH IBN SALÂM
Salam, Al- (newsp.), *see Et al Salam*
Salama, Johann **7**:347
Salāma ben Mevorakh **10**:420
SALAMAN (fam.) **14**:670
Salaman, Annette A. **14**:670
Salaman, Charles Kensington **14**:670
Salaman, Julia **14**:670
Salaman, Kate **14**:670
Salaman, Malcolm Charles **14**:670
Salaman, Myer Head **14**:671
Salaman, Nina Ruth **14**:671
- English literature **6**:784
Salaman, Peggy **2**:321
Salaman, Rachel **14**:670
SALAMAN, REDCLIFFE NATHAN **14**:670
SALAMANCA (city, Sp.) **14**:671
Salamander (zool.) **3**:18; **6**:36, 1002, 1304
Salamander, D. **10**:90
Salāmeh (Chr. fam.) **9**:1435
Salameh (vill., Er. Isr.) **15**:922
Salami Netofah (fam.) **16**:630
Salamis (city, Cyprus) **6**:15; **7**:869
Salamon (physic., Sp.) **6**:859
SALAMON, ERNÖ **14**:672
Salamon de' Rossi, *see* ROSSI, SALAMONE DE'
Salamons, Sir Julian Emanuel **3**:880
Salampsio (Judea), *see* SALOME ALEXANDRA
Salant, Beinush **14**:674
SALANT, JOSEPH SUNDEL BEN BENJAMIN BENISH **14**:673
- Lipkin, Israel **11**:279
- *see also:* MUSAR MOVEMENT
SALANT, SAMUEL **14**:673
- Diskin, Moses Joshua **6**:74
- Ereẓ Israel **9**:890
Salantai (cmty., Lith.) **14**:769
Salanter, Israel ben Ze'ev Wolf, *see* LIPKIN, ISRAEL BEN ZE'EV WOLF
Salas, M. **12**:1129
Salas, S.N. **5**:505; **12**:1129
Salaspils (concen. camp, Latv.) **10**:1467
Salat, Ze'ev Wolf **12**:868
Salaya, Juan de **16**:904
Salazar, Arturo Garcia **10**:1456
Salbīt (vill., Isr.) **14**:1211
Salces (tn., Fr.) **14**:353
SALCHAH (tn., Er. Isr.) **14**:674
Salchli, J.J. **8**:54
Saldae (tn., Alg.), *see* BOUGIE
SALE (leg.) **14**:675
- *Contents:*
- - General **14**:675
- - The Decision of the Parties **14**:675
- - Things not yet in Existence **14**:677
- - The Conditions of the Sale **14**:678
- - In the State of Israel **14**:680 **2**:216
- acquisition **2**:216
- agent **2**:352
- bill of **14**:1388
- converted into loan **11**:419
- custom as acquisition mode **12**:17; **12**:19
- dowry **6**:187ff
- duress **12**:1398
- gift **7**:560
- *keẓaẓah* **10**:935
- land **13**:1147ff
- lien and purchasers **11**:228
- *maẓranut* **11**:1153
- overreaching **12**:1391
- ownership **12**:1532
- paternal inheritance and age **13**:1357
- transfer of property **4**:341
- waiver **11**:1232
- *see also:* LEASE AND HIRE; MISTAKE; PROPERTY
Saleim (vill., Er. Isr.) **10**:893
Salem (city, Er. Isr.) **9**:1549
- Jerusalem **9**:1559
Salem (city, Mass.) **11**:1112; **11**:622
Salem (city, Oreg.) **12**:1451
Salem, A.B. **5**:627
SALEM, EMMANUEL RAPHAEL **14**:680
Salem, Raphael **14**:680
Sale of human beings, *see* SLAVERY; SLAVE TRADE
Sale of stolen animals, *see* THEFT AND ROBBERY
SALÉ-RABAT (twin tn., Mor.) **14**:680
- Abenatar family **3**:812
- Jewish quarter **10**:87
- *illus:* text
SALERNO (city, It.) **14**:683
- medicine **11**:1187
Salesky, Charles **12**:1222
SALFELD, SIEGMUND **14**:683
Salford (city, Eng.) **11**:859
Salicornia (bot.) **9**:225
Saliège, Mgr. **7**:36; **15**:1287
ṢALIḤ, ABRAHAM (Yem.) **14**:683
Ṣāliḥ, Abraham (Iraq) **8**:1453
Ṣāliḥ, Antuwān **9**:1039
Sāliḥ, Yaḥyā ben Jacob **7**:1037
ṢĀLIḤ, YAḤYÂ BEN JOSEPH (MAHARIS) **14**:683
- masorah **16**:1478
- Sa'adi, Judah **14**:542
- Salih ibn Yahya **14**:684
- Yemen **16**:746
Salih the Ayyubid (sult., Egy.) **3**:998
- holy places **8**:935
ṢĀLIḤ IBN YAḤYĀ IBN JOSEPH **14**:684
Sālim (vill., Er. Isr.) **14**:1266
Salina (q., Judea), *see* SALOME ALEXANDRA
Salinas, Abraham ben Yomtov de **3**:523
Salinas, Bonastruc ben Abraham de **3**:523
Salinger, Benjamin **8**:1439
SALINGER, JEROME DAVID **14**:684
- U.S. literature **15**:1577
Salins-les-Bains (tn., Fr.) **7**:45
SALISBURY (city, Rhod.) **14**:685
- Corfu immigrants **14**:1172
- *illus:*
- - text
- - Sephardi Hebrew Congregation **14**:149
Salisbury (city, N.C.) **12**:1220
SALIT, NORMAN **14**:685
Salix (bot.) **9**:225
SALK, JONAS EDWARD **14**:686
Salka (tn., Transj.) **9**:279
SALKIND, JACOB MEIR **14**:687
Salkind, Solomon **7**:964
SALKINSON, ISAAC EDWARD (Eliezer) **14**:687
- Shakespeare, translation **14**:1262
Sallāḥiyya building (Jer.), *see* St. Anne, Church of
Sallah Shabbati (movie picture) **10**:1070; **12**:462
- *illus:*
- - Topol, Chaim **12**:457
Sallam (9th cent., ling., Sp.?) **16**:1280
Sallām ibn Mishkam **10**:942
Saller, S.J. **9**:1525; **16**:1324
Sallis (Er. Isr.) **10**:892
Sallon, Ralph **5**:220
Salmah (s. of Nahshon) **12**:792
- *geneal. table:* **5**:1341
Salmah, Isaac **13**:583
Salman (11th cent., Ger.) **6**:818
Salmān, Faraj **9**:1042
Salmas (tn., Iran), *see* Shahpur
Salmasius, C. **8**:291
Salmeron, Alfonso **8**:54
Salmon (s. of Nahshon), *see* Salmah
SALMON (fam.) **14**:687
Salmon (fish) **6**:36
SALMON, ALEXANDER **14**:688
- travels **15**:1350
Salmon, Alfred **7**:626; **14**:687
Salmon, Barnett **7**:626; **14**:687
SALMON, SIR CYRIL BARNET **14**:688
Salmon, Gaston **12**:645
Salmon, Geoffrey Isidore Hamilton **14**:688
Salmon, Isidor **14**:688
Salmon, Isidore, *see* Salmon, Sir Samuel
Salmon, Julian **14**:688
SALMON, KAREL (Karl Salomon) **14**:688
Salmon, Sir Samuel **14**:688
SALMON BEN JEROHAM **14**:689
- *aliyah* **9**:511
Salmony, Alfred **3**:650
Salmu (deity) **14**:1531
Salo, Salo, *see* Roth, Salo
Salom, Israel **13**:107
Salom, Max **13**:1371
Salome (Herod's sister) **2**:595
- Alexandra and **2**:587
- Aristobulus III **3**:442
- Costobar **5**:990
- Cypros **5**:1179
- Herod I **8**:384
- Sholi, the Nabatean **12**:743
SALOME (step granddau. of Herod) **14**:689
- John the Baptist **8**:388; **10**:160
- *illus:*
- - text
- - with head of John the Baptist **6**:775
Salome, S.C. **8**:54
SALOME ALEXANDRA **14**:691
- Alexander Yannai **16**:714
- Hasmoneans **8**:632
- history chart **8**:766-767
- Nabateans **12**:742
- Simeon ben Shetaḥ **14**:1563ff
- warfare **16**:279
Salome bat Iakeimos (Er. Isr.) **7**:691
Salomo, Abraham **5**:1597
Salomo, Isaac **5**:1597
Salomon (educ., Holl.), *see* MULDER, SAMUEL ISRAEL
Salomon (fam.) **5**:1543
Salomon, Abraham **5**:952
SALOMON, ALBERT **14**:693
SALOMON, ALICE **14**:693
Salomon, Berthold, *see* JACOB, BERTHOLD
SALOMON, CHARLOTTE **14**:694
Salomon, Deborah **14**:696
Salomon, Edward S. **11**:1551; **16**:355
SALOMON, ERICH **14**:694
SALOMON, GESKEL **3**:609
- *illus:*
- - "Old Jewish Pedlar" (paint.) **3**:639
SALOMON, GOTTFRIED **14**:694
SALOMON, GOTTHOLD **14**:695
SALOMON, HAYM **14**:695
- banking **4**:178
- spying **12**:1069
- U.S. **15**:1591
- *illus:*
- - text
- - pages from letterbook **15**:1591
Salomon, Haym M. **14**:696
Salomon, Hirschel **10**:1159
Salomon, Isaac **16**:1222
SALOMON, JOEL MOSES **14**:696
- Brill, Jehiel **4**:1374
- *Ha-Levanon* **7**:1178
Salomon, Judith, *see* Cohen, Judith
SALOMON, JULIUS **14**:697
Salomon, Karl, *see* SALMON, KAREL
Salomon, Leah, *see* Mendelssohn,

Lea
Salomon, Mordecai **14**:696; **16**:1222
Salomon, Moses **16**:1222
Salomon, Otto **6**:462
Salomon, Rachel Franks, *see* Franks, Rachel
Salomon, Raphael **16**:989
Salomon ben Samuel **16**:1390
SALOMON-CALVI, WILHELM **14**:697
Salomon de la Tour, Gottfried, *see* SALOMON, GOTTFRIED
Salomon the Jew (11th cent., Sp.) **5**:266
Salomon of Hormuz **8**:976
SALOMONS, SIR DAVID **14**:697
- emancipation **6**:701
Salomons, Sir David Lionel **14**:698
Salomons, Israel Levin **6**:5
SALOMONS, SIR JULIAN EMANUEL **14**:698
Salomons, Levi **14**:697
Salomons, Philip **5**:310
SALOMONSEN, CARL JULIUS **14**:698
Salomonski, Martin **4**:648
SALOMONSOHN, H., *see* BRODY, HEINRICH
Salomon Trismosin **2**:544
Salon (tn., Fr.) **2**:37
Salon, Moses de **13**:1263; **15**:1322
Salona (loc., Yug.), *see* Solin
Salonik (journ.) **13**:1038
SALONIKA (city, Gr.) **14**:699
- *Contents:*
- - Introduction **14**:699
- - Byzantine Period **14**:699
- - Turkish Conquest-Sephardi Immigration **14**:700
- - 17th Century **14**:701
- - 18th-19th Centuries **14**:702
- - 19th-20th Centuries **14**:702
- - Holocaust period **14**:704
- - Contemporary Period **14**:707
- - Hebrew Printing **14**:707
- capitulations **5**:148
- Diaspora **6**:10
- dress **6**:216
- dyeing center **6**:328
- education **6**:420
- Greece **7**:872ff
- informers *haskamah* **8**:1367
- *Kahal Kadosh shel Ba'alei Teshuvah* **3**:174
- marriage custom **11**:1043
- Ottoman period **16**:1552
- Sephardi center **14**:1167ff
- Shabbetai Ẓevi **14**:1223; **14**:1234; **14**:1239ff
- textiles **15**:1039
- *illus:*
- - text
- - Ḥayyim Pinḥas dispensary **7**:877
- - memorial to Jews killed by Nazis **7**:882
SALONS (cultural and social gatherings) **14**:708
- Haskalah **7**:1434
SALONTA (tn., Rum.) **14**:709
Salsalah (Samar. wk.) **14**:750
SALSBERG, JOSEPH B. **14**:710
- communism **5**:806
- Ontario **12**:1408
- Russia **14**:498
- Toronto **15**:1263
Salsburgh, Abram **16**:516
Šalšelet (cantillation sign) **16**:1454
Salt (tn., Jor.) **13**:1511
SALT **14**:710
- Bible **6**:1416
- folklore **6**:1400
- Sodom **15**:72
- *illus:*
- - text
- - Dead Sea composition (chart) **9**:806
- *see also:* MAYIM AḤARONIM
Salt, Valley of (Er. Isr.) **6**:374
Saltbush (bot.) **13**:625
SALTEN, FELIX **14**:711
- *illus:* text
Salter, Ernst **13**:1367
Salting meat, *see* Kashering of meat
Salt Lake City (Utah) **16**:33
- *illus:*
- - Ransohoffs' shop **15**:1597
Saltpeter (mineral) **16**:1287
Saltsman, Max **13**:810; **15**:27
SALT TRADE AND INDUSTRY **14**:712
Saltykov-Shchedrin, Mikhail **14**:508
SALTZMAN, HARRY **12**:473
Saltzman, Maurice **5**:612
Salu (bib. fig.) **14**:1549; **16**:1026
SALUS, HUGO **14**:713
Salusque Lusitano (pseud.), *see* USQUE, SOLOMON
Salustri, Carlo Alberto, *see* Trilussa
Salutzki-Hardman, Y.B., *see* HARDMAN, JACOB BENJAMIN
Saluzzo (tn., It.) **14**:714
SALVADOR (fam.) **14**:714
Salvador (city, Braz.) **4**:96
Salvador, Francis (Lond. mer.) **14**:714
Salvador, Francis (Am. patr.) **5**:359; **14**:715; **15**:211; **15**:1586
- *illus:*
- - commemorative plaque **14**:715
Salvador, Jonah **14**:1583
SALVADOR, JOSEPH (schol., Fr.) **14**:715
- Montpellier **12**:283
Salvador, Joseph (Eng. mer.) **14**:714
Salvation
- Abrabanel, Isaac **2**:108
- Hemerobaptists **14**:1088
- Mendelssohn **13**:455ff
- Messiah and **11**:1408
- Neoplatonism **12**:958
- providence **13**:1280
- Reconstructionism **13**:1615
- sages on **14**:654
- Teacher of Righteousness **15**:886
- Thanksgiving Psalms **15**:1046
- *see also:* ESCHATOLOGY; REDEMPTION
SALVENDI, ADOLF **14**:716
Salvia (bot.) **9**:221
SALZ, ABRAHAM ADOLPH **14**:717
- *illus:*
- - F.Z.C. **16**:1165
Salzberg (tn., Pol.), *see* BOCHNIA
SALZBURG (city and prov., Aus.) **14**:717
- Host desecration **8**:1043
Salzinger, Kurt **13**:1345
Salzman, Joseph **15**:309
Salzman, Leibl, *see* MALACH, LEIB
Salzman, Leon **13**:1340
SALZMAN, PNINA **12**:705
SALZMAN, WILLIAM **14**:719
Salzmann, S. (bsmn., Er. Isr.) **7**:1007
Salzmann, Samuel Ezekiel **11**:426
Salzmann, Siegmund, *see* SALTEN, FELIX
Salzmann, Solomon **14**:1430
Salzwedel (city, Ger.) **4**:1301
Sama (amora) **3**:710; **11**:940
SAMAEL (name of Satan) **14**:719
- Angel of Death **2**:953
- demons **5**:1529
- eschatology **10**:588
- Eve **6**:980
- evil inclination **8**:1319
- Lilith **11**:247
- Tamar **15**:783
- Worlds, the Four **16**:642
- *see also:* SATAN
Samaias (Phar.) **14**:1374
Samakhos (prin. of Mesene) **9**:1157
SAMAKOF (Bul.) **14**:722
Samak River (Er. Isr.) **9**:180
Samal (kdm., Syr.) **2**:685; **16**:661
SAMAMA (Shemama), NESSIM **14**:722
- Tunisia **15**:1447
Samama, Salomon **14**:722
Samama, Samuel **12**:1517
SAMANDAR (Khazar tn., Cauc.) **14**:722
- Atil and **3**:823
Samara (city, Rus.), *see* KUIBYSHEV
SAMARIA (city, Er. Isr.) **14**:723
- Archaeology and Geography
- - agriculture **2**:393
- - archaeology **3**:306ff
- - architecture **3**:357
- - Ares **3**:407
- - Crowfoots' excavations **5**:1129
- - emperor worship **6**:729
- - geology **9**:201ff
- - ivory inscriptions **16**:662
- - mountains **9**:142
- - ostraca **9**:119; **12**:1510
- - - alphabet **2**:682
- - - Hebrew language **16**:1569
- - - numerals **12**:1255
- - - writing **16**:666
- - pillars **13**:522
- - pottery type **13**:941
- - *see also:* Sebaste
- History
- - Ahab **2**:435ff
- - Alexander the Great **2**:578
- - calf of **8**:1020
- - Crusader period **9**:268; **9**:269; **9**:272
- - Herod **8**:636; **14**:730
- - history chart **8**:766-767
- - Jerusalem **9**:1563
- - John Hyrcanus **8**:631
- - *Jund-Filasṭīn* **9**:261
- - legend on building **4**:276
- - Micah's prophecy **11**:1480ff
- - Omri **8**:596ff; **12**:1390
- - *Palaestine Prima* **9**:254
- - *Provincia Judaea* **9**:239
- - Roman period **8**:626; **8**:630ff
- - Sargon II **14**:880
- - Shalmaneser V **16**:1503
- *illus:*
- - Hellenistic round tower **3**:322
- - Israelite remains **2**:438
- - Nablus **9**:578
- - ostraca **2**:684; **3**:372 **12**:1509
- - sarcophagus **12**:1505
- *see also* Jehoahaz; SAMARITANS
Samaria (prov., Er. Isr.)
- Arab population **9**:1032
- Arab refugees **9**:451
- health services **9**:992ff
- human geography **9**:587ff
- Muslim life **9**:918
- Six-Day War **9**:411ff
Samaria (vill., Egy.) **6**:9
Samaritan Aramaic **3**:275
Samaritan Chronicles, *see* Chronicles, Samaritan
Samaritan Pentateuch, *see* PENTATEUCH, SAMARITAN
SAMARITANS **14**:725
- *Contents:*
- - History
- - - Until 1300 **14**:727
- - - 1300-1970 **14**:733
- - - Statistics **14**:736
- - Religion and Customs **14**:738
- - - Holidays and Festivals **14**:741
- - - Religious Ceremonies **14**:744
- - Samaritan Chronology **14**:748
- - - The Calendar **14**:748
- - - Historical Chronology **14**:750
- - Language and Literature
- - - Language **14**:752
- - - Literature **14**:753
- - In Islam **14**:757
- History
- - Alexander the Great **2**:577
- - Arab period **9**:264; **9**:265
- - Claudius **5**:601
- - Crusades **5**:1140
- - exile, Assyrian **6**:1035
- - Israel history **9**:247ff
- - Jerusalem revolt **9**:1407
- - John Hyrcanus **8**:631
- - Justinian **10**:478
- - Neapolis **12**:744
- - Second Temple **6**:1040
- Language and Literature
- - Abu al-Ḥasan of Tyre **2**:179
- - *al-Asāṭīr* **2**:511
- - Amram Darah **2**:893
- - Aramaic **3**:275
- - Dead Sea texts **5**:1401
- - Decalogue **5**:1438
- - Hebrew language of DSS **16**:1584
- - Markah **11**:999
- - Pentateuch, Samaritan **13**:264
- - *Philo (Pseudo)* **13**:409
- - pronunciation **13**:1122ff
- Beliefs and Practices
- - abortion **2**:99
- - amulet **2**:911; **2**:912
- - calendar **5**:50
- - *haftarah* **16**:1343
- - *kiddush ha-Shem* **10**:982
- - laws of cleanliness **4**:194
- - masorah **16**:1468
- - menstruation **12**:1148
- - *mezuzah* **11**:1476
- - Passover ritual **13**:164
- - Sabbath carrying **6**:851
- - *sukkah* **15**:494
- - synagogue **15**:599
- - *tefillin* **15**:898
- - Torah acceptance **4**:823
- Judaism and Polemics against
- - Abbahu **2**:36
- - Akiva's views **2**:492
- - Andronicus **2**:949
- - *avodah zarah* **3**:981
- - benedictions **2**:803
- - Jewish identity **10**:54
- - *kiddush ha-Shem* **10**:982
- - Minor Tractates **12**:49
- - nagid **12**:761
- - polemics against **3**:193
- - term for Christian **7**:411
- Settlements
- - Athens community **3**:817
- - distribution **9**:569ff
- - Dustan **6**:313
- - holy places **8**:936
- - Macedonians **8**:625
- - Rome **14**:241; **14**:244
- - Shechem **14**:1333
- *illus:*
- - Mount Gerizim encampment **7**:437
- - paschal lamb sacrifice **8**:934; **13**:169
- - script **2**:679
- - Torah scroll **13**:265
- *see also:* BABA RABBAH; CUTH; GERIZIM, MOUNT; SHAALBIM
SAMARITANS: MUSICAL TRADITION **16**:1555
SAMARKAND (city, U.S.S.R.) **14**:758
- Persia **13**:310
- *see also:* BUKHARA
Samarra (tn., Iraq) **8**:1449
Šamaš (deity) **5**:1020
SAMAU'AL BEN JUDAH IBN ABBAS (ibn Yaḥya al-Magribi) **14**:760

- Alfonsus Bonihominis **2:**607
- Ibn Kammuna **8:**1187
- Islamic polemics **4:**931
- Tabriz **15:**693
Samawa (tn., Iraq) **8:**1450
Samaw'al, Al (Islamic name for Samuel), *see* Shamwīl
Samᶜayas (fam., Syr.) **15:**645
SAMBARI, JOSEPH BEN ISAAC **14:**761
- chronicle of scholars **8:**560
- Jewish history **11:**349
- nagid **12:**759
SAMBATYON (leg. riv.) **14:**762
- Lost Tribes **15:**1005
- messianism **11:**1426
Sambenito (inq. garment) **11:**1455
SAMBERG, ISAAC (Aizik) **15:**1089
- motion pictures **12:**455
SAMBOR (tn., Ukr.) **14:**764
SAMBURSKY, DANIEL **14:**766
SAMBURSKY, SAMUEL **14:**766
- *illus:*
- - Oppenheimer, J. Robert, and **12:**1430
Sambutia (tn., Egy.), *see* SUMBAT
Samcho (lake), *see* Yam Samcho
SAMEGAH, JOSEPH BEN BENJAMIN **14:**767
SAMEKH (Heb. let.) **14:**767
- *parashah setumah* **16:**1407
Samekh Mem (name for Samael) **14:**721
Samengelof (angel)
- folklore **6:**1400
- Lilith **11:**246
- *illus:*
- - amulet **5:**1525
Samfield, Max **11:**1302
Samiel (angel), *see* SAMAEL
SAMINSKY, LAZARE **14:**767
- Society for Jewish Folk Music **15:**57
Samiro, S., *see* TZARA, TRISTAN
Samitca (fam.) **13:**1369
SAMKALDEN, IVO **14:**768
Samkush (Samkerch; Crimea) **5:**1103
Samlaić, Erich (Elisha) **16:**990
Sammern-Frankennegg (Nazi) **16:**351
Sammuel (angel), *see* SAMAEL
Samoga (tn., Transj.) **8:**631
SAMOGITIA (reg., Lith.) **14:**768
SAMOILOVICH, RUDOLPH LAZAREVICH **14:**769
- travels **15:**1350
Samokov (city, Bul.) **4:**1482
SAMOKOVLIJA, ISAK **14:**770
- Sarajevo **14:**871
- Yugoslavia **16:**874
- Yugoslav literature **16:**887; **16:**889
Samoobrona (orgn., Warsaw ghetto) **16:**349
Samos (tn., Gr.) **7:**868
Sampaio, Teixeira, Judith, *see* Teixeira de Sampaio, Judith
Sampler, Samuel **11:**1552
Sampson, I.K. **15:**209
SAMPTER, JESSIE ETHEL **14:**770
- U.S. literature **15:**1572
SAMRA, DAVID **14:**771
Samsi (q., Arab.) **15:**940
SAMSON (bib. fig.) **14:**771
- *Contents:*
- - General **14:**771
- - In the Aggadah **14:**773
- - In the Arts **14:**774
- Beth-Shemesh **4:**772
- Bible history **8:**584
- descendants, legendary **6:**576
- illuminated *maḥzorim* **11:**735
- Judges, Book of **10:**449
- nazirite **12:**908
- Philistines **13:**405
- Talmud **12:**905
- *illus:*
- - gates of Gaza **7:**1088
- - "Samson and Delilah" (drg., A. Mantegna) **5:**1473
- - Solomon J. Solomon's painting **15:**118
- *see also:* DELILAH
Samson (13th cent., ling.) **16:**1387
"Samson" (paint., S. J. Solomon) **15:**118
Samson, Hertz **9:**1240
Samson, Mink, *see* Jacobson, Mink Samson
Samson, Philip **16:**609
Samson, Solomon **4:**109
Samson, Veit **4:**109
Samson Agonistes (poem) **11:**1588
"Samson and Delilah" (drg., A. Mantegna) **5:**1473
SAMSON BEN ABRAHAM OF SENS (tos.) **14:**777
- *aliyah* **9:**273
- Isaac ben Abraham **9:**14
- Isaac of Dampierre **9:**31
- *tosafot* of Sens **15:**1280
Samson ben Bezalel **10:**1255; **10:**375
SAMSON BEN ELIEZER **14:**778
SAMSON BEN ISAAC OF CHINON (tos.) **14:**779
SAMSON BEN JOSEPH OF FALAISE (tos.) **14:**779
Samson ben Meir **15:**1203
Samson ben Pesaḥ **10:**287
SAMSON BEN SAMSON OF COUCY (tos.) **14:**779
- seals **14:**1079
Samson ben Samuel **13:**593
Samson ben Solomon **7:**264; **15:**1326
Samson ben Zadok **2:**85; **11:**1251
Samson de Mirabeau **11:**472
SAMSON HA-NAKDAN **14:**780
- linguistics **16:**1387
- masorah **16:**1474
Samson the Ḥasid, *see* BLOCH, SAMSON BEN MOSES
Samson of Baiersdorf **4:**352
Samson of Corbeil **5:**960
Samson of Erfurt **11:**569
Samson of Ostropol **10:**635
Samson of Troyes (tos.) **15:**1407
Samsonov, Samson **12:**456
Samsonovich brothers (bsmn., China) **7:**1331
Samsonschule (school, Ger.) **10:**462
Samson's Foxes (Isr. army) **9:**369
- *illus:*
- - bren-gun carriers **16:**321
Samson Zelig ben Jacob Joseph ha-Levi **11:**561
Samsu-ditana (k., Mesop.) **16:**1497
Samter (tn., Pol.) **3:**694
SAMTER, ERNST **14:**780
Samūᶜ, Al (vill., Er. Isr.) **6:**892
- I.D.F. reprisal raid **14:**1625
- Israel army **9:**404
- U.N. censure **15:**1556
Samual ha-Ḥazzan (Kar. poet) **10:**783
Samuda, Joseph d'Aguilar **14:**1413
SAMUEL (bib. fig.) **14:**780
- *Contents:*
- - Introduction **14:**780
- - Biblical Account **14:**780
- - Critical Evaluation **14:**783
- - in the *Aggadah* **14:**783
- - In Islam **14:**784
- - In the Arts **14:**784
- - Tomb of Samuel **14:**785
- Agag **2:**341
- Amalek **2:**788
- Arts **14:**917
- Chronicles **5:**522
- chronological chart **8:**766-767
- Eli **6:**613
- Elkanah **6:**676
- Hophni and Phinehas **8:**971
- Israelite monarchy **8:**586ff
- Korah **10:**1192
- Naziriteship of **12:**905,908 **12:**908
- priest **13:**1076
- priestly *mishmarot* **12:**92
- Samuel, Book of **14:**788
- Saul **14:**910ff
- tomb of **13:**514
- *illus:*
- - text
- - anointing of David **3:**28; **6:**285,1125 **12:**1351; **14:**793
- - beheading Agag **2:**341
- - Eli instructing the child Samuel **6:**614
- - God appearing to at Shiloh **3:**54
SAMUEL (amora) **14:**786
- astronomy **3:**797
- Babylonia **8:**650
- calendar **5:**46,47,49
- decision in disputes **5:**891
- gentiles **7:**411
- Johanan ben Nappaḥa **10:**145
- medicine **11:**1183ff
- Nehardea **2:**204
- non-Jewish law **6:**51
- Papi **13:**67
- Rav **13:**1577ff
- responsa **14:**84
- *Sefer Asaf ha-Rofe* **3:**675
- Shapur I **14:**1306
- Shela **14:**1354
- Talmud **11:**319
- vows **16:**228
- World to Come **12:**1356
Samuel (gaon) **7:**318
Samuel (paytan, Egy.) **13:**593
Samuel (13th cent., Ger.) **7:**1289
Samuel (paytan, Ger. or Fr.) **13:**593
Samuel (paytan, Sp.) **13:**593
Samuel (14th cent., Pol.) **5:**1026
Samuel (physic., Cracow) **13:**834
Samuel (moneychanger, Egy.) **4:**167
Samuel (r., Vilna) **6:**653
Samuel (fam., Eng.) **12:**1227
Samuel, Abraham (Eng. jeweler) **15:**519
Samuel, Abraham (r., Lith.) **11:**280
Samuel, Arthur Michael, *see* Mancroft, Arthur Michael Samuel
SAMUEL, BOOK OF **14:**788
- *Contents:*
- - Introduction **14:**788
- - Title, Authorship and Text **14:**788
- - Contents and Major Themes **14:**789
- - The Basic Building Units **14:**790
- - Pre-Deutoronomic Source **14:**791
- - The Deuteronomic Compiler **14:**795
- - Historical and Religious Value **14:**797
- Spinoza **15:**283
- *illus:*
- - Dead Sea Scroll **2:**712
- - Saul, suicide of **14:**915
Samuel, Denis de **14:**190
Samuel, Edwin (bnk., Eng.) **14:**797
SAMUEL, EDWIN, SECOND VISCOUNT (adminis., Isr.) **1:**36; **14:**800
- Zionist Commission **16:**1163
- *illus:*
- at Government House, Jerusalem **2:**57
Samuel, Emanuel **10:**305
Samuel, Frank **6:**766
Samuel, Godfrey **2:**57
SAMUEL, HAROLD **12:**706
- Nathan, Isaac **12:**853
Samuel, Herbert (r., Can.), *see* Sandheim, Herbert
SAMUEL, HERBERT LOUIS, FIRST VISCOUNT **14:**797
- Balfour Declaration **4:**131
- Ben-Yehuda **4:**568
- Deedes, Sir Wyndham **5:**1455
- Hajj Amin al-Husseini **9:**461ff
- Haycraft Commission of Inquiry **13:**31
- history chart **8:**766-767
- Israel history **9:**337f
- religion in Israel **9:**892
- Storrs, Ronald **15:**417
- Tiberias **15:**1133
- Zionism **16:**1081
- *illus:*
- - text
- - Abdullah ibn Hussein, and **10:**199
- - at Government House, Jerusalem, 1921 **2:**57
- - autograph **3:**917
- - Bols' "delivery note" for Palestine **3:**392
- - Churchill, Winston, and **5:**555
- - Feisal's letter **16:**1050
- - Government House Party, Jerusalem **9:**339
- - Hebrew University, opening ceremony **8:**221
- - inaugural speech **8:**471; **9:**601
- - inspecting Bedouin horsemen **9:**1021
- - Lawrence, T. E., and **10:**1489
- - Marks, Simon, and **11:**1009
- - Rishon le-Zion visit **14:**195
- - Schuster, Sir Arthur, and **14:**1012
- - Transjordan, declaration of independence **9:**339
Samuel, Hyman **16:**163
Samuel, Isaac **13:**583
Samuel, Joseph (of Cracow; r.) **6:**668
Samuel, Joseph (ed., Fr.) **13:**1032
Samuel, Julius **16:**452
Samuel, Lewis **5:**103; **14:**802
Samuel, Marcus (Eng. mer.) **4:**358
- petroleum and oil products **13:**346
Samuel, Marcus (Eng. fin.), *see* BEARSTED, MARCUS SAMUEL, FIRST VISCOUNT
Samuel, Marcus Richard, *see* Bearsted, Marcus Richard Samuel, Third Viscount
SAMUEL, MAURICE **14:**801
Samuel, Michael **7:**603
Samuel, Moses **4:**319
SAMUEL, RALPH E. **14:**802
Samuel, S. (Eng. trav.) **13:**918
Samuel, Sam **4:**358
Samuel, Saul (court J., Ger.) **5:**1010
SAMUEL, SIR SAUL **14:**802
- politics **13:**808
SAMUEL, SIGMUND **14:**802
Samuel, Stuart **14:**815
SAMUEL, SYDNEY MONTAGU **10:**316
- Jewish Chronicle **10:**40
Samuel, Theodore **12:**478
Samuel, Tomb of **14:**785
Samuel, Walter, *see* Bearsted, Walter Horace Samuel, Second Viscount
SAMUEL. WILFRED SAMPSON **14:**803
Samuel Avigdor "Tosfa'ah" **12:**967
Samuel bar Mar (gaon) **7:**316
Samuel bar Isaac (amora) **11:**1033
Samuel ben Abba ha-Kohen (amora), *see* SAMUEL
Samuel ben Abbahu (savora) **14:**920
Samuel ben Abraham **12:**65
Samuel ben Abraham de Ortas, *see* Samuel d'Ortas
SAMUEL BEN ALI (gaon) **14:**803
- Daniel ben Ḥasdai **6:**1123
- David ben Samuel **5:**1354

- Edessa 6:367
- gaonate 7:321; 7:323
- geonic hierarchy 8:678
- Maimonides 11:746; 11:759
- Moses of Kiev 12:433
Samuel ben Asher 3:808
SAMUEL BEN AVIGDOR 14:804
- Vilna controversy 16:143
SAMUEL BEN AZARIAH 14:805
Samuel ben Azriel of Landsburg 15:322
Samuel ben Baruch of Bamberg 4:149
Samuel ben Benveniste 15:1324
SAMUEL BEN DANIEL ABU RABI'A HA-KOHEN (gaon) 14:805
- David ben Abraham Maimuni 9:274
- gaonate 7:321
SAMUEL BEN DAVID (12th cent., r.) 14:805
Samuel ben David (13th cent., exil.) 6:1033
SAMUEL BEN DAVID (Kar. trav.) 14:806
- Gaza 7:342
- travels 15:1353
SAMUEL BEN DAVID MOSES HA-LEVI 14:806
- Bacharach, Jair Ḥayyim 4:48
Samuel ben David Naḥmias, *see* MOROSINI, GIULIO
Samuel ben Eliasaph 13:593
SAMUEL BEN ELIEZER OF KALVARIJA 14:807
Samuel ben Feibush 10:287
Samuel ben Gershom 7:513
Samuel ben Ḥama ha-Kohen (amora) 13:468
Samuel ben Hananel 5:156
SAMUEL BEN HANANIA 14:807
- gaonate 7:324
- Hananel ben Samuel 7:1253
Samuel ben Ḥayyim (tos.) 16:108
Samuel ben Ḥayyim Ḥaikel of Amdur 7:1510
Samuel ben Hezekiah ha-Levi 8:1324
Samuel ben Hoshana 5:1241
- Nathan ben Abraham 15:123
SAMUEL BEN HOPHNI (gaon) 14:807
- Abraham ben Nathan 2:153
- Bible exegesis 4:892
- financial deeds 16:1282
- gaonate 7:315ff
- Hai ben Sherira 7:1130
- history chart 8:766-767
- Jewish philosophy 13:433
- Judeo-Arabic 10:412
Samuel ben Isaac ha-Sardi, *see* SARDI, SAMUEL BEN ISAAC
Samuel ben Isaac the Spaniard 16:1341
Samuel ben Israel 13:647
Samuel ben Jacob (11th cent., scribe, Egy.) 5:*fcg.* 43
Samuel ben Jacob (ling.) 15:1327; 16:1394
SAMUEL BEN JACOB OF KELMY 14:808
- Ragoler 13:1513
Samuel ben Joseph 5:1534
Samuel ben Joseph ha-Kohen (gaon) 7:323
Samuel ben Joseph the Younger (tos.) 16:109
Samuel ben Judah (amora) 12:943
Samuel ben Judah (paytan) 9:22
Samuel ben Judah ibn Abbas, *see* SAMAU'AL BEN JUDAH IBN ABBAS
Samuel ben Judah ben Meshullam 15:1165
Samuel ben Judah of Marseilles 2:581; 4:363; 11:1057
- Abba Mari ben Eligdor 2:37
- astronomy 3:799; 3:800
- Provence 13:1264
- translations 15:1321
Samuel ben Kalonymus 6:838
SAMUEL BEN KALONYMUS HE-ḤASID OF SPEYER 14:809
- barnacle goose 4:247
- family 10:719; 10:721
- Isaac of Dampierre 9:31
- Judah ha-Ḥasid 7:1388
- *Shir ha-Yihud* 14:1416
- *tefillin* 15:898
Samuel ben Manasseh 4:1238
Samuel ben Mattathias 11:542
Samuel ben Maẓli'aḥ Marli, *see* MARLI, SAMUEL BEN MAẒLI'AḤ
SAMUEL BEN MEIR (Rashbam) 14:809
- apologetics 3:195
- Ashkenazi (Keren Shemu'el) 14:811
- Bible exegesis 4:893
- genealogy 7:382
Samuel ben Meir Latif 8:1324
Samuel ben Menahem 7:1509; 11:1248; 16:675
Samuel ben Meshullam Phoebus 11:1404
Samuel ben Moses 2:24
SAMUEL BEN MOSES AL-MAGHRIBĪ 14:812
- biblical text 6:91
Samuel ben Moses ha-Levi 13:1105
Samuel ben Moses of Evreux 12:433
Samuel ben Musa 8:1326
Samuel ben Nafusi of Palermo 13:29; 14:1495
SAMUEL BEN NAḤMAN 14:812
SAMUEL BEN NATRONAI 14:813
Samuel ben Rabbah (savora), *see* Samuel ben Abbahu
Samuel ben Reuben of Chartres 5:362
Samuel ben Saadiah ibn Danan 7:1121
SAMUEL BEN SAMSON 14:813
- travels in the Holy Land 9:1148
Samuel ben Samuel of Rome 8:1324
Samuel ben Shalom 13:593
SAMUEL BEN SHILAT (amora) 14:813
- masorah 16:1405
Samuel ben Simeon 13:593
Samuel ben Sofat 14:681
Samuel ben Solomon Kohen 12:424
Samuel ben Solomon Nasi 5:160
SAMUEL BEN SOLOMON OF FALAISE (tos.) 14:814
- title of nobility 15:1165
Samuel ben Solomon Sekili 5:1352
Samuel ben Talyon 15:123
SAMUEL BEN URI SHRAGA PHOEBUS 14:814
Samuel Benveniste, *see* BENVENISTE, SAMUEL
Samuel ben Yakar (Tov Elem) 6:628
Samuel ben Yose (amora) 16:852
Samuel Bronfman Biblical and Archaeological Museum (Jer.) 12:552
SAMUEL COMMISSION (inquiry com.) 14:815
Samuel d'Ortas 4:1233; 10:1593
Samuel Elijah Taub of Zwolen 10:858; 12:207
SAMUEL HA-KATAN (tan.) 14:815
- *Birkat ha-Minim* 2:841; 4:1035
Samuel ha-Kohen (gaon) 8:1152
Samuel ha-Kohen (*chelebi*, Egy.) 16:1535
Samuel ha-Kohen (r., Leb.) 15:1397
Samuel Ha-Kohen ben Josiah 13:202
Samuel ha-Levi (mer., Sp.) 15:1300
Samuel ha-Levi (kab.) 4:991
Samuel ha-Levi ben al-Dastur (gaon), *see* SAMUEL BEN ALI
Samuel Halevi Synagogue (Sp.) 15:1199
SAMUEL HA-NAGID (Ismail Ibn Nagrela) 14:816
- Albalia, Isaac 2:522
- al-Bazak 2:527
- Ali ben Amram 2:631
- Almeria, war 2:661
- astrology 3:791
- *Ben Mishlei* 16:531
- Granada 7:852
- Hai ben Sherira 7:1130
- Hebrew poetry 16:1619
- history chart 8:766-767
- Jehoseph Nagid 5:1291
- Jewish literature 11:327
- linguisitcs 16:1357
- Muslim Spain 8:660,666ff
- Nissim ben Jacob 12:1183
- poetry 13:685
- prosody 13:1215
- Spain 15:226
- special Purim 13:1399
- Zirids 16:1184
Samuel ha-Nakdan 4:1378
Samuel ha-Nasi 10:720
SAMUEL HA-SHELISHI BEN HOSHANA 14:818
Samuel Hayyim 16:1548
SAMUEL IBN 'ĀDIYA (al-Samaw'al ben Ghārid ben 'Ādiyā) 14:819
- Arabia 3:234
Samuel Ibn al-Barqūlī, *see* Ibn al-Barqūlī, Samuel
Samuel ibn Fodeila 11:573
Samuel ibn Sid, *see* SID, SAMUEL IBN
Samuel ibn Waqār 10:420; 15:1203
Samuel Isaac 12:784
Samuel Jachia, *see* DENIS, ALBERTUS
Samuel the Jew (apos.) 14:507
Samuel le Pointur, *see* Samuel ha-Nakdan
Samuel Levi, Prince of the Diaspora 5:616
Samuel Sir Morel (tos.), *see* SAMUEL BEN SOLOMON OF FALAISE
Samuel Netzky Adult Institute of Jewish Studies (U.S.) 7:861
- *illus:*
- - class 13:374
Samuel Noah of Safed 3:670
Samuel of Baghdad, *see* Ibn al-Barqūlī, Samuel
Samuel of Cadiz 5:4
Samuel of Derenburg, *see* SMOL
SAMUEL OF EVREUX (tos.) 14:819
Samuel of Fez (14th cent.) 2:607
Samuel of Fez (17/18 cent.) 6:839
Samuel of Indura 14:1303
Samuel of Kamenka 10:727
Samuel of Landshut 10:1412
Samuel of Lublin 3:840
Samuel of Merseburg 11:1393
Samuel of Messina 14:1495
Samuel of Mosul (12th cent., exil.)
- David ben Samuel 5:1354
- David ben Zakkai 5:1359
- exilarchate 6:1029
- Irbil 8:1462
- Maimonides 11:759
Samuel of Murcia 14:1060
Samuel of Norwich 10:475
Samuel of Primo 14:1366
Samuels, Ruth, *see* Campbell, Gay
Samuels, Samuel N. 7:226
Samuel Shmelke ben Mordecai 11:45
Samuelsohn, Simon 5:1034
Samuelson, Max 16:112
SAMUELSON, PAUL ANTHONY 14:820
Samuel Yaḥya, *see* DENIS, ALBERTUS
Samuel Yarḥina'ah (amora), *see* SAMUEL
Samuel Zanvil ha-Kohen 12:204
Samuel Ẓevi of Mukachevo, *see* Mukachevo, Samuel Ẓevi of
Samura (place, Iraq) 8:1447
SAN'A (city, Yem.) 14:820
- Haydan 7:1497;
- Iraq academies' support 16:741
- special Purim 13:1399
Sanafir (isl., Red Sea) 9:387
Sanamayn (vill., Jor.) 16:719
SANANDAJ (tn., Kurd.) 14:822
San Angelo (city, Tex.) 15:1036
San Antonio (clny., Arg.) 3:431
- *illus:*
- - *Fondo Communal* management 3:432
SAN ANTONIO (city, Tex.) 14:822
- Texas 15:1034ff
- *illus:* text
San Antioco (isl.) 14:875
- Roman catacomb 5:251
SANBALLAT I (gov., Samar.) 14:823
- Nehemiah 8:620ff; 11:55
SANBALLAT II (gov., Samar.) 14:823
- Alexander the Great 2:577
SANBALLAT III (gov., Samar.) 14:823
- Samaritans 14:728ff
Sanbatyon (leg. riv.), *see* SAMBATYON
Sanbenito (Inq. dress) 8:1405
- *illus:* 15:236
Sanberg, J. 15:1072
San Bernardino (city, Calif.) 5:56
Sanbornton (tn., N.H.) 12:1024
Sanches, Antonio 14:825
Sanches, Caspar, *see* Sanctius, Caspar
SANCHES, FRANCISCO 14:825
Sanchez (fam.) 11:1190
Sánchez, Alonso 14:826
Sanchez, Alvar, de Cartagena 13:4
SANCHEZ, ANTONIO NUÑEZ RIBEIRO 14:826
- Marranos 11:1024
- medicine 11:1192
- psychology 13:1343
Sánchez, Diego 15:248
SÁNCHEZ, GABRIEL 14:826
- banking 4:170
- Golluf, Eleazar 7:762
- Sanchez, Francisco 14:825
- Saragossa 14:865
Sanchez, Guillén 14:826
Sanchez, Isabel 5:468
Sanchez, Juan de Calatayud, *see* Golluf, Isaac
Sanchez, Juan de Pedro 14:826; 14:865
Sanchez, Juan de Sevilla, *see* Abrabanel, Samuel of Seville
Sanchez, Luis (15th cent.) 14:826
Sánchez, Luis (16th cent.) 5:265; 14:826
- banking 4:170
Sánchez, Pedro 14:826
Sancho III (k., Cast.) 15:1201
Sancho IV (k., Cast.)
- Abrabanel, Judah 2:102
- Abraham el-Barchilon 2:157
- Abulafia, Todros 2:195
- Cartagena Jewry 5:209
Sancho VI (the Wise) 15:1424

Sancta mater ecclesia (papal bull) **4:**1496
Sanctification, *see* KEDUSHAH
Sanctification of the Divine Name, *see* KIDDUSH HA-SHEM AND HILLUL ḤA-SHEM
Sanctius, Caspar **8:**55
Sancto Aquilino, Alexius **8:**55
Sanctuary, *see* TABERNACLE; TEMPLE
SANDAK (godfather) **14:**826
- chair of Elijah **6:**663
- circumcision **5:**571
- *illus:* text
SANDALFON (angel) **14:**827
- celestial hierarchy **2:**968
- Worlds, the Four **16:**642
Sandalwood **14:**1074; **15:**98
SAN DANIELE DE FRIULI (tn., It.) **14:**829
- *illus:*
- - synagogue Ark **15:**1255
Sandauer, Artur **13:**803; **14:**765
Sandbichler, Alois **8:**55
Sandek, *see* SANDAK
Sanden, Bernhard von (Jr.) **8:**54
Sanden, B. von (Sr.) **8:**54
Sander, Martin **9:**1207
Sander, Werner **10:**1592
Sanders, Leon **2:**823,829
SANDGROUND, JACK HENRY **14:**829
Sandgrouse (zool.) **9:**226
Sandheim (Samuel), Herbert **16:**550
SAN DIEGO (city, Calif.) **14:**829
- *illus:* text
Sandler, Harry N. **15:**790
SANDLER, JACOB KOPPEL **14:**830
Sandler, Joseph J. **13:**1340
Sandler, Steve **15:**310
SANDOMIERZ (tn., Pol.) **14:**831
- history chart (1712) **8:**766-767
- Lesser Poland **11:**48
Sandomir (tn., Pol.), *see* SANDOMIERZ
SÁNDOR, PÁL **14:**832
Sandoval, Manoel de **11:**301
SANDROW, EDWARD T. **14:**832
Sandström, Emil **13:**34; **15:**552; **16:**1093
Sandz (has. dyn.), *see* HALBERSTAM
SANDZER, ḤAYYIM BEN MENAHEM **14:**832
Sanehat Scroll **2:**387
Ṣan el-Ḥagar (Egy.), *see* ZOAN
San Fernando Valley (Calif.) **11:**503
SAN FRANCISCO (Calif.) **14:**833
- history chart (1849) **8:**766-767
- *illus:*
- - text
- - Temple Emanu-El **3:**453; **5:**56
San Francisco Conference **2:**824
San Francisco Gleaner (journ.) **13:**1051
San Gabriel Valley (Calif.) **11:**503
Sangara (ruler, Carchemish) **5:**161
Sangari, Isaac **10:**955
Sanger (fam.) **5:**1229
Sanger, Adolph L. **12:**1103
Sanger, H. **11:**1283
San Gimignano (tn., It.) **15:**1467
San Giusto, Luigi di **9:**1106
Sanguinetti, Abraham Ishmael **3:**834
SANGUINETTI, AZARIAH HAYYIM **14:**835
Sanhedria (sub., Jer.) **9:**1515
- cemetery **9:**1496
- Jerusalem **9:**1472
- necropolis **9:**1398
- pillars **13:**522
SANHEDRIN (tract.) **14:**839
- *Avodah Zarah* **3:**981
- *illus:* text
SANHEDRIN (J. high court) **14:**836
- General
- - community **5:**809
- - *gerusia* **7:**523
- - Ḥever ha-Yehudim **8:**438
- - magic **11:**706
- Composition and Functions **4:**720ff
- - abolishment **11:**1240
- - age limit **2:**345
- - *amoraim* **2:**873
- - codification of law **5:**632
- - Commandments, the 613 **5:**765f
- - death sentence **6:**1196
- - *eglah arufah*, performed by **6:**477
- - *halakhah* **4:**739
- - heads of **10:**372
- - languages, knowledge of **14:**1566
- - *nasi* **12:**834
- - ordination, required **14:**1140
- - procedure **13:**958; **13:**961
- - proceedings **2:**202
- - sages **14:**636ff
- - *takkanot* **15:**721
- - *tannaim* **15:**799
- - *urim* and *thumim* **16:**9
- - *zaken mamre* **16:**920
- History
- - Anan **2:**534
- - Great Synagogue **15:**630
- - Herod I **8:**375ff
- - Israel history **9:**238; **9:**241ff
- - Palestinian gaonate **12:**483
- - Pharisees **13:**364
- - Roman period **8:**636; **8:**637
- - Sadducees **14:**620
- - Simeon ben Shetaḥ **14:**1563ff
- Seats of
- - Bet She'arim **4:**766
- - Jabneh **9:**1176
- - Jerusalem **9:**1394
- - Usha **16:**17
- - Temple **15:**983
- Re-Establishment
- - Berab, Jacob **4:**583
- - Kook, A. I. **10:**1183
- - Maimon, J. L. **11:**741
- - Maimonides **11:**764
- - responsum on **14:**93
- *illus:*
- - sitting of **14:**839
- - Tombs, Jerusalem **3:**340
SANHEDRIN, FRENCH **14:**840
- anti-Semitism **3:**113
- Barruel, Augustin **4:**262
- Berr, Michel **4:**692
- Berr de Turique **4:**693
- chronological chart **8:**766-767
- "Elders of Zion" **6:**581
- history **8:**713ff
- loan transactions **12:**253
- Napoleon **7:**23; **12:**824
- seal **14:**1080
- Segrè, Salvatore **14:**1114
- synods **15:**634
- *illus:*
- - text
- - "Grand Sanhedrin des Israélites de France" (lith., E. Vernier) **8:**704
- - medal **12:**823
- *see also:* ASSEMBLY OF JEWISH NOTABLES
Sanhedrin, Tombs of, *see* Sanhedria
Sanhedrin Gedolah (geonic) **7:**322
Sanīʿ al-Dawla, *see* ABU AL-MUNAJJĀ SOLOMON BEN SHAYA
SANIELEVICI, HENRIC **14:**842
San Isidoro Bible (illum ms., Sp.), *see León Bible*
Sanim (vill., Er. Isr.), *see* Shalem Rabta
Sanitation **2:**805
- *see also:* HYGIENE
SAN JOSE (city, Calif.) **14:**843
San Juan (city, Puerto Rico) **16:**473, 1555
San Luis Obispo (city, Calif.) **5:**56
SAN MARINO (rep., It.) **14:**843
San Martín (city, Arg.) **11:**1347
San Mateo (tn., Sp.) **2:**535
San Miguel, Felige Scio de **4:**879
San Millán de la Cogolla (tn., Sp.) **12:**800
San Miniato (tn., It.) **15:**1467
San Miniato, da (fam.), *see* PISA, DA
SAN NICANDRO (tn., It.) **14:**843
- Almah **2:**659
- hymns **9:**1146
Sanoi (demon), *see* Snwy
SANOK (tn., Pol.) **14:**844
San Rafael (city, Arg.) **11:**1347
SAN REMO CONFERENCE **14:**845
San Saba (tn., Tex.) **15:**1036
Sansanoi (demon), *see* Snwy
Sanscrit (lang.) **16:**1414ff
Sanson (cartog.) **11:**927
Santa Clara (prov., Cuba) **5:**1148
SANTA COLOMA DE QUERALT (tn., Sp.) **14:**845
Santa Cruz (city, Calif.) **5:**56
Santa Cruz, Pedro de **14:**865
Santa Cruz de la Sierra (city, Bol.) **4:**1187
Santa Elena (stlmt., Arg.), *see* Wawelberg
Santa Fé (conv. fam.), *see* Abnarrabi
SANTA FE (prov., city, Arg.) **14:**846
- Argentina **3:**419ff
- ICA **10:**46
- *illus:*
- - Spiegelberg store **12:**1038
Santa Fé, Francisco de **11:**495; **14:**865
Santa Fé, Gerónimo de **14:**865; **15:**1270
Santa Fé, Juan de, *see* Abnarrabi, Joshua
Santa Fé de Bogotá (Colom.), *see* BOGOTÁ
Santa Maria (city, Braz.) **4:**1326
Santa Maria la Blanca (ch., Sp.) **15:**1205
- *illus:* **15:**612, 1199
Santa Maria Magdalena, Church of (Jer.) **9:**1416
Santa Maria Maggiore (ch., Rome) **12:**407
Santa Marta (city, Colom.) **5:**745
Santa Monica (tn., Calif.) **11:**503
Santangel, Fernando **14:**847
Santangel, Jaime **14:**847
SANTANGEL, LUIS DE **14:**847
- banking **4:**171
SANTARÉM (city, Port.) **14:**847
- Host desecration **8:**1043
SANTIAGO (city, Chile) **14:**848
- *illus:* text
Santiago (city, Cuba) **5:**1150
Santiago, Bento Dias **8:**1391; **15:**1301
Santiago, Moses **14:**681
Santillana, Marquis of **14:**849
"Santina" (medal, A. Zadikow) **16:**913
Santo (-v; tn., Hung.) **10:**108; **11:**442
Santo André (city, Braz.) **4:**1329
SANTOB DE CARRION **14:**849
- *Proverbios Morales* **10:**1349
- translations **15:**1329
Santo Domingo (Dominican Rep.) **6:**160
Santos (city, Braz.) **4:**1329
Sants (city, Pol.), *see* NOWY SACZ
SANÛʾ, YAʿQŪB (James) **14:**849
- Oriental literature **12:**1463
Sanua, Victor **15:**68
Sanuto, Marino **11:**925ff
Sanz (has. dyn.), *see* HALBERSTAM
Sanzolo, Yom Tov **8:**556
São Caetano do Sul (tn., Braz.) **4:**1329
São Diogo, Brotherhood of, *see* Brotherhood of São Diogo
São Francisco, Luiz de **8:**55
São Miguel (city, Braz.) **4:**1327
São Miguel Island (Azores) **4:**546
SÃO PAULO (Braz.) **14:**850
- *illus:*
- - text
- - ORT school **12:**1482
- *see also:* BRAZIL
São Tomé (isl.) **15:**487
São Vicente (city, Braz.) **4:**1324
Ṣapān, Mount (W. Asia) **4:**9
Šapattu (Babyl. term) **14:**562
Sapaudus (J. stlr., Fr.) **14:**921
Sapci Basi, *see* CARMONA, BEKHOR ISAAC DAVID
SAPERSTEIN, ABE **14:**852
- sport **15:**304
Saphein (loc., Er. Isr.), *see* ZOFIM
Saphet (tn., Er. Isr.), *see* SAFED
SAPHIR, JACOB **14:**852
- Brill, Jehiel **4:**1374
- Cairo *genizah* **16:**1334
- Dunedin **6:**273
- Faiyum **6:**1139
- Judah ben Shalom **16:**745
- Lost Tribes **15:**1005
- Vital, Ḥayyim **16:**176
- *illus:* text
SAPHIR, MORITZ (Moses) GOTTLIEB **14:**854
- *illus:* text
Saphir, Naomi, *see* SHEMER, NAOMI
Saphire, Saul
- Jephthah **9:**1344
- Joseph **10:**215
- Moses **12:**405
- Ruth **14:**523
- Samson **14:**775
- Solomon **15:**109
Saphirstein, Jacob **10:**76; **12:**1102; **13:**1054
SAPIR, EDWARD **14:**855
- anthropology **3:**38
- linguistics **16:**1400
SAPIR, ELIYAHU **14:**856
SAPIR, JOSEPH (Zion. ldr.) **14:**856
Sapir, Joseph (Yosef; Isr. polit.) **14:**856
- politics **9:**667,678ff; **14:**1627
Sapir, Meir **4:**632
SAPIR, PINḤAS **14:**857
- Israel politics **9:**671,678f
SAPIRO, AARON **14:**858
Sapirstein, Rosa **4:**374
Saporta (fam., Fr.) **11:**1190
Saporta, Antoine **11:**1190
SAPORTA, HANOKH **14:**858
Saporta, Ḥayyim Baruch **14:**1366
Saporta, Jean **11:**1190
Saporta, Louis **11:**1190
Saporta, Raphael **9:**1590
Sapphar (anc. loc., Yem.), *see* Ẓafār
Sapphire (gem) **13:**1010
Sappir (gem) **13:**1009
Saptai, Juda (leg. fig.) **10:**326
Sapur (k., Pers.) **11:**1183
Saqqarah (site, Egy.) **2:**685; **13:**403; **16:**659; **16:**667
Saqqiz (tn., Iran) **8:**1443
Sar (title) **15:**1164
Sarʿa (Arab vill., Isr.) **16:**1222
Sārā al-Qurayẓiyya **12:**1462
"Saraband" (paint., M. Louis) **3:**635
Sarābīt al-Khādim (site, Sinai) **2:**674; **16:**665

Sarach bat Asher (bib. fig.), *see* Serah bat Asher
Sarachek, Bernard **15:**303
SARACHEK, JOSEPH **14:**858
Saracopti, Joseph **9:**281
Ṣarafand (Er. Isr.), *see* ZAREPHATH
Ṣaraga, Elias **13:**1369
Ṣaraga, Lascăr (poet), *see* LAZAR, SAMSON
Ṣaraga, Samuel **13:**1369
SARAGOSSA (city, Sp.) **14:**858
- *Contents:*
- - Muslim Period **14:**858
- - The Jewish Quarter **14:**859
- - After the Christian Reconquest **14:**859
- - Results of the Disputation of Tortosa **14:**862
- - The Conversos in Saragossa **14:**865
- dyeing **6:**328
- imprisonment **8:**1305
- Inquisition **8:**1384ff
- Jewish cobblers' guild **16:**1287
- sick care **14:**1498
- Spain **15:**228
- *takkanot* **15:**735
- *illus:* text
Saragossi, Joseph **16:**1533
SARAH (bib. fig.) **14:**866
- Abimelech **2:**76
- adoption **2:**298
- Arts **2:**122
- concubinage **12:**1288
- Genesis **7:**389
- Isaac **9:**1
- matriarch **13:**181
- Rachel **13:**1487ff
- slander of Abraham **10:**1432
- *illus:*
- - carried by Asmodeus **3:**754
- - preparing food for the three angels **4:**938
- - told of God's command to sacrifice Isaac **4:**880
- *see also:* ABRAHAM
Sarah (Apoc. fig.) **15:**1184
Sarah (dau., J. H. Teomim-Frankel) **16:**628
Sarah Bas-Tovim, *see* BAS-TOVIM, SARAH
Sarah Eshet Ḥayil (bk.) **4:**137
Sarah of Wuerzburg **11:**1190
Sarai (bib. fig.), *see* SARAH
SARAJEVO (city, Yug.) **14:**869
- *Contents:*
- - General **14:**869
- - Trade Activities **14:**869
- - Historical Developments **14:**870
- - Rabbis and Jewish Learnings **14:**871
- - Jews in Literature and Arts **14:**871
- - Holocaust and After **14:**872
- museums **12:**543
- special Purim **13:**1399
- Yugoslavia **16:**871,877
- *illus:*
- - text
- - cemetery **16:**874
SARAJEVO HAGGADAH **7:**1100
- anthropomorphism **3:**58
- art **3:**523; **3:**593
- Babel, Tower of **4:**26
- Holy Ark **3:**458
- illuminated mss. **8:**1265
- Jerusalem **9:**1579
- Sodom and Gommorah **15:**73
- *illus:* **3:**456,462,530; **4:**1088; **5:***fcg.* 1067; **7:**205,1085,*fcg.* 1155,1346; **8:**1218,1272; **9:**1202,1285; **10:**204; **11:**885,1014,1157; **12:**379,1192; **13:**605,1602
Saralvo, Joseph **5:**694
Sarapis (deity)
- Hellenism **8:**294
- Jerusalem **9:**1406
- *see also:* Sarpanitum
SARASOHN, KASRIEL HERSCH **14:**872
Saratoga Springs (city, N.Y.) **15:**1649
SARATOV (city, Rus.) **14:**873
- Alexeyev, Alexander **2:**595
- Crémieux, Isaac **5:**1076
- history chart **8:**766-767
- Judaizers **10:**400ff
SARAVAL (fam., It., Ger.) **14:**874
Saraval, Abraham ben Judah Leib **14:**874
Saraval, Jacob ben Leib **14:**874
SARAVAL, JACOB RAPHAEL BEN SIMḤAH JUDAH **14:**874
- Mantua **11:**898
Saraval, Joseph, *see* Henriques, Gabriel
SARAVAL, JUDAH LEIB **14:**874
Saraval, Leon Ḥai **14:**874
Saraval, Nehemiah ben Judah Leib **14:**874
Saraval, Solomon Ḥai ben Nehemiah **14:**874
Saravia, Hadrian à **8:**55
Sarchi, Philip **8:**55
Sarcophagi, *see* OSSUARIES and SARCOPHAGI
Sarcophagus, Ahiram, *see* HIRAM (sarcophagus inscription)
Sardanapalos (k., Assyr.) **16:**1501
SARDI, SAMUEL BEN ISAAC **14:**875
- codification of law **5:**643
- *ḥiddushim* **8:**467
- Naḥmanides **12:**781
- *see also: Sefer ha-Terumot*
SARDINIA **14:**875
- Alghero **2:**621
- Cagliari **5:**14
- Cantoni, Lelio **5:**130
- capitulations **5:**150
- Inquisition **8:**1398
- Roman catacomb **5:**251
- Sea Peoples **16:**1501
- *illus:*
- - "Tower of the Jews", Alghero **2:**621
- *see also:* TUSCANY
SARDIS (Lydia) **14:**876
- Diaspora **6:**10
- Hanfmann's excavations **7:**1261
- inscriptions **16:**669
- Sepharad **3:**746; **14:**1164
- Shushan, road to **14:**1483
- synagogues **3:**521; **15:**599
- *illus:*
- - text
- - marble lions, synagogue **11:**263
- - ruins of ancient synagogue **3:**519
- - synagogue sculpture **6:**338
- *see also:* LYDIA, LYDIANS
Sarei ha-Elef (wk.) **14:**193
Sarezer (bib. fig.), *see* SHAREZER
Sarfati (name), *see also* Sarfaty; Sarphati; Serfaty; Zarefati; Zarfati
SARFATI (fam. name) **14:**878
Sarfati, Abraham (au., Sp.) **14:**878
Sarfati, Abraham (educ., It.) **6:**1231
Sarfati, Ben Zion **7:**515; **14:**874
Sarfati, Giosifante, *see* Sarfati, Joseph
Sarfati, Isaac (physic., It.) **14:**879
Sarfati, Jacob ben Solomon **14:**879
Sarfati, Joseph (Josiphon; Giosifante; Giuseppe Gallo) **14:**878
- poetry **13:**691
Sarfati, Joseph (apos.) **14:**879
Sarfati, Joseph ben Moses **14:**878
Sarfati, Joseph de Isaac **12:**625
Sarfati, Josiphon, *see* Sarfati, Joseph
Sarfati, Samuel (Gallo; Fr. physic.) **14:**878; **5:**601
Sarfati, Samuel (print., It.) **14:**879
- Ferrara **6:**1234
- printing **13:**1100ff
- Rome **14:**252
Sarfatti, Margherita **10:**306
Sarfaty (name), *see also* Sarfati; Sarphati; Serfaty; Zarefati; Zarfati
SARFATY (fam., Mor.) **14:**879
- name origin **14:**878
Sarfaty, Aaron **14:**879
Ṣarfaty, Abner Israel (d. 1884) **2:**516; **6:**1257 **14:**880
Sarfaty, Abner Israel (d. 1933) **14:**880
Sarfaty, Elijah ben Joseph ben Isaac **14:**880
Sarfaty, Isaac (d.c. 1600) **14:**879
Sarfaty, Isaac (d.c. 1660) **14:**879
Sarfaty, Israel Jacob **14:**880
Sarfaty, Raphael Menahem **14:**880
Sarfaty, Samuel **6:**1256
Sarfaty, Samuel ben Abraham **14:**879
Sarfaty, Solomon **11:**800; **14:**879
Sarfaty, Vidal (17/18 cent.) **14:**879
Sarfaty, Vidal (19/20 cent.) **14:**880
Sarfaty, Vidal ben Solomon ben Israel Jacob **14:**880
Sarfaty, Ẓemaḥ **14:**880
- teacher **2:**599; **15:**1444
Sargado, Ḥalaf ibn, *see* AARON BEN JOSEPH HA-KOHEN SARGADO
Sargenes (garment), *see* KITEL
Sargon (dyn. founder, Akkad)
- Akkad **2:**493; **2:**494
- birth legend **3:**466
- chronological chart **8:**766-767
- Mari **11:**974
- Mesopotamia **16:**1489ff
- Sumer **15:**512
- Ur **16:**3
SARGON II (k., Assyr., Babyl.) **14:**880
- Ashdod rebellion **3:**695
- Babylon **4:**32
- history **8:**605
- Israel kingdom exile **14:**728; **14:**736
- Mesopotamia **16:**1504
- war and warfare **16:**277
- *illus:* text
Sargonid (royal house, Assyr.) **16:**1504
Sarha, Adulammi, *see* EDELMANN, SIMḤAH REUBEN
"Sar ha-Birah" (amora), *see* JONATHAN BEN ELEAZAR
Sar ha-Panim (angel), *see* METATRON
Sarḥ asmaʾ al-ʿuqqār (wk.) **11:**779
SARID (tn., Er. Isr.) **14:**881
Sarid (kib., Isr.) **14:**881
- statistics **1:** place list
- *illus:*
- - roundabout milking of sheep **9:**782
Sarid u-Falit (journ.) **1:** newsp. list
Sariel (angel) **2:**962
Sarig, Naḥum **13:**47
Sarighshin (tn.), *see* ATIL
Ṣârim, Al- (loc., Er. Isr.) **14:**42
Sarique (fam.), *see* CHRIQUI
Saris, see EUNUCH
Sáriš-Zemplín (loc., Slov.) **5:**1195
SARKIL (Khazar fort) **14:**881
- Khazar settlement **10:**952
Sárközi, György **8:**1083
SARMAD, MUHAMMAD SAʿĪD **14:**882
- Oriental literature **12:**1465
Sarmas (vill., Rum.) **8:**1103
Sarmasel (vill., Rum.) **8:**1103
Sarmento, Jacob de Castro, *see* CASTRO SARMENTO, JACOB
SARMIENTO, PEDRO **14:**882
SARNA, EZEKIEL **14:**883
Sarna, Jacob Ḥayyim **14:**883
SARNA, NAHUM M. **1:**36
Sarner, Ferdinand L. **11:**1569
SARNOFF, DAVID **14:**884
- T.V. **15:**928
Sarnoff, Robert **14:**885
- T.V. **15:**928
SARNY (tn., Ukr.) **14:**885
SARON, GUSTAV **1:**36
- South Africa **15:**193
Sarona (stlmt., Er. Isr.) **9:**296; **9:**571
- government headquarters **9:**368
- Hoffmann, C. **15:**995
- Jaffa **9:**1256
- Tel-Aviv **15:**922
- Templers **9:**1256
Sarpanitum (deity) **16:**1497
- *see also:* Sarapis
Sarphati (name), *see also* Sarfati; Sarfaty; Serfaty; Zarefati; Zarfati
SARPHATI, SAMUEL **14:**886
- Amsterdam **2:**901
ṢARRĀF (Arab. bnk.) **14:**886
- Ottoman Empire **16:**1553
Sarrāf bāshī ("chief banker") **6:**1034; **14:**887
- appointed by the pasha **16:**1537
Sarraut, Colonel **9:**371
SARRAUTE, NATHALIE **14:**887
Sarrebourg (tn., Fr.) **11:**497,1452
- Saarbruecken **14:**555
SARREGUEMINES (tn., Fr.) **14:**888
- Alsace **2:**757
- Metz **11:**1452
- Saarbruecken **14:**555
Sar Shalom (fam., Egy.) **2:**151
Sar Shalom (12th cent., Pers.) **13:**310
Sar Shalom (14th cent., gram.) **16:**1388
Sar Shalom ben Abraham ben Mazhir **6:**1123
SAR SHALOM BEN BOAZ (gaon) **14:**888
- gaonate **7:**318
SAR SHALOM BEN MOSES HALEVI (gaon) **14:**889
- gaonate **7:**324
Sar Shalom ben Phinehas **8:**1447; **12:**835
Sarsur, see AGENCY (brokerage)
SARTABA (fort., Er. Isr.) **14:**889
Sartan (zodiac sign), *see* Cancer
Sarto, Giuseppe Melchiorre, *see* PIUS X
Sartorius, J. (Hebr., Holl.) **8:**55
Sartorius, J. (Hebr., Hung.) **8:**55
Sartre, Jean-Paul **12:**1033ff
Sarug, Isaac **11:**577
SARUG (Saruk), ISRAEL **14:**889
- Bacharach, Naphtali **4:**49
- Lurianic Kabbalah **10:**548; **10:**590; **11:**576
- Vital, Hayyim **16:**176
SARŪJ (tn., Turk.) **14:**890
Saruk, Israel **14:**890
ṢĀRŪM, ABRAHAM **14:**890
Saruq, Menahem Ben Jacob ibn, *see* MENAHEM BEN JACOB IBN SARUQ
Sarzec, Ernest de **16:**1507
SASA (kib., Isr.) **14:**891
- statistics **1:** place list
- *illus:*
- - *Haggadah* **9:**908
- - Palmaḥ attacking Arab irregulars **9:**686
Sásdi, Sándor **8:**1083
SASKATCHEWAN (prov., Can.) **14:**891
- colonization **10:**46

Saskatoon (city, Can.) **14:**892
SASLAVSKY, LUIS **12:**473
Sason, *see* SOLOMON BEN SAMSON
Sason, Aaron **10:**701
- Ḥayyim Shabbetai **7:**1512
SASOV (tn., Ukr.) **14:**892
Sasov (concen. camp) **16:**1218
Sasov, Jekuthiel Shmelke of, *see* Jekuthiel Shmelke of Sasov
Sasov, Moses Leib of, *see* MOSES LEIB OF SASOV
Sasover Rebbe (Isr.) **9:**899
Saśow (tn.), *see* SASOV
Sasporta, Hanokh, *see* SAPORTA, HANOKH
Sasportas (fam.) **12:**1446; **15:**1173
Sasportas, Abraham (N. Afr.) **16:**1187
Sasportas, Abraham (Holl.) **14:**894
Sasportas, Isaac **2:**622
SASPORTAS, JACOB **14:**893
- Abendanan, Saadiah **2:**68
- Amsterdam **2:**896
- arbitration in community **3:**730
- Barrios, Daniel Levi de **4:**259
- Bueno, Isaac **4:**1461
- Shabbetai Ẓevi **14:**1233
- *illus:* text
Sasportas, Joseph **13:**1449
Sasportas, Solomon **5:**1224
Sass, L. **5:**454
Sassanids (Pers. dyn.) **13:**307ff
Sassen, Willem **6:**520
Sasson, Aaron ben Isaac **14:**895
SASSON, AARON BEN JOSEPH **14:**894
Sasson, Abraham (kab.) **10:**549
Sasson, Abraham (print., Syr.) **2:**564
Sasson, Albert **12:**345
Sasson, Elijah (kab., Er. Isr.) **3:**1008
SASSON, ELIYAHU (Isr. dipl.) **14:**895
- Abdullah ibn Hussein **2:**57
- Vatican **16:**78
- *illus:*
- - Israel-Egypt General Armistice Agreement, 1949 **3:**479
Sasson, Joseph (r., It.) **2:**610; **14:**895
Sasson, Joseph ben Moses **14:**895
Sasson, Moses **11:**1215
Sasson, Randy (El Andaluz) **15:**306
Sasson ben Israel **4:**89; **8:**1452
SASSOON (fam.) **14:**896
- coat of arms **8:**339
- military service **11:**1553
- *geneal. tables:* text
- *illus:* text
Sassoon, Aaron **14:**899
Sassoon, Abdulla (Albert) **14:**899
- Gabbai, Ezekiel **7:**231
- Persian Jews **13:**317
- *illus:*
- - portrait **14:**896
Sassoon, Alfred Ezra **14:**901
Sassoon, Arthur **14:**899
Sassoon, ʿAzîza, *see* Gabbai, ʿAzîza
Sassoon, David S. (18/19 cent.) **14:**896
- Bene Israel, and **4:**498
- Bombay **4:**1193
- *illus:* text
Sassoon, David Solomon (19/20 cent.)
- book collection **4:**975
- family **14:**899
Sassoon, Sir Edward Albert **14:**900
Sassoon, Sir Edward Elias **14:**901
Sassoon, Elias **14:**900
Sassoon, Ellicé, *see* Sassoon, Sir Victor
SASSOON, SIR EZEKIEL **14:**901
- Kefar Yeḥezkel **10:**896
Sassoon, Flora, *see* Gabbai, Flora
Sassoon, Sir Jacob Elias **14:**900
Sassoon, Leontine **14:**901
Sassoon, Mordecai Moses **10:**552; **10:**642
Sassoon, Muzli (Mazal-Tov), *see* Ezra, Muzli
Sassoon, Sir Philip **14:**901
Sassoon, Rachel, *see* Ezra, Rachel
Sassoon, Reginald **15:**310
Sassoon, Reuben **14:**899
Sassoon, Sassoon David **14:**900
- Beer, Rachel **4:**380
Sassoon, Selina **14:**899
SASSOON, SIEGFRIED LORRAINE **14:**901
- Sassoon, Philip **14:**901
- *geneal. table:* **14:**898
- *illus:* text
Sassoon, Solomon **14:**899
Sassoon, Solomon (Suleiman) David **14:**901
- bibliophile **4:**975
Sassoon, Sybil **14:**896
Sassoon, Sir Victor (Ellice) **14:**901
- horse-breeder **15:**311
- Shanghai **14:**1293
Sassoon ben Sâlaḥ **14:**896
- Baghdad **4:**89
- Bushire **4:**1535
- Gabbai, Ezra **7:**231
Sassoon Spanish Haggadah (illum. ms.) **7:**1096; **8:**1264
- *illus:* **7:**1084, *fcg.* 1387
SATAN **14:**902
- Adam **2:**237
- Adam Kadmon **2:**249
- Angel of Death **2:**953
- Armilus **3:**476
- demons **5:**1525
- evil inclination **8:**1319
- Isaac and *Akedah* **9:**5
- Job, Book of **10:**111
- Joseph Della Reina **10:**240
- Judaism **10:**389
- Lilith **11:**248
- Mastema **11:**1119
- righteous **14:**182
- *Solomon, Wisdom of* **15:**120
- visions **16:**169
- worldly evil **7:**776
- *Zerubbabel, Book of* **11:**1412
- Zohar **16:**1203
- *illus:*
- - text
- - attempting to tip scales of judgment **11:***fcg* 619
- - fall from heaven **2:**970
- - temptation of Adam and Eve **6:**981
- *see also:* ANGELS AND ANGELOLOGY; BELIAL; SAMAEL
SATANOV (tn., Ukr.) **14:**905
- Shabbateanism **14:**1251
Satanov, Reuben **13:**218
SATANOW, ISAAC **14:**905
- literature **5:**1115
- Vital, Ḥayyim **16:**174
SATANOWSKI, MARCOS **10:**1511
Satanowski, Robert **13:**775; **13:**776
Satenstein, Bernard **15:**308
Satire, Hebrew, *see* PARODY, HEBREW
Satmar (city, Rum.), *see* SATU-MARE
Satmar (ḥas. dyn.)
- dynasties **1:** has. table
- ḥasidic music **7:**1425
- Israel **9:**899
- Teitelbaum, Joel **15:**909
- U.S. **7:**1399
- *illus:*
- - Rebbe at Western Wall **14:**908
- - Williamsburg Yeshivah **12:**1121
- *see also:* SATU-MARE
Satmar Rebbe, *see* Teitelbaum, Joel
SATINSKY, SOL **14:**906
SÁTORALJAÚJHELY (city, Hung.) **14:**906
Satorra (fam.), *see* STORA
SATRAP (ruler, Pers.) **14:**907
- Persia **13:**305
SATU-MARE (city, Rum.) **14:**908
- *illus:* text
- *see also:* Satmar (ḥas. dyn.)
Saturn (planet) **3:**796
- Lilith **11:**248
Saturnalia (Rom. fest.) **5:**191
SATZ, LUDWIG **15:**1090
- recordings **13:**1617
Saubert, Johann **4:**867
- Hebraist **8:**55
SAUCKEL, FRITZ (Ernst Friedrich Christoph) **14:**909
- *illus:*
- - Nuremberg Trial **16:**289
Saudek, Emil **5:**1209
Saudek, Erik **5:**1209
Saudi Arabia
- Arab League **3:**242
- Arab refugees **9:**449
- Armistice Agreements **3:**479
- frontier **9:**314
- Israel's relations with **9:**445
- Six-Day War **9:**408
- War of Independence **16:**306ff
- *see also:* ARABIA
Saugus (tn., Mass.) **11:**1112; **11:**622
SAUL (k., Isr.) **14:**909
- *Contents:*
- - General **14:**909
- - In the Aggadah **14:**914
- - In Islam **14:**916
- - In the Arts **14:**916
- - In Music **14:**918
- Abner **2:**87
- Afghanistan annals **2:**326
- Agag **2:**341
- Ahimaaz **2:**462
- Ahimelech **2:**465
- Amalekites **2:**789; **8:**345
- Amasa **2:**794
- Ammonites **2:**856
- anointing **3:**31
- David **5:**1318ff
- En-Dor **6:**738
- Eupolemus on **6:**964
- Geba **7:**349
- Gibeah **7:**549
- history chart **8:**766-767
- in the Arts **5:**1335; **14:**784
- kingship **8:**586ff; **10:**1012ff
- mental illness **11:**1372
- Nahash **12:**770
- Palti **13:**49
- realm designation **9:**111
- sacrifice **14:**606
- Samuel **14:**783ff
- Samuel, Book of **14:**789
- Ziba and **16:**1016
- *illus:*
- - text
- - David hiding from **13:**1326
- - dead on Mount Gilboa **7:**567
- - greeted with songs and dances **5:**1263
- - kingdom, limits of (map) **9:**114
- - Michal and **11:**1493
- - sending messengers after David **7:**229
- - threatening David with a spear **7:**196
Saul (Croatian), *see* Mar Saul
Saul, Anwar **8:**1452
SAUL BEN ANAN **14:**918
- Karaism **10:**765
Saul ben Batash **2:**9
Saul ben Netira **2:**154
SAULCY, LOUIS FÉLICIEN DE JOSEPH CAIGNART **14:**919
- Jerusalem **9:**1525
- Jewish art **3:**593
- Helena of Adiabene **8:**288
- numismatics **12:**1271
Saul ha-Kohen of Candia **2:**105
Saul Jedidiah Eleazar of Modzhitz **12:**208
Saul Judycz, *see* WAHL, SAUL BEN JUDAH
Saul of Tarsus, *see* PAUL OF TARSUS
Sault Sainte Marie (city, Ont.) **12:**1408
Saumur (tn., Fr.) **3:**23
Saunas (leg. fig.) **10:**326
Saurin, Jacques **8:**55
Šauška (deity) **12:**1170
Sava de-Mishpatim (rab. wk.) **16:**1195
SAVANNAH (city, Ga.) **14:**919
- U.S. **15:**1590
SAVERNE (tn., Fr.) **14:**920
- Alsace **2:**752ff
Savin, Moses **12:**1035
Savini, S. **16:**788
Savior, *see* MESSIAH
Savir (masorah version), *see Sevirin*
Savitt, Richard **15:**314
Savning, Hans **4:**877
Savoie (duchy, Fr.), *see* SAVOY
Savoir, Alfred **7:**147
Savonarola, Girolamo **12:**280
SAVORA, SAVORAIM (Babyl. schols.) **14:**920
- Aḥa of Shabḥa **2:**449
- *amoraim* **2:**865
- *Beẓah* **4:**786
- *Halakhot Pesukot* **7:**1171
- Jewish law **12:**122
- *kiddushin* **10:**987
- tradition **15:**1311
Savory (spice) **15:**269
- plant list **13:**625
SAVOY (duchy, Fr.) **14:**921
- Acqui Jews **2:**216
- Jews in **7:**17ff
Savra, Jacob **13:**712; **13:**720
SAVRAN (Bendery; ḥas. dyn.) **14:**922
- dynasties **1:** ḥas. table
Savran, David **14:**922
Savran, Moses Ẓevi **12:**785; **14:**922
Savran, Simeon Solomon **14:**922
SAVYON (tn., Isr.) **14:**922
- statistics **1:** place list
Sawelson, William **11:**1552
SAWICKI, JERZY **14:**922
Ṣawīl, Al-(tn., Yem.) **7:**1027
Sax-Bernhard, Gertrud (art.) **4:**677
Saxe, Michael **15:**303
Saxe-Meiningen-Hildburghausen (duchy, Ger.) **15:**1128
Saxe-Weimar Eisenach (duchy, Ger.) **15:**1128
Saxl, Fritz **3:**651
- archaeology **3:**301
SAXONY (state, Ger.) **14:**923
- Luther, Martin **11:**585
- mintmasters **12:**63
- *illus:* text
Sayce, A.H. **16:**1334
Saydon, P.P. **4:**887
Sayf Ibn Dhūi Yazan (k., S. Arab.) **9:**1038
Sayl al-Siyāgh (loc., Transj.) **13:**341
Saylūn (Er.Isr.) **14:**1402
Saymishte (camp, Yug.) **4:**428
Sayyid Ali Muhammad **9:**924
Sayyidunā Ali **8:**935; **9:**922
Sborowitz (firm, Cz.) **13:**1243
Scaccarium Aaronis (exchequer) **2:**22
Scacchi, Fortunato, *see* Schach, Fortunato
Scales, *see* BALANCE; WEIGHTS AND MEASURES
SCALIGER, JOSEPH JUSTUS **14:**925
- Hebraists **8:**55

- Hellenism and Jew **8:**291
Scandari (fam.), *see* ISCANDARI
Scandari, Abraham the Elder **9:**76
Scandari, Joseph **9:**76
Scandarani (fam.), *see* ISCANDARI
Scandinavia, *see* DENMARK; NORWAY; SWEDEN
SCANDINAVIAN LITERATURE **14:**925
- *Contents:*
- - Danish Literature **14:**925
- - Swedish Literature **14:**928
- - Norwegian Literature **14:**932
- - Major Authors **14:**934 **14:**925
- Bible translations **4:**877
- journalism **10:**304ff; **13:**1368
Scantrel, Félix André Yves, *see* SUARÈS, ANDRÉ
Scapegoat, *see* AZAZEL
Scapegoat's Gangway (Temple Mt.) **15:**964
Scarab seals **14:**1072
- *illus:*
- - "Hebron" **8:**227
- - Lachish **14:**1076; **16:**386
Scaramella, Gershom **9:**1148
Scarlatti, Alessandro **10:**460
Scarsdale (vill., N.Y.) **16:**464
Scaurus (Rom. sol.) **3:**407; **12:**742
- Hyrcanus II **8:**1145
SCEPTER **14:**935
Scerbo (Hebr.) **8:**55
Schaaf, Carlus **8:**55
SCHACH, FABIUS **14:**936
- Basle Program **4:**307
- *illus:*
- - F.Z.C. **16:**1165
Schach, Fortunato **8:**55
Schach, Leonard **5:**74
Schach, Miriam **14:**936
Schacherer-Elek, Ilona **12:**1376
Schachno, Charles **11:**498
Schachnowitz, S. **9:**1066
Schacht, Alexander **15:**301
Schacht, Hjalmar **14:**937
- *illus:*
- - Nuremberg Trial **16:**289
Schacht, Lawrence **6:**904
SCHACHTEL, HUGO-HILLEL **14:**936
- Zionist Congresses **16:**1178
SCHACHTER, HERSCHEL **14:**936
SCHACHT PLAN (Nazi emigration scheme) **14:**937
Schadaeus, Elias **8:**55
- Strasbourg printing **15:**424
SCHAECHTER, JOSEPH **14:**937
SCHAECHTER, MORDKHE **14:**938
- Territorial stlmt. **15:**1022
Schaefer, Johannes **13:**755
Schaefer, L.C. **8:**55
SCHAEFFER, CLAUDE F. A. **14:**938
SCHAEFFER, HANS **14:**939
SCHAFER, STEPHEN **14:**939
Schaferman Pästoresu, S. **14:**399
SCHAFF, ADAM **14:**939
Schaffa (vill., Morav.), *see* Safov
Schaffer, A. **16:**1508
Schaffer, Shepsel **4:**146
- *illus:*
- - F.Z.C. **16:**1165
SCHAFFHAUSEN (canton, city, Switz.) **14:**940
Schaffner, David **11:**1202
Schaken (city, Lith.), *see* SAKIAI
SCHALIT, ABRAHAM CHAIM **1:**36; **14:**940
- historiography **8:**565
SCHALIT, HEINRICH **12:**706
- music **12:**663
SCHALIT, ISIDOR **14:**940
- *illus:* **16:**1165
Schalith, I. **16:**632
Schalkowitz, A.L. **16:**148
Schallman, Aaron **14:**264
SCHAMES, SAMSON **3:**609
Schanfarber (r.) **15:**1207
Schanfeld, Josep **12:**38
SCHANKER, LOUIS **3:**609
- *illus:*
- - "Revolving Figures" (wdct.) **3:**639
SCHANZER, CARLO **13:**830
SCHAPERA, ISAAC **14:**941
Schapira (qtr., Tel Aviv) **15:**921
Schapira (name), *see also under* Schapiro; Shapira; Shapiro; Spero; Spira; Spiro
Schapira, Clara **16:**1165
SCHAPIRA, DAVID **13:**830
Schapira, E.I. **5:**432
SCHAPIRA, HERMANN (Ẓevi-Hirsch) **14:**941
- Hebrew University **8:**219
- Zionist Congress (5th) **16:**1168
- *illus:*
- - text
- - F.Z.C. **16:**1165
SCHAPIRA, NOAH **14:**943
Schapiro (name); *see also under* Schapira
Schapiro, Abraham **4:**807
Schapiro, A.J. **13:**1375
Schapiro, Boris **5:**169
SCHAPIRO, ISRAEL **14:**943
SCHAPIRO, JACOB SALWYN **14:**944
Schapiro, Meyer **3:**651
Scharf, Móric **15:**1155ff
Scharfstein, Asher **13:**1377
Scharfstein, Sol **5:**451
SCHARFSTEIN, ẒEVI **14:**944
- *illus:*
- - Histadruth Ivrith of America **13:**371
- - Pen Club, N.Y. **8:**211
- - writers' convention **8:213**
SCHARY, DORE **14:**944
- *illus:*
- - Skulnik, Menasha, and **14:**1650
Schatner, Mordechai **13:**1299
Schatz, Bezalel **14:**946
SCHATZ, BORIS **14:**945
- art in Ereẓ Israel **3:**576
- *illus:*
- - text
- - Bezalel School **4:**789; **9:**331
- - "Jeremiah" (rlf.) Fig. 89 **3**-ART
- - "Mattathias" (sculp.) **11:**1128
Schatz, Louise **14:**946
- art **3:**593
- *illus:*
- - "Lost Horizon" (wtrcl.) Pl.16 **3**-ART
Schatz, Rivka **7:**1420
Schatz, Zahava **14:**946
SCHATZ, ẒEVI **14:**946
SCHATZ-ANIN, MAX **14:**946
- *illus:*
- - Ukrainian Provisional National Council **15:**1515
Schatzki, Erich **2:**322
Schatzky, T. **4:**1355
Schatzman, Evry **3:**807
Schauder, Adolf **13:**909
Schauer, Dr.
- *illus:*
- - F.Z.C. (Bingen) **16:**1165
Schauffler, W.G. **8:**55
Schaulen (city, Lith.), *see* SIAULIAI
Schaulsohn, *see* FRAENKEL, LEVI BEN SAUL
SCHAULSON NUMHAUSER, JACOBO **14:**947
Schaumburg-Lippe (princip., Ger.) **11:**285
SCHAYES, ADOLPH (Dolph) **14:**947
- sport **15:**304
SCHECHTER, ABRAHAM ISRAEL **14:**947
- Houston **8:**1051
Schechter, Eva I. **14:**947
SCHECHTER, SOLOMON (Shne'ur Zalman) **14:**948
- Alexander, Morris **2:**575
- Cairo *genizah* **7:**405; **16:**1334
- Cambridge **5:**70
- Conservative Judaism **5:**903
- history chart **8:**766-67
- JTS **10:**96
- *kelal Israel* **10:**898
- Oral Law **12:**1444
- rabbinical conferences **13:**1461
- United Synagogue of America **15:**1673
- Zionism **16:**1141
Schechter, Mrs. Solomon **15:**1674
Schechtman, Eli **10:**997
Schechtman, J. **13:**1598
SCHECHTMAN, JOSEPH B. **14:**950
Schechtman, Oscar **15:**303
Schedel, Hartmann **9:**1580
Schedia (tn., Egy.) **6:**9
Scheer, Eva **14:**934
Scheff, Otto **12:**1375
SCHEFFLER, ISRAEL **14:**950
Schefftel, Rosalie, *see* Perles, Rosalie
Schefftel, S.B. **13:**293
SCHEFTELOWITZ, ISIDOR **14:**951
Schegez (journ.) **5:**219
Scheib, Israel, *see* ELDAD, ISRAEL
SCHEIBER, ALEXANDER **1:**36; **14:**951
Scheicher, Joseph **3:**84
SCHEID, ELIE **14:**952
Scheidt (Scheidius), Balth. **8:**55
Scheidt (Scheidius), Everard **8:**55
Scheidt, Samuel **9:**1361
Schein, Lasar, *see* SAINEANU, LAZAR
Schein, Samuel **16:**556
SCHEINERT, DAVID **7:**151
Scheinfeld, Aaron **11:**1588
SCHEINFELD, SOLOMON ISAAC **14:**952
- Louisville **11:**522
- Milwaukee **11:**1590
Scheinman, Arieh **4:**1363
Scheinman, Benjamin J. **11:**501
SCHELER, MAX FERDINAND **14:**952
- Jews in sociology **15:**62
SCHELLENBERG, WALTER **14:**953
SCHELLING, FRIEDRICH WILHELM JOSEPH **14:**953
- Einhorn, David **6:**531
- Kabbalah, Christian **10:**646
- philosophy, Jewish **13:**455
Scheltinga, Theodorus **8:**55
Schenck, Joseph **15:**311
SCHENECTADY (city, N.Y.) **14:**954
Schenk, Joseph M. **12:**449
Schenk, Max **4:**653; **14:**955
Schenk, Nicholas **12:**449
SCHENK, FAYE L. **14:**955
Schenken, Howard **5:**169
Schenker, Gitta **11:**1567
SCHENKER, HEINRICH **14:**955
Schenker, Zoltan **12:**1375
Schenweter, Julius **5:**1036
Schepps, Julius **5:**1232
Scherberk, S. **13:**1375
Schereschewski, E. **5:**743
SCHERESCHEWSKY, BEN ZION (BENNO) **1:**36
SCHERESCHEWSKY, SAMUEL ISAAC JOSEPH **14:**955
SCHERLAG, MARK **14:**956
Scherlogus, Paul **8:**55
Scherman, David E. **13:**484
Scherman, Harry **13:**1372
Scherping, Jacob **8:**55
Scherr, Isaac (Eisik) **6:**1292
Scher(t)zer(-us), J. Adam **8:**55
Scheuer, Edmund **7:**1239; **15:**1260
Scheuer, Herz **8:**401; **10:**790
Scheuer, Miriam **15:**366
Scheurer-Kestner, Auguste **6:**226
Scheveningen (tn., Neth.) **7:**1125
Schey, Philipp **10:**1220
Scheyer, Herts Abraham **10:**556
Schiassi, G.M. **9:**1361
Schiber, Chaim, *see* SHEBA, CHAIM
SCHICK, ABRAHAM BEN ARYEH LOEB **14:**956
SCHICK, BARUCH BEN JACOB **14:**956
- Haskalah **7:**1445
SCHICK, BELA **14:**957
SCHICK, CONRAD **14:**957
- Jerusalem **9:**1526ff
Schick, Elijah (Elinke Lider) **11:**213
Schick, Jacob **10:**473
Schick, Joseph **14:**959
SCHICK, MOSES BEN JOSEPH **14:**957
- Hungary **8:**1092
- *meḥiẓah* **11:**1235
- Silberstein, D.J.L. **14:**1535
SCHICKARD, WILHELM (Guillielmus) **14:**959
- Hebraists **8:** 55
Schidlowsky, Leon **5:**467
Schieber, Chaim, *see* SHEBA, CHAIM
Schiff (fam., Ger.) **7:**87
SCHIFF, DAVID TEVELE **14:**959
- *illus:*
- - London monument **11:**473
SCHIFF, DOROTHY **14:**960
- Backer, George **4:**57
Schiff, Frieda, *see* Warburg, Frieda
Schiff, Friedrich **8:**409
SCHIFF, HUGO **5:**387
SCHIFF, JACOB HENRY **14:**960
- AJC **2:**822
- *American Hebrew* **2:**821
- Galveston movement **7:**294
- history chart **8:**766-67
- JDC **2:**827
- Publication Society **10:**80
- railroads **13:**1519
- Schechter, Solomon **14:**949
- U.S. **15:**1604ff
- Warburg, Felix Moritz **16:**282
- *illus:*
- - JDC **2:**829
Schiff, John M. **15:**311; **15:**312
Schiff, Leon **11:**1201
SCHIFF, MEIR BEN JACOB HA-KOHEN **14:**962
- *hadran* **7:**1054
- *ḥiddushim* **8:**467
- Talmud novellae **11:**333
Schiff, Mortimer L. **15:**318
Schiff, Moses **14:**960
Schiff, Sydney, *see* HUDSON, STEPHEN
Schiffer, Feivel **9:**1203
Schifferstein, Victor E. **15:**316
SCHILDER, PAUL FERDINAND **14:**963
Schildkraut, Joseph **14:**965
SCHILDKRAUT, RUDOLPH **14:**964
- Gottesfeld, Chone **7:**820
- *illus:* text
SCHILLER, ARMAND **10:**316
SCHILLER, FRIEDRICH VON **14:**965
- Mendelssohn **11:**1329
- *The Bell* parodied **13:**133
- *Wilhelm Tell* in Hebrew **4:**575
Schiller, Herbert M. **16:**33
Schiller, L. **14:**1264

- Shakespeare **14:**1265
Schiller, Marcus **14:**829
SCHILLER, SOLOMON
14:966
- *illus:*
- - F.Z.C. **16:**1165
SCHILLER-SZINESSY, SOLOMON MAYER **14:**966
- Cambridge **5:**70
- Manchester **11:**858
- *illus:* text
SCHILLINGER, JOSEPH **12:**706
Schimmer, Gustav Adolf **13:**884
Schimen, B. **13:**1375
Schindler, Joseph **10:**862
- Szeged **15:**659
SCHINDLER, RUDOLPH M. **3:**366
SCHINDLER, SOLOMON **14:**967
Schindler, Valentin **8:**55
SCHIPER, IGNACY (Yiẓḥak) **14:**967
- historiography **8:**562
Schippenbeil (concen. camp) **15:**464
SCHIRMANN, JEFIM (Ḥayyim) **14:**968
- Abi Zimra's poems **2:**81
- Cairo *genizah* **16:**1338
- *Tarbiz* **15:**809
Schischa, Isaac, of Mattersdorf **4:**62
Schistosomiasis (disease) **14:**1502
Schizophrenia **11:**1374
Schlaposchnikow, Dr.
- *illus:*
- - F.Z.C. (Kharkov) **16:**1165
Schlaposchnikow, M.
- *illus:*
- - F.Z.C. (Kharkov) **16:**1165
Schlechter, Carl **5:**405
SCHLEGEL, DOROTHEA (Brendl), VON **14:**969
- family **11:**1326
- *geneal. table:* **11:**1325
- *illus:* text
Schlegel, Friedrich **11:**1326; **14:**969
Schleidan, J. **8:**55
SCHLEIERMACHER, FRIEDRICH **14:**970
- Bible criticism **4:**907
- theology, modern **15:**1108
Schleifer, Zaveli **3:**575
Schleisingerville (tn., Wis.), *see* Slinger
Schleisinweil, Bernard **16:**555
Schlemiel (journ.) **5:**219
Schlemiel (ne'er-do-well) **6:**1381
Schlesien (reg.), *see* SILESIA
Schlesingen, Abraham von, *see* Abraham von Schlesingen
SCHLESINGER (fam., court Js.) **14:**970
- railroads **13:**1519
- *see also:* MARGOLIOTH
SCHLESINGER (fam., mus. publs.) **12:**706
Schlesinger, Adolf Martin **12:**706; **13:**1366
SCHLESINGER, AKIVA JOSEPH **14:**971
- *aliyah* **9:**515
- Gutmann, David Meir **7:**988
Schlesinger, Béla, *see* SZENES, BÉLA
SCHLESINGER, BENJAMIN **14:**971
Schlesinger, Benjamin Wolf **14:**970
Schlesinger, Bernard **11:**1554
Schlesinger, Bruno Walter, *see* WALTER, BRUNO
Schlesinger, C. **4:**174
SCHLESINGER, FRANK **14:**972
SCHLESINGER, GEORG **8:**1433
Schlesinger, Ḥayyim ben Isaac, *see* KITTSEE, ḤAYYIM BEN ISAAC
Schlesinger, Heinrich **4:**376; **12:**706
SCHLESINGER, ISIDORE WILLIAM **14:**973
Schlesinger, Israel **14:**971
Schlesinger, Issachar **8:**180
Schlesinger, J. (bk. firm) **4:**1239
SCHLESINGER, JOHN **12:**453; **12:**473
Schlesinger, John Samuel **14:**973
Schlesinger, Joseph **13:**1374
SCHLESINGER, KARL **14:**973
Schlesinger, Marx (Markus) **14:**971
- Köszeg **10:**1220
Schlesinger, Marx (Mordecai) **14:**970
- Margulies **11:**964
Schlesinger, Max **2:**524
Schlesinger, Moritz Adolph **12:**706
Schlesinger, S. **11:**1297
Schlesinger, Simḥah Bunim ben Moses, *see* EGER, SIMḤAH BUNIM BEN MOSES
SCHLESWIG-HOLSTEIN (state, Ger.) **14:**973
- rabbinical jurisdiction **13:**1453
Schlettstadt (tn., Fr.), *see* SÉLESTAT
SCHLETTSTADT, SAMUEL BEN AARON **14:**974
Schleusner, J.F. **8:**57
Schlevogt, Paul **8:**57
Schlick, Moritz **10:**843
Schliefer, Jehiel Mikhel **14:**976
Schliefer, Moses **14:**976
SCHLIEFER, SOLOMON **14:**976
- anti-Fascist committee **3:**63
- Moscow **12:**366
Schlimazel (ne'er-do-well) **6:**1381
Schlock (city, Latv.), *see* Sloka
Schloegl, Nivard **4:**875
SCHLOESSINGER, MAX **14:**976
- Zionism **16:**1144
Schloezer, A.L. **14:**1148,1149
Schlosberg, Herzl J. **15:**209
Schloss, Arthur David, *see* WALEY, ARTHUR
Schloss, David Frederick **16:**251
Schloss, Moses **12:**1075
Schloss (Waley), Rachel Sophia **16:**251
SCHLOSSBERG, JOSEPH **14:**977
Schlosser, von **3:**593
Schmal, Felix **15:**307
SCHMELKES, GEDALIAH BEN MORDECAI **14:**977
SCHMELKES, ISAAC JUDAH **14:**978
- responsa **14:**91
Schmelkes, Moses **14:**978
Schmelt, Albrecht **13:**763
Schmelt Organization, *see* Dienststelle des Sonderbeauftragten der R.R.S.S.
SCHMELZ, USIEL OSCAR **1:**36
SCHMELZER, MENAHEM **1:**37
SCHMERLING, LOUIS **5:**387
SCHMID, ANTON VON **14:**978
- Bratislava **4:**1312
- Hebraists **8:**57
- Hebrew literature **8:**183
- Vienna **16:**131
Schmid, Franz **14:**978
Schmid(t), S. **8:**57
Schmidt, David, *see* Ephraim, David
Schmidt, H.H. **4:**910
Schmidt, J.A. **8:**57
Schmidt, J.F. **8:**57
Schmidt, Johann Lorenz **4:**873
SCHMIDT, JOSEPH **14:**979
Schmidt, Karl Benjamin **8:**57
Schmidt, Karl Ludwig **6:**80, 100ff
Schmidt, Lothar **8:**825
Schmidt, Menaḥem, *see* SHEMI, MENAḤEM
Schmidt, P.W. **4:**873
Schmidt, Simon, *see* BENADOR, URY
Schmidt College (Jer.) **9:**1460
SCHMIEDL, ADOLF ABRAHAM **14:**979
Schmitz, Ettore, *see* SVEVO, ITALO
SCHMOLKA, MARIE **14:**980
- Czechoslovakia **5:**1192
Schmoller, Hans P. **15:**1479
Schmookler, Michael **15:**310
Schmorak, A. **7:**384
Schmorak, Emil **16:**1131
SCHNABEL, ARTHUR **14:**980
Schnabel, Hieronymus W. **8:**57
Schnabel, Louis **5:**456
SCHNAITTACH (vill., Bav.) **14:**981
SCHNAPPER, BER **14:**982
Schnauss, H. L. **10:**1592
SCHNEEBERGER, HENRY WILLIAM **14:**982
SCHNEERSOHN (ḥas. fam.) **14:**982
- *see also:* SHNEUR ZALMAN OF LYADY
Schneersohn, Dov Ber, of Lyubavich **2:**17
Schneersohn, Ḥayyim Shneur Zalman **11:**617; **14:**1434
SCHNEERSOHN, ISAAC (cmty. ldr.) **14:**983
Schneersohn, Isaac Dov Baer **14:**1434
Schneersohn, Israel Noah **12:**1131; **14:**1435
Schneersohn, Joseph Isaac (19th cent.) **14:**1435
Schneersohn, Joseph Isaac (19/20 cent.) **14:**1435
- Riga **14:**174
- U.S. Ḥasidism **7:**1399
Schneersohn, Judah Leib **14:**1434,1436
Schneersohn, Levi Isaac **14:**1435
Schneersohn, Menaḥem Mendel (Rus.) **7:**1404; **14:**1434
Schneersohn, Menaḥem Mendel (U.S.) **14:**1435
- U.S. Ḥasidism **7:**1399
- *geneal. table:* **14:**981
Schneersohn, Samuel **14:**1435
Schneersohn, Shalom Dov Baer (1840–1908) **14:**1436
Schneersohn, Shalom Dov Baer (1866–1920) **14:**322, 1435
Shneersohn, Shemariah Noah **14:**1436
Schneersohn, Solomon (Shneur) Zalman **14:**1436
Schneider, Abram **11:**279
SCHNEIDER, ALAN (Abram Leopoldovich) **15:**1090
SCHNEIDER, ALEXANDER **12:**706
Schneider, Arthur **5:**1567,1572
Schneider, Howard **5:**216
SCHNEIDER, ISIDOR **15:**1574; **15:**1583
Schneider, Ken **15:**310
Schneider, Leonard Alfred, *see* BRUCE, LENNY
SCHNEIDER, MORDECAI BEZALEL **14:**983
Schneider, Teddy **15:**193
Schneider, Yoram **15:**314
SCHNEIDERMAN, HARRY **14:**983
SCHNEIDERMAN, ROSE **14:**984
Schneidermesser, Moses **11:**544
Schneir, Chaim **16:**151
Schneitscher (cmty. ldr., Ukr.) **14:**765
Schnelle (-lius), Sebald **8:**57
Schneller, Abba, *see* KHOUSHI, ABBA
Schneller, Ludwig **9:**1457
Schneur, Abraham **7:**216
Schneur, S.S. **7:**216
Schneur, Zalkind, *see* SHNEOUR, ZALMAN
Schnirer, Isaac **16:**1165
SCHNIRER, MORITZ TOBIAS **14:**984
- Birnbaum, Nathan **4:**1041
- Zionism **16:**1107
- *illus:*
- - F.Z.C. **16:**1165
Schnirer, Sarah **4:**742; **5:**597; **6:**427
Schniskes, K. **4:**1312
SCHNITZER, ADOLF **10:**1511
Schnitzer, Eduard, *see* EMIN PASHA
SCHNITZLER, ARTHUR **14:**985
Schnitzler, Johann **14:**985
Schnurrer (-Christ), F. **8:**57
Schocken, Gershom **7:**1008; **9:**1015; **14:**987
SCHOCKEN, SALMAN **14:**986
- Agnon, Shmuel Yosef **2:**369
- book collection **4:**975
- incunabula **8:**1322
- Institute for Medieval Hebrew Poetry **8:**1407; **16:**1338
- Shenhar, Yitzhak **14:**1377
Schocken, Simon **14:**986
Schocken Bible (illum. ms.)
- *illus:* **7:***fcg.* 395
Schocken department stores (Ger.) **5:**1545; **14:**986
- *illus:*
- - Chemnitz **11:**1323
Schocken Haggadah (15th cent., illum. ms., It.) **12:**83
"Schocken-Hebrew" (type) **15:**1488
- *illus:*
- - example **15:**1486
SCHOCKEN INSTITUTE (Isr.) **14:**987
- Brody, Heinrich **4:**1400
- Schocken, Salman **14:**986
- *illus:* text
Schocken Italian Maḥzor (illum. ms.) **11:**733; **14:***fcg.* 11
Schocken Soehne, I. (firm) **14:**986
Schocken Verlag Berlin (publ. house) **14:**986
Schoeffer, Nicolas **14:**1069
Schoem, Ira **13:**162
Schoen, David Dezsö **15:**1510
- Marton, Ernö **11:**1067
Schoen, Jacob **4:**1379
Schoenbaum, Eliezer Isaac, *see* ILNA'E, ELIEZER ISAAC
SCHOENBERG, ALEXANDER JULIUS WILHELM **5:**387
SCHOENBERG, ARNOLD **14:**988
- *Moses und Aaron* **12:**409
- *illus:* text
Schoenberg, Moses **2:**829
Schoenberger, Guido **3:**651
Schoenberger, Margaret, *see* MAHLER, MARGARET
Schoenblum, Samuel **10:**235
SCHOENERER, GEORG VON **14:**989
- Hitler's anti-Semitism **3:**83; **8:**782
Schoenfeld (Morav. fam.), *see* DOBRUSCHKA-SCHOENFELD
Schoenfeld, Avigdor, *see* SCHONFELD, VICTOR
Schoenfeld, Franz Thomas von, *see* Dobruschka-Schoenfeld, Moses
SCHOENFELD, JOSEPH **14:**990
Schoenfeld, William **13:**1345
Schoenfeld, Sam **15:**304
SCHOENHACK, JOSEPH **14:**990
Schoenhaus, A.L. **11:**886
SCHOENHEIMER, RUDOLPH **14:**990
Schoenlanke (tn., Pol.), *see* TRZCIANKA
Schoenstein, G. **5:**988
Schoenus (bot.) **8:**1311

Schoenwald, Irving **15:**306
SCHOEPS, HANS JOACHIM **14:**991
Schoessler, S. **16:**27
Schoettgen, J.Ch. **8:**57
Schoffmann, Gershon, *see* SHOFMAN, GERSHON
Schola Cantorum, Paris (mus. school) **2:**610
Scholars' Festival, *see* LAG BA-OMER
Scholarship, *see* EDUCATION; STUDY; WISSENSCHAFT DES JUDENTUMS
Scholasticism **13:**428
SCHOLBERG, KENNETH R. **1:**37
Scholem, Arthur **4:**654
Scholem, Erich **4:**654
SCHOLEM, GERSHOM GERHARD **1:**37; **14:**991
- historiography **8:**562
- Kabbalah, studies on **10:**648
- Rosenzweig **14:**301
- Zohar **16:**1215
Scholem, Siegfried **4:**654
Scholl (-ius), J.C.F. **8:**57
Scholtz, David **6:**1364
Scholtz, Samuel **4:**1380
Scholz, Hermann **8:**57
SCHOMBERG (fam.) **14:**992
- ships **14:**1413
Schomberg, Sir Alexander Wilmot **11:**1553; **14:**994
- *illus:*
- - portrait **14:**993
Schomberg, Henry **11:**1553; **14:**994
Schomberg, Isaac (physic.) **14:**994
Schomberg, Isaac (navy com.) **14:**994
Schomberg, Meyer Lo(e)w **11:**1553; **14:**992
Schomberg, Raphael (Ralph) **14:**994
- Aberdeen University **2:**71
- *illus:*
- - portrait **14:**993
Schonberg, Al, *see* SHEAN, AL
Schonfeld, Jozsef **16:**1121
Schonfeld, Solomon **14:**994
SCHONFELD, VICTOR **14:**994
- education **6:**448,765
- Orthodoxy **12:**1491; **15:**1673
Schonfield, H. J. **6:**734
Schonwald, Dave **12:**1353
School for Jewish Communal Work **6:**192
Schoolman, Albert P. **6:**444; **14:**995
SCHOOLMAN, BERTHA S. **14:**995
School of Montparnasse, *see* PARIS SCHOOL OF ART
Schools, *see* EDUCATION
Schopenhauer, Arthur **4:**593
Schor (name), *see also* Schorr
Schor (fam.), *see* WOLOWSKI
Schor, Abraham Ḥayyim **10:**336
SCHOR, ALEXANDER SENDER BEN EPHRAIM ZALMAN **14:**995
Schor, David **9:**1006
Schor, Elisha **16:**622
SCHOR, EPHRAIM SOLOMON (THE ELDER) BEN NAPHTALI HIRSCH **14:**995
Schor, Ḥayyah **16:**622
Schor, Ḥayyim **14:**396, 397
SCHOR, ILYA **3:**610
- *illus:*
- - bookplate for Kalman S. Goldenberg **4:**1223
- - silver *mezuzah* **11:**1475
- - Torah crown **3:**640
Schor, Jacob (Lith.) **4:**1362; **11:**588; **14:**996
Schor, Jacob (Slov.) **6:**511
Schor, Meir **4:**1394
Schor, Zalman Naphtali **16:**622
Schor, Ze'ev **11:**190
Schornstein, Max **5:**1538
Schornstein, M. Ch.
- *illus:*
- - F.Z.C. **16:**1165
Schorr (name), *see also* Schor
SCHORR, BARUCH **14:**996
SCHORR, FRIEDRICH **12:**706
Schorr, Israel **14:**996
SCHORR, JOSHUA HESCHEL **14:**996
- Albalag, Isaac **2:**521
- Auerbach, Ẓevi Benjamin **3:**843
- *He-Ḥaluz* **8:**255
SCHORR, MOSES (Mojżesz) **14:**997
SCHORR, NAPHTALI MENDEL **14:**998
Schorr, Osias, *see* SCHORR, JOSHUA HESCHEL
Schorr, R. J. **10:**341
Schorr, Zeev Wolf **8:**209
SCHORSCH, GUSTAV **14:**998
Schossberger, Eliezer **4:**1374
Schossberger, Janus **13:**1340
Schotanus, C. **8:**57
Schott, Benedict, *see* SCHOTTLAENDER, BENDET
Schottanus, A. **8:**57
Schotten, Samuel **7:**87; **11:**483
SCHOTTLAENDER, BENDET (Benedict) **14:**999
SCHOTTLAND, CHARLES IRWIN **14:**999
SCHOTZ, BENNO **14:**999
- *illus:* text
Schoyer, Alfred **4:**651
Schoyer, Raphael **9:**1280
SCHRAMECK, ABRAHAM **14:**1000
Schramm, David (Agricola) **8:**57
Schreckenfuchs, Erasmus Oswald **8:**57
SCHRECKER, PAUL **14:**1001
Schreiber (fam.), *see* SOFER
Schreiber, Benjamin **7:**929; **16:**1330
Schreiber, David (Zion.) **11:**612
Schreiber, David (writ.) **5:**558
Schreiber, E. (trans.) **5:**1297
Schreiber, Ephraim **11:**499
Schreiber, Geri, *see* SPINA, GERI
Schreiber, H. **10:**89
Schreiber, Jacob **14:**362
Schreiber, Joseph L. **3:**811
Schreiber, Julius (Koenigsberg) **10:**1129
Schreiber, Moses Aaron **8:**210
Schreiber, Simon **6:**469
Schreibman, Welwel **13:**1294
Schreier, Norbert **8:**57
Schreiner (Gal. fig.) **13:**345
Schreiner, Abraham **6:**232; **13:**345
SCHREINER, MARTIN (Mordechai) **14:**1001
Schreiner, Olive **15:**208
SCHREKER, FRANZ **4:**411; **12:**706
Schrenzel, Abraham, *see* RAPOPORT, ABRAHAM BEN ISRAEL JEHIEL HA-KOHEN
SCHRENZEL, MOSES **14:**1002
Schrenzilsh, Mordecai **13:**1554
Schreter, Zygmund **13:**116
Schrieber, Cornell **15:**1206
Schrift, Shirley, *see* WINTERS, SHELLEY
Schriftsetzer, Menahem **16:**148
"Schrijver", *see* MULDER, SAMUEL ISRAEL
Schrimm (tn., Pol.) *see* SREM
Schroeder, J. F. **8:**57
Schroeder, J.J. **8:**57
Schroeder, Nicolaus W. **8:**57
- Hebrew grammar **16:**1395
Schroth and Rathke (print.), *see* Rathke and Schroth
Schub, Esther **12:**456
SCHUB, MOSHE DAVID **14:**1002
Schubart, Christian Friedrich Daniel **16:**261
Schubert, H. F. W. **8:**57
SCHUBERT, KURT **14:**1003
SCHUBERT, LIA **5:**1273
SCHÜCK, JOHAN HENRIK EMIL **14:**1003
- Warburg, Karl Johan **16:**286
Schuckman, Albert **15:**303
SCHUDT, JOHANN JAKOB **14:**1003
- Hebraic studies **8:**57
- universities **15:**1676
Schuerer, Emil **8:**562
Schuette, Johann Heinrich **15:**1676
Schufftan, Leopold **15:**464
SCHUHL, PIERRE-MAXIME **14:**1004
SCHULBERG, BUDD WILSON **14:**1004
Schulenburg (tn., Tex.) **15:**1036
Schulhof, Esther **5:**1009; **11:**225; **14:**1005
SCHULHOF, ISAAC **14:**1004
Schulhoff, Erwin **14:**1005
SCHULHOFF, JULIUS **14:**1005
SCHULLER, GUNTHER **12:**706
SCHULMAN, ALAN RICHARD **1:**37
Schulman, Albert M. **8:**1362
Schulman, Isaac **12:**38
SCHULMAN, KALMAN **14:**1005
- cultural activities **15:**60
Schulman, Milton **15:**303
SCHULMAN, SAMUEL **14:**1006
SCHULMANN, ELEAZAR **14:**1007
SCHULSINGER, JOSEPH **7:**151
Schulstein, Moses **10:**382
Schult, J. **8:**57
Schulten, Carl **8:**57
SCHULTENS, ALBRECHT **14:**1007
- Hebraic studies **8:**57
- linguistics **16:**1394
Schultens, Heinrich Albert **8:**57
Schultens, J. J. **8:**57
Schultz, Gottschalk, *see* Praetorius, Abdias
SCHULTZ, SAMUEL **10:**1511
Schultze, V. **9:**1531
SCHULZ, BRUNO **14:**1008
Schul(t)z, J. C. F. **8:**57
Schulz, Julius **5:**1191
SCHUMACHER, GOTTLIEB **14:**1008
- Megiddo **11:**1222
Schumacher, Israel **15:**1081
SCHUMAN, WILLIAM HOWARD **14:**1008
Schumann, Horst **5:**85
- Auschwitz experiments **3:**855
- War Crimes Trials **16:**297
SCHUMANN, MAURICE **14:**1008
Schumann, Robert **9:**1344
Schünemann, C. H. **8:**57
Schupart, J. G. **8:**57
SCHUR, ISSAI (Isaiah) **14:**1009
Schur, W. **16:**1141
SCHUR, ZEV WOLF (William) **14:**1009
Schurman (n), Anna Maria **8:**56
Schürmann, Willem **6:**320
Schusser, Pessaḥ, *see* Shinar, Pessaḥ
SCHUSSHEIM, AARON LEIB **14:**1010
Schussheim, Marcus **15:**314
SCHUSTER (fam.) **14:**1010
SCHUSTER, SIR ARTHUR **14:**1012
- family **14:**1010
- physics **13:**490
- *illus:* text
Schuster, Claude **14:**1012
Schuster, Ernest Joseph **14:**1010
Schuster, Sir Felix **14:**1010
- *illus:*
- - portrait **14:**1011
Schuster, Francis Joseph **14:**1010
Schuster, Henry **14:**1010
Schuster, Joseph Samuel **14:**1010
Schuster, Judel Joseph **14:**1010
Schuster, Leo **14:**1010
Schuster, Louis **14:**1010
SCHUSTER, MAX LINCOLN **14:**1013
Schuster, Samuel **14:**1010
Schuster, Samuel Judah **14:**1010
Schutzbrief (H. Rom. Emp. doc.) **14:**1013
Schutzbuerger (protected subjects) **14:**167
SCHUTZBUND, REPUBLIKANISCHER (orgn., Aus.) **14:**1013
Schutzer, Paul **13:**485
SCHUTZJUDEN (protected Js.) **14:**1013
- Prussia **13:**1288ff
- *illus:* text
Schutzstaffeln (Nazi orgn.), *see* SS AND SD
Schuur, A. van den **4:**876
Schwab, Herbert M. **13:**912
SCHWAB, HERMANN **14:**1014
SCHWAB, JOSEPH J. **14:**1014
Schwab, J. P. **8:**56
SCHWAB, LÖW **14:**1015
SCHWAB, MOÏSE **14:**1015
- historiography **8:**564
Schwabacher (fam., Bav.) **15:**506
Schwabacher (fam., U.S.) **14:**834
Schwabacher, Henri Simon, *see* DUVERNOIS, HENRI
SCHWABACHER, SIMEON ARYEH **14:**1016
- Nathanson, J. S. **12:**867
- promotion of culture **15:**59
Schwabacher, W. **3:**301
SCHWABE, MOSHEH (Max) **14:**1016
Schwachman, Henry **11:**1201
SCHWADRON (SHARON), ABRAHAM **14:**1017
- autograph collection **3:**912
Schwaebisch Gmuend (city, Ger.) **16:**673
Schwager (bk. co.) **4:**1239
Schwager, Eduard **16:**1165
Schwager, L. **4:**973
Schwaner, Wilhelm **13:**1570
Schwartz (name), *see also* Schwarz
SCHWARTZ, ABRAHAM JUDAH HA-KOHEN **14:**1018
Schwartz, Abraham Nathan **12:**1035
SCHWARTZ, ABRAHAM SAMUEL **14:**1018
- *illus:*
- - Hebrew Pen Club, N.Y. **8:**211; **12:**1109
Schwartz, Albert **12:**1376
Schwartz, Arthur **15:**1059
Schwartz, Bernard, *see* CURTIS, TONY
Schwartz, Buky (Moshe) **14:**1070
- *illus:*
- - "White, from 0° to 180°" (sculp.) **14:**1065
Schwartz, Charleen **13:**1340
SCHWARTZ, DELMORE **14:**1018
- U.S. literature **15:**1576ff
Schwartz, Emanuel **13:**1345
Schwartz, Ḥayyim, *see* Shaḥor, Ḥayyim
Schwartz, Heinrich **5:**1195
Schwartz, Idel **15:**113; **15:**198
SCHWARTZ, ISRAEL JACOB **14:**1019

- Shakespeare **14:**1265
- translation **14:**1026
Schwartz, Izzy **15:**301
Schwartz, Joseph **13:**395
SCHWARTZ, JOSEPH HA-KOHEN **14:**1019
SCHWARTZ, JOSEPH J. **14:**1020
- *illus:*
- - Israel Bonds dinner, N.Y. **12:**1113
SCHWARTZ, LAURENT **11:**1125
Schwartz, Lew **13:**1372
SCHWARTZ, MANFRED **3:**610
SCHWARTZ, MAURICE (act.) **14:**1020
- Gottesfeld, Chone **7:**820
- Libin **11:**189
- Shakespeare **14:**1265
- *illus:* text
Schwartz, Maurice (r.) **11:**485
Schwartz, Morris (psych.) **13:**1340
SCHWARTZ, PHINEHAS (PINḤAS) SELIG HA-KOHEN (SIGMUND) **14:**1021
Schwartz, R. (soc.) **11:**563
Schwartz, Robert (sci.) **11:**1200
Schwartz, S. (poet) **16:**822
Schwartz, Sándor, *see* TISHBY, ISAIAH
Schwartz, Y. Y. **16:**822
Schwartzer, Benjamin **12:**367
Schwartzkoppen, Colonel von **6:**225ff
Schwartzman, M. **13:**1598
Schwartzman, Samuel **14:**527
Schwarz (name), *see also* Schwartz
Schwarz (fam.), *see* SHAHOR
SCHWARZ, ADOLF (Aryeh) **14:**1022
- Friedlaender, S. J. **7:**182
- Vienna rabbinical seminary **13:**1465
Schwarz, Anton **16:**918
Schwarz, Arthur Zechariah **14:**1023
Schwarz, Aryeh, *see* SCHWARZ, ADOLF
Schwarz, Benjamin **14:**1023
Schwarz, Cornelius **15:**996
SCHWARZ, DAVID **14:**1023
- aviation **2:**320
- stamps **15:**335
- *illus:* text
Schwarz, Gavro **16:**918
Schwarz, Gustave **10:**1498
Schwarz, Hannah, *see* Jaffe, Hannah
Schwarz, Ḥayyim, *see* Shahor, Ḥayyim
Schwarz, J. C. (Ger.) **8:**56
Schwarz, Joseph **10:**1170
Schwarz, Karl (art crit.) **3:**652
SCHWARZ, KARL HERMANN AMANDUS (math.) **14:**1024
SCHWARZ, LEO WALDER **14:**1024
- historiography **8:**564
- publishing **13:**1377
Schwarz, Ljudevit **16:**917
Schwarz, Mark **7:**1315
Schwarz, Peter, *see* NIGRI, PETRUS
SCHWARZ, RUDOLF **12:**707
SCHWARZ, SAMUEL **14:**1025
- Portuguese Marranos **13:**924
- Tomar **15:**1213
SCHWARZ, SOLOMON **14:**1025
- historiography **14:**499
Schwarz, Tamar, *see* Kollek, Tamar
Schwarz, Walter, *see* EVENARI, MICHAEL
SCHWARZ, YEHOSEPH **14:**1026
- Jerusalem **9:**1464
- travels **15:**1353
- *illus:* text
SCHWARZBARD, SHALOM (Samuel) **14:**1027
- *illus:* text
Schwarzbard Defense Council (Paris) **3:**386
SCHWARZ-BART, ANDRÉ **14:**1027
- *lamedvovnik* **10:**1368
SCHWARZBART, ISAAC IGNACY **14:**1028
- Union of General Zionists **7:**384
SCHWARZBERG, SAMUEL BENJAMIN **14:**1029
Schwarzblatt, Izrail **12:**1327
Schwarzburg (princ., Ger.) **4:**657
Schwarzenberger, Georg **10:**1495
Schwarzerd, Philipp, *see* MELANCHTHON, PHILIPP
Schwarzes Faehnlein (youth mvmt., Ger.) **16:**106
SCHWARZFELD (fam.) **14:**1029
Schwarzfeld, Benjamin **14:**1029
Schwarzfeld, Elias **14:**390,398,399,1029
Schwarzfeld, Moses (Moisi) **14:**399,1030
Schwarzfeld, Wilhelm **14:**1030
SCHWARZMAN, ASHER **14:**1030
Schwarzman, Gecel **15:**1421
Schwarzmann, Lev Isaakovich, *see* SHESTOV, LEV
SCHWARZSCHILD, KARL **14:**1031
Schwarzschild, Martin, *see* SCHWARZSCHILD, KARL
Schwarzschild, W. Harry, Jr. **14:**161
Schwarzschild, William H., Sr. **14:**161
Schweber, Samuel **5:**406
Schwefelberg, Veronica, *see* PORUMBACU, VERONICA
SCHWEID, ELIEZER **14:**1031
Schweidnitz (tn., Silesia), *see* SWIDNICA
Schweig, M. **14:**399
Schweig, Shemuel Yosef **13:**486
- *illus:*
- - "Plowing the Fields at Tel Yosef in the Jezreel Valley" (phot.) **13:**485
Schweiger, Hermann **15:**473
Schweiger, Moses **15:**473
SCHWEINFURT (city, Bav.) **14:**1031
- *illus:* text
Schweinfurt, Jacob **10:**179
Schweinfurth, George August **4:**143
SCHWEITZER (fam.) **14:**1032
Schweitzer, Albert **10:**1244
Schweitzer, Daniel **13:**821; **14:**1032
SCHWEITZER, EDUARD VON **14:**1032
Schweitzer, Helena, *see* Bresslau, Helena
Schweitzer, Miguel **13:**820; **14:**1032
Schweitzer, Recha, *see* FREIER, RECHA
Schweizerischer Israelitischer Gemeindebund (orgn.) **16:**1242
Schwenter, Daniel **8:**56
Schwerin (tn., Ger.) **11:**1163
SCHWERIN-GOETZ, ELIAKIM HA-KOHEN **14:**1032
- *illus:* text
SCHWIMMER, ROSIKA **14:**1033
SCHWINGER, JULIAN SEYMOUR **14:**1034
SCHWOB, MARCEL **14:**1034
Schwob, René **7:**147
Sciaki, Joseph (Pepo) **7:**887
Sciaky, Ḥayyim Isaac **11:**1159
SCIALOM, DAVID DARIO **14:**1035
Sciama, Dennis **3:**807
Sciatic nerve, *see Gid ha-nasheh*
Science **15:**892
- Jewish philosophy **13:**452
- Judaism and rise of **10:**397
- Kook, Abraham Isaac **10:**1186
- special providence **14:**137
- *illus:*
- - J.F.S. science class **11:**478
- *see also under individual sciences*
SCIENCE AND RESEARCH IN ISRAEL **9:**965
- UNESCO aid **15:**1565
- *illus:*
- - Bar-Ilan University **9:**971
- - expenditures on research and development (chart) **9:**973
- - Hebrew University, students engaged in research **9:**970
- - Negev Institute for Arid Zone Research **9:**966
- - professional manpower in research and development (chart) **9:**974
- - research and development finance sources (chart) **9:**973
- - research personnel in natural sciences and technology (chart) **9:**973
- - Technion, chemistry student engaged in research **9:**968
- - Weizmann Institute **16:**441
- - Weizmann Institute, nuclear physics department **9:**967
Science-Based Industries Development Corporation (Isr.) **9:**971
Science of Judaism, *see* WISSENSCHAFT DES JUDENTUMS
Scio, P. **8:**56
Scopus (place, Er. Isr.), *see* ẒOFIM
Scopus, Mount (Jer.)
- ancient vegetation **9:**1515
- Hebrew University **8:**219ff; **9:**1502
- Israel-Jordan armistice **9:**321; **9:**425ff
- Israel-Jordan clashes **9:**391; **9:**1497
- Mount of Olives **12:**481
- necropolis **9:**1532
- Six-Day War **14:**1630
- U.N. **15:**1548
- War of Independence **9:**1480
- Ẓofim **16:**1192
- *illus:*
- - Hebrew University campus **8:**222,225; **9:**956
- - Israel convoy at Mandelbaum Gate **9:**1490
- - "Jerusalem: Mount Scopus and Government House" (paint., D. Bomberg) **3:**555
- - sarcophagus **12:**1505
Scorpio (zodiac sign) **16:**1191
- *illus:* **5:**291
SCORPION **14:**1035
Scot (t), Michael **2:**928; **8:**56
SCOTLAND **14:**1035
- Edinburgh **6:**367
- Glasgow **7:**602
- *sheḥitah* legislation **14:**1341
- synagogues (Gr. Britain) **1:**syn. list
- *illus:*
- - text
- - Glasglow, Jewish Lad's Brigade parade **14:**1038
Scots, David **8:**56
SCOTT, CHARLES PRESTWICH **14:**1036
- Weizmann, Chaim **4:**132
Scott, Thomas **5:**1129
SCOTT, SIR WALTER **14:**1036
- *illus:*
- - Rebecca in *Ivanhoe* (engr.) **6:**779
Scottsdale (tn., Ariz.) **3:**450
Scotus, John, *see* Erigena, Johannes Scotus
SCOUTING **14:**1037
- *Contents:*
- - General **14:**1037
- - In Great Britain **14:**1037
- - In France **14:**1038
- - In Israel **14:**1040
- French resistance **13:**148
- youth movements **9:**977; **9:**981
- *illus:*
- - text
- - scout camp in Jerusalem **9:**979
- - Young Judaea camp **16:**860
SCRANTON (city, Pa.) **14:**1041
- Arzt, Max **3:**670
Screen Actors Guild (U.S.) **5:**133
SCRIBE **14:**1041
- books **4:**1228
- book tax **15:**850
- book trade **4:**1237ff
- Debdou Jews **5:**1428
- education **6:**392
- Ezra, the Scribe **6:**1104
- masorah **16:**1405
- Mesopotamia **16:**1493
- partner to usury **16:**29
- "scribe's error" and lien **11:**228,229
- *Sefer Torah* **14:**1100
- Talmud **15:**81
- tradition **15:**1311
- *geneal. table:* text
- *illus:*
- - text
- - inkwell, Persia **13:**313
- - Jerusalem Torah scribe **8:**771
- - *Megillat ha-Melekh* Esther Scroll **13:**1388-1389
- - school, Mari palace **11:**982
- - Yemenite Pentateuch (15th cent.) **16:***fcg.* 743
- *see also:* TIKKUN SOFERIM
Scribe, The (newsp.) **16:**565
Scribe, Augustin Eugène **11:**1466
Scribes (schols.), *see* SOFERIM
Script, *see* ALPHABET, HEBREW; CALLIGRAPHY AND WRITING MASTERS; WRITING, SCRIPTS, MATERIALS AND INSCRIPTIONS
"Script II" (paint., J. Tworkov) **3:**644
Scripta Hierosolymitana (journ.) **8:**224
Scripta Mathematica (period.) **7:**582
Scripture, *see* BIBLE
Scroll of Ahimaaz (bk.), *see Ahimaaz, Scroll of*
SCROLL OF ANTIOCHUS **14:**1045
- *Contents:*
- - General **14:**1045
- - Contents **14:**1045
- - The Author **14:**1046
- - The Language **14:**1047
- - Editions **14:**1047
- historiography **8:**555
SCROLL OF ESTHER *(Megillat Ester)* **14:**1047
- *Contents:*
- - Contents **14:**1047
- - Historicity **14:**1051
- - Interpretations **14:**1051
- - Recent Research **14:**1052
- - Canonization and the Greek Version **14:**1055
- canonization **4:**824
- Dead Sea Scrolls **5:**1399
- Esau **6:**857
- Esther **6:**906
- *Maccabees, Third Book of* **11:**661
- musical rendition **14:**1058
- Purim **13:**1390ff
- scribe **14:**1044
- Septuagint **4:**852
- Spinoza **15:**283
- *Targum Sheni* **15:**811
- *illus:*

– – text
– – embroidered scenes 6:911
– – European and Oriental 13:1388-1389
– – folkloristic depictions 6:911
– – illuminated 3:541, 543; 6:1399; 7:1545; 9:1101
– – Latin Bible, 12th cent. 12:733
– – *Megillat ha-Melekh* 13:1388-1389
– – *Moulins Bible* 10:1313
– – paper-cut (17th cent.) 13:63
– – silver cases 5:303
– – *tagin* 15:700
– – unrolling and reading of 11:1229
– – Yiddish version 2:702
– *see also:* ESTHER, ADDITIONS TO THE BOOK OF
Scroll of Ezra the Scribe 4:1513
Scroll of the Hasmoneans, see SCROLL OF ANTIOCHUS
Scroll of the Law, *see* SEFER TORAH
SCROLLS, THE FIVE 14:1057
– Arama, Isaac ben Moses 3:257
– books 4:1225
– canon arrangement 4:829
– Ecclesiastes 6:349
– Joseph Taitaẓak *(Leḥem Setarim)* 15:711
– Lamentations 10:1368ff
– *maḥzor* 11:732
– Ruth, Book of 14:522
– Scroll of Esther 14:1047
– Song of Songs 15:144
– Targum 4:849
– *illus:*
– – Esther, Scroll of 14:1048-1056
– – Esther scroll with *tagin* 15:700
– – *Midrash Ḥamesh Megillot* 11:1507
– – order of (table) 4:830
– – Song of Songs 15:145
SCULPTURE 14:1059
– *Contents:*
– – The Biblical and Talmudic Periods 14:1059
– – In the Middle Ages 14:1059
– – The 19/20th Centuries 14:1060
– – In Ereẓ Israel 14:1069
– Israel 9:1012
– *illus:* text
– *illus:* Ancient and Medieval
– – "Abraham's Bosom" 2:166
– – Adam and Eve 4:939
– – anthropomorphic pottery vessel 4:759
– – anthropomorphic sarcophagus lid 4:761
– – ape figurine 3:176
– – Aphrodite 3:510
– – Arch of Titus 15:1167
– – Artemis of Ephesus 5:12
– – Asherah figurine 3:704
– – Ashkelon synagogue screen 12:569
– – Astarte 3:318,504
– – Barbarians and Romans 4:206
– – bronze lion, second millenium B.C.E. 11:976
– – Capernaum synagogue 5:137-138; 6:948; 11:689; 13:44
– – Chorazin synagogue 5:493
– – Dabbūra *bet-midrash* lintel 13:1533
– – Ecclesia et Synagoga 3:91-94; 4:63; 6:347; 8:670
– – Eshtemoa synagogue 12:569
– – Greek mythology subjects in Ereẓ Israel antiquities 3:518; 4:770
– – Gush Ḥalav synagogue 6:337
– – Ḥaluẓah, relief fragment 12:929
– – Hammurapi stele 7:1245
– – Ḥathor 6:499
– – Hazor archaeological remains 7:1538
– – Hazor orthostat lion 11:263
– – headless prophyry statue, Caesarea 5:11
– – Holy Sepulcher church, frieze 9:1419
– – Jehu paying tribute to Shalmaneser 3:319
– – Jewish Sow libel 3:118
– – Jew with badge 4:63
– – Judith praying 10:454
– – Kalonymus house pillar, Mainz 7:459
– – Lamgi-Mari statue 11:972
– – lion's head, Kefar Birim 3:517
– – man on horseback, Bet She'arim 8:1007
– – Mari, goddess 11:984
– – Megiddo ivory tablets 11:1222
– – *menorah* 11:1355-1362
– – Merneptah stele 3:313; 6:497
– – "Moses" (G. Pisano) 12:406
– – Nike, Ashkelon 3:716
– – Nuremberg *Judenstain* 12:1275
– – Ostia synagogue architrave 12:1508
– – Peki'in synagogue 5:202
– – Philistine female deity 3:696
– – Ramses III 4:760
– – sarcophagi 12:1504,1505
– – Sardis synagogue 6:338; 11:263
– – Sennacherib's campaign against Hezekiah 3:319
– – seraph from Tell Ḥalaf 14:1180
– – Tang figurine of Semitic appearance 5:470
– – winged angel, Crusader 5:1145
– – winged lion 3:288
– *illus:* Renaissance and Modern
– – "Adam" (Rodin) 14:267
– – Alexander, Samuel (J. Epstein) 2:576
– – Anielewicz memorial (N. Rapaport) 3:3
– – "Archangel" (S. Lipton) 11:298
– – Ark of the Law (L. Kaish) 3:627
– – Ark of the Law and *menorah* (N. Azaz) 8:1466
– – Ascension (O. Freundlich) 7:169
– – Bamberger, Heinrich von 4:152
– – Barnert, Nathan 4:249
– – Basevi, George (T. I. Mazzoti) 4:289
– – Bat-Miriam, Yokheved (B. Lishansky) 4:326
– – Ben-Ami, Oved (Duda) 4:460
– – Ben-Yosef, Shelomo, monument 4:571
– – Ben-Zvi, Izhak (B. Lishansky) 4:578
– – Bergson, Henri (H. Kautsch) 4:621
– – Binger, Louis-Gustave 4:1009
– – "Blind Violinist" (ceramic, I. Ryback) 14:533
– – Bondy, Bohumil (Myslbek) 4:1206
– – Brandeis, Louis (E. Pratt) 4:1296
– – Broch, Hermann (I. Rothstein) 4:1385
– – Broken Man 3 (A. Kahane) 3:616
– – Burning Bush (H. Ferber) 15:625
– – "Burning Bush" (D. Palombo) 13:49
– – Capriccio (S. Etrog) 3:622
– – Chajes, Ẓevi Hirsch (I. Sors) 5:328
– – Chmielnicki, Bogdan 5:481
– – Chorin, Aaron (I. Guttman) 5:495
– – "Circus Woman I" (E. Nadelman) 12:754
– – Composition with Heads of Dolls (A. Brown) Fig. 109 3-ART
– – Construction in Space . . . (A. Pevsner) 3:564
– – Crow (L. Baskin) 4:302
– – Dachau camp memorial (N. Glid) 7:620
– – Dancing Girl (W. Zorach) 3:560
– – Daniel Sieff Research Institute (N. Rapaport) 16:440
– – "Devotion" (W. Zorach) 16:1221
– – Ecce Homo (J. Epstein) 6:829
– – Ezekiel's vision of the dry bones (B. Elkan) 6:1096
– – Fettling Shop 1 (Gh. Koenig) 3:634
– – Fleg, Edmond (Ch. Orloff) 6:1341
– – Gabirol, Solomon ibn (R. Armstrong) 7:244
– – "Gas Station" (G.Segal) 14:1106
– – Giving of the Law (Ghiberti) 5:1438
– – Gogh, Vincent van (J. M. Da Costa) 5:1221
– – Goldschmidt, Guido 7:728
– – Habakkuk (Donatello) 7:1015
– – Hananiah ben Teradyon (B. Elkan) 7:1255
– – Hashoah (B. Lishansky) 3:633
– – Hasmoneans (B. Elkan) 7:1459
– – Head of a Horse (G. Ehrlich) 6:513
– – Head of a Young Jew (N. Altman) 2:778
– – Hillel teaching a heathen (B. Elkan) 8:483
– – Hofmannsthal, Hugo von (bust) 8:812
– – Homage to Hieronymus Bosch (I. Tumarkin) Fig. 108 3-ART
– – Homage to Six Million (L. Nevilson) 3:635
– – Ḥuldah defenders memorial (B. Lishansky) 8:1063
– – Isaacs, Jorge 9:42
– – "I to the Hills" (B. Schotz) 14:1000
– – Ivan the Terrible (M. Antokolski) 3:556
– – Jefferson, Thomas (M. Ezekiel) 11:521
– – Jeremiah (Donatello) 9:1353
– – Jeremiah (B. Schatz) 3:*fcg.* 575
– – Jewish peddler 6:761
– – Jews with pointed hats (16th cent.) 5:159
– – Job (B. Elkan) 10:120
– – Johanan ben Zakkai (B. Elkan) 10:149
– – Judah ha-Nasi (M. Horn) 10:368
– – Judith and Holofernes (Donatello) 10:453
– – Kaposi, Moritz 10:755
– – Kohn, Samuel (bust) 10:1148
– – Krinitzi, Avraham (bust, N. Rapaport) 10:1261
– – Lazarus (J. Epstein) 6:829
– – Lieben, Adolph (bust) 11:214
– – Lucifer (J. Epstein) 6:829
– – Maharal (L. Saloun) 10:376
– – Maimonides and Judah Halevi (B. Elkan) 8:683
– – Marx, Karl Heinrich 11:1073
– – "Mattathias" (B. Schatz) 11:1128
– – *Menorah,* Knesset (B. Elkan) 6:675
– – *menorah* theme 3:227, 716, 947; 4:763, 768; 6:675, 821, 948, 1226; 7:934
– – Meskin, Aharon (Z. Ben-Zvi) Fig. 92 3-ART
– – Michaelis, Sir Max 11:1492
– – "Mother and Child" (M. Kottler) 10:1225
– – Mother and Child (Ch. Orloff) 6:528
– – Mount Sinai (Victor Ries) 5:59
– – Negev Sheep (Y. Danziger) 5:1298
– – Nude (M. Kogan) 10:1136
– – Offering (N. Kaz) 3:629
– – Oved, Moshe (J. Epstein) 12:1528
– – Player (E. Glicenstein) 7:618
– – Religious Liberty (M. Ezekiel) 3:556
– – Revere, Giuseppe Prospero 14:126
– – Roth, Cecil (H. Wald) 14:327
– – Salomon, Haym 14:696
– – sculpture at Mexico City (I. Danziger) Fig. 103 3-ART
– – sculpture at Miẓpeh Ramon (D. Feigin) 6:1206
– – sculpture at Naḥal Sorek (Sh. Haber) 7:1023
– – sculpture in welded iron (Y. Shemi) Fig. 104 3-ART
– – Segments (M. Kadishman) Pl. 20 3-ART
– – Shaw, George Bernard (J. Epstein) 3:555
– – Smuts, Jan Christian (M. Kottler) 15:205
– – Spinoza, Baruch, statue 15:276
– – Spirit of the Dance (W. Zorach) 3:559
– – Suasso, Antonio Lopez (bust) 15:467
– – Tablets of the Law (B. Elkan) 5:1448
– – Tel Ḥai Memorial (A. Melnikoff) 3:633
– – Temple Beth Abraham, Tarrytown, N.Y. (S. Simon) 16:465
– – Theseus (J. Lipschitz) 3:559
– – "Torso (Construction)" (A. Pevsner) 13:349
– – *Traustein,* Bingen 11:1041
– – Universal Peace (J. L. Butensky) 4:1538
– – Upward Journey (Th. Tewi) 3:643
– – "War and Peace" (C. Orloff) 12:1472
– – Warsaw ghetto uprising memorial (N. Rapaport) 16:351
– – Warsaw tombstone 15:1228
– – Washington, George (N. Aronson) 3:495
– – Whitman, Walt (Jo Davidson) 5:1366
– – Window (A. Caro) 5:192
– – Woman with Child (J. Epstein) 6:828
– – Wounded Woman (B. Reder) 3:637
– – Yad Vashem Memorial Hall (D. Palombo) Fig. 110 3-ART
– – "Young Girl" (W. Lembruck) 13:117
– – Zeid, Alexander (statue) 16:969
– – *see also:* ARCHAEOLOGY: MEDALS
Scutari (city, Alb.), *see* Üsküdar
Scythians (anc. people) 6:62
– Ashkenaz people 3:718
– Philistia invasion 13:403
Scythopolis (city, Er. Isr.), *see* BET(H)-SHEAN
SD (Nazi orgn.), *see* SS AND SD
S.D.S. (rad. orgn.), *see* Students for a Democratic Society
SEA, SONG OF THE 14:1070
– Av, The Ninth 3:938
– Exodus 6:1054ff
– Miriam 13:671ff
– Moses 12:375
– Samaritan marriage 14:746
– *mus. notations:* text
Sea Fisheries Institute (Isr.) 9:969
Se'ah (meas.) 16:377; 16:380,388ff

SEAL, SEALS **14:**1072
- *Contents*
- - Ancient Period **14:**1072
- - Post-Biblical Period **14:**1074
- engravers **12:**63
- inscriptions **16:**657ff
- jars **16:**660
- jewelry **13:**1012
- Legion, Tenth Roman **9:**239
- letters **11:**56
- Magen David **11:**688ff
- *illus:*
- - text
- - Abendana family **2:**65
- - American Jewish Historical Society **2:**826
- - Amsterdam Portuguese Jewish community **13:**482
- - Ashkenazi, Ẓevi Hirsch ben Jacob **3:**733
- - Charleston, S.C., Hebrew Benevolent Society **7:**376
- - Eliashib son of Eshyahu **16:**660
- - Eẓ Ḥayyim Yeshivah, Jer. **9:**1587
- - Gedaliah "in charge of the house" **7:**351
- - "Hebron" (Israelite) **8:**227
- - Hebron Sephardi community **9:**888
- - Jaazaniah **5:**418
- - Jerusalem emissary **14:**1359
- - Jotham **10:**302
- - Kishinev hatter (18th cent.) **10:**1064
- - Lachish jar handle **16:**386
- - Momet Tauros **10:**1421
- - Moses and Judith Montefiore Foundation **9:**1451
- - Persian Jewish doctor **4:**258
- - Pontoise, for documents of Jews **13:**849
- - Regensburg community **14:**35
- - scarab, Israelite **3:**509
- - "Seal of Solomon" **2:**913
- - *sheḥitah* seal for veal **14:**1342
- - Shema, servant of Jeroboam **9:**1374
- - tenth Roman legion **13:**1537
- - Trier, Hebrew **3:**396
- - Verona community **16:**113
- - Western Wall on Jerusalem community seal **16:**469
- - YHD (5/4 cent.) **9:**110
- *see also:* HERALDRY; SCULPTURE
Seal of MBD (amulets) **11:**696
Seal of Solomon, *see* MAGEN DAVID
Sea of Galilee, *see* KINNERET, LAKE
Sea of Reeds, *see* RED SEA
SEA OF THE TALMUD **14:**1081
- *see also:* STUDY; TALMUD
Sea Peoples **16:**1501
- *see also:* PHILISTINES
Sears, Roebuck (dept. store, U.S.) **5:**1546
SEASONGOOD (fam.) **14:**1082
Seasongood, Alfred **14:**1082
Seasongood, Lewis **14:**1082
Seasongood, Murray **5:**565; **14:**1082
Seasons, Four, *see Tekufah, tekufot*
SEATTLE (city, Wash.) **14:**1082
- Washington **16:**356
- *illus:* text
Sea well (Jer.) **9:**1539
Seba (bib. fig.) **12:**883
Seba (anc. reg., Sud.) **14:**587
SEBAG (fam. name) **14:**1083
Sebag, Hananiah **14:**1083
Sebag, Isaac ben Abraham **14:**1084
Sebag, Joseph, *see* Sebag-Montefiore, Joseph
Sebag, Judah ben Mas'ud **14:**1084
Sebag, Sarah, *see* Montefiore, Sarah
Sebag, Solomon **14:**1084
Sebag, Solomon ben Mas'ud ben Abraham **12:**275; **14:**1084
Sebag, Solomon ben Shalom **14:**1084
Sebag-Montefiore (fam.), *see* MONTEFIORE, SEBAG-MONTEFIORE
Sebag-Montefiore, Harold **12:**275
Sebag-Montefiore, Joseph **12:**275; **14:**1084
Sebag-Montefiore, Oliver **12:**275
Sebag-Montefiore, Robert **12:**275
Sebag-Montefiore, T.H. **12:**275
Sebag-Montefiore, William **5:**114
Sebaste (city, Isr.), *see* SAMARIA
SEBASTIAN, MIHAIL **14:**1084
Sebastianus, A. Nouzanus **8:**56
Sebastopol (city, Crimea), *see* SEVASTOPOL
Sebastos (harbor, Caesarea) **5:**6
SEBBA, SHALOM **3:**610
- *illus:*
- - "Shearing Sheep" (paint.) Fig. 94 3-ART
Sebestyén, Arpád **5:**1195
Seboim, Valley of (bib. site) **8:**1139
Sebomenoi **10:**55
Sebta (port, N. Afr.), *see* CEUTA
Sebti, Moses **16:**265
Sebutia, Caccelia **8:**56
Secco, M., *see* SMILANSKY, MEIR
Secession, law of (Ger.) *see Austrittsgemeinde*
Seckbach (fam.) **15:**790
Secker, Martin **13:**1370
Second Enoch (apoc. bk.), *see* ENOCH, SLAVONIC BOOK OF
Second Gaster Bible, see Gaster Bible, Second
SECONDHAND GOODS AND OLD CLOTHES, TRADE IN **14:**1085
- *illus:*
- - Florentine peddlers **13:**205
- - Monmouth Street, London **11:**475
- - Nuremberg peddler **13:**204
- - shoelace seller in New York **13:**207
Second International (orgn.) **15:**26
Second Leningrad Bible, see Leningrad Bible, Second
Second Nuremberg Haggadah (illum. ms.), *see Nuremberg Haggadah* (Second)
Second Passover, *see* PASSOVER, SECOND
Second Temple, *see* TEMPLE
Secret, François **10:**649; **13:**933; **16:**1214
Secretarii (offics., Sp.), *see Ne'emanim*
Secrets of Enoch (apoc. bk.), *see* ENOCH, SLAVONIC BOOK OF
Secret State Police (Ger.), *see* GESTAPO
Sectarian, *see* MIN
Sections, Jewish (org.), *see* YEVSEKTSIYA
SECTS, MINOR **14:**1087
- *Contents:*
- - Introduction **14:**1087
- - Bana'im **14:**1087
- - Hypsistarians **14:**1087
- - Hemerobaptists **14:**1087
- - Maghāriya **14:**1088
- Apocrypha **3:**185ff
- calendar **5:**50
- Christianity **5:**508ff
- Dead Sea Sect **5:**1408
- Essenes **6:**899
- Jewish Christian **10:**38
- Kariyah, al- **10:**791
- Pharisees **13:**363
- Protestant **13:**1247
- Rechabites **13:**1609
- Sadducees **14:**621; **14:**639
- Somrei Sabat **15:**139
- Therapeutae **15:**1111
Secueni (tn., Rum.) **14:**402
Secularization, *see* HASKALAH
SECUNDA, SHOLOM **14:**1089
Secureni (vill., Ukr.), *see* SEKIRYANY
Security (for loan), *see* SURETYSHIP
Security Service Law 1959 (Isr.) **9:**689
Securius, Pál **8:**56
Sedaca (orgn., Bordeaux) **4:**1244
Sedalia (city, Mo.) **12:**158
Sedan (tn., Fr.) **5:**360
Sedarim (journ.) **1:**newsp. list
Sedarim (Torah div.), *see Parashot ha-shavu'a*
Sedecla, *see* EN-DOR, WITCH OF
SEDEH BOKER (kib., midrashah, Isr.) **14:**1089
- Ben-Gurion **4:**511; **4:**512
- statistics **1:**place list
- *illus:*
- - text
- - Ben-Gurion in retirement **4:**514
Sedeh David (mosh., Isr.) **1:**place list
Sedeh Dov (airfield, Isr.) **9:**837
Sedeh Eli'ezer (mosh., Isr.) **1:**place list
SEDEH ELIYAHU (kib., Isr.) **14:**1090
- statistics **1:**place list
- *illus:*
- - new settlers under mosquito nets **9:**525
Sedeh Ilan (mosh., Isr.) **8:**1246
- statistics **1:**place list
Sedeh Moshe (stlmt., Isr.) **1:**place list **10:**48
SEDEH NAḤUM (kib., Isr.) **14:**1090
- Even-Shoshan **6:**986
- statistics **1:**place list
SEDEH NEḤEMYAH (kib., Isr.) **14:**1090
- statistics **1:**place list
Sedeh Uzziyyah (mosh., Isr.) **1:**place list
SEDEH WARBURG (mosh., Isr.) **14:**1091
- statistics **1:**place list
- Warburg, Otto **16:**288
SEDEH YA'AKOV (mosh., Isr.) **14:**1091
- Ha-Po'el ha-Mizrachi **7:**1321
- statistics **1:**place list
Sedeh Yizhak (mosh., Isr.) **1:**place list
Sedeh Yo'av (kib., Isr.) **1:**place list
Sedeh Ẓevi (mosh., Isr.) **1:**place list
Sedei Ḥemed (mosh., Isr.) **1:**place list
Sedei Ḥemed (wk.) **6:**734; **11:**1216
Sedei Terumot (mosh., Isr.) **1:**place list
Sedemot (periods.) **1:**newsp. list
SEDER (rab. term) **14:**1091
"Seder" (drg., Eva Meitner, Theresienstadt) Fig. 85 3-ART
Seder, Passover, *see* PASSOVER
Seder Birkat ha-Mazon (wk.) **16:**539
Seder Eliyahu (wk.), *see* TANNA DE-VEI ELIYAHU
Seder Eliyahu Rabbah (agg.), *see* AGGADAT BERESHIT
Seder Eliyahu Zuta (bk.) **5:**152; **11:**321; **11:**350
Seder Gan Eden (wk.) **12:**1457
Seder ha-Dorot (bk.) **8:**268
- bibliography **4:**971
- historiography **8:**559
- Jewish history **11:**349
Seder ha-Get (wk.) **5:**748
Seder ha-Tefilla (wk.) **11:**397,401; **13:**986
Seder Olam (wk., Jacob ben Samson) **9:**1223
SEDER OLAM (mid. wk.) **14:**1091
- chronology **16:**1263
- Jewish literature **11:**315
SEDER OLAM RABBAH (mid. wk.) **14:**1091
- historiography **8:**554
- *tannaim* **15:**800
- *illus:*
- - first page (Mantua, 1514) **8:**559
- *see also:* MIDRASH
SEDER OLAM ZUTA (mid. wk.) **14:**1093
- Davidic descent **5:**1344
- Jewish literature **11:**348
Seder Olam Zuta (wk., Nathan ha-Bavli) **2:**204
SEDEROT (tn., Isr.) **14:**1093
- statistics **1:**place list
Seder Rav Amram (prayer bk.) **2:**892ff
- *Al Ḥet* **2:**630
- codification of law **11:**330
- liturgy **11:**396ff
- prayer book **13:**985; **13:**986ff
Seder Tanna'im (wk.) **9:**1225
Seder Tefillah (prayer bk.) **13:**985
Seder Yiḥusei Tanna'im ve-Amora'im (lexicon) **10:**721
Seder Yoma (tract.), *see* YOMA
Sedima (tn., Isr.), *see* SHALEM
Sedom (bib. loc.), *see* SODOM AND GOMORRAH
Sedom (indus. site, Isr.) **1:**place list
Sedom Potash Works, *see* Dead Sea Potash Works
Sedot Mikhah (mosh., Isr.) **1:**place list
SEDOT YAM (kib., Isr.) **14:**1094
- statistics **1:**place list
- *illus:*
- - text
- - British army interrogation **9:**360
Sedrach, Apocalypse of (Chr. wk.) **14:**1256
SEDRAN (Sedransky), BARNEY **14:**1095
- sports **15:**302, 304
Sedres (Torah div.), *see Parashot ha-shavu'a*
Seduction **14:**1207
- commandments, the 613 **5:**769
- virgin **16:**160
- women's finery **13:**1012
- *illus:*
- - Amnon and Tamar **2:**860
- - Potiphar's wife and Joseph **10:**206
- *see also:* RAPE
Sedud (tn., Isr.), *see* SARID
SEDUVA (city, Lith.) **14:**1095
SÉE (fam.) **14:**1095
Sée, Camille **13:**813; **14:**1095
SÉE, EDMOND **7:**151
- family **14:**1095
Sée, Germain **14:**1095
Sée, Henri **14:**1095
SÉE, LÉOPOLD **14:**1095
Seeckt, Hans von **9:**1207
Seedorf, Hans Hartvig **16:**262
Seeds (bot.) **12:**170
SEEKERS AFTER SMOOTH THINGS **14:**1096
- Lion of Wrath **11:**276
- Prophet of Lies **11:**234
Seeligman, Isaac Leo (Arieh) **14:**1097
SEELIGMANN, SIGMUND **14:**1096
Seeligson, Henry **15:**1034; **15:**1035
Seeligson, Michael **8:**1050
Seerappen (concen. camp) **15:**464

Seer of Lublin, *see* JACOB ISAAC HA-ḤOZEH MI-LUBLIN
SEESEN (tn., Ger.) **14:**1097
– Brunswick **4:**1421
SEETZEN, ULRICH JASPER **14:**1097
Sefarad (period.) **15:**245
Sefaradim, *see* SEPHARDIM
Sefardi, Moisés (Mosé), *see* PETRUS ALFONSI
Sefarim (publ. firm) **13:**1376
Sefarim Ḥiẓonim (apoc.) **3:**181ff
Sefat Emet (prayer book) **3:**1018
Sefatenu (journ., Isr.) **1:**newsp. list
Sefatenu (journ., Rus.) **1:**newsp. list **13:**1047
Sefatenu (soc., Pal.) **4:**568
Sefat ha-Naḥal (wk.) **14:**1299
Sefat Yeter (wk., Ibn Ezra) **16:**1358,1384
Sefat Yeter (wk., Isaac ha-Levi) **16:**1387
Sefer Abudarham (wk.) **2:**181
Sefer Arukh (bk.) **8:**766-767
Sefer Arukh ha-Shalem (dict.) **8:**1269
Sefer Asaf ha-Rofe **3:**673; **12:**1198
Sefer Avisha (Samar. Bib.), *see* Abisha Scroll
Sefer Ba'al Shem Tov **9:**1056
Sefer Beri'at ha-Olam, see GENESIS, BOOK OF
Sefer Dikdukei ha-Te'amim **4:**467
Sefer Divrei Ha-Adon **7:**69-70
Sefer Eẓ ha-Da'at **16:**175
Sefer Gezerata (code) **5:**631
Sefer Giddul Banim **6:**460
Sefer ha-Agron **14:**552
– Hebrew language **16:**1613
– linguistics **16:**1347
Sefer ha-Anak **8:**1172; **11:**327
Sefer ha-Azarah, see TEMPLE SCROLL
Sefer Ha-Bahir, see BAHIR, SEFER HA-
Sefer ha-Berit (bib.), *see* BOOK OF THE COVENANT
Sefer ha-Berit (bk., Kimḥi) **3:**194; **11:**354
Sefer ha-Berit (bk., Horowitz) **6:**731
Sefer ha-Dikduk (wk., Ibn Janaḥ), *see Kitāb al-Tanqīḥ*
Sefer ha-Dikduk (wk., Tibbon) **16:**1358
Sefer ha-Dinim **12:**312
Sefer ha-Emunot (wk., Shem-Tov) **15:**1272
Sefer ha-Emunot ve-ha-De'ot (Saadiah), *see Emunot ve-De'ot*
Sefer ha-Eshkol **2:**146; **3:**843; **10:**342
Sefer ha-Galui **16:**1361,1386
Sefer ha-Hakhlamah, see Kitāb al-Tashwīr
Sefer ha-Halakhot **2:**601; **5:**638
– *illus:*
– – *siyyum* invitation **14:**1642
Sefer ha-Hashva'ah (wk., Ibn Janaḥ), *see Kitāb al-Taswi'a*
Sefer ha-Hashva'ah (wk., Solomon ben Joseph ben Job) **16:**1359,1387
Sefer ha-Haspakah **8:**1152
Sefer ha-Hassagah (wk., Ibn Janaḥ), *see Kitāb al-Mustalḥaq*
Sefer ha-Hassagah (wk., Obadiah ha-Sefardi) **16:**1359,1386
SEFER HA-ḤAYYIM **14:**1098
– Jewish mysticism **10:**515
Sefer ha-Ḥezyonot (Luria) **6:**1270
Sefer ha-Ḥezyonot (Vital) **16:**172
Sefer ha-Ḥillukim bein Anshei Mizraḥ ve-Ereẓ Yisrael **12:**27
Sefer ha-Hokhaḥah ve-ha-Re'ayah le-Haganat ha-Dat ha-Bezuyah, see Kuzari
Sefer ha-Ikkarim **2:**535ff
– apologetics **3:**196
– illustrated texts **8:**1270
– Jewish literature **11:**342
– Jewish philosophy **13:**449
– revelation **14:**124
– Tortosa disputation **15:**1272
– *illus:*
– – fifteenth century manuscripts **2:***fcg.* 555, 700; **5:**788
Sefer ha-Ittur **9:**12ff; **11:**331
Sefer ha-Iyyun **10:**538
Sefer ha-Kabbalah **8:**1159
– fiction **6:**1265
– geonim list **7:**318
– historiography **8:**556; **16:**1263
– Jewish literature **11:**348
Sefer ha-Kanah, see KANAH, BOOK OF
Sefer ha-Kundas **13:**133
Sefer ha-Kuzari, see Kuzari
Sefer ha-Ma'aneh **16:**1359, 1387
Sefer ha-Ma'asim li-Venei Ereẓ Yisrael **9:**266
Sefer ha-Ma'asiyyot **6:**1021; **6:**1264
Sefer ha-Mafte'aḥ **16:**1358,1383
Sefer ha-Maggid **16:**802; **16:**968
Sefer ha-Maharil **11:**1235
Sefer ha-Maḥbarot, see Maḥbarot
Sefer ha-Makor **16:**1358
Sefer ha-Manhig, see Manhig Olam
Sefer ha-Ma'or **2:**139; **8:**466
Sefer ha-Maslul, see Kitāb al-Tawti'a
Sefer ha-Meliẓah **15:**1337; **16:**1390
Sefer ha-Middot, see ORḤOT ZADDIKIM
Sefer ha-Mikhtam **5:**1352
Sefer ha-Mikkaḥ ve-ha-Mimkar **7:**1131
Sefer ha-Milḥamot **8:**466
Sefer ha-Minhagim (Klausner) **10:**1090
Sefer ha-Minhagot (Asher of Lunel) **12:**27
Sefer ha-Mishar (period.) **1:**newsp. list
Sefer ha-Mitzvot (Maimonides) **8:**1268; **11:**766
Sefer ha-Mitzvot (Ḥefeẓ ben Yazli'aḥ) **8:**242
Sefer ha-Mitzvot (Anan ben David) **2:**920
Sefer ha-Mitzvot (prayer bk.), *see Siddur* of Isaiah ben Uzziah ha-Kohen
Sefer ha-Mordekhai (wk.), see *Mordekhai*
Sefer ha-Musar (al-Ḍāhiri) **16:**746; **16:**959
Sefer ha-Musar (Kaspi) **11:**345; **16:**532
Sefer ha-Navon **7:**1378
Sefer ha-Ner **2:**367
SEFER HA-NEYAR **14:**1098
Sefer ha-Nikkud **16:**1384
Sefer ha-Niẓẓaḥon **11:**355; **12:**500ff
Sefer ha-Orah **10:**531; **14:**1375
Sefer ha-Pardes **6:**624; **14:**1375
Sefer ha-Peles, see Eshkol ha-Kofer
Sefer ha-Peli'ah **10:**539; **10:**541; **10:**639
Sefer ha-Ploiderzakh **13:**137
– *illus:*
– – "Editors' Meeting" **13:**130
Sefer ha-Ravyah **10:**137
Sefer Ḥaredim **3:**1009
Sefer ha-Razim, see RAZIM, SEFER HA-
Sefer ha-Refu'ot **3:**674
Sefer ha-Refu'ot shel Shem ben Noah **3:**674
Sefer ha-Rikmah (Ibn Janaḥ), *see Kitāb al-Luma'*
Sefer ha-Rikmah (wk., Tibbon) **16:**1358,1385
Sefer ha-Roke'aḥ **6:**592
– literature **11:**331
– *Sefer Ḥasidim* **7:**1388
Sefer ha-Shanah (annual, Pol.) **1:**newsp. list **12:**1051
Sefer ha-Shanah (journs., U.S.; Isr.) **1:**newsp. list
Sefer ha-Shanah ba-Amerikah shel Histadrut Benei Ereẓ Yisrael (journ.) **1:**newsp. list
Sefer ha-Shanah Bibliografyah Yehudit be-Polanyah (bibl.) **1:**newsp. list
Sefer ha-Shanah ha-Em ve-ha-Yeled (journ.), *see Ha-Em ve-ha-Yeled*
Sefer ha-Shanah le-Anaf ha-Beniyyah (journ.) **1:**newsp. list
Sefer ha-Shanah li-Kehillot ve-Irgunim (journ.) **1:**newsp. list
Sefer ha-Shanah li-Melekhet ha-Defus (journ.) **1:**newsp. list
Sefer ha-Shanah li-Yhudei Amerikah (journ.) **1:**newsp. list
Sefer ha-Shanah shel Ereẓ Yisrael (journ.) **1:**newsp. list
Sefer ha-Shanah shel ha-Ittona'im (journ.) **1:**newsp. list
Sefer ha-She'iltot, see She'iltot
Sefer ha-Shem **4:**793; **16:**1358, 1385
Sefer ha-Shetarot (Al-Bargeloni) **15:**735
Sefer ha-Shetarot (Hai) **7:**1129; **7:**1131
Sefer ha-Shoham **12:**417; **16:**1359,1387
Sefer ha-Shorashim (Abendanan) **2:**68
Sefer ha-Shorashim (Kimḥi) **10:**1002
Sefer ha-Shorashim (Tibbon) **16:**1358,1385
Sefer Ḥasidim, see ḤASIDIM, SEFER
Sefer ha-Tekhunah **3:**803
Sefer ha-Temunah, see TEMUNAH, THE BOOK OF
Sefer ha-Terumah **4:**278
Sefer ha-Terumot **5:**643
Sefer ha-Tikkunim **10:**534
Sefer ha-Tokhaḥat, see Kitāb al-Taswi'a
Sefer ha-Turim **11:**335
Sefer Ḥavakkuk ha-Navi **13:**129
Sefer ha-Yakar (wk.) **6:**169
– *illus:*
– – first page (14th cent., It.) **11:**1189
Sefer ha-Yalkut **2:**136
Sefer ha-Yashar (Bib.), *see* GENESIS, BOOK OF
Sefer ha-Yashar (bib. source bk.), *see* BOOK OF JASHAR
SEFER HA-YASHAR (anon. wk.) **14:**1099
– ethical literature **11:**344
– Falaquera, Nathan **6:**1140
– fiction **6:**1263
– *Poema de Yoçef* **10:**1349
– smaller midrashim **16:**1516
Sefer ha-Yashar (Jacob Tam) **15:**779,1279
– responsa **14:**86
Sefer ha-Yashar (Abraham ben Daniel) **2:**136
Sefer ha-Yesod **16:**1358,1385
Sefer ha-Yuḥasin **16:**904, 905
Sefer ha-Zekhut (Abraham of Posquières) **2:**139
Sefer ha-Zekhut (Naḥmanides) **12:**781
Sefer ha-Ẓerufim, see Kitāb al-Taṣārīf
Sefer ha-Zikhronot (Levita) **16:**1390
Sefer ha-Zikhronot (Nathanson) **11:**118
Sefer ha-Zikkuk, see Index Expurgatorius
Sefer ha-Zohar, see ZOHAR
Sefer ha-Ẓoref **14:**1247
Sefer he-'Arukh **16:**1389
Sefer Heikhalot **10:**500
– *see also:* MERKABAH MYSTICISM
Sefer Ḥikrei Lev (wk.) **7:**1541
– *illus:*
– – title page (Salonika, 1806) **13:**1109
SEFER ḤUKKEI HA-TORAH **14:**1099
Sefer Issur ve-Heter **2:**940
Sefer Josippon, see JOSIPPON
Sefer li-Yhudei Polanyah (journ.) **1:**newsp. list
Sefer Me'irat Enayim **6:**1158ff
Sefer Middot **11:**358
Sefer Milḥamot Adonai (Jacob ben Reuben) **3:**194
Sefer Milḥamot Adonai (Levi ben Gershom) **8:**1266; **8:**1267
– *illus:*
– – title page (Riva di Trento, 1560) **11:**93
Sefer Milḥamot YHWH, see BOOK OF THE WARS OF THE LORD
Sefer Mitzvot Gadol **12:**419
– codification of law **5:**643
– Colon, Joseph **5:**748
– Isaac of Corbeil **9:**22
– literature **11:**334
– *Megillat Sefer* **5:**227
– Stein, Isaac **15:**354
– *illus:*
– – second edition (1488) **8:**1333 **9:**1125
Sefer Mitzvot Katan **9:**21
– barnacle goose **4:**247
– codification of law **5:**644
– literature **11:**334
– *illus:*
– – Abraham ben Hezekiah's ms. (1395) **9:**21
Sefer Moznayim **16:**1353,1384
Sefer Otiyyot ha-Inyanim, see Kitāb Ḥurūf al-Ma'ānī
Sefer Otiyyot ha-No'ah (Ibn Ezra) **16:**1384
Sefer Otiyyot ha-No'ah ve-ha-Meshekh (Gikatilla) **16:**1382
Sefer Pitronei Millim, see Sefer ha-Meliẓah
Sefer Po'olei ha-Kefel (Ibn Ezra) **16:**1384
Sefer Po'olei ha-Kefel (Gikatilla) **16:**1383
Sefer Razi'el, see RAZIEL, BOOK OF
Sefer Rishon (Bib.), *see* GENESIS, BOOK OF
Sefer Sha'ashu'im **6:**1129; **11:**352
Sefer Sharḥ Shahin al ha-Torah **7:**1146; **10:**434; **14:**1258
– *illus:*
– – illuminated page **14:**1258
– – Zimri and Cozbi slain by Phineas **16:**1027
Sefer shel Rabbi Anshel, see Mirkevet ha-Mishneh
Sefer Shirei Zimrah **11:**817
Sefer Ta'amei ha-Mikra **16:**1474
Sefer Tagin **15:**700
Sefer Taḥkemoni (bk., al-Harizi), *see Taḥkemoni*
Sefer Tehillim (Tehillot), see PSALMS, BOOK OF
Sefer Toledot Yeshu, see TOLEDOT YESHU
SEFER TORAH **14:**1100
– *Contents:*
– – The Writing of the Scroll **14:**1100
– – Invalid and Disqualified Scrolls **14:**1102
– – The Duty to Possess a *Sefer Torah* **14:**1103
– – Other Uses **14:**1104
– General
– – Ark of Covenant **3:**465
– – Pentateuch **13:**262
– – Roman Jews **14:**247
– – synagogue **15:**579ff

- Laws of Writing **16:**670; **16:**1406
- - correct text **7:**1105ff
- - gold lettering **16:**670
- - photography **14:**92-3
- - scribe **14:**1043
- - square script **2:**706
- - *tagin* **15:**700
- Other Laws and Customs
- - burning of **10:**917
- - fastdays **6:**1192; **6:**1196
- - *hakkafot* **7:**1153
- - *ḥazakah* **7:**1523
- - *ḥerem* pronouncement **8:**355
- - heretics **8:**360
- - kissing of **10:**1074
- - marriage **11:**1028
- - oath administration **12:**1300
- - ornaments **15:**1255
- - purchase from gentiles **7:**592
- - reading **15:**1254
- - scroll **4:**1225; **4:**1227ff
- - Sephardi custom **14:**1170
- - *siyyum* of **14:**1642
- *illus:*
- - text
- - Ḥabad Ḥasidim, celebration on completion of writing **7:**1014
- - Israel stamp **9:**844-845
- - Samaritan **13:**265; **14:**737,739
- - script types (2/16 cent.) **2:**689-728
- - Simḥat Torah procession **9:**907
- - Yemenite scribe **14:**1044,1045
- *see also:* TIKKUN SOFERIM
Sefer Yashresh Ya'akov **13:**1478
Sefer Yehoshua **4:**14
Sefer Yere'im **11:**331; **15:**1280
Sefer Yeẓirah, see YEẒIRAH, SEFER
Sefer Yuḥasin **8:**556
- in Talmud **11:**1231
- Jewish history **11:**349
Sefer Zaḥot **16:**1358,1381,1417
Sefer Ẓaḥut ha-Lashon ha-Ivrit **14:**552
Sefer Zekharim u-Nekevot, see Kitāb al-Tadhkīr wa al-Ta'nīth
Sefer Zeraḥ **4:**137
Sefer Zikkaron **16:**1358,1385
Sefer Ẓurat ha-Areẓ (wk.) **2:**132; **3:**802; **7:**420
- *illus:*
- - page **13:**1102
Seff, Joseph **16:**1165
Seffer, G. A. **8:**56
Sefirah (weeks before Shavuot), *see* OMER
Ṣefirah, Joseph **14:**1104
ṢEFIRAH, SAADIAH BEN JOSEPH **14:**1104
Sefirat ha-Omer, see OMER
Sefire inscription **16:**657; **16:**666ff
SEFIROT (Kab. conc.) **14:**1104
- General
- - *Adam Kadmon* **2:**248
- - alchemy **2:**545ff
- - alphabet **2:**748; **2:**749
- - articles of faith **3:**659
- - concept of God **7:**661
- - *devekut* **5:**1598
- - dualism **6:**244
- - emanation **6:**696
- - eschatology **6:**881ff
- - imitation of God **8:**1293
- - gnostic designations **7:**638
- - *menorah* **11:**1367
- - Neoplatonism **12:**958
- - peace **13:**198
- - providence **13:**1282ff
- - Sabbath **14:**567
- - sacrifice **14:**615
- - *Shekhinah* **14:**1353
- - theology **15:**1108
- - Torah **15:**1237,1241
- - Worlds, the Four **16:**641
- Views and Literature
- - Abulafia, Abraham **2:**186
- - Alkabez **2:**636
- - *Aẓilut* **3:**1009
- - Azriel of Gerona **3:**1014
- - *Bahir, Sefer ha-* **4:**98ff
- - Cordovero, Moses **5:**968
- - Dov Baer of Mezhirech **6:**182
- - Gerondi, Jacob **7:**508
- - Jacob Koppel of Mezhirech **9:**1231
- - Luzzatto, M. H. **11:**602
- - *Ma'arekhet ha-Elohut* **11:**638
- - *Sefer Yeẓirah* **16:**783ff
- - Shabbetai Ẓevi **14:**1240
- - *Shi'ur Komah* **3:**57
- *illus:*
- text
- - diagramatic representation **10:**491-635
- *see also:* KABBALAH
Sefrou (city, Mor.) **12:**328
- Abitbol family **2:**80
- Elbaz family **6:**572
Sefunot (period.) **1:**newsp. list; **4:**472; **15:**56
Segal (fam.) **13:**1399
Segal, Abraham **15:**314
Segal, Abraham ben Model, *see* Riess, Abraham
Segal, Anshel **4:**1417
SEGAL, ARTHUR (art.) **3:**610
- *illus:*
- - "Self Portrait" (paint.) **3:**641
Segal, Arthur (writ.) **15:**209
Segal, Bat-Sheva, *see* Iussim Segal, Bat-Sheva
SEGAL, BERNARD GERARD **14:**1105
Segal, Carol **13:**1369
Segal, D. (nov.), *see* BASHEVIS SINGER, ISAAC
Segal, David **12:**1377
Segal, David bar Naphtali **8:**1368
Segal, Eisik, of Lemberg **7:**1338
Segal, Eliezer **14:**1106
SEGAL, GEDALIAH BEN ELIEZER **14:**1105
SEGAL, GEORGE **14:**1106
- *illus:* text
Segal, Hayyim ben Isaac **12:**215
Segal, H. C. **2:**821
- *illus:*
- - *The Israelite* **2:**821
Segal, Isaac, *see* Ḥarif Ha-Levi, Isaac Segal
Segal, Isaiah **10:**1173
SEGAL, ISRAEL BEN MOSES, OF ZAMOSC **14:**1106
Segal, Israel Isserl ben Isaac, *see* ISRAEL ISSERL BEN ISAAC SEGAL
Segal, Jacob **14:**1248
Segal, Jekuthiel Zalman, *see* Ḥarif Ha-Levi, Jekuthiel Zalman Segal
Segal, Joseph, *see* Ḥarif Ha-Levi, Joseph Segal
Segal, Joshua ha-Levi, *see* MEZAḤ, JOSHUA HA-LEVI
Segal, Judah Benzion **14:**1108
SEGAL, LOUIS **14:**1107
- *illus:*
- - protest against 1940 White Paper **15:**1632
Segal, Marc, *see* CHAGALL, MARC
Segal, Moses, *see* Ḥarif Ha-Levi, Moses Segal
Segal, Moses Ḥayyim **10:**1078
SEGAL, MOSES HIRSCH (ZEVI) **14:**1107
- linguistics **16:**1394
- mishnaic Hebrew **16:**1592
Segal, Phillip **15:**210
Segal, Phoebus **8:**1287
Segal, Lord Samuel **14:**1108
Segal, Simon **13:**120
Segal, Yakov **12:**456
SEGAL, YAKOV-YITSKHAK **14:**1108
Segal, Zev **6:**904
Segall, Berta **3:**301
Segall, Jacob **4:**1426
SEGALL, LASAR **14:**1108
- *illus:* text
Segalovicz, Clara **15:**1072
Segalowicz, Jehiel Moses **12:**186
SEGALOWITCH, ZUSMAN **14:**1109
Segalowitz, Benjamin **13:**1049
Segan ha-Kohanim (offic.) **9:**1320; **15:**974
Segan Leviyyah, *see* ISAAC BEN ELIEZER
Segarra, Arnold de **4:**213
Segelmesi, Judah **13:**587
Segev (rural stlmt., Isr.) **1:**place list
SEGHERS, ANNA **14:**1110
"Segments" (sculp., M. Kadishman) Pl. 20 **3**-ART
Segni, Lothair of, *see* INNOCENT III
Segol (cantillation sign) **16:**1440,1450,1454
Segond, Louis **4:**881
SEGORBE (city, Sp.) **14:**1110
SEGOVIA (tn., Sp.) **14:**1110
- Host desecration charge **8:**1043
Segrais, Jean Regnault de **15:**1168
SEGRE (fam.) **14:**1112
- Chieri **5:**422
Segré (tn., Fr.) **3:**23
Segre, Abraham ben Judah (Isr.) **14:**1112
Segre, Abraham ben Judah (It.) **9:**1145; **14:**1112; **15:**1455
Segre, Abraham ben Zerah **14:**1112
Segre, Alfredo **9:**1112
SEGRÈ, ARTURO **14:**1112
- family **14:**1112
SEGRE, BENIAMINO (math.) **11:**1125
Segre, Benjamin (schol.) **14:**1112
Segre, Cesare **9:**1114
SEGRÈ, CORRADO **14:**1112
- family **14:**1112
Segre, David **14:**714
Segre, Deodato Nethaneel **9:**1109
Segre, Dino, *see* PITIGRILLI
Segre, Elisha **14:**1112
SEGRÈ, EMILIO GINO **14:**1113
- family **14:**1112
SEGRÈ, GINO **14:**1113
- family **14:**1112
Segre, Guido **11:**1559; **11:**1568
Segre, Ḥayyim **14:**1112; **14:**1245
Segre, Ḥayyim Judah **9:**105
Segre, Jacob ben Isaac **13:**583 **13:**130; **14:**1112
Segre, Jacob ben Joshua Benzion **15:**1455
SEGRE, JOSHUA BENZION (1705-1797) **14:**1113
- Acqui **2:**216
Segre, Joshua Ben-Zion (1729-1809), *see* SEGRE, SALVATORE
Segre, Judah **14:**1112
Segre, Nethanel **14:**1112
Segre, Nethanel ben Aaron Jacob **14:**1112
SEGRÈ, ROBERTO **14:**1114
- family **14:**1112
Segrè, Salvador (1705-1797), *see* SEGRÈ, JOSHUA BENZION
SEGRE, SALVATORE (1729-1809) **14:**1114
Segub (bib. fig.) **9:**1269
Segullah (mosh., Isr.) **1:**place list
Segullot (remedies) **4:**6; **4:**7
Segura, Judah de **16:**1552
SEIBER, MÁTYÁS GYÖRGY **14:**1114
Seid, Ruth, *see* SINCLAIR, JO
Seidel(-ius), C. **8:**56
Seidel, Nathaniel **15:**462
Seidemann, Gustav **16:**1149
Seiden, Allan **15:**303
SEIDENFELD, MORTON **13:**1347
Seidenman, A. **13:**1597
- *illus:*
- - *Razsvet* staff **13:**1596
Seidenstücker, J. H. P. **8:**56
Seidenstücker, W. F. F. **8:**56
Seidl, Siegfried **4:**610; **15:**1115
Seidmann, J. **16:**1509
Seiferheld, J. L. **8:**56
Seifert, David **13:**116
Seiffert, Ernst, *see* TAUBER, RICHARD
SEIGEL, KALMAN A. **1:**37
Seineccerius, Nicolaus **8:**56
SEINI (vill., Rum.) **14:**1115
SEIPEL, IGNAZ **14:**1115
Seir (bib. fig.), *see* ESAU
Seir (anc. kdm.), *see* EDOM
SEIR, MOUNT (bib. regs.) **14:**1116
- Amalekites **2:**790
- Jibāl mountains **9:**596
- Karaites **13:**309
- physiography **9:**176
- Transjordan **15:**1316
- *see also:* EDOM
Se'irim (demons) **5:**1523
Seistan (reg., Asia) **10:**958; **13:**311
SEIXAS (fam.) **14:**1116
Seixas, Abigail, *see* Judah, Abigail
Seixas, Abraham Mendes (Eng.) **14:**1116
Seixas, Abraham Mendes (U.S.) **14:**1117
Seixas, Benjamin Mendes **12:**848; **14:**1117
Seixas, David G. **14:**1117
Seixas, Gershom Mendes **14:**1116
- historiography **8:**567
- New York City **12:**1069; **12:**1082
- universities **15:**1677
- U.S. anti-Semitism **15:**1648
- *illus:*
- - commemorative medal **7:**221
- - portrait **14:**1116
Seixas, Isaac Mendes **14:**1116
- *geneal. table:* **12:**849
Seixas, Moses Mendes **14:**1117; **15:**1305; **16:**360
- *illus:*
- - address to George Washington **14:**144
Seixas, Rebecca **7:**1354
Seixas, Sara **12:**848
Sejera (mosh., Isr.), *see* ILANIYYAH
SEJM (parl., Pol.) **14:**1117
- minority bloc **12:**41
- Nomberg, Hersh **12:**1210
- Ugoda **15:**1508
- Warsaw **16:**334
- Zionist Socialist Workers' Party **16:**1180
Sejmists (Rus.), *see* JEWISH SOCIALIST WORKERS' PARTY
Sekhakh (sukkah covering) **15:**493
Sekel, Shalom ben Isaac **16:**1295
Sekhel Tov (wk.) **11:**1307
Sekirah Ḥodshit (journ.) **1:** newsp. list
SEKIRYANY (vill., Ukr.) **14:**1118
Sela (bib. place, Edom) **2:**798; **6:**375; **10:**906; **12:**1305
- *see also:* PETRA
Sela (bldg. co., Isr.) **8:**542
Sela (coin, weight) **5:**719; **14:**1349; **16:**390
Sela, Michael **11:**1204
Sela Edom (loc., Transj.), *see* PETRA
Selah (bib. term) **12:**565; **13:**1321
Sela ha-Yehudim (tn., Crimea), *see*

CHUFUT-KALE
SELBSTEMANZIPATION (newsp.) **14:**1119
- Zionism **16:**1032
SELBSTWEHR (weekly, Cz.) **14:**1120
- Bar Kochba Association **4:**228
- press **13:**1026
- Weltsch, Felix **16:**446
Selbstwehr (period., Yug.) **13:**1026
Selby, David **10:**1492
Selchen, Mark **5:**113; **16:**551
SELDEN, JOHN **14:**1120
- Hebraist **8:**56
- Jewish law **8:**702
SELDES, GEORGE **14:**1121
Seldes, Gilbert **16:**157
SELDIN, HARRY M. **11:**1210
Selebi (vill., Er. Isr.) **14:**1211
Selek (bot.), *see* BEET
Selek, Jacob **13:**859
SELEKMAN, BENJAMIN M. **14:**1122
Selektion (Nazi murder procedure) **3:**855
- *illus:*
- - at Auschwitz camp **3:**863
Selemia (loc., Er. Isr.) **10:**881
SÉLESTAT (tn., Fr.) **14:**1122
SELEUCIA (city, Gaulanitis) **14:**1122
SELEUCIA (city, Mesop.) **14:**1122
- Babylon inhabitants **4:**32
- Diaspora **6:**11
SELEUCID ERA **14:**1123
- chronology **16:**1264
- *see also:* CALENDAR
Seleucids (dyn.) **8:**625ff
- Hellenistic states **8:**292ff
- history chart **8:**766-767
- Jerusalem **9:**1390
- Transjordan **15:**1317
- war and warfare **16:**278
- *illus:*
- - Antioch (plan) **3:**72
- - Antiochus VII's coin for John Hyrcanus **3:**75
Seleucus I Nicator (k.) **8:**766-767; **3:**71, 747; **14:**1123
Seleucus II Callinicus **3:**73
Seleucus III Soter **3:**73
SELEUCUS IV PHILOPATOR (k.) **14:**1123
- Apollonia **3:**187
- chronological chart **8:**766-767
- Erez Israel history **8:**628
- Temple **15:**958; **15:**980
Seleukeia (bib. site, Iran), *see* SHUSHAN
Self-abnegation, *see Bittul ha-Yesh*
SELF-DEFENSE **14:**1123
- *Contents:*
- - General **14:**1123
- - In Austria-Hungary **14:**1128
- - After World War I **14:**1128
- bloodguilt **4:**1119
- Giladi, Israel **7:**566
- Haganah **7:**1064
- Israel retaliatory raids **15:**1553ff
- *kiddush ha-Shem* **10:**985
- penal law **13:**227
- Podolia **13:**669
- pogroms **13:**697ff; **14:**446, 455, 457
- reaction to pogroms **8:**735
- Russia **15:**1412
- Siemiatycze **14:**1513ff
- Transylvania **15:**1344
- Ulla and Johanan on **15:**1521
- Uruguay **16:**14
- *illus:*
- - Bundist group, Pinsk, 1905 **4:**1503
- - J.D.L. rally **12:**1123
- - Minsk, soldiers convention **14:**448
- - N.Y., night patrol **15:**1646
- - Odessa group (1905) **14:**445
- *see also:* DEFENSE FORCES OF ISRAEL
Self-determination, Jewish **15:**42
- *see also:* AUTONOMY; TERRITORIALISM
"Self Portrait" (paint., B. Baruh) **3:**618
"Self Portrait" (paint., B. Kopman) **3:**632
"Self Portrait" (drg., L. Kossoff) **3:**631
"Self Portrait" (paint., A. Segal) **3:**641
"Self Portrait" (lith., E. Spiro) **3:**642
"Self Portrait in the Fruit Market" (paint., R. Guttmann) **7:**996
Selig, Allan **15:**302
Selig, Gabriel **15:**1677
Selig, Gottfried **10:**402
Selig, Ḥayyim **12:**627
Selig, Jacob (r., Hung.) **11:**811
Selig, Jacob (Pol. emis.) **5:**602
SELIG, PHINEAS **14:**1129
- Christchurch **5:**505
- New Zealand **12:**1130
Selig, William **12:**446
SELIGMAN (fam.) **14:**1129
- railroads **13:**1519
Seligman, Adolph **12:**1037
Seligman, Arthur **12:**1039
Seligman, Bernard **12:**1037
Seligman, Brenda **14:**1130
SELIGMAN, CHARLES GABRIEL **14:**1130
Seligman, David **14:**1129; **14:**713
Seligman, Edgar **12:**1375
SELIGMAN, EDWIN ROBERT ANDERSON **14:**1131
Seligman, Henry **5:**854
Seligman, Herbert **13:**1362
SELIGMAN, HERBERT SPENCER **14:**1131
Seligman, Isaac Newton **2:**821; **14:**1130; **15:**312
Seligman, J. and W. (bnks.) **4:**178
Seligman, Jesse **14:**1130
Seligman, Joseph **12:**1103; **14:**1129; **15:**1604; **15:**1607; **15:**1649
Seligman, Loeb **15:**407
Seligman, Margaret **11:**178
Seligman, Sigmund **12:**1037
Seligmann (fam., Ec.) **6:**361
Seligmann (fam., Ger.) **4:**173
Seligmann, Aron (trader) **6:**523
Seligmann, Aron (court J.) **6:**523
Seligmann, Aron Elias **4:**173
SELIGMANN, CAESAR **14:**1132
- Liberal Judaism **16:**110
Seligmann, Elias **6:**523
SELIGMANN, KURT **14:**1132
- Paris school **13:**114
Seligmann, Lemle **6:**523
Seligmann, Leopold **10:**1121
Seligmann, Liebmann **6:**523
Seligmann, Mayer **6:**523
Seligman of Bingen **9:**1080
SELIGSBERG, ALICE LILLIE **14:**1132
Seligsfeld, Zimra **10:**1038
Seligsohn, Julius (Berlin) **8:**897
Seligson, Julius (sport., U.S.) **15:**314
Seliḥah (*Amidah* ben.) **2:**840
SELIḤOT (litur.) **14:**1133
- *Akedah*, theme **9:**5
- announcement of **14:**1478
- Day of Atonement **3:**979
- Elul **2:**294
- Jerusalem theme **9:**1561
- *Minhag Elzos* **2:**753
- *piyyut* **13:**600
- prayer books **13:**987
- *Shovavim Tat* **14:**1460
- *teḥinnah* **15:**907
- Ten Days of Penitence **15:**1001
- variations **11:**398ff
- *illus:*
- - Averbuch's *Seliḥot* (1677) **13:**1103
- - Italian edition (1475) **15:**1483
- - service for a fast day in Frankfort, 1711 **6:**1193
- *mus. notations:* text
- *see also:* BAKKASHAH
SELIKOVITCH, GEORGE (Getzel) **14:**1135
Selim I (sultan)
- Erez Israel **9:**282
- Ottoman Empire **16:**1533
- Western Wall **16:**468
Selim II (sultan)
- caliph **5:**62
- Erez Israel **9:**287
- Nasi, Joseph **12:**838
SELJUKS (dyn., Turk.) **14:**1135
- Ereẓ Israel history **9:**262
Selke, Judah **4:**109
Selke, Naphtali Hirz ben Judah, *see* HIRSHEL, MEYER
Selleck, Samuel **12:**1035
SELLERS, PETER (Richard Henry) **14:**1136
SELLIN, ERNST **14:**1137
- Isaiah **9:**62
Selling, Ben **12:**1451
Sellman (Nazi crim.) **12:**956
Selma (city, Ala.) **2:**506
- *illus:*
- - civil rights march (1965) **12:**931
Selnik, Benjamin Aaron **10:**640
Seltman, Charles **3:**301
Seltman Maḥzor (ms.) **11:**731
Seltmann, L. **8:**802
Seltzer, Dov **6:**912
SELTZER, LOUIS BENSON **10:**316
Seltzer, Thomas **13:**1371
Selve, Georges de **11:**133
Selver, Paul **5:**1209
SELVINSKI, ILYA LVOVICH **14:**1137
Selz, Jane Weiller **15:**309
SELZ, OTTO **14:**1138
SELZNICK (fam.) **14:**1138
Selznick, David Oliver **14:**1138
Selznick, Lewis B. **11:**503; **14:**1138
Selznick, Myron **14:**1138
Selznick, Philipp **15:**68
S-e-m-a, *see* FALK, JOSHUA BEN ALEXANDER HA-KOHEN
Semach, Yomtob, *see* Ẓemaḥ, Yom Tov
Semaddar (mosh., Isr.) **9:**1175
S-e-m-a-g (bk.), *see Sefer Mitzvot Gadol*
Semah, David **12:**1465
SEMAḤOT (tract.) **14:**1138
S-e-m-a-k, *see* ISAAC BEN JOSEPH OF CORBEIL
Semakh (place, Er. Isr.), *see* Ẓemaḥ
Semamit (zool.) **7:**351
SEMAN, PHILIP LOUIS **14:**1139
Semanario Hebreo (weekly) **16:**15
Semana Trágica (pogrom) **3:**414
Semarang (city, Indon.) **8:**1363
Semendria (tn., Serb.), *see* Smederevo
Semi-Gotha (anti-Sem. wk.) **15:**1166
SEMIKHAH (laying of the hands; ordination) **14:**1140
- *Contents:*
- - Of Sacrifices **14:**1140
- - Of Judges, Elders, and Rabbis **14:**1140
- - In Medieval and Modern Times **14:**1142
- - Controversy on *Semikhah* Renewal **14:**1143
- - "Neo-*Semikhah*" and *Hattarat Hora'ah* **14:**1144
- - Modern Practice **14:**1146
- Babylonian *Amoraim* **2:**873
- Berab, Jacob **4:**583ff
- *Bet Hillel, Bet Shammai* **4:**738
- codification **5:**648
- conflict of opinion **5:**890
- emissaries **14:**1365
- Ereẓ Israel, 70 to 640 **9:**242; **9:**252; **9:**253
- Germany **7:**470
- Hillel and Shammai **8:**483
- Judah ben Baba **10:**343
- judges **4:**722
- Levi ben Ḥabib **11:**99
- Meir ha-Levi **11:**1247
- polemic literature **13:**794
- *yeshivot* **16:**768ff
- *illus:*
- - text
- - Anau, Phinehas, ordination certificate **2:**935
- - Briel, Judah ben Eliezer, rabbinical diploma **4:**1373
- *see also:* RABBI, RABBINATE
SEMILIAN, SAVIN SOLOMON **10:**316
SÉMINAIRE ISRAÉLITE DE FRANCE (educ. inst.) **14:**1147
- library **11:**192
- rabbinical seminaries **13:**1464
Seminaries, Rabbinical, *see* RABBINICAL SEMINARIES
Seminole (Ind. tribe, N. Am.) **16:**894
SEMITES **14:**1148
- Bronze Age **3:**42
- early Canaanite settlement **13:**473
- Mesopotamia **16:**1485ff
- monumental inscriptions **16:**657
- moon **12:**290
- names **12:**803ff
- Sumer **15:**512
- patriarchal history **8:**572
- Semitic languages **14:**1149
- *illus:*
- - semi-nomadic clan in Egypt **3:**311
- - Tang figurine **5:**470
SEMITIC LANGUAGES **14:**1149
- *Contents:*
- - Wider Background **14:**1149
- - The Semitic Family **14:**1149
- - Northwest Semitic **14:**1149
- - East Semitic **14:**1151
- - South Semitic **14:**1152
- - The Divisions of Semitic **14:**1153
- - Proto-Semitic **14:**1153
- - Relation of Hebrew to Other Semitic Languages **14:**1154
- - The Origin of Hebrew **14:**1156
- Arabic **3:**237
- Cooke, George Albert **5:**937
- Dillmann's studies **6:**47
- Hebrew **16:**1560
- Mesopotamia **16:**1494
- Phoenician **13:**480
- Semites **14:**1148
- Ugaritic **15:**1506
- *see also:* AKKADIAN LANGUAGE; ARAMAIC; CANAAN, LAND OF (Language and Script); ORIENTALISTS
Semler, Johann **4:**905
Semlin (tn., Yug.), *see* ZEMUN
SEMMEL, BERNARD **8:**549
Semo, Abraham **4:**1482
Semo, David **5:**970
Semol (journ.) **1:**newsp. list
Semolina (bot.) **4:**1333
Semol Yisre'eli Hadash (orgn., Isr.) **12:**1034
SEMON, SIR FELIX **14:**1157
SEMON, RICHARD WOLFGANG **14:**1157
Semosenko (sol., Ukr.) **13:**1194
Semukhim (hermeneutical rule) **8:**368
Semyatitski, H. **16:**819
Semyen (reg., Eth.) **6:**1147

SENAAH (loc., Er. Isr.) 14:1157
Senandaj (tn., Iran) 8:1443
Senappir (isl., Red Sea), *see* Sinafir
Sen Astruc de Noves, *see* ABBA MARI BEN ELIGDOR
SENATOR, DAVID WERNER 14:1158
- Jewish Agency 16:1103
- *illus:*
- - Jewish Agency Executive 10:28
SENATOR, HERMANN 14:1158
Sender (18th cent., Shab. r.) 13:1241
Sender, Alexander 14:635
Senderey, Israel, *see* DRAPKIN, ISRAEL
SENDREY, ALFRED 14:1158
Seneca, Lucius Annaeus, *see* SENECA THE ELDER; SENECA THE YOUNGER
SENECA THE ELDER 14:236
SENECA THE YOUNGER 14:1158
- attitude towards Jews 14:233
SENED, ALEXANDER 14:1159
Sened, Yonat 14:1159
Senegal (rep., Afr.) 9:441
Šene gerišin (cantillation sign), *see Gersayim*
Seneh (tn., Iran), *see* Senandaj
Seneh (journ.) 1:newsp. list
SENEOR, ABRAHAM 14:1159
- Abrabanel, Isaac 2:105
- Leon, Isaac de 11:27
- Olmedo 12:1369
- Senior, Solomon 14:1160
- Spain 15:241
- tax farming 16:1291
- Toledo 15:1205
- trade and commerce 15:1300
- Valladolid 16:61ff
Senepin (Hebr.) 8:56
Senever, Judah Loeb 10:466
Senguas, Eliahu Leib 2:531
Senica (tn., Slov.) 14:1678
SENIGALLIA (tn., It.) 14:1160
- special Purim 13:1399
Senior, Abraham (apos., Sp.), *see* SENEOR, ABRAHAM
Senior, Abraham (Mar., Port.), *see* TEIXEIRA DE SAMPAIO, ABRAHAM SENIOR
Senior, Augustin 5:745
Senior, David 14:1662
Senior, Isaac Ḥayyim, *see* Teixeira de Sampaio, Manuel
Senior, Jacob 14:1662
Senior, Jacob ben Moses 13:613
SENIOR, MAX 14:1160
SENIOR, SOLOMON 14:1160
Senir (kib., Isr.) 1:place list; 13:1534
Senir (riv., Isr.) 7:1123; 9:172
- *illus:*
- - Senir Valley 9:170
- *see also:* HERMON, MOUNT
Seniri, Isaac ben Judah ha-, *see* ISAAC BEN JUDAH HA-SENIRI
SENJIRLI (vill., Turk.), *see* Zenjirli
SENKO, YASUE 14:1160
SENLIS (tn., Fr.) 14:1161
SENNABRIS (loc., Er. Isr.) 14:1161
SENNACHERIB (k., Assyr., Babyl.) 14:1161
- General
- - Arts 8:454
- - chronological chart 8:766-767
- - Shemaiah 14:1374
- History 8:605ff
- - Achzib 2:213
- - Adrammelech's murder of 2:304
- - Ahikar 2:460; 2:462
- - Azor 3:1011
- - Ekron captured by 6:559
- - Eltekeh battle 6:688
- - Hezekiah 8:451ff
- - Jerusalem siege 16:1509
- - Mesopotamia 16:1504ff
- - Nineveh 12:1170
- - population 13:868
- - Sargon II 14:880
- - throne 15:1125
- - treasures of war 15:1361
- - war and warfare 16:276
- *illus:*
- - text
- - Hezekiah, list of tribute 12:573
- - Lachish siege 3:319
- - transportation of Jewish captives 5:213
Sennaya (tn., Crimea) 5:1103
Šenoa, August 16:886
Senoff, Herbert 15:313
SENS (tn., Fr.) 14:1163
Senses
- intellect and 8:1411
- Jewish philosophy 13:423
- *see also:* IMAGINATION
Senta (city, Yug.) 2:233
Sentencia-Estatuto (statute) 11:255
Senunit (journ.) 1:newsp. list
Seoul (city, S. Korea) 9:444
SEPHARAD (loc. term) 14:1164
- Ashkenaz and 3:719ff
- region 14:1164
- Sardis 14:876
- Spain 15:220
Sepharad (period), *see Sefarad*
Sepharadim, *see* SEPHARDIM
Sephardic Jewish Brotherhood of America (soc.) 14:1174
Sephardic Jewish Community of New York 14:1174
Sephardic pronunciation (Heb.) 13:1124ff; 14:1170; 16:1645
Sephardic Publishing Company 13:1039
Sephardi Great Synagogue (Jer.) 15:587
SEPHARDIM 14:1164
- *Contents:*
- - General 14:1164
- - Sephardi Diaspora 14:1167
- - Language 14:1168
- - Literature 14:1168
- - Religious Practice 14:1170
- - Distinctive Practices 14:1170ff
- - Eclipse of Sephardi Jewry 14:1171
- - After World War I 14:1172
- - Holocaust 14:1172
- - After World War II 14:1172
- - 20th Century 14:1172
- - In the U.S. 14:1173
- - In Ereẓ Israel 14:1174
- Community
- - contemporary Judaism 10:395
- - economic history 16:1297
- - England 6:754ff
- - - London 11:473ff
- - Hamburg-Altona 2:779; 7:1225
- - immigration to Israel 9:378
- - Israel 9:497ff; 9:887ff
- - Jerusalem community 9:1463
- - Marrano Diaspora 11:1019f
- - Netherlands 12:976ff
- - - Amsterdam 2:895ff
- - Salonika 14:700ff
- - Spanish nationality 15:244
- - United States 15:1586f
- - - New York 12:1062ff
- - - Seattle 14:1083
- - Zamora exiles 16:926
- Tradition
- - *Ascama* 3:677
- - cooking and food 6:1421ff
- - growth of culture 8:691ff
- - Ḥasidism controversy 7:1392
- - Kabbalah and *halakhah* 10:640
- - Ladino 10:1042
- - liturgy 11:400
- - masorah 16:1464ff
- - masoretic accents 11:1108ff
- - musical traditions 12:559
- - rabbinical office 13:1447; 13:1449
- - titles 15:1165
- - tombstones 15:1223
- - widow 16:495
- *illus:*
- - text
- - Jerusalem synagogues 9:1443,1444
- - Sephardi script types 2:697-698,721, 735-737
- - Sephardi Jew from Ereẓ Israel 6:217
Sephardi *Maḥzor* (bk.) 11:400
Sephardi Union (Er. Isr.) 9:659
SEPHARVAIM (anc. city) 14:1177
- Anammelech 2:918
Sepp, Alfred 12:1215
Sepph (tn., Er. Isr.) 14:626
SEPPHORIS (city, Er. Isr.) 14:1177
- battle site 16:281
- Crusader treaty 9:269
- En-Dor 6:739
- Ereẓ Israel, 70 to 640 9:239ff
- Galilee 7:266
- history chart (200) 8:766-67
- Jerusalem Talmud 15:773
- Judah ha-Nasi 10:367
- Mishnah 11:808
- statistics (moshav) 1:place list
- Yose academy 2:202
- *table:* principal *Amoraim* 2:871
Sep-Szarzyński, Mikolaj 4:885; 13:798
Septimania (reg., Fr.) 12:827
Septimania (city, Sp.) 15:221
Septimia Canotha (Rom. col.), *see* KENATH
Septimius Severus, *see* SEVERUS, SEPTIMIUS
SEPTUAGINT (Gr. trans. of Bib.) 14:1178
- General
- - Christian attitude to 4:926ff
- - Hebrew linguistics 16:1393
- - Hellenism 8:297; 8:299
- - New Testament 12:1060
- - Samaritan dispute 14:729
- - title of Genesis 7:386
- History
- - *Letter of Aristeas* 3:439
- - Pharos 13:366
- - Ptolemy Philadelphus (II), initiator of 13:1348
- Text and Translations
- - Aquila's Bible translation 9:243
- - Bible translations 4:851; 15:1318
- - canon, Bible 4:825; 4:834
- - Greek 8:291
- - Latin translations 4:857
- - original Hebrew text 2:47
- - Peshitta 4:859ff
- Judaism
- - Bible interpretation 8:1417
- - Jewish philosophy 13:425
- - law source 12:117
- - Torah 15:1238
- - Torah reading 15:1246
- Literature
- - Dead Sea Scrolls 5:1400
- - Hellenistic Jewish literature 2:590; 8:303
- - Jewish literature 11:312ff
- - Josephus Flavius 10:258
- - Lamentations, Book of 10:1371
- - Talmud 11:1229
- Themes
- - abortion 2:98
- - anthropomorphism 3:53
- - Apocrypha and Pseudepigrapha 3:181ff
- - God, concepts 7:652
- - *ḥaliẓah* 11:126
- - Psalter 13:1306
- *illus:*
- - Exodus (5th cent. ms.) 4:851
- *table:* Apocrypha books canonized 3:181
Septuagint, Cambridge (bk.) 4:854
Septuagint, Goettingen (bk.) 4:854
Sepulchers, *see* TOMBS AND TOMBSTONES
SEPÚLVEDA (tn., Sp.) 14:1178
Sequeira, Isaac Henrique 13:918
Sequeira, Jacob de, *see* RODRIGUES, BARTHOLOMEW
Sequerra, Semtob 13:926
SEQUEYRA, JOHN DE 14:1179
Sequoyah (Ind. chief, N. Am.) 4:888
Seradz (tn., Pol.), *see* SIERADZ
Serah bat Asher (bib. fig.) 9:78; 13:315
Serai (tn., Gr.) 7:879
Seraiah (scribe) 14:1042
SERAIAH (s. of Neriah) 14:1179
- quartermaster 4:266
SERAIAH (h. pr.) 14:1179
- history 8:617
- priest 13:1075
SERAIAH (sol.) 14:1179
SERAIAH (royal offic.) 14:1179
Serajevo (city, Yug.), *see* SARAJEVO
SERAPH (bib. serpent) 14:1179
- *illus:* text
Seraphim, *see* ANGELS AND ANGELOLOGY
Seraphim, P. H. 5:1533
Seraphis (Serapia; deity), *see* Sarapis; Sarpanitum
Serapion Brothers (lit. gr.) 14:1676
Serapis (deity), *see* Sarapis; Sarpanitum
Serarah (dyn. right, Mor.) 13:1451
Serarius, Nicolaus 8:56
Serbia (state, Balkans) 16:868
- Alliance Israélite 2:650; 2:651
- Berlin, Congress of 4:655
- emancipation 6:709ff
- *illus:*
- - Jewish badge decreed by the Nazis 4:72
- *see also:* YUGOSLAVIA
SERBIN, HYMAN 2:324
Serbo-Croatian (lang.) 4:885; 5:455;
ŞERBU, IERONIM 14:427
Ṣere (vowel) 16:1432,1449
Serebrenik (r., Lux.) 11:591
Serebryanski, Zalman 11:1282
Serebryansky (resist. ftr.) 12:54
Sered (lab. camp, Slov.) 13:147
Serédi, Justinianus 8:1103
SEREKH ("rule", D. S. Scrolls) 14:1180
- Yaḥad community 16:699
Serekh ha-Yaḥad, see DISCIPLINE, MANUAL OF
SERENI (Serena; Sereno; It. fam.) 14:1181
Sereni, Ada 14:1182
Sereni, Angelo 14:1181
SERENI, ANGELO PIERO 14:1181
Sereni, Emilio 14:1181
SERENI, ENZO ḤAYYIM 14:1181
- Givat Brenner 7:597
- Neẓer Sereni 12:1131
Sereni Haggadah (15th cent. ms., It.) 7:1049
Serenus (ps.-mess., Babyl.), *see* SEVERUS
SERERO (fam.) 14:1182
- *illus:* text
Serero, David 2:792
Serero, Emanuel 14:1183
Serero, Emmanuel ben Menahem 14:1182
Serero, Ḥayyim David (18/19 cent.) 14:1183
Serero, Ḥayyim David (20th cent.)

14:1184
Serero, Jacob 14:1183
Serero, Jonathan 14:1183
Serero, Joseph 14:1183
Serero, Joshua (17/18 cent. scribe) 14:1182
Serero, Joshua (18/19 cent., dayyan) 14:1183
Serero, Judah 14:1183
Serero, Judah Benjamin 14:1183
Serero, Mattathias (19th cent.) 14:1183
Serero, Mattathias (20th cent.) 14:1184
Serero, Mattathias ben Menahem (18th cent.) 14:1183
Serero, Menahem 14:1183
Serero, Menahem ben David 14:1183
Serero, Saul 14:1183
Serero, Saul ben David 14:1182
- Fez 6:1256
Seres (tn., Gr.), *see* SERRAI
Sereth (tn., Rum.), *see* SIRET
Serfaty (Serfati; name), *see also* Sarfati; Sarfaty; Sarphati; Ẓarfati; Ẓarefati
Serfaty, Mordecai 12:340
SERFATY BENAZAR, RAFAEL 13:830
Serfdom 2:398
Sergeyev-Bystrov, Captain 12:56
SERGHI, CELLA 14:422; 14:427
Sergius IV (pope) 13:852
Serhatlya, Suljo, *see* KRAUSS, FRIEDRICH SALAMO
SERING, MAX 14:1184
Serkin, Peter 12:707
SERKIN, RUDOLF 12:707
Serles, Moses 11:357
Serlin, Yosef 9:667
Sermide (tn., It.) 11:895; 13:1399
Sermon, *see* HOMILETIC LITERATURE; PREACHING
SERMONETA, JOSEPH BARUCH (GIUSEPPE) 1:37
Sermons of St. Gregory of Nazianzus (9th cent., Gr. ms.) 4:945
SERMONS TO JEWS 14:1184
- auto da fé 3:911
- Borromeo, Carlo 4:1258
- Browning's poem on 4:1412
- forced attendance 4:215
- papal bull enjoining 4:1496
- *illus:*
- - conversion sermon 3:201
- - "Vicente Ferrer Preaching" (paint., D. Morone) 6:1235
Sernet, Claude 14:423
Serock (tn., Pol.) 13:557
Seron (Sel. mil. comm.) 10:379
SEROR (fam.) 14:1185
Seror, Joseph (mer.) 14:1185
Seror, Joseph (r.) 14:1185
Seror, Raphael Jedidiah 2:623; 14:1185
Seror, Solomon 14:1185
Seror, Solomon ben Tobias 14:1185
Seror, Tobias 14:1185
Serota, Beatrice 13:812; 15:27
SERP (Rus.), *see* JEWISH SOCIALIST WORKERS' PARTY
Serpec (tn., Pol.), *see* SIERPC
Serpent, *see* SNAKE
Serpent, Copper, *see* COPPER SERPENT, THE
SERRAI (tn., Gr.) 14:1186
Serrarius, Peter 14:1233
Serravalle (tn., It.), *see* VITTORIO VENETO
SERRE, JEAN-PIERRE 11:1126
Serrero (name), *see* Serero
Serres (city, Gr.), *see* SERRAI
SERRES (vill., Fr.) 14:1186
- Chartres 5:362
Serri, Salvador 6:1234
Serrières Bible 4:881
Serubabel (newsp.) 14:1119
Serug (bib. fig., place) 12:789; 13:182; 15:1014
Serugin (ms.) 16:1434
Serungiya (vill., Er. Isr.) 7:1541
SERUSI (fam.) 14:1186
Serusi, Abraham (dipl.) 14:1186
Serusi, Abraham (cmty. ldr.) 14:1186
Serusi, David 14:1186
Serusi, Ḥai 14:1186
Serusi, Moses 14:1186
Serusi, Nissim 14:1186
ṢERUYA (fam.) 14:1187
Ṣeruya, Isaac 14:1187
Ṣeruya, Jacob 14:1187
Seruya, Solomon (mer., schol.) 14:1187
Ṣeruya, Solomon (states.) 14:1187
Servant
- anti-Jewish accusations 2:915
- labor law 10:1325ff
- prototype of 6:618
- tort liability 11:185
- *see also:* SLAVERY
SERVANT OF THE LORD (bib. term) 14:1187
- eschatology 6:869ff
- Isaiah 9:49; 9:65
Servants of Solomon (royal mers.), *see* SOLOMON, SERVANTS OF
Servatius, Robert 6:521
Servetus, Michael (Miguel) 5:66
Servi, Ferruccio 14:1187; 16:116
SERVI, FLAMINIO (Ephraim) 14:1187
Servi Camerae Nostrae, *see* SERVI CAMERAE REGIS
SERVI CAMERAE REGIS ("Servants of the Royal Chamber") 14:1187
- Aquinas, Thomas 3:229; 3:230
- Augsburg Jews 3:849
- German Jews 7:462
- Poland 13:712
- status of Jews 8:677
Service (rel.), *see* LITURGY; PRAYER
Service and Consumer Industries 16:1317ff
Serviel, Moses 14:1230
Servilius Galba, Publius 11:1547
SERVITUDES (leg. term) 14:1188
- laborers' rights 10:1323
- nuisance 12:1246
Sesame (bot.) 2:400; 6:1416; 12:1352; 15:269
- plant list 13:625
SESSA, KARL BORROMAEUS ALEXANDER 14:1190
- Hep! Hep! riots 8:330
SESSO, SALAMONE DA 3:524, 610; 7:742
Sestigers (lit. orgn.) 15:208
Seta (cmty., Lith.) 14:769
SETER, MORDECHAI 14:1190
- music 12:670
SETH (bib. fig.) 14:1191
- oil of mercy 12:1347
- *illus:*
- - text
- - at Adam's deathbed 2:247
Seth (deity) 3:784
- *see also:* BAAL WORSHIP
Seth, Concerning the Good Tidings of (Apoc. bk.) 2:245
Sethos I (Pharaoh), *see* SETI I
Seth-Typhon (deity) 7:888
SETI I (Pharaoh) 14:1192
- Asher tribe 8:579
- history chart 8:766-67
- *illus:*
- - stele 4:761; 8:580
Sétier (print., Fr.) 13:109
Sétiers, L. P. 8:56
Sétif (city, Alg.) 2:616
Settat (city, Mor.) 5:223
Settlement and Colonization Schemes (pre-State)
- General
- - agriculture 2:406ff
- - Alkalai, Judah 2:639
- - Brodsky, Abraham 4:1394
- - economic history 16:1311
- - Friedmann, Paul 7:193
- - Hirsch, Baron Maurice de 8:505
- - J.D.C. 2:828
- - Montefiore, Sir Moses 12:271
- - Netter, Charles 12:1001
- - Noah, Mordecai Manuel 12:1198
- - Oliphant, Laurence 12:1362
- - ORT 12:1481ff
- - Pines, Yeḥiel Michael 13:535
- - Rosenthal, Herman 14:293
- - Rothschild, Baron Edmond de 14:342ff
- - Warburg, Otto 16:287
- - Zionist Congresses 16:1164ff
- In Various Countries
- - Anatolia (Turkey) 16:287
- - Argentina 3:413ff,427ff
- - - Entre Ríos colonies 6:802
- - - Gerchunoff's *Gauchos Judíos* 7:434
- - - Maurício 4:1462
- - - Santa Fé colonies 14:846
- - Australia 11:1286
- - Bolivia 4:1188
- - Brazil 4:1325
- - - Raffalovich, Isaiah 13:1511
- - British Guiana proposal 7:997
- - Canada 2:412; 5:106
- - - Saskatchewan 14:891
- - Cyprus 5:1182
- - Dominican Republic 6:160
- - Ecuador 6:300
- - El-Arish 6:565
- - Ereẓ Israel (pre-Herzlian) 9:515; 14:343
- - - Bilu'im 4:998ff
- - - Ekron (Mazkeret Batyah) 11:1152
- - - Gederah 7:354
- - - Gilead 12:1362
- - - Ḥibbat Zion 8:463
- - - Mikveh Israel 11:1544
- - - Petaḥ Tikvah 13:336
- - - Rishon le-Zion 14:194
- - - Yemenites 16:743,752
- - - Zikhron Ya'akov 16:1019
- - Latin America 2:413
- - Madagascar plan 11:678
- - Mexico 11:1456
- - Midian scheme 7:193
- - New Zealand 8:1008; 12:1128
- - Peru 13:324
- - Poland 2:409
- - Rumania 2:411
- - Russia 14:438ff,468ff
- - - Belorussia 2:408
- - - Bessarabia 4:705
- - - Birobidzhan 4:1044ff
- - - Bobrovy Kut 4:1155
- - - Crimea 5:1107
- - - Kalinindorf 10:706
- - - Kherson 10:954
- - - Ukraine 2:407; 15:1514
- - - *Yevsektsiya* projects 16:780
- - Uganda scheme 15:1500
- - United States 2:411
- - - Am Olam colonies 2:861
- - - Ararat scheme 12:1199
- - - Baron de Hirsch Fund 4:254
- - - Galveston plan 7:294
- - - Iowa 8:1437
- - - Jewish Agricultural Society 10:35
- - - Kansas 10:738
- - - Louisiana 11:519
- - - Minnesota 12:39
- - - Missouri 8:1437
- - - Nebraska 12:912
- - - New Jersey 12:1029
- - - North Dakota 12:1221
- - Uruguay 16:13
- *illus:*
- - Argentina 2:414; 3:428, 429, 431
- - El-Arish, 16:1072
- - Ereẓ Israel
- - - Rishon le-Zion 14:194
- - - Menuḥah ve-Naḥalah 9:556
- - - Mikveh Israel 11:1544
- - Russia
- - - Birobidzhan, a street 8:742
- - - "Emes" collective farm, 14:470
- - - ICA colony, Bessarabia 10:45
- - - Jewish kolkhoz farmers 2:407-410
- - - Tel Ḥai farm, Crimea 14:469
- - - vine-growers, Crimea 5:1107
- - United States
- - - Ararat, foundation stone 4:1465
- - - North Dakota scheme, promotion poster 12:1219
- *see also:* JEWISH COLONIZATION ASSOCIATION; TERRITORIALISM
SETTLEMENT IN ISRAEL 9:546
- agriculture 9:773
- Ḥibbat Zion 16:1039ff
- historical survey 9:381
- human geography 9:572
- motives 9:508ff
- Negev 12:929
- Ruppin, Arthur 14:431
- Satmar rebbe's views 15:909
- Warburg, Otto 16:287ff
- Yemenite Jews 16:752ff
- *illus:*
- - Gerofit founder-members 9:980
- - Hefer Valley settlement 9:521
- - Kefar Yeḥezkel 12:436
- - Negbah 12:925
- - Neveh Yam 12:1019
- - Petaḥ Tikvah 13:337,338
- - tower and stockade model 9:550 15:405
- *maps:*
- - Negev 12:926
- *pop. tables:*
- - general statistics 9:473-496
- - population, 1700-1948 9:549
- - population and area, 1898 9:547
- - settlement figures, 1948-1970 9:551
- *see also:* ALIYAH
Settlement of Canaan, *see* CANAAN, LAND OF
"Settlement Regime" (Pal.) 14:128
Setton (fam., Jan.) 9:1274
SETUBAL (city., Port.) 14:1192
Setubal, "Messiah" of, *see* DIAS, LUIS
Setzer (print., Pol.) 11:544
Setzer, Aaron (print., Altona), *see* Aaron ben Elijah ha-Kohen
SE'UDAH (festive meal) 14:1192
- food 6:1415
- Purim 13:1392
- Sabbath 14:564
- *siyyum* 14:1642
SE'UDAH SHELISHIT ("third meal") 14:1195
- Ḥasidism 7:1400
- Sabbath 14:570
- synagogue 15:584
Se'udat David, *see* MELAVVEH MALKAH
Se'udat Yitro u-Moshe (rel. celebration) 14:1642
Seutter (cartog.) 11:927
SEVARAH (halakhic logic) 14:1195
- *Contents:*
- - General 14:1195
- - As Creative Source of General Legal Principles 14:1196

– – In the Amoraic Period **14:**1197
– codification of law **5:**630
– halakhic exegesis **8:**1419
– law source **12:**119
– rabbinical authorities **3:**910
– *see also:* TAKKANOT
SEVASTOPOL (city, Ukr.) **14:**1198
– Crimea **5:**1106ff
Seven Benedictions
– betrothal and marriage **11:**1032ff
– *minyan* required **12:**67
Seven Books of Histories against the Pagans (wk.) **12:**1477
Seven-Branched Light; a Reading Guide and Index (enc.) **6:**734
Seven Good Townsmen **7:**1492
– community agents **10:**1568
– endowments **8:**284
– exempt from overreaching **12:**1394
– *Landjudenschaft* **10:**1406
– public authority **13:**1351
– *see also:* BATLANIM; ELDER
Seven Noachide Laws, *see* NOACHIDE LAWS
Seven Shepherds (kab. conc.) **10:**575
Seven Species, *see* Species, the Seven
Seventh Brigade (Isr. army) **7:**1073; **9:**366; **16:**324
Seventh Vision of Daniel (Arm. apocalypse) **5:**1277
Seventy Nations, *see* NATIONS, THE SEVENTY
SEVENTY SHEPHERDS, VISION OF **14:**1198
– eschatological king **11:**1409
Seven Years' War **8:**766-67
"Seven Zamero sons" (burial vaults), *see* BENZAMERO
SEVER, ALEXANDRU **14:**423; **14:**427
Severance pay **7:**1005ff
Severan Emperors (Rom.) **9:**251
Severus (bp., Minorca) **12:**41
SEVERUS (ps.-mess., Babyl.) **14:**1199
– Natronai bar Nehemia **12:**887
– Umayyads **15:**1529
SEVERUS, ALEXANDER (emp., Rom.) **14:**1200
– *archisynagogus* **8:**649
– attitude to Jews **14:**230
– Ereẓ Israel **9:**251
– history chart **8:**766-767
– Samaritans **14:**731
SEVERUS, SEPTIMIUS (Rom. emp.) **14:**1200
– Aelia Capitolina visit **9:**1406
– attitude to Jews **8:**648
– Ereẓ Israel **9:**251
– history chart **8:**766-67
– Jerusalem excavations **9:**1536
– Jerusalem water supply **9:**1540
– Judah ha-Nasi **10:**368
Severus, Sextus Julius (Rom. comm.), *see* JULIUS SEVERUS
Severus, son of Antoninus (Rom.) **14:**1200
Severus Sammonicus **2:**111
SEVILLE (Sevilla; city, Sp.) **14:**1201
– *Contents:*
– – General **14:**1201
– – Muslim Period **14:**1201
– – Location of the Jewish Quarter **14:**1201
– – After the Christian Reconquest **14:**1202
– – Persecutions of 1391 **14:**1204
– – Decline of the Community **14:**1204
– – Conversos in Seville **14:**1205
– dyeing center **6:**328
– Inquisition **8:**1383
– seal **14:**1079
– Spain **15:**236
– *illus:*
– – text
– – Jewish quarter **10:**81
Sevirin (Masorah version) **16:**1423
SEVITZKY, FABIEN **12:**707
Sevodnya (newsp.) **14:**175
Šewa (vowel) **16:**1432,1447,1475
Sewer, Ignacy, *see* Maciejowski, Ignacy
SEX **14:**1206
– General
– – Ben Ze'ev's poem **13:**131
– – cancer **14:**1503
– – kabbalistic literature **10:**573; **10:**642
– – reproduction **4:**1018
– – sages on **14:**653
– – Shabbateanism **14:**1251
– – Tree of Knowledge **13:**78
– – vital statistics **16:**178ff
– Ethics **6:**935
– – artificial insemination **3:**661
– – biblical ethics **6:**935
– – concubine **5:**862
– – *derekh ereẓ* **5:**1551
– – family **6:**1165ff
– – holiness **10:**871
– – *Iggeret ha-Kodesh* **8:**1238
– – laws of *niddah* **12:**1141
– – regulations **13:**797
– – Sabbath **14:**562
– – slaves and owner **14:**1662
– – *taharat ha-mishpaḥah* **15:**703
– – *talmid ḥakham* **15:**747
– – virginity **16:**160ff
– – washing hands **12:**998
– *illus:*
– – woman showing menstrual stain to her husband **12:**1148
– – *see also:* BIRTH CONTROL; CELIBACY; CHASTITY; MARRIAGE; SEXUAL OFFENCES
Sextarius (Rom. meas.) **16:**388
Sexton, *see* SHAMMASH
SEXTUS EMPIRICUS (philos.) **7:**897
Sextus Florentinus (Rom. gov.) **13:**343
Sextus Julius Africanus **5:**49
SEXUAL OFFENSES **14:**1207
– General
– – abomination **2:**97
– – crime among Jews **5:**1093; **5:**1097
– – ethics **6:**935
– – gentiles **12:**1189
– – impurity **13:**1406
– – *Kiddush ha-Shem* **10:**978
– – Leviticus, Book of **11:**144
– – priests **13:**1081
– Types
– – adultery **2:**313
– – bestiality **13:**223
– – homosexuality **8:**961
– – incest **8:**1316
– – onanism **12:**1396
– – prostitution **13:**1243
– – rape **13:**1548
– Punishment
– – banishment **4:**165
– – imprisonment **8:**1302
– – *ketubbah* deprivation **8:**1127
– – *niddui* **8:**352
– *see also:* ABORTION; BIGAMY AND POLYGAMY; MARRIAGE, PROHIBITED; SEX
Seyfer Midos (Yid. wk.) **16:**804
Seyfried, C. **8:**56
Seyfried, H. **8:**56
SEYMOUR, DAVID **14:**1209
Seymour, Steve **12:**1376
SEYSS-INQUART, ARTHUR **14:**1209
– *illus:*
– – Nuremberg Trial **16:**289
Sezer, Robert **12:**1465
Sezon (anti-underground action, Er. Isr.), *see* "Saison"
SFARD, DAVID **14:**1209
Sfax (loc., Tun.) **15:**1435
Sfez, Batto **15:**1446
Sforno, Hananel **14:**1209
Sforno, Obadiah ben Israel **14:**1210
SFORNO, OBADIAH BEN JACOB **14:**1209
– *Akedah* **2:**483
– Averroes **3:**952
– Cesena **5:**314
Sforno, Solomon Shemaiah **14:**1211
Sgambati(us), Scipio **8:**56
Sha'afat (vill., Er. Isr.), *see* Shaʿfāt
Sha'ag, Abraham **9:**515
Sha'agat Aryeh (bk.) **7:**978
SHAALBIM (Shaalabbin; tn., Er. Isr.) **14:**1211
– synagogue **15:**599
Shaalbim (kib., Isr.) **14:**1211
– statistics **1:** place list
Sha'ali Serufah be-Esh (litur. wk.) **3:**938
SHAANAN, AVRAHAM **14:**1211
Shaaraim (bib. city, Isr.) **14:**1317
Shaarai Torah-Sons of Abraham (syn., Mass.) **16:**633
Shaaray Brocho (syn., N.Y.) **9:**548; **9:**572; **12:**1071
Sha'ar Efrayim (mosh., Isr.) **1:** place list
Sha'ar Efrayim (wk.) **3:**667
Sha'arei Avraham (inst., Isr.) **1:**place list
Sha'arei Beri'ut (journ.) **1:** newsp. list
Sha'arei Dura (wk.) **6:**262
Sha'arei Ḥabad (wk.) **7:**1413
Sha'arei Halakhot (journ.) **1:** newsp. list
Sha'arei ha-Ma'alot (wk.) **4:**1108
Sha'arei ha-Nikkud (wk.), *see Darkhei ha-Nikkud*
Sha'arei Ḥesed (qtr., Jer.) **9:**1462
Sha'arei Mizraḥ (journ.), *see La Puerta del Oriente*
Sha'arei Musar Haskel (poem), *see* MUSAR HASKEL
Sha'arei Orah (wk.) **10:**534
SHA'AREI SHEVU'OT (wk.) **14:**1212
– David ben Saadiah **5:**1354
Shaarei Shomayim (syn., Can.) **15:**1261
– *illus:* **15:**1263
Sha'arei Teshuvah (bk.) **11:**344; **16:**1207
Sha'arei Torat ha-Takkanot (wk.) **4:**1108
Sha'arei Ẓedek (qtr., Jer.) **9:**1460
Sha'arei Ẓedek (hospital, Isr.) **16:**254
– *illus:*
– – operating theater **9:**991
Sha'arei Ẓedek (wk.) **12:**248
Sha'arei Zion Hospital (Isr.) **9:**1257
Sha'arei Ẓion Public Library (Isr.) **4:**984
Sha'arei Ẓiyyon (wk.) **10:**641
Shaʿarei Ẓiyyon (newsp.) **9:**1466
– culture **9:**1014
– Hebrew newspapers **12:**1054
– statistics **1:**newsp. list
Shaarey Hashamayim (syn., N.Y.) **12:**1071
Shaarey Tefila (syn., N.Y.) **12:**1071; **12:**1079
Shaarey Zedek (syn., N.Y.) **12:**1071
Shaarey Zedek (syn., Mich.) **15:**625
Shaarey Zedek (syn., Winnipeg) **16:**549
– *illus:* **16:**550
Sha'ar ha-Aliyah (absorption center) **9:**536
SHA'AR HA-AMAKIM (kib., Isr.) **14:**1212
– statistics **1:** place list
– *illus:*
– – *Haggadah* **9:**908
Sha'ar ha-Gay (loc., Isr.) **11:**1405
Sha'ar ha-Gemul (wk.) **12:**781
– *illus:*
– – incunabulum (1490, Naples) **8:**1334
SHA'AR HA-GOLAN (kib., Isr.) **14:**1212
– statistics **1:** place list
– *illus:*
– – tower and stockade **9:**356,550
Sha'ar ha-Kalkalah (newsp.) **12:**1058
Sha'ar ha-Kavvanot (wk.) **10:**553
Sha'ar ha-Mayim (wk.) **2:**308
Sha'ar ha-Negev (dist., Isr.) **9:**576
Sha'ar ha-Negev (kib., Isr.) **7:**1059; **9:**553
Sha'ar ha-Shamayim (wk., Gerson of Arles) **6:**730
Sha'ar ha-Shamayim (wk., Herrera) **10:**528; **10:**549
Shaar Hashomayim (syn., Can.) **12:**285
– *illus:*
– – sermon **12:**284
– – wedding ceremony **12:**288
Sha'ar ha-Yiḥud ve-ha-Emunah (bk.) **14:**1437
SHA'AR ḤEFER (mosh., Isr.) **14:**1213
– statistics **1:** place list
Sha'ari, Yehudah **8:**1349
Sha'ariyyah (vill., Isr.) **13:**338
Sha'ar la-Kore he-Ḥadash (journ.) **1:** newsp. list
Sha'ar Menasheh (stlmt., Isr.) **1:** place list
Sha'ar Ẓiyyon (journ.) **1:**newsp. list
SHA'ATNEZ (forbidden mixture) **14:**1213
– bureau in Gateshead **7:**334
– camel's wool **5:**72
– Commandments, the 613 **5:**722
– flax **6:**1339
– hemp **8:**323
– Maimonides **11:**775
– *see also:* MIXED SPECIES
Shababo-Zain, Yeshu'ah **2:**608
SHABAD, ẒEMAḤ **14:**1214
– relief work **16:**735
Shaʿbān, Al-Malik al-Ashraf **9:**1423
Shabat, Oscar **5:**417
Shabats (tn., Serb.), *see* Sabac
SHABAZI, SHALEM **14:**1215
– folktales **6:**1382
– Kabbalah **10:**553
– poems **16:**746
– Yemen persecutions **16:**742
SHABBAT (tract) **14:**1215
– *Eruvin* **6:**850
– oils **12:**1351
– *illus:*
– – text
– – title page (Vilna, 1859) **14:**255
Shabbat (day), *see* SABBATH
SHABBAT BERESHIT **14:**1217
– *Barekhi Nafshi* **4:**218
– cooking and food **6:**1426
– *see also:* SABBATHS, SPECIAL; TRIENNIAL CYCLE
Shabbateanism, *see* SHABBETAI ẒEVI
SHABBAT HA-GADOL (special sabbath) **14:**1217
– *illus:* text
Shabbat ha-Ḥodesh **14:**573
Shabbat Ḥazon **14:**573
Shabbat hi mi-Lizok u-Refu'ah Kerovah Lavo (blessing) **7:**914
Shabbat Ḥol ha-Mo'ed **14:**573
"Shabbat in Safed" (paint., M. Castel) Pl. 7 **3**-ART
Shabbat Mevarekhim, *see* NEW MOON, ANNOUNCEMENT OF

Shabbat Nahamu 14:574
Shabbat Parah 14:573
Shabbat Rosh Hodesh 14:572
Shabbat Shalom (greeting) 7:914
Shabbat Shekalim 14:573
Shabbat Shirah 14:1071; 14:573
Shabbat Shuvah 14:572
- *illus:*
- - *Or Olam*, prayer 14:74
Shabbat Zakhor 14:573
Shabbes, Hershl 14:1512
Shabbetai (paytan) 13:595
Shabbetai, Hayyim, *see* HAYYIM (Ben) SHABBETAI
Shabbetai, Judah ibn 11:937
Shabbetai, Moses ben Hayyim 14:702
Shabbetai, Uri 14:673
Shabbetai Baer, *see* Baer, Shabbetai
Shabbetai ben Abraham 4:994; 12:67
Shabbetai ben Malkiel ha-Kohen 4:136; 5:860
Shabbetai ben Marinus 13:1578
Shabbetai ben Mattathias 8:1268
- *illus:*
- - *Bishop Bedell Bible* 4:*fcg.* 940; 8:1281
SHABBETAI BEN MEIR HA-KOHEN (Shakh) 14:1217
- Chmielnicki massacres 5:482; 5:483
- Ephraim ha-Kohen 6:812
- *Siftei Kohen* 5:1355
Shabbetai ben Moses 13:595
Shabbetai ben Raphael ben David of Makow 5:1363
Shabbetai ben Solomon 7:842
Shabbetai ben Yom Tov ibn Boded, *see* EHRLICH, ARNOLD BOGUMIL
Shabbetai Elhanan Ben Elisha, *see* DEL VECCHIO, SHABBETAI ELHANAN BEN ELISHA
Shabbetai ha-Kohen (r., Egy.) 11:894
Shabbetai Jonah 4:1270; 8:1170; 11:76; 14:90; 14:895
Shabbetai Lozinski (ship) 8:1250
- *illus:*
- - disembarkment 9:361
SHABBETAI OF RASZKOW 14:1219
Shabbetais, Hayyah, *see* Schor, Hayyah
SHABBETAI ZEVI 14:1219
- *Contents:*
- - Background of the Movement 14:1219
- - Shabbetai Zevi's Early Years and Personality 14:1222
- - The Beginning of the Movement 14:1224
- - Shabbetai Zevi in Smyrna and Constantinople 14:1227
- - The Movement in the Diaspora 14:1231
- - Shabbetai Zevi's Apostasy 14:1236
- - After the Apostasy 14:1237
- - The Shabbatean Kabbalah 14:1241
- - The Movement, 1680-1700 14:1243
- - In the 18th Century 14:1247
- History 8:693
- - *aliyah* 9:513
- - chart 8:766-767
- - emissaries 14:1366
- - imprisonment 8:1302
- - letter to bride 11:61
- - organized societies 8:441
- - seal 14:1080
- Places
- - Adrianople 2:309
- - Amsterdam 2:897
- - Busk 4:1536
- - Cochin 5:627
- - Germany 7:475
- - Istanbul 9:1091
- - Jerusalem and Gaza 9:290; 9:1437
- - Ottoman Empire 16:1550
- - Salonika 14:702
- - Syria 15:644
- - Venice 16:99
- Polemics 11:58; 13:794ff
- - Aboab, Samuel 2:94
- - Aboab da Fonseca, Isaac 2:95
- - Algazi, Solomon 2:610
- - Amigo, Abraham 2:847
- - Aryeh Loeb ben Samuel Zevi Hirsch 3:668
- - Ayllon, Solomon 3:996
- - Bacharach, Jair Hayyim 4:47
- - Barrios, Daniel de 4:259
- - Baruch ben David Yavan 4:277
- - Baruch of Kosov 4:281
- - Benjamin of Reggio 4:532
- - Benveniste, Hayyim 4:559
- - Bikayam, Meir 4:991
- - Bloch, Mattathias 4:1107
- - Bonafoux, Daniel 4:1198
- - Boton, Jacob 4:1270
- - Brudo, Abraham 4:1414
- - Buzaglo, Shalom 4:1545
- - Cardozo, Abraham 5:163
- - Costa, Athias, Solomon da 5:989
- - Cuenque, Abraham 5:1153
- - Damavandi, Samuel 5:1252
- - David ha-Levi 5:1355
- - Emden, Jacob 6:721
- - Escapa, Joseph 6:860
- - Eybeschuetz, Jonathan 6:1074
- - Falk, Jacob Joshua 6:1156
- - Galante, Moses 7:259
- - Hagiz, Moses 7:1122ff
- - Hayon, Nehemiah Hiyya 7:1501
- - Jehiel Michel ben Judah Leib he-Hasid 9:1314
- - Laniado, Solomon 10:1423
- - Lapapa, Aaron 10:1424
- - Malakh, Hayyim 11:818
- - Nathan of Gaza 12:861
- - Nehemiah ha-Kohen 12:939
- - Pinheiro, Moses 13:536
- - Primo, Samuel 13:1091ff
- - Prossnitz, Judah 13:1241
- - Sak, Jacob 4:1449
- - Sasportas, Jacob 14:894
- - Yakhini, Abraham 16:704
- - Zacuto, Moses 16:907
- - Zoref, Joshua Heshel 16:1222
- Doctrine and Practice
- - abrogation of Torah 15:1246
- - *Adam Kadmon* 2:248
- - antinomianism 3:70
- - Av, The Ninth 3:938
- - *Ba'al Shem* 4:7
- - *deus absconditus* 10:558
- - evil 10:586
- - *gematriot* 7:373
- - Kabbalah 10:548; 10:551ff
- - *Lekha Dodi* 2:635
- - Messiah 11:1419
- - providence 13:1283
- - Sambatyon 14:764
- - special Purim 13:1396
- - Trinity 7:672
- - visions 16:169
- - *zimzum* 10:593
- Influences
- - Bacharach, Naphtali 4:50
- - Doenmeh 6:148
- - Hasidism 7:1391; 7:1395
- - Israel Ba'al Shem Tov 9:1055
- - Jacob Koppel of Mezhirech 9:1231
- - Luzzatto, M. H. 11:601
- - *maggidim* 11:700
- - Molcho, Solomon 12:226
- - Nahman of Bratslav 12:783
- - *see also:* FRANK, JACOB, AND THE FRANKISTS
- Literature and Studies 6:1270
- - Hebrew parodies 13:131ff
- - homiletical literature 8:955
- - Kurzweil, Baruch 10:1303
- - Shazar, Zalman 14:1326
- *illus:*
- - Nathan of Gaza 12:862
- - portrait 8:691
- - *Shevet Musar* (1734) 8:959
- - Zhulavsky's Yiddish play 15:1067
- *see also:* MESSIANIC MOVEMENTS
Shabbezi, Shalem, *see* SHABAZI, SHALEM
Shabriri (demon) 2:111; 5:1528
Shabsazviniks, *see* SHABBETAI ZEVI
Shabsha (bib. fig.), *see* Seraiah
Shabtai, Y. 6:206
Shachter, Jacob 4:415
Shaci, Siman-Tov 16:1552
Sh-a-d-a-l, *see* LUZZATTO, SAMUEL DAVID
Shaddai, *see* GOD; GOD, NAMES OF
Shadganites (sect) 16:868
SHADKHAN (matchmaker) 14:1254
- folktale 6:1381
Shadmi, Nahum, *see* Kramer, Nahum
SHADMOT DEVORAH (mosh., Isr.) 14:1255
Shadov (city, Lith.), *see* SEDUVA
Shadov, Shalom 16:1013
Shadovsky, Israel Hayyim, *see* SHULMAN, VICTOR
SHADRACH, MESHACH, ABED-NEGO (bib. fig.) 14:1255
- Daniel 5:1277
- in the Arts 5:1276; 12:918
- Judah's virtue 10:332
- *Kiddush ha-Shem* 10:981
- Mordecai's genealogy 15:813
- Nebuchadnezzar 12:915
- *Prayer of Azariah* 15:154
- *illus:*
- - in the fiery furnace 2:960
Shadwan Island (Egy.) 14:1640
Shaf, I. 5:434
Sha'fāṭ (vill., Er. Isr.) 9:1487 9:1515; 14:1635
Shaffer, Louis 16:516
SHAFFER, PETER 14:1256
Shaffir, Moishe M. 5:112
Shafir (inst., Isr.) 1: place list
Shafir merukkam (embryo) 4:1020
Shafirov, Peter 12:360
Shafi't (school of Isl. law) 9:918
Shafner, Perry 12:1035
Shaftesbury, Anthony Ashley, Earl of 5:1464; 8:727
- Zionism 16:1070; 16:1154
SHAFTESLEY, JOHN MAURICE 1:37
Shaf ve-Yativ (anc. syn.) 2:34, 11:100; 12:935; 15:580ff
SHAG, ABRAHAM 14:1256
Shāghur, al- (tn., Er. Isr.) 9:274
SHAHAM, NATHAN 14:1257
Shahar (mvmt.) 9:981
Shahar (mosh., Isr.) 12:940
- statistics 1: place list
Shahar, David 9:1568
Shahari (lang.) 14:1153
Shahariah (He-Halutz training center) 4:197
SHAHARIT (morning prayer) 14:1257
- *Adon Olam* 2:296
- *Ahavah Rabbah, Ahavat Olam* 2:454
- *Akedah* 2:481
- *Amidah* 2:838
- *Ashrei* 3:736
- *Barukh she-Amar* 4:283
- Maimonides' Principles 3:656
- *pesukei de-zimra* 13:336; 16:987
- priestly blessing 13:1062
- Samaritan Sabbath 14:741
- *Shema* 14:1370
- variations in liturgy 11:393ff
- *see also:* MORNING BENEDICTIONS
Shaharit (newsp.) 16:972
- statistics 1: newsp. list
Shaharut (mag.) 5:457
SHAHIN (14th cent., poet) 14:1258
- iconography 8:1216
- Judeo-Persian literature 10:434
- *illus:*
- - text
- - paraphrase of the Pentateuch 2:733; 4:932; 12:395
- - *Sefer Sharh Shāhīn al ha-Torah* 16:1027,1182
Shāhīn, Hikmat 9:1039
Shahina (stew), *see* CHOLENT
Shahin Girai (Tatar khan) 2:340
Shahirbani, Manasseh ben Saliman 8:1452
Shahmat (newsp.) 1: newsp. list
SHAHN, BEN 14:1259
- editorial cartoons 5:220
- New York City 12:1122
- *illus:*
- - mosaic design for Mishkan Israel Synagogue, Hamden, Conn. 5:899
- - "Sacco and Vanzetti" (drg.) 3:561
- - Solomon holding a Bible 6:351
- - stained glass windows and Tablets of the Law, Temple Beth Zion, Buffalo 4:1466
Shahnamah (illum. ms.) 6:639
SHAHOR (fam.) 14:1260
Shahor, Hayyim 14:1260
- Augsburg press 3:850
- *haggadah* 7:1101
- Jaffe family 9:1258
- Kohen family 10:1138
- printing 13:1100
- typography 15:1479
- *illus:*
- - *Prague Haggadah* (1526) 13:1101
Shahor, Isaac 14:1261
- Augsburg press 3:850
Shahpuhr (Pers. ks.), *see* SHAPUR
Shahpur (tn., Iran) 3:1005; 13:312
Shahraban (tn., Iraq), *see* Muqdadiya
Shahr Rey (tn., Iran), *see* Rai
Shahu (soc.) 6:257
Shai (journ.) 1: newsp. list
Shaievitz, S. 16:819
Shaikevich, Nahum Meyer, *see* SHOMER
Shaikh Muwannis (vill., Isr.) 15:923
SHAKESPEARE, WILLIAM 14:1261
- English literature 6:777
- Florio, John 6:783
- in Hebrew 14:1262
- Jephthah 9:1343
- Lebensohn, Micah 10:1550
- Lopez 11:489
- *illus:* text
Sha-kh, *see* SHABBETAI BEN MEIR HA-KOHEN
Shakhna, Israel ben Shalom, *see* Israel ben Shalom Shakhna
Shakhna, Shalom, *see* SHALOM SHAKHNA BEN JOSEPH
Shakhnovich, G. 8:1348
Shaki (city, Lith.), *see* SAKIAI
SHAKI, ISAAC 14:1265
Shakna, Shalom, *see* SHALOM SHAKHNA BEN JOSEPH
Shakow, David 13:1340

Shakowitzky, N. **7**:334
Shakrai (agg. fig.) **15**:71
Shakurai (agg. fig.) **15**:71
Shakyai (Shakyay; city, Lith.), *see* SAKIAI
Shalag, *see* GORDON, SAMUEL LEIB
Shalakh (bird) **12**:1531
Shalat (service in Naḥal) **12**:767
SHALEM (locs., Er. Isr.) **14**:1265
- Jerusalem **9**:1379
- *illus:* text
Shalem, Asher ben Emanuel **14**:90
SHALEM, SAMUEL **14**:1266
Shalem, Solomon **4**:1485; **12**:795
Shalem Rabta (vill., Er. Isr.) **14**:1266
SHALEV, YITZHAK **14**:1266
Shali'aḥ (messenger), *see* AGENCY
Shaliat (loc., Ind.) **5**:55; **8**:1355
Shalim (deity), *see* Shulmanu
SHALISH (fin. trustee) **14**:1267
Shalishim (metal instrum.) **12**:564
Shalit, Abraham Jedidiah **13**:613
Shalit, Benjamin **10**:23,63
Shalit, Ilya **13**:1340
Shalit, Joseph ben Jacob **13**:1101
- Mantua **11**:897
- Provençal, Moses **13**:1259
- Riva **14**:196
- Sabbioneta **14**:586
Shalit, M. **16**:838
Shalita, I. **6**:735
Shalit case (Isr.) **10**:23,63
Shaliyah ibn Ṭīrūn ibn Nīn **6**:315
SHALKOVICH, ABRAHAM LEIB **14**:1268
- children's literature **5**:433
- publications **13**:1375
- Warsaw **16**:340
Shallekhet (journ.) **1**:newsp. list
Shallot (bot.) **13**:625
SHALLUM (k., Isr.) **14**:1269
- chronological chart **8**:766-767
- Hilkiah **8**:481
- history **8**:602
Shallum (k., Judah), *see* JEHOAHAZ
Shallum (h. of Huldah) **8**:1063
Shalma ben Tabia **14**:737
Shalmaneser III (k. Assyr.) **16**:1502
- Ahab **2**:437
- Carmel **5**:186
- history **8**:597ff
- image of Jehu **3**:306
- Karkar battle **10**:791
- *illus:*
- - Black Obelisk **3**:320
Shalmaneser V (k., Assyr.) **16**:1503
- Babylon **4**:31
- chronological chart **8**:766-767
- history **8**:605
- Hoshea **8**:1030
Shalmiah ben Phinehas **14**:734
Shalmon ha-Nasi **6**:1032
Shalom (cmty., Gr.) **7**:1512
Shalom (name for God) **7**:684
Shalom (name for Messiah) **11**:1411
Shalom (greeting) **7**:914
- *see also:* PEACE
Shalom (monthly, Arg.), *see Sholem*
Shalom (journ., Isr.) **1**:newsp. list
Shalom (journ., It.) **9**:1140; **13**:1037; **14**:253
Shalom (period., Turk.) **15**:1461
SHALOM, ABRAHAM (Salonika) **14**:1269
Shalom, Abraham (18th cent., It.) **13**:12
SHALOM, ABRAHAM BEN ISAAC BEN JUDAH BEN SAMUEL (Sp.) **14**:1270
- Albalag **2**:521
- philosophy **13**:450
- Tárrega **15**:825
Shalom, Isaac (Gr.) **10**:1430
Shalom, Isaac Effendi (Bosnia), *see* Effendi Shalom, Isaac
SHALOM, ISAAC I. (U.S.) **14**:1271
Shalom, Joseph **9**:1443
SHALOM, SHIN **14**:1271
- Brod, Max **4**:1387
- drama **6**:200
- Hebrew literature **8**:202
Shalom, Solomon Effendi, *see* Effendi Shalom, Solomon
Shalom, S.S. (ship) **9**:399; **9**:901; **16**:1024
SHALOM ALEICHEM **14**:1272
- *Contents:*
- - Life and Works **14**:1272
- - Development of His Works **14**:1278
- Berkowitz, Yitzḥak **4**:635ff
- Dobrushin **6**:144
- Kotik **10**:1221
- Ladino **10**:1351
- recordings **13**:1617
- Spector, Mordecai **15**:258
- stamps **15**:336
- Yiddish literature **16**:812
- Yiddish theater **15**:1065
- *illus:*
- - text
- - autograph **3**:917
- - "Dodie the Innkeeper" (illus., A. Kaplan) **10**:748
- - funeral **12**:1104
- - Gorshman's illustration **14**:1469
- - *Job of Mr. Green,* illustration **14**:490
- - Mendele Mokher Seforim, Ben-Ammi, Bialik, and **16**:809
- - Odessa Committee convention **12**:1329
- - Ohel production of *Ammekha* **12**:1343
- - Russian stamp **15**:335
Shalom Aleichem Folk Institute
- education, U.S. **6**:436ff
- *illus:*
- - students **12**:1105
SHALOM ALEIKHEM (greeting) **14**:1286
- greetings **7**:914
Shalom al Yisrael (wk.) **7**:1419
Shalom al Yisrael (epitaph) **15**:1222
Shalom Baer of Lubavich **8**:234; **11**:538
Shalom bar Mishael (gaon) **7**:318
Shalom ben Aaron ben Obadiah ha-Kohen **8**:1356
Shalom ben Abraham **4**:867
Shalom ben Obadiah ha-Cohen **5**:39ff
Shalom berakhah ve-tovah (greeting) **7**:914
Shalom Dov of Lubavich, *see* Shalom Baer of Lubavich
Shalom Joseph of Melnitsa-Podolskaya, *see* Friedmann, Shalom Joseph
Shalom Joseph of Spikov, *see* Friedmann, Shalom Joseph of Spikov
Shalom lekha (greeting) **7**:914
Shalom Mordecai ha-Kohen **4**:159
Shalom of Koidanov, *see* Koidanov, Shalom
Shalom of Safed, *see* MOSKOVITZ, SHALOM
Shalom of Wiener-Neustadt **2**:22
Shalom Shakhna ben Abraham, *see* Friedmann, Shalom Shakhna
SHALOM SHAKHNA BEN JOSEPH **14**:1286
- codification of law **5**:650
- Isserles, Moses **9**:1081
- Slonik, Benjamin **14**:1670
- *illus:* text
Shalom Shraga of Prohobyst **2**:140
Shalom Tower (bldg. Tel Aviv), *see* Migdal Shalom
Shalom Ulman Ḥarif of Lokenbach **10**:1103
Shalom Zakhar (custom), *see* SHOLEM ZOKHOR
SHALON, RAḤEL **8**:1433
"Shalosh", *see* PINELES, HIRSCH MENDEL BEN SOLOMON
Shalosh Se'udot, see SE'UDAH SHELISHIT
Shalshalah (wk.) **14**:754
Shalshelet ha-Kabbalah (wk.) **8**:1208
- fiction **6**:1265
- historiography **8**:556
- Jewish history **11**:349
- Tam ibn Yaḥya **15**:785
SHALTIEL, DAVID **14**:1287
Shalvah (mosh., Isr.) **1**:place list
Shalyat (loc., Ind.), *see* Shaliat
Shamah, Joseph **12**:1537
Sham'al (anc. reg.), *see* Ya'udi
Shamaᶜ River (Leb.) **9**:152
Shamash-shum-ukin **4**:32; **16**:1504
Shamayim (name for God) **7**:684
Shamdon (demon), *see* BEN TEMALYON
Shamerim, *see* SAMARITANS
SHAMGAR (bib. fig.) **14**:1288
- Deborah battle **8**:585
- Judges, The Book of **10**:445
- *see also:* DEBORAH
Shamhazzai (fallen angel) **12**:962; **12**:963
Shami (cmty. and rite) **9**:500; **14**:452; **16**:1535
SHAMI, YITZHAK **14**:1288
Shaming (insult) **8**:1408
SHAMIR (kib., Isr.) **14**:1289
- statistics **1**:place list
Shamir (worm) **8**:970; **15**:107
Shamir, Gabriel **11**:1167
- *illus:*
- - stamps, Israel **9**:843,844; **11**:1385
Shamir, Maxime **11**:1167
- *illus:*
- - stamps, Israel **9**:843,844; **11**:1385
SHAMIR, MOSHE **14**:1289
- drama **6**:205
- Hebrew literature **8**:204; **8**:206
Shamir, Yiẓḥak **11**:464
Shamiya, Al-(tn., Iraq) **8**:1450
SHAMMAH (bib. fig.; Edomite) **14**:1291
SHAMMAH (bib. fig.; s. of Jesse) **14**:1291
SHAMMAH (bib. fig.; s. of Agee) **14**:1291
SHAMMAH (bib. fig.; Harodite) **14**:1291
SHAMMAI (Ha-Zaken; tan.) **14**:1291
- chronological chart **8**:766-767
- codification of law **5**:632
- conflict of opinion **5**:890
- Hillel **8**:483
- siege of Jerusalem **3**:67
- *see also:* BET HILLEL AND BET SHAMMAI
Shammaites (schols.), *see* BET HILLEL AND BET SHAMMAI
SHAMMASH (sexton) **14**:1292
- *shulklapper* **14**:1477
- *tokheḥah* **15**:1192
- *illus:*
- - Lithuania **11**:387
- - *shulklapper's* mallet **14**:1477
Shammash, Yuspi **11**:359
Shamokin (boro., Pa.) **13**:230
Shamoon (fam.) **14**:1293
SHAMOSH, YIẒḤAK **12**:1466
Shamouti, see Jaffa orange
SHAMRI, ARIE **14**:1293
Shamshi-Adad I (k., Mesop.) **11**:978; **11**:979; **16**:1495
Shamshi-Adad V (k., Assyr.) **5**:331
Shamsky, Arthur **15**:301
Shamun, Joseph ibn, *see* Ibn Shamun, Joseph
Shamwīl (Islamic name for Samuel) **14**:784
Shanah be-Shanah (journ.) **1**:newsp. list
Shanah Tovah (greeting) **7**:916
Shandookh, Sasson ben Mordecai **10**:554
Shandukha (vill., Kurd.) **10**:1297
Shane, Joseph **15**:310
SHANGHAI (port, China) **14**:1293
- Zionism **16**:1127; **16**:1128
- *illus:* text
Shangi, Isaac ben, *see* Isaac ben Shangi
Shani, G. **3**:361
Shani, Isaac **10**:542
Shanji, David ibn **13**:1092
SHANKER, ALBERT **14**:1294
SHANKMAN, JACOB K. **14**:1294
Shannon, Joseph **14**:834
Shanwar Telis (name for Js., Ind.) **4**:493
Shaool, Anwar, *see* SHAUL, ANWAR
Shape ben Said **13**:595
SHAPERO, HAROLD **12**:707
SHAPERO, NATE S. **14**:1295
SHAPHAN (bib. fig.) **14**:1295
- Ahikam **2**:460
- Hilkiah **8**:481
Shapira (name), *see also under* Schapira; Schapiro; Shapiro; Spero; Spira; Spiro
SHAPIRA (fam., Has.) **14**:1295
- dynasties **1**:ḥas. table
- *hassagat gevul* **7**:1465
- printing **13**:1111
- Romm dispute **14**:255
Shapira, Aaron Simeon **14**:1297
SHAPIRA, ABRAHAM **14**:1296
- watchmen **9**:681
- *illus:*
- - Rothschild, Edmond de, and **14**:344
- - Transjordan Arab leaders and **9**:346
Shapira, Aryeh Leib (r.) **14**:1297
Shapira, Aryeh Leib (print.) **16**:1013
Shapira, Asher **15**:412
Shapira, Eliezer ben Zevi Elimelech **10**:1382; **14**:1295
SHAPIRA, ELIJAH BEN BENJAMIN WOLF **14**:1297
- Jaffe, Mordecai **9**:1264
Shapira, Hanina Lipa **16**:1013
Shapira, Ḥayyim **6**:233
Shapira, Ḥayyim Eleazar **2**:599; **12**:514; **14**:1296
Shapira, Ḥayyim Meir Jehiel **14**:1271
SHAPIRA, ḤAYYIM MOSHE **14**:1297
- Ha-Po'el ha-Mizrachi **7**:1322
- Israel politics **9**:664ff
- Mizrachi World Movement **12**:179
- National Religious Party **12**:881
- *illus:*
- - Druze Community leaders **9**:926
- - Jewish Agency Executive **10**:28
- - Knesset session **10**:1113
- - proclamation of the State of Israel **4**:513
SHAPIRA, ḤAYYIM NACHMAN **14**:1298
Shapira, Henrik, *see* Shara, Henrik
Shapira, Isaac **14**:956
Shapira, Isaac ben David ha-Kohen **5**:1029; **11**:547
Shapira, Isaac ben Noah Kohen, *see* ISAAC BEN NOAH KOHEN SHAPIRA

Shapira, Israel ben Nathan **16:**1347
Shapira, Jacob **16:**217
Shapira, Joshua Heschel **16:**1013
SHAPIRA, JOSHUA ISAAC BEN JEHIEL **14:**1299
Shapira, Leib **15:**13
SHAPIRA, MEIR **14:**1299
Shapira, Moses **14:**1665
Shapira, Moses William **7:**1349
Shapira, Myriam, *see* HARRY, MYRIAM
Shapira, Phinehas (print.) **14:**1665
Shapira, Raphael **16:**216
Shapira, Samuel (r.) **14:**1297
Shapira, Samuel Abba (print.) **14:**1665; **16:**1013
Shapira, Shalom Joseph, *see* SHALOM, SHIN
Shapira, Solomon **12:**514; **14:**1295
SHAPIRA, YESHAYAHU **14:**1300
Shapira, Ẓevi Hirsch **12:**514; **14:**1295
SHAPIRA FRAGMENTS **14:**1301
- Clermont-Ganneau **5:**605
Shapiro (name), *see also under* Schapira; Schapiro; Shapira; Spero; Spira; Spiro
Shapiro, Aaron Solomon **5:**1038
SHAPIRO, ABBA CONSTANTIN **14:**1302
Shapiro, Abraham Duber Cahana **8:**898
Shapiro, Alexander **15:**35
SHAPIRO, ARYEH LEIB BEN ISAAC **14:**1302
SHAPIRO, ASCHER HERMAN **14:**1303
Shapiro, A.Y. **16:**1654
Shapiro, Bernard **7:**1360
SHAPIRO, DAVID S. **14:**1303
SHAPIRO, EZRA Z. **14:**1303
- Basle Program **4:**308
- Cleveland **5:**612
Shapiro, Harry (natur.) **15:**1036
SHAPIRO, HARRY LIONEL (anthro.) **14:**1303
- anthropology **3:**40
Shapiro, Irving S. **16:**534
Shapiro, Israel **7:**929
Shapiro, Jacob Ẓevi **12:**1519
Shapiro, John D. **15:**311
Shapiro, Joseph ben Abraham, *see* CASE, JOSEPH BEN ABRAHAM
Shapiro, Judah J. **12:**871
Shapiro, Judah Meir ben Jacob Samson **14:**93
SHAPIRO, KARL JAY **14:**1304
- U.S. literature **15:**1578
SHAPIRO, LAMED **14:**1304
Shapiro, Lev **4:**1049
Shapiro, Levi Joshua, *see* SHAPIRO, LAMED
SHAPIRO, LIONEL **5:**115; **5:**116
Shapiro, Louis (jur.) **5:**900; **7:**1360
Shapiro, Louis K. (horse-breeder) **15:**311
Shapiro, Manheim Simeon **15:**68
Shapiro, Mathilde **3:**684
Shapiro, Maurice **11:**1203
Shapiro, Milton **12:**1025
Shapiro, M. M. **3:**684
Shapiro, Morris **15:**311
Shapiro, Moshe (Isr. polit.), *see* SHAPIRA, ḤAYYIM MOSHE
Shapiro, Naphtali Herz **5:**1038; **13:**1110
Shapiro, Neal **15:**311
Shapiro, Phinehas, *see* KORETS, PHINEHAS BEN ABRAHAM ABBA SHAPIRO OF
Shapiro, Rose **6:**465
Shapiro, Sam (soc.) **12:**1095
SHAPIRO, SAMUEL H. (law.) **14:**1305
SHAPIRO, SAUL BEN DOV **14:**1305
Shapiro, Y. (polit., Rus.) **6:**268
Shapiro, Ya'akov Shimshon **9:**677
Shapiro, Zalman Sender **10:**142; **10:**1221
Shapiro Vallentine (publ. co., Eng.) **5:**450; **13:**1374
- Silbermann, A. M. **14:**1534
Shapoff, Mose **15:**310
SHAPP, MILTON J. **14:**1305
Shapsh (deity) **4:**10
Shapshal, Serajah Khan **10:**776
SHAPUR I (k., Babyl.) **14:**1306
- Babylonian Jews **4:**40
- Jewish autonomy **6:**1025
- relations with Jews **8:**650
SHAPUR II (k., Babyl.) **14:**1306
- Babylonian Jews **4:**42
- Shushan **14:**1483
Shapur III (k., Babyl.) **14:**1306
Shaqīf, Al (tn., Er. Isr.) **9:**274; **9:**284
Shara, see JEWISH QUARTER
Shara, Henrik **12:**454
SHARʿAB (tn., Yem.) **14:**1307
Sharʿabī, Abraham **16:**746
Sharʿabī, Isaac **16:**746
Sharʿabī, Raphael **16:**746
SHARʿABI, SHALOM **14:**1307
- Abraham Gershon of Kutov **7:**1392
- Azulai, Ḥayyim **3:**1019
- Beth-El yeshivah **9:**293
- Kabbalah **10:**553ff; **16:**746
- mystical prayer **10:**629
- *illus:*
- - Bet El synagogue, Jerusalem **9:**1564
Shar'abi, Solomon (print.) **4:**498
Sharʿabim (tn., Yem.), *see* SHARʿAB
Sharaf (qtr., Jer.) **9:**1436
Sharaf, Judah **13:**1091; **14:**1245
Sharafāt (vill., Isr.) **4:**5
Sharaḥil Yaqbul (5/6th cent., comm.) **16:**898ff
Sharāt mountains (Transj.) **9:**596
Sharav (heat wave) **9:**1514; **9:**580; **9:**182
Sharecropping **10:**1534ff
SHAREF, ZE'EV **14:**1308
Sharett, Adah **14:**1309
SHARETT, MOSHE **14:**1309
- Ben-Gurion **4:**508; **4:**511; **6:**145
- foreign policy **9:**423; **9:**428
- Jewish Agency **16:**1083
- politics **9:**668ff
- request for arms **9:**388
- Uruguay **16:**16
- Vatican **16:**76; **16:**77
- *illus:*
- - text
- - autograph **3:**917; **9:**331
- - "Black Saturday" **10:**31
- - German-Israel reparations agreement **7:**499; **14:**72
- - giving evidence before UNSCOP **16:**1093
- - Herzlia Gymnasium class **11:**1448
- - Jewish Agency Executive **10:**28
- - Jewish Brigade members and **9:**359
- - London Round Table Conference **9:**359
- - proclamation of the State of Israel **4:**513
- - Technion, protest against non-Hebrew teaching **9:**331
- - Transjordan Arab leaders and **9:**346
- - visiting Aden transit camp **16:**750
Sharett, Rivkah **14:**1309
- *illus:*
- - with brother Moshe **14:**1310
SHARETT, YEHUDAH **14:**1313
SHAREZER (bib. fig.) **14:**1314
- Bethel-Sarezer **14:**34
SHARF, ANDREW **1:**37
SHARFMAN, ISAIAH LEO **14:**1314
SHARGOROD (tn., Ukr.) **14:**1314
- Transnistria **13:**669
Shargorodski, Lev **15:**1527
Shargorodski, Zalman ben Mordecai **10:**1063
Sharḥ (wk.) **10:**410
Sharḥ Eshet Ḥayil (wk.) **4:**137
Shari, Reuven **9:**1498
Shari'a Courts (Musl.) **9:**628ff; **9:**918ff
- *illus:*
- - Muslim religious judges **9:**922
- - session **9:**640
Sharigrad (tn., Ukr.), *see* SHARGOROD
Shark **6:**36
Shar-kali-sharri (k., Mesop.) **2:**493; **16:**1490
Sharm al-Māʿ (el-Moye; bay, Red Sea) **14:**1315
SHARM-EL-SHEIKH, TIRĀN ISLAND, and TIRĀN STRAITS **14:**1315
- airfield **9:**838
- Egyptian garrison **9:**387
- navigation rights **9:**390ff
- right to freedom of passage **9:**428
- Sinai Campaign **9:**390; **14:**1605,1607,1624
- Six-Day War **9:**408; **14:**1626,1636
- U.N. **15:**1552ff
- *illus:*
- - text
- - Israel stamp **9:**844-845
- - loading supplies onto frigate *Miznak* **14:**1604
- - Ras Nusrani shore battery **14:**1604
Sharon (city, Pa.) **13:**230
Sharon (plain, Isr.) **2:**387; **9:**125; **9:**127ff; **9:**216; **9:**572; **9:**579ff
- *illus:*
- - abraded seashore **9:**129
Sharon, Abraham, *see* SCHWADRON, ABRAHAM
Sharon, Ariel **14:**1629
SHARON, ARYEH **14:**1316
- urban workers' housing **3:**361
- *illus:*
- - cooperative housing project, Tel Aviv **3:**349
- - Technion Forum, Haifa **3:**351
- - Yad Mordekhai museum **16:**696
SHARONAH (mosh., Isr.) **14:**1317
- statistics **1:**place list
Sharp, Granville **8:**56
Sharp, Thomas **8:**56
Sharsheret (mosh., Isr.) **15:**916
- statistics **1:**place list
Sharshot ha-Kesef (wk.) **16:**1388
SHARUHEN (city, Er. Isr.) **14:**1317
- Tell el-Far'ah **8:**1141
- *illus:*
- - Philistine coffin lid **13:**401
- - stirrup case **13:**404
SHAS (T.) **14:**1317
- *see also:* TALMUD
Shasha (custom), *see* SHOLEM ZOKHOR
Shashrum (loc., Mesop.), *see* Shushara
SHAʿSHŪʿ, SALĪM **12:**1466
- Arabic literature **8:**1452; **9:**1041
Shasta (co., Calif.) **5:**56
Shasu (nomads) **2:**790; **15:**1316
Shatā (vill., Isr.) **4:**775
Shatlem (orgn., Isr.), *see* ILAN
Shatner, Mordekhai **5:**1455
Shatra (tn., Iraq) **8:**1450
Shatt en-Nil (canal), *see* CHEBAR
Shatz, Meir ben Isaac **13:**597
Shatzkes (fam.) **4:**1397
SHATZKES, MOSES **14:**1317
SHATZKES, MOSES AARON **14:**1318
SHATZKY, JACOB **14:**1318
Shaul (bib. fig., f. of Simeon) **14:**1549
SHAUL, ANWAR **14:**1318
- Oriental literature **12:**1464
Shauloff (fam.) **8:**340
Shaulyai (city, Lith.), *see* SIAULIAI
Shavei zion (6/5 cent., returnees to Isr.) **2:**834
SHAVEI ZION (mosh., Isr.) **14:**1319
- statistics **1:**place list
Shaving, *see* BEARD AND SHAVING
Shavli (city, Lith.), *see* SIAULIAI
Shavu'a ha-ben (circumcision ceremonial), *see Yeshua ha-ben*
Shavu'a Tov (greeting) **7:**914
SHAVUOT (fest.) **14:**1319
- General
- - Anan's calendar **2:**921
- - date **5:**52
- - folklore **6:**1392; **6:**1405
- - illuminated *maḥzorim* **11:**733 **11:**735
- - *Jubilees, Book of* **10:**324; **10:**325
- - kibbutz festival **10:**959
- Customs and Observances
- - children **7:**306
- - Commandments, the 613 **5:**764,768
- - cooking and food **6:**1424
- - dance festivals **5:**1270
- - Falashas **6:**1148
- - first fruits **6:**1313ff
- - Karaites **10:**779
- - night vigil **10:**642
- - *Omer* **12:**1382ff
- - Reform bar-mitzvah **15:**1310
- - sacrifice **14:**600ff,611
- - Samaritans **14:**742
- - *Targum Sheni* **15:**812
- - *Tikkun Lel Shavuot* **2:**635
- - tomb of Nahum **5:**1268
- Liturgy
- - *Akdamut Millin* **2:**479
- - *azharot* **3:**1007
- - Decalogue **5:**1446
- - Ruth, Book of **14:**1057; **14:**522
- *illus:*
- - text
- - *bikkurim* festival in a kibbutz **6:**1314,1315
- - carrying first fruits to Jerusalem **4:**993
- - festive folkdance **5:**1267; **7:**314
- - Gesher ha-Ziv festival **10:**962
- - *ḥallah*, traditional shape **6:**1419
- - paper-cut window decoration **6:**1394
- - "Shevousl," paper-cut **13:**65
- - synagogue decoration **6:**1368
- - *Tripartite Maḥzor* **2:***fcg.* 11
- - Western Wall pilgrims, 1967 **9:**901
- *see also:* FESTIVALS; PILGRIM FESTIVALS; SHELOSHET YEMEI HAGBALAH
"Shavuot" (paint., Oppenheim) **6:**1368
SHAW, ARTIE **12:**707
Shaw, George Bernard **6:**775
- *illus:*
- - bust, by Jacob Epstein **3:**555
- - Cameri production of *Saint Joan* **15:**1062
SHAW, IRWIN **14:**1322
Shaw, Nathan **15:**305
Shaw, Sir Sebag **10:**1495
Shaw, Thomas **8:**56
Shaw, Sir Walter **9:**344; **9:**1474; **13:**31

Shawbak (loc., Transj.) **15**:1318
- Crusaders **9**:268
- human geography **9**:596
Shaw Commission (1929, Pal.) **13**:31
Shawnees (Ind. tribe, N.Am.) **13**:229
Shay (Haganah intelligence service), *see* Sherut Yedi'ot
Shay (lit. suppl.) **4**:575
Sha'yā ibn Amaṣyā, *see* ISAIAH
Shayevich, Heinrich **8**:1348
Shaykh (cmty. ldr., N. Afr.) **5**:817
Shazar, Rahel, *see* KATZNELSON, RAḤEL
SHAZAR, SHNEUR ZALMAN **14**:1323
- as president **13**:1021
- Bernstein, Eduard **4**:684
- stamps **15**:335
- *illus:*
- - text
- - autograph **3**:917
- - Brazilian stamp **4**:1332
- - Druze judge sworn in **9**:925
- - Eshkol, Levi, and **6**:891
- - Israel Defence Forces generals with **14**:1634
- - Philippine ambassador and **13**:396
- - receiving first German ambassador to Israel **7**:502
- - Yod-Tet Kislev celebration **10**:883
Sh-a-z-ḥ-ah (bibliophile), *see* HALBERSTAM, SOLOMON ḤAYYIM
Shchebreshin (tn., Pol.), *see* SZCZEBRZESZYN
SHCHEDRIN (tn., Belor.) **14**:1327
Shchedrin, Mikhail Saltykov, *see* Saltykov-Shchedrin, Mikhail
Shchedrin, Rodion **13**:647
Shcherbakov, A.S. **6**:144; **6**:145
Sh.D. (demon) **5**:1532; **14**:1328
SHEALTIEL (bib. name) **14**:1328
- Zerubbabel **16**:1000
Shealtiel (16th cent., r.) **9**:1089; **16**:1547
Shealtiel ben Levi **13**:595
SHEAN, AL **15**:1090
SHEAR, MURRAY JACOB **5**:387
Sheara, Jacob Aben, *see* Aben Sheara, Jacob
She'arim (newsp.) **9**:1016; **12**:1056
- statistics **1**:newsp. list
"Shearing Sheep" (paint., Sh. Sebba) Fig. 943 **3**-ART
Shearith Israel (syn., Calif.) **14**:833
Shearith Israel (syn., Can.) **12**:284ff
- *illus:*
- - prominent members **12**:285
Shearith Israel Congregation (U.S.) **5**:276; **12**:1063,1068ff,1079; **14**:1173
- *illus:*
- - Central Park West building **12**:1070
- - Crosby Street building **12**:1069
- - Mill Street building **12**:1068
- - synagogue **14**:1175
Shear-jashub (bib. fig.) **9**:44
She'ar Sifrei de-Vei-Rav (wks.) **4**:401
SHE'AR YASHUV (mosh., Isr.) **14**:1328
- statistics **1**:place list
- *illus:* text
Sheba (anc. reg., Arab.), *see* SABEA
SHEBA, CHAIM **14**:1328
- medicine **11**:1203
Sheba, Queen of, *see* QUEEN OF SHEBA
SHEBA BEN BICHRI (bib. fig.) **14**:1329
- Amasa **2**:794
- Joab **10**:107
- source of revolt **8**:591
Shebaniah (priestly clan) **12**:89
- Tobiah **15**:1179
- unjust accusations **8**:1409
Shebitku (pharaoh) **15**:1152
SHEBNAH (bib. fig.) **14**:1329
- Ahaz **2**:455
- in the Arts **8**:454
- *illus:*
- - epitaph **6**:819
Sheboygan (city, Wis.) **16**:556
Shebreshin (tn., Pol.), *see* SZCZEBRZESZYN
Shebsel, see SHABBETAI ẒEVI
Shebuel (bib. fig.) **7**:511
Shecaniah (priestly clan), *see* Shebaniah
Shechem (bib. fig.) **7**:1249; **16**:277
SHECHEM (city, Er. Isr.) **14**:1330
- Abimelech **2**:77ff
- Adoniram **2**:295
- Ahab **2**:437
- archaeology **3**:306
- Baal-Berith **4**:1
- Bible history **8**:579ff
- city of refuge **5**:591
- fortifications **16**:275
- grape harvest feast **15**:496
- John Hyrcanus **8**:631
- Megiddo **11**:1227
- pictographic scripts **16**:654
- proscription **8**:347
- Simeon **14**:1548
- tribal center **15**:1383
- *illus:*
- - abduction of Dinah **6**:56
- *see also:* NABLUS
Sh-e-d-a-l, *see* LUZZATTO, SAMUEL DAVID
Shedemah (mosh., Isr.) **1**:place list
Shedemot (journ.) **10**:969
Shedia (loc., Egy.) **15**:581; **15**:595
Shedim (demons) **2**:251; **5**:1523; **7**:644
Shedletser Vokhnblat (journ.) **14**:1509
SHEDLOVSKY, THEODORE **11**:1210
Sheduva (city, Lith.), *see* SEDUVA
She'elah (ritual) **5**:47
She'elot u'Teshuvot,see RESPONSA
She'elot u'Teshuvot ha-Ramban (wk.) **12**:781
She'elot u-Teshuvot min ha-Shamayim (wk.) **9**:1233
SHEEP **14**:1333
- animal tales **3**:20
- dietary laws **6**:31
- *shofar* **14**:1442
- *kapparot* **10**:756
- sacrifice **14**:601ff
- *illus:*
- - Jacob's crossbreeding of Laban's flock (chart) **4**:1025
- - Jotham's seal **10**:302
- - Moses with his flock **12**:379
- - ram caught in thicket **11**:734
- - roundabout milking **9**:782
- - selection for tithe **11**:651
- - sheepshearing festival, Geva **10**:962
Sheepshead Bay (section, N.Y.C.) **12**:1107
Sheepshearing, Feast of (kib. fest), *see Ḥag ha-Gez*
Sheep's pool (Jer.) **9**:1398; **9**:1407; **9**:1539; **9**:1541
Sheer, Vincente, *see* Callahan, Mushy
Sheerah (bib. fig.) **4**:782
She'eris Yisroel (wk.) **16**:805
She'erit ben Saadiah Gaon **4**:1010; **14**:545
SHE'ERIT HA-ḤAZZAN (poet) **14**:1334
She'erit ha-Ḥazzan, the Splendor of Ḥazzanim, ben Shemariah, the Glory of Ḥazzanim **14**:1334
She'erit ha-Ḥazzan the Blind, the son of Japhet **14**:1334
She'erit ha-Levi **14**:1334
She'erit ha-Peletah (orgn., Ger.) **6**:76; **7**:497
She'erit Ya'akov (Orth. ldr.), *see* Franklin, Jacob
Shefā 'Amr (tn., Isr.), *see* SHEFARAM
SHEFARAM (tn. Isr.) **14**:1334
- Arab general survey **9**:1028
- human geography **9**:580
- Ottoman period **9**:285; 292
Shefa Tal (wk.) **10**:593
- *illus:*
- - hands as cosmic symbol **10**:514
SHEFAYIM (kib., Isr.) **14**:1335
- statistics **1**: place list
Shefer (mosh., Isr.) **1**:place list
Shefeyah (agr. school, Isr.), *see* ME'IR SHEFEYAH
Sheffa, Gershon **15**:314
SHEFFER, HENRY M. **14**:1335
SHEFFIELD (city, Eng.) **14**:1336
SHEFTALL (fam.) **14**:1336
- contractors **5**:935
Sheftall, Benjamin **7**:429;**14**:919,1336
Sheftall, Hannah, *see* Solomons, Hannah
Sheftall, Levi **14**:1336; **14**:919; **16**:360
Sheftall, Mordecai **14**:1336; **14**:919
Sheftall, Moses **14**:1337
Sheftall, Perla **14**:1336
Sheftall, Sheftall **14**:1337
Sheftel, H.J. **4**:591
SHEFTEL, MIKHAIL **14**:1337
Sheḥakim (journ.) **1**:newsp. list
She-Heḥeyanu (benediction)
- animals **3**:6
- *Barukh she-Petarani* **4**:285
- circumcision **5**:572
- Day of Atonement **5**:1380
- Three Weeks **15**:1124
SHEḤITAH (ritual slaughter) **14**:1337
- *Contents:*
- - Introduction **14**:1337
- - The *Shoḥet* **14**:1338
- - The Knife **14**:1338
- - The Act **14**:1338
- - Reasons Given for **14**:1339
- - Anti-Sheḥitah Movements **14**:1340
- - Stunning **14**:1341
- - Communal Aspects **14**:1342
- General
- - animal care **3**:5
- - economic history **16**:1286
- - Falashas **6**:1146
- - *gilgul* **7**:574
- - Ḥasidism **7**:1395,1401
- - *Ḥullin* **8**: 1069
- - illuminated manuscripts **8**:1285
- - livestock trade **11**:410
- - meat **11**:1162
- - Nazism **4**:682
- - Pentateuch **13**:240
- - place in cult **5**:1157
- - supervision (Jerusalem) **9**:889
- - tax **15**:839
- Laws
- - animal stunning **14**:93
- - blindness **4**:1091
- - Commandments, the 613 **5**:767
- - dietary laws **6**:28
- - *ḥazakah* **7**:1521
- - *nevelah* **12**:1019
- - *niddui* and negligence **8**:352
- - Polish law **13**:1296
- - scythe **4**:737
- - *takkanot ha-kahal* **15**:732
- - *talmid ḥakham* **15**:746
- - *Terefah* **15**:1016
- - women **14**:89
- *illus:*
- - text
- - *sheḥitah* and *bedikah* rules (1804) **6**:41-45
Sheḥitah knife, *see ḥalaf*
Sheḥitat Hullin (tract.), *see* ḤULLIN
Sheḥitat Kodashim (tract), *see* KODASHIM
She'ifatenu (period.) **4**:632
- statistics **1**:newsp. list
SHEIKH, ABRAHAM BEN SHALOM HA-LEVI AL- **14**:1344
Sheikh Abbas Bible, see Morgan Picture Bible
Sheikh 'Abdal 'Azīz (loc., Isr.) **14**:1630
Sheikh Abu Zarad (site, Isr.) **15**:806
Sheikh Faḍl inscriptions **16**:669
Sheikh Isḥāq Pasha, *see* Gabbai, Isaac ben David ben Yeshu'ah
Sheikh Jarrāḥ (qtr., Jer.) **9**:1487
- police headquarters **9**:1503
- Six-Day War **9**:1501; **14**:1630
Sheikh Sa 'ad (loc., Isr.) **10**:800
Sheikh Saydā (loc., Leb.) **14**:1508
Sheikh Zuwayd (loc., Er. Isr.) **14**:1629
She'iltot (wk.) **2**:449ff
- Berlin, Naphtali **4**:661
- codification of law **5**:634
- *Halakhot Pesukot* **7**:1171
- homiletical literature **8**:953ff
- Jewish literature **11**:330
- responsa **14**:87
- *Tanḥuma* **15**:795
Shein, Avraham **4**:571
Shein, Joseph **15**:1071
Sheinbah, Moshe **13**:1298
Sheinbaum, Moshe **13**:1377
Sheinboim, Yechiel **16**:149,150
Sheinin, Lev Romanovich **15**:452
SHEINKIN, MENAHEM **14**:1344
- Balta **4**:144
Sheinowicz, Josko (Joseph) **11**:541
Sheitel (headdress) **6**:220, 223; **8**:6
SHEKALIM (tract.) **14**:1345
- Jerusalem Talmud **15**:774
Shekalim, Shabbat, see Shabbat Shekalim
SHEKANZIB (tn., Babyl.) **14**:1347
SHEKEL (coin) **14**:1347
- *Contents:*
- - *Shekel* **14**:1347
- - *Ḥeẓi* and *Revi'a* **14**:1349
- - Other Denominations **14**:1349
- - In the Zionist Movement **14**:1349
- currency **5**:696ff
- Fiscus Judaicus **6**:1325
- Jewish War **9**:1399
- Lydia Jews **11**:622
- measures **16**:377; **16**:381ff,391
- Nehemiah's Temple tax **9**:1389
- redemption **5**:1560
- silver **11**:1431
- Temple **9**:1393; **15**:965
- Vespasian's decree **9**:238
- Zionist use **16**:1096ff; **16**:613
- *illus:*
- - text
- - Jewish War coins **5**:705-707; **9**:109
- - payment of half-shekel tax **14**:1346
- - weight **16**:377,379
"Shekel Day" (U.S.) **16**:1141
Shekelesh (anc. people) **13**:399
Shekel Yisrael (name for Isr.) **9**:111
Shekem (Zahal consumer network) **9**:691
Shekeẓ, see ABOMINATION
SHEKHINAH (Divine Presence) **14**:1349
- *Contents:*
- - General **14**:1349
- - In the Targums **14**:1350

- - In Talmud and Midrash **14:**1350
- - In Jewish Philosophy **14:**1352
- - In the Kabbalah **14:**1353
- General
- - hospitality **8:**1032
- - Lilith **11:**247
- - Metatron **11:**1445
- - ten journeys **12:**484
- - woman **16:**627
- Theology
- - anthropomorphism **3:**56
- - as Intellect **6:**695
- - eschatology **6:**882
- - exile **7:**275ff
- - providence **13:**1282
- - soul immortality **15:**178
- Mysticism and Prophecy
- - *devekut* **5:**1598
- - exile of, in Kabbalah **10:**616
- - Jewish gnosis **10:**507; 509ff, 515ff
- - Lurianic *tikkun* **10:**600
- - prophecy **13:**1176
- - *Ru'ah ha-Kodesh* **14:**366ff
- - *Sefirot* doctrine **10:**575
- - *Shi'ur Komah* **14:**1418
- - visions **16:**169
- - word **16:**635
- Places
- - pillar of cloud **13:**523ff
- - place of manifestation **3:**460
- - Tabernacle **15:**686; **15:**687
- - Temple **15:**947
- - Western Wall **16:**467
- Views on
- - Abelson **2:**63
- - Aḥa **2:**435
- - Ḥasidei Ashkenaz **7:**1379
- - ḥasidic thought **7:**1405
- - Judah Halevi **10:**363
- - Moses Ḥayyim Luzzatto **11:**600ff
- *see also:*PRESENCE, DIVINE; THRONE OF GOD
Shekhiv me-ra (sick person) **16:**519
- *see also: Goses*
Shekhunat Aḥvah (qtr., Tiberias) **15:**1133
Shekhunat Borokhov (tn., Isr.), *see* GIVATAYIM
Shekhunat Green (city, Isr.), *see* ḤOLON
Shekhunat ha-Yehudim, see JEWISH QUARTER
Sheki'at ha-Ḥammah, see Sunset
SHELA (amora) **14:**1354
- Jewish autonomy **6:**1025
- Rav **13:**1577
Shelah (bib. fig.) **15:**782
Sh-e-l-a-h (r.), *see* HOROWITZ, ISAIAH BEN ABRAHAM HA-LEVI
Shelah, pool of (E. Isr.), *see* SHILOAH, SILOAM
Shelakhmones (gifts; Purim), *see Mishlo'ah manot*
Shelamim (shelem), see Peace offering
Shelattim (journ.), *see Ha-Po'el ha-Vatik*
SHELEM, MATTITYAHU **14:**1355
Shelemiah (bib. fig.) **8:**624; **15:**957
Sheli'aḥ kolel (term for emis.) **14:**1359
Sheli'aḥ-Ẓibbur (kab.), *see* Baruch Sheli'aḥ-Ẓibbur Togarmi
SHELI'AḤ ZIBBUR (reader) **14:**1355
- *ḥazzan* **7:**1542
- music **12:**571
Sheliḥim (emissaries), *see* SHELUḤEI EREẒ ISRAEL
Shelish (meas.) **16:**379
Shelishi ba-Havurah (tit.) **7:**322
Shelley, Edgar P. **9:**829
Shelley, Percy Bysshe **6:**778; **16:**261
Shell Oil Company **4:**358; **5:**684
- *see also:* Paz
SHELOM BAYIT (domestic peace) **14:**1356
Shelomi (tn., Isr.) **9:**580
- statistics **1:**place list
Shelomoh (k.), *see* SOLOMON
Shelomo ha-Elkoshi, *see* EPSTEIN, ZALMAN
Shelomoh Yitzḥaki, *see* RASHI
Shelomo min ha-Adummim, *see* ROSSI, SALAMONE DE'
Shelomẓiyyon, *see* SALOME ALEXANDRA
SHELOSHET YEMEI HAGBALAH **14:**1357
SHELOSHIM (mourning) **14:**1357
- *see also:* MOURNING
Sheluḥat Noẓah ridge (Isr.) **12:**927
SHELUḤEI EREẒ ISRAEL **14:**1358
- *Contents:*
- - General **14:**1358
- - Historical Survey **14:**1361
- - Activities in the Diaspora **14:**1364
- - Ereẓ Israel Emissaries and Spiritual Movements **14:**1365
- - Emissaries' Activities on their Own Behalf **14:**1367
- - Historical Importance **14:**1367
- Ḥasidism **7:**1393
- Hebron **8:**232
- link with Israel **8:**729
- Ottoman period **16:**1536
- post Temple destruction **9:**243; **9:**256
- *illus:*
- - text
- - Altona receipt book for donations to Ereẓ Israel **3:**379
- - Hebron, Israel Halevi's credentials (1811) **9:**288
- - Hebron emissary's credentials **8:**728
- - Jerusalem letter of appointment **7:**1211-1214
- - Tiberias letter to Gibraltar community **7:**555
Sheluḥo shel adam kemoto (leg. conc.) **2:**349
SHELUḤOT (kib., Isr.) **14:**1368
- statistics **1:**place list
Sheluḥot (publ.) **1:**newsp. list **9:**580
Shelumei Emunei Yisrael (publ.) **1:**newsp. list
SHEM (bib. fig.) **14:**1368
- Abraham **2:**112
- Ceuta legend **5:**316
- Genesis **7:**395
- in the Arts **12:**1197
- Jacob **9:**1198
- Melchizedek **11:**1289
- Noah **12:**1191
- patriarchs **13:**182
- Semites **14:**1148
- Sumer **15:**515
- Tamar **15:**782
- tomb **12:**897
- *illus:*
- - text
- - covering Noah **6:**238; **9:**1285
Shem, ha- (wk.), *see Sefer ha-Shem*
SHEMA, READING OF **14:**1370
- *Contents:*
- - Introduction **14:**1370
- - Development of the Practice **14:**1370
- - The Laws of the Shema **14:**1372
- - In Jewish Thought **14:**1372
- General
- - *Berakhot* **4:**585
- - declaration of faith **10:**388
- - Jewish philosophy **13:**422
- - *kiddush ha-Shem* **10:**980
- - reward, punishment **14:**134
- - *Sefer ha-Ẓoref* **14:**1247
- - Torah study **15:**456; **16:**1278
- Laws and Customs
- - blind, the **4:**1091
- - Commandments, the 613 **5:**763
- - impurity **13:**1411
- - interruption **8:**966
- - laborer **10:**1323
- - language **10:**370
- - mourning **12:**488
- - *onen* **3:**23
- - recital **4:**737
- - *tefillin* **15:**904
- - washing hands **12:**998
- - *ẓiẓit* kissing **15:**744
- Prayer Form
- - *Ahavat olam* **2:**454
- - Amen preceding **2:**803
- - *Barukh Shem* **4:**284
- - benedictions **4:**485
- - *El Melekh Ne'eman* **6:**683
- - variations in liturgy **11:**393
- - *yozerot* **16:**865
- Recitation
- - *Arvit* **3:**665
- - day and night **5:**1371
- - *Hakhel* **7:**1149
- - Karaite rite **10:**781
- - *Kedushah* **10:**876
- - night prayer **12:**1157
- - public affairs **13:**1352
- - sacrifices **14:**608
- - Samaritan betrothal **14:**745
- - Temple **15:**786
- *illus:*
- - text
- - reciting before going to bed **8:***fcg.* 1015
Shema'atin (publ.) **1:**newsp. list
SHEMAIAH (bib. fig.) **14:**1374
- Baasha **4:**13
SHEMAIAH (sage) **14:**1374
- Bible interpretation **8:**1417
- Hillel **2:**201; **8:**482
- history chart **8:**766-767
- Jerusalem, siege of **3:**67
- Nebuzaradan **16:**1513
- Paschal lamb **15:**1309
- proselyte descent **13:**1186
- sages **14:**640
- Sennacherib **14:**1163
Shemaiah (gaon) **7:**323
Shemaiah (grands., Rashi) **13:**1559
Shemaiah (alchemist) **2:**548
Shemaiah ben Abraham Issachar Ber **9:**21
Shemaiah ben Delaiah (bib. fig.) **8:**622
Shemaiah ben Shecaniah (bib. fig.) **15:**956
Shemaiah ha-Shoshani **14:**1375; **15:**83
Shemaiah the Nehelamite (bib. fig.) **6:**1037; **11:**56
SHEMAIAH OF TROYES **14:**1374
Shemama, Nessim, *see* SAMAMA, NESSIM
Shemanski, Joseph **12:**1451
Shemariah ben Aaron ha-Kohen **13:**595
SHEMARIAH BEN ELHANAN **14:**1375
- Cairo *genizah* **16:**1341
- Four Captives **6:**1447ff
- gaonate, Egyptian **7:**323
SHEMARIAH BEN ELIJAH BEN JACOB **14:**1376
- articles of faith **3:**656
- Italy **9:**1122
Shemariah ben Mordecai **2:**155; **10:**349; **15:**264
Shemariah ben Simhah **10:**1160
Shemariah of Rabyuand **13:**595
Shemariahu ben Jacob of Grodno **11:**450
Shemed (bib. fig.) **11:**619
Shemen, see OILS
Shemen, Ben **15:**768
Shemen, Nachman **5:**113
Shemen edible oil factory (Isr.) **9:**341
- *illus:*
- - Haifa plant, 1925 **9:**342
SHEMER, NAOMI **12:**707
- music **12:**670
- Song of Jerusalem **9:**1590
Shemesh-Adom (city, Er. Isr.) **7:**265
Shem ha-Gedolim (wk.) **4:**971
Shem ha-Gedolim he-Ḥadash (wk.) **4:**972; **16:**248
Shem ha-Nikhbad, ha- (wk.), *see Sefer ha-Shem*
Shemhazai (angel) **2:**966
Shemhurish (demon) **5:**1531
SHEMI, MENAḤEM **14:**1376
- *illus:*
- - "View of Safed" (paint.) Pl. 4 3-ART
SHEMI, YEḤI'EL **14:**1376
- *illus:*
- - sculpture **14:**1067
- - welded iron sculpture Fig. 104 3-ART
Shemu'ah (leg. tradition) **15:**1309
Shemiel (angel) **2:**973
Shemini Aẓeret (fest.)
- Commandments, the 613 **5:**781
- prayer for rain **13:**1523
- Samaritans **14:**742; **14:**744
- Simḥat Torah **14:**1571
- Sukkot **15:**501
- *see also:* FESTIVALS
Shemittah, see SABBATICAL YEAR AND JUBILEE
Shemonah Perakim (wk.) **11:**764ff
- ethical literature **6:**940f; **11:**344
Shemonah She'arim (wk.) **10:**553
SHEMONEH ESREH (prayer) **14:**1376
- *see also:* AMIDAH
Shemot (bib. bk.), *see* EXODUS, BOOK OF
Shemot (discarded holy books) **7:**405
Shemot ha-Higgayon (wk.), *see Millot ha-Higgayon*
Shemot Rabbah (agg. Mid.), *see* EXODUS RABBAH
Shemtob, Ezekiel **4:**93
Shem Tov (mintmaster), *see* Bonnom
Shem Tov (nasi) **12:**835
Shem-Tov (r., Mor.) **14:**682
Shem Tov, Isaac ibn, *see* IBN SHEM TOV, ISAAC BEN SHEM TOV
Shem Tov, Joseph ben Shem Tov, *see* IBN SHEM TOV, JOSEPH BEN SHEM TOV
Shemtov, Victor **9:**680
Shem Tov ben Abraham ibn Gaon, *see* IBN GAON, SHEM TOV BEN ABRAHAM
Shem Tov ben Isaac Ardutiel, *see* SANTOB DE CARRION
Shem Tov ben Isaac ibn Shaprut **3:**195; **13:**52
Shem Tov ben Isaac of Tortosa **15:**1322
Shem Tov ben Joseph ibn Shem Tov, *see* IBN SHEM TOV, SHEM TOV BEN JOSEPH BEN SHEM TOV
Shem Tov Falcon, *see* Falkon, Shem Tov
Shem-Tov ibn Ḥalaz, *see* Ibn Ḥalaẓ, Shem-Tov
Shem Tov ibn Shem Tov, *see* IBN SHEM TOV, SHEM TOV
Shemuel Ben-Natan, *see* PEVZNER, SAMUEL JOSEPH
Shemurah maẓẓah, see MAẒẒAH
Shem ve-Yefet (period.) **13:**1528
Shem Ya'akov (bk.) **14:**1248
Shen (tort conc.) **3:**986ff; **15:**1273
Shenabazzar (Shenazzar; bib. fig.),

see SHESHBAZZAR
Shenaton Agudat Yisrael-Amerikah (journ.) **1**:newsp. list
Shenaton ha-Aguddah ha-Yisre'elit le-Shikkum (journ.) **1**:newsp. list
Shenaton ha-Histadrut (journ.) **1**:newsp. list
Shenaton ha-Hitaḥadut le-Khadduregel (journ.) **1**:newsp. list
Shenaton ha-Memshalah (journ.) **1**:newsp. list
Shenaton ha-Po'el (journ.) **1**:newsp. list
Shenaton Ha-sefer, see Jewish Book Annual
Shenaton ha-Student (journ.) **1**:newsp. list
Shenaton ha-Televizyah (journ.) **1**:newsp. list
Shenaton Ḥerut (journ.) **1**:newsp. list
Shenaton Hidrologi (journ.) **1**:newsp. list
Shenaton le-Mishpat Ivri (journ.) **1**:newsp. list
Shenaton Massadah (journ.) **1**:newsp. list
Shenaton Statisti le-Yisrael (journ.) **1**:newsp. list
Shenaton Yedi'ot Aḥaronot (journ.) **1**:newsp. list
Shenaton Yisrael le-Ommanut ha-Zillum (journ.) **1**:newsp. list
Shenayim Plus (journ.) **1**:newsp. list
Shên Chu'üan (poet) **12**:1465
Shenei Dimyonot (wk.) **16**:1152
Shenei Luhot ha-Berit (bk.) **8**:991ff; **11**:347
- ethical will **16**:531
- kabbalistic customs **10**:642
Shenei Ofarim (wk.) **4**:1389
Shenfield, Baruch **8**:185
Shengold Publishers (U.S.) **13**:1377
Shenhab, *see* IVORY
SHENHAR, YITZHAK **14**:1377
- drama **6**:202
Shenhud, S. **16**:826
Sheni va-Ḥamishi, see MONDAY AND THURSDAY
SHENKAR, ARIE **14**:1379
- *illus:*
- - Va'ad Le'ummi meeting **16**:50
SHENKER, BEN-ZION **12**:708
Shenkman, Stanley **5**:113
Sheol, see NETHERWORLD
Shepel (sol.) **13**:699
SHEPETOVKA (city, Ukr.) **14**:1379
Shepham Hariblah (boundary, Er. Isr.) **14**:153
Shepharam (tn., Isr.), *see* SHEFARAM
SHEPHATIAH BEN AMITTAI **14**:1380
- Amittai I **2**:849
- Amittai II **2**:850
- Apulian Jewry **3**:226
- Basil I **6**:90
- history chart **8**:766-767
SHEPHELAH (reg., Er. Isr.) **14**:1380
- Bliss's excavations **4**:1095
- geology **9**:216
- human geography **9**:584
- physiography **9**:142
Sh-e-ph-e-r, *see* RABBINOWITZ, SAUL PHINEHAS
Shepherd, Rezin **15**:1288
"Shepherds" (Crusaders), *see* PASTOUREAUX
Shepparton (city, Austr.) **11**:1286
Sheps (tn., Pol.), *see* SIERPC
Sheptitski (metropolitan, Ukr.) **14**:475
Sher, Isaac **14**:1669
Sher, Jacob **15**:311
Sher, Zelig **14**:526
Sher'ab (tn., Yem.), *see* SHAR'AB
Sherbrooke (city, Can.) **13**:1423
Sherden (anc. people) **13**:399
Sheresh (bib. fig.) **11**:668
Shereshevski (fam. name), *see also* Schereschewski (sky); Szereszewski
Shereshevski, Meir **14**:1513
Shereshevski, Zelig, *see* Sher, Zelig
Shereshevsky, Abraham Moses **8**:210
Shereshevsky, Simon **4**:633
Sheridan (tn., Wyo.) **16**:680
Sheridan, Richard Brinsley **6**:778
SHERIFF, NOAM **12**:708
- music **12**:671
Sherif Pacha **5**:1250
Sheringham, Robert **8**:56
SHERIRA BEN ḤANINA GAON **14**:1381
- Albaradani, Nahum **2**:525
- amulet **2**:911
- Bustanai **4**:1537
- gaonate **7**:315ff
- *Halakhot Gedolot* **7**:1169
- history **8**:555
- history chart **8**:766-767
- Jewish mysticism **10**:511
- Mesopotamian academies **3**:375
- Nehemiah bar Kohen Zedek **12**:938
- responsa **14**:84ff
- Sabbath arrest **8**:1301
- Talmud **15**:760ff
- *see also:* HAI BEN SHERIRA
Sherman (city, Tex.) **15**:1035
Sherman, Alexander (Allie) **15**:308
Sherman, C. Bezalel **15**:68
Sherman, Max **12**:1408
Sherman, Moshe **11**:1203
Sherman, William T. **7**:855; **15**:1649
Sherrill, Lewis J. **15**:1674
Sherry, Lawrence **15**:301
Shershevsky, *see* Shereshevsky
Shertok, Moshe, *see* SHARETT, MOSHE
Shertok, Ya'akov **4**:1000; **14**:1309
Shertok, Yehudah, *see* SHARETT, YEHUDAH
Sherut la-Am (orgn., Isr.) **9**:543
Sherut Yedi'ot (intelligence service) **7**:1070
Shesh (gem) **13**:1011
Sheshai (bib. fig.), *see* AHIMAN, SHESHAI, TALMAI
SHESHBAZZAR (bib. fig.) **14**:1382
- Babylonian exile **6**:1040
- David's lineage **5**:1340
- Ezra-Nehemiah, Book of **6**:1116
- history chart **8**:766-767
- Temple **15**:955
- Zerubbabel **16**:1000
SHESHET (amora) **14**:1383
- Isaac bar Rav Judah **9**:12
- Naḥman **5**:891
- Talmud **15**:756
Sheshet bar Idi (amora) **8**:1227
Sheshet ben Isaac of Saragossa **11**:748
Sheshna (gaon) **7**:318
Sheshonq (k., Egy.), *see* SHISHAK
Shestapol, Samuel **14**:1384
SHESTAPOL, WOLF **14**:1384
SHESTOV, LEV **14**:1384
SHETAR (deed, document) **14**:1385
- *Contents:*
- - Early Examples **14**:1385
- - Format **14**:1386
- - Shetarot Written Before Gentile Courts **14**:1387
- - Types of Document **14**:1388
- acquisition **2**:219
- bailment laws **14**:1456
- civil marriage **5**:597; **5**:598
- conflict of laws **5**:886
- custom validity **12**:15
- debt **3**:768ff; **6**:1014ff
- elucidation, interpretations **8**:1425ff
- evidence **16**:585ff
- forgery **6**:1432
- *ḥaliẓah* **11**:127
- *ḥazakah* **7**:1519
- imprisonment **8**:1304ff
- *iska* **12**:255; **13**:153; **16**:32,1283
- Jerusalem law **9**:1554
- law source **12**:118
- lien liability **11**:228ff
- loans **11**:415ff
- marriage **11**:1046
- negotiable bonds **3**:770
- oaths **12**:1300
- obligation **12**:1314
- overreaching **12**:1392ff
- service contract **10**:1328
- slavery **14**:1657ff
- surety **15**:525
- waiver **11**:1233; **11**:1234
- wills **16**:520ff
- *illus:*
- - Elephantine Aramaic papyrus **2**:684; **6**:607
- - land-lease deed, Bar Kokhba period **3**:375
- - marriage deed **2**:692, 736
- - papyrus deed **2**:711
- - sale of synagogue pew, deed (1792) **7**:1519
- - slave emancipation **14**:1663
Shetar ko'aḥ harsha'ah mishpati (emis. let.) **14**:1358
Shetarot, Sefer ha- (wks.), *see Sefer ha-Shetarot*
Shetar pitturin (emis. let.) **14**:1358
Shetar tena'ei ha-sheliḥut (emis. let.) **14**:1358
Shethay-Bozenai (gov., As. M.) **15**:831,956
Shetilim (period.) **5**:457; **13**:1047
Shetuki (child of unknown parentage) **11**:841
Shetulah (vill., Er. Isr.) **7**:270 **1**: place list
Shetulim (mosh., Isr.) **1**:place list
SHETZER, SIMON **14**:1390
Sheuerman, Leopold **8**:1438
Sheva (bib. fig.), *see* Seraiah
Sheva (anc. reg., Arab.), *see* SABEA
Sheva, S. **6**:207
Sheva Berakhot, see Seven Benedictions
Shevaḥim literature **7**:1415
SHEVAT (Heb. month) **14**:1391
- planting **2**:376
- *illus:* text
- *see also:* CALENDAR
Shevat, fifteenth of, *see* TU BI-SHEVAT
Shevchenko, T. **15**:1517
Shevet mi-Yhudah (bk.) **15**:1689
Shevet Musar (bk.) **14**:1248
- Ladino **10**:1349
- *illus:*
- - title page(1734)**8**:959
Shevet va-Am (publ.) **1**:newsp. list
Shevet Yehudah (bk.) **8**:1203
- fiction **6**:1269
- historiography **8**:556; **8**:557
- Jewish history **11**:349
- Jewish-Gentile relations **8**:696ff
Shevet Ẓedek (qtr., Jer.) **9**:501, 503
SHEVI'IT (mish. tract.) **14**:1391
- *illus:* text
Shevilei Emunah (bk.) **2**:551ff; **6**:730
Shevilei ha-Hinnukh (period.) **1**:newsp. list; **6**:442; **15**:1290
Shevilei Olam (wk.) **4**:1110
Shevilim (journ.) **1**:newsp. list
Shevilin (period.) **1**:newsp. list
Sheviv (period.) **5**:453; **16**:348
Shevlin, Arnold **16**:515
Shevo (gem) **13**:1010
"Shevousl" (paper-cut, Gal.) **13**:65
Shevreshiner, Jacob, *see* HOROWITZ, JACOB BEN ABRAHAM
Shevu'ah, see OATH
Shevu'a ha-Ben (pre-circumcision custom), *see* SHOLEM ZOKHOR
Shevu'ah Mi-Divrei Soferim (oath) **12**:1299
Shevu'at ha-Torah (oath) **12**:1299
Shevu'at Hesset (oath) **12**:1300
SHEVU'OT (tract.) **14**:1392
- *illus:* text
Shevut Teiman (publ.) **1**:newsp. list
Shevut Ya'akov (wk.) **14**:61
Shev ve-al ta'aseh (rab. enactment) **7**:1159
SHEWBREAD **14**:1394
- Bet Garmu **4**:731
- incense offering **8**:1314
- Leviticus, Book of **11**:146
- place in cult **5**:1161
- priests **13**:1077
- Tabernacle **15**:682
- Talmud **11**:1314
- *illus:*
- - text
- - Antigonus II coin **3**:66
- - Ark of the Law, Cracow **5**:1035
She-Yiḥyeh le-Orekh Yamim Tovim (address) **7**:918
Shezor (mosh., Isr.) **1**:place list
SHIBĀM AND KAWKABĀN (tns., Yem.) **14**:1396
- Yemen **16**:746
Shibbolei ha-Leket (bk.) **2**:938; **2**:939; **2**:940; **11**:334
Shibbolim (mosh., Isr.) **1**:place list
Shibbolim (journ.) **4**:499
Shibbolim (bi-weekly) **2**:478
SHI'BUDA DE-RABBI NATHAN (leg. conc.) **14**:1397
- *ha'anakah* **7**:1004
- wife's maintenance **11**:786
Shi'bud nekhasim (leg. conc.), *see* LIEN
Shibuta (zool.) **13**:507
Shiddukhin, see BETROTHAL
Shield (Torah), *see* BREASTPLATE
Shield (armor) **16**:269
Shield of David, *see* MAGEN DAVID
Shieren, Jacob, *see* BEN-AMI, JACOB
Shiflut, see HUMILITY
Shifman, Pinhas **6**:425
Shiggayon (Psalm superscription) **13**:1321
Shihāb, Iskandar **9**:1039
Shihāb al-dīn Ahmad ben Muhammad ben Ibrāhīm ibn Hilāl, *see* Ibn Hilāl, Shihāb al-dīn Ahmad ben Muhammad ben Ibrāhīm
SHIḤIN (city, Er. Isr.) **14**:1398
SHIHOR, SHIHOR-LIBNATH (geog. term) **14**:1398
Shi'ism (Isl. sect)
- Abdallah ibn Sabā' **2**:53
- 'Āshūrā' fast day **3**:739
- Ayyubids **3**:998
- Ereẓ Israel **9**:263; **9**:278
- Seljuks **14**:1135
- Umayyads **15**:1529
- Yemen **16**:742
Shikhḥah, *see* LEKET, SHIKHḤAH, AND PE'AH
Shikkun (housing co., Isr.) **8**:539; **9**:564
Shikkun Ammami (housing co., Isr.) **9**:564
Shikkun, Workmen's Housing Ltd. (Isr.) **9**:855
Shikkun Rassco (Jer.), *see* Rassco

Quarter **9:**1496
Shikkuẓ, see ABOMINATION
Shikkuẓ Meshomem (idol), *see* ABOMINATION OF DESOLATION
Shikla (J. sign) **2:**663; **15:**1440
Shikmonah (city, Er. Isr.) **7:**1134
Shiknāz (Ott. decree) **9:**1448
Shila (amora), *see* SHELA
Shila bar Avina (amora) **3:**767
Shilak-Inshushinak (k., Elam) **14:**1483
SHILA OF KEFAR TAMARTA (amora) **14:**1399
- judicial autonomy **4:**40
Shilhim (city, Er. Isr.) **14:**1317
Shillem (tribal clan) **12:**818
Shilling, D. **8:**56
Shillumim Corporation (Isr.) **14:**73
Shilo (publ. house) **5:**438
Shilo, M. **3:**395
SHILOAH, AMNON **12:**708
SHILOAH, REUBEN **14:**1399
- *illus:*
- - Armistice Agreement, 1949 **3:**480
SHILOAH, SILOAM (spring, vill., Er. Isr.) **14:**1399
- Village
- - Jerusalem **9:**1491; **9:**1507; **9:**1515
- - tombs **9:**1525; **16:**666
- - Yemenite Jews **9:**500,1460; **16:**749
- Spring
- - Hezekiah **8:**452
- - *mikveh* **11:**1543
- - pool **9:**1398; **9:**1407
- - water supply **9:**1538ff
- *illus:*
- - text
- - Daughter of Pharaoh Tomb **9:**1526
- - graves hewn out of rock **15:**1220
- - Hezekiah's tunnel **9:**1539
- - Royal Steward inscription **2:**679; **6:**819
- - Siloam tunnel **3:**316; **8:**603
- *see also:* Gihon; KIDRON
Shiloah Center (Isr.), *see* Reuben Shiloah Center for Middle Eastern and African Studies
Shiloah Inscription, *see* SILOAM INSCRIPTION
SHILOH (city, Er. Isr.) **14:**1401
- Ahijah the Shilonite **2:**460
- cultic center **5:**1163ff
- Eli **6:**613
- history chart **8:**766-767
- Nabi-Samwīl **14:**785
- priesthood **13:**1083
- sacrifice **14:**606
- Samaritans **14:**727
- Temple **15:**943
- tribal center **15:**1383
- Twelve Tribes **15:**1382
- *illus:*
- - Ark's route to Jerusalem **3:**464
Shiloh River (Er. Isr.) **9:**142
Shiloh Valley (Er. Isr.) **9:**588
Shilstone, E. **8:**564
Shiltei ha-Gibborim (bk., Joshua Boaz ben Simon Baruch) **10:**285
Shiltei ha-Gibborim (bk., Abraham ben David Portaleone) **13:**908
Shilton, Moses ben Jacob **13:**1547
Shimea (bib. fig.) **4:**321
Shimei (s. Gershon; bib. fig.) **7:**513
SHIMEI (s. Gera; bib. fig.) **14:**1402
- Benaiah **4:**458
- Mordecai **12:**309
- Solomon **15:**97
Shimkin, Leon **13:**1373
Shimkin, Naum Isaakovich **14:**917
Shimmel, M. **16:**819
SHIM'ON, JOSEPH BEN JUDAH IBN **14:**1403
- Aknin, Joseph **2:**501
Shimon, Max **15:**304
Shimon bar Yoḥai, *see* SIMEON BAR YOḤAI
SHIMONI (Shimonovitz), DAVID **14:**1404
- *illus:*
- - text
- - Writers' Assoc. in Israel **8:**205
SHIMRON (Cana. city) **14:**1407
- Levi ben Sisi **11:**100
Shimshai (Samar. offic.) **8:**619; **14:**45
Shimshelevich (Shimshi), Ẓevi **4:**577
Shimshon cement factory (Isr.) **4:**774
Shimshoni (wk.), *see Ḥibbur ha-Konim*
SHIN (Heb. let.) **14:**1408
- *illus:* text
- *see also:* ALPHABET, HEBREW
SHINAH, SELMAN **13:**830
- Oriental literature **12:**1463
Shinai (gaon) **7:**318; **10:**225
SHINAR (loc., Mesop.) **14:**1408
- Amraphel **2:**894
- Babel, Tower of **4:**22
- Sumer **15:**515
Shinar, Pessaḥ **3:**993
SHINDOOKH, MOSES BEN MORDECHAI **14:**1408
Shindookh, Sasson ben Mordecai **8:**1451 **14:**1406
Shinedling, A.I. **8:**568
Shinkali (port, Ind.), *see* CRANGANORE
Shinnar, Felix Eliezer **14:**72
- *illus:*
- - reparations agreement **7:**499; **14:**72
SHINWELL, EMANUEL, LORD **14:**1409
SHION (tn., Er. Isr.) **14:**1409
Shipbuilding, *see* SHIPS AND SAILING
SHIPHRAH AND PUAH (bib. figs.) **14:**1410
- Pharaoh **12:**372
- *illus:*
- - before Pharaoh **6:**285
SHIPLACOFF, ABRAHAM ISAAC **14:**1410
Shippur (Bib. sign), *see Otiyyot menuẓẓarot*
SHIPS AND SAILING **14:**1411
- Alexandrian Jewish seamen **16:**1276
- Hellenistic state **8:**294
- historical survey **9:**393ff
- Israel **9:**835; **16:**1023
- maritime law **11:**996
- Ophir traders **16:**1269
- Sidonians **14:**1506
- Solomon's trade **15:**98
- Tunisia **15:**1435
- *illus:*
- - Ashdod harbor **9:**837
- - Ballin, Albert, commemorative stamp **4:**139
- - Israel stamps **9:**844-845
- - maritime symbols, Archelaus coins **3:**333
- - sailing, world championships **15:**317
- - Zim freighter *Shiqma* **16:**1023
"Ship to settlement" policy (Isr.) **9:**394ff
S-h-i-r, *see* RAPOPORT, SOLOMON JUDAH LEIB
Shir (Psalm superscription) **13:**1319
Shir, M. **5:**458
Shira, Myer Hart de, *see* De Shira, Myer
Shirah, Shabbat, see Shabbat Shirah
Shirah le-Ḥayyim (bk.) **5:**783
Shirayim (ḥas. term) **7:**1402
SHIRAZ (city, Iran) **14:**1415
- Iran **8:**1439; **13:**310
- special Purim **13:**1399
- *illus:*
- - Oẓar ha-Torah school **6:**430
Shirei Musar Haskel (poem), *see* MUSAR HASKEL
Shirei Tiferet (poem) **8:**180; **12:**404; **13:**1225; **16:**461
Shirei Ẓiyyon (wk.), *see Songs of Zion*
Shir ha-Kavod (hymn), *see* ANIM ZEMIROT
Shir ha-Lamedin (piyyut) **4:**371
Shir Hamalos-Tsetl, see AMULET
SHIR HA-MA'ALOT (psalms) **14:**1415
- Psalms, Book of **13:**1319
Shir ha-Shirim (Bib.), *see* SONG OF SONGS
Shir ha-Shirim Rabbati (agg. Mid.), *see* SONG OF SONGS RABBAH
Shir ha-Shirim Zuta (wk.), *see Aggadat Shir ha-Shirim*
SHIR HA-YIḤUD (litur. poem) **14:**1415
- *Anim Zemirot* **3:**22
- Ḥasidei Ashkenaz **7:**1379
- mysticism, Jewish **10:**517
Shirim le-Tu be-Av (kib. litur.) **10:**960
Shirim u-Meḥolot le-Tu be-Av (kib. litur.) **10:**960
Shir shel ha-Otiyyot (wk.) **14:**552
Shir Yedidot (psalm superscription) **13:**1321
Shisha (bib. fig.), *see* Seraiah
SHISHAK (k., Egy.) **14:**1416
- Arad **3:**243; **3:**249
- battle **16:**276
- Beth-Shemesh **4:**773
- Ereẓ Israel expedition **8:**594ff
- history chart **8:**766-767
- Jeroboam **9:**1372
- Solomon's throne **15:**812
Shiskes, Joseph **4:**789
Shitah Mekubbeẓet (bk.) **3:**723; **11:**333
- *illus:*
- - title page (Amsterdam, 1721) **8:**465
Shīth (bib. fig.), *see* SETH
Shitrei Berurin, see Arbitration, Deed of
SHITRIT, BEḤOR SHALOM **14:**1417
- *illus:*
- - proclamation of the State of Israel **4:**513
Shittah, Shittim (bot.), *see* ACACIA
Shittim (tn., Moab), *see* ABEL SHITTIM
Shittuf (journ.) **1:**newsp. list
Shi'urim (leg. meas.) **10:**780
SHI'UR KOMAH (Kab. doctrine) **14:**1417
- anthropomorphism **3:**56ff
- Kabbalah **10:**501ff
- Maimonides **11:**766
- providence **13:**1283
- *Sefirot* doctrine **10:**569; **10:**571
Shivah, see MOURNING
Shivah Keru'im (soc.) **8:**441
Shivah Tuvei ha-Ir, *see* Seven Good Townsmen
Shivat ha-Ḥarash ve-ha-Masger Society (Er. Isr.) **13:**536
Shivat ha-Minim, see Species, the Seven
Shivat Zion (hist.), *see* Zion, Return to
Shivat Ẓiyyon (publ.) **1:**newsp. list
Shivḥei ha-Ari (bk.) **15:**1208
Shivḥei ha-Besht (bk.)
- Adam Ba'al Shem **2:**247
- fiction, Hebrew **6:**1271
- ḥasidic literature **7:**1415
- Israel Ba'al Shem Tov **9:**1050
- *Toledot ha-Ari* **15:**1208
- Yiddish literature **16:**809
Shivḥei R. Ḥayyim Vital (bk.), *see Sefer ha-Ḥezyonot*
SHIVTAH (city, Er. Isr.) **14:**1419
- Negev **12:**929
SHIVVITI (syn. plaque) **14:**1420
- *illus:*
- - European and Oriental plaques **14:**1420-1421
- - paper-cut **13:**44-45,63
- - Purim prayers and quotations **13:** *fcg.* 1390
- *see also:* MIZRAḤ
Shivviti amulets (Pers.) **2:**912
- *illus:*
- - amulet **2:**913
Shkhauri (lang.), *see* Shaḥari
Shkliar, E. **12:**659
SHKLOV (city, Belor.) **14:**1420
- Shneour's works **14:**1430
Shklov, Israel ben Samuel of, *see* ISRAEL BEN SAMUEL OF SHKLOV
Shklover, Baruch, *see* SCHICK, BARUCH BEN JACOB
Shklover, Hillel **10:**808
Shklover, Jacob **9:**1062
Shklover, Nathan, *see* NOTKIN, NATA
SHKLOVSKI, ISAAC VLADIMIROVICH **14:**1421
Shklovski, Joseph Samuilovich **3:**807
Shklovski, Victor **14:**513
Shkolnik, Levi, *see* ESHKOL, LEVI
SHKOP, SIMEON JUDAH **14:**1421
- Telsiai **15:**938
Shkuder, Israel **12:**654
SHLOM THE MINTMASTER **14:**1421
- Vienna **16:**122
SHLONSKY, ABRAHAM **14:**1422
- Alterman, Nathan **2:**774
- Hebrew literature **8:**200
- prosody **13:**1235
- *illus:*
- - Writers' Assoc. in Israel **8:**205; **16:**653
Shlumal (Shlumil), Solomon, *see* Dreznitz, Solomon Shlomel
S.H. Margulies Rabbinical School (It.) **9:**1140
Shmelke Ḥazzan (Hung.) **7:**747
Shmelke of Nikolsburg **14:**534
SHMERUK, CHONE **1:**37; **14:**1426
Shmire-Tsetl, see AMULET
Shmoneh ba-Erev (journ.) **1:**newsp. list
Shmuel (name), *see* Samuel
SHMUEL BUKH (wk.) **14:**1426
- Moses Esrim ve-Arba **12:**428
- Yiddish literature **11:**357; **16:**801
- *see also:* MELOKHIM BUKH
SHMUELEVITZ, ARYEH **1:**37
SHMUELI, EPHRAIM **14:**1427
SHMUELI, HERZL **12:**708
Shmuhler, Moses (Moshko) **13:**1297
Shmulevich, Solomon **14:**1089
Shmulevitsch, Issy, *see* Smith, Issy
Shmulovich, Dov Baer **15:**1233
- *illus:*
- - Warsaw mausoleum **15:**1231
SHMUSHKEVICH, YAACOV **14:**1428
Shneersohn (ḥas. fam.), *see* SCHNEERSOHN
Shneour, Yiẓhak-Isaac **14:**1428
SHNEOUR (Shneur), ZALMAN **14:**1428
- drama, Hebrew **6:**202
- Hebrew literature **8:**197
- *illus:*
- - Hebrew Pen Club **12:**1109
Shne'ur, Joseph **7:**216; **13:**1108

Shne'ur, Solomon 13:1108
SHNEUR ZALMAN OF (LIOZNA-)LYADY 14:1432
- Contents:
- - Shneur Zalman 14:1432
- - Schneersohn Family 14:1434
- - Kopys Branch 14:1436
- - The Ḥabad System 14:1436
- - The Tanya 14:1439
- - Successors to the Ḥabad system 14:1439
- Abraham ben Alexander Katz of Kalisk 2:133
- Abraham ben Dov of Mezhirich 2:140
- Avigdor ben Joseph Ḥayyim 3:964
- Ḥabad 7:1013
- Ḥasidism 7:1396ff
- history chart 8:766-767
- Naḥman of Bratslav 12:783
- religious life in Ereẓ Israel 9:890
- Torah study 15:457
- ẓimẓum 10:593
- Zusya of Hanipoli 16:1243
- geneal. table 14:981
- illus:
- - text
- - micrographic portrait 7:1013
- - Tanya (Slavuta, 1796) 7:1418
Shnorrer (beggar) 6:1381; 4:389
Shobab (bib. fig.) 4:321
Shobal (loc., Er. Isr.), see SHOVAL
Shobi (Ammon. k.) 2:856; 12:770
SHOCHAT, ISRAEL 14:1440
- defense forces 9:681
- illus: text
SHOCHAT, MANIA WILBUSHEWITCH 14:1441
- Ha-Shomer 7:1371
- Independent Workers Party 8:1348
Shochet, J. Louis 11:1480
Shochetman, Baruch, see SHOHETMAN, BARUCH
"Shoemaker" (wdct., S. Judovin) 14:1468
Shoemaking 5:1048; 7:972
- illus:
- - ḥaliẓah shoe 11:123,126
- - Jerusalem shop 9:1468
- - Jewish shoemaker, Poland 10:1241; 13:746
- - sandals, Masada 11:1090
- - shoemakers' cooperative, Poland 13:1781
- - Ukmerge school 15:1513
Sho'evah (mosh., Isr.) 1:place list
SHOFAR (ram's horn) 14:1442
- Contents:
- - General 14:1442
- - History and Description 14:1443
- - Sounds of the Shofar 14:1444
- - Use on the Holy Days 14:1444
- - Other Uses 14:1446
- - Reasons for Sounding the Shofar 14:1447
- Abbahu 2:36
- Akedah 2:481
- Commandments, the 613 5:767
- Elul 6:690
- fastdays 6:1192
- folklore 6:1392
- folk music 12:664ff
- ḥerem pronouncement 8:355
- illuminated maḥzorim 11:733
- Johanan ben Zakkai 10:153
- Jubilee 14:580ff
- music 12:565
- New Moon proclamation 12:290
- Rosh ha-Shanah 14:309ff
- Sabbath enactment 7:1159
- sacrifice 14:610
- Samaritans 14:757
- Satan 14:904
- Shofarot 14:1447
- synagogue art 15:597ff
- takkanah 15:717
- Temple destruction 9:238; 9:241
- illus:
- - text
- - Ashkelon synagogue sculpture 12:569
- - benediction, Seder Berakhot (1687) 4:486
- - Beth-Shean synagogue mosaic 13:905
- - Beth She'arim tombstone 6:821
- - blowing the 3:834; 7:468; 11:734; 14:306
- - capture of Jericho 3:517
- - Eshtemoa synagogue sculpture 12:569
- - ḥerem 3:930
- - oil lamp 12:1349
- - Ostia synagogue relief 12:1508
- - second-third cent. bas-relief 3:716
- - shulklapper's mallet 14:1477
- - Six-Day War 7:809
- - Villa Torlonia catacomb 15:569
- - warding off the demon 5:1524
Shofar (Temple collec. box) 9:1320; 15:966; 15:981
Shofar (period., Bul.) 14:237
Shofar (period., U.S.) 11:296
Shofar mahpakh (cantillation sign) 16:1413
SHOFAROT (litur.) 14:1447
- Rosh ha-Shanah 14:307ff
- see also: MALKHUYYOT; TEKI'ATA; ZIKHRONOT
Shofet (Kar. tit.) 15:1165
Shofet, Yedidyah 15:906
SHOFMAN, GERSHON 14:1448
- Elisheva's translation 6:671
- Hebrew literature 8:203
Shogeg (unintentional sin) 2:350
Shoghi Effendi Rabbani (Bahā'ī ldr) 9:924
Shoham (gem) 13:1010
Shoham, Ha- (wk.), see Sefer ha-Shoham
SHOHAM, MATTITYAHU MOSHE 14:1449
- drama, Hebrew 6:199
- Jerusalem theme 9:1566
SHOHAM, SHLOMO 5:1111,1112
Shoḥarei ha-Tov ve-ha-Tushiyyah ve-Doreshei Leshon Ever (soc.), see Ḥevrat Doreshei Leshon Ever
Shoḥarei Sefat Ever (soc., U.S.) 6:552
Shoḥat, Alexander 9:1056
SHOḤAT, ELIEZER 14:1452
Shoḥer Tov, see MIDRASH PROVERBS; MIDRASH SAMUEL; MIDRASH TEHILLIM
Shoḥet (rit. slaughterer), see SHEḤITAH
Shoḥet, Asher, see Asher Anschel ben Eliezer Shoḥet
SHOHETMAN, BARUCH 14:1452
Shoḥet u-vodek (tit.) 15:1164
Shokedah (mosh., Isr.) 1:place list
Sholal (fam.), see SOLAL
Sholal, Abraham ha-Kohen 6:303
SHOLAL, ISAAC HA-KOHEN 14:1452
- aliyah 9:281; 9:512
- Ascandarani's letter 9:75
- Jerusalem 9:285; 9:1426
- Reuveni, David 14:114
Sholal, Joshua (Leib) 13:355
SHOLAL, NATHAN (Jonathan) HA-KOHEN 14:1453
- Jerusalem 9:1426
Sholem (period.) 5:459
Sholem Aleichem (au.), see SHALOM ALEICHEM
Sholem Aleichem Folk Institute, see Shalom Aleichem Folk Institute
Sholem Aleichem School (Montevideo) 16:14
- illus: 16:12
Sholem Aleikhem (greeting), see SHALOM ALEIKHEM
Sholem Asch Museum (Isr.) 3:687
SHOLEM ZOKHOR (custom) 14:1453
- boy's birth 5:426
- circumcision 5:576
Sholi (Nabatean offic.) 12:742ff
Sholokhov, Mikhail 14:512
Sholom, Theowald 11:664
SHOMER (nov.) 14:1454
Shomer (kashrut inspector), see MASHGI'AḤ
Shomerah (mosh., Isr.) 1:place list
SHOMERIM (bailees) 14:1455
- Contents:
- - Biblical Classification 14:1455
- - Measure of Damages 14:1456
- - Principles of Liability 14:1457
- - Rights and Duties of a Bailee 14:1457
- - Modern Israel law 14:1458
- consecrated property 8:280
- guardian, unpaid 4:341ff
- laws origin 12:7
- lost property 11:505
- oath 12:1299
- partners 13:151
- pledge 13:640
- possession 12:1532
- restitution obligation 12:1313
- theft 15:1095
- transference of deposit 11:644
- unjust enrichment 15:1683
- see also: SHALISH
Shomerim (watchmen, Er. Isr.) 9:681
Shomerim la-Boker (hymn reciters) 4:116; 12:615
SHOMER ISRAEL (mvmt.) 14:1458
- Aguddat Aḥim 2:426
- assimilation 16:1329
- Bierer, Rubin 4:984
- Byk, Emil 4:1547
Shomer la-Boker (assoc.) 14:355
Shomer Ẓiyyon ha-Ne'eman (period.) 12:1048; 1:newsp. list
SHOMRAT (kib., Isr.) 14:1459
- statistics 1:place list
Shomrei Hadass Society (party, Hung.) 12:1489
Shomronim, see SAMARITANS
Shooting (sport) 15:313
Shopkeepers, Jewish 16:1287
Shor (fam.) 7:69
Shor (zodiac sign), see Taurus
Shor, Solomon ben Elisha 7:63
Shorashim (journ.) 1:newsp. list
Shorashim, Ha- (wk.), see Sefer ha-Shorashim
SHORE, DINAH (Francis Rose) 15:1090
SHORESH (mosh., Isr.) 14:1459
- statistics 1:place list
Shor ha-bar (agg. animal), see WILD BULL
Shor ha-Bor (Yid. theat.) 4:1392
Shorshei ha-Shemot (wk.) 16:908
Short, Renée 13:812
Shorthand, Hebrew, see ALPHABET, HEBREW
Shortmeqash, Ibn, see IBN MUHAJIR, ABRAHAM BEN MEIR
Shoshan (fam.), see BENSUSAN; IBN SHOSHAN
Shoshani, M., see RIBALOW, MENACHEM
Shoshani, Sa'adyah 7:1066; 13:1114
Shoshannah (bot.), see Lily
Shoshannah (period.) 5:41
Shoshannah, Samuel 7:1188
Shoshannat ha-Amakim (rural stlmt., Isr.) 1:place list
Shoshannim (Kar. gr., Er. Isr.) 3:946; 9:273,1412
Shoshi, Elijah, see Shushi, Elijah
Shostak, Eliezer 8:542
Shostakovich, Dmitri 3:157
Shoteh, see Idiot
Shoter (court secretary) 6:394
Shoub, Mac 10:308
SHOVAL (kib., Isr.) 14:1459
- statistics 1:place list
Shoval (publ.) 1:newsp. list
SHOVAVIM TAT (acrostic) 14:1460
- Kabbalah 10:642
- Seliḥot 14:1134
Shovevim (demonic offspring) 10:642
Showbread, see SHEWBREAD
Shoyer (fam.) 11:1588
Shpan, Shmuel 15:821
Shpitz, Naphtali Hirsch 13:931
SHPOLA (city, Ukr.) 14:1460
Shpoler Zeide, see ARYEH LEIB OF SHPOLA
Shraga Feivel of Goerits 16:304
SHRAGAI, SHLOMO ZALMAN 14:1461
- Jerusalem affairs 9:1498
- illus:
- - "Black Saturday" 9:362; 10:31
- - Rabbinical Council of America convention 13:1462
Shraga of Chortkov 5:497
Shreibman, Reuven, see Shari, Reuven
SHREIER, FEIWEL 14:1461
Shretelakh (mag.) 5:458
Shrew (zool.) 9:226
Shriftn (period., Arg.) 3:424
Shriftn (period., Urug.) 16:727
Shriftn (period., U.S.) 8:1238
Shriki (fam.), see CHRIQUI
Shrimski, Samuel 6:274
Shrine of the Book (Jer.) 9:1495; 12:552ff; 16:695
Shrines of the Holy Land, see HOLY PLACES
Shriqui (fam.), see CHRIQUI
Shriqui, Addy 5:504
Shriqui-Delevante, Jacob Addy 5:504; 14:633
Shrire, Valva 11:1203
SHRODER, WILLIAM J. 14:1462
Shrouds, Burial 4:1519
SHTADLAN (cmty. repr.) 14:1462
- Alsace-Lorraine 2:753
- community 5:811
- Court Jews 5:1008
- Roman Jews 14:245
- Spain 15:230
Shtark, Samuel 4:1436
SHTAYGER (mus. term) 14:1463
- ḥasidic niggun 7:1425
- maqām 11:937
- music 12:609ff
- mus. notations:
- - Ha-Shem malakh 13:1331
- see also: CANTILLATION
Shtegen (period.) 15:339
Shtemenko, S. M. 6:144
Shtern (journ.) 4:447; 12:53; 13:1048; 14:464; 16:780
SHTERN, ISRAEL 14:1466
- Khaliastre 10:936
Shtern, Sholem 5:113
SHTETL (tnship.) 14:1466
- Contents:
- - General 14:1466
- - Life in the Shtetl 14:1471
- - Dissolution of the Shtetl 14:1473
- economic structure 8:655ff
- Shklov 14:1430
- illus: text
Shtibl (syn.) 7:1401; 15:584
- see also: BET (HA-) MIDRASH
SHTIF, NAHUM 14:1473

Shtifzin (publ.) **10**:997
Shtoptsi (tn., Belor.), *see* STOLBTSY
Shtrigler, Mordecai **16**:833
Shtrom (period.) **8**:813; **10**:1303; **16**:816
Shua (bib. fig.) **10**:327; **12**:1395
Shuadit (J. lang.), *see* JUDEO-PROVENÇAL
Shu'al, see FOX
Shuʿayb (Musl. fig.), *see* JETHRO
Shub, David **16**:1132; **16**:1133
Shub, Katriel, *see* CHASANOWICH, LEON
Shubat-Enlil (city, Mesop.) **16**:1495
SHUBERT (fam.) **14**:1474
Shubert, Jacob J. **14**:1474
Shubert, Lee **14**:1474
Shubert, Sam **14**:1474
Shubshi, Elijah **7**:549
SHUCHAT, WILFRED **14**:1474
Shuchmacher, Yossele **9**:399
Shudrich, Y. **16**:819
Shukeiri, Ahmed **9**:1033; **9**:404; **9**:467; **9**:469; **14**:1625; **14**:1639
Shukrī al-ʿAsalī **9**:456
Shukr Kuḥayl (ps.-Mess.), *see* Judah ben Shalom
Shul, see SYNAGOGUE
Shulal (fam.), *see* SOLAL
Shulamit (Zion. orgn., Pol.) **14**:538
Shulamit (period., Ger.) **16**:474
Shulamit (journ., Isr.) **1**: newsp. list
Shulamit (weekly, U.S.A.) **4**:1135; **16**:1141
Shulamit (play) **16**:450
Shulamit Conservatoire (Er. Isr.) **9**:1006
SHULAMMITE (bib. name) **14**:1475 **14**:1475
- in the Arts **15**:151
Shulent (stew), *see* CHOLENT
Shulgi (rlr., Ur) **16**:1493
- kingdom expansion **16**:3
- Sumer **15**:513
SHULḤAN ARUKH (code, Joseph Caro) **14**:1475
- *Contents:*
- - Introduction **14**:1475
- - Isserles' Commentary **14**:1475
- - Opposition to Acceptance **14**:1475
- - Final Acceptance **14**:1476
- - Development of *Halakhah* **14**:77
General
- codification of law **5**:648; **7**:1166; **11**:335
- David ben Levi of Narbonne **5**:1352
- - Ladino **10**:1349
- - rabbinical office **13**:1447
- - Rashba **2**:308
- - Reischer, Jacob, views **14**:61
- - scope of topics **12**:132
- - Sephardi terms **14**:1167
- - Sirkes' attitude **14**:1620
- - Sofer, Moses **15**:79
- - tradition **15**:1310
- Commentators, and Works Based on **11**:336
- - Abukara, Abraham ben Moses **2**:184
- - Altaras' Ladino translation **2**:771
- - *Arukh ha-Shulḥan* (Epstein, Jehiel Michael) **6**:831
- - Bacharach, Jair Ḥayyim **4**:48
- - *Ba'er Heitev* (Ashkenazi, Judah) **3**:729
- - *Ba'er Heitev* (Isaiah ben Abraham) **9**:72
- - *Be'er ha-Golah* (Rivkes, Moses) **14**:197
- - *Darkhei Teshuvah* (Spira, Ẓevi Hirsch); **14**:1296
- - Dick, Isaac Meir, popular version **6**:22
- - *Erekh ha-Shulḥan* (Tayyib, Isaac) **15**:874
- - *Erekh Leḥem* (Castro, Jacob de) **5**:651
- - *Even ha-Ezer* (Lima, Moses) **11**:251
- - Eybeschuetz, Jonathan **6**:1074
- - Gaon of Vilna **6**:651
- - Gatigno, Ḥayyim Abraham **7**:337
- - *Gilyon ha-Shas* (Eger, Akiva) **6**:469
- - *Gilyon Rasha* (Eger, Solomon) **6**:473
- - *Ḥayyei Adam, Ḥokhmat Adam* (Danzig, Abraham) **5**:1297
- - *Ḥelkat Yo'av* (Weingarten, Joab) **16**:402
- - *Ḥinnukh Beit Yehudah* (Judah Leib ben Enoch Zundel) **10**:374
- - *Imrei Barukh* (Fraenkel-Teomim, Baruch) **7**:6
- - *Keẓot ha-Ḥoshen* (Heller, Aryeh Leib) **8**:306
- - *Kiẓẓur Shulḥan Arukh* (Ganzfried, Solomon) **7**:313
- - Lipschutz, Aryeh Leib **11**:293
- - *Magen Avraham* (Gumbiner, Abraham) **2**:129
- - *Maḥaẓit ha-Shekel* (Kolin, Samuel) **10**:1162
- - *Mishnah Berurah* (Israel Meir ha-Kohen) **9**:1070
- - *Penei Yehoshua* **5**:654 (Falk, Joshua) **6**:1158
- - *Peri Ḥadash* (da Silva, Hezekiah) **8**:457
- - *Peri Megadim* (Teomim) **15**:1011
- - *Pitḥei Teshuvah* (Eisenstadt, Abraham) **6**:548
- - Rema (Isserles, Moses; *Ha-Mappah*) **5**:650; **9**:1083
- - responsa **14**:89
- - *Sefer Yehoshua* (Joshua Heschel Babad) **4**:14
- - Shakh (Shabbetai ben Meir ha-Kohen) **14**:1218
- - Shapira, Isaac ben Noah **9**:27
- - Shneur Zalman of Lyady **7**:1415; **14**:1432
- - Taz (David ben Samuel) **5**:1354
- - Walkin, Aaron **16**:253
- - *Yad Efrayim* (Margolioth, Ephraim) **11**:964
- *illus:*
- - text
- - Israel stamp **9**:844-845
- - *Sefer Ḥikrei Lev* **13**:1109
- - sixteenth century print (Venice, (1594) **5**:195
- - title page (Lublin, 1635) **9**:1215
- *see also:* CARO, JOSEPH BEN EPHRAIM; HALAKHAH; JACOB BEN ASHER; RABBINICAL LITERATURE
Shulḥan Arukh ha-Rav (hal. wk.) **7**:1415
Shulḥani (exchange banker) **12**:244ff
SHULIM, JOSEPH ISIDORE **8**:550
SHULKLAPPER (type of sexton) **14**:1477
- *illus:* text
Shulkult (orgn., Pol.) **16**:341
Shullam, Samuel **10**:991
SHULMAN, CHARLES E. **14**:1478
Shulman, E. **7**:1366
SHULMAN, HARRY **14**:1478
SHULMAN, MAX **15**:1583
Shulman, Morton **12**:1408
Shulman, Nachum **12**:38
SHULMAN, VICTOR **14**:1479
Shulmanu (deity) **9**:1379
SHULSINGER, BEZALEL **14**:1479
- Abrass, Osias **2**:172
Shulsinger, Shlomo **6**:444
Shulsinger Brothers (publ., U.S.) **13**:1377
Shulsteyn, M. **16**:819
Shultz, Samuel **16**:67
Shul un Kultur Farband, see Educational and Cultural Union
SHULVASS, MOSES AVIGDOR **14**:1479
SHUM (abbrev., Rhine cmties.) **14**:1479
- *takkanot* **15**:264
Shumen (tn., Bul.), see KOLAROVGRAD
SHUMIATCHER-HIRSCHBEIN, ESTHER **14**:1481
- travels **8**:517
Shumlin, Herman **12**:1121
Shuna, Al-(vill., Isr.) **11**:793
Shunami, Shlomo **4**:972
Shunary, Jonathan **2**:745
SHUNEM (anc. city, Er. Isr.) **14**:1481
- Abishag **2**:79
- Jezreel Valley **10**:102
Shunrah (topog.) **12**:926
Shunya-Shumvata (loc., Babyl.) **13**:1384
Shuppim (bib. clan) **4**:523
Shuqba (vill., Isr.) **16**:237
Shuqbāh Cave (loc., Er. Isr.) **16**:237
Shur (bib. place) **7**:432
Shuraḥbīl ibn Ḥasana **9**:260
SHURER, HAIM **14**:1482
- drama **6**:203
Shurot (journs.) **1**: newsp. list
Shurrabi, Shalom **2**:631
Shurun, Y. **12**:406
Shuruppak (city, Mesop.) **16**:1485
- excavation **16**:1507
Shurūṭ, see OMAR, COVENANT OF
SHUSHAN (bib. site, Iran) **14**:1482
- tombs of Ezekiel and Ezra **2**:627
- *illus:*
- - Daniel's tomb **13**:302
Shushan Dokt (5th cent.) **15**:1337
Shushan Gate (Temple mt.) **15**:963
Shushan Purim (fest.) **13**:1390
Shushara (loc., Mesop.) **16**:1498
Shushi, Elijah **11**:894
SHUSHTAR (tn., Iran) **14**:1484
Shu-Sin (k., Mesop.) **16**:1494
Shuster, Joe **5**:216
Shuster, Zachariah **5**:543
Shutruk-nahhunte (k., Elam) **14**:1483
Shutu (nomads) **5**:100
Shuvah (mosh., Isr.) **1**: place list
Shuvah, Shabbat ("Sabbath of Repentance"), *see Shabbat Shuvah*
Shuval, Judith **15**:69
Shuvalsky, M. Moshe **14**:162
SHVADRON, SHALOM MORDECAI BEN MOSES **14**:1484
Shvartser, Benjamin **15**:1076
Shvartse Tume (Rus. tn.), *see* BELAYA TSERKOV
Shwartsman, D. **5**:794
Shweid, Mark **14**:1265
Shylock (Shakespearian fig.) **14**:1261*ff*
- *illus:*
- - Adler, Jacob, as **15**:1066
- - Irving, Henry, as **14**:1263
- - *Merchant of Venice,* scene **14**:1262
Si'aḥ (journ.) **1**: newsp. list
Si'aḥ (orgn., Isr.), *see* Semol Yisre'eli Ḥadash
Si'ah Bet (party, Isr.), *see* AḤDUT HA-AVODAH
Si'aḥ ha-Sadeh (bk) **5**:1587
Si'aḥ Yiẓḥak (bk.) **7**:1177
Siam (kdm.), *see* THAILAND
Siamun (Egy. ruler) **8**:592; **14**:1416
SIAULIAI (city, Lith.) **14**:1485
- *illus:* text
Siavouch Pasha (vizier) **4**:562
Sib'e (ruler, Egy.) **13**:1509
SIBERIA (reg., Rus.) **14**:1486
- Judaizers **10**:401
- *illus:*
- - Zionist exiles (1925) **16**:1139
SIBIU (city, Transyl.) **14**:1489
SIBONI (fam.) **14**:1489
Siboni, Aaron **14**:1489
Siboni, Abraham **14**:633
Siboni, David **14**:1489
Siboni, Joshua **14**:1489
Siboni, Shalom **14**:1489
Sibraim (anc. city, Syr.) **14**:1177
- Anammelech **2**:918
SIBYL AND SIBYLLINE ORACLES **14**:1489
- astrology **3**:789
- eschatological king **11**:1409
- Hellenistic Jewish literature **8**:304
- magic **11**:705
- philosophy, Jewish **13**:425
- Pseudo-Phocylides **13**:1335
- resistance literature **8**:302
Sicaricon (mish. term), *see* SIKARIKON
SICARII (pats., Er. Isr.) **14**:1491
- Abba Sikra **2**:43
- African refuge **2**:331
- Albinus, Lucceius **2**:34
- Ananias ben Nedebeus **2**:923
- Cyrene Jews **5**:1184
- Eleazar ben Ananias **6**:585
- Eleazar ben Jair **6**:590
- Festus, Porcius **6**:1247
- Sikarikon **14**:1529
- *see also:* ZEALOTS
SICHAR (city, Er. Isr.) **14**:1492
Sichel, Giuseppe **15**:1057
Sichel, Julius **11**:1197
Sichel, Philip **11**:498
SICHER, GUSTAV **14**:1493
- Prague **13**:975
Sicherheitsdienst des Reichsfuehrers (Nazi orgn.), *see* SS AND SD
Sichrovsky, Elise **14**:1493
SICHROVSKY, HEINRICH VON **14**:1493
SICILY **14**:1493
- *Contents:*
- - History **14**:1493
- - Juridical Status **14**:1494
- - Community Organization **14**:1494
- - Cultural Life **14**:1495
- - Expulsion **14**:1495
- agriculture **2**:402
- al-Bazak, Mazli'aḥ **2**:527
- *aliyah* **9**:512
- artisans **16**:1287
- Bonavoglia, Moses **4**:1201
- catacombs **5**:251
- Dienchelele **6**:24
- guilds **7**:972
- history chart (1492-93) **8**:766-767
- Inquisition **8**:1396
- metalworks **11**:1438ff
- Obadiah Bertinoro **11**:351
- papyrus **16**:658
- Sea Peoples **16**:1501
- tax **15**:839
- textiles **15**:1038
- universities **15**:1675
Sicily Island (La.) **11**:519
- Am Olam **2**:862
- Rosenthal's settlement **14**:293
SICK, PRAYER FOR **14**:1496
- *Adonai, Adonai, El Raḥum* **2**:294
- Holy Ark **3**:457
- *illus:*
- - in time of plague **11**:1196
- *see also:* NAME, CHANGE OF

SICK, VISITING THE **14:**1496
- charity **5:**347
- gemilut ḥasadim **7:**376
- communal amenities **2:**805
- *illus:*
- - text
- - *ḥevra kaddisha* jug **8:**445
SICK CARE, COMMUNAL **14:**1498
- communal amenities **2:**805
- *illus:*
- - treatment of the sick **11:**1192
- - visiting the sick **14:**1497
Sick Fund, *see* Kuppat Ḥolim
Sickingen, Franz von **14:**110
SICKNESS **14:**1499
- *Contents:*
- - Introduction **14:**1499
- - Lifetime Longevity **14:**1499
- - Morbidity **14:**1500
- *agunah* **2:**430
- blessing on recovery **7:**768
- change of name **12:**802
- *ḥazakah* **7:**1519
- *pikku'aḥ nefesh* **13:**510
- priests **13:**1078
- wife **8:**1124
- wills **16:**519ff
- *illus:*
- - amulet **2:**913
Sicut Judaeis (papal bull) **4:**1495
- Alexander III, IV **2:**568
- Calixtus II **5:**63
Sicyon (anc. tn., Gr.) **7:**868
SID, SAMUEL IBN **14:**1505
- Alashkar, Moses **2:**512
SIDCO (Isr.), *see* Science-Based Industries Development Corporation
Ṣiddunnu (port), *see* SIDON
Siddur, *see* PRAYER BOOKS
Siddur ha-Ari **10:**630
Siddur Maharid **14:**1434
Siddur of Isaiah ben Uzziah ha-Kohen **9:**74
Siddur of the Rabbi of Ruzhin (illum. ms., Ger.) **8:**1281; **11:***fcg.* 875
Siddur of Solomon ben Nathan of Sijilmossa **11:**397
Siddur Rashi **13:**986
- language **16:**1636
- liturgy **11:**397
- *maḥzor* **11:**737
- Shemaiah of Troyes **14:**1375
Siddur Rav Amram, see Seder Rav Amram
Siddur Rav Saadiah Gaon **14:**553
- liturgy **11:**397,401
- prayer books **13:**985
Siddur Troyes **11:**399
Side (city, As. M.) **13:**51
Sidelocks, *see* PE'OT
Siderokastron (tn., Gr.) **7:**875
Siderowf, Richard **15:**309
Sidilyo, Samuel ibn, *see* SID, SAMUEL IBN
Sidjelmessa (tn., Mor.), *see* SIJILMASSA
SIDNEY, SYLVIA **12:**473
- Cerf, Bennett **5:**312
SIDON (Phoen. port) **14:**1505
- capitulations **5:**148
- Crusader period **9:**268ff
- glass production **7:**606
- Lebanon **10:**1543
- Phoenicia **13:**471ff
- Solomon **15:**100
- *illus:*
- - Eshmun'azar sarcophagus **2:**680
SIDON, SIMEON **14:**1508
- Manoah of Narbonne **11:**892
Sidor, Karol **8:**1072; **5:**1196
Sidqa (Phil. k.) **3:**714; **13:**403
SIDRAH (Torah portion) **14:**1509
Sidrei mikrata' (cantillation signs) **16:**1470
Sidun, Joshua **2:**622
Siebenbuergen, *see* TRANSYLVANIA
Siebenbuerger Israelit (newsp.) **2:**519
Sieber, Franz Wilhelm **9:**1549
Sieber, Heinrich **4:**1312
SIEDLCE (city, Pol.) **14:**1509
- pogroms **13:**698
Sieff (fam.) **16:**438
- *illus:*
- - Daniel Sieff Research Institute **16:**439,440
SIEFF, ISRAEL MOSES, BARON **14:**1510
- *illus:*
- - Zionist delegation to Palestine (1918) **9:**336
SIEFF, REBECCA **14:**1511
- *illus:*
- - protest against Passfield White Paper **16:**1118
- - WIZO delegation to Twelfth Zionist Congress **16:**1101
- - Wizo executive **16:**594
Sieff Research Institute (Isr.), *see* WEIZMANN INSTITUTE OF SCIENCE
Siegburg (tn., Ger.) **4:**168
Siegel, Arthur **13:**484
SIEGEL, BENJAMIN ("Bugsy") **14:**1511
Siegel, Ida **15:**1264
Siegel, Jacob (writ.) **11:**357
Siegel, Jacob (sport.) **15:**312
Siegel, Jerry **5:**216
Siegel, Martin **16:**476
SIEGEL, SEYMOUR **1:**37
SIEGMEISTER, ELIE **14:**1512
Siegora, Moreno **9:**1165
SIEMIATYCKI, CHAIM **14:**1512
SIEMIATYCZE (tn., Pol.) **14:**1512
SIENA (city, It.) **14:**1514
- special Purim **13:**1397
- *illus:*
- - text
- - cantata for inauguration of synagogue **5:**123, 125
- *see also:* TUSCANY
SIERADZ (tn., Pol.) **14:**1515
Sierck (vill., Fr.) **11:**496
SIERPC (tn., Pol.) **14:**1516
- *illus:* text
Sierra, Justo **15:**255
SIERRA, SERGIO JOSEPH **14:**1517
- Turin **15:**1455
Sierra Leone (state, Afr.) **9:**441
SIESBY, GOTTLIEB ISASCHAR **14:**935
- journalism **10:**306
- Scandinavian literature **14:**928
Siete Partidas (bk.) **2:**605
- Spain **15:**230
SIEVERS, EDUARD **14:**1517
- poetry **13:**676
SIFRA (mid. wk.) **14:**1517
- *Bei-Rav* **4:**401
- Leviticus **11:**139
- literature, Jewish **11:**316
- *tannaim* **15:**799
- *see also:* MIDRASH; SIFREI
Sifra de-Adam ha-Rishon (bk.) **2:**247
Sifra de-Ẓeniuta (bk.) **4:**1545
- Zohar **16:**1194
SIFREI (mid. wk.) **14:**1519
- *Bei-Rav* **4:**402
- Hezekiah **8:**455
- Hillel ben Eliakim **8:**487
- Ishmael **9:**84
- literature, Jewish **11:**316
- Pardo, David Samuel **13:**93
- Satan **14:**903
- *Sifra* **11:**139; **14:**1517
- Simeon bar Yoḥai **14:**1552
- *tannaim* **15:**799
- usury **12:**246
- see also: MIDRASH; SIFREI ZUTA
Sifrei de-Vei Rav (bk.), *see* MEKHILTA OF R. SIMEON BEN YOḤAI
SIFREI HA-MINIM (bks.) **14:**1521
- *see also:* MIN
Sifrei Homerus (bks.) **8:**944
Sifrei Katan (bk.), *see* SIFREI ZUTA
Sifrei Sha'ashu'im (journ.) **1:**newsp. list
Sifrei shel Panim Aḥerim, see SIFREI ZUTA
Sifrei Tarshish (publ. firm. Isr.) **13:**1378
Sifrei Yerushalmi, see SIFREI ZUTA
SIFREI ZUTA (mid. wk.) **14:**1522
- Bar Kappara **4:**227
- Lydda school **15:**773
- *Midrash ha-Gadol* **11:**1515
- *tannaim* **15:**799
- *see also* SIFREI
Sifriyyat ha-Po'alim (publ. house, Isr.) **9:**857; **10:**970
Sifriyyat Tarmil (Ẓahal lit.) **9:**694
Sifroni, Israel, *see* ZIFRONI ISRAEL BEN DANIEL
Sifrut (publ. firm, Pol.) **13:**1345
Sifrut (journ.) **1:** newsp. list
Sifrut ha-Olam, Leksikon (wk.) **6:**735
Sifrut Ẓe'irah (period.) **1:**newsp. list. **12:**1469
Sifsufah (mosh., Isr.) **1:** place list
Siftei Ḥakhamim (wk.) **15:**520
Siftei Renanot (prayer bk.) **11:**400
- Ḥarizi **7:**1339
Siftei Yeshenim (wk.) **4:**971
Sigebert of Gembloux **8:**56
Sigelmann, Oscar Bloch **13:**1370
Sigenensis, Tilemanus **11:**927
SIGHET (town, Rum.) **14:**1523
- Teitelbaum, Jekutiel **5:**1591
Sighmar, ibn (fam), *see* Ibn Sighmar
Sighmar, Judah ibn, *see* Ibn Sighmar, Judah ben Joseph
Sigilla Veri (enc.) **6:**733
Sigismund I (k., Pol.) **7:**74
- Abraham Judaeus **2:**160
- chronological chart **8:**766-767
- Lesser Poland **11:**48
Sigismund II (August)
- Jews' autonomy **3:**924
- Lesser Poland **11:**48
- tax-farming **4:**1257
Sigismund III **16:**242
Sigler, Eugen, *see* RELGIS, EUGEN
SIGMAN, MORRIS **14:**1523
Sigmund Christian Geitler, *see* Jeiteles, Samuel
Signature, *see* AUTOGRAPHS
Signet rings **13:**1012
Signon (journ.) **1:** newsp. list.
SIGNORET, SIMONE **12:**474
Signs, *see* DIVINATION
Signs (Divine), *see* MIRACLE
SIGNS AND SYMBOLS **14:**1524
- paper-cuts **13:**61
- seals **14:**1072
- *illus:*
- - Lubaczow tombstone decoration **15:**1229
- - Zechariah's vision **16:***fcg.* 935
Sigoli, Simone **15:**1356
Sigonio, Carlo **8:**56
Sigoph (site, Er. Isr.) **14:**1410
SIGÜENZA (tn., Sp.) **14:**1527
Sihanouk, Prince Norodom **9:**444
SIHON (bib. fig.) **14:**1528
- aggadah **12:**1341
- Bible history **8:**577
- Israelites **12:**377
- proscription **8:**345ff
- Shamhazzai **12:**962
- Transjordan **15:**1316
- *illus:*
- - defeat by Israelites **2:**878
Sija (game) **9:**1038
SIJILMASSA (tn., Mor.) **14:**1528
Sijilmassi, Judah b. Joseph **14:**1528
Šik, Lavoslav **16:**874
Šik, Ota **3:**159; **5:**1202
Sik, Sándor **4:**883
SIKARIKON (mish. term) **14:**1529
- Judah ha-Nasi **10:**369
Sike, Henry **8:**58
SIKHNIN (tn., Er. Isr.) **14:**1530
- academies **2:**202
Sikhri, Isaac ben Moses ibn **5:**1534
SIKILI, JACOB BEN HANANEL **14:**1530
- Sicily **14:**1495
Sikkot (journ.) **1:**newsp. list
SIKKUTH AND CHIUN (deities) **14:**1531
- Amos **2:**884
SILANO (litur. poet) **14:**1532
- Apulia **3:**226
- Jerusalem emissary **16:**102
SILAS (fort. comm.) **14:**1532
SILAS (friend, Agrippas I) **14:**1532
SILAS (Babyl. sol.) **14:**1532
SILAS (comm., Tiberias) **14:**1533
Silber, Mendel **11:**520; **14:**665
Silber, Moses **11:**783
Silber, Saul **8:**216
Silber, Solomon M. **12:**38
SILBERBERG, MENDEL **14:**1533
Silberberg, Mendel B. **11:**501
Silberberg, Paul **11:**1440
SILBERBUSCH, DAVID ISAIAH **14:**1533
SILBERFARB, MOSES **14:**1533
SILBERG, MOSHE **14:**1534
- Jewish identity **3:**209
- *illus:*
- - Eichmann trial **6:**519
- - Supreme Court bench **9:**637
Silberman, Curt C. **2:**820
Silberman, Morton **14:**214
Silberman, Saul **15:**311
SILBERMANN, ABRAHAM MORITZ **14:**1534
SILBERMANN, ALPHONS **12:**708
Silbermann, Eliezer Lipmann **7:**1221; **12:**1049
SILBERNER, EDMUND **14:**1534
SILBERSCHLAG, EISIG **14:**1535
Silberstein, Abe, *see* SILVERSTEIN, ABE
SILBERSTEIN, DAVID JUDAH LEIB **14:**1535
Silberstein, Isaiah **14:**1535; **16:**51
Silberstein, Leib **16:**51
Silberstein, M. **16:**1328
SILBERSTEIN, SOLOMON JOSEPH **14:**1536
SILBERSTEIN-ÖTVÖS, ADOLF **10:**316
Silence (conc.) **16:**304
Silene (bot.) **6:**1365
SILESIA (reg.) **14:**1536
- Bernheim Petition **4:**681
- Czechoslovakia **5:**1188
- Familiants laws **6:**1162
- settlements, early **13:**710
- Shabbateanism **14:**1248
- *illus:*
- - Jewish badge decreed by the Nazis **4:**72
Silicate Brick Factory (Er. Isr.) **9:**341
SILIUS ITALICUS, TIBERIUS CATIUS ASCONIUS **14:**236
SILK **14:**1538
- Amalfi **2:**791
- Ankara **3:**24
- Babylonian trade **4:**38
- Bushire **4:**1535
- Catanzaro **5:**252
- Chalcis **5:**329

- Frederick II **7:**114
- industry pioneers **16:**1285
- Israel **12:**516
- Jaffa industry **9:**1255 **12:**516
- textiles **15:**1036ff
- weaving **5:**1046ff
- *illus:*
- - *tallit* **15:**744
Silk, Dennis **9:**1578
Silk City (N.J.), *see* PATERSON
Silkin, John (polit.) **14:**1540
SILKIN, JON (poet) **14:**1539
SILKIN, LEWIS, LORD **14:**1539
- Silkin, Jon **14:**1539
Silkin, Samuel **14:**1540
SILKINER, BENJAMIN NAHUM **14:**1540
- Hebrew literature **8:**211; **8:**213
Sill, *see* DOOR AND DOORPOST
Sillein (tn., Slov.), *see* ZILINA
Sills, Arthur J. **11:**1504
Sills, Beverly **12:**1122
Silluk (piyyut type) **13:**1205*ff*,1210
Silluk (leg., waiver) **11:**1232ff
Silluq (cantillation sign) **16:**1454
SILMAN, KADISH YEHUDA LEIB **14:**1540
Silman, M. **5:**434
Siloam (loc., Er. Isr.), *see* SHILOAH, SILOAM
SILOAM (OR SHILOAH) INSCRIPTION **14:**1540
- alphabet **2:**682
- archaeology **9:**1525
- Hezekiah **8:**452
- Old-Hebrew **16:**1569
- writing **16:**666
- *illus:*
- - plaster cast **3:**315
SILVA, ANTONIO JOSE DA **14:**1541
- drama **15:**254
Silva, Diego Núñez (physic.) **11:**825
Silva, Diogo da (monk) **10:**158
SILVA, FLAVIUS **14:**1542
- Masada **11:**1079
Silva, Francisco Maldonado de **13:**322
Silva, Hezekiah da, *see* HEZEKIAH BEN DAVID DA SILVA
Silva, Jacob da, *see* SILVA, RODRIGO MENDEZ DA
Silva, Jean Baptiste **11:**1190
Silva, João Mendes da **14:**1541
SILVA, JOSHUA DA **14:**1542
SILVA, RODRIGO MENDEZ DA **14:**1542
SILVA, SAMUEL DA **14:**1542
Silvain, Eugene **15:**1055
Silva Rosa, J. S. da **13:**1035
- *illus:*
- - Montezinos, David, and **12:**279
Silva Solis, Duarte da, *see* Solis, Duarte da Silva
Silva Solis, Francisco da, *see* Solis, Francisco da Silva
Silva Solis, Isaac (Fernando) da, *see* Solis, Isaac (Fernando) da Silva
Silver **11:**1428ff
- ancient currency **16:**1269
- jewelry **13:**1012
- Solomon's trade **15:**98
SILVER, ABBA HILLEL **14:**1543
- Ben-Gurion, David **16:**1061
- Cleveland **5:**610
- Judaism **10:**387
- U.S. **15:**1632
- Wise, Stephen **16:**567
- Zionism **16:**1088*ff*
- *illus:*
- - Biltmore Conference **15:**1633
Silver, Daniel J. **5:**610; **12:**871
Silver, David L. **7:**1348
SILVER, ELIEZER **14:**1544
- Cincinnati **5:**563
SILVER, HAROLD M. **14:**1545
Silver, Ivan **15:**311
SILVER, JESSE HAROLD **1:**37
Silver, Julius, Institute of Bio-medical Engineering **9:**972
Silver, Morris **12:**1025
Silver, Ray J. **6:**734
Silverberg, David **15:**151
Silverberg, Douglas **15:**309
Silverblatt, Howard, *see* DA SILVA, HOWARD
Silver City (Nev.) **12:**1017
Silverman (stlr., Can.) **2:**530
SILVERMAN, ALEXANDER **5:**387
- Pittsburgh **13:**570
Silverman, Joseph (r.) **12:**1091
Silverman, Joseph H. (mus.) **10:**1353
SILVERMAN, LESLIE **8:**1433
SILVERMAN, MORRIS **14:**1545
SILVERMAN, SAMUEL SIDNEY **14:**1546
SILVERMAN, SIME **10:**316
- newspapers **7:**901
Silvers, Herbert, *see* FERBER, HERBERT
SILVERS, PHIL **15:**1091
Silvers, Robert **15:**1578
Silversmith, Philip, *see* SILVERS, PHIL
Silversmiths **7:**971ff
SILVERSTEIN, ABE **14:**1546
- astronautics **2:**322
- Cleveland **5:**612
Silverstone, A. E. **14:**1394
SILVEYRA, MIGUEL DE **14:**1546
Silvia of Aquitania, St. **15:**1355
SILVIU, GEORGE **14:**427
Silwān (vill., Er. Isr.), *see* SHILOAH, SILOAM
Sima (amora), *see* Sama
SIMA, HORIA **14:**1547
SIMA, MIRON **3:**610
- *illus:*
- - "Hannah Rovina as Medea" (wdct.) **3:**644
- - Hannah Rovina in *Dybbuk* (wdct.) **6:**19
- - Kovner, Abba (drg.) **10:**1230
Simakho (w., Izates II), *see* Samakhos
Simancas (tn., Sp.) **3:**376
Simanei Or Zaru'a (bk.), *see Kiẓẓur Or Zaru'a*
Simanim (mnemonic device) **12:**187
- acrostics **2:**230
Simaniyyot (bib. signs), *see Otiyyot menuẓẓarot*
Simão da Fonseca, *see* ABOAB DA FONSECA, ISAAC
SIMCHONI (Simchowitz), JACOB NAFTALI HERTZ **14:**1547
SIMEON (bib. fig., tribe) **14:**1547
- *aggadah* **15:**1385
- Amalek **2:**790
- breastplate stone **13:**1008
- Genesis **7:**393
- Judah tribe **15:**1383ff
- Negev **3:**671
- settlement **8:**579; **9:**115
- *illus:*
- - text
- - parents and brothers **10:**1526
- - slaying Hamor and Shechem **7:**1250
Simeon I (h. pr.), *see* SIMEON SON OF ONIAS I
Simeon II (h. pr.), *see* Simeon son of Onias II
Simeon (h. pr.) **15:**1180
Simeon (Temple offic.), *see* Simeon of the House of Bilgah
Simeon (br., Onias IV) **12:**1404
Simeon (s., Hillel) **14:**643
- Azariah **3:**999
Simeon (tan.), *see* SIMEON BAR YOḤAI
Simeon (ḥas.) **12:**782
Simeon, Alter Israel (r.) **12:**59
Simeon, Testament of (Pseudepig.), *see* PATRIARCHS, TESTAMENTS OF THE TWELVE
Simeon Akiva Baer, *see* AKIVA BAER BEN JOSEPH
Simeon bar Giora, *see* BAR GIORA, SIMEON
SIMEON BAR ISAAC **14:**1551
- Abun **2:**197
- *Beraḥ Dodi* **4:**585
- chess **7:**305
- Eliezer ben Isaac of Worms **6:**623
- exile, meaning of **7:**284
- Kalonymus family **10:**719; **10:**721
Simeon Bar Kokhba (Kosevah), *see* BAR KOKHBA
SIMEON BAR YOḤAI (tan.) **14:**1551
- Academy on High **2:**208
- agriculture **2:**396
- Akiva **2:**489
- anti-Christological exegesis **3:**191
- Ben Temalyon **4:**555
- decisions in controversies **5:**891
- gentiles **7:**411
- halakhic midrashim **14:**1520
- Judah bar Ilai **10:**339
- labor **10:**1322
- Lag ba-Omer **8:**495; **10:**1357; **12:**1387
- *Mekhilta* **11:**1269
- Meron tomb **8:**921; **11:**1391
- mysticism **10:**508; **10:**533
- Peki'in **13:**216
- proselytes **13:**1186
- sages **14:**646
- *tannaim* table **15:**801
- Zohar **16:**1194; **16:**1198
- *illus:*
- - text
- - Lag ba-Omer dancing at Meron **5:**1270
- - tomb **8:**926
SIMEON BEN ABBA (amora) **14:**1553
Simeon ben Akiva **2:**490
Simeon ben Antipatros **10:**710
Simeon ben Azzai (tan.) **11:**1235
- *tannaim* table **15:**801
- Torah **15:**1239
Simeon ben Bathyra (tan.) **4:**324
SIMEON BEN BOETHUS (h. pr.) **14:**1554
- Boethusians **4:**1169
- Marianne **11:**990
Simeon ben Cathlas, *see* Simeon ben Katala
SIMEON BEN ELEAZAR (tan.) **14:**1554
- labor **10:**1322
- *tannaim* table **15:**801
SIMEON BEN GAMALIEL I **14:**1555
- Johanan ben Zakkai **9:**240
- Josephus **10:**252
- letters **11:**57
- sages **14:**643
- *tannaim* table **15:**801
SIMEON BEN GAMALIEL II (of Jabneh; 2nd cent. C.E., nasi) **14:**1556
- Akiva **2:**489
- biologist **4:**1028
- dancing **5:**1262
- decisions as **5:**891
- Greek **8:**296
- Jacob ben Korshai **9:**1221
- Meir **2:**459; **11:**1240ff
- peace **13:**196
- presidency **9:**249; **9:**250
- *tannaim* table **15:**801
- tombstones **15:**1222
SIMEON BEN ḤALAFTA (tan.) **14:**1557
- biologist **4:**1028
- *tannaim* table **15:**801
Simeon ben Ḥanina (tan.) **16:**858
Simeon ben Issac the Great of Mainz, *see* SIMEON BAR ISAAC
Simeon ben Isaac Halevi **2:**17; **3:**687
SIMEON BEN JEHOZADAK (amora) **14:**1558
Simeon ben Jeshua ben Sira, *see* BEN SIRA, SIMEON BEN JESUS
Simeon ben Johanan, *see* SIMEON THE JUST
Simeon ben Judah the Galilean **10:**355
- Zealot leadership **16:**949
SIMEON BEN JUDAH HA-NASI **14:**1558
Simeon ben Katala **6:**378
- Jacob ben Sosas **9:**1224
SIMEON BEN LAKISH (amora) **14:**1559
- decisions in controversies **5:**891
- gladiator **7:**599; **15:**292
- Johanan ben Nappaḥa **10:**145
- Judah Nesiah **10:**333ff
- theater **15:**1050
- Torah **15:**1236
SIMEON BEN MEGAS HA-KOHEN **14:**1561
SIMEON BEN MENASYA (tan.) **14:**1561
- Holy Congregation **8:**919
- *tannaim* table **15:**801
Simeon ben Mordecai **14:**1672
SIMEON BEN NANAS (tan.) **14:**1562
- *tannaim* table **15:**801
SIMEON BEN NETHANEL (tan.) **14:**1562
- *tannaim* **15:**798,801
SIMEON BEN PAZZI (amora) **14:**1562
Simeon ben Rabbi (tan.) **15:**801
SIMEON BEN SAMUEL OF JOINVILLE **14:**1563
SIMEON BEN SHETAḤ (tan.) **14:**1563
- capital punishment **5:**146
- Judah ben Tabbai **10:**353; **11:**56
- magic **11:**707
- Man of Lies **11:**233
- sages **14:**638
Simeon ben Solomon (ha-Sheni) ben Ẓemaḥ **6:**301
Simeon ben Solomon Duran, *see* DURAN, SIMEON BEN SOLOMON
Simeon ben Yannai **16:**711
Simeon ben Yosef ben Lakonya **16:**1200
Simeon ben Ze'ev Wolf **16:**143
- Samuel ben Avigdor **14:**805
Simeon ben Ẓemaḥ Duran, *see* DURAN, SIMEON BEN ẒEMAḤ
Simeon ben Zoma **15:**801
Simeon Cantheras (h. pr.) **4:**1169
- *see also:* SIMEON BEN BOETHUS
Simeon the Galilean, *see* Simeon ben Judah the Galilean
Simeon ha-Darshan **16:**706
Simeon ha-Gadol (the Great), *see* SIMEON BAR ISAAC
SIMEON HA-PAKULI (tan.) **14:**1565
- *tannaim* table **15:**801
Simeon ha-Shikmoni (tan.) **8:**468
SIMEON THE HASMONEAN **14:**1565
- Antiochus VII **3:**74
- Asaramel **3:**676
- Bethbasi battle **4:**736
- chronological chart **8:**766-767

- Dok **6**:153
- Great Assembly **7**:1456
- Hasmonean revolt **8**:629
- Jerusalem **9**:1392
- *Maccabees, Book of* **11**:658ff
- mausoleum **12**:206
- *nasi* **14**:643
- Ptolemy **13**:1349
- Temple **15**:958
- warfare **16**:279
- Wicked Priest **16**:486
- *geneal. table:* **7**:1457

SIMEON HA-TIMNI (tan.) **14**:1566
Simeon ha-Zaddik (qtr., Jer.) **9**:501,1461
Simeonis, Simeon **15**:1355
SIMEON THE JUST **14**:1566
- Alexander the Great **2**:577; **2**:578
- *Ben Sira, Wisdom of* **4**:550
- Jerusalem grave **8**:921; **9**:1459
- Lag ba-Omer **10**:1357
- Naziriteship **12**:906
- Synagogue, the Great **15**:629ff
- Temple **15**:958
- Torah study **15**:1239

Simeon Kayyara (gaon), *see* Kayyara, Simeon
Simeon of Gabara **10**:163
Simeon of the House of Bilgah **9**:1390; **12**:1403
SIMEON OF MIZPAH (tan.) **14**:1567
- *Yoma* tractate **16**:844

Simeon Safra (amora) **12**:478
Simeon Solomon (r., Rum.) **14**:922
Simeon Solomon of Bendery, *see* Bendery, Simeon Solomon of
Simeon Solomon Savran, *see* Savran, Simeon Solomon
Simeon son of Kimḥit (h. pr.) **10**:1009
SIMEON SON OF ONIAS I (h. pr.) **14**:1568
- Simeon the Just **14**:1566; **15**:629

Simeon son of Onias II (h. pr.)
- Onias III **12**:1403
- priests **13**:1086
- Simeon the Just **14**:1567; **15**:629
- Temple **15**:960

Simeon the Sorcerer, *see* Simon Magus
SIMFEROPOL (city, Ukr.) **14**:1568
Simḥah, see JOY
Simḥah bar Judah **11**:736
Simḥah ben Joseph of Poland **11**:351
SIMḤAH BEN JOSHUA OF ZALOZHTSY **14**:1568
- Naḥman of Horodenka **12**:787

Simḥah ben Naḥman of Gorodenka **2**:259
SIMḤAH BEN SAMUEL OF SPEYER **14**:1569
- Avigdor ha-Kohen **3**:963
- taxation **15**:857

Simḥah ben Samuel of Vitry **11**:331
- cantillation signs **16**:1417
- *Maḥzor Vitry* **16**:195

SIMḤAH BUNEM OF PRZYSUCHA **14**:1570
Simhah Bunem of Warka **16**:305
Simḥah ha-Kohen of Belgrade **2**:669
Simḥah Menaḥem ben Jona **16**:1014
Simḥah of London, *see* Soloveichik, Simhah ha-Levi
Simḥah Zimel ben Menahem Nahum **16**:148
Simḥat Aniyyim (wk.) **2**:775
Simḥat Beit ha-Sho'evah (kib. fest. playlet) **10**:960
Simḥat Beit ha-Sho'evah (fest.), *see* Water drawing, feast of
Simḥat Beit ha-Sho'evah u-Mo'adei ha-Mayim (kib. litur.) **10**:960
Simḥat Kohen (wk.) **10**:244
SIMḤAT TORAH **14**:1571
- *Attah Horeta Lada'at* **3**:833
- Bridegrooms of the Law **4**:1370
- cooking and food **6**:1426
- customs described **16**:690
- Diaspora **6**:1245; **6**:1246
- festival of **15**:502
- Holy Ark **3**:457
- Israel **9**:903
- Russian observance **15**:589
- Samaritans **14**:744
- *illus:*
- - text
- - Bridegroom of the Law cantata **12**:622
- - Bridegrooms of the Law chairs **4**:1370
- - Carpentras *Maḥzor* **11**:403
- - Cochin rite prayers **11**:401
- - dancing **5**:1269
- - *hakkafot* **7**:1154
- - Karaite hymns **10**:783-4
- - procession with Scrolls of the Law **9**:907
- - "Rejoicing of the Law . . ." (paint., S. A. Hart) **3**:547

"Simḥat Torah in the Synagogue (drg., B. Picart) **14**:1571
SIMḤONI, ASSAF **14**:1574
Simḥoni, Yehudit **14**:1574
Simic, V. **13**:34
Simittu (loc., Tun.), *see* Chemtou
Simkhas ha-Nefesh (wk.) **16**:804
SIMLAI (amora) **14**:1574
- *Sefer Yuḥasin* **11**:1232

Simla'i, R., *see* MOHR, MEIR
SIMLEUL-SILVANIEI (tn., Rum.) **14**:1575
SIMMEL, GEORG **14**:1575
- Joel, Karl **10**:134
- sociology **15**:64ff

Simmons, Barnett Abraham **11**:1552
Simoes, Isaac Lopes **13**:923
Simon, *see also under* SIMEON
Simon (br., Jesus) **10**:10ff; **16**:948
Simon (4th cent., bp.) **11**:1449
SIMON (fam.) **14**:1576
Simon, Abram **15**:631
SIMON, AKIBA ERNST **14**:1577
- *Akedah* **2**:484
- Israel **9**:899
- Rosenzweig **14**:301

Simon, Emanuel **15**:295
Simon, Felix **10**:317
SIMON, SIR FRANCIS EUGENE **14**:1578
Simon, Gustav **11**:591
SIMON, HEINRICH **10**:317
Simon, Henry **12**:1122
Simon, Herbert **14**:1576
- publishing **13**:1370
- typography **15**:1479

SIMON, HERBERT ALEXANDER **14**:1578
Simon, Jacob **14**:1579
SIMON, JAMES **14**:1578
- art collection **3**:648

SIMON, JEAN HENRI **14**:1579
Simon, Jean Marie Amable **14**:1579
SIMON, SIR JOHN **14**:1579
SIMON, JOSEPH (U.S.) **14**:1580
- Kentucky **10**:909
- Louisiana **11**:521
- peddling **13**:207
- trading **15**:1305

SIMON, JOSEPH (Hung.) **14**:1580
Simon, Julius (mer., U.S.) **12**:1021
SIMON, JULIUS (Zion. ldr.) **14**:1580
SIMON, SIR LEON **14**:1581
- *illus:*
- - Zionist delegation **9**:336

Simon, Maurice **14**:1582; **16**:1214
Simon, Max **5**:610
Simon, Mayer **14**:1579
Simon, Moritz Alexander **2**:468
- *illus:*
- - horticultural school, Ahlem **2**:468

Simon, Moses (Ger.) **6**:572
Simon, Moses (N.J.) **13**:161
Simson, Nathan **15**:1305
SIMON, NEIL **15**:1578; **15**:1584
Simon, Norma **5**:451
SIMON, NORTON **14**:1582
Simon, Oliver **14**:1576
- publishing **13**:1370
- typography **15**:1479

Simon, Paul **8**:1256
SIMON, RALPH **14**:1582
- Chicago **5**:417

SIMON, RICHARD **14**:1583
- Bible criticism **3**:809
- Hebraists **8**:58

Simon, Richard L. (publ.) **13**:1371; **14**:1013
Simon, Robert **13**:1371
Simon, Samuel **14**:1579
Simon, Schuschu, *see* Simon, Yakhin
SIMON, SHLOME **14**:1583
SIMON, SIDNEY **3**:610
- *illus*
- - Tarrytown, Temple Beth Abraham **16**:465

Simon, Simone **15**:1055
Simon, S. J. (card pl.) **5**:169
SIMON, TAMÁS **8**:1087
Simon, Therese **10**:317
Simon, Walter B. **15**:68
Simon, Yaakov **5**:453
Simon, Yakhin **16**:472
SIMONA (savora) **14**:1584
Simon ben Jacob of Trier **15**:1391
Simon ben Joachim, *see* SIMON, RICHARD
Simon ben Samuel **5**:159
Simon de Montfort **2**:533; **11**:471
Simon de Paris, *see* Simon, Mayer
SIMONE, ANDRÉ **14**:1584
Simonhoff (brs.) **11**:1478
Simoni, Simon **4**:176
Simonias (vill., Isr.), *see* SHIMRON
Simonides-Agrippa (s., Josephus) **10**:254
Simonini (informer) **4**:262
Simonis, J. **8**:58
Sim'oniya (vill., Er. Isr.), *see* SHIMRON
Simon Magus (magician) **10**:506
- Belial **4**:429
- Dustan **6**:314
- Gath **7**:335

Simon of Beit Arsham **16**:897
Simon of Trent **4**:315
- Trent **15**:1374
- *illus:*
- - alleged torturing **3**:97; **15**:1374
- - Frankfort broadsheet **3**:119
- - martyrdom of Trent Jews **7**:467
- - memorial card **2**:97

Simon of Trier **15**:1390
Simons, Abraham **7**:429
Simons, Charles C. **5**:1570; **5**:1572
SIMONS, DAVID (Neth.) **10**:1512
Simons, David W. (U.S.) **5**:1568; **5**:1570
Simons, L. (Neth.) **6**:320
- publishing **13**:1365

Simons, Leonard N. (U.S.) **5**:1571
SIMONSEN, DAVID JACOB **14**:1584
- Posnanski **13**:930

Simonsen, Jacob **14**:1584
Simonsky, Lawrence **15**:1264
Simonsohn, S. **8**:563
- Rieti **14**:170

Simon Stylites **3**:72
Simon the Tanner (N.T. Fig.) **9**:1250
Simplicia (wk.) **8**:1152
Simplizissimus (journ.) **5**:219
- *illus:*
- - anti-Semitic caricature **5**:177 **14**:1593

Sims, Zoot **12**:1122
SIMSON (U.S. fam.) **14**:1585
SIMSON, BERNHARD VON **14**:1586
- title **15**:1166

SIMSON, MARTIN EDUARD VON **14**:1586
- Simson, Bernhard von **14**:1586

Simson, Nathan **2**:822; **12**:1064
SIMSON, PAUL **14**:1587
Simson, Salomon **7**:224
Simson, Sampson (the elder) **14**:1585
- New York City **12**:1067ff

Simson, Sampson (the younger) **14**:1585
- historiography **8**:567
- universities **15**:1677

Simson, Solomon **14**:1585
Sin (site, Egy.) **14**:1593
- Ramses **13**:1544
- Sinai etymology **14**:1597

Sin (deity) **12**:290; **16**:3
- Sinai **14**:1597

SIN (conc.) **14**:1587
- General
- - Adam and mortality **11**:236
- - Book of Lamentations **10**:1371
- - *dibbuk* **6**:20
- - famine and drought **6**:1174
- - fear of sin **6**:1198
- - history of mankind **7**:645
- - man's nature **11**:844
- - netherworld **12**:998
- - resurrection **14**:99
- - *sitra aḥra* **10**:584
- - theology **15**:1105
- - worship **3**:977
- Atonement **3**:830
- - *Al Ḥet* **2**:629ff
- - *Avodah* **3**:977
- - Azazel ritual **3**:1000
- - death **5**:1420ff
- - expiation **10**:1039
- - fasting **6**:1191ff
- - forgiveness **6**:1433ff
- - God's justice and mercy **7**:669
- - *ḥibbut ha-kever* **8**:464
- - redemption **14**:4
- - repentance **14**:73
- - suffering **15**:486
- - *Tashlikh* **15**:829
- - wilderness **16**:512
- - *see also:* CONFESSION OF SINS
- Law
- - agency inapplicable **2**:349ff
- - cardinal offenses **8**:1318
- - duress **12**:1397
- - exclusion from community **3**:656
- - divorce **6**:128; **6**:129
- - impurity **13**:1406; **13**:1414
- - penal law **13**:222
- - rebuke and reproof **13**:1605
- Views and Attitudes
- - Cohen, Hermann **13**:461
- - Dead Sea Scrolls **15**:1046
- - Ḥasidism **7**:1404; **7**:1410
- - Kabbalah **11**:639
- - Mordecai Joseph Leiner of Izbica **9**:1159ff
- - Saadiah **13**:432
- *illus:*
- - *Tashlikh* ceremony **15**:829
- *see also:* GOOD AND EVIL; REWARD AND PUNISHMENT

Sin, original, *see* Original sin
SIN, WILDERNESS OF **14**:1593
Sin-ab-usur (Aram. name), *see* SHESHBAZZAR
Sinafir (isl., Red Sea) **14**:1315
SINAI (geog. reg.) **14**:1593
- *Contents:*
- - General **14**:1593
- - Pre-Biblical Period **14**:1595
- - Biblical Period **14**:1595
- - Post-Biblical Period **14**:1596

-- Modern Period **14:**1596
- Arab population **9:**1037
- Bedouin **9:**1045
- Bedouin and Israel guests **9:**1044
- British-Turkish negotiations **9:**307
- fisheries **9:**787
- frontier, Anglo-Turkish **9:**311
- geology **9:**194ff
- health services **9:**993
- history, early Bible **8:**573; **8:**576
- Jewish settlement **8:**415; **16:**1074
- mineral deposits **9:**812
- Naḥal Yam settlement **12:**767
- Negev **9:**132
- Sharm-el-Sheikh, Tiran **14:**1315
- Sinai Campaign **9:**389ff; **14:**1607
- Six-Day War **9:**408ff; **14:**1629
- U.N. and fedayeen raids **15:**1554ff
- *illus:*
-- desert vegetation **9:**227,229,234
-- Israel doctor examining Bedouin child **9:**1044
-- Jebel Mūsā **14:**1597
-- Leven's letter re settlement **10:**47
-- Mount Umm Shomar **9:**217
-- Paran Desert **13:**89
-- Sharm el-Sheikh **14:**1316
-- Sinai Campaign **14:**1601,1603
-- Six-Day War **14:**1627ff
-- *Tamarix mannifera* tree **11:**884; **15:**784
- *maps:* text
- *see also:* SINAI, MOUNT
Sinai (period., Ger.) **3:**838
Sinai (period., Isr.) **11:**741; **13:**1379
- statistics **1:**newsp. list
Sinai (annual, Rum.) **14:**399
- statistics **1:**newsp. list
Sinai (period., U.S.) **4:**146; **6:**531; **13:**1052
- *illus:*
-- cover (1858) **15:**1600
"Sinai" (term for amoraim) **2:**867
Sinai, Benjamin **8:**1076
Sinai, Mikhal ha-Cohen **3:**423
SINAI, MOUNT **14:**1597
- allegoric interpretation **3:**55
- Decalogue **5:**1435
- Hazeroth **7:**1531
- identification **14:**1595
- Moses **12:**374; **12:**376ff
- revelation at **14:**119ff
- Samaritan tradition **14:**743
- Tablets of Law **15:**690
- theophany **6:**1056ff
- tribal center **15:**1383
- wilderness **16:**513
- *illus:*
-- text
-- *Birds' Head Haggadah* **7:***fcg.* 875
-- fenced mountain **3:***fcg.* 907; **4:**430
-- Giving of the Law **2:***fcg.* 11; **4:**430; **5:**1436-1441; **7:***fcg.* 875, *fcg.* 1131; **8:**1218
-- major theories on site of (map) **6:**1043
-- Moses led by angel **2:**965
-- *Sarajevo Haggadah* **7:***fcg.* 1131
-- sculpture (V. Ries) **5:**59
-- Sharm el-Sheikh **14:**1316
- *maps:* text
Sinai ben Bezalel **10:**375
SINAI CAMPAIGN **14:**1600
- *Contents:*
-- Causes of the Campaign **14:**1600
-- The Campaign **14:**1605
-- The Aftermath **14:**1607
- Alexandrian Jews **2:**594
- Ben-Gurion **4:**511; **4:**512
- Dayan, Moshe **5:**1373
- Defense Forces **9:**697
- Eden, Anthony **3:**982
- historical survey **9:**388
- Kissufim **10:**1076
- Nasser **12:**842
- Turkey **15:**1463
- U.N. censure **15:**1554
- U.S. **15:**1666
- *illus:*
-- paratroopers at Mitla Pass **9:**379
Sinai Temple Museum (Los Angeles, U.S.) **12:**544
Sinani, Isaac **10:**776
Sinan Pasha **9:**76
Sinay, Gil **5:**467
Sinay, Hélène **10:**1496
SINCLAIR, JO **15:**1584
Sinda (site, Cyp.) **13:**400
SINDABAR (Sindabot, Sindbad; bk., lit. fig.) **14:**1607
- folklore **6:**1130ff, 1266, 1379
Sind ibn Ali **3:**801
Sindur (vill., Kurd.) **10:**1297
Sines (Saint) **11:**247
SINGAPORE (rep.) **14:**1608
- synagogues **1:**syn. list
- Zionism **16:**1127
- *illus:* text
SINGER, ABRAHAM **14:**1609
Singer, Al **15:**305
Singer, Bernard (writ.) **7:**1499; **12:**844
Singer, Bernat (Bernard; r.) **15:**473
SINGER, CHARLES JOSEPH **14:**1609
Singer, Clara **14:**1613
Singer, Dorothea Waley **14:**1610
Singer, E.F. **12:**1408
SINGER, GEORGE **12:**708
- Prague **13:**973
SINGER, HOWARD **15:**1584
SINGER, ISIDORE **14:**1610
- press **13:**1056
Singer, Israel **14:**1612
SINGER, ISRAEL JOSHUA **14:**1611
- Bashevis Singer **4:**293
- Khaliastre **10:**936
- *illus:*
-- *Literarishe Bleter,* editorial board **16:**818
-- Schwartz, Maurice, in *The Brothers Ashkenazi* **14:**1021
SINGER, JOSEF (ḥazzan) **14:**1612
SINGER, JOSEF (engin.) **2:**324
SINGER, JOSEPH (sol., Aus.-Hung.) **14:**1613
Singer, Joseph (polit., Can.) **15:**1264
Singer, Judah Veit, *see* Veit, Judah
SINGER, KURT **12:**708
- Juedischer Kulturbund **10:**462
Singer, Leo **14:**1609
Singer, Louis M. **15:**1264
SINGER, LUDVIK **14:**1613
- Czechoslovakia **5:**1189
Singer, Michael **16:**1141
SINGER, MILTON **14:**1613
Singer, Mirjam **5:**449
SINGER, PAUL **14:**1614
- in socialism **15:**35
SINGER, PESAḤ **14:**1614
Singer, S. (Aus.) **16:**1165
Singer, S. (Rum.) **16:**1134
Singer, Samuel (U.S.) **11:**1477
Singer, Shlome **11:**359
SINGER, SIMEON (r.) **14:**1614
- England **6:**762
- prayer book **13:**989
Singer, Simon (ḥazzan) **14:**1613
Singer, Simon (sport., U.S.) **15:**310
Singer, Vernon **12:**1408; **15:**1264
Singer, Y.Y. **7:**1499
SINGERMAN, BERTA **14:**1615
Singerman, Felix **4:**648
Singerman, Paulina **14:**1615
Singermann, Nora **14:**1615
"Singer of Zion," *see* JUDAH HALEVI
Singer's Prayer Book **11:**402
- Psalms **13:**1323
Single Gate (Jer.) **9:**1434
- *illus:*
-- general view **9:**1430
Singleton, Sir John (J.E.) **13:**33
- *illus:*
-- Anglo-American Enquiry Committee **16:**1089
Singriener, Hans **16:**131
Sington, Fred **15:**307
Siniansky, Simon **11:**1114
SINIGAGLIA (It. fam.) **14:**1615
Sinigaglia, Abraham Vita **14:**1615
Sinigaglia, Alina **12:**709
Sinigaglia, Jacob Samson Shabbetai **14:**1615
SINIGAGLIA, LEONE **12:**708
- family **14:**1615
Sinigaglia, Moses Elijah **14:**1615
Sinigaglia, Solomon Jedidiah **14:**1615
Sinim (port., Leb.), *see* TRIPOLI
ŠINKO, ERVIN **14:**1615
Sinneh (tn., Kurd.), *see* SANANDAJ
Sin offering **14:**600ff
- Commandments, the 613 **5:**766f,774f
- Day of Atonement **3:**977
- Leviticus **11:**140
- *see also:* Asham
Sinoi (angel), *see* Snwy
Sins, confession of, *see* CONFESSION OF SINS
Sinsheim (tn., Ger.) **4:**59
Sinsinoi (angel), *see* Snwy
Sin-uballit (deity), *see* SANBALLAT
Sinuhe, Story of (anc. Egy.) **6:**479; **6:**484
Sinyavski, Andrey **5:**1291; **14:**512
SINZHEIM, JOSEPH DAVID BEN ISAAC **14:**1616
- chronological chart **8:**766-767
- homiletical literature **8:**956
- Notables Assembly **3:**763
- Sanhedrin, French **14:**841
- *Sefer Ḥasidim* **2:**177
- Strasbourg printing **15:**424
- *illus:*
-- text
-- French Sanhedrin session (1807) **14:**841
Sion (mt., Jer.), *see* ZION
Sion (Zion. gr., Arg.) **16:**1123
Sion (newsp.) *see* DEN
Sion, Fathers of (Chr. cong.) **13:**1571
Sion, Sisters of (Chr. cong.) **13:**1571
Sion, Yael, *see* Dayan, Yael
Sionistichka Tribuna (Zion. orgn., Bul.) **16:**1109
Sionistsko-Sotsialisticheskaya Rabochaya Partiya (Rus.), *see* ZIONIST SOCIALIST WORKERS' PARTY
Sioux City (city, Ia.) **8:**1437
Sipley, Lewis Walton **13:**486
SIPONTO (tn., It.) **14:**1617
- Apulia **3:**227
- excavation **16:**1507
- Sepharvaim **14:**1177
- Sippar (city, Mesop.) **16:**1485
Sippud (Bib. sign), *see Otiyyot menuẓẓarot*
SIPRUTINI, EMANUEL **14:**1617
Sipyaghin (polit.) **11:**1148
Siq, Al- (gorge, Er. Isr.) **9:**177; **13:**341
- Crusaders **9:**268
Siqlāb River (Er. Isr.) **9:**178
Siracides (Apoc. work), *see* BEN SIRA, WISDOM OF
Sirah, Wisdom of, see BEN SIRA, WISDOM OF
Sirāj (wk.), *see Commentary to the Mishnah*
ŠiTaya (masor. term) **16:**1432
Sir Bevis of Hampton (wk.) **4:**1276
Sirbonic, Lake (Middle East) **14:**16
SIRET (tn., Rum.) **14:**1618
Sirgunya (vill., Er. Isr.), *see* Serungiya
SIRILLO, SOLOMON BEN JOSEPH **14:**1618
- Jerusalem Talmud **15:**777
Sirilyo, Samuel ibn, *see* SID, SAMUEL IBN
Sirion, *see* HERMON, MOUNT
Sirizli, Yom Tov ben Elijah, *see* ISRAEL, YOM TOV BEN ELIJAH
SIRKES, JOEL **14:**1619
- chronological chart **8:**766-767
- codification of law **5:**647; **5:**654
- Council of the Four Lands **5:**999
- *haggahot* **7:**1109
- *illus:* text
Sir Leon of Paris (tos.), *see* JUDAH BEN ISAAC
Sirluck, Ernest **16:**551
Sir Morel, *see* SAMUEL BEN SOLOMON OF FALAISE
Široký (polit., Cz.) **5:**1202
SIROTA, GERSHON **14:**1620
- *ḥazzanut* **7:**1444
- records **13:**1617
- *illus:*
-- concert for Sholem Asch **12:**660
Sis (bird), *see* SWIFT
SISEBUT (k., Sp.) **14:**1621
- forced conversions **3:**170
- Spain **15:**220
Sisenand (k., Sp.) **15:**220
SISERA (bib. fig.) **14:**1621
- Arts **5:**1432
- Benjamites **4:**525
- Jael **9:**1247
- Judges, The Book of **10:**445
- *illus:*
-- slain by Jael **9:**1247
Sisinnios (saint) **11:**247
Sisitsky, Alan **15:**319
SISKIND, AARON **14:**1622
Siskind, Edward **15:**308
Sisó, Astruc Jacob **4:**1530; **14:**1110
Sistan (reg.), *see* Seistan
Sister (fam. member) **6:**1167
Sisterhood Sabbath (Ref. Jud.) **14:**574
SISTERON (tn.,Fr.) **14:**1623
Sisters of Sion (Chr. cong.), *see* Sion, Sisters of
Sistine Chapel (Rome) **2:**244; **4:**939; **5:**1071; **10:**133,460
- *illus:*
-- "Creation of Adam" **5:**1068
-- "Deluge" **6:**1353
-- Jeremiah **4:**940
-- Joel **10:**133
SITBON (fam., Tun.) **14:**1623
Sitbon, Abraham **14:**1623
Sitbon, Joseph **14:**1623
Sitbon, Judah **14:**1623
Sitbon, Samuel **14:**1623
Sithon, Shaul **3:**421
Sitis (leg. fig.) **10:**129
Sitkov, Issachar **7:**1066
Sitnah (loc., Er. Isr.) **7:**432
Sitra aḥra (Kab. conc.)
- Kabbalah **10:**531; **10:**551
- Lurianic cosmogony **10:**596
- original sin **10:**608
- problem of evil **10:**584ff
Sitrei Otiyyot (kab. wk.) **16:**1196
Sitrei Torah (kab. wk.) **10:**494; **16:**1196
Sitriyyah (mosh., Isr.) **1:**place list
Sittenfeld, Julius **4:**654; **13:**1111; **13:**1373
Sittin, Al-(shrine, Er. Isr.) **14:**1402
"Sitting Old Man" (lith., J. Budko) **4:**1456
SIVAN (Heb. month **14:**1623
- *illus:* text

- *see also:* CALENDAR
Sivan, Aryeh **8:**206
Sivan, Twentieth of (fast day) **4:**1113; **5:**482
Sivan press (Isr.) **13:**1378
Si vera sunt (papal bull) **4:**1496
Sivitz, Herman **15:**1262
Sivitz, Simon **13:**569
SIX-DAY WAR **14:**1624
- *Contents:*
- - Background **14:**1624
- - The Arab Threat **14:**1626
- - Israel Strikes Back **14:**1628
- - Jerusalem and the Jordanian Front **14:**1629
- - The 2nd Day **14:**1630
- - The 3rd Day-the Capture of Jerusalem **14:**1635
- - The 4th Day-Israel's Forces Reach the Suez **14:**1636
- - The 5th and 6th Days-the Golan Heights Taken **14:**1637
- - After the Six-Day War **14:**1638
- Alexandrian Jews **2:**594
- Arab national movement **9:**468
- Arab refugees **15:**1550
- Borges' poems **15:**255
- cartoons **5:**178
- cease fire lines **9:**321
- Dayan, Moshe **5:**1374
- defense forces **9:**697
- Diaspora Jewry **16:**1062
- historical survey **9:**404ff
- Israel-Rumania relations **14:**416
- Jerusalem **9:**1498
- Kissufim **10:**1076
- Lebanon **10:**1545
- letters of Israel soldiers **11:**62
- migrations **16:**1527
- Nasser **12:**843
- partition plans **13:**39
- responsa concerning **14:**94ff
- Russia, Zionism in **16:**1139
- Sinai Campaign **14:**1607
- Temple Mount **15:**993
- Tiran Straits **14:**1316
- Turkey **15:**1063
- U.N.resolutions **15:**1556
- UNEF withdrawal **15:**1556
- U.S. government policy **15:**1666
- U.S. Jews **15:**1647
- U.S.S.R. stand **16:**1063ff
- Vatican **16:**78
- Western Wall **16:**472
- *illus:*
- - text
- - Agron (Mamilla) Road **9:**1497,1498
- - Arab family crossing Jordan **9:**450
- - Brussels demonstration **4:**422
- - Centurion tank unit **9:**696
- - dancing at the Western Wall **12:**672
- - Dayan and Hitler (cartoons) **3:**155-156
- - Dayan entering Jerusalem **9:**409
- - Egyptian stamp **12:**842
- - Eshkol meeting religious leaders **9:**410
- - Eshkol with soldiers **9:**409
- - Goren, Shlomo **7:**809
- - Hebron **8:**233,234
- - "Israeli extremists' appetite" (cartoon) **3:**135
- - Israel pre-war position (cartoon) **7:**328
- - Israel stamps **9:**844-845
- - Jerusalem, first anniversary of reunification **9:**1503
- - Jerusalem, Lions' Gate breakthrough **8:**777
- - Kefar Ḥabad bar-mitzvah celebration for orphans **9:**904; **10:**883
- - letter in *Sunday Times* **6:**86
- - Los Angeles mass rally **11:**503
- - paratroopers boarding plane **9:**695
- - Sharm el-Sheikh **14:**1316
- - tanks, Golan Heights **9:**409
- - Tel Aviv, filling sandbags **9:**406
- - U.N. (cartoon. Herblock) **4:**1111
- - U.N. Gaza force **7:**343; **9:**406
- - victory coin **5:**733
- - Warsaw, desecrated tombstone **13:**782
- - Washington, D.C., demonstration in support of Israel **16:**1145
- - Western Wall **9:**901, 1499
- - Western Wall wedding party **11:**1045
- - wounded soldier's arrival at Hadassah Hospital **9:**990
- - Zion Gate commemorative plaque **9:**1427
- *maps:*
- - text
- - Administered Territories **9:**623
- - cease-fire lines **9:**318
SIXTUS IV (pope) **14:**1641
- Avignon Jews **3:**966
- papal bull **4:**1496
- popes **13:**856
Sixtus V (pope)
- censorship **5:**277
- Inquisition **8:**1398; **8:**1400
- papal bull **4:**1496
- popes **13:**858
- *illus:*
- - censorship of the Talmud (1589) **5:**277
SIXTUS OF SIENA **14:**1641
SIYYUM (ceremony) **14:**1642
- *illus:* text
- *see also* HADRAN
Sjöbring, P. **8:**58
SJUF-Bladet (period.) **13:**1048
S. K. (nov.), *see* KOHN, SALOMON
Skaest, A. **16:**1509
SKALAT (tn., Ukr.) **14:**1642
Skandari, Abraham **5:**892
Skarbowe Niggunim (Pol. tunes), *see* MI-SINAI NIGGUNIM
SKARGA, PIOTR **14:**1643
SKARZYSKO-KAMIENNA (tn., Pol.) **14:**1644
- labor camp **5:**1214; **13:**767
Skating (sport) **15:**316
Skazinets (vill., Ukr.) **14:**1119; **15:**1333
SKEPTICS AND SKEPTICISM **14:**1644
SKIDEL (tn., Belor.) **14:**1645
SKIERNIEWICE (tn., Pol.) **14:**1646
Skiing (sport) **15:**317
Skin (meas.), *see Nevel*
Skin diseases **11:**143; **11:**1180
SKINK (reptile) **14:**1646
- dietary laws **6:**36
- *illus:* text
Skinner, Ralph **8:**58
Skins (animal) **15:**1036ff
Sklar, Isaac **8:**797
SKLARE, MARSHALL **14:**1647
Sklower, D. **6:**330
Skokie (sub., Chicago) **5:**415; **8:**1255
SKOLE (city, Ukr.) **14:**1647
Skolsky, Sidney **10:**307
SKOPLJE (Skopje; city, Yug.) **14:**1648
- Nathan of Gaza **14:**1241
- Yugoslavia **16:**872; **16:**880
- *illus:* text
Skorovey, Joseph Samuel **10:**399
SKOSS, SOLOMON LEON (Zalman Leib) **14:**1649
- Cairo *genizah* **16:**1336
- linguistic literature **16:**1376
Skotnicki, Alexander **13:**91; **13:**775
Skoulidhis, Manolis Georgiou **7:**887
Skulasson, Torlak **4:**877
SKULNIK, MENASHA **14:**1650
- recordings **13:**1617
- *illus:*
- - *Jacobowsky and the Colonel* **15:**1068
Skulsky, Shlomo **10:**268
SKUODAS (city, Lith.) **14:**1650
Skutsh, David **14:**1106
Skver (city, Ukr.), *see* SKVIRA
Skver (ḥas. dyn.), *see* TWERSKY
SKVIRA (city, Ukr.) **14:**1651
Skwarczyński, General **12:**1540
Skylark (bird) **6:**30
SLANDER **14:**1651
- ethics **6:**933
- flogging **6:**1349
- imprisonment **8:**1302; **8:**1303
- insult **8:**1409
- punishment **13:**1389
- Yose ben Zimra on **16:**857
- *see also:* LASHON HA-RA
Slanderers, *see* INFORMERS
Slánský, Rudolf **5:**1201; **13:**1026; **14:**1653
SLÁNSKÝ TRIAL **14:**1653
- Goldstuecker, Eduard **7:**750
- Israel-Czechoslovakian relations **9:**387; **9:**429
- Mapam **11:**914
- Simone, Andre **14:**1584
- Stalin **15:**328
Ślask (reg., central Eur.), *see* SILESIA
SLATKINE, MENAHEM MENDEL **14:**1655
Slaughter, Edward **8:**58
Slaughter, ritual, *see* SHEḤITAH
"Slaughterhouse" (paint., Chagall) **14:**1341
"Slaughterhouse" (paint., Y. Krize) Fig. 101 3-ART
Slaughter of stolen animals, *see* THEFT AND ROBBERY
Slavek (resist.), *see* Kozinets, Isay Pavlovich
Slave Labor (W.W.II), *see* FORCED LABOR
SLAVERY (leg.) **14:**1655
- abduction **2:**55ff
- adultery of "designated" slave woman **2:**314; **2:**316
- agricultural employment **2:**395
- *Avodah Zarah* **3:**981
- bailment laws **14:**1456
- brotherhood of man **11:**843
- Commandments, the 613 **5:**767f, 778
- debt bondage **6:**1008; **6:**1010; **12:**1312
- ethics **6:**933
- fraud against **7:**111
- freedom **7:**117ff
- gratuity on freedom **7:**1003
- *Haggadah,* Passover, and **7:**1079
- *ḥazakah* on slaves **7:**1521
- labor law and servant **10:**1325; **10:**1329
- lien **11:**230; **11:**231
- Minor Tractates **12:**49
- non-Jewish law, force of **6:**51
- overreaching **12:**1392ff
- Pentateuch **13:**246,254
- slave trade **14:**1660
- strangers and gentiles **15:**420
- surety **15:**524
- theft **5:**1098
- tort liability **11:**185
- witnesses **16:**586
- *illus:*
- - bill of emancipation **14:**1663
- - Joseph being sold **13:**354
- - Pithom and Ramses, building by Hebrew slaves **13:**1544
- *see also:* Servant
SLAVE TRADE (hist.) **14:**1660
- Agobard **8:**662
- Argentinian Jews **3:**415ff
- Cairo *genizah* **16:**1339
- Christian slaves **5:**546; **9:**1119
- Constantius II's prohibition **8:**653
- economic life **16:**1269
- Hurrian customs **12:**1288; **12:**1289ff
- Jewish slaves **7:**424
- Koran **10:**1198
- merchant class in ancient Israel **8:**614
- mythical Jewish role in **16:**1281
- Raphall, M. J. **13:**1551
- servants of Solomon **15:**116
- social structure of ancient Israel **8:**615
- tattoos **16:**664
- Toledo **15:**1203
- trade and commerce **15:**1297ff
- U.S. **12:**932
- Wise's position **16:**564
- *illus:* text
Slaveykov, P. R. **4:**886
Slavic languages **4:**884
- Hebrew linguistics **16:**1397
Slavin, Ḥayyim **7:**1072
Slavinski, Maxim **9:**1180
Slavkov u Brna (tn., Morav.), *see* AUSTERLITZ
Slavney, Morris **16:**556
Slavonia (reg. of Croatia, Yug.) **16:**868ff
Slavonic (lang.), *see* Slavic languages
Slavonic Book of Enoch, *see* ENOCH, SLAVONIC BOOK OF
Slavonic Countries **3:**720
SLAVSON, SAMUEL RICHARD **14:**1664
SLAVUTA (city, Ukr.) **14:**1665
- Talmud printing dispute **2:**129
- Vilna printing and **16:**148
Sławek (law.), *see* GROSSER, BRONISŁAW
SŁAWOJ-SKŁADKOWSKI, FELICJAN **14:**1665
SLAWSON, JOHN **14:**1666
- *illus:*
- - A. J. C. delegation to Pope Paul VI, 1964 **5:**543
Slaying (by sword) **5:**143
Sleep
- condition of soul **4:**1165
- criminal responsibility **13:**225
- synagogue **15:**593ff
- washing hands **12:**998
- *see also:* DREAMS
Sleidanus, J., *see* Schleidan, J.
SLEPIAN, JOSEPH **8:**1434
- Pittsburgh **13:**570
Slevogt, Paul, *see* Schlevogt, Paul
Sleznick, Eugene **15:**316
Slezsko (Reg., central Eur.), *see* SILESIA
Slimān al-Kāreh **13:**1451
Slimmer, Abraham **8:**1438
Sling (weapon) **16:**270
Šling, Otto **14:**1653
Slinger (tn., Wis) **16:**555
Slinin, Moshe **2:**837
SLIOZBERG, HENRY **14:**1666
- relief work **16:**734
Slobodka (tn., Ukr.) **12:**1326
- Kaunas **10:**847ff
SLOBODKA YESHIVAH **14:**1668
- Epstein, Moses **6:**835
- Hebron **8:**235; **9:**341
- Kaunas **10:**847
- Mussar movement **12:**536
- *yeshivot* **16:**769
- *illus:* text
Slobodnik, Wlodzimierz **13:**802
Slobotzki, E. **7:**92
Sloka (city, Latv.) **14:**173

Sloman, Charles **15:**1091
SLOMAN, HENRY (Solomon) **15:**1054,1091
Sloman, M. G. **11:**1285
Slomka, Samuel **10:**1540
SLOMOVITZ, PHILIP **10:**317
Slonik, Abraham **14:**1670
SLONIK, BENJAMIN AARON BEN ABRAHAM **14:**1669
- Podgaitsy **13:**666
Slonik, Faivel **14:**1670
Slonik, Jakel **14:**1670
SLONIM (city, Belor.) **14:**1671
- Baranovichi **4:**197
- ghetto **13:**770
SLONIM (ḥas. dyn.) **14:**1672
- dynasties **1:**ḥas. table
- ḥasidic music **7:**1423; **7:**1426
- Shapira, Joshua **14:**1299
- town **14:**1672
Slonim, Joel **16:**896
SLONIM, MARC **14:**516
Slonim, Reuben **15:**1264
Slonimer, Isaac **10:**724
Slonimer, Yoshe, *see* ALTSCHUL, JOSEPH
Slonimski, Alexander **14:**1675
SLONIMSKI, ANTONI **14:**1673
SLONIMSKI, ḤAYYIM SELIG **14:**1674
- *ha-Ẓefirah* **7:**1529; **16:**340
- Society for the Promotion of Culture **15:**58ff
SLONIMSKI, LEONID ZINOVYEVICH **14:**1675
SLONIMSKI, MIKHAIL LEONIDOVICH **14:**1675
SLONIMSKY, HENRY **14:**1676
SLONIMSKY, NICOLAS **12:**709
- Slonimski, Hayyim **14:**1675
- Slonimski, Leonid **14:**1675
Slonim Vort (newsp.) **14:**1673
Slonkovic, Martinus **8:**58
Sloss (fam.) **5:**56; **14:**834
Sloss, Louis **7:**224,520
SLOSS, MARCUS CAUFFMAN **14:**1676
- California **5:**56; **14:**834
Sloth, *see* Idleness
SLOTKI, ISRAEL WOLF **14:**1677
Slotki, Judah Jacob **14:**1677
Slotkin, James S. **3:**40
Slouschz, David Solomon **14:**1677
SLOUSCHZ, NAHUM **14:**1677
- Hammath synagogue **7:**1243
- Jerusalem **9:**1535
Slovak (lang.), *see* Slavic languages
SLOVAKIA (reg.) **14:**1678
- Church and Nazism **8:**914; **8:**915
- Holocuast **5:**1195; **8:**851; **8:**900
- Hungary **8:**1096
- partisans **13:**147
- Reik, Ḥavivah **14:**54
- *illus:*
- - Jewish badge decreed by the Nazis **4:**72
- *see also:* CZECHOSLOVAKIA
Slovak People's Party **15:**1155; **15:**1427
Slovenia (rep., Yug.) **16:**868ff
Slovensko (reg.), *see* SLOVAKIA
Slowacki, Juliusz **13:**798,799
Slowakei (reg.), *see* SLOVAKIA
Slowo Mlodych (period.) **7:**806
Sluck (tn., Belor.), *see* SLUTSK
SLUCKI, ABRAHAM JACOB **14:**1681
Sluter, Claus **9:**69; **9:**1360; **12:**406
SLUTSK (tn., Belor.) **14:**1682
- yeshivah **14:**1668
SLUTSKI, BORIS ABRAMOVICH **14:**1683
SLUTSKY, YEHUDA **1:**37
SLUTZKI, DAVID **14:**1684
Sluyser, Meyer **6:**321
Smadja (art.) **13:**118
Smadja, Pierre (sol.) **11:**1567
Smalridge, George **8:**58
Smaragd (gem) **13:**1009
Smederevo (tn., Yug.) **12:**1161; **16:**869
SMELA (city, Ukr.) **15:**1
SMELSER, NEIL JOSEPH **15:**1
SMEND, RUDOLPH **15:**2
Smendes (k., Egy.) **16:**658
Smerdis (k., Haran) **14:**728
Smichov (sub., Prague) **10:**1403
Smidovich (Sov. ldr.) **16:**779
SMILANSKY, MEIR **15:**2
SMILANSKY, MOSHE **15:**3
- Hebrew literature **8:**198
Smilansky, Yizhar, *see* YIZHAR, S.
Smirnov, V. N. **2:**420; **11:**220; **15:**39
Smith, Sir Archibald Levin **15:**312
Smith, Eli **4:**887
Smith, Frederick **8:**58
SMITH, SIR GEORGE ADAM **15:**4
- Assyrian archaeology **16:**1507
Smith, Goldwin **5:**110
Smith, Issy **11:**1553
Smith, John **8:**58 **8:**209
SMITH, JOHN MERLIN POWIS **15:**4
Smith, Joseph **16:**1154
Smith, Louis **15:**311
Smith, Miles **8:**58
SMITH, MORTON **15:**4
Smith, Pauline **15:**208
Smith, Thomas **8:**58
SMITH, WILLIAM ROBERTSON **15:**5
Smiths (craft) **16:**1270
Smithville (tn., Ont.) **8:**254; **12:**1408
SMN (pseud.), *see* HEILPRIN, PHINEHAS MENAHEM
Smnglf (angel), *see* Samengelof
Smofsky, Harry **11:**998
SMOIRA, MOSHE **15:**5
- *illus:*
- - Supreme Court bench **9:**637
Smoking **7:**1405; **15:**1176
SMOL (Samuel; court J., Ger.) **15:**6
SMOLAR, HERSH **15:**6
- Minsk **12:**55
SMOLENSK (city, Rus.) **15:**6
SMOLENSKIN, PEREZ **15:**7
- *Contents:*
- - Early Life **15:**7
- - Early Literary Career **15:**8
- - Founder and Manager of Ha-Shaḥar **15:**8
- - Financial Difficulties **15:**9
- - As Novelist **15:**9
- - Philosopher of Jewish Nationalism **15:**11
- - General Evaluation **15:**12
- Ahavat Zion **4:**984
- Beilinson **4:**398
- Ben-Yehuda **4:**568
- Braudes **4:**1316
- Brill, Joseph **4:**1375
- chronological chart **8:**766-767
- critic **5:**1118
- Guenzburg, Mordecai **7:**964
- Hacohen, Mordecai **7:**1038
- *Ha-Shaḥar* **7:**1366
- Haskalah **7:**1450; **8:**188
- Kadimah **10:**666
- Reform Judaism **16:**1037
- Shakespeare in Hebrew **14:**1263
- Vienna **16:**127
- *illus:*
- - *Ha-Shaḥar* (Vienna, 1868) **7:**1367
Smolenskin, Y. L. **7:**1368
SMOLI, ELIEZER (Smoler) **15:**12
Smollett, Tobias **6:**778
SMORGON (Smorgonie; tn., Belor.) **15:**12
Smouha, Ellis R. **12:**1376
Smrzovka (tn., Bohem.) **9:**1174
Smuggling **8:**1302; **16:**210
Smuḥa, Sasson, *see* HA-LEVI, SASSON BEN ELIJAH BEN MOSES
Smukler, David **15:**308
SMUTS, JAN CHRISTIAAN **15:**13
- Balfour Declaration **4:**135
- South Africa **15:**190ff
- Zionism **16:**1140
- *illus:*
- - Johannesburg presentation **15:**205
Smy (J. prophet) **4:**137
Smyrna (city, Turk.), *see* IZMIR
Smyslov, Vassili Vassilyevich **5:**407
Snail (zool.) **3:**19; **6:**38; **15:**913
- *illus:*
- - *tekhelet* **15:**914
Snaith, N. H. **4:**839
SNAKE (zool.) **15:**14
- dietary laws **6:**36
- Eve **6:**979
- evil inclination **8:**1319
- evolution **6:**1003
- paradise **13:**77ff
- viper reproduction **4:**1017
- *illus:*
- - Chrysanow tombstone **15:**1226
- - Dan emblem **12:***fcg.* 1259
- - enemies of Judah **16:**49
- - Seraph **14:**1180
- - temptation of Adam and Eve **2:**242; **4:**856, 1050
- *see also:* COPPER SERPENT, THE; POISON; SERAPH
Snake Pool (Jer.) **9:**1539; **9:**1541
Snapper, Isadore **11:**1200
SNEERSOHN, ḤAYYIM ẒEVI **15:**15
- *illus:* text
Sneezing **6:**1407
SNEH, MOSHE **15:**16
- Mapam **11:**914
- *illus:*
- - Haganah High Command **7:**1070
Snell, Harry **9:**344; **13:**31; **13:**32
Śniatyń (city, Ukr.), *see* SNYATYN
Snider, Edward M. **15:**316
Snife (bird) **6:**30
Snir, *see* HERMON, MOUNT
Snoeck, A. L. **11:**1167
Snow **9:**583
"Snow" (drg., Lesser Ury) **3:**552
Snow, C. P. **6:**782
Snowden, Earl of, *see* Armstrong-Jones, Anthony
Snow water **15:**19
S. N. S. (army gp., Er. Isr.), *see* Special Night Squads
Snuff **15:**1176
Snwy (angel) **6:**1400; **11:**246
- *illus:*
- - amulet **5:**1525
SNYATYN (city, Ukr.) **15:**17
Snydacker, Godfrey **5:**411
Snyder, A. Cecil **16:**1555
Snyder, Baron **3:**886
SNYDER, LOUIS LEO **8:**550
SO (k., Egy.) **15:**18
SOAP **15:**18
- crafts **5:**1052
- Jerusalem industry **9:**1423
- *illus:*
- - text
- - German factory near Danzig **13:**761
SOARE, IULIA **14:**421; **14:**427
SOAVE, MOISE **15:**19
Soba (loc., Er. Isr.) **13:**1439
Sobata (city, Er. Isr.), *see* SHIVTAH
SOBEDRUHY (tn., Bohem.) **15:**19
SOBEL, BERNARD **15:**1091
- public relations **13:**1361
SOBEL, JACOB ẒEVI **15:**20
Sobell, Michael **15:**311
Sobell, Morton **14:**280
SOBELOFF, ISIDOR **15:**20
- public relations **13:**1362
SOBELOFF, SIMON ERNEST **15:**20
Sobelsohn, Karl, *see* RADEK, KARL
SOBIBOR (concen. camp, Pol.) **15:**21
- Amsterdam Jews **2:**903
- Holocaust **8:**879; **8:**894
- Pechersky, Alexander **13:**201
- *illus:* text
- *see also:* CAMPS (CONCENTRATION AND EXTERMINATION)
Sobieski, Jan III (k., Pol.) **2:**149
Soble, James H., *see* SOBEL, JACOB ẒEVI
Soble, Kenneth D. **7:**1239
SOBOL, ANDREY MIKHAILOVICH **15:**22
Sobol, Louis **10:**307
Soborten (tn., Bohem.), *see* SOBEDRUHY
SOBOTKA, HARRY HERMAN **5:**387
SOBRE (neo-Nazi orgn.), *see* Sozialorganische Bewegung Europas
Sobremonte, Tomás Treviño de, *see* TREVIÑO DE SOBREMONTE, TOMÁS
Soccer (sport) **15:**298
- *illus:* **15:**293,298
SOCHACZEW (city, Pol.) **15:**23
- Host desecration **8:**1043
SOCHACZEW, ABRAHAM BEN ZE'EV NAHUM BORNSTEIN OF **15:**24
- dynasties **1:**ḥas. table
- responsa **14:**91
- Torah study **7:**1397
- Weingarten, Joab Joshua **16:**402
Sochatshever Tsaytung (period.) **15:**24
Social and Religious History of the Jews (bk.) **4:**254; **8:**562
Social behaviour, *see* Social life, Jewish
Social Credit (polit. mvmt., Can.) **5:**110
Social-Democratic Bund (party, Rus.) **2:**170
Social-Democratic Party (Ger.) **15:**25ff
Social Insurance, Israel **9:**994
SOCIALISM **15:**24
- *Contents:*
- - Introduction **15:**24
- - France **15:**25
- - Great Britain **15:**25
- - Germany **15:**25
- - The 1st International **15:**26
- - The 2nd International **15:**26
- - 1914-1939 **15:**26
- - Post World War II **15:**27
- - Eastern Europe **15:**28
- - Poland and Rumania **15:**29
- - United States **15:**29
- - Latin America **15:**32
- - Asia and Africa **15:**32
- - Anarchism **15:**32
- - Socialism and the Jews **15:**34
- Austria **3:**897
- Lassalle, Ferdinand **10:**1441
- Martov, Julius **11:**1067
- Marx, Karl **11:**1071
- politics **13:**807
- socialism, Jewish **15:**38
- Trotski's theory **15:**1406
- *Yevsektsiya* **16:**779
- *see also:* COMMUNISM
SOCIALISM, JEWISH **15:**38
- *Contents:*

- - The Beginnings of the Movement **15:**38
- - The Bund **15:**41
- - Zionist Socialism **15:**43
- - Europe Outside Russia **15:**46
- - The United States **15:**46
- - Relations with the Communist Party **15:**48
- - Pioneering Youth Movements **15:**50
- - Later Developments **15:**51
- Aguddat ha-Sozyalistim ha-Ivrim **2:**410
- Blum, Leon **4:**1138
- Borochov, Ber **4:**1256
- kibbutz movement **10:**964
- Lithuania **11:**371
- Mapam **16:**1010
- Po'alei Zion **13:**656
- Zhitlowsky, Chaim **16:**1010
- *illus:*
- - Workmen's Circle, early leaders **12:**1095; **16:**636
- *see also:* BUND; COMMUNISM; COOPERATIVES; JEWISH SOCIALIST WORKERS' PARTY
Socialism, Zionist
- Borochov, Ber **4:**1253ff
- Communist Movement and **5:**792ff
- Idelson, Abraham **8:**1225
- socialism, Jewish **15:**43
- Zhitlowsky, Chaim **16:**1011
- *see also:* MAPAI
Socialist League (Er. Isr.) **10:**969
Socialist Pro-Palestine Committee (1928) **4:**1138
Socialist Reich Party (neo-Nazi polit. party) **12:**954
Socialist Workers' Party (Isr.), *see* Mifleget Po'alim Sozialistim
Socialist Workers' Party, Jewish, *see* JEWISH SOCIALIST WORKERS' PARTY
Socialist Yiddish Schools (U.S.) **6:**436
Social Justice (mag.) **15:**1655
Social life, Jewish
- fourth to seventh centuries **8:**655
- Ḥasidism **7:**1390
- law and morality **10:**1480
- Muslim conquest of Erez Israel **8:**659
- old age **2:**346
- Poland **13:**718ff
- 16/17 centuries **8:**698
- Solomon **15:**100ff
- *Tohorot ha-Kodesh* **15:**1191
- Yemen **16:**743ff
- *see also:* ANTI-SEMITISM: ASSIMILATION
Social-Revolutionary Party (Switz.) **15:**29
SOCIAL SECURITY AND WELFARE IN ISRAEL **9:**993
- care for aged **2:**348
- family allowances **9:**865
- I. C. A.'s activities **10:**49
- sociology **15:**69
SOCIAL STRUCTURE OF ANCIENT ISRAEL **8:**609
- agriculture **2:**382ff
- Ahab's rule **2:**438
- *Am ha-Arez* **2:**834
- Chieftain **5:**420
- Commandments, the 613 **5:**769
- family **6:**1164ff
- old age **2:**346
- widow **16:**487
Social welfare, *see* CHARITY; PHILANTHROPY
Socianus, Faustus **11:**1337
Sociedad Agrícola Lucienville (Arg.), *see* Primera Sociedad Agrícola Israelita
Sociedad de Sociedades (Peru) **16:**1125
Sociadade Beneficente das Damas Israelitas (Braz.) **10:**1085; **14:**191
SOCIEDAD HEBRAICA ARGENTINA (orgn.) **15:**52
- A.M.I.A **2:**837
- Latin America **10:**1454
Sociedad Jacob Gordin (theat. gr., Arg.) **15:**1073
Sociedad Mercantil de Peleteros (Arg.) **7:**226
Societatea De cultura Israelita (Rum.) **4:**200
Société Biblique de Paris (Bib. soc.) **4:**969
Société d'Encouragement et de Secours (Fr.), *see* Comité de Bienfaisance Israélite de Paris
SOCIÉTÉ DES ÉTUDES JUIVES (Fr.) **15:**52
- Jewish studies **16:**577
- Kahn, Zadoc **10:**694
- learned societies **15:**54
SOCIETIES, LEARNED **15:**53
- *Contents:*
- - Early 19th-Cent. **15:**53
- - Later 19th-Cent. **15:**53
- - Publishing Scholarly Works **15:**53
Society, *see* ḤEVRAH, ḤAVURAH
Society for the Advancement of Judaism (U.S.) **13:**1616
SOCIETY FOR THE ATTAINMENT OF FULL CIVIL RIGHTS FOR THE JEWISH PEOPLE IN RUSSIA **15:**56
Society for Christian-Jewish Understanding (Ger.) **7:**498
Society for the Culture and Science of Judaism (Ger.), *see* VEREIN FUER KULTUR UND WISSENSCHAFT DES JUDENTUMS
Society for Ethical Culture (U.S.) **2:**276
Society for the History of the Jews in the Czechoslovak Republic **8:**564
SOCIETY FOR JEWISH FOLK MUSIC (St. Petersburg) **15:**57
- Achron, Joseph **2:**211
- Engel, Joel **6:**744
- Leningrad **11:**17
Society for Jewish Writers and Journalists (Pol.) **12:**1210
Society for Manual and Agricultural Work among Jews, *see* ORT
Society for Promoting Christian Knowledge (Bib. soc.) **4:**969
SOCIETY FOR THE PROMOTION OF CULTURE AMONG THE JEWS OF RUSSIA **15:**58
- *Contents:*
- - Foundation **15:**58
- - Ideological differences **15:**59
- - Publishing Activities **15:**59
- - Educational Activities **15:**60
- - Membership **15:**61
- - From the 1890s **15:**61
- Baratz, Hermann **4:**203
- history chart **8:**766-767
- education **6:**424
- Russia **14:**455,464
- scholarly publications **15:**53
- *illus:*
- - Nizhni-Novgorod exhibition **14:**441
Society for the Promotion of Handicrafts and Agriculture among Hungarian Jews **14:**1015
Society for the Promotion of Jewish Settlement (Rus.) **14:**468, 472
- Yevsektsiya **16:**780
Society for the Propagation of Enlightenment (Rus.), *see* SOCIETY FOR THE PROMOTION OF CULTURE AMONG THE JEWS OF RUSSIA
Society for the Protection of Artisans and Traders (Ger.) **3:**79
Society for the Protection of the Health of the Jews, *see* OZE
Society for the Safeguarding of the Health of the Jewish Population, *see* TOZ
Society for the Science of Judaism in the Netherlands, *see* Genootschap voor Joodsche Wetenschap in Nederland
Society for Spreading Artisan and Agricultural Work Among Jews, *see* ORT
Society for the Support of Agricultural Workers and Craftsmen of Syria and Erez Israel (Rus.) **12:**324
Society of American Historians **7:**721
Society of the Friends of Reform (Ger.) **14:**24
Society of Israelitic Christians (Rus.) **2:**570
Society of Jesus (Cath. order), *see* JESUITS
Society of Jewish Bibliophiles (U.S.) **15:**55
Society of Jewish Studies (Fr.), *see* SOCIÉTÉ DES ÉTUDES JUIVES
Society of Lovers of Hebrew (Rus.), *see* Ḥovevei Sefat Ever
Socin, Albert **5:**1595
SOCIOLOGY **15:**62
- Durkheim's views **6:**308ff
- economic history **16:**1307
- Friedmann, Georges **7:**191
- Gumplowicz's views **7:**976ff
- Jewish contributions **8:**743
- Orthodoxy's influence **12:**1487ff
- population **13:**886ff
- Protestant revivalism **13:**1254
- universities **15:**1680
- vital statistics **16:**178ff
- *see also:* DEMOGRAPHY
SOCOH or SOCO (tn. Er. Isr.) **15:**69
Socor, Matei **14:**414
Socrates (philos.)
- Ahithophel **2:**466
- influence of Bible **3:**444
Sod (kab. conc.) **2:**644; **10:**623ff; **13:**91
Soda (min.) **15:**18
Sodei Razayya (wk.) **10:**516; **10:**518
Söderberg, Hjalmar Emil Fredrik **14:**929
Sod ha-shelah (kab. term) **7:**576
Sodicky, Solomon **15:**305
Sodilkow, Moses Ḥayyim Ephraim of, *see* MOSES HAYYIM EPHRAIM OF SUDYLKOW
Sodom (indus. site, Isr.), *see* Sedom
SODOM AND GOMORRAH (bib. tns.) **15:**70
- *Contents:*
- - General **15:**70
- - In the Aggadah **15:**70
- - Modern Times **15:**72
- - In the Arts **15:**73
- homosexuality **8:**961
- *illus:*
- - text
- - men of Sodom **4:**943
Sodom, Mountain of, *see* Jebel al-Sudūm
Sodom Potash Works (Isr.) **15:**72
- mining and industrial sites **9:**595
Sodomy **15:**71
- Commandments, the 613 **5:**781
- ethics **6:**935
- imprisonment **8:**1302
- sexual offenses **14:**1207
Sod Shem ha-Meforash (wk.) **15:**999
Soeiro, Samuel **6:**175; **11:**857
Soemis (k., Emesa) **3:**1010
Soesmans, Loeb **7:**1124
SOEST (tn., Ger.) **15:**74
Soest, Benedict, *see* Meyers, Benedict
Soeurs de Reparatrice convent (Jer.) **9:**1459
Soeurs de Sion monastery (Jer.) **9:**1458
- *illus:*
- - Aelia Capitolina ruins **9:**1402
- - Ecce Homo arch **9:**1401
Soeurs du Sainte Rosaire convent (Jer.) **9:**1459
SOFAER, ABRAHAM **15:**1091
SOFER (fam.) **15:**75
- *geneal. table:* text
- *illus:* text
Sofer, see SCRIBE; SOFERIM
Sofer, Abraham **15:**76
Sofer, Abraham Samuel Benjamin Wolf **15:**75; **15:**79
- *geneal. table* **4:**1310
Sofer, Akiva **15:**76
Sofer, Emanuel **15:**814
SOFER, ḤAYYIM BEN MORDECAI EPHRAIM FISCHEL **15:**77
Sofer, Joseph **13:**218; **14:**1508; **15:**1353
Sofer, Meir **6:**46; **11:**897; **13:**1102
SOFER, MOSES **15:**77
- Abony synagogue **2:**98
- Ashkenazi, Moses David **3:**730
- Aszod, Judah **3:**811
- Fuld, Aaron **7:**217
- *ḥiddushim* **8:**467
- history chart **8:**766-767
- Lag ba-Omer **12:**1388
- *meḥizah* **11:**1235
- Rapoport, Benjamin **13:**1554
- responsa **14:**91
- Schwerin-Goetz **14:**1033
- *geneal. tables* **4:**1310; **15:**76
- *illus:* text
Sofer, Nahum **15:**694
Sofer, Naphtali Hirsch **14:**199
Sofer, Simeon **15:**75; **15:**79
- assimilation **16:**1329
- Ornstein, Jacob **12:**1474
- Shomer Israel **14:**1459
Sofer, Simḥah Bunem **6:**311; **10:**827; **15:**76
- *geneal. table* **4:**1310
Sofer, Solomon **15:**76
Sofer, Wolf **14:**958
Sofer, Zussman **14:**958; **15:**1532
SOFERIM (scholars) **15:**79
- Bible interpretations **8:**1417
- Bible redaction **4:**833
- *halakhah* elements **7:**1158; **7:**1161
- Jewish law periods **12:**121
- origin **4:**889
- Pentateuch **13:**263
- sages **14:**636ff
- *zaken mamre* **16:**920
- title rabbi **13:**1445
- *see also:* SCRIBE; SYNAGOGUE, THE GREAT
SOFERIM (minor tract.) **15:**81
- prayer books **13:**985
- writing of Bible **16:**1406
Sofer setam (scribe) **14:**1043
Soffer, Alfred **11:**1202
SOFIA (city, Bul.) **15:**81
- Bulgaria **4:**1482ff
- museums **12:**543
- Shabbateanism **14:**1239
- *illus:*
- - Jewish badge decreed by the Nazis **4:**72
Sogane (tn., Er. Isr.), *see* SIKHNIN
Soghd (anc. prov., As.) **15:**1336
SOGLOW, OTTO **15:**82

– *New Yorker* 5:216
– *illus:*
– – "The Little King" 5:216
Soharet (gem) 13:1011
Soher, A. *see* HOROWITZ, HAYYIM DOV
SOISSONS (tn., Fr.) 15:83
SOKAL (tn., Ukr.) 15:83
Sokhachev (city, Pol.), *see* SOCHACZEW
Sokher valley (Er. Isr.) 12:745
Sokho (tn., Er. Isr.), *see* SOCOH, SOCO
SOKOLKA (tn., Pol.) 15:84
– ghetto 13:769
Sokolli (Sokollu), Mehemet (Mohammed Pasha) 3:732; 12:839
Sokolnikov, G. 5:794
Sokoloff, Nikolai 5:612
Sokolovski, A. 16:1179
SOKOLOW, ANNA 15:85
Sokolow, Florian 12:844; 16:75
Sokolow, Marie 16:1165
SOKOLOW, NAHUM 15:85
– Arab nationalists 16:1077
– Balfour Declaration 4:132ff
– Feuerberg, Mordecai Ze'ev 6:1251
– Goldbloom, Jacob Koppel 7:707
– *Ha-Asif* 7:1011
– *Ha-Zefirah* 7:1529
– history chart 8:767
– *Izraelita* 9:1166
– Salvador, Joseph 14:716
– Vatican 16:74
– Warsaw 16:340
– Writers' Association 16:652
– *illus:*
– – F.Z.C. 16:1165
– – Protest against Passfield White Paper 16:1118
– – Thirteenth Zionist Congress 16:1173
– – Weizmann, Chaim, and 16:429
SOKOLOW PODLASKI (tn., Pol.) 15:89
Sokolsky, Melvin 13:484
Sol, Robert 5:452
Sola, de (fam. name), *see also:* DE SOLA
SOLA, DE (fam.) 15:90
– El Salvador 6:687
Sola, Aaron de 15:90
Sola, Abraham de 15:90
Sola, Benjamin de (physic.) 15:90
Sola, Benjamin de (Curaçao) 15:90
Sola, David de (Amst.) 15:90
Sola, David de (Colom.) 5:745
Sola, David Aaron de (Eng.) 15:91
– Canadian descendants 5:1562
– Sephardi music 12:650
– *illus:*
– – oil painting 5:1562
Sola, Isaac de 15:90
Sola, Juan de (Isaac) 15:90
Sola, Raphael Samuel Mendes de 15:90
SOLAL (fam., N. Afr.) 15:91
Solal, Isaac ha-Kohen, *see* SHOLAL, ISAAC HA-KOHEN
Solal, Maimon 15:91
Solar Cycle 5:43
SOLDI (-Colbert), EMILE-ARTHUR 15:92
– medalists 11:1165
– *illus:* text
Soldiers 6:850
– *see also:* MILITARY SERVICE; WAR AND WARFARE
Soldiers' Committees, Jewish, *see* Jewish Soldiers' Committees
Soldyck, Emile-Arthur, *see* SOLDI, EMILE-ARTHUR
SOLEL BONEH (coop., Isr.) 15:92
– cooperatives 5:947
– Histadrut 8:540
– labor economy of Israel 9:851ff
– *illus:* text
Soler, Antonio 10:1376
Sol ha-Zaddikah, *see* HATCHWELL, SOL
Solidarity (co-op., Pol.) 5:944
SOLIELI, MORDECAI (MAX) 15:93
– encyclopedias 6:734
– *illus:*
– – *Razsvet* staff 13:1595
Solin (vill., Yug.) 15:288; 16:870
SOLINUS, CAIUS JULIUS 14:236
SOLIS (fam., Port.) 15:94
Solis, Benjamin de 15:94
Solis, Diego da 15:94
Solis, Diogo da Silva; *see* Solis, Isaac da Silva
Solis, Duarte da Silva 15:94; 15:1166
Solis, Duarte Gomes de 15:94
Solis, Eleazar, *see* Solis, Henrique
Solis, Fernando da Silva, *see* Solis, Isaac da Silva
Solis, Francisco da Silva 15:94; 15:1166
Solis, Henrique 15:94
Solis, Isaac (Diego) da Silva 15:94
Solis, Isaac (Fernando) da Silva 15:94; 15:1166
Solis, Joseph de 15:94
Solis, Rodriguez 15:1301
Solis, Simão Pires 11:302; 15:94
Solis, Solomon da Silva 15:94
SOLIS-COHEN (U.S. fam.) 15:95
– *geneal. table:* text
Solis-Cohen, David da 15:95
Solis-Cohen, Emily da Silva Jr. 15:95
Solis-Cohen, Jacob da 15:95
Solis-Cohen, Jacob da Silva Jr. 15:95
Solis-Cohen, Judith da Silva 15:95
Solis-Cohen, Leon da 15:95
Solis-Cohen, Myer da Silva 15:95
Solis-Cohen, Solomon da Silva 15:95
Solitude 14:653
Solkhat (city, Crimea), *see* Stary Krym
Sollinger, Mrs. J.P. 16:131
Solly, Henry 8:385
Solnik, Benjamin Aaron ben Abraham, *see* SLONIK, BENJAMIN AARON BEN ABRAHAM
SOLODAR, ABRAHAM 15:96
Sologub, Feodor 14:507
Solomo, Meir (Maehir) 4:1230
SOLOMON (k., Isr.) 15:96
– *Contents:*
– – Kingdom 15:97
– – Economy and Society 15:100
– – The Wise King and Judge 15:103
– – In the Aggadah 15:105
– – In Islam 15:108
– – In the Arts 15:108
– General
– – ablution 2:84
– – God's revelation 14:118
– – history 8:591
– – history chart 8:766-767
– – Mari parallels 11:977
– – realm designation 9:111
– – warfare 16:271
– Administration 9:116
– – Beth-Shemesh 4:773
– – corvée workers 5:977
– – Dor 6:172
– – priestly divisions 12:89
– – proscribed population 8:346ff
– – servants of Solomon 15:116
– – Tadmor 15:697
– – Transjordan 15:1317
– Architecture and Temple
– – altar 2:762ff
– – archaeological evidence 3:306
– – architecture 3:336
– – fortresses in Negev 12:928
– – Jerusalem archaeology 9:1524
– – Megiddo 11:1227
– – Mount of Olives 12:483
– – priestly ritual 13:1083
– – Solomon's palace 8:1049
– – Temple 15:943
– Economic History
– – economic life 16:1269
– – fleet of Tarshish 15:825
– – Jerusalem 9:1382
– – merchant fleet 14:1411
– – metals and mining 11:1428ff
– – taxation 15:840; 15:841
– – Timna mines 15:1146
– – trade and commerce 15:1294ff
– Foreign Relations
– – Ammonites 2:856
– – Hiram 8:501
– King, Kingship 10:1012ff
– – Abiathar 2:71; 13:1080
– – Abishag the Shunammite 2:79
– – Adonijah 2:295
– – Ahijah the Shilonite 2:459
– – Ahimaaz 2:462
– – anointing 3:31
– – Benaiah 4:458
– – Jerusalem 9:1550
– – Joab 10:107
– – Nathan 12:846
– – Shimei 14:1403
– – throne 15:1124; 15:812
– Legend and Literature
– – alchemist 2:543ff
– – Asmodeus 3:755ff
– – Ecclesiastes 6:349
– – Ethiopia 6:943
– – Eupolemus 6:964
– – folktales 6:1382, 1383
– – Greek literature 7:894ff
– – in the Arts 15:151,985
– – Kings, Book of 10:1022ff
– – parables 13:73
– – Proverbs, Book of 13:1268
– – Psalms, Book of 13:1318
– – *Solomon, Testament of* 15:118
– – Song of Songs 15:147
– – wisdom literature 16:557; 16:558
– *geneal. table:* 5:1341
– *illus:*
– – text
– – entering Jerusalem 10:1024
– – enthroned 2:355; 5:1
– – folk-art portrait 8:1286
– – holding a Bible (drg., Ben Shahn) 6:351
– – holding scepter 16:901
– – Islamic representation 5:1334
– – Judgment 3:527; 4:968; 5:130; 8:*fcg.* 1271; 11:*fcg.* 683 and 1355; 1269; 14:1061
– – Megiddo fortress gateway 3:316; 8:591; 11:1223
– – Megiddo plan 11:1225
– – Queen of Sheba 13:1425
– – Temple plan 15:9441 987
– – throne 8:649
– – Torah breastplate (c. 1775) 4:1339
– *map:*
– – kingdom 9:115
– *see also:* DAVID
SOLOMON (fam., Austr.) 15:111
SOLOMON (fam., St. Helena and S.A.) 15:112
Solomon (fam., U.S.) 3:450
Solomon (schol., Fr.) 15:1290
Solomon (hazzan, Er. Isr.) 15:123
Solomon (exil.) 7:321 8:1446
Solomon (Pol.) 15:815
Solomon (stlr., Tas.) 15:830
Solomon (oratorio) 15:110
Solomon, Abraham (mer.) 8:1356
Solomon, Abraham (sol.) 12:1069
Solomon, Abraham (art.) 15:117
Solomon, Benjamin (S.A.) 15:112
Solomon, Benjamin (Austr.) 15:111
SOLOMON, BERTHA 15:113
Solomon, Crescas 5:1078
Solomon, Edward 15:113
Solomon, Edward Philip 15:113
Solomon, Elias (stlr., Que.) 13:1422
Solomon, Elias (Austr.) 13:808
SOLOMON, ELIAS L. (r., U.S.) 15:113
Solomon, Emanuel 2:259; 13:808; 15:111
SOLOMON, EZEKIEL (mer.) 15:114
– Michigan 11:1498
Solomon, Ezekiel (ed.) 13:1036
Solomon, G. (r., S.A.) 8:957
Solomon, Gus J. (jur.) 13:912
SOLOMON, HANNAH GREENEBAUM 15:114
– National Council of Jewish Women 12:869
Solomon, Haym, *see* SALOMON, HAYM
Solomon, Henry (philan.) 11:1393
Solomon, Henry (apos.) 13:819
Solomon, Henry (act.), *see* SLOMAN, HENRY
Solomon, Hyman Henry 13:909
Solomon, Isaac (mer.) 7:1191
Solomon, Isaac Abraham 8:1463
Solomon, Isidor 11:1285
Solomon, Israel 11:302
Solomon, James Hymie, *see* Reese, James Hymie
Solomon, Joel M. ben, *see* Ben Solomon, Joel M.
Solomon, Joseph (mer.) 15:112
Solomon, Joseph (Tas.) 15:830
Solomon, Judah (Tas.) 15:830
Solomon, Judah Moss (Austr.) 2:259; 13:808; 15:111
Solomon, Julius 11:1285
Solomon, Maestro 16:100
Solomon, M.G. (r., U.S.) 11:499
Solomon, Michael 15:117
Solomon, Moses 12:267
Solomon, Nahum 8:1430
Solomon, Nathaniel 15:112
SOLOMON, ODES OF (Chr. poems) 15:114
Solomon, P.S. (N.Z.) 3:839
SOLOMON, PSALMS OF (Pseudepig. collec.) 15:115
– apocalypse 3:180
– date 13:846
– Davidic dynasty 5:1344
– Hellenistic literature 8:304
Solomon, Rebecca 15:117
Solomon, Richard (S.A.) 15:113
Solomon, Richard (sci.) 13:1345
Solomon, Saul (mer.) 15:112
Solomon, Saul (polit.) 13:819; 15:112
– *illus:*
– – cartoon 15:112
Solomon, Saul (jur.) 15:113
SOLOMON, SERVANTS OF (bib. figs.) 15:116
Solomon, Sidney (print.) 15:1480
Solomon, Sidney III (sport.) 15:316
Solomon, Sidney Jr. (sport.) 15:316
SOLOMON, SIMEON 15:117
– *Song of Solomon* 15:151
SOLOMON, SOLOMON JOSEPH 15:118
– portraits 13:917
– *illus:* text
Solomon, Temple of (mosque, Jer.), *see* Al-Aqsa
SOLOMON, TESTAMENT OF (Pseudepig. wk.) 15:118
– translation 16:461
Solomon, Vabian Louis 2:259; 13:808; 15:111
Solomon, William Henry 15:113

SOLOMON, WISDOM OF (Apoc. wk.) **15:**119
- allegorical exegesis **4:**896
- God, concept of **7:**653
- Hellenistic literature **8:**304
- Jewish philosophy **13:**425
- Kings, Book of **10:**1024
- logos **11:**460ff
- Pseudo-Phocylides **13:**1335
- Septuagint **4:**853
- wisdom literature **16:**557; **16:**558ff
Solomon Abū al-Mu'allim, *see* Ibn Mu'allim, Abu Ayyub Sulayman
Solomon Adeni, *see* ADENI, SOLOMON BAR JOSHUA
Solomon al-Malaki **7:**338
Solomon Almoli, *see* ALMOLI, SOLOMON BEN JACOB
Solomon and Moses Almshouse (Eng.) **5:**349
Solomon Baḥye **12:**531
Solomon bar Raphael **13:**300
Solomon ben Aaron **10:**1318
Solomon ben Abba Mari Yarḥi **16:**1388
Solomon ben Abraham Adret, *see* ADRET, SOLOMON BEN ABRAHAM
SOLOMON BEN ABRAHAM OF MONTPELLIER **15:**121
- Maimonidean controversy **11:**749
Solomon ben Abraham of Urbino **16:**1360,1389
Solomon ben Amar of Sijilmassa **11:**796
Solomon ben Aroyo **9:**1294
Solomon ben Asher **10:**340
Solomon ben Azariah **3:**999; **5:**1389
Solomon ben Bouya'a (Buya'a) **4:**465; **11:**900
- *illus:*
- - *Keter Aram Ẓova* **11:**901
- - *Leningrad Bible* **3:***fcg.* 524
Solomon ben David (print.) **9:**1098
Solomon ben David (Kar.) **10:**295
Solomon ben Dov Baer **13:**1587
Solomon ben Elijah (astron.) **3:**801
SOLOMON BEN ELIJAH HA-KOHEN **15:**121
- Damascus **5:**1241
- gaonate **7:**323
Solomon ben Elijah Sharvit ha-Zahav ha-Levi, *see* Solomon Sharvit ha-Zahav
Solomon ben Ferrizuel **6:**1236
SOLOMON BEN ḤASDAI **15:**122
- Aḥa of Shabḥa **2:**449
- Sura **15:**522
Solomon ben ha-Yatom **3:**227
Solomon ben Isaac, *see* RASHI
Solomon ben Isaac (Aus.) **15:**1492
Solomon ben Isaac ben Meir Gaon **13:**595
Solomon ben Isaac ha-Nesiah **10:**1006; **11:**566
Solomon ben Isaac Nizza **7:**414
Solomon ben Isaac of Lisbon **14:**252
Solomon ben Jacob Almoli, *see* ALMOLI, SOLOMON BEN JACOB
Solomon ben Jacob of Brandenburg **4:**1302
Solomon ben Jehiel Michel **2:**166
Solomon ben Jeroḥam **11:**58; **13:**792; **16:**1634
Solomon ben Jesse (nasi) **6:**1033; **10:**295
Solomon ben Joseph ha-Kohen (gaon) **2:**144; **6:**650; **7:**323; **15:**122
Solomon ben Joseph ha-Kohen (r., Iraq) **10:**1285
Solomon ben Joseph ibn Ayyūb (Job) of Granada **3:**959; **4:**793; **16:**1359,1387
Solomon ben Josiah (Ḥasan; exil.) **3:**999
SOLOMON BEN JUDAH (gaon) **15:**122
- Al-Kazzâz, Manasseh **13:**1419
- Cairo *genizah* **16:**1338
- Fez **6:**1255
- gaonate **7:**322
- Kairouan **10:**698
- Nathan ben Abraham **12:**857
Solomon ben Judah **5:**365
Solomon ben Judah (print.) **8:**1323
- *illus:*
- - *Mishneh Torah* (1475) **8:**1328
SOLOMON BEN JUDAH HA-BAVLI **15:**124
- *Beraḥ Dodi* **4:**585
- *piyyut* **13:**597
- Rome, Hebrew poetry **14:**245
Solomon ben Judah of Cracow **8:**990
SOLOMON BEN JUDAH OF DREUX **15:**124
SOLOMON BEN JUDAH OF LUNEL **15:**124
Solomon ben Lavi **8:**1161; **15:**1324
Solomon ben Mazzal Tov **13:**595
SOLOMON BEN MEIR **15:**125
Solomon ben Meir ha-Levi of Karlin, *see* Karlin, Solomon ben Meir ha-Levi of
Solomon ben Menahem, *see* Frat Maimon
Solomon ben Moses **11:**345; **12:**776
Solomon ben Moses of Chelm **12:**1475
Solomon ben Moses of Melgueuil **3:**957; **15:**1323
Solomon ben Moses Trani, *see* Trani, Solomon ben Moses
Solomon ben Nathan (trans.) **15:**1326
Solomon ben Nathan (r., Mor.) **14:**1528
Solomon ben Nissim **5:**626
Solomon ben Obadiah **11:**754
Solomon ben Parḥon **6:**814; **16:**1358,1385
Solomon ben Sa'id **13:**595
SOLOMON BEN SAMSON (11th cent.) **15:**125
- Worms **16:**644
Solomon ben Samson (hist.), *see* Solomon ben Simeon
Solomon ben Samson (14th cent.) **11:**903
- *illus:*
- - Babylonian Talmud ms,1342 **11:**901
Solomon ben Samson ben Eliakim **15:**125
Solomon ben Samuel (Petit)
- Acre **2:**224; **9:**29
- David ben Abraham Maimuni **9:**274
- David ben Daniel **5:**1349 **12:**444
SOLOMON BEN SAMUEL (schol.) **15:**125
Solomon ben Samuel of Wuerzburg **8:**1267
Solomon ben Sar Shalom **13:**595
Solomon ben Shaya, *see* ABU AL-MUNAJJĀ SOLOMON BEN SHAYA
Solomon ben Simeon **8:**555
Solomon ben Simeon Duran, *see* DURAN, SOLOMON BEN SIMEON
Solomon ben Uri, *see* Strelisk, Solomon ben Uri of
Solomon ben Ya'ish **10:**420; **15:**1328
Solomon ben Yeruhim **16:**1471
Solomon ben Zahit **15:**1438
Solomon ben Zequi of Majorca **2:**613
Solomon Davin of Rodez **3:**801
Solomon de Braga, *see* Braga, Solomon de
Solomon de Sessa, *see* Ercole dei Fideli
Solomon di Trani *see* Trani, Solomon ben Moses
Solomon Enoch Ha-Kohen of Radomsko, *see* Radomsko, Solomon Enoch Ha-Kohen of
Solomon ha-Dayyan ben Formash **13:**1417
Solomon ha-Kohen (ps. mess.) **11:**1422; **12:**1307
Solomon ha-Kohen (Salonika) **12:**445
Solomon ha-Levi, *see* PABLO DE SANTA MARIA
Solomon ha-Levi (kab.) **4:**991; **7:**1512
Solomon ha-Levi ha-Zaken **14:**261
Solomon ha-Ma'aravi (Abunaha) **16:**1549
Solomon Ḥayyim of Koidanov, *see* Koidanov, Solomon Ḥayyim of
Solomon ibn Adret, *see* ADRET, SOLOMON BEN ABRAHAM
Solomon ibn Ayyûb, *see* Solomon ben Joseph ibn Ayyûb (Job) of Granada
Solomon ibn Fatir ha-Kohen **15:**1325
Solomon ibn Gabirol, *see* GABIROL, SOLOMON BEN JUDAH, IBN
Solomon ibn Job, *see* Solomon ben Joseph ibn Ayyub (Job) of Granada
Solomon ibn Melekh **2:**67; **10:**1002
Solomon ibn Okhana **13:**93
Solomon ibn Ẓur **9:**513
Solomon Isaac of Provence **11:**346
Solomon Jacob, *see* Suleiman Ibn Ya'qûb
Solomon Jacob of Kolin, *see* Ehrenstamm, Solomon Jacob
Solomon-Kitovras folk-legends **3:**755
Solomon of Dubna **7:**1416
Solomon of Radzymin **13:**1508
Solomon of Rome **8:**1269
Solomon of Soest **15:**74
Solomon of Straubing (tos.) **15:**428
Solomon of Tomaszow **13:**1297
Solomon of Treviso **15:**1380
Solomon of Troki **14:**1302
Solomon Petit, *see* Solomon ben Samuel (Petit)
SOLOMONS, ADOLPHUS SIMEON **15:**126
Solomons, Bethel **15:**313
Solomons, Ezekiel **12:**284
Solomons, Hannah **14:**1336
Solomons, Ikey **15:**830
Solomons, Israel (bk. collec.) **4:**1220
Solomons, Israel Levin (mer.) **4:**463; **8:**1356
SOLOMONS, JACK **15:**126
Solomons, Levi
- Detroit **5:**1566
- Michigan **11:**1498
- Montreal **12:**284
- Solomon, Ezekiel **12:**284
- trade **10:**219
Solomons, Rachel **10:**219
Solomon Seneor ben Ephraim, *see* SZERENCSÉS, IMRE
Solomon Sharvit ha-Zahav **4:**136; **15:**1325
Solomon Shlomel of Dreznitz **9:**513
Solomon's Labyrinth (alch. ms.) **2:**544
Solomon's Mines (loc., Er. Isr.) **15:**1146
Solomon's Pillars (rock facade, Isr.) **9:**592; **15:**1146
Solomon's Pools (loc., Er. Isr.) **9:**1472; **9:**1540; **9:**1541
Solomon's Seal
- *illus:*
- - amulet **2:**913
- - Capernaum frieze **5:**138
Solomon's Stables (Jer.) **13:**522; **15:**963
- *illus:*
- - single Gate **9:**1430
SOLOMON SULIMAN BEN AMAR **15:**126
Solomon Zalman ben Jeremiah Jacob **16:**1347
Solomon Zalman of Chelm **5:**371
Solomon Zalman of Volozhin **6:**1101
Sölösi, Pál **8:**58
SOLOTAROFF, THEODORE **15:**1578; **15:**1584
SOLOVEICHIK (fam.) **15:**127
- *geneal. table:* text
SOLOVEICHIK, AARON **15:**128
- family **15:**128
- Hebrew Theological College **8:**216
- *geneal. table* **15:**128
Soloveichik, Abraham **15:**127
Soloveichik, E. **12:**1323; **15:**59
Soloveichik, Elijah Zevi **15:**127
SOLOVEICHIK, ḤAYYIM **15:**129
- Agudat Israel **2:**422
- family **15:**127
- *ḥiddushim* **8:**467
- Katzenellenbogen **10:**830
- Soloveichik, Joseph Baer **15:**131
- Volozhin yeshivah **16:**216
- *geneal. table* **15:**128
- *illus:* text
Soloveichik, Ḥayyim Simḥah **15:**127
Soloveichik, Isaac ben Joseph **15:**127
Soloveichik, Isaac Ze'ev ben Joseph **15:**127
SOLOVEICHIK, ISAAC ZE'EV HA-LEVI **15:**130
- Eisenstadt, Menahem Ẓevi **6:**550
- family **15:**128
- *geneal. table* **15:**128
SOLOVEICHIK, JOSEPH BAER OF VOLOZHIN **15:**131
- *Akedah* **2:**484
- Jewish theology **15:**1109
- prophecy **13:**1180
- redemption **14:**8
- revelation **14:**125
- Soloveichik, Isaac Ze'ev **15:**130
- Volozhin yeshivah **16:**215ff
- *geneal. table* **15:**128
Soloveichik, Joseph ben Moses **15:**127
Soloveichik, Joseph Dov (r., U.S.), *see* SOLOVEITCHIK, JOSEPH DOV
Soloveichik, Joseph Dov ben Isaac Ze'ev **15:**127; **15:**130
Soloveichik, Joseph Dov ben Simhah **15:**128
Soloveichik, Joseph ha-Levi **15:**127
Soloveichik, Max, *see* SOLIELI, MORDECAI
Soloveichik, Moses ben Ḥayyim **15:**128,132
Soloveichik, Moses ben Isaac **15:**127
Soloveichik, Moses ben Simhah **15:**128
Soloveichik, Simḥah ben Joseph **15:**127
Soloveichik, Simḥah ha-Levi **15:**127
Soloveichik, Zalman **15:**127
Soloveitchik (bnk. Rus.) **4:**176
Soloveitchik, Ḥayyim, *see* SOLOVEICHIK, ḤAYYIM
SOLOVEITCHIK, JOSEPH DOV **15:**132
- family **15:**128
- Orthodoxy **12:**1490ff
- *geneal. table:* **15:**128
- *illus:*
- - Rabbinical Council of America

convention **13:**1462
Soloveitchik, Samuel **15:**128
Soloveitchik, Tonya **15:**132
Soloviev, S. M. **15:**133
SOLOVIEV, VLADIMIR **15:**133
Solowei, M. S. **16:**1165
Solowiesczyk, Aron **11:**1204
SOLTI, GEORG **12:**709
Soltz, A. **5:**794
Solvey, J. **11:**1284
Solyma (tn., Er. Isr.), *see* SHALEM
Solzhenitsyn, Alexander **14:**513
Somali (lang.) **14:**1149
Somalia (rep., E. Afr.) **9:**441
Somaliland (reg., E. Afr.) **8:**1311
Soman (fam.) **12:**1227
SOMARY, FELIX **15:**134
SOMBART, WERNER **15:**134
SOMBOR (city, Yug.) **15:**135
- *illus:* text
Somekh, Abdallah (Pers. flklr.) **6:**1382
SOMEKH, ABDALLAH BEN ABRAHAM **15:**135
- Nawi family **12:**899
Somekh, Sasson **9:**1041; **12:**1465
SOMEN, ISRAEL **13:**831
- Kenya **10:**910
Somi, Leone Ebreo de (di), *see* SOMMO, JUDAH LEONE BEN ISAAC
SOMLYÓ, ZOLTÁN **8:**1087
Somme le Roi (illum. ms.) **7:**196
Sommer (U.S. fam.) **14:**834
SOMMER, EMIL VON **15:**136
Sommer, G. C. **8:**58
Sommer, Michael **15:**308
Sommer, Siegfried **10:**1597
Sommerfeld (phys.) **13:**490
Sommerfelt, Aimée **14:**933
Sommerhausen, Zevi Hirsch **13:**132
SOMMERSTEIN, EMIL **15:**136
- Zionism **16:**1132
Sommi Portaleone, Leone de, *see* SOMMO, JUDAH LEONE BEN ISAAC
SOMMO, JUDAH LEONE BEN ISAAC **15:**137
- drama, Hebrew **6:**194
- Italian literature **9:**1108
- poetry **13:**692
SOMOGYI, BÉLA **15:**139
Somosi, P. János **8:**58
Somossi, János **8:**58
Somovit (concen. camp) **4:**1488
SOMREI SABAT (Chr. sect) **15:**139
Son, Rebellious (bib.), *see* REBELLIOUS SON
SONCINO (fam., print.) **15:**140
- Aldo Manuzio **2:**553
- Bible editions **4:**837ff
- book-art **3:**536
- printers' marks **13:**1095
- publishing **4:**1233; **13:**1365
- typography **15:**1480ff
- *geneal. table:* text
- *illus:*
- - *Arba'ah Turim* **3:**533
- - Ben Porat prayer book **8:**1327
- - *Maḥzor Minhag Roma* **8:**1327
- - Mishnah (1492) **8:**1328
- - *Mivḥar ha-Peninim* **8:**1332
- - *Sefer ha-Ikkarim* **5:**788
- - *Sefer ha-Maḥbarot* **4:**1235,1352
- - *Sefer Mitzvot Gadol* **8:**1333; **9:**1125
- - *Soncino Bible* **4:**840
Soncino, Eliezer **9:**1097; **15:**142
Soncino, Gershom (Egy.) **15:**142
Soncino, Gershom ben Moses (It.) **15:**142
- Brescia **4:**1353
- Hebrew printing **8:**1321; **8:**1324
- Istanbul **9:**1097
- Pesaro printing press **13:**329
- publishing **13:**1365
- Rimini **14:**186
- typography **15:**1481
- *illus:*
- - *Meshal ha-Kadmoni* **14:**657
- - printer's marks **15:**140
- - *Sefer ha-Maḥbarot* **16:**1192
Soncino, Ḥayyim Joshua **3:**728
Soncino, Israel Nathan **15:**142
- Abraham ben Ḥayyim, the Dyer **2:**143
SONCINO, JOSHUA **15:**143
- *illus:*
- - Mishnah (1492) **12:**98
Soncino, Joshua ben Menahem **15:**143
Soncino, Joshua Solomon **15:**142
- Abraham ben Ḥayyim, the Dyer **2:**143
- incunabula **8:**1321; **8:**1324;
Soncino, Menzlein, *see* Soncino, Gershom ben Moses
Soncino, Moses (Ger.) **15:**140
Soncino, Moses (Turk.) **15:**142
Soncino, Moses ben Joshua
- Ashkenazi, Judah **3:**728
- Bikayam, Meir **4:**991
Soncino, Samuel **15:**140
Soncino, Simon **15:**140
Soncino, Solomon ben Moses **8:**1325; **15:**142
Soncino Bible (illum. print) **4:**837
- *illus:* **4:**840
Soncino-Blaetter, Beitraege zur Kunde des juedischen Buches (period.) **4:**973
Soncino-Casal Maggiore *Maḥzor* (prayer bk.) **11:**399
SONCINO GESELLSCHAFT DER FREUNDE DES JUEDISCHEN BUCHES (soc.) **15:**143
Soncino Press (pub. firm, Eng.) **14:**1582
Soncinus, Hieronymus, *see* Soncino, Gershom ben Moses
Sonderabteilung (Nazi dept.) **11:**435
Sondereinsatzkommando (Nazi orgn.) **8:**1099
Sonderkommando (concen. camp orgn.) **3:**856
Sondheimer, Alexander **12:**1354
SONDHEIMER, FRANZ **15:**143
Sondheimer, Hillel Wolf **3:**688
Sondheimer, Joseph **12:**1354
Sondheimer, Moses Tobiah **15:**368
Song, *see* MUSIC
SONG, ANGELIC **15:**144
Song Festival, Hebrew, *see* Hebrew Song Festival (Isr.)
Song of Ascent (Ps.), *see* SHIR HA-MA'ALOT
Song of Deborah (Bib.) **5:**1431
Song of Moses, second (*Ha'azinu*) **12:**778
- *illus:*
- - Yemenite Pentateuch (15th cent.) **16:***fcg.* 743
Song of the Sea, *see* Sea, Song of the
Song of Solomon, *see* SONG OF SONGS
"Song of Solomon" (drg., S. Solomon) **3:**547
SONG OF SONGS **15:**144
- *Contents:*
- - The Character of the Song of Songs **15:**144
- - The Interpretation of the Song of Songs **15:**146
- - The Song as an Allegory **15:**147
- - The Song as a Drama **15:**148
- - The Song as a Cultic Liturgy **15:**148
- - The Literal Interpretations **15:**149
- - Authorship, Date, and Origin **15:**150
- - In the Liturgy **15:**151
- - In the Arts **15:**151
- *Aḥot Ketannah* **2:**470
- Akiva's views **2:**490
- allegorical interpretation **2:**643; **4:**896ff
- anthropomorphism **3:**56ff
- *Beraḥ Dodi* **4:**584
- canonization **4:**824
- Cansinos-Assens' version **15:**248
- Ibn Aknin **2:**501
- in the Arts **15:**108
- love **11:**527
- musical rendition **14:**1058
- poetry **13:**677
- Scrolls, The Five **14:**1057
- Septuagint **4:**855
- *Shiur Komah* **14:**1417; **14:**1418
- Solomon **15:**105
- Wisdom literature **16:**559
- *illus:*
- - text
- - initial-word panel **11:***fcg* 683
- - Rashi's commentary **4:**891
- - *Rothschild Maḥzor* **15:**99
- - Solomon enthroned **2:**355
- - "Song of Solomon" (drg., S. Solomon) **3:**548
Song of Songs, Aggadah of (wk.), *see* *Aggadat Shir ha-Shirim*
SONG OF SONGS RABBAH (agg. Mid.) **15:**152
- *Harugei Malkhut* term **15:**1007
- *illus:* text
- *see also:* MIDRASH
Song of Thanksgiving **13:**678
SONG OF THE THREE CHILDREN AND THE PRAYER OF AZARIAH **15:**154
Song of the Well **13:**677
Songs for Miscellaneous Festivals (kib. litur.) **10:**961
Songs of Sabbath Service (sec. scroll) **11:**1090
Songs of Unity (litur.), *see* SHIR HA-YIḤUD
Songs of Zion (wk.) **10:**360
Song Thrush (bird) **6:**30
Sonik (tn., Pol.), *see* SANOK
Sonnabend, Abraham M. **15:**315
Sonnabend, Roger **15:**315
Sonne, Avraham, *see* BEN YIẒḤAK, AVRAHAM
SONNE, ISAIAH **15:**154
- Hebraic studies **8:**218
SONNEBORN, RUDOLF GOLDSCHMIDT **15:**154
SONNEMANN, LEOPOLD **15:**155
Sonnenberg, Benjamin **13:**1360
Sonnenberg, Ber **4:**618; **16:**945
Sonnenberg, Fritz **5:**140
Sonnenberg, Max **5:**1547
Sonnenberg, Zundel **5:**1548
Sonnenfeld (stlmt., Can.) **14:**892
Sonnenfeld, Iulia, *see* SOARE, IULIA
SONNENFELD, JOSEPH HAYYIM BEN ABRAHAM SOLOMON **15:**155
- Agudat Israel **2:**424
- Diskin, Isaac Jeroham **6:**75
- Ereẓ Israel **9:**892
- *illus:*
- - Allenby and **2:**647
- - Masaryk, Thomas, and **11:**1092
SONNENFELD, SIGISMUND **15:**157
SONNENFELS, ALOYS VON **15:**157
Sonnenfels, Joseph von **10:**1493; **11:**1335ff; **15:**157
Sonnenschein, Rosa **16:**1165
Sonnenschein, William Swan **13:**1370
SONNENTHAL, ADOLF, RITTER VON **15:**158
Sonneschein, S.H. **8:**958
Sonneschmid, J.J. **8:**58
Sonnino, Joseph **16:**1122
SONNINO, SIDNEY **15:**159
- *illus:* text
Sonntag, C. **8:**58
SONNTAG, JACOB **6:**785; **6:**790
SON OF MAN **15:**159
- *Daniel, Book of* **11:**1408
Son of Man (mess.) **6:**874
- Messiah **11:**1410
Sonol (co., Isr.) **9:**795
Sonora (city, Calif.) **5:**56
Sonschein, R. **4:**176
Sonshine, Harry **15:**308
Sons of Bava (Jer. nobles), *see* Bava, Sons of
Sons of Benjamin (assoc., Er. Isr), *see* BENEI BINYAMIN
Sons of Darkness (D. S. scrolls), *see* SONS OF LIGHT
Sons of Heman (Bib.) **8:**320
Sons of Hezir, tomb of, *see* Hezir, tomb of sons of
Sons of Israel (syn., Mass.) **16:**634
Sons of Israel and David (syn., R.I.) **13:**1277,1278
- *illus:*
- - general view **13:**1278
SONS OF LIGHT **15:**160
- Davidic Messiah **16:**701
- War Scroll **16:**1559
Sons of man, *see* SON OF MAN
Sons of Zadok, *see* ZADOKITES
Sons of Zion (soc., U.S.), *see* B'nai Zion
SONTAG, SUSAN **15:**161
- U.S. literature **15:**1578
Sontheim (loc., Ger.) **8:**263
Sontheim, Tuviah **7:**1257
Sontheimer, Mayer **15:**1534
Soothsaying **3:**788; **15:**163
- *see also:* DIVINATION
Sophonim (lit. fig.) **6:**797
Sophronius (7th cent. patr.) **9:**261,264,1096,1408
Sophronius (16th cent., patr.) **9:**287
SOPRON (city, Hung.) **15:**161
Sopronkeresztúr (tn., Aus.), *see* DEUTSCHKREUTZ
Soprotimis (orgn., Arg.) **3:**414
Soqotri (lang.) **15:**1153
Sorani, Aldo **14:**197
SORAUER, PAUL KARL MORITZ **15:**162
SORCERY **15:**163
- Agrat bat Mahalath **2:**374
- Commandments, the 613 **5:**781
- extraordinary remedy **14:**1564
- lots **11:**513
- practical Kabbalah **10:**633
- Saul **14:**913
- Simeon ben Shetaḥ **14:**1564
- *see also:* MAGIC
Soref, Harry E. **11:**1588
Soreg (Temple fence) **15:**965
- *illus:*
- - Herod's Temple (model) **15:**960
- - plaque forbidding entry to gentiles **15:**964
SOREK, VALLEY OF (Er. Isr.) **15:**164
- human geography **9:**587
- Judah boundary **10:**330
- river **9:**141; **9:**1515
- Timnah **15:**1147
- vine of **16:**155
- Wadi al-Sarâr **4:**773
- *illus:*
- - text
- - valley, aerial view **9:**137
Sorek Nuclear Research Center (Isr.) **9:**797; **15:**93
Sorel, Felicia **5:**1272
SORGHUM (bot.) **15:**164
SORIA (city, Sp.) **15:**165

Soriano, Henri **9:**1096; **15:**1457
Soriano, Raphaelita Hilario **13:**396
Soriano, Victor **11:**1203
Soriano, Yom Tov **13:**597
Soroca, Abraham Abba-Joseph of, *see* Abraham Abba-Joseph of Soroca
SOROKI (Soroca; city, Mold.) **15:**166
SOROTZKIN, ZALMAN BEN BEN-ZION **15:**166
Sorrel, garden (bot.) **13:**625
Sors, Ivan **11:**1167
- *illus:*
- - Chajes, Ẓevi Hirsch (plaque) **5:**328
SOSIS, ISRAEL **15:**167
SOSIUS, GAIUS **15:**168
- Antigonus II **3:**67
- Seneca the Elder **14:**236
- Temple **6:**58
SOSKIN, SELIG EUGEN **15:**168
- Aaronsohn **2:**25
- *illus:*
- - text
- - El-Arish technical commission **5:**565
SOSNOWIEC (Sosnovets; city, Pol.) **15:**169
Sosúa (vill., Dominican Rep.) **2:**414; **6:**160
SOTAH (tract.) **15:**170
- *illus:*
- - text
- - ordeal of "waters of bitterness" **12:**1448
Sotah ("suspected wife"), *see* ORDEAL OF JEALOUSY
Soter, Jacob **5:**742
Soteriology, *see* Salvation
Sotsiale Meditsin (period.) **15:**1292
Sotsialisticheskaya Yevreyskaya Rabochaya Partiya, *see* JEWISH SOCIALIST WORKERS' PARTY
Soucek, Theodor **12:**956
Souchy, Jacob **13:**722
Souirah (port, Mor.), *see* MOGADOR
Souiri (Mor. polit.), *see* Chriqui, Joseph ben Mas'ud
Souk-Ahras (loc., Tunis) **15:**1431
SOUL **15:**172
- Concepts
- - beatitude **4:**359
- - Heaven and Hell **13:**84
- - intellect **8:**1411
- - light as symbol **11:**1301
- - pre-existence **10:**500ff; **11:**845
- - psychology **13:**1342
- - reward and punishment **14:**137
- - *Ru'aḥ ha-Kodesh* **14:**366
- - spirit and flesh **6:**243
- - union with God **2:**152
- - Worlds, the Four **16:**641
- Doctrines and Movements
- - Aristotelianism **13:**430ff
- - ḥasidic teachings **7:**1408
- - Jewish philosophy **13:**421
- - kabbalistic doctrine **10:**504
- - Lurianic cosmogony **10:**591
- - Maimonidean controversy **11:**748
- - Neoplatonism **12:**958ff
- Views
- - Crescas, Ḥasdai **5:**1084
- - Gabirol **7:**241
- - Hillel ben Samuel **8:**489; **13:**444
- - Ibn Da'ud **8:**1162
- - Ibn Ezra, Abraham **8:**1169
- - Ibn Ezra, Moses **8:**1173
- - Israeli **13:**434
- - Maimonides **11:**775
- - Philo **13:**427
- - Saadiah Gaon **13:**432; **14:**551
- - *Sefer Asaf ha-Rofe* **3:**674
- - Ẓaddik, Joseph ben Jacob ibn **16:**912
- *see also:* AFTERLIFE; BODY AND SOUL; SOUL, IMMORTALITY OF
Soul, Additional, *see* NESHAMAH YETERAH
SOUL, IMMORTALITY OF **15:**174
- *Contents:*
- - In the Bible **15:**174
- - In the Talmud **15:**175
- - In Medieval Jewish Philosophy **15:**176
- - In Modern Philosophy **15:**179
- - In Kabbalah **15:**180
- Concepts
- - article of faith **3:**655ff
- - fear of death **11:**236
- - Messiah **11:**412
- - netherworld **12:**996
- - resurrection **14:**96
- - source of belief **10:**389
- - symbolic expression **15:**569ff
- - *yahrzeit* **16:**703
- Views
- - Aaron ben Elijah **2:**12
- - Aristotelianism **3:**448
- - Gersonides **13:**446ff
- - Hillel ben Samuel **8:**489
- - Ibn Ezra, Abraham **8:**1169
- - Kabbalah **10:**613
- - *Kitāb Maʿānī al-Nafs* **4:**103
- - Maimonides **6:**1439; **11:**776
- - Mendelssohn, Moses **11:**1330ff
- - Naḥmanides **10:**527
- - Philo **13:**427
- - Sadducees **14:**621
- *see also:* AFTERLIFE; BEATITUDE; BODY AND SOUL; OLAM HA-BA; PARADISE; PLATO AND PLATONISM; REPENTANCE; REWARD AND PUNISHMENT; SOUL
Soul, Transmigration of, *see* GILGUL
SOULTZ (Sulz; tn., Fr.) **15:**181
SOUS (prov., Mor.) **15:**182
Sousa (fam.) **5:**1022
Sousse (loc., Tun.) **15:**1431ff
Soustelle, Jacques **7:**42
Souterliedekens (Du. psalter) **13:**1328
SOUTH AFRICA **15:**184
- *Contents:*
- - Settlement **15:**184
- - Immigration **15:**186
- - Legal and Social Status **15:**188
- - Communal Organization and Structure **15:**191
- - Social and Cultural Life **15:**197
- - Jews in the Armed Forces **15:**202
- - Economic Life and Social Structure **15:**202
- - Relations with Israel **15:**206
- General
- - Ashkenazim **3:**721
- - assimilation **3:**779
- - Committee for Refugees **6:**991
- - demography **5:**1494ff
- - Israel's relations with **9:**432
- - migrations to **16:**1520
- - population **8:**733
- - refugees, Jewish **14:**30
- - vital statistics **16:**183ff
- Jewish Life
- - communal organization **5:**824
- - education **6:**455
- - Habonim **8:**1243
- - Ha-Shomer ha-Ẓa'ir **7:**1376
- - ORT **12:**1483
- - press **13:**1049
- - rabbinate **13:**1453
- - *sheḥitah* legislation **14:**1341
- - Six-Day War volunteers **9:**543
- - student movements **15:**453
- - synagogues **1:**syn. list
- - theater **15:**1074
- - Zionism **16:**1140ff
- Occupations
- - law **10:**1502
- - medicine **11:**1203
- - military **11:**1554
- - mining **11:**1440
- - politics **13:**819ff
- - sugar industry **15:**488
- *illus:*
- - text
- - Bloemfontein, Baumann Brothers trading store **4:**1112
- - *kolel* emissary **7:**1211-1214
- - Solomon, Saul, in political cartoon **15:**112
- *pop. tables:*
- - text
- - postwar communities **5:**839
- *see also:* AFRICA; TRANSVAAL
South African Board of Jewish Education **6:**455
South African Jewish Board of Deputies **2:**573; **12:**854
- influence **15:**192ff
South African Jewish Chronicle **13:**1049
South African Jewish Times **6:**1217; **13:**1049
SOUTH AFRICAN LITERATURE **15:**207
- *Contents:*
- - Biblical Influences **15:**207
- - The Figure of the Jew **15:**208
- - The Jewish Contribution **15:**208
- - - Writers in English **15:**208
- - - Writers in Afrikaans **15:**210
- Jewish involvement **15:**202
South African War, *see* Boer War
South African Zionist Federation **16:**614 **12:**854;
South America, *see* LATIN AMERICA
SOUTHAMPTON (city, Eng.) **15:**210
South Arabia, *see* ARABIA
South Arabian (lang.) **16:**1398
South Bend (city, Ind.) **8:**1361
SOUTH CAROLINA **15:**211
- United States **15:**1586ff
- *illus:* text
- *pop. tables:* text
SOUTH DAKOTA **15:**213
- *pop. tables:* text
Southern Israelite (newsp.) **3:**825
Southern Jewish Weekly (U.S.) **6:**1316
Southern Yemen (rep., Arab.)
- Arab League **3:**242
- Israel's relations **9:**445
South Haven (city, Mich.) **11:**1500
South Orange (sub., N.J.) **6:**904
- *illus:*
- - Temple Beth El **4:**1005
Southsea (sub. Portsmouth, Eng.) **13:**919
South Wales Review (Gt. Brit.) **13:**1031
South-West Africa (terr.) **15:**184ff
SOUTHWOOD, JULIUS SALTER ELIAS, VISCOUNT **15:**213
SOUTINE, CHAIM **15:**214
- *illus:*
- - text
- - self-portrait **8:**749
Souza, De (fam., Jam.) **9:**1274
Sova, Antonín **5:**1207
SOVERN, MICHAEL IRA **15:**215
SOVETISH HEYMLAND (period.) **15:**215
- Sternberg, Jacob **15:**395
- *illus:* text
Soviano, Henry **13:**816
Sovietish Literatur (period.) **13:**1048
Soviet Union, *see* RUSSIA
Sovinform bureau (Rus.) **3:**62
Sowden, Lewis **15:**209
Soyer, Abraham **8:**212; **15:**216
Soyer, Isaac **12:**1122; **15:**217
Soyer, Moses **12:**1122
- *illus:*
- - "My Friends" (paint.) **15:**217
SOYER, RAPHAEL **15:**216
- New York **12:**1122
- *illus:*
- - text
- - "Transients" (study) **3:**561
- - "Village East" (paint.) **12:**1116
Sozialistischer Deutscher Studentenbund (rad. orgn.), *see* Students for a Democratic Society
Sozialorganische Bewegung Europas (Neo-Nazi orgn.) **12:**956
Sozusa (city, Er. Isr.), *see* APOLLONIA
Spaak, Paul-Henri **4:**424
SPACE AND PLACE **15:**217
- Crescas **13:**448
- Mendelssohn **11:**1330
- *Shekhinah*, presence of **14:**1351
- *ẓimẓum* doctrine **10:**589ff
- *see also:* PHILOSOPHY, JEWISH
SPAETH, JOHANN PETER (Moses Germanus) **15:**219
Spahn, Moe **15:**303
SPAIN **15:**220
- *Contents:*
- - Under Visigothic Rule **15:**220
- - Muslim Spain **15:**223
- - The Reconquest Period **15:**227
- - The Golden Age **15:**228
- - Beginning of the Christian Reaction **15:**231
- - The Persecutions of 1391 **15:**236
- - The Conversos **15:**237
- - Steps toward the Expulsion **15:**240
- - Cultural Life **15:**241
- - Modern Period **15:**244
- - Holocaust Period **15:**244
- - After World War II **15:**245
- - Spain and Israel Relations **15:**246
- General
- - Algerian communities **2:**612ff
- - *aliyah* **9:**512
- - capitulations **5:**150
- - Jewish quarter **10:**86
- - museums **12:**544
- - Provence influenced by **13:**1263
- - rites **11:**397
- - Sepharad **14:**1164
- - Sephardi Diaspora **14:**1167ff
- - slaves **14:**1661
- History
- - Christian period **8:**673ff
- - Civil War **8:**741
- - Crusades **5:**1141, 1143
- - Diaspora, Second Temple period **8:**640
- - history chart **8:**766-767
- - Jews' emigration to Ottoman Empire **16:**1532,1547ff
- - Latin America **10:**1448
- - Majorca **11:**795
- - population **13:**870ff
- - Tunisia **15:**1438
- - Umayyads **11:**894; **15:**1530
- Anti-Semitism **3:**107
- - Barcelona, Disputation of **4:**213
- - blood libel **10:**1359
- - disputations **6:**92
- - dress **6:**219
- - Ferrer, Vicente **6:**1235; **6:**1236
- - Tortosa, Disputation of **15:**1269; **15:**1270
- - Visigothic period **8:**657; **8:**661ff
- Inquisition and Expulsion **8:**1381; **8:**1384; **8:**1387ff
- - Abrabanel, Isaac **2:**105

- - anusim 3:173
- - Arbués, Pedro de 3:300
- - auto da fé 3:912
- - Av, the Ninth 3:936
- - expropriations 16:1284
- - Judaizers 10:398
- - limpieza de sangre 11:255
- - Marrano Diaspora 11:1019
- - New Christians 12:1022
- - Sephardim 14:1164
- Autonomy 3:923
- - adelantados (parnasim) 2:259
- - autonomy, judicial 3:929ff
- - Barcelona jurisdiction 4:210
- - communal organization 5:818
- - courts 4:726
- - education 6:405ff
- - finances 6:1281
- - guilds 7:972
- - hospital 8:1033
- - informers, regulations on 8:1366
- - Muslim period 8:660
- - nagid 12:758; 12:759
- - offenders 4:164
- - rabbi, rabbinate 13:1447ff
- - Rab de la corte 13:1468
- - synagogues 1:syn. list; 15:611
- - takkanot 14:725,735
- - taxation 15:839, 858
- Arts and Occupations
- - agriculture 2:402
- - banking 4:172
- - crafts 5:1048ff
- - goldsmiths 7:741
- - Ḥanukkah lamp 7:1290
- - illuminated manuscripts 8:1264
- - journalism 10:304
- - letter-writing 11:59
- - medicine 11:1190
- - mintmasters 12:62
- - moneylending 12:250; 12:254
- - printing 8:1325
- - publishing 13:1370
- - sculpture 14:1060
- - silversmithery 7:741
- - textiles 15:1038
- - trade and commerce 15:1297ff
- - typography 15:1480
- Scholarship and Literature
- - gaonate 7:324
- - ḥiddushin 8:465; 8:466
- - Ladino 10:1343ff
- - piyyut 13:597,600
- - poetry 13:681ff
- - prosody 13:1199,1211
- - resh kallah title 14:83
- - responsa 11:336
- - yeshivot 16:763
- Writings on
- - Abraham of Torrutiel 2:157
- - Alami, Solomon 2:509
- - Capsali, Elijah 5:152
- - Hayyat, Judah 6:1070
- - History of the Jews in Christian Spain 4:82
- - Jabez, Joseph 9:1173
- - Kayserling's studies 10:856
- - Levi-Provençal, Evariste 11:122
- illus:
- - text
- - Alfonso X of Castile 2:605
- - anusim at a Madrid auto da fe 3:171
- - Gerona, old Jewish quarter 7:506
- - Ḥanukkah lamps 7:1296,1297
- - hat, Jewish 4:66
- - Maimonides stamp 11:759
- - Toledo, El Transito synagogue 3:520
- pop. tables:
- - text
- - Burgos province before 1492 4:1513
- see also: PORTUGAL; SPANISH AND PORTUGUESE LITERATURE; and under individual towns
Spain, David 11:1202
Spalato (tn., Yug.), see SPLIT
Spalding, G.L. 8:58
Spalding, Robert 8:58
Spalter, Isaac 11:858
Span (meas.), see Zeret
SPANDAU (city, Ger.) 15:246
- Brandenburg 4:1301
- see also: BERLIN
SPANIER, ARTHUR 15:247
Spanier, Israel, see WECHSLER, ISRAEL
Spanier, Moritz 11:686
Spanier, Nathan 5:1007
Spaniolish (lang.), see LADINO
Spanish (lang.)
- Bible translations 4:878
- Jewish encyclopedias 6:733; 6:735
- Ladino 10:67,1342f
- Sephardim 14:1167
SPANISH AND PORTUGUESE LITERATURE 15:247
- Contents:
- - Biblical and Hebraic Influences 15:247
- - Image of the Jew in Spanish Literature 15:249
- - Conversos and Marranos 15:249
- - Modern Spanish Writers 15:250
- - Image of the Jew in Portuguese Literature 15:250
- - The Jewish Contribution to Spanish Literature 15:251
- - The Later Conversos 15:253
- - The Jewish Contribution to Portuguese Literature 15:254
- - The Jewish Contribution to Latin-American Literature 15:254
- - Contemporary Jewish Writers 15:255
- Consolaçam as Tribulacoens de Israel 8:556
- Jewish literature 11:326ff
- Ladino 10:1348
Spanish and Portuguese Synagogue (N.Y.C.), see Shearith Israel Congregation
Spanish and Portuguese Synagogue Jewish Welfare Board (Eng.) 13:379
Spanish cherry (bot.) 13:625
Spanish Civil War 15:244
Spanish rites 11:397
"Spanish Smiths" (paint., E. Josephson) 3:551
Spanish Synagogue (Venice) 16:101
Spanish Town (city, Jam.) 9:1273
Spannheim, F. (Sr.) 8:58
Spannheim, F. (Jr.) 8:58
Sparger, William 7:1548
Spark, Muriel 6:782
Sparks, Holy, see Niẓoẓot
SPARROW (bird) 15:256
- house sparrow 6:34
- Italian sparrow 6:30
SPARTA (anc. city state) 15:256
- Abraham and Spartans 2:117
- Judea 7:893
- Simeon the Hasmonean 14:1565
Spartakus (orgn., Warsaw ghetto) 16:348
Spartanburg (city, S.C.) 15:211
Sparzenstein, Baron von, see RICIUS, PAULUS
SPASSKY, BORIS 15:257
- chess 5:407
Spassovich D.V. 4:1114
Spaulding, Arthur W. 14:917
Speaker, Henry 7:860
Spear (weapon) 16:266ff
Spear, A. 12:1272
Special Committee to Investigate Israel Practices Affecting the Human Rights of the Population of the Occupied Territories (U.N.) 15:1561
Special Night Squads (Er. Isr.)
- attacks on terrorists 9:351
- defense 9:684
- Haganah 7:1068
- Wingate, Charles Orde 16:548
- illus:
- - mixed unit 9:685
Special Political Committee (U.N.) 15:1551
Species, the four, see FOUR SPECIES
Species, the seven
- barley 4:241
- fig 6:1272
- first-fruit 4:993; 6:1314
- honey 13:43
- olive 12:1364
- pomegranate 13:841
- vine 16:155
- wheat 16:480
- illus:
- - barley 4:242
- - fig 6:1273
- - pomegranate 3:322
- - vine 16:156
- - wheat 6:1332
- see also: FOOD
SPECTOR, JOHANNA 15:258
SPECTOR, MORDECAI 15:258
Spector, Robert 15:258
Speculative Kabbalah, see KABBALAH
Speculum Historiale (14th cent., illum. ms., Ger.) 10:485
Speech 6:946; 13:1119
Speech, Evil, see LASHON HA-RA
Speer, Albert 5:86; 13:756
- illus:
- - Nuremberg Trial 16:289
Spegel, Haquin 14:928
Speidelius, J. C. 8:58
Speightstown (tn., Barb.) 4:205
SPEISER, EPHRAIM AVIGDOR 15:258
- Abraham story 4:911
- historiography 8:562
- illus:
- - JPS Torah translation committee 10:80
SPEKTOR, ISAAC ELHANAN 15:259
- Ash, Abraham Joseph 3:694
- Jacob Lipschuetz 11:288
- sabbatical year 14:584
- secular study 16:217
- illus: text
Spellman, Frank 12:1376
Spells, see BLESSING AND CURSING; MAGIC
Spelman, Henry 8:58
Spelt 13:625; 4:1333; 16:481
SPENCER, JOHN 15:261
- Hebraist 8:58
- Jews 5:1463
Spender, Stephen 6:785
Spener, Philipp Jakob 15:219
Spengler, Oswald 7:445
Sperber, Alexander 12:1461; 16:1398
Sperber, Alfred Margul 14:414
Sperber, Hugo 10:1494
SPERBER, MANÈS 15:261
Sperling, Harry 16:1214
Sperling, M.S. 5:452
Spero (name), see also Schapira; Schapiro; Shapira; Shapiro; Spira; Spiro
Spero, Donald 15:312
Spero, George 13:812
SPERO, SHUBERT 15:262
SPEWACK, BELLA and SAMUEL 15:262
SPEYER (fam.) 15:266
- England 4:175
- financiers 13:1519
SPEYER (city, Ger.) 15:262
- banking 4:168
- charters to Jews 8:622
- Crusades 5:1134
- Germany 7:460
- history chart (1195-96) 8:766-767
- informers 8:1367
- Jewish trading privilege (1090) 16:1287
- persecutions 4:280
- synod 15:633ff
- Worms 16:644
- illus: text
- see also: SHUM
SPEYER, BENJAMIN 15:267
Speyer, Edgar 15:266
Speyer, Eduard Beit von 15:266
Speyer, Gustav 15:266
Speyer, Isaac ben Jacob 4:653
Speyer, Isaac Michael 15:266
Speyer, James 15:266
Speyer, J.M. 4:174
Speyer, Joseph Lazarus 15:266
Speyer, Lazarus Speyer 15:266
Speyer, Michael Isaac 15:266
Speyer, Philipp 15:266
Speyer, Philipp and Co. (bnk., U.S.) 4:174
Speyer-Elissen, J.L. 4:174
Speyer-Elissen, Lazard 4:174
Spheres, celestial 13:422; 13:430
- illus:
- - diagramatic representation 3:791
- - Sefirot 10:521,532
Sphinx 14:1073
Spicehandler, Daniel 15:1573
SPICEHANDLER, EZRA 1:38
SPICES 15:267
- Bible 6:1416
- Havdalah 7:1481ff
- industry at En-Gedi 6:742
- seder ceremonial food 7:1346
- spice trade 15:270
- tragacanth 15:1311
- illus:
- - balsam 4:143
- - blessing over 8:1315
- - cinnamon 5:566
- - cumin 5:1170
- - henna 8:326
- - tragacanth 15:1312
- see also: COSMETICS; INCENSE AND PERFUMES
SPICE TRADE 15:269
- Jewish merchants 4:1535
- Solomon 15:98
SPIDER (zool.) 15:271
Spiegel, Frederick 5:565
SPIEGEL, ISAIAH 15:271
Spiegel, Jacob (stlr., U.S.) 16:861
Spiegel, Jacob J. (jur.) 11:1115
SPIEGEL, LUDWIG 15:272
SPIEGEL, SAMUEL P. 12:474
SPIEGEL, SHALOM 15:272
- Akedah 2:482
SPIEGEL-ADOLF, MONA ANNA SIMONA 5:387
Spiegelberg (character, Schiller) 14:965
SPIEGELBERG, HERBERT 15:272
Spiegelberg, Solomon Jacob
- illus:
- - Santa Fe store 12:1038
Spiegelberg, Wilhelm 3:302
Spiegelberg, Willi (New Mex.) 12:1038
Spiegelblatt, A. 16:826
Spiegelman, Abraham Ẓevi 14:631
Spiegler, Mordecai 15:298
Spielmaenner, see Minstrels, Jewish
SPIELMAN (-N; fam., Eng.) 15:272
- military service 11:1553
Spielman, Adam 15:272
Spielman, Lady Emily 15:273
Spielman, Ferdinand 5:114

Spielman, Sir Isidore **6**:761; **15**:272
Spielman, Marion Harry Alexander **15**:272
- *illus:*
- - portrait **15**:273
Spielman, Sir Meyer Adam **6**:465; **15**:273
Spielman, Percy Edwin **15**:273
Spielmann (fam. Eng.) *see* SPIELMAN
Spielmann, Jacob Meir **10**:555
SPIELMANN, RUDOLF **5**:409
SPIELVOGEL, NATHAN **15**:273
- Ballarat **4**:138
SPIER, LESLIE **15**:274
- anthropology **3**:38
Spies, Twelve (Bib.) **12**:377
SPIKENARD (spice) **15**:274
- incense offering **8**:1315
- source **8**:1311
Spiller, James **15**:598
Spina, Alfonso de, *see* ALFONSO DE ESPINA
SPINA, GERI **10**:317
Spinalunga (Isl. It.) **16**:94
Spindel, Louis **15**:303
SPINGARN (U.S. fam.) **15**:274
Spingarn, Arthur Barnett **15**:275
Spingarn, Joel Elias **15**:274
Spinka (ḥas. dyn.) **1**:ḥas. table
Spinka, Isaac Eizik Weiss of **15**:275
Spinka, Jacob Joseph Weiss of **15**:275
SPINKA, JOSEPH MEIR WEISS OF **15**:275
"Spinners" (paint., M. Liebermann) **3**:551
Spinning (fabrics) **15**:1036
SPINOZA, BARUCH DE **15**:275
- *Contents:*
- - Life and Works **15**:275
- - His Philosophy **15**:278
- - Influence **15**:281
- - As Bible Scholar **15**:282
- General
- - alchemy **2**:547
- - chronological chart **8**:766-767
- - Spinoziana **4**:152
- - Wolfson's studies **16**:618
- Philosophy **11**:343ff; **13**:417; **13**:453
- - anthropomorphism **3**:56
- - imagination **8**:1290
- - revelation **14**:124
- - soul **15**:174
- Judaism
- - articles of faith **3**:659
- - biblical criticism **5**:1463
- - circumcision **5**:575
- - Commandments **5**:789
- - grammar **16**:1393
- - Kabbalah **10**:601
- - Torah **15**:1241; **15**:1246
- Life
- - Amsterdam **2**:897
- - Heidelberg university **15**:1676
- - heresy **8**:361
- - letters **11**:61
- - seal **14**:1080
- People
- - Aboab da Fonseca **2**:95
- - Abrabanel, Judah **2**:111
- - Andrade's polemics against **2**:947
- - Crescas, Ḥasdai **5**:1085
- - Mendelssohn, Moses **11**:1340ff
- - Nieto, David **12**:1152
- *illus:*
- - text
- - autograph **3**:918
- - portrait **8**:694
"Spinoza" (paint., A. Hirszenberg) **8**: 350
"Spinoza of chess," *see* RUBINSTEIN, AKIVA
Spira (fam. name), *see also* Schapira; Schapiro; Shapira; Shapiro; Spero; Spiro
Spira (ḥas. dyn.), *see* SHAPIRA
Spira, Aaron Simeon **14**:61
Spira, B. (Zion. ldr.) **16**:1165
Spira, Benjamin Wolf **12**:1420; **14**:61
Spira, Berechiah Berakh **10**:552
Spira, Elijah **14**:61
Spira, Ḥayyim Jacob **7**:76
Spira, Isaac **6**:1074
Spira, Jacob **8**:1071
Spira, Judah **15**:1141
Spira, Moses Isaac **12**:185
Spira, Nathan **10**:7
SPIRA (SPIRO), NATHAN NATA BEN SOLOMON **15**:284
- Berechiah Berakh **4**:598
- biblical exegesis **10**:623
- Ostropoler, Samson **12**:1517
- Vital, Ḥayyim **16**:175
- Zacuto, M. **16**:907
- *illus:*
- - *Megalleh Amukot* (Lemberg, 1795) **7**: 370
Spira, Shifra, *see* Oppenheim, Shifra
Spira-Wedeles, Moses Isaac **10**:1403
Spire (city, Ger.), *see* SPEYER
SPIRE, ANDRÉ **15**:284
- Zionism **16**:1114
Spire, Elie Vitte **3**:966
Spires (city, Ger.), *see* SPEYER
Spirit, *see* BODY AND SOUL; SOUL
"Spirit of the Dance" (Sculp., W. Zorach) **3**: 560
Spiritualism **10**:637; **14**:93
Spiritual man (kab.), *see* ADAM KADMON
Spiro (fam. name), *see also* Schapira; Schapiro; Shapira; Shapiro; Spero; Spira
Spiro (fam.) **7**:1
Spiro, David **10**:98
SPIRO, EUGEN **3**:610
- *illus:*
- - Horovitz, Vladimir (portrait) **8**:983
- - Huberman, Bronislaw (portrait) **8**:1056
- - Self-Portrait (paint.) **3**:642
SPIRO, KARL **5**:387
SPIRO, MELFORD ELLIOT **15**:285
- psychiatry **13**:1340
Spiro, Nathan ben Reuben **10**:550
Spiro, Nathan Nata ben Solomon, *see* SPIRA, NATHAN NATA BEN SOLOMON
Spiro, Solomon **10**:1384
Spisska Nova Ves (tn., Slov.) **8**:1076
Spišske Podhradie (tn., Slov.) **10**:1216
Spitz, Haiman Philip **11**:782
Spitz, Isaac **4**:1366; **12**:185
Spitz, Joseph **13**:162
Spitz, Mark **15**:314
Spitz, Moritz **11**:1590
SPITZ, RENE **15**:286
Spitz, R.J. **6**:321
Spitzer, Armin **10**:1174
Spitzer, Benjamin Solomon Zalman, *see* SPITZER, SOLOMON
Spitzer, Daniel **7**:448; **10**:305
Spitzer, Dov Beer **14**:1018
Spitzer, Franjo, *see* ŠINKO, ERVIN
SPITZER, FREDERICK **3**:611
SPITZER, HUGO (philos.) **15**:286
Spitzer, Hugo (Zion.) **16**:1077
SPITZER, KARL HEINRICH **15**:286
Spitzer, Leopold **15**:287
Spitzer, M. **15**:1488
Spitzer, Rudolf, *see* LOTHAR, RUDOLF
Spitzer, S. (Bib. trans.) **4**:885; **13**:798
Spitzer, Samuel (art collec.), *see* SPITZER, FREDERIC
SPITZER, SAMUEL (r.) **15**:287
SPITZER, SOLOMON **15**:287
- Ahavat Zion society **4**:984
- Maharam Shick **14**:958
- Nathanson, Joseph **12**:867
- Sofer, Moses **15**:79
Spitzer, Reb Zalman, *see* SPITZER, SOLOMON
SPIVACKE, HAROLD **12**:709
Spivak, Charles D. **5**:1545; **16**:729
Spivak, E. **14**:1278
Spivak, Naphtali **16**:682
SPIVAK, NISSAN **15**:288
Spivak, Sydney **11**:879; **13**:811; **15**:27
Spivakovski, Jacob **15**:1072
Splendour, Book of (wk.), *see* ZOHAR
SPLIT (city, Yug.) **15**:288
- Yugoslavia **16**:870
Spljet (city, Yug.), see SPLIT
SPOEHR, ALEXANDER **15**:290
- anthropology **3**:40
Spohr, Louis **12**:682
Spokane (city, Wash.) **16**:356
SPOLETO (tn., It.) **15**:290
- special Purim **13**:1397
Sponges **6**:38
Sponheim, Abbot of, *see* TRITHEMIUS, JOHANNES
Spontaneous generation **4**:1016
SPORN, PHILIP **15**:290
Sporrenberg, J. **16**:295
Sport ba-Olam (journ.) **1**:newsp. list
- *see also: Ha-Sport*
Sport ha-Boker (period.) **1**:newsp. list
Sport ha-Shavu'a (period.) **1**:newsp. list
Sport Kadduregel (period.) **1**:newsp. list
Sport la-Am (publ.) **1**:newsp. list
SPORTS **15**:291
- *Contents:*
- - Middle Ages **15**:292
- - Modern Era **15**:293
- - In Israel **15**:294
- - Jewish Sportsmen **15**:298
- Ha-Koaḥ (Vienna) **16**:127
- Israel **9**:1018; **9**:869; **9**:1496
- Maccabi World Union **11**:664
- *The Ring* **6**:1345
- *illus:*
- - text
- - Chess Olympics medal **11**:1174
- - first Maccabiah **11**:663
- - Greenberg, Hank **7**:904
- - Houdini **8**:1047
- - Israel basketball team in Moscow **12**:363
- - Israel stamps **9**:844-845
- - J.N.F. assembly in Riga **14**:174
- - Kaunas Maccabi soccer team **11**:377
- - Kosov soccer team **10**:1217
- - Mendoza, Daniel **11**:1348
- - Modi'in torch **12**:207
- - Olympic Games medal winners (table) **12**:1373ff
- - seventh Maccabiah **11**:663
- - Vilna sports festival poster **16**:145
- *see also:* HUNTING
Sport ve-Toto (period.) **1**:newsp. list
Sport Yisrael (period.) **1**:newsp. list
Spracker, Maurice M. **11**:1589
Sprecher, J.D. **8**:58
Spring, Michael **15**:316
Springer, Béla, *see* DÉNES, BÉLA
Springer, Daniel **8**:59
Springfield (city, Ill.) **8**:1255
SPRINGFIELD (city, Mass.) **15**:318
- *illus:* text
Springfield (city, Mo.) **12**:158
Springfield (vill., N.J.) **15**:1534
Springs (city, Transvaal) **15**:1340
- *illus:*
- - opening of new synagogue **15**:1340
Spring Valley (tn., N.Y.) **10**:1222; **12**:1127; **14**:214
Sprinzak, Dov Ber **15**:319
SPRINZAK, JOSEPH **15**:319
- Warsaw **16**:337
- Zionist Congress (12th) **16**:1171
- *illus:*
- - protest against Passfield White Paper **16**:1118
Spritzer, Victor **14**:523
Spying, *see* Espionage
Square script **2**:705
- *illus:*
- - script types **2**:711-728
Squash (sport) **15**:315
Squid (zool.) **6**:38
Squier (Squire, Squyer), Adam **8**:59
SQUILL (bot.) **15**:321
- plant list **13**:625
- *illus:* text
Squirrel (zool.) **14**:1078 (illus.)
Srebrek, Alexander **13**:1378
Srebrek, Joseph **13**:1378
Srebrek, Shlomo **13**:1378
Srebrek Publishing House (Vilna) **5**:434
Srednicki, Matla, *see* Kremer, Pati
SREM (tn., Pol.) **15**:321
Sri Lanka, *see* CEYLON
Środula (sub., Sosnowiec) **5**:1218
Srole, Leo **11**:1375ff; **13**:1340; **15**:68
SRP, *see* Socialist Reich Party
SS AND SD (Nazi org.) **15**:322
- *Contents:*
- - Until World War II **15**:322
- - The "Final Solution" **15**:324
- Auschwitz trials **3**:873; **3**:874
- camps **5**:77
- Gestapo **7**:527
- Heydrich, Reinhard **8**:448
- Himmler, Heinrich **8**:498
- Hoess, Rudolf **8**:806
- Holocaust **8**:854
- Kapo **10**:754
- Katzmann, Friedrich **10**:834
- Pohl, Oswald **13**:701
- *illus:*
- - Bergen-Belsen guards on trial **16**:295
- - Hulievca-Berezovca camp, report of execution **15**:1330
- - humiliation of Polish Jews **8**:855-860
- - Stroop, Juergen, in Warsaw ghetto **15**:442
- *see also:* R.S.H.A.
Staab, Abraham **12**:1037
Staab, Zadoc **12**:1037
STACHEL, JACOB **15**:324
Stacte (bot.) **8**:1314
Stade, Bernhard **16**:1397
Stadermann, Sigi **12**:672
Stadia (meas.) **16**:389
Stadio Israelita (orgn.) **10**:1454
Stadler, J. E. **8**:59
Stadler, L.J. **4**:1031
STADTHAGEN, JOSEPH **15**:325
Stadt-Schlaining (vill., Burgenland) **4**:1511
Staemmer, Christoph van **8**:59
Staff, Leopold **13**:798
Staff of Aaron, *see* ROD OF AARON

Staff of Moses, *see* ROD OF MOSES
Stagnelius, Erik Johan **14:**929
Stahl (fam., Guatemala) **7:**956
Stahl, Abram M. **12:**1024
STAHL, FRIEDRICH JULIUS **15:**325
STAHL, HEINRICH **15:**326
Stahl, Samuel **11:**1588
Stahlecker, Walter **8:**869 ; **11:**389
Stalin (city, Bul.), *see* VARNA
STALIN, JOSEPH VISSARIONOVICH **15:**326
- anti-Semitism **3:**148
- communism **5:**792ff
- Dimanstein **6:**48
- "doctors' plot" **6:**144
- Jewish culture **16:**1069
- Jewish nationhood **14:**460
- Kamenev, Lev **10:**727
- persecutions **14:**481
- Solomon, Mikhoels **11:**1531
- Soviet anti-Semitism **3:**149
- Trotski **15:**1405
- universities **15:**1679
- Zionism **16:**1139
- *illus:*
- - newborn State of Israel (cart.) **9:**424
Staliniri (vill., Rus.) **7:**428
Stalino (city, Ukr.), *see* DONETSK
Stalinskoye (Stalindorf; stlmt., Rus.) **2:**408 ; **14:**468 ; **15:**1518
Stallybrass, William Swan, *see* Sonnenschein, William Swan
"Stam" (type let.) **15:**1488
- *illus:*
- - Hebrew type face example **15:**1485
Stambler, Benedict **13:**1618
STAMFORD (city, Conn.) **15:**329
- *illus:* text
STAMFORD (tn., Eng.) **15:**328
- Crusades **5:**1140
Stamford Hill (sub., London) **11:**478,479,481
- *illus:*
- - shift of population **11:**479
Stamler, Jeremiah **11:**1202
Stamp duty (Isr.) **9:**757
STAMPFER, JEHOSHUA (Isr. stlr.) **15:**329
Stampfer, Joshua (r., U.S.) **13:**911
Stampfer, Judah **15:**1572
STAMPS **15:**330
- Israel postal services **9:**841
- Israel taxation **9:**749
- *illus:*
- - Austria
- - - Landsteiner, Karl **12:**1203
- - - Lieben, Robert von (1936) **11:**215
- - Brazil: Shazar (1966) **4:**1332
- - Czechoslovakia
- - - Prague Jewry (1967) **5:**1197
- - - Theresienstadt drawings (1968) **5:**1203
- - Denmark: Bohr, Niels **12:**1203
- - Egypt: Nasser, Gamal Abdul (1967) **12:**842
- - France:
- - - Natzweiler-Struthof concentration camp (1964) **12:**893
- - - Proust, Marcel (1966) **13:**1256
- - - Sarah Bernhardt (1945) **4:**678
- - Germany (East)
- - - camp memorials **4:**1445
- - - *Kristallnacht* **10:**1263
- - - Luxemburg, Rosa (1955) **11:**592
- - Germany (West)
- - - Albert Ballin **4:**139
- - - Ehrlich, Paul **12:**1203
- - - Lassalle, Ferdinand **10:**1442
- - - Oppenheimer, Franz (1964) **12:**1426
- - - Pappenheim, Bertha **13:**68
- - Hungary: Zamenhof, Ludwik Lazar **16:**925
- - India: Waldemar Haffkine (1964) **7:**1061
- - Israel **9:**844-845
- - - Balfour, Arthur James (1967) **9:***fcg.* 843
- - - Benei Akiva conference (1958) **4:**491
- - - Benjamin tribal emblem **6:**1450
- - - Bialik (1958) **4:**796
- - - Bilu jubilee (1952) **9:***fcg.* 843
- - - First Zionist Congress symbols (1960) **9:***fcg.* 843
- - - ibex (1967) **8:**1150
- - - Iraqi *aliyah* (1970) **8:**1455
- - - Israel Ba'al Shem Tov's *bet ha-midrash* (1960) **9:**1053
- - - Jewish War coinage (1948) **9:***fcg.* 843
- - - J.N.F. jubilee (1951) **9:***fcg.* 843
- - - Korczak, Janusz (1962) **10:**1200
- - - Maimonides (1953) **11:**759
- - - Memorial Day 5727 (1967) **9:**844-845
- - - Merḥavyah jubilee (1960) **11:**1385
- - - Mirage aircraft (1967) **9:**844-845
- - - Naphtali tribal emblem (1955) **12:**819
- - - national flag (1949) **9:**844-845
- - - Negev (1950) **12:**927
- - - Stamp Day issues **9:**843, 844
- - Poland
- - - Einstein, Albert **12:**1203
- - - Lodz ghetto **11:**431
- - - Majdanek death camp **11:**794
- - Russia: Metchnikoff, Elie **12:**1204
- - Spain
- - - Maimonides (1967) **11:**759
- - Surinam **15:**530
- - Sweden
- - - Baeyer, Adolf Von **12:**1203
- - - Lippmann, Gabriel **12:**1203
- - - Michelson, Albert Abraham **12:**1204
- - - Moissan, Henri **12:**1204
- - U.S.
- - - immortal chaplains memorial stamp (1948) **11:**1571
- - - Pulitzer, Joseph (1947) **13:**1302
Stancaro, Franciscus **8:**59
STAND, ADOLF **15:**337
- Mahler, Arthur **11:**725
- *illus:*
- - First Zionist Congress **16:**1165
Standard Jewish Encyclopaedia **14:**326
Standards Institution of Palestine **9:**967
STANDE, STANISLAW RYSZARD **13:**804
Standing Bear (Ind. chief) **12:**1374
Stangl, Franz **15:**21 ; **16:**298
Stanichka (vill., Rus.), *see* Kunikov
STANISLAV (city, Ukr.) **15:**337
- Auerbach, Arieh **3:**843
Stanislaver Nakhrikhten (newsp.) **15:**338
Stanislavsky, Konstantin **5:**338 ; **7:**1029
STANISLAVSKY, SIMON JUDAH **15:**339
Stanislawow (city, Rus.), *see* STANISLAV
Stanisloyer Gloke (newsp.) **15:**338
Stanmore (sub., London) **11:**479
- *illus:*
- - shift of population **11:**479
Stanss, David **13:**1107
Stapleton, Thomas **8:**59
Star, patron, *see Mazzal*
Star, Sol **12:**266
Starachowice (concen. camp) **13:**557
STARA ZAGORA (city, Bul.) **15:**340
Starck, H.B. **8:**59
Starckius, S.G. **8:**59
Stargazing **3:**789
Stark, Albert D. **15:**301,303
STARK, EDWARD **7:**1550
Stark, I. **15:**1575
Stark, Jacob **4:**1220
STARK, LOUIS **10:**317
Stark, Pesach, *see* STRYJKOWSKI, JULJAN
Stark, Rodney **13:**1251 ; **15:**68
Starke, H.B., *see* Starck, H.B.
Starke, S.G., *see* Starckius, S.G.
STARKENSTEIN, EMIL **15:**340
STARKEY, JOHN LLEWELYN **15:**340
Starkova, K.B. **11:**18
STAROBINSKI, JEAN **15:**341
STARODUB (city, Rus.) **15:**341
- Chernigov **5:**392
Star of David, *see* MAGEN DAVID
Star of Redemption (bk.) **14:**300
Star of Solomon **2:**911
STARO-KONSTANTINOV (city, Ukr.) **15:**341
Starominsky, Mordechai, *see* SETER, MORDECHAI
STARR, JOSHUA **15:**342
Stars
- as angels **2:**964
- day and night **5:**1376
- Host of Heaven **8:**1044
- moon, appeasement of **12:**290
Stary Bykhov (city, Rus.), *see* BYKHOV
Stary Krym (city, Crim.) **5:**1105
Stashev (tn., Pol.), *see* STASZOW
Stasov, Vladimir Vasilievich **3:**162
STASZOW (tn., Pol.) **15:**343
State, Oscar **15:**316
STATE COMPTROLLER OF ISRAEL **9:**617
State Jewish Theater (Moscow) **15:**1069 ; **15:**327
State Jewish Theater (Ukr.) **15:**1076
State List (party, Isr.) *see* Reshimah Mamlaḥtit
Statenbijbel (Du. Bib.) **4:**876
Staten Island (boro., N.Y.C.), *see* Richmond
State of Israel, *see* ISRAEL
State of Israel Bonds, *see* BONDS, STATE OF ISRAEL
Stations of the Cross (Jer.)
- *illus:*
- - Franciscans at First Station **9:**916
- - pilgrims at Third Station **9:**916
STATISTICS **15:**343
- *Contents:*
- - Official Statistics **15:**343
- - Jewish-Sponsored Data Collection **15:**345
- intermarriage **12:**164
- Israel Association **15:**56 ; **15:**347
- mental health **11:**1372
- synagogues **1:**syn. list
- Youth Aliyah **16:**862ff
- *see also:* VITAL STATISTICS
Statistics, Population, *see* DEMOGRAPHY
STATIUS, PUBLIUS PAPINIUS **14:**236
Statue of Liberty (N.Y.C.) **15:**1608
Status of the Jews, *see* DHIMMA, DHIMMI ; EMANCIPATION ; HISTORY ; MINORITY RIGHTS ; *and under individual towns and countries*
STATUS QUO ANTE (cmties., Hung.) **15:**347
Statute of Kalisz (charter) **4:**1187
Statutum de Judaismo (law, Eng.) **5:**127 ; **6:**751
- history chart **8:**766-767
STAUB, HERMANN **15:**347
Staunton (city, Va.) **16:**163
STAVI (Stawsky), MOSES **15:**348
- Kook, Abraham **10:**1183
Stavitsky, Michael A. **6:**904
Stavordale Bible (illum. ms.) **4:**64
Stavski, Avraham **3:**471 ; **9:**1181
Stawell (tn., Austr.) **11:**1285
Stealing, *see* THEFT AND ROBBERY
Stearns, Daniel Eckford **15:**301
Stechenberg, Jacob **15:**36
Steckelmacher (r.) **15:**265
Steel City (indust. zone, Haifa) **2:**226 ; **7:**1139
Steen, Cornelius van den, *see* Lapide, Cornelius à
Steenbach, J. **8:**59
STEFANESTI (tn., Rum.) **15:**348
- Aaron Samuel ha-Kohen **2:**23
Stefanesti (ḥas. dyn.) **14:**532
Stefen, Oskar **4:**808
Steierman (cmty. ldr.) **14:**765
Steiermark (prov., Aus.), *see* STYRIA
Steig, William **5:**220
STEIGER, ROD **12:**474
Steiger, Sam **3:**450
Steiger, Stanislaw **15:**348
STEIGER TRIAL **15:**348
- Waldmann, Israel **16:**250
Steigman, Jerakhme'el **15:**109
STEIMAN, BEYNUSH **15:**349
Steimatzky's Agency (publ. firm, Isr.) **13:**1378
Stein (fam., U.S.) **15:**790
Stein, Abraham **7:**348
STEIN, ARTHUR **15:**349
STEIN, AUGUST **15:**350
- Cechu-Zidu, Svaz **5:**267
- Czechoslovakia **5:**1191
Stein, Aviezri **15:**355
Stein, David **12:**215
STEIN, EDITH **15:**350
STEIN, EDMUND MENAHEM **15:**351
STEIN, ELIEZER LIPMAN **15:**351
Stein, Fortunee **15:**1045
Stein, Gabriel **15:**351
STEIN, GERTRUDE **15:**352
Stein, Harry **15:**303
STEIN, HENRI **15:**353
STEIN, HERMAN D. **15:**354
Stein, H.Z. **12:**214
STEIN, ISAAC **15:**354
Stein, Jacob **15:**135
STEIN, BARON KARL VOM ZUM **15:**355
Stein, Leo **15:**352 ; **15:**353
STEIN, LEONARD JACQUES **15:**356
- A.J.A. **2:**978
STEIN, LEONID **5:**409
Stein, Leopold **7:**89 ; **11:**403
Stein, Louis B. **15:**305
STEIN, LUDWIG **15:**356
- sociology **15:**66
Stein, M. (r., Lith.) **11:**1297
STEIN, SIR MARC AUREL **15:**356
- archaeology **3:**302
- China exploration **5:**468
- travels **15:**1351
Stein, Maurice **15:**63
Stein, Menahem **11:**1203
Stein, Menahem (educ.) **16:**340
Stein, Morris **13:**912
Stein, Moshe **12:**1518
Stein, Nathan **2:**820 ; **10:**1497
Stein, Robert **15:**308
Stein, Samuel **15:**308
Stein, Solomon **14:**1031

Stein, Theodore De **6**:1159
Steinach (tn., Ger.) **4**:352
STEINACH, EUGEN **15**:357
Steinamanger (city, Hung.), *see* SZOMBATHELY
STEINBACH, ALEXANDER ALAN **15**:358
STEINBACH, EMIL **15**:358
STEINBARG, ELIEZER **15**:358
- Yiddish literature **16**:820
Steinberg (cantor, Rus.) **12**:367
Steinberg, Aaron **15**:361
Steinberg, Abraham Menahem ha-Levi **14**:92
Steinberg, B. **11**:1569
Steinberg, Charles **15**:308
Steinberg, David (jur.) **7**:1239
Steinberg, David (sport.) **15**:308
Steinberg, H. **13**:1369
STEINBERG, ISAAC NAHMAN **15**:359
STEINBERG, JACOB **15**:361
- critic **5**:1121
- drama **6**:202
- literature **8**:197
STEINBERG, JOSHUA **15**:363
- Bible translator **4**:887
STEINBERG, JUDAH **15**:363
- Elisheva **6**:671
STEINBERG, MARTIN R. **11**:1210
STEINBERG, MAXIMILIAN OSSEJEVICH **12**:709
Steinberg, Meyer **15**:1338
STEINBERG, MILTON **15**:364
- *Akedah* **2**:484
- Elisha ben Avuyah **6**:670
Steinberg, Moses **4**:1398
Steinberg, Paul **15**:302; 308
Steinberg, Riva **11**:1567
Steinberg, Samuel **15**:1679
STEINBERG, SAUL **15**:365
- *New Yorker* **5**:220
- *illus:*
- - text
- - drawing **5**:218
STEINBERG, WILLIAM **12**:709
- Pittsburgh **13**:570
STEINBRUCH, AARAO **15**:365
- politics **13**:821
Steinbruch, Julia Vaena **15**:365
Steindorff, Georg **3**:302; **12**:1461
Steineck (fig., *Altneuland*) **11**:1013
STEINER, GEORGE **6**:785,790
STEINER, HANNAH **15**:366
- Czechoslovakia **5**:1192
- press **13**:1027
- Zionism **16**:1113
Steiner, Herman **5**:407
Steiner, J. **8**:59
Steiner, Jean-François **5**:677
Steiner, Lajos **5**:407
Steiner, Ludwig **15**:366
Steiner, Newman Leopold **15**:1264
Steiner, Rudolf **16**:1214
Steiner, Shaye **4**:1164
STEINER-PRAG, HUGO **3**:616
- Prague **13**:973
Steinersdorff, J. C. **8**:59
Steinfeld (fam.) **3**:450
Steinglass, Dora **4**:1105
Steinglass, Meyer **13**:1363
STEINGUT (fam.) **15**:367
Steingut, Irwin **15**:367
Steingut, Stanley **15**:367
Steinhardt, Akiva **15**:368
Steinhardt, Jacob **3**:250; **8**:505
STEINHARDT, JAKOB(paint.) **15**:367
- *illus:*
- - *Ḥad Gadya* (wdct.) **7**:1050
- - ḥasidic dance (wdct.) **7**:1415
- - "Street in Jerusalem" (wdct.) fig. 93 **3**-ART
- - ten plagues (wdct.) **13**:612
STEINHARDT, JOSEPH BEN MENAHEM **15**:368
- Banet, Mordecai **4**:159
- Berlin, David **4**:657
- Cleves *get* **5**:614
Steinhardt, Kreindel **15**:368
STEINHARDT, LAURENCE ADOLF **15**:369
STEINHARDT, MENAHEM MENDEL BEN SIMEON **15**:369
- Westphalia **16**:474
Steinhardt, Moses **15**:369
Steinhart (fam.) **5**:56
Steinhart, Arye L. **15**:521
STEINHAUS, HUGO DYONIZY **11**:1126
STEINHEIM, SALOMON LUDWIG **15**:370
- concept of God **7**:663
- Jewish equality **14**:973
- philosophy **13**:459
- prophecy **13**:1180
- revelation **14**:125
- Torah **15**:1242
- *illus:* text
STEINHERZ, SAMUEL **15**:371
Stein Iron Works (Isr.) **9**:328
Steinitz, Hans **13**:1053
STEINITZ, WILHELM **15**:371
- chess **5**:405; **5**:407
- *illus:* text
Steinkopf, Maitland **15**:1679
Steinman, A.(ed.) **12**:495
Steinman, Baynush **15**:372
Steinman, David B. **11**:1498
STEINMAN, ELIEZER **15**:372
- *illus:*
- - Writers' Assoc. in Israel **8**:205
Steinman, Jacob **15**:1214
STEINMETZ, CHARLES PROTEUS **15**:373
Steinmetz, J. A. **8**:59
Steinsalz, Adin **15**:768
Steinschneider, Daniel, *see* PROSSTITZ, DANIEL
Steinschneider, Malvine, *see* Husserl, Malvine
STEINSCHNEIDER, MORITZ **15**:374
- Asher, Abraham **3**:702
- book collection **4**:975
- Brody, Heinrich **4**:1399
- chess **5**:402
- Graetz, Heinrich **8**:561
- incunabula **8**:1322
- Jewish scholarship **16**:575
- Wolf, J. C. **16**:605
- Yiddish literature research **16**:826
Steinthal, Fritz **12**:505
STEINTHAL, HERMANN HEYMANN **15**:377
Steinweg, G. F. **8**:59
Steirischer Heimatschutz (S. S. orgn.) **13**:1576
STEKEL, WILHELM **15**:377
STEKELIS, MOSHE **15**:378
- archaeology **3**:39; **3**:302
Steklov, J. **5**:794
Stele of Hammurapi (Mesop.) **16**:1507
Stella (city, Sp.), *see* ESTELLA
Stellin (writ.), *see* POSENER, SOLOMON
STEMATSKY, AVIGDOR **15**:378
- *illus:*
- - text
- - pastel painting Pl. 10 **3**-ART
Stember, Charles **15**:68
Stempenyu (wk.) **14**:1278
STENCL, ABRAHAM NAHUM **15**:379
Stendahl, K. **8**:921
STENDAL (city, Ger.) **15**:379
- Brandenburg **4**:1301
- population **13**:880
Stendal, Moses **4**:867; **11**:357
Stengel, Erwin **13**:1340
Stengel, L. **8**:59
Stenhagen, G. **8**:59
Steniatyn (tn., Ukr.) **15**:84
Stenring, K. **16**:787
Stepan, David ha-Levi of, *see* David ha-Levi of Stepan
Ṣtephan (metropolitan of Sofia) **8**:915
Stephanus, Robert, *see* Estienne (Stephanus), Robert
Stephanus of Byzantium **7**:893
Stephen (1st cent. Chr. st.) **7**:712
Stephen III (pope) **13**:852
Stephen Báthory **11**:1309
Stephen of Avignon **3**:964
Stepney (dist., London) **6**:447,449
Stereochemistry **11**:1465
Sterility, *see* BARRENNESS AND FERTILITY
Sterilization **5**:85
Sterling, Marc **13**:116
Sterling, Seweryn **11**:1204
STERN (fam., Eng.) **15**:380
Stern (fam., Ger.) **15**:74
Stern (fam., U.S.) **5**:56; **13**:1519
Stern, Aaron Samuel **15**:300
STERN, ABRAHAM JACOB **15**:380
- inventor **8**:1430
- *illus:* text
STERN, ADOLPHE **15**:381
- Rumania **14**:391, 394ff
Stern, Sir Albert **15**:384
STERN, ALFRED **15**:381
STERN, ANATOL **15**:382
STERN, ARTHUR C. **8**:1434
STERN, AVRAHAM (Ya'ir) **15**:382
- Yellin-Mor, Nathan **16**:738
- *illus:*
- - "Wanted" poster **8**:1468
- *see also:* LOḤAMEI ḤERUT ISRAEL
Stern, Axel **4**:546
STERN, BERNHARD JOSEPH **15**:383
STERN, BEZALEL **15**:383
- Odessa school **16**:450
Stern, Clara Joseephy **6**:463; **15**:394
Stern, Curt **4**:1031
Stern, Daniel **15**:315
Stern, David (mfr.) **15**:435
Stern, David de (bnk.) **15**:380
Stern, Edgar B. **12**:1042
Stern, Sir Edward **15**:380
Stern, Emma **13**:120
STERN, ERICH **15**:384
Stern, Ernst **15**:1057
STERN, SIR FREDERICK CLAUDE **15**:384
Stern, Georges **15**:310
STERN, GERSHON **15**:385
STERN, GLADYS BRONWYN **15**:385
STERN, GRIGORI **11**:1556; **11**:1576
STERN, HANS **15**:385
Stern, Hermann de **15**:380
STERN, HORACE **15**:386
- Pennsylvania **13**:230
Stern, I. (poet) **16**:820
STERN, IRMA **15**:386
STERN, ISAAC (mus.) **15**:386
- Cultural Foundation **2**:817
- *illus:*
- - Israel Festival (1961) **9**:1007
Stern, Isaac (bnk.) **4**:177
Stern, Israel **14**:1265
STERN, JACQUES **15**:387
Stern, Jean **15**:311; **12**:1375
Stern, Jenö, *see* ZSOLDOS, JENÖ
STERN, JOSEPH (Hung.) **15**:387
STERN, JOSEPH ZECHARIAH (Lith.) **15**:387
- Gordon, Judah **7**:801
- *illus:*
- - funeral **14**:1485
STERN, JULIUS (cond.) **12**:710
STERN, JULIUS DAVID (publ.) **15**:388
- literature **11**:307
STERN, KURT GUNTER **15**:388
Stern, Laura Julia **15**:380
Stern, Lav **16**:1149
STERN, LINA SOLOMONOVNA **15**:388
- Anti-Fascist Committee **3**:64
- *illus:*
- - Jewish Anti-Fascist Committee **3**:63; **6**:1203
Stern, Louis (philos.), *see* STERN, WILLIAM
STERN, LOUIS (bsmn.) **15**:389
STERN, MALCOLM HENRY **15**:389
STERN, MAX (bsmn.) **15**:390
STERN, MAX EMANUEL (Mendel; writ.) **15**:390
- *Bikkurei ha-Ittim* **4**:993
Stern, Meir **10**:1117
STERN, MENAHEM **15**:390
Stern, Mikhail **15**:314
Stern, Mór (Bib. trans.) **4**:884
STERN, MORITZ **15**:390
- archives **3**:388
- historiography **8**:562
STERN, NOAH **15**:391
STERN, OTTO **15**:391
Stern, Paul **5**:169
Stern, Percival **12**:1042
STERN, PHILIP COHEN **15**:392
Stern, René **11**:1165
Stern, Salomo Gottlieb **4**:334
Stern, Samuel I. **14**:399
STERN, SAMUEL MIKLOS (Eng.) **15**:392
- Neoplatonic studies **12**:959
STERN, SIGISMUND **15**:392
Stern, Sydney James **15**:380
Stern, Viktor **5**:1191
STERN, WILLIAM **15**:393
- Koffka, Kurt **10**:1134
Sternbach, Leon **5**:1035
Sternberg (tn., Ger.) **8**:1043; **11**:1163
Sternberg, Ben **11**:1552
Sternberg, Ben-Zion **5**:1455
STERNBERG, ERICH-WALTER **15**:394
Sternberg, Fritz **15**:64
STERNBERG, JACOB **15**:395
- Botoshanski, Jacob **4**:1272
STERNBERG, JOSEF VON **15**:395
- *illus:*
- - on the set of *The Blue Angel* **12**:454
STERNBERG, KURT **15**:395
STERNBERG, LEV YAKOVLEVICH **15**:396
- anthropology **15**:1351
Sternberger, Leon **12**:1072
Sternberger, Moses **3**:824
Stern College (N.Y.) **16**:761
Sterne, Adolphus **15**:1034
STERNE, HEDDA **3**:611
STERNE, MAURICE **15**:396
- *illus:* text
Sterne, Samuel G. **15**:312
STERNE, SIMON **15**:397
Stern Group (orgn., Pal.), *see* LOḤAMEI ḤERUT ISRAEL
STERNHARZ, NATHAN **15**:398
- Naḥman of Bratslav **12**:783*ff*
STERNHEIM, CARL **15**:398
Sternhold Psalter **13**:1328
STERNSCHUSS, MOSHE **3**:611
- sculptor **14**:1070
STERN-TAEUBLER, SELMA **15**:399
- historiography **8**:562
- Taeubler, Eugene **15**:699

Stettenheim, Julius **7**:449
STETTIN (city, Pol.) **15**:399
Stettner, Henry **15**:1206
Stettner, Sam **15**:1206
Steubenville (city, Ohio) **12**:1345
Steuco, Agostino **8**:59
STEUERMAN, ADOLF RODION **15**:400
STEUERMANN, EDWARD **12**:710
STEUERNAGEL, CARL **15**:401
STEUSS, DAVID **15**:401
Steuss, Hendlin (12/13 cent.) **15**:401
Steuss, Hendlin (14/15 cent.) **15**:401
Steuss, Jacob **15**:401
Steuss, Jonah **15**:401
Stew **6**:1415
Stibium (metal), *see* Antimony
Stichkin, David **5**:467
Sticker, Josephine **12**:1375
STIEGLITZ (fam.) **15**:402
Stieglitz, Alexander **13**:1518; **15**:402
STIEGLITZ, ALFRED **15**:402
Stieglitz, Bernhard (Hirsch) **15**:402
Stieglitz, Heinrich **7**:449
Stieglitz, Johann **11**:1173
STIEGLITZ, JULIUS OSCAR **5**:388
Stieglitz, Ludwig **15**:402
Stieglitz, Nicolai **15**:402
Stier, Ewald R. **8**:59
Stier, G. **8**:59
STILES, EZRA **15**:403
- Carigal, Raphael **5**:180
- Hebraic studies **8**:59
Stiller, Mauritz **12**:456
Stiller, S.P. **16**:1015
STILLING, BENEDICT **15**:403
- medicine **11**:1197
Stilling, Jacob Benedict **15**:403
"Still Life" (paint., L. Marcoussis) **11**:943
"Still Life" (paint., M. Mokady) Pl.6 **3**-ART
Stillman, Saul **5**:611
Stillwater (city, U.S.) **12**:1353
Stindardul (period.) **14**:398
Štip (tn., Maced.) **16**:872; **16**:880
Stipulations, *see* CONDITIONS
Stiri din Lumea Evreească (period.) **14**:399,1084; **16**:1135
Stirling, Edward **15**:1054
Sto, Adrian **15**:1074
STOBBE, OTTO **15**:404
Stobi (city, Yug.) **16**:872
- *illus:*
- - synagogue column **12**:238
Stobnitsa (place, Pol.) **3**:224
Stock, Dov, *see* SADAN, DOV
Stock, Fradel **16**:822
Stock, Joseph **8**:59
STOCKADE AND WATCHTOWER **15**:404
- Defense Forces **9**:687
- history **9**:352
- *illus:*
- - text
- - Ein ha-Kore **9**:356
- - Massadah **11**:1116
- - Negbah **12**:925
- - Nir David **12**:1173
- - Sha'ar ha-Golan model **9**:550
- - She'ar Yashuv **14**:1328
- - Tirat Ẓevi **8**:757
- - woman guard **7**:1068
Stockerau (leg. loc.) **10**:326
STOCK EXCHANGE, TEL AVIV **9**:829
- *illus:* text
STOCK EXCHANGES **15**:405
- Amsterdam **2**:898
- *see also:* BANKING AND BANKERS
STOCKHOLM (city, Swed.) **15**:407
- library **11**:191
- *illus:* text
Stockton (city, Calif.) **5**:56
Stodolsky, Jacob **8**:1434
STOECKER, ADOLF **15**:408
- Bismarck **4**:1058
- Hep! Hep! slogan **8**:332
- history chart **8**:766-767
- opposition to **16**:111
- Westphalia **16**:475
STOICISM **15**:409
- Hellenistic period **8**:293; **8**:298
- Jewish literature **8**:304
- logos **11**:461
- Neoplatonism **12**:959
- Philo **13**:413ff
- rabbinic philosophy **13**:423
- sages **14**:651
Stokes, J.G. Phelps **15**:410
STOKES, ROSE PASTOR (Wieslander) **15**:410
Stol, Y. **16**:826
Stolberg, Balthasar **8**:59
STOLBTSY (tn., Belor.) **15**:411
STOLIN (city, Belor.) **15**:412
- *see also:* Karlin
Stolin (ḥas. dyn.) **1**:ḥas. table
Stolle, J. H. **8**:59
Stoller, Ezra **13**:484
Stolp (concen. camp, Pol.) **15**:464
Stolpce (tn., Belor.) *see* STOLBTSY
STOLYARSKI, PETER SOLOMONOVICH **15**:413
Stolypin, Peter Arkadyevich **16**:614
- Bogrov, assassin **4**:1172
Stolzenberg, A. **16**:822
Stomanyakov, Khristo **4**:1488; **8**:851
Stone (fam.) **5**:612
Stone (geol.) **11**:510; **16**:656
Stone (weight), *see 'Even*
STONE, DEWEY **15**:413
Stone, George Robert **15**:301
STONE, I.F. (Isidore Feinstein) **10**:317
STONE, IRVING **15**:1584
STONE, J.E. **11**:1278
STONE, JULIUS **15**:413
STONE, MICHAEL EDWARD **1**:38
Stone, Mickey, *see* MARCUS, DAVID DANIEL
Stone, Steven M. **15**:301
Stone age **9**:226
Stone of Bohan (anc. mon.), *see* Bohan
Stoning (leg.) **2**:313,316; **5**:142; **16**:161
- *illus:*
- - Achan **8**:346
- - Naboth **12**:747
STOPNICA (tn., Pol.) **15**:414
Stoppelman, Joseph F. **10**:306
STORA (Satorra; fam.) **15**:415
- family **4**:1274; **12**:1446; **15**:1173
Stora, Abraham **15**:415
Stora, Marcel **15**:1535
Stora, Paul **15**:415
Stora, Reuben **15**:415
Storace, Anna **4**:1289
STORAX (resin) **15**:415
- flora of Israel **9**:221
Storch, Hillel **15**:549
STORK (ornith.) **15**:416
Storm troops, *see* S.A.
STOROZHINETS (city, Ukr.) **15**:416
STORRS, SIR RONALD **15**:417
- Jerusalem **9**:1469; **9**:1472
- *illus:*
- - at Government House, Jerusalem **2**:57
- - Amery, Leopold, and **2**:833
- - Rothschild, James de, and **14**:346
Stoss, Veit **14**:1060
Stoypts (tn., Belor.) *see* STOLBTSY
STRABO **15**:417
- *androgynos* fable **2**:949
- Judaism **7**:889; **7**:894
STRACK, HERMANN LEBERECHT **15**:418
Stradela (site, Er. Isr.), *see* JEZREEL
Stradom (place, Pol.) **5**:1028
STRAKOSCH, MAURICE **12**:710
Strakosch, Salomon **15**:1041
STRANGERS AND GENTILES **15**:419
- Commandments, the 613 **5**:770
- *see also:* PROSELYTES
Strnagling **2**:316; **5**:144
Stránsky, Bedřich **13**:346
Stransky, Hugo **11**:1284; **16**:1022
STRANSKY, JOSEF **12**:710
STRASBERG, LEE **15**:421
Strasberg, Susan **15**:422
STRASBOURG (city, Fr.) **15**:422
- Alsatian history **2**:751ff
- Armleder bands **3**:484
- banking **4**:168
- Crusades **5**:1138
- Ennery, Jonas D' **6**:792
- library **11**:193
- museums **12**:544
- *illus:*
- - text
- - Agnon at the Hebrew Institute of University of **12**:940
- - Alsatian Museum, Jewish room **12**:545
Strasburg, Gabriel ben Aaron **7**:1107
STRASBURGER, EDUARD **15**:426
Strashun, David **15**:428
Strashun, Isaac **15**:427
STRASHUN, MATHIAS (Mattityahu) **15**:426
STRASHUN, SAMUEL BEN JOSEPH **15**:428
- Strashun, Mathias **15**:427
Strashun Library (Vilna) **15**:426*ff*
- *illus:* **16**:141
Strashunsky, Joel David, *see* LOEWENSTEIN-STRASCHUNSKY, JOEL DAVID
Strasser, Adolph **15**:30
Strassnitz (tn., Morav.) **7**:1010
Stratford (city, Ont.) **12**:1408
Straton II (k., Sidon) **5**:6; **14**:1507
Straton's Tower (tn., Er. Isr.), *see* CAESAREA
STRAUBING (city, Ger.) **15**:428
Strauch, Aegidius (Giles) **8**:59
Straucher, Benno **11**:725; **13**:122; **13**:809; **16**:213
Straus (name), *see also* Strauss
STRAUS (fam.) **15**:429
- department stores **5**:1546
Straus, Herbert A. **2**:820
Straus, Isidore **2**:125; **12**:1093; **12**:1103; **15**:429
- *illus:*
- - "Abraham and Straus" delivery wagons **2**:125
Straus, Jack Isidor **15**:431
Straus, Jesse Isidor **15**:431
Straus, Julius **14**:162
Straus, Lazarus **7**:613, **12**:1083; **15**:429
Straus, Lina **15**:430
Straus, Mike **13**:1361
Straus, Nathan (philan.) **2**:125; **15**:430
- *illus:*
- - "Abraham and Straus" delivery wagons **2**:125
- - Jerusalem health center cornerstone ceremony **15**:429
Straus, Nathan Jr. (journ.) **12**:1111; **15**:431
STRAUS, OSCAR **15**:432
- *illus:* text
Straus, Oscar Solomon **15**:430
- *American Hebrew, The* **2**:821
- Historical Society **2**:827
- Palestine settlement **9**:325
- politics **13**:821
- U.S. Jewish Committee **2**:822
Straus, Oscar Solomon ΙΙ **15**:432
STRAUS, RALPH **6**:790
Straus, Raphael **14**:37
Straus, Robert Kenneth **15**:431
Straus, Roger William **13**:1372; **15**:432
Straus, R. Peter **15**:431
Straus, Simon **8**:1362
Strausberg, Baruch Hirsch, *see* STROUSBERG, BETHEL HENRY
Straus Health Center (Jer.), *see* Nathan Straus Health Center
Strauss (name), *see also* Straus
Strauss, Alice **15**:436
STRAUSS, ARYEH LUDWIG **15**:433
STRAUSS, BENNO **8**:1434
Strauss, Berthold-Baruch **4**:975
Strauss, David **13**:1049
STRAUSS, EDUARD **5**:388
- Rosenzweig **14**:301
Strauss, Eliahu, *see* ASHTOR, ELIAHU
Strauss, Emil **13**:972
STRAUSS, GEORGE RUSSEL **15**:433
STRAUSS, GUSTAVE LOUIS MAURICE **6**:790
Strauss, Heinrich **4**:633
Strauss, Herbert D. **2**:317
Strauss, Johann **16**:111
Strauss, Joseph (art collec.) **12**:538
Strauss, Joseph (sol.) **11**:1552
STRAUSS, LEO **15**:434
STRAUSS, LEVI **15**:434
- San Francisco **5**:56; **14**:833; **14**:834
STRAUSS, LEWIS LICHTENSTEIN **15**:435
- Agricultural Society **10**:35
Strauss, Meyer, *see* STROUSE, MYER
Strauss, Seligman J. **16**:516
Stravinsky, Igor **2**:486; **10**:1376
Strazov (place, Cz.) **10**:1087
Strazzaria (term, It.), *see* SECONDHAND GOODS AND OLD CLOTHES, TRADE IN
Streane, A. W. **15**:768
Streckenbach, Bruno **8**:869
STRECKFUSS, ADOLF FRIEDRICH KARL **15**:436
"Street in Jerusalem" (wdct., J. Steinhardt) Fig. 93-ART
"Street in Shtetl" (drg., Z. Tolkatchov) **14**:1469
STREICHER, JULIUS **15**:436
- cartoons **5**:177
- *Der Stürmer* **15**:460
- *illus:*
- - *Der Sturmer* **3**:154
- - Nuremberg Trial **16**:289
STREICHMAN, YEḤEZKIEL **3**:611
- *illus:*
- - "Reclining Woman" (paint.) **3**:641
Streimel (headdress) **6**:220, 223
- *illus:*
- - hasidic boy **15**:*fcg.* 491
STREISAND, BARBRA **15**:437
STREIT, SHALOM **15**:438
Strelisk (ḥas. dyn.) **15**:438
Strelisk, Solomon ben Uri of **15**:438
STRELISK, URI BEN PHINEHAS OF **15**:438
- Greenberg, Uri Ẓevi **7**:906

Strelisker, David, *see* BROD, DOVIDL
STRELISKER, MARCUS **15:**438
Stretyn, Abraham of **15:**439
STRETYN, JUDAH ZEVI HIRSCH (Brandwein) OF **15:**438
- dynasties **1:** has. table
Streuch, Fabian **12:**1455
Strusand, Ira **15:**303
STRICH, FRITZ **15:**439
STRICK, JOSEPH **12:**474
Stricker, Paula **15:**440
STRICKER, ROBERT **15:**439
- Abeles **2:**61
- Revisionist Zionism **14:**129; **16:**1107
- Vienna **16:**127
- Volkspartei, Juedische **16:**213
- *illus:* text
Stridzberg, N. H. **8:**59
Striebow (Nazi) **7:**928
Striga (myth.) **11:**249
STRIGLER, MORDECAI **15:**440
- *illus:*
- - Yiddish writers group, Paris **16:**821
Strikes
- Arabs **9:**1474ff
- Histadrut **9:**882ff
- rabbinical attitude **10:**1323
- responsa on **14:**94
- socialism, Jewish **15:**41ff
- *illus:*
- - Jewish Protest Committee Against Pogroms, announcement **13:**695
- - New York garment workers **15:**1616,1617
- - New York teachers' rally **12:**1114
Strindberg, August **14:**929ff
- Wandering Jew **16:**262
Stripes, *see* FLOGGING
Stripping (legal) **2:**313
STRISOWER, LEO **15:**440
STRNAD, OSKAR **3:**366
Strogovich, Mikhail Solomonovich **10:**1501
STROHEIM, ERICH VON **12:**474
- *illus:*
- - in *Blind Husbands* **12:**450
STROOCK (fam.) **15:**441
Stroock, Alan **15:**441
Stroock, Hilda **15:**441
Stroock, Joseph **15:**441
Stroock, Louis S. **15:**441
Stroock, Marcus **15:**441
Stroock, Mark **15:**441
Stroock, Moses J. **15:**441
Stroock, Regina **15:**441
Stroock, Solomon Marcuse **15:**441
STROOP, JUERGEN (Josef) **15:**442
- Athens **3:**818
- Warsaw ghetto **16:**351
- *illus:*
- - Warsaw Ghetto liquidation report **16:**346
- - Warsaw Ghetto photographs **16:**345,346
- - Warsaw Great Synagogue **16:**337
STROUSBERG, BETHEL HENRY **15:**443
- railroads **13:**1519
Strouse, Irving **13:**1361
Strouse, Mark **12:**1017
STROUSE, MYER **15:**443
- Pennsylvania **13:**230
STRUCK, HERMANN **15:**443
- *illus:*
- - Barth, Jacob (lith.) **4:**262
- - Brainin, Reuben (etch.) **4:**1292
- - Cohen, Hermann (etch.) **8:**749
- - Einstein, Albert (drg.) **8:**749
- - Frischmann, David (drg.) **7:**202
- - Gernsheim, Friedrich (etch.) **7:**504
- - Gorelik, Shemarya (lith.) **7:**807
- - Guttmacher, Elijah (lith.) **7:**991
- - Hirschfeld, Georg (etch.) **8:**525
- - Hoffmann, David Zevi (etch.) **8:**809
- - Marshall, Louis (etch.) **11:**1060
- - Reines, Isaac Jacob (lith.) **14:**58
- - Schechter, Solomon (etch.) **14:**949
- - Shneour, Zalman (lith.) **14:**29
- - Soloveichik, Hayyim (lith.) **15:**129
- - Ussishkin, Menachem Mendel (etch.) **16:**23
- - Zweig, Arnold (etch.) **16:**1247
Struk (sol.) **13:**699
Struma (refugee boat) **8:**766-767; **8:**1249; **9:**353; **14:**404
Strumza, Hayyim Abraham **14:**1186
STRUNSKY, SIMEON **10:**317
Strupp, B. M. **11:**1240
Strupp, Gustav **11:**1240
Struthion Well (Jer.) **9:**1539
Struvius, Julius **8:**59
STRY (Stryj; city, Ukr.) **15:**444
STRYJKOWSKI, JULJAN **15:**446
STRYKOW (tn., Pol.) **15:**446
Strykow, Fishel of, *see* Fishel of Strykow
Strykow, Ze'ev Wolf ben Abraham of, *see* Ze'ev Wolf ben Abraham of Strykow
Strzyzow (tn., Pol.) **4:**15
Stuart, Moses **8:**59 **8:**209
Stubbs, J. N. **13:**31
Stubbs, Wolfran **8:**59
Stuckuis, Joannes Guilhelmus **8:**61
STUDENTS' ASSOCIATIONS, GERMAN **15:**447
- Burschenschaft **15:**1129
- Hep! Hep! riots **8:**330
- Jewish association **10:**804
- Viadrina (Breslau) **4:**1355
Students for a Democratic Society (orgn.) **12:**1031
STUDENTS' MOVEMENTS, JEWISH **15:**448
- *Contents:*
- - In Great Britain **15:**448
- - In France **15:**449
- - In the U.S. **15:**450
- - In Israel **15:**451
- - World Union of Jewish Students **15:**452
- Kadimah **10:**665
- *illus:*
- - Bar Kochba members **16:**1105
- - Berlin University **16:**1115
Student Zionist Organization (U.S.) **15:**451
Studer, Claire, *see* Goll, Claire
Studia Rosenthaliana (period.) **2:**904; **13:**1035
Studies in Bibliography and Booklore (period.) **8:**218; **15:**55
Studies in Torah Judaism (monographs) **16:**762
Studies on Jewish Life and Culture (journ.) **9:**1282
STUDY **15:**453
- *Contents:*
- - The Laws of Study **15:**456
- - Scope of Study **15:**456
- - Historical Aspects **15:**458
- History and Development
- - associations **8:**441; **15:**53
- - Ezra **8:**622ff
- - Hasidism **7:**1397ff
- - instruction development **8:**640
- - learned societies **15:**53
- - Ottoman Empire **16:**1549ff
- - Pentateuch **13:**257
- - Pharisees **13:**366
- - Rome **14:**245
- - sages **14:**638; **14:**647; **14:**649
- - Samaritans **14:**744
- - Spain **15:**224; **15:**242
- - tax exemption **15:**856
- - Temple **15:**983
- - title of rabbi **13:**1445
- - *see also:* YESHIVOT
- In Judaism **10:**391; **10:**393; **10:**395
- - fasting **6:**1194
- - fear of God **6:**1199
- - hasidic thought **7:**1405ff
- - labor **10:**1322
- - *mamzer* **11:**840
- - piety **13:**505
- - public affairs **13:**1352
- - purpose **13:**1463
- - *Shekhinah* **14:**1351
- - sin **14:**1593
- - study and action **9:**243
- - *talmid hakham* **15:**746
- - *Tohorot ha-Kodesh* **15:**1191
- Views on
- - Akiva **2:**491
- - Gersonides **14:**137
- - Johanan **16:**1278
- - Judah ha-Nasi **10:**370
- - *Ma'aseh Efod* (profiat Duran) **6:**301
- - Maimonides **5:**1551
- - Meir **11:**1242
- - Mendel of Kotsk **10:**1223
- - Rava **13:**1580
- - Simeon the Just **15:**1239
- - Volozhiner, Hayyim **16:**218
- *Halakhah*
- - *aliyah* **9:**509
- - covering of head **8:**5
- - marriage **11:**1028
- - mourning **12:**489ff
- - *niddui* and *herem* **8:**351
- - impurity **13:**1411; **13:**1413
- - *siyyum* **14:**1642
- - women **10:**1566; **16:**626
- In Midrash
- - Angel of Death **2:**953
- - David **5:**1328
- - *manna* **11:**886
- Prayer **13:**984
- - benediction over **4:**1036
- - *Kaddish* **10:**660
- - *Kedushah* **10:**876
- Methodology
- - Bible **4:**917ff
- - halakhah **7:**1156
- - Lithuania **11:**362ff
- - *pilpul* **13:**524
- - Rashi, use of **13:**1563
- - subject order **15:**767
- - *tosafot* **15:**1278ff
- In Art and Music **11:**735
- - melody in **15:**753
- *illus:*
- - amulet for learning of Torah **2:**907
- - angel rewarding good pupils **6:**387
- - children introduced to study of Torah **6:**386
- - "Examination" (paint., Oppenheim) **6:**393
- - Ez Hayyim Yeshivah Talmud lesson **16:**764
- - Gateshead Yeshivah **6:**421
- - *hadran alakh* **7:**1053
- - "*Heder*" (paint., E. Brandon) **6:**390
- - Lomza Yeshivah *Gemara* lesson **16:**762
- - pupils at U.S. yeshivah **6:**408
- - Rabban Gamaliel teaching **7:**297,1085
- - *siyyum* invitation **14:**1642
- - "Talmudists" (etch., Reiss) **3:**369
- - Talmud study **15:**753,754
- - "Teacher and Young Pupil" (paint., Kaufman) **3:**553
- - Yeshiva University, New York **6:**414; **16:**767
- *see also:* EDUCATION
STUERMER, DER (journ.) **15:**460
- cartoons, anti-Semitic **5:**177
- history **8:**737
- Holocaust **8:**837
- *illus:*
- - text
- - "Jews Are Our Misfortune" (April, 1929) **8:**833
- - ritual murder number (May, 1934) **3:**154
- *see also:* STREICHER, JULIUS
Stuhlweissenburg (city, Hung.), *see* SZEKESFEHERVAR
Stumpf, Carl **12:**679
Stumpp (art.) **4:**1319; **6:**674; **10:**921,1244; **12:**1010
- *illus:*
- - Roda Roda, Alexander (lith.) **14:**215
- - Toller, Ernst (lith.) **15:**1211
Stunning, electrical **14:**1341
Stupnicki, S. **6:**1411
Stur, Jan **13:**802
Sturgeon (zool.) **6:**36 **9:**1364
Sturgkh, Count Karl von **2:**277
Sturm, Albert **11:**298
Sturm, Ephraim **16:**860
Sturmabteilungen (Nazi orgn.), *see* S.A.
STURMAN, HAYYIM (d. 1938) **15:**461
Sturman, Hayyim (d. 1969) **15:**461
Sturman, Moshe **15:**461
Sturmhoefel, Nahida, *see* LAZARUS, NAHIDA RUTH
STUTSCHEWSKY, JOACHIM **15:**461
STUTTGART (city, Ger.) **15:**462
- textiles **15:**1041
- *illus:* text
STUTTHOF (concen. camp) **15:**464
- art **3:**575
Stuyvesant, Peter **12:**1062
- anti-Semitism **15:**1648
Stwosz, Wit, *see* Stoss, Veit
STYBEL, ABRAHAM JOSEPH **15:**465
- Agnon, S.Y. **2:**369
- children's literature **5:**436
- Frischmann, David **7:**201
- *Ha-Tekufah* **7:**1469
Style (bib. poetry) **13:**683
Stylus **16:**664
STYNE, JULE **15:**1091
STYRIA (prov., Aus.) **15:**465
- Host desecration **8:**1043
- Marburg **11:**992
- *see also:* AUSTRIA
SUARÈS, ANDRÉ **15:**466
SUAREZ (fam.) **15:**466
- Cairo **5:**31
Suarez, Edouard (19th cent.) **15:**466
Suarez, Edouard (20th cent.) **15:**467
Suarez, Felix **15:**466
Suarez, Leon **15:**466
Suarez, Raphael **15:**466
SUASSO (fam.) **15:**467
Suasso, Abraham Israel, *see* Suasso, Francisco Lopez
Suasso, Alvaro Lopez **15:**467
Suasso, Antonio Lopez (17th cent.) **15:**467
- title **15:**1165
- *illus:*
- - bust **15:**467
Suasso, Antonio Lopez (17/18 cent.) **15:**467
Suasso, Antonio Lopez (18th cent.) **15:**467
Suasso, Baron Isaac Lopes **14:**714
Suasso, Francisco Lopez **5:**935; **15:**467

Suasso, Isaac Lopez, *see* Suasso, Antonio Lopez
Suasso, Jacob Israel, *see* Suasso, Alvaro Lopez
Sūbā (place, Er. Isr.), *see* Soba
Subarians (ethnic gr.) **12:**1287; **16:**1484,1494
SUBBOTIN, ANDREY PAVLOVICH **15:**468
Subbotniki (Rus. sect) **10:**400
SUBCARPATHIAN RUTHENIA (reg., Ukr.) **15:**468
- Hungary **8:**1096
- shtetl **14:**1471
- *illus:* text
- *see also:* CZECHOSLOVAKIA
Subeita (city, Er. Isr.), *see* SHIVTAH
Subino, D. **10:**1498
Subordinate Legislation **15:**713
SUBOTICA (tn., Yug.) **15:**472
- *illus:* text
Subpoena, *see* ḤEREM BET DIN
SUBSTANCE AND ACCIDENT **15:**473
- form and matter **6:**1438
- pantheism in Kabbalah **10:**602
- *see also:* CATEGORIES
Substantives **16:**1581
Subverted city, *see* IR HA-NIDDAḤAT
SUCCESSION (inheritance) **15:**475
- *Contents:*
- - Order of Succession **15:**475
- - "Inheritance in the Grave" **15:**476
- - Primogeniture **15:**476
- - The Husband as Heir to his Wife **15:**477
- - The Wife's Rights to her Husband's Estate **15:**478
- - Inheritance Rights of Daughters **15:**478
- - Shetar Ḥaẓi Zakhar **15:**479
- - Proselytes as Heirs **15:**479
- - Devolution of Inheritance and Renunciation **15:**479
- - Debts of the Deceased **15:**479
- - Commorientes **15:**480
- - In the State of Israel **15:**481
- General
- - apostates **3:**214
- - Commandments, the 613 **5:**778
- - daughters of Zelophehad **16:**979
- - halakhic midrash **8:**1415
- - heirs as partners **13:**150
- - Karaite decision **10:**295
- - ordinance, 1923 **12:**143
- - public servant **10:**1327
- - proselytes **13:**1184
- - repayment to heirs **12:**1315
- - robber **15:**1097
- - *takkanot* **15:**717
- - waiver of rights **11:**1232
- - wills **16:**519ff
- Property
- - *apotropos* **3:**218
- - *ḥazakah* plea **7:**1516
- - leased property **10:**1536
- - lien on **11:**228; **11:**229
- - minimum amount **2:**396
- Marriage
- - civil marriage **5:**597
- - common law issue **12:**147
- - concubine **5:**865
- - husband and wife **8:**1124
- - intermarriage **12:**168
- - *ketubbah* payment **10:**929
- - levir **11:**124ff
- - time limitation **11:**252
- - widow **16:**491ff
- Child
- - adoption **2:**302
- - embryo **6:**720
- - firstborn **6:**1307
- - *mamzer* **11:**840
- - minimum legal age **13:**1357
- - provision for minors **13:**97*ff*
- - right to sell **14:**677
- Ancient Customs
- - Elephantine **6:**607
- - Hurrian **12:**1287ff
- - Mari **11:**986
Succession (of office) **13:**1355
Succession of Kings **10:**1014
SUCCOTH (tn., Egy.) **15:**482
- Pentateuch **13:**248
- seven clouds **13:**524
- Tjeku **13:**566
SUCCOTH (tn., Transj.) **15:**481
- metals **11:**1432
Succoth (fest.), *see* SUKKOT
SUCCOTH-BENOTH (deity) **15:**482
SUCEAVA (tn., Rum.) **15:**482
- Transnistria **15:**1334
Sucharczuk, Leon **14:**358
Suchowolsky, Yeḥezkel, *see* DANIN, YEḤEZKEL
Suckert, Kurt Erich, *see* Malaparte, Curzio
Sucre (city, Bol.) **4:**1188
Suczawa (tn., Rum.), *see* SUCEAVA
Sudan (state)
- Arab League **3:**242
- Israel **9:**441
- synagogues **1:**syn. list
Sudar, Kinyan (leg. conc.) **2:**219
Sudbury (city, Ont.) **12:**1408
Sudenburg (tn., Ger.) **11:**686
Sudomir (tn., Pol.), *see* SANDOMIERZ
Sudylkow, Moses Ḥayyim Ephraim of, *see* MOSES ḤAYYIM EPHRAIM OF SUDYLKOW
Sue, Eugène **16:**261
Sueddeutsche Warte (journ.) **15:**995
SUEDFELD, GABRIEL **15:**483
Suedfeld, Simon Maximilian, *see* NORDAU, MAX
SUESS, EDUARD **15:**483
Suess, Joseph, *see* OPPENHEIMER, JOSEPH BEN ISSACHAR SUESSKIND
Suesskind (Ger. J.) **10:**1120
Suesskind, Mordecai **7:**925
Suesskind, Walter **13:**973
SUESSKIND VON TRIMBERG **15:**483
- *illus:* text
Suetonio, Agostino **8:**61
SUETONIUS **15:**484
Suez (tn., Egy.)
- frontier, Egyptian-Turkish **9:**311
- Israel army shelling **9:**414
- Red Sea **14:**15
- Six-Day War **14:**1636,1639
- *illus:*
- - Gemini II photograph **14:**15
Suez Canal
- ancient use **14:**15
- Disraeli, Benjamin **6:**106
- Eden, Anthony **3:**982
- Egyptian armistice violations **3:**482
- Israel-Egyptian clashes **9:**414ff
- Israel shipping **9:**386; **9:**389; **9:**428; **15:**1553ff
- Sinai Campaign causes **14:**1605
- Six-Day War **14:**1630,1636
- U.S. shipping **15:**1665
- *illus:*
- - Disraeli and the 'Key of India' (caric.) **6:**106
- - Israel post **9:**420; **14:**1634
SUFFERING **15:**485
- in Jewish belief **4:**432; **4:**434
- Lamentations, Book of **10:**1372
- Messiah **11:**1411
- Naḥmanides on **12:**778
- problem of evil **7:**776; **7:**777
- reward and punishment **14:**135
- Sumerian influence **15:**515
- *see also:* GOD (Justice and Mercy)
Suffern (tn., N.Y.) **12:**1127
Suffolk (co., N.Y.) **12:**1108; **12:**1125
SUFISM (Isl. mysticism) **15:**486
- Abraham Maimuni **2:**151; **2:**152
- Abulafia, Abraham **2:**186
- Baḥya **13:**435
- communities in Israel **9:**918
- Jerusalem **9:**1435
- kabbalistic meditation **10:**631
- mysticism, Jewish **10:**512; **10:**529; **10:**553
- philosophy, Jewish **9:**104
Suftaya (fin. deed) **16:**1282
SUGAR, INDUSTRY AND TRADE **15:**487
- Jewish economic history **16:**1298
- Jewish merchants **4:**1535
Sugar cane (bot.) **5:**37
Sugarman, Lou(is) **15:**303
Sugerman, Sir Bernard **3:**886; **10:**1492
Sugiyot (collec.) **1:**newsp. list
Suhren, Fritz **13:**1583
SUICIDE **15:**489
- burial **5:**275
- *Kiddush ha-Shem* **10:**978,982
- mental illness **11:**1377
- prohibition **4:**1166
- society **6:**310
- York **16:**848
- *illus:*
- - Auschwitz camp inmates **8:**886
- - Jabotinsky's letter to a young man **9:**1183
- - Saul **14:**915
- - York, Clifford's tower **16:**849
Suicide squads (1955, Egy.), *see* Fedayeen
Suinthila (k., Sp.) **14:**1621
SUKENIK, ELIEZER LIPA **15:**491
- archaeology **3:**302
- Avigad, Naḥman **3:**961
- Bet Alfa synagogue **4:**710
- Dead Sea Scrolls **5:**1396
- Jerusalem Archaeology **9:**1535
- Thanksgiving Psalms **15:**1045
- War Scroll **16:**1558
- *illus:*
- - Dead Sea Scroll **5:**1401
Sukenik, Matitayahu **15:**492
Sukenik, Yigael, *see* YADIN, YIGAEL
Sukenik-Feinsod, Hasya **15:**492
Sukhostaver, Mordecai **7:**961
Sukhumi (city, Rus.) **2:**81
SUKKAH (booth) **15:**492
- agency inapplicable **2:**350
- Samaritans **14:**743
- Ushpizin **16:**19
- *illus:*
- - text
- - Amsterdam Jewish quarter **15:**499
- - embroidered hanging **7:**1385
- - 'In the Sukkah' (paint., M. Oppenheim) **3:**547
- - Jerusalem, Battei Varsha quarter **15:**501
- - Jerusalem portrayal **9:**1588
- - meal in **15:**496
- - papercuts **13:**44-45
- - preparation of **15:**495
- - Tel Aviv **9:**904
- - wall paintings **15:***fcg.* 491
- - *Pesaro Maḥzor* **11:**735
- - Sukhomi synagogue **7:**426
- *see also:* SUKKOT
SUKKAH (tract.) **15:**494
- *illus:* text
SUKKOT (fest.) **15:**495
- *Contents:*
- - In the Bible **15:**496
- - Critical Theories Concerning Origin **15:**497
- - In Rabbinic Literature **15:**498
- - Laws and Customs of Sukkot **15:**500
- - Hoshana Rabba **15:**501
- - Shemini Aẓeret **15:**501
- - Simḥat Torah **15:**502
- - In Art **15:**502
- General
- - Commandments, the 613 **5:**763,767f
- - Dionysus, Cult of, and **6:**61; **6:**62
- - folklore **6:**1392
- - Ḥanukkah, similarity to **7:**1283ff
- - *Jubilees, Book of* **10:**324
- - kibbutz harvest festival **10:**962
- - moon **12:**290
- - pilgrimage **13:**510ff
- - sacrifice **14:**601*ff*
- - Solomon **15:**104
- - year **16:**725
- sects
- - Falashas **6:**1148
- - Karaites **10:**779
- - Samaritans **14:**742; **14:**743
- Laws and Customs
- - Ecclesiastes **14:**1058
- - *etrog* **6:**947
- - food **6:**1426
- - Four Species rite **6:**1448
- - *Hakhel* ceremony **7:**1148
- - *hakkafot* **7:**1153
- - *halakhah le-Moshe mi-Sinai* ceremonies **7:**1167
- - Hoshana Rabba **8:**1026
- - *hoshanot* **8:**1028
- - Israel **9:**903
- - Johanan ben Zakkai **9:**241
- - *lulav* **11:**561
- - *sukkah* **15:**492
- - *Targum Sheni* **15:**812
- In Art
- - etrog containers **5:**309
- - illuminated *maḥzorim* **11:**733; **11:**735
- *illus:*
- - text
- - first page of prayers **11:**735
- - Four Species, Bar Kokhba coin **6:**1448
- - Four Species market, Tel Aviv **6:**950,1449; **12:**728
- - service at the Western Wall **6:**1245
- - *Simḥat Torah* **14:**1571*ff*
- - *sukkot* types **15:**493
- *see also:* FESTIVALS; PILGRIM FESTIVALS
Sukkot Valley (Isr.) **9:**589
Sulaiman, J.J. **14:**1294
Sulam (vill., Isr.) **14:**1482
Sulam, Moise **13:**1039
SULAMITH (period.) **15:**502
- Dessau **3:**1
- Hep! Hep! riots **8:**331
- press **13:**1056
- *illus:* text
Sulayim ibn Ruḥaym, *see* SALMON BEN JEROHAM
SULEIMAN I (the Magnificent) **15:**503
- Ereẓ Israel history **9:**282; **9:**287
- Jerusalem walls **9:**1426ff
- Jerusalem water supply **9:**1541
- Ottoman Empire **16:**1535
- *illus:*
- - Jaffa Gate inscription **9:**288
- - Jerusalem Old City gates **9:**1427-1432
- - Jerusalem Old City wall **9:**1517
- - public fountain, Jerusalem **9:**1434
Suleiman (pasha, Damascus) **2:**188
Suleiman (gov., Acre) **9:**294
Suleiman al-Qānūnī, *see*

SULEIMAN I
Suleiman ibn 'Abd al-Malik
- Jerusalem **9:**1425
- Ramleh **9:**262; **13:**1540
- Umayyads **15:**1529
Suleiman Ibn Ya'qūb **4:**1192
SULEIMANIYA (AL-) (prov., Iraq) **15:**504
- Kurdish Jews **8:**1456
Sūlim (vill., Isr.) **14:**1482
SULITA (vill., Mold.) **15:**504
Suliṭa (tn., Ukr.), *see* NOVOSELITSA
Sullam (period.) **6:**575
- statistics **1:**newsp. list
Sullam, Jacob **15:**1505
SULLAM, SARA COPPIO **15:**505
- Italian literature **9:**1109
- letters **11:**61
Sullivan (co., N.Y.) **12:**1127
Sullivan, Louis **2:**274
- synagogue **15:**620
- *illus:*
- - Anshe Maariv Synagogue, Chicago **15:**622
SULPICIUS SEVERUS **14:**236
- Bourges Jews **4:**1275
- Titus **15:**1169
Sultan, Abraham **14:**633
Sultāniyya (tn., Iran) **3:**1005
Sultan's Gate (Jer.), *see* New Gate
SULTANSKY, MORDECAI BEN JOSEPH **15:**506
- Crimean Karaites **5:**1104
- Poznanski, S.A. **13:**930
Sultan's Pool (Jer.) **9:**1434
Sulum (deity), *see* MARDUK
Sulz (cmty., Aus.) **16:**223
Sulz (tn., Fr.), *see* SOULTZ
SULZBACH (tn., Bav.) **15:**506
- *illus:* text
SULZBACH, ABRAHAM **15:**507
SULZBACH, WALTER **15:**508
- sociology **15:**66
Sulzbach brothers (bnks.) **4:**177
- railroads **13:**1519
Sulzbacher, I.M. **9:**1191
SULZBERGER, ARTHUR HAYS **15:**508
Sulzberger, Arthur Ochs **15:**509
Sulzberger, Cyrus Leo **15:**509
- *The American Hebrew* **2:**821
- Jewish Agricultural Society **10:**35
Sulzberger, David **2:**273
Sulzberger, Marion **11:**1201
SULZBERGER, MAYER **15:**509
- Adler, Cyrus **2:**273
- American Jewish Committee **2:**822
- book collection **4:**975
- Imber, Naphtali Herz **8:**1290
- Jewish Publication Society **10:**80
- *illus:*
- - A.J.C. delegation **2:**823
SULZER, SALOMON **15:**510
- Abrass, Osias **2:**172
- chronological chart **8:**766-767
- Vienna **16:**124
- *illus:* text
SUMAC (bot.) **15:**511
- plant list **13:**625
- spices **15:**269
Sumayr (mintmaster) **12:**64; **16:**1281
- - ʿAbd al-Mālik ibn Marwān **2:**55
Sumbal, Joseph Hayyim **13:**816; **15:**511
SUMBAL, SAMUEL **15:**511
- Marrakesh **11:**1016
Sumeil (vill., Er. Isr.) **15:**922; **15:**923
Sumeir (mintmaster), *see* Sumayr
SUMER, SUMERIANS **15:**512
- *Contents:*
- - Prehistory **15:**512
- - History **15:**512
- - Society **15:**513
- - Religion **15:**514
- - The Written Word **15:**515
- - Biblical Echoes **15:**515
- archaeology **16:**1507
- demons, demonology **5:**1521
- Garden of Eden **13:**78
- flood story **6:**1352
- Mesopotamia **16:**1484
- moon **12:**290
- poetry **13:**671ff
- Shinar **14:**1408
- Tammuz **15:**787
- Ur **16:**1
- warfare **16:**266
- *illus:*
- - Sumerian King List **3:**367
- - Ziggurat of Ur **16:**1
- *maps:*
- - text
- - Akkad and **2:**494
Sumerian (lang.) **14:**1151
- Mesopotamia **16:**1484
- Sumerian and Akkadian **2:**496
Sumerology **26:**1507
Summenhardt, Konrad **8:** 61
Summit (city, N.J.) **15:**1533
Summons, court **8:**356
SUMPTUARY LAWS **15:**515
- *illus:* text
Sumter (city, S.C.) **15:**211
Sumu-Yamam (k., Mari) **11:**978
Sun (tn., Egy.), *see* Sin
SUN **15:**516
- Bet Alfa mosaics **4:**713
- calendar **5:**43,47
- moon **12:**290
- *Sefirot* **10:**575
- solar eclipse **3:**789
- sundial **15:**519
- year **16:**724
- *illus:*
- - Abraham bar Hiyya's illustration of solar eclipse **3:**800
- *see also:* ASTRONOMY; DAY AND NIGHT; HOST OF HEAVEN
SUN, BLESSING OF THE **15:**518
- calendar reckoning **5:**47
Sunbal, Naḥman ibn **6:**1256; **12:**332; **16:**42
Sunbal, Samuel, *see* SUMBAL SAMUEL
SUNBAT (tn., Egy.) **15:**518
Sunbury (city, Pa.) **13:**230
"Sunday Afternoon" (paint., A. Bihari) **4:**990
Sunday Times (newsp.) **10:**1489
SUNDERLAND (city, Eng.) **15:**518
SUNDIAL **15:**519
Sundukov (sectarian) **10:**400
Sunnites (Isl. sect) **3:**998; **9:**263; **9:**918
Sunrise, *see Haneẓ ha-Ḥammah*
Sunset **5:**1376
Sun Yat-Sen **4:**1258
Suomi (state), *see* FINLAND
Super, Arthur Saul **10:**156
- children's literature **5:**450
- South Africa **15:**200
Super, I.J. **11:**1281
SUPERCOMMENTARIES ON THE PENTATEUCH **15:**520
Superior (city, Wis.) **16:**556
Superstitions **6:**1397
- Agobard **2:**372
- amulet **2:**906
- birth **4:**1051
- chiromancy **5:**477
- demonology **5:**1521
- divination **6:**111
- eclipse **15:**517
- evil eye **6:**997
- Hoshana Rabba **8:**1027
- Ibn Abi Zimra **5:**1357
- Kabbalah **10:**641
- *kapparot* **10:**756
- *niddah* laws **12:**1146
- *Sefer ha-Razim* **13:**1594
- sorcery **15:**163
- *Tokheḥah reading* **15:**1192
- *illus:*
- - Hoshana Rabba, looking at one's shadow **8:**1027
- *see also:* MAGIC
Supino, Igino **3:**651
Šuppiluliuma I (Hittite k.) **8:**788
- Mesopotamia **16:**1500
Šuppiluliuma II (Hittite k.) **8:**789
Supplication
- *Amidah* **2:**839
- *Bakkashah* **4:**116
- *taḥanun* **15:**702
SUPRASKY, YEHOSHUA **15:**521
Supreme Arab Committee, *see* Arab Higher Committee
Supreme Committee of Jewish Congregations (Neth.) **3:**766
Supreme Court (Isr.) **9:**632ff
- *illus:*
- - members **9:**637
Supreme Muslim Council (Er. Isr.) **9:**461ff
Suq al-Mnaḥḥsin (bazaar, San'a) **14:**820
Sūq al-Shuyūkh (tn., Iraq) **8:**1450
SURA (acad.) **15:**521
- General
- - gaonate **7:**315ff
- - *Haggadah* **7:**1091
- - Ḥuzal **8:**1137
- - mortgage **13:**642
- academies **2:**204
- - Mata Meḥasya **11:**1121
- - Nehardea **12:**935
- Personalities
- - Abraham ha-Baghdadi **2:**154
- - Ashi **3:**709
- - David ben Zakkai **5:**1358ff
- - Natronai bar Hilai **12:**886
- - Rav **13:**1576
- - Saadiah Gaon **14:**545
- *tables:*
- - *geonim* **7:**319
- - principal *amoraim* **2:**869
- *see also:* PUMBEDITA
Sura (Koran) **10:**1195
Sura (journ.) **1:**newsp. list
Surabaya (city, Indon.) **8:**1363
SURAT (city, Ind.) **15:**523
- India **8:**1356
Sūr-Báhir (vill., Er. Isr.) **9:**1515
- Bethlehem road **9:**1487
- Jerusalem reunification **9:**1507
- Six-Day War **14:**1630
Sūrdāsh (tn., Iraq) **15:**504
SURE, BARNETT **5:**388
SURENHUIS, WILHELM (Guilielmus) **15:**524
- Hebraists **8:**61
Surenhuysen, Wilhelm, *see* SURENHUIS, WILHELM
SURETYSHIP **15:**524
- *Contents:*
- - In the Bible and the Talmud **15:**524
- - Formation of Suretyship **15:**524
- - Arev and Arev Kabbelan **15:**525
- - Subatance and Scope **15:**526
- - Scope of the Surety's Liability **15:**527
- - Suretyship in Respect of Different Kinds of Obligations **15:**527
- - A Surety's Right of Recourse Against the Debtor **15:**527
- - Plurality of Sureties and Debtors **15:**528
- - In the State of Israel **15:**528
- bail **13:**959
- contractual obligation **5:**924; **5:**929
- debt repayment **6:**1011
- *Ḥerem ha-Ikkul* **8:**356
- orphan's debt **5:**888
- plurality of guarantors **12:**1315
- public body **13:**1353
- sacrifice **14:**601
- Saragossa *takkanah* **8:**1305
- validity **11:**643; **14:**601
- *see also:* LIEN
Surgery, Obstetrics, and Gynecology **11:**1201
SURGUN, ISAAC **15:**529
Surgun, Michael **4:**498
Suriano, Henry, *see* Soriano, Henri
Suriel (angel) **2:**963
Suriel, Moses, *see* Serviel, Moses
SURINAM (state) **15:**529
- Gabbai Izidro, Abraham **7:**234
- Marrano Diaspora **11:**1024
- population **13:**883
- settlement **2:**809
- sugar trade **15:**488
- synagogues **1:**syn. list
- territorialism **15:**1021ff
Surkis, Meshullam **5:**396
Surkis, Mordechai **4:**629; **4:**630
SUROWIECKI, WAWRZYNIEC **15:**531
Suruc (tn., Turk.), *see* SARŪJ
Šuruq (vowel) **16:**1432,1450
Survey, archaeological **3:**303
Susa (site, Iran), *see* SHUSHAN
SUSAN, ISSACHAR BEN MORDECAI **15:**531
SUSANNA AND THE ELDERS (apoc. wk.) **15:**532
- false witnesses **7:**1162
- Hellenistic Jewish literature **8:**304
- *illus:*
- - Susanna and the Elders **3:**184; **15:**533,534
Susholz, Alexander **14:**954
Susiana (reg., Iran), *see* ELAM
SUSITA (city, Er. Isr.) **15:**535
- coinage **5:**720
- Golan **13:**1532
- *see also:* DECAPOLIS
Susita, Mount (Isr.) **9:**171
Sūsiyya (vill., Er. Isr.) **15:**535
SUSMAN, MARGARETE **15:**536
Susman brothers (bsmn., Zambia) **16:**922
Suspended letters, *see Otiyyot teluyot*
Sussex, Augustus Frederick, Duke of, *see* Augustus Frederick, Prince
Susskind, Arthur **15:**306
SUSSKIND, DAVID **15:**1091
- television **15:**928
Susskind, Manfred J. **15:**307
Susslin, Israel ben Joel, *see* ISRAEL BEN JOEL
Sussman (fam.) **14:**834
Sussman (r., Regensburg) **2:**800
SUSSMAN, ABRAHAM **15:**536
Sussman, C. **10:**1001
Sussman, Eliezer **15:**609
- *illus:*
- - Bechhofen synagogue **4:**346; **15:**609
- - Horb synagogue **15:***fcg.* 622
SUSSMAN, EZRA **15:**536
Sussman, M.M. **11:**1203
Sussman, Norman **16:**556
Sutro (fam.) **5:**56
SUTRO, ABRAHAM **15:**536
- Leeser, Isaac **10:**1561
SUTRO, ADOLPH HEINRICH JOSEPH **15:**537
SUTRO, ALFRED **15:**538
Suttner, Baron von **16:**111
Suttner, Bertha, Baroness von **7:**171; **12:**1286
SUTZKEVER, ABRAHAM **15:**538
- *illus:*
- - *Yung Vilne* group **16:**821
SUWALKI (tn., Pol.) **15:**539
- He-Ḥalutz farm **8:**252
SUWALSKI, ISAAK **15:**540

Ṣuweida, A- (tn., Bashan) **9:**597
Suzanne, Robert **11:**120
SUZIN, SOLOMON MOSES **15:**540
- Navon, Jonah Moses **12:**898
Suzman, Elie **5:**1547
SUZMAN, HELEN **15:**541
Šváb, Karel **14:**1654
Svaz Čechů-židů (mvmt., Cz.), *see* ČECHŮ-ŻIDŮ, SVAZ
Svaz Slovenských Židov (mvmt., Slov.) **5:**267
Sveaborg (fort., Fin.) **6:**1296
Sverdlov, Abraham **11:**1558
SVERDLOV, YAKOV MIKHAILOVICH **15:**541
- stamp **15:**336
Sverdlovsk (city, oblast, Rus.) **14:**483
SVETLOV, MIKHAIL **15:**542
Světové rozhledy (journ.) **14:**1584
SVEVO, ITALO **15:**542
- Debenedetti **5:**1428
- Italian literature **9:**1112
Svihov (vill., Cz.) **10:**1087
SVIRSKI, ALEXEY IVANOVICH **14:**516
SVISLOCH (tn., Belor.) **15:**543
Svitavy (tn., Morav.) **12:**296
Svůj k svému (anti-Sem. mvmt.) **4:**1179
Svyatopolsk-Mirski (polit., Rus.) **16:**1137
SWABIAN LEAGUE (Ger.) **15:**544
SWADESH, MORRIS **15:**544
Swados, Harvey **15:**31
Swallow (bird) **9:**226
Swamp drainage, *see* LAND RECLAMATION IN ISRAEL
Swampscott (tn., Mass.) **11:**1112; **11:**622
Swan (bird), *see Tinshemet*
Swan, G. **8:**61
SWANSEA (city, Eng.) **15:**544
- *see also:* WALES
SWARSENSKY, HARDI (Bernhard) **15:**545
- Argentina **3:**424
Swarzedz (tn., Poznan) **6:**614; **13:**947
Swarzenski, George **3:**651
Swaythling, First Baron, *see* Montagu, Samuel
Swaythling, Lady **15:**314
Swaziland (state) **9:**441
SWEDEN **15:**545
- *Contents:*
- - Holocaust Period **15:**548
- - Contemporary Period **15:**550
- - Relations with Israel **15:**552
- capitulations **5:**150
- Church and Nazism **8:**915
- emancipation **6:**702ff
- Holocaust **8:**907
- Isaac, Aaron **9:**9
- migrations to **16:**1524
- museums **12:**544
- population **13:**887ff
- press **13:**1048
- Scandinavian literature **14:**928ff
- *sheḥitah* **14:**1341
- synagogues **1:**syn. list
- UNSCOP **15:**1688
- Warburg, Karl Johan **16:**286
Swedenborg, Emanuel **14:**929
Swedish literature **14:**928ff
Sweet, Joseph A. **7:**1239
Sweet calamus (spice), *see* CALAMUS, SWEET
Swenko (w., Lewko Jordanis) **11:**180
SWET, GERSHON **10:**317
Sweynheym, Conrad **8:**1319
Swichkow, Louis J. **11:**1590
SWIDNICA (tn., Pol.) **15:**553
Swidrichsen, M. **16:**1165
Swietochowski, Aleksander **13:**800
SWIFT (bird) **15:**553
- dietary laws **6:**34
Swift Current (city, Sask.) **14:**892
SWIG, BENJAMIN HARRISON **15:**553
- Weiler, Jack D. **16:**397
Swig, Simon **15:**553
Swimming **15:**313
- *illus:*
- - Kinneret, annual crossing **15:**297
- - seventh Maccabiah **11:**663
Swinarski, Arthur Marya **13:**802
Swinburne, Algernon Charles **6:**781
Swintila (k., Sp.) **15:**220
Swine, *see* PIG
Swislocz (tn., Belor.), *see* SVISLOCH
Swiss Literature, *see* FRENCH LITERATURE; GERMAN LITERATURE
Swit (orgn.) **16:**348
SWITZERLAND **15:**554
- *Contents:*
- - The Medieval Community **15:**554
- - Slow Steps Toward Emancipation **15:**556
- - Population **15:**558
- - Holocaust and Contemporary Periods **15:**559
- - Relations with Israel **15:**561
- - Arab terrorists **9:**416
- - French Revolution **7:**157
- - Hebrew MSS **11:**907
- - population **8:**733; **13:**885ff
- Communal Life
- - Alliance Israélite Universelle **2:**650
- - communal organization **5:**824
- - emancipation **6:**709
- - journalism **10:**304
- - livestock trade **11:**411
- - markets and fairs **11:**1003
- - military service **11:**1566
- - Orthodoxy **12:**1489
- - press **13:**1049
- - students'movements **15:**450ff
- - synagogues **1:**syn. list
- - trade **15:**1299
- Anti-Semitism
- - Aargau anti-Semitism **2:**3
- - Basle expulsions **4:**304
- - Berne expulsions **4:**675
- - Levy, Jonas Phillips **11:**159
- - *sheḥitah* **14:**1340
- Holocaust Period **8:**906; **8:**907
- - Church and Nazism **8:**915
- - Germany **7:**491
- - refugee statistics **14:**30
- *illus:* text
- *pop. table:* text
SWOPE, GERARD **15:**561
SWOPE, HERBERT BAYARD **15:**562
Sword (weapon) **16:**266ff
Swordfish **6:**38
Sycamina (tn., Er. Isr.), *see* HAIFA
SYCAMORE (bot.) **15:**562
- flora of Israel **9:**222
- Shephelah **14:**1380
SYDNEY (city, Austr.) **15:**564
- Montefiore, Joseph **12:**270
- *illus:*
- - Great Synagogue **3:**881
- - Hebrew Day School certificate of incorporation **6:**424
Sydney (city, Can.) **11:**998
Sydney Jewish News (newsp.) **13:**1025
Sydney Zionist Society (Austr.) **16:**1105
- Hebrew MSS **11:**900
Syene (fort., Egy.) **14:**1593
Sykes, Arthur Ashley **8:**61
Sykes, Henry **8:**61
Sykes, Sir Mark
- Balfour Declaration **4:**132
- British interests **9:**310ff
SYKES-PICOT TREATY **15:**565
- Balfour Declaration **4:**132
- frontiers, Ereẓ Israel **9:**312
- Palestinian interests **9:**308
- Zionists **16:**1079ff
Syllaeus (Nabatean), *see* Sholi
Sylvester I (pope) **9:**1119; **13:**851
SYLVESTER, JAMES JOSEPH **15:**567
Sylvester, Johannes **8:**61
SYLVIA, SARAH **15:**1091
- Johannesburg **10:**156
Symbolism, Jewish
- Hirsch's *mitzvot* interpretation **8:**513
- Kabbalah **10:**494
- Kabbalah and *halakhah* **3:**70
- Prophets **13:**1162
- *Sefirot* **10:**570ff
- visions **16:**167
SYMBOLISM, JEWISH (IN THE GRECO-ROMAN PERIOD) **15:**568
- *Contents:*
- - Common Symbols **15:**570
- - Pagan Devices **15:**571
- - Meaning **15:**573
- - Mystic symbolism in Judaism **15:**575
- Dura-Europa **6:**276
- Hellenistic Jewish art **8:**301
- laws, interpreted by **3:**69
- portal **13:**905
- Rome catacombs **5:**250ff
- tombstones **15:**1223
Symbols, *see* SIGNS AND SYMBOLS
Symmachus (Bib. trans.) **3:**54; **4:**853ff
SYMMACHUS BEN JOSEPH (tan.) **15:**578
Symons, Baron Lyon de **11:**477
Sympathetic magic **11:**711
Symphony of Psalms (mus. wk.) **13:**1328
SYNAGOGUE **15:**579
- *Contents:*
- - Origins and History **15:**579
- - - Until the First Century **15:**581
- - - First Century C.E. **15:**581
- - - Middle Ages **15:**583
- - - Modern Period **15:**584
- - In Halakhah **15:**591
- - - Design and Location **15:**591
- - - Furnishings and Interior Design **15:**592
- - - Proscribed Uses of the Synagogue and its Contents **15:**593
- - In Aggadah **15:**594
- - Architecture **15:**595
- - - The Architectural Problem of the Synagogue **15:**595
- - - The Earliest Synagogues **15:**595
- - - The Early Synagogues **15:**595
- - - The Transitional Type **15:**597
- - - Fifth-Century Synagogues **15:**598
- - - Outside Ereẓ Israel **15:**599
- - - From the Middle Ages to the 18th Century **15:**601
- - - In the 18th Century **15:**618
- - - In the 19th Century **15:**619
- - - Early 20th century **15:**620
- - - Contemporary Period **15:**620
- General
- - folklore **6:**1394
- - Samaritan **14:**741
- - Sephardi practice **14:**1170
- - *sheli'aḥ ẓibbur* **14:**1355
- - *takkanot* **15:**735
- - Western Wall **16:**468
- History
- - development, early **15:**983ff
- - Ereẓ Israel, 70 to 640 C.E. **9:**237; **9:**252; **9:**255ff
- - Ibrahim Pasha **9:**1447
- - Jerusalem, Mamluk period **9:**281
- - Muslim countries **5:**1606
- - Omar, Covenant of **12:**1379
- - origin **13:**980
- - Ottoman Empire **16:**1541
- - Rome **14:**241ff
- - Spain **15:**236
- - *Yevsektsiya* **16:**780
- Ancient Synagogues **3:**328
- - Aegina **3:**521
- - Al-Dikki **12:**181
- - Al-Ghariba **6:**139
- - Alexandria **2:**589
- - Arbel **3:**293
- - Bet Alfa **4:**710
- - Bet-Shean **4:**758
- - Bet She'arim **4:**766
- - Bet Yeraḥ **4:**780
- - Borion **10:**478
- - Caesarea **5:**12
- - Callinicum **2:**801
- - Capernaum **5:**139
- - Chorazin **5:**492
- - Cyprus **5:**1181
- - Dumuh **2:**253; **6:**268
- - Dura-Europos **6:**276
- - En-Gedi **6:**743
- - Eẓ ha-Ḥayyim (Turk.) **11:**878
- - Gaza **7:**341
- - Ḥammat Geder **7:**251
- - Hammath **7:**1243
- - Japhia **9:**1286
- - Jericho **9:**1369
- - Kazrin **13:**1533
- - Kefar Baram **10:**877
- - Masada **11:**1089
- - Meron **11:**1391
- - Midrash Ben Al-Nakawa **2:**672
- - Mount Zion **9:**1424
- - Nawā **12:**897
- - Ostia **12:**1506
- - Peki'in **13:**218
- - Salonika **14:**700
- - Sardis **11:**622; **14:**877
- - Shaf ve-Yativ (Nehardea) **12:**935
- - Synagogue of Severus **14:**1200
- - Temple area **9:**1425
- - Usha **16:**17
- - Watzinger's studies **16:**366
- Architecture and Art
- - architecture **3:**358
- - ark **3:**450
- - art in **3:**505ff
- - basilica structure **4:**300
- - *bimah* **4:**1002; **9:**1142
- - ceremonial objects **5:**288
- - decorative motifs **8:**652; **8:**653
- - *dukhan* **6:**267
- - Marmorek, Oscar **11:**1013
- - *menorah* **11:**1368
- - Nasna (Transyl.) **12:**840
- - pillars **13:**522
- - *shivviti* plaque **14:**1420
- - symbolic decoration **15:**568ff
- Customs
- - *Anim Zemirot* **3:**23
- - Av, Ninth of **3:**938
- - *bittul ha-tamid* **4:**1061
- - choir **5:**486
- - dedication ceremony **7:**1153
- - eternal lamp **12:**965
- - Falashas **6:**1147
- - *ḥazakah* of place **7:**1519
- - *ḥazzan* **7:**1542
- - *ḥuppah* **11:**1035; **11:**1041
- - impurity **13:**1411
- - Italy **9:**1142
- - *Kiddush* **10:**974
- - *mizraḥ* **12:**180
- - organ **12:**1453ff

-- preaching **13:**994
-- priestly watches **7:**1056
-- sanctity laws **14:**616
-- seating **2:**152
-- separation of sexes **11:**1234; **11:**1235
-- *shulklapper* **14:**1477
- As Communal Center **15:**583
-- archisynagogos **3:**335
-- *asarah batlanim* **4:**325
-- community **5:**810ff
-- education **6:**403ff
-- endowments **8:**284
-- gambling **7:**301
-- *klaus* **16:**766
-- libraries of (U.S.) **11:**191
-- London, United Synagogue congragations **15:**1671
-- *mishmarot* **12:**92
-- rabbinate, modern **13:**1448; **13:**1455
-- *shammash* (sexton) **14:**1292
-- *shtetl* **14:**1472
-- taxes **15:**867
-- worship and Pharisees **13:**364; **13:**366
-- *see also:* BET (HA-) MIDRASH
- Holocaust
-- Austria **3:**898ff
-- *Kristallnacht* **10:**1263
-- Poland **13:**752
- *see also:* LITURGY; and under individual towns and countries
- *illus:* text
- *illus:* Argentina
-- Buenos Aires **3:**422; **4:**1462; **14:**1173
- *illus:* Australia
-- Hobart (Tasmania) **15:**831
-- Melbourne
--- Adass Israel Synagogue **11:**1284
--- Toorak Synagogue **11:**1283
-- Perth **13:**322
-- Sydney, Great Synagogue **3:**881; **15:**563
- *illus:* Austria
-- Graz **7:**864
-- Hohenems **8:**815
-- Klagenfurt **10:**1086
-- Korneuburg **10:**1207
-- Krems **10:**1259
-- Mattersdorf **11:**1130
-- Vienna
--- Leopoldstaedt synagogue **16:**129
--- Sephardi synagogue **16:**129
- *illus:* Belgium
-- Brussels, Great Synagogue **4:**1424
- *illus:* Belorussia, *see under* Russia
- *illus:* Brazil
-- São Paulo **14:**851
- *illus:* Bulgaria
-- Nikopol **4:**1489; **12:**1161
-- Plovdiv, Yeshurun Synagogue **13:**653
-- Sofia, Central Synagogue **4:**1483
- *illus:* Canada
-- Calgary **2:**531
-- Hamilton, Ont. **7:**1239
-- Montreal **12:**284,288
-- Toronto
--- Holy Blossom Temple **5:**106; **15:**1261
--- Shaarei Shomayim **15:**1263
-- Winnipeg **16:**550
- *illus:* Chile
-- Santiago,
--- Bn'e Jisroel Synagogue **5:**463
--- Magen David Temple **14:**848
- *illus:* China
-- Kaifeng **5:**471; **10:**695
-- Shanghai **14:**1293
- *illus:* Cyprus
-- record of a 4th cent. synagogue reconstruction **5:**1183
- *illus:* Czechoslovakia
-- Austerlitz **3:**876
-- Bardejov **4:**217
-- Boskovice **4:**1262
-- Breznice **4:**1367
-- Brno **5:**1196; **12:**299
-- Budyně nad Ohří **4:**1458
-- Carlsbad **5:**183-184
-- Chroučovice **5:**1194
-- Hermanuv Mestec **8:**366
-- Holesov **8:**819
-- Hostoun **4:**1178
-- Lazne Kynzvart **10:**1520
-- Marienbad **11:**993
-- Nezdášov **10:**1171
-- Nitra **12:**1187
-- Opava **12:**1412
-- Pilsen **13:**528
-- Prague
--- Altneuschul **4:**1004; **13:**966,967; **15:***fcg.* 619
--- Klaus Synagogue **13:**973
--- Pinkas Synagogue, memorial wall **13:**976
-- Presov **13:**1022
- *illus:* Egypt
-- Alexandria, Eliyahu ha-Navi Synagogue **6:**502
-- Cairo, Ben Ezra Synagogue **5:**28,29
- *illus:* El Salvador
-- San Salvador **6:**687
- *illus:* England
-- Birmingham, Central Synagogue **4:**1038
-- Brighton **4:**1373
-- Bury St. Edmunds, Moyse's Hall **6:**751
-- Leeds, Belgrave Street Synagogue **10:**1561
-- Liverpool, Princes Road Synagogue **6:**765; **11:**410
-- London
--- Bevis Marks **11:**471; **14:**1167; **15:**620-621
--- first synagogue after readmission, plaque **6:**754
--- Great Synagogue **11:**475
--- St. Albans Place Synagogue, consecration **6:**757
--- St. John's Wood Synagogue **11:**480
-- Manchester, Great Synagogue **11:**859
-- Wallingford, Carmel College **6:**419
-- *see also. under* Scotland
- *illus:* Estonia
-- Tallinn **15:**742
- *illus:* Ethiopia
-- Woozaba **6:**1145
- *illus:* Finland
-- Helsinki **6:**1297,1298
- *illus:* France
-- Bayonne **4:**351
-- Belfort **4:**416
-- Besançon **4:**702
-- Béziers, foundation stone **4:**791
-- Carpentras **5:**203-207; **11:**1540
-- Cavaillon **5:**260; **7:**23
-- Isle-sur-la-Sorgue, L' **9:**105
-- Lunéville **11:**567
-- Metz, Great Synagogue **11:**1451
-- Nancy **12:**816
-- Paris
--- Don Isaac Abrabanel Synagogue **3:**341
--- Rue de la Victoire Synagogue **13:**105; **15:**620-621
--- Rue Pavée Synagogue **13:**108
-- Strasbourg **15:**423
-- Verdun **16:**109
- *illus:* Georgia (U.S.S.R.)
-- Kuolashi **7:**424
-- Sukhomi **7:**426
-- Tiflis **15:**1138
- *illus:* Germany
-- Aachen **2:**1
-- Altenstadt **2:**773
-- Amberg **2:**800
-- Ansbach **3:**32
-- Aschaffenburg **3:**687
-- Augsburg **3:**850
-- Baden-Baden **8:**845-848
-- Baiersdorf **4:**109
-- Bamberg **4:**149
-- Bechhofen **4:**346
-- Berlin
--- Fasanenstrasse Synagogue **3:**454; **4:**647,652; **10:**1264
--- Reform Synagogue **12:**265
-- Bingen **4:**1008; **11:**1041
-- Bochum **4:**1158
-- Bonn **4:**1210,1211
-- Bremen
--- Gartenstrasse Synagogue **4:**1346
--- new synagogue **4:**1347
-- Breslau **4:**1354
-- Bruchsal **4:**1412
-- Brunswick **4:**1421
-- Coburg **5:**619
-- Cologne **5:**740; **16:**498
-- Constance **5:**912
-- Cottbus **5:**991
-- Darmstadt
--- Bleichstrasse Synagogue **5:**1307
--- Landgraf-Georg-Strasse Synagogue **5:**1307
--- neo-oriental synagogue **7:**492
-- Dortmund **6:**176,177
-- Dresden **14:**924
-- Duesseldorf **6:**262
-- Duisburg **6:**265
-- Emden **6:**721
-- Erfurt **6:**838,839
-- Essen **6:**896,897
-- Frankfort a/M, Boerneplatz Synagogue **7:**89-91
-- Freiburg im Breisgau **7:**132
-- Fuerth **4:**344; **7:**215
-- Fulda **7:**218
-- Geroda **6:**1403
-- Goettingen **7:**690
-- Goslar **7:**816
-- Halberstadt **7:**1173
-- Hamburg
--- Bornplatz Synagogue **7:**1226
--- new synagogue **7:**1227
--- Portuguese Synagogue **7:**1228
-- Hameln **7:**1234
-- Hanau **7:**1257
-- Hanover **7:**501,1278,1279
-- Harburg **4:**1003
-- Heidelberg **8:**256
-- Heidingsfeld **8:**260
-- Heilbronn **8:**264; **10:**1265
-- Hildesheim **8:**475
-- Homburg **8:**943
-- Horb **15:***fcg.* 622
-- Kaiserslautern **10:**699
-- Karlsruhe **10:**796
-- Kassel **10:**812
-- Kiel **10:**989
-- Kissingen **10:**1075
-- Kitzingen **10:**1083,1084
-- Koblenz **10:**1121
-- Krefeld **10:**1251
-- Landau **8:**849; **10:**1385
-- Leipzig **10:**1591
-- Lueneburg **11:**557
-- Mainz **11:**790
-- Mannheim **10:**1264,1265; **11:**887
-- Marburg **11:**941
-- Munich
--- Central Synagogue **8:**738
--- New Synagogue **11:**1166
--- Ohel Yakob **12:**523
-- Nuremberg **12:**1276,1278,1280
-- Offenbach **12:**1335
-- Oldenburg **12:**1358
-- Osnabrueck, Rolandstrasse Synagogue **12:**1501
-- Pforzheim **13:**358
-- Regensburg **14:**36
-- Roedelheim **14:**220
-- Speyer **15:**265
-- Stuttgart **15:**463
-- Sulzbach **15:**507
-- Trier **15:**1390
-- Westheim **4:**344
-- Wiesbaden **16:**506
-- Worms **4:**1004; **7:**458; **13:**1561; **16:**644
-- Wuerzburg **16:**676
- *illus:* Greece
-- Athens **7:**873
-- Rhodes **14:**145
-- Salonika **14:**703
- *illus:* Hong Kong
-- Ohel Leah Synagogue **8:**964
- *illus:* Hungary
-- Baja **4:**112
-- Budapest
--- Dohany Street synagogue **4:**1451
--- fifteenth cent. synagogue, remains **8:**1091
--- Heroes' Synagogue **4:**1450
-- Debrecen **5:**1434
-- Györ **7:**1000
-- Hodmezovasarhely **8:**803
-- Kecskemet **10:**863
-- Kisvárda **10:**1077
-- Nagykanizsa **12:**766
-- Nyiregyhaza **12:**1291
-- Paks **13:**15
-- Papa **13:**59
-- Pecs **13:**203
-- Szeged **8:**1103; **15:**658
- *illus:* India
-- Alibag **8:**1351
-- Bombay
--- Kneseth Elijah Synagogue **4:**1193
--- Magen David Synagogue **4:**1193
-- Calcutta, Maghen David Synagogue **8:**1353
-- Chennamangalam **8:**1351
-- Cochin **8:**1352; **15:**336
-- Ernakulam, Theckoobagam Synagogue **5:**625
-- Kachangadi, dedication stone (1345) **5:**623
- *illus:* Iraq
-- Baghdad **4:**92; **8:**1459
- illus: Ireland
-- Belfast **4:**415; **8:**1466
-- Dublin, Adelaide Road Synagogue **6:**248
- *illus:* Israel
-- Arbel Valley **3:**293
-- Bene-Berak **9:**895
-- Bet Alfa **3:**511,513; **4:**711; **11:**989
-- Beth-Shean **13:**905
-- Capernaum **3:**461; **5:**136-138; **6:**948; **11:**689; **13:**44
-- Chorazin **5:**492-494
-- Eshtemoa **6:**893
-- Gaza **7:**340-341
-- Ḥammat Gader **7:**249,251
-- Hammath **3:**325 **7:**1243; **15:**574,575
-- Hebron **8:**229
-- Jericho, mosaics **2:**690; **9:**1370
-- Jerusalem
--- Beth El **9:**1564
--- Bukharan synagogue **4:**1472; **9:**503
--- Eliyahu ha-Navi Synagogue ruins **9:**1486
--- Hebrew University Synagogue

13:1575
- - - Hurvah 9:1445,1446,1485
- - - Ioannina Jews' Synagogue 8:1436
- - - Istambuli 9:1444
- - - Italian Rite Synagogue 5:869
- - - Johanan ben Zakkai 9:1444
- - - Karaite Synagogue, Old City 10:782
- - - Nisan Bak 9:1445,1480
- - - Ophel, dedicatory stone 3:335
- - - Porat Joseph 9:1443
- - - Ramban 9:1443
- - - Tiferet Yisrael, *see* Nisan Bak
- - - Yeshurun 9:1479
- - Kefar Baram 3:517; 10:878
- - Khirbat Kānif 13:1532
- - Lavi 10:1476
- - Ma'on 11:908
- - Masada 11:1085
- - Meron 11:1391
- - Naarah (plan) 12:737
- - Nazareth, "The Synagogue" 12:900
- - Nes Ẓiyyonah 12:968
- - Peki'in 5:202; 13:217
- - Qaṣrayn 13:1534
- - Safed
- - - Ha-Ari Synagogue 11:572; 14:629
- - - Isaac Aboab Synagogue 14:631
- - Tel Aviv 3:356
- *illus:* Italy
- - Alessandria 2:566
- - Ancona 2:942,943; 9:1128
- - Asti 3:785
- - Casale Monferrato 5:225-226
- - Conegliano (in Jerusalem) 5:869
- - Ferrara 6:1231
- - Florence 6:1359,1361; 15:620-621
- - Leghorn
- - - old synagogue 9:1139; 10:1571
- - - new synagogue 10:1572
- - Mantua 11:896,898
- - Merano 11:1381
- - Milan, new synagogue 11:1546
- - Modena 3:451; 12:202
- - Ostia 12:1507,1508
- - Padua 13:9,11
- - Parma 13:123
- - Pesaro Sephardi Synagogue 13:330
- - Pisa 13:562
- - Pitigliano 15:1469
- - Reggio Emilia 14:39
- - Rome
- - - Great Synagogue 14:247,250
- - - Piazza delle Cinque Scuole 14:245
- - Rovigo 14:354
- - Siena 14:1514
- - Trani 15:1314
- - Trieste 15:1393
- - Turin 15:1454
- - Venice
- - - Canton Synagogue 4:1003; 5:295; 16:98
- - - Great German Synagogue 3:453; 16:97
- - - Italian Synagogue 9:1135; 16:100
- - - Levantine Synagogue 16:99
- - Vercelli 16:107
- - Verona 16:114
- - Vittorio Veneto 3: *fcg* 462; 11:1235
- *illus:* Jamaica
- - Kingston 9:1273
- *illus:* Japan
- - Tokyo 9:1283
- *illus:* Latvia
- - Daugavpils (Dvinsk) 10:1464
- - Riga 14:176
- *illus:* Lithuania
- - Biržai 11:372
- - Jurbarkas 11:365, 366
- - Kaunas
- - - Hasidic Synagogue 11:383
- - - Yagshto Street Synagogue 10:847
- - Kedainiai 10:864
- - Ozery 12:1539
- - Panevezys, Karaite Synagogue 11:366
- - Plunge, Great Synagogue 13:653
- - Vezaitai 11:371
- - Vilkaviškis 16:135
- - Vilna
- - - Great Synagogue 16:142
- - - Khorshul 16:146
- - Žydikiai, *bet ha-midrash* 11:373
- *illus:* Morocco
- - Aroumiath 6:395
- - Demnate 5:1492
- - Fez 14:1183
- - Marrakesh 11:1018
- *illus:* Netherlands
- - Amsterdam
- - - Ashkenazi Synagogue 2:899
- - - Jacob Obrechtsplein Synagogue 6:688
- - - Lekstraat Synagogue 16:1119
- - - Liberal Synagogue 12:991
- - - New Synagogue 2:904
- - - Sephardi synagogue 2:897; 3:452
- - Hague, The
- - - main Ashkenazi synagogue 7:1125
- - - Sephardi (Portuguese) Synagogue 7:1124; 13:1061
- - Maastricht 11:1166; 12:979
- - Rotterdam 14:349
- *illus:* Netherlands Antilles
- - Curaçao, Temple Emanu-El 12:995
- *illus:* New Zealand
- - Auckland 3:840
- - Hokitika 12:1129
- - Nelson 12:1130
- *illus:* Norway
- - Trondheim 12:1223
- *illus:* Pakistan
- - Karachi, Magen Shalom Synagogue 13:15
- *illus:* Paraguay
- - Asunción 13:86
- *illus:* Persia
- - Isfahan 13:305; 15:620-621
- *illus:* Poland
- - Bedzin 4:374
- - Bialystok 4:808
- - Breslau 4:1354
- - Brody 4:1397
- - Checiny 5:369
- - Chelm 5:372
- - Chodorow 13:727
- - Chryzanow 5:534
- - Cracow
- - - medieval synagogue 5:1033
- - - Rema Synagogue 9:1083
- - Czestochowa 5:1213
- - Leczna 10:1555
- - Leszno 11:52
- - Lodz 11:429
- - Lublin, Maharshal Shul 11:545
- - Nasielsk 12:840
- - Ostroleka 12:1515
- - Pabianice 13:3
- - Piotrkow, Great Synagogue 13:556
- - Plonsk, Great Synagogue 13:651
Przedborz 11:693; 12:621; 13:1297
- - Przemysl, Sheinbach Synagogue 13:1298
- - Radom, Old People's Home 13:1501
- - Radymno 13:1506
- - Rawicz 13:1587
- - Sierpc 14:1516
- - Tarnow 15:820
- - Tykocin 15:1475
- - Warsaw, Great Synagogue 16:337
- - Wlodawa 16:598
- - Wyszogrod 16:682
- - Zamosc 16:927
- *illus:* Portugal
- - Oporto, Kadoorie Synagogue 12:1417; 13:924
- - Ponta Delgada (Azores) 13:925
- *illus:* Rhodesia
- - Bulawayo 4:1480; 14:149
- - Salisbury 14:149,685
- *illus:* Rumania
- - Arad 15:1341
- - Baia-Mare 4:108
- - Bucharest, Choir Synagogue 14:411,414
- - Cluj 5:618
- - Craiova 5:1058
- - Oradea Mare 12:1437
- - Timisoara 15:1144
- *illus:* Russia (incl. Belorussia, Ukraine)
- - Bendery 4:478
- - Chernovtsy 5:393
- - Grodno, wooden synagogue 7:925,927
- - Kiev 10:992
- - Kremenets 10:1256
- - Leningrad 11:15
- - Leshnev 11:45
- - Lutsk 11:587
- - Lvov
- - - Taz Synagogue 11:609
- - - Great Synagogue 11:611
- - Lyuboml 13:727
- - Mogilev 12:215
- - Moscow, Great Synagogue 12:366,367
- - Nemirov 12:947
- - Novogrudok 12:1238
- - Odessa 12:1321,1324
- - Olyka 12:1372
- - Oshmyany, Great Synagogue 12:1496
- - Pinsk, Great Synagogue 13:539,540
- - Pogrebishchenski 13:694
- - Rozdol 14:359
- - Sadgora 14:625
- - Shpola 14:1460
- - Tarnopol 15:816
- - Zholkva 16:1014
- *illus:* Scotland
- - Edinburgh 14:1035
- *illus:* Singapore
- - Chased El 14:1609
- *illus:* South Africa
- - Bloemfontein 12:1448
- - Cape Town 15:192
- - East London 6:341
- - Johannesburg
- - - Great Synagogue 10:156
- - - Park Synagogue 15:191,194
- - - Temple Emanuel 10:157
- - Kimberley 15:199
- - Port Elizabeth 13:910
- - Springs, Transvaal 15:1340
- *illus:* Spain
- - Barcelona, Casa Sefardita 4:212
- - Córdoba, Ramban Synagogue 5:964
- - Madrid 11:683
- - Toledo
- - - El Transito 3:520; 15:1201,1205
- - - Santa Maria la Blanca 8:685; 15:1199
- *illus:* Surinam
- - Joden Savanne 15:530
- *illus:* Sweden
- - Göteborg 7:819; 15:548
- - Norrköping 15:547
- - Stockholm 15:408
- *illus:* Switzerland
- - Basle 4:304
- - Bremgarten 15:559
- - Fribourg 7:170
- - Geneva 7:403
- - La Chaux-de-Fonds 10:1332
- - Lausanne 10:1471
- - Lengnau 2:3; 15:558
- - Lucerne 11:5513
- - St. Gall 15:559
- *illus:* Syria
- - Aleppo 15:636
- - Dura-Europos 3:28,451,461,515; 6:277-294; 15:571
- *illus:* Transjordan
- - Gerasa 7:434
- - Ma'on 6:604
- *illus:* Tunisia
- - Djerba 6:139
- - Gabès 15:1438
- - Hamam Lif 3:519; 15:572
- - Hara al-Seghīra 15:1434
- - Tunis 15:1433
- *illus:* Turkey
- - Istanbul
- - - Ahrida Synagogue 15:1460
- - - Ez Hayyim, Ortaköy 9:1091
- - - Karaite Synagogue 9:1092; 10:779
- - - Neveh Shalom, Beyoglu 9:1096
- - - Toferei Begadim synagogue 15:1461
- - - Yambol Synagogue 14:1169
- - - Yüksekkaldirm Synagogue 8:1093
- - Sardis 3:519; 14:877
- *illus:* Ukraine, *see under* Russia
- *illus:* United States
- - Albany, Ga. 7:429
- - Albany, N.Y. 7:782
- - Albuquerque, N. Mex., Temple Albert 12:1038
- - Allentown, Pa., Temple Keneseth Israel 13:230
- - Atlantic City, N.J., 3:826
- - Baltimore, Md.
- - - Lloyd Street Synagogue 4:146
- - - Temple Oheb Shalom 4:148
- - Boston, Mass.
- - - Mishkan Tefilla 4:1266
- - - Ohebei Shalom 11:1115
- - Brandeis University, 6:1226
- - Bridgeport, Conn. 4:1372
- - Brookline, Mass. 4:1265
- - Buffalo, N.Y. 4:1466
- - Charleston, S.C. 5:357; 15:212
- - Charleston, W.Va. 4:787
- - Chicago, Ill.
- - - South Shore Temple 5:1445
- - - Temple Rodfei Zedek 5:417
- - Cincinnati, O., Isaac Mayer Wise Temple 5:563; 12:1345
- - Cleveland, O.
- - - Fairmount Temple 5:607
- - - Tifereth Israel Temple 5:606
- - Columbus, O. 5:755
- - Dallas, Tex. 5:1231
- - Dayton, O. 5:1389
- - Des Moines, Ia. 8:1439
- - Detroit, Mich.
- - - Beth Aaron Synagogue 5:1567,1572
- - - Temple Beth El 5:1569
- - El Paso, Tex. 6:685
- - Englewood, N.J., Temple Emanu-El 12:1030
- - Evansville, Ind. 8:1361
- - Glencoe, Ill. 8:1256
- - Hamden, Conn. 5:899
- - Harrisburg, Pa. 7:1349
- - Houston, Tex. 8:1051
- - Indianapolis, Ind. 8:1362
- - Jackson, Calif. 15:1604
- - Jackson, Miss. 12:155
- - Jacksonville, Fla. 9:1191

- - Kansas City, Mo. **10:**739
- - Lakewood, N.J., Congregation Sons of Israel **4:**1005
- - Livingston, N.J. **6:**903
- - Los Angeles **11:**499,500
- - Milwaukee, Wis. **16:**556
- - Newark, N.J., Temple B'nai Abraham **12:**1029
- - Newport, R.I., Touro Synagogue **3:**454; **12:**1043
- - New York, N.Y.
- - - B'nai Jeshurun **12:**1072
- - - Central Synagogue **12:**1091
- - - Shearith Israel **4:**1418; **12:**1068,1069,1070; **14:**1175
- - - Temple Emanu-El **3:**344; **12:**1108
- - Oklahoma City, Temple B'nai Israel **12:**1354
- - Omaha, Nebr., Beth Israel **12:**1374
- - Philadelphia, Pa.
- - - Beth Shalom **13:**375
- - - Mikveh Israel **10:**691; **13:**371
- - Pittsburgh, Pa., Temple Sinai **13:**569
- - Portland, Oreg.
- - - Beth Israel **13:**911
- - - Park Street **12:**1451
- - Providence, R.I. **13:**1278
- - Richmond, Va. **14:**161; **16:**164
- - Rochester, N.Y. **3:**627; **14:**210
- - St. Louis, Mo. **12:**157; **14:**663,665
- - Saint Paul, Minn. **12:**38
- - San Antonio, Tex. **14:**823
- - San Diego, Calif. **14:**830
- - San Francisco, Calif. **3:**453; **5:**56; **14:**833,835
- - San Mateo, Calif. **5:**59
- - South Orange, N.J. **4:**1005
- - Springfield, Mass. **15:**319
- - Stamford, Conn. **15:**329
- - Tarrytown, N.Y. **16:**465
- - Wichita, Kan., Temple Emanu-El **10:**739
- - Wilmington, Del. **16:**533
- - Winston-Salem, N.C., Temple Emanuel **12:**1219
- - Worcester, Mass., Temple Emanuel **11:**114; **16:**633
- *illus:* Venezuela
- - Caracas **16:**92
- *illus:* Virgin Islands
- - St. Thomas **16:**164
- *illus:* Yugoslavia
- - Belgrade **16:**879
- - Pančevo **16:**875
- - Sarajevo **14:**872
- - Stobi **12:**238
- - Subotica **15:**472
- - Zagreb **16:**869,918
- - Zenica **16:**882
- *illus:* In the Arts
- - Altneuschul, commemorative stamp **5:**1198
- - Bevis Marks Synagogue (Paint., J.H. Belisario) **15:**620-621
- - Day of Atonement in a Dutch synagogue (drg., B. Picart) **3:**831
- - Day of Atonement prayers *(Kirchliche Verfassung der heutigen Juden)* **5:**1385
- - flower and foliage decoration on Shavuot (paint., M. Oppenheim) **6:**1368
- - *Golden Haggadah,* "Sister" to **2:**806
- - "Interior of a Synagogue at Safed" (paint., Y. Frenkel) Fig. 99 **3**-ART
- - raising of the Torah scroll (drg., B. Picart) **7:**1077
- - Rejoicing of the Law (paint., S. A.Hart) **3:**547
- - "Rosh Ha-Shanah in the Synagogue" (drg., B.Picart) **13:**497
- - "Simḥat Torah in the Synagogue" (drg., B. Picart) **14:**1571
- - "Synagogue" (paint., H. Bloom **4:**1132
- - "Synagogue in Jerusalem" (paint., S. Hirshenberg) **3:**627
- - "Synagogue in Safed" (paint., N. Gutman) **7:**988
- - "Synagogue in Safed" (paint., M. Levanon) Pl. 9 **3**-ART
- - Tishah be-Av scene (18th cent. engr.) **3:**937
- - "Yom Kippur in the Country" (lith., A. Levy) **5:**1383
- *see also:* ARK; ART (Synagogal); BIMAH; CEREMONIAL OBJECTS

"Synagogue" (paint., H. Bloom) **4:**1132
SYNAGOGUE, THE GREAT (hist. inst.) **15:**629
- *Aleinu le-Shabbe'aḥ* **2:**557
- gerusia **7:**523
- *halakhah* development **7:**1161
- legal traditions **15:**1311
- liturgy **11:**393
- Oral Law **11:**314
- Knesset, modern, and **10:**1112
- sages **14:**636ff
- *soferim* **15:**80
- *tikkun soferim* **15:**1139

SYNAGOGUE COUNCIL OF AMERICA, THE (orgn.) **15:**631
- Artz, Max **3:**670
- *illus:* text

"Synagogue Court" (phot., R. Vishniac **16:**166
"Synagogue in Jerusalem" (paint., S. Hirshenberg) **3:**627
"Synagogue in Safed" (paint., N. Gutman) **7:**988
"Synagogue in Safed" (paint., M. Levanon) Pl. 9 **3**-ART
Synagogue of Elijah (Cairo) **16:**1334
Synagogue of Elijah (Jer.), *see* Elijah, Synagogue of
SYNGALOWSKI, ARON **15:**632
Synod, Antioch (Chr.) **3:**72
Synod, the Great, *see* SYNAGOGUE, THE GREAT
Synodoros (saint) **11:**247
SYNODS **15:**632
- autonomy **3:**924
- Anjou rabbis and **3:**23
- Brunswick (1844) **4:**1422
- community **5:**818
- fines imposition **6:**1289
- France **7:**19
- Shum influenced by **14:**1480
- *takkanot* **15:**725
- Troyes **14:**1480
- *see also:* CONFERENCES; RABBINICAL CONFERENCES

Syntax (Heb. gram.) **8:**140
- Bible poetry **13:**683
- Dead Sea Scrolls **16:**1587
- mishnaic Hebrew **16:**1602ff
- *illus:*
- - diagrammatic constructions **8:**146-153

Syphilis (disease) **6:**515
Sypkens, Hendrik **8:**61
SYRACUSE (city, Sic.) **15:**634
- catacombs **5:**251
- special Purim **13:**1399

SYRACUSE (city, N.Y.) **15:**635
- New York **12:**1126

SYRIA **15:**636
- *Contents:*
- - Biblical and Second Temple Period **15:**636
- - From the Arab Conquest **15:**639
- - Contemporary Period **15:**646
- - Attitude Toward Israel **15:**647
- General
- - Diaspora **6:**10
- - dress **6:**216
- - history chart **8:**766-767
- - language **16:**1415ff
- - population **13:**871ff
- - synagogues **1:**syn. list
- Ancient Period
- - archisynagogos **3:**335
- - commerce **15:**1293ff
- - designation **9:**108
- - early Bible history **8:**572,577
- - Ereẓ Israel, 634 to 1099 **9:**259ff
- - Ereẓ Israel, Hellenistic-Roman period **8:**625; **8:**633
- - Hellenistic state **8:**292ff
- - Mari **11:**972
- - *Provincia Judaea* **9:**239
- - seals **14:**1072
- - Solomon's kingdom **15:**97
- - spices **8:**1311
- - Syro-Ephraimite War **2:**455
- - urban culture **5:**584ff
- - warfare **16:**268
- - *see also:* COELE-SYRIA
- Middle Ages
- - Jerusalem community **9:**1436
- - Mamluk rule **11:**834
- Modern Period
- - Alliance Israélite Universelle **2:**652
- - anti-Jewish discrimination **6:**71
- - Arab command, joint **14:**1605
- - Arab League **3:**242
- - Arab refugees **9:**448ff
- - armistice agreements (1949) **3:**479; **9:**377
- - frontier, Transjordan, Israel **9:**313
- - Israel clashes **9:**385; **9:**404ff
- - Israel War of Independence **9:**366ff; **16:**306ff
- - Security Council resolution, 1967 **9:**415
- - Six-Day War **9:**404ff ; **14:**1624
- - U.N. **15:**1546ff
- - Youth Aliyah **16:**862
- - Zionism **16:**1127
- *illus:*
- - text
- - Druze population (map) **9:**926
- - Franco-British frontier agreements, 1920-23 (map) **9:**316
- - Gadot, Syrian shell damage **14:**1631
- - Israel-Syria General Armistice Agreement, 1949 **3:**482
- - Israel-Syria negotiations, Maḥanayim, 1949 **3:**481
- - masoretic accents **11:**1109
- - Sasa, Ẓahal attack on Syrians **16:**326
- - Six-Day War **14:**1637

Syria and Phoenicia (Ptolemaic dist.) **8:**626
Syriac (lang.)
- Aramaic **3:**276
- Bar Hebraeus, Joḥanan **4:**222
- Bible translations **4:**858
- Cairo *Genizah* **16:**1335
- diacritical marks **16:**1430ff
- Hebrew linguistics **16:**1393
- inscriptions script **2:**687
- masorah **16:**1415ff
- neo-Aramaic **12:**949
- philosophy, Jewish **13:**428
- vocalization system **16:**1443

Syrian (Gr. philos.) **6:**164
Syrian Christians **9:**912; **9:**1439; **9:**1441
Syrian Orthodox Church (Isr.) **9:**912
- *illus:*
- - Holy Sepulcher **9:**914

Syria Palaestina (Rom. prov.) **9:**248
SYRKIN, JOSHUA (Grigory) **15:**650
SYRKIN, MARIE **15:**650
- Syrkin, Nachman **15:**653

SYRKIN, MOSES NAHUM SOLOMONOVICH **15:**650
SYRKIN, NACHMAN **15:**651
- Shazar, Zalman **14:**1324
- Zionist socialism **9:**519; **15:**43

SYRKIN, YAKOV KOVOVICH **5:**388
Syro-Ephraimite War **2:**455
Syro-Hexaplar (Bib. trans.), *see Hexaplar, Syro-*
Syrokomla, Wladislaw **13:**799
Systemalpatent (fam., laws, Bohem.) **6:**1163
Szabadka (tn., Yug.), *see* SUBOTICA
Szabatowki (school system) **16:**341
SZABÓ, IMRE **15:**654
Szabo, László **5:**406
SZABOLCSI, BENCE **15:**654
SZABOLCSI, LAJOS **15:**654
- *Egyenlöség* **6:**479

SZABOLCSI, MIKSA **15:**655
- *Egyenlöség* **6:**478

Szadów (city, Lith.), *see* SEDUVA
SZAJKOWSKI, ZOSA (Szajko Friedman) **15:**655
- history **8:**568

Szaki (city, Lith.), *see* SAKIAI
SZÁLASI, FERENC **15:**656
- Arrow Cross Party **3:**499

Szalit, Julius **15:**656
SZALIT-MARCUS, RACHEL **15:**656
Szamosujvár (tn., Hung.) **5:**618
Szancer, Wladislaw, *see* Ordon, Wladislaw
Szaniawski, Klemens, *see* JUNOSZA, KLEMENS
SZÁNTÓ, GYÖRGY **8:**1087
Szántó, István **8:**61
Szántó, Meir **12:**765
SZÁNTÓ, SIMON **15:**656
- press **12:**1333; **13:**1033

Szapiro, Rosa **13:**1503
Szapiro-Sawicka, Hanna **16:**353
Szarkowczyzna (vill., Belor.) **7:**624
Szarogrod (tn., Ukr.), *see* SHARGOROD
Szasz, Thomas **13:**1340
Szasza, Abraham **2:**518
Szászregen (tn., Rum.), *see* REGHIN
Szatmar (city, Rum.), *see* SATU-MARE
Szatmári, Ötvös István **8:**61
Szatmár-Némethi, Mihály **8:**61
Szatmarnemeti (city, Rum.), *see* SATU-MARE
Szatmárnémeti, Mihály **8:**61
Szatmárnémeti, Samuel **8:**61
Szatmáry, Orban Samuel **8:**61
Szatmáry, P. Daniel **8:**61
SZCZEBRZESZYN (tn., Pol.) **15:**657
Szczecin (city, Pol.), *see* STETTIN
Szczerbato, Joel **11:**589
SZCZERCOW (vill., Pol.) **15:**658
Szczupak, Yvette **9:**1516
Szebnia (lab. camp) **14:**538
Széchényi, Count **6:**1159
SZEGED **15:**658
- *illus:*
- - synagogue **8:**1103

Szegedi, István **8:**61
Szeghö, Ignaz **15:**1373
Székely, Béla **15:**1510
Szekely, Eva **12:**1376
Székely, István **8:**61
SZEKESFEHERVAR (city, Hung.) **15:**659
SZELL, GEORGE **12:**710
Szemiot, Alexander **8:**61

Szenczi Molnár, Albert **4**:883
- Hebraists **8**:61
SZENDE, PÁL **15**:660
Szendrei, Aladar, *see* SENDREY, ALFRED
SZENES, BÉLA **15**:660
SZENES, ERZSI **15**:660
SZENES, HANNAH **15**:661
- Banja Luka **4**:166
Szenice (tn., Slov.), *see* Senica
Szentesi, Rudolf, *see* KISS, JÓZSEF
Szentiványi, Márton **8**:61
SZENWALD, LUCJAN **13**:805
Szeö, Demeter **8**:1080
SZÉP, ERNÖ **15**:661
Szép Szo (period.) **8**:1239
Szeptycki, Andreas **8**:875,910
SZER, SEWERYN **15**:662
SZERB, ANTAL **15**:662
SZERENCSÉS, IMRE (Fortunatus) **15**:662
- Hungary **8**:1088
Szereszewski, *see also under* Schereschewsky, Shereshevsky
Szereszewski, Benjamin **4**:1362
Szereszewski, Michael **15**:663
SZERESZEWSKI, MOSES DAVID **15**:663
Szereszewski, Raphael **15**:663
Szerman, Abraham Isaac **7**:1550
SZERMAN, PINCHAS **7**:1550
Szerman, Szymon **3**:575
- *illus:*
- - "Market of the Lodz Ghetto" (paint.) Fig. 79 **3**-ART
SZERYNG, HENRYK **12**:710
SZIGETI, IMRE **3**:611
- *illus:*
- - "Lighting the Sabbath Candles" (drg.) **14**:567
SZIGETI, JOSEPH **12**:710
Szigligeti, Ede **8**:1079
Szigmondy, Samuel **8**:61
SZILÁGYI, GÉZA **15**:663
Szilágyi, Péter **8**:61
Szilágysomlyo (tn., Rum.), *see* SIMLEUL-SILVANIEI
SZILARD, LEO **15**:664
Szillassy (fam.) **11**:551
Szinérváralja (vill., Rum.), *see* SEINI
Szlovákia (reg.), *see* SLOVAKIA
Szmuszkowicz, Nechama **13**:113
Sznajder, Edward **13**:818
SZO, *see* Student Zionist Organization
SZOBEL, GÉZA **3**:611
SZOLD, BENJAMIN **15**:664
- Civil War, views on **4**:148
SZOLD, HENRIETTA **15**:665
- Hadassah **7**:1041ff
- Jewish Publication Society of America **10**:81
- Magnes, Judah Leon **11**:718
- Russian Night School **4**:148
- *illus:*
- - text
- - autograph **3**:918
- - Hadassah nurses **7**:1042; **16**:721
- - Kefar Szold **10**:893
- - London Round Table Conference **9**:353
- - Z.O.A. **15**:1623
SZOLD, ROBERT **15**:668
- Brandeis, Louis Dembitz **4**:1298
- U.S. Zionism **16**:1143
SZOLNOK (city, Hung.) **15**:669
Szombat (Shabbat; period.) **6**:796; **15**:473
- - history chart **8**:766-767
SZOMBATHELY (city, Hung.) **15**:669
SZOMORY, DEZSÖ **15**:669
Szpalski, Karol **13**:803
Szrensk (vill., Gal.) **14**:536
Sztafeta (newsp.) **12**:826
Sztejnbarg, Dina, *see* KOTARBIŃSKA, JANINA
SZTÓJAY, DÖME **15**:670
- Hungary **8**:1099
Sztutowo (concen. camp), *see* STUTTHOF
Sztybel, A.J., *see* STYBEL, ABRAHAM JOSEPH
Szuliawicz, Eliezer **11**:469
Szulwas, Moses Avigdor, *see* SHULVASS, MOSES AVIGDOR
Szumacher, I. **12**:454
Szurday, Robert **15**:1040
Szwalbe, Nathan **12**:844
SZWARC, MICHAEL **15**:670
Szwarcfus, Adam **13**:775
SZYDLOWIEC (tn., Pol.) **15**:670
SZYK, ARTHUR **15**:672
- anti-Nazi caricatures **5**:219
- *illus:*
- - Statute of Kalish (illum.) **3**:922
Szymański, Eduard **13**:802
Szyper, Henryk **13**:803
SZYR, EUGENIUSZ **15**:672

T

Ta'amei ha-Mikra, see CANTILLATION
Ta'amei ha-Mikra (wk.) **4:**573
Ta'amei ha-Mitzvot, see COMMANDMENTS, REASONS FOR
Taʿamra (Bedouin clan, Isr.) **9:**1045
TAANACH (city, Er. Isr.) **15:**673
– battle route **16:**270
– cuneiform letters **16:**1561
– Deborah battle date **8:**585
– letters **11:**55
– village block **9:**591
– *illus:*
– – drainpipe cistern **5:**579
– – moshavim in regional settlement area **9:**578
TA'ANIT (tract.) **15:**675
– *illus:* text
Ta'anit, Megillat (tan. wk.), *see* MEGILLAT TA'ANIT
Ta'anit Ester, *see* ESTHER, FAST OF
Ta'aniyyot (type of prayer bk.) **13:**987
Ta'aniyyot (tract.), *see* TA'ANIT
Ta'as (co., Isr.) **9:**684
– *illus:*
– – assembling hand grenades **9:**682
Ta'asiyyah u-Misḥar (journ.) **1:** newsp. list
Ta'asiyyah ve-Khalkalah (journ.) **1:** newsp. list
TABACHNIK, ABRAHAM BER **15:**676
Tabachnik, Shelomo, *see* BEN-YOSEF, SHELOMO
Tabak, Max **15:**339
TABAK, SOLOMON LEIB **15:**676
Ṭabāqāt-i-Nāsiri (chronicle, Pers.) **2:**327
Ṭabarī, Abu Jaʿfar Muhammad al- **4:**930
Tabarī, Ali al- *see* ALI IBN SAHL IBN RABBAN AL-TABARĪ
Tabarī, Sahl ibn Rabbān al-
– Ali ibn Sahl **2:**632
– mathematics **11:**1122
– medicine **11:**1187
Tabaristan (reg., Iran) **13:**312
Tabbur ha-areẓ ("navel of the earth") **9:**1558
– *see also:* EVEN SHETIYYAH
TABEEL, THE SON OF (bib. fig.) **15:**676
– Ahaz **2:**455
Tabenkin, Moshe **15:**678
TABENKIN, YIẒḤAK **15:**678
– Ben-Gurion **4:**508
– Po'alei Zion **16:**338
– *illus:*
– – Labor parties merger meeting **9:**677
Tabenkin, Yosef **13:**47
TABERNACLE **15:**679
– *Contents:*
– – Terminology **15:**679
– – Sources **15:**680
– – Materials **15:**680
– – The Tabernacle Proper **15:**681
– – The Tabernacle Completed and in Use **15:**683
– – Exegetical and Historical Problems **15:**684
– – The Theology of the Tabernacle **15:**686
– – In the Aggadah **15:**687
– altar **2:**761
– Arad temple **3:**244
– art **3:**506
– building of **4:**193
– cloud **13:**524
– divine presence **13:**1015ff
– Exodus, Book of **6:**1060ff
– Holy of Holies **10:**1322
– in the Arts **15:**984
– Kohathites **10:**1135
– Levites **11:**72; **12:**1249
– *menorah* **11:**1355
– metals **11:**1430ff
– Moses **12:**377
– Mount Gerizim **7:**437
– music **12:**559
– Numbers, Book of **12:**1249ff
– Pentateuch **13:**242ff
– priests **11:**141
– purification **11:**143
– revelation **14:**118
– Sabbath **14:**558
– Samaritan tradition **14:**751
– Temple **15:**946ff
– Twelve Tribes **15:**1383
– vessels **11:**846
– wooden furniture **16:**630
– *illus:*
– – text
– – Aaron with implements **6:**277
– – *Baraita de-Melekhet ha-Mishkan* **4:**193
– – Bezalel and Oholiab building the **4:**787
– – Bezalel stretching hides for **4:**786
– – cherubim **5:**398
– – disposition of the tribes **8:**566
– – *First Leningrad Bible* **3:***fcg.* 524
– – implements **4:**957,963,977 **5:**398; **6:**277; **7:***fcg.* 619 and 622; **8:**1275
– – sacrifice of birds **10:**1037
– – *tahash* identification **15:**703
– *see also:* CULT PLACES, ISRAELITE; TEMPLE
Tabernacles, Feast of, *see* SUKKOT
TABGHA (site, Er. Isr.) **15:**688
– holy places **8:**935
TABI (1/2 cent., slave) **15:**689
– slavery **14:**1657
Tabia ben Isaac **14:**734
Tabiah ben al-Doweik, *see* Ghazzāl
Tabiah ben Phinehas **14:**754
TABIB, AVRAHAM **15:**690
TABIB, MORDEKHAI **15:**690
– Yemen **16:**755
Tabitha (N.T. fig.) **9:**1250
Table hymns, *see* ZEMIROT
Table manners **6:**946
Table of nations, *see* NATIONS, THE SEVENTY
Table tennis **15:**314
– *illus:*
– – Barna, Victor **15:**313
TABLETS OF THE LAW **15:**690
– Ark **3:**460
– Jewish badge **4:**64
– *illus:*
– – as Jewish badge **4:**63
– – ceremonial object motif **4:**1340,1341,1466
– – handed down to Moses **2:***fcg.* 11; **3:***fcg.* 907; **4:**430; **5:**1436–1438; **7:***fcg.* 875 and 1131; **8:**1218
– – Knesset *Menorah* (sculp., B. Elkan) **5:**1448
– – Pentateuch alluded to **7:***fcg.* 875
– – *Perpignan Bible* **4:**967
– – *Regensburg Pentateuch* **14:***fcg.* 1323
– – *Sarajevo Haggadah* **7:***fcg.* 1131
– – Tarrytown, Temple Beth Abraham **16:**465
– *see also:* COVENANT
Tabnith (k., Phoen.) **14:**79; **16:**668
TABOR (tn., Bohem.) **15:**691
TABOR, DAVID **15:**692
TABOR, HARRY ZVI **1:**38; **15:**692
Tabor, Israel **15:**692
TABOR, MOUNT (Isr.) **15:**692
– Crusades **9:**269
– Jezreel Valley **10:**102
– physiography **9:**148
– Tabor **15:**691
– *illus:* text; **9:**149
TABOR (TÁBORI), PAUL **6:**791
Tabori, Yael **12:**672
Taborites (extremist Hussites) **4:**1175; **8:**1134
Tabor River (Isr.) **9:**151
Tabrimmon (bib. fig.) **4:**515; **14:**186
TABRIZ (city, Iran) **15:**693
– Azerbaijan **3:**1005
Tabrīzī (name), *see also* Tawrīzī
TABRIZI, MAHOMET ABU-BEKR-AT-BEN MAHOMET **15:**694
Tabszunsky, Jacob **12:**1519
Tabu **10:**866
Tabu (land registry, Isr.) **9:**555,749
Tabūl, Joseph ibn, *see* JOSEPH IBN TABŪL
Tabula Peutingeriana (geog. chart), *see* Peutinger table
Ṭabʿūn (site, Er. Isr.) **15:**1172
Tacapae (anc. tn., Tun.), *see* GABÈS
Tachauer (fam.) **15:**694
TACHOV (Tachau; tn., Bohem.) **15:**694
TACITUS (Rom. hist.) **15:**695
– anti-Jewish accusations **3:**190
– ass worship **3:**784
– Jewish war **10:**255
– Jews and Judaism **14:**233
– population of Jerusalem **13:**871
Tacoma (city, Wash.) **16:**356
Tacuara (mvmt., Arg.) **3:**416
– Neo-Fascism **12:**951
TADEF (vill., Syr.) **15:**696
Tadhkīr wa al-Ta'nīth, al- (wk.), *see Kitāb al-Tadhkīr wa al-Ta'nīth*
Tadi (apostle) **10:**15
Tadi Gate (Temple mt.) **15:**963
Tadić, J. **8:**563
Tadjer, Salis **4:**1494
TADMOR (city, Syr.) **15:**696
– Ereẓ Israel **9:**254
– Mari **11:**983
– Odenathus and Zenobia **12:**1318
Tadmuri, Isḥāq ben Ibrāhīm al-, *see* Al-Tadmurī, Isḥāq ben Ibrāhīm
Tadsheh Midrash, see MIDRASHIM, SMALLER
Tadzhir, Moses **4:**1485
TAENZER, ARNOLD (Aaron) **15:**699
TAEUBLER, EUGEN **15:**699
Taeubler, Selma, *see* STERN-TAEUBLER, SELMA
Tafīla (vill., Transj.) **9:**596
Tafilalet (reg., Mor.) **14:**1529
Tafrit (period.) **1:** newsp. list
Tafsir (wk.) **12:**951
Taft, William Howard **15:**1653
– *illus:*
– – protest against anti-Semitism **15:**1654
Taftafiyyah (angel) **11:**695
TAGANROG (city, Rus.) **15:**699
Tagblat (newsp., Rus.) **13:**1047
Tageblat (period., N.Y.C.) **6:**1331; **12:**1101; **14:**1135
Tagger, Theodor, *see* BRUCKNER, FERDINAND
Tagim (bibl.) **1:** newsp. list
TAGIN (letter ornamentation) **15:**700
– *illus:* text
– *see also:* MASORAH
TAGLICHT, DAVID ISRAEL **15:**701

- Vienna **16:**127
Tagrīb wa al-Tashīl, al- (wk.), *see Risālat al-Taqrīb wa al-Tashīl*
TAHAL (corp., Isr.) **15:**701
- South Korea **9:**444
- water **9:**770
TAḤANUN (prayer) **15:**702
- *Arvit* **3:**665
- mourning **12:**491
Taḥanunim (form of piyyut), *see* TEḤINNAH
Taharah (cleansing of dead), *see* TOHORAH
TAHARAT HA-MISHPAḤAH (fam. purity) **15:**703
- Karaites **10:**780
- *see also:* NIDDAH
TAḤASH (animal) **15:**703
- giraffe **6:**32
- Tabernacle **15:**681
Ta Hazei (wk.) **16:**1197
Taḥbiv (period.) **1:**newsp. list
Taḥburah ve-Tayyarut (period.) **1:**newsp. list
Taheb (Samar. mess.) **14:**738; **14:**751
Ṭahir al-Ṭabarī **9:**921
Tahiti (isl.) **14:**688
Taḥkemoni (bk.; al-Ḥarizi) **2:**627; **7:**1339; **11:**327; **13:**126
Taḥkemoni (wk.; Moses Bali) **4:**137
Taḥkemoni (journ.) **1:** newsp. list **11:**169
Taḥlifa ben Saul (amora) **7:**1154; **12:**187
Taḥpanḥes (port, Egy.) **4:**13 **9:**1351
Tahuel, Isaac **16:**56
Tahuel, Omar **16:**56
Taiber, Y. **13:**904
Tailor, Francis, *see* Tayler, Francis
TAILORING **15:**704
- *contents:*
- - England **15:**706
- - United States **15:**708
- - in Israel **15:**709
- crafts **5:**1046ff
- guilds **7:**972
- Israel industry **9:**823
- migrations **16:**1521
- modern economic history **16:**1315
- *sha'atnez* prohibition **14:**1213; **16:**1286
- *chart:* text
- *illus:*
- - N.Y. garment workers **15:**1616,1617
- - Poland **13:**746
- *see also:* TEXTILES
Taima (oasis, Arab.); *see* TAYMA
TAIMANOV, MARK YEVGENYEVICH **5:**404; **5:**409
Taima Stele **15:**940
Tainet (tell, Syr.) **15:**947
Taitazak, Hananiah **2:**669
TAITAẒAK, JOSEPH **15:**711
- Arollia, Isaac **3:**492
- Ashkenazi, Eliezer **3:**725
- Benjamin of Arta **4:**538
- Kabbalah and alchemy **10:**636; **10:**637
- Ottoman Empire **16:**1535
Taitaẓak, Judah **15:**711
Taitaẓak, Samuel **16:**1533
Taitaẓak, Solomon **15:**711
Ta'iz (tn., Yem.) **14:**1215; **16:**742
Tajar, Colonel **11:**1566
Tajik (J. lang.), *see* Judeo-Tajiki
Tājir (16th cent., r.) **6:**496
Tajnīs, al- (wk.), *see Kitāb al-Tajnīs*
Tajtelbaum, Niuta **16:**353
Takāyā (Musl. hostel) **9:**918
Takelma (Ind. tribe, N.Am.) **14:**855
Takhrikhim, see Shrouds, Burial
TAKKANOT (halakhic directives) **15:**712
- *Contents:*
- - Definition and Substance **15:**713
- - Legislation in the *Halakhah* **15:**714
- - Nature of Halakhic Legislation **15:**715
- - Rules of Legislation **15:**717
- - Role of the Public **15:**719
- - Annulment of *Takkanot* **15:**720
- - Until End of Tannaitic Period **15:**720
- - Amoraic Period **15:**721
- - Gaonic Period **15:**722
- - Post-Gaonic Times **15:**723
- - Different Centers **15:**724
- - Family Law **15:**726
- - Chief Rabbinate of Ereẓ Israel **15:**728
- Theory
- - *ascama* **3:**677
- - autonomy **3:**925
- - codification of law **5:**630
- - conflict of laws **5:**883ff
- - decision by majority **11:**805
- - interpretation **8:**1415
- - Jewish law, place in **12:**112ff
- - law and morality **10:**1481
- - law source **12:**119
- - status in *halakhah* **7:**1157ff
- - synods **15:**632ff
- - Usha **16:**19
- Application
- - assault **3:**760
- - child's maintenance **13:**97
- - custom **12:**9ff
- - debtor's property **6:**1013ff
- - Decrees, the 18 **13:**1409
- - *dina de-malkhuta* **6:**52
- - documents **14:**1390
- - encroachment safeguards **7:**1462ff
- - endowment witnesses **8:**285
- - *ḥaliẓah* and maintenance **11:**128
- - *ḥazakah* **7:**1522
- - *ḥerem bet din* **8:**355
- - *ḥerem ha-yishuv* **8:**355
- - imprisonment for debt **8:**1305ff
- - inheritance **15:**477ff
- - lien **11:**227ff
- - limitation of actions **11:**253;
- - loans **11:**418
- - penal law **13:**222ff
- - *prosbul* **13:**1181
- - rape **13:**1549
- - sumptuary laws **15:**515
- - *takkanat ha-shuk* **15:**1097
- - widow **2:**399; **16:**495
- - wills **16:**519ff
- Places
- - Candia **5:**152
- - Castile **2:**333; **7:**382
- - Germany **7:**465ff
- - Israel rabbinate **13:**958
- - Jerusalem, Mamluk period **9:**281
- - Lithuania **5:**1002
- - Moravia **12:**123
- - Shum **6:**186; **14:**1481; **15:**264
- - Toledo **9:**1066; **16:**529
- - Troyes **6:**627
- - Tunisia **15:**1443
- - *yeshivot* **16:**766
- Creation and Utilization
- - Abendanan, Samuel **2:**68
- - Abraham ben Avigdor **2:**134
- - Abraham ben Moses **2:**151ff
- - Eger, Akiva **6:**470
- - Epstein, Aryeh **6:**825
- - exilarch **6:**1031
- - *geonim* **7:**316
- - Hillel **8:**484
- - rabbinical authority **3:**910
- - Simeon ben Shetaḥ **14:**1564
- - Yellin, Yehoshua **16:**736
- *illus:* text
- *see also:* SEVARAH; TAKKANOT HA-KAHAL
TAKKANOT HA-KAHAL (communal regulations) **15:**728
- *Contents:*
- - Concept **15:**728
- - Source of Authority **15:**729
- - Majority and Minority **15:**730
- - Role of the Communal Representatives **15:**730
- - Scope of the *Takkanot* **15:**731
- - *Halakhah* and *Takkanot* **15:**731
- - *Takkanot* and Halakhic Authority **15:**732
- - Approval by a Distinguished Person **15:**732
- - Principles of Justice and Equity **15:**733
- - Interpretation of *Takkanot* **15:**734
- - *Takkanot ha-Kahal* and the Jewish Legal System **15:**734
- - Historical Aspects **15:**735
- *see also:* PUBLIC AUTHORITY; TAKKANOT
Takli, Judah Aaron **14:**1366
TAKU, MOSES BEN ḤISDAI **15:**737
- description of works **13:**793
- Ḥasidei Ashkenaz **7:**1378; **10:**518
Tal, E. P. **13:**1367
Tal, Israel **14:**1629
TAL, JOSEF **15:**738
- Moses, works on **12:**409
Tal, Justus **13:**1035
TAL, MIKHAIL **15:**739
- chess **5:**407
Talaat Pasha **16:**1080
Ṭalāl (k., Jor.) **8:**1131
Talara (tn., Peru) **13:**324
TALAVERA DE LA REINA (city, Sp.) **15:**739
- economic life **16:**1287
Talbiyah (qtr., Jer.) **9:**1516
- *illus:*
- - aerial view of public buildings **9:**1490
Talbiyah Hill (Jer.) **9:**1495
Talbot (tn., Austr.) **11:**1285
Talbot, H. F. **16:**1507
Talbot, James **8:**61
Talbottom (tn., Ga.) **7:**429
Taleh (zodiac sign), *see* Aries
Talent (anc. coin and wt.) **5:**696ff.; **14:**1347; **16:**377; **16:**381ff
Tales, *see* FICTION, HEBREW
Tales, folk **6:**1377f
Tales of Sendebar (bk.) **6:**1266
Taless (prayer shawl), *see* TALLIT
Talḥa (loc., Isr.), *see* TEL ḤAI
TALHEIM (vill., Ger.) **15:**740
TALION (leg. conc.) **15:**741
- assault **3:**758
- Pentateuch **13:**246; **13:**255
- punishment **13:**1387
- Sadducees **14:**621
- sin **14:**1590
Talita Kumi school (Jer.) **9:**1458
Talker, Bahais Joseph **12:**1465
Talker, Moses Daniel **12:**1465
Talks and Tales (period.) **5:**459
Tall, Abraham Levi ben Menahem **12:**1454
Tallahassee (city, Fla.) **6:**1363
TALLINN (city, Est.) **15:**742
- Estonia **6:**916ff
- *illus:* text
TALLIT (prayer shawl) **15:**743
- Aden **2:**264
- Av, The Ninth **3:**939
- cemetery prohibition **5:**272
- Day of Atonement **5:**1380
- flag **6:**1337
- kissing of **10:**1074
- marriage ceremony **11:**1036
- mixed species **14:**1214
- *onen* **3:**23
- priestly blessing **13:**1062
- Samaritans **14:**741
- *illus:*
- - text
- - *atarah* **9:**1057
- - eighteenth cent. engraving **4:**1161
- - ḥasidic boy **15:***fcg.* 491
- - New York religious articles shop **12:**1101
- - wedding ceremony **10:**986; **11:**1029, *fcg.* 1067
- *see also:* ẒIẒIT
TALLIT KATAN (fringed garment) **15:**745
- mixed species **14:**1214
- *tallit* **15:**744
- *see also:* ẒIẒIT
TALMACIU (vill., Rum.) **15:**745
Talmai (bib. fig.), *see* AHIMAN, SHESHAI, TALMAI
Talmai (bib. fig.; f.-in-law of Absalom) **2:**174; **2:**464
Talmei Bilu (mosh., Isr.) **1:**place list
Talmei Elazar (mosh., Isr.) **1:**place list
Talmei Menasheh (mosh., Isr.) **4:**387; **11:**1221
Talmei Yafeh (mosh., Isr.) **1:**place list
Talmei Yehi'el (mosh, Isr.) **1:**place list
Talmi, A. **5:**458
Talmi, Efraim **9:**1568
TALMI, IGAL **15:**746
Talmi, Menaḥem **5:**437; **9:**1568
Talmid (fam.) **9:**1218
Talmid, Jacob ben Ḥayyim, *see* JACOB BEN ḤAYYIM TALMID
TALMID ḤAKHAM (tit.) **15:**746
- Academy on High **2:**208
- *am-ha-areẓ* **2:**836
- honored in court **13:**954
- insult of **14:**1652
- mourning for **12:**489
- *niddui* **8:**350ff
- *takkanot ha-kahal* **15:**733
- tax **15:**842ff
- walking with **14:**179
- warning in criminal act **13:**227
- *see also:* ḤAKHAM
TALMON, JACOB LEIB **15:**749
TALMUD **15:**750
- General
- - *Enoch, Ethiopic Book of* **6:**796
- - history chart **8:**766-767
- - rabbinical literature **13:**1463
- - *siyyum* **14:**1642
- - *talmid ḥakham* **15:**746
- History
- - academies **2:**199
- - Babylonian supremacy **7:**1164
- - burning **15:**768
- - censorship **4:**215; **4:**482
- - codification of law **5:**633
- - development after Mishnah **10:**372
- - *geonim* **7:**316ff
- Structure
- - *Baraita* **4:**189
- - minor tractates **12:**49
- - Mishnah **12:**93
- - *Shas* **14:**1317
- - *Tosefta* **15:**1283
- - *see also under individual tractates*
- Methodology
- - allegory **2:**643
- - Bible exegesis **4:**889
- - conflict of opinion **5:**890
- - halakhic decision **7:**1164
- - halakhic exegesis **8:**1419
- - hermeneutics **8:**366
- - legal maxims **10:**1565
- - mnemonics **12:**187
- Study of
- - Abbaye **2:**45
- - age for study **15:**456

-- Ashkenazim **3:**720
-- cantillation **5:**128
-- *Ḥiddushim* **8:**464
-- *Kelalei Shemu'el* **14:**1505
-- Naḥmanides **12:**778
-- *pilpul* **13:**524
-- Samson of Chinon **14:**779
-- *She'iltot* **2:**449,450
-- Sherira Gaon **14:**1381
-- Soloveichik, Ḥayyim **15:**129
-- Tosafot **15:**1278ff
- Topics
-- alchemy **2:**548
-- animals **3:**7
-- animal tales **3:**20
-- anthropomorphism **3:**55
-- apocalypse **3:**180
-- apologetics **3:**190ff
-- art **3:**507ff
-- asceticism **3:**678
-- astrology **3:**789
-- astronomy **3:**796
-- *avot nezikin* **3:**986ff
-- bloodletting **4:**1119
-- Boethusians **4:**1169
-- capital punishment **5:**145
-- chameleon **5:**333
-- Decalogue **5:**1446
-- demons **5:**1526
-- dualism **6:**244
-- economic history **16:**1273
-- elephant **6:**603
-- eschatology **6:**879
-- ethical instruction **6:**940,941
-- flea **6:**1339
-- fly **6:**1369
-- folklore **6:**1376
-- free will **7:**129
-- gentile **7:**411
-- Jesus **10:**14
-- law and morality **10:**1481
-- magic **11:**706
-- mathematics **11:**1122
-- medicine **11:**1181
-- metals and mining **11:**1429; **11:**1433ff
-- *minyan* **12:**67
-- miracles **12:**74
-- music **12:**577
-- mysticism **10:**498
-- names **12:**807
-- oils **12:**1351
-- peace **13:**196
-- prophecy **13:**1175
-- proselytes **13:**1185
-- proverbs **13:**1273
-- providence **13:**1281
-- psychology **13:**1341
-- rabbi **13:**1445
-- rain **13:**1520ff
-- resurrection **14:**98
-- revelation **14:**119
-- reward and punishment **14:**134
-- Rome **8:**302; **14:**242
-- Satan **14:**904
-- *Shekhinah* **14:**1350
-- soul immortality **15:**175
-- synagogue **15:**583
-- weights and measures **16:**388
- Language
-- Arabic **3:**237
-- Aramaic **3:**277
-- English **6:**826
-- French **5:**410
-- Greek and Latin **7:**884; **8:**296
-- German **7:**729
-- Hebrew **16:**1591
- Editions
-- Adelkind, Israel Cornelius **2:**259
-- Bomberg, Daniel **4:**1195
-- incunabula **8:**1321ff
-- *Kiẓẓur Talmud* **13:**537
-- mss. **11:**903ff
-- printing dispute **7:**1465
-- Romm family **14:**255; **15:**1487
-- *Sefer ha-Ner* **2:**367
-- Shapira press **14:**1665
-- Soncino **15:**142
- Attitudes to
-- Abner of Burgos **2:**88
-- Catholic Church **5:**538
-- Christian attacks **8:**689ff
-- Falashas **6:**1147
-- Haskalah **7:**1436ff
-- Judaism **10:**384ff
-- Kabbalah **3:**70
-- Karaites **10:**774
-- Maimonides **11:**746ff
-- Nicholas Donin **6:**167
-- Reform **12:**1442
- *illus:*
-- text
-- animals (table) **3:**9-16
-- censorship order by Sixtus V **5:**277
-- Clavis Talmudica **4:**297
-- coins, denominations (table) **5:**721
-- *Ḥullin* (1719) **8:**1069
-- Jerusalem Talmud manuscript (1289) **15:**776
-- *Kiddushin* **11:**544; **15:**757
-- *The Living Talmud* **4:**1143
-- *Middot* **15:**970
- *mus. notations:* text
- *see also:* AMORAIM; MISHNAH; TALMUD, BABYLONIAN; TALMUD, BURNING OF; TALMUD, JERUSALEM; TANNA, TANNAIM
TALMUD, BABYLONIAN **15:**755
- *Contents:*
-- Methods of Study **15:**757
-- Scope **15:**758
-- Mishnah and Gemara **15:**758
-- Interpretation and Application **15:**759
-- Development and Conclusion **15:**760
-- Style **15:**762
-- The Text **15:**763
-- Minor Tractates **15:**763
-- Commentaries **15:**764
-- Manuscripts **15:**765
-- Editions **15:**766
-- Authority of Babylonian Talmud **15:**767
-- Influence **15:**767
-- Translations **15:**768
- General
-- *Aggadah* **2:**356
-- *amoraim* **2:**865ff
-- Babylonia **4:**34
-- date and editing **3:**709ff; **6:**852
-- Hebrew language **16:**1591
-- historical background **8:**656ff
-- Jewish law **12:**117; **12:**121; **12:**131; **12:**136
-- Jewish literature **11:**319ff
-- *Neḥutei* **12:**942
-- order of tractates, subject matter (chart) **15:**751
-- Palestinian criticism of **9:**1363
-- Persian Jewry **13:**308
-- Pirkoi ben Baboi **13:**560
-- Pumbedita **13:**1384
-- *savora, savoraim* **14:**921
-- Sura **15:**521
-- Yehudai ben Naḥman **16:**731
- Commentators **8:**464; **11:**328
-- Abraham of Montpellier **2:**146
-- Abulafia, Meir **2:**191ff
-- Aghmati, Zechariah **2:**367
-- Akiva Eger **6:**470
-- Alfasi **2:**600
-- *Arukh* **12:**859
-- Asher ben Jehiel **3:**708
-- *Beit Aharon* **2:**17
-- Benveniste, Ḥayyim **4:**561
-- Berlin, Isaiah **4:**659
-- Buzaglo, Shalom **4:**1545
-- Chajes, Ẓevi Hirsch **5:**327
-- *Ein Mishpat* **10:**285
-- *Ein Ya'akov* **8:**1177
-- Fraenkel-Teomim **7:**6
-- *Gilyon Maharsha* **6:**473
-- *Ha-Ma'or* **7:**509
-- Hananel ben Hushiel **7:**1252
-- Isaiah ben Elijah di Trani **9:**73
-- Isaiah ben Mali di Trani **9:**73
-- Joseph Samuel of Cracow **10:**246
-- Landau, Eleazar **10:**1387
-- Landau, Ezekiel **10:**1389
-- Maharal of Prague **10:**375ff
-- Maharam of Lublin **11:**547; **15:**1282
-- Maharam of Rothenburg **11:**1252
-- Maharam Schiff **15:**1282
-- Maharsha **6:**363; **15:**1282
-- Maharshal **11:**580
-- *Mareh Kohen* **4:**790
-- Meiri **11:**1258
-- *Migdanot Natan* **4:**1247
-- *Mikhtav le-David* **5:**1353
-- *Millon Shimmushi la-Talmud* **10:**805
-- *Nezer ha-Kodesh* **2:**14
-- *Nimmukei ha-Grib* **4:**56
-- Nissim ibn Shahin **12:**1183
-- *Penei Yehoshu'a* **6:**1156
-- Rabad **2:**138ff
-- Rabbenu Gershom **7:**512
-- Ramban **12:**779ff.
-- Ran **12:**1185
-- Rashba **2:**308
-- Rashbam **14:**811
-- Rashi **7:**1107; **13:**1564
-- Ritba **16:**846
-- Samuel ben Hophni **14:**807
-- *Sefer ha-Mikhtam* **5:**1352
-- *Shitah Mekubbeẓet* **3:**723
-- Strashun, Samuel **15:**428
-- *Tevu'ot ha-Sadeh* **5:**1587
-- Tosafot **15:**1278ff
-- Vilna Gaon **6:**656f
-- *Yefeh Einayim* **9:**1337
- *illus:*
-- text
-- *Bekhorot* (Frankfort, 1720) **13:**1106
-- *Derekh Ḥayyim* (Joseph ibn Yaḥya) **8:**1210
-- fourteenth cent. ms. **11:**901
-- *Middot* **15:**970
-- *Shabbat,* title page **14:**255
- *see also:* TALMUD; TALMUD, JERUSALEM
TALMUD, BURNING OF **15:**768
- General
-- censorship **5:**277
-- Christian countries **8:**689ff
-- history chart (1242,1553) **8:**766-767
-- Ibn Lev **14:**89
-- kabbalistic literature **10:**543
-- *see also:* ANTI-SEMITISM
- Church, Catholic **5:**539
-- bull **4:**1496
-- councils **5:**549
-- Clement VIII **5:**602
-- John XXII **10:**159
-- Julius III **9:**1124
-- Paul IV **13:**189
- France **7:**14
-- Anav, Zedekiah **2:**939
-- dirge commemorating **3:**938
-- Dominicans **6:**162
-- Donin, Nicholas **6:**167
-- Odo of Châteauroux **12:**1331
-- Paris **13:**105
-- Strasbourg **15:**424
- Germany
-- Luther, Martin **11:**584
-- Pfefferkorn **13:**355
-- Reuchlin **14:**108
- Italy
-- Bragadini, Alvise **4:**1288
-- Florence **6:**1359
-- Lodi **11:**424
-- Ravenna **13:**1582
-- Rome **14:**246ff
-- Tuscany **15:**1467
-- Venice **16:**97
- Poland
-- Baruch ben David Yavan **4:**277
-- Frankists **7:**59
-- Kamenets-Podolski **10:**725
- *illus:* text
TALMUD, DAVID L. **5:**388
TALMUD, JERUSALEM **15:**772
- *Contents:*
-- The Contents **15:**773
-- Characteristics **15:**774
-- Acceptance of the Two Talmuds **15:**775
-- Editions **15:**776
-- Commentaries **15:**777
- General
-- Academy of Sciences **9:**1049
-- Aḥa of Shabḥa **2:**450
-- *amoraim* **2:**865ff
-- Anav, Jehiel **2:**938
-- Aramaic **3:**270
-- as law source **12:**117; **12:**121; **12:**131; **12:**132
-- Cairo *genizah* **16:**1336
-- historical background **8:**656ff
-- Jewish literature **11:**318ff
-- Johanan ben Nappaḥa **10:**146
-- Lieberman, Saul **11:**218
-- mishnaic Hebrew **16:**1591
-- order of tractates, subject matter (chart) **15:**751
-- Piotrkow edition **13:**556
-- popularity **15:**766
-- redaction **9:**257 **15:**1132
- Commentators
-- Benveniste, Joshua Raphael **4:**562
-- Casès, Benjamin **5:**227
-- Elijah of Fulda **6:**648
-- Fraenkel, David **7:**3
-- Fraenkel-Teomim **7:**6
-- Ḥabib, Moses **7:**1026
-- Margoliot, Moses **11:**963
-- Sirillo, Solomon **14:**1618
- *illus:*
-- text
-- *Sedarim Zera'im* and *Mo'ed* (13th cent. ms.) **2:**937
-- title page (Krotoszyn, 1866/67) **10:**1279
- *see also:* TALMUD; TALMUD, BABYLONIAN
Talmud, Sea of the, *see* SEA OF THE TALMUD
Talmud de Benei Ma'arava, see TALMUD, JERUSALEM
Talmudic academies, *see* ACADEMIES IN BABYLONIA AND EREẒ ISRAEL
Talmudical College of Chicago **13:**1465
"Talmudists" (etch., L. Reiss) **3:**639
Talmud Katan (wk.), *see Sefer ha-Halakhot*
Talmud Leshon Ivri (wk.) **4:**573
Talmud Torah (conc.), *see* STUDY
Talmud Torah (school) **6:**413ff
- *ḥeder* **8:**241
- libraries of **11:**190
Talmud Torah (soc., Amst.) **2:**65; **2:**896
Talmud Yanka'i (wk.) **13:**136 **14:**303
- *illus:*
-- *Massekhet Amerika,* opening page **13:**127
TALNOYE (city, Ukr.) **15:**779
Talpioth (journ.) **1:**newsp. list
TALPIR, GABRIEL JOSEPH **15:**779
Talpiyyot (sub., Jer.) **9:**563

– ancient vegetation **9:**1515
– Jerusalem development **9:**1472
– *illus:*
– – early houses **9:**1477
– – *ma'barah* **11:**653
Talpiyyot (journ., Rum.) **1:**newsp. list
Talpiyyot (collec., Ukr.) **1:**newsp. list
TAL SHAHAR (mosh., Isr.) **15:**779
– statistics **1:**place list
Talut (k.), *see* SAUL
Tam (tort conc.) **3:**987ff
Tam, Isaac **15:**779
TAM, JACOB BEN MEIR (tos.) **15:**779
– Abraham the Proselyte **3:**195
– Apulian Jewry **3:**227
– Ashkenazim **8:**666
– barnacle goose **4:**247
– Bekhor Shor, Joseph **4:**410
– communal enactments **11:**805
– Crusader attack on **5:**1139
– dowry enactments **6:**186
– Dunash-Menahem dispute **6:**270
– genealogy **7:**382
– history chart **8:**766-767
– Ibn Ezra, Abraham **8:**1164
– Jacob ben Meir Levi **16:**788
– Jacob ben Samson **9:**1223
– lending money to gentiles **12:**248
– linguistics **16:**1361,1385
– marriage *takkanah* **15:**723
– Meshullam of Melun **11:**1403
– method of commentary **15:**765
– responsa **14:**86
– Samson of Falaise **14:**779
– *Sefer ha-Yashar* **14:**1099
– *takkanot* **15:**736
– *tefillin* **15:**899ff
Tam, Joseph **15:**779
Tam, Miriam **15:**779
Tam, Moses **15:**779
Tam, Solomon **15:**779
Tamad (loc., Sinai) **14:**1605
Tamah, Mordecai ben Isaac **10:**1592
TAMAKH, ABRAHAM BEN ISAAC HA-LEVI **15:**781
– *see also:* ABRAHAM BEN ISAAC HA-LEVI
Tamakh, Joseph **15:**782
Taman (port, Crimea) **5:**1105
TAMAR (bib. fig., w. of Er and Onan) **15:**782
– in *Aggadah* **10:**332
– levirate marriage **11:**122
– Onan **12:**1395
– widow status **16:**489
– *geneal. table:* **5:**1342
TAMAR (bib. fig., dau. of David) **15:**783
– Amnon **2:**860
– in the Arts **5:**1334
– *illus:*
– – rape **2:**860; **8:**1317
TAMAR (bib. fig., dau. of Absalom) **15:**783
TAMAR (bib. loc., Isr.) **15:**782
– Kenites **10:**907
– palm treee **13:**43
Tamar (bot.), *see* PALM
TAMAR, DAVID SHLOMO **1:**38
Tamar, Menaḥem **6:**658
TAMARES, AARON SAMUEL **15:**783
– Steinman, Eliezer **15:**372
Tamari, Joseph **13:**1258
TAMARISK (tree) **15:**784
– flora of Israel **9:**225; **9:**788
– manna **11:**883
– plant list **13:**625
– *illus:*
– – *Tamarix mannifera* **11:**884
– – Wadi Paran **9:**234
Tamarite de Litera (tn., Sp.) **6:**1236
Tamaroff, Mordecai, *see* TENENBAUM, MORDECAI
Tamentit (loc., Afr.) **10:**88; **15:**1418
Tamerlane **2:**563
Tamḥir (period.) **1:**newsp. list
Tamḥui (cmty. charity) **2:**805; **4:**388; **6:**159
– *illus:*
– – London, charity drum **5:**350
– – Spitalfields (London) soup kitchen **5:**346
– *see also:* CHARITY
TAM IBN YAḤYA, JACOB BEN DAVID **15:**785
– Ibn Yaḥya, David **8:**1208
TAMID (tract.) **15:**785
– Mishnah **12:**94
– *Yoma* tractate **16:**844
Tamid, see Burnt offering
Tamil (anc. lang.) **5:**621
Tamim, Dunash, ibn, *see* DUNASH IBN TAMIN
Tamir, Moshe **3:**593
Tamir, Shemuel Moshe **10:**840
TAMIRIS, HELEN **15:**786
TAMMUZ (deity) **15:**787
– Song of Songs **15:**148
TAMMUZ (Heb. month) **15:**788
– ḥasidic holiday **14:**1435
– *see also:* CALENDAR; TAMMUZ, FAST OF
TAMMUZ, BENJAMIN **15:**789
– Hebrew literature **8:**207
TAMMUZ, FAST OF (17th day) **15:**789
– Apostomos **3:**217
– fast days **6:**1191; **6:**1195
– Nathan of Gaza **14:**1226
– Shabbetai Ẓevi **14:**1235
– Titus **15:**1168
– *see also:* THREE WEEKS
Tamnugalt (vill., Mor.) **6:**190
TAMPA (city, Fla.) **15:**789
– Florida **6:**1362ff
Tampere (city, Fin.) **6:**1298
Tamrah (mosh., Isr.), *see* RAMAT ẒEVI
Tamsweg (tn., Aus.) **5:**181
Tamuda (city, Mor.), *see* TETUÁN
Tamworth (tn., Austr.) **3:**878
Tamzert (vill., N. Afr.) **3:**827
Tan (animal), *see* JACKAL
Tan, N. A., *see* BOGORAZ, VLADIMIR GERMANOVICH
T-a-n-a-g, *see* ABRAHAMS, ABRAHAM
Tanais (anc. tn., Bosphorus) **4:**1263
TANAKH (Bib.) **15:**790
– *see also:* BIBLE
Tanan, S., *see* Tanny, S.
Tananir (anc. sanct.) **10:**301
Tanbīh, al- (wk.), *see Risalat al-Tanbīh*
Tanburi, Issak, *see* Romano, Issac Fresco
Tancred (Crus. ldr.) **9:**267; **9:**271; **9:**1415
Tancred Tower (Jer.) **9:**1415
Táncsics, Mihály **8:**1079
Tandrup, Harald **14:**926
Tanenbaum, Marc **13:**1253
Tanenbaum, Sidney **15:**303
Tanfield, Elisabeth **8:**61
Tang, *see* ABRAHAMS, ABRAHAM
Tanganyika, *see* Tanzania, United Republic of
Tang-i Azao (8th cent., writ.) **10:**429
TANGIER(S) (city, Mor.) **15:**790
– Abrabanel **2:**104
– Azancot family **3:**998
– special Purim **13:**1399
Tangiz (Mamluk gov.) **9:**274
Tanḥum, Gershon **13:**1513
Tanḥuma (Mid.), *see* TANḤUMA YELAMMEDENU
TANḤUMA BAR ABBA (amora) **15:**793
– *Tanhuma-Yelammedenu* **11:**321
TANḤUMA YELEMMEDENU **15:**794
– *Aggadat Bereshit* **2:**366
– Casès, Benjamin **5:**227
– *Deuteronomy Rabbah* **5:**1584
– *Genesis Rabbah* **7:**401
– Hebrew alphabet **16:**786
– Jewish literature **11:**321
– *illus:*
– – title page (1595) **4:**113
– *see also:* MIDRASH
TANHUM BEN ELIEZER **15:**796
– Broda, Benjamin **4:**1388
TANḤUM BEN ḤANILAI (amora) **15:**796
TANḤUM BEN ḤIYYA (amora) **15:**797
– Aḥa **2:**435
– Hepher **8:**332
Tanḥum ben Ila (amora), *see* TANḤUM BEN ḤANILAI
TANḤUM BEN JOSEPH HA-YERUSHALMI **15:**797
– linguistics **16:**1360,1387
Tanḥum ben Joseph ha-Kohen **10:**233
Tanḥum ben Moses **4:**363
Tanḥum of Kefar Akko (amora), *see* TANḤUM BEN ḤIYYA
Tanḥum Yerushalmi, *see* TANHUM BEN JOSEPH HA-YERUSHALMI
Tanis (anc. city, Egy.), *see* ZOAN
"Tanit" (paint., J. Atlan) **3:**823
Tanja (tn., Mor.), *see* TANGIER(S)
TANNA, TANNAIM **15:**798
– academies **2:**200; **2:**203
– *aliyah* **9:**510
– *amoraim* **2:**865ff
– as aggadists **2:**363
– controversy restrictions **5:**891
– *halakhah* **7:**1163
– Jewish law periods **12:**121
– law and morality **10:**1481
– legal maxims **10:**1565
– liturgy **11:**393ff
– modes of scholarship **14:**651
– rabbinical authority **3:**910
– *tanna kamma* **4:**738
– Temple destruction **9:**238
– tradition **15:**1311
– *see also:* AMORAIM; BARAITA, BERAITOT; MISHNAH
TANNA DE-VEI ELIYAHU (mid. wk.) **15:**803
– *see also:* AGGADAT BERESHIT; MIDRASH
Tanna de-Vei Rav (wk.) **4:**402
Tanna of Safed (Mish. corrector) **7:**1106
Tannenbaum, E. **11:**62
TANNENBAUM, FRANK **8:**550
– criminology **5:**1110
Tannenbaum, Jacob, *see* TENNENBAUM, JACOB
Tanners' Gate (Jer.), *see* Dung Gate
Tannhauser, Siegfried **7:**133
Tannim (owl) **12:**1531
Tannim (tannin; reptile), *see* CROCODILE
Tanning **5:**1044ff
– *illus:* **9:**150; **15:**446
– *see also:* LEATHER INDUSTRY AND TRADE
Tanny, S. **5:**458
Tanqīḥ, al- (wk., Ibn Janaḥ), *see Kitāb al-Tanqīḥ*
Tanqīṭ, al- (wk., Ḥayyuj), *see Kitāb al-Tanqīṭ*
TANSMAN, ALEXANDER **15:**804
TANTA (tn., Egy.) **15:**804
Tantalus (Gr. myth. fig.) **12:**997
Tantura (vill., Isr.)
– Dar-Ṭanṭura **9:**291
– Dor **6:**173
– glass factory **7:**613 **9:**325
TANUJI (fam.) **15:**804
– politics **13:**816
– Tunisia **15:**1444
TANUJI, ISHMAEL HA-KOHEN **15:**805
– family **15:**804
TANUJI, JOSEPH BEN SHALOM HA-KOHEN **15:**805
– family **15:**804
Tanuji, Joshua **5:**817; **15:**805
Tanuji, Judah Cohen **15:**805
Tanuji, Justo Cohen **15:**805
Tanuji, Moses **15:**805
Tanuji, Shalom **15:**805
Tanur (waterfall, Isr.) **9:**177
Tanūs (fam.) **9:**1435
Tanya (wk.) **7:**1413; **14:**1433ff
Tanya Rabbati (wk.) **2:**938
Tanzania, United Republic of (Afr.) **9:**441; **9:**991; **9:**992
TANZHAUS (cmty. hall) **15:**805
– communal amenities **2:**805
Tanzman, Norman **11:**1504
Taos (co., N.Mex.) **12:**1037
Ta'oz (mosh., Isr.) **1:**place list
Taphath (bib. fig.) **5:**1340
Tapiero, Meir **14:**682
Tappan-dara (k., Sumurrum) **16:**1493
TAPPUAḤ (city, Er. Isr.) **15:**806
– *see also:* TEKOA
Taqqū' (vill., Isr.) **15:**916
Tarābāy (fam.) **9:**287
Tarābulus al-Shām (port, Leb.), *see* TRIPOLI
Tarāda (Koran fig.) **15:**108
TARAGAN, BEN-ZION **15:**806
Taragon, Elijah **5:**166; **14:**1248
TARANTO (city, It.) **15:**806
– Apulia **3:**226
– *illus:*
– – text
– – tombstones **3:**227; **9:**1123
Tarapiks (coin) **5:**721
TARASCON (tn., Fr.) **15:**807
Tar'ata (deity), *see* Atargatis
Tarat Umm Basīs (loc., Sinai) **14:**1606
Tar'av (almanac) **1:**newsp. list
TARAZONA (city, Sp.) **15:**808
Tarazona, Francisco **14:**865
Tarbit (leg. term) **16:**27
TARBIZ (period.) **15:**809
– historiography **8:**563
– publications **13:**1367
– Schirmann **14:**968
– statistics **1:**newsp. list
TARBUT (educ. orgn.) **15:**809
– Ataki **3:**812
– Berliand, Shlomo **4:**638
– education **6:**428ff
– Warsaw **16:**341
– *illus:*
– – central committee of the association, 1925, **4:**706
– – refugee kindergarten **14:**447
Tarbut (journ., Eng.) **1:**newsp. list
Tarbut (journ., Pol.) **1:**newsp. list
Tarbut (journ., U.S.) **1:**newsp. list
Tarbut Ve'Ḥinukh (publ. firm, Isr.) **13:**1366
Tardiola, Moses **3:**1015
TARES (bot.) **15:**809
TARFON (tan.) **15:**810
– Akiva **2:**489
– dialogue with Tryphon **5:**551
– honor for parent **13:**101
– reward and punishment **14:**135
– reward and study **12:**1356
Tarfon, Jacob **11:**486; **13:**583
Târgo-Jiu (concen. camp) **6:**1371; **14:**402; **15:**1336
Targu-Frumos (tn., Mold.), *see*

TIRGU-FRUMOS
TARGUM (Aram. trans., Bib.) **15:**811
– General
– – Anthropomorphism in **3:**53
– – Bible translation **4:**841
– – in Art **6:**297
– – Jastrow **9:**1297
– – preaching **13:**994
– – public reading of **11:**394
– – Samaritan language **14:**753
– – *Shekhinah* in **14:**1350
– – Song of Songs **15:**147
– – Torah reading **15:**1248
– – Talmud **11:**1229
– – Yemenite Jews **16:**757
– Targum Jonathan
– – anthropomorphism in **3:**53
– – Aramaic **3:**267
– – translation **4:**845ff
– Targum Joseph
– – Joseph ben Ḥiyya **10:**230
– Targum Onkelos **12:**1405
– – Akiva **2:**490
– – Aramaic **3:**267
– – Berliner's edition **4:**664
– – Bible **4:**842ff
– – Hebrew linguistics **16:**1393
– – Jewish literature **11:**312
– – Kasovsky's concordance **10:**809
– – masoretic notes **16:**1428
– – Rashi **13:**1561
– Targum Yerushalmi
– – anthropomorphism in **3:**53
– – Cairo *genizah* **16:**1337
– – Jewish literature **11:**313
– – translation **4:**845ff
– *illus:*
– – Targum Jonathan **4:**895
– – Targum Onkelos **4:**837, 843, 1190; **15:**1483
– – Targum Yerushalmi **2:**713
Targum Jews, *see* KURDISTAN
Targum Rishon (Esther) **15:**811; **15:**813
TARGUM SHENI (homiletic text) **15:**811
– *see also:* MIDRASH
TARGU-MURES (tn., Transyl.) **15:**813
Targu-Neamt (tn., Mold.), *see* TIRGU NEAMT
Ṭarḥa (cantillation sign) **16:**1457
Tarichaea (dist., Isr.) **7:**266; **11:**685
Tarija (city, Bol.) **4:**1188
Tarikah, Jedidiah (of Rhodes) **7:**876
Ṭāriq, Jacob ibn, *see* Ibn Ṭariq, Jacob
Tarj (tn., Yem.) **16:**741
Tarkinus (Rom. emp.), *see* TRAJAN, MARCUS ULPIUS
Tarlo, Joel **5:**169
Tarlo, Louis **5:**169
Tarlov, Malcolm **12:**1222
TARN, NATHANIEL **15:**814
TARNOBRZEG (tn., Pol.) **15:**814
Tarnóczi, Márton **8:**61
TARNOGROD (Tarnograd; vill., Pol.) **15:**815
TARNOPOL (city, Ukr.) **15:**816
– Babad, Joshua **4:**14
– *illus:*
– – text
– – Krochmal, Nachman, tombstone **10:**1270
Tarnopol, Israel ben Samuel of (r.), *see* Israel ben Samuel of Tarnopol
TARNOPOL, JOACHIM ḤAYYIM **15:**818
TARNOW (city, Pol.) **15:**819
– ghetto **13:**766
– *illus:* text
Tarnow, J. **8:**61
TARONJÍ Y CORTÉS, JOSÉ **15:**822
– Majorca **11:**803
TARRAGONA (port, Sp.) **15:**822
– Barcelona jurisdiction **4:**210
– council of **15:**231
TARRASCH, SIEGBERT **15:**824
– chess **5:**405
TÁRREGA (tn., Sp.) **15:**824
Tarrytown (tn., N. Y.) **12:**1127; **16:**464
Tarshīḥā (vill., Isr.), *see* MA'ALOT-TARSHIḤA
TARSHISH (bib. figs) **15:**825
TARSHISH (port) **15:**825
– Cadiz **5:**4
– Carmona **5:**190
– Phoenicia **13:**479
– silver **11:**1430; **11:**1433
– Tarsus **5:**562
– trade and commerce **15:**1295ff
– Tunisia **15:**1430
Tarshish (bk.), *see Sefer ha-Anak*
Tarshish (gem) **13:**1010
Tarshish Mediterranean Lines (co., Isr.) **9:**836
Tarsians (anc. people) **7:**970; **15:**582
TARSKI, ALFRED **15:**825
Tarsus (city, Syr.) **6:**10; **7:**721
TARTAKOVER, SAVIELLY GRIGORYEVICH **15:**826
Tartakow (tn., Ukr.) **15:**84
TARTAKOWER, ARIEH **15:**826
TARTAN (Assyr. offic.) **15:**827
Tartas, Isaac de Castro **8:**1392
Tartasi, Shem Tov ben Isaac **15:**1327
Tartimar (measure) **16:**388
TARTU (city, Est.) **15:**827
– Estonia **6:**916ff
Tartufari, Clarice **9:**1106
Tartuschi, Ibrahim **15:**270
Tarum (mosh., Isr.) **1:**place list
TARUTINO (vill., Ukr.) **15:**828
Taryag mitzvot, see COMMANDMENTS, THE 613
Tasārīf, al- (wk.), *see Kitāb al-Tasārīf*
Tashab (type of acrostic) **2:**230
Tashbeẓ (wk.) **6:**305
– *illus:*
– – title page (1741) **12:**978
Tashbeẓ (Ha-; period.) **1:**newsp. list
TASHKENT (city, Uzbek) **15:**828
– blood libel **14:**488
– Bukhara Jews **16:**40
– *see also:* BUKHARA
TASHLIKH (ceremony) **15:**829
– Rosh ha-Shanah **14:**310
– synagogue **15:**592
– *illus:* text
Tashlum Abudarham (wk.) **2:**182
TASHRAK (writ.) **15:**830
Tashrak (acrostic) **2:**230
Tashwīr, al- (wk.), *see Kitāb al-Tashwīr*
Taslitt, Israel Isaac **10:**268
TASMANIA (isl.) **15:**830
– *illus:* text
– *pop. table:*
– – Jewish communities **3:**877
– *see also:* AUSTRALIA
Tasso, Torquato **9:**1103; **9:**1577
Taswi'a, al- (wk.), *see Kitāb al-Taswi'a*
Tat (Armenian dialect) **9:**503
Tatef, Isaac ibn, *see* Ibn Tatef, Isaac
Tatic (J. lang.), *see* JUDEO-TAT
TATLIN, VLADIMIR E. **3:**611
Tats (J. tribe), *see* MOUNTAIN JEWS
TATTENAI (gov., Trans-Euphrates) **15:**831
– Babylonian exile **6:**1041
– Temple **15:**956
– Zerubbabel **16:**1000
TATTOO **15:**831
– Commandments, the 613 **5:**771
– inscriptions **16:**663
TAU, MAX **15:**832
Taub, Ezekiel ben Zevi-Hirsch **10:**858
Taub, Hayyim Jerahmeel **10:**858
Taub, Moses Aaron **12:**1244
Taub, Siegfried **5:**1191
Taub, Yiẓhak Isaac, *see* KALLO, YIZHAK ISAAC
TAUBE, MICHAEL **12:**711
– music **12:**669
Taubeles, J. **13:**1366
Taubenhaus, M. **14:**629
TAUBENSCHLAG, RAPHAEL **15:**832
TAUBER, RICHARD **12:**711
TAUBERBISCHOFSHEIM (tn., Ger.) **15:**832
– *illus:* text
– Joseph ha-Nakdan **10:**232
TAUBES, AARON MOSES BEN JACOB **15:**833
Taubes, Alexander **16:**73
TAUBES, ḤAYYIM ẒEVI **15:**833
Taubes, Isaac Eisik (Shor) **15:**833
Taubes, Jacob (r.) **15:**833
Taubes, Jacob (hist.) **15:**834
TAUBES, LOEBEL **15:**834
Taubes, Samuel **15:**833
Taubes, Shalom **15:**1151
Taubes, Shmelke **15:**833
– *illus:*
– – Jassy, oath *more judaico* (1886) **12:**1304
TAURAGE (city, Lith.) **15:**834
Taurida (prov., Rus.) **13:**696; **14:**1568; **15:**1514; **15:**1515
Tauroci, Isaac, *see* IṢAAC BEN TODROS
Tauroggen (city, Lith.), *see* TAURAGE
Taurīzī (name), *see* Tabrīzī; Tawrīzī
Taurus (zodiac sign) **16:**1191
– *illus:* **9:**1157
Taurus Mountains (Mesop.) **16:**1497
Tausen, Hans **4:**876
Tausig, Aloys **12:**711
TAUSIG, KARL **12:**711
TAUSK, VIKTOR **15:**835
TAUSSIG (fam.) **15:**835
Taussig (cmty. ldr., Rum.) **4:**656
Taussig, Edward David **15:**835
TAUSSIG, FRANK WILLIAM **15:**835
Taussig, Friedrich, *see* FRITTA
Taussig, Joseph Knefler **15:**835
Taussig, Sigmund **15:**1363
Taussig Neu-Greschel, Abraham **2:**163
TAUSTE (tn., Arag.) **15:**835
Tav (Heb. let.), *see* TAW
Tavern-keepers, *see* WINE AND LIQUOR TRADE
Tavi (tal. fig.) **8:**794; **10:**451
Tavia (fam.), *see* Yellin-Tavia
Taviya ben Darta **14:**753; **14:**756; **16:**1471
Tavra' (cantillation sign), *see Tevir*
Tav-Resh-Ayin-Vav (almanac), *see Tar'av*
Tavrig (city, Lith.), *see* TAURAGE
Tavriya (prov., Rus.), *see* Taurida
Tav-Shin (almanac) **1:**newsp. list
TAVUS, JACOB BEN JOSEPH **15:**836
– Judeo Persian **10:**433
Tavyomi (amora), *see* MAR BAR RAV ASHI
Tavyomi, Nahum Manasseh, *see* Guttentag-Tavyomi, Nahum Manasseh
TAW (Heb. let.) **15:**836
Tawa, Abraham **2:**623
Tawara (tn., Er. Isr.), *see* DOR
Tāwārij (tn., Iraq) **8:**1450
Tawfīq (loc., Golan) **14:**1638; **15:**648
Tawil, Abraham ben Isaac he-Ḥasid **13:**575
Tawilan (loc., Er. Isr.) **15:**941
TAWIOW, ISRAEL ḤAYYIM **15:**836
Tawrāt (Bib.), *see also* Tabrīzī
Tawrīzī (name), *see also* Tabrīzī
Tawrīzī, Abraham Meir **15:**837
TAWRĪZĪ, JUDAH MEIR BEN ABRAHAM **15:**837
Tawrogi (r., Ger.) **10:**1261
Tawwaḥ, Abraham **6:**306
TAX, SOL **15:**837
– anthropology **3:**40
TAXATION **15:**837
– *Contents:*
– – Historical Aspects **15:**838
– – Legal Aspects **15:**840
– – – The Biblical Period **15:**840
– – – The Talmudic Period **15:**841
– – – The Post-Talmudic Period in General **15:**843
– – – Yardsticks of Tax Assessment **15:**847
– – – Taxable Property **15:**848
– – – Place of Residence, Business, or Situation of Property **15:**851
– – – Date of Accrual of Liability **15:**852
– – – Tax Relief and Immunity **15:**854
– – – Methods of Tax Assessment **15:**858
– – – Tax Appeals **15:**863
– – – Adjudication and Evidence **15:**865
– – – Principles of Interpretation **15:**866
– – – Tax Collection Procedure **15:**868
– – – Ethics of Tax Payment **15:**870
– – – Halakhic Compilations of Tax Law **15:**871
– – – In the State of Israel **15:**872
– Anti-Jewish
– – Aquinas **3:**229
– – Lateran Council IV **10:**1446
– – *see also under* Countries
– Types
– – Archae **3:**300
– – *arikha* **4:**404
– – candle tax **5:**119
– – Catechumens **5:**253
– – circumcision, marriage, burial **13:**21
– – *Dhimma* **5:**1604
– – Fiscus judaicus **6:**1325
– – inheritance **8:**442
– – *Kharaj and Jizya* **10:**937
– – *Leibzoll* **10:**1588
– – markets and fairs **11:**1002ff
– – millet **11:**1582
– – Opferpfennig **12:**1412
– – *Presbyter Judaeorum* **13:**1014
– – seal-taxes **14:**1079
– – *sheḥitah* **10:**1211; **14:**1343
– – slaves **14:**1662
– – Tithes, Church **15:**1162
– Law
– – custom **12:**15; **12:**24; **12:**25
– – *dina de-malkhuta* **6:**51
– – domicile **6:**159
– – *ḥerem ha-yishuv* **8:**357
– – imprisonment for evasion **8:**1306ff
– – informer's prosecution **8:**1366; **8:**1372
– – law suits with Gentiles **5:**888
– – *takkanot ha-kahal* **15:**728
– – *talmid ḥakham* **15:**747
– Autonomy **3:**922ff; **12:**129
– – Ashkenazi, Bezalel **3:**723
– – Councils of the Lands **5:**995
– – exilarchate **6:**1032
– – finances **6:**1280ff
– – *Landjudenschaft* **10:**1405
– – *landrabbiner's* role **10:**1409
– – tax gatherer **5:**813; **5:**818

- - *see also:* PHILANTHROPY
- Countries
- - Afghanistan **2:**328
- - Alsace **2:**754
- - Austria **3:**888ff
- - England **6:**747
- - - Hereford **8:**344
- - France
- - - Béziers **4:**792
- - - Chinon **5:**475
- - - Paris **13:**106
- - - Strasbourg **15:**424
- - Germany
- - - Bamberg **4:**149
- - - Berlin **4:**641
- - - Middle Ages **7:**467
- - - Nuremberg **12:**1277
- - - Regensburg **14:**35
- - Greece **7:**872
- - Israel, Ancient
- - - Nehemiah **9:**1389
- - - Persian Period **8:**618; **16:**1272
- - - Second Temple period **8:**627ff
- - - 70 to 640 C.E. **9:**238ff
- - - 639 to 1099, Jerusalem **9:**265
- - - Solomon **15:**103
- - Italy
- - - ancient Rome **3:**336; **14:**242; **16:**1274
- - - Catanzaro **5:**253
- - - medieval Rome **14:**246
- - - Tuscany **15:**1467
- - Muslim lands **16:**1278
- - New Amsterdam **12:**1063ff
- - Poland **5:**1030
- - Portugal **13:**922
- - Spain
- - - Aragon **15:**1022
- - - Barbastro **4:**207
- - - Burgos **4:**1512
- - - Cervera **5:**314
- - - Saragossa **14:**860
- - - Toledo **15:**1202
- - - Tudela **15:**1425
- - Turkey **9:**1089; **15:**1458
- - - Ottoman Empire **13:**1451; **16:**1530
- *illus:*
- - Brandenburg-Ansbach decree **10:**1405
- - payment of half-shekel tax **14:**1346
- - weighing shekels for payment to Temple **11:***fcg.* 619
TAXATION IN ISRAEL **9:**749
- Sharef, Ze'ev **14:**1308
TAX GATHERERS **15:**873
- Abrabanel, Isaac **2:**105
- Alami, Solomon **2:**509
- Amulo **2:**915
- *arenda* **3:**402
- Diaspora **6:**11
- economic history **16:**1274
- finances **6:**1283
- grant to Polish Jews **4:**1257
- post-Temple destruction **9:**239
- witnesses **16:**586
- *see also:* BANKING AND BANKERS
Tax Museum (Isr.) **15:**872
Tayeb, Abraham (r., Tun.), *see* Tayyib, Abraham
Tayeb, Ḥayyim **15:**1444
Tayeb, Isaac, *see* TAYYIB, ISAAC BEN BENJAMIN
Tayler, Francis **8:**61
Taylor, Charles **16:**1335
Taylor, Edward **8:**61
Taylor, Elizabeth **12:**451,474; **15:**1082
Taylor, Herman **15:**305
Taylor, Jacob **8:**61
Taylor, Jeremy **8:**60 **6:**776
Taylor, John **8:**60
Taylor, Myron **6:**987
- *illus:*
- - memo re Bermuda Conference **8:**906
- - telegram re Evian Conference **6:**988
Taylor, R. **4:**887
TAYMA (tn., Saud. Arab.) **15:**874
- Arabia **3:**233; **3:**235
- inscriptions **16:**669
- Khaybar **10:**943
- Tema **15:**940
Tay-Sachs Disease **14:**1500
Tayyib, Abraham **2:**599; **15:**1443ff; **15:**805
TAYYIB, ISAAC BEN BENJAMIN **15:**874
ṬAYYIBA, AL- (tn., Isr.) **15:**874
- care center **9:**988
- Ephron **6:**816
- Hapharaim site **7:**1319
- Hepher **8:**332
- human geography **9:**575; **9:**579
- Ophrah **12:**1414
T-a-z (hal.), *see* DAVID BEN SAMUEL HA-LEVI
Taza (city, Mor.) **12:**336ff
Taẓash (kab. name) **10:**504
Taẓlil (bibl.) **1:**newsp. list
Tbilisi (city, Georgian S. S. R.), *see* TIFLIS
T. Carmi, *see* CARMI, T.
Tchemerinsky, Michael **16:**423
TCHERIKOVER, VICTOR (Avigdor) **15:**875
- historiography **8:**562
TCHERIKOWER, ELIAS **15:**876
- historiography **8:**568
Tcherikower, Eliezer **12:**360
Tcherniawsky, Charles **13:**116
TCHERNICHOWSKY, SAUL **15:**877
- Brainin, Reuben **4:**1292
- drama **6:**197
- Engels **6:**744
- Hebrew literature **8:**196
- prosody **13:**1232
- Writers' Association **16:**652ff
- *illus:*
- - text
- - fellow Hebrew writers **8:**199
- - Persky, Daniel, and **13:**321
- - Shneour, Zalman, and **14:**1431
- - Writers' Assoc. in Israel **8:**205
Tchernovitz, Jacob, *see* TSUR, JACOB
TCHERNOWITZ, CHAIM **15:**883
- Assaf, Simḥa **3:**756
- H.U.C.-J.I.R. **8:**218
- Odessah yeshivah **16:**770
- *illus:*
- - text
- - fellow Hebrew writers **8:**193
- - Hebrew writers convention, 1943 **8:**213
TCHERNOWITZ, SAMUEL **15:**884
- Dimanstein, Simon **6:**48
- *illus:*
- - Ukrainian Provisional National Council **15:**1515
TCHERNOWITZ-AVIDAR, YEMIMAH **15:**885
- *illus;*
- - Mrs. Molotov and **14:**497
"Teacher and Young Pupil" (paint., Kaufman) **3:**553
TEACHER OF RIGHTEOUSNESS (Qumran cmty. ldr.) **15:**885
- Apocalypse **3:**179
- Damascus Document **5:**1247
- Dead Sea sect **5:**1417
- eschatology **6:**876ff
- *Isaiah, Martyrdom of* **9:**72
- Lies, Man of **11:**233
- Lies, Prophet of **11:**234
- *pesher* revelation **13:**331; **13:**333
- Seekers after Smooth Things **14:**1096
- Thanksgiving Psalms **15:**1048
- Wicked Priest **16:**485
- Yaḥad **16:**699; **16:**701
- Zadok **16:**916
Teachers, Honor of **10:**917
TEACHERS' ASSOCIATION IN ISRAEL **15:**888
- education in Israel **9:**929
- Hebrew Language Committee **2:**205
- Technion controversy **15:**890
Teachers' Assocations, International Federation of, *see* International Federation of Teachers' Associations
Teachers' Institute (N.Y.) **16:**760
Teachers' Seminary for Girls (Austr.) **11:**1283
Teacher Training **7:**1441; **9:**951
Teal (zool.) **6:**30
Teaneck (TN., N.J.) **4:**612
Te'ashur (mosh. Isr.) **1:** place list
Te'ashur (bot.) **4:**1277; **5:**1178
Te'atron (journ.) **1:** newsp. list
Te'atron Ereẓ Yisre'eli (theat., Er. Isr.) **9:**1004; **15:**1061
Te'atron ha-Onot (theat., Isr.) **2:**673
Te'atron Ivri (theat., Er. Isr.) **9:**1004
Te'atron ve-Ommanut (journ.) **1:**newsp. list
Tebessa (tn., Alg.) **10:**88; **15:**1433
Tebi (slave), *see* TABI
Tebriz (city, Iran), *see* TABRIZ
Tebtunis (tn., Egy.) **6:**9; **12:**246
Tecanus (Techanus), *see* TEKA
Technical Aid Program, Israel **9:**435ff
TECHNION, ISRAEL INSTITUTE OF TECHNOLOGY (Isr.) **15:**889
- Abir, David **2:**79
- higher education **9:**952
- language of instruction controversy **9:**330
- science and research **9:**966ff
- *illus:*
- - text
- - chemistry research **9:**968
- - Churchill Auditorium **9:**955
- - new Forum **3:**351
- - old building **3:**347
- - protest against non-Hebrew teaching **9:**331,1000
- - student hostel room **9:**961
Technion Research and Development Foundations Ltd. (Isr.) **15:**891
TECHNOLOGY AND HALAKHAH **15:**892
- Sabbath **14:**567
- transplants **15:**1337
Tecuci (tn., Rum.) **14:**398
Teddy the Jewboy, *see* DAVIS, EDWARD
TEDESCHI (fam.) **15:**897
- Varna **16:**70
- *illus:*
- - laver and basin **14:**252
Tedeschi, Eliezer Laude **15:**897
TEDESCHI, GAD (Guido) **15:**897
- family **15:**897
- law **10:**1498
Tedeschi, Isaac Raphael **2:**943; **15:**897
Tedeschi, Marco **14:**714; **15:**897
TEDESCHI (Tedesco), MOSES ISAAC BEN SAMUEL **15:**898
- family **15:**897
Tedeschi, Nathan **15:**897
Tedesci, Solomon, *see* ASHKENAZI, SOLOMON
Tedesco (fam.), *see* TEDESCHI
Tedesco, David Vita **15:**897
Tedesco, Isaac **15:**897
Tedesco, Moses **15:**897
Tedesco-Finzi (fam.), *see* FINZI
Te'enah (bot.), *see* FIG
Tefaḥ (meas.) **16:**378,389
Tefillah, see AMIDAH; PRAYER
Tefillah (Psalm superscription) **13:**1320
Tefillat Arvit (*ha-Erev;* prayer), *see* ARVIT
Tefillat Geshem, see RAIN, PRAYER FOR
Tefillat ha-Derekh, *see* TRAVEL, PRAYER FOR
Tefillat ha-Ḥodesh (prayer bk. type) **13:**987
Tefillat ha-Yiḥud (prayer) **3:**25
Tefillat Tal, see DEW, PRAYER FOR
TEFILLIN (phylacteries) **15:**898
- *Contents:*
- - Order of Passages **15:**900
- - The Tefillin of the Dead Sea **15:**903
- General
- - Abraham **2:**115
- - acquisition from gentile **7:**592
- - amulets **2:**906
- - burial with corpse **4:**1522
- - Dead Sea finds **5:**1406; **12:**528
- - folklore **6:**1405
- - Karaites **10:**781
- - Lurianic cosmogony **10:**595
- - scribe **14:**1043
- - square script **2:**707
- - *tallit* **15:**743
- - *Talmid ḥakham* **15:**746
- - Talmud **11:**1315
- Laws
- - agency inapplicable **2:**350
- - Av, The Ninth of **3:**939
- - cemetery prohibition **5:**272
- - Commandments, the 613 **5:**763
- - festivals **6:**1246
- - *halakhah le-Moshe mi-Sinai* **7:**1167
- - heretics **8:**360
- - impurity **13:**1409; **13:**1411
- - laws of writing **16:**670
- - left arm **14:**179
- - minimum age **4:**245
- - mourning prohibition **3:**23; **12:**488ff
- - Sephardi practice **14:**1170
- - *tagin* **15:**700
- Prayer
- - *Ashrei* **3:**736
- - benedictions **4:**488
- - kissing of **10:**1074
- - *shema* **14:**1372
- *illus:*
- - text
- - eighteenth cent. engraving **4:**1161
- - Kefar Ḥabad bar mitzvah celebration **9:**904
- - *Shema* fragments, Murabba'at **14:**1371
Tefillin (tract.) **12:**49
Tefnakhte (k., Egy.) **15:**18
Tefuẓot, see DIASPORA
Tefuẓot Yisrael (journ.) **1:**newsp. list
Tegart Wall (fortification line, Isr.) **15:**92
Teglikhe Gazeten (newsp.) **13:**1053
Teglikher Herald (newsp.) **13:**1053
Tegucigalpa (city, Hond.) **8:**962
TEHERAN (city, Iran) **15:**905
- Iran **8:**1439
- Judeo-Persian literature **10:**437
- *illus:*
- - text
- - Alliance School for Girls **8:**1442
- - Zionist Federation leaders **13:**307
Teheran Children **7:**1531
Tehillah (Psalm superscription)

13:1321
Tehillim, see PSALMS, BOOK OF
TEḤINNAH (prayer) **15:**907
- liturgy **11:**394ff
- Yiddish translations **11:**356; **11:**358
- *illus:*
- - *Shloyshe Sheorim* (1838) **4:**318
Tehiru (Kab. conc.) **14:**1241
- *illus:*
- - flaring up of *Sefirot* **10:**597
Teḥiyyah (journ.) **1:** newsp. list
- *see also: Ha-Tehiyyah*
Teḥiyya, Ha- (soc., Pol.), *see* Ha-Teḥiyya
Tehiyyat ha-Metim (ben.), *see Gevurot*
Teḥiyyat Israel Society (Er. Isr.) **4:**566; **9:**999; **13:**535
Tehom, see DEEP, THE
Tehomi, Avraham **7:**1066ff; **8:**1466
Teḥumim (journ.) **1:** newsp. list
Teḥum Shabbat (leg. conc.), *see* ERUV
TEIF, MOSHE **15:**907
Teigh, Robert **8:**60
Teima (oasis, Arab.), *see* TAYMA
TEITEL, JACOB **15:**907
TEITELBAUM (fam.) **15:**908
TEITELBAUM, ABRAHAM **15:**1091
Teitelbaum, Abraham Aaron **15:**908
Teitelbaum, Benjamin, Joseph, *see* DEMBLIN, BENJAMIN
Teitelbaum. David **10:**401
Teitelbaum, Eleazar Nisan **15:**387; **15:**908
Teitelbaum, Elijah Bezalel **15:**908
Teitelbaum, Hananiah Yom Tov Lipa **15:**908
Teitelbaum, Ḥayyim Ẓevi **15:**908
Teitelbaum, Jekuthiel Judah (19th cent.) **5:**1591; **15:**908
Teitelbaum, Jekuthiel Judah (20th cent.) **15:**909
Teitelbaum, Joel (ish) **15:**909; **16:**1145
- *illus:*
- - at the Western Wall **14:**908
Teitelbaum, Moses ben Ẓevi **11:**293; **15:**908
Teitelbaum, Moses Joseph **15:**908
Teitelbaum, Nahum Ẓevi **15:**908
Teitelbaum, Samuel **15:**908
TEITELBOIM, VOLODIA VALENTIN **15:**910
- Chile **5:**467
- politics **13:**821
TEITLER, SAMUEL **10:**1512
TEITSH, MOISHE **15:**910
TEITZ, PINCHAS MORDECAI **15:**910
TEIXEIRA, PEDRO **15:**911
- travels **15:**1350
Teixeira, Samuel **3:**58; **5:**248
- *illus:*
- - tombstone **3:**54
TEIXEIRA DE SAMPAIO, ABRAHAM SENIOR (Diego) **15:**911
- trade **15:**1303
Teixeira de Sampaio, Judith **15:**467
Teixeira de Sampaio, Manuel (Isaac Ḥayyim) **15:**912
- banking **4:**172
- court Jews **5:**1009
- Suasso, Francisco **15:**467
- trade **15:**1303
- *illus:*
- - legal document **4:**177
TEIXEIRA PINTO, BENTO **15:**912
Teixera, D'Andrade Isaac **15:**467
TEKA (bnk.) **15:**913
- Vienna **16:**122
Tekes Ḥag ha-Asif (kib. litur.) **10:**960
TEKHELET (blue dye) **15:**913
- Korah **10:**1192
- Leiner, Gershon Henikh **9:**1160
- *illus:* text
Tekhelet-Lavan (youth mvmt.), *see* BLAU-WEISS
Tekhnikah u-Madda (journ.) **1:** newsp. list
Tekhunot Zakkut (wk.), *see Ha-Ḥibbur ha-Gadol*
Teki'ah (blowing of Shofar) **14:**309ff
TEKI'ATA (*Teki'ot;* litur.) **15:**914
- *piyyut* **13:**599
- *see also:* MALKHUYYOT; ROSH HA-SHANAH; SHOFAROT; ZIKHRONOT
Tekiata de-Vei Rav (litur.) **2:**557; **3:**833; **15:**914
Teki'at Kaf, see Handshake
TEKOA (city, Er. Isr.) **15:**915
- Amos **2:**879
- Simeon bar Yoḥai **14:**1553
Tekoah, Yosef **9:**421
Teku (reg., Egy.) **7:**816
Tekufah, Tekufot (season) **5:**43,46
- angels **2:**964
- astronomy **3:**798
- Bet Alfa mosaics **4:**713
- *illus:*
- - Bet Alfa mosaics **4:**711; **5:**45
- - Hammath synagogue mosaics **15:**574
- - *ketubbah* (Corfu, 1781) **5:**971
Tekufah de-Rav Adda (wk.), *see Baraita de-Rav Adda*
Tekufatenu (journ.) **1:** newsp. list
Tekufot u-Mazzalot (wk.), *see Ha-Ḥibbur Ha-Gadol*
TEKUMAH (mosh., Isr.) **15:**916
- statistics **1:** place list
Tekumah (soc., Pol.) **15:**1351
Tekumah (publ.) **1:** newsp. list
Tel . . . (arch. loc.), *see* Tells . . .
Tel-abib (city, Babyl.) **4:**35
TEL ADASHIM (mosh., Isr.) **15:**916
- statistics **1:** place list
Telaim (loc., Er. Isr.) **14:**912
Telamim (mosh. Isr.) **1:** place list
Telamim (journ.) **1:** newsp. list
Telamyon (tal. fig.), *see* BEN TEMALYON
Tel Arzah (suburb, Jer.) **9:**1472, 1519
Telassar (reg., Mesop.) **4:**728
TEL AVIV-JAFFA (city, Isr.) **15:**916
- *Contents:*
- - Background to History and Development **15:**918
- - 1909-1917 **15:**921
- - 1918-1939 **15:**921
- - 1939-1948 **15:**923
- - From 1949 **15:**924
- - The Tel Aviv Conurbation **15:**925
- Arab terrorist acts **14:**1639
- demography **5:**1513ff
- Dizengoff, Meir **6:**138
- exhibitions **9:**764
- Hacohen, Mordecai ben Hillel **7:**1039
- harbor **9:**832
- historical survey **9:**341
- history chart **8:**766-767
- human geography **9:**572ff
- Jewish religious life **9:**891ff
- local government **9:**605
- parodic *haggadah* **13:**137
- PBS broadcasting **15:**931
- riots, 1921 **9:**683
- Sokolow, Nahum **15:**86
- stock exchange **9:**829
- television and radio **15:**930
- *illus:*
- - text
- - Adloyada parade **9:**907
- - *Altalena* burning **16:**318
- - cooperative housing project **3:**349
- - Egged headquarters **5:**952
- - El Al Building **10:**798
- - *etrogim* market **6:**950,1449
- - Habimah Theater **7:**1031
- - Hebrew Book Fair **9:**1002
- - Herzlia Gymnasia, 1st graduating class **9:**931
- - Histadrut headquarters **8:**535
- - Independence Day celebrations **8:**1346
- - International Trade Fair (1970) **9:**818
- - Kadman Numismatic Museum **12:**549
- - Levant Fairs **9:**347,766
- - Mann Auditorium, Israel Philharmonic Orchestra **9:**1071
- - newspaper stand **9:**1016
- - Reading power station **9:**792
- - sailing, world championship competition **15:**317
- - Simḥat Torah, street celebration **14:**1573
- - stock exchange **9:**830
- - synagogue (Aba Elḥanani, designer) **3:**356
- - *tashlikh* ceremony **15:**829
- - temperatures, mean (table) **9:**189
- - Tu bi-Shevat celebration **9:**907
- - *ulpan* class **9:**965
- - University campus **15:**925
- - University library building **3:**351; **9:**956
- - view from northeast **9:**573
- - Zimriyyah concert **9:**1010
- *see also:* JAFFA
Tel Aviv Council of Social Agencies **13:**386
Tel Aviv Institute of Religious Jewish Music, *see* Jewish Religious Music, Tel Aviv Institute of
Tel Aviv Museum **12:**551; **15:**922
- *illus:*
- - Mokady exhibition **12:**224
Tel Aviv Philharmonic Choir **9:**1008
Tel Aviv School of Law and Economics **15:**925
Tel Aviv Trade Fair **9:**765
TEL AVIV UNIVERSITY **15:**925
- higher education **9:**957
- medical school **9:**989
- Wise, George **16:**563
- *illus:*
- - text
- - library building **3:**351; **9:**956
Tel Barukh (loc., Isr.) **9:**772
Telcs, Ede **11:**1167
TELECOMMUNICATIONS IN ISRAEL **9:**840
- Arab states **15:**1565
- cultural life **9:**1017
- PBS broadcasting **15:**931
- *illus:*
- - Nazareth telephone exchange **9:**841
Telegramot Aḥaronot (journ.) **1:** newsp. list
Teleki, Béla **4:**883
Telem (loc., Er. Isr.) **14:**912
TELENESHTY (Telenesti; tn., Mold.) **15:**927
Teleological argument (philos.) **7:**658; **10:**742; **12:**888; **12:**889; **12:**890
Telephone Services in Israel, *see* TELECOMMUNICATIONS IN ISRAEL
Telesin, Zalman **10:**707; **16:**826
Telesinus (5th cent., physic.) **7:**362; **13:**852
Telestikhon (*Telestich;* lit. style) **2:**230
TELEVISION AND RADIO **15:**927
- *Contents:*
- - In the U.S. **15:**927
- - In Europe **15:**929
- - In Israel **15:**930
- Israel
- - Arabic programs **9:**1029
- - cultural life **9:**1018
- - Hebrew pronunciation **16:**1646
- - religious life **9:**902
- South Africa
- - Schlesinger, Isidore William **14:**973
- U.S.
- - Sarnoff, David **14:**884
- *see also:* ADVERTISING; TELECOMMUNICATIONS IN ISRAEL
Telgener (print. press, Ger.) **4:**1113
TEL ḤAI (stlmt., Isr.) **15:**931
- defense forces **9:**683
- history chart **8:**766-767
- *illus:*
- - general view **9:**336
- - Memorial **3:**633
Tel Ḥai (pion. gr., Crimea) **5:**1107; **8:**249
- *illus:*
- - He-Ḥalutz group **14:**469
Tel ha-Shomer Hospital (Isr.) **9:**989; **15:**926
- *illus:*
- - mobile medical unit **9:**987
Teliša' (cantillation sign) **16:**1440
Teliša' gedolah (cantillation sign) **16:**1440,1454
Teliša' qeṭannah (cantillation sign) **16:**1440,1455
Tel-Kabar (vill., Kurd.) **10:**1297
Tel Kabbir (housing zone, Tel Aviv) **15:**924
TEL KAẒIR (kib. Isr.) **15:**932
- statistics **1:**place list
Tell Abu (Avital mt., Er. Isr.) **13:**1531
Tell al-Ru'ūs (mon., Er. Isr.) **9:**1254
TELL EL-AMARNA LETTERS **15:**933
- Akhenaton **2:**488
- archives **3:**368
- Ashtaroth **3:**737
- Borchardt, Ludwig **4:**1242
- clay inscriptions **16:**661
- history chart **8:**766-767
- Hebrew language **16:**1562,1565
- letters **11:**55
- Phoenicia **13:**474ff
- Semitic languages **14:**1150ff
- *illus:*
- - clay tablet **3:**370
Teller, Chester **12:**873
TELLER, EDWARD **15:**935
Teller, Hirsh Lazar, *see* TELLER, ẒEVI LAZAR
TELLER, ISRAEL **15:**936
- Zionism **16:**1133
TELLER, ISSACHAR BAER **15:**937
Teller, Leopold **15:**1056
TELLER, ẒEVI LAZAR **15:**937
- Silberbusch, David **14:**1533
Téllez, Gabriel de, *see* Tirso de Molina
Tell ʿIbbīn (mt., Transj.) **15:**1316
Tells . . . (arch. locs.)
- Abil **2:**60
- Abu-al-Qābūs **6:**892
- Abu Hawam **7:**1133
- Abu Hurayra **7:**432
- Abu Khanzīr **9:**180
- Abu Kharaz **9:**1172

- Abu Matar 2:382; 9:593
- Abu Nadā' 9:180
- Abu Salāih 16:1508
- Abu-Shūsha, *see* (tells) Jazar
- Abu Sifri 2:62
- Abu Sūs 2:62
- Achzib 2:213
- ʿAffuleh 12:1415
- al-Ahdab 7:295
- al-ʿAjjūl (N.Isr.) 2:917; 6:739
- al-ʿAjjūl (S. Isr.)
- - Bet Aglayim 4:710
- - glass vessels 7:604
- - goldsmiths and silversmiths 16:937
- - Hyksos 8:1143
- - inscriptions 16:654
- - mining 11:1433
- - Old Gaza 7:341
- - Petrie's work 3:330; 13:344
- - pottery 13:939
- al-Amarna, *see* TELL EL-AMARNA LETTERS
- al-ʿAmr 7:1347; 7:350; 14:1621
- al-Ashʿarī 6:110
- al-Badawiyya 7:1272; 14:1398
- al-Balāṭ 14:41
- al-Balāṭa 14:1330
- al-Baṭṭāshī 15:1147
- al-Bayḍā 2:214
- al-Birwa al-Gharbī 14:42
- al-Dibbīn 8:1244
- al-Duwayr 10:1332; 16:667
- al-Far'ah (Fari'ah; N. Isr.) 15:1153
- al-Farah (Fariʿa; S. Isr.), *see* (tells) Sharuhen
- al-Fukhkhār 2:223; 10:877
- al-Fūl 7:549; 14:1630
- al-Hajaj 11:724
- al-Ḥammām 2:62
- al-Ḥasī 2:677; 4:1095; 6:477; 13:343; 16:654
- al-Husn 4:757
- al-Ḥuwaylifa 16:1021
- al-Ifshar 8:332
- al-Jaynā 9:181
- al-Judayda 12:317
- al-Khalayfa 6:1103; 6:377; 16:45
- al-Khayr 14:16
- al-Makharkhas 2:917
- al-Malāt 7:549
- al-Maqbara 9:1172
- al-Maqlub 2:62
- al-Mazār 16:937
- al-Milḥ 3:249; 8:976
- al-Mutasallim 11:1222
- al-Muṭilla 15:648
- al-Najīla 7:335
- al-Naʿm 9:1175; 9:1277
- al-Naṣb (Naṣba) 4:383; 12:173; 13:400
- al-Qāḍī, *see* (tells) Dan
- al-Qaws 16:934
- al-Qidah 7:1535
- al-Radgha 14:1266
- al-Rāma 4:736
- al-Raʿs 3:696
- al-Rimah 9:1317; 16:1502
- al-Rumayla 4:773
- al-Ru'ūs 9:1254
- al-Sabʿ, *see* (tells) Beersheba
- al-Ṣāfī 7:335
- al-Saʿīdiyya 16:668; 16:934; 16:937
- al-Ṣārim 14:42
- al-Shalf 6:688
- al-Sharīʿa 7:432; 16:1021
- al-Sheikha 9:180
- al-Sheikh al-Riḥab 14:42
- al-Shihāb 15:1316
- al-Sulṭān 9:1365
- al-Urayna 7:335
- al-Yahūdiyya 8:1142; 11:31; 13:939
- ʿAmmātā 2:851; 16:934
- ʿAmr, *see* (tells) al-ʿAmr
- Arad 2:452; 3:244; 16:1569
- Arshaf 3:187; 9:268
- Ashtareh 3:737
- ʿAzāziyāt 14:1637
- Balameh 8:1151
- Balaybil 4:753
- Beersheba 2:452; 4:384; 16:660
- Beit (Bayt) Mirsim 3:306,330
- - agriculture 2:387
- - Albright's excavations 2:538
- - architecture 3:336
- - Bible history 8:578
- - Debir 2:212; 5:1429
- - Eglon 6:477
- - fortifications 16:276
- - Hyksos 8:1143
- - inscription 16:654
- - Philistines 13:400
- - Solomon's building 15:102ff
- Beth-Shean 4:757
- Dan 5:1260; 15:1556; 16:157
- Defneh 9:1351
- Deir (Dayr) al-ʿAzār 10:1046
- Deir ʿAllā 7:604; 13:400; 15:481
- Dimah 16:1508
- el-ʿAjjūl, *see* (tells) al-ʿAjjūl
- el-Amarna, *see* TELL EL-AMARNA LETTERS
- el-Atshana 2:508
- el-Far'ah, *see* (tells) al-Far'ah
- el-Ful, *see* (tells) al-Ful
- el-Jurn, *see* (tells) Goren
- el-Maskhutah 13:566
- el-Milḥ, *see* (tells) al-Milḥ
- el-Naṣb, *see* (tells) al-Naṣb
- el-Rimah, *see* (tells) al-Rimah
- el-Sabʿ, *see* (tells) Beersheba
- Erani (Erany) 6:479; 14:1595
- er-Ratabeh 13:567
- Fakhr 14:1637
- Fāra 13:88
- Farah (S. Isr.), *see* (tells) Sharuhen
- Faras 9:180
- Gat, *see* (tells) Erani
- Gath Hepher 7:336
- Gibbethon, *see* (tells) al-Malāt
- Goren 6:741
- Halaaf 2:304; 7:835
- Ham 7:1217
- Ḥarashim 2:451
- Ḥarīrī 11:972
- Ḥūm 5:139
- Iblakhiye 3:37
- Ibrāhīm 5:1175
- Iktanū 4:736
- Jamma (Jemmeh) 5:1131; 7:432; 11:1428; 11:1433; 13:343
- Jarīsha 7:336; 15:492
- Jazar 7:534
- Jokneam, *see* (tells) Qamūn
- Kābrī 10:657
- Kadadi 9:1249
- Kafrayn 2:62
- Kasila, *see* (tells) Qasīla
- Khaybar 10:943
- Khirbat al-Bayda 12:317
- Khirbat al-Ṣafṣāfa, *see* (tells) al-ʿAjjūl (N.Isr.)
- Kinrot 5:474
- Kisan 2:213
- Kurdani 3:176
- Magadim 3:327
- Maʿīn 11:907
- Makmish 3:327
- Malḥata, *see* (tells) al-Milḥ
- Maskhūṭa 15:482
- Megiddo 11:1222
- Mor (Murra) 3:696
- Nabī Mind 10:665
- Nebi Yunus 12:1168
- Nimrin 4:753
- Nimrūd 16:662; 16:667
- Nuffar 5:65
- Qadis 10:664
- Qamūn 10:166
- Qasīla (Qasīle) 3:306
- - Jaffa 9:1249; 10:1543
- - metals 11:1428
- - ostraca 2:682; 16:666
- - Philistines 13:399
- - pillar structure 13:521
- Qaṣr al-Zaʿfarān 10:866
- Quyunjiq 12:1168
- Rafāḥ 13:1510
- Rakhma 16:759
- Ramīth 13:1543
- Raš Abu Ḥumayd 7:591
- Ras el-Ain 3:176
- Rehov 16:654
- Rifaʿat 3:497
- Saʿīdiyya, *see* (tells) al-Saʿīdiyya
- Ṣandaḥanna 11:954
- Seilun 14:1401
- Shadūd 14:881
- Shalem 14:1266
- Sharuḥen
- - fortifications 16:273
- - goldsmiths and silversmiths 7:738
- - Hyksos 8:1141; 14:1317
- - ostraca 16:668
- - Petrie's excavations 3:330; 13:343
- - Philistines 13:399
- Sheikh al-Diyāb 3:814
- Taʿīnāt (Tainet) 3:306; 15:947
- Umm Ḥamād 16:937
- Urayma 10:1032
- Waqqās, *see* (tells) al-Qidah
- Yamma, *see* (tells) Jamma
- Yūsuf 9:180
- Zakariyeh (Zechariah) 2:462; 3:1004; 10:1335
- Zif 16:1181
- *see also:* Khirbat . . .

TEL MOND (mosh., Isr.) 15:937
- statistics 1:place list

TELSIAI (Telshi; Telschen; city; Lith.) 15:938
- *illus:* text

Tel Talpiot (period.) 1:newsp. list 10:827; 16:51

Tel Yehudah (camp, U.S.) 16:860
- *illus:*
- - Young Judaea members 16:860

TEL YIZḤAK (kib., Isr.) 15:939
- statistics 1:place list

TEL YOSEF (kib., Isr.) 15:939
- statistics 1:place list
- *illus:*
- - text
- - plowing the fields 13:485
- - Tnuva central dairy 15:1175

Telz (city, Lith. S.S.R.), *see* TELSIAI

Tel Ẓofim (kib., Isr.), *see* REVIVIM

Tel Ẓur (vill., Isr.) 6:987

Telz yeshivah (Lith.) 15:166; 15:938; 16:769

Telz yeshivah (U.S.) 4:1097; 15:939

Tema (Temai; bib. fig.) 9:89; 15:940

TEMA (loc., Arab.) 15:940
- moon worship 16:1505

TEMAN (bib. fig.; loc., Er. Isr.) 15:941
- Edom 6:370

Tembleque (tn., Sp.) 10:1359

Temerls, Eliezer Lipmann 15:941

TEMERLS, JACOB BEN ELIEZER 15:941
- Ḥanneles, Judah Leib 7:1272

Temes, Judit 12:1376

Temesvár (city, Transyl.), *see* TIMIȘOARA

TEMIANKA, HENRI 12:711

Temidi (Pal. lab. ldr.), *see* AHARONOVITCH, YOSEF

TEMKIN (fam.) 15:941

TEMKIN, ASHER 15:942

Temkin, Mordecai 15:941

Temkin, Moshe 15:941

Temol Shilshom (bk.) 8:203

Tempelgesellschaft (Ger. sect), *see* TEMPLERS

Tempesta, Antonio 9:1544

Templars (knight order)
- Athlit 3:821
- De la Cavalleria family 5:261
- Jerusalem 9:1416,1579

TEMPLE 15:942

Contents:
- - First Temple 15:943
- - - History 15:943
- - - Structure 15:946
- - - Ritual 15:952
- - - The Significance of the Temple for the People 15:954
- - Second Temple 15:955
- - - History 15:955
- - - Structure 15:960
- - - Ritual 15:969
- - - The Significance of the Temple for the People 15:983
- - - In the Arts 15:984
- General
- - ass worship 7:895
- - cattle consumption 16:1273
- - chronology 16:1266
- - divine presence 13:1017ff
- - economic life 16:1272
- - history chart 8:766-767
- - history of Ereẓ Israel 8:625
- - Leo and Ariel 16:1192
- - pillar symbol for 13:523
- - sacrifice 14:600ff
- - sacrilege 14:616ff
- - *semikhah,* ceremony of 14:1140
- - shewbread 14:1394
- - shofar 14:1443
- - *soferim* 15:80
- - Sukkot 15:497ff
- - synagogue 15:579ff
- - tax 15:838
- - *tikkun ḥazot* 15:1139
- - tithe 15:1161ff
- - Torah ornaments 15:1256
- First Temple
- - The Building
- - - Abraham 2:120
- - - Ahaz 2:455
- - - *Akedah* 2:481
- - - Arad temple 3:244
- - - architecture 3:357
- - - Cedars of Lebanon 10:1543
- - - David 5:1324
- - - Jachin and Boaz 9:1186
- - - Jehoiachin 9:1319
- - - Jeremiah 9:1350ff
- - - Jerusalem 9:1550
- - - Nathan 12:846ff
- - - Onias 12:1404
- - - Sidonians 14:1506
- - - Solomon 8:592ff; 15:99ff
- - - Solomon's Jerusalem 9:1383
- - - Tablets of Law 15:691
- - - Temple Mount 15:988
- - - Temple Scroll 15:997
- - - wooden furniture 16:630
- - Service 15:974ff
- - - *Ahavah Rabbah* 2:454
- - - altar encirclement 14:179
- - - anointing oil 3:31
- - - *Avodah* 3:976
- - - *Barukh Shem Kevod Malkhuto* 4:284
- - - choir 5:486ff
- - - Damascus document 5:1248ff
- - - Decalogue 5:1436
- - - *dukhan* 6:267
- - - First-Fruit offering 4:993
- - - fly miracle 6:1369
- - - genealogy 7:377
- - - Gibeonites 7:552ff
- - - *hakhel* ceremony 7:1149
- - - Heman 8:319

- - - high priest **8:**470
- - - *hoshanot* ceremony **8:**1028
- - - incense **8:**1310
- - - king's privileges **10:**1017
- - - Kohathites **10:**1136
- - - levites **11:**73
- - - levitical singers **3:**672; **3:**673; **13:**1316
- - - Manasseh, alien rites **11:**853
- - - Nethinim **7:**552ff
- - - *Omer* ceremony **12:**1383
- - - pilgrimage **13:**510ff
- - - prayer **11:**393; **13:**980
- - - priestly blessing **13:**1060
- - - priestly divisions **12:**89
- - - priestly immersions **2:**82
- - - priestly vestments **13:**1063
- - - prophets' attitude **13:**1172ff
- - - red heifer rite **14:**9
- - - Uriel **16:**7
- - - wood offerings **16:**630
- - Destruction
- - - Av, The Ninth of **3:**936
- - - Babylonians **16:**1513
- - - diminution of joy **10:**319
- - - Exile, Babylonian **6:**1037
- - - history **8:**615
- - - Psalm before Grace **7:**839
- - - refugees in Africa **2:**331
- Second Temple
- - The Building **15:**955
- - - Agrippa II **2:**417
- - - Alcimus **2:**549
- - - Antiochus IV **3:**74
- - - Apion's statement **3:**178
- - - archives **3:**375
- - - Babylonian exiles **6:**1039
- - - Chamber of the Lepers **11:**37
- - - Clermont-Ganneau **5:**605
- - - court session **13:**958
- - - Essenes **6:**900
- - - Ezra **8:**618ff
- - - genealogy **7:**379
- - - Hasmoneans **7:**1283
- - - Herod **8:**384; **9:**1394,1398
- - - history **8:**626ff
- - - Josephus and Zealots **16:**948
- - - measurements **11:**1504
- - - money changers **12:**243ff
- - - Monobaz and Helena **2:**267
- - - Nicanor's Gate **12:**1133ff
- - - Pompey **13:**846
- - - removal of *soriga* **11:**1230
- - - Shushan Gate **14:**1484
- - - Yaḥad community **16:**699; **16:**700
- - - Zerubbabel **16:**1000
- - Service
- - - *Amen* **2:**803
- - - *Ashrei* **3:**736
- - - Av, the Fifteenth of **3:**935
- - - high priest **8:**473; **8:**474
- - - lots, casting of **11:**511
- - - music **12:**565
- - - Nethinim **7:**552ff
- - - Pharisees **13:**366
- - - prayer **2:**839; **11:**393
- - - Sadducees **14:**620
- - Destruction
- - - ablution laws **2:**82
- - - astrology **3:**793
- - - Avelei Zion **3:**945
- - - Christian attitude **9:**1569ff
- - - Dio Cassius **6:**58
- - - *Ghriba* synagogue door **15:**1430
- - - Johanan ben Zakkai **10:**152
- - - Kamẓa and Bar Kamẓa **10:**732
- - - Karaites **10:**779
- - - Nine Days **12:**1168
- - - *Seder Olam Rabbah* **14:**1092
- - - *Shekhinah* **14:**1351
- - - Three Weeks **15:**1124
- - - Titus **15:**1168ff
- - - Ulla **15:**1521
- - - vessels **15:**1169
- - - Western Wall **16:**467
- Rebuilding
- - *Addir Hu* **2:**257
- - Akiva's optimism **2:**492
- - eschatology **6:**868
- - history, 70-640 C.E. **9:**237ff
- - Julian the Apostate **8:**653
- - messianic times **11:**1409
- - Reform Judaism **14:**24
- Halakhah and Aggadah cloud symbol **13:**524
- - Commandments, the 613 **5:**763f, 773f
- - destruction **16:**845
- - disqualifications for service **4:**1082ff
- - extension of precincts **4:**722
- - *hekdesh* **8:**279
- - *ḥerem* property **8:**345ff
- - *mikva'ot* in **11:**1541
- - Pentateuch **13:**239; **13:**244
- - proscribed town **8:**1471
- - purgation **5:**1384; **10:**1040
- - rabbinical literature **13:**1463
- - ritual impurity **13:**1406ff
- - sages' attitude **14:**641ff
- - Sanhedrin **14:**837
- - treasurer as corporate agent **10:**1568
- in the Arts **3:**506; **8:**1265; **9:**1578ff; **15:**108,1167,1171
- Literature
- - Apocrypha and Pseudepigrapha **3:**181
- - *Baruch, Apocalypse of* **4:**270
- - Dead Sea Scrolls **6:**878
- - Enoch, Ethiopic Book of **6:**796
- - Ezekiel's vision **6:**1089
- - Ezra-Nehemiah, Book of **6:**1114ff
- - Kings, Book of **10:**1024ff
- - *Lamentations Rabbah* **10:**1376
- Music **12:**560; **12:**566
- *illus:*
- - announcement of Sabbath **12:**573
- - Ark of the Covenant **3:**462
- - Day of Atonement service **16:**845
- - Dura-Europos wall paintings **6:**277; **9:**1581
- - eighteenth cent. engraving **11:**1505
- - entrance (reconst.) **3:**511
- - fifteenth cent. illumination **3:***fcg.* 988
- - Herodian masonry **3:**323
- - inscription prohibiting entry **9:**1555
- - *menorah* **11:**1355,1358
- - musical instruments **12:**569
- - Nicanor Gate **12:**1134
- - payment of the half-shekel tax **14:**1346
- - Perugino's painting **9:**1585
- - sacking of byPtolemy VI **10:**256
- - sacrifices **13:**327; **15:**786
- - *Sarajevo Haggadah* **7:***fcg.* 1131
- - shewbread on the golden table **14:**1395
- - *sukkah* wall painting **15:***fcg.* 491
- - thirteenth cent. icon **9:**1581
- *see also:* PRIESTS AND PRIESTHOOD; TABERNACLE; TEMPLE MOUNT; Temple Vessels
Temple Albert (syn., New Mex.) **12:**1038
- *illus:* **12:**1038
Temple Beth Abraham (syn., Tarrytown) **16:**465
Temple Beth-El (syn., Conn.) **15:**329
- *illus:*
- - exterior **15:**329
Temple Beth-El (syn., Tex.) **14:**822
- *illus:*
- - exterior **14:**823
Temple Beth El (syn., N.Y.) **12:**1071
Temple Beth Emeth (syn., Wilmington) **16:**534
- *illus:*
- - exterior **16:**533
Temple Beth-Israel (syn., Braz.) **14:**851
Temple Beth Israel (syn., Oregon) **16:**566
Temple Beth Israel Judaica Museum (Phoenix, U.S.) **12:**551
Temple B'nai Israel (syn., Okla.) **12:**1354
- *illus:*
- - *bimah* **12:**1354
Temple B'rith Kodesh (syn., N.Y.) **14:**210,211
- *illus:*
- - Ark of the Law **3:**627
- - exterior **14:**210
Temple Emanu-el (syn., Calif.) **14:**834
- *illus:*
- - exterior **5:**56
- - interior **14:**835
- - portable Ark **3:**453
Temple Emanu-el (syn., Curaçao) **12:**994
- *illus:* **12:**995
Temple Emanuel (syn., Mass.) **16:**633
- *illus:* **11:**1114; **16:**633
Temple Emanu-el (syn., Milwaukee) **11:**1589,1590
- *illus:*
- - exterior **16:**556
Temple Emanuel (syn., N.C.) **12:**1219
Temple Emanuel (syn., N.J.) **12:**1030
Temple Emanu-el (syn., N.Y.) **6:**525; **12:**1071; **12:**1079; **15:**620; **15:**623
- *illus:* **12:**1108
Temple Emanuel Museum (N.Y.) **12:**544
Temple Emanuel Museum (Providence) **12:**551
Temple Israel (syn., N.Y.) **12:**1079
Temple Keneseth Israel (Pa.) **13:**230
TEMPLE MOUNT **15:**988
- *Contents:*
- - In Jewish Law **15:**989
- - During the Period of the Temple **15:**989
- - Status after Destruction of Temple **15:**990
- *halakhah* **9:**1555
- Herod I **8:**384
- holy places **8:**921ff
- inscriptions **16:**669
- Islamic eschatology **6:**884
- *mikveh* **11:**1543
- modern sanctity **14:**617
- Muslim thought **9:**1575ff
- Six-Day War **14:**1635
- Suleiman's alterations **9:**1434
- Temple **15:**951ff
- Umayyads **15:**1529
- water supply **9:**1539
- Western Wall **16:**467
- Zion **16:**1030
- *illus:*
- - text
- - aerial view **9:**1413
- - Al-Aqsā Mosque **8:**931
- - Dome of the Rock **8:**931
- - Double Gate **9:**1429
- - Herodian wall and pavement **9:**1399
- - Mazar's excavations **9:**1533,1535
- - Ophel view **12:**1413
- - Single Gate **9:**1430
- - Triple Gate **9:**1429
- - Warren's excavations **9:**1522; **16:**333
- - Wilson's Arch **16:**535
- - Wolin Ḥasidim seal **14:**1077
Temple of Jupiter (Jer.), *see* Jupiter, Temple of
Temple of Solomon (mosque, Jer.), *see* Al-Aqṣa
Temple of Venus (Jer.), *see* Venus, Temple of
Templer, General (Brit. sol.) **9:**1033
TEMPLERS (Ger., sect.) **15:**994
- Haifa **7:**1136
- Jaffa **9:**1256
- settlements **9:**296
Temples
- Arad **3:**244
- Elephantine **6:**608
- Israelite **5:**1162
- Mesopotamian **16:**1511
- Phoenician **13:**480
Temple Sanctuary, *see* Holy of Holies
TEMPLE SCROLL (D. S. Scroll) **15:**996
- Bible **4:**834
- eschatology **6:**879ff
- Temple **15:**983
Temple Sinai (syn., Mass.) **16:**633
Temple Sinai (syn., N.Y.), *see* Bikur Cholim
Temple Sinai (syn., Pittsburgh) **13:**569
Temple Vessels
- Ahasuerus **2:**453
- Ahaz **2:**455
- altar **2:**760
- Antioch **3:**71
- Ark of Covenant **3:**464
- Bet Alfa mosaics **4:**713
- cherubim **5:**397
- Copper Scroll **5:**957
- Eleazar ben Yose **6:**600
- *menorah* **11:**1357
- metals and mining **11:**1428ff
- Temple of Jupiter **14:**244
- Titus **15:**1169
- *illus:*
- - Arch of Titus **15:**1167
- - *menorah* **11:**1355,1358
- - Samaritan Torah scroll **14:**739
- - *Shivviti* plaques **14:**1420-1421
Templin (tn., Ger.) **13:**842
Templo, Isaac, *see* Cordova, Isaac de
TEMPLO, JACOB JUDAH (ARYEH) LEON **15:**998
- *illus:* text
Templo, Solomon Judah Leão **15:**999
Templum Domini (church, Jer.) **9:**1579
Templum Solomonis, *see* Dome of the Rock
Temporary laws (Rus.), *see* MAY LAWS
Temptation **14:**653,904
Temuco (city, Chile) **5:**466
TEMUNAH, THE BOOK OF (kab. wk.) **15:**999
- abrogation of Torah **14:**1245
- antinomianism **3:**70
- eschatology **6:**882ff
- Kabbalah **10:**528
- visions **16:**169
TEMURAH (tract.) **15:**1000
- *illus:* text
Temurah (kab. conc.) **4:**267
Temurot (journ.) **1:**newsp. list
Tena, Luis de **8:**60
Tenai Bet Din (leg. conc.) **15:**1033
- *see also:* TAKKANOT
Tena'im (marriage conditions) **4:**754ff; **6:**186
Tenants, Protection of **7:**1518ff
- conflict of laws **5:**886
- eviction notice **7:**1006
- trespass safeguards **7:**1462
- *see also:* LEASE AND HIRE
Ten Commandments, *see*

DECALOGUE
TEN DAYS OF PENITENCE **15:** 1001
- *Avinu Malkenu* **3:** 973
- Elul **6:** 689
- opening of Holy Ark **3:** 457
- Samaritans **14:** 743
- *seliḥot* **14:** 1133
- *Shabbat Shuvah* **14:** 572
- *illus:*
- - *Avinu Malkenu* **3:** 973
Tendler, Lew **15:** 306
TENDLER, MOSES D. **15:** 1002
TENE, BENJAMIN **15:** 1002
Tenenbaum (name), *see also* Tennenbaum
Tenenbaum, A. **13:** 1596
Tenenbaum, Israel **4:** 1362
TENENBAUM, JOSEPH L. **15:** 1002
- anti-Nazi boycott **4:** 1281
TENENBAUM, JOSHUA **15:** 1003
TENENBAUM, MORDECAI **15:** 1003
- Barash **4:** 203
- Bialystock **4:** 809ff
- Warsaw ghetto **16:** 349
Tenenboim, Jacob **14:** 1509
Tenenboim, Moses **12:** 1285
Tenerife (Can. Is.) **5:** 117
Tenes (tn., Alg.) **2:** 613
Tenets of Faith, *see* ARTICLES OF FAITH
Tengiz (viceroy, Syr.) **9:** 1424
Tengiziyya Madrasa, Al- (theol. coll.) **9:** 1425
Tenje (vill., Croatia) **16:** 878
TEN LOST TRIBES **15:** 1003
- Baruch ben Samuel **4:** 279
- Bonafoux, Daniel **4:** 1199
- British Israelites **4:** 1381
- Eldad ha-Dani **6:** 576ff
- emissaries **14:** 1366
- exile, Assyrian **6:** 1035
- Falashas **6:** 1153
- fate of **7:** 420ff
- fiction, Hebrew **6:** 1262
- folktales **6:** 1382
- Georgian Jews **7:** 423
- Khorasan **2:** 326
- Kurdish Jews **10:** 1296
- Manasseh ben Israel **11:** 856
- messianism **11:** 1425; **14:** 1226
- Montezinos, Antonio de **12:** 278
- Nishapur **12:** 1176
- Sambatyon River **14:** 762ff
- Twelve Tribes **15:** 1385
- *illus:*
- - text
- - Hine's *Forty-Seven Identifications* . . . (1871) **4:** 1381
- - Shabbetai Ẓevi as Joshua Helcam **14:** 1245
TEN MARTYRS, THE **15:** 1006
- *Arzei ha-Levanon* **3:** 938
- Eleazar ben Shammua **6:** 598
- Hadrian, Publius Aelius **7:** 1054
- Hananiah ben Ḥakhinai **7:** 1254
- Samuel ha-Katan **14:** 816
- *illus:*
- - Hananiah ben Teradyon **7:** 1255
- - *Midrash Elleh Ezkerah* (1853) **7:** 1117
Ten Men of Leisure, *see* BATLANIM
Tenne (coop., Isr.) **5:** 950
Tennen, B. **16:** 788
TENNENBAUM, JACOB **15:** 1008
Tennenbaum, Meir **15:** 1008
Tennenbaum, Menahem **15:** 1008
Tennes (k., Sidon) **14:** 1506
TENNESSEE (U.S.) **15:** 1008
- *pop. tables:* text
Tennis **7:** 300; **14:** 875; **15:** 314
Ten Plagues, *see* PLAGUES OF EGYPT
Ten Plagues, Operation (War of Indep.), *see* Yo'av, Operation
Tent of Meeting, *see* TABERNACLE
Tenu'ah le-Yahadut shel Torah (orgn., Isr.) **16:** 4
Tenu'at ha-Meri ha-Ivri (resist. mvmt.) **9:** 688; **4:** 509; **11:** 465
Tenufah, see Wave Offering
Tenu'ot, see Vowels
Tenuvah (coop., Isr.), *see* TNUVA
Tenuvot (mosh., Isr.) **1:** place list
Te'o (animal) **4:** 1467
Te'omim (Zodiac sign), *see* Gemini
TEOMIM, AARON BEN MOSES **15:** 1010
- Bacharach, Jair Ḥayyim **4:** 48
- Shabbateanism **14:** 1253
Te'omim, Aaron Isaac **7:** 67
Te'omim, Abraham **4:** 1436
TEOMIM, ARYEH LEIB **15:** 1010
Teomim, Eliyahu David Rabinovich **9:** 890
Teomim, Jacob Moses **12:** 1244
Te'omim (Te'omim-Fraenkel) Jonah ben Isaiah **7:** 925; **11:** 1450
TEOMIM, JOSEPH BEN MEIR **15:** 1011
Teomim-Ashkenazi, Samuel **9:** 1336
Teomim-Fraenkel, Ḥayyim Jonah **6:** 469
Teomim-Fraenkel, Isaac Jair **5:** 484
Tepe Gawra culture **16:** 1484
Tepho (loc., Er. Isr.), *see* TEKOA
TEPLICE (Teplice-Šanov; city, Cz.) **15:** 1012
- Czechoslovakia **5:** 1200
Teplitz, Mordecai **11:** 357
Teplitz-Schoenau (city, Cz.), *see* TEPLICE
TEPPER, KOLYA **15:** 1013
TEPPER, MORRIS **15:** 1013
TERAH (bib. fig.) **15:** 1013
- Nimrod **12:** 1167
- patriarchs **13:** 182
- Sarah **14:** 866
- *illus:*
- - Abraham delivered to Nimrod **2:** 118
Terah (bib. loc.) **15:** 1014
Teraklin (journ.) **1:** newsp. list
Terakon de-Zimra (area, Er. Isr.) **4:** 292
Terakona (area, Er. Isr.) **4:** 292
TERAPHIM (idols) **15:** 1014
- divination **6:** 114
- Ephod **6:** 804
- inheritance **12:** 1289
- Rachel **13:** 1487ff
Terapyah Shimmushit (journ.) **1:** newsp. list
Terbent (loc.) **5:** 1550
TEREBINTH (bot.) **15:** 1015
- afforestation **9:** 221
- almond graft **12:** 171
- plant list **13:** 625
- *illus:*
- - text
- - "Little Switzerland" **9:** 235
- - Negev **9:** 234
Tered (bot.), *see* BEET
TEREFAH (dietary conc.) **15:** 1016
- categories **6:** 28,39
- eggs **6:** 47
- *halakhah le-Moshe mi-Sinai* **7:** 1167
- *Ḥullin* **8:** 1069
- Maimonides **11:** 761
- *see also:* DIETARY LAWS
Ter'ela (loc., Er. Isr.) **15:** 481
Ṭerem (cantillation sign), *see Gereš*
Terentius, J. Gerhardi **8:** 60
Terentius Phologombos, *see* JUDAH, SAMUEL BENJAMIN HELBERT
Terentyeva, Maria **16:** 87
Teresh (bib. fig.) **12:** 308
Terezín (tn.), *see* THERESIENSTADT
Terminology, religious **14:** 1170
Termissis (coin) **5:** 721
TERNI, DANIEL BEN MOSES DAVID **15:** 1017
- Bolaffi, Michele **4:** 1185
Terni, Mattathias Nissim **5:** 1485
Terni, Michael **13:** 12
Ternopol (city, Ukr.), *see* TARNOPOL
Terqa (tn., Mesop.) **11:** 977
TERRACINI, BENVENUTO ARON **15:** 1018
- Italian literature **9:** 1114
TERRACINI, UMBERTO ELIA **15:** 1018
Terra Sancta School (Jer.) **9:** 1494
- *illus:*
- - Hebrew University **9:** 1487
Terre Haute (city, Ind.) **8:** 1361
Terris, Sid **15:** 306
Territorial Federations of Communities, *see* FEDERATIONS OF COMMUNITIES, TERRITORIAL
TERRITORIALISM **15:** 1019
- History **8:** 751
- - archives **3:** 389
- - communist theory **5:** 793; **5:** 796ff
- - Hungary **16:** 1121
- - Po'alei Zion **13:** 657
- - Russia **15:** 1136
- - Uganda Scheme **15:** 1501
- - Zionism **16:** 1073ff
- - Zionist Congress (7th) **16:** 1168ff
- - Zionist socialists **15:** 44ff; **16:** 1179
- - Zionist split **16:** 1097
- Views
- - Borochov,Ber **4:** 1254
- - Churchill, Sir Winston **5:** 555
- - Glanz-Leyeles, Aaron **7:** 600
- - Lvovich, David **11:** 616
- - Steinberg, Isaac Nahman **15:** 359
- - Vozrozhdeniye **16:** 229ff
- - Zangwill, Israel **16:** 932
- - Zhitlowsky, Chaim **16:** 1010
Territur (isl., Ind.) **5:** 624
Terrorism, Arab, *see* Arabs (nationalism); Fataḥ, al; Fedayeen; Palestine Liberation Organization
Terry, Fred **12:** 945
TERTIS, LIONEL **12:** 711
TERTULIAN, NICOLAE **14:** 423; **14:** 427
Tertullian (Ch. F.) **3:** 784; **5:** 551; **6:** 85; **8:** 302
Tertz, Abram, *see* Sinyavski, Andrey
TERUEL (city, Arag.) **15:** 1022
- archaeology **3:** 332
- Host desecration **8:** 1043
- Inquisition **8:** 1384
Teruel, Abraham ben Solomon **16:** 365
Terumah (sacrifice), *see* Heave Offering
Terumah (journ.) **1:** newsp. list
Terumat ha-Deshen (bk.) **9:** 1080ff
TERUMOT (tract.) **15:** 1023
- *illus:* text
TERUMOT AND MA'ASEROT (tithes) **15:** 1025
- General
- - Alkalai on re-introduction **2:** 639
- - *amoraim,* paid to **2:** 874
- - banking **4:** 166
- - other gifts **13:** 1088
- - Talmud **11:** 651; **15:** 1023
- Halakhah
- - agency **2:** 349
- - *demai* **5:** 1486ff
- - impurity **13:** 1407,1412
- - Judah ha-Nasi and exemptions **10:** 369
- - *ma'aser sheni,* price change **5:** 887
- - *Pe'ah* **13:** 200
- - proscription **8:** 1471
- - Syria **15:** 639
- - uncleanness of hands **4:** 817
- - women and slaves **16:** 776
- *see also:* ḤAVER, ḤAVERIM; TITHE
Teruvtor (bot.) **5:** 1
TESCHEN (tn., Silesia) **15:** 1028
- Moravia **12:** 304
Tesha ba-Erev (mag.), *see Ha-Olam ha-Zeh*
Tesha Tesha Tesha (period.) **1:** newsp. list
Teshub (deity) **8:** 1115
Teshuvah, see REPENTANCE
Teshuvah (kab. conc.), *see Binah*
Teshuvah (prayer) **2:** 840
Teshuvot, see RESPONSA
Teshuvot Ḥakhmei Provence (responsa collec.) **5:** 1352
Teshuvot Yad Malakhi (responsa collec.) **11:** 817
Tĕsín-Cieszyn (dist., Morav.), *see* TESCHEN
Tessler, Brian **15:** 930
Testa (fam.) **5:** 464
Testament, *see* WILLS
Testament, New, *see* NEW TESTAMENT
Testament, Old, *see* BIBLE
Testament of Abraham (Apoc.), *see* ABRAHAM, TESTAMENT OF
Testament of Gad (Apoc.) **14:** 903
Testament of Job (Pseudepig.), *see* JOB, TESTAMENT OF
Testament of Moses (Apoc.), *see Moses, Testament of*
Testament of Rabbi Eliezer the Great (wk.) **2:** 208
Testament of the Twelve Patriarchs (Pseudepig.), *see* PATRIARCHS, TESTAMENT OF THE TWELVE
Testamentum Mosis (Apoc.), *see* Moses, Testament of
Testimony, *see* EVIDENCE; WITNESS
TET (Heb. let.) **15:** 1029
Tetiyev (tn., Ukr.) **13:** 700; **14:** 459
Tetmajer, Kazimierz Przerwa **13:** 798
Tetracomia (dist., Er. Isr.) **9:** 252
Tetradrachm (weight, coin), *see Sela*
Tetragrammaton, see GOD, NAMES OF
Tetrapla (Bib. trans.) **4:** 856
- Origen **12:** 1467
Tetrapylon (gate, Jer.) **9:** 1406
TETRARCH (gov.) **15:** 1029
Tetrateuch (bib. bks.) **13:** 232
TETUÁN (city, Mor.) **15:** 1029
- Abenatar, Jacob **3:** 813
- Jewish quarter **10:** 87
- special Purim **13:** 1399
- Tangier **15:** 791
- *illus:* text
Teubal, Ezra **12:** 1537
TEUCER OF CYZICUS **7:** 889; **7:** 897
Teucheira (J. cmty., Libya) **11:** 198
Te'udah (conc.) **3:** 199
Te'udah be-Yisrael (bk.) **11:** 117
Te'udke (epithet) **11:** 117
Te'urah (journ.) **1:** newsp. list
Teutsch-Khumesh (Bib.) **11:** 356
Tevah (Noah's), *see* ARK OF NOAH
Tevah (syn.), *see* ARK; BIMAH
Tevah, Victor **5:** 467
Tevai (journ.) **1:** newsp. list
Teva u-Veri'ut (journ.) **1:** newsp. list
Teveryah (tn., Isr.), *see* TIBERIAS
TEVET (Heb. month) **15:** 1031
- 28th, Sadducees deposed **14:** 1563

- *illus:*
- - text
- - *tekufat Tevet* **5:**45
- *see also:* CALENDAR
TEVET, SHABBETAI **15:**1032
Tevet, Tenth Day of (fast day)
- fasting **6:**1191; **6:**1195
- Holocaust victims **8:**917
- Karaites **10:**779
- Shabbetai Ẓevi's abolition of **14:**1229
Tevet Markah (mid. wk.), *see Meimar Markah*
Teveẓ (vill., Isr.), *see* Tūbās
Tevilah, see ABLUTION
Tevir (cantillation sign) **16:**1440,1454
- *mus. notations:*
- - masoretic accents **11:**1107
TEVUL YOM (tract.) **15:**1032
- *illus:* text
Tevunah (journ., Isr.) **1:**newsp. list
Tevunah (journ., Lith.) **1:**newsp. list
Tevunah (period., Prus.) **11:**280
- statistics **1:**newsp. list
Tevu'ot Shor (hal. comment.) **14:**995
Tevye and his Seven Daughters (motion picture) **12:**462
- *illus:*
- - Rodensky, Shmuel **12:**462
Tevye der Milkhiker ("Tevye the Milkman"; wk.) **6:**1382; **14:**1280
Teweles, David **15:**1033
Teweles, Heinrich **13:**973
TEWELES, JUDAH **15:**1033
- Afike Jehuda **2:**329
Teweles, Lipmann **15:**1033
TEWI, THEA **3:**611
- *illus:*
- - "Upward Journey" (sculp.) **3:**643
Texarkana (city, Tex.) **3:**459; **15:**1035
TEXAS **15:**1034
- *illus:*
- - Eshkol, Levi, visit **9:**405
- *pop. tables:* text
Texas Jewish Press (period.) **15:**1036
Texeda, Fernando de **5:**209
Texeira (fam. name), *see also:* Teixeira
Texeira, Myer Hart, *see* HART, MYER
Texeira de Mattos (fam.) **5:**1537
TEXTILES **15:**1036
- *Contents:*
- - In the Talmud **15:**1037
- - Medieval Period **15:**1038
- - In the Ottoman Empire **15:**1038
- - Eastern Europe **15:**1039
- - Central Europe **15:**1040
- - Great Britain **15:**1042
- - United States **15:**1042
- - In Israel **15:**1042
- Acqui Jews **2:**216
- Austrian Jews **3:**894
- clothing industry, U.S. **15:**1615
- crafts **5:**1044ff
- Israel industry **9:**823
- Lodz **11:**425ff
- Loew-Beer family **11:**445
- Russia and Poland **16:**1317 **16:**1274
- *illus:*
- - Kiryat Gat factory **9:**817
- - Maskit oriental gown **9:**822
- - New York garment workers **15:**1616,1617
- - ration books, Israel **9:**376
- *see also:* TAILORING
Textus (period.) **8:**224
Texts and Studies in Jewish History and Literature (wk.) **16:**1338
Tezuka, N. **9:**1283
Thaarup, Thomas **14:**927
Thabit, David **16:**1537
Thackeray, William Makepeace **6:**779
Thadamora (city, Syr.), *see* TADMOR
Thaddaeus (apostle), *see* Tadi
Thadden, Adolf von **12:**955
Thadden, Eberhard von **8:**860; **14:**150
THAILAND (state) **15:**1043
- Israel **9:**991
- *illus:* text
Tha'labī, Al- **4:**931
Thalassemia (disease) **14:**1501
THALBERG, IRVING GRANT **15:**1044
Thalberg, Joseph **15:**1045
THALBERG, SIGISMUND **15:**1045
Thalheimer, August **5:**1434
Thalheimer, Gates **15:**635
Thalhimer (fam.) **14:**161
Thalhimer, Isaac **16:**163
Thalhimer, William B. **14:**161
Thall, Burnett **15:**1264
Thall, Thelma **15:**314
THALLUS (au.) **15:**1045
- biblical history **8:**304
Thalman (bnk., U.S.) **4:**178
Thalman, Ernesto A. **15:**1549
Thamalla, Richard **15:**21
Thamara (Rom. fort) **15:**783
Thamna (toparchy, Er. Isr.) **9:**120
Thamud (tribe) **3:**943
Thamūdic (lang.) **3:**237
- Semitic languages **14:**1152
Thanksgiving, Song of, *see* Song of Thanksgiving
Thanksgiving offering **14:**603ff
THANKSGIVING PSALMS (D. S. Scroll) **15:**1045
- Dead Sea sect **5:**1409
- Psalter **13:**1312
- revelation of mysteries **13:**331
- Teacher of Righteousness **15:**888
- Yaḥad community **16:**701
- *illus:* **5:**1404-1406,1413
- *see also:* DEAD SEA SCROLLS
Thann (tn., Fr.) **2:**752
Thannhauser, Justin **3:**648
Thant, *see* U Thant
Thapsacus (city, Mesop.), *see* Tiphsah
Tharaud, Jean **15:**1048
THARAUD, JÉRÔME **15:**1048
Thassis, *see* SIMEON THE HASMONEAN
Thau, Yohanan **16:**1149
Thauros (13th cent., Fr.) **11:**565
Théas (archbp.) **7:**36
THEATER **15:**1049
- *Contents:*
- - Origins **15:**1049
- - Post-Biblical Period **15:**1049
- - From 1600 to the 20th Century **15:**1052
- - - England **15:**1052
- - - France **15:**1054
- - - Germany **15:**1055
- - - Italy **15:**1057
- - - Holland **15:**1057
- - - Russia **15:**1058
- - - United States **15:**1058
- - - Jews in the Musical **15:**1059
- - - The Jew as Entertainer **15:**1060
- - - Theater in Israel **15:**1061
- - Yiddish Theater **15:**1064
- - - United States **15:**1065
- - - London **15:**1068
- - - France **15:**1071
- - - Rumania **15:**1071
- - - Poland **15:**1071
- - - Latin America **15:**1073
- - - Israel **15:**1074
- - - South Africa **15:**1074
- - - Soviet Union **15:**1074
- - Capsules **15:**1077
- General
- - folk dramas **6:**1389
- - music **12:**659
- Hebrew
- - Cameri **5:**73
- - Gnessin, Menaḥem **7:**634
- - Habimah **7:**1028
- - Israel **9:**1003
- - Ohel **12:**1342
- - Sommo, Judah **15:**137
- Yiddish
- - Argentina **3:**423
- - Broder Singers **4:**1391
- - Fraye Yidishe Folksbine (U.S.) **6:**801
- - Odessa dramatic group **8:**517
- - Purim Shpil **13:**1396
- - Shakespeare **14:**1264
- - Vilna Troupe **16:**151
- *illus:*
- - text
- - Adler, Celia, in *The Women* **2:**271
- - Almagor, Gila, in *Laylah be-Mai* **6:**204
- - Altman's stage set for *Uriel Acosta* **5:**989
- - Ben-Amos, Immanuel, in *He Walked in the Fields* **5:**73
- - Bergner, Elizabeth, in *The Jewish Wife* **4:**617
- - Bernstein-Cohen, Miriam, in *Tura* **4:**690
- - Bertonoff, Yehoshua, in *Tevye the Milkman* **4:**700
- - Buchman, Naḥum, in *Ha-Adamah ha-Zot* **6:**196
- - Burstein family, in *The Megilla* **4:**1532
- - Caesarea **5:**9
- - *Eternal Jew* performance in Vilna ghetto **16:**145
- - Finkel, Shimon, in *Inherit the Wind* **7:**1032
- - Finkel, Shimon, in *Peer Gynt* **7:**1031
- - Friedman, Shraga, in *Inherit the Wind* **7:**1032
- - Habimah, members of original company **7:**1029
- - "Habimah" drama circle **12:**1160
- - Habimah performance of *The Dybbuk* **14:**465
- - Habimah Theater **7:**1031
- - Habimah Theater, cornerstone laying **7:**1028
- - Haifa, Municipal Theater **7:**1141
- - "Hannah Rovina as Medea" (wdct., M. Sima) **3:**644
- - Leoni, Myer, in *The Duenna* **11:**30
- - Marceau, Marcel **11:**942
- - Marcus, Rachel, in *Laylah be-Mai* **6:**204
- - Margalit, Meir, in *Ammekha* **12:**1343
- - Marx Brothers **11:**1076
- - Meron, Hannah
- - - in *Hedda Gabler* **11:**1392
- - - in *He Walked in the Fields* **5:**74
- - Meskin, Aharon, in *Be-Arvot ha-Negev* **6:**200
- - Mikhoels as King Lear **11:**1530
- - Moscow Jewish State Theater **12:**361
- - Mostel, Zero, in *Fiddler on the Roof* **12:**433
- - Reinhardt, Max **14:**60
- - Rovina, Hannah, in *Dybbuk* **6:**19; **14:**356
- - Schildkraut, Rudolph **14:**964
- - Schwartz, Maurice, in *The Brothers Ashkenazi* **14:**1021
- - *Shulamis,* poster **7:**716
- - Turkow family **15:**1464
- - *Uriel Acosta,* stage set **5:**989
- - Zemach, Nahum, in *The Eternal Wanderer* **16:**981
- - Ziegfeld, Florenz, and *Rosalie* rehearsal **16:**1018
- - *Zulu and the Zayda* rehearsal **14:**1650
- *see also:* DRAMA, HEBREW
Theater for Youth (Pol.) **15:**1072
Theater Journal und Familien Blatt (journ.) **13:**1055
Théâtre Sarah Bernhardt **4:**677
Theben, Abraham **15:**1093
THEBEN (MANDL), JACOB KOPPEL **15:**1093
THEBES (city, Egy.) **15:**1093
- Diaspora **6:**9
- history chart **8:**766-767
- *illus:*
- - Merneptah stele **3:**313
THEBES (city, Gr.) **15:**1093
- Greece **7:**868
THEBEZ (city, Er. Isr.) **15:**1094
THEFT AND ROBBERY **15:**1094
- *Contents:*
- - Civil Aspects **15:**1094
- - The Criminal Law **15:**1097
- - State of Israel **15:**1098
- agency **2:**350; **2:**352
- arbitration **3:**298
- bailees **14:**1455ff
- *Bava Kamma* **4:**339
- captives' redemption **12:**19
- Commandments, the 613 **5:**769,772
- consecrated property **8:**280
- despair (*ye'ush*) **16:**774ff
- ethics **6:**933,936
- gentiles **12:**1189ff
- graves **15:**1217
- *ḥazakah* **7:**1520
- imprisonment **8:**1302
- Israel **5:**1097
- land **13:**1146
- land encroachment **7:**1460
- *niddui* imposition **8:**354
- overreaching **12:**1391
- possession **12:**1532; **12:**1533
- prohibition validity **12:**120
- purchaser's compensation **12:**10; **16:**1288
- repayment obligation **12:**1313
- sacrifice **14:**601
- sale of theft **12:**10; **14:**678
- self-defense **6:**1071
- *Sikarikon* **14:**1529
- stealing and slaughtering **13:**223
- stolen goods **6:**1288
- synagogue **15:**584
- tax evasion **15:**870
- thief as witness **16:**586
- warning **13:**227
- work dismissal **10:**1328
- *see also:* ABDUCTION; OPPRESSION
Theism, *see* GOD
Theilhaber, Felix A. **13:**888
THÉMANLYS, PASCAL **7:**151
THEMISTIUS (philos.) **15:**1099
- intellect, doctrine of **2:**581
Theobald (Hebr.) **8:**14
THEOCRACY (polity) **15:**1099
Theodicy (conc.)
- Bible **7:**648
- justice **10:**477
- religious tale **6:**1380
- *see also:* GOD (Justice and Mercy); GOOD AND EVIL
THEODOR, JULIUS **15:**1100
- *Genesis Rabbah* **7:**401
Theodora (czarina) **4:**1493
Theodore (ruler, Transj.) **2:**850; **7:**433
Theodore, Adah Isaacs, *see* MENKEN, ADAH ISAACS
THEODORE OF MOPSUESTIA **15:**1100
- Old Testament **4:**926
Theodore Psalter (illum. ms.)

12:1351
Theodor Herzl (Zion. gr., Cz.) **16:**1112
Theodor Herzl (ship) **8:**1250
- *illus:*
- - at Haifa port **8:**767
- - Latin American immigrants arriving **9:**530
Theodor Herzl Memorial Home for the Jewish Sick (Eng.), *see* Herzl-Moser Hospital
Theodoric (Ostrogoth k.) **9:**1119
- history chart **8:**766-767
Theodosia (Gr. clny.), *see* FEODOSIYA
Theodosian Code **15:**1101
- Church councils **5:**547; **5:**549
THEODOSIUS (Samar.) **15:**1101
- Andronicus **2:**949
THEODOSIUS I (Rom. emp.) **15:**1101
- Callinicum incident **2:**801
- Ereẓ Israel **9:**257
- history chart **8:**766-767
- Jews **14:**230
- polygamy **12:**259
THEODOSIUS II (Rom. emp.) **15:**1101
- Antioch **3:**72
- Aurum Coronarium **3:**854
- Ereẓ Israel **9:**257
- history chart **8:**766-767
- Jews **14:**230
- Samaritans **14:**732
- synagogue building **8:**655
- Thrace and Illyria **4:**1480
THEODOSIUS OF ROME **15:**1102
Theodotion (pros.) **4:**853ff; **11:**312
THEODOTUS (Samar. poet) **15:**1102
- apologetics **3:**189
- Greek influence **8:**300
- Hellenistic Jewish literature **8:**304
Theodotus son of Vettenos **15:**583
THEOLOGY **15:**1103
- *Contents:*
- - Introduction **15:**1103
- - Theology in the Bible **15:**1104
- - Rabbinic Theology **15:**1105
- - Medieval Jewish Theology **15:**1106
- - Modern Jewish Theology **15:**1108
- General
- - Aristotelianism **3:**446
- - Jewish literature **11:**338ff
- - Kabbalah **10:**493; **10:**638
- - Maimonidean controversy **11:**745
- - physics **13:**488
- - Protestant anti-Semitism **13:**1251
- - revelation and heresy **8:**360
- Themes
- - eschatology **11:**1414
- - evil **7:**775ff
- - existentialism **6:**1041
- - holiness **10:**871
- - Providence **13:**1279
- - sin **14:**1587ff
- Views and Attitude to
- - Baruch Togarmi **4:**267
- - Finch, Sir Henry **6:**1285
- - Frankists **7:**59
- - *Ḥabad* **14:**1437ff
- - Ḥasidei Ashkenaz **7:**1379
- - Heschel, A. **8:**426ff
- - Islam **9:**97
- - Judaism **10:**392; **10:**394
- - Maimonides **11:**769ff
- - modern Orthodoxy **12:**1492
- - Philo **13:**411
- - rabbinical **15:**1239
- - *Zohar* **10:**533
- *see also* ARTICLES OF FAITH; BELIEF; PHILOSOPHY; PHILOSOPHY, JEWISH
Theomim (fam.) **7:**1
Theomin, D. E. **6:**273
Theophany
- altar **2:**764
- altar-building **5:**1168
- fire **6:**1303
- Moses **12:**374
- Sinai, Mount **14:**1598ff
- Tabernacle **15:**685
- Torah reading **15:**1253
Théophiliens (drama gr.) **5:**670
THEOPHILUS (Gr. au.) **7:**897
- Eupolemus' writings **6:**964
THEOPHILUS (h. pr.) **15:**1110
- Matthias **11:**1131
- Simeon ben Boethus **14:**1554
Theophrastus Bombastus ab Hohenheim, *see* Paracelsus
THEOPHRASTUS OF ERESOS **15:**1111
- Jews **7:**887
Theosophy, *see* KABBALAH
THERAPEUTAE (sect) **15:**1111
- allegorical exegesis **4:**896
- asceticism **3:**680ff
- *Job, Testament of* **10:**129
- Torah as organism **10:**622
Theresia von Picquigny, Joanna **16:**479
THERESIENSTADT (tn., ghetto) **15:**1112
- art **3:**568ff
- Fritta's paintings **7:**203
- gassing **16:**1332
- German Jews **7:**496
- ghetto **7:**544ff
- ghetto currency **5:**726
- Utitz, Emil, writings on **16:**35
- *illus:*
- - ghetto "bank note" **5:**726
- - ghetto children's drawings **5:**1203
- - "Living Quarters in the Theresienstadt Ghetto" (paint., O. Ungar) Fig. 83 3-ART
- - "Loading a Transport of Old People..." (drg., L. Haas) Fig. 81 3-ART
- - old people in the Theresienstadt Ghetto (drg., F. Bloch) Fig. 82 3-ART
Thermuthis (Egy. prin.) **12:**392
"Theseus" (sculp., J. Lipschitz) **3:**559
Thesouro dos Dinim (bk.) **11:**856
Thessaloniki (city, Gr.), *see* SALONIKA
Thessaly (reg., Gr.) **7:**868ff
Theudas (physic, Alex.) **11:**1183
THEUDAS (false prophet) **15:**1117
- messianism **11:**1420
Theudian (br., Doris) **4:**601
Theunitz, J. Antonii **8:**60
Theurgy **10:**632
- Neoplatonism **12:**958
Theurgic literature **10:**500,508
Thiasoi (Hellen. cmty.) **4:**1263
Thibaut II (count, Champagne) **7:**14
Thibaut IV (count, Campagne) **16:**195
THIEBERGER, FRIEDRICH **15:**1117
- press **13:**1029
Thiele, E. E. **8:**60
THIEME, KARL **15:**1117
Thierack (Reich offic.) **8:**854
Thiersch. H. W. J. **8:**60
Thietman (trav.) **15:**1355
THIONVILLE (tn., Fr.) **15:**1118
- Lorraine **11:**497
- Metz **11:**1452
Thirsch, Leopold **8:**60
Thirteen Attributes of God, *see* GOD (Attributes of)
Thirteen, The (nat. exec., Isr.), *see* Minhelet ha-Am
Thirteen Principles, *see* ARTICLES OF FAITH
Thirty-Seven, The (council, Isr.), *see* Mo'eẓet ha-Am
Thirty-Six Saints, *see* LAMED VAV ẒADDIKIM
Thisia (Gr. mystery play) **7:**887
THISTLES AND THORNS **15:**1118
- flora of Israel **9:**222
- plant list **13:**625
- weeds **16:**371
Thiyah (student orgn., U.S.) **15:**450
Thodah (disciple, Jesus) **10:**15
T'Hoen, Pieter **14:**784
Thomar (city, Port.), *see* TOMAR
Thomas (monk) **5:**1250
Thomas, John **16:**1153
Thomas, Max **8:**869
- Paris **13:**110
Thomaschewsky, Hulda **16:**1165
Thomashefsky, Bessie **15:**1121
THOMASHEFSKY, BORIS **15:**1120
- Sandler, Jacob Koppel **14:**830
Thomashefsky, Pincus **15:**1120
Thomas of Heraclea **4:**860
Thomason, George **8:**60
Thomasville (city, Ga.) **7:**429
THOMSEN, PETER **15:**1121
- Zionism **16:**1156
Thompson, Richard **8:**60
THON, ALBERT **15:**1121
Thon, Helen Hannah **15:**1123
THON, OSIAS (Jehoshua) **15:**1121
- Bet Yehoshu'a **4:**778
- Sejm **14:**1117
Thon, Sarah **15:**1123
THON, YA'AKOV YOḤANAN **15:**1123
- Va'ad Le'ummi **16:**51
- *illus:*
- - National Council meeting **9:**365
Thopas (place, Er. Isr.), *see* THEBEZ
Thorek, Max **11:**1201
Thorenburg (tn., Transyl.), *see* TURDA
Thorláksson, Gudbrandur **4:**877
Thorman, Simson **5:**606; **5:**609
Thorn (port, Pol.), *see* TORUN
THORN, SIR JULES **15:**1123
Thorndike, Herbert **8:**60
Thorne, William **8:**60
Thorns, *see* THISTLES AND THORNS
Thoth (deity) **8:**372
Thouars (tn., Fr.) **13:**704
Thought, Divine (kab. conc.) **10:**561ff
Thought, Jewish, *see* JUDAISM; PHILOSOPHY, JEWISH
"Thoughts, 1964" (paint., Alcopley) **3:**616
Thousand Families Settlement Scheme, *see Hityashevut ha-Elef*
Thrace (reg., Gr.) **8:**292
Thread (meas.), *see Ḥut*
"Three Calabrian Laborers" (paint., C. Levi) **11:**78
Three-Day March (Isr.) **15:**298ff
- *illus:*
- - Hebrew University students **9:**1020
- - Israel flags **11:**694
- - Mordechai, Doron **15:**297
- - Valley of the Cross camp **9:**1489
Three Lights (kab. conc.) **10:**563
"Three Peasants" (drg., J. Herman) **3:**557
THREE WEEKS (mourning period) **15:**1124
- Av, the Ninth of **3:**937
- Tammuz, Fast of **15:**789
Threshold, *see* DOOR AND DOORPOST
Throat **8:**7
THRONE **15:**1124
- kingship **10:**1013ff
- *illus:* text
THRONE OF GOD **15:**1125
- angelic song **15:**144
- anthropomorphism **3:**56
- *I Enoch* **3:**180
- mystical speculation **10:**497ff
- right side **14:**177
- Tablets of Law **15:**691
- Torah **15:**1236ff
- visions **16:**168
- Worlds, the Four **16:**642
- *see also:* KABBALAH; MERKABAH MYSTICISM; SHEKHINAH
Thuir (tn., Fr.) **14:**353
Thumann, Anton **11:**794
Thummim, see URIM AND THUMMIM
THUNDER AND LIGHTNING **15:**1127
Thunder Bay (dist., Ont.) **12:**1408
Thureau-Dangin, F. **16:**1507
Thuri, György **8:**60
THURINGIA (state, Ger.) **15:**1127
- Hillel of Erfurt **8:**490
- Sauckel, Fritz **14:**909
Thurston, E. Temple **16:**262
Thusurus (loc., Tunis), *see* Tozeur
Thutmose I **8:**1174
Thutmose III (Thutmosis; k., Egy.)
- Anaharath **2:**917
- Ara (ʿrn) **3:**231
- Ashtaroth **3:**737
- Ereẓ Israel cities **13:**868
- Gibbethon **7:**549
- Ibleam **8:**1151
- Megiddo **11:**1227
- Mesopotamia **16:**1499ff
- seals **14:**1073
- *illus:*
- - plants brought from Palestine **2:**385
Thyme (spice) **15:**269
- plant list **13:**625
Thysius, Antonius **8:**60
Tiamat (deity) **5:**1061; **11:**952
Tib'a (coin) **5:**721
Tibbon, Abraham ibn **15:**1130
- translations **15:**1322
TIBBON, IBN (Tibbonids; fam.) **15:**1129
- Hebrew language **16:**1624
- medicine **11:**1189
Tibbon, Jacob ben Machir ibn **15:**1130
- Astruc, Abba Mari **3:**808
- Averroes **3:**950
- Ibn Aflah **3:**799
- medicine **11:**1189
- quadrant **3:**787
- translations **15:**1322
Tibbon, Jacob ben Moses ibn **15:**1130
Tibbon, Jacob ibn **2:**513
Tibbon, Judah ben Saul ibn **15:**1129
- ethical literature **6:**925
- ethical wills **11:**345; **16:**531
- linguistics **16:**1358,1385
- mystical environment **10:**520
- Rabad **2:**136
- translations **15:**1319ff; **16:**1622
- *illus:*
- - *Mivḥar ha-Peninim* (1484) **8:**1332
Tibbon, Moses ben Samuel ibn **15:**1130
- astronomy **3:**799
- Avicenna **3:**959
- Themistius **15:**1099
- translations **15:**1321
Tibbon, Samuel ben Judah ibn **15:**1130

- Alconstantini, Enoch **2:**551
- Aristotelianism **3:**446
- Avicenna **3:**959
- beatitude **4:**362; **4:**363
- Béziers **4:**793
- Maimonides **11:**757; **11:**769ff
- *Musar Av* **16:**531
- philosophic exegesis **11:**346
- philosophy, Jewish **13:**444
- Providence **13:**1285
- Torah **15:**1240
- translations **15:**1320; **16:**1624
Tiberian Masorah **16:**1447
- Biblical Hebrew **16:**1571
- Cairo *genizah* **16:**1336
- Hebrew pronunciation **13:**1129
TIBERIAS (city, Isr.) **15:**1130
- General
- - *aggadah* **12:**997
- - earthquake **9:**171
- - Hammath **7:**1242
- - history chart (235-1837) **8:**766-767
- - Jerusalem Talmud **15:**773
- - Meir Ba'al ha-Nes **11:**1246
- - pillars **13:**523
- - population, Ereẓ Israel **13:**872
- - statistics **1:**place list
- History
- - Crusader period **9:**267ff
- - Ereẓ Israel, 70 to 640 **9:**239ff
- - Ereẓ Israel, 634 to 1099 **9:**261ff
- - Justus of Tiberias **10:**480
- - Mamluk provinces **9:**274
- - Nasi, Joseph **16:**1535
- - Ottoman provinces **9:**284ff
- Communal Life
- - Abulafia, Hayyim **2:**188
- - academy **2:**202
- - Ashkenazi community **9:**497ff
- - Bena'ah's academy **4:**457
- - Berab, Jacob **4:**584
- - community **5:**809
- - emissaries **14:**1359ff
- - *ḥalukkah* **7:**1215
- - ḥasidic settlement **7:**1392
- - *mikveh* **11:**1541
- - pilgrimage center **8:**922
- - religious life **9:**890ff
- - Sephardi settlement **14:**1175
- - special Purim **13:**1399
- *illus:*
- - text
- - letter to Gibraltar community (1748) **7:**555
- - Ma'abarah **9:**530
- - Maimonides' tomb **11:**764
- - Meir Ba'al ha-Nes tomb **9:**27; **11:**1246
- - Palestine stamp **15:**332
- - seawall of Lake Kinneret **10:**1035
Tiberias, Lake, *see* KINNERET, LAKE
Tiberius (Rom. emp.)
- Antipas, Herod **3:**76
- Ashdod **3:**696
- history chart **8:**766-767
- Jews **14:**229
- Tiberias **15:**1131
- *illus:*
- - Pontius Pilate's inscription **3:**323
TIBERIUS JULIUS ALEXANDER (procurator) **15:**1135
- Jewish rebels **5:**1134; **16:**949
- Philo **6:**17; **13:**411
- Titus **15:**1168
Tibet **8:**1311
TIBNI (k., Isr.) **15:**1135
Tibnīn (Crus. fort.) **9:**269
- Mamluk provinces **9:**274
- Ottoman provinces **9:**284
TIBULLUS, ALBIUS **14:**232; **14:**236
Tiburino, Isaac **12:**1227
Tiburtinus, *see* Plato of Tivoli
Ticho, Abraham Albert **15:**1136
TICHO, ANNA **15:**1136
- *illus:*
- - text
- - "Jerusalem Hills" (drg.) Fig. 95 3-ART
Ticho, Josef **4:**1262
Tidal (Hittite k.) **7:**693
Tidericus Judeus, *see* Judeus, Tidericus
Tidhar (mosh., Isr.) **1:**place list
TIDHAR, DAVID **15:**1136
Tidsi (tn., Mor.) **15:**182
Tidsskrift for Jødisk Historie og Litteratur (period.) **13:**1048; **14:**697
Tieffenbach, E. W. **15:**143
Tiehberg, Judah Moses **2:**561
TIEMPO, CÉSAR **15:**1137
Tiempo de Jerusalém (journ.) **3:**426
Tienen (tn., Belg.), *see* Tirlemont
TIENTSIN (city, China) **15:**1137
- Jewish community **5:**470
Tiepolo (art.) **9:**69
"Tiergarten, Berlin" (drg., L. Ury) **16:**16
TIETZ (Ger. fam.) **15:**1137
Tietz, Alfred **15:**1138
Tietz, Georg **15:**1137
Tietz, Hermann **15:**1137
Tietz, Leonhardt **15:**1137
Tietz, Martin **15:**1137
Tietz, Oskar **15:**1137
Tiferet (kab. conc.) **10:**570ff
- *Shekhinah* **14:**1353
- Torah **15:**1237
Tif'eret Binyamin (stlmt., Bashan) **9:**596
Tifereth Israel (syn., Mass.) **16:**633
Tifereth Jerusalem (tal. acad., N.Y.) **12:**1120
Tifereth Zion (orgn., Braz.) **16:**1124
Tiferet Israel Yeshivah (Jer.) **9:**1480
Tiferet Sión (orgn., Arg.) **3:**423; **16:**1123
- Diskin, M. J. J. **6:**75
Tiferet Yisrael (bk.) **11:**293
Tiferet Yisrael synagogue (Jer.) **7:**1458
- Arab Legion **9:**1486
- Ruzhin, Israel of **14:**527
- *illus:*
- - general view **9:**1445
- - Jewish Quarter of Old City **9:**1480
Tifḥa' (cantillation sign), *see* *Ṭippeḥa'*
TIFLIS (city, Georgia) **15:**1138
- Georgia **7:**424
Tiflisites (sect) **2:**183; **7:**423
Tifraḥ (mosh., Isr.) **1:**place list
Tiger, Theobald, *see* TUCHOLSKY, KURT
Tiger Hill (ship) **15:**923
- *illus:*
- - off Tel Aviv **2:**634
Tiger weasel (zool.) **9:**226
Tighina (city, Bess.), *see* BENDERY
Tighina Agreement (anti-J. action) **15:**1333
Tiglath-Pileser I (k., Assyr.) **16:**1502
Tiglath-Pileser III (k., Assyr.) **16:**1503
- Ahaz **2:**455
- Ammonites **2:**857
- Arameans **3:**255
- Ashtaroth **3:**737
- Babylon **4:**31
- Chaldeans **5:**331
- Dor **6:**172
- Exile, Assyrian **6:**1034
- Hannathon **7:**1272
- history **8:**603ff
- Israel tax **14:**736
- Menahem **11:**1303
- Sargon II **14:**880
- Tema **15:**940
- Transjordan **15:**1317
- warfare **16:**273; **16:**277
Tigra (riv.), *see* TIGRIS
Tigranes (Herod's grands.) **7:**601
Tigranes (Herod's great-grands.) **5:**760
Tigranes (the Great; k., Arm.) **4:**37
Tigranes IV (k., Arm.) **3:**474
Tigranes V (k., Arm.) **3:**474
Tigre (reg., Eth.) **11:**1153
Tigrid, Pavel **13:**1026
Tigrinya (lang.) **6:**1149
- Semitic languages **11:**1153
TIGRIS (riv.) **15:**1139
- Garden of Eden **13:**78
- Mesopotamia **16:**1490
- ʿUkbarā **15:**1512
- *illus:*
- - Sumer **15:**513
Tihanyi, Lajos **13:**113
Tih Desert (Sinai penin.) **13:**88
Tikhlal (siddur, Yem.) **13:**985ff
Tikkanta Shabbat (prayer) **12:**187
Tikkun (kabb. conc.) **10:**547
- Ḥasidism **7:**1405; **7:**1408ff
- Lurianic cosmogony **10:**588; **10:**596ff
- Lurianic Kabbalah **11:**578
- mystical prayer **10:**629
Tikkunei ha-Zohar (kab. wk.) **16:**1194; **16:**1197
- *Kisse Melekh* **4:**1545
- symbolism of *menorah* **11:**1368
Tikkun ha-Geshem, see RAIN, PRAYER FOR
TIKKUN HAẒOT (midnight prayer) **15:**1139
- Ḥayyim ben Abraham ha-Kohen **7:**1507
- kabbalistic influence **10:**642
Tikkunim (kab. prayers) **16:**908
Tikkun Leah (prayer) **15:**1139
Tikkun Leil Hoshana Rabba (wk.) **8:**1028
Tikkun Leil Shavuot **2:**635; **14:**1322
Tikkun Middot ha-Nefesh (bk.) **7:**243
- Alexander stories **2:**579
- ethical instruction **6:**940
- Jewish literature **11:**343
- philosophy **13:**435
Tikkun olam (kab. conc.) **14:**635
Tikkun Raḥel (prayer) **15:**1139
Tikkun shovevim (fast days), *see* SHOVAVIM TAT
TIKKUN SOFERIM (text changes) **15:**1139
- euphemism and dysphemism **6:**960
- scribes **14:**1044
- *soferim* **15:**80
- *see also:* MASORAH
Tikkun Tal, see DEW, PRAYER FOR
TIKTIN (fam., Pol.) **15:**1140
Tiktin (vill., Pol.), *see* TYKOCIN
Tiktin, Abraham **15:**1140
- Bloch, Herman **4:**1101
- *illus:*
- - portrait **15:**1141
Tiktin, Gedaliah **15:**1140
- Breslau **4:**1355
- Eger, Akiva **6:**473; **14:**1299
- Shapira, Joshua Isaac **14:**1299
Tiktin, Heinrich **14:**399; **15:**1140
Tiktin, Menahem **2:**24
Tiktin, Solomon **15:**1140
- Bloch, Herman **4:**1101
- *illus:*
- - portrait **15:**1141
Tiktiner, Khaym, *see* SIEMIATYCKI, CHAIM
Tiktiner, Rebekah **11:**358; **11:**359
TIKTINSKI (Lith. fam.) **15:**1141
Tiktinski, Abraham (18/19 cent.) **15:**1141
- Mir **12:**71
Tiktinski, Abraham (19th cent.) **15:**1141
Tiktinski, Ḥayim Leib **15:**1141
Tiktinski, Samuel (18/19 cent.) **15:**1141
Tiktinski, Samuel (19th cent.) **15:**1141
Tikulti-Ninurta I (k., Mesop.) **12:**1166
Tikvatenu (poem) **7:**1472
Tikva Records (co.) **13:**1618
Tikvath Jisrael (period.) **13:**1035; **16:**1119
Til, S. van **8:**60
Tilapia (fish) **9:**785
Til Barsip (city, Mesop.) **4:**728
Tilinger, Zygmund **10:**1306
TILLICH, PAUL **15:**1142
Tillim, see PSALMS, BOOK OF
Tilmun (isl.), *see* BAHREIN
TIMAGENES OF ALEXANDRIA **7:**889; **7:**897
Timaru (port, N.Z.) **12:**1128
Timbrel (mus. instr.) **13:**1319
Time, *see* CHRONOLOGY
TIME AND ETERNITY **15:**1142
- emanation **6:**696
- Mendelssohn **11:**1330
- *Sefirot* doctrine **10:**568
- see also: DAY AND NIGHT
TIMENDORFER, BERTHOLD **15:**1143
TIMISOARA (city, Transyl.) **15:**1143
- Aguilar, Diego d' **2:**427
- Amigo family **2:**847
- Transylvania **15:**1342ff
- *illus:* text
Timius of Cyprus **5:**1181
Timmins (tn., Ont.) **12:**1408
Timmurim (mosh., Isr.) **1:**place list
TIMNA (reg., Isr.) **15:**1145
- copper deposit **9:**798ff
- Elath's economy **6:**569
- geology **9:**199ff
- metals **11:**1428; **11:**1431
- temple, Egyptian **14:**1192
- *illus:*
- - text
- - chemical composition of ore (chart) **9:**802
- - copper mines **5:**378; **9:**172-173
- - schematic columnar section of area **9:**799
- - sulfuric acid plant **9:**798
Timna, Mt. (Er. Isr.) **15:**1146
TIMNAH (city, Er. Isr.) **15:**1147
- Gofnah **7:**691
- Samson **14:**771
TIMNATH-HERES (city, Er. Isr.) **15:**1147
- Joshua **10:**265
- Simeon ha-Timni **14:**1566
Timnath-Serah (city, Er. Isr.), *see* TIMNATH HERES
TIMOCHARES (Gr. au.) **7:**897
Timofey, *see* KOPELSON, ẒEMAḤ
Timor, M. **6:**735
Timoshin, *see* KOPELSON, ẒEMAḤ
Timpul (*Di Tsayt;* newsp.) **14:**398
Tin (met.) **11:**1433ff
Tindal, Matthew **5:**1464
Tingis (tn., Mor.) *see* TANGIER(S)
Tingstadius, Johan Adam **14:**929
- Hebraists **8:**60
TINNEIUS RUFUS **15:**1148
- Bar Kokhba revolt **9:**247
- Jerusalem ceremony **9:**1405
Tin Quarter (Jer.), *see* Shevet Ẓedek
Tinshemet (zool.) **12:**1530
- chameleon **5:**333
Tintoretto, Jacopo (paint.) **2:**123,244; **10:**460; **15:**110
- *illus:*
- - "Susanna and the Elders" **15:**534

– – "Visit of the Queen of Sheba to Solomon" **15:** 105
Tiomkin, Dmitri **12:** 451
TIOMKIN, VLADIMIR (Ze'ev) **15:** 1148
– Hacohen, Mordecai **7:** 1039
– *illus:*
– – Odessa Committee convention **12:** 1329
– – Ukrainian Provisional National Council **15:** 1515
Tiphsah (city, Mesop.) **11:** 1302
– Davidic borders **9:** 116
Ṭippeḥa' (cantillation sign) **16:** 1439,1454
Tippeḥa-ʾetnaḥ (cantillation sign) **16:** 1439
Tippoo Sahib (sult., Mysore) **6:** 111
TĪRA, AL- (vill., Isr.) **15:** 1149
– eastern Sharon **9:** 575
– health centre **9:** 988
– *illus:*
– – medical centre **9:** 990
TIRADO, JACOB **15:** 1150
– Amsterdam **2:** 896
– Caceres, Francisco de **5:** 3
Tiran (isl., straits), *see* SHARM EL-SHEIKH, TIRAN ISLAND, and TIRAN STRAITS
Tiran Basin (Isr.) **9:** 152
TIRASPOL (city, Mold.) **15:** 1150
– concentration camp **12:** 1457
Tirat Karmel (Haifa sub., Isr.) **9:** 579
– statistics **1:** place list
Tirat Shalom (stlmt., Er. Isr.) **9:** 572
Tirat Yehudah (mosh., Isr.) **1:** place list
TIRAT ẒEVI (kib., Isr.) **15:** 1150
– statistics **1:** place list
– *illus:*
– – text
– – "tower and stockade" **8:** 757
TIRGU-FRUMOS (tn., Mold.) **15:** 1151
TIRGU NEAMT (tn., Mold.) **15:** 1151
TIRHAKAH (bib. fig.) **15:** 1152
Tirishkan, Mordecai **4:** 865
– *illus:*
– – *Emunah omen* (1846) **13:** 1111
Tirlemont (tn., Belg.) **4:** 416
Tirmidhī, Al- **7:** 1052
Tirosh (mosh., Isr.) **1:** place list
Tirso de Molina **15:** 248
Tirzah (bib. Fig.) **16:** 979
– in the Arts **14:** 917
TIRZAH (city, Er. Isr.) **15:** 1153
– Jewish architecture **3:** 336; **3:** 357
– Omri **12:** 1390
Tisch, Elijah **12:** 1245
TISCHLER, HANS **12:** 711
TISCHLER, MAX **5:** 388
Tischler, Victor **13:** 115
Tish, der (Ḥas. conc.) **7:** 1425
– ḥasidic *niggun* **7:** 1424
Tishah be-Av (fast day), *see* AV, THE NINTH OF
Tishbi (wk.) **11:** 134; **16:** 1360,1390
Tishbi, Judah ben Elijah **2:** 150
TISHBY, ISAIAH **15:** 1153
– Kabbalah studies **10:** 648
– Zohar **16:** 1215
TISHRI (month) **15:** 1154
– New Year **12:** 1061
– pilgrimages to Jerusalem **12:** 483
– Rosh ha-Shanah **14:** 306ff
– *illus:* text
– *see also:* CALENDAR
Tishvits (vill., Pol.), *see* TYSZOWCE
TISO, JOSEF **15:** 1155
Tissard (us), François **8:** 60
Tissenbaum, Mariano **10:** 1502
Tisza, Kálmán **15:** 1155
TISZAESZLAR (tn., Hung.) **15:** 1155
– Allianz **2:** 654
– Austrian anti-Semitism **3:** 896
– Bloch, Joseph Samuel **3:** 199
– history chart **8:** 766-767
– Kossuth **10:** 1219
TITANS (myth. figs.) **15:** 1156
TITHE **15:** 1156
– *Contents:*
– – General **15:** 1156
– – Way of Processing and Spending **15:** 1158
– – According to Pentateuchal Sources **15:** 1159
– – In the Deuteronomic Code **15:** 1160
– – Second Temple Period **15:** 1161
– *am ha-areẓ* **2:** 834; **4:** 737
– Commandments, the 613 **5:** 767,775
– *demai* **5:** 1486
– *Demai* tractate **5:** 1486
– economic history **16:** 1274
– fourth year fruit **12:** 13
– gifts, other **13:** 1088
– *ḥazakah* of *ḥaver* **7:** 1522
– *hefker* **8:** 244
– Judah ha-Nasi **9:** 252
– *ma'aser sheni* **9:** 1555; **11:** 652
– *Ma'asrot* tractate **11:** 651
– new year **12:** 1061
– Pentateuch **13:** 251
– proscription **8:** 1471
– recitation **11:** 392
– Syria **15:** 639
– Temple **15:** 957
– Tu bi-Shevat **15:** 1419
– *illus:*
– – selection of lambs **11:** 651
– – tithing of produce **5:** 1487
– *see also:* TERUMOT AND MA'ASEROT
TITHES, CHURCH **15:** 1162
TITIEV, MISCHA **15:** 1163
Title page **7:** 1452
– *see also:* BOOKS; HAKDAMAH; PRINTERS' MARKS
TITLES **15:** 1163
– "Jewish bishop" **15:** 1390
– rabbi, rav **13:** 1445
– Torah reading **15:** 1253
Titles (letter crowns), *see* TAGIN
Titles, Hebrew Book, *see* HEBREW BOOK TITLES
TITLES OF NOBILITY **15:** 1165
Tito, Josip Broz **13:** 508
Tittmann, Harold H. **8:** 911
TITUS, ARCH OF **15:** 1167
– pope and Jews **14:** 250
– ritual art on **3:** 524
– Temple *menorah* **11:** 1363
– Titus **15:** 1169
– *illus:*
– – text
– – *menorah* **11:** 1355
– – State of Israel emblem **11:** 1366
Titus, Roy V. **14:** 376
Titus Flavius Clemens (Ch. F.), *see* CLEMENT OF ALEXANDRIA
Titus Flavius Domitianus (Rom. emp.), *see* DOMITIAN
TITUS FLAVIUS VESPASIANUS (Rom. emp.) **15:** 1168
– Berenice **4:** 601
– Dio Cassius **6:** 58
– Flavia Domitilla **6:** 1338
– history chart **8:** 766-767
– Jerusalem capture **9:** 1399
– Jewish prisoners **5:** 1134
– Jews **14:** 229
– Josephus Flavius **10:** 254
– Kittim **10:** 1082
– landholdings expropriated **2:** 395
– Neapolis **7:** 438
– Otranto **12:** 1521
– Taranto **15:** 806
– Temple **15:** 959
– *illus:*
– – Arch of Titus **11:** 1355; **15:** 1167
– – coin, Judean **5:** 714
Titus Livius (Rom. hist.), *see* LIVY
Tivata (vill., Er. Isr.) **15:** 874
Tiverton (tn., R.I.) **14:** 143
Tivoli (fam.) **4:** 173
Tivoli, Jacob **6:** 498
TIVOLI, SERAFINO DA **15:** 1171
– Ancona **2:** 945
– art **3:** 565
TIVON (loc., Er. Isr.) **15:** 1172
– Haifa **7:** 1134
– Hebrew pronunciation **16:** 1595
Tivra' (cantillation sign), *see Tevir*
Tivveryah, *see* TIBERIAS
Tiyāha, Al- (Bedouin tribe) **9:** 593
Tiyout (tn., Mor.) **15:** 182
Tizenkét Röpirat (period.) **9:** 1099
Tieker (people, Er. Isr.) **13:** 399
Tjeku (tn., Egy.) **13:** 566
TKATCH, MEIR ZIMEL **15:** 1172
– Second Temple period
Tkhine (Yid. prayer) **16:** 803
TLEMCEN (city, Alg.) **15:** 1172
– Agadir **2:** 340
– Alashkar, Joseph **2:** 511
– Al-Nakawa, Ephraim **2:** 672
– Ankawa, Abraham **3:** 25
– Inquisition refugees **16:** 1186
– Sasportas' appointment **13:** 1449; **15:** 1179
– Tunisia **15:** 1439
– *illus:* text
Tlomats (tn., Ukr.), *see* TLUMACH
Tlomatske 13, *see* Society for Jewish Writers and Journalists
TLUMACH (Tlumacz; tn., Ukr.) **15:** 1174
Tluste (tn., Ukr.), *see* TOLSTOYE
Tmanyini (slave traders) **3:** 415ff
TNUVA (coop., Isr.) **15:** 1174
– Histadrut **8:** 539
– labor economy **9:** 855; **9:** 862
– *illus:* text
Toad, *see* FROG
TOAFF (fam.) **15:** 1175
Toaff, Alfredo Sabato **15:** 1175
Toaff, Elio **15:** 1176
To'afot Re'em (wk.) **9:** 1084
Toasts (drinking) **16:** 540
Toaty (fam.), *see* Tuati
To'avat Miẓrayim (abominations) **2:** 97
TOB (bib. loc.) **15:** 1176
– Kerak **10:** 911
TOBACCO TRADE AND INDUSTRIES **15:** 1176
– Amsterdam Jews **2:** 897
– Baron, Bernhard **4:** 251
– economy of Israel **9:** 851
– excise duty **9:** 749,750
– ḥasidic attitude **7:** 1405
– Israel industry **9:** 823
– New York City **12:** 1084
Tobago, *see* Trinidad and Tobago
TOBENKIN, ELIAS **10:** 318
Tobey, Barney **5:** 220
Tobey, Dave **15:** 303,304
Tobi (schol., Babyl.) **11:** 1132
TOBIADS (fam.) **15:** 1178
– inscriptions **8:** 295; **16:** 668
– Jason and Menelaus **8:** 295
– Jerusalem **9:** 1389; **9:** 1390
– Second Temple period **8:** 627
– salvation **11:** 1408
– war and warfare **16:** 278
– *illus:*
– – palace ruins **3:** 338
– *see also:* Joseph Son of Tobiah
Tobiah (bib. fig.) **8:** 620ff; **8:** 627; **15:** 1179
Tobiah (3rd cent.B.C.E.) **8:** 627; **15:** 1179
Tobiah (15th cent. physic.) **15:** 1374
Tobiah, Land of (Transj.) **15:** 1178
Tobiah ben Daniel **12:** 857; **15:** 123
Tobiah ha-Levi **2:** 142
Tobiah the Physician (tal. fig.) **14:** 1657
Tobias (Apoc. fig.) **2:** 461; **15:** 1184
– *geneal. table:* **2:** 461
– *illus:*
– – return of **15:** 1185
TOBIAS, ABRAHAM **15:** 1180
Tobias, Isaac **15:** 1181
TOBIAS, JOSEPH **15:** 1181
TOBIAS, MOSES **15:** 1181
TOBIAS, PHILLIP VALLENTINE **15:** 1181
– anthropology **3:** 39
Tobias, Reuben **11:** 1286
Tobias, Captain William **11:** 880
Tobias ben Eliezer
– Bulgaria **4:** 1481
– Greece **7:** 873
– literature **11:** 322
– *Midrash Lekaḥ Tov* **11:** 1516
Tobias ben Elijah of Vienne **6:** 261; **16:** 133
Tobias ben Joseph **14:** 525
TOBIAS BEN MOSES HA-AVEL (Or ha-Ma'tik) **15:** 1182
– al-Baṣīr **4:** 301ff
– Avelei Zion **3:** 946
Tobias the physician, *see* COHN, TOBIAS BEN MOSES
Tobijah (bib. fig.) **15:** 980; **16:** 955
TOBIT, BOOK OF **15:** 1183
– Aḥikar the Wise **2:** 460
– Dead Sea scrolls **5:** 1402
– Hellenistic influence **8:** 298
– Hellenistic literature **8:** 304
– inheritance law **15:** 475
– lost tribe **15:** 1004
– magic **11:** 706
– Muenster's translation **12:** 506
– salvation **11:** 1408
– Septuagint **4:** 852
– wisdom **16:** 557; **16:** 560
– *illus:*
– – text
– – finding himself blind **16:** 689
"Tobit and the Angel Raphael" (paint., Pollaiuolo) **15:** 1184
Tobler, Oscar, *see* Jackson, Willie
Tobler, Titus **9:** 1521
Tobolsk (city., Sib.) **14:** 1486ff
Tobriner, Matthew **5:** 56; **14:** 834
TOBY, JACKSON **5:** 1110; **5:** 1113
TOCH, ERNST **15:** 1187
Toch, Herman **8:** 1430
TOCH, MAXIMILIAN **5:** 388
TOCHNER, MESHULLAM **15:** 1187
TODD, MIKE **12:** 474
– theater **15:** 1059
Todesco, Aaron Hirschl, *see* Wellisch, Aaron Hirschl
Todesco, Eduard **15:** 1188
TODESCO, HERMANN **15:** 1187
– textiles **15:** 1040
Todesco, Moritz **15:** 1188
Todos Ish Romi, *see* THEODOSIUS OF ROME
Todros ben Meshullam of Arles **3:** 469
Todros ben Samuel ha-Levi **14:** 1079
Todros Todrosi (trans.) **3:** 958; **15:** 1321
To'eleth Society (soc., Amst.), *see* Tongeleth circle
TOEPLITZ, OTTO **11:** 1126
To'evah, see ABOMINATION
Tof (drum) **12:** 565
Tofaḥ (meas.), *see Tefaḥ*
Toferei Begadim (syn., Istanbul) **15:** 1461
Tofeus Dobos, Mihály **8:** 60
Tofteh Arukh (poem) **16:** 909
Tog (newsp.), *see* JEWISH DAY
Togarmah (bib. loc.) **3:** 473

Togarmi, Baruch Shel'iaḥ-Ẓibbur, *see* Baruch Shel'iaḥ-Ẓibbur Togarmi
Togblat (period.) **11**:612
Togo (rep., Afr.) **9**:442
Tog un Nakht (wk.) **13**:321
Toḥelet (stlmt., Isr.) **1**:place list
TOHORAH (cleansing of dead) **15**:1188
- *illus:* text
TOHOROT (Mish. order) **15**:1189
TOHOROT (tract.) **15**:1190
- *illus:* text
TOHOROT HA-KODESH (bk.) **15**:1191
- Shabbateanism **14**:1248
To'im (wanderers) **5**:1135
Tojbenfeld, Konrad **6**:250
TOKAT (city, Anatolia) **15**:1191
Tokhaḥah, see REBUKE AND REPROOF
Tokhaḥat Megulah (wk.) **5**:61
TOKHEḤAH (bib. sections) **15**:1192
Tokheḥot Musar (wk.) **6**:1123
Tokhen Ezra (bk.), *see Horayat ha-Kore*
TOKYO **15**:1192
- Japan **9**:1281ff
- *illus:*
- - Jewish Community Center **9**:1281
- - synagogue **9**:1283
Tola (bib. figs.) **6**:329
- judge **10**:448
- son of Puah **9**:1076
Tola'at shani, see CRIMSON WORM
TOLAND, JOHN **15**:1193
- defense of Judaism **3**:198
- on Jews **5**:1464
- tolerance **8**:706ff
Tolansky, Samuel **13**:490
Tolcsva (tn., Hung.) **3**:730; **7**:626
Told (pseud.), *see* FEIWEL, BERTHOLD
TOLEDANO (fam.) **15**:1193
- Meknes **11**:1272
- *geneal. table:* text
Toledano, Aaron **15**:1195; **15**:792
Toledano, Abraham ben Aaron **15**:1195; **15**:792
Toledano, Abraham ben Baruch **15**:1194
Toledano, Baruch **15**:1196
Toledano, Baruch ben Joseph **15**:1193
Toledano, Culeman ben Abraham, *see* Toledano, Solomon ben Abraham
Toledano, Daniel (16/17 cent.) **15**:1193
Toledano, Daniel (17th cent.) **15**:1193
Toledano, Daniel ben Ḥayyim (17th cent.) **15**:1193
Toledano, Daniel ben Ḥayyim (17/18 cent.) **2**:516; **15**:1194
Toledano, Eliezer ben Jacob **8**:1325; **11**:303
- *illus:*
- - *Ḥiddushei ha-Torah* **8**:1329
- - *Perush ha-Berakhot ve-ha-Tefillot* **11**:301
Toledano, Eliezer ben Judah **15**:1194
Toledano, Ḥabib (17th cent.) **15**:1193
Toledano, Ḥabib (17/18 cent.) **15**:1194
Toledano, Ḥabib ben Eliezer **15**:1196
Toledano, Ḥayyim (17th cent.) **15**:1193
Toledano, Ḥayyim (17/18 cent.) **15**:1194
Toledano, Ḥayyim ben Baruch **15**:1194
Toledano, Ḥayyim ben Ḥabib **15**:1194
Toledano, Ḥayyim ben Joseph **15**:1196
Toledano, Ḥayyim ben Judah **15**:1195
Toledano, Ḥayyim ben Moses ben Baruch **15**:1194
Toledano, Jacob (Ma-ha-rit) **15**:1195
Toledano, Jacob ben Moses **15**:1197
TOLEDANO, JACOB MOSES **15**:1197
- *geneal. table:* **15**:1196
Toledano, Joseph (17th cent.) **4**:1461; **15**:1193
Toledano, Joseph (18th cent.) **15**:1196
Toledano, Joseph ben Daniel **15**:1194
Toledano, Judah **15**:1197
Toledano, Maimon **15**:1194
Toledano, Meir **15**:1196
Toledano, Moses (17/18 cent.) **15**:1194
Toledano, Moses (18th cent.) **15**:1196
Toledano, Moses ben Baruch **15**:1193; **15**:792
Toledano, Moses ben Daniel **15**:1195
Toledano, Moses ben Ḥayyim **15**:1194
Toledano, Raphael Baruch ben Jacob **15**:1197
Toledano, Samuel **15**:792
Toledano, Solomon **15**:1196
Toledano, Solomon ben Abraham **11**:1442
Toledano, Solomon ben Eliezer **15**:1195
Toledano, Zacheo **11**:303
TOLEDO (city, Cast.) **15**:1198
- *Contents:*
- - Early Jewish Settlement and Visigothic Period **15**:1198
- - The Jewish Quarter **15**:1198
- - Jewish Edifices and Ancient Remnants **15**:1199
- - Period of Muslim Rule **15**:1200
- - The Persecutions of 1391 **15**:1204
- - The Conversos of Toledo **15**:1205
- Abulafia, Samuel **2**:193
- Abulafia, Todros **2**:194
- Al-Nakawa **2**:672
- Inquisition **8**:1383
- Kabbalah **10**:524
- museum **12**:544
- Spain **15**:226
- synagogue **15**:611
- trade and commerce **15**:1300
- *takkanot* **15**:736
- Talavera de la Reina **15**:739
- *illus:*
- - text
- - Abulafia, Samuel, residence **2**:193
- - El Transito synagogue **3**:520; **15**:613
- - Santa Maria la Blanca synagogue **8**:685; **15**:612
TOLEDO (city, Ohio) **15**:1206
- Ohio **12**:1344
Toledo, Abraham de (poet)
- Bible in art **4**:933
- children's literature **5**:446
- Ladino **10**:1349
- literature **11**:358
- on Joseph **10**:213
- Sephardi literature **14**:1169
Toledo, Councils of **3**:170; **5**:546ff
- third **15**:220
- fourth **15**:1201; **15**:220
- sixth **15**:220
- eighth **15**:221
- tenth **15**:221
- twelfth **15**:221
- sixteenth **15**:222
- seventeenth **15**:1198; **15**:223
TOLEDO, MOSES DE **15**:1207
Toledot Adam (wk.) **2**:307
Toledot Aharon (wk.) **2**:23
TOLEDOT HA-ARI (wk.) **15**:1207
Toledot ha-Emunah ha-Yisre'elit (wk.) **16**:1349
Toledot ha-Sifrut ha-Ivrit ha-Ḥadashah (bk.) **10**:1339
Toledot Ya'akov Yosef (wk.) **7**:1392; **7**:1413; **9**:1056
- *illus:*
- title page (1780) **8**:960
TOLEDOT YESHU (wk.) **15**:1208
- Amulo **2**:915
- fiction, Hebrew **6**:1266
- Reuchlin, Johannes **14**:109
- suppressed in Spain **15**:238
TOLERANZPATENT (edict of tolerance) **15**:1209
- Austria **3**:892ff
- Galicia **16**:1326
- Joseph II **10**:218
- Moses Mendelssohn **11**:1335
- Vienna **16**:123
- *illus:*
- - text
- - medal **10**:218
- *see also:* FAMILIANTS LAWS
Tolerierte (tolerated Js., Aus.) **3**:892
Tolidah, al- (wk.) **14**:750,751; **14**:754
Tolkowsky, Dan **15**:1211
TOLKOWSKY, SHEMUEL **15**:1211
TOLLER, ERNST **15**:1211
- *illus:* text
Tolner, Yossele **15**:779
Tolosa, Vidal de **16**:136
Tolstoy, Count D. **13**:696
Tolstoy, Leo Nikolayevich **14**:508
- Berg **4**:607
- Epstein, Zalman **6**:837
- Gordon, Aharon **7**:792
TOLSTOYE (tn., Ukr.) **15**:1212
TOLUSH (writ.) **15**:1213
Tolvens, Arricha de, *see* Hollaender, Victor
TOMA, A. **14**:422; **14**:428
- Rumania **14**:414
TOMAR (city, Port.) **15**:1213
Tomashefsky, Boris, *see* THOMASHEFSKY, BORIS
Tomashov, M.B. **12**:1118
Tomashover Vokhenblat (newsp.) **15**:1215
TOMASHPOL (tn., Ukr.) **15**:1213
TOMASZOW LUBELSKI (tn., Pol.) **15**:1214
TOMASZOW MAZOWIECKI (city, Pol.) **15**:1214
- ghetto **13**:767
TOMBS AND TOMBSTONES **15**:1215
- *Contents:*
- - Tombstones **15**:1218
- - Art **15**:1222
- Tombs
- - David's dynastic tomb **9**:1382; **9**:1383
- - Herod **9**:1398
- - impurity **13**:1409
- - Jerusalem **9**:1393; **9**:1398
- - Jerusalem archaeology **9**:1525; **9**:1532
- - Kings **9**:1459
- - Helena of Adiabene **8**:288
- - Izates II **9**:1158
- - Mary, Church of **9**:1416
- - *menorah* **11**:1368
- - Mount of Olives **12**:484
- - Omar, Covenant of **12**:1379
- - Petra **13**:343
- - pillar **13**:522ff
- - Rachel **13**:1486
- - Virgin **8**:936
- Tombstones
- - Aden **2**:262
- - art, Jewish **3**:535
- - epitaphs **6**:818
- - holy places in Israel **8**:922
- - Lieben, Koppelman **11**:215
- - priestly engravings **13**:1062
- - Rome **14**:250
- - Toledo **15**:1199
- *illus:*
- - text
- - Abendana, Isaac Sardo **2**:67
- - Aboab Cardozo, Abigail **3**:527; **14**:1061
- - Al-Dayr, Petra **13**:341
- - Arab Legion desecration **9**:1485
- - Babel, Menachem **12**:1320
- - Basle **15**:555
- - Bet She'arim, Greek epitaph **6**:821
- - Brandys nad Laben **4**:1307
- - Calabria **5**:33
- - Castro, Mordochay Namias de **12**:994
- - Chernovtsy cemetery **5**:276
- - Crémieux, Isaac Adolphe **5**:1076
- - Daniel (Susa) **13**:302
- - Delmedigo, Joseph Solomon **5**:1480
- - Deutsch de la Meurthe, Henri **5**:1593
- - Elijah Gaon, Vilna **6**:654
- - Ephraim ben Israel al-Nakawa **15**:1173
- - Gans, David ben Solomon **5**:1198; **7**:311
- - German (1427) **3**:527
- - grave of a kohen, Prague (1786) **3**:528
- - Gruzdžiai (Lith.) cemetery **11**:365
- - Herzl, Theodor **8**:421
- - Ibrahim Tushtumur Mausoleum, Jerusalem **9**:1424
- - Jassy, old cemetery **9**:1294
- - Jericho, Middle Bronze Age **8**:571
- - Jerusalem
- - - Daughter of Pharaoh Tomb **9**:1526
- - - Mount of Olives cemetery **5**:273; **9**:1485
- - Joden Savanne **15**:530
- - Keysville, Calif. **15**:1599
- - Krochmal, Nachman **10**:1270
- - León tombstone **15**:225
- - Levi Isaac of Berdichev **11**:103
- - lion motif **11**:267
- - London, Ashkenazi cemetery **11**:473
- - Magna Graecia catacombs **2**:697
- - Maimonides **11**:764
- - Mainz (11th cent.) **2**:725
- - Mareshah, painting in Hellenistic tomb **11**:953
- - Mary, mother of Jesus **9**:1417
- - Marx, Karl **11**:1073
- - Meir Ba'al ha-Ness **9**:276; **11**:1246; **13**:1132
- - Meir ben Baruch of Rothenburg **11**:1250
- - Meisel, Mordecai **11**:1262
- - Mendes, Catulle **11**:1344
- - Meshullam ben Kalonymus **10**:719; **11**:1402
- - Monteverde catacomb epitaph **2**:723
- - Mount Herzl military cemetery **9**:368
- - Mt. Scopus sarcophagus **12**:1505
- - Nabi Shu'ayb **10**:20

- - Orléans epitaph **12:**1469
- - Prague
- - - ancient Jewish cemetery **5:**273
- - - pharmacists' guild sign **7:**973
- - - Zalman Ḥayyat (1629) **7:**971
- - Rabat, Malta **11:**831
- - Rachel **13:**1489
- - Rome, old Jewish cemetery **5:**271
- - Salonika, memorial to Nazi victims **7:**882
- - Samaria sarcophagus **12:**1505
- - Shabbetai ben Meir ha-Kohen **14:**1218
- - Shabbethai ha-Parnas **3:**890
- - Shalom Shakhna ben Joseph **14:**1287
- - Simeon bar Yoḥai **14:**1552
- - Simeon the Just **14:**1567
- - Strasbourg **15:**422
- - Taranto **3:**227; **9:**1123; **15:**807
- - Tauberbischofsheim cemetery **15:**833
- - Texeira, Samuel Senior **3:**54
- - Tortosa **2:**722; **15:**1270
- - Warsaw cemetery **13:**782
- - Wiener Neustadt **16:**504
- - Worms cemetery **16:**645
- - Yevanic square script **2:**723
- - Zechariah **9:**1392
- - Zemun cemetery **16:**990
- *see also:* BURIAL; CATACOMBS; CEMETERY; EPITAPHS
Tomekhei Temimim (yeshivah, Rus.) **14:**1435
Tomen (meas.) **16:**388
Tomer, Ben-Zion **6:**207
Tommaseo, Niccolò **9:**1128
Tomor (publ. firm, Vilna) **13:**1376
TOMSK (city, Rus.) **15:**1233
- Siberian Jews **14:**1486ff
Toms River (vill., N. J.) **12:**1030
Tongeleth circle (soc., Amst.) **2:**900; **12:**516
Tonypandy (tn., Wales) **16:**251
Toolamba (dist., Austr.) **11:**1286
Tooth (leg. conc.), *see* AVOT NEZIKIN; *Shen*
Toowoomba (tn., Austr.) **3:**878; **4:**1377
Top, Alexander **8:**60
TOPARCHY (admin. dist.) **15:**1234
Topaz (precious stone) **13:**1009
Topography of Israel, *see* PHYSIOGRAPHY OF ISRAEL
TOPOL, CHAIM **15:**1234
- *illus:*
- - in *Sallah Shabbati* **12:**457
TOPOLCANY (tn., Cz.) **15:**1234
- Czechoslovakia **5:**1202
TOPOLEVSKY, GREGORIO **15:**1235
Topovske Supe (internment camp) **8:**858
Toppel, Eta **15:**1071
TORAH **15:**1235
- *Contents:*
- - The Term **15:**1235
- - Origin and Preexistence **15:**1236
- - Nature and Purpose **15:**1238
- General
- - authority of interpretation **3:**908
- - Commandments, the 613 **5:**763ff
- - gentiles **12:**1189
- - *Kinyan Torah* **3:**984
- - letters of alphabet **2:**748ff
- - masorah **16:**1404
- - Pentateuch **13:**261
- - preceded Christianity **9:**1378
- - ritual and customs **3:**68
- - Tabernacle **15:**687
- - term **5:**1574
- - *zaken mamre* **16:**920
- Theology **15:**1104
- - belief as dogma **3:**655ff
- - Divine character **7:**646ff
- - Elijah ben Solomon **6:**654
- - evil inclination **7:**776
- - interpretations by God **2:**208
- - Jewish philosophy **13:**421
- - Judaism **10:**383ff
- - kabbalistic doctrine **10:**619ff
- - logos **11:**461ff
- - Lurianic cosmogony **10:**591ff
- - Maimonides **13:**442
- - man's nature **11:**845
- - Philo **13:**427
- - revelation **8:**992; **14:**119ff
- - Saadiah **13:**431
- - Sadducees and Pharisees **14:**621
- - sages **14:**640
- - tradition **15:**1308
- - Yudghanites **16:**868
- *illus:*
- - Torah scribe **8:**771
- *see also:* BIBLE; ORAL LAW
TORAH, READING OF **15:**1246
- *Contents:*
- - History **15:**1246
- - The Reading of the Torah Today **15:**1248
- - The Laws and Customs of Reading the Torah **15:**1253
- General
- - Cairo *genizah* **16:**1338
- - candles **5:**117
- - festive meal **10:**1565
- - *megillah* **11:**1228
- - *nagid* **12:**762
- - Ottoman Empire **16:**1542
- - Samaritans **14:**741ff
- - Shabbetai Ẓevi **14:**1228
- - title **13:**1445
- Reading and Translation
- - Bashyazi, Menahem **4:**297
- - Bible chant **12:**583
- - Falashas **6:**1148
- - *Ḥazak, Ḥazak ve-Nitḥazzek* **7:**1516
- - Ibn Quraysh, Judah **8:**1193
- - Karaite tradition **10:**784
- - liturgy **11:**394; **11:**402
- - Mahalla Al-Kubra **11:**723
- - masoretic accents **11:**1098; **16:**1406
- - *mishmarot* **12:**91; **12:**92
- - Targum **4:**841; **15:**811
- - *tokheḥah* **4:**1087; **15:**1192
- - *yad* **16:**692
- Law
- - blindness **4:**1091
- - cemetery prohibition **5:**272
- - gamblers **7:**300
- - head covering **8:**5
- - interruption **4:**1061ff
- - minimum age **4:**244
- - *minyan* **12:**67
- - mourner **12:**491
- - synagogue **15:**580ff
- - *tallit* **15:**744
- - vows **16:**228
- Occasions
- - Day of Atonement **5:**1379
- - fastdays **6:**1192
- - festivals **6:**1246
- - *Hakhel* **7:**1149
- - markets and fairs **11:**1002
- - Simḥat Torah **14:**1571ff
- - Sukkot **15:**497
- Aliyah
- - *aufrufen* **3:**849
- - benediction **4:**1036
- - birth of a girl **5:**426
- - bridegroom **11:**1042; **11:**1043; **11:**1044
- - bridegrooms of the Law **4:**1370
- - collections **14:**1364
- - *gomel* **7:**768
- - *maftir* **11:**685
- - *Mi she-Berakh* **12:**86
- - order of **7:**594
- - priest's priority **13:**1089ff
- - societies **8:**441
- *illus:*
- - text
- - bridegrooms of the Law, chairs **4:**1370
- - Kaifeng synagogue **5:**471
- - pointer *(yad)* **5:**295
- - *Porta Accentuum* (1715) **5:**128,129
- - triennial cycle (chart) **15:**1387
- *mus. notations:*
- - Italian rite cantillation **9:**1143
- - masoretic accents **11:**1100-1112
- *see also:* CANTILLATION; HAFTARAH; TRIENNIAL CYCLE
Torah, study of, *see* STUDY
Torah and Labor (mvmt.), *see* TORAH VA-AVODAH
Torah im derekh ereẓ (conc.), *see* *Torah ve-derekh ereẓ*
Torah Judaism, Movement for, *see* Movement for Torah Judaism
Torah lo ba-Shamayim (conc.) **3:**907; **3:**908
Torah mantle **15:**1260-1261
Torah min ha-Shamayim (conc.) **3:**907 **14:**120
Torah mi-Ẓiyyon (journ.) **1:**newsp. list; **2:**599
Torah Or (wk.) **10:**285
Torah Or academy (Holl.) **4:**1461
TORAH ORNAMENTS **15:**1255
- art **3:**524ff
- breastplate **4:**1335
- ceremonial art **5:**288
- crown **5:**1132
- desecration of **15:**585
- folklore **6:**1395
- *mitpaḥat* **4:**1228
- *yad* **16:**692
- *illus:*
- - text
- - binder **5:**291
- - breastplates **3:**542; **4:**1345; **5:**296; **11:**271; **15:***fcg.* 1259, *fcg.* 1262
- - cases **5:**289,472,473; **15:**1260-1261
- - crowns **3:**640; **5:**293, 1132; **11:**270; **14:**1649; **15:**1260-1261
- - mantle **5:**291; **15:**1260-1261
- - *parokhet* **3:**531; **5:**297,961; **9:**1187; **11:**273; **12:**549; **15:**1256,1260-1261
- - *rimmonim* **3:**530; **4:**1527; **5:**291,1444; **11:**269; **12:**725; **13:**311; **15:**1260-1261
- - *yad* **5:**295; **11:**267; **15:***fcg.* 1259; **16:**693
- - *see also:* CEREMONIAL OBJECTS
Torah Or ve-Derekh Ḥayyim (wk.) **4:**1388
Torah Scroll, *see* SEFER TORAH
Torah she-be-al Peh, see ORAL LAW
Torah she-bi-Khetav, see BIBLE; TORAH
Torah Shelemah (wk.) **10:**807
Torah Temimah (wk.) **6:**825
TORAH UMESORAH (educ. soc.) **15:**1259
TORAH VA-AVODAH (mvmt.) **15:**1259
- Great Britain **6:**449
- Ha-Po'el ha-Mizrachi **7:**1320
- kibbutz movement **10:**973
- Landau, Shemuel **10:**1398
Torah Vadaath (tal. college, N. Y.) **12:**1120
Torah ve-derekh ereẓ (conc.) **12:**1488
- Hirsch, S. R. **8:**510
- Rabbinical Seminary **13:**1459
- *yeshivot* **16:**771
Torai, H. **12:**765
Torat Emet (bk.) **16:**1454
Torat Ereẓ-Yisrael (journ.) **1:**newsp. list
Torat ha-Adam (wk.) **12:**781
Torat ha-Areẓ (journ.) **1:**newsp. list
Torat ha-Bayit (wk.) **2:**308
- codification of law **5:**644; **11:**334
- *illus:*
- - title page (Venice, 1607) **8:**76
Torat ha-Bayit ha-Kaẓer (wk.) **2:**308
Torat ha-Olah (wk.) **9:**1084
Torat Ḥattat (wk.) **5:**650; **9:**1083
Torat Ḥayyim (wk.) **7:**1512
Torat Kohanim (bib. bk.), *see* LEVITICUS, BOOK OF
Torat Kohanim (Mid. wk.), *see* SIFRA
TORBERG, FRIEDRICH **15:**1259
TORCHIN (Torczyn; tn., Ukr.) **15:**1259
Torczyner, Harry, *see* TUR-SINAI, NAPHTALI HERZ
Torda (tn., Transyl.), *see* TURDA
Torelli, Achille **9:**1105
Torgau (city, Ger.) **14:**923
Torgoff, Irving **15:**303
Toriel, Solomon **16:**787
Torino (city, It.), *see* TURIN
Tormah (tn., Er. Isr.), *see* RUMAH or ARUMAH
Tornimpapte, Alessandra, *see* GINZBURG, NATALIA
TORONTO (city, Can.) **15:**1260
- museum **12:**551
- *illus:*
- - text
- - Associated Hebrew Schools building **5:**107
- - Holy Blossom Temple **5:**106
TORQUEMADA, TOMÁS DE **15:**1264
- history chart **8:**766-767
- Inquisition **8:**1383ff
- Spain **15:**240
- *illus:* text
TORRE, ALFONSO DE LA **15:**1266
Torre, Joseph della **16:**131
Torre, Lelio Della **4:**878
Torre de Moncorvo (tn., Port.), *see* MONCORVO
Torres, David **2:**622
TORRÈS, HENRY **15:**1266
- Schwarzbard, Shalom **14:**1027
TORRES, LUIS DE **15:**1266
- America **2:**808
- travels **15:**1349
TORREY, CHARLES CUTLER **15:**1267
- Isaiah **9:**45
Torriano, C. **8:**60
Torrutiel, Abraham of, *see* Abraham of Torrutiel
"Torso (Construction)" (sculp., A. Pevsner) **13:**349
TORTOISE (zool.) **15:**1267
- dietary laws **6:**36
TORTOSA (city, Sp.) **15:**1268
- *illus:*
- - text
- - Hebrew epitaph **2:**722
TORTOSA, DISPUTATION OF **15:**1270
- General
- - apologetics **3:**196
- - confrontation **6:**92
- - history chart **8:**766-767
- - messianism **11:**1410
- - Saragossa **14:**862
- - Spain **15:**238ff
- - Tortosa **15:**1270
- Principals
- - Abbas, Moses **2:**39
- - Astruc ha-Levi **3:**810

-- Benedict XIII **4:**482
-- Ferrer, Vicente **6:**1236
-- Lorki, Joshua **11:**494
- Effects
-- Alcañiz Jews **2:**542
-- Alcolea Jews **2:**549
-- Barbastro Jews **4:**207
-- Gerona Jews **7:**506
- Literature **11:**355
-- Albo, Joseph **2:**535; **2:**536
-- *Shevet Yehudah* **8:**557
- *illus:*
-- "Vicente Ferrer Preaching" (paint., Morone) **6:**1235
TORTS **15:**1272
- *Contents:*
-- Principal Categories **15:**1272
-- The Basis of Liability-Negligence **15:**1273
-- No Liability Where no Negligence Exists **15:**1274
-- Indirect Damage **15:**1276
-- Unusual Damage by Cattle **15:**1276
-- Defenses to Negligence **15:**1276
-- Damage Committed by the Person and by his Property **15:**1276
-- Joint Tortfeasors **15:**1276
-- Israel Law **15:**1277
- *avot nezikin* **3:**986
- bailees **14:**1455
- Commandments, the 613 **5:**771
- condemned person **13:**961
- consecrated property **8:**280
- domains **14:**83
- execution **6:**1011
- gentile **7:**412
- lien **11:**228,229
- moral liability **12:**113
- nuisance **12:**1246
- obligations **12:**1311ff
- pleas **13:**631
- slaves **14:**1659
- *takkanah* **15:**715
- tractate *Nezikin* **12:**1132
- unjust enrichment **15:**1683
- waiver **11:**1232
- *see also:* DAMAGES; LIABILITY
Torture, *see* ORDEAL
TORUN (port, Pol.) **15:**1277
- concentration camp **15:**464
- Czechoslovakia **5:**1192
Toruńczyk, Henryk **13:**776
TOSAFOT (comments.) **15:**1278
- General
-- attitude toward Gentiles **7:**412
-- codification of law **5:**645
-- Dampierre yeshivah **16:**764
-- *hassagot* **7:**1466
-- *ḥiddushim* **8:**465; **8:**466
-- history chart **8:**766-767
-- Jerusalem Talmud **15:**776
-- literature, Jewish **11:**329
-- mishnaic Hebrew **16:**1591
-- Naḥmanides **12:**774,778
-- period of **5:**1143
-- Urbach's studies **16:**4
- Tosafists
-- Abraham of Toul **15:**1285
-- Asher ben Jehiel **3:**707
-- Avigdor ben Elijah ha-Kohen **3:**963
-- Baruch of Mainz **4:**280
-- Baruch of Worms **4:**278
-- David of Metz **11:**1450
-- Elhanan of Dampierre **6:**611
-- Eliezer of Bonn **6:**626
-- Eliezer of Chinon **5:**475
-- Eliezer of Metz **6:**628
-- Eliezer of Toul **6:**631
-- Eliezer of Touques **6:**631
-- Eliezer of Verona **6:**629
-- Elijah of Paris **6:**648
-- Ephraim of Regensburg **6:**812
-- Ezra of Montcontour **6:**1124
-- Ḥayyim ha-Kohen **7:**1508
-- Hezekiah of Magdeburg **8:**458
-- Isaac ben Abraham **9:**14
-- Isaac ben Meir **9:**23
-- Isaac ben Mordecai **9:**25
-- Isaac ha-Levi **9:**16
-- Isaac ha-Zaken **9:**31
-- Isaac of Chinon **5:**475
-- Isaac of Corbeil **9:**21
-- Isaac of Evreux **9:**38
-- Isaac of Prague **9:**20
-- Israel ben Joel **9:**1058
-- Jacob ben Joseph **16:**109
-- Jacob ha-Lavan **13:**339
-- Jacob of Chinon **5:**475
-- Jacob of Corbeil **9:**1233
-- Jacob of Coucy **12:**418
-- Jacob of Marvege **9:**1233
-- Jacob of Orleans **9:**1234
-- Jacob Tam **15:**779
-- Jehiel of Paris **9:**1312
-- Joseph Bekhor Shor **4:**410
-- Joseph Kara **10:**759
-- Joseph of Clisson **10:**226
-- Joseph of Troyes **10:**234
-- Judah ben Isaac **10:**345
-- Judah ben Kalonymus ben Meir **10:**348
-- Judah ben Kalonymus ben Moses **9:**20
-- Judah ben Nathan **10:**351
-- Judah ben Yom Tov **9:**23
-- Judah of Corbeil **9:**1233
-- Judah Segre **14:**1112
-- Mattathias of Chinon **5:**475
-- Meir of Ramerupt **11:**1255
-- Meir of Rothenburg **11:**1247
-- Meshullam of Melun **11:**1403
-- Moses ben Meir **6:**1231
-- Moses ben Yom Tov **12:**427
-- Moses of Coucy **12:**418
-- Moses of Evreux **12:**433
-- Moses of Pontoise **12:**416
-- Moses Taku **15:**737
-- Nethanel of Chinon **12:**972
-- Perez of Corbeil **13:**284
-- Petter ben Joseph **13:**348
-- Samson of Chinon **14:**779
-- Samson of Coucy **14:**779
-- Samson of Falaise **14:**779
-- Samson of Sens **14:**777
-- Samuel ben Ḥayyim **16:**108
-- Samuel ben Joseph **16:**109
-- Samuel ben Meir **14:**809
-- Samuel of Evreux **14:**819
-- Samuel of Falaise **14:**814
-- Solomon of Dreux **15:**124
-- Solomon of Straubing **15:**428
-- Yom Tov of Falaise **10:**351
- *see also:* TALMUD
Tosafot Ḥadashim (wk.) **4:**1110
Tosafot Yom Tov (wk.) **8:**312
- Adeni, Solomon **2:**266
- Elijah ben Moses **6:**659
- Jewish literature **11:**333
Toscanini, Arturo **8:**1056; **8:**983
Tosefet Arukh ha-Shalem (wk.) **3:**278
TOSEFTA (hal. wk.) **15:**1283
- Abramsky, Yeḥezkel **2:**171
- academy procedure **2:**203
- Albeck, Hanokh **2:**528
- *amoraim* **2:**865
- as law source **12:**117
- Baal-Meon **4:**5
- codification of law **5:**631
- Hebrew MSS **11:**903
- Jewish literature **11:**317
- Kasovsky's concordance **10:**809
- *Leviticus Rabbah* **11:**147
- Lieberman's work **11:**219
- *Moed* **12:**208
- *Nezikin* **12:**1132
- Pardo, David **13:**93
- *tannaim* **15:**799
- Zuckermandel's work **16:**1229
- *see also:* BARAITA; MISHNAH
Tosefta Yerushalmi (bk.) **4:**846
Toska, M. **13:**1242
Tostado, Alfonso de Madrigal **8:**60
Total Solution (Nazi plan), *see* FINAL SOLUTION
Totrossiah (Div. name) **10:**505
Tot Simedrea (metropolitan) **8:**915
Totul Pentru Ţară (Rum.), *see* IRON GUARD
Touansas (Js., Tun.) **15:**1442
Touati (fam. name), *see* Tuati
Toubi, Tawfiq **5:**808
Toubias (sol., 3rd cent. B.C.E.), *see* Tobiah
Toubin, Isaac **2:**819
TOUL (city, Fr.) **15:**1285
TOULON (port Fr.) **15:**1285
TOULOUSE (city, Fr.) **15:**1286
- Beaucaire community **4:**363
- Church council **5:**549
- Pastoureaux massacre **5:**1141
TOURAINE (prov., Fr.) **15:**1287
Touré, Sékou **9:**439
TOUREL, JENNIE **12:**711
TOURISM IN ISRAEL **9:**845
- Jerusalem
- *illus:*
-- Israel stamps **9:**844-845
-- Protestants visiting Jerusalem Garden Tomb **9:**916
-- Tiberias, modern hotel **9:**172-173
- *map:* text
Touro, Abraham **12:**1043
Touro, Isaac **12:**1043; **15:**1288
TOURO, JUDAH **15:**1288
- Montefiore, Sir Moses **12:**271
- Newport **12:**1043
- *illus:* text
Touro, Reyna **15:**1288
TOUROFF, NISSAN **15:**1289
- *illus:*
-- Hebrew Pen Club, N.Y. **8:**211
Touro Infirmary (U. S.) **8:**1039
Touro Synagogue (R.I.) **12:**1043 **15:**619
- *illus:*
-- Ark of the Law **3:**454
-- exterior **12:**1043
TOURS (city, Fr.) **15:**1290
- Touraine **15:**1288
TOUSSENEL, ALPHONSE **15:**1291
Tov, Moshe **10:**1455
Tovah, Judah Levi **6:**149
Tovbin, Mark **12:**454
Tovelei shaḥarit, *see* Hemerobaptists
Tov Elem, *see* Samuel ben Yakar
Tov Elem, Joseph ben Eliezer, *see* BONFILS, JOSEPH BEN ELIEZER
Tov Elem, Joseph ben Samuel, *see* BONFILS, JOSEPH BEN SAMUEL
TOVEY, D'BLOISSIERS **15:**1291
- history **8:**560
- *illus:*
-- *Anglia Judaica* (1738) **6:**755
Toviana, Abraham **10:**554
Tovija ben Abraham ha-Levi **14:**655
Tovim (cmty. ldrs.) **10:**1406
Toviss, Yvonna **15:**314
Tov ukur (title) **15:**1164
"Toward Jerusalem" (paint., M. Ardon) Pl. 8 **3**-ART
Towarzystwo Ochrony Zdrowia (orgn.), *see* OZE
Towarzystwo Ochrony Zdrowia Ludności Zydowskiej (orgn.), *see* TOZ
Tower and Stockade, *see* STOCKADE AND WATCHTOWER
Tower of Babel, *see* BABEL, TOWER OF
"Tower of Babel" (paint., Pieter Breughel the Elder) **4:**27
Tower of David (loc., Jer.), *see* David, Tower of
Towers, Pool of (Jer.), *see* Hezekiah, Pool of
TOWNE, CHARLES **3:**540; **3:**612
- *illus:*
-- "Norwich Cattle Fair" (paint.) **3:**545
Townley, James **8:**60
Town Planning (Isr.) **9:**622
Toynbee, Arnold **2:**425; **3:**775; **8:**779
TOZ (orgn.) **15:**1291
- Joint Distribution **2:**829
- Warsaw ghetto **16:**348
- *see also:* OZE
Toẓe'ot Ḥayyim (wk.) **4:**1263
Tozeur (loc., Tun.) **15:**1431
TRABOT (fam.) **15:**1292
- name of Sarfati **14:**878
Trabot, Azriel (16th cent.) **15:**1292
Trabot, Azriel (17th cent.) **15:**1292
Trabot, Jehiel **15:**1292
Trabot, Jehiel ben Azriel **5:**1485; **6:**1302; **15:**1292
Trabot, Nethanel **6:**25; **15:**1292
- choral singing **5:**124
- Graziano, Abraham **7:**865
- *illus:*
-- Mordecai ben Hillel ha-Kohen's commentary to the Mishnah **12:**313
Trabot, Perez **10:**429; **15:**1292
Trabot, Solomon **15:**1292
Trabotto (fam.), *see* Trabot
Trabotto, Rafael **15:**1292
Trachoma (disease) **4:**1093; **14:**1502
TRACHONITIS (prov., Bashan) **15:**1293
- Argob **3:**433
- Bashan **4:**292
- Herod and Nabateans **12:**743
- Herod's kingdom **8:**635
Trachtenberg, Beba, *see* IDELSON, BEBA
Trachtenberg, Herman **10:**1501
TRACHTENBERG, JOSHUA **15:**1293
Trachtenberg, Maximilian **10:**1171
Track-and-field (sport) **15:**315
- *illus:*
-- Copeland, Lillian **15:**315
-- Laskan, Henry **15:**315
Tractatus adversus Judaeos (wk.) **3:**851
Tractatus theologico-politicus (wk.) **15:**282ff
Tradai (city, Lith.), *see* TROKI
TRADE AND COMMERCE **15:**1293
- *Contents:*
-- In the Bible **15:**1293
-- Post-Biblical **15:**1296
-- Middle Ages to 18th Century **15:**1297
-- 19th and 20th Centuries **15:**1304
-- In the U.S. **15:**1305
- General
-- ancient merchant class **8:**614
-- market days **11:**1000
-- merchants **16:**1305
-- Muslim's attitude **8:**659
-- Pale of Settlement **13:**24
-- selection of **10:**1322
-- ships and sailing **14:**1411
-- *shtetl* **14:**1472
- Israel
-- Damascus-Akaba route **9:**245
-- economic life, ancient **16:**1269
-- foreign trade, modern **9:**759
-- Hellenistic period **8:**294
-- Mamluk period **9:**278
-- Red Sea route **14:**15
-- 634 to 1099 C.E. **9:**263; **9:**264
-- social structure **8:**614

- - Solomon's kingdom **15:**97
- - tithes, church **15:**1162
- - West Bank **14:**1638,1640
- Other Localities
- - Aden **16:**741ff
- - Africa **2:**334
- - Amsterdam **2:**897ff
- - Austria **3:**888ff
- - Avignon **3:**965
- - Bayonne **4:**350
- - Burgos **4:**1513
- - Bushire **4:**1535
- - Europe **16:**1286
- - Greece **7:**876
- - India **8:**1350ff
- - Lvov Jews **11:**608
- - N.Y., early period **12:**1064ff,1083ff,1109ff
- - Phoenicia **13:**475
- - Poland **13:**717
- - Radaniya **13:**1495
- - Regensburg **14:**35
- - South Africa **15:**203ff
- - Spain **15:**224ff
- - Toledo **15:**1200; **15:**1201
- Legal Aspects
- - custom, force of **12:**17
- - *Ḥerem ha-Ikkul* **8:**356
- - *Ḥerem ha-Yishuv* **8:**357
- - imprisonment for debt **8:**1305ff
- - legal person **10:**1568,1569
- - Medieval period **3:**921
- *illus:*
- - chicken vendor, Poland **13:**744
- - Cracow, agreement re commercial rights (1485) **5:**1029
- - Cracow, goose market **16:**1329
- - Cracow, Jewish merchants **5:**1039
- - Dublin, Jewish old clothes men **6:**249
- - fruit vendor, Poland **13:**743
- - Graaff Reinet trading station **15:**187
- - Grant's anti-Semitic General Order **15:**1651
- - Hungarian Jewish peddler **8:**1097
- - Israel clothing exports (table) **15:**710
- - Jewish blacksmith, Lithuania **11:**384
- - Jewish porter, Lithuania **11:**379
- - London
- - - Houndsditch **6:**764
- - - Monmouth Street **11:**475
- - - Petticoat Lane **6:**769
- - - Royal Exchange, plan **11:**470
- - Metz Jews' petition **11:**1450
- - New York, Lower East Side orange vendor **12:**1080
- - New York religious articles shop **12:**1101
- - Nuremberg hawker **12:**1277
- - Palestine and Israel statistics **9:**701-762
- - porters,Poland **13:**745
- - professional structure of urban populations between the two world wars (table) **5:**1055
- - regulation re taxes on trading in jewels **6:**1283
- - Russia, statistics (tables) **14:**435,451,472
- - Salt Lake City, Ransohoff's shop **15:**1597
- - secondhand goods man, Poland **13:**743
- - slaves redeemed from Jewish traders **14:**1661
- - water-carrier **8:**755
- *see also under individual trades*

Trade Unionism
- socialism **15:**26ff
- socialism, Jewish **15:**40ff
- tailoring **15:**708
- U.S. **15:**1616
- Zaritsky, Max **16:**938

Trade union organizations (Isr.), *see* JEWISH LABOR ORGANIZATIONS IN ISRAEL
Tradition (period.) **12:**1490; **13:**1051; **15:**1110
TRADITION **15:**1308
- Aḥad Ha-Am **2:**444ff
- *Avot* **3:**983
- commandments, discontinuation of **15:**171
- Commandments, the 613 **5:**760,761
- Conservative Judaism **12:**1444
- criticism **4:**908
- *halakhah le-Moshe mi-Sinai* **7:**1167
- Karaites **10:**777
- Mishnah **12:**97
- music **12:**555
- *see also:* FOLKLORE; KABBALAH ("tradition")

Traditional Judaism, *see* ORTHODOXY
Traeard, E. **8:**60
Traffic Magistrates' Courts (Isr.) **9:**639
TRAGACANTH (spice) **15:**1311
- plant list **13:**625
- source **8:**1311
- *illus:* text

Trager, David **15:**304
Trager, George L. **3:**40
Trager, Hannah **5:**451
Trager, Harry **11:**880
Tragic Week (Arg. pogrom), *see* Semana Trágica
Traianus, Marcus Ulpius (Rom. emp.), *see* TRAJAN, MARCUS ULPIUS
Trainin, Aron Naumovitch **10:**1501
Trainin, Paul **14:**479
Trains, *see* RAILROADS
TRAJAN, MARCUS ULPIUS (Rom. emp.) **15:**1312
- attitude to Jews **14:**230
- Carmel **5:**186
- Cyrenaican inscriptions **3:**332
- Cyrene **5:**1184
- Diaspora **6:**15
- Dio Cassius **6:**59
- Egypt **6:**489
- history **9:**245
- history chart **8:**766-767
- Nabatea **9:**121
- revolts against **8:**644
- Samuel ha-Katan **14:**816
- Transjordan **15:**1317
- warfare **16:**280
- *see also:* QUIETUS, LUSIUS

Trajan, Day of (J. holiday) **11:**1231
Trajan Decius (Rom. emp.), *see* Decius, Trajan
Traken (city, Lith.), *see* TROKI
Tralles (city, Turk.), *see* AYDIN
Tramer, Ludwig **13:**1340
TRAMER, MORITZ **15:**1313
Trance, *see* ECSTASY
TRANI (tn., It.) **15:**1313
- *illus:* text

Trani, Baruch ben Isaac di **2:**310
Trani, Isaiah ben Elijah (Younger), *see* ISAIAH BEN ELIJAH DI TRANI
Trani, Isaiah ben Mali (Elder), *see* ISAIAH BEN MALI DI TRANI
TRANI, JOSEPH BEN MOSES **15:**1314
- emissary **14:**1358

Trani, Joseph di **11:**1159
- Ottoman Empire **16:**1549

TRANI, MOSES BEN JOSEPH **15:**1315
- Alashkar, Solomon **2:**513
- Berab, Jacob **4:**583
- chief rabbinate **13:**1451
- responsa **11:**338

Trani, Solomon ben Moses **5:**30; **15:**1315
Tranmaehl, Martin **12:**1225
Transaction (legal) **5:**924
- *asmakhta* **3:**751ff
- custom **12:**17ff
- embryo **6:**720
- gift **7:**561
- Marranos **5:**885
- *see also* CONDITIONS; MISTAKE

Transactions (period.) **10:**53; **15:**54
Trans-Baikal (reg., Sib.) **14:**1487
Transcarpathian oblast (reg., Ukr.), *see* SUBCARPATHIAN RUTHENIA
Transcendence of God, *see* GOD
"Transfer" (Nazi Ger.), *see* HAAVARA
Transfer of property (legal), *see* ACQUISITION
Transference of souls, *see Ha'atakah*
Transfer of debt, *see* ASSIGNMENT
"Transferstelle" (ghetto fin. com.) **16:**342
Transgression, *see* SIN
"Transients" (study, R. Soyer) **3:**561
Transislanus, Johannes, *see* CAMPEN, JOHANNES VAN
"Transition" (paint., L. Krasner) **3:**634
Transition Law (Isr.) **9:**610; **9:**650ff
TRANSJORDAN **15:**1315
- General
- - frontier **9:**313
- - Frontier Force **9:**340
- - geology **9:**199ff
- - human geography **9:**595ff
- - Jewish Agency settlement plans **16:**1084
- - Manasseh tribal territory **11:**851
- - physiography **9:**173ff
- - trade, Arabian **9:**245
- History
- - Crusaders **9:**268
- - early Bible period **8:**573ff
- - Fakhr al-Din II **9:**287
- - Hellenistic-Roman period **8:**626ff
- - *Jund-Filasṭīn* **9:**261; **9:**264
- - Mamluk provincial organization **9:**274; **9:**277
- - Palestine, partition **13:**34
- - Solomon's kingdom **15:**97
- *illus:*
- - Jewish and Arab leaders' meeting, 1933 **9:**346
- - Jewish settlement, Wauchope's letter **9:**343
- - Samuel, Herbert, reading declaration of independence **9:**339

Transjordan (state), *see* JORDAN, HASHEMITE KINGDOM OF
TRANSLATION AND TRANSLATORS **15:**1318
- Arabic influence **16:**1622ff
- Aramaic into Hebrew **16:**1613
- Jewish literature **11:**340ff
- Jewish philosophy **13:**443
- *La'az* and liturgy **10:**1313
- *Mishlei Sindbad* **14:**1608
- Talmud **15:**768
- Targum **15:**811
- Tibbon **15:**1129

Translations, Bible, *see* BIBLE
Transliteration, *see* LA'AZ
Transmigration of souls, *see* GILGUL
TRANSNISTRIA (reg. Ukr.) **15:**1330
- *Contents:*
- - Jewish Population **15:**1330
- - Deportations to Transnistria **15:**1330
- - Concentration Camps and Expulsions **15:**1333
- - Aid Operations **15:**1335
- - Rescue and Assistance **15:**1335
- Antonescu, Ion **3:**163
- Balta **4:**144
- ghettoes **7:**545
- Podolia **13:**669
- Rumania **14:**401ff
- *illus:* text
- *maps:* text

TRANSOXIANA (reg., As.) **15:**1336
TRANSPLANTS (med.) **15:**1337
- autopsies **3:**933ff
- responsa **14:**93

Transport
- Austrian Jews **3:**894
- cart and chariot **5:**210
- railroads **13:**1517

TRANSPORTATION IN ISRAEL **9:**831
- historical survey **9:**393ff
- ICAO **15:**1564
- Jaffa-Jerusalem railroad **9:**1461
- Jerusalem **9:**1492ff
- *illus:*
- - text
- - Afulah-Nazareth road construction **9:**517
- - Ben-Gurion opening Eilat road **9:**380
- - statistics **9:**845
- - Zim freighter Shiqma **16:**1023

Transposition of letters (Bib. exeg.) **2:**776
Transubstantiation (Cath. doctrine) **3:**102; **8:**1040
TRANSVAAL (prov., S.A.) **15:**1340
- South Africa **15:**184ff
- *illus:* text

Transvaal Jewish Board of Deputies **12:**853
TRANSYLVANIA **15:**1341
- Rumania **14:**387ff
- *illus:* text

TRAPANI (city, Sic.) **15:**1346
TRASKE, JOHN **15:**1346
Tras-os-Montes (prov., Port.) **16:**135
TRAUBE, ISIDOR **15:**1347
TRAUBE, LUDWIG **15:**1347
TRAUBE, MORITZ **5:**388
TRAUBE, WILHELM **5:**388
Trauberg, Leonid **12:**456
Traustein ("marriage stone") **11:**693,1031,1041
TRAVEL, PRAYER FOR **15:**1347
- *gomel* blessing **7:**768
- *mishmarot* **12:**92
- *illus:* text

Travel, Sabbath **14:**94; **14:**567; **14:**741
TRAVELERS AND EXPLORERS **15:**1348
- *Contents:*
- - Jewish Travelers **15:**1351
- - Christian Travelers **15:**1354
- - Muslim Travelers **15:**1358
- Benjamin of Tudela **4:**535
- David d'Beth Hillel **5:**1360
- Jewish literature **11:**350
- *illus:*
- - Benjamin of Tudela, map of travels **4:**535
- - Bertinoro, Obadiah, map of journey **4:**698
- - Geldern, Simon von, drawing of the globe **7:**365
- - prayer for travel **15:**1348
- - *Travels and Adventures in Eastern Africa* (1836) **9:**43

TRAVELERS AND TRAVELS TO EREẒ ISRAEL **15:**1351
- *see also:* ITINERARIES OF EREẒ ISRAEL

TRAVNIK (tn., Yug.) **15:**1359
Trawniki (concen. camp) **8:**874
TREASURE, TREASURY **15:**1360
- Cairo *genizah* **16:**1333
- divination **6:**120
- Temple **15:**953ff,979ff
Treaties, international **5:**148 **16:**657
- *see also under individual names*
Treaty, *see* COVENANT
TREBIC (Trebitsch; tn., Morav.) **15:**1362
- archives **3:**387
- electoral rights **13:**832
- Holocaust period **5:**1199
- *illus:* text
TREBITSCH, ABRAHAM **15:**1363
Trebitsch, Arthur **15:**1364
TREBITSCH, MOSES LOEB BEN WOLF **15:**1363
- art **3:**539
TREBITSCH, NEHEMIAH (Menahem Nahum) **15:**1363
- Steinschneider, Moritz **15:**374
Trebitsch, S.(mfr., Vienna) **15:**1040
TREBITSCH, SIEGFRIED **15:**1364
TREBITSCH-LINCOLN, IGNATIUS TIMOTHY **15:**1364
TREBLINKA (concen. camp) **15:**1365
- *Contents:*
- - Treblinka I **15:**1366
- - Treblinka II **15:**1366
- - Acts of Resistance **15:**1369
- - The Aftermath **15:**1369
- gassing **16:**1332
- Holocaust **8:**879; **8:**894
Treblinka (wk.) **5:**677
Tredegar (tn., Wales) **16:**251
Tree Goose, *see* BARNACLE GOOSE MYTHS
Tree of Knowledge, Tree of Life **13:**77ff
- apple **3:**224
- fig **6:**1274
- olive **12:**1347
- *Sefirot* doctrine **10:**575
- *illus:*
- - Adam, Eve, and the serpent **2:**242
- - amulet **6:**998
- *see also:* ADAM
Trees
- cultic planting **8:**1228
- eclipse omen **12:**291
- ecology **4:**1029
- folklore **6:**1404
- mixed species **12:**170ff
- *orlah* **12:**1467
- Tu bi-Shevat **15:**1420
- *see also:* PLANTS
Trefouse (fam.), *see* TRÈVES
TREFOUSSE, HANS LOUIS **8:**550
Treiberman, Mendel **12:**1514
Treister, Leizer **14:**917
Treistman, Eliezer Leib **11:**430
Treistman, Simḥah **13:**1501
TREITSCHKE, HEINRICH VON **15:**1372
- Bamberger, Ludwig **4:**154
- Breslau, Harry **4:**1359
- Graetz, Heinrich **7:**847ff
- history chart **8:** 766-767
Trejwart (ed.), *see* Hescheles, Henryk
Trellis-writing **2:**47
TREMELLIUS, JOHN IMMANUEL **15:**1373
TRENCIN (Trencsén; tn., Cz.) **15:**1373
Trendl (game), *see Dreidl*
Trennungsorthodoxie (rel. trend, Ger.) **12:**1488
TRENT (city, It.) **15:**1374
- Bernardino da Feltre **4:**672
- history chart (1475) **8:**766-767
- Talmud censorship **5:**549
- Tyrol **15:**1491
- *illus:*
- - Apocryphal books canonized (table) **3:**181
- - Simon of Trent blood libel **3:**97,119; **7:**467
TRENTON (city, N.J.) **15:**1375
Trentschin (tn., Cz.), *see* TRENCIN
Trepp, Leo **12:**1359
Trespass, land, *see* HASSAGAT GEVUL
TREST (tn., Morav.) **15:**1376
Treu (fam.) **3:**539
Treuenburg, Jacob Bassevi von, *see* BASSEVI OF TRUENBERG, JACOB
Treuenfels, Abraham **15:**400
Treue Zionswaechter, Der (period.) **8:**477
Treuhandstelle (Nazi "trustee office") **13:**974
- *illus:*
- - clocks looted from Jews **13:**975
Treves (city, Ger.), *see* TRIER
TREVES (fam.) **15:**1376
Trèves, Abraham **15:**1376
Treves, Albert, Baron **15:**1166
Treves, Claudio **13:**815; **15:**27
Trèves, Eliezer, *see* Drifzan, Eliezer
TREVES, EMILIO **15:**1377
Treves, Gabriel **6:**1023
Treves, Giuseppe **13:**1368; **15:**1378
Treves, Ḥayyim ben Johanan **2:**470; **4:**1211
Treves, Isaac ben Gerson **6:**46
Trèves, Johanan (Ger.) **15:**1376
TREVES, JOHANAN BEN JOSEPH (r., It.) **15:**1378
TREVES, JOHANAN BEN MATTATHIAS (Fr.) **15:**1378
Trèves, Joseph (r., It.) **15:**1377
Trèves, Joseph (publ., Ger.), *see* Drifzan, Joseph
Trèves, Joseph ben Johanan (the Great) **15:**1376
Trèves, Joseph ben Mattathias **15:**1377
Treves, Mattathias ben Joseph (r., Fr.), *see* Mattathias ben Joseph
Treves, Moses ben Eliezer **15:**1391
Trèves, Naphtali Herz, *see* Drifzan, Naphtali Herz
Treves, Pellegrino **4:**463; **8:**1356
Trèves, Raphael (au.) **15:**1377
Trèves, Raphael Joseph (publ.) **15:**1377; **15:**1378
Treves, Sabbato Graziadio **15:**1455
Trevet, Nicholas, *see* TRIVETH, NICHOLAS
TREVIÑO DE SOBREMONTE, TOMÁS **15:**1379
TREVISO (city, It.) **15:**1380
Trevitsch (print.) **4:**654
TRÉVOUX (tn., Fr.) **15:**1380
- Lyons **11:**624
- Trabot family **15:**1292
Trial (law)
- autonomy, judicial **3:**928ff
- *bet din* **4:**719
- practice and procedure **13:**952
Trial of Jesus (bk.) **16:**552
Triangle, Little (area, Isr.), *see* Little Triangle
Tribal Courts (Isr.) **9:**1043ff; **9:**633
Tribas (fam.), *see* TRÈVES
Tribes, Lost Ten, *see* TEN LOST TRIBES
TRIBES, THE TWELVE **15:**1381
- General
- - apostles' number **3:**216
- - banners **4:**181; **6:**1334
- - Bible history **8:**578ff
- - biblical term **5:**894
- - intermarriage **15:**475
- - Jacob **9:**1193
- - Jacob's blessing **9:**1207
- - Lost Tribes **15:**1003
- - stones of the breastplate **13:**1007ff
- - tribal standards **8:**334
- - Urim and Thummim **16:**8,9
- - Zodiac Signs **16:**1191
- - *see also under individual tribes*
- Settlement **9:**115
- - Gerar, Land of **7:**432
- - inheritance **16:**980
- - levitical inheritance **13:**1082
- - lots **11:**510
- - monarchy **10:**1011ff
- - social structure **8:**609ff
- - Transjordan **15:**1316
- - wars of conquest **8:**348
- *illus:*
- - text
- - Abraham ben Jacob's map (1695) **11:**927
- - Asher territory **3:**700
- - Benjamin territory **14:**522
- - Dan territory **5:**1256
- - disposition around Tabernacle **8:**566
- - emblems **4:**181; **5:**57; **6:**1450; **8:**335; **12:**820, *fcg.* 1259
- - Ephraim territory **6:**807
- - Gad territory **7:**247
- - Israel stamp **9:**844-845
- - Issachar territory **9:**1075
- - "Jerusalem Windows" (M. Chagall) **4:**526; **5:**1258; **9:**1077
- - Judah territory **10:**327
- - levitical cities **11:**137
- - Manasseh territory **11:**852
- - Naphtali territory (map) **12:**820
- - Reuben territory (map) **14:**104
- - Robert's map (1750) **11:**929
- - Simeon territory (map) **14:**1548
- - Vesconte's map (14th cent.) **11:**925
- - Zebulun territory **16:**951
Tribuna (pub.) **13:**1047
Tribuna Evreeasca (period.) **9:**1295; **16:**1135
Tribuna Israelita (period.) **11:**1459
Tribune Sioniste (journ.) **13:**1026
Tribuswinkel (vill., Aus.) **3:**890
Tribute-offering, *see Minḥah*
Tricameron (temple, Jer.) **9:**1405
Trichinosis (disease) **14:**1502
Trieber, Jacob **3:**459
TRIENNIAL CYCLE (Torah readings) **15:**1386
- *Exodus Rabbah* **6:**1067; **6:**1068
- *Genesis Rabbah* **7:**400
- *haftarah* **16:**1344
- *Leviticus Rabbah* **11:**148
- sermons **13:**995
- Torah reading **16:**1406
- *tables:* text
- *see also:* TORAH, READING OF
TRIER (city, Ger.) **15:**1389
- banking **4:**168
- Council of 1227 **5:**548
- Crusades **5:**1137,1143
- Jews in fourth century **8:**657
- *illus:*
- - text
- - Synagoga statue **8:**670
Trier (fam.) **13:**1519
Trier, Abraham Solomon **7:**80
Trier, Ernst **6:**464
Trier, Herman **5:**1537
Trier, Louis **6:**903
Trier, Solomon Abraham **7:**88
Trier, Solomon Zalman **7:**217
TRIER, WALTER **15:**1392
- cartoonists **5:**219
Triesch (tn., Morav.), *see* TREST
TRIESTE (city, It.) **15:**1392
- special Purim **13:**1399
- *illus:* text
Trieste, Gabriele **13:**12
Trieste Haggadah **7:**1102
Triestino, Anonimo **9:**1112
TRIETSCH, DAVIS **15:**1394
- *illus:*
- - First Zionist Congress **16:**1165
Trigland, J. (Nepos) **8:**62
TRIKKALA (Trikala; city, Gr.) **15:**1395
- Greece **7:**875,880
Trikomia (tn., Egy.) **6:**9
Trilepton (coin) **5:**717
- *illus:*
- - Archelaus coins **3:**333
Triller (Bib. trans.) **4:**873
Trilles, Vincentius **8:**62
Trilling, Diana **15:**1396
TRILLING, LIONEL **15:**1395
- U.S. literature **15:**1578
Trilussa (poet) **9:**1107
Trinidad (city, Colo.) **5:**753
Trinidad and Tobago (W. Indies) **16:**473
- Israel's relations with **9:**444
- population, Jewish **10:**1451
- synagogues **1:**syn. list
- *illus:*
- - Port of Spain Zionist youth parade **16:**1126
Trinitarian Bible Society **4:**969
Trinity, Trinitarianism **7:**671
- Abraham and Angels **2:**123
- Kabbalah **10:**563ff
- Mendelssohn **3:**659
- Saadiah Gaon **3:**193
Trinquetaille (loc., Fr.) **3:**468
TRIOLET, ELSA **15:**1396
Tripartite Maḥzor (illum. ms.) **11:**732ff
- Solomon **15:**110
- *illus:* **2:***fcg.* 11, 355; **4:**1154; **11:***fcg'* 683
Triple Gate (Jer.) **9:**1433
- Temple **15:**963
- *illus:*
- - general view **9:**1429
TRIPOLI (port, Leb.) **15:**1396
- capitulations **5:**148
- Lebanon **10:**1543
- Muā'wiya **9:**264
- Sidonians **14:**1507
TRIPOLI (city, Libya) **15:**1397
- Arbib family **3:**294
- Artom, Elia **3:**663
- *ḥakham bashi* **13:**1451
- special Purim **13:**1399
- Tunisia **15:**1431
Tripoli *Maḥzor* (prayer bk.) **11:**400ff
Tripolis (Phoen. city) **13:**478
Tripolitania (reg., Libya)
- capitulations **5:**149
- dress **6:**219
- Libya **11:**198
- Ottoman period **16:**1536
Trisit (coin) **5:**721
Trisker ḥasidic dynasty, *see* TWERSKY
Trismosin, Salomon **2:**544
Tristan, L. **12:**455
TRISTRAM, HENRY BAKER **15:**1399
- pilgrimage **13:**518
TRITHEMIUS, JOHANNES (Tritheim) **15:**1400
- Hebraic studies **8:**62
Trito-Isaiah (prophet) **6:**870ff; **9:**48,62
TRIVALE, ION **14:**422; **14:**428
Triverzans (fam.), *see* TRÈVES
TRIVETH, NICHOLAS (Trivetus) **15:**1400
- Hebraic studies **8:**62
Trivus, I. **13:**1598
TRIWOSCH, JOSEPH ELIJAH **15:**1400

Triwusch, Abba Joseph **10:** 1090
TRNAVA (city, Cz.) **15:** 1401
- Czechoslovakia **5:** 1195; **5:** 1200
- *status quo ante* **15:** 347
- *illus:*
- - Pressburg community, treaty with (1717) **4:** 1312
Troeltsch, Ernst **8:** 744
Troestlin ha-Navi of Erfurt **10:** 514
Trogianus (Rom. emp.), *see* TRAJAN, MARCUS ULPIUS
Troitsky (Rus. schol.) **4:** 400
TROKI (city, Lith.) **15:** 1401
- Bashyazi, Elijah **4:** 298
Troki, Abraham ben Josiah, *see* ABRAHAM BEN JOSIAH TROKI
TROKI, ISAAC BEN ABRAHAM **15:** 1403
- apologetics **3:** 198
- Jewish-Christian disputation **6:** 96ff
Troki, Joseph ben Mordecai, *see* MALINOVSKI, JOSEPH BEN MORDECAI
Troki, Solomon of, *see* Solomon of Troki
Trollope, Anthony **6:** 780
Trommel Kaddish (litur. mus.) **10:** 663
Trondheim (city, Nor.) **12:** 1224
- *illus:*
- - synagogue **12:** 1223
Trop, Naphtali **4:** 1401
Troper, Morris C. **2:** 828
Troppau (city, Cz.), *see* OPAVA
Tropplowitz, Joseph, *see* HA-EFRATI, JOSEPH
Trost(-ius), Martinus **8:** 62
Trostyanets (tn., Ukr.) **13:** 669
- massacre **14:** 459
- pogroms **13:** 669; **13:** 700
Trotski, H. A. **3:** 360
TROTSKY, LEV DAVIDOVICH **15:** 1404
- military service **11:** 1556
- *illus:* text
Trout (fish) **6:** 36
Troy (city, Mo.) **12:** 157
Troy (city, N.Y.) **12:** 1126
Troy, Samuel Z. **14:** 161
TROYES (tn., Fr.) **15:** 1406
- history chart (1288) **8:** 766-767
- rabbinical conferences **15:** 725
- synod **15:** 633
- *illus:*
- - Ecclesia et Synagoga **6:** 346
Trubar, Primož **4:** 885; **16:** 885
Truce Commission for Palestine **15:** 1545
True Sisters (soc., U.S.) **7:** 110
True World, The (wk.) **5:** 270
Truffles (bot.) **12:** 553
- plant list **13:** 625
Trujillo (city, Peru) **13:** 324
TRUJILLO (tn., Sp.) **15:** 1408
Trujillo, Fernando de **6:** 356; **13:** 45
TRUMAN, HARRY S. **15:** 1408
- Commission on Higher Education **15:** 1681
- Jewish refugees **15:** 1658; **16:** 1088
- recognition of Israel **9:** 365
- Weizmann **16:** 1095
- Zionism **16:** 1176
- *illus:*
- - text
- - B'nai B'rith leaders **4:** 1146
- - newborn State of Israel (cartoon) **9:** 424
Truman Peace Center (Jer.), *see* Harry Truman Peace Center
TRUMPELDOR, JOSEPH **15:** 1410
- Alexandria Jewry **2:** 593
- Ben-Gurion **4:** 506
- defense forces **9:** 681
- He-Ḥalutz **8:** 248
- history **8:** 756
- Jabotinsky **9:** 1179
- Jewish labor organization **9:** 848
- Jewish Legion **10:** 69ff
- Melitopol **11:** 1292
- St. Petersburg **11:** 17
- *illus:*
- - text
- - Tel Ḥai before Arab attack **9:** 336
Trumpeldor, Ze'ev (Vladimir) **15:** 1410
Trumpeldor Labor Legion (Isr.), *see* GEDUD HA-AVODAH
Trumper, Naum **5:** 464
Trumpet (instr.) **12:** 563
- *illus:*
- - Bar Kokhba coins **12:** 569
Trunk, Isaac Judah **15:** 1413
TRUNK, ISRAEL JOSHUA **15:** 1413
TRUNK, YEḤIEL YESHAIA **15:** 1414
- Hershele Ostropoler **12:** 1516
- *Poyln* **16:** 824
Truro (tn., Can.) **11:** 998
Trustee (fin.), *see* SHALISH
Trustin, Harry **12:** 1378
TRUTH **15:** 1414
- Albalag **13:** 444
- "double truth" doctrine **2:** 521
- Mendel of Kotsk **10:** 1223
- Mendelssohn **11:** 1329ff
- miracles **12:** 74; **12:** 75ff
- peace **13:** 197
- Rosenzweig **14:** 301
- Tarski **15:** 825
Truth (period.), *see* HA-EMET
Trutnov (loc., Cz.) **15:** 1041
Trybuna (period.) **13:** 1500
Tryphon (2nd cent. B.C.E., sol.), *see* DIODOTUS-TRYPHON
TRZCIANKA (tn., Pol.) **15:** 1415
- Ash, Joel ben Meir **3:** 694
Tsayt (newsp. Pol.) **4:** 1502; **13:** 1042
Tsaytung (period. Gal.) **12:** 219; **16:** 1330
Tschernichowsky, Saul, *see* TCHERNICHOWSKY, SAUL
Tschernikhov, Joseph **6:** 1412; **15:** 1541; **16:** 148,1179
Tschlenow (qtr., Tel Aviv) **15:** 921
Tschlenow, Israel **16:** 1126
TSCHLENOW, JEHIEL (Yefim Vladimirovich) **15:** 1415
- Zionist Congress (6th) **16:** 1168
- *illus:*
- - Benei Zion meeting **12:** 359
- - Helsingfors Conference **16:** 1137
"Tse" (nov.), *see* BASHEVIS SINGER, ISAAC
Tsedaka (fam.) **14:** 735
Tsedaka, Japheth ben Abraham **14:** 735
- *illus:*
- - Ben-Zvi, Izhak, and **14:** 735
Tsederbaum, Iulii Osipovich, *see* MARTOV, JULIUS
Tsefoni, A. **14:** 502
Tsekhanov, Abraham ben Raphael Landau, of, *see* CIECHANOW, ABRAHAM BEN RAPHAEL LANDAU OF
Tseretheli, M. von **16:** 1508
TSFASSMAN, ALEXANDER NAUMOVICH **15:** 1416
Tshebiner Rav, *see* WIEDENFELD, DOV
TSHEMERISKI, ALEXANDER (Solomon) **15:** 1417
Tsholnt (stew), *see* CHOLENT
Tsidekel, see TALLIT KATAN
Tsimiskes (10th cent., Byz. emp.) **9:** 262
Tsion, Ilya Faddeyevich, *see* CYON, ELIE DE
Tsionistishe Shtime (newsp.) **16:** 1115
Tskhinvali (vill., Rus.), *see* Staliniri
Tsofnas Pane'akh (wk.) **8:** 1118
Tsolner (mer., Pol.), *see* VOLCHKO
Tsoyzmir (tn., Pol.), *see* SANDOMIERZ
Tsu Gezunt (greeting) **7:** 914
TSUR, JACOB **15:** 1417
Tsushtayer (gr., Gal.) **4:** 1197
Tsuzmir (tn., Pol.), *see* SANDOMIERZ
Tsvayer (lab. gr.) **4:** 1504
Tswey Khasidimlekh (bk.) **13:** 133
TUAT (oasis, Afr.) **15:** 1418
Tuati (fam.) **15:** 1418
Tubal (bib. loc.) **4:** 1060
TUBAL-CAIN (bib. fig.) **15:** 1418
- alchemy **2:** 542
- metal crafts **10:** 906; **11:** 1429,1431
Tūbās (vill. Isr.) **15:** 1094
- Six-Day War **14:** 1635
Tu be-Av (minor fest.), *see* AV, THE FIFTEENTH OF
Tubelski, Leonid Davydovich (plwrt.), *see* TUR BROTHERS
Tubiana, Abraham **2:** 622
Tubieni (site, Er. Isr.), *see* KERAK
TU BI-SHEVAT (minor fest.) **15:** 1419
- Ben Susan **15:** 532
- cooking **6:** 1427
- dance festival **5:** 1270
- Israel **9:** 903
- New Year for trees **12:** 1062
- *illus:* text
Tuch, Ernst **11:** 664
Tuch, Nathan **5:** 606
TUCHIN (vill., Ukr.) **15:** 1420
Tuchinka (loc., Belor.) **12:** 54
TUCHMAN, BARBARA WERTHEIM **15:** 1421
Tuchnor, Hannah **6:** 1344
TUCHOLSKY, KURT **15:** 1421
Tuck, Gustave **12:** 543
TUCKER, RICHARD **12:** 712
TUCKER, SOPHIE **15:** 1422
Tuckum (city, Latv.), *see* TUKUMS
TUCSON (city, Ariz.) **15:** 1423
- Arizona **3:** 449,450
Tucumán (city, Arg.) **3:** 409
Tuczyn (vill., Ukr.), *see* TUCHIN
TUDELA (city, Sp.) **15:** 1423
- goldsmiths **7:** 741
- Spain **15:** 228
- *takkanot* **15:** 735
- *illus:* text
Tudḫaliya (Hittite k.), *see* Tidal
Tudḫaliya IV (Hittite k.) **8:** 789
Tudor, Andrei **14:** 422
TUEBINGEN (city, Ger.) **15:** 1426
TUGAL, PIERRE **5:** 1273
Tugendhaft, W. **8:** 957
TUGENDHOLD, JACOB **15:** 1427
- apologetics **3:** 199
- state schools **16:** 399
Tugendhold, Wolf **15:** 1427
Tughril Bey (Seljuk ldr.) **14:** 1136
TUKA, VOJTECH **15:** 1427
Tukulti-Ninurta I (k., Assyr.)
- Babylon **4:** 31; **16:** 1501
- Mari **11:** 974
Tukulti-Ninurta II (k., Assyr.) **16:** 1502
TUKUMS (city, Latv.) **15:** 1428
Tulaylāt al-Ghassūl (site, Transj.) **9:** 591; **15:** 1316
TULCHIN (city, Ukr.) **15:** 1428
- Transnistria **15:** 1335
Tulchiner, Baruch, *see* BARUCH BEN JEHIEL OF MEDZIBEZH
Tulip (bot.) **6:** 1365
TŪL KARM (tn., Er. Isr.) **15:** 1429
- human geography **9:** 587ff
Tullāb al-ʾilm (Isl. mvmt.) **7:** 1052
Tulleberg, H. K. **8:** 62
Tulsa (city, U.S.) **12:** 1353
Tulūil Abu al-ʿAlayiq (loc., Er. Isr.) **9:** 1366,1369
Tulul al-Dhahab (site, Isr.) **11:** 724
- *see also:* PENUEL
Tulunids (rulers, Egy.) **9:** 1428
Tumah ve-Tohorah, see PURITY AND IMPURITY, RITUAL
TUMARKIN, IGAEL **15:** 1429
- *illus:*
- - sculpture **14:** 1067
- - "Homage to Hieronymus Bosch" (sculp.) Fig. 108 **3**-ART
TUMIN, MELVIN MARVIN **15:** 1429
Tummal (sanctuary, Mesop.) **16:** 1487
Tummat Yesharim (wk.) **15:** 785
Tumtum (leg. term) **2:** 949
TUNIS, TUNISIA **15:** 1430
- *Contents:*
- - Second Temple Period **15:** 1430
- - Under Arab Rule **15:** 1432
- - Hafsid Rule (1228-1534)
- - Under Ottoman Rule until the Modern Era **15:** 1441
- - 1900-1968 **15:** 1447
- - Attitude Toward Israel **15:** 1450
- Communal Life
- - Alliance Israélite **2:** 652
- - Aydan, David **3:** 994
- - communal organization **5:** 817,827
- - crime **5:** 1092ff
- - dress **6:** 219
- - marriage customs **11:** 1044
- - ORT **12:** 1485
- - politics **13:** 816
- - population **13:** 870
- - press **13:** 1041
- - special Purim **13:** 1399
- - synagogues **1:** syn. list
- - Zionist movement **16:** 1127ff
- Miscellaneous
- - Arab League **3:** 242
- - Baḥuẓim **4:** 102
- - capitulations **5:** 149
- - emigration **16:** 1527
- - Hafsids **7:** 1064
- - migration to Israel **9:** 499ff,538
- - Nazi occupation **4:** 1247
- - Omar, Covenant of **12:** 1381
- *illus:*
- - text
- - Great Synagogue **15:** 615
- - Jewish women from Gabès **7:** 234
- - man's embroidered skullcap Pl.11 **6**-DRESS
- - Oẓar ha-Torah pupil **6:** 428
- *pop. tables:* text
TUNKEL, JOSEPH **15:** 1452
- parody **13:** 139
Ṭūqān, Fadwa **9:** 1040ff
Ṭūqān, Ibrahim **9:** 1040ff
Tur, *see* JACOB BEN ASHER
Ṭūr, al-(Tur-A; vill., Er. Isr.) **12:** 482,484
- Bethphage **4:** 748
- Jerusalem boundary **9:** 1461,1515
Tur, El- (loc., Sinai) **14:** 1607
Ṭur ʿAbdīn (dialects) **12:** 948
Turbato corde (papal bull) **4:** 216,1496
- Spain **15:** 232
TUR BROTHERS (plwrts.) **15:** 1452
Turckheim (Alsace-Lorraine) **2:** 752
TURDA (tn., Transyl.) **15:** 1452
TURECK, ROSALYN **12:** 712
Turei Zahav (*Taz;* wk.) **5:** 1354
Ture Kardu (mts., Kurd.) **3:** 290
Turgeman (trans.) **13:** 995
Turgenev, Ivan Sergeyevich **14:** 508
- Epstein, Zalman, on **6:** 837
- Mark Antokolski **3:** 162
Turiel, Moses ibn **12:** 530
Turim (period.) **8:** 200

TURIN (city, It.) **15:**1453
- Cantoni, Lelio **5:**130
- Nice community **12:**1136
- special Purim **13:**1399
- *illus:* text
TURKA (city, Ukr.) **15:**1456
Turkestan
- Meshed *anusim* **2:**327
- spices **8:**1320
- *see also:* KHURASAN
TURKEY **15:**1456
- *Contents:*
- - Economic Activities **15:**1457
- - Demography **15:**1459
- - Cultural, Religious and Social Life **15:**1460
- - Jewish Communal Schools **15:**1460
- - Contemporary Situation **15:**1462
- - Karaites **15:**1462
- - Relations with Israel **15:**1462
- Political Life
- - Abenaes, Solomon **2:**64
- - Berlin, Congress of **4:**655
- - capitulations **5:**148
- - Ereẓ Israel, Ottoman **9:**282
- - Israel's relations **9:**433
- - Jerusalem **9:**1454
- - Jewish participation **13:**815
- - judicial autonomy **12:**141
- - military service **11:**1567
- - minority treaty **12:**45ff
- - Palestine mandate **9:**121; **11:**861
- - Zionism **16:**1127ff,1170
- Demographic Data
- - African Jews **2:**335
- - *aliyah* **9:**512
- - Austrian Jews **3:**891
- - Kurdistan **10:**1295
- - Sardis **14:**876
- - Seattle migrants **14:**1083
- - vital statistics **16:**188ff
- Miscellaneous
- - Alliance Israélite **2:**651
- - Angel, Shemayahu **2:**951ff
- - Casès, Benjamin **5:**227
- - Doenmeh sect **6:**148
- - dress, medieval **6:**216
- - I.C.A.'s activity **10:**48
- - Ladino *Haggadah* **7:**1103
- - Ladino press **13:**1038
- - Neo-Aramaic dialects **12:**948
- - printing, medieval **8:**1326
- - railroads **13:**1519
- - Shabbateanism **14:**1243
- - stamps **15:**330
- - Steinhardt, Lawrence Adolf **15:**369
- - synagogues **1:** syn. list
- - trade **15:**1302
- *illus:*
- - text
- - Constantinople
- - - Jewish quarter **5:**917; **9:**1087
- - - Jewish women Pl. 8 6-DRESS; **9:**1089
- - stamp, 1914 pictorial series **15:**331
- *pop. tables:* text
- *see also:* ASIA MINOR; OTTOMAN EMPIRE; *and under individual cities*
Turkey (bird) **6:**34
Turkish Petroleum Co. **9:**793
Türkiye Hahambashiligi (Turk.) **16:**1462
TURKOW (fam.) **15:**1463
- *illus:* text
Turkow, Itzhak **15:**1463
Turkow, Jonas **15:**1464
Turkow, Mark **15:**1464
Turkow, Zygmunt **15:**1463
- Kaminska, Ida **10:**730
- motion pictures **12:**454
Turks
- Khwarizmian **9:**269,273
- Tlemcen **15:**1173
Turku (city, Fin.) **6:**1297
Tur Malka (poet), *see* GREENBERG, URI ẒEVI
Tur Malka (dist., Judah), *see* HAR HA-MELEKH
Turnau (tn.), *see* TURNOV
Turnip (bot.) **16:**83
- plant list **13:**625
TURNOV (tn., Bohem.) **15:**1464
Turnus Rufus, *see* TINNEIUS RUFUS
TURÓCZI-TROSTLER, JÓZSEF **15:**1465
Turquoise (mineral) **13:**1009
Tur Shulḥan Arukh (wk.), *see* JACOB BEN ASHER
TUR-SINAI (Torczyner), NAPHTALI HERZ (Harry) **15:**1465
- Bible exegesis **4:**902ff
- linguistics **16:**1399
Tur Talga (mt.), *see* HERMON, MOUNT
Turtânu (Assyr. office), *see* TARTAN
Turteltaub, Wilhelm **14:**538
TURTLE DOVE **15:**1466
- dietary laws **6:**30,34
- sacrifice **10:**1036; **14:**600ff
TUSCANY (reg., It.) **15:**1467
- Inquisition **8:**1400
- Sea Peoples **16:**1501
- *illus:*
- - text
- - proclamation re ill-treatment of Jews (1668) **9:**1131
Tusch-Letz, S. J. de, *see* LEC, STANISLAW JERZY
Tushiah (schools) **6:**428
Tushiyyah (rural center, Isr.) **1:**place list
Tushiyyah (publ. house) **5:**433; **13:**1375; **14:**1269
Tushratta (k., Mitanni) **12:**1170
Tushtumur (emir) **9:**1424
Tuska, Mordecai **14:**210; **15:**1469
TUSKA, SIMON **15:**1469
- Memphis **11:**1302
Tustar (tn., Iran), *see* SHUSHTAR
Tustari, al-, *see* ABU SA'D AL TUSTARĪ
Tuta, (poet), *see* AMRAM DARAH
Tut-ankh-Amon (k., Egy.) **15:**1125
Tutânu (Assyr. sol.) **16:**1504
Tuthmosis (k., Egy.), *see* Thutmose
Tutunik (sol., Rus.) **13:**699
Tuvia, Ovadia **8:**1309
Tuvim, Abraham **12:**468
Tuvim, Judith, *see* HOLLIDAY, JUDY
Tuviyyah ha-Rofe, *see* COHN, TOBIAS BEN MOSES
Tuv Ta'am (wk.) **16:**1390
Tuwim, Immanuel **15:**1470
Tuwim, Irena **6:**735; **13:**802; **15:**1471
TUWIM, JULIAN **15:**1470
Tuzla (tn., Yug.) **14:**869
Tuzora (tn., Mold.), *see* KALARASH
Tversky, A. **16:**822
Twain, Mark **15:**1570ff
- Wandering Jew **16:**261
Twelve Patriarchs, Testament of the (Pseudepig.), *see* PATRIARCHS, TESTAMENT OF THE TWELVE
Twelve Prophets, The, *see* MINOR PROPHETS
Twelve spies, (Bib.), *see* Spies, twelve
Twelve Tribes, *see* TRIBES, THE TWELVE
Twena, Solomon **5:**41; **13:**1036
"Twenty-four" (r.), *see* MOSES ESRIM VE-ARBA
Twerski, Jacob **11:**1590
TWERSKY (ḥas. dyn.) **15:**1471
- dynasties **1:**ḥas. table
- U.S. settlement **7:**1399; **7:**1400
- *illus:* text
Twersky, Bernard **13:**1462
Twersky, David ben Mordecai, *see* DAVID OF TALNA
Twersky, Isaac **14:**1651
TWERSKY, ISADORE **15:**1473
Twersky, J. **6:**735
Twersky, Moïse **7:**148
Twersky, N. **13:**1378; **15:**465
Twersky, Y. (ḥas. ldr.) **14:**214
TWERSKY, YOHANAN **15:**1473
- Hebrew literature **8:**213
TWILIGHT **15:**1474
- *see also:* CALENDAR; DAY AND NIGHT
Twins **4:**1018
"Two Brothers, Tale of" (anc. Egy.) **6:**484
"Two-gun" Cohen, *see* COHEN, MORRIS ABRAHAM
TWORKOV, JACK **3:**612
- *illus:*
- - "Script II" (paint.) **3:**644
Tyard, Pontus de **7:**139; **8:**62
Tyché (Gr. deity)
- Aelia Capitolina **9:**1406
- emblem on coins **5:**718
- Hellenism **8:**294
TYCHSEN, OLAUS GERHARD (Oluf) **15:**1474
- art **3:**593
- Hebraic studies **8:**62
- Mecklenburg **11:**1163
Tydeman, B. F. **8:**62
TYKOCIN (vill., Pol.) **15:**1475
- imprisonment *takkanot* **8:**1307
- Tiktin family **15:**1140
- *illus:* text
- *see also:* BIALYSTOK
TYKOCINSKI, ḤAYYIM **15:**1476
TYKOCINSKI, JEHIEL MICHEL **15:**1477
Tykotsin (vill., Pol.), *see* TYKOCIN
Tyler (city, Tex.) **15:**1035
Tyler, Gus **15:**31
Tympe, Johann G. **8:**62
TYNDALE, WILLIAM **15:**1477
- Hebraic studies **8:**962
- translation **4:**869ff
Tyn nad Vltavou (tn., Bohem.) **10:**1170
TYNYANOV, YURI NIKOLAYEVICH **15:**1478
Typhon, Cult of **3:**784
TYPOGRAPHERS **15:**1478
TYPOGRAPHY **15:**1480
- incunabula **8:**1322
- Soncino Gesellschaft **15:**143
- *illus:* text
- *see also:* BOOKS; PRINTING; WRITING, SCRIPTS, MATERIALS, AND INSCRIPTIONS
TYRE (port, Leb.) **15:**1488
- Abulafia, Isaac **2:**189
- Alexander, siege **2:**577
- Crusades **9:**268,272,274
- cult in Israel **8:**596
- David and **5:**1322
- gaonate **7:**323
- glass vessels **7:**612
- Hiram **8:**501
- industry **15:**641
- Kingdom of Israel, and **2:**435ff; **10:**99
- Mamluk rule **9:**274
- Ottoman period **9:**284
- physiography **9:**131
- precious stones **13:**1009
- Sidon **13:**472ff; **14:**1506
- Solomon's trade **15:**98
- *tekhelet* **15:**914
- throne **15:**1125
- trade **15:**1294
- Zedekiah's revolt **16:**962
- Zemina, "elder" **2:**33
- *illus:*
- - throne **15:**1124
TYRE, LADDER OF (place, Isr.) **15:**1490
- physiography **9:**128ff
- *illus:*
- - chalk cliffs **9:**205
- - checkpost on Lebanese frontier **10:**1547
- - seacoast **7:**269
TYRE OF THE TOBIADS (fort., Transj.) **15:**1490
Tyrnau (city, Cz.), *see* TRNAVA
TYRNAU, ISAAC (Tyrna) **15:**1491
- Aaron of Neustadt **2:**22
- *hakkafot* **7:**1153
- Trnava **15:**1401
TYROL (prov., Aus.) **15:**1491
- Innsbruck **8:**1379
Tyrolean-Vorarlberg Insurrection, *see* HOFER, ANDREAS
Tyropoeon Valley (Er. Isr.)
- archaeology **9:**1521ff
- cheesemaking **5:**371
- commercial quarters **9:**1398
- Kidron **10:**988
- Temple **15:**963
Tyros (anc. place) **15:**1180
Tyshler, David **12:**1377
TYSMENITSA (Tysmienica; tn., Ukr.) **15:**1492
Tysziński, David **13:**648
Tyszko, Jan, *see* JOGICHES, LEON
TYSZOWCE (vill., Pol.) **15:**1492
- concentration camp **12:**1526
TZARA, TRISTAN **15:**1493
- Rumanian literature **14:**423
- *illus:* text
Tzelem (ḥas. gr.) **7:**1399
TZELNIKER, MEIR **15:**1071,1092
Tzohar (period.) **13:**1040

U

U.A.H.C., *see* UNION OF AMERICAN HEBREW CONGREGATIONS
U.A.R., *see* EGYPT (Modern Period)
Ubaid (vill. Mesop.) **16:**2, 1483
Ubaidians (anc. people, Mesop.) **16:**1483
Uballa (city, Iraq) **4:**310
ʾUbayd Allah al-Mahdi **2:**367; **5:**62
ʾUbaydiyya, Al-(loc., Er. Isr.) **2:**329; **10:**1032
- archaeology **9:**591; **10:**1035
- Beth-Shemesh **4:**774
UCEDA, SAMUEL BEN ISAAC **15:**1497
Uchill, I.L. **8:**568
Uchtmann, Alard **8:**62
UCKO, SIEGFRIED (Sinai) **15:**1498
- Offenburg **12:**1338
Udall (Uvedale), John **8:**62
Udall, Nicholas **6:**774
ʾUdayma, Al-(site, Transj.) **15:**1316
UDIM (mosh., Isr.) **15:**1498
- statistics **1:**place list
Udim (journ.) **1:**newsp. list
Udin, Sophia **3:**391
- Zionism **16:**1157
Udine (tn., It.) **7:**810
Udita (leg. term), *see Odaita*
UDLICE (vill., Bohem.) **15:**1499
Ueberall, Ehud, *see* AVRIEL, EHUD
Ueber das Wesen der...Chassidim... (wk.) **7:**1418
UEBERLINGEN (tn., Ger.) **15:**1499
- population **13:**877
Ueberlingen, Menlin of **15:**1499
Uebersitz kinder (educ. term) **6:**414
U.E.J.F., *see* Union of French Jewish Students
Uelsmann, Jerry **13:**485
U.E.P. (orgn., Rum.), *see* Union of Native Jews
UFA (city, Rus.) **15:**1500
Uganda (state, Afr.) **9:**442
- Baruch, Bernard **4:**269
- Cohen, Sir Andrew **5:**666
- Judaizing sect **10:**398
UGANDA SCHEME **15:**1500
- Aḥad Ha-Am **2:**442
- Balfour Declaration **4:**131
- Ben-Yehuda, Eliezer **4:**568
- Chamberlain, Joseph **5:**333
- failure **8:**751
- Greenberg, Leopold **7:**905
- Herzl **8:**417; **16:**1072ff
- history chart **8:**766-767
- Kharkov Conference **10:**941ff
- Nordau, Max **12:**1213
- Russia **14:**452
- socialism, Jewish **15:**45
- Tschlenow, Jehiel **15:**1415
- Zionist Congress (6th) **16:**1168
- Zionist split **16:**1097
UGARIT (anc. city) **15:**1501
- *Contents:*
- - Excavation **15:**1501
- - Early Stratigraphy **15:**1502
- - History-Middle Bronze **15:**1502
- - History-Late Bronze **15:**1502
- - Social Structure **15:**1505
- alphabet **2:**681
- Ashdod, reference to **3:**695
- clay inscriptions **16:**661
- cuneiform alphabet **16:**654
- ethics **6:**940
- kingship **10:**1012ff
- Mesopotamia **16:**1498
- Minoan contacts **8:**295
- royal archives **3:**369
- Schaeffer, Claude **14:**938
- *tekhelet* **15:**914
- temple **15:**951
- *illus:*
- - Baal of the lightning **4:**8
- *see also:* UGARITIC
UGARITIC (anc. lang.) **15:**1506
- cuneiform, Beth-Shemesh **4:**773
- Hebrew linguistics **16:**1298,1561
- Semitic languages **14:**1151
- term for virgin **16:**160
- *illus:*
- - abecedary **2:**678
- - Baal's message to Anath (tablet) **4:**11
- *see also:* UGARIT
Ugav (bib. instr.) **12:**565
Ugdulena, G. **4:**878
Uger, Isaiah **11:**431
U.G.I.F., *see* UNION GÉNÉRALE DES ISRAÉLITES DE FRANCE
UGODA (Pol., "Compromise") **15:**1508
Ugolino, Blasio **8:**62; **15:**767
U.H.C., *see* Jewish Family Services
UHERSKE HRADISTE (tn., Cz.) **15:**1509
- Moravia **12:**299
- Nazi deportation **15:**1510
UHERSKÝ BROD (tn., Morav.) **15:**1509
- Holocaust period **5:**1199; **10:**1308
Uhlemann, F. G. **8:**62
UHLMAN, FRED **3:**612
ʿUhūd, *see* OMAR, COVENANT OF
U.I.W.U., *see* United Israel World Union
U.J.A., *see* UNITED JEWISH APPEAL
Ujazd (tn., Pol.) **14:**831
Ujejski, Kornel **10:**1375; **13:**798
- Solomon poem **15:**109
Új Élet (newsp.) **4:**1454; **13:**1036
Ujhely (city, Hung.), *see* SATORALJAUJHELY
UJ KELET (newsp.) **15:**1510
- Israel **9:**1017
- Marton, Ernö **11:**1067
- Transylvania **15:**1343
- *illus:* text
Uj Kor (period.) **15:**1144
Ujpest (tn., Hung.) **11:**457
- *see also:* BUDAPEST
UJVÁRI, PÉTER **15:**1511
Újvidék (city, Yug.), *see* NOVI SAD
Ukazatel literatury o sionizme (wk.) **16:**1156
UKBA, MAR (amora) **15:**1511
- Samuel **14:**787
- Tunisia **15:**1434
UKBA, MAR (9/10 cent., exil.) **15:**1512
Ukban bar Nehemiah **6:**51; **12:**860
Ukban de Ẓuẓita, Mar **12:**860
ʿUKBARĀ (tn., Babyl.) **15:**1512
- Iraq **8:**1447
Ukbarites (sect) **10:**765
UKHMANI, AZRIEL **15:**1512
Ukin-Zer (k., Babyl.) **11:**1389
Ukla (meas.) **16:**388
Uklein, Simeon **10:**400
UKMERGE (city, Lith.) **15:**1513
- *illus:* text
UKRAINE **15:**1513
- *Contents:*
- - Development and Distribution of Jewish Settlement **15:**1514
- - Economic Situation **15:**1515
- - Hatred of the Jews **15:**1517
- - Period of Independent Ukraine and Jewish National Autonomy **15:**1517
- - Religious and Social Movements in Ukraine Jewry **15:**1518
- - After World War II **15:**1518
- agricultural settlement **2:**407; **8:**741
- Chmielnicki **5:**480
- Haidamacks **7:**1132
- Ḥasidism **7:**1394
- Kostomarov, Nikolai **10:**1219
- minority rights **12:**47
- partisans **13:**140ff
- Podolia **13:**667
- self-defense **14:**1125
- Silberfarb, Moses **14:**1533
- socialism, Jewish **15:**39
- theater **15:**1076
- Yiddish education **6:**434ff
- Zionist movement **16:**1138
- *illus:*
- - text
- - Soviet Jewish farmers **2:**407-410
- *see also:* POLAND; RUSSIA
Ukrainian (lang.) **4:**886
Ukrainian Academy of Science, Jewish Research Institute of, *see* Jewish Research Institute of the Ukrainian Academy of Science, Kiev
Ukrainian Jewish Provisional National Assembly **5:**876
- Ukraine **15:**1518
- *illus:*
- - Kiev conference **15:**1515
Ukva, Mar (amora) *see* UKBA, MAR
UKẒIN (tract.) **15:**1519
- *illus:* text
Ulan Bator (city, Mongolia) **12:**256
Ulan-Ude (city, Rus.), *see* VERKHNEUDINSK
ʿUlaymī, Mujīr al-Dīn al-, *see* Mujīr al-Dīn al-ʿUlaymī
Ulcerative Colitis (disease) **14:**1503
Ulenberg, Caspar **4:**874
Ulff, Levi **15:**1041
Ulfilas (Gothic bp.) **4:**872
ULIANOVER, MIRIAM **15:**1521
- Yiddish literature **16:**820
Ulica Żydowska, *see* JEWISH QUARTER
Ulif, Gershon, *see* ASHKENAZI, GERSHON
ULJUS, *see* University of London Jewish Union Society
ULLA I (amora) **15:**1521
- Eleazar ben Pedat **6:**597
- epigram on dates **16:**1276
- Isaac bar Rav Judah **9:**12
- *Neḥutei* **12:**942
ULLENDORF, EDWARD **15:**1521
Ullman (name), *see also* Ulman
Ullman, Cecily **6:**784
Ullman, T. S. **4:**420
Ullmann (fam.) **12:**39
ULLMANN, ADOLPH **15:**1522
Ullmann, David **13:**21
ULLMANN, ERNEST **15:**1522
- *illus:* text
Ullmann, J. L. (r., Aus.) **8:**815
Ullmann, Joseph **12:**36
Ullmann, Leo **10:**1252
Ullmann, Moritz **4:**176
ULLMANN, SALOMON **15:**1523
Ullmann, Solomon Zalman **4:**1058
Ullmann and Boskovitz (co., U.S.) **7:**225
Ulloa, Alberto **13:**34
ULLSTEIN (fam.) **15:**1523
Ullstein, Franz **15:**1523
Ullstein, Hans **15:**1523
Ullstein, Hermann **15:**1523
Ullstein, Leopold **10:**305; **15:**1523
Ullstein, Louis **15:**1523

Ullstein, Rudolf **15:**1523
ULM (city, Ger.) **15:**1524
- banking **4:**168
- Swabian League **15:**544
- War Crimes Trials **16:**298
Ulma (fam.), *see* GUENZBURG
Ulma, Seligman **2:**783; **11:**358
Ulma-Guenzburg (fam.), *see* GUENZBURG
Ulman (name), *see also* Ullman
ULMAN, ABRAHAM **15:**1525
Ulman, David **15:**1525
ULMAN, JOSEPH N. **15:**1525
Ulman, Shalom **15:**1525
Ulman, Solomon Zalman **6:**472
Ulmann (Ger. lit. fig.) **15:**1055
Ulmann, J. **8:**62
Ulmo, David, *see* Ullmann, David
ULPAN (lang. inst.) **15:**1525
- adult education **9:**964
- cultural life **9:**1000
- immigrant absorption **9:**538
- *illus:*
- - text
- - Tel Aviv class **9:**965
ULPIAN (Rom. jur.) **15:**1526
ULRICH, JOHANN CASPAR **15:**1527
- historiography **8:**560
- *illus:*
- - *Sammlung Juedischer Geschichten ...*, engraving **15:**557
Ulster, *see* IRELAND
Ulster (co., N.Y.) **12:**1127
Ulyanov, Vladimir Ilyich, *see* LENIN, VLADIMIR ILYICH
UMAN (city, Ukr.) **15:**1527
- Haidamacks **7:**1133
Umano (fam.) **2:**934
'Umāra ibn Wathīma **4:**931
'Umar ('Amr) ben Dayyan **2:**667
'Umar ibn al-Khattāb (caliph), *see* OMAR IBN AL-KHATTĀB
UMAYYADS **15:**1528
- attitude to Jews **8:**1444
- gaonate **7:**318
- Ereẓ Israel history **9:**261
- Jerusalem rule **9:**1425ff
- Kharaj and Jizya **10:**937
- Manṣūr, al- **11:**894
- Mazar's excavations **9:**1537
- palace remains **3:**329
- Spain **15:**224ff
- Syrian Jews **15:**639
- *illus:*
- - Temple Mount excavations **9:**1534,1535
- *see also:* ABBASIDS
Umayya ibn 'Abd al-Aziz, *see* IBN ABI AL-SALT
UMAYYA IBN ABI AL-SALT (Isl. fig.) **15:**1531
- Abrahamic tales **2:**121
- Balaam in Islam **4:**124
- Exodus interpretation **13:**363
Umbehoven of Dorlisheim **3:**483
Umbria (loc., It.) **12:**255
Umedana ("estimation"; leg. term) **16:**525
UMEJ, *see* World Union of Jewish Students
Um-el-'Amed (site, Isr.) **3:**270
Umma (city, Mesop.) **16:**1488
Umm al-'Awāmid (loc., Phoen.) **16:**668
Umm al-Dabr (city, Pal.) **11:**424
Umm al-Daraj (mt., Gilead) **9:**179; **15:**1316
Umm al Faḥm (vill., Isr.) **9:**588
- block **9:**143
- geology **9:**201
Umm al-Kitāb (Isl. scripture) **9:**92
Umm al-Qanāṭir (site, Er. Isr.) **12:**181; **13:**1532
Umman (med. offic.) **4:**1119
Ummān-Manda (Babyl., "barbarians"), *see* MEDES AND MEDIA
Ummayya, Ummayads (dyn.), *see* UMAYYADS
Umm Basīs (loc., Sinai), *see* Tarat Umm Basīs
Umm Jūnī (reg., Er. Isr.) **4:**782; **5:**1459ff; **15:**797
Umm-Qataf (loc., Sinai) **14:**1606,1629
Umm Qays (vill., Transj.), *see* Muqays
Umm Rashrash (site, Isr.), *see* ELATH
Umm Shaykhān (loc., Sinai) **14:**1606
Umm Turfa (loc., Sinai) **14:**1606
U.N., *see* UNITED NATIONS
Unabhaengiger Orden Bne Briss (orgn., Ger.) **15:**1143
Unayziyya cistern (Ramleh, Isr.) **13:**1540
U.N. bodies and agencies, *see under* UNITED NATIONS; UNRRA; UNSCOP
Uncia (weight), *see Unkiyyah*
Uncleanness, Ritual, *see* PURITY AND IMPURITY, RITUAL
"Unclean ones" (Arg. traders), *see* Tmanyini
Uncle Batya, *see* Linkov, G. M.
Unction, *see* ANOINTING
Undercharging, *see* ONA'AH
Underground, Zionist **4:**629
"Underground Shelter in Mile End" (drg., E. Kapp) **3:**629
Undzer ..., see also under Unser ..., Unzer ...
Undzer Shtime (period., Bergen-Belsen) **4:**612
Unemployment in Israel **9:**883*ff*; **16:**1303
U-NETANNEH TOKEF (litur.) **15:**1531
- Amnon, Rabbi **2:**861
- Book of Life **4:**1218
- Kalonymus ben Meshullam **11:**326
UNGAR, BENJAMIN **7:**1551
Ungar, Eliezer **15:**1532
UNGAR, JOEL OF RECHNITZ **15:**1532
Ungar, Otto **3:**575; **7:**203
- *illus:*
- - "Living Quarters in the Theresienstadt Ghetto" (paint.) Fig. 83 **3**-ART
Ungarisch Brod (tn., Morav.), *see* UHERSKY BROD
Ungarisch-Hradisch (tn., Cz.), *see* UHERSKE HRADISTE
Ungarlaendische Juedische Zeitung (newsp.) **13:**1036
- Bettelheim, Samuel **4:**777
Unger, Ephraim Solomon **3:**2
Unger, Erich **7:**706
UNGER, IRWIN **15:**1532
Unger, J. (ed., Pol.) **13:**1042
UNGER, JOSEF **10:**1493; **10:**1512
UNGER, MAX **12:**712
UNGERFELD, MOSHE **15:**1532
Ungern-Sternberg, Baron R. **13:**700
Ungnad, Karl **13:**868
Ungvár (city, Ukr.), *see* UZHGOROD
Uniates (Chr. cmty.) **9:**915
Unicorn (leg. animal) **3:**37; **15:**704
- *illus:*
- - ceremonial object motif **4:**1337
- - *Meshal ha-Kadmoni* **3:**19
Unidad Juvenil (pub.) **16:**1126
Uniev, Dosoftei **4:**882
Unio mystica (kab. term) **10:**613; **12:**958
UNION, OESTERREICHISCH ISRAELITISCHE **15:**1533
- Bloch, Joseph **4:**1104
Union Bank of Israel **9:**827
Union City (N.J.) **8:**1057; **15:**1534
Union City (Tenn.) **15:**1009
Unión Cooperativa Agrícola (Arg.) **3:**431
UNION COUNTY (N.J.) **15:**1533
- *illus:* text
Unión de Jóvenes Hebreos (youth mvmt., Venez.) **16:**1126
Union des Associations Culturelles de France et d'Algérie (orgn.) **5:**911
Union des Croyants Monothéistes **2:**616
Union des Étudiants Juifs de France, *see* Union of French Jewish Students
Union for Full Equality of the Jewish People in Russia **8:**437
UNION GÉNÉRALE DES ISRAÉLITES DE FRANCE (U.G.I.F.) **15:**1534
Union Internationale de la Presse pour la Paix **7:**171
Unión Israelita del Peru **16:**1125
Union Libérale Juive (Fr.) **5:**1594
UNION OF AMERICAN HEBREW CONGREGATIONS (U.A.H.C.) **15:**1536
- Bernheim, Isaac Wolfe **4:**679
- Board of Delegates of American Israelites **4:**1150
- Cincinnati **5:**563
- Eisendrath, Maurice **6:**543
- history chart **8:**766-767
- publishing **13:**1376
- *illus:*
- - Fairmount Temple, Cleveland, O. **5:**607
Union of French Jewish Students **15:**449
Union of General Zionists (polit. party) **9:**661
Union of Israel Synagogues, *see* Union of Synagogues in Israel
Union of Italian Jewish Communities **5:**130
Union of the Jewish Communities (Rum.) **14:**405ff
Union of Jewish Women (S.A.) **15:**195
Union of Jewish Women of Switzerland **4:**305
Union of Monotheistic Believers, *see* Union des Croyants Monothéistes
Union of Native Jews (Rum.) **14:**390; **15:**381; **16:**1134
Union of Orthodox Hebrew Congregations (Eng.) **12:**1491
- synagogue **15:**590
- United Synagogue **15:**1673
- *see also:* Adath Yisroel
UNION OF ORTHODOX JEWISH CONGREGATIONS OF AMERICA **15:**1537
- *hekhsher* **8:**287
- history chart **8:**766-767
- Orthodoxy **12:**1490
- publishing **13:**1376
- *see also:* RABBINICAL COUNCIL OF AMERICA
UNION OF ORTHODOX RABBIS OF THE UNITED STATES AND CANADA **15:**1537
Union of Progressive Synagogues **10:**396
- ***Haggadah*** **reform** **7:**1094
Union of Religious Communities (Pol.) **13:**779
Union of Rumanian Jews, *see* Uniunea Evreilor Români
UNION OF THE RUSSIAN PEOPLE (anti-Sem. mvmt.) **15:**1538
UNION OF SEPHARDIC CONGREGATIONS (U.S.) **15:**1538
- Sephardim **14:**1174
Union of Soviet Socialist Republics, *see* RUSSIA
Union of Synagogues in Israel **15:**588; **15:**591
Union of Zionist Revisionists, *see* REVISIONISTS, ZIONIST
Unión Po'alei Ẓedek (Arg.) **3:**425
Union Prayer Book (ref.) **4:**775; **13:**199; **13:**991
Union Régionale des Sionistes de l'Est de la France **16:**1114
Union Sioniste Française **16:**1115
Uniontown (city, Pa.) **13:**230
Unirea (newsp.) **4:**1441; **14:**414
United Arab Command **3:**242
United Arab Republic, *see* EGYPT (Modern Period)
United Artists (publ.) **13:**1379
United Boycott Committee of Poland **4:**1280
United Committee for Jewish Emigration (Ger.), *see* Emig-Direkt
United Federation of Zionist Youth in Russia **8:**255
United Hebrew Beneficial Society (U.S.) **5:**350
United Hebrew Charities, *see* Jewish Family Services
United Hebrew Congregation (syn., Mo.) **14:**662ff
- *illus:* **14:**665
United Hebrew Relief Association (U.S.) **5:**350
United Hebrew Sheltering and Immigrant Aid Society (U.S.), *see* UNITED HIAS SERVICE
United Hebrew Trades (U.S.) **6:**1214; **11:**1581
- history chart **8:**766-767
United Help, Inc. (U.S.) **2:**820
UNITED HIAS SERVICE (relief orgn., U.S.) **15:**1539
- New York City **12:**1098
- *illus:* text
United Israel Appeal, Inc. (U.S.), *see* KEREN HAYESOD
United Israel World Union (U.I.W.U. miss. soc.) **13:**1192
UNITED JEWISH APPEAL (U.S.) **15:**1540
- Friedman, Herbert A. **7:**186
- Keren Hayesod **10:**915
- *Malben* **11:**821
- philanthropy **13:**383
- Schiff, Frieda **16:**284
- U.S. Zionism **15:**1632; **16:**1146
- Weiler, Jack D. **16:**397
- *illus:*
- - text
- - Israel stamp **9:**844-845
- - Meir, Golda, addressing dinner **15:**1668
United Jewish Choral Societies of the United States and Canada **5:**488
United Jewish Education Board (Austr.) **11:**1277
UNITED JEWISH SOCIALIST WORKERS' PARTY (Rus., Pol.) **15:**1541
- Bolsheviks **14:**463
- Communist party **15:**48
- Lestschinsky, Jacob **11:**51
- Silberfarb, Moses **14:**1533
- socialism **10:**90
United Jewish Welfare Fund of Toronto (Can.), *see* Federation of Jewish Philanthropies
United Kibbutz (mvmt.), *see* HA-KIBBUTZ HA-ME'UḤAD
United Kingdom, *see* ENGLAND; IRELAND; SCOTLAND; WALES

UNITED NATIONS **15:**1543
- *Contents:*
- - Partition Resolution (1947) **15:**1543
- - War of Independence **15:**1544
- - Israel Membership **15:**1546
- - Jerusalem **15:**1547
- - Arab Refugees **15:**1549
- - Direct Negotiations **15:**1551
- - Armistice: First Phase **15:**1552
- - Sinai Campaign **15:**1554
- - Armistice: Second Phase **15:**1555
- - Six-Day War and After **15:**1556
- - Anti-Semitism **15:**1558
- - Jews in Arab Countries and U.S.S.R. **15:**1561
- - U.N. Bodies and Agencies **15:**1563
- General
- - Arab League **3:**242
- - armistice agreements **3:**478
- - Bernadotte, Folke **4:**669
- - Comay, Michael **5:**758
- - Committee of Jurists **12:**724
- - Eban, Abba **6:**344
- - genocide declaration **7:**409
- - Israel, establishment **9:**421,434
- - Israel experts **9:**436
- - Israel history **9:**365ff
- - minority rights **12:**48
- - Music Council **11:**1379
- - Palestine Mandate **16:**1091ff
- - Partition Plan **3:**243; **16:**76
- - refugees, Arab **9:**378; **9:**447ff
- - refugees, Jewish **14:**31
- - Relief and Works Agency (U.N.R.W.A.) **6:**991; **9:**1032ff
- - Trade Commission **4:**1144
- - truce supervision (UNTSO) **3:**480; **9:**377,1484
- - UNESCO **5:**231
- - UNICEF **7:**1345
- - "United Nations Sabbath" **14:**574
- - U.S. Jewry **2:**815
- - War Crimes Commission **16:**290ff
- Emergency Force
- - foundation **15:**1554ff
- - Gaza Strip **9:**1034
- - Israel-Arabs conflict **9:**390ff
- - Sinai Campaign **14:**1607,1624
- - withdrawal (1967) **9:**407ff
- *illus:*
- - text
- - Gaza Strip evacuation, 1967 **9:**406
- - Gromyko's speech (May 14, 1947) **14:**493
- - Security Council voting Israel's admission, 1949 **9:**426
- - Sharett, Moshe, hoisting flag of Israel **14:**1312
- - voting chart on partition of Palestine **9:**423
- *see also:* UNRRA; UNSCOP

United Palestine Appeal (U.S.A.) **10:**915; **15:**1632
- U.S. Zionism **16:**1146

UNITED RESTITUTION ORGANIZATION **15:**1567
- foundation **2:**820

United States Conference of Major Jewish Organizations, *see* CONFERENCE OF PRESIDENTS OF MAJOR AMERICAN JEWISH ORGANIZATIONS

UNITED STATES LITERATURE **15:**1568
- *Contents:*
- - Influence of Bible and Hebrew Culture **15:**1568
- - Image of the Jew **15:**1569
- Works on Palestine and Israel **15:**1572
- - The Jewish Contribution **15:**1573
- - Capsules **15:**1579
- *illus:*
- - *Deborah* (1855) **13:**1052
- - Hebrew Pen Club, N.Y. **8:**211
- - Hebrew writers convention (1943) **8:**213
- - *The Jew* (1823) **13:**1050
- - Lazarus, Emma **15:**1608
- - *New Yorker Juedische Zeitung*, first issue **13:**1054
- *see also:* UNITED STATES OF AMERICA (Culture)

UNITED STATES OF AMERICA **15:**1585
- *Contents:*
- - Colonial Jewry, 1654-1776 **15:**1586
- - Early Period, 1776-1820 **15:**1590
- - 1820-1880 **15:**1596
- - - Population, Immigration, and Settlement **15:**1596
- - - Social Life and Status **15:**1597
- - - Religious, Cultural, and Communal Activities **15:**1598
- - - The Civil War **15:**1601
- - - Post-Civil War Stability **15:**1603
- - 1880-1929 **15:**1608
- - - The Great Immigration **15:**1608
- - - Neighborhoods, Occupations, and Labor Movement **15:**1612
- - - Social and Cultural Life **15:**1618
- - - Immigrants and Natives; Religious Life **15:**1620
- - - Education **15:**1621
- - - Communal Structure and Leadership **15:**1622
- - - World War I, Nativism, and Prosperity **15:**1622
- - 1929-1945 **15:**1628
- - - The Impact of Depression **15:**1628
- - - Political Activity **15:**1630
- - - Religion and Education **15:**1631
- - - Communal Organization **15:**1631
- - - World War II and Zionism **15:**1632
- - 1945-1970 **15:**1635
- - - Population, Demography, and Economic Activity **15:**1636
- - - Status and Communal Structure **15:**1640
- - - Social and Cultural Place in American Life **15:**1641
- - - Religious and Cultural Life **15:**1642
- - - Culture and Education **15:**1644
- - - The Late 1960s **15:**1645
- - Anti-Semitism **15:**1648
- - - Colonial Period—Civil War **15:**1648
- - - Civil War Period and Thereafter **15:**1648
- - - Mass Immigration of the 1890s and After **15:**1650
- - - The 1920s **15:**1652
- - - The 1930s and World War II **15:**1655
- - - Post-World War II **15:**1656
- - Relations with Israel **15:**1657
- - - Introduction **15:**1657
- - - History of U.S.-Israel Relations **15:**1658
- - - Economic Relations **15:**1667
- Anti-Semitism **3:**126ff
- - American Jewish Committee **2:**824
- - Atlanta **3:**825
- - Birmingham **4:**1037
- - discrimination **6:**69
- - Frank Case **7:**73ff
- - Jewish Defense League **14:**1128
- - Miami **11:**1480
- - *numerus clausus* **6:**70; **12:**1269ff
- - race theory **13:**1485
- - U.N. on discrimination
- - U.S. negroes **12:**934 **15:**1559
- Communal Life
- - aged, care for **2:**347
- - Ashkenazim **3:**721; **3:**722
- - autonomy **3:**921
- - Bund **4:**1499; **4:**1505
- - coöperatives **5:**943
- - crime **5:**1092ff
- - demography **5:**1494; **5:**1507ff
- - divorce statistics **6:**136
- - fraternal societies **7:**110
- - Freemasons **7:**124
- - history **8:**723ff
- - hospitals **8:**1034
- - *landsmannschaften* **10:**1414
- - mental illness **11:**1373ff
- - organization **5:**829; **5:**847
- - Oriental Sephardim **14:**1173
- - philanthropy **13:**381
- - population **13:**866ff
- - Sephardi community **14:**1173ff
- - statistics **15:**344; **16:**177ff
- - student movements **15:**450
- Culture
- - archives **3:**383
- - children's Hebrew books **5:**437
- - children's literature **5:**450
- - children's Yiddish books **5:**440
- - choirs **5:**487
- - Hebrew language **2:**249
- - Hebrew literature **8:**208
- - Hebrew magazines **5:**457
- - Hebrew mss. **11:**907
- - Hebrew newspapers **12:**1052
- - historiography **8:**567
- - Jewish education **6:**437ff
- - Ladino press **13:**1039
- - magazines **5:**460
- - music **12:**661
- - night schools **4:**148
- - parody **13:**136ff
- - press **13:**1050ff
- - publishing **13:**1367
- - television, radio **15:**927
- - theater **15:**1058
- - universities **15:**1677; **15:**1679
- - university libraries **11:**193
- - U.S. literature **15:**1568ff
- - Yiddish education **6:**435
- - Yiddish literature **16:**821
- Economic Life and Professions
- - agriculture **2:**411; **16:**1317
- - banking **4:**177
- - economic history **16:**1321
- - glassmaking **7:**613
- - journalism **10:**303ff
- - law **10:**1491ff
- - metalwork **11:**1439
- - military service **11:**1550
- - peddling **13:**207
- - petroleum and oil **13:**346
- - press **13:**1049ff
- - publishing **13:**1371, 1376
- - railroads **13:**1519
- - secondhand goods **14:**1086
- - stock exchanges **15:**405
- - tailoring **15:**708
- - textiles **15:**1042
- - tobacco industry **15:**1177ff
- - trade and commerce **15:**1305
- - typography **15:**1478ff
- - wine and liquor **16:**546
- Emancipation **2:**810; **6:**700ff
- - Adams, John **2:**249 assimilation **3:**775
- - egalitarianism **8:**712ff
- - minority rights **12:**44
- - mixed marriages **8:**732
- - patterns of identity **10:**63
- Jewish Press
- - *Di Post* **4:**690
- - *Ha-Le'om* **7:**722
- - *Ha-Moreh* **7:**722
- - *Ha-Yom* **7:**722
- - *Hazofeh ba-Arez ha-Hadashah* **4:**690
- - *In-Zikh* **4:**1136
- - *Morgen-Journal* **4:**1136
- - *Yidishe Kultur* **11:**1428
- Judaism
- - Beth Jacob schools **16:**1260
- - chaplaincy **11:**1569
- - Conservative Judaism **5:**901ff; **10:**396
- - Hasidism **7:**1395
- - homiletic literature **8:**959
- - Jewish studies **16:**582
- - Judaizers **10:**398
- - Orthodoxy **12:**1490
- - proselytism **13:**1192
- - Protestant-Jewish relations **13:**1252; **13:**1253; **13:**1254
- - rabbinate **13:**1448, 1453ff
- - rabbinical conferences **13:**1461
- - rabbinical seminaries **13:**1465
- - Reform Judaism **14:**24
- - religious thought **8:**743
- - Sephardi day schools **14:**1174
- - *shehitah* **14:**1341
- - synagogue libraries **11:**191
- - synagogues **1:** syn. list; **15:**586; **15:**619ff
- - trends **10:**395, 396
- - *yeshivot* **16:**772
- Politics **13:**821ff
- - Church and Nazism **8:**916
- - Communism **5:**804
- - labor movement **10:**1324ff
- - Negro emancipation **12:**932ff
- - neo-Fascism **12:**952
- - neo-Nazism **12:**954
- - New Left **12:**1031
- - socialism **15:**29ff; **15:**47; **15:**51
- Relations with Israel **9:**422; **9:**429ff
- - military aid **9:**402ff, 694
- - Palestine Mandate **11:**862
- - Partition Plan **15:**1544
- - peace guarantees **9:**384
- - Sinai (Suez) Campaign **9:**389ff; **14:**1607
- - Truman and State Department **15:**1409
- Zionism **16:**1063; **16:**1141ff
- - Agudat Israel **2:**426
- - Bluestone, Joseph Isaac **4:**1135
- - Brandeis, Louis Dembitz **4:**1297ff
- - Habonim **8:**1241
- - Ha-Shomer ha-Za'ir **7:**1375
- - Jewish Legion **10:**73
- - Mizrachi **12:**180
- - ORT **12:**1485
- - Poale Agudat Israel **13:**656
- - Po'alei Zion **13:**658
- - Six-Day War volunteers **9:**543
- - Territorialism **15:**1020
- - United Jewish Appeal **15:**1540
- - Weisgal, Meyer Wolf **16:**410
- - Zion Commonwealth **2:**339
- - Zionist Emergency Committee **2:**504
- - Zionist movement **16:**1087ff
- Miscellaneous
- - Am Olam settlement **2:**861
- - Berihah **4:**630
- - capitulations **5:**150
- - Catholic Church **5:**542
- - Colonization Association **10:**46
- - Committee Sports for Israel **8:**330
- - immigration **6:**974; **16:**1520
- - longevity **13:**1499
- - psychology **13:**1344
- - refugees **14:**28ff
- - War Crimes Trials **16:**289ff
- *illus:*

- - text
- - Brandeis University 4:1300-1301
- - Bronx, N.Y., Sholem Aleichem School pupils 6:434
- - Camp Lejeune, N.C., lesson in Religion 6:411
- - Camp Morasha, a class 6:418
- - Chicago, Ill.
- - - the "ghetto" in 1915 5:413
- - - Maxwell Street district 5:412
- - Cincinnati, O., Hebrew Union College 6:416
- - Dallas, Tex., an "aleph class" 6:410
- - Denver, Colo.
- - - National Jewish Hospital for Consumptives 5:1543
- - - record re donation of land for synagogue 5:1542
- - Hanukkah play in a Hebrew school 7:1285
- - immigrants from Eastern Europe under auspices of HIAS 15:1539
- - Israel Hawk missiles 9:430
- - Levy, Uriah Phillips 11:165
- - New York, Yeshiva University 6:414
- - New York Jews protest against Palestine policy (1947))6:1059
- - Philadelphia, Pa., Gratz College 7:861
- - Poland, description of conditions in 1943 13:759
- - pupils at a yeshivah 6:408
- - Saint Paul, Mount Zion Hebrew Congregation charter 12:36
- - Senate's endorsement of a Jewish national home in Palestine 3:393
- - solidarity with Soviet Jews, press advertisement 4:503
- - trade with Germany, 1927-1937 (table) 4:1282
- *pop. tables:*
- - text
- - Alabama 1969 2:506
- - Alaska, 1969 2:513
- - Arizona, 1969 3:449
- - Arkansas, 1969 3:459
- - California, 1969 5:59
- - Colorado 5:754
- - Connecticut 5:897
- - Delaware, 1969 5:1469
- - Florida, 1970 6:1363
- - Georgia, 1968 7:429
- - Hawaii 7:1495
- - Idaho, 1968 8:1222
- - Illinois, 1970 8:1255
- - Indiana, 1968 8:1360
- - Iowa, 1968 8:1438
- - Jewish population
- - - by religion and state, 1967 5:1512
- - - 1850-1967 5:1501
- - Kansas 10:738
- - Kentucky, 1968 10:909
- - Louisiana, 1968 11:518
- - Maine, 1968 11:783
- - Maryland 11:1077
- - Massachusetts 11:1113
- - Michigan, 1968 11:1499
- - Minnesota, 1968 12:39
- - Mississippi, 1968 12:155
- - Missouri, 1968 12:157
- - Montana, 1968 12:267
- - Nebraska, 1968 12:911
- - Nevada, 1968 12:1017
- - New Hampshire 12:1024
- - New Jersey, 1968 12:1028
- - New Mexico, 1968 12:1037
- - New York City 12:1077, 1078
- - New York State, 1968 12:1125
- - North Carolina, 1968 12:1218
- - North Dakota, 1968 12:1221
- - Ohio, 1968 12:1344
- - Oklahoma, 1968 12:1353
- - Oregon 12:1451
- - Pennsylvania, 1968 13:229
- - postwar communities 5:839
- - Rhode Island, 1968 14:143
- - South Carolina, 1968 15:211
- - South Dakota, 1968 15:213
- - Tennessee, 1968 15:1009
- - Texas 15:1034
- - towns with 100,000 or more Jews, 1967 5:1514
- - Utah, 1968 16:34
- - Vermont, 1968 16:112
- - Virginia, 1968 16:163
- - Washington, 1968 16:356
- - West Virginia, 1968 16:475
- - Wisconsin, 1968 16:557
- - Wyoming, 1968 16:680
- *see also under indivudual states and cities*
UNITED SYNAGOGUE (orgn., Eng.) 15:1672
- Adler, Nathan Marcus 2:286
- archives 3:382
- Cohen, Sir Robert Waley 5:684ff
- England 6:757ff
- London 11:477
- Orthodoxy 12:1491
- rabbi's function 13:1452
- synagogue 15:1590
- *maps:* text
United Synagogue Book Service (U.S.) 13:1376
UNITED SYNAGOGUE OF AMERICA 15:1673
- Abbell, Maxwell 2:46
- Abramowitz, Herman 2:169
- Adler, Cyrus 2:273
- publishing 13:1376
- Rabbinical Assembly 13:1460
- synagogues 15:591
United Synagogue Youth (U.S.) 15:1674
United Zionist Federation (Ger.) 16:1116
United Zionist Organization (Braz.) 16:1124
United Zionists (U.S.) 4:1135
Unit One Hundred and One (Isr. army) 9:386
Unity of God, *see* GOD (Attributes of; Unity)
Uniunea Evreilor Romani (J. org., Rum.) 14:396, 399, 405, 416
Universal Anti-Semitic League (Rum.) 3:86
Universal Brotherhood Movement 10:97
Universalism
- Akiva 2:492
- Chosen People 5:498
- Genesis, Book o f 7:395
- Judaism 10:388; 10:390
- Kook, Abraham Isaac 10:1186
- message of Torah 15:1239
- Noachide laws 12:1189
- prophets 13:1161
Universal Jewish Encyclopedia 6:733
"Universal Peace" (sculp., J.L. Butensky) 4:1538
Universal Postal Union 15:1564
Universe, *see* World
UNIVERS ISRAELITE (period.) 15:1674
- Kahn, Leon 10:690
- Levaillant, Isaie 11:65
- press 13:1032; 13:108
Universitates (Rom. leg. term) 10:1567
UNIVERSITIES 15:1675
- *Contents:*
- - In the Middle Ages 15:1674
- - 17th and 18th Centuries 15:1676
- - Enlightenment 15:1677
- - Modern Period 15:1678
- - In the U.S. 15:1679
- - Jewish Studies 15:1682
- *numerus clausus* 6:69ff; 12:1263
- Odessa 12:1325
- U.S.S.R. 14:464, 475
- *illus:*
- - Berlin students' society 16:1115
- - Yeshiva University 16:760, 767
Universities' Zionist Council (Eng.) 15:449
Universities' Zionist Federation (Eng.) 15:448
University College, London 6:462
University of . . ., *see also under main word*
University of Judaism (U.S.A.) 10:96
University of London Jewish Union Society 15:448
University of the Negev 9:958
- *illus:*
- - Beersheba buildings 4:385
UNJUST ENRICHMENT 15:1683
Unkiyyah (weight) 16:388
UNNA, PAUL GERSON 15:1687
Unna, Raphael 5:35
UNO., *see* UNITED NATIONS
Unquillo (tn., Arg.) 5:966; 15:1688
UNRRA 15:1668
- Berihah 4:630ff
- Jewish refugees 14:29
UNSCOP (orgn.) 15:1688
- Ben-Gurion, David 4:509
- Eban, Abba 6:343
- historical survey 9:359
- Inquiry Commission 13:34
- Palestine problem 16:1092
- partition plans 9:314; 13:34; 13:37; 15:1659
- U.N. and 15:1544
- Va'ad Le'ummi 16:50
- *illus:*
- - Sharett giving evidence 16:1093
Unser . . . see also under Undzer . . ., Unzer . . .
Unser Shtime (newsp., Pol.) 10:1172
Untash-Gal (k., Elam) 14:1483
Untash-Huban (k., Elam) 14:1483
Unterbalbach (tn., Ger.) 11:1384
Unterberg, Israel 12:1085
- *illus:*
- - J.W.B. committee 12:873
Unterkapo (concen. camps) 10:755
UNTERMAN, ISSER YEHUDA 15:1688
- autopsies and dissection 3:933
- religious life in Israel 9:896
- transplants 15:1337
- *illus:*
- - kindling Hanukkah lights at the Western Wall 7:1285
- - Rabbinical Council of America 13:1462
- - Six-Day War, meeting religious leaders 9:410
- - Yeshivat ha-Kotel 9:898
Untermeyer, Alvin 15:311; 15:1690
UNTERMEYER, LOUIS 15:1689
UNTERMYER SAMUEL 15:1690
- anti-Nazi boycott 4:1281
Untertuerkheim (loc., Ger.) 15:1042
Unzer . . ., see also under Undzer . . ., Unser . . .
Unzer Ekspres (daily) 13:1042; 16:973
Unzer Fraynd (newsp.) 13:1041; 16:15
Unzer Gedank (mag.) 3:886; 13:1025
Unzer Journal (period.) 14:1673
Unzer Lebn (newsp.) 13:1041
Unzer Shtime (newsp., Fr.) 13:1032
Unzer Shtime (newsp., Latv.) 15:910
Unzer Tribune (pub.) 16:1126
Unzer Tsayt (period., U.S.) 4:1506; 13:1056
Unzer Tsaytung (period., Pol.) 13:557
Unzer Veg (period.) 13:1056
Unzer Vort (newsp., Fr.) 13:1032 16:1115; 16:640
Unzer Vort (pub., Mex.) 16:1125
Unzer Zeit (U.S. period), *see Unzer Tsayt*
U.O.B.B. (orgn., Ger.), *see* Unabhaengiger Orden Bne Briss
U.O.J.C.A., *see* UNION OF ORTHODOX JEWISH CONGREATIONS OF AMERICA
U.P.A., *see* United Palestine Appeal
Uphaz (bib. loc.) 11:1430
Upper Galilee (reg., Er. Isr.), *see* GALILEE
Upper Silesia, *see* SILESIA
Upper Volta (rep., W. Afr.) 9:442
Uprimny, Julius 16:445
Uprooter of Mountains (term for amoraim) 2:867
U.P.U., *see* Universal Postal Union
"Upward Journey" (sculp., Thea Tewi) 3:643
ʿUqba ibn Nafil 10:697
UR 16:1
- Edessa 6:367
- excavations 16:1507
- Genesis 7:388
- Mari 11:973
- Mesopotamia 16:1487
- moon cult 12:290
- Sumer 15:512ff
Ural Mountains (Asia) 14:1486
ʿUr al-Tahta (vill., Isr.) 4:747ff
Uranius, Henricus 8:62
Urarta, Urartu (state, Mesop.), *see* ARARAT
Urartians (anc. people, Mesop.) 16:1502,1503
URBACH, EPHRAIM ELIMELECH 16:4
- religious life in Israel 9:900
- *Tarbiz* 15:809
Urbach, Hinko 16:52
Urban II (pope) 13:853
- Crusades 9:267; 11:35
Urban V (pope), *see* BULLS, PAPAL
Urban VIII (pope) 13:858
Urban, Anna Weissbrucker 8:62
Urbana (city, U.S.) 8:1255
Urbanization
- ancient Israel 8:611ff
- demographic changes 5:1511
- *see also:* CITY
Urbanus, Rhegius H. 8:62; 7:1278
Ur-Bau (gov., Mesop.) 16:1491 13:1399
URBINO (tn., It.) 16:4
- Giovanni Maria 7:588
- special Purim 13:1399
- *illus:*
- - wedding pageant 15:1051
Urbino, Manfredo d', *see* D'Urbino, Manfredo

Urdun, Al (Urdunn; prov., Er. Isr.) **7:**267; **9:**261
Urena, Pedro Henriquez **6:**160
Urfa (city, Turk.), *see* EDESSA
Urfa (prov., Turk.) **9:**504
Urfals (Turk. Js.) **9:**504
Urga (city, Mongolia), *see* Ulan Bator
Urgench (city, Usbek S.S.R.) **15:**1336
Urhai (loc., Osroene), *see* Orhai
URI, AVIVA **3:**612
- *illus:*
- - landscape (drg.) Fig. 105 **3**-ART
Uri, J. **8:**62
URI, PIERRE EMMANUEL **16:**5
URIAH (the Hittite, bib. fig.) **16:**5
- Bath-Sheba **4:**321
- letter **11:**55
- status of *gerim* **15:**420
- *illus:*
- - David and Bath-Sheba **11:**633
URIAH (Uritah; 8th cent. B.C.E., H.Pr.) **16:**6
- Ahaz **2:**455
- priesthood **13:**1075
URIAH (Uriahu; 6th cent. B.C.E., porphet) **16:**6
- Elnathan ben Achbor **6:**684
- Jeremiah **9:**1349
URIAH (5th cent. B.C.E. Pr.) **16:**6
Uriahssohn, M. **16:**1165
URI BEN AARON HA-LEVI **16:**6
- printing-press **13:**1034
- Zholkva **16:**1015
Uri ben Joel ha-Levi of Bonn **6:**625
Uri ben Phinehas of Strelisk, *see* STRELISK, URI BEN PHINEHAS OF
URI BEN SIMEON OF BIALA **16:**6
- itinerary, illuminated **9:**1149
Uriel (bib. fig.) **10:**1137
URIEL (angel) **16:**7
- as archangel **2:**962
Uri'el (vill., Isr.) **7:**354
Urijah (bib. fig.), *see* URIAH
URIM (kib., Isr.) **16:**7
- statistics **1:** place list
Urim (journ.) **1:** newsp. list
URIM and THUMMIM (priestly vestment) **16:**8
- astrology **3:**792
- divination **6:**112ff
- ephod **6:**804
- Jerusalem expansion **9:**1554
- lots **11:**511
- prophecy **13:**1154
- Saul **14:**913
- sin **14:**1590
- *illus:*
- - answering a question **6:**112
- - priestly vestments **13:**1065
- - Torah breastplate **4:**1342
- *see also:* PRIESTLY VESTMENTS
Urim le-Horim (period.) **1:**newsp. list
URIS (fam., U.S.) **16:**9
Uris, Harold **16:**9
Uris, Harris **16:**9
URIS, LEON **16:**10
- U.S. literature **15:**1573ff
Uris, Percy **16:**9
Uritsky, M. **5:**794
Urkhān (Ott. sult.) **16:**1530
Urmia (tn., Iran), *see* RIZAIEH
Ūrmiyā (prophet), *see* JEREMIAH
Ur-Nammu (ruler., Mesop.)
- Mari **11:**974
- Mesopotamia **16:**1492
- Sumer **15:**513
- Ur **16:**3
- *illus:*
- - Ziggurat of Ur **16:**1
U.R.O., *see* UNITED RESTITUTION ORGANIZATION
Urraca (q., León, Castile) **6:**1236
Urrutia, Francis **9:**1497
Ursa Major (constellation) **3:**796
Ursa Minor (constellation) **3:**796
Urshu (Hurrian stronghold) **16:**1497
Ursicinus (Rom. comm.)
- Jerusalem Talmud **15:**775
- revolt against Gallus **9:**256
- Tiberias **15:**1132
- warfare **16:**281
- Yose, Jonah, and **16:**850
- Yudan **16:**867
Ursinus (anti-pope) **2:**801
Ursinus, J. H. **8:**62
URUGUAY (S. Am.) **16:**10
- *Contents:*
- - The Colonial Period **16:**10
- - The Modern Period **16:**10
- - - Institutional Development **16:**11
- - - Economy **16:**12
- - - Community Relations **16:**13
- - - Jewish Education **16:**14
- - - Religious and Cultural Life **16:**14
- - Relations with Israel **16:**15
- education **6:**457
- Latin American Jewry **10:**1449ff
- politics, Jews in **13:**821
- press **13:**1041
- socialism **15:**32
- synagogues **1:**syn. list
- UNSCOP **15:**1688
- Zionism **16:**1126
- *illus:* text
Uruk (city, Mesop.), *see* ERECH
Urukagina (k., Mesop.) **16:**1488
Urwaehlerzeitung (journ.) **4:**682
Ury, J., *see* Uri, J.
URY, LESSER **16:**16
- *illus:*
- - text
- - "Snow" (drg.) **3:**552
Ur-Zababa (ruler, Mesop.) **16:**1489
Urzidil, Jan **5:**1209
U.S.A., *see* UNITED STATES OF AMERICA
Usage (leg. term), *see* MINHAG
Usatges (Barcelona code) **4:**208
Uscudama (tn., Turk.), *see* ADRIANOPLE
USHA (tn., kib., Er. Isr.) **16:**17
- statistics **1:** place list
USHA, SYNOD OF **16:**17
- children, maintenance **12:**111
- Eliezer ben Jacob **6:**624
- historical chart **8:**766-767
- *tannaim* **11:**1240ff
"Ushering in the Sabbath" (paint., Oppenheim) **14:**560
USHPIZIN ("guests"; myst.) **16:**19
- *hoshanot* **8:**1029
- Sukkot **15:**501; **15:**502
- *illus:*
- - papercut **13:**44-45
ʿUSIFIYYA (loc., Isr.) **16:**19
- Druze village **5:**186
- synagogue **12:**181; **15:**598
- *illus:* text
Uskub (city, Yug.), *see* SKOPLJE
Uskudam (tn., Turk.), *see* ADRIANOPLE
Üsküdar (city, Turk.) **2:**523; **9:**1086
Uslaky-Rejto, Ildiko **12:**1377
USOV (tn., Morav.) **16:**20
USQUE, ABRAHAM **16:**21
- Ferrara **6:**1234
- printing **13:**1095
- Usque, Solomon **16:**22
- *illus:*
- - printers' marks **13:**1094
USQUE, SAMUEL **16:**21
- *Consolaçam as Tribulaçoens de Israel* **8:**556
- history **8:**696
- on Reformation **14:**22
- Usque, Abraham **16:**21
USQUE, SOLOMON **16:**22
- Usque, Abraham **16:**21
- Usque, Samuel **16:**21
Ussermann, Aemilian **8:**62
Ussher, James **8:**62
USSISHKIN, ABRAHAM MENAHEM MENDEL **16:**22
- Ben-Yehuda, Eliezer **4:**568
- He-Halutz **8:**247
- Kharkov conference **10:**941*ff*
- Language Committee **2:**206
- Zionist Commission **16:**1163
- Zionist Congress (9th) **16:**1170
- *illus:*
- - text
- - F.Z.C. **16:**1165
- - Keren Hayesod bld'g cornerstone ceremony **10:**916
Ussishkin, D. **9:**1525
"Ussishkin Fortresses" (stlmts., Isr.) **16:**26
- Dafnah **5:**1220
- Dan (kibbutz) **5:**1260
Ussoskin, Moshe **10:**916
U.S.S.R., *see* RUSSIA
Ustashi (Croatian fascists) **8:**869; **16:**917
USTEK (tn., Cz.) **16:**26
ÚSTÍ NAD LABEM (tn., Bohem.) **16:**27
- Czechoslovakia **5:**1200
Usufruct (leg. term)
- antichresis **3:**59
- *shekhiv me-ra* **16:**524
Uṣūl al- (wk., ibn Janaḥ), *see Kitāb al-Uṣūl*
Uṣūl wa al-Fuṣūl, al- (wk., Abu al-Faraj), *see Kitāb al-Uṣūl wa al-Fuṣūl fī al-Lugha al-ʿIbrāniyya*
USURY **16:**27
- *Contents:*
- - Biblical Law **16:**27
- - Talmudic Law **16:**28
- - Post-Talmudic Law **16:**31
- In *Halakhah*
- - Amram ben Sheshna **2:**892
- - antichresis **3:**59
- - by document **14:**1388ff
- - contracts, illegal **5:**930
- - *dina de-malkhuta* **6:**55
- - gain *(lucrum)* **12:**249
- - *halakhic* opposition to **16:**1277
- - *hekdesh* **8:**280; **8:**282
- - *iska* **14:**1389
- - legal fictions **16:**1282
- - legal person **10:**1569
- - lien **11:**228
- - orphans' money **12:**12
- - partnership **13:**153
- - pledge **13:**639; **13:**641
- - strangers **7:**412; **15:**419
- - usurer as witness **16:**586
- - wage delay compensation **10:**1327
- *see also:* BANKING AND BANKERS; MONEYLENDING
- In History
- - ancient Israel **16:**1269
- - anti-Semitism **3:**101
- - Aquinas, Thomas, on **3:**229
- - Assembly of Jewish Notables **3:**761ff
- - Bernardino da Siena **4:**672
- - Calvin, John **5:**66
- - Christian attitude to Jews **8:**673
- - economic doctrines **16:**1294
- - Germany **7:**461
- - Hurrian customs **12:**1290
- - image of the Jew **7:**443
- - Innocent III **5:**1139
- - Jacob of Orleans **9:**1234
- - Koran prohibition **10:**1199
- - Lateran Council, IV **10:**1446
- - medieval Jewry **16:**1289
- - Meir ben Simeon of Narbonne **3:**194
- - Monti Di Pietà **12:**279
- - papyri **8:**300
- - Poland **13:**729
- - Pomis' defense of **3:**196
U.S. War Refugee Board, *see* WAR REFUGEE BOARD
U.S.Y. (orgn., U.S.), *see* United Synagogue Youth
UTAH (U.S. state) **16:**33
- Bamberger, Simon **4:**156ff
- *illus:*
- - text
- - Salt Lake City **15:**1597
- *pop. tables:* text
UTENA (tn., Lith.) **16:**34
Utensils, *see* Vessels
Utes (Ind. tribe, N.Am.) **5:**754
U Thant (U.N. offic.)
- Armistice Agreements, 1949 **3:**482
- Six-Day War **9:**407ff; **14:**1626
- UNEF withdrawal **15:**1556
ʿUthmān (caliph)
- Abdallah Ibn Salām **2:**54
- Umayyads **15:**1528
ʾUthmān I (Ott.) **16:**1529
ʿUthmān III (sult.) **16:**1538
ʾUthmaniyya Madrasa, Al- (coll., Jer.) **9:**1425
UTICA (city, U.S.) **16:**34
Utica (loc., Tun.) **15:**1431
Utin, Nicolai **15:**28
Utitz (fam., Cz.) **16:**227
UTITZ, EMIL **16:**35
UTKIN, JOSEPH PAVLOVICH **16:**35
Utley, Francis Lee **13:**178
Utnapishtim (Bab. myth. fig.) **12:**730; **16:**1485
- Flood **6:**1352; **6:**1354; **12:**1192ff
Utopias, Zionist **16:**1159
UTRECHT (city, Holl.) **16:**36
Utrecht, Treaty of **3:**167
Utsyany (tn., Lith.), *see* UTENA
Utu (deity) **6:**1352
Utu-hegal (k., Mesop.) **16:**1492
- Ur **16:**3
Utyana (tn., Lith.), *see* UTENA
UVAROV, SERGEY SEMYONOVICH **16:**38
- Lilienthal, Max **11:**243
Uvdah, Operation (War of Indep.) **6:**568; **9:**377; **16:**313
Uvdot u-Misparim (period.) **1:**place list
Uvedale, John, *see* Udall, John
Uythage, C.C. **8:**62
ʾUyūn al-Shaʾīn (loc., Isr.) **14:**1410
Uz (bib. fig.) **12:**790
UZ (bib. land) **16:**38
- Armenia **3:**473
Uzal (bib. fig.) **16:**39
UZAL (bib. loc.) **16:**39
UZAN (fam., N. Afr.) **16:**39
Uzan, Michael (cmty., ldr.) **16:**39
Uzan, Michael (chem.) **16:**39
Uzan, Michel (au.) **15:**1449
Uzan, Solomon **15:**805; **16:**39
Uzan, Victor **16:**39
"Uz-Armenia" (loc., Anatolia) **3:**473
ʿUzayr (scribe), *see* EZRA
Uzayr, Al- (tn., Iraq) **8:**1450
UZBEKISTAN (rep., U.S.S.R.) **16:**39
- Bukharan *aliyah* **9:**503
- synagogue **15:**589
- *illus:*
- - text
U.Z.C. (orgn.), *see* Universities' Zionist Council
Uzedah, Samuel ben Isaac, *see* UCEDA, SAMUEL BEN ISAAC

U.Z.F. (orgn.), *see* Universities' Zionist Federation
UZHGOROD (city, Ukr.) **16:**41
Uziel, *see also under* Uzziel
Uziel (s., Ben Sira) **4:**549
UZIEL (Seph. fam.) **16:**42
Uziel, Abraham (poet) **16:**42
Uziel, Abraham **4:**1397
Uziel, Ben-Zion Meir Ḥai, *see* OUZIEL, BEN-ZION MEIR ḤAI
Uziel, David ben Ḥayyim **16:**42
Uziel, Ḥayyim **16:**42
Uziel, Isaac (r., Sp.) **11:**1215
Uziel, Isaac (trans., It.) **14:**1608
UZIEL, ISAAC BEN ABRAHAM **16:**42
- Aboab da Fonseca **2:**95
- Amsterdam **2:**896
Uziel, Jacob **13:**1038
Uziel, Joseph **16:**42
Uziel, Judah **6:**1256; **16:**42ff
Uziel, Judah ben Joseph **16:**42
Uziel, Judah ben Samuel **16:**42
Uziel, Rafael **13:**1038
Uziel, Solomon **16:**42
Uzielli, Gustavo **7:**422
UZZA AND AZA'EL (leg. figs.) **16:**43
- *nephilim* **12:**962; **12:**963
- *see also:* AZAZEL
UZZAH (bib. fig.) **16:**43
Uzzah (mosh., Isr.) **1:** place list
Uzzenu (periods.) **1:** newsp. list
Uzzi (Samar. h. pr.) **14:**751
UZZIAH (k., Judah) **16:**43
- Adar **2:**252
- agriculture **2:**391
- Carmel vineyards **5:**184
- Edom **6:**375
- Elath **6:**566
- history **8:**601ff
- history chart **8:**766–767
- Hosea **8:**1010ff
- Jerusalem **9:**1383
- Negev **12:**928
- Tobiads **15:**1178
- *geneal. table:* **5:**1341
- *illus:*
- - text
- - divided kingdom (map) **9:**117
- - reburial inscription **2:**712
Uzziel, *see also under* Uziel
Uzziel (amora) **8:**1111
Uzziel (k., Lost Tribes), *see* Addiel
Uzziel (fallen angel) **12:**962; **12:**963
Uzziel (fam., Gr., Isr.) **14:**707
Uzziel, Joseph **7:**254
Uzziel ben Kehat (bib. fig.) **10:**1135
- Samaritan priesthood **14:**734

V

Va'ad Adat ha-Sefaradim (orgn., Jer.), *see* Council of the Sephardi Community
Va'ad Arba Arazot, *see* COUNCILS OF THE LANDS
Va'ad ha-Hazzalah (rescue com.)
- archives 3:386
- Austrian Jews 3:901
- Kotler, Aaron 10:1222
- UNRAA 15:1688
- U.S. 15:1634
Va'ad ha-Hinnukh ha-Rashi (orgn.) 3:425*ff*
Va'ad ha-Kehillah (Jer., cmty. council) 9:1471; 9:1497
Vaad Hakehilot (Arg. orgn.) 3:417
Vaad Hakhamim (journ.) 1:newsp. list
Va'ad ha-Lashon ha-Ivrit, *see* ACADEMY OF THE HEBREW LANGUAGE
Va'ad ha-Yeshivot (orgn.)
- Grodzinski, Hayyim Ozer 7:928
- Israel Meir ha-Kohen 9:1070
- Israel *yeshivot* 16:772
- Sorotzkin, Zalman 15:167
Va'ad Kelali (cmty. council, Jer.) 9:892
Va'ad le-Ma'an ha-Mizrah (orgn.) 4:1160
VA'AD LE'UMMI (govt. body, Er. Isr.) 16:49
- adult education 9:964
- archives 3:388
- Asefat ha-Nivharim 9:684
- communal organization 9:608
- religious life 9:894
- Sephardim 14:1175
- sport 15:296
- Thon. Ya'akov Yohanan 15:1123
- *illus:*
- - text
- - final meeting 9:365
- - U.S. Senate's endorsement of a Jewish national home in Palestine 3:393
- *see also:* JEWISH AGENCY
Va'ad Medinat Lita, *see* Council of the Land of Lithuania
Va'ad Zemanni (govt. body, Er. Isr.) 15:1123; 16:49
Vaballathus (Rom. vassal) 12:1318
VAC (city, Hung.) 16:51
VADASZ, LIPOT 16:51
VAD RASHKOV (tn., Mold.) 16:51
Vadum Jacob (bridge, Isr.), *see* GESHER BENOT YA'AKOV
Vaez (fam., Alg.) 12:1446
VAEZ, ABRAHAM 16:52
Vaez, Jacob 16:52
Vafiadhis, Nikodemos 7:887
Vafopoulos, G. Th. 7:898
VÁGÓ, JÓZSEF 16:52
Vai'da-Voevod, Alexandru 14:394ff
Vainshtein, Lev 12:1377; 15:313
Vais (fam., Alg.), *see* Vaez
Vaivara (concen. camp) 6:917
Vajda, Béla 2:98
VAJDA, GEORGES 16:52
- Kabbalah and philosophy 10:537; 19:649
Vajda, István 12:1438
VAJS, ALBERT 16:52
Vakhnakht (custom), *see* SHOLEM ZOKHOR
Vakhtangov, Yevgeni 6:20; 7:1030
Val, Merry del 16:74
VALABREGA, CESARE 12:712
Valabrega, Daniel 15:1455
Valabrègue, Jules 10:1496
VALABRÈGUE, MARDOCHÉE GEORGES 16:53
Valckenier, S. 8:62
Valdeolivas (tn., Sp.) 16:1287
Valdheim (kolkhoz, Rus.) 4:1049
Valdivia (city, Chile) 5:466
VALEA-LUI-VLAD (stlmt., Bess.) 16:53
Valeanu, I. H., *see* WECHSLER, MAX
Valenca (fam.) *see* VALENSI
VALENCE (tn., Fr.) 16:53
Valenci, Samuel 16:42
Valencia (fam.), *see* VALENSI
VALENCIA (city, Sp.) 16:54
- *Contents:*
- - After the Christian Reconquest 16:54
- - The Persecutions of 1391 16:54
- - The Conversos 16:57
- Alconstantini, Moses 2:550
- Auto da Fé 3:912
- Isaac ben Sheshet Perfet 9:32
Valencia (city, Venez.) 16:91
Valencia, Diego de (monk), *see* Diego de Valencia
Valencia, edict of (1239) 15:231
Valenciano (fam.) *see* VALENSI
Valens (Rom. emp.) 9:257
VALENSI (fam.) 16:58
- Azemmour 3:1004
Valensi, Abraham 16:58
Valensi, Alfred 16:58
Valensi, Gabriel (inter.) 16:58
Valensi, Gabriel (sol.) 16:58
Valensi, Gabriel de Manuel (fin.) 16:58
Valensi, Henry 13:113
Valensi, Isaac ben David, *see* Balansi, Isaac ben David
Valensi, Joseph (r.) 16:58
Valensi, Joseph (polit.) 16:58
Valensi, Joseph (dipl.) 16:58
Valensi, Joseph (schol.) 16:58
Valensi, Moses (J. ldr.) 16:58
Valensi, Moses (dipl.) 16:58
Valensi, Raymond 16:58
Valensi, Rudolphe 16:58
Valensi, Samuel (sol.) 16:58
Valensi, Samuel (polit.) 16:58
Valensi, Samuel ben Abraham 16:58
- Alashkar, Moses 2:511
- Ibn Habib, Jacob 8:1176
Valensi, Théodore 16:58
Valensin, Eugene 16:1165
Valensis, T. 8:63
Valenstein, Lawrence 2:317
Valente, F. 4:878
VALENTIN, GABRIEL GUSTAV 16:59
- *illus:* text
VALENTIN, HUGO MAURICE 16:59
Valentinian III (Rom. emp.) 3:854; 14:230
Valera, Cipriano de 8:62; 4:879
Valera, Diego de 15:253
Valerianus (Rom. Emp.) 9:1406
Valerius, *see* Vonck, Cornelis Hugo
VALERIUS GRATUS (Rom. gov.) 16:59
- Anan ben Seth 2:922
- *illus:*
- - coins, Judean 5:711
Valerius Flaccus, L. 3:746
VALERIUS MAXIMUS (Rom. writ.) 14:236
VALERO (fam., Jer.) 16:60
Valero, Hayyim Aharon 16:60
Valero, Jacob 16:60
Valero, Joseph Moshe 16:60
Valéry, Paul Ambroise 5:1428
Valeton, J. P. P. 8:63
Valhalla (stlmt., Er. Isr.) 9:1256
Valis, Raphael 11:803
VALLADOLID (city. Sp.) 16:60 16:60
- Antunes family 3:167
- Badajoz 4:59
- Benveniste, Abraham 4:559
- education 6:412
- Ferrer, Vicente 6:1235
- informers 8:1367
- *takkanot* 15:725
Valladolid, Alfonso de, *see* ABNER OF BURGOS
Valladolid, Juan de 15:253
VALLAT, XAVIER 16:62
Valle, Federico Della 9:1101
VALLE, MOSES DAVID BEN SAMUEL 16:62
- Luzzatto, M. H. 11:601
- Shabbateanism 14:1251
Valle, Pietro della, *see* Pietro della Valle
Vallensis, Joannes 8:63
Vallentine (bk. firm) 4:1239
Vallentine, Isaac 13:1374
- navy service 11:1552
Vallentine Mitchell (publ. house) 5:450
Vallentine's Jewish Encyclopedia 6:734; 14:1534
Valley of the Cross (Jer.) 9:1515
- War of Independence 9:1480
Valley of Hinnom (Isr.), *see* GEHINNOM
Valley of Jehoshaphat (Er. Isr.), *see* JEHOSHAPHAT, VALLEY OF
Valley of the Titans, *see* Refaim Valley
Vallicrosa, Millas 14:875
Vallsecha, Gabriel de 11:917
Vallsecha, Juan de, *see* Ibn Rich, Hayyim
VALMASEDA (tn., Sp.) 16:63
Valois, Henry of (k., Fr.), *see* Henry III
Valois, Louis de, *see* Louis de Valois of Alais
VALONA (city, Alb.) 16:63
Valor, Road of (Er. Isr.), *see* Road of Valor
VALPARAÍSO (city, Chile) 16:64
Valperga, Tommaso di Caluso 8:63
VALRÉAS (tn., Fr.) 16:64
- Dauphiné 5:1315
- Vienne 16:133
Valriant (period.) 8:219
Valvasson, Yomtov 7:414
Valverdius, Bartholomaeus 8:63
Valvrojenski, Bernard, *see* BERENSON, BERNARD
VAMBERY, ARMINIUS (Vamberger, Hermann) 16:65
- stamps 15:335
- travels 15:1351
Vambery, Rustem 16:66
Vámoš, Gejza 5:1208
Vampires 11:708
Van (lake, Mesop.) 16:1502
Van Ameringen, M.L. 13:707
Van Buren (city, Ark.) 3:459
VANCE, ZEBULON BAIRD 16:66
Vancouleurs, Gerard de 3:806
VANCOUVER (city, Can.) 16:66
- British Columbia 4:1380
Vandals (people) 4:206
- Rome 14:244
Van Damm, Sheila 15:298
Van den Vondel, Joost 9:1343
Van Der Driesche, J.C., *see* DRUSIUS, JOHANN CLEMENS
Vandervelde, Émile 4:1138

Van de Velde (cartog.) **11**:931
Van de Water **16**:37
Van Diemen's Land, *see* AUSTRALIA
Van Dreunen, Meinardus **16**:37
Van Erpe, Thomas, *see* ERPENIUS, THOMAS
Van Eyck, Jan **9**:1580
Van Gelder, J. **16**:37
Van Geldern, Peira, *see* Heine, Betty
Van Geldern Haggadah (bk.) **8**:1287
Van Geldern Haggadah, "Sister" to (illum. ms.) **13**:172-173
Van Hard, Judith **4**:677
Van Helmont, Franciscus (Franz) Mercurius, *see* Helmont, Franciscus Mercurius van
Van Leer Jerusalem Foundation **9**:1490
Van Leyden, Lucas, *see* Lucas van Leyden
Van Limborch, Philipp **6**:96
Vannes Church Council **4**:1383
Van Nierop (fam.), *see* NIEROP, VAN
Van Noorden, Solomon **15**:1206
VAN OVEN (fam.) **16**:67
Van Oven, Abraham **16**:67
Van Oven, Barnard **16**:68
Van Oven, Joshua **16**:67
Van Oven, Lionel **16**:68
VAN PAASSEN, PIERRE **16**:68
Van Praag, Joe, *see* Praag, Joe Van
Van Praag, Lionel Maurice **15**:312
VAN PRAAGH, WILLIAM **16**:68
VAN RAALTE, EDUARD ELLIS **16**:69
VAN VRIESLAND, SIEGFRIED ADOLF (Zadok) **16**:69
- Zionism **16**:1118
VAN VRIESLAND, VICTOR EMANUEL **16**:69
Van Waesberge, Johannus **16**:37
Vapnyarka (tn., Ukr.) **15**:1335
Vara, La (newsp.) **14**:1174
Várad (city, Rum.), *see* ORADEA
Varano, G. **9**:1103
Varazdin (tn., Croatia) **16**:870
Vardi, David **7**:1029
- *illus:*
- - Habimah **7**:1029
Vardi, Herzl, *see* Rosenblum, Naphtali Herzl
Vardon (mosh., Isr.), *see* Menuḥah
Varenius, August **8**:63
VARGA, YEVGENI SAMOILOVICH **16**:69
Vargas, Jeronimo de, *see* Athias, Yom Tov
Varhayt (newsp.), *see Warheit*
Varlik Vergisi (tax) **15**:1458
VARLIN (Guggenheim, Willy) **3**:62
VARNA (city, Bul.) **16**:70
VĂRNAI, ZSENI **8**:1087
VARNHAGEN, RAHEL **16**:70
- Asser family **3**:766
- salon **14**:708; **14**:709
Varon, Benjamin, *see* Weiser, Benno
VARRO, MARCUS TERENTIUS **14**:232; **14**:236
VARSHAVSKI, ABRAHAM **16**:71
Varshavski, Y., *see* BASHEVIS SINGER, ISAAC
Varshavsky, Mark **7**:804
VARSHAVSKY, OIZER **16**:71
- *Khaliastre*, editor **10**:936
Varshever Ekspres (newsp.) **13**:1042
Vartashen (vill., Rus.) **3**:1005; **3**:1006
Varthema, Ludvico di **3**:235
Varus (Rom. gov.) **8**:636
- Aretas IV **12**:743
Varzager, S. **16**:826
Vásárhelyi, K. Péter **8**:63
VAŠEK, ANTON **16**:72
Vashiasky, Michal **12**:455
VASHTI (bib. fig.) **16**:72
- in the Arts **6**:908
- Scroll of Esther **14**:1047
- *Targum Sheni* **15**:812
Vasilevski, A. M. **6**:144
VASILKOV (city, Ukr.) **16**:73
Vaslinus (moneylender) **11**:892
VASLUI (city, Mold.) **16**:73
Vaslui (Ḥas. dyn.) **14**:387, 532
Vasseur, Joshua le **8**:63
Vatable (Vantablus), François **8**:63
Vater, J. Severin **8**:63
Vaterland (journ.) **16**:204
VATICAN **16**:73
- *Contents:*
- - The Vatican and the Zionist Movement **16**:73
- - The Vatican and the State of Israel **16**:76
- blood libel **4**:1120
- ecumenical council (1958) **15**:1645
- Hebrew mss. **11**:907
- Holocaust and Churches **8**:910
- Holocaust rescue **8**:907
- Judaism **10**:159
- library **11**:193
- Zionism **13**:572
- *illus:*
- - Poland, description of conditions in 1943 **13**:759
- *see also:* CHURCH, CATHOLIC; POPES
Vatican I, Council of **5**:549
Vatican II, Council of **5**:549
- Isaac, Jules Marx **9**:10
- John XXIII **10**:159
- Paul VI **13**:189
Vatican Arba'ah Turim (illum. ms.) **12**:602
VATKE, WILHELM **16**:79
VATRA DORNEI (tn., Rum.) **16**:80
Vaturi, Benjamin **13**:1483
Vaucluse (reg., Fr.) **3**:964
Vaud (canton, Switz.) **10**:1471
Vaudoncourt (loc., Fr.) **11**:496
Vaudrevange (tn., Fr.) **11**:496
VAUGHAN, FRANKIE **15**:1092
Vaughan, Henry **6**:778
Vaughan, Thomas **10**:646
Vaughan Williams, Ralph **9**:1589
Vaumeil (loc., Fr.) **14**:1623
Vauvert (tn., Fr.), *see* POSQUIÈRES
VAUX, ROLAND DE **16**:80
Vav (Hebr. let.), *see* WAW
Va-Yedabber Rabbah (agg. Mid.), *see* NUMBERS RABBAH
Va-Yelakket Yosef (journ.) **1**:newsp. list
Va-Yeshalleḥu Zuta, *see* SIFREI ZUTA
Va-Yiggash Yehudah (wk.) **7**:1272
Va-Yikra, *see* LEVITICUS, BOOK OF
Va-Yikra Rabbah (Mid.), *see* LEVITICUS RABBAH
Vayol, Hans **4**:1417
Vaz (fam., Jam.) **9**:1274
Vaz (fam., Nantes) **12**:817
Vaz, Diego **12**:1273
Vaz, Simḥah **4**:443
Vaz, Tome **8**:1407
Vaz Dias, Arnold **10**:306
Vázsonyi, János **16**:81
VÁZSONYI, VILMOS **16**:81
Vborevich, A. **11**:1556
Vecchi, de (fam.) **14**:241
Vecchi, Orazio **9**:1105
Vecchietti, Giambattista **10**:433
VECINHO, JOSEPH **16**:81
- astrolabe **3**:788
Vecker (newsp.), *see Veker*
Vedan (bib. loc.) **11**:1433
Vedelius, Nicolaus **8**:63
Veenendaal (tn., Holl.) **16**:37
Veesenmayer, Edmund **8**:1099
- Szálasi, Ferenc **15**:656
Vega, Garcilaso de la **15**:248
Vega, Joseph Penso de la, *see* PENSO DE LA VEGA, JOSEPH
Vega, Judah **16**:42
Vega, Lope de, *see* Lope de Vega
Vega, Manuel Rodrigues **15**:1302
Vega Enriques, Rachel de **5**:367
VEGETABLES **16**:82
- *Contents:*
- - Artichoke **16**:82
- - Celery and Parsley **16**:83
- - Colocasia **16**:83
- - Cress **16**:83
- - Turnip and Rape **16**:83
- Bible **6**:1416ff
- mixed species **12**:170ff
- *illus:*
- - *maror* **11**:1014
- - *sukkah* decoration **15**:*fcg.* 491
- - West Bank, cultivation under plastic cover **9**:786
- *see also:* LEGUMES
Vegetarianism **11**:1162
- Wormser, Sekel **16**:649
Vegetative soul (philos. conc.) **15**:173
Ve-ha-kohanim (litur.) **3**:980
- *mus. notations:*
- - *Mi-Sinai niggunim* **12**:151
Ve-Hayita Akh Same'aḥ (Heb. greeting) **7**:916
Vehe, M. **8**:63
Vehel, J. **14**:537
Ve-Hizhir (wk.) **2**:450
Veidt, Conrad **16**:262
Veigelsberg, Hugo, *see* IGNOTUS, HUGO
VEIGELSBERG, LEO **10**:318
VEIL **16**:83
- chastity **8**:6
- marriage **11**:1033
- Samaritan marriage **14**:746
Veil, Charles-Marie **16**:84
VEIL, LEWIS (Daniel) COMPIÈGNE DE **16**:84
Veil, Sir Thomas **16**:84
Ve-imru Amen (litur.) **2**:803
VEINBERG, MOISSEY SAMUILOVICH **16**:84
VEINER, HARRY **16**:85
- Alberta **2**:531
VEINGER, MORDECAI **16**:85
Veinstein, Nathan, *see* TERTULIAN, NICOLAE
VEIT (fam.) **16**:85
Veit, Benedict **4**:640
- Prussia **13**:1288
Veit, David **16**:85
Veit, Johannes (Jonas) **14**:970; **16**:86
Veit, Joseph **16**:86
Veit, Judah **16**:85
Veit, Levin **12**:64
VEIT, MORITZ **16**:86
Veit, Philipp (art.) **16**:86
- Mendelssohn, Moses **11**:1326
- Schlegel, Friedrich **14**:970
Veit, Philipp (bnk.) **16**:86
Veit, Simon **16**:85
- Schlegel, Dorothea **14**:969
Veit, Solomon **16**:85
VEITH, JOHANN EMANUEL **16**:86
Veith, Joseph **16**:87
Veker (newsp.) **4**:1500 **13**:1046
- Vilkaviskis **16**:135
VEKSLER, VLADIMIR **16**:87
Velasco (city, Tex.) **15**:1034
Veleslavinova Bible **8**:1135
Vélez de Guevara, Luis **15**:253
Veliki Bečkerek (city, Yug.), *see* ZRENJANIN
VELIZH (city, Rus.) **16**:87
- history chart **8**:766-767
Vellos (ship) **8**:1249
Vellum (parchment) **16**:659
Velosino, Fosue **13**:1613
Velt-Ayn, Velt-Oys (annual) **8**:1238
VELTWYCK, GERARD **16**:89
Velvele Brisker, *see* SOLOVEICHIK, ISAAC ZE'EV HA-LEVI
Velvel Zbarazher, *see* EHRENKRANZ, BENJAMIN (Wolf) ZEEB
Velyun (tn., Pol.), *see* WIELUN
Venclović, Gavril Stefanović **16**:885
Vendramin, Giovanni **16**:101
Vendrovsky, Zalman, *see* WENDROFF, ZALMAN
Venema, Herman **8**:63
Venereal disease **14**:1502
- *zavim* **16**:941
VENETIANER, LAJOS (Ludwig) **16**:89
Venetian Haggadah (bk.) **8**:1319
Venetus, F. G., *see* GIORGIO (Zorzi), FRANCESCO
VENEZIANI, EMMANUEL FELIX **16**:89
Venezis, Elias **7**:887
Venezky, Julian **4**:1204
VENEZUELA (rep.) **16**:90
- *Contents:*
- - Jewish Organizations **16**:91
- - Political Status and Ties with Israel **16**:92
- Israel **9**:435
- Latin America **10**:1450ff
- politics, Jews in **13**:821
- synagogues **1**:syn. list
- Zionism **16**:1126
- *pop. tables:* text
VENGEANCE **16**:93
- *see also:* BLOOD-AVENGER; BLOODGUILT
Vengerov, Semyon Afanasyevich, *see* WENGEROFF, SEMYON AFANASYEVICH
Vengrov(e) (tn., Pol.), *see* WEGROW
VENICE (city, It.) **16**:94
- *Contents:*
- - Emancipation **16**:98
- - Cultural and Social Life **16**:98
- - Hebrew Printing **16**:101
- - Holocaust Period and After **16**:102
- archives **3**:383
- Ashkenazi, Solomon **3**:732
- *banchi del ghetto* **16**:1291
- banking and bankers **4**:169
- book-art **3**:537
- ghetto origin **7**:542
- *ḥalukkah* **7**:1208
- history chart (1427, 1516) **8**:766-767
- Inquisition **8**:1400
- library **11**:193
- Luzzatto's apologetic **8**:700
- Marrano Diaspora **11**:1022
- Museums **12**:544
- Nathan of Gaza **14**:1239
- ricondotta **2**:404
- Shabbateanism **14**:1234
- tax **15**:839
- typography **15**:1481
- *illus:*
- - text
- - Bragadini's printers' mark **13**:1093
- - Canton Synagogue **4**:1003; **5**:295
- - Castellazzo's petition **5**:238
- - circumcision register **3**:383
- - Conigliano family, charter **9**:1132
- - decree re arms **3**:925

– – German Synagogue 3:453
– – Giustiniani press printers' mark 13:1093
– – ghetto 9:1127; 10:82
– – Italian synagogue 9:1135
– – Jewish museum 12:547
– – Spanish synagogue 15:617,618
– – Talmud burning, announcement 15:770
– – wedding ceremony, 18th cent. 11:1033
– – World War II refugees 14:28
VENICE HAGGADOT 7:1101
– Jerusalem in Art 9:1580
– illus: 2:878; 3:537; 7:1088; 10:211; 11:1410
Venisti, Raphael Isaac Meir Ibn 11:1159
Ve-nomar Amen (litur.) 2:803
VENOSA (tn., It.) 16:102
– catacombs 5:251
– epitaphs 6:819
– Silano 3:226
– yeshivah 16:764
Venta Prieta (vill., Mex.) 11:1460
VENTIDIUS, PUBLIUS (Bassus) 16:103
– Antigonus' war 3:66
– Malchus I 12:742
VENTSPILS (city, Latv.) 16:103
Ventura, David Shabbetai 16:121
Ventura, Elijah 16:121
Ventura, Jack 13:1038
VENTURA, MICHON (Moses) 16:103
– law 10:1492
VENTURA, MOÏSE 16:103
Ventura, Raphael Isaac 7:865
VENTURA, RUBINO 16:104
– illus: text
Venture, Mardochée 4:882
Venturozzo, Samuel 13:1258
Venus (planet) 3:796
Venus, Temple of (Jer.) 9:1405
Venusi, Johann Bernhard 8:63
VEPRIK, ALEXANDER MOISEYEVITCH 16:104
– music 12:660
VERA Y ALARCON, LOPE DE 16:105
Verb (Heb. gram.) 16:1562
– Arabic influence 16:1629
– biblical Hebrew 16:1577
– Dead Sea Scrolls 16:1587
– mishnaic Hebrew 16:1597
– Semitic languages 14:1154
– tables:
– – inflection 8:129-138
Verband bayerischer israelitischer Gemeinden (orgn.) 4:345
VERBAND DER DEUTSCHEN JUDEN (orgn.) 16:105
– history chart 8:766-767
Verband der Rabbiner Deutschlands (orgn.) 13:1455
VERBAND DER VEREINE FUER JUEDISCHE GESCHICHTE UND LITERATUR (assoc.) 16:106
VERBAND NATIONAL-DEUTSCHER JUDEN (orgn.) 16:106
Verber, Jacob 16:1330
Verbitzky, Bernardo 15:255
Verblovski, Gregori 10:1501
Verbo (Vrbové; cmty., Slov.) 14:1679
Verbrugge, Otho 8:63
VERCELLI (city. It.) 16:107
– illus: text
VERCORS (au.) 16:108
Verdi, Giuseppe 12:918
VERDUN (tn., Fr.) 16:108

– Lorraine 11:497
– illus: text
Verdun (city, Montreal) 12:286
VERDUN-SUR-GARONNE (vill., Fr.) 16:109
– Pastoureaux massacre 5:1141
VEREA, ADRIAN 14:420; 14:428
Vereeniging (tn., Transvaal) 15:1340
– Marks, Samuel 11:1009
Verein Deutscher Studenten (assoc.) 3:79
Verein fuer die Statistik der Juden (inst.) 15:66
Verein fuer Juedische Geschichte und Literatur (soc., Vienna) 10:1248
VEREIN FUER KULTUR UND WISSENSCHAFT DES JUDENTUMS (soc.) 16:109
– Germany 7:478
– Heine, Heinrich 8:272
– Hep! Hep! riots 8:331
– history chart 8:766-767
– learned societies 15:53
– Moser, Moses 12:371
VEREINIGUNG FUER DAS LIBERALE JUDENTUM IN DEUTSCHLAND (orgn.) 16:110
Vereinigung Traditionell-Gesetzestreuer Rabbiner (orgn.) 13:1455
Verein Juedischer Studenten 10:805
VEREIN ZUR ABWEHR DES ANTISEMITISMUS (orgn.) 16:110
Verein zur Foerderung der Handwerke der Israeliten (orgn.) 16:456
Verein zur Gruendung und Erhaltung einer Akademie fuer die Wissenschaft des Judentums (orgn.) 16:581
Vereker, John Standish Surtees Prendergast 8:470
Verestói, György 8:63
Verga, Judah ibn, see Ibn Verga, Judah
Verga, Solomon ibn, see IBN VERGA, SOLOMON
VERGELIS, AARON 16:111
Verguenza (Inq.) 8:1402
Veria (city, Gr.), see VEROIA
Veritas (orgn.) 2:61
Vérité Israélite (period.) 5:456
VERKHNEUDINSK (city, Rus.) 16:111
Verlag der juedischen Freischulen (soc.) 4:653
Vermigli, Pietro Martire, see Martyr, Peter
Vermillion (city, S.D.) 15:213
Vermin 6:1002
VERMONT 16:112
– pop. tables: text
Vermont, Abraham 3:423
VEROIA (city, Gr.) 16:112
– Diaspora 6:10
– Greece 7:879
VERONA (city, It.) 16:113
– archives 3:383
– Avigdor ben Elijah 3:963
– Charitable Societies 5:346
– educational regulations 6:417
– special Purim 13:1399
– illus:
– – text
– – Basevi printers' mark 13:1093
Veronese, Paolo 10:460; 12:408
– illus:
– – "Finding of Moses" (paint.) 12:407
Verrocchio (tn., It.) 7:588
Versailles Peace Conference
– Alliance Israélite 2:650; 2:653
– Comité des Délégations Juives 5:758

– Haffkine, M. W. 7:1060
– minority rights 12:43; 12:45
– Palestine mandate 11:861
– Zionism 16:1052ff
– illus:
– – Feisal's letter to Herbert Samuel re Zionism 16:1050
– – Jewish delegation 4:255
Versamelaar, de (newsp.), see De Versamelaar
Verschuir, Johannes Hendrik 8:63
Versegi, Ferenc 8:63 4:883
Vershilov, B. 15:1076
VERTOV, DZIGA 12:456; 12:474
Vertyuzhani (tn., Rum.) 14:402
Verus, see MARCUS, AARON
Verzhboloro (city, Lith.), see VIRBALIS
Vesaas, Halldis Moren 14:932
Vesalius, Andrea 11:1186
– Frigeis de Lazaro 7:197
Vesconte, Pietro 11:925
– illus:
– – map of Erez Israel, 14th cent. 11:925
Vesey, Gergely 8:63
VESOUL (tn., Fr.) 16:115
Vesoul, Héliot de, see Héliot of Vesoul
VESPASIAN, TITUS FLAVIUS 16:116
– Agrippa II 2:417
– Antipatris 3:78
– Bethleptepha 4:747
– Carmel 5:186
– Flavia Domitilla 6:1338
– Gofna 7:691
– history chart 8:866-767
– in the Arts 10:264; 15:1171
– Jews 14:230
– Johanan ben Zakkai 9:241; 10:152
– Josephus, Flavius 10:252ff
– repressive measures 9:238; 9:239
– tax on Jews 6:1325; 8:644
– Titus 15:1168
– warfare 16:280
– illus:
– – text
– – coins, Judean 5:713
Vessels
– ablution 2:83
– milk and meat 6:40
– mikveh 11:1534
– ritual purity 10:900
– illus:
– – immersion of food utensils in mikveh 11:1536
– – Passover kashering 13:164
Vessels, Breaking of (kab. conc.) 10:588; 10:594ff
VESSILLO ISRAELITICO, IL (journ.) 16:116
– press 13:1036
– Turin 13:502
– Vercelli 16:107
Vestali, Elisha 2:925; 16:174
Vestnik (period.) 13:975
Vestnik (mag., Rus.) 13:1046
Vestnik Evreiskoi Obshtchini (journ.) 13:1047
Vestnik Russkikh Yevreyev (newsp.) 15:59
Veszelin, Pál Kismariai 8:63
VÉSZI, ENDRE 8:1087
VÉSZI, JÓZSEF 16:117
VESZPREM (city, Hung.) 16:117
Veszprémi, B. István 8:63
Vetch (bot.) 13:625
Veterinary Institute (Isr.) 9:969
Vetranović, Mavro-Nikolo 16:885
Vevey (tn., Switz.) 10:1472
Veynes (tn., Fr.) 5:1315
Veyssière de la Croze (schol.) 2:89
Viable embryo 2:99
Viadana (tn., It.) 11:895
Via Dolorosa (route, Jer.) 9:1516

– Crusader times 9:1416
– illus:
– – Aelia Capitolina ruins 9:1401,1402
– – Ecce Homo arch 9:1401
– – Franciscans at First Station of the Cross 9:916
– – Lion's gate 9:1431
– – Pilgrims at Third Station of the Cross 9:916
Viadrina (assoc., Breslau) 4:1355
– Jacob, Benno 9:1207
Via Maris (trade route) 8:589
– Chinnereth 5:474
– Gesher Benot Ya'akov 7:525
– Hazor 7:1535
– human geography 9:568
– Solomon's kingdom 5:98
Via Nova (farm, Crimea) 7:356
Via Nova (road, Transj.) 15:1317
Viaţa Evreascā (newsp.) 13:1043
Viaţa Noastrā (newsp.) 9:1017
Viaţa Novuā (newsp.) 4:1441
VIBERT OF NOGENT 16:118
Viborg Manifesto 4:1413; 6:268
Viccars, John 8:63
Vicente, Gil 15:248
Vicente, Juan 8:1396
Vicenza (city, It.) 16:118
VICH (tn., Sp.) 16:118
Vichniac, Jacques, see GIVET, JACQUES
Vicilimus (pros.) 13:1187
Vicinho, Joseph 16:904
Vicinus, Joseph de, see Voisin, Joseph de
Vickar, Louis 14:892
Vicksburg (city, Miss.) 12:156
Vicky (cart.), see WEISZ, VICTOR
Victor Emmanuel III (k., It.) 16:1073
Victoria (q., Eng.)
– Disraeli, Benjamin 6:106
– Hechler, William Henry 8:237
– Montefiore, Sir Moses 12:272
Victoria (state, Austr.) 11:1277
– pop. tables:
– – Jewish population (1861-1961) 11:1279
– see also: AUSTRALIA; MELBOURNE
VICTORIA (city, Can.) 16:118
Victoria (city, Tex.) 15:1035
Victoria Cross (medal, Eng.) 11:1553,1554
Victoria Memorial Jewish Hospital (Eng.) 8:1034
Victorian Jewish Board of Deputies (orgn.) 11:1280
– Ashkanasy, Maurice 3:712
Victorian Zionist League 16:1105
Victor Porchetto de Salvatici, see PORCHETUS SALVAGUS
Vidaković, Milovan 16:885
Vidal (fam., Sp.) 15:1300
Vidal, Bonafos 16:119
VIDAL, CRESCAS 16:118
Vidal bar Judah 15:822
Vidal Bellsom, see MOSES BEN JOSHUA OF NARBONNE
Vidal ben Lavi, Don 10:3
Vidal ha-Sarfaty 14:879
– Uziel, Judah 16:42
VIDAL YOM TOV OF TOLOSA 16:119
– Caro, Joseph 5:198
Vida Nuestra (period.) 3:424; 13:1040
VIDAS, ELIJAH BEN MOSES DE 16:120
– chess condemned 5:403
– Safed Kabbalah 10:546
Viddui, see CONFESSION OF SINS
Viddui Bikkurim (recitation) 11:392
Viddui Ma'aser (recitation) 11:392
Videky, Alexander 15:1041

Videla, Gabriel Gonzalez **5:**467
VIDIN (city, Bul.) **16:**121
- special Purim **12:**1399
Vidor, Imre **15:**473
Vidric, Vladimir **16:**886
VIEIRA, ANTÔNIO **16:**121
- Jesuits **10:**8
Vieira, E. **8:**63
Viejos (parnasim, Sp.) **2:**259
Viener, Jacob M. **14:**162
VIENNA (city, Aus.) **16:**122
- *Contents:*
- - The Holocaust Period **16:**127
- - Postwar Period **16:**128
- - Hebrew Printing **16:**131
- General
- - Albert II **2:**530
- - Austrian Jews **3:**887ff
- - history chart (1670, 1792,1811,1882) **8:**766-767
- - population **8:**732
- - seal **14:**1080
- - trade route **15:**1298
- Anti-Semitism
- - expulsion of Jews **10:**1523
- - Host desecration **8:**1043
- - persecutions (1421) **16:**503ff
- Communal Activities
- - Aguilar, Diego d' **2:**427
- - Avigdor ben Elijah **3:**963
- - education **6:**423ff
- - press **13:**1033
- - stock exchanges **15:**406
- - textiles **15:**1040
- - Volkspartei, Juedische **16:**213
- - Zionism **16:**1106
- Institutions
- - archives **3:**381,387
- - library **11:**192; **11:**193
- - museums **12:**538
- - synagogue **15:**619
- - yeshivot **16:**764
- *illus:*
- - Bar Kochba members **16:**1105
- - boundary stone, 1656 **11:**692
- - humiliation of Jews (1938) **8:**847
- - "Judenbuch der Scheffstrasse" **3:**901
- - Ofner, Julius, memorial **12:**1339
VIENNA, CONGRESS OF **16:**131
- Arnstein family **3:**490
- Austrian Jewry **3:**894
- history chart **8:**766-767
- rights of Jews **8:**713ff
Vienna, Council of (1267, 1312) **5:**548; **6:**162
Vienna Economic Society **14:**973
Vienna Genesis (illum. ms.) **8:**1258
- Jewish art **3:**508
- Lot's wife **15:**73
- Moses **12:**407
- *illus:* **2:**122,364,956; **3:**515; **4:**524,730,944; **5:**1423; **6:**209,240,809; **9:**3,1171,1208; **10:**329; **13:**363,934,1525; **14:**105
Vienna Psychoanalytic Society **2:**272
Vienna School (arch.) **3:**301
VIENNE (tn., Fr.) **16:**132
Vienne, Council of (1311-12) **5:**549
Viereck, G.S. **16:**262
VIERTEL, BERTHOLD **16:**133
Vierteljahrsschrift fuer Musikwissenschaft (period.) **2:**277
Vietnam, North (rep.) **9:**445
Vietnam, South (rep.) **9:**445
- Israel aid **15:**1563
- *illus:*
- - *seder* for U.S. servicemen, Saigon **12:**876
View-Dos Vort (period.) **13:**1026
"View of Safed" (paint., M.Shemi) Pl.4 **3**-ART
Viewpoints (journ.) **16:**1110; **16:**640
VIGÉE, CLAUDE **16:**133
VIGENÈRE, BLAISE DE **16:**134
- Christian Kabbalah **10:**646
- Hebraists **8:**63
Vigevano, Giuseppe **5:**64
Vigier, Henri **3:**480
- *illus:*
- - Rhodes, April 1949 **3:**479
Vignal(-ius), Pierre **8:**63
Vigneria, Abramo della **16:**107
Vigneria, Angelo della **16:**107
Vigny, Alfred Victor de **7:**141; **9:**1343; **14:**774
Vijnita (tn., Ukr.), *see* VIZHNITSA
Viking Press (publ. house) **7:**974
Vikku'aḥ (bk.) **11:**354
Viladestes, Mecia de **11:**917
Vila Nova de Fozcôa (tn., Port.) **12:**241
VILA REAL (tn., Port.) **16:**134
Vileika (tn., Pol.) **13:**770
Vilenkin, N.M., *see* MINSKI, NIKOLAI MAXIMOVICH
Vilenski, Y.N. **10:**862
Vilenskiy Vestnik (journ.) **11:**66
Vilensky, Zev, *see* VILNAY, ZEV
VILKAVIŠKIS (tn., Lith.) **16:**135
Vilkomierz (city, Lith.), *see* UKMERGE
Vilkovo (tn., Bess.) **4:**705
Villa Alba (clny., Arg.) **3:**430
VILLADIEGO (tn., Sp.) **16:**136
VILLAFRANCA DEL PANADÉS (tn., Sp.) **16:**136
- Villefranche **16:**137
"Village East" (paint., R. Soyer) **12:**1116
Villagómez, Leonor Martínez de, *see* Martínez de Villagómez, Leonor
Villalobos, Francesco Lopez de **11:**1191
Villalpando, Juan Bautista **8:**65
Villanova (fam., Sp.) **15:**1300
Villanova, Arnaldo de **8:**65
Villa Real (tn., Sp.), *see* CIUDAD REAL
VILLAREAL (fam.) **16:**136
Villareal, Catherine da Costa **8:**339; **11:**61; **16:**137
Villareal, Isaac **16:**137
Villareal, José da **16:**136
Villareal, José da Costa **16:**137
Villareal, Manuel Lopez **16:**137
Villaroel, Isaac, *see* Villareal, Isaac
Villasandino, Alfonso Alvarez de **4:**79
Villa Torlonia (loc., Rome) **9:**1579
- *illus:*
- - catacomb **9:**1582; **11:**1361; **15:**569
VILLEFRANCHE-DE-CONFLENT (vill., Fr.) **16:**137
Villefranche-sur-Saône (tn., Fr.) **16:**137
Villemanya, Solomon Moses de **14:**353
Villeneuve-lès-Avignon (tn., Fr.) **12:**1165
Villeurbanne (loc., Fr.) **11:**625
Villimpenta, Marquis of, *see* Fano, Joseph da
VILLINGEN (tn., Ger.) **16:**138
Villon, François **7:**139; **6:**1162
VILNA (city, Lith.) **16:**138
- *Contents:*
- - The Early Settlement **16:**138
- - Scholarship and Communal Affairs **16:**140
- - 1860-1939 **16:**144
- - Hebrew Printing **16:**147
- - Holocaust Period **16:**148
- - Contemporary Period **16:**150
- blood libel **14:**488
- Gaon of Vilna **6:** 651
- ghetto **7:**545; **13:**770
- ghetto resistance **10:**1229; **16:**591
- *ḥalukkah* **7:**1208
- Ḥasidism **7:**1392
- Haskalah **7:**1447
- history chart (1889) **8:**766-767
- Lebensohn, Abraham Dov **10:**1548
- museums **12:**539
- Ponary massacre **13:**847
- rabbinical seminary **8:**724; **13:**1465
- Shneour, Zalman **14:**1428
- special Purim **13:**1399
- tailors **15:**705
- Torah study relays **15:**459
- Troki Karaites **15:**1403
- *illus:*
- - text
- - Gaon's tombstone **6:**654
- - *Khurbn Vilne* (1947) **10:**659
- - "Synagogue Court" (phot.) **16:**166
- - Yiddish writers group **16:**183
- - *Yung Vilne* group **16:**821
Vilna Gaon, *see* ELIJAH BEN SOLOMON ZALMAN
VILNA TROUPE (Yid. theat. co.) **16:**151
- theater **15:**1069*ff*
VILNAY, ZEV **16:**151
Vilner Tog (newsp.) **14:**63, 370
Vilnius (city, Lith.), *see* VILNA
Viña del Mar (city, Chile) **5:**465
VINAVER, CHEMJO **16:**151
VINAVER, STANISLAV **16:**889; **16:**891
VINAWER, MAXIM **16:**152
- Chagall **5:**318
- Duma **6:**268
- relief work **16:**734
- civil rights society **15:**56
- *Voskhod* **16:**226
- *illus:*
- - first Duma electors **14:**445
Vincennes (city, Ind.) **8:**1361
VINCENT, LOUIS HUGUES **16:**153
- Naarah **12:**736
- *illus:*
- - Cave of Machpelah plan **11:**672
"Vincent van Gogh" (sculp., J.M. Da Costa) **5:**1221
VINCHEVSKY, MORRIS **16:**153
- *Asefat Ḥakhamim* **3:**692
- *Ha-Emet* **7:**1058
- socialism, Jewish **15:**46
Vinci, L. **9:**1344
VINCZE, PAUL **16:**154
- *illus:*
- - text
- - medal for resettlement in England **6:**772
Vindava (city, Latv.), *see* VENTSPILS
Vindiciae Judaeorum (wk.) **3:**197,198
- *Aleinu le-Shabbe'aḥ* **2:**557
Vinding, J.Paul **8:**65
VINE **16:**155
- Commandments, the 613 **5:**778
- grape juice **12:**1444
- grapes **6:**1416
- Jewish symbolism **15:**569; **15:**570
- mixed species prohibition **12:**170ff
- *peret, olelot* **11:**3
- plant list **13:**619
- *illus:*
- - text
- - African student receiving instruction in Israel **9:**439
- - Dura Europos painting **15:**571
- - Reḥovot, plowing a vineyard **9:**781
- - Rishon le-Zion grape harvest **14:**194
- - Vilna Torlonia catacomb **15:**569
- - Zikhron Ya'akov, loading grapes for wine cellars **9:**781
- *see also:* WINE
Vineam Soreth (papal bull) **4:**1496
Vineberg (fam., Can.) **5:**104; **12:**1408
Vineberg, Arthur **11:**1202
Vinegar (food) **6:**1418
VINELAND (city, N.J.) **16:**157
- *illus:* text
VINER, JACOB **16:**158
Viner, Meir, *see* WIENER, MEIR
Vineyards, Feast of, *see Ḥag ha-Keramim*
Vinitski, M., *see* MEDEM, VLADIMIR
Vinitsky, D. **4:**697
VINNIKOV, ISAAC N. **16:**159
VINNITSA (tn., Ukr.) **16:**159
- Haidamacks **7:**1132
- Podolia **13:**668
Vinogradov (tn., Ukr.) **16:**414
Vinogradov, Konstantin, *see* SOBOL, ANDREY MIKHAILOVICH
Vinokur, Leonid **14:**479
Vinokurov, Eduard **12:**1377
Violanta (q., Arag.)
- Cervera Jews **5:**314
- Crescas, Ḥasdai **5:**1080 **8:**1366
- Spain **15:**238
- Teruel **15:**1022
Violet, Thomas **6:**753
Viper (zool.) **15:**15
- dietary laws **6:**36
- fauna of Israel **9:**226
Vipper, A.I. **4:**399
Virág, Benedek **4:**883
VIRBALIS (tn., Lith.) **16:**159
Virchow, Rudolf **16:**111
Virgil (Latin poet) **8:**302
Virgily, P., *see* KAHAN, BARUCH MORDECAI
VIRGIN, VIRGINITY **16:**160
- Commandments, the 613 **5:**769
- marriage **11:**1033ff
- *niddah* **12:**1144
- reproduction **4:**1018
- *see also:* CHASTITY; SEX
Virginia (city, Minn.) **12:**39
VIRGINIA (state, U.S.) **16:**162
- *illus:* text
- - *Pop. tables:* text
Virginia City (tn., Mont.) **12:**266
Virginia City (vill., Nev.) **12:**1017
VIRGIN ISLANDS **16:**164
- synagogues **1:**syn. list
- *illus:* text
Virgin's Fountain (Jer.) **9:**1540
Virgo (Zodiac sign) **16:**1191
- *illus:* **6:**689,690
Virnikowski, Abraham Mordecai **12:**1457
Virolleaud, C. **15:**1501
Virtue and Vice, *see* ETHICS
Visalia (city, Calif.) **5:**56
VISEUL DE SUS (tn., Rum.) **16:**165
Vishegrod (tn., Pol.), *see* WYSZOGROD
Vishnepolsky, Bezalel **14:**1264
VISHNEVETS (vill., Ukr.) **16:**165
VISHNIAC, ROMAN **16:**166
- *illus:* text
Vishniak, Mark **13:**819
Vishniets (vill., Ukr.), *see* VISHNEVETS
Vishnyak, G. **13:**1598
Visigoths
- Barbarians **4:**206
- forced conversion **3:**170
- Spain **15:**220ff
- Toledo **15:**1198; **15:**1201
- *see also:* ALARIC II
Visino, Mordecai **7:**43
VISIONS **16:**166
- *Contents:*
- - In Medieval Hebrew Literature **16:**167
- - Early Middle Ages **16:**168
- - Later Middle Ages **16:**169

- - Later Writings **16:** 169
- Apocalyptic literature **2:** 126ff
- Apocrypha and Pseudepigrapha **3:** 183
- ḥasidic vision literature **7:** 1415
- prophets and prophecy **13:** 1153ff
- *see also:* DREAMS; KABBALAH
"Visit of the Queen of Sheba to Solomon" (paint., Tintoretto) **15:** 103
VISSCHER, JACOBUS CANTER **16:** 170
VISSER, LODEWIJK ERNST **16:** 170
Visser 't Hooft, Willem **8:** 916
Vistula region (Pol.) **13:** 24
VITAL (It. fam.) **16:** 170
VITAL, DAVID BEN SOLOMON **16:** 171
- Commandments, the 613 **5:** 783
VITAL, ḤAYYIM BEN JOSEPH **16:** 171
- *Adam Kadmon* **2:** 249
- alchemy **2:** 545ff
- Bacharach, Naphtali **4:** 50
- eschatology **10:** 588
- hagiography **7:** 1120
- Jonah, Moses **10:** 178
- Joshua ibn Nun **10:** 288
- Kabbalah **11:** 347
- Lurianic cosmogony **10:** 590
- Lurianic Kabbalah **10:** 549
- magic **11:** 713
- messianism **11:** 1426
- soul, doctrine of **10:** 614ff
- Syria **15:** 644
- Torah study **15:** 457
- *illus:* text
- *see also:* LURIA, ISAAC BEN SOLOMON
Vital, Joseph **16:** 170; **16:** 171
Vital, Moses ben Joseph **16:** 170; **16:** 172
Vital, Moses ben Samuel **16:** 171
- Vital, Ḥayyim **16:** 174
VITAL, SAMUEL BEN ḤAYYIM **16:** 176
- Pinto, Josiah **13:** 553
- Vital, Ḥayyim **16:** 172ff
Vitale (fam., It.) **2:** 566
Vitale, Abraham **2:** 566
Vitale, Benjamin, *see* BENJAMIN BEN ELIEZER HA-KOHEN VITALE OF REGGIO
Vitale, Joseph de Sacerdoti **2:** 566
Vitale, Simon **15:** 1676
Vitale, Simone (Samuel) **2:** 566
Vitale de' Medici **14:** 1185
Vitali, G.B. **9:** 1344
Vitalis, Ḥayyim Felix **11:** 542
Vitalis de Boulogne **12:** 267
Vitalis of Marseilles **15:** 1285
Vital of Capestang **5:** 139
VITAL STATISTICS **16:** 177
- *Contents:*
- - Introduction **16:** 177
- - Mortality **16:** 179
- - Marriage and Divorce **16:** 182
- - Births **16:** 186
- - Natural Increase **16:** 189
- Arabs in Israel **9:** 1023ff
- Jewish population growth **8:** 721
- mixed marriages **8:** 731f
- *tables:* text
- *see also:* DEMOGRAPHY; DIASPORA; MIGRATION; POPULATION; POPULATION OF ISRAEL
VITEBSK (city, Belor.) **16:** 190
- Chagall, Marc **5:** 318
- *illus:*
- - text
- - Yevsektsiya *ḥeder* trial **16:** 780
Vitebsky, Josef **12:** 1377
Vitellius (Rom. Gov.) **5:** 60
- Nabateans **12:** 743
- Temple service **15:** 979
Viterbi, Grazadio **13:** 12
VITERBO (tn., It.) **16:** 193
Viterbo, Aegidius da, *see* EGIDIO DA VITERBO
VITERBO, CARLO ALBERTO **16:** 193
- press **13:** 1037
VITERBO, JEHIEL ḤAYYIM **16:** 193
- Sinzheim's responsa **14:** 1617
Viticulture (wine growing)
- economic life **16:** 1268*ff*
- Troyes **15:** 1406ff
Viticulturists' Association (co-op, Er. Isr.), *see* Hitaḥadut ha-Koremim
Vitkin, Jacob, *see* ZERUBAVEL,JACOB
VITKIN, JOSEPH **16:** 193
- call for pioneers **9:** 519
- history chart **8:** 766-767
- political activity **9:** 657ff
- *illus:*
- - Kefar Vitkin **10:** 895
Vitold (grand duke, Lith.) **13:** 716ff
VITORIA (tn., Sp.) **16:** 194
VITORIA, FRANCISCO DE **16:** 195
Vitré (tn., Fr.) **13:** 704
Vitringa, Campegius **8:** 65
VITRY(-en-Perthois; tn., Fr.) **16:** 195
Vitry-le-Brûlé (tn., Fr.), *see* VITRY
Vitry-le-François (tn., Fr.) **16:** 195
VITTA, CINO **16:** 196
Vittorio Eliano (apos.), *see* Eliano, Vittorio
VITTORIO VENETO (tn., It.) **16:** 196
- synagogue **15:** 618
- *illus:*
- - Ark of the Law **3:** *fcg.* 462
- - synagogue *meḥiẓah* **11:** 1235
Vivaldi, Antonio **10:** 460
VIVANTE, CESARE **16:** 196
Vivante, Vita **13:** 815
VIVANTI, DAVID ABRAHAM **16:** 197
- Ancona **2:** 943
- homiletic literature **8:** 957
- Tedeschi **15:** 897
VIVANTI CHARTRES, ANNIE **16:** 197
- Italian literature **9:** 1112
Vivas, Solomon, *see* SOLOMON BEN JUDAH OF LUNEL
Vivelin the Red **4:** 168
- *illus:*
- - legal document **4:** 170
Vivero, Gonzalo de **16:** 903
Vives (r., Ger.), *see* Webes
Vives (fam., Sp.), *see* ABENVIVES
VIVES, JUAN LUIS **16:** 197
Vives ben Joseph ibn Vives **2:** 70
Vives of Koblenz **10:** 1120
Viweg, C. **8:** 65
Vizaknai, U. Mihály **8:** 65
VIZHNITSA (tn., Ukr.) **16:** 198
VIZHNITZ (ḥas. dyn.) **16:** 199
- dynasties **1:** ḥas. table
- ḥasidic music **7:** 1424,1425
- Kosov **10:** 1217
- town **16:** 198
- Vizhnitzer Rebbe **9:** 899
- *illus:* text
- *see also under* Hager
Vizille (tn.,Fr.) **5:** 1315
Vizinus, Joseph, *see* Vicinho, Joseph
Vjazd (tn., Pol.) **15:** 671
Vlachich, Matthias Flacius Illyricus **16:** 886
VLADECK, BARUCH CHARNEY **16:** 200
Vladikavkaz (city, Rus.), *see* ORDZHONIKIDZE
Vladimirov, M. **5:** 794
VLADIMIR VOLYNSKI (city, Ukr.) **16:** 200
- Karlin dynasty **10:** 793
- Volhynia **16:** 206ff
VLADIVOSTOK (city, Rus.) **16:** 202
Vlasić, Petar **4:** 885; **16:** 885
Vlodavi (city, Pol.), *see* WLODAWA
Vlona (city, Alb.), *see* VALONA
Vloten, Willem van **8:** 65
Vocalization, Hebrew
- *al tikrei* **2:** 776
- Ben-Asher **4:** 465
- Ben-Naphtali **4:** 540
- biblical Hebrew **16:** 1571
- Buxtorf's studies **4:** 1543
- Cairo *genizah* **16:** 1335
- Levita, Elijah **11:** 134
- *illus:*
- - vowels, first Hebrew book (1485) **8:** 1327
- *see also:* MASORAH; PRONUNCIATIONS OF HEBREW
Vocational Training, Hadassah **7:** 1044; **9:** 881ff
Vocea aparătorului (newsp.) **9:** 1295
Vochenblatt (newsp.) **5:** 113
Vodă, Aron **6:** 718
Voelkermarkt (tn., Aus.) **5:** 181
VOET, ANDRIES **5:** 389
Voetius, Gysbertus **8:** 65
Vofsi, M. **14:** 479
VOGEL, ARTHUR ISRAEL **5:** 389
VOGEL, DAVID **16:** 202
Vogel, Georg **15:** 1115
Vogel, G. J. L. **8:** 65
VOGEL, SIR JULIUS **16:** 203
- Dunedin **6:** 274
- New Zealand **12:** 1130
VOGEL, KAREL **3:** 612
VOGEL, SIMON **11:** 1576
VOGEL, WLADIMIR **16:** 203
VOGELSANG, KARL VON **16:** 204
Vogelsangh, Reinerus **8:** 65
VOGELSTEIN (fam., Ger.) **16:** 204
Vogelstein, Heinemann **15:** 400; **16:** 204
- Liberal Judaism **16:** 110
Vogelstein, Hermann **14:** 166; **16:** 204
VOGELSTEIN, LUDWIG **16:** 205
Vogelstein, Max **16:** 205
- Rieti family **14:** 170
Vogelstein, Theodor **16:** 204
Vogelstein-Braun, Julie **16:** 205
Voghera Fano, Giorgio, *see* Triestino, Anònimo
Vogler, E. **16:** 819
Vogler, Henryk **13:** 803
Vogshol (period.) **15:** 676
VOGUE, CHARLES EUGENE MELCHOIR, COMTE DE **16:** 205
- Jerusalem **9:** 1521
Vohliner Lebn (newsp.) **14:** 357
Vohryzek, Viktor **5:** 1026
Voice of The Communities (period.) **5:** 829
Voice of the Defender (newsp.), *see Vocea aparătorului*
Voice of Israel (broadcasting service), *see* Kol Israel
Voice of Jacob (newsp., Austr.) **13:** 1056
Voice of Jacob (period., Eng.) **7:** 103; **13:** 1031
- Benisch, Abraham **4:** 521
- Sola, David Aaron de **15:** 91
- *illus:*
- - masthead (1841) **13:** 1027
Voice of Zion to the Diaspora (broadcasting service), *see Kol Ziyyon la-Golah*
Voisin, Joseph de **8:** 65
Vojvodina, (reg., Yug.) **12:** 1236; **16:** 868ff
- Zionism **16:** 1149
Vokaty, Veit (Ḥayyim) **11:** 1262
Vokhenblat (newsp.) **4:** 612 **13:** 1026
Volborth, J. Karl **8:** 65
Volcani, Raanan **6:** 571
Volcani Institute of Agricultural Research (Er. Isr.) **9:** 966
Volcano **14:** 1599
VOLCHKO (fin., Pol.) **16:** 205
- Poland **13:** 713; **13:** 718
Volgare (dialect), *see* JUDEO-ITALIAN
VOLHYNIA (reg., Ukr.) **16:** 206
- center of Ḥasidism **7:** 1392
Volin, Y. **8:** 1348
Volkman, Samuel **16:** 476
Volkovisker Lebn (newsp.) **16:** 212
Volkovyshki (tn., Lith.), *see* VILKAVISKIS
VOLKOVYSK (city, Belor.) **16:** 212
Volksgerichtshof (court) **10:** 1574
Volkshilf (period.) **13:** 1048
VOLKSPARTEI, JUEDISCHE (party, Aus.) **16:** 213
Volkspartei, Juedische (Ger.), *see* JUEDISCHE VOLKSPARTEI
Volleyball (sport) **15:** 316
VOLLI, GEMMA **16:** 213
Volney, C. J. **15:** 1357
Volo (city, Gr.), *see* VOLOS
Volodarsky, M. **5:** 794
Vologases I (k., Parth.) **6:** 1023
VOLOS (city, Gr.) **16:** 214
- Greece **7:** 875
Volotski, Joseph **10:** 399
Volovelski, Yehuda, *see* KARNI, YEHUDA
VOLOZHIN (city, yeshivah, Belor.) **16:** 214
- Berlin, Naphtali **4:** 661
- Lithuanian *yeshivot* **16:** 768
- Mir Yeshivah **15:** 1141
- Soloveichik, Joseph Baer **15:** 131
- Volozhiner, Ḥayyim **16:** 218
- Volozhiner, Isaac **16:** 219
- *Yeshivah* closed **14:** 1668
- *illus:* text
VOLOZHINER, ḤAYYIM BEN ISAAC **16:** 218
- Ḥasidism **7:** 1417
- Lithuanian *yeshivot* **16:** 768
- Soloveichik, Joseph **15:** 127
- Torah study **15:** 457
- Volozhin *Yeshivah* **16:** 214ff
VOLOZHINER, ISAAC BEN ḤAYYIM **16:** 219
- Lithuanian *yeshivot* **16:** 769
- Soloveichik, Joseph Baer **15:** 131
- yeshivah **16:** 215
VOLPA (tn., Belor.) **16:** 219
Volpe, Aaron G. **15:** 1262
VOLPE, ARNOLD **12:** 712
Volta, Upper (rep., Afr.) **15:** 1563
VOLTAIRE **16:** 220
- Adams, John **2:** 249
- anti-Jewish stand **3:** 112, 198
- history chart **8:** 766-767
Volterra (tn., It.) **15:** 1467
VOLTERRA (It. fam.) **16:** 221
Volterra, Abraham **16:** 221
Volterra, Bonaventura **16:** 221
VOLTERRA, EDOARDO **16:** 221
Volterra, Ḥayyim (Vita) ben Moses **16:** 221
Volterra, Lazzaro (Eliezer) **16:** 221
Volterra, Manuel **16:** 221
VOLTERRA, MESHULLAM BEN MENAHEM DA **16:** 221
VOLTERRA, VITO **16:** 222
Volume (meas.) **16:** 379
Volyn (reg., Ukr.), *see* VOLHYNIA
Volynets (sol.) **13:** 699
Volynov, Boris **2:** 322
VOLYNSKI, AKIM LEVOVICH

16:222
VOLZ, PAUL **16:**222
Von Bruehl, Heinrich **14:**924
Von Buelow (polit.), *see* Buelow, Berhnhard von
Vonck, Cornelis Hugo **8:**65
Vondel, Joost van de **3:**819; **4:**934
Von Dittel, Leopold **11:**1197
Von Freudiger, Phillip **5:**1197
Von Hebraz, Ferdinand **11:**1196
Von Hoenigstein, Adam Albert, *see* Hoenig, Adam Albert
Von Hohenheim, Philippus Theophrastus Bombastus, *see* Paracelsus
Von Laemel, Leopold, *see* Laemel, Leopold Von
Von Laemel, Simon, *see* LAEMEL, SIMON VON
Von Welsenburg, *see* BLOCH, IWAN
Von Westphalen, Jenny **11:**1071
Von Westphalen, Baron Johann Ludwig **11:**1074
Von Wisendangen, Jakob, *see* Ceporinos, Jakob
Voorburg (tn., Neth.) **7:**1125
Voorsanger, Elkan C. **11:**1570
VOORSANGER, JACOB **16:**223
Voos, Julius **12:**505
Voprinsky, Reyze **16:**822
Vorarbeiter (concen. camp term) **10:**755
VORARLBERG (prov., Aus.) **16:**223
- Innsbruck **8:**1379
Vorhand, M. **11:**811
Vormela (fauna), *see* Tiger weasel
Vormess, M. **11:**1561
VORONCA, ILARIE **16:**224
VORONEZH (city, Rus.) **16:**224
- Judaizers **10:**400ff
VORONOFF, SERGE **16:**225
Voroshilovgrad (city, Rus.), *see* LUGANSK
Vorsheimer, Johan, *see* FORSTER, JOHANN
Vorspan, Albert **11:**281
- sociology **15:**68
VORSPAN, MAX **16:**225
- history **8:**568
Vorst, L. **14:**350
Vorst (-ius), W. Hendrik van der **8:**65
Vorster (Vorsteimer), Johann, *see* FORSTER, JOHANN
VOS, ISIDOR H. J. **13:**831
Vosen, C. Hermann **8:**65
VOSKHOD (period.) **16:**225
- Dubnow, Simon **6:**253
- Gordon, Judah Leib **7:**800
- Landau, Adolf Yefimovich **10:**1385
VOSKOVEC, GEORGE **15:**1092
- Prague **5:**1193; **13:**973
Voss (-ius), Dionysius **8:**65
Vossius, Gerhard Jan **8:**65
Vossius, Isaac **8:**65
Votadio, *see* WANDERING JEW
VOTICE (tn., Cz.) **16:**227
Votive offering **14:**604
Votslavsk (city, Pol.), *see* WLOCLAWEK
Vovsi, Solomon, *see* MIKHOELS, SOLOMON
Vowels (Heb. gram.) **16:**1562
- biblical Hebrew **16:**1573
- diacritical marks **16:**1429
- mishnaic Hebrew **16:**1595
- Samaritan masorah **16:**1468
- Tiberian system **16:**1447
- *illus:*
- - Latin transliteration **8:**79
- - phonological status **8:**92
VOWS AND VOWING **16:**227
- annulment **2:**350
- Commandments, the 613 **5:**765,775
- consecrated property release **8:**282
- false vow justification **8:**1370
- flogging **6:**1349
- in Talmud **12:**920
- *Kol Nidrei* **10:**1166
- Nazirite vow **12:**907
- *niddui* **8:**352
- public custom **12:**22
- sacrificial **11:**1314
- *illus:*
- - administration of oath **14:**1393
- - cantonist's oath **14:**439
- - oath *more judaico* **12:**1302
- *see also:* OATH
Voz Hebrea (newsp.) **16:**15
VOZNESSENK (city, Ukr.) **16:**229
VOZNITSYN, ALEXANDER ARTEMYEVICH **16:**229
- Baruch ben Leib **15:**7
VOZROZHDENIYE (gr.) **16:**229
- Po'alei Zion **13:**657
- Silberfarb, Moses **14:**1533
Voz Sefardí (period.) **11:**1459
Vpered (newsp.) **2:**420; **11:**220
- Liebermann, A. S. **15:**39
Vrbové (cmty., Slov.), *see* Verbo
VRCHLICKÝ, JAROSLAV **16:**231
- Wandering Jew **16:**262
Vredenburg, Joel **3:**486
Vreveil (angel) **6:**797
Vriemont, Emo Lucius **8:**65
Vries, De (name), *see also* De Vries
Vries, Louis de **12:**984; **15:**1057
Vries, M. C. de, Jr. **11:**1167
Vriesland, Siegfried Adolf van, *see* VAN VRIESLAND, SIEGFRIED ADOLF
Vries S. Ph. de **16:**1118
VRIEZEN, THEODORUS CHRISTIAAN **16:**231
VROMAN, LEO **16:**231
Vronik (tn., Pol.), *see* WRONKI
Vsetin (tn., Cz.) **5:**1198; **10:**1308
VUGHT (concen. camp) **16:**232
- Amersfoort **2:**832
Vuković, Vladimir **5:**406
Vulcan foundries (Isr.) **8:**538
VULGATE (bib. trans.) **16:**232
- Apocrypha **3:**181; **3:**182
- Bible **4:**857
- Hebrew linguistics **16:**1393
- Jerome **9:**1377
- Lamentations, Book of **10:**1371
Vulliaud, Paul **16:**1214
VULTURES (zool.) **16:**232
- Dietary laws **6:**34f
- fauna of Israel **9:**226
- *illus:* text
- *see also:* KITE
Vyborg (city, Rus.) **6:**1296
VYGOTSKI, LEV SEMYONOVICH **16:**233
Vyskov (tn., Morav.) **12:**296
VYSOKOYE (city, Belor.) **16:**234

W

Wachenheimer, Fred, see FRIENDLY, FRED W.
Wachman, Marvin 15:1679
Wachnacht (custom), see SHOLEM ZOKHOR
Wachner, A. G. 8:65
WACHSTEIN, BERNHARD 16:237
- *haskamot*, use of 7:1453
- historiography 8:564
- *Kerem Ḥemed* 10:914
Wachtel, Charles 13:346
Wachter, Johann Georg 8:65; 10:647
- *illus:*
- - *Adam Kadmon* and *Ein-Sof* 10:647
Waco (city, Tex.) 15:1034
WADDINGTON, MIRIAM (DWORKIN) 1:38; 5:116
Wadi (val., loc., Er. Isr.)...
- Abu Khushayba 11:1434
- al-Biyar 9:1541
- al-Dhulayl 9:1170
- al-Ḥasā', see ZERED
- al-Iḥrayr 9:181
- ʿAllan 9:181
- al-Mawjib, see ARNON
- al-Nattuf, see WADI AL-NATTUF
- al-Qult, see (Wadi) Qilt
- al-Qurā 10:943
- al-Ṣarār, see SOREK, VALLEY OF
- al-Tāba 10:301
- al-Tufaḥ 8:226
- Amman 9:1170
- Arṭās 9:140
- Balameh 8:1151
- Bayḥan (Beihan; Aden), see BAYḤĀN
- Dāliya, see WADI DĀLIYA
- el-Arish 6:503; 16:656
- el-Kelt (Qelt), see (Wadi) Qilt
- er-Rababi 7:357
- er-Rumma 13:78
- Fāra, see PARAH, PERATH
- Fariʿa 9:141; 9:168; 9:201; 9:588
- Firān 14:80
- Hārūniyya 8:971
- Hawārith 8:241; 8:332
- Jawz (Joz; Juz), see Naḥal Egozim
- Kabāni 8:242
- Kannā 10:733
- Ma'ara 16:654
- Māliḥ 9:201
- Manāʿiyya 15:1145
- Murabba' (Murabbat) 16:658
- Mūsā, see Siq, Al-
- Nimrin (Transj.) 15:1316
- Nuwei'imeh 2:211
- Qilt
- - Achor, Valley of 2:211
- - Cozeba 5:1025
- - Hyena 8:1139
- - Jerusalem 9:1472
- Qumran, see QUMRAN
- Rafayd 14:80
- Rūbīn, see SOREK, VALLEY OF
- Salib (qtr., Haifa) 9:395f; 9:507; 9:672
- Shu'eib 9:220
- Suwayliḥ 9:1170
- Tumeilāt (Egy.) 7:816; 16:669
- Yābis 9:1172; 9:178
- Zarqā, see JABBOK
- *see also:* Naḥal
WADI AL-NATTUF (loc., Er. Isr.) 16:237
- mesolithic art 3:505
WADI DĀLIYA (val., Er. Isr.) 16:238
- Aramaic papyri 16:668
- Samaritan papyri 14:729
Waeijen, Johan van der 8:65
Wagenaar, H. A. 13:707
Wagenaar, Johann 14:918
WAGENAAR, LION 16:238
- Arnhem 3:486
Wageningen, J. van, see PRESSER, JACOB
Wagenseil, Helena Sybilla Möller, see Möller, Helena Sybilla Wagensail
WAGENSEIL, JOHANN CRISTOPH 16:239
- Hebraist 8:65
- toleration of Jews 8:702
- *illus:* text
Wagenstein, Angel 4:1494
Wages
- Israel labor economy 9:863; 9:876f
- labor law 10:1325f
- withholding of 12:1435
- working hours and custom 12:14
WAGG, ABRAHAM 16:240
- New York 12:1069
Wagg, Rachel, see Gomez, Rachel
WAGHALTER, IGNATZ 12:712
Wagman, Adam, see WAŻYK, ADAM
Wagner (Ger. indus.) 9:1257
Wagner, Carl Friedrich 16:241
Wagner, Christian 8:65
Wagner, Cosima 16:241
Wagner, Horst 8:860
WAGNER, RICHARD 16:240
- Joseph Joachim 10:110
- Levi, Hermann 11:81
WAGNER, SIEGFRIED 3:612
Wagtail, White (bird) 6:30
Wahb ibn Jiyath, see NETHANEL BEN ISAIAH
WAHB IBN MUNABBIH 16:241
- Jeremiah 9:1360
- Yemen 16:756
Wahl, Abraham (Abrashka) 16:243
WAHL, JEAN 16:242
Wahl, Meyer, see Kaẓin Elin Bogen, Meyer
WAHL, SAUL BEN JUDAH 16:242
- seal 14:1080
Wahl, Zevi Hirsch 12:1473
Wahle, Julius 7:451
Wahle, Otto 12:1375; 15:313
WAHLE, RICHARD 16:243
Wahltuch, Victor L. 5:406
Wahrmann (bk. trade firm) 4:1239; 4:973
WAHRMANN, ABRAHAM DAVID BEN ASHER ANSCHEL 16:243
WAHRMANN, ISRAEL 16:243
WAHRMANN, MORITZ 16:244
Wailing Wall, see WESTERN WALL
"Wailing Wall and Its Surroundings" (Drg., S. Schulmann) 9:*fcg.* 1531
Wais, Lunez 15:1446
Waisberg (name), *see also* Weissberg
Waisberg, Carl 12:1408
Waisberg, Harry 12:1408
Waislitz, J. 15:1072
Wais(s)man(n) (name), *see also* Weisman; Weissman
WAISMANN, FRIEDRICH 16:244
Waissman, Nathan 13:1370
Wajsowna, Jadwiga 12:1376
Wakar, Don Isaac, see Ibn Waqar, Isaac
Wakefield (tn., Mass.) 11:622
WAKEFIELD, ROBERT (Wakfeldus) 16:245
- Hebraist 8:65; 8:16
Wakefield, Thomas 8:64; 16:245
Wakf (Musl. rel. trust) see Waqf
Waks, Ḥayyim Eleazar 16:1348
WAKSMAN, SELMAN ABRAHAM 16:245
Walachia (reg., Rum.)
- Jewish silversmiths 7:742
- Rumania 14:386f
- Zionism 16:1132
- *see also:* BUCHAREST
Walafrid Strabo (schol.) 8:11
Walbe, Joel 12:670
WALBROOK, ANTON 12:475
Walbrzych (city, Šilesia), see Waldenburg
Walch (fam., Ger.), see WALLICH
Walch (bnk., Ger.), see David the Elder
Walch, Abraham 16:256
WALD, ARNOLD 16:246
WALD, GEORGE 16:246
- biology 4:1032
WALD, HENRI 16:247
WALD, HERMAN 3:612
- *illus:*
- - Johannesburg memorial 10:157
- - Roth, Cecil (bust) 14:327
WALD, JERRY 12:449; 12:475
WALD, LILLIAN 16:247
Wald, Meir, see YAARI, MEIR
Wald, Pinie 3:414
Waldeck-Rousseau, René 6:228f
Waldegrave, Countess, see Braham, Francis Elizabeth
WALDEN, AARON BEN ISAIAH NATHAN 16:248
WALDEN, HERWARTH 16:248
Walden, Joseph Aryeh Leib 16:248
Walden, Moses Menaḥem 16:248
Waldenberg, Eliezer Judah 14:93; 15:1337
Waldenburg (city, Silesia) 14:1538
Waldheim (stlmt., Er. Isr.) 15:995
WALDINGER, ERNST 16:249
WALDMAN, LEIBELE 7:1551
WALDMAN, MORRIS DAVID 16:249
WALDMANN, ISRAEL 16:250
- Steiger trial 15:349
Waldor, Milton A. 6:904
Waldstein, Charles, see WALSTON, SIR CHARLES
Waldstein, Emil 13:1028
WALDTEUFEL, EMIL 12:713
Waldteufel, Lazare 12:713
WALES (country) 16:250
- anti-Semitism 16:251
Walewski, Alexandre Florian Joseph Colonna 13:1492
WALEY (Eng. fam.) 16:251
Waley, Alfred Joseph 16:251
WALEY, ARTHUR 16:252
Waley, Dorothea, see Singer, Dorothea Waley
Waley, Elizabeth 16:251
Waley, Jacob 2:977; 16:251
Waley, Julia Matilda, see Cohen, Julia Matilda
Waley, Sigismund David 16:251
Waley, Simon 16:251
Waley, Solomon Jacob 16:251
Waley-Cohen (fam.) 5:661
Waley-Cohen, Sir Robert, see COHEN, SIR ROBERT WALEY
Walford, Bernard 15:830
Walid II (caliph) 15:1529
WALINSKY (fam.) 16:252
Walinsky, Adam 16:253
Walinsky, Louis Joseph 16:252

Walinsky, Ossip Joseph **16:**252
Wali Sitīn (shrine, Er. Isr.) **14:**1402
Walk, Neal **15:**303
Walkenburg, fortress of (Ger.) **5:**1139
WALKIN, AARON **16:**253
WALKOMITZ, SIMḤAH ḤAYYIM **16:**253
WALKOWITZ, ABRAHAM **16:**253
Wallace, Henry **15:**1410
WALLACE, MIKE (Myron Leon) **10:**318
WALLACH, ELI **15:**1092
Wallach, Louis, *see* Cross, Leach
Wallach, Meir Moiseevitch, *see* LITVINOV, MAXIM MAXIMOVICH
WALLACH, MOSHE (Moritz) **16:**254
WALLACH, OTTO **16:**254
WALLANT, EDWARD LEWIS **15:**1577; **15:**1584
Wallase, Lazer **2:**285
Walla Walla (city, Wash.) **16:**356
Wallenberg, Jacob **14:**928
WALLENBERG, RAOUL **16:**255
- Holocaust **8:**907
WALLENROD, REUBEN **16:**256
- Hebrew literature **8:**213
- *illus:*
- - Hebrew writers' convention, 1943 **8:**213
WALLENSTEIN, ALFRED **12:**713
WALLENSTEIN, MEIR **16:**256
Wallenstein, William Francis **4:**1479
Wallenstein, Z. **13:**203
Waller, Louis **10:**1493
Wallerstein, Immanuel **15:**68
Wallerstein, Joseph **14:**162
Wallerstein, Morton L. **14:**161
Wallerstein, Moses **8:**311
Wallerstein chronicle (forged ms.), *see* Ramshak chronicle
WALLICH (fam.) **16:**256
Wallich, Abraham **16:**257
Wallich, David Tevele ben Isaac **15:**1391
Wallich, Isaac **11:**359; **16:**257
Wallich, Joseph ben Meir **16:**256
Wallich, Judah Loeb **16:**257
Wallich, Moses **16:**257
Wallich, Nathaniel **15:**1351; **16:**257
Wallich, Solomon Emmanuel **16:**257
Wallin, G. **8:**64
Wallin, Johan Olof **14:**929
Wallish, Otte **9:**842
Wallteufel, Lazare, *see* Waldteufel, Lazare
Walmer, Lord Cohen of, *see* COHEN, LIONEL LEONARD, BARON
Walnut tree **13:**199
- plant list **13:**625
Walpurgis Night (in April) **12:**1389
Walreven, Didericus Adrianus **8:**64
Walstein, Victor **3:**459
WALSTON, SIR CHARLES **16:**257
- archaeology **3:**301
- art history **3:**650
Walt, Abraham, *see* LIESSIN, ABRAHAM
WALTER, BRUNO **16:**257
- Ben-Haim, Paul **4:**517
Walter, J. **8:**64
Walterboro (tn., S. C.) **15:**211
Walterius (apos., Fr.), *see* Gautier
Waltham (city, Mass.) **11:**1112
- *illus:*
- - A.J.H.S. library **11:**191
Walther (-us), C. **8:**64
Walther, F. **8:**64
Walther (-us), Michael **8:**64
WALTON, BRYAN **16:**258
- Hebraist **8:**64 **8:**17
- linguisitcs **16:**1394
- *London Polyglot* **4:**840
WALZER, RICHARD RUDOLF **16:**259
Wamba (k., Sp.) **15:**221
Wandering, *see* MIGRATION
WANDERING JEW (fig. in Chr. leg.) **16:**259
- D'Ancona's study **2:**944
- *The Second Scroll* (Klein) **10:**1097
- *illus:* text
WANDSBECK (dist., Hamburg) **16:**263
- *see also:* ALTONA; HAMBURG
Wandsworth, Lord, *see* Stern, Sydney James
Wanger, Walter **12:**463
Wankenheim (vill., Ger.) **15:**1426
WANNEH, ISAAC BEN ABRAHAM **16:**263
Wannfried, Menahem, *see* KATZ, MENAHEM
WANNSEE CONFERENCE (Nazi conference on Final Solution) **16:**264
- Austrian Jews **3:**900
- Bormann, Martin **4:**1250
- Eichman, Adolf **6:**518
- Heydrich, Reinhard **8:**448
- Hitler, Adolf **8:**785
- history chart **8:**766-767
- Holocaust **8:**855
- *illus:* text
Want, Moshe **7:**235
Wapella (tn., Sask., Can.) **14:**891
Wappenstein, Asher **11:**1167
Waqāsa (fam.), *see* WAQQĀṢA
Waqf (Musl. rel. trust) **9:**918ff
- Cairo synagogues **16:**1333
- Israel **8:**286
- land ownership **9:**1021
- Sharia court **9:**628
WAQQĀṢA (fam.) **16:**265
- Merinids **11:**1386
WAR AND WARFARE **16:**266
- *Contents:*
- - To the Destruction of the First Temple **16:**266
- - - Weapons **16:**266
- - - Fortifications **16:**273
- - Second Temple to 614 **16:**278
- General
- - lots **11:**510
- - peace **13:**197
- - Resheph (deity) **14:**81
- - treasures **15:**1361
- - types **14:**83
- - vengeance **16:**93
- Halakhic Aspects
- - Commandments, the 613 **5:**769
- - *ḥerem* **8:**347
- - holiness aspect **10:**868
- - Sabbath **6:**851
- History
- - Ark of Covenant **3:**463
- - court Jews **5:**1007ff
- - Jewish Legion (WW I) **10:**69
- - Judah Maccabee **10:**379
- - Roman-Jewish war **16:**1275
- - Sinai Campaign **14:**1600
- - Six-Day War **14:**1624
- - tribal cooperation **15:**1385 **14:**1640
- - War of Attrition (post 1967) **14:**1640
- - War of Independence **16:**306
- *illus:*
- - Lachish dagger **16:**655
- - Masada, iron arrows **11:**1091
- - Sinai Campaign **14:**1601-1604
- - Six-Day War **14:**1627-1637
- - Temple Scroll **15:**997
- - War of Independance **16:**307-330
Waraqa (6/7 cent., Chr. w.) **12:**508
Warbler (bird) **6:**34
WARBURG (fam., Ger., U.S.) **16:**281
- Westchester **16:**465
Warburg (fam., Swed.) **15:**547
Warburg (dist., Ger.) **13:**7
WARBURG, ABY MORITZ **16:**285
- archaeology **3:**301
Warburg, Edward Mortimer Morris **2:**828; **16:**285
Warburg, Emil **16:**288
Warburg, Felix Moritz **16:**282
- art collector **12:**544
- Kefar Warburg **10:**895
- *illus:*
- - Joint Distribution Committee **2:**829
Warburg, F. J. (publ., Eng.) **13:**1370
Warburg, Frederick Marcus **16:**284
Warburg, Frieda **16:**282ff
Warburg, Gerald Felix **16:**285
Warburg, James Paul **16:**282
WARBURG, KARL JOHAN **16:**286
Warburg, Nina, *see* Loeb, Nina
WARBURG, OTTO **16:**286
- Zionist Congress (7th) **16:**1169
WARBURG, OTTO HEINRICH (biochem.) **16:**288
- biology **4:**1032
Warburg, Paul Felix **16:**285
Warburg, Paul Moritz **16:**281
Warburg Institute (London univ.) **3:**651
Warchavchik, Gregori **3:**360
WAR CRIMES TRIALS **16:**288
- *Contents:*
- - Crystallization of the Principles of International Criminal Law **16:**288
- - Trials in the Allied Courts and Liberated Countries, 1943-1949 **16:**291
- - In Allied Courts **16:**293
- - In Various Countries **16:**295
- - In the Soviet Union Since 1961 **16:**297
- - In West German and Austrian Courts **16:**297
- - Punishment of Criminals Tried in West Germany and Austria **16:**300
- - Number of Nazi Criminals and Their Collaborators **16:**300
- - The Lesson of the Trials **16:**301
- Auschwitz trials **3:**873
- Austria **3:**899ff
- Eichmann trial **6:**521
- Goebbels, Paul Josef **7:**687
- Latvia **10:**1468
- Lithuania **11:**389
- Nuremberg trials **8:**884
- Reichszentrale fuer Juedische Auswanderung **14:**51
- Treblinka **15:**1372
- Zentrale Stelle der Landesjustizverwaltungen **16:**992
- *illus:*
- - text
- - Auschwitz trial **3:**873
- - Eichmann trial **6:**519; **9:**405
- *see also:* GENOCIDE CONVENTION
War criminals, *see* HOLOCAUST; NATIONAL SOCIALISM (Leaders)
Ward, *see* APOTROPOS
Warden (offic.), *see* GABBAI
"The Warden" (drg., J. Kramer) **10:**1237
WARENDORF (tn., Ger.) **16:**302
WARFIELD, DAVID **16:**303
WARHAFTIG, ZERAḤ **16:**303
- *illus:*
- - Druze community leaders and **9:**926
- - Six-Day War, meeting religious leaders **9:**410
Warheit (newsp.) **10:**51; **11:**1581
- Entin, Joel **6:**801
- Fishman, Jacob **6:**1331
Warium (anc. kdm.) **16:**1496
WARKA (ḥas. dyn.) **16:**303
- dynasties **1:**ḥas. table
Warka (city, Sumer), *see* ERECH
Warka, Isaac of **2:**561; **16:**151, 303
WARNER (fam.) **16:**305
Warner, Albert **16:**305
Warner, Harry **16:**305
Warner, Jack **16:**305
Warner, Levinius **8:**64
Warner, Sam **16:**305
Warning (leg.)
- assault **3:**758
- Commandments, the 613 **5:**761,783
- perjury **13:**289
- witness **13:**960
WAR OF INDEPENDENCE **16:**306
- *Contents:*
- - The First Phase **16:**306
- - - The Jewish Forces **16:**306
- - - Repelling the Arab Offensive **16:**307
- - - Jewish Forces Take the Initiative **16:**308
- - The Second Phase **16:**314
- - - The Arab Armies Invade **16:**314
- - - Until the First Truce **16:**315
- - - The First Truce **16:**322
- - - The "Ten Days" **16:**322
- - - Clearing the Road to the Negev **16:**326
- - - The Arab Liberation Army Driven Off **16:**328
- - - Expelling the Egyptians **16:**329
- History **8:**770; **9:**363; **9:**365ff
- - Arab National Movement **9:**465
- - United Nations **15:**1544ff
- Military Forces
- - Druze **9:**927
- - Haganah **7:**1073
- - Israel Defense Forces **9:**697
- - I.Ẓ.L. **8:**1466
- - Leḥi **11:**463
- - Maḥal **11:**722
- - Palmaḥ **13:**46
- People
- - Allon, Yigal **2:**655
- - Ben-Gurion, David **4:**509ff
- - Dayan, Moshe **5:**1373
- - Dori Ya'akov **6:**173
- - Marcus, David Daniel **11:**945
- - Yadin, Yigael **16:**694
- - *see also under names of individual commanders*
- Places
- - Jerusalem **9:**1480ff
- - Tel Aviv **15:**923
- - Tiberias **15:**1134
- - *see also under individual towns and places*
- Operations
- - Ben-Ami **16:**310
- - Dani **11:**620; **16:**323
- - Dekel **16:**324
- - Ḥameẓ **16:**310
- - Ḥiram **16:**328
- - Ḥorev **16:**329
- - Kilshon **16:**314
- - Lot **5:**1395; **15:**72
- - Maccabee **12:**441; **16:**314
- - Naḥshon **7:**1073; **9:**363; **16:**308
- - Uvdah **6:**568; **9:**377
- - Yevusi **16:**313
- - Yiftaḥ **16:**309
- - Yo'av (Ten Plagues) **9:**371 **14:**132; **16:**326
- *illus:*
- - text
- - *Altalena* incident **8:**1470

- - Arab Legion soldiers on Jerusalem Old City wall **9:**1483
- - Arab refugee camp, Jericho **9:**447
- - desecrated graves in Mt. of Olives Jewish cemetery **9:**1485
- - Eilat, hoisting of the Israel flag, 1949 **6:**567
- - Eliyahu ha-Navi Synagogue destruction **9:**1486
- - food convoy arriving in Jerusalem **9:**1483
- - General Armistice Agreements with Arab states (1949) **3:**479-482
- - Hurvah Synagogue destruction **9:**1485
- - Israel-Jordan General Armistice Agreement, 1949 **3:**479
- - Israel stamps **9:**844-845
- - Israel-Syria negotiations, Maḥanayim **3:**481
- - Jerusalem fighting **9:**366
- - J.N.F. stamp **15:**333
- - Negev Brigade memorial **12:**931
- - Neẓer Sereni defense **12:**1131
- - Shertok's letter re peace talks with Arab states **3:**478
- - Tel Ḥai memorial **15:**932
- - tombstones from Mt. of Olives used for Arab Legion barracks **9:**1485
- - water rationing in Jerusalem **9:**1482
- - Yeḥi'am **16:**728
- *maps:*
- - armistice demarcation lines 1949 **9:**318
- *see also:* ARMISTICE AGREEMENTS, ISRAEL-ARAB
Waronovski, Aaron D. A. **11:**540
WAR REFUGEE BOARD (U.S.) **16:**332
- American Jewish Committee **2:**824
- Holocaust **8:**907
- Joint Distribution Committee **2:**830
- United States **15:**1634
Warren (city, Ohio) **12:**1345
Warren (tn., R. I.) **14:**143
WARREN, SIR CHARLES **16:**332
- Jerusalem **9:**1521ff
- Warren's shaft (Jer.) **9:**1307
- Zionism **16:**1155
- *illus:*
- - text
- - Temple Mount excavations **9:**1522
WARRENS, ROSA **14:**935
Warrenton (tn., Va.) **16:**163
WARSAW (city, Pol.) **16:**333
- *Contents:*
- - Within the Duchy of Warsaw **16:**335
- - Within Congress Poland **16:**336
- - Social and Cultural Developments **16:**337
- - Jewish Press **16:**339
- - World War I and the Polish Republic **16:**341
- - Jewish Educational Institutions **16:**341
- - Hebrew Printing **16:**342
- - Holocaust Period **16:**342
- - First Mass Deportations **16:**349
- - Active Resistance **16:**350
- - Post-War Developments **16:**353
- demography **5:**1516
- Farbstein, Joshua **6:**1181
- Frankists **14:**1253
- history chart (1483) **8:**766-767
- Jewish population in 1914 **8:**732
- library **11:**191
- museum **12:**539
- Poland **13:**763
- tailors **15:**705
- *illus:*
- - text
- - Bund, 30th anniversary **13:**912
- - Bundist Youth Organization **13:**741
- - children at OSE camp **12:**1537
- - communal *seder* (1960) **13:**781
- - cooperative workshop **5:**943
- - desecrated tombstone **13:**782
- - Israel consulate **13:**781
- - Jewish couple, 19th cent. **13:**728
- - Jewish Museum **12:**545
- - *Literarishe Bleter* board **16:**818
- - Menuḥah ve-Naḥalah society **9:**556
- - Shmulovicz mausoleum **15:**1231
- - tombstones **15:**1227,1228
- *pop. tables:*
- - growth, 1781-1897 **13:**735
Warsaw Ghetto
- Anielewicz, Mordecai **3:**3
- art **3:**575
- Czerniakow, Adam **5:**1210
- Holocaust Remembrance Day **8:**916
- Lubetkin, Zivia **11:**538
- Nossig, Alfred **12:**1230
- Stroop, Juergen **15:**442
- uprising **8:**879; **8:**892ff
- Warsaw **16:**342
- *illus:*
- - Anielewicz (memorial) **3:**3
- - boy from **13:**757
- - building the wall **8:**869
- - "Old Jew with Children" (drg., R. Kramsztyk) Fig. 75 **3**-ART
- - plan **16:**347
- - stamp **15:**336
- - street **7:**544
- - Stroop, Juergen **15:**442
Warsaw Ghetto Memorial (1963) **11:**1370
Warsaw Jewish Historical Institute, *see* JEWISH HISTORICAL INSTITUTE, WARSAW
Warschauer, A. J. **5:**1034
Warschauer, H. **6:**330
WAR SCROLL (D.S. ms.) **16:**1558
- Arameans **3:**252
- calendar **5:**51
- Kittim **10:**1081
- *illus:* **5:**1417
- *see also:* DEAD SEA SCROLLS
Warshavsky, Shemuel, *see* YAVNE'ELI, SHEMUEL
WARSHAVSKY, YAKIR **16:**354
WARSHAWSKI, MARK **16:**354
- *illus:* text
Warshawsky, Abel **5:**612
Warshawsky, Alex **5:**612
WARSHAWSKY, ISAAC **16:**355
WARSKI-WARSZAWSKI, ADOLF **16:**355
Wars of the Lord, Book of the (bib. source bk.), *see* BOOK OF THE WARS OF THE LORD
Warszawa (city, Pol.), *see* WARSAW
Warszawski, Bunim **12:**186
Warszawski, Jakir, *see* WARSHAVSKY, YAKIR
Wartels, Nat **13:**1371
Wartha, Johann Paul **8:**64
Warthegau (Wartheland; reg., Pol.) **11:**432
Warthog (zool.) **9:**225
Wartski, Philip **6:**308
WARWICK (tn., Eng.) **16:**355
Warwick (city, R. I.) **14:**143
Wase (city, Egy.), *see* THEBES
Waser (us), Kaspar **8:**64
Waserman, Meir **5:**497
Washer, Sam **15:**1036
"Washermen" Tales (fable), *see* *Mishlei Kovesim*
WASHINGTON (state, U.S.) **16:**355
Washington (city, Pa.) **13:**230
Washington County (R.I.) **14:**143
WASHINGTON, D.C. (U.S.) **16:**356
- history chart (1847) **8:**766-767
- Library of Congress **11:**193
- *illus:*
- - text
- - Israel demonstrations **15:**1667; **16:**1145
- - 1940 protest **15:**1632
WASHINGTON, GEORGE **16:**359
- *illus:*
- - text
- - bust of Naum Aronson **3:**495
- - letter to Mikveh Israel Congregation, Philadelphia **13:**369
- - prayer for **15:**1595
- - Seixas' address **14:**144
WASHINGTON HAGGADAH **7:**1100
- *illus:* **6:** *fcg.* 651; **7:**1086; **8:**1271
Washington Heights (loc., N.Y.C.) **12:**1082; **12:**1108
- *illus:*
- - Yeshiva University building **12:**1106
Washukkanni (city, Mesop.) **16:**1498
Wasilkow (tn., Pol.) **15:**1475
WASIT (city, Iraq) **16:**361
- Iraq **8:**1447
Wasmuth, M. **8:**64
Wassenaar (tn., Neth.) **7:**1125
Wasserman, Augustine **11:**498
WASSERMAN, ELḤANAN BUNIM **16:**361
Wasserman, Joseph **16:**679
WASSERMANN, AUGUST VON **16:**362
- *illus:* text
WASSERMANN, JAKOB **16:**362
Wassermann, Moses **15:**462
WASSERMANN, OSKAR **16:**364
WASSERZUG (Lomzer), HAYYIM **16:**364
- music **12:**651
Wasserzug, Joseph **9:**1166
Wassilewsky, Nathan **16:**1165
WAT, ALEXANDER **16:**364
WATCHERS (bib. term) **16:**365
- angel **5:**1525
Watches, Priestly, *see* MISHMAROT AND MA'AMADOT
Watchmaking **7:**742
Watchmen, Jewish, Association of, *see* HA-SHOMER
Watchtower and stockade, *see* STOCKADE AND WATCHTOWER
Watchung (tn., N.J.) **15:**1534
WATEN, JUDAH **16:**365
Water **11:**1490
- *Mikveh* **11:**1534
- *see also:* BATH, BATHING; DEW; RAIN
Water Affairs Tribunal (Isr.) **9:**640
WATER AND IRRIGATION IN ISRAEL **9:**767
- agriculture **9:**776
- FAO **15:**1564
- Israel-Arab dispute **9:**385; **9:**403ff
- Jerusalem, **9:**1380; **9:**1471; **9:**1480; **9:**1537
- Jordan River diversion **14:**1625
- legislation **9:**653
- National Water Carrier **9:**767; **15:**649
- Negev **12:**929
- Rutenberg, Pinḥas **14:**516
- United Nations **15:**1553
- United States plans **15:**1665
- Yarmuk **16:**720
- *illus:*
- - text
- - Dan River **9:**231
- - dew nights, average values 1945-52 (table) **5:**1601
- - flash flood in the Negev **9:**185
- - Gibeon pool **7:**551
- - Hezekiah's tunnel **9:**1539
- - Ḥuleh Valley **8:**1065-1068
- - Jerusalem aqueduct **9:**1538
- - Jerusalem public fountains **9:**1433,1434
- - Jordan, meandering course **9:**153
- - Jordan delta **9:**157
- - Lake Kinneret **9:**170
- - National Water Carrier **11:**1274
- - rain clouds, Beth-Shean valley **9:**187
- - Ramleh, 'Unayziyya cistern **13:**1541
- - Senir **9:**170
- - Siloam tunnel **3:**316; **8:**603; **14:**1400
- - snowfall, Jerusalem (1968) **9:**188
- - Ta'anach drainpipe cistern **5:**579
- - water ration card (1920) **9:**1476
- - water rationing, Jerusalem **9:**1482
- - Yarmuk River **13:**1531; **16:**719
- - Yarmuk Valley **9:**157
- *maps:*
- - dew nights, annual number **9:**187
- - rainfall, 1921-60 means **9:**186
- *see also:* MEKOROT WATER COMPANY; TAHAL
Water Carrier, National (Isr.) **9:**767; **15:**649
- *illus:* **11:**1274
"Water-Carrier at the Town Well" (paint., M. Minkowski) **8:**755
Water drawing, feast of **15:**499
- *halakhah le-Moshe mi-Sinai* **7:**1167
- kibbutz festivals **10:**962
- *Ru'ah ha-Kodesh* **14:**365
- sacrifice **14:**611
- sages **14:**642
- *illus:*
- - embroidered hanging for a *sukkah* **7:**1385
- *see also:* Libation offering
Waterford (city, Ire.) **8:**1464
Waterfowl (fauna) **9:**226
Water libation, *see* Water drawing, feast of
Waterloo (city, Iowa) **8:**1437
Waterman Wise, James, *see* Wise, James Waterman
Waterman-Wise, Louise **16:**568
Watermelon (bot.) **11:**1293
- plant list **13:**625
Water Planning for Israel (corp., Isr.), *see* TAHAL
Water Polo (sport) **15:**313
Water Skiing (sport) **15:**316
Watertown (city, S.D.) **15:**213
Waterville (city, M.) **11:**782
Watson, Tom **7:**73
WATTĀSIDS (Mor. dyn.) **16:**365
- Morocco **12:**330
Wattenberg, William **14:**13
WATTERS, LEON LAIZER **16:**366
WATZINGER, CARL **16:**366
Wauchope, Sir Arthur G.
- Arlosoroff and **3:**470; **16:**1083
- high commissioner **8:**470; **9:**601
- sympathy for Jews **9:**345; **9:**348
- White Papers **16:**484
- *illus:* **8:**472
- - Daniel Sieff Institute **16:**439
- - laying the Habimah Theater cornerstone **7:**1028
- - letter to Chaim Arlosoroff re settlement in Transjordan **9:**343
Waugh, Evelyn **6:**781
Waukegan (city, Ill.) **8:**1255

Waukesha (city, Wis.) **16**:556
Wausau (city, Wis.) **16**:556
Wave offering **5**:1161; **14**:604
WAW (Heb. let.) **16**:367
Wawelberg (stlmt., Arg.) **16**:367
WAWELBERG, HIPOLIT **16**:367
Wawelberg, Ẓevi Hirsch **16**:367
Waw qeti'a (Heb. let.) **16**:1409
Wawrzecki, Tomasz **4**:1539
Wax **16**:663ff
Waxman, Franz **12**:451
WAXMAN, MEYER **16**:368
WAY, LEWIS **16**:368
- Aix-la-Chapelle **16**:132
- missionary activity **13**:1248
Wayfarers, *see* TRAVELERS AND EXPLORERS; TRAVELERS AND TRAVELS TO EREẒ ISRAEL
Wayne (sub. Paterson, N.J.) **13**:179
WAYNE, JOHNNY **15**:1092
Way of the land of the Philistines (road, Sinai penin.) **14**:1594
WAZYK, ADAM **13**:805
W.C.C. *see* World Council of Churches
Wealth **16**:1293,1308
Weapons **16**:266f
- *illus:*
- - Canaanite axe and bow **16**:270-271
- - dagger from Lachish **16**:655
Weasel (zool.) **9**:226
Weather
- climate of Israel **9**:1127
- drought **15**:675
- rain **13**:1520
- thunder and lightning **15**:1127
- world organization **15**:1565
- *see also:* FAMINE AND DROUGHT
Weatherford (city, Tex.) **15**:1035
Weathermen (orgn.) **12**:1032
Weaving **5**:1044
- Egypt **6**:11
- guilds **7**:971ff
- Jewish pioneers **16**:1286
- textiles **15**:1037
- *illus:*
- - carpet weaving, Morocco **12**:338
- - Moroccan Jewish artisan **5**:1043
- - new immigrant **5**:1049
Webb, Sidney James (Lord Passfield)
- *aliyah* restriction **9**:528
- Arab National Movement **9**:459
- Shaw Commission **13**:31
- White Papers **9**:344; **16**:483
Weber, Georg **14**:1006
WEBER, MAX (art.) **16**:369
Weber, Max (sociol.) **15**:67
Weber, P. **13**:1052
Webes (r., Ger.) **5**:1597
Wecelinus (pros.) **16**:1341
Wechsler (fam., Vienna), *see* HALFANAUS
Wechsler, Adrian, *see* VEREA, ADRIAN
Wechsler, Bernhard **12**:1359
WECHSLER, DAVID **16**:369
- psychiatry **13**:1340
- psychology **13**:1345
Wechsler, Elhanan Hillel **10**:555
Wechsler, Eliezer **7**:1188
WECHSLER, HERBERT **16**:369
Wechsler, Howard **15**:311
WECHSLER, ISRAEL **16**:370
Wechsler, Jacob **3**:592
WECHSLER, JAMES A. **10**:318
Wechsler, Joseph **2**:125
WECHSLER, MAX **16**:370
Wechsler, Uri Shraga Phoebus **7**:1188
Wecker (monthly) **10**:90
Weckerlin, C.F. **8**:64
Wedding, *see* MARRIAGE
"Wedding in Shtetl" (paint., S. Raskin) **14**:1467
Wedekind, Frank **7**:441; **14**:221
Wedell, Rachel P., *see* Lit, Rachel P.
WEDGWOOD, JOSIAH CLEMENT **16**:371
WEEDS (bot.) **16**:371
- plant list **13**:625
Weekblad voor Israëlieten (newsp.), *see Nieuwsblad voor Israëlieten*
Weeks, Feast of, *see* SHAVUOT
Weemes, John, *see* Wemyss, John
Wegner, G. **8**:64
WEGROW (tn., Pol.) **16**:372
Wehemibre Neko II, *see* NECO
Wehle, Gottlieb **7**:71
Wehle, Jonas Beer **7**:70; **8**:805
Weibershul (w.'s gallery, syn.) **11**:1235
- *see also: Ezrat Nashim;* MEḤIẒAH
WEICHERT, MICHAEL **16**:373
- Shakespeare **14**:1265
- Vilna Troupe **16**:151
WEICHMANN, HERBERT **16**:373
- Germany **7**:500
- Hamburg **7**:1229
Weidenbaum, Naphtali Herz ha-Levi **9**:890
Weidenfeld, Sir Arthur, *see* WEIDENFELD, SIR GEORGE
Weidenfeld, Dov Berish ben Jacob **14**:93
WEIDENFELD, SIR GEORGE **16**:374
WEIDENREICH, FRANZ **16**:374
WEIDMAN, JEROME (nov.) **16**:375
Weidmann, J. (Chr. Hebr.) **8**:64
Weidner, Jean **12**:989
WEIDNER, PAULUS **16**:375
WEIGAND, THEODOR **16**:375
Weiganmei(e)r, Georg **8**:64
WEIGEL, CATHERINE **16**:376
Weigel, Melchior **16**:376
WEIGERT, CARL **16**:376
WEIGERT, FRITZ **16**:376
Weightlifting **15**:292; **15**:316
WEIGHTS AND MEASURES **16**:376
- *Contents:*
- - Metrological Systems in the Bible and the Ancient Near East **16**:377
- - In the Talmud **16**:388
- agoranomos **2**:372
- agriculture **2**:395; **2**:396
- *Beit Midot* **4**:1389
- bronze weights **16**:661
- Commandments, the 613 **5**:769,779
- egg **6**:474
- inscriptions **16**:667
- inspection of shops **13**:796
- *mikveh* **11**:1536f
- olive **12**:1365
- *Leshon ha-Zahav* **2**:628
- Talmud **11**:1314
- *illus:* text
- *see also:* BALANCE; COINS AND CURRENCY
Weil (U.S. fam.) **11**:1498
WEIL, A. LEO **16**:392
Weil, Alexander, *see* WEILL, ALEXANDRE ABRAHAM
WEIL, ANDRÉ **16**:392
Weil, Baruch **6**:1414
Weil, Bernard S. **11**:1589
Weil, Clifford **14**:162
Weil, Edmund **13**:973
WEIL, ERIC **16**:392
WEIL, FRANK LEOPOLD **16**:393
- Jewish Welfare **12**:873
WEIL, GOTTHOLD **16**:394
WEIL, GUSTAV **16**:394
WEIL, JACOB BEN JUDAH **16**:395
- Augsburg **3**:849
Weil, Jedidiah **10**:795
WEIL, JIŘÍ **16**:396
WEIL, JOSEPH **8**:1434
Weil, Meir, *see* WEYL, MEIR BEN SIMḤAH
Weil, Moses **11**:1588
WEIL, NETHANEL BEN NAPHTALI ẒEVI **16**:396
Weil, Prosper **10**:1496
WEIL, R. ADRIENNE **8**:1434
Weil, Rolf **5**:417
Weil, S. (r., Hung.) **14**:906
Weil, Samuel **3**:825
Weil, Sidney **15**:301
WEIL, SIMONE **16**:396
Weil, Solomon **5**:755
Weil, Tiah, *see* Weil, Jedidiah
Weile, Moses ben Jacob **2**:898
Weiler (Judenrat head) **16**:201
WEILER, JACK D. **16**:397
Weiler, Moses Cyrus **10**:156; **15**:200
Weiler, Samuel **4**:1399
Weilerstein, Sadie Rose **5**:451
Weill, Alexandre (bnk.) **10**:1513
WEILL, ALEXANDRE ABRAHAM **16**:397
- socialism **15**:25
Weill, Georges **16**:398
Weill, Julien **11**:82; **14**:133
WEILL, KURT **16**:398
WEILL, MICHEL AARON **16**:398
Weill, Raphael **14**:834
WEILL, RAYMOND **16**:399
- Jerusalem **9**:1522ff
Weill, S. (r., Fr.) **11**:568
Weill, Shraga **3**:593
- Song of Songs **15**:151
Weill, Simon **3**:420
Weiller, André **11**:1562
Weiller, Mirjam **5**:455
- Zionism **16**:1150
Weimann (fam., Bohem.) **12**:443
Weimar (city, Ger.) **15**:1128
Weimar Republic **7**:483
Wein, Albert W. **11**:1167
Weinbaum, Abram **13**:117
Weinbaum, David **13**:1049
Weinbaum, Erich-Marx **13**:1049
WEINBAUM, MARK **10**:318
Weinberg, Abraham (psych.) **13**:1340
Weinberg, Abraham (r., Belor.) **14**:1671
Weinberg, Abraham (r., Er. Isr.) **14**:1672
Weinberg, Abraham ben Isaac Mattathias **14**:1671
Weinberg, Abraham ben Issachar **14**:1672
Weinberg, Adolf **4**:655
Weinberg, Ajzik **16**:212
Weinberg, Arthur **5**:376
Weinberg, Carl **5**:376
Weinberg, Dvora, *see* LAPSON, DVORA
Weinberg, Gladys **3**:302
Weinberg, Issachar-Aryeh **14**:1672
WEINBERG, JACOB (comp.) **16**:399
Weinberg, Jacob (r.) **14**:379
WEINBERG, JEHIEL JACOB **16**:399
- Orthodoxy influenced by **12**:1490
Weinberg, Miriam (poet) **5**:445
Weinberg, Noah **14**:1671
Weinberg, Samuel **14**:1671
WEINBERG, SAUL S. **16**:400
- archaeology **3**:302
WEINBERG, SIDNEY J. **16**:400
Weinberg, Solomon **14**:1671
Weinberg, Von **15**:1166
WEINBERG, ẒEVI ZEBULUN **16**:401
Weinberger, Ephraim **10**:681
Weinberger, Jacob **3**:450; **5**:57
WEINBERGER, JAROMIR **16**:401
- Brod, Max **4**:1387
Weinberger, Joshua Aaron Ẓevi **11**:959
Weinberger, Mordecai Azriel **11**:959
Weindling, B. **5**:1038
Weiner, Dan **13**:485
Weiner, Harold **13**:1361
Weiner, Henry **15**:1034
Weiner, Herbert **9**:906
Weiner, Joseph **15**:302
WEINER, LAZAR **12**:713
- *mus. notations:*
- - composition for synagogue **12**:665
WEINER, LEO **12**:713
Weiner, L. (socialist) **2**:421
Weiner, Mattityahu, *see* SHELEM, MATTITYAHU
Weiner, René **12**:544
WEINER, RICHARD **16**:401
- press **13**:1026
Weiner, T. **14**:666
Weiner, Yehudi **5**:487; **12**:713
Weingarten, Abba **11**:628
Weingarten, Ḥayyim Isaac **11**:628
Weingarten, Isaac Aaron **11**:628
Weingarten, Jacob Loeb **11**:628
WEINGARTEN, JOAB JOSHUA **16**:402
Weingarten, Joe **8**:1052
Weingarten, Johnny, *see* WAYNE, JOHNNY
Weingarten, Meir **16**:402
Weingarten, Shemariah **11**:628
Weingarten, Victor **13**:1362
Weinger, Mordecai, *see* VEINGER, MORDECAI
WEINHEIM (tn., Ger.) **16**:402
WEINHOUSE, SIDNEY **5**:389
WEININGER, OTTO **16**:402
Weinman (art.), *see* BEN-ZION
Weinmann, Charles **16**:404
Weinmann, Eduard J., *see* WEINMANN, JACOB
Weinmann, Fritz **16**:404
Weinmann, Hans **16**:404
WEINMANN, JACOB **16**:403
Weinmann, Johan **8**:64
WEINPER (Weinperlech), ZISHE **16**:404
Weinreb (r., Can.) **15**:1261
Weinreb, F. **7**:1125
Weinreich, Harold **15**:627
WEINREICH, MAX **16**:404
- Ashkenazi pronunciation **13**:1128
WEINREICH, URIEL **16**:405
WEINRUB, MATVEY **11**:1576
- Russia **14**:479
Weinryb, Baruch Abraham, *see* Rivkin, Boruch
WEINRYB, BERNARD DOV SUCHER **16**:406
- historiography **8**:562
WEINSHALL (fam., Er. Isr.) **16**:407
Weinshall, Abraham **16**:407
Weinshall, Ben Zion Ze'ev **16**:407
Weinshall, Jacob **16**:407
- Herod drama **8**:386
Weinshall, Vladimir, *see* Weinshall, Ben Zion Ze'ev
WEINSTEIN, AARON **16**:408
Weinstein, Baruch **10**:92
WEINSTEIN, BERISH **16**:408
Weinstein, David **5**:416; **5**:735
Weinstein, Laurence **16**:557
WEINSTEIN, LEWIS H. **16**:408
- Conference of Presidents **5**:871
Weinstein, Michael **16**:597
Weinstein, Miksa, *see* SZABOLCSI, MIKSA
Weinstein, Nathanael, *see* WEST, NATHANAEL
Weinstein, Rose M. **15**:305

Weinstein, Yeraḥmiel, *see* WEINSTEIN, AARON
WEINSTOCK, SIR ARNOLD **16:**409
WEINSTOCK, HARRIS **16:**409
- Sacramento **14:**598
WEINSTOCK, HERBERT **12:**713
Weinstock, Isadore **15:**306
Weinstock, Leon **5:**558
Weinthrop, Bud, *see* FLANAGAN, BUD
Weintraub (music.) **12:**650
Weintraub, Aaron Ze'ev, *see* AESCOLY, AARON ZE'EV
Weintraub, Jerzy Kamil **13:**802
Weintraub, Philip **15:**301
WEINTRAUB, SOLOMON **16:**410
- *mus. notations:*
- - introduction to confession of sins **12:**651
Weintraub, Wiktor **13:**803
Weintraub, Ẓevi Hirsch Alter **16:**410
- *scores:*
- - *Addir Hu* **2:**257
- - *Aleinu le-Shabbeah* **2:**556
Weirton (city, W. Va.) **16:**475
Weisbach, Werner **3:**650
WEISBERGER, BARBARA **5:**1273
WEISBERGER, BERNARD ALLEN **8:**550
Weise, Christian **12:**917
Weisel (states.), *see* MAGNUS, MARCUS
WEISENBURG, THEODORE H. **16:**410
Weisenfreund, Muni, *see* MUNI, PAUL
Weiser (city, Ida.) **8:**1223
Weiser, Artur **4:**909
Weiser, Benno **6:**361
- Latin America **10:**1455
Weiser, Max **6:**361
WEISGAL, MEYER WOLF **16:**410
- Weizmann Institute **16:**439
- *illus:*
- - Biltmore Hotel Conference **15:**1633
- - Zionist Organization of Canada convention **16:**1110
WEISGALL, HUGO **16:**411
Weisman (name), *see also:* Wais(s)man(n), Weissman
Weisman, Adele (writ., Can.), *see* WISEMAN, ADELE
Weisman, Harold **13:**1361
WEISS, ABRAHAM (schol.) **16:**411
Weiss, Abraham (collec.) **4:**1220
Weiss, A.H. **14:**1519
WEISS, ALBERT PAUL **16:**412
Weiss, André **10:**1496
WEISS, AURELIU **14:**423; **14:**428
Weiss, Berthold **16:**415
WEISS, DAVID **16:**412
Weiss, Edmund **3:**806
Weiss, Eduardo **13:**1340
Weiss, Endre, *see* VESZI, ENDRE
Weiss, E.R. **15:**1488
WEISS, ERNST **16:**412
Weiss, Isaac Eizik, *see* Spinka, Isaac Eizik Weiss of
WEISS, ISAAC HIRSCH **16:**413
- Bruell, Nehemiah **4:**1415
- history chart **8:**766-767
- Wiener Neustadt **16:**504
- Wissenschaft **16:**577
Weiss, Isaac Jacob **14:**93
- transplants **15:**1339
Weiss, Isaiah **16:**412
Weiss, Jacob Joseph, *see* Spinka, Jacob Joseph Weiss of
Weiss, Jadwiga, *see* Wajsowna, Jadwiga
Weiss, J.G. (schol.) **7:**1420
WEISS, JIŘÍ **12:**475
WEISS, JOSEPH JOSHUA **5:**389
WEISS, JOSEPH MEIR **16:**414
Weiss, Joseph Zevi **6:**469
Weiss, Kalman **14:**907
Weiss, Karl **7:**449
Weiss, Louise **10:**306
WEISS, MANFRÉD **16:**415
Weiss, Margaret **13:**486
Weiss, Martin **11:**794
Weiss, Max **5:**405
Weiss, Meir **8:**802
WEISS, PAUL **16:**415
WEISS, PETER **16:**415
Weiss, Robert, *see* Szurday, Robert
WEISS, SAMSON **16:**416
Weiss, Samuel (sci.) **11:**1200
WEISS, SAMUEL ARTHUR **16:**416
- sport **15:**308
Weiss, Samuel Ẓevi **16:**414
Weiss, Simon **15:**1034
Weiss, Ya'akov **8:**1469
Weissberg (name), *see also* Waisberg
WEISSBERG, ISAAC JACOB **16:**416
Weissberg, Leon **13:**117
WEISSBERG, MEIR (Max) **16:**416
Weissblum, Mordekhai **12:**1411
Weissbrucker, Anna Urban, *see* Urban, Anna
Weissenberg, Heinz **12:**406
WEISSENBERG, ISAAC MEIR **16:**417
WEISSENBERG, JULIA LAZAREVNA **12:**713
WEISSENBERG, SAMUEL ABRAMOVICH **16:**417
Weissenburg (tn., Ger.) **15:**544
Weissenburg (city, Rus.), *see* BELGOROD-DNESTROVSKI
Weissenfels (city, Ger.) **11:**1393
- synod **15:**633
Weissensee (tn., Ger.) **13:**877; **15:**1128ff
Weissenstein, Emanuel **15:**1041
WEISSER, JOSHUA **16:**418
Weisskopf, F.C. **5:**1193
WEISSKOPF, VICTOR F. **16:**418
Weissman (name), *see also* Wais(s)man(n), Weisman
Weissman, Barukh Mordekhai **10:**997; **14:**501
Weissman, Bernardo **15:**1073
Weissman, George **13:**1360
Weissman, Mişu **16:**1134
Weissman, Y.A. **16:**822
WEISSMANDEL, MICHAEL DOV **16:**418
WEISSMANN, ADOLF **12:**714
Weissmuller, Johnny **15:**313
WEISS-ROSMARIN, TRUDE **16:**419
Weisweiller, Alec **15:**311
Weisz, Dezso, *see* SZOMORY, DEZSO
Weisz, Eric, *see* HOUDINI, HARRY
WEISZ, MAX **16:**419
Weisz, Mór, *see* SZOMORY, DEZSŐ
Weisz, Richard **12:**1376
Weisz, Samuel, *see* Budaspitz, Samuel
WEISZ, VICTOR ("Vicky") **16:**419
Weiszburg, Chajjim **15:**1510
Weitenauer, Ignaz **8:**64; **4:**874
WEITER, A. **16:**420
WEITZ, JOSEPH **16:**421
WEITZ, NAPHTALI **16:**421
Weitz, Ra'anan **16:**421
Weitz, Yeḥiam **16:**421
Wei-Yang (city, China), *see* YANG-CHOU
Weizel, Mordecai, *see* ROSENBLATT, MORDECAI BEN MENAHEM
WEIZMAN, EZER **16:**422
- Palmaḥ **13:**48
WEIZMANN (Rus. fam.) **16:**422
- *illus:* text
Weizmann, Anna **16:**423
Weizmann, Benjamin **16:**426
WEIZMANN, CHAIM **16:**423
- *Contents:*
- - First Zionist Steps **16:**424
- - World War I **16:**427
- - The 1920s and 1930s **16:**430
- - World War II **16:**433
- - The Bevin Period **16:**434
- - First President of Israel **16:**436
- - As Chemist **16:**437
- General
- - archives **3:**390
- - family **16:**422
- - Hebrew University **8:**219
- - history chart **8:**766-767
- - letters **11:**61
- - Weizmann Institute **16:**438ff
- Politics
- - *aliyah* **9:**528ff
- - Arab National Movement **9:**458ff
- - as president **13:**1021
- - Balfour Declaration **4:**132ff
- - Biltmore Conference **4:**998
- - Italy **16:**1122
- - Knesset, First **9:**374
- - Manchester **11:**860
- - Revisionists **14:**128
- - South Africa **15:**206
- - Sykes-Picot Agreement **9:**310ff
- - U.N. and Jewish state **16:**1094
- - Vatican **16:**74; **16:**76; **16:**77
- - White Papers **16:**483
- - Zionism **16:**1033,1048f,1078f,1143
- - Zionist Commission **16:**1163
- - Zionist Congress (8th) **16:**1169
- Personalities
- - Balfour **4:**130
- - Brandeis, Louis **4:**1297
- - Churchill, Winston **5:**556
- - Dugdale, Blanche **6:**263
- - Goldmann, Nahum **7:**724
- - Jabotinsky **9:**1179
- - Lawrence, T.E. **10:**1488
- - Marks, Simon **11:**1010
- - Marmorek, Alexander **11:**1013
- - Mussolini, Benito **12:**718
- - Scott, C.P. **14:**1036
- - Sieff, Israel **14:**1510
- - Yahuda, Isaac Ezekiel **16:**703
- - Wise, Stephen **16:**567
- *illus:*
- - text
- - Aḥad Ha-Am's letter re Hebrew University **2:**445
- - Allenby **2:**647
- - autograph **3:**918
- - Balfour **4:**130
- - Biltmore Hotel Conference **15:**1633
- - Churchill's letter re Jewish Fighting Force **3:**394
- - Cunningham, Sir Alan **8:**472
- - Dallas, Texas **5:**1231
- - Daniel Sieff Research Institute **16:**439
- - Dori, Ya'akov, and Ben-Gurion **6:**173
- - Dugdale, Blanche **6:**263
- - Faisal and **9:**336
- - Hebrew University, foundation stone ceremony **8:**219
- - Hebrew University, opening ceremony **8:**221
- - inaugural speech **9:**615
- - Israel stamp **9:***fcg.* 843
- - Mond, Alfred, and **12:**242
- - parents **16:**423
- - presidential oath **9:**370
- - protest against Passfield White Paper **16:**1118
- - Round Table Conference **9:**353
- - Schuster, Sir Arthur, and **14:**1012
- - Thirteenth Zionist Congress **16:**1173
- - Transjordan Arab leaders and **9:**346
- - Truman, Harry S., and **15:**1409
- - Yershov, Paul, and **14:**497
- - Zionist Commission arriving in Palestine (1918) **16:**1163
- - Zionist delegation to Palestine (1918) **9:**336
Weizmann, Gita **16:**422
Weizmann, Hannah, *see* Weizmann, Anna
Weizmann, Ḥaya **16:**422
Weizmann, Michael (pilot) **16:**433
Weizmann, Mikhail (agron.) **16:**423
Weizmann, Moses (Moshe) **16:**423
Weizmann, Ozer **16:**422; **16:**423
Weizmann, Rachel-Leah **16:**422; **16:**423
Weizmann, Samuel **16:**423
Weizmann, Vera **16:**425,437
- *illus:*
- - protest against Passfield White Paper **16:**1118
Weizmann, Yeḥiel Mikhl, *see* Weizmann, Mikhail
Weizmann Institute for Zionist Research (Isr.), *see* Chaim Weizmann Institute for Zionist Research
WEIZMANN INSTITUTE OF SCIENCE (Isr.) **16:**438
- atomic research **9:**795ff
- higher education **9:**957
- science and research **9:**966ff
- Sieff, Daniel **14:**1510
- *illus:*
- - aerial view **3:**352
- - Erna and Jakob Michael Institute of Nuclear Science **9:**956
- - Nuclear Physics Department **9:**967
Weldon (tn., N.C.) **12:**1220
Weledniki, Israel Dov Baer of, *see* Israel Dov Baer of Weledniki
Welensky, Michael **14:**148
WELENSKY, SIR ROY (Roland) **16:**442
- Zambia **16:**923
Welfare committee (Rus.), *see* Community chest
WELFARE IN ISRAEL **9:**993
Weli Yetim (shrine, Er.Isr.) **14:**1402
Welkom (tn., S.A.) **12:**1448
Well, Song of the **13:**677
Welland (city, Ont.) **12:**1408
Wellbeing offering, *see* Peace offering
Wellesley (tn., Mass.) **11:**1112
WELLESZ, EGON JOSEPH **16:**442
WELLESZ, JULIUS **16:**442
"Well Furnished Desert" (paint., Y. Bergner) Fig. 107 **3-**ART
WELLHAUSEN, JULIUS **16:**443
- biblical criticism **4:**906ff
- Genesis, Book of **7:**390
- Pentateuch **13:**239
Welling, Georg von **10:**646
Wellington (city, N.Z.) **12:**1128
Wellisch, Aaron Hirschl **15:**1187
Well-poisoning libel
- Basle Jews **4:**303
- Benevento **4:**500
- Black Death **4:**1064
- Clement VI **5:**601
- Marlowe's drama **11:**1011
- Wuerzburg (1349) **16:**675
Wells (concen. camp) **7:**366
Wells (tn., Nevada) **12:**1018
Wells, Charles Jeremiah **6:**775
Wells, Mary **15:**512
Wells, Matt **15:**304

WELNER, PINCHES 16:444
Welsche, Aaron Hirschl, see Wellisch, Aaron Hirschl
WELSH, ARTHUR L. (Al) 16:444
- aviation 2:321
- illus:
- - in an early plane 2:320
WELT, DIE (weekly) 16:445
- Marmorek, Oscar 11:1013
- Werner, Siegmund 16:453
- Zionism 16:1107
Welten, Heinz 12:917
Weltfrei, Immanuel 13:1297
WELTSCH, FELIX (Baruch) 16:445
WELTSCH, ROBERT 16:447
- Bar Kochba Association 4:228
- Zionism 16:1112
Welt-Verband Shomre Shabbos (assoc.) 7:945
Welwart (partisan) 15:1235
Wembley (sub., London) 11:479
- illus:
- - shift of population 11:479
Wemyss (Weemes), John 8:64
Wen-Amon (Wenamun; Egy. trav.) 6:172; 6:359; 6:483
WENCESLAUS IV (emp., Ger.) 16:447
- Kara, Avigdor 10:758
Wendel, Harold 12:1451
WENDLAND, PAUL 16:448
WENDROFF, ZALMAN 16:448
Wengeroff, Ḥanan 16:449
Wengeroff, Isabel 16:449
WENGEROFF, PAULINE 16:449
WENGEROFF, SEMYON AFANASYEVICH 16:449
Wengeroff, Zinaida 16:449
Wengrow, Moses ben Isaiah 12:418
Weniger Maertersdorf (city, Aus.), see EISENSTADT
Wenrik, Johann G. 8:64
Wenzel Bible 4:873
WERBEL, ELIAHU MORDECAI 16:450
Werbelowsky, Joseph L. 13:1376
Werber, Abraham 16:1150
WERBER, BARUCH 16:450
- editor 4:1398
Werber, Jacob 4:1398
Werbermacher, Hannah Rachel, see LUDOMIR, MAID OF
Werbermacher, Monesh 11:553
Werbezirk, Gisela 15:1056
Werbiz (vill., Pol.) 16:206
WERBLOWSKY, RAPHAEL JUDA ZWI 1:38; 16:450
Werchert, M. 15:1072
Werdiger, Jacob 13:989
Werewolf 11:708
WERFEL, FRANZ 16:450
- illus:
- - Jacobowsky and the Colonel 15:1068
Werfel, Yiẓḥak, see RAPHAEL, YIẒḤAK
WERGELAND, HENRIK ARNOLD 16:452
- Norway 12:1223
- Scandinavian literature 14:932
Werich, Jan 15:1092
Werkleute (Zion. mvmt.) 7:1540
Werkner, Lajos 12:1375
Werko (tax, Er. Isr.) 9:749
Wermuth, Christian 11:1173
WERNER, ALFRED 1:38
- art 3:651
WERNER, ERIC 16:452
WERNER, HEINZ 16:453
Werner, K. 13:1255
Werner, Sacher 15:311
WERNER, SIEGMUND 16:453
- Ruth, work on 14:523
WERTH, ALEXANDER 10:318
WERTHEIM (Ger. fam.) 16:454
- illus: text
Wertheim, Abraham 16:454
WERTHEIM, ABRAHAM CAREL 16:454
- Amsterdam 2:900
Wertheim, A.J. 16:459
Wertheim, Arthur 16:454
Wertheim, Aryeh Leib 4:477
Wertheim, David 15:1633
Wertheim, George 16:454
Wertheim, M. 6:321
WERTHEIM, MAURICE 16:455
Wertheim, Naphtali Herz 13:9
Wertheim, S. 11:1284
Wertheim, Samson 7:1453
Wertheim, Simeon Solomon 4:477
Wertheim, Wolff 16:454
Wertheim Bible 4:873
WERTHEIMER, CHAIM ERNST 16:455
Wertheimer, David 10:1590
WERTHEIMER, EDUARD VON 16:455
Wertheimer, Herz (Hirsch) 14:1080
Wertheimer, Israel 3:688
Wertheimer, John 11:481
Wertheimer, Joseph 7:403
WERTHEIMER, JOSEPH, RITTER VON 16:456
- Allianz, Israelitische, zu Wien 2:654
- Austrian Jews 3:894
- education 6:462
Wertheimer, Leopold, see BRUNNER, CONSTANTIN
WERTHEIMER, MAX 16:456
WERTHEIMER, SAMSON 16:457
- chronological chart 8:766-767
- Worms 16:646
- illus: text
Wertheimer, Simon 8:234
WERTHEIMER, SOLOMON AARON 16:459
- Cairo genizah 16:1334
Wertheimer, Wolf 3:489; 8:469; 16:459
Wertheimer and Gompertz (bnks.) 4:177
Wertheimstein (fam.) 10:1590
Wertheimstein, Franziska von 7:447
Wertheimstein, Hermann von 16:459
Wertheimstein, Joseph von 16:459
Wertheimstein, Josephine von 7:447
Wertheimstein, Lazar von 16:459
Wertheimstein, Leopold von 13:1517; 14:1493
Wertheimstein, Sophie von, Baroness Todesco 7:447
WESEL, BARUCH BENDET BEN REUBEN 16:459
Wesel, Ben-Zion Albert 15:1452
Wesel, Moses 11:918
Weshesh (anc. people) 13:399
WESKER, ARNOLD 16:460
Wesley, John 11:409
Wessel, Henry 12:911
Wessel, J. 8:64
Wessel, Lewis 12:911
Wessely, Moses, see Josephs, Moses
WESSELY, NAPHTALI HERZ 16:461
- Berlin, Saul 4:663
- chronological chart 8:766-767
- David Tevele 5:1353
- Frederick II 8:956
- Hebrew literature 8:180
- Hurwitz, Judah 8:1118
- Levin, Ẓevi Hirsch 11:112
- literature, views on 5:1115
- Me'assef 11:1161
- prosody 13:1225,1226
- Shirei Tiferet 12:404
- illus: text
- see also: HASKALAH
WESSELY, WOLFGANG 16:463
WEST, NATHANAEL 16:464
- U.S. literature 15:1574
West Australian Zionist Society 16:1105
West Bank (reg., Er. Isr.)
- agriculture 9:783
- population 9:492
- Six-Day War 15:1574
- illus:
- - Arab family crossing Jordan 9:450
- - Arab refugee camp, Jericho 9:447
- - Arabs cultivating vegetables 9:786
- - convoy of trucks crossing Allenby Bridge 9:410
West Chester (boro., Pa.) 13:230
WESTCHESTER COUNTY (N.Y.S.) 16:464
- illus: text
Westcott, W. 16:787
WESTERBORK (concen. camp) 16:466
- Amsterdam Jews 2:903
- Netherlands 12:987f
- illus: text
Westerly (tn., R.I.) 14:143
Western Palatinate (reg., Ger.), see PALATINATE
Western Synagogue (London), see Westminster Synagogue
WESTERN WALL 16:467
- Amīn al-Husseini 9:462
- anti-Jewish riot (1929) 9:459
- Arab-Jewish clashes 9:1474
- Av, Ninth of 3:939
- Behar, Nissim 4:393
- chief rabbinate control 9:411
- commission of inquiry 16:1083
- excavations 3:327; 9:1516
- holy places in Israel 8:921f
- in the Arts 9:1578; 15:984
- inscriptions 10:469; 16:669
- kissing of 10:1075
- Madaba map 9:1543
- pilgrimage to 13:514
- prayers dispute, Jewish-Arab 9:343
- Psalms recitation 13:1325
- religious life 9:901
- seal motif 14:1081
- Simeon the Just 15:958; 15:963ff
- Six-Day War 14:1635
- illus:
- - text
- - aerial view 9:1439
- - after Six-Day War 9:1499
- -Austrian Jewish soldiers, W.W.I. 11:1565
- - Betar members on guard duty 9:1478
- - demonstration of solidarity with Soviet Jewry 9:434
- - first anniversary of the reunification of Jerusalem 9:1503
- - Ḥanukkah lights at 7:1285; 9:904
- - ḥasidic youths dancing 12:672
- - Israel stamp 9:844-845
- - Jewish Legion (1918) 10:72
- - Jews praying 9:1467
- - praying at (1967) 8:923
- - Priestly Blessing 13:1063
- - primitivist woodcut 4:115
- - sukkah wall painting 15:fcg. 491
- - Sukkot service 6:1245
- - Szatmár rebbe at 14:908
- - "Wailing Wall and Its Surroundings" (drg., S. Schulmann) 9:fcg. 1531
- - wedding party, 1967 11:1045
- - Wolin Ḥasidim seal 14:1077
- see also: TEMPLE MOUNT
"Western Wall" (paint., S. Alva) 2:785
WESTERWEEL, JOOP 16:472
- Habas' book 7:1018
Westfield (tn., N.J.) 15:1533
West Friesland (prov., Neth.) 12:976
West Galician Federation (Zion. faction) 16:1131
West Hartford (tn., Conn.) 5:898
Westheim, Paul 14:1069
WESTHEIMER, FRANK HENRY 5:389
Westhoffen (vill, Ger.) 2:754
West India Company 14:1662
WEST INDIES 16:473
- Bayonne Jews 4:351
- history chart (1654) 8:766-767
- Marrano Diaspora 11:1019
- slave trade 14:1663ff
- tax 15:840
West Kildonan (sub., Winnipeg) 16:551
Westminster Abbey (Lond.) 11:1370
Westminster Synagogue (London) 11:474
- illus:
- - takkanot 15:714
Westmount (city, Can.) 12:286
West Oak Lane-Mt. Airy (Pa.) 13:374
West Orange (sub., N.J.) 6:904
West Palm Beach (city, Fla.) 6:1363
WESTPHALIA (reg., Ger.) 16:473
- Bail, Charles-Joseph 4:110
- history chart 8:766-767
- Jewish Consistory 12:824
- seal of Consistory 14:1080
- textiles 15:1042
- illus: text
West Rogers Park (sub., Chicago) 5:415
WEST VIRGINIA (U.S.) 16:475
- pop. tables: text
Westwood (bor., N.J.) 4:612
Westwood (L.A.) 11:503
Weszelin, Kismariai Paulus, see Veszelin, Pál Kismariai
Wettach, Charles Adrien, see GROCK
WETTE, DE, WILHELM MARTIN LEBERECHT 16:476
- Bible 4:873; 4:906
- Pentateuch 13:236ff
Wetterau (reg., Ger.) 12:62
WETTSTEIN, FEIVEL HIRSCH 16:477
Wettstein, J. Jakob 8:64
Wetzel, Erhard 16:477, 1332
Wetzel, J.C.F. 8:64
WETZLAR (city, Ger.) 16:477
Wetzlar, Abraham, see Wetzlar, Karl Abraham
Wetzlar, Amschel 16:478
Wetzlar, Gustave 6:342
Wetzlar, Karl Abraham 16:478
Wetzlar, Leonore 16:478
Wetzlar, Solomon ben Simeon 16:478
WETZLAR VON PLANKENSTERN (fam.) 16:478
Wetzlar von Plankenstern, Gustav 16:479
Wetzlar von Plankenstern, Heinrich Adolf 16:479
Wetzlar von Plankenstern, Ignaz 16:479
Wetzlar von Plankenstern, Joanna, see Theresia von Picquigny, Joanna
Wetzlar von Plankenstern, Raymund 5:1300; 16:479
W.E.V.D. (radio station, N.Y.) 10:50; 12:1122; 13:1618
Wevelinghofen (tn., Ger.) 5:1137
Wewitzer, Ralph 15:1053
WEXLER, WILLIAM ABE 16:479
- Bnai Brith 4:1147

- Conference of Presidents **5:**871
Wey, William **11:**925
Weyers, Hendrik Engelinus **8:**64
Weyl, F., *see* Nozière, Fernand
Weyl, Isaac **10:**692
Weyl, Jacob Meyer **10:**692
WEYL, MEIR BEN SIMHAH **16:**479
Weymar, Daniel **8:**66
Weyssenburg (city, Transyl.), *see* ALBA IULIA
Whale (zool.) **3:**17; **6:**32
- *see also:* LEVIATHAN
Wharton (city, Tex.) **15:**1036
Wharton, Edith **15:**1571
WHEAT **16:**480
- Aaronsohn, Aaron **2:**25
- food **6:**1416
- plant list **13:**625
- rice **14:**155
- Solomon's trade **15:**99
- suitable fields for **16:**372
- tares **15:**809
- *see also:* FIVE SPECIES
Wheatear (bird) **6:**30
Wheeler, Burton K. **15:**1652
Wheeler, H.M. **8:**66
Wheeling (city, W. Va.) **16:**476ff
Wheelocke, A. **8:**66
Whipping, *see* FLOGGING
White, Charley (Anschowitz) **15:**304
White, D.H. **8:**1052
"White, From 0° to 180°" (sculp., B. Schwartz) **14:**1065
WHITE, HARRY D. **16:**481
White, J. **11:**1553
WHITE, MORTON **16:**482
White, Patrick **6:**776
White, Philip **15:**1264
WHITE, ROBERT MAYER **16:**482
White Church (tn., Rus.), *see* BELAYA TSERKOV
White Fathers Monastery (Jer.) **9:**1459
Whitefield (tn., Eng.) **11:**859
White Field (tn., Rus.), *see* BELAYA TSERKOV
Whitehall Conference (1655) **10:**7
Whitehead, Alfred North **15:**1110
"White House in the Desert" (paint., M. Gross) Pl. 17 3-ART
White magic, *see* MAGIC
Whiteman, M. **8:**568
WHITEMAN, PAUL **12:**714
- Gershwin, George **7:**518
WHITE PAPERS (docs.) **16:**482
- Arab National Movement **9:**464ff
- Atlee, Clement **3:**836
- Ben-Gurion, David **4:**508; **4:**509
- Bevin, Ernest **4:**784
- Chamberlain, Neville **5:**333
- Churchill **5:**556; **9:**338,523
- Haganah **9:**687
- "illegal" immigration **8:**1250
- immigration restrictions **9:**532
- Israel historical survey **9:**343
- Jerusalem protests **9:**1477
- Jewish rejection **16:**1058; **16:**1086
- partition plans **13:**34
- Passfield white paper **9:**528
- Rothschild, James Armand de **14:**347
- Zionism **16:**1082ff
- Zionist Congress (21st) **16:**1175
- *illus:*
- - Jewish legion veterans protest **9:**357,525
- - London protest against Passfield White Paper **16:**1118
- - protest rally outside Yeshurun Synagogue, Jerusalem **9:**1479
- - U.S. Zionist leaders protest **15:**1632
- *see also:* MANDATE FOR PALESTINE; PALESTINE, INQUIRY COMMISSIONS; ST. JAMES'S CONFERENCE
White Plains (city, U.S.) **16:**464
White Wagtail (bird), *see* Wagtail, White
White Terror (pogrom, Hung.) **8:**1095
Whiteville (tn., N.C.) **12:**1220
Whitlock, Lee A. **14:**162
Whitlock, Philip **14:**161
Whitman, Walt **15:**1570
Whittaker, John William **8:**66
Whittier, John Greenleaf **10:**459
Whittingehame College (Eng.) **6:**450
WHO (U.N. orgn.), *see* World Health Organization
Whole-offering, *see* Burnt offering
Wiat (city, Libya), *see* TRIPOLI
Wichita (city, Kan.) **10:**738
- *illus:*
- - Temple Emanu-El **10:**739
Wichita Falls (city, Tex.) **15:**1036
Wichmann, Malkah, *see* ESTHER (commun.)
Wichmannshausen, J.C. **8:**66
Wickedness, *see* GOOD AND EVIL
WICKED PRIEST (D.S. Scroll fig.) **16:**485
- Anan **2:**919
- Man of Lies **11:**234
- Teacher of Righteousness **13:**332; **15:**886; **15:**887
Wickenburg (tn., Ariz.) **3:**499
Wickes, W. **4:**839
Wickhoff, F. **3:**301
Wickliffe (city, Ohio) **12:**1345
WIDAL, FERNAND **16:**487
- stamps **15:**335
Widder, Dávid, *see* GISZKALAY, JÁNOS
WIDMANSTETTER, JOHANN ALBRECHT (Widmanstadius, Lucrecius) **16:**487
- Christian Kabbalah **10:**645
- Hebraists **8:**66
-library **11:**19
Widmarius, Abdias **8:**66
WIDOW **16:**487
- *Contents:*
- - General **16:**487
- - - In Early Legal Codes **16:**488
- - - As Title of Individuals **16:**489
- - - As a Socially Deprived Class **16:**490
- - - As a Description of a City **16:**491
- - In Jewish Law **16:**491
- - - Personal Status **16:**491
- - - Rights and Obligations **16:**491
- - - Rights Out of the Estate **16:**492
- - - Rights Against Purchasers **16:**492
- - - The Widow's Maintenance **16:**493
- - - Claim for Past Maintenance **16:**493
- - - Right to Earnings and Income **16:**493
- - - Expiration of Right to Maintenance **16:**494
- - - Ketubbah and Denial of Maintenance **16:**494
- - - The State of Israel **16:**495
- Bene Israel **4:**498
- Commandments, the 613 **5:**770, 775*f*
- conflict of laws **5:**883ff
- embryo **6:**719
- ethics **6:**933,936
- fraud against **7:**111
- inheritance rights **15:**478
- inheritance validation **5:**881
- insult **8:**1409
- intermarriage **12:**167
- *ketubbah* **2:**399; **11:**252
- levirate marriage **11:**122
- maintenance **8:**1120; **11:**784
- oath **12:**1300
- orphan **12:**1478ff
- pledge **13:**638
- protected in court **13:**636
- public servant office **10:**1327
- seven benedictions **11:**1040
- *illus:*
- - Erfoud widow in mourning attire **12:**492
- - holding "*halizah* shoe" **11:**123; **16:**776
Wiedemann, J., *see* Weidmann, J.
WIEDENFELD, DOV **16:**496
Wiedenfeld, Isaac **16:**496
Wiedenfeld, Jacob **14:**635; **16:**496
Wiedenfeld, Nahum **16:**496
Wieder, Emil **15:**821
Wieder, Jacob **14:**1115
Wieder, Judah **14:**1115
Wiedergutmachung, *see* RESTITUTION AND INDEMNIFICATION
Wiedersheim, Seligmann **11:**1451
Wieleck, H. **6:**321
WIELICZKA (tn., Pol.) **16:**496
Wieliczkier, Jacob **15:**1215
Wielka-Wola (vill., Pol.) **3:**828
WIELUN (tn., Pol.) **16:**496
Wien, Sir Philip **10:**1495
WIENER (fam., Belg.) **16:**498
- *illus:*
- - Maastricht synagogue medal **11:**1166
WIENER, ALEXANDER S. **16:**498
- Landsteiner, Karl **10:**1416
- medicine **11:**1200
WIENER, ALFRED **16:**499
- *haskamot* **7:**1453
Wiener, Aloys, *see* SONNENFELS, ALOYS VON
Wiener, Charles **16:**498
- *illus:*
- - medallion of Astruc **3:**808
Wiener, Frantz, *see* CROISSET, FRANCIS DE
WIENER, HAROLD MARCUS **16:**499
Wiener, Hirz ben Hirsch, *see* Lemon, Hartog de
Wiener, Jacques **11:**1171; **16:**498
- *illus:*
- - medal for the opening of the Cologne synagogue **16:**498
WIENER, JEAN **12:**714
WIENER, LEO **16:**499
Wiener, Leopold **16:**498
Wiener, Ludwig **13:**802
Wiener, M. (writ.) **14:**479
Wiener, Markus **10:**1220
WIENER, MAX **16:**500
WIENER, MEIR **16:**500
- Gurshtein, Aaron **7:**982
WIENER, NORBERT **16:**501
WIENER, PHILIP P. **16:**502
Wiener, Rene **12:**544
WIENER, SAMUEL **16:**502
Wiener, Theodore (stlr., U.S.) **10:**738
Wiener, Theodore (libr., r.) **16:**500
Wiener Allgemeine Zeitung (newsp.) **8:**399
WIENER GESERA (persecutions) **16:**502
- Albert V **2:**530
- Austria **3:**889
- historical list **8:**766 767
- Vienna **16:**122
WIENER LIBRARY **16:**503
- archives **3:**385
- Cohen, David **5:**668
- historical research **15:**54
- historiography **8:**566
Wiener Library Bulletin **15:**54
Wiener Morgenzeitung (newsp.) **13:**1033
- Abeles, Otto **2:**61
- Stricker, Robert **15:**440
- Vienna **16:**127
- Volkspartei **16:**213
- Zionism **16:**1107
WIENER NEUSTADT (city, Aus.) **16:**504
- Aaron of Neustadt **2:**22
- Albert II **2:**530
- Isserlein's yeshivah **3:**889
- *illus:* text
WIENIAWSKI, HENRI **16:**505
- stamps **15:**335
- *illus:* text
Wieniawski, Joseph **16:**505
WIERNIKORSKI, JUDAH **16:**506
WIERUSZOWSKI, HELENE **8:**550
Wierzbolow (city, Lith.), *see* VIRBALIS
Wierzyński, Kazimierz **13:**802
WIESBADEN (city, Ger.) **16:**506
- rabbinical conference **15:**634
- *illus:* text
Wiese, Kurt **7:**928
WIESEL, ELIE **16:**507
- theology **14:**139
Wiesendanger, Jakob, *see* Ceporinus, Jakob
Wiesengruen, Paul **15:**63
Wiesenthal, Simon **16:**131
Wieslander, Rose Pastor, *see* STOKES, ROSE PASTOR
WIESNER, JEROME BERT **16:**508
- universities **15:**1679
WIESNER, JULIUS VON **16:**508
Wife, *see* HUSBAND AND WIFE
Wife-Sister (anc. inst.) **7:**390
Wig, *see* HEAD, COVERING OF THE
Wiggen, Henry W., *see* HARRIS, MARK
WIGODER, GEOFFREY **1:**38
- encyclopedias **6:**734
WIHL, LUDWIG **16:**509
WIJNKOOP, DAVID **16:**509
Wiktor, Jan **13:**801
Wilamowitz-Moellendorf **15:**699
Wilbrand of Oldenburg **15:**1355
WILBUSCHEWITZ (fam.) **16:**509
Wilbuschewitz, Gedaliah **16:**509
- Rivlin, Joseph Joel **14:**201
Wilbuschewitz, Isaac **16:**509
Wilbuschewitz, Moshe **16:**510
Wilbuschewitz, Nahum, *see* Wilbush, Nahum
Wilbuschewitz, Ze'ev **16:**509
Wilbush, Nahum **14:**1442; **16:**510
Wild, K. **13:**1369
WILD BULL **16:**510
- iconography **8:**1222
- *tahash* **15:**704
Wilde, Oscar **6:**775
- Leverson, Ada **11:**70
- *Salomé* **14:**689
WILDENSTEIN (Fr. fam.) **16:**510
- art dealing **3:**648
Wildenstein, Daniel Leopold **16:**511
- horse breeding **15:**311
Wildenstein, Georges **16:**510
- *illus:*
- - medal in honor of **16:**511
Wildenstein, Nathan **16:**510
WILDER, BILLY **16:**511
WILDERNESS **16:**512
Wilderness of Ziph, *see* ZIPH
Wild Goat, *see* IBEX
Wild ox, *see* WILD BULL
WILDMANN, ISAAC EISIK **16:**513
Wile, Gabriel **14:**210
Wile, Joseph **14:**210
Wilensky, Julius M. **15:**329
Wilensky, Leo **16:**1165

WILENSKY, MICHAEL **16:**514
– linguistics **16:**1377
Wilensky, Miriam, *see* YALAN-STEKELIS, MIRIAM
WILENSKY, YEHUDAH LEIB NISAN **16:**514
Wilheimer, Jonah **13:**128
WILHELM, KURT **16:**515
– Conservative Judaism **9:**905
Wilhelma (stlmt., Isr.)
– Be'erot Yiẓḥak **4:**383
– Neḥalim **7:**1122
– Templers **15:**995
Wilhelm of Boldensele **15:**1356
Wilkansky, Meir **6:**571
Wilkansky, Yiẓḥak, *see* ELAZARI-VOLCANI, YIẒḤAK
WILKES-BARRE AND KINGSTON (tn., Pa.) **16:**515
– Pennsylvania **13:**230
Wilkins, David **8:**66
Wilkomitz, Simḥah Ḥayyim, *see* WALKOMITZ, SIMḤAH ḤAYYIM
Will (testament), *see* WILLS
Will, Divine, *see* GOD
Will, freedom of, *see* FREE WILL
Willard (Chr. Heb.) **8:**66
Willcocks Plan (rail route) **9:**307ff
Willemer, Johann **8:**66
WILLEN, JOSEPH **16:**516
Willen, Pearl Larner **16:**516
Willentz, David T. **11:**1504
Willentz, Robert **11:**1504
Willesden (dist., Lond.) **6:**449,476
– *illus:*
– – cemetery memorial **11:**476
Willet, Andrew **8:**66
William I (k., Neth.) **2:**900; **12:**981
William I (k., Prus.) **6:**956
William II (Ger. Kaiser)
– Augusta Victoria hospice **12:**484
– Chamberlain, Houston **5:**332
– Herzl, Theodor **8:**414; **16:**1070ff
– Ereẓ Israel visit **9:**323,1461
– Zionist Congress (3rd) **16:**1167
– *illus:*
– – arrival in Jerusalem **9:**323
– – meeting with Herzl **8:**417
William II (Rufus; k., Eng.) **3:**33; **11:**470
William III (of Orange; k., Eng.) **11:**1214
William V (Prin. of Orange) **5:**666
William of Austria, Duke **14:**1079
WILLIAM OF AUVERGNE **16:**516
– Gabirol's influence **13:**451
William of Mara **8:**14
William of Norwich **12:**1226
Williams, Sir Owen **15:**620
Williams, Reuben **15:**1036
Williams, Roger **3:**198; **8:**701, 712
Williamsburg (city, Va.) **16:**162
Williamsburg (section, N.Y.C.) **12:**1082; **12:**1107
– Satmar ḥasidim **15:**909
– *illus:*
– – Satmar Yeshivah **12:**1121
Willibald, St. **15:**1355
Willinger, J. **12:**1272
Williram of Ebersberg **4:**872
Willis, Arthur **8:**66
Willman, A. **14:**407
Willmet, Joannes **8:**66
Will of God, *see* GOD
Willoughby, Lord **15:**529
Willoughby College **15:**1678
WILLOW (bot.) **16:**517
– flora of Israel **9:**225
– Hoshana Rabba **8:**1026ff plant list **13:**625
– *see also:* FOUR SPECIES; HOSHANOT
WILLOWSKI, JACOB DAVID BEN ZE'EV **16:**518
– Jerusalem Talmud **15:**778
WILLS **16:**519
– *Contents:*
– – Mattenat Bari **16:**519
– – Mattenat Shekhiv me-Ra **16:**519
– – Meẓavveh Meḥamat Mitah **16:**521
– – Undertaking and Acknowledgment or Admission **16:**521
– – Mitzvah to Carry Out the Wishes of the Deceased **16:**522
– – Capacity to Bequeath **16:**523
– – Capacity to Benefit from a Bequest **16:**524
– – Subject Matter of the Bequest **16:**524
– – Form and Wording of Wills **16:**524
– – Interpretation of Wills **16:**525
– – Accrual of Rights under a Will **16:**526
– – Renunciation of Rights under a Will **16:**526
– – Fideicommissary Bequests **16:**527
– – Takkanot Concerning Wills **16:**527
– – Jerusalem Takkanot **16:**528
– – Takkanot Concerning Property of Spouses **16:**529
– – In the State of Israel **16:**529
– *apotropos* **3:**218
– bequest of body **3:**933
– embryo **6:**720
– expropriation of inheritance **5:**881
– firstborn inheritance **6:**1312
– *ḥazakah* **7:**1523
– Hurrian oral wills **12:**1289
– *see also:* SUCCESSION
WILLS, ETHICAL **16:**530
– Jewish literature **11:**345ff
– letters **11:**59
– *Naḥalat Avot* **11:**1252
– *Orḥot Ḥayyim* **12:**1457
Willstaedter, Elias **10:**795
WILLSTAETTER, RICHARD **16:**532
WILMINGTON (city, Del.) **16:**533
– *illus:* text
Wilmington (city, N. C.) **12:**1219
Wilna, Ḥayyim Nissim Yeruḥam **16:**534
WILNA, JACOB BEN BENJAMIN WOLF **16:**534
– Bikayam, Meir **4:**991
– Shabbateanism **14:**1247
Wilner, Arie (Jurek) **16:**350
Wilno (city, Lith.), *see* VILNA
Wilofski, Jacob, *see* WILLOWSKI, JACOB DAVID BEN ZE'EV
Wilshur, Curley **15:**306
Wilson, Charles, (Hebr.) **8:**66
WILSON, SIR CHARLES WILLIAM **16:**535
– *illus:*
– – text
– – Jerusalem, scenes **9:**1418,1433,1460,1467,1468; **14:**205
Wilson, Daniel **8:**66
Wilson, Henry **15:**1649
Wilson, John **6:**381; **8:**66
WILSON, SOL **3:**612
WILSON, WOODROW **16:**535
– Balfour Declaration **4:**134
– Brandeis, Louis **4:**1297
– King-Crane Commission **13:**30
– *illus:*
– – protest against anti-Semitic propaganda **15:**1654
Wilson's Arch (Jer.) **9:**1398
– Temple **15:**963
– Wilson, Sir Charles William **16:**535
– *illus:* **16:**535
Wimpfen, Alexander ben Salomo **11:**1252
Wimpfen, Suesskind **7:**84
Wimple (Torah orn.), *see* Binder
WINAWER, BRUNO **13:**805
Winawer, Chemjo, *see* VINAVER, CHEMJO
Winawer, Shimon Abramovich **5:**405
WINCHELL, WALTER **16:**536
WINCHESTER (city, Eng.) **16:**536
Winchester Bible (illum. ms.) **9:**1360
– *illus:* **8:**1
Winchevsky, M., *see* VINCHEVSKY, MORRIS
WINCKLER, HUGO **16:**537
Wind (tort conc.) **15:**1273ff
Windau (city, Latv.), *see* VENTSPILS
Winder, Ludwig **5:**1193; **13:**972
Windisch, Konrad **12:**956
"Window" (sculp., A. Caro) **5:**192
Windsheim (tn., Ger.) **15:**544
WINDSOR (city, Ont.) **16:**537
WINE **16:**538
– General
– – biblical period **6:**1417ff
– – Carmel Oriental **14:**194
– – Jewish symbolism **15:**570ff
– – Middle Ages **2:**401
– – Noah **12:**1193ff
– – Omar, Covenant of **12:**1379
– – Ottoman Empire **16:**1545
– – Samaritan marriage **14:**746
– – seals **14:**1072
– – taxation **15:**850
– – vermouth **16:**650
– Ritual
– – consecration to Temple **8:**279
– – *Havdalah* **7:**1481ff
– – *Kiddush* **10:**974
– – libations **5:**1161
– – sacrifices **14:**599; **14:**603
– Prohibitions
– – Commandments, the 613 **5:**776,777
– – gentiles **3:**980; **7:**412; **7:**413
– – heretics **8:**360
– – Koran **10:**1198
– – *mishmarot* **12:**91
– – Nazirite **12:**907
– – *onen* **3:**23
– – priest **13:**1080
– – Temple destruction **9:**238
– *illus:*
– – text
– – blessing over **13:**353
– – grapevine **16:**156
– *see also:* DRUNKENNESS; VINE
WINE AND LIQUOR TRADE **16:**541
– excise duty **9:**749,750
– Hart, Lemon **13:**269
– Russia **8:**719
Wineapple, Edward **15:**303
Wineman, David **14:**13
Winer, J. G. B. **8:**66
Winer, Lazar **5:**487
Wingate, Allan, *see* Deutsch, André
WINGATE, CHARLES ORDE **16:**547
– Defense Forces **9:**684
– En-Harod **6:**792
– historical list **8:**766-767
Wingate, Lorna **16:**548
Wingate Institute of Physical Culture (Isr.) **9:**1020
– sport **15:**296
Winghe, Claes (Nicholas) van **4:**876
Winick, Arnold **15:**310
Winizky, Ignacio **10:**1503
Winkelmann, Otto **8:**1099
Winkler (Chr. Hebr.) **8:**66
Winkler, E. **12:**765
Winkler, Isaac **16:**548
Winkler, Jacob **16:**548
Win(c)kler, J.F. **8:**66
WINKLER, LEO (Judah) **16:**548
– Vienna expulsion **16:**123
Winkler, Wolff **5:**34
Winnebago (Ind. lang., tribe, N. Am.) **15:**66,1498
Winnemucca (city, Nev.) **12:**1018
Winnetka (vill., Ill.) **5:**415; **8:**1256
WINNIK, HENRY ẒVI **16:**549
WINNINGER, SOLOMON **16:**549
WINNIPEG (city, Man.) **16:**549
Winograd, Neville **15:**308
Winogradsky, Isaac **15:**1081
Winsberg, Jacques **13:**118
WINSLOW, THYRA SAMTER **15:**1584
WINSTEIN, SAUL **5:**389
Winston-Salem (city, N.C.) **12:**1220
– *illus:*
– – Temple Emanuel **12:**1219
Winter, David A. **11:**556
Winter, Elmer L. **11:**1588
Winter, Ernst **10:**1180
WINTER, GUSTAV **16:**551
– press **13:**1026
WINTER, JACOB **16:**552
Winter, Lev **5:**1191 **16:**551
Winter, Max **15:**304
WINTER, PAUL (schol.) **16:**552
Winter, Paul (sport.) **12:**1376
Winter, Solomon **12:**1540
"Winter Landscape near Copenhagen" (paint., A. Gottschalk) **3:**623
WINTERNITZ, EMANUEL **12:**714
WINTERNITZ, MORITZ **16:**552
WINTERS, SHELLEY **12:**475
WINTERSTEIN, ALFRED **5:**389
Winterstein, Simon **13:**809
Winterstein, Simon **13:**809
Winthrop, Bud, *see* FLANAGAN, BUD
Wintner, Leopold **12:**39
WINTROBE, MAXWELL MYER **16:**552
Wintzenheim (tn., Fr.) **2:**754
Wirballen (city, Lith.), *see* VIRBALIS
Wirgin, W. **12:**1272
WIRSZUBSKI, CHAIM **16:**553
WIRTH, CHRISTIAN **16:**553
– euthanasia **16:**1332
WIRTH, LOUIS **16:**553
– sociology **15:**65
Wirth, Sophie **12:**36
WISCHNITZER, MARK **16:**554
– historiography **8:**562; **8:**568
Wischnitzer, Rachel **3:**651; **16:**555
WISCONSIN (state, U.S.) **16:**555
– university **15:**1680
– *illus:* text
– *pop. tables:* text
Wisconsin Jewish Chronicle (newsp.) **11:**1589
Wisdom, Divine, *see* GOD
WISDOM; WISDOM LITERATURE **16:**557
– *Contents:*
– – Connotation of Wisdom **16:**557
– – History of the Wisdom Tradition **16:**558
– – International Background and Setting **16:**558
– – The Wisdom of Books of the Hebrew Bible **16:**559
– – The Concept of Wisdom **16:**562
– Concept
– – demonic **2:**966
– – Judaism **10:**391; **10:**392
– – Neoplatonism **13:**429
– – philosophy, Jewish **13:**425
– – revelation **14:**119
– – Solomon **15:**103ff
– – Torah **15:**1236

- - treasure symbolism **15:**1361
- - word **16:**634
- Wisdom Literature
- - abomination origin **2:**97
- - adultery **2:**314
- - *Baruch, Book of* **4:**272
- - *Ben Sira, Wisdom of* **4:**551ff
- - biblical criticism **4:**910
- - Egypt, ancient **6:**484
- - Lamentations, Book of **10:**1372
- - proverbs **13:**1264
- - Proverbs, Book Of **13:**1268ff
- - *Wisdom of Solomon* **7:**653; **15:**119
Wisdom of Ben Sira (Sirach; bk.), *see* BEN SIRA, WISDOM OF
Wisdom of Solomon (bk.), *see* SOLOMON, WISDOM OF
Wise, Aaron **16:**566
WISE, GEORGE SCHNEIWEIS **16:**563
WISE, ISAAC MAYER **16:**563
- Albany **2:**524
- *American Israelite* **2:**821
- anti-abolitionist **12:**932
- Cincinatti **5:**563; **5:**565
- Einhorn, David **6:**531
- historical list **8:**766-767
- H.U.C. **8:**216
- Leeser, Isaac **5:**901
- paradigm of rabbi **13:**1456
- peddlers **15:**1597
- prayer books **13:**990
- Reform Judaism **14:**26
- slavery **15:**1602
- Tuska, Simon **15:**1469
- U.S. literature **15:**1569
- *illus:*
- - autograph **3:**918
- - *Deborah,* first issue **13:**1052
- - *The Israelite* **2:**821
Wise, James Waterman **16:**568
WISE, JONAH BONDI **16:**565
- *American Israelite* **2:**821
- *illus:*
- - *The Israelite* **2:**821
Wise, Justine, *see* Polier, Justine Wise
Wise, Leo **2:**821
- *illus:*
- - *The Israelite* **2:**821
Wise, Louise, *see* Waterman-Wise, Louise
WISE, LOUIS ELSBERG **5:**389
WISE, ROBERT **12:**475
WISE, STEPHEN SAMUEL **16:**566
- Brandeis, Louis **4:**1298
- New York City **12:**1092; **12:**1115
- Zionism **15:**1634; **16:**1141ff
- *illus:*
- - autograph **3:**918
- - Biltmore Conference **15:**1633
- - Marks, Simon, and **11:**1009
- - protest against 1940 White Paper **15:**1632
WISEMAN, ADELE **5:**115; **5:**116
- Bible in art **4:**937
Wiseman, Shlomo **5:**113
Wiseman, Thomas **6:**785
Wisendangen, Jakob von, *see* Ceporinus, Jakob
Wishnick, William **15:**312
Wiskitki (loc., Pol.) **13:**950
WIŚLICA (vill., Pol.) **16:**569
WISLICENY, DIETER **16:**569
- Athens **3:**818
- Europe **6:**966
- Greece **7:**879
- Salonika **14:**705
Wiślicki, Ḥayya Jacob **11:**426
Wismar (tn., Ger.) **11:**1163
Wisnaik, Jaime **5:**467
Wiśniowiec (vill., Ukr.), *see* VISHNEVETS
WIŚNIOWIECKI, JEREMI **16:**570
Wissembourg (tn., Fr.) **2:**752
WISSENSCHAFT DES JUDENTUMS **16:**570
- correspondence, 19th cent. **11:**60ff
- Dubnow, Simon **6:**256
- Haskalah **7:**1444
- Hirsch, S.R. **8:**513
- historiography **8:**561
- history **8:**725; **8:**726
- Judaism **10:**386
- Krochmal, Nachman **10:**1272ff
- modern rabbi type **13:**1454
- Torah study **15:**458
- Wessely, W. **16:**463
- Yiddish literature research **16:**826
- Zunz, Leopold **16:**1236ff
- *see also:* GESELLSCHAFT ZUR FOERDERUNG DER WISSENSCHAFT DES JUDENTUMS; HOCHSCHULE FUER DIE WISSENSCHAFT DES JUDENTUMS
Wissenschaftliche Zeitschrift fuer Juedische Theologie (period.) **16:**576
- press **13:**1056
WISSOTZKY, KALONYMUS ZE'EV **16:**584
Wisten, Fritz **15:**1057
Wiszmowice (loc., Pol.) **3:**843
Witbank (tn., Transvaal) **15:**1340
Witchcraft, *see* SORCERY
Witebsky, Ernest **11:**1200
Witgenstein, Field-Marshal **14:**531
Witkow (tn., Ukr.) **15:**84
Witkowitz Steel Works **7:**989
Witkowski, Georg **7:**1335; **7:**451
Witmund, Uri, *see* URI BEN AARON HA-LEVI
WITNESS **16:**584
- General
- - Commandments, the 613 **5:**769,779
- - imprisonment **8:**1302
- - *Makkot* tractate **11:**808
- - *takkanot ha-kahal* **15:**732
- - usury **16:**29
- Acceptability
- - gentile **7:**412
- - informers **8:**1372
- - oppression **12:**1436
- - self-incrimination **13:**634
- - shepherd **16:**1274
- - tax collector **15:**842
- - trustees **14:**1267
- - usurer **16:**31
- Procedure
- - interrogation **13:**960
- - judgment participation **13:**956
- - oath **12:**1298
- - perjury **13:**288
- - prosecution **13:**227
- Subject of evidence
- - *agunah* **2:**430
- - documents **14:**1386ff
- - duress **12:**1399
- - endowments **8:**285
- - lien liability **11:**228,230
- - loan cases **11:**419
- - New Moon **12:**1039
- - payments **13:**632ff
- - taxation **15:**865
- *see also:* EVIDENCE
Witold (duke, Lith.) **2:**403
- historical list **8:**766-767
Witt, Jan De **15:**277
WITTE, SERGEY YULYEVICH, COUNT **16:**590
- Herzl **16:**1072
Wittenberg, Henry **12:**1376
- *illus:* **15:**316
Wittenberg, Itzig, *see* WITTENBERG, YIẒḤAK
Wittenberg, Solomon **15:**28
WITTENBERG, YIẒḤAK **16:**591
- Poland **13:**774
- Vilna **16:**149
Witter, H.B. **3:**809
- Hebraists **8:**66
WITTGENSTEIN, PAUL **12:**714
Wittig, J. Sigmund **8:**66
Witting, Richard **4:**175
Wittkower, Eric D. **13:**1340
WITTKOWER, RUDOLF J. **16:**592
- art historians **3:**651
WITTLIN, JÓZEF **16:**592
Witwicki, Stefan **13:**798
Witzenhausen, Josef **2:**899; **4:**877; **11:**357
Witzenhausen, Uri, *see* URI (PHOEBUS) BEN AARON HA-LEVI
Witzhum, Hermann **13:**1049
Witzius, Hermann **8:**66
Wizeltir, Meir **8:**206
WIZEN, MOSHE AHARON **16:**592
Wiznitzer, A. **8:**563
WIZO (orgn.) **16:**593
- agricultural school **3:**994
- fundraising **13:**390
- health services **9:**985
- Israel politics **9:**663ff
- mobile libraries **11:**194
- Rumania **16:**1134
- Zionism **16:**1114ff
- *illus:*
- - text
- - Twelfth Zionist Congress delegation **16:**1101
Wizo bi-Medinat Israel (publ.), *see* *Ha-Ishah be-Yisrael*
W.J.C., *see* WORLD JEWISH CONGRESS
Wlen (cmty., Silesia), *see* Laehn
WLOCLAWEK (city, Pol.) **16:**596
WLODAWA (city, Pol.) **16:**597
- *illus:* text
Wlodzimierz (city, Ukr.), *see* VLADIMIR VOLYNSKI
Wloszczowa (loc., Pol.) **13:**950
WMO, *see* World Meteorological Organization
Woad, isatis (bot.) **13:**625
Woburn (city, Mass.) **11:**1112
Wockum, David J. **5:**1568
Wodianer (fam., Hung.) **13:**1369
Wodianer, Fülöp **13:**1369
WODZISLAW (tn., Pol.) **16:**599
Woeldicke, Marcus **8:**66
Woelfel of Komárom **15:**1166
Woelfflein of Schnaitach **12:**1498
Woerlitz (loc., Saxony) **3:**2; **15:**618
WOGUE, LAZARE ELIEZER **16:**599
- Bible translation **4:**882
- *l'Univers Israélite* **4:**882; **15:**1674
WOHL, HENRYK **16:**600
Wohl, Herman **5:**487
Wohlbrueck, Anton, *see* WALBROOK, ANTON
Wohlgemuth, Isaiah **16:**600
WOHLGEMUTH, JOSEPH **16:**600
- Bible scholar **4:**876
- Kitzingen **10:**1083
- rabbinical seminary **13:**1459
Wohlgemuth, Judah Ari **16:**600
Wohlmann, Judah Loeb **8:**385
Wohlwill, Immanuel **16:**109
Wojciechowski, S. **15:**348
WOJDA, CAROL FREDERICK **16:**601
Wojslawice (tn., Pol.) **10:**1242
Wojslawski, Zvi, *see* WOYSLAWSKI, ZEVI
WOLBERG, LEWIS ROBERT **16:**601
Wolborz (vill., Pol.) **13:**556
WOLBROM (tn., Pol.) **16:**601
Wolder(-us), David **8:**66
Wolezko (financier), *see* VOLCHKO
Wolf (Aus. fam.), *see* AUERBACH
WOLF (fam., U.S.) **16:**602
Wolf (stlmt. found.), *see* VOLCHKO
Wolf (16th cent., Aus.) **16:**223
WOLF (zool.) **16:**602
- dietary laws **6:**32
- fauna of Israel **9:**225
Wolf, Aaron ben Isaac Benjamin **9:**1314
WOLF, ABNER **11:**1211
WOLF, ABRAHAM (philos.) **16:**604
Wolf, Abraham (mfr.) **16:**602
Wolf, Adolf Grant **16:**608
Wolf, Albert **3:**594 **16:**603
Wolf, Aron (r., Fr.) **15:**425
Wolf, Benedict (Pinḥas) **3:**844
Wolf, Daniel **15:**1021
Wolf, Edwin **16:**603
Wolf, Edwin II **16:**603
- culture foundation **12:**871
- J.P.S. **10:**80
- *illus:*
- - JPS Torah translation committee **10:**80
Wolf, Elias **16:**602
Wolf, Emil **3:**807
Wolf, Francisca, *see* WOLF, FRUMET
Wolf, Frank **15:**1120
WOLF, FRIEDRICH **16:**604
Wolf, Friedrich August **16:**1236
WOLF, FRUMET **16:**604
Wolf(f), G. (Chr. Hebr.) **8:**66
WOLF, GERSON **16:**605
WOLF, GUSTAV **3:**613
Wolf, Ḥayyim Joachim of Eisenstadt **16:**604
Wolf, Immanuel **16:**109
Wolf, Israel **12:**63
Wolf(-ph), J.J. (Chr. Hebr.) **8:**66
WOLF, JOHANN CHRISTOPH **16:**605
- Bibliotheca Hebraea **12:**1421
- Hebraists **8:**66
Wolf, Johann W. **8:**67
Wolf, Joseph **15:**502
WOLF, LEIZER **16:**606
- *illus:* **16:**821
Wolf, Levi **16:**602
WOLF, LUCIEN **16:**606
- AJA **2:**977
- historical list **8:**766-767
- JHS **10:**53
Wolf, M. (polit.) **11:**382
Wolf, Meshullam Zalman ben Shalom **3:**840
Wolf, Morris **16:**603
Wolf, Moses **3:**842
Wolf, Phil **15:**305
Wolf, Phinehas **3:**841
Wolf, Rudolf **3:**806
Wolf, Samson **14:**1217
Wolf, Sandor **6:**547; **12:**538
Wolf, Simeon **3:**840
Wolf, Simeon (of Vilna) **9:**1082
Wolf, Simeon ben Abraham **5:**1036; **15:**76
WOLF, SIMON **16:**607
Wolf, Simon ben Meshullam **3:**841
Wolf ben Joseph of Dessau, *see* Wolf, Joseph
Wolf ben Samuel, *see* Ze'ev ben Samuel
Wolf-Catz, Helma **6:**321
Wolfe, Arthur **15:**310
Wolfe, Benjamin **14:**160
WOLFE, BERTRAM DAVID **16:**608
Wolfe, George (cart.) **5:**220
Wolfe, George (sport.) **15:**303
WOLFE, HUMBERT **16:**609
Wolfe, J. Robert **8:**67
Wolfe, Thomas **15:**1571ff
Wolfeer, Anton **11:**1197
WOLFENBUETTEL (tn., Ger.)

16:609
- Brunswick 4:1422
WOLFENSTEIN, ALFRED 16:610
Wolfers, Philip S. 12:4
WOLFERT, IRA 15:1584
Wolfer(d)us, Michael 8:67
Wolff (prof., Holl.) 16:37
WOLFF, ABRAHAM ALEXANDER 16:610
Wolff, Albert (law.) 10:1492
WOLFF, ALBERT LOUIS 12:714
Wolff, Baron (Rus.) 15:317
WOLFF, BERNHARD 16:611
- news agency 8:714
- *illus:*
- - portrait 8:707
Wolff, Gustav Wilhelm 14:1413
Wolff, Heinrich 15:996
WOLFF, HERMANN 12:714
Wolff, Johann H. 8:67
WOLFF, JOSEPH 16:611
Wolff, Louis, *see* WOLFF, ALBERT LOUIS
Wolff, Martin 10:1495
Wolff, Max 15:63
Wolff, Moritz 7:819
Wolff, Moses 4:1211
Wolff, Moses Benjamin 3:1
Wolff, Pauline Sterne 8:1051
Wolff, Phillip 7:348
Wolff, Pierre 7:147
Wolff, S. de 16:1119
WOLFF, THEODOR 16:612
Wolff, Umberto, *see* WOLFE, HUMBERT
WOLFF, WERNER 13:1347
Wolffe, Edgar 11:1562
Wolffe, Marc-Jean-Jérôme 11:1560
WOLFFSOHN, DAVID 16:612
- flag, creation of 6:1337
- Goldbloom, Jacob K. 7:707
- historical list 8:766-767
- Zionism 16:1073ff
- Zionist Congresses 16:1167; 16:1169
- *illus:*
- - F.Z.C. 16:1165
Wolffson, J. 5:335
Wolfner, József 13:1369
Wolfowitz, Jack 11:1203
WOLFOWSKI, MENAHEM ZALMAN 16:615
WOLFSBERG (tn., Aus.) 16:616
Wolfsberg, Oscar, *see* AVIAD, YESHAYAHU
WOLFSKEHL, KARL 16:616
- *illus:* text
WOLFSOHN, JULIUSZ 12:714
Wolfsohn, Wilhelm 7:449
WOLFSOHN-HALLE, AHARON 16:617
- Hebrew Literature 8:181
WOLFSON, HARRY AUSTRYN 16:617
WOLFSON, SIR ISAAC 16:619
- Hechal Shlomo 8:423
- United Synagogue 6:766; 15:1673
Wolfson, Louis E. 15:311
Wolfson College (Oxford, Eng.) 4:658; 16:619
WOLFSTHAL, CHUNE 12:715
Wolk, Myer S. 16:112
Wolk, Samuel 2:524
Wolkowicz, Samuel 12:844
WOLKOWISKI, JEHIEL BER 16:620
Wolkowysk (city, Belor.), *see* VOLKOVYSK
Wollaston, William 8:67
WOLLEMBORG, LEONE 16:620
Wollenberg, Albert 5:57
WOLLHEIM, GERT 3:568; 3:613
Wollrauch, Ch. 10:820
WOLMARK, ALFRED 16:620
Wolofsky, Hirsh 5:113
WOLOMIN (city, Pol.) 16:621
WOLOWSKI (Schor; fam.) 16:621
Wolowski, Franciszek 16:622
Wolowski, Franciszek Lukasz 16:622
- Frank, Jacob 7:69
Wolowski, Jan Kanty 16:622
Wolowski, Lipman 16:622
Wolowski, Louis François 16:622
Wolowski, Michael 7:69
Wolowski, Nathan 16:622
Wolowski, Solomon 16:622
Wołpa (tn., Belor.), *see* VOLPA
Wolpe, Berthold 15:1479
Wolpe, Henryk 13:803
WOLPE, STEFAN 12:715
WOLPER, DAVID LLOYD 12:475
Wolpert, Ludwig 7:743; 13:173
- *illus:*
- - Torah breastplate 4:1342
WOLSEY, LOUIS 16:622
- Cleveland 5:610
Wolski, Wlodzimierz 13:799
Wolters, Friedrich 7:449
Wolters, Ludovicus 8:67
Wolyn (reg., Ukr.), *see* VOLHYNIA
WOMAN 16:623
- *Contents:*
- - Terminology 16:623
- - Created Status 16:623
- - Family Status 16:623
- - Legal Status and Religious Participation 16:624
- - In Public Life 16:625
- - Attitude to Women 16:625
- - Status in Modern Ereẓ Israel 16:628
- General
- - Abraham of Sarteano 2:161
- - finery 13:1012
- - Garden of Eden 13:77
- - longevity 14:1499
- - magic 11:707
- - *mishmarot* 12:92
- - names 12:806
- - perfume 8:1310; 8:1313
- - Shabbetai Ẓevi 14:1229
- - Yemenite songs 16:757
- - Yose ben Zimra 16:857
- In Society 8:680
- - crime 5:1101
- - education of 6:397ff
- - election rights 13:1357
- - employment 9:887
- - *Ḥevrah* 8:441
- - Israel labor movement 9:879ff
- - kibbutz 10:968
- - military service 11:1567
- - Sumer society 15:514
- - Yemenite Jews 16:753ff
- Literature of
- - ethical 11:358
- - letter writing 11:61
- - Yiddish 11:356ff
- Halakhah
- - *apotropos* 3:219
- - Bible study 4:921
- - childbirth 13:510; 14:135
- - education 15:170
- - inheritance 16:522
- - mixed choirs 5:488
- - new moon 12:1039
- - *niddah* 12:1149
- - sanctification of Sabbath 10:974
- - *shema* 14:1372
- - slavery 15:1098
- - three commandments incumbent on 11:1039
- - trades enjoinder 10:1322
- - witness 16:585ff
- *illus:*
- - forced to undress prior to being shot by Nazis 13:757
- - woman showing menstrual stain to husband 12:1148
"Woman with Child" (sculp., J. Epstein) 6:828
Womb 14:94
"Women on the Beach of Jaffa" (paint., N. Gutman) Fig. 90 3-ART
Women's Court (Temple), *see Ezrat Nashim*
Women's Equal Rights Association (party, Isr.) 9:660
Women's Equal Rights Law (Isr.) 16:629ff
Women's Institute (N.Y.) 10:97
Women's International Zionist Organization, *see* WIZO
Women's League for Israel (N.Y.) 4:1092
Women's League of Ha-Po'el ha-Mizrachi (orgn.) 7:1321
Women's Mizrachi Organization 7:1321
Women Workers, General Council of (Isr.), *see* MO'EẒET HA-PO'ALOT
Wonders, *see* MIRACLE
WOOD 16:630
- inscriptions 16:662ff
- lots 11:510
Woodbine (borough, N.J.) 2:412; 12:1028; 16:157
- *illus:*
- - Baron de Hirsch Agricultural School 10:35,47; 16:158
Wood Chamber (Temple) 15:968
Wood Cock (bird) 6:30
"Wooden Bridge in the Kovno Ghetto" (drg., E. Lurie) Fig. 78 3-ART
Woodhead Commission (Pal.) 13:33
- Arab National Movement 9:463
- Jerusalem plans 9:1476
- Partition plans 9:319; 13:34; 13:35
- White Papers 16:484ff
- Zionists 16:1085
- *maps:*
- - Plan C 13:38
Woodland (city, Cali.) 5:56
Wood offerings 16:630
Wool 15:1036ff
- *sha'atnez* 14:1213
Woolf (nurse, Eng.) 11:1567
Woolf, Herbert M. 15:311
WOOLF, LEONARD SIDNEY 16:631
Woolf, Moses 8:1362
WOOLF, MOSHE 16:631
Woolf, Virginia 15:1479; 16:631
Woolin, Elias 12:1067
WOOLLEY, SIR CHARLES LEONARD 16:632
- Assyriology 16:1507
- Ur 16:2,1487
Woonsocket (tn., R.I.) 14:143
- *illus:*
- - synagogue 15:626
WORCESTER (tn., Eng.) 16:632
- Hereford community 8:344
- historical list 8:766-767
- Jewish Parliament 15:838
WORCESTER (city, Mass.) 16:633
- *illus:*
- - text
- - Temple Emanuel 11:1114
WORD 16:634
Word games 7:307
Word of God, *see* LOGOS
Wordsworth, William 6:774
Work, *see under* Labor
Workers' Bank (Isr.), *see* Bank ha-Po'alim B.M.
Workers, Jewish, *see* Proletariat, Jewish
Workers' Settlement, *see* MOSHAV
Workers' Theater of Palestine, *see* OHEL
Worki (tn., dyn.), *see* WARKA
Working and Student Youth, *see* HA-NO'AR HA-OVED VE-HA-LOMED
Working class, Jewish, *see* Proletariat, Jewish
"Work in the Present" (Zion. program) 8:318ff
WORKMEN'S CIRCLE (J. orgn.) 16:635
- Feigenbaum, Benjamin 6:1206
- New York City 12:1097
- socialism, Jewish 15:47
- *illus:*
- - text
- - early leaders and documents 12:1095; 15:43
Workum, Duffie 7:131
Worky (tn., dyn.), *see* WARKA
World
- Aristotelianism 3:447
- *Aẓilut* 3:1009
- center 9:1558
- providence 14:137
- space and place 15:219
- Torah 15:1237
World Alliance for Combatting Anti-Semitism (orgn.) 14:1281
World Association for Hebrew Language and Culture, *see* BRIT IVRIT OLAMIT
World Bible Contest (Isr.) 9:395
World Calendar 5:54
WORLD CONFERENCE OF JEWISH ORGANIZATIONS 16:636
World Council of Churches (WCC) 13:1250ff
World Council of Synagogues 15:1674
- Abbell, Maxwell 2:46
- synagogue 15:591
World Federation of Diamond Workers 13:708
World Federation of General Zionists 7:385
World Federation of Ha-Shomer ha-Ẓa'ir 7:1374
World Federation of YMHA's 12:877
World Health Organization (WHO) 15:1564
World Hebrew Union, *see* BRIT IVRIT OLAMIT
World History of the Jewish People (bk.) 8:567
WORLD JEWISH CONGRESS 16:637
- AJC 2:826
- anti-Nazi boycott 4:1281
- Arab lands, Jews in 15:1561
- Ashkenazy, Maurice 3:712
- Barou, Noah 4:256
- Comité des Délégations Juives 5:759
- Goldmann, Nahum 7:724
- interfaith advancement 13:1252
- Wise, Stephen 16:567
- *illus:* text
- Yefroykin, Israel 16:727
World Jewry (period.) 13:1031
WORLD LABOR ZIONIST MOVEMENT 16:639
World Meteorological Organization 15:1565
World Non-Sectarian Anti-Nazi Council 4:1282
World Over (period.) 5:460
World Parliament of Religions 13:1254
WORLDS, THE FOUR (Kab. conc.) 16:641
- Kabbalah 10:581; 10:615
World Sephardi Federation 14:1174

- Palestine **16:**1150
- Spain **15:**245
World Socialist Union of Jewish Workers - Po'alei Zion **13:**660ff
World to come, *see* OLAM HA-BA
World Union for Progressive Judaism **12:**265; **14:**27
World Union for the Propagation of Judaism **13:**1192
World Union of General Zionists **7:**384; **7:**385
World Union of Jewish Students (WUJS, UMEJ) **15:**449ff
- efforts for Soviet Jewry **14:**501
World War I
- African Jews **2:**335
- Balfour Declaration **4:**132
- Cohen, Sir Robert **5:**684
- demographic changes **5:**1493ff
- Monash, Sir John **12:**237ff
- population changes **13:**888ff
- *illus:*
- - Austrian Jewish soldiers at Western Wall **11:**1565
- - Jewish Legion at El-Arish **9:**335
- - Jewish Legion outside Jerusalem **10:**76
- - Jewish war orphans **8:**745
- - Lodz Jews with German soldier, 1915 **11:**430
- - *Managem,* yacht used for Nili information **12:**1164
- - Minsk, self-defense convention **14:**448
- - Palestine, Jewish refugees at Jaffa **9:**335
- - participation of Jewish soldiers (chart) **11:**1550
- - Riga Committee for assisting refugees **14:**173
- - Russia, refugees sheltered in synagogue **14:**447
- - Tarbut kindergarten for refugee children **14:**447
- - Turkey, Jewish soldiers **9:**335; **11:**1568
- - Willesden (London) Jewish cemetery, memorial **11:**476
- - Zion Mule Corps **10:**70; **11:**1555
World War II
- African Jews **2:**335
- "illegal" immigration **8:**1249
- J.D.C. **2:**830ff
- Jewish Brigade **10:**35
- Jewish history **8:**765
- Mussolini, Benito **12:**719
- Palmach **13:**46
- U.S. Jews **15:**1632
- *illus:*
- - Allied troops, expenditure in Palestine, 1939-1944 (table) **9:**720
- - Churchill's letter re Jewish Force **3:**394
- - Holocaust, spread of (map) **8:**895
- - Jewish Brigade Group **10:**36,37
- - Jewish Brigade members **9:**359
- - Jewish Brigade soldiers guarding German prisoners **9:**686
- - Jewish partisans **13:**141-142
- - Nazi persecution (map) **8:**843
- - Palestine immigration appeal **8:**766
- - Palestinian volunteers enlisting in British army **9:**358
- - participation of Jewish soldiers (chart) **11:**1550
- - partisan units and uprisings, Poland (map) **13:**141
- - refugees in Venice **14:**28
- - U.S. chaplain presenting Hanukkah gifts to servicemen **11:**1553
- - Willesden (London) Jewish cemetary, memorial **11:**476
- *pop. tables:*
- - age composition, pre-war **5:**1517
- - Jewish population in Soviet-annexed territories **14:**473
- - population, 1939 and 1946 **6:**973,975
- - postwar communities **5:**831-842
- *see also:* HOLOCAUST
World Zionist Organization, *see* ZIONISM
WORM (zool.) **16:**643
- dietary laws **6:**38
- evolution **6:**1002
Worm, Christian **8:**67
Worman, E.J. **16:**1337
WORMANN, CURT **16:**643
WORMS (city, Ger.) **16:**643
- archives **3:**387
- Crusades **5:**1137
- Germany **7:**460
- historical list **8:**766-767
- informers **8:**1367
- Rashi **13:**1558
- synagogue **15:**602ff
- synod **15:**633ff
- Torah study groups **15:**459
- *illus:*
- - text
- - Charles V's charter **7:**470
- - Meir of Rothenburg's tombstone **11:**1250
- - Rashi *bet ha-midrash* **13:**1561
- - register of transactions **6:**1280
- - synagogue **4:**1004; **15:**603
- *see also:* SHUM
WORMS, AARON **16:**647
- Lambert, Mayer **10:**1362
WORMS, ASHER ANSHEL **16:**647
- Heilbronn, Joseph **8:**265
Worms, Benedict de **16:**648
WORMS, DE (fam.) **16:**648
- coat of arms **8:**340
- *illus:*
- - coat of arms **8:**338
Worms, Emile **10:**1496
Worms, Gabriel Benedict de **16:**648
Worms, Baron George de **16:**648
Worms, Gustave Hippolite **15:**1055
Worms, Baron Henry de **16:**648
Worms, Jacob **5:**935
Worms, Jeanette, von, *see* Rothschild, Jeanette von
Worms, Maurice Benedict de **16:**648
WORMS, RENÉ **16:**649
Worms, Simeon Wolf **16:**648
Worms, Solomon Benedict de **16:**648
Wormser (U.S. fam.) **14:**838
- Arizona **3:**450
WORMSER, ANDRÉ (Alphonse-Toussaint) **12:**715
Wormser, B.H. **4:**61
Wormser, Michael **3:**450; **13:**481
WORMSER, OLIVIER BORIS **16:**649
WORMSER, SECKEL (Isaac Loeb) **16:**649
- Kabbalah **10:**555
- - *illus:* text
Wormser brothers (Ceylon) **5:**317
WORMS MAHZOR (illum. ms.) **11:**732ff
- *illus:* **8:**1219; **11:**732,*fcg.* 619; **14:**1217,1320; **16:**1191
WORMWOOD (bot.) **16:**650
- flora of Israel **9:**222
- orach shrub **12:**1436
- plant list **13:**625
WOROSZYLSKI, WIKTOR **13:**805
Worship (conc.)
- Commandments, the 613 **5:**771
- *devekut* **5:**1598
- hasidic teachings **7:**1408
- Islam **9:**93
- Karaites **10:**780
- Pharisee attitude **13:**366
- piety **13:**504
- Samaritans **14:**741
- study **15:**458
- synagogue **15:**579
- Temple **15:**943ff
- *see also:* PRAYER
Wortman, Marcos **3:**432
Wortsmann, Yecheskiel C. **16:**1165
Wotitz (tn., Cz.), *see* VOTICE
Wotizky (fam.) **16:**227
Wotton, William **8:**67
WOUK, HERMAN **16:**650
- U.S. literature **15:**1579
"Wounded Woman" (sculp., B. Reder) **3:**637
WOYSLAWSKI, ZEVI **16:**651
- *illus:*
- - Persky, Daniel, and **13:**321
- - Tchernichowsky and **8:**199
- - Writers' Ass'n in Israel **8:**205
W.R.B., *see* WAR REFUGEE BOARD
Wreaths, *see* CROWNS, DECORATIVE HEADDRESSES AND WREATHS
Wrede, Baron **6:**1297
WRESCHNER, ARTHUR **16:**651
Wreschner, Walter **16:**652
Wrestling **15:**317
Wright, Aldis **4:**976
Wright, Frank Lloyd **15:**626
- Adler, Dankmar **2:**274
- *illus:*
- - Beth Shalom Synagogue **15:**625
Wright, Peter **14:**815
WRITERS' ASSOCIATION IN ISRAEL **16:**652
- Burla, Yehuda **4:**1524
- cultural life **9:**1001
- *illus:*
- - text
WRITING (Scripts, Materials, and Inscriptions) **16:**654
- *Contents:*
- - Scripts and Materials **16:**654
- - Inscription **16:**665
- - In the Talmud and Halakhah **16:**669
- Bible **16:**1405
- Cairo *genizah* **16:**1334
- *mezuzah* **11:**1475
- Moses **12:**389
- seals **14:**1073
- *Sefer Torah* **14:**1100
- Sumerians **15:**515; **16:**1484
- *illus:*
- - text
- - ostraca **12:**1509,1510
- - scribe's inkwell **13:**313
- - scribe at work **14:**1043,1044,1045
- - *Sefer Torah* **14:**1101,1102
- - Sennacherib's prism **14:**1162
- *see also:* ABBREVIATIONS; ALPHABET, HEBREW; BOOKS; CALLIGRAPHY AND WRITING MASTERS; HEBREW LANGUAGE; Inscriptions; SCRIBE
Written Law, *see* BIBLE
Wroclaw (city, Pol.), *see* BRESLAU
WRONKI (tn., Pol.) **16:**672
WRONSKY, SIDDY **16:**673
Wschód (period.) **11:**612; **14:**313
- Zionism **16:**1132
Wucherer (usurer) **4:**168
WUENSCHE, AUGUST KARL **16:**673
Wuerfel, Andreas **8:**560
WUERTTEMBERG (state, Ger.) **16:**673
- Baden
- historical list **8:**766-767
- Hohenzollern **8:**816
- rabbinical office **13:**1454
- Stuttgart **15:**740
- Talheim **15:**740
- Vienna, Congress of **16:**132
Wuerttemberg, Antonia, Princess of, *see* Antonia, Princess of Wuerttemberg
Wuerttemberg Bible Institute **15:**1487
WUERZBURG (city, Bav.) **16:**675
- archives **3:**387
- Crusades **5:**1139ff
- Hep! Hep! riots **8:**331
- persecutions **4:**280
- proselyte of **10:**137
- *illus:*
- - deportation of Jews by Nazis **7:**495
Wuerzburger Rav, *see* BAMBERGER, SELIGMANN BAER
Wujek, J. **4:**885; **13:**798
WUJS, *see* World Union of Jewish Students
Wulf, Liebman Meyer **11:**1465
Wulf (fam.) **9:**1150; **15:**406
Wulff, Berend **5:**1010
Wulff, Cecily, *see* Eskeles, Cecily
Wulff, Liepmann Meyer **12:**64
Wulff, Moses Benjamin **5:**1010; **11:**225
Wulff, Moshe, *see* WOOLF, MOSHE
Wulfila (bp.), *see* Ulfilas
Wulkin, Hayyim **16:**217
Wulliger, M. **6:**734
Wulman, Leon **15:**1292
WUNDERBAR, REUBEN JOSEPH **16:**676
- Riga **14:**173
WUNDERLICH, FRIEDA **16:**677
WUPPERTAL (city, Ger.) **16:**677
- war crimes trials **16:**294
Wurm (act.) **15:**1055
Wurm, Bishop (of Wuerttemberg) **8:**915
WURZBURGER, WALTER S. **16:**678
Wurzel, Julius **5:**558
WURZWEILER, GUSTAV **16:**678
Wurzweiler School of Social Work **16:**761
Wust, Balthasar Christian **7:**91
W.V.H.A. (div. of SS) **15:**323
Wygnanski, Moshe **4:**734
Wygodsky, Jacob **11:**376
Wygodzki, Isaac **16:**687
WYGODZKI, STANISLAW **1:**38; **16:**678
Wyler, Veit **13:**1049
WYLER, WILLIAM **16:**679
- *illus:*
- - Wilder, Billy, and **16:**511
Wylkowyszki (tn., Lith), *see* VILKAVISKIS
Wylie, B. K. N. **9:**793
Wyman, Frederick, *see* Weinmann, Fritz
Wyneken, Gustav **4:**675
Wyner, Yehudi, *see* Weiner, Yehudi
WYNN, ED **12:**475
Wynn, Ida **11:**1284
WYNN, KEENAN **12:**476
Wynn, Samuel **11:**1283
Wynnefield (section, Pa.) **13:**374
WYOMING (state, U.S.) **16:**679
Wysoki (Nazi) **11:**389
Wysokie Litewskie (city, Belor.), *see* VYSOKOYE
Wyspiański, Stanislaw **13:**798
WYSZKÓW (tn., Pol.) **16:**680
WYSZOGROD (tn., Pol.) **16:**680
WYZANSKI, CHARLES EDWARD JR. **16:**682

X

Xabillo, Elijah Ben Joseph, *see* HABILLO, ELIJAH BEN JOSEPH
XANTEN (tn., Ger.) **16:**685
- Crusade massacre **5:**1137
- historical chart (1891) **8:**766-767
- *kiddush ha-Shem* **10:**984
- martyr's prayer **7:**464
Xativa (city, Sp.) *see* JÁTIVA
Xavier, Francis **8:**1355
Xenophobia **3:**113
XENOPHON OF LAMPSACUS **7:**898
Xenopoulos, Gregorios **7:**887
Xéré (fam., Mor.) **14:**633
Xerxes (k., Pers.), *see* AHASUERUS-XERXES
Xestes (Gr. meas.) **16:**388
Ximenes (fam.) **4:**172
- commerce **15:**1301
- spice trade **15:**270
- sugar trade **15:**487
Ximenes, André **15:**270
XIMENES, SIR DAVID **11:**1576
- Ximenes, Sir Morris **16:**686
XIMENES, SIR MORRIS **16:**686
- coat of arms **8:**339
- travellers **15:**1350
Ximenes, Tomáz **15:**270
XIMENES DE CISNEROS, FRANCISCO **16:**686
- Hebraists **8:**67
- Inquisition **8:**1388
Xosroes (k. Pers.), *see* Khosroes
Xous (bib. fig.) **5:**1174
Xullel, Maimon, *see* Solal, Maimon

Y

Y.A., *see* AHARONOVITCH, YOSEF
Ya'ad (journ.) **1**: newsp. list
Ya'ad Agricultural Development Bank (Isr.) **9**:827
Ya'af (airline co., Isr.) **9**:838
Yaakoviyyim (Doenmeh sect) **6**:149ff
YA'ALEH VE-YAVO (prayer) **16**:689
– *see also:* FESTIVALS; NEW MOON
Ya'arah (mosh., Isr.) **1**: place list
YAARI, ABRAHAM **16**:690
– anthology of Hebrew letters **11**:62
YAARI, MEIR **16**:691
YAARI, YEHUDAH **16**:692
– Yaari, Abraham **16**:690
Ya'arot ha-Carmel (stlmt., Er. Isr.) **5**:186; **9**:588
Yabajai, Gedaliah ibn **11**:485
Yabez, Joseph, *see* JABEZ, JOSEPH BEN ḤAYYIM
Yâbis (riv., Er. Isr.), *see* Wadi Yâbis
Yachdav United Publishers Co. (Isr.) **13**:1379
Yachting (sport) **15**:317
Yacov ben Yishma'el **14**:754
YAD (Torah orn.; memorial) **16**:692
in Art **5**:288
– Torah ornaments **15**:1257
– *illus:*
– – European and Oriental **5**:295; **11**:267; **15**:*fcg.* 1259; **16**:933
Yad'an Ma'ariv (annual) **1**: newsp. list
Yad Avshalom (tomb, Jer.), *see* Absalom, Tomb of
Yad Avshalom (bk.) **3**:257
YADAYIM (tract.) **16**:693
Yad Ben-Zvi (inst., Isr.) **4**:581
Yad Binyamin (rural center, Isr.) **1**: place list
Yad Chaim Weizmann (memorial area, Isr.) **16**:437
Yad ha-Ḥazakah (Maim. code), *see* MAIMONIDES (*Mishneh Torah*)
Yad ha-Ma'avir (sub., Tel Aviv) **15**:923
YAD ḤANNAH (kib., Isr.) **16**:694
– statistics **1**: place list
Yad ha-Rav Herzog (inst., Isr.) **11**:195
Yad ha-Rav Maimon (inst., Jer.) **9**:1495
YADIN, YIGAEL **16**:694
– archaeology **3**:303
– Avigad, Naḥman **3**:961
– *illus:*
– – Haganah High Command **7**:1070
– – Israel-Egypt General Armistice Agreement, 1949 **3**:479
Yadin, Yoseph **15**:492; **16**:696
Yadkovski, Ḥayyim Leib **10**:1106
Yad la-Banim (inst., Isr.) **13**:338
Yad la-Koré (bibls.) **1**: newsp. list
Yad la-Safran (journ.), *see Alim le-Bibliografyah u-le-Safranut*
Yadler, Ben Zion **11**:699
Yad Malakhi (bk.) **11**:338; **11**:817
YAD MORDEKHAI (kib., Isr.) **16**:696
– Anielewicz, Mordecai **3**:3
– statistics **1**: place list
– War of Independence **16**:316
– *illus:*
– – Anielewicz memorial **3**:3
– – Israel stamp **9**:844-845
– – triple wedding **11**:1050
Yad Nathan (mosh., Isr.) **1**: place list; **10**:1176
Y-a-d-o, *see* OLMO, JACOB DANIEL BEN ABRAHAM
Yad Ramah (bk.) **7**:212
Yad Rambam (mosh., Isr.) **1**: place list
YAD VASHEM (inst., Isr.) **16**:697
– archives **3**:386,391
– historiography **8**:566
– Holocaust Law **8**:916
– Holocaust publications **15**:56
– Jerusalem **9**:1495
– library **11**:195
– synagogue destruction **15**:585
– *illus:*
– – text
– – building containing eternal flame **9**:1488
– – Memorial Hall doors Fig. 110 **3**-ART
– – Righteous of the Nations medal **14**:184
Yad Vashem Bulletin (News; period.), *see Yediot Yad Vashem*
Yad Vashem Studies (period.) **16**:698
– statistics **1**: newsp. list
Yad Yiẓhak (bk.) **7**:626
Ya'el (vill. Er. Isr.) **15**:675
Yael (J. brigade) **3**:962
Yafa (site, Isr.) **9**:1286; **12**:181
Y-a-f-a-g, *see* GOLDBLUM, ISRAEL ISSER
Yaffe, Aryeh (Leyb), *see* KOENIG, LEO
Yaffe, Azriel Aharon **14**:1026
Yaffo (city, Er. Isr.), *see* JAFFA
Yafi'a (loc., Isr.), *see* JAPHIA
Yafil, Abraham **14**:1185
Yâfith ibn Ali, *see* JAPHETH BEN ALI HA-LEVI
Yagdil Torah (period., Belor.) **1**: newsp. list **2**:171; **16**:399, 1005
Yagdil Torah (journs., Eng., Ger., Ukr.) **1**: newsp. list
Yagel (mosh., Isr.) **1**: place list
Yagid-Lim (dyn. foun., Mari) **11**:977
Yagupsky, Máximo G. **13**:1370
YAGUR (kib., Isr.) **16**:698
– kibbutz *haggadah* **10**:959
– Passover service **14**:1313ff
Yagur (refugee boat) **8**:1253
Yagur Haggadah (kibb. litur.) **10**:960
Y-a-h-a-b-y ha-Nakdan, *see* JEKUTHIEL BEN JUDAH HA-KOHEN
YAḤAD (Qumran cmty.) **16**:698
– asceticism **3**:680
– Qumran **13**:1429
– sage's associations **14**:642ff
– Seekers after Smooth Things **14**:1096
– Serekh **14**:1180
– Sons of Light **15**:160
– Teacher of Righteousness **15**:885
– War Scroll **16**:1558
– Wicked Priest **16**:485
– Zadokites **16**:915
– *see also:* DAMASCUS, BOOK OF COVENANT OF; DEAD SEA SCROLLS; DEAD SEA SECT
Yahadut, *see* JUDAISM
Yahadut Polin (hist.) **1**: newsp. list
Yahal (kab.) **3**:1008
Yahalom (gem) **13**:1010
Yaham (loc., Isr.) **15**:69
Yahav (fin. co., Isr.) **9**:828
Yaḥaz (charity orgn.) **8**:232
Y-a-h-b-i, *see* JEKUTHIEL BEN JUDAH HA-KOHEN
Yaḥdav (publ.) **1**: newsp. list
Yaḥdû (schol.) **6**:314
Yaḥdun-Lim (k., Mari) **11**:977; **11**:983
– *illus:*
– – foundation inscription **11**:986
YAHIL, CHAIM **1**:38
YAHIL, LENI **1**:38
Yaḥiri (nomads) **7**:1494
Yaḥmur (zool.) **5**:1458
Yahoel (angel) **10**:519
YAH RIBBON OLAM (hymn) **16**:702
– Jewish literature **11**:328
YAHRZEIT (anniversary of death) **16**:702
– Adar *Rishon* **2**:251
– astrological explanation **3**:795
– *El Male Raḥamim* **6**:682
– greetings **7**:915
– Holocaust victims **8**:917
– *Kaddish* **10**:662
– *kever avot* **10**:934
– *memorbuch* reading **11**:1299
– memorial light **11**:1301
– Psalms **13**:1325
– *illus:*
– – condolence formula (table) **7**:915
– – *El Male Raḥamim* **6**:682
– – "*Yahrzeit* at the Front" (paint., M. Oppenheim) **ii**:1563
– *see also:* ADAR, THE SEVENTH OF; MOURNING
"*Yahrzeit* at the Front" (paint., M. Oppenheim) **11**:1563
Yahu (deity) **6**:608
Yahud (Judea), *see* Yehud
YAHÛD (Isl. term) **16**:703
– *see also:* HÛD
YAHUDA, ABRAHAM SHALOM **16**:703
– *illus:*
– – Hebrew writers' convention (1943) **8**:213
– – F.Z.C. **16**:1165
Yahuda, Isaac Ezekiel **16**:703
Yahudah Haggadah (illum. ms., Ger.) **7**:1097
– *illus:* **3**:*fcg.* 299; **14**:569
Yahûdî (Isl. term), *see* YAHÛD
YAHUDI, YUSUF **16**:704
– Judeo-Persian **10**:435
Yahudice (lang.) **15**:1462
Yahûdiyya (vill, Isr.) **16**:730
Yaḥyâ (nagid, Egy.), *see* ZUTA
Yaḥya (imam, Yem.) **16**:743
Yaḥya, Abu Isḥaq Ibrahim ben, *see* Zarkal
Yaḥya, Bonsenior ibn **5**:402
Yaḥya, David ben Gedaliah ibn **15**:1200
Yaḥya, Don (fam.), *see* Don Yaḥya
Yaḥya, Ibn (fam. name), *see also* Ibn Yaḥya
Yaḥya, Samuel, *see* DENIS, ALBERTUS
Yaḥya ben Abraham ben Saadiah al-Bashiri, *see* BASHIRI, YAḤYA
Yaḥya ben Joseph Ẓalaḥ, *see* Ẓalaḥ, Yehaiah ben Joseph
Yaḥyâ ben Yaḥyâ **11**:201
Yaḥyâ ibn Suleiman al-Ṭabîb, *see* ZECHARIAH BEN SOLOMON ROFE
Yaḥya ibn Yaish **2**:326
Yaḥyâ ibn Zakariyyâ, *see* JOHN THE BAPTIST
Yaḥyâ Sâliḥ ben Jacob, *see* Sâliḥ, Yaḥyâ ben Jacob
Ya'ir, *see* STERN, AVRAHAM
Ya'ir Nativ (wk.), *see Me'ir Nativ*
Ya'ish, Abraham ibn **9**:1090; **16**:1549
YA'ISH, BARUCH BEN ISAAC IBN **16**:704
– Avicenna **3**:959
– translations **15**:1322
Yaish, Don Isaac ibn **12**:530

Yaish, Jacob ibn, *see* Abenaes, Jacob
Ya'ish, Judah ibn **2:**607
Ya'ish, Moses ibn **7:**1025
Ya'ish, Solomon ibn, *see* ABENAES, SOLOMON
Yâjûj and Mâjûj, *see* GOG AND MAGOG
Yakar (13th cent. schol.) **16:**133
Yakar (Yakir), Joseph **4:**867; **11:**357
Yakar ben Samuel ha-Levi **13:**597
Yakhin (co., Isr.) **9:**854
Yakhini (mosh., Isr.) **1:** place list
YAKHINI, ABRAHAM BEN ELIJAH **16:**704
- Shabbetai Ẓevi **14:**1230; **14:**1243
YAKIR, YONAH **11:**1576
YAKNEHAZ (pseud., au.) **16:**705
YAKNEHAZ (litur.) **16:**705
- *Havdalah* **7:**1482
- *Kiddush* **10:**974
- *illus:*
- - mnemonic picture **2:**49
Yakobovits, Avraham Aryeh Leib, *see* AKAVYA, AVRAHAM ARYEH LEIB
Yakovlev, Y. **5:**794
Yakubson, B. **6:**267
YAKUM (kib., Isr.) **16:**705
- statistics **1:** place list
Yakum of Ẓerorot (pros.) **15:**491; **16:**854
YALAN-STEKELIS, MIRIAM **16:**706
- *illus:*
- - *Ba-Ḥalomi* (1962) **5:**446
Yaldabaot (Yalda Bahut; name for God) **7:**638
Yale University (U.S.) **4:**1219; **15:**1677
Yalkut (mid. anth.), *see* YALKUT SHIMONI
Yalkut Bar Mitzvah (play) **10:**960
Yalkut ha-Mikhvarot (journ.) **1:**newsp. list
Yalkut ha-Mizraḥ ha-Tikhon (journ.) **1:**newsp. list
Yalkut ha-Re'im (mag.) **1:**newsp. list; **14:**1289
Yalkut Ma'aravi (journ.) **1:** newsp. list
Yalkut Magen (journ.) **1:** newsp. list
YALKUT (ha-) MAKHIRI **16:**706
- *see also:* MIDRASH
Yalkut Moreshet (publ.) **1:**newsp. list
Yalkut Reuveni **10:**552,640
YALKUT SHIMONI (mid. anth.) **16:**707
- Jewish literature **11:**322
- *Yalkit ha-Makhiri* **16:**706
- *see also:* MIDRASH
Yalkut Tekhni (journ.) **1:**newsp. list
Yalkut Vohlin (hist.) **1:**newsp. list
YALON, HANOCH **16:**709
- Hebrew pronunciation **13:**1129
- linguistics **16:**1377
- Mishnah vocalization **16:**1337
YALTA (tal. fig.) **16:**710
YALTA (city, Crimea) **16:**710
- Crimea **5:**1106ff
Yalu (vill, Isr.) **2:**473
Yam (deity), *see* Yamm
Yamah shel Sedom, *see* DEAD SEA
Yamâma (city, Yem.) **7:**1027; **16:**741
Yaman (tn., Yem.) **7:**1027
Yamanî, Zechariah ben Sa'îd al- **16:**745
Yambol Synagogue (Turk.) **14:**1169
Yam ha-Aravah (ha-Melaḥ), *see* DEAD SEA
Yamḥad (anc. kingdom) **16:**1496
Yam ha-Talmud (conc.), *see* SEA OF THE TALMUD
YAMIM NORA'IM (high holydays) **16:**711
- *illus:*
- - Poznan community register **3:**381
- *see also:* TEN DAYS OF PENITENCE
Yaminites (tribal fed., Mari) **11:**982
Yam Kohelet (litur. poem) **14:**849
Yamm (deity) **3:**739; **4:**10; **11:**89
Yampol (tn., Rus.) **2:**23; **15:**1330
Yam Samcho (lake, Er. Isr.) **8:**1064
Yam Shel Shelomo (hal. wk.) **5:**652; **11:**333; **11:**580
Yam Suf, *see* RED SEA
Yanait, Raḥel, *see* BEN-ZVI, RAḤEL YANAIT
Yancyville (vill., N.C.) **12:**1219
YANG-CHOU (city, China) **16:**711
Yanka (gaon.), *see* Ravya
Yankton (city, S.D.) **15:**213
Yankwich, Leon **5:**57
YANNAI (amora) **16:**711
- Akhbarei **2:**487
- *shemittah* ruling **16:**1276
YANNAI (paytan) **16:**712
- *Az Rov Nissim* **3:**1014
- Cairo *genizah* **16:**1338
- Ephraim ben Jacob **6:**813
- historical list **8:**766-767
- liturgical poetry **11:**326
- messianic age **11:**1414
- prosody **13:**1204
- *illus:*
- - *Az Rov Nissim* **3:**1014
YANNAI, ALEXANDER (k., Judea) **16:**714
- arts **7:** 1457
- Avtalyon's teachers **3:**991
- coinage **5:**716
- crucifixion **5:**1134
- Dor **6:**172
- Hasmoneans **8:**632
- Hellenism **8:**296
- historical list **8:**766-767
- Lion of Wrath **11:**276
- Nabateans **12:**741ff
- Parthian Babylonia **4:**37
- Ptolemy Lathyrus **2:**922
- Qumran sect **5:**1249
- sages **14:**640
- Shamir's novel **14:**1289
- Simeon ben Shetaḥ **14:**1563
- war and warfare **16:**279
- Wicked Priest **16:**486
- *geneal. table:* **7:** 1457
- *illus:*
- - text
- - coins **3:**509; **5:**699; **8:**630
- - kingdom borders (map) **9:**118
Yannai ben Ishmael (amora) **16:**712
Yannai Rabbah (the Great; amora) *see* YANNAI
Yanoah (loc., Er. Isr.) **9:**1278
- *illus:*
- - Egyptian record of name **3:**313
Yanofsky, Daniel Abraham (Abe) **5:**406; **16:**551
Yanon ben Zemah **13:**597
Yanovsky, Jacob **7:**182
Yanshuf (zool.) **12:**1531
Yanûḥ (vill., Leb.) **9:**1278
Yanuka (wk.) **16:**1195
Yanuv (mosh., Isr.) **1:**place list
Yaoundé (tn., Cameroon) **9:**438
Yapahu (k., Gezer) **7:**535
Ya'qûb al-Mansûr, *see* Manṣûr, Abu Yusuf Ya'qūb al-
Ya'qub ibn Killis, *see* IBN KILLIS, ABU AL-FARAJ YA'QŪB IBN YŪSUF
Yâqûq (vill, Er. Isr.) **8:**1062
YARCHO, NOE (Noah) **16:**716
- Kaplan, Isaac **10:**750
- medicine **11:**1202
YARDENAH (mosh., Isr.) **16:**716
- statistics **1:** place list
Yarḥei Kallah (study months), *see* KALLAH, MONTHS OF
Yarḥina'ah, Samuel (amora), *see* SAMUEL
Yarḥiv (mosh., Isr.) **1:**place list
Yarḥon ha-Avodah (journ.) **1:**newsp. list
Yarḥon ha-Ḥazzanim (journ.) **1:**newsp. list
Yarḥon ha-No'ar ha-Musikali be-Yisrael (journ.) **1:**newsp. list
Yarḥon ha-Sport (journ.) **1:**newsp. list
Yarḥon Statisti la-Shetaḥim ha-Muḥzakim (publ.) **1:**newsp. list
Yarḥon Statisti le-Yisrael (publ.) **1:**newsp. list
Yari (nomads), *see* Yaḥiri
Yariḥ Azor (k., Ammon) **16:**666
Yarîm (tn., Yemen) **16:**741,746
Yarim-Lim (k., Iamhad) **11:**978; **16:**1496
YARKON (riv., Isr.) **16:**717
- Antipatris, springs of **3:**78
- geography **9:**571
- historical list **8:**766-767
- physiography **9:**127
YARKONAH (mosh., Isr.) **16:**718
- statistics **1:**place list
Yarkon-Negev line (Isr.) **12:**930
YARMOLINSKY, AVRAHAM (Abraham) **16:**718
YARMUK (river, Er. Isr.) **16:**718
- Arab-Israel conflict **7:**1241
- electric energy **9:**791
- frontier **9:**312ff
- geography **9:**595
- Jordan tributary **10:**192
- physiography **9:**167; **9:**179
- Transjordan **15:**1316
- *illus:*
- - El Ḥamme bridge **7:**1242
- - Golan Heights **13:**1531
- - river and basalt rocks **9:**157
Yarmukian Culture (Neolithic) **14:**1212
YARON, BARUCH **1:**38
YARON, REUVEN **16:**720
- Assyriology **16:**1508
Yaroshevski, S. **16:**226
YAROSLAVSKY, YEMELYAN **16:**720
Yârûn (vill., Er. Isr.) **8:**1471
Y-a-sh-a-r, *see* REGGIO, ISACCO SAMUEL
Yashar ben Ḥesed, *see* SAHL IBN FADL
Y-a-sh-a-r of Candia, *see* DELMEDIGO, JOSEPH SOLOMON
Yasher Ko'aḥ (greeting) **7:**914
Yashfeh (gem) **13:**1010
Yashresh (mosh., Isr.) **1:**place list
Yasinovski, Y. **16:**1136
Yâsir (7th cent., sol.) **11:**971
Yasmaḥ-Adad (ruler, Mari) **11:**978; **11:**979
YASSER, JOSEPH **16:**721
- music **12:**660
Yassi (amora), *see* ASSI
YASSKY, HAIM **26:**721
- *illus:* text
Yasuna, Elton **16:**634
Yas'ur (kib., Isr.) **1:** place list
Yates, Benjamin, *see* Goetz, Benjamin
Yates, Samuel **4:**1219
YATES, SIDNEY R. **16:**722
Yathrib (city, Arab.), *see* MEDINA
Yatom, see ORPHAN
Yatom, ibn al- (fam.), *see* Ibn al-Yatom
Yatom, Isaac ibn al-, *see* Ibn al-Yatom, Isaac
Yatrib (city, Arab.), *see* MEDINA
Yatzkan, Samuel Jacob **16:**341
Ya'udi (reg.) **14:**1151
Ya'udic (Sem. lang.) **14:**1151ff
Ya'uri (nomads), *see* Yaḥiri
Yaush (gov., Er. Isr.) **16:**677
Yavan, Baruch, *see* Yovon, Baruch
Ya'veẓ, *see* Jacob ben Isaac ben Eliezer ha-Levi
Ya'veẓ, *see* EMDEN, JACOB
Ya'veẓ, Ze'ev, *see* JAWITZ, ZE'EV
Yavne (Zion. gr., Fr.) **16:**1114
Yavne'el (tn., vill., Er. Isr.), *see* JABNEEL
YAVNE'ELI, SHEMUEL **16:**722
- Aḥdut ha-Avodah **2:**456
- labor problems **9:**329
YAVNEH (kib., Isr.) **16:**722
- *illus:*
- - reading Purim *megillah* **13:**1395
YAVNEH (tn., Isr.) **16:**723
- statistics **1:** place list
Yavneh (anc. city, Er. Isr.), *see* JABNEH
Yavneh (period., Hung.) **11:**721
Yavneh (journ., Gal.) **1:**newsp. list
Yavneh (journ., Isr.) **1:**newsp. list
Yavneh (publ. firm, Ger.) **13:**1374
Yavneh (publ. firm, Isr.) **13:**1378
Yavneh (school network) **6:**428ff; **16:**981
Yavneh (student orgn., Isr.) **9:**900; **15:**448ff
Yavneh-Yam (site, Er. Isr.) **13:**403
YAVNEH-YAM, LEGAL DOCUMENT FROM **16:**723
YAVOROV (city, Ukr.) **16:**724
Yawetz, Joseph, *see* JABEZ, JOSEPH BEN ḤAYYIM
Yazan (fam., Yem.) **16:**898
Yazîd (sult., Mor.) **2:**516; **15:**792
Yazîd (caliph) **15:**1528
Yazîd II (caliph) **15:**1529
Yazîd ibn-Abi Sufyân **9:**260
Yaẓiv Y. **5:**458
Yaẓiẓ (mosh., Isr.) **1:** place list
Yâzûr (vill., Isr.), *see* AZOR
Ybellin (fort., Er. Isr.), *see* JABNEH
YEAR **16:**724
- calendar **5:**44
Yeates, Thomas **8:** 67
Yeats, W.B. **6:**776
Yeb (city, Egy.), *see* ELEPHANTINE
Yeda Am (period.) **15:**55
- statistics **1:**newsp. list
Yeda Research and Development Co. (Isr.) **9:**971; **16:**428
Yedidah (educ. inst., Isr.) **1:** place list
Yedidiah (h. pr.), *see* THEOPHILUS
Yedidiah, Shelomo **4:**1220
Yedid Nefesh (piyyut) **3:**1008
YEDIDYAH (mosh., Isr.) **16:**726
- statistics **1:** place list
Yedies Fun Yivo (period.) **16:**839
YEDINTSY (tn., Mold.) **16:**727
- Lipkany **11:**278
Yedion, see Shenaton Yedi'ot Aḥaronot
Yedi'on ha-Aguddah le-Gerontologyah (journ.) **1:**newsp. list
Yedi'ot (journ.) **1:**newsp. list
Yedi'ot Arkhiyyon u-Muze'on ha-Avodah (journ.) **1:**newsp. list
Yedi'ot Beit Loḥamei ha-Getta'ot (journ.) **1:**newsp. list
Yedi'ot Beit Yiẓḥak Katznelson (journ.) **1:**newsp. list
Yedi'ot Ereẓ va-Emunah (journ.) **1:**newsp. list
Yedi'ot Genazim (journ.) **1:**newsp. list.;
YEDIOTH AHRONOTH (newsp.) **16:**727
- Carlebach, A. **5:**182
- Israel cultural life **9:**1016

- newspapers **12:**1057; **12:**1058
- statistics **1:**newsp. list
Yedi'ot ha-Ḥevrah le-Ḥakirat Ereẓ Yisrael va-Attikoteha (journ.) **1:**newsp. list
Yedi'ot ha-Kibbutz ha-Dati (journ.), *see Ammudim*
Yedi'ot ha-Makhon le-ḥeker ha-Shirah ha-Ivrit(journ.) **1:**newsp. list
Yedi'ot ha-Mazkirut (journ.) **1:**newsp. list
Yedi'ot ha-Tenu'ah le-Aḥdut ha-Avodah, see Le-Aḥdut ha-Avodah
Yediot P.A.I. (period.) **13:**656
Yedi'ot shel Hitaḥadut Olei Germanyah (period.) **16:**447
Yedi'ot Taḥanat ha-Nissayon (journ.) **1:**newsp. list
Yediot Yad Vashem (period.) **16:**697
- statistics **1:**newsp. list
Yedonyah ben Gemariah **6:**610
Yefeh Einayim (bk.) **9:**1337
YEFROYKIN, ISRAEL **16:**727
Yehaiah ben Joseph Zalah, *see* Zalah, Yehaiah
Y-e-h-a-l-e-l, *see* LEVIN, JUDAH LEIB
Yehareg ve-al ya'avor, see Offenses, Cardinal
Yehawmilk (k., Byblos) **16:**661
- *illus:*
- - Byblos stele **13:**476
Yehem (anc. loc.) **16:**269
Yeḥezkel of Zhitomir **12:**654
YEḤI'AM (kib., Isr.) **16:**728
- statistics **1:**place list
- *illus:* text
Yeḥidah (kab. conc.) **10:**611
Yeḥieli, Y. **5:**435
Yehiel Nahmany Sefardi, *see* CONSOLO, FEDERICO
Yeho'aḥaz (k., Judah), *see* AHAZ
YEHOASH (pseud.) **16:**728
- Yiddish literature **16:**800
- *illus:* text
Yehoshu'a (bib. fig.), *see* JOSHUA
YEHOSHUA, AVRAHAM B. **16:**730
- drama, Hebrew **6:**207
- Hebrew literature **8:**207
- Jerusalem theme **9:**1568
- *illus:*
- - *Laylah be-Mai* in Bimot Theater **6:**204
Yehoshua, Raphael **2:**328
Yehud (Judea) **8:**626; **8:**627; **9:**111; **10:**403
- *illus:*
- - coins **3:**322; **5:**698; **8:**625
- - map **9:**117
YEHUD (stlmt., Isr.) **16:**730
- Petaḥ Tikvah **13:**337
- statistics **1:** place list
- Yehuda (fam., Iraq) **11:**1133; **16:**736
Yehuda, Isaac **11:**1133
Yehuda, Shelomo Yeḥezkel **16:**736
Yehudah (govt. offic., Jaffa) **9:**1251
Yehudah (sect, Iran.), *see* YUDGHAN
Yehudah, Zevi **7:**1326
Yehudah vi-Yrushalayim (newsp.) **9:**1014; **9:**1466; **14:**697
- statistics **1:**newsp. list
YEHUDAI BEN NAḤMAN (Yehudai Gaon) **16:**731
- codification of law **5:**634; **11:**330
gaonate **7:**315; **7:**317
- *Halakhot Gedolot* **7:**1169
- *Halakhot Keẓuvot* **7:**1170
- *Halakhot Pesukot* **7:**1171
- Ḥanina Kahana ben Huna **7:**1266
- *Kallah* **10:**710
- responsa **14:**84
- Sura **15:**522
Yehud-el ʿArab (J. tribes), *see* BAḤUẒIM
YEHUDI BEN SHESHET **16:**732
- Dunash ben Labrat **6:**270; **11:**1306
- linguistics **16:**1354
Yehudi ha-Kadosh, *see* PRZYSUCHA, JACOB ISAAC BEN ASHER
Yehudit (period.) **4:**1316
Yeimar (amora) **2:**866. 870
Yeiva (zoharic fig.) **16:**1195
Yeivi, R., *see* JACOB JOSEPH OF OSTROG
Yeivin, I. **15:**809
YEIVIN, SHEMUEL **16:**733
- archaeology **3:**303
YEIVIN, YEHOSHUA HESCHEL **16:**733
Yekaterinodar (city, Rus.), *see* KRASNODAR
Yekaterinoslav (city, Ukr.), *see* DNEPROPETROVSK
YEKOPO (orgn.) **16:**733
- communal charity **13:**380
- Naiditsch, Isaac Asher **12:**796
- Yefroykin, Israel **16:**727
YEKUM PURKAN (prayer) **16:**735
- Abraham Maimuni **2:**151
- *geonim* **7:**317
- *resh kallah* **14:**83
Yekutieli, Yoseph **11:**662; **15:**295
Yelammedenu, Midrash, see TANḤUMA YELAMMEDENU
Yelin, Chaim **10:**849
Yelizavetgrad (city, Ukr.), *see* KIROVOGRAD
Yelizavetpol (city, Rus.), *see*
YELLIN (fam., Er. Isr.) **16:**735
Yellin, Aviezer **16:**737
Yellin, Avinoam **16:**738
Yellin, David **2:**205ff; **16:**736
- Hebrew pronunciation **16:**1645
- linguistics **16:**1378
- Va'ad Le'ummi **16:**51
Yellin, Simon **15:**304
Yellin, Thelma, *see* Bentwich, Thelma
Yellin, Yehoshua **5:**1295; **16:**735
YELLIN-MOR, NATHAN **16:**738
- Avnery's cooperation **3:**976
- Leḥi **11:**464
Yellin-Tavia (Pol. fam.) **16:**736
Yellow badge, *see* BADGE, JEWISH
Yellowhammer (zool.) **6:**30
Yema, (cmty., Sp.), see ALJAMA
Yemei Ẓiklag (bk.) **8:**206
YEMEN (country) **16:**739
- General
- - Arabia **3:**233
- - Arab League **3:**242
- - conversions **8:**677
- - history chart (1449–50) **8:**766-767
- - illuminated mss **8:**1263
- - Ottoman conquest **16:**1537
- - trade route **15:**1298
- Community
- - Aden Jews **2:**260ff
- - aliyah to Israel **8:**770; **9:**500ff; **9:**512; **9:**534
- - Avelei Zion **3:**946
- - demography **5:**1501; **13:**871ff; **16:**182ff
- - exilarchate **6:**1032
- - goldsmiths **7:**740
ḥakham bashi **13:**1451
- - *Iggeret Teiman* **11:**758
- - Israel community **9:**500ff; **9:**891; **9:**897; **9:**983; **9:**991
- - Jewish quarter **10:**85
- - literature **9:**1567
- - *nagid* **12:**763
- - Saphir, Jacob **14:**853
- - Shabbateanism **14:**1234; **14:**1236
- - sickness **14:**1501,1502
- - Yavni'eli's mission **9:**329; **16:**722ff
- Customs
- - cooking and food **6:**1421ff
- - dress **6:**219
- - folk music **12:**669
- - Hebrew pronunciation **13:**1122ff
- - liturgy **11:**397; **11:**401ff
- - marriage **11:**1045
- - masorah **16:**1478
- - masoretic accents **11:**1109
- - Psalm singing **13:**1333
- - Torah reading **16:**1413
- Israel relations
- - Armistice Agreements **3:**479
- - War of Independence **16:**306ff
- Personalities
- - Arusi, Abraham **3:**664
- - Kafaḥ, Yosef **10:**672
- - Shabazi, Shalem **14:**1215
- *illus:*
- - text
- - bride and groom **11:**1046, 1047
- - children in Jerusalem *ḥeder* **9:**897, 942
- - dress articles and jewels **6:***fcg.* 235
- - filigree ornamentation **7:**742
- - Genesis ms. (1496) **11:**903
- - Ḥanukkah lamp **7:**1294
- - immigrants at Givat Ye'arim **9:**577
- - immigrants at Rosh ha-Ayin **9:**379
- - operation "Magic Carpet" **9:**529
- - Temanic script types **2:**696,719-720,733-734
- - Torah scribe **14:**1044,1045
- - Torah scribe's art (15th cent.) **16:***fcg.* 743
- - varieties of Hebrew pronunciation (map) **13:**1124
- *pop. tables:*
- - refugee influx into Aden, 1946-47 **2:**263
- *mus. notations:*
- - text
- - Prophets cantillation **11:**1110
Yemen, Southern (rep.), *see* Southern Yemen
Yemenite Federation (polit. party, Isr.) **9:**374
"Yemenite Torah scribe" (etch., E. M. Lilien) **14:**1044
Yemin Moshe (qtr., Jer.) **9:**1516,1457
- *illus:*
- - Montefiore Foundation seal **9:**1451
- - windmill **9:**1451
Yemin Orde (vill., Isr.) **12:**1174; **16:**548
- *illus:*
- - high school class **9:**949
Yemma (vill., Er. Isr.), *see* JABNEEL
Yenisei (reg., Sib.) **14:**1487
Yenne (vill., Fr.) **14:**921
Yeraḥ ben yomo (cantillation sign) **16:**1455
Yeraqa, Afdah (Afidah) **10:**782
Yeraqa, Shabbetai **10:**782
Yeridah le-Ẓorekh Aliyyah (Has. conc.) **7:**1410
Yerim (tn., Yem.), *see* YARIM
Yeri'ot Shelomo (wk.) **11:**580; **15:**520
YEROḤAM (stlmt., Isr.) **16:**759
- statistics **1:**place list
- *illus:*
- - dam and water reservoir **9:**769
Yeruḥam ha-Koton, *see* BLINDMAN, YERUḤAM
Yerusalimchik, Nahum, *see* YUD, NAHUM
Yerushalayim (city), *see* JERUSALEM
Yerushalayim (yearbk.) **12:**1055
Yerushalayim (period.) **4:**1158; **16:**1330
- statistics **1:**newsp. list
Yerushalayim (journs., Isr.) **1:**newsp. list
Yerushalayim (journ., Pol.) **1:**newsp. list
Yerushalayim (kibb. litur.) **10:**961
Yerushalayim de-Lita (city, Lith.), *see* VILNA
Yerushalmi (kab. wk.), *see* ZOHAR
Yerushalmi, Abraham ben Josiah, *see* ABRAHAM BEN JOSIAH YERUSHALMI
Yerushalmi, Benjamin **11:**351
Yerushalmi, Josiah **2:**150
Yerushalmi, Shalom ben Solomon **15:**634
Yesha (mosh., Isr.) **1:** place list
Yeshayahu, Israel **9:**677
YESHEVAV THE SCRIBE (tan.) **16:**759
- ethics **6:**941
Yeshiva College (N.Y.) **14:**117; **16:**760
Yeshivah Kneset Israel, *see* SLOBODKA YESHIVAH
Yeshivah shel Ma'lah, see ACADEMY ON HIGH
Yeshivah Tikhonit (school, Isr.) **16:**772
Yeshivat ha-Kotel (Jer.) **4:**491
- *illus:*
- - *bet ha-midrash* dedication **9:**898
YESHIVA UNIVERSITY (N.Y.) **16:**760
- New York City **12:**1119ff
- Orthodox Judaism **10:**396
- Sephardic Studies Program **14:**1174
- universities **15:**1678
- U.S. yeshivot **16:**773
- *illus:*
- - Albert Einstein College of Medicine **8:**1037
- - cornerstone ceremony **12:**1106
- - studying the Talmud **6:**414; **16:**767
- *see also:* RABBINICAL COUNCIL OF AMERICA (RCA)
YESHIVOT (rab. seminaries) **16:**762
- *Contents:*
- - In Islamic Countries and in Western and Central Europe to the 15th Century **16:**762
- - The Shifting of Yeshivah Centers in the 15th-18th Centuries **16:**765
- - Organization and Inner Life **16:**766
- - Curriculum **16:**767
- - Degrees and Graduation **16:**768
- - Lithuania and Russia **16:**768
- - Yeshivot in the 20th Century **16:**770
- - Yeshivot in Ereẓ Israel **16:**771
- - In the United States **16:**772
- General
- - academies **2:**199
- - Councils of the Lands **5:**1002
- - education **6:**401ff
- - Ereẓ Israel **9:**891
- - Grodzinski, Ḥayyim Ozer **7:**928
- - Haskalah **7:**1442
- - *kazyonny ravvin* **10:**861
- - Lipkin, Israel **11:**279
- - married students **10:**1161
- - Musar movement **12:**534
- - pilpul **13:**526
- - rabbinical syllabus **10:**517
- - responsa **14:**83
- - *takkanot* **15:**735

- - wandering students **4:**390
- - Yevsektsiya **16:**780
- Countries
- - Algeria
- - - Maimonides rabbinical college **2:**623
- - Australia
- - - Sydney **3:**885
- - - Yeshivah Gedolah **3:**885
- - Austria
- - - Eisenstadt **6:**546
- - - Vienna **16:**124
- - - Wiener Neustadt **3:**889 **16:**504
- - Belorussia
- - - Baranovichi **4:**197
- - - Bobruisk **4:**1156
- - - Novogrudok **12:**1237
- - - Ruzhany **14:**526
- - - Slonim **14:**1672
- - - Tomekhei Temimim **6:**425; **7:**1014 **11:**538
- - - Torah v'Daas **6:**426 **11:**213; **14:**58
- - - Volkovysk **16:**212
- - Brazil
- - - Etz Haim **4:**1324
- - Bulgaria
- - - Nikopol **4:**1485 **12:**1160
- - Canada
- - - Montreal **6:**454
- - - Ner Israel **6:**454 **15:**1262
- - - Yesodei Hatoroh **15:**1262
- - Czechoslovakia
- - - Kosice **10:**1215
- - - Trnava **15:**1401
- - Egypt
- - - Abraham Monzon **16:**1550
- - - Bezalel Ashkenazi **16:**1550
- - - David ibn Abi Zimra **16:**1550
- - - Isaac Berab **16:**1550
- - - Jacob Castro **16:**1550
- - England
- - - Beth Hamedrash Heshaim **6:**446
- - - Chaye Olam **6:**450
- - - Etz Chaim **6:**448,450
- - - Gateshead **6:**429,448f; **7:**334
- - - Horomo **6:**450
- - - Ilford **6:**450
- - - Jews' College **10:**98
- - - Leeds **6:**448,450
- - - Liverpool **6:**448,450 **11:**409
- - - Manchester **6:**448,450
- - - Ohel Moshe vi-Yhudit **16:**577
- - - Sunderland **6:**450 **15:**519
- - - Torat Emet **6:**448,450
- - France
- - - Lunel **11:**566
- - - Marseilles **11:**1055
- - - Montpellier **12:**282
- - - Paris **13:**104; **13:**108
- - - Posquières **6:**407 **13:**931
- - - Strasbourg **15:**425
- - Germany **13:**1454
- - - Altona **2:**779
- - - Augsburg **3:**849
- - - Frankfurt on the Main **7:**86
- - - Fuerth **7:**215
- - - Halberstadt **7:**1173
- - - Mainz **11:**789ff
- - - Regensburg **14:**35
- - - Worms **16:**644
- - - Wuerzburg **16:**676
- - Georgia
- - - Ḥabad **14:**1435
- - Greece
- - - Arta **6:**420
- - Hungary
- - - Baja **4:**112 **14:**1033
- - - Bonyhad **4:**1213
- - - Khust **10:**958 **14:**958
- - - Sopron **15:**162
- - Iraq
- - - Baghdad **4:**86
- - - Beit Zilkha **4:**89
- - Israel
- - - Aḥuzat Ya'akov **13:**1462
- - - Belz **4:**453 **9:**1495
- - - Bet(h) El **7:**1392; **9:**293; **10:**553; **11:**1219; **14:**1360; **16:**746
- - - Ein Zeitim **16:**1549
- - - Eẓ Hayyim **10:**1222; **11:**1295; **14:**674
- - - Gedulat Mordecai **3:**1016
- - - ha-Darom **13:**1462
- - - Harry Fischel Institute **8:**424
- - - Hebron **14:**883
- - - Hesed le-Abraham **8:**234; **14:**378
- - - Isaac Sholal's **16:**906
- - - Kefar Ḥabad **10:**882
- - - Kefar Haro'eh **10:**884
- - - Kerem be-Yavneh **10:**31
- - - Lomza **11:**469
- - - Merkaz ha-Rav **10:**1183; **10:**1187
- - - Merom Zion **9:**1495
- - - Midrash ha-Gadol de-Parisi **9:**512
- - - Mir **6:**1290; **12:**71
- - - Netiv Meir **9:**1495
- - - Or ha-Ḥayyim **4:**217
- - - Or Zore'aḥ **4:**251
- - - Ponevezh **10:**684
- - - Porat Yosef **9:**1486; **9:**1495
- - - Safed **14:**629; **16:**1549
- - - Shevet mi-Yehudah **15:**1689
- - - Shevet u-Meḥokek **15:**1689
- - - Slobodka **8:**235; **9:**341; **14:**1668; **14:**883
- - - Spinka **15:**275
- - - Tiberias **15:**1133; **16:**1550
- - - Tiferet Yerushalayim **6:**75
- - - Torat Emet **8:**234
- - - Vizhnitsa **16:**199
- - - Yehivat ha-Kotel **4:**491
- - Italy **6:**418
- - - Bari **4:**223
- - - Conegliano **14:**170
- - - Leghorn **10:**1573
- - - Lucca **11:**549
- - - Metivta de Mata Roma **14:**245
- - - Neveh Shalom **6:**839
- - - Venice **16:**100
- - Japan
- - - Mir **9:**1282
- - Kurdistan
- - - Akrah **4:**205
- - - Amadiyah **4:**205
- - - Barazan **4:**205
- - - Mosul **4:**205
- - Lithuania
- - - Brest-Litovsk **4:**1360
- - - Grodno **6:**425; **7:**924
- - - Keneset Beit Yizḥak **10:**848; **14:**1668
- - - Kovno **10:**847
- - - Lomza **11:**469
- - - Mir **6:**1290; **12:**71; **15:**1141
- - - Ohel Yizḥak **13:**56
- - - Pinsk **15:**541
- - - Plunge **4:**1100; **13:**653
- - - Ponevezh **10:**683; **13:**55
- - - Radun **4:**445; **6:**425 **13:**1505
- - - Slobodka **10:**847ff; **12:**536; **14:**1668; **14:**883
- - - Slutsk **4:**447 **14:**1668
- - - Taurage **15:**834
- - - Telz **15:**166; **15:**938
- - - Volozhin **4:**445; **6:**425 **14:**1655; **15:**131; **15:**1141; **16:**214ff **16:**218; **16:**219
- - - Voronova **15:**166
- - - Zagare **16:**916
- - Moravia
- - - Boskovice **4:**1262
- - - Mikulov **11:**1531
- - - Šafov **4:**160
- - Morocco
- - - Fez **6:**1255
- - - Marrakesh **11:**1016
- - Netherlands
- - - Amsterdam **2:**899
- - - Eẓ-Ḥayyim **13:**287
- - Poland
- - - Beit Yosef **14:**1513; **16:**680
- - - Cracow **5:**1028
- - - Hakhmei Lublin **6:**429 **6:**550; **14:**1300; **14:**532
- - - Kalisz **16:**1347
- - - Kletsk **10:**1107
- - - Lublin **11:**542
- - - Makow **11:**811
- - - Ostrog **12:**1513
- - - Poznan **13:**950
- - - Staszow **15:**343
- - - Suwalki **15:**540
- - - Taḥkemoni **6:**429
- - Rumania
- - - Oybervisha **16:**165
- - - Siret **14:**1618
- - Russia
- - - Kol Ya'akov **12:**367
- - - Odessa **12:**1327
- - - Tomekhei Temimim **14:**1435
- - Scotland
- - - Glasgow **7:**602
- - Slovakia
- - - Bratislava **4:**1311
- - South Africa
- - - Johannesburg **6:**455 **10:**156
- - Spain
- - - Barcelona **4:**210
- - - Cordoba **5:**963
- - - Lucena **11:**550
- - Switzerland
- - - Eẓ Hayyim **10:**1472
- - Syria
- - - Damascus **5:**1241
- - - Hadrach **7:**1052
- - Tunisia
- - - Gabes **7:**234
- - - Kairouan **10:**697
- - Turkey **15:**1462
- - - Adrianople **16:**1549
- - - Aydin **3:**995
- - - Gheron **5:**1295
- - - Istanbul **9:**1088; **16:**1549ff
- - - Izmir **9:**1163
- - - Salonika **6:**420; **16:**1549ff
- - Ukraine
- - - Belz **4:**452
- - - Degel Torah **15:**1456
- - - Stanislav **15:**338
- - - Sorozhinets **15:**417
- - - Uzhgorod **16:**41
- - - Vizhnitsa **16:**199
- - Uruguay
- - - Ha-Rav Kook **16:**14
- - U.S.
- - - Beth Yehudah **16:**416
- - - Elizabeth **15:**1534
- - - Etẓ Chaim **6:**439 **16:**760
- - - Ḥafez Hayyim **12:**1120
- - - Lakewood **10:**1222
- - - Lubavich **12:**1120
- - - Mir **12:**1120
- - - Ner Israel **4:**146 **14:**379
- - - New Square **14:**214
- - - Rabbi Isaac Elchanan **6:**439 **16:**760
- - - Telz **15:**939
- - - Tifereth Jerusalem **12:**1120
- - - Torah Vadaath **12:**1120
- - Yugoslavia
- - - Belgrade **4:**426
- *illus:*
- - text
- - Bene-Berak **9:**895
- - Eẓ Hayyim (Jer.), seal **9:**1587
- - Gateshead **6:**421; **7:**334
- - Khust, students **10:**959
- - Mir, students (1929) **12:**71
- - New York, Satmar **12:**1121
- - Panevezys (Lith.), students **13:**55
- - Ponevezh, *kallah* months **10:**711
- - Radun, aid appeal **9:**1069
- - Slobodka **14:**1667
- - Tiferet Israel (Jer.) **9:**1480
- - U.S. yeshivah, students **6:**408
- - Yeshivat ha-Kotel, *shi'ur* **9:**898
- - Yeshiva University **6:**414; **16:**760
- *see also:* ACADEMIES IN BABYLONIA AND EREẒ ISRAEL; KOLEL; RABBINICAL SEMINARIES

Yesh Noḥalin (wk.) **16:**532
Yeshu'a (bib. fig.), *see* JOSHUA
Yeshu'a ha-Ben (custom), *see* SHOLEM ZOKHOR
Yeshurun (fam.), *see* JESURUN
Yeshurun (period., Bagh.) **4:**93; **7:**1047; **8:**1450
Yeshurun (period., Gal.) **16:**1730
Yeshurun (period., Ger.) **1:**newsp. list
Yeshurun (period., Rum.) **1:**newsp. list
YESHURUN, AVOT **16:**773
Yeshurun, Isaac **6:**258
Yeshurun Synagogue (Jer.) **6:**617; **11:**195; **15:**620,1674
- *illus:* **15:**623
- - protest rally against 1939 White Paper **9:**1479
Y-e-s-o-d, *see* JUDAH BEN ELIEZER
Yesod Dikduk (wk.), *see Sefer ha-Yesod*
Yesodei ha-Tevunah u-Migdal ha-Emunah (enc.) **2:**132; **6:**730
Yesod ha-Amrami (prayer bk.), *see Seder Rav Amram*
Yesod Mishneh Torah (wk.) **2:**538
Yesod Mispar (wk.) **16:**1358,1385
Yesod Olam (wk., Isaac ben Joseph Israeli) **3:**803; **9:**1062
Yesod Olam (drama, Moses Zacuto) **16:**908
Yesod Olam (kab. conc.), *see Ẓaddik*
Yesodot (mosh.) **1:**place list
Yesodot (period.) **8:**1241
YESUD HA-MA'ALAH (mosh., Isr.) **16:**773
- seal **14:**1081
- statistics **1:**place list
Yetiv (cantillation sign) **16:**1454
YE'USH (leg. conc.) **16:**774
- stolen property **12:**10
- theft and robbery **15:**1096
- *see also:* LOST PROPERTY
Yeushzon, B., *see* JUSTMAN, MOSHE BUNEM
Yev (city, Egy.), *see* ELEPHANTINE
YEVAMOT (tract.) **16:**775
- *see also:* LEVIRATE MARRIAGE
Yevanic (J. lang.), *see* JUDEO-GREEK
YEVOPO (orgn.) **16:**734
YEVPATORIYA (city, Crimea) **16:**778
Yevreyskaya Avtonomnaya Oblast (Rus.), *see* BIROBIDZHAN
Yevreyskaya Biblioteka (period.) **11:**16; **13:**1045; **15:**60; **16:**225
Yevreyskaya Entsiklopediya
- Berlin, Israel **4:**660
- encyclopedias **6:**732
- Efron, Ilya **6:**468
- Guenzburg, Baron David **7:**963
- historical chart **8:**766-767
- Katzenelson, Judah Leib **10:**832
- Leningrad **11:**16
- Russia **14:**455
- Wissenschaft des Judentums **16:**581
Yevreyskaya Rabochaya Khronika (period.) **11:**1059; **13:**839
Yevreyskaya Starina (period.) **4:**660; **6:**252; **10:**92; **11:**17

Yevreyskaya Stranitsa (period.) 15:1137
Yevreyskaya Tribuna (newsp.) 16:153
Yevreyskaya Zhizn (newsp.) 7:1332; 11:1058; 15:93; 16:227
Yevreyskiy Kavkazskiy Vestnik (period.) 16:407
Yevreyskiy Komitet Pomoshchi Zhertvam Voyny (orgn., Rus.), *see* YEKOPO
Yevreyskoye Istoriko-Etnograficheskoye Obshchestvo, *see* JEWISH SOCIETY FOR HISTORY AND ETHNOGRAPHY
YEVSEKTSIYA (orgn., U.S.S.R.) 16:779
- acrivity 14:463
- Agursky, Samuel 2:433
- Buchbinder, Nahum 4:1442
- communism 5:799
- Esther (M. Lifschitz) 6:913
- He-Ḥalutz 8:249
- historical chart 8:766-767
- history 8:743
- Tshemeriski, Alexander 15:1417
YEVTUSHENKO, YEVGENI ALEXANDROVICH 16:781
- Babi Yar 4:30
- *illus:*
- - *Babi Yar*, English translation 4:28
Yevusi, Operation (Isr. War of Indep.) 16:313
Yevzerichin, Zerubavel 14:1574
YEZD (city, Iran) 16:781
Yezdegerd I (k., Pers.) 4:46
Yezdegerd II (k., Pers.) 4:42
Yezdegerd III (k., Pers.) 11:940
Yeẓer ha-Ra' and *Yeẓer ha-Tov*, *see* INCLINATION, GOOD AND EVIL
YEZIERSKA, ANZIA 16:782
- U.S. literature 15:1573ff
YEẒIRAH, SEFER (wk.) 16:782
- *Contents:*
- - Contents and Structure 16:782
- - Time of Composition 16:785
- - Commentaries on Sefer Yeẓirah 16:786
- - Printed Editions and Translations 16:787
- General
- - Abraham 2:118
- - astrology 3:791
- - *Bahir, Sefer ha-* 4:98ff
- - golem 7:753ff
- - Judah Halevi 10:364
- - Kabbalah 10:507ff
- - mystical literature 11:347
- - zodiac 16:1191
- Commentators
- - Abulafia, Abraham 2:186
- - Donnolo, Shabbetai 6:168
- - Dunash ibn Tamim 6:272
- - Joseph ben Shalom Ashkenazi 10:236
- - Joseph ben Uzziel 10:238
- - Lonzano, Abraham 11:486
- - Saadiah Gaon 14:549
- - Sahula, Meir ben Solomon 14:658
YEẒIV PITGAM (piyyut) 16:788
Y H W H, *see* GOD, NAMES OF
Yibbum, *see* LEVIRATE MARRIAGE AND ḤALIẒAH
Yibnā (vill., Isr.) 9:1176; 16:723
Yidde'oni (wizard) 6:114
Yiddish..., *see also under* Yidishe
Yiddish Art Theater (U.S.)
- Adler, Celia 2:271
- Hirschbein and 8:517
- Libin's plays 11:189
- Mestel, Jacob 11:1428
- Schwartz' theater 14:1021ff; 15:1066
Yiddish culture
- assimilation 3:781
- communism 5:793ff
- Israel 9:1002
- Kiev 10:995
- New York City 12:1101
- Stalin's attitude 15:327ff
- U.S. 15:1618; 15:1620; 15:1627
- Workmen's Circle 16:635
Yiddishe Morgenpost (newsp.) 7:939
YIDDISHER KULTUR FARBAND (assoc., U.S.) 16:788
Yiddishkeit, *see* JUDAISM
YIDDISH LANGUAGE 16:789
- *Contents:*
- - The Speech Community 16:789
- - Sound System 16:790
- - Writing System 16:791
- - Grammar 16:791
- - Dialectical Differences 16:793
- - Historical Development 16:795
- - History of Yiddish Studies 16:797
- General
- - education 6:433ff
- - greetings 7:912
- - history 8:760ff
- - *Me'assef* 11:1161
- - Mendelssohn, Moses 11:1334; 11:1338ff
- - music, Jewish 12:657
- - radio and TV 15:929f
- - Shakespeare 14:1264
- - Vilna 16:147
- - *yeshivot* 16:771ff
- - Yiddisher Kultur Farband 16:788
- Linguistics
- - Beilinson, Moses Eliezer 4:398
- - dysphemisms 6:962
- - grammar 4:1042; 14:63
- - Hebrew language 16:1637
- - Jewish languages 10:67
- - linguistic development 10:67
- - Old French 10:424
- - pronunciations 13:1126
- - Shazar, Zalman 14:1327
- - Weinreich, Uriel 16:405
- - YIVO 16:837
- Struggle For
- - Agudat Israel 2:421
- - autonomism 3:920
- - Birnbaum, Nathan 4:1041
- - Bund 4:1501ff
- - Dubnow, Simon 6:254
- - Czernowitz conference 5:1211
- - Golomb, Abraham 7:763
- - Haskalah 7:1437ff
- - Lenin and 11:13
- - Levinsohn's objections 11:117
- - socialism 15:30ff; 15:42ff
- - Zhitlowsky, Chaim 16:1009ff
- Countries
- - Ashkenaz 3:721
- - Austria 3:892
- - Birobidzhan 4:1047
- - Russia 14:455, 464, 473, 483 16:779ff
- - South Africa 15:197ff
- *illus:*
- - Belorussia republic emblem 14:469
- - dialects (map) 13:1127
- - Russia, unofficial publications (1950s) 14:489
- *see also:* YIDDISH LITERATURE
YIDDISH LITERATURE 16:798
- *Contents:*
- - Introduction 16:798
- - Until the End of the 18th Century 16:800
- - - Bible in Yiddish Literature 16:800
- - - Liturgy 16:802
- - - Ethical Literature 16:803
- - - "Historical" Songs and Writings 16:804
- - - Transcriptions of German Works 16:805
- - - "Secular" Yiddish Literature in Italy 16:806
- - Modern Literature 16:807
- - - Until World War I 16:807
- - - After World War I 16:815
- - State of Research and Bibliography 16:826
- - - Up to the End of the 18th Century 16:827
- - - Modern Literature 16:830
- General
- - allegory 2:644
- - cultural life in Israel 9:1002
- - *Di Yidishe Folksbibliotek* 14:1274
- - Hebrew literature 8:176
- - Sadan, Dov 14:619ff
- - theater 15:1071
- - Warsaw 16:340
- - Wiener, Leo 16:499
- Movements
- - In-Zikh 8:1434
- - Workmen's Circle 16:635
- - YIVO 16:837
- - Yunge, Di 16:896
- Types and Examples
- - Bible translations 4:866
- - children's literature 5:439
- - encyclopedias 6:731; 6:735
- - Ḥasidic literature 7:1413
- - Jewish letters 11:55
- - Jewish literature 11:356ff
- - *Kol Mevasser* 10:1165
- - *Ma'aseh Book* 11:649
- - *Melokhim Bukh* 11:1292
- - press 13:1031; 13:1053ff
- - Purim Shpil 13:1396
- - *Shmuel Bukh* 14:1426
- - *teḥinnah* 15:907
- - *Ẓe'enah u-Re'enah* 16:967
- *illus:*
- - text
- - Broderzon's *Siḥat Ḥulin* 4:1392
- - Buenos Aires, exhibition 3:424
- - *Buovo d'Antona* (1541) 4:1276
- - *Der Moment* 12:235
- - *Dinstagishe Kurant* 13:1034
- - *Josippon* (1771) 10:296
- - *Khurbn Vilne* (1947) 10:659
- - *New Yorker Juedische Zeitung*, first issue 13:1054
- - *Sovetish Heymland*, 1st. issue 15:216
- *see also:* FOLKLORE; YIDDISH LANGUAGE
Yiddish Pen Club 3:687
Yiddish Press, *see* PRESS
Yiddish Press (newsp.) 16:551
Yiddish School Organization, *see* Central Yiddish School Organization
Yiddish Scientific Institute, *see* YIVO INSTITUTE FOR JEWISH RESEARCH
Yiddish Theater, *see* THEATER
Yidish . . ., *see also under* Yiddish . . .
Yidish Bukh (publ. house, Pol.) 13:785; 14:1209
Yidishe Bibliotek (period.) 16:340
Yidishe Filologye (period.) 14:64
Yidishe Folks-Bibliotek (annual) 13:1045
Yidishe Folksblat, Dos (period.)
- Kantor, Judah Leib 10:744
- press 13:1045
- St. Petersburg 11:16
- Shalom Aleichem 14:1273
- Zederbaum, Alexander 16:964
Yidishe Folks-Entsiklopedye 6:735
Yidishe Folkspartei in Poyln (party), *see* FOLKSPARTEI (POLAND)
Yidishe Folksshtime (newsp.) 15:445
Yidishe Folkstsaytung (newsp., Den.) 13:1049
Yidishe Folkstsaytung (newsp., Gal.) 15:834
Yidishe Folkstsaytung (period., U.S.) 13:1053
Yidishe Kultur (period.) 11:1149; 11:1428; 13:1056
Yidishe Kultur Lige (orgn.) 4:609
Yidishe Landvirtshaftlekhe Gezelshaft (soc.), *see* Yilag
Yidishe Prese (journ.) 4:1331; 13:1040; 16:640
Yidisher Arbayter, Der (newsp.), *see Der Yidisher Arbayter*
Yidisher Ekspres (period.) 13:1031
Yidisher Gezelshaftlekher Leksikon (*wk.*) 16:1159
YIDISHER KEMFER (Yiddisher Arbeiter; period.) 16:833
- Chasanowich, Leon 5:362
- Entin, Joel 6:801
- Marmor, Kalman 11:1012
- Pinski, David 13:550
- Po'alei Zion 13:659
- Press 13:1056
- U.S. Zionism 16:1042
- World Labor Zionist movement 16:640
Yidisher Kommunistisher Farband (orgn.) 15:1542
Yidisher Natsionaler Arbeter Farband (soc.) 13:659
Yidisher Selbsttetigkayt Kolektiv (theat. troupe, Lith.) 10:850
Yidisher Tageblat (newsp.) 13:1031
Yidisher Telefon (newsp.) 13:1031
Yidisher Visenshaftlikher Institut, *see* YIVO INSTITUTE FOR JEWISH RESEARCH
Yidisher Zhurnal (period.) 13:1031
Yidishes Folksblat, Dos (period.), *see Yidishe Folksblat, Dos*
Yidishe Shprakh (period.) 16:839
Yidishe Shriftn (journ., Pol.) 13:785; 14:370
Yidishe Shriftn (period., U.S.) 7:787
Yidishe Shtime (newsp., Eng.) 13:1031; 14:687
YIDISHE SHTIME, (newsp., Lith.) 16:833
- Kaunas 10:848
Yidishe Sotsiale Alleynhilf (orgn.) 13:772
Yidishes Tageblat (newsp., Pol.) 6:1295; 7:1498; 16:341
YIDISHES TAGEBLAT (newsp., U.S.) 16:833
- press 13:1053
- Sarasohn 14:873
Yidishe Tsaytung (journ., Carpathorus.) 13:1029; 16:1330
Yidishe Tsaytung (newsp., Urug.) 13:1041
Yidishe Velt (period.) 16:727
Yidishe Vochenshrift (lit. pub.) 13:1055
Yidish far Ale (journ.) 13:1295
Yidishkeyt, *see* JUDAISM
Yifat (kib., Isr.) 7:532
- statistics 1:place list
Yiftaḥ (kib., Isr.) 1:place list
Yiftaḥ, Operation (Isr. War of Indep.) 13:47; 16:309
Yiftah Brigade (Isr. army) 7:1073; 13:47; 16:318
YIGDAL (litur. hymn) 16:833
- authorship 3:656
- Immanuel of Rome 8:1296
- Leoni's tune 11:29
- *mus. notation;* text
Yiḥudim (kab.) 10:548
YIḤUS (fam. records) 16:835
- genealogy 7:383
- minimized in Aggadah 12:922
- *see also:* FAMILY; YUḤASIN
Yiḥya Saliḥ, Mori, *see* SALIḤ,

YAḤYA BEN JOSEPH
YIḤYE, ISAAC HA-LEVI **16:**836
- Yemen **16:**746
Yiḥye, Shalom Isaac ha-Levi **16:**836
Yikkavu ha-Mayim (bk.) **11:**346
Yilag (soc.) **2:**410
Yinchwan (city, China), *see* NINGSIA
Yinnon (mosh., Isr.) **1:**place list
YINNON, MOSHE **16:**836
- *Haynt* **7:**1499
Yirei Shamayim (sect) **14:**1087
Yirkā (vill., Isr.) **9:**589
Yiron (kib., Isr.) **1:**place list
YISA (orgn.), *see* Yidishe Sotsiale Alleynhilf
Yiscah (bib. fig.) **14:**867
Yishar Kohakha (congratulations) **7:**914
Yish'i (mosh., Isr.) **1:**place list
YISHTABBAḤ (litur.) **16:**837
Yishuv (Er. Isr.)
- General
- - Arab National Movement **16:**1076
- - history **8:**757; **9:**282; **9:**322
- - Palestine partition **13:**35
- - seals **14:**1081
- - socialism **15:**51
- - Zionist Congresses **16:**1175
- Community
- - *aliyah* **2:**633ff
- - Ashkenazim **9:**497ff
- - Bilu **4:**998
- - defense **9:**681f
- - Diskin, Moses **6:**74
- - *ḥalukkah* **7:**1207
- - ḥasidic influx **7:**1392
- - "illegal" immigration **8:**1248
- - Nili **12:**1162ff
- - old and new **9:**326ff
- - Revisionists **14:**128
- - revival of Hebrew **4:**566ff
- - "Saison" **7:**1071; **9:**356
- - women **16:**628
- - yeshivot **16:**771
- Defense Forces
- - Haganah **7:**1064
- - I.Z.L. **8:**1466
- - Leḥi **11:**463
- Political Life
- - autonomy **3:**927
- - capitulations **5:**150
- - Jewish Agency **10:**26ff
- - jurisdiction **3:**299
- - Va'ad Le'ummi **16:**49
- *illus: kofer ha-yishuv* coupons **9:**355
Yishuv Ereẓ Israel movement (Rum.) **9:**1294; **16:**1132
Yismaḥ Moshe (stlmt., Isr.), *see* Kiryat Yismaḥ Moshe
Yismaḥ Moshe (folksong) **12:**409
Yisra'eli, Ḥayyim **3:**959
Yissa Berakhah, see ELYASHAR, JACOB SAUL BEN ELIEZER JEROHAM
Yissum Research Development Company (Isr.) **9:**972
Yissurin shel ahavah, see Afflictions of love
Yivo Annual of Jewish Social Science (period.) **16:**839
YIVO INSTITUTE FOR JEWISH RESEARCH **16:**837
- archives **3:**384
- Argentinian branch **3:**423
- historiography **8:**568
- learned societies **15:**55
- library **11:**192
- music **12:**658
- Rejzen, Zalman **14:**64
- Rivkind, Isaac **14:**199
- Shtif, Nahum **14:**1474
- Sutzkever, Abraham **15:**539
- Tcherikower, E. **15:**876
- Yiddish language **16:**797f
- *illus:* text
YIẒḤAKI, ABRAHAM BEN DAVID **16:**839
- Anau, Phineas Ḥai **2:**935
- Galante, Moses **7:**259
- Ḥayon, Nehemiah Ḥiyyu **7:**1501
YIẒḤAKI, DAVID **16:**840
Yiẓḥaki, Isaac **16:**840
Yiẓḥaki, Jacob **4:**387; **12:**479
Yiẓhar (bot.), *see* OILS
YIZHAR, S. **16:**840
- Hebrew literature **8:**204; **8:**206
Yiẓhari, *see* Gerondi, Berechiah ben Isaac ha-Levi
YIZKOR (memorial prayer) **16:**842
- *illus:*
- - Frankfort *Memorbuch* **11:**1300
- *see also:* ASHKAVAH; AV HA-RAḤAMIM; HAZKARAT NESHAMOT
YIZRE'EL (kib., Isr.) **16:**842
- statistics **1:**place list
Yizre'el (encyc.) **2:**478
Yizre'el (newsp.) **13:**494
Ykhnovich, Mary **11:**1567
YKUF, *see* YIDDISHER KULTUR FARBAND
Ylla, *see* Koffler, Camilla
Y. M. C. A. (Jer.) **9:**1473; **9:**1491; **11:**195
- *illus:*
- - view from King David Hotel **9:**1478
Y.M.H.A. (U.S.), *see* Young Men's Hebrew Association
Y.M.H.A. and K.A. (U.S.), *see* Council of Young Men's Hebrew and Kindred Associations
Yo'av, Operation (Isr. War of Indep.) **9:**371; **9:**1484; **14:**132; **16:**326,311
YOD (Heb. let.) **16:**843
- *see also:* ALPHABET, HEBREW
Yode'ei Ḥen (kab. conc.) **10:**494
Yodefat (fort., Er. Isr.), *see* JOTAPATA
Yodefat (kib., Isr.) **1:**place list
Yoel, *see* ALMANZI, JOSEPH
Yoelson, Asa, *see* JOLSON, AL
YOFFE, ALTER **16:**843
Yoffe, Avraham **14:**1629
YOFFE, MORDECAI **16:**843
YOFFEY (fam.) **16:**843
Yoffey, Israel Jacob ben Abraham ha-Kohen **16:**844
Yoffey, Joseph ben Moses **16:**843
Yoffey, Joseph Mendel **16:**844
Yofiel (angel) **10:**508
Yoga (Ind. practise) **10:**631
Yoḥana (leg. fig.), *see* JANNES AND JAMBRES
Yokhani (period.) **16:**903
- statistics **1:**newsp. list
Yokne'am (mosh., urb. stlmt., Isr.), *see* JOKNEAM
Yokohama (city, Jap.) **9:**1280f
Yolande (q., Prov.) **13:**1261
Yolles, P.E. **11:**1588
Yollos, G. B. **15:**1538
YOMA (tract.) **16:**844
- *illus:* text
Yom ha-Aẓma'ut, *see* INDEPENDENCE DAY, ISRAEL
Yom ha-Kaddish ha-Kelali (Memorial Day, Isr.) **8:**917
Yom ha-Kippurim, see DAY OF ATONEMENT
Yom ha-Kippurim (tract), *see* YOMA
Yom ha-Sho'ah, *see* HOLOCAUST REMEMBRANCE DAY
YOM HA-ZIKKARON (Remembrance Day, Isr.) **16:**846
- *illus:*
- - Israel stamp **9:**844-845
Yom Kippur, *see* DAY OF ATONEMENT
"Yom Kippur in the Country" (lith., Levy) **5:**1383
YOM KIPPUR KATAN (fastday) **16:**846
- *Ashamnu* **3:**694
- kabbalistic influence **10:**642
Yom Tov, *see* FESTIVALS
Yom Tov (tract.), *see* BEẒAH
Yom Tov, Jacob ben David, *see* Jacob ben David ben Yom Tov
YOM TOV BEN ABRAHAM ISHBILI (Ritba) **16:**846
- Alconstantini, Moses **2:**550
- *ḥiddushim* **8:**466; **11:**332
- Ibn Migash **8:**1189
- Naḥmanides **12:**778
- Rashba **2:**307
- responsa **14:**86
- taxation **15:**867
Yom Tov ben Isaac **13:**597
Yom-Tov ben Perez Ẓarfati **8:**1324
Yom Tov Kahana bar Jacob (gaon) **7:**318; **14:**545
Yom Tov Lipmann, *see* Lipmann, Yom Tov
Yom Tov of Falaise (tos.) **10:**351; **13:**1559
YOM TOV OF JOIGNY (paytan) **16:**848
- Jacob of Orleans **9:**1234
Yom-Tov of London **4:**483; **12:**427
Yom Tov Sheni shel Galuyyot, see FESTIVALS
Yom Yom (newsp.) **12:**1058
Yonah, Menahem Simḥah Emmanuel de **11:**610
Yonkers (tn., N.Y.) **12:**1127; **16:**464
Yontev Bletlakh (period.) **16:**339
Yoreh De'ah (code), *see* SHULḤAN ARUKH
Yoreh De'ah (wk.), *see Sefer ha-Musar* (Kaspi)
YORK (city, Eng.) **16:**849
- historical chart **8:**766-767
- massacre **5:**1140; **8:**669
- Yom Tov of Joigny **16:**848
- *illus:* text
York (city, Pa.) **13:**229
YORK-STEINER, HEINRICH ELCHANAN **16:**849
- *illus:*
- - F. Z. C. **16:**1165
Yorktown Heights (tn., N.Y.) **16:**464
YOSE (amora) **16:**850
Yose (savora) **14:**920
Yose Banai, see Yose ha-Banai
YOSE BAR ḤANINA (amora) **16:**850
- Aḥa **2:**435
- Avira **3:**975
- Eleazar ben Yose **6:**600
Yose bar Saul (tan.) **7:**1154
Yose bar Zevida (amora) **16:**850; **16:**852
Yose bei Rabbi **14:**1556
YOSE BEN AKAVYAH (tan.) **16:**851
- economic life **16:**1273
- masorah **16:**1412
YOSE BEN AVIN (amora) **16:**852
- Akhbarei **2:**487
- fixing of calendar **5:**49
YOSE BEN DORMASKOS (tan.) **16:**852
Yose ben Eleazar (tan.), *see* YOSE HA-GELILI
YOSE BEN ḤALAFTA (tan.) **16:**852
- Akiva **2:**489
- apologetics **3:**191
- decisions **5:**891
- Dostai ben Yannai **6:**179
- history **8:**554
- Joseph of Huẓal **8:**1137
- *Kelim* tractate **10:**900
- right and left **14:**182
- Satan **14:**903
- *Seder Olam Rabbah* **14:**1091
- Sepphoris academy **2:**202
- sons of **12:**807ff
- *illus:*
- - *Seder Olam Rabbah* **8:**559
YOSE BEN JOEZER OF ZEREDAH (tan.) **16:**853
- Alcimus **2:**549
YOSE BEN JOHANAN HA-TANNA OF JERUSALEM **16:**854
YOSE BEN JUDAH (tan.) **16:**854
- Johanan ben Zakkai **10:**151
YOSE BEN KIPPAR (tan.) **16:**855
- Dostai ben Yannai **6:**179
YOSE BEN KISMA (tan.) **16:**855
Yose ben Levi **15:**596
YOSE BEN MESHULLAM (tan.) **16:**855
- Holy Congregation **8:**919
Yose ben Samuel **7:**323
Yose ben Yose (amora) **16:**856
YOSE BEN YOSE (litur. poet) **16:**856
- Abudarham **2:**182
- *Attah Konanta Olam* **3:**977
- historical list **8:**766-767
- liturgical poetry **11:**326; **13:**574; **15:**915
- prosody **13:**1210
- Yannai **16:**714
YOSE BEN ZIMRA (tan. amora) **16:**857
- *Akedah* **14:**903
YOSEF, OVADIAH **16:**857
- responsa **14:**94
Yosef Da'at (period.) **1:**newsp. list; **2:**311; **13:**1039
Yosef ha-Mekanne, *see* OFFICIAL, NATHAN BEN JOSEPH AND JOSEPH
Yosefiah (pros., Fr.) **13:**1188
Yose the Greek (kab.) **2:**194
Yose ha-Banai **12:**1332; **14:**630
YOSE HA-GELILI (the Galilean; tan.) **16:**857
- afterlife **12:**1357
- *Baraita of 32 Rules* **4:**194
- *illus:*
- - *Rylands Spanish Haggadah* **6:***fcg.* 619
YOSE HA-KOHEN (tan.) **16:**858
Yose Katnuta (Katonta, tan.) **16:**851; **16:**859
Yosele Solovey (bk.) **14:**1278
Yoseloff, Thomas **12:**1122; **13:**1371
Yose of Heidelberg (13th cent., gram.) **10:**232
Yose of Peki'in (Zohar fig.) **13:**217
Yose of Yokrat (amora) **16:**852
Yosh (plwrt.) **6:**206
Yoshivyah (mosh., Isr.) **1:**place list
Yoske, Joseph **10:**790
Yotam, Ẓvi, *see* Iussim, Henrique
Yotbat-Yodpat (bib. fig.) **16:**951
YOTVATAH (kib., Isr.) **16:**859
- playas of **12:**927
- statistics **1:**place list
- *illus:*
- - text
- - vegetable fields **10:**964
Young, M. H. de **14:**834
Young, Michael de, *see* De Young, Michael
Young, Robert **8:**68
Young, W. T. **9:**1448
"Young Girl" (sculp., W. Lehmbruck) **13:**117
"Young Girl Asleep" (paint., S. Delaunay-Terk) **13:**117
Young Guard (orgn.), *see* Ha-Mishmeret ha-Ze'irah

Young Guard (period.) **7:**1376
Young Hebrews (polit. mvmt.), *see* CANAANITES
Young Israel (period. Eng.) **5:**456; **5:**460; **7:**905
Young Israel (period., U.S.) **5:**457
YOUNG ISRAEL, THE NATIONAL COUNCIL OF (U.S.) **16:**859
- New York **12:**1097
- study **15:**450
Young Israel Viewpoint (newsp.) **16:**860
Young Jewry (mag.) **5:**457
YOUNG JUDAEA (orgn.) **16:**860
- Israel **9:**981
- scouting **14:**1037
- *illus:* text
Young Judaean (mag.) **5:**457; **16:**860
Youngman, Moshe, *see* YUNGMAN, MOSHE
Young Men of Zion (lab. mvmt.), *see* ẒE'IREI ZION
Young Men's Hebrew and Benevolent Society (Can.) **14:**891
Young Men's Hebrew Association **5:**665; **12:**877,1079,1093,1121 **15:**586,1533
- historical chart **8:**766-767
Young Montreal, *see* Billingkoff, Morris
Young Otto, *see* Susskind, Arthur
YOUNGSTOWN (city, O.) **16:**861
- Ohio **12:**1344
Youngstown (cmty., Ariz.) **13:**482
Youngstown Jewish Times (newsp.) **16:**861
Young Turks (revol. mvmt.) **5:**1593; **9:**456; **16:**1074,1553
Young Vilna (lit. gr.), *see* YUNG VILNE
YOUTH ALIYAH (Zion. mvmt.) **16:**861
- Austria **3:**899
- Betar **4:**715
- Beyth's leadership **4:**785
- Freund, Miriam **7:**167
- Hadassah **7:**1044
- Israel immigration **9:**531; **9:**539ff
- kibbutz movement **10:**964ff
- Szold, Henrietta **15:**667
- *illus:* text
Youth Corps (Isr.), *see* GADNA
Youth movements
- Germany **7:**493
- periodicals **5:**459
- *illus:*
- - Iḥud Habonim (chart) **8:**1242
- - youth accepted for training (table) **9:**543
- *see also:* SCOUTING
YOUTH MOVEMENTS IN ISRAEL **9:**976
- Benei Akiva **4:**490
- Betar **4:**714
- Ha-No'ar ha-Oved veha-Lomed **7:**1275
- Ha-Shomer Ha-Ẓa'ir **7:**1372
- He-Ḥalutz **8:**247
- Iḥud Habonim **8:**1240
- kibbutz movement **10:**969
- labor movement **9:**869
- scouting **14:**1037ff
- students' movements **15:**450ff
- *illus:*
- - badges **9:**977
- - members (chart) **9:**981
Youth of Zion (lab. mvmt.), *see* ẒE'IREI ZION
YOUTIE, HERBERT CHAYYIM **16:**865
Yovel, *see* SABBATICAL YEAR AND JUBILEE
Yovon, Baruch **15:**267
YOZEROT (piyyutim) **16:**865
- *piyyut* **13:**598
Yozpa, Jepthah Joseph **16:**646
YSANDER, TORSTEN **16:**866
Yshmael Haramḥi **2:**511; **14:**756
Ysleta (vill., Tex.) **15:**1036
Ytreberg, Nils A. **14:**933
Yuçaf de Ecija **15:**1203
YUD, NAHUM **16:**867
- Yiddish literature **16:**822
YUDAN (amora) **16:**867
Yudan ben Misatya ha-Kohen **13:**597
Yudel (ḥas. ldr.) **12:**784
Yudelevitch, David, *see* IDELOVITCH, DAVID
YUDGHAN (Yehudah; sect., Iran) **16:**867
- Judah ha-Parsi **10:**372
- Karaites **10:**764
- messianism **11:**1422
- Persia **13:**309
Yudin, T. I. **13:**1340
Yudlin, Vitali, *see* EISENSTADT, ISAIAH
YUDKIN, JOHN **5:**389
Yudkovitch (writ.), *see* TASHRAK
Yudubin (Yudovin), Shlomo **4:**1219; **12:**540; **16:**192
- *illus:*
- - "Old Synagogue" **14:**1469
- - St. Petersburg Jewish Ethnographical Expedition **12:**541
- - "Shoemaker" **14:**1468
Yuedels, Isaac ben Judah Loeb, *see* Isaac ben Judah Loeb Yuedels
Yugend (almanac) **6:**801
YUGOSLAVIA **16:**868
- *Contents:*
- - Until 1918 **16:**868
- - After 1918 **16:**873
- - Holocaust Period **16:**874
- - Contemporary Period **16:**881
- - Relations with Israel **16:**883
- General
- - historical list **8:**766-767
- - Israel relations **9:**428ff
- - minority treaty **12:**45ff
- - publishing **13:**1369
- - U.N. resolutions **15:**1557
- - UNSCOP **15:**1688
- Community
- - organization **5:**827
- - synagogues **1:**syn. list
- - Zionism **16:**1148ff
- Holocaust **8:**851ff
- - Church and Nazism **8:**915
- - partisans **13:**140; **13:**147
- - Pavelić, Ante **13:**192
- - Sephardim **14:**1172
- - War Crimes Trials **16:**289ff
- *illus:*
- - text
- - Jewish partisan unit **13:**146; **16:**885
- *pop. tables:* text
YUGOSLAV LITERATURE **16:**885
- *Contents:*
- - Biblical and Hebraic Influences **16:**885
- - Image of the Jew **16:**886
- - The Jewish Contribution **16:**887
- - Later Trends **16:**888
- - Jewish Themes **16:**889
- - Capsules **16:**890
- children's magazines **5:**457
- encyclopedias **6:**735
Yugoslav Zionist Federation **16:**1148
YUḤASIN (pedigrees) **16:**891
- priests **13:**1088ff
- Sanhedrin **14:**837
- *see also:* FAMILY; YIḤUS
Yulee (fam.), *see* YULY
YULEE, DAVID LEVY **16:**894
- Florida **6:**1361
- Levy, Moses Elias **11:**162
- *illus:* text
YULY (fam.) **16:**895
- Morocco **12:**339
Yuly, Elijah **16:**895
Yuly, Judah (18th cent.) **16:**895
Yuly, Judah (19th cent.) **16:**895
Yuly, Moses **16:**895
Yuly, Samuel **16:**895
Yuman (Ind. tribe, N. Am.) **15:**274
YUNGE, DI (lit. mvmt.) **16:**896
- In-zikh **8:**1434
- Leivick, H. **10:**1595
- Tepper, Kolya **15:**1013
- Yiddish literature **16:**814
Yunger Leninetz (period.) **13:**1048
Yunge Skauten (youth mvmt., Arg.) **8:**1243
YUNGMAN, MOSHE **16:**896
Yung Theater (Pol.) **15:**1072
YUNG VILNE (lit. gr.) **16:**896
- Yiddish literature **16:**819
Yung-Yidish (lit. gr.) **4:**1392
Yung Yidish (period.) **2:**280; **16:**816
Yung Yisroel (period.) **16:**896
Yūnis, ʿAbd **9:**1039
Yunis, Bathsheba **11:**1203
YUNKERS, ADJA **3:**613
Yūnus (bib. fig.), *see* Jonah
Yuryev (city, Est.), *see* TARTU
Yūshaʿ ibn Nūn (bib. fig.), *see* JOSHUA
YUSHKEVICH, SEMYON SOLOMONOVICH **16:**897
Yussufzai (Afghan tribe) **2:**326
Yust, Joseph **15:**1532
Yūsuf (bib. fig.), *see* JOSEPH
Yusuf (15th cent., Const.) **15:**1205
Yūsuf, Al-Malik al-Nāṣir **9:**1423
Yusuf al-ʿAskarī (Samar.) **14:**754
Yūsuf al-Baṣīr, *see* BAṢĪR, JOSEPH BEN ABRAHAM HA-KOHEN HA-RO'EH AL-
YŪSUF 'AS'AR YATH'AR DHU NŪWĀS (MASRŪQ) **16:**897
- Arabia **3:**236
- Eldad ha-Dani **6:**577
- Sabea **14:**587
Yusuf ibn Tāshfīn **2:**667; **15:**226
Yūsuf Yahūdi **10:**432
Yutah (vill., Er. Isr.) **10:**943
Yutar, Percy **10:**1502; **15:**205
Yuval (mosh., Isr.) **1:**place list
Yuval (journ.) **1:**newsp. list
Yuval (publ. firm) **12:**659; **13:**1374
Yuzovka (city, Ukr.,), *see* DONETSK
Yvel, Albert **15:**306
Y. Zeh, *see* ZMORA, YISRAEL

Z

Zaanaim (Zaananim; bib. pl.) **10:**907
Za'ar Ba'alei Hayyim (hal. conc.) **3:**6
Zabadānī Valley (Isr.) **9:**181
Zabaḥ, Isaac **4:**1461
Zabala, Bruno Mauricio de **16:**10
Zabara (fam.) **4:**701
Zabeilus (Arab ldr.) **2:**577
Zabern (tn., Fr.), *see* SAVERNE
Zabīd (tn., Yem.) **16:**898
Zabler, Jób **8:**68
Zabłotów (tn., Ukr.), *see* ZABOLOTOV
ZABLUDOW (tn., Pol.) **16:**901
- *illus:*
- - synagogue **15:**611
ZABOLOTOV (tn., Ukr.) **16:**901
Zabrody (tn., Pol.) **12:**186
ZABRZE (city, Pol.) **16:**903
Zabud (bib. fig.) **13:**1071ff
ZACH, NATHAN **16:**903
Zachanin (fief, Isr.) **14:**1530
Zachariah, Isaac **5:**505; **12:**1128
Zachariah al-Ḍahiri, *see* ZECHARIAH AL-DĀHIRI
Zacharias (7th cent., patr.) **9:**1407 **9:**1407
ZACHARIAS, JERROLD REINACH **16:**903
ZACHARIAS, JOHN **15:**1092
Zack, Léon **13:**115; **13:**117
Zack, S. **13:**1378
Zacks, Samuel **15:**1264; **16:**1111
Zacuth, Abraham, *see* ZACUTUS LUSITANUS
Zacuto (fam.) **2:**614
ZACUTO, ABRAHAM BEN SAMUEL **16:**903
- Aboab, Isaac **2:**93
- astronomy **3:**802; **3:**805
- historical list **8:**766-767
- Jewish history **11:**349
- medicine **11:**1191
- museum named for **15:**1213
- nautical instruments **14:**1413
- *Sefer Yuḥasin* **8:**268, 556
- Tunisia **15:**1441
- *illus:*
- - text
- - autograph **3:**918
- - calendar conversion chart (1568) **5:**53
ZACUTO, MOSES BEN MORDECAI **16:**906
- Basilea, Solomon **4:**299
- Benjamin of Reggio **4:**531
- drama **6:**194; **11:**328
- Gediliah, Abraham **7:**354
- Kabbalah **10:**553; **10:**641
- poetry **13:**691
- Shabbateanism **14:**1235
Zacuto, Samuel **16:**904
ZACUTUS LUSITANUS **16:**909
- Amsterdam **2:**896
- medicine **11:**1191
- *illus:* text
ẒADDIK (righteous man) **16:**910
- General
- - community leadership **8:**723ff
- - fall of **6:**662
- - genealogy **7:**383
- - Ḥabad **7:**1013; **14:**1436ff
- - Ḥasidism **7:**1393ff
- - kabbalistic role **10:**494
- - Naḥman of Bratslav **12:**782,786
- - piety **13:**504
- - resurrection **14:**99
- Views on
- - Apta, Meir **3:**224
- - Ba'al Shem Tov **9:**1055
- - Baruch of Medzibozh **4:**279
- - Dov Baer of Mezhirech **6:**182ff
- - Dynow, Ẓevi **6:**332
- - Elimelech of Lyzhansk **6:**661ff
- - Jacob of Lublin **9:**1228
- - Jacob of Polonnoye **9:**1229
- *see also:* ADMOR; RIGHTEOUSNESS
Ẓaddik (kab. conc.) **10:**570ff
ẒADDIK, JOSEPH BEN JACOB IBN **16:**911
- attributes of God **7:**659
- categories **5:**254
- form and matter **6:**1438
- Maimonides **11:**769
- microcosm doctrine **11:**1502
- nature **12:**889
- Neoplatonism **12:**960; **12:**961
- philosophy **13:**437
- problem of evil **7:**777
- prosody **13:**1218
- soul **15:**172
- soul immortality **15:**177
- translations **15:**1323
Ẓade (Heb. let.), *see* ṢADE
Zadek, Adolph **5:**1545
Zadek, Frederick **5:**1543
Zadek, Hyman **5:**1543
Zadik, Don Solomon **7:**1345
ZADIKOW, ARNOLD **16:**913
- art **3:**575
- *illus:* text
ZADKINE, OSSIP **16:**914
- *illus:*
- - "Heroic Orpheus" (sculp.) **14:**1063
Zadok (bib. fig.; h. pr.)
- Abiathar **2:**71ff
- Ahitub **2:**466
- Eleazar **6:**584
- founder of Zadokites **16:**915
- in the Arts **15:**110
- Nathan **12:**846
- priesthood **13:**1072ff
- Solomon **15:**96
Zadok (bib. fig.; scribe) **15:**957
Zadok (disciple of Antigonus) **14:**620
ZADOK (1st cent., tan.) **16:**914
Zadok II (1st cent., s. of Eliezer) **16:**915
Ẓadok (12th cent., schol.) **2:**224
Zadok (15/16 cent., r.) **10:**228
Zadok (fam.) **15:**1201
Zadok, Ḥayyim **9:**676, 677
Zadok bar Mar Yishi **7:**317
Zadok ben Josiah **12:**857
Zadok ben Shemariah **10:**373; **14:**1247
ẒADOK HA-KOHEN OF LUBLIN **16:**915
Zadokite Fragments (wk.), *see* DAMASCUS, BOOK OF COVENANT OF
ZADOKITES **16:**915
- asceticism **3:**680
- Cairo *genizah* **16:**1335
- Dead Sea sect **5:**1412
- Qumran community **6:**66
- seekers **14:**1096
- Teacher of Righteousness **15:**885
- term for Christian **7:**411
- Wicked Priest **16:**486
- Yaḥad community **16:**699
ZADOK THE PHARISEE **16:**916
- messianism **11:**1420
- Zealot revolt **16:**947
Zadok the Physician **15:**1172
Ẓafār (anc. loc., Yem.) **16:**897ff
Ẓafenat Pa'ne'aḥ (wk.) **15:**520
Zafrana, Abraham ben Gabriel **13:**575
Ẓafririm (mosh., Isr.) **1:**place list
Ẓafriyyah (mosh., Isr.) **1:**place list
ZAGARE (tn., Lith.) **16:**916
Zagayski, Michael **4:**976; **5:**311
Zager (tn., Lith.), *see* ZAGARE
Zagłebia (concen. camp) **10:**1309
Zagora (vill., Mor.) **12:**327
Zagorodski, Y. **15:**86
Żagory (tn., Lith.), *see* ZAGARE
ZAGREB (city, Yug.) **16:**917
- Pavelić, Ante **13:**192
- Yugoslavia **16:**870
- *illus:* text
Zaglembia (tn., Pol.) **10:**1310
Zagury, Yaḥia **5:**224
Zagzagael (angel) **2:**968
Zahal, *see* DEFENCE FORCES OF ISRAEL
Ẓahalah (sub., Tel Aviv) **15:**923
Ẓahallal ben Nethanel Gaon **16:**787
ẒAHALON (fam.) **16:**919
Ẓahalon, Abraham ben Isaac **16:**919
Ẓahalon, Jacob ben Isaac **16:**919
- bloodletting **4:**1119
- medicine **11:**1194
Zahalon, Mordecai ben Jacob **2:**935; **16:**919
Ẓahalon, Yom Tov benAkiva **16:**919
Ẓahalon, Yom Tov ben Moses **2:**189, 596; **16:**919
Zahavi, David **12:**670
Ẓāhir, al- (11th cent., caliph) **6:**1197; **9:**262
Ẓāhir, al-Malik al- (12/13 cent.) **3:**998
Ẓāhir al-Omar **2:**188, 224, 398; **9:**290ff; **15:**1133
Ẓāhir Sayf-al-Dīn Jaqmaq, al-, *see* Jaqmaq, al-Ẓāhir Sayf-al-Dīn
Zahīrt (tn., Iraq) **8:**1449
Zāhirz Zakariyyā al-, *see* Zakariyyā al-Zāhirz
Zaḥot (wk.), *see Sefer Zaḥot*
Ẓaḥut ha-lashon (lang. conc.) **16:**1614ff
Ẓaḥzaḥot ("splendors"), *see* Three Lights
Zaʿīm, Ḥusnī al- **15:**646
Zaire, Republic of, *see* CONGO, DEMOCRATIC REPUBLIC OF
Zaitchikoff, Chaim **11:**1555
Zaitsev (fam.) **10:**993
Zajednica (period.) **16:**888
Zak, Baruch Joseph **10:**1125
ZAK, EUGÈNE **3:**614
- art **13:**120
Zak, Jacob, *see* JACOB BEN BENJAMIN ZE'EV
Zakar-Baal (k., Byblos) **16:**658
Zakariyyā al-Ẓāhirż **8:**1463
Zakarpatskaia oblast (reg., Ukr.), *see* SUBCARPATHIAN RUTHENIA
Zakay, David **5:**1316
Zaken ha-Yehudim (tit., Tun.) **5:**817; **12:**764; **15:**1441
ZAKEN MAMRE **16:**920
- punishment purpose **13:**1387
- warning **13:**227
Zakhar (gram. term.) **16:**1422
Zakharov, Marshal **14:**1638
ZAKHO (tn., Kurd.) **16:**920
- Kurdish Jews **8:**1456
Zakhor, Shabbat, see Shabbat Zakhor
Zakhu (tn., Kurd.), *see* ZAKHO
Zakir (anc. k.) **10:**1015; **16:**666
Zakkai (tan.) **5:**2
Zakkai (Babyl. exil.) **4:**1537
Zakkai ben Azariah **3:**999
- Basra **8:**1447
- Mosul **12:**444
Zakkay, Benjamin Aaron **12:**1465
Zaks, Moshe **16:**1148
Ẓalaḥ, Joseph **10:**553

Ẓalaḥ, Yehaiah ben Joseph **13:**989; **14:**90
Zalcman, Shmuel **5:**484
ZALESHCHIKI (city, Ukr.) **16:**921
Zalis, Henri **14:**423
Zalizky, Moshe, *see* CARMEL, MOSHE
Zalman, Ephraim **6:**251
Zalman ben Ze'ev **6:**232
Zalman Nakdan, *see* Jekuthiel ben Isaac ha-Kohen
Zalmati, Solomon
- books **4:**1233
- Híjar **8:**474
- incunabula **8:**1325
- Játiva **9:**1300
Ẓalmona, Joseph **5:**373
Ẓalmon River (Isr.) **9:**151; **9:**171
Zalmunna (bib. fig.), *see* ZEBAH AND ZALMUNNA
Zalozhtsy, Simḥah ben Joshua of, *see* SIMḤAH BEN JOSHUA OF ZALOZHTSY
Zaltman, Moses ben Judah **10:**721
Zaltman, Ẓevi, *see* Yehudah, Ẓevi
ZALUDKOWSKI, ELIJAH **7:**1551
Zaludkowski, Noah **7:**1551
Zaluszowska, Catherine, *see* WEIGEL, CATHERINE
Zalutsky, P. **5:**794
ZAM, ZVI HERZ **16:**921
- military service **11:**1555
ZAMARIS (1st. cent., sol.) **16:**922
- Trachonitis **15:**1293
ZAMBIA (Afr. rep.) **16:**922
- relations with Israel **9:**443
- synagogues **1:**syn. list
Zambri (4th cent., magician) **13:**852
ZAMBROW (Zambrov; tn., Pol.) **16:**923
Zambrowski, Joshua **16:**925
ZAMBROWSKI, ROMAN **16:**924
ZAMBROWSKY, TSEMACH MENACHEM **16:**925
- Mizrachi **12:**179
- *sheḥita* **5:**107
ZAMENHOF, LUDWIK LAZAR **16:**925
- *illus:*
- - text
- - autograph **3:**918
ZAMENHOF, STEPHEN **11:**1211
Zametkin, Laura, *see* HOBSON, LAURA Z.
Zamir, Emanuel **12:**670
Zamir, Ẓvi **13:**48
Zamir choir (Mex.) **11:**1459
Zammārīn (site, Isr.) **16:**1019
Zammatto, Aiessandro **13:**12
Zamojski, Jan **16:**926
ZAMORA (city, Sp.) **16:**926
- La Guardia, Holy Child of **10:**1359
Zamora, Andreas de León **8:**68
ZAMOSC (city, Pol.) **16:**926
- *illus:*
- - text
- - deportation **4:**454
ZAMOSC, DAVID **16:**928
- children's literature **5:**431
ZAMOSC, ISRAEL BEN MOSES HALEVI **16:**929
- Ḥasidism **7:**1417
- Moses Mendelssohn **11:**1329
ZAMZUMMIM (bib. gr.) **16:**929
Zandberg, Yitzhak **15:**1072
Zandvoort (vill., Neth.) **7:**1008
Zandz (ḥas. dyn.), *see* HALBERSTAM
Zanetti (Zanetius; fam.) **13:**1099
- *illus:*
- - *She'elot u-Teshuvot*, Bezalel Ashkenazi, (1595) **3:**724
Zanetti, Francesco **14:**252
Zangen (mil. farm, Rus.) **8:**250
Zangen (journ.) **10:**821
ZANGWILL, ISRAEL **16:**930
- Ayrton, Hertha **3:**997
- *Badḥan* **4:**75
- Churchill **5:**555
- Cowen, Joseph **5:**1024
- history chart **8:**766-767
- Imber, Naphtali **8:**1290
- I.T.O. **16:**1069
- Territorialism **15:**1019ff
- Zionist Congress (7th) **16:**1169
- *illus:*
- - autograph **3:**918
- - portrait **6:**784
Zangwill, Louis **16:**932
Zangwill, Moses **16:**930
Zangwill, Oliver Louis **16:**932
Zanjābad (tn., Iraq), *see* Kifri
ZANOAH (Bib. cities) **16:**933
Zanoah (mosh., Isr.) **16:**933
- statistics **1:**place list
Zanolini, Antonio **8:**68
Zanta (10th cent., moneyer) **12:**60
ZANTE (isl., Gr.) **16:**933
Zanvil, Samuel **15:**439
Zanz (ḥas. dyn.), *see* HALBERSTAM
Zanzibar (rep., Afr.), *see* Tanzania, United Republic of
Zaphenath-Paneah (bib. fig.), *see* JOSEPH
ZAPHON (city, Er.Isr.) **16:**934
- Tell al Sa'idiyya **16:**937
- Transjordan **15:**1316
ZAPOROZHE (city, Ukr.) **16:**934
Zaprudy (labor camp) **10:**1123
Zaqef (cantillation sign) **16:**1439
Zaqef gadol (cantillation sign) **16:**1424,1430
Zaqef qaṭan (cantillation sign) **16:**1454
Zar, Mordekhai **11:**1400
Zar'a (Samar. h. pr.) **6:**314
Zaragoza (city, Sp.), *see* SARAGOSSA
Zarai, Yoḥanan **9:**1591
ZARASAI (city, Lith.) **16:**935
Zarchi, A.L. **11:**522
ZARCHI, ISRAEL **16:**935
ZARCHIN, ALEXANDER **16:**935
- *illus:*
- - Eilat desalination plant **9:**772
ZARCO, JUDAH **16:**936
Zardiāwa (tn., Iraq) **15:**504
Zardiel, Moses, *see* ABZARDIEL, MOSES
Zarefati (name), *see also:* Sarfati; Sarfaty; Sarphati; Serfaty; Ẓarfati
Ẓarefati, Joseph (art.), *see* JOSEPH HA-ẒAREFATI
Ẓarefati, Joseph ben Samuel, *see* Sarfati, Joseph (Josiphon)
Ẓarefati, Raphael ben Joshua **13:**12
Zarekhanut Shittufit (journ.) **1:**newsp. list
ZAREPHATH (city, Isr.) **16:**936
Zarepath, widow of (bib. fig.) **6:**640
ZARETHAN (site, Isr.) **16:**936
- metals and mining **11:**1432
- Transjordan **15:**1316
Zaretski, Joseph **12:**1127
ZARETZKI, ISAAC **16:**937
Zarfati (name), *see also:* Sarfati; Sarfaty; Sarphati; Serfaty; Ẓarefati
Zarfati, Abraham (17/18 cent.) **2:**310 **4:**407
Ẓarfati, Abraham ben Solomon (15/16 cent.) **15:**1377
Ẓarfati, Isaac **2:**309; **5:**860
- Ottoman Empire **16:**1532
- pilgrimage **9:**280
Ẓarfati, Joseph Ḥayyim ben Aaron Strasbourg **18:**1323
Ẓarfati, Mordecai ben Ruben **8:**1324
Zarfati, Perez, *see* Trabot, Perez
Zarfati, Reuben **10:**540
Zarfati, Solomon ben Pereẓ **8:**1324
Zarfati, Solomon ben Pereẓ Bonfroi **8:**1324
Ẓarfati, Yom-Tov ben Pereẓ, *see* Yom-Tov ben Pereẓ Ẓarfati
Zarḥi, Simeon **9:**1333
Ẓarīf al-Ṭūl (Arab poetry) **9:**1038
ZARISKI, OSCAR **16:**937
Zar'it (vill., Isr.) **7:**270
ZARITSKY, MAX **16:**938
ZARITSKY, YOSSEF **16:**938
- *illus:*
- - "Jerusalem" (wtrcl.) Pl. 3 **3-**ART
Zark, Judah **13:**563
Zarka, Joseph ben Isaac **16:**939
Zarka, Solomon **5:**1306
Zarkal (astron., Sp.) **15:**1200
Zarkhy, Alexander **12:**456
ZARKO (Zarka), JOSEPH BEN JUDAH **16:**939
- linguistics **16:**1388
Zarlin (site, Isr.), *see* JEZREEL
Zaromb, S. **16:**819
Zarphatic (lang.), *see* JUDEO-FRENCH
Zarqā (tn., Jor.) **9:**472; **9:**596
Zarqa' (cantillation sign) **16:**1440,1454
Zarqā Ma'īn River (Isr.) **9:**164
Zarqā River, *see* JABBOK
Zarudny, A.S. **4:**400
ZARZA, SAMUEL IBN SENEH **16:**939
ZARZAL (Zarzab), ABRAHAM IBN **16:**939
Zarzal, Pharez ben Abraham ibn **16:**939
Zarzecze (loc., Pol.) **12:**1512
Zasanie (city, Pol.) **13:**1299
Zasavica (vill., Yug.) **16:**876
Zasio, András **8:**68
Zaskovitzer, Samuel ben Joseph, *see* STRASHUN, SAMUEL BEN JOSEPH
Zaslani, Reuben, *see* SHILOAḤ, REUBEN
Zaslavl (city, Ukr.), *see* IZYASLAV
Zaslavl case **3:**200
Zaslavski **11:**431
ZASLAVSKY, DAVID **16:**940
Zaslavsky, Rudolf **15:**1073
Zaslaw (concen. camp) **14:**844
Zaslofsky, Max **15:**303
Zasmir, Jekuthiel Asher Zalman Ansel **15:**387
Zastavna (tn., Ukr.) **16:**940
ZATEC (tn., Bohem.) **16:**941
Zatolovsky, Devorah, *see* Dayan, Devorah
Zatzman, Joseph **11:**998
Zauba'a (demon) **5:**1532
Zav (male impurity) **13:**1405; **16:**941
Zavah (female impurity) **12:**1142; **13:**1405
Zavdi'el (mosh., Isr.) **1:**place list
Zavertse (city, Pol.), *see* ZAWIERCIE
ZAVIM (mish. tract) **16:**941
Zavit (gr., Isr.) **15:**1062
Zavodiel (kab. name) **10:**504
Ẓavva'at Rabbi Eliezer (bk.), *see* ORḤOT ḤAYYIM
Ẓavva'at Rabbi Yehudah he-Ḥasid (wk.) **10:**352
Zawadski, Peter **16:**342
Zawarnice (concen. camp) **16:**1218
Zawāyā (Musl. inst.) **9:**918,1424
Zawichost (tn., Pol.) **8:**893
ZAWIERCIE (city, Pol.) **16:**942
- Wolbrom **16:**602
Zāxó dialect **12:**949
ZAY, JEAN **13:**831
Zayantshik, Elijah Ḥayyim **13:**135
Zaydi (Isl. dyn.) **16:**741ff
Zaydl Rovner, *see* MOROGOWSKI, JACOB SAMUEL
Zayen, Yusuf, *see* Zu'ayin, Yusuf
Zayet, Isaac **5:**265
ZAYIN (Heb. let.) **16:**943
Zaynab (Isl. fig.) **2:**667; **10:**943; **11:**971
Zaynab of Aghmāt (11th cent.) **2:**667
Zayyafi (agg. fig.) **15:**71
ẒAYYAḤ, JOSEPH BEN ABRAHAM IBN **16:**943
- Kabbalah **10:**543
Zbara, Nathan **10:**997
ZBARAZH (tn., Ukr.) **16:**944
Zbaszyń (concen. camp) **16:**166
Zbitkower, Ber, *see* Sonnenberg, Ber
Zbitkower, Judith **16:**945
ZBITKOWER, SAMUEL **16:**944
- Bergson family **4:**618
ZBOROV (city, Ukr.) **16:**945
- special Purim **13:**1399
ZDUNSKA-WOLA (tn., Pol.) **16:**945
Zdzięciól (tn., Belor.), *see* DYATLOVO
Zeal, *see* JEALOUSY
ZEALOTS (sect) **16:**947
- Abba Sikra **2:**44
- African refuge **2:**331
- Alexander **2:**587
- Anan **2:**919
- Ben Ẓiẓit ha-Kassat **4:**576
- Herod I **8:**384
- Johanan ben Zakkai **10:**152
- Josephus and Cyrene revolt **10:**254
- lots, casting of **11:**512
- Masada **11:**1078ff
- Phinehas **9:**1306; **16:**1026
- Qumran Sect **14:**327
- warfare **16:**280
- Yaḥad community **16:**701
- *illus:*
- - Masada *mikveh* **11:**1087
- *see also:* PHARISEES; SICARII
Zebadiah son of Asahel (bib. fig.) **3:**672
Zebadiah son of Ishmael (bib. fig.) **9:**1327
ZEBAH AND ZALMUNNA (bib. fig.) **16:**950
- Judges, Book of **10:**447
Zebid (tn., Yem.), *see* Zabid
ZEBIDAH (fam.) **16:**950
Zebidah, Abraham ben Judah **16:**950
Zebidah, Isaac **16:**950
Zebidah, Jacob ben Isaac **16:**950
Zebidah, Judah **16:**950
Zebidah, Yosef **16:**950
Zeboiim (bib. loc.) **15:**70
Zebra **6:** 32
"Zebras" (M. Hirshfield) **3:**629
Zebudah (bib. fig.) **14:**386; **16:**951
Zebul (bib. fig.) **2:**77
ZEBULUN (bib.fig., tribe) **16:**950
- blessing **15:**1385
- breastplate stone **13:**1008
- fisherman **6:**1326
- *ḥillazon* **15:**913
- Issachar **9:**1075ff
- Nabī Sabālan **8:**1113; **8:**936
- settlement of tribe **8:**580
- shipping **14:**1411
- tomb of **14:**1508
- *illus:* text
Zebulun (sailing gr., Isr.) **9:**1019
Zebulun, Testament of (Pseudepig.), *see* PATRIARCHS, TESTAMENTS OF THE TWELVE
Zebulun Valley **9:**292; **9:**572; **9:**579ff
- *see also:* HAIFA; JEZREEL, VALLEY OF
ZECHARIAH (bib. fig., h. pr.) **16:**952
- Nebuzardan **12:**919
ZECHARIAH (bib. fig., k.) **16:**953
- assassination **8:**602

- history chart **8**:766-767
- Ibleam **8**:1151
ZECHARIAH (bib. fig., son of Jeberechiah) **16**:953
ZECHARIAH (bk.; prophet) **16**:953
- *Contents:*
- - Chapters 1-8 **16**:953
- - Chapters 9-14 **16**:956
- - In Later Sources **16**:958
- - In the Aggadah **16**:958
- ass **3**:784
- eschatology **6**:869ff
- messianic figures **11**:1409
- Minor Prophets **12**:48
- rebuilding of Temple **16**:1001
- Satan **14**:902
- tomb **3**:358; **12**:484; **13**:522
- *illus:*
- - text
- - *Cervera Bible* **16**:*fcg.* 935
- - *menorah* in Zechariah's vision **2**:642
- - tomb **3**:339; **9**:1392; **13**:513; **15**:1221
Zechariah (tax-farmer) **15**:873
Zechariah (physic., Babyl.) **11**:1183
ZECHARIAH AL-ḌĀHIRI **16**:959
- Mansurah, Sa'adiah **11**:894
- Yemen **16**:745
Zechariah ben Ali **2**:631
ZECHARIAH BEN AVKILUS **16**:959
- emperor worship **6**:585
- Kamza legend **10**:732
ZECHARIAH BEN BARACHEL **16**:960
- Aleppo **2**:562
- *gaon* **7**:321
- Maimonides **11**:746
- Samuel ben Ali **14**:803
Zechariah ben ha-Kazzav **4**:835
Zechariah ben Joseph **3**:1009
Zechariah ben Saadiah **5**:55
Zechariah ben Saʿīd al-Yamanī, *see* Yamanī, Zechariah ben Saʿid al-
ZECHARIAH BEN SOLOMON-ROFE **16**:960
ZECHARIAH MENDEL BEN ARYEH LEIB **16**:960
Zechariah Mendel ben David of Lissa **5**:1353
Zechariah Meshullam (bib. fig.) **16**:958
Zechariah Zaksel Ashkenazi **5**:194
Zeckendorf (fam.) **3**:450
Zedad (loc., Cana.) **5**:100
Zedakah (paytan) **13**:597
ẒEDAKAH (charity) **16**:961
- charity **5**:340ff
- permissible hatred **7**:1473
- Sodom **15**:70
- *Solomon, Wisdom of* **15**:119ff
- *see also:* RIGHTEOUSNESS
Ẓedakah ben Judah **12**:424
Ẓedakah gedolah, see Community Chest
Zedek, see JUSTICE
ZEDEKIAH (bib. fig., k.) **16**:961
- Book of Lamentations **10**:1370
- Elnathan ben Achbor **6**:684
- history **8**:608
- history chart **8**:766-767
- in the Arts **12**:917
- Jeremiah **9**:1351
- Psametic II **12**:920
- slavery **14**:1657
- *geneal. table:* **5**:1341
ZEDEKIAH (bib. fig., s. of Chenaanah) **16**:964
ZEDEKIAH (bib. fig., s. of Maaseiah) **16**:964
- Ahab ben Kolaiah **2**:439
- Babylonian exile **6**:1037
Zedekias (9th cent., physic.) **11**:1187
ZEDERBAUM, ALEXANDER **16**:964
- *Ha-Meliẓ* **7**:1232
- *Kol Mevasser* **10**:1165
- Kovner, Abraham Uri **8**:1369
- Lifshits, Shiye-Mordkhe **11**:237
- Society for the Promotion of Culture **15**:58ff
- *illus:*
- - Odessa Committee convention **12**:1329
- - Kattowitz Conference **10**:820
Zederbaum, Joseph **16**:927
ZEDNER, JOSEPH **16**:965
- Asher, Abraham **3**:702
Ẓedoki (sectarian), *see* MIN
Ẓedukim (sect), *see* SADDUCEES
Zeeb (Midianite princ.), *see* OREB AND ZEEB
ZE'EIRA (amora) **16**:966
- Abba **2**:30
- Abba bar Zemina **2**:33
Ze'eir anpin (kab. conc.) **10**:569; **10**:599
Ze'elim (loc., Isr.) **9**:772
- statistics **1**:place list
ZE'ENAH U-RE'ENAH (wk.) **16**:967
- Crehange, Alexander **5**:1072
- Jewish literature **11**:357
- Yiddish literature **16**:801
Ze'ev (cart.), *see* Farkas, Yaacov
Ze'ev, Aaron **5**:437
Ze'ev, Jehiel **13**:16
Ze'ev ben Judah Leib **13**:666
Ze'ev ben Samuel **12**:1359
Ze'evi, Ḥayyim Abraham Israel **2**:672; **14**:378
- Azulai, Isaac **3**:1016
Ẓe'evi, Raḥavam **13**:48
Ze'ev Wolf ben Abraham of Strykow **5**:561
Ze'ev Wolf ben Judah **10**:350
Ze'ev Wolf of Zbaraz **9**:514
ZE'EV WOLF OF ZHITOMIR **16**:968
Zefa-Efʿeh (site, Isr.) **9**:595,809; **12**:930
Ẓefat (tn., Isr.), *see* SAFED
ZEFIRA, BRACHAH **16**:968
Zegbib, Masʿūd **5**:915
Zehner, David **6**:1329; **13**:833
Zehner, Sarah, *see* Fishel, Sarah
Zeichik, H.H. **14**:955
ZEICHNER, OSCAR **8**:551
ZEID, ALEXANDER **16**:968
- *illus:* text
Ẓeidah la-Derekh (wk.) **15**:520
Zein, Joshua **12**:907
Zeira (amora), *see* ZE'EIRA
ZEIRA, MORDECHAI **16**:969
Ze'ir anpin (conc.), *see Ze'eir anpin*
Ẓe'irei Agudat Israel (mvmt.) **2**:421
- *illus:*
- - Jaroslaw conference, 1932 **9**:1289
Ze'irei ha-Mizrachi (orgn.) **10**:1398; **16**:1114
ẒE'IREI ZION (mvmt.) **16**:970
- Ha-Shomer ha-Ẓa'ir **7**:1372
- He-Ḥalutz **8**:247
- labor **10**:1331
- socialism, Jewish **15**:50
- Warsaw **16**:338
- world movement **16**:639
- *illus:*
- - Riga group **10**:1466
- *see also:* Z.S.
ZE'IRI (ben Ḥinna; amora) **16**:972
Ze'irim (Cath. order) **7**:47
Zeisler, Fanny, *see* BLOOMFIELD-ZEISLER, FANNY
Zeist (tn., Holl.) **16**:37
ZEIT, DIE (newsp.) **16**:973
- press **13**:1031
Zeitan (mosh., Isr.) **1**:place list
Zeitgeist (publ. house, Ger.) **13**:549
ZEITLIN, AARON **16**:973
- Hebrew literature **8**:214
- Shakespeare **14**:1265
- Yiddish literature **16**:820
ZEITLIN, HILLEL **16**:974
- *Khaliastre* **10**:936
- Utopian Zionism **16**:1152
- Warsaw ghetto **16**:348
Zeitlin, Israel, *see* TIEMPO, CESAR
ZEITLIN (Zeitlis), JOSHUA **16**:975
- Haskalah **7**:1446
ZEITLIN, SOLOMON **16**:975
- historiography **8**:562
ZEITLIN, WILLIAM (Ze'ev) **16**:976
- Zionism **16**:1156
Zeitschrift (period., Rus.) **13**:1048
Zeitschrift des Deutschen Palaestinavereins (journ.) **5**:1595
Zeitschrift fuer Demographie und Statistik der Juden (publ.) **4**:1074; **13**:1032
Zeitschrift fuer die Geschichte der Juden (journ.) **7**:696
Zeitschrift fuer die Geschichte der Juden in Boehmen und Maehren (hist. review, Cz.) **13**:1029
Zeitschrift fuer die Geschichte der Juden in der Tschechoslowakei (journ.) **7**:696
Zeitschrift fuer die Geschichte der Juden in Deutschland (review) **5**:1595; **8**:563; **13**:1373
Zeitschrift fuer die religioesen Interessen des Judenthums (journ.) **7**:80
Zeitschrift fuer die Wissenschaft des Judentums (period.) **16**:110; **16**:570
Zeitschrift fuer Hebraeische Bibliographie (journ.) **4**:972,1400
Zeitschrift fuer rationelle Medicin (journ.) **8**:325
Zeiwald, Israel **15**:339
Zekharim u-Nekevot (wk.), *see Kitāb al-Tadhkīr wa al-Ta'nīth*
Zekharyah (mosh., Isr.) **1**:place list
Zekher Ẓaddik li-Verakhah (epitaph) **7**:918
Zekhor le-Avraham (wk.) **15**:520
ZEKHUT AVOT (merit of the fathers) **16**:976
- patriarchs **13**:184
- prosperity of wicked **7**:776
- *see also:* KEVER AVOT; YIḤUS
Zekhuto Yagen Aleinu (epitaph) **7**:918
Zela (bib. place) **10**:1063; **14**:909
Ẓelafon (mosh., Isr.) **1**:place list
Zelany (sol., Rus.) **13**:699
Zelbshuts (orgn.) **14**:1473
Zelcer, S., *see* GROSSER, BRONISLAW
Zelea-Codreanu, Corneliu **14**:394
ZELECHOW (tn., Pol.) **16**:978
Ẓelem (tn., Aus.), *see* DEUTSCHKREUTZ
Ẓelem (kab. conc.) **10**:611
Zeleny, F. **8**:68
Zelevinski, N. **5**:453
Zelig, Phinehas **10**:1433
Zeligs, Dorothy Freda **5**:451
Zelikovich, B. (Rus.) **5**:803; **15**:1541; **16**:1179
Zelikovich, Elimelekh (Avner) **7**:1065
Zelikovitch, G. **8**:958
Ẓelilim (journ.) **1**:newsp. list
Ẓelil va-Omer (journ.) **1**:newsp. list
Zelinsky-Codreanu, Ion **8**:1130
ZELK, ZOLTÁN **8**:1087
Zelka, Dan **16**:903
Zell (vill., Ger.) **3**:694
Zeller, A.C. **8**:68
ZELLERBACH (fam.) **16**:979
- California **5**:56
Zellerbach, Anthony **16**:979
Zellerbach, Harold Lionel **16**:979
Zellerbach, Henry **16**:979
Zellerbach, Isadore **16**:979
Zellerbach, Jacob C. **16**:979
Zellerbach, James David **16**:979
Zellerbach, Marks **16**:979
Zellerbach, William J. **16**:979
Zellermayer, Julius **13**:1340
ZELOPHEHAD (bib. fig.) **16**:979
- daughters **16**:1425
- Hepher **8**:332
ZELOW (tn., Pol.) **16**:980
Zeltner, G.G. **8**:68
Zeltner, Henry **13**:1360
Zeltner, Louis **13**:1360
Zeltzer, Israel **7**:806
ZELVA (Zelwa; tn., Belor.) **16**:981
Zemach (name), *see also:* Zemaḥ
Zemach, Abraham **11**:1499
ZEMACH, BENJAMIN **5**:1273
ZEMACH, NAHUM **16**:981
- *illus:*
- - Habimah original company **7**:1029
- - Rovina, Hannah, and Menahem Gnessin **7**:634
ZEMACH, SHLOMO **16**:982
Zemaḥ (name), *see also:* Zemach
Ẓemaḥ (paytan), *see* MENAHEM BEN JACOB
Ẓemaḥ (gaon) **7**:323; **8**:964
Ẓemaḥ (Kar. acad. head, Jer.) **9**:266
Ẓemaḥ (place, Er. Isr.) **9**:312; **15**:92
Ẓemaḥ, Abraham (17th cent.) **11**:83
Zemaḥ, Abraham (19th cent., comp.) **2**:311
Ẓemaḥ, David **8**:1452; **9**:1041
Ẓemaḥ, Hayyim **16**:176
Ẓemaḥ, Jacob (r., Port.) **4**:1288
Ẓemaḥ, Jacob (philan.), *see* JACOB BEN ẒEMAḤ BEN NISSIM
ẒEMAḤ, JACOB BEN ḤAYYIM (kab.) **16**:984
- Shabbetai Ẓevi **14**:1225
- Vital, Hayyim **16**:174
Ẓemaḥ, Yom Tov **11**:1442; **16**:746
Ẓemaḥ, Ẓevi Hirsh **11**:1492
Ẓemaḥ bar Isaac (gaon) **7**:318; **15**:522
Ẓemaḥ bar Kafnai (gaon) **7**:318
ẒEMAḤ BEN ḤAYYIM (gaon) **16**:985
- Eldad ha-Dani **6**:577
- gaonate **7**:317
Ẓemaḥ ben Isaac (gaon), *see* Ẓemaḥ bar Isaac
ẒEMAḤ BEN PALTOI (gaon) **16**:985
- gaonate **7**:318
- *Halakhot Gedolot* **7**:1169
Ẓemaḥ ben Shahin, *see* Ibn Shahin, Ẓemaḥ
Ẓemaḥ ben Solomon **2**:893; **6**:1031
Zemah ben Yanon ha-Hazzan **13**:597
Ẓemaḥ David (wk., David Gans) **8**:559; **8**:697; **11**:349
Ẓemaḥ David (wk., David De'Pomis) **13**:845
- *illus:*
- - title page (1587) **13**:845
Ẓemah Ẓedek (has. ldr.), *see* Schneersohn, Menaḥem Mendel
ẒEMAḤ ẒEDEK BEN ISAAC (gaon) **16**:985
Zeman, Kamil, *see* OLBRACHT, IVAN
Zemannim (journ.) **1**:newsp. list
ZEMARAIM (city, Er. Isr.) **16**:985
Ẓemarkad (mystic "name") **4**:268
ZEMBA, MENAHEM **16**:986
Ẓemed (meas.) **16**:381
Zemer (zool.), *see* ANTELOPE
Zemina ("elder", Tyre) **2**:33

ZEMIROT ("songs") 16:987
- folksongs 6:1384
- hasidic music 7:1423
- *mus. notations:*
- - text
- - *villancico* form 12:623
- - *Ẓur mi-shello akhalnu* 9:1145
- *see also:* PESUKEI DE-ZIMRA
ZEMUN (tn., Yug.) 16:989
- Yugoslavia 16:868ff
- *illus:* text
ZEMURRAY, SAMUEL 16:991
Zendel, Gabriel 13:118
Zengi, ʿImād al-Dīn 6:367
Zenica (tn., Yug.) 14:869
- *illus:*
- - synagogue 16:882
Zenjirli (site, Turk.)
- Kilamuwa inscription 16:666
- language 14:1151
- Temple 15:951
Zeno (offic., Egy.) 16:992
- Caesarea 5:6
- Tobiah 15:1179
Zeno (Gr. philos.) 15:409
Zeno (Byz. emp.) 14:732
ZENO, PAPYRI OF 16:991
Zenobia (q., Palmyra), *see* ODENATHUS AND ZENOBIA
Zenobius (archit.) 9:1406
ZENODORUS (tetrarch) 16:992
Zenoff, David 12:1018
"Zentral" (publ. firm), *see* Merkaz
Zentralausschuss fuer Hilfe und Aufbau (orgn., Ger.) 13:380
ZENTRALE STELLE DER LANDESJUSTIZVERWALTUNGEN (Ger. orgn.) 16:992
- War Crimes Trials 16:297ff
Zentralstelle (Nazi office) 13:974
ZENTRALSTELLE DER FUERSORGE FUER KRIEGSFLUECHTLINGE (orgn., Aus.) 16:993
Zentralverein der Amerikanischen Zionisten (orgn., U.S.) 16:1141
Zentral-Verein deutscher Staatsbuerger juedischen Glaubens (orgn.), *see* CENTRAL-VEREIN DEUTSCHER STAATSBUERGER JUEDISCHEN GLAUBENS
ZENTRAL-WOHLFAHRTSTELLE DER DEUTSCHEN JUDEN (orgn.) 16:993
- Berlin 4:646
- Caspary, Eugen 5:228
- Germany 7:485
- philanthropy 13:380
Zenwirth, Yehoshua, *see* BAR-YOSEF, YEHOSHUA
Zephaniah (witch), *see* EN-DOR, WITCH OF
Zephaniah (h. pr.) 13:1075
ZEPHANIAH (prophet) 16:994
- eschatological writings 6:866
- Minor Prophets 12:48
- tomb 14:1508
- *illus:*
- - Latin Bible (13th cent.) 16:49
Zephaniah (f., Josiah) 16:955
Zephath (Cana. city), *see* HORMAH
Zephon (city, Er. Isr.), *see* ZAPHON
Zeppelin (airship) 2:320
ZERAH (s., Judah) 16:995
- Judah 14:1549
- Tamar 15:782
- *geneal. table* 5:1342
ZERAH (Edomite chief) 16:996
ZERAH (s., Simeon) 16:996
- Simeon 14:1549
ZERAH (levite) 16:996
ZERAH BEN NATHAN OF TROKI 16:996
- Manasseh ben Israel 15:1403
ZERAH THE CUSHITE (bib. fig.) 16:996
- Asa 8:595
- Zerah 16:996
ZERAHIAH BEN ISAAC HA-LEVI 16:997
- Astruc ha-Levi 3:810
- Saragossa 14:862
- Spain 15:238
- Tortosa disputation 15:1271ff
- translations 15:1323
Zeraḥiah ben Isaac ha-Levi Gerondi, *see* GERONDI, ZERAHIAH BEN ISAAC HA-LEVI
Zerahiah ha-Yevani 14:1099
Zeraḥyah (mosh., Isr.) 1:place list
ZERA'IM (Mish. order) 16:997
- enlargement on 12:131; 12:132
- Jerusalem Talmud 15:774
Zera'im (period.) 1:newsp. list 5:460
Zeramim (journ.) 1:newsp. list
ZERBST (city, Ger.) 16:998
ZERED (riv. val., Er. Isr.) 16:998
- Edom border 6:369
- physiography 9:163; 9:177
- Transjordan 15:1316
Zereda (demon) 5:1528
ZEREDAH (tn., Er. Isr.) 16:998
- Jeroboam 9:1372
- see also: ZARETHAN
Zererah (place, Er. Isr.), *see* ZARETHAN; ZEREDAH
Zeresh (bib. fig.) 15:812
Zeret ("span"; meas.) 16:378; 16:389
Zerffi, Gustáv 8:1081
Zerika *(amora)* 14:634
Zer-Kavod, M. 16:1509
Zerlin, Rebekah 11:1190
Zerneikov, Adam 2:248
Zerniewski, Anton 7:68
Zeromski, Stefan 13:800
Ẓeror Mikhtavim (journ.) 1:newsp. list
Ẓeror Mikhtavim li-She'elot ha-Ḥinnukh ha-Meshuttaf (journ.) 1:newsp. list
Ẓerorot (tort conc.) 3:987
Zeruah (bib. fig.) 9:1371
Zeru'ah (mosh., Isr.) 1:place list
Zerubavel (stmt., soc., Rus.) 16:1000
ZERUBAVEL, JACOB 16:999
- *illus:*
- - Ukrainian Provisional National Council 15:1515
- - Yiddish writers group, Vilna 16:813
ZERUBBABEL (bib. fig.) 16:1000
- chronological chart 8:766-767
- exile, Babylonian 6:1040
- Great Synagogue 15:629
- messianism 11:1420
- Nehemiah 12:937
- Samaritans 14:728
- Sheshbazzar 14:1382
- Temple 15:955
- Zechariah 16:955
- *Zerubbabel, Book of* 16:1002
- *geneal. table:* 5:1341
- *see also:* DAVID, DYNASTY OF
ZERUBBABEL, BOOK OF 16:1002
- fiction, Hebrew 6:1261
- messianism 9:326
Zerubbavel (wk., Levinsohn) 11:118
Zerubbavel (play, Lilienblum) 9:326
Ẓerufah (mosh., Isr.) 1:place list
Zerufim, ha- (wk.), *see* *Kitâb al-Taṣârif*
Zeruiah (bib. fig.) 2:79; 3:672; 10:106
- *geneal. table:* 5:1342
Zeterbaum, M. 10:90
Ẓet ha-kokhavim (nightfall) 5:1376
Zetkin, Clara 15:26
Zetlin, Mikhail Osipovich 14:513
Zeus Casius (sanct., Egy.), *see* BAAL-ZEPHON
Zeus of Carmel (deity) 5:186
Zeus Olympius (deity)
- Antiochus IV 9:1391
- Jerusalem sanctuary 3:74
- *Shikkuẓ Shamem* 2:98
Zev (art.) 13:120
Zevadiah (paytan) 13:597
Zevaḥ (sacrifice) 5:1165
Ẓeva Haganah le-Israel, *see* DEFENCE FORCES OF ISRAEL
ZEVAḤIM (tract.) 16:1002
- sacrifice 14:599; 14:607
- *illus:* text
Zevaḥ (ha-) todah, *see* Thanksgiving offering
Zeved ha-Bat (celebration) 16:989
Ẓevi (zool.) 5:1458
Ẓevi, A. 9:1139
ZEVI, BRUNO 16:1004
- *illus:*
- - text
- - Garibaldi Bridge, Rome 3:341
Ẓevi, Esther 14:1240
Ẓevi, H. (pseud.), *see* HAZAZ, ḤAYYIM
Ẓevi, Jochebed, *see* Ẓevi, Esther
Ẓevi, Samuel 15:1377
Ẓevi, Sarah 14:1224
Ẓevi, Shabbetai, *see* SHABBETAI ẒEVI
Ẓevi ben Israel 9:1050
Ẓevi ben Jacob 9:1259
Ẓevi ben Joseph 5:372
Ẓevi ben Moses Abraham 14:1523
Zevid (amora) 2:866, 869
Ẓevi Elimelech of Blazowa 14:325
Ẓevi Elimelech of Dynow 14:1295
Ẓevi ha-Levi ben Nethanel 12:972
Ẓevi Hirsch ben Abraham 10:1140; 11:741
Ẓevi Hirsch ben Benjamin 7:929
Ẓevi Hirsch ben Ḥayyim 13:1107
Ẓevi Hirsch ben Simeon ha-Kohen 16:1012
ẒEVI HIRSCH FRIEDMAN OF LESKO 16:1004
Ẓevi Hirsch of Kamenka, *see* KAMENKA, ẒEVI HIRSCH OF
ẒEVI HIRSCH OF NADWORNA 16:1005
Ẓevi Hirsch of Romanov 10:724
Ẓevi Hirsch of Zamosc 9:1079
Ẓevi Hirsch of Zhidachov 7:1414
Ẓevi Hirsh of Zborov 16:945
Ẓevi Migdal (orgn.) 3:415
Zevin, Benjamin David 13:1372
Zevin, Israel Joseph, *see* TASHRAK
ZEVIN, SOLOMON JOSEPH 16:1005
Zevina ("elder"), *see* Zemina
Ẓevi of Przysucha 14:1570
Ẓevoyim, Mount (Er. Isr.) 8:1139
Zevulun Sea-Farers' Society (Er. Isr.) 9:835
ZEYER, JULIUS 16:1006
Zey Greit (period.) 13:1048
Zeynati (fam., Isr.) 13:218
ZGIERZ (Zgerzh; city, Pol.) 16:1006
ZGURITSA (Zgurit ,a; vill., Mold.) 16:1007
Zhagare (tn., Lith.), *see* ZAGARE
ZHDANOV (city, Ukr.) 16:1008
Zhdanov, A.A. 6:144; 6:145
Zheleznyak, Maxim 15:1527
Zheleznyak, Yokheved, *see* BAT-MIRIAM, YOKHEVED
ZHERNENSKY, MOSHE ELIYAHU 16:1008
Zhetel (tn.,Rus.), *see* DYATLOVO
ZHIDACHOV (has. dyn.) 16:1009
- dynasties 1:ḥas. table
ZHIDACHOV (city, Ukr.) 16:1008
Zhidovin, Skhariya 10:399
Zhikhlinski, Reisel 16:819
Zhirkova, Elizaveta, *see* ELISHEVA
ZHITLOWSKY, CHAIM 16:1009
- diaspora nationalism 16:1067
- minority rights 12:43
- Schwarzberg 14:1029
- *illus:*
- - Peretz, Isaac Leib 16:814
ZHITOMIR (city, Ukr.) 16:1011
- massacre (1941) 16:211
- rabbinical seminary 8:724; 13:1465
- self-defense 14:1126
ZHITOMIRSKI, ALEXANDER MATVEYEVITCH 12:715
- Jewish music 15:57
Zhizn (period.) 12:721
ZHMERINKA (city, Ukr.) 16:1013
- *illus:* text
Zhmud-Samogitia (reg., Lith.), *see* BIRZAI
ZHOLKVA (city, Gal.) 16:1014
- Shabbateanism 14:1251
- *illus:*
- - text
- - synagogue 15:608
ZHURAVNO (tn., Ukr.) 16:1016
ZIBA (bib. fig.) 16:1016
Zibiah (bib. fig.) 4:384
Zichron Ephraim (syn., N.Y.) 12:1079
Ziddim-Zer (bib. place) 10:885
ẒIDDUK HA-DIN (burial service) 16:1016
ŽÍDEK, PAVEL 16:1017
Zidon (Phoen. port), *see* SIDON
Židov (period.) 16:918 16:1150; 16:1151; 16:918
Zidovska Smotra (period.) 11:207; 16:1150; 16:888
ZIDOVSKA STRANA (polit. party, Cz.) 16:1017
Židovska Svijest (newsp.) 16:1018; 16:1150
Židovské Listy pro Čechy, Moravu a Slezsko (period.) 13:1027
Židovské Zprávy (period.) 13:1027
ZIEGFELD, FLORENZ 16:1018
- theater 15:1085
- *illus:* text
Ziegler, Bernhard 11:585
ZIEGLER, IGNAZ 16:1018
Ziegler, Jacob 11:928
Zielonka, David L. 15:790
Ziemian, Joseph 5:448
Ziereis, Franz 11:1136
Zieriksee, Amandus van, *see* Amandus van Zieriksee
Zietil (tn., Lith.), *see* DYATLOVO
Ziff, William Bernard 13:1371
Ziffer, Moshe 14:1070
Zifroni, Elishama 6:46
Zifroni, Gavriel 7:1033; 7:1036
ZIFRONI, ISRAEL BEN DANIEL 16:1019
- books 4:1235
- Di Gara 6:46
- *Haggadah* 7:1101
- printing 13:1102
- *Toledot Aharon* 2:22
Zifroni, Moses Elishama 16:1019
Ziggurat (temple tower), *see* Ziqqurat
Zikhron Hava'at ha-Omer (kib. litur.) 10:960
Zikhron Moshe (qtr., Jer.) 9:328,1462
Zikhrono li-Verakhah (epitaph) 7:918
ZIKHRONOT (litur.) 16:1019
- *akedah* in 2:481
- *Attah zokher* 3:833
- Rosh ha-Shanah 14:307
- *see also:* MALKHUYYOT; TEKIʿATA

Zikhronot (annals) **2:**205
Zikhronot, ha-(wk.), *see Sefer ha-Zikhronot*
Zikhronot Devarim shel ha-Aguddah ha-Meditzinit ha-Ivrit (journ.) **1:**newsp. list
Zikhronot ha-Akademyah la-Lashon ha-Ivrit (annual) **1:**newsp. list; **2:**207
ZIKHRON YA'AKOV (vill., Isr.) **16:**1019
- Nili archives **6:**1210
- statistics **1:** place list
- *illus:*
- - text
- - Aaronsohn home **12:**1163
- - loading grapes for wine cellars **9:**781
- - rest home **13:**1612
Zikim (kib., Isr.) **1:**place list
Zikkaron (wk.), *see Sefer Zikkaron*
ZIKLAG (tn., Er. Isr.) **16:**1020
Ẓiklag (kib., Isr.), *see* Lahav
Ẓiklon (journ.) **1:**newsp. list
Zilber, Leib **15:**1214
Zilberberg, Fishl **13:**648
Zilberberg, Moses Judah Leib **10:**1433
Zilberberg, Moses Leib Benjamin **14:**1516
Zilberg, Benjamin A., *see* KAVERIN, BENJAMIN ALEKSANDROVICH
Zilberman, Alexandru, *see* SEVER, ALEXANDRU
ZILBERTS, ZAVEL **16:**1021
ZILBOORG, GREGORY **16:**1021
- criminology **5:**1108
ZILINA (tn., Slov.) **16:**1022
- Czechoslovakia **5:**1200
Zilis (port, Afr.), *see* ARCILA
ZILKHA (fam., bnk.) **16:**1022
Zilkha, Abdulla **16:**1023
Zilkha, Ezra **16:**1023
Zilkha, Khedoury **16:**1022
Zilkha, Maurice **9:**1192,1193
ZILKHA, NAʿIM **16:**1023
Zilkha, Selim **16:**1023
Zilkhah Bank (Syr.) **15:**646
Zill, Egon **12:**893
Zillah (bib. fig.) **2:**233; **15:**1418
Zillisheim (tn., Als.-Lor.) **2:**754
Ẓillum, see ha-Ẓillum
ZILPAH (bib. fig.) **16:**1023
- Jacob **9:**1192,1193
- tribes of **15:**1384
Ẓilẓelei Shema (journ.) **1:**newsp. list
ZIM (navig. co., Isr.) **16:**1023
- labor movement **9:**860
- shipping in Israel **9:**836
- *illus:* text
Zim, Jacob **11:**1167
ZIMBALIST, EFREM **16:**1024
Zimbalist, Efrem Jr. **16:**1024
Zimberknopf, J. **7:**1103
Zimberlin, John **3:**483
Zimel, Simḥah **12:**53
Zimlin, Levi Reuben **13:**135
Zimman, Harry **12:**1378
ZIMMELS, HIRSCH JACOB **16:**1025
Zimmels, Julius **7:**133
ZIMMERLI, WALTHER **16:**1025
ZIMMERMAN, CHARLES SASCHA **16:**1025
ZIMMERMAN, HARRY M. **16:**1026
Zimmerman, Robert, *see* DYLAN, BOB
Zimmermann (cartog.) **11:**930
Zimmermann (print.) **4:**1312
ZIMMERN, SIR ALFRED **16:**1026
Zimmun (ben.) **7:**839ff
Zimna, Zimona ("elder"), *see* Zemina
Zimra, Ibn (fam., Sp.), *see* Ibn Zimra
Zimrat (mosh., Isr.) **1:**place list
Zimrat ha-Areẓ (journ.) **1:**newsp. list
ZIMRI (s., Salu) **16:**1026
- al-Sāmarī **14:**757
- Simeonites **14:**1549
- *illus:*
- - text
- - slain by Phinehas **13:**467
ZIMRI (k., Isr.) **16:**1027
- chronological chart **8:**766-767
Zimri (Babyl.), *see* ZAMARIS
Zimridda (k., Sidon) **14:**1505
Zimri-Lim (k., Mari) **11:**975ff; **16:**1496
Zimriyyah (choir fest.) **9:**1008; **12:**672
- *illus:*
- - festival concert **9:**1010
Zimron, Joseph **5:**915
Ẓimẓum (kab. conc.) **10:**547; **10:**588ff
- Abraham Kohen de Herrera **8:**392
- Bacharach, Naphtali **4:**50
- Baruch of Kosov **4:**281
- Dov Baer of Mezhirech **6:**183ff
- ḥasidic thought **7:**1403; **14:**1438
- Joseph Moses of Salositz **10:**246
- Luzzatto, Moses Ḥayyim **11:**601
- Menahem Mendel of Vitebsk **11:**1311
- Naḥman of Bratslav **12:**785
- Ricchi, Raphael **14:**154
- Shabbateanism **14:**1241
- *illus:*
- - *Ein-Sof* **10:**574
- - flaring up of *Sefirot* **10:**597
Zin (river, canyon, Isr.) **9:**136; **12:**927
Ẓinabri (city, Er. Isr.),*see* SENNABRIS
ZINBERG, ISRAEL (Sergei) **16:**1028
Zinn, Abe **12:**1039
Zinn, Harold **2:**321
ZINNEMANN, FRED **12:**476
Ẓinnor (cantillation sign), *see Zarqaʿ*
Ẓinnorit (punctuation mark) **16:**1461
ZINOVIEV, GRIGORI YEVSEYEVICH **16:**1029
- Kamenev, Lev Borisovich **10:**726; **16:**1029
- Po'alei Zion **15:**49
- Trotsky **15:**1405
Zinovyevsk (city, Ukr.), *see* KIROVOGRAD
Zion (Jer., name) **9:**1379; **16:**1032ff
- in music **9:**1589
- Lamentations, Book of **10:**1370
Zion (Jebusite citadel, Jer.) **9:**1382
- *illus:*
- - site **9:**1384
ZION (mt., Jer.) **16:**1030
- Armageddon **3:**472
- eschatology **6:**866ff
- holy places **8:**921ff
- Jerusalem **9:**1549
- Mamluk period **9:**1425
- religious center **9:**1496
- topography **9:**1515
- *illus:*
- - Church of the Dormition **8:**929
- - David's tomb **8:**924
- - east view **9:**1465
- - Hall of the Last Supper **8:**930
- - wedding **11:**1048
- - Zion Gate **9:**1427
Zion (periods., Ger.) **13:**1033
- Hebrew newspapers **12:**1048
Zion (quarterly, Pal.) **1:**newsp. list **8:**563; **15:**55
Zion (orgn., Belgrade) **16:**1148
Zion (soc., Bucharest) **4:**655
Zion (soc., Lvov) **11:**612
Zion, Bat (name, Jer.), *see* Bat Zion
Zion, Me'assef (journ.) **1:**newsp. list
Zion, Return to **8:**615
- Artaxerxes I **3:**646
- Artaxerxes II **3:**647
- Cyrus **5:**1185
- Darius I **5:**1304
- exile, Babylonian **6:**1039
- Ezra **6:**1104
- *Ezra, Greek Book of* **6:**1110
- Ezra and Nehemiah, Book of **6:**1115
- Haggai **7:**1112
- Ingathering of the Exiles **8:**1373
- Isaiah **9:**64
- Jerusalem **9:**1384
- Jeshua **10:**1
- Judea **10:**403
- Malachi **11:**815
- Nehemiah **12:**936
- Persia **13:**306
- Samaritans **14:**728
- Sanballat **14:**823
- Sheshbazzar **14:**1382
- suffering as precursor **10:**1369
- Tattenai **15:**831
- Temple **15:**942
- Zechariah **16:**953
- Zerubbabel **16:**1000
- *illus:*
- - Jerusalem at the time of Nehemiah (map) **9:**1387
- - *Yehud* coins **3:**3222; **5:**698; **8:**625
- - Yehud province, borders (map) **9:**121
Zion, Sons of (soc.), *see* B'nai Zion
Zion, Yedi'ot (journ.) **1:** newsp. list
Zion College (Cincinnati) **16:**564
Zion Gate (Jer.) **9:**1433
- *illus:*
- - general view **9:**1428
Zion Hall (Jer.) **9:**1462
Ẓioni (fam., Latv.) **11:**555
Ẓioni, A., *see* ELAZARI-VOLCANI, YIẒḤAK
Ẓioni, Aaron Zelig **11:**555
Ẓioni, David **11:**555
Ẓioni, Isaac **11:**555
Ẓioni, Menaḥem, *see* MENAḤEM ẒIYYONI
Ẓioni, Naphtali **11:**555
Zionides (poems) **10:**1010
ZIONISM **16:**1031
- *Contents*
- - The Word and its Meaning **16:**1032
- - Forerunners **16:**1033
- - Ḥibbat Zion **16:**1037
- - Ideological Evolution **16:**1042
- - - Political Zionism **16:**1042
- - - Cultural and "Synthetic" Zionism **16:**1046
- - - Post-War Consensus and Differentation **16:**1051
- - - Between Pogroms and Holocaust **16:**1054
- - - The Relation to the Arabs **16:**1056
- - - After the Holocaust **16:**1058
- - - The State of Israel **16:**1060
- - - Tensions in the U.S. and the U.S.S.R. **16:**1062
- - - Ideological Problems in Israel **16:**1064
- - - Non-Zionist and Anti-Zionist Trends **16:**1066
- - - Autonomists and Yiddishists **16:**1066
- - - Religious and Secular Nationalism **16:**1067
- - - Territorialism and Agricultural Settlement **16:**1068
- - - Soviet Jewish Culture **16:**1069
- - Zionist Policy **16:**1069
- - - The Herzl Period **16:**1070
- - - Transition Period **16:**1073
- - - The Young Turks **16:**1074
- - - The Arab Problem **16:**1075
- - - Struggle for the Future **16:**1077
- - - Words and Deeds **16:**1080
- - - War and Holocaust **16:**1086
- - - Years of Decision **16:**1087
- - - The U.N. Investigates **16:**1091
- - - The U.N. Decision **16:**1094
- - Zionist Organization **16:**1096
- - In Various Countries
- - - Australia and N.Z. **16:**1105
- - - Austria **16:**1106
- - - Bulgaria **16:**1108
- - - Canada **16:**1109
- - - Czechoslovakia **16:**1111
- - - France **16:**1113
- - - Germany **16:**1115
- - - Great Britain **16:**1116
- - - Holland **16:**1118
- - - Hungary **16:**1120
- - - Italy **16:**1122
- - - Latin America **16:**1123
- - - N. Africa and Asia **16:**1127
- - - Poland **16:**1129
- - - Rumania **16:**1132
- - - Russia **16:**1136
- - - South Africa **16:**1140
- - - U.S. **16:**1141
- - - Yugoslavia **16:**1148
- - Zionist Utopias **16:**1151
- - Christian Zionism **16:**1152
- - Zionist Bibliography **16:**1155
- General
- - archives **3:**388
- - Germany, resettlement **7:**498
- - Jerusalem in literature **9:**1565ff
- - Mendelssohn, Moses **11:**1335
- - Rosenzweig on **14:**303
- - Schwadron, Abraham **14:**1017
- - Zionism, term **4:**1040
- Pre-Herzlian
- - Alkalai, Judah **2:**638
- - Baruch, Joseph Marcou **4:**275
- - Bilu **4:**998
- - Eisler, Edmund **6:**553
- - Ereẓ Israel settlement plans **9:**298
- - He-Ḥalutz **8:**247
- - Hess, Moses **8:**431
- - Ḥibbat Zion **8:**463
- - Judah Halevi **10:**357
- - Kadimah **10:**665
- - Kalischer, Ẓevi Hirsch **10:**708
- - Kaspi, Joseph ibn **10:**810
- - Krochmal, Nachman **10:**1272
- - Pinsker, Leon **13:**545
- - pogroms **13:**701
- - Rothschild family **14:**334
- - *Selbstemanzipation* **14:**1119
- History **9:**773
- - *aliyah* **2:**633 **9:**515ff
- - apologetists **3:**200
- - Arab National Movement **9:**455ff
- - Balfour Declaration **4:**130ff; **4:**131
- - Basle Program **4:**306ff
- - Biltmore Program **4:**997
- - Birobidzhan alternative **4:**1047
- - border, Ereẓ Israel **9:**312
- - chronological chart **8:**766-767
- - Churchill, Sir Winston **5:**555
- - cultural Zionism **9:**996ff
- - economic factions **16:**1322
- - Haganah **9:**683ff
- - Helsingsfors Program **8:**318ff
- - ingathering of the exiles **8:**1373
- - Jewish Brigade Group **10:**36
- - Jewish Colonial Trust **10:**42
- - kibbutz movement **10:**964
- - law of return **10:**1485
- - mandate for Palestine **11:**862
- - minority rights **12:**44ff
- - Minsk Conference **12:**58
- - Nili **12:**1162ff
- - Palestine, Inquiry Commissions **13:**30
- - Palestine Partition **13:**34

- - Petrograd Conference 13:344
- - San Remo Conference 14:845
- - self-defense 14:1126
- - shekel 14:1349
- - Sykes-Picot Treaty 15:566
- - Uganda scheme 15:1500
- - UNSCOP 15:1688
- - White Papers 16:482
- - Wilson, Woodrow 16:535
- - Zionist Congresses 16:1164ff
- - *see also:* ISRAEL (Political Life and Parties); Socialism, Zionist
- Other Movements and Zionism
- - Agudat Israel 2:421ff
- - Alliance Israélite 2:650; 2:653
- - anti-Semitism and 3:137; 3:138; 3:148
- - Bund 4:1500ff
- - Catholicism 5:599; 13:572 16:73
- - Christianity 5:514
- - communism 5:792ff; 16:779ff
- - Conservative Judaism 5:903
- - Esra 6:896
- - Israel Communist Party 5:807ff
- - Joint Distribution Committee 2:829
- - Liberal Judaism (Ger.) 16:110
- - neo-Fascism 12:951
- - Pittsburgh Platform 13:571
- - P.P.S. 13:951
- - Protestant churches 13:1250ff
- - Reconstructionism 13:1616
- - Socialism 15:26ff
- - socialism, Jewish 15:43ff
- - students' movements, Jewish 15:448ff
- - Tarbut 15:809
- - Territorialism 15:1019ff
- Opposition
- - Adler, Hermann 2:278
- - American Council for Judaism 2:820
- - Anglo-Jewish Association 2:978
- - Cohen, Sir Robert Waley 5:684
- - Dubnow, Simon 6:254
- - Duehring, Karl 6:260
- - Grodzinski, Ḥayyim Ozer 7:928
- - Hirsch, S.R. 8:514
- - *Izraelita* 9:1166
- - Lenin 11:14
- - Liber, Maurice 11:187
- - Lishkah Sheḥorah 13:1478
- - Montefiore, Claude 12:268
- - Mussolini 12:718
- - Protestrabbiner 13:1255
- - Satmar rebbe 15:909ff
- - Shapira, Ḥayyim Eleazar 14:1296
- - Stalin 15:328
- - Trotski 15:1406
- - Zhitlowsky, Chaim 16:1010
- Countries
- - Australia 3:882f
- - Austria 3:896ff; 12:879
- - Canada 5:108
- - Czechoslovakia 13:971ff
- - England 6:760ff; 16:1171
- - Ereẓ Israel 15:919; 16:49
- - France 7:39
- - Georgia 7:425
- - Germany 7:482; 13:1455
- - India 4:498; 5:627
- - Iran 13:318
- - Iraq 8:1450
- - Latin America 10:1455
- - Libya 11:204
- - Lithuania 11:370ff; 16:147
- - Morocco 12:342ff
- - Poland 13:749
- - Rumania 14:406
- - Russia 14:452ff
- - South Africa 15:190ff
- - Turkey 15:1457; 15:1461
- - United States 15:1632
- - - Aḥuzah society 7:313
- - - Farband Labor Zionist Order 6:801
- - - Labor Zionist Organization 10:1331
- - - New York 12:1100ff
- - - Zionist Congress (12th) 16:1171
- - - Zionist Organization 16:1178
- - Uruguay 16:11
- - Yugoslavia 11:207; 14:872
- Zionist Organizations
- - Democratic Fraction 5:1492
- - Ezra (Rus.) 4:505
- - Ha-Po'el ha-Mizrachi 7:1320
- - Ha-Shomer ha-Ẓa'ir 7:1372
- - Hebrew education 8:255
- - He-Ḥaver 8:255
- - Hitaḥadut 8:781
- - Jewish Agency 10:26
- - Jewish National Fund 10:77
- - *Juedische Turnerschaft* 11:664
- - Keren Hayesod 10:914
- - Maccabeans, Ancient Order of 11:656
- - Maccabi World Union 11:664
- - Mizrachi 12:175ff
- - National Religious Party 12:880
- - Palestine office 13:40
- - Pioneer Women 13:555
- - Po'alei Zion 13:656
- - Revisionists, Zionist 14:128
- - scouting 15:931
- - television and radio 15:931
- - Torah va-Avodah 15:1259
- - United Jewish Appeal 15:1540
- - United Jewish Socialist Workers Party 15:1541
- - WIZO 16:593
- - World Labor Zionist Movement 16:639
- - Ẓeirei Zion 16:970
- - Zionist commission 16:1163
- - Zionist Socialist Workers' Party 16:1179
- - Zionist-Socialist Workers' Union 4:1253
- - Z.S. 16:1224
- Personalities
- - Aḥad Ha-Am 2:441ff; 8:191
- - Amiel, Moshe Avigdor 2:846
- - Arlosoroff, Chaim 3:470
- - Bar-Ilan, Meir 4:505
- - Ben-Gurion, David 4:505
- - Ben-Yehuda, Eliezer 4:565ff
- - Ben-Zvi, Izhak 4:577
- - Berlin, Sir Isaiah 4:658
- - Berlin, Naphtali Ẓevi 4:662
- - Bernstein, Pereẓ 4:688
- - Birnbaum, Nathan 4:1040
- - Borochov, Ber 4:1253ff
- - Brandeis, Louis 4:1297
- - Braunstein, Menahem 4:1320
- - Brodetsky, Selig 4:1392
- - Buber, Martin 4:1429ff
- - Feiwel, Berthold 6:1215
- - Frumkin, Israel Dov 7:211
- - Glasner, Moses Samuel 7:604
- - Goldbloom, Jacob K. 7:706
- - Goldman, Nahum 7:724
- - Gordon, Aharon David 7:790
- - Gruenbaum, Yiẓḥak 7:944
- - Herzl, Theodor 8:407
- - Jabotinsky, Vladimir 9:1178
- - Katznelson, Berl 10:834
- - Klausner, Joseph 10:1095
- - Kook, Abraham Isaac 10:1182
- - Lilienblum, Moses 11:242
- - Maimon, Judah Leib 11:739
- - Motzkin, Leo 12:477
- - Namier, Sir Lewis 12:1213
- - Nobel, Nehemiah Anton 12:1200
- - Nordau, Max 12:1213
- - Nurock, Mordechai 12:1282
- - Rabinowitz, S. J. 13:1478
- - Ruppin, Arthur 14:430
- - Samuel, Maurice 14:801
- - Sharett, Moshe 14:1310
- - Silver, Abba Hillel 14:1543ff
- - Simon, Sir Leon 14:1581
- - Smolenskin, Perez 15:11
- - Sokolow, Nahum 15:86ff
- - Spire, André 15:284
- - Syrkin, Nachman 15:651ff
- - Tamares, Aaron 15:783; 16:22
Trumpeldor, Joseph 15:1410
- - Tschlenow, Jehiel 15:1415
- - Ussishkin, Menahem 16:22
- - Warburg, Otto 16:287ff
- - Weizmann, Chaim 16:423
- - Wise, Stephen 16:566ff
- - Wolffsohn, David 16:612
- Non-Jewish Supporters, *see* Christian Zionists and Friends of Israel
- Press and Publishing
- - Hebrew newspapers 12:1047ff
- - Juedischer Verlag 10:463
- - press 13:1025ff
- Judaism
- - Ḥasidism opposition to 7:1397; 7:1398
- - Hebrew language 12:144
- - Jewish identity 10:61ff
- - Jewish law 12:141
- - Jewish studies 16:580
- - Judaism and nationalism 10:394
- - liturgy on 11:403
- - messianism 11:1412,1415
- - redemption 14:9
- - Torah 15:1243ff
- *illus:*
- - Alkalai's *Harbinger of Good Tidings* 2:640
- - A.Z.E. Council rally for a Jewish Palestine 15:1659,1661
- - Benei Zion group, Moscow 12:359
- - Biltmore Hotel Conference 15:1633
- - *Der Judenstaat* 8:415
- - *Die Welt*, first issue 16:445
- - exiles in Siberia 14:1487
- - exiles in Uzbekistan 16:40
- - Federation of American Zionists convention (1908) 15:1623
- - Ha-Teḥiyyah Zionist Youth convention 13:543
- - J.C.T. subscription announcement 10:43
- - J.C.T. founders' share 3:394
- - Kishinev, Zionist committee, 1920 10:1068
- - Minsk Zionist Conference (1902) 12:57
- - political prisoners in Belorussia 14:409
- - Poltava Zionist Committee 13:840
- - protest against 1940 White Paper 15:1632
- - Second Zionist Congress 16:1169
- - *shekel* membership card 14:1348
- - Soviet anti-Semitic cartoon 14:492
- - territorial proposals, 1919 (map) 9:316
- - Transjordan, Wauchope's letter re settlement in 9:343
- - Twenty-Third Zionist Congress 9:379
- - Warsaw Kadimah organization 16:338
- - Warsaw *shekel* certificate (1912) 16:1171
- - Zionist delegation to Palestine 1918 9:336
- - Zionist Organization of America conventions (1915, 1939) 15:1623; 16:1177
ZIONIST COMMISSION 16:1163
- Cowan, Joseph 5:1024
- Eliash, Mordecai 6:616
- Zionism 16:1081ff
- *illus:* text
ZIONIST CONGRESSES 16:1164
- General
- - Basle 4:304ff
- - Basle program 4:306,308
- - holy places 16:74
- - Jewish Legion 10:75
- - partition plans 13:35
- - shekel 14:1349
- - sport 11:664
- - Territorialism 15:1019ff
- - Uganda scheme 15:1500
- - Youth Aliyah 16:862
- - Zionism 16:1033ff
- Personalities
- - Bar-Ilan, Meir 4:224
- - Baruch, Joseph 4:275
- - Belkowsky, Ẓevi 4:440
- - Ben-Gurion, David 4:506; 4:508; 4:509
- - Birnbaum, Nathan 4:1040
- - Bluestone, Joseph 4:1135
- - Braudes, Reuben 4:1317
- - Bruck, Grigori 4:1413
- - Buchmil, Joshua 4:1446
- - Cohn, Arthur 5:695
- - Farbstein, Joshua 6:1181
- - Feiwel, Berthold 6:1215
- - Goldmann, Nahum 7:724;
- - Gronemann, Samuel 7:931
- - Herzl, Theodor 8:418ff; 16:1044
- - Ish-kishor, Ephraim 9:80
- - Nordau, Max 12:1211
- - Schur, Zev Wolf 14:1009
- - Tepper, Kolya 15:1013
- - Wolffsohn, David 16:613
- - Zangwill, Israel 16:930
- *illus:*
- - text
- - athletes at Sixth Zionist Congress 15:291
- - Basle municipal casino 4:306
- - Basle Program 4:307
- - commemorative medal 4:380
- - eighteenth, Prague 16:1097
- - First Congress, invitation signed by Herzl and Ehren Preis 16:1045
- - First Congress symbol 9:*fcg.* 843
- - London Conference, 1920 10:915
- - membership card 3:388
- - *shekel* Zionist membership card 14:1348
- - Twenty-Third Zionist Congress 9:379
- - WIZO delegation to Twelfth Congress 16:1101
- - WIZO executive members 16:594
- *see also:* JEWISH AGENCY; KATTOWITZ CONFERENCE; ZIONISM
Zionist Council of New Zealand 16:1105
Zionist Federation of America 16:1147
Zionist Federation of Australia and New Zealand 16:1105
Zionist Federation of Germany, *see* Zionistische Vereinigung in Deutschland
Zionist Federation of Great Britain and Ireland, *see* English Zionist Federation
Zionistisches A-B-C Buch (wk.) 16:1159
Zionistische Vereinigung in Deutschland (orgn.) 16:1115ff
- Germany 7:486
Zionist Organization in Germany 16:1116
ZIONIST ORGANIZATION OF AMERICA (Z.O.A.) 16:1178
- United States 15:1635
- Zionism 16:1143
- *illus:*
- - text

- - eighteenth annual convention, Boston (1915) **15:**1623
Zionist Organization of Canada **16:**1109
- *illus:*
- - delegates to 1950 convention **16:**1110
Zionist Organizations, *see also under* ZIONISM (Countries)
Zionist Record (newsp.) **13:**1049; **16:**1140
Zionist Review (journ.) **7:**781; **13:**1031
Zionist Revisionist Movement of Canada **16:**1110
Zionists, Christian, *see* Christian Zionists and Friends of Israel
Zionist Socialist Federation of the workers of Ereẓ Israel, *see* AḤDUT HA-AVODAH
Zionist Socialist Labor Party (Pol.) **16:**1131
Zionist Socialist Party (Rus.), *see* Z.S.
ZIONIST SOCIALIST WORKERS' PARTY (S.S.; Rus.) **16:**1179
- socialism, Jewish **15:**45
- United Jewish Socialist Workers' Party **15:**1541
- Vozrozhdeniye and **16:**230
- Z.S. and **16:**1224
Zionist-Socialist Workers Union (Rus.) **4:**1253
Zionist Society of Mesopotamia (Iraq), *see* Aguddah Ẓiyyonit le-Aram-Naharayim
Zion Mule Corps (W.W.I.)
- Ben-Gurion, David **4:**506
- history **8:**756
- history chart **8:**766-767
- Levontin, Zalman David **11:**153
- military **11:**1553
- Trumpeldor, Joseph **15:**1412
- Zionist movement **16:**1050
- *illus:*
- - in Egypt, 1915 **10:**70
- - unit **11:**1555
ZIPH (city, Er. Isr.) **16:**1181
Ziphion (city), *see* ZAPHON
Ziphronah (stlmt., Cana.) **5:**100
ZIPPER, GERSHON **16:**1181
Zipper, Jacob **5:**113
Zipper, Moshe **11:**1167
ZIPPORAH (bib. fig.) **16:**1182
- in the Arts **12:**404
- Jethro **10:**18
- Moses **12:**374
- *illus:*
- - text
- - with Moses, sons and Aaron **12:***fcg.* 427
Zippor ha-Nefesh (journ.) **1:**newsp. list
Zippori (city, mosh.), *see* SEPPHORIS
Ẓippori River (Isr.) **9:**152
Ziqqurat (Babyl. tower) **4:**23, 24
- Mesopotamia **16:**1492
- Nebuchadnezzar II **16:**1505
- Temple altar **15:**949
- Ur **16:**1
- *illus:*
- - Ziqqurat of Ur **16:**1
Zircon (min.) **13:**1010
ZIRELSON, JUDAH LEIB **16:**1183
ZIRIDS (Berber dyn.) **16:**1183
- Tunisia **15:**1433
Zirndorfer (publ. firm) **13:**1373
Ẓir Ne'eman (period.) **15:**817
Ziskes, Eliezer **13:**935
Ziskind, Jacob **6:**1161
Ziskind, Raphael **4:**663
ZISLING, AHARON **16:**1184
- *illus:*
- - proclamation of the State of Israel **4:**513
ZISSU, ABRAHAM LEIB **16:**1185
- Antonescu **3:**164
Zissu, Theodore **16:**1185
ZITNITSKY, PINCAS LAZARO **10:**318
ZITRON, SAMUEL LEIB **16:**1186
Zittel (tn., Lith.), *see* DYATLOVO
Ziusudra (myth. fig.), *see* Utnapishtim
Ziv (bib. month) **5:**48; **16:**725
Ziv, Nahum Velvel **5:**1564
Ziv, Simḥah Zissel **5:**1564
Ziva rabba (kab. term) **10:**361
Zivḥei Kohen (wk.) **6:**29
ẒIVION (journ., U.S.) **16:**1186
- *illus:*
- - Workmen's Circle leader **12:**1095
Ziyādat, Allah I (emir) **2:**366
Ziyādat, Allah III (emir) **2:**367
ZIYANIDS (Berber dyn.) **16:**1186
Ẓiyyaḥ, Joseph ben Abraham ibn, *see* ẒAYYAḤ, JOSEPH BEN ABRAHAM IBN
Ziyyat, Isaac **11:**27
Ẓiyyon (journ., Gal.) **1:**newsp. list
Ẓiyyon (journ., Ger.) **1:**newsp. list; **14:**997
Ẓiyyonei Zion (faction, Zion. mvmt.) **15:**1500
Ẓiyyon ha-lo tishali (poem) **10:**361
Ẓiyyon he-Ḥadash (journ.) **1:**newsp. list
Ẓiyyoni, Menaḥem, *see* MENAḤEM ẒIYYONI
Ziz (bird)
- Angel of Death **2:**953
- earth **6:**340
- iconography **8:**1222
- *illus:*
- - *Ambrosian Bible* **4:**360
Ẓiẓit (tract.) **12:**49
ẒIẒIT (fringes) **16:**1187
- Abraham **2:**115
- Amram Ḥasida **2:**893
- Commandments, the 613 **5:**764
- Eisenstadt custom **6:**547
- *Hashkivenu* benediction **7:**1370
- Ḥasidim **7:**1415; **7:**1417
- Karaites **10:**781
- Leiner, Gershon Henikh **9:**1160
- mixed species in **14:**1214
- *niddui* **8:**353
- *Numbers, Book of* **12:**1250
- Pentateuch **13:**248
- *talmid ḥakham* **15:**746
- Talmud **11:**1315
- *tekhelet* **15:**913
- textiles **15:**1037
- *illus:*
- - Polish Ḥasid **6:***fcg.* 238
- - *tallit* **15:**744
- *see also:* TALLIT; TALLIT KATAN
Zizyphus (bot.) **9:**788
ZLATOPOL (tn., Ukr.) **16:**1188
ZLATOPOLSKY, HILLEL **16:**1188
- *illus:*
- - Ukrainian Provisional National Council **15:**1515
Zlochover, Fischel **16:**1014
ZLOCISTI, THEODOR **16:**1188
- *illus:*
- - First Zionist Congress **16:**1165
Złoczów (tn., Ukr.), *see* ZOLOCHEV
Zloczow, Issachar of, *see* ISSACHAR DOV BAER BEN ARYEH LEIB OF ZLOCZOW
Zlotina, Rachel **11:**1558
Zlotnick, Yehuda Leib, *see* AVIDA, YEHUDA LEIB
Zlotopolsky, Saveli **15:**29
Zlotorevsky, Isidor **14:**1264
ZMIGROD NOWY (vill., Pol.) **16:**1189
ZMORA, YISRAEL **16:**1190
Zmudz (reg., Lith.), *see* SAMOGITIA
ZNOJMO (Znaim; tn., Morav.) **16:**1190
Z.O.A., *see* ZIONIST ORGANIZATION OF AMERICA
ZOAN (city, Egy.) **16:**1190
- building of **6:**1046
- Goshen **7:**816
- Hebron **8:**226
- Ramses **13:**1545
Zoar (loc., Transj.) **15:**1318
- Bela **15:**70
- Dead Sea **5:**1393
- Kenites **10:**907
Z.O.B. (partisan gr., Pol.) **13:**144; **13:**774
- Anielewicz, Mordecai **3:**3
- Cracow **5:**1039
- Cukierman, Itzhak **5:**1153
- Nossig, Alfred **12:**1230
- Warsaw ghetto **16:**350
Zobel, Moritz **16:**445
ZODIAC (astrol.) **16:**1191
- Bet Alfa mosaics **4:**713
- illustrations **4:**1225
- kabbalistic literature **3:**794
- *maḥzor* **11:**731 **11:**732; **11:**735
- synagogue art **15:**598ff
- *illus:*
- - text
- - Aquarius **11:**732; **14:**1391
- - Aries **12:**1175
- - astrological sphere **3:**788
- - Cancer **15:**788
- - *Canon of Avicenna* **8:**1283
- - Capricorn **11:**732; **15:**1032
- - ceremonial object motif **4:**1343; **5:**293
- - fourteenth cent. *maḥzor* **5:**51
- - Gemini **14:**1624
- - Hammath-Tiberias synagogue mosaic floor **15:**574
- - kabbalistic drawing, 17th cent. **11:**692
- - *ketubbah* **5:**971; **6:**1375; **10:***fcg.* 939*f*; **11:**129
- - Leo **3:**935
- - Libra **6:**690; **15:**1154
- - Pisces **2:**251
- - Sagittarius **10:**1071
- - Scorpio **5:**291
- - *Scroll of Esther* **3:**543; **13:**1388-1389
- - *Sefer ha-Maḥbarot* **4:**1235; **8:**1297
- - Taurus **9:**1157
- - Virgo **6:**689,690
- *see also:* ASTROLOGY; ASTRONOMY
Zoffany, John **3:**540
Ẓofim (scouts, Isr.), *see* Histadrut ha-Ẓofim be-Israel
ZOFIM (place, Er. Isr.) **16:**1192
- *see also:* Scopus, Mount
Zofingen (tn., Switz.) **15:**554
ẒOFIT (mosh., Isr.) **16:**1193
Ẓofiyyah (educ. inst., Isr.) **1:**place list
Zohar (fort, Er. Isr.) **5:**1394
Zohar (mosh., Isr.)
- gas field **9:**794
- statistics **1:**place list
ZOHAR (kab. wk.) **16:**1193
- *Contents:*
- - Form of the Zohar **16:**1194
- - Unity of the Work **16:**1199
- - Translations **16:**1213ff
- - Scholarship **16:**1214ff
- General
- - Apocalypse influence **3:**181
- - *Aẓilut* **3:**1010
- - history chart (1286; 1558-60) **8:**766-767
- - Moses **12:**401
- - mystical literature **11:**347ff
- - Postel's translation **13:**932
- - Satires on **13:**132
- - Zerah **16:**996
- Aspects and Concepts
- - abortion **2:**99
- - *Adam Kadmon* **2:**248
- - Akedah **2:**483
- - alchemy **2:**544
- - antinomianism **3:**70
- - articles of faith **3:**659
- - astrology **3:**794
- - astronomy **3:**803
- - Commandments, the 613 **5:**783
- - demons, demonology **5:**1529
- - eschatological teaching **6:**880ff
- - hagiography **7:**1119
- - Judaism **10:**387
- - Kabbalah **10:**532ff
- - kabbalistic psychology **10:**609ff
- - Lilith **11:**247
- - love and fear of God **11:**529
- - magic **11:**712
- - Messiah **6:**881
- - music **12:**604
- - providence, in **13:**1282
- - Raphael **13:**1549
- - Raziel **13:**1592
- - Sabbath **14:**568
- - sacrifices **14:**615
- - Samael **14:**721
- - *Shi'ur Komah* **3:**57; **14:**1418
- - Uriel **16:**7
- - visions **16:**169
- - Worlds, the Four **16:**641
- Authorship and Authenticity
- - Basilea, Solomon **4:**299
- - Emden, Jacob **6:**723
- - Isaac ben Samuel **9:**29
- - Moses de Leon **12:**425ff
- - Simeon bar Yoḥai **14:**1553
- - Zacuto, Abraham **16:**905
- Commentaries
- - Aaron Selig of Zolkiew **2:**24
- - Ashlag, Yehudah **4:**1306
- - Azulai, Abraham ben Mordecai **3:**1018
- - Azulai, Abraham ben Israel **3:**1018
- - Buzaglo, Shalom **4:**1545
- - Cordovero, Moses **5:**968; **10:**546
- - history chart (1286) **8:**766-767
- - Joseph ibn Tabûl **10:**244
- - *Kadmut Sefer ha-Zohar* **11:**571
- - Mehlsack **11:**1236
- - Vital, Hayyim **16:**175
- - Zacuto, Moses **16:**907
- - *see also:* KABBALAH
Zohar (journ.) **1:**newsp. list
Zohar, Uri **12:**462
- illus:
- - *Three Days and a Child* **12:**460
Zoharariel (kab. name) **10:**504
Zohar Ḥadash (kab. wk.) **16:**1194
- parody **13:**132
- Zacuto, M. **16:**907
ZOHARY, MICHAEL **16:**1215
Zoheleth (bib. loc.) **13:**1070
Zoilus (tyrant, Er. Isr.) **5:**6
ZOLA, ÉMILE **16:**1216
- Dreyfus **6:**227
- French literature **7:**144
- history chart **8:**766-767
- *illus:*
- - text
- - *J'Accuse* (*L'Aurore*, Jan. 13, 1898) **6:**225
ZOLD, MARTON **11:**1576
Zolf, Falik **16:**551
Zolkiew (city, Gal.), *see* ZHOLKVA
ZOLLER, ISRAEL **16:**1217
ZOLLSCHAN, IGNAZ **16:**1217
ZOLOCHEV (tn., Ukr.) **16:**1218
Zolotkoff, Leon **5:**417